A DICTIONARY OF
SOUTH AFRICAN ENGLISH
ON HISTORICAL PRINCIPLES

EDITORIAL STAFF

MANAGING EDITOR
Penny Silva

EDITORS
Wendy Dore, Dorothea Mantzel, Colin Muller,
and Madeleine Wright

A DICTIONARY OF SOUTH AFRICAN ENGLISH

ON HISTORICAL PRINCIPLES

OXFORD UNIVERSITY PRESS

in association with
THE DICTIONARY UNIT FOR SOUTH AFRICAN ENGLISH

1996

Oxford University Press, Walton Street, Oxford OX2 6DP
Oxford New York
Athens Auckland Bangkok Bogota Bombay
Buenos Aires Calcutta Cape Town Dar es Salaam
Delhi Florence Hong Kong Istanbul Karachi
Kuala Lumpur Madras Madrid Melbourne
Mexico City Nairobi Paris Singapore
Taipei Tokyo Toronto
and associated companies in
Berlin Ibadan

Oxford is a trade mark of Oxford University Press

Published in the United States
by Oxford University Press Inc., New York

© Dictionary Unit for South African English 1996
First published by Oxford University Press 1996

All rights reserved. No part of this publication may be reproduced,
stored in a retrieval system, or transmitted, in any form or by any means,
without the prior permission in writing of Oxford University Press.
Within the UK, exceptions are allowed in respect of any fair dealing for the
purpose of research or private study, or criticism or review, as permitted
under the Copyright, Designs and Patents Act, 1988, or in the case of
reprographic reproduction in accordance with the terms of the licences
issued by the Copyright Licensing Agency. Enquiries concerning
reproduction outside these terms and in other countries should be
sent to the Rights Department, Oxford University Press,
at the address above

This book is sold subject to the condition that it shall not, by way
of trade or otherwise, be lent, re-sold, hired out or otherwise circulated
without the publisher's prior consent in any form of binding or cover
other than that in which it is published and without a similar condition
including this condition being imposed on the subsequent purchaser

British Library Cataloguing in Publication Data
Data available

Library of Congress Cataloging in Publication Data
Data available
ISBN 0-19-863153-7

1 3 5 7 9 10 8 6 4 2

Typeset in Swift and Hollander
by Latimer Trend Ltd, Plymouth

Printed and bound in Great Britain by
Bookcraft (Bath) Ltd., Midsomer Norton, Somerset

ACKNOWLEDGEMENTS

THE Dictionary Unit has received major financial support from the Human Sciences Research Council (1970-5), the Department of National Education (1976-94), and the Department of Arts, Culture, Science and Technology (1994-). The Council and administration of Rhodes University have also provided assistance and support in many ways, for which we are grateful.

The publication of the dictionary was made possible by generous donations from the Anglo-American and De Beers Chairman's Fund, First National Bank, the Gencor Trust, the Gold Fields Foundation, the Molteno Brothers Trust, the PG Foundation, and Mr Gavin Relly. Their contribution is greatly valued.

We owe a great debt to colleagues at the Oxford University Press: to Rob Scriven, Senior Commissioning Editor (Dictionaries), Kendall Clarke, and Kate Wandless in Oxford, for their management of the business of publication, and to Kate McCallum, Managing Director of OUP South Africa, for her assistance in this process; to John Simpson, Chief Editor of the *Oxford English Dictionary*, and his staff for their unfailing willingness to check sources, give opinions, and share their expertise; to Jeffery Triggs, manager of the North American reading programme in Madison, New Jersey, for offering his computing skills, time, and energy via the Internet for the conversion of this text into Standard Generalized Markup Language for typesetting, and for the enthusiasm he has shown in both formal and informal ways. We particularly wish to record our deep gratitude to Edmund Weiner, Deputy Chief Editor of the *Oxford English Dictionary*, and honorary consultant during the preparation of this dictionary, for the many hours of his own time which he so graciously gave to the project; for his critical reading of the entire text over four years; for his invaluable suggestions and comments at the various stages of editing—the later stages via the Internet, an education which led to the transformation of our lexicographical processes; for his co-ordination of the process of transmitting the text to Oxford via North America; and, especially, for his friendship and warm encouragement.

We would like to express our thanks to those institutions, companies, and individuals who generously responded to our requests for specialized information, who contributed data regularly, or who gave assistance in other ways:

Prof. M. V. Aldridge, Ms K. Barber (OUP Toronto), R. J. Bouch, Prof. A. P. Brink, Mrs E. Brink (Schonland Herbarium, Albany Museum), Dr R. W. Burchfield, Dr R. Chernis, Miss D. Child, Prof. J. Combrink (Stellenbosch University), L. F. B. Cornelius (Natal Education Department), Mr D. Dabengwa (Minister of Home Affairs, Zimbabwe), Dr T. R. H. Davenport, A. Davids, Dr W. J. de Klerk (Albany Museum), J. H. de Lange (South African Film, Video, and Sound Archives), Prof. Hans den Besten (University of Amsterdam, the Netherlands), M. Derry (Gold Fields Foundation), Prof. A. de Villiers, Don Africana Library (Durban), East London Public Library, the late Prof. V. S. Forbes, D. M. Franklin, A. Goldstuck, M. Green, M. M. Hacksley and his staff (National English Literary Museum), Dr M. Haron (University of the Western Cape), Prof. R. K. Herbert (University of the Witwatersrand), Prof. E. Higgins (Vista University), Dr M. Hirst (Kaffrarian Museum, King William's Town), Prof. J. B. Hlongwane (University of Zululand), Ms J. Hobbs, Ms E. Horwitz (Witwatersrand University Press), H. Hurwitz (Manel), Prof. E. R. Jenkins (Vista University), Johannesburg Public Library, Miss M. Jooste (Mendelssohn Collection, Library of Parliament), Killie Campbell Africana Library (University of Natal), K. Kirkman (Nooitgedacht Agricultural Research Station), A. Klaaste, D. Kramer, Dr V. Krohn, R. A. Laing, M. D. Lawrie, C. Leigh (Johannesburg Public Library), G. Levin, J. P. K. Lotter (Joint Matriculation Board), Dr N. A. C. McNaught, Prof. B. M. Mini (University of Fort Hare), Dr B. Moore (Australian National Dictionary Centre, Canberra), Dr R. Morris (Foundation for Research Development), Mossgas, Prof. E. Mphahlele (University of the Witwatersrand), Prof. C. T. Msimang (University of South Africa), J. Mullen (SABC), D. Mutasa (University of South Africa), Natal Teachers Society, S. Naum, Nietvoorbij Wine Research Institute, J. Orr (SABC), Dr H. Orsman

(Victoria University, Wellington, New Zealand), B. G. Paterson, Dr J. Pauw, Prof. J. B. Peires MP, Mrs H. Phillips, Port Elizabeth Football Association, Port Elizabeth Public Library (Africana Section), Dr K. Prinsloo (Human Sciences Research Council), Queenstown Public Library, Prof. E. H. Raidt (University of the Witwatersrand), Dr W. Ramson (Australian National Dictionary Centre, Canberra), Dr P. E. Raper (Human Sciences Research Council), Mr G. Robinson (Dalro), Mrs A. Ryan, R. Simpson, Dr A. Sitaram (University of Durban Westville), P. Slabolepszy, the late Prof. J. Smuts, South African Library (Cape Town), South African National Defence Force, South African Police Services, B. N. Stark (South African Breweries), J. Taylor, Ms H. P. Thomson (United Tobacco Company), Mrs H. Tilney, Dr K. Tomaselli (University of Natal), Prof. A. Traill (University of the Witwatersrand), Transvaal Education Department, Ms S. Triggs, R. van der Elst (South African Association for Marine Biological Research), Prof. J. van der Westhuizen (University of Cape Town), G. van Rooyen, Dr D. van Schalkwyk and his staff (Woordeboek van die Afrikaanse Taal), Prof. P. G. J. van Sterkenburg (University of Leiden), R. H. Wakefield (Portacamp), Ms A. Warring, R. J. B. Wilson (SABC), N. B. Wynne (Natal Sharks Board).

At Rhodes University, Grahamstown: Prof. F. G. Butler; Dr D. S. Henderson, Dr K. S. Hunt; J. C. S. Lancaster; H. A. Long; Dr M. A. H. Smout; Dr R. van der Merwe; *Computing Centre*: S. Bangay, B. Bonnevie, T. J. Bouwer, I.S . Dore, F. Jacot-Guillarmod, D. Wilson; *Dept of African Languages*: Prof. P. T. Mtuze, Dr J. S. Claughton; *Dept of Afrikaans and Nederlands*: Prof. A. B. Bosch, T. Huisamen, Prof. E. R. van Heerden; *Dept of Anthropology*: Prof. C. de Wet, Dr R. C. G. Palmer, Prof. M. G. Whisson; *Dept of Botany*: the late Dr A. Jacot-Guillarmod; *Dept of English*: Prof. M. van Wyk Smith; *Dept of Geography*: O. West (cartographer); *Dept of Geology*: Prof. J. M. Moore; *Dept of History*: Dr J. Cobbing, Prof. P. R. Maylam, Miss B. M. Nicholls; *Dept of Human Movement Studies*: Prof. P. A. Scott; *Dept of Journalism*: Prof. G. Stewart, L. Strelitz, M. Cooper; *Dept of Law*: Professors J. G. Grogan, A. J. Kerr, I. D. Schafer, and Mrs S. Maclennan; *Dept of Linguistics and English Language*: Prof. V. A. de Klerk, Dr D. H. Gough, Mr D. McLean; *Dept of Zoology and Entomology*: Professors A. J. F. K. Craig, P. E. Hulley, C. D. McQuaid; *Institute for Social and Economic Research*: Prof. P. A. McAllister; *Institute for the Study of English in Africa*: Professors L. W. Lanham, L. S. Wright, P. S. Walters; *International Library of African Music*: Mr A. Tracey; *J. L. B. Smith Institute for Ichthyology*: Dr P. Skelton; *University Library*: J. M. Berning; Ms S. Rowoldt and her staff at the Cory Library.

The editors acknowledge with gratitude the considerable debt owed to this dictionary's predecessors, particularly *Africanderisms* (1913), the pioneering dictionary by Charles Pettman; D. R. Beeton and Hele Dorner's *Dictionary of English Usage in Southern Africa* (1975); and the four editions (1978–91) of *A Dictionary of South African English* by Jean Branford.

Many hundreds of South Africans, from schoolchildren to pensioners, contributed material to the competitions we ran nationwide, in collaboration with *Personality magazine* (1970) and Radio South Africa (1991 and 1992); others wrote spontaneously, offering observations on South African English, and enclosing press-cuttings or references to texts. Much of what they contributed will be found in this dictionary, and we thank them, and express the hope that interest in and awareness of South African English will be stimulated by this publication.

Users of the dictionary will no doubt encounter errors and inaccuracies: these are the responsibility of the editorial staff, and should not be attributed to those whose help we have acknowledged here. Corrections, comments, and illustrative material (e.g. providing earlier or later examples of a word's use) would be valued. Correspondence should be addressed to: The Editor, Dictionary Unit for South African English, Rhodes University, PO Box 94, Grahamstown 6140, South Africa.

PREFACE

THIS dictionary is the product of twenty-five years of work, and contains the accumulated and synthesized insight, skills, knowledge, and resourcefulness of many people. Three who made most significant contributions are no longer working in the Dictionary Unit: William Branford initiated the project and guided it for close to two decades, and Jean Branford and Margaret Britz worked on it for much of that time. In addition the employees of the Dictionary Unit for South African English, those acknowledged above for the assistance they have so generously given the project, and the many hundreds of unnamed South Africans who have telephoned, written, or stopped staff members in the street with snippets of information have all contributed to the text, whose threads are too tightly interwoven to be distinguishable as the work of any one individual.

The present shape of the dictionary particularly reflects the combined work of the small editorial staff, which, over four years, reworked the material they had inherited from others, and added over 2,500 new entries. While all staff members participated in every facet of the work, each also became skilled in particular areas—Wendy Dore in styling, Dorothea Mantzel in bibliography and natural history, Penny Silva in history, Colin Muller in African languages and management of the computer network. Through communal decision-making the editors decided upon policy and developed new methodology.

Begun in 1969 during the height of the apartheid era, the dictionary records the vocabulary of English in South Africa over 300 years: from the late sixteenth to the late twentieth century. The work was completed at the end of 1994, the year of the country's first democratic elections.

In compiling the text, the editors have made a conscious attempt to give voice not only to the documented utterances of powerful men, but also to the daily speech of ordinary people—men, women, and children—who are identified as 'informants' in the text and acknowledged by name wherever possible. Illustrations have thus been gleaned not only from the printed word, but also from overheard conversations, and from ephemeral sources such as letters, handbills, and radio and television broadcasts.

The dictionary attempts to map and illustrate the complex landscape of that variety of English which is particular to South Africans—words borrowed from the many languages of South Africa, English words which have acquired particular senses here, and words coined for local phenomena. A few words and phrases which are not South African in origin, but which have a particular significance for South Africans (e.g. *constructive engagement*, *Sullivan (principles)*, and *Eminent Persons Group*), have been included.

South African English (*S. Afr. Eng.*) is the property not only of South Africa's relatively small number of English-speakers (about 10% of the population), but also of the much greater number of people who use English as a second or third language. All varieties of English are represented in this dictionary, and the provenance of regional or 'group' vocabulary is provided wherever a word is not widely familiar to South Africans. If these descriptions sometimes seem uncomfortably like racial labels, this is because the Group Areas Act ensured that for over forty years people were geographically segregated along racial lines; 'separate development' ensured that varieties of English developed separately, the vocabulary or English usage of each group being only partially understandable to others. Typical of this breakdown in comprehension is the use of the word *late* (deceased), which is used in general English only attributively ('my late father'), but is usually heard in 'township' English in the predicative ('my father is late'). The separation by racial or linguistic group is reflected also, for instance, in the two headwords *bhuti* and *boetie* ('brother') documenting use in two different communities. The scrapping of apartheid legislation and the broadening of non-racial schooling is likely to lead to a blurring of the linguistic barriers of the past.

In any country where many languages rub shoulders, there is a great deal of 'code-switching', or *ad hoc* borrowing, between languages. Many borrowings are not yet truly integrated into *S. Afr. Eng.*, but the decision has been taken to record such words, often marked as unassimilated (‖), in order to document the *S. Afr. Eng.* vocabulary as comprehensively as possible.

South Africans are notorious for their inferiority complex about all things South African, and this is true too of their own English. Time and time again the Dictionary Unit has been accused of 'writing a dictionary of slang'. This dictionary does, of course, include colloquialisms, slang, and vulgarisms; however, it is hoped that readers will be pleasantly surprised by the age, creativity, and variety of the standard vocabulary recorded here. Many words which the average South African would perceive as standard international English have been identified by colleagues beyond South Africa's borders as being peculiar to *S. Afr. Eng.*, and everyday words such as *advocate* and *attorney*, *bond* (mortgage), *cubby-hole* (of a car), *gem squash*, *geyser* (hot-water tank), and *to motivate (a project or proposal)* are used there in senses which are perplexing to English-speakers elsewhere.

The task of describing borrowed words has presented its own set of challenges:

DUTCH, SOUTH AFRICAN DUTCH, AND AFRIKAANS BORROWINGS

In documenting the words borrowed from the Dutch–South African Dutch–Afrikaans continuum, a decision had to be taken as to how to describe the various stages in this continuum. 'Dutch' has been used of words used in Holland in the same form and sense, and 'South African Dutch' of Dutch words which were either used in a new sense, or reflected South Africanized spelling forms, or were coined for South African phenomena. 'Afrikaans' is applied from about 1870—the beginning of the decade of the 'Taalbeweging', or 'Language Movement'. Some scholars would disagree, placing the birth of Afrikaans at an earlier date—the 1850s, or even the 1820s.

Because of the changing orthography of South African Dutch and Afrikaans over the centuries, many words borrowed by *S. Afr. Eng.* appear archaic to the modern Afrikaner. For example, in *S. Afr. Eng.*, *kopje* is still frequently used for the modern Afrikaans *koppie*, *krantz* is the usual form for *krans*, and *veldskoen* is more frequently used than the modern Afrikaans *velskoen*. The principle applied in this dictionary has been to select the most commonly used *S. Afr. Eng.* form as the headword, despite the preferred modern orthography in the source language. One exception to this rule is the word *dagha* (mortar), the Afrikaans derivative of the original Xhosa *ukudaka*. Despite the frequent occurrence in *S. Afr. Eng.* of the spelling *dagga*, the editors decided that the headword form would be *dagha*, in order to avoid confusion with *dagga* (cannabis), and to indicate the difference in pronunciation between the two words.

When the spelling of a borrowed word causes difficulties in English, *S. Afr. Eng.* has tended to simplify the orthography, or even alter it radically. An example of this alteration is found in the treatment of two Afrikaans homophones (both pronounced 'bray')—*bry* and *brei*. In *S. Afr. Eng.* these tend to be spelled *brei*, and *bray* or *brey* respectively.

Some borrowed words are used extensively in speech, but the written form has not been standardized. For example the word *leguan/legevaan* is found in many spelling forms, and the editors decided to standardize the spelling as *leguaan*.

An additional complexity has been the considerable influence of the Khoi-San and Malayo-Javanese languages on Afrikaans. The relevant etymologies present these origins in as much detail as possible, but difficulties have been experienced, particularly in orthography; for example, in the Khoikhoi languages, most of which are no longer spoken, there may be a great deal of variation in the way in which a given word has been represented. In such cases, several alternative forms are provided in the etymology.

An interesting feature of *S. Afr. Eng.* borrowing from Afrikaans has been a tendency in recent years to ignore the process of simplification and alteration, and to return to Afrikaans orthography. Sometimes this selfconscious 'correctness' has been misplaced, as in the case of *tackie*, which, mistakenly interpreted as being Afrikaans in origin, is often spelled *takkie*, or even *tekkie*.

BORROWINGS FROM THE SINTU (BANTU) LANGUAGES

The deeply resented adoption by the National Party government of the word *Bantu* as a racial designation for black people (from 1953 to 1978) has resulted in widespread rejection of this word among black South Africans, and avoidance of it by whites, even when it is used technically of the 'Bantu' languages. Despite the established international use of *Bantu*, several prominent black South African academics have stated a preference for the form *Sintu* (which reflects the Nguni prefix *isi-*, denoting language and culture). The question has generated lengthy discussion and some dissension among the Unit's staff. Our decision has been to use the terms in tandem in this edition. It is possible that *Bantu* will one day re-enter the South African scholarly vocabulary when some of the pain and anger of the apartheid era has receded.

The Sintu words borrowed by *S. Afr. Eng.* have frequently been simplified, losing features such as clicks, 'g' indicating voice, 'h' indicating aspiration, and prefixes indicating concord: thus in *S. Afr. Eng.* the Xhosa *mngqusho* is often (g)*nush*, the Xhosa *ingcibi* is often spelled *incibi* and the Xhosa and Zulu *ugonothi* has become *kanoti*, the Xhosa *ibhunga* has become *Bunga*, and the Zulu *umasikanda* is *maskanda*. The Sintu vowel /a/ may be interpreted as /ɒ/: for instance, the Zulu *bansela* is represented as *bonsella*. Largely for typesetting reasons, the implosive 'b' has not been distinguished from 'bh' in this text.

English-speakers display confusion over the complex prefixes and concords which are an integral part of the Sintu languages. There is little understanding of the numerous noun classes which exist (each requiring particular prefixes), or of the singular and plural prefixes, which are often used interchangeably in *S. Afr. Eng.* Only when a Sintu word is totally assimilated is there any consistency. In such words the prefix is either dropped (*bonsella, donga, moochi, tollie*), or is perceived as an integral part of the word (*amatungulu, impala, indaba, induna*). Some borrowings still display ambivalence—for instance *iqabane*, or the older *umpakati*, which is most commonly used either as *pakati* or *amapakati* (the latter being the plural form in the Nguni languages, but commonly used as either singular or plural form in *S. Afr. Eng.*). Other borrowings (e.g. *abakwetha*) are still highly fluid, displaying a plethora of forms, including a variety of singular and plural prefixes (which are used at random by English-speakers). Systematizing such words has proved to be a highly complex task, from choosing the headword form to describing singular and plural usage, and new systems have had to be developed to describe them. For example, a new method of treating singular and plural variants (see *Hurutshe*) was developed, which necessarily differs from the way in which these are treated in the *Oxford English Dictionary*. In order to clarify how the Sintu noun prefixes are applied, and to explain the relationship between singular and plural prefixes, many such prefixes are included as entries in this dictionary.

As is the case with Afrikaans borrowings, there has been a tendency towards 'correctness' in recent years, manifested for example in the reintroduction of prefixes before words which had become simplified as a result of assimilation ('the *Xhosa*' becoming 'the *amaXhosa*', and 'the *Zulus*' 'the *amaZulu*', for instance), or in a reversion from an Anglicized spelling to the accepted orthography of the source language (e.g. *baSotho* rather than *Basuto*, *Mfengu* for *Fingo*).

The existence of a wide range of pronunciation-spellings, encountered in the writings of those unfamiliar with the Sintu languages, has necessitated numerous cross-references in this dictionary, which, it is hoped, will assist and not distract.

P. M. S.

April 1995

CONTENTS

Dictionary Unit Staff, 1969–95	xii
Board of Directors, Dictionary Unit for South African English, 1995	xiii
The Dictionary Unit for South African English	xiv
English in South Africa	xvii
Maps: South Africa, 1910 to March 1994	xx
South Africa from April 1994	xx
The Pronunciation of English in South Africa	xxi
Key to the Pronunciation	xxv
Styling Conventions	xxvi
List of Abbreviations	xxviii
Proprietary Names	xxx
THE DICTIONARY	1
Select Bibliography	827

DICTIONARY UNIT STAFF, 1969–95

EDITORS-IN-CHIEF

William Branford	(Honorary Editor, 1969–June 1988; Senior Author, July 1989–90)
Malcolm Hacksley	(Acting Editor, July 1988–Dec. 1989)
Penny Silva	(Acting Editor, Jan. 1990–June 1991; Editor, July 1991–)

EDITORIAL AND RESEARCH STAFF

Jean Branford	(Assistant Editor, 1971–8; Associate Editor, 1979–June 1989)
Michael Breetzke	(Research Assistant, Feb.–Apr. 1994)
Margaret Britz	(Assistant Editor, 1977–June 1991)
Wendy Dore	(Associate Editor, Dec. 1989–Nov. 1995)
Lalage Gough	(Assistant Editor, 1990)
Malcolm Hacksley	(Associate Editor, 1991)
Raewyn Hill	(Assistant Editor, 1987)
Sally Hunt	(Assistant Editor, 1988)
Rachael Johnston	(Research Assistant, 1994)
Peter Kota	(Editorial Assistant, 1969)
Irene Künz	(Editorial Assistant, 1987–8)
Vanessa Limbrick	(Assistant Editor, 1989–90)
Dorothea Mantzel	(Associate Editor, 1989–)
Betty McLeod	(Editorial Assistant, Feb.–June 1970)
Colin Muller	(Associate Editor, May 1990–April 1995)
Jane Pargiter	(Editorial Assistant, 1982–4)
Abigail Paton	(Editorial Assistant, 1988–9)
Susan Pattison	(Assistant Editor, 1987)
Alan Pitt	(Editorial Assistant, 1988)
Armanda Santos	(Assistant Editor, 1987–8)
Penny Silva	(Assistant Editor, Aug. 1970–3, Oct.–Dec. 1989)
Lucy Smith	(Research Assistant, Apr.–May 1994)
John Walker	(Assistant Editor, Jan. 1973–Apr. 1976)
Madeleine Wright	(Associate Editor, Mar. 1990–)

CLERICAL STAFF

Margaret Britz	(July 1971–6)
Anita Coetzee	(1986–9)
Nova de Villiers	(1976–7)
Pat Holgate	(1990–3)
Joseph Jadi	(1987–91)
Jane Rist	(1990–2)
Beverley Taylor	(July–Dec. 1993)
Tracey Wild	(Dec. 1989–94)

BOARD OF DIRECTORS, DICTIONARY UNIT FOR SOUTH AFRICAN ENGLISH, 1995

Dr Michael Smout (Chair)
Professor Guy Butler
Mark Franklin
Professor Buyiswa Mini

Professor Edith Raidt
Professor Malvern van Wyk Smith (Vice-Chair)
Achmat Davids

Eve Horwitz
Professor Peter Mtuze
Penny Silva (Executive Director)

THE DICTIONARY UNIT FOR SOUTH AFRICAN ENGLISH

THE EARLY YEARS: ESTABLISHMENT AND CONSOLIDATION

In mid-1968 William Branford, then the Professor of English Language at Rhodes University, Grahamstown, initiated a pilot project on South African English, beginning with the collection of citations which illustrated South African English words in context, and employing one part-time editorial assistant, Peter Kota, during 1969.

In 1970 a research grant from the Human Sciences Research Council meant that the project could continue for a further three years. With an office in the Drostdy Barracks, an early nineteenth-century stone building on the campus, the Dictionary Unit was initially a project of the English Institute (subsequently the Institute for the Study of English in Africa) at Rhodes University, of which William Branford was Director. Charles Pettman's *Africanderisms: A Glossary of South African Colloquial Words and Phrases and of Place and Other Names* (1913), and C. P. Swart's 1934 thesis, a supplement to Pettman's work, provided a set of data which formed a useful starting-point, supplemented by the South African entries in the *Oxford English Dictionary* and its supplement. A great deal of material was gathered from the public during a competition for the best list of South African English words which was run in *Personality* magazine.

During the first half of 1970 the first full-time professional researcher, Betty McLeod, was employed for a period of six months. Penny Silva continued this data-gathering work and began compiling entries in August 1970. She was joined by Jean Branford in 1971. By the end of 1973 a working system had evolved, and the first 1,000 entries had been written for a planned dictionary of South African English, to be compiled on historical principles. An editorial committee under the chairmanship of Professor William Branford was drawn from the Rhodes University academic staff. In the Progress Report of July 1971, it was noted that two drafts were prepared for each word—one for 'the Dictionary proper..and one for the Pocket version'. This dual system of drafting was subsequently discontinued.

The staff of the Dictionary Unit has usually been small: there was one full-time researcher in 1970; one full-time and one part-time researcher and a clerical assistant between 1971 and 1975; and one full-time researcher and an editorial assistant between 1976 and 1981. While many worked in the Unit for relatively short periods of time, continuity was provided by two editors who together made a major contribution to the Unit: Jean Branford from 1971 until her retirement in June 1989, and Margaret Britz from 1971 until June 1991. In 1988 Malcolm Hacksley (now the Director of the National English Literary Museum in Grahamstown) was appointed Acting Editor, followed by Penny Silva in 1990. During 1990 the staff complement was expanded to five full-time and two part-time researchers, two typists, and a clerical assistant, in order to prepare for the editing of the large *Dictionary of South African English on Historical Principles* during the following four years. From 1991–4 the staff consisted of five editors (one being part-time), a typist, and a clerical assistant, with additional temporary assistance from graduate students.

In Report No. 3 of the dictionary project (*Towards a Dictionary of South African English*, September, 1971), which offered drafts of fifty entries as 'a sample of work in progress and ... a basis for criticism, comments and suggestions' (p. 1), William Branford described the aim of the project as being 'to provide an historical record of the South African element in the English vocabulary from its first appearances in the language down to the present day'. He expressed the hope that a Pocket Dictionary would be ready for publication in 1973, with the publication of 'the Dictionary proper ... some years after that'.

By 1976 the publishing programme of the Unit had changed somewhat, the short-term goal being the compilation of an interim (unpublished) text of between one and two thousand entries, primarily for the sponsors of the project (by this time the Department of National Education). In the preface to this interim text, titled *Voorloper* ('one who walks ahead', 1976), William Branford described the Unit's aims as being first the production of 'a Dictionary of South Africanisms in English, designed as a project substantially independent of the main dictionary, and with about three thousand main entries'; and, secondly, 'a *Dictionary of South African English on historical principles* ... containing perhaps between 5,000 and 15,000 headwords treated in *extenso*'.

Voorloper consisted of 921 pages, and offered about 1,000 entries, compiled principally by Penny Silva and John Walker under the supervision of the Editorial Committee (September 1976). The shape of the entries was based on the style of the *Oxford English Dictionary*, with full etymologies, and numerous illustrative contexts for each sense. The entries contained in *Voorloper*, together with those in its companion volume, *Agterryer* ('one who rides behind'), which was produced in 1984 and contained entries compiled by Margaret Britz, Jean Branford, Jane Pargiter, and William Branford, provided a basis for the preparation and editing of the *Dictionary of South African English on Historical Principles* (DSAE: Hist).

The planned 'Dictionary of South Africanisms in English' was published in 1978 as Jean Branford's *Dictionary of South African English*, by Oxford University Press in Cape Town. This general readers' dictionary, which, in addition to the standard vocabulary, includes colourful colloquial and slang expressions, and often quirky or humorous illustrative citations, is, in the compiler's own words in the preface, 'intended to be useful; but, unlike many, . . . intended also to give pleasure and amusement' (p. vii). Descriptive rather than prescriptive, the text is characterized by labels which indicate register or provide information on regional or group use. The dictionary draws the reader's attention to semantic links between South African English and world English, comparing terms used in South Africa with those found, for example, in the English of Britain, the United States, Jamaica, or Nigeria. It also provides many internal links, providing access to synonyms within the South African English lexicon. Many (specially marked) notes on South African English usage are included. Four editions of this dictionary have appeared, the most recent (1991) being co-edited by William Branford—who also edited the *South African Pocket Oxford Dictionary* (1987 and 1994), adapting the text for the local reader and adding entries for South African words.

William Branford's foresight in initiating research on South African lexicography, and his perseverance in securing the funding, year by year, to support this work, filled a gap in world English dictionary-making, and the continuing contribution by both William and Jean Branford, over three decades, established South African English lexicography as a scholarly discipline, both nationally and internationally.

THE DICTIONARY UNIT'S NEW LEGAL STATUS

In 1985 the Unit, after twenty years of *ad hoc* and uncertain financial support, was given the assurance of regular funding by the Department of National Education. In June 1991, after lengthy negotiations between the university and the department, the Rhodes University Dictionary Unit became 'The Dictionary Unit for South African English (Association incorporated under Section 21)', a company not for gain, with a nationally representative Board of Directors. In 1992 the Dictionary Unit moved from the Drostdy Barracks, its home for twenty-three years, to a wing of the St Peter's Building, an imposing red brick Victorian edifice which had formerly been the home of the sisters of the Community of the Resurrection. The Unit is associated with Rhodes University as a research institute receiving an annual grant from the state—from the Department of National Education until April 1994, and subsequently from the Department of Arts, Culture, Science, and Technology. The Unit's task was initially defined as 'the continuous and comprehensive collecting, arranging and storing in a lexicographically workable form of the vocabulary of the English language as used in Southern Africa and the editing and publication of the collected materials in the form of a Dictionary of South African English on Historical Principles, as well as periodical revision and updating of the text thereof and other research and publications associated therewith' (Memorandum of Association, 1991). Its broadened function now includes the production of a range of dictionaries for the South African market, and the planned establishment of teaching courses in lexicography at various levels.

The first challenges facing the new company were those of computerizing the work (most of which existed only as typed or handwritten copy), and planning an efficient computer system. A local area network was established, linking each editor to the database and to the other editors, and giving access to various printers, the CD-ROM version of the Oxford English dictionary (which enables rapid searches of this twenty-volume work), and, most significantly, to the electronic highway, the Internet.

The network, and particularly access to the Internet, transformed the way in which the lexicographers operated. The 'e-mail' facility enabled fast and efficient correspondence with a range of consultants, including authorities in various specialist fields, and lexicographers at the Bureau of the Woordeboek vir die Afrikaanse Taal (Dictionary of the Afrikaans Language) in Stellenbosch (Western Cape), and, internationally, with dictionary-makers in Amsterdam, Canberra, Wellington, Toronto, and New Jersey. Most significantly, 'email' gave rapid access to the then co-editors of the *Oxford English Dictionary* (*OED*), in Oxford, John Simpson and Edmund Weiner.

The Unit had forged links with the Oxford University Press (OUP) Dictionary Department in the 1970s. Robert Burchfield, then editor of the *OED*, had visited Grahamstown in 1974; Jean Branford acted as a consultant for the *OED*'s second edition; William Branford became a member of the Editorial Board of that dictionary in 1984. The Delegates of the Press accepted the *DSAE: Hist* for publication in 1983, but the project had not been completed. William Branford maintained contact with Edmund Weiner of the *OED*, who, in 1987, had agreed to act as lexicographical consultant to the Unit.

In 1990 the Editorial Board of the Unit requested the then Acting Editor, Penny Silva, to renew negotiations towards the publication of the *DSAE: Hist*. In September 1990 she thus visited the OUP in Oxford, discussed the contract, and spent several days in the Dictionary Department, working through drafts for the *DSAE: Hist* with Edmund Weiner, identifying methodological problems, and in the process undergoing an informal, short, but highly formative training in the complexities of *OED* styling. The Internet, and Edmund Weiner's generosity, enabled the long-distance continuation of this training, which had a considerable impact upon the reshaping and writing of the *DSAE: Hist* between 1991 and the end of 1994. As well as providing advice on methodology, Edmund Weiner and his co-editor John Simpson gave opinions on the 'South African-ness' of particular words or expressions, and they and their colleagues were helpful in checking bibliographical information. Always willing to exchange data freely, the editors provided the Unit with new material in the form of entries which had been compiled for the third edition of the *OED*, and citations ante-dating or supplementing the material in the *DSAE: Hist*. In return the Dictionary

Unit assisted Oxford by supplying South African English material, answering queries, and checking drafts for the third edition of the *OED*, which is planned for 2005.

At the beginning of 1991 the final editing and writing of material for the *DSAE: Hist* began, and in July of the same year the publication project was approved by OUP's Delegates.

The following four years proved to be a continual training process, resulting often in the frustration of having to restyle material already 'completed', as the editors worked their way slowly from A to Z. With a core staff of only five editors—Penny Silva, Colin Muller, Wendy Dore, Dorothea Mantzel, and (part-time) Madeleine Wright—each editor participated in all areas of lexicography, including continual data-gathering, the drafting of new entries, correspondence with consultants, proofreading, and acquiring basic skills in computer-system use. Temporary research assistants were hired for specific tasks, according to the dictates of the deadline.

Once the editing and content proofreading of the *DSAE: Hist* had been completed at the end of 1994, the Internet proved its value yet again, acting as the vehicle for the transfer of the text to OUP in Oxford. The WordPerfect files were first sent by File Transfer Protocol to Jeffery Triggs (the manager of OUP's North American reading programme in New Jersey), who had generously offered to reformat the files in Standard Generalized Markup Language (SGML) so that they would be more easily accessible to the typesetters. Prior to the transfer of the full text to New Jersey in January 1995, sample files were sent for experimentation, Jeffery Triggs creating a suite of software to manage the process. The word-processed text was first converted into ascii files, while preserving the typesetting information. This information was then converted into tags which indicated structural elements, and the data was checked for accuracy. Once the conversion process had been completed, the reformatted data were transferred to Oxford on the Internet for typesetting.

THE DICTIONARY UNIT'S PLACE IN 'THE NEW SOUTH AFRICA'

With the twenty-five-year project of the *DSAE: Hist* completed, the Dictionary Unit for South African English has moved into a new phase of its history. The status of English has been changing since 1990, when it became the language of negotiation between the government of F. W. de Klerk and the ANC—negotiation which subsequently widened into national talks of an inclusive nature. The elections of April 1994 heralded the introduction of an interim constitution which established eleven official languages. Despite its being only one of these official languages, English is the *de facto* language of communication at central government level, and in many regions. There is thus a growing need for a range of English dictionaries which are suited to the diverse South African community.

Over the next decade the Unit will turn its attention to 'indigenizing' several dictionaries for primary schools, for both first- and second-language speakers of English, altering wording and illustrative sentences to suit the local reader, and adding definitions for appropriate South African vocabulary items.

Although at the time of writing only the province of Gauteng has announced its decision concerning the vexed question of the language of instruction (each school in Gauteng being given the freedom to choose for itself), the demand for accessible dictionaries of English for all age-groups and levels of expertise is likely to increase.

P. M. SILVA

April 1995

REFERENCES

Agterryer: An Interim Presentation of Materials for a Dictionary of South African English on Historical Principles. 1984. 2 vols., Grahamstown: Rhodes University.

Branford, Jean. 1978. *A Dictionary of South African English.* Cape Town: Oxford University Press. Revised edns. 1980, 1987, and, with William Branford, 1991.

Branford, William (ed.). 1987. *South African Pocket Oxford Dictionary.* Cape Town: Oxford University Press.

Pettman, Charles. 1913. *Africanderisms: A Glossary of South African Colloquial Words and Phrases and of Place and Other Names.* London: Longmans, Green & Co.

Progress Reports. 1970–94. Grahamstown: Dictionary Unit for South African English. Unpublished.

Swart, C. P. 1934. 'A Supplement to the Rev. Charles Pettman's *Glossary of South African Colloquial Words and Phrases and of Place and Other Names*'. M.A. diss., University of South Africa.

Towards a Dictionary of South African English. 1971. Report No. 3 of the Dictionary Committee. Grahamstown: Rhodes University.

Voorloper: An Interim Presentation of Materials for a Dictionary of South African English on Historical Principles. 1976. Grahamstown: Institute for the Study of English in Africa, Rhodes University.

ENGLISH IN SOUTH AFRICA

In the South African context English has been both a highly influential language and a language influenced, in different ways and to different degrees, by processes of adaptation within the country's different communities.

Recent estimates based on the 1991 census (Schuring 1993) indicate that approximately 45 per cent of the South African population have a speaking knowledge of English (the majority of the population speaking an African language, such as Zulu, Xhosa, Tswana, or Venda, as home language). The number of individuals who cite English as a home language appears to be, however, only about 10 per cent of the population. Of this figure it would seem that at least one in three English-speakers come from ethnic groups other than the white one (in proportionally descending order, from the South African Indian, Coloured, and Black ethnic groups). This figure has shown some increase in recent years.

THE COMING OF THE ENGLISH

Records indicate that English people made initial contact with southern Africa prior to the period of formal British colonization of the area (Silva 1996). From the sixteenth century onwards, for instance, English explorers and traders who visited the region began to introduce a vocabulary describing the land and its people.

More lasting experiences of the area are also on record during this early period (Burman 1986). In the late seventeenth century a group of English sailors was wrecked on the Natal coast, and settled (in the present region of the coastal city of Durban) amongst the native inhabitants (probably Zulu), by whom they were amicably received. The sailors learned the language and customs of the local people, and explored and traded extensively over a relatively large area. While some were rescued after a few years of what appears to have been an adventurous but comfortable life, a few remained behind, forming what could possibly be regarded—a hundred years before the formal commencement of British colonization—as the first permanent settlement of English-speakers in southern Africa. Xhosa oral lore also tells of English-speaking castaways (including a civilian woman by the name of Bessie) who were absorbed into a particular clan, apparently in the late eighteenth century. To this day there exists a Xhosa clan with the name 'abelungu', the Xhosa term for white people.

Besides these early encounters, three initial historical phases in the formal establishment of English-speakers in South Africa may be discerned (Lanham 1982):

1. Following Britain's initial occupation of the Cape Colony in 1795, the first major establishment in 1820 of approximately 4,000 British immigrants on farms along the Eastern Cape frontier. These settlers were mostly from southern England, and primarily of working-class or lower-middle-class backgrounds. During the formation of a classless frontier society with few attachments to the home country, a 'settler English' developed which merged features of the various English dialects originally spoken by the settlers (a strongly influential dialect being Cockney), and which also revealed features indicative of extensive interaction with the Dutch farming community already established in the area.

2. The second major settlement of approximately 4,000 British immigrants in the colony of Natal between 1849 and 1851. Unlike the 1820 settlers, these immigrants, the 'Byrne settlers', were typically of middle- and upper-middle-class origin, and predominantly from the north of England. This group also appears to have maintained stronger ties with Britain than did the 1820 settlers (Branford 1991).

3. From 1870 onwards, the discovery of gold and diamonds, and the industrial revolution, which led to further British immigration, extensive urbanization, and the emergence of a stratified urban society. In terms of variety of English, the most affluent class in this context was associated with an externally focused British standard—Received Pronunciation. The variety of English which had developed in Natal, however, emerged as the basis of a local norm for the aspiring middle class, while Eastern Cape English assumed a low status, and became associated with working-class speech.

LANGUAGE STATUS

English was declared the sole official language of the Cape Colony in 1822 (replacing Dutch), and the stated language policy of the government of the time was one of Anglicization of the region. On the formation of the Union of South Africa in 1910, which united the former Boer republics of the Transvaal and Orange Free State with the Cape and Natal colonies, English was made the official language together with Dutch (which was replaced by Afrikaans in 1925). During the height of the era of Afrikaner nationalism and apartheid, as well as after the establishment of the Republic of South Africa in 1961, this policy continued, the African languages being accorded no official status. However, in the 'independent homelands' (established as part of the apartheid policy of 'separate development'), English rather than Afrikaans was typically utilized by homeland authorities as an official language, together with one or more African languages of the region. Since the first democratic elections in 1994, under the terms of the new interim constitution English is now but one of eleven official languages in the 'new South Africa' (the others being Afrikaans, Zulu, Xhosa, siSwati, Ndebele, Southern Sotho, Tswana, Northern Sotho, Venda, and Tsonga).

THE INFLUENCE OF ENGLISH

English is presently established throughout South African society, amongst individuals from a variety of linguistic and ethnic backgrounds (although less so in the rural than the urban areas, and amongst the working class). Especially amongst the educated, English functions as a lingua franca, and is a primary language of government, business, and commerce. It is a compulsory subject in all schools, and is the preferred medium of instruction in most schools and tertiary institutions (the only other medium of instruction at advanced levels at present being Afrikaans). In terms of societal influence it is clear that English has spread far beyond the domain of those of British origin (Mesthrie 1993).

Amongst the African majority, English has typically been seen as the language of liberation and black unity (as opposed to Afrikaans, which has been perceived as the language of the oppressor). Very few Africans, however, presently reveal complete language shift to English away from African languages. While English functions as the language of prestige and power, an African language is typically maintained as a solidarity code. According to the latest census figures, while 33 per cent of Africans have a knowledge of English, only about 1 per cent cite English as a home language.

The initial spread of English amongst Africans took place during the colonial era, through mission education which enabled a high standard of English amongst a privileged minority. Subsequently, however, the apartheid policy in general, and the discriminatory Bantu Education policy in particular, resulted in a poor acquisitional context, with restricted access to English, and little opportunity to develop appropriate abilities in the language. Consequently a major educational and societal challenge has been to improve access to English amongst the African majority.

Amongst whites as a whole, 89 per cent appear to have a speaking ability in English. Amongst white Afrikaners, despite negative sentiments towards English earlier in this century, an ability in the language has become essential, given its general societal status and the lack of popular support for Afrikaans. Such speakers typically reveal superior abilities in English than native English speakers do in Afrikaans, and there is some evidence of language shift towards English amongst those who were previously Afrikaans-speakers.

For 'Coloureds' whose traditional language was Afrikaans, English has become increasingly influential since the early nineteenth century (Mesthrie 1993). While complete language shift to English *has* occurred in this group, this appears to be a trend only amongst more affluent and educated individuals. In total, 51 per cent of 'Coloureds' indicated a speaking knowledge of English in the 1991 census.

For South Africans of Indian origin there has been considerable language shift towards English, which has almost completely replaced the traditional Indian languages as home language. Census figures indicate that 99 per cent of South Africa's Asian population (the majority of whom are of Indian descent) know English.

English has also had a strong influence on the languages of South Africa, and an enormous stock of English words has been adopted into Afrikaans and the African languages. The pervasiveness of code-switching—the mixing of English and another indigenous language—is perhaps the strongest indication of the impact of English. Such mixing has for many speakers become a linguistic norm, reflecting a dual identity of membership of both the élite and the specifically African groups. Consider the following example of code-mixing, with Zulu, English (italics), and Afrikaans (bold), recorded in Soweto:

I-Chiefs isidle nge-*referee's optional time, otherwise* ngabe ihambe **sleg. Maar** *why* benga *stopi* this system *ye-injury time*? (Mfusi 1989: 31)

Chiefs [a local soccer team] have won owing to the referee's optional time, otherwise they could have lost. But why is this system of injury time not phased out?

VARIETIES OF ENGLISH

Given the discussion so far, it should be clear that there is presently considerable (and overlapping) variation in the manifestation of English in South Africa. First, one may distinguish between various 'ethnic varieties', such as 'Coloured', Black, South African Indian, and Afrikaans English, besides White South African English as traditionally defined. Each of these varieties in turn extends on a continuum from 'broad' to more 'cultivated' varieties (depending on the educational level and social status of its speakers), with these varieties becoming less distinct at higher levels of education. An additional overlay of variation is the distinction between first and second language varieties.

Amongst white English-speakers there has been a traditional threefold distinction between 'Conservative', 'Respectable', and 'Extreme' South African English (Lanham 1982). Conservative South Africa English is based on the (now dated) British norm of Received Pronunciation; Respectable English is an indigenously developed norm, typically found amongst the white English-speaking middle class; while Extreme South African English is associated with the lower classes and low educational levels.

Conservative South African English, as a variety based on externally rather than internally (and therefore ethnically) based norms, appears to have emerged as a prestigious variety or model across all ethnically based varieties. Many English newsreaders, no matter what their ethnicity, typically use something approximating this on radio and television. However, indigenously developed and more ethnically marked varieties, especially black accented English, appear to becoming more acceptable, and are increasingly found on television and radio news broadcasts.

INFLUENCES ON ENGLISH

Indigenization or nativization is the process through which a language is accommodated and adapted to its speakers and their circumstances. In a country where English is acquired and used in a variety of different contexts, as it is in South Africa, the indigenization of English reflects particular socio-historical processes which have resulted in the emergence of the varieties discussed above. As in other parts of the globe, therefore, 'new Englishes' have come into being in South Africa, reflecting the peculiarities of the South African situation and its people. Consider the following examples illustrating selected grammatical features of various varieties:

General South African English

(a) 'Busy' as a marker of the progressive: 'I'm busy cooking.'
(b) Reduplication of adverb 'now' as 'now-now', which denotes either 'immediately' or 'soon'.

African English

(a) Use of indefinite article before certain 'non-count' nouns: 'He was carrying a luggage.'
(b) Use of 'can be able' for 'can': 'I can be able to do it' (Gough 1995).

'Coloured' English

(a) Use of 'the dative of advantage': 'I'm gonna buy me a new car.'
(b) Use of 'do' or 'did' in unemphasized statements and questions: 'I did tell him to come.' 'Who did throw that?' (Mesthrie 1993: 31).

South African Indian English

(a) Use of 'y'all' as second person plural pronoun.
(b) Retention of ordinary question order in indirect questions with the verb 'be': 'I don't know what's that.' (Mesthrie 1989: 6).

THE FUTURE OF ENGLISH

Despite the popular support English has among the masses, there is an attitude among the intelligentsia that the dominance of English entrenches present unequal power relations in the country. It is held that English is not a neutral language, as some would believe, but that it effectively discriminates against the majority of the country's citizens. In South Africa such thinking appears to be reflected in a shift in state policy towards emphasizing multilingualism and the rights of indigenous languages against English as a prerequisite for democracy.

An alternative response to the simple rejection of English has been to valorize the indigenous varieties of English. As opposed to imposed, externally focused, standards, many authors have emphasized the future emergence of a specifically South African norm, reflecting influences and changes from the other languages of South Africa.

More generally, perhaps, understanding the future of English within South Africa is not so much a question of what variety of English will emerge, but rather of whether an appropriate learning context can be constructed which enables English to be a language of access and empowerment.

D. H. GOUGH

Department of Linguistics and English Language, Rhodes University

REFERENCES

Branford, W. R. G. 1991. 'Sociocultural factors and syntax'. Unpublished paper, Grahamstown: Rhodes University.

Burman, J. 1986. *Shipwreck! Courage and Endurance in the Southern Seas*. Cape Town: Human and Rousseau.

Gough, D. H. 1996. 'Black English in South Africa', in V. De Klerk (ed.), *English Around the World: Focus on Southern Africa*. Amsterdam: John Benjamins.

Lanham, L. W. 1982. 'English in South Africa', in R. Bailey and M. Görlach (eds.), *English as a World Language*. Ann Arbor: University of Michigan Press.

Mesthrie, R. 1988. 'South African Indian English: Some Characteristic Features', *English Usage in South Africa*, 19/1: 1–11.

—— 1993. 'South African English', *English Today*, 9/1: 27–33.

Mfusi, M. J. H. 1989. Soweto Zulu Slang: A Sociolinguistic Study. Hons. diss., University of South Africa.

Schuring, Gerhard K. 1993. 'Sensusdata oor die tale van Suid-Afrika in 1991'. Unpublished working document, HSRC: Pretoria.

Silva, P. M. 1996. 'Lexicography for South African English', in V. De Klerk, (ed.), *English Around the World: Focus on Southern Africa*. Amsterdam: John Benjamins.

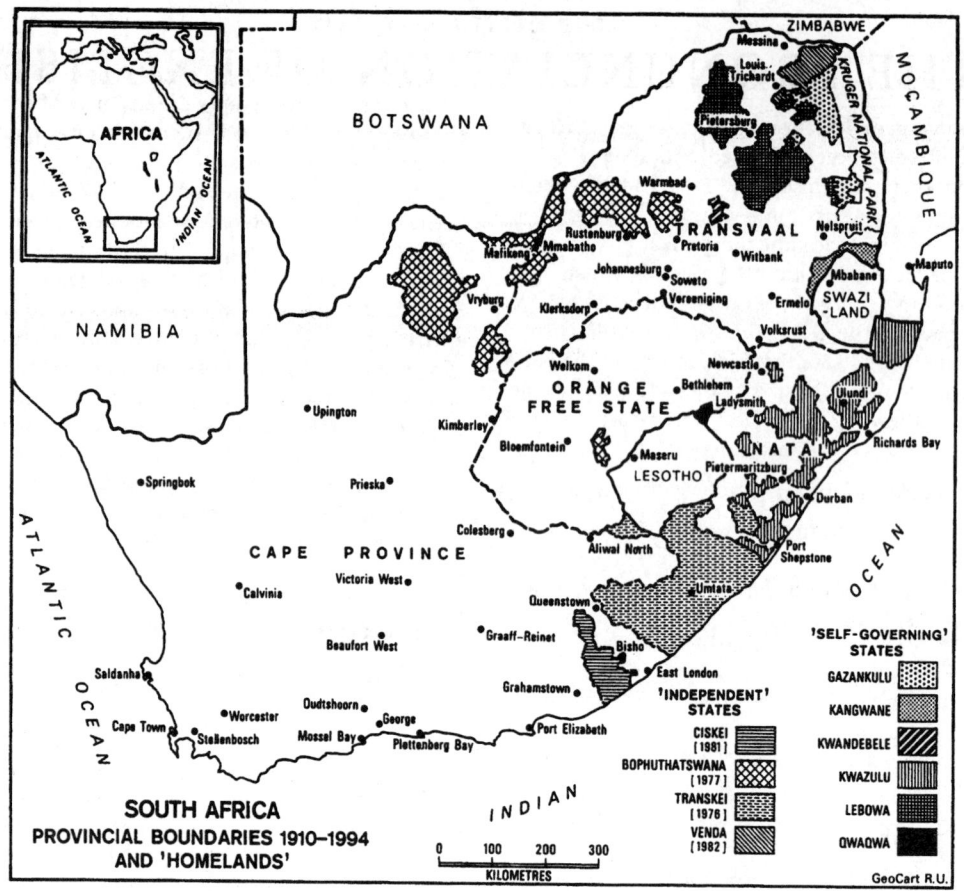

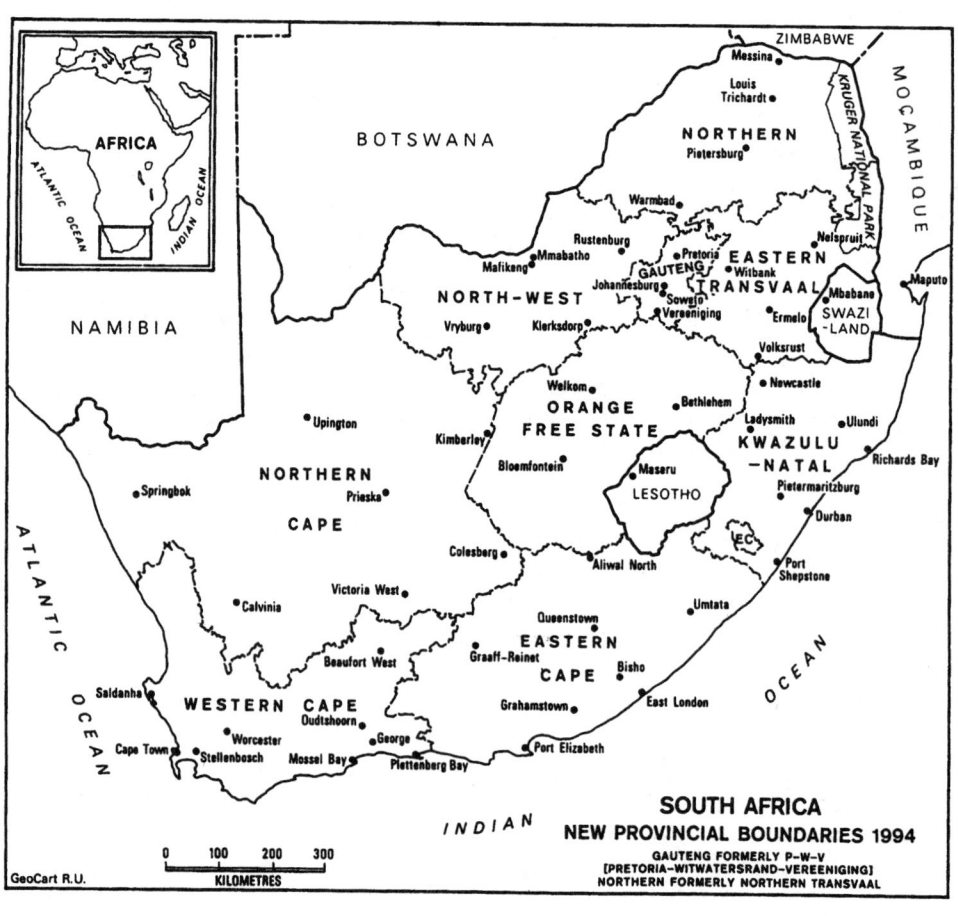

THE PRONUNCIATION OF ENGLISH IN SOUTH AFRICA

INTRODUCTION

There is no one, typical South African English accent as there is one overall Australian English accent. The variety of accents within the society is in part a consequence of the varied regional origins of groups of native English speakers who came to Africa at different times, and in part a consequence of the variety of the mother tongues of the different ethnic groups who today use English so extensively that they must be included in the English-using community.

The first truly African, native English accent in South Africa evolved in the speech of the children of the 1820 settlers who came to the Eastern Cape with parents who spoke many English dialects. The pronunciation features which survive are mainly those from south-east England with distinct Cockney associations. The variables (distinctive features of pronunciation) listed under A below may be attributed to this origin. Under B are listed variables of probable Dutch origin reflecting close association and intermarriage with Dutch inhabitants of the Cape. There was much contact with Xhosa people in that area, but the effect of this was almost entirely confined to the vocabulary. (The English which evolved in the Eastern and Central Cape we refer to as Cape English.)

The next large settlement from Britain took place in Natal between 1848 and 1862 giving rise to pronunciation variables pointing more to the Midlands and the north of England (List C). The Natal settlers had a strong desire to remain English in every aspect of identity, social life, and behaviour. Until well into this century, therefore, British English shaded into Natal English, an accent less well defined than Cape English. Of interest is the recent spread of certain features of Natal English through the community of native English speakers in South Africa.

Standard southern British English (SSB) (the so-called 'received pronunciation' of the well educated with high social status) became socially significant in South African society generally from 1880 onwards in the great flow of immigration from, mainly, Britain and Europe to the diamond- and gold-fields. In the new towns and cities in these areas it overshadowed all local 'Englishes' with a social meaning of authority and high social status in the stratified class societies which were evolving. It became the 'standard' to be imitated by all who aspired to higher status (Barney Barnato, the self-made mining magnate, was one of these). The social influence of SSB was retained in South Africa until the Second World War. Even in the 1960s and 1970s, news readers of the SABC were expected to speak in this way; a BBC correspondent as late as 1973 commented on the 'impeccably upper middle-class' accents of the announcers. In 1971 an English professor of Wits University commented cynically: 'The English-speaking population is touchy only in its uncritical reverence for received English pronunciation.' The sounds of most vowels and some consonants of SSB are indicated in the lists of pronunciation variables in the Key to Pronunciation.

There is a residue of South African English (*S. Afr. Eng.*) variables, not obviously traceable to origins associated with Lists A to C, which have a high incidence of occurrence; some serve to identify South Africans abroad. Termed General *S. Afr. Eng.* variables (List D), a number are probably products of trends in language change arising within the pronunciation system itself.

The English speech of the Dutch in the Western Cape had an accent at least as old as that of Cape English, strongly influenced by Dutch pronunciation—usually in coexistence with high levels of competence in every other aspect of English usage. Afrikaans English today ranges from an accent heavily impregnated with features of Afrikaans pronunciation to what is basically a native English accent with only traces of the hallmarks of Afrikaans English (Afk. E). The latter are found in List E below.

Black South Africans make up the largest body of English-users in South Africa with their own distinctive accent. African English (Afr. E) was initially a product of education in mission schools in the nineteenth century, mainly in the Cape, where an élite received a high-quality education. The industrialization of South Africa saw an ever-increasing number of people with a need for English and a growing number of private and state schools were meeting this need. Afr. E became self-fertilizing in the forty years of isolation created by apartheid and some obvious direct transfers from African-language pronunciation have hardened into an Afr. E pronunciation which the great majority of black South Africans are now using. A selection of the most prominent features is found in List F.

Indian English (Ind. E) was introduced by, or evolved within, the groups of indentured labourers and immigrants coming to Natal from 1860 onwards. Until well into this century, Ind. E pronunciation was characterized by variables typical of the Indian English of India. In recent generations, however, Ind. E has progressively moved away from the influence of Indian languages, coinciding with a shift to English as the language of the home. English is, in fact, the only language really known by younger South African Indians. The distinguishing feature of Ind. E today is the extent to which it excludes the most typical *S. Afr. Eng.* variables and approximates the local standard. Some surviving variables of Ind E which may be heard are given in List G.

The so-called Coloured community has had a use for English going back well into the nineteenth century. Col. E in the Western Cape is almost universally paired with Afrikaans in competent bilingualism and the majority of its many characterizing properties are similar to those of Afk. E.

THE VARIABLES OF S. Afr. Eng. PRONUNCIATION

Variables characterize accents and serve as differentials between different accents. As a term, 'variable' reflects the variation associated with each: the phonetic properties of a variable are present in different degrees of prominence in different idiolects (the speech patterns of individuals). Moreover, a variable may, idiolectally, vary in prominence according to situation, for example, between formal and informal occasions. In the varying degrees of prominence in different speakers, a variable is often a point where the language is changing, a 'phonetic trend' advancing in successive generations (as in variable C8 below), or receding (variable A5 below).

The variables listed below are shown in their association with social or regional groups, or, in two cases, their probable historical origins. They are selected for their significance in differentiating accent types. They are described according to their articulatory properties, for example the position of the tongue in the mouth. Where symbols are used (between slashes) they are those found in some recent British dictionaries, such as the *Collins English Dictionary*, and represent the vowel and consonant sounds of SSB. SSB was formerly a significant accent in South African society and, in that it still exercises some control over native English speakers, it is provided as a basis for comparison. It supplies reference-points in the phonetic (articulatory) description of the sounds of English in South Africa.

Note Most English diphthongs, such as /aɪ/ in *time*, have two vowel qualities, the first being a recognizable vowel, the second a gliding movement of the tongue away from the vowel in the direction of /ɪ/, for example, in the case of /aɪ/.

A. Variables of British origin in Cape English

Cape English provides the basis of Extreme South African English (Ext. S. Afr. Eng.) which is widely distributed in the society and is the most typically local of native English pronunciation patterns.

1. /ɑː/ in *Martin, pass*.
   Tongue further back than in SSB and raised with weak lip-rounding. *Martin* is heard as 'Morton', *garden* as 'Gordon'. (George Bernard Shaw spelt Cockney 'r' as 'aw'.)
2. /eɪ/ (SSB has a more central vowel than the /e/ shown here.)
   In *play, Cape*.
   Tongue lower and further back (approximating 'u' in *but*) with greatly weakened glide. (Cockney '*pline Jine*' for plain Jane.)
3. /əʊ/ in *no, show*.
   Initial vowel is, as in 2. /eɪ/, a central vowel followed by weakened glide with no lip-rounding. (Eliza Doolittle's 'nah' for *no*.)
4. /aɪ/ in *nice, why*.
   Tongue further back and raised towards 'o' of *pot*. Shortened glide. (Cockney 'moy' for *my*.)
5. /aʊ/ in *round, cow*.
   Tongue further forward and raised, close to SSB 'a' in *hat*. Glide is weakened and unrounded. This variable has receded greatly in the past half century.

B. Variables of probable Dutch origin in Cape English

6. /r/ (In SSB a resonant sound without trilling having no sound in post-vowel position—except if another vowel follows.)
   In *press, Grahamstown, really, hairy*: a single strike of the tongue against the upper teeth ridge, but can be a trill (rolled).
7. /p,t,k/ In SSB these are aspirated—released with audible breath flow—when introducing a stressed syllable.
   In *pattern, attack, conquer*: unaspirated as in Afrikaans (no free breath flow after release).

C. Variables associated with Natal

8. /aɪ/ in *nine, slide*.
   Glide is greatly weakened or completely lost and the vowel is more fronted and tenser. (*Five times five* heard as 'faav taams faav'.)
9. The backing, bunching, and possible lowering of the tongue in vowels before a following /l/, which is word-final or followed by a consonant.
   Most noticeable in:
   cold with a vowel similar to *cock*
   bell, elf, the latter sounding like 'Alf'
   cull with an effect similar to *cold* above
   milk with a vowel closer to /ʊ/
10. /ɜː/ in *hurt, Durban*.
    The tongue is raised and fronted with some lip-rounding.
11. /uː/ in *you, too*.
    The tongue is central and high with lip-rounding largely lost.

D. General S. Afr. Eng. variables

These variables are distributed widely in native English accent patterns in South Africa, being major contributors auditorily to the 'South African accent'. The source and phonetic development of these variables is less clear than those in other lists:

12. /ɪ/ in *spirit, limit, sit*.
    Central and lower tongue /ə/ in S. Afr. Eng.
    In S. Afr. Eng. /ɪ/ complements /ə/, occurring when adjacent to the consonants present in *kiss, sick, ring, rich* and after 'h' (*hit, his*) and when word-initial (*in*). There are exceptions to and variation in this complementation, notably either /ɪ/ or /ə/ in *pin, wind*. For /ɪ/ see variable 19.

13. /ɪ/ word-final in *happy, any* is /i/ which is raised, tenser and longer.
14. /ɛ/ in *head, bent*.
    Raised tongue; *yes* is heard as 'yis'.
15. /ɛə/ in *there, scarce*.
    The vowel is shorter, the glide is lost. The vowel is the same or similar to that in 14 /ɛ/.
16. Word-final, unstressed syllables in SSB *chicken, wanted, candid* are stressed (louder) and have a prominent lower central /ə/ vowel.
17. /ɔː/ in *forty, paws*.
    Raised tongue, shortened, more lip-rounding.
18. /ɔɪ/ in *boy, point*.
    Vowel similar to variable 17 with higher, tenser, more prominent glide.
19. /ɪ/ complementing /ə/, in *kiss, ring, hit*.
    Raised tongue, more front and tenser. Approaching Afrikaans 'ie' in *siek*.

E. Variables of Afrikaans English

20. High diphthongal glides /aɪ/, /əʊ/, /eɪ/. (See variables 2, 3, 4.)
    The glides are high and prominent, to /i/ and /u/. /a/ is low, fronted and tense. /ə/ and /e/ are, phonetically, low fully central /ə/.
21. /r/ (See variable 6.) In Afk. E it is trilled (rolled), but may be just a single strike of the tongue. It is sounded word-finally, and after a vowel before a consonant (*four, part*), which is distinctly Afk. E.
22. /h/ word-initial in *hair, hot*.
    /h/ is voiced as in Afrikaans with some breathiness.
23. Intrusive /h/ between vowels in sequence.
    (The /h/ is voiced and breathy.) As in 'cha(h)os', 're(h)act'.
    Often the only evidence of the Afrikaans mother-tongue in highly competent English-users, hence a shibboleth identifying Afk. E.
24. /æ/ in *carry, happy*.
    Tongue raised higher than /ɛ/: *cattle* heard as *kettle*.
25. /ɪ/ Tongue is high front and tenser /i/ in *ticket, rich*, complementing lowered, central /ə/ in *sit, little* as with the variable 12.
    In stressed monosyllabic words it may be a long vowel, e.g. *It is* is heard as 'Eat ease'.

F. Variables of African English

26. /ɜː/ (a central vowel in SSB and *S. Afr. Eng.*) in *sir, heard, nurse*.
    A front vowel close to SSB /e/ (*head*) substitutes in Afr. E together with loss of length hence *nurse* is heard as 'ness'.
27. The vowel length distinction of native English is lost in apparently random alternation of long and short versions of a vowel, hence:
    heat heard as 'hit'
    pull heard as 'pool'
    sport heard as 'spot'
    heart heard as 'hut'
28. Unstressed syllables with /ə/ quality in the last syllables of *teacher, wanted, enter*, and the first syllables of *attack, return*, are fully stressed with an /a/ quality vowel or a pronunciation spelling, hence:
    in *father* both syllables have the same vowel quality, the same stress and the same length; similarly *return* with the same two /e/-quality syllables.
29. /ɪ/ The central vowel /ə/ complementing /ɪ/ as described in variable 12 in, for example, *sit, simple, did*, is absent in Afr. E. Both are pronounced with /ɪ/ or tongue-higher /i/. Hence the variable in *live*, compounded with the loss of vowel length, is heard as 'leave'.
30. /æ/ in *cat, matter* has the /ɛ/-quality of African languages, hence the loss of distinctions such as *head : had* and *kettle : cattle*.

G. Variables of South African Indian English

31. Reduction of certain diphthongs. Most dipthongs in SSB and *S. Afr. Eng.* have prominence and length on the vowel before the glide. Ind. E reduces the vowel in length and prominence in an overall faster tempo.
    /aɪ/ in *my, five* is noticeably shorter with equal prominence to /a/ and /ɪ/.
    /eɪ/ in *Bombay, taking* is reduced to a pure vowel with the quality of phonetic /e/.
32. /v/ and /w/ in *vine, wine* are conflated in a labial articulation (the lips approaching each other) lacking both the friction of /v/ and the raising of the back of the tongue of /w/.
33. Shift in the main stress in words. Examples:
    'interested' instead of in*terested*,
    'celebrate' instead of *celebrate*.

DISTINGUISHABLE ACCENTS IN SOUTH AFRICA

SSB pronunciation conveyed high social prestige and correctness in speech behaviour to a wide sector of South African society until the Second World War. The ability to use and distinguish this accent from a 'local standard' is now given to but a few by virtue of age, British associations, or theatrical aspirations. The local standard, termed Conservative South African English, is recognizably South African, but remains close to SSB. However, a pronunciation pattern apparently conveying to post-war generations all the social meaning of Cons. *S. Afr. Eng.*, now includes the 'Natal variables' (List C). Variables C8 and 9 are advancing with considerable prominence in all native English communities in South Africa. Television commercials give evidence that in 1995 they have reached the speech of young children: 'faav' for five in the Stasoft commercial and 'Malrose' as the name of Melrose cheese. The term Respectable *S. Afr. Eng.* is applied to this version of local 'standard English' and the Natal variables widen the phonetic gap between SSB and Cons. *S. Afr. Eng.*

With a long history of social stigma, which the mining society firmly entrenched, Extreme *S. Afr. Eng.* comprises essentially the Cape English variables (Lists A and B) complemented by General *S. Afr. Eng.* variables (List D) and, variably, Afk. E variables. This accent type is receding in SA society; variables A5 and B6 have been significantly reduced in recent generations. It is maintained in groups which value the 'macho' image (schoolboys, in particular) and the 'typical South African' identity. It is still common in the older generations in the Eastern Cape where it has long been the local vernacular.

An overall Afk. E pronunciation pattern typified by the variables of List E is less and less the speech pattern of native speakers of Afrikaans. A growth in competent English–Afrikaans bilingualism coincides increasingly with native English accent types described above with, nevertheless, variables such as E23 often remaining as markers of descent-group identity. In the 1990s a uniform Afk. E pronunciation with all the variables of List E in prominence is likely to correlate with one, or a combination of, the following: age over 50 representing socialization at a time when the English–Afrikaans divide cut deepest into white South African society; low socio-economic status; residence in predominantly Afrikaans-speaking communities with little contact with native English speakers.

In the 1990s the English pronunciation of black South Africans (Afr. E) covers the whole range from virtually native English pronunciation of a small minority to a pronunciation pattern taken over almost entirely by African-language norms. Many intermediate versions exist, but the majority of idiolects present the characterizing variables in List F which are drawn from a central core of Afr. E pronunciation norms, being the variables most likely to mark even highly competent Afr. E.

With the ascendancy of English as the home language of the Indian community, Ind. E has rapidly shed its salient Indian-language features and in pronunciation approximates more and more to a local native English pattern. For the better educated this comes close to Cons. *S. Afr. Eng.* It is noteworthy that the Natal variables are not usually in evidence and there is little or nothing of Ext. *S. Afr. Eng.* Traces of the earlier Ind. E are found in the variables of List G which also occur in the English of India.

Variables for the English of the Coloured community are not listed although the pronunciation pattern is readily recognized in South Africa. The basis is Afrikaans, although there are characterizing variables of Coloured Afrikaans which, however, are not usually carried over into English. There is a good deal of variability within Col. E with certain Cape English variables, notably A3, to be found in the speech of those who would claim English as home language—usually in the higher socio-economic ranks. Col. E intonation remains the main characterizing feature which is not derived from English or Afrikaans. It is, in sound, the sustained high pitch of terminal syllables in assertions as well as questions.

L. W. LANHAM

Professor Emeritus
Rhodes University

KEY TO THE PRONUNCIATION

Pronunciation is given using the symbols of the International Phonetic Alphabet.

The pronunciations given here are those in use in the educated speech of South Africans whose home language is English. The illustrative examples given have been taken, as far as possible, from the general English vocabulary; for notes on how the South African pronunciation of these words differs from that of the educated speech of southern England (the 'Received Standard'), see page xxi.

I. CONSONANTS

b, d, f, k, l, m, n, p, t, v, z *have their usual English values.*

/g/ *as in* go /gəʊ/
/h/ *as in* ho! /həʊ/
/r/ *as in* run /rʌn/, terrier /'terɪə/
/(r)/ *as in* her /hɜː(r)/
/s/ *as in* see /siː/, success /sək'ses/
/w/ *as in* wear /wɛə/
/j/ *as in* yes /jes/
/θ/ *as in* thin /θɪn/, bath /bɑːθ/
/ð/ *as in* then /ðen/, bathe /beɪð/
/ʃ/ *as in* shop /ʃɒp/, dish /dɪʃ/
/tʃ/ *as in* chop /tʃɒp/, ditch /dɪtʃ/
/ʒ/ *as in* vision /'vɪʒn/
/dʒ/ *as in* judge /dʒʌdʒ/
/ŋ/ *as in* singing /'sɪŋɪŋ/, think /θɪŋk/
/ŋg/ *as in* finger /'fɪŋgə/

Not found in general English use

x *as in* Afk. gaan /xɑːn/, berg /bɛrx/, Ger. ach /ax/, Sc. loch /lɒx/
c *as in* Afk. liedjie /'lici/
/ɬ/ *as in* Zulu hlala /'ɬala/, Welsh Llanelly /ɬa'neɬi/
/ʄ/ *as in* Zulu indlela /in'ʄeːla/

Symbols in parentheses are used to denote elements that may be omitted either by individual speakers or in particular phonetic contexts: e.g. bottle /bɒt(ə)l/, bedonnerd /bə'dɒnə(r)t/. Final (r) indicates that some speakers articulate this sound even when it is followed by a consonant: e.g. broeder /'brudə(r)/.

II. CLICKS

/ǀ/ dental, *as in* Zulu cela /ǀela/ (similar to the English sound of disapproval, 'tsk, tsk')
/ǂ/ palatal, *as in* Zulu qala /ǂaːla/
/ǁ/ lateral, *as in* Zulu xola /ǁɔːla/ (similar to the clicking sound made to encourage a horse)

III. VOWELS AND DIPHTHONGS

Short

/ɪ/ *as in* pit /pɪt/
/e/ *as in* pet /pet/
/æ/ *as in* pat /pæt/
/ʌ/ *as in* putt /pʌt/
/ɒ/ *as in* pot /pɒt/
/ɔ/ *as in* Xhosa Pondo /'pɔːndɔ/
/ʊ/ *as in* put /pʊt/
/ə/ *as in* another /ə'nʌðə/
/(ə)/ *as in* beaten /'biːt(ə)n/
/i/ *as in* Afk. riem /rim/, Zulu indaba /in'daːba/, Fr. si /si/
/a/ *as in* Afk. man /man/, Zulu amasi /a'maːsi/, Fr. mari /mari/
/œ/ *as in* Afk. rus /rœs/
/u/ *as in* Afk. boet /but/, Fr. douce /dus/
/y/ *as in* Afk. nuut /nyt/, Fr. tu /ty/
/ɛ/ *as in* Afk. berg /bɛrx/, Fr. sept /sɛt/

Long

/iː/ *as in* bean /biːn/
/ɑː/ *as in* barn /bɑːn/
/ɔː/ *as in* born /bɔːn/
/uː/ *as in* boon /buːn/
/ɜː/ *as in* burn /bɜːn/
/eː/ *as in* Afk. venster /feːnstər/, Zulu indlela /inʄeːla/, Ger. Schnee /ʃneː/
/aː/ *as in* Afk. vader /'faːdər/, Zulu lala /'laːla/, Ger. Tag /taːk/
/yː/ *as in* Afk. suur /syːr/, Ger. grün /gryːn/

Diphthongs, etc.

/eɪ/ *as in* bay /beɪ/
/aɪ/ *as in* buy /baɪ/
/ɔɪ/ *as in* boy /bɔɪ/
/əʊ/ *as in* no /nəʊ/
/aʊ/ *as in* now /naʊ/
/ɪə/ *as in* peer /pɪə/
/eə/ *as in* pair /peə/
/œɪ/ *as in* Afk. muis /mœis/
/iœ/ *as in* Afk. keur /kiœr/
/ʊə/ *as in* tour /tʊə/
/aɪə/ *as in* fiery /'faɪərɪ/
/aʊə/ *as in* sour /saʊə/

The incidence of main stress is shown by a superior stress mark /'/ preceding the stressed syllable, and a secondary stress by an inferior stress mark /ˌ/, e.g. Bamangwato /ˌbamaŋ'gwaːtɔ/. A mark under a consonant indicates a syllabic consonant, e.g. /m̩'biːzɔ/.

C. N. MULLER

STYLING CONVENTIONS

Some entries may deviate from the conventions outlined below, which are provided only as a general guide to the use of this dictionary.

Entries are in alphabetical order. Capital letters, apostrophes, hyphens, and spaces between words are not taken into account when alphabetizing entries. A complex entry is subdivided first by part of speech and then by sense. Elements of an entry are given in the following order (an entry not necessarily containing every element):

Headword. An entry begins with a headword, the central form of the word which is the subject of the entry. The headword is given in large bold roman against the left-hand margin. The initial letter is not capitalized, unless the word normally has an initial capital. If two spelling forms enjoy similar support, they may share headword status. A word may have separate entries for its different parts of speech. Such headwords are distinguished by their part of speech, and are normally arranged in the sequence *n.* (and *adj.*) before *v.* If two or more headwords have the same spelling and the same part of speech, superscript numerals are introduced. One main entry is chronologically before another; a cross-reference is before a main entry.

The symbol ‖ precedes any item not fully assimilated into South African English (*S. Afr. Eng.*).

Pronunciation. The pronunciation of a headword is given in International Phonetic Alphabet notation (see previous page), between slashes. The standard *S. Afr. Eng.* pronunciation is given first. Notes on pronunciation may be given as part of the etymology of the word (where orthography is affected), or as a separate encyclopædic note.

Part of speech. A part of speech is given in italics after the pronunciation, and is normally abbreviated. One entry may have many parts of speech. A part of speech may also accompany subordinate entries such as phrases and derivatives.

Labels. Labels are in italic, followed by a full stop. A label which informs all senses follows the initial part/s of speech; one which informs a single sense precedes that sense. Specialist subject labels are always capitalized; other labels have a small initial letter, but may be capitalized to avoid confusion between part of speech and label. Currency labels (e.g. *obs. exc. Hist.*) precede labels indicating specialist subjects (e.g. *Diamond-mining, Mineralogy, Pathology*); these are followed by labels of attitude (e.g. *offensive, derog.*), register (e.g. *slang, colloq.*), and frequency (e.g. *rare*). Offensive and derogatory terms, while included, have been clearly marked as such.

Variant spellings. Variant spellings are listed alphabetically in bold roman after the part of speech (and label); they are preceded by 'also'. Variant spellings which contain brackets appear where they would if the brackets were omitted. Only clearly aberrant spellings are excluded from the list. Significant differences in initial and medial capitalization are noted, but hyphenation is generally unremarked. Current variant spellings may be given before those no longer in use. Variant spellings may also be grouped (as 'Forms') according to distinctive patterns of development: variant spellings in each group are given in alphabetical order, and groups are given in chronological order. Each group is identified by a Greek character (α, β, etc.), and substantiated by a unique set of citations. Not every variant spelling is supported by the citations shown.

Singular and plural forms. If a word does not follow a standard English pattern of plural formation, the plural form is listed in bold roman after the variant spellings, preceded by 'pl.'. Where multiple plural forms occur, the more common forms are given first. An entry is normally under the most common singular form of the word, even if one or more of the plural forms appears to be more widely used. Where singular and plural forms have different prefixes, cross-references have been provided; there are also entries for many of the more common prefixes. If a headword has many plural forms as well as many singular forms, and some of these are used interchangeably in *S. Afr. Eng.*, a division into groups marked '*sing.*', '*sing.* and *pl.*', and '*pl.*' replaces a list of variant spellings (although the most common plural form may still be given first). The entry is supported by a single set of citations.

Etymology. The etymology of a word is given in square brackets. An etymology which informs all senses of a headword is given before any subdivision of the entry. An etymology which is specific to a single sense is given before the definition for that sense. The full etymon (primary or root word) is given in italics or, if itself a main entry, in small capitals.

Definition (signification). The definition of a headword is given in roman; it may be a single unit, or divided into many senses. Stylistic information is given with the definition, and may include reservations about the use of the word (e.g. 'Not in polite use'), information about who uses it (e.g. 'Esp. among South Africans of Indian descent'), regional usage (e.g. 'In KwaZulu-Natal'), etc.

Ordering of senses. Each entry is chronologically arranged, first by part of speech and then by sense. If a headword has many senses, each sense is preceded by a number or letter in bold; each sense begins on a new line, on the left-hand margin, and is followed by a set of citations. If it is unclear which sense a citation supports, continuous senses are followed by a single set of citations.

Within an entry, a capital letter (**A**, **B**) is used for each part of speech represented by the headword, and an arabic numeral (**1**, **2**) for each sense within that group; if the distinction between these senses is a fine one, lower case letters (**a**, **b**) may be used instead of arabic numerals. Senses marked **1**, **2** may have subdivisions (marked **a**, **b**), and further subdivisions (marked **i**, **ii**). The italic lettering (*a*), (*b*) is used for the divisions encountered under combinations or collocations, as well as for further subdivisions. Numbered senses which fall into distinct semantic or other patterns may be grouped by large roman numerals (**I**, **II**).

Inflected forms. Where variation in the termination of a word results in distinctive diminutive, feminine, comparative, or superlative forms, these may be given in bold roman immediately after the main definition, or as an encyclopædic note.

Combinations and collocations. Combinations and collocations of which the headword is the main (or first) element are listed at that headword, in bold roman. They may be given as a separate subdivision, or immediately after the main definition. The headword is repeated within each combination or collocation. If a combination requires more detailed treatment, or is independent of the bulk of the entry, it is listed as a separate entry.

Phrases. Phrases of which the headword is the main element are listed at that headword, in bold italics. They may be a separate subdivision, or continuous with the main definition.

Derivatives. Derivatives formed by the addition of a simple suffix (e.g. -ly, -ness) are treated as subordinate items. They are given in their place in the entry in bold roman, preceded by 'Hence' or 'So'. Most derivatives are in a separate, unnumbered section at the end of an entry, followed by a single chronologically arranged set of supporting citations. A part of speech is provided for each derivative.

Cross-references. A definition may include cross-references. A cross-reference to a main entry is in small capitals, and one to a subordinate item is in italic (followed by the relevant main entry, in small capitals). In a cross-reference, the relevant numbered sense is always specified in plain type; the part of speech is given only if this is necessary to distinguish the main entry being referred to. A cross-reference has the same capitalization as the entry to which it refers. If multiple cross-references are provided, synonyms are given before less closely related words; within each group of cross-references, items are arranged alphabetically. This dictionary contains three main types of cross-reference:

If there is exact synonymy between headwords, only one headword is defined. A list of synonyms follows the definition; each of these synonyms is defined only by cross-reference to that headword, although (if ambiguity is possible) the scientific name of the referent may be repeated. Derogatory and offensive words have individual definitions and no cross-references.

If there is a strong link—but not full synonymy—between words, this is indicated by 'cf.' (compare). 'Cf.' is also used if a headword is better understood by contrasting it with another headword.

If crossing to another headword will provide useful (or complementary) information, a cross-reference is introduced by 'See also'.

Encyclopædic notes. An encyclopædic note is used to expand upon any item of information given. It is in a smaller typeface, indented from the left hand margin.

Citations (quotations). Citations form the basis for the definitions provided, and are given in a smaller typeface than these definitions. Sets of citations illustrate the historical use of each word from its earliest recorded occurrence up to the present day. An effort has been made to provide a reasonably spaced sequence of citations for each headword, and to validate the date of utterance or publication provided for each citation. For each sense (or subdivision thereof), citations are arranged in chronological order. The first citation in each set is indented from the left-hand margin. The date is given in bold typeface; where a date of death has been used, sources are dated 'ante' the date of death, and where external evidence has led to the determination of a probable date of publication, sources are dated '*circa*' that year. Wherever possible, the person actually responsible for the citation is named in small capitals: this includes the author of a work published in a periodical or in an edited collection of material. Where an institution was the issuing source, the title of the work is given first, followed by the name of the institution in roman in parentheses. Published titles are italic, unpublished titles roman (followed by a full stop). Informal sources are in italic, and may be preceded by a named source person. Although most sources referred to in citations are listed in more detail in the Select Bibliography, the short reference used in the citation is usually sufficient to identify the text or edition used. Where the date of utterance differs from the date of publication of the edition used, the latter is given in round brackets immediately after the title. The numbering of volumes and parts (or sections) reflects the numbering used in the source documents: these are either in upper- and lower-case roman, or in arabic numerals preceded by 'Vol.' and 'No.' respectively. A page number is given wherever possible. Although extraordinary typefaces have been standardized on italic and some extraneous material has been omitted (omissions are indicated by an ellipsis), care has always been taken to remain true to the author's intent.

W. D. DORE

ABBREVIATIONS

Abbreviations which are listed below in italic may sometimes be printed in roman type, and vice versa. They may also appear with or without an initial capital, depending on their context.

Some abbreviations which are common in English (and whose meaning is readily understood) are excluded from this list. Where two or more abbreviations occur as a group, reference should be made to each element.

If a full form and its abbreviation both end with the same letter, the end stop has generally been omitted. Plural forms are included in this list.

Abbreviation	Meaning
a (before a date)	before, not later than
abbrev.	abbreviated, abbreviation (of)
absol.	absolute, -ly
Acct	account(s)
ad.	adaptation (of)
adj.	adjective, -tival
adjs	adjectives
Admin.	administration
adv.	adverb, -ial
advs	adverbs
advt	advertisement
Afk.	Afrikaans
Afk. E	Afrikaans English
Afr.	Africa, -n
Afr. E	African English
Agric.	agriculture, -al
Amer.	American
A.N.C., ANC	African National Congress
Ann.	annual, annals
anon.	anonymous
Anthropol.	anthropology, -ical
app.	apparently
App.	Appendix
Archeol.	archeology
Archit. (as label)	in architecture
Archit. (in titles)	architecture, -al
Assoc.	association, associated
attrib.	attributive, -ly
Austral.	Australian
Autobiog.	autobiography, -ical
Biog., Biogr.	biography, -ical
bk(s)	book(s)
Bot.	botany, -ical
Brit.	British, Brittanica
Brit. Eng.	British English
Bros.	brothers
c (before a date)	circa
C. (as 19th C.)	century
Catal.	catalogue
Cent.	century
cf.	compare
Chem.	chemical
Chron.	chronicle(s)
Civ.	civilization(s), civilized
Co.	company
cogn.	cognate
Col.	colony, -ies, colonial
Col. E	Coloured English
Coll., Collect.	collection
colloq.	colloquial, -ly
comb.	combination(s), combining
Comm.	committee
Commiss.	commission
Compar.	comparative
Cons. S. Afr. Eng.	Conservative South African English
Constit.	constitution, -al
Contemp.	contemporary
Contrib.	contribution
Corresp.	correspondence
Cycl.	cyclopædia
Decentral.	decentralization
Dept	department
derog.	derogatory, derogatorily
Descr.	description(s)
Dev.	development
dial.	dialect, -al
Dict.	dictionary
dim.	diminutive
Dir.	directory
Dis.	diseases
Disc.	discovery, -ies
Doc.	documentary, document(s)
Du.	Dutch
E.	East, -ern
Econ.	economic(s), economy, economical
ed.	edition, editor, edited
Edin.	Edinburgh
eds	editors
Educ.	education, -al
ellipt.	elliptical, -ly
Encycl.	encyclopedia
Eng.	English
Engin.	engineers, engineering
Environ.	environmental
E. Prov.	Eastern Province (South Africa)
Equat.	Equatorial
erron.	erroneously
esp.	especially
Esq.	esquire
Est.	establishment, established
et al.	and others
etc.	and the rest
etym.	etymology, -ical
exc.	except
Exec.	executive
Exped.	expedition(s)
Explor.	exploration(s), exploratory
Ext. S. Afr. Eng.	Extreme South African English
fem.	feminine
fig.	figurative, -ly
fr.	from
Fr.	French
freq.	frequent, -ly
Furn.	furniture
G.	German
Gard.	gardeners'
Gaz.	gazette
Gen.	general
Geog., Geogr.	geography, geographic, -al
Geol.	geological
G.H.	Good Hope
Gk	Greek
Gloss.	glossary
Govt	government
Gt	great
Hist. (as label)	in a historical context
Hist. (in titles)	history, -ical
Hort., Horticult.	horticulture, -al
Hse	house
Ibid.	in the same book or passage
i.e.	that is
I.L.A.M.	International Library of African Music, Grahamstown
Illust.	illustrated, illustrations
imp.	imperative, -ly
Imp.	imperial
Ind.	India, -n
Ind. E.	Indian English
Indust.	industry, -ies, industrial
Info.	information
Inst.	institute
int.	interjection, -al
Int.	interior
Internat.	international
intrans.	intransitive, -ly

ABBREVIATIONS

Intro., Introd.	introduction	*Parl.*	parliamentary	*sc.*	namely
It.	Italian	part.	partial	*Scot.*	Scottish
		perh.	perhaps	*Sci.*	science, scientific
(Jeffreys)	quoted from M. D. W. Jeffreys: see Bibliography	pers.	person, -al	Sect.	section
		Pers.	Persian	Sel.	select, -ed, selection(s)
		(Pettman)	quoted from C. Pettman: see Bibliography		
Jhb.	Johannesburg			Sep.	separate
joc.	jocular, -ly			sing.	singular
Jrnl(s)	journal(s)	Pg.	Portuguese	Sn	southern
		Phil.	philosophical	Soc.	society, social
K.W.V.	*Ko-operatieve Wijnbouwers Vereniging* (Co-operative Winegrowers Association)	Philol.	philological	sp.	spelling, species (singular)
		Philos.	philosophical		
		phr(r).	phrase(s)	Sp.	Spanish
		Pict.	pictorial	*spec.*	specific, -ally
		pl., *pl.*	plural	spp.	species (plural)
		Pl.	plate	SRC	Students' Representative Council
		pl. n. (phr.)	plural noun (phrase)		
L.	Latin	Pop.	popular		
Lang.	language(s)	ppl adj.	participial adjective	SSB	Standard Southern British English
Lett.	letters	pple	participle		
Ling.	linguistic(s)	Prac.	practical	St	Saint
Lit.	literary, literature	prec.	preceding (word or entry)	Stat.	statute(s), statutory
loc.	locative			Std	standard
Ltd	limited	*pref.*	prefix	Str.	street
		Pref.	preface	subsp.	subspecies
m.	metre	prep.	preposition	suff.	suffix
Mag.	magazine	prob.	probably	Suppl.	supplement
Mem.	memoirs, memorial, memories	Proc.	proceedings	*S.W. Afr.*	South-West Africa, -n
		Proclam.	proclamation	(Swart)	quoted from C. P. Swart: see Bibliography
Meth.	Methodist	Prog.	progress		
Mil.	military	pron.	pronoun		
Misc.	miscellaneous, miscellany	Prov.	Province		
		Pty	proprietary	tr.	translation (of), translator, translated
ml	millilitre				
Mod.	modern	Quart.	quarterly		
		quot., quots	quotation(s)	Trad.	tradition(al)
n.	noun			trans.	transitive
N.	North, -ern	R.	royal	Trans.	transactions
Napac	Natal Performing Arts Council	Rd	road	transf.	transferred (sense)
		Rec.	record(s)	Trav.	travels, traveller
Narr.	narrative, narration	Ref.	reference	Treas.	Treasury
Nat.	national, natural	Reflect.	reflections	Treat.	treatment
N.E.L.M.	National English Literary Museum, Grahamstown	Reg.	register, regulation(s)	trs	translators
		Regul.	regulation(s)	Tvl	Transvaal
No.	number	Rel.	relations	U.K.	United Kingdom
nr	near	rel. to	related to	Univ.	university
ns	nouns	Reminisc.	reminiscences	unkn.	unknown
N.U.M.	National Union of Mineworkers	Rep.	report, representative	U.S.(A.)	United States (of America)
Nusas	National Union of South African Students	Rep. of S. Afr.	Republic of South Africa	usu.	usually
		Res.	residence	v.	verb, -al
N.Z.	New Zealand	Rev.	review	var(r).	variant(s) of
		rev.	revised	vbl n.	verbal noun
obs.	obsolete			Vet.	veterinary
Observ.	observation	S.	South	Vol.	volume
occas.	occasionally	S. Afr.	South Africa, -n	vols	volumes
OED	*Oxford English Dictionary*, 2nd edition	S. Afr. Du.	South African Dutch	Voy.	voyage(s)
		S. Afr. Eng.	South African English		
Off.	Official	S.A.I.R.R.	South African Institute of Race Relations	W.	West, -ern
O.F.S., OFS	Orange Free State			Yr(s)	year(s)
Ord.	Ordinance(s)				
orig.	original, -ly	S.A.R. & H.	South African Railways & Harbours	Zoo., Zool.	zoology, -ical
P.A.C.	Pan-African(ist) Congress				
		Sat.	Saturday		

PROPRIETARY NAMES

This dictionary includes some words which are or are asserted to be proprietary names or trade marks. Their inclusion does not imply that they have acquired for legal purposes a non-proprietary or general significance nor any other judgement concerning their legal status. In cases where the editors have some evidence that a word is used as a proprietary name or trade mark this is indicated, but no judgement concerning the legal status of such words is made or implied thereby, and accordingly the editors disclaim and disavow any liability arising from the inclusion of such words.

AAC /eɪ eɪ 'siː/ *n. hist.* Initial letters of *All-African Convention*, a confederation of black political movements founded in 1935 to co-ordinate resistance to Prime Minister J.B.M. Hertzog's bills for the disenfranchisement of the Cape's black voters. See also HERTZOG BILLS.

Later absorbed by the Non-European Unity Movement (see NEUM).

[1935 *Rand Daily Mail* 17 Dec. 20 About 400 delegates from all parts of the Union .. are attending a special all-African Convention in the Bathu Location, Bloemfontein, to discuss the Native Bills.] 1941 C.A. KUSE in *Bantu World* 1 Mar. 4 We will have no constituted cooperation with political organisations like the A.A.C. 1959 E. MPHAHLELE *Down Second Ave* 188 It was later in 1955 that I joined the African National Congress (ANC). I had for some years been torn between it and the All-African Convention (AAC). 1963 M. BENSON *Afr. Patriots* 86 Another question that disrupted African unity was whether the A.A.C. should continue. Despite hot opposition from A.N.C. leaders, Jabavu obtained majority support in advocating its permanence ... The emergence of this rival organization, coming on top of the A.N.C.'s failure to lead the opposition to the Hertzog bills, shocked some of its members into a decision. 1989 *Reader's Digest Illust. Hist.* 339 The threat to the Cape vote provoked a broad revival of African political activity, and on 16 December 1935, more than 400 delegates from every corner of South Africa .. gathered in Bloemfontein for the founding conference of the All-African Convention. The leading lights of the AAC were Professor Davidson Jabavu and Dr Alfred Xuma.

aag var. AG.

aai-aai var. AI-AI.

aalie var. ARLIE.

aandblom /'ɑːntblɔm/ *n.* Forms: α. **avondbloem, avond-bloom, avont-bloem**; β. **aandblo(e)m, aantblom**. Also with initial capital. Pl. -me, -s, or unchanged. [Afk., earlier S. Afr. Du. *avondbloem*, fr. Du. *avond* evening + *bloem* flower.] Any of several species of plant of the Iridaceae having flowers which exude a strong scent at dusk and in the evening, esp. those of the genera *Gladiolus* (see GLADIOLUS), *Hesperantha*, and *Ixia* (see IXIA); AANDBLOMMETJIE; EVENING FLOWER.

α. 1795 C.R. HOPSON tr. *C.P. Thunberg's Trav.* I. 286 The *Ixia cinnamomea* (*Avondbloem, Canelbloem*) opens every evening at four, and exhales its agreeable odours through the whole night. 1822 W.J. BURCHELL *Trav.* I. 186 It being then nearly dusk, the delightful fragrance of the Avond-bloem (evening flower) began to fill the air, and led to the discovery of the plants. 1834 *Makanna* (anon.) II. 149 The rich jasmine-like fragrance of the 'avond-bloem', came in luscious breathings from the more deep and shadowy glens. [1847 J. BARROW *Reflect.* 218 Above all .. must be noticed a beautiful little humble ixia, which the Dutch call the *avond-bloom* (the evening flower); it is the modest *Ixia cinnamomea*, which, having concealed itself during the day within its brown calyx, now expands its small white blossoms, and perfumes the air, throughout the night, with its fragrant odour.] 1890 [see IXIA]. 1904 *Argus Christmas Annual* (Cape Colony Sect.) 20 The scent of the avond-bloom, whose modest brown bells perfume the air. 1913 H. TUCKER *Our Beautiful Peninsula* 92 The sanguine-stained 'painted lady,' as she usurps with her flaunting gaiety the slopes over which her sad-hued, divinely-scented cousin, the avondbloem, held inconspicuous sway. 1927 *Chambers's Jrnl* (U.K.) Mar. 190 Wild flowers, from the stately arum lily .. to the modest *avondbloem*, which at night perfumed the whole veld with its fragrance.

β. 1890 A. MARTIN *Home Life* 21 Another of our favourites was the *aantblom* .. whose lovely flowers range through all possible shades of rose-colour and orange, from the deepest to the palest tints of pink and yellow, down to the purest white. 1932 *Grocott's Daily Mail* 9 Jan. 3 The flowers which form the subject of these delightful fantasies are Flames, Morning Flowers, Aandbloems. 1964 J. MEINTJES *Manor House* 35 The exotic aandblom, or evening flower, which opened at night and permeated the house with its delicious fragrance. 1988 LE ROUX & SCHELPE *Namaqualand* 58 *Hesperantha bachmannii*, Aandblom. This plant name has changed from *Hesperantha angusta* ... Found in Namaqualand .. and also eastwards to Somerset East. *Ibid.* 150 *Sutera tristis*, Aandblom, .. The flowers give off a strong scent at dusk. 1991 *Weekend Post* 6 Apr. (Leisure) 7 In the Tsitsikamma we used to find aandblomme growing in profusion amongst the grasses on the sandy flats near the mouth of the Groot River ... The blooms of *G. liliaceus* are brownish in colour, changing to purple or mauve in the evenings when they also have a very strong perfume. Another aandblom (*Gladiolus tristis*) has pale cream or greenish-yellow blooms with purple or brown markings running from the tips of the petals into the throat of the bloom. They become heavily scented at night.

aandblommetjie /'ɑːntˌblɔməki/ *n.* Formerly also **avond-bloemetjie, avond-blommetje, avond-bloomje**, etc. [Afk. *aandblom*, see prec. + -IE.] AANDBLOM.

1861 'A LADY' *Life at Cape* (1963) 10 As we pause upon these heights .. the scent of the avond bloemetjies is fragrant in the air. 1868 W.H. HARVEY *Genera of S. Afr. Plants* 375 *Hesperantha*, .. Colonial name 'Avondbloomjes'. 1902 H.J. DUCKITT in M. Kuttel *Quadrilles & Konfyt* (1954) 15 The hills overlooking Groote Post are scented of an evening with lovely sprays of *avond bloemetje*, or evening flower. 1906 B. STONEMAN *Plants & their Ways* 197 *Hesperantha*, ('Avond-Bloemetjes') ... Flowers white or yellow. The sepals frequently red outside. Delightfully scented at evening when their insect guests are abroad. 1915 R. MARLOTH *Flora of S. Afr.* IV. 145 *H. falcata* (Avond bloemetje, generally pronounced 'aandbloem'). 1917 — *Common Names* 3 Aandblom, (Avond-blommetje). Several sweet-scented Iridaceae, especially species of *Hesperantha* ... At the Knysna and further east the name — is applied to *Gladiolus tristis*, which is scentless in daytime, but exhales a strong perfume in the evening. 1927 *Farming S. Afr.* 171 How often does one see .. the beautiful 'painted ladies' or 'aandblommetjies' adding scent to the garden in the evening. 1970 [see EVENING FLOWER]. 1974 *Motorist* Aug. 35 No less imaginative were the names of some of the flowers — vetkousies, weeskindertjies, aandblommetjies and duikerwortel. 1982 A. MORIARTY *Outeniqua Tsitsikamma* 62 *Hesperantha falcata*, Aandblommetjie. Found in grassy clearings in the forests around George ... *Hesperantha lutea*, Geel aandblommetjie .. bears bright yellow flowers with tan colouring on the back of the outer tepals. *Ibid.* 70 *Gladiolus permeabilis*, .. Aandblommetjie.

‖**aanneming** *n. obs.* Also **anneming**. [Afk.] Confirmation or admission to church membership in the Dutch Reformed Church.

1851 R. GRAY *Jrnl of Bishop's Visitation* II. 23 It happens to be the Sunday appointed for their 'aanneming,' or confirmation, which is without the imposition of hands. 1868 W.R. THOMSON *Poems, Essays & Sketches* 170 The time of *aanneming* approaches. Both are passed as fit candidates for the church. 1871 J. MACKENZIE *Ten Yrs* (1971) 19 In one family there may be children for baptism; children for 'aanneming,' or admission to church-membership, and children who are now men and women who are going to be married. 1909 H.E.S. FREMANTLE *New Nation* 228 All over South Africa the Dutch Church applies an ingenious but effective compulsion of its own, by declining either to admit to confirmation (anneming) young people who cannot read and write, or marry those who have not been confirmed.

aantblom var. AANDBLOM.

aapjesdoorn var. APIESDORING.

‖**aapsekos** /'ɑːpsəkɔs/ *n.* Formerly also **aapsekost, aap z'n kost**. [Afk., *aap* ape + possessive particle *se* + *kos* food; see quot. 1977.] KERSHOUT sense 2.

1913 C. PETTMAN *Africanderisms* 18 Aapsekost, .. *Gardenia Rothmannia*. 1917 R. MARLOTH *Common Names* 3 Aap z'n kost, Gardenia Rothmannia. An eastern forest tree with large white flowers and large woody fruit. 1970 M.R. LEVYNS in *Std Encycl. of Sn Afr.* I. 1 Aapsekos, Kershout. Candlewood. (*Rothmannia capensis* = *Gardenia capensis*). Its flower is creamy white, with dark spots in the tube, and it has a heavy, sweet scent. The inedible fruit is large and globose and woody. 1977 E. PALMER *Field Guide to Trees* 291 Aapsekos, .. Fruit eaten by baboons and monkeys, hence common names, aapsekos meaning 'monkeys' food', and bobbejaanappel 'baboon apple'. 1984 R.J. POYNTON *Characteristics & Uses of Sel. Trees* 105 Aapsekos .. *Rothmannia capensis*.

aar *n. obs.* [Afk., transf. use of Du. *aar* contracted form of *ader* vein.] An underground watercourse, often indicated on the surface by greener or stronger plant growth.

1872 E.J. DUNN in A.M.L. Robinson *Sel. Articles from Cape Monthly Mag.* (1978) 40 On the road .. we are quite amazed at the number of 'water aars' that traverse the country in all directions — some marked by lines of bushes, others by low ridges of black rock. [1893 H.A. BRYDEN *Gun & Camera* 443 Here in limestone formation they had, even in time of drought, a good water supply, which, by opening up fresh veins ('aars,' the Boers call them), they had largely augmented.] 1906 *Education Gazette* Vol.6 No.2, 28 The farmers of the Karoo have long used differences of vegetation as surface indications of dolerite dykes or water *aars.* **1920** F.C. CORNELL *Glamour of Prospecting* 74 In the stone-strewn aars that are a feature of this country these little birds take advantage of their marvellous protective colouring.

‖**aarbossie** /ˈɑː(r)bɔsi/ *n.* Formerly also **aarbosje.** [Afk., *aar* underground watercourse + *bossie* (earlier *bosje,* see BOSCHJE) bush.] Any of several plants supposed to flourish above artesian rivers, including *Selago* and *Walafrida* of the Selaginaceae, *Limeum* (Aizoaceae), *Oligomeris* (Resedaceae), and *Pollichia* (Illecebraceae); WATER-FINDER. Cf. *vleibos(sie),* see VLEI sense 2.

1896 R. WALLACE *Farming Indust. of Cape Col.* 87 The aarbosje, or 'water-finder', *Selago leptostachya* .. is a useful forage plant for goats, being a stand-by in times of drought. [**1902** *Patriot-Woordebk* (1968) 1 *Aarbossi,* .. Schrub [*sic*] showing underground watercourses.] **1906** F. BLERSCH *Handbk of Agric.* 254 The valuable schaap boschjes belong to the Pentzia group, and the aar boschje most praised has the scientific name Selago leptostachya. **1913** C. PETTMAN *Africanderisms* 18 *Aarbosje,* .. *Selagolepta stachya* .. sometimes called 'water-finder' .. generally grows above an underground watercourse. **1917** R. MARLOTH *Common Names* 3 *Aarbossie,* .. Sub-shrub of the Karoo, growing preferably in localities holding subterranean water, hence often found along underground fissures or dykes where water circulates. **1966** C.A. SMITH *Common Names* 55 *Aarbossie,* In the eastern Karoo, the name used in a 'generic' sense for plants .. from their alleged preference for habitats said to overlie subterranean water in a fissure or artery. **1975** *S. Afr. Panorama* Jan. 36 Some of the flora which are indigenous to the proposed Karoo parks ... Aarbossie (waterfinder bush) [etc.].

aarde-wolf var. AARDWOLF.

aardroos /ˈɑː(r)truəs/ *n.* Pl. **-rose** /-ruəsə/. [S. Afr. Du., *aard* earth + *roos* rose.]

1. Any of several plant parasites, esp. *Cytinus sanguineus* of the Rafflesiaceae and *Hyobanche sanguinea* of the Scrophulariaceae, with vividly-coloured red flowers projecting just above the ground near the host plant. See also EARTH-ROSE, *skilpadblom* (SKILPAD sense b).

1795, 1809 [see EARTH-ROSE]. **1913** C. PETTMAN *Africanderisms* 19 *Aardroos,* .. Thunberg applies this name to *Phelipaea sanguinea,* but it is now applied — and much more appropriately as far as colour is concerned — to the thick-stemmed, rosy-red, root parasite, *Hyobanche sanguinea.* **1970** M.R. LEVYNS in *Std Encycl. of Sn Afr.* I. 2 *Aardroos,* (*Cytinus sanguineus.*) A parasite, of the family *Cytinaceae,* which lives on the roots of a number of different plants which act as hosts. It has no green leaves, and its .. flowers are orange or scarlet. They appear close to the host.

2. Any of several species of dwarf PROTEA, esp. *P. acaulos.*

1965 S. ELIOVSON *S. Afr. Wild Flowers for Garden* 265 *P[rotea] minor.* Aardroos ... This species was only discovered about 10 years ago in the Bredasdorp and Caledon divisions of the south-western Cape. **1966** C.A. SMITH *Common Names* 56 *P[rotea] minor* .. *P. acaulos* and *P. aspera* are the original aardroos of the district and the name is said to date from about the middle of the 18th century. **1984** BOND & GOLDBLATT *Plants of Cape Flora* 372 Protea .. acaulos (L.) Reichard — (*aardroos*); shrub with trailing branches from underground rootstock, flowers yellow to pink.

aardvark /ˈɑːdfɑːk/ *n.* Forms: α. **aardvaark, aardvark, aard-varké, aard-varken;** β. **erdvark, erdverk.** Also with initial capital. Pl. **-s, -e,** or unchanged; (*obs.*) **-en.** [S. Afr. Du., fr. Du. *aarde, erd* earth + *vark* pig. (The modern Afk. form is *erdvark.*)] The ant-eater *Orycteropus afer* of the Orycteropodidae, an insectivorous burrowing mammal of nocturnal habits with a long, tapering muzzle and sparsely-haired body; ANTBEAR; ANT-EATER sense 1; EARTH-HOG; EARTH-PIG. Also *attrib.*

α. **1786** G. FORSTER tr. *A. Sparrman's Voy. to Cape of G.H.* I. 270 The *aard-varken,* or earth-pig, which, probably, is a species of *manis.* **1795** [see ANT-EATER sense 1]. **1827** G. THOMPSON *Trav.* II. 86 The Aardvark is about four feet and a half in length, and occasionally is found to weigh upwards of 100 lbs. It .. lives entirely upon ants. **1847** J. BARROW *Reflect.* 146 The aard-varké, or earth-hog (the *Myrmecophaga Capensis*), is also very common, undermines the ground, and seldom appears but in the night. **1878** T.J. LUCAS *Camp Life & Sport* 86 In the category of strange creatures to be found in this district, I must not omit the ant-bear, or 'aard-vark' (earth pig), which not only inhabits the frontier, but is spread over all parts of the interior. **1896** R. WALLACE *Farming Indust. of Cape Col.* 68 They [*sc.* termites] are greedily sought after and *devoured* .. by a large ungainly looking quadruped with a long snout, called the ant-eater or 'aard-vark.' **1901** W.L. SCLATER *Mammals of S. Afr.* II. 220 The aard-vark .. use their tails to thump the ground near the ants' nest and so cause a panic within .. make an opening in the side of the ant-heap and then collect the ants by means of their sticky tongues. **1929** [see ANT-EATER sense 1]. *c***1936** *S. & E. Afr. Yr Bk & Guide* 1101 Nearly every ant-heap in the karroo has a widely gaping mouth on its Southern side, this point of attack being selected by the *aard vark,* either because it is next to the habitation of the queen-ant or because the structure is not baked quite as hard as where it is exposed to the full rays of the sun. **1949** H.C. BOSMAN in L. Abrahams *Unto Dust* (1963) 149 He was the kind of white man who, if he was your neighbour, would think it funny to lead the Government tax-collector to the aardvark-hole that you were hiding in. **1988** C. & T. STUART *Field Guide to Mammals* 162 The Aardvark resembles no other mammal occuring in southern Africa, with its long pig-like snout, elongated tubular ears, heavily muscled kangaroo-like tail and very powerful, stout legs which terminate in spade-like nails. **1990** J. KNAPPERT *Aquarian Guide to Afr. Mythology* 19 *Aardvark,* In African folklore the aardvark, or ant-bear, has a good name not only because it is unafraid of armies of soldier ants but also because it digs diligently searching for food all night, an example and model for lazy cultivators. **1991** M. NEL in *Personality* 11 Mar. 26 Like the Aardvark's sense of smell for ants, Nick's knowledge of theatre is intuitive.

β. **1796** E. HELME tr. *F. Le Vaillant's New Trav.* III. 392 This ant-bear is called in the colonies *erd-verken* (earth hog). **1924** [see ANTBEAR]. **1959** L.G. GREEN *These Wonders* 207 That creature of obscure origin, that champion tunneller of the veld, the erdvark or ant-eater. This pig-shaped freak is not rare, but is seldom captured.

aardwolf /ˈɑː(r)tvɔlf, ˈɑːdwʊlf/ *n.* Also **aardewolf,** and with initial capital. [S. Afr. Du., fr. Du. *aarde* earth + *wolf* wolf. (The modern Afk. form is *erdwolf.*)] The hyaena-like mammal *Proteles cristatus* of the Protelidae, which feeds mainly on insects; *maanhaar jackal,* see MAANHAAR. Cf. WOLF *n.*[1]

1833 *Penny Cyclopaedia* I. 4 The genus proteles contains but a single species, the *Aard-wolf,* or earth-wolf (*Proteles cristata*), so called by the European colonists in the neighbourhood of Algoa Bay, in South Africa ... The size of the aard-wolf is about that of a full-grown fox. **1835** A. STEEDMAN *Wanderings* II. 114 In its habits and manners the Aard-wolf resembles the fox: like that animal it is nocturnal, and constructs a subterraneous burrow, at the bottom of which it lies concealed during the daytime. **1871** [see TIGER-WOLF]. **1881** P. GILLMORE *Land of Boer* 205 There is a very pretty little hyaena to be found up in these localities, called by the natives 'aard-wolf.' .. It is about the size of a jackal, possesses a bright fawn-coloured coat, handsomely marked with black lines. **1900** W.L. SCLATER *Mammals of S. Afr.* I. 82 The aard wolf .. is a slow animal and can be run down by an active man, and is easily outpaced by dogs. **1913** C. PETTMAN *Africanderisms* 20 *Aardwolf,* .. An animal about the size of a fox, occupying an intermediate position between the jackals and the hyenas. *c***1936** *S. & E. Afr. Yr Bk & Guide* 1072 The *Aard-wolf* (*proteles cristatus*), often called 'maanhaar jackal', stands about 18 inches in height and is of a brown colour with a few dark markings. **1973** *Farmer's Weekly* 9 May 10 In this territory, there is a long list of protected game .. Aardwolf, bat-eared fox, dikdik. **1980** J. HANKS *Mammals* 52 *Aardwolf, Proteles cristatus.* Dog-like carnivore with a sloping back ... Mainly nocturnal, but may be seen at any time of the day. **1982** *S. Afr. Panorama* Jan. 39 Also extremely rare is the aardwolf whose continued existence is dubious. **1988** *Grocott's Mail* 29 Jan. 3 The aardwolf is a particularly interesting carnivore, not only because it feeds almost exclusively on termites but also because, throughout its African distribution, it feeds primarily on termites of the genus Trinervitermes.

aarlie var. ARLIE.

aaskies var. EKSKUUS.

‖**aasvoel** /ˈɑːsfʊəl/ *n.* Forms: α. **aars-vogel, aasvogel, asphogel, asse vogel, assvogel, astvogel, asvogel;** β. **aasvoel, aasvoël.** [fr. Afk. *aasvoël,* earlier Du. *aasvogel* (pl. *-vogelen*) *aas* carrion + *voël, vogel* bird.]

a. Any of several vultures, esp. the Cape vulture *Gyps coprotheres* of the Accipitridae, but occas. the whitebacked vulture *G. africanus.* Also *attrib.,* and *fig.* See also *Cape vulture* (CAPE sense 2 a).

α. **1834** A. SMITH *Diary* (1939) I. 149 29 Piet Whitefoot had .. said that the white men were like crows and aasvogels; that though many were together the approach of one man caused them all to fly. **1838** —— *Jrnl* (1975) 243 A neighbouring chief .. had arrived with the Asse vogels (warriors) to beg for meat. [*Note*] It is customary, we found, to call the warriors Asse vogels, especially when they are begging meat from the king. **1852** H. WARD *Jasper Lyle* 2 Like any demons waiting for their prey, the asphogels, the gigantic vultures of South Africa, keep watch over the bivouac. **1853** F.P. FLEMING *Kaffraria* 70 Called by the Hottentots the Astvogel, which answers to the .. Sociable Vulture, in plumage and colour. **1878** T.J. LUCAS *Camp Life & Sport* 221 The hideous asvogels or common vultures were so gorged that they cared only to tear out the eyes here and there. **1886** [see GEDAAN sense 1]. **1890** A. MARTIN *Home Life* 250 The aasvogel, a repulsively ugly, bald-headed, bare-necked bird of the .. vulture type, is very common in South Africa. **1899** G.H. RUSSELL *Under Sjambok* 222 The men of this country are like the aars-vogel .. that feeds upon it. [**1908** HAAGNER & IVY *Sketches* 1 The Aasvogel of the Boers. Birds with an unprepossessing appearance and an evil smell, they are, nevertheless, exceedingly useful in clearing the veld of carrion.] **1913** J.J. DOKE *Secret City* 103 If I don't find her to-morrow, .. I'll shoot you, like an aasvogel that you are! **1925** F.C. SLATER *Centenary Bk of S. Afr. Verse* (1946) 232 *Aasvogel,* Large vulture ... Head and upper parts of neck dirty white; back and wings ashy mottled with brown. Scarce now. **1931** G. BEET *Grand Old Days* 16 The aasvogel has the credit of being the most long-sighted bird in the world. **1957** D. GRINNELL-MILNE *Baden-Powell at Mafeking* 66 Only the haunting notes of the Last Post sounded across the quiet veld, where the scavenging *aasvogel* picked the bones of dead horses. **1979** E. DRUMMOND *Burning Land* 100 They also heard the desolate cries of the *aasvogels* as they circled high above a distant spot, waiting to descend on whatever lay breathing its last below them.

β. **1935** H.C. BOSMAN *Mafeking Rd* (1969) 21 Overhead a lonely aasvoël wheeled, circling slowly round and round without flapping his wings. **1948** A.C. WHITE *Call of Bushveld* 133 Farmers who adopt the abhorrent practice of poisoning wildebeest or zebra carcasses to thin out lions, hyenas and jackals, exterminate a number of aasvoëls at the same time ... The latter serve an excellent purpose as scavengers and do little harm. **1968** K. MCMAGH *Dinner of Herbs* 27 On the distant horizon a pall of dust still hung curtaining the sky while aasvoels flapped their wings and fought over the wealth of carrion. **1976** S. CLOETE *Chetoko* 34, I am not a welcome figure. I even know what I am called. Coetzee the *aasvoël*. It is not easy to be an undertaker. **1985** *Style* Oct. 55 In exile the mind would roam through .. the wide wheel of the aasvoel, a witgat tree.

b. With defining words designating various species of aasvoel, as **black -, koning -** /ˈkʊənəŋ -/ [Afk., *koning* king], **swart -** /swart -/ [Afk., *swart* black], **white aasvoel**: see quots.

α. **1839** W.C. Harris *Wild Sports* 196 *Vultus Fulvus*, and *Vultus Auricularis*: White and **Black Aas-vogel** of the Cape Colonists. [**1908** Haagner & Ivy *Sketches* 4 There is another fairly well-known species, the Black Vulture, called by the Boers the **Koning Aasvogel** (King Vulture) .. which is considerably scarcer than the ordinary Aasvogel. c**1808** C. von Linné *System of Natural Hist.* VIII. 11 The Dutch colonists call this species *swarte aas vogel*, dark carrion-bird.] **1913** C. Pettman *Africanderisms* 577 *Zwart aasvogel*, .. *Otogyps auricularis*. See Koning aasvogel. **1839** [white aasvoel: see quot. at black aasvoel above].

AB /ei'bi, ɑː'biə/ *n.* [Initial letters of *Afrikaner Broederbond.*] Broederbond sense 1.

1972 *Evening Post* 30 Sept. 8 There is a periodic outcry against the Afrikaner Broederbond (AB for short), which, it is alleged, controls the Government. **1981** *E. Prov. Herald* 23 Apr. 2 To vote for Nats is to support AB-dominated Govt, says Smuts. **1990** *Sunday Times* 15 July 18 The AB is yesterday's issue. So it is curious that Mr Hans S— should have elevated it into a principle justifying his resignation from the DP.

aba- /aba/ *pref.* A Xhosa and Zulu plural noun prefix found in some words originating in these languages, sometimes shortened to **ba-**.

For examples, see abakwetha, abalumbi, mlungu. In Xhosa and Zulu, the singular of words beginning *aba*- is formed by replacing this prefix with *um*- or *umu*-; in *S. Afr. Eng.* this pattern is not always observed, and words in the plural form are sometimes treated as singular nouns, an *-s* being added to form the English plural. See also um-.

abafana pl. form of umfaan.

abafazi pl. form of umfazi.

abafundis(i) pl. form of umfundisi.

abakhaya pl. form of mkhaya.

abakhulu pl. form of mkhulu.

abakweta dance var. kwetha dance.

abakwetha /ˌabaˈkweːtə, -ta/ *n.* Pl. usu. unchanged, or *-s*. Forms: α. **amakweta, amaquati, amaqueta, magwetha, makweta, maqueta, maqweta** (pl. unchanged or -s); β. **abakhwetha, abakweta, abakwetha, bakweta** (pl. unchanged or -s); γ. **mkhwetha, mkweta, mkwetha, umkhwetha, umkwetha** (pl. unchanged or -s); **khwetha, kweta, kwetha** (pl. -s). [Xhosa *abakhwetha* such initiates (sing. *umkhwetha*). For notes on the variety of pl. forms, see aba-, ama-, ba-, ma- pref.³, m-, and um-.]

1. Freq. used collectively. A Xhosa initiate to manhood, ritually circumcised and isolated from other people for a prescribed period. Also *attrib.* See also ikhankatha, ikrwala, tshila. Cf. intonjane.

The rare unprefixed forms usu. appear in *attrib.* contexts.

α. **1833** S. Kay *Trav. & Researches* 75 In the afternoon we strolled over the plain to a neighbouring hamlet to see the *amaquati*, or circumcised. **1835** A. Steedman *Wanderings* I. 54 A number of boys confined within a circular enclosure, whose bodies were daubed over with white clay .. the *Amaquati*, or newly circumcised, who are not permitted, for a certain period after the operation, to associate with the other inhabitants of their village. **1966** I. Vaughan *These Were my Yesterdays* 40, I knew something outrageous would come of this junketing around with cloaks and daggers like makwetas or hula dancers. **1970** S.E. Natham *Informant, Cape Town* Amaqueta. Young African (Xhosa) man going through period of initiation. **1971** *Sunday Times* 11 Apr. (Suppl.) 6 Still trying to spot those amakwetas? No woman must see them during their initiation. **1973** *E. Prov. Herald* 23 Jan. 8 On another occasion the script called for Boesman and Lena to walk past two 'maquetas' in the dry Scabi riverbed. **1985** L. Sampson in *Style* Dec. 44 He has a few tribal scars painted across his face with Maqweta paint. **1989** *Grocott's Mail* 17 Mar. 1 A group of magwethas .. were going through initiation exercises on the farm.

β. **1860** W. Shaw *Story of my Mission* 460 The sons of Christian natives, who have attained the age considered suitable for circumcision, almost invariably seek an opportunity to desert their homes and join one of the parties of *abakweta*. **1866** W.C. Holden *Past & Future* 183 Which state of initiation is called ubukweta, the boys themselves being termed abakweta. **1891** *Stat. of Cape of G.H.* 1889–93 (1894) 254 Act To prohibit the Native Dances known as the 'Abakweta' and 'Intonjane' Dances. **1920** S.M. Molema *Bantu Past & Present* 122 The young men who were undergoing the rites were known as makoloanyane among the Bechuana, and abakweta among the Xhosa-Zulu peoples. **1955** J.B. Shephard *Land of Tikoloshe* 59 Until their wounds are healed Abakhwetha do no work, but later .. they help to herd cattle but do not mix with the younger Khwedinis. **1976** *Daily Dispatch* 20 Aug. (Suppl.) 4 According to the custom, the initiates or 'Abakhwethas', were not supposed to appear in public. **1978** *Post* 20 July 1 Mr Tambo was lured by companions to go to the 'Mguyo' dance — a drinking party for the 'Abakhwethas'. **1993** *Daily Dispatch* 6 Aug. 11 (caption) These abakhweta were .. sauntering down the main road near Bridle Drift Dam, East London.

γ. **1937** B.J.F. Laubscher *Sex, Custom & Psychopathology* 84 At the *Abakweta* ceremony particular attention is paid to acts of disobedience of which the *mkweta* has been guilty during his childhood years. **1967** J.A. Broster *Red Blanket Valley* 126 The initiation period lasts two to three months, and during this time the initiate or umkhwetha (plural abakhwetha) lives in isolation in a specially constructed grass hut. **1978** *Daily Dispatch* 17 Aug. 8 A 'Mkhwetha' has died .. after allegedly eating poisonous food at a circumcision school in the bush. **1980** E. Joubert *Poppie Nongena* 41, I grew up with these customs. I took food to a young buti — when he was um-kwetha. **1988** *E. Prov. Herald* 13 Feb. 3 Protests against the presence of an initiate (mkhwetha) as a State witness led to the postponement of a trial in the Port Elizabeth Regional Court this week.

δ. **1950** A.W. Burton *Sparks from Border Anvil* 181 The 'Kwetas' went into seclusion in the forest.

2. Among Xhosas: the initiation period or ritual symbolizing passage into manhood; ubukwetha. Also *attrib.* See also circumcision sense 1.

β. **1937** C. Birkby *Zulu Journey* 282 'Abakweta' initiation ceremony in the Transkei, with the novices wearing reed masks and skirts. **1937** [see γ quot. at sense 1]. **1973** *Prog. through Sep. Dev.* (Info. Service of S. Afr., New York) 14 An important milestone in a tribal society is a young man's initiation into manhood. The Xhosa call this ritual the Abakwetha which is part of youths' education. **1979** *E. Prov. Herald* 2 Feb. (Indaba) 2 Some go so far during their abakhwetha period to attend functions, appearing there well-dressed before returning to the bush. **1980** E. Joubert *Poppie Nongena* 41 The most important of these beliefs is the abakwetha, or the man-making ritual. Ibid. 42 We never knew what they did to the boys in the bush, that they can cut the foreskin to make men of them. We just knew it was abakwetha.

γ. **1955** J.B. Shephard *Land of Tikoloshe* 60 His khwetha blanket, his grass hat and even the hut where he had sheltered, were burned to ashes, symbolizing the obliteration of his past. **1991** *Settler* Vol.65 No.1, Only after initiation does he play any part in tribal life. He is recognized as a man after he has attended Khwetha school.

Hence **abakhwetha** *v. trans.*, (*passive*) to undergo initiation into manhood.

1970 S.E. Natham *Informant, Cape Town* Quedien. Young African (Xhosa) man before he has been amaqueted. **1993** J. Bursey *Informant, Grahamstown* From the Saturday morning, after they've been 'abakwethed', they're not allowed to drink anything until he comes back to change the dressing for them.

abalongo, abalo(o)ngu pl. forms of mlungu.

‖**abalumbi** /ˌabaˈlʊmbi/ *pl. n.* Also **abberlomba**, and with initial capital. [Zulu, 'wonder-workers, magicians', pl. prefix aba- + -lumbi one who does wonders, fr. *lumba* do wonders.] A term (formerly) used by black people of whites, alluding to their technological and scientific achievements.

1887 A.A. Anderson *25 Yrs in Waggon* II. 144 The natives state the gold was worked and the forts built by the white men that once occupied this country, whom they called Abberlomba (men who made everything). **1956** A. Sampson *Drum* 156 There is a large vocabulary of African words to describe Europeans, including *abalumbi* (magicians), *izinjada* (wildcats), and the Zulu phrase *abandlebe zikhanya ilanga*, meaning 'those whose ears reflect the sunlight.' **1962** M. Brandel-Syrier *Black Woman* 128 The God of the Europeans is the new great witchdoctor, more potent, knowledgeable and accessible .. than the old Gods; the God from whom, no doubt, Europeans derive their 'strength' ... One of the words for Europeans is *Abalumbi* (magicians).

abalungu pl. form of mlungu.

abaMbo pl. form of mbo.

abangoma pl. form of sangoma.

Abantu, abaNtu varr. bantu *n.* sense 1.

abanumzane pl. form of umnumzana.

aba-s-eMbo, Abasembu pl. forms of mbo.

abatagati pl. form of tagati *n.*

Abatembu pl. form of tembu.

abathakathi pl. form of tagati *n.*

abba /ˈæbə, ˈabə/ *v. trans.* [Afk., ad. Khoikhoi *awa*.] To carry (a child) on one's back. Also *attrib.* Found most often in speech.

1913 C. Pettman *Africanderisms* 21 Abba, .. To carry on the back as a mother does her child. [**1945** L.G. Green *Where Men Still Dream* 135 Each section of the plant, as it grows, carries another section on its back as it were, and the Bushmen called it in their language the 'Abba' plant because it reminded them of the manner of their women in carrying babies in skin sacks on their backs.] **1971** P.J. Silva *Informant, Grahamstown* You look tired — I wish I could abba you all the way home. **1974** *S. Afr. Panorama* Apr. 39 The name given to this new industrial growth point is Babelegi, a word which in Setswana is derived from 'abba': to carry a baby on one's back ... At Babelegi industrialists and workers really 'abba' each other. [**1978** *Argus* 19 Apr. .. The word abba .. has an interesting rebirth in the recent use of the term 'abbahart' in Afrikaans for the piggy-back heart operation.] **1986** D. Case *Love, David* 75 Had David not been carrying Stumpy, he would surely have abba-ed me at least part of the way. **1991** B. Dean *Informant, Kenton-on-Sea* (*Eastern Cape*) Another girl, abbaing her baby on her back, went and sat with the boys.

abberlomba var. abalumbi.

‖**abdas** /ˈabdas/ *n.* [fr. Pers. *ābdast* ablution before prayer, *āb* water + *dast* hand.] In the Cape Muslim community: the ritual washing of a corpse.

1937 *Argus* in I.D. Du Plessis *Cape Malays* (1944) 30 The ceremonial ablution known as *abdas* then follows. The body is washed and persistently massaged with hot water until all the limbs are as soft and pliant as those of a living person. **1949** E. Hellmann *Handbk on Race Rel.* 595 A bench and a bath are brought into the room, and the corpse, its face towards Mecca, is washed and cleaned. These ablutions are known as *abdas*. **1953** DU PLESSIS & LÜCKHOFF *Malay Quarter* 39 The clothes of the dead man are removed and the body washed. This ceremonial ablution is known as *abdas* or *ayer sumbaiyang* is used for the purpose. **1985** *S. Afr. Panorama* Jan. 24 The death of a Cape Malay is an occasion of profound solemnity ... After death follows the ablution ceremony, the *abdas*.

abe- /abe/ *pref.* A Xhosa and Zulu plural noun prefix found in some words originating in these languages.

For an example, see MLUNGU. In Xhosa and Zulu, the singular of words beginning *abe-* is formed by replacing this prefix with *um-* or *umu-*; in *S. Afr. Eng.* this pattern is not always observed, and words in the plural form are sometimes treated as singular nouns, an *-s* being added to form the English plural. See also UM-.

abe(h)lungu pl. form of MLUNGU.

ablou, hasie, aboel, hasie see HASIE sense 3.

absolution *n. Law.* In full *absolution from the instance* [tr. Du. *absolutie van de instansie*]: a form of judgement by which allowance is made for the re-institution of proceedings once further evidence has been obtained (the plaintiff's claim not having been established to the satisfaction of the court).

1892 C.J. DE VILLIERS in H. Juta *Index to Cases in Supreme Court of Cape of G.H.* (1973) IX. 279 It has never been understood that a defendant is bound to accept absolution from the instance if the evidence given at the trial is of such a nature as to entitle him to judgement in his favour. In such a case he would .. be quite entitled to object to absolution. **1896** *Stat. of Natal* (1900) Act 39 of 1896, 11 The Judge presiding at a trial with a jury shall be entitled, if he considers there is no evidence upon which a jury may reasonably find for the plaintiff, to withdraw the case from the jury and enter a judgement of absolution from the instance in favour of the defendant. **1910** *E. Prov. Herald* 8 June, Unless he was satisfied on this point it was absolutely no use to go on with the proceedings any further. There must be absolution from the instance, with costs. **1934** C.P. SWART *Supplement to Pettman*. 1 *Absolution from the instance*, .. A form of judgement granted, where the plaintiff has not established his claim to the satisfaction of the court, enabling him, on obtaining better evidence, to institute proceedings de novo. **1960** J.J.L. SISSON *S. Afr. Judicial Dict.* 5 By long practice in the courts of South Africa *absolution from the instance* has acquired a wider range than it possessed in the Dutch courts. The latter courts confined this form of judgement to those cases in which a plea in abatement would be successfully pleaded according to the practice of the English courts. **1970** *Rand Daily Mail* 12 Nov. 3 He granted the plaintiff absolution from the instance, which means that the woman might at some other time, and in changed circumstances, re-open her case. **1987** *E. Prov. Herald* 20 Mar. 1 He gave a judgement of 'absolution', meaning that should Mr B– be able to bring evidence that Mrs P-'s husband knew about the contract, he could present it to the court.

absolve *v. trans. Law.* In full *absolve (someone) from the instance* [see prec.]: to grant (a defendant) provisional acquittal, pending a possible re-institution of proceedings.

1844 *Graham's Town Jrnl* 10 Oct. 3 Defendants absolved from the instance with costs, – subject to review by the Supreme Court. **1982** A.P. BRINK *Chain of Voices* 521 The Court consequently absolves the 10th prisoner Pamela from this instance. **1990** *E. Prov. Herald* 9 Feb. 1 The couple were absolved from the instance by the magistrate at the end of evidence by members of the congregation.

abuti var. AUBUTI.

accrual *n. Law.* In full *accrual system*: the system which applies to a marriage out of community of property in terms of an ANTENUPTIAL CONTRACT, by which (at the dissolution of that marriage) the spouse whose estate shows no financial growth, or less than that of the estate of the other spouse, may claim half of the difference between the accrued values of the respective properties from that spouse.

The system was introduced in terms of the Matrimonial Property Act of 1984.

1984 *Act 88* in *Govt Gaz.* Vol.229 No.9322, 3 At the dissolution of a marriage subject to the accrual system, .. the spouse whose estate shows no accrual or a smaller accrual than the estate of the other spouse, .. acquires a claim against the other spouse or his estate for an amount equal to half of the difference between the accrual of the respective estates of the spouses. **1985** *Fair Lady* 6 Mar. 32 Spouses married according to the accrual system have independent control and ownership of their own assets. **1986** *Reader's Digest Family Guide to Law* 252 Spouses in a marriage out of community of property, that was entered into before the coming into operation of the Matrimonial Property Act of 1984, are able to have their marriage governed by the accrual system without having to apply to court. All they need do is have a contract drawn up by a notary, in which they agree that the accrual system shall apply to their marriage.

ace /eɪs/ *n. slang.* Also **eis**. [Etym. obscure: perh. fr. Austral. Eng., referring to the single mark on a playing card; reinforced in S. Afr. Eng. by the similarity in sound between 'ace' and Afk. *eie* (in the phr. *op jou eie* on your own).] In the phr. *on one's ace*: on one's own, alone.

Also Austral. and N.Z. Eng. The spelling 'Uys' (quot. 1972) is a play on an Afrikaans surname pronounced 'ace'.

1972 R. MALAN *Ah Big Yaws* 53 There can be a certain isolationist pride in doing things on your Uys. **1975** *Darling* 9 Apr. 95 The groovy okies what you can connect with there if you happen to rock along on yore eis. **1985** P. SLABOLEPSZY *Sat. Night at Palace* 12 He shouts from the bladdy bench we mustn't crowd him! (*He laughs scornfully*) The oke's on his ace – we mustn't crowd him!

ACF *n.* Also **A.C.F.** [Initial letters of *Active Citizen Force*.]

1. *hist.* ACTIVE CITIZEN FORCE sense 1. Also *attrib.*

1939 *Cape Times* 17 Nov., The expansion of the ACF units of the Cape Command to war establishment has meant a vast amount of work for officers of the command. **1952** *Rand Daily Mail* 28 Nov. 8 A.C.F. defaulters too severely caned, says Guardian. **1979** MARTIN & ORPEN *S. Afr. At War* 347 In a war-weary world, initial voluntary response to appeals for men to join the ACF was poor.

2. ACTIVE CITIZEN FORCE sense 2. Also *attrib.*

1960 *Natal Mercury* 4 Apr. 3 The A.C.F. suffered its first casualty in the Cato Manor 'siege' last night. **1975** [see DRONKLAP].

ach var. AG.

acha, acha(a)r varr. ATJAR.

achtdag-geneesbos var. AGTDAEGENEESBOS.

achterborg /ˈaxtə(r)bɔː(r)x/ *n. Law.* [Du., *achter* rear, behind + *borg* guarantor, surety.] One who stands surety for an indemnity; rear surety.

1934 C.P. SWART *Supplement to Pettman*. 1 *Achterborg*, .. A Roman-Dutch term signifying, rear surety, surety for an indemnity. **1960** J.J.L. SISSON *S. Afr. Judicial Dict.* 10 *Achterborg*, rear surety; surety for an indemnity, a person who gives security for the deficiency after the excussion of the debtor or other surety. **1977** *Friend* 2 June (Suppl.) 3a, *Achterborg* .. a person who gives security for the deficiency after the excussion of the debtor or other surety.

achterhuis var. AGTERHUIS.

achterkamer var. AGTERKAMER.

achteros var. AGTEROS.

achter ox /ˈaxtə(r) ɒks/ *n. phr. Obs. exc. hist.* [Part. tr. S. Afr. Du. *achteros* (see AGTEROS).] AFTER-OX sense 1.

1882 J. NIXON *Among Boers* 172 The two most powerful oxen in the span are chosen as the 'achter', or pole oxen. **1944** J. MOCKFORD *Here Are S. Africans* 65 If the way was rough or dangerous, he would walk beside the achter oxen, or run up and down the length of the team, exhorting each member of it by name.

achterrijder var. AGTERRYER.

achter sjambok var. AGTER SJAMBOK.

achtertang, -tong varr. AGTERTANG.

Achterveld var. AGTERVELD.

Active Citizen Force *n. phr.*

1. *hist.* A division of the Union Defence Forces; ACF sense 1. Also *attrib.* See also CITIZEN FORCE sense 1, U.D.F. *n.*[1]

1912 *Act 13* in *Stat. of Union* 198 The Citizen Force shall comprise three divisions:- I. The Active Citizen Force II. The Citizen Force Reserve III. The National Reserve. **1926** M. NATHAN *S. Afr. from Within* 136 The Defence Act .. created an Active Citizen Force, and rendered every citizen of European descent liable from his seventeenth to his sixtieth year to render personal service in defence of the country in any part of South Africa within or without the Union. **1941** [see CITIZEN FORCE sense 1]. **1948** *Story of Jhb. Stock Exchange* (Comm. of Jhb. Stock Exchange) 83 Then suddenly .. sporadic street fighting developed into open revolt and civil war ... The regiments of the Active Citizen Force were mobilised for action and Burgher commandos and police detachments were brought to the Rand to restore order. **1967** M.S. GEEN *Making of S. Afr.* 220 The Government declared martial law, called up the Active Citizen Force, and forced the leaders of the strike to surrender. **1983** J. KEEGAN *World Armies* 525 After discussion with the British government, a Union Defence Force was established by the Defence Act of 1912. From the outset the permanent force was fairly small (2500 mounted police in five regiments and five batteries of artillery), but to be supplemented by a much larger reserve of some 25,000 formed into an active citizen force of embryonic regiments. **1989** *Reader's Digest Illust. Hist.* 347 When South Africa declared war on Germany, the Permanent Force was made up of 3 350 officers and men. There were 14 600 part-time soldiers in the Active Citizen Force. **1990** *Bulletin* (Centre for Science Dev.) Nov.-Dec. 3 Blacks were not entitled to the provisions of the Citizen Force and Active Citizen Force Regulations which pertained to white soldiers.

2. A division of the reserve forces of the South African Defence Force to which men are posted after completing their national service; ACF sense 2. See also CITIZEN FORCE sense 2.

1981 *S. Afr. Panorama* July 42 The South African Army is a veritable people's army, like the armies of Switzerland and Israel. Only a small percentage of its members belong to the Permanent Force. The rest are servicemen or hail from the Active Citizen Force or Commandos. *c*1988 *S. Afr. 1987-8: Off. Yrbk* (Bureau for Info.) 256 They qualify for appointment in the Active Citizen Force Reserve where under normal circumstances, they have no active training or service commitments.

actuarius /ˌaktjuˈɑːrɪəs, ˌæktjuˈɛərɪəs/ *n.* Also **actuaris**. [Afk., fr. L., secretary, clerk.] An officer of the Synod of the DUTCH REFORMED church (see quot. 1843); ACTUARY.

1831 *S. Afr. Almanac & Dir.* 135 Synod of the Reformed Church ... Rev. A. Faure Actuaris and Quaestor. **1843** *Ordinance 7* in *Stat. Law of Cape of G.H.* (1862) 618 An actuarius synodi shall be appointed from amongst the ministers, .. the actuarius being charged, – a) With transcribing during the sitting of the general church assembly .. b) With conducting the correspondence .. c) With the care of the synodal papers and books, besides the synodical repertory .. d) With framing and continuing a systematical registry in an alphabetic form of the 'acta synodi.' **1866** *Cape Town Dir.* 55 The Synodical Commission is composed of the Moderator, the Scriba, the Actuarius, five acting ministers, and three elders or retired elders nominated by the Synod. **1934** *Friend* 19 Apr. (Swart), The Actuarius informed the meeting that the commission had obtained legal advice and that it was in favour of the Synod's decision. **1974** *Cape Herald* 14 Sept. 2 An Actuarius or registrar (the Rev. Dawid Botha of Bellville).

actuary *n.* [Calque formed on Afk. *actuarius.*] ACTUARIUS.

1970 *Evening Post* 17 Oct. 1 In 1963, when Mr Vorster became Minister of Justice Dr Vorster became Actuary of the Cape Synod of the NG Kerk. **1974** *Sunday Times* 27 Oct. 15 *(caption)* The new moderature of the general synod of NGK .. Dr. F.E.O'B. Geldenhuys (actuary), Dr. J.D. Vorster (assessor). **1987** L. FLANAGAN in *Weekly Mail* 12 June 3 Dominee .. now holds the position of actuary.

Adamastor /ædəˈmæstə/ *n.* [fr. Gk *adamastos* untamed, wild.] A mythological giant spirit inhabiting Table Mountain and symbolizing the confrontation between Europe and Africa.

The figure of Adamastor was adopted from Graeco-Roman mythology, and was believed by the early Portuguese explorers to brood over the Cape of Storms.

1823 J.E.V. ARAGO *Narr. of Voy. round World*, When reflecting on the numerous victims whom this sea has engulphed, I cannot read without the liveliest emotion the episode of the giant Adamastor, in the poem of Camoens. **1877** W.J. MICKLE tr. *L. De Camoen's Lusiad* 133 After a voyage of five months, with continued storms, they arrive in the latitude of the Cape. Apparition of Adamastor, the giant of the Cape of Storms. **1910** D. FAIRBRIDGE *That Which Hath Been* (1913) 18 A wild south-easter succeeded the night of calm ... 'It is Adamastor,' said Bergh, 'the spirit of Table Mountain greets his Excellency and shrieks a welcome.' **1930** R. CAMPBELL *Adamastor* (1950) 34 The low sun whitens on the flying squalls. Against the cliffs the long grey surge is rolled, where Adamastor from his marble halls threatens the sons of Lusas as of old. **1941** C.W. DE KIEWIET *Hist. of S. Afr.* 2 The Portuguese had regarded the Cape with feelings of suspicion and superstition ... To them it was the cape of Adamastor, the vengeful spirit of storms who in the Lusiad had appeared at dead of night to Vasco da Gama, predicting the woes that would befall those that sailed on to India. **1958** F.G. BUTLER in R.M. Macnab *Poets in S. Afr.* 5 Look on Africa, leap through the line .. of her coasts, inland from Adamastor's roar. **1973** S. GRAY *Writers' Territory* 181 Da Gama anthropomorphoses Table Mountain .. into the shape of Adamastor, the giant who personifies the spirit of the Cape for any sailor running into a south-easter there on a stormy night. **1988** G. CORNWELL in *NELM News* May 1 Camoen's portrayal of Da Gama's encounter with Adamastor .. a symbol of the confrontation between Europe and Africa in the often violent context of colonialism. **1991** F.G. BUTLER *Local Habitation* 147 Apart from the superb creation of Adamastor, Africa itself did not touch him into song.

Adam fig *n. phr.* Also **Adam's fig.** [tr. Du. *Adamvijg.*] The large, brown fig *Ficus carica*, a native of southern Europe which was introduced to the Cape during the second half of the 17th century. Also *attrib.*

1913 C. PETTMAN *Africanderisms* 22 *Adam fig*, A large brown variety of fig is thus designated in South Africa. **1967** E.M. SLATTER *My Leaves Are Green* 5 Behind the house lay the big orchard that grew juicy brown Adam figs, early peaches, pomegranates, golden apricots, quinces and apples. **1974** *S. Afr. Panorama* Apr. 16 From these Adam's figs the famous 'block figs' of Prince Albert are made. **1977** F.G. BUTLER *Karoo Morning* 145 He would allow us to pillage his enormous Adam fig tree.

addada var. HADEDA.

adiate /ˈædɪeɪt/ *v. trans.* and *intrans. Law.* [Apparently irreg. fr. L. *adīre* to approach + Eng. v.-forming suffix *-ate.*] To accept (an inheritance) as the beneficiary of a will.

1898 H.H. JUTA *Sel. of Leading Cases* 111 If the survivor has adiated and accepted benefits under the will. **1915** R.W. LEE *Roman-Dutch Law* 286 If he [*sc.* the 'extraneus heres'] accepted or acted as heir, he was said to 'adiate' the inheritance (*adire hereditatem*), and from that moment was in the position of a universal successor. **1945** *S. Afr. Law Jrnl* LXII. 555 A person can be relieved from the consequences of adiation if he has adiated under a just and probable ignorance of his legal rights, but the mere fact that an heir who has adiated *bona fide* thought that such adiation would be of greater benefit to him that it turns out to be is not a sufficient reason for granting him relief. **1960** J.J.L. SISSON *S. Afr. Judicial Dict.* 22 The instituted heir was not bound to accept the inheritance; he might repudiate it, or take time to deliberate, or adiate it. **1977** C.J. CLAASSEN *Dict. of Legal Words & Phrases* I. 49 If the instituted heir, well knowing whether he has acquired a right to the inheritance by last will or *ad intestato*, disposes of any part of the inheritance, he is considered as adiating, unless he declares that he does so merely out of kindness, or unless he has received judicial permission to do so.

adiation /ædɪˈeɪʃən/ *n. Law.* [ADIATE + Eng. *-tion* suffix expressing the sense 'the action or process of'.] The acceptance (of an inheritance) as the beneficiary of a will.

1829 in J.W. Knapp *Rep. Cases Privy Council* (1831) I. iii., Adiation (*aditio in hereditatem*) is a question more of intention than action. **1945** [see ADIATE]. **1960** J.J.L. SISSON *S. Afr. Judicial Dict.* 22 *Adiation*, a term adopted from the Roman law signifying the acceptance of an inheritance by the heir ... *Adiation* is a mode of election and may be resiled from. **1977** C.J. CLAASSEN *Dict. of Legal Words & Phrases* I. 49 The *adiation* 'consists in the intention which may be indicated, not only by words, but by actions'.

administration board *n. phr. Hist.* Often with initial capitals. A regional government structure responsible for implementing INFLUX CONTROL regulations and other laws which affected black people living outside the 'homelands'; BAAB. Also *attrib.* See also *pass office* (PASS sense 4).

Constituted in 1971, the boards were first known as 'Bantu Affairs Administration Boards' (see BAAB), then renamed 'development boards' (see DEVELOPMENT BOARD) in 1984, before being abolished in July 1986. Often combined with the name of the region served, e.g. *East Cape Administration Board* (abbrev. *ECAB*), *West Rand Administration Board* (abbrev. *WRAB*).

1971 *Act 45* in *Govt Gaz.* Vol.72 No.3127, 2 Act To make better provision for the administration of Bantu Affairs outside the Bantu homelands, and for that purpose to provide for the establishment of Bantu Affairs Administration Boards. *c*1980 *S. Afr. 1979: Off. Yrbk* (Info. Service) 227 Qualified Blacks can now buy houses from the administration boards. **1980** *Rand Daily Mail* 31 Oct. 1 Three people were wounded when two handgrenades were hurled at the West Rand Administration Board offices in Soweto. **1984** [see DEVELOPMENT BOARD]. **1985** PLATZKY & WALKER *Surplus People* 58 Each year the Administration Board attempts to rid Cape Town of Africans (who may have been in the area for many years) having no formal shelter. **1986** *Learn & Teach* No.7, 9 Mrs Voyiya .. built a new shack in a new squatter camp right next to the Administration Board offices in Nyanga township. **1987** *Race Rel. Survey 1986* (S.A.I.R.R.) I. 341 Employers used to have to pay a monthly levy in respect of each African employee to the administration (and later development) boards. **1987** *New Nation* 5 Mar. 1 They had used an administration board vehicle to carry out arrests and the board's office to interrogate and assault people.

administrator *n. hist.* Often with initial capital. [Special senses of general Eng. *administrator* one who administers.]

a. Prior to UNION in 1910: the chief executive officer of any territory in South Africa which was situated beyond the borders of the Cape Colony and had been annexed by the Crown.

1875 *Constit. Amendment Law* in G.W. Eybers *Sel. Constit. Doc.* (1918) 199 Enacted by the Administrator of the Government of Natal, with the advice and consent of the Legislative Council thereof. **1882** *Tvl Advertiser* 14 Jan. 1 In the civil capacity of Administrator of the Transvaal. **1900** H.C. HILLEGAS *Oom Paul's People* 55 Sir Owen Lanyon, a man of no tact and an inordinate hater of the Boers, succeeded Shepstone as administrator of the Transvaal in 1879. **1946** S. CLOETE *Afr. Portraits* 121 Meanwhile, in March, 1879, Sir Owen Lanyon, a soldier by profession, who knew nothing of administration and spoke no Dutch, replaced Shepstone as administrator of the Transvaal. **1973** K.H.C. MCINTYRE in *Std Encycl. of Sn Afr.* IX. 611 He [*sc.* Sir T. Shepstone] proceeded to the Transvaal .. annexed that Boer republic to the Crown and as Administrator made tentative efforts to introduce his own administrative system.

b. Between 1910 and 1994: the chief executive officer of one of South Africa's four provinces.

1909 *S. Afr. Act* in G.W. Eybers *Sel. Constit. Doc.* (1918) 536 In each province there shall be a chief executive officer appointed by the Governor-General in Council, who shall be styled the administrator of the province, and in whose name all executive acts relating to provincial affairs therein shall be done. **1926** M. NATHAN *S. Afr. from Within* 127 In terms of the South Africa Act, an administrator, to hold office for five years, was appointed in each of the new Provinces. **1936** *Cambridge Hist. of Brit. Empire* VIII. 689 Each original colony was to retain its identity as a Province of the Union with an Administrator at its head. This officer is appointed for five years and may not be removed in the interim except by the Governor-General in Council for cause assigned, which must be communicated to both Houses. *c*1936 *S. & E. Afr. Yr Bk & Guide* 140 The chief executive officer is the Administrator assisted by a Council, elected for three years by those entitled to vote for the House of Assembly. Four members, chosen by the Council, form the Executive Committee. **1943** L. SOWDEN *Union of S. Afr.* 150 General Smuts appointed him Administrator (a post analogous to Governor) of the Transvaal Province. **1957** *Act 33* in *Stat. of Union* 372 'Administrator', in any law passed since the establishment of the Union, means the Administrator of the province for or in respect of which that law was enacted. **1967** M.S. GEEN *Making of S. Afr.* 217 The Administrator is the head of the provincial system of government. He is appointed by the State President for a period of five years, and is eligible for reappointment. **1974** A.P. CARTWRIGHT *By Waters of Letaba* 143 In 1917 Mr Simon Bekker, then the Administrator of the Transvaal, initiated a system of farm schools. **1989** *Cape Times* 12 Jan. 6 The refusal of the Administrator of the Cape .. to accede to the wishes of East London to open one of the city's most popular beaches to all races. **1990** *Sash* Vol.33 No.1, 23 In Cape Town, pensioners held placards which told their story outside the administrator's garden party. This led to a meeting with the administrator and Cape Provincial Administration officials.

advice office *n. phr.* Any of several centres established and staffed by the BLACK SASH (sense b), offering assistance with legal and other problems, particularly those caused by apartheid laws. Also *attrib.* Cf. AID CENTRE.

1962 B. WILKS in *Black Sash* June 27 Since January, 1956, twenty-six thousand Africans (26,000) have been 'endorsed out' of the Western Cape under the Bantu Urban Areas Act ... In 1958, in an effort to give advice and assistance to some of these unfortunate people, the Black Sash established the Athlone Advice Office. **1973** *Survey of Race Rel.* (S.A.I.R.R.) 164 The Athlone Advice Office in Cape Town, run jointly by the Black Sash and the S.A. Institute of Race Relations commented .. 'The establishment of an official aid centre might be expected to have rendered an independent Advice Office redundant, but this office feels needed as much as ever.' **1983** C. SAUNDERS *Hist. Dict.* 27 The Sash's .. 'advice offices' in urban centres .. tried to help Africans with such problems as influx control, unemployment, contracts, housing, and pensions. **1990** *Sash* Vol.33 No.1, 23 Advice office workers from East London and Port Elizabeth, as well as Cape Town, attended and were able to report on the situation in those centres. *Ibid.* 26 On Monday, 12 February 1990, the day on which Nelson Mandela came home to Johannesburg, the waiting room in the advice office was full.

advocate *n. Law.* [Special sense of general Eng.] A lawyer who pleads the cause of a client in the South African Supreme and Appeal Courts; used as a title before a surname, often abbrev. as **Adv.** See also SC. Cf. ATTORNEY.

Used also in *Scot. Eng.* Cf. *Brit. Eng.* 'barrister'.

1832 *Graham's Town Jrnl* 20 Apr. 68 John Marr, European, was arraigned alternatively for Rape and Incest, and was defended by Mr. Advocate van Ryneveld. **1849** *De Zuid-Afrikaan* in J. Crwys-Williams *S. Afr. Despatches* (1989) 19 Silence was at length procured, and after the spectators had been addressed by Mr Ebden, Sr., Mr. Sutherland, and Mr. Adv. Ebden, the crowd separated. **1934** N. DEVITT *Mem. of Magistrate* 126 The Magistrate .. has risen .. from a junior post in the Union public service. His qualifications for the position are either those of an advocate or attorney. **1940** E. BRIGHT in Baumann & Bright *Lost Republic* 97 Mr A. Fischer .. was actually an eminent advocate – but in those days there was no prohibition against practising both at the Bar and Side-Bar. **1950** [see ATTORNEY]. **1958** A. SAMPSON *Treason Cage* 21 'This is something which I as an accused feel with deep resentment,' said Advocate Slovo, conducting his own defence. *Ibid.* 34 [M-] .. had practised illegally for several years as an advocate. **1978** S. KENTRIDGE *Informant, Johannesburg* The South African Advocate is the equivalent of the English barrister. The official designation .. is an advocate of the Supreme Court .. the term is also used as a description of a particular function of a barrister's calling, namely the conduct of cases in court ... The .. peculiarity of the South African usage .. is its use as an appellation ... It is very common .. to hear a member of the bar described as 'Advocate Jones'. It is however an undesirable usage. **1979** A.P. BRINK *Dry White Season* 111 In the face of strong opposition from Adv De Villiers the magistrate ruled that the court would .. consider their affidavits as evidence. **1982** [see ATTORNEY]. **1987** J. JOUBERT in *Style* Mar. 89 Advocate P.J. Wessels, now a senior judge. **1987** *Star* 29 Oct. 13 [He] is in South Africa to contribute to the .. debate .. over the fusion of the Bar and Side-bar. Advocates in South Africa are generally against fusion, while most attorneys would like the right to argue cases in the Supreme Court. **1990, 1992** [see ATTORNEY].

Af /æf/ *n. Derog.* and *offensive.* Also with small initial. [Abbrev. of AFRICAN *n.*[1] sense 1.]

1. A demeaning term for a black person.

1976 J.F. BURNS in *New York Times* 22 June 13 A common feature of the conversation with the whites was the use of pejoratives to refer to blacks ... In English-speaking households, the words 'natives', or 'Afs' were common. **1978** *Sunday Times* 21 May 14 Yes, I know it sounds daft, getting worked up about a stray Af ... You can't tell me a Jo'burg Af doesn't pick up a smattering of English and/or Afrikaans. **1980** D. BECKETT in *Bloody Horse* No.2, 13 Honestly, *no one* is more anxious to see the afs get what is due to them than we are. **1986** *Style* Dec. 41 Newcomers were conspicuous as they bit their tongues turning garden boy into gardener, girl into maid, boys into men, Afs into blacks and South West into Namibia. **1989** *Informant, Grahamstown* This is my dairy book – you know, I keep a record of the milk production per day, otherwise the Afs steal it. **1990** *Frontline* Jan. 29 The sayings of the Ex-colonials: What I don't like about the hairybacks is that they're so bloody rough on the Afs. **1990** R. MALAN *My Traitor's Heart* 41 In my teens, everyone knew that all 'Afs' smoked dope.

2. *comb. nonce.* **Aftax** [blend of *Af* and Eng. *taxi*], a derogatory term for a black-owned taxi of a particular type.

A perceived euphemism for the offensive term *kaffir-taxi* (see KAFFIR *n.* sense 2 e).

1983 T. MCALLEN *Kyk Daar*, In order to qualify for the label *Aftax* the vehicle has to be of original American manufacture and at least twenty years old ... To own an *Aftax* carries status and wealth. To drive it requires courage and fortitude, second to none.

‖**afdak** /ˈafdak/ *n.* [Afk., *af* down + *dak* roof.] A lean-to; occas., a roughly-constructed building.

1970 E. MUNDELL *Informant, Pearston (E. Cape)* The sheep are under the afdak (shed). **1970** J.V. WINTERS *Informant, Kimberley* Nice house, except for the afdak (lean-to – usually room added on to house at below usual roof height). **1987** G. VINEY *Col. Houses* 40 Behind the *voorhuys* was .. a backroom .. , a kitchen and two pantries which may or may not have been *afdaks*. **1991** *Bulletin* (Centre for Science Dev.) Jan., Many of the houses have 'afdakkies' in their backyards where additional family members or friends live. **1993** C.M. KNOX *Informant, Cape Town* His slave lived in an afdak down there because he was coloured and this guy was white.

afdelingsbestuur see BESTUUR sense 2.

affected *ppl adj. Hist.* [Special sense of general Eng. *affected* influenced, acted upon.] Of or pertaining to any organization which is deemed by the State President to be politically influenced from abroad, and is thus prohibited from receiving foreign money with which to further its aims. Usu. in the collocation **affected organization.**

1974 *Act 31* in *Govt Gaz.* Vol.105 No.4222, 3 If the State President is satisfied that politics are being engaged in by or through an organization with the aid of or in co-operation with or in consultation with or under the influence of an organization or person abroad, he may, .. by proclamation in the *Gazette* declare that organization to be an affected organization ... No person shall .. ask for or canvass foreign money for or on behalf of an affected organization .. receive money from abroad for or on behalf of an affected organization. *c*1980 *S. Afr. 1979: Off. Yrbk* (Dept of Info.) 323 The Affected Organisations Act of 1974 provides for the prohibition of the receipt of money from abroad for certain organisations which are declared to be affected organisations. **1987** *Weekly Mail* 22 May 14 The government's moves to block foreign funding dates back to 1974 when it passed the Affected Organisations Act. The first bodies declared affected were the Christian Institute .. and the National Union of South African Students. **1987** *New Nation* 10 Sept. 5 The government promptly declared it [*sc.* Nusas] an affected organisation, preventing it from raising money overseas and slashing its budget by 90 percent.

Africaander var. AFRIKANER.

Africaaner Bond, etc. varr. AFRIKANDER BOND.

Africaans var. AFRIKAANS.

Africa, for see FOR AFRICA.

African *n.*[1] and *adj.*[1] [Special senses of Eng. *African.*]

A. *n.*

1. A black person of African descent; cf. BLACK *n.* sense 1 b. See also ASIAN, COLOURED, WHITE *n.* sense 2. Also *attrib.*

'African' was never an official term during the apartheid era, but was used (until replaced by 'black') by black people of themselves, and by those who opposed apartheid.

See note at BLACK *n.* sense 1 b.

1696 J. OVINGTON *Voy. to Suratt* 54 The Art of Poysoning is what these *Africans* do very commonly exceed in, and to which they are generally propense upon any occasional Quarrel or Abuse. **1804** R. PERCIVAL *Acct of Cape of G.H.* 205 It is not unusual to see eight or nine children .. adding to the domestic comforts by squalling and domineering over those of the slaves; for the first lesson they are taught is their superiority over the unfortunate Africans. **1824** W.J. BURCHELL *Trav.* II. 9, I doubt whether the most accomplished performer in Europe, feels .. a gratification greater than that which I received on witnessing the pleasure which my music afforded to a kraal of simple Africans. *a*1827 D. CARMICHAEL in W.J. Hooker *Botanical Misc.* (1831) II. 50 The African requires nothing but instruction to render his intellectual, as well as his mechanical talents, equal to those of the European, who has so long oppressed him, under the plea of his being an inferior animal. **1833** S. KAY *Trav. & Researches* 331 Those of the poor Africans who are constantly engaged in a course of warfare, keep their spears, and shields, (&c.), always at hand. **1843** J.C. CHASE *Cape of G.H.* 270 In fifty years more the Cape colony .. will be an object on which even the debased and fallen mind of the African cannot look without astonishment. **1871** J. MACKENZIE *Ten Yrs* (1971) 509 It is the custom for even educated persons to include 'all these Africans' and 'all these black people' in some sweeping statement. **1902** G.M. THEAL *Beginning of S. Afr. Hist.* 256 It was impossible for the European without losing self respect to labour side by side with the African. **1931** W.A. COTTON *Racial Segregation* 18 My main concern is to secure on behalf of the Africans a righteous settlement of the problem that is created by white immigration. **1941** A. MAQELEPO in *Bantu World* 15 Feb. 5 We are confused as to whether we are to be described as Kaffirs, Coloureds, Bantu, Negroes or even Africans ... To be called an *umuntu* is far too general, but to call us African or Negro is honourable and precise. *c*1949 *Survey of Race Rel. 1948–9* (S.A.I.R.R.) 6 Whereas formerly the African had no other aspiration than to be a South African, today he is more and more imbued with the idea of African nationalism and freedom from the control of the white man. **1950** H. GIBBS *Twilight* 109 Africans (Natives) especially are losing their fear of VD and tend to cast whatever little discretion they ever had in this connection completely to the winds. **1955** [see PROCLAIM]. **1959** L. LONGMORE *Dispossessed* 317 The terms African, Bantu and Native will be used as synonymous terms when discussing the Negroes of South Africa. All white people in South Africa, whether or not born in Europe, are referred to as Europeans. **1961** T. MATSHIKIZA *Choc. for my Wife* 119 It was around here .. that many bitter battles have been fought between Africans and non-Africans for the cattle and the land that we possessed .. the non-Africans wanted meat. **1962** L.E. NEAME *Hist. of Apartheid* 157 Several of the English-language papers had adopted the practice of referring to the Natives as 'Africans'. **1964** [see AFRIKANER *n.* sense 2 a]. **1985** PLATZKY & WALKER *Surplus People* 98 They wanted to impose more rigid divisions within the dominated black population, to separate off coloureds and Indians and Africans from each other, and then to divide the African population along even finer, ethnic lines. **1988** E. VOSLOO in *Femina* May 143 Mrs Malan compared the Afrikaner and the *Afrikaan* (African). Both, she said, had suffered the trauma of urbanisation and the painful adjustment to a new way of life. **1989** J. HOBBS *Thoughts in Makeshift Mortuary* 17, I won't have you using any of those other awful words for blacks. 'African' is what they prefer, I'm told. **1990** *Sunday Times* 18 Feb. 12 He [*sc.* Nelson Mandela] refers to 'Europeans' and 'Africans', the terminology in use when he was arrested .. in August 1962. But he corrects himself immediately. **1990** J. MCCLURG in *Star* 11 Sept. 11 Over the years we have seen 'native' .. go through 'Bantu' and 'African' to end up as 'black'.

2. Any person born or living in Africa.

1786 G. FORSTER tr. *A. Sparrman's Voy. to Cape of G.H.* I. 59, I arrived at the house of farmer *Van der Spoei*, who was a widower, and an African born. **1795** A. MACKENZIE in G.M. Theal *Rec. of Cape Col.* (1897) I. 46 It is composed of six members who are European Africans who regulate every thing in the most despotick manner and have monopolised all the public Offices. **1812** A. PLUMPTRE tr. *H. Lichtenstein's Trav. in Sn*

Afr. (1928) I. 31 All the address of our European waggon drivers vanishes entirely before the very superior dexterity in this way shown by the Africans. **1827** G. THOMPSON *Trav.* I. 78 This town owes much of its prosperity and embellishment to Captain Stockenstroom, who, though an African born, and educated entirely in the Colony, has been long distinguished. **1879** E.L. PRICE *Jrnls* (1956) 330 We dined with .. the Dutch Minister ... No coarseness or roughness, either – but only the absence of all those naughty superfluities of form and ceremony, wh. so *mar* the English life to us Africans and wh. make one feel as if in a strait jacket. *Ibid.* 378 Rain at last! .. The frogs are 'snoring' loudly, .. and the little rills and rivers running everywhere. Such *delicious* sounds, as only we poor thirst-weary Africans can appreciate. **1926** R. CAMPBELL in *Voorslag* (1985) 68 What a preposterous figure the white African makes who in order to hypnotise himself into believing in his mental superiority to the blacks is *forced* to retard the blacks *artificially* from entering into competition with him. **1948** O. WALKER *Kaffirs Are Lively* 213 'I am an African,' said General Smuts, during the 1947 Session. **1952** Z. MOTHOPENG in *Drum* July 10 People will be treated irrespective of colour. Everyone in Africa would be an African. We want to smash prejudices. **1960** E.G. MALHERBE in H. Spottiswoode *S. Afr.: Rd Ahead* 146 After all, we are White Africans. Africa is our only home and we shall have to learn to get on with the rest of Africa, or perish. **1973** *Sunday Tribune* 1 Apr. 20 If they can't see themselves as White Africans or simply as Africans, then their hearts are just not going to be in separate and equal development .. or anything else. **1979** W. EBERSOHN *Lonely Place* 21 'We are all Africans,' he had often told Yudel. 'We should be able to communicate with other Africans.' **1988** P. LAWRENCE in *Saturday Star* 9 July 11 An African is anyone who, to quote Sobukwe again, 'owes his only loyalty to Africa.' .. Whites can, by a positive act of identification with the indigenous majority, thus become Africans in the .. ideological sense. **1990** *Sunday Times* 13 May (Mag. Sect.) 6, I love the way South Africans do not flinch from being called Africans any more. **1990** K. NHLAPO in *New African* 3 Sept. 10 As Africans (I use this term in an inclusive sense) we must perpetuate our own true culture.

B. *adj.*

1.a. Of or pertaining to Africa; applied both to black people (as in general English) and, esp. in the past, to persons born or living in Africa, but of European extraction; characteristic of, or pertaining to, such persons; AFRIKANDER *adj.* sense 2.

1786 G. FORSTER tr. *A. Sparrman's Voy. to Cape of G.H.* I. 16 The Europeans are apt to conceive rather unfavourable ideas of the politeness of the African colonists. **1802** W. SOMERVILLE *Narr. of E. Cape Frontier* (1979) 45 The victorious party .. counted above a hundred dead bodies – a sight which in the breast of any but an African boor would have excited sorrow. **1821** C.I. LATROBE *Jrnl of Visit* 207 This is said to be the first time, that any African descendants from Europeans have suffered death for crimes deemed capital in Europe. *Ibid.* 416, I never felt disposed to take an African nap after dinner. **1827** G. THOMPSON *Trav.* I. 4, I travelled with Mr. Theunissen, a substantial African landholder. **1837** 'N. POLSON' *Subaltern's Sick Leave* 149 These orders were carried into effect by Captain Andreas Stockenstrom, a gentleman of Swedish and African extraction. **1841** B. SHAW *Memorials* 85, I found great assistance in laying hold of the long tail of my African horse, when, through fatigue, he was unable to carry me. **1854** M.R. ROBINSON *Report upon Cathcart's Plan for Eastern Frontier* in *Cape of G.H. Annexures* 3 These allotments and privileges are very limited for an African stock farmer. **1990** *Sunday Times* 30 Sept. 20 President De Klerk skilfully and subtly cast himself as an African leader.

b. Special collocations.

i. In the names of plants and animals: **African ant-eater**, see ANT-EATER sense 1; **African oak** *obs.*, STINKWOOD sense a; **African sandalwood**, see SANDALWOOD; **African tiger** *obs.*, the TIGER (sense 1), *Panthera pardus*; **African wattle**, the HUILBOOM, *Peltophorum africanum*.

1811 R. STOPFORD in G.M. Theal *Rec. of Cape Col.* (1901) VIII. 25 This timber called Stinkwood or **African Oak** has been found to be in many respects equal to the English Oak for all purposes of Ship Building. **1812** A. PLUMPTRE tr. *H. Lichtenstein's Trav. in Sn Afr.* (1928) I. 207 An excellent meal, which we took lying at the foot of an African oak, at least a century old. **1829** C. ROSE *Four Yrs in Sn Afr.* 3 The shade, thrown by the trailing branches of the African oak through which gleams of sunny light find their way. **1838** [see SHEEP'S TAIL FAT]. **1913** C. PETTMAN *Africanderisms* 24 *African oak, Ocotea bullata* is sometimes so called because of the acorn-like appearance of its fruit. See Stinkwood. **1846** R. MOFFAT *Missionary Labours* 153 In one of my early journeys, I had an escape from an **African tiger** and a serpent. **1911** D.B. HOOK *'Tis but Yesterday* 8 The skin of Majesty was that of the African 'tiger' which was the badge of the highest rank. [**1973** S. CLOETE *Co. with Heart of Gold* 113, I wished to shoot a tiger. Not our African spotted tiger – leopard, as they say – but a real one with stripes.] **1972** I.C. VERDOORN in *Std Encycl. of Sn Afr.* V. 652 *Huilbos*, **African wattle** ... This tree with its showy, lemon-yellow flowers and wattle-like foliage belongs to the family *Leguminosae*. **1988** A. HALL-MARTIN et al. *Kaokoveld* 14 Other tree species associated with the termitaria are .. buffalo thorn .. and African wattle.

ii. African Dutch (*obs.*), freq. used *attrib.*: (*a*) DUTCH *n.* sense 2 a; (*b*) ***The African Dutch*** (*pl.*): *the Dutch* (DUTCH *n.* sense 1).

1812 A. PLUMPTRE tr. *H. Lichtenstein's Trav. in Sn Afr.* (1928) I. 93 The concise, yet expressive, African Dutch language, in which the relation was given. **1829** C. ROSE *Four Yrs in Sn Afr.* 11 Eyes of dry lustre, betraying that at some distant period a sprinkle of black blood had mingled with and tainted the pure descent of the African Dutch. **1900** W.S. CHURCHILL *London to Ladysmith* 135 This Boer farmer was a very typical character, and represented to my mind all that was best and noblest in the African Dutch character.

2.a. Used of a black person, esp., in the South African context, as opposed to a 'coloured', Asian, or white person; of or pertaining to black people. Cf. BLACK *adj.* sense 1.

1832 *Graham's Town Jrnl* 10 Aug. 127 To hire, an African Slave Girl who understands all descriptions of House work. [**1900** G.W. LINES *Ladysmith Siege* 67 One of our young ladies, a refugee from Dundee, is so refined in her language, that she never uses the word 'blackguard,' but substitutes 'African Sentinel.'] **1929** *Workers' Herald* 7 Sept. 1 The Voice of African Labour. *c***1948** H. TRACEY *Lalela Zulu* 9 It carried the African Labour Battalions on their way to France. *c***1949** [see sense A 1]. **1959** B. BUNTING *Story behind Non-White Press* 2 *The World* is run by an African editor and an African staff, but overall supervision is exercised by whites and .. the paper is controlled by white capital. **1964** [see AFRIKANER *n.* sense 2 a]. **1971** *Daily News* 4 Mar. 11 African areas could have their own official languages alongside English and Afrikaans. **1983** *Frontline* Sept. 27 She is 'coloured ... but I'm married to an African man'. **1988** G. MOKOE in *Pace* Apr. 62 Prof Mokgokong's move also eased another frustration pertaining to African medical practitioners; production of enough African general practitioners to serve the country's large African population. **1990** T. DANIELS in *New African* 3 Sept. 2 The fighting broke out last weekend between supporters of local rival soccer clubs, one primarily African and the other mainly coloured.

b. Special collocations. **African beer**, TSHWALA sense a; **African print**, *German print* (see GERMAN). Also *attrib.*

1974 *Drum* 8 Aug. 27 The BIC has the monopoly for brewing and distributing **African beer** in all major townships. **1990** *Weekend Post* 29 Sept. 11 Everything we shot for the pot we shared with the local folk, and they always invited us to drink African beer with them. **1976** *Star* 12 June, The woman in the flowery **African print** dress standing on the platform at Naledi Hall, Soweto, stared down into the crowd. **1983** J. MORTIMER in *Star Today* 15 Nov. 3 The old man in African-print skirt waited impatiently at the side of the highway. **1986** *Fair Lady* 5 Mar. 55 The white trouser suit she is wearing, .. combined with a vivid African print blouse and traditional beaded headdress and necklace.

Hence (sense A 1) **Africanerdom** *n. nonce*, black African people collectively. Cf. AFRIKANERDOM.

1941 A. MAQELEPO in *Bantu World* 15 Feb. 5 There is an unfortunate position created today for many who are not *Africans* but claiming a place in Africanerdom.

African *n.*[2] and *adj.*[2] *Obs.* [tr. Du. *Africaan(sche)* African, Afrikaner, Afrikaans.]

A. *n.* AFRIKANER *n.* sense 2 a.

1786 G. FORSTER tr. *A. Sparrman's Voy. to Cape of G.H.* I. 115, I formed an acquaintance and even friendship with Mr. Daniel Ferdinand Immelman, a young African. **1790** tr. *F. Le Vaillant's Trav.* I. 151 My tent .. was under the particular care of an old African, named *Swanepoel.* **1797** LADY A. BARNARD *S. Afr. Century Ago* (1925) 120 Our Dutch friends are safe lodged in the Castle till a ship is ready to take them to Batavia – silly, bold, foolish people! No African was ever known to live there. **1832** *Graham's Town Jrnl* 18 May 81 In the *Zuid Afrikaan*, No. 109 .. you may read these words, 'we Africans differ with the Irish not only in Language but in Sentiments.' .. All the advantages that have been afforded to the Africans have been thrown away, and .. they still differ as much from Irish .. as their fathers when they were sent out from Holland for their good behaviour.

B. *adj.* AFRIKAANS *adj.*

1796 E. HELME tr. *F. Le Vaillant's Trav. into Int.* II. 378 One of them, Dina Sagrias-de-Beer, .. was one of the most beautiful African ladies I had ever seen. **1812** A. PLUMPTRE tr. *H. Lichtenstein's Trav. in Sn Afr.* (1928) I. 217 We stopped at the house of a family, by name Marx .. the youngest daughter .. struck us all, for really dazzling beauty. If the African young women had as much politeness and education as they have native charms, they would be perfectly irresistible. **1836** R. GODLONTON *Introductory Remarks to Narr. of Irruption* 198 The intercourse .. between the English and Dutch inhabitants has been attended with the most important results. The African farmer on the border is quite a different character from that portrayed some twenty or thirty years ago. **1941** N. DEVITT *Celebrated S. Afr. Crimes* 22 This land was to be: '.. the unmolested property of the African burghers (Africaansche burgers) .. which land can never be .. ceded to any other white Power whatever.'

Africana /ˌæfrɪˈkɑːnə/ *n.* [Eng., fr. neut. pl. form of L. adj. *Africanus* African.] Books, manuscripts, art, furniture, and artefacts connected with Africa, and in particular southern Africa, specifically, those items of value or interest to collectors. Also *attrib.*

Used also in general Eng.

1908 *Davis & Sons catal.* (title) Africana: a list of work [*sic*] dealing with South Africa. **1926** M. NATHAN *S. Afr. from Within* 299 The Rand Club is the best residential club, and has an excellent library, with a special collection of Africana. **1937** M. ALSTON *Wanderings* 191 A library of some 2000 books which contained a valuable collection of Africana. **1943** *Africana Notes & News* Dec. 4 Africana is a word of many different meanings; to one it means books and other printed or manuscript material, to another it means objects other than books. For *Africana Notes and News* it is used in its widest sense, covering prints, maps .. books, pamphlets .. furniture, weapons, pictures and bygones of all kinds – it is restricted only from a geographical point of view; it denotes not the whole of Africa but only Southern Africa. **1951** D. HELLER *In Search of VOC Glass* 21 The second incident .. relates to an out-of-hand sale of Africana held early in 1938. **1963** D. GODFREY *Enchanted Door* 20 The late Frank Thorold, Africana dealer, of Johannesburg, had this definition of Africana. 'I take it to mean books, artistic items, statues, pictures and other objects relating to Africa – primarily, we in South Africa consider it to relate to Africa south of the Sahara, but I think the whole of Africa can rightly now be included, although such items in Rhodesia are now called Rhodesiana.' **1968** C.J.D. HARVEY in D.J. Opperman *Spirit of Vine* 293 William J. Burchell, author of the famous *Travels in the Interior of South Africa* (1822), than which perhaps no book is dearer to the heart of any true Africana enthusiast. **1974** *The 1820* Vol.47 No.2, 21 Africana is the term used for all those items, large and small, of historical importance and interest to southern Africa, although not necessarily made or manufactured in this country. **1987** L. CAPSTICKDALE in *S. Afr. Panorama* Aug. 41 Africana is defined as any book, document, artefact, painting or object associated with the discovery, exploration, development and life of South Africa and its peoples of all races in the past 500 years. **1990** *Flying Springbok* July 16 Africana history buffs will be further informed about turn-of-the-century events concerning the Republican forces' invasion of the Cape. **1991** *S. Afr. Panorama* May-June 18 Little is known about the development of boeremusiek before 1930 when the first records of *Die Vyf Vastrappers* .. were released by Columbia under the Regal label. Today the recordings of this band are Africana.

African Coast Fever *n. phr. Obs. Pathology.* EAST COAST FEVER.

1905 D. HUTCHEON in Flint & Gilchrist *Science in S. Afr.* 340 Dr. Koch showed that African Coast Fever differs from Texas Fever ... It has since been found, although not recognized by Koch, that .. the blood of cattle immune to African Coast Fever is not infective ... The local lesions in certain organs are quite different in African Coast Fever from those seen in Redwater. [**1910** A.B. LAMONT *Rural Reader* 95 Other diseases, such as African East Coast fever, are spread by means of ticks.] **1914** S.P. HYATT *Old Transport Rd* 139 The African Coast Fever .. wiped out ninety-seven per cent. of the cattle owned by white men. **1916** *Farmer's Weekly* 27 Dec. 1618 Several deaths occurred amongst cattle on A's farm, and the Veterinary Department, suspecting African coast fever, had the cattle affected removed to another of A's farms. **1955** J.H. WELLINGTON *Sn Africa: Geog. Study* II. 79 East Coast fever, or 'African Coast fever', a very virulent and highly fatal form of piroplasmosis.

Africanda var. AFRIKANDER.

African daisy *n. phr.* Any of several daisy-like flowering plants of the Asteraceae, esp. of the genera *Arctotis, Gerbera*, and *Dimorphotheca*. See also NAMAQUALAND DAISY.

1731 G. MEDLEY tr. *P. Kolb's Present State of Cape of G.H.* II. 225 *Bellis Africana*, .. i.e. African Daizy, with naked Foot-Stalks and cut leaves. **1974** *Daily Dispatch* 29 June 4 Dimorphotheca, the African daisy sown now where it is to flower will produce dwarf compact plants to flower in September and October. **1985** *Fair Lady* 3 Apr. 137 Rake in a couple of bags of compost and a few large packets of African Daisy seed .. over as wide an area as you can water ... You'll have a once-in-a-lifetime spring garden. **1989** [see NAMAQUALAND DAISY]. **1990** *Weekend Mail* 14 Sept. 6 I'm all for African daisies (Dimorphotheca) ... I marvel at the ease with which they grow. **1994** *Weekend Post* 22 Oct. (Leisure) 7 Displays of spring flowers such as the dimorphothecas (African daisies), lampranthus (vygies), arctotis, gazanias and many bulbs.

Africander *n.*[1] var. AFRIKANDER.

Africander *n.*[2] var. AFRIKANER.

Africanderdom var. AFRIKANERDOM.

Africanderism var. AFRIKANERISM.

Africanderland var. AFRIKANDERLAND.

Africanism /ˈæfrɪkənɪzm/ *n.* [AFRICAN *n.*[1] sense 1 + Eng. suffix *-ism*, forming the name of a system or theory.] A philosophical and political creed based on the belief that black African values should predominate in Africa and that black Africans should achieve political control without assistance from whites. See also PAC. Cf. BLACK CONSCIOUSNESS.

1952 Z. MOTHOPENG in *Drum* July 10 The present basis of the struggle is Africanism – we must broaden the basis. **1957** W.M. HAILEY *Afr. Survey* 251 It seems advisable on this occasion to give prominence to the use of the term 'Africanism' rather than 'nationalism'. **1959** *Cape Times* 14 Apr. 8 Africanism can be accepted as a solution in one sense, viz. that Africa in future must belong to the Africans, that is to those peoples who have chosen Africa as their home. **1963** M. BENSON *Afr. Patriots* 243 'Africanism' had an obvious emotional appeal especially to younger men, not only in a negative retaliation to Afrikaner nationalism but in positive identification with what was happening in other African countries. **1986** P. MAYLAM *Hist. of Afr. People* 184 Africanism in the 1940s found its main institutional expression in the ANC's Youth League. **1986** *Sowetan* 17 Nov. 2 More than 1 000 SA Black Municipal and Allied Workers delegates yesterday adopted Africanism as a 'guiding factor' in the black liberation struggle. **1988** P. LAWRENCE in *Saturday Star* 9 July 11 Africanism .. sees the struggle in South Africa as primarily a struggle against colonialism and for 'national liberation and self-determination' of the indigenous people. **1990** *Weekend Argus* 17 Feb. 13 Some .. proclaim a policy of 'non-racialism' and others .. a more racially exclusive one of 'Africanism'.

Africanist /ˈæfrɪkənɪst/ *n.* and *adj.* [AFRICAN *n.*[1] sense 1 + Eng. suffix *-ist*, designating a follower or adherent of (a philosophy), or forming an adj.]

A. *n.* An African nationalist who advocates or supports a socio-political system based on AFRICANISM. Also *attrib.*

1956 *New Age* 5 July 1 The cry 'Azikwelwa' .. has held together the longest and most complete boycott ever ... Some of the boycotters, who are leading 'Africanists', have voiced the demand that the [bus] company abandon the route. **1958** A. SAMPSON *Treason Cage* 87 The Africanists believed that Africans must 'go it alone', and that they alone could achieve their own liberation. *Ibid.* 98 The most formidable critics within Congress were the 'Africanists' .. their argument boiling down to the old cry of 'Africa for the Africans'. **1978** T.R.H. DAVENPORT *S. Afr.: Mod. Hist.* 285 Recriminations between the two wings, the leftists and the Africanists, resulted ... At the Transvaal A.N.C. conference, in November 1958, Robert Sobukwe led a walk-out ... In March 1959, the Pan-Africanist Congress was formed. **1988** P. LAWRENCE in *Saturday Star* 9 July 11 Africanists are sharply critical of the Freedom Charter, a document accepted by both the ANC and the UDF. **1990** M. NTSOELENGOE in *City Press* 4 Mar. 9 Africanists throughout the world are commemorating the death of Robert Mangaliso 'Wonderboy' Sobukwe, who had a vision of a new non-racial South Africa.

B. *adj.* Of or pertaining to the philosophy of AFRICANISM.

1962 A.J. LUTHULI *Let my People Go* 185 The clash between Congress as a whole and its 'Africanist' membership was becoming difficult to contain ... The number of Africanists was small, but they were vocal. **1990** *Frontline* Mar.-Apr. 14 What of the Africanist and Black Consciousness lines, like return of the land? **1990** P. LAWRENCE in *Star* 11 Sept. 11 Dr Jordan offers a critical explanation for the Africanist break-away which led to the PAC, the most serious of the revolts against communists.

Africanize *v. trans.* [AFRICAN *n.*[1] sense 1 + Eng. v.-forming suffix *-ize* to make (African).]

1. To make (a person or organization) more African in character, as by replacing the prevalent western (or 'white') ethos, lifestyle, goals, or attitudes of this person or organization with those of black Africans. Often *passive*.

Used also in general Eng.

1970 *Survey of Race Rel.* (S.A.I.R.R.) 24 In many smaller towns .. there are few Coloured people ... An inter-departmental committee had completed an examination of the possibility of reclassifying such of these people as had become Africanized. **1970** *Daily News* 18 Dec. 13 From a thriving little place .. it has a new, unhurried tempo, a bit more dust, .. more animals in the street, particularly miserably thin, pitiful dogs. For better or for worse it has become Africanised. *c***1985** F.G. BUTLER in *Eng. Academy Rev.* 3 174 Afrikaners are being anglicised; English are being Afrikanerised; Africans are being westernised, and everybody is being Africanised. **1987** *Argus* 8 July 6 Mr Mcanyana also suggested institutions such as Wits should 'Africanise' themselves ... Academic material must be seen to be addressing the need of indigenous populations.

2. To restructure (an organization) by replacing white employees with black personnel.

1973 *Drum* 8 Jan. 10 The complete machinery of Bantustans must be Africanised to such an extent that after some years of training we will not need the Whites.

Hence **Africanization** *n.*; **Africanizing** *vbl n.*

1970 *Daily News* 14 May, Understandably, employers feel they are the best judges of how fast their staff can be promoted and – remembering the chaos that has accompanied over-fast Africanisation in some other countries – proceed cautiously. **1975** *E. Prov. Herald* 19 June 3 The Africanisation of teaching personnel or the employment of teachers in active sympathy with Black aspirations was a prerequisite for the Africanisation of curricula at the Black universities. **1984** E. MPHAHLELE *Afrika my Music* 7 Africanisation should not mean merely employing more African teachers; curricula and syllabuses should increasingly be Africa-based, instead of constantly singing the triumphs of Western civilisation. **1990** *Sunday Times* 1 July 22 Having started the Africanising of the classic, everyone promptly forgets it again, leaving the play littered with Anglicisms which now sound irrelevant. **1991** W. BREYTENBACH in *Sunday Times* 6 Jan. 19 There are five typical fears: of drastic suffering; of declining law and order; of loss of status and influence; of expendability through Africanisation or affirmative action; and fear of revenge.

African Lily *n. phr. Rare.* AGAPANTHUS.

[**1789** W. AITON *Hortus Kewensis* I. 414 *Agapanthus*, .. African blue Lily. Nat. of the Cape of Good Hope. **1882** *Garden* (U.K.) 20 May 356 A variety of the African Lily, in which the leaves are marked longitudinally with stripes of yellow.] **1898** SMITH BROS. *Horticulture* 268 African Lily (*Agapanthus umbellatus*). **1967** E. ROSENTHAL *Encycl. of Sn Afr.* 10 *Agapanthus* or *African Lily*, A strong plant with a showy umbel of blue flowers above a mass of thick sword-shaped leaves.

Africanor var. AFRIKANER.

African time *adv. phr.* and *n. phr.* [AFRICAN *adj.*[1] sense 1 + Eng. *time*.]

Often affectionately jocular, but may be seen as offensive.

A. *adv. phr.* According to a perception of time which leads to unpunctuality.

1963 K. MACKENZIE *Dragon to Kill* 32 Two-fifteen African time means four o'clock.

B. *n. phr.* A perception of time which leads to unpunctuality; *black time*, see BLACK *adj.* sense 1 d. Also *attrib.* Cf. *Indian time* (see INDIAN *n.* sense 2 b).

1974 *Schoolgirl Informant, Grahamstown* Communion this morning ... Real African time set-up here ... The service was at 7.30 and at eight o'clock the first person rocks up. **1983** F.G. BUTLER *Bursting World* 103 It seemed straightforward enough: five p.m. on Tuesday and Thursday afternoons ... It was the first occasion I found myself on the receiving end of what is affectionately known as African time. **1987** M. MOTANYANE in *Tribute* Feb.-Mar., When a friend or business partner .. is late .. do you accuse them of keeping African time or do you wait for an explanation? **1990** *Sunday Times* 2 Dec. 23 'African time' – that measure endemic in this continent where a fixed appointment to meet is no more than a vague indication of the possibility of a meeting, and a rough estimate of

Afrika /ˈɑːfrikə/ *int.* and *n.* [In the Sintu (Bantu) languages, 'Africa'.]

A. *int.* A political slogan of the African National Congress and other African nationalist groups. See also AMANDLA. Cf. IZWE LETHU, MAYIBUYE.

1958 A. SAMPSON *Treason Cage* 14 The crowds shouted '*Afrika*!' when the Bishop had finished, and the groups gradually thinned. *Ibid.* 24 'Afrika! Sons and daughters of Africa, just as the sun rises in the East, it is sure that through all our vicissitudes we will achieve the aims of the Freedom Charter.' 1960 [see IZWE LETHU]. 1962 A.J. LUTHULI *Let my People Go* 210 The Road to Freedom is via the Cross. Mayibuye! Afrika! Afrika! Afrika! 1963 [see IZWE LETHU]. 1990 G. SLOVO *Ties of Blood* 289 'They say more than four thousand have defied so far.' 'Afrika,' shouted Moses' neighbour. 1990 T. MATTHEWS et al. in *Newsweek* 19 Feb. 25 The cop walked up, then, as Mandela braced himself, he flipped a thumbs-up salute, whispered 'Afrika,' and walked away.

B. *n.*

1. In the phrr. *Afrika sign*, *Afrika salute*, the African National Congress salute of a clenched fist with raised thumb.

Subsequently largely replaced by the 'Black Power' salute of a raised clenched fist.

[1952 *Drum* May 35 (*caption*) Dr Dadoo, President of the Indian Congress, and Dr Moroka, President of the African Congress, making the Africa Sign on the platform at the meeting.] *Ibid.* Nov. 15 (*caption*) First women volunteers released in Durban make the 'Afrika' salute to the welcoming crowd. 1954 *Ibid.* Feb. 10 (*caption*) Albert J. Luthuli President-General of the African National Congress, gives the 'Afrika' sign to delegates at conference. 1958 A. SAMPSON *Treason Cage* 11 They cheered and thumped on the sides of the van, while bare grey arms giving the '*Afrika*' thumbs-up salute emerged between the bars.

2. An Africanized spelling of 'Africa'. So **Afrikan** *n.* and *adj.*, AFRICAN *n.*[1] and *adj.*[1]

[1964 see OPERATION MAYIBUYE.] 1981 B. MFENYANA in M. Mutloatse *Reconstruction* 294 When we dare to deal with the black language arts, the Black European Vernacular in Southern Afrika, we have to bear in mind the following. *Ibid.* 295 The latter [*sc.* language creoles] became more prominent after colonists came into contact with the Afrikan peoples. *Ibid.* 296 Adjustment to anything the westerners would throw at them became almost a reflex action on the part of the Afrikans.

Afrikaan(d)er *n.*[1] var. AFRIKANDER.

Afrikaan(d)er *n.*[2] var. AFRIKANER.

Afrikaans /ˌafrɪˈkɑːns/ *n.* and *adj.* Formerly also **Africaans, Afrikaansch**. [Afk., fr. earlier Du. *Afrikaansch* 'African'.]

A. *n.* A language of southern Africa, and particularly South Africa, which has evolved from dialects of seventeenth century Dutch; AFRIKANDER *n.* sense 6; TAAL sense 1 a. Also *attrib.* See also kitchen Dutch (KITCHEN *n.* sense 2), SOUTH AFRICAN DUTCH *n. phr.* sense 1.

With English, an official language of the Republic of South Africa until 1994; now one of eleven official languages. Frequently abbrev. to *Afriks* by English-speaking schoolchildren when referring to the school subject.

[1900 A.H. KEANE *Boer States* p.xix, Taal, Cape Dutch, called by the Netherlanders *Afrikaansch*.] 1908 E. *London Dispatch* 20 Oct. 4 (Pettman), I have always regarded (high) Dutch as my mother tongue and *Africaans* (low Dutch) as a hodge-pot sort of a language. 1924 G. BAUMANN in Baumann & Bright *Lost Republic* (1940) 103 Over a pipe of tobacco we spoke to each other freely in Afrikaans. 1925 *Act* 8 in *Stat. of Union* 24 The word 'Dutch' .. is hereby declared to include Afrikaans. 1926 [see NEDERLANDS]. c1928 BOTHA & BURGER *Grammar of Afrikaans* 1 What is Afrikaans? It has been called by all sorts of names — a patois, a debilitated form of Dutch, a Hottentot language, kitchen Dutch, .. a mere dialect spoken by the uneducated, etc., etc. Its official recognition as a language came very long after it had in reality been the spoken tongue of the population. 1936 *Cambridge Hist. of Brit. Empire* VIII. 859 In 1925 a joint sitting of both Houses of Parliament resolved to amend the Act of Union so as to make Afrikaans one of the official languages, co-equal for all purposes with English and Dutch. 1948 A. PATON *Cry, Beloved Country* 265 *Afrikaans*, The language of the Afrikaner, a much simplified and beautiful version of the language of Holland, though it is held in contempt by some ignorant English-speaking South Africans, and indeed by some Hollanders. 1949 L.G. GREEN *In Land of Afternoon* 90 The people who spoke the pre-Afrikaans of that period were the farmers of Stellenbosch and the Drakenstein valley. 1954 H. NXUMALO in J. Crwys-Williams *S. Afr. Despatches* (1989) 31 The fat Zulu warder said in broken Afrikaans: 'He's mad, sir,' He gave the man a hard slap in the face .. 'On your way ... voetsak!' 1960 G. LISTER *Reminisc.* 5 He also wrote humorous verse, and an effort in Afrikaans, called *Kaatje Kekkelbek*, is almost the earliest printed example of the language. 1960 in J. Crwys-Williams *S. Afr. Despatches* (1989) 334 A helmeted European miner .. took turns with the Basuto boss-boy to shout down the microphone in Afrikaans, English and Basuto. 1968 J. LELYVELD in Cole & Flaherty *House of Bondage* 18 Many Africans pass as Coloreds. Ernest was too dark to expect to have an easy time but .. his Pretoria upbringing had made him perfectly fluent in Afrikaans, the language most Coloreds speak. 1973 *Informant*, Grahamstown My matric subjects are English, Afriks, Geography, Agrics, Biology and Maths. 1976 N. ASHFORD in J. Crwys-Williams *S. Afr. Despatches* (1989) 412 Up to 10,000 students .. carried banners with slogans denouncing the use of Afrikaans such as 'Down with Afrikaans', 'We are not Boers' and 'Viva Azania'. 1977 *Sunday Times* 29 May (Mag. Sect.) 4 There is no longer even a pretence of language equality in official and semi-official circles, and most of the communication, both written and oral, is blandly conducted through the medium of Afrikaans. 1987 *Frontline* May 24 That the so-called coloured immigrants are present in Australia in some force is evident from the fact that Afrikaans is listed as a community language in Melbourne along with Italian, Greek, Croatian, Vietnamese etc. 1990 R. GOOL *Cape Town Coolie* 97 'Why aren't you working?' he asked, in the racy sing-song Afrikaans peculiar to Malay fishermen. 1990 W. SMITH *Golden Fox* 142 Nobody in South Africa with political aspirations could survive without fluency in Afrikaans, the language of the politically dominant group. 1990 *Informant*, Grahamstown I've only got Afriks composition next, so I can't work.

B. *adj.* Of or pertaining to the Afrikaner people, their way of life, ideas, or language; AFRICAN *adj.*[2]; AFRIKANER *adj.* See also AFRIKANER *n.* sense 2 a.

1916 *E. Prov. Herald* 24 Dec. 7 He dwelt on the change from the time when it was an offence if one dared to speak of an Afrikaans people or nation. c1928 BOTHA & BURGER *Grammar of Afrikaans* Pref., This Afrikaans Grammar .. is intended to supply the long-felt want of some kind of guide to the study of Afrikaans by English-speaking people. 1940 *Forum* 7 Sept. 3 Let us forget the bioscopes in the city and visit the Reddingsdaadbond-bioscopes. There is no 'God Save the King' there, and the atmosphere is genuine Afrikaans. *Ibid.* 13 Oct. 19 Several new Afrikaans student organisations had sprung up as a result of a dislike of 'the totally un-Afrikaans fuehrer principle' introduced by the O.B. 1957 D. JACOBSON *Price of Diamonds* 124 A deep Afrikaans voice at the other end of the line had said: 'Good morning, Mr Gottlieb, we picked up a kaffir last night for not having a proper pass.' 1963 S. CLOETE *Rags of Glory* 235 Afrikaans words like trek, kop, donga, dorp and drift — hill, gully, village, and ford — used by the war correspondents, brought the African veld into the parlours of Brixton and the pubs of Highgate. 1973 *Star* 8 June 13 It has been said our tendency to apologise for things that are Afrikaans is proof of this inferiority complex. We are ashamed, for instance, of Afrikaans music. 1978 P.-D. UYS in S. Gray *Theatre One* 141 He was so Afrikaans — Rugby-God-Rugby-Beer ... He even spoke English like a Van der Merwe joke — 'Ag no sis man Anna sis.' 1988 *S. Afr. Panorama* Feb. 24 It was an experience to behold — in the heart of a Black state in southern Africa, homage being paid to the Afrikaans language and the voice of Black choirs singing traditional Afrikaans songs at the top of their voices. 1990 D. BECKETT in *Frontline* Jan. 12 There are people who are so Afrikaans that you could pick them out in the street in Alaska. 1990 M. VAN RENSBURG in *Style* Nov. 119 Personally, I don't lead a particularly traditional Afrikaans life.

Hence **Afrikaansness** *n.*, the state of being Afrikaans.

1978 A.P. BRINK *Rumours of Rain* 162, I know you're trying to free yourself from your own Afrikaansness, but you won't ever succeed.

Afrika Mayibuye see MAYIBUYE.

Afrikander /ˌafrɪˈkɑːndə(r), ˌæfrɪˈkændə/ *n.* and *adj.* Forms: α. Africanda, Africander, Afrika(a)nder; β. Afrika(a)ner, Afrikaner. [See AFRIKANER.]

A. *n.*

1. *Obs.* variant of AFRIKANER *n.* sense 2 a.

2. *Obs. exc. hist.* COLOURED *n.* sense a. Also *attrib.*

α. 1823 W.W. BIRD *State of Cape of G.H.* 73 Slaves at the Cape may be divided into three classes: the Negro, the Malay, and the Africander ... The last and most valuable class of slaves is the African-born slave, — the produce of an European, or of a Cape Dutchman, and of a slave girl. *Ibid.* 74 The Africander slave girl would consider herself disgraced by a connection with the Negro. 1847 'A BENGALI' *Notes on Cape of G.H.* 71 The 'Africanders', or Half-castes, make good servants, but the men are all more or less pilfering thieves. 1861 LADY DUFF-GORDON *Lett. from Cape* (1925) 24 My landlady is Dutch; the waiter is an Afrikander, half Dutch, half Malay, very handsome, and exactly like a French gentleman, and as civil. 1900 A.H. KEANE *Boer States: Land & People* 86 The term 'Afrikander,' which is now extended to all 'country-born' whites, was originally coined to designate this very class of Boers, who were known or supposed to be touched with this (yellow) tar-brush. 1917 S.T. PLAATJE *Native Life* 279 The Natives and the Cape coloured Afrikanders were not alone in tendering loyal offers of service to the Government.

β. 1968 E.A. WALKER *Hist. of Sn Afr.* 84 Half-castes or Afrikaners, a growing class, who were household slaves and often the confidantes of their masters and mistresses. 1986 M. PICARDIE in S. Gray *Market Plays* 93 Imagine that this is the voice of the coloured people who were once themselves called Afrikaners.

3. One born in South Africa of European descent; a white inhabitant of South Africa. Also *attrib.*

α. 1834 *Cape of G.H. Lit. Gaz.* July 103 The number of matches that have taken place between the fair Africanders (the general term for natives of European descent ..) and 'Indians,' proves that their attractions are appreciated. 1851 H. RABONE in A. Rabone *Rec. of Pioneer Family* (1966) 103 You should see how I astonish some of the Dutch folks, and even the English Afrikanders too. 1866 J. LEYLAND *Adventures* 9 The Africandas are the descendants of English and other settlers. 1870 C. HAMILTON *Life & Sport in S.-E. Afr.* 229 Europeans born in this colony are called Africanders. 1880 *Volkstem* 9 Jan. 1 It is .. an insult which every citizen, be he Africander or European, Boer or Englishman, should resent in unmistakable terms. 1882 J. NIXON *Among Boers* 311 The selfish policy of the English Africanders; the internal squabbles of the white settlers, and their lack of energy. **1892** [see AFRIKANDER BOND]. **1895** *Star* 31 Dec. 1 Afrikanders! A meeting of all men born in South Africa of *European descent* will be held at Standard Restaurant. **1897** F.R. STATHAM *S. Afr. as It Is* 139 In the adoption of the expression 'Afrikander' a somewhat bold departure was made ... The word .. has come to signify, all those Europeans, no matter what their original nationality or birthplace, who regard South Africa as their home. **1899** [see BOER sense 1 a]. **1900** H.C. HILLEGAS *Oom Paul's People* 1 The Afrikander class comprises those persons who were born in the country but of European descent, while the Uitlanders are the foreigners who are, for the most part, only temporary residents. **1903** J.C. EVERETT *Easy Anglo-Afrikander Taal Guide* 8 The *patois* which is in general use, and which the Anglo-Afrikander must acquire to be understood. **1904** *Argus Christmas Annual* (Cape Colony Sect.) 38 The physique of the native-born Afrikander – by that no distinction is made, and Dutch, Scotch, English, Irish, etc., are included – is admirably suitable for the rugged athleticism of the football arena. **1912** *The Jrnl* 31 Oct. 4 If a Dutch Afrikander spoke so, it would be decried as treacherous, but it comes safely from an English born Afrikander. **1940** F.B. YOUNG *City of Gold* 385 The Walker joke came, at last, to the quick ears of a shrewd, scrubby man named Joe Robinson, a bankrupt Afrikander shop-keeper from the Cape.

β. **1940** W. ADENDORFF in *Forum* 7 Sept. 3 The dictionary describes Afrikaner as being a white South African. **1943** I. FRACK *S. Afr. Doctor* 115 It is not pleasant for the English-speaking Afrikaner to be reminded, day after day, that he is unwanted and that his future is very uncertain. **1948** A. PATON *Cry, Beloved Country* 265 *Afrikaner*, The name now used for the descendants of the Boers. Some large-minded Afrikaners claim that it has a wider connotation, and means white South Africans, but many Afrikaans-speaking and English-speaking South Africans would object to this extension of meaning. **1950** J.B.M. HERTZOG in H. Gibbs *Twilight* 210 His membership of this anti-English movement of necessity compelled him to depart from the policy of national unity, which included the English-speaking Afrikaner. **1966** T.R.H. DAVENPORT *Afrikaner Bond* 326 The word *Afrikaner* and its variants could be used more naturally in the late nineteenth century to describe any white South African than is the case in the mid-twentieth.

4. (One of) an indigenous breed of cattle, red in colour and with large spreading horns; *Cape ox*, see CAPE sense 2 a. Also *attrib.* See also BONSMARA.

α. **1837** 'N. POLSON' *Subaltern's Sick Leave* 152 Cattle, both Afrikaander and vader-land or crossed, thrive generally over the whole Colony, and would be productive stock if properly managed. **1852** *Durban Observer* 9 Jan. (Pettman), The *Africander* is a very tall, ponderous, large-horned breed of cattle. *c***1911** C.A. POPE in S. Playne *Cape Col.* 424 To those accustomed to the improved breeds the Afrikander appears full of faults, being narrow, uneven, and flat-sided, with a decided lack of fleshy covering to fill up the angularities. **1921** *E. Prov. Herald* 9 Mar. 11 Afrikanders .. exhibited excellent show condition and form. **1937** H. SAUER *Ex Afr.* 195 Of the genus trek ox, the red Afrikander is a long way ahead of all other breeds ... He is a fine upstanding bullock, with long, wide, spreading horns, and stands higher than any European ox. **1950** H. GIBBS *Twilight* 154 Afrikander cattle have yet to gain the quality of cattle in Northern countries. **1967** E.M. SLATTER *My Leaves Are Green* 14 The oxen were not easy to acquire, but in the end we got together a team of twenty powerful red Afrikander beasts with humped backs and spreading horns. **1971** *S. Afr. Panorama* July 5 Africander cattle, the only breed indigenous to South Africa, have always been the foundation of the country's beef industry. **1977** *Family Radio & TV* 11 May 32 Africanders, *Bos indicus*, originated in Central Asia and crossed to this continent as long as 2000 years ago with various nomadic tribes. **1982** M. MZAMANE *Children of Soweto* 183 His neck was as thick as an Afrikander bull's, with jugular veins jutting out. **1990** R. STENGEL *January Sun* 13 Sailors who landed at the Cape six years before Columbus discovered America reported seeing such cattle with Khoisan tribesmen. The Africander has a large, floppy dewlap and a coffin-shaped head .. its distinctive horns .. twist downward, giving them the appearance somehow of being upside down. **1990** *Weekend Post* 6 Oct. (Leisure) 7 A local variant of the breed known in this country as Nguni or Africander.

β. *a***1951** H.C. BOSMAN in L. Abrahams *Unto Dust* (1963) 137 He'll say that his Afrikaner cattle are in a bad way with the heart-water. **1988** R. BILLET in *Farmer's Weekly* 1 Jan. 7 They initially bought four registered Brahman bulls which they used on Afrikaner, Hereford, and Simmentaler crosses. **1990** *Sunday Times* 1 July 22 The Afrikaner ox is the most recognisable beast of burden here.

5. Variant of AFRIKANER *n.* sense 1.

6. *obs.* AFRIKAANS *n.* Also *attrib.*

α. [**1882** C.L. NORRIS-NEWMAN *With Boers in Tvl* 2 Before .. the close of the last century the different languages and dialects had become less used and spoken, and a kind of Dutch patois, now termed Afrikander Dutch, was and is now in the O. F. State and Transvaal, .. spoken by the inhabitants.] **1886** G.A. FARINI *Through Kalahari Desert* 434 A little nigger .. said in Afrikander, 'That is Mr. Scott's .. house'. **1887** A. WILMOT *Poetry of S. Afr.* 229, I spoke to her in broken Dutch Or damaged English with a touch of 'Afrikander' in it. **1901** G.M.G. HUNT (*title*) A Handy Vocabulary, English-Afrikander, Afrikander-English. **1910** J.H.H. DE WAAL (*title*) Africander Grammar. *Ibid.* 1 The Africander alphabet consists of 22 letters. *Ibid.* 6 The tendency of most writers who have made use of the Africander language has been to spell phonetically. *Ibid.* 7 Differences in spelling between Dutch and Africander. [**1931** see JIM FISH.]

7. Either of two indigenous breeds of sheep, orig. derived from the same breed but subsequently adapted to different feeding conditions: the ***Namaqua Afrikander*** (see NAMAQUA *n.* sense 2), and the RONDERIB. Also *attrib.*

α. **1887** A.A. ANDERSON *25 Yrs in Waggon* I. 271 When outspanned, it was taken down to the water .. to obtain milk and purchase the large Africander sheep. **1897** 'F. MACNAB' *On Veldt & Farm* 55 The Count laid great stress on the importance of feeding the veldt in rotation; first with goats .. then with Afrikander sheep .. then with Kaffir cattle; lastly with Afrikander or Friesland. **1911** D.B. HOOK *'Tis but Yesterday* 158 Jan kept the woolled sheep on his property, while Charles had the Africander sheep, and they were not allowed to mix. **1925** H.J. MANDELBROTE tr. *O.F. Mentzel's Descr. of Cape of G.H.* II. 56 The average dead weight of the Afrikander sheep is about 65 lbs. **1936** *Cambridge Hist. of Brit. Empire* VIII. 17 Native cattle and sheep, obtained by barter from the Hottentots, formed the basis for the stock of the early colonists. The breeds that were developed were in both cases indicated as 'Afrikaanders', to distinguish them from imported European types. **1945** [see PERSIAN]. **1968** [see BLINKHAAR *n.*²].

β. **1946** S. CLOETE *Afr. Portraits* 26 At the age of nine he left home with his grandfather, father, his uncles Gert and Theunis, their families, a flock of nearly thirty thousand Afrikaaner sheep and a few hundred horses and cattle.

B. *adj. obs.*

1. AFRIKANER *adj.*

α. **1822** W.J. BURCHELL *Trav.* I. 274 Their industry .. excited .. some jealousy and unkindness in the behaviour of their Africaander neighbours towards them. **1837** [see SETTLER sense 2 a]. **1849** E.D.H.E. NAPIER *Excursions in Sn Afr.* II. 29 We were .. obliged to conform in every respect to the usual slow, tortoise-like 'Africander' movements of treking. **1881** [see BOERESS]. **1892** *The Jrnl* 20 Sept. 2 He is a trustworthy, honourable and steadfast landvader, who if elected, will send the Hollanders away, and set up a purely Afrikander Government. **1900** W.S. CHURCHILL *London to Ladysmith* 120 Think of a great Afrikander Republic – all South Africa speaking Dutch. **1913** [see Pettman quot. at AFRIKANERDOM sense 1]. **1924** L. COHEN *Reminisc. of Jhb.* 15 An Africander accent you couldn't cut with a knife without blunting it. **1930** *Friend* 25 Aug. 14 Misgivings as to the women's franchise also exercise party adherents who condemn it as socialistic and opposed to Afrikander traditions.

2. AFRICAN *adj.*¹ sense 1 a.

α. **1840** W. PITT *Cabin Boy* 149 There were .. horse races, cricket matches, the swell, prime of life, bang up and Africanda societies, balls, fêtes champetres contrasted with arduous services. **1881** *E. London Dispatch & Frontier Advertiser* 12 Jan. 2 We should like this journal to be as 'Africander' as possible in all saving the ugly euphony of the term. **1910** J. RUNCIE *Idylls by Two Oceans* 16 Roger, the Africander collie, trotted gaily to the swinging strides of the rand miner.

Afrikander Bond /ˌafrɪˈkɑːndə(r) ˈbɔnt/ *n. phr. Hist.* Also **Africaaner Bond**, etc. [Afk., *Afrikander*, var. AFRIKANER *n.* sense 2 a + *bond* league, association.] A political party at the Cape between 1880 and 1911, originally established as a pan-Afrikaner movement, and later supporting the all-inclusive white nationalism which led to UNION in 1910; BOND *n.*² sense 1. Also *attrib.*

1884 *Times* (Canada) 6 Mar. 6 The Afrikaner Bond .. was sending petitions that the Basutos should be handed back to the British Government. **1888** *Cape Punch* 25 Jan. 62 The present Government should know as much about sleepers as anyone in South Africa – regular old Afrikander Bond sleepers too. **1892** J.E. RITCHIE *Brighter S. Afr.* 123 The Afrikander Bond, a political organization, was founded in 1881 ... An Afrikander is considered as such by the Bond who, whether by birth or adoption, considers Africa as his home, and its interests as his own. The object of the Bond, as defined by its general committee, is .. the formation of a South African nationality, by means of union and co-operation. **1896** PURVIS & BIGGS *S. Afr.* 171 Closely associated with Mr Rhodes' Premiership was the Africander Bond .. at present the most important political association in South Africa. **1900** H.C. HILLEGAS *Oom Paul's People* 243 In Cape Colony there is an organization called the Afrikander Bond which recently has gained control of the politics of the colony, and which will undoubtedly be supreme for many years to come. **1915** J.K. O'CONNOR *Afrikander Rebellion* 20 One of the greatest blights that ever made itself known in South Africa was the Afrikander Bond, which incubated the germ of racialism. **1926** M. NATHAN *S. Afr. from Within* 47 It was at this period [*sc.* 1890] that the Afrikander Bond became an active force in Cape politics. **1936** *Cambridge Hist. of Brit. Empire* VIII. 492 In 1879 S.J. du Toit .. launched in *Die Patriot* a project for the establishment of a new organisation to be called the Afrikander Bond. **1946** S. CLOETE *Afr. Portraits* 274 Rhodes formed an alliance with Hofmeyr's Africaaner Bond, persuading him that their ends were his own – a United South Africa. **1966** T.R.H. DAVENPORT *Afrikaner Bond* p.ix, The Afrikaner Bond was thus the chief lineal ancestor to both the government party and the major opposition party of mid-twentieth century South Africa. **1974** D. ROOKE *Margaretha de la Porte* 101 In a few years' time when the elections were held he might be the President of the Transvaal; and later when the Afrikander Bond had achieved its aim of union, the Prime Minister of South Africa. **1986** P. MAYLAM *Hist. of Afr. People* 154 The conference .. decided little more than to support Progressive candidates in the forthcoming Cape election against the Afrikaner Bond-dominated South African Party. **1990** R. GOOL *Cape Town Coolie* 5 One of my grandfathers had been a founder of one of the country's most progressive institutions – the *Afrikaner Bond*. *Ibid.* 19 The *Stellenbosch Van Der Merwes* .. had more than a hand in the beginnings of the Great Trek, and later in the formation of the liberal *Afrikaner Bond*.

Afrikanderdom var. AFRIKANERDOM.

Afrikanderism var. AFRIKANERISM.

Afrikanderize var. AFRIKANERIZE.

Afrikanderland *n. obs.* Also **Africanderland**. [Afk. *Afrikander*, var. AFRIKANER *n.* sense 2 a +

Eng. *land*.] Afrikaners collectively; the areas inhabited by Afrikaners. See also AFRIKANERDOM sense 1.

1899 *Grocott's Daily Mail* 10 July 2 We have had enough delay .. ; let us have some deeds. The wisest counsels of Africanderland are present in our midst. Let us see that we make use of them. **1937** C.R. PRANCE *Tante Rebella's Saga* 149 Once again the Worldly Hope of progress in the backwoods of Afrikanderland had gone.

Afrikaner /ˌafrɪˈkɑːnə(r), ˌæf-/ *n.* and *adj.* Forms: α. **Africaner, Africanor, Afrika(a)ner**; β. **Africa(a)nder, Afrikaander, Afrikander.** [Afk., fr. S. Afr. Du. *Africander*, fr. Du. *Afrikaan* African + suffix *-(d)er* signifying 'belonging to'.]

A. *n.*

1. Any of several species of indigenous flowering plants of the Iridaceae, esp. of the genus *Gladiolus*, but also of *Homoglossum* and *Antholyza*. Also *attrib.*, and with distinguishing epithets designating different species, as **mauve Afrikaner, pink Afrikaner, small brown Afrikaner**, etc. See also GLADIOLUS.

α. **1801** J. BARROW *Trav.* I. 25 The Gladiolus, which is here called Africaner, is uncommonly beautiful with its tall waving spike of striped flowers. **1810** G. BARRINGTON *Acct of Voy.* 341 The *Africaner*, is uncommonly beautiful with its tall waving spike of striped flowers, and has also a fragrant smell. That species of a deep crimson is still more elegant. **1970** M.R. LEVYNS in *Std Encycl. of Sn Afr.* I. 185 *Large brown afrikaner, Aandpypie. Ribbokblom. Kaneelblom.* (*Gladiolus grandis*) ... This afrikaner is sweetly scented at night ... *Small brown afrikaner*, (*Gladiolus maculatus*). This is a more common plant, with smaller flowers than the large brown afrikaner ... *Mauve afrikaner, Sandpypie.* (*Gladiolus carinatus*). **1985** A. TREDGOLD *Bay between Mountains* 161 There were afrikaners, painted ladies, proteas and many other flowers on the hills.

β. **1861** 'A LADY' *Life at Cape* (1963) 36 The smell of the sugar and buchu bushes, and the pungent odour of the bulbs and Africander lilies peeping out under their skirts, are the best cures I know for a nervous headache. **1904** *Argus Christmas Annual* (Cape Colony Sect.) 19 The thin red line of 'Afrikanders,' far flung among the stones. **1912** *Cape Times* 14 Sept. 9 (Pettman), Called by some people the *Mauve Afrikander*, this beautiful flower may be found here growing from 3 to 4 feet high, with as many as ten or twelve flowers on a stem. **1913** H. TUCKER *Our Beautiful Peninsula* 70 It becomes garden-gay with .. the pale blue and delicate rose of afrikanders and pypjes. **1917** R. MARLOTH *Common Names* 4 *Africander*, (Afrikaander). Various species of *Gladiolus* and *Antholyza*, especially in the South West. **1933** J. JUTA *Look Out for Ostriches* 20 Sometimes we found the rarer, cocoa coloured *Afrikanders*, a delicate member of the large gladiolus family. **1937** M. ALSTON *Wanderings* 38 The largest and most beautiful Afrikander lilies she had ever seen. **1954** M. KUTTEL *Quadrilles & Konfyt* 86 Lettie Duckitt .. remembers seeing Miss North painting the scarlet Africanders at Groote Post.

2.a. A Dutch-speaking (or later Afrikaans-speaking) white inhabitant of South Africa, usu. of Dutch, German, or Huguenot descent; AFRICAN *n.*[2]; DUTCHMAN sense 1 a. Also *attrib.* See also BOER sense 2, SOUTH AFRICAN DUTCH *n. phr.* sense 2.

α. **1820** T. PHILIPPS *Lett.* (1960) 57, I could not help reflecting on the characters of the Africaners (as they call themselves, distinguishing those who come from even any part of Europe as Vaderlandvolk or Fatherland People). **1824** W.J. BURCHELL *Trav.* II. 619 Africaanders, or Afrikaaners. **1834** *Makanna* (anon.) I. 188 That inseparable companion of a Dutch Boer, his 'roer', (or gun — and by the by, the weapon of that sort used by an 'Africanor' is no plaything, being of a make between a blunderbuss and a musket). **1850** J.D. LEWINS Diary. 52 No appearance yet of Van Staade. Afrikaner like. **1905** R. FENTON *Peculiar People* p.vi, As General Piet Joubert said to me one day: 'We are Afrikaaners, not Dutchmen.' **1964** N. NAKASA in J. Crwys-Williams *S. Afr. Despatches* (1989) 345 I'm not even sure that I could claim to be African. For if I were, then I should surely share my identity with West Africans and other Africans in Kenya or Tanganyika. Yet it happens to be true that I am more at home with an Afrikaner than with a West African. **1968** W.K. HANCOCK *Smuts* II. 239 The entire cultural life of Afrikaners was beginning to bear the Broederbond stamp of Afrikanervolkseenheid. Its meaning was that the Afrikaners were by themselves a nation. **1970** *Daily Dispatch* 20 June 20 Mr Terblanche told the audience: 'The Afrikaner has to defend South Africa at its borders while the Englishman and the Jew sit at home with their millions of rands.' **1980** N. FERREIRA *Story of Afrikaner* 89 The young new nation became aware of itself the moment its language was born. Afrikaans, the language, was the birthcry of the Afrikaner. It gave him his name. **1983** A. SPARKS in J. Crwys-Williams *S. Afr. Despatches* (1989) 446 They came, many of the 'ooms' and 'tannies', in Mercedes-Benzes, for the Afrikaner is no longer the underdog in South Africa that he once was. **1988** *South* 21 July 16 'If any national group in South Africa today could understand the language of the Freedom Charter, it should be the Afrikaner,' said Malan. **1990** D. VAN HEERDEN in *Sunday Times* 10 June 8 Some talk of Afrikaners; others detest the term and prefer Boere. **1990** R. STENGEL *January Sun* 40 Since light-skinned Coloureds were virtually impossible to differentiate from Afrikaners, the Population Registration Act of 1950 emphasized association and ancestry as the principal ways of establishing who was white. **1991** K. OWEN in *Sunday Times* 24 Feb. 21 Somewhere in the 60s the Nationalists took the Afrikaners as a people across a moral precipice.

β. **1822** W.J. BURCHELL *Trav.* I. 21 All those who are born in the colony speak that language [*sc.* Dutch], and call themselves Africaanders, whether of Dutch, German or French origin. **1829** C. ROSE *Four Yrs in Sn Afr.* 1 The elder Africanders keep a sore sullen distance. [*Note*] The designation by which the Cape-born Dutch are distinguished. **1837** 'N. POLSON' *Subaltern's Sick Leave* 80 Most of the 'Kapenaars,' as the Dutch and other natives of Cape Town delight to call themselves, in contradistinction to the other native white inhabitants of the colony whom they style 'Afrikaanders,' have some sort of business or another to attend to. **1852** A.W. COLE *Cape & Kafirs* 165 The Africanders, blessing on their simple souls, don't walk through a quadrille, or glide through a polka; but they pound away with feet and arms. **1861** 'A LADY' *Life at Cape* (1963) 34 To see women of this stamp .. turn up their chiselled noses, at good-natured, and by no means vulgar Africanders, .. is one of the saddest proofs of insular pride and power of human conceit. **1902** E. WALLACE in J. Crwys-Williams *S. Afr. Despatches* (1989) 194 The dream of the United Afrikander nation is dying hard. **1903** H. ELFFERS *Englishman's Guide to Cape Dutch* 6 From Cape Point to the Rhodesian wilds, and wherever the Afrikander roams, it is the same language with but little local idiom. **1913** *Times Lit. Suppl.* (U.K.) 24 July 309 Dutch remains the great influence in the English spoken by Africanders. **1926** R. CAMPBELL in *Voorslag* Vol.1 No.2, 9 In Dutch churches I have collected much evidence .. and I understand that the Almighty is Dutch, a real old Afrikander. **1937** C.R. PRANCE *Tante Rebella's Saga* 47 A rascally Irish 'rooinek' whose real name had been Pat Murphy till he changed it to Piet van der Merwe when he turned Afrikander to fight against Cromwell's England in Paul Kruger's 'Freedom War'. **1949** L.G. GREEN *In Land of Afternoon* 212 Kaapenaars, the people of the Cape Peninsula called themselves in the seventeenth century and long afterwards. The farmers beyond the Cape Flats were 'Afrikaanders'. **1966** T.R.H. DAVENPORT *Afrikaner Bond* 326 To the nineteenth-century reader, *Afrikaner* and its semi-anglicized form *Africander* carried a cultural nuance not present in the geographical though not yet politically meaningful term *South African*. **1990** R. STENGEL *January Sun* 33 By the late eighteenth century, the Cape community had formed its own distinctive identity. The people were known as Boers — farmers — and they called themselves Afrikanders, later Afrikaners, the people of Africa.

b. With qualifying word: **New Afrikaner**, a person of Afrikaans descent who rejects the conservative and insular aspects of white Afrikaans-speaking society (see also ALTERNATIVE); **super Afrikaner**, see quot. 1991.

α. **1986** *Style* July 63 The hostess .. sends a frantic eyebrow signal to the **New Afrikaner**. Van, a large, jolly dynamo in a navy-and-grey striped suit with matching navy-and-grey striped tie (made in Germany, acquired in Windhoek), instantly comes to the rescue. **1989** C. DU PLESSIS in *Style* Dec. 153 Stark, easily recognisable Afrikaner symbols and metamorphosised metaphors .. reflect .. the 'New' Afrikaner writer's attitute towards his heritage: .. Kappie-kommando tannies with faces like hogs, regimented AWB-types, a grotesque Anglo-Saxon .. swallowing a black man. **1990** *Top Forty* July 12 Republic Day ... On a day that is usually noted for its solemnity, pomp and Afrikaner nationalism, a bunch of 'new' Afrikaners put together an irreverent gathering of musos in the Woodstock style, calling it 'Houtstok', probably because the day's significance made them feel quite *naar*. **1990** R. MALAN *My Traitor's Heart* 127 New Afrikaners .. were people of the most civilized sort. They holidayed in Europe, collected art, drank fine Cape wines, and appreciated the best in books — especially the works of Breyten Breytenbach. **1991** A. VAN WYK (*title*) The Birth of a New Afrikaner. *Ibid.* 27 A stereotype **'super' Afrikaner** .. may best be defined as an uncompromising Afrikaans-speaking Christian Nationalist and uncritical apartheid supporter ... Most of them were either members or supporters of the secret *Afrikaner Broederbond* ... According to the yardstick of the 'supers' I didn't qualify as a 'true' Afrikaner.

3. [Named for the clan founder, *Jager Afrikaner* (d. 1823).] OORLAM *n.* sense 2. Also *attrib.*

α. **1840** J. TINDALL *Jrnl* (1959) 19 In company with our two friends we set off at 8 p.m. to visit the outpost of the Afrikaners at Jerusalem. **1842** *Ibid.* 32 The Afrikaners reside 9 days northward of Nosasanabis, and have taken possession of a part of Damaraland. **1856** *Ibid.* 35 Adjoining the Eastern boundary of the Bundel Zwarts are the Africaners, a part of the tribe of which Jonker is the chief. **1877** *Sel. Comm. Report on Mission to Damaraland* 54 Within the tract of country .. two tribes of Namaquas, the Afrikaaners and the Gobabis people, are living. **1905** G.W. STOW *Native Races of S. Afr.* 327 The Africaanders belonged to a large tribe of Hottentots who were at one time called Jagers or the Hunters, and who lived within a hundred miles of Capetown, near the rugged Witsenberg range of mountains. **1930** I. SCHAPERA *KhoiSan Peoples* 347 In the same way, the Afrikaners .. an Orlam tribe, are said to be an old branch of the present !Aman or Bethanie Hottentots .. who formerly lived between the Berg and the Olifants River in Cape Colony. **1969** [see OORLAM *n.* sense 2]. **1987** D. HAARHOFF in *Eng. Academy Rev.* 4 28 His cries at birth were lost in war cries against the Afrikaner Nama.

4. Variant of AFRIKANDER *n.* sense 3.

5. Variant of AFRIKANDER *n.* sense 7.

6. Variant of AFRIKANDER *n.* sense 4.

7. Variant of AFRIKANDER *n.* sense 2.

8. *rare.* Any South African, irrespective of colour, language, or descent.

α. **1973** A. SMALL in *Weekend Post* 24 Mar. 1, I would want 'Afrikaner' now to translate as 'African', just as 'Amerikaner' translates as 'American'. In this sense we are all Afrikaners (when we are described in Afrikaans), whether we be black, blue, pink, or what have you. **1980** *Het Suid-Western* 13 June, The Rev Martin Kota, of the Church of Christ, gave a talk on the unity of 'all Afrikaners, white, black, brown or yellow'.

9. Either of two plant species of the genus *Tagetes*, family Asteraceae, indigenous to Mexico: *T. erecta* (also known as *African marigold*), or *T. minuta* (also known as *kleinafrikaner*); see also *khaki bush* (KHAKI *adj.* sense 1 b).

α. **1981** *Het Suid-Western* 18 Feb. 2 Khaki bush and afrikaners .. are members of the genus Tagetes.

B. *adj.* Of, pertaining to, or descriptive of Afrikaans-speaking people; AFRIKAANS *adj.*; AFRIKANDER *adj.* sense 1; cf. BOERE sense 1 a. See also DUTCH *adj.* sense 1.

α. **1950** H. GIBBS *Twilight* 230 In every respect, at all times, the children of Afrikaner people are to be kept separate from all others in South Africa, including the children of English-speaking people. **1953** LANHAM & MOPELI-PAULUS *Blanket Boy's Moon* 46, I have seen, Moruti, that most of the police and the men who work on the railway, and on the trams, seem to be of the Afrikaner nation. **1969** S. UYS in J. Crwys-Williams *S. Afr. Despatches* (1989) 396 The rousing of the Nationalist rank and file out of its apathy, the whole emotional mobilisation of the Afrikaner nation, is generating political intemperance and intolerance. **1983** A. SPARKS in *Ibid.* 446 He also noted that the Bible is abundant in its approval of the preservation of a people's heritage – and mampoer, after all, is a piece of Afrikaner culture ... A band struck up, featuring a concertina and guitar, playing the bouncy waltzes and quicksteps of traditional *boeremusiek*, the music of the Voortrekkers. **1983** [see ENGELSMAN sense 2]. **1988** *South* 21 July 16 Afrikaner history was a parallel of what was happening at present in liberation politics. **1990** R. MALAN *My Traitor's Heart* 127 Five hundred tuxedoed members of the High Afrikaner Establishment. **1991** A.C. LOBAIDO in *Sunday Star* 21 July (Review) 5, I find it hard to argue with Terreblanche's dissertation of the Boer claim, via international law, for an Africaner nation.

Hence (all nouns, from sense A 2 a) **Afrikanerhood, -ness, -ship, -skap** [Afk. *-skap* -ship].

1956 J.C. VAN ROOY in M. Rogers *Black Sash* 148 Those who are Afrikaans-speaking, of Protestant faith, of clean character, who are firm in the principle of maintaining their Afrikanerhood. **1971** *Sunday Times* 14 Nov. 15, I have had occasion in the past to draw attention to the increasing Afrikanerness of the Progressive Party. **1972** *Daily Dispatch* 26 July 14 Mr Vorster and his party politicians are busy exploiting the Afrikanerskap of the Afrikaner for their own party's political purposes. **1973** *Weekend Post* 30 June 22 Although they spoke Afrikaans they had no claim to Afrikanership, he said.

Afrikanerdom /ˌafrɪˈkɑːnə(r)dəm, -dəm/ *n.* Formerly also **Africanderdom, Afrikanderdom.** [AFRIKANER *n.* sense 2 a + Eng. abstract suffix of state *-dom.*]

1. The Afrikaner people; Afrikaners collectively, esp. in a nationalistic or political sense; AFRIKANERISM sense 1. See also AFRIKANDERLAND, BOERDOM, VOLK sense 3 b.

1893 *Standard* (U.K.) 21 Apr. 6 The sympathy of Africanderdom. **1899** P.A. MOLTENO *Sel. from Correspondence* (1981) 122 Conversations which I have had since leaving London strengthen my conviction that the 'Dominion of Afrikanderdom' bogey .. i.e. the fact of a bellicose and armed South African Republic .. is *the* argument and justification which is relied upon for the war. **1900** *Standard & Diggers' News* in M.M. Cleaver *Young S. Afr.* (1913) 89 The great cause of Afrikanderdom, the unity of the race from Capetown to the Zambesi, the mighty principle for which we are now struggling. **1911** BLACKBURN & CADDELL *Secret Service* 313 It may be that the unwanted sight of uniforms and the presence of the symbolism of war excited young Afrikanerdom. **1913** C. PETTMAN *Africanderisms* 23 *Africanderdom*, .. That section of the people of South Africa animated by the Africander spirit and ideals. **1930** L. BARNES *Caliban in Afr.* 118 Afrikaner supremacy must be protected, even .. 'at the cost of injustice to the native.' That, in its naked crudity, is the final answer of Afrikanerdom to the native question. **1941** *Bantu World* 22 Feb. 4 'The members of the Ossewa Brandwag are, and shall always be, the storm troopers of Afrikanerdom,' said Mr O. Pirow. **1948** *Press Digest* No.7, 48 The movement had nothing to do with politics but .. was nevertheless being of service in uniting Afrikanerdom at a critical moment. **1950** H. GIBBS *Twilight* 179 Having started by announcing itself in favour of a republic, the OB was stated by van Rensburg to be 'the core and concentration of Afrikanerdom'. **1955** G. SARON in Saron & Hotz *Jews in S. Afr.* 382 All the ills of 'Afrikanderdom' were attributed to 'British-Jewish capitalism'. **1960** A.D. LAZARUS in H. Spottiswoode *S. Afr.: Rd Ahead* 91 These miseries have not been brought upon the Indian people by the present government or even on the insistence of Afrikanerdom generally. **1976** *Sunday Times* 1 Aug. 15 The disappearance of Afrikanerdom as an exclusive White group as we know it today will be the prelude to the downfall, too, of the White English speakers as a separate group, although their language will be preserved as an official language. **1981** S. UYS in *Rand Daily Mail* 27 Feb. 9 Afrikanerdom, of course, has never been the monolith that some people have liked to think it is: Afrikaners are a contentious people. *c*1985 F.G. BUTLER in *Eng. Academy Rev.* 3 167 It is possible that there is a profound change taking place within Afrikanderdom itself. **1987** *Weekly Mail* 17 July 7 Some adherents of apartheid regard the Dakar talks 'as an act of betrayal, not only to the apartheid state but also to the community of Afrikanerdom'. **1990** D. VAN HEERDEN in *Sunday Times* 10 June 8 He called Mr Terre Blanche .. 'the rock of Afrikanerdom who will lead us into the struggle'.

2. The ethos of the Afrikaner people, 'Afrikanerness'; Afrikaner nationalism; AFRIKANERISM sense 2. See also *Afrikanerhood, -ness, -ship, -skap* at AFRIKANER.

1915 J.K. O'CONNOR *Afrikander Rebellion* 87 The Republic would welcome any person of any European nationality provided that he adopted the principles of Afrikanderdom. **1915** D. FAIRBRIDGE *Torch Bearer* 134 Where is the sacred spirit of Afrikanderdom? **1926** S.G. MILLIN *S. Africans* 156 There was a spirit of Afrikanerdom abroad. **1959** H.F. VERWOERD in *Hansard* 27 Jan. 55 The United Party .. members said the immigrants should come to plough National Afrikanerdom under. **1963** A. DELIUS *Day Natal Took Off* 4 When all these excitements were over .. and the inevitable onward grind of Afrikanerdom and Afrikaans had started up again, we began to wonder. **1972** [see BYWONER sense 2]. **1976** V. ROSENBERG *Sunflower* 153 Herman Bosman's reaffirmation of his Afrikanerdom was more the result of an overwhelming rediscovery after years spent in a nationality vacuum. **1982** *E. Prov. Herald* 13 July 3 Afrikanerdom did not exclude South Africanism, rather it enriched it and steered it forward on an independent path. **1990** *Bulletin* (Centre for Science Dev.) Nov.-Dec. 3 The war has again been invoked, this time in the general ideological discourse of the far right who see themselves as the true custodians of Afrikanerdom.

Afrikanerism /ˌafrɪˈkɑːnərɪzm/ *n.* Formerly also **Africanderism, Afrikanderism.** [AFRIKANER + Eng. n.-forming suffix *-ism.*]

1. ?*obs.* AFRIKANERDOM sense 1.

1884 *Pall Mall Gaz.* (U.K.) 9 Oct. 2 Shall we throw in our lot with Afrikanderism, abjuring our nationality for evermore? **1892** *Review of Reviews* 15 Jan. 53 The further cry of Afrikanderism 'South Africa for the South Africans.' **1899** P.A. MOLTENO *Sel. from Correspondence* (1981) 88, I see the Cape Times is openly urging hostilities being commenced not only against the Transvaal but against 'Africanderism'. **1930** L. BARNES *Caliban in Afr.* 238 Afrikanerism is wooing with insidious energy all white settlers between Cape Agulhas and the Nile. **1934** A.J. BARNOUW *Lang. & Race Problems* 33 Dutch culture was no longer feared as a menace to Afrikanerism, and the Hollanders ceased to be distrusted as importers of its insidious blessings. **1936** [see VIERKLEUR]. **1974** *Sunday Times* 6 Oct. 8 The day of the 'velskoen' mentality is past ... While staying within the margin of censorship, we have urged Afrikanerism towards the future.

2. *obs.* AFRIKANERDOM sense 2.

1891 *Saturday Rev.* 17 Jan. 59 The .. apology for Afrikanderism which Sir Gordon Sprigg included in his speech on Imperial Federation. **1899** M. MARQUARD *Lett. from Boer Parsonage* (1967) 36 When the public opinion of England is once against this Afrikanderism, one wonders where it may lead to! **1909** R.H. BRAND *Union of S. Afr.* 9 The spirit of Dutch Africanderism on the one hand and of British dominance on the other, has caused the current of national feeling to flow in separate channels. **1924** L.H. BRINKMAN *Glory of Backveld* 146 You will find, at election time, that there is a great show of flag-wagging on the English side, and a counter-blast of 'Africanderism' and 'taal' on the Dutch side. **1930** L. BARNES *Caliban in Afr.* 239 The conscience of the civilised world as a whole has declared emphatically against Afrikanerism in all its forms. **1934** A.J. BARNOUW *Lang. & Race Problems* 26 This language [*sc.* Afrikaans] is to the Nationalists the hall mark of their Afrikanerism.

3. A characteristic feature of the Afrikaans language occurring in South African English; an Afrikaans word, idiom or phrase when used in South African English. Cf. SOUTH AFRICANISM sense 1.

1909 *The State* Dec. 701 (Pettman), If an English boy learns Dutch he is apt to acquire what are popularly called Dutchisms or *Africanderisms*. **1959** *Cape Argus* 21 Nov. 11 Among the words that fall in this category of Afrikanerisms are bobotie, gousblom. **1970** W.S. MACKIE in *Std Encycl. of Sn Afr.* I. 188 By Afrikanerisms we mean Afrikaans words and idioms that have been taken over into South African English. **1974** *Daily Dispatch* 30 Oct. 1 Colloquialisms and Afrikanerisms are playing an ever greater part in South African English – particularly in the language spoken by the country's English-speaking school-children. It appears that the age of Afrikanerisms is now in full swing in South African English.

Afrikanerize /ˌafrɪˈkɑːnəraɪz/ *v. trans.* Formerly also **Afrikanderize.** [AFRIKANER *n.* sense 2 a + Eng. v.-forming suffix *-ize.*] To assimilate (someone) into the Afrikaner community; to bring (something) under the control or administration of Afrikaners; to make (language) more Afrikaans, in form or pronunciation.

1905 LORD A. MILNER in C. Headlam *Milner Papers* (1933) II. 552 A separate Afrikander nation and State, comprising, no doubt, men of other races, who are ready to be 'afrikanderized'. **1955** SARON & HOTZ *Jews in S. Afr.* 207 Of those who fought on the Boer side, some were Jewish burghers who had become thoroughly Afrikanerized. **1960** *20th Century* July 63 The Nationalists sought to Afrikanerize the white trades unions. **1977** *Sunday Times* 29 May (Mag. Sect.) 4 Similarly, coloured schools have been systematically 'Afrikanerised', so that today 60 per cent of the people who speak Afrikaans in this country are non-white. **1979** [see Daily Dispatch quot. at FORTYPERCENTERS]. **1981** *E. Prov. Herald* 23 Apr. 2 It was decided that English-speakers needed to be 'Afrikanerised.' **1985** [see AFRICANIZE sense 1]. **1989** *Sunday Times* 29 Oct. 28 Not even Afrikaners married to English-speaking wives are allowed membership unless she has been 'Afrikanerised'.

Hence **Afrikanerization** *n.*; **Afrikanerizing** *vbl n.*; also *attrib.*

1947 *Forum* 5 Apr. 5 The Afrikanerizing of the cities .. had gone ahead by leaps and bounds. **1952** E.H. BURROWS *Overberg Outspan* 190 The afrikanerizing influence she exerted on her husband. **1952** B. DAVIDSON *Report on Sn Afr.* 158 The 'Afrikanerization' of public life and education 'in the Christian National sense'. **1960** [see DUAL-MEDIUM]. **1970** *Sunday Times* 22 Mar., There is a very real danger of a greater Afrikanerisation of our youth, which will mean that the heritage and culture of the English-speaking section will be lessened and diluted.

Afrikaner Party see HERTZOGITE.

Afrino /æfˈriːnəʊ/ *n.* [Blend of S. Afr. Du. *Afrikander* (see AFRIKANDER *n.* sense 7) + Eng. *Merino.*] (One of) a hardy local sheep breed, a cross between Afrikander and Merino stock, yielding both wool and mutton. Also *attrib.* See also AFRIKANDER *n.* sense 7.

1980 *E. Prov. Herald* 17 Dec. 4 All the courses will be held at Grootfontein except for the Afrino sheep course, which will be held in Carnarvon. **1982** *S. Afr.*

afslaer /ˈafslɑːr, ˈafslaə/ n. Also formerly **afslager**. [Afk., earlier Du. *afslager*.] An auctioneer.

1882 C. Du Val *With Show through Sn Afr.* I. 199 An elderly gentleman carrying on the business of an 'Afslager' (auctioneer). 1943 I. Frack *S. Afr. Doctor* 135 If the 'Afslaer' said they were sold, they remained sold.

afslag /ˈafslax/ n. *Obs. exc. hist.* [Afk., 'reducing auction', *af* down + *slag* beating.] Downward bidding, an early Dutch method of auctioning in which, after upward bidding (see OPSLAG sense 2) has stopped, the auctioneer names a much higher price, then lowers it bit by bit, the first person to accept a price becoming the buyer unless the figure falls to the level of the first bid, in which case the first bidder is obliged to become the buyer. See also STRYKGELD.

1927 C.G. Botha *Social Life in Cape Col.* 99 The method of selling immovables at such sales differed somewhat to that of other countries. The property was first of all sold by *opslag*, advance bidding, and then put up again and sold by *afslag*, or downward bidding. 1965 [see OPSLAG sense 2]. 1981 P. Dane *Great Houses of Constantia* 119 First the house .. came up for sale, by the traditional method of '*opslag en afslag*' — the rise and fall of the hammer, where the bidding opens twice and the best price is accepted.

afslager var. AFSLAER.

after-chest n. *obs.* [Calque formed on Afk. *agterkis* (earlier S. Afr. Du. *achterkist*).] AGTERKIS.

1824 W.J. Burchell *Trav.* II. 397, I had scarcely been ten minutes on my waggon, before Mollemmi came and took his seat on the after-chest. 1838 J.E. Alexander *Exped. into Int.* I. 2, I bought an excellent waggon, complete, with a tilt, fore and after chests, side cases, water kegs, yokes, &c., for 60l.

after-clap n. *Obs. exc. hist.* [Calque formed on S. Afr. Du. *achterklap*, *achter* rear + *klap* flap.] The canvas curtain hanging at the rear of a covered wagon. Cf. FORE-CLAP, KLAP n.²

1850 R.G.G. Cumming *Hunter's Life* I. 23 'Fore-clap' and 'after-clap,' which is the colonial name for two broad canvas curtains, that form part and parcel of the sail, and hang in the front and rear of the waggon, reaching to within a few inches of the ground. 1913 C. Pettman *Africanderisms* 24 After-clap, The canvas curtain hanging at the back of the wagon. 1942 S. Cloete *Hill of Doves* 392 He was mending the afterclap of the wagon, stitching it up where it was torn.

after-ox n. *hist.* [Calque formed on S. Afr. Du. *achteros*, *achter* rear + *os* ox.]

1. One of the hindmost pair in a team of draught oxen; ACHTER OX; AGTEROS. Cf. FRONT OX.

1822 W.J. Burchell *Trav.* I. 303 As these two were a serious loss to the team, one being my best 'after-ox', Philip was desirous of riding back in search of them. 1831 *Graham's Town Jrnl* 30 Dec. 1 For Sale, on Commission, a New Waggon, .. a span of Oxen, 2 black after Oxen .. and 2 plots of ground in Graham's Town. 1844 [see FLAUW]. 1857 T. Shone *Diary*. 15 June, Henry bought from Wm. Banks 6 Oxen, he paid for 2 after Oxen £14.0.0. 1864 T. Baines *Explor. in S.-W. Afr.* 54 They had brought the expected oxen from Lamert, but .. there was not a fore nor after ox among the lot, and without them it would be impossible to go forward. 1878 P. Gillmore *Great Thirst Land* 335, I do not think I have another bullock that would treck as an after-ox. 1881 —— *Land of Boer* 251 Among the loose cattle was a magnificent after-ox .. a splendid beast, very fat. 1907 J.P. Fitzpatrick *Jock of Bushveld* (1909) 233 Achmoed and Bakir, the big after-oxen who carried the disselboom contentedly through the trek .. heaved together. 1914 [see SCOTCH CART]. 1934 B.I. Buchanan *Pioneer Days* 97 The hook to which the trektouw was fastened was pulled out of the disselboom, and the rest of the span went on, leaving the whole weight of the wagon on the two after oxen. 1967 E.M. Slatter *My Leaves Are Green* 125 The after oxen had the worst of it — they had to hold back the wagon and steady its mad rush.

2. *comb.* **after-ox sjambok** /-ˌʃæmbɒk/ *obs.*, AGTEROS SJAMBOK.

1896 C. Brownlee in F.G. Butler *When Boys Were Men* (1969) 143 An after-ox sjambok was used to accelerate their exit from the house.

after-rider n. *hist.* [Calque formed on S. Afr. Du. *achter-rijder*.] AGTERRYER sense 1.

1824 [see AGTERRYER sense 1]. 1856 J. & M. Churchill *Merchant Family in Natal* (1979) 74, I took horse in company with a young man and Kaffir 'after-rider' to 'Pretoria' a new Dorp lately begun about a hundred miles E.N.E. from Mooi River Dorp. a1868 J. 'Montgomery *Reminisc.* (1981) 127 Then I told my after-rider, Plaatje Rooibaadje, to lead some of our horses down the hill, while we continued slowly to retreat. 1875 C.B. Bisset *Sport & War* 47, I could not afford an 'after-rider', but it so happened that my second horse required no one to lead him. 1898 G. Nicholson *50 Yrs* 181, I had a Hottentot 'afterrider' with me and was armed with a good double gun. 1907 W.C. Scully *By Veldt & Kopje* 27 An alert-looking Hottentot was assigned to me as an after-rider and guide. 1913 C. Pettman *Africanderisms* 21 The English colonists have simply translated the term [*sc.* achterrijder] and speak of their 'after-rider'. 1931 V. Sampson *Kom Binne* 146 A Hottentot boy, known as an after-rider, followed the cart on horseback, for the purpose of opening gates on the road, and attending to the horses in the Dorp. 1944 J. Mockford *Here Are S. Africans* 72 The guns were piled up in charge of the coloured after-riders at the two milk trees at the Boer encampment. 1953 K. Larson *Talbots, Sweetnams & Wiggills*. 31, I left Plaat-Berg on horseback alone, although it is customary in the Cape to have a young boy to ride with a traveller. The Dutch call him an 'after-rider'.

after sjambok n. phr. *Obs.* [Part. calque on S. Afr. Du. *achteros sjambok*; see AGTEROS SJAMBOK.] AGTEROS SJAMBOK.

1838 T. Shone *Diary*. 17 Nov., I hung up two after sambucks to dry for the use of my waggon. 1878 T.J. Lucas *Camp Life & Sport* 43 There is generally a third performer sitting .. in front of the waggon, whose business it is to punish the wheelers with an 'after sjambok', or thick strip of sea-cow hide. 1914 S.P. Hyatt *Old Transport Rd* 273 An 'after-sjambok', a bullock sjambok, seven feet long.

‖**afval** /ˈaf fal/ n. [Afk.] OFFAL.

1951 S. van H. Tulleken *Prac. Cookery Bk* 123 Head Trotters and Tripe (Afval) of a Sheep. 1978 *Sunday Times* 19 Feb. 8 The superb food which will always be the food of her childhood. She makes waterblommetjiebredie, bobotie, afval, and while I was there was in the process of cooking a myriad of crayfish.

ag /ax, ʌx/ *int.* Also **aag**, **ach**, **agh**, **og**. [Afk., earlier S. Afr. Du. *ach*.] An exclamation expressing impatience, irritation, exasperation, sympathy, resignation, sadness, nostalgia, or pleasure. Freq. in the phrr. *ag man* and *ag shame*: see MAN *int.* and SHAME.

1833 *Cape of G.H. Lit. Gaz.* 1 Mar. 37 The former exclaimed — 'By what right, by what law have you outraged' — 'Ach, duiveltje,' vociferated Noot, interrupting the concluding sentence. 1892 'Marian' in *Cape Illust. Mag.* Dec. 115 'Ach! but that must have been old Slambie,' he exclaimed. 1900 M. Marquard *Lett. from Boer Parsonage* (1967) 71 Where does the need come in for such needless casting of fuel in the flames. Ach – it is all too sad. 1913 D. Fairbridge *Piet of Italy* 64 Ach, what, man? What should I do in France? The Cape is good enough for me. a1920 O.E.A. Schreiner in D.L. Hobman *Olive Schreiner* (1955) 22 Ach, how nice it is outside! 1936 C. Birkby *Thirstland Treks* 47 Ja, we left the old village. Ag, nice village and I liked it. 1959 [see EINA *int.*]. 1963 J. Packer *Home from Sea* 126 'Og, she's tame, that mooi animal,' said Ben, who loved and admired her. 1978 [see AFRIKAANS *adj.*]. 1989 'K. Lemmer' in *Weekly Mail* 3 Nov. 13 'Ag, the green and gold looked so lovely against the black of his tuxedo,' she sighed. 1993 *Sunday Nation* 8 Aug. 6 De B— said he once earned R800 a week as a crane-driver. 'But ach, the drink got to me and I lost that job.'

agapanthus /ˌægəˈpænθəs/ n. Also with initial capital. Pl. usu. unchanged. [Modern L., fr. Gk *agape* love + *anthos* flower.] Any of several plants of the Liliaceae native to Africa, esp. *Agapanthus africanus*, with umbels of white, blue, or lilac flowers, and sword-shaped leaves; the species so named; AFRICAN LILY; BLUE LILY. Also *attrib*.

1789 [see BLUE LILY]. 1817 *Botanical Cabinet* I. 42 Agapanthus Minor .. a native of the Cape of Good Hope .. differs from umbellatus both in leaves and flowers. 1868 W.H. Harvey *Genera of S. Afr. Plants* 348 Agapanthus, These are well known garden favourites. One is very common on the sides of Table mountain. 1874 G.M. Hopkins *Jrnl* (1937) 214 A splendid thick-stemmed carnation-coloured lily called valotta .. in the greenhouse next to an agapanthus. 1913 D. Fairbridge *Piet of Italy* 182 He looked up and saw Nissa standing in the doorway, her arms filled with scarlet crassulas and blue agapanthus lilies. 1924 —— *Gardens of S. Afr.* 86 Neither Romneya nor Agapanthus have been given a drop of water for months, and yet they are flourishing. 1948 [see RED-HOT POKER]. 1967 E. Rosenthal *Encycl. of Sn Afr.* 10 Agapanthus or African Lily, A strong plant with a showy umbel of blue flowers above a mass of thick sword-shaped leaves. 1988 N. Gardiner in *S. Afr. Garden & Home* June 108 An unbroken wave of pale blue sweeps through in late spring, brought about by many thousands of agapanthus which make a spectacular sight, rivalling any bluebell woods. 1989 *Woman's Focus* (Spar) 2 Agapanthus are bulbous plants with several stems attached to a hard underground plate-like stem with roots below.

agh var. AG.

agika var. IGQIRA n.²

agretjie /aˈxreki/ n. Also **agrietjie**, **aigretje**, **aigrettje**. [Afk., fr. Fr. *aigrette* 'egret, tuft of plumes' (prob. via Du.): see quot. 1966.] Any of several species of plant of the genus *Tritonia* of the Iridaceae which are characterized by feathery tufts of flowers, esp. *T. undulata*.

1902 H.J. Duckitt in M. Kuttel *Quadrilles & Konfyt* (1954) 15 Among them, the crimson gladioli, the proteas of all kinds, the aigrettje or little aigrette. 1913 C. Pettman *Africanderisms* 25 Aigretje, (.. this name was in French transferred from the bird to the crest of feathers which adorned its head.) The Western Province name of a wild-flower. 1966 C.A. Smith *Common Names* 58 Agretjie (agrietjie), From the French 'Aigrette' and refers to the arrangement of the flowers along the flowering rachis, a fanciful resemblance to the projecting head plumes of an egret. *Tritonia undulata*. 1970 M.R. Levyns in *Std Encycl. of Sn Afr.* I. 221 Agretjie, .. A small but attractive plant of the family Iridaceae, widespread in the coastal strip of the Western Cape Province from Namaqualand southwards.

agricultural demonstrator n. phr. A black official trained at an agricultural school and employed to teach improved farming methods, esp. in black rural areas. Cf. *extension officer* (see EXTENSION).

1937 C. Birkby *Zulu Journey* 253 Agricultural demonstrators are drawn from the ranks of the pupils at Tsolo School. In the early years, indeed, practically every youngster who passed the examination was made a demonstrator and sent out into the fields among his fellow tribesmen. **1942** *Off. Yrbk of Union 1941* (Union Office of Census & Statistics) 404 Selected students from these schools [of agriculture] are appointed as agricultural demonstrators or extension officers, and work under the supervision of trained European supervisors. **1949** E. HELLMANN *Handbk on Race Rel.* 185 The Native agricultural demonstrator secures the right from Native farmers in his area to use certain plots ... These are worked in an up-to-date-manner with implements supplied by the Department of Native Affairs. **1955** J.B. SHEPHARD *Land of Tikoloshe* 106 The headman .. called in an African Agricultural Demonstrator to vet his horse.

agrietjie var. AGRETJIE.

agtdaegeneesbos /ˌaxtdɑː(ə) xəˈniəsbɔs/ *n.* Also **agt-dag-geneesbos**, and (formerly) **achtdag-geneesbos**. [Afk., *agt* eight + *dae* days + *genees* healing + *bos* bush.] Any of several aromatic shrubs formerly used for their supposed healing properties. See also *pokkiesblom* (POKKIES sense 2).

1917 R. MARLOTH *Common Names* 4 *Achtdag-genees bos*, Three quite different shrublets have been pointed out to us by native herbalists under this name, all used as tea, probably on account of certain aromatic properties: *Hermannia hyssopifolia* (Stercul.); *Lobostemon fruticosus* (Borag.) also called Dauwwormbos; and *Psoralea decumbens* (Papil). **1934** *Sunday Times* 28 Sept. (Suppl.) 12 There is .. a shrub with small blue tubular flowers called the 'agt-dag-geneesbos' (eight-day healing bush). **1972** BEETON & DORNER in *Eng. Usage in Sn Afr.* Vol.3 No.2, 6 *Agtdaegeneesbos*, .. (*Psoralea decumbens*) struggling [*sic*] plant of the fam[ily] *Leguminosae*, sub-fam[ily] *Lotodeae*; the early settlers used the plant to make an ointment for treating skin ailments.

agterhuis /ˈaxtə(r)heɪs, -hœis/ *n. Archit.* Formerly also **achterhuis**. Pl. **-e** /-ə/. [Afk., *agter* rear, behind + *huis* house.] AGTERKAMER. Cf. VOORHUIS.

1926 P.W. LAIDLER *Tavern of Ocean* 79 Straight ahead through the voorkamer was the *achterhuis* or back room, with once again one or more chambers on either side. **1952** G.M. MILLS *First Ladies of Cape* 42 Approached through the front door was the voorkamer or front room, on either side of which were sleeping apartments. Beyond the voorkamer was the achterhuis or back room. **1963** R. LEWCOCK *Early 19th C. Archit.* 7 A central front door, often under an ornamental gable, gave access to a 'voorkamer' or front room ... Behind the 'voorkamer', and often separated from it by only a screen, was the 'achterhuis', or back room. **1977** *S. Afr. Panorama* Aug. 32 The magnificent teak and yellowwood screen dividing the *agterhuis* (backroom) from the *voorkamer* (front part of the large central room) was still in fine condition. **1991** *Best of S. Afr. Short Stories* (Reader's Digest Assoc.) 147 In early Cape-Dutch designs, the front door .. opened directly into a large room called the *voorhuis* or *voorkamer* (front room). A wooden screen provided privacy in the rear part of the room which became known as the *agterkamer* (back room) or the *achterhuis*.

agterkamer /ˈaxtə(r)ˌkɑːmə(r)/ *n. Archit.* Formerly also **achterkamer**. [Afk., *agter* rear, behind + *kamer* room.] The second reception room in a traditional Cape Dutch house, often separated from the VOORKAMER or parlour by a wooden screen, and freq. with access through a back door; AGTERHUIS; GAANDEREIJ.

1913 J.J. DOKE *Secret City* 134 The achterkamer on the right hand at least was still intact, and the stoep, although deep in water, was built of stone and might resist the flood. **1936** C. BIRKBY *Thirstland Treks* 218, I have always been as much at home scrambling about the falls as in the *agterkamer* of the farmhouse. **1963** J. PACKER *Home from Sea* 23 A spacious *voorkamer* — or entrance hall — leads into the *agterkamer* which is the true living room of the house. **1976** *Weekend Argus* 26 June 1 (*advt*) A large agterkamer/playroom with authentic fire-place. **1976** G. & G. FAGAN in *Optima* Vol.26 No.2, 74 Two small rooms built at the back of the agterkamer (dining-hall) seemed atypically situated. *Ibid.* 75 The voorkamer, agterkamer and reception room had all been painted dark green. **1984** *Cape Times* 11 Apr., Westoe retains much of its original woodwork including yellow-wood ceilings, single panelled yellow-wood and teak doors, and a restored screen between the voorkamer and the gandereij (agterkamer). **1987** G. VINEY *Col. Houses* 82 The folding screen which once divided the *voorkamer* from the *agterkamer* has long since disappeared, leaving a great hall or gallery. **1991** [see AGTERHUIS].

‖**agterkis** /ˈaxtə(r)kəs/ *n. hist.* Also **achterkist**. [Afk., earlier S. Afr. Du. *achterkist*, *achter* rear + *kist* chest.] A storage chest, traditionally placed at the rear of the trek-wagon; AFTER-CHEST. See also WAKIS.

1868 W.R. THOMSON *Poems, Essays & Sketches* 184 Turn the family in to roost securely and comfortably for the night in the inside space between that [*sc.* the voorkis] and the *achterkist*. **1922** J.G. FRASER in F.G. Butler *When Boys Were Men* (1969) 207 On the front of the wagon, between the sides, was the front box (the *voorkist*), and at the back the *achterkist*, or hind-box — into which boxes of all sorts of requisites for the journey could be packed. **1936** E. ROSENTHAL *Old-Time Survivals* 12 In the *voorkis* and the *agterkis* — the 'front cupboard' and the 'back cupboard' — innumerable necessaries for the journey can be stowed. **1948** H.V. MORTON *In Search of S. Afr.* 83 The .. trek wagon was really a caravan in which people lived as they travelled. This meant the addition of several features unknown to the European wheelwright, the katel, or bed, and the voorkis and agterkis, the front and rear chests or kists. **1971** BARAITSER & OBHOLZER *Cape Country Furn.* 221 The Voorkis (the chest in front of the wagon) is bigger and has sloped front and sides, whereas the agterkis (the chest at the back of the wagon) is smaller and square. **1991** [see VOORKIS].

‖**agteros** /ˈaxtə(r)ɔs/ *n. hist.* Also **achteros**. Pl. **-se** /-sə/, **-sen**. [Afk. (earlier sp. *achteros*), *agter* rear + *os* ox.] AFTER-OX sense 1. Also *attrib.* Cf. VOOROS.

1896 R. WALLACE *Farming Indust. of Cape Col.* 269 As many as five spans are sometimes yoked to a waggon to get it out of the mud. The 'voor-ossen' and 'achter-ossen,' or the first and last pair, being picked specimens, used to be worth in the good old early days as much as £16 each, and the whole span would average about £12. **1913** C. PETTMAN *Africanderisms* 21 *Achteros*, .. One or other of the last pair in a span of oxen. **1937, 1977** [see VOOROS]. **1994** M. ROBERTS tr. *J.A. Wahlberg's Trav. Jrnls 1838–56* 58 The agteros-yoke broke.

‖**agteros sjambok** /ˌaxtə(r)ɔs ʃamˈbɔk, -ˈʃæmbɒk/ *n. phr. Hist.* Also **achteros sambok**, **achter-oss sjambok**, etc. [Afk., fr. S. Afr. Du. *achteros sjambok*; see AGTEROS and SJAMBOK.] A short thick hide whip, used to control the draught oxen nearest the wagon; AGTER SJAMBOK; *after-ox sjambok* (AFTER-OX sense 2); AFTER SJAMBOK.

1822 W.J. BURCHELL *Trav.* I. 87 The shambok employed by waggon-drivers, and called *Agter-os-shambok*, (or the shambok for managing the after pair of oxen) is of the same form as the other, but of double the length, and as much thicker as the hide will admit it. **1832** [see CULPABLE HOMICIDE]. **1883** M.A. CAREY-HOBSON *Farm in Karoo* 115 George had .. armed himself with the 'achter os sjambok,' or whip made of thick rhinoceros hide. **1894** E. GLANVILLE *Fair Colonist* 145 He rolled up his sleeves, and drew from the waggon an achter-oss sjambok, a fearful weapon, used for lashing the hindmost oxen, thick at the butt as a man's wrist. **1900** B. MITFORD *Aletta* 57 Gideon had him tied to the waggon-wheel and thrashed him with an *agteros sjambok*, till he should promise not to ask for the girl any more. **1947** E.R. SEARY *S. Afr. Short Stories* 228 *Agterossambok*, A short whip for the oxen nearest the wagon, thicker than the ordinary *sweep* or long whip.

agterryer /ˈaxtə(r)ˌreɪə(r)/ *n.* Also **achterrijder**, **achterryder**, **agter rijer**, **agter-ruiter**, **agter-ruyter**, **agter-ryder**, **agterryer**. [Afk., formerly S. Afr. Du. *achter-rijder* (*-ruiter*, *-ryder*, *-ryer*), *achter* rear + *rijder* rider.]

1. *hist.* A mounted groom or other attendant; a military servant, or batman; AFTER-RIDER. Also *attrib.*

1824 W.J. BURCHELL *Trav.* II. 132 Two boors on horseback, attended by two Hottentot *achter-ryders*, or according to colonial pronunciation *achter-ryers* (after riders) passing by, halted ... These *achter-ryders* .. correspond .. to many of our English grooms. **1833** *Graham's Town Jrnl* 7 Feb. 3 The commando then proceeded in the dark, each warrior followed sometimes at a distance of 50 to 100 paces by his 'squire', or agter-ryder, who carried his musket for him in such a manner as to be entirely unprepared for any sudden attack. **1835** C.L. STRETCH Journal. Mar., W. Simmons was obliged to take their guns from them and arm their 'agter ruyters' 8 in number who behaved well and succeeded in taking 85 head of cattle from about 1000 caffres. **1835** T.H. BOWKER Journal. 5 Apr., He was wounded through the hand by an assagay also an agter rider had his thigh broken by a ball from the Kafirs. **1839** W.C. HARRIS *Wild Sports* 333 In the course of the forenoon, we were met by a farmer from Beaufort, on the Karroo, with a Hottentot achter ryder, or footman. **1846** J.C. BROWN tr. *T. Arbousset's Narr. of Explor. Tour to N.-E. of Col.* 212 He arrives amongst them on horseback, a gun on his shoulder, and followed by a young *agter ruiter*, their kind of groom. **1868** W.R. THOMSON *Poems, Essays & Sketches* 152 His only companion was a young Hottentot *achterryder*, who, with all the liveliness of his race, had been entertaining his master. **1874** in A.M.L. Robinson *Sel. Articles from Cape Monthly Mag.* (1978) 224 A solitary journey on horseback with an attendant *achterryder* on a sumpter horse and an occasional 'off-saddle', to give the animals a 'roll in the dust' to refresh them withal. **1882** C.L. NORRIS-NEWMAN *With Boers in Tvl* 183 My 'achter' rider .. divested the three horses of their saddles and accoutrements. **1887** A. STOCKENSTROM in F.G. Butler *When Boys Were Men* (1969) 59 A bushboy, one of the Agterryders of the escort, came running down the mountain, shouting out in the distance that the whole party was murdered. **1900** M. MARQUARD *Lett. from Boer Parsonage* (1967) 56 His pathetic stories of the faithful old 'achterrijder' Valentyn cooking his *keteltje*, — keeping his horses - .. all these were to me most interesting. **1911** D.B. HOOK *'Tis but Yesterday* 100 Piet .. was armed with his bow and arrows, and mounted on a pony as 'achter-ruiter' to Jan. **1937** F.B. YOUNG *They Seek a Country* 523 Sixty-six armed men were there, with thirty Hottentot *achter-ryders* leading the spare horses, and the ten Zulus driving home the stolen cattle. **1937** H. KLEIN *Stage Coach Dust* 125 The sheriff then ordered three of his 'agter rijers' (native servants) to drag the body into a slight declivity alongside the road. **1946** V. POHL *Adventures of Boer Family* 155, I pretended to be an *agterryer* belonging to a British patrol and said that the officer had told me to ask for these things and that he would pay for them in the morning. **1955** L.G. GREEN *Karoo* 66 Fraser visited them on horseback, accompanied by an elder and an *agterryer*, a groom leading a pack-horse which carried bedding, clothes, food and Communion plate. **1968** F.G. BUTLER *Cape Charade* 13 If only Klaas were free, he could be your guide, and your agter-ryder! **1970** P.J. VENTER in *Std Encycl. of Sn Afr.* I. 253 *Agterryers*, Coloured batmen ... 'Agterryer' is .. a military term, and it is the South African word for the time-honoured custom of having military servants or batmen. **1982** [see BURGHER sense 4]. **1989** *Reader's Digest Illust. Hist.* 246 The Boer practice of going to war accompanied by a coloured or African *agterryer* (batman) who tended the horses, collected firewood, cooked and generally saw to the chores that needed doing about the camp.

2. *fig.* One filling a subordinate position and thereby reinforcing the position of those in authority. Also *attrib.*

1962 A. FUGARD *Notebks* (1983) 50 Another important person in terms of getting things organised was the 'agter-ryer' — the tough bully singled out by the warder to help him keep the other prisoners in order. Every section had its agter-ryer. **1972** R. De Villiers in *Argus* 25 Mar. 9 Who keeps on emphasising the necessity of maintaining the separate identity of the Afrikaner people? Who is responsible for the top-dog attitude with its concomitant 'agter-ryer' tag? **1976** *Sunday Times* 10 Oct. 6 In a big prison in the Transvaal all the 'agterryers' (boss-boys) in a big span .. were Big Five. **1977** *E. Prov. Herald* 18 Nov. 2 The coloureds and the Indians, nearly three million in all, will have to be content with a kind of agterryers' role in so-called white South Africa.

agter sjambok /ˈaxtə(r)ʃambɒk, -bɔk/ *n. phr. Obs.* exc. *hist.* Also **achter sjambok**. [S. Afr. Du.] AGTEROS SJAMBOK.

1821 C.I. Latrobe *Jrnl of Visit* 356 A hard flogging .. with the achter-shambock, the thickest whip cut out of the hippopotamus skin, and used to beat the shaft-oxen. **1859** 'B.A.' in *Cape Monthly Mag.* VI. Nov. 269 These roystering revelers .. plied the 'achter sjambok' with vigorous effect. **1860** A.W. Drayson *Sporting Scenes* 16 He .. exchanges his long whip for a short strip of seacow-hide, called the 'achter-sjambok' with which he touches up occasionally the two wheelers. *a*1875 T. Baines *Jrnl of Res.* (1964) II. 15 They turned the cattle from the dam and, had not Jan gone to the assistance of the herds with his agter zambok, would have prevented them from drinking. **1994** M. Roberts tr. *J.A. Wahlberg's Trav. Jrnls 1838–56* 63 Sent Ia to find my hat and agtersjambok, lost yesterday.

agterskot /ˈaxtə(r)skɔt/ *n.* [Afk., *agter* after + *skot*, on the analogy of *voorskot* (see VOORSKOT).] The final payment made to a farmer for a crop or wool clip, being the total amount due for the season less the advance payments (the VOORSKOT and MIDDELSKOT). Also *attrib.*, and *fig.*

1944 *Cape Argus* 18 May 7 More than 1,000 persons went to Rustenburg .. from many parts of the Transvaal to receive back pay (agterskot) for tobacco sold to the Magaliesberg Co-operative Tobacco Planters Association. **1950** *Cape Argus* 8 Sept. 8 The country is reaping an 'agterskot' in reverse from devaluation. **1958** *Cape Times* 12 Dec. 8 An *agterskot* amounting to £31,000 is being paid to lucern seed farmers in Oudtshoorn district. **1970** S.S. Brand in *Std Encycl. of Sn Afr.* I. 223 The product may .. be sold only to the control board, but the price producers are paid, usually in the form of an advance (*voorskot*), and a final payment (*agterskot*) depends on the average price realised by the control board for all sales from the pool into which individual producers deliver their produce. **1973** *E. Prov. Herald* 13 Dec. 23 South African gold mines are receiving prices on average for their gold approaching the high levels of July and September because of the agterskot — that is the payment of gold sold from reserves at the free market price. *c*1976 H. Flather *Thaba Rau* 179 She added a token of water to the drinks. 'Just an *agterskot* as we say in South Africa'. **1978** *Farmer's Weekly* 2 Aug. 85 The interest on *agterskot* moneys amounts to R1,2 million. **1984** *Ibid.* 2 Mar. 77 A supplementary payment (*agterskot*) will be paid out on most wool types at the end of the season. **1991** *E. Prov. Herald* 5 Jan. 4 Mohair farmers got the bad news first this year. There will be no agterskot.

agterslag /ˈaxtə(r)slax/ *n.* Also **achter-slag, agterslaag**. [Afk., *agter* rear + *slag* whiplash.] The short section of whiplash joining the main thong of a whip to the strip of buck-hide forming the fine end (or VOORSLAG).

[**1850** R.G.G. Cumming *Hunter's Life* I. 25 The invariable whip .. consisting of a bamboo pole upwards of 20 feet in length, with a thong of about 25 feet, to the end of which is sewn with 'rhiem-pys,' or strips of dressed steinbok-skin, the 'after-slock,' and to this again is fastened the 'fore-slock'.] **1922** S.C. Cronwright in O. Doughty *Early Diamond Days* (1963) 28 The agterslag tough and the voorslag keen Came from the royal koodoo. **1925** F.C. Slater *Shining River* 232 *Agterslag*, The thong of a whip. **1937** H. Klein *Stage Coach Dust* 91 Without warning the voorslag broke at the junction of the agterslag, and the released riem coiled back at lightning speed. **1937** [see VOORSLAG]. **1968** *Farmer's Weekly* 3 Jan. 96 Agter slags 75c. **1973** *Ibid.* 13 June (Suppl.) 39 Boermaak Riems, 10 ft. R5,00; cheaper quality R3,60; Strops R3,00; Agterslaags R1,35; Voorslaags 86c doz. **1991** *Best of S. Afr. Short Stories* (Reader's Digest Assoc.) 45 A long handle of bamboo was attached to the 'whip', a cylinder of about 2,5m long often made of sable antelope or giraffe skin; next came the thong or *agterslag*, thinner and about a metre long; to it was tied a longer whiplash or *voorslag*, made of kudu or bushbuck hide.

agterstel /ˈaxtə(r)stel/ *n. Obs.* exc. *hist. Wagon-making.* [Afk. (earlier S. Afr. Du. *achterstel*), *agter* rear + *stel* undercarriage, chassis.] The rear part of the chassis of a wagon, including the back wheels. See also ONDERSTEL. Cf. VOORSTEL.

1822 W.J. Burchell *Trav.* I. 150 Those parts belonging to, and joined with, the fore pair of wheels, are denominated the *voor-stel*; and those to the after pair, the *agter-stel*. *Ibid.* 152 The agterstel and voorstel are, in their movement, independent of each other; being held together only by the langwagen, which by its joint, moves either way. **1972** L.G. Green *When Journey's Over* 46 They made every part from *disselboom* to *agterstel*.

agtertang /ˈaxtə(r)taŋ/ *n. Obs.* exc. *hist. Wagon-making.* Formerly also **achtertang, achtertong**. [Afk., *agter* rear + *tang* tongs.] A forked wooden link coupling the rear axle structure (or AGTERSTEL) of a wagon to the central beam or LONG-WAGON; TANG. Cf. VOORTANG.

[**1899** G. Lacy *Pictures of Trav., Sport & Adventure* 6 The 'trek-touw' (hide-rope to which the yokes are fastened) of the other wagon was made fast to the 'after-tongue,' and all our Kafir servants .. dragged at it to slow the wagon down.] **1913** C. Pettman *Africanderisms* 21 *Achtertong*, .. A wooden fork that passes up from the hind axle to the long-wagon, fastening them together. **1919** *Dunell, Ebden & Co.'s Price List* Aug. 35 Achter tongs 5/0 rough, 7/0 dressed. **1958** A. Jackson *Trader on Veld* 37 Coupled with the vehicle-building industry was the manufacturing of coach and wagon felloes, yokes, spokes, disselbooms, achter en voortang .. and other parts. **1967** E. Rosenthal *Encycl. of Sn Afr.* 12 *Agtertang*, Portion of a wagon holding the back axle to the 'long wagon'. **1977** F.G. Butler *Karoo Morning* 89 The wheels were exactly like those of a real big wagon, so was the undercarriage, the 'voortang' and the 'agtertang' — everything authentic from the brake to the disselboom.

‖**Agterveld** /ˈaxtə(r)felt, -fɛlt/ *n.* Also **Achterveld**, and with small initial. [Afk. (earlier S. Afr. Du. *achterveld*), *agter* back + *veld* countryside (see VELD).] BACKVELD *n.* sense a.

1812 A. Plumptre tr. *H. Lichtenstein's Trav. in Sn Afr.* (1928) I. 105 The Agterveld, as it is called, that is the thinly inhabited northern part of the district. **1833** *S. Afr. Almanac & Dir.* 166 The inhabitants, being all graziers, are under the necessity of migrating annually with their flocks to the Grass or Agterveld. **1873** *Cape Monthly Mag.* VI. 276 (*title*) In the Achterveld. **1958** A. Jackson *Trader on Veld* 29 If you wore velschoens, drank Cape Smoke and wore corduroy trousers you could never leave the 'Achterveld'. **1974** *Sunday Tribune* 24 Nov. 5 Neighbouring farmers in this close-knit community, who live in what the wealthy Boland wheat growers refer to as the agterveld, were stunned by the shooting.

AHI /eɪ eɪtʃ ˈaɪ/ *n.* [Abbrev. formed on Afk. *Afrikaanse Handelsinstituut, Afrikaanse* attrib. form of *Afrikaans* see AFRIKAANS *adj.* + *handels* commercial + *instituut* institute.] An organization of Afrikaans business leaders, representative of all branches of commerce, industry, mining, and finance. See also SAKEKAMER.

1985 [see RANDLORD sense 2]. **1987** A.D. Niemandt in *Nat. State of Emergency* (S. Afr. Govt) 10 Maintaining the State of Emergency in its present form is regarded by the AHI as conducive to improve business confidence, and essential to help stabilise the labour market and prevent labour unrest. **1988** *New Nation* 10 Mar. 14 The Afrikaanse Handels Instituut (AHI), the Federated Chamber of Industries and the Associated Chambers of Commerce.

‖**ai** /aɪ/ *int. colloq.* [Etym. unkn.: perh. Afk.; or fr. Xhosa *hayi*, Zulu *hhayi* no.] An exclamation expressing strong emotion such as amazement, consternation, pity, or regret. Cf. AIKONA *int.*, HAAI.

1900 H. Blore *Imp. Light Horseman* 214 Ai! There was an art in reloading when you sat astride of a galloping pony and the wind blew past your ears. **1939** S. Cloete *Watch for Dawn* 11 Ai, he was a slim thief. One would have to go very far to find a more cunning man. **1955** A. Delius *Young Trav.* 110 Oom Thys sighed. 'Ai, yes. It's a bad business.' **1963** A. Fugard *Blood Knot* (1968) 113 Zach: I'm telling you man, Morrie, not even Minnie .. (*pause*) .. ai .. ai .. ai! What the hell has happened to old Minnie. **1989** J. Hobbs *Thoughts in Makeshift Mortuary* 8 'Ai, Missie Rose, my baby,' Lindiwe mourned, rocking herself backwards and forwards.

aia var. AYAH.

ai-ai /ˈaɪaɪ/ *n. slang.* Also **aai-aai**, and with initial capitals. [Etym. unkn.; perh. fr. Xhosa *hayi*, Zulu *hhayi* no; or fr. Eng. *A.A.* initial letters of *absolute alcohol*.] In urban (esp. township) English: either methylated spirits or absolute alcohol, when taken as a drink or used for lacing drinks. See also BLUE TRAIN sense 2.

1969 *Post* 16 Feb., A nip of 'Ai-Ai' sells in Soweto shebeens for 25 cents and some queens have been offloading it at 15 cents ... Soweto police uncovered the secret of the killer drink known in the townships as 'Ai-Ai', alias 'The Aeroplane' or 'Mpala Mpala' — that has claimed 14 lives in recent weeks. Confiscated liquor — taken in a raid near Baragwanath — was .. identified .. as 'absolute alcohol'. **1970** *Post* 18 Jan. 13 One sip of ai-ai was enough to kill 2 boozers. A wild booze-swigging orgy .. ended tragically this week when a couple collapsed and died in an Orlando West shebeen after drinking a scale of maiza doped with deadly ai-ai. **1985** *Pace* Sept. 4 Have you heard that Ai-ai [or] Flymachine is gaining popularity once more as one of the special beverages in the townships? .. The many current drinkers of Flymachine have forgiven it for killing seven old ladies five years ago, who took too much of Ai-ai. If you don't know what Flymachine is, sorry, it is the blue methylated spirits. **1985** K. Ngwenya in *Drum* July 76 We do not see those people dressed in tatters and drinking mbamba and aai-aai (methylated spirits) as human beings who have characters, emotions and loved ones.

aid centre *n. phr. Hist.* Also with initial capitals. A government office through which black people charged with INFLUX CONTROL offences were channelled. Cf. ADVICE OFFICE.

Although proposed as early as 1964, aid centres were first established in 1971; they were closed upon the repeal of the Black Labour Act in July 1986. Persons referred to aid centres were either assisted with finding employment (if they were legally entitled to be in the urban area), or sent to the 'homelands'.

1964 *Act 42* in *Stat. of Rep. of S. Afr.* 355 Any Bantu who is arrested or convicted on a charge of having contravened or of having failed to comply with .. the provisions of this Act .. may .. be admitted to an aid centre established by or for a labour bureau and approved by the Director and be dealt with in the manner prescribed. **1970** H. Suzman in *Hansard* 23 Feb. 1670 Thousands of Africans are going to be sent back, either by the Bantu Commissioner's courts or by the aid centres when they start functioning. **1973** [see ADVICE OFFICE]. **1978** *Survey of Race Rel.* (S.A.I.R.R.) 387 The Minister of Bantu Administration and Development gave the following figures for Africans referred to each Aid Centre during 1976. No. referred to centre .. 188 608. Not subsequently prosecuted .. 91 631. Assisted to find employment .. 20 871. Returned to homelands .. 38 544. **1981** *E. Prov. Herald* 11

aigret(t)je var. AGRETJIE.

aikona, haikona /(h)aɪˈkɔːnə, -na/ adj. and int. Forms: α. ikona, i'kona; β. haikhona, haikon(n)a, hayik(h)ona, hayi khona, hy 'khona, hykona; γ. aikhona, aikona, ai-kôna, ayikona. [Fanakalo, fr. Xhosa *hayi*, Zulu *hhayi* no, not + Xhosa *kona*, Zulu *khona* here, there.]

‖**A.** *adj.* No; not any; not.

α. [1882 C. Du Val *With Show through Sn Afr.* II. 145 Sir Owen Lanyon .. promised that a Kaffir runner leaving with despatches should bear it; but intelligent 'Ikona Mali' (No Money), and two others of his fraternity who at later intervals were also despatched .. were but broken reeds.] 1941 N. Devitt *Celebrated S. Afr. Crimes* (1945) 120 'Hands up!' The robber shouted 'Ikona hands up!' swung round and fired.

β. 1899 S.T. Plaatje *Boer War Diary* (1973) 1 No thunder. Haikonna terror; and I have therefore got ample opportunity to sit down and think.

γ. 1963 M. Kavanagh *We Merry Peasants* 142 He was immediately indignant to be considered as youthful as that: '*Aikona* piccanin, madam.'

B. *int. colloq.* An emphatic negative: 'No', 'certainly not', 'never'. Cf. AI, HAAI.

α. 1901 P.T. Ross *Yeoman's Lett.* 92 (Swart), We spotted a Kaffir village and riding to it, enquired at every kraal for eggs, but, alas, they had none, 'I'kona', signifying the negative. 1911 Blackburn & Caddell *Secret Service* 70 He passed the detective office and whispered 'Ikona' — that most comprehensive negative in any language. 1936 P.M. Clark *Autobiog. of Old Drifter* 173, I was asked to address the meeting. '*Ikona*!' said I. 'Nothing doing!' 1941 'R. Roamer Esq.' in *Bantu World* 15 Feb. 5 Fancy expecting me .. to be a stay-in .. when all young girls were dancing and having a nice time. Ikona! 1952 H. Klein *Land of Silver Mist* 26 John flatly refused to sleep outside. 'Ikona, baas. Too many snakes and skellums ... Me sleep inside, baas.' 1982 *Sunday Times* 19 Dec. (Mag. Sect.), He took one look at it and said: 'Ikona! Non molto bene.'

β. *a*1931 S. Black in S. Gray *Three Plays* 142 Abraham: Vell, I von't beat you. Tell me. Jeremiah: Haikona, baas. 1965 J. Bennett *Hawk Alone* 212 The eldest African listened politely and when Babby was finished he shook his head. 'Haikona, Baas,' he said. 1979 F. Dike *First S. African* 18 No daughter of mine is going to waste her life away on a tsotsi. Not after all the education I've given her. Hayi khona. 1982 *Pace* Nov. 222 He was not going to be outdone. No! Never! Haikhona! S'true's God! 1988 J. Khumalo in *Pace* Nov. 8 Haikona! This is no fake, brother.

γ. 1959 G. & W. Gordon tr. F.A. Venter's *Dark Pilgrim* 102 'Aikona!' He shakes his head with a decisive gesture. 'You take the money; I take the baskets.' 1969 A. Fugard *Boesman & Lena* 16 Boesman: You mean that day you get a bloody *good* hiding. Lena: *Aikona*! I'll go to the police. 1971 *E. Prov. Herald* 15 Sept. 13 If that is the way to teach a boy to speak his home language then, aikona. I'd rather he didn't learn it. 1982 *Voice* 18 July 4 Aikhona, Chief Leabua Jonathan! You simply cannot get away with it so easily. 1989 J. Hobbs *Thoughts in Makeshift Mortuary* 48 You think would I bring you trouble? Aikona! 1991 P. Slabolepszy *Braait Laaities.* 8, I know what you thinking, you thinking — This guy—? Aikona! 1991 *Sunday Times* 7 Apr. 14 *The Big Time* .. is living up to its promise ... Frank Opperman is creating an enduring character in the combative hero Chris Karedes, with his explosive '*Aikona*!' when things aren't going right. He could start a new craze for the word.

Hence **aikona** *v. trans.*, to say 'aikona' to someone.

1985 H. Prendini in *Style* Oct. 39 What's your case? Don't aikona me, my china.

aina var. EINA.

ainga var. INJA.

aiya, aja varr. AYAH.

aju(i)ntje var. UINTJIE.

‖**Akademie** /ˌakaˈdɪəmi/ n. [Afk.] Shortened form of *Suid-Afrikaanse Akademie vir Wetenskap en Kuns* (South African Academy of Arts and Sciences), an organization which promotes the Afrikaans language and culture. Also *attrib.*

Established in 1909, it was known until 1942 as the *Suid-Afrikaanse Akademie vir Taal, Lettere en Kuns* (South African Academy of Language, Literature and Arts).

1936 E. Rosenthal *Old-Time Survivals* 6 The leading cultural body of the Afrikaans-speaking section of the populace, the Afrikaanse Akademie. 1971 *Daily Dispatch* 20 May 9 Uys Krige received the Akademie Prize for translated work 'Spaans Amerikaanse Ballades.' 1973 *Weekend Post* 30 June 1 A faculty member of the Akademie expressed the hope that politics was not being dragged into its activities ... It is understood that some akademie members disagree with the judge's verligte attitude. 1983 C. Groenewald in *S. Afr. Panorama* Apr. 26 The Akademie was extended in 1942 to incorporate the sciences as well as medicine and engineering.

akadijs var. AKKEDIS.

akarwanie, akervanie varr. AKKEWANI.

AK 47 n. [Eng.; abbrev. of Russian *Avtomat Kalashnikova* (fr. the name of its designer, M.T. Kalashnikov), model *1947*.] Used allusively as a symbol of revolutionary activity. Also *attrib.*

This automatic assault rifle was standard issue to UMKHONTO WE SIZWE soldiers.

1987 S. Sole in *Frontline* Oct.-Nov. 26 The streets would become a mass of people running, singing, chanting and doing the AK47 shuffle. 1990 *New African* 18 June 3 The crowd often burst into chants of Sayco slogans like 'Forward to battle!', 'Viva AK 47!' and 'Viva Samora Machel!' 1990 D. Van Heerden in *Sunday Times* 16 Sept. 21 If you 'suspend' violence but keep a loaded AK-47 behind your back, you are engaging in double-talk.

‖**akkedis** /akəˈdəs/ n. Formerly also **akadijs, hagurdis.** Pl. **-se** /-sə/. [Afk., earlier S. Afr. Du. *akadijs*, ad. Du. *hagedis* lizard, gecko.] Any of several species of lizard.

1864 T. Baines *Explor. in S-W. Afr.* 270, I have never again seen the Voetjes Slang (four footed snake) or Slang Hagurdis (snake lizard) which I once sent home from Mooi River in the Trans Vaal. 1896 J.M. Kerdic in *Scientific African* Mar. 78 *Akadis*, or properly *hagedis*, is a very vague definition, as the name is applied to all species of lizards. 1913 C. Pettman *Africanderisms* 25 *Akadijs*, The common name of a small lizard which runs with great rapidity among the bushes. 1975 S. Roberts *Outside Life's Feast* 26 Jan did not spot the akkedis on the stone when we went past ... He can't notice things.

akkewani /akəˈvaːni/ n. Also **akarwanie, akervanie, akkerwani,** and with initial capital. [ad. Malay *akar wangi, akar* root + *wangi* fragrant, a name for the grass *Vetiveria zizanoides*.] The grass *Cymbopogon marginatus* of the Poaceae (subfamily Panicoideae), with odorous roots.

1856 L. Pappe in *Cape of G.H. Almanac & Annual Register* 341 The creeping fibrous roots of this grass have a peculiar and rather ferulaceous smell. By the name of Akarwanie they are known to most colonists, and serve as a sure preventive against the destruction of wearing apparel, etc. by moths and other noxious vermin. 1887 *S.W. Silver & Co.'s Handbk to S. Afr.* 156 *Akervanie, Andropogon Iwaracanusa,* the creeping fibrous roots of which have a peculiar fragrance. 1913 C. Pettman *Africanderisms* 26 *Akkewani*, .. A plant .. the many thread-like roots of which have a somewhat peculiar and not unpleasant scent, and, when dried, are placed among woollen articles to preserve them from moth. 1917 R. Marloth *Common Names* 5 *Akkewani*, .. The rootstock of *Cymbopogon marginatus* ... Aromatic, used medicinally. 1966 C.A. Smith *Common Names* 59 *Akke(r)wani*, .. *Cymbopogon marginatus* ... Probably introduced by the Malays from the East where the original form functioned for an allied species with an aromatic rootstock.

alamachtig, -magtig, -matjes varr. ALLEMAGTIG.

albacore /ˈælbəkɔː/ n. [Transf. use of Eng. *albacore* a name for the tuna *Thunnus alalunga* of the Scombridae and related species; see HALF-CORD.] The YELLOWTAIL (sense a), *Seriola lalandii*.

1890 A.G. Hewitt *Cape Cookery* 11 The Best Fish for Boiling. Stokvisch, geelbek, cabeljauw, galjoen, albacore, mackerel, elft, steenbrasem, hamburger, seventy-four. 1913 [see HALF-CORD]. 1930 C.L. Biden *Sea-Angling Fishes* 69 The name of albacore is associated in other countries with a large species of oceanic fish not visiting South African waters, but as *Seriola lalandii* is commonly known throughout the Cape as the albacore, the changing of that popular local name is not desirable. 1947 K.H. Barnard *Pict. Guide to S. Afr. Fishes* 116 Yellowtail; Albacore (*Seriola lalandei*) ... In False Bay the record seems to be one of 55 lbs. weight, but larger ones are caught in the West Indies, where the fish is known as the Amber-jack ... Albacore has become corrupted in the Cape fishermen's parlance to Half-cord. 1957 S. Schoeman *Strike!* 108 The most distinctive feature of the yellowtail is .. its yellow tail. It is also known as an albacore. 1967 [see HALF-CORD]. 1975 J.L.B. Smith in *Std Encycl. of Sn Afr.* XI. 563 *Yellowtail. Albacore,* .. Fish rarely seen on the west coast ... It is taken in vast numbers by nets, and is one of the best angling fishes.

Albanian *adj.* and *n.* Also **Albanyen**. [Regional name *Albany* + Eng. adj.- and n.-forming suffix *-an* 'of or belonging to (a place)'.]

A. *adj. obs.* Of or pertaining to the Albany district of the Eastern Cape.

1822 G. Barker *Journal.* 31 Dec., The Report of the Sunday school society for Albany, the Report of the Albanyen track society & Report of the Albanyen Missionary Society were read.

B. *n.* A resident of this district.

1828 T. Philipps *Lett.* (1960) 196 We Albanians petitioned for leave to distil from Grain about 18 months ago. 1832 *Graham's Town Jrnl* 20 Apr. 67 To the Doctor we are, as Albanians, under the greatest obligation for the interest he took in our welfare, when we were left to ourselves, labouring under every difficulty from disappointments, rust, drought, &c. and which we ought never to forget. 1989 *Grocott's Mail* 6 Oct. 10 (*letter*) Come on, academics and others in a similar situation, put your money where your mouths are. 'Albanian'.

Hence **Albaniana** *n. nonce*, matters concerned with Albany.

1834 *Cape of G.H. Lit. Gaz.* Mar. 35 Odds and ends from a Settler's Scrap-book. Albaniana. No. 1. Precious Stones in Albany.

albert-koord see quot. 1913 at HALF-CORD.

a le wereld var. ALLEWERELD.

‖**algemene handelaar** /ˌalxəmɪənə ˈhandəlaː(r)/ *n. phr. Hist.* Also **algemeene handelaar, algemene handelaren, allegemene handelaar.** [Afk., *algemene* general + *handelaar* trader.] GENERAL DEALER sense 1. Also *attrib.*

1898 W.C. Scully *Between Sun & Sand* 26 Above his head was a large signboard bearing the legend: 'Nathan Steinmetz, Allegemene Handelaar.' 1920 R.Y. Stormberg *Mrs Pieter de Bruyn* 20 Two poor Scotch boys who work all hours of the day and night at that untidy old Produckten and Algemene Handelaren shop. 1937 C.R. Prance *Tante Rebella's Saga* 122 Has any novelist yet taken as her hero the pioneer-trader, the 'General Dealer, Algemene Handelaar'? 1949 L.G. Green *In Land of Afternoon* 44 Some of the stores down in the village have modern windows, others are the traditional Cape algemene handelaars. 1955 G. Aschman in *Saron & Hotz Jews in S. Afr.* 123 Julius Ascher, another *algemeene handelaar*, .. was also honorary secretary of the Oudtshoorn Turf Club. **1974** *S. Afr. Panorama* Apr., At one time the 'algemene handelaar' was as much a part of the South African countryside as the sunshine and the wide, open spaces. **1976** V. ROSENBERG *Sunflower* 20 The Jeppe counterpart of the 'algemene handelaar' that served the farmers' needs in Potchefstroom was tailored to the specific needs of the suburban housewife.

alie var. ARLIE.

alikreukel /ˌaliˈkriœkəl, -ˈkrɪəkəl/ *n.* Also **aliekruikel, alikriek, alikrok, alikruikel, allekruk, olikreukel,** and (formerly) **aricrickel, arikreukel, arikrikkel, arikruikel.** Pl. unchanged, or -s. [Afk. *alikruik, arikreukel* fr. Du. *alikruik*, applied in Holland to a periwinkle, a species of the Littorinidae.] The mollusc *Turbo sarmaticus* of the Turbinidae, eaten as seafood and used as bait; OLLYCROCK. Also *attrib.*

1913 C. PETTMAN *Africanderisms* 13 *Arikreukel*, (D. *kreukel*, a fold.) A well-known shell-fish. **1945** H. GERBER *Fish Fare* 70 Periwinkle, Arikruikel. Boil these snail-like shells in boiling salt water or wine stock. **1958** L.G. GREEN *S. Afr. Beachcomber* 129 Another large shellfish which is often eaten at the Cape is the alikruikel or arikruikel, a sort of giant periwinkle found in huge quantities ... Riversdale farmers make alikruikel biltong. **1969** J.H. DAY *Guide to Marine Life* 159 Turbo sarmaticus Linn. 'Cape turban-shell or alikreukel'. False Bay to the Transkei. **1970** [see OLLYCROCK]. **1973** J. RABIE in S. Gray *Writers' Territory* 172 One may dive down to .. perlemoen clinging on trembling tendrils of reefs, amber-red alikreukel and crayfish in deep gullies. **1979** SNYMAN & KLARIE *Free from Sea* 22 Tough but very tasty, alikreukels are considered a great delicacy by lovers of shellfish. **1982** [see Kilburn & Rippey quot. at OLLYCROCK]. **1985** A. TREDGOLD *Bay between Mountains* 18 The shell fish on which they [*sc.* strandlopers] feasted included perlemoen, aliekruikels, mussels and perdevoetjies (limpets). **1986** M. VAN WYK *Cooking the S. Afr. Way* 17 Alikreukel pancakes ... Place alikreukel in saucepan, cover with cold water and boil for about 20 minutes ... Mince cooked alikreukel. **1987** *Informant, Jeffrey's Bay* The alikroks are very tough so you first mince them very fine, then fry them in a bit of butter with onions.

alla wereld var. ALLEWERELD.

Alleen Blankes see BLANKES ALLEEN.

allegemene handelaar var. ALGEMENE HANDELAAR.

allekruk var. ALIKREUKEL.

‖**allemagtig** /ˌaləˈmaxtəx/ *int.* Forms: α. **alamagtig, allamag, -maghtag, -magtag, alle maaghte, allemag, -maghte, -magtie, -magtig;** β. **alamachtig, allamach, -machta, -machtag, -machte, -machtig, allemach, -macht, -machtag, -machte, -machter, -machtig, almachte, -machtig;** γ. (Euphemisms) **alamatjes, alla mopsticks, alle maskas, allemastig.** Also with initial capital. [Afk. *allemagtig, allamagtig*, earlier Du. *allamachtig, alla* oh + *magtig* mighty; or Afk. *almagtig*, earlier Du. *almachtig* almighty.] An exclamation of surprise, alarm, horror, or reproach, equivalent to 'good Lord'. Cf. ALLEWERELD, MAGTIG.

Often used by writers to suggest Afrikaans dialogue.

α. **1837** J.E. ALEXANDER *Narr. of Voy.* II. 70 An old Hottentot sat down .. and swore with a round oath (almagtig) that he would not go back. **1866** J.W.D. MOODIE *Soldier & Settler* 150 If you ask them, why they want to leave you, their usual answer is, 'Alamagtig! mynheer, I have been here for a *whole year*.' **1882** C. DU VAL *With Show through Sn Afr.* I. 195 £100 per month for waggons. Alle maaghte! Jumping Jerusalem! **1899** [see ENGELSMAN sense 1]. *c***1929** S. BLACK in S. Gray *Three Plays* (1984) 79 Allamag, he runs so fast I get soemaar giddy when I see him. **1949** C. BULLOCK *Rina* 30 'Allemagtig!' shouted Piet. 'You've broken the wagon.' **1959** J. MEIRING *Candle in Wind* 32 'Allemagtig!' exclaimed Martha, 'How did she manage it?' **1963** K. MACKENZIE *Dragon to Kill* 86 'Oooo! Yirra! Allemagtig!' said Margaret, hopping from one foot to another. **1971** *Daily Dispatch* 22 Sept. 15 (advt) Allemagtig! 33 Lovely acres fronting large pool on Gonubie River with some 9 acres super lands. *c***1976** H. FLATHER *Thaba Rau* 227 Trudie burst out laughing. '*Alamagtig*', she exclaimed, 'What a thing to say!'

β. **1853** W.R. KING *Campaigning in Kaffirland* 291 Dutchmen flocked round .. drawling out the constant exclamation Allamachtig! Allamachtig! **1880** E.F. SANDEMAN *Eight Months in Ox-Waggon* 361 The meeting listened .. to the explanations, but with many a muttered 'Almachte', and occasional nods and winks of disbelief. **1908** S. BLACK in S. Gray *Three Plays* (1984) 112 Lady M: Go and tell Sophie to stop that gramophone. Frikkie (*alarmed*): O-o-o allamach, if I tell her that ... **1910** J. RUNCIE *Idylls by Two Oceans* 50 They would not let him pluck the birds himself. Allemachtig! Certainly not. **1911** L. COHEN *Reminisc. of Kimberley* 325 'Alamachtig', ejaculated poor Leroux, opening his mouth and eyes to their fullest extent, and wishing himself dead. **1924** —— *Reminisc. of Jhb.* 167 'Sir Drummond has had his digit shot off.' '*Alamachtig!*' sighed the Boeress, to whom the strange word signified something more serious than a finger, 'I do feel so sorry for his poor wife.' **1935** P. SMITH *Platkop's Children* 67 'Allamachta!' 'Tisje said, 'If it isn' Bram Laata! Grayshus sake! Get into bed!'

γ. **1913** C. PETTMAN *Africanderisms* 26 *Alamagtig*, (D. *almachtig*, almighty.) A common expletive. *Alamatjes, Alamastig, Alamopsticks*, are forms of the word employed by those who have scruples about using the word *Almagtig*, and salve their consciences by these variations. **1920** R.Y. STORMBERG *Mrs Pieter de Bruyn* 49 He is mildly incredulous, and says something like 'Alla Mopsticks — what genius is he, pray?' **1937** C.R. PRANCE *Tante Rebella's Saga* 171 A London couple .. insisted on paying a shilling each to wash simultaneously in separate baths! Allemastig! Why two shillings for man and wife, when they could quite modestly have shared a bath at sixpence each? **1944** —— *Under Blue Roof* 141 Electric cookery! Allemastig! It is an uncanny thought savouring almost of ungodliness, with the possibility of electric shock in punishment. **1970** N. CONWAY *Informant, Rhodesia (Zimbabwe)* Alle maskas for Alle Magtig.

alles sal regkom /ˌaləsal ˈrɛxkɔm, ˌʌləsal -, -ˈrexkɔm/ *phr. colloq.* Also **alles sal regt kom, alles zal recht kom(m)en.** [Afk., fr. Du. *alles* everything + *zal* will + *recht* right + *komen* come; see also quot. 1913.] 'All will be well', an optimistic, consolatory, or now often ironical saying; cf. *all will come right* (see COME sense 1). See also *moenie panic (nie)* at MOENIE sense 2, and *môre is nog 'n dag* (MÔRE sense 2).

[**1870, 1882** see COME sense 1.] **1899** A. WERNER *Captain of Locusts* 99, I shall be back by dark .. Goodbye: and cheer up — Alles zal regt kom! **1913** J. BRANDT *Petticoat Commando* 147, I do believe the Dutch South African saying, 'Geduld en moed, alles sal reg kom' ('Patience and courage, everything will right itself'), is responsible to a great extent for the South African indifference to duty. It was first spoken by President Brand .. no one could have foreseen that the first part .. would fall into disuse and be forgotten, .. and the second, 'Alles sal reg kom,' would be made an excuse for a sort of lazy optimism, by which anything could be justified which comes easiest. *c***1929** S. BLACK in S. Gray *Three Plays* (1984) 117 Cicely .. : You see darling, life arranges things properly in the end? Van K. (*strong accent*): Alles sal reg kom if you only wag 'n bietjie. **1939** S. CLOETE *Watch for Dawn* 20 All is explained in my letters and things will come right. Ja, alles sal reg kom, of this I am certain. **1946** V. POHL *Adventures of Boer Family* 77 The wagon .. stopped exactly opposite President Brand's statue; and as I looked up at it someone quoted the statesman's famous motto, 'Alles zal recht komen'. **1959** J. MEIRING *Candle in Wind* 73 We all hope things will get better. Maybe they will. Alles sal reg kom, they say. [**1968** G. CROUDACE *Black Rose* 57 Alles sal reg kom, Emily, as the Dutchmen say. Everything will be all right.] **1973** R. DE VILLIERS in *Argus* 5 May 12 'Moenie worry nie — alles sal reg kom' is the mood. The rest of the world, Africa in particular, is in a mess ... We .. are just fine. **1986** *Style* Feb. 30, 101 Reasons for staying in South Africa ... 14. Alles sal regkom. **1990** P.D. UYS in *Drum* Dec., South Africa has .. a great and generous population that can make the future work. If only we don't panic. Alles sal regkom.

‖**alles van die beste** /ˌaləs fan di ˈbɛstə, -ˈbestə/ *phr. colloq.* [Afk., *alles* everything + *van* of + *die* the + *beste* best.] Used as a toast, or to wish someone well, 'all (of) the best'.

1959 J. PACKER *High Roof* 65 But no, Mr Day wasn't like that. He raised his glass. 'To you and your wife, Mr Day. Alles van die beste!' **1972** *Argus* 28 Oct. 15 There are handshakes, warmly grasped elbows and deep, meaningful looks. Totsiens! Alles van die beste, oom! **1991** M.R. HOWELLS *Informant, Port Elizabeth* Sincerely, and Alles Van Die Beste to you & yours.

allewereld /ˌalə ˈvɛːrəlt, ˌʌlə -/ *int.* Also **a le wereld, alla wereld.** [Afk., *allewêreld, allawêreld* fr. Du. *alla* oh + *wereld* world.] An exclamation of surprise, alarm, wonder, or admiration, equivalent to 'good heavens' or 'goodness gracious'. Cf. ALLEMAGTIG.

Often used by writers to suggest Afrikaans dialogue.

1883 O.E.A. SCHREINER *Story of Afr. Farm* 95 'He says he could kill himself quite easily if he wants to ... ' 'A le wereld', said Trana: and then they went to sleep. **1898** W.C. SCULLY *Vendetta* 28 Uncle, I am sick, very sick. After I eat my heart goes just like an old churn — and I dream — *Alle Wereld*, how I dream. **1900** H. BLORE *Imp. Light Horseman* 168 '*Allewereld*, sieur' said Quguza admiringly, employing one of the Dutch expletives, 'if this be your skill then I need not fear.' **1913** A.B. MARCHAND *Dirk, S. African* 8 (Swart), But alle wereld! your mountain roads are steep. **1926** P. SMITH *Beadle* (1929) 212 Then she roused herself with a gentle 'al-le-wereld!' and said: 'See now, my child!' **1937** C.R. PRANCE *Tante Rebella's Saga* 181 Allewereld! There was so much noise altogether that the parents drove up to see what was wrong. **1959** J. PACKER *High Roof* 14 Allewereld! What a shambles. That's the worst storm I've met in ten years. **1961** D. BEE *Children of Yesterday* 230 Allewêreld we ran away sometimes! I can see them coming at me in my dreams. **1976** S. CLOETE *Canary Pie* 98 Africa was big. *Alla-Wereld*, only his people knew how big it was. **1989** J. HOBBS *Thoughts in Makeshift Mortuary* 208 Allewêreld, a rebel, is it?

alliteral *adj. Obs. Grammar.* [Eng., fr. *alliterate.*] Characterized by alliteration; an attribute first applied by the Revd W.B. Boyce to the Sintu (Bantu) group of languages. See also CONCORD.

1833 S. KAY *Trav. & Researches* 280 There is .. one remarkable peculiarity in the language, which renders it difficult of acquirement by Europeans; and which, as my worthy brother Missionary Mr. Boyce observes, may be termed 'the *euphonic* or *alliteral* concord. One principal word in a sentence governs the initial letters or syllables of the other words ... Changes must be made in the initial letters or syllables of the word which is governed by this euphonic concord.' **1850** J.W. APPLEYARD *Kafir Lang.* 26 The alliteral class forms the second and principal division of South African languages. **1864** M. MÜLLER *Science of Lang.* II. 12 The Kafir, or, as Appleyard calls them, alliteral languages.

all over *adv. phr. Colloq.* Everywhere. Hence as *n. phr.*

Used as a noun phr. in *U.S. Eng.*

1937 [see GARDEN sense 1]. **1956** D. JACOBSON *Dance in Sun* 7 There were cars, we saw from the registration plates, from all over. **1979** *Drum* Jan. 28 With spectacles and parted hairstyle Chief Patrick M— may look like a clerk, country teacher or preacher but .. his government has spread fear all over. **1984** *Frontline* May 39 The way the darkies actually speak is full of

English and Afrikaans all over, not to mention tsotsitaal. **1986** *Weekly Mail* 21 Nov. 2 Just then a bottle and a rock landed beside us. The next moment the police were shooting all over. **1987** L. COUTTS in *E. Prov. Herald* 22 Aug. 1 There were bodies all over. A lot of the people were still trapped inside the bus.

all will come right see COME sense 1.

almachte, -machtig varr. ALLEMAGTIG.

already *adv.* [Eng., influenced by Afk. *al* already, yet, before, now.] Used redundantly, or in deviant word or time sequence, for emphasis, or in order to indicate or reinforce the perfective.

    1891 J.P. LEGG in *Cape Illust. Mag.* I. 95 'Already' is used much oftener than Englishmen would use it, and frequently tacked on to a sentence needlessly; for instance, an Englishman would say 'I have done it;' an Africander, 'I have done it already.' **1916** S. BLACK in S. Gray *Three Plays* (1984) 207 Maudie: .. (*To Van Kalabas*) Have you been in London long? Van K: Amper three months already. Halford: From South Africa, I presume? **1920** R.Y. STORMBERG *Mrs Pieter de Bruyn* 47 If I were a man and your ma was fifty-five already I should still be mad for her. *c*1929 S. BLACK in S. Gray *Three Plays* (1984) 108 Frikkie: Who was her father? Sophie: Corporal Smith. Frikkie: Jah, I had my suspicions a long time already. *a*1931 *Ibid.* 170 Abraham: Oy veh, but I gave you a donation last month already. **1959** J. MEIRING *Candle in Wind* 8 The old Baas had told her to pay for the sugar and coffee she had bought three weeks ago already! **1973** *Informant*, Grahamstown He bought the fish-shop last year already. **1975** 'BLOSSOM' in *Darling* 12 Feb. 119 'Smooching, hell,' he grins. 'This is the "Back to Nature" road we on already so soon?' **1982** *Staffrider* Vol.5 No.1, 34 Mphahlele realized this in the fifties already. **1989** J. HOBBS *Thoughts in Makeshift Mortuary* 274 'We're just checking all the houses on this street for illegals.' 'You won't find any in my khaya ... I sacked my girl for drinking last year already.' **1991** *S. Afr. Panorama* May-June 30 The water is already 45 m deep a mere 800 m offshore, making it the ideal habitat for game fish.

alternative *adj.* Also with initial capital. [Special sense derived from general Eng. *alternative* 'purporting to represent a preferable or equally acceptable alternative to that in general use or sanctioned by the establishment' (*OED*).] In the n. phrr. *alternative Afrikaans*, *alternative Afrikaner*, *alternative Afrikanerdom*: of or pertaining to a way of life opposed to the perceived traditional values of Afrikaans society, esp. regarding apartheid attitudes and policies.

    1988 'K. DE BOER' in *Frontline* Apr.-May 34 The last year or so the whole movement towards Alternative Afrikaans has gained momentum, an exciting baken in the life of a language that is the home language of millions, of which more than half is not classified as white. **1989** 'A. LETOIT' in *Weekly Mail* 27 Jan. 23 I'm tired of the label 'alternative Afrikaners'. It doesn't mean anything any more. **1989** *Style* Feb. 36 The term Alternative Afrikaners is apparently too provocative, too Engelse Pers and too glib. However, until someone comes up with something better — Reborn Afrikaners? — there's a lot of moving and shaking going on among the volk. *Ibid.* 45 He's one of those in the Outer Siberia of Alternative Afrikanerdom, who are seen as having gone rotten. **1989** *Weekend Post* 30 Dec. (Leisure) 5 Alternative Afrikaans music also made its mark during the year, with artists like Johannes Kerkorrel and Andre Letoit ruffling a few establishment feathers. **1990** B. RONGE in *Sunday Times* 16 Dec. (Mag. Sect.) 6 Will the boere-yuppies of tomorrow be hanging the hats and veldskoens of Johannes Kerkorrel or Joos Tonteldoos and other 'alternative Afrikaner' icons on the walls?

Hence **alternative** *n.*, an Afrikaner open to new ways of thinking and living. See also *New Afrikaner* (AFRIKANER *n.* sense 2 b).

1989 *Style* Feb. 38, I discover that even Alternatives grow up with a feeling of always having to compete with the English. 'You have to show them,' is an expression I become familiar with.

altydbos /ˈalteɪtˌbɔs/ *n.* Formerly also **altijd bos**, **altijd boschje**. [Afk., *altyd* always + *bos* bush: see quot. 1913.] The dwarf bush *Staavia radiata* of the Bruniaceae, found mainly in the Western Cape.

    1913 C. PETTMAN *Africanderisms* 28 Altijd Boschje, .. *Staavia radiata*, Thun. So called because the bush may be found in flower well-nigh the year through. **1917** R. MARLOTH *Common Names* 6 Altijdbos, .. A dwarf shrublet of the Flats and lower hills of the South West, with virgate shoots and persistent white flower-heads. **1972** BEETON & DORNER in *Eng. Usage in Sn Afr.* Vol.3 No.2, 8 Altydbos, .. Low bush of the fam. Bruniaceae, with slender, heath-like leaves and small flower-heads wh. superficially resemble daisies. **1983** M.M. KIDD *Cape Peninsula* 192 *Staavia radiata* ... Altydbos. Dense shrublet, .. common at most altitudes; Jan.-Dec.

a luta continua /əˈluːtə kɒnˈtɪnjuə/ *phr.* Also **aluta continua**. [Pg., *a* the + *luta* struggle, fight + *continua* continues.] 'The struggle continues', a political rallying-cry. Also *ellipt.* **aluta**. Cf. DIE STRYD DUUR VOORT.

Part of the international language of resistance, particularly in Portuguese-speaking countries.

    1982 M. MZAMANE *Children of Soweto* 116 We've been shut indoors for far too long. To tell the truth, my own nerves have been on edge, too. But what the hell! *Aluta*! **1987** *Pamphlet* (Hindu Students Soc.), Harassment, Detentions and Bannings will not solve the problems of our country. The Struggle Continues! A luta continua. **1987** *Pace* July 11 Some of our white brothers .. have come to realise that their destiny is tied up with our destiny and their freedom is inextricably bound to our freedom. Together we shall rise and Aluta Continua. **1989** S. MABASO in *City Press* 19 Feb. 2 'Aluta continua' — the struggle continues — were the first words uttered by 52-year-old black consciousness exponent Simon Nkosi when he was freed this week after 13 years in jail. **1991** K. OWEN in *Sunday Times* 22 Sept. 29 The [peace] accord has shifted the struggle from the military arena to the political, and to that extent it represents a normalisation of South African society. But *a luta continua*.

ama- /ama, ʌmʌ/ *pref.* A Xhosa, Zulu, and Ndebele plural noun prefix found in some words originating in these languages. Cf. MA- *pref.*³ For examples, see *amadoda* (INDODA), AMAJAHA, and *amakwenkwe* (INKWENKWE).

In Xhosa, Zulu, and Ndebele, the singular of words beginning with *ama-* is formed by replacing this prefix with *i-, ili-*, or *in-*. In *S. Afr. Eng.* this pattern is not always observed: words in the plural forms are sometimes treated as singular nouns, an *-s* being added to form the English plural; at other times, the unprefixed form of the word is used with or without pl. *-s*. See also I-, ILI-, IM-, and IN-.

amaas *n.*¹ var. MAAS.

amaas /əˈmɑːs/ *n.*² *Pathology.* [Perh. fr. Xhosa *imasisi* measles, ad. Du. *maselen*.] A mild disease caused by the smallpox virus, occurring esp. among the black peoples of southern Africa.

    1911 *E. London Dispatch* 14 Nov. 4 (Pettman), It was reported to the Council that the late Trooper .. was suffering from *Amaas*. **1912** A.W. HODSON *Trekking Great Thirst* 109 Dr. Rutherford is of opinion that the sickness at Otse is *amaas*, or Kaffir milk-pox. **1972** E.H. CLUVER in *Std Encycl. of Sn Afr.* VI. 90 The relative prevalence of smallpox among the Bantu is attributable .. also to the fact that the disease commonly occurs in a mild form known as *amaas*. This may go unrecognised, although the infection is caused by the true smallpox virus, which when conveyed to Europeans will cause the very serious disease in unvaccinated persons.

amaaz var. MAAS.

Amabambo pl. form of MBO.

amabandla pl. form of IBANDLA.

amabele var. MABELA.

Amabhaca pl. form of BHACA.

‖**Amabhulu** /amaˈbuːlʊ/ *pl. n.* Also **amaBhulu, Amabula, Amabulu, Amahulu, Maboela**, and with small initial. [Xhosa *amaBhulu* 'Boers' (sing. *iBhulu*), ad. Afk. *Boer* Afrikaner.] Among Xhosa-speakers, a derogatory name for:

1. Afrikaners. Cf. AMABHUNU sense 1, BOER sense 4 a, MABURU.

    1852 [see AMANGESI]. **1967** E.M. SLATTER *My Leaves Are Green* 179 Dingane killed some of the Maboela (the Boers) at his kraal. **1976** M. THOLO in C. Hermer *Diary of Maria Tholo* (1980) 76 They had said, 'You are Amabhulu (Boers) and you will go to other Amabhulu and sit around and say "Hulle is mal." (They are mad.)' **1980** *Staffrider* Vol.3, No.1, 46 The Boers don't feel a thing about us but we are all children like their children. Our parents here at Crossroads are being chased by the amaBhulu.

2. White people. Cf. AMABHUNU sense 2, BOER sense 5.

    1983 *Frontline* June 29 Whitey, 'abelungu' in terms of the dictionary, is more often 'amabulu' — initially 'boers' but now meaning any white man.

‖**Amabhunu** /ˌamaˈbuːnʊ/ *pl. n.* Also **AmaBhunu, Amaboona, Amabuna, Amabunu, Bhuna, ma Bunu**, and with small initial. [Zulu *amaBhunu* 'Boers' (sing. *iBhunu*), ad. Afk. *Boer* Afrikaner (see BOER sense 4). See also AMA-.] Among Zulu-speakers, a derogatory name for:

1. Afrikaners. Cf. AMABHULU sense 1. Also *attrib.*

Also occas. used as a sing. n. (see quot. 1974).

    1883 B. MITFORD *Through Zulu Country* 314 One chief told me he would like nothing better than to be allowed to lead an *impi* against the *Amabuna* (Boers). **1895** H. RIDER HAGGARD *Nada* 199 Now it is, my father, that the white men come into my story whom we named the Amaboona, but you call the Boers. **1898** B. MITFORD *Induna's Wife* 147 Tidings came which were weighty indeed. The Amabuna were advancing into the land of Zulu. [*Note*] Boers. **1949** O. WALKER *Proud Zulu* (1951) 36 In their hearts no Zulu trusted the white man, least of all the 'Amabunu,' the Dutch farmers with their harsh guttural voices and their lust for land. **1961** D. BEE *Children of Yesterday* 229 When will the Amabunu (Boer) Government be beaten? When will your people win? When will an English Government win? **1972** J. McCLURE *Caterpillar Cop* (1974) 140 There was talk, he added in hushed tones, that despite speaking English, the boy was actually an *amaboona*. A Boer. **1993** G. McINTOSH in *Sunday Times* 20 June 23 'Amabhunu' can have the hint of a 'smear' in it rather as the words 'Vaalpens' (Transvaler), 'soutie' (white English-speaking South African) and 'hairyback' (Afrikaner) have.

2. White people. Cf. AMABHULU sense 2.

    1988 'A. AMAPHIXIPHIXI' in *Frontline* Apr.-May 33 The youth refer to all white people as AmaBhunu (boers). One could be an English liberal running some alternative educational structure or an Italian artisan building homes in black areas. All of them are labelled boers.

3. The police. Cf. BOER sense 6.

    1991 on M-Net TV 22 Sept. (Carte Blanche), It was clear who the enemy was — Amabunu — the police.

amabooto(es) pl. form of IBUTHO.

Amabriquas pl. form of BRIQUA.

Amabula, -bulu varr. AMABHULU.

Amabuna, -bunu varr. AMABHUNU.

amabuthi, amabut(h)o pl. forms of IBUTHO.

Amacaleka(s) pl. form of GCALEKA.

amacanquas pl. form of INKWENKWE.

Amadhlambi var. NDLAMBE.

amadhlozi, amadlosi, amadlozi(s) pl. forms of IDLOZI.

amadoda pl. form of INDODA.

amadodana see INDODA.

amadodas, amadodo pl. forms of INDODA.

amadoombies, amadumbi(e)s pl. forms of MADUMBI.

amadumbe, -dumbi varr. and pl. forms of MADUMBI.

Amafengu pl. form of MFENGU.

amafufunyane var. MAFUFUNYANA.

Amagaleka, Amagcaleka(s) pl. forms of GCALEKA.

Amagesi var. AMANGESI.

amageu var. MAHEWU.

Amaglezi var. AMANGESI.

amagoduka pl. form of GODUKA.

amagogo pl. form of GOGO n.¹

amagogog pl. form of GOGOG.

Amagonakwaybie, -kwebi varr. GQUNUKHWEBE.

amagqi(g)ha, amagqira n.¹, **amagqirha** pl. forms of IGQIRA n.²

amagqira n.², **amagqwira** pl. forms of IGQWIRA.

Amagqunukwebe, -kwebi, Amagunuquabi varr. GQUNUKHWEBE.

amaGwamba pl. form of MAGWAMBA.

amagxagxa pl. form of IGXAGXA.

Amahahabi pl. form of RHARHABE.

amahen var. MAHEM.

amahewu var. MAHEWU.

amaHlose, amahlosi, a'Mahlozi, amahlozi pl. forms of IDLOZI.

Amahlubi pl. form of HLUBI.

Amahulu var. AMABHULU.

‖**amajaha** /ama'dʒaxa/ n. Also **amajaka, machaha, majaha,** and with initial capital. Pl. unchanged, or **-s**. [Zulu, 'strong (young) men' (sing. *ijaha*). For notes on sing. and pl. forms, see AMA- and MA-.] A young warrior.
  1835 A. SMITH *Diary* (1940) II. 78 The commando of Dingan was composed partly of machaha and partly of men. 1897 F.W. SYKES *With Plumer in Matabeleland* 53 An old native woman, who witnessed the deed, .. greatly admired the boy's courage, and spoke of him as a true 'Amajaka' (warrior). 1930 S.T. PLAATJE *Mhudi* (1975) 36, I suffered from awful hallucinations, I saw all over again the butcheries at Kunana and the terrible faces of the ferocious majahas (soldiers). 1988 *Drum* Mar. 10 Sibanyoni is one of the most popular warriors in Swaziland. He .. has taken part in many traditional ceremonies including those held at the Royal Residence. He is one of Amajaha ka Mswati III — the King's regiment called Lindimpi.

amajita var. and pl. form of MAJITA.

‖**amajoni** /ama'dʒɔni/ pl. n. Also **jonis, majoni.** [Xhosa and Zulu, 'soldiers', pl. prefix AMA- + *joni* ad. Eng. *Johnny.*] A Xhosa and Zulu name for:
  1. *hist.* British soldiers. See also ROOIBAADJIE sense 1.
    1891 B. MITFORD *Romance of Cape Frontier* 252 When the *amajoni* are mustered .. the trumpet is blown. 1913 C. PETTMAN *Africanderisms* 29 *Amajoni,* The Natal natives' name for the English soldiers. 1967 E. ROSENTHAL *Encycl. of Sn Afr.* 16 *Amajoni,* Native nickname for British soldiers, derived from the word 'Johnnie'.
  2. Any soldiers.
    1973 *Informant,* George Oh madam please lend me five bob. Amajoni stole all my Pick and Pay [sc. groceries]. 1981 K. GOTTSCHALK *Informant,* Cape Town 'Amajoni' has expanded its meaning. It is now by no means restricted to white soldiers. To the contrary, freedom fighters are referred to as 'amajoni' as in that popular song for funerals, 'angena amajoni', etc. 1990 L. JAMJAM *Informant,* Grahamstown Wellington doesn't know English properly — when he says to Robbie 'here come soldiers' he says 'here come jonis'.

Amakakabi pl. form of RHARHABE.

Amakasa pl. form of XHOSA.

‖**amakhafula** /ˌamaka'fʊːla/ pl. n. Also **(ama)kafula,** and with initial capital. [Zulu, 'contemptible or ill-mannered persons' (sing. *ikhafula*), fr. *khafula* 'to spit out, shout abuse at', fr. ideophone *khafu* of spitting, of talking inconsiderately. The word's similarity in sound to KAFFIR causes some confusion (see quots 1913 and 1961) but is prob. coincidental.] 'Barbarians': among Zulus, a contemptuous name for people considered to be uncivilized, esp. those from outside the speaker's home area; applied in the nineteenth century to Zulu soldiers from Natal who collaborated with the British, and more recently used of migrant workers, and as a general term of abuse.
  1894 B. MITFORD *Curse of Clement Waynflete* (1896) 235 Of those yonder — those red cattle and the *amakafula,* who are aiding them to fight against us — there will soon be not one left alive — not one. [Note] Natal natives. 1898 —— *Induna's Wife* 222 The English at Tegwini had undertaken to interfere in this quarrel, and had crossed the Tugela with a large *impi* of Amakafula. 1913 C. PETTMAN *Africanderisms* 29 *Amakafula,* (Z. *i Kafula,* Zuluized form of the word Kaffir, applied by the Zulus proper to the Natal natives.) An opprobrious name for natives resident in Natal. 1961 D. BEE *Children of Yesterday* 12 He ran to the gate .. and, picking up a clod, hurled it at Madévaan. 'Kaffer! Kafula!' he screamed. 1980 S. SEPAMLA in M. Mutloatse *Forced Landing* 81 Quite likely Amakhafula, who lived here sometime back, in their effort to reduce the dust .. from the nearby mine-dump, must have poured down ash and water to lay it to sleep over the years.

amakhaya n.¹ pl. form of KAYA.

amakhaya n.² pl. form of MKHAYA.

amakhenkwe pl. form of INKWENKWE.

amakholwa pl. form of KHOLWA.

amakhosi pl. form of INKOSI n.

amakhowe pl. form of IKHOWE.

amakhwenkwe pl. form of INKWENKWE.

Amakosa(e), Amakosas pl. forms of XHOSA.

amakosi pl. form of INKOSI n.

Amakosina n. obs. Also **Amakosîna, Amakosinae, Ammakosina.** [ad. Xhosa *emaXhosini* 'among the Xhosa.'] *Xhosaland,* see XHOSA n. sense 1 c.
  1812 A. PLUMPTRE tr. H. Lichtenstein's *Trav. in Sn Afr.* (1928) I. 309 The tribe .. call themselves Koossas, or Kaussas, but to their country they give the name of Ammakosina. 1829 C. ROSE *Four Yrs in Sn Afr.* 78 The tribe that occupies the country on the eastern frontier .. is named Amakosae and their country is called by them Amakosina. 1834 T. PRINGLE *Afr. Sketches* 505 That tribe of Caffers whose territory is now divided from the colony by the river Keisi, or Keiskamma, are, in their own language designated the Amakósa, and their country Amakosîna.

Amakosoe, Amakosse pl. forms of XHOSA.

amakrwala pl. form of IKRWALA.

‖**amakula** /ama'kuːla/ pl. n. *Derog.* Also **amaKula, ma coola, m'kula's,** and with initial capital. [Zulu, pl. prefix AMA- + -*kula* ad. of COOLIE sense 1. For explanation of occas. redundant Eng. pl. suffix -s, see AMA-, M-, MA-.] Among Zulu-speakers: an insulting name for people of Indian origin.
  1953 LANHAM & MOPELI-PAULUS *Blanket Boy's Moon* 169 Some of his own race, some of the Zulus, and even some of the hated amaKula. c1963 B.C. TAIT *Durban Story* 207 The Zulus derided the meagre physical stature of the Indians and dubbed them 'Ma Coola'. 1971 *Post* 16 May 5 (letter) Why do most Africans refer to Indians and Coloureds as 'Boesmans' and 'm'kula's'? These are everyday terms of abuse used by a majority of people.

Amakunugubi var. GQUNUKHWEBE.

amakwedini pl. form of KWEDINI.

amakwenkwana see INKWENKWE.

amakwenkwe pl. form of INKWENKWE.

amakweta var. ABAKWETHA.

amalaita /æməˈlaɪtə, amaˈlaɪtə/ pl. n. *Hist.* Also **amalaaita(s), amalaaitas, amalayita, amal(e)ita, amelitas, lieta, malaita,** and with initial capital. [Zulu *amalayitha* or S.-Sotho *malaeta* thugs, robbers; etym. dubious: prob. formed on Zulu AMA- (or MA- *pref.*³) + -*layitha* to pay up, ad. Eng. *light (up),* initially used among Zulu-speakers as tr. of Zulu *khanyisa* to pay up, lit. 'light up' (with one's shining money); or perh. ad. Eng. *moonlighter* (see quot. 1934); or *Allrighter* (see quot. 1980). For explanation of forms with Eng. pl. suffix -s, see AMA- and MA- *pref.*³] Urban gangs once notorious for committing a variety of crimes, usu. violent; members of these gangs. Freq. *attrib.* Cf. SKEBENGA, TSOTSI sense 1.
  1903 *Ilanga* 8 May 3 No Christened natives have taken part in a faction fight, or defied the Government, nor has a murder of them; nor do they obstruct Europeans in the locations, nor form lieta gangs in towns. [1908 *Rand Daily Mail* 11 Sept. 7 Some three years ago the Amalaita made its appearance. The nucleus was a number of piccanins, mainly Basuto or Magatese. *Ibid.* see ZULU.] 1910 *Rand Daily Mail* 8 Nov. 3 No reason can be assigned for the murder, which is theoretically set down to the wanton blackguardism of an amalaita gang. 1934 N. DEVITT *Mem. of Magistrate* 143 This gang was akin to the gangs which are known in Johannesburg to-day as 'Amalaita', a name the natives have themselves created. I believe the origin of this name to be European. Natives have been told of the doings of the Irish 'Moonlighters' ... The contraction 'M'lait' is probably derived from this word, the prefix 'Ama' being a Zulu plural prefix. c1936 *S. & E. Afr. Yr Bk & Guide* 242 Playing fields .. should assist in the dissolution of the gangs of hooligans, known as the *Amalayita,* which infest some of the larger towns .. due to the want of outlet for superfluous energy. 1949 J. MOCKFORD *Golden Land* 102 Gangs, such as the *amalaitas* of Johannesburg, exist for Bantu esprit de corps and for all the crimes known to man. 1951 *Drum* Oct. 8 Then there are other lesser gangs like the Amalaita, who consist mostly of Vendas from the Northern Transvaal. Many of them work during the week as domestic servants in the suburbs, but at week-ends they roam the middle of the city in big gangs. 1952 B. DAVIDSON *Report on Sn Afr.* 117 The *amalaitas* .. were not suppressed at all: they persisted through the 'twenties and 'thirties, only to merge, in the 'forties, with the *tsotsis,* or 'narrow-trouser boys', of contemporary Johannesburg. 1959 E. MPHAHLELE *Down Second Ave* 101 These people came to be known as malaita — Sotho for ruffians ... The malaita assaulted people .. raped women and girls. 1971 *Drum* Mar. 38 [He] photographed the Amalaita fights outside Pretoria. It was a barbaric Sunday

pastime. **1980** D.B. COPLAN *Urbanization of African Performing Arts.* 143 The most significant offshoot of the Ninevites was Johannesburg's first organized group of 'juvenile delinquents.' The *Amalaita* took their name from the way in which Zulu native police pronounced 'Allrighters,' a term for the Ninevites. They were mostly young Basotho who joined together to resist the pass laws. **1986** P. MAYLAM *Hist. of Afr. People* 150 Organised groups, such as *amalaita* gangs, became involved in the liquor traffic ... *Amalaita* gangs began to operate in the eastern suburbs of Johannesburg from 1906. **1987** S. ROBERTS *Jacks in Corners* 62 The *Amalaaitas*, with their trousers caught at the knee with steel bands and their heavy sticks and their handkerchiefs tied at the corners and worn on their heads could kill you with a single blow.

Amamfengu pl. form of MFENGU.

amamPondo pl. form of PONDO.

Amampondumisi var. MPONDOMISE.

AmaNdabele, -Ndebele, -Ndebeli pl. forms of NDEBELE.

amandla /a'maːnɡ̊a, ə'maːnɡ̊ə/ int. Also **amandhla**. [Xhosa and Zulu.] 'Power', 'strength', a political rallying-cry used by liberation groupings, esp. the African National Congress. See also AFRIKA *int.*, VIVA.

'Amandla!' usu. elicits the response 'ngawet(h)u' or 'awet(h)u' ('is ours').

1961 *ANC pamphlet* in H.H.W. De Villiers *Rivonia* (1964) 77 With your support we will win. Amandla ngawethu! **1973** *E. Prov. Herald* 2 Nov. 3 An historic summit meeting of homeland leaders drew to a close yesterday with a crowd .. giving the Black Power salute and shouting in reply to Chief Gatsha Buthelezi's amandla (power) ngawetu (is ours). **1977** *Rhodeo* (Rhodes Univ.) 30 Sept. 3 Suddenly he bellowed *Amandla!* at the crowd, holding his fist in the air. Twenty thousand voices roared back as one: Ngawethu (The power is ours), raising clenched fists above their heads. **1979** [see AZAPO]. **1983** *Daily Dispatch* 25 Nov. 1 Before stepping from the witness box to go to the cells below, Niehaus raised his fist and shouted 'amandla' (power). People in the public gallery responded with 'awethu' (ours). **1986** M.O. MTSHALI in S. Ndaba *One Day in June* 90 The black mob has raised its black fists into an ominous flag of our freedom; its voice rises into a unison of Amandla! Amandla! Ngawethu! Ngawethu! Power to the People! Power to the People! **1990** *Weekly Mail* 9 Mar. 1 Bophuthatswana police had been responding to shouts of 'Viva ANC!' and 'Amandla!' with clenched fists. **1990** G. NEVILL in *Sunday Times* 30 Dec. 1 Remember, the future is certain. It is the past that's unpredictable. Amandla/Vrystaat.

Hence **amandla** *n.*, a shout of 'amandla'.

1989 J. HOBBS *Thoughts in Makeshift Mortuary* 409 Rose's pallbearers approach the other side of the grave and put her coffin down in silence, no 'Amandla!' here. **1990** K. PATHER in *Cue* 5 July 2 Ja well, you've seen it all you say; lots of amandlas, toyi-toyi and just another struggle story line. **1994** D. FORREST in *Weekly Mail & Guardian* 16 Sept. 29 Questions from the floor to 'our ministers' reflected subterranean tensions but did not seek to confront or embarrass. For the ministers' loud 'amandlas' and then their plain speaking, and the subdued response, it was a strange and touching spectacle.

amaNdlambe var. NDLAMBE.

‖**Amangesi** /amaˈŋɡeːsi, -ŋɡeː-, -zi/ *pl. n. Obs. exc. hist.* Also **Amagesi, Amaglezi**, and with medial capital. [Xhosa *amaNgesi* (sing. *iNgesi*), Zulu *amaNgisi* (sing. *iNgisi*), ad. Eng. *English*.] Among speakers of Nguni languages: the English; English-speakers.

1852 H. WARD *Jasper Lyle* 176 The Kafirs chuckled at hearing the *Amabulu* [printed *Amahulu*] and the *Amaglezi* — (the Boers and the English) — were 'barking at each other like dogs.' **1855** G. BROWN *Personal Adventure* 250 All the spruits of the Keiskama .. are being scoured by the 'Amagesi' — English. **1981** B.

MFENYANA in M. Mutloatse *Reconstruction* 299 And then AmaNgesi came to Anglicise everybody, resulting in Fanakalo, African and Boere English.

AmaNgqika pl. form of NGQIKA.

Aman Kozas pl. form of XHOSA.

amantombazana pl. form of INTOMBAZANA.

amapagate var. UMPAKATI.

amapagati, -pakate, -pakati(e), -phakathi pl. forms of UMPAKATI.

Amaponda, -pondo pl. forms of PONDO.

Amapondomisi var. MPONDOMISE.

amaqaba pl. form of QABA.

amaqabane, -bani pl. forms of IQABANE.

amaqira var. and pl. form of IGQIRA *n.*²

amaquabane pl. form of IQABANE.

Amaquabe, -quabi varr. QWABE.

amaquati, -queta varr. ABAKWETHA.

Amararabe pl. form of RHARHABE.

amarewu var. MAHEWU.

amarsa var. MAAS.

amarwela var. of IKRWALA.

amas var. MAAS.

Amascosa pl. form of XHOSA.

amasi var. MAAS.

‖**amasoka** /amaˈsɔːka, -ɡa/ *pl. n.* Also **amosoka**. [Xhosa, 'young unmarried men' (sing. *isoka*).] Used collectively:

1. Young unmarried men considered old enough to court women; womanizers.

1952 H. KLEIN *Land of Silver Mist* 48 The boys, now known as amosoka — swains — are smeared with red clay and fat and are given new blankets and karosses. They are taken to a cattle kraal where they are lectured by the elders .. in their duties as men and then dispersed to their home kraals. **1962** W.D. HAMMOND-TOOKE *Bhaca Soc.* 95 Young men boast of their escapades and are proud of being called amasoka (bachelors loved by many girls). The accredited lover is a frequent visitor at the girl's kraal, where he is given food and hospitality. **1987** *Pace* Nov. 4 Amasoka better look before they leap. There was this dandy of a dude who left nothing under a skirt untouched.

2. *transf.* Migrant workers separated from their families.

1976 M. THOLO in C. Hermer *Diary of Maria Tholo* (1980) 173 The people streaming into Guguletu were full of two warnings. Firstly the Bhacas — we now call them the amasoka or bachelors — were on the warpath.

amaSwati pl. form of SWATI sense 2.

amatagati var. and pl. form of TAGATI *n.*

amatangula var. AMATUNGULU.

Amatebele pl. form of MATABELE.

Amatembu pl. form of TEMBU.

amathonga, -thongo pl. forms of ITONGO.

amatikati pl. form of TAGATI *n.*

amatingoola, -gula varr. AMATUNGULU.

amatola pl. form of ITOLA.

Amatonga *n.*¹ pl. form of ITONGO.

Amatonga *n.*² pl. form of TONGA.

amatongo pl. form of ITONGO.

amatontos pl. form of INDODA.

amatungulu /əˌmɑːtʊŋˈɡuːlu/ *n.* Also **amatangula, amatingoola, amatingula, amatum-gula,**

amatungula, amatunguli, armatingoola, itungulu, umatungulu, and with initial capital. Pl. unchanged. [Zulu, earlier form of *amathungulu* (sing. *ithungulu*) the fruits of *umthungulu*, the shrub *Carissa macrocarpa*. For an explanation of sing. use of Zulu pl., see AMA-.] The shrub *Carissa macrocarpa* of the Apocynaceae; its large, edible, scarlet fruit; MATINGOLA; *Natal plum*, see NATAL sense b; *wild plum* sense (e) (see WILD sense a); also called NUM-NUM. Also *attrib.*

1836 N. ISAACS *Trav.* (1936) I. 43 The third, which the natives called armatingoola, grew on the thorn tree, which throws out a white blossom exceedingly pretty; its fruit resembles in shape the European plum; its skin is thin, and it contains a great number of seeds. **1856** *Cape of G.H. Almanac & Annual Register* 283 The wild fruits, as the itungulu, the Cape gooseberry, and a species of fig, are much esteemed and make delicious preserves. **1859** [see *Natal plum* (NATAL sense b)]. **1876** H. BROOKS *Natal* 168 The native name of this plant is *Amatungulu*, and the botanical name *Arduinia grandiflora*. **1887** J.W. MATTHEWS *Incwadi Yami* 40 Tramping along the narrow Kafir path .. we had to push aside fantastic wreaths of tangled convolvuli .. and whilst avoiding the wild date trees on the one hand, had on the other to shun the prickly thorns of the crimson-fruited *amatungula*. **1894** R. MARLOTH in *Trans. of S. Afr. Phil. Soc.* p.lxxxiv, *Carissa grandiflora* (amatungulu). **1917** — *Common Names* 6 Amatungulu, .. An evergreen shrub of the eastern districts, with forked spines, glossy leaves, white, sweet-scented flowers and large edible fruit (berries). *Ibid.* 61 *Natal plum*, Amatungulu. **1953** B. FULLER *Call Back Yesterday* 110 Sometimes, they would look for amatungulu plums, though these were not really popular on account of their thorns. *c*1963 B.C. TAIT *Durban Story* 83 Clumps of wild date-palms and wild bananas, with here and there a wild fig tree, grew among the scrub and Amatungula, coarse grass and rushes. **1970** HEARD & FAULL *Cookery in Sn Afr.* 473 Little girls collecting the *amatungula* berries to make our delectable jelly. **1972** [see *Natal plum* (NATAL sense b)]. **1973** O.H. SPOHR tr. F. Krauss's *Trav. Jrnl* 59 *Carissa grandiflora* .. amatungulu .. a bush with white sweet-smelling flowers and red gooseberry-like berries with a pleasant flavour. **1986** J. CONYNGHAM *Arrowing of Cane* 23, I scan the slope of cane, palms, amatungulu and wild bananas and, in the distance, the hump of bush. **1989** [see *Natal plum* (NATAL sense b)]. **1991** M. HAZELL in *Grocott's Mail* 22 Feb. 8 *Carissa macrocarpa* — Amatungulu with its glossy green foliage and attractive white flowers.

AmaXhosa pl. form of XHOSA.

AmaXosa var. and pl. form of XHOSA.

amaZooloo, -Zoulah, -Zoulou, -Zulu *n.* pl. forms of ZULU *n.* sense 1 a.

amaZulu *adj.* var. ZULU *adj.* sense 1.

amba, amber varr. HAMBA.

AME /eɪ em ˈiː/ *n.* Also **A.M.E.** [Initial letters of *African Methodist Episcopal* (Church).] In full *AME Church*: a branch of the African-American church of the same name. See also ETHIOPIAN.

1903 E. NUTTALL *Private Circular.* (Wesleyan Methodist Church of S. Afr.), Transfer of Members to or from A.M.E. Church and Ethiopian Associations. **1904** *Declaration of Bishops* (Afr. Methodist Episcopal Church), The delegates came, affiliation was effected, and the A.M.E. Church formally invited to begin operations in South Africa. **1941** *Bantu World* 1 Feb. 9 The A.M.E. Church Choir under Rev. Lethoba .. rendered fine musical items. **1952** *Drum* July 27 Rev. William B. Modikoane, of the A.M.E. Church. *c*1967 G.Z. LETHOBA *Afr. Methodist Episcopal Church in S. Africa.* 28 He [*sc.* Rev. Dwane] proposed that the A.M.E. Church in South Africa should secede from the A.M.E. Church of America and join the Anglican Church. **1970** *Std Encycl. of Sn Afr.* II. 54 In 1896 the Rev. James M. Dwane brought about the incorporation of most of the members of the Ethiopian Church into the African Methodist Episcopal Church (A.M.E.), a branch of an American Negro church. **1988** *Pace* Apr. 28, I made history as the first white woman to join the AME (African Methodist Episcopal) church.

American kitchen *n. phr.* [Prob. orig. general Eng.; now no longer in use except in S. Afr. Eng.] A fitted kitchen. Also *attrib.*

1966 H. BECK *Meet Cape Wines* 37 The contributions which the U.S.A. has made to such comfort as we may enjoy in modern life must be fully acknowledged. The American kitchen bears witness to them. Even washing up is not the imposition it used to be. **1971** *Daily News* 23 Jan. 13 *(advt)* Large panelled lounge with fireplace, large American fitted kitchen. **1971** *E. Prov. Herald* 26 Jan. 22 *(advt)* Bathroom, separate toilet, American kitchen with breakfast nook. **1977** J. SIKAKANE *Window on Soweto* 32 Some Soweto houses are equipped with a radiogram, a dining suite, an American kitchen scheme and a refrigerator. **1990** *Homefinder* 20 Apr. 6 *(advt)* French doors leading to La Cotta tiled private pool area. White American kitchen. **1991** F.G. BUTLER *Local Habitation* 184, I decided to convert the old club buttery into an American kitchen for her.

Ammakosae pl. form of XHOSA.

Ammakosina var. AMAKOSINA.

Amokosa pl. form of XHOSA.

amosoka var. AMASOKA.

‖**amper** /ˈampə(r)/ *adv.* [Afk., fr. Malay *ampir* nearly.] Nearly, almost.

1913 C. PETTMAN *Africanderisms* 30 *Amper*, .. This word, introduced by the Malays, is in common use in Cape Dutch and among English residents in districts where Dutch prevails. **1916** [see ALREADY]. **1968** A. FULTON *Dark Side of Mercy* 13 This is a cruel country. It happens like this amper every day.

‖**amper-baas** /ˈampə(r)ˌbɑːs/ *n. colloq.* Pl. **-base** /-bɑːsə/. [Afk., *amper* (see prec.) + *baas* (see BAAS senses 2 and 3).] 'Almost-boss', an ironic name for someone who (though not white) is perceived to behave like a stereotypical white person, or to aspire to power of some kind. Also in dim. form **amper-baasie** [see -IE]. See also BAAS.

1952 *Drum* Apr. 7 *(by-line)* 'Amperbaas'. **1982** M. MZAMANE *Children of Soweto* 22 Monty was very light-complexioned. 'Amper Baasie' or 'Rooi Nek' we sometimes called him. When Pakade was angry with him .. he always likened him to a Boer. **1982** *Voice* 30 May 4 Is Lofty A— asleep like Rip Van Winkle or is he so taken up with the idea of being amper-baas that he overlooks all these facts of life in our current South Africa? **1984** A. DANGOR in *Staffrider* Vol.6 No.1, 17 Appointed Assistants Mrs Muriel Meraai Mr Reginald Baatjies. 'What's he saying now?' 'He's the boss, Muriel and Reggie are the amper-base.'

anaboom /ˈænəbʊəm, ˈana-/ *n.* Pl. **-bome** /-bʊəmə/. [Afk., fr. Nama *ana* name for this tree + Afk. *boom* tree.] ANATREE.

1961 PALMER & PITMAN *Trees of S. Afr.* 148 The ana tree or anaboom is one of the largest trees of the northern Transvaal, a great spreading blue-green giant .., one of the very noblest of the great Acacia race. **1970** M. TYACK *S. Afr.: Land of Challenge* 303 Acacia trees (Anabome and Kameeldoringbome) whose roots tap the underground supply of water seeping through the sands. **1977** E. PALMER *Field Guide to Trees* 122 Flowers in spikes; pods orange to red brown, much twisted (Zululand west to SWA) *A. albida* Anaboom. **1980** [see ANATREE].

anatree /ˈænətriː, ˈana-/ *n.* Also **anna tree**, and with initial capital. [Nama *ana* name for this tree + Eng. *tree*.] A species of tall thorn-tree, *Acacia albida* of the Leguminosae, which bears large, edible pods; ANABOOM; also called APIESDORING. Also shortened form **an(n)a**.

1856 C.J. ANDERSSON *Lake Ngami* 27 The principal trees thereabouts are the ana and the giraffe-thorn (*acacia giraffæ*). **1864** T. BAINES *Explor. in S.-W. Afr.* 42 Halting before the house under the most magnificent anna-trees (a kind of thorn) I had seen in the country. **1877** *Sel. Comm. Report on Mission to Damaraland* 11 Amongst the trees the Anna, often 80 feet high, is the most conspicuous. **1886** G.A. FARINI *Through Kalahari Desert* 257 We camped under some 'anna' trees — immensely tall trees, with wide-spreading branches, bearing large fruit of a beautiful scarlet colour when opened, and no less delicious to the taste than attractive to the eye. The fruit is full of seeds, which are also edible. **1915** W. EVELEIGH *S.W. Afr.* 57 The handsome Ana tree, *Acacia albida*, is found. The fruit of this remarkable tree is a legume. The beans, when ripe and dry, are used for fodder for cattle. **1917** R. MARLOTH *Common Names* 6 *Ana tree, Acacia albida*. One of the largest species of the genus, the crown being up to 100 feet in diameter. Frequent along rivers of tropical Africa ... The large pods form a very nutritious food for all kinds of stock. **1961** PALMER & PITMAN *Trees of S. Afr.* 148 The flowers of the ana tree grow in long creamy spikes. **1973** W.F.E. IMMELMAN et al. *Our Green Heritage* 274 There are many species of trees which occur naturally in certain bushveld areas which are important as fodder .. *Capparis* spp. (witgat), .. *Rhus* spp. (karee trees), *Acacia giraffae* (Camel-thorn), *Acacia albida* (ana tree) and various other acacias. **1980** *E. Prov. Herald* 30 Apr. 9 Anaboom/Ana Tree and Koorsboom/Fever Tree might as well have had thorn added to complete the umbrella of uniformity. **1988** A. HALL-MARTIN et al. *Kaokoveld* 11 Along watercourses which cut through the rugged terrain the dominant trees are mopane, the scented thorn .., the ana tree or winter thorn (Acacia albida) and leadwood.

ANC *n.*[1] Also **A.N.C.** [Initial letters of *African National Congress*.] South Africa's oldest and largest nationalist organization, founded in Bloemfontein in 1912 as the *South African Native National Congress*, and renamed the *African National Congress* in 1923; also called CONGRESS (sense 1). Also *attrib.*

The ANC's stated aims include the fostering of a broad, non-ethnic nationalism and the establishment of a democratic political system. In 1956 the FREEDOM CHARTER was formally adopted as the organization's manifesto. Banned from April 1960 to February 1990, and with its leadership in exile, the ANC used armed resistance as part of its strategy from 1961: see UMKHONTO WE SIZWE. The organization became the majority party in the Government of National Unity in 1994.

[**1923** *Resolution of Annual Conference* in Karis & Carter *From Protest to Challenge: Protest & Hope 1882–1934* (1972) I. 298 It is resolved that the South African Native National Congress shall henceforth be known and described for all intents and purposes as 'The African National Congress.'] **1952** *Rand Daily Mail* 27 Nov. 12 The recommendations were adopted by the conference of the A.N.C. and S.A.I.C., and the course of action followed during the defiance campaign was mainly that prescribed in these recommendations. **1958** *Ibid.* 15 Apr. 1 A.N.C. calls off 'stay home' protest. The African National Congress called last night on all its supporters .. to return to their jobs to-day. **1962** A.J. LUTHULI *Let my People Go* 89 It was originally called the South African Native National Congress. I shall refer to it here .. as 'Congress', or as the A.N.C. **1967** P.C. PELSER in *Hansard* 1 June 7024 These terrorists who are returning now are to a great extent the fruits of the undermining activities of the A.N.C., the P.A.C., S.W.A.P.O. and the communists. **1969** M. BENSON *At Still Point* (1988) 103 Then she said, 'The A.N.C. has a new plan. We must use violence to achieve our freedom. It is the only way!' **1970** *Rand Daily Mail* 1 Oct. 7 On hearing the sentence, he .. gave the clenched fist salute of the A.N.C. **1977** *Rhodeo* (Rhodes Univ.) 30 Sept. 7 Both the ANC and the PAC were banned as from April 1960 under the specially-introduced Unlawful Organizations Act, and from then on a pattern of revolutionary violence began to emerge. **1982** D. TUTU *Voice of One* 20 The main opposition party in South Africa, the African National Congress (ANC), moved away from non-violent strategy in 1961, after the Sharpeville massacre. **1986** M. DU PREEZ in *Sunday Times* 12 Jan. 18 Seventy-four years after its founding, 25 years since opting for the armed struggle, the ANC this week promised to turn more ploughshares into swords for what it believes is the last great assault against white nationalism. **1987** *E. Prov. Herald* 25 Apr. 1 The African National Congress would seize any opportunity for 'a negotiated resolution of the conflict in our country', the president of the ANC, Mr Oliver Tambo, is quoted as saying. **1988** C.A. MOKOENA in *Inside S. Afr.* June 8 Is there any difference between the ANC and AWB? The only difference is, the one is white, the other black. **1990** G. SLOVO *Ties of Blood* 223 In the end it had been inevitable that she would join the Party. Most Africans of her age were in the ANC but since whites were not admitted that option was closed to her. **1990** P. CULL in *E. Prov. Herald* 3 Feb., State President F.W. de Klerk threw down the gauntlet yesterday, unbanning the ANC, PAC and South African Communist Party. **1990** *Weekly Mail* 21 Sept. 7 Since February the ANC, an organisation geared to opposition, has had to start grappling with the reality of power or potential power.

ANC *n.*[2] *colloq.* Also **A.N.C.** [Initial letters of *antenuptial contract*.] A popular name for the ANTENUPTIAL CONTRACT.

1970 H.H. HERMANS *Law my Master* 42 After marriage, there is no way of changing the marital relationship, unless perhaps after arranging a collusive divorce .. followed by a subsequent marriage after execution of an A.N.C. **1976** *Darling* 22 Dec. 14, I purchased all the furniture in our house and when we were married by ANC he undertook to provide furniture to the value of R3 000. **1979** *Fair Lady* 29 Aug. 15, I was married by ante-nuptual [*sic*] contract, yet my property was never returned to me. What is the value of an ANC if a husband is forcibly able to retain his wife's property? **1985** *Ibid.* 27 Nov. 14 Hats off to Mr Justice Johan Kriegler who during a recent divorce case awarded a woman (with an ANC) a share of her husband's estate on the grounds that she gave him loyal service for 20 years. **1988** L. TAGER in *Pace* Oct. (Queen) 15 Parties to a marriage may enter into an ante nuptial contract (ANC). This is a special kind of contract, which has to be concluded before the marriage ... The ANC is the mechanism to exclude the husband's marital power.

ANCYL /ˈænsɪl/ *n.* [Acronym formed on *African National Congress Youth League*.] The youth organization of the ANC, founded during the 1940s, banned in 1960, and re-launched in 1990, when it merged with and incorporated the South African Youth Congress (see SAYCO). Also *attrib.*

1992 A. BRIDGE *Informant, Soweto* The ANCYL 'Civic Assoc.' call on every resident of zone 2 Diepkloof to attend the mass meeting which will be on 29 May 1991; venue: Joe Slovo-Roma. **1993** *Natal Witness* 8 Apr. 3 The African National Congress Youth League (ANCYL) commemorated the death of Mkhonto we Sizwe .. cadre Solomon Mahlangu in style at the Wadley Stadium on Tuesday ... The ANCYL diverted from its usual political programme in order to give the day a new emphasis. **1993** *Sunday Times* 25 Apr. 21 ANCYL deputy president .. says the youth form the core of the 56 percent of the population that is unemployed and the 64 percent that is illiterate. **1993** *City Press* 12 Dec. 1 At least a dozen ANCYL members have been slain and their comrades have vowed to take bloody revenge if the SDU is not disbanded.

‖**anderskleuriges** /ˌan(d)ə(r)sˈkliœrəxəs/ *pl. n.* Also **anderkleuriges**. [Afk., *anders* other + *kleur* colour + n.-forming suffix *-ige* + pl. *-s*.] 'Those of another colour': used by whites of black and COLOURED people (an ironic use of apartheid terminology).

Common in speech, perh. avoiding use of the term NON-WHITE.

1978 *Sunday Times* 4 June 17 Some Afrikaans writers .. have indeed pleaded over the years for the language to become common coin. They have emphasised the contribution made by anderkleuriges whose language, after all, it also is. **1979** *Ibid.* 18 Nov. 6 She told him, not very politely, to go to the hole in the wall around the back. He was only five and couldn't even reach the hole in the wall, where anderskleuriges had to queue. **1980** *Ibid.* 2 Nov. 5 What were the English-speaking children offered, never mind the so-called anderskleuriges? **1981** *Rand Daily Mail* 18 June 3 The Afrikaans-speaker's hyper-exclusivity had brought him to the position where it had become difficult, if not unthinkable, for him to admit people of other colours (anderkleuriges) to within his ranks.

angel's food *n. phr.* Also **angels' food**, and with initial capitals. Fruit salad.

1891 H.J. DUCKITT *Hilda's 'Where Is It?'* 212 Salad (Guava Salad, or 'Angel's Food'). (A favourite Cape dish.) **1912** *Bloemfontein Post* 7 Sept. 16 (Pettman), We were fortified by luscious coffee and mystic trifle, and angel's food, and ambrosia, and spiced stars. **1913** A. GLOSSOP *Barnes's S. Afr. Hsehold Guide* 103 Fruit Salad or Angel's Food. **1951** S. VAN H. TULLEKEN *Prac. Cookery Bk* 242 Angels' Food. Peel 6 oranges very thickly, .. cut into very thin slices; peel and slice 10 bananas, 8 guavas .. 1 pineapple. Sprinkle $1\frac{1}{2}$ cups sugar over, and just before serving, add 1 wineglass sherry. **1970** G. WESTWOOD *Bright Wilderness* 139 Bowls full of sliced paw-paw, oranges, grenadillas, bananas and pine-apples. 'Angel's food,' said Nan. 'A Ball would not be complete without Angel's Food.' **1973** *Farmer's Weekly* 9 May 98 The Cape can provide good fruit salads. Angels' food consists of alternate layers of sliced guava and orange. **1973** on Radio South Africa 11 Nov. (Test the Team), 'What is the old-fashioned name for fruit salad?' 'We used to call it angels' food.'

Anglikaans /ˌæŋglɪˈkɑːns/ *n.* Also **Englikaans**. [Blend of Eng. *Anglo* (or *English*) + Afk. *Afrikaans*.] A hypothetical language resulting from the mixing of English and Afrikaans.

1934 *Cape Argus* 9 June (Swart), It was suggested at a meeting of the Johannesburg English Association that a language called 'Anglikaans' might be the future language of South Africa. **1972** *Cape Times* 8 Jan., What is Anglikaans? Does it consist in the jocular use of Afrikaans words and accents by the English-speaking? Does it extend to the serious use of Afrikaans words, such as trek and spoor, already incorporated into English? .. If Anglikaans includes .. South Africanisms of every variety, is there any likelihood that Anglikaans will eventually become the dominant South African vernacular? **1972** 'M.S.' *Informant, Graaff-Reinet* The farming community here use 'slag' quite commonly in this 'Anglikaans' that is spoken on the farms. **1977** W. STEENKAMP in *Cape Times* 5 Dec. 13 We in South Africa have our own dialect too, of course, which is known as 'Englikaans.' I cannot help wondering, though, what will happen to Englikaans's various sub-dialects in this age of mass communication. I think particularly of a rare specimen I can only call 'Xhonglish', which is found in Transkei. **1981** V.A. FEBRUARY *Mind your Colour* 156 He uses the language of the poor, that peculiar mixture of English and Afrikaans which I shall refer to as Englikaans. **1987** R. CUTLER in *Style* Mar. 28 It might be a smart solution to the major white lingo problem to allow Anglikaans to become official as soon as possible. **1989** *Weekend Post* 26 Aug. 11 If that main-man what counts among the taal-tiffies, Dr Samuel Johnson, could hear military Englikaans he would get a skrik and probably strek the troopies like a blougat two-liner, but William Shakespeare would feel bakgat about it.

Hence **Anglikaner**, also **Englikaner**, an English-speaking South African; also *attrib.*

1982 M. SPRING in *Star* 19 Sept. 10 Denis Worrall, who is now our country's ambassador to Britain, has rightly been saying for years that intelligent Englikaners are cursed with the disease of negativism ... Back in the early '60s and the mid-'70s, when we experienced similar civil unrest, .. exoduses of Englikaner liberal intellectuals began: 15000 South Africans emigrated in 1961, 26000 in 1977.

‖**Anglisisme** /ˌaŋxləˈsəsmə/ *n.* [Afk., 'Anglicism'.] A word or expression of English origin used in Afrikaans (often in an adapted form) in the place of an existing Afrikaans word or expression.

1972 *Cape Times* 1 Aug., (*editorial*) Perhaps current admonitions against the use of anglisismes in Afrikaans are based on the mistaken assumption that where two languages mingle the weaker will go to the wall. **1984** *Frontline* Feb. 33 They're most unhappy that the waiters don't speak Afrikaans, which seems odd since their own Afrikaans consists of so many Anglisismes that my highschool Afrikaans teacher would have rapped their knuckles. **1986** *Weekend Argus* 29 Nov. (Suppl.) 7 They were replying to an irate listener who had complained about the intrusion of Anglisismes into Afrikaans. No language can remain pure, they said. Each one must borrow from the others.

Anglo /ˈæŋgləʊ/ *n.* Short for *Anglo American Corporation of South Africa Limited*, the largest mining and financial house in southern Africa; sometimes used allusively (see quot. 1989) as a symbol of powerful business interests. Also *attrib.* In *pl.*, the shares of this company.

Registered as a public company in 1917.

1971 C.J. JUTA in *New Nation* June 11 Despite increases in the tonnages milled at all mines of the Anglo Group, except East Daggafontein, only three of the Group's goldmines managed to improve their working profits during June (1970) quarter. **1989** D. GOULD in *Dictionaries II* 248 A South African English informalism that should be added is *Anglo* 'the Anglo-American Corporation'. It is found in the South African English expression *Anglo will provide* .. which is a bittersweet one-liner among South Africans asked about the country's long-range prospects. **1993** *Daily News* 7 Dec. 14 (*caption*) Anglos and De Beers glitter. **1993** J.O. THOMPSON in *Weekly Mail* Oct. (Suppl.) 4 Together with De Beers, Anglo spends about R3,3-million a year on more than 1 200 disadvantaged students at private schools, in pre-university bridging programmes, and on vocational scholarships at universities and technikons. **1994** B. COHEN in *Weekly Mail* 18 Mar. 14 Despite the unbundling of Anglo's newspaper interests, a chronic monopoly still exists in the English press.

Anglo-Boer War /ˌæŋgləʊ bʊə ˈwɔː/ *n. phr.* [Eng. *Anglo-* + Afk. *Boer* (see BOER sense 2) + Eng. *war*.]

1. *hist.* The war of 1899–1902 between the British and the Boers; occas., any other conflict between the British and the Boers; BOER WAR sense 1; *Engelse Oorlog*, see ENGELS *adj.* sense 3; SOUTH AFRICAN WAR. Cf. VRYHEIDSOORLOG.

See note at SOUTH AFRICAN WAR.

1900 *Westminster Gaz.* (U.K.) 4 May 11 A large proportion of the money hoarded up, as a consequence of the Anglo-Boer War, will be set into circulation. **1913** J. BRANDT *Petticoat Commando* p.ix, I have tried to give the public some idea of what was done by Boer women, during the great Anglo-Boer war, to keep their men in the field and to support them in what proved to be a hopeless struggle for independence and liberty. **1920** R.H. LINDSEY-RENTON *Diary* (1979) 8 Talks a lot about the War, but it is the South African War, or the Anglo-Boer War as it is called out here. **1929** H.A. CHILVERS *Out of Crucible* 162 The Anglo-Boer war had a disastrous effect on Johannesburg and the goldfields. *a***1930** G. BAUMANN in Baumann & Bright *Lost Republic* (1940) 157 To this day we are still suffering from the effects of the Jameson Raid and the Anglo-Boer War. **1933** W.H.S. BELL *Bygone Days* 328 The conclusion of the Anglo-Boer war was the beginning of a new era, a wonderful transition from the old state of things to the new. **1950** H. GIBBS *Twilight* 21 The year is 1888: the first Anglo-Boer War is in progress. **1955** D.L. HOBMAN *Olive Schreiner* 112 The Boer War at the turn of the century, which should properly be called the Anglo-Boer War, was a prologue to the tragic drama which opened in 1914. **1974** *S. Afr. Panorama* June 47 After the Anglo-Boer War conditions in the former Boer republics were critical. Families were left without fathers or roofs over their heads. **1976** *Drum* June 31 We were not rich, but my father had enough to look after us. After the Anglo-Boer War he could help some of the destitute Boers with food and some money. **1980** D. CHILD *Portrait of Pioneer* 127 On 11 October 1899 war was declared between Britain and the Transvaal. This second Anglo-Boer War had been preceded by months of rising tension and fruitless negotiation. **1985** PLATZKY & WALKER *Surplus People* 80 Tensions between the Transvaal Boers and the British-dominated mining and industrial companies over who was to control and direct the wealth of the Witwatersrand led to the outbreak of the Anglo-Boer War in 1899. **1990** *City Press* 3 June 2 Mandela has spoken of the armed struggle continuing, and we are not waiting for our women and children to be murdered like they were by the British in the Anglo-Boer War.

2. *fig. rare.* Conflict between English- and Afrikaans-speaking people. See also BOER-BRIT, BOER WAR sense 2.

1972 *Sunday Times* 23 Apr., While Tuesday was largely devoted to the aftermath of last week's 'third Anglo-Boer war' on the language issue and economic matters, Wednesday was mostly taken up by several confrontations.

Angola Boer /æŋˌgəʊlə ˈbʊə, -ˈbuːr/ *n. phr. Hist.* [See BOER sense 2.] In the *pl.*, used collectively: a group of Boers who migrated to south-western Angola and settled there in 1881; *Dorsland trekker*, see DORSLAND.

1943 D. REITZ *No Outspan* 104 He followed a faint track which he optimistically called the Road of the Angola Boers. He said it was the route taken by the Thirstland Trekkers when they passed through forty-five years ago. **1944** 'TWEDE IN BEVEL' *Piet Kolonel* 125, I expressed a certain amount of surprise at his decision not to return to his parents, because family ties are nowhere more binding than amongst the Angola Boers. **1970** G.P.J. TRÜMPELMANN in *Std Encycl. of Sn Afr.* I. 426 At their own request approximately 2,000 of the Angola Boers were moved by the South African government to South-West Africa in 1928. **1976** O. LEVINSON *Story of Namibia* 98 In 1928 most of the Thirstland Trekkers (or Angola Boers as they are also known) who had survived this monumental journey — together with their descendants — were brought back from Angola and settled in various parts of northern and eastern Namibia. **1977** *Sunday Times* 9 Oct. 17 An Afrikaner, descended from the Dorsland Trekker 'Angola Boers', notes that most Portuguese are sending their children to Afrikaans schools. 'Perhaps .. the ties with the Angola Boers still survive.'

anijswortel, anise wortel varr. ANYSWORTEL.

anker /ˈaŋkə(r), ˈæŋkə/ *n. Obs.* exc. *hist.* [Du., liquid measure of 38.8 litres.] A unit of liquid measurement formerly in use at the Cape, equivalent to 7,5 to 8,5 imperial gallons (36 to 38 litres), being a quarter of one AUM; the vessel containing this amount. Also *attrib.* See also STUKVAT.

1833 *S. Afr. Almanac & Dir.* 41 Liquid Measure: 16 Flasks, equal to 1 Anker – 4 Ankers equal to 1 Aum. **1843** J.C. CHASE *Cape of G.H.* 192 An Anker is equal to $9\frac{1}{2}$ Dutch gallons or about $7\frac{11}{12}$ths Imper. **1861** *E. Prov. Yr Bk & Annual Register* 61 An anker is equal to $9\frac{1}{2}$ Dutch gals., or about $7\frac{7}{11}$ im. *c***1936** *S. & E. Afr. Yr Bk & Guide* 1009 1 anker = $9\frac{1}{2}$ Dutch Gallons = $7\frac{1}{2}$ Eng. Gals. **1964** L.G. GREEN *Old Men Say* 100 Look up the market prices in the *Cape Argus*, and you will find that as late as 1859 .. Dutch weights and measures were .. in everyday use ... Measurers of capacity were the 'anker' and the 'legger' barrels and casks. **1968** W. KEMPEN in D.J. Opperman *Spirit of Vine* 285 *Anker*, An eight-gallon barrel. Origin unspecified, but no connection with 'anchor'. **1971** R. RAVEN-HART (tr. F.A. *Bolling's Oost-Indiske Reise-Bog*) *Cape G.H. 1652–1702* I. 144 That same day the Captain announced that whoever first sighted land would receive a fresh-milk cheese, a new hat .. a little keg ('Anker') of brandy, and 4 Rixdollars in cash. **1972** [see LEAGUER].

anna-tree var. ANATREE.

anneming var. AANNEMING.

antbear *n.* [Named for a fancied resemblance to a bear.] AARDVARK. Also *attrib.*

1796 E. HELME tr. *F. Le Vaillant's New Trav.* III. 392 This ant-bear is called in the colonies *erd-verken* (earth hog). **1810** G. BARRINGTON *Acct of Voy.* 323 The creature called the *ant bear* .. feeds upon them (ants); and as his tongue .. can be suddenly darted out to a length of two feet, he imbibes a great number of these little insects at once. **1835** J.W.D. MOODIE *Ten Yrs* I. 254 The ant-bears, which are much better furnished with strong claws for penetrating the indurated clay of a dry climate. **1876** T. STUBBS Reminiscences. 7 Many a poor Settler nearly broke his neck by tumbling into Ant Bear holes, that were covered with grass. **1880** [see MEERCAT sense 1]. **1907** J.P. FITZPATRICK *Jock of Bushveld* (1909) 245 Once they caught an ant-bear in the open, and there was a rough-and-tumble. **1911** P. GIBBON *Margaret Harding* 81 Paul's store was an abandoned ant bear's hole across which there trailed the broad dry leaves of a tenacious gourd. **1924** G. BAUMANN in Baumann & Bright *Lost Republic* (1940) 112 They were discussing the enormous speed at which an 'erdvark' (ant-bear) dug itself in. *c***1936** *S. & E. Afr. Yr Bk & Guide* 1101 The ant-bear (*orycteropus afer*) .. is an animal with a long body, some 6 feet in length, sparsely covered with black hair. Its snout, ears and tongue are also enormously long, and its legs and tail strong and short; the former being well adapted to digging. It lives upon insects and nearly every ant-heap in the Karroo has a widely gaping mouth on its Southern side, this point of attack being selected by the *aard vark.* **1967** E.M. SLATTER *My Leaves Are Green* 181, I came round a thick bush and there, at the side, was a big hole made by Isimbamgodi (the antbear). **1970** *Evening Post* 20 Oct. 3 An African hunter apparently suffocated after chasing a small buck down an antbear hole. **1977** [see *flecked* (FLECK)]. **1982** *S. Afr. Panorama* Dec. 12 Lesser animals, some of them nocturnal, include antbear, mongoose, porcupine .. and civet cats. **1990** *Ibid.* July-Aug. 20 The burrow of the ant-bear (*Orycteropus afer*) serves as a pleasant abode with a favourable temperature for a score of 'lodgers'.

ant-cat *n. obs.* [tr. Afk. *mierkat*, see MIERKAT.] MEERKAT.

1901 W.S. SUTHERLAND *S. Afr. Sketches* 73 Jimmy and her fraternity .. are known to the Colonists by the Dutch name of Meer-Kat, (that is Ant-Cat). **1925** F.C. SLATER *Shining River* Glossary, *Meerkat*, Ant-cat.

ant-eater *n.* [Transf. use of general Eng. *ant-eater* a name used of any of several quadrupeds of the order *Edentata*.]

1. The AARDVARK, *Orycteropus afer.*

Often (esp. formerly) called *African ant-eater, Cape ant-eater,* or *great ant-eater.* Cf. *scaly ant-eater* (see sense 2 below).

1795 C.R. HOPSON tr. *C.P. Thunberg's Trav.* I. 137 The *anteater*, or aardvarken (*myrmecophaga*), digs large holes in the earth, in which in the day time he lies secure from his enemies. **1809** [see EARTH-PIG]. **1827** G. THOMPSON *Trav.* I. 50 Our horses were in continual danger of falling or breaking their legs, from the innumerable holes of ant-eaters, porcupines, and jackals. *Ibid.* 111 We ran no small risk of being overset by the excavations of the great ant-eater, which were sometimes sufficiently large to admit a man and horse into them. **1834** T. PRINGLE *Afr. Sketches* 227 The African ant-eater (*orycteropus*, or *myrmecophaga capensis*), called *aard-vark*, or earth-pig, by the colonists, from its habit of burrowing in the earth — a shy and timid creature, which lives entirely upon ants. **1847** 'A BENGALI' *Notes on Cape of G.H.* 80 The '*Aard-vark*' or 'great anteater' burrows the numerous holes found in the sands in the interior. **1871** J. MCKAY *Reminisc.* 15 He fell up to his armpits into one of those large holes which have been formed most likely by some species of ant-eater, and which are plentifully scattered over the plains in this colony. **1929** J.G. VAN ALPHEN *Jan Venter* 283 'It's an *aardvark*,' cried Grobbelaar. It was a hefty specimen of Cape ant-eater with a three-foot body, digging itself in. **1959** [see AARDVARK]. **1989** *Motorist* Aug., Look out for the potholes made by ant-eaters, or washaways caused by rain.

2. With defining word, **scaly ant-eater**: the pangolin *Manis temminckii* of the Manidae.

1918 S.H. SKAIFE *Animal Life* 251 The scaly ant-eater is closely related to the aard-vark ... The upper part of its body is encased in hard, horny scales. *c***1936** *S. & E. Afr. Yr Bk & Guide* 1101 The *scaly ant-eater* (*manis temminchi*) is found in Cape Colony, the Orange River Colony and to the North, and the porcupine is spread over Africa generally. **1959** C. LAGUS *Operation Noah* 172 Also known as the Scaly Anteater, the South African Pangolin is as peculiar in appearance as the Aardvark. It looks like a gigantic animated fir cone, with a thick tail added. **1985** C. WALKER *Signs of Wild* (1987) 29 Pangolin ... Other names in English: Scaly Anteater, Temminck's Pangolin. **1987** *Hit* Feb. 14 If you kill a scaly ant eater, you immediately cut off its head because a pregnant woman is not supposed to see it as she could bear a child with a similar head shape.

antenuptial contract *n. phr. Law.* A contract drawn up by a notary between two persons intending to marry, by which each retains full control over his or her separate property under the accrual system (in terms of the Matrimonial Property Act of 1984), and by which the community of property, and of profit and loss, are excluded; ANC *n.*[2] See also ACCRUAL. Cf. COMMUNITY OF PROPERTY.

1822 LORD C. SOMERSET in *Stat. of Cape of G.H.* (1862) 63 In case any .. natural-born subject of the United Kingdom of Great Britain and Ireland shall enter into the marriage state within this settlement, without making a previous marriage settlement (called, in the colonial law term, antenuptial contract), his property .. shall be administered and divided according to colonial law. **1843** J.C. CHASE *Cape of G.H.* 129 All persons who do not marry under an 'antinuptual contract' [*sic*] are supposed to have entered into that state in 'community of goods'. **1861** J.S. MAYSON *Malays of Capetown* 25 The Cape Colonial Law, with regard to the disposal of property, differs greatly from the laws which obtain elsewhere; e.g. a man (whether Dutch or English, Malay or South African) marrying in the colony, without an antenuptial contract .. marries in 'community of property'. **1887** *S.W. Silver & Co.'s Handbk to S. Afr.* 328 When there has been no ante-nuptial contract or previous settlement entered into, the effect of the marriage at the Cape is to introduce what is called 'community of property'. **1926** M. NATHAN *S. Afr. from Within* 309 Upon marriage, all property is shared equally by the spouses, unless different provisions are made by an ante-nuptial contract, which usually provides that each spouse is to hold his or her property separately and is not to be responsible for the debts of the other. **1930** [see COMMUNITY OF PROPERTY]. *c***1936** *S. & E. Afr. Yr Bk & Guide* 1046 Rather more than a quarter of the marriages solemnized in the Union are under Antenuptial Contract. **1945** WILLE & MILLIN *Mercantile Law of S. Afr.* 20 In the absence of any ante-nuptial contract, the spouses are married in community of property, and of profit and loss, and the husband obtains the marital power. **1972** *Evening Post* 29 Apr. 2 Under present law, a woman married without an ante-nuptial contract remains a ward of her husband for the rest of her life. **1983** *Fair Lady* 7 Sept. 23 As a general rule, where the marriage is by antenuptial contract, on divorce, the spouses retain their separate property and the wife is entitled to whatever settlements were promised to her in the antenuptial contract. **1987** G. VINEY *Col. Houses* 99 When Melck remarried after the death of his first wife he took out an antenuptial contract — a most unusual step in those days [*sc.* 1778]. **1990** C. LAFFEATY *Far Forbidden Plains*, 'This Community of Property business — is that the way most people get married?' 'Yes, because if they don't it means they have to hire a lawyer to draw up an Antenuptial Contract and that's expensive.'

ant-heap *n.* [Eng. *-heap*, instead of the more common *-hill*, is prob. the result of the influence of S. Afr. Du. *mierhoop* ant-hill (*mier* ant + *hoop* heap).]

1. An ant-hill constructed by ants or termites to house their colonies. Also *fig.*

1835 T.H. BOWKER Journal. 27 Mar., Made cartridges mended my gun again tried a shot or two at an Antheap. **1866** E.L. PRICE *Jrnls* (1956) 212 He found the Matebele-refugees (women) making the floor of his fine new house — smearing it with [the] hard black earth of some antheap and then polishing it with smooth round stones in their own fashion. **1870** C. HAMILTON *Life & Sport in S.-E. Afr.* 219 In many parts of the colony so numerous are the ant-heaps that it is difficult to go many places without meeting them. **1878** T.J. LUCAS *Camp Life & Sport* 103, I have seen on the frontier a large ant-heap converted into a series of ovens by scraping out holes at different points at the sides; the ant-heap is then heated in the usual way. **1882** LADY F.C. DIXIE *In Land of Misfortune* 34 With a sudden floundering movement he toed the ground over a high ant-heap and came down with a heavy crash into a deep gully or pit. **1889** 'A HOUSEWIFE OF THE COLONY' *Col. Hsehold Guide* 57 Large ant-heaps are often scooped out in country parts, and make good ovens, a stone daubed around with earth, securing the door opening. **1899** B. MITFORD *Weird of Deadly Hollow* 110 Ant-heaps, stones, and that greatest peril of all — meercat-holes. **1910** A.B. LAMONT *Rural Reader* 28 Many of you have seen the holes in ant-heaps and on the road-sides where the ant-bear has been digging. **1918** [see *daghaing* (DAGHA *v.*)]. **1925** L.D. FLEMMING *Crop of Chaff* 11 Antheaps are more common than bushes in the Orange Free State. *c***1936** [see AARDVARK]. **1943** D. REITZ *No Outspan* 116 One morning I watched a bull elephant .. rubbing the under part of his neck against one of those tall ant-heaps that stand over ten feet high. **1950** D. REED *Somewhere S. of Suez* 73 We have received a position of equality and freedom, not only among the other States of the Empire but among the other nations of the world. Shall we now throw away all these advantages to get back to our old antheap? **1979** S.H. SKAIFE *Afr. Insect Life* 47 The fortress homes of termites, the so-called 'ant-heaps', or termitaria, are a characteristic sight in Africa. **1987** [see MEERKAT].

2. *noncount.* The fine soil and other material from an ant-hill, pulverized and used to make floors, tennis-courts, and other hard ground surfaces. Also *attrib.* See also DAGHA *n.*, *misvloer* (see MIS sense 3).

1880 [see DAGHA *n.* sense a]. **1913** C. PETTMAN *Africanderisms* 31 *Ant-heap*, The earth brought to the surface by the so-called white ants (Termites) is employed, under this designation, to floor rooms, tennis courts, etc. When properly prepared it gives a smooth, hard surface eminently suitable for such purposes. **1916** L.D. FLEMMING *Fool on Veld* (1933) 88 Hadn't we spread a quarter of an inch of antheap over these stubborn deposits, watered and rolled it, and pretended that it was as beautiful a pitch as could be found? **1936** P.M. CLARK *Autobiog. of Old Drifter* 92, I hired a hut constructed of *dagga* — that is, ant-heap mixed with cowdung. **1940** F.B. YOUNG *City of Gold* 21 None of these three noticed Janse standing framed in the doorway, or heard his step on the ant-heap floor when he entered. **1952** F.J. EDMONSTONE *Where Mists Still Linger* 11 The womenfolk would thatch the hut with grass from the veld; then antheap, well watered and stamped down, was used for the floor. **1975** LEVICK & MULLINS *'Prep' Story* 23 Two antheap tennis courts were made in the .. garden. **1977** F.G. BUTLER *Karoo Morning* 67 He surfaced it with ant-heap and old unbaked bricks, employing his children as draught animals to drag a six-foot section of railway line back and forth and to and fro, to level it.

anti var. AUNTIE.

anti-apartheid /ˌænti əˈpɑːtheɪt/ *adj.* [Eng. prefix *anti-* against + APARTHEID.] Of or pertaining to (organized groups working in) opposition to institutionalized apartheid; against apartheid.

1963 K. MACKENZIE *Dragon to Kill* 129 He now took little active interest in politics except to give this annual Christmas party to which anyone concerned in the anti-apartheid struggle was welcome. **1965** G.

SHORT *Trevor Goddard Story* 75 The first move in the anti-apartheid campaign was made well before the Springboks arrived. **1970** *Std Encycl. of Sn Afr.* I. 461 It is necessary, at the outset, to exclude from anti-apartheid movements the legitimate political opposition parties in South Africa, such as the United Party. [*Ibid.* 462 One of the many organisations based in London and operating against the South African authorities is the Anti-Apartheid Movement (A.A.M.) so called, which was formed in 1960 for the specific purpose of opposing apartheid in South Africa.] **1977** N. GORDIMER in *Quarry '77* 81 My novels are anti-apartheid, not because of my personal abhorrence of apartheid, but because the society that is the very stuff of my work reveals itself. **1987** *Cape Times* 11 Apr. 2 Anti-apartheid campaigners have launched a 'spring offensive' against companies with links with South Africa. **1987** *New Nation* 1 Oct. 4 Attended by over 1 000 delegates — twice as many as the organisers expected — it was the largest convention of anti-apartheid whites ever staged in the country. **1993** H. TYSON *Editors under Fire* 11 The first waves were designed to alienate our Afrikaans readers, many of whom were still anti-apartheid in their political views.

Hence **anti-apartheid** *n.*; **anti-apartheider** *n.*

1972 *E. Prov. Herald* 9 Oct. 2 New management revival for US anti-apartheiders. **1990** D. BECKETT in *Frontline* Sept. 30 Joe comes from an environment where anti-apartheid was a holy cause. *Ibid.* He's moved into a whole new realm — beyond anti-apartheid, or post post-apartheid.

Anti-CAC /ˌænti siː eɪ ˈsiː/ *adj. hist.* Also **Anti-C.A.C.** [Eng. prefix *anti-* against + initial letters of *Coloured Advisory Council.*] Of or pertaining to the ANTI-CAD organization.

1963 M. HORRELL *Action, Reaction* 4 A section of the Coloured people .. established an Anti-C.A.C. movement, which later changed its name to the Non-European Unity Movement. **1989** *Reader's Digest Illust. Hist.* 396 The formation of the Coloured Advisory Council (CAC) by the Smuts government in 1943 brought this split [in the 'coloured' community] clearly into the open, with the almost immediate formation of an Anti-CAC (later Anti-CAD) organisation.

Anti-Cad /ˈæntiˌkæd/ *n. hist.* Also **Anti-C.A.D.** [Eng. prefix *anti-* against + acronym formed on *Coloured Affairs Department.*] A committee formed in 1943 (as Anti-CAC) by leading members of the 'coloured' community who refused to collaborate with the newly-created Coloured Advisory Council. Also *attrib.* See also ANTI-CAC, NEUM.

1949 E. HELLMANN *Handbk on Race Rel.* 517 The Non-European Unity Movement .. draws most of its support from the Coloured community, including the Anti-C.A.D. movement (i.e., Anti-Coloured Advisory Council: their slogan being 'Anti-Coloured Affairs Department'). **1952** 'KAAPENAAR' in *Drum* Dec. 10 He is said to be the real brains behind the Anti-Cad and Unity Movements. **1953** *Drum* Oct. 14 The Anti-C.A.D. is dead because it is, in essence, a negative body pledged to a policy of boycott and political non-collaboration. **1959** [see NEUM]. **1971** *Rand Daily Mail* 19 Feb., The Unity Movement .. was formed in 1943 by the merging of the two other Non-White radical groups, the Anti-Coloured Affairs Department Movement (Anti-C.A.D.) and the All African Convention. **1989** *Reader's Digest Illust. Hist.* 396 The Anti-Cad group, with its broader view of the liberation struggle, did attain greater unity with African freedom groups. **1990** *Staffrider* Vol.9 No.1, 10 The New Unity Association was a breakaway group of the United Movement, itself a splinter group of the All United Alliance, a sub-committee of the Anti-Cad.

anysdruppels see DRUPPELS sense b ii.

anyswortel /aˈneɪs ˌvɔ(r)t(ə)l/ *n.* Also **anijswortel, anyse wortel,** and formerly also part. tr. **anise wortel.** [S. Afr. Du., fr. Du. *anijs* anise + *wortel* root.] Any of several species of plant of the genus *Annesorrhiza* of the Umbelliferae, having edible, anise-flavoured tubers.

1790 tr. *F. Le Vaillant's Trav.* II. 85 Two other roots of the size of one's finger, but exceedingly long .. are to be met with in the colonies, where they are known, one under the name of *anys-wortel*, and the other under that of *vinkel-wortel*. **1795** C.R. HOPSON tr. *C.P. Thunberg's Trav.* I. 149 The root of Anise (*anys-wortel*) was eaten here roasted, and tasted well; it is either roasted in the embers, or boiled in milk, or else stewed with meat. **1809** J. MACKRILL Diary. 56 Anise Wortel and Gatagey, Tentandria umbelliferous plants, the Dutch eat thʳ Roots. **1822** [see SWARTLAND]. [**1837** ECKLON & ZEYHER *Enumeratio Plantarum Africae* 344 *Annesorhiza capensis* ... Incolis: Vlackte Anyswortel ... *Annesorhiza montana* ... Incolis: Berg Anyswortel.] **1856** L. PAPPE in *Cape of G.H. Almanac & Annual Register* 341 Annesorhiza Capensis. Ch Schltdl. (Umbelliferae) The turnip-like root of this umbelliferous plant is very nutritious and has been used for many years past as food by the natives and colonists who call it Anise-root (Anijs-wortel). **1868** W.H. HARVEY *Genera of S. Afr. Plants* 141 Biennials or perennials, with aromatic roots; *Anyswartel* [*sic*] of colonists. **1917** R. MARLOTH *Common Names* 6 *Anijswortel, Annesorrhiza montana* and *A. macrocarpa*. Perennial plants .. gathered at the beginning of summer and used as a vegetable, tasting somewhat like parsnips. **1966** C.A. SMITH *Common Names* 63 The probabilities are that the name Anyswortel gained currency for one or more species of *Annesorrhiza* during van Riebeeck's time, though the name was only mentioned some 45 years later. **1971** L.G. GREEN *Taste of S.-Easter* 82 The sweetish suikerwortel or anyswortel, rather like the parsnip of civilisation, was another Cape root that helped to cure scurvy.

apartheid /əˈpɑːtheɪt/ *n.* [Afk., 'separateness'.]

1. *hist.*

a. The National Party government's policy of racial segregation at all levels. Also *attrib.*, and (*punning*) **apart-hate, departheid**. See also *parallel development* (PARALLEL sense 1), SEPARATE DEVELOPMENT.

1944 D.F. MALAN in *Star* 25 Jan., To ensure the safety of the white race and of Christian civilisation by the honest maintenance of the principles of apartheid and guardianship. **1950** H. GIBBS *Twilight* 35 It is worth noting that the Nationalist Government is pledged to support a policy of *apartheid*, segregation, under which the native shall have certain areas in which to develop his own community and culture, which will be removed from the European zones. **1952** B. DAVIDSON *Report on Sn Afr.* 76 On the policy of *apartheid* — the saving of white supremacy in the face of all the facts that it could not be saved without national suicide — the Nationalist came to power. **1952** G. MAGWAZA in *Drum* Aug. 11 She .. was faced with the signs 'Non-Europeans Only' and 'Europeans Only' on the entrance leading to the platform steps ... But it all started looking like departheid when she saw a mass United Nations down the platforms, where passengers of all races rubbed shoulders. **1955** E. DE S. BRUNNER in *Pol. Science Quarterly* Sept. 372 It must be remembered that the Dutch Reformed Church furnishes strong religious support to the apartheid policy. **1960** A. HEPPLE in H. Spottiswoode *S. Afr.: Rd Ahead* 81 The Nationalists claim that South Africa's choice is between *apartheid* ('separate development') and integration, describing the former as a policy of opportunity for every man within his own race group in racially reserved areas. **1968** J. LELYVELD in Cole & Flaherty *House of Bondage* 8 Eventually — or so the theory of *apartheid*, at its most preposterous, holds, the entire urban black population will melt back into tribal reserves. **1970** E. KAHN in *Std Encycl. of Sn Afr.* I. 472 The word 'apartheid' .. came into common use only in 1948, though it had been used by academics and men in public life, especially in National Party circles, from the mid-thirties as a synonym, with a less pejorative tang, for segregation. **1979** [see BAASSKAP]. **1980** [see MISSUS sense 2 b]. **1980** S. JENKINS in *Rand Daily Mail* 19 June 9 Apartheid wasn't being dismantled but was merely undergoing some kind of transformation. This is the new apartheid, which I call neo-apartheid. **1986** P.W. BOTHA in *Cape Times* 1 Feb. 19 We have outgrown the outdated colonial system of paternalism as well as the outdated concept of apartheid. **1986** M. TSEDU in *Sowetan* 30 Dec. 4 We could swim in the same sea water .. but the little shower, where there would be no contact at all, was taboo. That's apartheid in reformist South Africa. **1987** *S. Afr. Digest* 10 July 2 The abolition of discriminatory legislation and the moves towards political power-sharing have followed the first steps that were taken to dismantle apartheid: the opening of public facilities. **1988** N. MOLOTO in *New Nation* 10 Mar. 13 Hearken and hurry to the pavements of Soweto the cities of apart-hate. **1990** *Daily Dispatch* 17 Apr. 1 The government .. had no intention of summarily scrapping cornerstones of apartheid like the Population Registration Act and the Group Areas Act without putting something in their place. **1990** O. MUSI in *Drum* Dec. 18 From one corner one blonde matron was saying in a voice which would have done any mezzo-soprano proud .. 'I don't believe in *apart-hate*, but .. '. **1990** R. MALAN *My Traitor's Heart* 6 A final solution for the 'native question' .. was apartheid, a gridlock of more than a hundred laws designed to keep blacks and whites forever separate and to ensure, not at all coincidentally, that blacks remained in their God-ordained place, hewers of wood and drawers of water, forever and ever. **1991** G.J. CHURCH in *Time* 22 July 12 Apartheid was always an unworkable as well as immoral system whose breakdown was inevitable. **1991** N. MANDELA in *Ibid.* 5 Aug. 12 Apartheid may be mortally wounded but its heart has not yet stopped beating.

b. With defining words denoting various forms of apartheid: **beach apartheid; big apartheid** or **grootapartheid** /ˈxruət-/ *rare* [Afk., *groot* big, prob. tr. Eng. *grand*], GRAND APARTHEID; **klein apartheid** /ˈkleɪn/ [Afk., *klein* small], **small apartheid,** PETTY APARTHEID. Also *attrib.*

1960 *Star* 8 Aug. 1 Members of the Provincial Council's commission on **beach apartheid** proposals for the Cape coast left here today for Kleinemond. **1978** P. LANGE in *E. Prov. Herald* 7 Mar. 1 The Administrator of the Cape, Dr Munnik, is to be invited to inspect Port Elizabeth's beaches in the light of a request to do away with beach apartheid. **1988** B. STREEK in *Cape Times* 20 Jan. 2 The Progressive Federal Party yesterday backed the call by the leader of the Labour Party, Mr Allan Hendrickse, for a boycott of the Dias Festival unless all beach apartheid was lifted. **1970** M. TYACK *S. Afr.: Land of Challenge* 135 The Government's idealistically motivated desire to 'unscramble' the South African ethnic 'omelette', into a constellation of nation-states for the White and the main Bantu peoples ... This 'grand design' (popularly referred to as '**Big Apartheid**'). **1972** *Sunday Times* 22 Oct. 16 Addressing a meeting in Stellenbosch, Mr Vorster repeated that he did not know 'what petty or big apartheid is — for me there is just apartheid and nothing else.' **1989** W. SWING in *Sunday Times* 3 Dec. 27 While the main pillars of Verwoerdian **grootapartheid** remain, there is daily erosion which varies widely from place to place. **1968** W.K. HANCOCK *Smuts* II. 512 The pinpricks which some people called '**klein apartheid**' .. job-reservation for whites, the shutting down of artisan training for blacks, the imposition upon Cape Town of separate racial railway carriages and post office queues. **1972** *Sunday Times* 5 Nov. 17 Mr. Vorster is convinced that there is no such thing as petty or klein apartheid. **1982** *Rand Daily Mail* 25 Feb. 11 As he said in his book, 'Credo van 'n Afrikaner': 'If **small apartheid** is completely eliminated, big apartheid becomes superfluous, stupid and unnecessary.'

2. *transf.* Any system, policy, or action which segregates people, whether based on caste, religion, gender, class, or any other social category.

[**1955** *Times* (U.K.) 5 July 6 The Archbishop of Canterbury, Dr. Fisher, drew a parallel yesterday between the political *apartheid* which he has seen in South Africa, separating the nation, and ecclesiastical *apartheid* which prevented unity among the churches.] **1984** *Drum* Sept. 20 The innocent Ndebele tribe is being intimidated by the majority Shona tribe to welcome a one party state in Zimbabwe. It is 'pure apartheid' to leave a Shona in the driver's seat and shooting [*sic*] an Ndebele in the back seat. **1987** G. SILBER in *Style* Nov. 52 Apartheid: System of institutionalised discrimination applied to South African citizens wishing to visit Australia. **1989** *Cape Times* 10 July 6 Religious fundamentalism and 'ecclesiastical apartheid' were behind much of the strife in the modern world, whether it be Islamic or Jewish in the Middle East, or Christian in Ulster, the Archbishop of Canterbury, Dr Robert Runcie said. **1990** *Sunday Times* 11 Nov. 24 Caste system is India's apartheid.

Hence (*nonce*) **apartheid** *v. intrans.*, to blame apartheid for every misfortune; **apartheid, apartheidish** *adjs*; so **apartheidist, apartheiditis** *ns*.

1952 L.E. NEAME *White Man's Afr.* 54 At heart all South Africans are Apartheidists. **1956** A. SAMPSON *Drum* 33 Over there, there's a cemetery for non-Europeans. Of course, it's very apartheid, even when you're dead! **1982** *Voice* 30 May 4 He is a protegé of apartheidists who has surprised even the proponents of this rotten ideology of apartheid. **1989** *Informant, Grahamstown* It sounds like he's going to take an apartheidish view of language, but it's not so. **1989** *Argus* 14 Aug. 7 Afrikaans railway employee .. has an acute illness called 'apartheiditis' ... He said he could not go to work because his co-workers' racism .. had sickened him. **1991** D. BECKETT in *Sunday Star* 3 Feb. (Review) 2 It boils down to blaming apartheid for every ill under the sun or moon. He's down there now, apartheiding away.

Apdusa /æpˈduːsə/ *n.* Also **APDUSA**. Acronym formed on *African People's Democratic Union of South Africa*, an organization founded in 1961 as a break-away group of the NEUM.

1971 *Rand Daily Mail* 19 Feb., The detainees are members either of the Non-European Unity Movement or of a splinter group of that organisation, the African People's Democratic Union of South Africa (Apdusa). **1972** *Drum* 15 Jan. 10 The headquarters of Apdusa — the African People's Democratic Union of South Africa — had gone into exile with its president, Isaac Bagani Tabata, when he fled to Zambia in 1964. **1984** R. DAVIES et al. *Struggle for S. Afr.* 313 The Tabata leadership formed an individual membership organisation affiliated to the NEUM in January 1961. This was the African Peoples' Democratic Union of South Africa (APDUSA). **1989** *Poster, Pietermaritzburg* Don't vote .. issued by Apdusa. **1990** *Graffiti, Cape Town* Viva APDYM. Viva APDUSA.

apiesdoring /ˈɑːpisˌduərəŋ, ˈɑːpiːz-/ *n.* Also **aapjesdoorn, apiesdoorn.** [Afk., earlier S. Afr. Du. *aapjesdoorn, aap* ape + -IE + euphonic *-s-* + *doorn* thorn.] Any of several trees of the genus *Acacia* of the Leguminosae, with high, leafy crowns, esp. *A. albida, A. burke, A. galpinii* and *A. welwitschii*; MONKEY THORN. Also *attrib.* See also ANATREE.

1917 R. MARLOTH *Common Names* 7 *Apiesdoorn, Acacia Welwitschii* and *A. Burkei*. Large trees .. with numerous straight spines (also on the old wood). **1937** S. CLOETE *Turning Wheels* 165 Further away were four tall apiesdoorns, which from their size, must have been hundreds of years old. **1944** C.R. PRANCE *Under Blue Roof* 27 The aapjesdoorn forest choking the pass behind. **1958** R.E. LIGHTON *Out of Strong* 3 Their farm sloped down from weathered dolomite ridges dotted with white stinkwood trees to the banks of a river shaded by huge apiesdorings. **1966** C.A. SMITH *Common Names* 63 *Apiesdoring*, .. Several species of *Acacia* which afford effective cover to the small blue-black-faced monkeys. **1973** *Star* 19 June 19 An Acacia Galpinii — or apiesdoring — near Naboomspruit. This particular specimen is almost 80ft high. **1976** [see SOETDORING sense 1]. **1991** [see MONKEY THORN].

APK /eɪ piː ˈkeɪ, ɑː piə ˈkɑː/ *n.* [Initial letters of Afk. *Afrikaanse Protestantse Kerk*.] The Afrikaans Protestant Church, a conservative breakaway from the Nederduitse Gereformeerde Kerk (see NGK), having an exclusively white membership.

1987 *Cape Times* 10 July 2 The new breakaway Afrikaanse Protestantse Kerk (APK) now has six ministers, according to church sources in Pretoria. **1987** 'K. DE BOER' in *Frontline* Oct.-Nov. 42 A plattelandse skou is still something not to be missed, irrespective of whether you belong to the AWB, the APK, the BBB or the Vrymesselaars. **1990** *Sunday Times* 14 Oct. 4 In spite of the breakaway to the APK, the NG church remains the only Afrikaner institution that has not yet split irrevocably along party political lines.

Apla /ˈæplə, ˈaplə/ *n.* [Acronym formed on *Azanian People's Liberation Army*.] The military wing of the Pan Africanist Congress. Also *attrib.* See also AZANIA, PAC, POQO.

[**1976** *E. Prov. Herald* 29 Sept. 1 An organisation known as the Azania Liberation Army was recruiting people in Soweto for guerilla training outside South Africa.] **1988** *Daily Dispatch* 29 July 23 The Apla unit attacked the South African forces with hand grenades and followed up with automatic gunfire when fire was returned. **1988** P. LAWRENCE in *Saturday Star* 9 July 11 Similar uncompromising attitudes may be maturing in the camps of the PAC army, the Azanian People's Liberation Army (Apla). Its recruits are reported to chant a chilling slogan: 'One settler, one bullet.' **1990** *City Press* 4 Feb. 2 He said it was unrealistic to expect the PAC to disband its army, the Azanian Peoples' Liberation Army (Apla), as it was formed to meet certain national objectives. **1991** L. KAUNDA in *Natal Witness* 28 Mar. (Echo) 5 Apla continued to operate and said most of their missions were reported as ANC missions by the police and the press, or were totally unreported.

apotheek var. APTEEK.

appelblaar /ˈapəlblɑː(r)/ *n.* [Afk., *appel* apple + *blaar* leaf.] The deciduous shrub or small tree *Lonchocarpus capassa* of the Fabaceae, with grey-green, drooping leaves similar to those of the apple tree.

1961 O. LEVINSON *Ageless Land* 137 West of the Pan grow tambotie, wolf's thorn, appelblaar, date, wild fig, marula and makalanie palm. **1972** *Pamphlet, Etosha National Park* The dry, deciduous bushes consist mainly of Mapani, but to the east and further away from the pan a large variety is found, such as tambootie, wolf's-thorn, wild fig, wild date, 'appelblaar'. **1984** J. ONDERSTALL *Tvl Lowveld & Escarpment* 114 *Lonchocarpus capassa*, Apple-leaf, Rain Tree, Appelblaar. The common name implies a similarity to the apple tree but they are not related, the apple having simple leaves, whereas those of *Lonchocarpus* are compound.

Appel-der-liefde *n. obs.* Also **Appel de liefde**. [S. Afr. Du., transf. use of Du. *appel-der-liefde* (*appel* apple + *der* of + *liefde* love), applied to the tomato.] CAPE GOOSEBERRY.

1843 J.C. CHASE *Cape of G.H.* 152 That abundant and delicious fruit the *Physalis Peruviana*, called here the Cape Gooseberry, or Appel de Liefde. **1856** L. PAPPE in *Cape of G.H. Almanac & Annual Register* 345 Although this plant, the *Cape Gooseberry* (Appel der Liefde) cannot .. be called indigenous being a native of South America, yet it has become so common in the country that it is found now in most shady localities, where it grows perfectly wild. **1917** R. MARLOTH *Common Names* 7 *Appel-der-liefde*, In Holland this name is applied to the tomato, but here to the Cape gooseberry.

Apple Express *n. phr.* A narrow-gauge steam train, originally serving the Langkloof fruit-growing area of the Cape province, and later a tourist attraction. Also *attrib.*

1963 M.G. MCCOY *Informant, Port Elizabeth* The boys went off with the cub pack for the day on the 'apple express' as far as Loerie. **1974** *The 1820* May 17 Exactly 70 years after the first tiny trains started running on Port Elizabeth's 'Apple Express' railway, powerful diesel locomotives have been introduced to modernise what is probably the busiest and most useful narrow-gauge line in the world. **1979** *Family Radio & TV* 28 May 54 The trio of veteran engines of the 'Apple Express' continue to pull their loads of fruit along the 120 km of track between Assegaaibos, Joubertina and Avontuur. **1982** *E. Prov. Herald* 20 Sept. 1 It's 'Apple 2, Runners 1' after the Apple Express walked Saturday's third .. Great Train Race ... When it reached the first station, the Apple was lagging behind and the back of the last runner could just be seen in the distance ... But the Apple Express won. **1988** A. ERASMUS in *Ibid.* 25 Aug. 3 It will be full steam ahead for the Apple Express on Saturday, September 17, when the ninth .. Great Train Race is run. **1990** *Weekend Post* 20 Oct. 6 The Apple Express and all those other special trains can keep their green or brown-and-cream paintwork.

apprentice *n. hist.* [Special sense of general Eng. *apprentice* one learning a craft or trade while bound to serve the employer for a fixed period.] An indentured servant (usu. a former slave, or the child of a slave) registered with a particular master (often the former slave-owner) for a fixed number of years; frequently a euphemism for 'slave' (see quot. 1934); INBOEKSELING. Also *attrib.*

1820 in G.M. Theal *Rec. of Cape Col.* (1902) XII. 128 Return showing the Population and Cattle in the Possession of Individuals at the Cape of Good Hope. Christians: .. Free Blacks, Hottentots, Negro Apprentices, Slaves. **1835** G. CHAMPION *Jrnl* (1968) 10 The slaves, (apprentices rather, for now the Colony is free from the evil of slavery, in name,) we were told were eager for instruction. **1836** *Ordinance 3* in *Cape of G.H. Govt Gaz.* 3 June 2 And be it further enacted, that .. the said Commissioners .. shall jointly with the Master or Mistress of the said Apprentice, execute and sign a form of Indenture, to contain such provisions and covenants for the protection of the interest of such Apprentice. **1837** 'N. POLSON' *Subaltern's Sick Leave* 108 The servants on the farms and in the houses of the Boers are chiefly free apprentices (late slaves), and some Hottentots. **1841** J. COLLETT Diary. II., Hired Adonis free Aprentice to day for one year @ 6 Rd. **1852** M.B. HUDSON *S. Afr. Frontier Life* 252 There was only one exception to the general insurrection, in the person of an old emancipated Mozambique apprentice, who gave undoubted evidence of the guilt of the whole Hottentot population. **1928** E.A. WALKER *Hist. of S. Afr.* 282 Some of the commissioners closed the inquiry .. and returned home (with a black apprentice bought on the scene of their labours). **1934** C.P. SWART Supplement to Pettman. 6 *Apprentice*, .. Originally it meant a slave retained legally in servitude for a term of years after manumission. Afterwards the word became more elastic in meaning, signifying freedmen and captives held in servitude indefinitely and illegally. **1949** O. WALKER *Proud Zulu* (1951) 37 He proclaimed all the land up to the Tugela as his in addition to the 40,000 cattle plundered and 1,000 'apprentices', young Zulu children, orphaned by war, whom the Dutch vrous demanded for their share of booty as labour in their households. **1973** J. MEINTJES *Voortrekkers* 55 The British .. decided to implement abolition on 1 December 1834, compromising only by allowing slaves to remain with their masters for the next four years as apprentices — on probation as it were. **1986** P. MAYLAM *Hist. of Afr. People* 130 The Ndzundza Ndebele chiefdom was broken up and its people given over to boer farms as apprentice labour. **1989** *Reader's Digest Illust. Hist.* 126 Although the importation of slaves was banned in 1807, it was not until 1834 that slaves were officially granted their freedom, and even then they were obliged to work as 'apprentices' for their former owners — unpaid — for a period of four years.

apprentice *v. trans. Hist.* [As prec.] To register (someone, often a former slave or the child of a slave) as the indentured servant of a particular master for a fixed period; BOOK; INBOEK.

1816 G. BARKER Journal. 25 Jan., A Hottentot woman .. had resided a long time with a certain Boor and had cohabited with a slave of his, by whom she had several children; the Boor had driven her away & deprived her of the man with whom she had so long lived that he might take a slave woman to wife, that the Boor might gain slaves, (the children of the

Hottentot being free) her children were detained by the Boor & apprenticed after the usual manner. **1836** *Ordinance 3* in *Cape of G.H. Govt Gaz.* 3 June 1 In order that Persons in this Colony desirous of obtaining the Services of Children from the said Instituition may be enabled to exercise a legal authority over them, it is necessary that some Persons be authorized to act as Guardians for and on behalf of such Children, with power to apprentice or otherwise provide for them as to their said Guardians may appear most expedient. **1857** [see INBOEK sense 1]. **1863** LADY DUFF-GORDON in F. Galton *Vacation Tourists* (1864) III. 213 She is 'apprenticed', a name for temporary slavery, and is highly spoken of as a servant, as the Caffres always are. **1887** *S.W. Silver & Co.'s Handbk to S. Afr.* 29 Sir John Cradock issued a proclamation empowering each landdrost in his respective district to seize upon any Hottentot child, of the age of eight years, whose parents had been in his service at the period of his birth, and apprentice him to whomsoever he pleased for a term of ten years. **1913** C. PETTMAN *Africanderisms* 224 *Inbooking*, .. The anglicized form of the word used by the Dutch in the Transvaal for a system of apprenticing natives that was open to great abuse. **1946** [see INBOEK sense 1]. **1963** P. HINCHLIFF *Anglican Church* 15 In 1836 the Children's Friend Society sent 700 destitute and neglected children to the colony. These youths had been rescued from a life of delinquency in the London slums and were apprenticed to the farmers at the Cape. **1980** J. COCK *Maids & Madams* 175 San women and children were captured by both Xhosa and Dutch farmers who wanted servants. San adults sometimes 'apprenticed' their children to Dutch farmers when they were 'in a famished state'.

Hence **apprenticing** *vbl n.*

1904 H.A. BRYDEN *Hist. of S. Afr.* 279 A large number of Bechuanas were deported to Cape Colony proper, where they were 'apprenticed' among Dutch farmers. This deportation and forcible apprenticing .. is little better than a form of slavery.

apprenticeship *n. hist.* [See APPRENTICE *n.*] The system of forced labour whereby a person, usu. a former slave or the child of a slave, was indentured to serve a particular master for a fixed period; *inboeking*, see INBOEK.

1816 G. BARKER Journal. 6 Jan., Three children of one of the men, he said, were apprenticed to his late master, but without stating to him the nature of the apprenticeship, or the reason why he kept them, or even asking his consent. **1826** [see OPGAAF sense 1]. **1836** *Ordinance 3* in *Cape of G.H. Govt Gaz.* 3 June 2 And be it further enacted, that .. such Apprenticeship is to continue in force until the Child, if Male, shall have attained the Age of Twenty one Years, and, if Female, until such Female shall have attained the age of Twenty-one Years, or shall be married .. except in such case in which it shall be considered expedient by the .. Commissioners to limit the Apprenticeship to a shorter period. **1892** W.L. DISTANT *Naturalist in Tvl* 25 The poor wretches have often been bound to an apprenticeship of 21 years (which they did not comprehend), any attempts to escape being met with savage floggings and shootings. **1896** [see *inboeked* at INBOEK]. **1951** H. DAVIES *Great S. Afr. Christians* 14 The new Ordinance either removed or mitigated such disadvantages as: the legal disability to hold land, the pass system, summary imprisonment, and forced labour and apprenticeship. **1973** J. MEINTJES *Voortrekkers* 55 The Boers liked the system of apprenticeship and were to maintain it for years to come, but the British refused to see this as anything but glorified slavery, and were to make this accusation for decades. **1989** *Reader's Digest Illust. Hist.* 126 Not all former slaves left their masters at the end of the period of apprenticeship.

appy /'æpi/ *n. colloq.* Also **appie**. [Formed on Eng. *apprentice* + (informal) n.-suffix *-y* (or *-ie*).] An apprentice. Also *fig.*, a greenhorn.

1985 *Sunday Times* 27 Oct. (Mag. Sect.) 10 All you need do is pop down to the local garage and charm the appies into lending you a couple of chamois leathers. **1989** *Ibid.* 14 May 5 I've got all my pay slips going back to when I was an appy. **1991** M. KANTEY *All Tickets* 19 Being woken up at 03h00 to drink neat cane by appies on their way to trade tests in Pretoria. **1993** *Natal Witness* 6 Jan. 3 Jockey fined for hitting appie. **1993** *Informant, Grahamstown* That lecturer is a bladdy appy.

apricot sickness *n. phr. Pathology.* [tr. Afk. *appelkoossiekte, appelkoos* apricot + *siekte* sickness; see quot. 1949.] Diarrhoea occurring in summer; any intestinal or gastro-intestinal infection.

1945 *Cape Times* 27 Jan. 11 Apricot sickness is most troublesome when the entire gastro-intestinal tract is affected; that is to say, when there is vomiting as well as diarrhoea. **1949** L.G. GREEN *In Land of Afternoon* 156 Apricot sickness .. is an inevitable complaint during the fruit season ... The illness gained its name because apricots were the first spring fruits which the early Cape farmers produced. They suffered from the familiar griping pains and diarrhoea, and rightly blamed the apricots. **1958** R.E. LIGHTON *Out of Strong* 51, I said nothing about eating marulas. Better leave them alone: they make your lips sore and may give you apricot sickness. **1974** *Sunday Times* 24 Nov. (Mag. Sect.) 2 The 'trots', a 'runny tummy', 'Apricot sickness' or 'gastric flu'. **1983** J.A. BROWN *White Locusts* 160 In the height of summer not a week passed but an infant died of what they called 'the apricot sickness'. The milk sold from door to door by Boer farmers was suspect.

April Fool *n. phr.* [See quot. 1906.] Any of several bulbous plant species of the Amaryllidaceae, esp. *Haemanthus rotundifolius*, with two large, almost circular leaves which lie flat on the ground during the winter months.

1906 B. STONEMAN *Plants & their Ways* 192 *Haemanthus*, 'The April Fool' merits its name, as we think when we find that what we took to be a single flower is really a dense umbel of many flowers surrounded by bright red bracts. **1950** M.M. KIDD *Wild Flowers* Pl.15, *Haemanthus rotundifolius* .. (Amaryllidaceae). 6–8 in.: common; Feb.-Mch. Leaves 2, large, opposite, almost circular. *April Fool.* **1967** G. HARESNAPE in C.M. Booysen *More Tales of S. Afr.* 148 There were the everlastings whose petals formed stiff rosettes above their leaves, the blood red April Fools. **1970** M.R. LEVYNS in *Std Encycl. of Sn Afr.* I. 492 *April Fool*, (*Haemanthus rotundifolius*.) .. Towards the end of summer .. a stout, red flowering axis is put up. The umbel of flowers is surrounded by a number of fleshy red bracts, which are a little shorter than the flowers. **1988** M. BRANCH *Explore Cape Flora* 38 Beautiful fire lilies and April fools have appeared as if from nowhere to bloom in the ashes.

apron *n. obs.* [Special senses of general Eng.] **1.** An article of traditional African dress consisting of a flap or thongs of softened hide suspended from the hips at the front or back. Cf. KAROSS sense 2, MUTSHA.

1691 BROWNE in R. Raven-Hart *Cape G.H. 1652–1702* (1971) II. 388 The men have litle bit of skin which hangs befor their privie members, and the women a kind of apron. **1786** G. FORSTER tr. *A. Sparrman's Voy. to Cape of G.H.* II. 283 She was clad in the usual manner with a sheep-skin *pellisse*, and a well greased raw leathern apron .. and could boast of as broad and flat a nose as any Hottentot lady whatever. **1824** W.J. BURCHELL *Trav.* II. 563 They wear the same *dress* as the Hottentots; but call the 'fore-apron,' by the names of *makkaabi* or *moteeno* (motayno), and the 'hinder apron,' by that of *museesi* (moosaysy). **1827** G. THOMPSON *Trav.* II. 417 They [*sc.* Zulus] wear an apron of hide about the middle; and it becomes so pliable and soft, from frequent rubbing, that it has quite the appearance of cloth. **1835** A. SMITH *Diary* (1940) II. 285 The common jackal apron, a cap of skin with bead ornaments and a tail covered with beads fixed to the top. **1841** B. SHAW *Memorials* 21 The females wear a little apron, ten or twelve inches in length, and as many in breadth, to which are appended six or eight chains of copper or iron. **1898** *Chambers's Jrnl* (U.K.) 8 Jan. 95 His only dress consisted of a monkey skin muchi, or apron, and in his hand he carried a rifle.

2. *Hottentot apron*, see HOTTENTOT *n.* sense 6 b.

1905 G.W. STOW *Native Races of S. Afr.* 31 These people .. appear to have adopted among themselves the name of '*Khai*', which is also the same as that given to the natural apron for which the women of pure Bushman and Hottentot races be distinguished.

‖**apteek** /ap'tɪək/ *n.* Formerly also **apotheek**. [Afk. (Du. *apotheek*).] A pharmacist's shop, a chemist. See also HUIS-APOTHEEK.

1873 W.L. SAMMONS in A.M.L. Robinson *Sel. Articles from Cape Monthly Mag.* (1978) 263 *Shop Signs* or Figures do not appear to be very prevalent in Cape Town, but there are a few. One of the purest brightest and best is '*The Golden Angel*', at the '*Engel Apotheek*', in Loop-street. **1911** L. COHEN *Reminisc. of Kimberley* 391 When I reached the hamlet I was in great pain, and a Boer inhabitant directed me to a small building on which was written 'apotheek.' **1926** P.W. LAIDLER *Tavern of Ocean* 13 A house within the ramparts was turned into a compact *Apotheek*, or chemist's shop. **1975** W. STEENKAMP *Land of Thirst King* 138 For many years the only formal medical help the average farmer possessed was what he called his 'apteek', or pharmacy. **1980** *Rand Daily Mail* 20 Nov. 12 Every dorp will have a mall soon in spite of the fact that there is only one short shopping street from the apteek at one end to the take-away eats at the other.

Arab *n.* [Special sense of general Eng.] Esp. in Natal: a Muslim of Indian descent, usu. of the wealthier merchant class. Also *attrib.* See also PASSENGER.

Also used elsewhere.

1885 *Law 3* in *Stat. Law of Tvl 1839–1910* (1910) I. 135 Relating to Coolies, Arabs, and other Asiatics ... This law shall apply to the persons belonging to one of the native races of Asia, including the so-called Coolies, Arabs, Malays, and Mohamedan subjects of the Turkish Empire. **1888** C. DU VAL in M. Fraser *Jhb. Pioneer Jrnls* (1985) 29 We entered Johannesburg before daylight .. to find ourselves .. surrounded by the usual crowd of early buyers, English, Dutch, Arabs, Coolies, Kaffirs, and even Chinese. **1897** J. BRYCE *Impressions of S. Afr.* (1969) 298 The other class [of Indian people], less numerous, but better educated and more intelligent, consists .. of so-called 'Arabs' – Mohammedans, chiefly from Bombay and the ports near it, or from Zanzibar – who conduct retail trade, .. and sometimes become rich. **1901** *Natives of S. Afr.* (S. Afr. Native Races Committee) 7 India (with Zanzibar) also supplies another class of immigrants in the 'Arab' retail dealers of the colony, who are mostly Mohammedans from Bombay and the neighbouring ports. **1913** *Indian Opinion* 29 Mar. 73 The magistrate expressed his opinion that fresh Licences to Arab traders should be prohibited, and suggested that existing Arab stores should be closed down. **1957** M. DESAI tr. *M.K. Gandhi's Autobiog.* 108 Coolie .. became a common appellation for all Indians. The Musalman merchant would resent this and say: 'I am not a coolie, I am an Arab,' or 'I am a merchant,' and the Englishman, if courteous, would apologize to him. *c*1963 B.C. TAIT *Durban Story* 207 The white colonists, through ignorance and lack of interest, referred to all Indians as coolies ... When educated, intelligent Bombay merchants and shipowners came upon the scene with cargoes of rice and condiments for sale .. the townsfolk learned to discriminate between .. 'Arab merchants' and 'coolie shopkeepers'. **1989** *Reader's Digest Illust. Hist.* 225 Known as Arabs or 'Passengers', and most of them Muslims from the State of Gujarat, they began to arrive in the 1870s and constituted the upper stratum of Indians in southern Africa.

archaar var. ATJAR.

arem var. ARM.

aricrickel, -kreukel, -krikkel, -kruikel varr. ALIKREUKEL.

arlie /'ɑːli/ *n.* Also **aa(r)lie, alie.** [Afk. *alie*, abbrev. of *albaster* marble + -IE; or ad. Eng. *all(e)y*.]

Esp. in the speech of children: a marble. Also *attrib*. See also GHOEN sense a, IRONIE.

1970 D. HANSEN *Informant*, Durban, I rouksed ten aarlies today (I won ten marbles today). 1970 J. GREENWOOD *Informant*, Johannesburg Let's play arlies (marbles). 1985 *E. Prov. Herald* 27 Feb. 1 Gleefully showing yesterday's winnings in the 'arlie patch' is .. a Sub B pupil at Grey Junior School. 1988 D. HIRSON in Bunn & Taylor *From S. Afr.* 96 Marbles: alies malies ghoens glassies puries smokies ironies twos castles tens twenties shy up. 1990 *Fair Lady* 6 June 111 'How do you know when marble season starts?' I ask as they stagger off to school with bank bags bulging with ironies and alies.

arm /ɑːm, 'arəm/ *n. slang*. Also **arem**. [Special sense of general Eng., or Afk. *arm* arm; see quot. 1989.] A large roll of marijuana (see DAGGA *n.*² sense 1). Cf. COB *n.*²

1967 *Drum* 27 Aug. 7 Arem (arm): One rand parcel of dagga. 1974 in *Eng. Usage in Sn Afr.* Vol.5 No.1, 11 These *stops* or rather the *boom* for the *stop* .. come in varying parcels from a *finger* .. to a *bale* and an *arm*. 1979 *E. Prov. Herald* 5 June, It contained four 'arms' of dagga. An 'arm' weighs about 2 kilograms. 1981 *Het Suid-Western* 18 Feb. 1 He noticed her handbag, and on inspection found it contained several 'arms' of dagga. 1989 *E. Prov. Herald* 7 Dec. 1 Major Du Plessis said a dagga 'arm' is a thick roll of dagga about as long and as thick as a man's arm.

armatingoola var. AMATUNGULU.

‖**arme** /'ar(ə)mə/ *adj*. Also **arm, armen**. [Afk. (earlier Du.), attrib. form of *arm* poor.] Poor, needy, unfortunate; usu. an expression of pity.

[1838 J.E. ALEXANDER *Exped. into Int.* I. 73 Ver doem de government! it presses us in upon every side; we de armen boeren (the poor farmers) pay for everything.] 1901 *Grocott's Penny Mail* 17 Apr. 3 We are so often called upon to record ever-recurring acts of fiendish treachery on the part of the arme boer, that they have become monotonous. 1911 *Farmer's Weekly* 11 Oct. 170 Increased production .. was not to be brought about by putting down the 'arme blanke' nor was it going to be brought about in the towns or by farming by proxy. 1931 V. SAMPSON *Kom Binne* 298 Two Boers standing on the stoep, watching him go with varied emotions ... 'Arme man (poor man),' said Mrs Von Tonder, with feminine sympathy. 1941 N. MASIBA in *Bantu World* 22 Feb. 8, I really felt sorry for him. 'Arme man.' Girls! we ought to sympathize. 1979 F. DIKE *First S. African* 11, I feel sorry for him now, arme ou, I mean I really ripped him off, and on top of that he bought me this bottle of scotch. 1987 *Pace* May 4 Suddenly the cat is out the bag and the arme ngamlas from Europe are startled.

Armscor /'ɑːmzkɔː/ *n.* Also **ARMSCOR**. [Blend formed on *Armaments Corporation*.] A parastatal corporation which, in collaboration with its subsidiaries, develops and produces munitions for the local and export markets. Also *attrib*.

1968 P.W. BOTHA in *Hansard* 8 May 4871 There is a registered company which uses an expression by way of reference, fairly similar to 'Armscor'. 1977 *Ibid.* 21 Feb. 1849 The Bill under discussion seeks to accomplish the amalgamation of the Armaments Board and Armscor. 1979 *Evening Post* 10 May 3 The development of the G5 was recently completed by Armscor as prescribed by the chief of the army. 1986 *E. Prov. Herald* 27 Nov. 1 An Armscor spokesman said last night that it was not policy for Armscor to comment on the sales or purchases of arms. 1989 *Weekly Mail* 15 Dec. 6 A missile range built by the parastatal armaments corporation, Armscor, five years ago to test its rockets and bombs. 1990 *Armed Forces* Nov. 27 The Armaments Corporation of South Africa Ltd. (ARMSCOR) has a proven record. With the end of the border war and foreseeable budget cuts in the defence Armscor will be forced to increase its exports in weaponry and other manufactured goods. 1991 *Weekly Mail* 1 Feb. 10 Military sources said yesterday it was very probable that some of the 200 G5 mobile howitzers bought from Armscor by Iraq have already been put to use in this week's land battles.

arpuse var. HARPUIS.

arvie /'ɑːvi/ *n. colloq*. Also **arvey, avie**. [Formed on Eng. *afternoon* + (informal) n.-suffix *-ie* (or *-y*).] Esp. in the speech of children: afternoon.

c1971 *Informant*, Grahamstown Can I come and play by Justin this arvie? 1974 'BLOSSOM' in *Darling* 9 Oct. 95 I'm there by the municipal baths one arvey trying to catch a tan. 1975 *Ibid.* 12 Apr. 95 'See you s'arvey, then? Around about five?' 'OK,' I reckon through my teeth. 1977 J. McCLURE *Snake* (1981) 44 Tell me who doesn't wear his best casuals at the weekend? On Saturday arvie, or Sunday? 1992 E.M. JOYCE *Informant*, Port Elizabeth, I have just, more or less, done my shells for a meeting this arvie. Two big fam[ilie]s .. needed lots more time on them.

ASB /eɪ es 'biː, ɑː es 'bɪə/ *n.* [Afk., abbrev. formed on *Afrikaanse Studentebond*, *Afrikaanse* attrib. form of *Afrikaans* (see AFRIKAANS) + *studente* attrib. and combining form of *student* student + *bond* association, league.] A union of Afrikaans university students to which Afrikaans-medium campuses were historically affiliated.

1955 T.B. DAVIE *Education & Race Rel.* (Hoernlé Mem. Lecture 1955) 10 Since 1933 .. the Afrikaans-medium universities have disaffiliated themselves [from NUSAS] have joined a new and separate organization, Die Afrikaanse Studentebond (A.S.B.). 1969 *Survey of Race Rel.* (S.A.I.R.R.) 221 The Afrikaanse Studentebond (ASB), which the Afrikaans-language universities support, .. held its annual congress .. in Pretoria. 1977 *Daily Dispatch* 3 Aug. 10 Too often the Afrikaanse Studentebond congresses are forums for verkramptheid. But this week an ASB congress on law heard some sound common sense. 1982 *Drum* Nov. 51 Only the ASB remain relatively unchanged by the upheavals of 1976. And the gulf between the Afrikaner student organisation and the others is massive. 1987 *Weekend Argus* 26 Sept. 16 The Afrikaanse Studentebond (ASB), cultural and political home of the cream of Nationalist Afrikaner youth over decades, has come to the end of the road.

asbos /'asbɔs/ *n.* Formerly also **asbosch, as(ch)-bosje**. [Afk., *as* ash + *bos* (earlier *bosch, bosje*, see BOSCHJE) bush.] Any of several species of shrub of the genus *Psilocaulon* of the Mesembryanthemaceae, which when burnt yields an ash rich in alkali; ASH BUSH. See also *lidjes ganna* (GANNA sense 2).

Used in the past in soap-making (see BOER SOAP) and the curing of tobacco.

1860 J. SANDERSON in *Jrnl of Royal Geog. Soc.* XXX. 247 The raisins are prepared by the aid of an alkali — the ash of a plant which grows only in the colony, and is used also for making soap: it is known as aschbosje, or ashbush. 1910 A.B. LAMONT *Rural Reader* 260 The asbos is the common bush of the High Veld, where it is burnt and the ash used by the people in place of soda. 1913 C. PETTMAN *Africanderisms* 302 A potash salt obtained by burning a small karoo bush with cylindrical fleshy leaves, known as the 'Asbosje' (ash bush). The salt thus obtained is used as a lye in the manufacture of the coarser Boer or Kaffir tobacco as it is called. 1926 P.W. LAIDLER *Tavern of Ocean* 97 Soap was made from the fat of cattle and sheep, and the ash of the kanna bush, the *asbosch* of the backveld. 1958 [see BOERSEEP]. 1973 M.A. COOK *Cape Kitchen* 104 The lye was obtained by burning various sorts of 'lye-bush' growing in the veld, e.g. asbos (*Psilocaulon* species) or gannabos (*Salsola* species), several of which yielded an alkaline ash.

aschkoek, asch-kook varr. ASKOEK.

ash bush *n. phr.* [tr. Afk. *asbos*.] ASBOS.

1860, 1913 [see ASBOS]. 1958 F.G. BUTLER in R.M. Macnab *Poets in S. Afr.* 12 Ashbushes grew dim in smudges of smoke. 1977 — *Karoo Morning* 203 There, among the ashbushes and the mimosa, I prayed with a passionate earnestness.

ash cake *n. phr. Rare*. [tr. Afk. *askoek*.]
1. ASKOEK sense 1.
Used also in *U.S. Eng*.

c1929 L.P. BOWLER *Afr. Nights* 37 If I did subsist almost entirely on 'ash-cakes,' and often sleep on the bare ground, it was an excellent training for the adventurous life to come. 1949 [see KARBONATJIE].
2. ASKOEK sense 2.
1950 [see ASKOEK sense 2].

ash cookie *n. phr*. [Calque formed on Afk. *askoekie*.] ASKOEK sense 1.

1880 F.G. BROWNING *Fighting & Farming* 314 Another way of making bread is what is called an 'ash cookie'. It is something akin to an Australian 'damper' ... Having waited till the wood fire has burnt right down, the cookie is placed upon the ground, the ashes being cleared away and heaped upon it, when it is left till it becomes hard on top, when it is done. 1937 B.H. DICKE *Bush Speaks* 274 The trader, with the exception of hunter's ash-bread, roaster and ash-cookies, which were always a success, had himself an expert knowledge regarding bread-making.

Asian *n.* and *adj. Hist*. [Special uses of general Eng. *Asian* one from India, Pakistan, or any other part of Asia; of or pertaining to Asia.]
A. *n.* One classified as an Asian in terms of apartheid legislation; esp., a South African of Indian or Pakistani descent; ASIATIC *n*. See also CLASSIFY, INDIAN *n.* sense 2.

Used esp. in, or with reference to, official terminology. 'Asian' was the last official term used during the apartheid era to refer collectively to people whose ancestral origins were in Asia; previously such people had been known as 'Asiatics', or were viewed in smaller groups according to whether their ancestors were Indian, Chinese, etc.

1952 [see *Group Areas Act* (GROUP AREA *n. phr.* sense 2 a)]. 1970 [see Survey of Race Rel. quot. at EXIT PERMIT]. 1972 *Sunday Times* 15 Oct. (Mag. Sect.) 4 Allow me to thank the Johannesburg City Council for changing the signs 'Coloureds and Asiatics' to 'Coloureds and Asians' on its buses. 1974 *E. Prov. Herald* 19 July 5 The rising generation of Asians in South Africa used English as a mother-tongue. 1988 A. VAN WYK in *S. Afr. Panorama* May 38 The first Asians came to South Africa in 1860 as contract labourers for the developing sugar and tea industries ... There are about 913 000 Asians in South Africa of whom the majority — 583 320 — are Hindu. 1990 *Weekend Argus* 9 June 13 He no longer exists as a white, coloured, black, Indian, 'Other Asian', Chinese, Griqua or whatever other category Pretoria's racial overlords would care to label him.

B. *adj*. Of or pertaining to the group officially designated as 'Asians'; ASIATIC *adj*. See also INDIAN *adj*. sense 2.

c1970 [see GROUP AREA *n. phr.* sense 1]. 1975 *S. Afr. Panorama* Dec. 2 Today Afrikaans is spoken by over five million white, Coloured, Asian and Black South Africans. 1980 C. HERMER *Diary of Maria Tholo* 2 An Asian area is in the middle of 'coloured' land, and furthest away from the city centre are the three townships for Cape Town's black residents. 1990 *Bulletin* (Centre for Science Dev.) Vol.2 No.1, 8 The Asian population is .. confined mainly to a single region, Natal.

Asiatic *n.* and *adj. Offensive. hist*. [Special uses of general Eng.]
A. *n.* ASIAN *n*.

1882 C. DU VAL *With Show through Sn Afr.* I. 214 The introduction of Indian labour is much to be regretted, as the Asiatic is of a repellent and uncongenial character. 1885 *Law* 3 in *Stat. Law of Tvl 1839–1910* (1910) I. 135 Relating to Coolies, Arabs, and other Asiatics ... This law shall apply to the persons belonging to one of the native races of Asia, including the so-called Coolies, Arabs, Malays, and Mohamedan subjects of the Turkish Empire. c1936 *S. & E. Afr. Yr Bk & Guide* 240 In May, 1932, the Union Government passed the Transvaal Asiatic Land Tenure Act which forbids future ownership of land by Asiatics, and occupation of proclaimed land, in the Transvaal, except where the minister may authorise. 1941 *Bantu World*

15 Feb. 9 Benoni Magistrate's court on January 31 was crowded to the doors with Europeans, Asiatics, Coloureds and Bantu. **1942** *Off. Yrbk of Union 1941* (Union Office of Census & Statistics) 984 Asiatics – Natives of Asia and their descendants; mainly Indians. **1948** *Act 47* in *Stat. of Union* 390 Asiatic Laws Amendment Act ... 'Asiatic' means any member of a race or tribe whose national home is in Asia, other than a Turk, or a member of the Jewish or the Syrian race or a person belonging to the race or class known as the Cape Malays. **1948** *Press Digest* No.5, 35 Our ancestors gave their blood for South Africa, and why must we, their descendants, allow Asiatics to conquer our land. **1952** *Drum* Mar. 27 We Chinese are just Asiatics, and are not welcome, according to law, either in European or non-European areas. **1956** *Off. Yr Bk of Union No. 28, 1954–55* 679 The amended racial definitions are as follows: .. Asiatics – natives of Asia and their descendants, mainly Indians and Pakistani, with a few thousand Chinese. **1956** E. HELLMANN in M. Rogers *Black Sash* 38 We must find a way in which all the different peoples of South Africa – Europeans, Coloureds, Asiatics and Africans – can co-exist. **1961** T. MATSHIKIZA *Choc. for my Wife* 68 The advertisements offer: 'Europeans only.' 'Asiatics Welcome.' **1970** *E. Prov. Herald* 4 Sept., Asiatics – the White man's term for the 600 000 Indians (and a few other Asians) who are the majority 'minority' in Durban and Natal Province. **1972** *Drum* 8 Sept. 53 Away, we say, with the potpourri of names such as Native, Coloured, Asiatic etc., – all under the negative sign of Non-White – from here on we want to be known as Blacks. **1972** *Sunday Times* 15 Oct. (Mag. Sect.) 4 Apart from being a semantic oddity, the word Asiatic was offensive to Indians.

B. *adj.* ASIAN *adj.*

1897 *E. Prov. Herald* 2 Apr., It is understood that the Asiatic Law is to be enforced. All Coolie traders, being Indians, will be given three months to dispose of their stocks. **1908** *Act 35* in *Stat. of Tvl* 356 'Coloured person' shall mean any African or Asiatic native or any other person who is manifestly a coloured person. **1912** *Indian Opinion* 21 Sept. 316 Mr Smith asked what had been done in respect of the Council's resolution some time ago concerning Asiatic trading. **1941** C.W. DE KIEWIET *Hist. of S. Afr.* p.v, I have devoted relatively little space to the Cape coloured people or to the Asiatic population. **1952** *Drum* Nov. 11 It is 'alleged' that the Council has organised Tsotsis to commit atrocities during strikes arranged by the A.N.C. – like the burning down of Asiatic shops in Newclare. **1955** E. DE S. BRUNNER in *Pol. Science Quarterly* Sept. 374 No Coloured or Asiatic family may live in a white or African neighbourhood. **1960** J.J.L. SISSON *S. Afr. Judicial Dict.* 69 A woman, born in India of a Cape Malay mother and an Asiatic father, and who lived as one of the Cape Malay community of Johannesburg, held to be a person 'belonging to the class known as Cape Malays'. **1976** *Leader* 5 Mar. 4 Runjeeth, an Asiatic male adult, whose further names and occupation are to the Plaintiff unknown, formerly residing at Umkomaas, Natal.

asigie var. ASSEGAI.

Askari /æs'kɑːri, as-, əs-/ *n. hist.* [Transf. sense of East African Eng. *askari* (fr. Arabic), a black police officer or soldier.] A 'turned' UMKHONTO WE SIZWE soldier serving in the South African police force, esp. in operations against the African National Congress. Also *attrib.*

1989 *Weekend Post* 18 Nov. 1 Vlakplaas was a camp to train ANC defectors ... The defectors, known as 'Askaris', were integral members of assassination teams. **1989** *Weekend Argus* 25 Nov. 11 The members of the 'hit squad' .. known as Askaris have disbanded ... The Askaris were former ANC operatives who had switched sides. **1990** D. BERESFORD in *Weekly Mail* 27 Apr. 10 The farm was manned by some 18 'Askaris' – 'rehabilitated terrorists' – under his command, whose job was to track down ANC infiltrators. **1990** KOCH & RICKARD in *Weekly Mail* 14 Sept. 1 M— was arrested by two askaris (turned guerrillas used by the police for counter-insurgency work) inside the OK Bazaars store in West Street, Durban. **1991** *Advertisement* (ANC) in *E. Prov. Herald* 16 Apr. 7 All counter-insurgency units such as the CCB, Askaris, Koevoet etc. should be publicly disbanded. **1993** *Sunday Nation* 8 Aug. 15 Members of a regiment credited with such missions as the Sasol bombing joined the infamous Askari unit of the South African police at Vlakplaas ... For the first time since they switched sides, they spoke .. about their lives on both sides of the struggle.

askies var. EKSKUUS.

askoek /'askʊk, -kuk/ *n.* Formerly also **asch-koek, asch-kook**. Pl. unchanged. [Afk., *as* ash + *koek* cake.]

1. A dough-cake baked in embers; ASH CAKE sense 1; ASH COOKIE; ROASTER-CAKE sense a; ROOSTERKOEK sense b. Cf. COOKIE, STORMJAER sense 1.

1900 F.R.M. CLEAVER in M.M. Cleaver *Young S. Afr.* (1913) 54, I have re-acquired all my old veld craft, and know the exact turn to which to bake a stormjager or aschkoek. **1908** *E. London Dispatch* 10 July (Pettman), J— S— who jumped a bag of *askoek* from a transport wagon, was sentenced to a month's hard labour. **1920** F.C. CORNELL *Glamour of Prospecting* 305 That Hottentot was a perfect Oliver Twist. He made asch-kook of the meal and devoured it, whilst we sat and partook of the smell. **1972** L.G. GREEN *When Journey's Over* 43, I wanted no finer bread than *askoek*, the famous cake of coarse flour and water, with a pinch of salt, laid on glowing embers. **1981** *Sunday Times* 1 Mar. (Mag. Sect.) 5 Their first taste of such delicacies as askoek, potbrood or putu. **1986** M. VAN WYK *Cooking the S. Afr. Way* 97 Askoek. Use the same dough, but bake directly on the coals or in the ashes.

2. *fig. rare.* In the dim. form **askoekie**: a flat river-stone resembling an ash-cake; ASH CAKE sense 2.

1950 E. ROSENTHAL *Here Are Diamonds* 197 A quaint word of Afrikaans origin, which English-speaking diggers also came to employ, was derived from the fact that the flat water-worn stones bore a likeness to a certain kind of Boer pastry. They were (and are) known as 'askoekies' or 'ash-cakes'.

asphogel var. AASVOEL.

assagaay, assagai, assagi(e), etc. varr. ASSEGAI.

‖**asseblief** /ˌasə'blif/ *adv.* Formerly also **assumblief**. [Afk., reduced form of Du. *als het u belieft* 'if it pleases you'.] Please.

Usu. used in Eng. texts to suggest Afrikaans dialogue.

1913 D. FAIRBRIDGE *Piet of Italy* 26 Lift me up then, Da'ood, assumblief toch. I would see inside the door. **1913** C. PETTMAN *Africanderisms* 34 *Asseblief*, (D. *Als het ubelieft*, if you please.) This is the common Cape contraction of the Dutch phrase. *c*1963 B.C. TAIT *Durban Story* 31 'Some water, asseblief,' they falter. **1973** *Cape Times* 11 Jan. 7 No Signal fires or litter, asseblief. **1982** M. MZAMANE *Children of Soweto* 91 'Sindi, get into the car, *asseblief tu*', he said. **1988** A. KENNY in *Frontline* Apr. 21 There is a conspicuous lack of Platteland courtesy. In the shops and pubs, words like 'asseblief' and 'thank you' are rare.

assegai /'æsəgaɪ/ *n.* Also **assagai, assegaai**, and (formerly) **asigie, assagaay, assagay(e), assagi(e), assag(u)y, assaig(a)i, assaygay, asseagi, assega(a)y, assega(i)e, asseger, assegie, assiguie, azaguay, hasagaye, hassagai, hassagay(e), hassaguay, hassegai.** [Pg. *azagaia*, ad. Arabic *az-zaghayah*, fr. *al* the + Berber *zagayah* lance, spear. The word occurs in early Du. as *hasegaij* or *hassegaai.*]

1.a. A spear with a pointed, sharpened iron tip, and a wooden shaft which is either short, for stabbing, or long, for throwing; UMKHONTO sense 1. Also *attrib.*

A weapon used by African and Khoikhoi peoples from early times.

1625 S. PURCHAS *Hachluytus Posthymus* (1905) II. 263 One of them with a woodden Assagay (sharpe at the point) in his hand, threatened to shoot at one of our men. **1677** T. HERBERT in R. Raven-Hart *Before Van Riebeeck* (1967) 121 They have little Art in War, their weapon commonly is an Azaguay or Javelin headed with Iron. **1731** G. MEDLEY tr. *P. Kolb's Present State of Cape of G.H.* I. 241 The Hassagaye is a Sort of Half-Pike. The Shaft of it is a Taper-Stick, of the Length and Thickness of a Rake-Handle. 'Tis arm'd at the thickest End with a little thin Plate of Iron, tapering to a Point, and very sharp on the Edges. **1776** F. MASSON in *Phil. Trans. of Royal Soc.* LXVI. 296 They were all armed with hassaguays, of which every one had eight or ten in his left hand. **1786** G. FORSTER tr. *A. Sparrman's Voy. to Cape of G.H.* I. 194 Here and there .. a man will furnish himself with a javelin .. : this is called a *hassagai*. **1798** B. STOUT *Narr. of Loss of Ship 'Hercules'* 35, I requested the chief to order some of his people to shew me how they used their assaygays. This is a spear of about four feet six inches in length, made of an elastic wood, and pointed with iron. **1809** J. MACKRILL Diary. 63 Assagay is a hottentot Javelin, consists of an Iron spear hollowed out on each side about six Inches long, this spear is fastened with thongs of Leather to a slender round stick five feet long made of the Assagay wood or Curtisea faginea and tapers towards the End. **1821** *Missionary Notices* 120 The assagy, which is a sort of spear fixed to the end of a tapering shaft, is in general use. *a*1823 J. EWART *Jrnl* (1970) 50 A long spear called a hassagai which they throw in the manner of a javelin, with great certainty to the distance of fifty or sixty paces. **1837** F. OWEN *Diary* (1926) 8 A large party of them overtook us, .. armed with guns and assegais. **1841** B. SHAW *Memorials* 23 The weapons used, as well in warfare as upon these occasions, are the kerrie, a stick two or three feet in length, with a large knob at one end; the assagai, or spear, and the bow and arrows. **1849** N.J. MERRIMAN *Cape Jrnls* (1957) 38 The assegai is a poor match for the musket, and yet under cover of the bush these fellows are formidable. **1851** J.F. CHURCHILL Diary. (Killie Campbell Africana Library MS37), A body of Caffirs with their assegais & shields were sent into the reeds to beat up the Buck that were generally so plentiful there. **1866** J. LEYLAND *Adventures* 55 The blade of the assaigi, varies from nine to twelve inches in length; the handle is from five to six feet long, and half-an-inch in thickness. **1879** C.L. NORRIS-NEWMAN in J. Crwys-Williams *S. Afr. Despatches* (1989) 46 We could hear the hoarse cries of the enemy, and the rattle of their knob-kerries and assegais against their shields. **1884** B. ADAMS *Narr.* (1941) 117 All were armed with assegaies – long spear with blade barbed like a fish hook – and some .. had guns. **1876** T. STUBBS Reminiscences. I. 57 We found Mr Henderson lying on his face, with one hand holding an Assegie wound in his stomach. **1897** F.R. STATHAM *S. Afr. as It Is* 64 The destroying weapon was the long-bladed assegai, a weapon as terrible in the hands of a Zulu as the two-edged broad sword in the hands of a Roman soldier. **1912** AYLIFF & WHITESIDE *Hist. of Abambo* 8 Adopting the Zulu model, he divided his army into regiments, and armed them with the short stabbing assagai. **1926** M. NATHAN *S. Afr. from Within* 19 Chaka, who lived until 1828, .. introduced their short stabbing assegai as their destructive weapon. *c*1948 H. TRACEY *Lalela Zulu* 9 In recent times the Zulus have brought firearms to their faction fights instead of assegais only. **1973** J. MEINTJES *Voortrekkers* 75 They used three types of spear or assegai: one for stabbing with a blade of about twelve inches and a short shaft up to thirty-six inches long. The second had a shorter blade and a somewhat longer shaft of up to forty-eight inches, also a stabbing weapon. Then there was the throwing spear with a small blade of up to six inches on the end of an iron tang of eight inches or more. **1985** *Cape Times* 30 Sept. 1 Lamontville residents said warriors took to the streets with fighting sticks and assegais, beating up people and smashing windows. **1991** W. MBHELE in *Weekly Mail* 15 Mar. 2 Inkatha loyalists poured out of the hostel rooms brandishing pangas, spears, firearms and assegais.

b. *fig.*

1949 O. Walker *Proud Zulu* (1951) 172 'This is an assegai in the king's back,' said the indunas turning away. The ultimatum was thrust in their hands, but they would not take it. **1988** L. Shaw in *Style* July 95 If you can read the stars, you can work to avert the assegais that are heading for our country. **1990** M. Tyala in *Sunday Times* 19 Aug. 15 Messrs Mandela and Buthelezi need to send clear signals down to the grassroots operatives that Inkatha and the ANC may be political adversaries but they are not enemies. It worked in Zimbabwe, and I am willing to bet my assegai it will work here.

2. Ellipt. for ASSEGAI WOOD.

1887 J.C. Brown *Crown Forests* 122 Assegai, Grows from seed, and also shoots from the stump; is used for waggon wood; becomes useful after 7 or 8 years growth. **1887** [see BORRIE sense 2]. **1905** D.E. Hutchins in Flint & Gilchrist *Science in S. Afr.* 392 *Curtisia faginea* (Assegai) Medium-sized trees prized for wagon-making. **1907** T.R. Sim *Forests & Forest Flora* 48 Hard horny seeds like those of the Yellow-woods, Black Ironwood, Wild Olive, Assegai, Olinia etc. do not readily germinate even in cultivation. **1919** *Dunell, Ebden & Co.'s Price List* Aug. 35 Colonial Wagon Wood ... Spokes. Assegai. 1½in. Cape Cart, 1/2½. *c*1936 *S. & E. Afr. Yr Bk & Guide* 320 The principal species composing these forests and the main uses of their woods are as follows: .. *Curtisia faginea* Assegai: Waggon building. *Ocotea bullata* Black Stinkwood or Laurel: A furniture wood. **1955** [see *white pear* (WHITE *adj.* sense 2)]. **1960** G. Lister *Reminisc.* 80 Native forest trees such as Yellow-wood, Stinkwood, Assegai and Kaffirplum were also tried but have not grown well. **1989** *Conserva* July 4 The wood of species like yellow-wood, stinkwood, assegai and iron-wood, names to conjure with, was in everyday use. **1991** H. Hutchings in *Weekend Post* 23 Feb. (Leisure) 7 Although fairly slow to mature, the assegai is a delight to the eye from an early age and eventually grows into a very large, handsome tree.

3. STEEKGRAS sense b.

1986 *Farmer's Weekly* 13 June 18 Usually, they select plants that retain their palatability longer, such as redgrass, assegaai and wild oatgrass.

assegai /ˈæsəgaɪ/ *v. trans.* Also **hasagaye**, etc. [fr. prec.] To wound or kill (someone or something) with an assegai. Often *passive*.

1804 R. Percival *Acct of Cape of G.H.* 87 General Vandeleur though very well mounted, in making away from a party of them [*sc.* the Boschman Hottentots] narrowly escaped being hasagayed or killed with their spears. **1837** J.E. Alexander *Narr. of Voy.* I. 354 The Kaffirs, not contented with burning the house, and driving off what they could of his property, had assegaied dogs, pigs and poultry; and the smell was intolerable. *a*1858 J. Goldswain *Chron.* (1949) II. 163 They were assegaied, and Charles was shot in the back. **1879** *Cape Argus* 5 June, Suddenly the Zulus appeared .. and the party jumped on their horses .. leaving the Prince, who was assegaied by the Zulus. **1882** Lady F.C. Dixie *In Land of Misfortune* 373 It is my belief that if every Zulu in Zululand were in this tent all assegaing you at once, you would sleep through it all. **1893** 'Harley' in *Cape Illust. Mag.* June 378 It's not all beer and skittles campaigning – even when you are not being assegaied. **1925** F.W. Grenfell in S. Clarke *'Vanity Fair'* (1991) 90 He was assegaid in seventeen places. **1933** W. Macdonald *Romance of Golden Rand* 128 A Zulu force rushed in and assegaied a large number of the detachment as they came out of the tents. **1949** C. Bullock *Rina* 48 It did not matter to them whether a buck died a painful death impaled on a stake in a camouflaged game-pit, or was caught in a net and assegai'd. **1950** D. Reed *Somewhere S. of Suez* 269 The Zulu lives long and if you give a penny to an ancient sitting on the kerb in Durban today you may place it in the hand that assegai'd that Prince. *c*1960 E.M. Jones in J.B. Bullock *Peddie – Settlers' Outpost* 38 Sergeant-Major Benn's body was found, assegaied, and brought to Fish River Mouth Camp for burial. **1968** D.R. Edgecombe Letters of Hannah Dennison. 244 He earned his living as a merchant. He was assegaied on 13 May 1866. **1971** *The 1820* Vol.43 No.10, 14 'Iqawa loku', he said. 'He was a very brave man.' But, of course, he was eventually assagaied.

assegai wood /ˈæsəgaɪ ˌwʊd/ *n. phr.* [ASSEGAI *n.* + Eng. *wood*; so named as their wood was thought to have been commonly used to make spears.] The wood of the trees *Curtisea dentata* of the Cornaceae and *Grewia occidentalis* of the Tiliaceae; the trees themselves; ASSEGAI *n.* sense 2; HASSAGAI HOUT. See also KRUISBESSIE.

1795 C.R. Hopson tr. *C.P. Thunberg's Trav.* I. 181 The spear is fastened with thongs of leather to a slender round stick, five feet long, made of the *Assagay wood* (*Curtisia faginea*), and tapering towards the end. **1804** R. Percival *Acct of Cape of G.H.* 148 The hasagay wood is much used for wagon wheels, rafters for houses ... It resembles mahogany, and the planks make excellent flooring for houses. **1812** A. Plumptre tr. *H. Lichtenstein's Trav. in Sn Afr.* (1928) I. 270 A short stick of Hassagai wood, so cut, that a knob is made at the end by a part of the thick root of this stem. [*Note*] *Curtisea faginea*, a wood something of the nature of mahogany. **1879** [see DISSELBOOM]. **1896** R. Wallace *Farming Indust. of Cape Col.* 123 Assegai wood is the most valuable of the waggon woods ... It is 'extremely tough and strong, heavy and elastic, close-grained and durable, if exposed to only moderate damp.' The colour is bright red, but it soon fades if exposed to the air. **1917** R. Marloth *Common Names* 8 *Assegai-wood, Curtisia faginea*. A large handsome tree with beautiful foliage. Wood tough and strong, highly esteemed for wagons. **1931** V. Sampson *Kom Binne* 139 The kerrie .. was made of hard assegai-wood, a most dangerous bludgeon. **1958** S. Cloete *Mask* 84 This wagon .. was heavy and immensely strong, being built of selected and seasoned assegai wood, wild pear, blackwood, stink- and iron-wood. **1971** L.G. Green *Taste of S.-Easter* 45 Assegai-wood, hard as oak and like mahogany in appearance, made handsome furniture. **1976, 1987** [see CROSS-BERRY]. **1989** *Conserva* Vol.4 No.4, 4 The wood of species like yellow-wood, stinkwood, assegai and ironwood, names to conjure with, was in everyday use for buildings, farm implements, the wagons and carts of pioneers, in the early mines, and even as firewood.

asse vogel var. AASVOEL.

Assocom /ˈæsəkɒm/ *n.* Also **ASSOCOM**. Blend formed on *Association of Chambers of Commerce (of South Africa)*.

1970 *Rand Daily Mail* 28 Sept. 11 The manpower survey conducted by Assocom (Association of Chambers of Commerce) – which was published last week – had disclosed a shortfall of 35000 employees in just one sector alone. **1986** N.S. Ndebele in Bunn & Taylor *From S. Afr.* (1988) 221 The Association of Chambers of Commerce of South Africa (ASSOCOM) .. commissioned Professors J.A. Lombard and J.A. du Pisanie to provide 'academic help' in drawing up an ASSOCOM memorandum called 'Removal of Discrimination Against Blacks in the Political Economy of the Republic of South Africa.' **1989** *E. Prov. Herald* 9 Mar. 5 Assocom regional congress to be held in Grahamstown ... An Association of Chambers of Commerce (Assocom) regional congress will be held in Grahamstown this weekend.

assous /aˈsəʊs/ *n.* [Afk., unkn.; thought by some to be ad. Du. *ansjovis* anchovy.] SPIERING.

1902 J.D.F. Gilchrist in *Trans. of S. Afr. Philological Soc.* XI. iv. 224 (Pettman), We have hitherto considered names for which derivations can be suggested ... There are a few .. for which no plausible derivation can be discovered. These are bafaro, assous, zeverrim. **1913** C. Pettman *Africanderisms* 36 *Assous*, The name given at Hout Bay to the fish known elsewhere as Spiering. **1949** J.L.B. Smith *Sea Fishes* 325 *Atherina Breviceps* Cuvier. *Silverside. Assous* or *Spierintje* (Cape). *Whitebait* (Knysna) ... Body transparent, difficult to see in the water.

assumblief var. ASSEBLIEF.

assvogel, as(t)vogel varr. AASVOEL.

atcha(r) var. ATJAR.

A-team /ˈeɪ tiːm/ *n.* [Named for U.S. television series *The A-Team*, which featured an extra-legal group fighting injustice.] A name chosen by several groups of right-wing black vigilantes having the expressed aim of keeping order in the townships. See also VIGILANTE.

1986 *Learn & Teach* No.3, 1 In other townships vigilantes have different names – the A-Team in Tumahole, the Pakathis in Thabong, the Amabutho in Durban, the Mbhokhoto in KwaNdebele and the 'fathers' in Cape Town. **1987** *Ibid.* No.1, 38 In the townships there has been no peace ... Vigilante groups started all over the country. In Moutse there was the Imbokotho. In Tumahole there was the A-Team and in Durban there was the Amabutho. **1987** *New Nation* 30 July 9 In Chesterville, women arranged all-night vigils to protect their children against the vigilante A-Team which had the backing of Inkatha. **1989** T. Gqubulu in *Weekly Mail* 17 Feb. 3 The child army fought physical battles with the municipal police – 'Green Beans' – and right-wing vigilantes called the 'A-Team'. **1990** *Weekend Post* 31 Mar. 6 It was a media myth that the forces tapping into the violence were merely political. The Wild Dogs, the Ninjas and the A-Team were just some groups with no political agenda at all.

atjar, atchar /ˈatʃa(r), ˈatʃɑː(r), ˈætʃə/ *n.* Also **acha, acha(a)r, archaar, atcha(r), atjaar, attjar**, and with initial capital. [Afk., fr. Malay *achar* relish, fr. Pers. *āchār* pickles.] A spicy pickle or relish of sliced or chopped vegetables or fruit, eaten usu. with curried dishes. Also *attrib.* Cf. SAMBAL.

In the form 'achar', also *Indian Eng.*

1798 S.H. Wilcocke tr. *J.S. Stavorinus's Voy. to E. Indies 1768–71* I. 237 When green, it [*sc.* the mango] is made into *attjar*; for this, the kernel is taken out, and the space filled up with ginger, pimento, and other spicy ingredients, after which it is pickled in vinegar. **1902** H.J. Duckitt *Hilda's Diary of Cape Hsekeeper* 63 Red Cabbage Pickle (Atjaar). **1927** C.G. Botha *Social Life in Cape Col.* 57 The condiments as 'atjar' made from apricots or from chillies, 'blatjang' and 'sambal' are too well known to dilate on. **1947** L.G. Green *Tavern of Seas* 65 Atjar (the red cabbage pickle of the Malays). **1950** H. Gerber *Cape Cookery* 75 Serve potatoes or rice separately, and round off the dish by serving as well beetroot salad or atjar. **1959** E. Mphahlele *Down Second Ave* (1965) 32 We missed going to the market to work for a few shillings for bread and *atcha* – mango boiled in 'hot' red curry mixture – during school recess. **1971** *Fair Lady* 24 Nov. 92 The older children buy three slices of bread on which they have *achaar* – a type of chutney spread – and an orange. **1985** *S. Afr. Cookbk* (Reader's Digest Assoc.) 380 *Atjar*, A Malay condiment of blended fruit and spices, similar to chutney but containing chunks of whole fruit. **1988** *Drum* Apr. 78 A tasty new addition to the .. family of top quality prepared meat products is Achar Polony ... Real chunky Achar is included in the recipe. **1993** *Star* 22 July 16 Fry boerewors in a frying pan and eat with stiff 'pap' which you cover with a thick tomato and onion gravy. For extra spiciness add 5 ml mango atchar to your gravy.

Attaqua /əˈtakwə/ *pl. n. Hist.* Also **Ataquas, Attaquas**. [Khoikhoi.] Collectively, the members of a Khoikhoi people formerly resident in what is now the Western Cape.

As is the case with many names of peoples and groups in *S. Afr. Eng.*, this word has been found only in plural uses; however, it may be that it has also been used in unrecorded singular forms.

1731 G. Medley tr. *P. Kolb's Present State of Cape of G.H.* I. 71 The *Attaquas* are possess'd of but a very indifferent Soil, and but ill provided with Water. For which Reason they live in little Troops at a considerable Distance from one another, in Parts the most commodious. **1795** C.R. Hopson tr. *C.P. Thunberg's Trav.* I. 308 Farther to the northward, and near the large valley, through which one must pass in order to go to Lange-kloof and the adjacent country, occurs the district of the *Ataquas Hottentots*, which is mountainous and abounds in grass. **1977** T.R.H. DAVENPORT *S. Afr.: Mod. Hist.* 4 Others [*sc.* Khoikhoi] spread towards the eastern Cape coast, .. into the Fish and Sundays river valleys, and then migrated either eastwards (the Gona) or westwards (the Attaqua, Hessequa, Chochoqua and others) in the direction of the Cape peninsula. **1989** *Reader's Digest Illust. Hist.* 227 Descendants of the early white trekboers and the Outeniqua and Attaqua Khoikhoi.

attorney *n.* [Special sense of general Eng.] A lawyer, usu. a member of a practice, who handles matters such as cases in the lower courts, conveyancing, and the drawing up of legal documents, as well as briefing an ADVOCATE in any matter to be dealt with in the Supreme Court.

Cf. *Brit. Eng.* 'solicitor'.

1846 *Natal Witness* 6 Mar., These are to certify that Robert Lester, Esq., has been duly admitted and enrolled to practise as an Advocate and Attorney before the District Court of Natal. **1846** *Ibid.* 13 Mar., A short discussion took place in respect of the propriety of one attorney preparing his brief and handing it to another to act as advocate. **1924** G. BAUMANN in Baumann & Bright *Lost Republic* (1940) 97 The attorney for the opposition was Mr Abraham Fischer, the one lawyer in the Free State who had been eminently successful in all land cases. **1936** E. ROSENTHAL *Old-Time Survivals* 30 Attorneys close their offices, the courts only sit in matters of great urgency, and everybody concentrates on holidaying. **1945** WILLE & MILLIN *Mercantile Law of S. Afr.* 65 Where an attorney was said to have procured a partnership with his client by the exercise of undue influence .. the client was held disentitled to claim the attorney's share of the profits. **1950** H. GIBBS *Twilight* 190 In 1914 he entered the Civil Service; three years later he joined a firm of attorneys; in 1918 he became an advocate. **1958** B. BENNETT *This Was a Man* 14 Upington did not have to sit in his office .. waiting for the brief that never seemed to come .. until an attorney's knock on the door started him on the road to fame and fortune. **1960** C. HOOPER *Brief Authority* 186 The women .. are to be legally defended. The attorney is a Mrs Muller. **1982** G. RANDELL *Gentlemen of Law* 27 Grahamstown Supreme Court cases in which he was the instructing attorney ... He certainly took pains to ensure that the advocate he briefed was in his opinion the right man for the job. **1990** *Weekend Post* 27 Oct. 11 Advocates and attorneys belong to separate professions. Attorneys have 'rights of audience' only in magistrate's courts and are denied the right to appear in Supreme Courts, which is held exclusively by advocates. The corollary is that an advocate or counsel may not offer their services directly to the public and may only accept briefs or instructions in any legal matter from an attorney ... Attorneys are general practitioners, concerned with drafting documents and advice, conveyancing transactions and preparing cases for trial. **1992** C. RICKARD in *Weekly Mail* 9 Oct. 13 Against the background of the unedifying squabble between advocates and attorneys about who may appear in the supreme court .. [he] argues that the new Bill [*sc.* Admission of Advocates Amendment Bill 1992] is unnecessary since existing legislation allows attorneys temporary rights of appearance under certain circumstances.

‖**au** /aʊ, aːʊ/ *int.* Also **auw, awu, ow.** [fr. Zulu and Xhosa *awu*.] Among Zulu- and Xhosa-speakers: HAU.

1857 D. LIVINGSTONE *Missionary Trav.* 88 Sebituane .. asked why they had wished to kill him; he had never attacked them, never harmed their chief: 'Au!' he continued, 'the guilt is on your side.' **1899** B. MITFORD *Weird of Deadly Hollow* 72 'Au!' cried the Kafir, contemptuously. **1907** J.P. FITZPATRICK *Jock of Bushveld* (1909) 250 The other voices dropped out, only to be heard once in a while in .. that briefest of all comments — the kaffir click and 'Ow!' **1949** O. WALKER *Proud Zulu* (1951) 19 Auw! A man who did not have his soul in cattle was not Zulu, was less than a man. **1956** D. JACOBSON *Dance in Sun* 76 'Au!' he exclaimed, gaining enthusiasm .. 'Lovely bed for boy!' **1963** A.M. LOUW *20 Days* 239 'Dangerous weapons? Illicit liquor?' asked the policeman. 'Au, my baas!' The grey-beard was shocked at the idea. **1979** M. MATSHOBA *Call Me Not a Man* 81 '*Awu*, Monde. Don't exaggerate,' she cooed, pretending not to believe the sincerity of the compliment. **1982** [see MTSHANA]. **1983** *Pace* Oct. 70 The government is to launch a no-mercy campaign against .. Soshanguve residents who refuse to use trains ... Awu! Woe unto those who shun Putco. **1992** T. PEMBA in *Weekly Mail* 24 Apr. 32 'Awu Gaba,' he says, praising him by his totem.

auboetie var. OUBOETIE.

aubuti /əʊˈbʊːti/ *n.* Also **abuti, aubhuti,** and with initial capital. [S. Sotho, fr. Afk. *ou boetie*, see OUBOETIE.] 'Brother': a respectful term of address, used esp. among Sotho-speakers when speaking to an older man; also used as a title. Cf. BHUTI, OUBOETIE sense 1.

1965 [see BOETIE sense 2]. **1981** B. MFENYANA in M. Mutloatse *Reconstruction* 299 Aubhuti Mbhele noted as early as 1900 that terms like ikomityi .. have already found a home in Africa. **1990** M.L. NAWA in *Staffrider* Vol.9 No.1, 68 Haike abuti Andrew, like abuti Benjamin Moloise, you did, what you did, because they did, what they did, to you.

auck var. AUK.

Auckland Park *n. phr. Colloq.* [So called after the Johannesburg suburb in which the organization's headquarters are situated.] SABC.

1989 *Weekly Mail* 20 Oct. 35 The SABC has never fallen into the trap of being nice to 'terrorists' and if it weren't for those blundering foreign television crews telling the people to throw stones at police vans, South Africa would probably ascend straight up to heaven. Well, at least Auckland Park would. **1990** *Weekend Argus* 17 Feb. 3 Although senior executives firmly maintain that there has been no 'hot-line' communication between Tuynhuys and Auckland Park since Mr. P.W. Botha left office, the SABC remains the government's strongest propaganda arm. **1990** D. GORDON in *Sunday Times* 18 Nov. 19 This year, Auckland Park has suffered many Afrikaans TV flops with dubbed French and German soaps proving to be a big yawn. **1991** D. CAPEL in *Personality* 2 Sept. 18 Is Auntie Auckland Park trying to indoctrinate its viewers into accepting a 'new world order' — complete with *kommuniste* .. - by using the highly unethical method of subliminal messages on its news logo?

‖**auk** /aːʊk, aːʊg/ *int.* Also **auck, aug.** [fr. Zulu and Xhosa *awu-ke, awu* (see AU) + emphatic enclitic formative *-ke*.] Among Xhosa- and Zulu-speakers: HAU.

1907 J.P. FITZPATRICK *Jock of Bushveld* (1909) 403 He would .. give a click of disgust, a quick shake of the head, and say: 'Aug! Ang-a-funa!' ('I do not desire it!') **1959** G. & W. GORDON tr. *F.A. Venter's Dark Pilgrim* 24 One of them says softly, with wonder in his voice: 'Auk! This is the city of the white man; this is the city of the gold.' [**1967** L. VAN DER POST in C.M. Booysen *Tales of S. Afr.* 102 'Auck! Auck!' Umtumwa exclaimed in Sindakwena. 'He goes the long way to the great sleep.']

aum /ɔːm, əʊm, aʊm/ *n. hist.* Also **awm, ha(u)m.** [Englished form of Du. *aam* liquid measure of 155,2 litres; a cask.]

a. A unit of liquid measurement formerly in use at the Cape, usu. equivalent to 30 to 34 imperial gallons (136 to 154 litres); a vessel of this capacity. See also ANKER, LEAGUER sense a.

Not exclusively *S. Afr. Eng.* Confusion as to the volume represented by an aum and other measures appears to have resulted partly from the difference between Dutch and English gallons, a Dutch gallon being approx. $\frac{5}{6}$ of an English gallon.

1731 G. MEDLEY tr. *P. Kolb's Present State of Cape of G.H.* I. 355 Besides the Governor's Salary and Board — Wages, his Excellency is likewise allow'd by the company for his Household, Monthly .. 1 Aum of *African* Wine; 8 Quarts of Brandy; 16 of Canary. **1798** S.H. WILCOCKE tr. *J.S. Stavorinus's Voy. to E. Indies 1768–71* I. 545 The muscadel fetches sixty and seventy rixdollars, and the constantia-wine from sixty to seventy-five rixdollars the awm. [*Note*] A leager is nearly four awms, and an awm contains about forty English gallons. **1800** LADY A. BARNARD in D. Fairbridge *Lady Anne Barnard* (1924) 242 Out of the quantity of Constantia Wine which is delivered annually to Government from the two Farms, General Dundas thought it proper last Year to reserve Ten Aums to be Disposed of as he pleased. **1802** J. PRINGLE in G.M. Theal *Rec. of Cape Col.* (1899) IV. 140, I have the honour to inform you that I have as usual reserved Sixty Aums of Constantia Wine. **1833** *S. Afr. Almanac & Dir.* 41 16 Flasks, equal to 1 Anker. 4 Ankers equal to 1 Aum. 4 Aums, equal to 1 Leaguer. **1861** *E. Prov. Yr Bk & Annual Register* 61 An aum is equal to 38 Dutch gals., or about $31\frac{2}{3}$ gals. im. **1863** W.C. BALDWIN *Afr. Hunting* 369 He helped considerably to lighten our half-aum of Pontac. **1955** A. DELIUS *Young Trav.* 95 They heard names such as leaguers, pipes, aums, half-pipes and hogsheads and stared at vast quantities of barrelled wine and brandy. **1965** A. GORDON-BROWN *S. Afr. Heritage* IV. 21 Illustration 45 shows the original bill of lading for the shipment of aums of Constantia wine from Table Bay to London. **1986** W. STEENKAMP *Blake's Woman* 83 Soon she was ticking off things like sacks of coffee and flour, chests of tea, bags of salt, half an aum of Cape Brandy.

b. With qualifying word designating part of an aum: **half-aum.** Also *attrib.*

1786 G. FORSTER tr. *A. Sparrman's Voy. to Cape of G.H.* I. 40 The red Constantia wine sells for about sixty rixdollars the half awm. **1798** S.H. WILCOCKE tr. *J.S. Stavorinus's Voy. to E. Indies 1768–71* II. 69 The farming of the wine consists herein, that whoever is the farmer has the exclusive right of selling wine and spirituous liquors in smaller quantities than by the half-awm. **1806** J. BARROW *Trav.* II. 317 This wine sells at the Cape for 70 or 80 rixdollars the half aum, a cask which ought to contain 20 gallons. **1829** C. ROSE *Four Yrs in Sn Afr.* 116 The boors left a half aum (a cask) of brandy wine in the bush, and we drank it, and the rest drank more than I did, and got drunk. **1860** J. SANDERSON in *Jrnl of Royal Geog. Soc.* XXX. 247 The price of this liquor, a very coarse fiery spirit, known in South Africa as 'Cape smoke,' is 7l. or 7l. 10s. per halfaum. **1873** A. EDGAR in *Friend* 27 Nov., They discovered a prize .. in the shape of a half-aum of Cape brandy, or 'smoke' as they termed it ... The cunning old tipplers had hurled the half-aum into a deep pool of water with the intention of visiting their old friend at night. **1913** W.W. THOMPSON *Sea Fisheries of Cape Col.* 9 What they could not sell was to be handed over to the Company for the garrison at .. 8 gl. the half-aum for train oil. **1926** P.W. LAIDLER *Tavern of Ocean* 37 On 16th June, 1663, the authorities seized four half-aums of Batavia arrack, all that was left of eleven smuggled ashore. *c*1936 *S. & E. Afr. Yr Bk & Guide* 1009, 1 aum = 30 Dutch Gallons = $31\frac{2}{3}$ Eng. Gals. **1972** [see LEAGUER].

auntie *n.* Also **anti, aunti, aunty,** and with initial capital. [Eng., influenced by Afk. *tannie*.] Not referring to a blood relation:

1.a. Indicating respect: an older woman; cf. TANNIE sense 3 b; also used as a title, with a first name or surname.

[**1882** S. HECKFORD *Lady Trader in Tvl* 262, I heard him whisper to his grandmother, 'If the aunt' (Little Boers call all women 'aunt') 'won't buy it, what shall I do with it?'] **1946** V. POHL *Adventures of Boer Family* 112 Dudley, much perplexed, asked mother what 'the auntie' was cross about. *c*1966 J. HOBBS in *New S. Afr. Writing* No.3, 161 Perspiring aunties scurry back and forth with cups of coffee and mounds of glistening braided koeksisters. **1977** J. SIKAKANE *Window on Soweto* 36 Your mother had .. succesfully borrowed a few coins from the 'auntie' next door. **1979** *Sunday Times* 7 Oct. (Mag. Sect.) 1 Our English-speaking fellow-countrymen have thought it wise to copy this custom and .. my children's little English-speaking friends are also told to say 'hullo to the auntie' and to open the door for 'the uncle'. **1979** W. EBERSOHN

Lonely Place 26 Scolded by some of the old aunties for siding with the Communists. **1979** [see FAT-KOEK]. **1980** [see MME]. **1980** M.P. GWALA in M. Mutloatse *Forced Landing* 101 At the door I was met by the house servant, MaZungu, an elderly auntie who did all the household chores. **1987** M. MASIPA in *Pace* May (Suppl.) 3 If the aunty who sells fruit at a street corner manages to send her son to a medical school his success is the success of the nation. **1988** E. MALULEKE in *Drum* Jan. 16 The yard had been swept, the toilet was clean and sparkling and garbage got rid of. He had done a better job than the aunties and boys I always hired. **1988** *Pace* Apr. 4 The auntie whose daughter was not lucky decided to seek out the auntie whose daughter had captured the jackpot.

b. As a form of address: TANTE sense 3.

In Afrikaans substituted for the second person pronoun 'you' as a respectful form of address (see quot. 1903).

1903 J.D. KESTELL *Through Shot & Flame* 105 'Auntie can make bread or vetkoek (dampers) of it, just as you think fit.' **1939** *Outspan* 6 Oct. 65 'I'm having some golf practice, boys. Everyone plays golf in Pretoria.' 'You'll be playing Bobby Locke before long, Auntie.' **1964** G. GORDON *Four People* 408 'Put in the money, Auntie,' the child urged anxiously, and she heard the voice shouting again, 'Put in your tickey, can't you?' **1972** *Drum* 22 Mar. 29, I asked who it was. Someone said: 'Me, aunty. I want some milk.' I thought it was my neighbour's children. **1976** M. THOLO in C. Hermer *Diary of Maria Tholo* (1980) 165 'But who are we burying?' 'Auntie, it's best for you to go and find out for yourself.'

2. *shebeen queen*, see SHEBEEN sense 2; used as a title, with a first name or surname.

1970 M. DIKOBE Marabi Dance. 7 George had been engaged to play the piano for the two days by Auntie Ma-Ndlovu. The drinks, Skokiaan and other concoctions, were sold in a room adjoining. **1971** *Post* 7 Feb. 1 Cops raced to a Diepkloof shebeen when they heard James Bond had spent the night there. The 'Auntie' confirmed this. **1976** [see NIPINYANA]. *a***1977** K.M.C. MOTSISI in M. Mutloatse *Casey & Co.* (1978) 64 They have at last decided to license the aunties who have, through all the dry years, been slaking our thirsts by serving us under the counter. **1981** *Daily Dispatch* 15 Sept. 12 Imagine 'Aunties' who have not gone far with their schooling, battling with figures for the general sales tax! **1983** J. JOHNSON in *S. Afr. Speaks* 30, I managed to stay with an auntie who was selling liquor ... I helped this auntie with her shebeen, meantime trying to get a job. [**1985** *Drum* Jan. 34 We'll get enough exercise elbowlifting at Aunt Peggy's.]

3. *rare.* Used euphemistically: a nanny.

1984 *Sunday Times* 8 July (Suppl.) 10, R318 Return: Including 7 nights accommodation on S.A.A. from Johannesburg or Durban. Children and Aunties stay free with every couple in separate rooms.

ausei, **ausi(e)**, **ausisi** varr. OUSIE.

Australian bug *n. phr.* The cottony cushion-scale *Icerya purchasi* of the Coccoideae, which attacks plants, esp. citrus trees.

This pest was introduced from Australia in the late nineteenth century.

1877 *Alice Times* 11 May, The Australian Bug is not likely to have in the Colony either a long life or a merry one. Its new-found enemy the 'Lady Bird' is multiplying exceedingly, it is said. **1887** E.A. ORMEROD (*title*) Notes on the Australian Bug. **1889** — *Notes & Descr. of Injurious Farm & Fruit Insects* 70 The soft, cushiony, white-ribbed Scale insects, commonly known as the Australian Bug (the Cottony Cushion Scale of North America), ranks amongst the most destructive of the insect pests hurtful to trees and shrubs in S. Africa, although little more than fifteen years have elapsed since this pest was first observed in the Colony. **1892** W.L. DISTANT *Naturalist in Tvl* 88 High veld .. arboriculture is in danger by the arrival of the Coccid, or so-called 'Australian Bug' (Icerya purchasi), which has ruined many trees and shrubs. **1918** S.H. SKAIFE *Animal Life* 154 The Australian bug was a very serious pest here at one time, and threatened the whole of the citrus-growing industry. **1937** *Handbk for Farmers* (Dept of Agric. & Forestry) 992 *Australian Bug*, .. *Icerya purchasi*, Mask. Mature females pouch-like, stationary, about 1/4 inch long. **1967** E. ROSENTHAL *Encycl. of Sn Afr.* 156 *Dorthesia*, Insect pest, also known as Australian Bug, introduced into Cape Colony in 1873, where it did immense damage to trees. **1973** B. SMIT in *Std Encycl. of Sn Afr.* IX. 505 The Australian bug spread to all countries where citrus was being grown, but everywhere it was brought under control by the ladybird beetle. **1990** *Weekend Post* 23 June (Leisure) 7 Many of the suckling insects like Australian bug, scale and mealy bug seem to zero in on plants which are under stress due to having dust-clogged pores.

australopithecine /ˌɒstrələʊˈpɪθəsaɪn/ *n.* and *adj.* Also with initial capital. [AUSTRALOPITHECUS + Eng. n.- and adj.-forming suffix *-ine*.]

A. *n.* Pl. **-s**, **-cinae**. A member of the genus *Australopithecus*, the family of southern man-apes.

1947 R. BROOM in *Pan-Afr. Congress on Prehist.* 111 In the near future we hope to get further specimens which will help us to decide whether the Australopithecines and man arose from a Proconsul-like group or from a still earlier and less anthropoid group. **1947** W.E. LE GROS CLARK in *Pan-Afr. Congress on Prehist.* 113 The Australopithecinae represent an extinct group of the Hominoidae which must be associated with the line of hominid evolution rather than with that leading to the modern large apes. **1962** R. MASON *Prehist. of Tvl* 94 Within .. the last million years hominid evolution may have followed a progression from australopithecines to pithecanthropines, whose earliest known representatives appear to be about thirty-five thousand years old. *Ibid.* 96 If australopithecines used weapons they were merely extending a well-known aspect of animal behaviour, for a variety of birds, insects and mammals use tools. **1970** P.V. TOBIAS in *Std Encycl. of Sn Afr.* I. 609 Most anthropologists today consider that the differences are of such an order that it is best to regard all the australopithecines as members of a single genus with several species. **1978** R.R. INSKEEP *Peopling of Sn Afr.* 27 [*Australopithecus*] *africanus* is often referred to informally as the gracile (slender) australopithecine in contrast to the robust species. **1984** A. TURNER in *S. Afr. Jrnl of Science* LXXX. 201 Dart's claims for the bone-tool using, meat eating and homicidal habits of the australopithecines of the Transvaal caves had a significant effect on ideas about human evolution. **1989** *Reader's Digest Illust. Hist.* 11 *Australopithecus africanus* .. lived between one and three million years ago ... More discoveries followed, helping to fill the gaps between the *australopithecines* and modern man.

B. *adj.* Of or pertaining to a member of the genus *Australopithecus*.

1957 R.A. DART in *3rd Pan Afr. Congress on Prehist.* 164 There are nearly 7 times as many baboon as australopithecine fragments and only 1 out of 376 bone fragments is australopithecine. However at least 45 baboon and 5 australopithecine creatures are represented in the remains recovered: 9 times as many baboons as australopithecines.

Australopithecus /ˌɒstrələʊˈpɪθəkəs/ *n.* [Name coined by R.A. Dart, modern L. *australis* southern + Gk *píthēkos* ape (see Dart quot., 1925).] An extinct genus of small-brained, bipedal hominids living in southern and eastern Africa between one and four million years ago. Also *attrib.* See also MRS PLES, SALDANHA sense 2.

1925 *Star* 5 Feb., Why was 'Australopithecus africanus' something that was ceasing to be an animal but could not be described as the 'Pithecanthropus erectus' of Java has been, as something which was becoming a man? **1925** R.A. DART in *Nature* 7 Feb. 199, I propose tentatively, then, that a new family of *Homo-simiadae* be created .. and that the first known species of the group be designated *Australopithecus Africanus* in commemoration first, of the extreme southern and unexpected horizon of its discovery, and secondly of the continent in which so many new and important discoveries have been made, thus vindicating the Darwinian claim that Africa would prove to be the cradle of mankind. **1959** J.D. CLARK *Prehist. of S. Afr.* 62 The first adult *Australopithecus* specimen ... Believing it to be rather different from the *Taung child*, Broom gave it the distinct generic name of *Plesianthropus Transvaalensis*. Now .. anatomists are agreed that only one generic form is represented in the Man-ape remains, but that two specific forms exist — Australopithecus and a later, more specialized form *Paranthropus*. **1967** E.H. LENNEBERG *Biol. Foundation of Lang.* 258 If the modern apes do not talk, this is no evidence against the possibility that *Australopithecus* had some potential for a primitive form of speech-like communication. **1978** R.R. INSKEEP *Peopling of Sn Afr.* 27 Today, all the South African man-apes are accommodated in a single genus *Australopithecus* containing two species, *africanus* and *robustus*. **1984** *S. Afr. Panorama* Aug. 35 Dr Dart's find enabled Dr Robert Broom to establish beyond any doubt the significance of the discoveries at Sterkfontein, Kromdraai and Swartkrans .. of fossil remains of hundreds of *Australopithecus* man. **1988** *Cape Times* 5 Dec. 6 Bones recovered from the Swartkrans cave suggest that Homo erectus or Australopithecus robustus cooked on fires, sought heat from them or used them to frighten predators as long as 1,5 million years ago. **1990** *Sunday Star* 23 Dec. (Review) 8 Makapansgat is one of three South African sites to yield remains of Australopithecus africanus. **1994** S. ARMSTRONG in *Sunday Times* 18 Sept. 22 Professor Dart claimed the Taung child — which he named Australopithecus africanus — was the missing link between apes and man.

Auteniqua, **Auteniquois**, **Autinegua**, **Autinicqua** varr. OUTENIQUA.

auw var. AU.

AV /eɪˈviː, ɑːˈfɪə/ *n.* [Afk., initial letters of *Afrikaner Volkswag*, *Afrikaner* (see AFRIKANER *n.* sense 2 a) + *volks* people's + *wag* guard.] An extreme right-wing, largely Afrikaner, political-cum-cultural movement. Also *attrib.*

1984 *Daily Dispatch* 9 May 1 The rightwing Afrikaner Volkswag (AV) — formed at an emotion-charged meeting in Pretoria last Friday has come in for severe criticism. **1985** *Frontline* Aug. 37 Virginity for youngsters is an ideal one would expect at an AV conference. **1986** *Race Rel. Survey 1985* (S.A.I.R.R.) 11 A member of the AV .. said .. that the AV was born because the Afrikaner had to maintain his cultural identity.

avie var. ARVIE.

avo /ˈævəʊ/ *n. colloq.* Shortened form of *Avocado pear*. Also *attrib.*

1983 *Rand Daily Mail* 16 Sept. 12 The avo and biltong and the bean soup .. followed by .. the Cape dishes and the denningvleis. **1986** *Cape Times* 26 Feb., Beware of green avos ... The SA Avocado Growers' Association has warned people against buying immature avos. **1986** J. WHYLE in S. Gray *Market Plays* 164 There was honey on the avo and we were stoned and Ricky kept saying Eastern Province avos are really sweet. **1987** *E. Prov. Herald* 4 June 13 Avos 35c each. **1988** H. PRENDINI in *Style* June 102 We're talking Blairgowrie, Westdene, Mondeor. The land of the slasto patio, the curlicued burglar guard, the avo dip. **1992** A. FORROW on TV1, 24 Oct. (Amanda's Way), You can always have a spare avo on hand to do your garnish afterwards. **1993** C. EDEN in *Food & Home* Aug. 138 Tell Pantie you don't want 20 avos all at once, and his face crumples in pain.

avondbloem, **avondbloom(je)**, **avontbloem** varr. AANDBLOM.

avond-bloemetjie, **-blommetje**, etc. varr. AANDBLOMMETJIE.

AWB /eɪ dʌbəljuː ˈbi, ɑː vɪə ˈbɪə/ *n.* [Abbrev. formed on Afk. *Afrikaner Weerstandsbeweging*, 'Afrikaner Resistance Movement', *Afrikaner* (see AFRIKANER *n.* sense 2 a) + *weerstand* resistance + linking phoneme *-s-* + *beweging* movement.]

A militant, white, right-wing organization founded in 1973; a member of this organization. Also *attrib.*, *transf.*, and *comb.* **AWB-type** *adj.* See also STORMVALK.

1974 *E. Prov. Herald* 17 Oct. 18 The leader of the AWB is Mr Eugene Terreblanche, an ex-policeman. **1975** *Sunday Times* 23 Nov. 2 The Afrikaner-Weerstandsbeweging (Afrikaner Resistance Movement — AWB) .. has been concentrating on infiltrating and recruiting supporters among police and defence officers. **1980** *Survey of Race Rel. 1979* (S.A.I.R.R.) 16 It was reported that the AWB aimed to scrap democracy and favoured a return to a boererepubliek ... It claimed it intended becoming a political party. **1987** L. WROUGHTON in *Pretoria News* 15 June 6 The AWB leader claims not to be a political party leader nor does he aim to become a representative in Parliament but rather a national movement alongside 'his people'. **1988** *Afr. Contemp. Record 1986–7* 737 Although there were no proven cases of the AWB having been involved in vigilante attacks on Black activists and White liberals, allegations were frequently made that its paramilitary [wing], the *Brandwag*, was behind such attacks. **1988** V. KHUMALO in *Pace* May 17 AWB-type treatment outside a Hillbrow all-night grill ... A platteland punch that felt like it came from the bowels of earth clipped his eye which promptly ballooned inside its socket. **1990** T. MATHEWS et al. in *Newsweek* 19 Feb. 22 Eugene Terre'Blanche, head of the Afrikaner Resistance Movement, a white-supremacy group best known by its Afrikaans initials AWB, says, 'We will restore law and order with force and create a state for the *volk*.' **1990** *Sunday Times* 12 Aug. 17 An NP/ANC coalition will usurp all power and suppress the living daylights out of AWBs, PACs, CPs, Azapos, Democrats and anyone else who dares express a dissenting view. **1990** *Weekend Post* 18 Aug. 2 The PAC was seen as an uncompromising, hard-line non-conciliatory party, referred to by a number of respondents as a 'black AWB'.

awethu see AMANDLA.

awm var. AUM.

awu var. AU.

ayah /ˈaɪə/ *n. obsolescent.* Also **aia**, **a(i)ya**, **aja**, and with initial capital. [Indian Eng., fr. Pg. *aia* nurse (fem. of *aio* tutor).]

Also *Indian Eng.* Offensive to some.

1. A child's nurse, usu. a COLOURED or black woman; a term of respect for an elderly 'coloured' woman.

1806 J. BARROW *Trav.* II. 102 The poor children scramble as well as they can among the slaves .. each, in the better sort of families, having its proper slave, called its aya, a Malay term, borrowed, perhaps, from the Portuguese or Italian, signifying nurse or protectress. **1861** P.B. BORCHERDS *Auto-Biog. Mem.* 37, I returned to Stellenbosch, telling .. of what I had seen and experienced .. to the amazement of my 'ayah,' or nurse, the kind, good-hearted Leonora, a native of Bengal. **1882** T. HAHN *Address S. Afr. Public Library* 36 One word about the Dutch *patois* of this Colony ... We learn this *patois* first from our nurses and ayahs. **1891** J.P. LEGG in *Cape Illust. Mag.* I. 96 'Tiffin' and 'ayah' are to be met with in England, but in the Cape they are more generally used. **1905** J. DU PLESSIS *1000 Miles in Heart of Afr.* 88, I required a wash-up as much as when (so runs the legend) my *ayah* once regaled me, a boy of two, on a dish of pumpkin, which I devoured, not with mouth and fingers only, but with eyes and nose and cheeks and clothes as well. **1913** C. PETTMAN *Africanderisms* 37 *Ayah* or *Aja*, .. was introduced by the Portuguese into India and was thence imported at an early date into the Cape. **1930** [see MOSADI]. **1935** P. SMITH *Platkop's Children* 152 Presently Katisje met another ayah an' stood showin' her the perambilator [*sic*]. An' the other ayah said how wonderful it was. **1944** I.D. DU PLESSIS *Cape Malays* 47 The Malays played an important part in life at the Cape during the 19th century. The women did the cooking and washing and acted as *ayahs* to the children. **1964** L.G. GREEN *Old Men Say* 133 Some of the Cape families who have clung to their homes through the centuries have cooks whose great-grandfathers were slaves on the same estates. These old aias (from the Portuguese word aya) are treated with great respect. They carry the old Cape cuisine in their heads, from *frikkadel* and *sosaties* to *geelrys* and *doekpudding*. **1975** *Argus* 17 Sept. 28 Mrs le Roux also recalls how her aia (nursemaid) brewed a wonderful gharra beer from the clusters of tiny berries of the gharrabos.

2. A title or term of address, sometimes used in conjunction with the woman's first name.

1888 A. BRIGG *Sunny Fountains & Golden Sands* 105 We generally called her 'old Ayah,' a title she herself preferred, not only as one of some honour amongst the people, but as describing the character in which she liked to be known, that of a professional nurse. **1908** I.W. WAUCHOPE *Natives & their Missionaries* 4 A female Native was called 'Meid,' i.e. girl, or as a term of endearment 'Ou-ma,' i.e. grandmother or 'Ayah.' **1927** [see OUTA sense 2]. **1953** U. KRIGE *Dream & Desert* 47 When she started imitating Outa Adoons or Aia Rosie, they would laugh (including Outa Adoons and Aia Rosie) till the tears came. **1955** A. DELIUS *Young Trav.* 100 Frank told him that Outa and Aia were general names for more elderly coloured men and women respectively. **1981** F. MALHERBE in V.A. February *Mind your Colour* 35 The Coloured labourer, the farm-hand, has hitherto enjoyed the greatest attention in our literature ... The relationship, 'baas-boy', with its 'Ja, Baas', and 'Nee Baas' .. should not necessarily be interpreted as denigrating — this also applies to the terms 'outa' and 'aia', the earlier forms of respect.

ayikona var. AIKONA.

azaguay var. ASSEGAI.

Azania /əˈzeɪnɪə/ *n.* [Gk (by the first century A.D.; see quot. 1912), prob. fr. Arabic *Zanj* a dark-skinned African, but see also quot. 1933. The element *zan-*, prob. derived from *Zanj*, appears also as a prefix in *Zanzibar*, and as an infix in *Tanzania*.

Edward Lane, in his *Arabic-English Lexicon* (1955) describes *Azzanj* or *Azzenj* as 'a certain nation of Blacks', quoting ancient Arabic sources as follows: 'Their country is beneath, and to the south of, the equinoctial line; and beyond them is (said to be) no habitation, or cultivation: .. some say their country extends from the western parts of Africa nearly to Abyssinia .. and part of it is on the Nile of Egypt'.

J.H. Soga, in *The South-East Bantu (Abe-Nguni, Aba-Mbo, Ama-lala)* (1930) suggests that *Zenj* was the ancient term for 'Bantu': 'There is little doubt that all east coast tribes, from Somaliland down to Sofala, were in ancient times called "Zenj".' By the year 880 the inhabitants of the east coast of Africa were being referred to as 'Zenj' by Abu Zayed-Hassan of Syraf. The name continued to be used until 1154, when Abu Abdullah al Idrisi called them by the double designation of 'Zenj' and 'kaffir', meaning 'heathen'.]

Among members of the BLACK CONSCIOUSNESS and AFRICANIST movements: South Africa; a free, non-racial South Africa.

Waugh's 'Azania' (see quot. 1932) is a fictitious island off the east coast of Africa. As a name for South Africa, 'Azania' was taken from classical geography and may have been first publicly suggested in 1959 (see Van Jaarsveld quot., 1990).

[**1854** W.B. DONNE in W. Smith *Dict. of Greek & Roman Geogr.* I. 354 *Azania*, .. Another name for the maritime region of eastern Africa .. from the promontory of Aromata, lat. 11°N, to that of Rhaptum, lat. 2°S. The Mare Azanium .. skirted this whole region. **1912** W.H. SCHOFF (tr. *Periplus of Erythraean Sea* [*c* A.D. 60, author unkn.]) in B. Davidson *Old Afr. Rediscovered* (1959) 133 Two days sail beyond, there lies the very last market town of the continent of Azania, which is called Rhapta. **1932** E. WAUGH *Black Mischief* (1952) 12 He proclaimed the island a single territory and himself its ruler ... Until now it had been scored on the maps as Sakuyu Island; Amurath renamed it the Empire of Azania. **1933** G.W.B. HUNTINGFORD in *Antiquity* VII. 153 At some period between the Stone Age and medieval times a civilization .. left traces over a large part of East Africa ... This civilization I propose to call 'Azanian'. [*Note*] From ἀζανία, the name given by classical geographers to East Africa from Cape Guardafui to the southern limit of the known world (about lat. 10°S) ... The word may mean 'the dried-up country', from ἀζαίνω, 'I am dry'. *cf.* azaniae nuces, 'dried-up pine-cones', Pliny, *Nat. Hist.* XVI, 44.] **1968** *Afr. Research Bulletin* Vol.5 No.6, 1102 The [PAC] statement described his death as 'a tragic loss ... His heroic death .. will always inspire the revolutionary youth of Azania.' **1970** [see POQO]. **1976** N. ASHFORD in J. Crwys-Williams *S. Afr. Despatches* (1989) 412 Banners with slogans .. such as .. 'We are not Boers' and 'Viva Azania' (the name given to South Africa by black nationalists). **1977** *Rhodeo* (Rhodes Univ.) 30 Sept. 3 At the end of each [song] the orator shouted *One Azania* and the barrelling, echoing response *One Nation* rolled out. **1979** *Sunday Times* 27 May 16 Azania has been adopted as a name for South Africa by some radicals. Originally, it was used by the mapmakers of ancient Egypt to describe all the unknown territories to their south. **1984** M. KA MYEZA in *Frontline* Mar. 38 The term [Azania] represents a society free of oppression and exploitation where there will be no regard for race. Azania will be an anti-racist society with no whites, coloureds, Indians or Africans — just Azanians who belong to the human race. **1987** *Frontline* Feb. 4 To the UDF the very term 'Azania' is a hostile shibboleth (and latterly there are tales of youngsters being beaten up for using the wrong word in the wrong company). **1988** J. GROBLER *Decisive Clash* 156 The name 'South Africa' was regarded by the PAC as a 'racist colonial name ... ' They therefore gave it a new name, Azania, which they claimed to mean Black man's country. **1990** F.A. VAN JAARSVELD in *Sunday Times* 20 May 14 In 1959 Peter Raborko of the Pan Africanist Congress proposed the name Azania. While the PAC has never officially accepted the name, it has found wide favour among a cross-section of black groups. **1990** A. GOLDSTUCK *Rabbit in Thorn Tree* 18 The ANC never refers to South Africa as Azania — that is a term employed by the black-consciousness movements, such as the Pan-Africanist Congress and the Azanian People's Organisation. **1990** *Style* May 35 Somewhere between the Utopian republics of Azania and Boerania lies the real South Africa, a land where hope and fear lie on either side of the faultline of change. **1990** T. PHAKE in *Star* 11 Sept. 8 The Black Consciousness Movement of Azania believes that all the miseries and hardships of our people will be solved when we implement a one-party state in Azania, or rather when we establish a democratic anti-racist and scientific socialist workers' republic of Azania.

Azanian /əˈzeɪnɪən/ *adj.* and *n.* [AZANIA + Eng. n.- or adj.-forming suffix *-an*.]

A. *adj.*

1. Of or pertaining to AZANIA or its inhabitants.

[**1932** E. WAUGH *Black Mischief* (1952) 39 Guards, Chiefs and tribesmen of the Azanian Empire. The war is over.] **1933** [see AZANIA]. **1968** *Afr. Research Bulletin* Vol.5 No.6, 1102 A member of the revolutionary command of the PAC .. had been killed .. by Portuguese forces in Mozambique ... The statement described his death as 'a tragic loss .. to the Azanian Revolution.' **1976** *Evening Post* 18 Oct. 1 The demonstrators were members of the 'ad hoc committee to support the just struggle of the Azanian people.' **1982** C. BUTLER in *Grocott's Mail* 21 May 7 A suggestion for next year's theme. Instead of 'Happily Haydn', 'Melodiously Mendelssohn' or 'Ecstatically European' .. why not 'Simply South African', or 'Absolutely Azanian'? **1990** R. MALAN in *Cosmopolitan* Apr. 158 On the wall is the Azanian flag, the flag that might have been South Africa's had Biko lived, and BC triumphed.

2. *comb.* **Azanian People's Liberation Army**, see APLA; **Azanian People's Organization**, see AZAPO; **Azanian Students' Movement**, see AZASM; **Azanian Students' Organization**, see AZASO.

B. *n.* An inhabitant of AZANIA.

[1970 B. DAVIDSON Old Afr. 195 In the hinterland the Azanians were probably Bantu-speaking peoples as well; although this does not settle their racial type.] 1977 Weekend World 17 July 131 (letter) God is on our side ... 'Concerned Azanian', Thaba 'Nchu. 1979 M. MATSHOBA Call Me Not a Man 96 One day we shall all overcome these divisions and live as South Africans. No! As Azanians, because South Africans have been divided for three centuries. 1984 H. MALOBELA in Drum Jan. 42 No right-thinking black, Indian or coloured Azanian can sit down and think that the Nats will one day give us a place in the sun. 1990 Frontline Feb. 18 If the 'doors of learning' are to be spurned by 'blacks' (presumably Azanians), should we infer that ignorance and prejudice .. are more in keeping with black aspirations?

Azanla /ə'zænlə, ə'zɑːnlə/ n. [Acronym formed on *Azanian National Liberation Army*.] The military wing of the *Black Consciousness Movement of Azania*, formed in 1984, the smallest of the resistance movements. See *Black Consciousness Movement* (BLACK CONSCIOUSNESS sense 2). Also attrib.

1990 City Press 3 June 2 Azania accused released on bail. Seven alleged Azanian National Liberation Army (Azanla) cadres facing terrorism charges in Klerksdorp were released on bail this week. 1993 'S.M.' in Mayibuye Sept. 5 The fantasy of co-opting MK, Apla and Azanla or integrating them with the SADF and SAP because the former are democratic forces and their image will be tarnished by mixing with forces which protected apartheid for decades. 1994 A. TRENCH in Weekly Mail 18 Mar. 8 The Azanian National Liberation Army (Azanla), the armed wing of the Black Consciousness Movement, has claimed responsibility for the gruesome attack ... Azapo says the attack was not in line with Azanla's normal activities: infrequent, low-profile incidents, normally involving petrol bomb attacks on soft targets.

Azapo /ə'zɑːpəʊ/ n. [Acronym formed on *Azanian People's Organization*.] A BLACK CONSCIOUSNESS movement formed in 1978; a member of this organization. Also attrib.

1978 Daily Dispatch 2 May 2 A new black national organisation, the Azania People's Organisation (Azapo), has been formed in Roodepoort. 1979 Voice 30 Sept. 2 Amandla! we say. We congratulate the Azanian Peoples' Organisation (Azapo) for their courage in convening the organisation's First Congress at the weekend. 1981 R. MOKGOATLHENG in Rand Daily Mail 6 Apr. 1 Azapo condemns in the strongest terms the detention of its president and other executive members. 1985 Pace Sept. 66 Azapo too, like other Black Consciousness organisations before it, has played an important role in the local civil rights movement. 1987 M. MASEDI in Frontline Apr. 5 The participation of Azapo and other Black conciousness espousing formations is based on three major principles, viz. anti-capitalism, anti-racism and the restoration of land to its rightful owners. 1990 P. GARSON in Weekly Mail 8 Feb. When Beyco was launched in February the 'Azapos' allegedly launched an attack at the meeting, which led to retaliation, murders on both sides and a spiral of revenge and retribution. 1990 City Press 4 Mar. 9 Azapo believes it is well placed to bring about unity between the PAC and the ANC. 1990 [see Sunday Times quot. at AWB].

Azasco see AZASM.

Azasm /ə'zæzəm, ə'zɑːsəm/ n. [Acronym formed on *Azanian Students' Movement*.] An organization founded in 1983 as the student wing of AZAPO, supporting the ideology of BLACK CONSCIOUSNESS.

Subsequently renamed *Azasco* (see quot. 1991).

1984 Survey of Race Rel. 1983 (S.A.I.R.R.) 62 The Azanian Students' Movement (AZASM) was inaugurated in Pietersburg in July .. a reaction to the movement of AZASO from black consciousness to non-racialism. 1987 M. MAIVHA in Star 7 May 3 A Soweto man whose family is identified with the Azanian People's Organisation (Azapo) and Azanian Students' Movement (Azasm) has been murdered by youths alleged to be political opponents of black consciousness. 1990 R. MALAN in Cosmopolitan Apr. 160 I .. asked the comrades' permission to interview a teenage member of Azasm — the Azanian Students' Movement, the youth wing of the BC movement. 1990 Varsity Voice Apr. 4 Supporters of the Azanian Students Movement (Azasm) chanted 'Liberals out! One Settler, One Bullet!' at last year's demonstration against the presence of Dr Frederick Van Zyl Slabbert on campus. 1991 Frontline May 17 For many years, Wits (like Natal and other varsities of their ilk) refused to recognise Azanian Students' Movement (Azasm), now Azanian Students' Convention (Azasco).

Azaso /ə'zɑːsəʊ/ n. [Acronym formed on *Azanian Students' Organization*.] A grouping founded in 1979 to represent black university students, and later affiliated to the United Democratic Front (see UDF n.²).

Although initially seen by some as a replacement for the banned SASO, this organization opposed black consciousness; to avoid confusion on this point, it was renamed SANSCO in December 1986.

1980 Survey of Race Rel. 1979 (S.A.I.R.R.) 546 In November a national organisation representing the interests of black university students, the Azanian Students' Organisation (AZASO) was formed. 1981 Voice 29 July 3 The Azanian Students Association (Azaso), officially switched from the Black consciousness philosophy to that of non-racial 'progressive and democrat' stance, at the weekend. 1982 Argus 12 July 3 A national campaign to draw up an education charter .. was launched by the Azanian Students' Organisation .. last week. Azaso represents black tertiary level students. 1984 Rhodeo (Rhodes Univ.) Oct. 3 Both Cosas and Azaso also work closely with non-student organisations — trade unions and community groups. 1985 A. AKHALWAYA in Frontline Dec. 25 The Congress of SA Students (Cosas) emerged as Freedom Charter supporting organisations. Later, the Azanian Students' Organisation (Azaso) was launched as the spiritual successor to Saso. 1987 J. DOWSON in Argus 1 Sept. 11 Known until last December as the Azanian Students' Organisation (Azaso), Sansco, like Nusas, is a UDF affiliate and supports the principles contained in the Freedom Charter.

∥**azikhwelwa** /ˌazi'kweːlwa/ int. hist. Also azikwelwa. [In the Nguni languages, lit. 'they are not ridden': neg. prefix a- + -zi- they + -khwel- mount, ride + passive suffix -wa.] 'We won't ride', during the 1950s, a rallying cry used by black commuters boycotting bus services in protest at high tariffs.

1956 New Age 5 July 1 Evaton's 11 months of struggle against increased bus fares has been closer to a little war than a boycott. Its 58,000 residents .. have faced assaults, attacks on their homes, arrests, provocation and threats, but the cry 'Azikwelwa' (Don't ride — don't get on) has held together the longest and most complete boycott ever. 1957 Drum Mar. 24 Azikhwelwa! For all its fierce passion and aggressive power, this slogan of the bus boycott in Johannesburg and Pretoria is in the Passive Voice. No one uses the Active Voice forms of 'Ningazikhweli!' (Don't board them) and 'Angizikhweli' (I don't board them). a1978 K.M.C. MOTSISI in M. Mutloatse Casey & Co. (1978) 81 'Azikhwelwa!' she shouted. 'We won't board the buses,' she interpreted for herself. Just like at the meetings. 1980 J. MATTHEWS in M. Mutloatse Forced Landing 35 Their cry was, 'Burn the buses!' Then there were those few who whispered, 'Accept the terms.' But there were also the many who defiantly said 'Azikwelwa! We will not ride!' 1981 E. WEINBERG Portrait of a People 166 It was decided to boycott the buses. 'Azikwelwa' (they shall not be ridden!) became the cry all along the Witwatersrand, in Alexandra, Sophiatown and Randfontein, and in Pretoria as well. 1989 R. FINLAYSON Changing Face of isiXhosa (Unpubl. thesis, Unisa) 6 Azikhwelwa they are not being boarded i.e. buses, now means 'boycott' or 'strike'. 1989 Reader's Digest Illust. Hist. 391 As they walked they sang and chanted slogans such as 'asinamali' ('we have no money') and 'azikwelwa' ('we will not ride'). 1994 Grocott's Mail 2 Sept. 8 The boycott was called when Putco increased bus fares by a penny. For three months the residents said 'Azikhwelwa!' (we will not ride) and walked the ten miles to work until fares were lowered again.

B

ba- /ba/ *pref.* A Sotho and seTswana plural noun prefix found in some words originating in these languages.

For examples, see BAKWENA, BATLHAPING. In Sotho and seTswana, the singular of words beginning *ba-* is formed by replacing this prefix with *mo-* or by dropping it. In *S. Afr. Eng.* this pattern is not always observed, and words in the plural forms are sometimes treated as singular nouns, an *-s* being added to form the English plural, or (esp. in the names of peoples), the noun stem, with neither prefix nor *-s*, being used as a collective plural. See also MO-.

BAAB /bɑːb/ *n. hist.* Also **Baab**. [Acronym formed on the initial letters of *Bantu Affairs Administration Board.*] Esp. during the 1970s: ADMINISTRATION BOARD. Also *attrib.*

1974 *Grocott's Mail* 3 Sept. 3 'As the law stands at the moment, a black person born in a rural community remains classified as a farm labourer for the rest of his days regardless of whether he has a matric or even a higher educational qualification,' said Mr. Dennis Bush, local director of the BAAB. **1977** J. SIKAKANE *Window on Soweto* 51 The ruling of Soweto was taken over in July 1973 by the Bantu Affairs Administration Boards (BAAB), a specially created government machine. *Ibid.* 52 Rents, liquor and the labour levy as the sole sources of revenue for the BAAB's [*sic*]. General taxation does not subsidise the development of facilities in the neglected townships. **1985** PLATZKY & WALKER *Surplus People* 5 They were informed by the police and the Baab that they were to be moved to a place called Glenmore. [Note] The shortened name for Bantu Affairs Administration Board.

baadjie /ˈbaɪki/ *n.* Also **baatj(i)e, badjie, batje**. [Afk., ad. Malay *baju* jacket.]
1. *obs.* A jacket.

1861 *Cape Monthly Mag.* in Du Plessis & Lückoff *Malay Quarter* (1953) 49 They wear a shirt, with sleeves left wide and open at the wrists .. and *baatjies*, or hip-jackets, in the pockets of which their hands are inserted in a very Frankish fashion. **1896** R. WALLACE *Farming Indust. of Cape Col.* 162 The inhabitants were supposed to be all Boers, dressed in fustian if they were fairly well off, in leather crackers and *batjes* if less well to do. **1913** C. PETTMAN *Africanderisms* 39 *Baatje*, .. This word was introduced into South Africa either by the Malays or by the sailors of the Dutch East India Company. It has made a permanent place for itself in the vocabulary of the Dutch sailor, *baatje* being the name that he gives to his jacket. In South Africa it is applied to almost every description of short coat. **1936** L.G. GREEN *Secret Afr.* (1974) 130 Even their language has not been entirely lost, for many an exotic Malay word is heard in the daily speech of South Africans both of Dutch and English descent. Words like *pondok* (a hovel) and *blatjang* (a relish), *mebos* (preserved fruit), *baatje* (a jacket) and *sjambok* (a whip) are Malay words. **1949** [see CRACKERS]. [**1953** DU PLESSIS & LÜCKHOFF *Malay Quarter* 59 Those who came from Java in the early part of the eighteenth century must have worn the dress described by Valentyn in 1726: a sarong swathed round the lower limbs, turban and badju (coat) over a silk or cotton garment.]

2. [So called after the jacket worn in the past by long-term male prisoners.] A long-term prison sentence; cf. BLUE-COAT sense 2. See also BLOUBAADJIE sense 2 a.

1974 in *Eng. Usage in Sn Afr.* Vol.5 No.1, 9 *Bandiete* .. graduate from short sentences 2–4 and 4–8 (years) to the pinnacle of a *coat* or *baadjie* (both widely used, recalling the former 'blou baadjie' worn by long termers). A *coat* means 9 to never.

baager var. BAGGER.

‖**Baai** /baɪ, bɑːɪ/ *n. colloq.* [Afk., 'bay'; see also BAY.] *Die Baai, the Baai*: Port Elizabeth (see PE). Also *attrib.*

Usu. used in reporting Afrikaans speech.

1975 *S. Afr. Panorama* Jan. 12 The Transvaal was populated largely by farming folk. They had to travel hundreds of kilometres to 'Die Baai' (Port Elizabeth) for essentials. **1980** *E. Prov. Herald* 30 Oct. 1 Baai boys 'kap dit uit' to top ... In a recorded programme on the Afrikaans service, the boys from 'die Baai' took it away with the foot tapping rhythms of their music that is as ethnic as boerewors and biltong. **1982** *S. Afr. Deciduous Fruit Grower* in *S. Afr. Digest* 18 June 9 The route the fruit follows from the Langkloof to Port Elizabeth is no easy one and Port Elizabeth, or simply the *Baai* (the bay) as it is affectionately known in that part of the world, has had to adapt in many ways to the peculiarities of its interior. [**1991** C. BARRETT in *Weekend Post* 5 Jan. 7 A group of campers from Philipstown, near De Aar, who transported some of their gear in a sheep truck, also said it was *lekker in die Baai*. **1993** see IBHAYI.]

baaija, -je varr. BAIE.

baaiscope var. BIOSCOPE.

Baaite var. BAYETE.

‖**baaken** /ˈbɑːkən/ *n. hist.* Also **bak(k)en, barcon**. [Du., beacon.]
1. BEACON *n.* sense 1.

1796 E. HELME tr. *F. Le Vaillant's Trav. into Int.* I. 35 (Pettman), We were told this morning that somebody had planted a *baaken* (a stake) upon our estate. **1801** J. BARROW *Trav.* I. 78 If one farmer is supposed to have put down his *baaken*, or stake, or land-mark, a little too near to that of his neighbour, the *Feld-wagt-meester* or peace-officer of the division, is called in, by the latter, to pace the distance, for which he gets three dollars. **1821** C.I. LATROBE *Jrnl of Visit* 157 Mounting a pony, I rode with Brother Leitner up the hill towards the Jagersbosch, to see the boundary-stones or baakens. **1833** *Graham's Town Jrnl* 3 Jan. 1 That no person may plead ignorance of the boundaries of the Estate of Cradock's Town, independant of the Bakkens required by Law, large whale-bones are placed on the most conspicuous parts of the property. **1838** J. COLLETT *Diary.* I. 8 June, Busy to day defining the Line and planting Barcons with Botha. **1847** J. BARROW *Reflect.* 161 It appeared to me so lovely a spot .. that I was tempted to declare I would erect there my *baaken*, or landmark, and solicit from the Governor possession of it, either as a free gift or by purchase. **1913** C. PETTMAN *Africanderisms* 38 *Baaken*, .. In addition to its general sense of 'beacon', this word was also applied to the stake which, in the early days of the Colony, was driven into the ground by the applicant for a farm, at the place where he proposed to build his homestead.

2. BEACON *n.* sense 2.

1809 R. COLLINS in G.M. Theal *Rec. of Cape Col.* (1900) VII. 20 It is within half an hour's ride of Governor Van Plettenberg's baaken, a stone which yet contains part of the inscription made on it in the year 1778.

3. *Transf.*, and *fig.*

1979 M. PARKES *Wheatlands* 37 The name 'Baakens' was given to the dam after a certain labourer had been thrown off a mule in the vicinity and the other man, as a joke, built a 'baaken' (beacon) to mark the spot. **1988** 'K. DE BOER' in *Frontline* Apr. 26 Majubadag. An inspiring baken in the Afrikaner history when the Boer forces surprised and routed the English column on Majuba.

baang var. BANG.

baar /bɑː(r)/ *n.* and *adj.* Pl. **ba(a)ren**. [Du., prob. ad. Malay *baharu* new, inexperienced.]
A. *n. obs.* A novice, newcomer, or raw military recruit. See also BARI, MOMPARA.

1868 [see OORLAM *n.* sense 1]. **1913** C. PETTMAN (tr. *N. Mansvelt's Idioticon*) *Africanderisms* 38 *Baar*, .. The word has come down from the days of the Dutch East India Company; the men who had seen considerable service were called *Oorlammen* (Mal. *orang lami*, old person), while the recruits were called *Baren* (Mal. *orang baru*, new hand). In India and also at the Military Academy at Breda the word seems to be used in the sense of green, inexperienced. In sailor language it also indicates a novice. **1919** M. GREENLEES tr. *O.F. Mentzel's Life at Cape in Mid-18th C.* 80 In the end, between thirty and forty men, most of them baaren, being driven to it by hunger and distress, made a plot together and planned to desert.

B. *adj.* Obs. exc. *hist.* Stupid; untaught. Cf. OORLAM *adj.* sense 2.

1881 [see OORLAM *adj.* sense 2]. **1913** C. PETTMAN (tr. *N. Mansvelt's Idioticon*) *Africanderisms* 38 *Baar*, .. The word is employed of both men and animals; in the former case it has the meaning of unskilful, untrained. **1980** [see OORLAMS sense 2].

baardman /ˈbɑːtmən, ˈbɑːrtmən/ *n.* Also **baartman**, and with initial capital. Pl. unchanged. [Afk., *baard* beard + *man* man.] Also in dim. form **baardmannetj(i)e** /-manəki/.
1. Any of various fishes with barbels on the lips and/or chin. **a.** The marine fish *Umbrina canariensis* of the kob family (Sciaenidae). **b.** The freshwater fish *Barbus andrewi* of the Cyprinidae; also called YELLOWFISH (sense a).

In Smith and Heemstra's *Smiths' Sea Fishes* (1986), the name 'baardman' is used for *Umbrina canariensis*.

1853 L. PAPPE *Synopsis of Edible Fishes* 16 *Umbrina capensis* .. Baardmannetje. Snout obtuse ... , lower jaw shortest with a barbel ... Measures from 2 to $2\frac{1}{2}$ feet, and is reputed for its delicious flesh. **1893** [see PAMPELMOESIE]. **1902** J.D.F. GILCHRIST in *Trans. of S. Afr. Philological Soc.* XI. iv. 226 Baardman ... *Umbrina capensis*. **1907** *E. London Dispatch* 5 Dec. (Pettman), *Baartman* (white-fish, barbel, catfish), a well-known ugly species of the family *Siluridae*. **1913** W.W. Thompson *Sea Fisheries of Cape Col.* 138 A very similar species, but not much esteemed for eating, is the White-visch or Baardman (Barbus capensis) which is fairly plentiful at times in the Breede and Dwars Rivers. **1930** [see BAFARO]. **1951** L.G. Green *Grow Lovely* 91 The baardman has a feeler under the jaw. **1972** *Grocott's Mail* 17 Mar. 3 He gave me to understand that the baardman were also about. These wily fish are seldom taken in any numbers although they are often seen in the waves close inshore. **1982** *S. Afr. Fishing* Apr.-May 10 At present the surf areas are .. providing most of the action in the form of baardman, steenbras, elf, leerfish and cob. **1992** V. Kabalin in *Afr. Wildlife* Vol.46 No.2, 201 We would like to see an immediate cancellation of this .. privilege until it can be scientifically proven that this .. open season has no ill effect on the sustainable stock in the Bay of yellowtail, kob, baartman, elf and steenbras.

2. A small bird, *Sporopipes squamifrons*, so called because of moustache- or beard-like stripes on its throat.

Also occas. called *scaly weaver*.

1913 C. Pettman *Africanderisms* 39 *Baardmannetje*, The name refers to its black moustache. This bird is also called the Scaly feathered finch. **1967** E. Rosenthal *Encycl. of Sn Afr.* 30 *Baardman* .. or *Scaly Weaver*, One of the commonest little birds of dry areas. **1985** G.L. Maclean *Roberts' Birds of Sn Afr.* 714 Identification: Small .. forecrown black, scaled white (hence 'Scaly-feathered') .. below whitish with bold black malar stripes (good field character, hence 'Baardmannetjie').

3. [See quot. 1966.] The flowering plant *Melasphaerula ramosa* of the Iridaceae.

1917 R. Marloth *Common Names* 8 *Baard'mannetje, Melasphaerula graminea*. Allied to *Gladiolus*. **1966** C.A. Smith *Common Names* 68 *Baardmannetjie*, .. Flowers cup-like with long tapering segments. The unusually long points of the segments suggest the vernacular name, literally 'bearded little man'. **1983** M.M. Kidd *Cape Peninsula* 152 *Melasphaerula ramosa*. Iridaceae. *Baardmannetjie*. 200–500mm, frequent in shade on the slopes of Table Mountain, Lion's Head, and Karbonkelberg.

baari(e) var. BARI.

baas /bɑːs/ *n.* Also **baase, bas(s)**. Pl. **-es, -e** /-ə/. [Du. (later Afk.), master.] Master, official, employer, owner, manager, supervisor, sir, boss. Cf. AMPER-BAAS, MASTER sense 2, SIEUR.

Now offensive to many. Esp. in the past, used of or to a white male, indicating the speaker's perception or acknowledgement of the other's superior social status. Sometimes used reluctantly or ironically. See also GROOT BAAS sense 1, KLEINBAAS, OUBAAS.

I. Used as a common noun.

1. *obs.* A naval or military officer; a civil official.

[**1598** J. Davys in R. Raven-Hart *Before Van Riebeeck* (1967) 20 The Flemmings fled before them like Mice before Cats, throwing away their weapons most basely. And our Baase, to save himself stayed aboord. **1625** S. Purchas *Hachluytus Posthymus* (1905) II. 306 Our Baase, (for so a Dutch Captaine is called) chose a Master of Mis-rule by the name of Kesar.] **1786** G. Forster tr. *A. Sparrman's Voy. to Cape of G.H.* I. 55 The owner or bailiff (or as they call him there, the *baas*) presented me with a glass of a strong-bodied wine. **1861** P.B. Borcherds *Auto-Biog. Mem.* 22 This old gentleman was the superintendent (*baas*) of the Company's outpost, and had the supervision of the extensive public woods at River Zonder End.

2. The owner and master of a home, farm, or business, and employer of the servants or labourers who work there; a manager or supervisor; *hist.*, a slave-owner or slave-master.

1821 C.I. Latrobe *Jrnl of Visit* 189 The good-natured *baas* of the adjoining farm, coming out to meet us, offered to supply us with as much sweet milk, as we might want. **1839** W.C. Harris *Wild Sports* 329 Pipe in mouth, the portly Baas, or master, presently sallied forth, and .. I inquired how many days' journey it was to the Great River. **1857** *Cape Monthly Mag.* II. Oct. 206 Enter a coloured servant. 'Is your baas in?' His baas was in, but was engaged. **1872** C.A. Payton *Diamond Diggings* 137 If he is a 'good baas,' his own 'boys' will frequently bring him relatives or friends who will offer their services. *a***1878** J. Montgomery *Reminisc.* (1981) 91 The farmer had been to a sale and purchased a slave girl and her child; her man was sold to another baas, and so they were separated. **1882** C. Du Val *With Show through Sn Afr.* II. 211 We .. got on to some farm tracks, which eventually landed us at a native kraal, the 'Baas' of which, an old Basuto of decidedly unprepossessing appearance, was the proprietor. **1897** J.P. Fitzpatrick *Outspan* 194 When I called again one boy came out. I asked him who was his baas, and he brought me to your hut. **1905** P. Gibbon *Vrouw Grobelaar* 50 'If I were the baas,' said the yellow man, 'I would turn out the young men to walk round the fields at night, with buckets to hit with sticks, and make a noise'. **1919** M. Greenlees tr. *O.F. Mentzel's Life at Cape in Mid-18th C.* 159 At one o'clock the bell is rung to recall to their labours the workmen and slaves, attended by their 'baase,' or overseers. **1919** R.Y. Stormberg *With Love from Gwenno* 73 To-day the two native boys had permission to leave early ... On such occasions the young 'baases' finish up the kraaling between them. **1932** G.B. Shaw *Adventures of Black Girl* 18 Doing justice and shewing mercy is only a small part of life when one is not a baas or a judge. **1939** R.F.A. Hoernlé *S. Afr. Native Policy* 141 He casts aggressive scowls .. at the Natives, in order to remind them that he is their 'baas' and they are his servants, and that it will go hard with them if they forget it. **1949** L. Hunter *Afr. Dawn* 75 He found out too that all the White men did not treat the 'boys' in their gangs as he had been treated by his 'baas'. The majority got more work from their gangs by kindly treatment. **1953** Lanham & Mopeli-Paulus *Blanket Boy's Moon* 36 Best off are those African men or women who work as house-servants; for sometimes the white Baas will allow a man's wife to live with him in the quarters, in exchange for her labour in the washing of clothes. **1962** F.C. Metrowich *Scotty Smith* 24 They told him that it was the property of Jan Coetzee. 'The baas,' they explained, 'has ridden ahead, as we are not far from the house'. **1974** *Drum* 8 July 42 Dr B— is the 'boy' because the hospital at which he works falls under the diocese of Zululand and Bishop Z— is the 'Baas' because he is the only man who can hire and fire him. **1988** *Frontline* Nov. 27 We do not pick up bottles only. We also pick up bones. Our black baas sells the bottles and bones in Pretoria. He pays us R5 per drum. **1990** *Frontline* Mar.-Apr. 33 Swerwers — coloured-cum-bushmen people who've lived this land for centuries and now spend their days trudging in search of a baas who'll let them squat until he needs them no longer. **1990** M.M. Hacksley (tr. E. van Heerden) in *Lynx* 190 Rations had been meagre, likewise cash for clothes and shoes, and the hand of the Baas had been stern and stingy. But it was a fine farm.

3. Any white male. Cf. MASTER sense 2.

Now often offensive to the one so addressed.

1882 J. Nixon *Among Boers* 27 He is a servant and he accepts his position. A white man is always 'baas' (tr. boss) — the Dutch for master. **1897** J.P. Fitzpatrick *Outspan* 111 The ladies and the baases, he said, could take the footpath along the mountains over the krantzes and avoid the two drifts. **1913** D. Fairbridge *Piet of Italy* 174 'My! It's Piet, eh?' he said .. 'An' I thought it was a baas!' **1939** R.F.A. Hoernlé *S. Afr. Native Policy* 16 The main lesson which the Native child has to learn in order to be fitted for its place 'in a subordinate society,' is that every White is a *baas* (master, boss); and that it is best to keep on good terms with a *baas*. **1951** O. Walker *Shapeless Flame* 191 Every man with a white skin in this country is a baas. No wonder South Africans scurry back to it, sunshine apart, after they have been voyaging. **1968** Cole & Flaherty *House of Bondage* 21 Police, magistrates, courts — all the apparatus of the law reinforces the already absolute power of the white *baas* and his madam. **1969** A. Fugard *Boesman & Lena* 22 Go on! Why don't you hit me? There's no white baases here to laugh. **1979** *Het Suid-Western* 12 Oct., Let us not look for insults where none are intended. Let us also be careful not to use words like 'baas', 'Hotnot' or 'plural' that in themselves give offence. **1980** N. Ferreira *Story of Afrikaner* 100 'Please baas, have you got a job for me? Give me a job,' he half-pleaded, half-demanded. 'I'm sorry,' I said, 'I work for a baas myself,' and nearly bit off my tongue. **1987** *Weekly Mail* 23 Oct. 8 Maybe the offended *baases* would have strung poor Kani up a tree for all to see what happens to an uppity black.

4. A member of the ruling class; the highest authority in any country, town or region; the 'top-dog'.

1888 *Cape Punch* 16 May 70 Make due reverence Councillors as I pass, For till this day week I am Grahamstown's *baas*. **1955** A. Delius *Young Trav.* 16 We don't take orders from anybody. We are our own 'Baas', as we say .. and so we don't like people calling us colonials as if we took orders from somewhere else. **1962** L.E. Neame *Hist. of Apartheid* 132 The white man is baas in South Africa. **1974** *Sunday Times* 23 Feb. 6 The attitude .. stems from some sort of briefing they receive from their fellows when they arrive in this country on how to get the most out of their new state of being 'baases' by putting the 'Bantu' in his place. **1981** *Drum* June 120 We are all South Africans, but it's hard for us to wish Gerrie Coetzee good luck. He is white and baas. **1983** *S. Afr. Digest* 20 May 22 Coloureds and Indians would either have to accept their own homelands or else live in South Africa under the white 'baas'. **1983** *Frontline* May 35 They think the boere have lost, so they must vote Swapo because the U.N. is baas now and the U.N. is on Swapo's side.

5. One who, because of his superior strength, abilities or achievements, is able to command or demand deference from others.

1963 S. Cloete *Rags of Glory* 424 The mean old bitch thought herself so fine just because she owned a farm and he was only a bywoner. Ja, she would see who was baas now. **1970** *Forum* Vol.6 No.2, 47 Listen to this fool. Punish a kaffer and he cries out. They think they can take advantage of you, but he knows who's baas now. **1986** S. Sepamla *Third Generation* 53, I will treat you nice so long as you follow suit. Shit on my head and I'll show you who is the *baas*. **1988** 'K. De Boer' in *Frontline* Jan. 28 Naas is baas and Botha is best, was the cry of the winter of '87. But the end of the year established a new superstar in the Afrikaner galaxy. **1990** R. Stengel *January Sun* 82 The blacks regarded the Indians as *baases* — which the Indians usually insisted on being called — and sometimes wryly referred to them as 'black Afrikaners'.

II. Used as a form of address.

6. 'Master'. Often in the phr. ***my baas***. Cf. MENEER sense 4.

'My baas' is more deferential than 'baas' used alone. Cf. *my baasie* (see BAASIE sense 1 a).

1786 G. Forster tr. *A. Sparrman's Voy. to Cape of G.H.* 219 To this he answered as quick as thought, *Ja, Baas, (Yes, Master,)* got up in an instant. **1812** [see GROOT BAAS sense 1]. **1827** T. Philipps *Scenes & Occurrences* 39 The Caffer .. moved about the room with all the dignity of the Peruvian chief, uttering in an undertone 'baas' the Dutch for master. **1838** J.E. Alexander *Exped. into Int.* I. 13 'What say ye?' replied my man, without the affix of mynheer or baas, (master). 'Ye, to me!' cried the Boor. 'I'll teach you better manners. I'll get you punished.' **1875** C.B. Bisset *Sport & War* 75 A little tottie of my troop, named Hendrik Dragonder, caught hold of me by the pouch belt and pulled me back saying Vacht, bass, or Wait master. **1876** F. Boyle *Savage Life* 32 'Me your Kaffir, *baas*,' says he; 'give me *briefje* to Mr. Jardine after breakfast, and he pay me £2?' **1899** 'S. Erasmus' *Prinsloo* 28 His Kaffir, Sixpence, called him out and said, 'Baas, that is the great Scotty Smith, the horse thief — I know him well'. **1910** J. Buchan *Prester John* (1961) 38 She dropped me a curtsy. 'This is your room, Baas,' she said in very good English in reply to my question. **1929** D. Reitz *Commando* 109 To the right was another British column moving parallel with us, which caused our native Charley to remark, 'Baas, those English people don't know the road to Pretoria'. **1936** Williams & May *I Am Black* 27 The white man said suddenly: 'Do you want work?' Shabala turned back and stood respectfully before him. 'Yes, Baas,' he said. **1946** P. ABRAHAMS *Mine Boy* (1954) 72 Paddy shot out his hand. Xuma shook it. The grip was the grip of two strong men. 'Have you money.' 'No, baas.' 'Don't call me baas. Here.' **1958** A. FUGARD *Dimetos & Two Early Plays* (1977) 128 Over here it is '*Baas*'. Do you understand? Just: yes *baas*, no *baas*, please *baas*, thank you *baas* .. even when he kicks you on the backside. **1961** —— *Notebks* (1983) 21 Two coloured men came to the door. Trying to get flat No.4. 'That way,' I said. 'Thank you, baas. Thank you, my baas.' **1973** S. SMITH in *Sunday Times* 29 Apr. 13, I talked to quite a few Black people ... Most of them called me baas or master. I know they called me those things because I am White. **1979** A.P. BRINK *Dry White Season* 162 They laid our table, brought up our children, emptied our chamber pots, called us Baas and Miesies. We looked after them and valued their services, and taught them the Gospel. **1986** *Learn & Teach* No.5, 35 We are not trained. If that man made trouble at all, all I could say is, 'Yes baas, no baas, anything you want, baas'. **1987** S.A. BOTHA in *Frontline* Oct.-Nov. 13 No black warder is ever given charge over white prisoners. I've heard a black warder addressing white cons as 'baas'. **1994** R. MHLABA in *Weekly Mail & Guardian* 13 May 14 We are going to rule this country and make sure that no black man uses the word 'baas' to a white man. Those days are gone.

7. Used in the third person, as a deferential form of address. Cf. BAASIE sense 1 a.

1824 W.J. BURCHELL *Trav.* II. 178 Pushing open an old door nearly falling off its hinges, our page said; 'Here is where baas is to sleep.' **1912** F. BANCROFT *Veldt Dwellers* 48 The baas must come and eat; see, I have brought in the broiled chops from the fat buck the baas shot before sun-up yesterday. **1924** G. BAUMANN in Baumann & Bright *Lost Republic* (1940) 138 'Don't you remember me, Baas? I neglected my duty' (or 'I was cheeky to my Baas', or something or other) 'and you gave me a flogging.' **1933** W.H.S. BELL *Bygone Days* 237 If Baas only knew what a schelm place it is Baas would never have come here. **1956** D. JACOBSON *Dance in Sun* 37 'Baas', he said slowly, 'it's a letter to another missus that I want you to read to me'. He added, reminding me: 'The baas said that he would read the letter to me.' **1961** T. MATSHIKIZA *Choc. for my Wife* 85 Baas mistakes me for someone else, perhaps baas makes a mistake. **1971** J. MCCLURE *Steam Pig* (1973) 213 My baas is sure the wire he going by that bottom side?

III. Used with a surname, first name, or nickname.

8. As a title.

Sometimes used by one white person of another, when speaking to a Black or 'coloured' person.

1824 W.J. BURCHELL *Trav.* II. 94 Our Bushman .. pointed out a distant table-mountain, on the other side of which, they said, we should find the residence of a boor whom they called *Baas Jacob*. **1898** W.C. SCULLY *Vendetta* 32 Baas Gideon is my baas. But it was not an accident; baas Stephanus shot my baas with his own gun. **1920** R.Y. STORMBERG *Mrs Pieter de Bruyn* 65, I am Marianna's sister, mem, wot werks by Baas Pieter's mother. **1930** N. STEVENSON *Farmers of Lekkerbat* 262 'Hi, you!' he said to a native .. 'There is an old woman who lives in a hovel, near where the *baas* Eloff Loubser lived.' **1959** J. MEIRING *Candle in Wind* 6 It was that old Baas O'Brien again, Rosie screamed. Who did the old Baas think he was, she asked, refusing to give her credit again? **1964** J. BENNETT *Mr Fisherman* (1967) 24 'Johnson!' she called ... The cook-boy shuffled out .. 'You can lay the table. We won't wait for Baas Faraday.' **1978** *Weekend Post* 11 Mar. 3 The city's Deputy Mayor .. has proclaimed himself as 'Baas Ted' in a newspaper advertisement — and he has upset the coloured community. 'He has branded himself as a racist,' said .. Mr Peter Mopp. **1987** S. VAN DER MERWE in *New Nation* 23 Apr. 11 Baas Piet gave him promotion — to become his good farm induna. **1990** *Sunday Star* 23 Dec. (Review) 6 A black man in the audience asks whether he can call the Overvaal MP Comrade Koos. 'You can call me Baas Koos,' says the beefy Afrikaner.

9. As a form of address.

1961 T. MATSHIKIZA *Choc. for my Wife* 37 'Can you drink, jong, hey?' 'Yes, Baas Smitty.' 'You can't drink, you.' **1987** J. MATLOU in *Staffrider* Vol.6 No.4, 40 Matlou called his boss by the name 'Baas Dick! Baas Dick!' **1991** T. MAKAMBA in *E. Prov. Herald* 14 Mar. 5 This business about reform holds nothing for us, except that we could now say 'thank you baas De Klerk' to cause us to be able to legally buy back our land that was robbed from us.

Hence **baas** *v. trans.*, to call (someone) 'baas'; **baasdom** *n.*; **baashood** *n.*

1892 *The Jrnl* 12 Jan. 3 One night .. he saw a number of bovines in the field 'Klaas! ..' 'Ja, baas.' 'Take those cattle to the skit at once.' 'Maar, baas,-' 'Don't baas me, take them off.' **1930** L. BARNES *Caliban in Afr.* 194 Any danger of white political supremacy being jeopardised by native numbers is still remote ... The current alarms .. are the work of benighted politicians who suppose baashood to be best nourished on fear and hatred of the native. **1948** H.V. MORTON *In Search of S. Afr.* 4 If you are white, you are a 'baas,' and if you have been accustomed to servants in your youth, you feel again the desire, so firmly implanted in the nursery, to be worthy of baas-dom. **1994** C.J. DRIVER *In Water-margins* 19 'I said he couldn't clean my car if he "Baas"-ed me,' my brother said, *sotto voce*.

baas-boy /ˈbɑːsbɔɪ/ *n.* [BAAS + BOY sense 1 a.]

1. BOSS-BOY. Also *attrib.*

1953 LANHAM & MOPELI-PAULUS *Blanket Boy's Moon* 97 He was able to get work at Nourse Mines, and before long became a baas-boy underground. **1961** D. BEE *Children of Yesterday* 12 It was Madévaan, baas-boy or headman of the farm, Bhekuyise's father. **1979** M. MATSHOBA *Call Me Not a Man* 34 She was the 'head girl', if that is a suitable feminine gender for *induna* or 'baasboy'. **1982** *Staffrider* Vol.4 No.4, 14 At work not even one of his Africans understands these two official languages. Not even his baasboy, Chrissie. **1990** *Pace* May 15 Joe was dressed to kill in his famous 'izimbadada' (handmade sandals synonymous with hostel inmates), .. brown overalls, .. baas-boy cap and colourful earrings. **1993** [see MANTSHINGILANE].

2. A derogatory term for one who collaborates with the authorities, i.e. 'boy of the baases', a play on sense 1.

1987 *New Nation* 5 Mar. 11, I don't think that you consider yourself as black, or if you do you must be a kind of 'baasboy'. **1987** *Ibid.* 17 Dec. 9 We want to make it clear to 'baas-boy' Lucas M— that his 'rule' is illegitimate. **1990** *Pace* May 36 Sothos are stigmatised as thieves and police informers and 'baas-boys'. With these forces at work, tribal conflicts erupt.

baase var. BAAS.

baasie /ˈbɑːsi/ *n.* Also **basie**, and (formerly) **baasje**. [Afk. (earlier Du. *baasje*), 'little master', *baas* see BAAS + dim. suffix -IE.]

1. As a term of address.

a. Often in the phr. ***my baasie***. An affectionate, respectful, placatory, supplicatory, or ironic term of address; KLEINBAAS sense 3; KLEINBASIE sense 2. Cf. BAAS sense 6. See also NONNIE sense a.

Now often offensive to the one addressed. Used by some black and 'coloured' people to a white male, regardless of his age.

1899 G.H. RUSSELL *Under Sjambok* 259 But drink, Baasie, drink, and the koss will soon be ready. **1951** A. O'DOWD in B. Sachs *Herman Charles Bosman* (1971) 154 An aged, respectful voice sounded over Paul's shoulder. 'Hau! My basie, why you shoot little piccanin?' **1953** LANHAM & MOPELI-PAULUS *Blanket Boy's Moon* 254 Should the Police, or the Customs Guards come knocking on the lavatory door, call out with confidence, 'Coming, my Baasie'. **1954** H. NXUMALO in J. Crwys-Williams *S. Afr. Despatches* (1989) 314 He asked for my address and tribe. He then recited something very long to the white official who was writing in a big book opposite him ... The only words I recognised .. were my first name and 'five foot, baasie'. **1958** S. CLOETE *Mask* 91 You, young baasie, are like the tree. So will you live, with many resting under the shadows of your branches in old age. **1960** J. COPE *Tame Ox* 23 'Have you ever in your life seen a crack in the sky, Outa Flip?' he asked his companion. Without thinking, the old coloured man answered: 'Ja, my basie.' *Ibid.* 27 To them, the child was 'Basie' — the little Baas. They touched their foreheads to him; as servants they recognised his destiny. **1964** V. POHL *Dawn & After* 77 As I was leaving the house, old January said to me, 'Basie, you had better leave the gun at home, the scouts are about and may shoot you if they find you are armed'. *c*1964 B. ROSE in *New S. Afr. Writing* No.1, 65 Baasie, spare a penny, Spare a penny for our kwela As we dance upon the pavement. **1978** *Sunday Times* 5 Nov. (Mag. Sect.) 5 A black beggar sidled up to me and said: 'My basie, can you give me 20 cents for a loaf of bread?' **1979** M. MATSHOBA *Call Me Not a Man* 72 A youth in 'Lee' denim overalls, checkered shirt and perched white 'sporty' sun hat was teasing the whites: 'Hey, *baasie*!' Some of the stone faces showed signs of response. **1982** *E. Prov. Herald* 20 Sept. 8 Any farm child knows the subtle difference between baas and basie. Many a farmer's son worked hard to rid himself of the title of basie, often used to address him until well into middle age or perhaps until the 'oubaas', the farmer, died. **1985** P. SLABOLEPSZY *Sat. Night at Palace* 45 September (*to Vince*): Please, baas. I get into very big trouble. (*Turning to Forsie, the submissive approach*) Asseblief, my basie. I must lock up here. **1989** J. HOBBS *Thoughts in Makeshift Mortuary* 344 Ag, sorry, my basie ... Don't shoot, my basie. I could get full of holes, and then what?

b. In the third person, showing deference to the (young) person so addressed. Cf. BAAS sense 7.

1911 *The State* Dec. 642 (Pettman), See what Outa caught for the baasjes near the Klip Kop this afternoon, a nice little berg schilpad.

2. As a common noun. A white boy or young man; a son (or younger brother) of a man seen as master; KLEINBAAS sense 2; KLEINBASIE sense 1. Cf. BAAS senses 2 and 3.

1957 H.J. MAY in *S. Afr. P.E.N. Yrbk 1956–7* 51 He said, 'it is the Other Baasie'. That was how he used to refer to Johan. I was Klein Baasie, the little master and Johan was the other little master. **1973** J. COPE *Alley Cat* 25 'The basie hit you in the face.' 'That was nothing.' **1994** [see PASOP *v.*].

baasskap /ˈbɑːs(s)kap/ *n.* [Afk., *baas* see BAAS + suffix *-skap* -ship.] Domination, esp. by whites of other groups. Also *attrib.*

1935 *Cape Times* 8 Nov. 8 Let us focus our attention on the fact that the primary consideration is whether Afrikanerdom will reach its ultimate destiny of bossism (baasskap) in South Africa. **1946** *Forum* 9 Nov. 27 'Baasskap' .. means the perpetual subservience of one individual group to another. **1955** [see NAT *adj.* sense 2 a]. **1956** D. JACOBSON *Dance in Sun* 139 He has exposed the tenacity and duplicity of my own feelings of white baasskap — my own 'liberal' intolerances, my own assertion of where his place should be, and where mine. **1957** [see BANTU EDUCATION]. **1960** A.J. LUTHULI in H. Spottiswoode *S. Afr.: Rd Ahead* 112 We should never forget that much of our suffering under *baasskap apartheid* had its genesis at Union and during the lifetime of the first Union Government under General Botha. **1970** *Cape Times* 4 June, The Progressive Party believes merit should be the criterion by which men are judged; the three *baasskap* parties believe that criterion should be colour. **1977** *Sunday Times* 27 Feb. 15 One might have to change vocabulary and a few attitudes in public — from 'baasskap' to 'apartheid' to 'separate development'; from 'kaffir' to 'native' to 'Bantu' to 'black'. **1978** *Cape Times* 11 Apr. 6 'Non-baasskap areas' plan for SA. **1979** C. VAN DER MERWE in *Frontline* Dec. 17 Flytalers react to the term tsotsi-taal in more or less the same way one might expect P.W. Botha to react if you told him his policy was Baasskap, or even Apartheid. It's out, gone, yesteryear's name, something to be lived down. **1983** C.W. EGLIN in *Hansard* 18 May 7354 If the Government's entrenchment of one-party majoritarianism and White baasskap in

South Africa is disturbing and unacceptable, .. I find the Government's cynicism towards the Coloured and Indian people quite appalling. **1989** S. Johnson in *Weekly Mail* 1 Sept. 7 The CP's blend of *baasskap*, xenophobia, and concern for the 'little' white man is a powerful thing to behold in its natural habitat, which is undeniably expanding. **1990** *City Press* 11 Feb. 5 An inferior type of education, known as Bantu Education, and designed to relegate the Africans to a position of perpetual servitude in a baasskap society. **1992** N. Mandela in *Sunday Times* 8 Mar. 23 The age of lies, disinformation and CCB assassination squads has to be put behind us forever. There can be no revival of the hated pass laws, the Group Areas Act and the obnoxious signs on buses ... There can be no going back to baasskap.

Hence (*nonce*) **baasskap** *v. trans.*, **baasskapism** *n.*, **baasskapize** *v. trans.*, **baasskapper** *n.*, **baasskappy** *adj.*

1966 L.G. Berger *Where's Madam* 62, I get all baaskaapy [*sic*] and yell at him, 'Get up man while I'm talking to you. Get up, get up'. **1972** *Sunday Times* 10 Sept. (Mag. Sect.) 11 The majority of the electorate are people who heartily believe in baasskap ... Unless a radical change of outlook takes place the Nationalists will continue to rule. Their party is by no means the exclusive home of baasskappers. **1974** *Sunday Times* 8 Sept. 13 The dream of Afrikaner rule — of just over two-million Afrikaners baasskapping it over 20-million other South Africans — is only a temporary one. **1982** *Pace* Oct. 162 The campaign was aimed at the projection of the African personality and the rejection of 'baaskapism'. **1985** *Frontline* May 3 The Afrikaans ones are left free to baasskapise the black universities while the English-speakers fiddle around in an ivory limbo.

Baastaerd var. BASTARD.

baatj(i)e var. BAADJIE.

baba *n.*[1] var. BARBER.

‖**baba** /ˈbaːba/ *n.*[2] Also **bab'**, **babe**, **babo**. [Zulu, voc. case of *ubaba* father (pl. *obaba*).] Esp. among Zulu-speakers: 'father'; used when speaking to or of an older black male who is not necessarily related to the speaker. Cf. BAWO, NTATE, TATA.

Also used in Eng. in other African countries, derived from the equivalent word in other Sintu (Bantu) languages.

1. Used as a respectful term of address.

1836 A.F. Gardiner *Journey to Zoolu Country* 91 Bāba — (Father) — used in reply, as 'Yearbo Bāba,' 'Yes, Father.' The same term is also used by inferiors of all ranks to them above them. **1857** J. Shooter *Kafirs of Natal* 97 The normal government is patriarchal, a tribe being only a larger family, of which the chief may be regarded as father: '*baba*', my father, is in fact, one of the titles by which he is addressed. **1875** D. Leslie *Among Zulus* 80 He was greeted with a perfect storm of 'Bayete' and 'Yebo Baba.' **1899** B. Mitford *Weird of Deadly Hollow* 234 'Ewa 'Nkose — Hau! Baba' replied the woman, showing a splendid set of 'ivories' as she caught the piece of tobacco he flung at her. [*Note*] 'Baba', lit. 'father' — a Kaffir form of expressing thanks. **1941** Barrett & Benson in *Bantu World* 22 Feb. 5 Inside the bus he still shows the passenger 'Plenty more seats at the back baba,' all the time busy dodging the poor man by drawing out his wallet from the inside of his (the passenger's) coat. **1952** A.S. Massiye in *Drum* July 23 'Baba, the bride-price .. is .. killing me,' she cried. **1964** *Drum* Nov. 19 He kept muttering: 'Baba, Baba' to his proud father. **1973** J. Cope *Alley Cat* 38 'Baba!' the child whispered ... Her father went down on one knee. **1989** L. Maimane in *Staffrider* Vol.8 No.1, 23 'What's the matter, baba?' the nurse asked nonchalantly, tilting her head. **1990** *Sunday Times* 12 Aug. 7, I am agonising over how to address the man. Madiba, Comrade Nelson, Baba (Father), Chief, Com (short for comrade) — there is such a plethora of salutations in use here that plain Mr Mandela sounds out of place. **1994** on TV1, 31 Aug. (Honeytown), 'Guys, I want this concert to be real hot!' 'Right, baba.'

2. Used as a title, usu. before a name, occas. with a common noun.

1975 *Sunday Times* 2 Nov. (Mag. Sect.) 2 Baba Piet shouted at me and kicked me out of his office. As I was walking away he yelled: 'Hey tsotsi, do you want a job?' I have worked for him ever since. **1982** *Drum* Mar. 38 Cry Babies. Ingrates who just can't appreciate what everloving baba mlungu is doing for them. *c*1985 G. Hippert in *Eng. Alive '86* 55 It hurts baba to be confronted by a white in metallic blue — demanding identification. **1987** *Learn & Teach* No.5, 17, I knocked on the door for Bab'uMantshingelane to let me in. **1990** M. Melamu in *Lynx* 277 It was an all-weekend affair, and was the noisiest show on earth. Certainly, at Wanderers it relegated Baba Mkhize's Zionist sessions to second place. *Ibid.* 278 Baba Mkhize, who took umbrage at these activities of the devil, as he described them, when he was about God's work.

3. Used as a common noun, sometimes in the deferential mode in which the one being spoken to is addressed in the third person.

1976 A. Delius *Border* 266, I greeted her, and she said, 'Am I grown so old then, the Baba does not know me?' **1981** M. Mutloatse in *Staffrider* Vol.3 No.4, 41 'It can't be! Father! My long-lost Baba!' a man exclaimed. **1987** L. Beake *Strollers* 56 Inside the hut, her husband, Johnny's own Baba, snored gently. **1989** — *Cageful of Butterflies* 32 His own Baba still had many fine, white teeth.

4. In *comb.* **baba-ka-** [Zulu *-ka-* of], 'father of'; placed before the name of a child of the person addressed, and used respectfully.

1971 *Drum* Aug. 53 Hey baba-ka-Mbutana, the money is too much in the house. We must do something about it.

babala /bəˈbɑːlə/ *n.* [ad. S. Sotho *baballa* to provide with.] Any of several species of millet, esp. *Pennisetum glaneum*, *P. typhoideum*, or *P. americanum*. Also *attrib.*

1929 *Farming in S. Afr.* Oct. 324 (Swart), It is his opinion that December is quite early enough for even such varieties as 'Potchefstroom Paarl', and February for .. sorgum (soetriet), and the different varieties of manna, 'babala' for instance. **1956** *Off. Yrbk of Union 1954–5* (Bureau of Census & Statistics) 520 N'Yati or Babala (Cattail millet) is grown by the Natives as a grain, and is used for porridge meal as well as for malt for the brewing of kaffir-beer. **1968** *Farmer's Weekly* 3 Jan. 89 Babala seed. Machine-cleaned, free from all foreign matter, at R2.35 per 100lb. **1975** *Informant, Dohne (Eastern Cape)* Babala (known in the U.S. as Pearl millet, also called Cattail millet, Bullrush millet, candle millet and Penicillaria ..) is of unknown origin but has been grown in Asia and Africa since prehistoric times. **1988** R. Billet in *Farmer's Weekly* 1 Jan. 7 Bana, a vigorous-growing and drought-resistant grass (said to be a cross of babala and Napier), is grown on 85 ha, and Red Top Candy (a sorghum) and babala on 150 ha.

babalaas /ˈbabəlas, -lɑːs/ *n.* and *adj. Slang.* Also **babala(a)z**, **babalas**, **babalazi**, **babbala(a)s**, **babbela(a)s**, **babelaas**, **bubblejas**. [Afk., ad. Zulu *ibhabhalazi.*]

A. *n.*

a. A hangover; *noncount*, the unpleasant after-effects of drinking. Also *attrib.*, and *fig.* See also NADORS.

1946 in E. Partridge *Dict. of Underworld* (1950) 15 *Babbeljas.* A hangover: (after a debauch): South Africa. C.20. Letter of May 23, 1946; by 1940, low s. Afrikaans word; lit. 'bubble-arse'? **1959** L. Longmore *Dispossessed* 218 Regular customers are usually given a free drink on certain occasions in order to remove what is called *babalazi* (dulling after-effects of carousal or drinking bout). **1970** K.M. Brand *Informant, East London* I've got babelaas after the party last night. **1970** J.R. Bennett *Informant, Krugersdorp* I've got a terrible babalas from last night. **1973** *Cape Herald* 22 Sept. B1 The price of a bout at the Bacchanalian altar is still the groggy head, unsteady hand, furred tongue, rubber knees and the floating stomach — the age old 'babbelas'. **1977** [see DOP *v.*[2]]. **1980** M. Matshoba in M. Mutloatse *Forced Landing* 111 His hands shook violently when he lit and shielded the flame. 'Ei! Babalaz has me.' **1986** L. Sampson in *Style* May 103 Here at the bottom end of the market, among the rough and tumble of heavy drinkers, of Honey Gold and nips of brandy and skokiaan and Tassies, there is evidence everywhere of people whose lives have been ruined by drink. On Monday morning the atmosphere is fuzzy with babbelas. **1987** P.A. Page in *Frontline* May 34 This time the throbbing babalaas of unqualified democracy, even the obsequious hysteria seems a little fuzzy round the edges. **1991** P. Morris *Informant, Gouritsmond* Bubblejus: a hangover. **1992** on M-Net 9 Nov. (Egoli), I can't believe it! You girls have got babalaas. **1993** S. Dikeni in *House & Leisure* Nov. 12 Just as the wine helped them praise 'their' town, the babalaas blues woke them up penniless and foul-tempered. Woe if you asked them the following day, 'How's life in Victoria West?'

b. *comb.* **babalaasdop** /-ˌdɔp/ [Afk., *dop* a drink, see DOP *n.* sense 3 a.], a drink taken to help a hangover; 'the hair of the dog'; also called REGMAKER.

1952 'Skappie' in *Drum* Nov. 6 Sometimes you are invited for a special meal or your first drink on a Monday morning is 'on the house' — often known as a 'babalaas dop'. **1977** D. Muller *Whitey* 30 The child gravely nodded his head and raised an index finger to those who called his name on their way to the kitchen to buy their morning wine: the old babalaas-dop, the hair of the dog.

B. *adj.* Hung-over; suffering from the effects of a hangover.

1969 A. Fugard *Boesman & Lena* 14 Look at you! *Babalas!* .. from yesterday's wine. Yesterday you were drunk. One or the other. Your whole life. **1970** M.C. Duffy *Informant, Durban* He was completely babbelas after the party. **1973** *Ilanga* 10 Nov., For backache, Body pains and that Babbalas feeling! .. Pills wash out kidney and bladder. See it working — watch it come out blue. *a*1977 K.M.C. Motsisi in M. Mutloatse *Casey & Co.* (1978) 74 'You keep that babalaas bek of yours shut before I bash it in with this pot,' 'Ma Tladi had fumed at her husband. **1990** P. Cullinan in M. Leveson *Firetalk* 10, I used to call the roll on Monday mornings ... If I thought that a man was too shaky, babelaas — hungover, I would point at him and say 'Skokiaan', meaning that he had been at the local firewater. **1991** L. Howard *Informant, Port Elizabeth*, I had partaken too much of the local witblitz and woke up feeling baballas.

Hence **babalaased** *adj.*, hung-over, suffering from a hangover.

1979 N. Motana in *Staffrider* Vol.2 No.2, 47 Lesiba: (*Examines Fred*) You look babalaazed pal. Fred: Of course! Our host gave us a lot of wine. **1987** N. Mathiane in *Frontline* Oct.-Nov. 33 If the bootleggers had not been there, the kids would have run out of stock, slept, woken up babbelaased, and gone home.

Babaton var. BARBERTON sense 2.

babbie-shop /ˈba-, ˈbæbiʃɒp/ *n.* Also **babi-shop**, **bobby-shop**, and with initial capital. [Etym. unkn.; perh. ad. Hindi *babu* clerk + Eng. *shop*.] An offensive name for an Indian trader's store or business.

1976 H. Lawrence in *Sunday Times* 21 Nov. (Extra) 2 Indian businessmen in Cape Town are up in arms ... In his interview, Mr M— used the term 'babbie-shop' which is regarded by Indian people in the same manner as Coloured people regard the term 'hotnot'. **1979** *Voice* 4 Mar. 7 The life to be seen in the myriad little streets of the area .. teenagers standing on the corner invariably near a Babi-shop singing the latest songs. **1987** P. Jooste in *Fair Lady* 25 Nov. 142 The group of Gus-Seep's acquaintances, known to us as the Rough Element, took up their loud game of dominoes on the pavement outside the bobbyshop.

babe var. BABA *n.*[2]

Baberton var. BARBERTON sense 2.

babiaan var. BAVIAAN.

babiaanbout var. BOBBEJAANBOUD.

babiaantj(i)e var. BOBBEJAANTJIE.

babiaan-touw var. BAVIAAN'S TOUW.

Babiana /bæbɪ'ɑːnə, babɪ-/ *n.* Also with small initial. [See quot. 1936.] BOBBEJAANTJIE. Also *attrib.*

1821 C.I. LATROBE *Jrnl of Visit* Glossary, *Bavians-blom*, Is a name given to various species of Babianas. **1835** *Penny Cyclopaedia* III. 226 Those strange Babianas which one so seldom sees in their beauty in our English gardens. **1887** J.F. SEWELL *Private Diary* (1983) 76, I took out some Babiana bulbs with my fork. **1906** B. STONEMAN *Plants & their Ways* 197 *Babiana*, Flowers usually regular, frequently violet, sometimes milk-white or sulphur-yellow. **1936** E.C. LLEWELLYN *Influence of Low Dutch* 166 *Babiana* (1835), a genus of bulbo-tuberous Iridaceae with handsome purple, yellow, or scarlet flowers; the modern Latin name is an adaptation of the Afrik. *babianer*, i.e. baboon plants, so named because their tubers are eaten by baboons. **1970** M.R. LEVYNS in *Std Encycl. of Sn Afr.* I. 628 *Babiana, Bobbejaantjie*, Sixty species of this flower of the family *Iridaceae* are native to South Africa. **1991** D.M. MOORE *Garden Earth* 195 Dwarf, drought-tolerant shrubs .. are common. So too are plants with underground storage organs (bulbs, corms and rhizomes) such as *Haemanthus, Oxalis* and *Babiana* (named after the Afrikaans term for the baboon, *bobbejaan*, which digs up the corms for food).

babiantje var. BOBBEJAANTJIE.

babian touw var. BAVIAAN'S TOUW.

babi-shop var. BABBIE-SHOP.

babo var. BABA *n.*²

baboeti(e) var. BOBOTIE.

baboon rock *n. phr.* Rocky, non-arable land.

1936 *Cambridge Hist. of Brit. Empire* VIII. 815 Grout's probably too conservative estimate of 50 000 as the native population of the three reserves, Inanda, Umvoti and Umlazi, gave nevertheless a density of 55 persons per square mile, or $11\frac{1}{2}$ acres of mixed arable land and 'baboon rock' per individual. **1941** C.W. DE KIEWIET *Hist. of S. Afr.* 71 Although Natal had its share of 'baboon rock' and barren soil, the proportion of good land was higher than in the Cape Colony. **1965** *Informant, George* No wonder she can't make a living growing potatoes: 90% of that farm is baboon rock. **1990** T. WILD *Informant, Grahamstown* The scenery [in Israel] .. has been very much like the Transvaal except for all the olive trees and stretches of baboon rock for 500 m – $1\frac{1}{2}$ km at a time.

baboon spider *n. phr.* [Prob. tr. S. Afr. Du. *baviaan spinnekop*; see quots 1905 and 1968.] Any of several large, hairy, burrowing spiders of the Theraphosidae, including the genera *Harpactira, Ceratogyrus, Pterinochilus*, and *Harpactirella*; BAVIAAN SPIDER; BAVIAAN SPINNEKOP. Also *attrib.*, and (occas.) *fig.*

1905 W.F. PURCELL in Flint & Gilchrist *Science in S. Afr.* 179 The members of the principal genus, *Harpactera*, are locally known as 'Baviaan Spinnekoppen' (Baboon spiders), either because baboons are supposed to be fond of them or on account of the resemblance of the velvet-padded feet to the fingers of a monkey. **1936** C. BIRKBY *Thirstland Treks* 317 An old hunter once told me the secret of how Bushman poison is made .. how they caught big 'baboon spiders', pounded them .. then spread the paste out to lie for three nights in the light of the full moon the while they muttered weird incantations over it. **1963** S.H. SKAIFE *Naturalist Remembers* 76 A large black baboon spider, .. a big hairy brute with fangs nearly a quarter of an inch long and a spread of legs that would almost cover the palm of the hand. *Ibid.* 77 The baboon spider .. had taken refuge in the slipper and bit me when my toe squeezed it ... The pain passed off very quickly; there was no swelling, and within a quarter of an hour all effects of the bite had disappeared. **1968** J.H. YATES *Spiders of Sn Afr.* 155 The large female .. was thickly covered with soft, dark-grey hair and it is this feature, together with the smooth grey padding on the under surface of the legs – a padding similar to that on the fingers of a baboon – that has given this species its name. **1973** *Cape Times* 27 Jan. (Weekend Mag.), The great baboon spider .. can inflict a painful bite, but will never do so unprovoked. **1979** J. LEDGER *S.H. Skaife's Afr. Insect Life* 330 The formidable baboon spider, black and hairy, with red round the mouth and with a stout body about an inch and a half long. **1980** *Sunday Times* 26 Oct. (Mag. Sect.) 1 There are no squeals of revulsion when .. Marc or .. Paul present their mother with a large hairy baboon spider. She's far more likely to say: 'Ooh give it to me! What a beautiful Ceratogyrus. Nearly as big as my hand!' **1982** A.P. BRINK *Chain of Voices* 399 Only Adonis, shifty old baboon-spider that he was, gave us trouble. **1987** *E. Prov. Herald* 11 Apr. 5 'Flatties' are not to be confused with baboon spiders, which only occasionally wander indoors. They are those heavy-bodied, flesh-brown jobs with long, angular legs ... The 'baboons' are favourite victims of large wasps which paralyse them and hide them in shallow holes. **1987** G. NEWLANDS *Spiders & Scorpions*, Very little is known about baboon spider venoms and their natural history.

babooti(e), babot(e)e, babotie varr. BOBOTIE.

baby *n. hist. Diamond-mining.* Also with initial capital. [See quot. 1886.] A machine used for sifting diamondiferous gravel on diamond diggings. Also *attrib.*

1870 *E. Prov. Herald* 2 Sept., Swinging sieves, called 'babies' are now in use on the fields. **1886** J. NOBLE *Cape of G.H.: Off. Handbk* 219 The invention of the 'baby' derives its name neither from its association with the 'cradle,' nor from its swinging motion suggestive of infancy, but from its inventor, an American named Babe who was digging at the river about 1870. **1887** J.W. MATTHEWS *Incwadi Yami* 175 Third in order came the 'baby' ... Three screens, somewhat similar to those used by bricklayers in making mortar, were suspended by reins (leather thongs) almost horizontally to four posts, and were kept in agitation by hand, the reins of course giving full play for 'pulsation'. **1891** R. SMITH *Great Gold Lands* 70 After the excavation has been made with pick and shovel, the boulders and large stones are thrown aside, and the gravel secured is taken to a sifting machine called a 'baby'. This consists of an oblong sieve, swinging by four thongs or chains from four upright poles, and inclined slightly, so that the pebbles may roll over it. **1922** S.G. MILLIN *Adam's Rest* 96 There was the cost of working materials – sieves, buckets, shovels, picks, a windlass, a 'baby' (a cradle-like affair for separating sand from pebbles) – nothing very elaborate. **1931** G. BEET *Grand Old Days* 28 The inventor of the South African type of cradle, or 'baby' was .. J.L. Babe. Of him it used to be jocularly remarked that he was the only Babe who had ever rocked his own cradle. **1948** H.V. MORTON *In Search of S. Afr.* 275 Earth and gravel from the claim was first thrown into a wooden frame with swing rockers fitted with meshes of varying sizes. As a native rocked the frame, which is called the 'baby', a stream of water helped to break up the deposit as it was shaken through the grid. **1950** E. ROSENTHAL *Here Are Diamonds* 196 The word 'Baby' .. Pettman defines as 'a sifting machine used on the Vaal River diamond diggings in the process known as dry-sorting'. **1968** J.T. MCNISH *Rd to Eldorado* 123 A Californian gold digger in the person of J.L. Babe found his way to the diamond fields of South Africa ... His invention of the Baby sifting appliance was an improvement of the first three-tier sieves in use. **1970** *Std Encycl. of Sn Afr.* II. 628 The 'baby', although primitive in design, nevertheless proved so satisfactory that it became popular at the river diggings, where it is still used. **1980** A.J. BLIGNAUT *Dead End Rd* 69 Rubble was bouncing with a clatter off the zinc ends of sieves swaying in wooden frames. They called them dummies and babies.

baby *v. trans. Diamond-mining.* [fr. prec.] To sift (diamondiferous gravel) in a swinging sifting machine known as a baby. Usu. *passive.*

1886 J. NOBLE *Cape of G.H.: Off. Handbk* 219 The average quantity of maiden ground that one man can excavate per day is about one and a half loads of rough gravel and sand, which after being 'babied,' yield half a load of pebbles to be washed. **1913** C. PETTMAN *Africanderisms* 41 Ground which had been sifted by the above machine [*sc.* the baby] was said to have been 'babied'. **1945** N. DEVITT *People & Places* 142 The sifting machine most of them had brought with them for use on the dry diggings .. was called 'baby'; they spoke of the ground having been 'babied'. **1968** J.T. MCNISH *Rd to Eldorado* 144 One and a half loads of rough gravel and sand, which, after being 'babied' yielded only half a load of gravel fit to be washed.

Hence **babied** *ppl adj.*

1919 M.M. STEYN *Diary* 148 We threw the screened or 'babied' gravel into the cradle where the stuff was rocked whilst being washed.

bacbacery var. BOKMAKIERIE.

Bac(c)a var. BHACA.

Bachapin var. BATLHAPING.

bachelor quarters *n. phr.* Also **bachelors' quarters**. HOSTEL sense 1 a.

1963 A.M. LOUW *20 Days* 114 Enog .. walked swiftly in the direction of the bachelors' quarters where lived the amasoka – the wifeless ones, who either had no wife, or had not the permission to bring a wife from the homelands to live in Cape Town. **1970** *Cape Times* 5 June, Black 'labour force units' are tolerated in urban 'bachelor quarters' while their 'superfluous appendages' are removed from their 'dwelling units' and 'repatriated' to 'resettlement camps'. **1971** *Rand Daily Mail* 16 Feb., It was a terrible choice either to live in with his family without work-facilities or live in bachelors' quarters and have the security of working for people he knew. **1979** *E. Prov. Herald* 16 Feb. (Suppl.) 7 Hundreds of people were occupying bachelor quarters illegally, and these men were not only staying there with their wives and children but were not paying any rent. **1980** E. JOUBERT *Poppie Nongena* 187 What will become of you when tata-ka Bonsile has to move to the bachelor quarters and you have no roof over your heads? **1987** *Frontline* Feb. 13 He lived in the bachelor quarters at PE's Kwazakele township ... The undiluted squalor of the ablution blocks, the desperate attempts at privacy by men of all ages shoved into a dormitory-like existence, the single, bare light bulb, grey walls, cement floors .. this is the ghetto to beat all ghettoes.

Bachuana pl. form of BECHUANA.

backbakiri var. BOKMAKIERIE.

Backlokwa, -loqua varr. TLOKWA.

backveld /'bækfelt, -fɛlt/ *adj.* and *n.* Also **backveldt**. [Part. tr. Afk. *agterveld*, see AGTERVELD.]

A. *adj.* Of or pertaining to (isolated) rural communities; hence, unsophisticated, rough. Often in the collocation ***backveld Boer*** *derog.*, an unsophisticated rural Afrikaans-speaking person. Cf. PLATTELAND *adj.*

[**1827** G. THOMPSON *Trav.* II. 115 That the back-country boors of former times were many of them as savage, indolent, and unprincipled as Mr. Barrow has described, cannot be questioned.] **1900** A.C. DOYLE *Great Boer War* (1902) 111 The British had inflated and sent up a balloon, to the amazement of the back-veldt Boers. **1902** E. WALLACE in J. Crwys-Williams *S. Afr. Despatches* (1989) 194 The malcontents were confident of the success of the Republican forces and, at the worst, of European intervention, and so they played that waiting game which so happily fits the back-veldt indolent. **1905** *Spectator* (U.K.) 7 Jan. 5 We do not see why the low European or the back-veld Dutchman should be given a right to a decision on matters which they do not profess to understand. **1915** D. FAIRBRIDGE *Torch Bearer* 295 'It is incomprehensible,' he went on, 'that there should be any back-veld Boer so credulous as to believe that Germany would leave South Africa a Boer Republic if she became the dominant power.' **1931** G. BEET *Grand Old*

Days 84 There was naturally a good sprinkling of backveld Boers on the Diamond Fields at this time, and their ways were often artless and childlike. **1937** [see *bond* v. (BOND *n.*[1])]. **1943** I. FRACK *S. Afr. Doctor* 106 Notwithstanding these obvious disadvantages of making Afrikaans the sole objective of the curriculum, the tendency continues in our backveld and backward schools. **1944** [see MÔRE sense 2]. **1957** D. GRINNELL-MILNE *Baden-Powell at Mafeking* 63 Whilst a single agent .. might have kept his news secret, a score or more spreading rumours over the Marico had ensured that even the most ignorant back-veld Boer knew about the mines. **1978** A.P. BRINK *Rumours of Rain* 313 In their previous post in a very small backveld congregation, people had objected to the idea of a *dominee* taking part in something as worldly as sport, so he'd had to give it up. **1982** *E. Prov. Herald* 19 Apr. 7 Backveld Americans are every bit as quick at spotting smut in literature as South Africans, but 'Romeo and Juliet' – censored in some Transvaal country schools according to a Herald report – has so far escaped them. **1985** [see TAKHAAR]. **1986** *Pretoria News* 24 Sept. 13 Bosman is probably best known for his Marico stories, in which Oom Schalk Lourens evokes the image of the so-called 'backveld Boer' with matchless humour and compassion. **1991** F.G. BUTLER *Local Habitation* 105 The results of the 1948 election and the government which the backveld vote put into power did give me some cause for reflection.

B. *n.* Often with initial capital.

a. Rural areas, often considered unsophisticated or unprogressive because remote from towns and their influence; AGTERVELD; GOPSE sense 1 a; cf. BUNDU sense 1. See also PLATTELAND *n.* sense a, VELD sense 4.

1911 *E. London Dispatch* 8 Nov. 6 (Pettman), In what way will a few visitors from the *back veld* equip the boys and girls for the battle of life. **1913** V.R. MARKHAM *S. Afr. Scene* 31 The smoke of an approaching locomotive twice or thrice a week is a real event in the Back Veld, the smaller Dorps turning out in force at the wayside stations. **1920** [see DORP sense a]. **1925** L.D. FLEMMING *Crop of Chaff* 58 Wish I could collect and keep all the food offered me in one day here and stow it away in my pantry on the backveld. **1928** N. STEVENSON *Afr. Harvest* 13 He was backveld born and backveld bred, and he did not alter his ideas easily. *c*1936 *S. & E. Afr. Yr Bk & Guide* 226 The joint findings of the Commission suggest measures to lessen the isolation of the back-veld and to afford increased and improved instruction in agriculture among the men and in home-making among the women. **1940** F.B. YOUNG *City of Gold* 239 Pretoria might still be more English than the English, but the back-veld was Dutch to the marrow. **1946** T. MACDONALD *Ouma Smuts* 50 She knew the tide of racial feeling in the rural areas, in the backveld where life was slow like the pace of an ox. **1958** A. JACKSON *Trader on Veld* 28 During my 12 years' sojourn in the Backveld, I learnt not only to speak but to write the 'Taal' fluently. **1960** C. HOOPER *Brief Authority* 198 We found it a trifle confusing; but nobody else did. Complex things can become very simple in the backveld. **1989** B. GODBOLD Autobiography. 84 There were no nurses, but only a couple of so-called medical orderlies, men of low-grade intelligence from the backveld. **1991** F.G. BUTLER *Local Habitation* 105 Perhaps Babylon is better than backveld.

b. The people inhabiting remote rural areas.

1949 C. BULLOCK *Rina* 32 He looked at me gloomily with a professional air like the quack doctor who frightened half the backveld into being vaccinated with tinned milk.

Hence **backvelder** /-ˌfeldə(r)/ *n.*, one from the backveld; a rustic or unsophisticated person; TAKHAAR sense b. Cf. *plattelander* (see PLATTELAND).

1911 *E. London Daily Dispatch* 28 Oct. 3 (Pettman), Mr. -'s work will have considerable value as tending .. to present the rugged *backvelder* in his true colours. *c*1911 S. PLAYNE *Cape Col.* 460 *Ons Land* .. also has a considerable amount of information for farmers in each issue, and its advent is eagerly hailed by the out-of-the-way backvelders. **1927** *Workers' Herald* 17 May 5 Even yet there were some back-velders in this country who have never seen a bicycle or a town larger than Volksrust. **1930** L. BARNES *Caliban in Afr.* 46 The backvelder has for many years been going through an elaborate system of tuition, the object of which was to impress indelibly upon him that the British are the root of all offence. **1934** N. DEVITT *Mem. of Magistrate* 29, I came much in contact with the people whom the Rand papers of late years call 'Backvelders'. The use of this word is probably not intended offensively, but it to my mind indicates a superiority complex on the part of the users which in my opinion is misplaced. **1944** 'TWEDE IN BEVEL' *Piet Kolonel* 50 Did we from henceforth learn our manners, poor ignorant backvelders that we were? **1955** W. ILLSLEY *Wagon on Fire* 26 When Katrina Deventer, a fair wisp of charm and culture, had announced that she was leaving Cape Town with all its attractions, for marriage with the uncouth backvelder, Frikkie van der Byl, her friends reckoned that she had taken leave of her senses. **1964** J. MEINTJES *Manor House* 119 These backvelders have today largely disappeared, but at that time one still found numbers of them: naive, primitive, uneducated and in some cases even idiots. **1974** A.P. BRINK *Looking on Darkness* 122 With the handful of other Coloured and Indian students I occasionally discussed my problems, but they'd all grown up in cities and regarded me, not without some condescension, as a backvelder. **1985** *E. Prov. Herald* 22 July 8 I'm a backvelder, a plattelander, a country bumpkin if you like. **1991** F.G. BUTLER *Local Habitation* 105 A backvelder born, like myself, often has a stubborn belief that God made the country and man made the town.

Bacloqua var. TLOKWA.

Bacquains var. BAKWENA.

BAD /bæd, bi(:) eɪ 'di:/ *n. hist.* Also **B.A.D.** Acronym formed on the initial letters of (Department of) *Bantu Administration and Development*, an earlier name for the Department of Co-operation and Development (see CO-OPERATION AND DEVELOPMENT). Also *attrib.*

1968 J. LELYVELD in Cole & Flaherty *House of Bondage* 12 An African has to be in his grave for his right to remain in the 'white area' to be beyond challenge. In Johannesburg this existential license is dispensed on Market Street in Rooms 45 and 46 of the Bantu Affairs Department (called BAD, for short). **1968** *Post* 4 Feb. 9 What the B.A.D. thinks 'reasonable' is not what the widows think of this arrangement. **1971** *Post* 23 May 7 So annoyed was BAD Minister M.C. Botha, he accused Mrs. Suzman of lying. **1973** *Drum* 22 Jan. 2 In all walks of life there are the goodies and the BADdies. We've had more than our fair share of the BADdies. **1974** *Drum* 8 Aug. 11 Mr Ndaba switched to a new job – as an information officer for BAD. Then he left the country. **1977** J. SIKAKANE *Window on Soweto* 32 Traders are hounded by BAD officials to move to the homelands.

bad friends *pl. n. phr.* [Calque formed on Afk. *kwaaivriende* (see KWAAI sense 1 b).] Enemies; *kwaai-vriende*, see KWAAI sense 1 b.

1952 J. TUNCE in *Drum* Feb. 23 We became bad friends with my mother-in-law. She would not allow me in her house. **1972** Radio South Africa 9 Mar., At such moments you forget you're bad friends. They are bad friends with me. **1987** C. NAIDOO in *Sunday Times* 12 Apr. 21 She refused to be named, saying Tzaneen was too small to make bad friends. **1987** *Informant, Grahamstown*, I don't know why she wants to be bad friends with me. I've got nothing against her.

‖**badimo** /ba'di:mu/ *pl. n.* Also **badzimo, barimo**, and with initial capital. [Sotho, gods, ancestral spirits (sing. *modimo*, see MODIMO).] Esp. among Sotho-speakers: ancestral spirits. See also ITONGO, MODIMO.

Quot. 1857 is in the context of a people living to the north of South Africa.

[**1857** D. LIVINGSTONE *Missionary Trav.* 316 He had just come from attending the funeral of one of his people, and found that the great amount of drum-beating that takes place on these occasions was with the idea that the Barimo, or spirits, could be drummed to sleep. *Ibid.* 331 One of my men of that tribe, on experiencing headache, said, with a sad and thoughtful countenance, 'My father is scolding me because I do not give him any of the food I eat.' I asked where his father was. 'Among the Barimo,' was the reply.] **1905** W.H. TOOKE in Flint & Gilchrist *Science in S. Afr.* 92 The be-Chuana .. believe in a chief spirit, Morimo, powerful and malicious, but which .. seems to bear no ancestral relation to his worshipper. They also, like the Kafirs, believe in the spirits of the dead ba-rimo, with which the priests or senyaka have intercourse. **1960** C. HOOPER *Brief Authority* 123, I used to dream of the voices of the badimo, and winding tracks among the hills taking me on journeys. **1962** M. BRANDEL-SYRIER *Black Woman* 132 A very important Church minister .. goes to the City Hall and places a wreath there. Isn't he thinking of his ancestors? But if I slaughter a goat to my Badimo, I am excommunicated. **1976** S. FUGARD *Rite of Passage* 13 At night the *badimo*, the spirits of the ancestors, came and mocked. They laughed at the white man and his stupidity. **1981** M. MUTLOATSE in *Staffrider* Vol.3 No.4, 42 The gusty sounds of mhalamhala were running through the blood vessels of the comrades ... It was just no coincidence: it had been planned, long planned by the badzimo. **1988** M. MANYANYE in *Pace* May 22 We know what we are worshipping because we know that our ancestors, whom we call 'badimo' are mediators between us and our God, whom we call 'Modimo'. We know 'Badimo', you know 'Jesus'.

badja var. BHAJIA.

badjie var. BAADJIE.

bafana pl. form of UMFAAN.

bafaro /bə'fɑ:rəʊ, ba-/ *n. obsolescent.* Also **pufaro.** [Unkn.] The wreckfish *Polyprion americanus* of the Polyprionidae.

In Smith and Heemstra's *Smiths' Sea Fishes* (1986), the name 'wreckfish' is used for this species and for the family to which it belongs.

1902 J.D.F. GILCHRIST in *Trans. of S. Afr. Philological Soc.* XI. iv. 224 (Pettman), We have hitherto considered names for which derivations can be suggested ... There are a few, however, for which no plausible derivation can be discovered. These are bafaro, assous, zeverrim. **1913** C. PETTMAN *Africanderisms* 42 *Bafaro*, The Cape Peninsula name for *Polyprion prognathus*. **1930** C.L. BIDEN *Sea-Angling Fishes* 98 The almost total disappearance of the pufaro (*Polyprion americanum*) and baardman (*Umbrina capensis*) from False Bay. **1951** [see SANCORD]. **1972** BEETON & DORNER in *Eng. Usage in Sn Afr.* Vol.3 No.2, 13 *Bafaro*, Black Bess, stone bass, wreck fish: type of rock-cod, found over a wide ocean area, in deep water fr the Cape to Natal, often in the neighbourhood of wrecks; grows to 2m.

bafo pl. form of MFO.

bafok var. BEFOK.

Bafokeng pl. form of MOFOKENG.

bafowethu pl. form of MFOWETHU.

bafta /'bæftə/ *n. hist.* [Eng. (usu. as *baft*), prob. ad. Pers. *baft* woven, wrought.] A coarse, cheap fabric, usu. of cotton.

Orig. of oriental manufacture, but later made in Britain for export, esp. to Africa.

Also *Indian Eng.*

1806 [see BOSLEMMER]. **1831** J. COLLETT Diary. I. 61, 6 lb. Sugar & 16 Ell Bafta 5/4. **1856** *Cape of G.H. Almanac & Annual Register* 61 Sheetings, Skirtings white and brown Punjums, white and brown Baftas. **1862** 'A LADY' *Life at Cape* (1963) 82 They .. sedulously avoid any allusion to business .. because they don't want to bore us about punjums and baftas, and the fall in wool and feathers. **1920** K.M. JEFFREYS tr. *Memorandum of Commissary J.A. de Mist* 244 Goods requisitioned from India .. : slaves, spices, pepper, coffee, tea, porcelain, .. cotton thread, blue baftas, .. ginghams, and all sorts of coarse calicoes. **1954** M. KUTTEL *Quadrilles & Konfyt* 33 The tailor .. was kept busy making two suits a year of blue 'Baftas' for each slave. **c1963** B.C. TAIT *Durban Story* 50 The ceiling was made of bafta — a strong calico which, alas! in time sagged in the centre and became the playground of rats and mice. **1972** A.A. TELFORD *Yesterday's Dress* 18 Most of the materials are unfamiliar to us, for they represent textiles produced on Eastern looms. Names like 'sampouris', 'bafta', 'bethelis' and 'taffacela' abound in the lists of the day.

Bafuking pl. form of MOFOKENG.

bafundisi pl. form of UMFUNDISI.

Bafurutse pl. form of HURUTSHE.

bag *n.* [Eng.] An official unit of measurement (usu. of grain), representing 70 kg (and formerly 200 lb). See also POCKET.

Crop yields are often calculated in bags per morgen.

a1930 G. BAUMANN in Baumann & Bright *Lost Republic* (1940) 95 Mealies were 2s.6d. a bag. **1930** [see LAND sense 1]. **1937** *Handbk for Farmers* (Dept of Agric. & Forestry) 667 The proportion of the world's crop of maize produced in South Africa is small ... The mean yield per morgen is a little less than 5 bags in South Africa. **1942** *Off. Yrbk 1941* (Union Office of Census & Statistics) 982 Weights prescribed for a 'Standard Bag' of Agricultural Products ... Mealie rice or maize grit .. 190 lb. **1958** [see DHAL]. **1972** *Farmer's Weekly* 21 Apr. 12 On lands which were specially treated during the experiment we expect crops in excess of 4500 kg/ha (50 bags a morgen). **1975** *Economist Measurement Guide* 71 Bag or muid: .. Rhodesia and South Africa .. Wheat, rye, maize, millet and sorghum = 200 lb = 90.718 kg. Barley and oats = 150 lb = 68.039 kg. **1987** *Frontline* Feb. 33 Farm labourers .. were paid next to nothing (some farmers actually paid a grown man with children R20 a month — and a bag of mealie meal).

Bagatla pl. form of KGATLA.

bagel /ˈbeɪg(ə)l/ *n.* Also **beigel, beygl.** [Special sense of general Eng. *bagel,* fr. Yiddish *beygl,* a hard, ring-shaped bread-roll.] A (usu. derogatory) nickname given to a young Jewish man of the moneyed class who affects a distinctive nasal mode of speech and flashy dress. Cf. KUGEL. Also attrib.

[**1957** D. JACOBSON *Price of Diamonds* 51 'Not a gentleman at all,' he called Gottlieb, and a *beigel,* a traitor.] **1981** J. MULLINS in *Fair Lady* 2 Dec., A male kugel is called a bagel ... [He] gets his name from a round piece of dough with a space in the middle. He originates in Johannesburg and as soon as he is mobile he migrates to 1st Beach, Clifton ... Bagels are round as the result of too much spoonfeeding, too many trips to the fridge, and living too near to a delicatessen. **1984** *Argus* 10 July 15 Further on a kugel and her bagel whined past. 'Lissen, doll.' **1986** *Style* June 61 No bagel this one so he avoids the lion's tooth slung on a gold chain resting on a hairy chest. **1988** *Sunday Times* 3 Apr. (Mag. Sect.) 42 'Don't worry,' he said, seeing her concern. 'I can tell you're going to take to this like a kugel to a bagel.' **1989** M. BRAND in *Fair Lady* 25 Oct. 93 These buzz words have gone decidedly off. You run the risk of being mega-unfash if you use them .. *Amazing. Bagel. Camp .. Kugel* (borderline case) [etc.].

bagger /ˈbægə, ˈbɑːgə/ *n.* ?obs. Also **baager, bagre, barga, barger, begger, pagger,** and with initial capital. [Prob. fr. L. *pagrus* bream, but see quot. 1731.]

1. Any of several marine and estuarine fish species: BARBEL sense 2.

1731 G. MEDLEY tr. *P. Kolb's Present State of Cape of G.H.* II. 210 'Tis probable, that *Pagger* is a Derivative from the Latin Word *Paco* .. for there is, on the Back of it, near the Head, a Sort of Horn or Prickle, of a poisonous Nature. **1801** J. BARROW *Trav.* I. 31 The *Bagre*, a second species of *Silurus*, commonly caught in the bay, is considered as poisonous. **1802** TRUTER & SOMERVILLE in G.M. Theal *Rec. of Cape Col.* (1899) IV. 398 We caught a fish in the river of about 3 feet 8 inches large, a large flat head somewhat like the bagger, and of a taste like the eel. **1804** R. PERCIVAL *Acct of Cape of G.H.* 44 The bagre, a very bad species of fish, and supposed to be of a poisonous quality. [**1906** J.G. SCHEUCHZER tr. *E. Kaempfer's Hist. of Japan* I. 84 Four fishermen came .. with Hayes and Beggers on board of us ... We bought none but dismissed them.] **1913** C. PETTMAN *Africanderisms* 42 *Bagger* or *Barger, Galeichthys folicepts.* The appearance of this fish creates a prejudice against it; it is, however, of a delicate eel-like flavour. **1949** [see BARBEL sense 2]. **1951** L.G. GREEN *Grow Lovely* 89 The bagger, or barbel .. tasted to Pappe like eel and deserved consideration in spite of its ugly appearance. **1967** E. ROSENTHAL *Encycl. of Sn Afr.* 100 *Cape Barger* or *Sea Barbel,* .. Common all round the South African coast. **1968** J.L.B. SMITH *High Tide* 35 There was the Bagger (barbel) much dreaded because it has a poisonous spine on the back of its head ... One of the Governor's slaves was stabbed in the hand while netting it at night.

2. Any of several freshwater fish species: BARBEL sense 3. Occas. with a distinguishing epithet, as **platkop bagger** /ˈplatkɔp-/ [Afk., *plat* flat + *kop* head], **rock bagger.**

1835 A. SMITH *Diary* (1940) II. 160 The bagre the same as that found in the Orange River inhabits the Marique; one, moderately large, caught today. **1878** T.J. LUCAS *Camp Life & Sport* 197 Perhaps one's capture would be .. a huge 'Barga' (evidently a Silurus), with its monstrous head adorned with bristling feelers .. running up to twelve or fourteen pounds in weight. **1893** *Trans. of S. Afr. Phil. Soc.* VIII. i. p.xcviii, It is universally known as the 'Rock baager', because, unlike its much larger, mud-loving congener, it chiefly haunts rocky spots. **1967** E. ROSENTHAL *Encycl. of Sn Afr.* 100 *Mud-barbel* or *Platkop Barger,* The best-known South African river species north of Cape.

Baharootzi(e), Baharutse, Baharutsi(e), Baharutzi, Bahuruts(h)e, Bahurutsi, Bahurutze pl. forms of HURUTSHE.

‖**baie** /ˈbaɪə/ *adj.* and *adv.* Also **baaija, baaije, baing, ba'je, banja, banje, banya, beyae, bonya, bye.** [Afk., earlier S. Afr. Du. *banje,* fr. Malay *banyak* many, much, plenty.]

A. *adj.* Much, many.

1815 J. CAMPBELL *Trav. in S. Afr.* 120 He offered to bring the water of two neighbouring fountains to water his ground; but all his arguments made no impression on the lazy boor, who said it was *bye* (or superfluous) trouble. **1850** J.D. LEWINS *Diary.* 15 Aug., Watering every thing. Lovely day. Tseu says beyae ewes are in lamb. **1899** *Natal Agric. Jrnl* 31 Mar. 4 'Banje,' much, is a word of Malay origin. **1945** N. DEVITT *People & Places* 144 A common word is 'banja' or 'baie'. It is from the Malay and means very, much, or many.

B. *adv.* Very; very much.

Usu. in Afrikaans phrases. See also *baie dankie* (DANKIE sense 1 b).

1855 G.H. MASON *Life with Zulus* 201 The two Zulus .. had lived for some months on the coast, and had therefore become tolerably familiar with the coast Caffres (Fingoes), whom they described as Bonya-skellom Fingoe (rascally Fingoes). **1863** E.L. PRICE *Jrnls* (1956) 149 His sufferings increased fearfully .. each morning as we enquired into his case, he wd. shake his head dolefully & say 'Groetman banja sick!' — 'Greatman is *very* sick!' **1884** B. ADAMS *Narr.* (1941) 215 He said he did not want anything for his trouble — would rather not take anything — as I was such a *banya mooi baas* — very good master. **1911** L. COHEN *Reminisc. of Kimberley* 323 'What's the matter, Leroux?' '*Baaije siek*' (very ill) complained the Boer. 'I cannot eat, am sick of a morning, have pains in my legs, back, and head.' **1913** J.J. DOKE *Secret City* 256 Wait, there's a good soul, until you are quite strong, baaija sterk. **1915** D. FAIRBRIDGE *Torch Bearer* 62 'Baing mooi' murmured the audience courteously, 'Very pretty!' **1920** R.Y. STORMBERG *Mrs Pieter de Bruyn* 13 Love to all.

Ba'je haastig, Gwenno. **1964** L.G. GREEN *Old Men Say* 59, I was drinking tickey beer, But I took too much, dear murrer, .. And my money disappear, Now I cannot pay John Campbell, And my kop is baing seer. **1990** *Top Forty* July 12 A bunch of 'new' Afrikaners put together an irreverant gathering of musos ... *Baie* nice. Cultural transmutation, and colloquial backbiting at its dusty best.

bai-nbai var. BY-AND-BY.

bajalo var. BOJALWA.

bajia var. BHAJIA.

bak see BAKGAT *adj.* and BAKKIE sense 1.

Bakalahadi, -hari varr. KGALAGADI.

Bakatla(s), Ba-Katlha pl. forms of KGATLA.

bakbakiri var. BOKMAKIERIE.

baken var. BAAKEN.

bakeoven *n. hist.* Also **bak oven.** [Calque formed on Du. *bakoven* or Afk. *bakoond* oven.] BAKOOND sense 1.

1934 *Cape Argus* 21 June (Swart), The good housewife of those days used to judge the heat of her oven by holding her hand in the bak oven. **1960** J. COPE *Tame Ox* 159 The ceilings of smoke-darkened polished bamboos, an old-fashioned bake-oven and pot-hooks and roasting-spit in the kitchen. **1968** *7 Castle Hill, Port Elizabeth* (pamphlet) 10 A brick corbelled bakeoven is set deeply into the stony hillside which provides the house with a solid foundation.

Bakgalagadi, -galis varr. KGALAGADI.

bakgat /ˈbakxat, ˈbʌkxʌt/ *adj., int.,* and *adv.* *Slang.* [Afk., ultimate orig. unkn.; perh. *bak* baking + *gat* hole, the theory being that the best bread was baked by the old method of making a fire in a hole; or perh. *bak* fine, 'A1' + *gat* hole, (slang) arse.]

A. *adj.* Good, excellent, fine, pleasing.

1965 C. HOOGENDIJK *Informant, Welkom* Hereby enclosed please find the following valuables: 2 Bakgat snaps. Thanks a lot for the photo. **1970** M. BENNETT *Informant, Krugersdorp* Bakgat — tops, fine. **1975** J.H. PICARD in *Eng. Usage in Sn Afr.* Vol.6 No.1, 36 If everything is in order they will feel *bakgat* (fine). **1980** *Sunday Times* 4 May (Mag. Sect.) 8 She is offering a glass of her favourite wine, .. which is 'bak'. 'Bak' is her word for anything that pleases her .. movies, friends, theatre and her brother.] **1985** P. SLABOLEPSZY *Sat. Night at Palace* 18 Vince: (*fondling his boots*): Bakgat, hey? Fibreglass bottoms. West Germany wore these things in the last World Cup. **1989** *Weekend Post* 26 Aug. 11 If that main-man what counts among the taal-tiffies, Dr Samuel Johnson, could hear military Englikaans he would get a skrik .. but William Shakespeare would feel bakgat about it. **1989** *Sunday Tribune* 17 Dec. 1 It may cost as much as your very own game reserve, but as the only one of its kind in the country, it's a real bakgat bakkie! **1990** *Fair Lady* 23 May 68 Whether he's lovingly lampooning the platteland, .. or making *bakgat* ads, people fall about laughing. **1992** D. EVANS in *Sunday Times* 17 May 26 Neither of them have the kind of *bakgat* confidence you might expect from the top contenders. Both are expecting an epic duel in this year's up-run.

B. *int.* An exclamation of approval, pleasure, etc.

1969 A. FUGARD *Boesman & Lena* 32 Boesman's alright. Two bottles and a pondokkie. Bakgat! **1971** *Informant, Grahamstown* A try! Bakgat! **1989** *Sunday Times* 15 Jan. 9 Johan leant against the wooden balustrade. 'Now imagine having a sundowner here with this view, eh?' 'Bakgat!' Clearly Stoffel could imagine. **1992** S. GUTKNECHT in *Sunday Times* 19 Apr. (Mag. Sect.) 28 Entertainer David Kramer thinks *bakgat* is great. 'It's totally expressive,' he says. 'It defines a feeling of exhilaration and carries far more weight than a word like amazing.'

C. *adv.* Well, perfectly.

Bakgatla, **Bakhatla** pl. forms of KGATLA.

Bakhurutse pl. form of HURUTSHE.

bakken var. BAAKEN.

bakkie /ˈbaki, ˈbʌki/ n. [Afk., *bak* container, load-bearing part of a truck + dim. suffix -IE.]
1. A bowl; any small container. Also shortened form **bak**. See also BOTTERBAK.

1893 H.P. BARNETT-CLARK in *Cape Illust. Mag.* Vol.4 No.6, 217 'Water? Why don't you carry a bottle of it with you?' She took up a *bakje* or mug, and .. set off to the duck pond. 1958 A. JACKSON *Trader on Veld* 41 All farms had wells .. from which water was drawn by means of windmills or 'bakkies pumps', a chain of rotating buckets driven by a mule or a horse walking round and round. c1967 J. HOBBS in *New S. Afr. Writing* No.4, 68 Oom Franz's eldest .. took to joining Klein Hannes behind the fowl-hok at five to twelve, carrying a bakkie of laying mash as an excuse. 1970 K. NICOL *Informant, Durban* That bak (bakkie) is too small to hold a decent quantity of tea. 1971 *Informant, OFS,* I put the oysters in a bakkie and in the deep-freeze. 1990 M.G. GILBERT *Informant, Ladybrand* John remembered my biscuit bakkie so he had one — I put some biscuits & sweets in a [packet] for the journey. 1991 *Informant, Port Elizabeth* I'm going to bring a bakkie for your false teeth. 1991 G. ZWIRN in *Settler* Vol.65 No.2, 11 Strictly speaking, *bakkie* means a container but through extension, it has come to mean any kind of receptacle, from a baking-tin to a trough.

2. A light truck, a pick-up; a 4-by-4 vehicle. Also *attrib.,* and (occas.) *fig.*

1968 *Farmer's Weekly* 3 Jan. 98 (*advt*) Bakkies! Bakkies! Bakkies! All makes and sizes. 1971 *Farmer's Weekly* 12 May, (*advt*) Firestone build their bakkie tyres with the same triple-strength method as their heavy duty truck tyres. 1972 C. BRITZ *Informant* At 8.30 a.m. I get sent here to Outjo — another 125 miles. And 4 full drums of diesel in a bakkie all the way back. 1975 *E. Prov. Herald* 18 June 17 Aviation history was made here yesterday when South Africa's very own 'aerial bakkie' took off and landed ... 'We had in mind what can be called a "bush" aircraft — an aerial bakkie,' said the general manager of Atlas. 1976 M. THOLO in C. Hermer *Diary of Maria Tholo* (1980) 81 It was a red van, a bakkie, with a canopy on top, and she recognised it as belonging to .. one of our biggest shebeen queens. 1985 J. LAWRENCE in *Style* Dec.-Jan. 63 He sent a telegram to Rolls-Royce in London .. declaring that he would rather buy a Japanese bakkie than anything British. 1986 *Motorist* 1st Quarter 51 This front-wheel-drive, half-ton bakkie has two derivatives — the only difference being engine size. 1989 P. LEE in *Sunday Times* (Mag. Sect.) 26 Feb. 36 The bakkie is synonymous with the local farmer out on his plaas, .. bags of mealies and his workers in the back. 1990 *Sunday Times* 10 June 7 Higgens .. was the first to meet the four-by-four bakkie driven by neighbours rushing to the rescue, refusing to let them out of the cab until he recognised them. 1990 R. MALAN *My Traitor's Heart* 103 On drunken Saturday nights, he sometimes roamed the countryside in his bakkie, his pickup, poaching rabbits and steenbok. 1991 *E. Prov. Herald* 7 Feb. 15 (*advt*) A bakkie building sand, crusher grit or top soil. We also supply stock bricks ... A bakkie load (one ton) building sand from R40. 1991 G. ZWIRN in *Settler* Vol.65 No.2, 11 Bakkie, This word is colloquial SAE for a light truck or delivery van.

Hence (sense 2) **bakkie** v. trans. nonce, to transport by bakkie.

1988 J. TAYLOR in *Inside S. Afr.* July 31, I asked if he could not sell me a ton [of grapes] and rail them up to me ... They arrived one day at Pretoria Station .. from where they were bakkied at once to Broederstroom.

bakkis /ˈbak kəs/ n. hist. Pl. -kiste /-kəstə/. [Afk., *bak* bake + *kis* chest.] A lidded wooden trough, or box on legs, in which dough was formerly made and kneaded.

1963 W. FEHR *Treasures at Castle of G.H.,* Yellow wood dough mixer or baking trough (bakkis). 1971 BARAITSER & OBHOLZER *Cape Country Furn.* 255 One finds this large box on legs on which dough was kneaded and the baked loaves of bread were stored ... The lid of the bakkis is detachable ... Bakkiste have neither handles nor hinges. 1973 M.A. COOK *Cape Kitchen* 68 Bakkiste are found in two sizes — the farm-house or large size, .. and the town-house or small size ... The writer has heard it stated that the true bakkis had a loose lid, whereas the type with a hinged lid was really a broodkis, used for storing loaves. 1974 [see *S. Afr. Panorama* quot. at KOSKAS]. 1975 *S. Afr. Panorama* Jan. 14 The housewife of that era had to bake her own bread, hence the large 'bakkis' (dough bin) against one wall. 1981 *S. Afr. Garden & Home* June 54 Her 'desk' — a yellow-wood and stinkwood *bakkis* or baker's trough.

‖**bakkop** /ˈbakɔp/ n. [Afk., *bak* bowl + *kop* head, so named for the shape of its spread hood.] The Cape cobra (see CAPE sense 2 a), *Naja nivea.* Also *attrib.*

1935 H.C. BOSMAN *Mafeking Rd* (1969) 85 For a bite from a bakkop or a puff-adder or a ringhals, a sharp knife and permanganate of potash crystals are nearly always efficacious. 1948 — in L. Abrahams *Unto Dust* (1963) 32 Her eight-year-old daughter had been bitten by a snake; they couldn't tell from the fang marks if it was a ringhals or a bakkop. 1980 A.J. BLIGNAUT *Dead End Rd* 50, I thought that he was pleased that the Bushman, who was as sly as a bakkop snake, was about to be put in his place.

Baklokwa var. TLOKWA.

Bakoena, Bakone varr. BAKWENA.

bakoond /ˈbakʊənt, ˈbakuənt/ n. [Afk., *bak* bake + *oond* oven.]
1. A brick or clay oven, usu. with a vaulted roof and iron door, either built into the side of a wide kitchen hearth, or as a free-standing structure outside a house; BAKEOVEN; DUTCH OVEN. Also *attrib.*

1951 H.C. BOSMAN in L. Abrahams *Bekkersdal Marathon* (1971) 65 Because of the crack .. the bakoond wasn't so good for baking bread in, any more. 1968 *7 Castle Hill, Port Elizabeth* (pamphlet) 13 (*caption*) Bakoond. 1970 L.G. GREEN *Giant in Hiding* 107 Every old cottage has the traditional *bakoond,* the country oven of rounded clay built into the kitchen and projecting from the end of the building. 1973 *Farmer's Weekly* 25 Apr. 44 Until recently bread was still baked in the spacious bakoond .. in the enormous chimney stack. 1976 *Weekend Argus* 26 June, A perfectly proportioned timber beamed lounge with bakoond idiom fireplace and a huge stoep offleading. 1981 J. KENCH *Cape Dutch Homesteads* 108 The farmer and his family and friends could sit .. warmed by the heat from the old Dutch *bakoond* and the stove under the great yellowwood beam supporting the inner wall of the kitchen. 1985 *Frontline* May 21 Clockwise from top left: Marico postmaster in front of *bakoond.*

‖**2.** *fig. rare.* A form of punishment, similar to running the gauntlet.

In Afrikaans, 'bakoond' has the *fig.* meaning of 'bottom' or buttocks.

1981 *E. Prov. Herald* 5 Nov. 44 His daughter, aged 13, had suffered physical pain and emotional upheaval from being put through the 'bakoond' — a form of punishment in which pupils had to crawl through the legs of their peers who slapped them on the buttocks as they progressed down the line.

Bakora see quot. 1841 at TLOKWA.

bakore /ˈbak ʊərə, -uərə/ pl. n. Colloq. [Afk., *bak* bowl + *ore* ears.] Large, protruding ears.

1970 S. SPARKS *Informant, Fort Beaufort* That poor little boy's protruding ears are real bakore and he is very self-conscious about it. 1978 *Darling* 30 Aug. 123 And you at the back with the bak ore, quit screeching 'Change the ref!' willya. 1985 D. KRAMER in *Cosmopolitan* May 102 For two bob one of the Krynauw brothers .. would .. shave my head with an electric clipper ... My bakore then protruded like two lilies from the side of my head and if I blushed they would turn a bright pink and glow in the dark. 1991 A. SHEPHERD on *Radio 5,* 8 Feb., I think it's a guy with incredibly big bakore on the back of a bakkie.

bak oven var. BAKEOVEN.

Bakwena /baˈkweːna, bəˈkwenə/ pl. n. Forms: α. **Bacquains, Bakoena, Bakone, Bakuena, Bakuéna, Bakwain(s), Bakwena(s), Ba-Kwena, Baquaina, Baquana, Baquans;** β. **Kwena.** [SeTswana, BA- + *Kwena,* perh. the name of an ancestral chief (lit. 'crocodile', the totem of these people). For an explanation of unprefixed forms and forms with -s, see BA-.] (The) members of a Tswana people living mainly in the western Transvaal North West Province and Botswana. Also *attrib.* See also BAMANGWATO, TSWANA sense 2 a.

The unprefixed form 'Kwena' is found mainly in academic contexts.

As is the case with many names of peoples and groups in *S. Afr. Eng.,* this word has been found only in plural uses; however, it may be that it has also been used in unrecorded singular forms.

α. 1835 A. SMITH *Diary* (1940) II. 75 Perhaps Baquana was originally derived from Quana and implies 'they of the crocodile,' or the chief might have had his name from that reptile and the people were called so as the people of that chief. 1839 W.C. HARRIS *Wild Sports* 230 We resolved to proceed immediately to the country of the Bakone, or Baquaina, where camelopards were reported .. to be very abundant. 1857 D. LIVINGSTONE *Missionary Trav.* 13 The different Bechuana tribes are named after certain animals ... The term Bakatla means 'they of the monkey', Bakuena, 'they of the alligator'; Batlapi, 'they of the fish'; each tribe having a superstitious dread of the animal after which it is called. 1866 J. LEYLAND *Adventures* 196 Koselensi, Sechele's brother, for some time had the management of a section of the Bakwains located about ten miles from Kolobeng. 1871 J. MACKENZIE *Ten Yrs* (1971) 247 Here dwell the Mkololo .. who in their northward journey conquered the Bankweketse, the Bakwena, and other tribes in that region. 1881 [see COMMANDO sense 3]. 1905 *Native Tribes of Tvl* 102 Setyeli or Secheli, chief of the Bechuana tribe called Ba-Kwena, who lived on the Koloberg near the western border in the Potchefstroom district. 1928 [see KGATLA]. 1930 S.T. PLAATJE *Mhudi* (1975) 87 Six Bechuana .. had come in overnight, bringing tribute from the loyal Bakwena — another Bechuana tribe which venerates the crocodile. 1939 N. DEVITT in *Outspan* 26 May 83 The Bakwena, for instance, are the 'People of the Crocodile'. The tribesman is loyal to his 'siboko' or tribal name. 1949 C. BULLOCK *Rina* 27 You might find some strange things there among the BaKwena, the Crocodile people. 1951 R. GRIFFITHS *Grey about Flame* 50 The people of this land are known as the BaKwena. Once they were mighty warriors and took tribute up and down the country. 1969 *40th Annual Report* (S.A.I.R.R.) 19 It .. considered ... the Batlharos, the Bakwena, Ba-Mohapo and other 'black spot' removals. 1985 PLATZKY & WALKER *Surplus People* 385 The government is 'motivating people to move voluntarily'. But if, as the Bakwena of Mogopa were told, they refuse to move voluntarily, they will be moved by GG trucks.

β. 1977 T.R.H. DAVENPORT *S. Afr.: Mod. Hist.* 7 The Kwena .. dispersed during the sixteenth century from a centre in the western trans-Vaal, and spread westwards .. and south-eastwards. 1986 P. MAYLAM *Hist. of Afr. People* 120 In the mid-nineteenth century the Kwena were the most powerful and prominent of the Tswana chiefdoms.

bakwet(h)a var. ABAKWETHA.

Balala /bəˈlaːla, ˌbaˈlaːla/ pl. n. Hist. [SeTswana, lit. 'serfs', 'servants', 'inferior people' (sing. *molala*).] (The) members of a dispossessed and impoverished Khoisan hunter-gatherer people living in a relationship of servitude to the BATLHAPING. Also *attrib.*

As is the case with many names of peoples and groups in *S. Afr. Eng.*, this word has been found only in plural uses; however, it may be that it has also been used in unrecorded singular forms.

1846 R. MOFFAT *Missionary Labours* 2 Connected with each of the towns among that people, there are great numbers of what are called 'Balala,' poor ones, who stand in the same relation to the Bechuanas as the Bushmen formerly stood in to the Hottentots, and whose origin doubtless was of the same nature. **1907** W.C. SCULLY *By Veldt & Kopje* 202 The spoil was handed over to the 'Balala' — 'the people who are dead' — wretched outlaws or waifs of annihilated clans, who wandered, weaponless and without clothing, over the veldt. **1908** J.M. ORPEN *Reminisc.* 124 The inhabitants of the Kalahari are mainly Balala, who are impoverished Bechuana people and, in a measure, in servitude to Bechuana chiefs, who partly use them to collect furs and skins for them. **1986** P. MAYLAM *Hist. of Afr. People* 46 The Tlhaping were known to have taken into clientage Balala hunter-gatherers. The Balala were expected to supply labour for the Thlaping, who in turn gave the Balala a chance to create their own herds by supplying them with cattle.

balast-mandje var. BALLASMANDJIE.

Balemba pl. form of LEMBA.

‖**balie** /ˈbɑːli/ *n. hist.* [Afk., large tub, cask.]
a. A tub, butt, or vat. Also *attrib.*

Balies were used in Cape Dutch kitchens and in wine-making.

1955 L.G. GREEN *Karoo* 105 On lonely farms the grapes are still pressed in the *balies* (large vats) with bare feet. Some days later the liquid *mos* is passed into the old *brandewynketel* or still, made to very much to same pattern as those used by Tennessee 'moonshiners'. **1971** BARAITSER & OBHOLZER *Cape Country Furn.* 263 A selection of large and small teak vats (balies) with and without lids were used in the household. **1973** M.A. COOK *Cape Kitchen* 79 The consideration of water storage leads on naturally to the subject of tubs or balies of all sorts. Their uses and names are legion. In the 18th Century they were made of teak, usually bound with brass hoops. **1974** *S. Afr. Garden & Home* June 31 Vats or *balies* in common use in the Cape kitchen ... The largest member of the family of balies was the water butt. **1981** *S. Afr. Panorama* July 47 The inlaid pearwood kist, on which rests a wooden Voortrekker *balie* (water carrier), was [her] first Africana furniture purchase. **1984** B. JOHNSON-BARKER in *Wynboer* June 72 He even bathed that night, using the enamel bucket and the balie that his wife made the pekel in, so he came out a bit salty and with the invigorating tang of vinegar.

b. With distinguishing epithet denoting a particular type of balie: **botterbalie** /ˈbɔtə(r)-/ [Du., *botter* butter], a butter-vat; **melk balie** /ˈmɛlk-/ [Du., *melk* milk], **milking balie**, a milking-vat; **pekelbalie**, see PEKEL sense 2; **teegoedbalie** /ˈtiəxut-/ [Du., *teegoed* 'tea things'], a washing-up basin; **trapbalie** /ˈtrap-/ [Afk., *trap* tread, crush underfoot], a wine-pressing vat; **vleisbalie** /ˈfleɪs-/ [Du., *vleis* meat], a vat for pickling meat; **voetebalie** /ˈfutə-/ [Du., *voete* feet], a foot bath; **waterbalie** /ˈvɑːtə(r)-, ˈwɔːtə/ [Du., *water* or Eng. *water*], a water butt.

1973 M.A. COOK *Cape Kitchen* 79 Next in size were the little **botterbalies**, which were provided with lids kept in place by two short lugs. **1971** BARAITSER & OBHOLZER *Cape Country Furn.* 257 Milking was done into a **melkbalie**, a small tub bound by two iron hoops and generally made of teak. **1973** M.A. COOK *Cape Kitchen* 79 The smallest of all were the milking balies. **1971** BARAITSER & OBHOLZER *Cape Country Furn.* 263 The shallowest of all vats is the **Teegoedbalie**. It is a small two-handled vat used both as a tray and as a basin for washing cups and saucers in. **1975** *S. Afr. Panorama* Jan., Items such as a .. 'pekelbalie' (tub for pickling meat) and on the boekenhout table in the middle stood a 'teegoedbalie' used for washing dishes. **1971** L.G. GREEN *Taste of S.-Easter* 204 The **trapbalies** were cleaned and the wagons came up to the cellar door loaded with baskets of grapes. **1981** P. DANE *Great Houses of Constantia* 100 A wine-press with all its accoutrements, a '*trap balie*' for treading grapes, vats filled with wine, .. ten empty leggers, [etc.]. **1971** BARAITSER & OBHOLZER *Cape Country Furn.* 263 One of the most important was the meat pickling vat (**Vleisbalie** or Pekelbalie). This was a large, round or oval balie with brass or iron hoops ... Not to be forgotten is the vat in which the head of the house took comfort soaking his feet, the **Voetebalie**. **1973** M.A. COOK *Cape Kitchen* 79 Voetebalies .. usually were slightly larger and had two lugs to allow them to be carried round. Although the old Cape houses lacked bathrooms most families .. were most particular about going to bed with clean feet. **1971** L.G. GREEN *Taste of S.-Easter* 54 Perhaps the most typical Sandveld items are the wooden kitchen tubs, casks, **waterbalies** and butter churns. **1974** *S. Afr. Garden & Home* June 30 The contents of the kitchen right from iron utensils to copper and brass, wooden kitchenware, furniture, water *balies* (vats) [etc.].

‖**ballasmandjie** /baˈlasˌmaɪŋki/ *n.* Also **balast-mandje, ballas mantje, ballast-mandje**. Pl. **-s**, or unchanged. [Afk. (earlier Du. *ballastmandje*), *ballas* ballast, load + *mandjie* small basket.] A bushel basket or lug, used for picking grapes or other fruit.

1873 *Cape Monthly Mag.* VII. 209 A large heap of papers .. which, years ago, had been deposited in a large basket (*ballast-mandje*) on the loft, where they still were. **1910** D. FAIRBRIDGE *That Which Hath Been* (1913) 108 In the hot vineyards the ballast-mandjes would be heaped with grapes by the hands of every available man, woman and child on the farm. [**1915** —— *Torch Bearer* 142 A ballast basket of apricots had arrived from a friend, and all day would Mrs. Roux be making preserve, also fig (komfyt), because unless you picked the green figs that very day they would ripen too much.] **1919** M.M. STEYN *Diary* 253 Old friends of the country .. send their Cape Town friends baskets of fruit; these baskets or 'ballas mantje,' held twice as much as an ordinary basket. *a***1930** G. BAUMANN in Baumann & Bright *Lost Republic* (1940) 93 Mr and Mrs Lopey welcomed me on my arrival, Mrs Lopey immediately spotting the 'balasmandje' (bushel basket) of grapes. **1977** *Darling* 16 Mar. 36 At Laborie in Paarl, pick grapes for your wine, rest with your loaded ballasmandjie on the mossy steps of the old cellars.

Balobedu, -belu pl. forms of LOBEDU.

baloi pl. form of MOLOI.

BaLovedu pl. form of LOBEDU.

Bamangwato /ˌbamaŋˈgwɑːtɔ, -təʊ/ *pl. n.* Forms: α. **Bamang(o)ato, Bamanguato, Bamangwatese, Bamangwato, BamaNgwato, Bamanwhato, Bawangwato.** β. **Ngwato.** [SeTswana, BA- + *Mangwato* (orig. sense uncertain).] (The) members of the largest people of the Tswana group, living mainly in Botswana. See also TSWANA sense 2 a. Also *attrib.*

The Bamangwato were originally part of the BAKWENA people.

The unprefixed β form 'Ngwato' is found mainly in academic contexts. A singular form, **'Mangwato**, has been found in one source (see quot. 1896).

α. **1835** A. SMITH *Diary* (1940) II. 32 When in the Bamanguato country a lion sprung over a kraal at least six feet high. **1857** D. LIVINGSTONE *Missionary Trav.* 10, I went northwards to visit the Bakaa and Bamangwato and the Makalaka living between 22° and 23° south lat. **1871** [see MOLOI]. **1896** H.A. BRYDEN *Tales of S. Afr.* 127 Seventy wagons and more now stood beside the Crocodile, whose owners, .. awaited the return of two deputies sent to Khama, Chief of Bamangwato, through whose country they first had to pass. *Ibid.* 157, I had also in my outfit .. a 'Mangwato, a capital fellow at languages, and understood Zulu and Dutch. **1900** H.C. HILLEGAS *Oom Paul's People* 13 Khama is the paramount chief of the Bawangwato, whose territory is included in the British Bechuanaland protectorate, situated about one thousand miles due north from Cape Town. **1928** E.H.L. SCHWARZ *Kalahari & its Native Races* 223 As the nation grew, other sections hived off, under separate seretos ... The last to hive off were the Batawana, who are an offspring of the Ba-Mangwato, or Khama's people. **1931** O. LETCHER *Afr. Unveiled* 122 The Bamangwato is a tribe inhabiting Bechuanaland on the eastern fringe of the Kalahari desert. **1937** C. BIRKBY *Zulu Journey* 315 The Bamangwato, the people whom Khama ruled so wisely, have reduced another tribe, the Masarwas, to a state of serfdom. **1949** J. MOCKFORD *Golden Land* 103 Serowe, royal capital of the Bamangwato — the most numerous and influential tribe in Bechuanaland. **1950** H. GIBBS *Twilight* 57 Beside him sat one or other of the younger Bamangwatese maidens. **1975** W.F. LYE *Andrew Smith's Jrnl 1834–6* II. Index, *bamaNgwato*, (Rendered Bamangato, Bamanwhato etc.) Major division of the Tswana descending from the Kwena. **1978** *Drum* Feb. 6 Sir Seretse was allowed to return from Oxford to Botswana on condition he did not make claims to the Bamangwato throne, which was hereditarily his. **1987** M. HOLMES in *Leadership* Vol.6 No.4, 49 In 1950 the Labour government arbitrarily ruled that Seretse Khama was not fit to lead the Bamangwato tribe and should remain in Britain. **1990** *Sunday Times* 1 July 3 The engagement has already upset leaders of Botswana's powerful Bamangwato tribe.

β. **1986** P. MAYLAM *Hist. of Afr. People* 45 The Ngwato were the second chiefdom to break away from the Kwena in the late eighteenth century.

bamboo var. BAMBUS.

bamboo fish *n. phr.* [Prob. tr. S. Afr. Du. *bamboesvis(ch)*; see Pettman quot. 1913.] The STREPIE, *Sarpa salpa.*

[**1887** *S.W. Silver & Co.'s Handbk to S. Afr.* 183 *Bamboes visch*, .. A rich and delicate fish, but scarce in Cape Town. Caught in Saldanha Bay, where it is dried and salted.] **1913** C. PETTMAN *Africanderisms* 43 *Bamboo fish, Box salpa.* A fish which lives among the Sea bamboo .. and large Sargassa. It feeds only upon algae. **1913** [see Fairbridge quot. at DIKKOP sense 3]. **1949** [see STREPIE]. **1955** C. HORNE *Fisherman's Eldorado* 210 False Bay anglers .. would not link the names karanteen or sasa with the fish they know as bamboo fish, but Natal anglers, who know this fish as karanteen and bamboo fish, would probably not experience a similar difficulty, although the name sasa, which originated on the Wild Coast, would come less readily to them than to East London anglers. **1951**, **1958** [see MOOI NOOITJE]. **1971** [see STREPIE].

bambus *n. obs.* Also **bamboo, bamboos(e), bambous.** Pl. **-ses, -es.** [Etym. unkn.; perh. fr. Du. *bamboes* bamboo.] A cylindrical wooden vessel used by Khoikhoi peoples to hold liquids and, with a skin tightly stretched over its mouth, as a drum. See also ROMMELPOT.

1821 *Missionary Notices* 121 Some of the Namacquas make bambooses to contain their milk. **1822** J. CAMPBELL *Trav. in S. Afr. Second Journey* I. 46 They brought us three bamboosses. [*Note*] A bamboos is a deep wooden vessel, something in shape like a tea-canister, but cut out of a block of wood. **1822** W.J. BURCHELL *Trav.* I. 407 The jug, or jar, which they call a bambus, is made in the form of a short cylinder, having the mouth or neck contracted generally to about two-thirds. Their most usual capacity is about a gallon. **1824** —— *Trav.* II. 65 *The drum* was nothing more than a *bambus* or wooden jug having a piece of wet parchment strained over the top, and containing a little water. **1838** [see MOER *n.*[1] sense 1]. **1841** B. SHAW *Memorials* 23 The household utensils are chiefly the bamboos or wooden milk-pail, the calabash, and a kind of wooden spoon. *Ibid.* 25 The rommel pot is a bamboo over which a piece of skin is tightly stretched, and is used as a drum at their [*sc.* the Namaquas'] public dances. *Ibid.* 85 Having partaken of no dinner, I was very faint; a bamboo of milk was brought me. **1844** J. BACKHOUSE *Narr. of Visit* 565 Bambouses .. are a sort of jars made of willow-wood. **1846** R. MOFFAT *Missionary Labours* 39 Sometimes a kind housewife would hang a bamboos, or wooden vessel filled with milk, on a forked stick, near my head, that I might .. drink during the night. **1853** F.

GALTON *Narr. of Explorer in Tropical S. Afr.* 66 A wooden 'bamboose,' a sort of bucket. **1872** E.J. DUNN in A.M.L. Robinson *Sel. Articles from Cape Monthly Mag.* (1978) 48 Taking this lump of fibre in their fingers, they dip it into the 'bamboos' or wooden bowl of milk. **1934** P.R. KIRBY *Musical Instruments of Native Races* (1965) 14 The true Hottentot drum consisted of either a *bambus* or wooden milk-jug, or a clay pot, over which a piece of sheepskin or buckskin was tied.

bamvoosie /bam'vʊsi/ *n.* [Formed on Afk. *bamboesvis* + -IE.] The STREPIE, *Sarpa salpa*.

1971 *E. Prov. Herald* 15 July 16 The Eastern Cape bamvoosie (derived from Bamboo fish) is known in Natal as the Karanteen and in other parts as the streepie.

ban *n. hist.* [Special sense of general Eng.] BANNING ORDER.

1963 K. MACKENZIE *Dragon to Kill* 10 Chief Mbula is coming down from Queenstown ... First meeting since his ban ended. **1971** *Seek* June 15 Does the ordinary churchman realise what a ban means? It means that the person concerned, who has not been found guilty of any crime in any court, is for five years socially dead. He may not leave his magisterial district without a special permit, which is only very sparingly granted. He may not attend any social functions of any kind. He may not speak in public; he may not write to the Press. **1971** *Rand Daily Mail* 25 Jan. 11 Mr Ramgobin was banned for five years. This was his first public speech since the ban expired. **1982** M. MZAMANE *Children of Soweto* 94 She had already served one five-year banning order .. but the government had subsequently decided to lift her ban. **1988** P. CULL in *E. Prov. Herald* 25 Feb. 1 A community leader from Oudtshoorn .. has also been restricted. The ban extends to the issuing of Press statements on behalf of the 17 organisations.

ban *v. trans. Hist.* [As prec.] Usu. *passive*, of a person: to be placed under restrictions in terms of security legislation. Cf. LIST, RESTRICT, UNBAN.

1953 *Drum* Aug. 9 Albert J. Luthuli .. is at present banned from attending any public gathering and from visiting 21 magisterial districts. *c***1968** J. COPE in *New S. Afr. Writing* No.5, 134 He's just been released from jail, and he's banned and can't meet people. It must be bloody lonely for him. **1969** A. PATON *Kontakion* 90 Because Bill was banned, only one person could speak to him at a time; otherwise he would have been taking part in a 'gathering', and could have been arrested on the spot. **1971** *Seek* June 15 In my opinion and that of many others, many of those banned are not guilty of any serious offence against the State. **1977** J. SIKAKANE *Window on Soweto* 65 In 1963 both Lawrence and Rita were banned, which means being subject to restriction orders, not allowed to continue working or travel outside one's home district. **1985** *Weekly Mail* 22 Nov. 1 After her visit yesterday, Mrs Mandela spoke briefly to the press. She is banned and cannot be quoted. **1990** *Weekend Argus* 17 Feb. 12 Their real opponents were in jail, banned or otherwise prevented from airing their views and desires.

Hence **banned** *ppl adj.*, and *absol.*, 'banned people'.

1971 *Seek* June 15 It is a remarkable thing that one so rarely hears prayers offered for the banned in the ordinary services of the parish churches. **1974** *Drum* 22 July 10 'I was slightly better off than other banned people,' he said. 'It was possible for me to attend church and meet people.' **1977** A. ROSCOE *Uhuru's Fire* 226 The voice reserved for the banned, the muzzled, the exiled, .. the detained. **1990** R. STENGEL *January Sun* 196 The movie is a bootleg tape of an American cable television movie ... It is technically illegal to show because Mandela is a 'banned' person. Listening to the words of a banned person is a violation of the Internal Security Act.

banana *n. colloq.* Also with initial capital. [Alluding to the perception of Natal as the country's main banana-producing region.]

1. *Attrib.*, referring jocularly to the province of Natal (now KwaZulu-Natal).

[**1915** J.K. O'CONNOR *Afrikander Rebellion* 17 The old cry of 'Afrika voor de Afrikanders' and the weak joke referring to the eating of bananas in Natal were resuscitated .. in 1904.] **1970** *Drum* Feb. 15 He left for Durban where he formed a trio ... They were an immediate hit in the banana province. **1971** *Daily Dispatch* 28 Sept. 24 Apart from a few bumps and bruises and a natural feeling of tiredness they were all fit when they got off the 'Banana Special' on Sunday night. **1985** L. DU BUISSON in *Avenue* May 33 You are now entering Banana Republic: Danger Natal Fever: Casino. **1988** G. SILBER in *Style* May 65 *(caption)* The independent Banana Republic of Natal .. where bananas flourish in the tropical haze and all people are equally tanned on the beaches. **1990** *Sunday Times* 8 July 1 Banana slip. Western Province beat Natal 27–21 in the semi-final at Newlands. **1990** H.P. TOFFOLI in *Style* Nov. 50 Young Durban movers there's a whole lot of shaking going on in banana country.

2. Special Comb. **banana boy**, often with initial capitals, a nickname for a man or boy born or resident in KwaZulu-Natal; in *pl.*, the residents of KwaZulu-Natal collectively; cf. NATALIAN *n.*; **Banana City**, a jocular nickname for Durban, KwaZulu-Natal's largest city; DURBS; **Banana Express**, a narrow-gauge steam train running along the southern coast of KwaZulu-Natal; also *attrib.*; **banana girl**, a nickname for a girl or woman born or resident in KwaZulu-Natal; **Banana Land**, also with small initials, the province of KwaZulu-Natal; hence **Bananalander**, one born or living in KwaZulu-Natal.

1956 N. GORDIMER in D. Wright *S. Afr. Stories* (1960) 69 Young white men brought up in the strong Anglo-Saxon tradition of the province of Natal are often referred to, and refer to themselves, as '**banana boys**', even though fewer and fewer of them have any connection with the dwindling number of vast banana estates that once made their owners rich. **1974** *Argus* 2 July 18 Natal? Oh yes, that's where they call the inhabitants Banana Boys because it's the territory which produces all South Africa's bananas. **1985** J. THOMAS in *Fair Lady* 1 May 20 In April I went to the independent Homeland of Natal to speak to the banana boys. **1991** *Weekend Post* 7 Sept. 1 The big-hearted Aussie, who's headed for Natal, has been granted 'local player' status – a bonus that will have the 'banana boys' smiling all the way. **1994** 'T. COBBLEIGH' in *Sunday Times* 2 Jan. 19 Nicest place in the country to be just now is ... Johannesburg! During the school holidays, the city so scorned by Kaapies and Banana-boys acquires a leisurely atmosphere, almost an elegance of its own. **1972** *Drum* 8 Nov. 43 Collecting beauty crowns comes sort of naturally with this peach from the **Banana City**. She is Miss Durban, Miss South Africa 1971, Miss Chamber of Commerce, Miss Natal and Miss Ambi Look. **1982** *Voice* 31 Jan. 1 Suspense is about all that scores of soccer fans who live outside the Banana City, will be left with today ... The next best alternative to being physically present at Umlazi Stadium, in Durban, today is to .. ogle the epic on the magic 'goggle-box'. **1987** G. MOKAE in *Pace* Oct. 59 Start packing and make your move to Durban ... If you have never set your feet in the 'Banana City' before, you ain't seen nothing yet. **1982** *S. Afr. Panorama* Sept. 40 Then there was the filming of the **Banana Express**. On the Sunday .. there were plenty of passengers but no sun. **1987** D. MARCH in *E. Prov. Herald* 29 Apr. 15 The Banana Express winds along the coast, passing across the sturdy steel bridge over the lovely Izotsha Lagoon before reaching Shelly Beach. **1987** *Fair Lady* 28 Oct. 18 It's the Banana Express, one of the country's last narrow-gauge steam trains ... Former Californian railman Rob Allingham plays the Banana Express guard. **1954** *Bantu World* 8 May (Suppl.) 11 In the few crowded hours of her visit to Johannesburg, Durban's '**Banana Girl**' was given a pretty good idea of the city's musical and stage talent. [**1928** R. CAMPBELL in *Collected Poems* (1949) 243 In fair **Banana Land** we lay our scene – South Africa, renowned both far and wide For politics and little else beside.] **1967** E. ROSENTHAL *Encycl. of Sn Afr.* 35 Natal is jocularly referred to as 'Bananaland.' **1971** *Daily Dispatch* 15 Sept. 9 You're wrong if you think 'banana land' is Natal. The banana image cultivated by the lads up the coast is a false one. Call them the sugar boys if you like, but banana boys, no. **1988** C. MITCHELL in *Personality* 6 June 12 This .. Durban City Councillor .. has been the driving force behind preparing the young men from Bananaland for their military duties. **1968** C.J.D. HARVEY in D.J. Opperman *Spirit of Vine* 299 One must remember that Campbell was a 'Bananalander' by birth and upbringing.

banddoom var. BANDOM.

bandhla var. IBANDLA.

bandiet /ban'dit/ *n. Prison slang.* Pl. **-e** /-ə/, **-s**. [Afk. (fr. Du., robber, brigand).] BANDIT. Also *attrib.*

[**1920** S. BLACK *Dorp* 162 All he knew was that his house had been broken into and rifled by 'some bandiet' of a Kafir, that his cook had been felled by a knob-kierie.] **1974** *Eng. Usage in Sn Afr.* Vol.5 No.1, 9 *Bandiete* .. graduate from short sentences *2–4* and *4–8* (years) to the pinnacle of a *coat* or *baadjie*. *Ibid.* 13 *Katkop*, .. originates from *Central* [*sc.* Prison] where bread is cooked in distinctive small brown loaves looking like a 'cat's head'. Itinerant bandiete have universalised the term now. **1981** H. LEWIN *Bandiet* (facing p.11) *Bandiet*, an Afrikaans word meaning *convict*. No longer in official use because considered derogatory. Unofficially – i.e. in common use throughout South African jails – a prisoner is called a *bandiet*. Plural *bandiete*. *Ibid.* 14 It was only as a prisoner – as a bandiet in a South African jail – that I could begin to realise what life is like for most South Africans. **1984** D. PINNOCK *Brotherhoods* 70 When a boy first enters the reformatory he is placed in the '*strafkoshuis*' (cells) for about two weeks to 'cool off'. Then he is sent to work for about three months in the fields, where he becomes part of the *bandiet* workforce. **1989** *Weekly Mail* 27 Oct. 2, I used to take gangs from the prison there ... The Agnes mine also uses *bandiets* to work on top of the mine. They still do it. In fact everybody here uses *bandiets*.

bandit *n.* Pl. **-s**, **-ti**. [Calque formed on Du. *bandiet* robber, brigand.] A convict or prisoner; BANDIET.

1795 C.R. HOPSON tr. *C.P. Thunberg's Trav.* I. 237 *Robben Island* is situated at the entrance of the harbour ... It is become the retreat of chameleons, quails, and prisoners for life (called here *banditti*). **1799** LADY A. BARNARD *S. Afr. Century Ago* (1925) 218 Towards night .. water rose so many feet .. as to .. go near to drown .. all the *bandits* in the lower courtyard. **1837** J.E. ALEXANDER *Narr. of Voy.* II. 297 Two redoubts were .. marked out; and with .. a party of banditti, as the Dutch call convicts .. the bush was soon cleared away for these works. **1851** R. GRAY *Jrnl of Bishop's Visitation* II. 177 The Boers not unfrequently shut their doors in his face, telling him he is a 'bandit' or convict. **1927** C.G. BOTHA *Social Life in Cape Col.* 27 They were .. the banditti from the East Indies who had been sent to the Cape to serve out their term of imprisonment. **1967** J.G. DAVIS *Hold my Hand* (1969) 22 Two tame bandits were walking ahead of him, unguarded, carrying sickles, returning from their hard labour in Mahoney's garden. **1980** *E. Prov. Herald* 7 Oct. 1 A gang of armed convicts went on a 'terror spree' ... Nobody had bothered to inform farmers that there had been a jailbreak and armed 'bandits' were on the loose.

bandom /'bantɔm/ *n. Mining.* Also **banddoom**, **ban(d)tom**, **banta(h)m**. [Afk., *band* band, hoop + *om* around.] See quot. 1913.

1891 R. SMITH *Great Gold Lands* 72 A curiously marked pebble that is streaked with a succession of parallel rings, from which it has received the descriptive name of 'banddoom,' or band round. **1906** *Tvl Leader* 8 Sept. 17 (Pettman), At a few feet he struck a layer of *bantoms*. The digger set to work washing these, and in a short while had a 22-carat stone, followed by another of less weight. **1913** C. PETTMAN *Africanderisms* 44 *Bandom*, .. A curiously marked pebble which is striated with a succession of parallel rings. The specific gravity of this stone is almost identical with that of the diamond, so that where this stone is found the diamond is confidently expected. **1917** BEET & TERPEND *Romance & Reality of Vaal Diamond Diggings* 50 The 'bantom' is so called from a corruption of a Dutch word meaning 'band-around' ... There exists a 'banthorn' on the Brazilian fields, and some consider the term 'bantom' to have come from thence, along with the usual corruptions in transit. **1920** F.C. CORNELL *Glamour of Prospecting* 15 A wonderful beach where the pebbles .. were very much larger .. chalcedonies, jaspers, and banded ironstones (the bandtom of the digger). *a***1930** G. BAUMANN in Baumann & Bright *Lost Republic* (1940) 152 The grubby tobacco-bag .. contained large 'bantams', crystals and other washed stones. [*Note*] A river-stone with barrel-like markings — round and water-washed. **1950** E. ROSENTHAL *Here Are Diamonds* 195 Mr. Van Vreeden believes that the oldest word peculiar to South African Diggerdom is 'bantom' (not bantam), which goes back almost to the year 1869 when the first finds were made. It has nothing to do with the small fowl, but means 'band om' i.e., the pebble has a 'band' or ribbon 'om' or round it. **1968** J.T. MCNISH *Rd to Eldorado* 119 Diggers searched eagerly for stones indicative of the presence of diamonds, but chiefly for a sight of 'bandoms' as the Boers called them .. which Britishers named 'bantams' and gutteral Germans 'bandooms'. *Ibid.* 128 Many claims known to be valueless, even lacking the usual indications of diamonds being there, were salted with promising material such as garnets, bantoms, blinkklippies and cats-eyes. **1971** A.E. SCHOCH in *Std Encycl. of Sn Afr.* IV. 32 Alluvial diamonds often occur together with beautiful, hard, water-worn pebbles ... Striped types with a 'band' around are called bantams by the diggers. **1980** A.J. BLIGNAUT *Dead End Rd* 68 The bantams, those smooth pebbles with fire in their hearts, promised much and soon. We were working a patch of ground from which the best diamonds on that field were being won. **1991** *Sunday Times* 21 Apr. 13 They .. have their own language — which includes words like 'bantams' and 'yellows'.

bang /baŋ/ *adj. colloq.* Also **baang**. [Du.] Scared, afraid. See also BANGBROEK.

1856 R.J. MULLINS Diary. 18 Dec., Rode on and found the Kei very full ... When we others .. were safely through, we looked back and saw Mr Waters on his charger looking very 'bang.' **1899** B. MITFORD *Weird of Deadly Hollow* 69 Baang, are you? And what the devil are you baang of? **1963** L.F. FREED *Crime in S. Afr.* 105 When he [*sc.* a ducktail] says that he is 'bang the ore will take a jerry', he intends to imply that he is afraid the police may find out. **1969** A. FUGARD *Boesman & Lena* 38 When the robot said go there at Berry's corner I was nearly bang in my broek. **1970** D. PINCUS *Informant, Bloemfontein*, I was bang to get up in the middle of the night to close the window. **1970** C.S. HENDRY *Informant, Somerset West* I'm so bang I'm going to dop [fail]. **1977** F.G. BUTLER *Karoo Morning* 94 'Tell me, Knaggs, are you afraid of Butler?' 'Of course not.' ... 'Knaggs is "bang" of Butler!' 'I'm not.' **1987** *Fair Lady* 18 Feb. 92 'Don't be a fool,' shivering in the shallows .. 'there are currents and things.' 'I'm too *bang* anyhow,' I said, my courage deserting me at armpit level. **1991** G. DE BEER *Informant, Port Nolloth (N. Cape)* She's so bang of heights.

bangalala /ˌbaŋgaˈlaːla, ˌbaŋgəˈlɑːlə/ *n.* Also **i-bangalala, uBangalala**, and with initial capital. [Zulu *u(lu)bangalala, ibangalala.*] An aphrodisiac, usu. prepared from the powdered roots of certain species of *Rhynchosia*, or from a decoction of the roots in milk; the living plant. Also *attrib.*

A word used in the names of certain patent medicines and herbal remedies.

1959 L. LONGMORE *Dispossessed* 45 Many stimulants are taken in urban areas to increase sex desires. Among these are Bangalala powder, Spanish Fly, Vuka-vuka ndoda, and Umzalisi, besides other chemical substances obtained from European chemists. **1966** A.T. BRYANT *Zulu Medicine* 61 The uBangalala herb enjoys a particularly high reputation, one of its roots being boiled in milk and a little of the decoction drunk from time to time. **1970** *Post* 8 Feb. 9 A little heap of coarse yellow powder, done up in a twist of brown paper .. that's Bull Khotso's secret. It's the muti this amazing 90-year-old inyanga relies on for the energy to satisfy his 23 wives ... Ibangalala, he calls the muti. It has a faint liquorice smell and a pleasant, spicy taste. **1976** *Label on medicine bottle, Umtata* Sok special bangalala mixture ... Recommended for Physical weakness & renewed energy. **1987** *City Press* 26 Apr. 6 (*advt*) Herbs specialist. Problem solver of love, sex, business, have babies, love potions .. Ubangalala powders.

bangbroek /ˈbaŋbruk, -brʊk/ *n. colloq.* Pl. **-e** /-ə/, **-s**. [Afk., *bang* afraid + *broek* (or occas. S. Afr. Eng. *broeks*) trousers.] A coward, a 'scaredy cat'; cf. BANGIE. See also BANG, PAPBROEK.

1913 C. PETTMAN *Africanderisms* 45 *Bangbroek*, A coward, a poltroon. **1945** N. DEVITT *People & Places* 142 This word 'bang' is from the Dutch. A bangbroek, for instance, is a coward. **1970** C. BANACH *Informant, Port Elizabeth* She's such a bangbroek that she won't even swim across the river. [**1986** *Sunday Star* 9 Nov. 7 As he left camp he taunted Maritz with the words 'Totsiens, bangbroek' (goodbye, coward).] **1990** *Sunday Times* 25 Feb. 19 Must be doing wonders for the sales of Imodium (take two tablets to avoid nasty accidents) among the *bangbroeke*. **1991** *People* 10 Apr. 2 'I was pleading with the guy. I begged him to keep the Cressida and just let me off in one piece,' he confessed. 'But don't call me bangbroeks till you've tried it yourself!' **1993** R. MCNEILL in *Sunday Times* 7 Nov. 21 Now the series is being rescreened on TV1, but at a time when even fewer people are likely to see it ... It's absurd, but the *bangbroeke* evidently still rule at Auckland Park.

bangie /ˈbaŋi/ *n. rare.* [BANG + Eng. suffix *-ie* (forming nouns used informally).] In urban (esp. township) slang: a coward; cf. BANGBROEK.

1973 P. BECKER in *The 1820* Vol.46 No.7, 32 A better-type shebeen is where 'Bangies' hang out, as the tsotsis say, referring to the customers who go there in groups, for fear of clashing with teenage thugs.

Bangoaketse, Bangwaketse, -waketze pl. forms of NGWAKETSE.

banja, banje varr. BAIE.

bank see BANKIE sense 2.

banket /baŋˈket, ˈbæŋkət/ *n. Mining.* Also **banquette**. [Du., see quot. 1937.] A name given by early gold-prospectors to gold-bearing conglomerates of quartz pebbles bound by siliceous cement. Also *attrib.*

1886 *Diamond Fields Advertiser* in J. Crwys-Williams *S. Afr. Despatches* (1989) 81 Banket or Almond reef, the same as Witwatersrand, has been discovered in large quantities at Schoonspruit. **1887** *Chambers's Jrnl* (U.K.) Apr. 284 The conglomerate .. is a peculiar formation of almond-shaped pebbles, pressed into a solid mass in a bed of rock of an igneous nature, and is called 'Banket' on account of its resemblance to a favourite Dutch sweetmeat known in England as almond rock. The 'Banket' is also rich in gold. **1897** H. RAYMOND *B.I. Barnato* 121 The first mines were worked literally from the outcrops of the reefs in the open, and the conglomerate rock or banket which contained the gold was crushed in small batteries with light stamps. **1913** V.R. MARKHAM *S. Afr. Scene* 44 The unique gold deposits of the Rand are to be found in conglomerate pebble beds called banket, tipped at an angle of between 30 and 70 degrees. **1933** W.H.S. BELL *Bygone Days* 131 The banket reef was quite new to geologists and they could not bring themselves to believe that it was anything more than a surface deposit. **1937** H. SAUER *Ex Afr.* 145 'Banket' .. should probably be spelt *banquette*, a term commonly used by the Dutch South Africans to distinguish a certain class of sweets — nuts, almonds, cloves, etc. — coated with sugar and variously coloured and all separate. The Boers applied the word to the conglomerate reefs of the Rand, because the conglomerate, on the outcrop, disintegrates into a mass of smooth quartz pebbles .. resembling the sweets. **1946** S. CLOETE *Afr. Portraits* 183 The formation in which gold is found on the Rand is called 'banket' ... The gold is mixed up in conglomerate beds, composed of quartz pebbles bound together by siliceous cement containing iron pyrites, in reefs which dip down to tremendous depths. **1951** *Off. Yrbk of Union 1949* (Union Office of Census & Statistics) 938 The name 'banket' .. refers specially to the ore taken from the oxidized zone. **1969** A.A. TELFORD *Jhb.: Some Sketches* 6 On the Reef [gold] was first found in the conglomerate or 'banket'. **1979** J. GRATUS *Jo'burgers* 19 They had already beaten him to some fine property with plenty of gold-bearing banket ore just beneath the surface and therefore cheap to mine. **1984** A. WANNENBURGH *Natural Wonder of Sn Afr.* 24 The real wealth of the Witwatersrand lay in the conglomerates, which locally were called 'banket'.

bankie /ˈbaŋki, ˈbʌŋ-/ *n.* [Afk., *bank* bench + dim. suffix -IE.]

1. A step-like rocky ledge; a terrace.

1882 J. NIXON *Among Boers* 265 We drove down a steep hill, over a series of steps caused by horizontal strata of rocks cropping out in ledges across the face of the hill. The road wound down the steps, or 'bankies' as they were called. **1924** G. BAUMANN in Baumann & Bright *Lost Republic* (1940) 90 Bruwer had gone a mile lower down, and adopted a beacon on a 'bankie' (small bank of earth) two feet high. **1967** W.A. DE KLERK *White Wines* 22 The high trellises .. have yielded up to 21 tons to the morgen. We use weed-killers for the *bankies*.

2. A small bench or stool. Also *attrib.*, and occas. without dim. suffix as **bank**. See also *riempie(s)bank* (RIEMPIE *n.* sense 2), and RUSBANK.

1959 J. MEIRING *Candle in Wind* 39 Martha Alberts sat on a bankie by the stove, staring at nothing. **1965** K. THOMPSON *Richard's Way* 98 There were a few small bankie stools clumped round the big fireplace beside an antique copper vat which held logs. **1971** BARAITSER & OBHOLZER *Cape Country Furn.* 111 In this particular case the bank as a whole is crude and it is difficult to know how old it is. **1980** F. CHISHOLM in *Cape Times* 9 Jan. 5 The attentive audience sat spellbound on uncomfortable school bankies. **1980** *Grocott's Mail* 26 Sept. 16 (*advt*) Dressing table, Riempie bankie, Electric stove, [etc.]. **1988** D. SAMUELSON in *Fair Lady* 16 Mar. 137 The old woman noticed that the child was watching her and beckoned her to come and sit on the bankie.

banning *vbl n. Hist.* [fr. BAN *v.*] The action of putting restrictions on a person in terms of security legislation; the state of being banned; RESTRICTION sense 1. Also *attrib.*

1971 *Rand Daily Mail* 16 Mar. 1 Shanthie Naidoo, the Indian woman whose exit permit cannot be used because she has been refused permission to leave Johannesburg, waits with quiet courage in the eight-year isolation of rigid banning. **1973** [see *boerehater* at BOEREHAAT]. **1977** *E. Prov. Herald* 29 Nov. 2 A Government that had to rely increasingly on bannings, detentions and the suppression of basic freedoms to cope with opposition to its policies was clearly in deep trouble. **1985** T. HEARD in J. Crwys-Williams *S. Afr. Despatches* (1989) 459 Banning has been described as civil death, since it restricts a person's movements and association ... Anyone who quotes a banned person is in big trouble. **1990** T. MATHEWS et al. in *Newsweek* 19 Feb. 24 The campaign gave him his first taste of real action, his first arrest, his first banning. **1990** [see MDM].

banning order *n. phr. Hist.* [BANNING + Eng. *order* injunction.] **a.** A document setting out the terms under which an individual's freedom of movement, association, speech, and action are restricted, and issued by ministerial decree in terms of security legislation. **b.** The conditions under which a 'banned' person is restricted. Also *transf.*, and *joc.* In both senses also called BAN *n.*, *restriction order* (see RESTRICTION sense 2).

The principal Acts in terms of which the Minister of Justice might impose a banning order were the Suppression of Communism Act, which introduced the concept in 1950, and the Internal Security Act.

1962 A.J. Luthuli *Let my People Go* 214, I had seven days' grace before the banning order took effect. **1974** *Daily Dispatch* 22 Feb. 16 We could not carry our drink out of the lounge ... When we saw the banning order just served verbally upon Mr Klaas could not be lifted we marched out and went to Cream Bowl Restaurant. **1979** *Survey of Race Rel. 1978* (S.A.I.R.R.) 102 On 11 May Mr Justice Philips in the Pretoria Supreme Court in an important judgement found that Ms Sheila Weinberg was guilty of contravening her banning order by having lunch with a friend; this constituted a social gathering. **1982** [see BAN *n.*]. **1983** C. Saunders *Hist. Dict.* 20 The typical 'banning order' .. restricted an individual to a magisterial district, required him or her to report regularly to the police, prevented anything said by the person from being quoted, .. and prevented him or her from meeting socially with more than one person at a time ... There was no appeal to the courts against a banning order, which was usually for five years, often renewed thereafter. **1990** *Weekend Argus* 17 Feb. 4 From 1959 onwards, he was served with a series of banning orders and was frequently arrested for not being in possession of a resident's permit. **1991** C. St Leger in *Sunday Times* 26 May 12 Both Dr Naude and the institute fell under the scrutiny of the security police and he was served with a banning order which effectively gagged him for 15 years.

banquette var. BANKET.

bansela var. BONSELLA.

banta(h)m var. BANDOM.

Bantoe /ˈbantu/ *n. offensive.* [Afk. pronunciation-spelling of BANTU.]

Used satirically, as a response to perceived patronizing attitudes among Afrikaans-speakers.

1. *obsolescent.* BANTU *n.* sense 1 (*offensive*).

1969 A. Fugard *Boesman & Lena* 25 You're one of the good Bantoes hey. I can see it. **1978** [see KAFEE].

2. *comb.* **Bantoedorp** /-dɔrp/ [Afk., *dorp* town], also in dim. form **Bantoedorpie** [see -IE], TOWNSHIP *n.* sense 2 a; **Bantoetaal** /-tɑːl/, pl. **-tale** /tɑːlə/ [Afk., *taal* language], BANTU *n.* sense 3.

*c*1970 C. Desmond *Discarded People* 155, I drove down the road and .. asked someone where this '**Bantoedorp**' was. **1981** *Voice* 18 Mar. 4 The LDC wanted to move his father's subjects to a new 'Bantoe dorpie' against their will. **1990** *Frontline* Mar.-Apr. 13 The blacks don't like to speak to them in Afrikaans; they want to speak English or **Bantoetaal**. **1978** M.J. Mtsaka *Not his Pride* 12 I'm not sure what that means, but if it was an insult all those whites who know Bantoetale would have stopped long ago.

bantom var. BANDOM.

Bantu /ˈba(ː)ntʊ, ˈbɒntu, ˈbæntu/ *adj.* and *n.* Also **Ba-ntu.** [Coined by W.H.I. Bleek, formed on elements found in varying forms in a number of Sintu (Bantu) languages: pl. prefix *ba-* denoting persons or people + n. stem *-ntu* person, as in Zulu *abantu* persons, people, humanity, sing. *umuntu* person, human being; cf. MUNTU).]

The offensive nature of this word as used to designate black African people under apartheid has led to its being offensive to many in all senses. The word tends to be avoided even as a scientific name for the language group, and the term SINTU is used by some in the academic community. The passing of time might remove the stigma attached to 'Bantu'. Cf. MUNTU.

A. *adj.*

1. 'Of or pertaining to an extensive group of negroid peoples inhabiting the equatorial and southern regions of Africa, and of the languages spoken by them' (*OED*); SINTU *adj.*; cf. BLACK *adj.* sense 1.

1862 W.H.I. Bleek *Comparative Grammar* 4 The South African division of the Bâ-ntu family of languages consists of one large middle body, occupying almost the whole known territory between the tropic of Capricorn and the equator. **1871** J. Mackenzie *Ten Yrs* (1971) 493 The Ba-ntu Family of Languages. The Kaffir language belongs to an extensive family of languages, which occupy (as far as our knowledge goes) the whole of the South African continent. **1888** D.C.F. Moodie *Hist. of Battles & Adventures* I. 578, I see that it is the fashion with many eminent ethnologists to call this collection of tribes the 'Bantu' tribes. As a Zulu linguist, I respectfully object to this. Bantu, or 'Abantu.' Abantu simply means 'people' in Zulu, and is used in this sense, 'Abantu bamhlope' *i.e.*, white people — and 'Abantu bamnyama' — *videlicet* — black people. **1905** W.H. Tooke in Flint & Gilchrist *Science in S. Afr.* 81 The Bantu tongue is an agglutinative polysyllabic, prefix-pronominal language of which the most salient features are the noun classes and the concord. **1907** W.C. Scully *By Veldt & Kopje* 167 The evangelisation and education of Bantu natives. **1926** W.A. Cotton *Race Problem* 23 We may desire that the pure Bantu race, in various groups, may be preserved, developing along lines most suitable to its own peculiar qualities. **1937** B.H. Dicke *Bush Speaks* 7 Their laws and customs did not only originate with their Bantu forbears, but with Semitic and other races. **1941** E.N.N. Msuthwana in *Bantu World* 1 Feb. 5 The high objective of combining Bantu languages should find grounds for feasibility. **1955** E. de S. Brunner in *Pol. Science Quarterly* Sept. 368 Numerically most important are the Native Africans, about nine million strong, divided among numerous tribes, most of which are of the Bantu group. **1976** West & Morris *Abantu* 7 Most social scientists would not use the term Bantu in anything other than a linguistic sense, and it certainly does not denote an ethnic group. **1983** U. Ndoma in *Jrnl of Afr. Lang. & Ling.* Vol.5 No.1, 105 The author of this monograph has attempted to locate and trace reflexes of earlier Bantu (Tshiluba) forms in present-day American language and culture. **1986** *Rhodes Newsletter* (Grahamstown) Dec. 6 The object of the research is to explore the sub-typologies within the Bantu language family so as to characterize better the Bantu family of languages.

2. *obsolescent. offensive.* Senses related to racial groupings.

a. Also with small initial. Designating one who is a member of a negroid people of South Africa; BLACK *adj.* sense 1 a.

See note at sense B 1. Cf. MUNTU sense 1.

1902 G.M. Theal *Beginning of S. Afr. Hist.* 95 Freedom from care to anything like the extent that is common to most individuals of our own race tended to make Bantu females as well as males far happier on the whole than white people. **1934** J. van der Poel *Educ. & Native* 2 By no body of persons in South Africa should the issues of Native education be more realistically confronted nor more passionately discussed than by an association of professional teachers having Bantu as well as European members. **1939** D.D.T. Jabavu in *Report of Proceedings of Natives Rep. Council* (UG10–1939) 5 We assume, Mr Chairman, in this respect that the Bantu people are considered a section of the population of South Africa as well and this announcement made the Natives hopeful of an era of solid progress and sympathetic consolidation of their welfare. **1948** H.V. Morton *In Search of S. Afr.* 155 From Cape Town to Port Elizabeth the traveller sees thousands of Cape Coloured ... But upon this road he is definitely moving into Bantu country. **1961** *Sunday Times* (U.K.) in *S. Afr. Speaks* (1962) 10 Bantu people must be protected against the social dis-integration associated with influx to the white cities. **1970** *Daily News* 12 July, (*advt*) Reliable Bantu Driver required for Durban office. **1986** D. Bradfield in *Grocott's Mail* 13 May 5 As my driver walked out of the shop he was confronted by five bantu teenagers demanding money from him.

b. i. Designating areas, facilities, services etc. intended for use by the black people of South Africa.

1934 D.D.T. Jabavu *Lovedale Sol-Fa Leaflet No.17* 4 When the Bantu township .. was first settled as a suburb of the Rand Municipality, the late Enoch Sontonga .. was a teacher. **1964** *Act 67* in *Stat. of Rep. of S. Afr.* 21 (1) There is hereby established .. (c) a district labour bureau — (i) in the office of every Bantu affairs commissioner. **1973** *Farmer's Weekly* 30 May (Suppl.) 31, 25 Bantu houses, church and school .. Bantu shop, shed for 23 cows. **1977** *World* 27 Sept. (Suppl.) 7 'Our own small staff is working closely with these independent companies in order to gain valuable experience in the field,' said Mr T van Heerden, head of Bantu Television. **1982** *Voice* 9 May 9 Bantu Education, Bantustans, Bantu Affairs Commissioner — the word Bantu has indeed become part and parcel of apartheid structures in South Africa. **1987** *E. Prov. Herald* 2 Apr. 10 Archbishop Tutu studied .. from 1950 to 1954 at Pretoria Bantu Normal College to be a teacher.

ii. Special collocation. **Bantu area**, an area officially set aside as residential or agricultural land for the use of black people.

1959 *Act 46* in *Stat. of Union* 522 'Bantu area' means any area consisting of land referred to in sub-section (1) of section *twenty-one* of the Native Trust and Land Act, 1936 (Act No. 18 of 1936), or any scheduled native area as defined in that Act. **1961** T. Matshikiza *Choc. for my Wife* 44 Why should they come to Orlando to the segregated Bantu area to see natives doing Shakespeare by candlelight. **1971** *Daily News* 8 Mar. 4 In the Bantu reserve I saw areas which were nothing but patches of red sand, whereas in the areas where there are Whites there is abundant grass to be seen. If we are to start it must be in the Bantu areas. **1971** *Argus* 5 June (Weekend) 5 It is this social upheaval in African society that is undoubtedly a major factor in creating the 'sub-culture of violence' in South Africa's urban Bantu areas. **1973** T. Bell *Indust. Decentral.* 12 The Bantu areas of South Africa thus comprise some 12.14 per cent of the country's land area .. and in 1965 contained approximately 25.6 per cent of the total population.

B. *n.*

1. *offensive.* Also **Abantu**, **abaNtu** and with small initial. Pl. unchanged, or **-s.** A black African; originally so-named as a speaker of one of the Bantu languages, but subsequently an ethnic designation; BANTOE sense 1 (*offensive*). See also BLACK *n.* sense 1 b.

Between 1953 and 1978 'Bantu' was one of the four major official ethnic designations, the others being 'Asian', 'Coloured', and 'White'. Originally a neutral term used also by blacks of themselves, 'Bantu' became increasingly unacceptable once it had become a part of the terminology of apartheid. See note at BLACK *n.* sense 1 b.

*c*1862 L. Grout *Zulu-Land* 60 The numerous tribes which occupy this broad section of southern and central Africa .. form but a single group in the larger divisions of the African race ... Some would call it the *Kafir* ... *Zingian* .. is another term which some of the learned have used, and *Bantu* another by which to designate the race. **1896** Purvis & Biggs *S. Afr.* 83 About the same time that the European commenced his inroad upon the regions below the Zambesi from the south, the dark-skinned Bantu was bestirring himself for his descent upon the land of the Hottentot and the Bushman from the north. **1909** O.E.A. Schreiner *Closer Union* (1960) 24 Our vast, dark native population consists largely of Bantus, who were already in South Africa when we came here; of a few expiring yellow varieties of African races, and a small but important number of half-castes. **1917** S.T. Plaatje *Native Life* 64 History does not tell us of any other continent where the Bantu lived besides Africa. **1918** H. Moore *Land of Good Hope* 43 The various native races of South Africa are generally classed together by the name Bantu, which means 'people'. **1925** D. Kidd *Essential Kafir* p.v, The title [*sc.* kaffir] is often used in South Africa as a synonym for the word native, and it is in this sense that it is used here. It is thus equivalent to the word Bantu. **1932** *Grocott's Daily Mail* 31 Mar. 4 The Joint Council of Europeans and Bantu for the Zoutpansberg District has instructed me to convey to you their emphatic protest against the imposition on the Native people of the above Bill. *c*1936 *S. & E. Afr. Yr Bk & Guide* 33 The Bantu, a name rather of linguistic than race significance, which form the vast majority of the native population over the Southern half of the Continent, derive from the mingling of the pure negro and the Hamitic strains in ever varying proportions. **1939** D.D.T. JABAVU in *Report of Proceedings of Natives Rep. Council* (UG10–1939) 5 It is hoped .. that there will be no half-hearted enthusiasm or any retraction in the bestowal of complete liberties generally acknowledged as legitimate claims of the Bantu in the present political machinery. **1941** W.M.B. NHLAPO in *Bantu World* 18 Jan. 9 One of the many institutions that Bantus really need just as much as Europeans do, is an aged home. *Ibid.* 22 Feb. 5 He was carried shoulder high down Main Street by some Bantu singing beautifully our sacred national anthem. **1943** 'J. BURGER' *Black Man's Burden* 47 The inhabitants of the Reserves are the Bantu. The word 'Bantu', like the word 'English', gives a linguistic rather than a racial description. **1952** *Drum* Nov. 10 They exhort the 'Bantu,' as they call Africans, to keep to themselves and have nothing to do with Indians. **1953** *Act 47* in *Stat. of Union* 258 In this Act, unless the context otherwise indicates – (i) 'Bantu' shall be synonymous with 'native'. **1960** A.J. LUTHULI in H. Spottiswoode *S. Afr.: Rd Ahead* 117 On their [*sc.* the National Party Government's] maxim: 'Do it yourselves, Bantus', Africans were to assume greater responsibility for paying for their welfare services and public services. **1962** L.E. NEAME *Hist. of Apartheid* 157 In Government circles the word Africans is now never used. The Blacks are called Bantu and sometimes Natives, but never Africans. **1967** in PLATZKY & WALKER *Surplus People* (1985) 65 It is accepted Government policy that the Bantu are only temporarily resident in the European areas of the Republic for as long as they offer their labour there. **1972** *Daily Dispatch* 8 Jan. 12 Once they were Kaffirs, then they were Natives, Africans, Non-Whites, Bantus. **1973** *Sunday Tribune* 1 Apr. 20 Non-Bantu means non-people and clearly refers to things like Whites. **1973** *Daily Dispatch* 6 Aug. 8 They [*sc.* members of the government] use the word 'black' or 'African' when discussing the indigenous peoples of this continent if they live outside South Africa's borders or in already sovereign independent states within them, but the name changes to 'Bantu' to describe South African blacks. **1976** *E. Prov. Herald* 31 Dec. 2 The Department of Bantu Education is in search of a new name because the word 'Bantu' has become offensive to the African people. **1978** *Daily Dispatch* 15 Mar. 1 A 'Bantu' will not be called a 'plural' after all. He or she will simply be known as 'black,' in terms of the new Government vocabulary. **1979** M. MATSHOBA *Call Me Not a Man* 8 Here, how I wish for the good old days when Bantus were Bantus and knew their place. **1980** *Voice* 20 Aug. 14 If indeed abaNtu as we know them today helped found and fashion this advanced urban culture, that should explain, partly I concede, why they have adjusted so speedily to the 20th century city groove. **1981** *Ibid.* 18 Oct. 4 He needs to be reminded that even the gospel of apartheid never used the kaffir terminology officially. It opened the evolutionary chapter with Native, then moved to Bantu, next Plural, and today something in between Cooperation and Black. And who knows tomorrow it might be just plain South African. **1983** C. SAUNDERS *Hist. Dict.* 22 'Bantu' was disliked by Africans themselves because of its associations with apartheid and inferior treatment, and 'a Bantu' and 'Bantus,' forms often used, were grammatical nonsense. **1986** *Style* Dec. 41 The only good bantus, commies, liberals and Engelse were dead ones. **1989** B. RONGE in *Sunday Times* 26 Feb. (Mag. Sect.) 8 Have you contrived to abolish words like native, bantu and plural from your vocabulary forever? Yes? Nice work! **1991** A. MAIMANE in *Weekly Mail* 15 Feb. 17 A simple way for them to decide whether a person who looked African should be classified coloured was to stick a comb in their hair: if it stayed put, they were fourth-class 'bantu' and not second-class kleurlings.

2. *noncount.* A family of related southern African languages including Ndebele, sePedi, Shona, siSwati, Sotho, seTswana, Venda, Xhosa, Zulu, etc.; SINTU *n.* Usu. *comb.* **Bantu-speaker** *n.*, a person who speaks one of these languages; **Bantu-speaking** *ppl adj.*, being a speaker of one of these languages.

1948 H.V. MORTON *In Search of S. Afr.* 171 The traveller who .. wishes to see the Bantu-speaking native in his primitive tribal conditions, should motor from Grahamstown through the enormous territory which is divided by the river Kei into the Ciskei and Transkei. **1951** *Report of Commission on Native Education* (UG53–1951) 9 In the Union the Bantu-speaking tribes as groups do differ in physical type .. from other aboriginal peoples. **1972** L.G. GREEN *When Journey's Over* 123 Fanagalo has .. been called Pidgin Bantu, Basic Bantu, Basic Zulu, Isilololo and Silinguboi. **1983** *Sunday Times* 18 Sept. (Lifestyle) 9 The people of Mapungubwe were Bantu-speaking, part Negroid, part East African and they must have been an indigenous group. **1984** P.R. BENNETT in *Jrnl of Afr. Lang. & Ling.* Vol.6 No.2, 200 Okoth-Okombo argues that prenasalized stops in Luo are inherited, not borrowed from Bantu. **1986** P.A. MCALLISTER Xhosa Beer Drinks. 42 Central Bantu-speaking groups such as the Bemba, Nyakyusa, Ndembu and Lamba. **1989** *Reader's Digest Illust. Hist.* 62 *'Bantu'*, which means 'people' is the scientific name for the language group to which all South African Africans, except the Khoisan, belong. **1990** *Sunday Times* 8 July 18 Archaeological evidence proves that Bantu-speakers have lived in the Transvaal since at least the 5th century AD. **1991** J. COULTER in *Weekend Post* 4 May (Leisure) 3 The arrival of the Khoikhoi .. and the Bantu-speakers with their cattle-owning and cultivating culture.

3. *noncount. nonce.* Used in place of the name of any of these languages; *Bantoetaal*, see BANTOE sense 2.

1963 A. FUGARD *Blood Knot* (1968) 174 The gate was open, God, your sun was too bright and blinded my eyes, so I didn't see the notice prohibiting. And 'beware of the dog' was in Bantu, so how was I to know, Oh Lord.

Hence **Bantoid** *adj.*; **Bantudom** *n.*; **Bantuized** *adj.*, (of language) adapted to the pronunciation and grammar of a Sintu (Bantu) language; **Bantu-ologist** *n.* *?nonce*, an anthropologist specializing in the study of the culture of Sintu-speaking (Bantu-speaking) peoples.

1929 H.S. MSIMANG in *Workers' Herald* 7 Sept. 3 It's very clear that the existing state of affairs cannot last unless Bantudom is doomed to everlasting slavery. **1929** [see NGUNI *adj.* sense 1]. **1941** W.M.B. NHLAPO in *Bantu World* 1 Feb. 9 A wave of unparalleled satisfaction and enthusiasm burst out on Bantudom to learn that at long last Europeans no longer look upon us as a child people. **1955** *Report of Commission for Socio-Economic Dev. of Bantu Areas* (UG61–1955) 84 Some Bantu-ologists consider that the average family in certain bushveld and lowveld parts of the Bantu Areas, derives its whole nourishment from such 'veld' foods for more than two months per year. **1983** R.M. RICHARDS in *Jrnl of Afr. Lang. & Ling.* Vol.5 No.2, 205 Such behaviour in verbal systems seems to widespread in Bantu/Bantoid languages.

Bantu beer *n. phr. Obsolescent. offensive.* [BANTU *adj.* sense 2 b + Eng. *beer.*] TSHWALA. Also *attrib.*

1962 *Act 63* in *Stat. of Rep. of S. Afr.* 1005 'Bantu beer' means – (a) the drink generally known as kaffir beer and commonly brewed by Bantu from kaffir corn or millet or other grain; and (b) any other fermented liquor which the State President may from time to time by proclamation in the *Gazette* declare to be Bantu beer. **1962** J. SCOTT in *Capricorn High School Mag.* 42 We visited .. an experimental plant for the brewing of Bantu beer. **1968** COLE & FLAHERTY *House of Bondage* 141 Bantu beer .. is a thick, sour-tasting drink, purplish in color, and containing only a piddling two per cent of alcohol. The beer comes in waxed half-gallon cartons that look like milk containers. **1968** J. LELYVELD in *Ibid.* 9 The state raises much of the money with which it runs the townships – and, thus, holds down white taxes – by brewing the concoction known as Bantu beer and operating all drinking establishments where black men can legally imbibe. **1970** HEARD & FAULL *Cookery in Sn Afr.* 466 Kaffir beer, the traditional drink of the various Bantu tribes, is not to be confused with the new Bantu beer, a powder and water preparation sold on the Rand and in most South African urban areas and now supplied through the various Beer Halls for the Africans. **1971** *Sunday Times* 31 Oct. 17 The Bantu Beer Unit of the CSIR Requires: Two Senior Biochemists. **1972** *Std Encycl. of Sn Afr.* VI. 266 Approximately 90% of the Kaffir-corn consumed in South Africa goes as malt and meal into the brewing of Bantu beer. Apart from home brewing, over 455 million litres are brewed annually in the breweries of local authories, mining companies, and large-scale employers of Bantu labour. **1977** [see SMALL TIME]. **1980** C. HERMER *Diary of Maria Tholo* 34 The Administration Board operated beerhalls selling 'jabulani' or 'bantu beer' mainly to migrants. **1988** *Farmer's Weekly* 1 Jan. 89 Redcorn malt. For making Bantu beer.

Bantu commissioner's court see COMMISSIONER'S COURT.

Bantu Education *n. phr. Hist.* Now *derog.* Also with small initials. [BANTU *adj.* sense 2 b + Eng. *education*; or tr. Afk. *Bantoe-onderwys.*] Under apartheid, the official system of education for black South Africans, initiated by the first Bantu Education Act (1953). Also *attrib.*

In official circles, education for blacks was usu. termed 'native education' up to the early 1950s, 'Bantu education' from then until the late 1970s, and 'black education' thereafter; among left-wing groupings, however, 'Bantu Education' remained a common name for the black education system. The former Department of Bantu Education was renamed the *Department of Education and Training* (see DET) in 1978.

1951 *Report of Commission on Native Education* (UG53–1951) 131 We now turn to the question why it should be *Bantu Education* ... Educational practice must recognise that it has to deal with a Bantu child, i.e. a child trained and conditioned in Bantu culture, endowed with a knowledge of a Bantu language and imbued with values, interests and behaviour patterns learned at the knee of a Bantu mother. These facts must dictate to a very large extent the content and methods of his early education. **1957** N. MANDELA *No Easy Walk* (1965) 49 An inferior type of education, known as Bantu education, and designed to relegate the Africans to a position of perpetual servitude in a baasskap society, is now in force in all African primary schools .. and will be introduced to all secondary and high schools as from next year. **1960** Z.K. MATTHEWS in H. Spottiswoode *S. Afr.: Rd Ahead* 191 He will cling to the idea of education without the adjective 'Bantu' until the day which he knows must surely come when he rejoins the mainstream of free education. **1962** A.J. LUTHULI *Let my People Go* 47 Bantu education came into effect in 1954. It is a specialised type of education designed exclusively by Europeans exclusively for Africans. **1968** J. LELYVELD in Cole & Flaherty *House of Bondage* 14 When the late Hendrik Verwoerd introduced the system of Bantu Education – which seeks to decree what a black child can learn, from whom, and where – he made clear that there would be no place for the African in the white community, except in specified forms of labour ... If the black man refuses to consider a multiracial solution when he finally reaches the point of decision in South Africa, that will be proof that Bantu Education accomplished its aim. **1971** BEHR & MACMILLAN *Education in S. Afr.* 406 State expenditure for 1960–61 was R12,46 per Bantu pupil. In the Cape Province it was for the same period R144,57 per white pupil ... This method of financing Bantu Education has proved inadequate. **1977** *Drum* Sept. 2 To hell with Bantu education, the students say. But, unlike their parents who said the same thing, the students mean it. **1977** J. SIKAKANE *Window on Soweto* 39 The twenty years of 'Bantu Education' have attempted to produce mentally retarded African graduates who cannot think beyond their repressed Blackness. **1978** *S. Afr. Panorama* Feb. 16 The .. President-designate, Chief Minister Lucas Mangope .. also attacked 'Bantu Education', and announced that his first major programme of reform was 'to prepare a blueprint for educating people who are just human beings and nothing fancy like Bantus.' **1981** *Pace* Sept. 33, I am a graduate of the 1976 uprisings in Soweto, the result of enforced Bantu Education and the use of Afrikaans as a medium of instruction. **1987** E. MOLOBI in *Frontline* Mar. 27 Where Bantu Education attempted to instil an acceptance of oppression, People's Education attempts to develop a critical awareness of the world. **1990** T. MATHEWS et al. in *Newsweek* 19 Feb. 24 Mandela grew up at a time when well-born South African blacks were given rigorous, moralistic, missionary educations. This puts him light-years ahead of dimmer, township revolutionaries who have apartheid's deliberately inferior, raise-no-expectations, Bantu education forced upon them. **1991** R.W. JOHNSON in *Sunday Times* 10 Feb. 21 The curse of Verwoerd lies heavy upon the country: decades of Bantu education have done their dreadful work.

bantustan /ˈbɒn-, ˈbæntuˌstæn, ˈbantuˌstɑːn/ *n.* [Formed by analogy with Eng. *Pakistan, Hindustan*, etc.; see BANTU *n.* (sense 1) and -STAN.]

1. *obs.* As a proper noun: The putative name of a proposed black state inside the boundaries of South Africa.

[**1949** J.S. FRANKLIN *This Union* 188, I should like to remind Hon. Senators that back of and beyond our Bantu Hindustan there lies the Continent of Africa with its 250 millions of black-skinned people.] **1949** *Round Table* June 208 A great Bantu State or group of States to which at least one ingenious thinker has affixed the term 'Bantustan'. **1949** E.H. BROOKES in *Survey of Race Rel. 1947–8* 2 The word 'apartheid' .. has proved as ambiguous as its predecessor 'segregation'. It has been interpreted .. as being the creation of a new large Bantu state. Some speakers have referred to it as 'Bantustan'. **1951** J.D.L. KRUGER *Bantustan: Study in Prac. Apartheid* 19 The proposed area which is contemplated as the non-white State .. will be referred to as Bantustan. **1952** *Rand Daily Mail* 1 Dec. 8 Dr. Malan, the leader and architect of apartheid and Bantustan, has sidestepped the issue once again. **1960** M. BALLINGER in H. Spottiswoode *S. Afr.: Rd Ahead* 22 Even those Nationalists who fear the new idea of Bantustan .. still maintain an attachment to this conception of a home for Africans where alone they might enjoy rights of domicile and property.

2. Now only *derog.* Often with initial capital. HOMELAND sense 1. Also *attrib.*

1954 *Observer* (U.K.) 20 June 4 The 'Bantustan' conception of the Nationalist intellectuals and the Dutch Reformed Church .. means the absolute division of South Africa into Black and White territories. **1959** H.F. VERWOERD in *Hansard* 27 Jan. 62 If Britain can establish something that the United Party describe as a Bantustan inside South Africa, and can do so with their blessing .. why cannot the Union of South Africa .. say:— We are giving the Bantu as our wards every opportunity in their areas to move along a road of development. **1962** L.E. NEAME *Hist. of Apartheid* 159 The Opposition in Parliament, and the public, promptly called these Bantu national units 'Bantustans'. **1968** COLE & FLAHERTY *House of Bondage* 98 There are three tribal colleges for blacks, administered by whites, and located only in the Bantustan reserves. **1973** *Drum* 18 Jan. 27 The White man tells us about bantustans, and do you know what he says when he is with his White brother? He says 'daar sal die Bantu Staan in the Bantustan and he won't progress further than that.' **1976** *Sunday Times* 31 Oct. 16 Not a single country, apart from South Africa, recognises Bantustan sovereignty. **1978** *Ibid.* 5 Mar. 16 The primary objective of this 'bantustan' or 'homeland' policy is to create a legal basis for treating the black urban population as foreigners in a country which belongs to them just as much as to the whites. **1979** *Voice* 30 Sept. 3 We have witnessed with dismay the calculated dissection of our country into bantustans. The disembodiment of the country into separate worthless 'independent' and subservient entities — the culmination of the apartheid policies. **1980** *Rand Daily Mail* 23 Aug. What were once the 'reserves' became 'Bantustans', then the 'homelands'; now they are 'national states'. **1984** E. AARVIK in *Daily Dispatch* 13 Dec. 18 Blacks are expected to exercise their political ambitions in unviable, poverty-stricken, arid bantustan homelands, ghettoes of misery, inexhaustible reservoirs of cheap black labour, bantustans into which South Africa is being balkanised. **1985** *Weekly Mail* 28 June 15 The organisation's continuing stand for a united, non-tribal, non-Bantustan South Africa helps to make it a deadly enemy to the Government. **1985** PLATZKY & WALKER *Surplus People* 18 The Status Acts conferring independence on the bantustans say that every person who is a citizen of the bantustan in terms of any law 'shall cease to be a citizen of South Africa'. **1985** *Ibid.* [see NATION]. **1987** *Frontline* Aug.-Sept. 30 They [*sc.* the chiefs] are so closely identified with bantustan power structures — structures inimical to mainstream black political thought — that oblivion is an option they ought to consider. **1988** 'VUSI' in *Pace* June 12 The Zambians .. are the vanguard of Frontline States. Their anti-apartheid, anti-bantustan stance is very well known. **1990** *Weekly Mail* 9 Mar. 2 'Away with bantustans!' 'Away with Mangope, forward to a democratic South Africa!'

Hence **Bantustania** *n.*, *Drum* magazine's satirical collective name for the 'homelands'; see also *-stania* (-STAN); so **Bantustanian** *n.*, a black South African; and *adj.*, of or pertaining to a Bantustan; see also *-stanian* (-STAN); **Bantustanism** *n.*, the policy of balkanising South Africa.

1974 *Drum* 8 Mar. 45 At times I wonder if a Bantustanian has any right to think at all. That is why my Bantustanian brain is in a muddle. *Ibid.* 8 Apr. 32 Once every year the witches of Bantustania have a get-together. **1979** M. MATSHOBA *Call Me Not a Man* 185 The Act established councils along tribal lines through which Apartheid and Bantustanism were forced down the people's throats through the manipulation of the appointed chiefs. **1982** *Voice* 24 Jan. 4 Bantustanism far from solves some of the burning issues in South Africa.

banya var. BAIE.

Bapedi see PEDI.

Baquaina, Baquan(s) varr. BAKWENA.

Bara /ˈbærə, ˈbara/ *n. colloq.* [Abbrev. of *Baragwanath.*] A nickname for Baragwanath Hospital, Soweto. Also *attrib.*

1974 K.M.C. MOTSISI in *Drum* 22 Dec. 44 He tells me that Kid Bles is admitted to the Repair House (Bara Hospital) after he gets himself knifed at a gumba-gumba session way out in Naledi. *a***1977** K.M.C. MOTSISI in M. Mutloatse *Casey & Co.* (1978) 132 Next time the quack and nurses call around this 'Bara' bed of mine they will find me singing — *Show me the way to go home* with a smile as wide as a two-up of maiza. **1988** S. DE FAY in *Frontline* Jan. 10 This was a night at Baragwanath, Africa's largest hospital. I went to Bara to find out why white doctors work there. **1990** *New African* 18 June 4 We saw how many babies were coming in, and how many died ... 'One can't say it is symptomatic of the lack of doctors .. because it is happening at other black hospitals like Bara (Baragwanath),' said one doctor. **1991** N. MBATHA in *Pace* Feb. 39 Taxi owners operating between Merafe, Bara and Johannesburg received a letter .. ordering them to stop transporting commuters.

Baralong var. BAROLONG.

barba var. BARBER.

Barbarton var. BARBERTON sense 2.

barbel /ˈbɑːb(ə)l/ *n.* Pl. unchanged, or **-s**. [Transf. use of Eng. *barbel* a type of fish, fr. Fr. *barbel* a whisker-like appendage found, usu. in pairs, beside the mouths of certain fish, ad. L. *barba* beard.]

The common name 'barbel' and the generic name *Barbus* (YELLOWFISH) are sometimes confused (see quot. 1930 at sense 3); quot. 1838 may more correctly belong at sense 3.

1. A freshwater fish of the Cyprinidae.

1838 J.E. ALEXANDER *Exped. into Int.* II. 204 Among other fish caught here were two which seemed to be novel: one .. had a purse or bag-like mouth, and eleven rays to the dorsal fin, was evidently a barbel (barbus), but peculiar from having its nose produced and rounded, like the Cyprinus Narus. **1867** *Blue Bk for Colony 1866* FF19, The Stormberg Spruit and other streams abound in barbel, white, and yellow fish, which are excellent food.

2. Any of several marine and estuarine fishes of the Plotosidae (barbel-eel) and Ariidae (sea barbel) families, of the order Siluriformes, with fleshy filaments hanging from their mouths and poisonous fin spines; BAGGER sense 1; BARBER sense 2; CATFISH sense 3.

1850 R.G.G. CUMMING *Hunter's Life* I. 217 They captured lots of mullet and barbel, averaging from one to four pounds in weight. **1907** *E. London Dispatch* 7 Oct. (Pettman), *Barbel*, or more correctly 'catfish'. **1913** C. PETTMAN *Africanderisms* 46 *Barbel* or *Barber*, (1) The East London name for the fish *Galeichthys feliceps*. See Catfish. (2) A freshwater fish. **1930** C.L. BIDEN *Sea-Angling Fishes* 283 Apart from the sting ray, if ever there is a fish of the sea one should treat with great caution it is the barbel. **1949** J.L.B. SMITH *Sea Fishes* 108 *Plotosus anguillaris*, .. *Barbel-eel. Barber* ... Despite the repulsive appearance of the fish, the flesh is excellent and wholesome ... *Tachysurus feliceps*, .. *Barbel. Barber. Sea-Barbel. Catfish. Bagger.* **1967** E. ROSENTHAL *Encycl. of Sn Afr.* 100 *Mud-barbel* or *Platkop Barger*, The best-known South African river species north of Cape ... *Cape Barger* or *Sea Barbel* .. is common all round the South African coast. **1983** *Cape Times* 9 July 11 When they did pick up a reef which produced a few red roman or stumpnose, it was not long before hordes of small sharks and barbel devoured the entire catch. **1994** *SA Commercial Marine* Sept.-Nov. 32 Mr Drew Hunter .. has started the first tag-and-release programme of one of this country's most arresting fish — Galeichthyes feliceps, better known as the barbel ... According to Dr [Deon] Rall, regular ingestion of Galeichthyes feliceps could have excellent lesion regenerative propensities ... The [Breede River] Lodge's chief chef .. had produced a number of haute cuisine platters incorporating barbel ... According to a Sea Fisheries spokesman only the sea barbel has spines, but both sea and fresh water [barbel] have whiskers.

3. Any of several freshwater fishes of the Bagridae, Clariidae, Schilbeidae, Amphiliidae, and Malapteruridae families of the order Siluriformes, characterized by fleshy filaments hanging from the mouth; BAGGER sense 2; CATFISH sense 2. See also BARBER sense 1 b.

*a***1875** T. BAINES *Jrnl of Res.* (1964) II. 134 The River abounded with fish, of which the principal was the barbel — *Silurus capensis* — I think; a wide-mouthed creature, whose insatiate jaws repeatedly caused the birds we shot to disappear beneath the surface. **1893** H.A. BRYDEN *Gun & Camera* 463 We were particularly successful among the barbel. This fish (*Glanis silurus*) grows to enormous weight and size in the larger African rivers. **1897** J.P. FITZPATRICK *Outspan* 113 It [*sc.* the river] .. carried samples of dressed stone and Portland cement to the barbel and crocodiles of Ingwenye Umkulu, thirty miles away. **1920** F.C. CORNELL *Glamour of Prospecting* 306 We had an alleged meal at midday by the river, where Gert caught a small barbel ... With the aid of the pea flour, and the bacon frizzled on a prospecting shovel, we ate it, bones and all. **1930** C.L. BIDEN *Sea-Angling Fishes* 286 There are about a thousand species of harmless, soft-finned, freshwater barbels which are called 'cat-fish' in some countries. To avoid confusion due to local names, the South African fresh-water barbel is *Clarias* of family Siluridae. The name 'barbel' would have been more properly applied to the many species of *Barbus* and allied genera of the Cyprinidae were it not that the name is used throughout South Africa for the Silurids. **1946** L.G. GREEN *So Few Are Free* 174 Many people in South-West Africa prefer Swakopmund to any of the Union's seaside resorts. They catch whiskered barbel from the iron jetty. **1964** G. CAMPBELL *Old Dusty* 147 Barbel we know can travel overland. We have heard the 'clop-clop-clop-clop' as they smack their way with tail and fins over rocks from pool to pool, and they are said to be able to travel long distances by land. **1967** R.A. JUBB *Freshwater Fishes* 131 Species of *Clarias*, catfish or barbel, ..

are notorious for the length of time they can live out of water ... Even in well-oxygenated water .. they eventually die if prevented from going to the surface to take gulps of air and expel vitiated air. **1988** C. NORMAN in *S. Afr. Panorama* Dec. 41 Monster barbel or catfish are the country's biggest freshwater fish and are found wherever the water is not too cold.

barber /ˈbɑːbə/ *n.* Also **ba(r)ba**. [ad. S. Afr. Du. *baber* barbel.] Any of several marine and freshwater fishes. **1.** Freshwater: **a.** The *Clanwilliam yellowfish* (see YELLOWFISH sense b), *Barbus capensis*. **b.** The airbreathing catfish *Clarias gariepinus* of the Clariidae; also called BARBEL (sense 3). **2.** Marine: BARBEL sense 2.

1848 H.H. METHUEN *Life in Wilderness* 67 (Pettman), A few fish called *barbers*, of a long and eel-like sort, with whiskers or feelers, were caught in the river. **1873** F. BOYLE *To Cape for Diamonds* 207 Here I first learned to eat the *barba*, a prodigy of fishes, and to love it. Do you know the bull-head, the miller's thumb, we used to catch at home? .. Fancy this ugly beast of any size between a half-pound and two hundred-weight; give it great teeth more cutting than a pike's; adorn its big mouth with four long beards, and you will have the barba. **1876** —— *Savage Life* 285 My sleepy friend declined with emphasis to help. He said a barba was a something cross between a toad, a sand-eel, and a pug dog; and he wouldn't stir for one of the three, nor for the lot combined. **1889** 'A HOUSEWIFE OF THE COLONY' *Col. Hsehold Guide* 32 The Baba. In some parts of the colony this fish, almost without bones, during some seasons of the year is caught in the muddy banks of the rivers. Its flavour resembles that of an eel, being very rich. **1892** NICOLLS & EGLINGTON *Sportsman in S. Afr.* 135 *The Cat Fish*, (*Clarias capensis*) — *Barbel* or *Barber* of the Cape Colonists ... The 'Barber' is the commonest of the South African freshwater fish, and may be found in almost every river and dam throughout the country. **1913** C. PETTMAN *Africanderisms* 47 *Barber*, .. A large freshwater fish, considered by some to be good eating. In appearance it is by no means prepossessing, the long fleshy filaments which hang from the corners of its mouth giving it a rather repelling appearance. **1929** J. STEVENSON-HAMILTON *Low-Veld* 126 Some of the bottom feeders find a secure winter refuge immersed in the mud ... It is possible to secure, by digging, numbers of perfectly healthy specimens, usually of the catfish tribe, commonly known as barbers. **1945** H. GERBER *Fish Fare* 72 *Barbel* or *barber*, This very ugly fish, with its hideous 'moustache' has no scales. It is found in the Orange River. It is similar to the freshwater catfish of the southern United States. **1989** E. BURSIK in *Ski-Boat* Jan.-Feb. 21 The comp[etition] .. was structured to force anglers to catch as many of the dozens of available species as possible — bream ('drie kol'), barbers, squeakers and many others.

Barberton /ˈbɑːbətən/ *n.* [Name of an Eastern Transvaal town.]

1. [These plants are abundant in the Barberton area.]

a. In full ***Barberton daisy***: the perennial plant *Gerbera jamesonii* of the Asteraceae, bearing large, daisy-like flowers on long stems; *Transvaal daisy*, see TRANSVAAL.

1906 B. STONEMAN *Plants & their Ways* 115 When several bracts surround a head of flowers, as in *Protea*, the Barberton daisy, and others of their tribe, they form an *involucre*. **1932** R. MARLOTH *Flora of S. Afr.* III. 282 The best known species is *Gerbera Jamesoni* from the Eastern Transvaal, commonly called Barberton daisy, now cultivated in many varieties of colour and foliage. **1956** H.F. WERNER in *Jrnl of Bot. Soc. of S. Afr.* XLI. 17 *Gerbera jamesonii* (Compositae) ('Barberton Daisy'): $1\frac{1}{2}$ — 2 ft. Scarlet. October to March. A very well-known plant. **1960** C. LIGHTON *Cape Floral Kingdom* 61 The Barberton daisy is known .. as the daisy from the Barberton district of the Transvaal, but outside the Union our Barbertons are commonly called gerberas. **1987** *S. Afr. Panorama* Sept. 19 The famous Barberton daisy has been grown and hybridised world-wide, but many lowveld gardeners prefer the original form with its orange-red flowers. **1989** *Gardening Questions Answered* (Reader's Digest Assoc.) 324 Barberton Daisy ... Summer flowering perennials which have hairy, mid-green leaves and bear daisy-like flowers on long, stiff stems. **1991** *Farmer's Weekly* 25 Jan. 92 Barberton Daisies: Immediate post-free despatches 10 plants R40.

b. With distinguishing epithet designating a specific variety of Barberton daisy: **Mountain Barberton**, *Gerbera welwitschii*.

1953 J. HOYLE *Some Flowers* 8 The Mountain Barberton is found in grasslands at high elevation. Flowers are clear yellow and about 1 in. across.

2. Also **Babaton, Baberton, Barbarton,** and with small initial. In urban (esp. township) slang: an illicitly-brewed raw liquor. Also *attrib.* Cf. MBAMBA.

1948 E. HELLMANN *Rooiyard* 48 At the present time *babaton* comes first in popularity, with *shimeya* or *shimeyani* as close second. **1950** *Report of Commission to Enquire into Acts of Violence Committed by Natives at Krugersdorp* (UG47–1950) 10 Illicit concoctions are still being brewed on a large scale. They consist chiefly of skokiaan, shimayane, barberton, etc. **1951** A. O'DOWD in B. Sachs *Herman Charles Bosman* (1971) 153 The street was full of the nauseating smell of Barberton ... There would be a liquor raiding squad later that night. **1960** J.J.L. SISSON *S. Afr. Judicial Dict.* 84 The ingredients of *barberton* drink are uncertain, but it must contain yeast and mealie-meal. A policeman's evidence that a concoction of which he produces a sample is *barberton* is *prima facie* proof of this fact. **1963** B. MODISANE *Blame Me on Hist.* (1986) 35 She turned our home into a shebeen, worked fourteen hours a day brewing and pressing home brews called skokiaan and barberton, and from the proceeds she educated me to high school level. *a***1968** [see MBAMBA]. **1972** *Drum* 8 Mar. 13 Every boozer who has downed methylated spirits or barberton knows the gnawing fear of going blind or mad. **1979** *Sunday Post* 8 July 7 Depending on the kind of shebeen .. the brandy might be spread thin and mixed with all sorts of things — methylated spirits, tobacco, molasses, calcium carbides, pineapple, bread, potatoes — to make tshopase, uhamba, (Barberton) and skokiaan. **1982** *Fair Lady* 1 Dec. 188 Blacks weren't allowed to buy 'white man's liquor' in those days (this only became legal in 1962) and the drink served was known as Barberton — a concoction made of bread, malt, sugar, yeast and warm water .. strictly illegal, of course. **1987** M. MELAMU *Children of Twilight* 9 Baba Nhlapo had three great passions: horse-racing, an illicit brew called 'Barberton', and fish-and-chips, in that order.

barboon var. BOERBOON.

barcelia, barcella varr. BASELA *n.*

barcon var. BAAKEN.

barga, barger varr. BAGGER.

bari /ˈbɑːri/ *n. slang.* Also **baari(e), barrie, barry, ibari.** Pl. **-s, -ies,** or (occas.) **iibari.** [Township slang (or Isicamtho), perh. fr. BAAR; but see also quot. 1963.] A rural person who is still in the process of being assimilated into urban life; a 'country bumpkin', unsophisticated person, or one lacking in astuteness. See also BAAR. Cf. MOEGOE, MOMPARA sense 1.

1963 WILSON & MAFEJE *Langa* 21 All of them are stigmatized as uncouth countrymen, iibari by the townsmen proper ... Ibari .. is also associated by some informants with barbarian ... After the film of *The Barbarians* the tsotsis in Johannesburg are said to have taken over the word and applied it to the new generation of country men who are in the process of being absorbed in town ... The iibari mostly have at least a little education .. but they come from the country and have not yet been assimilated. *a***1977** K.M.C. MOTSISI in M. Mutloatse *Casey & Co.* (1978) 65 'Who needs a licence to sell booze or drink. Like needing a licence to buy food and permission to eat it. Those papers are for baaries man,' Fatty .. would have said. **1981** [see *Voice* quot. at GEMORS sense b]. **1982** D. BIKITSHA in *Rand Daily Mail* 14 Oct. (Eve) 5 If you were a man-about-town and 'clever' or 'fly' as some of the adjectives of this new slanguage described, you spoke tsotsi taal. If you used the old hackneyed vernaculars you were termed a 'barry,' 'mogo,' 'streepkop,' 'jackaja,' 'kararow' or plain yokel. **1983** *Drum* Apr. 10 'The people of Soweto say we are "baris"' ... A 'bari' is a country bumpkin, a yokel. Somebody who is not with it. **1983** G. MVUBELO in *Natal Mercury* 8 June, Some people don't speak the township lingo. There are the 'baris' or the 'moegies'. They are the dumb ones, who just speak the vernacular. **1987** N. MATHIANE in *Frontline* Oct.-Nov. 34 In the street it is either joining the gang (carrying knives, harrassing girls and getting drunk) or be seen as a 'barrie' (bum) and be humiliated for not being 'with it'.

barimo var. BADIMO.

baroe, barroe /bəˈruː/ *n.* Also **baroo, barou, barup.** [Khoikhoi.]

a. Any of several species of the plant *Cyphia* of the Campanulaceae, with an edible, tuberous rootstock.

1795 C.R. HOPSON tr. *C.P. Thunberg's Trav.* II. 102 Besides the above-mentioned plant called Kon or Gunna, they use two others, viz. one called Kamekà, or Barup, which is said to be a large and watery root; and another called Ku, which is likewise, according to report, a large and succulent root. **1897** [see KAMBRO]. **1913** C. PETTMAN *Africanderisms* 48 *Baroo, Cyphia volubilis.* The Hottentot name of this watery bulb, which is much esteemed by them for the moisture which it contains even in seasons of protracted drought. **1924** L.H. BRINKMAN *Glory of Backveld* 53 The barroe is a bulb the size of a fowl's egg, full of sweet, delicious milk. **1966** C.A. SMITH *Common Names* 70 *Bar(r)oe*, A modification of a native name for certain species of Cyphia. The tuberous roots have a watery, but pleasantly sweet taste. **1971** L.G. GREEN *Taste of S.-Easter* 91 A school magazine published years ago .. contains practical advice on the veldkos of the Nieuwoudtville district, the baroe and voëlvoet dug out by trekboers, shepherds and schoolboys. **1976** [see KAMBRO].

b. With a distinguishing epithet designating a particular species of baroe: **bergbaroe**, see BERG sense 1 b ii; **bosbaroe** /ˈbɔs-/, and formerly **boschbaroe** /ˈbɔʃ-/ [Afk., *bos*, formerly *bosch*, see BOSCH], *Cyphia sylvatica*; **veldbaroe** /felt/ [Afk., *veld* uncultivated countryside], *Cyphia undulata*.

1893 P. MACOWAN in C.A. Smith *Common Names* 160 **Bosch Barroe** dug up and eaten by school boys. **1966** C.A. SMITH *Common Names* 160 *Bosbar(r)oe, Cyphia sylvatica* ... Stem and branches twining. Leaves entire or finely-toothed; flowers solitary, white. *Ibid.* 81 **Veldbar(r)oe**, *Cyphia undulata*. .. Tuber large, succulent and juicy. Stems slender, twining ... Flowers bilabiate, rosy or white, sweetly scented. The species was first recorded by Ecklon (1828) ... The vernacular name is derived from the habitat of the plants. **1972** BEETON & DORNER in *Eng. Usage in Sn Afr.* Vol.3 No.2, 17 There are several recognised species: bergbaroe (*Cyphia assimilis*), (*C. bulbosa*), bosbaroe (*C. phyteuma*), (*C. sylvatica*), .. veldbaroe, [etc.].

Barolong /ˈbærəlɒŋ, ˈbaralɔŋ/ *n.* Pl. usu. **Barolong(s), Rolong.** Forms: α. *sing.* **Morolong** (rare); *sing.* and *pl.* **Baralong, Barolong, B(o)rolong;** β. *sing.* and *pl.* **Rolong.** [SeTswana, pl. form of *Morolong* a member of this people, orig. the name of an early leader, see α quots 1905 and 1979, also β quot. 1970. For an explanation of sing. and pl. forms, see MO- and BA-.] A member of a Tswana people acknowledging Morolong as common ancestor, and living mainly in the North West Province and Botswana. See also HURUTSHE, TSWANA sense 2 a. Also *attrib.*, passing into *adj.*

α. [**1802** TRUTER & SOMERVILLE in G.M. Theal *Rec. of Cape Col.* (1899) IV. 404 He had been with the well known Cornelis Kok on a journey through the dorp Patania and Litakoe to the Barrolow nation.] **1824**

W.J. BURCHELL *Trav.* II. 304 They informed me that Makrakki, the chief of the Maibues, a division of the Barolong tribe, had fled. **1827** G. THOMPSON *Trav.* I. 182 The fourth speaker, Insha, a Barolong, began by recommending that the Bechuanas should wait until the Mantatees appeared, and then attack them. **1833** *Graham's Town Jrnl* 16 May 2 He made an excursion against the Borolongs, and came near to the chief Mahura, of the Batlapiis, who is exceedingly afraid of him. **1840** C.A. KINLOCH in *Echo* 26 Oct. 2 Thaba-'nchu, or as it is more generally called, Morocco, is a place of considerable size, containing, it is said, upwards of 6 000 inhabitants, the remnants of a once flourishing tribe called the *Borolong*. **1857** D. LIVINGSTONE *Missionary Trav.* 122 There had been some fighting between these Barolongs and the Boers, and .. capturing of cattle on both sides ... It was the first time that I ever heard of cattle being taken by the Bechuanas. **1872** *Encycl. Brit.* XVII. 814 In the southern-eastern portion of the State, and entirely surrounded by it, is a small native territory, of which the principal village is Thaba-nchu, where 10 000 of the Barolong tribe reside, peacably ruled by their chief according to their own laws. **1882** [see BURGHER sense 4]. **1888** *Encycl. Brit.* XXIII. 518 These western and south-western tribes (Barolongs, Batlapins, Bakwenas, Bakhatlas, etc.) are all Bechuanas. **1899** R. DEVEREUX *Side Lights on S. Afr.* 92 The Baralongs are, physically speaking, an inferior race, not conspicuous for either muscle or energy, but they are an amiable people, and remarkably quick to adopt the ideas and habits of civilisation. **1900** S.T. PLAATJE *Boer War Diary* (1973) 68 Kaffir beer to a common Morolong is 'meat vegetables and tea' rolled into one, and they can subsist entirely on it for a long time. **1905** *Native Tribes of Tvl* 16 The Baralong take their name from their earliest recorded chief Morolong, under whom, according to tradition, they migrated from a country in the far north, probably the region of the lakes, about 1400 AD. **1917** S.T. PLAATJE *Native Life* 242 But all were agreeably surprised to find that beyond slight damage to the housetops there were no casualties among the Barolongs. **1926** M. NATHAN *S. Afr. from Within* 52 The station of the Moffats was at Kuruman, and they laboured principally among the people, (the Barolong) near Mafeking. **1943** 'J. BURGER' *Black Man's Burden* 217 Unlike Basutoland, with its uniform population, Bechuanaland contains a number of tribes, such as the Bamangwato, the Bakhatla, the Barolong, and the Bakwena. **1951** P. ABRAHAMS *Wild Conquest* 175 'This one brought the news.' 'An Ndabele?' 'No, a Barolong.' **1957** D. GRINNELL-MILNE *Baden-Powell at Mafeking* 22 The soil was so stony, the land so arid that the Baralongs had long since found a name for it in their native tongue. They called it Mafeking — a Place of Stones. **1979** P. MILLER *Myths & Legends* 173 The second tribe were skilled metal workers, and took the name of ba-Rolong from their leader, Morolong (the black-smith). **1985** PLATZKY & WALKER *Surplus People* 74 In the Orange Free State freehold title among Africans was confined to a few Barolong farms that were not bought out by whites. **1989** J. CRWYS-WILLIAMS *S. Afr. Despatches* 169 Members of the 'Black Watch' (armed Baralongs from the 'native stadt').

β. **1940** P.R. KIRBY *Diary of Dr Andrew Smith* II. 142 This native was probably taken to England by the Wesleyan missionaries. [**1970** M. WILSON *1000 Yrs before Van Riebeeck* 8 Oral tradition, recorded in 1843, celebrates the skill in metal-work of an early Sotho ancestor. He was Rolong the forger .. iron and the hammer .. were the symbols .. of his lineage ... Calculating from genealogies he lived in the thirteenth century.] **1976** WEST & MORRIS *Abantu* 119 Among the better-known of the 50-odd Tswana tribes are the Ngwato, Kwena, Tswana, Ngwaketse, Kgatla, Thlaping, Rolong and Hurutshe. **1980** LYE & MURRAY *Transformations* 90 All Barolong acknowledge their descent from a common ancestor Morolong ... But there has been no united Rolong political community since the latter half of the eighteenth century. **1986** P. MAYLAM *Hist. of Afr. People* 113 Warden in 1851 assembled a combined force of troops, white farmers, Griqua, Kora and Rolong, and launched an attack on Moletsane's Taung as the prelude to a move against Moshoeshoe.

baroo, barou, barup varr. BAROE.

barrie, barry varr. BARI.

barroe see BAROE.

barsaala, -seela varr. BASELA *n.*

baruti pl. form of MORUTI.

bas var. BAAS.

basadi pl. form of MOSADI.

basala var. BASELA *n.*

Basatos pl. form of MOSOTHO.

basela /ba'se(:)la, -lə/ *n.* Also **barcelia, barcella, barsaala, barseela, basala, baseila, bas(s)ella, bazella, bazello, bhasela, pasel(l)a, passela,** and with initial capital. Pl. unchanged. [Prob. fr. Xhosa *bhasela*, Zulu *basela*, see BASELA *v.*

There is no firm evidence to support the theory that these words were derived fr. Eng. *parcel*, or fr. Du. *baas* master, giving rise to Xhosa *ndibhasele* 'behave to me like a *baas*'. The form with initial *p* is from Afk.]

1.a. BONSELLA sense 1 b.

1825 T. PHILIPPS *Lett.* (1960) 238 There were several other minor chiefs .. they are great beggars and end every visit with Barcelia, Barcelia (presents). **1829** C. ROSE *Four Yrs in Sn Afr.* 88, I sat with them, wrapped in my horseman's cloak .. the Chief .. offered me two horses or three oxen for it; and finding that his offers made no impression requested it as a 'Barseela'. **1833** S. KAY *Trav. & Researches* 285 While riding past Hinza's residence today a number of young girls came running out of the different huts, crying, *Basala, basala*, 'A present, a present.' **1835** J.W.D. MOODIE *Ten Yrs* II. 250 A number of women and children .. followed us for several hundred yards entreating us with their most winning graces for 'basella,' or presents. **1835** A. STEEDMAN *Wanderings* I. 17 A wandering band of Caffers .. surrounded us with very menacing applications for a *barsaala*. **1844** J. BACKHOUSE *Narr. of Visit* 240 We were frequently met by Caffers who come running down the hills .. calling out, 'Bassella,' which signifies A present. **1852** H. WARD *Jasper Lyle* They .. held out two pairs of hands, uttering the old imperative demand peculiar to Kafirs, 'Baseila,' — 'Gift.'

b. BONSELLA sense 1 a.

1835 A. STEEDMAN *Wanderings* I. 17 Galeyka, an old chief, .. pressed us to remain with him during the night, in expectation, no doubt, of receiving a handsome *barsaala*. **1836** A.F. GARDINER *Journey to Zoolu Country* 238 Procured some very indifferent amas, for which however a bazella (present) was asked. **1912** W. WESTRUP *Land of To-Morrow* 127, I heard an old girl ask you to stick on an extra tickey as a pasella. **1963** A.M. LOUW *20 Days* 97 He handed the papers back to Twelve, who received them in his two cupped hands as he would a basella, but with an expression of bewilderment on his face. **1974** A.P. BRINK *Looking on Darkness* 54 They gave me some pasella fo' good behaviour en' so I got out befo' my year was out.

2. *fig.* BONSELLA sense 2.

1900 *Grocott's Penny Mail* 2 July 3 The commando .. being .. thrown in with 'Slim Piet's' successor and Snyman as a sort of 'basella'. **1991** *S. Afr. Panorama* May-June 45 Outa's schooling went only as far as standard two and a half — the half was a 'pasella' from the school-master from being such a bright pupil, he chuckles.

3. BONSELLA sense 3.

1905 *E. London Dispatch* 1 Apr. I happened to enter our local stamp shop the other day, just in time to hear a native demanding a 'basela' on a penny stamp he had purchased. **1912** W. WESTRUP *Land of To-Morrow* 127 The old dame accepted her flannelette, and a few sweets as the inevitable pasella and went on her way rejoicing. **1913** C. PETTMAN *Africanderisms* 48 *Basela*, .. and the word *Bansela* .. are practically synonymous .. though this word seems to be more frequently applied to a something thrown in after a purchase has been made. **1920** S. BLACK *Dorp* 46 The coloured customers would still prefer Mahomet .. his 'pasellas', his compliments, his sympathy. **1955** *Report of Commission for Socio-Economic Dev. of Bantu Areas* (UG61–1955) 91 The habit of giving a 'pasela' .. is on the wane. **1979** F. DIKE *First S. African* 4 Also, I've got this pyramid handkerchief .. here, your bhasela for buying this jacket.

Hence **basela** *adv.*, 'for free', gratuitously; *bonsella*, see BONSELLA. Cf. MAHALA *adv.*

1925 *E. Prov. Herald* 19 Sept. 9 Accused asked her if she wanted some oranges. Witness said 'Yes, if you give me one "basella"'.

basela /ba'se(:)la, -lə/ *v. obs.* Also **baseila, basella, bassaala, bazaala, bossala.** [Prob. fr. Xhosa *bhasela* give a present (to), and Zulu *basela* beg for, make strong demands for (lit. 'kindle a fire for', fr. *basa* kindle + applied form suffix *-ela*).] To give (a present). See also BONSELLA (esp. sense 1 b).

Always reporting the speech of Xhosa- or Zulu-speaking people, in the imperative.

a. *intrans.*

[**1809** R. COLLINS in G.M. Theal *Rec. of Cape Col.* (1900) VII. 70 Several kraals .. were seen, from which the people issued on our approach, crying *nyasela incosee* (pray give me Sir).] **1825** T. PHILIPPS *Lett.* (1960) 268 When we were a little more acquainted, 'Basella, Basella' soon followed, which signifies 'Give me a present'. **1833** S. KAY *Trav. & Researches* 48 *Bassaala, bassaala* (give, give us a present) accompanied every salute. **1837** F. OWEN *Diary* (1926) 14 His first salutation was the usual one 'Basela,' give me a present.

b. *trans.*

1878 T.J. LUCAS *Camp Life & Sport* 214 They crawled up to my feet, begging in the most abject manner for tobacco. 'Bazaala Tobaka', they cried.

Bashootoo, Bashuta(s) pl. forms of MOSOTHO.

basics *n. colloq.* [fr. *basic training*.] The initial period of military training undergone by all national servicemen in the South African defence force.

1979 *Darling* 7 Feb. 32 During your basics you don't get your head down till about 10 pm, and stand-to is at four in the morning. **1981** *Fair Lady* 8 Apr. 7 'Basics' is tough, and your son will never be able to tell you what it's really like .. just as later on you will hear very little about what it's like 'somewhere on the Border'. **1986** J. WHYLE in S. Gray *Market Plays* 170 After two months I found myself getting fit and confident. Then towards the end of basics something happened. **1991** R. FRAGOSO *Informant, Pretoria* Roofie: .. Somebody who has just started his army service, i.e. is doing basics. Army colloquialism.

basie var. BAASIE.

basket *n.* [Special sense of general Eng.] A container of closely-plaited grass or reeds, used (esp. in the past) in rural African homesteads to hold milk; *milk-basket*, see MILK sense 1.

1790 tr. *F. Le Vaillant's Trav.* II. 4 Narina .. sent me a basket of goats-milk, which she knew I was very fond of. **1801** J. BARROW *Trav.* I. 70 (Pettman), In the evening they sent us in return some baskets of milk. **1829** C. ROSE *Four Yrs in Sn Afr.* 168 In the evening, the people from the adjoining kraals flocked around us fearlessly, bringing baskets of sweet and sour milk for sale. **1829** [see DOCTOR sense 1 a]. **1835** A. STEEDMAN *Wanderings* I. 56 Milk and millet were produced .. my looking rather squeamishly at the greasy basket which contained the former. **1860** W. SHAW *Story of my Mission* 413 A large milk-sack and some small baskets of platted grass cunningly constructed to hold liquids. **1866** W.C. HOLDEN *Past & Future* 284 The milk is not served up in a very 'lordly dish,' but usually in a dirty calabash, or basket. **1956** F.C. METROWICH *Valiant but Once* 108 A solitary Kaffir came into the camp, ostensibly to sell a basket of milk.

Basotho pl. form of MOSOTHO.

Basotho blanket /bəˈsuːtu -/ *n. phr.* [See MOSOTHO.] A multi-coloured, traditionally patterned blanket, worn round the shoulders by Basotho men and women.

Ceremonial blankets are presented and worn as a mark of honour.

1957 B. FRASER *Sunshine & Lamplight* 5 Particularly lovely were the Basuto blankets, which were mostly of light colouring with attractive patterns in all the brighter shades. **1969** I. VAUGHAN *Last of Sunlit Yrs* 81 The only sign of life appeared to be the odd Basuto horseman, .. galloping past, with his coloured Basuto blanket floating behind him. **1973** *Seek* July 2 After the service he was officially received by the people and solemnly clothed in a Basotho blanket. [*c*1976 see MOSOTHO.] **1987** J. DEACON in *S. Afr. Panorama* May 13 The famous Basuto blankets, worn summer and winter, were initiated by Lord Fraser of Lonsdale and manufactured in Harrismith. Motifs on ceremonial blankets represent royalty. **1989** J. HOBBS *Thoughts in Makeshift Mortuary* 166 Their blankets fall almost to their shoes like long capes. It is impossible not to look dignified in a Basotho blanket.

Basotho hat /bəˈsuːtu -/ *n. phr.* [See MOSOTHO.] A conical hat, woven of reeds, with a decorative 'topknot', traditionally worn by Basotho men.

1973 *Daily Dispatch* 16 June 19 (*advt*) Grass Mats; Basuto Hats; Wooden Curios. **1973** *Seek* July 2 At another place he was vested in cape, mitre, and crozier consisting of Basotho hat, blanket and stick! [*c*1976 H. FLATHER *Thaba Rau* 38 He had always found the Basutos pleasing to the eye, .. the women wearing gay *doeks* .. the men the traditional straw hats.] **1989** J. HOBBS *Thoughts in Makeshift Mortuary* 60 A photograph of King Moshoeshoe beaming under a conical straw Basotho hat worn with third world panache above a well-cut navy suit and club-striped tie. [**1990** *Sunday Times* 21 Oct. (Mag. Sect.) 78 There are ID books, security passes, disposable nappies, grass Lesotho hats, Teddy bears, sleeping-bags aplenty.]

Basotho pony /bəˈsuːtu -/ *n. phr.* [See MOSOTHO.] A hardy mountain pony bred in Lesotho from the Cape horse. See also *Cape horse* (CAPE sense 2 a), *Nooitgedacht pony* (NOOITGEDACHT).

1877 LADY BARKER *Yr's Hsekeeping* 75 G— has become possessed, .. of an aged and long-suffering Basuto pony. **1882** LADY F.C. DIXIE *In Land of Misfortune* 187 Most of them [*sc.* the horses] were little more than ponies, the biggest standing about 14.2, and the smallest 13 hands. This last was a Basuto pony ... a tough little specimen, who could stand any amount of hard work and long distances. **1896** R. WALLACE *Farming Indust. of Cape Col.* 313 Basuto ponies stand about 14 to 14½ hands at the withers, and are extremely hardy, active and sure-footed. They are reared in a hilly rugged country. **1910** A.B. LAMONT *Rural Reader* 66 The chief breeds of riding horses in South Africa are the English thoroughbred, the Arab horse, the Cape horse, and the Basuto pony. **1940** V. POHL *Bushveld Adventures* 18 His horse was a wonderful swimmer, like most Basuto ponies. **1955** W. ILLSLEY *Wagon on Fire* 47 A horseman, mounted on a Basuto pony, threaded his way over the mountain path that was almost obliterated by long dry grass. **1977** *Fighting Forces of Rhodesia* No.4, 27 Over generations, the Basuto pony has acquired a resistance to most common diseases in Southern Africa and this, combined with its ability to survive on the indigenous grasses while on trek or on operations, makes it the ideal type for days in the bush. **1988** *Personality* 29 Feb. 32 Known as one of the toughest, yet most mild-mannered of horses anywhere, the Basuto pony can be traced back to the Arab and barb horses brought to the Cape by missionaries and explorers. Today this animal is the number one form of transport in Lesotho. **1989** J. HOBBS *Thoughts in Makeshift Mortuary* 166 Basotho ponies .. have a good percentage of Arab blood in their veins. **1989** [see *Nooitgedacht pony* (NOOITGEDACHT)]. **1990** J. THERON in *Farmer's Weekly* 22 June (Sporting Horse) 14 In 1830, Moshoeshoe, the King of the Basuto nation, came in contact with the Cape Horse and began assembling hundreds of them in Basutoland. By 1860 almost every Basuto was mounted and it was from there the Basuto pony was developed.

bass var. BAAS.

bassaala var. BASELA *v.*

bassella var. BASELA *n.*

Bassutos pl. form of MOSOTHO.

Bastard /ˈbaːstəd/ *n.* and *adj.* Also **Baastaerd, Bastaard,** and with small initial. [Calque formed on S. Afr. Du. *bastaard* one of mixed racial ancestry, fr. Du. *bastaard, baster* 'bastard'.]

A. *n.*

1. *hist.* A person of mixed ethnic origin, usu. Khoikhoi and white or Khoikhoi and black; BASTER *n.* sense 1. Also *attrib.* See also BASTARD HOTTENTOT, COLOURED *n.* sense a, GRIQUA, HOTTENTOT sense 4 a.

Current until the late 19th century, the name was accepted as a title of distinction.

During the nineteenth century, groups of Bastards migrated northwards and formed new communities recognised as distinct clans (the largest of which became known as Griquas and Basters).

1786 G. FORSTER tr. *A. Sparrman's Voy. to Cape of G.H.* II. 27 We fixed our resting-place at the distance of a few gun-shots from a clan of *bastards*, or *Hottentot-Caffres*, who are the offspring of the mixture of both these nations. **1790** tr. *F. Le Vaillant's Trav.* II. 163, I mean to speak of the natural children which have sprung from an intercourse of the Whites with the female Hottentots, or between these same women and the negroes. They are commonly known at the Cape under the appellation of *Bastards*. **1810** G. BARRINGTON *Acct of Voy.* 188 When a Hottentot woman is connected with a white man, the result of such an alliance .. are beings of a very different nature from the unmixed Hottentot ... These people always acquire the degrading epithet of *Bastaards*. **1818** LORD C. SOMERSET in G.M. Theal *Rec. of Cape Col.* (1902) XII. p.iii, The intercourse between the descendants of Europeans and Hottentot women and between the latter and the various classes of slaves has produced a new breed of man here known by the name of Bastard. **1827** G. THOMPSON *Trav.* I. 151 The missionary traveller Mr. Campbell .. gave the name of *Griquas* to this infant community. They had previously been known (as indeed they still are among the Dutch colonists) by the uncouth appellation of *Bastaards*. **1837** 'N. POLSON' *Subaltern's Sick Leave* 128 The best route .. is from Graham's Town to Fort Beaufort, thence to Balfour on the Kat River, the capital of a settlement of *Baastaerds* (or half castes) and Hottentots. **1853** F.P. FLEMING *Kaffraria* 8 A very large proportion of those, who now are styled Hottentots, are, more properly speaking, a race who have sprung from an intermixture between the original Hottentots and the Europeans, and are locally known as Griquas or Bastaards, which latter title they much prefer themselves, and even seem to be proud of it. **1866** J. LEYLAND *Adventures* 32 The territory, of which Phillipolis is the principal town, is inhabited by the Griquas, or Bastards; the latter name is derived from the fact of their being a mixed breed between the Dutch and Hottentot. **1882** S. HECKFORD *Lady Trader in Tvl* 149 The kaffirs are bad as a rule; but there is a class of half-castes between white and Hottentot blood, here called 'bastards,' in which very excellent servants may be found. **1896** R. WALLACE *Farming Indust. of Cape Col.* 402 The *'Cape-boys'* form a mixed so-called 'bastard' class, descended from a variety of races. **1896** PURVIS & BIGGS *S. Afr.* 88 The Mixed races, the Cape 'boys' and other cross-breeds, including the Griquas and Bastards (who have descended from the union of Negro-slave and Boer or other unnatural union), number only about a quarter of a million. **1902** W. DOWER *Early Annals of Kokstad* 5 Among the Dutch of the Colony, they [*sc.* the Griquas] were long known as *'The Bastards,'* a descriptive title given with greater regard to fact than to courtesy. **1924** S.G. MILLIN *God's Step-Children* 65 The offspring of Hagar were beginning to seed the wilderness .. becoming a nation ... They called themselves proudly the Bastaards. **1946** S. CLOETE *Afr. Portraits* 104 The Bastaards — and proud of it — were a mixed race of Hottentots, Bushmen, and Eastern blood leavened with that of some of the less admirable whites. **1950** D. REED *Somewhere S. of Suez* 90 Griquas were called Bastards until a Scots clergyman persuaded them to change the name. **1968** J.T. MCNISH *Rd to Eldorado* 2 Friction grew owing to the whites taking unto themselves the daughters and even the wives of slaves, a practice which resulted in the creation of a race they called the 'Bastards'. **1976** R. ROSS *Adam Kok's Griquas* 13 The Bastards were those who could not claim to be Christian, but who were integrated into the colonial cash economy other than as tied farm-labourers or as slaves. They were transport riders, day-labourers, craftsmen, and most frequently, small farmers, living without title to their lands beyond the current frontier of white expansion. **1986** P. MAYLAM *Hist. of Afr. People* 27 After his [*sc.* Maqoma's] expulsion the expropriated land became a reserved area for Khoi and 'Bastards', known as the Kat River Settlement.

2. *Obs.* exc. *hist.* REHOBOTH.

1877 *Sel. Comm. Report on Mission to Damaraland* 80 The Damaras will consent to the Bastards continuing to live at Rehoboth, and would even agree to its being placed in the 'Reserve'. *c*1936 *S. & E. Afr. Yr Bk & Guide* 176 The Bastaards are descendants of a cross of Cape European and British farmers and hunters and Hottentots. They number about five thousand and live in the Rehoboth District. **1944** *S. Afr. Law Reports* 19 In the Rehoboth Gebied, for example, 'Bastard' is an appellation which burghers apply to themselves with pride. **1961** O. LEVINSON *Ageless Land* 53 From 1700 to 1870 a new immigration of three different tribes took place. These were the Hereros, the Orlams (a second wave of Hottentots who came from the Cape aross the Orange River) and the Bastards. **1969** J.M. WHITE *Land God Made in Anger* 196 The Basters are proud of their 'Baastard' descent and do not resent their name. None the less they usually figure in modern literature under the polite designation of 'Rehobothers'. **1973** *Observer* (U.K.) 2 Sept. (Colour Suppl.) 56 Hereros, Ovambos, Damaras, Kaokovelders, Bushmen and Rehobothers (until recently known as the Bastards).

B. *adj.* BASTER *adj.* See also *bastard galjoen* (GALJOEN sense 2), *bastard hartebeest* (HARTEBEEST sense b).

1913 C. PETTMAN *Africanderisms* 49 *Bastard geelhout*, .. *Podocarpus elongata* — The real Yellow wood being *P. Thunbergii*. **1971** BARAITSER & OBHOLZER *Cape Country Furn.* 75 They are made of kareehout, the wood of the bastard willow, and were inlaid with klapperbos, the wood of a small indigenous shrub. *Ibid.* 268 The syringa and bastard willow (karree). **1989** [see CABBAGE TREE].

bastard gemsbok *n. phr. Obs.* [(Part.) tr. S. Afr. Du. *baster* hybrid, cross + *gemsbok* see GEMSBOK.] The ROAN ANTELOPE, *Hippotragus equinus*. Cf. GEMSBOK sense 1.

1835 A. SMITH *Diary* (1940) II. 155 The bastard gemsbok again seen here in little herds. **1839** W.C. HARRIS *Wild Sports* 223 Another rare species — the roan antelope, or bastard gemsbok .. being utterly destitute of speed, may be ridden to a stand-still without difficulty. **1850** [see ROAN ANTELOPE]. **1887** *S.W. Silver & Co.'s Handbk to S. Afr.* 171 The roan antelope .. is also becoming very scarce ... It is also called the bastard gemsbok. [**1900** W.L. SCLATER *Mammals of S. Afr.* I. 217 *The Roan Antelope*, Bastard Gemsbok or Bastard Eland of the Dutch Colonists.]

Bastard Hottentot *n. phr. Hist.* Also with small initials. [fr. S. Afr. Du., see BASTARD and HOTTENTOT.] A member of a people of mixed Khoikhoi, white, and black African origin. See also BASTARD *n.* sense 1, GRIQUA sense 1, HOTTENTOT sense 4 a. Also *attrib.*

1790 tr. *F. Le Vaillant's Trav.* II. 202 Klaas .. informed me that four bastard Hottentots were concealed in my camp, and that he suspected them to be spies sent by the planters of Bruyntjes-Hoogte. **1801** TRUTER & SOMERVILLE in G.M. Theal *Rec. of Cape Col.* (1899) IV. 402 We perceived that the Bastard Hottentot Vigilant had made his escape. **1820** *Missionary Notices* 219 There are so many bastard Hottentots, and slaves, and Bushmen without the Word of God. **1827** G. THOMPSON *Trav.* II. 88 He told me that many of the Bastard-Hottentots in the vicinity had absconded, under the apprehension that I was a military officer, come to press men for the Cape corps. **1835** [see GRIQUA sense 1]. *a***1838** A. SMITH *Jrnl* (1975) 37 We proceeded to Boschies Spruit, the residence of a bastard Hottentot who emigrated several years ago from the colony and purchased the farm he now possesses for one hundred Rix dollars. *a***1858** J. GOLDSWAIN *Chron.* II. (1949) 164 They are caled the Fingo Levey but theas wich I had was Hottentots or Barsterds Hottentots and the[y] will not fight with the Hottentot Rebles. **1868** W.R. THOMSON *Poems, Essays & Sketches* 206 They .. engaged several Bastard Hottentots, and got together the necessary provisions. **1876** F. BOYLE *Savage Life* 210 On the diamond-fields we knew very well, and respected, the Bastard Hottentots, though — or because — they retain little of their ancestors, not even their language. **1892** J.E. RITCHIE *Brighter S. Afr.* 120 The Cape rejoices in an aristocracy of skin, and the white man .. will never be ruled by Malays, or bastard Hottentots, or Kaffirs. **1925** H.J. MANDELBROTE tr. *O.F. Mentzel's Descr. of Cape of G.H.* II. 126 Bastard-hottentots — the offspring of male slaves and hottentot women — sometimes make good labourers, but pure-bred hottentots, never. **1976** R. ROSS *Adam Kok's Griquas* 13 'Bastaard-Hottentots' .. were considered by the whites to be of mixed origin, having either one slave or one white ancestor. In fact, however, the term denoted a social rather than a genetic status ... They were transport riders, day-labourers, craftsmen, and most frequently, small farmers, living without title to their lands beyond the current frontier of white expansion.

Baster /ˈbastə(r)/ *n.* and *adj.* Also with small initial. [S. Afr. Du., half-caste, fr. Du. *bastaard, baster* bastard.]
A. *n.*
1. *hist.* BASTARD sense 1.

1790 tr. F. Le Vaillant's *Trav.* II. 344 These Boshmen .. far from being a distinct species .. are only a promiscuous assemblage of mulattoes, negroes and mestizos, of every species, and sometimes of Hottentots and Basters. **1962** F.C. METROWICH *Scotty Smith* 196 Scotty really enjoyed himself exercising magisterial authority over the Hottentots, Basters and Bushmen who came under his jurisdiction.

2. REHOBOTH. Also *attrib.*

1936 A.J. GOLDBLATT in J.J.L. Sisson *S. Afr. Judicial Dict.* (1960) 85 In this territory the term '*baster*' when it is ascribed to a person's race is well known to refer to the members of the Rehoboth Bastard Community. **1952** L.G. GREEN *Lords of Last Frontier* 202 Basters, the people of the Rehoboth 'republic' in South West Africa call themselves — not without pride. Now the Afrikaans word 'baster' means bastard, but it also means half-caste. These people are half-castes. **1966** J.P. VAN S. BRUWER *S.W. Afr.: Disputed Land* 28 During the second half of the 19th century a small group of people known as Basters entered the Territory. They were the descendants of white fathers and Khoi mothers in the north-western districts of the Cape Colony ... They .. spoke Afrikaans. **1971** [see CLASSIFICATION]. **1976** CUBITT & RICHTER *South West* 9 Last to appear on the scene were the Basters, descendants of early Dutch colonists at the Cape. They .. settled at Rehoboth under their kaptein Hermanus van Wyk in 1870 ... There is no innuendo in the word 'Baster', which is not translatable into the English 'bastard'. **1985** *E. Prov. Herald* 12 July 3 Afrikaners, coloureds and Basters belonged to the same ethnic tribe, a Deputy Minister told the National Assembly of the interim government here [sc. in Windhoek] yesterday. **1990** *Sunday Times* 11 Feb. 2 'I will be there on Monday,' he said defiantly, demanding that Namibia's 35 000 Baster people be granted the autonomy he claims is due under a 1976 SA Act of Parliament. **1990** *Tribute* Sept. 144 The Basters of Rehoboth were another wave of immigration (numbering little more than 17,500 today) from the 19th-century Cape Colony. They came to occupy land that many other Namibian groups claimed. Cattle raids between the Basters and the indigenous communities were the order of the day. Even after independence the Basters are clamouring for a separate 'homeland'.

B. *adj.* Qualifying the names of numerous plants which are similar in appearance to the original variety, but inferior in quality; BASTARD *adj.*

Rarely used in the original sense of 'hybrid'.

1966 C.A. SMITH *Common Names* 72 *Baster*, .. The term most commonly used in the sense of 'mock' or 'false' and then implying lack of superior qualities. In this sense the term 'baster' is found in the names of timber trees, with which it was most probably first associated. The earliest record with this meaning is *basteranyswortel* recorded by Burchell in 1811. **1972** BEETON & DORNER in *Eng. Usage in Sn Afr.* Vol.3 No.2, 19 *Baster*, .. Used in compound common names of plants & trees implying: likeness or similarity in appearance or habit but inferior in quality, usu applied to timber trees, eg *bastergeelhout* .. ; likeness in habit or appearance but lacking some product, eg basteralwyn. **1990** S. ROWLES in *Weekend Post* 16 June (Leisure) 5 A highlight .. was a sighting of a *baster kokerboom* (*Aloe pillansii*), the rarest plant in the Richtersveld.

bastersaffraan see SAFFRAAN sense b.

Basuta(s) pl. form of MOSOTHO.

Basuto, Basutu varr. and pl. forms of MOSOTHO.

Basuto(o)s pl. form of MOSOTHO.

Batammakas var. TAMMAKA.

Batclapi, Bathlaping varr. BATLHAPING.

bat-eared fox *n. phr.* The small southern African mammal *Otocyon megalotis*, with silver-grey coat, black legs and face, and large ears.

1975 *Dict. of Eng. Usage in Sn Afr.* 16 *Bat-eared fox*, .. Small harmless fox with relatively large ears. **1985** C. WALKER *Signs of Wild* (1987) 53 The bat-eared fox is not, as its name implies, a true fox. **1989** *Weekend Argus* 4 Mar. (Our Living World) 8 Four of South Africa's loveliest animals — the endangered riverine rabbit, the cheetah, vervet monkey and the bat-eared fox. **1990** *Afr. Wildlife* Vol.44 No.5, 316 The bat-eared fox is perhaps the most engaging of the five members of the dog family occurring in South Africa. Its appeal derives in part from its appearance, with its disproportionately large ears.

Bat(h)onga pl. form of TONGA.

batje var. BAADJIE.

Batklaka pl. form of KGATLA.

ba-Tlaro, Batlaroo varr. BATLHARO.

Batlhaping /ˌbatlaˈpɪŋ/ *n.* Pl. usu. unchanged, or *-s.* Forms: α. (pl. unchanged, or *-s*) Bachapin, Batclapi, Bathlaping, Batlapee, Batlapeng, Batlapi(i), Batlapin(g), Bathlaping, Batopeen; β. (pl. only) Matchappees, Matchlhapee; γ. (pl. unchanged) Thlaping, Tlhaping. [SeTswana *baTlhaping*, pl. n. prefix BA- (rarely MA- *pref.*²) + *tlapi* fish + loc. suffix *-(e)ng*; this can be literally interpreted as 'they of the (place of the) fish'. For notes on sing. and pl. forms, see BA-.] A member of a Tswana people, living mainly in the Northern Cape, who have a fish as their totem; BRIQUA. See also TSWANA sense 2 a. Also *attrib.*

The unprefixed form 'Tlhaping' is used mainly in modern academic contexts: see γ quots.

α. **1822** W.J. BURCHELL *Trav.* I. 364 By barter for beads and tobacco they annually obtain from the Bachapins (called *Briquas* or Goat men in the Hottentot language) a number of cattle. **1833** *Graham's Town Jrnl* 16 May 2 The chief Mahura, of the Batlapiis is exceedingly afraid of him. **1835** A. SMITH *Diary* (1940) II. 34 A native visited our encampment. He was a Batlapi and lived at a kraal not far distant. **1839** W.C. HARRIS *Wild Sports* 63 The scattered inhabitants of this part of the country are the remnants of various Bechuana tribes .. and consist principally of the Barolong, Wangkets, Batlapi and Baharootzi. **1857** D. LIVINGSTONE *Missionary Trav.* 13 The different Bechuana tribes are named after certain animals ... The term Bakatla means 'they of the monkey'; Bakuena, 'they of the alligator'; Batlapi, 'they of the fish'; each tribe having a superstitious dread of the animal after which it is called. **1871** J. MACKENZIE *Ten Yrs* (1971) 58 The Bataping tribe had been broken up, and were scattered over the country under 'head-men'; the power of the supreme chief being considerably in abeyance. **1887** J.W. MATTHEWS *Incwadi Yami* 257 A region which, if it had not been for the wonderful discovery of diamonds, would yet have been the home of the half-caste Griqua, the indolent Batlapin, the marauding Koranna, the pigmy Bushman and the pioneer Boer. **1931** G. BEET *Grand Old Days* 35 Chief Jantje, of the Batlapins, was also a cause of great vexation to the early diggers. **1971** *Rand Daily Mail* 6 Mar. 11 Strong resistance by members of the Batlhaping tribe at Majeng, near Taung, against being moved by the Department of Bantu Administration and Development from land it has occupied for the past 62 years. **1976** B. ROBERTS *Kimberley* 61 The Keate Award .. gave the Barolong and BaTlhaping tribes certain land. **1990** *Sunday Times* 27 May (Mag. Sect.) 6 The Batlaping tribe, who were moved (with their livestock) from the area .. now want to return.

β. **1827** G. THOMPSON *Trav.* I. 80 The marauding horde of strange people, who were now plundering and destroying the Bechuana tribes to the northward .. were fast approaching the country of the Matchlhapee tribe. *Ibid.* 85 Campbell calls them *Matchappees*, and Burchell *Batchapins*.

γ. **1970** M. WILSON *1000 Yrs before Van Riebeeck* The Tlhaping traded metal, and the expedition of 1801 was disconcerted to find that Tlhaping knives were preferred to the trade knives offered. **1975** *Std Encycl. of Sn Afr.* II. 106 Tswana is .. spoken .. by various tribes, among which are the Rolong, Thlaping, Ngwaketse, Ngwato, Kwena and Kgatla. **1980** LYE & MURRAY *Transformations* 41 The most southerly-placed Tswana, the Tlhaping ... The Kora named these Tlhaping 'Briqua', Goat People. **1986** P. MAYLAM *Hist. of Afr. People* 126 The Tlhaping had lost vast areas of land through the 1884 London Convention and the 1886 Land Commission.

Batlharo /ˌbaˈtla(ː)rɔ, bəˈtlaːrəʊ/ *pl. n.* Also Batlharos, ba-Tlaro(s), Batlaroo. [SeTswana *baTlharo*, BA- + *-Tlharo* (orig. sense unknown). For an explanation of the variation in forms, see BA-.] (The) members of a Tswana people living mainly in the Kuruman region of the Northern Cape. Also *attrib.* See also TSWANA sense 2 a.

As is the case with many names of peoples and groups in S. Afr. Eng., this word has been found only in plural uses; however, it may be that it has also been used in unrecorded singular forms.

1839 W.C. HARRIS *Wild Sports* 55 Several armed natives of the Barolong and Batlaroo tribes, branches of the Bechuana, visited us. **1905** W.H. TOOKE in Flint & Gilchrist *Science in S. Afr.* 92 The be-Chuana are .. remarkable for their honesty, a virtue which has been noticed from Livingstone's time (among the ba-Kwena and ma-Kololo) to the present day among the ba-Tlaro. **1969** *40th Annual Report (S.A.I.R.R.)* 19 It .. considered, among other things .. the Batlharos, the Bakwena, Ba-Mohapo and other 'black spot' removals.

Batlokua var. TLOKWA.

Batswana pl. form of MOTSWANA.

battle-axe *n.* [Special sense of general Eng.] A weapon traditionally carried by African men, usu. having a triangular blade.

1841 B. SHAW *Memorials* 49 Their weapons are the keerie, battle-axe, and assagai; which last differs somewhat from that of the Bechuanas and Kaffirs. **1846** R. MOFFAT *Missionary Labours* 91 A quiver containing poisoned arrows, is hung from the shoulder, and a battle-axe is held in his right hand. **1866** J. LEYLAND *Adventures* 65 The battle-axe is ingeniously formed in the shape of a triangle, and fastened to an handle made of hard wood, or from the horn of the Rhinoceros. **1896** H.A. BRYDEN *Tales of S. Afr.* 162 In front of a large .. circular hut were gathered some thirty headmen of various ages, all standing, and all armed with long spears, battle-axes, or bows and arrows. **1961** T.V. BULPIN *White Whirlwind* 248 From the work places of the armourers came the ominous swishing sound they made as they sharpened the points of spears, or the edges and barbs of battle-axes. **1975** D. WOODS in *Daily Dispatch* 13 June 12 The young men .. pick up their battle-axes and set out singing to chop up a rival gang from another area ... The battle-axes are home-made. The blade is a sharpened piece of iron .. with one end hammered firmly round the end of a wooden shaft. **1991** [see Maclennan quot. at *Natal code* (NATAL sense a)].

Battopeen var. BATLHAPING.

baugh-um var. BOCCHOM.

baum slang var. BOOMSLANG.

Bavenda pl. form of VENDA.

baviaan /ˌbaviˈɑːn, ˌbævi-/ *n. obsolescent.* Also **babiaan, bavian, bawian, bovian.** [Du., baboon; see BOBBEJAAN.]

1.a. The CHACMA, *Papio ursinus.*

1731 G. MEDLEY tr. *P. Kolb's Present State of Cape of G.H.* I. 202 In the Choice of Roots and Fruits for Food they follow .. the *Bavian*, a Sort of Ape; and will not taste of any Sort which those creatures do not feed upon. **1790** tr. *F. Le Vaillant's Trav.* I. 138 An ape, of that kind so common at the Cape, under the name of *bawians.* **1822** W.J. BURCHELL *Trav.* I. 45 A large kind of monkey, with a long greenish-brown fur, (*Cercopithecus ursinus*), called *Baviaan* by the colonists, inhabits this mountain. **1886** G.A. FARINI *Through Kalahari Desert* 102 Here some bovians (large monkeys ..) attacked me, coming quite close and showing their great teeth. **1918** S.H. SKAIFE *Animal Life* 271 The baboon, or *baviaan*, is too common and too well known to need description. Troops of them live in caves in steep rocky *krantzes.* **1973** S. CLOETE *Co. with Heart of Gold* 156, I told you the baviaans would take your mealies.

b. *fig. derog.* An idiot, a fool. See also BOBBEJAAN sense 1 b.

1838 J.E. ALEXANDER *Exped. into Int.* I. 73 Now we cannot lift a hand to a Hottentot baviaan (ape) without having to go before the magistrate for it. **1896** H.A. BRYDEN *Tales of S. Afr.* 225 Sooner than think myself akin to such a race as that little dressed-up *baviaan* (baboon) my husband has been telling you of, I would disown my own blood.

‖**2.** As a qualifier, esp. in plant names, often signifying species unsuitable for human consumption, or associated with baboons: see quots. See also BOBBEJAAN sense 2.

1917 R. MARLOTH *Common Names* 9 *Baviaansappel*, A gall on *Asparagus strictus* ... *Baviaanskers*, = Bergcypres. *Baviaansklauw*, = Luisjes. *Baviaanskost*, *Hydnora africana* ... *Baviaansoor*, *Eriospermum latifolium* ... *Baviaansstaart*, *Barbacenia retinervis* ... *Baviaans-uintje*, v. Uintje and Monkey-bulb. **1966** C.A. SMITH *Common Names* 77 *Baviaanskers*, *Euclea polyandra* ... One of the earliest of S. Afr. plant names beyond the confines of the late 17th century Colony. **1985** [see PAINTED LADY].

3. *rare.* BOBBEJAANTJIE.

[**1795** see BOBBEJAANTJIE.] **1986** J. & I. RUDNER (tr.) in V.S. Forbes *Carl Peter Thunberg 1772–5* 158 The *Gladiolus plicatus* appears to be the most favourite plant with those that live near the Cape, for which reason also this plant is known by the name of the *baviaan.*

baviaan bout var. BOBBEJAANBOUD.

baviaan spider *n. phr. Obs.* Also **baviaans spider.** [Part. tr. S. Afr. Du. *baviaan spinnekop*, see BAVIAAN SPINNEKOP.] BABOON SPIDER.

1918 S.H. SKAIFE *Animal Life* 170 Best known, perhaps, of all the South African spiders are the huge, black, baviaans spiders. They sometimes reach a length of two inches ... Their fangs are very long and sharp. **1920** F.C. CORNELL *Glamour of Prospecting* 232 The huge 'baviaan' spider provided one of these [poisons] ... These venomous insects were pounded between stones and the resultant paste exposed to the light of the moon for several nights.

baviaan spinnekop /baviˈɑːn ˌspənəkɔp/ *n. phr. Obsolescent.* Also **babiaan spinnekop**, etc. Pl. **-koppen** /-ən/, **-s.** [S. Afr. Du., *baviaan* baboon + *spinnekop* spider. (The modern Afk. form is *bobbejaanspinnekop*.)] BABOON SPIDER.

1879 *Queenstown Free Press* 21 Nov. (Pettman), I have seen here a rare spider, called by the natives *Baviaan spinnekop.* It is covered with hair, looks like a crab when running, and .. has formidable fangs between the eyes half an inch long. **1905** [see BABOON SPIDER]. **1958** I. VAUGHAN *Diary* 8 Where the outspan place is are many spiders. The babiaan spinneskops [*sic*] with long brown hair on them. [**1971** *Informant, Grahamstown* 'What's the big, hairy spider that jumps?' 'A bobbejaan spinnekop.']

baviaan's touw *n. phr. Obs.* Also **babiaan-touw, babian touw, baviaan's tauw, baviaanstouw, baviaan's-tow, baviaan-touw, bavianstau, bavians tow,** and with initial capitals. Pl. **-e.** [S. Afr. Du., *baviaan* baboon (+ Eng. possessive *-'s*) + *touw* rope.] MONKEY-ROPE. See also BAVIAAN sense 2.

[**1773** C.P. THUNBERG in C.A. Smith *Common Names* (1966) 134 Incolis, Bavian's tou.] **1790** tr. *F. Le Vaillant's Trav.* II. 243 Even the smallest branches of the trees, shot forth filaments that hung down to the earth ... These filaments, which are almost innumerable, bear no leaves, and the natives call them *bavians tow*, or *bavians ropes*, because .. apes climb to the tops of the trees in order to reach the fruit of the plants. **1821** C.I. LATROBE *Jrnl of Visit* 213 Bushrope, or bavianstau, a species of creeper resembling a rope, grows here in abundance, and nearly envelopes some of the loftiest trees, to the destruction of their growth and beauty. **1824** W.J. BURCHELL in C.A. Smith *Common Names* (1966) 134 *Baviaanstouw*, Caulis funiformis (like cables or large ropes). **1844** J. BACKHOUSE *Narr. of Visit* 151 A vine was climbing among the trees; it had heart-shaped leaves and slender branches which are used for cordage; it is called Baviaan-touw, *Baboon-rope.* **1861** 'A LADY' *Life at Cape* (1963) 44 We also came across .. the baviaan's tauw, or 'baboon ropes' ascending and descending in cord-like ladders from many a monarch of the ravines. **1877** J.F. SEWELL *Private Diary* (1983) 21 Gillespie's Two Sons .. were cutting Babian Tou in the Beach Bush. **1883** M.A. CAREY-HOBSON *Farm in Karoo* 48 They soon pulled themselves up the almost perpendicular pathway by the Baviaans touw or monkey rope, .. a climbing plant that grows in great profusion in many of the South African kloofs. **1906** B. STONEMAN *Plants & their Ways* 130 *Secamone* (Bavian's Touw), *Asclepias* (the milk bush) .. and all their family have their pollen in masses. **1914** *Farmer's Annual* 301 A C.P. correspondent sends a specimen of 'Baviaans's Touw' and asks for advice as to the best means of eradication. **1949** J. ROSE-INNES in F.G. Butler *When Boys Were Men* (1969) 271 Picking our way among great trees, draped with moss and festooned with a tangle of wild vine and *babiaan-touw.*

bavian var. BAVIAAN.

bavyantje var. BOBBEJAANTJIE.

Bawangwato var. BAMANGWATO.

Bawenda pl. form of VENDA.

bawian var. BAVIAAN.

‖**bawo** /ˈbɑːwɔ/ *n.* [Xhosa, voc. case of *ubawo* father.] Usu. among Xhosa-speaking people: 'father'; used also as a title or term of address or reference. Cf. BABA *n.*[2]

1949 L. HUNTER *Afr. Dawn* 60 'I should have known that no son of mine would take part in heathen practices.' Nomhle laughed. 'Yes, *Bawo*, .. I was suprised that you did not let him explain to you.' **1963** WILSON & MAFEJE *Langa* 87 Bawo is now used by a man to his father, formally, and to no one else ... *Tata* is used in the extended sense by both men and women, for father's brothers and senior men, but not *bawo* as it was traditionally. **1963** A.M. LOUW *20 Days* 129 The child .. began to cry shrilly. The mother put him down and shouted: 'It is that he sees the spirit of his bawo — father.' **1976** R.L. PETENI *Hill of Fools* 67 Bawo Langa, why don't you act with firmness in this? Surely you have the right to order your daughter to honour her promise? **1984** M. CILIBE in *Staffrider* Vol.6 No.1, 3 'Mdange! Mdange!' the old man called ... Mdange appeared from the door, quivering, his eyes bloodshot ... 'You were calling me, Bawo?' asked Mdange rhetorically.

Baxa var. BHACA.

Bay *n. colloq.* [Shortened form of *Algoa Bay.*] Usu. ***the Bay***: **a.** Port Elizabeth (see PE). **b.** Algoa Bay, on the shores of which Port Elizabeth was built. Also *attrib.*

Port Elizabeth is colloquially known in Xhosa as *iBhayi* (see IBHAYI), and in Afk. as *die Baai* (see BAAI).

1820 G. BARKER Journal. 17 Apr., Mr Bailey's party left the Bay for their location. **1820** W. SHAW Diary. 4 June, Preached twice during the week to the soldiers and Settlers at the Bay. *a***1827** D. CARMICHAEL in W.J. Hooker *Botanical Misc.* (1831) II. 281 We left the Bay early in the morning, and halted about ten o'clock at the Swartkop River. **1838** T. SHONE Diary. 3 Nov., We started from the bay at quarter past 7 o'clock in the evening for Swarts Kop. **1866** E. WILSON *Reminisc.* 41 In the month of October, 1861, a gentleman was stopped on the Bay road, and robbed of a very valuable gold watch and chain. **1873** F. BOYLE *To Cape for Diamonds* 46 So devious was the journey under these circumstances, that passengers from 'the Bay' did not hope to reach their journey's end before the eighth day. **1890** A. MARTIN *Home Life* 45 Only a day's journey from 'the Bay,' as Port Elizabeth, like San Francisco, is familiarly called. **1891** W. SELWYN *Cape Carols* 159 They bear their sad burden, of so little worth, To the jail, where Bay charity fans her small fire. **1911** *Farmer's Weekly* 22 Mar. 12 The S.S. 'Galician' has just landed at Port Elizabeth three very fine bulls ... Visitors to the Bay show will be able to see them on application. **1937** H. SAUER *Ex Afr.* 27 We headed for Port Elizabeth, or 'The Bay,' as the town was then universally called in South Africa. **1958** [see DIAMOND FIELDS]. **1976** *E. Prov. Herald* 17 June 18 Crunch in Bay economy cuts employment. Port Elizabeth and Uitenhage factories .. retrenched more workers between January and March this year than in corresponding periods over the past five years. **1986** *Sunday Times* 13 July 27 Another record for the 'boys from the bay' is that both Gerber and Serfontein captained the South African Schools XV. **1991** *Grocott's Mail* 26 Feb. 4 Splashing out at the Bay. The organisers of the '91 Port Elizabeth Festival, to be called Port Elizabeth Splash, have appealed to the hinterland for participation.

bay and bay var. BY-AND-BY.

Bayete /baˈjeːte/ *int.* and *n.* Forms: α. **Biatt, Byat(e), Byatt, Byatu;** β. **Baaite, Bayet(e), Beyete;** γ. **Bayede.** [fr. Zulu *bayede*, dial. form of *balethe* 'bring them (*sc.* the enemy)'.]

A. *int.*

a. 'Hail', the Zulu royal salute; also extended as an honour to prominent persons or high officials. Also *attrib.*

α. **1835** A. SMITH *Diary* (1940) II. 62 After waiting about ten minutes we were apprised by the exclamations 'Byat! Byat!' that he (i.e. Mazilikatze) was approaching from an inner enclosure. **1875** C.B. BISSET *Sport & War* 209 The Zulus .. presented a native salute to the Prince .. by simultaneously raising the right hand above the head and all exclaiming Biatt! at the same moment; it means King or Father. **1893** J.F. INGRAM *Story of Gold Concession* 40 A deep but subdued shout of 'Byatu!' ('Our King') rose from the warriors.

β. **1837** F. OWEN *Diary* (1926) 72 These men praise their king for his bounty, shaking their fingers in the air, making hizzing noises with their teeth and shouting out Bayet 'Our Father.' **1846** R. MOFFAT *Missionary Labours* 140 Whenever he rose or sat down, all within sight hailed him with a shout, Baaite! or Aaite! followed by a number of his high sounding titles. **1855** J.W. COLENSO *Ten Weeks in Natal* 103 A grand welcome awaited us, as we drew up – all the men of the kraal being assembled at the entrance, and uttering with one voice the royal salutation 'Bayete!' **1895** H. RIDER HAGGARD *Nada* 43, I went down on my knees before him and gave the royal salute, Bayéte, and so I stayed. **1905** R. PLANT *Zulu in Three Tenses* 69 You know quite well what your royal salutation is; Bayete is the one great word with which you always greeted your king. **1930** S.T. PLAATJE *Mhudi* (1975) 34 The king, with more than usual dignity, acknowledged the royal salute of 'Bayete' from thousands of leather-lunged Matebele. **1952** *Drum* Apr. 23 'Pula! Pula!' 'Bayete! Bayete!' These are the cries that welcomed Queen Elizabeth II, then Princess Elizabeth, and the rest of the Royal Family wherever they met their loyal African subjects. **1971** *Sunday Tribune* 5 Dec. (Mag. Sect.) 23 King Goodwill Zwelithini responded with an unscheduled speech to the roars of 'Bayete' from about 30 000 people. **1973** [see IMBONGI sense 1]. **1987** L. DELLATOLA in *S. Afr. Panorama* May 23 No Zulu would ever stand upright before him, or fail to hail him at all times with the royal praise-greeting of 'bayete'.

γ. **1940** P.R. KIRBY *Diary of Dr Andrew Smith* II. 72 Bayede, Hail, King. **1949** O. WALKER *Proud Zulu* (1951) 33 Their spears went up and with united thunder that split the concave they roared out the royal salute: 'Bayede!' **1978** A. ELLIOTT *Sons of Zulu* 36 As they died, the victims shouted the royal salute of 'Bayede!' to their 'father, Chief Shaka.'

b. In modern contexts, applied rather more loosely, indicating approval or support.

β. **1986** *Sunday Star* 28 Sept. 18 Bayete! It's 'Shaka' the Great, the right mix to make an international hit. **1990** *Sunday Tribune* 14 Jan. (Today) 7 South African music is finally starting to come into its own. Bayete Mango Groove!

γ. **1983** T.S. MASILELA in *Drum* June 23 Bayede ... !! you two brothers of the late conqueror. I salute your progressive opinion.

B. *n.* The Zulu royal salute; an utterance of this salute. Also *attrib.*

β. **1866** W.C. HOLDEN *Past & Future* 119 The Queen .. approached, and we saluted her with our 'bayete'. **1885** H. RIDER HAGGARD *King Solomon's Mines* 118 The old man made a deep obeisance, and murmured the word 'Koom, Koom,' which .. was their royal salute, corresponding to the Bayéte of the Zulus. **1898** B. MITFORD *Induna's Wife* 22 She drew near to the King, then halted, and, with hand upraised, uttered the 'Bayéte.' **1906** H. RIDER HAGGARD *Benita* 126 To no son of his shall his people give the Bayéte, the royal salute. **1972** *Sunday Times* 2 Apr. (Mag. Sect.) 7 The assembled company paid her the high Zulu honour of the royal Bayete salute.

Bayonian /beɪ'əʊnɪən/ *n. Obs.* exc. *hist.* [BAY + Eng. n.- and adj.-forming suffix *-onian.*] A resident of Port Elizabeth. Hence the back-formation **Bayonia** *n.* (*nonce*), Port Elizabeth (see PE).

1832 *Graham's Town Jrnl* 30 Mar. 55 Sir, In the letter of 'A Bayonian,' in your last week's number, there is a very proper allusion to the unaccountable Ordinance which annexes this Township, or District .. to that of Uitenhage. **1871** J. MCKAY *Reminisc.* 3 Instead of a standing camp when morning broke, the Bayonians had nothing to look upon but the trenches which had been dug around the tents. **1882** C. DU VAL *With Show through Sn Afr.* I. 161 The business men did not exhibit that nervous hurry which predominates with 'the Bayonians'. **1891** R. SMITH *Great Gold Lands* 41, I had heard a good deal of Uitenhage, a town within an hour's reach by rail, to which the Bayonians (so the Port Elizabeth people are called) go now and then for a change. **1891** W. SELWYN *Cape Carols* 155 Each thievish loafer prowling Deems it a jolly lark To keep Bayonians growling O'er pillage in the dark. **1897** G.A. PARKER *S. Afr. Sports* 14 Cape Town, King, and Kimberley took part [in the tourney] with the Bayonians. **1902** *The Jrnl* in *Grocott's Mail* (24 Sept. 1982) 2 On Wednesday night last, there arrived at Grahamstown a particularly neat and compactly built motor car .. , having on board its owner Mr W. Alcock, a most popular Bayonian. *Ibid.* 26 Aug., Bayonia has always struck us as having a council that is lavish in contracting municipal debt .. however, we suppose that the ratepayers of Port Elizabeth will know their own business. **1913** W.W. THOMPSON *Sea Fisheries of Cape Col.* 26 (Swart), Port Elizabeth – the Liverpool of South Africa as Bayonians proudly term it. **1975** *Weekend Post* 25 Oct. (TV Post) 10 At that time many Bayonians (Port Elizabethans) were conscious of their noses, especially those who had reason to go near the Baakens River. **1984** *Ibid.* 28 Jan. (Mag. Sect.) 1 'Bayonians' were beginning to realise .. that Humewood could offer .. most enjoyable seashore recreation.

baywhoner var. BYWONER.

bazaala var. BASELA *v.*

bazella, -zello varr. BASELA *n.*

BBB *n.* [Abbrev. of Afk. *Blanke Bevrydingsbeweging*, 'White Liberation Movement', *blanke* white + *bevryding* liberation + linking phoneme *-s-* + *beweging* movement.] A political movement of the far right wing, advocating among other things the removal of blacks from 'white' areas, and the repatriation of Jews. Also *attrib.*

The movement was banned from November 1988 to February 1990.

1987 *Pretoria News* 17 June 1 The posters, produced by a rightwing group called the 'Blanke Bevrydingsbeweging' (BBB), had been removed. **1988** *E. Prov. Herald* 23 Mar. 8 The Government yesterday threatened to take action against the Afrikaner Weerstandsbeweging (AWB) and the Blanke Bevrydingsbeweging (BBB) unless they stopped their 'dangerous incitement of emotions and intimidatory actions'. **1990** *Sunday Times* 11 Feb. 5 Four BBB guys don't even get a chance to unfurl their banners before announcements about airport regulations and muscled policemen ensure national security. **1992** R.H. DU PRE *Making of Racial Conflict* 164 *Blanke Bevrydingsbeweging*, (BBB) – Founded in 1987 by Prof Schabort; based on 'refined Nazism'. Will repatriate Jews and Blacks if it came [*sic*] to power.

BC *n.* Also **B.C.** [Initial letters of *Black Consciousness.*] BLACK CONSCIOUSNESS sense 1. Also *attrib.*

1981 S. SEPAMLA in *Staffrider* Vol.4 No.3, 43 Some of these critics are BC adherents. It appears they have not understood the meaning of black consciousness ... It is the man in the street – how he understands BC – that I feel we must listen to. **1982** *Voice* 25 Apr. 4 (*letter*) Why BC excludes Whites ... My dear brother has confused B.C. with Liberalism. **1983** A. MOKOENA in *Rand Daily Mail* 14 Sept. 7 It was never intended to lead people down the cul de sac of racial exclusivism ... The recent interpretation of BC .. smacks of revisionism. They have revised the original idea of BC that South Africa belonged to everyone, black or white, and now say it belongs to blacks only. **1984** M. KA MYEZA in *Frontline* Mar. 38 Meshack Mabogoane raised the long dormant head of Africanism, in a critique of Black Consciousness and of BC's standard-bearer AZAPO. **1985** N. GONIWE in *Weekly Mail* 20 Dec. 10 (*letter*) I won't say anything about his portfolio within the BC movement. **1987** F. KRÜGER in *Weekly Mail* 12 June 30 The headstone .. proclaims the BC slogan: 'One Azania One Nation.' **1988** *Frontline* Oct. 31 BC and Africanists have needed each other to survive at all against the non-racial Cosatu giant. **1990** R. MALAN *My Traitor's Heart* 247 BC supporters have been attacked on the street and expelled from schools ... Members of the BC youth movement have been abducted and murdered. **1991** *Frontline* May 17 A culture of intolerance then developed ... There are a number of recorded incidents of violence against BC exponents by Charterists on campuses.

BCM *n.* [Initial letters of *Black Consciousness Movement.*] BLACK CONSCIOUSNESS sense 2. Also *attrib.*

1987 *New Nation* 10 Sept. 7 BCM had to face the brunt of persecution in the seventies. It was never a planned and developed political organisation, never a substitute for the ANC or the PAC. Rather it was an association of like-minded people. **1990** *City Press* 17 June 11 The PAC, BCM and Azapo could unite, but not with the ANC because it is not ready to throw away the Freedom Charter. **1990** M. TYALA in *Sunday Times* 12 Aug. 2 With the advent of such new players as the UDF, black youth parted ways. Some remained with the more militant BCM while others joined the ranks of the then banned ANC through surrogate organisations. **1991** *Frontline* May 17 BC students found themselves subsidising Charterist activities. The inverse, however, did not hold, thanks to the university's non-recognition of the BCM. **1994** T. GRUNDY on Radio South Africa 27 July (Radio Today), There are still 52 BCM members in so-called exile in Zimbabwe.

beacon *n.* [Calque formed on Du. *baaken.*] A survey marker, or marker of ownership.

1. A post, stone, peg, or natural feature used to mark the boundaries of individually-owned land, or, less frequently, of provinces or states; BAAKEN sense 1.

1809 EARL OF CALEDON in G.M. Theal *Rec. of Cape Col.* (1900) VII. 185 Half an hour's walking .. from the house or beacon whence it [*sc.* the farm] is supposed to be measured. **1850** J.E. METHLEY *New Col. of Port Natal* 55 The beacons .. marked and numbered, gave an appearance of civilization in this unfortunately unmeasured country. **1854** *Minutes of Proceedings To Enquire into Existing Pound Regulations* in *Cape of G.H. Annexures* 109 The Committee find that the Petitioners complain .. Of the non-erection of proper Beacons on the boundaries of Farms. **1859** *Cape Town Weekly Mag.* 11 Feb. 39 Mr. Austen, the superintendent of the native Reserve in the Wittebergen, met Field-cornet Olivier on Thursday last, by the Governor's direction, and placed the last beacon on the Orange River, where the new boundary-line between the Basutos and the Free State terminates. **1878** *Crown Lands Act* in A. Douglass *Ostrich Farming* (*c*1881) 196 The expenses of survey, erection of beacons, and of the title-deeds, to be paid at any time the government may fix. *c***1881** A. DOUGLASS *Ostrich Farming* 238 Insist on seeing all corner and angle beacons, and .. find out whether any of these are disputed by the neighbours. *Ibid.* 239 An excellent plan is to whitewash all beacon stones; everybody in the farm then soon gets to know the boundaries. **1893** 'AFRICANUS' in *Cape Illust. Mag.* Vol.3 No.11, 417 The beacon, and ruins of the hut, still stand at the top of the zig-zag path leading up to it. **1905** G. BAUMANN in Baumann & Bright *Lost Republic* (1940) 242 Moffat .. said in his 'Omschryving' .. that the first beacon stood in a certain magnetic direction from this point, and then proceeded to describe the other beacons of the farm. **1924** *Ibid.* 107 The beacon should have been some four or five hundred yards nearer the original farm ... This my calculation and plotting verified, and it was also in accord with the old 'Omschryving'. **1927** C.G. BOTHA *Social Life in Cape Col.* 78 Beacons had to be fixed to show the boundaries and an old law laid down the death penalty for those found removing another man's beacons. **1934** C.P. SWART Supplement to Pettman. 9 *Beacon*, In its South African application this word, influenced by the Afrikaans 'baken', means a natural or artificial erection, used as a landmark or distinguishing point for the purpose of defining the division of land into portions, such as beacons defining the boundaries of farms (usually a stake driven into the ground), lots, erven, claims or water-rights. **1951** R. FARRAN *Jungle Chase* (1957) 46 It is necessary to mark off with clear lines and beacons through the bush square one-mile blocks which are registered as claims with the Mining Commissioner. **1969** I. VAUGHAN *Last of Sunlit Yrs* 88 It concerns an action involving an allegation that a beacon had been moved, and evidence as to the beacon's original position was vital to the case. **1972** *Daily Dispatch* 29 July

4 The beacons of new farms, still unfenced, were piling up on the veld. **1984** R.C. Fisher in Martin & Friedlaender *Hist. of Surveying & Land Tenure* I. 61 We should note that the extent of a modern land parcel is also demarcated by beacons. This raises the question: was this the case in van Riebeeck's time?

2. *rare.* An inscribed stone claiming possession of colonial land for the mother-country; BAAKEN sense 2. See also PADRAO.

1941 C.W. De Kiewiet *Hist. of S. Afr.* 25 Not van Plettenberg's beacon, nor any frontier or treaty line, nor any neutral belt availed in keeping white and black apart.

3. A trigonometrical station or point.

1962 *S. Afr. 1:50,000 Sheet 3326 AC Alicedale* (Trig. Survey Office), (*caption*) Trig. Beacons (Number to right and height below). **1989** *Weekend Post* 11 Nov. (Leisure) 4 You walk mostly on the crest of the range .. but the path deprives you of the final peak of the Oliewenberg ... You are forbidden to leave the trail to get to the beacon.

beacon *v. trans.* Usu. in the phr. ***to beacon off*** [calque formed on S. Afr. Du. *afbaken* delimit, demarcate]. To survey (land) and mark (the boundaries of a property). See also BEACON *n.* sense 1.

1872 J.L. Babe *S. Afr. Diamond Fields* 34 A great many diamonds had been picked up there; so we beaconed off a claim and returned to camp. **1883** *Pall Mall Gaz.* (U.K.) 16 Nov. 2 The boundary has never been beaconed off. **1904** H.A. Bryden *Hist. of S. Afr.* 108 The Boers, as they spread northwards beyond the Vaal River, .. beaconed out for themselves farms, built houses [etc.]. **1913** [see OUTSPAN *n.* sense 1]. *c*1936 *S. & E. Afr. Yr Bk & Guide* 26 A prospective tax on excess land beaconed off, a deterrent which seems to have been fairly effective, although many farms were reduced on survey. **1937** C.R. Prance *Tante Rebella's Saga* 41 A Commission to beacon-off their land roughly into farms for some of the burghers who were trekking away in swarms. **1962** A.P. Cartwright *Gold Miners* 61 The regulation under which a *mijnpachtbrief* was registered gave the owner of the land, or the purchaser of his mining rights, the right to beacon an area equal to about one-tenth of the total area of the farm on which he could conduct mining operations himself.

be-ah var. BEE-AH.

beast *n.* [Eng., influenced by S. Afr. Du. *beest* head of cattle.]

1. A domesticated bovine animal; a cow, ox, or bull.

A standard usage in *S. Afr. Eng.*

1812 A. Plumptre tr. *H. Lichtenstein's Trav. in Sn Afr.* (1928) I. 132 They called .. horned cattle *beasts*, the whole family of the antelopes *boks*. **1827** G. Thompson *Trav.* II. 350 If a person steal a cow, and slaughter it at his kraal, every one implicated is obliged to pay a beast to the plaintiff. **1841** J.W. Appleyard *War of Axe* (1971) 6 They had just slaughtered a beast at the great place and were busy preparing for eating. **1852** T. Shone Diary. 24 Aug., The Rebels have taken all The Cattle from the Police station on the Waay Plaats yesterday, they cannot Find the spur of the Beast. *c*1881 A. Douglass *Ostrich Farming* 205 Where sweet veldt cattle are brought on to sour veldt, a considerable per-centage suffer. The best and most simple remedy is a quart of linseed oil with a wine-glass of turpentine for a full-grown beast, and half the amount for a young beast. **1913** H. Tucker *Our Beautiful Peninsula* 75 Slaughter-houses flow unceasingly with the blood of slain beasts. **1923** G.H. Nicholls *Bayete!* 121 'My daughter is worth eight cattle,' he said. 'But if she is worth eight beasts now she was worth eight beasts six months ago.' **1936** R.J.M. Goold-Adams *S. Afr. To-Day & To-Morrow* 125 The unavoidable breeding of very poor quality beasts by natives and the poorer farmers, Dutch and English. **1955** V.M. Fitzroy *Dark Bright Land* 40 Their tribal custom is, to barter cattle for a bride, and the more considerable the maiden's father in the tribe, the richer the fee in beasts does he demand. **1964** *Drum* Nov. 19 The guests drank 100 gallons of beer and ate two beasts. **1975** W.M. MacMillan *My S. Afr. Yrs* 135 He reckoned that 1,000 morgen (which is over 2,000 acres) would support only 300 beasts, presumably cattle. **1985** *Probe* Nov. 18 It was hard to drive at night without finding horses, donkeys, beasts sharing roads with licensed vehicles. **1986** P.A. McAllister Xhosa Beer Drinks. 42 Among the Pedi 'beer is nearly always the medium of sacrifice' though it was sometimes accompanied by a beast (Monnig 1967, 61). **1990** *City Press* 11 Feb. 6 When he goes to Qunu the people there have promised to give him beasts and sheep to be slaughtered to thank the Dlomo ancestors. **1993** *Pace* July 2 We darkies are fond of expensive funerals .. our bills include buying of beasts, cakes, cooldrinks, caskets and hiring of expensive cars to ferry mourners.

2. *comb.* **beast-kraal** *obs.* [see KRAAL *n.* sense 3], *cattle kraal* (see KRAAL *n.* sense 3 b i). Also *attrib.*

1803 J.T. Van der Kemp *Trans. of Missionary Soc.* I. 437 In the centre of the kraal there is a large circular area, fenced by trees, cut down and laid in the manner of an abbatis. Into this beast-kraal, all the cattle belonging to the kraal are driven at evening and milked. **1821** C.I. Latrobe *Jrnl of Visit* 268 Close to the dwelling, was the beast-kraal. **1833** *Graham's Town Jrnl* 14 Mar. 2 They .. went to the beast-kraal gate, and my father went to the house.

Bechannas, Bechouanas pl. forms of BECHUANA.

bechu var. BESHU.

Bechuana /betʃw'ɑːnə, betʃu'ɑːnə/ *n. Obsolescent* exc. *hist.* Pl. usu. unchanged, or -s. Forms: α. (*pl.* only) **Boetshoenas, Bootchuannas, Bōōtshooānās, Bootshuanas, Buc(h)uanas, Mōōtshooānās**; β. (*pl.* only) **Bos(c)huanas, Boshuanah, Botchuana's, Botschuanas**; γ. (*pl.* only) **Beetchuanah, Beetshuanas, Betcuana, Betshoenas, Beuchuanas, Bichuana(s), Bituanas**; δ. *sing.* **Bechuan, Betj(o)uana, Mo(t)chuana**; *sing.* and *pl.* **Bechuana**; *pl.* **Bachuana, Bechannas, Bech(o)uanas, Bec(h)wana.** [Englished form of seTswana *baTswana*, see MOTSWANA; or perh. representing obs. seTswana pronunciation of an earlier form of *baTswana*; for an explanation of sing. and pl. forms, see MO- and BA-.]

1.a. A member of any of several Sotho-Tswana peoples inhabiting the interior of southern Africa; CHUANA sense 1 a. **b.** TSWANA sense 2 a. Also *attrib.*, passing into *adj.*

During the 19th century 'Bechuana' and 'Kaffir' often meant SOTHO and NGUNI respectively. 'Bechuana' has been replaced in *S. Afr. Eng.* by 'Tswana' (usu. meaning a seTswana-speaking South African) and 'Batswana' (often meaning the citizens of Botswana, but see MOTSWANA).

α. **1801** W. Somerville *Narr. of E. Cape Frontier* (1979) 123 Briqua is a name unknown to them, but applied to them by the Kora Hottentots — they call themselves Bōōtshooānās or Mōōtshooānās — for they hardly make any distinction in the articulation of these two letters. **1821** *Missionary Notices* 119 They differ much from the Caffers and Bootchuannas on the east, as also from their nearest neighbours, the Damaras on the west. **1834** J.C. Chase in A. Steedman *Wanderings* (1835) II. 171 The Beuchuanas, a peculiarly mild race, .. amiable, courteous, and much-civilized. **1875** C.B. Bisset *Sport & War* 170 About the year 1830 some of the dispersed native tribes from the interior of Africa migrated into the Cape Colony ... The tribes were called Munatees and Bucuanas.

β. **1818** Lord C. Somerset in G.M. Theal *Rec. of Cape Col.* (1902) XII. 112 Those tribes the Boshuanas, Ghonas, and Briquas .. have been very peaceable towards the Colonists. **1822** *Missionary Notices* 214 One of these visitors having frequently travelled amongst the Manketsens, Boschuanas, and Marootzes, to the north and north-east of Griqua Town, gave us much more information respecting that country.

γ. **1824** W.J. Burchell *Trav.* II. 26 In her ear are two small copper ornaments of Bichuana manufacture. *a*1838 A. Smith *Jrnl* (1975) 187 Locusts form with the Bituanas not an uncommon article of food, and .. are by no means disrelished by these natives. **1884** *Cape Law Jrnl* I. 223 These are the .. interior Basuto tribes and those in the Transvaal Territory and Colonial Basutos, including the Barolongs of the Orange Free State and the Beetshuanas or Batlapins of Griqualand West and also the Griquas.

δ. **1827** G. Thompson *Trav.* I. 91 The fourth speaker, Insha, a Barolong, began by recommending that the Bechuanas should wait until the Mantatees appeared, and then attack them. *Ibid.* 158 The marauding horde .. were now plundering and destroying the Bechuana tribes to the northward. **1832** *Graham's Town Jrnl* 24 Feb. 34 In 1824 and 1825, the Bechuanas were in a most wretched condition. They had been attacked by the Mantatees, who .. are reputed cannibals. The Griquas also .. made inroads upon them. **1835** D. Lindley in D.J. Kotze *Lett. of American Missionaries* (1950) 87 We shall make use of a Mochuana, who speaks Dutch very well, as our interpreter. **1835** G. Champion *Jrnl* (1968) 10 The range of mts separating the Caffre from the Betjouana country. *Ibid.* 35 Striking difference between the Kaffers & Betjouanas. **1837** R. Giddy in B. Shaw *Memorials* (1841) 227, I have now to take leave of this people, having received orders from the Committee to remove to the Bechuana Mission. **1845** S. Dennison in D.R. Edgecombe, Letters of Hannah Dennison. (1968) 202 Mrs Cambell wishes Elizabeth to stay with her untill she is confined so we will not see her in the betcuana Country untill July. [**1857** D. Livingstone *Missionary Trav.* 200 The name Bechuana seems derived from the word Chuana — alike or equal — with the personal pronoun Ba (they) prefixed; and therefore means fellows or equals. Some have supposed the name to have arisen from a mistake of some traveller, who, on asking individuals of this nation concerning the tribes living beyond them, received the answer, Bachuana, 'they (are) alike;' meaning, They are the same as we are'.] **1860** W. Shaw *Story of my Mission* 399 The 'Kwahlamba' .. forms the impracticable and almost impassable boundary which has for ages separated the Bechuana nations of the more inland districts, from the Kaffirs of the coast country. **1867** E.L. Price *Jrnls* (1956) 266 She uttered a sort of low *howl* when I said that Robert was dead & then she went away without begging a single thing — which is of course a remarkable event for an untaught Mochuana. **1871** J. Mackenzie *Ten Yrs* (1971) 106 He could be an orthodox Mochuana and a good Christian at the same time. *Ibid.* 501 There are cabins in the United Kingdom .. which are certainly less comfortable in every point of view than a well-built Bechuana hut. **1895** A.H. Keane *Africa* II. 241 Tribal groups belonging either to the Bechuana, or to the Zulu-Kafir division of the Southern Bantus. **1895** [see MOSOTHO]. **1905** W.H. Tooke in Flint & Gilchrist *Science in S. Afr.* 92 The be-Chuana are .. remarkable for their honesty, a virtue which has been noticed from Livingstone's time. **1905** *Native Tribes of Tvl* 131 The Basuto and Bechuana .. are both moderately developed people, generally well-built, wiry and active, but slight in figure. **1916** *Act 1* in *Stat. of Union* 2 Section *five* of Act No. 28 of 1898 .. is hereby amended by .. the addition after the word 'Koranna' of the following words:— 'Griqua, Zulu, Bechuana, Swazi, or any member of any aboriginal tribe or race of Africa.' **1930** S.T. Plaatje *Mhudi* (1975) 21 Two centuries ago the Bechuana tribes inhabited the extensive areas between Central Transvaal and the Kalahari Desert. *a*1951 H.C. Bosman *Willemsdorp* (1977) 55 The flat-boy .. was one Pieta, a Bechuana whose brown-boot-polish complexion was several degrees lighter than Mhlopi's own. **1965** J.D. Jones in *Setswana Dict.* (1982) p.vi, The sound represented by *c* and its aspirated relative *ch* is rarely if ever heard among the northern Becwana. **1967** E.M. Slatter *My Leaves Are Green* 33 Dogs were barking, and the native labourers, Fingos, Xosa, Bechuanas .. and others, were singing round their own fires. **1973** J. Cowden *For Love* 26 Reverend James Archbell .. came from Yorkshire in 1818 to be a missionary amongst the Baralong tribe in Bechuana Country (the

Transvaal of today) ... He and his wife .. were the first to publish a book – a reader for the Tswana people. **1986** P. MAYLAM *Hist. of Afr. People* 44 The label 'Bechuana' was developed by whites in the nineteenth century and was often applied very loosely to cover all the African peoples of the interior. **1989** J. CRWYS-WILLIAMS *S. Afr. Despatches* 14 On an up-country visit .. Thompson observed a general assembly of the tribes making up the Bechuana nation, which was called together at Kuruman to meet the threat of the advancing Mantatees.

2. Only in *sing.* δ forms with *Be-*: SETSWANA. Also *attrib.*

δ. **1826** R. MOFFATT *(title)* A Bechuana Catechism. **1833** W. SHAW in B. Shaw *Memorials* (1841) 235 The English, Dutch, Kaffir, and occasionally the Bechuana languages are used, as the means of conveying instruction to this people. **1835** G. CHAMPION *Jrnl* (1968) 19 They speak a little in the language. The language is the Betjouana. **1841** B. SHAW *Memorials* 38 The language [*sc.* Xhosa], which is radically the same as the Bechuana, save when interrupted by clicks, is soft and agreeable. **1864** J.M. BOWKER *Speeches & Sel.* 3 The Hottentots and Bushmen .. are the remnants of two distinct nations, whose languages bear no affinity to either Kafir or Bechuana. **1957** A. GORDON-BROWN *S. Afr. Yrbk & Guide* 208 The Bechuana are of Bantu stock and speak Bechuana. **1979** — *Settlers' Press* 57 William Binnington Boyce and James Archbell .. in the face of formidable difficulties, produced respectively grammars of the Kafir and Bechuana languages.

beck var. BEK.

beckbecary var. BOKMAKIERIE.

becreep *v. trans. Obs.* Also **becrep**, **becroup**, **bekr(u)yp**. [Calque formed on Du. *bekruipen*, prefix *be-* near, next to + *kruipen* to creep. From the spellings *becroup*, *bekruyp*, and *bekryp* it is clear that this word was sometimes borrowed directly from the Du. and sometimes Englished to *becreep*.] To stalk, creep up on (someone or something). So **becreeper** *n.*, stalker.

1796 E. HELME tr. *F. Le Vaillant's Trav. into Int.* I. 255 (Pettman), The Boshmen are generally considered as the best bekrypers. **1838** J.E. ALEXANDER *Exped. into Int.* II. 8 The watchful monster did not charge as we expected, being young, and made off before we had time to *becreep* it. *a***1858** J. GOLDSWAIN *Chron.* I. (1946) 118 My gun in her hand readey to give it to me in cace aney Kaffer or Kaffers should trie to becrep us. **1860** A.W. DRAYSON *Sporting Scenes* 75 Elephants would catch me; tigers (i.e. leopards) becroup (i.e. stalk) me; snakes bite me. *a***1875** T. BAINES *Jrnl of Res.* (1964) II. 155 Andries, arriving soon after, told us our shots had frightened away the ostrich he was 'bekruyping'. *Ibid.* 160 Andries and John were out from dawn till after sunset, and becrept and shot two wildebeestes.

becreeping *vbl n. Obs.* [As prec.] Stalking. Also *attrib.*

1824 W.J. BURCHELL *Trav.* II. 56 On the head of one man I remarked an unusually large fur cap .. of a shape extending far behind the head ... This was for the purpose of .. enabling the wearer .. to approach the animal within reach of his arrow. It is called a *be-creeping cap* (Bekruip-muts); and is only worn when in pursuit of game. **1868** J. CHAPMAN *Trav.* II. 110 What we call stalking the Boers have a much more correct term for – be-kruiping, or be-creeping.

becroup var. BECREEP.

Becwana pl. form of BECHUANA.

bedonnerd /bəˈdɔnə(r)t/ *adj. slang.* Also **bedonderd**, **bedonnered**. [Afk.] Wilfully obstinate, contrary; out of temper; crazy; BENEUKT.

1969 A. FUGARD *Boesman & Lena* 12 Sugar's not enough man. I want some real sweetness. Then you can be as *bedonnerd* as you like. **1974** *Drum* 8 Apr. 7 Some people think I'm bedonderd when I say I want to be ruled by a government of Africans. But they just don't blerrie understand. **1978** P.-D. UYS in *Theatre One* 149 Anna: Down? Do I look down? Molly: Sort of bedonnerd, yes. **1985** [see BEFOK]. **1987** R. SARGEANT in *Grocott's Mail* 30 Apr. 2 It's a crazy play – I think the best word to describe it is that marvellous Afrikaans word 'bedonnered'. [**1990** R. GOOL *Cape Town Coolie* 2 'These people,' he said in a strong *Platteland* Afrikaans, 'are mad!' – He used the colloquial word, *bedonderd*. – 'They all want to be coloured!']

be down see DOWN sense b.

bee-ah /ˈbiːɑː/ *n.* Also **be-ah**, **beeyah**, **bi-ah**. [Joc. pronunciation-spelling of *beer*, coined by *Drum* magazine columnist K.M.C. Motsisi.] In township English: beer.

1966 K.M.C. MOTSISI in *Post* 16 Jan. (Drum) 19, I order two bee-ahs and a nip. **1968** P. SEGOLA in *Lizard* No.2, I knew he would feel better, after two quarts of cold bi-ahs. 'Don't make me bi-ahs this time Jack ... I'd like scales maiza.' I must confess, he knew all the spots. **1978** *Drum* 22 Apr. 27, I tell him that we should go to Aunt Peggy's joint and debate this matter over a ha-ja of the mahog and maybe a be-ah or two as I know that he is very fond of be-ahs. **1979** M. MATSHOBA *Call Me Not a Man* 64 Why didn't you let us know you were out? We would have bought you a lot of 'beahs'. **1981** B. MFENYANA in M. Mutloatse *Reconstruction* 294 By the time he's through I've already downed four beeahs at Sis Nota's grog-house.

bee-cuckoo *n. obs.* [So named because of its cuckoo-like behaviour; see quot. 1927.] Also **bee-cuckow**. HONEY-GUIDE.

1786 G. FORSTER tr. *A. Sparrman's Voy. to Cape of G.H.* II. 186 The *bee-cuckow*, (*Cuculus indicator*) .. deserves to have more particular notice taken of it in this place. **1802** W. BINGLEY *Animal Biog.* (1813) II. 125 The Bee Cuckoo, in its external appearance, does not much differ from the common sparrow. **1835** [see HONEY-RATEL]. **1905** G.W. STOW *Native Races of S. Afr.* 86 They had also a most useful ally and assistant in carrying out this work, in the honey-bird – the 'Bee cuckoo' of Sparrman and called 'honing-wijzer', the honey-guide, by the Hottentots and Dutch.

beefsteak mushroom *n. phr.* [Transf. use of Eng. *beefsteak mushroom* a name for *Fistulina hepatica*.] Either of two species of large edible mushroom:

a. Freq. with distinguishing epithet **Natal beefsteak mushroom**: IKHOWE.

*c***1948** *S. & E. Afr. Yr Bk & Guide* 313 The Natal Beefsteak Mushroom or I-kowe (*Schulzeria umkowaan*). **1954**, **1972**, **1987** [see IKHOWE].

b. (*rare.*) *Boletus edulis* of the Boletaceae.

1982 FOX & NORWOOD YOUNG *Food from Veld* 233 *Boletus edulis* .. , known as *stone mushroom*, *beefsteak mushroom*, or *cow mushroom*, is edible and occurs in the western Cape Province.

beer-boep /ˈbɪə bʊp, -bup/ *n. colloq.* [Eng. *beer* + BOEP *n.*[2]] A beer-drinker's pot-belly; one who has a pot-belly. See also BOEP *n.*[2]

1980 *Sunday Times* 9 Mar. (Mag. Sect.) 5 Our duelling figures have been ruined by beer-boeps. **1984** *Fair Lady* 30 May 7 South Africa is fast becoming a nation of .. 'fat slobs'. They strut around our beaches with awful 'beer boeps' hanging over their swim shorts. **1985** *Cape Times* 5 Aug., In any South African pub the beer *boeps* seldom outnumber those who can see their navels without looking in a mirror. **1989** P. LEE in *Sunday Times* 22 Jan. (Mag. Sect.) 45 Picture the typical South African sports spectator. He normally sports a beer boep, has a beer can clutched firmly in his hot sweaty hand .. and .. you might even spot the odd naartjie among his cushions and umbrellas. **1990** *Sunday Times* 5 Aug. 13 Its not past our local rugger-buggers to pitch up for that special occasion .. with their shirts unbuttoned to the navel and flaunting a beer boep. **1990** *Personality* 3 Dec. 22 'I saw the report,' another beer boep told us, wiping the trickle of hops-in-liquid-form from his mouth.

beer-drink *n.* In both urban and rural African society: a traditional social or ceremonial gathering for the drinking of beer; BEER-DRINKING. Also *attrib.*

1879 R.J. ATCHERLEY *Trip to Boerland* 68 They were going to a 'beer-drink', and were totally out of these commodities; we were rich, would we make them a present of some? **1891** T.R. BEATTIE *Ride through Transkei* 67 When a 'beer-drink' is on at any particular kraal they will not have to wait long for their neighbours to help them to get rid of the good stuff. **1905** P. GIBBON *Vrouw Grobelaar* 46 Perhaps it began at a beer-drink with some boasting by the young men before the girls. **1913** C. PETTMAN *Africanderisms* 53 The natives are in the habit of gathering on frequent occasions for the purpose of drinking 'Kaffir beer' ... Such a gathering is known as a *Beer drink.* **1929** J.G. VAN ALPHEN *Jan Venter* 32 There was a beer-drink last night, and they got playful. Somebody insulted somebody else's sister, and kerries began to fly. **1937** B.J.F. LAUBSCHER *Sex, Custom & Psychopathology* 200 Fights at urban location beer-drinks leading to serious assaults are not uncommon. **1948** H.V. MORTON *In Search of S. Afr.* 181 The great social event of the Transkei, as of all native territories, I gathered, is what is called 'a beer drink'. **1948** O. WALKER *Kaffirs Are Lively* 178 Children scavenge the streets, learning the lore of the faro-dens, *marabi* beer-drink dances, prostitutes' hide-outs. **1953** LANHAM & MOPELI-PAULUS *Blanket Boy's Moon* 22 Father Moruti, I freely promise that I will go no more at night from beer-drink to beer-drink. **1960** J.J.L. SISSON *S. Afr. Judicial Dict.* 86 *Beer drink*, in terms of Act No. 32 of 1909 (C.), s. 11, and Proclamation No. 36 of 1914, means a gathering of natives who assemble together for the purpose of drinking beer. **1971** *Daily Dispatch* 25 Sept. 1 Four Pondo tribesmen were killed when a 100-strong faction clashed with a group of 25 men in the Nyati area ... The skirmish followed a beer drink. **1980** C. RUKUNI in M. Mutloatse *Forced Landing* 176 'T-h-i-r-t-y cents! Do others buy beer at all or do they wait for you?' .. That was how his wife always talked before he went off for a beer-drink. **1986** P.A. MCALLISTER Xhosa Beer Drinks. p.vii, The main theoretical argument is that beer drinks may be regarded as 'cultural performances' in which social reality or 'practice' is dramatised and reflected upon ... Beer drinks are dominated by verbal communication of various kinds. **1990** *Weekend Post* 1 Dec. 4 He .. conducted research for his PhD on the social significance of beer drinks and oratory in the Xhosa community.

beer-drinking *vbl n.* [Special sense of general Eng.] BEER-DRINK. Also *attrib.*

1899 A. WERNER *Captain of Locusts* 171 Then, to Nono's dismay, she said that all the men had gone to a beer-drinking on the other side of the valley. **1940** F.B. YOUNG *City of Gold* 358 When he reached the kraal it soon became clear that the beer-drinking season, which lasts for several months, was in full swing. **1986** P.A. MCALLISTER Xhosa Beer Drinks. 4 Davies (1927) had published a three page article on Bomvana beer-drinking customs.

beerhall *n.* [Special sense of general Eng.] A public establishment in a black township where sorghum beer is sold, and which is run by the State or by a municipal authority. Also *attrib.*

[**1900** *Stat. Law of Sn Rhodesia 1899* II. 90 'Beer Hall Licences' may be issued to brewers of beer manufactured in Southern Rhodesia for the sale of such beer by retail.] **1942** *Cape Times* 24 Dec. 7 The shebeeners of large townships naturally press for the abolition of municipal beer-halls. **1942** *Report of Native Affairs Commission to Enquire into Working of Provisions of Natives (Urban Areas) Act Relating to Use & Supply of Kaffir Beer* 4 The beerhall system in South Africa originated in Natal ... In 1908 the Natal Beer Act (No. 23 of 1908) was passed ... Official reports in the following year commented favourably on the operation of the Act at Durban and Pietermaritzburg where beer-halls had been established. **1950** [see SHEBEEN sense 2]. **1951** *Drum* Oct. 6 Tired of drinking Kaffir Beer at the Municipal Beer Hall, many Africans move along to where they can have doctored beer with a kick in it. **1958** *Rand Daily Mail* 9 June 5 A beer hall in Daveyton, costing £105,000 is expected to yield a surplus of £725,680 by next year – the Law says some of this must be spent on social services. **1962** A.J. LUTHULI

Let my People Go 63 The beer hall has become for us — and especially for the women — a symbol of legal robbery by whites. **1970** [see BANTU BEER]. **1977** J. SIKAKANE *Window on Soweto* 35 Where, then, does the money come from to keep the beerhalls and liquor stores busy with customers and thriving with money to finance the wastelands of the Bantustans? **1980** E. JOUBERT *Poppie Nongena* 308 The black people in the Cape Town locations are rising, they are burning down buildings, smashing the beer halls, overturning cars and stoning the buses. **1986** *Learn & Teach* No.3, 32 'We hated the beerhalls.' said Mrs Sibanda. 'Our children were dying because of the beerhalls. On payday some men never went home. They went to the beerhalls. Then they drank until they had no money left.' **1990** W. BOTHA in *Frontline* Sept. 21 'I think this beer hall must be changed into a church,' Shabalala says. 'I don't like these things — they cause only trouble.'

beesem-riet var. BESEM-RIET.

Beetchuanah pl. form of BECHUANA.

beetj(i)e var. BIETJIE.

Beetshuanas pl. form of BECHUANA.

beeyah var. BEE-AH.

befok /bə'fɔk/ *adj. slang*. Also **bafok**, **bevok**, and (*attrib*) **befokte**. [Afk. *befok* (attrib. form *-te*) 'fucked'.] Not in polite use. Messed up, 'screwed up'; 'not right in the head'. Cf. BOSBEFOK.

1979 F. DIKE *First S. African* 22 Hey, but Mtshiselwa is bafok ... Max: You know Mtshiselwa is not very clever, and he is not foolish either. **1980** A. DANGOR in M. Mutloatse *Forced Landing* 165 Go and do your *befokte* shouting somewhere else. A man can't even get a decent night's sleep here. **1985** *Frontline* Aug. 54, I don't suppose it'll ever end. It'll go on until the blacks get the vote, and then we're befok ... Of course guys who spend long enough living in the bush end up bedonderd, but that's just normal army befok, it's not bossies like from war.

begger var. BAGGER.

‖**begrafnisrys** /bə'xrafnəs,reɪs/ *n*. Formerly also **begrafenisrijs**(t). [Afk. (earlier S. Afr. Du. *begrafenisrijst*), *funeral rice*, *begrafnis* funeral, burial + *rys* rice; see quot. 1913.] *yellow rice*, see YELLOW sense c.

1913 C. PETTMAN *Africanderisms* 54 *Begrafenisrijst*, Rice prepared with turmeric ... A reference to the custom, still in vogue in country districts, of providing a meal for those who had come long distances to be present at the funeral, though now .. used quite apart from funerals. **1927** C.G. BOTHA *Social Life in Cape Col.* 66 When a hot course of poultry or meat was given it was usual to serve 'yellow' rice with it. This was rice coloured by borrie with raisins added. Such a dish received the name of 'begrafenis rijs', or funeral rice. **1972** L.G. GREEN *When Journeys Over* 70 After a funeral there was always the special *begrafnisrys*, yellow rice with raisins. [**1981** *Flying Springbok* Sept. 55 Typical South African dishes: the 'sosaties' or kebabs are usually eaten, with yellow rice ('begrafnisrys' in Afrikaans meaning 'funeral rice').]

beigel var. BAGEL.

beitje var. BIETJIE.

beiwoner var. BYWONER.

bek /bek/ *n. colloq*. Also **beck**, **bêk**. [Afk.]
1. Beak; muzzle; in expressions indicating irritation, the human mouth.

1913 C. PETTMAN *Africanderisms* 54 *Bek*, .. In Cape Dutch this word is frequently used in the same sense as the English slang word 'cheek' — 'Hou, uw bek'. 'Shut up!' 'Don't be cheeky!' **1916** *Farmer's Weekly* 27 Dec. 1580 Jackasses. Just arrived per Clan Chisholm Castle ... Colours: All Black with white bellies and wit beks. **1970** J. GOOSEN *Informant*, Queenstown I'll keep his 'bek' shut (I'll silence him). **1971** *Informant*, Grahamstown One of them [*sc*. the birds] loved grapes and he used to have his bek dripping with purple sap in the garden.

2. In the expression **hou jou bek** /ˌhəʊ jəʊ -/ [Afk., *hou* hold + *jou* your + *bek* mouth], shut up!

1913 [see sense 1]. *c*1929 S. BLACK in S. Gray *Three Plays* (1984) 108 Camelia: Shuee! Here comes two ladies. Frikkie (*to Sophie*): Hou jou bek! ... Sophie: Shut up yourself. **1959** J. PACKER *High Roof* 175 'Hou jou beck!' he stormed suddenly. 'I don't believe anything of this!' **1971** *Personality* 5 Mar. 78 'Hou jou bek!' 'Kafirboetie!' 'Liberalist!' ... Our boys would have to drag up some better guns than that. **1979** A. HOUSE in *Staffrider* Vol.2 No.1, 9 'I'm not drunk. I don't drink.' 'Shut up. Hou jou bêk, Hotnot.' **1984** W. STEENKAMP in *Cape Times* 3 Mar., Hate mail continues to land on my desk. The latest .. *He's Coming To Get You. Hou Jou Bek*.

bekmakeri var. BOKMAKIERIE.

bekr(u)yp var. BECREEP.

Bele(n)ryna, Bel-en-ry-na varr. BELLERYNA.

bell *v. trans. Colloq*. Also **bel**. [Derived fr. Eng. 'give (someone) a bell', prob. influenced by Afk. *bel* to ring, telephone.] To telephone (someone).

1974 *E. Prov. Herald* 15 Mar. 25 (*advt*) Man, you want a farm? .. Please bel me by Kirkwood 1412. **1975** 'BLOSSOM' in *Darling* 25 June 111 One day after I been there two weeks or so, Mr F gets belled by he's everloving wife to jol out to the supermarket and pick up some sugar. **1976** *Ibid*. 1 Sept. 115 OK so we'll fix it for Saturday night then. I'll bel some of the chicks meanwhile and organise the graze.

Belleryna /ˌbelə'reɪnə, -na/ *n*. Also **Belenryna, Bel-en-ry-na, Bell en Ry Na, Beleryna**, and with small initial. [Afk. *bel en ry na* 'telephone and ride to', punning on Eng. *ballerina*.] A woman acting as a telephone contact for national servicemen needing transport between cities under the RIDE SAFE scheme. Also shortened form **Belle**.

1979 *E. Prov. Herald* 3 May 5 There were two Bell en Ry Na contacts in Port Elizabeth and three in Uitenhage. **1981** *Outeniqualander* 25 June 5 If you are going on a journey and could give a troopie or soldoedie a lift, please phone the Belerynas. National Servicemen looking for a lift should also phone the Belerynas. **1982** *E. Prov. Herald* 9 Nov. 1 Any belle could be fired without notice. 'How can that be if this is voluntary work?' **1983** *Ibid*. 16 May 9 Bellerynas — women who man telephones to organise lifts for national servicemen — from the Eastern Cape will meet in Graaff-Reinet on Saturday to discuss their problems with the national body of the movement.

bel(l)tong, belting, -tongue varr. BILTONG.

benauwdheid *n. obs*. Also **benaawdheit, benaudheid**. [Du., *benauwd* tight in the chest, suffocating + *-heid* -ness.] Anxiety; constriction, shortness of breath.

1883 O.E.A. SCHREINER *Story of Afr. Farm* 107 She smiled kindly at Bonaparte .. quickly returning with a bottle of red drops in her hand. 'They are very good for "benaawdheit"; my mother always drinks them,' she said, holding the bottle out. **1898** W.C. SCULLY *Vendetta* 27 She put her head in through the doorway. 'Pa, — it is Aunt Emerencia's wagon; she is sure to be coming for some more medicine for her *benaudheit*.'

beneukt /bə'niœkt, -'niːək(t)/ *adj. slang*. Also **beneeked, beneuk**, and (*attrib*.) **beneekte**. [ad. Afk. slang *beneuk* (attrib. form *-te*) contrary, bad-tempered (fr. *neuk* hit, push, deceive).] BEDONNERD.

1963 P.R. LUND *Informant*, Port Elizabeth, I think your Mom has told you that I have left [the company] as I had begun to realize that it was wragties a beneekte joint. **1969** A. FUGARD *Boesman & Lena* 69 We're whiteman's rubbish. That's why he's so beneeked with us. **1970** A.L. RUSSELL *Informant*, Johannesburg Beneuk. Very difficult. **1980** S. ROBERTS in *Bloody Horse* No.2, 57 He sprayed stink sulphur all over the flowers in the flower show she had organized ... She stayed beneukt for so long about the stink and the spoilt flower show.

benoudhijds druppels see DRUPPELS sense b i.

berg /bɜːg, bɛrx, beəx/ *n*. Pl. unchanged, *-e* /-ə/, or *-s*. [Du.]

1.a. A mountain or mountain range. Also *attrib*.

1823 W.W. BIRD *State of Cape of G.H.* 99 Others send them over the berg, or mountains. **1841** B. SHAW *Memorials* 27 To Cape Town school — o'er *bergs* and knowes, They sent the tawney-coloured boy. **1865** T. LEASK *S. Afr. Diary* (1954) 2 The wind was blowing down the berg, almost cutting us thro'. **1882** LADY F.C. DIXIE *In Land of Misfortune* 251 A winding pass, high up on the Berg, ... was the only means of passage from this side of the Drakensberg into the interior. **1899** B. MITFORD *Weird of Deadly Hollow* 244 Another day I was out on the berg with the goats .. when I saw a huge tiger. **1902** C.R. DE WET *Three Yrs War* 24 As there was no water to be obtained nearer than a mile from the berg, we suffered greatly from thirst. **1911** L. COHEN *Reminisc. of Kimberley* 304 Around it soar beautiful inviting bergs of diversified colour, fine mountains touching the skies. **1929** D. REITZ *Commando* 122 The British appeared above the berg an hour or two later. **1936** E. ROSENTHAL *Old-Time Survivals* 24 The journey .. is carried out in patriarchal style, the farmer accompanying his black herdboys over the 'berge' or mountains, camping by night on the wayside with his flocks. **1949** L.G. GREEN *In Land of Afternoon* 21 A krantz is not merely a cliff, but a steep, rocky place near the summit of a berg. **1963** S. CLOETE *Rags of Glory* 344 When dawn broke later over the dark mass of the berg, the Boers found themselves under fire from which there was no protection. **1989** B. GODBOLD *Autobiography*. 127, I longed to go up into the wall of the main berg, but the horses deserved the two days rest.

b. *comb*.

i. In the names of mountain peoples: see BERG DAMARA. See also BERGENAAR, BERGIE sense 2.

ii. In the names of fauna and flora usu. of mountain origin, or displaying a preference for a mountain habitat: **berg adder** /-ædə/ [Du., *adder* adder], the venomous snake *Bitis atropos* of the Viperidae; also *attrib*.; cf. *berg slang*; **bergaster**, the shrub *Lachnaea filamentosa* of the Thymelaeaceae; **bergbaroe** /-bəru:/ [Afk., *baroe* see BAROE], any of several species of the plant *Cyphia* of the Lobeliaceae, esp. *C. assimilis, C. bulbosa*, and *C. volubilis*, distinguished from other varieties of *Cyphia* by an inedible tuber; see also BAROE; **bergbas** /-bas/, formerly also **bergbast**, [Afk., *bas* bark (earlier S. Afr. Du. *bast*)], the bark of the trees *Colpoon compressum* and *Osyris lanceolata* of the Santalaceae, used in tanning leather; one of these trees; also *attrib*.; **berg canary**, also **berg-canarie**, *obs*. [part. tr. S. Afr. Du. *bergcanarie*], any of several species of canary of the Fringillidae, esp. the black-throated canary *Serinus atrogularis*, and the black-headed canary *S. alario* (BLACKHEAD sense 1 b); BERGIE sense 1; also called SYSIE (sense a); **berg cypress**, the *mountain cypress* (see MOUNTAIN), *Widdringtonia nodiflora*; **berggans** /-xans/, pl. **-ganse** /-xansə/ [Afk., *gans* goose], the Egyptian goose *Alopochen aegyptiacus* of the Anatidae; *mountain goose*, see MOUNTAIN; **berggansie** /-xansi/ [Afk., *berggans* + dim. suffix -IE; see quot. 1966], an aromatic Karoo bush of the genus *Pentzia* (family Asteraceae); see also *Karoo bush* (KAROO sense 2); **berghaas** *obs*. [S. Afr. Du., *haas* hare], the SPRINGHAAS, *Pedetes capensis*; **bergklapper** /-klapə(r)/ [fr. Du. *klappen* to rattle, clap], (*a*) the plant *Tetraria secans* of the Cyperaceae; (*b*) the plant *Montinia caryophyllaceae* of the Montiniaceae; **berg leguaan**, see LEGUAAN; ‖**berglelie** /-lɪəli/ [Afk., *lelie* lily], the KNYSNA LILY (sense b), *Cyrtanthus purpureus*; **berg lily**, any of several species of bulbous plants bearing lily-like flowers and growing on mountain slopes, esp. *Galtonia candicans* of the Liliaceae; *Cape hyacinth*, see CAPE sense 2 a; **bergpruim** /-prœɪm/ [Afk., *pruim* plum], the shrub *Ochna pretoriensis* of the Ochnaceae; **berg roos** /-ruəs/ [Afk., *roos* rose], the shrub *Protea nana* of the Proteaceae; ||**bergskilpad** /-ˌskəlpat/ [Afk., *skilpad* (earlier Du. *schildpad*) tortoise], the tortoise *Geochelone pardalis* of the Testudinidae; cf. SKILPAD; ||**berg slang** /-ˈslaŋ/ [Afk. (fr. Du.) *slang* snake], see quot.; cf. *berg adder*; **berg sprew** *obs.* [see SPREW], see quot.; **berg swallow, -zwaluw** *obs.* [S. Afr. Du., *zwaluw* swallow], the European bee-eater *Merops apiaster* of the Meropidae; **berg sysie**, see *dik-bek sysie* (SYSIE sense b); **berg tea**, also **berg thee** /-tiə/ [Du., *thee* tea], any of several plants used as a substitute for tea, or for medicinal purposes; see also BUSH TEA; **berg-tiger** *obs.*, the TIGER (sense 1), *Panthera pardus*; **berg wolf** *obs.* [Afk., *wolf* hyaena], the spotted hyaena, *Crocuta crocuta* of the Hyaenidae.

1818 C.I. LATROBE *Jrnl of Visit* (1905) 89 A wood-keeper .. had lately lost his life by the bite of a **Berg-adder**. **1821** G. BARKER Journal. 22 Sept., Rode to Salem to day .. killed a Berg adder (mountain adder) near Salem. **1834** T. PRINGLE *Afr. Sketches* 279 The berg-adder, though much smaller in size .. is generally considered not less deadly, and it is the more dangerous from its being less easily discovered and avoided. *c***1911** S. PLAYNE *Cape Col.* 77 Beware of the Berg adder ... A beautiful creature he may be, but he is one to be avoided, as his bite is commonly fatal. **1937** *Guide to Vertebrate Fauna of E. Cape Prov.* (Albany Museum) II. 76 *Berg-Adder*, .. similar to puff-adder in form, but smaller and with different markings. **1950** W. ROSE *Reptiles & Amphibians* 306 Less frequently seen is the Berg Adder .. a smaller Viper, which may be found on the levels as well as on the mountains ... A very irascible snake. **1964** L.G. GREEN *Old Men Say* 167 Although there are twenty-five species of snakes in the Peninsula, only the Cape yellow cobra, the *rinkals*, puff adder, berg adder, and the back-fanged *boomslang* and *skaapsteker* are deadly. **1971** *Rand Daily Mail* 12 Jan. 1 The Hartebeespoort snake expert .. said there was no satisfactory serum for berg adder bites. **1988** *Cape Times* 4 Nov. 1 President P W Botha's son .. is in the intensive-care unit of 2 Military Hospital, Wynberg, after being bitten by a berg adder. **1970** *Std Encycl. of Sn Afr.* II. 280 **Berg-aster** (*Lachnaea filamentosa*), Low shrub of the family *Thymelaeaceae* with branches covered by overlapping leaves. **1910** *S. Afr. Jrnl of Science* VI. 98 The plant which is locally known as '**bergbarroe**,' is not edible, while the tubers of three other species of Fockea, called 'Kambarroe,' are eaten raw by the natives or turned into preserves by the rural housewife. **1917** R. MARLOTH *Common Names* 9 *Berg [barroe]*, *F. capensis*, (Prince Albert district) is very large but not edible. **1972** [see BAROE sense b]. **1982** A. MORIARTY *Outeniqua Tsitsikamma* 172 *Cyphia volubilis, Aardboontjie, Bergbaroe.* A slender plant which twines through grasses and shrubs. It has a tuberous rootstock and snowy white or pinkish-mauve flowers. **1892** W.L. DISTANT *Naturalist in Tvl* 43 The best and strongest tanning-material in the Transvaal appears to be the leaf of a tree (Colpoon compressum), called by the Boers '**Berg bas**'. We obtained our largest supplies — on the hills of the Waterberg district. **1908** J.M. ORPEN *Reminisc.* 13 Tanning liquor .. we used to make, by soaking, the bruised leaves and bark of a bush called 'bergbast'. **1957** *Handbk for Farmers* (Dept of Agric.) I. 339 Tanning by means of Bark and 'Bergbas' ... The 'bergbas' tree is chopped off — stem, leaves and all. Use a barrel .. cover the bottom with the leaves ... 'Bergbas' gives a light yellowish colour to the leather, while mimosa bark gives a dark reddish colour. **1966** C.A. SMITH *Common Names* 86 *Bergbas*, The bark (Afr.: bas) obtained from *Osyris abyssinica* ... Common on the Magaliesberg and its spurs. **1983** K.C. PALGRAVE *Trees of Sn Afr.* 156 *Santalaceae* (The sandalwood and bergbas family). **1861** 'A LADY' *Life at Cape* (1963) 28 The Pietje and the **Berg canary** are not unlike London sparrows in plumage, but they sing with great vigour, and are capital birds to put together in a large cage especially if you have a good English canary to conduct the orchestra. **1867** E.L. LAYARD *Birds of S. Afr.* 200 *Amadina Alario* ... Berg-canarie of Colonists, lit. Mountain Canary. **1905** *Westminster Gaz.* (U.K.) 9 Oct. 10 Patches of **berg cypress** .. afford splendid cover for that magnificent antelope the eland. **1913** C. PETTMAN *Africanderisms* 56 *Berg cypress, Widdringtonia cupressoides.* A shrub growing on the mountains from Cape Town to Natal. **1966** C.A. SMITH *Common Names* 88 *Berg cypress, Widdringtonia cupressoides* (Cape). **1889** H.A. BRYDEN *Kloof & Karroo* 93 The big **berg gans** (mountain goose) (*Chenalopex ægyptiacus*), .. a magnificent fellow, whose harsh noisy 'honk' warns us of his whereabouts. **1931** R.C. BOLSTER *Land & Sea Birds* 181 The Berg Gans, so-called because he sometimes nests among rocks, is a true goose in that he is essentially a land-feeder, his diet being grass, and a good walker. **1937** [see *mountain goose* (MOUNTAIN)]. **1949** L.G. GREEN *In Land of Afternoon* 176 Then a green slope going down to a vlei; and a berggans coming up to look at the hunters and leading all the wild duck away. **1933** *Farming in S. Afr.* Nov. 435 (Swart), **Berg-gansie** (Pentzia sphaerocephala) is excellent, especially in somewhat hilly country. **1966** C.A. SMITH *Common Names* 88 *Berggansie, Pentzia punctata* ... The shortly stalked aromatic discoid heads of some allied species are said to be a favourite food of geese. **1786** [**berghaas**: see SPRINGHAAS]. **1796** C.R. HOPSON tr. *C.P. Thunberg's Trav.* II. 182 In the mountains .. resides a kind of jumping rat (*Jerboa Capensis*) which the farmers considered as a species of hare, and called it *Berghaas* or *Springhaas*. **1806** J. BARROW *Trav.* I. 26 We saw here .. a quadruped called the *Berghaas* or mountain hare. **1913** C. PETTMAN *Africanderisms* 57 **Berg-klapper**, .. *Montinia acris* is known by this name because of the rattling noise which the seeds make in the dry capsule. **1966** C.A. SMITH *Common Names* 90 *Bergklapper, Teraria secans* ... When the large spikes are pressed between the fingers a snapping report (Afk. klap) is produced. **1917** R. MARLOTH *Common Names* 10 **Berglelie**, *Vallota purpurea.* Frequent on the Outeniqua mts., generally known as Knysna lily. **1932** [see KNYSNA LILY]. **1934** C.P. SWART Supplement to Pettman. 11 *Berglelie*, .. So called by the Dutch farmer as it grows in mountainous regions. The bulbs of the plant are very poisonous, causing severe gastro-intestinal disturbance in animals. **1966** C.A. SMITH *Common Names* 90 *Berglelie*, .. With large, showy and ornamental umbels of lily-like flowers, frequenting kloofs or the open slopes of hills. **1961** *Redwing* (St Andrew's College, Grahamstown) 3 In the marsh was .. an occasional clump of stately **berg lilies** or white galtonias. *c***1968** S. CANDY *Natal Coast Gardening* 73 Berg Lily ... A Drakensberg lily which must have a dormant season. The 'bells' are only an inch long, and hang in tall, widely-spaced spikes. **1971** *Reader's Digest Complete Guide to Gardening* II. 394 Berg lily ... This species bears erect racemes of drooping, bell-like, green-tinged, white flowers in late summer. **1973** *E. Prov. Herald* 18 July 22 Until last summer I had never consciously seen Galtonia candicans (Berg Lily). **1993** [see *Cape hyacinth* (CAPE sense 2 a)]. **1967** E. ROSENTHAL *Encycl. of Sn Afr.* 55 **Bergpruim**, .. Shrub or tree up to 20 feet. Wood hard, handsome. [*a***1823 berg roos**: J. EWART *Jrnl* (1970) 71 A plant rising to the height of six or seven feet, called the mountain rose, from the resemblance its leaves bear to those of the rose bush.] **1913** C. PETTMAN *Africanderisms* 57 *Berg roos*, .. *Protea nana vel rosacea* is so named in the Cape Peninsula. **1911** *The State* Dec. 642 (Pettman), See what Outa caught for the baasjes near the Klip Kop this afternoon, a nice little **berg schilpad**. **1844** J. BACKHOUSE *Narr. of Visit* 167 A boy died here a few days ago, in consequence of the bite of a small species of Viper, *Vipera inornata* called in the colony, **Berg Slang**, *Mountain Snake*. *c***1808** C. VON LINNÉ *System of Natural Hist.* VIII. 358 At the Cape, they call this bird **berg-sprew**, mountain starling; or *roogevlerk sprew*, red-winged starling. **1822** W.J. BURCHELL *Trav.* (1953) I. 259 One was a Bee-eater, known commonly by the name of **Berg Zwaluw** (Mountain Swallow), which scarcely differed from the European species. **1887** A.A. ANDERSON *25 Yrs in Waggon* II. 213 That beautiful bird the berg swallow, the size of a dove, with a brilliant golden copper-colour plumage on the back, and light salmon colour and sky-blue breast. *c***1860** L. PAPPE *Florae Capensis* I. 257 (Pettman), This is the **Berg thee** of the colonists. **1913** C. PETTMAN *Africanderisms* 57 *Berg thee*, .. (1) *Geranium incanium*. (2) Riversdale District, *Cyclopia Vogelii, Harv.* **1982** FOX & NORWOOD YOUNG *Food from Veld* 47 Plants from which infusions of the leaves are prepared include the following: Aspalathus spp. e.g. *A. linearis* — Rooibos: Athrixia spp.; .. *Dicoma anomala; Geranium incanum* — berg tea. **1834** T. PRINGLE *Afr. Sketches* 263 The **berg-tiger** has not, so far as I know, been distinctly classed by naturalists. **1911** D.B. HOOK *'Tis but Yesterday* 53 They were real 'berg-tigers,' the finest we have in South Africa, full grown, and very well fed. **1844** J. BACKHOUSE *Narr. of Visit* 102 The Wolf of the Cape country is the Hyena, of which two species are found in the Colony: *Hyena crocuta*, the spotted hyena, sometimes called **Berg Wolf**, *Mountain Wolf*, .. and *Hyena villosa*, the Straand Wolf.

iii. In place names: see quots.

1849 N.J. MERRIMAN *Cape Jrnls* (1957) 52 On Sunday I .. administered the Holy Communion to about 7 persons in the little school room, just below the Didima berg. **1914** C. PETTMAN *Notes on S. Afr. Place Names* 16 Roodehoogte, Rooiberg, Wittebergen, .. Blauwberg, .. Sneeuwberg .. are all of them names that tell us something of the impressions made by the places or natural features so named upon those who first gave the names. **1971** *Std Encycl. of Sn Afr.* III. 318 Colesberg was founded in 1830 ... It lies some distance away from the mountain called Torenberg ('tower mountain'). **1989** P.E. RAPER *Dict. of Sn Afr. Place Names* 557 *Underberg*, .. The name is descriptive of its position under (at the foot of) the Hlogoma or Hlokoma, a peak. **1991** [see BUSH *n.*[1] sense 2 a].

2. ***The Berg***, occas. also with small initial: The Drakensberg mountain range, esp. those areas which are in KwaZulu-Natal. Also *attrib.*

1851 J.F. CHURCHILL Diary. (Killie Campbell Africana Library MS37) 7 May, Supplied a Trader with some articles who was going over the Berg. **1862** J.S. DOBIE *S. Afr. Jrnl* (1945) 31 On starting again rode to the highest point of the range and had a view of 'The Berg' (Drakensberg). **1882** C.L. NORRIS-NEWMAN *With Boers in Tvl* 39 He then travelled over the Berg to Natal. **1897** J.P. FITZPATRICK *Outspan* 51 Among the transport-riders the condition of the Berg — as the spurs of the long Drakensberg range of mountains are called colloquially — is always a fruitful topic of conversation. **1912** W. WESTRUP *Land of To-Morrow* 48 An exceedingly prosperous farmer of advanced ideas who had a magnificent place close under the berg in Natal. **1926** M. NATHAN *S. Afr. from Within* 197 The longest river is the Orange, which takes its rise in the Drakensberg or Quathlamba range (generally known as the 'Berg'). **1937** H. SAUER *Ex Afr.* 59 On account of the difficulty of crossing the Berg by ox-wagon and of the tsetse-fly in the low country, we decided to leave the wagon and team at Mac Mac. **1944** J. MOCKFORD *Here Are S. Africans* 71 The total number of wagons that crossed the Berg during the Great Trek is estimated at more than one thousand. **1951** O. WALKER *Shapeless Flame* 215 Down in Port Natal the Dragon Mountains were known as the 'Berg' and when a rare wind blew in winter, that had a knife edge on it, people looked wise and said there was snow on the Berg. **1970** *Daily News* 9 May, Nearer the Drakensberg the veld was invisible under a thick mantle of snow, while the 'Berg itself and its foot-hills have been transformed into a winter wonderland. **1973** J. COWDEN *For Love* 26 As do most people born in Natal, I regard the 'Berg' as my personal heritage. The great Mountains of the Dragon curl in ancient silence round 'The Garden Province' that rolls from them .. to the Indian Ocean. **1986** *Sunday Star* 9 Nov. (Travel) 1 An overnight stay with all meals — and these are invariable multi-course affairs — at a first-class 'Berg' hotel costs around R50. **1990** *Motorist* 2nd Quarter 4 They'll be spending days traversing the 'berg' and spending nights in the hut in the vicinity of Mont-aux-Sources.

Berg Damara /ˈbɜːg ˌdæmərə, ˈbɛrx ˌdamərə/ *n. phr.* Also **Bergdama**. [Afk. *Bergdamara, berg* mountain + DAMARA.] A member of a negroid people of Namibia.

1842 J. TINDALL *Jrnl* (1959) 31 Berg Damaras .. speak the Namaqua dialect ... Many of them are servants to the Namaquas, who overburden them neither with work, food or wages. *a***1867** C.J. ANDERSSON *Notes of Trav.* (1875) 97 Some Berg Damaras whom we had captured, declared that we should find them [*sc.* the Namaquas] in a range of hills no great way off, and which we could distinctly see from our camp. **1902** G.M. THEAL *Beginning of S. Afr. Hist.* 31 Thus the people called Berg Damaras .. are Bantu by blood, though they speak a Hottentot dialect, and resemble Bushmen in their habits. **1915** W. EVELEIGH *S.W. Afr.* 163 The Bergdamaras, who for many years inhabited the mountainous district of Western Damaraland, constitute a fascinating ethnological problem. They are Bantu by blood, Hottentot by language, and Bushmen by habit. **1928** H. VEDDER in *Native Tribes of S.W. Afr.* 39 In the old days the chief centres of the Berg Damaras were the inaccessible Auas and Erongo Mountains, the Otjair Highlands and the Brandberg. From those times dates the name !Hom-dama, Berg Damaras. **1930** I. SCHAPERA *KhoiSan Peoples* 3 The Bergdama, also inhabiting South-West Africa, are racially a true negro people, different in appearance from both the Bushmen and the Hottentots. **1956** A.G. MCRAE *Hill Called Grazing* 126 This derelict appeared to be a Berg Damara, a tribe with hardly any tribal cohesion, who were looked upon as slave people by the Herero and other more powerful tribes. **1966** [see KLIPKAFFIR]. **1971** I. GOLDBLATT *Hist. of S.W. Afr.* 12 The origin of the Berg Damaras is unknown. They inhabited the central and northern parts of the country, but from the earliest times, those who could not hide in the mountains had been subdued and made the slaves of the Namas. **1986** W. STEENKAMP *Blake's Woman* 6 In Damaraland lived various black tribes: the Ovaherero, the Ovambo, the Ovahimba, the Bergdamara and others. **1988** A. HALL-MARTIN et al. *Kaokoveld* 55 The Dama, also known as Damara or Bergdama, are a mysterious people whose origins and ethnic relationships are obscure. They have negroid features, but speak a Khoisan language.

Bergenaar /ˈbɛrxənɑː(r)/ *n. hist.* Also **Bergener**. [S. Afr. Du., 'mountain dweller', *berg* mountain + n.-forming suffix *-enaar*.] Usu. in *pl.*: A group of Griqua rebels who lived in mountain strongholds, surviving often by armed robbery. Also *attrib.*

1824 MEVILL in J. Philip *Researches* (1828) II. 81 A number of disaffected people now began to leave the country to join the *Bergenaars*, or Mountaineers. **1825** W. THRELFALL in B. Shaw *Memorials* (1841) 340 It had been previously reported, that Mr. Archbell and some of his people had been killed by the Bergenaars. **1834** T. PRINGLE *Afr. Sketches* 359 Certain bands of banditti, of mixed colonial and African lineage .. had recently fixed themselves in the fastnesses of the Stormberg mountains, and had from that circumstance obtained the name of Bergenaars (mountaineers). *a***1875** T. BAINES *Jrnl of Res.* (1964) II. 19 Her daughter was detained in servitude by the Bergenaars or mountain Hottentots. **1877** J. NOBLE *S. Afr.* 80 The disorganized bodies under the names of Barolongs, Basutos, Mantatees, Korannas, Bergeners, and Bushmen. **1908** J.M. ORPEN *Reminisc.* 194 In July 1824, Waterboer was again employed .. to proceed with a force against the Bergenaars, who .. were robbing and massacring the Basutos and Bechuanas and selling their children to whites. **1976** A. DELIUS *Border* 139 The half-caste Griquas — related to the Bergenaar banditry here — fought a battle far to the North against a vast, pouring horde of cannibal people called the Mantis. **1980** LYE & MURRAY *Transformations* 40 By 1822 a more dangerous rebellion propelled the majority of the Griqua from their settlements ... These new rebels took the name of *Bergenaars* (Mountain people) because they lurked in the hill country to the east and west of Griqualand, from whence they preyed on their neighbours.

‖**berghaan** /ˈbɛrxˌhɑːn, ˈbɜːg-/ *n. obsolescent.* [S. Afr. Du., *berg* mountain + *haan* cock.]

1. The BLACK EAGLE, *Aquila verreauxii.*

1844 J. BACKHOUSE *Narr. of Visit* 488 Three species of Eagle occur in South Africa .. [including] *Aquila vulturina*, the Berghaan. **1867** [see DASSIEVANGER]. **1889** H.A. BRYDEN *Kloof & Karroo* 273 Suddenly, starting as if from space, comes soaring above us a great black mountain eagle. We know him at once for a berghaan (cock of the mountain) or dassie-vanger (coney-eater). **1937** M. ALSTON *Wanderings* 81 They [*sc.* black eagles] would descend and circle round and round the mountain-side in search of rock rabbits — hence the Dutch names of 'dassievanger' or 'berghaan' (for they are never found far from mountains). **1967** W.A. DE KLERK *White Wines* 98 Above the rocky spires of Drostersberg the *berghaan* soars.

2. The bateleur eagle, *Terathopius ecaudatus* of the Accipitridae; INGQANGA.

1867 E.L. LAYARD *Birds of S. Afr.* 18 *Helotarsus ecaudatus* ... *Le Bateleur* .. *Berghaan* (cock of the mountains) of the Colonists. **1893** A. NEWTON *Dict. of Birds, Berghaan,* (Mountain-cock), the name given to some of the larger Eagles, and especially to the beautiful *Helotarsus ecaudatus* .. by the Dutch colonists in South Africa. **1910** J. BUCHAN *Prester John* (1961) p.viii, A brace of white *berghaan* circled far up in the blue.

bergie /ˈbɜːgi, bɛrxi/ *n. colloq.* Also with initial capital. [BERG + Eng. suffix *-ie*, denoting an inhabitant of a place; or formed in Afk., *berg* mountain + -IE.]

1. (*obs.*) *berg canary*, see BERG sense 1 b ii.

1923 HAAGNER & IVY *Sketches* 146 Another good little songster is the Yellow-rumped Seed-eater (or 'Black-throated', as it is usually called — *S. Angolensis*) .. exceedingly common in the Brandfort and Kroonstad Districts, Orange Free State, and Pretoria District, Transvaal, in which latter locality it is known as the 'Bergie'.

2. In the Western Cape: a vagrant living on the mountain slopes above Cape Town; any vagrant. Cf. OUTIE.

1952 *Drum* Feb. 8 The 'Bergies' who live on the slopes of Devil's Peak .. are in a class by themselves. **1959** J. PACKER *High Roof* 59 Sometimes he had camped out in a mountain cave with the bergies, who stood high in nobody's esteem and were always being chivvied by the foresters because they were vagrants and likely to set the bush on fire. **1964** M. MURRAY *Under Lion's Head* 3 Some of these people [*sc.* Hottentots] probably, had hide-outs along the bush land of the Green and Sea Point coast, or, like our *bergies* of today, behind the boulders of the Lion's Head. **1972** *Argus* 10 Aug. 10 Sea Point is a Riviera for most of the won't-works. Even the Bergies come down to do their shopping ... Bergie women smelling of drink frequently come to the door begging. **1973** *E. Prov. Herald* 9 May 1 The police immediately suspected that someone other than a Coloured mountain-dweller (a 'Bergie') had committed the crime. **1982** *Cape Times* 15 Apr. 11 Cape Town's vagrants or bergies are not confined to the mountainside areas but are living in large number in the elite suburbs of Rondebosch and Claremont. **1987** [see DRONK]. **1990** *Weekend Post* 3 Feb. (Leisure) 4 Bergies of all colours .. zigzag across the road.

berg sysie see *dik-bek sysie* (SYSIE sense b).

berg wind *n. phr.* [BERG + Eng. *wind.*] A hot, dry wind originating over the high central plateau of South Africa and blowing towards the coast. Also *attrib.*

1876 J.F. SEWELL *Private Diary* (1983), May 13, .. Wind from North being the first 'Berg' wind of the season. **1893** E. NICHOLSON in *Cape Illust. Mag.* Vol.4 No.7, 241 She .. was vainly trying to lose in sleep the monotonous boom of the hot Berg Wind. **1905** C.M. STEWART in Flint & Gilchrist *Science in S. Afr.* 40 Another factor which considerably modifies the climates of the coast districts is to be found in the fairly frequent occurrence of hot, dry Föhn-like winds all along the coast from Walfish Bay to Durban. The disturbing effect of these 'Berg winds,' as they are termed, on the temperature curve is most marked in the winter months of April to September. **1907** T.R. SIM *Forests & Forest Flora* 38 This is known as the 'berg' winter wind of the Midland Conservancy coast districts, and the hot winter winds of the Eastern districts; it usually blows for two or three days in succession, after which time the heated atmosphere naturally rises and gives place to cooler breezes. **1923** *S. Afr.: Land of Outdoor Life* (S.A.R. & H.) 4 The towns along the south-east and east coasts have occasional hot or berg winds. *c***1936** *S. & E. Afr. Yr Bk & Guide* 99 The hot or 'Berg' winds are a feature of the coastal climate, they may blow for 2 or 3 days and cause great oppression. *c***1939** *Off. Yrbk of Union 1938* (Union Office of Census & Statistics) 40 These 'bergwinds', as they are called along the south coast, at times cause a practical inversion of the seasons. **1955** A. DELIUS *Young Trav.* 123 The Eastern Province suffered a great deal from the whipping, irritating southeaster and hot, northerly Berg wind — so called because it comes from the scorched interior, bringing with it the heat of the mountain rocks. **1971** *Daily Dispatch* 11 May 10 If you were complaining about the hot berg wind in East London yesterday .. just thank your lucky stars you were not in Egypt in the old days with a strong Khamsin blowing. **1973** J. COWDEN *For Love* 100 The wind always blew around the mountain, but sometimes it was a Berg wind, warm and dry, and the lassitude it produced in us was also apparent in the eagles. **1990** *Weekend Post* 2 June 2 Berg wind conditions kept East London and Port Elizabeth firemen busy fighting several grass fires today. **1990** G. CANDY in *Staffrider* Vol.9 No.2, 62 Where berg winds blow, grass withers wombs abort and blossom lies like dung.

Hence **berg windy** *adj. nonce.*

1963 M.G. MCCOY *Informant, Port Elizabeth* It was a very hot day, berg windy, and the car had had a following wind all the way up.

Bericqua var. BRIQUA.

berinjela var. BRINJAL.

berry wax *n. phr.*

a. *hist.* A high quality wax produced by boiling the berries of *Myrica cordifolia* of the Myricaceae, used for polishes and candles by early colonists.

[**1789** LADY A. BARNARD in Lord Lindsay *Lives of Lindsays* (1849) III. 396 The vegetable wax which the Vrow Alleng's slaves were stewing from berries, of which I saw a stock of green dull candles made.] **1831** *S. Afr. Almanac & Dir.* 102 The quantity and quality of the undermentioned Cape Produce which passed the Market from January 1, to November 30, 1828 .. Berry wax 164 pounds. **1857** 'J.S.H.' in *Cape Monthly Mag.* I. May 265 Mr. Feeney .. has written a description of the growth of *M. Cordifolia*, and the preparation of the berry wax. **1897** EDMONDS & MARLOTH *Elementary Botany* 169 The genus *Myrica*, of which *M. cordifolia* and others supply the berry-wax. **1913** R. MARLOTH *Flora of S. Afr.* I. 133 The layer of wax on the berries of some species [of *myrica*] is so considerable that it is technically exploited. The farmers boil the berries with water, strain the hot mixture and allow the melted wax to solidify. The *berry wax* (myrica wax) is of a pale greenish colour and considerably harder than beeswax. **1917** [see WAX-BERRY]. **1927** *Off. Yr Bk of Union 1925* (Union Office of Census & Statistics) 474 *Berry Wax*, This is obtained from the berries of *Myrica cordifolia*, a shrub growing on the coast sands in the neighbourhood of Cape Town. It is used locally for floor polish .. and is also suitable for soap manufacture. *c***1936** *S. & E. Afr. Yr Bk & Guide* 302 *Berry Wax*, obtained from the berries of the *Myrica cordifolia*, is used locally for making various polishes. A few tons are exported annually, its value at S.A. port being about 1s per lb. **1955** [see MARKET MASTER]. **1964** L.G. GREEN *Old Men Say* 100 Aloes and acorns were on sale, and berry wax for candles.

b. *rare.* WAX-BERRY sense b.

1913 H. TUCKER *Our Beautiful Peninsula* 75 The red marbles of the berry-wax gleam against the white background.

besembos /ˈbɪəsəmˌbɔs/ *n.* Formerly also **bessing bosch, bezem bosch.** [Afk. (earlier S.

Afr. Du. *bezembosch*), *besem* broom + *bos* bush.] Any of various shrubs from which brooms are made, esp. several species of *Rhus* of the Anacardiaceae.

1907 T.R. SIM *Forests & Forest Flora* 42 The usual abundant presence of Bessing-bosch (Rhus erosa and Rhus dregeana). **1913** C. PETTMAN *Africanderisms* 58 *Bezem bosch*, (D. *bezem*, a besom, broom.) *Rhus dregeana* and *R. erosa* are so named because their rigid branches are used as brooms. **1973** *E. Prov. Herald* 28 Mar. 4 Along the eastern and north-eastern mountain and ridge route, besembos, leucoisidea, ironwood and the exotic nasella, have come in. **1987** M. POLAND *Train to Doringbult* 35 The dust from the wheels spiralled out, coating the brush and *besembos*.

besem-riet /ˈbɪəsəmˌrit/ *n. obsolescent.* Also **beesem-riet**, **besom-riet**, **bezem-riet**, and with initial capital. [Afk. (earlier S. Afr. Du.), *besem* broom + *riet* reed.] Any of several species of reed-like plants of the Restionaceae used in the manufacture of brooms.

1795 C.R. HOPSON tr. *C.P. Thunberg's Trav.* I. 295 Of the *Restio dichotomus* (*Beesem-riet*) brooms were made to sweep the floors with. **1809** J. MACKRILL Diary. 59 Besem-riet — for Brooms — Restio dichotomus. **1888** P. MACOWAN in C.A. Smith *Common Names* (1966) 98 (Kaalblad may be) easily made harmless by simple thrashing with a bundle of besemriet. **1896** R. WALLACE *Farming Indust. of Cape Col.* 96 Some farmers boil 'besom-riet,' *Restio scoparius*, .. and administer the decoction. It has no medicinal value. **1966** C.A. SMITH *Common Names* 97 *Besemriet*, Various species of Restionaceae ... The brooms made from the culms are very durable.

beshu /ˈbeːʃu/ *n.* Also **bechu**, **betshu**, **iBeshu**, **ibetshu**, **ibheshu**. [fr. Zulu *ibeshu* (pl. *amabeshu*); see also I-.] A hide flap covering the buttocks, worn esp. by Zulu men on ceremonial occasions. Cf. MUTSHA.

1949 O. WALKER *Proud Zulu* (1951) 19 Cattle were their bride-price, their security ... They were hides for their great war-shields ... They were betshus to cover their buttocks and aprons to cover the pregnant women. **1955** E.A. RITTER *Shaka Zulu* 18 He now donned the umutsha, and the ibetshu (an apron of soft skin and similar size) to cover his buttocks. **1967** O. WALKER *Hippo Poacher* 101 At the weekend the girls would usually shuffle up in their best bead aprons, and the young men in their courting *betshus* of black and white and brown and white calf-skins. **1974** C.T. BINNS *Warrior People* 208 The *iBeshu* is usually made of dressed calf-skin, cut to a length of about 15 inches, with a breadth of approximately 12 inches, and acts as a loosely hanging apron which covers the buttocks. This is also suspended from the belt. **1986** *New Nation* 17 July 13 Traditional dancers better start shaking the dust from their 'beshus' and 'gumboots' for dance competitions to be held .. at Manyeleti Beer Garden. **1994** B. KHUMALO in *Weekly Mail & Guardian* 1 July 26 Walt [Disney] and his hangers-on at Ster Kinekor .. were launching a dubbed version of .. *The Lion King*. This was intended to be a real jungle event, with the invitation encouraging me to come dressed in either a black tie or traditional dress. For me traditional dress would have been a loincloth and an *ibheshu* — you've seen it in all the bad 'Zooloo' movies. The problem was that I don't have the masochistic inclination to walk around in a loincloth in the cold.

beskuit /bəsˈkœit, -ˈkeɪt/ *n. noncount.* Also **biskute**. [Afk.] Rusked bun. See also BOEREBESKUIT, *commando beskuit* (COMMANDO sense 1 c), HARDE BESKUIT.

*a***1868** J. AYLIFF *Jrnl of 'Harry Hastings'* (1963) 83 Very soon a nice clean black girl came out .. with basons of smoking coffee and some hard buns, but they called them 'biskute'. **1938** *Star* 1 Dec. 12 Pannekoeke, braaiwors, melktert, mosbolletjies, beskuit and coffee could be had in plenty and everyone thoroughly enjoyed themselves. **1955** A. DELIUS *Young Trav.* 102 With tea there was always served either preserved oranges or melon, known as *konfyt*, or hard, white rusks called *beskuit*. **1965** C. VAN HEYNINGEN *Orange Days* 70 They rode away .. with their Mauser rifles slung on their backs and their bandoliers round their chests — their rations, mostly biltong and beskuit, in their saddle-bags. **1977** *Sunday Times* 24 Apr. (Mag. Sect.) 5 Mrs Greyvenstein .. used to bake the best beskuit for church bazaars. **1987** E. BADENHORST in *Flying Springbok* Aug. 22 Zola sits quietly warming her hands on a mug of tea and nibbling *beskuit* in the kitchen.

besluit /bəˈslœit, -ˈsleɪt/ *n. Hist. Law.* [Afk.] A resolution, law, or ordinance of the Transvaal Republic. Cf. WET.

1899 A.E. HEYER *Brief Hist. of Tvl Secret Service* 15 According to Volksraad besluit £10,000 annually are granted for Secret Service. **1912** H.H. JUTA *Reminisc.* 103 The Legislative body passed a law or 'besluit' that any free and independent burgher refusing to accept a Government appointment offered to him should be fined. **1919** M.M. STEYN *Diary* 325 They .. passed a resolution in the 'Volksraad' as follows: 'No action of the High Court shall over-ride any action of our "besluits" (ordinances).' **1936** *Cambridge Hist. of Brit. Empire* VIII. 574 The Second Volksraad .. a legislature which could and did alter even old-fashioned laws by resolution (*besluit*) at a single sitting. **1977** T.R.H. DAVENPORT *S. Afr.: Mod. Hist.* 66 They insisted on a three-quarters majority for every law passed, and .. three months between the first tabling of a measure and its enactment ... This .. led to the short-cut practice of making laws by besluit (resolution) of a simple Volksraad majority.

besom-riet var. BESEM-RIET.

bessing bosch var. BESEMBOS.

best *adj. colloq.* [Calque formed on Afk. *beste* favourite.] Favourite. Also *absol.* Cf. WORST.

Esp. common in children's speech.

1971 J.W. BRANFORD *Informant, Grahamstown* What's your best subject? — mine's history — and what's your best occupation? **1974** D. VESCO in *Daily Dispatch* 19 July (Indaba) 10 Please pass my regards to my best family. **1989** *Informant, Cape Town* The picture of the peacock is my best. It really looks beautiful. **1990** *Weekend Argus* 17 Feb. (Junior Argus) 2 My best singer is Glen Madeiros. I would like to have his address. **1991** [see WORST].

‖**bestuur** /bəˈstyːr/ *n.* Also with initial capital. [Afk.]

a. The government or administration of a predominantly Afrikaans-speaking area; the executive of an (Afrikaans) organization. Also *attrib.*

1885 *Pall Mall Gaz.* (U.K.) 12 May 8 Stellaland will be governed by the Bestuur under the advice of Captain Trotter and Vincent. **1936** C. BIRKBY *Thirstland Treks* 230 The Bestuur, as the organization became known, planned to divide the 3 000 morgen that composed Cannon Island into erfs of from eight to ten morgen in size. **1936** E.C. LLEWELLYN *Influence of Low Dutch* 171 *Bestuur* .. was a term borrowed to describe the government or administration in the Dutch-speaking parts of South Africa as distinct from the English. *c***1949** CURREY & SNELL *Threat to Freedom* (Standing Comm. of Assoc. Church Schools) 3 At this conference an Institute of Christian National Education .. was established, and its executive (bestuur) was instructed to draw up a statement of the principles of 'Christian National Education'.

b. With distinguishing epithets denoting different types of administration: **afdelingsbestuur** /afˈdiələŋs -/, also **Afdelings Bestuur**, [Afk. (fr. Du.), *afdeling* division + linking phoneme *-s-*], the divisional committee of a political party; ‖**dagbestuur** /ˈdaxbəstyːr/ [Afk., *dag* day], the management committee or executive of a political party; also *attrib.*; **hoofbestuur** /ˈhuəf-/ [Afk., *hoof* head, chief], the head committee or national executive of a political party.

1934 *Star* 2 Feb. (Swart), This was the gist of resolutions passed at a meeting of the **Afdelings Bestuur**. **1943** I. FRACK *S. Afr. Doctor* 92 The 'afdelingsbestuur' or district committee had its headquarters in Helfontein, and consisted of delegates from each little branch in the district. **1956** M. ROGERS *Black Sash* 54 The '**Dagbestuur**' of the Transvaal Nationalist Party was to consider the 150 applications for senatorships. **1972** *Sunday Times* 5 Mar. 5 Mr Cuyler .. is a member of the Transvaal Dagbestuur. **1980** *Evening Post* 11 Nov. 8 The .. *dagbestuur* election .. will take place on November 29. **1990** *Daily Dispatch* 19 July 15 The chairman of the DP's 'Dagbestuur' .. said the party was being placed on an immediate election footing. **1991** *E. Prov. Herald* 18 July 1 The election of the NWC — effectively the ANC's 'Dagbestuur' or 'shadow cabinet' — is at the top of the agenda. **1934** *Argus* 9 Mar. (Swart), This meeting wishes to express its approval of the agreement between the **Hoofbestuur** and General —, but with the clear understanding that the principles of the Party will be maintained in the new constitution.

Betcuana pl. form of BECHUANA.

Betj(o)uana var. BECHUANA.

‖**betoger** /bəˈtʊəxə(r)/ *n. colloq.* [Afk.] A political demonstrator.

Used ironically in *S. Afr. Eng.*, making fun of the pejorative use of the word in bureaucratic Afrikaans.

1971 *Rhodeo* (Rhodes Univ.) 13 May 4 I desperately needed some material for my weekly funnies, and in order to crack a few jokes at your expense and that of my attorney. Love and kisses, all you blerrie betogers. **1981** *Seek* Sept. 4 All that was seen of the game was an unruly crowd of 'betogers', with (horrible to relate) a man wearing a dog collar, out there in front egging them on! .. Now if there is one thing in this country that rouses the ire more than a 'betoger', it is a 'betoger' wearing a dog collar. **1987** S. ROBERTS *Jacks in Corners* 55 Also, perhaps in cosmic defiance, I grow my hair very long. Some people think I am a *betoger*. But I am not.

Betshoenas pl. form of BECHUANA.

betshu var. BESHU.

better *v. trans.* [fr. BETTERMENT.] To manage (an area) as part of a BETTERMENT scheme.

1985 PLATZKY & WALKER *Surplus People* 46 The percentage of bantustan land 'bettered' is no longer reported in official documents.

betterment *n. hist.* [Special sense of general Eng.] Usu. *attrib.*, esp. in the following phrr.: ***betterment area***, a proclaimed area in a black reserve in which a betterment scheme was applied (see also RESERVE); ***betterment scheme***, a scheme, introduced in 1939, for the improvement of agricultural land in black reserves, including the consolidation of homesteads into villages, the rotation of crops, and the limitation of stock; an instance of the implementation of this scheme.

1948 H.V. MORTON *In Search of S. Afr.* 182 We went to 'betterment areas' where a whole village had been persuaded to fence its land and kill off half its cattle with encouraging results. **1949** E. HELLMANN *Handbk on Race Rel.* 186 A more direct attack on the problem of agricultural re-education was begun in 1939 with the inauguration of the 'betterment area' scheme ... The inhabitants of certain rural wards were asked to agree to the voluntary limitation of their stock to the carrying capacity of the land. **1955** J.B. SHEPHARD *Land of Tikoloshe* 145 There are over nine hundred locations in the Transkei, but I couldn't say how many have been proclaimed as Betterment areas. **1981** *Pace* Sept. 16 Thousands of people .. have been moved within homeland boundaries because of the introduction of the so-called 'betterment scheme' — controlling the use of the land by zoning off areas for agricultural and for residential use. **1985** PLATZKY & WALKER *Surplus People* 9 Under betterment, tribal areas are divided into residential and agricultural land. Instead of living in scattered homesteads close to fields, people are clustered into villages on poorer soil such as hill tops, while the rest of the land is divided into fields suitable for growing crops, forestry (wood lots) or grazing. *Ibid.* 46 In many parts of bantustans such as Gazankulu and Lebowa one may drive only a kilometre or so between betterment areas and rural villages which have had to absorb thousands of landless people evicted from white-owned farms or former tenants of black spots. **1990** E. KOCH in *Weekly Mail* 30 Mar. 11 During the 1950s the village .. was turned into a betterment scheme, part of the new Nationalist government's grand plan to ensure that black villagers would remain on their tribal lands ... Betterment schemes like these were fiercely resisted in most parts of the country, where peasants saw these as gross interference in their traditional way of life.

Beuchuanas pl. form of BECHUANA.

‖**beukenhout** /'biœkənhəʊt/ *n.* Also **beukehout**. [Du., *beuke(boom)* beech(tree) + linking phoneme *-n-* + *hout* wood.] BOEKENHOUT. Also *attrib.*

1831 *S. Afr. Almanac & Dir.* 211 Felling of Timber: Keurboom and Beukenhout this month, Oak in March or April. **1887** J.C. BROWN *Crown Forests* 237 Beukenhout, 2d; Essenhout 2d. **1907** T.R. SIM *Forests & Forest Flora* 10 The kinds which have been worked to any extent are .. Sneezewood, Real Yellow-wood, Outeniqua Yellow-wood, *Faurea arborea* under the name of Beukenhout. **1917** R. MARLOTH *Common Names* 11 *Beukehout*, Several species of *Faurea*, viz. *F. saligna* (Tr. Rhod.); *F. Galpinii* (Zoutpansberg); *F. speciosa* (No.). The Cape beech (Myrsine) is sometimes called *Wit.* **1944** C.R. PRANCE *Under Blue Roof* 74 Between the sundial and the rain-gauge towers the giant ruin of a 'beukenhout' tree, shaped like a rough-hewn ebony cross. **1966** *Cape Times* 24 Sept. (Weekend Mag.) 9 Some other species have not done well. A beukenhout has pined.

bevok var. BEFOK.

bewaarplaats /bə'vɑː(r)ˌplɑːts/ *n. Hist. Law. Mining.* Also **bewaarplaatz, bewaarplats**. Pl. **-en**. [S. Afr. Du., transf. use of Du. *bewaarplaats* place of storage, fr. *bewaren* to store safely + *plaats* open piece of land.] A piece of land on which mining was not permitted, granted to claim-holders by the Transvaal Republican government for surface use only (see quots 1960 and 1977). Also *attrib.*

1895 *Star* 26 Dec. 4 The Railway Commissioner, the Landdrost, and the Commandant of Pretoria are members of a syndicate whose avowed object is or was to wrest from the companies their right to the bewaarplaatsen. **1899** A. MILNER in C. Headlam *Milner Papers* (1931) I. 345 The *Bewaarplaatzen* were sites on which grants had been made for surface rights such as the storing of water, piling of waste ore, etc. **1913** C. PETTMAN *Africanderisms* 58 *Bewaarplatsen*, .. In South Africa this term is applied to certain pieces of land granted under Government licence to be used as dumping places for debris or slimes from the mines ... Licences for such *bewaarplatsen* ceased to be issued in 1902. **1928** E.A. WALKER *Hist. of S. Afr.* 568 The Nationalists and Labour men .. censured the ministry for giving half the *bewaarplaatsen* funds to the owners of the surface lands instead of keeping the whole. *c*1936 *S. & E. Afr. Yr Bk & Guide* 382 *Bewaarplaatsen* (Dutch for *depository* or *store house*) are areas secured by various mining companies in the early days of the Rand for the purpose of dumping tailings, etc., but carrying with the surface rights no claim to underlying minerals. **1960** J.J.L. SISSON *S. Afr. Judicial Dict.* 93 Under the Transvaal Gold Law .. certain areas of land were given out by Government to claim-holders as storage sites, or for the purpose of depositing tailings .. , or for erecting settling tanks or pans .. , or for storing ores; the areas so given out were called *bewaarplaatsen*; the holder of a *bewaarplaats* acquired only a right to use the surface of the land. **1977** *Friend* 2 June (Suppl.) 3a, The Transvaal Gold Law of 1898, repealed in 1908, had the term *Bewaarplaats*. This meant a depository. The Transvaal Republic in the times of Paul Kruger gave certain areas of land to claim-holders for use as storage sites.

beyae var. BAIE.

Beyete var. BAYETE.

beygl var. BAGEL.

bezem bosch var. BESEMBOS.

bezem-riet var. BESEM-RIET.

‖**bezitrecht** /bə'sət 'rext/ *n. Hist. Law.* [S. Afr. Du., 'right of possession', *bezit* possession + *recht* right.] Indisputable title granted to a holder of land where legal evidence of transfer or title was lacking. Also *attrib.*

1893 T. REUNERT *Diamonds & Gold* 153 There is another method by which indefeasible title may be obtained .. called *bezitrecht* .. which means right of possession; .. it has only recently been introduced into the Gold Law. **1896** *Star* 14 Oct. 4 A statement dealing with 'Bezitrecht Titles'. **1933** W.H.S. BELL *Bygone Days* 125 The tenure was made more secure by the grant of what was called 'bezitrecht', which conferred an almost complete title upon the holder. Many years after, the holder was permitted to obtain a freehold title to Government stands. **1951** — *S. Afr. Legal Dict.* 154 In the early days of the Gold Fields, .. it frequently happened that transfers were passed which were not perfectly regular, or powers of attorney were mislaid ... To obviate the risk of defeat of title through some such irregularity or formal flaw, this certificate of *bezitrecht* was introduced. **1977** *Friend* 2 June (Suppl.) 3a, *Bezitrecht* meant the 'right of possession', and also a certificate of title granted by the Transvaal Government confirming and assuring the title already held by the registered owner of a *mijnpacht* (a mining area granted under lease in the Transvaal), water-right or other mining right.

Bhaca /'bɑːka, 'bala/ *n.* Also **Bac(c)a, Baxa**. Pl. **ama-, -s**, or unchanged; rarely **aba-**. [Xhosa (orig. Zulu) *iBhaca* a member of the Bhaca people (pl. *amaBhaca*), fr. v. *bhaca* hide. For an explanation of varying plural forms, see AMA-.] A member of a Xhosa-speaking people of the Nguni group, having their traditional home on the mountainous plateau of Griqualand East. Also *attrib.* See also GUMBOOT DANCE.

The Bhaca people was formed from refugee groups fleeing south along the eastern coast during the nineteenth century (see MFECANE).

*c*1847 H.H. DUGMORE in J. Maclean *Compendium of Kafir Laws* (1906) 8 In consequence of the repeated formidable inroads of the Amampondo and the Amabaca (the tribes of Faku and Ncapai), nearly the whole tribe has migrated to the country watered by the upper branches of the Kei. **1866** W.C. HOLDEN *Past & Future* 144 The Amabaca are the latest great division, and are formed out of the remnants of several tribes after the wars of Utshaka. **1872** *Wesleyan Missionary Reports* 81 We have been surrounded with war and rumours of war. At one time we thought the Amabaca tribe would be scattered. **1912** AYLIFF & WHITESIDE *Hist. of Abambo* 4 The Amabele were attacked by the Bacas, but the Abasa-kunene looked on at the defeat of their neighbours and rendered no help. **1941** C.W. DE KIEWIET *Hist. of S. Afr.* 73 Kafirland, where dwelt the Ama-Xosa, the Tembu, the Pondo, the Xesibe, and the Ama-Baca. **1954** W.D. HAMMOND-TOOKE in A.M. Duggan-Cronin *Bantu Tribes* III. v. 13 The name Baca is derived from the verb *ukubhaca* (to flee) and refers to the flight from Natal from Tshaka's displeasure. **1962** — *Bhaca Soc.* p.vii, The Bhaca are of particular interest to ethnographers and linguists concerned with South Africa because they provide a link between northern and southern Nguni types. **1971** P. MAYER *Townsmen or Tribesmen* 3 For practical purposes the three million Xhosa-speakers .. — the Xhosa proper, Mfengu, Thembu, Mpondo, Mpondomise, Bhaca, Bomvana — can be regarded as one group divided into tribes or sub-tribes. **1982** M. MZAMANE *Children of Soweto* 86 Their more peace-loving cousins, the Bacas, .. had made the gumboot dance famous and were employed by the City Council as nightsoil men. **1990** *Weekend Post* 24 Mar. 5 The removal of nightsoil and refuse is handled almost exclusively by members of the Baca tribe, who originate from Lusikisiki in Transkei ... [He] could not say how the amaBaca came to be nightsoil removers.

bhajia /'badʒ(j)ə/ *n.* Also **badja, bajia**. Pl. **-s**, or unchanged. [fr. Urdu *bhajya*.] Esp. in the English of South Africans of Indian descent: CHILLI-BITE.

1970 *Leader* 24 July 10 While preparing batter for bhajias and bondas, always heat a tablespoonful of ghee and pour it with batter for the extra taste. **1982**, **1990** [see CHILLI-BITE]. **1990** J. NAIDOO *Coolie Location* 65 My mother made him some badja and tea.

bhasella var. BASELA *n.*

bhola var. BULA.

bhoma var. BOMA.

bhula var. BULA.

Bhuna var. AMABHUNU.

bhuti /'bʊti/ *n.* Also **bhut', buti**, and with initial capital. [Xhosa, vocative form of *ubhuti* (pl. *obhuti*), fr. Afk. *boetie* (see BOETIE).] 'Brother': a polite title and term of address or reference used, esp. among speakers of Sintu (Bantu) languages, when speaking to a man. Cf. AUBUTI, SISI sense 1.

a. A term of address; cf. BOETIE sense 2.

1961 T. MATSHIKIZA *Choc. for my Wife* 62 'Morning, morning, Bhuti,' using the polite form of address. [**1963** WILSON & MAFEJE *Langa* 89 *uButi* (from the Afrikaans 'boetie', brother) has all but replaced the traditional *umkhuluwe* .. in town ... In the country, among the Xhosa speaking groups who circumcise, uncircumcised boys address all those already circumcised as *buti* irrespective of their relative ages ... Women also use *buti* to senior contemporaries.] **1979** [see ENKOSI]. **1979** F. DIKE *First S. African* 29 The parents of men never say 'bhuti' to their sons, even when they are circumcised ... To us you will always be a boy, to us you'll die a boy. **1984** M. CILIBE in *Staffrider* Vol.6 No.1, 4 'Hey! Hey! Bhuti, stand in the queue!' The caller had on a headsman's uniform. Mdange looked from side to side at all the queues to his utter confusion. **1988** Z.C. NDABA in *Staffrider* Vol.7 No.1, 21 We appreciate your care for us Bhuti. But I must say that we are not all impressed by what you have done.

b. A title.

1976 R.L. PETENI *Hill of Fools* 17 'No, bhut' Duma,' he said in a calm voice. 'I see you don't understand.' **1980** E. JOUBERT *Poppie Nongena* 42 After Plank had been to the bush we who were younger no longer called him Plank, but buti Plank, to show respect.

c. A common noun.

1980 [see ABAKWETHA sense 1].

bi-ah var. BEE-AH.

Biatt var. BAYETE.

Bible desk *n. phr.* Also with small initial. A reading-desk with a sloping top (which may be hinged to provide storage space beneath) and a ridge to rest a book upon.

1960 G.E. PEARSE *18th C. Furn.* 176 The Bible desk was an essential piece of furniture in every Cape home and several have been preserved. **1960** J. CorE *Tame Ox* 130 He remembered with awe the four black chairs and black table and a bible-desk inlaid with a star in ivory. **1965** M.G. ATMORE *Cape Furn.* 206 Bureaux of Slant top desks ... Another type which had appeared .. , probably in Italy in about 1650, also had a hinged sloping front but in this case the hinges were at the back and the flap was lifted only to gain access to the storage space below ... In South Africa these have come to be known as 'Bible desks'. **1971** BARAITSER & OBHOLZER *Cape Country Furn.* 18 The other interesting piece of furniture found in both town and country houses is the 'lessenaar'. This is seldom described as a Bible desk but the inventory states whether or not it has a base ... The Bible desk was situated in one of the front rooms other than the reception room ... Some were made of ebony. *Ibid.* 209 The Bible desk is made either of yellowwood of perhaps cedarwood and, as in most cases, the lectern is detachable. **1981** P. DANE *Great Houses of Constantia* 135 A teak and satinwood bible-desk.

BIC /biː aɪ 'si/ *n. hist.* Also **B.I.C.** Initial letters of *Bantu Investment Corporation*, a government body promoting industrial and other development in the homelands. Also *attrib.* See also HOMELAND.

Founded in 1959, it was renamed the *Corporation for Economic Development* in 1977.

[**1960** *State of Union 1959–60* 99 To promote industrial and other undertakings and to act as a development, financial and investment institution among Bantu in the Bantu reserves, the Government introduced in 1958 the Bantu Investment Corporation Bill, which has since been passed by Parliament.] **1970** *Daily News* 7 May, BIC's five-year plan envisages four African homeland growth points through the country. **1971** *S. Afr. Panorama* Nov. 43 The Bantu Investment Corporation of South Africa Limited .. has developed into a large organisation ... The managing director of a bus service in the Tswana Homeland .. payed [*sic*] back his loan of R152 000 with the B.I.C. within 21 months. **1974** *Drum* 8 Aug. 27, I became suspicious of the activities of the Bantu Investment Corporation when an offer of a bottle store was made to me. The message was brought to me by a newsman who assured me that the BIC would finance me. *c***1978** *S. Afr. 1977: Off. Yrbk* (Dept of Info.) 512 The primary objective of the CED (known as the Bantu Investment Corporation (BIC) prior to 15 June 1977 and established in 1959) embraces the promotion of economic viability in the Black homelands. **1988** S. MOTAU in *Frontline* Feb. 22 Mr Masinga says the corporation is viewed as a 'disguised B.I.C. (Bantu Investment Corporation)'.

Bichuana(s) pl. form of BECHUANA.

bidow, biedouw varr. BIETOU.

biekie var. BIETJIE.

biesie /'bisi/ *n.* Also **biese.** [Afk.] A rush- or reed-like plant. Also *attrib.*

1933 *Star* 30 Dec. (Swart), Between these dunes small pools of water are visible, overgrown with healthy-looking 'biesies'. **1964** L.G. GREEN *Old Men Say* 219 *Biese* are bulrushes, and Jan was some forgotten character who lived among the bulrushes. **1970** M. VAN RENSBURG *Informant, Grahamstown* Biesie mat. Mat made of rushes or reeds. **1984** T.F.J. VAN RENSBURG *Intro. to Fynbos* 6 Restios are wiry, reed-like plants (mainly Restionaceae) that occur in leafless, evergreen tussocks. They are often called reeds or 'biesies'.

bietjie /'bɪki, 'bici, 'bitʃi/ *n.* and *adv. Colloq.* Also **beetj(i)e, beitje, biekie, bietje.** Usu. *'n bietjie* [Afk. 'n a + *biejtie* (earlier Du. *beetje*) little, a bit]: a little, some.

A. *n.*

*c***1838** A.G. BAIN *Jrnls* (1949) 196, I learned ein kleene beitje And left, with wisdom just as full As gekke tanta Meitje. **1913** C. PETTMAN *Africanderisms* 59 *Bietje* or (dial.) *Biekie*, .. A little, a small portion or space. **1920** R. JUTA *Tavern* 144 De days I maak watermelon konfeit, en van der Hum brandy-vine, I says my praers in Dutch, to bring, mar, ein beitje luck to de brandy-vine. **1973** Y. BURGESS *Life to Live* 10 Wait a bietjie, Mr Levy said, pronouncing the word 'beechie' as the Cape Coloureds do. **1989** P. LEE in *Sunday Times* 26 Feb. (Mag. Sect.) 36 Consider the humble Vellie. Originally crudely crafted from a stukkie vel and net 'n bietjie leather, the velskoen has become one of the country's greatest treasures.

B. *adv.*

1943 *Week-End News & Sunday Mag.* 20 Mar. 4 We is hoping jou will nort be too hard on Dok Malan bekos he is er ou mense an hij is er beetje lopsided. **1977** S. ROBERTS in E. Pereira *Contemp. S. Afr. Plays* 239 But it's my weekend too. I want to relax. Bietjie relax. Why must I go driving round now? **1968** F.G. BUTLER *Cape Charade* 5 'Do you speak English?' .. ''n Bietjie — a little. I got it from my mother, Kaatje Kekkelbek.' **1983** [see DRONK].

bietou /'bitəʊ/ *n.* Also **bidow, biedouw, bieto(u)w, bitou, bitto.** [Afk., fr. Khoikhoi.] Any of several plants of the Asteraceae, some toxic, others nutritious, esp. *Chrysanthemoides monilifera* and species of *Dimorphotheca*, and *Osteospermum.* Also *attrib.* See also *bush-tick berry* (BUSH-TICK sense 2).

1831 *Cape of G.H. Lit. Gaz.* 21 Sept. 224 Osteospermum. Bidow. **1856** L. PAPPE in *Cape of G.H. Almanac & Annual Register* 344 Osteospermum pisiferum Lin. (Compositae) The bony kernels or seeds are enclosed within an oblong berry-like fruit which, though small, is eaten by the inhabitants and called by them *Biedouw besje.* **1883** O.E.A. SCHREINER *Story of Afr. Farm* 130 The bitto flower has been for us a mere blur of yellow; we find its heart composed of a hundred perfect flowers. **1914** *Farmer's Annual* 131 Any extra succulent plant may cause an attack [of tympany], such as lucerne or clover, and the effects of 'bietow' are only too well known to the majority of farmers. **1917** R. MARLOTH *Common Names* 11 Bietouw, (Biedouw). Several quite different plants of the order Compositae bear this name. In the coast districts it is *Osteospermum moniliferum* ... This plant is poisonous ... In Calvinia the same name is applied to a valuable stock-food, viz., *Tripteris sinuata* ... In the Eastern Prov. it is *Dimorphotheca Ecklonis* (otherwise known as the *Van Staden's daisy*), a poisonous herb. **1973** J. RABIE in S. Gray *Writers' Territory* 169 In July and August the first wild flowers already steal the show. First the rosy viooltjies, then yellow bietou and sorrel and blue bobbejaantjies, and at last gladioli and the whole spectrum of gousblomme. **1987** [see BUSH-TICK sense 2]. **1988** *E. Prov. Herald* 6 Feb. 5 It is a good thing boug[ainvillea]s apparently do not go rampant in their adopted home like .. our bietou (Monilifera chrysanthemoides) in Australia.

Big Five *n. phr.* A collective name coined by hunters for the five largest and most dangerous African mammals: the rhinoceros, elephant, buffalo, lion, and leopard. Also *attrib.*

[**1987** *Cape Times* 7 July (Time Share) 3 The Big Five — elephant, rhino, kudu, lion and leopard .. have given Mabula Bush Lodge a quality unique.] **1988** *S. Afr. Panorama* May 14 South Africa is the only country where the 'Big Five', namely elephant, white rhino, buffalo, lion and leopard can still be hunted. **1990** P. CANDIDO in *Weekend Argus* 9 June 16 He said it was about time the Department of Conservation was given more clout to control the hunting of the 'Big Five'. **1993** *Here's What You Should Know about S. Africa's New R50 Banknote* (South African Reserve Bank) (*pamphlet*) The new banknotes .. depict the 'big five' animals .. The R50 note has a lion as the main motif ... The R20 note will feature an elephant ... The R10 note will have the rhinoceros as motif ... The R100 note will feature the buffalo ... The R200 note will have a leopard on the front. **1994** D. MCDONALD in *Afr. Wildlife* Vol.48, No.3, 13 The traditional 'big five' of ecotourism — lion, leopard, elephant, rhino and buffalo — will be joined by the new 'big five' of the South African environment: housing, electricity, water, sewerage and refuse removal.

Big Flu see 'FLU.

Big Hole *n. phr.* A vast man-made excavation in the city of Kimberley (Northern Cape), formerly the Kimberley Diamond Mine, but disused since 1914.

1925 *E. Prov. Herald* 24 July 8 The Prince made an unofficial visit to Kimberley's 'big hole,' 1,700 feet deep. **1936** L.G. GREEN *Secret Afr.* 226 Before leaving Kimberley I motored with Mr. Grimmer to a place rich in memories, the 'Big Hole' of the abandoned Kimberley Mine. Here is the largest open working man has ever dug: a gigantic funnel in the earth. *c***1937** *Our Land* (United Tobacco Co.), The 'Big Hole,' Kimberley, is over 3,500 feet deep and is stated to be the deepest open excavation in the world. **1967** E. ROSENTHAL *Encycl. of Sn Afr.* 287 Digging was concentrated at Colesberg Koppie ... The Koppie was literally dug away, and the gigantic pit, now referred to as the 'Big Hole', came into existence. **1970** P.C. WINTERS in *Std Encycl. of Sn Afr.* II. 317 *Big Hole*, Kimberley .. is 1,600 yds in circumference, with a diameter of 1,520 ft. from north to south and 1,490 ft. from east to west. It occupies an area of 38 acres .. to a depth of 1,200 ft. **1971** *Daily Dispatch* 10 July (Suppl.), Diamond City Celebrates. Mining at the Big Hole came to a halt in 1914 — 25 400 000 metric tons of Kimberlite and 14.5 million carats of diamonds after its discovery. **1989** *Personality* 13 Mar. 38 As you fly over Kimberley, the Big Hole stares up at you like a gaping eye. It's deserted now. **1990** *Weekend Post* 23 June (Leisure) 3 Our three-day safari included a four-hour stop-over at Kimberley to view the Big Hole and museum.

bijter var. BYTER.

Biko Day /'biːkəʊ deɪ, 'biːkɔ -/ *n. phr.* The 12th of September, the anniversary of the death in police custody in 1977 of Steven Biko, a leading figure in the *Black Consciousness Movement* (see BLACK CONSCIOUSNESS sense 2). Also *attrib.*

1984 *Daily Dispatch* 13 Sept. 7 Yesterday was the anniversary of the death of the black consciousness leader, Mr Steve Biko, who died in detention in 1977. Student organisations had called for the commemoration of Biko Day. **1984** *Grocott's Mail* 14 Sept. 1 Stonings boycotts and unrest mark Biko Day. **1989** *Weekly Mail* 15 Dec. 11 Two months ago its [*sc.* the BCM's] 'Biko Day' celebrations and stayaway failed to attract a mass following. **1991** L. MARTIN in *E. Prov. Herald* 2 Apr. 6 The country needs to investigate the official list of public holidays, and I look forward to holidays such as Sharpeville Day, Soweto Day, and Biko Day being recognised paid holidays.

biliary fever *n. phr. Pathology.* [Perh. tr. Afk. *galkoors*, *gal* bile + *koors* fever.] Either of two tick-borne diseases characterized by fever and jaundice. **a.** In horses: equine piroplasmosis, caused by the blood parasite *Babesia equi* and transmitted by the red tick *Rhipicephalus evertsi*. **b.** In dogs: canine piroplasmosis, caused by the blood parasite *Babesia canis* and transmitted by the common dog tick *Haemaphysalis leachi* and a species of brown tick, *Rhipicephalus sanguineus*. In speech often shortened to **biliary.** Cf. TICK-BITE FEVER.

1905 D. HUTCHEON in Flint & Gilchrist *Science in S. Afr.* 344 Equine piroplasmosis, commonly known throughout South Africa as Biliary fever, was first observed in Natal in 1883 by Wiltshire, who named the malady Anthrax Fever. **1937** *Handbk for Farmers* (Dept of Agric. & Forestry) 503 Biliary fever is a name applied to a disease in dogs and two distinct diseases in horses, all caused by different parasites which closely resemble the redwater parasite of cattle ... Biliary fever in horses is caused by two different kinds of parasites, of which, however, only one is frequent in South Africa. **1974** R. CLARK in *Std Encycl. of Sn Afr.* X. 302 *Protozoal diseases*, Biliary Fever (Afk. galkoors) is a term used to describe certain diseases which affect horses and dogs and which are transmitted by ticks. **1978** *Argus* 7 Apr. 8 The disease attacked the liver, and first indications were a rise in temperature. The symptoms were similar to those of biliary. **1979** T. GUTSCHE *There Was a Man* 196 264 He mentioned the astonishing discovery that Trypan Blue used for staining, had proved a specific against biliary fever. **1989** J. DU P. BOTHMA *Game Ranch Management* 183 Babesiosis is the scientific name of the diseases that are known as redwater in cattle and biliary fever in dogs and horses. The parasites (*Babesia* species) occur in the red blood cells of the hosts and cause severe anaemia, with concurrent high fever, listlessness and jaundice. **1991** J.B. WALKER in *Onderstepoort Jrnl of Vet. Research* Vol.58 No.2, 87 Thus far the only *Haemaphysalis* species in southern Africa known to be a vector of any pathogens in *H. leachi*. It transmits *Babesia canis*, causing canine biliary fever, a disease that is frequently fatal.

bilingual *adj.* [Special sense of general Eng.; *bilingual* came to be used of Afrikaans and English exclusively because they were the dominant languages among the ruling white group.] Of a person, proficient in English and Afrikaans; of a document, label, etc., printed in English and Afrikaans; of an organization or institution, offering its services in both English and Afrikaans; TWEETALIG. Also *fig.*

From the creation of the Union of South Africa in 1910 until 1925, Dutch and English were the two official languages; in 1925 Afrikaans replaced Dutch as the second official language, and in 1994 eleven official languages were recognized.

[**1909** *S. Afr. Act* in *Stat. of Union* 72 Both the English and Dutch languages shall be official languages of the Union, and shall be treated on a footing of equality.] **1911** G.J. Du Preez in *Farmer's Weekly* 11 Oct. 3 A paper such as yours .. must be bi-lingual. The greatest number of the farming population cannot appreciate your paper as it is uni-lingual. **1913** V.R. Markham *S. Afr. Scene* 168 The first of those propositions and one always forgotten by the extremists, both Dutch and English, is the fact that the country is bi-racial and bi-lingual; the Dutch-speaking population, it is estimated, being 60 per cent. of the whole. **1938** *Star* 8 Dec. 19 'I like to think of it as a kind of bilingual beard! This,' pointing to the white, 'is the fine, old mature language of the English, and this' — stroking the black — 'the strong young virile language of the Afrikaner.' **1943** 'J. Burger' *Black Man's Burden* 44 Classification of Europeans According to Language (1936). 66% of the total population is classed as bilingual. 53% of the urban population has English as a mother tongue. 41% of the urban population has Afrikaans as a mother tongue. **1950** H. Gibbs *Twilight* 174 In 1908, while Attorney-General and Minister of Education in the first Free State Cabinet, he was responsible for introducing the Act by which every child had to be bilingual. **1979** *E. Prov. Herald* 6 Apr., Farm Manager required for dairy farm. Should be bilingual and must speak Xhosa. **1990** A. Sachs in *Weekly Mail* 2 Feb. 23 South Africa is now said to be a bilingual country: we envisage it as a multi-lingual country. **1990** R. Stengel *January Sun* 150 An American arrives at Jan Smuts airport in Johannesburg. Van der Merwe (the generic surname in all Afrikaner jokes), the customs official, asks him if he speaks any other languages besides English. The man says, 'Yes, I speak French, Spanish, and German.' Van der Merwe replies, 'Oh, so you're not bilingual?' **1994** on TV1, 18 Oct. (Good Morning South Africa), There will be a bilingual news update at 8 o'clock.

Hence **bilingual** *n. nonce* (used ironically), Afrikaans; **bilingualism** *n.*, proficiency in English and Afrikaans.

*c*1936 *S. & E. Afr. Yr Bk & Guide* 36 The census of 1926 ... As compared with the figures of 1921, a very considerable increase in bi-lingualism is indicated. **1939** *Outspan* 6 Oct. 23 She is thoroughly and completely at home in English and Afrikaans, a perfect example of bilingualism. **1943** I. Frack *S. Afr. Doctor* 103 The incessant stressing of bilingualism by the politicians really means unilingualism. The country must learn Afrikaans even if it is killed in learning it. **1952** [see VAT sense 1]. **1976** V. Rosenberg *Sunflower* 12 His bilingualism and his administrative abilities were utilised during pleasant sojourns at the Cape. *c*1988 *S. Afr. 1987–8: Off. Yrbk* (Bureau for Information) 34 Afrikaans replaced Dutch as the other official language in 1925 and bilingualism was encouraged in the public service. **1990** *Weekly Mail* 21 Dec. (Suppl.) 31 Experiments with bilingualism have already been done in Afrikaans literature through ventures like *Forces Favourites*.

billtong, bill tongue, bill-tung varr. BILTONG.

bilt var. BULT.

biltong /ˈbɪltɒŋ, ˈbəl-/ *n.* Forms: α. **billtong, bill-tongue, bill-tung, biltong(ue)**; β. **bel(l)-tong, belting, beltongue, bel tong(ue)**; γ. **bultong, bültong**. [S. Afr. Du., fr. Du. *bil* buttock, rump (fr. which the meat is often taken) + *tong* tongue (referring to the long, narrow shape of the strips of meat).]

1. Salted dried meat in strips, usu. lean beef, venison, or ostrich-meat, but sometimes other game, or fish; TASSAL sense a. Also *attrib.*, and *transf.* See also BOKKEM.

Usu. *noncount*, but see α quot. 1890, and γ quot. 1883.

α. **1815** A. Plumptre tr. *H. Lichtenstein's Trav. in Sn Afr.* (1930) II. 77 He lived almost entirely upon dried mutton and biltong. **1827** T. Philipps *Scenes & Occurrences* 213 The remainder of the beams were tastefully festooned with .. long strips of *bill tongue*, that is, narrow slices of beef salted and dried in the sun. **1832** *Graham's Town Jrnl* 25 Oct. 170 Jan Aron, alias Jan Bastaard: Storebreaking, with intent to Steal; and Theft, in stealing 8 lbs of soap, 8 pieces of Biltong, and 200 dried Peaches. **1855** J.W. Colenso *Ten Weeks in Natal* 161, I found the house .. hardly endurable .. from the quantity of fresh *biltong*, or flesh cut off in strips from an animal ... The pieces of raw meat were hung up inside in the open roof to dry. **1875** C.R. Bisset *Sport & War* 13, I saw Englishmen buying pieces of biltong from the Dutch about the size of your thumb for half a crown, and it made a very good meal for the day. **1890** A.G. Hewitt *Cape Cookery* 42 To Cure Biltong. Have the biltongs cut at the butchers as he knows the best pieces for the purpose; they are cut from the shoulder and should weigh 3 or 4 lbs. **1891** H.J. Duckitt *Hilda's 'Where Is It?'* 11 'Biltong.' (An old Cape way of curing and drying meat.) **1903** R. Kipling *Five Nations* 201 Ah there, Piet! — be'ind 'is stony kop, With 'is Boer bread an' biltong, an' 'is flask of awful Dop. **1920** F.C. Cornell *Glamour of Prospecting* 30 We had good horses and travelled light, with a few roster-kooks and some biltong, by way of provisions. *Ibid.* 132 The heat .. seemed to be drying the very blood up in our veins, and converting us into biltong. **1943** D. Reitz *No Outspan* 83 Baas, baas, the old missus says you must come at once, someone has stolen all the biltong (dried meat) from the clothesline in the back yard. **1950** H. Gerber *Cape Cookery* 95 Biltong. Cut the meat into strips and rub it with salt. Allow it to lie for 2 to 3 days in a basin, placed in a cool spot. After 3 days salt the meat once more and brush off all surplus salt. Hang it up in a shady place to dry. **1971** *Sunday Times* 14 Nov. (Mag. Sect.) 7 'Jake' Jacobs himself .. emerges as a biltong-tough natural leader with inherent sensitivity. **1973** *Weekend Post* 14 Apr. 3 The word 'biltong' was becoming part of the Hebrew language. Former South Africans living in Israel are believed to have encouraged the introduction of biltong to Israel. **1974** *E. Prov. Herald* 27 Feb. 5 An ambitious scheme .. is aimed at putting an end to the large scale dumping of bananas in years of over-production — by turning the fruit into a form of 'biltong'. **1983** D.A.C. Maclennan *Reckonings* 17 You licked your lips in the biltong weather. **1986** *E. Prov. Herald* 14 June 5 That is the biltong party. They are busy drying out like a piece of biltong. Parliament must adjourn so that the members on the other side of the House can go hunting. **1989** P. Lee in *Sunday Times* 22 Jan. (Mag. Sect.) 45 He normally sports a beer boep, has a beer can clutched firmly in his hot sweaty hand, carries a cooler-box jammed with carry-packs and biltong. **1991** *Leisure Books Catal.* Apr.-June 19 Recipes are included, such as biltong quiche, biltong potbread, .. Traditional SA fare at its very best.

β. *a*1827 D. Carmichael in W.J. Hooker *Botanical Misc.* (1831) II. 273 In lieu of bread, they sometimes use the flesh of various animals, salted and dried in the sun ... Which they call 'Belltong'. **1849** N.J. Merriman *Cape Jrnls* (1957) 66 Had it not been .. for the Beltongue sandwiches .., I should have suffered both from hunger and thirst before reaching Graaff Reinet. **1860** A.W. Drayson *Sporting Scenes* 144 We .. had a little beltong meat dried in the sun for supper. *a*1868 J. Ayliff *Jrnl of 'Harry Hastings'* (1963) 98 After a good supper of dried meat which they call 'beltong' and milk, we lay ourselves down. **1872** C.A. Payton *Diamond Diggings* 153, I must not forget to mention a favourite food of the Boers — 'beltongue' or jerked meat — the flesh of springbuck, blesbuck, wildebeest, and other large game, cut into thick strips, and dried in the sun by hunters who are too far from the markets to bring in the game fresh. **1884** B. Adams *Narr.* (1941) 107 A good supply of Bel Tongue and bread was set before us ... Bel Tong .. is seldom found in the houses of Englishmen. It is made from beef .. cut into long strips and dried. **1892** W.L. Distant *Naturalist in Tvl* 32 In a campaign he only requires some dried meat — beltong — attached to his saddle, and a bottle of hollands or water. **1898** G. Nicholson *50 Yrs* 251 Their favourite 'naama' (meat), with which the trees and bushes around were festooned in strips, in process of becoming 'belting' in the dry and fervid atmosphere.

γ. **1883** O.E.A. Schreiner *Story of Afr. Farm* 86 Did not Tant' Sannie keep in the loft 'bultongs' and nice smoked sausages? *Ibid.* 100, I was older than you when I used to eat 'bultong' in my mother's loft. **1897** H.A. Bryden *Nature & Sport*, The flesh of the hartebeest is fairly palatable, darkish in colour and makes good bültong (sundried flesh), though not so good as the bültong of springbok or koodoo. **1914** W.C. Scully *Lodges in Wilderness* 48 We cut up and salted the meat preparatory to its being packed together and rolled in sacking. Next day it would be hung out on lines to dry into 'bultong'. **1961** D. Bee *Children of Yesterday* 16 He was eating a piece of sundried ostrich meat, known as bultong.

2. *comb.* **biltong curtain** [by analogy with Eng. *Iron Curtain*], a jocular name for the borders of South Africa; **biltong farmer, -hunter, -jackal**, one who hunts game in order to obtain meat for the making of biltong.

1979 *Daily Dispatch* 12 May 6 The China Syndrome .. is more than .. simple-minded entertainment. The subject is a hot one beyond this **biltong curtain**. **1949** L.G. Green *In Land of Afternoon* 66 In 1937 it became illegal to sell game biltong in the Cape Province ... The ban .. slowed up a slaughter which had been in progress ever since the modern rifle reached South Africa. It put the '**biltong farmer**' also known as the 'biltong jackal' out of business. **1937** C. Birkby *Zulu Journey* 110 The year before last 150 shooting licences were given to the '**biltong hunters**'. **1939** H. Klein in *Outspan* 3 Nov. 25 He was one of the old-time professional biltong hunters, who lived for the three short winter months when .. he could roam the plains shooting for lion pelts and biltong. **1971** H. Zeederberg *Veld Express* 74 We call this part of the country the 'Springbok Flats'. Twenty years ago, heads of three to four hundred were quite common, and it is still a paradise for biltong hunters. **1949** [**biltong jackal**: see quot. above].

bio /ˈbaɪəʊ/ *n. colloq.* Shortened form of BIOSCOPE (senses 1 a and b). Also *attrib.*

1918 H. Baumann *Informant, Bloemfontein* 23 Sept., In the afternoon took the *nurses* and patients to the Bio & tea. **1934** C.P. Swart Supplement to Pettman. 13 Instead of saying 'I am going to the pictures or the cinema,' South Africans say 'I am going to the bio(scope).' **1963** A. Fugard *Blood Knot* (1968) 125 Both of us hates Oudtshoorn, man ... There's only two bios here. **1977** F.G. Butler *Karoo Morning* 120 Ernest and Alice .. had reservations about letting their offspring haunt the 'bio'; for what was the 'bio' .. but a mass-produced version of the theatre ... The first 'bio' I saw was 'Charley's Aunt.' **1979** *Sunday Times* 8 July (Extra) 2 We jam-pack our bios to the ceiling, sit shoulder-to-shoulder with our black broers — and applaud a bloody good show! **1990** J. Naidoo *Coolie Location* 192 Sometimes we used to scrape together enough to make up our bio fare.

bio-café /ˈbaɪəʊˌkæfeɪ/ *n. hist.* [Compound of BIO + CAFÉ.] A cinema-cum-tearoom, offering continuous film-screenings, at which patrons might enjoy light refreshments while seeing a film; CAFE-BIO; SOPPIES; *tearoom bio(scope)*, see TEAROOM sense 2. Also *attrib.* See also BIOSCOPE.

[**1949** H.C. Bosman *Cold Stone Jug* (1969) 111 And that evening I went into a bioscope café. And I went and sat down next to a girl ... I was an ex-con and I was sitting next to her for an hour in a bioscope café, and she dressed all in pink.] **1963** A. FUGARD *Notebks* (1983) 87 In Johnnie's heyday the 'Pop Bio Café' was still in existence – the grey flickering screen, sweet smell of green cold-drink, the waitresses. **1977** *E. Prov. Herald* 22 June 5 The Dolphin .. was previously run as the Ster 400 and before that as a bio-cafe, the Roxy. **1981** *Cape Times* 22 Dec. 8 On her day off she goes down town to a bio cafe. She has seen The Sound of Music 30 times. **1990** *Sunday Times* 4 Mar. (Mag. Sect.) 64 My grandfather owned one of the first movie houses in Johannesburg – the 'Palm Court' ... It became the 'Tearoom Bioscope' or Biocafé as they were known then ... Sadly the 70's saw the last of these biocafés, which became known as 'fleapits' at the end.

bioscope /ˈbaɪ(ə)skəʊp/ *n.* Also **baaiscope**. [Obs. Eng., cinema projector, fr. Gk *bios* life + *skopein* to look at; the continued use of the word in S. Afr. Eng. was no doubt reinforced by Afk. *bioskoop* movies, cinema.]

1. *obsolescent.*

a. A motion-picture film; BIO. Also *attrib.* Cf. FLIEK.

[**1898** *The Jrnl* 19 Mar. 2 Albany Hall. To-Night (Saturday), And following Nights. James's Bioscope and micro-Phonograph Entertainment.] **1902** *Star* 1 June, The bioscope entertainment to be given on Saturday next .. promises to be bright and enjoyable. **1916** L.D. FLEMMING *Fool on Veld* (1933) 92 His face, very naturally, went ashy white – a sort of whiteness you meet in bioscopes, or in William Le Queux's novels. **1920** S.C. CRONWRIGHT-SCHREINER Letter. 15 Aug., The building is large, with a big dining room & a free 'kinema' (bioscope) running all day. **1965** C. VAN HEYNINGEN *Orange Days* 14 With an eyebrow cocked up interrogatively, like a comedian's on the bioscope. **1965** J. BENNETT *Hawk Alone* 106 That night he took her to a very bad cinema show (in South Africa they called them bioscopes then, and still do: it is only by the more sophisticated people that they are called the movies, or the flicks). **1979** *Sunday Times* 8 July 3 They could get out on Friday night to the church coffee bar .. and see religious bioscopes. **1984** [see MARABI sense 2]. **1989** B. GODBOLD Autobiography. 48 The first bioscope (the word 'cinema' came into use much later) was shown in the same hall. **1990** D. BECKETT in *Frontline* Mar.-Apr. 12 The German is a technician on holiday, with a bioscope accent.

b. A cinema, or motion-picture house; BIO. See also BUGHOUSE. Also *attrib.*

Often used without an article (see quots. 1974, 1986, 1989).

1905 *Rand Daily Mail* 1 Mar. 6 Rees' Popular Bioscope. Hundreds turned away on Saturday night. **1915** *Cape* 8 Oct. 19 They extended to her facetious invitations to the theatre and the bioscope. **1929** J.G. VAN ALPHEN *Jan Venter* 171 All these ladies might very well have stepped out of some such garden-party as he had seen depicted in illustrated papers, or at the bioscope. **1939** J.G. CHALMERS in *Outspan* 13 Oct. 71 The boy who lives in this age of wireless and bioscopes presents the same difficulty and demands the same just treatment as he who appears to have been less favoured in past days. **1940** [see AFRIKAANS *adj.*]. **1943** 'J. BURGER' *Black Man's Burden* 91 In the largest urban locations there are recreation grounds, a cinema (still called 'bioscope' in South Africa), social centres, and clubs. **1950** H. GIBBS *Twilight* 155 No bioscope opens on Sundays. **1951** L.G. GREEN *Grow Lovely* 151 The bioscope became a regular part of Cape Town's life in 1903, when the Tivoli opened and included films in every variety programme. **1974** *Drum* 8 Apr. 35 My hobbies are reading, listening to the radio, going to bioscope, soccer .. and travelling. **1975** *Friend* 28 July 8 Thousands of juvenile lovers in their unisex velskoens .. all heading for the 'baaiscope' at the top of their voices. **1980** J. COCK *Maids & Madams* 163 We can't be expected to sit in a bioscope (cinema) with such smelly people. **1986** B. SIMON in S. Gray *Market Plays* 117, I was coming out of bioscope after a musical picture. **1988** E. MPHAHLELE *Renewal Time* 101 'Coloured' people have better houses; .. go to the bioscope, the 'coloured' people sit at the back and we blacks are put right in front. **1989** J. HOBBS *Thoughts in Makeshift Mortuary* 76 All they talked about .. was boyfriends and makeup and who was going to bioscope with whom on Saturday. **1990** *Sunday Times* 4 Mar. (Mag. Sect.) 65 A mini-museum of moviehouses, authentic in its detail right down to the heavy velvet curtains, retrieved from a bioscope about to close down.

c. *rare.* With distinguishing epithet. **little bioscope, mini-bioscope**: television.

1971 *Daily News* 8 Mar. 13 First it was Dr. Albert Hertzog and his opposition to the 'little bioscope'. **1971** *Personality* 28 May 30 It seems to me only fair that if the 'little bioscope' is to be allowed to insinuate itself into everyone's homes on the Sabbath, the big bioscope should be allowed the same privilege. **1977** *E. Prov. Herald* 1 July 15 Dr Albert Hertzog .. who called television an 'immoral mini-bioscope' .. will make his television debut soon.

2. *fig.* A spectacle; entertainment.

1953 LANHAM & MOPELI-PAULUS *Blanket Boy's Moon* 204 Dost Ghulam watched with interested eyes the bioscope which Nature provided on the windscreen of the motor car. **1956** A. SAMPSON *Drum* 80, I watched a faithless husband hiding under the table from his wife, while his friends chased his mistress out of the window. 'Big bioscope,' said a fat man, shaking beside me. **1969** A. FUGARD *Boesman & Lena* 36 The ou trying to catch his donkey? Or the other one running around with his porridge looking for a fire to finish cooking it? It was Bioscope man! **1981** *Sunday Times* 1 Mar. (Mag. Sect.) 5 We had become, Steenkamp and I, part of the Cape Town bioscope. **1986** L. SAMPSON in *Style* May 103 It is .. a real bioscope. What they don't buy, and what they don't do. Oi, sometimes a person can hardly believe it.

biriani, biryani varr. BREYANI.

biscop var. BISKOP.

bishop *n.* Ellipt. form of BISHOP-BIRD.

The *ellipt.* form 'bishop' is now more common than 'bishop-bird' among bird-watchers, and is frequently used with distinguishing epithets.

1923 HAAGNER & IVY *Sketches* 120 The Golden Bishop .. builds a similar nest to that of the Red Bishop. **1936** E.L. GILL *First Guide to S. Afr. Birds* 27 *Golden Bishop-bird*, Taha Bishop. [**1953** D.A. BANNERMAN *Birds W. & Equat. Afr.* II. 1415 When not breeding the Fire-crowned Bishops go about in small flocks.] **1980** J.O. OLIVER *Beginner's Guide to our Birds* 77 Like the weavers, the bishop males are beautifully coloured ... After breeding, the bishops leave their nesting places to winter elsewhere. **1984** G.L. MACLEAN *Roberts' Birds of Sn Afr.* 733 The technical difference between a bishop and a widow is that a male widow replaces its rectrices (tail feathers) in the pre-breeding moult, while a bishop does not ... *Red Bishop .. Euplectes orix. Ibid.* 734 *Firecrowned Bishop* (Blackwinged Bishop) .. *Euplectes hordeaceus. Ibid.* 735 *Golden Bishop .. Euplectes afer.*

bishop-bird *n.* [Perh. so named because of the scarlet and black plumage of *Euplectes oryx*.] Any of several birds of the genus *Euplectes* of the Ploceidae, esp. *E. oryx*; BISHOP. Freq. also with distinguishing epithet.

1884 LAYARD & SHARPE *Birds of S. Afr.* 463 We have not thought it necessary to separate these two Bishop Birds specifically. **1900** STARK & SCLATER *Birds of S. Afr.* I. 127 In winter the Bishop Birds collect in flocks sometimes numbering thousands of individuals. **1923** HAAGNER & IVY *Sketches* 118 The Red Bishop-Bird or Kaffir-fink (*P[yromelana] oryx*), too well known in its brilliant plumage of orange-scarlet and black to need any description. **1937** M. ALSTON *Wanderings* 84 The particular joys of this spot were .. the scarlet bishop-birds on an island, absorbed in weaving their nests, and, like leaping flames, flying backwards and forwards from the mainland. **1950** E.L. GILL *First Guide to S. Afr. Birds* 30 *Yellow Bishop-bird*, A larger bird .. than the Red Kaffir-vink, with .. shining yellow in place of scarlet. **1961** *Redwing* (St Andrew's College, Grahamstown) 17 In one vlei close to our house thousands of red bishop birds used to nest every summer; however, fires have burnt off most of the reeds and last year I didn't find a single bishop bird's nest. **1970** G.J. BROEKHUYSEN in *Std Encycl. of Sn Afr.* II. 345 The weavers, the Cape weaver for instance, or the red bishop-bird, build a very complicated nest like a closed basket, which sometimes has a short tubular entrance. **1986** L.B. HALL in *Style* July 97 From the bushes red bishop birds rise up in fright, like small flying embers.

biskop /ˈbəskɔp/ *n.* Also **biscop**. Pl. usu. unchanged. [Afk., etym. dubious: perh. 'bishop', see quot. 1913, or ad. of Du. *beestkop*, see quot. 1930 (sense 1); see also POENSKOP.]

1. Either of two species of seabream: **a.** The *black musselcracker* (see MUSSELCRACKER sense 2), *Cymatoceps nasutus*. **b.** The *white musselcracker* (see MUSSELCRACKER sense 2), *Sparodon durbanensis*. Cf. sense 2.

[*a*1827 D. CARMICHAEL in W.J. Hooker *Botanical Misc.* (1831) II. 267 The common and the red *Steinbrassen*, the *Boskop*, the *Hottentot fish*, the *Roman fish*.] **1902** J.D.F. GILCHRIST in *Trans. of S. Afr. Philological Soc.* XI. iv. 227 (Pettman), Biscop, Poeskop. *Chrysophrys* sp. **1913** C. PETTMAN *Africanderisms* 60 *Biscop*, .. A variety of *Chrysophrys*. The name is supposed to have reference to the curiously grave appearance which the large head and peculiar facial features of this fish give to it. **1923** *S. Afr.: Land of Outdoor Life* (S.A.R. & H.) 240 The biskop is the prince of winter fish round and about the Cape Peninsula, and as long as it is played on light sporting tackle with fair methods it has no rival aspirant to that rank. **1930** C.L. BIDEN *Sea-Angling Fishes* 257 'Biskop' is the fishermen's corruption of the very old Dutch name 'beestkop', meaning animal- or beast-head. **1951** L.G. GREEN *Grow Lovely* 91 Other fish based on the same ribald principles were the biskop and the fransmadam, the latter an ugly customer with large black eyes. **1971** *Argus* 4 June 10 The musselcracker or biskop is inclined to shake the bait once or twice before taking it.

2. With distinguishing epithet designating a particular species of biskop: **black -**, **blou -** [Afk., *blou* blue], **blue biskop**, the *black musselcracker* (see MUSSELCRACKER sense 2), *Cymatoceps nasutus*; **white biskop**, the *white musselcracker* (see MUSSELCRACKER sense 2), *Sparodon durbanensis*.

1930 C.L. BIDEN *Sea-Angling Fishes* 262 When an angler lands his first large **black biskop** he is so impressed with the huge, bluntly-shaped, almost human head that he stands aghast at this extraordinary creature. **1945** H. GERBER *Fish Fare* 51 Musselcrackers or *Biskops*. These fish are greatly prized by anglers as game fighting fish. The White kind goes up to .. 64 lbs and the black or **blou biskop** to about 120 lbs. **1949** [**blue biskop**: see Smith quot. at MUSSELCRACKER sense 1]. **1930** C.L. BIDEN *Sea-Angling Fishes* 259 False Bay netters sometimes find a few large biskop in their hauls ... Boatmen seldom catch the **white biskop** out at sea, for it is essentially a rock or surf anglers fish. **1990** [see STOMPKOP].

biskute var. BESKUIT.

bitou var. BIETOU.

bitter apple *n. phr.* [Transf. use of Eng. *bitter apple* a name for the European species *Citrullus colocynthis*; or tr. S. Afr. Du. *bitterappel*.]

1. *obs.* TSAMMA.

1862 HARVEY & SONDER *Flora Capensis* II. 493 *Citrullus*, .. *C. vulgaris* ... *Hab.* In the sands of the Cape downs .. and of similar localities ... Pepo the size of an apple or of a child's head. When edible or sweet it is called water-melon or Kaffir water-melon; when bitter, it is the *bitter apple* or *wild water-melon* of the colonists. **1868, 1887** [see *kaffir water melon* (KAFFIR *n.* sense 2 e)]. **1913** C. PETTMAN *Africanderisms* 61 *Bitter apple*, .. This name is also given to *Citrullus vulgaris*.

2. Any of several shrubs of the Solanaceae bearing bitter fruits shaped like small apples, esp. *Solanum aculeastrum* and *S. hermannii*; GIFAPPEL sense 2.

1911 *E. London Dispatch* 31 Aug. (Pettman), The bush commonly known as snake-berry or bitter apple. **1913** C. PETTMAN *Africanderisms* 61 *Bitter apple*, The fruit of several species of *Solanaceae* are so called. **1953** J. HOYLE *Some Flowers* 32 The Bitter Apple is found all over Africa. **1970** M.R. LEVYNS in *Std Encycl. of Sn Afr.* II. 349 *Bitter Apple*, Apple of Sodom. Gifappel. (*S. sodonaeum* [*sic*] var. *hermanii; Solanum aculeastrum*) The popular names apply to both these species. **1983** M.M. KIDD *Cape Peninsula* 128 *Solanum hermanii* (=S. sodomaeum var. hermanii). Solanaceae. *Apple of Sodom, Bitter Apple, Gifappel.* A branching shrub up to 1m.

‖**bitterbossie** /ˈbətə(r)ˌbɔsi/ *n.* [Afk., *bitter* bitter + *bos* bush + -IE.] BITTER KAROO. Also *attrib.*, and (occas.) **bitterbos.**

1917 R. MARLOTH *Common Names* 12 *Bitter bossie, Chrysocoma tenuifolia.* A small shrublet hardly a foot high, which now prevails in many parts formerly occupied by the Schaapbos (*Pentzia*). The animals do not eat it on account of its bitter taste, but the flower tops are a welcome food when herbage is scarce. **1937** *Handbk for Farmers* (Dept of Agric. & Forestry), The most reliable methods of preventing the disease is not to allow pregnant ewes and goats access to 'bitterbossie veld' for a period of at least 14 days before they are due to lamb, and for at least 14 days after lambing. [**1973** E. LEROUX in S. Gray *Writers' Territory* 145 Bitterbos and Karoo stretch to the horizon where a blood-red sun sets.]

bitter bush *n. phr.* [tr. Afk. *bitterbos.*] BITTER KAROO.

1891 in C.A. Smith *Common Names* (1966) 107 When the ewes have to feed on .. bitter bush .. the milk must be poisonous, and the lambs suffer from bloedpens. **1971** *Golden Fleece* (S. Afr. Wool Board) June (Suppl.) 8 Chrysocoma tenuifolia – bitter bush. **1973** *E. Prov. Herald* 28 Feb. 4 Unpalatable thorny types such as bitter bush, thorny figs, buchu karoo bushes and karoo thorn types are to be found on the western Karoo route.

bitter-einder /ˌbətərˈeɪndə(r)/ *n.* [Afk., formed on S. Afr. Eng. (or the orig. U.S. Eng.) *bitter-ender* die-hard. It is probable that *bitter-ender* entered S. Afr. Eng. towards the end of the Anglo-Boer War, at approx. the same time as it was taken into S. Afr. Du. as *bitter-einder.* The comparatively recent borrowing of *bitter-einder* into S. Afr. Eng. is perhaps an attempt at 'correctness', based on the misconception that *bitter-ender* was derived fr. Afk.]

1. *hist.* BITTER-ENDER. Also *attrib.*

1946 E. ROSENTHAL *General De Wet* 89 It was noticeable that more and more began to side against the 'Bitter-Einders', as they were called. **1960** L.M. THOMPSON *Unification of S. Afr. 1902–10* 17 The events of the war had left a bitter legacy of divisions within Afrikanerdom – between Transvaalers, Free Staters, and the Cape Colonials, and between bittereinders (bitter enders) who had fought to the end, hensoppers (hands-uppers) who had passively accepted British rule, and National Scouts who had actively assisted the British forces. **1977** T.R.H. DAVENPORT *S. Afr.: Mod. Hist.* 156 Conciliation was necessary to heal the rifts within Afrikanerdom between the bitter-einder and the National Scout. **1980** *Cape Times* 29 Mar. 8 History – and the future – belonged to the hollow-eyed men of the veld, the *bitter-einders* who against unbelievable personal and military odds carried on the fight to the bitter end. **1982** [see BURGHER sense 4]. **1990** D. VAN HEERDEN in *Sunday Times* 10 June 11 The son of one of the bittereinder Boer leaders who refused to sign the Vereeniging Peace Treaty in 1902, Dr Naudé was named after General Christiaan Frederick Beyers.

2. *Fig.*, and *transf.* One who holds out to the end; a die-hard.

1970 M. BENNETT *Informant, Krugersdorp* Bittereinders. People who hang about after the party is over. **1975** *Sunday Times* 12 Oct. 16 This acceptance comes from many countries (communist regimes and a few bitter-einders excepted). **1986** *Style* Sept. 6 The evening (or morning) ended with a few chosen *bittereinders* moving off to Melvyn Minnaar's house for a Sunday morning champagne breakfast. **1989** H.P. TOFFOLI in *Style* Feb. 40 It's this healthy tradition of voluble Boere diehards – bittereinders – who speak their minds no matter what the cost, that the *Vrye Weekblad* in its stated editorial policy clearly sees itself as part of. **1990** *E. Prov. Herald* 9 Feb. 5 It's with the bittereinders that you will have to reckon if you want to give away the freedom of the Afrikaner. This nation will not be led to the abattoir. **1990** *Sunday Times* 7 Oct. 7 Armed police dismantled the last homes and loaded the furniture and livestock of black *bittereinders.* **1990** *Sunday Times* 14 Oct. 25 All that is left is for the *bittereinders* to drink the pub dry after its reopening.

bitter-ender *n. hist.* [Orig. U.S. Eng., die-hard: see prec.] A Boer who refused to surrender towards the end of the ANGLO-BOER WAR; BITTER-EINDER sense 1. Also *attrib.* Cf. HANDS-UPPER sense 1 a. See also *white button* (WHITE *adj.* sense 2).

1915 J.K. O'CONNOR *Afrikander Rebellion* 6 As far back as 1902 when the ink in which the Vereeniging Treaty had been inscribed was scarcely dry, there were ominous signs of disaffection among a section of the Dutch people, who were pleased to call themselves 'bitter-enders'. **1916** E.H. SPENDER *General Botha* 127 Their leaders still proved the most obstinate 'Bitter-enders' – just as now .. they still resist most obstinately the mingling of their racial influence with that of the British stock. **1937** C.R. PRANCE *Tante Rebella's Saga* 34 The Colonel was instructed confidentially to ascertain what Oom Gideon's price would be to .. go home to his farm in a blaze of glory as the last Free State 'bitter-ender' to stand out against Pax Britannica. **1949** A. KEPPEL-JONES *S. Afr.: Short Hist.* 138 Others who surrendered – 'hands-uppers' – thought the continued resistance madness and felt that the 'bitter-enders' would be responsible for the ruin of their country. **1974** K. GRIFFITH *Thank God We Kept Flag Flying* 377 There were still about 22 000 Boers fighting on the veldt. They are known in the Republic of South Africa as 'the bitter-enders'. **1978** M. VAN WYK SMITH *Drummer Hodge* 222 Ex-Boer Generals Botha and Smuts accepted the spirit of an imperial family of nations in which South Africa could play her part ... But there were also the 'bittereinders' ('bitter-enders'), who had pledged eternal enmity to all things British. **1981** *Cape Times* 12 Sept. 9 There can be little doubt that it was British Army policy – explicit or otherwise – to shoot bitter-ender Boer prisoners out of hand in the final phase of the South African War. **1988** A. SHER *Middlepost* 239 Swanepoel had been a *bitter-ender*, fighting on long after the official surrender, committing legendary acts of bravery. **1990** *Bulletin* (Centre for Science Dev.) Nov.-Dec. 3 Many other popular books .. glorified the Boer generals and 'bitterenders' and railed against the injustices of the concentration camps.

bitter Karoo *n. phr.* Also with small initials. [Afk. *bitter* bitter + KAROO.] In full ***bitter Karoo bush***, formerly ***bitter Karoo boschje***: the pernicious shrub *Chrysocoma ciliata* of the Asteraceae; BITTERBOSSIE; BITTER BUSH. See also KAROO sense 2.

1896 R. WALLACE *Farming Indust. of Cape Col.* 94 The bitter Karoo bosje, *Chrysocoma tenuifolia Berg* .. is only eaten in times of scarcity, as it produces stomach and biliary disorders. **1910** A.B. LAMONT *Rural Reader* 258 Bitter karoo spreads rapidly, and is not eaten by stock except when other food is scarce. **1913** A. GLOSSOP *Barnes's S. Afr. Hsehold Guide* 316 Extirpate the bitter Karoo boschje, Rhenoster bush, .. lalybloem, 'drinkgras', [etc.]. **1933** G.A. GILL in *Farming in S. Afr.* May 190 Bitter Karroo is now also recognised to have poisonous properties. **1937** *Handbk for Farmers* (Dept of Agric. & Forestry) 396 Overstocking should be avoided, as this induces a strong growth of steekgras and bitter Karroo. **1948** H.V. MORTON *In Search of S. Afr.* 257 There is the bitter Karoo bush, which has a yellow flower, and the Vaal Karoo, which is a greyer version of the bitter. **1971** *Golden Fleece* (S. Afr. Wool Board) June (Suppl.), Where grassveld is overstocked or grazed injudiciously with sheep, shrubs such as Karroo bush, (pentzia spp.) and bitter Karroo (Chrysocoma tenuifolia) often form the dominant vegetation.

bitter-melon *n.* [Eng., prob. shortened form of BITTER WATERMELON.] TSAMMA.

1828 T. PRINGLE *Ephemerides* 90 The bitter-melon, for food and drink, Is the pilgrim's fare by the salt lake's brink. [*Note*] A wild fruit found in the deserts. [**1844** J. BACKHOUSE in C.A. Smith *Common Names* (1966) 109 A round, poisonous bitter melon, *Citrullus amara*, about five inches in diameter is abundant in this country.] **1913** C. PETTMAN *Africanderisms* 61 *Bitter-melon*, .. *Citrullus vulgaris Sch.* See also Tsama water-melon. **1917** R. MARLOTH *Common Names* 12 *Bittermelon, Citrullis vulgaris*, var. *amara.* (*Wild coloquint*). Frequent in the Karoo and Kalahari regions. **1982** FOX & NORWOOD YOUNG *Food from Veld* 167 *Citrullus lanatus* ... *Common names*: English – *bitter melon*, [etc.].

bitter watermelon *n. phr. Obs.* Also **bitter watermeloen.** [tr. S. Afr. Du. *bitterwaatlemoen*, *bitter* bitter + *waatlemoen* watermelon.] TSAMMA.

*c***1822** W.J. BURCHELL in C.A. Smith *Common Names* (1966) 109 Bitter water Meloen. Cat. Geogr. Sub. 2128. **1857** D. LIVINGSTONE *Missionary Trav.* 48 These melons are not, however, all of them eatable; some are sweet, and others are so bitter that the whole are named by the Boers the 'bitter water-melon'. **1890** P. MACOWAN in C.A. Smith *Common Names* (1966) 109 The *Bitter-watermelon* .. is of some medicinal value. [**1966** C.A. SMITH *Common Names* 109 *Bitterwaatlemoen*, .. *Citrullus lanatus*: In general character like the cultivated watermelon .. but smaller ... The pulp is intensely bitter and has apparently been known since early colonial days for its purgative properties.]

bitto var. BIETOU.

Bituanas pl. form of BECHUANA.

bla var. BRA.

blaasop /ˈblɑːsɔp/ *n.* Also **blaaz-op, blas(s)op, blos op.** Pl. **-s**, or unchanged. [Afk., earlier S. Afr. Du. *blaazop*, fr. Du. *opblazen* to inflate.]

1. *obs.* Any of several species of forest-dwelling grasshoppers of the Pneumoridae, the males having greatly distended abdomens which serve as resonance chambers; GHONYA; OPPBLAZER.

1786 G. FORSTER tr. *A. Sparrman's Voy. to Cape of G.H.* I. 312 Here were .. insects of that peculiar genus .. pneumora ... Their abdomen, one single small gut excepted, is always found empty, and at the same time quite pellucid, as well as blown up and distended; on which account they are called *blaaz-ops* by the Colonists, and are said to live on nothing but wind. **1853** F.P. FLEMING *Kaffraria* 77 The *Pneumora*, or as they are styled by the Dutch, 'the Blos Op,' are also common, and by their loud buzzing noise often attract notice to their large inflated bodies, which are of the most beautiful light green tints, spotted all over with silver. **1918** S.H. SKAIFE *Animal Life* 65 The peculiar green *blaasop* also belongs to this family. The distended, bladder-like abdomen of the male probably serves to increase the volume of the sound made by this insect.

2. Any of a number of poisonous sea fishes of the Tetraodontidae which are able to inflate their bodies into nearly spherical shape (see quot. 1986); BLAASOPPIE.

[**1853** L. PAPPE *Synopsis of Edible Fishes* 8 This fish (*Blaasopvisch; Balloonfish; Toadfish*) is never found in Table Bay, but is very common in the bays to the east of it.] **1902** J.D.F. GILCHRIST in *Trans. of S. Afr. Philological Soc.* XI. iv. 227 (Pettman), Blassop, Toad-fish (E. London). *Tetrodon honkenyi.* **1913** W.W. THOMPSON *Sea Fisheries of Cape Col.* 159 Tetrodon honkenyi .. Blaasop; Toad-fish (East London). **1930** C.L. BIDEN *Sea-Angling Fishes* 279 Men catching blaasop .. at Simonstown, and not knowing the fish, fried and ate some with fatal results ... Blaasop is known as 'swell-fish' by Americans. **1947** L.G. GREEN *Tavern of Seas* 36 It should not be necessary to warn anyone that the blaasop's liver contains a deadly poison, for the appearance of the fish is so revolting that I cannot imagine anyone even considering eating one. **1953** *Drum* Mar. 31 They catch anything, from sharks to sardines, and lots of little fat blasops. **1959** M.W. SPILHAUS *Under Bright Sky* 44 Sometimes the boys catch blaasop, and they are *Deadly Poison!* **1968** J.L.B. SMITH *High Tide* 24 Poisonous and dangerous creatures are generally the best known. Because of their peculiar appearance and characteristics, blaasops have attracted attention from the earliest times. **1976** *E. Prov. Herald* 18 Nov. 37 Even blaasops have been known to chew through nylon with their parrot like beaks. **1986** SMITH & HEEMSTRA *Smith's Sea Fishes* 894 Blaasops (or puffers) are so called because they can inflate their body by swallowing water (or air) to form an almost spherical, generally spiny ball to deter predators ... The skin, liver and particularly the ovaries of most (perhaps all) species of tetradontids contain a potent alkaloid poison called tetraodotoxin. **1993** R. VAN DER ELST *Guide to Common Sea Fishes* 377 Blackback blaasop, reference to its colour and ability to inflate itself.

3. Any of several species of burrowing frog of the genus *Breviceps* of the Microhylidae, characterized by their tendency to inflate themselves when alarmed. See also DONDER PADDA sense b, RAIN FROG.

1908 'BATRACHOS' in *E. London Dispatch* 23 Oct. 5 Another very curious frog is the 'Blas-op' .. [which] spends most of his time underground, coming only to the surface after very wet weather. **c1939** S.H. SKAIFE *S. Afr. Nature Notes* 208 A frog that .. blows itself up like a bladder when it is annoyed .. is called a *blaasop*. **1950** W. ROSE *Reptiles & Amphibians* 8 The number of eggs deposited varies greatly, from the twenty or so of the Chirping Frog or the Blaasop to the 24 000 odd of the Leopard Toad. **1973** *S. Afr. Panorama* Sept. 50 The Blaasop (*Breviceps adspersus adspersus*) often digs its way into a white-ant hill, and then comes out with the first rains. **1993** [see RAIN FROG].

blaasoppie /ˈblɑːsɔpi/ *n.* [Afk., *blaasop* see BLAASOP + -IE.] BLAASOP sense 2.

1983 M. DU PLESSIS *State of Fear* 95 It was an odd thing, bristling all over with stiff spines, and with its little whitish belly enormously puffed out. 'It's a *blaasoppie*, Frans,' Papa said. **1987** *Sunday Times* 15 Feb. 16 The Foreign Minister, Mr Pik Botha, should not puff himself up like a *blaasoppie* over the US Presidential Committee report on sanctions tabled this week.

blaatgham var. BLATJANG.

blaauwbok var. BLAUWBOK.

blaau(w)bosch var. BLOUBOS.

blaauwkop koggelmander see KOGGELMANDER sense 2.

blaauwkop koggelmannetjie see KOGGELMANNETJIE sense 2.

blaauw schimmel see SKIMMEL.

blaauw-tong var. BLAUWTONG.

blaawbok, blaawebock varr. BLAUWBOK.

blaaz-op var. BLAASOP.

black *n.* and *adj.* [Special senses of general Eng.]

A. *n.*

1. A relatively dark-skinned person, in any of the following senses (some of which are also in general Eng. use):

a. A member of any of the darker-skinned peoples of South Africa. See also sense B 2. Cf. sense c.

1616 A. CHILDE in R. Raven-Hart *Before Van Riebeeck* (1967) 85 The 17- 18- and 19th dayes wee mad way with ouar mene to remmedye and wattar ouar shepes and everey day expectinge ffreshe vetteles from the blackes to refreshe ouar mene butt they browte us nott aney. **1790** tr. F. *Le Vaillant's Trav.* I. 127 In this place there are two separate baths, one for the blacks, and another for the whites. **1815** G. BARKER Journal. 30 July, B^r P preached in the morning to about 70 blacks & B^r W to about 60 whites, & in the afternoon it was reversed. **1852** A. ESSEX in A. Rabone *Rec. of Pioneer Family* (1966) 19, I have no fear of either Hottentots or Kaffirs, and consequently no hatred towards them, but the pseudo-philanthropists and the self-righteous missionaries .. have no sympathy to spare for the plundered, ruined, bereaved Colonists, because all their attention is taken up by the Blacks among whom it is questionable if they have done any good. **1915** D. FAIRBRIDGE *Torch Bearer* 73 'What blacks?' he asked breathlessly. 'Kaffirs or Hottentots?'

b. A dark-skinned person of African origin, belonging to a people whose home language is of the Sintu (or Bantu) group; *hist.*, during the apartheid era, one classified as a 'Black' person; cf. AFRICAN *n.*[1] sense 1. See also *black black* (sense B 1 d), CLASSIFY, NON-BLACK.

'Black' has replaced 'African' (see AFRICAN *n.*[1]) as the (presently) most widely accepted term. In apartheid legislation, 'Black' was the last official racial designation applied to black African people, earlier terms being 'Native' (see NATIVE *n.* sense 1) and 'Bantu' (see BANTU *n.* sense 1), each in turn being judged offensive because used in apartheid terminology. See also KAFFIR sense 2 b (*derog.* and *offensive*). Cf. ASIAN, COLOURED, WHITE.

1696 J. OVINGTON *Voy. to Suratt* 283 This fair Country which the Blacks inhabit, is blest with a Soil as pregnant as the Days are pleasant. **1795** C.R. HOPSON tr. *C.P. Thunberg's Trav.* I. 262 If the mother is a Black or a Hottentot, but the father a Christian, who requires it to be baptized, it is baptized. **1819** G.J. ROGERS in G.M. Theal *Rec. of Cape Col.* (1902) XII. 159 No blacks to be suffered hereafter between the Fish river and a supposed line continued to the sea from where the Ghonap inclines towards the Fish River. **1824** W.J. BURCHELL *Trav.* II. 480 Mattivi's younger brother, *Mahura* whom I have before noticed as a young man of remarkably handsome countenance as a black. **1828** T. PHILIPPS *Lett.* (1960) 337 Chaka declares for universal dominion over the Blacks, hopes we will not assist the Kaffers. **1846** J.M. BOWKER *Speeches & Sel.* (1864) 258, I fear the blacks themselves will be left to cram that doctrine down the throats of our descendants with the bullet and the assegai. **1861** H. RABONE in A. Rabone *Rec. of Pioneer Family* (1966) 123, I have not the slightest disgust to blacks, or browns, can touch them, nurse them, and get on very well with their race. **1871** J. MCKAY *Reminisc.* 1 We for the first time saw veritable blacks in a state of nudity. **1880** *Alice Times* 16 Jan., Poor old Moirosi – hang it we are anti-black, but who could not admire that stubborn old dog? **1896** *Star* in J. Crwys-Williams *S. Afr. Despatches* (1989) 107 The great majority were whites, the Sisters in charge of the kaffir ward only having had three blacks under their care. **1921** W.C. SCULLY *Harrow* 47 'Well', he said, 'the arming and employment of blacks in this war may be right, or it may be wrong.' **1941** C.W. DE KIEWIET *Hist. of S. Afr.* 37 The effects of that disturbance were seen in friction and war between whites and blacks, in internecine struggles between the tribes themselves. **1968** J. LELYVELD in Cole & Flaherty *House of Bondage* 18 The men who work in that office are supposed to be expert at telling a white from a brown from a black. **1973** J. MEINTJES *Voortrekkers* 16 The name Kaffir is today offensive, but then it applied specifically to the blacks of the Eastern Cape, namely the ama-Xhosa nation. **1977** B.J. VORSTER *Letter to Voters* (pamphlet), It is our policy that the Blacks should govern themselves, that the Coloureds and Asians should manage their own affairs and should be co-responsible for matters of mutual interest. **1980** C. HERMER *Diary of Maria Tholo* 159 This term 'kaffir' .. was a derogatory one for a black person. It was replaced in South African usage by 'native', then 'bantu' and latterly 'black'. **1980** *Rand Daily Mail* 17 Nov. 8 Mr Bernstein was not in possession of the permit which non-blacks require to enter Soweto and other black areas. **1981** *Flying Springbok* Dec. 26 South Africa is building houses for Blacks and Browns at the rate of 5000 a month. **1983** H. OPPENHEIMER in *Rand Daily Mail* 12 Oct. 11 The advantages of coloured and Indian representation in Parliament are .. to be bought at the cost of further alienation of the blacks.

c. A member of a people or group which was disadvantaged by apartheid laws, i.e. a member of any but the white group. Cf. sense a, and NON-WHITE *n.*

Distinct from sense b above: see note at sense B 3.

1953 G. MAGWAZA in *Drum* Apr. 29 I've tried a couple of collective nouns for the lot: Non-Europeans, non-whites and whatnot. I'm fed up with these negatives ... I'm now toying with *blacks* and *non-blacks*. **1968** J. MAYET in *Drum* Sept. 8, I sometimes get the weird sensation that to the Whites who sit in their offices dreaming up new gimmicks to harass us and deciding where they should kick us out of or into next, we Blacks are not even people. **1970** *News/Check* 10 July 8 It is most significant that numbers of Coloured and Indian students are now beginning to identify with Africans – actually calling themselves 'blacks' and declaring that 'black is beautiful'. **1973** *Drum* 22 May 63, I am a Coloured ... I am not Black and I don't want to be included as a Black. **1973** *Evening Post* 14 July 1 More and more 'Blacks' (Africans, Coloureds and Indians) are reaching the limits of their patience. **1977** J. SIKAKANE *Window on Soweto* 13 In these areas moneyed Blacks composed of Africans, Indians, Chinese, Coloureds, Japanese, Malayans and Pakistanis built a famous beautiful township known as Sophiatown. **1986** P. MAYLAM *Hist. of Afr. People* 193 Whereas Africanism had tended to exclude Indians and coloureds, the black consciousness movement was keen to incorporate them as blacks. **1988** S. VOLLENHOVEN in *Frontline* Apr. 15 My mother objected to being called black and insisted she was coloured. **1989** *Reader's Digest Illust. Hist.* 487 Black, Person whose skin colour is not white. However, apartheid ideology refers only to Africans as 'blacks', and coloured, Indian and African people together as 'non-whites'. This book uses mainly the first definition.

d. Special Comb. **black-on-black** *adj.*, applied to violent or exploitive action seen as perpetrated by black people against black people; often in the phr. *black-on-black violence*; cf. *white-on-black* (see WHITE *n.* sense 2 b).

See note at FACTION.

1986 *Financial Mail* 13 June 6 Black-on-black violence erupts once again in Cape Town's squatter camps. **1986** *Rhodeo* (Rhodes Univ.) Aug. 11 The ideological impact of SABC television news coverage cannot be overestimated. Decontextualised scores of so-called 'black-on-black' violence and other 'black aggression' would seem to the average viewer to justify military and police intervention. **1987** 'A. AMAPHIXIPHIXI' in *Frontline* Mar. 38 Is it wrong to be exploited by whites and right when it is black-on-black exploitation? **1987** *New Nation* 5 Nov. 6 The conflict has been passed off as another case of inter-tribal and 'black-on-black violence'. **1988** *Now Everyone Is Afraid* (Catholic Inst. for Internat. Rel.) 67 The state likes to use terms like 'black-on-black violence' or 'faction fights' to describe internal township conflict. Words like these are used to place the blame for the violence with the black community rather than the apartheid system. **1989** *Reader's Digest Illust. Hist.* 480 A new and devastating form of killing that was primarily reserved for what became known as 'black-on-black' violence: the murder of alleged African collaborators. **1990** *Sunday Times* 1 Apr. 7 Black-on-black incidents have also been reported. Black shoppers who defied the boycott were forced to eat detergent and steel wool .. , residents claim. **1990** *City Press* 17 June 11 The black-on-black violence .. involves Inkatha, ANC, PAC and BCM members. **1990** *Sash* Vol.33 No.1, 19 It will become generally known .. that the conflict is not a matter simply of black on black violence or even simply of a UDF/Inkatha struggle for power but that there are many complicating factors.

2. *Ostrich-farming.* A long black feather from a cock ostrich, taken from the place where the wing joins the body. Also *attrib.* See also ONDERBAATJIE. Cf. BLACK BUTT.

c1881 A. DOUGLASS *Ostrich Farming* 75 The black and drab feathers .. protect the quill feathers for the first four months of their growth. *Ibid.* 82 The blacks and drabs should each be run into seven different lengths, with a bunch each of broken feathers, and one each of floss. **1896** R. WALLACE *Farming Indust. of Cape Col.* 235 'Black' is the long growth on the part of the wing near to the junction with the body of the male .. and 'drab' is the corresponding growth on the female ... Blacks were very irregular, and .. rates on the average declined — long and medium, 10s. to 15s. per lb., and medium and medium short about 15 per cent. **1909** J.E. DUERDEN in *Agric. Jrnl of Cape of G.H.* XXXIV. 523 Blacks .. include the first and second rows of wing coverts of the cock, and also the feathers sometimes plucked from the upper borders of the humerus. **1911** O. EVANS in S. Playne *Cape Col.* 55 Two rows of blacks .. act as guards over the prime whites.

B. *adj.*

1. Of or pertaining to dark-skinned people of African origin whose home languages belong to the Sintu (Bantu) group. Cf. AFRICAN *adj.*[1] sense 2 a.

a. Applied to a person or persons: belonging to a people whose language is of the Sintu (Bantu) group (cf. sense A 1 b).

1795 C.R. HOPSON tr. *C.P. Thunberg's Trav.* I. 136 A traveller who has not been provident enough to bring water with him, has no other resource .. than strictly to examine, whether any black shepherds are to be found attending their master's flocks in the neighbourhood. **1828** G. BARKER Journal. 11 Nov., The fourth case, was for stealing, a black boy. **1837** J.E. ALEXANDER *Narr. of Voy.* I. 333 Even the little black urchins in the streets were calling out to one another, .. 'There goes the Kaffir! shoot him dead!' **1847** J. BARROW *Reflect.* 143 A black boy and a smart Hottentot took charge of my horses. **1853** T. SHONE Diary. 12 Jan., I see a black man flogged. He got 50 lashes. **1905** P. GIBBON *Vrouw Grobelaar* 85 Ask an old wise Kafir, not a young one that has forgotten the wisdom of the black people and learned the foolishness only of the white. **1936** WILLIAMS & MAY *I Am Black* 149 You know how we Zulus look with scorn upon the other black people of the land ... Now I say to you that all the tribes of all the nations are but one people, the Black People. **1942** U. KRIGE *Dream & Desert* (1953) 119 We white South Africans have no real confidence in ourselves, we're afraid our black countrymen might use those weapons against us later. **1961** T.V. BULPIN *White Whirlwind* 304 These fellows from the Cape are black or coloured, but the Matabele hate them, so they are in the same cart as us. **1969** A. FUGARD *Boesman & Lena* 20 Lena: It's a hard life for us brown people hey. Boesman: He's not brown people, he's black people. **1970** N.D. THEBEHALI in *Post* 5 May 5 When I call myself a Bantu, a White man is thrilled; and when I call myself a Black man, a White gets angry. **1975** *S. Afr. Panorama* Dec. 2 Today Afrikaans is spoken by over five million white, Coloured, Asian and Black South Africans. **1986** *E. Prov. Herald* 10 Apr. 2 The municipality fired 215 black workers at the hostel and employed coloured labourers in their place. **1991** *Census 91* (Central Statistical Service) (*pamphlet*), 'Black language' means any language of the Black population groups, e.g. North Sotho, Xhosa, Zulu, etc.

b. Of, pertaining to, intended for, or predominantly used by those whose home language is of the Sintu (Bantu) group.

1949 A.G. BARLOW in *Hansard* 24 May 6462 There is no one man who does not shiver in his shoes when he thinks of this great black problem we have in this country that may overwhelm us at any time. **1961** T. MATSHIKIZA *Choc. for my Wife* 75 That conversation took me back to Black South Africa where I had become used to, and grown to love, being called 'black' man. **1973** *E. Prov. Herald* 27 Mar. 1 Many of those in the queue became angry and .. Mr Percy T—, manager of Computicket, personally came out of the stadium to escort them to one of the 'Black' gates. **1975** S. ROBERTS *Outside Life's Feast* 42 'I thought you were not allowed to use negative terms like non-white ... I thought your radical-liberal boyfriend insisted on positive statements.' .. 'Had I said a black cinema hall, .. you would have asked me if the décor was black.' **1979** *Sunday Times* 10 June (Business Times) 29 Knowledge of black languages and experience in instructional work and driving will be an advantage. **1980** *Govt Gaz.* Vol.182 No.7147, 5 The performance of the functions of a messenger according to Black law in respect of the exercise of the judicial power of any person on whom such power has been conferred. **1982** *Pretoria News* 21 Sept. 14 (*advt*) Black Salespeople. Here is your chance to join the leaders in the black furniture trade. *c*1985 C. GARDNER in *Eng. Academy Rev.* 3 82 The phrase 'the black experience' is less common now than it was five or seven years ago, but it retains a great deal of pregnant and precise meaning. **1986** *Grocott's Mail* 23 May 10 The detention of people involved in the arena of black education is becoming the order of the day. **1988** G. RATHBONE in *Cape Times* 8 Jan. (Suppl.) 8 If one isn't playing indigenous 'black' sounds, one generally has to play to a white audience, and vice versa. **1989** A. DONALDSON in *Style* Aug. 98 The industry, to put it mildly, is huge: Investment in black taxis is estimated at R3000-million.

c. Of a town or area: in the v. phr. *to go black*, to be officially incorporated into a HOMELAND.

1974 *E. Prov. Herald* 2 Aug., Peddie declared Black village ... It was business as usual yesterday after an announcement .. that the village would go Black from September. **1978** *Weekend Post* 28 Oct. 8 The town went black in 1975, a year before Transkei's independence.

d. As a distinguishing epithet in Special Comb. **black-belt** *nonce*, an area or areas in which black townships are situated (see TOWNSHIP sense 2 a); also *attrib.*; **black black** [*black* 'dark skinned, of African origin, speaking one of the Sintu (Bantu) group of languages as home language' (see sense a) + *black* 'one who is not white' (see sense A 1 c)], a dark-skinned person of African origin and whose home language belongs to the Sintu (Bantu) group; see also note at sense 3; AFRICAN *n.*[1] sense 1; **black danger**, SWART GEVAAR sense 1; **black market**, the black consumer market; also *attrib.*; **black time**, AFRICAN TIME *n. phr.*

1968 COLE & FLAHERTY *House of Bondage* 61 Rush-hour trains to the white suburbs are rarely more than three minutes apart. Similar trains to **black-belt** destinations lag as much as half an hour apart. **1987** D. TUTU *Informant, Cape Town* Isn't 99 [-year leasehold] mainly for **black blacks**? **1988** N. MATHIANE in *Frontline* Oct. 31 When applying for overseas scholarships, the Indians get the bulk of the money because they are studying Masters and fancy degrees while the black-black is battling on a first degree maybe. **1969** M. BENSON *At Still Point* (1988) 84 You know, Miss Dawson, you liberals ought to worry about us Afrikaners. *We* are the ones faced with the **black danger** and UNO. **1986** *Sunday Times* 13 Jul. (Business Times) 16 (*advt*) **Black market** toiletries ... This means taking over a product group whose flagship is a generic name in the Black Market. **1990** A. CLARKE in *Frontline* Sept. 26 Was he trying to impress me that he was working around the clock? .. Was it something to do with '**black time**'?

2. Of or for the various darker-skinned peoples of South Africa; cf. BROWN *adj.* sense 3. See also sense A 1 a.

1841 B. SHAW *Memorials* 87, I am happy, however, to state, that in my journey to Cape Town, and other places, I have held service where white and black people were mingled in the same congregation. **1854** R.J. MULLINS Diary. 5 On Tuesdays and Fridays the bishop has a 'black' school in the evenings, well attended. I heard an old Malay woman read a chapter of St. Luke in Dutch. **1953** G. MAGWAZA in *Drum* Nov. 51 The whites would like to know how black people want to be called ... They're Africans, but this is not as inclusive as 'black' or 'white.' All black people are not Africans, just as all white people are not English!

3.a. Of a person or persons from any of those groups which were historically disadvantaged by apartheid laws, i.e. from any but the white group; cf. NON-WHITE *adj.* sense 1. See also sense A 1 c.

This use of 'black', with its ideological connotations, is distinct from that in sense 2. Since the early 1970s it has been part of the philosophy of the *Black Consciousness Movement* (see BLACK CONSCIOUSNESS sense 2), emphasizing (as grounds for political solidarity) the common predicament of those who were discriminated against under apartheid; it has met with mixed responses from those whom it is used to describe.

1970 *Daily News* 9 June, Students at the University of Natal Medical School .. have decided to call themselves 'Black' rather than 'non-European' students. **1970** *E. Prov. Herald* 4 Sept., Blacks — a term used more and more by non-Europeans, who hate the term 'non-Whites' and who are developing a 'Black Power' concept that they hope will unite Africans, Coloureds, Malays and Indians in a solid 'Black' front opposing White domination. **1972** *Argus* 10 Aug. 3 The amendment .. asked the council to reject Black consciousness as well as the term 'Black' and expressed the party's association with the term Coloured. **1973** *Survey of Race Rel.* (S.A.I.R.R.) 25 It is recognised that not all Coloured people and Asians — or indeed Africans — wish to be referred to as 'Black'; but the consensus of opinion appears to be that this term is preferable to 'Non-White'. **1973** *Argus* 16 June 4 Why, for example, did the Coloured student call himself Black. 'He is Black because he is positively not White,' Mr Small said. **1987** *Drum* Apr. 44 Hassan Mall .. is South Africa's first black judge. **1988** E. BONELLE in *Black Enterprise* Vol.13, 17, I am a Coloured woman who prefers to be called Black simply because I identify with my ancestors and my granny, a Black woman, reared me. **1989** T. BOTHA in *Style* Dec. 161 The Malays came. They saw. They were conquered ... Children learn the Arabic of old, while old men greet you with the black handshake of the young. **1990** D. BECKETT in *Frontline* Mar.-Apr. 22 I've heard that some coloured people like to be called 'black' ... I mean people who are classified 'coloured' but consider themselves 'black'. **1990** R. MALAN *My Traitor's Heart* 182 The court was so white, so Western, and Simon so black — or more truly, so African. The psychiatrist who ultimately testified in the Hammerman's defense was also 'black', also a victim of apartheid — but he was Indian, not African, and as culturally alien from Simon as I was.

b. Pertaining to, intended for, or predominantly used by groups which were historically disadvantaged by apartheid laws, i.e. by all but the white group; NON-WHITE *adj.* sense 2.

1970 Minutes of Meeting. (Rhodes University S.R.C.) 3 May, At a recent Student Body meeting the students of the Black section of the University of Natal voted to change the name of their institution from UNNE (University of Natal Non-European) to UNB (University of Natal Black Section). **1972** J. SCOTT in J. Crwys-Williams *S. Afr. Despatches* (1989) 407 You .. enter the station your end, then come back along the platform to the point where the black coaches end and the white ones begin. I'll meet you there and we can talk about how the different races are finding one another. **1974** *Cape Times* 3 Jan. 8 Is it my sense of humour that makes me think that 'the Coloured people', or Black South Africa on the whole, need not feel too bad about their incapacity. **1976** *Cape Herald* 6 July 4 Double shifts up in Black schools. In one year double shift classes in Coloured schools increased by 140. **1978** J. ESSOP in *Argus* 23 Jan. 10, I couldn't go to the 'black' station via the 'white' entrance and had to go via Strand Street. **1979** *E. Prov. Herald* 21 Mar. 10 The black coaches need to be re-coupled so that they can arrive at the black sections of the stations at the journey's respective ends. **1985** PLATZKY & WALKER *Surplus People* 80 The Act tried to encourage black people to think of themselves as 'coloured' and 'Indian' and 'African', rather than as blacks or workers or oppressed people who had many problems in common. **1988** T. ANDERS in *Star* 9 Aug. 5 A local Indian businessman was recently given back the R100 he had paid for a .. raffle ticket because the right-wing school management board decided it would not accept 'black money'.

black bream *n. phr.* The GALJOEN (sense 1), *Coracinus capensis.*

1949 [see DAMBA]. **1955** C. HORNE *Fisherman's Eldorado* 16 The fish known in the Cape as galjoen becomes damba in the Eastern Province-Transkei littoral, and galjoen or black bream in Natal. **1979** SNYMAN & KLARIE *Free from Sea* 30 *Galjoen, Highwater, Damba, Blackbream, Blackfish.* Aptly named after that stately Spanish sailing vessel – the galleon – and unique to South African waters. **1984** [see BLACKFISH sense 1]. **1985** [see GALJOEN sense 1].

black butt *n. phr. ?Obs. Ostrich-farming.* A feather with a black butt-end, taken from between the tail and the tail covert of a cock ostrich. Cf. BLACK *n.* sense 2. See also TAIL.

1896 R. WALLACE *Farming Indust. of Cape Col.* 235 Black Butts .. were 2s. per lb. dearer. **1909** J.E. DUERDEN in *Agric. Jrnl of Cape of G.H.* XXXIV. 524 The feathers intermediate between the tails and tail coverts are known as *Tails, Black Butts* (B.B.).

Black Circuit *n. phr. Hist.* A circuit court held in 1812 which heard charges brought by missionaries against a number of Cape farmers accused of having ill-treated their black servants. See also CIRCUIT COURT.

[**1909** C.D. HOPE *Our Place in Hist.* 101 The occasion [*sc.* of circuit courts] was chosen by the friends of the Hottentots to bring accusation of cruelty and ill-treatment against every white man whose servants complained of any grievance. These 'Black Assizes' lasted for three years, and far the greater number of cases were proved to be based on false evidence or on foolish exaggeration.] *c***1934** M. ANDREWS *Story of S. Afr.* 25 Two missionaries brought charges of great cruelty and even of murder against a number of farmers ... The effect of 'the Black Circuit,' as the court of 1812 was called, was to turn the farmers against the missionaries and British methods of administering justice. **1936** *Cambridge Hist. of Brit. Empire* VIII. 285 The first Circuit in 1811 was uneventful ... The second, which set out from Cape Town in September 1812, was destined to make history. Expressly charged with the investigation of numerous missionary complaints in addition to several Crown prosecutions, it has become well known as the 'Black' Circuit. **1955** L. MARQUARD *Story of S. Afr.* 111 In 1811, circuit courts .. were instituted to visit the districts periodically. It was a much-needed reform .. but its use by the missionaries in the so-called Black Circuit of 1812 made it unpopular with frontiersmen, who were not accustomed to a legal system that interfered between them and their servants. **1963** W.M. MACMILLAN *Bantu, Boer & Briton* 8 Two of the earliest assertions of authority, the Black Circuit of 1812, and the execution of white men for a rebellion at Slagter's Nek in 1815, are long remembered grievances. **1967** E. ROSENTHAL *Encycl. of Sn Afr.* 62 'Black Circuit,' Name given by Cape Colonists to a Circuit Court held in 1812 ... The Black Circuit caused much ill-feeling, and was regarded as a major cause of the Great Trek. **1970** *Std Encycl. of Sn Afr.* II. 352 'Black Circuit,' Special session of the Circuit Court of the Cape of Good Hope exclusively for the trial of whites who, according to two missionaries of the London Missionary Society, had murdered or maltreated Hottentots. **1973** J. MEINTJES *Voortrekkers* 25 A Circuit Court was launched in 1811 by Lord Caledon, admirable in intent and non-racial, but soon to become notorious as the Black Circuit.

Black Consciousness *n. phr.* Also with small initials.

1. A political ideology which defines as 'black people' all those who have been disadvantaged under apartheid, and which urges them to be strongly aware of their common experience of racially-based oppression, thus developing political solidarity, formulating ideas, and taking action independently (esp. of the ideas and actions of whites, whether sympathetic or not); BC. Also *attrib.*

'Black Consciousness' emerged in the late 1960s among black university students who were dissatisfied with the attitudes of their white liberal colleagues in student organizations. It rejects all white political initiatives as inevitably slanted, criticizes the African National Congress and the South African Communist Party for the class basis to their ideologies, and differs from AFRICANISM in not reserving the label 'black' for people of the Sintu language-groups and in not insisting on Africanization as a primary aim for post-apartheid South Africa. See also BLACK *n.* sense 1 c, and BLACK *adj.* sense 3.

1972 *Daily Dispatch* 26 July 14 We fear the Nationalists still do not perceive the full significance of the new black consciousness. **1973** *Survey of Race Rel.* (S.A.I.R.R.) 26 Members of Black Consciousness organizations, in particular students, have rejected White liberals. *a***1977** S. BIKO in S. Ndaba *One Day in June* (1986) 29 What is Black Consciousness? In essence this is an attitude of mind and a way of life ... Its unadulterated quintessence is the realisation by the black man of the need to rally together with his brothers around the cause of their oppression – the blackness of their skin – and to operate as a group in order to rid themselves of the shackles that bind them to perpetual servitude. **1977** A. BOESAK *Farewell to Innocence* 12 Getting rid of an implanted slave mentality is central to the philosophy of Black Consciousness. **1978** *Daily Dispatch* 24 May 11 Chief Sebe said black consciousness was nothing more than 'apartheid in reverse'. **1981** *Voice* 10 June 5 Black Consciousness therefore can not be called a racist philosophy since it seeks to eradicate such inequalities and conflicts in our society and establishes an open and egalitarian society. **1983** C. SAUNDERS *Hist. Dict.* 26 Black Consciousness .. was much criticised by the *African National Congress* for placing too much emphasis on race, for being elitist and out of touch with the masses, and for not accepting the *Freedom Charter.* The PAC was more sympathetic, even claiming, without justification, that it was responsible for the introduction of Black Consciousness into South Africa. Several former members of the PAC were .. among the leading figures in the Black Consciousness Movement. **1986** P. VAN NIEKERK in *New Statesman* (U.K.) 13 June 21 The chief proponent of Black consciousness, the Azanian People's Organisation (AZAPO) has widespread popular support in Soweto, symbolically the most important of all the Black townships. **1987** *New Nation* 23 Apr. 9 The Black Consciousness (BC) theorists tried to avoid racial or ethnic concepts. Blackness was defined by oppression, not race, and could embrace Indians and coloured people as well as Africans ... Whites who wished to contribute .. should confine themselves to attempting to 'conscientise' their white compatriots. **1990** A. DANGOR in *Staffrider* Vol.9 No.2, 33, I have developed from a position of commitment to Black Consciousness in the seventies to non-racialism in the eighties but I still believe that the values of black self-assertion and emancipation put forward by Black Consciousness are relevant to me today if they do not preclude upholding a non-racial political philosophy. **1991** F.G. BUTLER *Local Habitation* 188 Aelred Stubbs, a charming, elongated Etonian devoted to the cause of black consciousness, and a great admirer of its leader, Steve Biko.

2. *comb.* **Black Consciousness Movement**, a collective name for those organizations subscribing to the principles of Black Consciousness; the actions of these groups, esp. those aimed at increasing the support given to Black Consciousness; BCM. See also BPC.

1977 *Daily Dispatch* 3 Aug. 9 The identification of the committee with the black consciousness movement was .. referred to in an article yesterday in Die Transvaler. **1977** *Times* (U.K.) 20 Oct. 1 The South African Government, in an effort to suppress the country's black consciousness movement and stifle domestic criticism of its racial policies, yesterday banned 18 anti-apartheid organizations, closed two newspapers and arrested between 50 and 70 black leaders. **1982** *E. Prov. Herald* 6 Nov. 3 The organisation gave financial assistance to the ANC, PAC and various other organisations known collectively as the Black Consciousness Movement. **1987** *Star* 2 Jan. 13 The exiled Black Consciousness Movement urged 'solidarity in the ranks of the oppressed'. **1987** M. BENSON *At Still Point* (1988) 243 Steve Biko and other young Blacks from that area [*sc.* the Eastern Cape] were to found the Black Consciousness Movement, helping to inspire the 1976 uprising when Black schoolchildren in Soweto confronted heavily armed police. **1991** *E. Prov. Herald* 17 May 5 Mr Pityana was a leading figure in the Black Consciousness movement in the late 60s and 70s .. a co-leader with the late Steve Biko.

black eagle *n. phr.* Also with initial capitals. The large eagle *Aquila verreauxii* of the Accipitridae, black with a white 'V' on back and rump; BERGHAAN sense 1; DASSIEVANGER; *Kaffrarian eagle*, see KAFFRARIAN; VERREAUX'S EAGLE. Also *attrib.*

1908 HAAGNER & IVY *Sketches* 55 The powerful Black Eagle (*Aquila verreauxi*), called by the Boers the Dassievanger (dassie-catcher) from its fondness for Rock-rabbits. **1918** [see DASSIEVANGER]. **1936** E.L. GILL *First Guide to S. Afr. Birds* 128 *Black Eagle, Dassievanger, Verreaux's eagle,* .. A large and fine eagle, jet black all over except for a white band down the centre of back and rump. **1937** M. ALSTON *Wanderings* 81, I came upon two large eagles, the Verreaux's or black eagles – 'les Caffres' of Le Vaillant. **1964** L.G. GREEN *Old Men Say* 163 King of the more than one hundred and fifty species of Cape Peninsula birds .. is the black eagle or *dassievanger.* **1973** J. COWDEN *For Love* 38 Known in South Africa as the Black Eagle, Witkruis arend (white cross eagle), Dassie-vanger (dassie catcher) and, by the Zulus, as uKozi .. it is found now only in the mountain vastnesses and is not often seen. *Ibid.* 52 Nature .. allows only one egg to play a part in perpetuating the black eagle species. Even if both eggs hatched, only one would live. **1990** *Weekly Mail* 6 July (Weekend Mail) 13 The magnificent Black Eagle lives in mountainous territory all over Africa – from the Cape to Arabia.

blackfish *n.* [Transf. use of Eng. *black fish* a name given to several varieties of fish; see quot. 1984.] In KwaZulu-Natal (and formerly in the Eastern Cape):

1. The GALJOEN (sense 1), *Coracinus capensis.*

1905 H.E.B. BROOKING in *E. London Dispatch* 8 Apr. 3 Shaped much like the black-fish or galjeon. **1930** [see HIGHWATER]. **1949**, **1971** [see DAMBA]. **1979** [see BLACK BREAM]. **1984** *Cape Times* 13 Jan. (Funfinder) 12 Facts about galjoen are: .. Those taken near rocks are almost black (also known in Natal as blackfish or black bream).

2. *?obs.* The marine cavebass, *Dinoperca petersi* of the Dinopercidae.

1913 C. PETTMAN *Africanderisms* 61 *Black-fish,* .. In Natal the name is applied to *Dinoperea queketti.* **1947** K.H. BARNARD *Pict. Guide to S. Afr. Fishes* 106 *Queketts Blackfish,* (Dinoperca queketti) ... A well-known Natal fish remarkable for the high, square-cut soft dorsal fin. **1949** J.L.B. SMITH *Sea Fishes* 199 *Dinoperca Petersii ... Lantern Fish. Butterbream* (Pondoland). *Butterfish. Blackfish.*

black, green, and gold *n. phr.* and *adj. phr.* Also **black, gold and green**. The colours of the African National Congress, used allusively of that organization or of its members.

A. *n. phr.*

1990 D. VAN HEERDEN in *Sunday Times* 16 Sept. 21 Listening to ANC leaders one gets the impression they – and only they – are as innocent as lambs ... The only righteous people in Gomorrah wear black, green and gold.

B. *adj. phr.*

[**1963** M. BENSON *Afr. Patriots* 116 The parade was the biggest ever seen in Johannesburg: 20,000 Africans with a few people of other races followed the two brass bands and the leaders carrying the flags –

the A.N.C.'s black green and gold flag waved alongside those of the victorious Allies. **1989** *Weekly Mail* 15 Dec. 27 Dressed in black, green and gold skirts, the choir sang: 'Listen when the children speak'.] **1992** 'HOGARTH' in *Sunday Times* 26 Apr. 24 Comrade MP .. Pierre C— .. left the DP for black, gold and greener pastures this week.

blackhead *n.* Also with initial capital.
1. [Transf. use of Eng. *black-head* a name given to various bird species.] Either of two bird species:
a. *obs.* In Natal, any of several species of bulbul, esp. *Pycnonotus barbatus* of the Pycnonotidae. See also TOPPIE *n.*¹

> **1899** R.B. & J.D.S. WOODWARD *Natal Birds* 21 Boys often call this bird [*sc. Pycnonotus layardi*] the 'Blackhead'. **1913** C. PETTMAN *Africanderisms* 62 *Blackhead*, (1) In Natal *Pycnonotus layardi* is so named. **1923** HAAGNER & IVY *Sketches* 86 These Bulbuls .. are known by various 'local' or vernacular names such as 'Tiptol' in the Eastern Cape, .. 'Topknot' or 'Black Head' in Natal.

b. In the Eastern Cape, the canary *Serinus alario* of the Fringillidae; also called *berg canary* (see BERG sense 1 b ii).

> **1913** C. PETTMAN *Africanderisms* 62 *Blackhead*, .. in the Eastern Province of the Cape Colony the *Alario alario* is so called. See Berg canarie. **1923** HAAGNER & IVY *Sketches* 147 A favourite little songbird is the dainty little Mountain Canary (*Alario alario*) familiarly called the 'Black-head' by the schoolboys of the Eastern Cape Province. **1936** E.L. GILL *First Guide to S. Afr. Birds* 18 Mountain Canary, Blackhead, Swartkoppie, Bergkanarie; *Alario alario*. **1958** I. VAUGHAN *Diary* 52 They are cape canarys, blackheads and geel sysies. Now he has 20 blackheads. **1962** W.R. SIEGFRIED *Some Protected Birds* (1967) Pl.169 *Mountain Canary, Black-headed Canary, Black-head*. A familiar bird of the dry western areas and a popular cage-bird.

2. In the n. phrr. *Blackhead Persian* and *Blackheaded Persian* [see PERSIAN], a hardy non-woolled sheep with a black head and neck, and white body; PERSIAN. Also *attrib.* See also DORPER *n.*², VAN ROOY.

The breed is used principally in cross-breeding, and for improved mutton production.

> **1953** *S. Afr. Stockbreeder & Farmer Ref. Bk* 230 The non-woolled sheep are mostly fat-tailed, e.g. the indigenous Namaqua and Ronderib Afrikaner, the Blackhead Persian and the van Rooy. *Ibid.* 231 The Blackhead Persian found to-day in South Africa is superior to its progenitors found in Arabia and Somaliland ... Blackhead Persian stud sheep have been registered in the South African Stud Book since its inception in 1906. **1955** J.H. WELLINGTON *Sn Afr.: Geog. Study* II. 69 Non-woolled sheep .. such as the Blackhead Persian, the Africander, [etc.]. **1957** [see DORPER *n.*²]. **1966** [see PERSIAN]. **1973** W.J. HUGO in *Std Encycl. of Sn Afr.* VIII. 509 The Black-headed Persian has made a very important contribution to the development of Karakul breeding in South Africa.

black jack *n. phr.* [Special senses of general Eng.] Also with initial capitals.
1. [Perh. comparing the shape of the black seed with a bludgeon, in U.S. Eng. called a *blackjack*.] The weed *Bidens pilosa* of the Asteraceae; its barbed black seed. Also *attrib.*

> **1877** LADY BARKER *Yr's Hsekeeping* 130 An innocent-looking plant, .. bearing a most aggravating tuft of little black spires, which lose no opportunity of sticking to one's petticoats in myriads. They are familiarly known as 'black jacks', and can hold their own as pests with any weed of my acquaintance. **1900** O. OSBORNE *In Land of Boers* 171 It was discovered that I had harvested a few loads of 'black jack' grass, that harpooned around, crawled through blankets and clothes, and jabbed into everybody with such ferocity that I was condemned to cast the whole hayrick and a-half away. **1931** O. LETCHER *Afr. Unveiled* 39 The burrs and black-jacks had been carefully picked out of the neatly rolled putties. **1956** P. BECKER *Sandy Tracks* 118 We struggled through groups of prickly-pear, a dense growth of burrs and blackjacks, and an entanglement of branches and undergrowth. *c***1957** D. SWANSON *Highveld, Lowveld & Jungle* 65 The tiny spiteful spines of blackjack plants insinuated themselves into his legs and ankles. **1974** *Grocott's Mail* 9 Apr., The paths are full of blackjack and weeds. **1981** *Fair Lady* 9 Sept. 242 The herbaceous border is well under control and there's never a dandelion or blackjack in sight. **1990** *Grocott's Mail* 2 Mar. 9 Although the Black jack is widely regarded as a pest, it is also one of the most widely used weeds of cultivation and the young shoots and leaves can be eaten as a vegetable.

2. *slang.* [See quot. 1966.]
a. A derisive name for a township municipal policeman. Also *attrib.* See also COUNCIL POLICE.

> **1966** K.M.C. MOTSISI in *Post* 30 Jan. (Drum) 16 There are the Municipal cops who the township wits call Black Jacks, so called because of their black uniform. **1977** P.C. VENTER *Soweto* 125 A Black Jack is Soweto's wry nickname for a non-white member of the municipal police, a force primarily concerned with administrative duties and the collection of accumulated rent. **1977** [see ILLEGAL *adj.*]. **1983** *City Press* 9 Oct. 1 The journalists protested against .. 'blackjacks' who attacked squatters, churchmen and members of the Press in Katlehong this week, leaving several hurt. **1987** *Pace* Oct. 4 There was this half-baked Soweto Town council cop who was pleading with people to stop calling them 'black jacks' ... These cops used to dress in black uniforms and as a result they were called 'black jacks' ... Today they wear green attire ... Somebody has responded to their plea. He calls them 'green beans'. **1989** M. TYALA in *Sunday Times* 29 Jan. 7 The blackjacks quickly earned a reputation for ruthlessness and bad manners. Scores of deaths in the Vaal Triangle alone were attributed to blackjack and kitskonstabel guns. **1990** [see Malan quot. at GREEN BEAN].

b. With distinguishing epithet: **flying black-jack**, *?nonce*, a member of the municipal flying squad.

> **1969** O. MUSI in *Post* 15 June 14 Three 'flying blackjacks' in their new vans will .. speed out to your rescue.

Black Napoleon *n. phr.* A name given to the Zulu chief Shaka (d. 1828) because of his ability as a military strategist and the fear he invoked as a conqueror.

> [**1882** W.R. LUDLOW *Zululand & Cetewayo* 190 He had an illegitimate son, whose name was Tschaka, or 'the bastard.' This child .. was destined to be the 'Napoleon' of South Africa.] **1963** A. KEPPEL-JONES *S. Afr.: Short Hist.* 58 The rise of the 'Black Napoleon', Shaka. *c***1963** B.C. TAIT *Durban Story* 8 Shaka .. had devastated the country ... The Cape colonists called him 'Black Napoleon'. **1970** *Std Encycl. of Sn Afr.* II. 212 Shaka, the 'black Napoleon', perfecting the method of attack. **1981** GRÜTTER & VAN ZYL *Story of S. Afr.* 22 Tshaka has aptly been called the Black Napoleon, for he introduced an unheard-of state of military readiness, personally leading his men on many battlefields ... The men were efficiently trained, as in a modern army. **1982** *Pace* Feb. 150 Trying to find ways to resurrect the 'Black Napoleon,' Tshaka.

black peril *n. phr.* Also with initial capitals. [Prob. tr. Afk. *swart gevaar*.]
1. *Obs. exc. hist.*
a. Usu. *attrib.*, a euphemism for (sexual) assault on a white woman by a black man. **b.** One who is guilty of such an assault.

> [**1902** *Volkstem* 10 May 13 *Zwarte gevaar*, Vrouw te Bloemfontein aangerand.] **1908** D. BLACKBURN *Leaven* (1991) 106 The more the kafir was enlightened — the nearer he was brought to moral and intellectual equality with the white — the less likely was he to be a 'Black Peril'. **1911** *Farmer's Weekly* 4 Oct. 115 This system of employing men in our households is pernicious and has led to a considerable number of the 'black peril' cases. **1913** V.R. MARKHAM *S. Afr. Scene* 279 Another difficult and unpalatable subject, which raises the most acute and violent of all racial antipathies, namely what are known as 'black peril' cases. That attacks of this character on white women should rouse Europeans to the highest pitch of fury is most comprehensible. **1923** G.H. NICHOLLS *Bayete!* 244 The news of the Black Peril outrage, occurring as it did to the person and in the house of such a well-known and important lady as Mrs Stultz, caused a hysteria of leading articles in the Press. *Ibid.* 245 The recommendation of the Black Peril Commission regarding the employment of black male domestics should be at once made law. [**1924** E.T. JOLLIE *Real Rhodesia* (1971) 276 Rhodesia has a good record as to Black Peril cases, but there is no doubt that as the native becomes more sophisticated the danger increases.] **1980** D.B. COPLAN *Urbanization of African Performing Arts.* 143 By 1908, their [*sc.* the Amalaita's] membership and activities were changing in response to the commanding social issue of the day, the 'Black Peril.' The Black Peril controversy ostensibly centered on the rising crime rate among Blacks ... In particular, Whites expressed fear of sexual assaults on White women, so many of whom spent their days in close contact with male African domestic servants.

2. SWART GEVAAR sense 1.

> **1960** C. HOOPER *Brief Authority* 21 We whites .. imprison ourselves in the stale airs of our spiritual laager; we man the defences .. against a long dead Black Peril. **1972** *Daily Dispatch* 1 Mar. 1 These rights were scrapped by white South Africa in the light of what they call 'the black peril' or 'swart gevaar' or simply their fear of being swamped by hordes of blacks. **1973** Y. BURGESS *Life to Live* 137 The talk at the time was of the 'Swart Gevaar', the Black Peril, which some thought referred to some new kind of disease, and that, in a way, was how the coiners of the ugly phrase meant it. **1974** [see *To the Point* quot. at SWART GEVAAR sense 1]. **1985** *Time* 5 Aug. 12 The Botha reforms have helped convince the right wing that the President is not sufficiently aware of *die swart gevaar* (the black peril). **1990** G. SLOVO *Ties of Blood* 106 The Nationalist Party which had gone to the polls on the twin slogans of 'Segregate the Black' and 'Save the Poor White', formed a coalition with the Labour Party. Together they came into office dedicated to fighting the black peril. **1990** *Ibid.* [see NAT *n.* sense a]. **1991** [see SWART GEVAAR sense 1].

Black Pimpernel *n. phr. Colloq.* [BLACK + Eng. *pimpernel* someone elusive and much sought after, alluding to the *Scarlet Pimpernel*, the name given to Sir Percy Blakeney, a heroic character created by Baroness Orczy.] A nickname given by news reporters to Nelson Mandela during his period in hiding in 1961.

> **1962** *Guardian* (U.K.) 9 Aug. 7 The man who has become known as the 'Black Pimpernel of South Africa'. **1989** *Weekly Mail* 13 Oct. 6 In March 1961 he [*sc.* Nelson Mandela] went into hiding to defy his banning order, but emerged at the Pietermaritzburg All-in-Africa conference and was made honorary secretary of the All-in-National Council. Nicknamed the 'Black Pimpernel', he remained underground for the next 17 months. **1990** *City Press* 11 Feb. 6 He and Sisulu travelled around the country secretly organising the strike and Mandela (nicknamed the Black Pimpernel) remained a fugitive for the next 17 months. **1990** T. MATHEWS et al. in *Newsweek* 19 Feb. 25 He gave interviews from phone boxes to reporters, who started calling him the Black Pimpernel. **1993** H. TYSON *Editors under Fire* 10 He could not know while he was the dashing, active 'Black Pimpernel' ('They seek him here, they seek him there ...') that he was soon to become the world's most famous prisoner.

Black Sash *n. phr.* [Named for the broad black sashes worn by members at protest vigils as a symbol of mourning.]
a. *obs.* A protest campaign by the Women's Defence of the Constitution League, organized in opposition to the disenfranchisement of 'coloured' voters, and characterized by members wearing black sashes as they stood in silent protest. Also *attrib.*

1955 *Sunday Times* in M. Rogers *Black Sash* (1956) 99 What can the majority do but protest again and again? This is what the Women's Defence of the Constitution League has been doing, through the Black Sash movement. **1956** *Friend* in *Ibid.* 64 Bloemfontein's 'Black Sash' women members of the Defence of the Constitution League were here, there and everywhere in the city yesterday.

b. A name given by the Press to the Women's Defence of the Constitution League, and adopted as its official title; SASH *n.* Also *attrib.* See also SASH *v.*

The Black Sash works for the protection and advancement of civil rights through protest, research, and the maintenance of a network of advice offices (see ADVICE OFFICE).

1956 M. ROGERS *Black Sash* 227 The Women's Defence of the Constitution League decided at this conference .. in the light of the changed constitutional circumstances to change its name to 'The Black Sash.' **1962** A.J. LUTHULI *Let my People Go* 213 A further meeting was fitted in in Rondebosch – the Black Sash wanted me. **1970** E.D. STOTT in *Std Encycl. of Sn Afr.* II. 353 With the passing of the Senate Act, the Black Sash turned its attention to all other legislation considered unjust or a deprivation of civil rights and liberties, which it was constituted to uphold. **1978** *Daily Dispatch* 14 July 1 The Black Sash is a women's protest organisation formed in the 1950's to draw attention to injustices in South African society. **1980** E. JOUBERT *Poppie Nongena* 237 She considered the Black Sash people and the Legal Aid that Mrs Retief once said would help her. **1987** *New Nation* 2 Apr. 2 Nobel Prize for Sash? The Black Sash has been nominated for the 1987 Nobel Peace Prize – becoming the first South African organisation to be nominated for the prestigious award. **1990** *E. Prov. Herald* 5 Mar. 4 She said .. the Black Sash .. should retain its independent role of monitoring and fostering human rights, rather than seeking political power or influence.

Hence **Black Sash** *v. trans.*, SASH *v.*; **Black Sasher** *n. phr.*, a member of the Black Sash; *Sasher*, see SASH *n.*; **Black Sashing** *vbl n. phr.*; **Black Sashism** *n. phr.* (*rare*), the practices, ideals, and policies of the Black Sash.

1955 J. MERVIS in M. Rogers *Black Sash* (1956) 72 Black Sashism has become accepted practice in South Africa. **1955** [see JEUGBOND]. **1956** M. ROGERS *Black Sash* 57 By the time he had been 'black sashed' twice, he managed to raise a smile, and looked the women straight in the face. **1956** *Melbourne Herald* (Australia) in *Ibid.* 70 At a ceremonial opening of a police barracks, the Minister of Justice, Mr C.R. Swart, scrambled over a fence to avoid walking through the Black Sashers' gauntlet. **1956** P. WOLSTENHOLME in *Ibid.* 256 These things are best left to the women, who after all tackle all the hardest jobs, such as street collecting and Black Sashing. **1965** W. JACKSON in *Black Sash* Vol.9 No.2, 32 As I stood around shivering, I noticed a long line of Black Sashers standing at the edge of the quay-side. **1971** J. ROBERTSON *Liberalism in S. Afr.* 141 The Black Sashers were initially concerned with the preservation of the Constitution and with promoting the unity of the white races in South Africa.

black south-easter *n. phr.* Also with initial capitals. Esp. in the Western Cape: a violent south-easterly wind, cold and usually accompanied with heavy rain. Also *attrib.* Cf. CAPE DOCTOR.

1847 'A BENGALI' *Notes on Cape of G.H.* 13 The black South Easters, as they are called, and which blow occasionally in winter, are exceedingly violent and gloomy, and are justly considered unhealthy. **1913** C. PETTMAN *Africanderisms* 63 *Black south-easter,* .. A violent south wind heavily laden with saline and other matter, prevalent at certain seasons of the year round the South African coast. **1949** J. MOCKFORD *Golden Land* 24 When there is an ordinary south-easter, an old citizen will remark that the Devil is smoking today. But when it is a black south-easter, blowing great guns and tumbling cloud, then, he will say, it is the Devil and van Hunks. **1976** A.P. BRINK *Instant in Wind* 47 The popularity of this thatching in the Cape must be ascribed to an effort to avoid the grave accidents which may result from heavier roofing being ripped off by the notorious 'Black South-easter' winds raging in this region. **1977** *Cape Times* 23 Dec. 8 A black south-easter .. roaring from ocean to ocean, struck the south-western corner of the sub-continent, causing millions worth of damage in orchards and vineyards. **1981** *Fair Lady* 25 Mar. 49 A black south easter coming up the south Atlantic caused heavy rain ... A black south easter is a cold moist wind (the normal south easter is warm and dry) which caused a high pressure system to move over the interior. **1985** A. TREDGOLD *Bay between Mountains* 102 The wind from the SSE, the black south-easter, is one of the most dangerous, .. for it comes up suddenly with great force from the open sea and builds up huge waves. **1990** *Weekend Argus* 10 Feb. 5 Pedestrians outside Cape Town Civic Centre struggle to make their way against the black south-easter. At times it became almost impossible for people to walk on the Foreshore.

black spot *n. phr. Hist.* Often with initial capitals. [BLACK + Eng. *spot* area, place.] A freehold area occupied by black people but surrounded by land designated for white occupation, and thus destined for expropriation and re-zoning in terms of Group Areas legislation; land in designated 'white' areas which was occupied by black people. Also *attrib.* Cf. *white spot* (see WHITE *adj.* sense 1 d). See also RESETTLEMENT.

[**1941** E.H. BROOKES in *Bantu World* 25 Jan. 4 There are still a good many Native-owned farms and settlements .. entirely surrounded by a European area, and .. sometimes referred to as 'black islands'.] **1951** *Natal Mercury* 13 Apr. 11 [The Mayor] will ask the Minister if Durban is to receive any of the money the Minister recently announced would be set aside for the elimination of 'black spots.' **1956** A. SAMPSON *Drum* 229 Johannesburg spread out like an avalanche, surrounding Sophiatown with European townships. Europeans resented the 'black spots' in their midst. **1960** A.J. LUTHULI in H. Spottiswoode *S. Afr.: Rd Ahead* 116 In rural areas African freehold lands that are surrounded by white farms are by law 'Black Spots', which must be vacated by Africans when so ordered by the Government. **1965** E. MPHAHLELE *Down Second Ave* 176 Like Sophiatown, the township must move because it is a 'black spot' – too near whites. **1968** COLE & FLAHERTY *House of Bondage* 52 In South Africa today a 'black spot' is an African township marked for obliteration because it occupies an area into which whites wish to expand. The township may have been in existence for fifty years and have a settled population of twenty-five or fifty or seventy-five thousand people. **1969** *Survey of Race Rel.* (S.A.I.R.R.) 119 Farms acquired by Africans prior to 1936 are considered to be part of the scheduled areas if they adjoin existing Reserves; but if they are surrounded by white-owned land they are officially regarded as black spots. **1977** *Daily Dispatch* 17 Nov. 4 The National Party's parliamentary candidate .. has pledged to speed up the removal of 'black spots' in the white corridor of land between the Ciskei and Transkei. **1985** PLATZKY & WALKER *Surplus People* 15 'Black spot' and 'squatter' are two particularly loosely applied and confusing terms. For some officials any area to be removed is labelled as 'black spot' .. regardless of the actual legal standing of either place or person. *Ibid.* 44 'Black spot' is used to describe African freehold land and land owned by Church or mission stations leased to individual Africans; in both cases land falling within what the government has defined as the white area. **1986** P. MAYLAM *Hist. of Afr. People* 174 Although long since outlawed, 'black spots' have only been eliminated on a large scale since about 1960. **1988** *E. Prov. Herald* 10 Feb. 2 More than 3,5 million people had been uprooted from 'black spots.' **1990** *New African* 11 June 4 'Black spots' – black freehold land that was acquired before the 1913 Land Act and which fell within areas designated as white.

Blackstan see -STAN.

blacktail *n.* Pl. usu. unchanged, occas. -s. [Transf. use of general Eng. *black-tail* a name for certain varieties of fish.] In the Eastern Cape and KwaZulu-Natal: the edible seabream *Diplodus sargus capensis* of the Sparidae; DAS sense 2 a; DASSIE sense 2 a.

The name 'blacktail' is used for this species in Smith and Heemstra's *Smiths' Sea Fishes* (1986).

1905 *E. London Dispatch* 29 July 7 A few friends fishing in the Buffalo River .. had some excellent sport taking .. a black fish of about 9 lbs. and *black-tail* of about $2\frac{1}{2}$ lbs. **1906** *Ibid.* 6 Mar. 7 The biggest I caught on these rocks was a fine *dasje* (black-tail) weighing $7\frac{1}{2}$ lbs. **1949** J.L.B. SMITH *Sea Fishes* 269 *Diplodus sargus* ... *Das. Dassie* .. *Kolstert. Blacktail* ... About the best fighter of our inshore angling fishes ... Weight for weight the Blacktail has twice the vigour of any trout. **1955** [see DASSIE sense 2]. **1971** *Farmer's Weekly* 12 Sept. 85 When fishing for night feeders like stumpnose and big blacktail (anything up to 2 kg) I use a 1/0 hook. **1975** *E. Prov. Herald* 30 Jan. 13 The tidal pools were nursery areas for several species of fish which were not nurtured in the river estuaries. This included the popular baitfish strepie, and blacktails. **1987** [see DASSIE sense 2]. **1993** R. VAN DER ELST *Guide to Common Sea Fishes* 348 Blacktail, a reference to the distinctive saddle on the caudal peduncle.

black thorn *n. phr.* [Prob. tr. Afk. *swarthaak*, *swart* black + *haak* hook.] Either of two acacias of the Fabaceae:

a. *rare.* The thorn tree *Acacia nilotica*, with a sweet scent.

1966 C.A. SMITH *Common Names* 111 *Black thorn, Acacia nilotica.* **1973** I.C. VERDOORN in *Std Encycl. of Sn Afr.* IX. 266 *Red-Heart, Black-thorn* ... (*Acacia nilotica* = *A. benthami.*) Thorn-tree with a spreading round canopy, belonging to the family *Leguminosae*, subfamily *Mimosoideae*. It is characterised by the straight pods which turn blackish when ripe.

b. The deciduous tree *A. mellifera*, esp. subsp. *detinens*, with large curved thorns in pairs and hard, red timber; also called HAAKDORING (sense 1).

1992 *Weekend Post* 6 June (Leisure) 7 R1,05c: *A. mellifera*, black thorn. Named *mellifera* (honey-bearing) for its plentiful nectar, it provides good fodder and, once it has grown, shade. **1992** D.M.C. FOURIE in *Philatelic Services Bulletin* 61 *Acacia mellifera Black thorn,* The black thorn is a valuable fodder and provides good shade once it has developed into a tree ... Two subspecies are recognised in the black thorn. The most common of the two is subsp. *detinens* which has a wide distribution range.

black turf see TURF.

bladdy /ˈblædi/ *adj.* and *adv. Slang.* Also **blady**. [Pronunciation-sp. of the Eng. expletive *bloody*, reflecting a pronunciation influenced by Afk. but common among Eng.-speakers. See also BLEDDY.]

See note at BLEDDY.

A. *adj.* BLERRY *adj.*

1973 Y. BURGESS *Life to Live* 61 The kids .. stretch you to bladdy blazes, you never the same again. **1977** S. ROBERTS in E. Pereira *Contemp. S. Afr. Plays* 232 It's the weekend ... he couldn't get through a Saturday without his bladdy bottle. **1978** A.P. BRINK *Rumours of Rain* 31 Where you think I get change for two rand, bladdy fool? **1985** P. SLABOLEPSZY *Sat. Night at Palace* 37 Delicate wafer. Tiny ripples for artistic effect. I mean, this isn't just sommer a chip any more – it's a bladdy twentieth-century work of art! **1989** A. SHER *Middlepost* 68 You gave me such a damn-bladdy fright, you bastard. **1990** *Style* May 37, I asked Van Tonder about the swastikas. 'Ag man,' he said, 'those bladdy things. I keep telling people, we're not Germans, we're Boere.'

B. *adv.* BLERRY *adv.*

1974 B. SIMON *Joburg, Sis!* 129 They walk around there with their long hair and their tight jeans and so bladdy filthy dirty man. **1977** C. Clayton in *Contrast 43* Vol.11 No.3, 23 He .. laughed loudly, shouting in her ear, 'Too bladdy drunk, old Alice, too bladdy drunk.' **1984** *Sunday Times* 1 Apr. (Mag. Sect.) 27 If I say that to the whites, they'll bladdy laugh at me! **1987** M. Poland *Train to Doringbult* 190 It's been so bladdy boring with Kobie and them away. **1991** P. Slabolepszy Braait Laaities. 9 Boikie: .. Why don't you show me what you've got? Moira: I'm not bladdy showing anybody anything!

blah var. BRA.

||**blanke** /'blaŋkə/ *n.* Also with initial capital. [Afk.] A white person; often joking or ironic, making fun of official terminology. Also *attrib.* Cf. NIE-BLANKE. See also BLANKES ALLEEN, SLEGS VIR BLANKES.

1949 M. Fortes in *Hansard* 24 May 6451 There is perhaps an agreed dictionary definition of the word 'European' and the word 'Blanke'. **1966** L.G. Berger *Where's Madam* 113 The courtroom was a bare brick structure with .. the body of the court divided by a high brick partition running along its length to divide the Blankes from the Nie-Blanke spectators. [**1968** Cole & Flaherty *House of Bondage* 150 The Dutch Reformed Church maintains separate churches for the different races. But they are not alone. *Net Vir Blankes* is figuratively written on many a South African church door, not all of them Boer.] **1971** *Daily Dispatch* 5 May 10 (*cartoon*) Patrons accompanied by blankes must ensure that the latter have reference books duly stamped by the proper authority. **1972** *Sunday Times* 1 Oct. 2 The most significant fact of this policy .. was that it meant the acceptance by the party of the principle of sharing power – 'not Blanke baas-skap, not Black supremacy, but a sharing of power and a safe-guarding of rights.' **1981** *Rhodeo* (Rhodes Univ.) May, The prevalent cross-calvinistic-pseudo-patriotic attitude divides our nation into whites/blankes /coloureds/blacks/Indians/english/afrikaners/etc/etc /etc. **1988** [see NIE-BLANKE].

||**Blankes Alleen** /ˌblaŋkəs a'liən/ *n. phr.* Also with small initials. [Afk., *blankes* white people + *alleen* only.] *Attrib.*, '(for) white people only', often used ironically; cf. SLEGS VIR BLANKES. Also *attrib.* See also BLANKE.

In the past, this was the Afrikaans wording found on racially-restrictive signs.

[**1957** D. Jacobson *Price of Diamonds* 46 'This is my place,' Fink said, with another glance around the booking-office at the timetables and the railway maps on the walls, the sign that said: '*Europeans Only/Blankes Alleen*.'] **1988** *Sunday Tribune* 31 Jan. (Today) 7 The news is not good. Huns and Visigoths have overrun our formerly fair and *blankes alleen* beaches. [**1989** J. Hobbs *Thoughts in Makeshift Mortuary* 59 The gritty pavement with the .. green-painted oil drum rubbish bins and the *Whites only/Alleen blankes* signs.] **1991** A. Maimane in *Weekly Mail* 3 May 18 Calvinists who believe that their *blankes-alleen* divinity gives them the right to oppress other races.

blanket *n. Obsolescent. Offensive* and usu. *derog.* [fr. U.S. Eng. (referring to the Native Americans); see also quot. 1913.] *Attrib.*, *comb.*, and in phrr.: designating black Africans who wear the blanket as a garment and who cling to their traditional way of life; therefore meaning 'unsophisticated', 'rural'. Cf. DRESSED.

a. *Attrib.*, passing into *adj.* Designating an unsophisticated, rural black person, esp. in the offensive phrr. ***blanket boy***, ***-kaffir***, ***-native*** (see also RAW, RED *adj.* sense 2 b ii), and ***blanket vote(s)***, the collective black vote in South Africa.

1892 B. Mitford *'Tween Snow & Fire* p.xxxvi, There were a few muttered jeers about .. getting into the assembly on the strength of 'blanket votes'. **1903** Lord A. Milner in *Indian Opinion* 23 July 4 Cross issues and totally irrelevant considerations .. gather round the question, such as .. the eccentricities of what is known as the 'Blanket' vote in the Cape Colony. **1904** *Daily Chron.* (U.K.) 13 May 3 The 'compound' system is essentially degrading even for 'blanket' Kaffirs. **1913** C. Pettman *Africanderisms* 64 *Blanket vote*, The collective Kaffir vote is thus designated. The reference is, of course, to the blanket which has gradually but generally superseded the more dignified Karos .. as an article of apparel among the natives. **1920** R.H. Lindsey-Renton *Diary* (1979) 12, I saw a few Kaffir kraals inhabited by what are called 'blanket kaffirs', that is those who clothe themselves in blankets and not in modern civilised garb. **1928** E.A. Walker *Hist. of S. Afr.* 544 The tendency had .. been to raise the franchise qualification to keep out the blanket kaffir. **1943** [see DRESSED]. **1948** E. Hellmann *Rooiyard* 103 Some women regard the custom with contempt as being performed only by 'red' or 'blanket' Natives and not by educated Natives. **1953** Lanham & Mopeli-Paulus (*title*) Blanket Boy's Moon. **1958** A. Fugard *Dimetos & Two Early Plays* (1977) 127 Tobias: I'm not frightened of work. Guy: There, you see, old Blanket-boy's got guts. **1963** K. Mackenzie *Dragon to Kill* 140 Look at them in those countries up north – ordinary blanket kaffirs and they have independence already. **1973** P.A. Whitney *Blue Fire* 83 They had come to be set apart from the black population and had fared better in the Cape Peninsula than the 'blanket native,' so recently from the reservation.

b. In the phr. ***man of the blanket*** (*nonce*), *blanket boy* (see sense a).

1968 A. Fulton *Dark Side of Mercy* 16 Her beer was spoken of with longing wherever men of the blanket gathered, not only in mountain homelands, but far afield as the compounds of the Reef goldmines.

Hence **blanketeer** *n. nonce*, *blanket boy* (see sense a).

1928 N. Devitt *Blue Lizard* 149 (Swart), The Golden City and its ways had turned these natives from 'blanketeers' in all their pristine manliness and innocence, into black dudes, with a tendency to emulate the white man's vices.

blaps /blaps, blʌps/ *n. colloq.* Pl. **-es**. [Afk., blunder.] A blunder or mistake; a mess.

1970 *Informant, Pietersburg* He made a big blaps of what was once a nice picture. **1979** *Sunday Times* 8 Apr. 16 An Artes Award should be made to the SABC for committing .. 'the biggest protocol "blaps" of the year': Failure to invite Pretoria's mayor to the awards night. **1985** *Ibid.* 17 Nov. (Mag. Sect.) 37 Slip of the tongue. Why, oh why, do we make those embarrassing verbal blapses .. ? **1989** J. Allan in *Ibid.* 11 June 4 Most of the Household Names walked off the set, shaking their heads in disbelief at the *blapses* they'd made. **1994** P.S. Walters *Informant, Grahamstown*, I lie awake at night thinking of all the blapses I've made during the day.

blarry var. BLERRY.

blas(s)op var. BLAASOP.

blatjang /'blatjaŋ, 'blatʃaŋ/ *n.* Formerly also **blaatgham, blatcham, blatchang**. [Afk., fr. Malay *belachan* a shrimp and fish condiment.

It is probable that in late 19th century Afk. this word still had two meanings: A. Pannevis's *Afskrif van Lys van Afrikaanse Woorde en Uitdrukkings* (1880) defines 'Bladjang' as being made of dried chillies and stewed dried apricots in vinegar; H.C.V. Leibbrandt's *Het Kaapsch Hollandsch* (1882) lists 'Balachan' and 'Blatchong', both with the same meaning as the Malay *belachan*; and the *Woordelijst van het Transvaalsch Taaleigen* (1890) includes 'Blatjang', defined as 'een zeker gerecht' (a certain dish).]

A tangy sauce made of dried fruit (usu. apricots) and chillies cooked in vinegar; chutney. Also *attrib.*

1890 A.G. Hewitt *Cape Cookery* 86 Cape Blatcham. 1 lb. of chillies, 1 table spoonful salt, ½lb. almonds ... Mix all the ingredients and boil in 3 bottles of vinegar to the required consistency. **1891** H.J. Duckitt *Hilda's 'Where Is It?'* 12 'Blatjang.' (Malay. Appetising condiment.) **1891** J.P. Legg in *Cape Illust. Mag.* I. 96 The word 'Blatjang' no doubt has an Indian origin and the same may be said of 'Chutney,' though this can hardly be claimed as an exclusively Cape word. **1902** H.J. Duckitt *Hilda's Diary of Cape Hsekeeper* 69 Blatjang made this way will keep for a year. I have sent it to England several times, and have had orders for another supply from those who prefer it to chutney. **1913** C. Pettman *Africanderisms* 65 *Blatcham* or *Blatjang*, .. A relish made with dried apricots, peaches, quinces, raisins, chillies, vinegar, etc. **1913** *D.S.G. Bk of Recipes* 52 Blaatgham. 1lb. dried apricots boiled to a pulp. 1lb. chillies (ground) [etc.]. **1932** *S. Afr. Medical Jrnl* in *Personality* (27 Aug. 1970) 160 (*advt*) Mrs Ball's Chutney .. is a variety of the old Cape 'blatjang' sauce, prepared from dried fruits and sugar, of a consistency similar to the blatjangs so popular some generations ago. **1947** L.G. Green *Tavern of Seas* 65 Blatjang (the Malay condiment of apricots soaked in vinegar, red chillies and coriander seeds). **1950** H. Gerber *Cape Cookery* 126 Blatjang. Slice 1 onion and dry it in the oven. Then pound it. Boil 1 pound dried apricots until they are soft .. add the onions and some chilli powder to make it hot. **1951** S. van H. Tulleken *Prac. Cookery Bk* 264 Blatchang. **1958** A. Jackson *Trader on Veld* 43 Here and there 'Blatjang' (a sort of chutney) was made from dried apricots, raisins, curry powder, cloves and other ingredients. **1964** L.G. Green *Old Men Say* 130, I always wander through the home industries section of the Cape Show to examine the many chutneys, *atjars* and *blatjangs* set out there. **1975** *Weekend Post* 20 Sept. (Parade) 14 Blatjang, a type of chutney originally made by the Malay slaves, contains peaches, raisins, quinces, dried apricots, vinegar and other ingredients. **1978** *Sunday Times* 26 Mar. 6 Blatjang sauce is made by mixing together fried chopped onions, chopped garlic, chutney, tomato sauce, ketjap, brown sugar and sambal celek. **1988** F. Williams *Cape Malay Cookbk* 61 Malay blatjang is essentially a tangy chilli sauce ... This traditional blatjang should not be confused with ordinary chutney.

blauwbok *n. hist.* Pl. unchanged, or **-ke** /-ə/. Also **blaa(u)wbok, blaawebock, blaubock, blauwboc, blauwe bok, blaw-bock**. [S. Afr. Du., *blauw* blue + *bok* antelope, goat.]

1. Either of two antelopes of the genus *Hippotragus*:

a. The extinct South African antelope *H. leucophaeus*, in the past found only in the south-western Cape; BLOUBOK; BLUE BUCK sense 2; TZEIRAN.

[**1731** G. Medley tr. *P. Kolb's Present State of Cape of G.H.* II. 114 The Blew Goats are shap'd like the Tame, but are as large as an *European* Hart. Their Hair is very short and of a delicate Blew .. their Beards, which are pretty long, add not a little to their comliness.] **1786** G. Forster tr. *A. Sparrman's Voy. to Cape of G.H.* II. 219 The *blaauw-bok* is also one of the large species of *gazel*. **1790** tr. *F. Le Vaillant's Trav.* II. 130 My hunter stopping all of a sudden, called out to me that he perceived a *blaw-bock*, a blue goat .. the most curious and beautiful species of antelope that Africa produces ... This antelope has been described by Pennant under the name of the *blue antelope*, and by Buffon under that of the *tseiran*. **1821** C.I. Latrobe *Jrnl of Visit* 561 *Blaubock, Antilope leucophaea*. This is a large animal and very different from the little one of the Zuureveld. **1832** *Penny Cyclopaedia* II. 88 The Blauwbok .. is six feet in length. **1905** W.L. Sclater in Flint & Gilchrist *Science in S. Afr.* 122 The Blaauwbok (*Hippotragus leucophæs*), an antelope resembling the Roan, but somewhat smaller and without the black face markings, was even then on the verge of extinction; the last one of which we have any record having been obtained by Lichtenstein, a German traveller, in 1799. *c*1936 *S. & E. Afr. Yr Bk & Guide* 1094 The great *blauwbok* (*H. leucophoeus*), nearly related to but somewhat smaller than the roan antelope, was once very common in the Swellendam district, but has long been exterminated, probably since about 1800. **1948** A.C. White *Call of Bushveld* 89 Several species or sub species of zebra have disappeared and so has the blaauwbok. The extinct zebras and blaauwbok were probably merely varieties of the respective species to which .. they belonged. **1989** D. Day *Encycl. of Vanished Species* 191 The first African animal to disappear in historic times was the Blue Buck or Blaauwbok

(*Hippotragus leucophaeus*), a relative of the Roan and Sable Antelopes, which lived only in Zwellendam province of the old Cape Colony and became extinct within eighty years of its discovery.

b. The ROAN ANTELOPE, *H. equinus*. Also *attrib.*

1866 J. LEYLAND *Adventures* 116, I was anxious to obtain a specimen of the Bastard Gemsboc (Antelope Leucophaea) or Roan Antelope, also known as the Blauwboc. **1874** A. EDGAR in *Friend* 4 June, What was my joy to find that the animal when it emerged from the tree was a large 'blaauwbok ram'. **1900** W.L. SCLATER *Mammals of S. Afr.* I. 216 Blaauw-bok of the colonists, not to be confounded with the Blaauw bokje or little blue buck (*Cephalophus monticola*). **1936** E.C. LLEWELLYN *Influence of Low Dutch* 163 *Blauwbok* (1786) is named from its colour, blue, an effect produced by its black hide showing through its ashy-grey hair.

2. The *blue duiker* (see DUIKER sense 1 b), *Philantomba monticola*.

1834 T. PRINGLE *Afr. Sketches* 273 The *blaauwbok*, or pigmy antelope .. seldom exceeds ten inches in height. **1835** J.W.D. MOODIE *Ten Yrs* II. 139 The woods also abound with large wood-antelopes, and an elegant little antelope not more than a foot in height, called the 'blaawe bock,' or blue buck. **1837** 'N. POLSON' *Subaltern's Sick Leave* 123 A blauwbok, a very beautiful pigmy antelope .. of a bluish slate colour (whence its name.) These diminutive animals frequent the thick woods which they seldom quit, but run from bush to bush a few yards distance and round in circles. [**1900** W.L. SCLATER *Mammals of S. Afr.* I. 163 *The blue duiker*, Blaauwbok or Kleenebok of the Dutch colonists .. [is] the smallest of South African antelopes ... The alarm cry is a sharp whistling shriek.]

blauw bosch var. BLOUBOS.

blauwkop koggelmander see KOGGELMANDER sense 2.

blauw schimmel see SKIMMEL.

blauwtong /ˈblaʊtɔŋ/ *n. Obs.* exc. *hist. Pathology.* Also **blaauw-tong**. [S. Afr. Du., *blauw* blue + *tong* tongue.] BLUE TONGUE.

1896 R. WALLACE *Farming Indust. of Cape Col.* 382 Autumn fever, or 'blaauw-tong' is a form of influenza which is thought to be nearly allied to horse-sickness, .. that local form of it which affects the head and tongue more particularly. **1913** C. PETTMAN *Africanderisms* 67 Sometimes the swelling is confined to the tongue and gives rise to that form of the sickness known as *blauwtong* or blue-tongue. **1979** T. GUTSCHE *There Was a Man* 21 He [*sc.* A. Theiler] identified and described the historic Blaauwtong (Blue Tongue) in sheep.

blaw-bock var. BLAUWBOK.

bleary var. BLERRY.

bleddy \"bledi\ *adj.* and *adv. Slang.* Also **bleddie**. [Afk. *bleddie*, fr. Eng. *bloody*; see also BLERRY.]

This orthography is generally used to represent the pronunciation of Afrikaans-speakers, as is BLERRY; BLADDY is the form most often used to represent the pronunciation of English-speakers.

A. *adj.* BLERRY *adj.*

1963 A.M. LOUW *20 Days* 173 The Coloured girl fell back screaming and swearing: 'You bleddie witvrou!' [**1972** *Sunday Times* 12 Mar. 17 An Afrikaner stopped and spat in her face and said: 'Jou bleddie koelie' (You bloody coolie).] **1973** *Cape Times* 27 Jan. (Weekend Mag.) 3 Othello is a Cape Coloured and Desdemona his 'bleddy white bitch'. **1977** [see OUTIE]. **1989** E. ABRAHAMS in *Sunday Times* 19 Feb. 9 Mr Poggenpoel could not keep his plan to himself. He told his friends ... 'But they are not my friends any longer, the *bleddy* tattle-tales. They told the nurse what I intended to do.' **1989** J. HOBBS *Thoughts in Makeshift Mortuary* 314 Who do you think I am, a bleddy gigolo?

B. *adv.* BLERRY *adv.*

1973 J. COPE *Alley Cat* 30 You take what God gave you .. ? You don't want to be bleddy white? **1985** J. THOMAS in *Fair Lady* 1 May 20 'Ag siestog Wallaby, that's now bleddy funny,' he chortled.

bleekbok *n. obs.* [S. Afr. Du., *bleek* pale + *bok* antelope, goat.] A STEENBOK of a pale colour, mistakenly believed to be a separate species; *vaal rhebok* sense (*a*), see RHEBOK sense 2; *vlaksteenbok*, see VLAKTE sense 2.

1786 G. FORSTER tr. *A. Sparrman's Voy. to Cape of G.H.* II. 223 The colour of it [*sc.* the vlaksteen-bok] was a very pale-red or a mouse-colour, .. on which account it was likewise said to be called by some the *bleekbok*, or *vaale ree-bok*. **1839** W.C. HARRIS *Wild Sports* 386 The *Vlachte Steenbok* (Tragulus Rufescens), and the *Bleekbok* (T. Pediotragus) appear to be merely varieties of this Antelope, and not distinct species. **1900** W.L. SCLATER *Mammals of S. Afr.* I. 173 *Raphicerus campestris*, .. Steinbok, or more correctly Steenbok, Vlaktebok and Bleek-bok of the Colonists, Dutch and English.

bleesmol var. BLESMOL.

blerry /ˈbleri/ *adj.* and *adv. Slang.* Also **blarry**, **bleary**, **blerrie**, **blirry**. [ad. Eng. *bloody*, reflecting the pronunciation of Afk.-speakers; see also BLEDDY. Cf. Austral. Eng. *plurry*.] 'Bloody'.

See note at BLEDDY.

A. *adj.* An epithet expressing emotion ranging from irritation to fury; BLADDY *adj.*; BLEDDY *adj.*

1920 R.Y. STORMBERG *Mrs Pieter de Bruyn* 10 His oral whip-lashing of indolent servants is sometimes overheard. What's the meaning of 'blirry domkop'? **1949** O. WALKER *Wanton City* 61 You black skellums ... Where's our blerry scoff, eh? **1956** [see DUTCHMAN sense 1 b]. *c***1957** D. SWANSON *Highveld, Lowveld & Jungle* 64 'You all right, Hansie?' 'Ach man' Swart said, feeling at his damaged arm 'Just a blarry scratch.' **1964** G. GORDON *Four People* 140 Don't be a blerry fool. **1982** M. MZAMANE *Children of Soweto* 185 Ag, these *blerry* native names, they so difficult! How do they ever manage to pronounce them? **1986** *Anon. Handbill* A heavy blerrie Commie cold front to the North East. Expected temperatures: hot for blerrie Commies. **1990** *Weekly Mail* 21 Dec. 35, I mean, your speciality is who's doing what to who in the northern suburbs .. and the *blerrie* editor says write me something on the masses marching.

B. *adv.* An intensifier, ranging in meaning from 'very' to 'unspeakably', 'appallingly', 'completely'; BLADDY *adv.*; BLEDDY *adv.*

1949 H.C. BOSMAN *Cold Stone Jug* (1969) 47 When I is blue like what I is now, then I says you can maar keep me locked up in the old boob as long as you blerrie well like. **1954** J. WILES *Moon to Play With* 218 'Ag, demmit,' said Johannes, 'you're blerry mad.' **1972** [see Drum quot. at OU *n.* sense 1 a]. **1973** Y. BURGESS *Life to Live* 75 That's what's wrong with you church people, you all so blarry narrow-minded! **1975** *Darling* 12 Feb. 119 I'm that blerry hot already, I couldn't care. **1980** A. DANGOR in M. Mutloatse *Forced Landing* 162 You don't have to blerrywell hit him! **1988** *Style* May 55 Actress Shaleen Surtie-Richards is irrepressibly full of life. 'Sies, I'm blerrie disgusted with you,' she tells me.

bles /bles/ *n.* Pl. **-se** /-ə/. [Du., blaze (of a horse).] A white blaze on the face of a horse or other animal. Also *attrib.*, passing into *adj.*

Common in speech.

[**1824** see BLESBOK]. **1832** *Graham's Town Jrnl* 13 Dec. 193 1 brown Mare, with a white bles, two white legs. **1837** 'N. POLSON' *Subaltern's Sick Leave* 128 The game found here consists of immense herds of *blesbok* or *bontibok*, so called from the blaze or *bles* on their faces. **1880** *Alice Times* 27 Feb., Strayed ... A Chestnut mare, with kol bles, marks of reim on both knees, branded A.P. on left side of neck. **1905** W.L. SCLATER in Flint & Gilchrist *Science in S. Afr.* 134 The Blesmol (*Georychus capensis*) .. is common in gardens where it ravages bulbs and potato tubers; it is so called from the 'bles' or white spot on the top of its head. **1906** A.H. WATKINS *From Farm to Forum* 55 Those are his 'bles' (white-faced) horses; but where has he come by a splinter new spider like that? **1913** [see BLESHOENDER]. **1940** BAUMANN & BRIGHT *Lost Republic* 231 There were blesbok, called so because of the 'bles' or white mark right down their noses.

blesbok /ˈblesbɔk/ *n.* Also **blessboc**, **blessbok**, **blesse-bôk**, **bliss bock**. Pl. unchanged, or **-s**. [S. Afr. Du., *bles* blaze + *bok* antelope, goat; see quot. 1824.] The antelope *Damaliscus dorcas phillipsi* of the Bovidae; BLESBUCK. Also *attrib.*

See note at BONTEBOK.

1824 W.J. BURCHELL *Trav.* II. 335 The *Blesbok* is so called, from having a white mark on its forehead, similar to that which, in horses, is termed, in Dutch, a *bles*, and by English horsemen a *star*, or *blaze*. **1827** [see BONTEBOK]. **1835** T.H. BOWKER Journal. 26 Apr., Bliss Bocks Quaggas & other game to be found here. **1863** LADY DUFF-GORDON in F. Galton *Vacation Tourists* (1864) III. 190 Yesterday Captain D— gave me a very nice caross of blessbok skins which he got from some travelling trader. **1871** J. MCKAY *Reminisc.* 14 Throughout the greater part of the plains frequented by blesboks, .. the sunbaked hills or mounds of clay formed by the white ants occur. **1882** J. NIXON *Among Boers* 119 The blesbok is a larger and clumsier antelope than the springbok. Its head looks almost too heavy for its body, and it never takes long leaps like the springbok. **1896** R. WARD *Rec. of Big Game* 83 Formerly to be numbered by hundreds of thousands, the beautiful Blesbok has in the last twenty years grown very scarce indeed. *a***1936** E.N. MARAIS *Soul of Ape* (1973) 82 The vast herds of bontebok (*Damaliscus pygargus*), blesbok (*Damaliscus albifrons*) .. are on the verge of extinction or have vanished because they were unable to exist in the Bushveld which lay as a harbour of refuge before them. **1940** [see BLES]. **1949** J. MOCKFORD *Golden Land* 216 With the springbok were battalions of wildebeest, and brigades of blesbok. **1973** *Farmer's Weekly* 30 May (Suppl.) 25 Live Blesbok for sale at R24 each. **1988** A. VAN WYK in *S. Afr. Panorama* Oct. 45 The blesbok .. has a reddish brown body colour, with a white face blaze that is divided by a narrow transverse brown band between the eyes. **1991** *Personality* 5 Aug. 27 Blesbok with blood staining their white blazes after they gored each other because of the stress of confinement. **1994** M. ROBERTS tr. *J.A. Wahlberg's Trav. Jrnls 1838–56* 64 First skoft 4 hours through immense plains covered with blesbok (my first).

blesbuck \"blesbVk\ *n.* Also **bless-buck**. Pl. unchanged, or **-s**. [Part. tr. S. Afr. Du. *blesbok*.] BLESBOK. Also *attrib.*

1839 W.C. HARRIS *Wild Sports* 289 Large troops of bles-bucks, or white-faced antelopes, a pied species that we had rarely met with before. **1840** C.A. KINLOCH in *Echo* 26 Oct. 2 We halted a couple of days between the Riet and the Caffer River, in order to hunt the Gnoo and the Blesbuck (Gazella Albifrons) which we found in large herds. **1857** T. SHONE Diary. 26 Sept., I went to A. Forbes, paid for A Bless Buck skin 14/-. **1879** R.J. ATCHERLEY *Trip to Boerland* 73 The bless-buck .. is so named on account of the white mark or 'blaze' upon the face. **1891** R. WARD *Sportsman's Handbk* 123 In the .. Orange Free State and the Transvaal, herds of Blesbucks, Springbucks, and Black Wildebeests, are still to be met with. **1900** P.J. DU TOIT *Diary* (1974) 10 First excitement. Bles-buck. What fun! a troop of about 40 were coming towards us ... A regular volley was fired in amongst them knocking over four besides wounding several other and a donkey. *c***1936** *S. & E. Afr. Yr Bk & Guide* 1083 The *Blesbusk* (*D. albifrons*; Dutch, *blesbok*). Height about 39 inches; colour and shape very similar to that of the bontebuck, but white markings less acute excepting on the face, which shows a prominent, pure white blaze, whence the name. **1948** H.C. BOSMAN in L. Abrahams *Unto Dust* (1963) 140 A four-ounce linen bag with the picture on it of a leaping blesbuck — the trade-mark of a well-known tobacco company. **1971** *Farmer's Weekly* 12 May 11 Because of the strong resemblance between the Bontebok and the Blesbuck .. early writers often confused the two species. **1992** *S. Afr. Panorama* Mar.-Apr. 50 (*caption*) Perfect harmony — blesbuck (*Damaliscus dorcas phillipsi*) and impala (*Aepyceros melampus*) grazing on a hillside.

bleshoender /ˈbleshʊnə, -hunər/ *n.* [Afk., *bles* blaze + *hoender* fowl, chicken.] The coot *Fulica cristata* of the Rallidae, a water fowl characterized by a white blaze on the forehead.

1913 C. PETTMAN *Africanderisms* 67 *Bles hoender*, .. A water-fowl with a *bles* or white spot on the head; it is often found on *vleis*. **1923** HAAGNER & IVY *Sketches* 257 The .. Bles Hoender .. is of a general dark ash-brown or sooty colour throughout ... It flies well and is an expert diver. **1969** [see DUIKER sense 2 a]. **1977** *S. Afr. Panorama* Oct. 25 The sanctuary is mainly a heronry, but one can also see .. red-knobbed coots, better known in South Africa as 'bleshoenders'. **1980** *Daily Dispatch* 5 Nov. 12 There were coots (bleshoenders), tiny dabchicks, cormorants and Egyptian geese.

bleskop /ˈbleskɔp/ *n. colloq.* Pl. **-pe** /-ə/. [Afk., *bles* bald + *kop* head.] A bald-headed person; a bald head.

1966 I. VAUGHAN *These Were my Yesterdays* 97 Her father .. cut her plaits off. Said to barber, 'Cut short. Can't have hair and brains — one or other. Brains better for her, she so plain.' Barber said to father, 'You are only an old Bleskop how can you know.' **1970** M. WOLFAARDT *Informant, Stilfontein* Your Dad is a real bleskop. (Your dad is bald). **1981** *Fair Lady* 14 Jan. 98 He is our Standard two teacher ... That one there — look, behind the fat lady in the pink dress — the one with the *bleskop* see? *He's* my teacher. **1988** ADAMS & SUTTNER *William Str.* 28 We were playing ball in the street and a ball goes against his head, he had a big head with a bles kop.

blesmol /ˈblesmɔl/ *n.* Formerly also **bleesmol**, **bles-moll**. Pl. **-le** /-ə/. [S. Afr. Du., *bles* blaze + *mol* mole.] Any of several species of molerat of the Bathyergidae, characterized by white markings on the face and head, esp. **a.** the *Cape mole-rat* (see MOLERAT sense 2), *Georychus capensis*; and **b.** the SAND-MOLE, *Bathyergus suillus*. In both senses also called BLES-MOLE. Cf. GOLDEN MOLE.

[**1776** F. MASSON in *Phil. Trans. of Royal Soc.* LXVI. 305 There is another species of the animal, called by the Dutch Bles-moll, which inhabits the hard ground; but seldom exceeds the size of the common European mole.] **1786** G. FORSTER tr. *A. Sparrman's Voy. to Cape of G.H.* II. 195 The one sort [of mole] .. is most common round about the *Cape*; and from the white spots on its head is called *bleesmol*, and is the *mus Capensis* of Messrs. Pennant, Schreber, and Pallas. **1795** C.R. HOPSON tr. *C.P. Thunberg's Trav.* I. 263 The second, called the Blaze-fronted Mole (*Bles Moll, Marmota Capensis*), is smaller, and white with brown spots. **1822** [see MOLERAT sense 1]. [**1901** W.L. SCLATER *Mammals of S. Afr.* II. 74 *Georychus capensis*, .. Mus capensis .. Bathyergus capensis .. Georychus capensis ... Thunberg .. described [it] as *Marmota capensis* ... Vernacular name .. Blesmol of Dutch colonists.] *Ibid.* 75 The blesmol is found both in the uncultivated, sandy districts and also in cultivated grounds and gardens, where it burrows [in] much the same fashion as the sand-mole, throwing up heaps of earth at intervals. **1905** [see BLES]. **1912** [see GOLDEN MOLE sense a]. **1918** S.H. SKAIFE *Animal Life* 256 The *blesmol* is about half the size of the sand-mole, brown in colour, and there is a white patch on the front of its head that gives it its name. **1939** —— *S. Afr. Nature Notes* 167 There are several different species of mole-rats, from the large sand-mole .. to the smaller brown and white mole-rats of our gardens and the blesmol. **1967** E. ROSENTHAL *Encycl. of Sn Afr.* 64 Although regarded as a curse by the farmers, it [*sc.* the blesmol] does at least usefully break up hard ground. Allied to the Blesmol is the wholly grey Mole Rat. [**1990** see *Cape mole-rat* (MOLERAT sense 2).]

bles-mole *n. obs.* [Part. tr. Afk. *blesmol.*] BLESMOL.

1913 C. PETTMAN *Africanderisms* 112 The Bles-mole, *Georychus capensis*, closely resembles *Bathyergus* but is much smaller, and is a great nuisance in gardens. The popular name refers to the white face of the animal. **1924** D. FAIRBRIDGE *Gardens of S. Afr.* 172 Spanish Irises grow readily, but must be taken up after the flowers have died off, to save them from the ravages of the bles-mole. *c***1936** *S. & E. Afr. Yr Bk & Guide* 134 Peculiar to South Africa are, among Rodentia, Blesmoles and Springhares.

blessboc, -bok, blesse-bôk varr. BLESBOK.

blij stil var. BLY STIL.

blik /blək/ *n.* [Afk., tin.]

‖**1.** BLIKKIE.

1913 C. PETTMAN *Africanderisms* 67 Small tin cans, used by labourers to carry tea or coffee in, are known as *bliks*. **1920** R.Y. STORMBERG *Mrs Pieter de Bruyn* 89 A native working in a garden had thoughtlessly thrown a blik (tin) over the fence, and this had hit the horse sharply on its eye.

2.a. Tin, the metal. Also *attrib.*

1973 M.A. COOK *Cape Kitchen* 109 (*caption*) Two graters for lemon rind, nutmeg etc. Made of blik. **1981** *Frontline* May 15 'Blik' is Afrikaans for tin and is a reference to the homemade tin guitar used by the Coloureds of the Western Cape. It was with a slightly more sophisticated version — but also blik — that Kramer began his musical career at the age of twelve. **1986** [see sense b below]. **1988** K. NGWENYA in *Drum* Mar. 92 Jonathan Butler was born 25 years ago in Athlone, Cape Town. It is where he made his first 'blik' guitar — an old fish oil tin strung with nylon fishing gut. **1990** E. HOLTZHAUSEN in *Sunday Times* 16 Dec. 7 The pint-sized singer whose 'blik' guitar and Boland ballads have become as synonymous with South Africa as biltong and potjiekos.

b. *transf.*

i. In full ***blik music***: a style of popular music featuring a metal-bodied guitar as accompaniment to the voice, associated esp. with composer and musician David Kramer. Also *attrib.*

1981 *Frontline* May 15 Kramer's music is as difficult to label as the man himself. 'But if you have to give it a name let's call it blik'. **1982** M. SWIFT in D. Kramer *Short Back & Sides* Foreword, The raucous, aching strains of David Kramer's 'blik' are belting into the homes of all South Africans. **1982** *Fair Lady* 24 Feb. 95 Kramer's current obsession is with a sound he calls 'blik' — the sound you get from cheap guitars ... He has listened to many of Hugh Tracey's recordings of blik music. **1986** D. KRAMER in *Sunday Times* 5 Jan. 9 When I started out, people often used to ask me what my music was called. I told them it was 'blik' — you know, like a blik guitar or banjo. **1988** —— in *Flying Springbok* Apr. 27 It was a creative relationship between David Kramer — king of Boland *blik* — and Taliep Petersen. **1989** D. KRAMER in *ADA* No.7, 9 Because I was talking about 'blik' music, I went to America and came back with a silver guitar.

ii. *comb.* **blik-based** *nonce*, founded on this style of music.

1986 M. LE CHAT in *Sunday Times* 20 July (Mag. Sect.) 32 He .. embarked on a *blik*-based career that saw him end up as a social commentator who was '*almal se pêl*'.

‖**blik-huis** /ˈbləkhœis, -heɪs/ *n.* Pl. **-e** /-ə/. [Afk., *blik* tin + *huis* house.] A house constructed of corrugated iron: either a prefabricated wood-and-iron structure, or a squatter's makeshift home. See also TIN.

1949 J. MOCKFORD *Golden Land* 250 Nine miles south of Pretoria is General Smuts's 'blik-huis' (tin-house) at Irene, where he farms. General Smuts calls his house a 'blik-huis' because, originally, it was a British Army cantonment of corrugated iron. **1987** *South* 2 July 5 They have now been further angered by .. another rent increase expected in September for 'blikhuise' which the residents say 'is not worth it'.

‖**blikkie** /ˈbləki/ *n.* [Afk., *blik* tin + -IE.] A can or similar container made of tin; BLIK sense 1.

1912 H.H. JUTA *Reminisc.* 10 Below the cart, from the axle, swung a fair-sized 'blikkie' — a tin cannister. *c***1929** S. BLACK in S. Gray *Three Plays* (1984) 58 The only French I know I learnt off a condensed milk blikkie. **1958** A. JACKSON *Trader on Veld* 35 A favourite meal in the shop consisted of a *blikkie gember konfijt*, or *blikkie sardines* (tin of preserved ginger or a tin of sardines) accompanied by half a pound of sugared biscuits.

Blikkies- /ˈbləkiːz/ *combining form. Colloq.* [By analogy with BLIKKIESDORP.] A pejorative element in fictitious place names, meaning 'one-horse', insignificant, or 'dreary'.

1982 *Sunday Times* 18 Apr. (Mag. Sect.) 1 A holiday on the cheap .. only if Mum is agreeable to doing all the work she .. does at home on a camping site in Blikkiesbaai. **1982** *Grocott's Mail* 25 June 1 Modern buildings like some of those in High Street .. make the place look more like Blikkiesfontein than the fountainhead of English culture in South Africa. **1982** E. PLATTER in *Fair Lady* 3 Nov. 344 'Interesting, unusual, striking' .. can tide you over anything from the top growths to a plonk de plonk from the Overblikkiesberg Co-operative.

Blikkiesdorp /ˈbləkiːzˌdɔːp/ *n. colloq.* [Afk., *blikkie* 'little tin' (prob. alluding to houses of corrugated iron, see BLIK-HUIS) + linking phoneme *-s-* + *dorp* town.]

1. The imaginary epitome of an insignificant, dreary, 'one-horse' town. See also BLIKKIES- and DORP sense a.

[**1959** J. MEIRING *Candle in Wind* 118 'Hello Blikkiesdorp,' he called, and his little friends yelled with glee. 'Hello, Smartie!' Lena called back, with a good humour she did not feel.] **1962** J. TAYLOR 'Hennie van Saracen'. (*lyrics*) One day outside Blikkiesdorp I got out of control, And I ended up in Bree Street, with my tank stuck up a pole. **1971** *Fair Lady* 6 Sept. 103 Are you bored stiff by that routine job somewhere in Blikkiesdorp? **1972** *Daily Dispatch* 27 May 12 (*cartoon*) Just imagine, hey, if — instead of Blikkiesdorp — we land up in the Seychelles. **1974** on Radio South Africa 20 June (Encounter), What about the people in the main urban areas? You can't tell them to go and live in Blikkiesdorp. **1979** *Sunday Times* 9 Dec. (Mag. Sect.) 2 Around Blikkiesdorp or wherever .. simple minds are not known for their deep insight into race relations. **1984** E.K. MOORCROFT in *Grocott's Mail* 10 Apr. 17, I can see no merit at all in debating who said what about the Hon. Member of Blikkiesdorp's buffalo-hunting trip when you are supposed to be debating the budget. **1990** J.G. DAVIS *Land God Made in Anger* 304 The good old Afrikaner farmers and housewives of Blikkiesdorp — they're just simple God-fearing folk. **1990** *Weekend Argus* 24 Nov. 1 What was billed as 'the most spectacular outdoor event seen in South Africa' had as much spark as Guy Fawkes at Blikkiesdorp.

2. Any slum area or shanty-town; a run-down black residential area; *onderdorp*, see DORP sense b.

1970 B.C. MARITZ *Informant, Port Elizabeth* The poor whites live in Blikkiesdorp. **1977** *Het Suid-Western* 12 Sept., Mrs .. N— and Mrs .. B— live in Blikkiesdorp — the Bantu area of tin houses next to Rosemoor. **1978** *Speak* Vol.1 No.5, 55 The location houses in which his pupils lived, the hungry children from Blikkiesdorp in his school. **1980** E. JOUBERT *Poppie Nongena* 14 They lived in Blikkiesdorp, which was Upington's shanty-town or location. All kinds of people, except whites, were living there. **1990** *Sunday Times* 5 Aug. 10 The poorer kids — who live in what is known to Krugersdorp locals as 'Blikkiesdorp' — gave most of their earnings to their parents.

Blikoor /ˈbləkʊə(r)/ *n. colloq.* Pl. **-o(o)re** /-ʊərə/, **-oors**. [Afk., *blik* tin + *oor* ear.] A nickname for an inhabitant of the Orange Free State; (*rare*) an inhabitant of the Transvaal. Also *attrib.*

1899 *Cape Times* 24 Nov. 7 (Pettman), Their Transvaal brethren do not hesitate to admit that the *Blikoors* (nickname of Free Staters) are the best body of men round Ladysmith. **1913** C. PETTMAN *Africanderisms* 68 *Blikoor*, .. One of several nicknames given to the Transvaalers by the Dutch of the Cape Colony, and subsequently applied by the Transvaalers to their brethren of the Orange Free State. [**1934** *Star* 1 May 13 For the past 50 years and more Free Staters have been known among Dutch-speaking South Africans as Blikore (tin ears) and Transvaalers as Vaalpense, the latter so called after a certain native tribe of that name who lived in the Transvaal.] **1945** N. Devitt *People & Places* 144 The country people of the two Republics for long years had nicknames for each other. The Transvalers were called 'Vaalpense' (grey-bellies), the Free Staters 'Blikoore' (tin ears). **1967** E. Rosenthal *Encycl. of Sn Afr.* 64 *Blikoor*, .. Nickname given traditionally to the Orange Free State and Transvaal Boers, but also applied by the Transvalers to the Orange Free Staters. **1980** *Sunday Times* 12 Oct. 20 Freestaters do occasionally become hot under the collar over matters political. Hence the squabble over who should succeed .. as administrator of the blikoor province. **1990** *Weekend Post* 23 June 20 Eastern Province overran Free State .. in Bloemfontein on Saturday ... EP's win puts the coastal men back into the hunt for the coveted gold cup while the 'Blikore' are surely now also rans.

bliksem /ˈbləksəm/ *n.*, *int.*, *adj.*, and *adv. Slang.* Also **bliksom**, **bluxom**. [Afk., lit. 'lightning'.] Not in polite use.

A. *n.*

a. A scoundrel, blighter, 'bastard'; DONDER *n.* sense a.

1950 E. Partridge *Dict. of Underworld Slang* 47 *Bliksem*, .. A rogue. *c*1957 D. Swanson *Highveld, Lowveld & Jungle* 64 'The little bliksom,' Klaussens said, staring down at the crumpled, inert body. **1977** A. Roscoe *Uhuru's Fire* 226 All you bliksems look the same. **1983** *Drum* Aug. 31 These township bliksems are all communists and agitators. **1986** L.B. Hall in *Style* July 97 'Koos man, these blerrie horseflies are chewing me alive.' Smack, slap. 'The bliksems.' **1991** J. Dewes in *E. Prov. Herald* 10 Dec. 5 A bluxom can .. be a person who makes himself objectionable for any number of reasons: slander, theft, forgetfulness, failure to pay a debt or failure to buy a round of drinks.

b. A term of address equivalent to 'bastard', 'scoundrel'; BLIKSKOTTEL sense 2 a; DONDER *n.* sense b.

1954 J. Wiles *Moon to Play With* 224 'Bliksem! Vuilgoed!' she screamed ... Then she was chasing them up the street, shouting and waving her arms at them. **1965** K. Mackenzie *Deserter* 43 The next time the axle came down it splashed some surface water towards them. 'You *bliksem*!' James shouted, jumping backwards out of the way. **1973** Y. Burgess *Life to Live* 144 His 'girl-friend' swore at him, called him 'bliksem', which means, innocuously enough, lightning, fed him sleeping pills and tied him to the bed. [**1984** S. Gray *Three Plays* 135 Katoo: Make it six, jou bliksem. Abraham: No, I couldn't do it, really, really. Where's my profit?]

c. An utterance of this word.

1990 J. Naidoo *Coolie Location* 153 She's really a civilized chick. You know, no fuckings, no blerry's, no voetseks, no bliksems.

d. In the phr. ***to donner the bliksem out of*** [see DONNER *v.*], 'to beat the hell out of'.

1993 A. Goldstuck in *Rhodent* (Rhodes Univ.) 28 *Pik Botha* ... Pastimes include poetry, classical music, eastern philosophy, and donnering the bliksem out of anyone who checks him skeef.

B. *int.* An expression of frustration, anger, or disgust. See also DONDER *int.*

1963 A. Fugard *Blood Knot* (1968) 151 (*Zach lunges suddenly, but Morris escapes*) Zach: Bliksem! Wait, Morrie! Wait! **1982** [see DUIWELTJIE]. **1983** A. Sparks in J. Crwys-Williams *S. Afr. Despatches* (1989) 447 Oom Daniel was overwhelmed by his success. '*Bliksem* — bloody hell,' he kept muttering ... 'My worst mampoer won the prize'. **1990** J. Clegg in *Sunday Times* 24 Dec. 11 If there's criticism of something I've written .. bliksem! It's eina! **1991** J. Dewes in *E. Prov. Herald* 10 Dec. 5 British technicians .. first became acquainted with the word when one accidentally collided with a South African, not only hurting the South African's nose but also treading on his toes. 'Bluxom!' said the South African, rubbing his nose and hopping on one foot.

C. *adj.* Also (*attrib.*) **bliksemse**. Damned.

1975 S. Roberts *Outside Life's Feast* 85 It was blarry good luck for him there was a bliksemse lawaai coming from the bathroom an' we somaar walk in. **1987** *Rhodes SR Scene* (Grahamstown) May 2 (*cartoon*) Go, and darken my door no more! .. The bliksem liberal voted Nat!

D. *adv.* Used as an intensifier; cf. BLERRY *adv.*

1977 Fugard & Devenish *Guest* 20 One thing I do know, his medicine is bliksem strong. **1983** J. Cronin *Inside* 8 At fifteen he became office boy at Katzenellenbogen's .. where he learned: .. The GPO telegram charge is reckoned per word. A word is 15 letters max. You have to drop *one l* from Katzenellenbogen Inc or *Hear me boy?!* nex'time *you's* gonna pay extra one word charge your bliksem self.

Hence **bliksem** *v. trans.*, to curse (something) with the word 'bliksem'; to beat (someone) up.

1980 M. Mutloatse in *Staffrider* Vol.3 No.4, 40 'Well, if this bugger gets up he's going to moer us again; or his chommies will get here and bliksem us to pieces.' **1991** J. Dewes in *E. Prov. Herald* 10 Dec. 5 Inanimate things can .. be bluxomed with ease: an obstinate wheelnut, a cigarette lighter that won't work, a letter from a creditor, or a dog barking at dead of night. **1991** D. Boswell *Informant, Giyani* (*N. Tvl*) I'm warning you. Don't gooi me grief because I'm not in the mood ... I'll bliksem you.

‖**blikskottel** /ˈblək,skɔt(ə)l, -d(ə)l/ *n.* [Afk., *blik* tin + *skottel* dish.]

1. *rare.* A tin basin. Cf. SKOTTEL sense 1.

1958 A. Jackson *Trader on Veld* 46 On his return he prepared them for a great surprise, and gathering the family in his rondavel, called for a 'blikskottel' (tin basin).

2. *slang.* An abusive form of address:

a. A euphemism for BLIKSEM *n.* sense b.

1959 A. Delius *Last Division* 74 Where have you come from, you villain! You bloody old bastard, Blikskottel, Hotnot! **1975** S. Roberts *Outside Life's Feast* 58, I had to send him to clean himself and had to maar start the breakfast myself. I said listen here you blikskottel if you do this again you're out.

b. An expletive expressing disgust or anger.

1973 J. Cope *Alley Cat* 30 Blikskottel! She's got to have sense knocked into her foken head, sooner the better.

bliksom var. BLIKSEM.

blinkaar /ˈbləŋkɑː(r)/ *n.* Also **blinkhaar**. [Afk., *blink* shining + *aar* spikelet, ear.] In full ***blinkaar grass***: the silvery grass *Stipagrostis uniplumis* of the Poaceae (sub-family Arundinoideae). See also BUSHMAN GRASS.

1968 G. Croudace *Silver Grass* 8 His private cattle stood knee-deep in the fine shining grass. This was the grass that the Boer hunters called *blinkhaar*, likening it to the gleaming hair of the blonde daughters they had left behind in South Africa. **1975** W.B. Miller in *Std Encycl. of Sn Afr.* XI. 321 Vegetation is very sparse and consists of arid shrub grass-land and some good stands of blinkaar grass (*Aristida uniplumis*).

‖**blinkblaar** /ˈbləŋkblɑː(r)/ *n.* [Afk., *blink* shining, glossy + *blaar* leaf.] Any of several species of indigenous trees or shrubs with glossy leaves, esp. *Rhamnus prinoides* of the Rhamnaceae.

1913 C. Pettman *Africanderisms* 68 *Blinkblaar*, .. *Rhamnus prinoides*, a shrub with glossy, shining leaves. **1937** F.S. Laughton *Sylviculture of Indigenous Forests* 61 *Rhamnaceae. Rhamnus prinoides*, .. (*Blinkblaar*) is a shrub, sometimes 15 feet in height, which occurs occasionally throughout the forests. **1944** H.C. Bosman in L. Abrahams *Cask of Jerepigo* (1972) 157 Then there was the bush ... Swarthaak and blinkblaar and wag-'n-bietjie. **1951** N.L. King *Tree-Planting* 70 *Rhamnus prinoides* (*Blinkblaar*), A widely dispersed shrub with shiny leaves, dark green above, paler below. Suitable for hedges. Grows almost anywhere except in the driest parts. [**1966** C.A. Smith *Common Names* 112 *Blinkblaar(boom)*, Several unrelated arboreous or arborescent species of which the leaves have a characteristic glossy or polished appearance.] **1970** M.R. Levyns in *Std Encycl. of Sn Afr.* II. 364 *Blinkblaar(bos)*, The best-known bearer of this name is *Rhamnus prinoides*, a thornless shrub of the family *Rhamnaceae*, having shining, dark green, simple leaves. **1977** E. Palmer *Field Guide to Trees* 208 *Rhamnus*, .. A famous magic tree believed to have protective powers. Also known as blinkblaar (shiny leaf). **1990** *Weekend Post* 3 Mar. (Leisure) 7 The darker greens which were used as fillers were *Rhamnus prinoides* (blinkblaar), an indigenous shrub which grows along river banks ... The shiny leaves and lasting qualities of this plant have made it popular with florists.

‖**blinkblaar-wag-'n-bietjie** /,bləŋkblɑː(r) ˈvaxəbɪki/ *n.* [Afk., see BLINKBLAAR and WAG-'N-BIETJIE.] The *buffalo thorn* (see BUFFALO sense 2), *Ziziphus mucronata*.

1951 N.L. King *Tree-Planting* 72 *Zizyphus mucronata* (*Blinkblaar Wag-'n-bietjie*), A small, bushy tree armed with strong recurved thorns. **1961** [see *buffalo thorn* (BUFFALO sense 2)]. **1970** M.R. Levyns in *Std Encycl. of Sn Afr.* II. 364 *Blinkblaar-Wag-'n-bietjie*, .. (*Ziziphus mucronata*.) Tall shrub or tree of the family *Rhamnaceae*, having dark green, glossy leaves. The stipules develop into sharp thorns — one straight, the other recurved, which make sudden contact with the species an unpleasant experience — hence the name 'wag-'n-bietjie' (Afrikaans for 'wait a bit') and the English vernacular name sometimes used: 'come-and-I'll-kiss-you'.

blinkhaar *n.*[1] var. BLINKAAR.

blinkhaar /ˈbləŋk(h)ɑː(r)/ *n.*[2] Also with initial capital. [Afk., *blink* glossy + *haar* hair.] A silky-haired RONDERIB sheep. Also *attrib.*

Considered by some to be the true Ronderib sheep, those without silky hair being seen as not bred to type.

*a*1878 J. Montgomery *Reminisc.* (1981) 110 Some of the farmers from the New Hantam arrived on their way to Graham's town ... I persuaded them not to continue their journey, as the Kafirs had broken out ... They stayed, and I became the purchaser of the whole of their produce, and 400 blinkhaar ewes at Rds. 2 each. **1937** *Handbk for Farmers* (Dept of Agric. & Forestry) 199 In certain individual sheep was observed the occurrence of coarse opaque, brittle, kempy fibres .. in contrast to the soft silky hair of the greater majority. This difference of covering is submitted to be the origin of a sub-division in Ronderib sheep, namely the 'Blinkhaar' and the 'Steekhaar'. **1945** [see PERSIAN]. **1966** [see BOERBOK]. **1968** G. Croudace *Black Rose* 78 Your indigenous flocks, your fat-tailed blinkhaar Afrikanders.

blink klip *n. phr. Obs.* Pl. **-pe** /-ə/, **-pers** /-ərs, -əz/. [S. Afr. Du., *blink* shiny, glossy + *klip* stone.]

1. *noncount.* Micaceous iron ore, formerly used (in powdered form) by certain African peoples as a cosmetic.

1827 G. Thompson *Trav.* I. 226 Hundreds of pack-oxen were continually moving off to the westward, loaded with the most valuable effects of the inhabitants .. red paint-stone, powder of the *blink-klip*, corn, carosses, &c. **1835** A. Smith *Diary* (1940) II. 27 When the corn is young they will not kill elephants; they think the corn will burn up. They cannot go and get red clay or blink klip before harvest.

2. KLIP *n.* sense 2.

1893 T. Reunert *Diamonds & Gold* 6 The attention of everyone in that neighbourhood was turned to seeking *blink klippe* .. and during the following year several diamonds were picked up on the banks of the Vaal. **1920** F.C. Cornell *Glamour of Prospecting* 54 They were looking for 'blink klippers' (bright stones) in a sand river, and finding them too, lots of them. **1923** *S. Afr.: Land of Outdoor Life* (S.A.R. & H.) 82 Another and remarkable discovery of diamonds was made ... Some 'blink klippe' as the Boers called them, were found early in 1871.

‖**blink klippie** /ˈbləŋ,kləpi/ *n. phr. Obs.* exc. *hist.* Formerly also **blink klippije**. [Afk., *blink klip* (see prec.) + dim. suffix -IE.] KLIP *n.* sense 2.

blirry var. BLERRY.

bliss-bock var. BLESBOK.

blister bush *n. phr.* [See quot. 1966.] The plant *Peucedanum galbanum* of the Apiaceae, which blisters the skin on contact; *wild celery*, see WILD sense a. Freq. also **blistering bush**.

  1917 R. MARLOTH *Common Names* 122 P[*eucedanum*] *Galbanum*, ... Blistering bush, wild celery. 1932 WATT & BREYER-BRANDWIJK *Medicinal & Poisonous Plants* 134 *Peucedanum galbanum*, Wild celery, Blistering bush .. is taken as an abortifacient and blisters the skin on contact. 1966 C.A. SMITH *Common Names* 113 *Blistering bush, Peucedanum galbanum* (Cape) ... Severe blistering of the skin follows on contact with bruised leaves. 1970 [see *wild celery* (WILD sense a)]. 1983 *Flying Springbok* Apr. 41 Suitable plants have been superseded by more dominant species like .. blister bush (Peucedanum galbanum). 1988 M. BRANCH *Explore Cape Flora* 36 Crushed leaves of blister bushes cause painful, long-lasting brown blisters. These appear after two to three days but only if the skin is exposed to sunlight. If you touch a bush, cover the skin to keep it dark.

blits /blǝts/ *n.* Also **blitz**. Shortened form of WITBLITS (sense b).

  1977 *Family Radio & TV* 19 Sept. 51 Tradition at the heart of a Boer way of life will become a crime — for *witblitz*-making will be entirely illegal ... Thirty-five litres of the already strong *mos* make only 1,5 litres of *blitz*. 1984 *Cape Times* 29 Feb., The Cape's cleverest concocters of mind-blowing booze will be gathering at the Worcester Open-Air Farm Museum .. to determine who brews the finest blits of them all ... Distillers .. will compete for the honour of being crowned South Africa's first official champion witblits distiller.

blitskommando see KOMMANDO sense 1 b.

block *n.* [Special sense of general Eng. *block* a large sub-division of land.] A large area of agricultural land consisting of a number of farms owned by one person or company, and forming a single unit.

  1937 C. BIRKBY *Zulu Journey* 187 He employs 18 farm managers to run 18 blocks of farms — some of them immense holdings — ranging from Basutoland to Portuguese East Africa. 1978 A.P. BRINK *Rumours of Rain* 198 Calitz had set to work immediately, profiting from the drought to buy up, through intermediaries, a vast block of farms at ridiculous prices. Almost in the centre of the block was our family farm. 1988 *Personality* 16 May 36 Later he bought other farms, and eventually owned a block of 5 000 hectares, as well as other properties.

blocked rand see RAND sense 3 b.

‖**bloedpens** /'blutpens, 'blʊt-/ *n. Pathology.* [Afk., *bloed* blood + *pens* stomach.] A type of dysentery affecting domestic livestock, esp. lambs. Also *attrib.*

  1891 [see BITTER BUSH]. 1911 *Farmer's Weekly* 4 Oct. 127 (advt) Little's Fluid Dip ... Experienced Farmers have proved Little's Fluid to be a certain cure for and preventative of Bloed-Pens in Lambs. 1914 *Farmer's Annual* 133 In some districts it is known by the farmers as 'Bloedpens', owing to the blood-coloured appearance of the lining membrane of the stomach, which is highly congested, or a purple colour, and presents a soft, flabby appearance. 1937 *Handbk for Farmers* (Dept of Agric. & Forestry) 491 Bloedpens is a disease occurring in lambs in the first week of life. The symptoms are .. abdominal pain and usually a diarrhoea. 1957 *Handbk for Farmers* (Dept of Agric.) III. 366 The unmistakable signs of 'bloedpens' are seen when a carcase is opened: the intestines are filled with gas and the mucous membrane of the small intestine is swollen, dark red, and is bloody over large areas. 1970 D.M. MCMASTER *Informant, Cathcart (E. Cape)* The Afrikaans words for vaccines are used more than the English equivalents even by English-speaking farmers — e.g. the vaccine against lamb dysentery is always called bloedpens vaccine. 1976 MÖNNIG & VELDMAN *Handbk on Stock Diseases* 23 Lamb Dysentery (Bloedpens) .. is an acute gastro-enteritis of lambs during the first few days of life. It is caused by *Clostridium welchii* and occurs in areas with a severe winter.

bloedsap /'blʊtsap, 'blʌt-/ *n.* Also **bloed SAP**, and with initial capital. Pl. **-sappe** /sapǝ/. [Afk., *bloed* blood + *sap* a member or supporter of the United Party; see also quot. 1983.] An ultra-conservative, dyed-in-the-wool member or supporter of the former United Party (see UP); a supporter of the politics of Jan Smuts and Louis Botha; an Afrikaner supporting a predominantly English-speaking political party and not the National Party. Also *attrib*. See also SAP *n.*[1] sense 2 b. Cf. *bloednat* (see NAT *n.* sense b).

  1971 *Sunday Times* 27 June 6 The United Party .. cannot take any heart from the result. It is clear that many 'bloedsappe' did not only vote for the HNP, but in fact joined the HNP. 1972 *Star* 7 Nov. 5 Leaf-blight which, like the 'Bloedsap' (ultra-conservative UP supporter) would always be with you. 1974 [see ENGELS *n.* sense 3 b]. 1977 *Sunday Times* 29 May 16 So after 44 years we again have a South African Party. Born at a bloedsap convention .. and committed, apparently, to a kind of semi-detachment from the NP, its membership reflects the longings, prejudices and habits of a passing generation. 1983 C. SAUNDERS *Hist. Dict.* 159 Many Afrikaners remained bloedsappe, .. (literally blood South African Party men, i.e. those with a hereditary loyalty to Botha and Smuts). 1986 P. LE ROUX in Burman & Reynolds *Growing Up* 188 He .. explained that he was merely a *bloedsap* — that is, that his father, who was a strong Smuts supporter, would never forgive him should he vote for the National Party, and that he himself would never do anything to harm the party. 1990 K. O'MALLEY in *Frontline* Feb. 2 On the right are old Bloedsappe and NRP supporters, many of whom are more anti-Nat (or anti-Afrikaans) than anything else. 1991 A. VAN WYK *Birth of New Afrikaner* 13 To be an Afrikaner and not to vote Nat was to be out of step with the vast majority and labelled 'not a good Afrikaner'. Of course there were *bloedsappe*, that small coterie of ever-willing Afrikaners who had been supporting English-oriented political parties since the days of Louis Botha ... They were either regarded as politically wayward, or tolerated as *verdwaaldes* (strayed ones) who would one day come to see the light of true Boer patriotism. *Ibid.* 69 Virtually alone in his stand, he was more than a *bloedsap* (Sap by inheritance), he firmly believed that the Nationalist policies were wrong and never hesitated to tell us so. 1991 D. BECKETT in *Sunday Star* 3 Feb. (Review) 5 Doc is a renowned Bloedsap, a Smuts man ... So how did he reach the top arena where a Sap was once as low a form of life as a Kommunis?

bloedstillende druppels see DRUPPELS sense b i.

bloem(m)etjie var. BLOMMETJIE.

‖**blombos** /'blɔmbɔs/ *n.* [Afk., *blom* flower + *bos* bush.] Any of several species of low coastal shrubs producing a profusion of scented flowers, esp. *Metalasia muricata* of the Asteraceae.

  1917 R. MARLOTH *Common Names* 13 *Blombos, Metalasia muricata*. One of the most frequent shrubs of the coastal districts. 1924 *Off. Yrbk of Union* 1923 (Union Office of Census & Statistics) 46 The low bush and scrub on the sandy flats is comprised mainly of .. the blombos .. *Metalasia muricata*. 1934 C.P. SWART *Supplement to Pettman*. 46 *Blombos*, .. A low shrub growing on the sandy flats is so called on account of its beautiful growth of flowers. 1966 C.A. SMITH *Common Names* 114 *Blombos*(sie), Species of a number of unrelated genera which produce a profusion of white flowers. 1970 M.R. LEVYNS in *Std Encycl. of Sn Afr.* II. 374 *Blombos, (Metalasia muricata)* Widespread shrub of the family compositae ... The flowers are scented and are much favoured by bees in search of honey. 1987 T.F.J. VAN RENSBURG *Intro. to Fynbos* 17 Among the single stem low shrubs, the blombos (*Metalasia* spp.), with its dense white, yellow or pink flowers is often striking. 1989 *Weekend Post* 11 Nov. (Leisure) 4 There are always many small plants to catch your attention. Bright blue lobelias, red everlastings and white blombos are a few.

blomkoolganna see GANNA sense 2.

‖**blommetjie** /'blɔmǝki, -ci/ *n.* Formerly also **bloem(m)etje, blommetje**. [Afk., *blom* (earlier Du. *bloem*) flower + dim. suffix -IE.]

1. A small flower. Also *attrib.*

  1904 *Argus Christmas Annual* 12 (Pettman), There was that wonderful valley of the lake with the *bloemetjes* and the scent-laden *avond bloem*. 1913 D. FAIRBRIDGE *Piet of Italy* 46 And all roun' me hedges of pink roses an' purple bloemmetjes. 1924 —— *Gardens of S. Afr.* 119 The Government .. is .. prohibiting the uprooting or sale of a few of the more rare bulbs and plants — but it is easier to make such a law than to enforce it on the flower-sellers, to whom every flower is just a blommetje. 1936 E. ROSENTHAL *Old-Time Survivals* 13 Examine a good one [*sc.* wagon] carefully and you will notice quaint little ornaments in many colours painted along the sides of the frame. These are the traditional 'blommetjies' or flowers on which the conservative farmer insists, just as did his 'oupa'. 1949 L.G. GREEN *In Land of Afternoon* 127 Many farmers rightly insist on the traditional hand-painted blommetjie decorations on wheels and sides, the same bunches of flowers that have adorned wagons for more than a hundred years. 1990 S.I. Ross *Informant, Grahamstown* The buses are decorated with carvings and tassles and blommetjies and bells — you wouldn't believe it.

2. Ellipt. for WATERBLOMMETJIE (sense a).

  1981 *S. Afr. Panorama* Dec. 21 The demand for blommetjies has shot up to such an extent that their natural habitat, the *vleis* or marshlands of the Cape, are being positively denuded.

blood *n. Ostrich-farming.* [See quot. 1913.] In full *blood feather*: a partly grown feather from the wing of a cock ostrich, with blood still in the shaft. See also PRIME.

  1873 F. BOYLE *To Cape for Diamonds* 193 It is very rare to find tame 'bloods' — as these first feathers are called — that will bear comparison with the wild. 1874 W.G. ATHERSTONE in De Mosenthal & Harting *Ostriches & Ostrich Farming* (1877) 205 He then picked out a blood-feather, very beautiful, which, on being cut, bled a little, but .. without it being felt. 1877 DE MOSENTHAL & HARTING *Ibid.* 225 The finest white wild 'blood-feathers' .. are worth more than double. 1880 S.W. Silver & Co.'s *Handbk to S. Afr.* 234 Chicken plumes are worth 5s., and blood feathers from 35l. to 45l., or even 60l. a lb. 1886 G.A. FARINI *Through Kalahari Desert* 134, I .. plucked out his best feathers — all 'bloods,' though not very long, the season being early. *Ibid.* 328 'What's a blood feather, Jan?' 'One that's pulled out with blood in the pen. The tame ones are cut. If they were pulled out, they would never grow again.' 1913 J.E. DUERDEN in *S. Afr. Agric. Jrnl* VI. 656 Partly grown feathers with the blood within them are known as blood feathers, or, technically, as 'bloods'.

blood sickness *n. phr. Obs. Pathology.* [tr. S. Afr. Du. *bloedziekte*, see BLOODZIEKTE.] Any of several diseases affecting the circulatory system in livestock, some being communicable to human beings; BLOODZIEKTE.

[1795 C.R. Hopson tr. *C.P. Thunberg's Trav.* I. 151 The bloody sickness (*blaar* or *bloodziekte*) is a disease of the cattle, in which the veins all over the body are extremely turgid.] 1838 J.E. Alexander *Exped. into Int.* I. 145 Balli was suffering under the disease called blood sickness. Sheep occasionally get this, which is a corrupted state of the blood ... The disease is very often communicated to those partaking of the impure flesh. *a*1867 C.J. Andersson *Notes of Trav.* (1875) 229 Neither have sheep succeeded; those that have been imported from Damaraland, or elsewhere, have for the most part succumbed to a disease designated the 'blood-sickness'.

bloodwood *n.* [See quot. 1971.] KIAAT.
1913 C. Pettman *Africanderisms* 70 Bloodwood, The Transvaal name of *Pterocarpus angolensis*. 1971 Baraitser & Obholzer *Cape Country Furn.* 279 Kiaat is a medium sized tree ... The wood has a light brown colour and because it exudes, when cut, dark red juice, it is also known as blood wood. 1990 M. Oettle in *Weekend Post* 29 Dec. (Leisure) 7 *Pterocarpus angolensis*, kiaat or bloodwood.

bloodziekte *n. Obs. Pathology.* Also **bloodzichte**. [Part. tr. S. Afr. Du. *bloedziekte*, fr. Du. *bloed* blood + *ziekte* sickness.] BLOOD SICKNESS.
1795 [see BLOOD SICKNESS]. [1798 S.H. Wilcocke tr. *J.S. Stavorinus's Voy. to E. Indies 1768–71* II. 64 The *blaar*, or *bloedziekte*, is a disorder, in which the veins all over the body become extremely turgid.] 1835 A. Smith *Diary* (1939) I. 241 The disease called *bloodzichte* is sometimes very common about Latakoo during the months of Feby, March and April ... First appears like the swellings occasioned by muskitoe bites, then gets puffy and a black spot appears .. which ulcerates.

blos op *var.* BLAASOP.

bloubaadjie /ˈblǝʊbaɪki, -ci/ *n.* [Afk., *blou* blue + *baadjie* jacket (see BAADJIE).]
1. *colloq.* A provincial traffic officer.
1970 C. Mans *Informant, Cape Town* You mustn't go too fast on the National road, because there are a lot of bloubaadjies. 1972 R. Malan *Ah Big Yaws* 36 Surrenly, unmar revue murra, Ah seizes blow-bard-chiennarkin tyellyew Ah storts nippon strauce. [Suddenly, in my rearview mirror, I sees this bloubaadjie — and I can tell you I starts nipping straws.] 1974 *Het Suid-Western* 17 Oct. 2 Every time a bloubaadjie stops a car and issues a speeding ticket .. the Government loses another vote.
2. *Prison slang.*
a. The blue jacket worn in the past by long-term male prisoners serving an indeterminate sentence. See also BAADJIE sense 2.
1972 *Sunday Times* 24 Sept. 5 Mr Justice Theron at the Rand Criminal Sessions declared R— an habitual criminal and ordered him the 'blou baadjie' or blue jacket worn by convicts serving the indeterminate sentence of nine to 15 years. 1974 [see BAADJIE sense 2].
b. *transf.* A long-term male prisoner: BLUE-COAT sense 1.
1980 *Cape Times* 9 Jan. 5 Four battle-scarred shaven ex- 'Bloubaadjies' — long term prisoners — had heard a noise emanating from the darkened building and decided to investigate. 1987 S. Roberts *Jacks in Corners* 171 Laetitia dreamt she was a photographer, snapping at *bloubaadjies* breaking stones in a prison yard.

blou biskop see BISKOP sense 1 b.

bloubok /ˈblǝʊbɒk/ *n. hist.* [Afk., earlier S. Afr. Du. *blauwbok*, see BLAUWBOK.] The BLAUWBOK (sense 1 a), *Hippotragus leucophaeus*.
1971 *Farmer's Weekly* 12 May 11 The bloubok (*Hippotragus leucophaea*) which had a distribution similar to that of the bontebok, was together with other species of game, completely exterminated at the end of 1799. 1982 *E. Prov. Herald* 27 July 13 The numbers of most species have been appreciably reduced so we can consider ourselves lucky that only three species have been exterminated. These are the quagga, bloubok, and Cape lion. 1987 *Conserva* Apr. 15 The bloubok is not known to have survived beyond about 1800 and was apparently the first of the recent African mammals to become extinct.

bloubokkie /ˈblǝʊbɒki/ *n.* [Afk., *bloubok* (*blou* blue + *bok* antelope, goat) + dim. suffix -IE.] The *blue duiker* (see DUIKER sense 1 b), *Philantomba monticola*.
[1951 A. Roberts *Mammals* 323 *Guevei caerula caerula*, Blue Duiker, Bloubokkie.] 1973 *Cape Times* 13 Jan. (Mag. Sect.) 4 The little Blue Duiker, or the Bloubokkie, which is the smallest South African antelope, as small as a hare in fact. 1978 *Het Suid-Western* 20 Sept., Ruthless people have been shooting at and allowing their dogs to hunt down the tiny herd of rare little bloubokkies.

bloubos /ˈblǝʊbɒs/ *n.* Formerly also **blaau(w)bosch, blauw bosch**. [Afk. (earlier S. Afr. Du. *blauwbosch*), *blou* blue + *bos* bush.] Any of several small trees or shrubs of the genus *Diospyros* of the Ebenaceae, esp. *D. lycioides*; BLUE-BUSH. Also *attrib.*
1907 T.R. Sim *Forests & Forest Flora* 14 On the rich alluvial soil along the dry river beds there are, however, occasional trees of Mimosa (Acacia horrida), Karreeboom (Rhus lancea), Blaauwbosch (Royena). 1911 *Farmer's Weekly* 15 Mar. 1 On the farm are .. many Olive wood, karree and Blaauwbosch Trees and Bushes. *a*1930 [see BLUE-BUSH]. 1961 Palmer & Pitman *Trees of S. Afr.* 133 The bloubos differs greatly in appearance in various parts of the country, varying from a shrub a couple of feet high to a small sized timber tree. 1971 L.G. Green *Taste of S.-Easter* 161 No mean botanist, he could recognise most of the South African bee plants from the boerboom to the bloubos to the water-bessie and dopperkiaat. 1977 E. Palmer *Field Guide to Trees* 263 The commonest *Diospyros* species, particularly familiar in parts of OFS and Karoo; valued for shade, shelter, bark for tanning ... Widely known as bloubos (blue bush).

bloukop koggelmander see KOGGELMANDER sense 2.

bloukop koggelmannetjie see KOGGELMANNETJIE sense 2.

bloupak /ˈblǝʊpak/ *n. colloq.* Pl. **-ke** /-kǝ/. [Afk., *blou* blue + *pak* suit.] KITSKONSTABEL.
A term used in those black urban areas in which auxiliary policemen wear blue uniforms.
1987 A. Ismail in *South* 9 July 7 There have been a number of reported clashes between special constables called 'bloupakke' and residents. A number of people have appeared in court recently charged with .. attacks on 'bloupakke'. 1988 *Now Everyone Is Afraid* (Catholic Inst. for Internat. Rel.) 20 There are important differences between kitskonstabels and municipal police. 'Kitskonstabels' is a slang term for special constables. In the townships they are also known as blue lines, blou pakke (blue suits), lindekhayas (home guards) and many other nicknames. 1990 D. Beckett in *Frontline* Apr. 13 On local politics, he explains there are two factions: the bloupakke – police auxiliaries – are 'for the whites' and the comrades are 'for zabalaza' – liberation or revolution ... Twice we come across bloupakke in royal-blue fatigues, rifles in hand and cartridge belts on waist.

Blourokkie /ˈblǝʊrɒki/ *n. phr.* Also with small initial. [Afk., 'little blue dress', *blou* blue + *rok* dress + -IE.]
1. *Prison slang. rare.* [Prob. by analogy with Afk. *bloubaadjie* the blue jacket worn in the past by long-term male prisoners (see BLOUBAADJIE).] A female habitual criminal, sentenced to an indeterminate period in gaol; this sentence. See also BLUE-COAT sense 1.
1969 A. Fugard *Boesman & Lena* 7 Oppas they don't get you. Blourokkie next time they catch you stealing.
2. *colloq.* [Named for the sky-blue uniform of the sect.] A name given to a woman belonging to the Pentecostal 'Latter Rain' or 'Spade Reën' sect.
[1972 A.V. Krige in *Std Encycl. of Sn Afr.* VI. 555 The women .. wear a uniform consisting of a sky-blue dress worn well below the knee, with headdress to match ... This uniform ensures that they are modestly and neatly dressed, independently of changing fashions.] 1981 E. Collier in *Rand Daily Mail* 13 Jan. 5 New hats which, they claimed, made them look like members of the 'Blou Rokkies', the religious sect in which members wear long blue coats, black stockings and little blue hats perched on their heads. 1987 A.N. Bell in *Fair Lady* 25 Nov. 7 You have .. sold out to the nappies and recipes brigade. Nothing, not one single item in your latest effort, would ruffle the blouest of blourokkies in this fair land.

blue *adj.* and *n.* [Special senses of general Eng.]
A. *adj.*
1. *Geology. Diamond-mining.* [See quot. 1882.] Of or pertaining to the unweathered diamond-bearing soil lying beneath the surface or 'yellow' soil.
1872 O.E.A. Schreiner in *Eng. in Afr.* (Mar. 1974) 17 The men at work in the claims below seem mere moving specks, as they peck at the hard blue soil. 1882 J. Nixon *Among Boers* 152 The rock now worked is known as the 'blue rock'. It is loosely-textured rock of a dull blue colour, looking like a solidified mud. 1897 F.R. Statham *S. Afr. as It Is* 190 The yellow soil from which they had been extracting diamonds came to a stop ... Instead there was a pale blue gravel which seemed the end of everything. Really it was the beginning, for the blue soil turned out to be the true home of the diamond. 1939 M. Rorke *Melina Rorke* 57, I had no interest in diamonds themselves — the stones were so common that they were frequently scuffed out of the 'hard blue' refuse from the mines, which formed our lovely garden walks. 1978 M. Hartmann *Shadow of Leopard* 8 By late 1873 they had gathered enough money to acquire several claims — all of them containing the blue clay or Kimberlite — which a few geologists said would be rich in the precious stones.
2. *slang.* [Transf. use of Eng. *blue* intoxicated, drunk.] Under the influence of marijuana; *boomed up*, see BOOM *n.* See also GEROOK.
1949 [see *boomed up* (BOOM *n.*)]. *a*1951 H.C. Bosman in V. Rosenberg *Almost Forgotten Stories* (1979) 102 When you smoke good dagga you get blue in quite a number of ways. 1963 L.F. Freed *Crime in S. Afr.* 92 The gangsters describe each other as being 'blue' when under the influence of dagga. [1978 see KAARTJIE sense 1.]
B. *n.*
1. *Geology. Diamond-mining.* Ellipt. for BLUE GROUND.
1873 *Diamond Field* in B. Roberts *Kimberley* (1976) 123 Diggers have gone down into the blue and report the finds are improving. 1886 J. Noble *Cape of G.H.:*

Off. Handbk 194 The extent of this hard rock is as yet unknown; though not quite all the 'blue' has been removed to this level, it has been recently ascertained that the basaltic rock encircles the entire mine. **1888** *Cape Punch* 4 Apr. 199 The blue, *i.e.* the Kimberley diamondiferous 'blue'. **1891** R. SMITH *Great Gold Lands* 64 At the surface the precious 'blue' is run in trucks by an endless rope to the drying grounds, which are some miles away, and some square miles in extent. **1913** C. PETTMAN *Africanderisms* 71 The dark, greyish-blue soil which forms the matrix in which the diamonds are found .. is also called 'blue-clay' or simply 'the blue'. **1924** G. BAUMANN in Baumann & Bright *Lost Republic* (1940) 84 The diamond fields had been worked down to the 'blue,' and many diggers, thinking they had struck 'country rock', abandoned or sold their claims. *c***1936** *S. & E. Afr. Yr Bk & Guide* 499 Permits can be obtained and a few hours profitably passed in inspecting the original hole, the first washing, when the mud is taken from the disintegrated blue and the machinery for crushing the hard lumps of blue. **1963** O. DOUGHTY *Early Diamond Days* 94 'Blue' – meaning diamondiferous soil.

2. [fr. sense A 2.] In *pl.*, ***the blues***: a state of mind and emotion resulting from marijuana-smoking.

1963 L.F. FREED *Crime in S. Afr.* 208 'Blues' were divided into three categories. There were the 'terror blues', the 'recognising blues' and the 'happy blues'. Two were self-explanatory, but the 'recognising blues' represented a state in which the addict felt that he knew everybody around him and that he was not lonely.

blue-back *n. hist.* [See quot. 1965.] A bank-note issued by the South African (Transvaal) Republic in 1865; a bank-note of the Free State Republic. Also *attrib.*

The blue-back became notorious for failing to hold its face value.

1867 *Blue Bk for Col. 1866* JJ39, The only means of payment are *blue-backs*, which are almost useless in the Colony. **1870** *E. Prov. Herald* 14 Jan., A diamond .. was exhibited for sale on our market this morning. It was held in, as not more than ninety-five bluebacks were offered for it. **1872** J.L. BABE *S. Afr. Diamond Fields* 64 Lillienveld and Webb .. purchased this farm .. for £2,000 in 'bluebacks' (Orange Free State currency). **1882** C. DU VAL *With Show through Sn Afr.* II. 216 He supposed 'the reign of bluebacks would return', an allusion to the paper currency in circulation under the former Boer Government, the value of which depreciated to an extraordinary extent, and became actually more or less fictitious. **1893** *Cape Illust. Mag.* Vol.4 No.8, 284 [The Republic] left behind it an empty exchequer, a floating debt represented by 'bluebacks' worth 3/6 in the £, and a long list of arrear salaries. **1896** [see GELD sense a]. **1900** *Daily News* 17 Sept. 5 President Kruger has deserted them, taking all the gold, and leaving them only 'blue-backs'. **1919** M.M. STEYN *Diary* 146 We were asked if we wished to pay in cash or 'blue-backs' – 'blue-backs' were Free State Government Notes. **1928** E.A. WALKER *Hist. of S. Afr.* 332 At the end of the wars £126 000 in paper were in circulation; the £5 'blueback' was worth £3. **1940** F.B. YOUNG *City of Gold* 213 The Republican paper currency was worth as little as its 'goodfors,' pound 'blue-back' notes were fetching a shilling apiece. **1965** T.V. BULPIN *Lost Trails of Tvl* 101 The government had run right out of hard cash and had been forced to print £10 500 in notes. These were crudely and hastily printed on blue foolscap paper and were promptly named 'bluebacks'.

bluebok *n. obs.* Also **bluebock**. [Part. tr. *blauwbok*, see BLAUWBOK.] The *blue duiker* (see DUIKER sense 1 b), *Philantomba monticola*.

1821 C.I. LATROBE *Jrnl of Visit* 237 A bluebock, one of the smallest antelopes ... The fur of the bluebock is remarkably fine; brown, changing with a blueish grey. **1835** J.M. BOWKER Journal. 5 Feb., Nothing could they find but some blue boks and a duiker. **1842** R. GODLONTON *Sketches of E. Districts* 29 The rietbok, the elegant little bluebok, and several others of the antelope tribe, are often met with. **1894** E. GLANVILLE *Fair Colonist* 70 The ferns that grew there moved suddenly, and a little bluebok stepped into view.

bluebottle *n.* [Prob. fr. Austral. Eng. (the *Australian National Dictionary* records a context from 1911 in which the word is used in this sense).] The Portuguese man-o'-war, the marine siphonophore *Physalia physalis*, characterized by a blue, balloon-like float, and trailing tentacles which inflict painful, sometimes dangerous stings. Also *attrib.*

1918 S.H. SKAIFE *Animal Life* 11 The well-known bluebottle, or Portuguese man-o-war .. consists, not of one animal, but of a number joined together .. it is a colony of animals ... Those cast up on our shore are generally from one to two inches across. **1947** L.G. GREEN *Tavern of Seas* 143 A seashore strewn with physalia, better known as blue-bottles or Portuguese men-'o-war, is no place for bare feet ... The pain a blue-bottle can inflict is maddening. **1972** *Daily Dispatch* 16 Feb. 1 Warm waters and easterly winds have brought sporadic oil and blue bottles to East London's beaches. **1982** *Weekend Argus* 4 Dec. 1 Bluebottle tendrils are up to two metres long. They contain tiny arrow-like barbs which penetrate the flesh and contain poison which causes intense irritation and swelling. **1990** *Style* July 105 The clan have retired to the sparkling pool in the garden (planned to circumvent the bluebottle and wind problem).

blue buck *n. phr.* Pl. unchanged. [tr. S. Afr. Du. *blauwbok*, see BLAUWBOK.]

1. The *blue duiker* (see DUIKER sense 1 b), *Philantomba monticola*. Also *attrib.*

1809 R. COLLINS in G.M. Theal *Rec. of Cape Col.* (1900) VII. 14 Abounding in .. almost every description of animal from the diminutive blue buck to the towering elephant. **1834** J.C. CHASE in A. Steedman *Wanderings* (1835) II. 205 Antelope skins, especially those of the blue buck, the *antilope pygmea*, a favourite and costly ornament, used for the head dress of the Caffer belles. **1841** B. SHAW *Memorials* 37 Their head-dress, worn only on particular occasions, is made of the fur of the beautiful blue buck. **1893** J. NOBLE *Illust. Off. Handbk of Cape & S. Afr.* 62 The diminutive bluebuck, not bigger than a rabbit. **1937** H. SAUER *Ex Afr.* 51 The antelope family ranges from the tiny cerulean antelope or blue-buck – so small that one can put him into one's coat pocket, and found only in the wooded coastal districts of South Africa – to the giant eland. **1949** L. HUNTER *Afr. Dawn* 160 Dainty blue buck picked their way along the game paths that meandered through the thick undergrowth. **1975** *Friend* 30 July 8 There stood a bluebuck, surely the daintiest and most beautiful thing I had ever seen. **1981** J.B. PEIRES *House of Phalo* 6 The main purpose of the hunt was to obtain rare skins (bluebuck, for instance) and ivory for armlets.

2. *hist.* The BLAUWBOK (sense 1 a), *Hippotragus leucophaeus*.

*c***1902** F.C. SELOUS in C.J. Cornish *Living Animals of World* I. 250 The *bluebuck*, which appears to have been entirely confined to the mountainous districts of the Cape Peninsula, became extinct during the first decade of the last century. **1983** R.H.N. SMITHERS in Skinner & Smithers *Mammals of Sn Afr. Subregion* 698 Some writers who travelled further east and north-east of the Cape .. gave drawings of the 'blue buck' which were obviously based on the roan ... Roberts .. went so far as to include this 'intermediate' in his list of extinct species as the Karoo blue antelope, *Ozanna aethiopica*. It is much more likely .. that *O. aethiopica* never actually existed. **1987** T.F.J. VAN RENSBURG *Intro. to Fynbos* 51 The bluebuck, quagga and Cape Lion have long been extinct. **1989** [see BLAUWBOK sense 1 a].

Blue Bull *n. phr. Colloq.* [Prob. tr. Afk. *Blou Bul*, the word *blou* (blue) alluding to the team's blue jerseys, and *bul* (bull) alluding to the physical strength of the players.] Usu. in *pl.*: The Northern Transvaal provincial rugby team. *sing.* A member of this team. Also *attrib.*

1982 *Sunday Times* 5 Sept. 1 His relentless Blue Bulls machine beat Western Province 27–22 in yesterdays 'shadow final' for the Currie Cup .. in Pretoria. **1985** *E. Prov. Herald* 16 Apr. 20 The Blue Bulls will meet Free State .. on April 24. **1990** M. CHANNER in *Sunday Times* 12 Aug. 19 His finest hour as a Blue Bull undoubtedly was that 1969 Currie Cup final. **1991** I. GAULT in *Sunday Times* 22 Sept. 34 The booing of the Blue Bulls turned to cheers for the same side when it was obvious which team were going to take the honours.

blue-bush *n.* [tr. Afk. *bloubos*.] BLOUBOS. Also *attrib.*

*a***1930** G. BAUMANN in Baumann & Bright *Lost Republic* (1940) 142, I came across a shallow 'vlei', on the outer edge of which stood a solitary *blaaubosch* (blue-bush). *Ibid.* 235 In winter time we cut supple blue-bush sticks, and bent them into bows. **1973** J. COPE *Alley Cat* 57 Blue-bush and vaal-kameel thorns grew in the river bed. **1977** [see BLOUBOS].

blue-coat *n. Prison slang.* [tr. Afk. *bloubaadjie*, see BLOUBAADJIE.]

1. A long-term male prisoner serving an indeterminate sentence, usu. after having been declared an habitual criminal; BLOUBAADJIE sense 2 b. See also BLOUROKKIE sense 1.

1949 H.C. BOSMAN *Cold Stone Jug* (1969) 12 In prison the blue-coat occupies a position of some degree of importance. A blue-coat is even higher than a murderer. **1976** V. ROSENBERG *Sunflower* 57 In prison, the murderer, unlike the blue-coat, does not wear a distinctive garb. He is not dressed by the authorities in a way to single him out from the other convicts.

2. An indeterminate prison sentence; BLUE-JACKET; COAT; cf. BAADJIE sense 2.

1949 H.C. BOSMAN *Cold Stone Jug* (1969) 11 He goes back to prison to serve the indeterminate sentence all over again. As they say in prison, he goes back to do his second blue-coat. **1975** *Sunday Times* 15 June 3 If I give myself up, I want to know that I'm not going to get a bluecoat (indeterminate sentence).

blue crane *n. phr.* The blue-grey crane *Anthropoides paradisea* of the Gruidae; INDWE sense 1; STANLEY CRANE.

The national bird of South Africa. Also occas. called *paradise crane*.

1801 J. BARROW *Trav.* I. 256 These [nests] were judged to be at least sufficiently large .. for the large blue cranes that sat by the river's side near them. **1822** W.J. BURCHELL *Trav.* I. 508 During the day, I had been employed in preparing the skin of the large blue crane. **1867** E.L. LAYARD *Birds of S. Afr.* 303 *Anthropoides Stanleyanus* .. *Blue Crane* of Colonists. Entirely of a leaden-blue, with the exception of the upper portion of the head, which is white, and the ends of the long drooping plumes of the wings, which are black. **1899** B. MITFORD *Weird of Deadly Hollow* 230 Fowls scratched and clucked around the kitchen door, among them the lanky, stilted figure of a blue crane, caught young, and easily domesticated. **1899** R.B. & J.D.S. WOODWARD *Natal Birds* 174 Blue or Stanley Crane. **1911** *Daily Dispatch* 1 Mar. (Suppl.) 12 Parrots, knysna loeries, jackal buzzards and blue cranes are examples of Ciskei's rich birdlife. **1931** R.C. BOLSTER *Land & Sea Birds* 108 The Blue Crane, which is gregarious in winter, likes open plains, with water near at hand. Its food is small reptiles, fishes, large insects, especially locusts and grasshoppers, roots, and seeds. **1967** E. ROSENTHAL *Encycl. of Sn Afr.* 129 The *Blue* or *Stanley Crane* belongs to the Highveld and can be easily tamed. **1987** *S. Afr. Digest* 8 May 13 South Africa also has a number of symbols derived from its wildlife ... The springbok appears on the R1 coin, the protea on the 20c coin and the blue crane on the 5c coin. **1991** J. CULLUM in *Weekend Post* 30 Mar. 3 The survival of South Africa's national bird, the blue crane, is in the balance, say ornithologists and conservationists ... The blue crane is found only in South Africa. **1994** D. ALLAN in *Afr. Wildlife* Vol.48 No.4, 8 The International Red Data Book is being revised ... The draft of this revision includes the Blue Crane as a 'globally threatened species'.

blue fish *n. phr.* Any of several species of marine fish, so called for a blueish element in their colouring. **1.** The PAMPELMOESIE, *Stromateus fiatola*. **2.** Either of two species of sea chub of the Kyphosidae: **a.** *Kyphosus bigibbus*; see also *bastard Jacob Evertson* sense (*b*) (JACOB EVERTSON sense 3); **b.** *K. cinerascens*. **3.** Either of two species of seabream of the Sparidae, *Pachymetopon* spp.: **a.** the BRONZE BREAM (sense b), *P. grande*; **b.** the HOTTENTOT (*n.* sense 2 a), *P. aeneum*.

1905 H.E.B. BROOKING in *E. London Dispatch* 7 Aug. 2 The blue fish is partly herbivorous, partly carnivorous in its feeding, and, so far as I know, is only caught with ascidion (rock-bait) upon our part of the coast. **1949** J.L.B. SMITH *Sea Fishes* 276 *Pachymetopon grande* ... *Blue Hottentot* (Cape). *Hottentot* (Knysna). *Das. John Brown. Jan Bruin* (South Coast). *Fatfish. Vetvis. Butterfish* (Eastern Cape). *Bluefish. Butter Bream* (East London — Transkei). *Bronze Bream. Copper Bream. Damkokker* (Transkei — Natal). *Ibid.* 303 *Stromateus fiatola* ... *Butterfish. Cape Lady. Pampelmoes. Bluefish.* **1971** *Evening Post* 5 Jan. 22 Anglers had a good run of bluefish at Bonza Bay. **1986** *Daily Dispatch* 21 May 4 Anglers are reminded that one is only permitted to catch five of the protected species — for example two bluefish and three shad per day.

blue ground *n. phr. Geology. Diamond-mining.* [See quot. 1920.] Eruptive diamondiferous rock which occurs in vertical cylindrical pipes (see PIPE), often having a diameter of several hundred feet, and of unknown depth; BLUE *n.* sense 1; KIMBERLITE. See also GRIQUAITE, HARDEBANK.

Blue ground is more compacted and often darker in colour than the looser, weathered layers of *yellow ground* (see YELLOW sense b) above it.

1882 C. DU VAL *With Show through Sn Afr.* I. 82 Digging, delving, and filling up with the precious 'blue ground' huge iron buckets. **1886** J. NOBLE *Cape of G.H.: Off. Handbk* 192 The 'blue ground' .. far from being barren of diamonds .. yielded even better returns than the upper layers of 'yellow ground'. **1900** H.C. NOTCUTT *How Kimberley Was Held* 31 The great ten-foot tunnel that stretches right away through the rock from the shaft to the blue-ground. **1905** G.F. WILLIAMS in Flint & Gilchrist *Science in S. Afr.* 320 In the case of the Kimberley mines, the diamond-bearing rock or blue ground has been forced up through the geological strata ... This rock was described by Professor Henry Carvill Lewis as 'a phorphyritic volcanic peridotite of basaltic structure,' which he named kimberlite — a name now generally accepted by geologists. **1911** *E. Prov. Herald* 11 Dec., They were now sinking Kimberley mine another thousand feet and to the surprise of many croakers they had struck blue ground at the 3,500 feet level under granite. **1920** R.H. LINDSEY-RENTON *Diary* (1979) 36 The diamonds are found in what is known as 'blue ground', the soil being of a colour which might by a stretch of imagination be called pale blue. This soil is found in 'pipes'. **1931** G. BEET *Grand Old Days* 98 Blue ground was conveyed from the mines and spread out on large open spaces, .. allowed to disintegrate by exposure to the elements .. over a period of from six to eighteen months. **1956** [see FLOOR]. **1965** D. ROOKE *Diamond Jo* 169 When they reached the blue ground, they abandoned the claims, thinking that they had reached the end of the diamondiferous ground. **1971** G.S. SWITZER in *Nat. Geog. Mag.* Dec. 864 The material in which diamonds are found is a dark, basic rock called kimberlite, after the famous mines in the vicinity of Kimberley, South Africa; miners call it 'blue ground'. **1983** *Motorist* 1st Quarter 13 The area surrounding Kimberley is mainly blueground owned by De Beers Consolidated Mines or privately. **1985** A.J.A. JANSE in Glover & Harris *Kimberlite Occurrence & Origin* 23 When diggers found that much harder compact blue ground underlay the yellow ground, many sold out because they thought that they had reached the bottom of the depression and thus the end of the diamondiferous ground.

blue-jacket *n. colloq.* [tr. Afk. *bloubaadjie*, see BLOUBAADJIE.] BLUE-COAT sense 2.

1970 *Post* 15 Mar. 25 Cancer M—'s habit of stealing cars landed a blue jacket (9–15 years' jail) on his shoulders this week. **1972** P. DRISCOLL *Wilby Conspiracy* 14 He was from Port Elizabeth and was doing the first year of a bluejacket for sticking some whore with a knife.

blue lily *n. phr.* [tr. Afk. *bloulelie.*] AGAPANTHUS.

1789 W. AITON *Hortus Kewensis* I. 414 *Agapanthus*, .. African blue Lily. Nat. of the Cape of Good Hope. Cult. 1692, in the Royal Garden at Hampton-court. **1982** A. MORIARTY *Outeniqua Tsitsikamma* 15 Blue lily (*Agapanthus praecox* ..) forms large clumps.

blue mottled *n. phr. Obs.* In full ***blue mottled soap***: BLUE SOAP.

[**1804** R. PERCIVAL *Acct of Cape of G.H.* 98 A species of soap made from the fat of beef and sheep, with the ashes of some particular plants; it resembles in appearance a bluish mottled marble.] **1891** H.J. DUCKITT *Hilda's 'Where Is It?'* 170 Shred half a pound of blue mottled soap in a jug. **1900** O. OSBORNE *In Land of Boers* 176 Cutting off a cube from the bar of best blue mottled, I grabbed one of my newest flannel shirts, soused it in the water, and then — dropped the soap into the river. **1913** A. GLOSSOP *Barnes's S. Afr. Hsehold Guide* 269 Sunlight soap for general wearing apparel, 'blue-mottled' for household linen; &c. **1928** J.W.N. MOLLER *What Every Housewife Should Know* 86 Blue Mottled Soap.

blue pointer *n. phr. ?Obsolescent.* Also with initial capitals. [Transf. use of Austral. Eng. *blue pointer* the shark *Isurus glaucus*; the shark *C. carcharias* is called *white pointer* in Austral. Eng.] In KwaZulu-Natal: the great white shark, *Carcharodon carcharias* of the Lamnidae.

1949 J.L.B. SMITH *Sea Fishes* 49 *Blue-Pointer* (Durban). *White-Pointer* or *Man-Eater* (General). **1958** L.G. GREEN *S. Afr. Beachcomber* 96 No one ever scoffs at the carcharodons, which include Durban's blue pointers and the true man-eater or great white shark. **1973** *Cape Times* 13 Jan. (Weekend Mag.) 3 Later on the same day two Blue Pointers (or White Deaths as they are called in Australia) were caught close to the shore between Macassar Beach and the Strand. **1973** J.L.B SMITH in *Std Encycl. of Sn Afr.* IX. 605 *Man-eater* (*Carcharodon carcharias*), .. In Natal it is called the blue-pointer, elsewhere the white-pointer or the white death shark or the great white shark.

Blue Sky *n. phr. Hist. Prison slang.* [Unkn.] A nickname for the Cinderella Prison in Boksburg (Gauteng Province). Also *attrib.* Cf. SUN CITY.

The prison was closed down on 31 March 1983.

*c*1948 H. TRACEY *Lalela Zulu* 54 No one seems to know for certain why the Zulus gave the name 'Blue Sky' to the gaol at Boksburg, near Johannesburg ... It may be American in origin. **1952** *Drum* Sept. 15, I did a nine-month stretch at the Cinderella Prison (Blue Sky) in Boksburg. **1953** A. MOGALE in *Drum* Oct. 33 All you have to do is to let me loose .. and you won't have to serve a term at 'Blue Sky'. **1990** O. MUSI in *Frontline* Jan. 18 A stone's throw away from the famed Boksburg Lake and two stones' throw away from Blue Sky prison, where many a friend has been a guest of the state.

blue soap *n. phr.* [Shortened form of *blue mottled soap.*] A coarse, hard, blue-marbled soap used in both kitchen and laundry, made by stirring a mixture of washing blue, caustic soda, and starch into the cooling soap; BLUE MOTTLED.

Orig. made from animal fat and plant lye. See also GANNA.

1956 A. LA GUMA in *New Age* 27 Sept. 6 Once a week is washing day. A scrap of hard blue soap and a scrubbing brush are issued, and everybody gets down at the ditch across the middle of the yard to do their clothes. **1963** A. FUGARD *Blood Knot* (1968) 100 Her mother did washing. Connie used to buy blue soap from the Chinaman on the corner. **1975** *E. Prov. Herald* 5 July 9 Self-raising flour, yeast, long bars of blue soap and washing powder. **1976** M. VAN BILJON in *Sunday Times* 16 May (Mag. Sect.) 4 Women who could still make a cake of blue soap, smooth as marble, delicately mottled and veined with blue. **1982** J. DAVIDS in Chapman & Dangor *Voices from Within* 98 My words slid like a ball of hard blue soap into the tub to be grabbed and used by you to rub the clothes. **1985** L. SAMPSON in *Style* Feb. 103 Ag, the blue soap you get nowadays. It isn't soap at all. **1988** A. DANGOR in Bunn & Taylor *From S. Afr.* 198 She had long ago stopped using the harsh, carbolic-based Blue soap so commonly used in the township.

blue tick *n. phr.* [So called for the colouration of the unengorged female tick.] Any of several ticks of the genus *Boophilus* of the Ixodidae (esp. *B. decoloratus*), which transmit REDWATER (sense 1), GALLSICKNESS (sense 1 a), and spirochaetosis, esp. among cattle.

1886 F.R. SCHAUBLE in E.A. Ormerod *Notes & Descriptions of Injurious Farm & Fruit Insects* (1889) The common huge Blue Tick. **1911** *Farmer's Weekly* 22 Mar. 22 Whilst at Graaff-Reinet Show, he picked four ticks off one of the prize animals ... The fourth was the blue tick, which carries redwater. **1918** S.H. SKAIFE *Animal Life* 180 The blue tick .. is one of the commonest of our ticks. It is also of great importance, as it spreads redwater fever and gallsickness among cattle. **1937** *Handbk for Farmers* (Dept of Agric. & Forestry) 515 One-host Ticks ... To this group belongs the blue tick (*Boophilus decoloratus*). **1978** *Daily Dispatch* 16 Aug. (Agric. Review) 16 The blue tick is the main transmitting agent for anaplasmosis and redwater. **1989** J. DU P. BOTHMA *Game Ranch Management* 196 In the case of one-host ticks, such as the blue tick, the larva moults on the host into a nymph, re-attaches onto the same host and engorges. **1991** J.B. WALKER in *Onderstepoort Jrnl of Vet. Research* Vol.58 No.2, 85 *Genus Boophilus*, .. Members of this small, but economically important, genus are commonly known as blue ticks ... The common blue tick, *Boophilus decoloratus*, is the species that is most frequently implicated in the transmission of 3 cattle parasites: .. also, *Anaplasma marginale* and *A. centrale*, causing gallsickness.

blue tongue *n. phr. Pathology.* Also with initial capitals. [tr. S. Afr. Du. *blauwtong*, see BLAUWTONG.] Either of two viral diseases of livestock, transmitted by gnats: **a.** A disease (esp. of sheep) characterized by swelling of the lips and tongue, and bluish discoloration of the mucous membrane of the mouth; TUNG-ZIEKTE. **b.** DIKKOP sense 2 a. In both senses also called BLAUWTONG. Also *attrib.*

1863 J.S. DOBIE *S. Afr. Jrnl* (1945) 86 Blue tongue .. (.. a swelling of the tongue and lips which prevents the poor beast from eating). **1887** H. RIDER HAGGARD *Jess* p.viii, It's a beautiful veldt .. no horse sickness, no blue-tongue. **1905** *Nature* 4 Sept. 502 Catarrhal Fever of Sheep: Blue Tongue. **1911** [see MARITZBURG]. **1914** *Farmer's Annual* 131 *Blue-tongue*, or Malarial Catarrhal Fever, is a disease which was formerly responsible for much loss; recently, however, a preventative vaccine has greatly reduced its dangers. *c*1936 *S. & E. Afr. Yr Bk & Guide* 354 *Blue Tongue* is restricted to certain areas of the Union, which can only be used in consequence during the dry months ... The discovery of a vaccine by Sir A. Theiler has done much to bring the disease under control. **1953** U. KRIGE *Dream & Desert* 177 Death, like a hailstorm in the wheat, rinderpest among the cattle, blue tongue among the sheep, could come at any moment. **1960** J. COPE *Tame Ox* 133 'The jackals took many, my basie. Other died of blue-tongue, gall-sickness,' a headman said. **1967** E. ROSENTHAL *Encycl. of Sn Afr.* 153 *Dikkop* (*Thick head*), Disease of horses, accompanied by the swelling of the tissue under the skin. It may take the form of swelling of the tongue, for which reason it is also known as Blue Tongue. **1969** *Grocott's Mail* 28 Mar., (advt) Merino Hamels ... Innoculated against Blue Tongue and Pulpy Kidney. **1976** MÖNNIG & VELDMAN *Handbk on Stock Diseases* 69 Bluetongue is a virus of sheep and sometimes of cattle ... Horsesickness and bluetongue usually occur in the same areas, because the same insects (gnats) that transmit the one virus also transmit the other. **1982** *S. Afr. Panorama* Sept. 6 Onderstepoort Veterinary Research Institute in Pretoria is leading the world in developing cattle disease vaccines ... Vaccines against blue tongue, lumpy skin disease and Rift Valley fever are manufactured nowhere else. **1988** SMUTS & ALBERTS *Forgotten Highway* 180 If you didn't trek with your sheep in winter, those sheep would be far more likely to suffer from blue tongue, and especially tribulosis.

blue train *n. phr.*
1. Usu. with initial capitals. [So called for the colour of the livery.] A luxury passenger train, inaugurated in 1946, which runs between Cape Town and Pretoria. Also *attrib.*

1948 *Press Digest* No.7, 50 Just travel in the blue train and you will see. **1949** J. MOCKFORD *Golden Land* 250 Pretoria is linked with Cape Town by the Blue Train, the fastest Train in South Africa. **1959** M.W. SPILHAUS *Under Bright Sky* 88 Instead of catching the Blue Train to Jo'burg from the ship, he has arranged to go on round the coast to Durban. **1966** *Cape Argus* 19 Sept. 1 A 'Substantial Plot' to derail the Blue Train between Worcester and Touws River where the railway line passes through a tunnel, was mentioned. **1979** B. ZURNAMER *Locomotives of S. Afr. Railways* 87 In 1933, the dining car Protea, was placed into service ... Protea was not painted in the official livery of imperial brown, but in a combination of blue and cream. The colour scheme was so appealing that the Limited and Express were painted blue and cream in 1935 – the colour scheme of the present Blue Train. **1979** *S. Afr. Railways & Harbours Handbk* 93 The war .. delayed the start of the operations of this luxurious train ... Finally, in 1946, the Blue Train was officially inaugurated by the then Minister of Transport. **1988** N. PATTERSON in *Cape Times* 11 Jan. 7 The five-star hotel on wheels, the Blue Train.

2. *slang.* Also with initial capitals. [So called for the colour of methylated spirit, which, because it is toxic, is dyed blue and made unpalatable (drinkers using bread to strain it); a play on sense 1 (see quots 1982 and 1984).] Methylated spirit when taken as an alcoholic drink; VLAM sense a. See also AI-AI.

1980 *Sunday Times* 4 May 19 He said people also drank ethylated spirits – which has replaced methylated spirits or 'blue train'. **1982** R. JOSEPH in *Sunday Times* 28 Feb. 19 The one-way 'blue train' of death – blue train is the name meth drinkers give their habit. **1984** *True Love* Nov. 77 Despite romantic allusions to .. 'riders of the blue train' (methylated spirits) their lives are squalid and lonely, often passed in a blur of alcohol. **1987** L. BEAKE *Strollers* 71 Saturdays the money was less, so they had to drink Blue Train, and methylated spirits made them mean, man, real mean. **1988** *Weekend Argus* 19 Mar. 17 I'm drunk. I'm riding the Blue Train ... I drink meths to keep me warm.

blushing bride *n. phr.* Also with initial capitals. [Unkn.; perh. influenced by the Afk. name *skaamblom, skaam* shy + *blom* flower; see quot. 1977.] The shrub *Serruria florida* of the Proteaceae; its drooping, pale pink flowers. Also *attrib.*

1917 R. MARLOTH *Common Names* 13 *Blushing bride, Serruria florida.* One of the .. rarest flowers of S.A., known only from one of the valleys of the upper Bergriver (Franschhoek). Flowering in winter. **1949** L.G. GREEN *In Land of Afternoon* 74 To the delight of botanists .. the 'Blushing Bride' has reappeared in the Kloof fairly recently ... The delicate shrub has pink flowers, the colour of a blush. According to Franschhoek custom, a man takes off his hat when he encounters the 'Blushing Bride'. **1955** K.A. THOMPSON *Great House* 213 The small, frail looking pink protea called the Blushing Bride .. was supposed to be extinct when he found it flowering in a tiny kloof in the Fransch Hoek Mountains. **1973** *Argus* 30 June 1 The bride .. carried blushing bride proteas and orchids. **1976** [see SUGARBUSH]. **1977** *S. Afr. Panorama* May 31 The 'blushing bride' .. bears the name of *Serruria florida* after the Dutch botanist, J. Serrurier. The story goes that young Franschhoek farmers used to wear a 'blushing bride' as a buttonhole when they went courting, and the deeper pink, the more serious their intentions. **1987** T.F.J. VAN RENSBURG *Intro. to Fynbos* 43 Many fynbos species, such as .. the blushing bride .. are completely dependent on fire for regeneration. **1990** *Weekend Post* 17 Feb. (Leisure) 7 Blushing brides are difficult to grow under ordinary garden conditions. **1992** [see MARSH ROSE].

bluxom var. BLIKSEM.

bly stil /bleɪ ˈstəl/ *int. phr. Colloq.* Formerly also **blij stil.** [Afk. (earlier Du. *blij stil*), *bly* to remain, stay + *stil* quiet.] A command: 'be quiet', 'shut up'.

1924 L. COHEN *Reminisc. of Jhb.* 225 His Honour glared, sneezed and grunted harshly, loudly, reprovingly, 'Blij stil!' (Be quiet!) **1959** J. MEIRING *Candle in Wind* 21 'Bly stil', she snarled at them, and they recognised her voice and were quiet. **1975** S. ROBERTS *Outside Life's Feast* 16 Kaptein had started howling and jumping and wagging and bouncing bum-up when he saw them at the window, and Mrs Luyt had yelled, bly stil. **1989** H. HAMANN in *Scope* 24 Mar. 56 'Bly still!' I heard someone hiss in a harsh whisper. Thud! The sandbag fell again. **1990** *Sunday Times* 4 Mar. 5 She was hushed by the audience and told to 'Bly stil,' 'Sit' and 'Sssssh'.

bo- /bɔ/ *pref. colloq.* [Sotho pl. marker before names and kinship terms.] Used in urban (esp. township) English before names, to mean 'and co.', 'the likes of', '*et al.*'.

[**1962** W.S. MANQUPU in *Star* 22 Feb. 14 The lorry used as a pick-up van is called the 'Khwela-Khwela,' as the police call out 'Khwela, bo, khwela!' ('Ride, man, ride!')] **1982** [see Sepamla quot. at EXCUSE-ME]. **1988** *Learn & Teach* 19 Nomsa also worried about the fines taxi drivers get from the 'bo-Chacklas' or the traffic cops, as they are called. **1989** *Pace* Dec. 4 The pamphlet .. adds that the leadership position is for the learned and not for bo 'Dom Jan' and bo 'Ja Baas'. **1990** *City Press* 11 Mar. 7 Bo-Tat'u-Mandela, Tat'uSisulu etc. **1990** O. MUSI in *City Press* 20 May 9 The famed St Peter's School in Rosettenville .. has produced the likes of yours truly and a host of lawyers, doctors and music giants such as bo Hugh Masekela.

boardman *n. obs.* In urban (esp. township) English: a member of the advisory board of a black township. See also UBC.

Advisory boards were established by Act 79 of 1961.

1968 *Golden City Post* 11 Feb. 2 Two former veteran Kwa Thema boardmen who were getting an allowance of R13 a month as sitting members are following up their defeat in the elections .. with expensive Supreme Court actions costing several hundred rands in a bid to change the results. **1968** *Drum* Sept. 26 A tradition of Advisory Boardmen is that they fought individual cases of people in trouble with Influx Control or eviction. **1969** *Post* 10 Aug. 7 Would you say that the former boardmen did a better service to the people of Soweto than the UBC? **1971** *Ibid.* 3 Oct. 17 Boardman Petrus Mnguni said Sunday beer lounges would certainly draw people away from shebeens.

Boar tobacco var. BOER TOBACCO.

Bob, as true as see TRUE sense b.

bobbejaan /ˌbɔbəˈjɑːn/ *n.* Also **bobijan**. Pl. **-jane** /-jɑːnə/. [Afk., fr. Middle Du. *babiaen* (Du. *baviaan*) baboon.]
‖**1.**
a. The CHACMA, *Papio ursinus.*

1959 J. PACKER *High Roof* 106 On their last afternoon the Coloured caddy said: 'Listen to the bobbejaan – up there in the krans.' He looked .. seeing the old sentinel of the baboon troop. **1965** J. BENNETT *Hawk Alone* 42 'Come up and have a go at the bobbejane,' said Gord. **1966** C.A. SMITH *Common Names* 130 Each animal .. ranked high in their .. tribal taboos, and no Hottentot would eat the meat of any of them. The 'bobbejaan', they held, was too much like a man. [**1986** M. LE CHAT in *Sunday Times* 20 July (Mag. Sect.) 32 It's a song called *Bobbejaan, Bobbejaan*, a tale of weekends in Worcester when he would be taken up to the hill above the town to see a baboon on a chain.]

b. *fig. derog.* Usu. with initial capital: A nickname for one held to be a fool. See also BAVIAAN sense 1 b.

In certain contexts used with racist overtones.

1937 C.R. PRANCE *Tante Rebella's Saga* 177 On the spot of course Oom Jan was unanimously and uproariously crowned with the nickname 'Bobbejaan' which means 'Baboon,' and the shame of it so ate into his soul that he sold his farm and trekked away to far south-west Africa. **1942** S. CLOETE *Hill of Doves* 239 And what are you, Adonis? Ja, that's what you are, an old bobbejaan of a man, an old baboon .. a disgrace to your nation. *c*1957 D. SWANSON *Highveld, Lowveld & Jungle* 64 'The little bliksom,' Klaussens said, staring down at the crumpled, inert body ... 'Go and get that other bobijan.' **1965** C. VAN HEYNINGEN *Orange Days* 36 One day a small skinny piccanin turned up to look for work; when asked what his name was, he said 'Maargat', but he was renamed 'Bobbejaan' (monkey) to which he answered cheerfully. **1971** *Sunday Times* 10 Oct. (Mag. Sect.) 5 Addressing an African bringing tea into the studio, he said: 'What is your name? Bobbejaan? Oh, Willem. Willem Bobbejaan.'

2. As a qualifier, esp. in plant names, often designating species unsuitable for human consumption, or associated with baboons: **bobbejaanappel** /-apəl/ [Afk., *appel* apple], KERSHOUT sense 2; **bobbejaankos** /-kɔs/ [Afk., *kos* food], see quot. 1966; **bobbejaanstou** /-ztəʊ/ [Afk., *tou* rope], MONKEY-ROPE; **bobbejaanuintjie** /-ˈœɪŋki/, BOBBEJAANTJIE. See also BAVIAAN sense 2.

1972 PALMER & PITMAN *Trees of Sn Afr.* III. 2061 The distinctive fruits .. become soft when ripe and are eaten by baboons and monkeys, hence the common names 'aapsekos' and '**bobbejaanappel**'. **1966** C.A. SMITH *Common Names* 132 Several unrelated species .. are regarded as inferior as a source of food .. for human beings, hence **bobbejaankos**. **1983** D. HUGHES et al. *Complete Bk of S. Afr. Wine* 16 [The Khoikhoi] had no settled community or agriculture, living meagrely off shellfish and fruit, including the berries of a wild vine, Rhoicissus capensis, later to become popularly known as '**bobbejaanstou**', or monkey creeper. **1971** L.G. GREEN *Taste of S.-Easter* 91 You can tell the **bobbejaanuintjie** by its lovely flowers.

‖**bobbejaanboud** /bɔbəˈjɑːnˌbəʊt/ *n. hist.* Formerly also **babiaanbout, baviaan bout**, etc. [Afk., *bobbejaan* (ad. S. Afr. Du. *baviaan*) baboon + *boud* (fr. Du. *bout*) haunch, rump.] A gun-stock with a large cheek-piece resembling a baboon's haunch; any firearm with this stock. Also *attrib.* See also ROER sense a.

1864 T. BAINES *Explor. in S.-W. Afr.* 280 Until he should become the happy owner of the 'Babijaana' (Baboons), a contraction of 'Baviaan's bout' (Baboon's thigh, the colonial term for a musket), he could enjoy nothing else. **1905** [see SNAPHAAN]. **1913** C. PETTMAN *Africanderisms* 40 *Babiaanbout*, The old-fashioned, muzzle-loading musket; the name refers to its shape. **1971** F.V. LATEGAN in *Std Encycl. of Sn Afr.* IV. 520 This particular shape of the stock with its large cheek-piece was nicknamed colloquially 'bobbejaanboud' (baboon-thigh). **1977** *E. Prov. Herald* May 14 One of the earliest of these Cape guns to become so popular as to generate a nick-name for itself was the long barrelled 'Bobbejaanboud'. This versatile weapon .. was a smooth bore, muzzle-loader .. and could be loaded with practically anything from a solid slug to half a palm full of coarse sand. **1980** *Farmer's Weekly* 2 July 60 There must still be hundreds of antique *bobbejaanboud* flintlocks still in existence about which the regular collectors know nothing. **1990** *Caption, 1820 Settlers' Memorial Museum (Grahamstown)* A typical 'bobbejaanboud sterloop' smooth-bore with a 45" barrel. The nickname referred to the heavy butt which was shaped like a baboon's thigh.

bobbejaan spanner /bɔbəˈjɑːn -, bɔbəˈdʒan -/ *n. phr.* Also **bobiaan-spanner**. [Part. tr. Afk. *bobbejaansleutel*, monkey-wrench (tool patented by C. Moncky), *bobbejaan* baboon, monkey + *sleutel* wrench, spanner.] A monkey-wrench or shifting spanner.

1961 D. BEE *Children of Yesterday* 229 Nigel put down the bobbejaan spanner and mopped his brow ... 'I understand this machinery, Oom.' *c*1966 M. JABOUR in *New S. Afr. Writing* 92 Ouma was always prepared for any eventuality. In the black bag .. she kept bandages and medicine, needle and thread, and even a bobbejaan spanner. **1976** *Grocott's Mail* 21 May 6 (*advt*) The Messenger of the Court has attached the following assets, namely: 1 Wheelbarrow, 1 Bin, 1 Bobbejaan Spanner, 1 Chisel. **1984** T. BARON in *Frontline* Feb. 17 Sylvester grabbed his chin, swivelling it from side to side with fingers hard as a bobbejaan spanner. **1989** J. EVANS in *Personality* 29 May 15 Woe betide anyone who sneaks into the pound at the dead of night with a *bobbejaan spanner* to make a quick adjustment.

bobbejaantjie /ˌbɔbəˈjaɪŋki, -ci/ *n.* Formerly also **babiaantj(i)e, babiantje, bavyantje, bobbejantje**, and with initial capital. [Afk., contraction of *bobbejaanuintjie*, fr. S. Afr. Du. *babiaan uyntje*, fr. Middle Du. *babiaen* or Du. *baviaan* baboon + *uien* bulb, tuber + dim. suffix -IE; see also quot. 1917.] Any of several species of cormous plant of the genus *Babiana* of the Iridaceae, with blue, white, purple, yellow, or scarlet flowers; BABIANA; BAVIAAN sense 3; *bobbejaanuintjie*, see BOBBEJAAN sense 2.

[**1795** C.R. HOPSON tr. *C.P. Thunberg's Trav.* I. 285 The baboons of Table Mountain .. feed also upon the pulpous bulbs of several plants ... The *Gladiolus plicatus* appears to be the most favourite, .. for which reason .. this plant is known by the name of the *Baboon*.] **1857** 'HORTULANUS' in *Cape Monthly Mag.* I. June 350 South Africa abounds with many fine genera of the *Irideæ*, varying in form and colour. A few of those are frequent in the Cape gardens, and generally known by the names of *Afrikaanders, Bavyantjes*, &c. **1917** R. MARLOTH *Common Names* 8 *Babiaantje, Babiana* (several species). The baboons (baviaan, mostly pron.: babiaan) unearth the corms (so-called bulbs) for food. **1949** [see KALKOENTJIE sense 2]. **1957** L.G. GREEN *Beyond City Lights* There are *gousblom* of many colours, scarlet *bobbejaantjies*, white arums and *rooipypies*. **1958** F.T. PRINCE in R.M. Macnab *Poets in S. Afr.* 80 In the hidden dew The unbelievably keen perfume Of the Babiaantjie. **1964** J. MEINTJES *Manor House* 35 These children always accompanied us on our walks to collect wild flowers: kalkoentjies, viooltjies, bobbejaantjies, freesias and the exotic aandblom. **1973** J. RABIE in S. Gray *Writers' Territory* 169 In July and August the first wild flowers already reveal the show. First the rosy viooltjies, then yellow bietou and sorrel and blue bobbejaantjies. **1974** *Cape Times* 28 Sept. (Suppl.) 1 The orchards north of the Outeniquas are covered with blossoms. There are .. 'bobbejaantjies' by the million in the veld.

bobby-shop var. BABBIE-SHOP.

bobiaan-spanner var. BOBBEJAAN SPANNER.

bobijan var. BOBBEJAAN.

bobotie /bəˈbuːti, bəˈbʊəti/ *n.* Also **baboeti(e), babooti(e), babote(e), babotie, boobootie, bobotee, boebooti**. [Afk., earlier S. Afr. Du. *boebooti, boboti*, prob. ad. Malay *bumbu* curry spices. N. Mansvelt's *Proeve van een Kaapsch-Hollandsch Idioticon* (1884) traces the origins of this word to Malay *boemboe* 'prepared curry powder', while both the *Patriot Woordeboek* (1902) and S.J. du Toit's *Afrikaanse Taalskat* (1908) acknowledge the word's eastern origins.]

a. A traditional dish (probably of Malay origin), made of lightly curried minced meat baked with a savoury custard topping. Also *attrib.*

1870 'A LADY' in *Cape Monthly Mag.* I. Oct. 224 '*Babootie*' and '*frickadel*' and '*potato-pie*' are great improvements upon the minced meats of England. **1883** O.E.A. SCHREINER *Story of Afr. Farm* 62, I will let my Kaffirs take you out and drag you, till there is not one bone left in your old body that is not broken as fine as bobootie-meat, you old beggar! **1891** H.J. DUCKITT *Hilda's 'Where Is It?'* 12 'Bobotee.' (A delicate Indian minced curry. Malay or Indian. My mother's Recipe.) *Ibid.* 13 One ounce of tamarinds soaked in half a pint of boiling water, then strained, and the juice used for Bobotee, Sasaties, and Curries instead of vinegar, gives a very pleasant acid flavour. **1900** *Graaff Reinet Budget* 23 July (Pettman), All the writing in the world will not induce Cape Colonials to forgo .. their carbonaatjes, *boobootis*, and sassatjes. **1913** D. FAIRBRIDGE *Piet of Italy* 237 He was dining contentedly on bobotie and rice, washed down with blue-bean coffee. **1927** [see KERRIE sense 1]. **1944** [see BREDIE sense a]. **1950** *Cape Times* 6 June 16 Something typically South African like babotie. **1963** S. CLOETE *Rags of Glory* 363 Babotie and rice, sweet potatoes and pumpkin followed by a milk tart and watermelon konfyt. **1969** D. CHILD *Yesterday's Children* 33 Exotic dishes introduced by Malay cooks from the East .. such as *bobotie* (a delicate minced curry), *bredie* (meat stew with green beans or tomatoes) and *sasaties* (morsels of lamb or mutton soaked in curry sauce and then grilled on skewers), have become traditional South African dishes. **1973** *Cape Times* 11 July 10, 1001 ways with mince — babotie, spaghetti bol., frikkadels, meat loaf, cottage pie. **1977** *S. Afr. Panorama* Dec. 35 The first bobotie recipe was published as early as 1609. Thus this exotic dish from the Orient became a Cape Malay speciality over the years, and the basic recipe underwent many variations. **1981** *Flying Springbok* Sept. 54 Bobotie is a mixture of minced mutton, curried, salted, with pepper and turmeric added and some chutney, baked with a sort of soft crust of milk and egg. **1983** *Rand Daily Mail* 16 Sept. 12 The baboetie is excellent. The spicing was outstanding, slightly piquant but never fiery. **1986** *Style* Mar. 12 The ethnic, spicy, Malay chicken curry and bobotie, rich with almonds and judiciously spiked with ginger and coriander and star anise. **1986** M. VAN WYK *Cooking the S. Afr. Way* 61 Foreign visitors are often taken aback when they sample dishes like curry and bobotie for the first time. The curiously tasty mixture of sweet and savoury — achieved by adding dried peaches, apricots, raisins — is peculiarly South African. **1991** *Argus* 29 Aug. 19 The recipes brought in by the Dutch pioneers had been vastly improved by the Malay influence — who introduced locals to boboties, bredies and biryanis, fruit and vegetable chutneys and atjars.

b. With distinguishing epithets designating various types of bobotie: **fish bobotie, lamb bobotie, pilchard bobotie, sultana bobotie**.

1964 L.G. GREEN *Old Men Say* 121 **Fish babotie**, a baked fish pudding, or fish bredie, would not be out of place on an all-Cape menu. **1978** *Daily Dispatch* 2 Aug. 5 The meal .. started with pickled herring .. and fish babotie. **1981** *Fair Lady* 9 Sept. 179 A menu that included butternut soup, fish bobotie, tomato bredie and brandy tart and cream. **1987** *Grocott's Mail* 25 Aug. (Coastal News) 4 Fish bobotie ... 2 Large cans Pilchards (plain or middle-cut) 2 medium onions. **1890** A.G. HEWITT *Cape Cookery* 37 **Lamb Babotee** ... Cut the meat from a leg of lamb, mince, and put into a pot. **1974** *E. Prov. Herald* 23 Aug. 29 **Pilchard bobotie**. **1984** L. SAMPSON in *Style* July 117 Sunday lunch is a feast, snoek kedgeree, **sultana bobotie**, lamb tripe and trotters, roast suckling pig, yellow rice.

boca var. BUCHU.

bocal var. BOKAAL.

bocchom /ˌbɔˈxɔm/ *int.* Also **baugh-um, bochom, boor-hoom, borchem**. [Englished form of Afk. *bô-gom*, which is echoic in origin.] A word used in imitation of the bark of a baboon.

1904 *Argus Christmas Annual* (Orange River Col. Sect.) 13 Baboons barked at him from the heights. 'Baughbaugh-baugh-um.' They barked incessantly. **1925** K. FAIRBRIDGE in F.C. Slater *Centenary Bk of S. Afr. Verse* 70 He [sc. the baboon], a patient sentinel, Shouts 'Boorhoom!' to th' offended sky To show that all is well. Hence **bocchom** *v. intrans.*, (of a baboon) to bark; **bocchom** *n.* the bark of a baboon or an imitation of this bark.

1922 S.C. CRONWRIGHT-SCHREINER in F.C. Slater *Centenary Bk* (1925) 62 Let the whip with its lightning crack Startle the buck from its lair in the kloof, while the baboons 'borchem' back! **1970** J. MCINTOSH *Stonefish* 9 Some way off, baboons bocchomed, and threw stones because the place they lived in had been invaded. **1994** R. MILJO on TV1, 30 Oct. (50/50), Come on, Damien, give us your best bochom.

bockenhout var. BOEKENHOUT.

Bocke-veld var. BOKKEVELD.

boco var. BUCHU.

body-feather *n. Ostrich-farming.* [See quot. 1909.] A feather taken from the body, rather than from the wings or tail, of an ostrich. Also *ellipt.*, **body**. See also FEATHER sense a.

*c*1881 A. DOUGLASS *Ostrich Farming* 97 The body feathers should be curly, rich in colour, with a shiny gloss on them. **1896** R. WALLACE *Farming Indust. of Cape Col.* 235 The short and medium are the body feathers. **1909** J.E. DUERDEN in *Agric. Jrnl of Cape of G.H.* XXXIV. 513 The feathers covering the body generally are known to farmers as *body-feathers* and are too small to be used commercially. *Ibid.* 519 By the time the birds are a year old nearly all the body-feathers show the drab colour of the juvenal plumage. **1955** G. ASCHMAN in Saron & Hotz *Jews in S. Afr.* 130 They quickly learnt the names of all the the different types of feathers .. bodies .. drab-cut bodies .. female bodies. **1956** P.J. BOTHA in *Farmer's Weekly* 14 Mar., The market for .. utilitarian body feathers has shown a handsome improvement in price.

boeb var. BOEP *n.*[1]

boebooti var. BOBOTI.

boedelhouder /ˈbʊdəlˌhəʊdə(r)/ *n. Law.* Also **boedelhouer**. [Du., *boedel* estate + *houder* holder. (The modern Afk. form is *boedelhouer*.)] See quot. 1960. See also COMMUNITY OF PROPERTY.

1833 *Ordinance 105* in *Stat. Law of Cape of G.H.* (1862) 290 The predeceasing spouse shall by will or other lawful instrument have appointed the tutor of his or her minor children and the administrator (boedelhouder) of the joint estate of such spouses during the minority of such children. **1934** C.P. SWART *Supplement to Pettman*. 16 A boedelhouer is .. executor, guardian and administrator of the joint estate during the minority of the children. **1960** J.J.L. SISSON *S. Afr. Judicial Dict.* 96 A boedelhouder is the survivor of persons married in community of property, whom the first-dying has by last will appointed executor, guardian and administrator of the joint estate during the minority of the children. In this manner community of property continues between the survivor and the children until the majority of the children. **1977** *Friend* 2 June (Suppl.) 3a, How do you like the expressive term *Boedelhouder* — the survivor of persons married in community of property?

Hence **boedelhouderschap** /-skap/ *n.* [Du., *-schap* state of being, '-ship'], continued community of property between the survivor of a joint estate and any minor children.

1833 in *Stat. Law of Cape of G.H.* (1862) 293 The administration by the survivor of two spouses during the minority of the children of the predeceased spouse (boedelhouderschap). **1960** J.J.L. SISSON *S. Afr. Judicial Dict.* 97 The use of the word *boedelhouder* in a will was held not to imply *boedelhouderschap* in the technical sense. **1980** M.M. CORBETT et al. *Law of Succession* 460 Continued community of property (*voortgezette gemeenschap, boedelhouderschap*) may be established by antenuptial contract, .. by mutual will or by the separate will of the first-dying ... Division of the community between the surviving spouse and the children takes place when the youngest child reaches majority.

Boedelkamer *n. obs.* Also **Boodle Kaamer**. [Du., *boedel* property, estate + *kamer* chamber.] The court dealing with insolvent estates at the

Cape of Good Hope, esp. under the rule of the Dutch East India Company.

1806 *Cape Town Gaz. & Afr. Advertiser* 5 Apr., His Excellency has been pleased to determine, that the Boedelkamer, or Chamber for Regulating Insolvent Estates, shall consist, for the future, only of two Members. **1809** H. ALEXANDER in G.M. Theal *Rec. of Cape Col.* (1900) VI. 477 The Orphan Chamber or Desolate Boedelkamer, for the purpose of promoting their respective administrations, may be in want. *a***1823** J. EWART *Jrnl* (1970) 41 A court called the Boodle Kaamer, comprised of a president and two members, has the regulating of all insolvent estates.

boego(e) var. BUCHU.

Boejesman var. BOSJESMAN.

boekenhout /ˈbʊkənhəʊt, ˈbukən-/ *n.* Also **bockenhout, boeken houtt, buchenhout, bucku-hout.** [S. Afr. Du., fr. Du. *beuke(boom)* beech (tree) + linking phoneme *-n-* + *hout* wood.] Any of several trees resembling the European beech, esp. the Cape beech *Rapanea melanophloeos* of the Myrsinaceae, and *Faurea saligna* of the Proteaceae; the wood of these trees; BEUKENHOUT. Also *attrib.* See also *Cape beech* (CAPE sense 2 a).

1790 tr. *F. Le Vaillant's Trav.* II. 241 The indolence of the planters suffered it to decay entirely, so that at present it is considered as a lost species. This tree, at the Cape, is named *boeken houtt.* **1815** J. MACKRILL Diary. 119 Sideroxylon Melanophleum is the Bucken Wood of the Boors .. Boeken Hout. **1860** J. SANDERSON in *Jrnl of Royal Geog. Soc.* XXX. 246 On the plain, sprinkled over with sugarbush, mimosa, boekenhout, &c., were the few houses forming the village of Rustenburg. **1887** A.A. ANDERSON *25 Yrs in Waggon* I. 42 The Pongola Bush .. is a beautiful forest of fine timber-trees. Some of the most valuable are the Bosch Gorrah, .. Ebenhout, .. Bockenhout, no regular grain. **1906** H. RIDER HAGGARD *Benita* 84 The square-face — as Hollands was called in those days, from the shape of the bottle — was set upon the rough table of speckled buchenhout wood. **1934** *Star* 17 Mar. (Swart), Boekenhout is greatly used for pick handles and for picture frames, book-ends, and similar things. **1951** N.L. KING *Tree-Planting* 70 *Rapanea melanophloeos (Boekenhout)*, A hardy tree with thick leathery leaves. Usually occurs on the margins of forests from Cape Town to Zululand and eastern Transvaal. **1961** PALMER & PITMAN *Trees of S. Afr.* 218 The tree received its name, boekenhout, or beech, from the resemblance of the wood to the European beech. **1975** *S. Afr. Panorama* Jan. 14 Furniture was mainly of wood indigenous to the Transvaal such as tambotie, boekenhout (South African beech), [etc.]. **1982** *Ibid.* Dec. 13 Other flowering sub-tropical plants and trees are wild fig, .. *boekenhout*, knobthorn. **1991** H. HUTCHINGS in *Weekend Post* 23 Feb. (Leisure) 7 Useful trees for background, windbreak or shade planting are *Rapanea melanophloeos* (boekenhout) and *Sideroxylon inerme* (milkwood).

‖**boekevat** /ˈbʊkəfat, ˈbukə-/ *n.* [Afk., *boek* book + linking phoneme *-e-* + *vat* take (up).] The custom of family devotions, observed by protestant Afrikaners, usu. in the evening. See also HUISGODSDIENS.

1970 E. MUNDELL *Informant, Pearston (E. Cape)* Very few people still practise boekevat (divine service at home). **1974** *E. Prov. Herald* 29 Aug. 16 When I was a small boy on the farm in the Free State my father observed the old Boer custom of 'boekevat' performing religious devotions after the evening meal. The books of course, were the Bible and the hymn book. **1984** E. PLATTER in *Fair Lady* 18 Apr. 79 Faith had always played an integral part in the .. household, and there was *boekevat* every night. **1991** A. VAN WYK *Birth of New Afrikaner* 43 We would not have gone to sleep without *boekevat* (family prayers), because my mother would have had her Bible ready for the ritual.

boekhoo var. BUCHU.

boem-slang var. BOOMSLANG.

boendoes var. BUNDU.

boep /bʊp, bup/ *n.*[1] *Prison slang.* Also **boeb, boop.** [ad. U.S. slang *boob*, fr. *booby* shortened form of *booby-hutch* jail.] Prison. Also *attrib.*

1970 S. SMUTS *Informant, Cape Town* A thief is put in the boep (prison). **1974** [see BOOM *n.* sense 1]. **1983** J. CRONIN *Inside* 16 Listen man, I'm in boeb For something I hardly didn't do. **1987** [see SUN CITY]. **1990** C. GOEDHALS *Informant, Port Elizabeth* When you see a guy walking around with short hair, a pair of pants and a shirt and carrying an old suitcase you know: this guy's just come out of boep.

boep /bʊp, bup/ *n.*[2] *colloq.* [Shortened form of Afk. *boepens* paunch, fr. Du. euphemism *boegpens, boeg* bow (of ship etc.) + *pens* (colloq.) stomach, paunch.] A paunch or potbelly. See also BEER-BOEP.

1976 P. SOLDATOS in *Darling* 9 June 34 For heaven's sake, if you're fat don't wear your trousers tight. Everywhere we've got to look at three layers of boep sticking out. **1976** *Het Suid-Western* 22 Dec. 2 We .. firmly believe in Father Christmas. We don't see him as a red faced old pagan with an enormous 'boep' a cotton wool beard and reindeer that land on your roof. **1980** *Daily Dispatch* 3 May 8, I see what I'd never registered before — the sloppiness of white South Africans .. the safari suits, or the shorts and T-shirts which seldom meet over bulging 'boeps'. **1988** P. PAGE in *Frontline* Jan. 29 No beer drinker worth his boep would feel at ease swigging the product of a company that was not enlightened and concerned and committed. **1991** H. DUGMORE in *Personality* 5 Aug. 19 The customers on this night are a mixed bag — from boep-heavy-boere to svelte sophisticates.

Hence **boepie** *adj. nonce.*

1990 *Personality* 3 Dec. 22 Who wants to exist on a mere glass of wine or beer — and that's for a whole *day*? Grief, definitely not our boepie pal.

Boer /bʊə, buːr/ *n.* Also with small initial, and (formerly) **Boor.** Pl. **-s, -e** /-ə/. [Du., farmer. All senses are also found in Afk.

The pl. 'boere' is a recent form in *S. Afr. Eng.*, first appearing in the 1970s, which suggests that the word was 're-borrowed' from Afrikaans because of the new senses it had acquired in that language.]

1.a. A farmer; a rural Dutch- or Afrikaans-speaking person; *plaasboer*, see PLAAS sense 1 c.

Almost without exception referring to a Dutch- or Afrikaans-speaking farmer, this sense gradually widened to include all rural Dutch-speaking people (see quots. 1896 and 1900).

Used *attrib.* in *S. Afr. Du.* and Afk., as well as in *S. Afr. Eng.*, to designate domestic products or foodstuffs typically or mainly produced by early colonists, usu. having the meaning 'home-made' or 'country-style': see BOER BRANDY and BOER BREAD. Used also to mean 'indigenous' in the names of plants and animals: see BOERBOK, BOERBOOM, BOERBOON, BOERBULL. See also BOERE sense 2.

1776 F. MASSON in *Phil. Trans. of Royal Soc.* LXVI. 282 The boors informed us, the summers are often so unkindly, that their wheat is blighted while in ear, so that they purchase corn with their cattle from the low-country farmers. **1786** G. FORSTER tr. *A. Sparrman's Voy. to Cape of G.H.* I. 50, I am just returned home .. having had occasion to visit several African *boors* .. a set of hearty honest fellows, who, though they do not, indeed, differ in rank from our Swedish peasants, .. are yet for the most part extremely wealthy. **1797** LADY A. BARNARD *S. Afr. Century Ago* (1925) 53, I think the Boers, or farmers, of the country, as far as I have seen or heard of them, a better charactered race than the people of Cape Town. **1810** G. BARRINGTON *Acct of Voy.* 178 A true Dutch peasant, or boor, as he styles himself, has not the smallest idea of what an English farmer means by the word comfort. *a***1823** J. EWART *Jrnl* (1970) 91 The Cape Boors or Farmers almost all of whom were originaly [*sic*] of Dutch or German extraction .. are perhaps the most huge and unwieldy of any race of men in the world. **1821** *Missionary Notices* 22 In consequence of my having come as the minister of the English Boors, they allow that it is a part of my duty to teach them also. **1837** 'N. POLSON' *Subaltern's Sick Leave* 142 The Dutch settlement .. increased, and farmers (or Boers as they are here called), the pioneers of civilization, gradually proceeded farther into the interior and established themselves. **1841** *Cape of G.H. Almanack & Annual Register* 387 Who among us does not remember the frontier boer of 1820, barefoot and clad in sheepskins, his wife covered (not dressed) in voerchitz, their dwelling houses wretched and unfurnished — and yet with all this conspicuous for their hospitality and kindness. **1852** M.B. HUDSON *S. Afr. Frontier Life* 234 The word 'Boer' is synonymous with the English 'Farmer', and is applied to every Agriculturist or Grazier. **1896** R. WALLACE *Farming Indust. of Cape Col.* 398 The word 'Boer' is the Dutch for a tiller of the ground, but its meaning in South Africa has been extended to cattle breeders as well as to cultivators, and 'it is frequently used in the plural form to signify the whole rural population of European blood speaking the Dutch language.' **1899** D.S.F.A. PHILLIPS *S. Afr. Recollections* 28 When he inhabits a town he is no longer called a Boer (which is the Dutch for 'farmer'), but an Africander of Dutch, German or English extraction. **1936** *Cambridge Hist. of Brit. Empire* VIII. 319 The Boers of the eighteen-thirties — and almost without exception the Trekkers were 'boers', that is to say frontier stock-farmers — had a definite character of their own. *c***1936** *S. & E. Afr. Yr Bk & Guide* 225 The voortrekkers, although always known as Boers or farmers, were hardly so in fact. They were, in the first instance, mainly hunters. **1950** H. GIBBS *Twilight* 125 In 1832 news comes that Crown lands .. must be sold by auction. To the Government this is only a means of raising badly needed revenue; to Boers, Afrikaner farmers, it means they must pay for what they had believed their birthright. **1979** J. GRATUS *Jo'burgers* 7 The country in which the gold was discovered was sparsely populated by farmers of Dutch descent (the Boers) who resisted the idea of having their peaceful lives disturbed. **1980** S. JENKINS in *Rand Daily Mail* 19 June 9 There is still a cultural gap between the traditional, largely rural Boers and the new, sophisticated Afrikaners who were the children of the 1948 revolution. **1989** J. SPARG in *Daily Dispatch* 13 July 3 Patrick Mynhardt's presentation .. was a hilarious but poignant evocation of life among the Marico farmers of yesteryear .. the traditions, prejudices and indomitable spirit of the 'boere' of the isolated bushveld. **1991** C. LEONARD in *Weekly Mail* 1 Feb. 6 It was the 'Boere' versus the boere: white policemen against white farmers. **1991** G. ZWIRN in *Settler* Vol.65 No.2, 10 A Boer was a farmer of Dutch descent, whose chief interest was growing crops and breeding cattle. **1991** H. JANSEN in *Sunday Times* 14 July 4 Charlie, the black boer of Delmas .. began life as a herdboy.

b. *obs.* With distinguishing epithet designating a particluar type of farmer: **cattle boer**; **corn boer**, a wheat-farmer or an agriculturalist; **melkboer** /ˈmelk-/ [Afk., *melk* milk], a dairy-farmer; **post boer**, a farmer paid by the British colonial government to convey mail, usu. once a fortnight, between his farm and the next post on a mail route; **schaapboer** /ˈskɑːp-/ [Du., *schaap* sheep], a sheep-farmer; **vee-boer**, see VEE sense 2; **wine boer**, WINE FARMER.

1827 G. THOMPSON *Trav.* I. 66 Where he resides, had been formerly occupied by an extensive **cattle boor**, who had left a memorable monument of his residence in a prodigious dunghill just in front of the house. **1786** G. FORSTER tr. *A. Sparrman's Voy. to Cape of G.H.* II. 249 In their company .. came to this a place [*sic*] a husbandman, or, as they are usually called here, a **corn-boor**, from the country near Cape Town. **1823** W.W. BIRD *State of Cape of G.H.* 48 The corn-Boer complains that, when there is an abundant harvest, the supply of wheat sent into Cape Town .. far exceeds the demand. **1827** G. THOMPSON *Trav.* II. 122 The poorer class of corn boors near Cape Agulhas, and other parts of the Caledon district, are many of them more rude in their manners. **1951** L.G. GREEN *Grow Lovely* 16 The old **melkboer**, Joachim Reyneke, .. settled near the foot of this hill late in the eighteenth century. **1809** LORD CALEDON in G.M. Theal *Rec. of Cape Col.* (1900) VII. 189 Relays of **Post Boors**, which it is found necessary to hold in readiness for the purpose of keeping up a fixed mode of communication between Cape Town and the Country Districts. **1912** *S. Afr. Agric. Jrnl* July 61 (Pettman), These plants were known to the veeboer or **schaapboer** as the cause of the troubles they produce, long before any scientific investigation of their properties had been made. **1786** G. FORSTER tr. *A. Sparrman's Voy. to Cape of G.H.* II. 329 This tract of country . . was so well inhabited, (chiefly by **wine-boors**) that I could not find room for distinguishing all the farms with the usual circular mark in my map. **1822** W.J. BURCHELL *Trav.* I. 179 We arrived at the house of a wine-boor, named Marais, a man of a religious turn, and a friend of my fellow-travellers. **1823** W.W. BIRD *State of Cape of G.H.* 43 The price of Cape wine of one year old, bought from the wine boer, is now under fifty rix-dollars. **1835** G. CHAMPION *Jrnl* (1968) 11 He was a wine boor (or farmer) living upon the products of his vineyard.

c. *obs.* Ellipt. for BOER TOBACCO.

1881 'LOOKER ON' in *Diggers' Ditties* (1989) 15 I've gin and a pipeful of Boer. **1897** F.W. SYKES *With Plumer in Matabeleland* 103 A half-pound cake of black tobacco fetched £2, whilst a handful of 'Boer' was greedily bought in at 5s. **1900** *Westminster Gaz.* (U.K.) 14 July 8 A smoker may keep his pipe going from early morning till late at night if he uses good 'Boer'.

d. In the idiomatic expression ***'n boer maak 'n plan*** /ə 'buːr mɑːk ə ˌplan/ [Afk., 'a farmer makes a plan']: in a crisis a creative solution may always be found. Also *attrib.* Cf. *maak 'n plan* (see MAAK sense 2).

1982 *Daily Dispatch* 11 Jan. 6 Farm wisdom permeates our language. 'n Boer maak 'n plan is the automatic response to any situation regarding thought or discussion. I've heard it said sardonically in an operating theatre when the power supply failed. **1985** *Fair Lady* 16 Oct. 24 They have . . forgotten the one central motto upon which this country rests as it always has done and always will — *'n Boer maak 'n plan* — and he is far, far better at it than Machiavelli ever dreamt of being. **1987** J. BARHILL in *Frontline* Mar. 25 Already the small family farm is more cost conscious than corporate farms and . . it is plain to see where the expression ''n boer maak 'n plan' comes from. Machines are held together with baling wire, chicken manure is fed to cattle and the cow dung goes on the lands. **1989** J. MICHELL in *Style* Feb. 79 A lot of products out here are merely utilitarian in nature because the attitude is, ''*n boer maak 'n plan* and if you don't like it you can get lost'. **1990** *Style* Feb. 30 Karen's platteland upbringing gave her . . a unique *'n-boer-maak-'n-plan* philosophy towards fashion.

2. *obs.* exc. *hist.* A Dutch-speaking colonist at the Cape; subsequently, a Dutch-speaking inhabitant of southern Africa, esp. of the Transvaal, Free State and Natal republics; SETTLER sense 1. See also sense 4 below, AFRIKANER sense 2 a, BOERDOM, BOERESS, BOERLAND, BOER REPUBLIC, BOER WAR, BURGHER sense 1 a.

1800 LADY A. BARNARD in D. Fairbridge *Lady Anne Barnard* (1924) 227, I do not think the Boers after what has passed will be turbulent in a hurry again. **1825** G. BARKER Journal. 25 July, On the road I baptised the child of a Boer at his particular request, the first time I had Baptised the child of a Colonist. **1837** 'N. POLSON' *Subaltern's Sick Leave* 111 There were and still are Boers too in this province, but the generality of the population is British. **1844** E.L. KIFT Letter. 17 Oct., From all that I hear respecting the Orange River & Natal Boers I am much inclined to think that ere long there will be a 'kick up' of a serious nature between them & the Govt. **1857** D. LIVINGSTONE *Missionary Trav.* 98 Two centuries of South African climate have not had much effect upon the physical condition of the Boers. They are a shade darker, or ruddier, than Europeans, and are never cadaverous-looking, as descendants of Europeans are said to be elsewhere. **1867** E.L. PRICE *Jrnls* (1956) 253 Oh one does so weary of these Boer farms! — for there is so little to interest one after one has once studied bread-making &c &c. **1878** A. AYLWARD *Tvl of Today* 41 South Africa is the home of the Boer. He is ever and always the domesticated South African settler; and therefore, as a rule, we find him a farmer and a herdsman, a flockmaster or a minister of the Dutch Church — but seldom or never a storekeeper or a middleman. **1880** E.L. PRICE *Jrnls* (1956) 408 The Boers are generally *so* proud in their behaviour to the natives. They count them infinitely beneath them — but there is nothing of this seen among these children in school. **1899** *Natal Agric. Jrnl* 31 Mar. 5 'Boer', which may be taken to mean a Cape colonist of Dutch or French descent is now an accepted English word. **1915** J.K. O'CONNOR *Afrikander Rebellion* 10 The townsman has a habit . . of classing all kinds of Dutch people in South Africa under the general name of Boers. **1922** J. GALSWORTHY *Forsyte Saga* 527 'The Boers are only half-civilised,' remarked Soames; 'they stand in the way of progress. It will never do to let our suzerainty go.' **1937** C. BIRKBY *Zulu Journey* 21 These armies of black warriors delivered a number of crushing defeats to the Boers in the early thirties and blocked Boer colonisation in their territory until December 16, 1838, when the Boers finally won a great victory over the Zulu army of King Dingaan. **1946** T. MACDONALD *Ouma Smuts* 32 By now the Boer term has disappeard and has been substituted by the term Afrikaner. To-day there are far more Afrikaners in the towns than on the land. **1949** L.G. GREEN *In Land of Afternoon* 15, I came across this old definition of a Boer: 'It signifies a European by descent whose vernacular is the Taal and who uses familiarly no literary European language. It does not denote race of necessity; the Boer may be French, Dutch, German, or of any other blood . . neither does it denote occupation. The Boer is often a farmer and stock-owner; but he may also be a hunter, trader, the president of a republic. He remains a Boer still while the Taal remains his only speech.' *a***1951** H.C. BOSMAN *Willemsdorp* (1977) 8 The colonists at the Cape had been welded into that homogeneous entity that constitutes a new nation. They were not Hollanders; they were Boers. **1966** C.A. SMITH *Common Names* 144 Their descendants . . became widely dispersed over the interior as farmers and being predominantly Dutch-speaking, the term 'boer' became synonymous with this latter class, now spelled with a capital initial letter (Boer). **1989** *Reader's Digest Illust. Hist.* 5 Blacks, British, Boers . . and blood; the history of our troubled country is steeped in the stuff, as Africans fought one another, the Boers fought the British, and both fought the Africans.

3. *hist.* A soldier of the Dutch- or Afrikaans-speaking forces fighting against British forces, esp. during the ANGLO-BOER WAR. Also *attrib.* See also BOER-BRIT, BROTHER BOER.

1882 C.L. NORRIS-NEWMAN *With Boers in Tvl* 301 'The behaviour of the Boers has won them the respect of many who formerly held them in contempt. Hardly an officer is there who has had anything whatever to do with our late enemies but is very favourably impressed with them.' **1897** F.R. STATHAM *S. Afr. as It Is* 4 If the skipper . . happens to be an officer of the Naval Reserve, he is not long, when once Madeira is passed, in finding sympathisers for his views about 'the Boers.' **1900** R. KIPLING in J. Crwys-Williams *S. Afr. Despatches* (1989) 162 The Boers had established themselves very comfortably among these rock-ridges and scrub-patches, and the 'great war' drizzled down to long shots and longer stalking. **1900** A.W. CARTER *Informant, Ladybrand* 8 Feb. 1 It was practically a drawn battle, the Boers failing to dislodge the British but not being routed from the field. **1910** J. BUCHAN *Prester John* (1961) 132, I remembered a story of an escaped prisoner during the war who had only the Komati River between him and safety. But he dared not enter it, and was recaptured by a Boer commando. **1926** M. NATHAN *S. Afr. from Within* 102 In August, Kitchener issued a proclamation threatening such Boer leaders as were captured with perpetual banishment. **1933** W.H.S. BELL *Bygone Days* 249 The problem that the General Staff are now investigating is how the Boer commandos towards the end of the war . . still raided British communications with persistent mobility. **1946** T. MACDONALD *Ouma Smuts* 83 General Smuts was made a Field-Marshal. It was an unique honour. It had been given to a one-time Boer general who had fought against Britain. **1977** L. SELLERS in *Sunday Times* 6 Nov. (Mag. Sect.) 3 The final irony, with the Boers winning the peace so quickly after losing the war, is briefly but nicely touched on. **1989** W. EBERSOHN in *Cosmopolitan* Apr. 200 At the Treaty of Vereeniging, only six out of the 60 members of the Boer contingent were in favour of rejecting the terms and continuing the war.

4. An Afrikaner.

a. A pejorative name for an Afrikaner, used esp. by black South Africans. Also *attrib.* Cf. AMABHULU sense 1.

1956 D. JACOBSON *Dance in Sun* 39 'I knew the baas wasn't a Boer', the African said ... If he had approached me on the strength of my not being an Afrikaner, or Boer as he preferred to put it, he had been foolhardy and reckless. **1960** J. COPE *Tame Ox* 57 South Africa, to her, was the land of the *maburu* (Boers). However many others lived there, it was still so. **1968** COLE & FLAHERTY *House of Bondage* 51 Boer farmers need cheap labor and it is a convenience that the Boer-dominated Government has a steady supply of prisoners available for rent at low cost. **1974** J. MATTHEWS *Park* (1983) 31 'The white people are not all bad. It's only the Boere,' she said. **1977** S. STANDER *Flight from Hunter* 68 'P.E. Leroux,' he read on a credit card. 'Hey, his name's Leroux, he's a bloody Boer, man.' **1977** J. SIKAKANE *Window on Soweto* 40, 1954 was the year of the formal switch to Bantu Education for all African children. I remember hearing our parents talking about it, saying 'the Boers were wanting to indoctrinate African children into being perpetual slaves of the white man.' **1979** A.P. BRINK *Dry White Season* 257 A sombre black figure rose from the dining table. 'Who is this kaffir?' asked Father-in-law ... 'Why don't you tell the boer who this kaffir is?' asked Stanley. **1980** *Sunday Times* 9 Mar. 5 Immediately one is aware of the inherent antagonism towards the Boer, that pejorative word used by coloureds to express their contempt. **1985** *Saspu National* Vol.6 No.2, 15 And now we are old, what will we get? Those boers who used us — what will they do for us now that we are old. Nothing. Niks. **1990** *Weekend Argus* 14 July 15, I was scared to death and thought I would never get out of Soweto alive, especially after Dhlomo had introduced me as a 'Boer' when we visited a shebeen one night. **1990** J. NAIDOO *Coolie Location* 153 She speaks English to him, only English ... You know, .. no voetseks, no bliksems, no hey jongs, no pas ops ... She never, never uses a single word of the Boer language.

b. An affectionate and humorous name used by Afrikaners of themselves.

1973 *Weekend Post* 17 Feb. 9 We sit in Africa and we are not Africans ... We go to England and we find out that we are Boers who try to live like the English here under the Southern Cross. **1989** M. DU PREEZ in *Style* Feb. 40 There's always suspicion about leftie Boere. If you're a Boer and you hate apartheid and side with the majority you're considered unbalanced and unstable. **1990** *Cosmopolitan* Apr. 169 He . . began to feel resentful of being treated like a token *boer*, covering the stereotypical stories on the Broederbond, *broedertwis*, the church and so on. **1990** R. MALAN *My Traitor's Heart* 127 The great Boer poet [*sc.* Breyten Breytenbach] spent the sixties in exile in Paris and most of the seventies in a South African prison, paying for his role in a quixotic 'terrorist' plot.

c. A name used by right-wing Afrikaners of all Afrikaners sharing a similar outlook; cf. BOEREVOLK. Also *attrib.*

1978 *Sunday Times* 30 Apr. 7 The Afrikaner cannot afford to allow a wedge to be cunningly driven between English and Afrikaner by catering only for a Boer homeland. **1985** A. GOLDSTUCK in *Weekly Mail* 2 Aug. 7 No longer, storms Terre'blanche, will the boer be a slave to the small political smurfs . . who are nothing but the backscratchers of . . international Jewry. **1988** J. BOEKKOOI in *Frontline* Oct. 23 Within the ranks of the far Right, a question rages . . : 'Mirror, mirror, on the wall, Who's the purest Boer of all?'

.. For some of the ultra-right a 'Boer' is a descendant of a Trekker, as opposed to an 'Afrikaner' .. those Cape Afrikaners who stayed behind in comfort .. talking English with the imperialists. **1990** *Sunday Times* 22 Apr. 1 Boerestaat Party leader Robert van Tonder confirmed this week that so-called 'Boer commandos' were being formed on a regional basis 'with commandants in every town and generals overseeing every region'. **1990** *Sunday Times* 19 Aug. 2 It was one of the closest confrontations yet ... The 3000 black and coloured marchers began streaming past a street lined with armed Boers who have never minced words over their hatred for communists and the ANC. **1990** R. VAN TONDER in *Style* Oct. 121 The Boers won't stand for it. There will be a civil war ... The armed forces and the police are almost all Boer boys.

5. A pejorative name for a white South African. Cf. AMABHULU sense 2.

1956 A. SAMPSON *Drum* 207 When he went to the Coloured school, he was singled out for teasing. 'Wit boer!' they called him. 'Why don't you go to a white school, eh?' **1974** J. MATTHEWS *Park* (1983) 55 'What about your Maureen, the one who can pass?' ... 'They stay in Parow ... Her children go to a white school.' 'She married to a boer?' Freda asked incredulously. **1984** D. BECKETT in *Frontline* Feb. 36 Overall, he says, there are plenty of white people putting in good and honest efforts. The trouble is that the blacks always believed the worst ... 'They just say "Rubbish, man, the Boere rob us".' **1986** E.E. BELLINGAN in *Daily Dispatch* 3 Apr. 8 Mr M— .. generalises, it appears, by referring to all white South Africans as 'boere'. The way he uses it has the same derogatory connotations as the word 'kaffir' has to the black man. **1991** *E. Prov. Herald* 20 Mar. 11 He said J— had found Mr K—, and decided to rob him. He protested, but J— said the 'boer had a lot of money.'

6. A pejorative name for a member of the South African security forces, including any member of the police force, prison service, or defence force; in *pl.*, the police force, prison service, or defence force. Cf. AMABHUNU sense 3.

1970 S. SMUTS *Informant, Cape Town* The boere threw the drunkard in the van. **1977** D. MULLER *Whitey* 49 'The police were in the house, Uncle Ben,' Willy explained, his face sullen. 'They have just gone away.' 'The boere, eh.' **1978** *Daily Dispatch* 20 Mar. 7 He said the talks centred around .. the withdrawal of South African troops ... 'But we never sat with the Boere and they were too scared to sit with the terrorists,' he said. **1978** *Swapo Military Council* in *Sunday Times* 12 Mar. 1 Tasks of the Regional Commander Nondonga ... 5. To ensure that the seizure of a boer prisoner of war is made a 'practice.' **1980** C. HOPE *A Separate Development* (1983) 138 I'm thinking myself safe and sound .. when the *boere* smash through the door and haul me off to the big hotel. **1983** *Rand Daily Mail* 19 Oct. 5 Unknown assailants .. accused him of being a spy for the Security Forces .. a 'puppet supplying information to the Boers'. **1985** *Ibid.* 14 Feb. 2 A coded message .. stated that a Maritzburg man, Mr Ben L—, had been eliminated because he was 'the guy who handed two comrades to the Boers'. **1989** *Daily Dispatch* 4 Apr. 1 They had been instructed by their regional commander in Angola to .. 'observe if the Boers (SADF) had been restricted to base.' **1989** *Weekly Mail* 1 Sept. 4 The young man .. began to recite, his words addressed to the government: 'When the children play *Comrades and Boere* (police), and they all want to be the comrades, then I know — you will surrender.' **1990** M. DJASI in *Sunday Times* 4 Mar. (Extra) 10 We have to be vigilant against the boers (white government forces) in South Africa. **1990** GARSON & MALUNGA in *Weekly Mail* 30 Mar. 4 Police said they opened fire in 'self-defence' after a crowd .. had attacked them, shouting 'kill the *boers*'. **1991** [see sense 1 a].

7. *hist.* Usu. *pl.* A pejorative name for the South African government. See also PRETORIA sense 1 a.

1976 *E. Prov. Herald* 19 Nov. 17 A Coloured school principal who is a member of the liaison committee in his town .. said he had been told his home was stoned because 'I work with the Boere'. **1977** *Sunday Times* 27 Nov. 8, I am by no means predicting a Boer-Soviet pact. But can we afford to neglect this possibility completely? **1982** *Voice* 18 July 4 Aikhona, Chief Leabua Jonathan! You simply cannot get away with it so easily by blaming your sins on poor Pretoria. It is simply not correct that the violence in your country .. is the sole creation of the 'Boers'. **1986** *Herald* (Zimbabwe) in *Cape Times* 24 Jan. 6 The fact that the Boers have now been able to successfully engineer a coup against an African leader they do not like is an indication of the seriousness with which frontline states should treat the dangers of apartheid. **1989** *Weekly Mail* 27 Oct. 26 'I don't think the boers (government) will allow the rally to be advertised, let alone permit it,' said club member Jozi. **1990** *Sunday Times* 18 Feb. 5 Within ANC ranks people who spoke to 'the Boere' were treated with suspicion by hardliners who preferred 'war-war' to 'jaw-jaw'.

Boer-bashing /ˈbʊəbæʃɪŋ/ *vbl n.* Also with small initial. [BOER sense 4 + fig. use of Eng. *bashing*, as found in *Paki-bashing*.] Fierce and unrelenting criticism of Afrikaners, or of South Africans.

1986 C. BARNARD in *Daily Dispatch* 10 Mar. 8 Yank-bashing is the thing at present ... It makes a change from the worldwide boerbashing that South Africans have been subjected to in the past year. **1986** *E. Prov. Herald* 19 Aug. 8 In some ways, the Afrikaner .. almost alone may be deemed generically repulsive without causing offence to the arbiters of decency. The phrase 'Boer-bashing' connotes not intolerance but something admirable in and of itself. **1989** *Weekly Mail* 3 Nov. (Suppl.) 1 If the reader was hoping to find slogans and improbably easy answers, and another session of Boer-bashing, *Memory of Snow and of Dust* will come as a big disappointment.

boer-bean /ˈbʊəˈbiːn/ *n.* [Part. tr. Afk. *boerboon*, see BOERBOON.]

1. *obs.* In full ***boer-bean tree***: the coral tree or (*offensive*) KAFFIRBOOM. Also *attrib.*

1906 B. STONEMAN *Plants & their Ways* 38 What protects the bud in *Erythrina* (Boer bean tree)?

2.a. BOERBOON.

1951 N.L. KING *Tree-Planting* 71 *Schotia brachypetala* (Boerbean). A much-branched tree found in dry scrub forest in eastern Cape, Natal, Zululand and Transvaal. Bears clusters of bright scarlet flowers on the stem or branches. **1991** C. URQUHART in *Weekend Post* 16 Mar. (Leisure) 1 A tree which grows on his farm — the boerbean.

b. With distinguishing epithets designating particular species of boer-bean, as **bush boer-bean**, **dwarf boer-bean**, **Karoo boer-bean**, **weeping boer-bean**: see quots. Also *attrib.*

1983 K.C. PALGRAVE *Trees of Sn Afr.* 275 *Schotia afra* .. Karoo boer-bean ... *Schotia brachypetala* .. Weeping boer-bean. *Ibid.* 276 *Schotia capitata* .. Dwarf boer-bean. *Ibid.* 277 *Schotia latifolia* .. Bush boer-bean. **1989** C. KURSCHELD in *S. Afr. Panorama* Apr. 41 Other favourites are the white stinkwood, .. the small-leaved Karroo boer-bean tree (*Schotia afra* var. *angustifolia*) and many more. **1989** *Conserva* July 23 She writes of the tree in her garden — a boerboon (*Schotia brachypetala*, the weeping boer-bean) which she planted.

boerbeschuit, **boerbeskuit** varr. BOEREBESKUIT.

Boer biscuit /ˈbʊəbɪskɪt/ *n. phr. Obsolescent.* Also with small initial. [Calque formed on Afk. *boerebeskuit.*] BOEREBESKUIT.

Unlike BESKUIT and BOEREBESKUIT, 'Boer biscuit' does occur with pl. *-s*.

1882 S. HECKFORD *Lady Trader in Tvl* 30 The father said a long grace in Dutch, and then the mother helped all to milk and biscuits — the hard bread is called Boer biscuit here. *Ibid.* 309 Hendrik managed to get some Boer biscuits from this man. **1902** C.R. DE WET *Three Yrs War* 9 The provisions .. of meat .. or else of sausages and 'Boer biscuits'. [*Note*] Small loaves manufactured of flour, with fermented raisins instead of yeast, and twice baked. **1914** W.C. SCULLY *Lodges in Wilderness* 25 As we did not mean to be luxurious, our commissariat list only included coffee, sugar, salt and 'Boer-biscuits' (a kind of coarse but exceedingly palatable rusk). ***a*1920** O.E.A. SCHREINER *From Man to Man* (1926) 111 One morning .. Baby-Bertie was kneeling in the pantry, making Boer biscuits. **1929** J.G. VAN ALPHEN *Jan Venter* 145 Hester van Aarder and her mother had baked a huge batch of Boer biscuits. **1944** J. MOCKFORD *Here Are S. Africans* 101 Before Lord Methuen was allowed to go to a British hospital, Mrs de la Rey killed and cooked a fat chicken which she sent to his tent with some Boer biscuits. **1951** S. VAN H. TULLEKEN *Prac. Cookery Bk* 12 Boer Biscuit. Make yeast in the morning, using 2 yeast cakes, and doubling ingredients as given for yeast cake sponge or 'zoet zuurdeeg.'

boer biskuit var. BOEREBESKUIT.

boerboel var. BOERBULL.

‖**boerbok** /ˈbuːrbɔk/ *n.* Pl. **-ke** /-ə/. [Afk., *boer* (applied to indigenous plants and animals) + *bok* goat, antelope.] BOER GOAT.

1966 C.A. SMITH *Common Names* 151 Neighbouring farmers bought progeny of crosses with blinkhaar-boerbok as stud rams, and about 1853 a small lot of these crosses were brought to Graaff-Reinet. **1972** L.G. GREEN *When Journey's Over* 56 Bokkeveld and Bokveld were not named after boerbokke; they were once alive with springbok, not goats. **1976** *Daily Dispatch* 6 Feb. (Suppl.) 2 They pointed out a boerbok and asked him to slaughter it. **1984** B. JOHNSON-BARKER in *Wynboer* Feb. 62 There happened to be a boerbok in the voorkamer at the time, .. but nobody threw a stick at it, or even shouted at it.

boerboom /ˈbuːrbuəm/ *n.* Also **boorbom**, **burbom**. [Contracted form of S. Afr. Du. *boerboon* (*-boom*) 'farmer's bean (tree)': see next.] BOERBOON. Also *attrib.*, and occas. with distinguishing epithet.

***a*1858** J. GOLDSWAIN *Chron.* (1946) I. 76 As soon as the Cattle came up to a Burbom .. Tree they Cattle returned back and .. we saw that in this tree thear must be a Kaffer. **1868** T. STUBBS Men I have Known. 19 A sort of huts were made under the flat topt Boorbom trees. **1972** *S. Afr. Garden & Home* Oct. 145 Among these trees are .. the thorny boerboom and the Kei apple tree. **1982** *E. Prov. Herald* 16 Sept. 11 The vegetation in the park, mainly spekboom, sneezewood, karoo boerboom and guarri is a unique tangle of creepers and trees.

boerboon /ˈbuːrbuən, ˈbʊə(r)-/ *n.* Also **barboon**, **boer-boen**, **boerbon**, **boereboon**, **boorbon**, **bourbon**, **burben**. Pl. **-s**. [S. Afr. Du., *boer* (applied to indigenous plants and animals) + *boon* bean; prob. so named because the seeds were widely used by Dutch colonists as a foodstuff and in making a coffee-like beverage.] Any of several species of tree of the genus *Schotia* of the Fabaceae, esp. *S. afra*, an evergreen flowering tree which produces pods of edible seeds resembling broad beans; these seeds; BOER-BEAN sense 2 a; BOERBOOM; BOERBOONTJIE sense 1; *Cape walnut* sense (*b*), see CAPE sense 2 a. Also *attrib.* See also *Hottentot('s) bean (tree)* at HOTTENTOT *n.* sense 6 a.

1809 J. MACKRILL Diary. 74 Thunberg's Guaiae africana, is the Scotia Speciosa (Wilde Boorbon). **1812** J.T. VAN DER KEMP *Acct of Caffraria* 63 There also grows the boereboon, called by the natives ingaem. **1832** *Graham's Town Jrnl* 18 May 80b, Now on hand, a small quantity of superior Cyder, Bourbon Coffee, and York Hams. **1833** *Ibid.* 2 May 3 A green boereboon stick, about the length of my arm, with the bark still on it. **1844** J. BACKHOUSE *Narr. of Visit* 172 Among the trees is the *Theodora speciosa*? called Boerboon, *Farmers-bean*, bearing gay, crimson flowers. **1846** J.M. BOWKER *Speeches & Sel.* (1864) 207 The trees under which he formed his bower, .. those very Bourbon trees are dead, and our grievances remain unredressed! **1875** C.B. BISSET *Sport & War* 163 Charles Somerset .. was taking out the honeycomb from the hollow of a large barboon or bean tree. **1908** F.C. SLATER *Sunburnt South* 11 At the foot of the valley ran a rivulet, along which *boer-boens*, ruddy with blood-like blossoms, .. grew in delightful profusion. **1917** R. MARLOTH *Common Names* 13 *Boerboon*, This name is applied to the four species of the genus *Schotia*, the young seeds being edible like beans. Trees with showy flowers. **1964** A. ROTHMANN *Elephant Shrew* 33 There are miles and miles of bush .., gnarled ghwarrie trees, 'boerboon' with its showy red flowers and flat pods and above all elephant's food or 'spekboom'. **1973** *E. Prov. Herald* 30 July 14 The heartwood of the boerboon or Cape Walnut (*Schotia latifolia*) polishes well and makes a most attractive small table. **1987** M. POLAND *Train to Doringbult* 57 For each goat shorn the shearer would toss a round tan boerboon into a tin — a tally of his day's work. **1989** [see Conserva quot. at BOER-BEAN sense b].

boerboontjie /ˈbuːrbɔɪŋki/ *n.* Also **boerboontje**, **bourboontjie**. [S. Afr. Du., BOERBOON + dim. suffix -IE.]

1. *obs.* BOERBOON.

1831 *S. Afr. Almanac & Dir.* 84 Bosche Bourboontjie. **1848** C.J.F. BUNBURY *Jrnl of Res. at Cape of G.H.* 101 The *Boerboontjes* (*Schotia speciosa*) a leguminous shrub with beautiful scarlet flowers growing in clusters out of the old wood.

2. A variety of broad bean.

1913 C. PETTMAN *Africanderisms* 73 *Boerboontjes*, In the Midlands a variety of broad bean is so named. **1970** C. DE VILLIERS *Informant, Bloemfontein* Boerboontjies are tasty in soup.

Boer brandy /ˈbʊə ˌbrændi/ *n. phr. Hist.* Also **Boers' brandy**, and with small initial. [BOER sense 1 a + Eng. *brandy*.] Brandy distilled privately by individual farmers. Also shortened form **Boers**. See also CAPE BRANDY.

1832 *Graham's Town Jrnl* 24 Feb. 33 W.R. Thompson Will hold a Public Sale on Monday next the 27 instant of a variety of fresh Goods, .. Cape and Boers' Brandy [etc.]. **1864** T. SHONE Diary. 18 Nov., Yesterday Henry gave me a pint of boar Brandy. **1866** E. WILSON *Reminisc.* 41 We discovered a number of Natives .. drinking freely in the canteen, of Boer brandy, or, as it is generally called here, 'Cape Smoke'. **1872** C.A. PAYTON *Diamond Diggings* 106 He starts for the Fields with his big waggon, his team of oxen .. and a good stock of maize flour, tobacco, and 'Boer brandy'. **1884** *Queenstown Free Press* 22 June (Pettman), The price of a glass of *Boers* or whisky is sixpence, though the former costs the hotel keeper considerably less than half the price of the latter. **1900** B. MITFORD *Aletta* 11 Boer brandy, when pure and well matured, is about the best liquor in the world, and this was the best of its kind. **1977** *Family Radio & TV* 19 Sept. 51 The creation of this Boer brandy has been a dying art since the '20s when intervention by the newly formed KWV became essential because the standards of 3 000 farmers making and marketing their own recipes were often disastrous ... Even legal Boer brandy heard the death sentence in 1964 when the KWV ruled that no more private licences would be issued.

Boer bread *n. phr. Obs.* Also **Boers' bread**, and with small initial. [Part. tr. Afk. *boerebrood; boer* farmer('s) + Eng. *bread*.] Home-made bread, usu. brown or whole-wheat; BOEREBROOD. Also *attrib.*

1876 F. BOYLE *Savage Life* 23 The calls of appetite we had satisfied between-whiles with potted meat, sardines, *biltongue* or dried flesh, boer-bread, coffee, and miscellaneous articles. **1877** LADY BARKER *Yr's Hsekeeping* 318 The only thing which at all daunted us was some freshly made Boers' bread, of the colour of sponge, the consistency of clay, and the weight of pig-iron. **1882** S. HECKFORD *Lady Trader in Tvl* 213, I could make the whole party laugh by saying how I tried to make bread myself, and how bad it was. That .. led to my being asked whether the Boer bread was not nice. **1903** R. KIPLING *Five Nations* 201 Ah there, Piet! — be'ind 'is stony kop, With 'is Boer bread an' biltong, an' 'is flask of awful Dop. **1914** L.H. BRINKMAN *Breath of Karroo* 98 The Predikant's larder was replenished with biltong, butter, huge loaves of Boer bread and dried sausages. **1925** H.J. MANDELBROTE tr. *O. Mentzel's Descr. of Cape of G.H.* II. 143, I maintain that 'boer bread' is tastier and more nourishing than the rye-bread of Amsterdam. **1933** W. MACDONALD *Romance of Golden Rand* 205 There was not a shop of any kind in the camp, and the only article of food procurable was some rather stale Boer bread.

Boer-Brit /bʊəˈbrɪt, buːrˈbrət/ *adj.* Also **Boer /Brit**. [BOER sense 3 + *Brit* abbrev. of Eng. *Briton*; alluding to the protagonists in the Anglo-Boer War of 1899–1902.] Of or pertaining to tension or antagonism between English- and Afrikaans-speakers in South Africa. See also ANGLO-BOER WAR sense 2.

[**1971** *Grocott's Mail* 6 Sept. 3 Kids are sick and tired of the old Boer and Brit politics.] **1973** *Daily Dispatch* 12 Mar. 10 Such legacies of the Boer-Brit tensions as lack of respect for another man's language and cultural traditions. **1984** R. LEAVER in *Frontline* Mar. 39 The new phenomenon .. is striking an enormously healthy nail into the coffin of the old Boer/Brit split, and into the tradition of ethnic politics in South Africa. **1989** *Evening Post* 25 Jan. 2 The ongoing correspondence .. reveals a remarkable degree of intolerance among some English and Afrikaans speakers towards each other's language ... Will this Boer-Brit nonsense never die? **1990** *Sunday Times* 4 Mar. 14 When Nelson Mandela flies to talks in Lusaka about the policy of a future ANC government, are the old Boer-Brit antagonisms now merely ancient history and irrelevant? **1991** *Grocott's Mail* 10 Sept. 9, I did so hope that with all the civic and social bridge-building we must attend to in our little valley we might at last have forgotten our hoary Boer/Brit hang-ups.

boer-brood var. BOEREBROOD.

boerbull /ˈbuːrbəl, ˈbʊəbʊl/ *n.* Also **boerboel**, **boerbul**, and with initial capital. [fr. Afk. *boerboel, boer* (as in BOER HOUND) + *boel* fr. Du. *bul* (as in *bulhond* mastiff, bulldog).] A large dog of a cross-breed between European mastiff, bull-mastiff or Great Dane, and indigenous southern African dogs. Also *attrib.* See also BOER HOUND.

[**1899** B. MITFORD *Weird of Deadly Hollow* 129 Two great smooth-haired dogs — powerful Boer mastiffs — who had followed him, proceeded to coil themselves at his feet. **1951** H.C. BOSMAN in L. Abrahams *Jurie Steyn's Post Office* (1971) 62 I've got an old Boer bulldog that's chased just about everything in his time.] **1965** J. BENNETT *Hawk Alone* 145 One morning the dogs — they had a crossbred ridgeback and a boerboel — had put up a rooikat. **1971** D. MARAIS in *Std Encycl. of Sn Afr.* IV. 55 Some other types are found in South Africa that can be recognised as independent breeds: the Boer hound, the Boer mastiff or Boerbull and the Kaffir dog. **1974** A.P. CARTWRIGHT *By Waters of Letaba* 123 He bred these dogs by crossing collies with the stout-hearted 'Boer bull'. **1987** G. SILBER in *Frontline* Mar. 9, I reach a farmstead and a black Boerbul terrier with a build like a Sumo wrestler waddles out to greet me. **1991** D. CARTE in *Sunday Times* 26 May (Mag. Sect.) 38 The Shepherd is by far the most versatile working dog. The army also likes Dobermans, Rottweilers, Border Collies (for nose work) and a Boerbull-mastiff cross. **1992** C. MARAIS in *Scope* 13 Nov. 64 Pik .. plans to speak in Right-wing heaven tonight. The AWB and their affiliates have vowed to rip his head off and feed it to their boerbulls.

Boerdom *n. obs.* [BOER sense 2 + Eng. abstract suffix of state *-dom*.] Boers collectively, esp. in a nationalistic or political sense. See also AFRIKANERDOM sense 1.

1869 *E. Prov. Herald* in F.A. van Jaarsveld *Awakening of Afrikaner Nationalism* (1961) 66 Boerdom is down just now, and it must accept the situation. It is clearly understood that both the Free State and Transvaal can exist only on sufferance. **1873** F. BOYLE *To Cape for Diamonds* 32 In 1835 .. the bolder spirits of Boerdom, impatient of a hated rule, conceived the adventurous project of escaping from it across the Orange River. **1882** C. DU VAL *With Show through Sn Afr.* II. 145 Breathless narrations of their hair-breadth escapes in attempting to run the gauntlet of encircling Boerdom. **1884** *Pall Mall Gaz.* (U.K.) 15 Oct. 6 Boerdom develops faster than British progress. **1888** *Cape Punch* 8 Feb. 69 The unholy alliance between Brandy, Brass, and Boerdom. **1901** *Grocott's Penny Mail* 9 Jan. 3 His thorough knowledge of Krugerism, Bondism and Boerdom generally, and of the mischievous potentialities of the Steytler-Sauer-&-Cronwright-Schreiner gang, make him the man of the hour. **1903** E.F. KNIGHT *S. Afr. after War* 281 Repeatedly I hear expressions of regret the Mr. Chamberlain was not taken through these beautiful rich vales of the granary of the Transvaal, the heart of Boerdom and cradle of 'Dopperdom,' instead of across the treeless, desolate, high veldt that lies between Potchefstroom and Mafeking. **1911** BLACKBURN & CADDELL *Secret Service* 12 The tragedy .. had filled Boerdom with horror. **1924** L. COHEN *Reminisc. of Jhb.* 45 Rotten eggs have played a conspicuous and revolutionary part in the early history of the Rand. An unwholesome ovum had much to do with the downfall of Boerdom. **1941** C.W. DE KIEWIET *Hist. of S. Afr.* 125 His successor, President F.W. Reitz, believed that all Boerdom should stand united against the British paramount power.

boere /ˈbuːrə, ˈbʊərə/ *adj.* [Afk. *boere-*, combining form of *boer* farmer, Afrikaner; in most of the examples below, this form will have been deduced from combinations borrowed from Afk. which contain it (as BOEREBESKUIT, BOEREBROOD, etc.).]

1.a. Of or pertaining to the Afrikaner community; cf. AFRIKANER *adj.*

1970 *Daily News* 12 May, Many other good 'boere' names had been maliciously changed, he said. **1978** *Sunday Times* 20 Aug. 14 If you travel a few miles further through the koppies, you get to Linden, which is called the Boere Houghton. It is a kind of Afrikaner bantustan. **1980** R. GOVENDER *Lahnee's Pleasure* 18 Suddenly this big Boere cop stopped me. I pulled up one side and I told the kids, duck away in the back. **1981** B. MFENYANA in M. Mutloatse *Reconstruction* 299 Those nannies and farm 'boys' who toiled for the Dutch immigrants from 1700 onwards played a big part in the formation of creole or local Dutch, Afrikaans, isiBhulu ... Then amaNgesi came to Anglicise everybody, resulting in Fanakalo, African and Boere English. **1984** *Fair Lady* 18 Apr. 94 They dressed in charming country clothes, sandals, flowered cottons and cheesecloth. 'A bunch of earnest Boere hippies'. **1987** *E. Prov. Herald* 5 Sept. 2 The popular image of the AWB was 'boere cowboys' who broke up meetings, intimidated people, and took the law into their own hands. **1988** *Style* May 6 Port Elizabeth has become the happy breeding ground of the Boere Kugel. **1990** G. GILL in *Sunday Times* 22 Apr. 20 The Mother Grundys can sleep easy in their beds tonight ... controversial boere-rocker shocker Johannes Kerkorrel is leaving the country.

b. Special collocations. **boere concertina**, BOEREKONSERTINA; **boerenooi**, see NOOI sense 2; **boerenooientjie**, see NOOIENTJIE.

1972 P. BECKER in *Star* 17 Mar. B6 Basie .. strove all his adult life to master Rimsky-Korsakov's 'Servilia' [*sic*] on a **Boere concertina** only to die eventually in abject disillusionment. **1981** *Family Post* 3 Oct. 4 Neels himself is heard on both the English and the 'boere' concertinas. **1990** *Weekend Post* 8 Dec. 7 (*caption*) Boeremusiek 'is for everybody', they say. Women too, as Mrs Hettie Breytenbach shows with her Boere concertina.

2. Country-style, rural; used by or associated with farmers; 'home-grown', indigenous. See note at BOER sense 1 a.

1974 *Daily Dispatch* 20 July 8, I could still savour the memory of gorgeous 'boere' coffee served on the trains 20 years ago. **1977** *Family Radio & TV* 28 Apr. 47 Some have generators, one woman uses gas and the others just use the good old boere paraffin lamp. **1980** *Farmer's Weekly* 2 July p.ii, (*advt*) The Boere Truck. Tough & Versatile .. [it] incorporates many features for profitable farming. **1981** [see GOMPOU]. **1982** D.

KRAMER *Short Back & Sides* 46, I once played for a band in a Boland hotel. We played waltzes and foxtrots and a bit of boerebop as well. **1985** *Cape Times* 4 Oct. 6 There is also a coach house and stable, .. an early 'boere' dwelling-house and a primitive herdman's house. **1989** *Daily Dispatch* 5 June 12 The two worlds of music — forties jazz and boeremusiek — sometimes .. intermarry into a type of boere-jazz. **1990** *Motorist* 1st Quarter 16 Sarah has had the still in her family for thirty-five years and is teaching her grandson .. the in's and out's of this great boere tradition. **1990** *Sunday Times* 11 Feb. 9 A sports promoter has challenged fans of the beloved 'boere' sport, kennetjie, to promote the game and support a worthy cause.

boerebeskuit /ˈbuːrəbəˌskeɪt, -skœit, ˈbʊərə-/ *n. noncount.* Also **boerbeschuit, boerbeskuit, boer biskuit**, and with initial capital. [Afk., *boere* see BOERE + *beskuit* (earlier *beschuit*) rusk.] Traditional, country-style rusked bun, either sweetened or unsweetened; BOER BISCUIT. See also BESKUIT.

1905 J. DU PLESSIS *1000 Miles in Heart of Afr.* 32 The *boerbeschuit, biltong, meebos,* and *moskomfijt* of South Africa are now requisitioned, and .. make life (culinarily speaking) endurable. **1930** M. RAUBENHEIMER *Tested S. Afr. Recipes* 59 Boer Biskuit (Unsweetened Rusks) ... Knead the 'Biskuit' rather late .. as there is always a risk of the dough turning sour overnight. **1936** C. BIRKBY *Thirstland Treks* 75 The *trekkers* will not have bread to eat with their coffee, but they can have *boer beskuit*, the rough biscuit of the veld, in the ashes of the camp fire. **1949** L.G. GREEN *In Land of Afternoon* 164 Nagmaal often meant leaving the farm for weeks at a stretch ... There were new clothes to be made, shoes to be mended, boerebeskuit and loaves to be made for the trek. **1958** R.E. LIGHTON *Out of Strong* 13 Tant Hendrina and their mother ranged in their talking from boer beskuit and the dutch oven it was baked in, to servant problems and knitting patterns. **1958** [see BOERMEEL]. **1963** A.M. LOUW *20 Days* 27 He had pushed aside his meagre old man's breakfast of hot milk and dried boerebeskuit. **1978** *Sunday Times* 20 Aug. 15 There, Andre Greyvensteyn, with the help of his mother, used the kitchen oven to make the company's first product — boere-beskuit. **1984** *Cape Times* 31 Mar. 11, I always thought one of the best customs of the *volk* was the breakfast habit of black coffee and *Boerebeskuit*, taken at 5am. **1987** B. ORPEN in *E. Prov. Herald* 7 May 2 It was a day for 'boerbeskuit' and home-brewed coffee simmering on coals under sunny skies, as farming life came to a halt in the small community.

‖**boerebrood** /ˈbuːrəbrʊət/ *n.* Also **boer-brood**. [Afk., *boere* see BOERE + *brood* bread.] BOER BREAD. Also *attrib.*

1862 'A LADY' *Life at Cape* (1963) 89 Indeed, I quite won the heart of the hostess by my devotion to her butter and boer-brood. **1941** *Star* 3 Feb. 7 A soldier's rations must include bread or a substitute for bread ... In this war it is real bread, similar to the 'boere-brood' baked everywhere in the Union. **1976** *E. Prov. Herald* 24 Mar. 14 (*advt*) Boerebrood loaf tins — 37 cm x 14 cm x 10 cm — large.

boeredans /ˈbuːrədɑːns/ *n.* [Afk., *boere* see BOERE + *dans* dance.] OPSKOP sense a.

1985 A. GOLDSTUCK in *Frontline* Feb. 19 Leaping towards him comes the radical swing king of the boeredans, he of the furious pace and the ostentatious prance ... Old timers and young rebels, tannies and cherries, are all at home at the boeredans. **1985** W. VANVOLSEM in *Sunday Times* 3 Feb. 5 A Boeredans .. in a platteland dorp had to be cancelled .. when a hotel manager's plan to bring in concertinas and banjos instead of a disco DJ and stroboscopic lights to lure the town's young to an evening of fun fell flat. **1986** *Cape Times* 8 Feb. 3 One of the highlights for passengers .. will be a 'boeredans' on the historic town's railway station platform.

boerehaat /ˈbuːrəhɑːt/ *n.* Often with initial capital. [Afk., 'hatred of Boers', *boere* see BOERE + *haat* hatred. Coined as an emotive political slogan by P.W. Botha (of the National Party) during the election campaign of 1972.] Hatred of Afrikaners as a group. Also *attrib.* Cf. *Engelsehaat* (see ENGELS *n.* sense 2 b). See also HAAT *n.*

1972 *Sunday Times* 26 Mar. 9 Boerehaat Campaign. UP shocked by Nat bid to stir up hatred. **1972** M. KUIPER in *Times* (U.K.) 18 Apr. 7 Locally and nationally the opposition United Party (UP) is being accused of *boerehaat* (hatred of the Afrikaner) and said to be bent on the destruction of the Afrikaner and everything he stands for. **1972** *Daily Dispatch* 12 May 10 The word 'Boere-haat' is appearing throughout the country, since it was introduced by Mr. P.W. Botha, during his campaign of the recent Oudtshoorn parliamentary by-election. **1981** [see *Engelsehaat* (ENGELS *n.* sense 2 b)]. **1984** *Cape Times* 23 Feb., 'Anything that's a waste of money is a scandal,' insisted Mr Bamford. 'Boerehaat!' called a Nationalist MP. **1986** *E. Prov. Herald* 12 Apr. 2 Amid cries of 'boere-haat', the Progressive Federal Party MP .. slammed Afrikaans-accented TV interviewers and called for a service 'in our language which can be an example to our children, and teach them to speak decent English.'

Hence **boerehater** /-hɑːtə(r)/ *n.*, one who hates the Afrikaner; *nonce*, one who hates farmers; **boerehating** /ˈbuːrəhɑːtɪŋ, -heɪtɪŋ/ *ppl adj.*

1972 *Sunday Times* 26 Mar. 9 The United Party will be depicted as being a party in the grip of 'boerehaters'. **1973** *Cape Times* 2 June 8 People who object to bannings are not necessarily *Boerehaters*, whose only desire is the downfall of Afrikanerdom. **1973** *Sunday Times* 1 Apr. 16 Hardly less breathtaking is the .. suggestion that Sir D— (allegedly a great Boerehater himself) is now the target of 'Boerehating jingoism.' **1984** *Daily Dispatch* 13 July 5 'The preponderance of evidence (laid before the select committee investigating the matter) was dead against the farmers,' declared Mr Frank le Roux .. of the Conservative Party. 'You're a boere hater,' shouted a Nationalist. **1993** J. SCOTT in *Cape Times* 25 Feb. 11 Louis Stofberg (CP, Sasolburg) revealed that 'the most expensive plot ever sold in Bloemfontein was sold to a Chinese' ... 'It was probably sold by a CP,' remarked someone ... 'You're a *boerehater*,' CP members shouted back.

boerejongens /ˈbuːrəˌjɔŋəns/ *pl. n.* [Afk., *boere* see BOERE + *jongens* young men.] Hanepoot grapes preserved in brandy; *Kaapse Jongens*, see KAAPSE sense 3. Cf. BOEREMEISIE sense 2.

1980 [see BOEREMEISIE sense 2]. **1986** M. VAN WYK *Cooking the S. Afr. Way* 122 Brandied grapes (Boerejongens). Enough ripe, firm Hanepoot grapes to fill a 1 *l* jar.

boerekommando see KOMMANDO sense 1 b.

boerekonsertina /ˈbuːrəkɒnsəˌtiːnə/ *n.* [Afk., *boere* see BOERE + *konsertina* concertina.] A concertina with twenty keys, each of which produces only one note, unlike an English concertina, each key of which produces two; *boere concertina*, see BOERE sense 1 b. See also BOEREMUSIEK.

1980 *E. Prov. Herald* 27 Oct. 13 And his big surprise? A genuine boerekonsertina. This is more tricky to play. It has only 40 notes against the usual 80, has a more gentle tone, but is ideal for certain pieces. **1985** A. GOLDSTUCK in *Frontline* Feb. 21 There are two basic concertinas — one is known as the boere konsertina, very simple with 20 keys. One key is one note whether you push in or pull out.

boerekos /ˈbuːrəkɔs, ˈbʊərə-/ *n.* [Afk., *boere* see BOERE + *kos* food.] Farm cooking, esp. that of Afrikaners; traditional country-style food. Also *attrib.*, and *fig.*

1977 *Darling* 16 Mar. 86 Between Riviersonderend and Mossel Bay is a small village called Albertinia, whose Albertinia Hotel was renowned for its hand-written menus and superb *boerekos*. **1979** *Sunday Times* 20 May 5 'I'm training on boerekos, not vegetables,' Kallie mumbled through a forkload of meat this week. 'I'm a man, not a bloody buck.' **1983** *Ibid.* 26 June 34 A hotel in the Free State platteland recently offered the following 'country fare' ... Main Course: Instant mashed potato served with one of those plastic sausages made of ersatz meat. Whatever happened to old-fashioned, wholesome *boerekos*? **1987** *Fair Lady* Mar. 7 From a *regte boerekos* family I have slowly had to change to a more economical way of providing a meal. **1990** *E. Prov. Herald* 27 Feb. 9 They are The Kerels, their music described variously as *boerekos*-bop, *boere*-punk, or *potjiekos*-pop. **1994** G. WILLOUGHBY in *Weekly Mail & Guardian* 8 July 38 The GM specializes in *egte boerekos* of a rather grand kind, but *boerekos* nevertheless.

‖**boereliedjie** /ˈbuːrəliki, -lici/ *n.* [Afk., *boere* see BOERE + *liedjie* see LIEDJIE.] An Afrikaans folk song, or a modern song in this style; also called LIEDJIE. Cf. VOLKSLIED sense 2.

1971 *S. Afr. Panorama* Nov. 25 In Europe .. a pot-pourri of 'Boereliedjies' proved the most popular — traditional songs such as 'Daar kom die wa' (There comes the wagon), 'Ou tante Koba' (Old Aunt Koba). **1973** *Cape Times* 11 June 11 The British public lapped up his *boere liedjies*. **1980** *Sunday Times* 11 May (Mag. Sect.) 9 Anton still writes 'boereliedjies', though cynical ones.

‖**Boerematriek** /ˈbuːrəmətrɪk, -matˌrik/ *n. joc.* Also with small initial. [Afk., *boere* see BOERE + *matriek* abbrev. *matrikulasie*, fr. Eng. *matriculation*.] A nickname for confirmation in the Dutch Reformed churches; BOER MATRICULATION. Also *attrib.*

1922 M.E. MARTINIUS *Sketch of Dev. of Rural Educ. 1652–1910 (pamphlet)* 51 Church membership was regarded by many farmers as the consummation of learning, and hence came to be termed jocularly 'boerematriek'. **1970** H.M. MUSMECI *Informant, Port Elizabeth*, I attended a boerematriek ceremony in church yesterday, during which my son was confirmed. **1973** A. COETZEE in *Std Encycl. of Sn Afr.* IX. 286 In days gone by .. the whole spiritual development of the child was directed towards attaining full membership of the Church, and confirmation was considered as the attainment of both full adulthood and full responsibility in the community. So much value was attached to this that confirmation is still jocularly referred to as 'Boerematriek'. **1981** *S. Afr. Panorama* Mar. 34 Religious and educational instruction went hand in hand, for to be confirmed children had to have mastered the process of learning. Without *boerematriek* (farmer's matric) one was not a full-fledged member of the community.

Boeremeal var. BOER MEAL.

boeremeel var. BOERMEEL.

boeremeisie /ˈbuːrəˌmeɪsi, ˈbʊərə-/ *n.* [Afk., *boere* see BOERE + *meisie* girl.]

1. An unsophisticated country girl; an Afrikaner girl; MEISIE sense 2; *plaasmeisie*, see PLAAS sense 1 c. Also *attrib.* See also BOERESEUN.

[**1972** *Grocott's Mail* 28 Jan. 3 The magazine is richly illustrated in the traditional rag magazine style and has numerous colour and black and white photographs of the 'Boeremeisies,' the rag queen finalists.] **1973** *Cape Times* 30 July 1 'I'm a ware [*sc.* real] boeremeisie, I love porridge' ... She polished off a plate of the hotel's best. **1976** *Darling* 27 Oct., The story of how a young, sweet *boeremeisie* came out of the wilds of Witbank, went to London and became Miss World. **1981** *Sunday Times* 25 Oct. (Mag. Sect.) 1 Beneath the natural-as-a-suntan boeremeisie exterior there is a razor-sharp intellect. **1985** L. SAMPSON in *Style* Feb. 100 Suddenly there are a lot of boeremeisies around. It has become hugely chic to produce some ethnic background. **1989** *You* 16 Nov. 13 'Boeremeisie' Patsy Kensit steals Mel's heart — but only in the film Lethal Weapon II.

2. *fig.* Always in *pl.*: Brandied apricots. Cf. BOEREJONGENS.

1978 *Daily Dispatch* 26 July 11 Her book is packed with goodies from 17th and 18th century Cape kitchens — sambals, breidies and Boeremeisies (brandied apricots). **1980** *S. Afr. Digest* 31 May, The French ..

bequeathed an unrivalled legacy to Cape cookery in the form of *boerejongens* and *boeremeisies* (literally, farmers' boys and farmers' girls), which were grapes and apricots preserved in brandy. **1992** G. ETHERINGTON in *Weekend Post* 6 June 5 Boeremeisies .. are a .. subtle blend, combining the succulence of sweet apricots with that country brandy known as witblits – a marriage made in heaven.

boeremusiek /ˈbuːrəmy̆ˌsik, -məˌsik, ˈbʊrə-/ *n.* [Afk., *boere* see BOERE + *musiek* music.]
1. *Music.* Popular light music, often for dancing, usu. based on Afrikaans folk music and played by a small band which usu. includes a concertina or piano accordion; SAKKIE-SAKKIE *n.* sense a; *skoffel jazz*, see SKOFFEL *n.*[2] sense 2. Also *attrib.* See also BOEREORKES, LANGARM, OPSKOP sense a, VASTRAP *n.* sense 1 a.

1952 *Cape Times* 27 Sept. 4 The music blared forth, real *boeremusiek* which sent the whole crowd dancing. **1965** E. MPHAHLELE *Down Second Ave* 66 She was always complaining .. the landlord; the weather; the noise her neighbours made whenever they played 'Boere musiek' – Afrikaner music – on weekends. **1971** *S. Afr. Panorama* Nov. 22 For years it was Boeremusiek (a lively type of folk music) which constituted Afrikaans music with its concertinas, accordions and guitars. **1979** *Capetonian* July 15 We want music everywhere, indoors and outdoors, from string quartets to boeremusiek, jazz to Malay choirs. **1981** D. KRAMER in *Frontline* May 14, I must look to South African folk music – boeremusiek, Cape Malay music and the wealth of indigenous African music. **1983** [see Sparks quot. at AFRIKANER *adj.*]. **1988** C. DE JAGER in *E. Prov. Herald* 11 Aug. 1 The result of the SABC boereorkes competition .. was called a 'farce' by some boeremusiek musicians yesterday .. and had shocked the boeremusiek world. **1990** *Weekend Post* 8 Dec. 6 Boeremusiek, like all authentic folk-music, is always vibrantly alive, extravagantly gay but at the same time full of indefinable sadness ... Sneering at boeremusiek is practically a trade mark of people to whom it is important to think of themselves as avant garde and intellectually superior. **1991** *S. Afr. Panorama* May-June 18 The experts will tell you that there are two kinds of boeremusiek today, namely, traditional and modern. The moderns hived off during the 50s and 60s when Hendrik Susan and other band leaders added drums, the piano accordion, and electronic and electric instruments to the traditional menu. Today the concertina is not always the leading instrument; this role is sometimes usurped by the violin, guitar or piano accordian. The new development did not please all the lovers of boeremusiek and today the adherents of the respective trends have formed their own separate associations. *Ibid.* 20 When one thinks about boeremusiek, the concertina (alias Christmas worm, wailing worm or donkey's lung) is the first instrument that comes to mind. **1994** *Weekly Mail & Guardian* 13 May 9 Nico Carstens took over from Ray Phiri with his accordion and *boeremusiek*.

2. *fig.* A heated discussion among Afrikaners; Afrikaner policies or demands.

1973 M. VAN BILJON in *Star* 30 June 6 Amid all this boeremusiek, the cool trumpet blow by Professor Marius Wiechers sounded a better note. While offering no solutions, he pointed out that the homeland might not want all these urban Africans. **1986** 'LOYAL MOSOTHO' in *Sowetan* 19 June 8 Lesotho is very poor and depends heavily on RSA and as long as this continues she will have to dance to 'boere-musiek' because unless she does this Basotho will suffer.

Boerenasie /ˈbuːrəˌnɑːsi/ *n.* [Afk., *boere* see BOERE + *nasie* nation.]
1. The Afrikaner group or 'nation'; cf. VOLK sense 3 b.

*c*1949 CURREY & SNELL *Threat to Freedom* 10 For both the Natives and Coloured people of the Union the foundations of the education supplied them is to be both Christian and National. This is to be the task of European people of South Africa, but – adds the Beleid – there is a special duty laid on the 'Boerenasie' as the 'senior European trustee'. **1955** E. DE S. BRUNNER in *Pol. Science Quarterly* Sept. 383 It believes that .. the Afrikaner must be insulated from outside influences. Thus they believe the Boerenasie will be built up. **1958** *Ikwezi Lomso* Sept. 4 This is apartheid in action. This is the jackboot placed squarely on the neck of the African population. It is a foretaste of what the Boerenasie has in store. **1960** E.G. MALHERBE in H. Spottiswoode *S. Afr.: Rd Ahead* 149 Verily South Africa has become the land of the corrugated iron curtain behind which the Boerenasie hopes to work in splendid isolation. **1977** F.G. BUTLER *Karoo Morning* 255 To Palestine with all Jews. Don't buy from them ... They are great enemies of the Boerenasie because they are international.

2. *hist.* The name of a far right-wing political organization with Nazi or neo-Nazi sympathies. Also *attrib.*

1950 H. GIBBS *Twilight* 179 Other new parties of Nazi sympathy and structure moved into the field ... Among these was the *Handhawersbond* (the League of Upholders) ... Then there were the *Volksparty*, and *Die Boerenasie* (the Boer nation) and *Die Boerevolk*. **1972** *Sunday Times* 24 Sept. 7 A lieutenant-general in the Right-wing Boerenasie organisation 11 years ago, claimed this week that he was a double agent. He said he infiltrated Boerenasie to smash an anti-Jewish neo-Nazi ring in South Africa. **1979** W. EBERSOHN *Lonely Place* 25 He was mixed up in some lunatic secret society, dedicated to saving South Africa for the white man ... The name they went by was Boere Nasie.

boereorkes /ˌbuːrəɔː(r)ˈkes, ˌbʊrə-/ *n.* Also with initial capital. Pl. **-te** /-tə/. [Afk., *boere* see BOERE + *orkes* orchestra, band.] A band which includes a combination of concertina or piano accordion, mouth organ, fiddle or guitar, and percussion, and plays Afrikaans popular music; ORKES. Also *attrib.* See also BOEREMUSIEK sense 1.

[**1938** *Star* 1 Dec. 12 There was dancing in the clubhouse to a Boere orchestra.] **1944** 'TWEDE IN BEVEL' *Piet Kolonel* 103 There were items from the Boere Orkes. **1951** H.C. BOSMAN in L. Abrahams *Bekkersdal Marathon* (1971) 115 All my daughter does, she moves in Voortrekker costume in time to the Boere-orkes music – and you simply can't keep your feet still when it's Boere-orkes music. **1977** G. HUGO in *Quarry '77* 91 The real hit of the show is this rather superior ou in a boereorkes; he's on the konsertina and he's into the whole virtuoso kick; swinging the old squeezebox round. **1982** D. KRAMER *Short Back & Sides* 24 It was easy to understand why so many boereorkeste had come to pose on this beach .. for the photograph on their next long-playing dance album. **1986** *Cape Times* 7 Feb., (advt) Delheim Harvest Festival '86 .. Opening – Spitbraai and Boere orkes. **1991** *S. Afr. Panorama* May-June 18 These pupils of the John Vorster Technical High School won last year's competition for the best junior boereorkes (band). **1994** [see LANGARM *n.*].

Boereperd var. BOERPERD.

boereraat /ˈbuːrərɑːt, ˈbʊ(ə)rə-/ *n.* Also **boereraad.** Pl. **-rate** /-ə/. [Afk., *boere* see BOERE + *raat* remedy.] A folk medicine or home remedy; HUISMIDDEL. Also *attrib.*, and *fig.* See also BOSSIEMIDDEL, HUIS-APOTHEEK, (*old*) *Dutch medicine* (DUTCH *adj.* sense 2).

[**1943** I. FRACK *S. Afr. Doctor* 123 In the country .. one gets them [*sc.* cancers] very late .. after the usual course of Boereraadjies and Dutch Medicines.] **1958** [see GROENE AMARA]. **1974** 'BLOSSOM' in *Darling* 11 Sept. 119 Use a face-pack once a week .. mainly I use ouma's *boereraat*; mud, lemon juice and egg-white. **1976** *S. Afr. Panorama* May 25 There are just as many mampoer 'boererate' (country remedies) as leaves on a peach tree. **1980** C. BARNARD in *Daily Dispatch* 1 Sept. 6 The ever-popular 'medical' column .. purportedly .. written 'by a doctor' .. gives the most sophisticated boererate (home remedies) in reply to problems put by readers. **1983** J.A. BROWN *White Locusts* 199 'We have our *boererate*,' said Joubert mildly. It was the same remark he had made in Pretoria when he gave Christiaan his Mauser. **1988** M. NEL in *Personality* 25 Apr. 56 After a very expensive consultation for an unexpected ailment he threw in a bit of 'boereraat' (homely advice) which turned out to be the best cure. **1989** D. SMUTS *Folk Remedies* Preface, Folk remedies are as old as man himself ... 'Boererate' originated in times of struggle and isolation on far-flung farms, in oxwagons crossing an unknown interior. **1990** *Personality* 19 Nov. 14 She helped Nelson Mandela cure his TB with 'boereraad' medicine.

Boereseep var. BOERSEEP.

boereseun /ˈbuːrəsiœn/ *n.* Also **boerseun.** [Afk., 'farmer's boy', *boere* see BOERE + *seun* boy, son.] An Afrikaner boy or man; a farm-boy, a 'son of the soil'; *plaas-seuntjie*, see PLAAS sense 1 c. Also *attrib.* Cf. SEUN. See also BOEREMEISIE sense 1.

1947 *Monitor* 21 Mar. 16 This literary masterpiece, written by a simple 'boerseun.' **1972** *Sunday Times* 24 Sept. (Mag. Sect.) 3 Some of our English friends are still flirting with an overseas beau (Kêrel). The boereseun has no time for this kind of deceit. **1979** M. MATSHOBA *Call Me Not a Man* 52 They are going to get it from baas Koos because I'm the only baas on this farm. This is one boereseun they must take a long time to forget. **1980** C. BARNARD in *Daily Dispatch* 21 Apr. 81 He told me what his labourers earned, how they were housed, and what was expected of them. He also told me what was expected of me as a good neighbour and boereseun. **1986** *Style* Feb. 62 Which brilliant schizoid boereseun sharpened his satirical tongue on his childhood pals in Pinelands? Pieter-Dirk Uys. **1988** *Femina* Mar. 88 He was a *boereseun* brought up on a farm. He loved animals, the veld, sunsets, everything South African. **1990** *Weekend Argus* 14 July 15 Afrikaner heads ANC in Cape Town ... A boereseun leaps the great divide.

boeresport /ˈbuːrəspɔrt, ˈbʊərəspɔːt/ *n.* Also with initial capital. Pl. unchanged, occas. **-s.** [Afk., *boere* see BOERE + *sport* sport, games, amusements.] A social gathering at which traditional Afrikaner games are played; any game traditionally played by Afrikaners (e.g. JUKSKEI (sense 2 a), and KENNETJIE). Also *attrib.*, and *transf.*

1958 L.G. GREEN *S. Afr. Beachcomber* 29 The Strand beach saw the first organised tournaments of jukskei, the national boeresport. **1968** *Fair Lady* 30 Oct. (Suppl.) 6 Before she married a farmer, Sarie lived in the city. So she was pretty hopeless at the local boeresport. **1970** *Argus* 24 Dec. 21 The New Year boeresport are to be held on The Strand main beach again this year ... There will be the toutrek (tug-o'-war) and kussingslaan (cushion fights on greased poles). **1977** *Sunday Times* 28 Mar., Oom Skraal Piet said that sex .. was 'the oldest boeresport in South Africa!' – outdating jukskei and kennetjie by at least four generations. **1982** *S. Afr. Panorama* Aug. 37 Afterwards there was *boeresport*, and the programme was rounded off with a traditional barn dance. **1989** *Sunday Tribune* 17 Dec. 13 The volk settled in for a day of Boeresport and festivities while piped Boeremusiek blared from speakers along the shores.

Boeress /ˈbʊəres, ˈbuːres/ *n. hist.* [BOER sense 2 + Eng. feminine suffix *-ess.*] A Boer woman.

1852 D. LIVINGSTONE in I. Schapera *S. Afr. Papers* (1974) 53, I feel grumpy when I think of a big fat Boeress lying on my sofa and drinking coffee out of my wife's coffeepot. **1881** *E. London Dispatch & Frontier Advertiser* 12 Jan. 2 It is also now stated that the Boeresses in the Transvaal have declared their intention to cut the throat of any Englishman they have the chance of attacking. The vrouws are really very wanting in the usages of polite 'Africander' life. **1924** [see β quot. at ALLEMAGTIG]. **1965** D. ROOKE *Diamond Jo* 37 She was laughing. 'I'm not a stupid Boeress to be taken in by you.' **1974** —— *Margaretha de la Porte* 272 On the afternoon of February 19th 1896 I saw the strangled body of a Boeress's slave.

Boerestaat /ˈbuːrəstɑːt/ *n.* [Afk., *boere* see BOERE + *staat* state.] A proposed Afrikaner state within South Africa to accommodate those of ultra-conservative outlook; NATIONAL STATE sense 2; VOLKSTAAT.

1985 *Weekend Argus* 26 Jan. 3 The latest plot to 'save' South Africa has surfaced in print ... The idea is to give the whole of Transvaal, Free State and northern Natal to the 'Boerestaat'. **1987** *Race Rel. Survey 1986* (S.A.I.R.R.) I. 140 'My people, the boeremense, are entitled to their land in South Africa.' .. Mr Terre'Blanche said that Jews, Indians or any non-Christians could be permitted residence within the boundaries of the 'boerestaat', but would be excluded from government. **1988** *Scope* 6 May 32 Although the core of the AWB's being is the establishment of a 'Boerestaat', they realise they cannot go it alone and thus the only criteria for membership are being White and Christian. **1990** *Sunday Times* 4 Mar. 24 The Afrikaners have only the Boerestaat as their fatherland; they have no other place to be loyal to, no other language. **1991** J. BORGER in *Focus on Afr.* Apr.-June 31 Orania was bought earlier this year by a group of Afrikaner intellectuals and businessmen. They want it to be the capital of a new Afrikaner Republic, the *Boerestaat*, which will take up most of Cape Province and about a third of the total area of South Africa.

Hence **Boerestater** /-ˌstɑːtə(r)/ *n.*, one advocating the creation of such a state.

1990 *Sunday Times* 22 Apr. 2 The militant approach of the Boerestaters was more to his liking.

boeretjie var. BOERTJIE.

‖**boeretroos** /ˈbuːrətruəs/ *n. colloq.* [Afk., *boere* see BOERE + *troos* comfort, consolation.] Coffee.

1970 H.M. MUSMECI *Informant, Port Elizabeth* This coffee is really refreshing. Now I know why it is called boeretroos. **1977** *E. Prov. Herald* 13 Apr. 3 South Africa's traditional 'boeretroos,' a good cup of coffee, is entering the super luxury price market. **1980** *Sunday Times* 3 Aug. (Mag. Sect.) 4 Steaming libations of delicious, aromatic coffee! Afrikaners have enshrined their deep attachment to it by vocabularising it as 'Boeretroos' (Boer's solace). **1988** J. ALLEN in *Sunday Times* 7 Aug. 4 She's tough as kudu biltong. Soft as a *boere beskuit* soaked in sweet strong *boeretroos*.

Boereverneuker var. BOER VERNEUKER.

Boerevolk /ˈbuːrəfɔlk, ˈbʊərə-/ *n.* [Afk., *boere* see BOERE + *volk* people.]

1. The Afrikaner people, esp. the more nationalistic and conservative section of the Afrikaner people; cf. VOLK sense 3 b; BOER sense 4 c. Also *attrib.*

1940 *Star* 12 Nov. 3 Not only the political party .. would see to it that the 'Boerevolk' secured their rights .. there would also be the great non-political organisation of the 'Boerevolk' – the Ossewa Brandwag. **1972** *Evening Post* 9 Sept. 9 When the Broederbond Government speaks of the 'White nation of South Africa' it means only the 2 000 000 Afrikaners or 'Boerevolk'. **1983** F.E.O'B. GELDENHUYS in *Optima* Vol.31 No.3, 154 Again the church saw to it that it became the anchor and rallying point of the disorientated *Boerevolk* in the alien, urban atmosphere. **1987** A. KENNY in *Frontline* June 34 Forget about the AWB rallies with flaxen-haired little girls gazing up at three-legged swastikas and Terre'-Blanche pounding on the big Boerevolk drum. **1987** L. WROUGHTON in *Pretoria News* 15 June 6 Mr Eugene Terre'Blanche demands nothing but the land he believes his people, the Boerevolk, are entitled to. **1990** *Weekend Post* 26 May 1 He said the ANC hated the 'Boerevolk' and the 'white nation' and demanded their land, but the Government saw fit to negotiate with it. **1993** *Natal Witness* 13 Apr. 3 Rudolf said he was commmitted to a peaceful resolution of the problems of the country. But .. the demands of the Boerevolk (Boer nation) for the return of the Boer republics and the restoration of their freedom were being ignored.

2. *hist.* See quot.

1950 H. GIBBS *Twilight* 179 New parties of Nazi sympathy and structure moved into the field, attracting considerable support among young Afrikaners ... The *Handhawersbond* .. the *Volksparty*, and *Die Boernasie* (the Boer Nation) and *Die Boerevolk*.

Boerevrou /ˈbuːrəfrəʊ, ˈbʊərə-/ *n.* Also **Boerevrouw, Boer-vrou(w)**, and with small initial. Pl. **-e** /-ə/, occas. **-en** /-ən/. [Afk., *boere* see BOERE + *vrou* (earlier *vrouw*) woman, wife.] An Afrikaner woman, usu. a farmer's wife of conservative outlook. Also *attrib.* See also VROU.

1883 M.A. CAREY-HOBSON *Farm in Karoo* 172 Wishing the Boer vrouw good morning, our friends made their escape as quickly as politeness permitted. **1896** — *At Home in Tvl* 359 It does seem a pity that a good-looking fellow like you should be dangling after .. a great, ugly Dutch Boer vrouw. **1920** R.Y. STORMBERG *Mrs Pieter de Bruyn* 5 Two or three months' cooling down of my bridal exuberance at last sees me solidifying into a staid young Boer vrouw. **1940** F.B. YOUNG *City of Gold* 22 'My husband, of course, is English ... But I am pure Dutch – a regular Boer vrou.' **1943** L. SOWDEN *Union of S. Afr.* 148 She remained, and was proud to remain, a *Boere vrou* (Boer woman) like her ancestors. And there is still more of the *Boere vrou* in her than of the scholar or the statesman's wife. **1948** V.M. FITZROY *Cabbages & Cream* 157 What she did wear in the garden, if it was hot, was a large and shapeless Boerevrou sun-bonnet. **1955** — *Dark Bright Land* 122 The boerevrouwen were plainly dressed, and elaborately capped; their sunbonnets, handmade of linen or lawn, were most intricately tucked, ruffled, and embroidered. **1970** M. DONOVAN in J.W. Loubser *Africana Short Stories* 60 The Boer-vrou and her husband could not understand him. **1976** S. GRAY in *Quarry '76* 121 The kindly boerevrou led me down mudslides where for that night I had one rondavel and one candle. **1989** N.H.C. SMITH in *Frontline* Nov. 36 The spectacle of a Boerevrou 'doing what is natural' in public would result in her being very sternly rebuked. **1992** R.H. DU PRE *Making of Racial Conflict* 166 *Kappiekommando*, Formed out of the AWB for the 'boervrou' to take up the fight beside her husband like the Voortrekker women of old.

boerewors /ˈbuːrəvɔrs, -vɔːs, ˈbʊrəvɔːs/ *n.* Formerly also **boerwors, boer worst**. [Afk., *boere* see BOERE + *wors* (earlier *worst*) sausage.]

1. A popular traditional sausage, usu. a coarsely-ground mixture of beef and pork seasoned with various spices; BOERIE; also called WORS (sense 1). Also *attrib.* See also *braaiwors* (BRAAI *n.* sense 4).

[**1913** A. GLOSSOP *Barnes's S. Afr. Hsehold Guide* 320 Farmer's Sausages ... To make 4 lb.: Take $3\frac{1}{2}$ lb. beef, and $\frac{1}{2}$lb. fat pork, put it through the sausage machine.] **1930** M. RAUBENHEIMER *Tested S. Afr. Recipes* 107 Boer Worst (beef sausage). **1937** *Handbk for Farmers* (Dept of Agric. & Forestry) 1171 Sausage (Boerwors). 10 lb. beef 5 lb. pork or mutton fat (tail fat) 4 tablespoons ground coriander (1 oz.) 4 tablespoons salt (2 oz.). **1949** L.G. GREEN *In Land of Afternoon* 63 Boerewors .. may be defined as a game sausage dating back years before the Great Trek; a sausage in which the meat has been pounded with a wooden stamper rather than minced. Modern boerewors, which is not to be despised, is usually a mixture of lean beef with pork fat, seasoned with wine or vinegar. **1956** A.G. MCRAE *Hill Called Grazing* 74 I'd bought a yard-and-a-half of boerwors, the coarse Boer sausage which I love. *c*1965 *State of S. Afr. 1965* 107 *Boerewors* is the sausage that reigns supreme throughout the country. **1966** L.G. BERGER *Where's Madam* 57 At night the braaivleis really came into its own, with flickering flames, soggy salads in chipped enamel basins and a million yards of mottled pink boerewors. **1974** *E. Prov. Herald* 28 Aug. 32 Boerewors, our typical South African sausage, is a mixture of beef and pork and even fat game flavoured with coriander, ground clove, ground peppercorn, thyme, sage with vinegar, salt and pepper to taste. **1980** A. PATON *Towards Mountain* 207 Prayers were said over the wagons, meat and *boerewors* were cooked over the fires, nostalgic Afrikaner *liedjies* were sung. **1984** R. KENYON in *Reader's Digest* Jan. 39 There is little delicacy in dealing with boerewors. In its raw state, you grapple with it like a snake charmer – great untamed metres of slippery, blotchy, pink python. **1989** *Sunday Times* 19 Nov. (Mag. Sect.) 10 Pavement boerewors wagons .. started as a novelty, became a craze, then a nuisance and then a headline story as the cops moved in asking for a licence. **1990** T. MKHWANAZI in *Weekly Mail* 2 Feb. 23 Our hostess left and re-entered the room with a bowl of pap and another of boerewors – testimony to the ironic merging of the culture of indigenous people of Namibia with the culture of their arch enemies. **1991** *Natal Mercury* 2 Apr. 2 Boerewors casings are imported from New Zealand.

2. *Fig.*, always *attrib.*, designating things made in or pertaining to South Africa, or people who are typically South African.

1974 *Sunday Times* 12 May 28 Instead of producing 'boerewors Westerns', the company will now concentrate on South African War films for TV. **1975** *Evening Post* 21 Jan. 4 She is soon to start filming a 'boerewors' Western, 'My Naam is Dingetjie', which is a send-up of the Trinity films. **1979** *Sunday Times* 2 Sept. (Mag. Sect.) 1 He came back to South Africa for four tours before the boerewors curtain dropped on him. **1990** L.R. DOWLING in *Fair Lady* 11 Apr. 41 How would I describe myself? I'm a *boerewors meisie*. But also someone who likes to believe that fairies exist.

boer goat /ˈbʊəgəʊt, ˈbuːr-/ *n. phr.* Also with initial capital. [Part. tr. Afk. *boerbok*, see BOERBOK.] (One of) a hardy, indigenous goat breed, well adapted to arid terrain which is not suited to sheep farming; BOERBOK. Also *attrib.*

1896 R. WALLACE *Farming Indust. of Cape Col.* 323 The Boer goat, which is termed the native goat to distinguish it from the recently imported Angora, is a strong, coarse, hardy energetic animal, strongly resembling the English goat. **1916** *Rand Daily Mail* 1 Nov. 3 (*advt*) Boer goats, kapaters, medium, 11s.6d. to 14s.; Boer goats, kapaters, best, 16s. to £1 1s. **1948** *George & Knysna Herald* 4 June 3 Monthly Stock Fair Summary of entries to date: 355 Prime Boer Goats. **1966** I. VAUGHAN *These Were my Yesterdays* 110 One of Xhosa dogs gets loose, rushes to attack the boer goats of tribesmen. Goats butt wildly against Sir Harry Smith's horse. **1966** [see BOKHORINKIE]. **1975** W. STEENKAMP *Land of Thirst King* 64 The Boer goat, on the other hand, supplied good velskoen-leather. **1980** *Farmer's Weekly* 30 July 68 He has since satisfied himself that Boergoats, properly run, can be a paying proposition on thorn veld. **1983** F.G. BUTLER *Bursting World* 37, I recall two efforts by the 'Hearties' .. to melt or break up their iceberg of a warden. The first was to introduce a large and odoriferous stray boergoat into his flat late one afternoon before he returned. **1991** D. BARRY in *Farmer's Weekly* 25 Jan. 18 There's tremendous scope for exporting embryos .. from our top Angora goats, Boergoats, Dormer sheep and certain cattle breeds.

boer hound /ˈbʊəhaʊnd, ˈbuːr-/ *n. phr.* Also with initial capital. [Calque formed on Afk. *boerhond* 'boer dog', *boer* (applied to indigenous plants and animals) + *hond* dog.] An indigenous cross-bred dog similar to the BOERBULL.

1895 H. RIDER HAGGARD *Nada* 27 His father was a Boer hound, the first that came into the country. *c*1904 E.L. PRICE *Jrnls* (1956) 56 Mother & I began ascending toward the house when out rushed 3 or four huge Boer-hounds straight for us, & a big Boer behind them – evidently not anxious to call them back. **1939** S. CLOETE *Watch for Dawn* 122 In all the district there was no dog as large or as savage as Bothma's; it was a regtig Boer hound of the best strain that had been kept pure without admixture. **1946** V. POHL *Adventures of Boer Family* 96 Dudley .. went unarmed on his journeys, relying only on his own courage and resource, on Plaatjie and on a fierce half-bred Boer hound. **1964** V. POHL *Dawn & After* 141 We were accompanied by Bosveld, a mongrel .. , and a large Boerhound of sorts called Bull. **1971** [see BOERBULL].

boerie /ˈbʊri/ *n. colloq.* [Formed on BOEREWORS + Eng. (informal) n.-forming suffix -IE.] BOEREWORS sense 1.

1994 *Sunday Times* 23 Jan. 28 (*advt*) Everyone knows that spitting, hissing sizzle sound of boerie in a braai grid. And the smell .. it's enough to drive a ou crazy with desire. **1994** M.J. MCCOY *Informant, Grahamstown*

There's chicken and boerie, David. Which do you want?

Boerland /ˈbʊəˌlænd/ *n. hist.* [BOER sense 2 + Eng. *land*.] Any territory under Boer occupation or sovereignty. See also BOER REPUBLIC.

1866 E.L. PRICE *Jrnls* (1956) 249 Mariqué — Boer-land ... Dear Jeanie, .. Here we are in the Mariqué now with the Mackenzies .. because the children were so delicate still & so in want of a change. **1878** A. AYLWARD *Tvl of Today* 27 He gives an instance of this, as seen by him at Victoria West, which was then, and still is, as much a piece of Boerland as if situated north of the Vaal river. **1879** R.J. ATCHERLEY *(title)* A Trip to Boerland. **1882** C. DU VAL *With Show through Sn Afr.* I. 256, I did not expect to realize modern Constances and Marmions while 'trekking' through Boerland. **1896** 'S. CUMBERLAND' *What I Think of S. Afr.* 121 It remained until I had the honour of meeting Oom Paul for me to discover that Boerland's Grand Old Man had nothing in common with their greatness. **1909** LADY S. WILSON *S. Afr. Mem.* 112 There is no doubt the women were a powerful factor in Boerland. Even a Britisher married to a Dutch woman seemed at once to consider .. the Transvaal as his fatherland. **1969** F. GOLDIE *River of Gold* 23 A photograph of the Volksraad building with three donkeys ruminating in the shade of the veranda. Its caption reads, 'At least, in Boerland, they keep their asses out of Parliament.'

Boer Matriculation /ˌbʊə mətrɪkjuːˈleɪʃən, ˌbur -/ *n. phr.* [Calqued on Afk. *boerematriek*.] BOEREMATRIEK. Also in shortened form **Boer Matric**. See also MATRICULATION.

1924 L.H. BRINKMAN *Glory of Backveld* 193 The child was taught to read the Bible and to write in a way, so as to qualify him for confirmation as a member of his church. This 'Confirmation' or 'Boer Matriculation' as it came to be called, was the *pons asinorum* of the young farmer, and when once through it, his education is complete. **1934** C.P. SWART Supplement to Pettman. 17 *Boer Matric*, .. Jocularly applied to the confirmation of members of the D.R. Church. In order to qualify as members, candidates have to attend a special course of lectures .. and are subsequently submitted to a stiff oral examination.

Boer meal /ˈbʊəmiːl/ *n. phr.* Also **Boeremeal**, and with small initial. [Calque formed on Afk. *boermeel*, see BOERMEEL.] A grade of wheat flour between white flour and whole-wheat flour in texture; BOERMEEL; *plaasmeel*, see PLAAS sense 1 c. Also *attrib.*

1873 F. BOYLE *To Cape for Diamonds* 141 Average prices at that time on the markets were as follows:— Boer meal (cheap at this moment) 42s. per muid (200 lbs). [**1878** H.A. ROCHE *On Trek in Tvl* 110 (Pettman), Bread we could not get, only the Boer's meal, i.e. the flour of the country.] **1886** *Barberton Herald* 20 July 1 A.J. Crawford & Co., Preparatory to removing their Stores to Barberton and Eureka City, offer sound Mealie Meal at 12/- with sack included: Boer Meal 15/-. **1892** A. SUTHERLAND in *Cape Illust. Mag.* Vol.3 No.4, 131 What could one expect when one had nothing to make it [*sc.* the pudding] of but Boer-meal, crushed Ship's biscuits, and spring-bok fat. **1897** R.S.S. BADEN-POWELL *Matabele Campaign* 399, I found a little tea and Jackson some Boer meal (coarse flour). Of the latter we made a really very good porridge, and had a few spoonsful round and a sip of tea. **1907** *Zululand Times* 5 Jan., *(advt)* Always in stock or to arrive: Boer Meal, Bran, .. Mealie Meal. **1914** S.P. HYATT *Old Transport Rd* 36 Up till the outbreak of the war, the average wage of a good driver had been three pounds a month with 'Cape boy rations' — a pound of Boer meal a day, a pound of tinned meat a week, coffee, sugar and as much Kaffir meal as he wanted. **1920** [see PAP *n.* sense 1]. **1936** M. HIGHAM *Hsehold Cookery* (1941) 271 Wholemeal Bread. This is made exactly as above, but of course, wholemeal flour (unsifted Boer meal) .. may be used. **1942** S. CLOETE *Hill of Doves* 19 Lena memorized the things she had to get ... A bag of Boer meal, and a gallon of paraffin for her grandmother; and she was not to put the paraffin near the Boer meal. **1949** *Cape Times* 24 Sept. 8 We used to get on farms the boermeal bread made from wheat, and nothing but wheat. **1955** [see KOEKIE sense 1]. *c***1963** B.C. TAIT *Durban Story* 55 Cape flour, brought to Natal in 100 lb. bags, was expensive, so the careful housewife reserved this for pastry-making and baked her bread from Boer meal, imported or obtained from 'Maritzburg, which she sifted with the precious Cape flour. **1987** *Personality* 4 Nov. 29 The shop's the same as it was when my *oupa* bought it more than 70 years ago ... Several of the old pine shelves contain a wealth of .. boxes of old Dutch remedies, *sak-tabbak*, boer-meal and tinned pilchard.

boermeel /ˈbʊəmiəl, ˈbuːr-/ *n.* Also **boeremeel**. [Afk., *boer* farmer('s) + *meel* meal, flour.] BOER MEAL. Also *attrib.*

1958 L.G. GREEN *S. Afr. Beachcomber* 24 They always loaded the wagon with a cask of good wine, coffee, a bag of boeremeel for bread, eight air-tight paraffin tins of boerebeskuit, and plenty of ox-biltong. **1970** BEETON & DORNER in *Eng. Usage in Sn Afr.* Vol.1 No.1, 18 *Boermeel*, .. Grade of wheat flour containing a higher proportion of wheat germ than white flour, but a lower proportion than whole-wheat flour. **1971** L.G. GREEN *Taste of S.-Easter* 87 When you come to the sweets .. you find a typically South African recipe. There among the canary, date and other puddings is a boermeel pudding. **1976** S. CLOETE *Chetoko* 85 They bought mealie-meal, *boermeel*, tea, coffee, sugar.

Boerperd /ˈbʊəpɛːrt, ˈbuːr-/ *n.* Also **Boereperd**. Pl. **-e** /-pɛːrdə/, **-s**. [Afk., *boer* (applied to indigenous plants and animals) + *perd* horse.] A recognized breed of utility horse dating from the early eighteenth century; BOER PONY. Also *attrib.* See also *Cape horse* (CAPE sense 2 a), *Nooitgedacht pony* (NOOITGEDACHT).

1970 *Grocott's Mail* 24 Nov. 4 *(advt)* 5-Gaited Boerperd Stallion. **1971** *Farmer's Weekly* 12 May 104 Meadows Boerperd Stud ... Vonk the sire (Skimmel) .. is a former South African Boerperd Champion. **1973** *Ibid.* 9 May 21 Research included .. study of part-bred horses which included the Old Cape Horse from which the Boerperd originates. 'After a thorough study of the Old Cape Horse it became abundantly clear to me that the well-loved Boerperd was rapidly dying out in its true form.' **1973** *Grocott's Mail* 30 Oct. 3 There are only two breeds of gaited horses in South Africa. These are the almost indigenous Boerperd which dates back to the time of Lord Charles Somerset, and the American saddle horse. **1984** *Daily Dispatch* 10 Oct. 1 A hundred horses will be American saddlers worth thousands of rands. Other breeds will include Arabs and Boerperds. **1989** [see *Nooitgedacht pony* (NOOITGEDACHT)]. **1990** J. THERON in *Farmer's Weekly* 20 Apr. (Sporting Horse) 13 People often refer to any old farm horse as a 'Boerperd'. However, there's a big difference between the pedigree Boerperd and the wanderabouts. **1990** *Ibid.* [see BOER PONY].

Boer pony /bʊə ˈpəʊni/ *n. phr.* [tr. Afk. *boerperd*.] BOERPERD.

1915 *Rand Daily Mail* 1 Feb., Most everyone who went through the South African war will agree .. that the Boer pony was vastly superior for the mounted arm of the service than the imported horse. [**1916** *Farmer's Weekly* 20 Dec. 1451 *(advt)* For Sale or Exchange. Three well bred Boer Mares ... Two are well-matched and trained to harness.] **1940** J. BUCHAN *Memory* 118, I used .. horses of all kinds from half-broken Argentines and Texans to handy little Boer ponies. **1963** S. CLOETE *Rags of Glory* 145, I got good ones, real Boer ponies. Two tripplers. All about fifteen hands. Short-coupled, good bone. The usual dash of Spanish and Arab blood. **1990** J. THERON in *Farmer's Weekly* 20 Apr. (Sporting Horse) 14 At the time of the Boer War .. large numbers were still to be found on farms. They were inbred Cape Horses and were generally known as 'Boerperde' or 'Boer Ponies'.

Boer Republic /ˌbʊə rəˈpʌblɪk/ *n. phr. Hist.* [BOER sense 2 + Eng. *republic*.] Any of several independent Boer states constituted during the nineteenth century (but particularly the South African Republic): **a.** The South African Republic: ZAR. **b.** The Orange Free State; see also FREE STATE *n. phr.* **c.** Any of several small, short-lived states, including Vryheid, Natalia, Stellaland, Goshen, Winburg, and Utrecht. In all senses also called *Dutch Republic* (see DUTCH *adj.* sense 2). See also BOERLAND.

1878 A. AYLWARD *Tvl of Today* 29 It is not a little interesting to remark the hold education has taken in the Orange Free State, essentially a Boer republic. **1913** J. BRANDT *Petticoat Commando* 107 The Boer Republics had no organised force. In the event of war against natives or against some foreign Power, the burghers were called up from their farms .. to fight for home and fatherland. **1926** M. NATHAN *S. Afr. from Within* 165 He [*sc.* Jameson] frustrated a Boer raid into his territory, only to become a raider in his turn — thereby endangering peace between Great Britain and the Boer Republics. **1937** C. BIRKBY *Zulu Journey* 145 Henry Cloete .. was sent to Natal as a special commissioner immediately the old Boer republic of Natalia struck its flag. **1955** D.L. HOBMAN *Olive Schreiner* 113 In due course the two Boer Republics were also annexed to the Crown, but the Transvaal was restored to independence after the victory of the Boers over the British at the battle of Majuba Hill in the first Anglo-Boer War, in 1881. **1961** T.V. BULPIN *White Whirlwind* 150 Utrecht, an odd little town which until recently had ranked itself among the capitals of the world, for it had been the political centre of one of the several Boer republics in South Africa. **1973** J. MEINTJES *Voortrekkers* 20 Without this faith in God there would have been no Great Trek, no Boer Republics and no Boer Wars. **1982** *S. Afr. Panorama* May 6 In the Boer republics of the Transvaal and Orange Free State, Dutch was the written language and Afrikaans the spoken language. **1988** *Afr. Contemp. Record 1986–7* 720 Since the days of the old Boer Republics in the 19th Century no Indian was allowed to remain in the Free State for longer than 24 hours. **1990** *Weekly Mail* 8 June 1 For years Van Tonder has used his isolated farm .. as the headquarters from which to wage a battle for the restoration of the old Boer Republics.

Boers see BOER BRANDY.

Boers' brandy var. BOER BRANDY.

Boers' bread var. BOER BREAD.

‖**Boerseep** /ˈbuːrsiəp, ˈbʊəsɪəp/ *n.* Also **Boereseep**. [Afk., *boer* farmer('s) + *seep* soap.] BOER SOAP.

1958 A. JACKSON *Trader on Veld* 26 Other items of barter were homemade 'Boereseep' (Boersoap) made from the fat or tallow of sheep and a sodium substance extracted from the ubiquitous 'asbos'. **1980** J. COCK *Maids & Madams* 223 Candles and soap, both had to be made ... Often during the evening they would roll and knot wicks in preparation for candle-making next day or cut the 'Boerseep' into handy household squares for washing purposes.

boerseun var. BOERESEUN.

Boer soap /ˈbʊəsəʊp/ *n. phr. Hist.* [Prob. part. tr. Afk. *boerseep*, see BOERSEEP.] Home-made boiled soap of animal fat and vegetable-lye or soda; BOERSEEP.

1902 H.J. DUCKITT in M. Kuttel *Quadrilles & Konfyt* (1954) 22 We are often supplied with a piece of Boer soap from Berg River for rubbing on any hard material we want to stitch with our machine, without blunting our needle. **1920** R.Y. STORMBERG *Mrs Pieter de Bruyn* 57 I've known Pieter say that half an hour in her society is like shaving with boer soap: plenty of lather, but it makes a man sore. **1929** *Farming in S. Afr.* Sept. 259 (Swart), Boer Soap as made in the olden days when our grandmothers used the Gannabossie, was a tedious process. **1958** [see BOERSEEP]. **1968** K. MCMAGH *Dinner of Herbs* 28 She also had for sale fine Boer-soap should one wish to indulge in the luxury of washing one's shirt and sluicing away the dust and sweat of hard travel.

boertjie /ˈbuːrci, ˈbʊə(r)ki/ *n.* Also **boeretjie**, and with initial capital. [Afk., *boer* Afrikaner + -IE.] A name for an AFRIKANER (sense 2 a), usu. *derog.* but also used affectionately. Also *attrib.*

1971 *Informant, Grahamstown* Please send me a photo of Paul with his short hair — I can't imagine him like that — I suppose he looks just like a 'boertjie' now! **1979** F. DIKE *First S. African* 8 Solly insulted Thembi and he called me boertjie. I'm a man too, he can't say things like that. **1983** *Informant, Grahamstown* You can't possibly buy that hat — you'll look like a proper boertjie. **1988** *Pace* Dec. 4, I was booked into some slum hotel in some boertjie dorpie in the Free State. **1990** P. FENSTER in *Sunday Times* 22 July 6 TV's S— R— and his boertjie wife Trudi ... Trudi looks for all the world like her own description of herself — 'a protected Boertjie from clean, white Pretoria'.

Boer tobacco /ˌbʊə təˈbækəʊ/ *n. phr.* Also **Boar tobacco**, **Boers' tobacco**, and with small initial. [Part. tr. S. Afr. Du. *boertabak*, *boer* farmer('s) + *tabak* tobacco.] Home-cured tobacco, made for chewing, smoking, or use as snuff; BOER sense 1 c. Also *attrib.*

1832 *Graham's Town Jrnl* 13 Jan. 12 Public Sale ... Brazil Tobacco, Boers' do., Raisins. **1842** J. COLLETT Accounts. II., Shoemakers Tacks, red Handk., Boers tobacco. **1857** T. SHONE Diary. 11 Sept., Bought from R.d Bradfield ½lb of boers tobacco, paid /6 for it. **1864** *Ibid.* V. 84 J.K. gave me a foot of Boar tobacco. **1873** F. BOYLE *To Cape for Diamonds* 80 Collarless, barearmed, unshorn, he puffed coarse boer tobacco from a short clay pipe. **1882** C. DU VAL *With Show through Sn Afr.* II. 191 They thought a golden opportunity for a little speculation in the Boer tobacco line had arrived; so roll upon roll of the dried leaves purchased from a local trader were piled up. **1896** M.A. CAREY-HOBSON *At Home in Tvl* 76 There was a large roll of Boer Tobacco, a small square board for cutting it upon, with a knife lying open, all ready. **1924** L. COHEN *Reminisc. of Jhb.* 23 These men who had been used to scanty pay — oft deferred — and whose only pleasures consisted of the delights found in coffee, dop brandy and Boer tobacco. **1941** C.W. DE KIEWIET *Hist. of S. Afr.* 251 Poor wine unattractive to foreign palates, bad brandy, good only for the Kafir trade, Boer tobacco or the notorious 'Pondo' leaf which caused experienced smokers to blanch. **1968** K. MCMAGH *Dinner of Herbs* 25 The smell of that delightful shop remains with me to this day, compounded as it was of the aroma of brown sugar, leather, soap, great twists of Boer tobacco and spices. *c*1976 H. FLATHER *Thaba Rau* 114 You'd have been squatting on your mealie patch, smoking your Boer tobacco, and watching you wife do the work — happy as a moron. **1986** W. STEENKAMP *Blake's Woman* 83 Twists of vicious-looking Boer tobacco.

Boer verneuker /ˈbʊə fə(r)ˌnɪəkə(r), -niœk-, ˈbuːr-/ *n. phr. Hist.* Also **Boereverneuker**, **Boer vernoeker**, **Boer vernuker**, and with small initial. [S. Afr. Du., *boer* a rural Dutch- or Afrikaans-speaking colonist + *verneuk* see VERNEUK + agential suffix *-er*.] An unscrupulous trader or confidence-trickster who took advantage of unsophisticated country people. See also VERNEUK.

1863 *Queenstown Free Press* 24 Feb., The 'boer vernukers' buy up as rashly and indiscriminately as ever. **1875** *Era* in Saron & Hotz *Jews in S. Afr.* (1955) 307 Israelitish boereverneukers try to persuade the farmers not to improve their properties but simply to confine themselves to sheep-shearing. **1879** R.J. ATCHERLEY *Trip to Boerland* 65 The Natal traders and Boer verneukers (literally swindlers of Boers) began to perceive that if they did not take a decisive step, their trade with the Transvaal would soon be lost. **1898** J.F. INGRAM *Story of Afr. City* 172 A class of middleman sprung up, who speedily earned for himself the title of 'Boer-vernucker', whose exalted mission it was to save each contracting party from the other, and, oftentimes by sharp practice, feather his own nest, to the serious disadvantage of both sellers and buyers. **1911** L. COHEN *Reminisc. of Kimberley* 64 The versatile Leo was looked up to as a marvel of cleverness and honesty by the myriads of Yiddisher Boer vernoekers (Boer besters) .. 'doing pizness' being, as a rule, fatal to the unsophisticated Dutchman. **1924** — *Reminisc. of Jhb.* 48 Dutchmen in those days .. fell easy prey to the experienced and versatile Boer-*verneuker* — who cheated them right and left. **1940** F.B. YOUNG *City of Gold* 57 A man of his word who gave value for money and not one of those *Boer-verneukers* who lived on his sharper wits and exploited their ignorance. **1968** K. MCMAGH *Dinner of Herbs* 61 That such dishonesty was indeed practised may be gathered from the fact that traders were quite openly named 'Boer verneukers', Boer cheaters.

Hence **Boerverneukery** /ˌbʊəfə(r)ˈnɪəkəreɪ, -niœk-, ˌbuːr-/, **Boer verneuking** /-fə(r)ˈniœkɪŋ/ *vbl ns* [both either derived from their S. Afr. Du. equivalents, or formed in Eng. on *boer verneuker*], the trickery or deception practised by such a trader; also used *fig.* in modern political contexts.

1911 L. COHEN *Reminisc. of Kimberley* 92 Before the financier came to Kimberley he was an honest Free State trader in the Boer winkle and wool-buying vocation, which two professions combined are sometimes called Boer verneuking. **1955** T.V. BULPIN *Storm over Tvl* 106 Another way of money making common on the Rand, and especially popular among the central European element, was what was known as 'Boerverneukery' or swindling farmers. **1973** *Weekend Argus* 7 Apr. 14 There is one thing worse than no change at this stage and that is hopes and aspirations which are aroused and not fulfilled. That kind of disillusionment, which will be ascribed to plain 'boereverneukery,' can lead to anger, bitterness and much worse. **1984** *Daily Dispatch* 27 June 1 The Conservative Party accused the National Party yesterday of 'boereverneukery' over the advertisements it published .. which were supposed to have been an apology.

Boer-vrou(w) var. BOEREVROU.

Boer War /ˌbuə ˈwɔː/ *n. phr.* [BOER sense 2 + Eng. *war*.]

1. ANGLO-BOER WAR sense 1. Also *attrib.*

1893 *Brown's S. Afr.* 209 The town served as the base of the British military operations during the disastrous Boer war and the treaty of peace was signed here in 1881. **1900** A.C. DOYLE *Great Boer War* (1902) 19 With the experience of the first Boer war behind them, little was done, either in tactics or in musketry, to prepare the soldier for the second. **1913** *Times Lit. Suppl.* (U.K.) 24 July 309 The Boer War added many South African words for good to the English language. **1920** R.H. LINDSEY-RENTON *Diary* (1979) 28 In the course of the journey crossed the Modder River of Boer War fame. **1936** H.F. TREW *Botha Treks* 81 It was an extraordinary fact that during the Boer War our Australian bushmen, who were nearly all young farmers, strongly objected when the order was given to burn farms. **1943** D. REITZ *No Outspan* 57 Now followed the Boer War of 1881. Under the Leadership of Paul Kruger and Piet Joubert, the Transvaalers rose in arms against Great Britain. *a*1951 H.C. BOSMAN *Willemsdorp* (1977) 8 In each small town there is a Boer War cemetery: women and children of the concentration camps lie there. **1955** D.L. HOBMAN *Olive Schreiner* 112 The Boer War at the turn of the century, which should properly be called the Anglo-Boer War, was a prologue to the tragic drama which opened in 1914. **1967** J.G. DAVIS *Hold my Hand* (1969) 46 He would have a fit when he knew, and Jake an Englishman at that! A Rooinek! Pappa was still fighting the Boer War. **1969** J. MEINTJES *Sword in Sand* 19 On the 8th August, 1881, the Vierkleur was again hoisted in Pretoria after a comparatively brief British occupation and a brisk war, known as the First War of Independence, or the First Boer War. **1973** [see BOER REPUBLIC]. **1980** N. FERREIRA *Story of Afrikaner* 27 Life was good in President Kruger's Transvaal Republic. But then came 1899 and the Boer War. **1987** M. BADELA in *City Press* 13 Mar. 7 They have long hankered for the land that was given to their forefathers by Paul Kruger before the Boer War.

2. *fig.* Friction between Afrikaans- and English-speaking people, or among Afrikaners. See also ANGLO-BOER WAR sense 2.

1978 S. VOS in *Sunday Times* 2 Apr. 1 The day the third Boer War broke out. An Englishman stood outside his luxury penthouse during Afrikaans television programmes and sang 'There'll always be an England' and one line from 'Rule Britannia', a Durban judge was told. **1980** *Sunday Times* 23 Nov. 29 Boer War over boeremusiek. 'I don't think the judging was correct. My band and that of my opponent .. were the only two who played the genuine boeremusiek.' **1985** H. PIENAAR in *Frontline* Aug. 37 Oom Jaap .. insisted that nothing had changed, that the Anglo-Americans were still fighting the Boer War.

boerwors(t) var. BOEREWORS.

‖**Boesman** /ˈbusman, ˈbʊs-/ *n. Derog.* and *offensive.* [Afk., prob. ad. Eng. BUSHMAN; some believe that the word is fr. Du. *Bosjesman*, but the change in the first vowel-sound makes this unlikely.] An insulting term for a 'coloured' person. Also *attrib.*

1959 J. MEIRING *Candle in Wind* 40 Do you think I want all the people pointing at me and laughing in my face, for letting that little Boesman-meid get hold of him? **1961** D. BEE *Children of Yesterday* 72 When the man asked for his money an ugly scene developed and the native made the mistake of calling William a Boesman (Bushman) to his face. **1971** [see AMAKULA]. **1982** C. VAN WYK in *Staffrider* Vol.5 No.1, 36 My mother is a boesman meid a kaffir girl a koelie aunty who wears beads of sweat around her neck and chains around her ankles. **1989** D. BECKETT in *Frontline* Apr. 25 'Do you want the boesmans in town?' 'Nee my baas.' **1990** [see KORANNA sense 2].

boesmangras /ˈbʊsmanxras, ˈbus-, ˈbʊsmən-/ *n.* Also **boesmansgras**, and with initial capital. [Afk., *boesman* bushman (+ linking phoneme *-s-*) + *gras* grass.] BUSHMAN GRASS.

1932 M. HENRICI in *Farming in S. Afr.* Apr. 5 The plants sampled were the following: *Aristida ciliata* Fine Twa grass ... *Aristida obtusa* Boesmangras. **1934** C.P. SWART Supplement to Pettman. 18 *Boesmangras*, .. The Aristida obtusa, a shrub native to Namaqualand, formerly occupied by Bushmen. **1955** J.D. SCOTT et al. in D. Meredith *Grasses & Pastures* 291 *Aristida* ... Common names for the genus are numerous. Among the best known are 'Steekgras', 'Bushman grass', 'Boesmangras' and 'Twa(a)gras', each with several descriptive adjectives for individual species. **1966** C.A. SMITH *Common Names* 148 *Boesman(s)gras*, To-day a general name for a large number of species of *Aristida*. **1974** J.M. COETZEE *Dusklands* 124, I know what it is like, it is like *rooigras*, it is a kind of *rooigras*. I will call it *boesmansgras*. **1991** G.E. GIBBS RUSSEL et al. *Grasses of Sn Afr.* 326 *Stipagrostis obtusa*, .. Kortbeen-boesmangras. Compact and densely tufted.

boet /bʊt, but/ *n. colloq.* Also with initial capital. [Afk., fr. Du. (Zealand dialect) *boet* youngster.] See also OUBOET.

1. 'Mate', 'pal', 'friend', 'buddy': used familiarly or affectionately of or to a man or boy:

a. As a term of address. Cf. BOETIE sense 2.

1920 R.Y. STORMBERG *Mrs Pieter de Bruyn* 59 This is the great day, Boet. Lucie said you could have your first meal to-day. **1949** H.C. BOSMAN *Cold Stone Jug* (1969) 48 What do you want to pick on us for, Boet? .. It's not us, man. **1976** J. MCCLURE *Rogue Eagle* 114 'Hey! Where's my snuff?' Steyn demanded. 'Sorry, *boet* — I'm coming, man, I'm coming.' **1988** S.A. BOTHA in *Frontline* Apr.-May 25 'You coming with, boet?' George's friend asked me. **1991** A. JAY on Radio 5, 4 Jan., I'd like to live in New York for a couple of years, to age quickly. Ja boet, it's true.

b. As a term of reference.

1974 B. SIMON *Joburg, Sis!* 146 Anyway, he hooks up with me and won't let me go, says I'm his boet, his china, his all-time mate.

2. 'Brother': used before a man's first name as an informal title; BOETA sense a. Cf. BRA sense 1.

1920 R.Y. STORMBERG *Mrs Pieter de Bruyn* 35 'You see, Boet Gavie, it's this way,' he said. *a*1968 D.C. THEMBA in E. Patel *World of Can Themba* (1985) 79 Boet Mike said, 'Straight.' And they brought a bottle of brandy that looked like guilty blood. 1971 *Drum* July 50 Boet Joe knows better than me. He was a great champ. 1980 M.P. GWALA in M. Mutloatse *Forced Landing* 99 Sorry, *boet* Dan. I did not mean it.

3. Brother; used familiarly or affectionately of or to one's brother:

a. As a term of reference. Cf. BOETIE sense 1 a, BROER sense 5.

1974 'BLOSSOM' in *Darling* 8 May 91 'What you mean ouma?' My *boet* gives out a hang of a cackle. 1976 *Ibid.* 4 Feb. 87 One shark's tooth what my *boet* gives me for my last birthday. 1979 *E. Prov. Herald* 5 Feb. 12 Beloved father of John and Helen and darling *boet* of Charles, Leslie and Kevin. 1986 *Crux* Aug. 43 Now there was this little laaitie, David . . . One day he pulls out to take some grub to his *boets* in the army. 1989 Informant, Port Elizabeth, I was hoping that the bus would be full so that my *boet* could drive me up to Grahamstown.

b. As a term of address.

1983 F.G. BUTLER *Bursting World* 240 Jeff turns his head, and says in a loud voice: 'Hi, Boet! Don't forget! Give my love to Mom and Dad; tell them not to worry.'

4. *fig. rare.* An Afrikaner: BROEDER sense 4.

1976 J. MCCLURE *Rogue Eagle* 179 'Well, you know the *boets*,' Tagg said, smiling to show he understood any prejudice on Buchanan's part. 'Afrikaners are an emotional lot.'

boeta /ˈbʊta, ˈbuta/ *n. colloq.* Also with initial capital. [Afk., elder brother, chum, pal; see also BOET.] 'Brother': an informal or familiar title or term of address.

a. Used as a title: BOET sense 2. Also *attrib.*

1965 E. MPHAHLELE *Down Second Ave* 31 A man was passing. It was Boeta Lem (Brother Blade), as we boys called him. 1975 *Sunday Times* 23 Mar. (Extra) 4 'At the moment I do not know where I stand,' explained Mr P. L— who is known in the village as 'Boeta Man'. 1980 A. DANGOR in M. Mutloatse *Forced Landing* 163 'Ow, *Boeta* Harry, don't you trust me?'

b. Used as a term of address. See also BRA sense 2 b.

1969 A. FUGARD *Boesman & Lena* 37 There was something else in the fire, something rotten. Us! Our sad stories, our smells, our world! And it burnt Boeta.

boetabessie /ˈbʊtaˌbesi, ˈbuta-/ *n.* [Afk., *boeta* see prec. + *bessie* berry; see quot. 1966.]

1. The bush-tick berry (BUSH-TICK sense 2), *Chrysanthemoides monilifera.*

1917 R. MARLOTH *Common Names* 13 *Boetabessie, Osteospermum moniliferum.* 1966 C.A. SMITH *Common Names* 151 *Boetabessie,* Strictly the drupaceous achenes of *Chrysanthemoides monilifera* s.sp. *pisifera* . . . Also heard as a literal translation *Brotherberry.* The name refers to the unusual arrangement of the 3 to 5 juicy fruits which are radially disposed in the manner, like brothers in the same bed. Boeta here is an illiterate rendering of *boetie* (brother). 1988 R. LUBKE et al. *Field Guide to E. Cape* 174 The first vegetation . . as one moves away from the shore is Dune Thicket. Along the margin of the scrub the dominant shrubs . . generally include *Chrysanthemoides monilifera* (boetabessie).

2. *fig. rare.* Usu. with initial capitals, **Boeta Bessie.** [Punningly, by conflation of *boeta* with Afk. *boete,* a fine or penalty, and *bessie* with the female given name *Bessie.*] A jocular name for a meter-maid or traffic warden.

1984 J. RYAN in *E. Prov. Herald* 23 June 4 Bonn's equivalent of our Boeta Bessies hand out 15 000 pink slips a year to three-and-a-half thousand vehicles belonging to the *Corps Diplomatique.*

boetebossie /ˈbʊtəˌbɔsi/ *n.* Formerly also **boete-bosch, boete bosje, boetebossi,** and with initial capital. [Afk., *boete* a fine or penalty + *bossie* (earlier *bosch, bosje* see BOSCHJE) bush; see quot. 1906.] The noxious weed *Xanthium spinosum* of the Asteraceae, a native of tropical America.

1906 W.S. JOHNSON *Orangia* 14 Why are the seeds so spiny? The boete bosje will answer that question. Its little seeds stick so closely in a sheep's wool that they ruin the fleece, and therefore any one who allows this plant to flourish on his farm must pay a boete, or fine. 1913 C. PETTMAN *Africanderisms* 74 *Boetebossi* or *Boeteklis,* . . *Xanthium spinosum.* 1917 R. MARLOTH *Common Names* 14 *Boetebossie,* (Boeteklis). *Xanthium spinosum* (Burweed). 1966 C.A. SMITH *Common Names* 151 The Cape Government . . passed legislation making the eradication of this burweed compulsory on pain of a fine or boete . . . The ready reaction of the countryside to this radical step is seen in the spontaneity with which it coined the name *Boetebossie* for the weed. It is significant too, that this name has been taken over into English without change, although sometimes rendered as Boetebosch. 1977 *E. Prov. Herald* 28 Nov. 4 It is alarming to see to what extent Scotch thistle is taking over in the district, and 'he did not even want to mention Boetebossies'. 1980 A.J. BLIGNAUT *Dead End Rd* 18 Even if our sheep were full of boete-bossies they would still win.

boetie /ˈbʊti, ˈbuti/ *n. colloq.* Also **boeti, bootie, buttie,** and with initial capital. [Afk., 'little brother' (see BOET + -IE.)]

1. A brother.

a. Used as a term of reference, usu. for a brother who is still a teenager and living at home. Cf. BOET sense 3 a.

1867 E.L. PRICE *Jrnls* (1956) 253 'Tis the ruling principle of every action, I think — love for the 'vrow & kinderen' — 'the man & the kinderen' — the buttie & Sisi'. 1962 J. TAYLOR 'Hennie van Saracen'. (lyrics) When I went back home To go and say goodbye To Mom and Dad and boetie They all began to cry. 1970 J.R. BENNETT *Informant, Krugersdorp* How old is your boetie? 1977 C. HOPE in S. Gray *Theatre Two* (1981) 36 You heard of my *boetie,* Poulie —? And *ou* Abba and those jollers? 1981 *Fair Lady* 14 Jan. 98 'I haven't got a daddy . . . My boetie is the man in the house.' 'How old is he?' 'Sixteen.' 'And you?' 'Fifteen.' 1986 M. PICARDIE in S. Gray *Market Plays* 94, I was the youngest, you see. My boeties and sussies were all at school.

b. An affectionate form of address.

1913 C. PETTMAN *Africanderisms* 74 *Boeti,* A pet name often given to the eldest or favourite son. 1988 J. FERGUSON in *New Nation* 14 Jan. 10 Boetie's on the Border Still fighting for the country.

2. 'Brother': a familiar form of address to any man or boy. Cf. BHUTI sense a, BOET sense 1 a.

1903 E. GLANVILLE *Diamond Seekers* 270 There's a lot of things you don't know, bootie. 1920 R.Y. STORMBERG *Mrs Pieter de Bruyn* 60 In great distress Gabriel leans over, puts his arms around the boy, says again: 'But my little Boetie, don't do that.' 1958 S. CLOETE *Mask* 167 The child was wailing now. Mina comforted him. 'Fear not, little brother . . . Fear not, my boetie.' 1965 K. MACKENZIE *Deserter* 101 'What is it *boetie*?' Japie asked the Basuto . . 'Aubuti, look,' The assonance between the Afrikaans and the Sotho words of brotherly affection was one of several jokes that had grown up between the two men. 1975 *S. Afr. Panorama* Oct. 20 Amid cheers of 'Very good, Boetie!' these youngsters had a go at 'kussingslaan' (a pillow fight on a beam). *a*1977 K.M.C. MOTSISI in M. Mutloatse *Casey & Co.* (1978) 121 There are more and more Simons invading the city to come and beg. You find them at the cinemas, in the streets, at the railway station: 'Boetie give me a sixpence to go home.' 1988 'K. DE BOER' in *Frontline* Apr. 26 Boeties, unless somebody else starts formulating really challenging alternative ideals and dreams, we're in for a nasty bit of *volksontwaking* in the near future.

3. *derog.* **boetie-boetie:** partisan behaviour. Also as *adj.,* in cahoots, over-friendly.

1956 D. JACOBSON *Dance in Sun* 73 Frank found that he and the other were boetie-boetie again, confidential. 1971 *Daily Dispatch* 2 Oct. 12 Most people voted according to tribal lines. It was a question of 'boetie-boetie'. Voters were not influenced by what the candidates said in their meetings.

4. *obsolescent. Offensive* to many. In the Eastern Cape: a term used for a black male employee. Cf. SISI sense 1 b.

1973 *Headmistress's letter, Grahamstown* Warning: Only 'Boeties' in [school] overalls should be allowed to carry luggage into the Houses at the beginning of term.

5. *fig.* A political fellow-traveller. See also KAFFIRBOETIE.

1973 Y. BURGESS *Life to Live* 120 The men in the bar . . agreed that the country was going to the dogs, that the Commies, the kaffirs, and the 'boeties', that is, brothers, of both, had taken over. 1987 R. DU PREEZ in *Sunday Times* 12 Apr. 1 Singer Mara Louw was telephoned and threatened with death by a woman who accused her of being an 'ANC boetie'.

6. *fig.* A generic nickname given to an Afrikaner, or to an aggressively masculine male. Also used ironically.

1973 F. CHISHOLM in *Cape Times* 30 June 7 The driver was a typical gun-happy South African with his Lee Enfield in a rack behind the seat, continually clapping on brakes, anxious to blaze away at every living thing he saw. The Prince was finally able to quell boetie's destructive ardour. 1992 H. TYRRELL in *Weekly Mail* 24 Apr. 24 Change in this country has not come about from waiting until big *boetie* and his business cronies are ready to throw out some crumbs.

Boetshoenas pl. form of BECHUANA.

bo-excuse-me pl. form of EXCUSE-ME.

bogadi /bɔˈxaːdi/ *n.* Also **bohadi, bohali.** [SeTswana and Sotho, cattle given in fulfilment of a marriage contract. 'Bogadi' is the seTswana and Northern Sotho orthography, while 'bohadi' is the Southern Sotho orthography used in South Africa, and 'bohali' is that used in Lesotho.]

Pronunciation of the three forms 'bogadi', 'bohadi', and 'bohali' is identical.

1. In Sotho and Tswana society: LOBOLA *n.* sense 1.

1882 J. MACKENZIE in A.J. Dachs *Papers of John Mackenzie* (1975) 81 My argument was that if the parents of the bride stood up in the Church and 'gave their daughter away' and signed a book or register to that effect, there was *no place* for '*bogadi*' or wife-buying; the transaction was complete. 1905 [see LOBOLA sense 1]. 1943 'J. BURGER' *Black Man's Burden* 62 Perhaps the most important aspect of that law [sc. civil] is that of lobolo or bogadi, the marriage dowry system.

2. In Sotho and Tswana society: LOBOLA *n.* sense 2.

1930 S.T. PLAATJE *Mhudi* (1975) 52 No male relatives to arrange the marriage knot, nor female relations to herald the family union, nor no uncles of the bride to divide the bogadi (dowry) cattle as, of course, there were no cattle. 1950 H. GIBBS *Twilight* 73 He has not managed to pay the *bogadi* — the marriage purchase price made in cattle — to the bride's family. 1953 LANHAM & MOPELI-PAULUS *Blanket Boy's Moon* 19 You know very well you have no cattle to pay bohali — dowry — for a rich wife: the father might demand twenty-five head of cattle. 1968 A. FULTON *Dark Side of Mercy* 18 No man is prepared to lose a good wife for whom he has paid bohali and so lose good cattle, especially when she is young and fertile and will have other children. 1970 M. DIKOBE *Marabi Dance.* 48 If you give him the home brew, he won't get drunk quickly and will be shy to say how many cattle he will pay for bogadi. 1976 WEST & MORRIS *Abantu* 150 Marriage, in common with that among most other

African peoples, was legalized by the transfer of bridewealth, called bohadi, from the groom's family to that of his bride. **1988** M. Nkotsoe in *Staffrider* Vol.7 No.3, 375 The couple could not raise enough money for bogadi. Cattle had decreased and the man's parents were too poor to meet the required number of cattle. **1988** Spiegel & Boonzaier in Boonzaier & Sharp *S. Afr. Keywords* 47 Paying bohali .. emerged as a major mechanism whereby people coped with the exigencies of migrant labour and the repeated absence of breadwinning husbands, fathers and sons for periods of up to two years at a time. **1989** J. Hobbs *Thoughts in Makeshift Mortuary* 398 He doesn't have to pay bohali, that is cows, for you.

boggerall /ˈbɔgərɔl/ *n. slang.* Also **bokkerol**. [Indicating Afk.-speakers' pronunciation of Eng. *bugger all* nothing.] 'Bugger all', nothing.

Freq. used jocularly, or to indicate the reported speech of Afrikaners.

1965 P. Baragwanath *Brave Remain* 99 Both looked at Babyface who was deep in thought. 'How much does he know?' 'Boggerall ..' the two replied. **1980** J. Scott in *Cape Times* 18 Apr. 9 'A litre of milk costs 41c,' he [*sc.* the Minister of Agriculture] said. 'To subsidize it by one cent amounts to 50 percent of *bokkerol*' ... Mr B— objected to the word *bokkerol*. 'I shall say "bugger nothing", then'. **1984** *Frontline* Feb. 26 The govt. was really hot on this whole issue of trying to make like the larnies and the bushies and the darkies actually had boggerall to do with one another. **1989** *Weekly Mail* 15 Dec. 7 If a man gets sick and does not go out, no money. If he gets hurt he gets 'boggerall'.

boguera /bɔˈgweːra/ *n.* Also **bogwera**. [SeTswana *bogwéra*.] Ritual male circumcision, an aspect of the Tswana initiation ceremony. See also circumcision sense 1. Cf. boyale.

1857 D. Livingstone *Missionary Trav.* 146 All the Bechuana and Caffre tribes south of the Zambesi practise circumcision (*boguera*), but the rites observed are carefully concealed. **1867** E.L. Price *Jrnls* (1956) 261 One of Sechele's sons ran off to the Circumcision the other day ... Sechele summoned him & told him to tell his Teacher why he went to the *Boguéra*. **1870** [see boyale]. **1871** J. Mackenzie *Ten Yrs* (1971) 375 The rite of circumcision is administered throughout Bechuana-land to boys between perhaps eight and fourteen years of age ... No honourable marriage could take place with a man who had not gone through the 'boguera' or initial ceremony. **1905** W.H. Tooke in Flint & Gilchrist *Science in S. Afr.* 91 Like most Bantu the be-Chuana practise circumcision (boguera) which is performed at the age of puberty. **1951** H. Davies *Great S. Afr. Christians* 105 An open break with the tribe took place in 1865 when the ceremony of *boguera* or circumcision was to be held. **1974** A.J. Dachs *Papers of John Mackenzie* 5 Among the ritual observances of the Tswana which attracted the immediate attention of missionaries were the initiation ceremonies of bogwera and bojale, whereby the youths and maidens of the chiefdom were elevated in rank to adults.

bohadi, -hali varr. bogadi.

boialloa, boïálloa varr. bojalwa.

boïalloa, bojala varr. boyale.

bojalwa /bɔˈjaːlwa/ *n.* Also **bajalo, boialloa, boïálloa, bojal(o)a, boyalwa**. [SeTswana *bojalwa*, S. Sotho *bojaloa* beer.] Among seTswana- and S. Sotho-speakers:

1. *obs.* honey-beer.

1824 W.J. Burchell *Trav.* II. 552 They .. possess the art of making a beverage .. from honey and water put into a state of fermentation by the addition of a certain root or by the dregs of a former preparation. This beverage is called *boïálloa* by the Bachapins, and is well known to the Hottentots by the Dutch name of *honing-bier* (honey-beer). **1834** T. Pringle *Afr. Sketches* 509 A sort of mead, called honey-beer by the Hottentots, and boialloa by the Bechuanas, is used both by these tribes and the Caffers.

2.a. tshwala sense a. **b.** tshwala sense c.

1826 A.G. Bain *Jrnls* (1949) 57 We were invited to drink a beverage called Bajalo or Beer made from the Caffre Corn. **1850** R.G.G. Cumming *Hunter's Life* I. 323 The king .. ordered 'boyalwa' or native beer, to be placed before them. **1874** [see *emmerful* (emmer)]. **1960** C. Hooper *Brief Authority* 123 He placed a jug of bojalwa, kaffir beer, on the table. **1975** M. Mutloatse in *Bolt* No.12, 18 You rouse yourself early only to guzzle bojalwa heh! **1982** *Pace* May 34 This is mageu and not bojalwa, which skokiaan and those others are. **1986** [see tshwala]. **1990** G. Slovo *Ties of Blood* 143 Around him are the remains of last night's festivities — the half-empty plates of food and the formerly full bottles of *bojaloa* now drained to the last drop.

Bojesman var. Bosjesman.

bok /bɔk/ *n.* [S. Afr. Du. (later Afk.), antelope, goat fr. Du. *bok* horned animal.]

1. Pl. unchanged, **-s**, or **-ke** /-kə/.

‖**a.** An antelope: buck *n.*[1] sense 1 a. Also *attrib.* See also bokkie sense 2.

1812 A. Plumptre tr. *H. Lichtenstein's Trav. in Sn Afr.* (1928) I. 133 They called .. the whole family of the antelope boks. **1835** A. Smith *Diary* (1940) II. 84 A large bok of yellowish colour with indistinct white spots seen towards the base of the Cashan hills. **1837** 'N. Polson' *Subaltern's Sick Leave* 122 The sportsman will find zebras and a large bok with long spiral horns. *Ibid.* 123 These bok are very easily floored with shot and are slow on foot. **1845** W.N. Irwin *Echoes of Past* (1927) 235 He is becoming a splendid shot, and is now stationed in a right good hunting Country where Buffaloes, Boks, etc., are to be met with. **1862** Lady Duff-Gordon *Lett. from Cape* (1925) 113 Old Klein has just sent me a haunch of bok, and the skin and hoofs, which are pretty. **1864** — in F. Galton *Vacation Tourists* 190 The excellence of the Caffre skin-dressing and sewing is, I fancy, unequalled; the bok-skins are as soft as a kid glove, and have no smell at all. **1877** Lady Barker *Yr's Hsekeeping* 6 The Museum is well worth a visit .. [and] contains numerous specimens of the great '*bok*' family. **1880** E.F. Sandeman *Eight Months in Ox Waggon* 273 Guinea fowls .. form a very relishing change from the never-varying menu of bôk or mealie pap. **1887** *S.W. Silver & Co.'s Handbk to S. Afr.* 188 The nearest man fired a shot at a bok as he leaped out of a large bush. It was but a snap shot, and missed. **1972** *Drum* 8 Mar. 26 Alfred Jacobs could not contain his jubilation. He jumps to the air like a bok. **1993** C. Eden in *Food & Home* Aug. 138 A good South African male can produce a braai anywhere on this planet; all he needs is a couple of sticks, a box of Blitz and an unsuspecting bok in a nearby bush.

b. With distinguishing epithets designating different species of antelope: see blauwbok, bleekbok, blesbok, bluebok, bontebok, boschbok, duikerbok, *elandbok* (eland sense 2), gemsbok, grysbok, klip-bok, *pronkbok* (pronk sense 1), *quagga bok* (quagga sense 2), rhebok, rietbok, rooibok, springbok sense 1, steenbok, *vlaktebok* (vlakte sense 2), waterbok. See also buck *n.*[1] sense 1 b.

2. Pl. **-s, -ke** /-kə/. A goat: buck *n.*[1] sense 2. See also bokkie sense 2.

[**1835** T.H. Bowker Journal. 2 July, Row between the Fingoos & hottentots om bokke one man confined.] **1920** F.C. Cornell *Glamour of Prospecting* 51 Both of them cleared off in the early morning and .. brought in a big goat between them ... 'Baas,' he said, ' .. I did not pay for this bok, he was a present!' **1975** *Daily Dispatch* 13 June 13 To take the child now — it's not a lamb. A bok is a bok, but a person is a person, and you don't do things like this to a person. **1990** Barrett & Grant in *Weekend Post* 1 Dec. 1 Angora rams .. are drawing bids of only R70 at auctions, goats as little as R10 ... Prior to the auction a farmer said he would be 'pleased to get R20 a *bok*'.

3. *transf.*

a. *slang. rare.* A sweetheart. See also bokkie sense 1.

1950 H. Gibbs *Twilight* 27 If a woman becomes the *bok* of a petty gangster, she is regarded as more fortunate than many. [**1982** D. Bikitsha in *Rand Daily Mail* 14 Oct. (Eve) 5 A woman went by such titles [in Isicamtho]: moll, cherrie, wibbit, ganda, slang, shows, gezu, bok, mathara and others.]

b. *colloq.* Pronounced /bɒk/. Also **'Bok**, and usu. with initial capital. Abbrev. of *Springbok*, see springbok sense 2 a. Also *attrib.*

With pl. -*s*, often referring to the South African rugby team.

1970 *Cape Times* 30 May, His grandson, Brian Lewis, is a baseball 'Bok', much to granddad's pride. **1971** *Rand Daily Mail* 31 May 8 For the first time ever, a Bok cricket team beat the Australians. **1974** *Sunday Times* 27 Oct. 1 The 1974 Springbok rugby team are flying to France ... The Boks are ready for anything — on and off the field. **1981** *E. Prov. Herald* 10 Mar. 4 Bok colours and trip overseas for PE schoolboy. **1990** *Weekend Post* 30 June 3 He went on to gain his Bok colours as a Northern Transvaal player.

c. *slang.* In the phr. *to be (a) bok for*, to be game for, or enthusiastic about.

1970 K. Nicol *Informant, Durban* Despite the cold he was bok for a swim. **1975** 'Blossom' in *Darling* 29 Jan. 103 I'm a bok for having fun and all, but I'll have to keep this one quiet. **1975** S. Roberts *Outside Life's Feast* 60 'Your sister's a dare-devil isn't she,' laughed Mrs Nel. 'Lennie says she's a bok for anything.' **1985** G. Verdal in *Argus* 24 Jan. (Tonight) 5 I'm a bok for anything. **1989** *Sunday Times* 15 Jan. 9 Johan sat down ... 'Who's bok for a beer?' **1989** I. Vladislavić *Missing Persons* 113 Boshoff's a bok for mounting a counter attack. **1990** *Weekend Post* 14 July (Leisure) 1 The East Cape Game Management Association, always a bok for sport, decided to have a fund-raiser to coincide with its game fair.

d. *slang.* A hero; a masculine or athletic male.

1973 Y. Burgess *Life to Live* 16 His dashing nickname he had bestowed on himself, she was sure, for he was not, never could have been, any young girl's idea of a 'bok', or charmer. **1975** *Darling* 12 Apr. 95 Seems he rocks over from Vredies to challenge the local pinball boks, and it also seems he already won a pile of bread off them. **1986** *Style* Oct. 132 This inspired Frenchman, who scattered architectural masterpieces all around the Cape, was a rather weary old *bok* by the time he did The Drostdy at Graaff-Reinet. **1990** *Frontline* Jan. 23 'You're too bold,' said the youth, 'and our future's in hock If you try to enfranchise whoever. Maybe coloureds and Indians will say you're a bok, But we don't think it's too bloody clever.'

boka var. buchu.

bokaal /bɔˈkɑːl/ *n.* Also **bocal, bok(h)al**. Pl. **-s, -en**. [Du., beaker.] A large goblet, often decoratively engraved and sometimes lidded, used for drinking toasts and (occas.) as a loving cup.

[**1827** G. Thompson *Trav.* II. 118 Even .. the richest, and most polished class of Cape Dutch gentry, are still but too frequently disgraced by hard drinking and riotous mirth — and the *pokaalie* cup .. too often drowns both reason and refinement.] **1870** 'S.R.N.' in *Cape Monthly Mag.* I. Nov. 306 One of the principal guests rises and holding in his hand a 'bokhal' filled to the brim. **1904** *Cape Times Christmas No.* 15 (Pettman), One hour later we were in the old voorhuis together drinking *bokals* and making the rafters ring with song and tale and laughter. **1910** D. Fairbridge *That Which Hath Been* (1913) 81 The glou-glou of the wine as they poured it into the *bokaal* at each guest's elbow. **1927** C.G. Botha *Social Life in Cape Col.* 41 Before the guests rose from the table the health of the family was drunk by passing round a large 'bokaal,' or loving cup, which seldom held less than a pint ... This large drinking glass made of the finest glass or crystal, was often beautifully engraved and had some appropriate motto or verse. **1951** D. Heller *In Search of VOC Glass* 74 Types of V.O.C. glasses said to be genuine consist of goblets (bokalen) and baluster and/or knopped-stem wineglasses. **1966** M. Kuttel *Hildegonda Duckitt's Bk of Recipes* 2 At Groot Constantia there would be great dinners in the enormous diningroom,

bokbaai vygie /ˌbɔkbaɪ ˈfeɪxi/ *n. phr.* [Afk. place name *Bokbaai* 'Buck Bay' + VYGIE.] Any of several species of succulent plant of the genus *Dorotheanthus* of the Mesembryanthemaceae, esp. *D. bellidiformis*, with brilliantly-coloured, daisy-like flowers; BUCK BAY VYGIE; also called VYGIE. Also *ellipt.*, **bokbaai**.

1962 S. ELIOVSON *Discovering Wild Flowers in Sn Afr.* 30 One should drive a little beyond Darling to Ysterfontein by the sea to see the brilliant Bokbaai Vygie (*Dorotheanthus*) winking in the sunlight. 1963 M.G. MCCOY *Informant, Port Elizabeth* We had a long walk in Settlers' Park, all the Namaqualands are out, & the sparaxis & bobbejantjies, .. oh! & acres of bokbaai vygies. *Ibid.* Lots of bokbaai & Namaqualand daisies. 1965 S. ELIOVSON *S. Afr. Wild Flowers for Garden* 290 *Dorotheanthus*, .. This small genus of 6 species contains one of the most brilliant edging annuals .. *D. bellidiformis*, the *Bokbaai Vygie*. 1972 *S. Afr. Garden & Home* Oct. 30 *Bokbaaivygie* (mesembryanthemum) is a classical drought-resistant plant. 1985 *Fair Lady* 3 Apr. 137 The flashy dayglo hues of the mesems — the bokbaais, lampranthus, suurvy and drosanthus — look their best against .. an open sky. 1991 H. HUTCHINGS in *Weekend Post* 30 Mar. (Leisure) 7 In spring and summer ground-cover annuals like portulaca, bokbaai vygies and perennial gazanias will create a carpet of brilliance. 1993 *Calendar order form* (Cape Nature Conservation & Museums), The bokbaaivygie (*Dorotheanthus bellidiformis*) of the West Coast grows quickly after rain, produces flowers and seeds in abundance, and then dies off to survive the dry period in seed form.

bokbaard /ˈbɔkbɑː(r)t/ *n.* Also **bokbaart**, and with initial capital. [Afk. (fr. Du. *boksbaard, bokkebaard*), *bok* goat + *baard* beard.]
1. Any of several unrelated species of plant with flowers or flowering parts resembling the beard of a goat, esp. the grass *Festuca caprina* of the Poaceae (sub-family Pooideae). Also *attrib.*

1896 *Agric. Jrnl of Cape of G.H.* in C.A. Smith *Common Names* (1966) 154 An argument with a farmer about bokbaard grass. 1898 *Ibid.*, Known by the local name of Bokbaard .. [it] seems to be essential to sheep farming. 1908 *Report S.A.A.A. Science* 209 *Festuca caprina*, Nees, locally known as 'bok-baard' a grass remaining green through the severe winter, yields excellent herbage on the mountain slopes. 1917 R. MARLOTH *Common Names* 14 Bokbaard, Festuca caprina (grass). 1966 C.A. SMITH *Common Names* 153 *Bokbaard*, Several unrelated plants, including some grasses go by this name because of some suggestion of the beard (Afr.: baard) of the goat, conveyed by some structure of the inflorescence. [1991 G.E. GIBBS RUSSELL et al. *Grasses of Sn Afr.* 169 Festuca caprina Bokbaardgras.]
2. *colloq.* A goatee or tufted beard; BOKBAARDJIE. Also *attrib.*

1913 C. PETTMAN *Africanderisms* 75 Bokbaard, .. A chin beard like that of a goat. [1958 I. VAUGHAN *Diary* 20 They call him Jonny Bok becos he has a beard like a goat.] 1973 K. TAYLOR on *Radio South Africa* 6 June, Here's what Shakespeare said — Shakespeare, the bokbaard of Stratford-on-Avon. 1978 P. STRAUSS in *Contrast* 46 Vol.12 No.2, 6 They're absorbed in the visit Of Mistah Pan the wood-god, Squatting on goat-legs ... Nodding his bokbaard wise-sheep face, A male without troubles. 1982 C. HOPE *Private Parts* 45 A bokbaard tapering to an exquisite point adorned his chin.

bokbaardjie /ˈbɔkbɑː(r)ki, -ci/ *n. colloq.* [Afk., *bokbaard* (see prec.) + -IE.] BOKBAARD sense 2.

c1966 J. HOBBS in *New S. Afr. Writing* 119 'And a beard like a tramp ..' 'But it's a bok-baardjie, Pa. All my friends are growing them.' 1991 'M.E.O.' in *Weekend Post* 13 Apr. (Leisure) 6, I first grew my beard at the age of 21 and .. it was a mess: mutton-chop whiskers, a straggly moustache and a *bokbaardjie*, all separated by skin as smooth as a baby's bottom.

bok-bok /ˈbɔkbɔk/ *n.* Also with initial capital. [Afk. fr. Du. The intended sense of *bok* is uncertain. The name is derived from a formula recited in the game, the Afk. version being 'Bok, bok, staan styf, hoeveel vingers op jou lyf?', (Bok, bok, stand firm, how many fingers on your body?). The game, believed to be of great antiquity, is known in Britain as 'Hey cockalorum'; the name 'Buck-buck' has also been recorded.

In the *Satyricon* of T. Petronius Arbiter (d. A.D. 66), a man, riding on another's back and hitting him on the shoulder with his fingers, asks '*Bucca, bucca, quot sunt hic?*' (Bucca, bucca, how many are here?). In this context the meaning of *bucca* is not known. Its usual sense is 'mouth' or 'cheek', but it can also mean 'bigmouth'; here, it may be related to the Sanskrit *bukka* he-goat, or be borrowed from a Germanic word represented in modern Du. by *bok* goat, or in Old Eng. by the word *búc* belly, body, trunk.]
A boys' game, with several variations, in which the players of one team fling themselves onto the other team in an attempt to make them collapse, either jumping one at a time onto the bent backs of opposing team members, or attempting to topple a pyramid composed of the other team.

See note at NOW-NOW.

1936 E. ROSENTHAL *Old-Time Survivals* 20 'Bok-Bok', One of South Africa's most popular games among boys. The basic idea, and even the quaint Dutch formula, spoken before the heap of youngsters collapses on the ground, is traceable far back into the Middle Ages. 1944 'TWEDE IN BEVEL' *Piet Kolonel* 55 He played boat races, scissors with the Colonel on the billiard table, bok-bok with teams of which every member was bound his weight. 1967 E. ROSENTHAL *Encycl. of Sn Afr.* 67 Bok-Bok, Popular name of a game played by boys in South Africa ... One player stands against a wall, while others form a chain, jumping over each other until the whole group collapses. 1975 D. WOODS in *Cape Times* 7 Feb. 12 The whole ethos of bok-bok predicates that some poor ou must always be up against a tree .. to absorb the impact of the leap. Then again, the leaper, who is basically seeking a superior or privileged position, is allowed to crash down on to the bent back of one of the lesser players. 1982 D. KRAMER *Short Back & Sides* 52, I grew up under the heavy hand Of the cane and the dominee I grew up in this government plan Playing bok-bok and toktokkie. 1985 W. SMITH *Burning Shore* 5 Michael was teaching the other new chums how to play the game of Bok-Bok ... One team formed a human pyramid against a wall of the mess, while the other team attempted to collapse them by taking a full run and then hurling themselves on top of the structure. 1988 T.J. LINDSAY *Shadow* (1990) 187 Before long they had formed two teams and were playing bok-bok, one team forming a scrum around one of the plane trees, the other hurling themselves at it after a run up one at a time.

bok-bok-makirie var. BOKMAKIERIE.

bokdrol /ˈbɔkˌdrɔl/ *n. slang.* Pl. -s, -le /-ə/. [Afk., *bok* goat + *drol* dropping.]
1. *fig.* A chocolate-coated peanut.

1970 A.H. NEWEY *Informant, Stutterheim* Bok drols. A vulgar usage, synonym for chocolate-coated peanuts (goat droppings). 1972 BEETON & DORNER in *Eng. Usage in Sn Afr.* Vol.3 No.2, 39 *Bokdrol*, .. Coll. name applied to a peanut dragee by schoolchildren.
2. Goat droppings; any droppings which resemble these. See also DROL.

1972 BEETON & DORNER in *Eng. Usage in Sn Afr.* Vol.3 No.2, 39 Bokdrol, .. Pellet of the dung of buck. 1983 B. JOHNSON-BARKER in *Wynboer* Aug. 72 In the little cave .. nothing happened except that perhaps another layer or two was added to the bokdrolle on the floor. 1986 *Informant, Durban* That pony-tail looks like a bokdrol on the top of your head.

Boke-veld var. BOKKEVELD.

bokhal var. BOKAAL.

bokhorinkie /ˈbɔkˌhʊərəŋki/ *n.* Formerly also **bokhoorntje**. [Afk., *bok* goat + *horing* horn + dim. suffix -IE; see quot. 1966.] Any of several species of creeping plant of the Asclepiadaceae, some of which bear edible seedpods.

1913 C. PETTMAN *Africanderisms* 75 Bokhoorntjes, .. Applied indiscriminately to the follicles of various *Asclepiadaceae* in the Riversdale District. 1966 C.A. SMITH *Common Names* 155 Bokhorinkie, Name applied to a few species, not from the shape of their fruits, but from the nature of their leaves ... The leaves are spirally turned in their upper half in a manner suggestive of the horns of certain wild buck or the boergoat. 1975 W. STEENKAMP *Land of Thirst King* 130 There are two kinds of stapelia the old people used to eat, and others known to me only by their colloquial names: the 'bokhorinkies' (goat's horns), the seedpods of a certain creeper, which are eaten while still green.

bokkem /ˈbɔkəm/ *n.* Also **bokking**, **bok(k)om**, **bokkum**. [Du. *bokking*, *bokkem* smoked herring.] Esp. in the Western Cape: a salted, dried, and sometimes smoked whole fish, usu. a small mullet (see HARDER); the flesh of a fish prepared in this way.

Occas. called *Cape biltong* or *fish biltong*. See also BILTONG.

1866 L. PAPPE *Synopsis of Edible Fishes* 19 They [sc. mullets] make good table-fish, but are more frequently salted or smoke-dried (Bokkoms) like the Herring. 1891 H.J. DUCKITT *Hilda's 'Where Is It?'* 92 The small dried and salted herring commonly called at the Cape 'Bokom,' is very good when done this way. 1910 D. FAIRBRIDGE *That Which Hath Been* (1913) 82 He has a good appetite now — though he is still lean as a *bokking*. c1936 M. VALBECK *Headlong from Heaven* 33 She eats snoek and bokkoms and what not before she goes to bed. 1945 H. GERBER *Fish Fare* 16 The term *bokkems* was originally applied to salted and air-dried harders, but now many other kinds of fish are prepared in the same way. 1955 A. DELIUS *Young Trav.* 99 After a hearty breakfast of oatmeal porridge, eggs and some dried salt-fish called *bokkems*, Dick went out. 1969 J.R. GRINDLEY *Riches of Sea* 68 Some harders and maasbankers were hung to dry as 'bokkoms' in the wind and sun on lines stretched between posts near the fishing villages. 1970 H. DE VILLIERS in *S. Afr. Panorama* June 8 Some people call it 'Cape biltong', but as a rule it is better known as *bokkem* — delicious dried fish which is peculiar to the Western Cape Province ... I met an expert on bokkems ... 'Here we concentrate on haarder, stumpnose, steenbras, elf (shad) and "doppies" (small silver fish). Bokkems are also often made from marsbanker.' 1972 [see DOPPIE sense 2]. 1990 M.M. HACKSLEY (tr. E. van Heerden) in *Lynx* 183 There were some farmers a man simply did not work for if he could possibly help it. They were the sjambok farmers who paid you nothing but bokkems and mealiemeel and trouble. 1993 [see HARDER].

bokkerol var. BOGGERALL.

Bokkeveld /ˈbɔkəfɛlt, -fɛlt/ *n.* Formerly also **Bo(c)ke-veld**, **Bokkeveld**, **Bokveld**, and with small initial. [fr. *Bokkeveld*, name of region in the Western Cape, fr. S. Afr. Du., *bokke* combining form of *bok* goat, antelope + *veld* open, undeveloped countryside; see also VELD sense 2 c.] Usu. *attrib., comb.*, and in *phrr.*: *Bokkeveld bed, -Series, -times* (*Geology*), designating a geological group of the Cape System comprised of alternating beds of shale and sandstone, situated in the valleys between the Cape foldmountains, and dating from the Lower Devonian age; *Bokkeveld Karoo*, that part of the Karoo closest to the Bokkeveld (or Ceres district); see also KAROO senses 1 a and b.

The area known as the Bokkeveld is comprised of the Warm (Afk. *Warme*) Bokkeveld, the lower-lying basin surrounding the town of Ceres, and the Cold (Afk. *Koue*) Bokkeveld, the higher-lying area to the north of that town.

[**1790** tr. *F. Le Vaillant's Trav.* II. 446, I quitted *Verkeerde Valey* on the twenty-first, and was now entering into another country, the *Boke-veld*, (plain of spring-bok).] **1822** [see SPAN *n.*[1] sense 1]. **1844** J. BACKHOUSE *Narr. of Visit* 520 Two of them, are said, some years ago, to have shot a white man on the Bokkeveld Karroo. **1896** R. WALLACE *Farming Indust. of Cape Col.* 54 The *Bokkeveld beds* rest conformably upon the coarse gritty sandstones of the Table Mountain sandstone series. They consist principally of soft micaceous deposits of various colours, abounding in fossil trilobites and other *Devonian* forms of extinct marine mollusca. Numerous Devonian fossils occur in argillaceous shales which rest on the Bokkeveld beds in the *second belt of mountains.* **1920** E.H.L. SCHWARZ *Thirstland Redemption* 41 The rocks from which the sediments were derived were old sandstones and slates of the Table Mountain and Bokkeveld series. **1972** J.H. WELLINGTON in *Std Encycl. of Sn Afr.* V. 163 The Cape System comprises three main lithological units: the Table Mountain Series, the Bokkeveld and the Witteberg Series ... In the Bokkeveld Series, which has a thickness of about 750 metres in the type area, the succession consists of 5 thicker shale beds alternating with 4 thinner sand-stones, the series forming most of the lower ground in the Cape topography. **1972** E.P. PLUMSTEAD in *Std Encycl. of Sn Afr.* V. 8 Early Lycopodiales like *Leptophloem* .. are found .. in the upper Bokkeveld beds, especially near Grahamstown. **1976** A.R. WILLCOX *Sn Land* 43 In Bokkeveld times (late Silurian or early Devonian) plant life crept ashore. **1988** SMUTS & ALBERTS *Forgotten Highway* 21 To the north the circle is completed by the outlying hills of the Cold Bokkeveld, which are crossed .. by a route .. to that desert gate of the Bokkeveld Karoo well named Karoo Poort.

Hence **Bokkevelder** *n.*, one from the Bokkeveld.

1957 L.G. GREEN *Beyond City Lights* 144 Lichtenstein noted the strength and active habits of the Bokkevelders, and put it down to the healthy climate.

bokkie /ˈbɔki/ *n.* [Afk., kid, *bok* antelope, goat + -IE.]

All senses are more common in speech than in written contexts.

1. *colloq.* An affectionate form of address, usu. for a woman; as a common noun, a girl(friend). See also BOK sense 3 a.

1959 A. MEIRING *Candle in Wind* 113 Someone bumped into her. 'Sorry, Bokkie,' he said, leering at her. 'Where are you going, Bokkie?' he asked. **1963** A.M. LOUW *20 Days* 91 'No, no, bokkie .. ,' he said imploringly. 'I didn't mean that. Come, come and let me love you.' **1963** A. FUGARD *Blood Knot* (1968) 115 Morris: .. Now imagine, if there was a woman, and you want to say something to her, what would you say? Go on. Zach: Cookie .. or .. Bokkie. **1977** D. MULLER *Whitey* 81 She .. laid her head against his chest. 'Not now, Bokkie,' she said softly. 'I'm so tired. Please let me go.' **1980** E. PATEL *They Came at Dawn* 48 Can't you see that blerry whitey, met a black bokkie? .. See them kissing. **1982** D. KRAMER *Short Back & Sides* 61, I need new tyres, need new shocks, Need to phone my bokkie from that tickey box. **1988** [see GOOI sense 1 b]. **1990** R. GOOL *Cape Town Coolie* 59, I 'eard you living in the Cape now ... Ow's all those Coloured *bokkies*? **1990** [see GOOSIE sense 2].

2. A small antelope; a small goat. See also BOK senses 1 a and 2.

1975 S. ROBERTS *Outside Life's Feast* 90 She stood soft. A bokkie. Afraid. Listening to me with round eyes. **1993** D. SÜLTER *Informant, Grahamstown* It's obviously translated from Afrikaans. They talk about some bokkie and its 'antlers'.

3. A member of the South African Infantry (SAI); the flash and headdress badge (depicting a springbok) of this unit. Cf. SPRINGBOK senses 2 b and 5.

1975 J.H. PICARD in *Eng. Usage in Sn Afr.* Vol.6 No.1, 36 During exercises there is a wealth of typically Afrikaans-inspired English military jargon in evidence: the infantry are called *bokkies* as a term of endearment, whilst the 'scorn term' is *bokkoppe* toting *ketties* (rifles). **1985** W. STEENKAMP in *Cape Times* 17 July, The Army seems to have a thing about shrinking headdress badges, even though these are potent tools for generating unit spirit. The Infantry Corps used to wear a large 'bokkie' which is now half its previous size and almost invisible.

bokking, bokkom, bokkum varr. BOKKEM.

bokmakierie /ˈbɒkməˌkiri, ˈbɔk-, -ma-/ *n.* Formerly also **bac(k)bakiri, back-my-keerie, bakbakiri, beckbecary, bekmakeri, bok-bok-makirie, bokmakary, bok-ma-keirie, bokmakeri(e), bok-makerij, bokmakerrie, bokmakir(r)i(e).** [S. Afr. Du., onomatopoeic: imitative of the call of the male bird and the immediate response of the female.] A large green, yellow, and black shrike, *Telophorus zeylonus* of the Malaconotidae; KOKKEWIET sense b. Also *attrib.*

1834 *Cape of G.H. Lit. Gaz.* Apr. 52 A rivulet .. flows through it [*sc.* the Kloof] with a trickling murmur that mingles well with the .. cry of the beckbecary, and the twittering of the graceful sugar-birds. *a***1839** C.W. SMITH *Christopher Webb Smith* (1965) 22 Bokmakary Thrush. **1852** T. PRINGLE in Godlonton & Irving *Narr. of Kaffir War of 1850–51–52* 247 Pleasant the rest under the orange boughs — to listen to the cry of the *buck-my-keerie* (whip-poor-will). **1856** R.E.E. WILMOT *Diary* (1984) 131 The wonderful duet which the cock and hen bokmakierie keep up will most assuredly attract his notice as he wanders among the protea groves of Wynberg and Claremont. **1867** E.L. LAYARD *Birds of S. Afr.* 161 *Bacbakiri* ... Its loud call of 'bacbakiri', its imitative powers, and bright plumage, render it one of the most conspicuous birds of the colony. **1888** *Cape Punch* 4 Apr. 203 Do you see those bokmakiries? Do you hear their melody? **1908** HAAGNER & IVY *Sketches* 98 The well-known Bakbakiri .. is easily recognisable by its yellow and green plumage and black chest-band. [**1910** D. FAIRBRIDGE *That Which Hath Been* (1913) 106 Overhead a green and yellow bird cried 'Bok, bok, bok,' to a distant mate, whose melodious response, 'makeri, makeri,' echoed dreamily through the warm air.] *c***1933** J. JUTA in A.C. Partridge *Lives, Lett. & Diaries* (1971) 153 The haunt of .. the brilliant *Bokmakierie*, golden, yellow and black, with a ringing clear call, sung in duets by the inseparable pairs but sounding like a single voice. **1937** M. ALSTON *Wanderings* 36 The green and gold of the bakbakiri shrike shone from many a fence. **1949** L.G. GREEN *In Land of Afternoon* 106 In the English countryside the peacock's cry announces changing weather; in the Cape the call to heed is that of the bokmakierie. **1983** K.B. NEWMAN *Newman's Birds* 380 *Bokmakierie, Telophorus zeylonus.* Common resident ... The calls are duets between both sexes and are variable, e.g. 'bok-makiri', 'kok-o-vit', 'bok-bok-chit', 'wit, wit-wit' or 'pirrapee-pirrapoo', each sequence repeated at about three-second intervals. **1987** J. QUEST *Burning River* 14 Two bokmakieries tok-tokked and kwirred at each other outside. **1990** *Weekly Mail* 4 May 21 Since Tuesday, the country's external radio service has been broadcasting only to Africa, the rest of the .. world catching its doleful call sign — the call of the bokmakierie .. — only by .. chance.

bokom var. BOKKEM.

Bokveld var. BOKKEVELD.

Boland /ˈbuəlant/ *n.* Formerly also **Bovenland.** [Afk. (earlier S. Afr. Du. *bovenland*), *bo* upper + *land* land, region; an area of the Western Cape.] Usu. *attrib.*, designating places in and characteristic of the area of the Western Cape lying to the west of the Hex River Mountains.

[**1822** W.J. BURCHELL *Trav.* I. 88 Over the whole colony the words *boven* (upper), and *boven-land*, are used to signify those parts of it which are nearer to Cape Town, and often Cape Town itself; while *onder* (under), and *onderveld*, are the terms applied in contradistinction.] **1950** H.C. BOSMAN in S. Gray *Makapan's Caves* (1987) 141, I think of a little Boland dorp with white houses and water furrows at the side of the streets and oak-trees. **1968** H. FRANSEN in D.J. Opperman *Spirit of Vine* 200 We arrive at the typical Boland wine cellar: a long thatched building .. next to the homestead .. grouped with the other outbuildings on the *werf* and provided with gables like the dwelling.

Hence **Bolander** *n.*, one who lives in, or comes from, the Boland.

1934 G.G. MUNNIK *Mem. of Senator* 115 The woman .. said, 'You dirty Bolander, do you beat my husband?' **1972** *Sunday Times* 15 Oct. (Mag. Sect.) 14 They portray glimpses of farming practices, social usages and habits of life that set the Bolanders apart from the rest of Afrikanerdom. **1977** *Cape Times* 23 Dec. 8 The Bolanders, the Kapenaars, too, one could say, have learnt to live with it for some ten generations now. **1985** *S. Afr. Panorama* May 7 The Bolanders (uplanders) have been cultivating the vine for three centuries.

bolermakissie var. BOLLEMAKIESIE.

‖**bolla** /ˈbɔla/ *n.* [Afk., bun (hair-style), ad. Du. *bol* ball, pate, crown of a hat.]

1. *colloq.* Hair worn in a bun. Also **bollatjie** /-ki/ [see -IE].

1971 G. BAYMAN on Springbok Radio 2 Feb., Bolla — the bun worn at the back of the head by Cape Malay women. **1973** *Cape Times* 8 May 7 A time not so long ago, when the 'onion look' was in vogue. A tight little *bollatjie* of hair at the top of the *kop*. Enough to make you cry. **1983** P.-D. UYS in *Sunday Times* 18 Sept. 6 The Japanese are very small and I can't wear heels or my bolla here.

2. KOSSITER.

1979 HEARD & FAULL *Our Best Trad. Recipes* 96 When Malays speak of koeksisters they mean bollas. These are made like koeksisters but are round and rolled in sugar and green and red coconut.

bollemakiesie /ˈbɔləmaˌkisi, -mə-/ *adv.* and *n.* *Colloq.* Also **bolermakissie, bol(la)makiesie.** [Afk., somersault; *bolle* fr. Du. *bol* (see prec.) + *makiesie* orig. unkn.]

A. *adv. fig.* Head over heels, somersaulting.

*c***1929** S. BLACK in S. Gray *Three Plays* (1984) 102 Van K: He's gone Home. Sailed on the mailboat. Bunked. Lady M: Bunked? Van K: Yes and I'm bunkered. Stymied. Off-side. Bolermakissie. **1985** D. KRAMER in *Cosmopolitan* May 102 Anita Kriel lived next door. She was in matric and I was probably in Standard 2 or 3 when I fell bollemakiesie in love with her. **1991** —— on M-Net TV 3 Apr., It went bollamakiesie over the telephone wires.

B. *n.* A somersault. Also *fig.*

1970 H.M. MUSMECI *Informant, Port Elizabeth* Look at the children turning bolmakiesies on the lawn. **1970** S. SPARKS *Informant, Fort Beaufort* The children were doing bollemakiesies on the grass. (Head-over-heels.) **1971** *Informant, Grahamstown*, I can do bollamakiesie backwards. **1975** S. GRAY *Local Colour* 40 Remember the old days you and the oubaas played bolmakiesies with the garden shears and my auntie put Dettol on your toes, the good old days. **1993** *Daily News* 14 Jan. 12 If the CP did become involved in planning talks and then multi-party negotiations, it would be a very public admission that it was wrong. 'The price of this bollemakiesie is: "Koos, you were right. So were you, Koos ... So were you Andries, Chris, [etc.]" That means a helluva climb-down,' said Mr van der Merwe.

Hence (*nonce*) **bollemakies** *v. intrans.*, to turn somersaults.

1982 J. KRIGE in *Staffrider* Vol.5 No.2, 20 They would play all over the farm whether it was bollemakissing from the rafters into the haystack or mucking about in the cowsheds.

‖**boloyi** /bɔˈlɔːji/ *n.* [S. Sotho, fr. *loya* to bewitch.] Witchcraft. Cf. TAGATI *n.* sense 3. See also MOLOI.

1987 *Pace* Oct. 4 Whoever said whites don't believe in the nefarious practice that darkies zealously indulge in when everybody is asleep. Ag man! You know mos what I mean — boloyi (witchcraft).

boma /ˈbəʊmə, ˈbɔːmə, -ə/ n.¹ [East Afr. Eng., fr. Swahili, stockade, enclosure; specific and extended senses have developed in S. Afr. Eng.] An enclosure.

1. A thorny fence or defensive barrier.

Also *East Afr. Eng.*

1906 H. RIDER HAGGARD *Benita* 244 To leave their camp was not easy, since they had made a thorn boma round it, to protect them in case the Makalanga should make a night sally. 1990 J. HEALE *Scowler's Luck* 34 Mrs van Wyk had scurried her girls into finding enough thorny branches to build a 'boma' for defence.

2. An open, usu. circular, fenced space in the REST CAMP of a game reserve or safari lodge, used for meals and social gatherings; LAPA n. sense 2.

1968 M. DOYLE *Impala* 55 The flames shot up, illuminating the curved reed wall of the *boma* and the trunk of the shadowing ironwood tree. 1980 *Signature* July 16 It opened in 1975 with four small rondawels, a drop loo in a 'boma' and a shower which was a rose stuck on the end of a hosepipe lodged in a tree on a hillside. 1988 *Fair Lady* 22 June (Suppl.) 34 It's back to the comfort of your cottage, .. and a later dinner around the fire in the dramatic setting of the reed-enclosed boma. 1990 L. VAN HOVEN in *S. Afr. Panorama* May-June 27 Food and drink .. taste just that much better when served in the boma (traditional reed shelter) around a huge, smouldering fire.

3.a. A stockaded enclosure in which game animals are kept for their protection.

Also *East Afr. Eng.*

1971 *Grocott's Mail* 8 June 3 The recently-acquired buffalo male and female from Addo have made their home in a kloof near the reserve picnic area, although they revisit the boma each night. 1982 *E. Prov. Herald* 16 Aug. 3 A ranger said yesterday the elephants would be kept in a boma for a while before being released. 1988 *S. Afr. Panorama* May 18 Capturing game on a ranch near Swartwater in the northern Transvaal. Game lots are rounded up by helicopter and driven into a boma. 1990 *Daily Dispatch* 19 July 8 The hippos' natural feeding area beside their water habitat has fenced off and they were attracted with food through an opening into a boma.

b. With distinguishing epithet: **cattle-boma**, an enclosure for cattle; also called KRAAL (n. sense 3 a).

Also *East Afr. Eng.*

1973 *The 1820* Vol.46 No.9, 36 Many ancient Zulu traditions will survive. You can tell the number of wives a man has by counting the huts surrounding his cattle-boma.

4. *fig.* A mental or social barrier. Cf. LAAGER n. sense 4.

1988 J. MICHELL in *Style* Mar. 46 Privileged people who gallop ahead of the herd are compelled to construct barriers and admit only the trusted few. Within her mental boma the chosen meet an entirely different Jessie. 1990 *Sunday Times* 27 May (Mag. Sect.) 20 Excited readers in London provoked the jackals at home to bay for his blood from their Calvinist bomas and in South Africa the book was banned.

boma /ˈbɔːma, ˈbɔːmə, ˈbəʊmə/ n.² Also **bhoma**, and (*sing.* only) **iboma**. Pl. **ama-** /ama-/. [Xhosa *ibhoma* fruit orchard, used erroneously in Xhosa instead of *ibhuma* seclusion hut. In S. Afr. Eng., this usage is reinforced by confusion with BOMA n.¹] The seclusion hut or lodge occupied during CIRCUMCISION rituals by initiates from the same clan.

1963 WILSON & MAFEJE *Langa* 106 The essential acts .. are (i) purification .. ; (ii) seclusion and circumcision in a *boma* 'built in the bush'; (iii) the burning of the *boma*, purification, feasting, and admonition ... An initiate's hut, a *boma*, is built beforehand. 1964 G. GORDON *Four People* 16 When his uncle had buried the little piece of skin .. and had dressed the wound .. Philemon, now an umkhwetha, entered the *boma*. 1976 R.L. PETENI *Hill of Fools* 122 Bhuqa and five other boys of his age-group entered the circumcision school or went to the forest ... The bhoma in which they were to live for about three months was hidden from their village but was within easy reach of it. 1989 *Weekend Post* 9 Dec. 7 (caption) *Abakwetha* .. next to their *iboma* (hut). *Ibid.* Once initiation is complete, their clothing and *amaboma* (huts) are burnt, and new clothes are put on to signify the start of adult life.

bombela /bɒmˈbelə, bɒmˈbe(ː)la/ n. Also **bombella**, **mbombela**, and with initial capital. [Unkn.; prob. Zulu *bombela* head for (a foreign place), perh. rel. to *ibombo* direction or bearings one takes on journeying.] Either of two types of transportation carrying black migrant workers between home and work:

a. A (railway) bus.

1934 R.M. AGAR-O'CONNELL in Stokes & Wilter *Veld Trails* 109 Twelve months' exile at the mines and in the train and *bombela* (railway 'bus). 1949 L. HUNTER *Afr. Dawn* 99, I would have been able to get home today but the *bombela* was very late owing to trouble on the road. 1952 H. KLEIN *Land of Silver Mist* 28 One of the huge railway road motor service buses, called 'bombelas' by the Natives throughout South Africa, drew up outside the store in a cloud of dust. Pondos, homeward bound from a spell on the Rand gold mines, climbed out.

b. A train; more recently, a commuter train. Also *attrib.*

1964 G. GORDON *Four People* 261 Hundreds of them .. hastily bundled their blankets, clothing and other belongings and caught the 'mbombela', or workers' train, home to the Transkei. 1970 G. WESTWOOD *Bright Wilderness* 8 All those who were grown up found it more profitable to go to a recruiting office and join the Bombella train, that took them to Egoli, Johannesburg, the city of gold. 1980 B. LESHOAI in M. Mutloatse *Forced Landing* 130 The third class Mbombela coaches were crammed with other men from Lesotho and the Cape. 1988 D.P. KUNENE in Bunn & Taylor *From S. Afr.* 406 She went to the station whenever the *bombela* train was coming, either with its new recruits from farther south, or with the weary returned ones who had just completed the *joyini* of twelve months or more. 1990 [see PASS sense 2]. 1990 *Weekly Mail* 21 Sept. 9 Back in the Fifties a few people did leap out of windows when *tsotsis* terrorised the *bombelas* that connected the various Orlandos (before the acronym Soweto was coined) with Jo'burg. Those raids were .. just plain criminal, as were the two last week on the same trains.

bombing *vbl* n. *Music.* [See quot. 1980.] Nguni male-voice choral work incorporating the forceful singing of chords, a stylistic effect characteristic of (esp. early forms of) MBUBE. Also *attrib.* See also NGUNI n. sense 1 a.

1957 D. RYCROFT in *Afr. Music* Vol.1 No.4, 33 One of the oddest and loudest forms of African noise to be heard nightly in some of the larger South African towns is described by its makers as 'Zulu Male Traditional Singing' .. when speaking to non-Zulus. Such singing, by small, all male, choirs and the restrained kind of strutting dance or slouch which goes with it is, however, a new tradition ... Among the singers themselves it is called 'Bombing' ... The conductor .. executes vigorous and precisely timed signals, both manual and vocal, for the attack of each choral yell. Explosive fortissimo chords result ... Any evening .. in Johannesburg, small groups of Bombing enthusiasts are to be heard rehearsing. 1978 [see INGOMA BUSUKU]. 1980 D.B. COPLAN *Urbanization of African Performing Arts.* 335 Zulu and Swazi migrants .. expressed their new urban identity in *ingoma ebusuku* competitions. During the 1940's the competing groups were known as 'bombing' choirs: their .. choral yells were intended to sound like the wartime aircraft shown on bioscope newsreels ... 'Bombing' was an urban but non-Western form.

bomshoza pl. form of MSHOZA.

Bomvana /ˌbɒmˈvɑːnə, ˌbɒmˈvɑːna/ n. Pl. unchanged, **ama-** /ama-/, or **-s**. [fr. the name of the clan's first leader, *Bomvana* 'little brownish one'.] A member of an Nguni people speaking a dialect of Xhosa and living mainly in the Transkei (now the north-eastern part of the Eastern Cape). Also *attrib.*

1828 W. SHAW *Diary.* 29 June, The tribes beyond the Bashee to the Umtata, near the coast are called Amabomvana, .. together they form a considerable body of people, but seem to possess less spirit and activity than the Caffres, and they are comparatively a poor people. 1901 *Natives of S. Afr.* (S. Afr. Native Races Committee) 14 The Xesibese in Matatiele; the Bomvanas in Elliotdale; the Bechuanas in Griqualand West. 1952 H. KLEIN *Land of Silver Mist* 31 Every writer on Pondoland, all of whom have been intrigued by the origin of the pale-skinned Abelungu who are scattered in the rugged hill country of the Bomvanas. 1970 *Std Encycl. of Sn Afr.* II. 405 The Bomvanas originally belonged to a larger Xhosa tribe, the Amatshezi, but were driven out of Pondoland early in the 19th century, and were thus separated from the main body of their people. 1972 *Daily Dispatch* 10 Aug. 14 A very pretentious Bomvana Once slipped on a piece of banana. 1973 *Evening Post* 27 Jan. 2 The juvenile Prophetess, Nongquase, who had been protected, was conducted to the Great Place of Moni, .. Chief of the Bomvana people residing beyond the Bashee River. 1981 *Bona* Jan. 22 By becoming chieftainess of the Amabomvana tribe, she automatically becomes a member of the Transkeian Parliament.

boncella var. BONSELLA.

bond /bɒnd/ n.¹ [Shortened form of *mortgage bond*.] The usual term for a mortgage. Also *attrib.* See also KUSTINGBRIEF.

Used also in *Scot. Eng.*

1827 *Reports of Commissioners upon Finances at Cape of G.H.* II. 103 The bank was authorized from these sources to discount at six per cent per annum the vendue rolls, .. and private bonds called 'kustings'. 1904 *Argus Christmas Annual* (Competitions Sect.) p.vii, Money was borrowed, and when the building was finished the family were soon domiciled therein, it being found that the interest on the 'Bond,' as the mortgage was called, amounted to less than a rent would be. 1937 [see below]. 1944 G. DENOON in *S. Afr. Law Jrnl* 287 In 1823 transfer and bond forms were translated into English ... As no exact equivalent for kustingbrief was found in English, the translated kustingbrief forms were also headed 'Mortgage Bond'. 1990 [see HELPER]. 1992 A. HOGGE on Radio South Africa 14 May (Radio Today), That would suggest a drop in interest across the board — including our bond rates? 1992 *Sunday Times* 16 Aug. (Business Times) 1 Others will use the spare cash to .. pay off their bonds faster. 1992 *Weekly Mail* 4 Sept. 6 Ducking any questions on the bond boycott, the Association of Mortgage Lenders would say only that a meeting was to be held today. 1993 E.M. JOYCE *Informant*, Port Elizabeth Sold his house on Show House on Sun[day] for the R162,000 ... Hope it all goes off without a hitch as the house buyer must get a Bond but only for approx. R90,000. It will be pos[sib]ly end May before he gives occupation. 1994 *Style* Oct. 22 My investment advisor .. cost me marginally less than the bond on my home. *Ibid.* 31 An abnormally huge monthly bond repayment on the triple-storey building.

Hence **bond** *v. trans.*, to mortgage (a property); also *passive*, and *transf.* (of the mortgagor).

1937 C.R. PRANCE *Tante Rebella's Saga* 124 Those golden days of backveld trade are gone. The Land Bank took over most of the old bonds, and the new settler is for the most part bonded up to his neck from the start. 1960 J. COPE *Tame Ox* 26 The farm was already bonded, but the lawyer Kalk gave Nico credit to put up a wind-pump and buy sheep.

Bond /bɒnd, bɔnt/ n.² [Afk., league, fellowship.]
1. *hist.* Shortened form of AFRIKANDER BOND. Also *attrib.*

1886 *Pall Mall Gaz.* (U.K.) 22 Apr. 3 Whether the continued affiliation of the Bond beyond the boundary of the colony was advisable. 1897 F.R. STATHAM *S.*

Afr. as It Is 141 The Bond was not long in claiming equal treatment for the English and Dutch languages, and succeeded in making its claim good. **1909** LADY S. WILSON *S. Afr. Mem.* 2 At the Cape the Bond party grew so strong it bid fair to elbow out the English altogether. **1919** M.M. STEYN *Diary* 267 Because of .. pernicious pandering to the ignorant portion of our people, by those who should know better, I refuse to join the Bond, alias the South African Party. **1936** *Cambridge Hist. of Brit. Empire* VIII. 630 Mr Merriman and the South African Party, the name which the Bond had adopted in 1903, were returned to power with large majorities in both houses. **1946** T. MACDONALD *Ouma Smuts* 13 Isie Krige heard the greybeards talking on the stoep about Cecil John Rhodes, the Englishman, and about Jan Hofmeyr of the Cape Dutch Bond. **1974** D. ROOKE *Margaretha de la Porte* 131 The Bond had been formed in the Cape, originally to promote the use of the Dutch language but now was directed towards bringing about union in South Africa.

2.a. Shortened form of BROEDERBOND. Also *attrib.*

1950 H. GIBBS *Twilight* 200 Its critics state that the Broederbond seeks to gain control of South Africa. So does the Bond. **1972** *Argus* 16 Sept. 1 In a 90-minute attack on the Broederbond, the chairman of the HNP, Mr Jan J–, became the first ex-member to divulge Bond secrets. **1972** *Sunday Times* 24 Sept. 17 Membership of the Bond is restricted to White males over 25 who must be Afrikaans-speaking, Protestant, and professing members of one of the three Afrikaner churches. **1982** *E. Prov. Herald* 30 June 2 Professor Terblanche said: 'I think it is quite possible that the Broederbond will split and if it splits that will be the end of the bond, of course.' **1990** D. VAN HEERDEN in *Sunday Times* 17 June 12 Documents circulated among branches tried to pave the way for radical changes but even the Bond seems to have been caught napping by the speed and the extent of the F W revolution.

b. *comb.* **Bondsraad** /-rɑːt/ [Afk., linking phoneme *-s-* + *raad* council], the general congress of the Broederbond. Also *attrib.*

1972 *Sunday Times* 23 Apr. 3 The Broederbond's *Bondsraad* (general congress) was specially convened to elect a successor to Dr. Piet Meyer. **1978** *Ibid.* 8 Oct. 1 About 1000 delegates from all over South Africa attended the biennial Bondsraad meeting on the farm on Tuesday.

Hence **Bondite** *n. rare*, a member of the Afrikander Bond: BONDSMAN.

1898 *Daily News* 23 July 5 Bondites are largely influenced in the adoption of obstructive tactics by the desire to obtain the maximum parliamentary allowance.

Bondel /ˈbɔndəl/ *n.* Shortened form of BONDELSWART. Also *attrib.*

1922 *Report of Administration on the Bondelzwarts Rising* (UG30–1922) 14 On approaching Guruchas we were met and stopped by three Bondels one of whom was armed with a mauser rifle and a bandolier of cartridges. **1936** *Cambridge Hist. of Brit. Empire* VIII. 697 Both the official and the Namaqua captain were shot, and this was the signal for the rising of the Bondels tribe. **1971** J.A. BROWN *Return* 16 Would anyone choose to live in such a God-forsaken land? Even the Nama did not live there by choice and the Witboois and Bondels had all come from the south .. driven out of better lands. **1990** K. PATHER in *Cue* 5 July 2 Abraham Morris .. is the Bondel leader who returns from exile across the Orange River. In response to 'destroy the Bondels' – a 1922 South African campaign .., Morris leads his people into rebellion.

Bondelswart /ˈbɔn(d)əlswart, -swɑːt/ *n.* Also **Bondelswaart**, **Bondelzwa(a)rt**, **Bondle Zwa(a)rt**, **Bundelswaart**. Pl. unchanged, or -s. [Afk., earlier S. Afr. Du., fr. Du. *bondel* bundle + *zwart* black.] A member of a Nama people living in Namibia and Namaqualand, and originally one of the Oorlam groups (see OORLAM *n.* sense 2); BONDEL. Also *attrib.* See also NAMA *n.* sense 1.

The members of this people called themselves *Gami-nun* or *Kami-nun*.

1826 R. HADDY in B. Shaw *Memorials* (1841) 167 To-day the chief of the Bondle Zwaart, .. from the Warm Bath, Great Namacqua-land, visited us. *a***1838** A. SMITH *Jrnl* (1975) 291 He is commonly known by the name of *Abram* and his tribe is denominated Kamiquis or *Bondel Zwart*. **1838** J.E. ALEXANDER *Exped. into Int.* I. 125 Here I now found .. the chief Abram, of the Bondelzwart (bundle of blacks) Namaquas. **1842** J. TINDALL *Jrnl* (1959) 41 Missionaries are wanted; not one of the above-named tribes is supplied except the Bondelswarts. **1877** *Sel. Comm. Report on Mission to Damaraland* 102 The Bondelzwaarts' territory has an area of 15,000 square miles, .. and this estimate does not include the veldt occupied by either the Afrikaaners, or the Bastards. **1887** A.A. ANDERSON *25 Yrs in Waggon* I. 256 The inhabitants are of various tribes, called the Namaquas, Veld-scoondrawers, Bundelswaarts, Hottentots. **1922** *Report of Administration on the Bondelzwarts Rising* (UG30–1922) 1 With the close of the Rebellion against the German Government certain leaders of the Bondelzwarts were proscribed from further residence in this Territory [*sc.* Namibia] and betook themselves to the north-western portion of the Cape. **1928** E.H.L. SCHWARZ *Kalahari & its Native Races* 194 Many half-breeds occur throughout South West Africa, the Bondelswarts, for instance. These were Oorlams, or people who had gone down to the Cape in the early days and had become contaminated with white blood. **1943** D. REITZ *No Outspan* 93 The area we passed through is inhabited by the Bondelswart tribe of Hottentots. **1966** J.P. VAN S. BRUWER *S.W. Afr.: Disputed Land* 20 There were also the Gaminun or Bondelswarts just north of the Orange River, and the Nara-nin or Topnaars in the area of the lower Kuiseb River. **1973** J. COPE *Alley Cat* 80 They were superstitious, though Jonkman, a Bondelswart, half white, prayed and read his Bible by the fire at night. **1982** *Voice* 18 July 9 One German author described the Bondelzwarts as: 'Skilful horsemen, slightly built, almost unbeatable in field duty and accurate marksmen'. **1987** B. LAU *Namibia in Jonker Afrikaner's Time* 5 The other brothers founded the *!Kami≠nûn* or *Bondelswarts*, the *‖Haboben* or *Veldskoendraers*, .. and the *‖Khau/gôan* or *Swaartboois*. **1990** K. PATHER in *Cue* 5 July 2 The play takes as its focus the resistance of the Bondelswarts people of Southern Namibia.

bondhoek var. PONDOK.

Bondle Zwa(a)rt var. BONDELSWART.

Bondsman /ˈbɒndsmən, ˈbɔnts-/ *n. hist.* Also **Bondman**. [Afk. *bond* see BOND *n.*[2] + linking phoneme *-s-* + Eng. *man*.] A member of the AFRIKANDER BOND; *Bondite*, see BOND *n.*[2].

1884 *Times* (U.K.) 6 Mar. 7 The views of many members returned to Parliament as Bondsmen. **1885** LADY BELLAIRS *Tvl at War* 412 Half of the seventy-four members of the present House of the Cape Parliament are Bondsmen, having the power of framing the laws. **1898** *Daily News* 22 Mar. 5 Two Progressives were elected, and one Bondman. **1900** *Grocott's Penny Mail* 11 July, For a Bondsman, he is a decent fellow, of no real political ability, and simply foisted on two Governments. **1936** E.C. LLEWELLYN *Influence of Low Dutch* 71 The adherents or members of the Afrikander bond were known as *Bondsmen*. **1971** L.H. THOMPSON in *Oxford Hist. of S. Afr.* II. 304 The Bond never had a majority in the House of Assembly and, although individual Bondsmen sat in cabinets, no Bondsman was ever Prime Minister.

So (*rare*) **Bondswoman** *n.*.

1921 W.C. SCULLY *Harrow* 59 These papers show why you are being sent; these papers show you to be a Bondswoman, a rebel and a traitor.

bone *n.* [Special senses of general Eng.]

1. DOLOS sense 1. Usu. in *pl.*

1849 J.D. LEWINS Diary. 3 Oct., Consulted for fun the Mantatee doctor with his bones, who for a sixpence told me as many lies as he spoke words. **1898** B. MITFORD *Induna's Wife* 38 Now cast me 'the bones', Lalusini, that I might know what success, if any, lieth before me. **1929** J. STEVENSON-HAMILTON *Low-Veld* 221 For 'smelling out' purposes it is nowadays usual for witch doctors to invoke the assistance of 'the bones.' **1936** WILLIAMS & MAY *I Am Black* 147 Gugugu the witch-doctor .. read the omens by fire, by the gall of an ox, by bones, and by many potent medicines. **1946** S. CLOETE *Afr. Portraits* 224 We have cast the bones and they say that she is guilty. **1958** — *Mask* 89 The future is foretold by the manner in which the bones fall ... The bone which represents .. the thrower, is the knuckle joint of the aardvark or antbear ... The knuckle bone of a hyena represents the forefathers ... The beak of a vulture or eagle gives direction ... Each bone has four positions. Upright means walking, upside down means sick or dead, falling on the left side means resting or watchful. On the right, since this is the assegai or striking arm, means that the person whose fortune is being told is helpless and in danger. **1964** [see DOEKUM]. **1968** COLE & FLAHERTY *House of Bondage* 153 If the bones indicate that the patient suffers a tormented spirit, .. the case is beyond the Herbalist's competence and he passes it on to .. the diviner. **1974** C.T. BINNS *Warrior People* 261 There is a wide variety in the bones themselves, but basically they consist of astragalus bones, to which there may be added the claw of a lion, .. cowrie shells or the bones of a bird. Each bone has its own particular praise name. **1974** *Drum* 8 Apr. 32 'Let lightning smite me in two .. if these my bones should ever tell even half a lie,' and old Dabula wipes the sweat from his furrowed brow. **1980** A.J. BLIGNAUT *Dead End Rd* 74 He had studied the lie of the bones in the sand where they had come to rest as he shook them out of his meerkat-skin pouch. **1987** *Personality* 21 Oct. 12 Monica went through the ceremony of blowing on the bones. Then .. she told me my bones were 'healthy'.

2. *comb.* (objective) **bone-thrower** *n.*, a diviner; **bone-throwing**, **bone-tossing** *vbl ns*, divining. See also *to throw (the) bones* (THROW sense 2).

1917 S.T. PLAATJE *Native Life* 323 The lower middle-class Boers attach great weight to the guesses of native **bonethrowers**. **1955** D.C. THEMBA in J. Crwys-Williams *S. Afr. Despatches* (1989) 323 If the bone-thrower says he'll show up the bastard who's been slinging lightning at me, I expect him to swing that bolt of lightning right back. **1971** P. BECKER on Radio South Africa 14 Nov., People like diviners and bone-throwers, prophets and exorcisers of evil spirits. **1980** M. MELAMU in M. Mutloatse *Forced Landing* 51, I don't see that I matter so much for Georgina to take the trouble of going to a *nyanga* on my account. If she goes to bone-throwers, that's her own *indaba*. **1980** A.G.T.K. MALIKONGWA in *Staffrider* Vol.3 No.1, 34 He is .. a great bone thrower. His bones speak with great precision. **1967** *Post* 23 July 15 The young pretty sangoma has made her **bone-throwing** business one of the most successful in the country. **1982** P. WILHELM in *Staffrider* Vol.5 No.1, 19 This is not a war of bone-throwing, Comrade Bula. This is the twentieth century. We fight with guns, not spears. **1939** M. RORKE *Melina Rorke* 114 The blowing and **bone-tossing** went on for about a quarter of an hour.

boney /ˈbəʊni/ *n. slang.* Also **bony**. [Prob. formed on Eng. *boneshaker* bicycle without rubber tyres, decrepit vehicle + (informal) n.-forming suffix *-y*.] A bicycle; a motor-cycle.

1970 J.R. BENNETT *Informant, Krugersdorp* Bony: Bicycle. This bony rides lekker. **1976** *Bike S. Afr.* Oct., When your bony is mif and dirty do you .. get *the moer in*? **1983** A. GOLDSTUCK in *Frontline* Oct. 58 Screaming along on a souped-up boney with your goose holding on tightly was a social statement. **1984** W. STEVENSON in *Sunday Times* 29 Jan. (Life Style) 9 We don't want heavy ous in our club. They mustn't have a criminal record and they must have boneys bigger than 750cc. **1991** C. SAMMY *Informant, Adelaide (E. Cape)* Boney: Bicycle. **1992** [see SMAAK].

bonga *n. obs.* [fr. Xhosa and Zulu verb, see BONGA *v.*; in Xhosa and Zulu the noun form is *isibongo* (pl. *izibongo*), see ISIBONGO.] In the context of traditional African society: declamatory praise. Also *attrib.* See also ISIBONGO sense 2.

1898 B. MITFORD *Induna's Wife* 14 The roars of *bonga* which greeted his appearance mingled with the howling of the gang of witch doctors and the shouting and blows of the royal guard. *Ibid.* 135, I understood the ways of kings, .. and so, disarming, I crept forward, the words of *bonga* rolling out thick and fast the while.

||**bonga** /ˈbɔːŋga/ *v.* [Xhosa and Zulu.] See also IMBONGI. Esp. in the context of traditional African society:

1.a. *trans.* To laud or to criticize (someone, something, or some action), through the medium of declaimed poetry.

1937 [see sense 2]. **1959** L. LONGMORE *Dispossessed* 100 The bride sat down and an old man, her grandfather's brother, stood up to bonga her with izibongo, that is, to laud her with her praises. **1970** M. KUNENE *Zulu Poems* 13 African .. poets did not only praise socially approved acts, but condemned socially repugnant ones as well. The word '*bonga*' (to praise) .. is exchangeable with the word condemn.

b. *intrans.* To perform a declamatory poem.

1983 *Grocott's Mail* 18 Mar. 14 The Xhosas love and respect their poets. In the old days when the chief's council was stuck with a difficult issue, the 'mbongi' would be called to 'bonga' loudly.

2. *comb.* **bonga-name**, praise name. See also ISIBONGO sense 1.

1937 B.H. DICKE *Bush Speaks* 35 After the konza-names come 'bonga'-names (praise-names) which are mostly animal names.

bongo var. MBONGO.

bongolo /ˈbɔŋgɔlɔ/ *n.* Also **bongol(a)**. [Xhosa and Zulu *imbongolo* mule, donkey.] A mule.

1911 *Queenstown Weekly Review* 25 Nov. (Pettman), [He] has been appointed one of the official Judges of the South African Judges Association, his speciality being mules, and none knows a *bongolo*. **1918** C. GARSTIN *Sunshine Settlers* 114 'Picanin', said Umsuaz, who is a linguist, and has the English. 'Old missus *bongola* go way in bush; by'm-by come back along picanin *bongola*'. **1947** C.R. PRANCE *Antic Mem.* 100 The Rustenburg O.C. Transport was ordered to assemble all his bongolas in a kraal where each in turn was to be thrown, hobbled, gagged, saddled, and tried-out for remount duty by hard-case bronco-busters. **1965** P. BARAGWANATH *Brave Remain* 126 The *bongols* are yours whenever you require them. I will .. assist you in dividing the bag of mealie-meal into two loads.

bonsella /bɒnˈselə/ *n.* Also **bansela, boncella, bonsela(h), bonzel(l)a, pansella, umbhanselo.** [fr. Zulu *bansela* express thanks in tangible form, or *umbanselo* a small gift (perh. fr. *bansa* be additional, give + applied form suffix *-ela*).]

1.a. A gratuity, reward, bonus, or present given in return for some service, for good behaviour, or, less often, in anticipation of these; occas., a bribe; BASELA *n.* sense 1 b.

1901 A.R.R. TURNBULL *Tales from Natal* 23 Instruct one of the inmates to catch us some fish. They know how to do so for a bansela, though they never do so on their own account. **1907** J.P. FITZPATRICK *Jock of Bushveld* (1909) 207 Few drivers could have handled so top-heavy a load without capsizing – he had received a bansela for his skill. **1908** D. BLACKBURN *Leaven* 56 He .. gladly yielded to their demand for a handful of sugar as a 'bonsella' for having carried out an instalment of their compact. **1911** BLACKBURN & CADDELL *Secret Service* 50 There is .. one form of active service which the 'illicit' expects from the recipients of his bonsellas: a sharp look out for poachers. **1948** O. WALKER *Kaffirs Are Lively* 35 Very occasionally he would allow a tribesman to keep a few shillings as a *bonsella*, or bonus. **1954** K. COWIN *Bushveld, Bananas & Bounty* 175 It had been his custom to give his boy Mafuta (Fat One) a boncella of 2s. 6d. every time he sold a given number of day-old chicks. **1970** M. DIKOBE *Marabi Dance.* 99 This missus made me wash everything in the house ... Here is an old shirt she gave me for bansela – gift. **1979** J. GRATUS *Jo'burgers* 164 'Give you a few little buttons as bonselah, nè?' Harry denied that anyone gave him any bonus to do or not to do anything. **1980** *Het Suid-Western* 18 June, He invited her to take a picture of him giving a 'bonsella' to a 'very decent' maid-servant who had completed a year's domestic service. **1985** *Sunday Times* 15 Sept. (Mag. Sect.) 8 A small *bonsela* of 50 000 dollars, which went with Pia's request that Pope John Paul II christen her bundle of joy, .. didn't have the desired effect. **1986** *Drum* Mar. 19 The other reason the people .. are up in arms, is that they see the move as a sort of bonsella for KwaNdebele for having accepted independence.

b. A present requested and given as a gesture of friendliness or good will; BASELA *n.* sense 1 a.

1920 R.Y. STORMBERG *Mrs Pieter de Bruyn* 62 The natives of Nooitgedacht are amiably putting themselves in my way for a bonsella.

2. *fig.* 'Something for nothing': a stroke of luck; something over and above what was expected, needed, or due; BASELA *n.* sense 2.

1947 C.R. PRANCE *Antic Mem.* 5 We had for long eked-out bully beef with skinny captured sheep as a 'bonsella' from a kindly Providence. **1971** *Sunday Times* 27 June 2 Because Africans contribute less than one per cent of the total income tax now paid, they did not qualify for a single M.P. Thus, written into the constitution, was a 'bonsella' of an initial 16 African M.P.s. **1972** C. FORTUNE on Radio South Africa 18 Mar., That's a bonsella for Natal, isn't it – they get one for the shot and 4 because a no-ball was bowled. **1978** *Weekend Argus* 16 Sept. 1 Big-fight fans get a bare-breasted bonsella ... An unscheduled strip-tease brought fans to their feet between preliminary bouts last night. **1982** *Drum* Nov. 21 As icing on the cake, he also gets a tax-free allowance of R4 830, a free or subsidised house and one to two snazzy cars as bonsella. **1991** *Sunday Times* 3 Feb. 3 Crossword bonsella for nine. Nine lucky readers can splash out this weekend after winning R445 each in consolation prizes.

3. A small extra (usu. sweets) thrown in by a shopkeeper as a mark of good will, or as an incentive to future trade; BASELA *n.* sense 3. Also *attrib.*

1954 P. ABRAHAMS *Tell Freedom* 67 My favourite buy was a pennyworth of coconut icing and a pennyworth of bread. I usually got a handful of roasted peanuts as *bonsella*. Without the *bonsella*, the 'come again' token, no little boy would shop at the same place twice. **1963** M. KAVANAGH *We Merry Peasants* 68 They were only the 'bonsella' sweets. Every Black customer expected a couple or more as a 'bonsella,' a give-away or discount on the newspaper twist of sugar he or she had bought. **1966** L.G. BERGER *Where's Madam* 7 The soft-eyed piccanins of four or five years old .. with a silver tickey in their pink palms, ask for 'six beeg peaches, missus and a bonsella' – the free one being quickly eaten. **1970** C.B. WOOD *Informant, Johannesburg* Give me some 'lekkers' (sweets) as a 'bonzela' (free gift). **1981** C. BARNARD in *Daily Dispatch* 16 Nov. 8 The housewives would come out to haggle over the fish and, if they bought enough, might be given a ready-cooked kreef as a bonsella.

Hence **bonsella** *adv.*, *basela adv.* (see BASELA *n.*).

1983 *Pace* Dec. 119 'We do not issue any certificates bonzella,' said Mr Stander. 'Every man who goes through this training must deserve his certificate.'

Bonsmara /ˌbɒnsˈmɑːrə/ *n.* [Blend formed on the names of *Jan Bonsma*, a major figure in the development of the cattle breed, and of the *Mara Research Station*, at which the breed was developed.] (One of) a breed of beef cattle developed for local conditions by crossing the Shorthorn, Hereford, and Afrikander breeds. Also *attrib.* See also AFRIKANDER *n.* sense 4.

1970 J. VAN MARLE in *Std Encycl. of Sn Afr.* II. 409 The Bonsmara is not yet officially recognised as a pure breed, but a Bonsmara Cattle-Breeders' Society was established in 1964. **1973** *Daily Dispatch* 12 May 18, 152 Bonsmara type cows (in calf). 119 Bonsmara type calves (some to be weaned). 26 Bonsmara heifers. **1981** J. JOUBERT in *E. Prov. Herald* 23 Mar. 13 It took years of experimenting with the Afrikanders, Herefords and Shorthorns before he [*sc.* Bonsma] was satisfied he had the ideal admixture for adaptability to local conditions, fertility, acceptable milk production and docility. Other desirable Bonsmara characteristics are their high heat tolerance and because of their smooth coats and thick skins, an ability to repel ticks, the causes of heartwater. **1987** H. GOOSEN in *S. Afr. Panorama* May 43 His most important achievement is the development of the hardy, tick-resistant Bonsmara cattle, a beef breed eminently suited to South African conditions. **1991** M. OETTLE in *Weekend Post* 9 Feb. (Leisure) 7 Bonsmara cattle ... It [*sc.* the breed] has from the first been produced on the principle of performance testing – the only breed in the world raised on this principle.

bont /bɔnt, bɒnt/ *adj.* Also (*attrib.*) **bonte**. [Du. (and Afk.), gaudy, motley, variegated.]

1.a. Variegated or pied.

A dominant colour is sometimes indicated: see quots 1881, 1886, and 1925.

1846 J.M. BOWKER *Speeches & Sel.* (1864) 222 We veered off .. by the bont bushes .., firing at them whenever we got behind one. **1881** *Alice Times* 14 Jan., In the Municipal Pound, at Seymour, .. will be sold .. 1 Vaal Bont Ox, small halfmoon in the right ear. **1886** G.A. FARINI *Through Kalahari Desert* 295 This is a *zwart bont* (dark spotted) [giraffe]; they are thicker and heavier than the *witte bont* (white spots), but not so long. **1892** *The Jrnl* 9 July 2 Red and white cow, mostly red, little white under belly, and bont on both hips, white patch on forehead. **1913** C. PETTMAN *Africanderisms* 77 *Bont*, .. Variegated, motley. **1925** S.G. CRONWRIGHT-SCHREINER in F.C. Slater *Centenary Bk of S. Afr. Verse* 62 The great buck-wagon, our 'desert ship,' With its four-ton heavy load, And its rooi-bont span and the Wagon-Whip, Is coming along the road. **1971** [see BONT-LEGGED TICK]. **1982** *E. Prov. Herald* 11 Nov. 15 A small group of grazing bontebok begin to take up their characteristic heat-defeating stance ... The buck certainly are 'bont', a handy Afrikaans word meaning brightly colourful or multicoloured.

||**b.** An element in the names of birds and mammals: **bonte elsje** *obs.* [S. Afr. Du., fr. Du. *elsje*, awl (for the shape of its bill)], the avocet *Recurvirostra avosetta* of the Recurvirostridae; **bonte vos** *obs.* [S. Afr. Du., fr. Du. *vos* fox], see quot.; **bont korhaan**, *black korhaan* (see KORHAAN sense 1 b); **bont-skilpad** /-ˌskəlpat/ [Afk., *skilpad* tortoise], the angulate tortoise, *Chersine angulata* of the Testudinidae; **bontspan** /-ˌspan/ [Afk., *span* team], see quot.

1884 LAYARD & SHARPE *Birds of S. Afr.* 673 The **Bonte Elsje**, *lit.* 'pied cobbler's awl,' occurs periodically in the colony in small flocks. **1844** J. BACKHOUSE *Narr. of Visit* 89 A **Bonte Vos**, *Spotted Fox*, a fine animal of the jackal tribe, crossed our path among the sand-hills in the forenoon. *c*1939 S.H. SKAIFE *S. Afr. Nature Notes* 45 The angulated tortoise, or **bont-skilpad**. **1967** E. ROSENTHAL *Encycl. of Sn Afr.* 69 **Bontspan**. Oxen of varying colours. The word is also applied to a mixture of meats roasted on a spit.

2. *colloq.* Esp. in the Eastern Cape: gaudy; colourful.

1970 *Informant, Grahamstown*, I liked the dress, but she said it was a little too bont for a formal occasion. **1970** H. MOFSOWITZ *Informant, Bloemfontein* The bont apron was very pretty. Bont – colourful. **1971** G. MASSYN *Informant, Grahamstown* Some friends .. sent her a Baby-gro suit, but it is very thin, so now I put it on under the little 'bont' dress you made. **1990** G. HEWITT *Informant, Grahamstown* Gee, Shirley V—'s wearing a bont dress this morning. **1993** I.S. DORE *Informant, Grahamstown* Go and have a look at the guy on TV if you want to see a really bont tie.

bontebok /ˈbɔntəbɔk/ *n.* Formerly also **bonta bock, bonteboc(k), bont(i)bok, buntebo(c)k**. Pl. unchanged, or occas. **-s, -ke** /-kə/. [S. Afr. Du., attrib. form of *bont* parti-coloured + *bok* antelope, goat.] The antelope *Damaliscus dorcas dorcas* of the Bovidae, now found only in the south-western Cape; BONTEBUCK. Also *attrib.*

Of the same genus and species as the BLESBOK (see quot. 1990), and similar in appearance. Historically the bontebok occurred in the western Cape, extending eastwards only as far as Mossel Bay, and reports of sightings beyond that area indicate confusion between bontebok and blesbok (see quot. 1837).

1776 F. MASSON in *Phil. Trans. of Royal Soc.* LXVI. 287 There is a fine species of antelope, which inhabits only here, called by the peasants Bonte Bock; something larger than a fallow deer, very shy, but not very swift. 1786 G. FORSTER tr. *A. Sparrman's Voy. to Cape of G.H.* I. 277, I have never seen the *bonte-boks* live otherwise than in large herds on the plains, and these were at least half as tall again as the *bosch-bok*. 1796 C.R. HOPSON tr. *C.P. Thunberg's Trav.* II. 44 The young Bonteboks are at first of a reddish brown colour, but, in time, become spotted with white. 1827 G. THOMPSON *Trav.* I. 95 Among the antelopes I observed a species .. called the *bles-bok*. It much resembles the *bonte-bok*, which is found in the vicinity of Swellendam. 1837 'N. POLSON' *Subaltern's Sick Leave* 128 North of the country of the Amakosa Kafirs is an immense extent of undulating downs styled the 'Bontibok Flats,' from the number of bonti or blesbok that are found there. 1866 J. LEYLAND *Adventures* 81 Its colour is so beautiful, and markings so distinct, as to give rise to the name of Bonteboc or Painted Goat. 1897 H.A. BRYDEN *Nature & Sport* 273 The bontebok (Alclaphus pygargus), or pied antelope .. resembles very strongly its near relative, the curious blesbok... The bontebok first attracts the eye by the singularity of its colouring, the downward slope of the hind-quarters, the pronounced hump, and somewhat heavy, ungainly shape. 1947 L.G. GREEN *Tavern of Seas* 154 The bontebok has a glossy, purple-brown coat like a plum. A white patch on the rump, and a continuous white blaze down the whole face are the only marks by which you may tell a bontebok from a blesbok. 1974 *E. Prov. Herald* 7 Sept. 6 Even more serious is the plight of the bontebok. There are only about 700 of these animals left, only 400 of which are living in protected reserves in the Cape. 1990 SKINNER & SMITHERS *Mammals of Sn Afr. Subregion* 627 The species *D. dorcas* must have had a wide and continuous distribution ... Through climatic changes .. it became split into two populations which .. have diverged in character, leading to the recognition of the two subspecies .. the bontebok, *D. d. dorcas*, and the blesbok *D. d. phillipsi*.

bontebuck *n. ?obs.* Pl. **-s**, or unchanged. [Part. tr. S. Afr. Du. *bontebok*.] BONTEBOK.

1809 R. COLLINS in G.M. Theal *Rec. of Cape Col.* (1900) VII. 58 Two bontebucks of the smaller species were killed. 1822 *Game Law Proclamation* in *Stat. Law of Cape of G.H.* (1862) 59 No holder of such licence .. shall be at liberty to shoot or kill any elephant, sea-cow (hippopotamus), bontebuck. 1839 W.C. HARRIS *Wild Sports* 303 At every step incredible herds of bontebucks .. were performing their complicated evolutions. 1861 P.B. BORCHERDS *Auto-Biog. Mem.* 23 Another reminiscence .. was my seeing .. Mr. Theunissen .. setting off with a wagon .. to see the number of bontebucks then abounding in that part of the country. 1949 J. ALLEN *Memoirs*. 42 On the wide plains I saw Bonte Buck.

bonte tick var. BONT TICK.

bonte veld(t) var. BONTVELD.

bontibok var. BONTEBOK.

bont-legged tick /ˈbɔntlegd ˌtɪk/ *n. phr.* Also **bont-leg tick**. [Afk. *bont* parti-coloured + Eng. *legged* + *tick*.] Any of several species of tick of the genus *Hyalomma* of the Ixodidae, characterized by red legs with pale yellow bands at the joints. Also *attrib.* Cf. BONT TICK.

This tick causes TICK-BITE FEVER, and transmits Crimean-Congo haemorrhagic fever.

1970 E. CRABBE in *Outpost* 223 Leon had lost some 15lbs in weight and was suffering from bont-legged tick sores of some severity. 1971 POTGIETER & DU PLESSIS *Animal Life in Sn Afr.* 219 Bont-leg tick, (*Hyalomma* spp.). Has a very wide distribution over Africa, and there seem to be several different species and varieties, so that it is difficult to name it precisely. It is well known in South Africa, however, because of its 'bont' legs... Recently it has been found to transmit sweating sickness and tick-bite fever. 1981 *E. Prov. Herald* 3 Mar. 1 Congo fever is transmitted by the 'hyalomma' or 'bont-leg' tick, of which 26 species are found throughout South Africa. 1984 L. VERGNANI in *Sunday Times* 23 Sept. 9 Railway employee Mr Frans Theart was bitten by a bont-legged tick. 1984 I. HORAK in *Grocott's Mail* 11 Dec. 19 The bont-legged tick measures about five to six millimetres, has a dark brown to black body and its legs are banded with red and white.

bontrockie var. BONTROKKIE.

bontrok *n.* Perh. *?obs.* [Afk., *bont* parti-coloured + *rok* garment.] In the Western Cape: either of two species of seabream of the Sparidae: **a.** The ZEBRA, *Diplodus cervinus hottentotus*. **b.** *Lithognathus mormyrus*; *sand steenbras*, see STEENBRAS sense b.

1902 [see BONTROKKIE]. 1913 C. PETTMAN *Africanderisms* 77 Bontrok, .. The Mossel Bay name of a species of *Dentex* referring probably to its varied colouring. 1930 C.L. BIDEN *Sea-Angling Fishes* 237 Family Sparidae: species *Diplodus* (or *Sargus*) *cervinus* (Lowe) ... Local names: Luderitz — Mossel Bay — Wildeperd. Knysna — Wildeperd; Bontrok. 1947 K.H. BARNARD *Pict. Guide to S. Afr. Fishes* 152 Zee-basje or Bontrok (*Lithognathus mormyrus*), a similar but smaller fish. 1949 J.L.B. SMITH *Sea Fishes* 269 *Diplodus trifasciatus* ... Streepdassie. *Wildeperd*. (Cape). Bontrok (Knysna). Ibid. 273 *Lithognathus Mormyrus* ... Seebas. Bontrok. Severrim (Cape).

bontrokkie *n. obs.* Also **bontrockie, bontrokje**. [Afk., *bontrok* see prec. + dim. suffix -IE; named for the black, white, and chestnut coloration of the male bird.] The stonechat, *Saxicola torquata* of the Turdidae.

1902 J.D.F. GILCHRIST in *Trans. of S. Afr. Philological Soc.* XI. iv. 221 (Pettman), The name Bontrok .. is perhaps derived from some supposed resemblance to the *Bontrokje*, a species of stonechat. 1923 HAAGNER & IVY *Sketches* 26 The Bontrockie may be found flitting about the banks of a spruit (stream) or perching on the ant-heaps and stones of the open veld.

bont tick /ˈbɔn tɪk, ˈbɒn-/ *n. phr.* Also **bonte tick**, and with initial capital. [Afk. *bont* parti-coloured + Eng. *tick*.] Any of several species of tick of the genus *Amblyomma* of the Ixodidae, esp. *A. hebraeum*, characterized by a patterned shield; *heartwater tick*, see HEARTWATER sense 2. Cf. BONT-LEGGED TICK.

Bont ticks transmit HEARTWATER in cattle, sheep and goats, and TICK-BITE FEVER in humans.

c1881 A. DOUGLASS *Ostrich Farming* 17 The large Bonte tick .. produces terrible sores on all animals. 1900 C.P. LOUNSBURY in *Cent. Dict. Suppl.* (1909) 41 The tick of greatest importance, because of its injuries to stock, is *Amblyomma hebraeum* Koch, commonly known as the bont tick. 1911 *Farmer's Weekly* 22 Mar. 22 Whilst at Graaff-Reinet Show, he picked four ticks off one of the prize animals. One of them was the well-known bont tick, which carries heart-water and East Coast fever. 1914 [see HEARTWATER sense 1]. 1937 [see *heartwater tick* (HEARTWATER sense 2)]. 1955 J.B. SHEPHARD *Land of Tikolosha* 144 They do not connect the bont-tick, the red-legged tick, and all the other parasites which dipping helps to destroy, with East Coast fever and Red Water. 1974 B. SMIT in *Std Encycl. of Sn Afr.* X. 500 Bont Tick, (*Amblyomma hebraeum*). This variegated tick is .. easy to identify because of the conspicuous markings on its shield ... The legs are banded as in the bont-leg tick. 1977 *E. Prov. Herald*

30 Feb. 10 Recent research at Rhodes had shown that certain chemicals secreted by fed male bont ticks effectively attracted unfed males and females and nymphs but not larvae. 1991 J.B. WALKER in *Onderstepoort Jrnl of Vet. Research* Vol.58 No.2, 82 Genus *Amblyomma* Koch, 1844 .. is distributed world-wide. The majority of these bont ticks .. are .. large, colourful species.

bontveld /ˈbɔntfelt, -fɛlt/ *n. rare.* Formerly also **bonte veld(t)**. [S. Afr. Du., *bont* see BONT + *veld* open, undeveloped countryside.] Savanna; flat, open grassland dotted with low-growing shrubs and trees. See also VELD sense 3 c.

1835 C.L. STRETCH *Journal*. 27 Apr., We were sadly harrassed by the broken ground which to use Jervis's expression was 'bonte veldt' that is so thickly covered with mimosa that we felt the effects of his guidance on our shins and arms. 1868 J. CHAPMAN *Trav.* II. 16 The intervening country, if not the usual *bonte-veld* or *eland-veld*, .. consists of a succession of sandy bults or ridges. 1986 H. VAN RENSBURG in *S. Afr. Panorama* May 29 In those days the centre of what is now the City of Pretoria, was covered in trees. We called it the 'bontveld' (varicoloured veld). Clumps and groups of trees, with open spaces in between, gave to the whole the appearance of a park.

Bonus Bond *n. phr. Hist.* [So called because the purchase of a bond entitled one to participate in a monthly draw for cash prizes.] A government bond sold (from 1977 to 1984) to raise funds for defence purposes. Also *attrib.*

1977 *Govt Gaz.* Vol.146 No.5693, 1 Defence Bonus Bonds ... Purpose of the issue. The bonds are issued for the partial financing of the Republic's expenditure on defence. 1978 *Evening Post* 9 Oct. 1 An ouderling .. said .. that if the general synod had found the bonus bond scheme to be against the law of God then bond buying was unquestionably a sin. 1979 *S. Afr. Panorama* Oct. 30 When R20 000 was won by Koos H— .. in the sixth South African Bonus Bond prize draw, he lived for eight months in blissful ignorance of the fact. 1983 *S. Afr. Digest* June 4 The Prime Minister, Mr P W Botha, has pledged to drop the Bonus Bond scheme if alternative ways could be found of raising money for defence and other purposes.

bony var. BONEY.

bonya var. BAIE.

bonzel(l)a var. BONSELLA.

boo *n. Obs.* Ostrich-farming. [Etym. dubious; perh. ad. Fr. *beau* beautiful.] TAIL. Usu. in *pl.*

c1881 A. DOUGLASS *Ostrich Farming* 91, 11 Bdls 14 oz. white Boos; 4 Bdls 10 oz. femina Boos; 4 Bdls 6 oz. drab Boos. 1896 R. WALLACE *Farming Indust. of Cape Col.* 235 Boos of all kinds were in good demand, and generally 5s. per lb. higher ... 'Boos' is used to distinguish the short and stumpy tail feathers of both birds — white from the male and drab from the female.

boocho var. BUCHU.

Boodle Kaamer var. BOEDELKAMER.

booitjie var. BOYKIE.

Boojesman var. BOSJESMAN.

book *v. trans. Obs. exc. hist.* Often in the phr. **to book in** [calque formed on Afk. *inboek*, see INBOEK]. APPRENTICE *v.*

1888 D.C.F. MOODIE *Hist. of Battles & Adventures* II. 255 The children of the natives killed on the commando were '*booked*' for a number of years, until they had reached a certain age, but they were seldom released when they reached that period. 1977 T.R.H. DAVENPORT *S. Afr.: Mod. Hist.* 58 Bring to trial not only those who maltreated servants, but those who 'booked in' the children of Bushmen or other aboriginals for service.

Book of Life *n. phr.* [Perh. a wry transf. use of the biblical *book of life* the record of the names of those inheriting eternal life.] A comprehensive personal identity document, including marriage-, driving-, and firearm-licences; cf. ID. Also *attrib.*

This document was introduced in 1972; initially for whites only (cf. PASS sense 3), it was in general use from 1986.

1971 *Sunday Times* 14 Nov. 5 The six foolscap-page form which people in South Africa will have to complete for the 'Book of Life' — the Government's new super-identity card — will pry deeply into personal affairs. **1972** *E. Prov. Herald* 2 Feb. 5 Book of Life forms now available. The new system of population registration and identification was launched yesterday. **1977** *Het Suid-Western* 2 Feb. (back page), Only driver's licences that are in the book of life identity document will be recognised as valid by this time next year. **1983** *Rand Daily Mail* 10 Nov. 5 He was aware a Book of Life was required to cast a referendum vote, but he was against being issued a Book of Life because it classified him according to race. **1986** *Drum* Aug. 55 The euphoria about the death of the old dompas has waned and in its wake comes the new Book of Life — complete with fingerprints maybe. **1990** J.G. DAVIS *Land God Made in Anger* 235 All South Africans .. have to carry the so-called Book-of-Life. An identification document. It contains all the bearer's details, his date and place of birth, his address, his marriage, everything of an official nature that he's done in his life.

bookoo var. BUCHU.

boom /'buəm/ *n. slang.* [Afk., lit. 'tree'; perh. fr. TREE OF KNOWLEDGE; see quots 1949 and 1952.]
1. DAGGA *n.*[2] sense 1. Also *attrib.*

1946 H.C. BOSMAN in L. Abrahams *Cask of Jerepigo* (1972) 203 A practice indulged in by every unregenerate South African criminal — white, native, coloured or Indian — is that of dagga ('boom') smoking. **1946** [see PILL]. **1949** H.C. BOSMAN *Cold Stone Jug* (1969) 46 The first time I heard convicts talk about dagga they referred to it as 'boom'. I wanted to know why. They said, well, you know, 'boom' is the Afrikaans word for a tree ... Then they said it meant tree of knowledge. **1952** 'MR DRUM' in *Drum* Sept. 12 Scientifically known as Indian hemp, dagga is called bhang in India, .. Kif in North Africa, .. Marihuana in Spanish America ... Derived from Hottentot Dachab, it is known in the slang as 'garnja', 'locoweed', 'baccy,' 'giggleweed,' 'ganga,' 'love weed,' 'reefers,' 'zoll,' 'tokwaan,' 'bangi,' 'hoenderpoort,' "Nsangu,' 'tree of knowledge,' 'parcel,' "n katjie,' 'stops,' 'boom,' 'tarrie,' 'weed' and 'No. 1.' **1971** *Daily Dispatch* 4 Sept. 6 Most widely used names in South Africa are pot, grass, weed, tea or boom. **1974** in *Eng. Usage in Sn Afr.* Vol.5 No.1, 10 Here the common boop terms invariably have further significance for the *rokers* i.e. those who smoke *boom* (dagga — occasionally *weed* or *tree*). **1979** *Cape Times* 1 Dec. 11 Many of the youths, ignored by the older gangsters, begin to smoke 'boom' (dagga), to impress them. **1985** [see STOP sense 1]. **1986** M. PICARDIE in S. Gray *Market Plays* 79 Jesus, I'm mad this morning, no more dagga, no more boom, no smoking on duty. **1988** P. WILHELM in *Staffrider* Vol.8 No.3, 77 We bought from him *dagga*, the weed, *boom*: that which I had always associated with precipitation into blackness.

2. *comb.* **boom boy**, DAGGA-ROOKER; **boomskuif** /-skeɪf/ [Afk., *skuif* see SKYF], ZOL *n.* sense 1 a; **boomstop** /-stɔp/ [Afk., *stop* see STOP], STOP sense 1 a; **boom tea**, an infusion of marijuana.

1974 *Eng. Usage in Sn Afr.* Vol.5 No.1, 11 For the rokers — the **boom-boys** — hand rolling is essential unless the *boom* and *snout* are mixed in a pipe ... The **boom-skuif** is held firmly between the fingers closer to the knuckle than normally and the smoke is then drawn in through cupped hands. **1980** E. PATEL *They Came at Dawn* 25 Sometimes the end of the boomskuif precipitously hangs onto the edge of my lips. **1977** D. MULLER *Whitey* 16 The magic of the jupe and the boomskuif was wearing thin. Body and soul were shrivelling. **1974** [**boomstop**: see *Eng. Usage in Sn Afr* quot. at STOP sense 1]. **1971** *Cape Times* 20 July 1 She and a boy friend went to a party .. They went into a barn .. and drank '**boom tea**' (tea made from dagga). Some of them were 'feeling a bit funny'.

Hence **boomed (up)** /'buəmd ('ʌp)/ *adj.*, BLUE *adj.* sense 2; **boomy** /'buəmi/ *adj.*, habitually intoxicated as a result of smoking marijuana.

1949 H.C. BOSMAN *Cold Stone Jug* (1969) 47 'Blue' was the most usual way of talking about one being under the spell of dagga, but there were other expressions, like 'geswael', 'boomed up'. **1964** M.E. McCOY *Informant, Port Elizabeth* A crazy drawing of a really boomy ou dragging a woman along. **1983** *Informant, Cape Town* Whole bloody pack of boomy ones that lot — boomed up the whole time.

boom /buːm, ?buːm/ *v. intrans.* [Eng.; or fr. Afk. *brom*, sometimes represented as *broom* in Eng., see BROM *v.*] BROM *v.* sense 1. Hence **booming** *vbl n.*

1897 S.C. CRONWRIGHT-SCHREINER in F. Goldie *Ostrich Country* (1968) 17 When the breeding season approaches one will hear the cock bird 'booming' like the roar of a lion. **1912** *S. Afr. Agric. Jrnl* Jan. 24 (Pettman), In the characteristic *bromming* or *booming* of the cock during the pairing season, the neck becomes greatly inflated by the filling of the foodpipe with air. **1987** O. PROZESKY *Wrath of Lamb* p.ii, By day the cock-ostrich boomed low to the hen he was courting.

boom dassie see DASSIE sense 1 c.

boomslang /'buəmslaŋ/ *n.* Also **baum slang**, **boem-slang**, and with initial capital. Pl. **-e** /-ə/, **-s**, or unchanged. [S. Afr. Du., *boom* tree + *slang* snake.] The venomous arboreal snake *Dispholidus typus* of the Colubridae; TREE-SNAKE. Also *attrib.*

1796 C.R. HOPSON tr. *C.P. Thunberg's Trav.* II. 23 A serpent, called Boomslang, was said to get into the trees, and swallow the birds it found there. [**1804** R. PERCIVAL *Acct of Cape of G.H.* 171 The boem snake, or tree snake, from five to ten feet long, .. supports itself from the branches of trees, and waits for its prey passing under.] **1837** J.E. ALEXANDER *Narr. of Voy.* I. 343 One of the dogs pointed in a strange manner. Young Botha called out '*Boom slang!*' (a tree snake,) and was preparing to shoot it. **1852** A.W. COLE *Cape & Kafirs* 243 There is also .. the boem-slang (or tree-snake), less deadly, one of which I once shot seven feet long. **1878** T.J. LUCAS *Camp Life & Sport* 241 Among the most brilliantly coloured, the Baum slang (the tree snake), .. resplendent with bright tints of green and gold. **1886** G.A. FARINI *Through Kalahari Desert* 61 Be careful of snakes, for there are often some of the *boom slange* here, and they are very poisonous. **1910** A.B. LAMONT *Rural Reader* 35 Others such as the boomslang, frequent bushes and trees in search of birds. **1929** F.C. SLATER *Sel. Poems* (1947) 116 Cobras with stars and adders in bright rings, Boomslangs that fly from tree to tree sans wings. **1955** [see *black mamba* (MAMBA sense 2)]. **1971** *The 1820* Vol.43 No.10, 20 Skaapstekers and boomslange are venomous, but they are back-fanged snakes and not aggressive, so we do not worry about them. **1982** *E. Prov. Herald* 6 Nov. 2 There was no serum for boomslang bites in Port Elizabeth, so it had to be specially flown in from Johannesburg. **1991** Ibid. 7 Feb. 1 The luckless boomslang was a male .. and two females ... This boomslang .. was normally found in trees but in the mating season would be found on the ground. **1991** [see MAMBA sense 1].

‖**boontjiesop** /'bɔɪŋkiˌsɔp/ *n.* [Afk. (ad. Du. *bonensoep*), *boon* bean + dim. suffix -IE + *sop* soup.] A thick soup, made usu. with dried haricot beans.

[**1913** A. GLOSSOP *Barnes's S. Afr. Hsehold Guide* 37 Witte Boonen Soep (White Bean Soup), Cape. Wash rather more than 1/2 pint of haricot beans.] **1964** L.G. GREEN *Old Men Say* 121 There is thick bean soup, the *boontjiesop* of many a farmhouse; but I think that came from Europe. **1972** *Cape Times* 9 Nov. 7 The '*boontjiesop*' and Kupugani biscuits were to my liking. [**1975** W. STEENKAMP *Land of Thirst King* 18 A good solid railway meal in the dining-saloon, with the menu proclaiming 'Potage de St. Germain' on the left and bluntly the Afrikaans version, 'Boontjiesop', on the right.] **1977** *Fair Lady* 8 June (Suppl.) 14 Boontjiesop — Cape Malay Bean Soup. 500 gr dried haricot beans; 3 litres water; [etc.]. **1986** *Motorist* 3rd Quarter 48 In the diningroom, .. 'boontjiesop' and 'braised Karoo lamb' are unlikely ever to be off the menu. Nothing could be more traditional!

boop var. BOEP *n.*[1]

Boor var. BOER.

boorbom, boorbon varr. BOERBOOM, BOERBOON.

boor-hoom var. BOCCHOM.

boorie var. BORRIE.

Bootchuannas pl. form of BECHUANA.

booti var. UBUTI.

bootie var. BOETIE.

Bootshooānǎs, -shuanas pl. forms of BECHUANA.

Bop /bɔp/ *n. hist.* [Abbrev. of seTswana *BophuthaTswana* this 'homeland', lit. 'gathering of the Tswana', *bo-* denoting progression + *-phutha* gather together, collect + *Tswana* (see TSWANA).]
1. *colloq.* The former Republic of Bophuthatswana, a 'homeland' with territories in both the Orange Free State and the Transvaal; the government of Bophuthatswana; cf. *Tswanaland* (see TSWANA sense 2 b). Also *attrib.* See also HOMELAND.

1982 *Pace* Nov. 47 No members of the United Nations, except South Africa, recognises BophphphphphuthaTswana [*sic*] ... Bop had adopted the attitude that as long as they recognise themselves as a country and a nation, they couldn't care a hoot for world recognition. **1987** *Financial Mail* 22 May 40 Bophuthatswana .. is blocking Tswanas from obtaining the new South African identity document by instructing them to first renounce their Bop citizenship. **1988** S. MOLAKENG in *Frontline* Apr.-May 20 Bophuthatswana has run ten years as an independent sovereign state ... Some people who reject it out of hand, have come up with a sweet abbreviation for it. They call it 'Bop' ... There is a hell of resentment towards Bop. **1990** *Sunday Star* 11 Mar. 14 Most of Bop's unrest of recent years has stemmed from attempts to incorporate further segments of territory into its jigsaw borders. **1990** *Weekend Post* 29 Sept. 8 The ANC still saw Bop as 'a bastard child of apartheid' and insisted on its reincorporation.

2. Used *attrib.* in the special collocations *Bop Air*, *-Radio*, *-TV*: Bophuthatswana's national airline, radio service, and television service.

1984 *Frontline* May 38 Koos, we all ought to be very proud of Bop TV, because it shows once again how South Africa is way ahead of the world. Who else has ever produced a TV Station which only ouens of one race are meant to see? **1986** *Star* 23 Apr. 19 South African Airways has trained air hostesses for Bop Air — but it says it cannot find 'suitable' candidates for its own flights. **1987** *E. Prov. Herald* 28 May 6 Harry Cohen, the only coloured DJ with Metro, moved over from Bop Radio.

borchem var. BOCCHOM.

Border *n.* Also with small initial. [Special senses and uses of general Eng. *border* limit or boundary.] Usu. *the Border*:
1. That region of the Eastern Cape lying south of the Great Kei river and east of the Katberg river. Also *attrib.*

Historically, the region adjoining the boundary of the Cape Colony. See also FRONTIER.

1832 *Graham's Town Jrnl* 30 Mar. 55 Public Meeting in Caffreland ... A number of respectable persons from Albany attended the meeting, and appeared greatly interested in the proceedings, as also in the evident progress making in the conversion and civilization of the border Caffres. **1852** M.B. HUDSON *S. Afr. Frontier Life* 181 The Graham's Town Board of Defence have of late To the governor sent, representing the state Of the country again; how the reigning disorder, And Hottentot treason have crippled the Border. **1886** J. NOBLE *Cape of G.H.: Off. Handbk* 102 King Williamstown, or 'King,' as it is sometimes shortly termed, ranks as an important commercial centre. It has also the chief command of the native trade, extending beyond the Border and north to Basutoland. **1893** H.B. SIDWELL *Story of S. Afr.* 122 From the loss of the year 1857 the Kafir tribes have never recovered ... Years of quiet followed the great unrest on the border. **1913** C. PETTMAN *Africanderisms* 80 *Border, The*, The Districts of King Williamstown and East London are often spoken of as 'The Border' or 'The Frontier', because they are situated between the Colony proper and the native territories. **1969** I. VAUGHAN *Last of Sunlit Yrs* 48 A wave of nostalgia for the little Border villages, the rolling grass hills, the cheerful chattering Bantu. **1970** *Daily Dispatch* 6 June 8 It is worth noting that this is more than the anniversary of the 1820 Settlers. It is also the birthday of the Border. **1979** *S. Afr. Panorama* July 27 The region is commonly called The Border – that part of the Eastern Cape Province where White and Black first made contact two centuries ago this year, in 1779, when the White settlement at the Cape of Good Hope was 127 years old. **1986** *E. Prov. Herald* 19 Aug., The Border selectors did the unexpected when they axed their prolific points scorer centre Peter Ker-Fox. **1990** *Weekly Mail* 2 Feb. 9 Several small Border towns are clashing with local authorities over the right to protest. In Tarkastad, west of Queenstown, the town council is desperately trying to end a consumer boycott.

2. Special Comb. **border area**, a declared area, situated on the borders of a HOMELAND, in which concessions are offered to industry in order to attract investment and development; **border industry**, a white-owned industry established on the South African side of the boundary of a homeland, in terms of the National Party government's policy of decentralization; also *attrib.*

1955 *Report of Commission for Socio-Economic Dev. of Bantu Areas* (UG61-1955) 140 A **border area** is .. one where development takes place in a European area situated so closely to the Bantu Areas, that families of Bantu employees engaged in that development, can be established in the Bantu Area in such a way that the employees can lead a full family life. **1959** H.F. VERWOERD in *Hansard* 29 June 9432 White South Africa will have two industrial legs, the one being the White industry deep in the White interior and the second the industries owned by White people and employing the Bantu labour coming from the Bantu areas because these industries are in the border areas. **1960** — in T. Bell *Indust. Decentral.* (1973) 42 By the concept of 'border areas' is meant those localities or regions near the Bantu areas, in which industrial development takes place, through European initiative and control, but which is so situated that the Bantu workers can maintain their residences and family lives in the Bantu areas ... Those regions within approximately 30 miles of the Bantu areas may be regarded as border areas. **1969** *Survey of Race Rel.* (S.A.I.R.R.) 97 Assistance by the State .. led to the establishment of 135 new industrial concerns and to the expansion of 74 existing concerns in border areas. **1971** *Daily Dispatch* 24 May 1 Among the substantial hand-outs to be offered to industrialists prepared to move away from the established areas are a seven-year tax holiday for industries in the border areas and a ten-year tax free period for homelands industries. **1986** P. MAYLAM *Hist. of Afr. People* 181 A number of black townships in white urban areas have been demolished and their occupants removed to new townships in 'homeland' border areas, from where Africans commute to their places of work. **1959** H.F. VERWOERD in *Hansard* 29 June 9432 The **Border industries**, which will also be White industries in the White area, although Bantu will come across the border of their own territory to work there – those industries will absorb the majority of these 14,000,000 Bantu. **1962** A.J. LUTHULI *Let my People Go* 201 The Bantustan planners .. offer a solution to the desperate poverty of the Reserves. They propose to establish 'border industries'. White industrialists are invited to place factories on the edges of the destitute Reserves. The bait is cheap labour. **1968** *Green Bay Tree (pamphlet)* p.xxxix, It is trying to meet the problem – and also its own desperate desire to get some black workers out of South African cities – by its policy of encouragement for 'border industries.' **1970** E. KAHN in *Std Encycl. of Sn Afr.* I. 483 One of the methods used from mid-1961 to promote the apartheid ideal has been the encouragement of 'border industries' in White areas close to the reserves, to which the Bantu workers can return at night or the week-ends. **1973** T. BELL *Indust. Decentral.* 123 The border industries policy cannot be convincingly explained in terms of objectives like redistributing income, shortening travelling distances within urban areas, maintaining communal ties intact, or alleviating the social evils associated with large population concentrations. **1983** *S. Afr. 1983: Off. Yrbk* (Dept of Foreign Affairs & Info.) 205 In the early 1960s the Government .. launched a programme in terms of which various incentives are offered industrialists to start new enterprises in areas just outside the border of the national states or to move their businesses from the metroplitan regions to these areas so that jobs could be taken to the work-seekers ... These projects and investments do not seem to have generated sufficient economic development in the national states ... In the period 1972 to 1975 .. 36,8 per cent [of the 100 000 young men and women who entered the labour market in the Black states every year] had found jobs in 'border' industries, while the rest were potential migrant workers or remained unemployed. **1987** *New Nation* 6 Aug. 16 She helped organise strikes against the border industry system by which employers closed factories in urban areas and moved them to rural regions where they could draw on vast cheap labour resources. **1988** A. FISCHER in Boonzaaier & Sharp *S. Afr. Keywords* 131 Because it was committed to the establishment of so-called 'border industries' (which meant that industrial developments remained within 'white' South Africa), the government spent only a fraction of the sum which Tomlinson had recommended for this diversification [*sc.* of economic activity within the Reserves].

3. *hist.*

a. Those areas in which military contact took place between the South African Defence Force and members of Umkhonto we Sizwe (or the South West African People's Organization), esp. the border of Namibia with Angola. See also *boys on the border* (BOY sense 2 c), OPERATIONAL AREA.

1978 *Pace* Dec. 61 'What do you think, Mrs Maponya,' I ask. 'Should the blacks help to fight on the border?' **1979** *Paratus* Jan. 36 The men on the border are isolated from their families for periods of up to three months or more and are separated from home by vast distances. **1981** *Fair Lady* 8 Apr. 7 You will hear very little about what it's like 'somewhere on the Border'. He doesn't need official warnings about security. **1987** M. MAARTENS *Ring around Moon* 19 On the border ... We don't know exactly where. The last we heard, he was somewhere deep in Angola. **1988** P. WILHELM *Healing Process* 23 Better, perhaps, than the deadly monotony of camp life under severe discipline – or a posting on the Border, that ill-defined ring around South Africa.

b. *Attrib.*, in the following Special Combinations: **border duty, border literature, border story, border war.**

1979 *Darling* 7 Feb. 24 By now, literally thousands of young men have been called-up for army training and will eventually report for **Border duty. 1979** *Daily Dispatch* 18 Oct. 7 The number of South African troops doing 'border duty' could be significantly reduced two years from now even if there is no international agreement on South West Africa .. head of the armed forces in the territory, said yesterday. **1986** *Sunday Times* 13 July (Lifestyle) 4 Should men be employed before border duties commence, they will receive automatic salary increases in their absence. **1987** H. SCHOLTZ Circular. (HAUM Literary) 2 Sept., He has now moved away from that poetic type of prose to write a gripping, relevant youth novel depicting the ravages of war; a novel that could well be described as **'border literature'**. **1988** BUNN & TAYLOR *From S. Afr.* 27 'Border' literature is that emergent genre associated specifically with the experience of young white conscripts forced to defend apartheid in the various wars on the borders of Namibia, Angola, Zimbabwe and Mozambique. **1986** *Pretoria News* 24 Sept. 13 A collection of 18 so-called **'border' stories**, this little work provides the reader with a rare insight into the everyday vicissitudes of our pesent-day crop of young men in uniform. **1990** D. GORDON in *Sunday Times* 28 Oct. 1 The SABC launched the programme in 1961, at the start of mandatory national service ... 'The show's popularity grew as the **border war** developed.'

Border, boys on the see BOY sense 2 c.

borehole *n.* [Transf. use of general Eng. *borehole* a hole drilled as an ancillary process in mining, oil drilling, etc.] A well drilled to tap underground water and furnished with a windmill, an engine, or occas. a hand-pump to bring the water to the surface. Also *attrib.*

A common feature in gardens and on farms in dry areas.

1911 *Farmer's Weekly* 15 Mar. 4 The water supply comes from a 16ft. windmill over a borehole tested to yield at least 96,000 gallons of water per day, and this water is pumped into a cement reservoir. **1920** R.H. LINDSEY-RENTON *Diary* (1979) 30 Every farm and nearly every house in the dorps have had a bore hole made with a pump driven by a windmill erected on it so that as long as the wind blows they can get a fairly good supply of water. **1946** H.C. BOSMAN *Mafeking Rd* (1969) 121 In time of drought .. you have been standing at the borehole all day, pumping water for the cattle, so that by the evening water has got a bitter taste for you. **1978** A.P. BRINK *Rumours of Rain* 195 The borehole is getting weaker too. There's a man coming today to look for water. Perhaps we can sink a new hole. **1982** *Rhodeo* (Rhodes Univ.) 6 Apr. 8 The water is supplied by a poor borehole service – as opposed to the permanent river that presently feeds Mgwali. **1989** J. HOBBS *Thoughts in Makeshift Mortuary* 302 Every few hundred metres, clustered like ticks round borehole windmills, were settlements of mud-brick houses and corrugated iron lean-tos.

borer *n.* [Special sense of general Eng. *borer* an insect which bores through wood.] In full ***borer beetle***: the furniture beetle *Anobium punctatum* of the Anobiidae. Also *attrib.*

1879 R.J. ATCHERLEY *Trip to Boerland* 238 At the hotel I had an excellent opportunity of noticing the depredations caused by an insect called the 'borer'. **1887** J.W. MATTHEWS *Incwadi Yami* 323 Coffee enterprise seemed dying out fast, no planting going on, the trees suffering from an insect, the 'borer'. **1899** W.H. BROWN *On S. Afr. Frontier* 316 The native woods in the country are attacked by a small beetle, commonly known as the borer, which is brown in colour and about a quarter of an inch in length. **1899** A. WERNER *Captain of Locusts* 68 The Administration bungalow did not, as yet, boast a ceiling – concluded from the softly descending showers of yellow dust, that the 'borer' had got into them – reflected that he ought to have them tarred or painted at the first opportunity. **1905** J. DU PLESSIS *1000 Miles in Heart of Afr.* 54 An insect called the borer drills holes into your house's beams and rafters and uprights. **1987** J. KENCH *Cottage Furn.* 169 *Borer beetle*, The common furniture beetle, *Anobium punctatum*, responsible for the small round holes found in woodwork. These are the flight holes of the mature insect ... Known especially in the U.K. as woodworm. **1990** *Weekend Post* 8 Dec. 1 The 'borer beetle certificate', which was .. commonly issued when a house was sold, also had limited value.

bori(e) var. BORRIE.

Borolong var. BAROLONG.

borrie /ˈbɔri/ n. Also **boorie, bori(e), borri.** [Du., fr. Malay *boreh* turmeric.]

1. Turmeric, the yellow spice derived from the powdered root of the plant *Curcuma longa* of the Zingiberaceae.

[1798 S.H. WILCOCKE tr. *J.S. Stavorinus's Voy. to E. Indies 1768-71* II. 136 The emperors [in Java] sometimes make criminals condemned to death fight with tigers. In such cases, the man is rubbed with *borri*, or turmeric.] 1847 'A BENGALI' *Notes on Cape of G.H.* 84 The 'Turmeric' (*bori*) is found in quantities in the Stellenbosch district. [1925 H.J. MANDELBROTE tr. *O.F. Mentzel's Descr. of Cape of G.H.* II. 39 Among other imports are pepper, ginger, 'burri-burri', sugar-candy, castor-sugar, cotton-wool and cotton yarns, wax candles and 'chiaten' wood for beams.] 1927 [see BEGRAFNISRYS]. 1950 [see FISH OIL]. 1975 G. WESTWOOD *Ross of Silver Ridge* 105 Make bobotie for lunch ... Serve it with yellow rice, that is, rice cooked with sugar, salt, a knob of butter, a handful of raisins and a teaspoon of borrie — that's what you call turmeric. 1977 *Oppidan* (Rhodes University) Sept. 4 Add tomato, 2 teaspoons of masala, 1 teaspoon bori, stir and leave for a minute. 1988 F. WILLIAMS *Cape Malay Cookbk* 8 Borrie, .. Ground spice obtained from the dried root of a plant related to ginger. It has a slightly bitter taste and care should be taken not to exceed the amount recommended in a recipe ... Borrie is .. used in curries, pickled fish and sosaties and for colouring yellow rice.

2. Used *attrib.* of vegetables, fruit, and trees with reference to the yellow colour of the flesh or wood, as *borriepatat* /-paˌtat, pə-/ [Afk., *patat* sweet potato] or *borrie sweet potato*, and *borrie yellow* (sometimes simply *borrie*), LEMON WOOD.

1887 A.A. ANDERSON *25 Yrs in Waggon* I. 42 The Pongola Bush .. is a beautiful forest of fine timber ... Ebenhout, a sort of ebony; Borrie yellow, Bockenhout, no regular grain; Assagaai, used for spear handles; [etc.]. 1906 B. DAVY in C.A. Smith *Common Names* (1966) 159 The Lemonwood or Borie. 1949 L.G. GREEN *In Land of Afternoon* 62 Very sweet and yellow is the borrie patat. 1970 *Pickstone's Catal.* 12 Quinces will succeed almost anywhere ... We no longer propagate the well-known Borrie variety as it is a very poor bearer unless skilfully pruned. 1971 *Argus* 4 May 4 (caption) Mr Joe Nel .. shows two giant 'borrie' sweet potatoes grown in his garden. 1977 *Darling* 16 Mar. 186 Mrs Malan's Stewed Sweet Potatoes. If available the fat yellow borrie-patat. Peel and slice them and stew gently in a little butter. 1983 M. VAN BILJON in *Sunday Times* 6 Mar. (Mag. Sect.) 16 To serve with snoek, put whole sweet potatoes (ask your green-grocer for 'borriepatats') into a oven pre-heated to 200 deg C. 1986 *Cape Times* 6 Feb., (advt) Borrie Sweet Potatoes 39c per kg.

∥**borsdruppels** /ˈbɔːsdrəpəlz, ˈbɔrsdrœpəls/ *pl. n.* Also **borstdroppels, borstdruppels.** [Afk., *bors* (fr. Du. *borst*) chest + *druppels* drops.] A home-remedy for the relief of asthma and other chest complaints. See also DRUPPELS.

*a*1900 *Lennon's Dutch Medicine Handbk* 18 Borsdruppels, This excellent remedy .. loosens and breaks the phlegm, clears the chest and relieves the spasms of coughs, croup and bronchitis in both adults and children. 1919 *Dunell, Ebden & Co.'s Price List* Oct. 20 Borst Droppels 3/6. 1934 *Sunday Times* 1 June (Swart), Why should Oom Piet, who had for years bought his borsdruppels just as regularly and from the same place as he ordered his tobacco now be prevented from doing so? 1943 [see HOFFMANSDRUPPELS]. 1958 E.H. BURROWS *Hist. of Medicine* 191 Bors droppels (Elixir pectorale, Chest Drops): used for all lung complaints, colds and coughs. 1975 W. STEENKAMP *Land of Thirst King* 138 For many years the only formal medical help the average farmer possessed was what he called his 'apteek', or pharmacy, which consisted of a fitted tin trunk containing such time-honoured specifics as Hoffman's Drops, a cough remedy known as 'Borstdruppels' (chest drops), Polgras Pills, 'Rooi Laventel' (lavender drops) and, naturally, the inevitable blue bottle of castor oil. 1989 D. SMUTS *Folk Remedies* 28 Cough mixture. Mix some honey and a few drops of borsdruppels thoroughly and eat a quarter of a teaspoonful every now and again.

bos see BOSCH.

bosbaroe see BAROE sense b.

bosbefok /ˈbɔsbəfɔk/ *adj.* Army slang. Also **bosbevok.** [Afk., *bos* bush + *befok* 'fucked', deranged; coined by members of the S. Afr. Defence Forces.] Not in polite use. BOSSIES. Cf. BEFOK.

1979 P. WILHELM in *Staffrider* Vol.2 No.3, 15 Border duty. It was noon and the *ous* were just sitting around, most of them bosbefok, drinking hot beer. 1979 *Rhodeo* (Rhodes Univ.) 25 Feb. 7 The Rhod Pseud. This cat hails from up north, and is into aggro basically. They are also into having a good time when they aren't bos-bef-k. 1985 H. PRENDINI in *Style* Oct. 40 Specific army terms include 'going bossies' and 'bosbevok' literally meaning bush-buggered and no longer capable of coping.

bosberaad /ˈbɔsbəraːt/ *n. Pl.* **-berade** /-bəraːdə/. [Afk., *bos* bush + *beraad* deliberation, consultation.] A 'bush summit', a meeting of leaders at a retreat which is remote from urban centres, intended to provide participants with the chance to focus on difficult issues undisturbed. Cf. INDABA sense 1.

1990 *E. Prov. Herald* 4 Apr. 3 President F W de Klerk and his cabinet began a two-day working session 'somewhere in the Boland' yesterday to discuss the political situation in South Africa and to develop strategies. This is the third 'bosberaad' (bush deliberation) Mr De Klerk has held with his Cabinet since he became State President in September last year. 1992 G. BRAY in *Sunday Times* 13 Sept. 17 Either that, or those much-heralded bosberade are actually occasions for secret, hushed-up lobotomies. 1992 A.A. FERRAR in *Afr. Wildlife* Vol.46 No.4, 151 The business of the 'Corporate Bosberaad' is booming ... When our leaders are presented with a real challenge, they readily resort to the veld to provide the inspiration and peace that are necessary for tough creative decision-making. 1993 J. SCOTT in *Cape Times* 25 Feb. 11 Mr Van der Merwe .. painted a picture of .. evil-doers overrunning South Africa while the State President shuffled his cabinet or held bosberade.

bosbevok var. BOSBEFOK.

bos-boc(k), bosbok varr. BOSCHBOK.

∥**bosch, bos** /bɔʃ, bɔs/ *n.* Also **bosh.** [Du. *bosch*, Afk. *bos*, forest, bush.]

1. *noncount.* BUSH *n.*[1] sense 1 a. Also *fig.*

1816 G. BARKER *Journal.* 15 Apr., Assisted in making a path toward Lombard's Post, thro' the bosch & at the drift. 1834 T. PRINGLE *Afr. Sketches* 214 After proceeding a mile or two down the river, we struck into a path on the left hand, which led us into the bosom of the jungle, or *bosch*, as it is termed in this country. 1862 LADY DUFF-GORDON *Lett. from Cape* (1925) 113 The people are burning the veld all about ... The ashes of the bosch serve as manure for the young grass, which will sprout in the autumn rains. 1905 H. BOLUS in C.A. Smith *Common Names* (1966) 159 (Bosch) includes a great variety of plants, the short shrubs of the Karroo, the knee-high boschjes of the Western Province, the dwarf trees of the mimosa type, the dense scrub of our coasts, and the majestic timber trees of our natural forest. 1982 *Daily Dispatch* 11 Jan. 6 You can spot the mistakes of the newcomer down the road who bought that piece of *bos* they call a farm. 1990 *Style* June 109 If you disappear into the *bos* .. you have no claim to the doctorate.

2. *obs.* BUSH *n.*[1] sense 2 a.

1820 J. AYLIFF *Journal.* 19 On the 24th they were found Dead a very little Distance from their home in a Bosch. 1828 T. PRINGLE *Ephemerides* 191 At length, we fairly tracked him into a large *bosch*, or straggling thicket of brushwood and evergreens.

3. *comb.*

a. *obs.* In the names of fauna, usu. indicating a preference for a bushy habitat: *boschvogel*, the bulbul *Andropadus importunus* (called 'sombre bulbul' in G.L. Maclean's *Roberts' Birds of Sn Afr.*, 1993); *boschbok, boschvark,* see as main entries.

1884 LAYARD & SHARPE *Birds of S. Afr.* 204 The 'Boschvogel' as it is called, is not very rare in the neighbourhood of Cape Town, and also occurs at the Knysna. 1901 STARK & SCLATER *Birds of S. Afr.* 66 The Boschvogel is seldom found away from the dense bush, and owing to its sombre colour and shy habits is not easily seen or discovered.

b. An element in place names, as *Boschheuwel, Rondebosch, Stellenbosch.* See also BUSH *n.*[1] sense 2 b.

1951 L.G. GREEN *Grow Lovely* 136 The Alabama-bos where the Malays held their annual picnics. 1989 P.E. RAPER *Dict. of Sn Afr. Place Names* 471 Rondebosch, .. Suburb of Cape Town ... The name, Dutch for 'round thicket' refers to a circular clump or grove of trees on the banks of the Liesbeek known at the the time of Van Riebeeck as 't ronde doorn bosjen', 'the round thorn bush'.

boschbok /ˈbɔʃbɔk/ *n. Obs. exc. hist.* Also **bosboc(k), bosbok, bosch-bock, boshbock.** *Pl.* **-ke** /-ə/, **-s,** or unchanged. [S. Afr. Du., *bosch* bush + *bok* antelope, goat; so called because it favours thickets and undergrowth.] BUSHBUCK. Also *attrib.*

1786 G. FORSTER tr. *A. Sparrman's Voy. to Cape of G.H.* I. 270 The *bosch-bock*, or wood-goat, .. is a species of antilope or gazel, which has been hitherto unknown to all the cultivators of natural history ... This animal has obtained the name it bears, in consequence of its being the only one among the gazels in Africa, which may be properly said to live in the woods and groves. 1790 tr. F. Le Vaillant's *Trav.* II. 244 These woods abounded likewise with two species of antelopes, not at all wild: the bos-boc, which I had seen in other places. 1806 J. BARROW *Trav.* I. 390 Every thicket is filled with the beautiful bosbok, or Bush deer, remarkable for its spotted haunches. 1834 T. PRINGLE *Afr. Sketches* 76 The boschbok oft would bound away. 1837 'N. POLSON' *Subaltern's Sick Leave* 123 In most of the woods about this part of the Colony is to be found boschbok, a very handsome species of antelope, with short spiral horns and his flank dappled. They frequent the thickest bush. 1866 J. LEYLAND *Adventures* 2, I crept along silently and cautiously, expecting every moment to see a Boschboc (*Tragelaphus Sylvatica*) spring from the bush. 1939 J.F. BENSE *Dict. of Low-Dutch Element in Eng. Vocab.* 19 Boschbok. 1786. An antelope of S. Africa, the Bush-buck. 1994 M. ROBERTS tr. *J.A. Wahlberg's Trav. Jrnls 1838-56* 24 Boschbok, 1 redbuck, little birds.

bosch dassie see DASSIE sense 1 c.

Boschie see BOSJESMAN sense 1.

∥**boschje, bossie** /ˈbɔʃi/ *n.* Also **bosje.** [Du., *bosch* bush + dim. suffix -*je* (Afk. *bossie, bos* bush + dim. suffix -IE), 'little bush'. Cf. BOSCH.] A bush.

1822 W.J. BURCHELL *Trav.* I. 23 A small number of the more remarkable indigenous plants are sometimes admitted to the honor of a place in their gardens: .. and it is a curious fact, that, among the colonists, these have not even a name, but, when spoken of, are indiscriminately called bosjes (bushes). 1880 N. MANSVELT in *Cape Monthly Mag.* III. 147 The well-known Cape Flats, which .. offer to the traveller nothing but the monotonous aspect of the almost unvarying 'bossies.' 1905 H. BOLUS in C.A. Smith *Common Names* (1966) 159 The knee-high boschjes of the Western Province. 1940 V. POHL *Bushveld Adventures* 24 No other weapon than the full-leafed branch of a melkbossie might be employed on the attack, and more often than not your bossie was smashed on your own head before the enemy had been subdued. 1972 *Star* 1 Apr. 7 Watch the dawn dribble pink over the bossies. 1973 O.H. SPOHR tr. *F. Krauss's Trav. Jrnl* 12 It was a pleasure to botanise along the slopes of Table Mountain and Devil's Peak among the flowering bushes (bosjes). **1988** O. OBERHOLZER *Ariesfontein to Zuurfontein*, From here one could see bossies and stones scattered amongst open patches of ground. Just the occasional 'doringdraad' fences cut their loneliness. **1991** J. COULTER in *Weekend Post* 4 May (Leisure) 3 This they did by bending saplings from the *bosje* (bush) and then covering them with thatching grass collected by the women.

boschjestroop var. BOSSIESTROOP.

boschjesveld var. BOSVELD.

boschlemmer var. BOSLEMMER.

Boschman var. BOSJESMAN.

Boschman Hottentot *n. phr. Obs.* Also **Boscherman Hottentot**, **Boschjies Hottentot**, etc. [Part. tr. S. Afr. Du. *Bosjesman* (see BOSJESMAN) + *Hottentot* (see HOTTENTOT).] Both elements usu. in *pl.*: a name given to the indigenous peoples by the early Dutch settlers at the Cape.

The name was probably applied to both KHOIKHOI and SAN indiscriminately; cf. KHOISAN sense 1.

1776 F. MASSON in *Phil. Trans. of Royal Soc.* LXVI. 311 We met a party of Dutchmen, who had been about 150 miles to the Northward of Bockland, destroying the Boschman Hottentots. **1790** tr. *F. Le Vaillant's Trav.* II. 68 Arrows, which I took from one of the Boshmen Hottentots. **1795** C.R. HOPSON tr. *C.P. Thunberg's Trav.* I. 157 The Boshiesmen Hottentots inhabit the most indifferent, poor, bare, and cold part of this southernmost point of Africa. **1804** R. PERCIVAL *Acct of Cape of G.H.* 87 The Boschermen Hottentots, who now are well known to be the aborigines of this country, .. will keep up with a horse at full speed for a considerable time. *Ibid.* 201 They [*sc.* the colonists] are subject to the warfare of the Caffrees and Boschjies Hottentots, who .. look with detestation and abhorrence on the Dutch boors. *a*1823 J. EWART *Jrnl* (1970) 32 Little or none of the country has as yet been explored but is supposed to be inhabited .. by tribes of Bosjesmen Hottentots.

boschsuiker *n. obs.* [S. Afr. Du., *bosch* bush + *suiker* sugar.] BOSSIESTROOP. Cf. BOSSUIKER.

1910 D. FAIRBRIDGE *That Which Hath Been* (1913) 115 Naartje-peel, spices, brandy, bosch-suiker — she had blended them in varying proportions again and again, but only to feel baffled and mortified. *Ibid.* 317 *Bosch-suiker*, A syrup obtained from the flowers of the Protea.

Boschuanas pl. form of BECHUANA.

boschvark /'bɔʃfark, -faːk/ *n.* Also **bosch vaark**, **bosch-varken**, **bos-vark**. Pl. **-varke** /-farkə/, **-varkens**. [S. Afr. Du. *boschvark*, later Afk. *bosvark*, fr. Du. *bosch* bush + *varken* pig; so called because it favours thickets and undergrowth.] BUSHPIG.

1786 G. FORSTER tr. *A. Sparrman's Voy. to Cape of G.H.* II. 23 This day I saw, for the first time, a herd of *bosch-varkens*, or, as they are likewise called, *wilde-varkens* .. in their wild uncultivated state. **1834** T. PRINGLE *Afr. Sketches* 277 The *bosch-vark*, or wood-swine .. a fierce animal, and armed with dangerous tusks, which protrude like those of an elephant. **1844** J. BACKHOUSE *Narr. of Visit* 213 The Bosch vark, Bush pig .. is about 2 1/2 feet high and 5 feet long, and has a tubercular excrescence covered with coarse hair on the face. **1900** W.L. SCLATER *Mammals of S. Afr.* I. 276 Bosch-varks are found most abundantly in broken hilly country where there is dense shade and plenty of water. **1918** S.H. SKAIFE *Animal Life* 259 Like most other wild pigs, the *bosch-vark* will fight fiercely when brought to bay. **1936** E.C. LLEWELLYN *Influence of Low Dutch* 164 *Boschvark*, .. A species of wild pig; so named from its habitat, from Du. *bosch*, bush, and *vark*, pig. **1968** L.G. GREEN *Full Many Glorious Morning* 227 A *bos-vark*, a bush pig and that one must have weighed two hundred and fifty pounds.

bosch veld var. BOSVELD.

bosh var. BOSCH.

Bosh(ees)man var. BOSJESMAN.

Boshman's grass var. BUSHMAN GRASS.

Boshuanah, **Boshuanas** pl. forms of BECHUANA.

bosje var. BOSCHJE.

Bosjesman *n. obs.* Forms: α. Boschjesman, Bosheesman, Boshie(s)-man, Boshis-man, Bosje(s)man, Bossies Mann, Bosyesman; β. Bosch(e)man, Boshman; γ. Bo(e)jesman, Boojesman. [Du., *bosch* or (dim.) *bos(ch)je* bush + linking phoneme -s- + *man* man; orig. meaning 'bush man' or bandit, *Bosjesman* was a Du. name for a member of the SAN people (see quot. 1992).]
1. Pl. **-man(n)s**, **-men**. SAN sense 1. So (*obs.*) **Bosjes menschen** or **Bosjes people** *n. phrr.*, **Bosjes woman** *n. phr.*, and **Boschie** *n.* [see -IE]. Also *attrib.*, and *fig.* Cf. BUSH *adj.*[2]

α. **1786** G. FORSTER tr. *A. Sparrman's Voy. to Cape of G.H.* I. 197 There is another species of Hottentots, who have got the name of *Boshies-men*, from dwelling in woody or mountainous places. *Ibid.* II. 31 He had caught .. three old Boshies-women with their children, with an intention to take them home to his master for slaves. **1795** C.R. HOPSON tr. *C.P. Thunberg's Trav.* I. 132 These Hottentots were *Boshiesmen*, of a dark brown complexion. **1795** F. KERSTEINS in G.M. Theal *Rec. of Cape Col.* (1897) I. 168 They are incessantly harrassed by the Bossies Manns (a Species of Hottentots). **1798** EARL MACARTNEY in S.D. Naudé *Kaapse Plakkaatboek* (1950) V. 141 The Bosheesmen are to be .. left in possession of their just rights and habitations and are not to be molested .. on any pretence whatsoever. **1799** LADY A. BARNARD *Lett. to Henry Dundas* (1973) 187 There is something singularly delicate in the make of the Boshie men, their arms so finely turned — hands so small. **1804** R. PERCIVAL *Acct of Cape of G.H.* 95 The Boschies are looked upon as of a more cruel, hardened and savage disposition than the Hottentots at the Cape. **1812** A. PLUMPTRE tr. *H. Lichtenstein's Trav. in Sn Afr.* (1928) I. 56 The Bosjesman race. [*Note*] A tribe of savage Hottentots who lurk about among the shrubs and bushes, whence they sally out to plunder travellers. **1828** *Ordinance* 49 in *Stat. Law of Cape of G.H.* (1862) 128 It shall and may be lawful for the Governor of this colony .. to authorise and direct the admission into the colony of any Kafirs, Gonaquas, Tambookies, Griquas, Bosjesmen, Bechuanas, Mantatees, Namaquas, or other natives of the interior of Africa. **1847** J. BARROW *Reflect.* 174 A singular people, known by the name of Bosjesman, from their living and concealing themselves among the bushes or thickets. [**1873** W.G. ATHERSTONE in A.M.L. Robinson *Sel. Articles from Cape Monthly Mag.* (1978) 99 The Boer .. called it simply 'kaup', .. the home of the ostrich and the wild baboon, and the still wilder men of the rocks and bush, *die bosjes menschen*.] **1876** F. BOYLE *Savage Life* 3 The diamond country was haunted by the Bushmen or Bosjesmen, and kindred tribes. [**1992** *Weekend Post* 15 Aug. (Leisure) 5 The Khoikhoi, their nearest relatives, called her people San; the Dutch named them Bosjemans. They themselves had no name for their ethnic group, referring by name only to their own bands and the few other bands they knew.]

β. [**1773** J. COOK in J. Hawkesworth *Acct of Voy.* III. 386 All .. are friendly and peaceable, except one clan that is settled to the eastward, which the Dutch call Boschmen, and these live entirely by plunder, or rather by theft.] **1790** tr. *F. Le Vaillant's Trav.* I. 326 He took the field, at the head of his people, to repel the Boshmen who came to disturb his repose. **1798** LADY A. BARNARD in Lord Lindsay *Lives of Lindsays* (1849) III. 457, I cannot think this was a real Boschewoman, her countenance had so much of the Hottentot mildness in it. **1800** W. JOHNSTON tr. *Fra Paolino's Voy. to E. Indies* 448 In the interior parts there is a kind of wild Hottentots, called Boshmen. **1819** G.M. KEITH *Voy.* 42 Locusts are .. esteemed excellent food by the Boshmans, by whom they are dried and kept for use. **1827** *Reports of Commissioners upon Finances at Cape of G.H.* 42 That unfortunate race of men called 'Boschmen'. **1838** J.E. ALEXANDER *Exped. into Int.* I. 51 Leopards and Boschmans are sometimes troublesome in this district. *Ibid.* II. 196 It is believed in the land that some of the Bosch-people can change themselves into wolves or lions when they like. *Ibid.* 197 A Boschwoman carrying a child on her back. **1854** H. MILLER *Footprints of Creator* (1870) 156 It is only the squalid savages and degraded boschmen of creation that have their feeble teeth and tiny stings steeped in venom.

γ. **1821** *Missionary Notices* Dec., Bojeman's tribe, who appear to be very numerous in this quarter. **1832** *Graham's Town Jrnl* 25 Oct. 172 Petrus Klaas, .. Jonker Keizer, .. Boojesmen or Bushmen. **1968** F.C. METROWICH *Frontier Flames* 10 Coenrad's hatred of the English was well known. He told Gaika they were 'the Boejesmans of the sea.'

2. *rare.* SAN sense 2.

α. **1907** C. DICKENS *Reprinted Pieces* 106 His cry of 'Qu-u-u-u-aaa!' (Bosjesman for something desperately insulting, I have no doubt).

Bosjesmansthee *n. obs.* Also **Bosjesman's thee**, **Bosjes-man's-thé**. [S. Afr. Du., *Bosjesmans* combining or possessive form of *Bosjesman* (see BOSJESMAN) + *thee* tea.] BUSHMAN'S TEA.

[**1837** ECKLON & ZEYHER *Enumeratio Plantarum Africae* 152 *Methyscophyllum glaucum* .. Frutex 8-12 pedalis; incolis: Bojesmansthee.] **1847** L. PAPPE in C.A. Smith *Common Names* (1966) 149 It grows about the Zwartkeirivier, where it is a favourite beverage with Bushmen and others, who also chew it, and call it Bojesmansthee. **1860** HARVEY & SONDER *Flora Capensis* I. 463 *Methyscophyllum* .. is the 'Bosjesman's-thee' of the colonists. The leaves, chewed to excess by the Bosjesmen, have intoxicating effects: a moderate infusion is said to be good as tea, and also as a remedy for asthma. **1868** W.H. HARVEY *Genera of S. Afr. Plants* 53 *C.[atha] edulis* .., The 'Bosjes-man's-thé' of the colonists. **1913** C. PETTMAN *Africanderisms* 82 *Bosjesmans thee*, *Catha edulis*, Forsk. .. An infusion of its leaves is used for coughs, asthma, etc. A rare shrub in South Africa known only from the Queenstown and Cathcart districts.

bosjesthee *n. obs.* [S. Afr. Du., *bos(ch)je* see BOSCHJE + linking phoneme -s- + *thee* tea.] BUSH TEA.

1861 LADY DUFF-GORDON *Lett. from Cape* (1925) 65 A cup of 'bosjesthee' (herb tea).

bosjestroop var. BOSSIESTROOP.

bosj(i)esveld var. BOSVELD.

Boskop /'bɒskɒp, 'bɔskɔp/ *n.* [Place name.] Usu. *attrib.* (passing into *adj.*), *occas. predicative*: descriptive of the early type of human indicated by the late Pleistocene skull found at Boskop in the North West Province (in what was formerly the Transvaal) in 1913.

'Boskop man', originally described as *Homo capensis*, is now regarded as a species of *Homo sapiens* from which the Khoisan peoples are probably descended.

1915 *Nature* 5 Aug. 615 The Boskop man was of the Neanderthal race, but more advanced in intelligence. **1930** C.G. SELIGMAN *Races of Afr.* (1939) 48 Whether the Boskop skull .. represents an undifferentiated Boskop-Khoisan type, or .. is itself a derivative with the Khoisan of a less differentiated proto-Boskop type, is uncertain. **1970** M. WILSON *1000 Yrs before Van Riebeeck* 4 Sometimes the short hunters described were the light-skinned people with tiny hands and feet, familiar in the south here as Bush-Boskop in type, and sometimes they were short, dark, heavily built negroes, with clumsy hands and feet, more resembling pygmies than Bush-Boskop. **1974** *E. Prov. Herald* 21 Aug. 10 [Raymond Dart] said that Boskop man found in different parts of southern Africa was the ancestor of the Bush-Hottentot type and that there existed a Boskop strain in the African population. **1974** C.T. BINNS *Warrior People* 18 The Boskop Skull found in 1913 on a Transvaal farm. 'A pure-blooded Homo Sapiens,' according to Dr Bryant, 'and should be regarded as an ancient member of the stock now represented in S. Africa by Bushmen and Hottentot .. divergent branches which have arisen from a common stock and in a collateral line of descent from the Negroes.' **1985** G.T. NURSE et al. *Peoples of Sn Afr.* 42 To equate a proto-Khoisan stage with the existence of the 'Boskop' race would be misleading on various grounds (Singer 1958). **1989** *Reader's Digest Illust. Hist.* 19 According to the researchers, the Boskop race was uniquely southern African, and by the middle 1900's at least seven distinct races, each with their own particular traits and cultures, had been identified as being ancestors of 'Boskop' man.

Hence **Boskopoid** /ˈbɒskəˌpɔɪd, ˈbɔskəpɔɪd/ *adj.* (also with small initial) [Eng. adj.-forming suffix *-oid* 'having the form or nature of, resembling' (*OED*)].

1926 *Bantu Studies* II. 219 Comparison has been made mainly with the Boskopoid remains from Zitzikama reported upon .. during the last two years, and with the descriptions of the original Boskop remains. **1936** *Cambridge Hist. of Brit. Empire* VIII. 21 Again, stone culture deposits of earlier facies and date than those of the Bushmen have quite recently yielded, at Fish Hoek in the Cape Peninsula, a skeleton belonging to the extinct racial type now termed 'Boskopoid'. **1970** B. DAVIDSON *Old Afr.* 29 Bushmen, very rare in modern Africa, may represent the only close link with 'boskopoid' populations of remote antiquity. **1977** T.R.H. DAVENPORT *S. Afr.: Mod. Hist.* 10 The Cape was thinly populated by sallow-skinned boskopoid hunter-gatherers and herders when the permanent white settlement began in 1652. **1989** *Reader's Digest Illust. Hist.* 19 Experts reconstructed a 'typical' skull complete with what they referred to as 'Boskopoid' features.

boslemmer /ˈbɔsleməə(r)/ *n. hist.* Formerly also **boschlemmer**. [Afk. (earlier S. Afr. Du. *boschlemmer*), *bos* bush + *lemmer* blade of knife.] HERNHUTTER. Also *attrib.*

1806 *Cape Town Gaz.* 8 Feb. (Suppl.), Public Sale. On Monday & Tuesday the 24 & 25 of Feb. 1806 there will be sold at the farm of Jacobus Redelinghuis, .. Boslemmer-knifes .. blue and white Baftas. **1819** W. ANDERSON in G.M. Theal *Rec. of Cape Col.* (1902) XII. 168 Common Tools. — Hatchets, .. Files, Knives (Boslemmers). **1821** C.I. LATROBE *Jrnl of Visit* 191 For a fine fat sheep, Mr Snyman was satisfied to take two Gnadenthal knives, called here boschlemmers, the goodness of which has long recommended them to the inhabitants of the colony. **1971** L.G. GREEN *Taste of S.-Easter* 158, I asked Anna about some knives of unfamiliar design and she told me they were boslemmers from the Genadendal mission; they were really farmer's knives, useful for rough work in a kitchen. **1972** —— *When Journey's Over* 29 The missionaries were teaching their flock tanning, the craft of the tinsmith and blacksmith, wagon-building and the manufacture of the celebrated Moravian knives known as boslemmers or Hernhutters.

BOSS /bɒs/ *n. hist.* Also **Boss**, **B.O.S.S.** Acronym formed on the initial letters of *Bureau of* (or *for*) *State Security*, a government agency set up in 1969 for the administration of national security. Also *attrib.*

Having become discredited, BOSS was replaced in 1978 by the Department of National Security (see DONS), and in February 1980 by the National Intelligence Service (see NIS). The security function has since been incorporated into the South African Police.

1969 S. UYS in J. Crwys-Williams *S. Afr. Despatches* (1989) 395 Explaining with almost child-like simplicity to his Worcester audience the implications of the Bureau for State Security (BOSS), Dr. Hertzog said: 'If one of BOSS's authorised officials in Worcester is cross with you, he can lock you up for as long as he likes.' **1969** O. MUSI in *Post* 15 June 14 You've probably read about B.O.S.S. The letters stand for the Bureau of State Security. **1971** *Rand Daily Mail* 16 Mar. 10 Public servants and nationalist politicians had become alarmed about the activities of BOSS, which they felt was developing into a 'super political police force'. **1972** *Sunday Times* 27 Feb. 4 General van den Bergh objects to being called the boss of BOSS. His organisation, he says, is the Bureau *for* State Security, and not *of* State Security, so he is not going to play speaks any more with newspapers which use the word BOSS. **1973** P. DRISCOLL *Wilby Conspiracy* 127 'BOSS'. Numbly he repeated the silly-sounding acronym. The Bureau of State Security, the powerful and faceless organization that controlled intelligence and secret police work. **1974** [see SHAKA'S SPEAR]. **1979** [see DONS]. **1985** J. ESMOND in *Staffrider* Vol.6 No.2, 26 It was a standing joke that if you yawned at a meeting *Boss* would have a photograph of all your fillings. **1990** A. GOLDSTUCK *Rabbit in Thorn Tree* 33 In the 1970's .. the notorious Bureau of State Security, or BOSS, was a byword for 'Big Brother' watching us. **1993** J. TURNER on Radio South Africa 28 Apr. (Radio Today), It seems more likely that it would have been BOSS if he had been killed by a hit squad. He had been harrassed by BOSS and the Security Police.

bossala var. BASELA *v.*

boss-boy *n. offensive.* [Eng. *boss* + BOY sense 1 a.] A black man in charge of a team of mineworkers or other labourers; a black foreman or caretaker; BAAS-BOY sense 1. Cf. INDUNA sense 1 b. See also BOY senses 1 a and b.

1906 *Daily Chron.* (U.K.) 11 Apr. 3 One white man in the mine is expected to 'boss' forty blacks or Chinese, which he cannot do with safety, in fact the black 'boss-boy' is left to do much of the blasting. **1923** G.H. NICHOLLS *Bayete!* 119 Munyati was the boss-boy on the farm, a man of forty-five years of age. **1925** [see MABALANE]. **1936** WILLIAMS & MAY *I Am Black* 169 To be a boss-boy was a great honour. It meant that he had charge over twelve or fifteen black men. **1952** *Drum* Mar. 33 Very often the boss boys, themselves Africans, are tough and ruthless with the labourers, for if they are not they lose their jobs. **1960** J.J.L. SISSON *S. Afr. Judicial Dict.* 100 A native *boss boy* is not necessarily a 'servant' as there defined, as *prima facie* the term *boss boy* would seem to indicate supervision rather than 'handicraft or other bodily labour'. **1962** A.J. LUTHULI *Let my People Go* 218 On the affected farms, African men — some are no more than boys — dig potatoes with their bare fingers. 'Boss-Boys' and overseers stand over them with whips, which they do not hesitate to use. **1973** *E. Prov. Herald* 26 Mar. 1 The ceiling for supervisors (known as boss boys) of whom there are about 8 000 will increase from R68 per month to R104. **1980** M. LIPTON in *Optima* Vol.29 No.2, 99 On the job, workers were subjected to strict and often aggressive supervision by White miners and Black 'boss boys'. **1985** J. IMRIE *Informant, Chamber of Mines* In respect of the term 'Boss Boy'. The leader of a team of underground mineworkers is officially and generally called a team leader (Fanakalo: tim lida) on gold mines and an mpati (pronounced mpahtee and meaning supervisor) on collieries. **1988** *Style* May 55 She relies heavily on the sweat of the backroom chaps with the picks and shovels, an indispensable team led by what is still known, anachronistically, as a Bossboy.

bossie var. BOSCHJE.

‖**bossiedokter** /ˈbɔsiˌdɔktə(r)/ *n. colloq.* [Afk., *bos* bush, shrub + -IE + *dokter* doctor.] A pejorative name for a herbalist or naturopath. Cf. HERBALIST.

The usual Afrikaans term for a herbalist is *kruiedokter* [*kruie* herbs].

1934 C.P. SWART Supplement to Pettman. 22 *Bossiedokter*, (A. bos, shrub; dokter, doctor). A herbalist is so designated by the Boers. **1949** L.G. GREEN *In Land of Afternoon* 49 Herbalists have always flourished in the Cape. The *bossie dokter* was at work before Van Riebeeck arrived; and he is still willing to prescribe for almost any ailment. **1970** H.M. MUSMECI *Informant, Port Elizabeth* Our Bantu servant believes that the bossiedokter will cure him. **1977** *Sunday Times* 9 Oct. 15 Some .. don't think much of naturopaths, it seems. Alluding to the herbs they use, they call them 'bossie dokters' — bush doctors. **1991** *Best of S. Afr. Short Stories* (Reader's Digest Assoc.) 104 The roots, leaves and bark or many plants were used to treat specific disorders, and a *bossiedokter* (herb doctor) .. was often in demand ... Not all the traditional plant 'cures' helped, of course, and some could actually be dangerous.

‖**bossiemiddel** /ˈbɔsiˌməd(ə)l/ *n.* Also **bossiesmiddel**. [Afk., *bos* bush + -IE + *middel* remedy.] A home remedy, usu. made of herbs. See also BOERERAAT. Also *fig.*

1929 D. REITZ *Commando* 17 He said, 'You see, my boy, we Boere don't hold with those new-fangled ideas; our herbal remedies (*bossie-middels*) are good enough.' **1930** L. BARNES *Caliban in Afr.* 128 In the same spirit the modern Afrikaner clutches the *bossiemiddel* of white privilege as the solvent of every difficulty and panacea for every ill. **1987** W. STEENKAMP *Blockhouse* 24 'Bossiesmiddels,' he said. 'Herbal remedies. That's what cures a man.' **1990** C. LAFFEATY *Far Forbidden Plains* 205 A blind eye was now being turned to the treatment of prisoners with herbal remedies by their own people. 'Afterwards .. they will be able to blame the sickness on the bossiemiddels of the Boers.'

bossies /ˈbɔsiːz, -is/ *adj. colloq.* [Afk., fr. *bosbefok* (see BOSBEFOK).] Traumatized or crazed as a result of the stress of experiencing military action in a war zone; BOSBEFOK. Also *transf.*

1979 *Informant, Grahamstown* Here's Richard, this bossies ou I was telling you about — thinks he's still in the army. **1983** D. BECKETT in *Frontline* Feb. 32 What .. of all those rumours about troops who went 'bossies' — bush mad? **1985** *Frontline* Aug. 54, I don't know about these guys who are meant to go bossies after service. I don't know anyone who is really gone in his head because of contacts ... Of course, guys who spend long enough living in the bush end up bedonderd, but that's just normal army befok, it's not bossies like from war. **1987** *Fair Lady* 21 Jan. 144 The SADF, when in doubt psychologically, reverted to *bossies*; 'The *ou* that knifed his girlfriend? *Nooit*, he's okay, a bit *bossies* but quite *lekker* basically.' **1987** M. POLAND *Train to Doringbult* 86 'It's time to go home. I'm getting *bossies* in this place.' Andrew laughed ruefully. 'Like the army.' **1988** *Personality* 7 Nov. 27 The border women share a .. horror of becoming women who have gone 'bossies' — sans hairbrush, sans make-up and sans the latest range from Foschini. **1991** T. BARON in *Sunday Times* 5 May 27 He never needed to go into the bush to become *bossies* because he was, surely, born that way. He is very high octane.

Bossies Mann var. BOSJESMAN.

‖**bossiestroop** /ˈbɔsiˌstruəp/ *n.* Formerly also **bos(ch)jestroop**. [Afk. (earlier S. Afr. Du. *boschjesstroop*), *bos* bush + -IE + *stroop* syrup.] The (syrup prepared from the) nectar of the flowers of *Protea repens* of the Proteaceae, used as a sweetening agent, and (formerly) as a cough medicine; BOSCHSUIKER. Also *attrib.* See also SUGARBUSH.

[**1797** LADY A. BARNARD *S. Afr. Century Ago* (1925) 55 In the same box you will find .. a small specimen of the syrup of the sugar tree; I could not make the box contain a quart, which I was sorry for. **1850** *Cape Monitor* 8 Nov., List Of Prize Prices ... Bush Syrup (or Boschjes Syrop, made from the flowers of The Protea Bush) for the finest dozen bottles .. £1.10.0.] **1913** C. PETTMAN *Africanderisms* 83 *Bosjestroop*, .. This syrup, which is used for the relief and cure of coughs, is made by boiling the mixed honey and dew taken in the early morning from the calyx of *Protea mellifera*. **1917** [see SUGARBUSH]. **1927** C.G. BOTHA *Social Life in Cape Col.* 101 In those parts where the sugarbush or species of protea abounded the sweet watery liquor, which filled the flower during its inflorescence, was collected and prepared by inspissation into a delicious syrup known as 'Boschjesstroop.' **1955** L.G. GREEN *Karoo* 105 Sugar was often a luxury on remote farms. Honey was the usual substitute, though some were able to secure *bossiestroop*, the thin syrup found in certain protea flowers. **1973** M.A. COOK *Cape Kitchen*

46 The Cape waffle was eaten with honey or with bossiestroop (syrup boiled up from the flowers of *Protea mellifera*, now reclassified as *P. repens*). **1980** [see SUIKERBOS]. **1988** M. ROBINS in *Argus* 1 Sept. 17 Bottles of wild grape jelly, *bossiestroop* and wild cucumber preserves perch next to specimens of their plant derivatives. **1988** M. BRANCH *Explore Cape Flora* 4 The early settlers .. discovered that if they placed the flower-heads of the *sugarbush* protea face down, they could collect buckets full of sweet nectar to use as syrup, known as 'bossiestroop'.

‖**bossuiker** /'bɔs sœikə(r)/ *n*. [Afk. (fr. Du. *borstsuiker, borst* chest + *suiker* sugar), 'barley sugar'; cough lozenge.] See quot. 1947. Cf. BOSCHSUIKER.

[**1916** S. BLACK in S. Gray *Three Plays* (1984) 229 Peace: Hum! What's this stuff? It looks like dynamite. Van K: That's bosch-sugar! Peace: What are you doing with bosch-sugar? Van K: I eat it. Try a piece.] **1947** L.G. GREEN *Tavern of Seas* 72 The sweet shop in Long Street, where a St. Helena woman named Rachel Thompson presided over a gorgeous array of Cape sweets ... There were burnt almonds, bossuiker (a sort of sugarstick), the aniseed flavoured dumily-klontjies and almond rock. **1951** — *Grow Lovely* 72 The Malay quarter, source of the cookery secrets that have survived the centuries. There, too, the origin of the old Cape sweets and pastries seen in the shop windows may be traced, the tammeletjie and bossuiker, kraakelen and sugared mebos. **1971** — *Taste of S.-Easter* 157 When I first went there as a school boy I was interested only in the golden tammeletjies and the striped bossuikers.

boss up *int. phr. Obs*. [ad. S. Afr. Du. *pas op*.] PAS OP *int. phr*.

1835 T.H. BOWKER *Journal*. 7 Aug., They fired a kafir fire in the top of the Clugh where the blackguards are watching us, boss up. **1892** NICOLLS & EGLINGTON *Sportsman in S. Afr*. 81 Extra precaution should be observed, or, as the Dutch hunters say, 'boss up.' **1913** C. PETTMAN *Africanderisms* 83 *Boss up!*, A corruption of the Cape Dutch *Pas op!* — Take care! look out! [**1928** N. STEVENSON *Afr. Harvest* 194 He .. silenced the old woman by saying: 'Bos op, Auntie; you had better see to the supper, which .. is burning.'

Hence (nonce) **boss up** *v. phr. trans*. [perh. influenced by Eng. *boss* to manage, control], to take care of (someone), to supervise (someone); cf. PASS-UP sense b, PASOP *v*.

1884 C. DU VAL *With Show through Sn Afr*. I. 38 They [sc. the quay porters] are not enthusiastically devoted to hard work, but do not appear to be altogether unwilling if put in the right groove and kept well 'bossed up.'

bos-vark var. BOSCHVARK.

‖**bosveld** /'bɔsfɛlt, -fɛlt/ *n*. Formerly also **bos(ch)jesveld, bosch veld, bosjiesveld**. [Afk. (earlier S. Afr. Du. *boschveld, boschjesveld*), *bos* bush + *veld* (open) countryside.]

1. Usu. with initial capital, designating a particular area.

a. *obs*. The inland area to the north-east of the Cape Peninsula.

1822 W.J. BURCHELL *Trav*. I. 119 This division of the district, on the northern side of the mountains, is called Bosjesveld (Bushland, or the Bushy Country); .. that name was probably, at its first imposition, characteristic of the nature of the country.

b. *the Bosveld*: the Bushveld, see BUSHVELD sense 1. Also *attrib*.

1882 J. NIXON *Among Boers* 249 From the top we took our last glimpse of the fertile and warm 'Boschveld,' and turned our faces towards the less tempting, arid plains of the high country. **1888** *Encycl. Brit*. XXIII. 518 Transvaal has been divided into three .. distinct natural regions ... These are .. the *Hooge veld*, .. the *Banken veld*, .. the *Bosch veld* or bush country, .. with an altitude of 3 000 to 4 000 feet and an area of 60 000 square miles. **1902** J. VAN WARMELO *On Commando* 43 Some hours north of Middelburg one suddenly leaves the high plateau of the Boschveld for a difficult road that curves steadily downwards between two high mountains. **1970** A. CONNOLLY *Informant, Bloemfontein* We are going to spend the winter months at a holiday resort in the Bosveld, as it is warmer there in winter. **1983** *Daily Dispatch* 11 May 6 In the picturesque bosveld town of Ellisras, party workers also mixed amicably but this changed for a short while when news of the scuffle and argument .. spread through the vast Waterberg constituency. **1989** D. VAN HEERDEN in *Sunday Times* 18 June 2 Sweating profusely on one of the coldest nights of the Bosveld winter, Mr Terre Blanche practically begged the CP not to oppose him at the polls.

2. BUSHVELD sense 2. Also *attrib*.

1896 R. WALLACE *Farming Indust. of Cape Col*. 96 The introduction of livestock to the 'boschjesveld' (bush country) has destroyed the balance of nature. [**1914** C. PETTMAN *Notes on S. Afr. Place Names* 22 Among Dutch place names must be included those which are applied to various localities as being descriptive of the character of the veld: e.g., Boschveld (bosch, bush), [etc.].] a**1928** C. FULLER *Trigardt's Trek* (1932) 97 Across the bosveld stretches a dark line formed by a string of high green trees. This marks the course of the Olifants River. **1963** A.M. LOUW *20 Days* 17 Glowing against the plain plaster walls the sultry bosveld dramas, the eternities of Karroo landscape, the studies of Native life. **1975** *Sunday Times* 7 Dec. (Mag. Sect.) 15 There are plenty of wealthy men around who will tell you with a nostalgic sigh that they built an empire on nothing more than the cattle farm they inherited in the bosveld. **1985** D. GARSIDE in *Staffrider* Vol.6 No.2, 15 Let your little incisors Bite through the fat, the uppermost crust With its bosveld and koppies. **1990** *Daily News* 20 Apr. 1 He .. bought the bull because of its shorter sheath which would not catch in South African bosveld, its hardiness and its fertility.

3. Special Comb. **bosveld garnaal** /- xar'nɑ:l/ (pl. **garnale** — /xar'nɑ:lə/) [Afk., *garnaal* prawn], *mopani worm* (see MOPANI sense 3).

1986 *Sunday Star* 8 June 5 It was the **Bosveld-garnale** ('Bushveld prawns' or, more accurately, mopani worms) .. that brought the crowds. **1991** *Personality* 6 May 24 Visualise a peculiar little bushveld delicacy called, aptly, *bosveld garnale* (bushveld prawns) .. otherwise known as mopani worms.

Hence **bosvelder**, *bushvelder n*. (see BUSHVELD).

1986 *Sunday Times* 12 Jan. 13 Outsiders must not accuse us of having a border mentality. We are simply hardened *bosvelders*.

Bosyesman var. BOSJESMAN.

Botchuana's pl. form of BECHUANA.

boterblo(e)m, boterboom varr. BOTTERBLOM, BOTTERBOOM.

Botha's Babe /ˌbʊətəz 'beɪb/ *n. phr. Hist. Colloq*. Also **Botha Babe**. [See quot. 1980.] SOLDOEDIE; usu. in *pl*., used collectively.

1971 *Daily Dispatch* 1 June 1 Botha's Babes, the Army girls who came all the way from George to show their paces, were hot favourites with the crowd. **1974** *Het Suid-Western* 12 Sept., The Civil Defence College gave a demonstration of simple self-defence methods, using seven Botha Babes as models. **1978** *Sunday Times* 23 Apr. 3 The college trains women in behind-the-line jobs such as telecommunications, releasing men for active service. It was started at the suggestion of Mr Botha and the girl soldiers are known as 'Botha's Babes.' **1980** *E. Prov. Herald* 4 Dec., Military rules .. have had to be re-interpreted at the South African Army Women's College in George ... Every year about 500 'Botha's Babes' pass through the college, which was opened in 1971 by Mr P.W. Botha, then Minister of Defence.

‖**botho** /'bʊːtʊ/ *n*. [Sotho, humanity, kindliness, mercy.]

a. Esp. among Sotho-speakers: UBUNTU sense a.

1979 *Voice* 6 Oct. 9 Botho means crying and sympathising with other children. Botho means knowing you are a child of the people not of Mr so-and-so. **1982** M. MZAMANE *Children of Soweto* 153 Bra P. possessed that rare quality Africans call *ubuntu* or *botho*, which is the sum total of human values as Africans understand them.

b. As an element in the *comb*. **ubuntu-botho**: see UBUNTU sense b.

Botlokoa var. TLOKWA.

Botschuanas pl. form of BECHUANA.

botsotsos /bɔ'tsɔtsɔs/ *pl. n. Slang*. Also **botsosos, potso-tsos**, and with initial capital. [Isicamtho, fr. Sotho and seTswana, n. prefix *bo-* + *-tsotso*, prob. ad. TSOTSI + Eng. pl. suffix *-s*.] Esp. in township Eng.: narrow stove-pipe trousers worn by girls and women.

1978 *Voice* 8 Nov. 2, I am worried about our Black sisters ... It gave me a frightening shock to see some of them wearing the so-called 'Botsotsos', with horrible make-ups [sic] on their faces, going around with Whites. **1981** K. MASHISHI in *Staffrider* Vol.3 No.4, 7 Guide us to righteousness Take us back to our Africa Away from the Botsotsos Back to our tradition Away from skyscrapers.-**1982** *Pace* June 133 Nomvula Madesi will have nothing of the Goray Skirt, 'I stick to my potso-tsos, sorry baby.' **1982** W.S. MTHETHWA in *Staffrider* Vol.5 No.2, 9 Some chicks in see-through dresses and botsotsos, some in typical traditional dresses and some dressed as responsible ladies. **1983** I.T. MNISI in *Frontline* Sept. 6 The old generation used to wear skins of animals, but today we see miracles. People wear 'Botsotsos'. This is the moment of civilization.

‖**botterbak** /'bɒtə(r)bak/ *n. hist*. Pl. **-ke** /-kə/. [Afk., *botter* butter + *bak* bowl.] A rectangular wooden dish in which freshly-churned butter was worked. See also BAKKIE sense 1.

1971 BARAITSER & OBHOLZER *Cape Country Furn*. 257 The watery lumps of butter are then transferred to a wooden botterbak. **1973** M.A. COOK *Cape Kitchen* 100 When the butter had 'come' as the saying is, the buttermilk was strained off and the butter was tipped out into the botterbak. This was traditionally made of *waboom*. .. The botterbak was made out of one piece of wood. **1974** *Reader's Digest* Dec., Objects that became obsolete more recently: house and kitchen gadgets like the *botterbak* — the rectangular wooden dish in which butter was served with a *spaan* or scoop. **1989** *Afr. Wildlife* Vol.43 No.3, 159 Another traditional household use of the waboom was in the construction of butter-bowls or 'botterbakke' used in the butter-making process.

botterbalie see BALIE sense b.

botterblom /'bɒtə(r)blɒm/ *n*. Formerly also **boter bloem, boterblom**. Pl. **-me** /-mə/. [Afk. (fr. Du. *boterbloem*), *botter* butter + *blom* flower; see quot. 1966.] Any of several species of flowering plants of the Asteraceae, Iridaceae, or Ranunculaceae; now applied esp. to species of *Gazania*, but also to *Arctotis* and *Sparaxis*; BUTTER-BLOEM. Also *attrib*. See also GAZANIA, GOUSBLOM, SPARAXIS.

1913 C. PETTMAN *Africanderisms* 83 *Boter bloem*, .. *Gazania pinnata* var. *integrifolia*. The flower is yellow, and an infusion of the whole plant is used as a preventative of miscarriage. **1917** R. MARLOTH *Common Names* 14 *Boterblom*, Applied to a number of different plants. *The Geel* — (E: buttercup) is *Ranunculus pinnatus*, one of the few indigenous species of the genus. The *Wit* — is *Dimorphotheca pluvialis*. Some yellow composites bear the same name, e.g., *Gazania pinnata*. **1966** C.A. SMITH *Common Names* 169 *Botterblom*, .. From the original Du. *boterbloem* ... Although the common name was almost certainly prompted in Holland by the colour of the sepals, its application to the Arctotidae was almost certainly influenced at the Cape by the very old traditional belief that the normal presence of these plants in the natural pastures increased the butter yield of milk of cows grazing on them. **1968** F.G. BUTLER *Cape Charade* 46 A botterblom. Does nothing in this magnificent setting of mountains and abysses impress you more than this common wild flower? **1986** N. CHARTON *Informant, Grahamstown* There are fields of yellow daisies – botterblomme we call them or Butter Flowers. **1987** *S. Afr. Panorama* Mar. 43 From August to October South African and foreign visitors are attracted in their thousands to this spectacle to revel in the red splashes of *Gazania krebsiana (botterblom).* **1988** M. BRANCH *Explore Cape Flora* 14 Botterblom sparaxis grows in marshy areas.

botterboom /ˈbɔtə(r)buəm/ *n.* Formerly also **boterboom.** Pl. **-s, -bome** /-buəmə/. [Afk. (earlier S. Afr. Du. *boterboom*), *botter* butter + *boom* tree; see quot. 1822. C.A. Smith reports that 'children slide down hillsides on the stout slippery and buttery .. stems' (*Common Names of S. Afr. Plants*, 1966, p.170).] **a.** The deciduous succulent *Tylecodon paniculatus* of the Crassulaceae; BUTTER-TREE. **b.** Any of several similar trees.

1822 W.J. BURCHELL *Trav.* I. 192 An arborescent species of *Cotyledon* was curious and remarkable. In growth, it resembled a small tree, having a disproportionately thick fleshy trunk. It was called the *Boterboom* (Butter-tree) probably from the soft fleshy nature of its trunk and branches. **1844** J. BACKHOUSE *Narr. of Visit* 113 The Cotyledons have thick, succulent leaves and stout, soft stems: some of them are arborescent shrubs of about eight feet high: they are called in the Colony Boter-booms, *Butter trees.* **1897** P. MACOWAN in C.A. Smith *Common Names* (1966) 170 The curious 'Boterboom' well-known from Worcester right up to Clanwilliam. **1917** R. MARLOTH *Common Names* 15 *Boter'boom, Cotyledon paniculata.* A deciduous succulent of the Little Karoo and similar tracts. Stem stout and fleshy. Leafless in summer. **1929** *Farming in S. Afr.* Feb. 1279 Spineless Cactus, Botterboom (Cotyledan [*sic*] paniculata), .. pumpkins or potatoes can be used in the place of prickly-pear. **1937** *Handbk for Farmers* (Dept of Agric. & Forestry) 462 The following (*Cotyledon*) plants may be responsible for krimpsiekte: .. *Cotyledon fascicularis* .. (botterboom). **1966** C.A. SMITH *Common Names* 170 In South West Africa, the name *botterboom* is applied to the taller thick-stemmed succulent *Cyphostemma cramerianum* .. ; and *C. juttae* .. because of the resemblance of the thick trunks to those of *Cotyledon paniculata.* **1988** P. DU TOIT in Smuts & Alberts *Forgotten Highway* 183 Rode donkeys and *botterboom*, a thick plant, butterbush, which becomes nice and slippery when you slide down a rocky slope on pieces of its trunk. **1992** *S. Afr. Garden & Home* Dec. 100 Another good container plant is the *botterboom, Tylecodon paniculatus.*

‖**botterspaan** /ˈbɔtə(r)spɑːn/ *n. hist.* Pl. **-spane** /-ə/. [Afk., *botter* butter + *spaan* scoop.] A wooden spatula or scoop used in Cape Dutch kitchens for working freshly-churned butter.

1971 BARAITSER & OBHOLZER *Cape Country Furn.* 259 With the botterbak goes the botterspaan or wooden butter-hand, consisting of a wide, spade-like paddle with raised edges and a thick handle. **1973** M.A. COOK *Cape Kitchen* 111 *Butter-Scoop,* Wooden spatula for working freshly churned butter. Also known as a botterspaan.

bottlebrush *n.* [Transf. use of general Eng. *bottlebrush* a name applied to various plants and flowers.] Any of several shrubs or trees of the Greyiaceae and Proteaceae, bearing brush-like flowers. Usu. with a distinguishing epithet: **mountain bottlebrush**, *(a) Natal bottlebrush; (b)* the winter-flowering shrub *Greyia flanaganii* of the Greyiaceae; **Natal bottlebrush**, the ornamental shrub or small tree *Greyia sutherlandii* of the Greyiaceae; **red bottlebrush**, the colourful low shrub *Mimetes cucullatus* of the Proteaceae; **silver-leaved bottlebrush** *rare*, the shrub *M. argenteus* of the Proteaceae; **Transvaal bottlebrush**, the gnarled shrub *Greyia radlkoferi* of the Greyiaceae.

Greyia flanaganii is also occas. called *Flanagan's bottlebrush* or *kei bottlebrush.*

1951 S. ELIOVSON *Flowering Shrubs & Trees* 86 *Greyia sutherlandii,* **Mountain bottlebrush.** This semi-deciduous shrub is most suitable for the rockery, for it comes from the mountain slopes of South Africa, particularly Natal. *c***1968** [see *Natal bottlebrush*]. **1972** *S. Afr. Panorama* Jan. 21 (*caption*) Mountain Bottle Brush near the Shelf. **1972** *Evening Post* 11 Mar. 6 The mountain bottlebrush (Greyia flanaganii) flowers in winter. **1907** J.M. WOOD *Handbk to Flora of Natal* 33 *Greyia Sutherlandi* is a handsome flowering tree of the upper districts, and is sometimes known as the **'Natal Bottle Brush'**. **1917** R. MARLOTH *Common Names* 15 *Bottle-brush,* (Na), *Greyia Sutherlandii.* **1951** N.L. KING *Tree-Planting* 68 *Greyia sutherlandi (Natal bottle brush),* A shrub or small tree with brilliant red flowers. Occurs on kranses and rocky ground in the high rainfall belt of Natal and eastern Transvaal at an altitude of 3, 500 feet or more. *c***1968** S. CANDY *Natal Coast Gardening* 53 *Greyia sutherlandi,* 'Mountain Bottlebrush'. 'Natal Bottlebrush'. A small native tree flowering in summer. **1970** M.R. LEVYNS in *Std Encycl. of Sn Afr.* II. 464 *Bottle-brush,* .. (*Greyia sutherlandii.*) Shrub or small tree of the family *Melianthaceae,* having a pale bark and large, broad, simple leaves, cordate at the base and with a toothed margin. The bright scarlet flowers are produced about June and are borne in dense racemes. **1972** *Evening Post* 11 Mar. 6 Another indigenous shrub is the Greyia sutherlandii or Natal bottlebrush. **1983** K.C. PALGRAVE *Trees of Sn Afr.* 548 *Greyia sutherlandii,* .. Natal bottlebrush. **1972** *Evening Post* 11 Mar. 6 Another indigenous shrub with red flowers is the Greyia sutherlandi or Natal bottlebrush. It has an interesting, rather gnarled growth habit and bears red flowers in early spring. **1991** *Ornamental Trees & Shrubs of Afr. Calendar, Natal Bottlebrush, Greyia sutherlandii* has been grown in Europe for more than a century but is less familiar to South African gardeners. **1991** *Light Years* Vol.2 No.3, 8 The Natal bottlebrush flames against the lush green of the hills. **1970** M.R. LEVYNS in *Std Encycl. of Sn Afr.* II. 464 **Bottle-brush, Red.** Colourful, low shrub, .. common on lower mountain slopes in the south-west portion of the Cape Province ... The flowers are regular and consist of four whitish perianth lobes, each with an anther at its apex. The stiff red styles are exposed as the flowers open. **1973** BEETON & DORNER in *Eng. Usage in Sn Afr.* Vol.4 No.2, 39 *Red bottle-brush,* .. (*Mimetes lyrigera*) .. low shrub of the Proteaceae, found on the lower mountain slopes on the s-wst Cape Province. **1987** T.F.J. VAN RENSBURG *Intro. to Fynbos* 17 Other smaller shrubs in the mountain fynbos are bottlebrushes (*Mimetes*) [etc.]. **1973** M.R. LEVYNS in *Std Encycl. of Sn Afr.* IX. 160 Rare species of *Mimetes* are .. *M. argentia* (the '**silver-leaved bottlebrush**') [etc.]. **1977** E. PALMER *Field Guide to Trees* 205 **Transvaal bottlebrush**, *G. radlkoferi* .. ; often confused with *G. sutherlandii* but leaves densely felted below, especially when young. **1984** J. ONDERSTALL *Tvl Lowveld & Escarpment* 128 *Greyia radlkoferi,* Transvaal Bottlebrush ... As rugged as its rocky, mountain environs, it is often gnarled and crooked, with very rough bark.

bottleneck *n. slang.* [Special senses of gen. Eng. *bottleneck* the neck of a bottle.] **a.** A mixture of marijuana, tobacco, and other substances, pressed into the broken-off neck of a bottle and smoked through the bottle mouth; cf. PIPE sense 2 a. **b.** The broken-off neck of a bottle, used as a pipe in this way; cf. *dagga pipe* sense (*a*), see DAGGA *n.*[2] sense 3 b. Also *attrib.*

1977 [see *dagga pipe* (DAGGA *n.*[2] sense 3 b)]. **1987** *Scope* 20 Nov. 41 White pipes were on the menu that morning. Dagga and mandrax mixed into a lethal bottleneck combo. **1988** [see *dagga smoker* (DAGGA *n.*[2] sense 3 b)]. **1992** *South* 27 Feb. 4 There's no room for theorising or analysis at bottleneck level.

bottle store *n. phr.* A shop at which liquor is sold for consumption off the premises; a wine-merchant's shop or 'off licence'. Also *attrib.* See also OFF-SALES.

1862 G.H. MASON *Zululand* 17 (Jeffreys), One of the first [of my old aquaintances] I met with was driving a carriage and a pair of horses; .. another, who formerly kept a small bottle store, was a wholesale exporter. **1897** H. RAYMOND *B.I. Barnato* 88 It was said that Merriman had formerly kept, or had been interested in the profits of a bottle store, that is, an off-licenced liquor shop. **1916** *E. Prov. Herald* 22 July 6 Touching on the bottle stores, the Committee considers that special officers under the control of the Resident Magistrate and closely in touch with the Police should be entrusted with power to issue or refuse liquor permits. **1952** *Drum* June 10 Africans .. are not allowed to buy wine in the bottle-stores; so they get Coloured workers to buy it for them, or brew Skokiaan or 'Kill-me-quick' for their weekend drinking. **1961** T. MATSHIKIZA *Choc. for my Wife* 30 She worked in the bottle store serving the blacks who had liquor permits, and whites who required none. **1978** *Het Suid-Western* 20 Sept., Bottle stores are now the last shops left in South Africa that practice racial segregation with separate entrances and separate counters, depending on your skin colour ... The poor bottle store man has no alternative, or else he is in grave danger of losing his liquor licence. **1984** D. PINNOCK *Brotherhoods* 15 Liquor prohibition was ended in terms of the Liquor Amendment Act of 1961 ... The Act granted all races the right to buy liquor at bottle-stores. **1991** G. ZWIRN in *Settler* Vol.65 No.2, 11 *Bottle store,* Colloquial SAE for a British-type of off-licence, viz. a shop where liquor is sold for consumption off the premises. **1993** *Sunday Times* 25 Apr. 13 A number of off-licences (the curious name for bottle-stores in Britain) pride themselves on keeping homesick South Africans .. supplied of their favourite tipple.

bouchu, boughou *varr.* BUCHU.

bourbon, bourboontjie *varr.* BOERBOON, BOERBOONTJIE.

Bovenland *var.* BOLAND.

bovian *var.* BAVIAAN.

boy *n.*

1. *offensive.* [Transf. use of general Eng. *boy* a male servant.]

a. An insulting term for a black African male, used irrespective of his age, occupation, or social position; also used as a term of address; BOYKIE sense 2; *Native boy,* see NATIVE *n.* sense 1 c. Cf. GIRL sense a, JONG *n.* sense 2 a, UMFAAN sense 2.

1812 A. PLUMPTRE tr. *H. Lichtenstein's Trav. in Sn Afr.* (1928) I. 118 A Hottentot .. expects to be called by his name if addressed by any one who knows it; and by those to whom it is not known he expects to be called Hottentot (which he pronounces *Hotnot*) or boy. **1839** W.C. HARRIS *Wild Sports* 15 We .. were amused .. by the drunken merriment and boisterous singing of a lame Irish cobbler, who was 'keeping it up' .. with two Hottentot 'boys,' neither of whom was under fifty years of age. **1855** J.W. COLENSO *Ten Weeks in Natal* 2 Our Kafir 'Boy' sleeps in the stable, not in the kitchen; I could not get reconciled to that un-English custom; and now he has begged that his wife may come. **1863** LADY DUFF-GORDON in F. Galton *Vacation Tourists* (1864) III. 215 Yes, madam, it is shocking here how people treat the blacks. They call quite an old man 'boy', and speak so scornfully. **1880** E.F. SANDEMAN *Eight Months in Ox-Waggon* 20 Every coloured man, irrespective of age, be he six or sixty, is called a boy throughout the colony. **1894** E. GLANVILLE *Fair Colonist* 76 'What is your name, John?' – all black men being Johns when they are not Boys. **1920** S.M. MOLEMA *Bantu Past & Present* 266 The average white man of South Africa .. seems even unwilling to call the black man by his name, delighting rather in calling him 'that Kaffir', 'this Kaffir', 'the big Kaffir', or some other kind of Kaffir. His black servants, no matter what their age may be, he always calls 'boys'. *a***1931** S. BLACK in S. Gray *Three Plays* (1984) 159 Rebecca: 'Ere, give me a chair too, Boy. Jeremiah: Madam, my godfathers and godmothers baptised me not Boy, but Jeremiah. **1943** F.H. ROSE *Kruger's Wagon* 29 We in South Africa call all our manservants 'boys', even when they are grown up and quite old men. **1955** J.B. Shephard *Land of Tikoloshe* 76, I don't call him 'Jim' or 'Boy' but 'Umteto', his real name. That is polite. **1966** L.G. Berger *Where's Madam* 78 Never address your servant in any other way or by any other name but the one originally given to you as his name. 'Boy', 'Jim', (or 'Mary' to females) as a form of address gives much more offence than is generally realised. **1971** *Post* 2 May 1 Chief Gatsha Buthelezi was called 'boy' by a provincial cop. **1980** A. Paton *Towards Mountain* 158 At long last the use of the words 'boy' and 'girl' as forms of address is going out, though not so fast as it might be. **1986** [see Af sense 1]. **1989** *Frontline* Mar. 26 I .. brought Winston, my boy, a half-dozen beers which he distributed amongst his colleagues. **1990** *Ibid.* Jan. 19, I had introduced my own father to the son of a local (white) shopkeeper, .. and he had scrutinised my father and then turned to me to say: 'Your father looks like a nice boy.' **1992** *Weekly Mail* Apr. 24 32 Some of the correspondents who helped him with bursaries referred to him as a 'boy' ... 'That was a different era ... Sometimes we had to live with the term in order to survive.'

b. With distinguishing epithet indicating the occupation of the person so designated: **bed(ding)-boy**, a bedding attendant on a train; **boss-boy**, see as a main entry; **bucket-boy**, one who removes night soil (see also bucket system); **dagha-boy**, also **daka-boy**, a man employed to mix cement or concrete (see dagha *n.* sense a); **delivery-boy**, a man delivering goods to customers on a bicycle or motor-cycle; **flat-boy**, a male domestic servant usu. employed to clean in an apartment block; **house-boy**, a male domestic servant; **ice-cream boy**, a man selling ice-creams from a small cart (usu. mounted on a bicyle); **kitchen-boy**, a kitchen labourer, usu. in a hotel or other institution; **mine-boy**, a labourer on a mine. Also ***cook-boy, garden boy, office-boy, tea-boy, watchboy, yard-boy***, etc. Cf. *location boy* (see location sense 3 c), *medicine boy* (see medicine sense 2).

1952 *Rand Daily Mail* 24 May 5 From the Coloured '**bedding boy**' to the ticket examiner they couldn't be nicer. **1952** *Drum* Sept. 13 The smuggler with a modest organization often depends upon bedding boys on the railways. **1956** N. Gordimer in *Best of S. Afr. Short Stories* (1991) 221 The bed boy found her this morning, dead in her bed. She never answered when the steward came round with coffee, you see. **1964** J. Bennett *Mr Fisherman* (1967) 10 He worked on the railways, too, as a bedding boy, although he was old for the job, and did a spell on the Blue Train and on the Orange Express. **1990** G. Slovo *Ties of Blood* 55 She .. dabbed at her nose with a handkerchief which she then replaced in her pocket. 'I do hope those **bucket boys** realise how utterly selfish they are being,' she said. **1907** J.P. Fitzpatrick *Jock of Bushveld* (1909) 219, I sent Jim back to his place under the waggon, and told the **cook-boy** to give him the rest of my coffee. **1953** Lanham & Mopeli-Paulus *Blanket Boy's Moon* 271 A friend of mine is cook-boy to a white man in Houghton. **1960** R. Byron in D. Wright *S. Afr. Stories* 30 Cook-boy to a wealthy family in Parktown. **1989** J. Hobbs *Thoughts in Makeshift Mortuary* 17 She had never allowed Sarah to talk about 'the cookboy' or 'the washgirl'. 'They're fully-grown adults,' she instructed. 'Charlie is a cook, not a cookboy.' **1970** L. Mangewatywa *Informant, Durban* **Dakaboy**. A man who mixes cement and ground or concrete. **1983** N. Ndebele in *Staffrider* Vol.5 No.3, 42 A typical South African scene ... A white man is looking on, standing with his hands in his trousers pockets watching his African 'daka boys' pushing wheelbarrows and throwing bricks, one at a time. **1988** E. Makwela in *Pace* June 47 Madambi was recruited by one of the Johannesburg's building construction companies where he was a 'daga boy'. **1993** [see mantshingilane]. **1951** *Natal Mercury* 5 Apr. 2 (*advt*) Native **Delivery Boy** seeks work. **1966** *Cape Argus* 26 May 24 (*advt*) Cycle delivery boy, respectable married Coloured male, wages R11 per week. **1970** *The 1820* May 25 A Zulu delivery boy labouring with about two dozen pints of beer in the carrier at the front of his bicycle, crashed into the kerb and came an awful perler. **1985** P. Slabolepszy *Sat. Night at Palace* 24, I am sitting on my delivery bike at Europa. 'Delivery Boy of the Month – August 1978'. **1963** L.F. Freed *Crime in S. Afr.* 99 The native 'shebeen queens' ply the **flat-boys** with home-brewed barberton. **1976** V. Rosenberg *Sunflower* 217 A black, dressed in one of those short canvas suits that are the standard uniform for 'flat boys', cleaned from dark corners cigarette-ash and 'stompies'. **1980** C. Hope *A Separate Development* (1983) 217 Houseboys, garden boys, skinny legged flat-boys, knock-knees circled by green or red or blue piping of their baggy shorts. **1948** A. Paton *Cry, Beloved Country* 149 He is sure that the one .. was an old **garden-boy** of Mary's. Mary had to get rid of him for some trouble or other. **1953** D. Rooke *S. Afr. Twins* 54 Sophia and Kondulu and the garden-boy joined in the chase. **1966** A. Fugard *Notebks* (1983) 138 During a game in the garden yesterday our neighbour's small daughter pretended she was a white housewife and her brother that he was an African garden-boy. **1979** A.P. Brink *Dry White Season* 97, I became a garden boy in Booysens. Not bad people, and I had my own room in the yard. **1988** *Pace* Dec. 74 He died shortly after I arrived, which changed my plans and forced me to work as a garden boy to an Afrikaans couple. **1993** [see mantshingilane]. **1832** *Graham's Town Jrnl* 13 Jan. 9 Wanted, a Servant as **House Boy**, preference will be given to a Member of the Temperance Society. **1893** *Standard & Diggers' News* in *Sunday Times* 4 Sept. (Mag. Sect.) 23 Beware of your houseboy .. for under the innocent front may be lurking and lying the passions of the panther, and worse! **1908** M.C. Bruce *New Tvl* 22 If he wants money for any special purpose, he goes for six months to town as houseboy, on a farm as labourer, or to a mine. **1919** M.M. Steyn *Diary* 119, I was up at five, had a delicious cup of coffee brought to my bedside by the houseboy. **1926** M. Nathan *S. Afr. from Within* 233 These Zulu men took with the greatest readiness to the work of 'house-boys', including such tasks as in European communities were ordinarily alloted to nursemaids, chambermaids and scullery-maids. **1937** C. Birkby *Zulu Journey* 33 The Zulu wore the red-hemmed shorts and jumper of the 'houseboy'. **1941** *Bantu World* 1 Feb. 8 With Bon Ami, your houseboy is able to give an 'extra shine' to all this cleaning. **1951** D. Lessing in D. Wright *S. Afr. Stories* (1960) 99 She .. called for the houseboy, to whom she handed the groceries and meat for removal. **1953** [see girl sense a]. **1976** J. Becker *Virgins* (1986) 20 Sometimes a neighbouring houseboy, his white cotton jacket discarded, would sit with them in his shirtsleeves. **1986** P. Maylam *Hist. of Afr. People* 150 Many entered domestic service, which tended to be dominated by African men, the so-called 'houseboys', in these early years of the century. **1972** *Daily Dispatch* 3 June, A Chinese diplomat was called an honorary white and an Italian diplomat a 'Mafia **ice-cream boy**.' **1941** 'R. Roamer Esq.' in *Bantu World* 29 Mar. 4 Our English is so simple that even **kitchen boys** can read it. **1946** P. Abrahams *Mine Boy* (1954) 108 Rubbing shoulders with the often-blanketed giants, were the small, smooth houseboys and kitchen-boys. **1958** A. Fugard *Dimetos & Two Early Plays* (1977) 122 You mean the hotel? That's the nearest I got to a job. They didn't need any musicians ... 'But we've got an opening for a kitchen boy.' **1974** J. McClure *Gooseberry Fool* (1976) 164 The public will always suspect the coon, but Swart's friends would know that a liberal like him isn't going to be carved up by his own kitchen boy. **1987** *Learn & Teach* No.5, 3 Sisulu – who had worked as a miner, a factory worker and a 'kitchen boy' – was now an estate agent. **1990** J. Naidoo *Coolie Location* 19 It was so easy to recall the frequent complaints my mother made about the various 'kitchen boys'. **1907** J.P. Fitzpatrick *Jock of Bushveld* (1909) 215 Presently a long string of about fifty time-expired **mine-boys** came in sight. **1941** *Bantu World* 1 Feb. (Suppl.) 2 Virile young men, the Reef 'mine boys' on holiday at home. **1946** P. Abrahams *Mine Boy* (1954) 55 'The compound is in Langlaagte,' Johannes said softly. 'all the mine boys must live in compounds.' **1968** *Farmer's Weekly* 3 Jan. 99 Business near mine compounds in Welkom area, doing mainly Native trade with mine boys. **1956** A. La Guma in *New Age* 4 Oct. 6 Some of the long-term prisoners are put to work as yard-boys, **office-boys** and cooks, positions of comparative ease and coveted by their less fortunate fellows. **1972** *Cape Argus* 10 Aug. 3 Mr Cloete said that if Coloured people were to be sent to embassies abroad, they would be relegated to duties such as **tea boys** and cleaners. **1982** *Fair Lady* 1 Dec. 180 This big, charismatic man, who once worked as a 'tea-boy', now has executives from the liquor industry falling all over themselves to court him. He's a born entrepreneur with a style all his own. **1963** in L.F. Freed *Crime in S. Afr.* 286, I opened the window. I saw the accused ... I told him I could call the **watchboy** if he did not go. **1956** [*yard-boy*: see quot. at *office-boy* above].

c. *comb.* **boy's meat**, also **boys' meat**, cheap cuts of meat bought for black servants or employees; *maid's meat*, see maid sense 2. Cf. dog's meat.

1936 M. Higham *Hsehold Cookery* (1941) 56 *Leg*, or *Veiny Piece*: Used for soups and stews. Frequently sold to Kaffirs as 'Boys' Meat'. **1968** Cole & Flaherty *House of Bondage* 72 When the lady of the house phones in her weekly meat order she simply says ' .. throw in a few pounds of boysmeat.' (The 'boy', of course, is the male African the meat is intended for. In the eyes of the whites, no African ever becomes a man. Until he reaches his teens he is a pickaninny; thereafter, until he dies of old age, he is merely 'boy'.) **1969** M. Benson *At Still Point* (1988) 153 Steak, fruit .. a celebration for Dan .. after more than a year of mealiepap and 'boy's meat'. **1974** *Rand Daily Mail* 28 Jan. 4 It used to be offensively described as 'boys meat' or 'servants meat' – the current euphemism is often 'staff meat'. Inside the packs it is still the same old thing: some lean meat, lots of fat and varying amounts of bone. **1976** J. Becker *Virgins* (1986) 19 They dipped .. into the two pots, of mealie-meal and stewed meat. It was called 'boy's meat' by Susan when she ordered it from the butcher. **1982** M. Mutloatse in *Best of S. Afr. Short Stories* (1991) 437 Servants' meat (or 'boys' meat). **1987** N. Mkhanze in *True Love* Mar. 46 A piece of chuck ('boy's meat') and mieliepap for supper. **1989** J. Hobbs *Thoughts in Makeshift Mortuary* 83 She was overweight, of course; ate too much putu and the cheap fatty meat you people so picturesquely call 'boy's meat'.

2. Always in *pl.*, ***the boys***:

a. *rare.* [Special sense of general Eng. *the boys* a group of criminals.] A collective name for 'tsotsis' (see tsotsi sense 1).

1956 [see taal sense 1 b].

b. Soldiers collectively, esp. guerillas fighting for a black resistance movement.

1978 *Voice* 16 Dec. 10 People in the rural areas say that they have been instructed by the 'boys' (guerillas) to refrain from voting or risk certain death. **1979** *Time* 31 Dec. 23 The Boys in the Bush. Employing classic hide-and-seek guerilla tactics, the 'boys,' as they are affectionately called by villagers who harbor them, have achieved control over much of the countryside. **1979** *Sunday Times* 29 July (Mag. Sect.) 1 I've told the locals to tell the boys – the name the Africans use to describe the terrorists – not to come near me because if I see them I will be obliged to report them. **1982** J. Frederikse *None but Ourselves* 60 In 1976 the boys came from the south ... They said, 'Do you know us?' And I said 'I just heard that there were boys around.' Then they said, 'We are the boys, we are the comrades, we have come to struggle together with you.'

c. In the n. phr. ***boys on the border***: soldiers involved in conflict on South Africa's borders. See also border sense 3.

1982 *Sunday Times* 25 July 28 When some blacks talk about 'our boys on the border', they are more than likely referring to the ANC's Umkhonto We Sizwe or Swapo's guerrillas. **1983** *Ibid.* 9 Oct. (Lifestyle), I was called on a little while back to produce a cake for the boys on the border. **1985** *Scope* 23 Aug. 42 The sort of war our Boys on the Border may face in the rest of 1985. **1987** H. Prendini in *Style* Feb. 35 Live audiences have included boys on the border, the disabled, the Vroue Landbou Vereeniging and the cattle farmers at Senekal's Dairy Festival.

Hence (sense 1) **boy** *v. trans. nonce*, usu. *passive*: to be addressed as boy.

1965 E. MPHAHLELE *Down Second Ave* 152, I was 'Jimmed' and 'boy-ed' and 'John-ed' by whites.

boyale /bɔˈjɑːle/ *n. hist.* Also **boïalloa, bojala, boyali, byale**. [SeTswana.] An initiation ceremony, usu. involving clitoridectomy, formerly undergone by Tswana girls at the age of puberty. See also DOMBA, INTONJANE. Cf. BOGUERA.

1827 G. THOMPSON *Trav.* II. 165 The celebration of a .. festival called *Boïalloa*, when all the young girls, on attaining the age of thirteen, go through certain ceremonies, after which they are admitted to the rank of women. **1846** R. MOFFAT *Missionary Labours* 66 The females have also their *boyali* at the same age, in which they are under the tuition of matrons, and initiated into all the duties of wives. **1857** D. LIVINGSTONE *Missionary Trav.* 149 A somewhat analogous ceremony (boyale) takes place for young women, and the protegees appear abroad drilled under the surveillance of an old lady to the carrying of water. **1870** *Cape Monthly Mag.* I. 285 Whilst the festival of circumcision among the Bechuanas (*Boguera*) has received frequent mention by missionaries and travellers, the analogous ceremony (*Bojala*), conducted about the period of puberty in the other sex, has not received the attention and investigation it deserves. **1871** J. MACKENZIE *Ten Yrs* (1971) 378 During the administration of 'boyali,' the rite initiatory to womanhood, the girls are assembled every day in the town, under the leadership of two or more old women, who instruct them in all the duties of their future life. **1876** — *Papers* (1975) 44 Circumcision or 'boyale', now bereft of the sanction and support of the chief, will sooner or later pine away in the cold and die. **1975** A.J. DACHS *Papers of John Mackenzie* 5 Among the ritual observances of the Tswana which attracted the immediate attention of missionaries were the initiation ceremonies of bogwera and bojale, whereby the youths and maidens of the chiefdom were elevated in rank to adults. **1979** J. GRATUS *Jo'burgers* 52 Trouble with you girls who've not had byale, circumcision. You know nothing about the world but you think you know everything.

boyalwa var. BOJALWA.

boykie /ˈbɔɪki/ *n. colloq.* Also **booitjie, boytjie**. [Eng. *boy* + Afk. suffix -IE.]

1. A boy or young man; a 'whizz-kid' or 'wonder-boy'; an affectionate term for a man of any age.

1974 A.P. BRINK *Looking on Darkness* 222 You Cape boytjies are softies. But we'll get you right, don't worry. **1979** P.-D. UYS in *Darling* 11 July 81 This little newspaper boytjie who I've known for years ... I said 'How are you?' 'No,' he said, 'I'm alright.' **1981** *E. Prov. Herald* 30 Apr. 3 '[Vaalwater] boys have narrower shoulders .. because there is no swimming bath in their town', a woman complained ... This, she said, was why the Vaalwater 'booitjies' couldn't do push-ups. **1983** *Financial Mail* 29 July 29 Frankly, there are going to be those in the business community who will wonder after all this shooting from the hip talk about the 'boykie from Brits'. **1983** T. BARON in *Frontline* Sept. 51 In the long run, I'd back him against the smartest business boykies you can find: sharp lawyers from New York, Greek tycoons with tankers, Army quartermasters. **1987** *Pace* May 4 This guy has changed his name. He is using the name of his South African boss. What a boytjie. **1987** *Sunday Times* 21 June (Mag. Sect.) 60 Me fly a Lear jet? Wouldn't I be just one macho boykie, the most macho boykie around! **1988** G. SILBER in *Style* Dec. 30 Looking as self-conscious as a Barmitzvah boykie and talking in an accent as flat as a matzo cracker. **1990** *Sunday Times* 11 Feb. 9 First in line to accept the challenge was Klerksdorp-trained 'boykie' and talk show host John Berks. **1990** C. GREEN on TV1, 1 June (Cyril Green Show), Gerhard Smith, the boykie that I work with, the co-producer. **1994** R. MALAN in *Sidelines* Dec. 29 Testosterone-crazed boykies from the VV and AWB.

2. BOY sense 1 a.

1978 *Het Suid-Western* 2 Aug., The days when you glibly talked about 'kaffirs' and 'hotnots' are over in South Africa. The same goes for 'boytjie', 'the girl' when you mean your domestic .. and all the rest of those derogatory appellations. **1986** S. SEPAMLA *Third Generation* 128 'You will have to speak the truth, boykie! Hear me?' Solly remained quiet not knowing what to say.

BPC *n. hist.* Initial letters of *Black People's Convention*, an organization coordinating the activities of supporters of the *Black Consciousness Movement* (see BLACK CONSCIOUSNESS sense 2). Also *attrib.*

1974 *Survey of Race Rel.* (S.A.I.R.R.) 172 Mrs Winnifred Kgware was unanimously elected first national president of the BPC. **1976** *E. Prov. Herald* 11 Nov. 5 The main charge against the nine accused alleges their involvement — and that of Saso and BPC — in a conspiracy to bring about revolutionary change in South Africa. **1977** *Daily Dispatch* 22 Aug. 1 Black consciousness leader Steve Biko and Mr Peter Jones of BPC reportedly arrested by Security Police in Grahamstown at weekend and now being held in Port Elizabeth. **1979** *Sunday Post* 26 Apr. 1 Two state witnesses in the East London BPC trial were this week sentenced to six months' jail for refusing to give evidence. **1985** M. TLALI in *Fair Lady* 26 June 107 The martyr lay in state in a 'casket' draped in the black T-shirts of the BPC movement. **1991** *Drum* Dec. (Then & Now) 14 Most important .. was the emphasis on Black Consciousness, and pride in being black. The BPC was founded in 1972, and symbolizing the shift in attitudes and thinking was a woman, Mrs Winifred Kgware, who became its president.

bra /bra, brɑː/ *n. colloq.* Also **bla(h)**. [Shortened form of Eng. *brother*; *bl-* forms result from the regular change of /r/ to /l/ found when English words are used in the Nguni languages.]

1. Mainly in urban (esp. township) usage: 'Brother': an informal or familiar title, used with a first name, nickname, or full name, usu. when speaking to or of a black man. Cf. BOET sense 2, MFOWETHU sense 1, SIS *n.*[2]

1956 *Drum* Apr. 61 Story by 'bra' D. Can Themba. Pictures by 'bra' Gopal S. Naransamy. **1963** B. MODISANE *Blame Me on Hist.* (1986) 13 'Look, Bra-Bloke, this is money,' Lloyd said. **1974** K.M.C. MOTSISI in M. Mutloatse *Casey & Co* (1978) 56 He has a nipinyana of 'madolo' which is the name non-voters prefer to call wine and which wine he buys from Bra Victor at the bottle store attached to this beer garden. **1980** M. MELAMU in M. Mutloatse *Forced Landing* 44 She told me that Bra Rufus .. who drives the huge Buick taxi, has graciously usurped my conjugal responsibilities. **1988** J. SEROKE in *Staffrider* Vol.7 No.3, 304 In the early seventies, black poets withdrew from a poetry reading at Wits University. You were invited to read too, bra Sipho. **1990** *New African* 18 June 13 Pat Matshikiza, affectionately known as Bra Pat to his many fans and colleagues. **1993** [see α quot. at FANAKALO].

2. 'Mate', 'buddy', 'pal', 'friend': an informal or familiar term of address or reference to a man or boy.

a. Mainly in urban (esp. township) speech: used as a term of reference. Cf. BRICATE sense b.

1974 *Drum* 22 Sept. 10 Like, you and your bra's move into a koesta where ander mannes are doing their thing. **1979** F. DIKE *First S. African* 37 'Which Carla are you talking about?' ... 'Oh Carla is 'n bra, he works at the docks.' **1984** H. ZILLE in *Frontline* Mar. 12 If you are driving your own car and have an accident with a taxi, he will come with his bras and make you a hospital case in no time. **1987** *New Nation* 3 Dec. 10 Bassist and vocalist Mac Mackenzie turns from the microphone to his 'bras' onstage.

b. Orig. mainly in township slang, but now widespread: as a term of address. Often in the phr. ***my bra***. Cf. BOETA sense b, BRICATE sense a, BRO, BROER sense 1.

1978 C. VAN WYK in *Staffrider* Vol.1 No.2, 36 Bob: I'm even tired of that mosque of yours; that noise over the loudspeaker. Ebrahim: Believe in Allah, my bra and that will no longer be noise. **1980** M. MELAMU in M. Mutloatse *Forced Landing* 41 They are talking full-blast, real township style. No inhibitions, my bla. **1983** W. SCHWEGMANN in *Frontline* Feb. 52 Any whitey with a camera is plagued by pleading voices: 'Hey brother .. bra .. baas .. here, baas .. take my picture .. for front page.' **1987** [see PIPE sense 2]. **1987** *Informant, Jeffrey's Bay* Hey bra, how's the surf? **1989** J. HOBBS *Thoughts in Makeshift Mortuary* 272 His cousin .. said, 'Listen, bra, I've got my Ma coming for a few days and I'll need your bedroom.'

3. MAIN MAN.

1974 *Drum* 22 Sept. 10 There was this .. ou .. who used to bully me, take my money, beat me up ... He was like one of 'Die manne', and I had no alternative ... If you're one of 'die bra's' no one else is going to mess you around.

4. A man; a 'guy'.

1978 C. VAN WYK in *Staffrider* Vol.1 No.2, 36 Heit fana. Ek sê, who's the other bra? **1984** *Drum* Jan. 6 When he was 17 years old a Mafia member took him .. to the house of the Mafia 'grootkop' ... The member was told .. : It is not the right time now. Bring the 'bra' tonight.

5. A black man who is acknowledged to be particularly street-wise and adept at making the most of urban life while remaining part of working-class black society.

Such a person is distinguished partly by the adoption of attitudes, behaviour, and language (see *tsotsi-taal* at TSOTSI sense 2) rooted in township life rather than in traditional African society or in modern western society.

1983 *Natal Mercury* 8 June, Q: Why was that word 'bra' so important? A: Because it's saying to the cop: 'Hey man, I'm black like you.' .. Also, it's showing him that he's dealing with a bright guy, someone who is 'one of the boys'. Q: You mean not all blacks call each other 'bra'? A: .. Some people don't even speak the township lingo ... They are the dumb ones, who just speak the vernacular. You can't regard them as 'bras' ... The youngsters don't speak the lingo properly any more, but they look up to a *grootman* who is a bra. **1984** *Drum* Sept. 26 Dave Mokale was what we all called a bra. A real mjieta who could swing ... He left teaching to join bantustan politics, but he still remained a bra.

braai /ˈbraɪ/ *n.* [Shortened form of *braaivleis*, see BRAAIVLEIS.] Barbecue.

1.a. An informal outdoor gathering at which meat is grilled over an open fire; BRAAIVLEIS sense 1; BRAAIVLEISAAND; VLEISBRAAI. Also *attrib.*, and occas. *fig.*

1959 *Cape Times* 11 Apr. 4 Chicken Braai at Somerset West. **1963** M.G. MCCOY *Informant, Port Elizabeth* All of us went out to Bushy Park at 11 for a braai. **1969** I. VAUGHAN *Last of Sunlit Yrs* 31 After some argument, we all .. decide to go off to German Bay for a swim and a braai. **1970** *Halls Committee Minutes* (Rhodes University) 26 Oct. 3 Students should acquaint themselves with Municipal regulations regarding the holding of braais. **1975** *Darling* 1 Oct. 31 Don't let the kids gallop around with braai forks — there's always someone who gets maimed or branded. **1976** V. ROSENBERG *Sunflower* 213 The menu in the Bosman-Vorster camp comprised braai chops, 'stywepap' and 'vetkoek', all washed down with claret. **1978** *Sunday Times* 3 Aug. (Mag. Sect.) 3 It's braaivleis time! Bring out the charcoal, fix up the grid. Isn't it good to be South African and enjoy a braai! **1978** A.P. BRINK *Rumours of Rain* 148 In the evening we had guests at a *braai* beside the pool until after midnight. **1984** *Reader's Digest* Jan. 43 A braai isn't a braai without boerewors. **1989** *Sunday Times* 19 Nov. (Mag. Sect.) 10 The rest of the world has Gorbachev and his *glasnost* initiative, and we have De Klerk and his *boerewost* [*sic*] initiative but yet I cannot help wondering if somehow we are not still headed for a braai. **1990** W. BOTHA in *Frontline* Sept. 19 You know, our Zulu men's kingdom is beer and braai meat. **1990** B. RONGE in *Sunday Times* 2 Dec. (Mag. Sect.) 8 If there are bean sprouts on the salads, you are at a relevant braai. **1993** [see BOK sense 1 a].

b. With distinguishing epithets designating different types of braai according to:

i. The method used: **newspaper braai**, a braai using tightly-rolled newspaper as fuel; **spit-braai**, a braai at which a pig, sheep, or other animal is roasted on a spit.

1988 H. PRENDINI in *Style* June 105 Like the man who invented the **newspaper braai** .. he gets an immense kick out of using whatever comes to hand. **1982** *Het Suid-Western* 22 Dec., Spectators at Saturday's gathering who attended a delightful **spit-braai** after the drill. **1989** *Weekend Post* 16 Dec. 1 A mammoth spit braai .. will be held in Bathurst.

ii. The food grilled: **chicken braai**, **fish braai**, **oxbraai**, **pork-braai**, etc.

1972 *Grocott's Mail* 17 Nov. 3 A **chicken braai** and dance, with no political speeches .. will be held for United Party supporters and friends. **1977** *Darling* 8 June 120 One of my greatest pleasures in life is a **fish braai** during the summer holiday when fresh fish is abundant. **1983** *E. Prov. Herald* 12 Jan. 6 On Wednesday night delegates will attend a 'fishtrek' and fishbraai. **1988** E. WITHERS in *Fair Lady* 22 June (Suppl.) 15 Another chapter deals with the increasingly popular fish braai. **1980** *Sunday Times* 25 May 11 Inviting Hindus to an **oxbraai** is tantamount to inviting Muslims or Jews to a **pork braai**.

2.a. Any of several types of structure in which a fire is made for the outdoor grilling of meat.

These may be stone or brick fireplaces or portable wood, gas or charcoal grills.

1962 J. TAYLOR 'Hennie van Saracen'. (*lyrics*) As we sits round the braai, chewing boerewors, My Dad says 'You're famous Son'. **1970** *Argus* 3 Oct. 18 Entertain your friends on the patio with its built-in braai. **1972** *Sunday Times* 2 Sept. (Mag. Sect.) 4 Someone grabbed our braai and sosaties and vanished into the night. We did not mind the loss of the food so much, as the loss of the braai. **1976** *Daily Dispatch* 24 Aug. 16 Lovely to look at, delightful to own. South entry, north-facing home with secluded outdoor living around the pool and braai. **1990** *Sunday Times* 29 Oct. (Mag. Sect.) 38 While the ladies prepare the salads and the mieliepap, the small talk around the braai is the same as the big talk. Farming.

b. Occas. with distinguishing epithet designating the type of structure so used: **gas braai**; **skottel-braai**, see SKOTTEL sense 2.

1993 *Getaway* Nov. 28 (*advt*) Ken and Angela Self with their tent, sleeping bags, gas braai and the rest of their gear set off to take on the challenge of Africa.

3. *noncount.* Meat grilled over an open fire; BRAAIVLEIS sense 2.

1972 *Cape Times* 29 Apr. 2 Braai, cooked in the garden, was served in the restored 'keller' which is shortly to be opened as a restaurant. **1976** *Sunday Times* 16 May (Mag. Sect.) 4 Unlike the ladies there, who are obviously accustomed to that kind of meat, .. I stuck to the braai. **1986** D. CASE *Love, David* 25 'Smell that braai!' Oupa said. 'Yes,' David replied. 'It makes you hungry.'

4. *comb.* **braai area**, an outdoor area including a fireplace on which meat may be grilled; **braai pack**, also **braai pak**, an assortment of braai meats or chicken pieces; **braai pit**, a hole in the ground in which a fire may be made for grilling meat; **braai wood**, twigs and small logs suitable for braai fires; **braaiwors** /-vɔ(r)s/ [Afk., *wors* sausage], sausage, esp. BOEREWORS.

1979 *E. Prov. Herald* 31 Oct. 11 Skill shows .. in the neatly handsome brickwork used in the **braai area**. **1987** *Uniform* 7 Apr. 2 The braai area is used on weekends for braai and potjiekos feasts. **1989** J. HOBBS *Thoughts in Makeshift Mortuary* 76 The back yards were too small to accommodate even a modest swimming pool and braai area. **1977** *E. Prov. Herald* 10 Feb. 11 (*advt*) Farmer Brown chickens ... Now you can get them in special **Braaipaks**. **1989** J. EVANS in *Personality* 9 Oct. 23 The locals were out in force with picnic hampers of beer and braai packs. **1990** *Weekend Post* 8 Dec. 12 Braai packs or picnic lunches can be bought at the farm. **1984** B. MOLLOY in *Style* Nov. 140 God help anyone who usurps their favourite **braai pit**. **1987** A. SOULE et al. *Wynand du Toit Story* 4 Around noon Wynand built a fire in their braai pit. **1985** *Cape Times* 4 Oct. 6 He arrives .. clutching cushions, sun-umbrella, portable braai, radio, .. *padkos* and **braai wood**. **1989** *Flying Springbok* Oct. 108 Small-time entrepreneurs were selling .. braai wood, making a packet from the occasion. **1938** 'MRS GOSSIP' in *Star* 1 Dec. 12 Pannekoeke, **braaiwors**, melktert, mosbolletjies, beskuit and coffee could be had in plenty.

Hence (*nonce*) **braai-ish**, **braai-y** *adjs.*

1970 *Informant, Grahamstown* 'I kiss your hand.' 'Don't, it's all braai-y.' **1979** *Sunday Times* 4 Mar. (Mag. Sect.) 3 It had a very nice braai-ish flavour.

braai /'braɪ/ *v.* Formerly also **bry**. [Afk., fr. Du. *braden* to roast, grill.]

a. *trans.* To grill (meat) over a fire, usu. in the open air. Also *absol.*

1891 E. GLANVILLE *Fossicker* 166 At last three remained about the fire 'brying' bones on the coals. **1913** C. PETTMAN *Africanderisms* 92 *Brying*, .. To toast meat on a fork, or to roast it in the ashes. **1941** A.G. BEE *Kalahari Camp Fires* (1943) 36 They had made a more than usually splendid fire, and perhaps it was the beauty of this that made them 'braai' the bones instead of leaving such process to the boys. **1959** *Cape Argus* 10 Mar. 9 Bring and braai your own meat. **1970** *Evening Post* 17 Oct. (Suppl.) 6 Braai (grill) over glowing coals until brown on one side then turn and grill other side which is thickest, until brown and cooked but juicy. **1974** *E. Prov. Herald* 16 May 1 Delegates and guests forsook the cuisine of the upper floors for good old 'pap en vleis' braaied in the hotel's parking basement.

b. *intrans.* To hold a barbecue.

1963 M.G. MCCOY *Informant, Port Elizabeth* We all braaied for lunch of course. **1973** M. PHILIP *Caravan Caravel* 28 A group of men were getting their barbecue fires going. 'That's what we must do, Dad,' said Peter longingly. 'We must braai often. We hardly ever do it.' **1983** G. SILBER in *Sunday Times* 28 Aug. (Mag. Sect.) 18 People come to Bapsies to braai and sit on blankets and dop and buy their kids orange Mirandas and purple candy-floss and shrivel-wrapped hamburgers. **1987** *Pace* May 50 You'll often find the three Mhlongo boys braai-ing in the park.

Hence **braaied** /braɪd/ *ppl adj.*, of food: grilled over an open fire; **braaier** /'braɪə/ *n.*, one who braais; **braaiing** /'braiɪŋ/ *vbl n.* Also *attrib.*, and *fig.*

1973 *E. Prov. Herald* 7 Feb., The Oudtshoorn Golf Club has invited the Free State vleisbraai champions .. to compete .. in a Vleisbraai competition against local braaiers. **1975** *Scope* 10 Jan. 61 The sun browns you gently — no Natal beach *braaing* here. **1977** *Sunday Times* 27 Feb. 15 'Braai-ing' is a lifestyle with certain old familiar problems: nowhere to sit where ants can't get you, nowhere to stand where gusts of smoke can't sting your eyes. **1978** Z. ROOS in *Darling* 1 Feb. 82, I think chicken pieces for a braai *must* be precooked for success. I know lots of expert braaiers don't agree. **1978** *Sunday Times* 19 Feb. 5 No wonder .. that Johannesburg braaiers were upset .. that an uitlander from England had been asked to help judge the Southern Transvaal championships. **1981** *Fair Lady* 9 Sept. 242 The sacred Sunday pastime of braaiing. **1984** *Reader's Digest* Jan. 42 Altogether there were 3 600 entries, including many braaiers with their own home-made boerewors. *Ibid.* 43 Those who never seem to manage braaing without a Guy Fawkes display of pyrotechnics. **1988** G. SPENCE in *Sunday Times* 10 Jan. 56 Stories abound about how he spent weeks as a kid camping on riverbanks and feasting on braaied cane rats. **1989** S. JOHNSON in *Laughing Stock* Sept.-Oct. 10 My eldest brother, erstwhile repository of braaiing traditionalism, sheepishly snuck a 'Blitz' beneath his ailing coalbed. **1991** C. URQUHART in *Weekend Post* 16 Mar. (Leisure) 1 Well braaied chops, sausage and steaks. **1993** *Flying Springbok* Apr. 123 The outer layer toughens slightly and, with the heat of the coals, crispens and traps in the tender flesh. The technique is great with just about any braaied fish.

braairibbetjie see RIBBETJIE.

braaivleis /'braɪfleɪs/ *n.* Pl. **-es**. [Afk., shortened form of *braaivleisaand* (see BRAAIVLEISAAND).]

1. BRAAI *n.* sense 1 a. Also *attrib.*

1939 A.W. WELLS *S. Afr.: Planned Tour* 410 Some Afrikaans words are used in English conversation, e.g ... *braaivleis*. **1950** H. GIBBS *Twilight* 155 A *braaivleis*, the Afrikaner open-air party where chops and sausages are cooked over an open wood fire — similar to the American barbecue — is a feature of summer evenings. **1951** [see OUTSPAN *n.* sense 1]. **1958** R.E. LIGHTON *Out of Strong* 3 Everyone .. gathered later at the farm for .. the great braaivleis when boerewors and meat were roasted over pits of glowing redwood. *c***1965** *State of S. Afr. 1965* 107 At outspan fresh meat was grilled on an open fire, known as braaivleis; but this word is now used for festive occasions and even for official functions held out of doors when meat is grilled over the open fire. **1968** P. SAUER in D.J. Opperman *Spirit of Vine* 353 A dinner-jacket at a braaivleis would look as ridiculous as casual clothes at a formal reception. **1971** *Daily Dispatch* 6 Feb. 8 In the smoke control regulations planned for the Johannesburg municipal area, residents will be permitted to have braaivleises in their gardens. **1975** *Darling* 1 Oct. 30 The main advantage of a braaivleis is that the South African male actually regards it as his privilege to cook the meat. **1986** *Vula* July 39 Bullets, teargas and sjamboks, pangas and necklaces .. those icons of our own insanely vicious society .. are as deeply a part of us, of our precious 'way of life' and 'culture', as braaivleises and Chevrolets. **1990** R. MALAN *My Traitor's Heart* 107 You must understand that a braaivleis is no mere barbecue. It is a profound cultural ritual.

2. *noncount.* BRAAI *n.* sense 3.

1943 *Week-End News & Sunday Mag.* 20 Mar. 4 Er Gooie Afrikaans Bankwet wid such tings to eat as lekker sosaartjes, boerewors, braaivleis, vetkoekies, etsettera, etsettera. **1953** [see VOLKSPELE]. *c***1965** [see sense 1]. **1966** F.G. BUTLER *S. of Zambesi* 20 Opened last month by our M.P.C. with a speets on nashonil prowgriss followed by braaivleis and brandy. **1977** P.C. VENTER *Soweto* 97 Have a friendly chat, share a few jokes. Braaivleis and porridge will be served at no extra cost. **1981** *E. Prov. Herald* 30 Apr. 3 At lunchtime the enticing aroma of braaivleis, curry and frikkadels hung in the air. **1986** *S. Afr. Panorama* Feb. 16 Bacon and eggs, fried onions and tomatoes and delicious bread rolls, or pap and braaivleis — who could ask for anything more!

braaivleisaand /'braɪfleɪsˌɑːnt/ *n. obsolescent.* [Afk., *braai* grill + *vleis* meat + *aand* evening.] BRAAI *n.* sense 1 a.

1934 *Star* 6 Apr. (Swart), On the kopjes at Cottesloe tomorrow evening the congregation of the Dutch Reformed Church at Vrededorp will take part in a 'braaivleisaand'. **1936** E. ROSENTHAL *Old-Time Survivals* 20 (*caption*) 'Braaivleisaand', or 'Roast Meat Evening': An old South African Dutch custom, which includes the public roasting of meat in the embers at night. **1939** *Outspan* 22 Sept. 42 (*advt*) Traditional as our Braaivleisaand. The hospitable, mellow flavour of this fine old Brandy. **1949** L.G. GREEN *In Land of Afternoon* 67 Just as typical as biltong is the country braaivleisaand. This form of hospitality is now so widespread that many people have sheltered fire-places built in their gardens. **1953** [see VOLKSPELE]. **1955** W. ILLSLEY *Wagon on Fire* 70 A card of attractive design .. was an invitation to support a 'braaivleisaand' in aid of the orphanage fund.

Braak /brɑːk/ *n.* [S. Afr. Du., fr. Du. *braak(land)* fallow (land).] ***The Braak***: A public square in Stellenbosch, Western Cape Province, formerly a military parade and fair ground, and now a proclaimed historical monument.

1861 P.B. BORCHERDS *Auto-Biog. Mem.* 26 These bodies of cavalry used to exercise annually in the village, on the 'Braak', now Queen's-square. **1934** *Friend* 9 Feb. (Swart), *Braak*, .. The historical square in Stellenbosch. A unique event was the firing of a royal salute of twenty-one guns from the famous signal cannon of the Braak. **1957** L.G. GREEN *Beyond City Lights* 197 One open space which Stellenbosch has preserved since the early days is the Braak (the 'fallow land') where the old cavalry manouevred. **1959** A. GORDON-BROWN *Yr Bk & Guide to Sn Afr. 1960* 375 In the centre of the town is a large grass-grown square known as the Braak – set aside in 1703 as a military parade ground, and in the early days the scene of the annual village fair. **1974** *E. Prov. Herald* 13 Sept. 14 The Braak in Stellenbosch .. was proclaimed as a square with all the surrounding facades, even if some of these were not old. **1978** *Reader's Digest Illust. Guide to Sn Afr.* 54 Today's Stellenbosch is perhaps even more beautiful than when the governor first founded it. He never saw the oak trees in their maturity, or the main thoroughfare .. lined with houses .., or the town square, the Braak, with its arsenal, parades, quaint houses, inns and churches.

braak /brɑːk/ *adj.* [Afk., fr. Du.] Fallow.

1937 *Handbk for Farmers* (Dept of Agric. & Forestry) 702 In earlier days there used to be included in the system an 'ouland' period of one to two years, between the sowing year and the 'braak' year.

braak /brɑːk, brɒk/ *v. trans.* Also **brak**. [Afk., fr. Du. *braken* to plough land and leave it unsown.] To plough or turn over (fallow land).

1937 *Handbk for Farmers* (Dept of Agric. & Forestry) 701 The crop that comes up serves for grazing purposes until August-September, when the soil is braaked deep. *Ibid.* 702 The system of sowing half of the arable land to grain and of 'braaking' or fallowing the other half in preparation for the following year's crop, is now the rule. **1970** D.M. MCMASTER *Informant, Cathcart (E. Cape)* To brak over a land is to plough it roughly for the first time after the crop has been reaped ... The pronunciation is 'brok' to rhyme with 'lock'.

braaking /ˈbrɑːkɪŋ/ *vbl n.* [See prec.] The ploughing of fallow land.

1896 R. WALLACE *Farming Indust. of Cape Col.* 468 *Ploughing* of virgin soil or 'braaking' is done in September after rain. If rain does not come, braaking is impossible at that season. **1913** C. PETTMAN *Africanderisms* 84 *Braaking*, .. The term applied to the ploughing of virgin soil. **1937** *Handbk for Farmers* (Dept of Agric. & Forestry) 705 'Braaking' or fallow ploughing is done from June to August; if chaff is added, braaking must be early ... Deep braaking is more effective than shallow braaking.

braakland /ˈbrɑːklænd/ *n.* [Afk., a piece of land, a field, fr. S. Afr. Du. *braak* fallow + *land* land.] See quot. 1913.

1913 C. PETTMAN *Africanderisms* 84 *Braakland*, Land which has been ploughed for the first time, or which has been lying fallow for several years. **1929** *Farming in S. Afr.* Apr. 44 He would naturally first make use of all the kraalmanure he has available on his farm, which is invariably applied to the 'braakland' that is to carry wheat. **1937** *Handbk for Farmers* (Dept of Agric. & Forestry) 706 Normally it is not necessary to cultivate the braakland again until seeding time, when the soil is shallow ploughed ... Dry cultivation is justifiable only when done with the object of eradicating weeds .. occurring in braaklands.

‖**braambos** /ˈbrɑːmbɔs/ *n.* Formerly also **braambosch**. [Afk., earlier S. Afr. Du. *braambosch*, transf. use of Du. *braambos(ch)* any of several European species of bramble; fr. *braam* bramble + *bos(ch)* bush.] Any of several species of bramble of the genus *Rubus* (family Rosaceae), esp. *R. pinnatus*. Also *attrib.*

1856 L. PAPPE in *Cape of G.H. Almanac & Annual Register* 345 The fruit of the *Bramble* or *Blackberry* bush (Braambosch), ripens in the month of January. **1868** —— *Florae Capensis* 12 The fruit of this species of *Bramble* or *Blackberry-bush* (Braambosch) is equal in flavour and taste to that of Europe. **1913** C. PETTMAN *Africanderisms* 84 *Braambosch*, .. *Rubus pinnatus*, the Cape bramble. **1966** C.A. SMITH *Common Names* 171 *Braambos(sie)*, The qualifying word (braam) is the original Dutch (English: bramble) for several species of *Rubus* in Holland, and transferred to the Cape to the indigenous *Rubus pinnatus* .. with subsequent extensions to cover other indigenous and naturalized introduced species. **1971** L.G. GREEN *Taste of S.-Easter* 177 He had tried all the medical remedies of the Cape countryside; pomegranate root for tape-worms, braambos roots boiled in water for diarrhoea.

brack, brackbush varr. BRAK, BRAK-BUSH.

bracket var. BRICATE.

brady var. BREDIE.

brae, braeing varr. BRAY *v.*², BRAYING.

braid *v.* var. BRAY *v.*²

braid *ppl adj.* var. BRAYED.

braiding var. BRAYING.

brak /bræk/ *adj.* and *n.*¹ Also **brack**. [Du. and later Afk. *brak* alkaline; Afk. *brak* alkalinity.

During the 16th century *brak* was borrowed from Dutch into Brit. Eng. as 'brack', but having been replaced by 'brackish', 'brack' is now *obs.* except in S. Afr. Eng.]

A. *adj.* Of water or soil: brackish, alkaline, containing an excess of mineral salts.

1796 C.R. HOPSON tr. *C.P. Thunberg's Trav.* II. p.xii, *Brakwater* is water stagnating in valleys and low places; it contains a kind of brine, and tastes more or less saltish. **1827** G. THOMPSON *Trav.* I. 447 We procured each of us a draught of very brack water. *a***1858** J. GOLDSWAIN *Chron.* (1949) II. 186, I said that in the sum[m]er that there was no water and that was was brak even in the winter. *a***1873** J. BURROW *Trav. in Wilds* (1971) 42 The water here is in pits and very *brak*, no (or very little and wild) game, and altogether very dull. **1887** A.A. ANDERSON *25 Yrs in Waggon* I. 76 I .. came to a very large brak pan, at least four miles in circumference, called Great Chue Pan. **1898** G. NICHOLSON *50 Yrs* 113 Probably the majority of waters tapped in this part of the country by the artesian or any other process would turn out more or less 'brak'. **1910** A.B. LAMONT *Rural Reader* 19 When it contains too much of certain substances, of which salt and soda are the chief, it is called 'brak' water. **1914** *Farmer's Annual* 318 Storage of brak water with free access to air, in open tanks, would not improve the quality of such water. **1920** F.C. CORNELL *Glamour of Prospecting* 50 Although but a day's ride from Van Rhyn's Dorp, the region is a very solitary and deserted one, much of the land being brak (alkaline) and unfit for stock to run on. **1931** H.D. LEPPAN *Agric. Policy* 42 A noteworthy feature of brak soils is the fact that high concentration of soluble salts generally coincides with richness in plant food, so that these soils are characterised by high potential fertility. **1942** J.A. BROWN *One Man's War* (1980) 53 We grope our way to the mess and swill down tepid, brak tea and white bread turned brown and gritty. **1951** H.C. BOSMAN in S. Gray *Makapan's Caves* (1987) 174 He wondered what those lands were like ... Maybe it was just *brak* soil, and with *ganna* bushes. **1969** I. VAUGHAN *Last of Sunlit Yrs* 57 The Residency was a small three-roomed cottage to which every drop of water – heavily brak – was sleighed every day from a distant well. **1975** *E. Prov. Herald* 6 Aug. 4 When salt bush was used plenty of drinking water should be available and should contain as little brak salt as possible. **1989** D. BRISTOW in *Weekly Mail* 21 Apr. 29 All the water is *brak*, which means it tastes like old swamp water, but you get used to it.

B. *n.*

1. Alkalinity or 'brackishness' of both soil and water.

1877 *Sel. Comm. Report on Mission to Damaraland* 11 Even the locomotive must have pure water, and when nothing but 'brak' is found, costly appliances are required for its distillation. **1897** 'F. MACNAB' *On Veldt & Farm* 72 It seemed that a good deal of 'brak' was in the soil. **1920** E.H.L. SCHWARZ *Thirstland Redemption* 35 Extreme care .. must be exercised in dealing with irrigated land; it has happened again and again that brak has risen on shallow soil by excessive waterings. **1931** H.D. LEPPAN *Agric. Policy* 42 Brak is commonly known as 'alkali' in America and other countries. It refers to the presence of soluble salts in the soil in sufficient concentration to injure plants. **1963** S. CLOETE *Rags of Glory* 414 But we have water – very fine, clear water with no trace of brak. **1966** C.A. SMITH *Common Names* 173 On such places only a brack-tolerant vegetation will flourish.

2. Alkaline soil, used in the past for roofing; often *attrib.*, esp. in the phr. ***brak roof***.

1890 A. MARTIN *Home Life* 82 The ground must be 'brack', a peculiar kind of soil which, though loose and friable, is not porous. This brack is often used to cover the flat roofs of the houses. *Ibid.* 94 It .. gave me the first experience of a big rain – and of the *brack* roof. **1940** E. BRIGHT in Baumann & Bright *Lost Republic* 207 The house she had come to had a 'brak' roof and a mud floor.

3. Ellipt. for BRAKBOS.

1892 *The Jrnl* 9 July 1 (*advt*) The veld is good Karoo and Granaat Plains with a Lot of Mimosa Valleys, Brak and Ganna. **1966** C.A. SMITH *Common Names* 173 Where special properties of a brack came to be recognized, .. it was soon enough 're-classified' to meet that new economy. **1974** *Farmer's Weekly* 2 Feb., Grazing consists of healthy karoo bushes, brak, ganna.

4. *rare.* A piece of alkaline ground.

1914 E.N. MARAIS *Rd to Waterberg* (1972) 23 This farm looks more like a barren brak than the luxuriant pasturage it once was.

Hence **brakish** *adj.*; so **brakishness** *n.*

1884 B. ADAMS *Narr.* (1941) 83 Nearly all the springs in that part of the country were brakish and entirely unfit for use. **1936** H.F. TREW *Botha Treks* 95 On arrival every man and horse was able to get a good drink of brakish water. **1958** A. JACKSON *Trader on Veld* 41 The water was excellent, with no sign of the brakishness so prevalent in that part of the country.

brak /brak/ *n.*² [Afk., fr. Du. *brak* setter.] A mongrel dog; BRAKKIE sense b. Also *attrib.*

1951 H.C. BOSMAN in L. Abrahams *Jurie Steyn's Post Office* (1971) 114 Patrolman Devenhage landed out one with his boot that sent the yellow brak pup flying through the door. **1961** D. BEE *Children of Yesterday* 94, I thought of my little dog – just an ordinary brak he is – and that dreadful loneliness seemed to leave me. **1969** *Personality* 5 June, You can keep any old brak you like you lucky dog. Let the snobs have their borzois and afghans. **1969** A. FUGARD *Boesman & Lena* 24, I had a dog. In Korsten. Just a brak. **1986** D. CASE *Love, David* 65 'Rich people don't buy mongrels!' Dadda sneered and added most disgustedly: 'That dog's a brak!' **1989** F.G. BUTLER *Tales from Old Karoo* 148 At his feet lay two equally careless-looking dogs of the large non-species which we call *brak*.

brak *v.* var. BRAAK *v.*

brakbos, brakbossie /ˈbrakbɔs(i)/ *n.* Formerly also **bra(c)k-bosch, brak-boschje**. [Afk., *brak* see BRAK *adj.* and *n.*¹ + *bos(sie)* (earlier *bosch(je)*, see BOSCHJE) bush.] Any of several species of salinaceous plants which flourish in alkaline soil and are palatable to livestock, esp. shrubs of the genera *Salsola* and *Atriplex*; BRAK *n.*¹ sense 3; BRAK-BUSH. See also GANNA sense 1, SALTBUSH sense a.

1824 W.J. BURCHELL *Trav.* II. 21 The soil .. was covered principally with such shrubs and plants as afford *alkali*: these were the *Kanna-bush*, and another whose name of *Brak-boschjes* (Brackish Bushes) indicates that their nature has been well observed by the inhabitants. **1886** G.A. FARINI *Through Kalahari Desert* 439 The poor oxen were obliged to be content with feeding on a shrub called *brak bosch* – the pulpy leaves of which have a strong taste of salt. **1890** A. MARTIN *Home Life* 48 The brack-bosch .. with blue-green leaves, and blossom consisting of a spike of little greenish tufts. **1917** R. MARLOTH *Common Names* 15 *Brak'bos*, (Salt bush). Several species of *Atriplex* are useful food-plants for stock. *A. Halimus* is the common indigenous salt-bush, frequent along the banks of rivers and on brackish ground of the drier districts. **1927** E.E. Mossop in Smuts & Alberts *Forgotten Highway* (1988) 65 The parched and black-stemmed 'vygie' and the brakbos on a hill with weathered furrows like the kindly lines on an aged mother's face. **1948** H.V. Morton *In Search of S. Afr.* 257 The brack-bosch .. is bluey green. **1955** L.G. Green *Karoo* 133 *Brakbos*, another typical bush, is almost identical with the salt-bush of the Australian sheep-runs. **1966** C.A. Smith *Common Names* 173 The brakbossie possessed individually distinctive properties and qualities which the stock-owners recognized by giving each a specific common name. **1973** Y. Burgess *Life to Live* 155 Nel .. was not as overcome at the sight of the Karoo, of the brakbossies and driedorings, or even the aloes, .. as she thought she would be. **1988** [see VYGIE].

brak-bush *n. obs.* Also **brackbush**. [(Part.) tr. Afk. *brakbos*.] BRAKBOS.

1844 J. Backhouse *Narr. of Visit* 502 When first our oxen were under the necessity of eating brak-bushes, we felt a little dismay, but now we looked out anxiously for a brak-place. **1863** J.S. Dobie *S. Afr. Jrnl* (1945) 122 He picked up some seed of brackbush (considered good for sheep).

brak ganna see GANNA sense 2.

‖**brakkie** /ˈbraki/ *n.* Also **brakje**. [Afk., mongrel (applied in transf. derog. sense to a person), *brak* see BRAK *n.*² + dim. suffix -IE.]

a. A derogatory term for a person.

1883 O.E.A. Schreiner *Story of Afr. Farm* 291 'Tant' Trana,' I said, 'you've married a Kaffir's dog, a Hottentot's "brakje"'. **1900** H. Nisbet *For Right & England* 159 (Pettman), Must they walk down the hills while the Rooibaatjes march up and make mince-meat of them? Have these *brakjes* not bayonets to plunge into us and turn our insides out?

b. A mongrel dog: BRAK *n.*²

1906 *E. London Dispatch* 12 Apr. 7 All they had to depend on was three small 'brakkies' (mongrel dogs) and their own kerries. **1913** C. Pettman *Africanderisms* 85 *Brakje*, .. As employed in the Cape Colony this word is almost exactly equivalent to the English words, mongrel, cur.

Branch *n. colloq.* Ellipt. for SPECIAL BRANCH. Also *attrib.*

1977 J. Sikakane *Window on Soweto* 76 He should not be surprised when the Special Branch called. The Branch men did call. *c***1985** K. Sole in *Eng. Academy Rev.* 3 9 The Branch say he's dangerous a terrorist of the foulest kind, and lock him up incessantly. **1990** 'Nhlanhla' in M. Kentridge *Unofficial War* 74 When you're a politician, (Special) Branch treat you more carefully. They don't assault you unless you have a provocative conversation ... They can keep you .. for months, even years, just to keep you out of the way. **1990** 'David' in *Ibid.* 75 The police are not all the same. The security police — Branch — they're clearly anti-comrade, even the black cops. *Ibid.* 75 While I was there I was not interrogated at all. Branch came four times, but only for five minutes.

brand /brant, ?brænd/ *n.* Formerly also **brandt**. [Afk., earlier S. Afr. Du.]

1. *obs. noncount.* Usu. reporting *S. Afr. Du.* or Afrikaans speech: fire.

1861 Lady Duff-Gordon *Lett. from Cape* (1925) 68 Capt. Davis jumped up and shouted '*Brand!*' (fire), rushed off for a stout leather hat, and ran down the street. **1919** M. Greenlees tr. *O.F. Mentzel's Life at Cape in Mid-18th C.* 124 There was a light shining from a little battery on shore; .. they mistook its light for the one on Robben Island, and steered accordingly. A moment afterwards the look-out man began to shout 'Brand! Brand!'

2.a. An area of land on which the grass has been burned. See also BURN.

1893 E. Nicholson in *Cape Illust. Mag.* Vol.4 No.6, 206 Great patches of dead black scarred the hill sides, until the wind carried away the burnt grass ... Soon a faint green tinged the *brands* as the young grass began to shoot. **1899** *Natal Agric. Jrnl* 31 Mar. 4 'Brand,' a burn, is very commonly used in connection with spring, autumn, and protecting burnings of grass. **1906** G.B. Beak *Aftermath of War* 112 This is capable of keeping animals which are not working in fair condition until the 'brandts' or burnt patches, are sufficiently strong for use. **1912** *S. Afr. Agric. Jrnl* July 38 (Pettman), A similar statement is made of *brands* where the young grass withers as the result of dry weather. **1929** J. Stevenson-Hamilton *Low-Veld* 57 Hunters know how eagerly game moves on the brand, and each year on the Eastern border of the Kruger National Park, the Portuguese natives .. burn the veld on their side as early as possible, and they may thus tempt the animals over to the fate awaiting them. **1949** L.G. Green *In Land of Afternoon* 176 Clusters of reeds, patches of brand where you will be lucky to find any buck exposing itself. **1970** E. Mundell *Informant, Pearston (E. Cape)* The sheep are grazing on the brand. (Veld that was burnt and is now budding).

b. *comb.* **brandgras** /ˈbrantˌxras/ *n.* [Afk., *gras* grass], see quot. 1966. See also BRANDBOSSIE.

1966 C.A. Smith *Common Names* 176 *Brandgras*, Sometimes used as a general term for all grasses which flourish on burnt (Afr.: brand) veld. Sometimes with specific reference to *Danthonia lanata* (Geo) and *Ehrharta duro* (Geo). Both species are rather coarse grasses, but as the result of burning sour mountain veld, the young growth affords excellent grazing.

‖**brandblaar** /ˈbrantblɑː(r)/ *n.* Forms: α. **brand blaad, brandblad**; β. **brandblaar, brandblare(n)**. [Afk. (earlier S. Afr. Du. *brandblad*), *brand* burn, fire + *blaar* (Du. *blad*) leaf, (Du. *blaar*) blister.] Either of two plant species, *Knowltonia capensis* and *K. vesicatoria* of the Ranunculaceae, with leaves which cause blistering on the skin.

α. **1795** C.R. Hopson tr. *C.P. Thunberg's Trav.* I. 292 The *Adonis Capensis* and *Atragene vesicatoria* (*Brandblad*) used instead of *Cantharides*: these plants grew on the sides of the mountains and hills. **1809** J. Mackrill Diary. 57 Medicinal plants of the Cape ... Adonis Capensis, Brand blaad — Blisters.

β. **1868** L. Pappe *Florae Capensis* 1 *Knowltonia vesicatoria*, ... The bruised herb, when applied to a painful part, raises a blister. It is therefore recommended in rheumatism, ischias, lumbago, and similar affections ... The plant is found in almost every part of the Colony, and from its effects is well known by the name of *Brandblaren*. **1917** R. Marloth *Common Names* 15 *Brandblaren, Knowltonia vesicatoria*. Leaves employed as a vesicant. **1966** C.A. Smith *Common Names* 176 *Brandblaar (blare)*, .. The vernacular name is prompted by the blistering (Afr.: brand) property of the leaves (Afr.: blare). **1972** Beeton & Dorner in *Eng. Usage in Sn Afr.* Vol.3 No.2, 34 *Brandblaar*, .. (*Knowltonia capensis*) lit: burn-leaf.

‖**brandboontjie** /ˈbrantˌbʊiŋki, -ci/ *n.* [Afk., *brand* burn + *boon* bean + dim. suffix -IE.] The climber *Mucuna coriacea* of the Fabaceae, with pods covered in stinging hairs.

1917 R. Marloth *Common Names* 15 *Brandboontjie, Mucuna coriacea*. Tropical. Pods clothed with sharp-pointed stinging hairs. **1940** V. Pohl *Bushveld Adventures* 81 Since .. they often brushed against brand-boontjies, a poisonous bean that sets up intense irritation and itching of the skin, their heads and necks were almost hairless. **1966** C.A. Smith *Common Names* 176 *Brandboontjie, Mucuna coriacea* ... The hairs can be extremely irritating to the skin and the pain may last for a week or more.

‖**brandbossie** /ˈbrantˌbɔsi/ *n.* Formerly also **brand-bos(ch)je**. [Afk., *brand* fire, burn + *bossie* (earlier *bosje, boschje*, see BOSCHJE) bush; see quots 1868 and 1917.] The fern *Mohria caffrorum* of the Schizaeaceae, which appears soon after veld is burned.

1868 L. Pappe *Florae Capensis* 44 In some parts of the Colony, the dry leaves are pulverised, and with fat made into an ointment, which is cooling, and very serviceable in burns and scalds. The vernacular name of this plant is *Brand-boschjes*. **1913** C. Pettman *Africanderisms* 86 *Brandbosjes*, .. *Mohria Thurifraga*. **1917** R. Marloth *Common Names* 15 *Brandbossie, Mohria caffrorum*. Not a shrub but a small deciduous fern of the South West; the leaves appear in great numbers after a bush fire when the shrubby vegetation .. has been destroyed. **1966** C.A. Smith *Common Names* 176 *Brandbossie*, .. *Mohria caffrorum* ... A fern, and one of the earliest plants to come up on burnt veld. **1973** Hancock & Lucas *Ferns of Witwatersrand* 36 *Mohrua caffrorum*, .. *Common names*: Scented fern; parsley fern; brandbossie.

‖**brandewyn** /ˈbran(d)əveɪn/ *n.* Also **brandywijn, brandywyn, brannewyn**. [Afk., fr. Du. *brandewijn*, (*ge*)*brande* distilled + *wijn* wine.]

1. Brandy; BRANDYWINE; also called CAPE BRANDY. Also *attrib.*

1806 J. Barrow *Trav.* I. 384 The bruised grapes, the undergrowings, the stalks and expressed husks, with the lees or dregs of the new wine, are thrown together into larger vessels ... From trash like this is most of the ardent spirit manufactured which is sold in the Cape under the name Brandewyn. **1835** T. Pringle in F.C. Metrowich *Valiant but Once* (1956) 74 They produced their provisions for supper, consisting chiefly of dried bullock's flesh, which they seasoned with a moderate *zoppjé*, or dram, of colonial *brandewyn*, from a huge horn slung by each man in his wagon beside his powder-flask. **1838** A.G. Bain *Jrnls* (1949) 196 'Snt half so good as Brandywyn. **1844** J. Backhouse *Narr. of Visit* 597 Few of the Boors in the vicinity, who make Brandewyn, or Cape brandy, will sell it to the Hottentots. **1850** T. Baines in S. Stander tr. *A.P. Brink's Brandy in S. Afr.* (1973) 101 In consideration for this kindness Mynheer requested a zoupie brandewyn for himself and friends. **1920** R. Juta *Tavern* 21 We stole some of de Baases brandy-wijn, a drink a lort from de brandy-wijn and orl de morning we go be in the sun. *a***1931** [see PHUZA *n.* sense 1]. **1937** F.B. Young *They Seek a Country* 413 One or two of the men rode over to pay their respects and drink a cup of tea-water or a *brandewyn soopie*. **1959** J. Packer *High Roof* 62 Bok watched her hurry away with the catch-me-charlie waggle that went to his head like brandywyn. What a girl! **1974** G. Jenkins *Bridge of Magpies* 43 He'll live to be a hundred. No women, no brannewyn. **1980** *Capetonian* Jan. 26 Die master en die merrem come home unexpected from die airport en found me en my friends jolling in hul living room en drinking hul bes' *brandewyn*. **1983** T. McAllen *Kyk Daar*, He immediately made a detour to the nearest Bottle Store to acquire a half-jack of brandewyn. **1990** C. Leonard in *Sunday Times* 2 Nov. 28 For the past 40 years Bapsfontein .. has been synonymous with country and western, with braaivleis, sunnyskies and brandewyn.

2. *comb.* **brandewynbos** /-ˌbɔs/ [Afk., earlier S. Afr. Du. *brandewynbosch*), *bosch* bush], the MORETLWA, *Grewia flava*; ‖**brandewyn ketel** /-ˈkɪətəl/ [Afk. (fr. Du.) *ketel* kettle], a copper still, used for brandy distillation. See also KETTLE.

1822 W.J. Burchell *Trav.* I. 364 They [*sc.* Hottentots] are fond of *brandy*, but their distance from the Colony prevents their being gratified to the extent of the wishes or means. An attempt at distilling a spirit from the berries of, what they therefore call, the **Brandewyn-bosch** (Brandy-bush) had succeeded. **1966** C.A. Smith *Common Names* 176 *Brandewynbos*, .. The vernacular name is derived from the use of the fruits in distilling a liquor or an inferior brandy (Afr.: brandewyn). **1937** C.R. Prance *Tante Rebella's Saga* 137 He had relied too much on his '**brandewyn-ketel**' (his private still) for the brewing of peach-brandy, potato-gin, and 'mampoer' from the wild fruits of the bush, and now that was getting dangerous. **1955** L.G. Green *Karoo* 105 Later the liquid *mos* is passed into the old *brandewynketel* or still, made to very much the same pattern as those used by Tennessee 'moonshiners.'

‖**brandlelie** /ˈbrantliəli/ *n.* [Afk., *brand* fire + *lelie* lily.] FIRE LILY.

1917 R. Marloth *Common Names* 15 *Brandlelie, Cyrtanthus angustifolius*. In many localities not flowering unless the ground has been cleared by a veld fire.

1965 S. Eliovson *S. Afr. Wild Flowers for Garden* 93 *C. tuckii* var. *transvaalensis, Brandlelie* ... These flowers are said to have been confused with 2 other red-coloured species, *C. angustifolius* and *C. contractus*, but may be distinguished readily from both of these. **1974** P. Clarke in S. Gray *On Edge of World* 35 There is the possibility of finding, in these charred areas, the flower called the 'Brandlelie'. These flowers look like symbolical tongues of the fire blood-red against the black, fire-ravaged shrubbery. **1983** M.M. Kidd *Cape Peninsula* 216 *Cyrtanthus ventricosus* ... *Brandlelie* ... Common in the south; [flowers] Dec.-May, usually after fires.

brandmeester *n. obs.* [Du., *brand* fire + *meester* master.] A fire warden.

*c*1795 W.S. Van Ryneveld in G.M. Theal *Rec. of Cape Col.* (1897) I. 250 Brand Meesters, persons to procure assistance, in case of fire. **1799** F. Dundas in G.M. Theal *Rec. of Cape Col.* (1898) II. 329 The Brandmeesters or Fire Wardens are, when the alarm is given for fire, immediately to repair to the fire with their staffs of office. **1926** P.W. Laidler *Tavern of Ocean* 83 Brand meesters were instituted, whose duty it was to secure all possible assistance in cases of fire, and to give orders to the burgher sergeants and to the freed slaves who worked the engines.

brandsick *adj.* and *n. Obs. Pathology.* Also **brand sic**. [Englished form of S. Afr. Du. *brandziekte*, see BRANDSIEKTE.]

A. *adj.* BRANDSIEK.

1835 C.L. Stretch Journal. 2 Apr., Our adjutant .. was .. directing the soldiers to cut the throat of a Brand Sick Calf — least [*sic*] the Enemy would thereby retain provision, or as he designated it '*Suport*'. *a***1875** T. Baines *Jrnl of Res.* (1964) II. 166 John had fallen in with a poor brandsick blesbok ewe, unable to rise, and had slaughtered it.

B. *n.* BRANDSIEKTE.

1863 T. Shone Diary. 20 May, Is sheep as got the brand sic. **1887** A.A. Anderson *25 Yrs in Waggon* I. 129 Many of the antelope species are subject to brandsick, and hundreds die.

brandsiek /'brantsik/ *adj. Pathology.* [Afk.] Suffering from scab; BRANDSICK *adj.*

1948 H.C. Bosman in L. Abrahams *Unto Dust* (1963) 28 'You never saw such a lot of brand-siek sheep in your life', the predikant was saying, 'as what Chris Haasbroek brought along as tithe'. **1970** H.M. Musmeci *Informant, Port Elizabeth* That poor horse is very brandsiek.

brandsiekte /'brantsiktə/ *n. Pathology.* Formerly also **brandt-sickte, brandt-siekte, brandziekte, brunt sickta**. [Afk. (earlier S. Afr. Du. *brandziekte*), *brand* burn, fire + *siekte* disease.] Scab or mange, a highly contagious notifiable skin disease of livestock, esp. sheep, caused by a mite; BRANDSICK *n.* Also *attrib.* See also *khaki brandziekte* (KHAKI *adj.* sense 1 b).

[**1790** W. Paterson *Narr. of Four Journeys* 48 At this season many die of a disease, which they term, the Burning Sickness, in which they lose most of their hair.] **1795** C.R. Hopson tr. *C.P. Thunberg's Trav.* I. 168 We were told that infectious distempers frequently prevailed among the cattle here, and that the *brandziekte* was not uncommon. **1806** J. Barrow *Trav.* I. 218 They are subject also to a cutaneous disease that works great havoc among the bovine tribe. It is called by the farmers the brandt siekte, or burning disease. **1835** A. Steedman *Wanderings* I. 139, I took out my rifle and shot it [*sc.* the gnu], when it proved to be greatly diseased with what the Colonists call the *Brandt-sickte*. **1847** *Ordinance 16* in *Stat. Law of Cape of G.H.* (1862) 832 No sheep affected merely with the disease commonly called *brandziekte* or goat with the disease called the scurvy shall be destroyed unless with the owner's consent. **1866** J. Leyland *Adventures* 86 A disease, called by the Boers 'brunt sickta,' or burnt sickness, .. sometimes breaks out and makes sad havoc amongst them. **1877** *Alice Times* 9 Feb., 1 Red Ox, very low condition, brandziekte along the back and shoulders. **1896** R. Wallace *Farming Indust. of Cape Col.* 367 Scab or Brandziekte in sheep .. [is] the result of an abnormal and unhealthy condition of the skin due to irritation created by myriads of microscopic mite-like insects or acari. **1910** A.B. Lamont *Rural Reader* 118 The worst enemy of the South African sheep farmer is scab or 'brandziekte,' which, as we have learned, is spread by a mite. **1955** L.G. Green *Karoo* 146 The farmers did not take kindly to woolled sheep. They argued that such sheep were more liable to scab; and indeed there are many references to 'brandziekte' in early documents. **1977** Fugard & Devenish *Guest* 29 This brandsiekte is beginning to get out of hand, you know. Castor oil for cows .. that's what I know about. **1980** P. Schirmer *Concise Illust. S. Afr. Encycl.* 19 *Scab* (brandsiekte), a mite-induced, mange-like disease which infects sheep.

brandsolder /'brantsɔldə(r)/ *n. Hist. Archit.* Formerly also **brand zolder, brandt-solder**. [Afk., fr. S. Afr. Du. *brandzolder, brand* fire + *zolder* loft; lit. 'fire-loft'.]

1. A layer of bricks or clay laid over a ceiling to catch burning thatch in the event of fire. Also *attrib.*

1832 *Graham's Town Jrnl* 20 Jan. 13 (advt) Fire Risks on the following moderate scale ... Fourth class, — trebly hazardous which includes all thatched buildings, *whether having a Brand Zolder or not* .. £0 15 0 For every £100 insured. **1833** *S. Afr. Almanac & Dir.*, (advt) Fire Premiums. First Class of Assurances. Thatched Buildings .. 15s.0d. Thatched Buildings with Brandzolder .. 12s.0d. **1845** *Cape of G.H. Almanac & Annual Register (advt)* De Protecteur Fire and Life Assurance Company ... Allowances made, as formerly, for substantial Brandzolders. **1896** M.A. Carey-Hobson *At Home in Tvl* (1896) 456 The brandt-solder ('solder' means attic, and 'brandt' something about 'burning') is a combination of the two; a layer, four or six inches thick, of clay and mud is laid upon reeds or laths which form the ceiling, and over this again is the many-gabled, high-pitched roof of thatch. **1938** C.G. Botha *Our S. Afr.* 75 To secure the house against destruction by fire should the inflammable thatch catch alight, a thickness of brick laid in clay was placed above the boarded ceiling. This 'brandzolder' gave coolness to the rooms below. **1954** K. Cowin *Bushveld, Bananas & Bounty* 69 Just before the roof itself went on, the upper side of the ceiling was covered with a layer of brandsolder ... The early Dutch settlers had first used this mixture of damp earth and straw for protection against fire under a thatched roof, but our version of it, made with soil and cement, was chiefly to keep the rooms cool. **1963** R. Lewcock *Early 19th C. Archit.* 383 The technique of laying a 'brand-solder' of clay over the ceiling to act as a fire-proofing seal between the roof construction and the rooms below survived sporadically for many years, and was even adopted with thatch and shingles by some of the immigrant thatchers. **1971** [see SPAANSRIET]. **1973** M.A. Cook *Cape Kitchen* 19 *Brandsolder*, This was a layer of well-worked clay laid over the ceiling, about 5 or 7,5 cm (2" or 3") thick; in large houses near Cape Town, however, a thin soft-burnt brick was sometimes used instead ... The brandsolder was an excellent safeguard in case of fire. **1979** Duminy & Adcock *Reminisc. of Richard Paver* 87 As the house is strongly barricaded and a *brandsolder*(?) made to cut off communication between the thatch and the rooms below, I have no fear but that, with the protection of the Almighty, we shall be safe. **1989** F.G. Butler *Tales from Old Karoo* 91 A strip of coir mat had been laid across the mud of the *brandsolder*, on either side of which was stored abundant furniture and junk of two or three generations.

2. *rare.* A loft or attic in the space above this layer; cf. SOLDER.

1913 C. Pettman *Africanderisms* 87 *Brandzolder*, .. A loft immediately under the thatch of a building, with a thick mud or brick floor, to protect the under part of the building should the thatch catch fire. The *Brand-zolder* is usually used for the storage of farm produce. **1949** L.G. Green *In Land of Afternoon* 82 Search your attic or brandsolder, for a complete copy of Ritter's Almanac .. would be worth as much as any Cape Triangular.

brandt var. BRAND.

brandt-sickte, -siekte varr. BRANDSIEKTE.

brandt-solder var. BRANDSOLDER.

brandwag /'brantvax/ *n.* Formerly also **brandwacht**. Pl. **-wagte** /-vaxtə/. [Afk. (fr. Du. *brandwacht*), *brand* fire + *wag* guard.]

1. *hist.* A picket, sentry, or outpost.

1895 *Cape Times Christmas No.* 45 The Boers .. adopted a very effective system of outposts ... Such parties were known as the 'Brand Wacht,' the term probably being a relic of the old custom of giving the alarm by means of beacon fires. **1899** F.R.M. Cleaver in M.M. Cleaver *Young S. Afr.* (1913) 35, I am duly installed under a Veldcornet, and to-night will take my spell of brandwacht (sentry) by sitting behind the wagons smoking. **1900** P.J. Du Toit *Diary* (1974) 32 Three Transvaal burghers .. who had joined the English, were following the trail of the laager, and not being aware of our presence, rode straight into our brandwacht. **1913** C. Pettman *Africanderisms* 86 *Brandwacht*, .. An old term which was revived during the Boer War of 1899–1902. It had reference to the old custom of giving alarm by means of beacon fires, but it was applied by the Boers to the system of outposts adopted by them during the war. **1940** F.B. Young *City of Gold* 186 Out on the veld, in a wide perimeter, strong outposts (or *Brandwagte*) kept watch and guard. **1946** E. Rosenthal *General De Wet* 23 Commandant-General Joubert had himself envisaged the possible coup, and had ordered a special guard or brandwacht to be kept. **1980** A.J. Blignaut *Dead End Rd* 58 We camped on the slope of the koppie that evening and the brandwag reported that the enemy was preparing for an attack at dawn.

‖**2.** Freq. with initial capital. [Prob. so named after the Ossewa Brandwag, see OB *n.*[1]] The armed guard of the *Afrikaner Weerstandsbeweging* (see AWB).

1986 *Weekend Argus* 8 Mar., This, he says, is why the Boere-brandwag wing has now been started so that every Boer could be part of the resistance of the volk. The brandwag is also supposed to help when 'gangs of murderers descend on us.' **1986** P. Van Niekerk in *New Statesman* (U.K.) 11 Apr. 17 At his public meetings Terre' Blanche has been wildly cheered, while calling for the establishment of a Brandwag — his own armed vigilante group. **1988** *Scope* 6 May 30 Already members of the Brandwag, the AWB's civil guard, are doing combat training at secret rendezvous. **1988** C. Legum in *Afr. Contemp. Rec. 1986–7* B737 Although there were no proven cases of the AWB having been involved in vigilante attacks on Black activists and White liberals, allegations were frequently made that its paramilitary, the *Brandwag*, was behind such attacks.

brandy bush *n. phr.* [tr. S. Afr. Du. *brandewyn-bosch, brandewyn* brandy + *bosch* bush.] The MORETLWA, *Grewia flava.*

1822 W.J. Burchell *Trav.* I. 364 They [*sc.* Hottentots] are fond of *brandy*, but their distance from the Colony prevents their being gratified to the extent of their wishes or means. An attempt at distilling a spirit from the berries of, what they therefore call, the Brandewyn-bosch (Brandy-bush) had succeeded. **1955** [see *rosyntjiebos* (ROSYNTJIE sense 2)]. **1972** Palmer & Pitman *Trees of Sn Afr.* II. 1439 Farmers in the Transvaal once made .. a brandy known as mampoer from the fermented fruits, and here the species [*sc. Grewia flava*] is widely known as 'brandy-bush'. **1982** Fox & Norwood Young *Food from Veld* 351 *Grewia flava* ... Common names: English — *brandy bush, raisin tree, wild plum.* **1987** F. Von Breitenbach *Nat. List of Indigenous Trees* 126 *Grewia flava*, ... Velvet Raisin, Wild Raisin, Raisin Tree, Brandy-bush.

brandy-wijn, brandywyn varr. BRANDEWYN.

brandywine *n. obs.* [Calque formed on Du. *brandewijn*, see BRANDEWYN. Also found in Brit. Eng. until the end of the 17th century.] BRANDEWYN sense 1.

1804 R. PERCIVAL *Acct of Cape of G.H.* 205 When he drinks he constantly uses that poisonous hot spirit called brandy-wine, or geneva when he can procure it. *a***1823** J. EWART *Jrnl* (1970) 15 From the refuse of the wine press, a strong spirit is distilled called brandy wine, in general use by the boors and the farmers. *a***1827** D. CARMICHAEL in W.J. Hooker *Botanical Misc.* (1831) II. 274 When a boor has returned from Capetown with a cask of brandywine, which he seldom forgets, the news spreads like wildfire. **1829** C. ROSE *Four Yrs in Sn Afr.* 116 The boors left a half aum (a cask) of brandy wine in the bush, and we drank it, and the rest drank more than I did, and got drunk. **1834** W.H.B. WEBSTER *Narr. of Voy. to Sn Atlantic Ocean* 279 They asserted with the most innocent faces imaginable, that they had only been drinking 'the bloom-sucker's health in a glass of brandy-wine; for he was a brave, good man.' *a***1862** J. AYLIFF *Jrnl of 'Harry Hastings'* (1963) 83 She told the shopman to give us a little refreshment out of some decanters of brandywine which stood on the counter. **1939** S. CLOETE *Watch for Dawn* 42 To make this feast there had been a great killing: of oxen, of sheep, of goats; of chickens, ducks, geese and turkeys ... There was wine and brandywine and peach brandy.

brandziekte, brand zolder varr. BRANDSIEKTE, BRANDSOLDER.

brannewyn var. BRANDEWYN.

Bratwah var. VATUA.

bray *n.* var. BREI *n.*

bray *v.*[1] var. BREI *v.*[2]

bray /breɪ/ *v.*[2] *trans.* Also **brae, braid, brei,** and (often) **brey.** [Englished form of S. Afr. Du. *breien* to prepare skins, fr. Du. *bereiden* to prepare (the mod. Afk. form being *brei*).] To soften (leather) by scraping, twisting, and working it until it is pliable. Also *comb.* **bray-paal** /-pɑːl/ [S. Afr. Du. *paal* pole], a device upon which leather thongs are worked by being hung and twisted by means of a heavy weight; *braying-pole*, see BRAYING sense 2.

1822 W.J. BURCHELL *Trav.* I. 351 Such an apparatus is called by them, and by the colonists, who also make use of it, a *Brey-paal.* [Note] The trunk of a tree is fixed up near the hut, for the purpose of preparing (or as they call it *breyen*) leathern *riems.* **1833** *Graham's Town Jrnl* 25 Apr. 4 She was tramping (or *breying*) some skins. **1837** [see RIEM sense 1 a]. **1849** J.D. LEWINS Diary. 20 Nov., Bester offers to bray & tan my sheepskins on the half. **1851** T. SHONE Diary. 11 Apr., Boy Jack was braying a bush buck skin for whip cord. **1863** *Queenstown Free Press* 3 Mar., The native was *sentenced* to be pegged out to a *bray paal* and receive 25 lashes with a stirrup leather. **1863** LADY DUFF-GORDON in F. Galton *Vacation Tourists* (1864) III. 192 The .. Hottentots can't 'bray' the skins as the Caffres do; and the women who did mine .. let them dry halfway in the process, consequently they don't look so well. **1913** A. GLOSSOP *Barnes's S. Afr. Hsehold Guide* 318 Proceed to brei between the hands or (if a cow or ox skin) by treading out with the bare feet. **1925** S.C. CRONWRIGHT-SCHREINER in F.C. Slater *Centenary Bk of S. Afr. Verse* 61 The hardy Boer .. cut the strip And brei'd and rolled and hammered it round to make the Wagon-whip. **1946** H.C. BOSMAN in L. Abrahams *Unto Dust* (1963) 164 Anything would be straight enough for him — even if it was something as twisted as a raw oxhide thong that you brei with a stick and a heavy stone slung from a tree. **1961** S. CLOETE in *Best of S. Afr. Short Stories* (1991) 288 It gave him great pleasure to brey the skins, to cut them and fit them. *Ja*, he made the children's shoes and his wife cut their nails. **1994** *Grocott's Mail* 20 Sept. 5 (*caption*) Captain Trapps .. explains various ways of breying hides to young 'Settlers'.

Hence **brayer** *n.*, a scraper, used to work skins.

1945 N. DEVITT *People & Places* 118 Lying beside the skeleton was the property of the dead man. A grinding stone and a fine specimen of a skin 'breyer' — made of bone, well-shaped.

brayed /breɪd/ *ppl adj.* Also **braid, brei'd.** [See BRAY *v.*[2]] Of leather: worked, softened.

1850 J.D. LEWINS Diary. 2 May, Bought a brayed sjambok fm. Ezra for 2/-. **1858** T. SHONE Diary. 29 Sept., She gave me a small braid buck skin. **1887** A.A. ANDERSON *25 Yrs in Waggon* I. 140 The young girls came decked out with a profusion of beads worked upon well-brayed leather, forming aprons. **1898** W.C. SCULLY *Vendetta* 60 A warm cape of brayed lambskin which she was in the habit of wearing in cold weather. **1907** — *By Veldt & Kopje* 198 His clothing was of brayed skin; his muscular arms were bare to the elbow. **1913** A. GLOSSOP *Barnes's S. Afr. Hsehold Guide* 318 Good farm harness line is made from brei'd ox skins. **1936** WILLIAMS & MAY *I Am Black* 14 He .. had clothed his magnificent body with a short apron of yellow brayed buckskin. **1956** P. BECKER *Sandy Tracks* 70 An old man was tanning a brayed antelope skin with the palms of his hands. **1964** B. TYRRELL in *Natal Mercury* 24 Oct., Dress comprises a spade-shaped back-skirt of brayed goatskin, apron of angora goatskin .. and eight more body rings made of grass twists. **1970** *Evening Post* 14 Nov. (Mag. Sect.) 1 The tight band of her skirt .. was deeply kilted to the knees and made from brayed skin.

brayer *n.* see BRAY *v.*[2]

braying /ˈbreɪɪŋ/ *vbl n.* Also **braeing, braiding, bre(y)ing.** [fr. BRAY *v.*[2]]

1. The process or action of working skins.

1848 H.H. METHUEN *Life in Wilderness* 259 (Pettman), A process commonly termed *braiding* which they perform by constantly rubbing it [*sc.* the skin] in their hands, greasing it, and thumping it with large sticks or stones, till it becomes soft and pliable. **1896** R. WALLACE *Farming Indust. of Cape Col.* 438 Braying is the simple and largely mechanical process by which raw hides are prepared for the making of the rough white leather-harness in use in the country districts of the Colony, and of .. 'rims' or powerful leather ropes. **1913** A. GLOSSOP *Barnes's S. Afr. Hsehold Guide* 318 In breing unsalted fat only must be used, and hard fat is the best. **1937** H. SAUER *Ex Afr.* 193 Buffalo, giraffe, hippo, or rhinoceros hide .. is trimmed to about the thickness of a lady's finger and made very pliable and supple by a process of 'braying' or constant rubbing by a greasy hand.

2. *comb.* **braying-pole** *n.*, *bray-paal* (see BRAY *v.*[2]).

1937 *Handbk for Farmers* (Dept of Agric. & Forestry) 1104 Such a riem is 70 to 80 yards in length. It is looped over the beam of a breying-pole or a strong branch of a tree.

breadfruit *n.* [See quot. 1972.] In full ***breadfruit tree***: BREAD TREE.

[*a***1827** D. CARMICHAEL in W.J. Hooker *Botanical Misc.* (1831) II. 265 The stem of the *Zamia cycadaefolia*, when stripped of its leaves, resembles a large *Pine-apple*. It is called the *Hottentot Bread-fruit*. These people bury it for some months in the ground, then pound it, and extract a quantity of farinaceous matter of the nature of *Sago*.] **1908** 'PHLOEOPHAGUS' in *E. London Dispatch* 24 Dec. 3 Our local Cycads .. are commonly called 'Kafirbread,' 'Breadfruit tree,' 'Bread palm,' or simply 'palm.' **1913** C. PETTMAN *Africanderisms* 88 *Breadfruit, Encephalartos caffer, Lehm.* The name sometimes given in the Eastern Province to this and other members of the *Cycadaceae* family. [*c***1969** E. GLEDHILL *E. Cape Veld Flowers* 38 *Encephalartos altensteinii*, .. *Cycad, Kaffir Bread Fruit.*] **1972** BEETON & DORNER in *Eng. Usage in Sn Afr.* Vol.3 No.2, 46 *Breadfruit tree*, .. Several species of *Encephelartos* .. with stout, round trunks & a crown of long, spiny pinnate leaves; the pith of the cone-like fruit of species such as *E. caffer* & *E. altensteinii* or *E. transvenosus* is used by Ba[ntu] to make bread.

bread palm *n. phr.* [Perh. tr. Afk. *broodpalm.*] Esp. in the Eastern Cape: BREAD TREE.

1908 'PHLOEOPHAGUS' in *E. London Dispatch* 24 Dec. 3 Our local Cycads .. are commonly called .. 'Bread palm.' **1913** C. PETTMAN *Africanderisms* 88 *Bread-palm*, Another Eastern Province name for the *Cycadaceae.* **1977** E. PALMER *Field Guide to Trees* 66 *Bread Palm, Encephalartos longifolius* ... Uniondale to Albany districts on inland sourveld hills and mountains, grassy slopes, kloofs. **1982** FOX & NORWOOD YOUNG *Food from Veld* 37 Encephalartos spp., e.g. *E. longifolius* — bread palm — pith used by Hottentots, rhizomes eaten raw or roasted by San.

bread tree *n. phr.* [tr. S. Afr. Du. *broodboom*, see BROODBOOM.] Any of several species of cycad of the genus *Encephalartos* of the Zamiaceae, esp. *E. altensteinii* and *E. longifolius*; BREADFRUIT; BREAD PALM; BROODBOOM; *Hottentot('s) bread* sense (a), see HOTTENTOT *n.* sense 6 a. See also MODJADJI sense 3.

1786 G. FORSTER tr. *A. Sparrman's Voy. to Cape of G.H.* I. 347 On a height near the uppermost farm on *Zeekoe-rivier* grew the *bread-tree* (*brood-boom*) of the Hottentots, discovered by Professor *Thunberg*, and of which he has given a description and drawing by the name of the *Cycas Caffra.* **1795** C.R. HOPSON tr. *C.P. Thunberg's Trav.* I. 201 The Bread tree Zamia caffra is a species of palm, which grows on the hills, below the mountains, on these tracts. It was of the height and thickness of a man at most, very much spread, and single. It is out of the pith, (medulla) of this tree that the Hottentots contrive to prepare their bread. **1834** T. PRINGLE *Afr. Sketches* 204 The Hottentot bread-tree, a species of palm. **1917** R. MARLOTH *Common Names* 16 *Bread-tree, Kaffir-. Encephalartos caffer, E. Lehmanni, E. Allensteinii*, etc. The pith contains starch and is turned into a food by the natives, like sago. **1965** S. ELIOVSON *S. Afr. Wild Flowers for Garden* 222 *Encephalartos*, Cycad, Bread Tree, Broodboom. The *Cycads* are said to be living fossils in that they are descendants of a primitive type of vegetation that covered the earth long before the time of early man. **1977** E. PALMER *Field Guide to Trees* 64 *Bread Tree, Encephalartos altensteinii* ... Eastern Cape, from Bushman's River .. eastwards and northwards to southern Natal border, coastal bush and forest. **1988** H. GOOSEN in *S. Afr. Panorama* Mar. 35 Thunberg had observed how the Hottentots were preparing a crude type of bread from the stem of a tree-like plant. The popular name *bread-tree* derives from this incident. **1990** R. STENGEL *January Sun* 11 The cycad is known as the .. bread tree in English. The plant's pith yields a starch that was used to make bread by de la Rey's ancestors, the Boers, the country's first white settlers.

breakfast run *n. phr.* An early morning motorcycle rally, held usu. on a Sunday.

1979 *Darling* 7 June 17 Breakfast Run. Every Sunday, several hundreds of people from all around Johannesburg crawl from their beds at the crack of dawn .. and gather at Fourways to go on the now traditional Breakfast Run to Hartbeespoort Dam. Sunday wouldn't be Sunday without the gleaming groups of bikes heading down the Pretoria road. **1982** *Drum* July 43 More and more township dudes are laying down big bucks on the latest high-powered mean machines. And recently they held their first 'breakfast run', roaring out of Soweto in the chill morning air. **1984** *Sunday Times* 29 Jan. 9 For bikers, the Breakfast Run has become a Sunday morning institution. **1989** *Grocott's Mail* 21 Mar. (Coastal News) 2 Five motorcyclists .. took a 'Breakfast Run' down to Port Alfred from Johannesburg.

breakwater *n. hist.* Often with initial capital. [Special sense of general Eng.] ***The breakwater***: The former Breakwater Convict Station (Cape Town), established in 1860 for long-term prisoners with hard labour. Also *attrib.*, and used allusively with reference to a sentence with hard labour, often in the phr. ***on the breakwater***.

The prison was situated at the docks, and prisoners worked on the construction of the breakwater.

1866 *Cape Town Dir.* p.xiii, Bondfield, Patrick. Overseer, Breakwater, 17 Napier Street. Bowlan, John. Constable (Breakwater). **1872** J.L. BABE *S. Afr. Diamond Fields* 62 The best thing he can do is .. steal something and be sent to the breakwater, where he will be provided for by the State. **1888** *Cape Punch* 31 Aug. 107 'Why was not de heaby swell arrested?' he asked indignantly 'No need for that,' Mr *Cape-Punch* replied, 'don't you see he was already on the breakwater?'

1899 A. WERNER *Captain of Locusts* 157 His sons — all that were not killed — were on the break water at Cape Town. **1899** G.C. GRIFFITH *Knaves of Diamonds* 34 I'll lay you ten years on the Breakwater to a thousand pounds .. that I'll take that little lot [*sc.* diamonds] through. **1911** L. COHEN *Reminisc. of Kimberley* 184 The thief was given in charge, .. fifteen thousand pounds' worth of diamonds were found, he got five years' well deserved punishment on the breakwater. **1913** A.B. MARCHAND *Dirk, S. African* 317 (Swart), 'Clear case of fraud I understand' said the other, 'shouldn't wonder if it meant the Breakwater.' **1924** L. COHEN *Reminisc. of Jhb.* 189 A report in a Kimberley newspaper of the trial was headed, 'Sweet Innocence', and O'Flynn went down to the breakwater for five years, convicted of an offence never committed by him. **1934** C.P. SWART Supplement to Pettman. 24 *Breakwater, to send to the*, A term formerly often used throughout South Africa to signify imprisonment. Long-term prisoners, who were sentenced to imprisonment with hard labour, were usually sent to work at the breakwater in Cape Town. **1944** 'TWEDE IN BEVEL' *Piet Kolonel* 170 The Break Water in Cape Town will be paradise for hard labour in comparison with this. **1952** H. KLEIN *Land of Silver Mist* 123 The famous old South African colleges, the Cape Town Breakwater and Pretoria Tronk. Illicit gold buying, illicit diamond buying, horse-thieving, and such-like degrees. **1963** O. DOUGHTY *Early Diamond Days* 146 Laughing gaily, drinking merrily, smiling serenely, but all the time with the shadow of the breakwater haunting them and phantoms of prison warders grinning over their shoulders. **1983** J.A. BROWN *White Locusts* 51 From the deck of the docked *American* it was possible to see the breakwater convicts labouring.

bredie /ˈbriːdi, ˈbrɪədɪ/ *n.* Also **brady**, **brédé**, **brede(e)**, **breede**, **bre(e)di**, **breidie**. [Afk., earlier S. Afr. Du., perh. fr. Pg. *bredo* any of several species of the widely distributed plant *Amaranthus* which is sometimes cooked as a vegetable; see quots 1815 to 1870.]

a. A stew or ragout of meat (usu. mutton) with vegetables. Also *attrib.*, and occas. *fig.*

1815 A. PLUMPTRE tr. *H. Lichtenstein's Trav. in Sn Afr.* (1930) II. 82 *Breedi* signifies in the Madagascar tongue *Spinage*; the word is brought hither by the slaves, and at present, throughout the whole colony, every sort of vegetable which, like cabbage, spinage or sorrel, is cut to pieces and dressed with Cayenne pepper is included under the general term *Breedi*. **1831** *S. Afr. Almanac & Dir.* 210 Cape turnip .. seldom produces more than leaves for *bredi*, when sown during the summer months. **1870** 'A LADY' in *Cape Monthly Mag.* I. Oct. 224 All sorts of vegetable 'breedies,' are importations from India. **1890** A.G. HEWITT *Cape Cookery* 30 Almost any vegetable may be made into Brédé. Pumpkin, water eeintjes, vet kousies, tomatoes, cabbage, cauliflower, &c. *Ibid.* 31 All brédés must be served with boiled rice. **1891** H.J. DUCKITT *Hilda's 'Where Is It?'* p.ix, First stew the meat and Onions together, .. then add Cauliflower, Green Beans, Potatoes, or any vegetable you like. Meat and vegetables done in this way are called by the Malay cook a 'Bredee'. *Ibid.* 14 Bredees are not to be made in deep saucepans, but in flat pots. **1910** D. FAIRBRIDGE *That Which Hath Been* (1913) 41 'He asked my permission to marry .. my cook. I couldn't refuse, though,' with a sigh, 'I have never had such bredees and sasaties since.' **1927** C.G. BOTHA *Social Life in Cape Col.* 56 In many homes to-day the old Cape cooking prevails ... What may be considered typical South African foods .. originated in the East, such as various stews known as 'bredie,' 'soesaties', .. and 'bobotie.' **1933** W.H.S. BELL *Bygone Days* 40 For dinner we had as a rule some kind of stew or 'brady' and probably pumpkin fritters or some other easily made pudding. **1944** I.D. DU PLESSIS *Cape Malays* 27 About a dozen words seem to have been a direct importation from the East. Most of these refer to Malay dishes such as *bredie, sosatie* and *bobotie*, which are still popular at the Cape. **1950** H. GERBER *Cape Cookery* 87 Allow the bredie to simmer until the meat is almost tender. Add the chopped suring (sorrel) leaves and the coarsely diced potatoes and continue to simmer the bredie until the potatoes are soft. **1969** D. CHILD *Yesterday's Children* 33 The typical Dutch fare was augmented by more exotic dishes introduced by Malay cooks from the East. Some of these, such as .. *bredie* (meat stew with green beans or tomatoes) .. have become traditional South African dishes. **1973** H. BECK in *Farmer's Weekly* 25 Apr. 101 The Cape bredie is a stew in which the vegetable has been reduced to a fairly thick consistency ... Tomato is the most popular among these bredies. **1980** *Fair Lady* 7 May 195 So what's new about stew? asks Erica Platter, risking her reputation to reveal the truth about bredie: it's fatty lamb dressed as holy cow. **1981** *Pretoria News* 26 Nov. (Town Suppl.) 2 Pieter-Dirk Uys .. attempts far too much in this dissertation on kugels, South African society, health hydros, gigolos and a bredie of other subjects. **1985** [see CAPE MUSLIM *n. phr.*]. **1990** *You* 24 May 52 A decent bredie, whether cabbage, green bean, waterblommetjie, or tomato, remains a firm favourite. **1994** *Weekend Post* 16 July (Leisure), Bredie, a traditional Cape dish, is made from meat and vegetables, simmered slowly together for full flavour. Mutton or lamb are used for bredie and the cuts are rib, breast, neck or shank. Add only a small amount of water. A bredie is often served in the pot in which it was cooked.

b. With distinguishing epithet signifying a particular type of bredie according to the ingredients used: **bean** - or **boontjes bredie** /ˈbʊɪŋkis-/ [Afk., *boon* bean + dim. suffix -IE], a bredie made using either dried- or green beans; **cabbage bredie**; **cauliflower bredie**; **green bean bredie**, a bredie made using green beans; also called *bean bredie*; **hotnotskoolbredie**, see HOTNOT sense 4; **pumpkin bredie**; **tamatiebredie** /təˈmɑːti-/ [Afk., *tamatie* tomato], or partially translated **tomato bredie**; **waterblommetjie bredie**, see WATERBLOMMETJIE sense b; **wateruintjie bredie**, see WATERUINTJIE sense b; **wortelbredie** /ˈvɔː(r)təl-/ [Afk., *wortel* carrot], see quot. 1970. See also quot. 1890 (sense a above).

1889 'A HOUSEWIFE OF THE COLONY' *Col. Hsehold Guide* 27 **Bean Brede**. Prepare the meat as in the cabbage brede, but instead of cabbage use some beans (French), cut into short pieces ... For tomato brede see tomato stew, which is prepared in the same way. **1979** *Sunday Times* 31 Oct. (Mag. Sect.) 1 We eat. Bean bredie with rice, mutton crisply potroasted with potatoes, beetroot salad [**1988** see quot. under *wortelbredie* below]. **1891** H.J. DUCKITT *Hilda's 'Where Is It?'* 14 **'Boontjes Bredie**.' (Dry Bean Stew. Cape or Malay.) **1889** 'A HOUSEWIFE OF THE COLONY' *Col. Hsehold Guide* 27 **Cabbage Brede**. This is a favourite colonial dish, but it is rich and not easily digested. **1892** 'MARIAN' in *Cape Illust. Mag.* Dec. 112 After the two had partaken of hot coffee, and cabbage brady, cooked in the choicest style, they felt considerably better. **1955** V.M. FITZROY *Dark Bright Land* 97 Mevrouw Baard, the landlady, was a notable cook, and her cabbage bredie, saffroned rice with raisins in it, and curried bobotie were tasty and satisfying, and the white wine refreshing. **1994** *Weekend Post* 16 July (Leisure), Cabbage bredie. Use recipe above [*sc.* for Cauliflower bredie], but use one medium cabbage, finely shredded, .. and omit water, as cabbage draws a lot of water. **1994** *Weekend Post* 16 July (Leisure), **Cauliflower bredie**. 2 onions .. 1kg mutton thick rib .. 5ml crushed dried chillis .. 1 large cauliflower, broken into florets .. 3 potatoes. **1951** S. VAN H. TULLEKEN *Prac. Cookery Bk* 171 **Green Bean Bredee**. This is a meat dish and a favourite dish in South Africa. **1970** *Evening Post* 17 Oct. (Mag. Sect.) 3 Green bean bredie. 2 lb breast or ribs mutton 3 cups sliced green beans 4 sliced potatoes ($\frac{1}{2}$inch thick slices) 1 large sliced onion 2 oz butter or dripping 6 whole cloves. **1994** *Weekend Post* 16 July (Leisure), Green bean bredie. 750g neck of mutton .. 2 onions .. 750g to 1 kg sliced green beans .. potatoes. **1994** *Ibid.*, **Pumpkin bredie**. 1kg dry pumpkin .. 700g fat mutton .. onions .. fresh ginger .. chilli. **1947** L.G. GREEN *Tavern of Seas* 59 She made every variety of bredie, the stews that the Malays brought to the Cape; especially the **tamatie bredie**. **1979** *Capetonian* May 7 Malay curry, tamatie bredie, bobotie — you name it, we've got it and it all originated in the Cape. **1986** B. STREEK in *Cape Times* 16 May 11, I would have thought that by now the names waterblommetjie-bredie and tamatiebredie were as South African as Table Mountain .. and that these .. should be called that in any language. **1889** [**tomato bredie**: see quot. at *bean bredie* above]. **1913** *D.S.G. Bk of Recipes* 18 Tomato Brady ... Part of the forequarter of mutton ... Place the meat in a saucepan with a little butter ... Stir in some onions .. and brown it. **1941** FOUCHÉ & CURREY *Hsecraft for Primary Schools* 11 Tomato Bredie. $\frac{1}{2}$lb. ribs of mutton, $\frac{1}{2}$oz. fat, 1 small onion, 1 lb. tomatoes, seasoning ... All bredies are cooked in this way. Any vegetables may be used. **1994** *Weekend Post* 16 July (Leisure), Tomato bredie. 1,5kg breast of lamb or mutton .. 2 onions .. 1kg ripe tomatoes, skinned and chopped .. 2 medium potatoes. **1970** HEARD & FAULL *Cookery in Sn Afr.* 489 **Wortelbredie** is the traditional funeral dish. **1971** *Sunday Times* 31 July (Mag. Sect.) 7 A decidedly South African flavour, from boerewors, wortelbredie, to snoek kedgeree. **1988** F. WILLIAMS *Cape Malay Cookbk* 95 The mourners are usually provided with something to eat. In the past, this would have been wortel and ertjie bredie or sugar bean bredie.

Hence **bredie** *v. trans. nonce*, to make (something) into a bredie.

1994 G. WILLOUGHBY in *Weekly Mail & Guardian* 8 July 38 The accent here is on the fresh-boiled, bredied or blommetjied. The dishes have names like 'snoek paté Houtbaai' and 'ostrich Oud[t]shoorn'.

Breede River yellowwood see YELLOWWOOD sense 2 c.

breeker var. BREKER.

brei /breɪ, bʁeɪ/ *n.* Also **br(a)y**, **brey**. [See BREI *v.*[2]] A guttural 'r' in speech (as in French), common esp. in the Malmesbury district of the Western Cape.

The normal *S. Afr. Eng.* pronunciation is /breɪ/; /bʁeɪ/ is used in imitation of the sound made by those who brei.

1957 L.G. GREEN *Beyond City Lights* 166 People of the Western Province wheat belt have an unmistakeable *bry*, a rolling of the letter 'r' ... I am told that this *bry* is a Huguenot legacy. **1963** M. KAVANAGH *We Merry Peasants* 14, I suspected an over-emphasized *'Kaapse bry*,' the rolling 'r' that distinguishes a Cape Afrikaner from those of the other provinces ... 'You don't have to get Trrrransvaal' guinea fowl ...' (There was the bry again!) **1970** F. PHILIP *Informant, Johannesburg* The smous had a *'brei'* .., a rolling mixture of Yiddish and Afrikaans. **1971** *Personality* 11 June 43 Smuts, for all his immense gifts, would have been another loser. His face was somewhat expressionless and he spoke with a harsh, grating Malmesbury bray. **1979** *Capetonian* May 9 The official languages will be Afrikaans, English and Xhosa. All school-children will .. be compelled to take at least two years of Swartland bry, gammatjietaal and Namaqualand singsong. **1983** *Sunday Times* 18 Sept. (Mag. Sect.) 32 She has a soft Boland *brei* that becomes comically pronounced when she expresses alarm. **1990** R. MALAN *My Traitor's Heart* 25 Ben's speech was haunted by the brei — a roll of the r that harked back to French, a language unspoken in South Africa for almost two centuries.

brei *v.*[1] var. BRAY *v.*[2]

brei /breɪ, bʁeɪ/ *v.*[2] *intrans.* Also **br(a)y**. [Altered form of Afk. *bry* fr. Du. *brijen*, fr. *brouwen* to speak thickly.] To pronounce the letter 'r' in the back of the throat, as in French.

See note at BREI *n.*

1955 A. DELIUS *Young Trav.* 93 He .. had a curious way of making his 'r' sounds into a throaty 'g'. 'Listen to Oom Thys braying!' cried Elise. **1985** J. CLOETE in *S.-Easter* Oct.-Nov. 28 Some of them *bry*; it is a typical characteristic of Swartland Afrikaans, the rolled 'r' coming deep out of the throat. **1986** *Cape Times* 22 Jan., We spent six years there, and one in Malmesbury — but when we began to 'brei' Mum pulled us up.

brei'd var. BRAYED.

breidie var. BREDIE.

breing var. BRAYING.

breker /ˈbrɪəkə(r)/ *n. colloq.* Also **breeker**. [Afk., 'destroyer', fr. *breek* to break + agential suffix *-er*.] A tough, destructive, or aggressive man. Also *attrib.* See also MAIN MAN.

1970 M. BENNETT *Informant, Krugersdorp* Breker. Tough young man. **1975** *Sunday Times* 2 Mar. 3 The Nationalist newspaper reported that 'Oom Willie' is used to tussles. He was not called 'the breker of the north' for nothing. *Ibid.* 7 Sept. 17 'Breeker' tactics – a short cut to title! .. A breeker is South African slang for a tough guy .. a champion street-fighter. An expression for an 'ou who can put the head and boot in better than the next ou'. **1979** *Capetonian* May 6 When the Joburg boys cribbed our Parow ous and put oranges on *their* aerials – the Cape Town brekers went one better and put green fur on top of their dashboards. **1979** *E. Prov. Herald* 18 Sept. 14 My son is not a mummy's boy, but he is a gentle person ... Are the 'breekers' who are to be his instructors and superiors going to have fun breaking him? **1982** D. KRAMER *Short Back & Sides* 62 Budgie, Budgie and the band, .. Budgie a breker on his 50cc He played Peter Gunn in the key of E. **1983** *Sunday Times* 8 May (Mag. Sect.) 25 You get the *brekers* who reckon this is going to be an A-1 way to get the cherries and donner the big okes, maybe even the teachers, my pal. **1987** *Fair Lady* 21 Jan. 144 The leftover Fifties hoodlums creating the incidents were not *totally cooled out* ... They were *very heavy brekers*.

brenjal, -jela varr. BRINJAL.

Brequa var. BRIQUA.

brey *n.* var. BREI *n.*

brey *v.* var. BRAY *v.*[2]

breyani, biryani /briˈjɑːnɪ, breɪ-, bir(ɪ)-/ *n.* Also **biriani, b(u)riyani**. [Urdu *biryānī*, ad. Pers. *biryān* fried, roasted.]

a. A dish of Indian origin consisting of spicy rice and lentils with vegetables, fish, chicken, or mutton. Also *attrib.*

Used also in other varieties of English.

1952 *Drum* May 40 (advt) Curry meals our speciality Whenever you are in town do drop in for a cup of tea Wednesday is biryani day. **1961** Z. MAYAT in J.B. Branford *Dict. of S. Afr. Eng.* (1987) 29 Biriani is the dish royal amongst all the exotic rice dishes of India, and remains 'the dish' to serve .. to welcome house guests on their first day, or .. the main course of the menu in formal entertaining. **1971** L.G. GREEN *Taste of S.-Easter* 154 All the good old Cape cookery books cry out for coriander; in blatjang and peach pickle, slamse wors and buriyani. **1977** *Darling* 16 Mar. 86 Let's use our breyani and curry spices, our fruits, game and fish, and create brand-new indigenous dishes, which we can set proudly before any gourmet. **1977** M.P. GWALA *Jol'iinkomo* 57 Grey Street, Tripe Breyani isn't on your menu, why? **1985** *Style* Apr. 30 A large Indian family sit over pots of briyani which they have brought wrapped in newspaper. **1985** *S. Afr. Cookbk* (Reader's Digest Assoc.) 380 *Biriani*, An Indian dish of meat, fish or chicken with rice, lentils, eggs and spices. **1990** *Fair Lady* 6 June 105 A very popular Indian dish, biriani is traditionally served on festive occasions. It consists of partly cooked rice and curry which are then layered together before continuing to cook.

b. *fig.* Esp. among South Africans of Indian descent: ***breyani every day***, endless success or fortune.

1986 F. KARODIA *Daughters of Twilight* 42 'Too expensive. For that kind of money they should be eating biryani every day.' Ma chuckled at his reference to the exotic dish. **1992** R. MESTHRIE *Lexicon of South African Indian English* 88 *To want biryani everyday*, .. To expect good fortune or success all the time.

breying var. BRAYING.

bricate /brɪˈkeɪt, brə-, ˈbrɪkət/ *n. slang.* Also **bracket, bricade, briekade**. [Isicamtho; ultimate origin unkn.] 'Friend', 'mate', 'buddy', 'pal', used informally or familiarly:

a. As a term of address. Cf. BRA sense 2 b.

1963 B. MODISANE *Blame Me on Hist.* (1986) 57 'Heit, bricade', he said, 'this is my cheerie; take a walk, friend, this cheerie is a rubberneck.'

b. As a term of reference. Cf. BRA sense 2 a.

1966 K.M.C. MOTSISI in *Drum* 30 Jan. They (the ghost squad) are always asking for the fare for a nip of port from each of the guys they meet in the street and which guy happens to be their 'bricate'. **1974** 'QUINTON' in *Drum* 22 Sept. 10 If you beat him, he goes to fetch his brackets, and you get a hiding.

Hence **bricateskap** /-skap/ *n.* [Afk. *-skap* -ship], friendship.

1978 M. MUTLOATSE *Casey & Co.* Thank-u to Bra Stan for your briekadeskap & warmth.

brief /brif/ *n. hist.* [Afk., letter. See also BRIEFIE.] Any of several types of (official) letter or note, including a letter of credit, or a pass; BRIEFIE sense 1. See also *slagter's brief* (SLAGTER sense b).

1849 N.J. MERRIMAN *Cape Jrnls* (1957) 69 He .. took me to an aged Boer, who .. simply asked where is 'de brief' (the letter), on presenting which, he perused it and said – It was right and I might stop. **1909** LADY S. WILSON *S. Afr. Mem.* 107 The inhabitants .. have to put all their stores at the disposal of the burghers .. The owners only received a 'brief' or note of credit on the Transvaal Government at Pretoria, to be paid after the war. **1945** N. DEVITT *People & Places* 139 A 'commandeer brief' was a document setting out the names and addresses of burghers to be called up for active service or containing a list of supplies, animals or transport to be requisitioned. **1974** P. GIBBS *Hist. of BSAP* II. 92 A curfew operated in the towns and no native was allowed abroad after 9 pm unless he had a 'brief', written hurriedly by his employer usually on an odd scrap of paper, authorizing him to be away from his quarters.

briefie /ˈbrifi/ *n.* Formerly also **briefje**. [Afk., (earlier Du. *briefje*), *brief* letter + dim. suffix -IE.]

1. *obs.* BRIEF.

1873 F. BOYLE *To Cape for Diamonds* 318 A dam-keeper, who brought up two horses and three oxen, captured from a drove of fifty or more, found drinking at the dam without a briefje. **1876** —— *Savage Life* 32 'Me your Kaffir, baas,' says he; 'give me briefje to Mr. Jardine after breakfast, and he pay me £2?' **1896** H.L. TANGYE *In New S. Afr.* 284, I desire to send a letter to one of my friends at Selukwe, so I take advantage of the travelling post-office – that is, I stop one of a party of boys and give him a 'briefie,' as it is called in Kaffir pigeon English (and in Flemish!) **1899** *Mafeking Mail* 7 Nov., We're besieged by the blooming old Boers, .. They've sent us in briefjes by scores .. Saying 'Surrender'. **1913** C. PETTMAN *Africanderisms* 88 *Briefje*, .. A note or letter; sometimes it is used of the 'Pass' which a native must have when passing from one part of the country to another with stock.

2. *hist.* A note or licence given by a land-owner to a digger, usu. at a small fee, entitling him to the freehold of a claim, and constituting a lease in perpetuity. Also *attrib.*

1910 J. ANGOVE *In Early Days* 26 The original diggers at Du Toit's Pan held their claims by right of a note, or licence, issued by the owner of the farm, termed a 'briefje', hence the claims held under these titles were known as 'briefje claims.' **1924** S.G. MILLIN *God's Step-Children* 93 A little corrugated iron shed, at the open window of which, before a deal table, sat a red-faced man writing an official looking paper. It was he, thought Kleinhans, who probably gave people the briefje – the licence – to dig. **1931** G. BEET *Grand Old Days* 52 Some of the brighter knights of the shovel got the better of the guileless and bewildered owner by .. obtaining, at a cost of 7s. 6d. each, concessions or claim 'briefjes,' which occasioned a heap of trouble afterwards. **1950** E. ROSENTHAL *Here Are Diamonds* 199 Today the word 'Briefie' .. no longer stands merely for a claim held under the original Orange Free State Diamond Law of 1871, but is often used by farmers for ordinary deeds of transfer. **1968** J.J. MCNISH *Rd to Eldorado* 134 A man named Meyer .. gave a digger named Prinsloo a 'briefie' to work section H.5 on the Harrisdale Estate, and found a few hours later he had thereby lost to his own syndicate diamonds worth, then, £100,000. *Ibid.* 220 There was uproar and defiance, the diggers refusing to comply, many now producing the scores of 'briefies' they had got .. giving them the right to seek for diamonds for all time. **1976** B. ROBERTS *Kimberley* 20 We paid down our money, and he granted us 'briefies' (written licences) in acknowledgement. This is the origin of what are known as 'briefie claims'. They constituted to all intents and purposes leases in perpetuity.

briekade var. BRICATE.

Brigua, Brikwa varr. BRIQUA.

brinjal /ˈbrɪndʒəl, -dʒɔːl, -dʒɒl/ *n.* an *adj.* Also **berinjela, brenjal, brenjela, bringal, bringall, bringaul, brinjel(a)**. [fr. Pg. *beringela* egg-fruit.]

A. *n.* The aubergine or eggplant, *Solanum melongena* of the Solanaceae; the plant bearing this fruit.

Also *Indian Eng.*

1804 R. PERCIVAL *Acct of Cape of G.H.* 142 The nopal or prickly pear which feeds the cochineal insects, is in abundance; as also bringalls and different kinds of cole and cabbages. **1843** *Cape of G.H. Almanac & Annual Register*, In very rich ground sow capsicum, chili-pepper, eggplant (Bringal), sweet bazil, tumato, okro, etc. **1891** R. MONTEIRO *Delagoa Bay* 54 Sometimes they bring a few fresh beans or bunches of cabbages, or Berinjelas (the fruit of the egg-plant and most delicious when cut in slices and fried in butter or oil). **1907** J.M. WOOD *Handbk to Flora of Natal* 90 Less well-known species are the Egg-plant or Brinjal. **1936** M. HIGHAM *Hsehold Cookery* (1941) 139 Brinjal or Egg Plant (Aubergine). **1950** H. GERBER *Cape Cookery* 98 Baked stuffed Brinjals. Choose plump fruits, and allow one halved brinjal per person. Without peeling the brinjal scoop out the pulp. **1977** *Fair Lady* 8 June (Suppl.) 30 Peel and coarsely chop brinjals. Sprinkle with salt and stand for 20 minutes. Drain brinjals and add to curry. **1990** *Weekend Post* 14 Apr. (Leisure) 6 Brinjals, also known as eggplants or aubergines, can be used in many dishes. **1994** *S. Afr. Garden & Home* Sept. 135 Pickled brinjals.

B. *adj.* Of the colour of a brinjal, 'aubergine'.

1988 A. PILLANS in *S. Afr. Panorama* May 23 A brinjal pillar? Splashes of pale rose, ox-blood, brick, ochre and taupe wherever you look! T-h-i-r-t-y s-e-v-e-n kinds of marble and granite!

Briqua /ˈbrɪkwa, -wə/ *n. Obs.* exc. *hist.* Also **Bericqua, Brequa, Brigua, Brikwa**. Pl. **-s**, unchanged, or (rarely) **Amabriquas**. [Etym. unkn.; perh. fr. Khoikhoi *birikwa* goat-men, see quot. 1857.] BATLHAPING. Also *attrib.*

1790 W. PATERSON *Narr. of Four Journeys* 121 Colonel Gordon .. intended to direct his course to the eastward in search of a nation, called Brequas, of the Caffer tribe. **1801** W. SOMERVILLE *Narr. of E. Cape Frontier* (1979) 107 Another range not very lofty seen E and West thro' which we penetrated into the Country of the Briquas. **1818** LORD C. SOMERSET in G.M. Theal *Rec. of Cape Col.* (1899) XII. 112 Those tribes the *Boshuanas, Ghonas*, and *Briquas*, who hitherto have been very peaceable towards the Colonists. **1822** W.J. BURCHELL *Trav.* I. 423 His father was a Briqua (or Bachapin). **1833** *Graham's Town Jrnl* 25 Apr. 2 Four of our people returned from Tamboekie land, bringing the news that the Tamboekies had been attacked by a party of people, called Amabriquas. **1857** D. LIVINGSTONE *Missionary Trav.* 201 The different Hottentot tribes were known by names terminating in kua, which means, 'man', and the Bechuanas simply added the prefix Ma- denoting 'a nation': they themselves were first known as Briquas or 'goat-men'. **1861** P.B. BORCHERDS *Auto-Biog. Mem.* 73 As we were approaching the Beriqua, now better known as the Boshuanah or Beetchuanah country, it was desirable that interpreters should be obtained. **1980** LYE & MURRAY *Transformations* 41 The most southerly-placed Tswana, the Tlhaping ... The Kora named these Tlhaping 'Briqua', Goat People.

British Indian *n. phr. Obs.* exc. *hist.* Esp. during the years 1902–1910: one of Indian or Pakistani descent, resident in South Africa but claiming the protection due to a British subject.

1904 *Indian Opinion* in Bhana & Pachai *Documentary Hist. of Indian S. Afr.* (1984) 96 In spite of nearly two years of British rule, the Orange River Colony remains closed against British Indians, no matter what position they may occupy. **1906** *Indian Opinion* 15 Sept. 657 The following is the text of the cablegram sent to the Viceroy of India:- British Indians alarmed at Asiatic Ordinance passing through Legislative Council Transvaal Ordinance degrading insulting reduces Indians to worse status than that of pariahs. **1909** J.J. DOKE *M.K. Gandhi* 56 The work of British Indians on the battle-fields of South Africa, has received some recognition. Their dead have been honoured. **1912** *The Jrnl* 31 Oct. 4 The 'Volkstem' .. says it is an open secret that the object of Mr. Gokhale's visit is to obtain on behalf of British Indians certain privileges which South Africa has meant to deny to all Asiatics without distinction. **1917** S.T. PLAATJE *Native Life* 26 Violent laws like the Immigration Law (against British Indians and alien Asiatics) and the Natives' Land [Act] were indecently hurried through Parliament to allay the susceptibilities of 'Free' State Republicans. **1926** M. NATHAN *S. Afr. from Within* 117 The British Indians, .. led by Mr M.K. Gandhi, led a powerful agitation against the registration statute, and a 'passive resistance' movement was inaugurated, which ultimately assumed large proportions. [**1946** V. WETHERELL *Indian Question* 9 The treatment of Britain's Indians had been one of the complaints against the old Transvaal Government. Surely their lot would improve now they are Britain's own?] **1951** *Off. Yrbk of Union 1949* (Union Office of Census & Statistics) 1109 At the Imperial Conference held in 1921 .. a resolution was passed which .. expressed the opinion that in the interests of the solidarity of the British Commonwealth it was desirable that the rights of British Indians to citizenship should be recognized. **1976** B. PILLAY *Brit. Indians in Tvl 1885–1906* p.xi, Why then is the history of British Indians in the South African Republic, better known as the Transvaal, somewhat different from that of overseas Indians elsewhere in the empire?

briyani var. BREYANI.

bro /bru(ː)/ *n.* Also **bru**. [Shortened form of BROER.] 'Brother': an informal or familiar term of address; also in the phr. ***my bro***. Cf. BRA sense 2 b.

1979 M. MATSHOBA *Call Me Not a Man* 182 'Is that fair?' 'Naw.' 'That's it, bro. But there's also a second reason.' **1987** *Scope* 6 Nov. 32 What about a *skyf*, bro? *Ibid.* 34 'I could have been gripped by the *Boere* ... And then?' ' Sorry, bro.' **1989** M. BRAND in *Fair Lady* 25 Oct. 92 *My bru*, my brother; friend; comrade.

Broderbond var. BROEDERBOND.

broeder /ˈbrʊdə(r), ˈbrudər/ *n.* [Du., brother.]
1. Esp. in the context of Afrikaner society: a brother. Cf. BROER sense 5.

1786 G. FORSTER tr. *A. Sparrman's Voy. to Cape of G.H.* I. 65 He looked .. very good-humoured, as well as his lively and *plaisirige broeder*, but was not able to say much. **1972** *Sunday Times* 5 Nov. 4 Broeders and sisters have I none, but this man's Broeder is my father's son. Who am I?

2. A term of address or reference to a fellow member of a religious community or congregation.

1798 LADY A. BARNARD in Lord Lindsay *Lives of Lindsays* (1849) III. 431 'This grate,' said he, 'and all the iron-work, is my broeder's making; he got the bars, and fashioned it himself.' **1841** B. SHAW *Memorials* 272 Broeders, (brethren), this is our state. By nature we are blind and know not God. **1935** H.C. BOSMAN in V. Rosenberg *Almost Forgotten Stories* (1979) 62 The Ouderling held up his hand .. 'Broeders', he said. 'Let us not judge Koenrad Wiurm too harshly.'

3. Usu. with initial capital.
a. Short for BROEDERBONDER; occas. also used as a title.

1972 *Weekend Post* 27 May 2 'How, then, can a top Broeder be entrusted with such a very important assignment?' **1972** *Sunday Times* 24 Sept. 11 One wonders who is in control of education in the Transvaal. Is it the Administrator and his executive, or is it Broeder K- .. ? **1973** *Ibid.* 4 Feb. (Mag. Sect.) 3, I must admit that in the past I have been bored by the Broeders and their Ku-Klux complexion. **1976** [see ENGELS *n.* sense 2 a]. **1981** *E. Prov. Herald* 23 Apr. 1 This powerful clique 'supervises the implementation of Broeder policies, sees that Broeders get effective control of key areas, .. and advises Cabinet Ministers on policy matters' according to .. a book which exposed the workings of the Broederbond. **1988** J. LE MAY in *Inside S. Afr.* May 12 By the 1960s he held numerous directorships and was also chairman of several companies, including Volkskas, the bank founded by Broeders. **1989** M. MANLEY tr. *L.M. Oosthuizen's Media Policy & Ethics* 93 Free from ideology, propaganda and slogans, inhibitions, maniuplation by state presidents, ministers, *broeders*, generals and big-time captialists. **1990** *Sunday Times* 15 July 18 The not so spooky Broeders. To the extent that the Broederbond still plays any political role at all, it is a benign one. **1993** R. MCNEILL in *Sunday Times* 4 Apr. 19 As a harbinger of the new spring of 'independent' Broeder-free television it was very ordinary indeed.

b. *attrib.* Of or belonging to the Broederbond or Broederbonders.

1972 *Sunday Times* 24 Sept. 11 A cousin of Broeder boss Dr. Andries Treurnicht slapped down the broederbond this week. **1981** *E. Prov. Herald* 23 Apr. 2 Broeder doctors were urged not to send patients to Roman Catholic hospitals. **1984** *Ibid.* 11 June 7 The town council is .. divided down the middle in what amounts to a 'Broeder' split.

4. *fig. rare.* An Afrikaner; BOET sense 4. See also AFRIKANER sense 2 a.

1975 *Sunday Times* 27 July 20 The Voortrekker spirit flickered in the north this week ... A dim memory .. of the time when protest ran strongly in the veins, and broeder thumped broeder with a point of principle.

Hence **broederskap** /ˈbrudə(r)skap/ *n.* [Afk. *-skap* -hood, -ship], brotherhood, comradeship; membership of the BROEDERBOND (sense 1).

1979 *Voice* 4 Mar., In a flash of broederskap Gerry is reported as saying Kallie can sommer stay in the same hotel as his opponent, John Tate. Tate is Black. **1988** 'K. DE BOER' in *Frontline* May 38 Scarcely had this been achieved and broederskap restored (if we are to believe the Press), than a new problem arose surrounding the collection of short stories. **1989** 'HOGARTH' in *Sunday Times* 3 Dec. 26 It seems that Mr Wynand Malan's membership of the Broederbond came up for discussion at a recent conclave of DP leaders. One wonders .. whether his *broederskap* really still needs to cause such alarm.

Broederbond /ˈbrʊdə(r)bɔnt, ˈbrudə(r)-/ *n.* Also **Broderbond, Broederbund**. [Afk., short for *Afrikaner Broederbond, Afrikaner* (see AFRIKANER) + *broeder* brother + *bond* league, fellowship.]
1. An exclusive (originally secret) organization promoting the economic and political interests of Afrikaners; AB; BOND *n.*[2] sense 2 a. Also *attrib.* See also BROEDER sense 3.

The Broederbond was established in 1918, with membership open (by invitation only) to male Afrikaners of a particular political persuasion.

1944 J.C. SMUTS in H. Gibbs *Twilight* (1950) 202 It is clear that the Broederbond is a dangerous, cunning, political, Fascist organization of which no public servant, if he is to retain his loyalty to the State and Administration, can be allowed to be a member. **1950** H. GIBBS *Twilight* 201 The history of the Afrikaner Broederbond (Band of Brothers) is one of the most fantastic of the 20th century. *Ibid.* The mysterious organization called the Broederbond, whose members pursued their business in the darkness of intrigue and whose ambitions were served by a fanatical devotion. **1950** D. REED *Somewhere S. of Suez* 66 The Broderbond, a band of brothers .. of which General Hertzog said in 1935: 'We now have to do with a secret political society accessible to and existing only for Afrikaans-speaking members, the moving spirits of which are out to govern South Africa over the heads of the English-speaking people among us.' **1952** [see GREAT TREK sense 1]. **1952** *Rand Daily Mail* 2 Dec. 11 The choice before South Africa was clear — a Broederbond .. or a united South Africa marching in step with the great Commonwealth of Nations. **1962** L.E. NEAME *Hist. of Apartheid* 71 The Broederbond, a secret society pledged to place Afrikaners in all important positions in the State. **1963** A. DELIUS *Day Natal Took Off* 47 The stock bogey of opposition politics, the Afrikaner Broederbond .. a kind of cultural and political Mafia among the Afrikaners. **1972** *Weekend Post* 27 May 2 Judging from information which had leaked out, the Broederbond was not well-disposed towards the English-speaker and his cultural heritage. **1972** [see Argus quot. at SAP *n.*[1] sense 2]. **1981** *E. Prov. Herald* 23 Apr. 1 South Africa's R3 000-million a year meat indsutry nestles in the beefy palm of the Broederbond — the country's powerful and secret Afrikaner organisation. **1990** T. MATHEWS et al. in *Newsweek* 12 Feb. 10 The secret Broederbond (Brotherhood) of elite white Afrikaners is pushing forcefully for reform, in the name of the survival of white society.

2. *transf.* Any exclusive grouping, esp. one operating secretively and having a lot of power within a particular field or organization.

1980 *Daily Dispatch* 6 May 6 Mr Rupert Lorimer of Orange Grove .. accused Mr B.H. W— of Carletonville of being a 'member of the mealie mafia' ..'I say he belongs to the mealie Broederbond.' **1982** *E. Prov. Herald* 26 Aug. 5 Opus Dei, which has been described as 'a kind of Catholic Broederbond,' claims to have .. 75 000 members in 80 countries. **1985** *Fair Lady* 6 Feb. 82 Botha then accused B— of running a black broederbond — the mud that his black political enemies also continually sling in his face. **1990** D. VAN HEERDEN in *Sunday Times* 10 June 8 The Afrikaner Volkswag .. is a sort of respectable umbrella organisation — the Broederbond of the right wing. **1990** *Sunday Times* 24 June 2 The party [*sc.* the South African Communist Party] does not see itself as a 'Broederbond' within the ANC.

Hence **Broederbondism** *n.*, the attitudes and actions of the Broederbond.

1960 J.H. COETZEE in H. Spottiswoode *S. Afr.: Rd Ahead* 68 The bogy of Afrikaner-nationalism, Afrikaner-calvinism and Afrikaner broederbondism, always kept alive by the press and hammered on by political machinations.

Broederbonder /ˈbrʊdə(r)bɔndə(r), ˈbrudə(r)-/ *n.* Also with small initial. [Afk., *Broederbond* (see prec.) + *-er* suffix denoting a member of (an organization, or group of believers).] A member of the Broederbond; BROEDER sense 3; BROER sense 4; BROTHER sense 1. Also *attrib.*, and *fig.*

1952 *Rand Daily Mail* 2 Dec. 11 Most of the Cabinet and most Nationalist members of the Parliament belonged to the Broederbond, which now aimed at nominating only Broederbonders as candidates for the general election. **1964** M.G. MCCOY *Informant, Port Elizabeth* Parliament has just re-opened, & Dr. V[erwoerd] has admitted to being a Broederbonder. **1979** *Sunday Times* 18 Feb. 10 The control of South Africa is in the hands of a few thousand broederbonders of limited talent: A national disaster. **1981** *Ibid.* 25 Jan. 23 English-speaking civil servants banished to backwaters to make way for Nat or Broederbonder pals. **1982** *Daily Dispatch* 4 May 9 Mr Billie .. was one of the founder-members of the Ciskei National Independence Party .. and usually referred to himself as one of the Ciskei's 'broederbonders'. **1987** *New Nation* 12 Feb. 6 Businessmen, church and student leaders travelled to Lusaka to meet the ANC. Even a Broederbonder made the pilgrimage to Lusaka — a move which angered Botha. **1990** R. MALAN *My Traitor's Heart* 27 Broederbonders, members of the Brotherhood, the secret society of Calvinists and apartheid zealots that constituted the spine of the Afrikaner power structure.

Broederkring /ˈbrʊdə(r)krəŋ, ˈbrudə(r)-/ *n. hist.* [Afk., *broeder* brother + *kring* ring, fraternity.] A fraternity of ministers of the black Dutch Reformed churches.

The Broederkring changed its name to *Belydende Kring van die Nederduitse Gereformeerde Kerke* (Confessing Fraternity of the Dutch Reformed Churches) in 1983.

See note at DUTCH REFORMED.

1980 *E. Prov. Herald* 8 Oct. 11 Members of the Broederkring — a progressive ministers' fraternity of the black churches — see this as further evidence of a mounting campaign against them. **1981** *Rand Daily Mail* 25 Mar. 8 The NGK's growing concern at the influence of the Broederkring, a fraternity of black ministers of the black Dutch Reformed churches. **1984** *Survey of Race Rel. 1983* (S.A.I.R.R.) 630 The (African) NG Kerk in Afrika asked its ministers not to join the Broederkring, which is not recognised by the (white) NG Kerk either. The (coloured) Sendingkerk is reported to be seeking a better understanding of the movement, while the (Indian) Reformed Church in Africa is divided in its views.

broedertwis /ˈbrʊdətwəs, ˈbrudə(r)-/ *n.* Also with initial capital. [Afk., 'a quarrel between brothers', *broeder* brother + *twis* quarrel.]
1. A split in the ranks of Afrikanerdom, caused by political, religious, or other differences. Also *attrib.* See also AFRIKANERDOM sense 1.

1965 C. VAN HEYNINGEN *Orange Days* 2 The call which brought the author's father to South Africa was itself a product of this broedertwis, amongst the Transvaal Afrikaners, for in addition to the political and personal jealousies that kept them divided, there was religious strife. **1978** WILKINS & STRYDOM *Super-Afrikaners* 40 Only 12 years after the Boer War, with heartbreak and grief still deep in Afrikaner hearts, the stage was being set for an even more traumatic experience — *Broedertwis*, brother taking up arms against brother. **1981** *Sunday Times* 8 Mar. 16 There's a nasty smell of cordite in the air as this broedertwis election gets under way. **1986** C. WILSON in *New Statesman* 30 May 17 The tension has produced new divisions among the whites, blurred the traditional political lines between English and Afrikaans speakers and splintered Afrikaner unity. This fragmentation is encapsulated in a single Afrikaans word with particularly bitter connotations: *broedertwis* — a fight among brothers. **1990** *E. Prov. Herald* 28 May 1 President F W de Klerk yesterday accused the Conservative Party leadership of carrying out a 'total campaign of incitement'. This held the danger of placing the party 'irrevocably on a slippery slide to a morass of violent "broedertwis"'. **1992** S. VAN DER MERWE in *South* 27 Feb. 13 While the referendum may temporarily increase the level of .. broedertwis, it will bring it to a head and it will abate after that.

2. *transf.* Friction between individuals or interest-groups.

1979 *Frontline* Dec. 21 It [*sc.* Inkatha] has also become the centre of a ferocious black broedertwis which shades its white equivalents to the level of incidental tiffs. **1982** S. MOTJUWADI in *Drum* May 39 Although I will concede that there is a discordant note of broedertwis across the colour border, I still maintain that it is nothing new. **1987** *Drum* July 12 When the brotherly love soured into broedertwis, the Ciskei turned into a scenario that could have been a cloak and dagger espionage dream for a Hollywood film scriptwriter.

‖**broek** /brʊk, bruk/ *n.* [Afk., pair of trousers.]
1. *Attrib.* and *comb.* **broek band** /-bænd/, ‖/-bant/ [Afk. *broekband* waistband], the waistband of a pair of trousers; **broek kaross** /-kəˈrɒs/ [fr. Khoikhoi *karo-s* skin cloak], a Nama or Khoikhoi petticoat made of animal skins; see also KAROSS sense 1.

1877 T. BAINES *Gold Regions of S.-E. Afr.* 113 Blocks three feet square were got out at '**Broek band**,' *i.e.* 'Waist' deep. **1838** J.E. ALEXANDER *Exped. into Int.* I. 96 The women wore skin petticoats, or the Namaqua **broek karosse**, consisting of a prepared sheep or goat skin, so arranged, as to depend from the waist in a broad oval flap behind, and in front to be only a few inches in depth.

2. Trousers; panties or knickers. Also **broekie** [see -IE], and *attrib.* Cf. BROEKIES, BROEKS.

1937 C.R. PRANCE *Tante Rebella's Saga* 96 Oom Jurie disappeared behind the screen, reappearing presently in shirt-sleeves .. only to be summarily bundled back again with summary .. orders to 'Mak af your shirt and broek'. **1966** I. VAUGHAN *These Were my Yesterdays* 109 Anna, my vrouw, sees my legs are just like matchies and not for running without a broek to cover them. **1969** A. FUGARD *Boesman & Lena* 25, I didn't even have on a *broek* or a petticoat when we started walking. **1975** 'BLOSSOM' in *Darling* 1 Oct. 111 Take a squizz down here by my broek-elastic. See that terrible ugly scar .. I'll never be able to hold my head up in a bikini .. again. **1993** *Informant, Grahamstown* Hey, there's somebody's broekie here. Who's lost a broekie?

broekielace /ˈbrʊkɪ leɪs/ *n. Archit.* Also **broekieslace**. [Afk. *broekie* panties, knickers + Eng. *lace.*] Victorian-style ornamental wrought-iron work, used on verandahs, or as fencing; decorative woodwork. Also *attrib.*

1980 *Cape Times* 30 Aug., Authentic Victorian charm in select oak lined avenue. Tralies Broekielace and marble fireplaces. **1981** *Rand Daily Mail* 18 June 2 One particularly memorable feature of those houses is the beautiful wrought iron fencework or 'broekielace' that adorns so many gardens. **1989** F.G. BUTLER *Tales from Old Karoo* 164 As you can see, our house has .. that broad stoep, with the elaborate broekielace woodwork all round. **1990** *Weekend Post* 3 Feb. (Leisure) 4 Some of Long Street's roofscapes are a joy to behold, with their gracious 'broekie-lace' balcony railings (some even have roof-top railings), Victorian pilasters, fancy gables, statues and gargoyles. **1991** *S. Afr. Garden & Home* Aug. 80 The broekie-lace was brought from the Karoo where it was hand-carved over 100 years ago.

broekies /ˈbrʊkiːz, ˈbrukis/ *pl. n.* [Afk. *broekie* panties, knickers + Eng. pl. suffix *-s.*] Women's or girls' panties or knickers; BROEKS sense b. Also *transf.*, and *fig.* Cf. BROEK sense 2.

1961 D. ROOKE *Lover for Estelle* 94 There were cries of goodbye and the little girls blew kisses to us; they had on new print dresses and broekies that Estelle had made for them. **1969** *Informant, Grahamstown* The Guildhall Banquet was magnificent: all those footmen standing around in their satin broekies. **1971** 'SAFIJOROQ' *As for Truth* 21 We were all busy looking at a lady on the platform ... She was sitting like this and you could see right up to her broekies. **1986** *Cape Times* 17 Jan., I don't see this as a place where everyone 'bares their broekies' the whole time. There is also a lighter human side to things. **1987** H. PARKER in *Pretoria News* 18 June (Tonight) 3 Having walked alone from Graaff-Reinet .. she screams out her shame — she had to tear up her 'broekies' to bind up her bloody feet. **1988** J. RAPHAELY in *Femina* May 152 Satin broekies under their three-piece suits *nogal!*

broeks /brʊks/ *pl. n. Colloq.* Also **brooks**. [Afk. *broek* pair of trousers + Eng. pl. suffix *-s.*]
a. Trousers or slacks for either sex. Cf. BROEK sense 2.

1861 *Queenstown Free Press* 4 Dec. (Pettman), Socks of course he wore none, and the tanned *broeks* had slightly contracted in their washing. **1913** C. PETTMAN *Africanderisms* 91 *Broeks*, .. The common form of the word among the English colonists of the Eastern Province of the Cape Colony; a pair of trousers. [**1958** I. VAUGHAN *Diary* 38 A new man teacher has come to teach. We call him *broeks* becos he wears such wide trousers.] **1963** [see OUTJIE]. **1980** A. DANGOR in M. Mutloatse *Forced Landing* 162 'Just get away from here before I bogger you up too!' 'Orraaight, don't piss in your *broeks!*' **1989** J. HOBBS *Thoughts in Makeshift Mortuary* 174 You had to drop your broeks and sit down quick so as not to look down the hole into the blackness. **1990** *Sunday Times* 22 Apr. (Mag. Sect.) 5 Michelle B— with her brooks.

b. BROEKIES.

*c*1966 M. JABOUR in *New S. Afr. Writing* 96 'He pushed me down, he threw mud on me, and,' she paused dramatically, 'he wanted to pull my broeks down.' **1973** *Fair Lady* 7 Mar. 19 My little one's 'broeks' which show ever so slightly when she marches off to school. **1975** *Darling* 29 Jan. 103, I get to be fitted out (frilly pink tutu, pink satin *broeks* and tinsel crown). **1978** [see MERREM sense 1].

broem vogel var. BROMVOËL.

broer /bruː(r)/ *n.* [Afk., fr. Du. *broeder* brother.] 'Brother'.
1. *colloq.* An informal or familiar term of address, often in the phr. ***my broer***. Also in dim. form **broertjie** /ˈbruːrki/ [see -IE]. Cf. BRA sense 2 b.

1912 F. BANCROFT *Veldt Dwellers* 110 'Look at my old shoes, *broertjie*,' she stretched out a foot clad in a well-worn pair of veldtschoens. **1969** LENNOX-SHORT & LIGHTON *Stories S. African* 63 Alle heil, *broer* .. see you tomorrow at the funeral. **1987** S.A. BOTHA in *Frontline* Oct.-Nov. 9 Don't you worry, my broer, this isn't boep. Wait until you get to Central. Oh, yes, my broer, then you'll check what's potting. **1989** *Sunday Times* 5 Nov. (Mag. Sect.) 31 When he gets to know you better .. he calls you *broer*, as in 'Hey, broer, what do you think?' or 'That's a great idea, broer.' **1990** B. COHEN in *Weekly Mail* 22 June (Suppl.) 7 Or Wally Onetime, looks like he had a rough night, who wakens to a glorious day in Bamboesbaai: 'Howzit my broer. Let's go fishing.' **1992** S. GUTKNECHT in *Sunday Times* 19 Apr. (Suppl.) 28 I'll check you later, broer.

2. *obs.* Used as a title before a man's first name.

1913 C. PETTMAN *Africanderisms* 91 *Broer*, .. This word is frequently employed in folk-lore tales and ordinary conversation as Uncle Remus — Mr. Chandler Harris' friend — uses the word 'Brer'. Instead of Brer Fox, Brer Rabbit, etc., we have Broer Jakhals, Broer Wolf, etc.

3. A friend or compatriot. Also *fig.*

1938 F.C. SLATER *Trek* 59 Twelve volleys from the belching roer, The trekker's trusted friend and broer, Had rattled harshly. **1979** *Sunday Times* 8 July (Extra) 2 We jam-pack our bios to the ceiling, sit shoulder-to-shoulder with our black broers. *Ibid.* 26 Aug. 3 My white broer was sitting there laughing. He had a great sense of humour. **1981** B. MFENYANA in M. Mutloatse *Reconstruction* 299 Now the white maponisa took a while to adjust to Mdantsane, coined by their own broers in the first place.

4. BROEDERBONDER. Also used as a title.

1950 H. GIBBS *Twilight* 209 The Broers are said to have realized that in future they would have to seek stronger control over the machinery of government. **1952** B. DAVIDSON *Report on Sn Afr.* 154 In the Parliament which elected Dr. Malan as Prime Minister it is said on reasonably sound evidence that more than four-fifths of all the members of the Nationalist and Afrikaner Parties were Broers, or brothers of the Bond. **1994** *Noseweek* No.10, 10 Broer D— they kept on as chief executive.

5. *colloq.* A brother. Cf. BOET sense 3 a, BROEDER sense 1.

1977 C. HOPE in S. Gray *Theatre Two* (1981) 40 Bring your broer's friend here and let's check his knife then. **1990** J. NAIDOO *Coolie Location* 177 'Ja, you know I had a long talk with my broer, Hafez, the other day. **1992** N. MBATHA in *Pace* Aug. 53 There were two warders, brothers, who proved particularly adverse toward him. 'The Kleynhans broers had their knives out for me,' he recalls.

6. *slang.* MAIN MAN.

1987 L. BEAKE *Strollers* 38 It was them what started it — the Spider Men. Wanted us to be lighties, you know, join the gang ... They kept after us. My uncle, .. he's one of the Broers, jy weet, high up, jy weet. He says it's family, man.

broken veld see GEBROKEN VELD.

Brolong var. BAROLONG.

brom /brɔm/ n. [Transf. use of Afk. *brom* to growl; see also BROM v.] The deep, booming call of a cock ostrich. See also *bromming* (BROM v.)

　1933 J. JUTA *Look Out for Ostriches* 71 Nothing stirred, and the only sound was the distant *brom* of a cock ostrich. 1968 F. GOLDIE *Ostrich Country* 21 The cry, or *brom*, is confined to the cock. Each cry consists of three booms, two short followed by one long, which reverberate across the veld. This *brom* can only be uttered while the bird is standing still. 1969 — *River of Gold* 59 Even experienced hunters often mistake the *brom* of an ostrich for a lion's roar. The female has no voice at all ... But the male bird makes up for her. He roars just like a lion.

brom /brɔm/ v. Also **broom**. [Afk., fr. Du. *brommen* to drone, hum, grumble, mutter.]

1. intrans. Of a cock ostrich: to make a booming call; BOOM v.

　[1838 J.E. ALEXANDER *Exped. into Int.* I. 121 The male ostrich sits on the nest .. during the night, the better to defend the eggs from jackals and other nocturnal plunderers; towards morning he *brommels* or utters a grumbling sound, for the female to come and take his place.] 1890 A. MARTIN *Home Life* 128 The departed hen was evidently his favourite wife; and disconsolate at her loss, he ran restlessly about the camp for some time, *brooming* repeatedly. 1912 [see BOOM v.] 1968 P. PAGE in F. Goldie *Ostrich Country* 62 That night I heard the old bird *bromming*, a sound almost like a faint lion's roar. 1970 M. HOBSON *Informant, Tzaneen*, I heard the cock ostrich '*brom*' in the 'Kamp' this morning. 1977 F.G. BUTLER *Karoo Morning* 82 He could make the most impressive bass sounds, coming deep out out of his throat and chest like a 'volstruis bromming'.

2.a. intrans. To grumble or complain.

　1976 *Informant, Grahamstown* He didn't bring me back my car so I had to walk to the hairdresser's, *bromming* all the way I can tell you. 1987 M. OLIVIER in *Fair Lady* 11 Nov. 126, I seldom get really angry; I tend to *brom* and *boom* and end up going to bed with a migraine.

b. trans. To say (something) in a grumbling fashion.

　1979 'BLOSSOM' in *Darling* 16 May 131 'You still on that phone ..?' 'She doesn't have to pay blerry phone bills ..' *broms* the ole man from behind the paper.

Hence (sense 1) **bromming** /ˈbrɔmɪŋ/ vbl n., also **brooming**, (the action of producing) the sound made by a cock ostrich (see BROM n.).

　1890 A. MARTIN *Home Life* 110 After a good rain, ostriches soon begin to make their nests; the males become very savage, and their note of defiance — *brooming*, as it is called by the Dutch — is heard in all directions. 1912 *S. Afr. Agric. Jrnl* Jan. 24 (Pettman), In the characteristic *bromming* or *booming* of the cock during the pairing season, the neck becomes greatly inflated by the filling of the foodpipe with air. 1948 H.V. MORTON *In Search of S. Afr.* 119 The sound he [sc. the male ostrich] makes in the breeding season has often been mistaken for the roar of a lion and is called 'brooming'.

‖**brommer** /ˈbrɔmə(r)/ n. [Afk. (perh. fr. Du. *bromvlieg*), blowfly, bluebottle, fr. *brom* to hum, buzz.] Any of several blow-flies of the Calliphoridae; BRUMMER FLY.

　c1939 S.H. SKAIFE *S. Afr. Nature Notes* 68 Among the most deadly enemies of the caterpillars are certain hairy stout-bodied flies about the size of the common 'bluebottle' (*brommer*). 1970 H. VAN RENSBURG *Informant, Port Elizabeth* Brommer. Blowfly. 1971 *Informant, Grahamstown* Oh no, not another brommer in the house — they make such a noise.

bromvoël /ˈbrɔmfʊəl/ n. Obs. exc. hist. Formerly also **broem vogel**, **bromfogel**, **brom(me) vogel**, **brom-voegel**. [Afk., *brom* (fr. Du. *brommen*) to growl, mutter + *voël* (earlier Du. *vogel*) bird; see also quot. 1867.] The hornbill *Bucorvus leadbeateri* of the Bucerotidae; RAINBIRD sense 2; TURKEY BUZZARD.

　1827 G. THOMPSON *Trav.* II. 353 If a person kill by accident a mayhem, (or Balearic crane) or one of those birds which the Colonists call *brom-vogel*, .. he is obliged to sacrifice a calf or young ox in atonement. 1835 A. STEEDMAN *Wanderings* I. 236 They are considered sacred amongst the Caffers, and are called by the Colonists, Bromme Vogels, from their singular cry, which is deep and harsh. 1853 [see TURKEY BUZZARD]. 1867 E.L. LAYARD *Birds of S. Afr.* 228 *Bucorvus Abyssinicus* ... *Brom-Vogel* of Colonists ... Common on the Eastern Frontier ... They get their name from the droning cry they utter. 1918 S.H. SKAIFE *Animal Life* 240 The hornbills are .. mostly found in forested regions, but some, such as the *bromvogel* or ground hornbill, frequent open country. 1939 [see LIGHTNING BIRD]. 1940 V. POHL *Bushveld Adventures* 66 The drowsy kuwees of the grey luries, the deep drumming of the bromvoels in the distance .. intensified the slumbering spirit that brooded over all. 1994 M. ROBERTS tr. *J.A. Wahlberg's Trav. Jrnls 1838–56* 35 Bromfogel. He throws his food up into the air and allows it to fall into his gullet.

bronze bream n. phr. Any of three species of seabream of the Sparidae (esp. *Pachymetopon grande*), so called from their colouring: **a.** The HOTTENTOT (n. sense 2 a), *P. aeneum*. **b.** *P. grande*; BLUE FISH sense 3 a; DAS sense 2 b; HOTTENTOT n. sense 2 c; JANBRUIN sense b; JOHN BROWN sense c. **c.** The JOHN BROWN (sense d), *Polyamblyodon germanum*. In all senses also called COPPER BREAM.

　In Smith and Heemstra's *Smiths' Sea Fishes* (1986), the name 'bronze bream' is used only for *Pachymetopon grande*.

　1947 K.H. BARNARD *Pict. Guide to S. Afr. Fishes* 157 Bronze Bream, Natal Hottentot, Pachymetopon aeneum. 1949 [see BLUE FISH]. 1971 *Farmer's Weekly* 12 May 85 When fishing for rockcod, galjoen, stumpnose, copper bream, bronze bream, or any fish which makes an immediate beeline for the rocks it is hard to better a medium outfit. 1972 [see DAS sense 2]. 1989 *Stanger Mail* 4 Aug. 16 One unusual species observed was a German fish (No 183.27 in Smith's Sea Fishes) which weighed 1,7kg. According to Rudi van der Elst, this fish is perpetually and wrongly identified as a bronze or copper bream. 1993 R. VAN DER ELST *Guide to Common Sea Fishes* 355 *Pachymetopon grande* ... Bronze bream, a reference to its metallic colouration and to *breme*, an old French name for a similar freshwater fish.

broodboom /ˈbruətbuəm/ n. Also with initial capital. Pl. **-bome** /-buəmə/. [S. Afr. Du., *brood* bread + *boom* tree.] BREAD TREE.

　1786 [see BREAD TREE]. 1965 S. ELIOVSON *S. Afr. Wild Flowers for Garden* 223 *E. altensteinii*, Broodboom, Bread Tree. This is a tall-stemmed tree which grows to the height of about 15 or 20 feet and comes from the eastern Cape. 1966 C.A. SMITH *Common Names* 179 Broodboom, Several native species of *Encephalartos* ... The vernacular name was first recorded for *E. caffer*. 1981 *Grocott's Mail* 29 Sept. 1 My own particular appeal is for a small reserve in the Albany area for Endangered species of the cycad family (Broodboom). 1984 J. ONDERSTALL *Tvl Lowveld & Escarpment* 28 The name Broodboom ('bread tree') is derived from the fact that the pith in the stems of some cycads yields an edible starch. 1988 K. SUTTON in *E. Prov. Herald* 23 July 4 Cycads, or broodbome, are hardly the glory of the floral kingdom. 1990 [see RANDLORD sense 1].

brooks var. BROEKS.

broom var. BROM v.

brother n. [Special senses of general Eng., influenced by the use of the equivalent words in Afk. and the Sintu (Bantu) languages.]

1. [tr. Afk. *broeder*.] BROEDERBONDER.

　1950 H. GIBBS *Twilight* 203 It [sc. the Broederbond] was a sort of secret Star Chamber .. whose aim .. was .. the promotion of the interests of a smaller section, especially the 'Brothers' and their friends.

2. [tr. of various words for 'brother' in languages of the Sintu (Bantu) group.] Esp. among speakers of Sintu (Bantu) languages: a man with the same surname, or a recent common ancestor. Cf. SISTER.

Used also, as elsewhere, as a term of address or reference to any black man.

　1953 D. JACOBSON *Long Way from London* 107 Harry Grossman knew enough to know that 'brother' in this context could mean anything, from the son of one's mother, to a friend from a neighbouring kraal. 1960 J. COPE *Tame Ox* 177 The two black men were 'brothers', they said. That meant they were cousins or clansmen or maybe no closer than belonging to the same sub-tribe. 1966 L.G. BERGER *Where's Madam* 66 In my innocence I thought they were his 'brothers'. When the number of 'brothers' got to about 20, I dropped to the fact that anyone who came from the same village was considered a 'brother'. 1978 A. ELLIOTT *Sons of Zulu* 167 In real life all the boys and girls of contemporary age belonging to the same clan regard each other as brothers and sisters and all the joint *parents* are their parents. 1990 *Weekend Mail* 13 July 5 In the old days, you did not need to know who someone bearing your name was or where he or she came from. Anyone who bore that name was your brother or sister.

Brother Boer n. phr. Obs. exc. hist. [Eng. brother + BOER sense 3.] During the Anglo-Boer War: a nickname for the Boer forces, or for an individual Boer soldier. See also BOER sense 3.

　1903 R. KIPLING *Five Nations* 194 'Oo'd dared to answer Brother Boer's attack. For there might 'ave been a serious engagement. 1937 G.F. GIBSON *Story of Imp. Light Horse* 120 Old Brother Boer showed good-natured humour and humanity on many occasions which have not been forgotten even after long years. [1947 C.R. PRANCE *Antic Mem.* 135 His horsemanship and his simple friendliness quickly endeared him to his Brother Boer.] 1979 T. PAKENHAM *Boer War* (1982) 274 Hamilton ordered these suicidal counter-attacks to be stopped. Brother Boer could be dealt with in due course.

Brow /braʊ/ n. colloq. Also '**Brow**. [Abbrev. of *Hillbrow*.] **The Brow**: A nickname for Hillbrow, a densely-populated high-rise suburb of Johannesburg.

　1975 *Sunday Times* 15 June 3 'I hailed the first cab I saw and asked him to head for the "Brow" (Hillbrow),' he said. 1984 *Ibid.* 29 Jan. (Life Style) 9 Most of the time we just jorl to the 'Brow and suss the scene out. 1989 *Scope* 24 Mar. 46, I got to know the notorious 'Brow at the age of 12, where it nurtured me and let me suckle its poisonous breast and get fat on corruption. It's a place where only the tough survive.

brown adj. and n. Also with initial capital. [Eng.; in certain senses, perhaps influenced by Afk. *bruin(mense)* 'coloured' (people).]

A. adj.

1. hist. Of the KHOIKHOI. Also used absol.

　1837 J.E. ALEXANDER *Narr. of Voy.* I. 322 A long wagon would pass .. drawn by a span of ten or fourteen oxen under the guidance of a voorloper, a brown boy. 1926 P.W. LAIDLER *Tavern of Ocean* 3 Saldanha's men collided with the Hottentots ... This affray laid the foundation of the bad feeling between the brown and white. 1968 K. MCMAGH *Dinner of Herbs* 27 He allowed the old Hottentot to take charge. It was the old brown man who gave the orders.

2. COLOURED ppl adj. sense a.

a. As a qualifier in the following n. phrr.: **brown Afrikaner** [prob. tr. Afk. *bruin Afrikaner* 'coloured' Afrikaner (see AFRIKANER)], a 'coloured' person; **brown Nat** [see NAT], a 'coloured' member of the National Party; **brown people** [tr. Afk. *bruinmense* 'coloured' people], a collective name for the 'coloured' community.

　1898 W.C. SCULLY *Vendetta* 95 He had heard that 'brown people' were whipped in Cape Town if they stole, which was quite right if they stole when they were not hungry. **1924** S.G. MILLIN *God's Step-Children* 216 'My house is full,' she said obstinately. 'And I cannot find room for brown people.' **1960** J.P. VAN S. BRUWER in H. Spottiswoode *S. Afr.: Rd Ahead* 52 The political development of the Bantu on the one hand, and the political development of the Brown People (usually referred to as Coloureds) and the Indians on the other hand. **1969** A. FUGARD *Boesman & Lena* 20 Lena: It's a hard life for us brown people hey. Boesman: He's not brown people, he's black people. **1970** S. PIENAAR in *E. Prov. Herald* 4 Nov. 15 Language, culture, religion, you have got your Coloured poets .. in Afrikaans. Their music is linked to Afrikaans. In all these respects they are 'brown Afrikaners'. **1973** T. SWARTZ in *Ibid.* We reject the concept of Black consciousness or identification with any other race. 'So naturally we do not want to be known as "Brown Afrikaners".' **1973** *Weekend Post* 30 June 3 Coloured academic and political leaders in the Cape have reacted to Dr Connie Mulder's statement this week that they will never be 'Brown Afrikaners' by telling him sharply that they have no wish to be called by that name. **1973** *Cape Times* 21 June 11 The chairman of the Student's Representative Council, Mr Christoff Pauw, believes that as a starting point Whites must be prepared to share political power with 'the Brown people'. **1975** G.J. GERWEL in T. Sundermeier *Church & Nationalism* 71 The 'brown Afrikaner' idea finds very few adherents these days. This is partly due to the Afrikaner's (at times rude) rejection of the idea, but also to the fact that Afrikanerdom is identified as an oppressive force. **1981** *E. Prov. Herald* 13 May 8 The coloureds are 'brown Afrikaners' who may yet in the future be accepted as such. Their culture is substantially Western. **1982** *Rand Daily Mail* 25 Feb. 4 For 34 years the National Party had rejected, despised and disenfranchised the brown people. **1990** R. STENGEL *January Sun* 40 The Coloured, one of South Africa's four main racial categories, are sometimes known as 'brown Afrikaners' because they are descended from mixed parentage and generally speak Afrikaans as their first language. Since 'light-skinned' Coloured were virtually impossible to differentiate from Afrikaners, the Population Registration Act of 1950 emphasized association and ancestry as the principal ways of establishing who was white. **1991** *E. Prov. Herald* 19 June 1 An embattled Labour Party drove back a no-confidence motion proposed by the 'brown Nats' yesterday by 43 votes to 40. **1992** G. DAVIS in *Weekly Mail* 16 Apr. 27 A brown Nat is a stupid Nat. **1995** C. LAWRANCE in *Natal Witness* 3 Jan. 7 Japie, the brown builder.

b. Simple adjectival uses.

1960 D.P. DE V. GRAAFF *(broadsheet)*, Let us get away from the idea at once that we can sit in a White citadel and quarrel about what shall be done about the Black and brown peoples outside, as our Nationalist friends want to do. **1960** [see MALAY *adj.*]. **1972** *Evening Post* 19 Aug. 4 South Africans' attitudes and actions were conditioned by race and colour. There were White South Africans, 'off-White' South Africans, Brown South Africans and Black South Africans. **1973** *Weekend Post* 30 June 3 We Coloured people are South Africans, not Brown South Africans.

3. *obs.* Of any group which is not white; cf. BLACK *adj.* sense 2.

1906 W.S. JOHNSON *Orangia* 5 Some hungry little Bushman might drive several of them [*sc.* oxen] off .. or .. a mob of angry Kaffirs .. might even rush in and try to steal or kill ... Many a boy, not older than you .. had to use his rifle and take away a brown man's life rather than lose his own.

4. Of any of several dark-skinned groups which are not African.

1977 *Std Bank Review* Apr. 2 Considerations outside the realm of economic policy dictated .. much higher outlays on improved social services, housing and education of the country's brown and black population. **1978** *S. Afr. Digest* 8 Sept. 9 Referring to accusations that the Indian and Coloured communities had rejected the new constitutional proposal, Mr Botha said there was no one who could say that South Africa's Brown peoples had rejected the plan. **1989** *Weekend Post* 4 Nov. 14 The aim of the negotiations will be a constitution with which the broad majority of South Africans — black, white and brown — can identify and in which they can share fully. **1990** C. ST LEGER in *Sunday Times* 17 Feb. 12 Jonathon S— is nearly three years old. Officially he is neither white, black nor brown. Until now, he's been a non-person. **1993** H. TYSON *Editors under Fire* 13 Black editors and brown editors took different sides from each other in their debates with white editors, who also adopted a variety of positions.

B. *n.*

1. A 'coloured' person (see COLOURED *n.* sense a).

1861 H. RABONE in A. Rabone *Rec. of Pioneer Family* (1966) 123, I have not the slightest disgust to blacks or browns, can touch them, nurse them and get on very well with their race. **1973** *Cape Times* 30 June 8, I believe that 99 per cent of Browns don't give two hoots for White South Africa's security, but they would all welcome freedom of the individual. **1975** *Het Suid-Western* 6 Aug. 2 Now the Council has set about preventing the Browns from attending a drive-in cinema. **1977** *S. Afr. Panorama* May 11 As for the constitutional position of the Browns and Asians — and of the urban Blacks — that will have to be handled in ways still to be properly explored. **1981** *Flying Springbok* Dec. 25 Compulsory education for Blacks and Browns is being phased in as rapidly as numbers of teachers and classrooms permit. **1990** *Weekend Post* 5 May 10 'I'm staying here,' called a Nationalist member. 'Then we will reclassify you,' offered Mr Curry. The Nationalist member could be an honorary brown.

2. *Military.* Always in *pl.*: A colloquial name for the brown uniform of the South African National Defence Forces; cf. NUTRIA. Also with qualifier, **bush-browns**.

1979 *National Serviceman, Informant* Browns are hell to iron. You've got to have sharp lines straight up the sleeves and overall pants, leg-pockets and all. **1982** *Weekend Argus* 18 Dec. 16 When the deejay in bush-browns gets the music going, there's exuberance in his boots, and Heideveld's communal sportsfields become an outdoor dance floor. **1983** C. VON KEYSERLINK in *Frontline* Feb. 37 The Defence Force has stopped issuing most trainees with 'stepouts,' as the smart uniforms are known, and now specifies 'browns' as suitable gear for outings. **1983** *Evening Post* 28 Mar. 3 Recently, Navy authorities in Pretoria gave the official go ahead for the traditional blue uniforms to be phased in again as working dress ... There had been an argument about browns being more flammable than the cotton used in blues. **1984** *Fair Lady* 14 Nov. 136 At the end of the day .. you see the men, now out of their heavy browns, wandering around the barracks talking to each other. **1990** S. MURRAY in *Staffrider* Vol.9 No.2, 73 A maid begins To hang surburban washing. Flapping in the late March sun, Army browns rise and fall. **1993** A. VINASSA in *Femina* Sept. 50 A Buffel full of soldiers dressed in browns sits parked on the pavement.

brown ear tick *n. phr.* The parasitic tick *Rhipicephalus appendiculatus* of the Ixodidae, the transmitter of several diseases, including EAST COAST FEVER; BROWN TICK. Also *attrib.*

1972 BEETON & DORNER in *Eng. Usage in Sn Afr.* Vol.3 No.2, 48 *Brown tick,* .. Alt. brown ear tick. **1991** J.B. WALKER in *Onderstepoort Jrnl of Vet. Research* Vol.58 No.2, 95 Cattle that are heavily infested with *R. appendiculatus* may develop a syndrome known as brown ear tick toxicosis.

brown tick *n. phr. Obsolescent.* BROWN EAR TICK.

1905 D. HUTCHEON in Flint & Gilchrist *Science in S. Afr.* 340 *Transmission of African Coast Fever,* This fever can be transmitted by the 'Brown Tick,' *Rhipicephalus appendiculatus.* **1910** A.B. LAMONT *Rural Reader* 46 Ticks annoy all kinds of stock by sucking their blood ... They .. are named after their colours — red, blue, brown and 'bont' (variegated). **1918** S.H. SKAIFE *Animal Life* 181 There are several species of brown ticks in this country ... They .. act as carriers of the east coast fever germs, and .. are also capable of carrying red-water fever and gallsickness. **1937** *Handbk for Farmers* (Dept of Agric. & Forestry) 516 The most important of these ticks are the brown tick (*Rhipicephalus appendiculatus*) which transmits East Coast fever and the bont tick .. which transmits heartwater. **1957** *Ibid.* (Dept of Agric.) III. 483 Each of the three stages — larvae, nymphs and adults — require a separate host for feeding ... The brown tick .. and the bont tick .. constitute examples of this group. **1971** POTGIETER & DU PLESSIS *Animal Life in Sn Afr.* 220 The brown tick transmits redwater and gall-sickness as well as East Coast fever.

bru var. BRO.

bruindulsies see DULSIES.

brummer fly *n. phr. Obs.* [ad. Afk. *brommer* (see BROMMER) + Eng. *fly.*] BROMMER.

1913 C. PETTMAN *Africanderisms* 92 *Brummer fly,* .. An insect somewhat like the common housefly, but considerably larger. It is useful in the destruction of locusts. **1924** *Chambers's Jrnl* (U.K.) XIV. 314 The brummer fly (*Wolfahrtia brunis palpis*) lays its eggs in the neck of the locust.

brunt sickta var. BRANDSIEKTE.

brusher *n.* Pl. unchanged. [Unknown.] Esp. in KwaZulu-Natal: the *white musselcracker* (see MUSSELCRACKER sense 2), *Sparodon durbanensis.*

1913 C. PETTMAN *Africanderisms* 92 *Brusher,* The Natal name for a large species of *Sargus.* **1930** C.L. BIDEN *Sea-Angling Fishes* 180 A larger fish that is evidently the Cape white biskop, otherwise known as 'brusher' at Natal. **1949** J.L.B. SMITH *Sea Fishes* 268 *Sparodon durbanensis* (Castlenau) ... *Brusher* (Eastern Cape — Natal). **1955** C. HORNE *Fisherman's Eldorado* 210 Natal anglers, differing from those at Port Elizabeth, call the black one musselcracker or John Cracker, the brilliant blue and silver fish they name Brusher ... Many Natal anglers would probably correctly associate the names of white biskop and black biskop with the fish they know as brusher or musselcracker. **1970** *Daily News* 5 Oct. 5 Highlight spot of the past week's fishing in and around Durban has again been the South Pier, from which some excellent catches of brusher — Sparodon Durbanensis .. have been made in deep water around its end. **1970** *Sunday Times* 8 Feb. (Mag. Sect.) 5 A catch of reef fish topping 700 lb., a mixed bag of springer, soldier, rock cod, brusher and just about a bit of everything. **1990** M. HOLMES in *E. Prov. Herald* 14 Sept. 18 In those days the Natalians knew poenskop as musselcracker. The musselcrackers were in turn known as brushers. **1993** R. VAN DER ELST *Guide to Common Sea Fishes* 369 *Sparodon durbanensis* .. white musselcracker, brusher, white biskop.

bry *n.* var. BREI *n.*

bry *v.*[1] var. BREI *v.*[2]

bry *v.*[2] var. BRAAI *v.*

bubblejas var. BABALAAS.

buchenhout var. BOEKENHOUT.

buchu /ˈbʊxʊ, ˈbʊxu, ˈbuxu/ *n.* Forms: α. **boego(e), boocho, b(o)uchu, boughou, buchee, bucho.** β. **boekhoo, bookoo, bucca, buckee, bucku, buk(k)u**; γ. **boca, boco, boka.** [Khoikhoi.] **1.a.** Any of several aromatic plant species of the family Rutaceae, esp. of the genera *Agathosma* and *Diosma*; the products of these plants. Also *attrib.*

Buchu leaves were pounded into a powder by the Khoikhoi and used cosmetically, mixed with sheeps' fat, on their bodies. Buchu has also been used to heal bruising, and infused for digestive ailments.

α. **1731** G. MEDLEY tr. *P. Kolb's Present State of Cape of G.H.* II. 249 The last mention'd *Spiraea* is call'd, by the *Hottentots, Buchu.* **1790** tr. *F. Le Vaillant's Trav.* I. 375 After rubbing their bodies with grease, they had besprinkled themselves with a kind of red powder, made of a root named in the country *boughou,* and which has a very agreeable odor. **1824** *Boekhoo Plant* in *Stat. Law of Cape of G.H.* (1862) 78 Any person who may be convicted .. of tearing up the Boekhoo (Boego) plant .. shall be deemed guilty of a misdemeanor. **1841** B. SHAW *Memorials* 114 On beginning this station in 1816, many of the people were so disagreeably greasy, and so strongly scented with boocho, that I have frequently become ill with the effluvia of a congregation. **1867** *Blue Bk for Col. 1866* JJ11, The quantity of buchu this year, of which there are about 100 bales of an average weight of 170lbs, ready for export, has been very plentiful. **1913** *Union Gaz.* Vol.14 No.427, 556 It is hereby notified for general information that the season for the collection of Buchu (*Barosma* species) from Crown Lands and Forest Reserves .. will .. be the period 15th January to 28th February in each year, inclusive. **1968** G. CROUDACE *Silver Grass* 72 In the afternoon, out came the rouge-pots of ox-horn and the tortoise-shells filled with powdered buchu and other fragrant herbs. **1973** *Cape Times* 12 Apr. 2 Buchu is frequently used for medicinal purposes. The demand for the product has increased considerably ... This has made buchu an export product that may contribute significantly to the country's income. **1987** T.F.J. VAN RENSBERG *Intro. to Fynbos* 31 Buchu (especially *Agathosma* spp.), .. is used on a large scale in medicines and as an oil base for perfume. **1988** M. BRANCH *Explore Cape Flora* 41 Buchu is the name given to a whole group of scented plants with oil glands dotted on their leaves. The most important are the *Agathosma* species.

β. **1786** G. FORSTER tr. *A. Sparrman's Voy. to Cape of G.H.* I. 184 The plants used for this purpose [*sc.* of smearing their bodies] are different species of the *diosma*, called by the Hottentots *bucku*, and considered by them as possessing great virtues in curing disorders. **1795** C.R. HOPSON tr. *C.P. Thunberg's Trav.* I. 309 They besmear themselves with grease, and powder themselves all over with the fetid substance called *Bucku*, or the powdered leaves of the *Diosma*. **1821** C.I. LATROBE *Jrnl of Visit* 225 we found the larger species of bukku, one of the most aromatic, medicinal plants in the country, and justly esteemed for its healing properties. **1824** [see α quot. above]. **1827** G. THOMPSON *Trav.* II. 35 For cuts and bruises they use the leaves of the buku, and one or two other plants, with good effect. **1847** J. BARROW *Reflect.* 209 The strong smell of his *bucca* (diosma); and the grease with which he smears his body, are sure to give notice to the lion that he is a morsel ready basted for eating. **1906** B. STONEMAN *Plants & their Ways* 234 *B[arosma] crenata* is the true 'Buku'. **1907** T.R. SIM *Forests & Forest Flora* 77 Boekhoo was not protected til 1824, but its powdered leaves, mixed with charcoal and fat are mentioned as a favourite cosmetic among the Hottentots during the first Governor's regime.

b. With distinguishing epithet designating a particular species of buchu: **berg buchu** /ˈbɜːg, ˈbɛrx-/ [Afk., *berg* mountain], *Agathosma ciliaris* or *A. betulina*; **false buchu**, *A. ovata*; **steenbok buchu** /ˈstiənbɔk/ [see STEENBOK], *A. ciliata*; **wild buchu**, *Diosma hirsuta*.

α. **1978** *Sunday Times* 3 Nov. (Mag. Sect.) 5 There are three kinds of buchu: the round leaf type .. the oval leaf buchu which he cultivates; and the '**berg buchu**'. **1989** K. SUTTON in *E. Prov. Herald* 23 Oct. 4 (*caption*) *Agathosma ovata*, an inland variety of the pungent shrub, also known as the **false buchu**. **1949** L.G. GREEN *In Land of Afternoon* 55 The long or oval leaf, also known as **steenbok buchu**, comes mainly from the Tulbach and Swellendam areas. **1983** M.M. KIDD *Cape Peninsula* 74 *Diosma hirsuta* ... **Wild Buchu**.

2. *comb.* ‖**buchu asyn** /-aˌseɪŋ/, **-azijn**, **-azyn** [Afk., *asyn* vinegar, fr. Du. *azijn*], **buchu brandy**, and **buchu essens** [Afk., 'essence']: medicinal preparations in which buchu leaves have been steeped.

1822 W.J. BURCHELL *Trav.* I. 479 This Boekoe (or **Buku**) **azyn** is made by simply putting the leaves of some kind of diosma into a bottle of cold vinegar, in which they are left to steep. **1913** C. PETTMAN *Africanderisms* 93 *Buchu azijn*, .. A domestic medicine prepared by macerating buchu leaves in vinegar. **1919** *Dunell, Ebden & Co.'s Price List* Oct. 20 Buchu Azijn, pints, 12/6. **1927** C.G. BOTHA *Social Life in Cape Col.* 103 The Hottentots placed great faith in the use of *Buchu Asyn* (Buchu Vinegar) as a wash to cleanse and heal a wound. **1949** [see GROENE AMARA]. **1972** BEETON & DORNER in *Eng. Usage in Sn Afr.* Vol.3 No.2, 49 *Buchu vinegar*, .. Alt. boegoe-asyn, infusion obtained by soaking the leaves of a certain species of *Agathosma* in vinegar, & used for medicinal purposes. **1821** C.I. LATROBE *Jrnl of Visit* 218 Her head received such a severe contusion, that .. she lost her recollection, and was in much pain. Some relief was afforded by an application of **bukku-brandy**. **1831** P. GAUGAIN Diary. 88 Embrocation for the Rheumatism 1 Bottle of Boco Brandy. **1866** T. SHONE Diary. 11 Sept., T. Shone gave me a half a bottle of Boka Brandy. **1878** T.J. LUCAS *Camp Life & Sport* 136 A coarse kind of spirit, termed 'Bucca brandy', made, I believe, from the seeds of a bush of the name, growing in the Veldt. **1968** C.J. ORFFER in D.J. Opperman *Spirit of Vine* 195 South Africans have for generations attached a particular value to kukumakranka brandy, buchu brandy [*printed* buchy], clove brandy, etc. **1977** *Daily Dispatch* 22 Aug. 6 Who hasn't heard of buchu brandy as a cure for stomach aches? **1988** A. DANGOR in *Staffrider* Vol.7 No.3, 92 The boegoe-brandy burned fiercely into the laceration Jan's weapon had left on his back. **1991** E. SWIEGERS in *S. Afr. Consumer* 1st Quarter 28 Buchu brandy, white dulcis and Jamaica ginger — their pungent smells conjure up images of yesteryear, but beware, these remedies may well be harmful. **1919** *Dunell, Ebden & Co.'s Price List* Oct. 20 **Buchu Essenz**, pints, 32/6.

Buchuanas pl. form of BECHUANA.

buck *n.*[1] [Calque formed on S. Afr. Du. *bok*, see BOK.]

1. Pl. **-s**, or unchanged.

a. Any antelope, whether male or female; venison; BOK sense 1 a. Also *attrib.*

1829 C. ROSE *Four Yrs in Sn Afr.* 82 The men were sitting round the fire with their dogs and arms about them, and two freshly killed bucks had been the sport of the day. **1841** J.M. BOWKER *Speeches & Sel.* (1864) 105 At least 500 Kafirs had been clearing the hunting grounds of the Hottentot settlement at the Kat River of game, killing between 300 and 400 bucks. **1851** J.F. CHURCHILL Diary. (Killie Campbell Africana Library MS37) 11–19 Apr., Saw a Buck in the cool of the morning but my Friends did not succeed in getting a shot at it. **1858** T. SHONE Diary. 1 July, For dinner Potatoes and fry'd buck no tea. **1860** [see IMPUNZI]. **1878** T.J. LUCAS *Camp Life & Sport* 203 An avant-garde formed of two or three single bucks, precedes the rest at full speed taking the most surprising leaps into the air in succession. **1900** B. MITFORD *Aletta* 129 He was fond of sport and had intended to ask for a day or two's leave to join a buck hunt on one of the farms. **1919** R.Y. STORMBERG *With Love from Gwenno* 5 We had all sorts of nice weird things to eat — .. venison — which they call 'buck.' **1925** D. KIDD *Essential Kafir* 318 Every bush was searched, and the 'buck' were driven out. [*Note*] The word, thus used, will sound absurd to British sportsmen. In South Africa wild animals of certain species are classed as 'buck', without regard to sex. **1967** E.M. SLATTER *My Leaves Are Green* 31 The buck moved round us in enormous herds — buff-coloured kudu with their huge frames, eland with beautiful spiral horns. **1970** *Argus* 24 Dec. 2 A great number of buck, snakes and birds succumbed in the raging fire. **1974** [see Herald quot. at FARM *v.*] **1975** *S. Afr. Panorama* July 47 While travelling around the reserve on the dirt roads a visitor may be surprised at the sight of .. antelope amidst tall grass or of a buck hobbling across the veld.

b. With distinguishing epithets designating particular species of antelope: see BLESBUCK, BLUE BUCK, BONTEBUCK, BUSHBUCK, DIKER-BUCK, GEMSBUCK, GRYSBUCK, HARRIS BUCK, KLIP-BUCK, RED-BUCK, REEDBUCK, RHEBUCK, RIETBUCK, ROEBUCK, ROOIBUCK, SPRINGBUCK, STEENBUCK, STEMBUCK, STONEBUCK, *trekbuck* (see TREK sense 12 b), WATERBUCK. See also BOK sense 1 b.

1832 *Graham's Town Jrnl* 13 July 112 The old denizens of the wilderness, Bush-bucks, Riet-bucks, and Bucks with every variety of prefix have disappeared.

2. Pl. **-s**. A goat; BOK sense 2. Also *attrib.*

Used also in *U.S. Eng.*; *obs.* in *Brit. Eng.*

1832 M. BOYCE in *Graham's Town Jrnl* 15 June 98 The old man immediately went away as he was in haste, managing, however, to finish half a 'buck', which I had just purchased and killed. **1838** J. COLLETT Diary. I. 7 July, rode this Evᵍ to Vandervyfers to purchase caparter Bucks. **1854** R.J. MULLINS Diary. 5 May, I have got 47 bucks (goats) now, so we shall not be without animal food; they are fine and young. **1902** H.J. DUCKITT *Hilda's Diary of Cape Hsekeeper* 282 For Hoarseness in Children.- Blue-gum leaves fried in buck-fat or *goat-lard*, with a little turpentine to soften it, rubbed into the chest, or applied on a linen rag as a plaster, is excellent. **1913** J.J. DOKE *Secret City* 91 Goats, or 'bucks', as we call them, are the most stupid of animals. **1968** K. MCMAGH *Dinner of Herbs* 24 We suffered exceedingly when we had buck-fat plasters put on our chests and some meddlesome old crone suggested that we be rubbed with honey back and front. **1987** N. RIDDICK *Informant, George* Every time I caught those bucks, over at my place, nobody would tell me who was the owner.

buck *n.*[2] *obs.* [tr. Afk. *bok* the body of a cart or wagon; or transf. use of Eng. dial. *buck*, in the same sense.]

1. BUCK-RAIL.

1875 'P.' in A.M.L. Robinson *Sel. Articles from Cape Monthly Mag.* (1978) 186 We dismounted the buck, and by the aid of our newly acquired friends we soon ran the heavy frame-work across the river. **1879** R.J. ATCHERLEY *Trip to Boerland* 83 The damage done to the waggon was serious: .. the 'buck,' or overlapping grating, was broken off and the dissel-boom was split in two. **1913** C. PETTMAN *Africanderisms* 93 The side-rails of the wagon, which help to give compactness to the load, are known as the 'buck' of the wagon.

2. BUCK-WAGON.

1919 J.Y. GIBSON in *S. Afr. Jrnl of Science* July 3 Substituting the buck for the kap-tent, the men engaged in the carrying trade, leaving their families at home. **1919** *Dunell, Ebden & Co.'s Price List* Aug. 35 Buck beams, Colonial Hickory, Rough, per cube 18/0.

buck *n.*[3] *colloq.* [Transf. use of colloq. U.S. Eng. *buck* a dollar.] RAND sense 3 a.

1975 S.S. MEKGOE *Lindiwe* (1978) 14 Beejay: (*Counting the money*) Let's see, (*Flipping through the money*) how much? Hmm! Four thousand bucks? **1975** *Rhodeo* (Rhodes Univ.) Vol.29 No.6, 2 A fair number of *kugels* are managing to infiltrate the Rhodes Campus .. all dolled up to the nines. You can't buy that clobber for under fifty bucks. **1982** *Drum* July 69 They are offering anything you want on HP. For a few bucks deposit they deliver the goods. **1987** *Scope* 6 Nov. 32 Yvonne was a 60-buck all-nighter, but for Jimmy the street-girls were free. **1989** F. DE VILLIERS in *Weekly Mail* 20 Jan. 14, I propose that our national currency be known as the 'buck' ... We're already talking like that anyway in all South African languages. **1991** P. SLABOLEPSZY Braait Laaities. 15 Boikie: I pay 120 — cash! Moira: You paid cash? Boikie: 120 Bucks.

Buck Bay vygie /ˌbʌkbeɪ ˈfeɪxi/ *n. phr. Rare.* [Part. tr. Afk. *bokbaai vygie.*] BOKBAAI VYGIE.

[**1962** S. ELIOVSON *Discovering Wild Flowers in Sn Afr.* 44 *Bokbaai Vygie, Buck Bay Daisy.*] **1965** —— *S. Afr. Wild Flowers for Garden* 290 *D[orotheanthus] bellidiformis* (*D. criniflorus*) Bokbaai vygie, Buck Bay vygie. **1970** *Cape Argus* 3 Oct. (Mag. Sect.) 13 The seeds of .. mesembrianthemums (Buck Bay vygies) were sent to Kew Gardens in England.

buck doctor *n. phr. Obs.* [Calque formed on Afk. *bokdokter*, *bok* goat (cf. BUCK *n.*[1] sense 2) + *dokter* doctor. Said to have been a nickname first given to a particular veterinary surgeon, D. Hutcheon, who, at the turn of the century, was well known for his campaign for the eradication of 'lungsickness'.] A veterinary surgeon.

1896 R. WALLACE *Farming Indust. of Cape Col.* 277 One farmer, in all seriousness, associated the increase of disease with the presence of *the Veterinary Advisor* — familiarly called the 'Bok' or 'Buck-doctor.' **1913** C. PETTMAN *Africanderisms* 94 *Buck doctor*, .. The name by which the Government veterinary surgeon is known among the rural population of the Midlands, because the earliest efforts of these 'Vets' were directed to the stamping out of contagious lung disease among goats.

buckee var. BUCHU.

bucket *n. Obs.* exc. *hist.* [Special sense of general Eng.] A measure of approx. 5 kg or 12 lbs by weight, used esp. in measuring farm produce.

1850 J.D. LEWIN's Diary. 21 May, Got 2 buckets potatos from Wilgemoed's. **1889** 'A HOUSEWIFE OF THE COLONY' *Col. Hsehold Guide* 124 Boil [the pork] in say three gallons of water, 1 bucket of salt, 1 oz cloves, 2 lbs brown sugar and 2 tablespoonsful potash. **1904** *Argus Christmas Annual* (Competition Sect.) p.vii, The charge per 'bucket' varies, but the weight should be 10 lbs. for onions and 12 lbs. for potatoes. [**1958** A. JACKSON *Trader on Veld* 45 Two 25-lbs. 'buckets of mealies', one bucket (25 lbs.) of unsifted boermeal.] **1986** *Fair Lady* 16 Apr., Pine-e-apples, swe-et pine-e-apples, three for a bob, fresh potatoes, shilling a bucket.

bucket system *n. phr.* The sanitation system used in those townships and shack settlements which are without water-borne sewerage.

1952 B. DAVIDSON *Report on Sn Afr.* 88 Sanitation is on the 'bucket system' – urine and excrement being regularly lifted in buckets, that is, and carried away outside. **1968** COLE & FLAHERTY *House of Bondage* 54 Toilets were outside and used the bucket system. Hired crews were supposed to pick up and replace the buckets every few days. **1985** *Saspu National* Vol.6 No.2, 11 At a meeting to protest against the bucket system, residents decided to go and dump the buckets at the administration board. **1988** M. MOSIMANE in *Pace* Apr. 28 The 'Third World' lifestyle of the township which still uses the bucket system and communal water taps. **1990** *Weekly Mail* 11 May 6 The bucket system is still in use. **1994** on M-Net TV 6 Oct. (M-Net Cares), They were using the bucket system. We have upgraded it – now they are using a water-borne system.

buck-my-keerie var. BOKMAKIERIE.

buck-rail *n. hist.* [Eng. *buck* the body of a cart or wagon (see BUCK *n.*[2]) + Eng. *rail.*] The side rail of a wagon; BUCK *n.*[2] sense 1. Also *attrib.*

1896 H.A. BRYDEN *Tales of S. Afr.* 182 The tent I've fastened on to the buck-rail. **1897** J.P. FITZPATRICK *Outspan* 41 Key dropped off the buck rails, as the drivers shouted their 'Aanhouws' to the cattle to give them a breather. **1907** —— *Jock of Bushveld* (1909) 456 They had enticed him on to the waggon, as he lay half unconscious between bursts of delirium, had tied him down flat on his back, with wrists and ankles fastened to the buckrails. **1911** D.B. HOOK *'Tis but Yesterday* 16 'Water vatje' full of water on the 'buck-rail'. [*Note*] Rails running parallel to the sides of the wagon extending over the wheels. **1939** M. RORKE *Melina Rorke* 82 The African wagon is a huge affair with buck-rail bed, eight feet wide by sixteen feet long, covered with a tarpaulin well soaked in paraffin wax. **1955** W. ROBERTSON *Blue Wagon* 35 The wagon canted over at an angle with the buckrails below the surface [of the water].

bucksail *n.* [Calque formed on Afk. *bokseil, bok* body of wagon + *seil* canvas.] A large tarpaulin or canvas used as a covering for a wagon or its load, as a temporary shelter, or as protection for a motor vehicle, etc. Also *attrib.* See also SAIL.

1882 S. HECKFORD *Lady Trader in Tvl* 11 The one was an open buck-waggon .. with a tarpaulin, or what is here called 'a buck-sail,' thrown over it to protect the goods. **1882** C.L. NORRIS-NEWMAN *With Boers in Tvl* 188 Most of the men lived in or under the waggons, covered with large buck-sails, or else in temporary sheds made with the same. **1897** R.S.S. BADEN-POWELL *Matabele Campaign* 436 A buck-sail stretched over the tilts of two [wagons] gave a shady room between, in which we sheltered from the midday heat. **1914** S.P. HYATT *Old Transport Rd* 134 That little Scotch cart of ours .. would carry all the kit and stores for quite a long expedition; with a small bucksail over it, we could easily rig up a shelter in case of rain. **1929** J.G. VAN ALPHEN *Jan Venter* 151 A huge buck-sail was stretched against the side of the waggon, forming room shelter on the east side. **1937** H. KLEIN *Stage Coach Dust* 140 A hasty shelter was rigged up under a buck-sail thrown across the stranded transport wagon. **1940** F.B. YOUNG *City of Gold* 365 Yankee Moore, whose store – a bucksail tent furnished with a counter of empty Rynbende gin-cases was .. the busiest commercial establishment at de Kaap. **1951** [see DROPPER]. **1969** F. GOLDIE *River of Gold* 46 The couples began to crowd onto the bucksail dance floor. **1979** *Farmer's Weekly* 21 Mar. 126 Sails & Tents. Brand new Heavy duty Bucksail, 7 m x 9 m. **1982** *Ibid.* 5 Nov. 147 (*advt*) (a) Bucksails: Available in green only. Our sail material is ideal for hard work. (b) Vinyl: Available in all colours. Ideal for lorries, transport packing and hard work.

bucku var. BUCHU.

bucku-hout var. BOEKENHOUT.

buck-wagon *n. hist.* [tr. Afk. *bokwa, bok* the body of a wagon + *wa* wagon; or formed in S. Afr. Eng. fr. Eng. dial. *buck* the body of a wagon + *wagon* a vehicle for the conveyance of loads.] A large transport wagon with a strong frame and rails, used for transporting heavy loads; BUCK *n.*[2] sense 2.

Also *U.S. Eng.*

[**1864** N. WEBSTER *American Dict. of Eng. Lang.*, *Buckwagon.*] **1870** H.H. DUGMORE *Reminisc. of Albany Settler* 15 The days of buck-waggons were still far off. **1875** 'P.' in A.M.L. Robinson *Sel. Articles from Cape Monthly Mag.* (1978) 184 The road .. takes a sharp turn to the right, making it a difficult matter to steer sixteen bullocks with a heavy buck wagon behind them. **1887** A.A. ANDERSON *25 Yrs in Waggon* I. 57 Enormous 'buck-waggons' are now made for the diamond fields. They require twenty oxen, and contain a sitting, a bedroom, and a kitchen, and a huge canvas covers the whole. **1893** F.C. SELOUS *Trav. & Adventure* 13, I bought a roomy buck-waggon .. with a half tent, or covered-in compartment to sleep in the back. **1900** H. BLORE *Imp. Light Horseman* 21 The command encamped at the station was housed in a caravan of about sixty white-hooded buck waggons, each capable of holding a family. **1914** W.C. SCULLY *Lodges in Wilderness* 183 Andries arrived bringing – not the comfortable, tilted, spring-wagon, – but the strong, heavy, tentless 'buck' wagon. **1922** S.C. CRONWRIGHT-SCHREINER in F.C. Slater *Centenary Bk of S. Afr. Verse* (1925) 61 The great buck-wagon, our 'desert-ship' With its four-ton heavy load And its rooi-bont span and its wagon-whip Is coming along the road. **1937** H. KLEIN *Stage Coach Dust* 18 Travelling on the buck-wagon was extremely dangerous. This type of farm wagon has its brake control situated at the back, in the form of a long wooden bar stretching across the two back wheels. **1963** POLLOCK & AGNEW *Hist. Geog.* 108 Ox wagons were of two main types. The first was large buck wagon from 18 to 22 feet long, 5 to 7 feet wide, either with a half tent or no tent at all, holding a great deal of cargo of up to three tons. **1971** H. ZEEDERBERG *Veld Express* 48 His buckwagons were fitted with cross-wise seats, which gave accommodation for three persons on either side. **1983** *S. Afr. Panorama* Apr. 18 When the diamond fields were discovered in the 1860's, the buck- and transport wagon was used to transport heavier loads. **1990** *Weekend Argus* 29 Sept. 13 Another consignment of gold .. was loaded on to a buckwagon guarded by Veldkornet Steyn and a small bodyguard.

Bucuanas pl. form of BECHUANA.

buffalo *n.* Also **buffalow.** [Transf. use of Eng. *buffalo* (in *OED* first denoting the Asian buffalo, 1588).]

1. The undomesticated bovine *Syncerus caffer* (family Bovidae); BUFFEL sense 1 a; *Cape buffalo,* see CAPE sense 2 a. Also *attrib.*

1699 W. ROGERS in W. Dampier *New Voy. round World* (1705) II. 109 Buffaloes and Bullocks only are kept tame. **1731** [see BUFFEL sense 1 a]. **1798** S.H. WILCOCKE tr. *J.S. Stavorinus's Voy. to E. Indies 1768–71* I. 558 The wild animals, which are found in the country, and among which the lion, the tiger, the leopard, the buffalo, and the ape are enumerated, are now far removed from the Cape, and are seldom seen near it. **1824** W.J. BURCHELL *Trav.* II. 250 The name of buffalo, presents another example of the misapplication of European names to the wild animals of Southern Africa. **1834** T. PRINGLE *Afr. Sketches* 270 The buffalo is a very formidable and powerful animal. He is considerably larger than the domestic ox. **1847** J. BARROW *Reflect.* 160 One of the farmer's Hottentots brought down a large male buffalo (Bos Caffer), the strongest and the fiercest of the bovine genus. **1858** T. SHONE Diary. 13 Jan., Henry and the boy's was hunting the Buffalow. **1900** W.L. SCLATER *Mammals of S. Afr.* I. 258 The buffalo is generally reckoned the most dangerous of South African animals. **1955** A. DELIUS *Young Trav.* 151 There were brown wooly buffaloes, big dangerous-looking creatures. **1990** SKINNER & SMITHERS *Mammals of Sn Afr. Subregion* 685 Disease and climatic factors affecting the habitat, rather than predation, are the most serious factors regulating buffalo numbers.

2. *comb.* **buffalo bird** *?obs.* [prob. tr. S. Afr. Du. *buffelvogel, buffel* buffalo + *vogel* bird], OXPECKER; **buffalo thorn** [prob. tr. S. Afr. Du. *buffelsdoorn, buffel* buffalo + linking phoneme *-s-* + *doorn* thorn], the small indigenous tree *Ziziphus mucronata* subsp. *mucronata* of the Rhamnaceae; BLINKBLAAR-WAG-'N-BIETJIE; *buffelsdoorn,* see BUFFEL sense 1 b; CAT-THORN sense 2 b; also called WAG-'N-BIETJIE.

1836 A.F. GARDINER *Journey to Zoolu Country* 113 Observed the **buffalo-birds** very busily employed, perched upon the backs of the oxen; they are generally found where cattle or buffaloes are numerous, living upon the insect which they find in their coats; they are larger than a swallow, with a thick red bill. **1857** D. LIVINGSTONE *Missionary Trav.* 545 Buffalo-birds act the part of guardian spirits to the animals. [**1896** H.A. BRYDEN *Tales of S. Afr.* 236 Numbers of the weaver birds (*Bubalornis erythorhyncus*) always found associating with buffalo, are here ... A few white egrets, apparently as fearless of the great quadrupeds as the *buffalo birds,* add beauty to the scene.] **1824** W.J. BURCHELL *Trav.* II. 20 Our good-fortune conducted us by a solitary **Buffalo-thorn** (*Buffel doorn*) where we found a small pond of fresh water. **1917** R. MARLOTH *Common Names* 16 *Buffelsdoorn,* (Buffalothorn), *Zizyphus mucronata.* Bears several other names, e.g. *Wacht-een-bietje.* **1929** J. STEVENSON-HAMILTON *Low-Veld* 50 The trees are mainly acacias or buffalo thorn (Zizyphus mucronata), equipped for the most part with an armament of hooks and spikes which must be seen to be believed. **1958** R.E. LIGHTON *Out of Strong* 100 In the hollows the apiesdorings spread their branches above copses of rough-barked, russet-leaved tambootie trees and glossy green buffalo thorns. **1961** PALMER & PITMAN *Trees of S. Afr.* 259 The buffalo-thorn, or as it is more frequently known, the blinkblaar-wag-'n -bietjie, is a familiar tree or shrub in many parts of South Africa. **1976** *E. Prov. Herald* 21 Oct. 4 Invader plants that caused the greatest problem in the mountainous parts of the Eastern Karroo Region were the broom bush, taaibos or kraaibossie, leucosidea, rhinoceros bush, resin bush and buffalo thorn. **1990** L. VAN HOVEN in *S. Afr. Panorama* May-June 27 The main kraal of the mighty .. Zulu king, Shaka, among hills and buffalo-thorn. **1991** *Best of S. Afr. Short Stories* (Reader's Digest Assoc.) 104 The buffalo thorn .. was another source of medicine. A poultice of the powdered and baked roots was applied to relieve pain, and skin infections were treated with a paste made from the leaves.

buffalo grass *n. phr.* [Perh. tr. Afk. *buffelsgras, buffel* buffalo + linking phoneme *-s-* + *gras* grass; or Eng., see quot. 1966.]

1. Any of several broad-leafed fodder or lawn grasses of the Poaceae (subfamily Panicoideae):

a. Any of several species of the genus *Panicum*. See also sense 2 below. **b.** *Stenotaphrum secundatum; coarse quick*, see QUICK sense 2; *coastal buffalo grass*, see sense 2 below; *grove quick*, see QUICK sense 2; QUICK sense 1 b; *seaside quick*, see QUICK sense 2. **c.** Any of several species of the genus *Setaria*. In all senses also called *buffel(s)gras* (see BUFFEL sense 1 b).

1868 J. CHAPMAN *Trav.* II. 457 The Buffalo-grass has a large broad, corrugated leaf, and is greedily eaten by horses and cattle. **1917** R. MARLOTH *Common Names* 34 *Buffalo [grass], Stenotaphrum glabrum, .. Setaria sulcata, .. Panicum laevifolium* (Buffelgras), .. *Panicum hirsutissimum.* **1918** J.W. BEWS *Grasses & Grasslands* 158 *P[anicum] hirsutissimum* Buffalo Grass ... *P. laevifolium* Buffalo Grass, or Old Land's Grass. *Ibid.* 160 *S[etaria] sulcata* Buffalo Grass. **1955** L.K.A. CHIPPINDALL in D. Meredith *Grasses & Pastures* 9 The common names of grasses in South Africa are best described as a menace ... Their popularity seems to increase in proportion to the welter of confusion surrounding appellations such as .. 'Buffalo Grass' or 'Buffelsgras'. **1966** C.A. SMITH *Common Names* 181 *Buffalo(quick)grass*, A vernacular name applied to several grasses which were said to be grazed by the buffalo. **1971** J.P. BOTHA in *Std Encycl. of Sn Afr.* IV. 602 Among the useful fodder grasses of the veld are .. rooigras .. ; panic or buffalo-grasses (genus *Panicum*); .. Bushman grasses. **1987** *Fair Lady* 18 Feb. 93, I walked around the house .. when I saw the overturned dustbin ... I .. baulked at the teabags and orange peels on the buffalo grass around the door. **1991** G.E. GIBBS RUSSELL et al. *Grasses of Sn Afr.* 314 *Stenotaphrum secundatum* ... Buffalo grass. **1992** H. HUTCHINGS in *Weekend Post* 24 Oct. (Leisure) 7 Fine lawns such as kweek can be cut to a length of about 10mm, whereas coarser grasses like kikuyu and buffalo should not be less than 25mm to 30mm.

2. With distinguishing epithet designating a particular species of buffalo grass: **blue buffalo grass**, SKAAPPLAAS sense a; **coastal buffalo grass**, *Stenotaphrum secundatum* (see sense 1 b above); **elbow buffalo grass**, *Panicum subalbidum*; **Natal buffalo grass**, *P. natalense*; **small buffalo grass**, *P. coloratum*; **sweet buffalo grass**, *P. schinzii*; **white buffalo grass**, *P. coloratum*.

1971 J.P. BOTHA in *Std Encycl. of Sn Afr.* IV. 603 **Blue buffalo-grass** (*Cenchrus ciliaris*) is palatable and strongly drought-resistant. **1986** *Farmer's Weekly* 25 July 49 Blue buffalo grass (Molopo strain), *Cenchrus ciliaris*, is a drought-resistant type, which does well in low-rainfall areas with warm to hot climate. **1992** F.P. VAN OUDTSHOORN *Guide to Grasses* 76 *Cenchrus ciliaris*, Blue Buffalo Grass. *Ibid.* 122 *Stenotaphrum secundatum*, **Coastal Buffalo Grass** ... Commonly used for course lawns. **1991** G.E. GIBBS RUSSELL et al. *Grasses of Sn Afr.* 242 *Panicum subalbidum* ... **Elbow buffalo grass.** *Ibid.* 240 *Panicum natalense* ... **Natal buffalo grass.** **1990** SKINNER & SMITHERS *Mammals of Sn Afr. Subregion* 685 They [*sc.* buffalo] are selective feeders in the rainy season .. with preference for grasses such as red grass, .. **small buffalo grass**, *Panicum coloratum*; buffalo grass, *P. maximum.* **1902** D. VAN WARMELO *On Commando* 77 Our horses often grazed on the **sweet buffalo grass** that always grows under the trees. **1992** F.P. VAN OUDTSHOORN *Guide to Grasses* 241 *Panicum schinzii*, Sweet Buffalo Grass ... It is .. good for making hay and silage. **1991** G.E. GIBBS RUSSELL et al. *Grasses of Sn Afr.* 236 *Panicum coloratum* ... **White buffalo grass.** **1992** F.P. VAN OUDTSHOORN *Guide to Grasses* 236 *Panicum coloratum*, .. White Buffalo Grass ... Preferred by white rhinoceros, roan, buffalo and reedbuck.

buffel /ˈbəfəl/ *n.* Also **buffle.** [S. Afr. Du. (later Afk.), buffalo; the first citation is perh. the obs. Eng. *buffle*.]

1.a. *?obs. rare.* The BUFFALO (sense 1), *Syncerus caffer.*

1731 G. MEDLEY tr. *P. Kolb's Present State of Cape of G.H.* II. 109 Buffles or Buffaloes are numerous in the Cape countries. They are larger than the *European* Buffles, and of a brown Red. **1881** 'W.H.P.G.' in *Cape Monthly Mag.* IV. June 382 Still, there are buffels in some numbers.

b. *comb.* **buffel(s)gras** /-ˌxras/ [Afk., *gras* grass], or partially translated **buffel grass** /-ˌgrɑːs/, BUFFALO GRASS; **buffel(s)doorn** *obs.* [S. Afr. Du., *doorn* thorn], the *buffalo thorn* (see BUFFALO sense 2), *Ziziphus mucronata.*

1915 R. MARLOTH *Flora of S. Afr.* IV. 22 **Buffelgras.** **1917** —— *Common Names* 35 *Buffelgras, Panicum laevifolium; P. maximum; Pennisetum cenchroides, Setaria culcata.* **1931** E.P. PHILLIPS *S. Afr. Grasses* 72 *Panicum maximum* (Guinea grass or Buffels gras) is a good pasture and hay grass. **1937** *Handbk for Farmers* (Dept of Agric. & Forestry) 409 Buffelsgras, known also as Ubabe .. is a sweet-veld grass. **1955** J. CLEARY *Justin Bayard* 182 Between the patch of buffel grass and the grey-blue slate was a small strip of fine sand. **1958** *Austral. Encycl.* IV. 126 Introduced species [of] .. fodder plants .. from Africa, veldt .. buffel (Cenchrus ciliaris) .. grasses. **1987** LUBKE & LA COCK *Vegetation & Ecology of Kwaaihoek: Site of Dias Cross (pamphlet)*, A characteristic grassland community dominated by *Sporobolus virginicus* (brakgras) and *Stenotaphrum secundatum* (seasidequick, buffelsgras) occurs on the northwestern side of the promontory. **1822** W.J. BURCHELL *Trav.* I. 317 The next was filled chiefly with Zwartebast (Black-bark), Karreehout, and **Buffeldoorn** (Buffalo-thorn). **1894** R. MARLOTH in *Trans. of S. Afr. Phil. Soc.* p.lxxxiv, *Zizyphus bubalinus* (Buffel's doorn). **1917** [see *buffalo thorn* (BUFFALO sense 2)].

2. *Military.* Usu. with initial capital. An armoured, mine-proofed troop carrier with a V-shaped body, used by the South African defence forces. Also *attrib.* See also CASSPIR, ELAND sense 2, HIPPO, OLIFANT, RATEL sense 2, SPOOK *n.* sense 2.

1980 *Daily Dispatch* 21 July 1 An infantry-man in an armoured Buffel troop carrier spotted three insurgents in the bush, and the patrol opened fire when they started to run away. **1985** *Cape Times* 2 Oct. 1 Police and soldiers in three Casspirs and two Buffel armoured personnel carriers took up position opposite the gate. **1986** *Sunday Times* 16 Mar. 14 Unique problems .. which led to South Africa becoming a pioneer and world leader in building mine-resistant troop vehicles. Most notable among these are the well-known Buffel troop carriers. **1987** [see TOYI-TOYI *v.* sense 1]. **1990** *Weekly Mail* 2 Feb. 25 We'd interrogate him ... Maybe we tie him to the front of the Buffel and do a little bundu-bashing. **1993** J. SLOVO *Informant, Johannesburg* The enemy has the Casspirs, .. the enemy has the buffels, .. but we have the majority.

bugger *n. slang.* [Short for RUGGER-BUGGER.]

In *S. Afr. Eng.* 'bugger' usu. has no sexual connotations, and is used more freely than in other forms of English.

1.a. RUGGER-BUGGER. **b.** As a form of address: 'mate', 'friend'; often in *pl.*

1985 *Rhodian 84–5* (Rhodes Univ.), There are among the stereotypes those poor, confused individuals who have no particular identity, who float between bungy and bugger. **1988** N. DEAN in *Style* June 136 *Buggers*, What we all would be if we could drink eight beers a night without falling over. The term 'buggers' does not refer to sexual practices, but comes from 'rugger-buggers'. Few play rugby, though (throwing the barmaid's T-shirt around the room doesn't count). Buggers puke out of res windows; get off with other people's girlfriends and wrestle each other to the ground at beerstubes.

2. *comb.* **bugger-chick**, the compliant girl-friend of an aggressively masculine man.

1988 N. DEAN in *Style* June 136 *Bugger-chicks*, .. Drink Esprit, wear pink takkies, have perfectly tanned belly-buttons and often show a startling generosity in dispensing sexual favours to their men's friends. Bugger chicks respond most satisfactorily to the ritual Ladies Night cry, 'A bottle of champagne to the first girl to give me her bra'. **1989** *Informant, Cape Town* Well, take your shoes off then – be a buggerchick. **1989** *Informant, Grahamstown* You know how the bugger-chicks always dress with these surfer T-shirts and make-up.

bughouse *n.* A run-down or second-rate cinema.

Also *Austral.* and *Brit. Eng.*, but first used in *S. Afr. Eng.* (see Beale quot. 1984).

1967 E. PARTRIDGE *Dict. of Slang & Unconventional Eng.* 1030 *bug house*, .. A second-rate cinema: South Africa: since ca. 1920. Cyrus A. Smith, in letter of July 17, 1946. **1970** S.E. NATHAM *Informant, Cape Town* Bughouse. Old cinema. **1970** *Informant, Pietersburg* Bughouse. Bioscope. **1984** R. SADOWSKY in *Sunday Times* 29 Jan. 19 In those days .. admission to the local 'bug house' (bioscope) was a 'zack' (sixpence). **1984** P. BEALE *E. Partridge's Dict. of Slang & Unconventional Eng.* 147 *Bug house*, A second-rate cinema: S. Africa: since c. 1920. **1985** A. GOLDSTUCK in *Frontline* Feb. 20 When he was about 8, the Joburg 'bughouses' used to play a 'magical sound' before the curtain went up for the movie. **1994** *Style* May 14 Clarence is something of a kung fu movie junkie and takes in chop-socky triple features at the local bughouse when he's not working at a Detroit comic book shop.

buikplank /ˈbœikplaŋk/ *n. Hist. Wagon-making.* Pl. **-e** /-ə/. [S. Afr. Du., fr. Du. *buik* belly + *plank* board.] The bottom boards of a wagon.

1822 W.J. BURCHELL *Trav.* I. 149 At the end of the month my waggon was finished and sent home ... The planks of the bottom (*buik plank*) were two inches thick. **1857** C.J. ANDERSSON *Lake Ngami* 27 (Pettman), The enraged brute struck his powerful horn into the *buik plank* (the bottom boards) with such force as to push the wagon several paces forward. **1868** W.R. THOMSON *Poems, Essays & Sketches* 184 He can cook his supper under the *buikplank*, serve it up to his wife and children on the *voorkist*, and then turn the family in to roost securely and comfortably for the night in the wide space between that and the *achterkist.* **1907** T.R. SIM *Forests & Forest Flora* 68 A loop of Onderstel means wood sufficient and of the description required to complete a wagon, minus the bed, or 'buikplank', or rails. **1919** J.Y. GIBSON in *S. Afr. Jrnl of Science* July 6 Burchell described his wagon with some minuteness, and his description is available to students of history. Its general scheme was divided thus: .. IV., the Boven Stel: (1) *Buik-plank*, or floor. **1974** A.A. TELFORD in *Std Encycl. of Sn Afr.* X. 568 To achieve the elasticity necessary in a vehicle traversing rough and trackless country, the wagon consisted of three main parts, loosely held together to allow play between them: the chassis, the bottom boards (*buikplanke*), and the body.

‖**buitekamer** /ˈbeɪtəˌkɑːmə(r), ˈbœɪtə-/ *n. Archit.* Formerly also **buitenkamer.** [Afk. (earlier Du. *buitenkamer*), *buite* outside + *kamer* room.] An outside room, occas. an out-building but usu. a part of a dwelling with access to the exterior.

1913 A.B. MARCHAND *Dirk, S. African* 8 (Swart), He stowed it away in the buitekamer, the sleeping-place kept for way-faring men. **1919** M.M. STEYN *Diary* 129, I had what was called a 'buiten kamer' (outside room). **1948** H.C. BOSMAN in L. Abrahams *Unto Dust* (1963) 50 Why my wire-cutters are rusting in the buitekamer from disuse, is not because the border is better patrolled than it was in the old days. **1973** *Fair Lady* 30 May 14 In her buitekamer .. was always the smell of moist moss, of earth and the mingling scent of flowers.

buk(k)u var. BUCHU.

‖**bula** /ˈbʊːla, ˈbuːlə/ *v. intrans.* Also **bhola, bhula.** [fr. Zulu v. *bhula* beat, hence (transf.) consult a diviner, prophesy (the transf. senses arising because of a method of divining in which the inquirer raps the ground with a stick in response to the diviner's statements).] *to throw (the) bones*, see THROW sense 2. Also *comb.* **bula dance.**

1893 J.F. INGRAM *Story of Gold Concession* 38 The King's chamberlain presently came out and announced that Nazaza would bula, or prophesy, that night at moonrise. **1949** J. MOCKFORD *Golden Land* 106 The *bula* dance .. is still performed, deep in the heart of Zululand ... Here the most terrible of all tribal

bulala /bʊˈlɑːlɑ/ *v.* Also **bullala**. [Common to the Nguni languages.]

‖**1.** Reporting Xhosa or Zulu speech:
a. *trans.* To kill (someone).

 1882 J. NIXON *Among Boers* 97 While we were seated drinking beer, a cry was raised, 'Bulala umtagatie' (kill the sorcerers). **1949** C. BULLOCK *Rina* 106 'Wena ikona kuluma!' thundered Jones, threatening in his vilest kitchen-kaffir to 'bulala' Ratisi if he should speak to anyone about our fight. [**1990** STANSFIELD & TYALA in *Sunday Times* 19 Aug. 2 It was after this incident that the whispers began: 'Bulalani amaBhunu, Kill the Boers.']

b. *intrans. imp.* 'Kill'.

 1899 A. WERNER *Captain of Locusts* 164 Though he knew very little Zulu, he knew what bulala meant, and he heard that shouted right and left, if he heard nothing else. **1937** S. CLOETE *Turning Wheels* 26 The sound of firing had increased; he could hear the shouts of the Kaffirs. Their wild cries of Bullala .. Bullala. Kill .. kill. **1959** G. & W. GORDON tr. *F.A. Venter's Dark Pilgrim* 190 'Bulala!' roars the mob. The explosion into movement is so violent that the foremost men are overthrown. **1964** H.H.W. DE VILLIERS *Rivonia* 63 The Zulu war cry 'Bulala' (kill) can still stir them into a frenzy of uncontrolled aggression and murder. **1982** *E. Prov. Herald* 26 June 1 The terrified man broke through the crowd and fled downhill, followed by hundreds of Zulus, many armed with sticks. The cry 'bulala' (kill) rang out again and again.

2. *comb.* **bulala lamp** /bʊˈlɑːlɑ -/, a battery-charged head-lamp used in hunting.

 1952 H. KLEIN *Land of Silver Mist* 161 He did his lion shooting at night by the light of a 'bulala lamp', an electric killing lamp fixed to an elastic band around his head, which flashed a powerful beam of light into the lions' eyes, dazzling them momentarily and giving him time to get in his shot. **1961** D. BEE *Children of Yesterday* 213 Nigel .. adjusted the light on his hat. It was connected to a battery-case in his left breast-pocket and was of the type commonly known as the bulala-lamp.

bully *n. obs.* [Etym. unkn.] The canary *Serinus sulphuratus* of the Fringillidae; *geel sysie*, see SYSIE sense b. Also *attrib.*

 In G.L. Maclean's *Roberts' Birds of Sn Afr.* (1993), the name 'bully canary' is used for *S. sulphuratus*.

 1908 HAAGNER & IVY *Sketches* 84 The Large Yellow Seedeater (*Serinus sulphuratus*), the 'Geel-seisje' and 'Bully' of the Colonial boys.

bult /bəlt/ *n.* Also **bilt**. Pl. **-s**; formerly **-en**. [Afk., hump.] A low ridge or sandy hillock. See also RANDJIE.

 'Bult' occurs as an element in place names, as *Bultfontein, Doringbult, Van Heerden's Bult.*

 1852 C. BARTER *Dorp & Veld* 96 They [*sc.* the lions] retreated slowly up the *bult*. **1864** T. BAINES *Explor. in S.-W. Afr.* 371 We crossed the seringa bult at a narrower place. **1868** [see BONTVELD]. **1900** A.W. CARTER *Informant, Ladybrand* 8 Feb., We slipped along until I thought we were safe enough behind a bult, cut the wire and drove across the veldt to Pohl's farm. **1902** D. VAN WARMELO *On Commando* 147 Against the sides of the mounds (bulten) the cattle were moving in black dense masses. **1928** E.H.L. SCHWARZ *Kalahari & its Native Races* 31 Behind the marsh fringing the stream on the south side, there now appeared a low bult, some twenty-five feet high. **1936** C. BIRKBY *Thirstland Treks* 91 No vice that a highway can have is lacking in the road … It twisted and turned, it laboured over bults, it lost itself in the wilderness on either side. **1941** A.G. BEE *Kalahari Camp Fires* (1943) 56 Poultney and Drake took their horses again and rode out towards a big 'sand bult' or sand-dune covered with fine trees. **1951** H.C. BOSMAN in L. Abrahams *Bekkersdal Marathon* (1971) 151 How do you know that the line you marked out on the other side of the bult is in a straight line from here? Can you *see* through a bult — a bult about fifty paces high and half a mile over it? **1987** M. POLAND *Train to Doringbult* 9 The light, just rising cobra-coloured up above the *bult*, was fading out to green, to white. Still the ridge was dark.

bultong, bûltong varr. BILTONG.

Bundelswaart var. BONDELSWART.

bundu /ˈbʊndu/ *n.* Forms: α. **bundu**; β. **boendoes, bundus** /ˈbʊnduːz/. Also with initial capital. [Etym. unkn.; perh. Shona *bundo* grasslands.

 The *-oe-* spelling form is used by those who perceive the derivation to be Afk. Despite the similarity between 'bundu' and U.S. Eng. 'boondocks' (fr. Tagalog *bundok*), it is unlikely that there is any relationship between the two words.]

'The back of beyond': any area remote from cities and civilization; GOPSE sense 1 b; GRAMADOELAS; cf. BACKVELD *n.* sense a. Also *attrib.*, and *comb.* (*nonce*) **bunduland**. See also BUSH *n.*[1] sense 3.

 The pl. form 'bundus' is found mainly in the Eng. of speakers of Sintu (Bantu) languages.

 α. **1939** *Outspan* 29 Sept. 25, I was stationed out in the bundu and I had to shoot all my meat. **1948** O. WALKER *Kaffirs Are Lively* 7 After a certain amount of dignified safari-like preparations I headed north for the 'Bundu' of the Transvaal. **1949** L. HUNTER *Afr. Dawn* 218 'Now, we'd better find out where we are Butch.' 'At the back o' beyond it looks like.' 'Yes, we certainly seem to be properly in the bundu.' **1954** K. COWIN *Bushveld, Bananas & Bounty* 17, I had thought we were standing on a *bult* in the bundu as we were speaking, but as he pointed out, at least we were only twenty miles from the nearest dorp. **1965** C. VAN HEYNINGEN *Orange Days* 96 The dorp where we lived was a mining town, practically in the bundu. **1970** A. THERON *More S. Afr. Deep Freezing* 173 The bundu means any lonely inaccessible part of the South African veld. **1981** B. MFENYANA in M. Mutloatse *Reconstruction* 298 Now the migrants from Egoli play the same role, bringing 'high culture' and town talk to the bundu. **1972** *Daily Dispatch* 30 Mar. 14 A .. message would have gone around, even up to remote **bunduland**, scrubtown or shanty. **1984** J. BROOKS in *Sunday Times* 23 Sept. 1 The bundu wedding of the year took place at sunset yesterday in a riverside tree-house. **1988** M. WAGAMOLOTO in *New Nation* 30 June 25 Tired of watching children from the bundu, kept illiterate while others wait to reap their sweat. **1991** *Sunday Times* 14 July 17 We in the bundu pay towards city dwellers' television and radio enjoyment, yet we receive no TSS transmissions. **1994** F.G. BUTLER in *Financial Mail* 16 Sept. (Suppl.) 30 Oxford and Cambridge were founded and still flourish in the British bundu.

 β. **1973** *Drum* 22 Jan. 18 He can work in the big city for the wife and children he left in the bundus. **1977** *Ibid.* Aug. 39 People outside King Williamstown found themselves without the valuable services of their only doctor after she had been banished to the bundus in the region of Tzaneen in the Northern Transvaal. **1978** *Daily Dispatch* 27 July 14 Amazing what those housewives get up to out there in the boendoes! **1985** *Sunday Times* 10 Nov. (Mag. Sect.) 15 We're living in a modern society, you know … it's hard for us to be different unless we go back to the bundus. **1986** B. NTLEMO in *Pace* May 49 It becomes obvious to those who meet him that he may live in the bundus, but the bundus don't live in him. **1990** F. KHUMALO in *Weekly Mail* 4 May 11 The Kosi Bay Nature Reserve, a haven for those who are tired of cities and hanker after the tranquility of the *bundus*.

bundu bash *n. phr.* [fr. next; a play on colloq. Eng. *bash* lively party.] A celebration, party, or concert in the country. Also *attrib.*

 1984 *Daily Dispatch* 4 June 2 A bundu bash with a difference .. to mark the opening of the Bloukrans Pass Tollgate. **1985** *Style* Dec. 41 A Botswana bundu bash that had the bride boating up the Chobe River .. to take her vows in a treehouse atop an ancient fig tree. **1989** J. LA MONT in *Sunday Times* 26 Feb. 2 British music circles are abuzz with plans for a mammoth bundu bash concert to celebrate the King of Swaziland's 21st birthday. **1990** R. RANGONGO in *New African* 3 Sept. 9 Traditional dancing, rasta music, a massive braai, and real beer highlighted Sipho Mchunu's bundu bash along the banks of the Tugela River.

bundu-bash *v. intrans. Colloq.* [BUNDU + colloq. Eng. *bash* to hit or beat (something).] To force one's way through rough and difficult terrain; to go out into the wilds. Also *fig.*

 1970 V.R. VINK *Informant, Florida* We spent our holidays bundu-bashing (on safari in the bush). **1972** *Star* 22 June 21 'Bundu-bashing' in pursuit of live game to sell … A four-wheel drive vehicle is completely worn out after two seasons of this work on his game ranch. **1975** J. MCCLURE *Snake* (1981) 139 Pity the old man's away bundu-bashing, you two should get on famously. **1976** *E. Prov. Herald* 8 June 5 About 600 people of all ages are expected to go 'bundu bashing' near Port Elizabeth .. for the Eastern Province Wildlife Society's annual snare hunt. **1976** *Cape Times* 21 Feb. 10 He blazed the homeward trail, and a generation of young poets came swearing and bundu-bashing behind him; in love with their hateful homeland. **1985** *Sunday Times* 11 Aug. (Lifestyle) 5 Bundu-bashing on the Botswana border?

Hence **bundu-basher** *n.*; **bundu-bashing** *vbl n.*, travel through very rough or difficult country; also *attrib.*

 1972 *Caravan* May 37 The bundu bashing Beira bunch are going west. This time they will be blazing a trail to Angola. **1973** *Evening Post* 14 July (Parade) 1 Track racing and .. the far-flung bundu-bashing type of rally. **1974** *Farmer's Weekly* 4 Dec. 44 The most rugged bundu-basher in the world! **1982** *S. Afr. Panorama* Dec. 12 At Sabi Sabi, 'bundu bashing', as game viewing is called in South Africa (*bundu* = bush) is an excitement that makes the visitor .. feel that he/she has truly arrived in 'darkest Africa'. **1984** C. ST LEGER in *Sunday Times* 26 Feb. 1 South Africans should be able to view Prince Charles doing a bit of bundu-bashing next month. He will be wandering over the desert sands in search of the Kalahari Bushmen. **1985** *Style* Oct. 95 Many are the options for the would-be bundu basher who wants to taste primitive, unspoilt Africa. **1989** B. LUDMAN *Day of Kugel* 100 'He keeps going off to the bundu … What does he do out there, Stephen?' 'I've no idea, anyway, he's picked a funny time for bundu bashing.' **1990** [see BUFFEL sense 2].

bundustan see -STAN.

Bunga /ˈbʊŋɡə/ *n.* Also with small initial. [fr. Xhosa *ibhunga* private consultation, council of a chief.]

1. *hist.* Any of several councils of chiefs constituted in 1895 for the administration of various districts in the eastern regions of the Cape.

 The Glen Grey Act (Act 25 of 1894) provided for local government structures in the form of district councils.

 1906 G. CALLAWAY in *E. & W. Mag.* (India) 425 The annual meeting of the 'Bunga,' or representative council for certain native districts, is held. **1912** *E. London Dispatch* 2 May 4 (Pettman), The *Bunga* has jurisdiction over an area fifty per cent larger than Basutoland and containing three times as many inhabitants. **1952** *Drum* Apr. 9 The All African Convention .. insisted that its members should have no truck with things like local councils, location advisory boards, Native representative councils and bungas. **1970** *Daily Dispatch* 16 Mar. 11 The Bungas .. were 'dummy' institutions created for the 'enslavement of the Africans', the Minister of Justice in the Transkei, Chief George Matanzima said.

2.a. *hist.* The General Council, and subsequently the Parliament, of the Transkei. Also *attrib.* See also NATIONAL ASSEMBLY.

*c*1911 B.H. Dodd in S. Playne *Cape Col.* 653 The local government of the Territories is in the hands (under the Union Parliament) of a body known as the Transkeian General Council, or 'Bunga'. *c*1936 *S. & E. Afr. Yr Bk & Guide* 656 A measure of self-government has been accorded to the natives in the form of a *General Council* called the 'Bunga', with which has been amalgamated since January, 1931, the *Pondoland Council.* 1941 C.W. De Kiewiet *Hist. of S. Afr.* 199 The Bunga or Transkeian General Council of 1895 was to be the forerunner of a greater measure of native self-government so that the benefits of Victorian liberalism should be bestowed on her Majesty's black subjects as well. 1955 A. Delius *Young Trav.* 137 The fair-sized stone building of the *Bunga*, the United Transkeian General Council. 1963 M. Benson *Afr. Patriots* 104 He [*sc.* Oliver Tambo] passed his Junior Certificate with a first class, and as a result the Bunga, the Transkei Tribal Council which normally only provided scholarships for sons of important people, gave him a scholarship not only to finish at St. Peter's, but to go on to Fort Hare College. 1981 *Sunday Times* 16 Aug. 8 A former member of the old Transkei Bunga (parliament), Mr Mbeki senior was ANC leader in the Eastern Cape. 1986 P. Maylam *Hist. of Afr. People* 164 The Bunga's members consisted of the twenty-six district magistrates, three paramount chiefs, and three representatives from each district council. 1987 *Drum* Dec. 22 My father as Paramount Chief of east Pondoland was deep in Bunga politics. 1990 *E. Prov. Herald* 18 Jan. 8 When Verwoerd wished to implement the Bantu Authorities Act in 1955, he knew that he had to make a breakthrough with the Transkeian Bunga, he had to convince the Transkeian Bunga.

b. The Transkeian parliament house in Umtata.

1931 *Nat. Geog. Mag.* Apr. 412 It is truly the Transkeian natives' own homeland, as witness Umtata's bunga, or Parliament House. 1969 I. Vaughan *Last of Sunlit Yrs* 142, I had been to the Bunga, the native Parliament, where, under the guidance of European Magistrates, each of whom was responsible for a portion of the Large Native Reserve, the Bantu Councillors met in debate. 1975 *Sunday Times* 7 Dec. 21 The brave new flag of Africa's youngest independent Black state will fly from the Bunga in Umtata next year.

bungalow *n.* [Special senses of general Eng. *bungalow*: orig., a temporary or lightly-built structure; in modern usage, a one-storied house.] A (usu.) one-storied building used for temporary, periodic, or rotating accommodation.

1. *Military.*

a. The living-quarters of men on military service.

1944 'Twede in Bevel' *Piet Kolonel* 54, I struck metal and out from under the bed skidded the lid of a small boot polish tin. 'What,' asked Colonel Lewis, 'are these receptacles littering the floor of the bungalow?' I had no idea. 1972 [see rope]. 1984 *Fair Lady* 14 Nov. 132 The sprawling web of base camps looks as though it popped up over-night ... Everything looks severely functional — and temporary: pre-fab bungalows. 1986 J. Whyle in S. Gray *Market Plays* 173 What was frightening was life out of work hours. We lived in a large bungalow where we were liable to unofficial initiation by the oumanne. 1991 F.G. Butler *Local Habitation* 138 On an Information Officer's course I felt particularly lucky to find myself in the same bungalow as his brother.

b. *comb.* **bungalow captain**, the leader of the group of men living in a bungalow.

1981 *Rand Daily Mail* 25 Apr. 1 Troops began leaving about midnight on Thursday after some had held a meeting. He said some 'bungalow captains' had complained about the shortage of hot water in the showers.

2. A holiday cottage, esp. one which is lightly built.

1955 A. Delius *Young Trav.* 149 There is a whole string of camps of thatched bungalows with restaurants where people spend the night. 1970 S.E. Natham *Informant, Cape Town* Bungalow. Small holiday house. 1975 *Dict. of Eng. Usage in Sn Afr.* 37 *Bungalow,* .. In S. Afr. E. a small, usu. rustic building, consisting of one or more rooms with cooking & bathing facilities, at a holiday resort. 1989 *Sunday Times* 19 Nov. (Mag. Sect.) 117 Sleep cosy at night in the rustic timber bungalows nestling close to the riverside. 1991 *Ibid.* 10 Mar. 23 The cost of a sea view at Clifton is now being pegged at nearly R2,9-million .. the price being asked for a wooden bungalow overlooking Fourth Beach. 1992 *Weekend Post* 12 Sept. (Holiday Playground) 2 Holiday resorts which offer holiday flats, bungalows, caravan sites, and camping sites.

3. *Prison slang.* See quot.

1992 E. Bulbring in *Sunday Times* 20 Sept. 3 The 'bungalows' (cells) at Diepkloof awaiting-trial section are run by a 'rep' who holds the position by virtue of his strength.

bungi /ˈbʌŋgi/ *n. slang.* Also **bungie, bungy.** [Prob. ad. Hindi *bhang* hemp, cannabis, or fr. slang *bunge*, ad. Ndebele *im-banje* marijuana. The expression appears to have originated on the campus of Rhodes University, Grahamstown.] Esp. among university students: one who rejects middle-class values and who is characterized by unconventional dress and behaviour, and often by the use of drugs, esp. marijuana. Also *attrib.*

1981 *Rhodeo* (Rhodes Univ.) 19 Oct. 2 My life was ruined. I was no longer cool. Jogging's hit the bungy scene. 1985 *Rhodian 84–5* (Rhodes Univ.) 8 Two broad categories, familiarly known as the 'bungies' and the 'rugger-buggers' form distinct social apartheid on campus, and there is no love lost between them ... Bungies are the flower-children of the 80's. 1988 N. Dean in *Style* June 101 Dope distinguishes bungies from other students and the bungie really comes alive only when the roach is furtively passed around the darkened room. 1988 *Sunday Times* 7 Aug. 14 Chameleon-like changes — a leather clad biker while she was at Wits, a confirmed 'bungi' wearing Indian cotton dresses and leather sandals to be part of the left circle at Rhodes. 1989 R. Palmer in *Rhodos* (Rhodes Univ.) May 4 Compared with the majority of the mourners in their bungi-rigs or Webster Memorial T-shirts I was over-dressed in my two-piece dark grey suit and navy tie. 1991 *Rhodeo* (Rhodes Univ.) Apr. 14 One student who asked why he was being searched, was given the reply 'I don't need an excuse to search a bungie' by .. the officer in question.

bunny chow *n. phr.* [*bunny* prob. ad. Hindi *banya*, fr. Gujerati *vaniya* one of a Hindi caste of merchants and traders + *chow* food (colloq. Eng., fr. Chinese); see G. Varma quot. 1984.] A take-away food consisting of a hollowed-out half-loaf of bread filled with vegetable or meat curry. Also *attrib.*

Esp. common in Natal.

1972 *Notice in shop window, Durban* Bunny chow 20 cents. 1979 *Darling* 4 Apr. 68 *Take-aways*: .. Middle Class — Chinese, pizza, Kentucky fried. Lower Class — Bunny chow, hot chips. 1982 J. Reddy in *Staffrider* Vol.5 No.1, 10 He stood there dipping bits of bread into the bunny chow. The hollowed out bread filled with thick, spicy bean curry, tasted delicious. 1984 G. Varma in *Daily News* 16 Jan., Your readers may be interested to know that this tavern [*sc.* the Queen's] gave birth to the 'Bunny Chow' ... I asked a friend to bring some lunch for me. Since we had no containers, I asked him to cut the bread at the crust, .. scoop out the soft portion and fill it with curry ... In those days all Gugerati Hindu businessmen were called 'Banias', so we called our take-away lunches 'Bunia Chow'. On my return to Durban in 1981 after an absence of over 25 years, I noted 'Bunny Chow' had become a household name. 1984 *S. Afr. Digest* 16 May 1 Bunny chow, the most popular food at many Durban take-aways today. All the bunny chow maker does is to dig out the inner, soft part of a loaf of bread and fill the hollow with curry. 1986 *Cape Times* 15 Jan. 7 That old Cape favourite Bunny-Chow — a loaf of bread stuffed with snoek or curry. 1986 *Fair Lady* 5 Mar. 24 The shared act of eating anything from pizza to a bunny chow (although those are rather better with beer) is .. sensual. 1992 *Handbill, Grahamstown* Now open. Houston's take-aways ... Toasted sandwiches ... Bunny chows ... Samp & Beans.

buntebo(c)k var. bontebok.

burben var. boerboon.

burbom var. boerboom.

burgar, burger varr. burgher.

burgeright var. burgher right.

burgermeester /ˈbɜːgəmɪəstə/ *n.* Also **burgemeester,** and with initial capital. [ad. Du. *burgemeester* mayor, magistrate, *burg* town + euphonic *-e-* + *meester* master; the form *burger-* prob. resulted from a misconception among English-speakers that the first element of the term was the Du. word *burgher* citizen (of a town). Cf. burgher.]

1.a. *obsolescent.* The mayor of a town. **b.** *hist.* A chief magistrate; also used as a title before a surname.

[1731 G. Medley tr. *P. Kolb's Present State of Cape of G.H.* I. 339 Three Regent Burgher-Masters, Magistrates at the *Cape*, chosen annually out of such as are not in the Company's Service, come in and assist in the Tryal.] 1902 D. Van Warmelo *On Commando* 35 Again I went to Warmbad for some weeks with Mr Burgermeester Potgieter and his family. 1915 D. Fairbridge *Torch Bearer* 226 'Mynheer burgermeester -' He turned to the mayor and checked suddenly before the stricken look on Johannes Roux's face. 1920 R.Y. Stormberg *Mrs Pieter de Bruyn* 19 His talk .. is .. a rambling catalogue of frightful slander against .. the Mayor ... When last we called, all the burgemeester's sins were spread out.

2. Special Comb. **burgermeester's chair**, also **burghermeester's -, burgomeester's -, burgomaster's chair**: an ornate, round chair with circular arms and back, a caned seat, and six legs.

1960 G.E. Pearce *18th C. Furn.* 54 *Figure 62* shows a wheel chair at Groote Schuur, a type often known as a Burgomaster's chair. It is circular in plan supported by six curved or cabriole legs ... Ball turning occurs in the stretchers or rails which link the legs together, an arrangement resembling the spokes of a wheel, which, no doubt, suggests the name wheel chair ... The curved back is supported on four uprights ... The seat is caned. 1965 M.G. Atmore *Cape Furn.* 61 *Burgomeester or wheel chairs* ... This unusual type of chair, which was popular in Holland at the end of the 17th Century is difficult to relate to any earlier European style and was probably an Eastern form. 1971 L.G. Green *Taste of S.-Easter* 49 'Burgomaster chairs' were made at the Cape; round 'compass' chairs with cane seats and six legs banded together. 1981 *Garden & Home* June 136 In one of the lengthy passages is this burgermeester's chair of Dutch origin and carved from one piece of wood. 1987 G. Viney *Col. Houses* 180 Amongst the curios which survive here are Lobengula's seal, a *burghermeester's* chair (which makes a surprise reappearance in the library of the Queen's Dolls' House).

Burgerraad /ˈbɜːgərɑːt, -rɑːd/ *n.* Also **Burgherraad, Burgerrad,** and with small initial. Pl. **-rade(n)** /-rɑːdən/, occas. **-raade** /-rɑːdə/. [S. Afr. Du., fr. Du. *burgher* citizen + *raad* council (see also raad). Cf. burgher.]

1. *Obs.* exc. *hist.* burgher senate sense a; a member of this authority. See also raad sense 1.

*c*1795 W.S. Van Ryneveld in G.M. Theal *Rec. of Cape Col.* (1897) I. 245 The first of the Burgerraden was President, and the Secretary paid by the College itself was also a Burgher. 1796 J. Smuts et al. in *Ibid.* 379 The Burgherraden, among many other functions, are also charged with the care of the Windmills and of the Conduits to the Public Pumps. 1827 *Reports of Commissioners upon Finances at Cape of G.H.* I. 48 In the following year this number was increased to four, under the appellation of 'Burger Raaden,' or burgher council, and their jurisdiction was extended to civil cases. **1862** *Court of Policy Resolutions* in *Stat. Law of Cape of G.H.* p.lxx, It was resolved to approve the regulations made by Burgerraden regarding .. the use of water descending from Table Mountain.

‖**2.** [Afk.] A citizen's council as formed by the AWB.

1986 *Weekend Argus* 8 Mar., Mr Terre'Blanche claims the AWB has now been organised in 'burgerrade' throughout the country.

burgher /'bɜːɡə/ *n.* Also **burgar**, **burger**, and with initial capital. [Du. Cf. Eng. *burger* borrowed during the 16th century fr. Du. *burger.*]

1. *hist.*

a. A Dutch colonist at the Cape, esp. under the Dutch East India Company; a townsman, with all the rights and duties of a citizen. Also *attrib.* See also BOER sense 2, FREE BURGHER.

Also used by the Dutch in Ceylon (Sri Lanka).

1731 G. MEDLEY tr. *P. Kolb's Present State of Cape of G.H.* I. 45 The Directors put a Stop to all Commerce with the Hottentots on the Company's Account; and ordered that all Supplies of Provisions for them should be bought up among their own Burgers at the *Cape*. **1798** S.H. WILCOCKE tr. *J.S. Stavorinus's Voy. to E. Indies 1768–71* II. 56 Reviews, both of horse and foot, are held every year, in the town [*sc.* Cape Town] for the burghers, and at *Stellenbosch* and *Zwellendam* for the farmers belonging to the colony. **1804** R. PERCIVAL *Acct of Cape of G.H.* 102 A number of excellent horses belonging to the wealthy burghers and principal people of Cape Town are thickly scattered on each side. **1824** W.J. BURCHELL *Trav.* II. 120 He went escorted by a cavalry party of twenty-two *Burghers* (or Citizens; as the Dutch colonists are frequently termed) and their attendant Hottentots. **1833** *Graham's Town Jrnl* 28 Feb. 3 When the Hottentots complain that white people have taken all their lands from them, they say it is not the Hottentots' country it is the country of the Burghers. **1900** [see FIELD CORNET sense 1]. **1925** H.J. MANDELBROTE tr. *O.F. Mentzel's Descr. of Cape of G.H.* II. 100 The burgher population of the Town is made up of Europeans of South African birth and of immigrants from Holland or Germany. **1926** P.W. LAIDLER *Tavern of Ocean* 23 Children of the Company's servants and those of burghers, born in lawful wedlock, were considered native burghers. **1944** J. MOCKFORD *Here Are S. Africans* 78 The bulk of the Dutch population was still in the Cape – the burghers of the towns and the farmers whose life was among the immovable orchards and vineyards planted by their fathers. **1955** [see LANDDROST sense 1]. **1971** [see COMMANDANT sense 1]. **1971** *Personality* 14 May 27 Since only *burghers* were liable to military duty, illegitimate children were free of that burden ... Filled with the stern Puritan spirit the authorities had laid down the condition that only those born in lawful wedlock could be *burghers*. **1981** *Grocott's Mail* 7 Aug. 1 Piet Retief was a greatly respected and influential community leader, Commandant of the local burger commando. **1988** D. HUGHES et al. *Complete Bk of S. Afr. Wine* 190 Louis Michel Thibault .. abandoned a career as a designer of military fortifications to devote himself to the graceful embellishment of the local Burgher architecture.

b. *comb.* **burgher councillor**, *burgher senator* (see BURGHER SENATE).

1952 G.M. MILLS *First Ladies of Cape* 24 There had been an official welcome attended by the burgher councillors, officials and members of the burgher militia. **1976** G. & G. FAGAN in *Optima* Vol.26 No.2, 70 He was by now prominent in the community; serving as burgher councillor, captain in the burgher cavalry and as a member of the church council.

2. A citizen; in mod. usage, often ironic.

1819 H. ELLIS in G.M. Theal *Rec. of Cape Col.* (1902) XII. 350 Our English Burghers would no doubt equal their Dutch fellow Colonists in courage, and would have stronger motives for loyalty to the paramount, which to them would be the mother country. **1844** E.L. KIFT Letter. 5 Sept., From what I know of Grahamstown folk, there is nothing but *Martial Law* ... Nothing short of Martial law will do any thing with my fellow Burghers. **1856** R.E.E. WILMOT *Diary* (1984) 37 The Totties were utterly routed and the place dismantled and granted to a young English burgher who keeps a shop near and treated us to an account of the affair. **1861** P.B. BORCHERDS *Auto-Biog. Mem.* 223 The lad has now closed his fifteenth year .. and the following morning would entitle him to be a burgher (citizen) of his native country, and to be inscribed as such on the rolls of the colony. **1888** *Cape Punch* 29 Feb. 117 'Would you deign to favour your humble Burgher with a few minutes' conversation?' 'Not now, mynheer,' he replied. *c*1936 [see RAAD sense 1]. **1939** R.F.A. HOERNLÉ *S. Afr. Native Policy* 127 An Indian .. who has no ambition but to be a citizen, a *burger*, of South Africa, in the same sense as a White South African. **1970** *News/Check* 29 May 8 While solid burghers heaped disapprobation on them, the student protests with their imprint of 'made in Europe', had a curious air of irrelevancy. **1987** *Personality* 21 Oct. 30 The burghers of South Africa's ostrich capital. **1991** R. MINOGUE in *Frontline* May 20 A lot of people smoke dope, including otherwise law-abiding, taxpaying burghers.

3. *hist.*

a. A civilian member of a local militia unit, mounted, armed, and usu. without formal uniform; (influenced by sense 4) a Boer soldier, see quot. 1900. See also COMMANDO senses 1 a and 4. Also *attrib.*

1828 W. SHAW Diary. 5 July, Arrived safely at Mount Coke last night, and heard that Major Dundas with fifty Burghers had left this place for the interior on Friday. **1832** *Graham's Town Jrnl* 13 Apr. 62 Early the next morning the cattle were sent to the Deba flat, under the protection of the Hottentot Burghers, whilst the troops and boers went eastward towards the *spruits* of the Buffalo. **1837** J.E. ALEXANDER *Narr. of Voy.* I. 346, I sat as a member of two or three courts-martial at Port Elizabeth on burghers who were insolent to their officers, or refused to mount guard. **1859** *Cape Town Weekly Mag.* 28 Jan. 27 A large commando will again go out against Mahura and the other minor Bechuana tribes, on the 1st February next. The burghers have already been commandeered, and are preparing to turn out. **1871** J. McKAY *Reminisc.* 20 We had no pursuing enemy after us; the road was full for miles behind us with levies, burghers, and cattle. **1884** B. ADAMS *Narr.* (1941) 155 The C.M. Rifles did considerable execution with their double-barrelled carbines; and the Burghers, I believe, did not waste a single round of their ammunition. **1893** 'HARLEY' in *Cape Illust. Mag.* Vol.4 No.10, 376 The farmers were called on to volunteer for service .. to form a burgher corps. Burghers were to bring their own horses, and, if they preferred, their own arms. **1900** A.W. CARTER *Informant, Ladybrand* 8 Feb., The house .. was surrounded by burghers watering their horses, trying to buy fruit, vegetables, bread, meat & anything that was to be had. **1911** D.B. HOOK *'Tis but Yesterday* 18 The settlers were constantly ordered out as burghers to repel the Kaffirs. **1929** D. REITZ *Commando* 19, I was seventeen years old and thus too young to be enrolled as a burgher. *a*1930 G. BAUMANN in Baumann & Bright *Lost Republic* 170, I found the British Tommies and their Burgher guards sitting on the ground together, hobnobbing. *Ibid.* 183 There was no discrimination, when commandeering Free State Burghers, as to whether their origin was English, German or any other nationality. *a*1951 H.C. BOSMAN *Willemsdorp* (1977) 95 That was how the men of his people had ridden to war half-a-century ago – Transvaal Boers and Free State Boers and Cape rebels – a handful of burghers ranging in age from schoolboys to octogenarians, with no uniform but their farm clothes.

b. *comb.* **burgher camp**, CONCENTRATION CAMP; also *attrib.*; **burgher duty**, military service demanded of citizens; **burgher force**, a militia or citizen army whose members could be called on to act together in their own region for purposes of mutual defence (see quot. 1846).

1902 *Postmark, Middelburg* **Burgher Camp** 24 Feb. 1902 Middelburg. **1913** J. BRANDT *Petticoat Commando* 151 In the Burgher Camps Department, as the headquarters of the Concentration Camps in Pretoria were called, there were men at work for us too, men who by smuggling through statistics of the high mortality and other facts connected with the Camps, strengthened the hands of the pro-Boers in England. **1934** N. DEVITT *Mem. of Magistrate* 44 A mile or so out of town was the large burgher camp. *Ibid.* 45 One day Lord Kitchener rode unexpectedly up to the gate of the burgher camp hospital accompanied by two of his staff. **1832** *Graham's Town Jrnl* 31 Aug. 140 The Path maker, an officer never above the rank of a farmer, and whose services are gratuitously exacted, under the head of **Burgher duty.** *a*1858 J. GOLDSWAIN *Chron.* (1949) II. 9 When we are caled out to do burger dutey we have to find our hone Horses & guns etc. etc. and we are paid when caled out on burger dutey by the hour at one shilling and three pence pur houer for the first day and one fifth less for every day that we might be out at the same time. **1881** *Encycl. Britannica* XII. 313 They complained that while doing burgher duty he had not received the same treatment as others who were serving in defence of the colony. **1846** J.W. APPLEYARD *War of Axe* (1971) 40, I received a letter from Mr. Shaw stating that war was decided upon in Cape Town, and that an express had gone out to the Country districts to call out the **Burgher force.** **1846** [see COMMANDANT sense 1]. **1846** J. HARE in *Imp. Blue Bks* Command Paper 786–1847, 108 The question of calling out the Burgher force to act in their own wards for the mutual defence of their neighbours I did not hesitate a moment about. **1850** J.E. METHLEY *New Col. of Port Natal* 36 At Pietermaritzburg many of the respectable inhabitants are formed into a burgher force, on the same principle, and similar in equipment to the English yeomanry. **1851** T. SHONE Diary. 5 Mar., The news in the paper is that the army and the Burgher force beats all they come nigh. **1877** R.M. BALLANTYNE *Settler & Savage* 347 Soon after the arrival of Colonel Smith, burgher forces were collected. **1877** C. ANDREWS Reminiscences of Kafir War 1834–5. 7 Grahamstown was thronged with Hottentot battalions, Burgher forces from Graaf Reinet and other districts, and troops of the line. **1976** D.M.B. PRESTON *Story of Frontier Town* 10 In 1828 the Fetcani were defeated and dispersed by a Burgher force under Colonel Somerset at Umtata.

4. *hist.* An (Afrikaans) citizen of a Boer Republic. Cf. UITLANDER *n.* sense b.

1882 C.L. NORRIS-NEWMAN *With Boers in Tvl* 48 He had never been able to check the constant warfare going on between the Basutos on the one hand, and the Baralong and the Burghers on the other. **1895** [see UITLANDER *adj.* sense 1]. **1897** F.R. STATHAM *S. Afr. as It Is* 19 During the thirty-five years of Panda's chieftainship, from 1838 to 1873, the Zulus and the burghers of the South African Republic lived on reasonably good terms. **1900** H.C. HILLEGAS *Oom Paul's People* 148 The difficulty with the Englishmen here is that they want to be burghers and at the same time retain their English citizenship. **1920** R.Y. STORMBERG *Mrs Pieter de Bruyn* 51, I wonder how it is that, his father being a Republican burgher and his mother a Dutchwoman, he can carry so much of an Imperial air. **1936** *Cambridge Hist. of Brit. Empire* VIII. 573 As 1896 wore on into 1897, bad times frayed the nerves of all, burghers, Uitlander rank and file, and magnates alike. **1970** *Cape Times* 19 May, Jack Hindon, a Scotsman, came to South Africa .. and became a fully fledged and enfranchised *burger* of the Transvaal Republic in 1895. **1971** H. ZEEDERBERG *Veld Express* 138 Vague rumours of unrest among the natives in Mashonaland had reached the Republic, but the burghers were not particularly interested. **1982** *Sunday Times* 4 Apr. 23 Plans are afoot to commemorate these and other Anglo-Boer War heroes. At an unveiling ceremony last week, maquettes of the 'banneling', the 'burgher', the 'bittereinder', and the 'agterryer', were shown.

Hence (sense 4) **burgheress** *n. hist.*, a female burgher; (senses 1 a and 2) **burghership** *n.*, the status or condition, rights, and privileges of citizenship; (senses 1 a and 3) **burghery** *n. hist.*, burghers collectively.

1807 Earl of Caledon in G.M. Theal *Rec. of Cape Col.* (1900) VI. 244 Letters of Burghership. 1815 *Afr. Court Calendar* Letters of burghership R100,00. 1858 'F' in *Cape Monthly Mag.* III. Mar. 148 Redress sometimes came for the complaints .. of the Burghery, or of the subordinate servants. 1861 P.B. Borcherds *Auto-Biog. Mem.* 25 The next day the signal guns were fired .. to call upon the militia (burgery) to proceed with all speed to Cape Town, in order to assist the garrison in the defence of the colony. 1861 E. *Prov. Yr Bk & Annual Register* 41 By Act 8, 1856, of the Colonial Parliament, the privilege of buying landed property has been conceded to foreigners without the possession of a deed of Burghership. 1865 E. *Prov. Herald* 27 July 3 These Fingoes were required to take out certificates of burghership which would effectually protect them from the stringent application of the pass-system. 1901 C.G. Dennison *Fight to Finish* (1904) 90 Dear burgheresses, pray for your husbands, encourage them to go to the front.

burghermeester's chair var. *burgermeester's chair* (see BURGERMEESTER sense 2).

Burgherraad var. BURGERRAAD.

burgher right *n. phr. Hist.* Also **burgeright**. [tr. S. Afr. Du. *burgherreg*, *burgher* see BURGHER senses 1 a and 2 + *reg* right.] The status of citizenship, with all its attendant rights and privileges. Also *attrib.*

1820 G. Barker Journal. 17 Nov., A number of the people came and complained that I witheld from them their baptismal cirtificates, and by that means prevented them from claiming their Burger right, or Citizenship. 1877 A. Jeppe *Tvl Bk Almanac & Dir.* (1976) 36 Burgher Right and Franchise of the White Population — Persons born in the State who have reached the age of 21, or who have resided in the State for one year and are in possession of fixed property have the burgher right, which can also be purchased on payment of £7 10s. on arrival in the country. 1899 *Volkstem* 5 Oct. 1, Ward no. 1 Burgherright Erven, running from Scheidings Street. 1899 [see SMEERLAP]. 1926 P.W. Laidler *Tavern of Ocean* 23 From time to time the Council granted burgher rights to those who desired to settle in the country, and to Company's servants taking their discharge. 1926 M. Nathan *S. Afr. from Within* 236 Law No. 3 of 1885 was passed, whereby they were prevented from obtaining burgher rights, were forbidden to acquire real property, and were to reside in definite localities assigned to them by the Government. 1974 A.P. Cartwright *By Waters of Letaba* 43 The founding fathers of the old Republic, the Voortrekkers, were each entitled to take up a farm. This 'burgher-right', as it was called, entitled a man to 'not more than' 6 000 morgen.

burgher senate *n. phr. Hist.* Also with initial capitals. [tr. S. Afr. Du. *burghersenaat*, *burgher* see BURGHER senses 1 a and 2 + *senaat* senate.]

a. A council of up to seven citizens responsible for civic affairs, instituted by the Dutch East India Company at the Cape and dissolved in 1827; BURGERRAAD sense 1. Also *attrib.* See also BURGHER sense 1.

1796 J.H. Craig in G.M. Theal *Rec. of Cape Col.* (1897) I. 402 A letter I wrote to the Burgher Senate and to the Landrosts in the country districts. 1801 H.H. Smith in *Afr. Court Calendar*, Burgher Senate, A. Fleck Esqre President, H.A. Truter Esqre, P.L. Cloete Esqre, O.U. Bergh Esqre, I.F. van Reenen Esqre, I.I. Vos Esqre, Mr D.P. Haupt — Secretary. 1807 *Ibid.*, A Town-house, in which the Burgher Senate, or the Council of Burghers meet for transacting business relative to the interior police of the town. 1819 *Ibid.* 65 Wardmasters shall take care .. that there are no gambling, nor any other houses, inconsistent with morality and good order; and on discovering such to exist they shall report this same to the Fiscal and to the President of the Burgher Senate. 1822 W.J. Burchell *Trav.* I. 73 The Stadhuis, or Burgher Senate-house, is a large, handsome building, appropriated to the transacting of public business of a civic nature. 1827 *Reports of Commissioners upon Affairs at Cape of G.H.* I. 48 The burger senate originated in the appointment of two persons by the Commissioner Van Goens in the year 1657, to deliberate in criminal matters. 1861 P.B. Borcherds *Auto-Biog. Mem.* 1 The widow of Petrus Johannes de Wit, formerly a member of the court of matrimonial and petty civil cases, orphan board, and burgher senate. 1960 M. Muller *Art Past & Present* 112 The *Michaelis Gallery* in Greenmarket Square was the old Burgher Watch House, built in 1755. Later it became the meeting-place of the Burgher Senate. 1965 A. Gordon-Brown *S. Afr. Heritage* I. 14 It housed the watch until 1796 when it became the council chamber of the Burgher Senate.

b. *transf.* The building in which this council met.

1920 R. Juta *Tavern* 20 Georgiana, who had stopped behind at the Cape at her express desire, had come down to the Burgher Senate. 1951 L.G. Green *Grow Lovely* 65 Cape Town has often had to defend its Parade vigorously against encroachments. The Burgher Senate was busy resisting building schemes two and a half centuries ago.

Hence **burgher senator** *n. phr.*, a member of this senate; **burgher councillor**, see BURGHER sense 1 b.

1796 J.H. Craig in S.D. Naudé *Kaapse Plakkaatboek Deel V* 24 The Burgher Senators shall employ such a number of watchmen as the extension of the town and necessity requires.

burgomeester's -, **burgomaster's chair** varr. *burgermeester's chair* (see BURGERMEESTER sense 2).

buriyani var. BREYANI.

burn *v. trans.* and *intrans.* [Special sense of general Eng.] To eradicate old grass from the open countryside by controlled burning, usually once a year after the first spring rainfall, as part of an overall system of grazing management. See also BRAND sense 2 a, *veld burning* (VELD sense 5).

In *Austral., N.Z.*, and *N. Amer. Eng.*, 'burn off'.

1812 A. Plumptre tr. H. Lichtenstein's *Trav. in Sn Afr.* (1928) I. 185 It is common to burn the lands every year, by which means they are manured, and the foundation laid for a wholesome vegetation. 1832 *Graham's Town Jrnl* 30 Mar. 54 The growth of the grass is so rapid, that what was burned in September and October is now eight feet high. 1833 *S. Afr. Almanac & Dir.* p.xlvii, The fields should be burned this month, observing to perform this operation at times when rain may be expected. 1840 J. Collett Diary. II. 3 Mar., Burning our Grass to day (being in its present state useless). 1893 E. Nicholson in *Cape Illust. Mag.* Vol.4 No.6, 206 The Free State sheep farmers came down to burn for their winter pasture. Great patches of dead black scarred the hill sides. 1907 J.P. Fitzpatrick *Jock of Bushveld* (1909) 289 'Niggers burning on the slopes; confound them!' Francis growled. They habitually fire the grass in patches .. in order to get young grass for the winter or the early spring. 1937 *Handbk for Farmers* (Dept of Agric. & Forestry) 397 If the veld is burned when the grass is in an active state of growth deterioration is certain to result.

Hence **burn** *n.*, **burning** *vbl n.*, controlled burning; also *attrib.*

1965 D. Howell in *Farmer's Weekly* 8 Dec. 31 The pattern of treatment which today is recommended .. is a season's rest prior to burning and a swift sharp burn which should take place after the first effective spring rains of an inch. 1971 C.L. Wicht in *Std Encycl. of Sn Afr.* IV. 539 Burning must .. be carried out in accordance with a scientifically determined system, adapted to each specific veld-type, and be strictly controlled. 1974 C.R. Van der Merwe in *Ibid.* X. 45 There are cases .. where a certain amount of burning is necessary for proper veld management, but then it should be carried out .. in spring, shortly after the first good rains. 1993 D. & P. Irwin *Field Guide to Natal Drakensberg* 2.5 Research .. has included the monitoring of grassland species composition under a variety of different burning schemes. The results have been used to formulate the burning programmes which are currently in practice.

burri-burri see quot. 1925 at BORRIE.

Buschie *n. obs.* [Formed on Du. *boschjesman* (see BOSJESMAN) + Eng. (informal) n.-forming suffix *-ie*.] A Khoisan bandit. See also KHOISAN sense 1. Cf. BUSHY.

1731 G. Medley tr. P. Kolb's *Present State of Cape of G.H.* I. 90 A Sort of *Hottentot Banditti* ... These are Troops of abandon'd Wretches, who finding the Laws and Customs of their Countries to be too great Restraints upon their Inclinations, repair to the Mountains ... They are called *Buschies*, or High-way Men. *Ibid.* 269 The honest Hottentots abhor those *Buschies*. 1936 E.C. Llewellyn *Influence of Low Dutch* 169 The early equivalent [of 'Bushman'] *Buschie* (1731), applied to a sort of Hottentot bandit, still shows the form of the Du. *boschjesman*.

busch tea var. BUSH TEA.

bush *n.*[1] and *adj.*[1] [Eng., influenced by S. Afr. Du. *bosch* and its senses, see BOSCH.]

A. *n.*

1.a. *noncount.* The thick vegetation covering any uncultivated area; BOSCH sense 1.

[1698 see BUSHMAN sense 1 a. 1731 see BUSH-CAT.] 1827 T. Philipps *Scenes & Occurrences* 80 Our road lay principally through bush. [*Note*] A term used by the inhabitants and very appropriate, for it is neither timber nor brushwood but a growth peculiar to this country. 1835 C.L. Stretch Journal. 29 Mar., They were carelessly sitting down near some bush. The enemy, perceiving their negligence, effected their destruction with very little trouble. 1843 R. Godlonton in J.C. Chase *Cape of G.H.* (1967) 46 The Fish River here pursues its course through a deep but broad valley in some places greatly encumbered with bush. 1853 F.P. Fleming *Kaffraria* 32 Those parts of Kaffraria, which are clothed by nature with this so called 'bush', are almost impervious to European invaders. 1860 D.L.W. Stainbank Diary. (Killie Campbell Africana Library KCM8680) 2 Feb., 2 Kafirs making path through bush to top of hill where I intend building. 1882 O.E.A. Schreiner *Diamond Fields.* 83 Right down to the walls & the little hill behind, is all covered with bush, right to the very top. 1882 J. Nixon *Among Boers* 147 Soon after inspanning, we emerged onto a plain covered with our old friend 'bush' instead of grass. 1964 A. Rothmann *Elephant Shrew* 33 There are miles and miles of bush, a dense, impenetrable mass of num-num, thorn bushes, taaibos, gnarled gwharrie-trees. 1972 *Grocott's Mail* 12 May 4 Medium-sized building plot, preferably with some natural bush. 1991 F.G. Butler *Local Habitation* 52 Interesting things were always being done, such as bush being cleared for new lands, sheep-shearing, harvesting, and above all, dam-building.

b. *Attrib.* and *comb.* **bushfire**, cf. *veldfire* (see VELD sense 2 b); **bush hat**, a military-style cloth hat with a narrow, floppy brim; **bush jacket**, a belted cotton jacket, often khaki, usu. with buttoned pockets; also called *safari jacket* sense (a), see SAFARI; **bush knife**, a large, heavy hunting-knife; **bush pay** *hist.*, a special allowance paid to soldiers on *border duty* (see BORDER sense 3 b); **bush soil**, (usu. in the Eastern Cape) the dark, friable soil found in bush country and valued by gardeners.

1911 *Farmer's Weekly* 4 Oct. 126 Farmers are beginning to complain of drought, and the number of **bush fires** that have raged in the vicinity of Grahamstown indicates that the country is getting dry. 1975 *E. Prov. Herald* 13 Nov. 3 Firemen .. were busy this morning trying to prevent a large bushfire which is burning in the Chatty River Valley near the old Uitenhage road from spreading to a nearby house. 1988 *Cape Times* 11 Jan. 7 A raging bushfire at Leeukoppie near Llandudno caused fearful home owners to start evacuating their homes on Saturday afternoon. 1961 D. Bee *Children of Yesterday* 211 They entered through the open door and Nigel removed the beloved **bush-hat** from his head. **1987** *Personality* 7 Oct. 16 Pieter Groenewald still wears his olive-green military bush hat when he doses the sheep or inspects for wheat rust. **1990** *Sunday Times* 14 Oct. 12 Their placards .. were also messages of hate. 'The first kaffir in my school I will shoot dead,' said one, carried by a youngster sporting a bush hat. **1966** F.G. BUTLER *S. of Zambezi* 27, I called a full indaba of headmen and of foremen, sat like Solomon in my canvas chair between them, in a clean **bush-jacket** and best topee, with a drunken interpreter swaying behind my throne. **1978** D. SMUTS in *Fair Lady* 19 July 43 A big black woman in a white bush jacket stood up at a poetry reading in Constantia one night and brought the house down. **1988** M.M. CARLIN in *Frontline* Apr.-May 15 Kenneth Kaunda, in his early days wore a bush jacket with a spotted scarf, exactly like a Northern Rhodesian farmer. **1971** *Daily News* 15 Feb. About 1 000 tribesmen armed with battleaxes, spears and **bush knives**. **1983** B. MASEKO in *Staffrider* Vol.5 No.3, 2 Before the van came to a halt, the two men, bush knives in their hands, alighted. The cyclist saw the bush knives, abandoned his bicycle and ran for dear life. **1986** *Daily Dispatch* 26 Feb. 4 Charges include .. attempting to murder a man with sticks, bush knives and a firearm. **1979** *E. Prov. Herald* 26 Oct. 1 Some of the soldiers complained to reporters that they were owed '**bush pay**' (border camp allowance) and extra leave. **1981** *Cape Times* 27 June 7 He will receive not only his full military pay .. but also the standard SADF camp allowance — commonly known as 'bush pay' — of several rands a day which is paid for service within the operational area. [**1982** A. VILJOEN in *E. Prov. Herald* 27 Aug. 1 The Zimbabwean government had the South African force numbers, ranks, salaries and bush allowances of the three white soldiers killed in south-eastern Zimbabwe last week.] **1974** *Informant, Grahamstown* **Bush soil** is soil that you get for your garden. You get it from the bush. It's very dark. **1991** *E. Prov. Herald* 7 Feb. 15 (*advt*) Bush soil: For better clean quality bush soil phone the oldest name in the game.

2.a. Pl. **-es**, or (rarely) unchanged. A forest or thicket; BOSCH sense 2.

A sense formerly found in *Brit. Eng.* but now *obs.*

[**1823** G. BARKER Journal. 7 Dec., We then sat down to a cold dinner, in a bush, about 120 [persons].] **1829** W. SHAW Diary. 14 May, The Cwanguha is a high point of land, on the summit of which is a rather extensive timber Bush. **1833** *Graham's Town Jrnl* 7 Feb. 3 One would suppose that a bush in which flocks of sheep and herds of cattle are taken care of, there must be space sufficient for men to pass. **1857** R. GRAY *Jrnl of Visitation to Diocese of Grahamstown* 15 We proceeded on our way, passing by, shortly after leaving the Fort, Burn's Hill, a dense bush close by the Keiskamma. **1860** W. SHAW *Story of my Mission* 401 The smaller bush or woods, found in all parts of the country, supply all their wants for fuel, and for implements of war and agriculture. *a***1867** C.J. ANDERSSON *Notes of Trav.* (1875) 318 We only passed two insignificant bushes. In traversing the last wood, which offered no impediment to our vehicle, I observed the singular fact that nearly every tree of a certain species was all but destroyed. **1871** J. MCKAY *Reminisc.* 15 We had arrived at a path or road in a dense bush, through which a wagon might with difficulty pass. **1888** *Castle Line Handbk & Emigrant's Guide* 69 The soil .. having been covered to a large extent by a thick forest of trees (usually termed 'bush') for many years, is in parts richly charged with decayed vegetable matter. **1971** *Rand Daily Mail* 27 July 5 Six safes and a stolen light delivery van had been found by the police in a bush near a Pretoria African township. **1991** F.G. BUTLER *Local Habitation* 52 There was the silhouette of Rhebokberg and the tree-lined course of the Great Fish River, the dam, the poplar bush and the lands.

b. An element in place names, esp. in the Eastern Cape, e.g. *Assegai Bush, Fish River Bush, Kowie Bush*. See also BOSCH sense 3 b.

3. *noncount.* Usu. ***the bush***: undeveloped, largely uninhabited country; country in its natural state. Also *attrib.* See also BUNDU, BUSHVELD sense 2, VELD sense 2 a i.

Used also in *Austral. Eng.* (1790).

1829 C. ROSE *Four Yrs in Sn Afr.* 146 When the wife of a Kaffer dies, he becomes unclean, leaves the kraal, and lives in the bush for a certain time. **1841** B. SHAW *Memorials* 247 He used to drive us into the bush, but to-day he is come to speak God's word to us. **1845** J.M. BOWKER *Speeches & Sel.* (1864) 173 The invincible might of British troops, supported by the courage of a colonial population accustomed to conflict in the bush. **1852** M.B. HUDSON *S. Afr. Frontier Life* 151 The Seventy-fourth, raw to the bush, made a bungle. **1877** R.M. BALLANTYNE *Settler & Savage* 84 The prospect, as I've heard father say to mother .. is a life in the bush — by which I suppose he means the bushes. **1933** W.H.S. BELL *Bygone Days* 36 The bush had a great attraction for us. Whenever our other duties permitted we made tracks for the bush. **1944** J. MOCKFORD *Here Are S. Africans* 25 After spending a night or two in the bush, where wild beasts glared and growled, they were glad to return to the bosom of the van Riebeek family. **1976** S. CLOETE *Chetoko* 9 The scene was in a way symbolic: the old Africa meeting the products of civilization on the floor of a store in the bush. **1991** J. SHEPHERD-SMITH in *Sunday Tribune* 19 May 5 The bush camp is only for bush purists. Toilet facilities are a toilet roll, a spade and a clearing far from the campsite. **1994** P. GIRD in *Sunday Times* 18 Sept. 3 She wants to come back. She fell in love with the bush.

4. Esp. in traditional Xhosa society: in the expression ***to go to the bush***, to take part in the traditional period of initiation during which young black men withdraw from their communities after undergoing circumcision. See also *circumcision school* (CIRCUMCISION sense 2).

1976 M. THOLO in C. Hermer *Diary of Maria Tholo* (1980) 22 We saw a big group of youths going to the bush up the road carrying loads of bushes and sticks like they do when they are going to slaughter and use a lot of fire. **1980** E. JOUBERT *Poppie Nongena* 41 Three of the boys went together to do abakwetha. They go into the bush to do the ritual, and that is why we call it going to the bush for short.

B. *adj. derog.*

1. Inferior; rough-and-ready; uncivilized.

Not exclusively *S. Afr. Eng.*

1974 *Sunday Express* 30 June 20 She has stamped out crime to the zing of a flaying sjambok and the rule of her dreaded makgotlas — unofficial tribal-type bush courts. **1982** *E. Prov. Herald* 17 June 1 He had to be shown that the law would not tolerate his kind of 'bush justice', two Grahamstown judges said yesterday. **1982** *Reader* Dec. 7 They sometimes bring people to their own courts called the 'bush courts'. People who are found guilty get beaten in public. **1983** *Pace* Oct. 52 The President has found .. a politically-aware community that calls his Zwelitsha establishment a 'Bush Government.' **1983** F.G. BUTLER *Bursting World* 269 The wind had blown my bush-carpentry to pieces, and sleet was screaming through the window. **1986** M. MABUSELA in *E. Prov. Herald* 20 June 3 A New Brighton 'bush mechanic' was found guilty .. of stealing an assortment of car tools, worth R5 200. **1987** 'A. AMAPHIXIPHIXI' in *Frontline* May 27 Many felt strongly that giving in to bush discipline would degrade that status of the committees and pave the way for more lawlessness and anarchy. **1988** J. KHUMALO in *Pace* June 8 Eminent scientists are .. baffled by WHO's curious romance with witchcraft. To them working alongside these Bush Doctors is infra dig. **1988** *R.S.A. Policy Review* (Bureau of Information) Vol.1 No.1, 46 Black educationalists' fears that differentiated curricula could mean inferior apartheid or bush education.

2. Special collocations. **bush college, bush university**: *derog.*, any of several universities founded by the government for exclusive use by blacks, 'coloureds', and Indians, in terms of Act 45 of 1959 which made non-racial universities illegal. See also TRIBAL COLLEGE.

1976 A.P. BRINK *Mapmakers* (1983) 140 The 'black' universities, where libraries are under strict control and students constantly surveilled by Security Police, and where academic qualifications are often secondary to political convictions, are generally referred to as '**Bush Colleges**'. **1978** *Sunday Times* 26 Mar. 12 Blacks had entered universities like his, which had been called 'bush colleges', with resentment because they had been 'forced' to go to them. **1983** *University Apartheid* (Nusas) (*pamphlet*), The Extension of University Education Act .. provided for the complete segregation of universities by establishing separate campuses, under strict state control, for black students. Today, the campuses of Fort Hare, Turfloop, Western Cape and Durban-Westville, known as 'bush colleges', fall into this category. **1987** J. GERWEL in *New Nation* 5 Mar. 19 UWC was created as a bush college under apartheid, but it has managed to outgrow this and become an open university. **1988** M. FAIRALL in *Fair Lady* 3 Feb. 58 Then came her years at the 'bush college' on Durban's Salisbury Island, .. predecessor of the Indian Campus of the University of Durban-Westville. **1988** G. MOKAE in *Pace* Apr. 62 When the Medical University of Southern Africa (Medunsa) was started in 1978, cynics saw it as another political still birth of apartheid .. a 'bush college'. **1991** P. MAURICE in *Weekly Mail* 28 Mar. 33 Sached .. established itself in 1959 by offering assistance to about 60 students who refused to go to 'bush' colleges. **1992** *New Nation* 7 Aug. 9 The process of transforming South Africa's black universities — once disparagingly referred to as bush colleges — is proceeding with vigour. Several .. are preparing themselves for a new role in a democratic society. This includes breaking away from their apartheid 'masters' and forging much closer relationships with both the local and the international community. [**1983** *Pace* Dec. 140 If they could not get a place at Wits or some other established universities, they would sacrifice their future academic careers rather than go to 'those **bush university**-colleges'.] **1987** *New Nation* 10 Sept. 5 Despite mass protest and huge international support, the 'open' universities were closed and the bush universities were established. **1988** *Drum* Sept. 10 Who's fooling whom at this bush university? .. The never never world of the self created Moretele University in Hammanskraal, Bophuthatswana. **1991** *Weekly Mail* 24 May 2 Leaving school to become a teacher of mathematics and science, he returned to his studies .. when he enrolled for a BSc at a 'bush' university, Turfloop.

3. In the v. phr. intrans. ***to go bush***, to lose the veneer of civilization by living in the bush or country.

1978 G. LANGLEY in *Sunday Times* 2 Apr. (Mag. Sect.) 2 Memories of earlier days, when he was young and strong, riding the hills bareback, following the cattle as they wandered, going 'bush' and sleeping rough like the pioneers of old. **1982** J. PLATTER in *Signature* July 25 Many of them are kind enough to .. patiently bring me up to date on the state of the world. But I sense their sympathy for one who has gone mildly 'bush' in the four years I've been a wine farmer. **1985** *Style* Oct. 52 The Englishman's contact with the land has always been uneasy. Some go bats. Some go bush.

Bush *adj.*[2] and *n.*[2] [fr. BUSHMAN.]

A. *adj.* Of or pertaining to the SAN people; frequently an element in special collocations, as **Bush-boy**, a San boy or man, and **Bush-woman**. Cf. *Bosjes-menschen* (see BOSJESMAN sense 1).

1790 W. PATERSON *Narr. of Four Journeys* 71 An excursion to the Hantum .. called the Boshmens' Land, from its being inhabited by the Bush Hottentots .. a very different people from the other peaceable and well-disposed inhabitants of this region. **1821** E.S. PIGOT Journal. 45 The Bush boy took off all the gentlemen; we danced more, then he took off the Ladies, made us laugh very much. **1824** W.J. BURCHELL *Trav.* II. 96 Another of the Bushwomen complained that this *baas* had compelled her son to remain in his service against his wish. *Ibid.* II. 128 The people were unable to proceed any farther, and .. were of opinion that the Bushboy was dying. **1828** T. PRINGLE *Ephemerides* 85 Afar in the Desert I love to ride, With the silent Bush-boy alone by my side. **1829** C. ROSE *Four Yrs in Sn Afr.* 105 In his time, the Bush people were still numerous, scattered over the country in small parties. **1835** A. STEEDMAN *Wanderings* II. 22 We ..

found extremely useful the services of an active young Bush-boy, named Cupido. *a*1838 A. SMITH *Jrnl* (1975) 146 We were visited by a considerable number of Bush-women, but by no means could we succeed in getting a glimpse of their countrymen. **1841** J.E. ALEXANDER in B. Shaw *Memorials* 33 Once on a time, a certain Namacqua was travelling in the company of a Bush-woman, carrying a child on her back. **1841** B. SHAW *Memorials* 100 One man, and a poor bush-boy, died of thirst, as died also seven of their dogs. **1874** D. LIVINGSTONE *Last Jrnls* I. 89 In 1841 I saw a Bushwoman in the Cape Colony with a round stone and a hole through it. **1878** T.J. LUCAS *Camp Life & Sport* 207 The Boer, finding he had missed the cock bird, jumped into his wagon again, sending his bush-boy after the wounded female. **1887** [see AGTERRYER sense 1]. **1907** W.C. SCULLY *By Veldt & Kopje* 232 The child had been dragged out from under the flaming roof by an old Bushwoman. **1928** E.H.L. SCHWARZ *Kalahari & its Native Races* 174 In most cases .. children of Bechuana with Bushwomen remain with the former. **1955** V.M. FITZROY *Dark Bright Land* 52 At Capt. Moresby's dance last evening .. we was diverted by the performance of a half-breed bush boy. **1975** [see *Hottentot apron* (HOTTENTOT sense 6 c)]. **1991** F.G. BUTLER *Local Habitation* 191 Bored stones .. beautifully shaped by millions of years in river beds or long-since shifted shores, searched for, and found by a 'Bushman', or, more likely, Bush woman, and then patiently pierced by boring with a harder stone .. from either side.

B. *n.* A name given to the languages of the KHOISAN peoples. Also *attrib.*

1928 E.H.L. SCHWARZ *Kalahari & its Native Races* 177 Their language is sometimes Bush, but more often a jargon of Sechuana. **1977** R. ELPHICK *Kraal & Castle* 13 It is unlikely that even an approximate date for the Khoikhoi genesis can be obtained through linguistic research, even in the improbable event of a reliable glottochronological date being obtained for the divergence of proto-Khoikhoi from Central 'Bush'. **1985** G.T. NURSE et al. *Peoples of Sn Afr.* 106 The !Kung are the principal speakers of what used to, and may yet again, be called the 'Northern Bush' languages. *Ibid.* 108 The Nharo .. are speakers of a 'Central Bush' or Tshu-Khwe language, one of the Hottentot (Khoi) language family ... The 'Southern Bush' languages are spoken by the G!aokx'ate in Namibia and by the more numerous !Xo in Botswana.

bush baby *n. phr.* [See quot. 1884.] Any of the lemur-like primates of the Lorisidae, esp. *Otolemur crassicaudatus* and *Galago moholi*; NAGAPIE; NIGHT-AAPPIE; NIGHT-APE.

Some specialist sources see 'bush baby' and 'night-ape' as synonymous, referring to both local species of the Lorisidae; others advocate the use of 'night-ape' for the thick-tailed bushbaby *Otolemur crassicaudatus*, and 'bush baby' for the smaller *Galago moholi*; while yet a third view is that the 'bush baby' is *O. crassicaudatus*, and the 'night-ape' *G. moholi*. In general usage the words are used interchangeably.

1835 A. SMITH *Diary* (1940) II. 160 *Galago maholi* is the Bush Baby or nag-aapie. **1884** J.S. LITTLE *S. Afr.: Sketch Bk* I. 31 The bush baby .. resembles a monkey in its general characteristics. Its squeal is unpleasantly similar to the cry of an infant in piteous distress. **1901** A.R.R. TURNBULL *Tales from Natal* 81 The occasional cry of a bush-baby alone broke the awful silence. **1913** C. PETTMAN *Africanderisms* 98 *Bush-baby*, .. This pretty little animal is scarcely larger than a rat; it has exquisitely soft fur, large dark-brown eyes, and round erect ears. It makes an engaging pet. **1929** J. STEVENSON-HAMILTON *Low-Veld* 70 The queer little fluffy, long-tailed bush babies, with their pointed inquisitive snouts, .. spend their time amid the foliage of the largest and most dense-leafed of the evergreen trees. **1953** R. CAMPBELL *Mamba's Precipice* 140 It seemed that there was a little child sobbing in a tree to his left. It sounded almost human but he knew it must be a bush-baby or lemur. **1967** S.M.A. LOWE *Hungry Veld* 108 The sleepers stirred at the loud yell of a bush baby. 'Clap, clap, clap. Wah! wah! wah!' were the strange noises these furry, wide-eyed little creatures made. **1971** D.J. POTGIETER et al. *Animal Life in Sn Afr.* 351 There are two night-apes or bush-babies in Southern Africa, the night-ape or large grey bush-baby (*Galago crassicaudatus*) .. and the bush-baby (*Galago senegalensis*). **1983** *Nat. Geog. Mag.* Mar. 370 A nocturnal insect hunter, the big-eyed bush baby rarely leaves the trees in which it lives. **1990** SKINNER & SMITHERS *Mammals of Sn Afr. Subregion* 145 The colloquial names bushbaby for this species and night ape for the smaller species are commonly used in the Subregion.

bushbok *n. obs.* Also **bushbock**. [Part. tr. S. Afr. Du. *boschbok*, see BOSCHBOK.] BUSHBUCK. Also *attrib.*

1821 C.I. LATROBE *Jrnl of Visit* 196 The road .. led through a forest of large bushes or various kinds, among which we started .. a bushbock antelope. *a*1827 D. CARMICHAEL in W.J. Hooker *Botanical Misc.* (1831) II. 287 A sort of turban made of the skin of the *Bushbock*, and shaped like the watering-caps of our dragoons. **1850** N.J. MERRIMAN *Cape Jrnls* (1957) 230 A partridge, a pheasant, a bushbok or hare Perhaps I may add to our evening's fare. **1860** W. SHAW *Story of my Mission* 383 The spring-bok, bush-bok, hartebeest, and qwagga, were frequently met with in troops and flocks in the grassy country of the neutral territory. **1877** R.M. BALLANTYNE *Settler & Savage* 269 Advancing down the kloof .. the leopard soon came in sight of a fine bushbok ... But the bushbok was not within spring-range.

Bushboy see BUSH *adj.*[2]

bushbuck *n.* Also with initial capital. Pl. unchanged, or -s. [tr. S. Afr. Du. *boschbok*, see BOSCHBOK.] The antelope *Tragelaphus scriptus* of the Bovidae, which favours bushy terrain; the meat of this antelope; BOSCHBOK; BUSHBOK; BUSH-GOAT sense 1. Also *attrib.*

1803 J.T. VAN DER KEMP in *Trans. of Missionary Soc.* I. 440 They always cover their heads with a cap, made of the skin of an animal, which they call babala, and the Colonists bush-buck. **1832** [see BUCK *n.*[1] sense 1 b]. **1836** A.F. GARDINER *Journey to Zoolu Country* 382 We soon .. reached an inhabited district, which was first indicated by a bushbuck, almost exhausted, crossing our path. **1865** D. LIVINGSTONE *Zambesi* 343 In the mornings and evenings the pretty little bush-buck (*Tragelaphus sylvatica*) ventures .. out of the mangroves, to feed. **1896** R. WARD *Rec. of Big Game* 194 The thicket-loving Bushbuck is still to be found plentifully in the southern portions of Cape Colony, the Trans-Kei, Natal, and along the south-eastern littoral wherever bush and covert flourish. **1910** J. BUCHAN *Prester John* (1961) 42 The great sport was to stalk bush buck in the thickets, which is a game in which the hunter is at small advantage. I have been knocked down by a wounded bush-buck ram. *c*1936 *S. & E. Afr. Yr Bk & Guide* 1096 The Cape Bushbuck (*tragelaphus sylvaticus*; Dutch *boschbok*). Height about 2 feet 10 inches; weight about 100 lbs ... Horns up to 14 inches, spiral .. and rough at the base. **1951** A. ROBERTS *Mammals* 311 *Tragelaphus* ... This genus comprises the smallest members of the subfamily [*sc.* Tragelaphinae] and are known as the true Bushbucks ... They occur only where there is dense cover near water. **1986** J. CONYNGHAM *Arrowing of Cane* 51 We are .. having bushbuck for supper. **1991** *Personality* 5 Aug. 29 Too many animals suffer and die for the supposedly humane alternative of game trading ... Species that easily succumb to these stresses [*sc.* of 'unnatural confinement, unfamiliar noises, smells, extremes of temperature and hunger and thirst'] are .. reedbuck, bushbuck, red hartebeest, [etc.].

bush cart *n. phr. Hist.* [BUSH *n.*[1] sense 3 + Eng. *cart.*] A two-wheeled ox-drawn vehicle for warfare in rough terrain. Also *attrib.*

These vehicles were issued to the Army in 1936 by the Minister of Defence, Oswald Pirow, but were never used.

1943 L. SOWDEN *Union of S. Afr.* 104 No one ever called them anything but bush carts — two-wheelers, made mostly of steel, said to be uncapsizable and drawn by a pair of oxen. **1946** T. MACDONALD *Ouma Smuts* 109 Pirow .. became famous (or notorious) for his bush-cart defence system ... When Pirow showed his true colours and voted anti-war his bush-carts became a laughing stock for cartoonists and reporters. **1948** *E. Prov. Herald* 24 Jan. 3 The last seven of the bush carts ordered for the army by Mr O. Pirow .. will be sold at a War Stores Disposal Board auction ... More than 200 have already been sold and others are still being used by the U.D.F. for the carting of garbage. **1968** E.A. WALKER *Hist. of Sn Afr.* 846 Non-Europeans would surely ask what prospects of political advancement there would be for them, and fear .. that their progress was likely to be even slower than that of Pirow's famous bush-carts. **1972** L.G. GREEN *When Journey's Over* 47 Pirow's ludicrous bush carts were built in Paarl. **1984** N. ORPEN *Cape Town Rifles* 93 At solemn discussions held in the Prime Minister's office in October 1937 Mr Pirow seriously put forward the claims of .. the 'bushcart'. It was an ox-drawn tumbril-like vehicle with which all battalions were to be equipped for bush fighting.

bush-cat *n. obs.* [Prob. tr. S. Afr. Du. *boschkat*, *bosch* bush, forest + *kat* cat. See also quot. 1731.] The serval, *Felis serval* of the Felidae.

1731 G. MEDLEY tr. *P. Kolb's Present State of Cape of G.H.* II. 127 There is another sort, call'd the Bush-Cat, from its keeping mostly in Bushes and Hedges. 'Tis spotted something like a Tiger, and is the largest of all the Wild Cats in the *Cape* Countries. **1780** G. FORSTER in *Phil. Trans. of Royal Soc.* LXXI. 2 The common Bush-cat of the Cape. **1821** C.I. LATROBE *Jrnl of Visit* 358 A dragoon gave me the skin of a bush-cat .. a fierce, but beautiful animal, about three feet and a half feet long. **1860** D.L.W. STAINBANK Diary. (Killie Campbell Africana Library KCM8680) 26 Jan., A great many fowls have been taken off by the bush cats out of the hen-house.

Bushesman var. BUSHMAN.

bush-goat *n. obs.* [BUSH *n.*[1] sense 1 a + *goat* tr. Du. *bok* goat, buck.]

1. BUSHBUCK.

1865 *Athenaeum* (U.K.) No.1948, 279 Dr. Gray gave notice of the skull of a new species of Bush Goat, proposed to be called *Cephalophus longiceps*.

2. [See quot. 1908.] The warbler *Camaroptera brachyura* of the Sylviidae.

In G.L. Maclean's *Roberts' Birds of Sn Afr.* (1993), the name 'bleating warbler' is used for this species.

1908 HAAGNER & IVY *Sketches* 79 This Warbler is called the Bush-goat on account of the plaintive goat-like call to which the bird gives utterance. **1931** R.C. BOLSTER *Land & Sea Birds* 139 *Green-backed Bush Warbler*, .. Glass-eye, .. Bush Goat, Tailor Bird. **1936** E.L. GILL *First Guide to S. Afr. Birds* 63 *Greenbacked Bush-Warbler*, .. The name 'Bush-goat' refers to its bleating call-note. **1937** M. ALSTON *Wanderings* 221 The green-backed bush-warbler, .. the little bird known as the 'bush-goat' in Natal, because the note he utters might easily be mistaken for that of a goat kid.

bush lory *n. phr. Obs.* Also **bush lori**, **bush louri**, etc. [Calque formed on S. Afr. Du. *boschloerie*, see BOSCH and LOERIE.] The *Narina trogon* (see NARINA *n.*[2]), *Apaloderma narina*. Cf. LOERIE.

1835 A. STEEDMAN *Wanderings* I. 189 Here also the bush-lori, as it sat upon the branch of some umbrageous tree in lonely solitude, uttered its deep and melancholy note. **1867** E.L. LAYARD *Birds of S. Afr.* 61 *Apaloderma Narina*, .. *Bushloorie* of Colonists ... Found throughout forests and wooded kloofs in all the eastern portions of the colony. About the Knysna it is scarce; but wherever found it exhibits the same shy creeping habits. **1897** H.A. BRYDEN *Nature & Sport* 93 In our deepest and bushiest kloof another very perfect bird of plumage crept secretly about the thickets. This was the bush lory (*Trogon narina*), a rare bird, whose wonderful scheme of colour — green and brightest carmine — made one burn to possess it. **1908** 'AL FRESCO' in *E. London Dispatch* 4 Dec. 4 Who does not know the raucous call of the bush-lourie?

bush louse *n. phr. Obs.* exc. *hist.* [Calque formed on S. Afr. Du. *boschluis*, *bosch* see BOSCH + *luis* tick.] BUSH-TICK.

1821 C.I. LATROBE *Jrnl of Visit* 526 Bushlouse, resembling the *Acarius ricinus*. **1822** [see RHINOCEROS BIRD]. **1838** J.E. ALEXANDER *Exped. into Int.* I. 192 A troublesome and small red bodied tormentor with eight legs, called a bush louse. **1850** C.W. POSSELT *Zulu Companion* 10 Take off [*sc.* from the horses] the bush-lice, and kill them. **1882** S. HECKFORD *Lady Trader in Tvl* 9 The common domestic insect of this part of the world, namely, the 'tick' or 'bush-louse', as it is called by the Boers. **1973** O.H. SPOHR tr. *F. Krauss's Trav. Jrnl* 62, I first had to undress and brush my whole body to free myself from the ticks, ixodes, called bushlice by the Boers.

Bushman *n.* Also **Bushesman**. [tr. Du. *Bosjesman*, see BOSJESMAN. See also quot. 1841.]

1.a. SAN sense 1. Also *attrib.*

See note at SAN sense 1.

1698 W. DAMPIER *New Voy. round World* II. 108 A small Nation of Savage People, called by our English *Wild Bushmen*; that live in Caves and in holes of Rocks ... They are of low stature, tawny colour'd, with crisped Hair. **1804** R. RENSHAW *Voy. to Cape of G.H.* 19 This dignity .. must be acquired by feats of courage .. ; a prince must have killed a lion, a bear and a Bosjesman, or (as we say) Bushman. **1826** G. BARKER Journal. 7 Sept., The Sum of 64 Rds 4 Sk collected for the Bushmen at Philippolis under the instruction of Mr Clark. **1835** A. STEEDMAN *Wanderings* I. 147 The term Bushmen, or Bosjesmen, has been applied to these people by the European Colonists, in consequence of their wandering habits of life. **1841** B. SHAW *Memorials* 27 The race of people called Bushmen, are thus designated from the place of their residence, which is among the bushes; or from the concealed manner in which they make an attack either to kill or plunder. *Ibid.* 30 The Bushmen neither cultivate the ground nor breed cattle, but for *animal food* are dependant upon the chase or theft. **1843** *Cape of G.H. Almanac & Annual Register* 430 In a few years the race of Bushmen will be extinct, not simply by death, but by amalgamation with other and more useful tribes of natives in the Colony. **1856** *Ibid.* (Annual Advertiser) 73 Kafir Karosses and Assegais, Bushmans Bows and poisoned arrows and numerous other specimens of African curiosities. **1876** F. BOYLE *Savage Life* 3 The diamond country was haunted by the dreaded Bushmen or Bosjesmen, and kindred tribes, whose poisoned arrows flew unseen by night against every intruder. **1882** C.L. NORRIS-NEWMAN *With Boers in Tvl* 20 The nomad Bushmen, the original inhabitants of the soil, were either obliged to leave it, being robbed of all they possessed by the stronger nations, sought the protection of the new-comers, or relapsed entirely into a wild life, being hunted and killed wherever and whenever found. **1911** D.B. HOOK *'Tis but Yesterday* 43 A Bushman trooper laughingly imitating the ferocity of the little swordsman in leather 'crackers,' who rode at him like the very devil! **1928** C.H.L. HAHN in *Native Tribes of S.W. Afr.* 82 The Hottentots, Hereros and Ovambos state that on their arrival the Bushmen were found in occupation and that the latter must have been living here ever since the creation of man. **1936** *Cambridge Hist. of Brit. Empire* VIII. 20 The Bushmen are not mentioned in the Cape Records as a separate people until about 1685. In general the early settlers made no attempt to distinguish them clearly from the Hottentots ... The Bushmen are typically short in stature, averaging about five feet, with slender limbs, small hands and feet, and poorly developed bodies. **1950** J. SACHS in B. Sachs *Herman Charles Bosman* (1971) 164 Bushman art .. shows affinities to oriental art where colour is used for decorative rather than realistic purposes. **1971** [see FIELD COMMANDANT]. **1984** *Evening Post* 22 Aug. 4 The role of Bushman women, whose husbands were in the army, had also undergone considerable changes. **1989** *E. Prov. Herald* 27 Dec. 10 As to why Bushmen should be called San, these people do not possess a common language, nor a single name for themselves ... We might as well use the name the Khoi folk used. **1990** W. STEENKAMP in *Frontline* Dec. 19 At least two of my ancestors had their lives saved by Bushmen, and I object to 'San', which means 'robber'. It's a hell of a label to hang on an innocent people who were the original South Africans.

b. *comb.* **Bushman bells**, see quot. 1913; **Bushman painting**, a rock painting made with various natural pigments, and believed to have had religious significance; **Bushman's bottom**, see quot. 1969; **Bushman's potato**, (*a*) see quot. 1886; (*b*) see quot. 1982.

1905 G.W. STOW *Native Races of S. Afr.* 110 The last instruments we shall notice were those which have been termed **'Bushman bells.'** **1913** C. PETTMAN *Africanderisms* 99 *Bushman bells*, Hollow spheres made of skin with small stones inside; large ones were fastened by the Bushmen to the upper arm and shoulders, while smaller ones were fastened on the belt and worn round their waists at dances. The noise they make is like peas in a bladder. **1883** O.E.A. SCHREINER *Story of Afr. Farm* 11 They sat under a shelving rock, on the surface of which were still visible some old **Bushman-paintings**, their red and black pigments having been preserved through long years from wind and rain by the overhanging ledge. **1905** W. ANDERSON in Flint & Gilchrist *Science in S. Afr.* 269 It is .. often very difficult to distinguish the authentic Bushman paintings from the reproduced copies of later days. **1946** M.S. GEEN *Making of Union of S. Afr.* 212 It is almost impossible to estimate the age of the Bushman paintings with any degree of accuracy. **1973** A.R. WILLCOX in *Std Encycl. of Sn Afr.* IX 73 The rock paintings of Southern Africa are generally called 'Bushman' paintings, and it is certain that most of them were the work of the Bushmen. **1989** S. VAN DER TOORN in *Motorist* Nov. 21 Stick figures, elongated eland, bows and arrows. The legacy of Bushmen paintings provide a fragile link with our past. **1969** J.M. WHITE *Land God Made in Anger* 106 There are dozens of genera of mesembryanthemums .. and the genus which is most commonly met with in the northern Namib is *Lithops*, known to the Afrikaners as **Bushman's Bottom**. **1886** G.A. FARINI *Through Kalahari Desert* 106 The **'Bushman's potato,'** a bulbous plant, with green leaves spotted with brown, which contained a good deal of water. I tasted the root, and found it a little bitter, but not unpleasant. **1982** FOX & NORWOOD YOUNG *Food from Veld* 232 Fungi *Terfezia claveryi*, .. Common names: English — *Bushman potato, Kalahari truffle, truffle* ... In size and colour these truffles resemble potatoes and they have been recorded in dry and sandy localities between the northern Cape and the Mediterranean.

2. SAN sense 2. Also *attrib.*

1835 W.B. BOYCE in A. Steedman *Wanderings* II. 280 One of these men interpreted my interpreter's Caffre into the Bushman language, and, for the first time, one hundred and twenty of these wanderers heard the words of everlasting life. **1850** J.W. APPLEYARD *Kafir Lang.* 15 *The Bushman family* includes the several dialects which are spoken by the wandering tribes called *Bushmen*. **1862** W.H.I. BLEEK *Comparative Grammar* 1 The *Bushman* tongue is as yet too insufficiently known to allow us to assign it to its proper place in a general classification of languages. **1869** — in R. Noble *Cape & its People* 277 Many nouns in Bushman vary in their terminations according to their position or use. **1874** J.M. ORPEN in *Folklore* (1919) XXX. 146 He sent another bird, the tinktinki .. -qinqininyq in Bushman. **1908** — *Reminisc.* (1964) 21 The Bushman language is quite full of sounds of unique character, which we call clicks, and queer combinations of explosive sounds and deep gutterals. **1923** D.F. BLEEK *Mantis & his Friends* Intro., This volume appears in English only, but I intend publishing a small edition of the same tales in Bushman as soon as possible. **1951** [see GNU *n.*[1] sense a]. **1960** *Times* (U.K.) 31 May (S. Afr. Suppl.) p.xv, Afrikaans also borrowed from .. the Hottentot and Bushman tongue. **1973** *Sunday Times* 27 May 4 When enunciated with the appropriate clicks this word amounts to an emphatic negative in the Bushman language. **1980** *Daily Dispatch* 24 July 7 Bushman Bible may be doomed ... Tsumkwe Kung, the language of Rev Weich's translations is one of three main branches of the Bushman language. **1981** G.B. SILBERBAUER *Hunter & Habitat* 4 'Bushman' distinguishes neither a language or even a family of languages ... Traill (1978) concluded that there are five separate language families among those of the yellow southern African hunter-gatherers. **1986** M. PICARDIE in S. Gray *Market Plays* 93 Go back, back to the time when dark skins, crinkly hair, flat nose, thick lips, talking Malay, or Hottentot or Bushman or even Xhosa didn't matter.

3. *Derog.* and *offensive.* COLOURED *n.* sense a. Also *attrib.*

1954 M. GANDHI in *Drum* Feb. 14 The term commonly used for Indians, Coloureds and Africans is respectively 'Coolie,' 'Bushman' and 'Kaffir.' **1961** D. BEE *Children of Yesterday* 107 A big Native had said to him there, 'Sit at the back, Bushman' — the most deadly insult a native can give a Coloured man in South Africa. **1971** *Sunday Times* 27 June 13 The other children ganged together and kept calling me 'Bushman'. I was afraid to go to school. **1978** A. ESSOP *Hajji* 28 Myrtle was a blowsy woman, tall, frizzy-haired ... She was often abusively referred to by women as 'that Bushman bitch'. **1986** M. PICARDIE in S. Gray *Market Plays* 87 You Hottentot rubbish ... You Bushman piece of dirt.

Bushman grass *n. phr.* Also with small initial. [tr. S. Afr. Du. *boesmangras*, see BOESMANGRAS.] A general term for any of several species of grass of the genera *Aristida*, *Stipa*, and esp. *Stipagrostis* of the sub-family Arundinoideae (family Poaceae); BOESMANGRAS. See also STEEKGRAS sense a, TWA-GRASS. Formerly also **Boshman's grass**.

1789 W. PATERSON *Narr. of Four Journeys* 63, I found many new species of Gramina, particularly that which the Dutch call Boshman's Grass, from the use made of it by that people, who eat the seed of it. **1790** *Ibid.* 134 The grass with which these Birds build, is called the Boshman's grass; and I believe the seed of it to be their principal food. **1857** A. WYLEY *Rep. Min. Struct. Namaqualand* App. 44 There the various kinds of Bushman grass prevail, almost to the exclusion of every other plant. **1883** [see TOA-GRASS]. **1915** R. MARLOTH *Flora of S. Afr.* IV. 19 *Stipa* (bushman grass). **1920** E.H.L. SCHWARZ *Thirstland Redemption* 16 The ground is covered with soil or sand; when it rains, grass ('Bushmangrass,' *Aristida brevifolia*) springs up quickly and withers, covering the surface with seed, for use in the next rains. **1930** I. SCHAPERA *KhoiSan Peoples* 9 The great plains .. are covered with tough sun-bleached Bushman grass (*Aristida brevifolia*). *c*1936 *S. & E. Afr. Yr Bk & Guide* 528 Bushman Grass .. is extraordinarily drought resisting. **1957** *Handbk for Farmers* (Dept of Agric.) III. 637 In the Western Karoo, bushmen-grasses and other species, such as *Enneapogon* .. may be used. **1971** *Golden Fleece* (S. Afr. Wool Board) June (Suppl.) 71 In the dry north-western Cape, Bushman grass (Stipagrostis spp.) and allied types on sandy soil form the climax. **1977** *Farmer's Weekly* 23 Nov. 12 Most important grass variety is bushman grass — perfect grazing for cattle. **1991** G.E. GIBBS RUSSELL et al. *Grasses of Sn Afr.* 329 *Stipagrostis zeyheri* .. subsp. *macropus* .. Bushman grass.

Bushmanland *n.* [BUSHMAN sense 1 a + Eng. *land.*]

1. A name for that region of the Northern Cape Province considered to be the historical home of the SAN (Bushman) people.

1790 W. PATERSON *Narr. of Four Journeys* 71 An excursion to the Hantum .. called the Boshmens' Land, from its being inhabited by the Bush Hottentots .. a very different people from the other peaceable and well-disposed inhabitants of this region. **1819** *Missionary Notices* June 205 In a few days I shall commence a journey to the Bushman Land. **1841** B. SHAW *Memorials* 27 The Bushman-land .. is a vast desert of a week's journey, situated between the Khamies Mountains and the Great Orange River, and is very thinly inhabited. **1913** [see TWA-GRASS]. *c*1936 *S. & E. Afr. Yr Bk & Guide* 527 Between Kakamas and Springbok, in the heart of Bushmanland, lies the notable French R.C. Mission of Pella. **1961** L.E. VAN ONSELEN *Trekboer* 70 Bushmanland has been described by many travellers as a desert with a rainfall so erratic that when a Pauw or wild turkey bathes itself in a dust bath .. this is looked upon as a sign that rain might fall.

2. *?hist.* A name given to a reserve situated along the South West African (now Namibian) border with Botswana, created for the SAN (Bushman) people of Namibia.

1964 *Report of Commission of Enquiry into S.W. Afr. Affairs 1962–3* (RP 12–1964) 99 The Commission .. recommends:- .. That homelands be created for the Bushmen .. i) the portion of the Western Caprivi .. for the Barakwengo Bushmen; and ii) Bushmanland .. for the other Bushmen. **1970** W.B. MILLER in *Std Encycl. of Sn Afr.* II. 612 *Bushmanland,* .. The name .. proposed by the Odendaal Commission of Inquiry into South-West African Affairs for a region which is to be set aside as a homeland for the Bushmen of South-West Africa. **1989** P.E. RAPER *Dict. of Sn Afr. Place Names* 80 *Bushmanland,* .. The name is .. applied to an area some 230 km long between Hereroland and Kavango in South West Africa/Namibia .. next to the Botswana border, with Tsumkwe as its main centre.

Bushmanoid *adj.* Also with small initial. [BUSHMAN + Eng. adj.-forming suffix *-oid* 'having the form or nature of, resembling' (*OED*).] Of or resembling a Bushman (see SAN sense 1).

1940 *Jrnl R. Anthrop. Inst.* 15 The Bushmanoid races are not negroid stock. **1959** J.D. CLARK *Prehist. of S. Afr.* 99 Or else both represent parallel specializations from an ancestral proto-bushmanoid stock. **1970** B. DAVIDSON *Old Afr.* 195 This racial tribe may have been bushmanoid or negroid. **1988** H. ANGULA in B. Wood *Namibia 1884–1984* 109 In the Old Stone Age, states Murphy, the population of Ethiopia seems to have included groups of 'Bushmanoid' peoples who lived in the northern, eastern and western portions of the country.

Bushman rice *n. phr.* [BUSHMAN sense 1 a + Eng. *rice*; see quot. 1913.] Any of several species of termite of the order Isoptera; more commonly, their larvae which resemble rice and are eaten by the SAN (Bushman) people; *Hottentots rice,* see HOTTENTOT *n.* sense 6 a; RYSMIER. Also **Bushman's rice**.

[**1797** EARL MACARTNEY in G.M. Theal *Rec. of Cape Col.* (1898) II. 99 The proper Bosjesmen .. feed upon .. ant eggs which they call Rice, & which serve them for a great part of their food.] **1827** G. THOMPSON *Trav.* I. 432 There are two species of ants which they chiefly feed upon – one of a black and the other of a white colour. The latter .. is, from its appearance, called by the boors 'Bushman's rice.' This rice has an acid, and not very unpleasant taste. **1886** G.A. FARINI *Through Kalahari Desert* 107 Kert went into a transport of joy at finding some 'Bushman's rice' – a species of ant, with broad black heads and long fat bodies ... Taking a handful of these he poured them into his mouth and chewed them with the greatest gusto. **1896** G.M. THEAL *Portuguese in S. Afr.* 12 The ordinary food of these people consisted of roots, berries, wild plants, locusts, larvae of ants – now commonly called Bushman rice by European colonists. **1905** G.W. STOW *Native Races of S. Afr.* 59 The Bushman-rice, as it was termed by the Dutch, or chrysalides of white ants obtained from the ants' nests, was merely gathered in such quantities as sufficed for daily use. **1913** C. PETTMAN *Africanderisms* 99 *Bushman rice,* The larvae of several species of termites are sometimes so called, because in appearance they are not unlike rice grains and were a favourite article of food with the Bushmen. **1948** MRS HOW in E. Rosenthal *Afr. Switzerland* 206 In the old days the .. Bushmen .. took the white pupae from inside the ant-heaps (known as Bushman Rice) and roasted them on hot stones. Unroasted pupae are said to be excellent for poultry and very fattening. **1955** L.G. GREEN *Karoo* 23 They feasted on the roasted white ants called 'Bushman rice'. **1967** E. ROSENTHAL *Encycl. of Sn Afr.* 87 *Bushman rice,* Name applied to the eggs of certain types of termites, for this reason known to the Boers as 'rysmier'. They closely resemble rice in appearance, and were actually eaten by the Bushmen.

Bushman's candle *n. phr.* [BUSHMAN sense 1 a + Eng. possessive *'s* + Eng. *candle.*] Any of several succulent shrubs of the genus *Sarcocaulon* of the Geraniaceae, yielding a flammable, resinous secretion, esp. *S. patersoni*; CANDLE BUSH; *Hottentot's candle,* see HOTTENTOT sense 6 a; KERSBOS *n.*[1] Also *attrib.*

1909 *Gardener's Chron.* (U.K.) 11 Dec. 401 (Pettman), Two Sarcocaulons (*Geraneacea*) whose thick cuticle .. is rich in hydrocarbons and burns with a yellow, smoky flame; it is commonly known as the *Bushman's candle.* **1915** W. EVELEIGH *S.W. Afr.* 65 The typical *Sarcocaulon rigidum,* the Candle-bush or Bushman's candle. This plant has specially adapted to meet the conditions of the desert; .. Layers of corky tissue, impregnated with a mixture of fat, wax, and resin, form the bark ... It burns steadily like a wax candle with a yellow, smokey flame, even when cut fresh from the ground. **1966** C.A. SMITH *Common Names* 149 The plants were used by the early Bushmen for providing fire, for the plants give a bright blaze on ignition, even when green. Facetiously spoken of as Bushman's candle. **1968** G. CROUDACE *Black Rose* 91 Here and there were clumps of Bushman's candles, a straggling shrub that burns and sputters with a smoky, yellow flame. **1976** O. LEVINSON *Story of Namibia* 4 The waxy untidy shrub *Sarcocaulon rigidum* or 'Bushman's Candle', with its sharp pointed spines that are modified stalks of former leaves. **1992** P. CULLINAN *Robert Jacob Gordon* 78 (*caption*) *Sarcocaulon l'heritieri* (often referred to as 'Bushman's candles').

Bushman's friend *n. phr.* [BUSHMAN (sense 1 a) + Eng. possessive *'s* + Eng. *friend.*] An open-bladed hunting knife. Cf. HERNHUTTER.

1880 E.F. SANDEMAN *Eight Months in Ox-Waggon* 348 A 'Bushman's Friend,' as the cheap open-bladed knives are designated, which are chiefly used for skinning and killing game, and any other rough purpose. **1907** J.P. FITZPATRICK *Jock of Bushveld* (1909) 113 Catching the buck by the head, held it down with one knee on its neck and my Bushman's Friend in hand to finish it. **1964** G. CAMPBELL *Old Dusty* 138 'No, Inkosi, I don't want money, but if you will give me that knife in your belt, I will watch them and tell you what happens.' I had a spare 'Bushman's friend' in my kit, so agreed to the Swazi's terms. **1984** *Bagpipe* (St Andrew's College, Grahamstown) 12 Sept. 12 What went wrong I don't know, but Dooley burst out of his class room and dashed down the stairs, with Terry Lloyd after him with a 'Bushman's Friend'.

Bushman's poison *n. phr.* [BUSHMAN + Eng. possessive *'s* + Eng. *poison.*] In full ***Bushman's poison bush***: any of several species of the toxic plant *Acokanthera* of the Apocynaceae, formerly used by the San in making poison for their arrows; *Hottentot's poison bush,* see HOTTENTOT *n.* sense 6 a. See also GIFBOOM sense b.

[**1885** A. SMITH *Contrib. to Materia Medica* 40 The Bushmen take the wood of the plant and pound it to a rough powder, which they put into a clay pot and boil for some time, keeping the lid on as the fumes are noxious, .. till it is reduced to a cupful of a glutinous fluid ... The poison is ready. It is a brownish substance such as you see in a bee-hive.] **1911** *E. London Dispatch* 10 Nov. 6 (Pettman), This is the *Bushman's poison bush* (*Acocanthera venenata*). **1913** C. PETTMAN *Africanderisms* 100 *Bushman's* or *Hottentot's poison bush, Acocanthera venenata.* This plant was used by the Bushmen in making poison for their arrows. The Kaffirs use it for the cure of snake-bites. **1973** *Weekend Post* 30 June 6 A shrub often seen in Port Elizabeth gardens is the indigenous Acokanthera venenata or 'bushman's poison' tree. **1973** [see *Hottentot's poison bush* (HOTTENTOT sense 6 a)]. **1976** U. VAN DER SPUY *S. Afr. Shrubs & Trees for Garden* 65 *Acokanthera oppositifolia* .. Bushman's Poison Bush, Gifboom ... Found in the eastern Cape from the Port Elizabeth area into Natal, usually at the edges of forests near the coast. **1981** VAHRMEIJER & STEYN *Poisonous Plants* 110 The Bushman's poison bush is a shrub or tree up to 6m high and has milky, white latex. **1988** J. MUNDAY *Poisonous Plants in S. Afr. Gardens & Parks* 22 *Bushman's poison,* .. *Poison tree, Winter sweet.* Several species of this genus are indigenous to South Africa and one or two are cultivated.

Bushman's rice var. BUSHMAN RICE.

Bushman's tea *n. phr.* [tr. S. Afr. Du. *Bosjesmansthee,* see BOSJESMANSTHEE.] Any of several aromatic shrubs whose leaves are used to make medicinal teas, esp. *Catha edulis* of the Celastraceae and *Stachys linearis* of the Lamiaceae; BOSJESMANSTHEE; *Hottentot('s) tea,* see HOTTENTOT *n.* sense 6 a.

1913 C. PETTMAN *Africanderisms* 100 *Bushman's tea, Catha edulis, Forsk.* The leaves of this plant when chewed to excess are intoxicating. **1917** R. MARLOTH *Common Names* 80 *Bushman's Tea, Catha edulis.* A tree widely spread in eastern Africa, from Egypt to the Cape ... Contains the stimulating alkaloid katine. **1970** M.R. LEVYNS in *Std Encycl. of Sn Afr.* II. 616 *Bushman's-tea, Kaffir tea.* (*Athrixia phylicoides.*) A slender, diffusely branched shrub of the family *Compositae,* this is confined to bushy places in the eastern parts of South Africa. *Ibid.* 617 *Bushman's-tea, Vaaltee. Dassiebos. Jakob-jong.* (*Stachys rugosa.*) A species belonging to the family *Labiatae,* it is an erect perennial and grows up to 2 ft. high. **1982** FOX & NORWOOD YOUNG *Food from Veld* 149 *Catha edulis* .. (*Methyscophyllum glaucum*). *Common names*: English – *Abyssinian tea, African tea,* .. *Bushmen's tea, wild tea.*

bushpig *n.* Pl. **-s**, or unchanged. [tr. S. Afr. Du. *boschvark,* see BOSCHVARK.] The wild pig *Potamochoerus porcus* of the Suidae; BOSCHVARK.

1844 J. BACKHOUSE *Narr. of Visit* 213 The Bosch vark, Bush pig .. is about 2 1/2 feet high and 5 feet long, and has a tubercular excrescence covered with coarse hair on the face. **1891** R. WARD *Sportsman's Handbk* 122 In Natal are found the Bushbuck, reedbuck .. Klipspringer, Bush Pig, and Leopard. *c***1936** *S. & E. Afr. Yr Bk & Guide* 1071 The wholesale trapping of them [*sc.* the leopards] .. has allowed Baboon and Bush Pig to multiply to such an extent that grave damage to cultivation results. *Ibid.* 1078 The *Bush Pig* or *River Hog,* .. This is about the same size as the Wart Hog, but is not plentiful in South Africa. **1948** A.C. WHITE *Call of Bushveld* 215 The bushpig is a perfect nuisance to Europeans who make an attempt to cultivate the lands and produce crops. **1970** C.M. VAN DER WESTHUIZEN in *Std Encycl. of Sn Afr.* II. 624 *Bush pig,* (*Potamochoerus porcus*) ... Unlike the warthog, it is nocturnal in habit. **1986** *Weekend Argus* 9 Aug. 5 Rush hour traffic and early morning golfers were stopped in their tracks when a bush pig made a surprise appearance in central Port Elizabeth. **1991** K. URQUHART in *Weekend Post* 16 Mar. (Leisure) 1 They would see about 20 different nocturnal animals and birds which live in the hills and valleys .. including bushpig, Cape and spring hares, porcupine, antbear, skunks. **1994** A. CRAIG in M. Roberts tr. *J.A. Wahlberg's Trav. Jrnls 1838–56* 63 Warthog *Phaeocochoerus aethiopica,* here clearly distinguished from bushpigs.

bush tea *n. phr.* Formerly also **busch tea**. [Prob. tr. S. Afr. Du. *bosjesthee,* see BOSJESTHEE.] A tea made from the dried leaves and twigs of various aromatic shrubs, esp. *Aspalathus linearis,* and *Cyclopia* species; the shrubs themselves; BOSJESTHEE. See also *berg tea* (BERG sense 1 b ii), HONEY TEA, *rooibos tea* (ROOIBOS sense 1). Cf. BUSHMAN'S TEA.

Widely used as a drink, this tea is believed by some to have medicinal properties.

1768 *Holyoke Diaries* (1911) 30 Began to take Bush Tea. **1838** J.E. ALEXANDER *Exped. into Int.* I. 141 He regaled Mr. Schmelen and myself on boiled salt beef and bush tea. **1857** R. GRAY *Jrnl of Visitation to Diocese of Grahamstown* 66 He tells me that he is living upon mealies and upon bush tea for which he pays 6d. a lb. **1889** 'A HOUSEWIFE OF THE COLONY' *Col. Hsehold Guide* 12 The Cape bush tea is better when used alone for being made in an earthenware teapot; it requires being stewed awhile before using. **1902** 'X.C.' *Everyday Life in Cape Col.* 122 In most of these Colonial stores 'bush' tea can be bought. It costs sixpence a pound, looks like the clippings of a privet hedge, including the twigs, and is said to be a tonic. **1907** J.P. FITZPATRICK *Jock of Bushveld* (1909) 81 We had .. nothing to drink but bush tea — that is, tea made from a certain wild shrub with a very strong scent. **1916** *Farmer's Weekly* 20 Dec. 1472 (*advt*) Supplied direct to the consumer. Raisins, Dried Fruits, Bush Teas, Grape Vinegar. **1919** *Dunnell, Ebden & Co.'s Price List* 30 *Tea* .. Colonial ... Ordinary Bush, per lb. 1 3/4d. **1928** N. STEVENSON *Afr. Harvest* 12 The English and Dutch nations were blending extraordinarly well, as, for instance, China and *busch* tea blended to give an excellent flavour. *c*1936 *S. & E. Afr. Yr Bk & Guide* 324 Bush Tea (Rooibosch tea), *Aspalathus sp.* obtained from the Cederberg is quite generally used in the Western Province as a beverage and possesses recognized tonic properties. **1949** L.G. GREEN *In Land of Afternoon* 55 Bush tea is popular in the fashionable cafes of the United States. They call it 'Kaffir tea' over there. *c*1951 [see HONEY TEA]. **1958** A. JACKSON *Trader on Veld* 36 Rooibos (bush) tea was another popular line carried by the vrugtesmous, a very cheap and healthy herb from the Cedarberg and elsewhere, much used by our farmers in sickness and in health. **1971** [see HONEY TEA]. **1979** HEARD & FAULL *Our Best Trad. Recipes* (1979) 19 As for South Africans today, many like to mix bush tea with ordinary tea, anything up to half of each; while thousands drink it as their forefathers did. **1982** FOX & NORWOOD YOUNG *Food from Veld* 225 Other edible *Fabaceae* (*Leguminosae*): .. The 'bush tea' with the finest aroma is said to be *Cyclopia buxifolia* ... *Aspalathus linearis* .. is used as a 'bush tea' in the Piquetberg district. **1989** J. HOBBS *Thoughts in Makeshift Mortuary* 17 They crooked their little fingers above their mug handles and took dainty sips with pursed lips at their strong sweet bush tea, just as her mother did at her fine Ceylon. **1994** [see *vlei tea* (VLEI sense 2)].

bush-tick *n.* Also **bush tic.** [BUSH *n.*[1] + Eng. *tick.*]

1. Any of several species of tick; BUSH LOUSE.

1856 *Cape of G.H. Almanac & Annual Register* 283 The most troublesome insect to man and beast is called the bush tick. **1856** C.J. ANDERSSON *Lake Ngami* 20 Besides myriads of fleas, our encampment swarmed with a species of bush-tick. **1889** F. GALTON *Trav. in S. Afr.* 11 We employed ourselves in picking bush tics from our persons, for the bushes swarmed with them. **1966** C.A. SMITH *Common Names* 163 *Bosluisblom (-metjie), (Erica viridipurpurea)* ... Flowers in clusters of fours. This disposition and their shape are rather suggestive of a nest of bushticks. **1988** J.S. SMITH in *Style* May 58 You might come across him engaged in the absorbing business of removing bush ticks from the back of his knees.

2. *comb.* **bush-tick berry**, the shrub *Chrysanthemoides monilifera* of the Asteraceae; its fruit; BOETABESSIE; also called BIETOU.

1865 HARVEY & SONDER *Flora Capensis* III. 436 A large bush .. the Colonial name is Bush-tick Berry. **1913** C. PETTMAN *Africanderisms* 101 *Bush-tick berry,* The fruit of *Osteospermum moniliferum, Linn.* **1917** R. MARLOTH *Common Names* 17 *Bushtick berry,* One of the names of *Osteospermum moniliferum.* **1966** C.A. SMITH *Common Names* 183 *Bushtick berry, Chrysanthemoides monilifera.* **1970** M.R. LEVYNS in *Std Encycl. of Sn Afr.* II. 315 *Bush-tick berry. Brother berries. Bietou. Boetebessie. Bokbessie,* .. Shrub widespread in South Africa. **1982** FOX & NORWOOD YOUNG *Food from Veld* 128 *Bush tick berry,* .. The purple fruits of this little tree, juicy and with a bony kernel are sweet and palatable and are eaten by children ... At one time they were much sought after by Hottentots. **1987** T.F.J. VAN RENSBURG *Intro. to Fynbos* 16 The bush-tick berry or bietou .. may sometimes provide extra colour with its bright yellow flowers.

bushveld /'bʊʃfelt, -fɛlt/ *n.* Also **bush veldt.** [Part. tr. Afk. *bosveld,* see BOSVELD.]

1. Usu. with initial capital, ***the Bushveld***: the hot and dry region of the Northern Transvaal and Eastern Transvaal, the low-lying part of which is also called the LOWVELD; *the Bosveld,* see BOSVELD sense 1 b. Also *attrib.*

1878 A. AYLWARD *Tvl of Today* 44 It is unnecessary for me here to go at great length into the distinction of Highveld and Bushveld. It is sufficient for the purpose of this narrative to state that northward and eastward from Lydenberg, Bushveld and Lowveld are convertible terms. **1887** A.A. ANDERSON *25 Yrs in Waggon* II. 61 The principal portion of the Transvaal, north of Pretoria in the Zoutpansberg and Waterberg districts, is called the bush veldt, where most of the farmers living on the high veldt, between Potchefstroom and Pretoria, trek at the close of the autumn. **1899** D.S.F.A. PHILLIPS *S. Afr. Recollections* 28 The High Veld .. was formerly only inhabited during the summer by nomadic Boers, who trekked with their sheep and cattle to the Bush Veld before the inclement winter season. **1907** J.P. FITZPATRICK *Jock of Bushveld* (1909) 15 Perched on the edge of the Berg, we overlooked the wonder-world of the Bushveld, where the big game roamed in thousands and the 'wildest tales were true'. **1936** *Cambridge Hist. of Brit. Empire* VIII. 14 Bush Veld as a proper name indicates the region with this type of vegetation in the northern Transvaal, regardless of the fact that there are large areas of bush veld in Rhodesia, Bechuanaland and the Mandated Territory. **1945** [see KOP-EN-POOTJIES]. **1975** *E. Prov. Herald* 21 May 16 Mr Jooste's research into the antecedents of mampoer took him to various areas in the Western and Northern Transvaal Bushveld where he visited some of the licensed distillers. **1987** C. HOPE *Hottentot Room* 45 Mona May was a brilliant young high-jumper from the Bushveld, who at sixteen had already cleared just under two metres and trained, it was said, back home by competing against a tame springbok.

2. Countryside composed largely of bush, often of a thorny or scrubby character; BOSVELD sense 2. See also BUSH *n.*[1] sense 3.

1882 C. DU VAL *With Show through Sn Afr.* I. 267 It is necessary to 'trek' with the stock for some months to other pasturages in the 'bush Veld', where the herbage retains its sweetness and freshness. **1901** *Contemp. Rev.* (U.K.) Mar. 333 An efficient guide, whose knowledge of the dense bushveld proved of great value. **1919** M.C. BRUCE *Golden Vessel* 87 The farm was most beautifully situated, with a horse-shoe of mountains behind, and lovely, rolling bush-veld in front. **1944** J. MOCKFORD *Here Are S. Africans* 10 We cannot entirely ignore the events any more than the hunter can ignore the changing bushveld when he is on the spoor of kudu or waterbuck, lion or elephant. **1968** *Farmer's Weekly* 3 Jan. 93 (*advt*) Abundant sweet veld grazing and edible bushveld. Cattle in super condition all year round. **1975** J.P.H. ACOCKS *Veld Types* 28 *Tropical Bush and Savanna Types (Bushveld),* .. This veld type occupies the plains, at altitudes between 150 and 600 m above the sea .. and replaces the valley bushveld in the deep valleys. **1989** *Weekend Post* 7 Oct. 3 It was considered vital to conserve the Baviaanskloof because it was the meeting place of four major veld types — mountain fynbos, valley bushveld, Knysna forest and Cape grassveld.

3. *comb.* **bushveld prawn** [prob. tr. Afk. *bosveld-garnaal,* see BOSVELD sense 3], *mopani worm* (see MOPANI sense 3).

1986 *Sunday Star* 8 June 5 'Bushveld prawns' or, more accurately, mopani worms. **1991** *Personality* 6 May 24 A peculiar little bushveld delicacy called, aptly, *bosveld garnale* (bushveld prawns). Or, brace yourselves, otherwise known as mopani worms.

Hence **bushvelder** /'bʊʃfeldə/ *n.,* an inhabitant of the bushveld; *bosvelder,* see BOSVELD. Cf. *Lowvelder* (see LOWVELD).

1976 V. ROSENBERG *Sunflower* 44 Herman Bosman .. was distinctly a transient, whose almost discourteous lack of interest in the socio-cutural activities of the Bushveld .. widened the gulf between him and the adult Bushvelders.

bush war *n. phr.* [BUSH *n.*[1] + Eng. *war.*] A guerilla war, esp. that waged for over two decades by the South African Defence Forces in northern Namibia. Also *attrib.* Occas. **bush warfare.**

1941 C. BIRKBY *Springbok Victory* 95 The whole operation, for which Brig. Dan Pienaar was awarded the D.S.O. immediately, was an almost flawless model for a bush-war raid. **1979** *Evening Post* 10 May 3 The R4 will, particularly in bush war conditions, be a more effective weapon than the R1. **1981** *E. Prov. Herald* 9 July 3 At least 700 people have died this year in the bush war in the operational area in northern South West Africa. **1984** *Rand Daily Mail* 9 Feb. 1 South Africa's Minister of Foreign Affairs .. said .. yesterday that a ceasefire was 'in practice at this moment' in southern Angola amid 'a very promising climate' for an extended halt to the bush war. **1987** *E. Prov. Herald* 15 June 9 The outcome of the current constitutional dispute is unlikely to have much impact on the 21-year bush war waged by Swapo in the far-north of the territory. **1989** H. HAMMAN in *Scope* 10 Mar. 56 They are acknowledged by friend and enemy alike as without equal — anywhere — when it comes to bush warfare. **1990** *Sunday Times* 27 May 6 They .. fought with South African forces against Swapo guerillas in the Caprivi bush war, killing hundreds of Swapo insurgents in 16 years of combat. **1992** on Radio South Africa 9 Aug. (News), The twenty-three year pre-independence bush war on the border of Namibia and Angola.

bush-willow *n.* [BUSH *n.*[1] + Eng. *willow.*] Any of several species of tree of the genus *Combretum* (family Combretaceae), with catkin-like flowers and drooping foliage. Occas. with distinguishing epithet, as **red bush-willow** (*Combretum apiculatum*). See also ROOIBOS sense 2.

1913 C. PETTMAN *Africanderisms* 102 *Bush willow,* Both *Combretum erythrophyllum* and *C. Salicifolium* are known by this name. **1917** R. MARLOTH *Common Names* 89 The so-called *'Bushveld [Willow]'* or *Bush [Willow]* is *Combretum salicifolium.* **1961** PALMER & PITMAN *Trees of S. Afr.* 244 Closely resembling the common vaderlandswilg is the bush-willow, *Combretum caffrum,* of the Eastern Province and the Transkei. It is never found far from water, and .. is a common sight overhanging streams ... One of the most beautiful of the Combretums is *Combretum erythrophyllum,* the bush-willow. **1970** B. DE WINTER in *Std Encycl. of Sn Afr.* II. 626 The bush-willows are generally characterised by small flowers borne in cylindrical spikes or spherical heads ... There are about 20 species of bush-willow in South Africa, found in the more-or-less frost-free, subtropical areas. **1988** A. HALL-MARTIN et al. *Kaokoveld* 12 The baobab (*Adansonia digitata*), red bushwillow (*Combretum apiculatum*), tamboti. **1992** T. VAN RENSBURG in *S. Afr. Panorama* Mar.-Apr. 8 The Transvaal Bushveld is home to species such as the bush-willows (*Combretum* spp.), mopani, .. and wild fig.

Bushwoman see BUSH *adj.*[2]

bushy *n. Derog.* and *offensive.* [fr. BUSHMAN + Eng. (informal) n.-forming suffix *-y.*] HOTTENTOT sense 4 b. Also *attrib.* Cf. BUSCHIE.

1984 *Frontline* Feb. 26 There are bushies living all over the 'white' suburbs like Observatory and Woodstock .. and apartheid in CA is even more of a gemors and a generally lost cause than in Joeys. *Ibid.* 27 The black guys hop off and look at the bushy driver like they're waiting for him to tell them the score. **1987** *Sunday Times* 12 Apr., He loved rugby and played for a top Durban club until team mates said he was 'a bushy'. **1988** *Pace* Dec. 4 I've heard of swart gevaar and rooi gevaar, but coloured teachers in this one bushy kasie have gone one better. **1989** J. HOBBS *Thoughts in Makeshift Mortuary* 198 I'm a bushy. Not quite black and not quite white.

busy *adj.* [Special uses of general Eng. *busy* occupied, actively engaged.]

1. [Found in general Eng., but very common in S. Afr. Eng., influenced by Afk. *besig om te* (+ v.) expressing continuous action.] Used predicatively: 'in the process of', often used redundantly, esp. in the case of stative verbs, as 'He was busy sleeping in his bed'.

1841 J.W. APPLEYARD *War of Axe* (1971) 6 They had just slaughtered a beast at the great place and were busy preparing for eating. **1859** *Cape Town Weekly Mag.* 21 Jan. 12 The people are .. busy considering the question of union with the Transvaal Republic under President Pretorius. **1896** [see CAMP *n.*[2]]. **1911** *Farmer's Weekly* 15 Mar. 12 At present they [*sc.* Parliament] were busy dealing with the matter [*sc.* the establishment of agricultural schools] in the Executive Committee. **1924** [see FAT CAKE]. **1949** H.C. BOSMAN *Cold Stone Jug* (1969) 124 Slangvel had pulled up his jersey above the level of his eyes, and was busy trying to jerk it off his head and shoulders. *a***1951** H.C. BOSMAN *Willemsdorp* (1977) 102 How flat that sounded, Mavis thought. Here was her mother just busy dramatising herself. **1968** K. MCMAGH *Dinner of Herbs* 96, I rushed in and found the two infants busy having convulsions – as though there was not enough trouble that day. **1970** *Farmer's Weekly* 21 Apr. 70 (*advt*) Dormer 4 tooth ewes with 22 lambs (busy lambing). **1974** *Drum* 8 July 58 The mourners are busy singing like this: 'Nearer My God to Thee,' very sad indeed. Kid Tebello, I notice, is busy whispering I know not what into some non-voters ears. **1983** N.S. NDEBELE *Fools* 27 You are busy working your heart out at the white man's, and your children are busy running wild. **1990** S.A. BOTHA in *Frontline* Feb. 10 The woman was very bad indeed .. wrecked and racked on the golden vine, sodden beyond sensibility, and busy dying.

2. [Influenced by Afk. *besig met*.] In the phr. ***busy with***, engaged upon.

1930 *Friend* 25 Aug. 12 Farmers are already busy with burning the veld, and there are signs of the grass growing. **1949** H.C. BOSMAN *Cold Stone Jug* (1969) 11, I believe there are some men in the Swartklein Great Prison to-day busy with their fourth blue-coat. **1978** *Fair Lady* 8 Nov. (Suppl.) 13 The Defence Force is busy with a project where artists and entertainers will be employed by them.

butchery *n.* [Eng., influenced by Afk. *slagtery* butcher's shop (fr. Du. *slachterij* abattoir).] A butcher's shop, where meat is sold to the public.

1890 in B. Fuller *Call Back Yesterday* (1953) (facing page) 118 (*name in photograph*) Estcourt Butchery. **1912** *S. Afr. 'Inquire Within'* (Cape Times) 28 (*advt*) Orange River Butchery ... Beef, Mutton, Veal, Lamb and Poultry always on hand. Orders promptly delivered to all parts of the town. **1950** H. GIBBS *Twilight* 113 They own general stores, restaurants, garages, butcheries, mineral water stores, bakeries, eating-houses, laundries, and cinemas. **1959** L. HERRMAN *Note on Cape Idiom* 242 The equivalent in English is 'butcher shop' or 'butcher's shop'. The word butchery may be applied in English to a slaughter house, but rarely, if ever, is it used for a place where meat is sold. **1968** *Farmer's Weekly* 3 Jan. 99 (*advt*) Two butcheries for sale. On popular South Coast. Great opportunities. **1971** *Drum* Aug. 53 He had then been given a little butchery by the council in Jabavu. He had no meat blocks or choppers. **1987** M. POLAND *Train to Doringbult* 191 An old black man came out of the butchery on the corner. The fly screen banged behind him. He clutched a packet of chicken feet under his arm. **1990** *Pace* May 23 The only business which survived the looting were two bottle stores, three general dealers, a butchery, a garage and ironically three funeral parlours. **1993** C. PRETORIUS in *Flying Springbok* June 35 A wonderful butchery in White River .. offered such delicacies as pineapple and apricot boerewors.

buti var. BHUTI.

butter-bloem *n. obs.* Pl. **-en**. [Part. tr. Afk. *botterblom*.] BOTTERBLOM.

1915 D. FAIRBRIDGE *Torch Bearer* 36, I went into a field behind the house, and I counted seventeen varieties without moving from one spot ... 'Cream-coloured flowers like lilies –' 'Butter-bloemen –' .. the mayor flung himself thankfully into the talk.

butter-tree *n.* [tr. Afk. *botterboom*.] The BOTTERBOOM (sense a), *Tylecodon paniculatus*.

1822, 1844 [see BOTTERBOOM]. **1972** *S. Afr. Garden & Home* Oct. 26 The 'butter-tree' (Cotyledon paniculata), the wild sweetpea, elephant's foot and many, many others. **1987** T.F.J. VAN RENSBURG *Intro. to Fynbos* 22 Along the West Coast the vegetation is much sparser. Shrubs such as .. the butter-tree (*Cotyledon paniculata*) are found here.

buttie var. BOETIE.

button *n. slang.* [Prob. a transf. use of U.S. Eng. *button* 'a small quantity of narcotic'.]

a. Among drug-users: a methaqualone tablet (trade name *Mandrax*), often crushed and smoked with dagga (marijuana): see *white pipe* (PIPE sense 2 b).

[**1979** see STOP sense 1 a.] **1980** *Ibid.* 12 Sept. 4 Glossary of gang slang ... *Button*, Mandrax tablet. **1982** *Sunday Times* 4 July 21 After selling the cameras, the two men bought 15 'buttons' (mandrax tablets), which they crushed and smoked. **1985** *Drum* Dec. 26 He .. received money from time to time and was able to smoke 30 to 40 'white pipes' a day containing two 'buttons' (mandrax tablets). **1986** *Cosmopolitan* Dec. 83 We call mandrax tablets 'buttons'. You crush them up and smoke them with zoll through a broken bottle neck. **1990** [see ZOL *n.* sense 2]. **1991** J. ANDERSON in *Focus on Afr.* July-Sept. 82 There are dealers on every street corner, selling a potent mix of cannabis and 'buttons' – white mandrax tablets. According to Deon Daniels, resident DJ at the Base, the drug problem runs deep. 'The Mandrax drug is easily obtainable ... And the little kids are smoking it.' **1993** *Fair Lady* 21 Apr. 76 Mandrax ... The 'buttons' as the drug is called on the street are often hidden in the seams of saris. 'Buttons' are produced in Bombay at a cost of about 30 cents a tablet. In South Africa the same tablet is sold .. for R20.

b. *comb.* **button-kop** /-kɔp/ *n.* [Afk. *kop* head, as in U.S. Eng. *-head* user of (a drug)], a Mandrax user.

1984 *Cape Times* 19 Apr., When a 'button-kop' (Mandrax user) like me puts out his hand, he needs immediate help ... Mandrax .. is the most readily available and the most used drug in Cape Town. **1991** C. BROSTER *Informant, Cape Town* Button kop. Mandrax addict. That guy's really hooked; a total button kop.

button spider *n. phr.* [See quot. c1939.] Any of several species of spider of the genus *Latrodectus* (family Theridiidae), esp. *L. mactans*, the only S. African spider having a poisonous bite which is dangerous to humans. Also *attrib.*

1936 L.G. GREEN *Secret Afr.* 232 While the most deadly type of button spider (*Latrodectus indistinctus*) does not seem to occur in the city of Cape Town, other species are often found in houses. They have small, round, shiny black bodies, and many display a red spot on the underside or the back. *c***1939** S.H. SKAIFE *S. Afr. Nature Notes* 221 The name 'button spider' apparently refers to the rounded abdomen, something like an old-fashioned shoe-button. The scientific name, *Latrodectus indistinctus*, means the 'secret biter with the indistinct markings.' **1947** L.G. GREEN *Tavern of Seas* 122 One spider in the Cape Peninsula possesses venom four times more virulent, bulk for bulk, than that of the cobra ... As far as the scientists know, only the female button spider is deadly. **1967** R.F. LAWRENCE in E. Rosenthal *Encycl. of Sn Afr.* 528 The bite of only one species in South Africa is dangerous to man, the 'button spider' *Latrodectus*, and serum against the poison is prepared in most of the tropical and semi-tropical countries it inhabits. **1968** J.H. YATES *Spiders of Sn Afr.* 125 The scientific name for the button spider was, for many years, *Latrodectus indistinctus* ... Recent investigations reveal that our *indistinctus* is identical with the *L. mactans* or black widow spider of America, the *Katipo* of New Zealand and the red backed spider of Australia, Arabia and other countries. All these spiders are now regarded as varieties of the *L. mactans*. **1973** *Weekend Argus* 14 Feb. (Mag. Sect.) 6 If you are going to carry anti-button-spider serum in your knapsack whenever you go out of town, then you might just as well carry anti-mamba [serum], anti-adder serum, anti-cobra serum, anti-boomslang serum. **1984** C. GROENEWALD in *S. Afr. Panorama* Mar. 46 Remains of beetles are often found in the nest of the button spider. **1991** I. & F. DE MOOR *Informants, Grahamstown* Button spider – Black widow spider.

buttonwood *n.* [Etym. unkn.] The KRUISBESSIE (sense b), *Grewia occidentalis*.

1970 M.R. LEVYNS in *Std Encycl. of Sn Afr.* II. 633 *Buttonwood*, Kruisbessie ... Common throughout South Africa in places that are not particularly dry. **1987** [see CROSS-BERRY].

BWB /ˈbiː dʌbəljuː ˈbiː, bɪə vɪə ˈbɪə/ *n.* [Afk., initial letters of *Boere Weerstandsbeweging* 'Afrikaner Resistance Movement'.] The military wing of the extreme right-wing Afrikaner Boerestaat Party. Also *attrib.*

1992 R.H. DU PRE *Making of Racial Conflict* 165 *Boere Weerstandsbeweging (BWB)*, Military wing of the Boerestaat Party. Breakaway from AWB. Its leader, Andrew Ford, was allegedly the target of a rightwing assassination plot in 1991. **1992** *Natal Witness* 30 Dec. 2 BWB leader .. Andrew Ford said the BWB will not hesitate to take the law into its own hands to restore a Boer state. **1993** A. FORD in *Ibid.* 9 Jan. 3 The BWB acknowledges only one Wit Wolwe leader and that is Mr Barend Strydom.

by *prep.* [Eng., influenced by Afk. *by* beside, with, at.] 'At'; 'beside', 'alongside', 'near', 'in', 'with', or 'to'.

Less common among first-language speakers of English than among those who speak English as a second language.

1822 J. HANCOCK Diary. 80 Was he at the shooting match by your place. **1872** 'Y.' in *Cape Monthly Mag.* V. Sept. 182 We often hear such expressions as 'by the house,' meaning 'at home'. **1872** in A.M.L. Robinson *Sel. Articles from Cape Monthly Mag.* (1978) 284 'I saw him *by* Mr Smith's house' has a frightfully adhesive force. **1891** J.P. LEGG in *Cape Illust. Mag.* I. 95 The little word 'by' is often used in a way foreign to English proper as 'by the station,' or 'by the house.' This of course is a direct translation of the Dutch Idiom. **1913** *Muir College Mag.* in *Weekend Post* (9 Mar. 1974) 2 Don't say that you have done your exercise, when you have not, but that you left it 'by' the house. **1916** S. BLACK in S. Gray *Three Plays* (1984) 201 Maria: I must have my money, baas. Van K: I can't pay. Maria: Then I go by the court. **1928** N. STEVENSON *Afr. Harvest* 183 You can speak freely. Uncle Frikkie is by Burghersrust. I am alone. **1965** J. BENNETT *Hawk Alone* 168 The sergeant there by Sandflats says he started her up to bring her in and she's run a bearing so bad it sounds like it's coming through the block. **1972** *Grocott's Mail* 17 Mar. 4 Pigeon loft, R70. Can be viewed by 58 Somerset Street. **1979** W. EBERSOHN *Lonely Place* 70 'Where did you live then?' 'By old-boss Marthinus farm, my boss.' **1984** S. GRAY *Three Plays* 133, I can' stand being a Boer anymore, I mus' work so hard! I want to be an Afrikaner and live by the city. **1986** W. SHARF et al. in Burman & Reynolds *Growing Up* 262 A stroller is someone who don't sleep by his house – he sleeps in the street. He don't eat by his house – he eats by the bins. **1989** [see NIGHT-ADDER]. **1991** *Informant, Grahamstown* 'Where are your children now?' 'By my husband.'

byale var. BOYALE.

by-and-by *n. Obs.* exc. *hist.* Also **bai-nbai, bay and bay, by-and-bye**. [fr. *mbayimbayi* (ad. Eng. *by and by*, see quot. 1913), in the Nguni languages 'cannon', 'field gun', with spelling remodelled to the Eng. root.] Among some Nguni peoples: a field gun, or its shell.

1857 J. SHOOTER *Kafirs of Natal* 112 They have had experience of warfare with Europeans, and retain a lively recollection of the guns and horses of the boers ... They believe that the fearful *by-and-bye* eats up everything – grass, stones, rocks – and why not *amadoda*? **1893** B. MITFORD *Gun-Runner* p.xxiv, We laugh at their *bai-nbai*. What are guns, big or small, against the broad shields and devouring spears of the ever-conquering Amazulu? **1894** C.H.W. DONOVAN *With Wilson in Matabeleland* 234 They used to call common shells 'by-and-byes', because they could see the smoke, and by and by a shell would explode in their midst. **1913** C. PETTMAN *Africanderisms* 103 *By and By*, The name by which cannon are known to the natives of Natal. It is said that inquiring in the early days what these cannon were, they were informed that they would learn *by and by*, hence the name, which seems to the native to represent the noise of the explosion – a primitive striving after meaning. **1994** M. ROBERTS tr. *J.A. Wahlberg's Trav. Jrnls 1838–56* 44 The Kaffers call a cannon 'bay and bay'; the name is said

Byat(e), Byatt, Byatu varr. BAYETE.

bye var. BAIE.

byock /ˈbaɪɒk/ n. Ostrich-farming. Also **byok**. [Etym. unkn.; the It. bajocco 'brown' entered Eng. in the 16th C. as byock or baiock, meaning 'a small Italian copper coin', but any relationship with this word seems unlikely.] A black and white wing-feather from a cock ostrich; FANCY sense 1. See also PRIME.

1877 J. DE MOSENTHAL Ostriches & Ostrich Farming 226 Byoks. White, with black spots. **1896** R. WALLACE Farming Indust. of Cape Col. 235 Dark Femina, 5s. and 10s. per lb. higher. Byocks steady ... 'Byock', said to be a corruption of a foreign word for black and white, denotes the parti-coloured feathers from the wing of the male; only a few are found on each bird. **1902** Agric. Jrnl of Cape of G.H. XX. 721 Byocks £4.10.0 – £6.0.0. **1909** J.E. DUERDEN in Agric. Jrnl of Cape of G.H. XXXIV. 523 Towards each extremity of the wing in the cock, the white wing quills pass gradually into the black feathers, and four or five feathers at each end are a parti-colour of black and white. They are generally very attractive plumes, and are known as fancies or byocks, and classed as long and short. **1930** [see FANCY sense 1]. **c1936** S. & E. Afr. Yr Bk & Guide 340 An exceptionally good bird should yield from 20 to 26 ozs. of feathers and should give from 60 to 62 long whites and byocks. **1967** E. ROSENTHAL Encycl. of Sn Afr. 90 Byocks, Type of ostrich feather, taken from the wing of a male, and of two colours.

‖**byter** /ˈbeɪtə(r)/ n. Formerly also **bijter**. [Afk. (earlier Du. bijter), byt bite + agential suffix -er.] The small shallow-water blenny, *Parablennius cornutus* of the Blennidae.

In Smith and Heemstra's *Smiths' Sea Fishes* (1986) the name 'horned blenny' is used for this species.

1913 C. PETTMAN Africanderisms 59 Bijter, The Cape name of Blennius cornutus, L. **1947** K.H. BARNARD Pict. Guide to S. Afr. Fishes 185 Common Cape Blenny, Bijter (Blennius cornutus), .. Dark brown or chestnut, sometimes faint pale bars or blotches. **1949** J.L.B. SMITH Sea Fishes 344 Blennius cornutus ... Byter. Blenny ... Gives sharp nips. **1966** J.L.B. & M.M. SMITH Fishes of Tsitsikama Coastal National Park 112 Blenny. Byter. Blennius cornutus.

bywoner /ˈbeɪvʊənə(r)/ n. Also **baywhoner, beiwoner, bywohner, bywonner, by-wooner**. [Afk., by (earlier Du. bij) with, at + woon dwell, reside + agential suffix -er.]

1. hist. A landless white tenant-farmer or foreman, giving his labour in exchange for the right to occupy and work a portion of farm land on his own account. Also attrib. See also POOR WHITE. Cf. LABOUR TENANT.

1886 J.J. AUBERTIN Six Months in Cape Col. & Natal 235 Then there is what are called the Baywhoner tribe among the Dutch .. that live upon the landowners, their friends. **1889** H.A. BRYDEN Kloof & Karroo 253 A beiwoner (a sort of sub-farmer on the estate of a richer farmer, who is expected to perform certain duties for the privilege of running his stock). **1896** R. WALLACE Farming Indust. of Cape Col. 481 'Bijwoners', who are frequently the hangers-on or poor relatives of some local magnate, grow tobacco and other crops on the share system. **1908** M.C. BRUCE New Tvl 5 The poor relations occupy the position of servants above that of the kafirs and help in the work on the farm. They build themselves a cottage a little distance off and have won the name of 'by-woner.' **1926** M. NATHAN S. Afr. from Within 226 Many farms are let on a profit sharing system to whites, who are neither owners nor tenants, but are remunerated by a certain share of the annual produce ... These persons are called 'bywoners'. **1928** [see NATIONAL SCOUT]. **1936** Cambridge Hist. of Brit. Empire VIII. 804 There emerged a landless class of Europeans who lived as 'bywoners' on the farms of others or sought unskilled work in the towns. **1946** T. MACDONALD Ouma Smuts 62 The poorest man in South Africa is the bywoner (the squatter on the farm), usually a poor white. **a1951** H.C. BOSMAN Willemsdorp (1977) 97 To be a lorry driver was to be a king. That was how he felt about it, after the poverty and the misery and the degradation of his life as a bywoner. **1975** W.M. MACMILLAN My S. Afr. Yrs 133 The tenants were traditionally called 'bywoners', men who live beside others (the landowners) and, as the name indicates, they were squatters without secure tenancy rights or for the most part any rights whatever. **1988** J. SHARP in Boonzaier & Sharp S. Afr. Keywords 84 Increasing tensions between large landowners, small farmers and landless bywoners in the rural Transvaal as early as the 1880s. **1990** D. VAN HEERDEN in Sunday Times 16 Sept. 21 The real Children of Verwoerd are the ones now conducting a reign of terror in black townships. A whole generation steeped in the culture of an underclass ... Discriminated against, denied dignity, treated like bywoners in the country of their birth.

2. Fig., and transf. A socially inferior, dispossessed, or dependent person (or thing); a parasite. Also attrib.

1872 in A.M.L. Robinson Sel. Articles from Cape Monthly Mag. (1978) 283 Of all the 'bywohners' hanging on to the skirts of the language there is only one to which we have a decided aversion — to wit, that symbol of Oily-Gammon- Iago-Judas-Iscariotism, 'slim.' **1966** C.A. SMITH Common Names 280 The bushes perform a useful function in that they shelter other plants — 'bywoners' (= squatters) as they were termed by Marloth — which would otherwise have been grazed or trampled out of existence. **1972** R. DE VILLIERS in Argus 25 Mar. 9, I don't blame English-speaking people who refuse to be content with a kind of 'bywoner' position which is implicit in the whole philosophy of Nationalist Afrikanerdom as the older and senior 'partner', as the dominant group. **1974** Sunday Tribune 28 Apr. 20 This province [sc. Natal] will remain the bywoner of national politics unnoticed and unsung. **1978** Sunday Times 20 Aug. 15 An economic bywoner in his own land, he sat on the sidelines of a massive economic expansion spearheaded by English-speaking South Africans. **1980** Ibid. 16 Mar. 15 Dr Treurnicht leads this band. They accommodate their new English allies with difficulty, as bywoners. **1983** [see GROUP AREA n. phr. sense 1].

Hence **bywonerskap** /-skap/ n. [Afk. -skap -ship].

1912 H.H. JUTA Reminisc. 148, I firmly believe that the evil and pernicious system of 'by-woonerschap' is more responsible for the manufacture of the poor white than anything else.

[left column top, continuation] to be derived from the English expression 'by and by', and the story is that once during a commando the Kaffers came quite near to the English troops, at which the officers, shewing the canon, used this expression by way of saying that they would soon make them clear off.

C

caama var. KAMA.

Caapie var. CAPEY.

Caapmen var. KAAPMANS.

cabaljao var. KABELJOU.

cabbage *n*. slang. [Named for the green colour of the banknote: cf. Eng. and N. Amer. slang *cabbage money*.] In urban (esp. township) English: a ten-rand banknote.
  1984 M. MTHETHWA in *Frontline* July 28 Their pockets and wallets and purses are thickly lined with stacks of 'cabbages' and 'chocolates' — ten and twenty-rand banknotes. **1992** — in *Pace* Aug. 38 'Cabbages' and 'chocolates' (R10 and R20 notes in township parlance) exchange hands in seconds at another shelter. **1994** WILHELM & NAIDOO in *Sunday Times* 1 May 15 Notes all have different names: a R10 is a *cabbage* (because it is green) or a *tiger*.

cabbage tree *n. phr*. [See quots 1987 and 1989.] KIEPERSOL.
  1868 J. CHAPMAN *Trav*. II. 447 One of the most remarkable of the Natal trees is our only representative of the Ivy family, and is known as the Cabbage-tree, and to the Dutch as the Nojes-boom (*Cussonia*). **1907** T.R. SIM *Forests & Forest Flora* 55 Softer woods there certainly are .. and these, such as the Kaffir-tree (Erythrina), the Cork tree (Commiphora), and the Cabbage tree (Cussonia), are too soft for planking. **1954** U. VAN DER SPUY *Ornamental Shrubs & Trees* 105 *Cabbage tree*, Evergreen tree growing to between 15 and 30 ft and of erect growth. In some species the stem sends out no branches near the bottom, but a few at the very top. **1987** *E. Prov. Herald* 28 Mar. 6 Cussonias, or Cabbage Trees, are a small branch of the large family of *Araliaceae* ... The name cabbage tree comes from the cabbage-like colour of some species. **1989** *Skipper* Vol.3 No.7, 9 Why is the *Schefflera umbellifera* called a Bastard Cabbage Tree? It indicates the tree's relationship to the real Cabbage Trees (*Cussonia* species). The name likens the big clusters of large leaves to those of a cabbage. **1991** *Weekend Post* 5 Jan. 11 He was against the aerial spraying of herbicides. Indigenous trees such as milkwoods and cabbage trees (kiepersol) were damaged or destroyed.

cabeliau, -jauw, -jou, cableow varr. KABELJOU.

cac var. KAK *n*.

Caca, a la see quot. 1816 at KAK *n*.

caddie var. CATTY.

cadel var. KATEL.

cadenza *n*. [It is likely that the expression originated in Danny Kaye's humorous 1940s recording 'The Little Fiddle'.] Usu. in the expression *to have a cadenza*: to show extreme agitation.
  1991 D. CAPEL in *Personality* 2 Sept. 18 The Conservative Party is having a cadenza about 'subliminal messages' on the SABC's news logo. [**1995** G. HUGHES *Informant, Johannesburg*, 'Cadenza' is one of the most used and unlisted words in S.A.E. I remember noticing it shortly after my arrival [from Britain] in '66.] **1995** on TV1, June (*advt*) My mother can't cook ... Oh, what a huge cadenza!

Caepmans var. KAAPMANS.

cafar var. KAFFIR.

café /ˈkæfeɪ, -fi/ *n*. Also **caf(fi)e**. [Special sense of general Eng. *café* 'a tea-shop or coffee house', a sense formerly current in S. Afr. Eng., but now usu. replaced by *coffee-shop*.] A shop selling sweets, cigarettes, newspapers, perishables, and basic groceries, and staying open after normal hours; GREEK; KAFEE; TEAROOM sense 1. Also *attrib*.
  1957 B. O'KEEFE *Gold without Glitter* 79 Number Twelve set off on the sixteen mile journey .. with as little concern as the city dweller when he strolls down to the corner café to buy a packet of cigarettes. **1969** M. BENSON *At Still Point* (1988) 188 'Last Wednesday evening,' he said, 'on your way to dinner .. , you stopped at a café to buy sweets.' **1974** *Sunday Times* 3 Nov. (Mag. Sect.) 3 The local cafe is the same throughout South Africa — a cluster of canned foods, sweets, cigarettes, cold drinks. **1975** *Ibid*. 9 Mar. (Mag. Sect.) 10 The cafe-owners' complaint that half-cents are hard to come by is partially valid in that there has been a shortage. **1978** *Staffrider* Vol.1 No.4, 10 Forlorn junction dorps .. where caffies have deep-fried burgers. **1986** S. SEPAMLA *Third Generation* 73 Ya, just a dorpie with one street: cafe, groceries, .. bottle-store, garage, bakery and the police station just behind the main street. **1989** T. BOTHA in *Style* June 108 A love story about the long open road, putting foot, fly-bitten caffies, *ver verlate vlaktes* as well as the art of sleepdriving at 120km/h. **1991** C. BARRETT in *Weekend Post* 12 Jan. 8 As the years marched on, the corner grocer evolved in[to] a café or general dealer.

cafe-bio /ˈkæfeɪ ˈbaɪəʊ/ *n. hist*. [Compound of CAFÉ + BIO.] BIO-CAFÉ.
  1976 *Family Radio & TV* 21 Nov. 6 It's farewell to Durban's last cafe-bio, closing because the building's to be demolished. Strange, I've always thought cafe-bios were demolished by the public as one sat there. **1981** *Sunday Times* 10 May (Mag. Sect.) 7 Oh, my cafe-bios of long ago, would that you were still here. **1987** S.B. FINE in *Star* 24 Oct. (Weekend) 4 On Saturdays .. we would hurry down to .. the cafe-bio. With 'Continuous Performances', it did not matter if we arrived late. 'Tea-coffee-cooldrink-icecream' the waitress would intone.

café de move-on /ˌkæfeɪ də ˈmuːvɒn/ *n. phr*. [Joc. pseudo-French formation, referring both to the mobile nature of the cart and to the need to 'move on' when so ordered by the authorities.] A small mobile canteen catering for the needs of workers at their places of work, and able to change its venue rapidly to escape the attention of officialdom. See also KOFFIE KAR.
  c1929 S. BLACK in S. Gray *Three Plays* (1984) 99, I rader go by die cafe der move-on for er oulap coffee en er Scots bun. **1936** A.G. THOMPSON in *Afr. Observer* Vol.4 No.4, 59 In a corner of the compound a tailor with his sewing machine is patching trousers. There is a 'Cafe de move on' from which bread and lemonade can be obtained. **1952** B. DAVIDSON *Report on Sn Afr*. 132 The *café de move-on* is necessary to the workers of Moroka .. if they are not to go without food throughout the day, or are to bring their daily meal with them ... The *café de move-on* .. failed, and fails, to meet the requirements of 'municipal order'. After all, it is no more than a street canteen, .. where natives buy bread or cake and coffee. *Ibid*. 133 The municipal authorities .. declared war on the *cafés de move-on*, and said that these little coffee-carts must vanish from the streets ... The authorities began prosecuting the owners of *cafés de move-on* who had failed to move on. [**1990** *City Press* 4 Feb. 6 Bessie .. was running a profitable pavement shebeen in the city. It was never situated in the same place for any length of time, but often changed venues — a sort of tavern de-move-on.] **1992** A. SWERDLOW on Radio South Africa 23 Aug., Cafés de move-on and hot-dog stands.

caffer, caffer-boom, caffer-corn varr. KAFFIR, KAFFIRBOOM, KAFFIRCORN.

Caffer fair *n. phr. Obs*. [*Caffer* obs. name for a member of the Xhosa people (see KAFFIR *n*. senses 1 b and c) + Eng. *fair*.] Any of a series of trade fairs instituted by the colonial government of the Cape to promote trade between colonists and Xhosas on the eastern frontier. Also *attrib*.
  Held at regular intervals from 1821 until 1834; esp. at Fort Willshire.
  1827 T. PHILIPPS *Scenes & Occurrences* 203 Several of the Caffer Fair dealers had arrived from Grahamstown. **1835** A. STEEDMAN *Wanderings* I. 35 The arrival of settlers from England on the eastern frontier .. led at last to an unrestricted intercourse through the Caffer fair, which was established in 1821 at Fort Willshire. **1955** V.M. FITZROY *Dark Bright Land* 61 Sophia and me from home three days with Papa, to visit a Caffer Fair ... They come with elephants' teeth, wild beasts skins, horns and the like to barter for knives, beads and such trinkets.

caffie var. CAFÉ.

caffir, caffir boom varr. KAFFIR, KAFFIRBOOM.

Caffrarian var. KAFFRARIAN.

caffre(e), caffre(e)-corn varr. KAFFIR, KAFFIRCORN.

Caffrian *adj. obs*. KAFFRARIAN.
  [**1786** G. FORSTER tr. A. Sparrman's *Voy. to Cape of G.H*. I. 190 These shells are commonly sold for not less than a sheep a piece, as it is said they are to be had no where else upon the most distant coast of Caffria.] **1899** tr. H.C.D. Maynier in G.M. Theal *Rec. of Cape Col*. (1899) IV. 293 The General, always desirous to be on good terms with the Great Caffrian Nation .. I again took upon me to go to the Chief Ghyka.

cafir, cafre varr. KAFFIR.

cake *n. obsolescent*. [Calque formed on Du. *koek* (later Afk. *heuningkoek*) honeycomb.] In the phrr.

cake of honey, honey cake, honey in the comb.

a1858 J. GOLDSWAIN *Chron.* (1949) II. 60 We all eat until we ware satisfied and Nelson thought that the cakes of huney wich he had left in the tree was ful three fut long. **1883** M.A. CAREY-HOBSON *Farm in Karoo* 147 The latter had brought with him a small piece of rag, which he set fire to .. to make a little smoke, and thus stupefy the bees .. to rob them of as many cakes of honey as the party could consume. **1949** L.G. GREEN *In Land of Afternoon* 160 Such nests yield enormous cakes of honey weighing up to three hundred pounds. *Ibid.* 161 Coloured people in the Piketberg Sandveld .. prefer honey cakes containing young bees.

calabash /ˈkæləbæʃ/ *n.* Also **calabass, calibash.** [Special senses of general Eng. *calabash* any of several gourds, or their (dried, hollowed-out) fruits; ad. Sp. *calabaza* prob. fr. Arabic *qar'ah yabisah* dry gourd.]

1. *obs. rare.* [Named for the shape of the tree's fruits.] The baobab tree, *Adansonia digitata* of the Bombacaceae.

1810 J. MACKRILL Diary. 88 The Baobab, or Adansonia, the Calabash of Africa, the largest tree in the World .. is totally distinct from the Cresentia or American Calibash tree. **1817** J. LEYDEN *Hist. Acct of Disc. & Trav. in Afr.* I. 201 The other tree is the baobab, which he called calabash, remarkable not for its height, which does not exceed sixty feet, but for its prodigious thickness.

2. As in general English, the fruit of the bottle gourd *Lagenaria siceraria* of the Cucurbitaceae (see MARANKA) when used as a receptacle, but in the following combinations peculiar to *S. Afr. Eng.*: **calabash milk**, curdled milk prepared in a calabash; see also MAAS sense 1; **calabash pipe**, a tobacco pipe made of a small gourd; occas. also *ellipt.*, **calabash.**

1900 E.E.K. LOWNDES *Every-Day Life* 87 This [*sc.* stamped mealies], with '**calabash milk**' forms the staple Kaffir food. **1956** F.C. METROWICH *Valiant but Once* 197 She .. gave him a basin of coffee, some calabash milk and some flour porridge sprinkled with sugar. **1967** E.M. SLATTER *My Leaves Are Green* 209 Calabash milk lay in clotted heaps on the floors and the granary huts were still smouldering. **1979** HEARD & FAULL *Our Best Trad. Recipes* 15 The hollow calabash shells .. were used as containers for all kinds of things, some fitted with lids. Some of these gourds were for the making of calabash milk, or sour milk. **1910** J. RUNCIE *Idylls by Two Oceans* 12 Stretching out his hand to a pipe rack, the man reached down a **calabash** [**pipe**] and filled it brimful with the sun-dried Transvaal. **1913** C. PETTMAN *Africanderisms* 104 *Calabash pipe*, A pipe the bowl of which is made from the shell of a peculiarly shaped calabash. **1957** L.G. GREEN *Beyond City Lights* 125 South Africans have never taken to the calabash pipe, though it gives a cool, slow smoke lasting for an hour. **1969** I.D. COLVIN in Lennox-Short & Lighton *Stories S. African* 130 He himself did nothing except sit on his stoep with a keg of Hollands .. or some other potent spirit by his side, a bocal in his hand and a large calabash pipe in his mouth.

calandra /kəˈlændrə/ *n.* Also **calander.** [ad. Du. *kalander* grain weevil.] The vineyard weevil *Phlyctinus callosus* of the Curculionidae; its larva; also called KALANDER *n.*[1]

1896 R. WALLACE *Farming Indust. of Cape Col.* 148 The insect pest of the vineyard known by the name of the *calander, Phlyctimes callosus*, has been successfully checked at Groot Constantia by the application of a moderate dressing of lime to the soil. **1905** C.D. LOUNSBURY in Flint & Gilchrist *Science in S. Afr.* 367 Next to Phylloxera, the most important insect pest of the grape vine are Otiorrhynchid beetles, known by the farmers as 'calanders'. **1929** *Handbk for Farmers* (Dept of Agric.) 571 The Vine Calandra is well-known to wine-farmers. **1968** C.J. ORFFER in D.J. Opperman *Spirit of Vine* 90 It is surprising to learn that the calandra of the grapevine, which is an indigenous pest at the Cape, did not at first give much trouble. **1970** C. KOCH in *Std Encycl. of Sn Afr.* II. 250 True weevils (Curculionidae) ... Many species are pests, such as .. the Cape vine-calandra (*Phlyctinus*). **1973** M.S. LEROUX in *Ibid.* V. 308 The most important pests [to which South African grapes are subject] are the mealy bug .. ; calandra or snout-beetle (*Eremnus, Phlyctinus* and *Bustomes*).

calcoon var. KALKOENTJIE.

calibash var. CALABASH.

califa var. KHALIFA.

cama var. KAMA.

camassie var. KAMASSI.

cambeass var. KOMBERS.

camberoo var. KAMBRO.

Camdeboo /ˈkæmdəbuː/ *n.* Also **Kamdeboom,** and with small initial. Ellipt. for *Camdeboo stinkwood*, see STINKWOOD sense b. Also *attrib.*

1916 *Farmer's Weekly* 20 Dec. 1456 For Sale. Direct from lathe, Kamdeboom and Castaai Yokes, 3s.6d. double stapled 4s. each. **1991** *Splash* Vol.4, 43 Walking through the forest of yellowwood, stinkwood, assegai, camdeboo, wild pear and Cape Chestnut, is a unique experience.

cameel-doorn var. KAMEELDORING.

camel *n. obs.* [Calque formed on S. Afr. Du. *kameel*, see KAMEEL.] CAMELEOPARD. Also *attrib.*

1837 'N. POLSON' *Subaltern's Sick Leave* 139 The princely zerapha or giraffe in bevies ... These camels (as they are technically termed by travellers in the interior) go off at an awkward and not very fast gallop. **1886** G.A. FARINI *Through Kalahari Desert* 294 'Yah!' interposed the veldt-cornet, 'it's always hard on the horses if the camel sees or smells them at a distance.' [*Ibid.* 304 The double-ended camel-birds .. are seen only in the k'gung forest, and then only in the parts where the stately giraffe makes his home, and this is why they are called 'camel-birds,' or 'giraffe-birds'.] **1897** SELOUS & BRYDEN *Trav. & Big Game* 170 (Pettman), The Boers as soon as they became acquainted with the tall giraffe, forthwith dubbed it in their quaint way, 'kameel' — *the camel*; and as the camel the giraffe is still known throughout the length and breadth of the South African hunting veldt. **1913** C. PETTMAN *Africanderisms* 105 *Camel*, The Anglicized Dutch name for the Giraffe (*kameel*) generally employed by South African hunters. **1936** [see KAMEEL].

cameleopard *n. obs.* Also **cameleopardalis.** [General Eng., ad. (influenced by Eng. *leopard*) of mod. L. *camelopardus, -pardalis*, fr. Gk *kamelos* camel + *pardalis* leopard. This term survived in S. Afr. Eng. long after it had disappeared elsewhere.] The giraffe, *Giraffa camelopardalis* of the Giraffidae; CAMEL; KAMEEL. Also *attrib.*

1802 TRUTER & SOMERVILLE in G.M. Theal *Rec. of Cape Col.* (1899) IV. 393 We passed in the night the place where on the 29th of October we had seen the cameleopards. **1806** J. BARROW *Trav.* I. 349 He boasted that, in one excursion, he had killed seven cameleopardales and three white rhinosceroses. **1819** G.M. KEITH *Voy.* 69 Among the quadrupeds of this country are antelopes, .. buffaloes, cameleopards. **1827** G. BARKER Journal. 27 Jan., Went to see a Camel Leopard which a man had caught when quite young. **1838** J.E. ALEXANDER *Exped. into Int.* II. 200 The word was passed that two cameleopards were in sight, .. two of these most graceful and long necked animals were seen gazing towards us, and 'craning' over the tops of the bushes. **1840** C.A. KINLOCH in *Echo* 9 Nov. 5 Shifting our camp by short marches of ten or twelve miles, we continued to hunt the Eland and the Camel-leopard. **1841** B. SHAW *Memorials* 312 The *giraffe*, or cameleopard, is found in Great Namacqua-land. **1850** N.J. MERRIMAN *Cape Jrnls* (1957) 133 The cameleopard-soled veldschoons in which I had trusted, turned out quite a failure. a1875 T. BAINES *Jrnl of Res.* (1964) II. 47 A wooden sheath, round which were plaited three bands of cameleopard's hair.

camel-thorn *n.* Also with initial capitals. Pl. unchanged, or **-s.** [Calque formed on S. Afr. Du. *kameeldoring*, see KAMEELDORING.] In full ***camel-thorn tree***: any of several species of *Acacia* tree, esp. *A. erioloba* of the Fabaceae; *giraffe acacia*, see GIRAFFE; KAMEELDORING; MOKAALA. Also *attrib.* See also *vaaldoring* (VAAL sense 2).

1824 W.J. BURCHELL *Trav.* II. 292 Some scattered trees of Camel-thorn, or *Mokaala*, gave a most picturesque and remarkable character to the landscape. **1821** *Missionary Notices* Dec., Comfortably screened from the scorching rays of the sun, under the spreading boughs of a large *Camel Thorn*, which stands close to the river. **1834** [see FOUNTAIN]. **1838** J.E. ALEXANDER *Exped. into Int.* II. 115 We gladly off-packed, after seventeen miles, under a mighty camel thorn, opposite the junction of the two rivers. **1846** R. MOFFAT *Missionary Labours* 34 Near a very small fountain, which was shown to me, stood a camel thorn-tree (Acacia Giraffe). **1871** E.J. DUGMORE Diary. 9 There are some very beautiful camel-thorn about here. We do not see them in the Colony. They are larger than our mimosa. **1896** M.A. CAREY-HOBSON *At Home in Tvl* 91 A fine specimen of the camel thorn (Acacia horrida), the tree so often noticed by travellers .. on account of the large amount of grateful shade which even one tree will afford. **1907** W.C. SCULLY *By Veldt & Kopje* 226, I did not then make for the camp, but for a low ridge to the northward, on which a number of 'camel-thorn' trees were visible. **1917** R. MARLOTH *Common Names* 17 *Camel Thorn, Acacia Giraffae.* A tree of slow growth but of large dimensions when fully developed. Wood dark brown and very hard. **1977** F.G. BUTLER *Karoo Morning* 41 A portion of earth under some old camelthorns was levelled and covered with a wagon sail: this was the dance floor. **1980** *S. Afr. Panorama* Dec. 46 Crimson cascades of bougainvillea and gaudy red-blooming avenues of flamboyants or umbrella-like camel-thorns. **1990** *Grocott's Mail* 2 Mar. 9 Both the Camel Thorn and the Mimosa tree exude a gum which can be chewed as a sweet, while the seeds of both make good coffee substitutes. **1991** J. HUNTLEY in *Sunday Star* 16 Feb. (Weekend) 4 Elephants habitually push or bump these camel-thorn trees to get at the highly nutritious pods.

camile-dorn var. KAMEELDORING.

camp *n.*[1] [General Eng. *camp* encampment, in several transf. uses.]

1.a. *hist.* A name given to any town which grew out of a temporary mining settlement, esp. Johannesburg.

1873 F. BOYLE *To Cape for Diamonds* 78 Pniel could not be called a town, for it has but a few hundred inhabitants. Village it is not, .. none could describe it as a settlement, seeing no person or thing therein is settled ... Pniel, by official designation, is a 'camp'. Just a camp it is indeed, and one very disorderly. **1908** D. BLACKBURN *Leaven* (1991) 124 Dane went into 'camp', as most of the old hands still call Johannesburg. **1933** [see BOER BREAD].

b. *comb.* **camp fever** *Pathology*, see quot.

1970 BEETON & DORNER in *Eng. Usage in Sn Afr.* Vol.1 No.1, 25 *Camp fever*, .. Traditional name for 'enteric', formerly very common among the mining community at Kimberley & in Johannesburg in the early days, owing to poor water supplies.

2. *hist.* Also with initial capital. Shortened form of CONCENTRATION CAMP. Also *attrib.*

1901 E. HOBHOUSE *Report of Visit to Camps* 3, I am anxious to submit to you without delay some account of the Camps in which the women and children are concentrated. **1902** BURGER & REITZ in E. Hobhouse *Brunt of War* 108 Still more pitiable was and is the lot of these families in the women's camps — several of which camps are situated in the coldest winter (*sic*) and most stormy places in our land, namely at Belfast, Middelburg, Standerton, and Volksrust. **1902** E. HOBHOUSE *Brunt of War* 86 Exposure and rough camp life have seriously affected Mrs. Hertzog's health. **1933** W.H.S. BELL *Bygone Days* 358 They set about their investigation in a very methodical and thorough manner; they never announced their intention of visiting a camp beforehand; they made surprise visits in nearly every case. They visited every concentration camp in South Africa. **1941** N. DEVITT *Concentration Camps* 15 The first camp is believed to have been erected in July 1900 near Mafeking whither came refugees from the western areas with their families and stock. **1957** A.C. MARTIN *Concentration Camps* 21 The diseases were not confined merely to the camps established by the British. They were causing havoc in the camps of the Boers. **1979** T. PAKENHAM *Boer War* (1982) 495 The camps have left a gigantic scar across the minds of the Afrikaners: a symbol of deliberate genocide.

3.a. Shortened form of REST CAMP.

1948 H. WOLHUTER *Mem. of Game Ranger* 86, I heard some elephants trumpeting .. not far from the present 'Gorge' camp. *Ibid.* 189, I drove up to within a few feet of the recumbent animal, and told the boys to load it onto the lorry and we would take it home as meat for the camp. **1948** A.C. WHITE *Call of Bushveld* 180 This section of visitors demand luxury hotels in the camps, a full measure of telephone communication, bioscope and dance halls. **1951** T.V. BULPIN *Lost Trails of Low Veld* 274 Three new ranger camps were established to administer the new areas. *Ibid.* 277 In the old days people came to camp and rough it and enjoy the glamour of the wilds ... Now .. mankind demands luxury and the camps have followed the demand ... Inner-spring mattresses and snug bungalows in place of a sleeping bag and the twinkling stars. **1972** *Etosha Nat. Park (brochure)*, It is .. essential to reach the gate at least half an hour before sunset in order to be in the camp in time. **1975** *E. Prov. Herald* 14 Jan. 1 An elderly lioness .. is jealously guarding her new home from intrusion by visitors to the camp. **1988** M. SPENCE in *Motorist* 4th Quarter 4 The Namutoni camp .. is open throughout the year.

b. *comb.* **camp-attendant**, **camp-superintendent**.

1948 H. WOLHUTER *Mem. of Game Ranger* 154 One of the native **camp-attendants**, then working in the Rest Camp, might be in league with the poachers. *Ibid.* 187 The **camp-superintendent** had sent me a message to say that this particular party had failed to return to camp.

4. Any of several short periods of annual military duty, usu. compulsory after completion of national service. Also *attrib.* See also CITIZEN FORCE.

[*c*1936 *S. & E. Afr. Yr Bk & Guide* 476 The commonage of this town [*sc.* Worcester] has been chosen by the military authorities as being healthy and suitable for military purposes, two Defence Force Camps being held here annually before the late war.] **1977** *E. Prov. Herald* 31 May, From January next year all national servicemen would do 24 months' continuous training followed by eight annual camps of 30 days each. **1979** *Fair Lady* 5 Dec. 65 The second of Kim's three camp call-ups. **1986** J. CONYNGHAM *Arrowing of Cane* 126 The khaki envelope arrived with my afternoon tea ... B Company, Natal Fusiliers will be doing a ninety-day camp in the operational area, beginning next month. **1988** *Student Advisor's Circular* (Rhodes Univ.), If notice is given well in advance, students should not find themselves being called up for training camps during term time. **1990** *Weekly Mail* 21 Dec. (Suppl.) 11 An 18-month sentence at Zonderwater Prison for refusing to do a one-month camp. **1991** *Weekend Post* 6 Apr. (Leisure) 5 As a SA 'troopie' doing a three-month camp at Mpacha, one of my duties was to sign visitors to the base.

Hence (sense 4) **camper** *n.*, a member of the Citizen Force called up for a short period of military duty.

1984 *Fair Lady* 14 Nov. 133 Home for months at a time to thousands of national servicemen and 'campers', sector one zero is in the operational area.

camp *n.*[2] [Calque formed on Afk. *kamp* paddock or run.]

a. A large enclosed field used as pasture; a paddock. Also *attrib.*

1877 *Queenstown Free Press* 25 Sept., He purchased three birds to establish a 'camp' at Somerset East in 1853. *c***1881** A. DOUGLASS *Ostrich Farming* **205** A farmer with a troop of cattle, if he buys others, should always put them in a camp by themselves for at least three months before he allows them to mix with his own. **1896** *Cape Argus* 2 Jan. 6 Marked improvements are taking place on most farms, especially with regard to wire-fencing, farmers being busy subdividing their farms into camps. **1900** E.E.K. LOWNDES *Every-Day Life* 90 Sometimes three or four large pieces will be divided off for the convenience of keeping cattle or ostriches separate; these are not called fields, a term you never hear in this part, but 'camps'. **1925** L.D. FLEMMING *Crop of Chaff* 44 There are two kinds of Orange Free State fences — boundary fences and your own camp fences ... Your own camp fences you put up yourself. **1930** [see *sweetveld* (SWEET sense 2)]. **1941** E. ROUX in *Bantu World* 18 Jan. 5 He had gates in the fences so that he could drive the cattle into whichever camp he pleased. **1977** F.G. BUTLER *Karoo Morning* 216 Get out of this camp, double quick. It's the bull's camp. **1988** *Farmer's Weekly* 1 Jan. 17 Mr Minnaar makes maximum use of 52 camps with rotational grazing and all have stock-proof fencing 1 m high. Each camp is rested for nine to 14 months.

b. With defining words designating a particular type of camp according to its use: **grazing camp**; **land camp** [see LAND], an enclosed field for the cultivation of crops; **ostrich camp**, see OSTRICH; **shelter camp**; **veld camp**, see VELD sense 5.

1968 *Farmer's Weekly* 3 Jan. 93, 150 Morgen irrigable rich river loam lands. Sweet veld, 10 **land** and **grazing camps**, each with its own water supply. **1921** W.C. SCULLY *Harrow* 159 When the enemy became .. bolder .. in their raids, what were called **'shelter camps'** were formed and to these all remaining animals were ordered to be sent.

camp *v. trans.* Usu. in the phr. *to camp off* [calque formed on Afk. *afkamp* (often found in the construction *kamp .. af*)]: To divide land and enclose it with fences, creating paddocks. Often *passive*.

1913 C. PETTMAN *Africanderisms* 106 *Camp off a farm, To*, To make enclosures. **1968** *Farmer's Weekly* 3 Jan. 31 The rest of the farm will be camped off in due course and eventually there will be 16 camps to accommodate the system. **1973** *E. Prov. Herald* 20 Sept. 29 There is an old house and fowl sheds on the property, which is camped and has a borehole.

Hence **camping** *vbl n.*

1937 *Handbk for Farmers* (Dept of Agric. & Forestry) 139 Improvement of natural veld can be brought about by means of the systematic camping of veld, and the judicious grazing of such camps.

can *n.* [Calque formed on Afk. *kan* jar, vessel for holding liquids.] A measure or container for wine, now usu. a two-litre glass bottle. See also VAATJIE sense 2 b.

1972 *Het Suid-Western* 13 Apr. 1 More than a dozen full bottles and several gallon cans, as well as a large quantity of empty wine bottles were found. **1976** *Ibid.* 10 Mar., The four of them sat in the kitchen drinking a can of wine Mrs Bothma had bought. **1977** D. MULLER *Whitey* 23 An elderly woman was decanting wine from a six-bottle can into a row of sparkling pint bottles ... Several full cans of wine stood on the floor. *Ibid.* 44 He looked at the can of cheap dark sherry, wondering if he would get a turn. **1979** *Sunday Times* 2 Feb. (Mag. Sect.) 2 After waiting endlessly on a bleak sandy stretch for a young man to return from a house to where he'd hastened with a can of wine and promises of crayfish, I withdrew from the lists. **1987** *Investing Today (pamphlet)*, Traditional stoneware 'cans' holding 500ml of mampoer will .. join the festive season market at about R17. **1991** J. PAUW *In Heart of Whore* 44 Get to a bottle store before closing time, buy 12 beers and a two-litre can of wine, find a peaceful place in the great outdoors, have a braai, fall over and sleep.

canary-biter *n. obs.* [tr. S. Afr. Du. *kanariebijter.*] The FISCAL (sense 2), *Lanius collaris*. Also (part. tr.) **canari-byter**, **canary byter**.

1795 C.R. HOPSON tr. *C.P. Thunberg's Trav.* I. 293 *Fiscal* and *Canary-byter* were the appellations given to a black and white bird (*Lanius collaris*) .. common in the town. [*c***1808** C. VON LINNÉ *System of Natural Hist.* VIII. 342 It [feeds] .. occasionally upon young birds; a circumstance well known to Colonists at the Cape, who call it *zwarte canari byter* or *bonte canari byter*, (black or spotted bird-killer).] **1822** W.J. BURCHELL *Trav.* I. 18 The loud and clear whistle of the canari-byter (canary biter) .. is heard from afar, its notes being very remarkable. **1822** J. LATHAM *Gen. Hist. of Birds* II. 23 The Canary-biter, or Fiscal-bird ... The tail feathers in the cinerous species are twice as broad as in the Fiscal. [**1913** see FISCAL sense 2. **1936** see FISKAAL.]

cancer bush *n. phr.* [tr. Afk. *kankerbos*, see KANKERBOS.] Any of several species of shrub of the genus *Sutherlandia* of the Fabaceae, esp. *S. frutescens*; KANKERBOS.

Formerly used medicinally for colds and stomach complaints, and believed to be a cure for cancer.

1888 A. SMITH *Contrib. to Materia Medica* 95 *Sutherlandia frutescens .. Cancer bush.* This shrub has been brought forward recently as a remedy for cancer. **1913** C. PETTMAN *Africanderisms* 106 *Cancer bush, Sutherlandia frutescens, R. Br.* This plant was supposed by the Dutch to be a remedy for cancer. **1917** R. MARLOTH *Common Names* 18 *Cancer Bush, Sutherlandia frutescens.* A half-shrub, 2–4 feet high ... A much esteemed remedy, for various purposes, among the natives. Clinical experiments have not shown any specific action on cancer. **1949** *Cape Argus* 9 July (Mag. Sect.) 3 This is where the .. cancer bushes and chincherinchees for his rockeries are raised. **1966** E. PALMER *Plains of Camdeboo* 277 The early settlers .. used .. the pretty little *Sutherlandia humilis* — the cancer bush — not only for cancer but for flu. **1973** *Weekend Post* 28 Apr. 6 Sutherlandia frutescens .. is commonly called the cancer bush – a rather unfortunate name for such an attractive shrub. **1988** M. BRANCH *Explore Cape Flora* 22 The grey leaves of the cancer bush are split into many leaflets that can fold, and which are also less likely to be damaged by strong winds.

candelabra *n.* [Special senses of Eng.; named for the shape of the plant or inflorescence.] As a qualifier, usu. in the n. phrr.:

1. ***candelabra flower***: any of several species of bulbous plant of the genus *Brunsvigia* of the Amaryllidaceae, esp. *B. orientalis*, bearing a large number of pinkish-red flowers on an umbel; also called SORE-EYE FLOWER (sense a). See also CHANDELIER sense 1.

1868 W.H. HARVEY *Genera of S. Afr. Plants* 382 *Brunsvigia*, Plants with large bulbs, popularly 'Candelabra Flowers.' **1910** *E. London Dispatch* 27 May 5 (Pettman), Brunsvigia or *candelabra flower* — pinkish red, on long pedicels, and not too many of them. *c***1911** S. PLAYNE *Cape Col.* 47 The lilies of the genus Brunsvigia are called by Cape colonists 'Candelabra flowers', because their columns or stems, which are crowned with numerous stalked flowers, all curve upwards and present their cups to the sky bearing much resemblance to a branched candlestick. **1964** G. CAMPBELL *Old Dusty* 48, I shall soon find myself going out to commune with the candelabras and leonotis. **1988** M. BRANCH *Explore Cape Flora* 32 The large dry head of the candelabra flower rolls over the veld like a ball, dropping seeds as it goes.

2. ***candelabra euphorbia***, ***-tree***: any of several cactus-like trees of the genus *Euphorbia* of the Euphorbiaceae, esp. *E. ingens*. See also CHANDELIER sense 3.

[**1834** T. PRINGLE *Afr. Sketches* 209 The lofty candelabra-shaped euphorbias towering above the copses of evergreens.] **1936** C. BIRKBY *Thirstland Treks* 317 The Bushmen of the Namaqualand borders use a mixture of snake poisons, spiders and the sticky juice of the candelabra euphorbia, the big cactus that you see everywhere in Thirstland. **1966** C.A. SMITH *Common Names* 185 *Candelabra tree, Euphorbia ingens* (Lowveld) ... A succulent arborescent with spiny, deeply 4-angled branches and masses of small yellow 'flowers'. **1973** BEETON & DORNER in *Eng. Usage in Sn Afr.* Vol.4

No.1, 10 *Candelabra tree*, .. (*Euphorbia ingens*) .. Succulent tree with single trunk & dense branches; round candelabra shaped crown. **1985** *S. Afr. Panorama* Feb. 33 There is a cactus-like candelabra tree shaded by a flat-topped wild syringa. **1994** *House & Leisure* June 101 The massively branched candelabra tree, *Euphorbia ingens*, is 10 metres high.

3. *candelabra aloe*: the plant *Aloe candelabrum* of the Liliaceae; CHANDELIER sense 2.

1966 *Lantern* Sept. 23 She has used the natural object as a motif ... For the next, we suggested a candelabra aloe. **1966** C.A. SMITH *Common Names* 185 *Candelabra aloe, Aloe candelabrum*: Trunk tall. Leaves in a terminal crown, spiny on the margins; inflorescence candelabra-like. **1986** P. PIETERSE *Day of Giants* 72 You must crush the leaves of the candelabra aloe and put the sap in the wound.

candle bush *n. phr.* BUSHMAN'S CANDLE.

1890 [see KERSBOS *n.*[1]]. **1898** W.C. SCULLY *Between Sun & Sand* 115 No matter how bright the fire of candle bushes, the scherm was lonely at night. **1906** B. STONEMAN *Plants & their Ways* 276 Plants are thorny and succulent, with underground storage systems. *Acacia horrida* (karroo thorn), *Portulacaria afra* (Spekboom), *Sarcocaulon* (Candlebush) .. serve as examples. **1917** R. MARLOTH *Common Names* 18 *Candle bush, Sarcocaulon Burmanni*. A low spiny succulent of the arid regions (flowers white). Burns, even when fresh, like a torch. **1957** L.G. GREEN *Beyond City Lights* 173 The duineveld is covered with reeds and taaibos shrubs, with the large candle-bushes standing alone like trees. **1966** E. PALMER *Plains of Camdeboo* 258 The men cut long forked sticks, spiked on the fork a Candlebush which burns like paraffin, and .. moved quickly from clump to clump, burning off the noors spines. **1971** M.R. LEVYNS in *Std Encycl. of Sn Afr.* III. 17 *Candlebush, Kersbos, Boesmankers.* (*Sarcocaulon burmanii.*) Small, spiny shrub, much-branched ... The old leafstalks become hard and spiny after the blade has withered. The bark is much compressed and wax-impregnated, so that when dry it is highly inflammable and will burn like a torch. **1991** *S. Afr. Panorama* Jan.-Feb. 39 Descriptive flower-names are like music to the ear .. candle bush, cat's tail, desert rose and many more.

candlewood *n.* [tr. Afk. *kershout*, see KERSHOUT.] Either of two species of forest tree or shrub: **1.** The KERSHOUT (sense 2), *Rothmannia capensis*. **2.** The KERSHOUT (sense 1), *Pterocelastrus tricuspidatus*.

*c***1968** J. COPE in *New S. Afr. Writing* No.5, 124 'What kind of tree is this?' 'Looks like candle-wood, or a garra.' **1972** M.R. LEVYNS in *Std Encycl. of Sn Afr.* VI. 370 Other common names of *R. capensis* are candlewood and wild gardenia. **1974** *Motorist* Nov. 12 About 0,5 km from the restaurant an outdoor museum is situated among the beautiful yellowwood, milkwort, candlewood and stinkwood trees. **1984** R.J. POYNTON *Characteristics & Uses of Sel. Trees* 119 Candlewood .. *Pterocelastrus tricuspidatus, Rothmannia capensis.* **1987** T.F.J. VAN RENSBURG *Intro. to Fynbos* 20 Low bushes such as candlewood (*Pterocelastrus tricuspidatus*), sea guarri (*Euclea racemosa*), glossy currant (*Rhus lucida*) and coastal saffron (*Cassine maritima*) often occur in patches. **1991** *Ornamental Trees & Shrubs of Afr. Calendar, Rothmannia capensis*, known in the Cape as Candlewood, is an extremely decorative tree with creamy, fragrant, tubular flowers about 5cm long.

cane *n.* In full *cane spirit(s)*: a popular spirit distilled from sugar-cane, first produced commercially during the 1960s. Also *attrib.*

1965 W. PLOMER *Turbott Wolfe* 62 They were both very far gone in raw cane-spirit, kindly supplied by the lady. **1966** *Cape Argus* 27 Sept. 2 The Government was aware of the increasing competition wine farmers were experiencing .. from beer as well as from cane spirits. **1970** *Forum* Vol.6 No.2, 27, I got a borrel of brandy this morning and then me and a pal of mine went to the saloon and got a half-jack of cane just now. **1972** *Sunday Tribune* 16 July 3 He and Mr D— had sat on the veranda of a friend's house and drunk a two-thirds full bottle of cane spirit and three bottles of sweet wine. **1975** *Darling* 12 Feb., Hot water melon, no shade to keep it cool isn't a blerry joke man. Let alone trying to catch a sluk of your cane and coke. **1981** *Sunday Times* 3 May 41 As they say in the cane spirit advertisement, Mr P W Botha can stay as he is, or he can change to ... **1981** *Cape Times* 22 Dec. 8 She does fancy a few little luxuries. She fancies a chocolate now and again and a bit of Cane at the weekends. **1983** M. DU PLESSIS *State of Fear* 160, I heard the ugly clamour of people getting drunk at eleven o'clock in the morning; suppose it's cane they drink, or gin. **1987** [see PORT JACKSON].

cane rat *n. phr.* [Named for its habitat and diet.] The large rodent *Thryonomys swinderianus* of the Thryonomyidae.

1876 H. BROOKS *Natal* 116 The cane-rat or ground-rat that feeds upon the sugar-canes is properly more of a porcupine than a rat. **1891** R. RUSSELL *Natal* 34 There are also jackals, wild or hunting-dogs .. cane-rats, hares, rabbits, rock-rabbits, and field and house rats and mice. **1907** J.P. FITZPATRICK *Jock of Bushveld* (1909) 339 There were the cane rats .. as big and tender as small suckling-pigs. **1931** *Guide to Vertebrate Fauna of E. Cape Prov.* (Albany Museum) I. 18 *The Cane-Rat*, A stout animal with no true fur, the hairs being very coarse and bristly like small quills, a short rat-like tail, short rounded ears and blunt snout ... They strip the bark of trees and are very destructive to sugar cane. **1971** C.M. VAN DER WESTHUIZEN in *Std Encycl. of Sn Afr.* III. 17 *Cane-rat*, Inhabits dense vegetation in the vicinity of water. **1990** SKINNER & SMITHERS *Mammals of Sn Afr. Subregion* 228 Agricultural development in the growing of crops such as maize, sugar-cane and pineapples has greatly improved the habitat for the greater canerat and .. they can be a problem.

Cango /ˈkæŋgəʊ/ *n. Obs.* exc. *hist.* Also **Kango**. [Name of a region on the southern slopes of the Swartberg, Oudtshoorn district (fr. Khoikhoi *kango* wet mountain).] A brandy produced in the Oudtshoorn district of the Western Cape. Also *attrib.* See also CAPE BRANDY.

1870 [see DOP *n.* sense 2 a]. **1871** *Diamond News* in *Diggers' Ditties* (1989) 4 I'd have drunk a whole gallon 'Cango' If the canteens had given me trust. **1874** 'P.' in A.M.L. Robinson *Sel. Articles from Cape Monthly Mag.* (1978) 168 These [dainties], washed down with a stiff glass of the 'cognac of the country' yclept 'cango', proved a capital supper. **1880** F.G. BROWNING *Fighting & Farming* 119 Two fellows had been drinking pretty freely (principally 'cango' and 'Cape smoke') and became very quarrelsome. **1889** H.A. BRYDEN *Kloof & Karroo* 84 Cango .. is the best kind of colonial-made brandy; it is of rich yellow colour, is produced in the Oudtshoorn district, and when matured, is really a very reasonable substitute for the more expensive foreign liquors. **1891** H.J. DUCKITT *Hilda's 'Where Is It?'* 134 Dissolve three pounds of candied sugar in six bottles of good brandy (*best Cango will do*). **1899** B. MITFORD *Weird of Deadly Hollow* 87 After a good supper, washed down by plenteous libations of Cango brandy and strong coffee, pipes were lit. **1962** A.P. CARTWRIGHT *Gold Miners* 115 A wine merchant's advertisement in 1892 gives us this list of prices: 'Pure Dop Brandy 2s. 6d. a bottle, Best Cango 3s. a bottle, .. Gin 5s. 6d. a flask'. **1983** D.E. SCHAEFER in *Optima* Vol.31 No.2, 86 Favourite drinks among the diggers were Bass light ale, Hennessey's Battle Axe brandy, Irish whiskey, Kango brandy, Spengler's Red gin, Letterstedt's Dop brandy and Guinness stout.

canna *n.*[1] var. GANNA.

canna *n.*[2] var. KANNA *n.*[2]

canna *n.*[3] var. KANNA *n.*[3]

canne doet var. KANNIEDOOD.

canteen *n. Obs.* exc. *hist.* Also **cantine**. [Special sense of general Eng. *canteen* a shop in a military camp or garrison town which sells provisions and liquor to the soldiers.]

a. A liquor shop; a public house. Also *attrib.*

1809 EARL OF CALEDON in G.M. Theal *Rec. of Cape Col.* (1900) VI. 490, I venture to recommend that a salary of 1,000 Rix Drs. pr. annum should be attached to his [*sc.* the Town Major's] Office; .. this .. being the salary which was attached to the Superintendance of Canteens, an appointment formerly held by that of Town Major. **1828** G. BARKER Journal. 6 May, Attended the court against a Canteen man, or retailer of Spiritous liquors, for retailing spirits contrary to Law and illicit traffic. **1835** G. CHAMPION *Jrnl* (1968) 19 Now & then companies pass by apparently just from the canteen (grog shop) .. singing & shouting, cursing & swearing. **1846** *Natal Witness* 10 Apr., Can D'Urban continue to exist with its present number of canteens, — and how many have died within the last three months of *delirium tremens*? **1852** C. BARTER *Dorp & Veld* 9 (Pettman), The inns sadly need reformation — they are in fact little better than *canteens*. **1862** LADY DUFF-GORDON in F. Galton *Vacation Tourists* (1864) III. 155 The so-called Hottentots are earning 2s. 6d. a day, with rations and wine. But all the money goes to the 'canteen' in drink. **1872** C.A. PAYTON *Diamond Diggings* 130 Small establishments for the retailing of liquors, not giving board and lodging, are called 'canteens,' and they are legion; for any man with fifty pounds in his pocket can start a canteen, if only on a very small scale. **1897** J.P. FITZPATRICK *Outspan* 188 The canvas canteens were crowded, and the bare spaces around them were strewn with empty bottles and victims of injudicious zeal. **1910** *E. Prov. Herald* 16 Apr., The report of the Transvaal Liquor Commission which will shortly be laid before Parliament recommends the establishment of Government Canteens for the sale of kaffir beer to natives. **1918** *Cape Argus* in J. Crwys-Williams *S. Afr. Despatches* (1989) 221 Representatives of the local licensed victuallers, .. in the interest of combating the epidemic, consented to close all bars, canteens and bottle stores for the supply of liquor .. until November 1. **1952** H. KLEIN *Land of Silver Mist* 122 A camp was established. Corrugated iron buildings sprang up. Canteens and gambling dens dotted the veld. **1962** A.P. CARTWRIGHT *Gold Miners* 55 He .. had shared drinks with Harrison and Walker in Koos Malan's primitive canteen. *Ibid.* 76 There were the same heavily loaded wagons pulled by teams of gaunt oxen, .. the same canteens set up in tents to sell Cape brandy and Nellmapius's 'Hatherley' gin. **1983** *Sunday Times* 4 Sept. (Mag. Sect.) 22 By 1895 there were 1 000 canteens between Krugersdorp and Nigel. Drunkenness was common and led to murders, faction fights and deaths from alcoholic poisoning.

b. *comb.* **canteen-keeper**, the proprietor of a public house; **canteen-keeping** *vbl n.*, also *attrib.*

1832 *Graham's Town Jrnl* 13 Jan. 11, I contend that a **Canteen keeper** can be as respectable a man, and as useful a member of Society as the 'True African'. **1843** *Cape of G.H. Almanac & Annual Register*, Jolly, John, canteenkeeper, east-barracks. **1878** T.J. LUCAS *Camp Life & Sport* 126 The canteen-keeper, who was the chief drain upon the pocket of the diamond seeker. **1882** [see *Natal rum* (NATAL sense a)]. **1933** W. MACDONALD *Romance of Golden Rand* 123 It was soon found that the canteen keepers were bribing the natives, and giving them liquor for diamonds. **1955** V. DE KOCK *Fun They Had* 153 A Jew canteen-keeper, who had picked up his riding .. in the United States army. **1972** *Grocott's Mail* 1 Feb. 3 He became Grahamstown's first canteen-keeper when he opened his canteen or 'grog shop' (as canteens and bars were sometimes called) at his house on erf No. 24. **1833** *Graham's Town Jrnl* 21 Mar. 2 Stamps us as one of the most Brandy-loving, **canteen-keeping** people in existence.

Capab /ˈkeɪpæb/ *n.* Also **CAPAB**. Acronym formed on *Cape Performing Arts Board*, a body established in 1962 to produce and promote theatre, opera, ballet, and music in the (then) Cape Province. Also *attrib.* See also NAPAC, PACOFS, PACT.

1965 W.J.B. SLATER in M. Grut *Hist. of Ballet* (1981) 196 We are expected to provide on a professional basis for the four expensive arts to a comparatively small population distributed in hundreds of towns and villages over an enormous area ... CAPAB will therefore need a much larger income in the future. **1970** *Argus* 24 Dec. 3 After dancing her way through many countries in the past 10 years, Cape Town-born Veronica Esterhuizen has come back to dance in her own country – for Capab Ballet. **1973** A. HARTMAN in *Std Encycl. of Sn Afr.* VIII. 377 An orchestra of 46 musicians was formed by the Cape Performing Arts Board (Capab) to play for opera and ballet performances in the new Nico Malan Opera House. **1980** A. & A.R. HOFFMAN *They Built Theatre* 168 Now that Pact, Capab and Pacofs are sponsored by the State, their provinces, and local authorities, it is possible for these groups to 'go to town' on all their productions, and losses are expected as a necessary part of cultural development. **1989** *Style* Feb. 41 His cabaret *Piekniek by Dingaan* .. turned establishment hair grey in the cautious corridors of Capab.

caparran var. KAPARRANG.

capa(r)ter var. KAPATER.

Cap Classique /ˌkap klaˈsiːk/ *n. phr.* [Fr., *Cap* Cape (see CAPE) + *classique* classic.] Shortened form of METHODE CAP CLASSIQUE. Also *attrib.*

1992 I. VON HOLDT in *Sunday Times* 6 Sept. 13 Paul Cadiau, wine educator, writer and graduate oenologist from France .. was full of praise for the Cap Classique wines. 'The name is beautiful – it tells everyone what it is, and it personalises the wine.' **1992** *Style* Nov. 92 Cap Classique Celebration, a brunch in which 12 local producers of sparkling wine will be presenting about 20 top-notch sparklers.

Cape *n.* [Ellipt. for *Cape of Good Hope*.]
1. ***The Cape***: A name for **a.** the Cape of Good Hope; **b.** *hist.* the Cape Colony; *the Colony*, see COLONY; **c.** the (Western) Cape Province; **d.** the Cape Peninsula; **e.** Cape Town. In all senses also called KAAP. Also *attrib.* See also FAIREST CAPE.

In 1994 the Cape Province was divided into three new provinces, the Western Cape, Eastern Cape, and Northern Cape.

[**1589** in W.S.W. Vaux *World Encompassed by Sir Francis Drake* (1854) 251 From *Jaua Maior* we sailed for the cape of *Good Hope* ... This Cape is a most stately thing, and the fairest Cape we saw in the whole circumference of the earth, and we passed by it the 18. of June [1580].] **1667** J. MILTON *Paradise Lost* Bk II. Line 637, They on the trading flood, Through the wide Ethiopian to the Cape, Ply stemming nightly toward the pole. **1696** J. OVINGTON *Voy. to Suratt* 289 The *third* thing observable at the *Cape*, was the Profit and Advantage which that Plantation affords the *Dutch*. **1731** G. MEDLEY tr. *P. Kolb's Present State of Cape of G.H.* I. 23 The First [Colony] is at the *Cape*, where are the Grand Forts, and the Capital City, call'd also the *Cape*; in which, and about it, are many genteel Buildings, with all sorts of Accommodations. **1773** P. CARTERET in J. Hawkesworth *Acct of Voy.* I. 8, I thought it better to run the risk of a few hard gales off the Cape, than remain longer in this unhealthy place. **1786** G. FORSTER tr. *A. Sparrman's Voy. to Cape of G.H.* I. 8 The town itself is the only one in the whole colony, and is properly called the *Cape*, though this name is often injudiciously given to the whole settlement. **1798** S.H. WILCOCKE tr. *J.S. Stavorinus's Voy. to E. Indies 1768–71* I. 558 The wild animals, which are found in the country, .. are now far removed from the *Cape*, and are seldom seen near it. *Ibid.* II. 56 The more distant farmers, required forty days (or rather nights, for they always travel by night), to ride their waggons to the *Cape*. **1810** G. BARRINGTON *Acct of Voy.* 152 The Cape, or principal district, is mostly composed of that peninsula, whose Southernmost projection was called by the Portuguese navigators, the *Cape of Storms*. *a***1827** [see SPEKBOOM sense 1]. **1828** J. PHILIP *Researches* I. 19 Cape Town is termed *'The Cape'* by the colonists. **1841** B. SHAW *Memorials* 15 The salubrity of the Cape climate attracts a great number of persons from India, who reside for a time in Cape Town or its vicinity, for the recovery of their health. **1852** E. RUTHERFOORD in J. Murray *In Mid-Victorian Cape Town* (1953) 21 If we were once to leave the dear old Cape I am afraid we should never see it again. **1859** *Cape Town Weekly Mag.* 21 Jan. 12 All idea of re-annexation to the Cape appears to have vanished into thin air and the people are consequently busy considering the question of union with the Transvaal Republic. **1888** *Cape Punch* 8 Feb. 69 By dint of sheer hard work the Cape Croesus – and by 'Cape' Mr. *C.-P.* refers to the whole colony – has raised himself to his present position. **1891** H.J. DUCKITT *Hilda's 'Where Is It?'* 127 Boiled *snook* or cabeljou [*printed* cabeljon], if at the Cape, or any white fish will do. **1913** D. FAIRBRIDGE *Piet of Italy* 300 It's glad enough they'll .. get back to the Cape .. but for my part I'm enchanted with Durban. **1941** C.W. DE KIEWIET *Hist. of S. Afr.* 1 It was renamed the Cape of Good Hope. But its fame and importance grew till it was familiarly called the Cape, without danger of confusion with the numberless other capes of the earth's surface. **1953** 'AMPERBAAS' in *Drum* Apr. 6 Coming to Johannesburg from the Cape thirty years ago, I tried to find a job. **1965** A. GORDON-BROWN *S. Afr. Heritage* 13 By 1800 the town had pushed up towards the mountain ... 'The Cape' had become 'Cape Town'. **1971** *Std Encycl. of Sn Afr.* III. 23 Before Union, 'the Cape' popularly stood for the Cape Colony, the political entity which, at the time of Union (1910) became the Cape Province. The same appellation therefore stood and still stands for the Cape of Good Hope, which also conveys the double meaning of a mere promontory and a whole province. Furthermore, the 'Cape' may mean the Cape Peninsula, or even, in popular parlance, Cape Town, as well as the magisterial district of the Cape, commonly known as the Cape district. Finally, 'the Cape' may refer to the Cape division, the area under the jurisdiction of the Cape Divisional Council. **1982** *E. Prov. Herald* 27 July 13 In the Republic there are an estimated 16 000 species of wild flowers which include the renowned Cape flora, one of the richest assemblages of plants in the world. **1990** R. GOOL *Cape Town Coolie* 173 He had once wanted .. to merge himself with the Cape, to belong here in Cape Town.

2. Special Comb.
a. Plants and animals: **Cape ant-eater**, see ANT-EATER sense 1; **Cape ash**, the ESSENHOUT (sense a), *Ekebergia capensis*; **Cape beech**, the tree *Rapanea melanophloeos* of the Myrsinaceae; also called BOEKENHOUT; **Cape box**, the tree *Buxus macowanii* of the Buxaceae; **Cape buffalo**, the BUFFALO (sense 1), *Syncerus caffer*; **Cape bulbs**, see quot. 1966; **Cape canary**, the seed-eating bird *Serinus canicollis* of the Fringillidae; also called SYSIE (sense a); **Cape cedar**, the CLANWILLIAM CEDAR, *Widdringtonia cedarbergensis*; **Cape chestnut**, *wild chestnut* sense (b), see WILD sense a; **Cape cobra**, the venomous cobra *Naja nivea* of the Elapidae; BAKKOP; *yellow cobra*, see YELLOW sense a; see also MFESI, and RINKHALS sense 1; **Cape cormorant**, the marine bird *Phalacrocorax capensis* of the Phalacrocoracidae; *trek-duiker*, see DUIKER sense 2 b i; **Cape cow** *obs.*, see quots; **Cape dikkop**, see DIKKOP sense 1 a i; **Cape dune molerat**, see MOLERAT sense 2; **Cape ebony**, either of two tree species, (*a*) *Heywoodia lucens* of the Euphorbiaceae; (*b*) *Euclea pseudebenus* of the Ebenaceae; **Cape fox**, the mammal *Vulpes chama* of the Canidae; **Cape francolin**, the game bird *Francolinus capensis* of the Phasianidae; **Cape fur seal**, the seal *Arctocephalus pusillus* of the Otariidae; **Cape gannet**, the MALGAS, *Morus capensis*; also *attrib.*; **Cape golden mole**, see GOLDEN MOLE sense b; **Cape grysbok**, see GRYSBOK; **Cape hare**, the hare *Lepus capensis* of the Leporidae; *vlakte haas*, see VLAKTE sense 2; **Cape hartebeest**, see HARTEBEEST *n.* sense b; **Cape heath** *obs.*, a collective name for various species of heath-like plants indigenous to the Cape Peninsula; **Cape hen**, the white-chinned petrel *Procellaria aequinoctialis* of the Procellariidae; **Cape holly**, the tree *Ilex mitis* of the Aquifoliaceae; **Cape honeysuckle**, the TECOMA, *Tecomaria capensis*; **Cape horse**, a hardy horse bred predominantly from Oriental and English stock, from which two indigenous breeds, the BOERPERD and the BASOTHO PONY, were developed; **Cape hunting dog**, the *wild dog* (see WILD sense b), *Lycaon pictus*; **Cape hyacinth**, *berg lily* (see BERG sense 1 b ii); **Cape jasmine**, also **Cape jassamine**, **-jessamine**, any of several sweet-scented flowering plants of the genus *Gardenia*; also called KATJIEPIERING; **Cape laburnum**, the plant *Crotalaria capensis* of the Fabaceae; **Cape lark** *obs.*, the KALKOENTJIE (sense 1), *Macronyx capensis*; **Cape lilac**, (*a*) the SYRINGA (sense a), *Melia azedarach*; (*b*) the *deurmekaarbos* (see DEURMEKAAR sense 2), *Ehretia rigida*; **Cape lion**, an extinct subspecies of lion, *Panthera leo melanochaites*; **Cape lobster**, CRAYFISH; **Cape mahogany**, either of two tree species, (*a*) *Natal mahogany* sense (*a*), see NATAL sense b; (*b*) STINKWOOD sense a; its wood; **Cape marigold**, NAMAQUALAND DAISY; **Cape molerat**, see MOLERAT sense 2; **Cape mountain zebra**, see *mountain zebra* sense (*a*) at MOUNTAIN; **Cape otter** (now usu. **Cape clawless otter**), the otter *Aonyx capensis* of the Mustelidae; **Cape ox** *obs.*, AFRIKANDER *n.* sense 4; **Cape parrot**, the endangered parrot *Poicephalus robustus* of the Psittacidae; **Cape partridge**, see PARTRIDGE sense 1 b; **Cape pheasant**, see PHEASANT sense b; **Cape pigeon**, the mottled black and white Pintado petrel, *Daption capense* of the Procellariidae; **Cape pondweed**, WATERBLOMMETJIE sense a; **Cape Riesling**, RIESLING sense 1; **Cape robin**, the common garden bird *Cossypha caffra* of the Turdidae; JAN FREDERIK; **Cape saffron**, (*a*) the plant *Sutera atropurpurea* of the Scrophulariaceae; (*b*) the tree *Cassine peragua* of the Celastraceae; **Cape sandalwood**, see SANDALWOOD; **Cape sheep** *obs.*, freq. with qualifying word, **large-tailed Cape sheep**, *fat-tailed sheep*, see FAT-TAILED sense a; **Cape sparrow**, the sparrow *Passer melanurus*; MOSSIE (sense 1 a); **Cape tiger**, the TIGER (sense 1), *Panthera pardus*; **Cape trumpet flower**, the TECOMA, *Tecomaria capensis*; **Cape vulture**, the endangered vulture *Gyps coprotheres* of the Accipitridae; also called AASVOEL (sense a); **Cape wagtail**, the commonest and most widely distributed of the southern African wagtails, *Motacilla capensis*, noted for its lack of fear of humans; also called QUICKSTERTJE; **Cape walnut**, (*a*) STINKWOOD sense a; (*b*) BOERBOON; **Cape wigeon** *obs.*, the teal *Anas capensis* of the Anatidae; **Cape willow** *?obs.*, the tree *Salix capensis* of the Salicaceae.

1989 *Gardening Questions Answered* (Reader's Digest Assoc.) 333 *Ekbergia, Ekbergia capensis* ... Also known as **Cape ash**. **1993** L. BROWN in *House & Leisure* Dec. 77 In Africa tree and roof may be one and the same. A giant Cape ash is the traditional heart of this thoroughly modern dwelling. **1961** PALMER & PITMAN *Trees of S. Afr.* 262 The **Cape beech** or boekenhout is one of the most variable of all South African trees. **1984** A. WANNENBURGH *Natural Wonder of Sn Afr.* 94 Some species – including white pear, .. Cape beech and Cape holly – are among the main trees in most Outeniqualand forest types. **1951** N.L. KING *Tree-Planting* 66 *Buxus macowani* (**Cape box**), .. A small and extremely slow-growing tree with small shiny leaves. **1961** PALMER & PITMAN *Trees of S. Afr.* 196 The Cape box occupies a unique position among South African trees for its timber is one of the very few exported from the Union. **1731** G. MEDLEY tr. *P. Kolb's Present State of Cape of G.H.* II. 109 A **Cape-Buffalo** is enrag'd at the Sight of red cloth, and at the Discharge of a Gun near him. **1910** A.B. LAMONT *Rural Reader* 82 These strong shoulders and short horns are still seen in the Cape buffalo. **1984** A. WANNENBURGH *Natural Wonder of Sn Afr.* 97 Red hartebeest, bontebok, Cape buffalo and spotted hyena disappeared from the coastal plains. **1992** C. STUART in *Afr. Wildlife* Vol.46

No.6, 279 Most of the imported animals are red forest buffalo .. or red forest buffalo/Cape buffalo hybrids ... This has serious implications for pure Cape buffalo stocks in South Africa. **1949** L.G. GREEN *In Land of Afternoon* 72 Australia grows **Cape Bulbs** in huge quantities. **1966** C.A. SMITH *Common Names* 186 *Cape bulbs*, A general term formerly commonly used in literature to indicate those groups of the more showy of the native monocotyledonous plants, chiefly belonging to the families Liliaceae, Amaryllidaceae, Haemadoraceae and Iridaceae. **1795** M.A. PARKER *Voy. round World* 141 To those who are amateurs of birds, I can, from experience, recommend the **Cape Canary**, the plumage of which is much like our green linnet. **1867** E.L. LAYARD *Birds of S. Afr.* 201 The Cape canary is a common bird throughout the colony, congregating in flocks on the open and ploughed lands, and feeding on grains and seeds of all kinds. **1890** A. MARTIN *Home Life* 18 The Cape canary is a greenish bird, with a very pretty soft note, quite different from the piercing screech of his terrible yellow brother in English homes. **1940** BAUMANN & BRIGHT *Lost Republic* 234 There were lots of little birds that we caught in traps .. but none, except the Cape canary, could sing nicely. **1983** K.B. NEWMAN *Newman's Birds* 436 *Cape Canary, Serinus canicollis* ... Song a series of loud, rolling warbles and trills. **1815** J. MACKRILL Diary. 120 The Shrub called the **Cape Cedar** is the Cupressus Iuniperoides. **1880** *S.W. Silver & Co.'s Handbk to S. Afr.* 125 They are patches of Cape Cedar .. and this is the only locality in which the tree is found. **1904** D.E. HUTCHINGS in *Agric. Jrnl of Cape of G.H.* Feb. 2 In size and appearance the Cape Cedar much resembles *Cedrus atlantica* ... The Cape Cedar produces an abundance of good seed and is easily propagated. **1971** J.A. MARSH in *Std Encycl. of Sn Afr.* III. 134 *Cedar, Clanwilliam. Cape (pencil) cedar.* **1912** *E. London Dispatch* 12 Apr. 7 (Pettman), It is very seldom that the **Cape chestnut** and the Wild fig become altogether devoid of leaves. **1951** N.L. KING *Tree-Planting* 66 *Calodendrum capensis, (Cape Chestnut)*, A large deciduous tree which bears masses of pink flowers in summer. **1991** *Ornamental Trees & Shrubs (calendar)*, *Calodendrum capense* — literally 'the beautiful tree of the Cape' — the Wild, or Cape Chestnut — was nominated as tree of the year in 1989. **1910** F.W. FITZSIMONS *Snakes of Sn Afr.* 74 The **Cape Cobra** (*Naia flava*) .. is by far the commonest species of Cobra inhabiting South Africa. **1943** B. ADAMS in *Outspan* 27 Aug. 32 As I looked down to where I would land (I was in the air) I saw a five-foot yellow Cape cobra. **1963** S.H. SKAIFE *Naturalist Remembers* 114 The Cape Cobra is a more dangerous reptile to tackle than the puff adder. **1988** M. BRANCH *Explore Cape Flora* 37 The Cape cobra may be yellow, brown or black. It is fast moving and usually retreats down a hole or under rocks. **1906** STARK & SCLATER *Birds of S. Afr.* IV. 6 **'Cape Cormorant'** of some authors. **1913** C. PETTMAN *Africanderisms* 109 *Cape cormorant, Graculus capensis, Gray.* **1969** J.R. GRINDLEY *Riches of Sea* 92 Vast numbers of sea birds occur in the seas off South Africa and nest on isolated islands near the coast... The commonest species are Cape cormorants (Phalacrocorax demersus). **1987** R. CRAWFORD in *Conserva* Oct. 6 The Cape cormorant is another species that breeds only along the Southern African coast ... Cape cormorants often feed in large flocks on dense shoals of small fish in near-surface waters. **1896** R. WALLACE *Farming Indust. of Cape Col.* 255 The **Cape Cow**, bred in the Cape Peninsula, belongs to a mixed breed famous for milking qualities. **1910** A.B. LAMONT *Rural Reader* 88 The Cape cow is the result of a combination of breeds, the hardy Afrikander qualities being combined with the characteristics of the Friesland, the Ayrshire, the Jersey, and other milking breeds. **1913** C. PETTMAN *Africanderisms* 110 **Cape ebony**, Both *Euclea pseudebenus* and *Heywoodia lucens* are so named. **1950** [see ESSENHOUT]. **1957** L.G. GREEN *Beyond City Lights* 10 The man spoke fondly of the Knysna evergreens, the scarlet-flowering kaffirboom of the Amatola range, .. the Cape ebony and Cape mahogany. **1961** PALMER & PITMAN *Trees of S. Afr.* 137 *Euclea pseudebenus*, the heartwood of which yields the jet-black, fine-grained, and durable wood known as Cape ebony, is confined almost entirely to the water courses of the north-west Cape and South West Africa. **1982** [see OLIENHOUT]. **1951** A. ROBERTS *Mammals* 200 The **Cape Fox** is not ordinarily a destructive animal .. and seldom does any harm to domestic small stock. **1985** C. WALKER *Signs of Wild* 49 *Cape Fox*, .. The only true fox to be found in southern Africa. **1988** A. HALL-MARTIN et al. *Kaokoveld* 32 The Cape fox is more secretive and more strictly nocturnal than either the aardwolf or bat-eared fox. **1971** *Evening Post* 12 June (Weekend Mag.) 1 He also breeds the **Cape francolin**, the Free State Swainson .. and the Orange River francolin. **1985** G.L. MACLEAN *Roberts' Birds of Sn Afr.* 175 *Cape Francolin* ... *Distribution*: Winter rainfall area .. *Status*: Common resident. **1911** *E. London Dispatch* 7 Sept. 5 (Pettman), Three young examples of the **Cape** sea-lion or **fur-seal** (*Otaria pusilla*). **1958** L.G. GREEN *S. Afr. Beachcomber* 139 Cape fur seals are not so amenable to training as other species. **1990** SKINNER & SMITHERS *Mammals of Sn Afr. Subregion* 525 Uncontrolled exploitation of the Cape fur seal which continued late into the 19th century led to the diminution of numbers. **1913** C. PETTMAN *Africanderisms* 111 **Cape gannet**, *Sula capensis*. **1936** E.L. GILL *First Guide to S. Afr. Birds* 186 *Malgas, Cape gannet* ... This is the gannet of the South African guano islands, on .. which it breeds in crowded acres, producing a substantial proportion of the annual harvest of guano. **1988** R. LUBKE et al. *Field Guide to E. Cape* 267 There is a large Cape Gannet colony on Bird Island. **1810** G. BARRINGTON *Acct of Voy.* 282 They have the **Cape hare.** **1853** F.P. FLEMING *Kaffraria* 66 It is the well-known *Lepus-Capensis*, or Cape hare, and its common local cognomen among the Dutch is the Vlakte Haas. *c*1936 *S. & E. Afr. Yr Bk & Guide* 1101 The Cape hare is light brown and somewhat smaller than the English hare. **1990** SKINNER & SMITHERS *Mammals of Sn Afr. Subregion* 171 Apart from the fact that the original specimen .. came from the Cape of Good Hope, the Cape hare is by no means associated particularly with this part of Africa. **1852** A.W. COLE *Cape & Kafirs* 30 Land covered with an innumerable variety of **Cape heaths** in full bloom. **1868** W.H. HARVEY *Genera of S. Afr. Plants* 216 *Erica*, .. A vast genus of over 400 species, the greater number of which are South African, and well known in European gardens as 'Cape Heaths'. **1893** *Brown's S. Afr.* 149 This part of the country may be regarded as the natural home of the Cape heaths. **1775** DALRYMPLE in *Phil. Trans. of Royal Soc.* LXVIII. 408 An uncommon birdlike **Cape hen.** **1809** 'G. VALENTIA' *Voy. & Trav.* I. 50 Cape hens have appeared, and very large flights of birds. **1867** E.L. LAYARD *Birds of S. Afr.* 360 The 'Cape Hen' is a constant resident in Table Bay, though the majority leave us at one season of the year to breed. **1937** M. ALSTON *Wanderings* 27 The Cape Hen .. with its albatross-like flight .. swept into the bay and away again. **1958** L.G. GREEN *S. Afr. Beachcomber* 105 The Cape hen, a very common black petrel with a white bill and chin. **1985** G.L. MACLEAN *Roberts' Birds of Sn Afr.* 22 *Whitechinned Petrel* (Cape Hen). **1917** R. MARLOTH *Common Names* 40 **Holly, Cape**, *Ilex mitis*. A stately tree with glossy foliage, from Table Mountain to the Drakensberg and beyond. **1957** L.G. GREEN *Beyond City Lights* 12 It was the show piece of a 'fairy glen' filled with tree ferns, Cape holly and red alder. **1984** [see quot. at *Cape beech* above]. **1883** M.A. CAREY-HOBSON *Farm in Karoo* 141 They had brought in from the wood some branches of a beautiful scarlet flowering shrub which George called the **Cape Honeysuckle.** **1951** N.L. KING *Tree-Planting* 71 *Tecomaria capensis, (Cape honeysuckle)*, .. Bears masses of large, brick-red flowers in spring. Also used as a climber. **1990** M. HAYTER in *Flying Springbok* July 119 Indigenous blue plumbago and bright Cape honeysuckle sprawl in the shade of coral trees, wild figs and oaks. **1804** R. RENSHAW *Voy. to Cape of G.H.* 56 The **Cape-horses** are small, but remarkably swift. **1837** 'N. POLSON' *Subaltern's Sick Leave* 164 The Cape horses are the quietest and most gregarious in their habits I have ever seen. Kickers and biters are almost unknown. **1882** J. NIXON *Among Boers* 33 Cape horses have a wonderful amount of endurance. They will go through work which will knock an English horse up in three days. **1973** J. MEINTJES *Voortrekkers* 106 This was a formidable band of men, firmly seated on their Cape horses, their rifles on their backs. **1990** J. THERON in *Farmer's Weekly* 20 Apr. (Sporting Horse) 13 Cape farmers kept on breeding with their original Oriental stock and a distinct inbred Cape Horse emerged that was renowned world wide as a military mount. **1887** *S.W. Silver & Co.'s Handbk to S. Afr.* 169 Another very remarkable animal is the **Cape Hunting Dog** (*Lycaon pictus*) .. which combines to a great extent the structure of the dog and hyaena. **1963** S. CLOETE *Rags of Glory* 378 Packs of Cape hunting dogs — yellow, marked irregularly with black and white, their bat ears pricked — galloped over the veld in pursuit of anything they could kill. **1990** SKINNER & SMITHERS *Mammals of Sn Afr. Subregion* 429 Often referred to as the Cape hunting dog, there seems no good reason why Cape should be retained as the species has a wide distribution in Africa south of the Sahara ... Hunting dog is acceptable, but wild dog is widely used and well entrenched. **1993** *House & Leisure* Oct. 126 Galtonia (**Cape Hyacinth** or berg lily) and St. Joseph's lilies. **1760** ELLIS in *Phil. Trans. of Royal Soc.* LI. 932 The **Cape Jasmine** .. is the most rare and beautiful shrub, that has yet been introduced into the European gardens. **1776** J. SCHAW *Jrnl of Lady of Quality* (1921) 246 We were admiring a row of cape jessamine, which even now is covered with flowers. **1804** J. BARROW *Trav.* II. 82 The *Gardenia Thunbergia*, or the wild Cape Jessamine, being in the height of its blossom, gave out so powerful a scent, that, in the evening, it could be felt [*sic*] at the distance of several miles. **1822** T. PHILIPPS *Lett.* (1960) 117 A thick shrubbery of geraniums, Cape Jassamine, and Palma Christi. **1879** MRS HUTCHINSON *In Tents in Tvl* 27 Cape Jasmines, looking like large hollies, grow in the bush, their white star-like flowers tipping their dark glossy branches. **1971** *Horticultural Terms* (Dept of Nat. Educ.) 34 *Cape jasmine*, (Gardenia, *Gardenia jasminoides*). **1973** *Weekend Post* 28 Apr. 6 The Crotalaria capensis is the well known **Cape Laburnum**, which is a much daintier plant that becomes covered with butter-yellow flowers in spring. **1991** H. HUTCHINGS in *Weekend Post* 23 Feb. (Leisure) 7 By using some of the faster-growing kinds like .. *Calpurnia* (Cape laburnum) .. create a micro-climate favourable for the cultivation of the others. **1821** C.I. LATROBE *Jrnl of Visit* 562 **Cape-lark**, *Alauda Capensis*. **1838** J.E. ALEXANDER *Exped. into Int.* I. 160 The Cape lark whirred aloft, and dropt to the ground with its melancholy note. **1913** C. PETTMAN *Africanderisms* 111 *Cape lark, Macronix capensis*. **1868** W.H. HARVEY *Genera of S. Afr. Plants* 49 *M[elia] Azedarach* .. the **'Cape Lilac'** or 'Pride of China', is cultivated throughout the colony, and partly naturalized. **1906** B. STONEMAN *Plants & their Ways* 31 In *Cassia* and the Cape Lilac they [*sc.* lenticels] extend across the stem. **1966** C.A. SMITH *Common Names* 187 *Cape lilac, Ehretia rigida* ... The plants bear masses of lilac to lilac-blue flowers on drooping branches and in general appearance the plants .. are suggestive of the European lilac. **1987** F. VON BREITENBACH *Nat. List of Indigenous Trees* 171 *Ehretia rigida*, .. *Puzzle Bush*, Cape Lilac. **1951** L.G. GREEN *Grow Lovely* 143 The **Cape lion** has vanished from the Cape almost without trace ... [It] seems to have been a sub-species, larger than the northern lion and with a black mane. **1976** A.R. WILLCOX *Sn Land* 113 In one of the Robberg caves was found a lion's shoulder blade (from its size probably from the extinct Cape lion). **1987** T.F.J. VAN RENSBURG *Intro. to Fynbos* 51 The bluebuck, quagga and Cape Lion have long been extinct. **1989** D. DAY *Encycl. of Vanished Species* 177 The last Cape Lion sighted in Cape Province itself was killed in 1858, but the last of the subspecies was hunted down and shot by General Bisset in Natal, in 1865. **1795** C.R. HOPSON tr. *C.P. Thunberg's Trav.* I. 240 The **Cape lobster** (*Cancer arctos*) .. has no large claws and is craggy all over, and covered with erect prickles. It has a strong and not very agreeable taste. **1902** H.J. DUCKITT *Hilda's Diary of Cape Hsekeeper* 47 'Crayfish,' or 'Kreeft,' is also plentiful all through the summer. We also call it 'Cape lobster.' **1913** W.W. THOMPSON *Sea Fisheries of Cape Col.* 51 The 'Cape lobster', as it is sometimes called, although it does not possess the huge claw for which its European congener is so famous, is a most valuable asset of the Cape fishing industry. **1955** [see CRAYFISH]. **1990** S. GRAY in *Staffrider* Vol.9 No.1, 50 Mounds of yellow rice, studded with whole abalones, Red Romans, bordered by mussels ... A Cape lobster on top. **1843** R. GODLONTON in J.C. Chase *Cape of G.H.* (1967) 48 The **Cape mahogany**, or stinkwood, is not found in Albany. **1913** C. PETTMAN *Africanderisms* 112 *Cape mahogany, Trichilia emetica.* The flowers of this tree which open in November are strongly scented. **1887** [see STINKWOOD sense a]. **1929** J. STEVENSON-HAMILTON *Low-Veld* 37 The umkudhlu, or Cape mahogany tree (*Trichilia emetica*) does not attain the height of the umtoma, about thirty feet being its limit in the Low-Veld. **1957** [see quot. at *Cape ebony* above]. **1984** *S. Afr. Panorama* Feb. 38 One of the most beautiful of all indigenous trees is the Cape Mahogany (rooi-essenhout) *Trichilia emetica.* **1971** *Farmer's Weekly* 12 June 55 It is called the African Daisy, Cape Daisy, **Cape Marigold** or Star of the Veld. **1989** [see NAMAQUALAND DAISY]. **1900** W.L. SCLATER *Mammals of S. Afr.* I. 108 The **Cape otter** .. is often found near the sea, in places where there are no streams. **1918** S.H. SKAIFE *Animal Life* 266 The Cape otter is a large dark-brown animal found only on the banks of streams and lakes. **1973** C.M. VAN DER WESTHUIZEN in *Std Encycl. of Sn Afr.* VIII. 403 The giant Cape or clawless otter (*Aonyx capensis*) is the largest of all Old World otters. **1990** SKINNER & SMITHERS *Mammals of Sn Afr. Subregion* 446 Two species occur on the continent, the Cape clawless otter, *A. capensis*, and the Zaire clawless otter, *A. congica.* **1807** *Afr. Court Calendar*, The heavy draught work of the colony is chiefly performed by oxen. The **Cape ox** is distinguished by his long legs, high shoulders, and large horns. **1821** C.I. LATROBE *Jrnl of Visit* 561 Cape-ox *is a variety of Bos Taurus.* **1921** H.J. MANDELBROTE tr. *O.F. Mentzel's Descr. of Cape of G.H.* I. 59 The Cape oxen are more suited for this purpose than horses, and when the Hottentots trek from place to place large caravans of oxen can be seen laden with huts and various utensils. **1931** *Guide to Vertebrate Fauna of E. Cape Prov.* (Albany Museum) I. 168 *Poicephalus robustus*, **Cape Parrot** ... Occurs in coastal and inland forests. **1970** O.P.M. PROZESKY *Field Guide to Birds* 148 *Cape Parrot*, .. This robust parrot is the largest in Southern Africa. **1991** E. KOCH in *Weekly Mail* 15 Mar. (Suppl.) 15 Rare birds that nest in the forests include the Cape parrot, Cape barn owl, the extremely vulnerable ground hornbill and the mangrove kingfisher. **1798** S.H. WILCOCKE tr. *J.S. Stavorinus's Voy. to E. Indies 1768–71* II. 31 We saw .. the birds called '**cape pigeons**'. **1853** W. RABONE in A. Rabone *Rec. of Pioneer Family* (1966) 43 Some Cape pigeons flew round the ship all day ... They are beautifully speckled black and white, about the size of a pigeon. **1878** T.J. LUCAS *Camp Life & Sport* 13 We left St. Helena and had now reached the zone frequented by the beautiful Cape pigeon, with its butterfly flight and handsomely speckled wings, flitting restlessly and unceasingly in our wake. **1906** STARK & SCLATER *Birds of S. Afr.* IV. 486 The Cape Pigeon is one of the commonest of the Petrels found in Cape seas ... To the east of Table Bay the Cape Pigeon is apparently a good deal less plentiful. **1985** G.L. MACLEAN *Roberts' Birds of Sn Afr.* 15 *Pintado Petrel* (Cape Pigeon) .. *Daption capense.* **1982** FOX & NORWOOD YOUNG *Food from Veld* 93 *Aponogeton distachyos*, .. *Common names*: English — *Cape asparagus*, **Cape pond weed**, *water onion.* **1990** *Menu, Dept of Nat. Education* Pumpkin Fritters, Cape Pondweed Stew, Stewed Fruit. **1988** D. HUGHES et al. *Complete Bk of S. Afr. Wine* 98 The grapes and the juice of **Cape riesling** have to be carefully handled, as this cultivar is particularly prone to oxidation which causes a slight browning of the wine ... Not only are Cape Riesling wines delightful to drink when young, but with selected plant material, fruit of optimum ripeness, and expert wine making, wines of special quality, which have good ageing potential, can be produced. **1867** E.L. LAYARD *Birds of S. Afr.* 132 This is the **Cape 'robin'**, and decidedly deserves the name. It is common in all the gardens .. pouring out a short, robin-like song. **1923** HAAGNER & IVY *Sketches* 170 The commonest member of the Robin-Chats is the 'Cape' species (*Cossypha caffra*) called the Cape Robin or Jan Fredric. **1960** J. COPE *Tame Ox* 88 Voices answered from the bush, quietly, like the note of the Cape robin. **1988** J. HUNTLY in *Saturday Star* 9 July (Weekend) 20 The piles of cut branches also attracted many white-eyes, .. Cape robin and a few others. **1897** EDMONDS & MARLOTH *Elementary Botany* 162 The flowers of *L. crocea* are called **Cape-saffron** (*Geele bloemetjes*). **1906** B. STONEMAN *Plants & their Ways* 260 *L. crocea* is called 'Cape Saffron' (Geele bloemetjies). **1949** L.G. GREEN *In Land of Afternoon* 51 Chest complaints are often treated with a dagga tincture, or geelblommetjie tea (Cape saffron) or Protea syrup. **1987** F. VON BREITENBACH *Nat. List of Indigenous Trees* 414 *Cassine peragua* .. *C. capensis*, .. Cape Saffron, Bastard Saffron. **1731** G. MEDLEY tr. *P. Kolb's Present State of Cape of G.H.* II. 65 The most remarkable Thing in the **Cape-Sheep** is the Length and Thickness of their Tails; the Tail of a *Cape*-Sheep weighing from 15 to 20 pounds. **1790** tr. *F. Le Vaillant's Trav.* II. 80 The sheep which the savages breed in the eastern parts are of a species known under the name of the *Cape sheep.* **1833** *S. Afr. Almanac & Dir.* 195 The old prejudice which formerly existed in favor of the common large tailed Cape sheep is fast disappearing before the indubitable evidence .. of the superiority of Woolled Sheep. **1833** *Graham's Town Jrnl* 18 Apr. 2 Many are procuring cross-bred rams, and the 'large-tailed' Cape sheep seems gradually losing ground in their estimation. **1834** W.H.B. WEBSTER *Narr. of Voy. to Sn Atlantic Ocean* 269 Every one has heard of the immense tails of the Cape sheep, but the formation of them is not so well known. They consist of a mass of very nice sweet fat. **1852** A.W. COLE *Cape & Kafirs* 28 Cape sheep in general are very extraordinary animals. They have no wool, but a sort of coarse shaggy hair, and in shape strongly resemble goats. **1891** H.J. DUCKITT *Hilda's 'Where Is It?'* p.ix, The tail of the native Cape sheep — which is composed entirely of fat .. — when minced and melted out, supplies the Cape housewife with a very good substitute for lard. **1913** C. PETTMAN *Africanderisms* 115 *Cape sheep*, A parti-coloured, lop-eared animal, with a large proportion of rough, wiry, brown hair among its wool. **1958** L.G. GREEN *S. Afr. Beachcomber* 90 A century ago farmers in the district were selling a pure oil, made from the tails of Cape sheep. **1905** W.L. SCLATER in Flint & Gilchrist *Science in S. Afr.* 138 The next family, the true Finches (*Fringillidae*) is not a dominant one in South Africa. It includes the **Cape Sparrow** (*Passer arcuatus*) which, though closely resembling the familiar English bird in appearance and ways, is really distinct, its back being cinnamon-red without any traces of the darker brown streaks characteristic of the European form. **1908, 1963** [see MOSSIE sense 1]. **1966** E. PALMER *Plains of Camdeboo* 196 Here it [*sc.* the English house sparrow] is on Cranemere, occupying the traditional homes of the swallows, ousting our own Cape sparrows from their old territory about the house. **1993** A. WHITLOCK in *Weekend Post* 19 June 3 Last month, Bob the Cape sparrow began venturing further away from the Schumann family home, but soon ran into difficulties when well-meaning but misguided people caged him when he visited their home. **1829** C. ROSE *Four Yrs in Sn Afr.* 27 The beautiful spotted form of the **Cape tiger** is sometimes to be met with in the dusk, gliding through the thicket. **1834** T. PRINGLE *Afr. Sketches* 158 We had once heard the peculiar growl, or *gurr* of the Cape tiger (or leopard). **1877** R.M. BALLANTYNE *Settler & Savage* 63 The more timid of the settlers .. see an elephant, a buffalo, or a Cape 'tiger' in every bank and stump and stone. **1887** *S.W. Silver & Co.'s Handbk to S. Afr.* 191 Elephants and Cape tigers (leopards) may .. both be found in the Colony. The latter have their homes in the recesses of the mountains. **1986** J. & I. RUDNER (tr.) in V.S. Forbes *Carl Peter Thunberg 1772–5* 278 The Cape tyger is small, and about the size of a dog. **1844** J. BACKHOUSE *Narr. of Visit* 251 Here I first saw in blossom, that beautifully scarlet-flowered climber, the **Cape Trumpet-flower**, *Tecoma capensis*, which is very abundant in bushy places in Caffraria. **1849** *Wesleyan-Meth. Mag.* V. i. 61 Here, also, is a beautiful climber, bearing scarlet flowers, called the Cape trumpet-flower; (*tecoma capensis*). **1966** C.A. SMITH *Common Names* 189 *Cape trumpet flower, Tecomaria capensis.* **1936** E.L. GILL *First Guide to S. Afr. Birds* 133 **Cape Vulture**, .. This is the vulture of the Cape Province ... Its general colour is a pale hoary brown, the quills nearly black. **1984** *Daily Dispatch* 9 May 1 The Department of Nature Conservation .. reported that the 42 dead vultures found on a farm in the Elliot district have been identified as the endangered Cape Vulture. **1990** W. & N. DENNIS in *Personality* 3 Sept. 49 Because of its huge wingspan and weight, the Cape vulture needs considerable space for its running take-offs and landings. **1822** W.J. BURCHELL *Trav.* I. 30 In most countries there are some few birds to which man has allowed the privilege of approaching him without molestation ... At the Cape, the familiarity of .. the **Cape wagtail** is greatly owing to the same cause. **1905** [see QUICKSTERTJE]. **1970** O.P.M. PROZESKY *Field Guide to Birds* 260 *Cape Wagtail*, One of the tamest and most familiar birds in South Africa. **1990** *Conserva* May 18 The dramatic drop in hoopoe and Cape-wagtail populations was noticed in time. **1887** [**Cape walnut**: see STINKWOOD sense a]. **1973** [see BOERBOON]. **1893** H.A. BRYDEN *Gun & Camera* 405 A very near relative of the red-billed teal .. is the **Cape wigeon** (*Mareca capensis*). **1906** STARK & SCLATER *Birds of S. Afr.* IV. 139 The Cape Widgeon .. appears to be everywhere a scarce bird and to have been but seldom met with. **1940** A. ROBERTS *Birds of S. Afr.* 37 *Notonetta capensis Cape wigeon.* **1856** A. WILMOT *Diary* (1984) 26 As for monkeys we saw plenty in the mimosas and **Cape willows** lining the road. **1913** C. PETTMAN *Africanderisms* 116 *Cape willow, Salix capensis*, growing upon the banks of rivers and streams in all parts of the Colony. **1961** PALMER & PITMAN *Trees of S. Afr.* 199 The most common wild willow in South Africa is *Salix capensis* ... The Cape willow varies in height from a bush to a tree 30 feet high. **1977** E. PALMER *Field Guide to Trees* 81 *Wild Willow, Salix capensis* .. Cape willow.

b. Products originating from (or manufactured at) the Cape: **Cape aloe** *obs.* exc. *hist.*, a pharmaceutical product obtained by tapping and drying the juice of the plant *Aloe ferox*; **Cape beer** *obs.*; **Cape biltong**, see BOKKEM; **Cape diamond**, a name used in the grading of diamonds for a stone with a yellowish colour (see also sense 3 below); **Cape dop**, see DOP *n.* sense 2 c; **Cape furniture**, esp. in the phr. ***old Cape furniture***, furniture made during previous centuries, usu. of indigenous woods, in a style blending Dutch and English tradition; see also sense 3 below, and CAPE DUTCH *adj. phr.* sense 2 b; **Cape Madeira** *obs.* exc. *hist.*, a sweet dessert wine similar in type to Madeira; see also CAPE WINE; **Cape ruby**, the semi-precious garnet, often found in association with diamonds; **Cape silver**, silverware dating from *c*1730 onwards; also *attrib.*; **Cape wagon** *hist.*, a large, loosely-constructed transport wagon, drawn by either horses or oxen; **Cape white**, a white diamond.

1798 S.H. WILCOCKE tr. *J.S. Stavorinus's Voy. to E. Indies 1768–71* II. 84 The **Cape aloe** is more transparent, and equal, if not superior, in quality, to those sorts, sold under the denominations of aloe succotrine, and aloe hepatica. **1861** P.B. BORCHERDS *Auto-Biog. Mem.* 16 In 1761, he produced the first sample .. of Cape aloes, extracted on his farm at Swellendam. **1926** P.W. LAIDLER *Tavern of Ocean* 141 Cape aloe was exported to London, but was not in very great demand. **1824** *Tariff of Stamps* in *Stat. Law of Cape of G.H.* (1862) 75 Privileges and Licences .. Licence for brewing **Cape beer**, d.o. 600 Rds. **1831** *S. Afr. Almanac & Dir.* 57 Licence for Auctioneers ... Brewing Cape Beer 600 — Retailing Cape Beer 133,16. **1883** 'A CAPE COLONIST' *Cape Malays* 7 Malays are .. as a rule sober, consuming sometimes Cape beer, inasmuch as their religion forbids them to take any intoxicating drinks. **1926** P.W. LAIDLER *Tavern of Ocean* 27 Four years later it was publicly notified that Jan de Wacht, burger, was to have the sole right to brew Cape beer of as much malt and hops as the Company might be able to supply him with. **1876** F. BOYLE *Savage Life* 21 In every digging known, large stones are apt to be 'coloured' or 'off-colour', and as we turned out so many of them our **Cape diamonds** early got a bad reputation. **1959** L.E. VAN ONSELEN *Cape Antique Furn.* 20 This foot is often found supporting **Cape furniture** and does not resemble any foot of overseas origin. **1965** M.G. ATMORE *(title)* Cape Furniture. **1991** D. GALLOWAY in *Weekend Argus* 26 Jan. 18 Most of the old Cape furniture, from beds and dressers to kists and riempie chairs, was collected from second-hand shops and homes and restored by Jolene. **1764** MRS KINDERSLEY *Lett.* (1777) 57 The vintage is in autumn which is about March and April, when a considerable quantity of wine is made; the white they call **Cape Madeira**. *c***1795** D. CAMPBELL in G.M. Theal *Rec. of Cape Col.* (1897) I. 137 A white Wine called Cape Madeira, .. the quality is somewhat between the Teneriffe and Madeira wines. **1804** R. PERCIVAL *Acct of Cape of G.H.* 187 The next wine in estimation to the Constantia is a kind of Muscadel, or as they call it here Cape Madeira. The colour of this wine is a deep violet, and the appearance thick and muddy. **1847** 'A BENGALI' *Notes on Cape of G.H.* 89 The wines from the Fransche Hoek, Paarl, and Drakenstein are from the Muscadel, a green grape, and are known in exportation under the deservedly unpopular names of 'Cape Sherry', and 'Cape Madeira'. **1920** K.M. JEFFREYS tr. *Memorandum of Commissary J.A. de Mist* 204 *The Cape grapes* .. produce, besides the universally famous Constantia wines, various other kinds of very healthy and delicious wines, known under the names of Cape Madeira, Cape Malaga, medicinal wine, steen wine, vintint and others. **1950** M. MASSON *Birds of Passage* 74 The Tulbagh Valley .. rich in corn, fruit and grapes, was particularly renowned for pleasant wine known as 'Cape Madeira'. **1974** A.P. BRINK *Dessert Wine* 85 The Cape Governor himself, that fashionable and fastidious gentleman Lord Charles Somerset, expressed his high opinion of Cape Madeira in no uncertain terms! *c***1936** *S. & E. Afr. Yr Bk & Guide* 430 The **Cape Ruby**, or *Precious Garnet*, common in diamondiferous deposits, are cut in Kimberley. **1968** G. CROUDACE *Black Rose* 29 Meanwhile, Jeremy had collected a glass full of garnets — the worthless Cape rubies — but not a single diamond with which they are so often associated. **1972** D.J.L. VISSER in *Std Encycl. of Sn Afr.* V. 124 *Pyrope*, the magnesium-aluminium garnet, is ruby-red in colour and is found in Southern and Central Africa, together with diamond ... It is also known as Cape ruby. **1949** L.G. GREEN *In Land of Afternoon* 200 **Cape silver** only began to acquire a special value after Union, when shrewd people from all parts of the country flocked to Cape Town for the Parliamentary session .. and heavy buying sent up the prices. **1965** A. GORDON-BROWN *S. Afr. Heritage* II. 16 Cape Silver has become of recent years very popular with collectors even though at first sight it may appear plain and uninteresting by comparision with contemporary European silver. **1991** S. WELZ in *Light Yrs* Vol.2 No.3, 11 A Cape stinkwood and beefwood armoire .. recently sold for R52 000. Examples with more elaborate carving and Cape silver fittings would be expected to sell for far more. **1798** LADY A. BARNARD *S. Afr. Century Ago* (1925) 65 The conveyance .. was a **Cape waggon**; any other sort of carriage in this country it is impossible to think of for such an excursion. **1838** J.E. ALEXANDER *Exped. into Int.* I. 9 It is the custom to sing the praises of the Cape waggons, their strength, their great length and pliability, preventing their upsetting; .. but I confess I am no friend to the slow three-mile-an-hour progress of this conveyance, and its 'stick-in-the-mud' propensities. **1890** A. MARTIN *Home Life* 69 These Cape waggons, clumsy as they look, are splendidly adapted to the abrupt ups and downs of the country over which they travel. **1928** L.P. GREENE *Adventure Omnibus* 252 The Cape Wagon careened from side to side like a derelict in a heavy sea. **1972** A. SCHOLEFIELD *Wild Dog Running* 66, I could see Filey and the Beggs already aboard another Cape wagon. **1931** G. BEET *Grand Old Days* 4 Seen strange signs and wonders; have conjured up visions of bucketfuls of lovely **'Cape whites'** of all shapes and sizes, and of priceless worth. **1965** D. ROOKE *Diamond Jo* 87 And in Africa the diamonds were waiting for men ... They were strewn on the banks of the rivers and hidden in pipes beneath the ground: the glorious Cape whites, the yellows.

3. Ellipt. for: *Cape diamond*, see sense 2 b above; *Cape furniture* (esp. in the phr. ***old Cape***), see sense 2 b above; *Cape hides; Cape leather* or CAPESKIN, see quot. 1956; *Cape stocks and shares; Cape wine; Cape wool.*

1884 *York Herald* (U.K.) 23 Aug. 7 Wool Markets ... Capes are without improvement. **1884** *Pall Mall Gaz.* (U.K.) 1 Oct. 5 Capes .. were practically unsaleable at the beginning of this week. **1916** *Farmer's Weekly* 20 Dec. 1518, I am certain that for all long combing Capes, at least if there were any, they would easily make a thick penny more than last series. **1921** B.E. ELLIS *Gloves & Glove Trade* 58 Real Cape gloves are usually bark-tanned .. but many gloves sold as 'Capes' are tawed and dyed by the dipping process. **1931** G. BEET *Grand Old Days* 124 It weighed $229\frac{1}{4}$ carats, in shape a perfect octahedron, and deeply tinged with yellow, and was classed as a second Cape. *c***1936** *S. & E. Afr. Yr Bk & Guide* 464 Constantia is the home of the famous wine, once commonly known as 'Cape'. **1940** G.F.H. SMITH *Gemstones*, The classification adopted for diamonds is as follows: (*a*) blue-white, (*b*) white, (*c*) fine silver Cape, (*d*) silver Cape, (*e*) light Cape, (*f*) Cape, (*g*) dark Cape, (*h*) fine light brown, [etc.]. **1956** *Glossary Leather Terms* (British Standards Institution) 7 *Cape*, Originally a soft, grain gloving or clothing leather made from South African hair sheep skin; now any similar leather made from hair sheep skin, but not finished leather made from E.I. native vegetable tanned hair sheep skin. **1957** *Handbk for Farmers* (Dept of Agric.) III. 226 The trade still grades the skins high — many as 'Capes'. **1965** M.G. ATMORE *Cape Furn.* 230 Many dealers in new furniture trade in old furniture as part payment and this may include odd pieces of Cape. **1968** S. TOLANSKY *Strategic Diamond* 94 Numerous groups of secondary classifications by colour exist. Starting with white, the off-white (usually brown-tinged) are called cape, these merge through various grades to light yellows, then .. to orange, then ultimately to opaque black. **1971** J. MCCLURE *Steam Pig* (1973) 93 It was all imbuya or stinkwood from the Knysna forests and the designs solid Early Cape. **1977** *Weekend Post* 18 June (Suppl.) 2 Diamonds occur naturally in five different shapes and nine colours — four of white and five yellow (Cape) — as well as the fancies, like reds, greens and blues. **1987** G. VINEY *Col. Houses* 54 The stinkwood and yellowwood cupboard on a stand is Cape, as are the two Cape Louis chairs.

Hence **Capian** *adj. obs.*, of or pertaining to the Cape; **Capeite** *n. obs.* [Eng. suffix *-ite* denoting (one) connected with or belonging to], KAAPENAAR sense 1.

1731 G. MEDLEY tr. *P. Kolb's Present State of Cape of G.H.* II. 9 The Reader needs not be told, that the *Cape* — or *Capian*-Settlement, as it is sometimes call'd, takes its Name from the *Cape*, which makes a Part of it ... In the Year 1712 the *Capian*-Colony was .. considerably extended. **1731** *Ibid.* [see LANDDROST sense 1]. **1869** [see PRIDE OF TABLE MOUNTAIN].

Cape boy *n. phr. Obs. exc. hist. Offensive.* [CAPE + BOY.]

1. A man of mixed ethnic ancestry (usu. partly white), esp. from the western Cape. See also COLOURED.

1882 C. DU VAL *With Show through Sn Afr.* I. 271 Travelling 'up country' with a two-wheeled Cape Cart, accompanied only by his driver, a 'Cape boy'. **1896** R. WALLACE *Farming Indust. of Cape Col.* 9 Fifteen 'Cape boys' — the name applied to the 'off colour' labourer irrespective of age — are all the men employed regularly. **1900** B.M. HICKS *Cape as I Found It* 144 In this class we may put the 'Cape boys', who .. are the result of the mixture which always takes place where black and white blood meets. **1911** [see EUROPEAN *n.*]. **1911** H.H. JOHNSTON *Opening Up of Africa* 182 There is at the present day, as the descendants of these slaves, a considerable population of 'Cape boys' (a mixture of Hottentots, Kafir, Fanti, Makua, Malagasy and whites), and Malays who are Muhammadans. **1929** J.G. VAN ALPHEN *Jan Venter* 30 Because the coloured or Cape boy has a strain of European blood, he gets almost all the privileges of the white man, including a parliamentary vote. **1931** G. BEET *Grand Old Days* 75 The Cape boy, Damon, Fleetwood Rawstorne's cook, was a perfectly reliable servant when sober, but a perfect nuisance when 'under the influence'. **1942** J.A. BROWN *One Man's War* (1980) 89, I heard a Cape boy singing in a soft melodious voice, picking out his accompaniment on a guitar. **1958** S. CLOETE *Mask* 86 He hired two more Cape boys — a driver named Philip and a boy, Hendrik, to act as voorlooper — to lead the oxen. **1968** L.G. GREEN *Full Many Glorious Morning* 191 The sounds of the old Hunter's Road; the clatter of ox horns, the voices of the Cape boys.

2. An immigrant to the Cape from St. Helena; his or her descendants.

1882 C. DU VAL *With Show through Sn Afr.* I. 43 The island of St. Helena has added a bastard black element whose descendants are known as Cape boys. **1911** L. COHEN *Reminisc. of Kimberley* 13 Hindoos, Hottentots, Negroes from Mozambique, Cape boys from St Helena, Half Breeds from Anywhere.

3. Any black or 'coloured' soldier from South Africa who participated in the campaign against the Matabele in Rhodesia (now Zimbabwe).

1896 F.C. SELOUS *Sunshine & Storm* 59 This force was .. augmented by about 150 Cape Boys, chiefly Amaxosa Kafirs and Zulus. **1896** *Spectator* (U.K.) 2 May 629 A Cape 'boy' fighting at Bulawayo is .. a coloured native enlisted and drilled within the Colony. **1897** R.S.S. BADEN-POWELL *Matabele Campaign* 147 First came an advance Force comprising the two corps of Cape Boys. Robertson and Colenbrander's Cape Boys are natives and half-castes from the Cape Colony, mostly English-speaking, and dressed and armed like Europeans. **1933** S.G. MILLIN *Rhodes* (1936) 197 There were also the troops under Goold Adams, the Bechuanas, the Cape Boys, and the friendly natives. **1946** S. CLOETE *Afr. Portraits* 155 He neglected to add the troops under Major Gould Adams or the Bechuanas or the Cape Boys or the Dutch Freebooters. **1961** T.V. BULPIN *White Whirlwind* 306 On his own he had already unofficially organised what was half-jocularly known as Colenbrander's Cape Boys. This was simply a small scouting and defensive force of 150 men, Coloureds, Xhosas and Zulus.

4. A member of the Cape Boy Contingent, a body of 'coloured' men who served with the British in the defence of Mafeking.

1900 E. ROSS *Diary of Siege of Mafeking* (1980) 135 Last night, Currie and his Cape Boys occupied a trench about 200 yards in advance of their extreme outpost, and .. so got the better of the enemy's snipers. **1917** S.T. PLAATJE *Native Life* 245 The 'Cape Boys' fought with distinction and maintained their reputation right up to the end of the siege. [**1920** S.M. MOLEMA *Bantu Past & Present* 287 The Cape Boy Contingent was another body of coloured men who helped in the defence of Mafeking. These served with the Police Force.] **1935** R.S. GODLEY *Khaki & Blue* 46 A Cape boy .. came forward, suggesting that if he were given a horse he would attempt to ride through the rebels. **1957** D. GRINNELL-MILNE *Baden-Powell at Mafeking* 152 The lurid terms used by the hard-fighting Cape Boys in the Brickfields when the Boers over the way sang out and called them 'bastards'.

Cape brandy *n. phr.* [CAPE + Eng. *brandy*.] Brandy produced at the CAPE. Also *attrib.* See also BOER BRANDY, BRANDEWYN sense 1, CANGO, CAPE SMOKE, DOP *n.* sense 2 a ii.

*c***1795** *Revenue Returns* in G.M. Theal *Rec. of Cape Col.* (1897) I. 134 The Privilege of selling in the same said manner by small measures the Cape Brandy. **1804** R. PERCIVAL *Acct of Cape of G.H.* 189 Besides wine the farmers make a great quantity of strong fiery spirit which they call brandy-wine, and British Cape brandy ... On inquiry I found that the planters principally extract it from the husks and stalks of compressed grapes by distillation. **1832** *Graham's Town Jrnl* 27 Jan. 20, I am a canteen keeper, and I glory in the name! .. I have been the humble means of dispensing more real and direct happiness in one hour, and that with plain Cape Brandy, than all your humbug of schools and societies will do in a century. **1850** [see CAPE

SMOKE]. 1864 T. SHONE *Diary.* 17 Nov., Henry gave me a glass of wine, and a pint of cape brandy, I am unhappy. 1873 F. BOYLE *To Cape for Diamonds* 16 The mere sight and smell of Cape brandy produced on me, as on others, a feeling of hatred towards the whole human race, and a wish that I never had been born. 1891 H.J. DUCKITT *Hilda's 'Where Is It?'* 134 Peel very thinly ten oranges and ten lemons. Put the peel on four bottles of good Cape brandy, add four pounds of white sugar. 1896 *Cape Argus* 2 Jan. 5 A native wagon-driver, who had been partaking freely of Cape brandy, was driving his master's wagon out to the farm along the Cradock road, when he fell off under the wheel. 1908 F.C. SLATER *Sunburnt South* 19 He produced a bottle of Cape brandy and a jug of water from an adjacent cupboard, and mixing two tolerably stiff soopjes handed one to me, and we pledged each other with the usual Dutch expression — *gezondheid.* c1936 *S. & E. Afr. Yr Bk & Guide* 305 Cape Brandy, now almost invariably distilled from pure wine, is an excellent spirit, in many cases equal to good French brandy. 1949 J. MOCKFORD *Golden Land* 217, I have known men who, after seeing a red elephant in the bush .. were ready to explain it away by blaming the Cape Brandy or the African Sun. 1958 A. JACKSON *Trader on Veld* 44 Crude Cape brandy was very cheap ... They were fond of mixing it with buchu, aniseed or other herbs, and also liked 'Gember brandewyn' (Ginger brandy). 1967 E.M. SLATTER *My Leaves Are Green* 200 A blast of Cape brandy struck me as he came closer .. it explained all Cooke's arrogance and his recklessness. 1973 *Sunday Times* 12 Aug. (Mag. Sect.) 12 The prices of the good old days — best Cape brandy at 7s. 6d. a gallon, finest French champagne at 60s. a dozen quart bottles. 1989 *Sun* Aug. 25 The first course, a superbly blended mousse of pheasant and truffle, flavoured with Cape brandy and served with brioche. 1990 *Tribute* Apr. 47 (*advt*) The story of Cape brandy can be traced back to 1659 when the first wine was pressed, a mere seven years after Jan van Riebeeck had established his refreshment station on the shores of Table Bay.

Cape cart *n. phr.* [Calque formed on S. Afr. Du. *kapkar*, fr. Du. *kap* hood (mistaken for *Kaap* Cape) + *kar* cart.] A two-wheeled hooded carriage, drawn by between two and eight horses or mules. Also *attrib.*

1832 *Graham's Town Jrnl* 16 Feb. 29 For Sale, an excellent Cape Cart, on springs with a set of four horse Harness. 1862 LADY DUFF-GORDON *Lett. from Cape* (1925) 93 Nothing but a Cape cart, Cape horses, and a Hottentot driver, above all, could have accomplished it. 1873 F. BOYLE *To Cape for Diamonds* 48 The Cape cart holds three persons besides the driver. It runs on two wheels, with a light wooden body, like our English tax-cart. A canvas awning, lined with green baize, is supported on iron stanchions. 1895 A.B. BALFOUR *1200 Miles in Waggon* 11 A Cape Cart .. is a most fascinating kind of vehicle on two wheels, holding four persons, all facing the horses, the whole being covered with one large hood. 1900 M. MARQUARD *Lett. from Boer Parsonage* (1967) 131 Father's pass was: 'This to allow the Rev. Marquard to return to his clerical duties. One kaffir boy, 2 horses and one cape cart.' 1920 R. JUTA *Tavern* 262 Driving in by Cape-cart (a light two-wheeled vehicle, introduced by the Huguenots, and reminiscent of the farm carts of Normandy). 1924 [see GELD sense b]. 1937 C.R. PRANCE *Tante Rebella's Saga* 152 Quagga whose foals might be ridden down, picked up and suckled on a donkey-mare for sale to a Rand Magnate, for a Cape-cart team. 1951 L.G. GREEN *Grow Lovely* 41 This grim, inevitable symbol of justice [*sc.* portable gallows] had followed by ox-waggon the gay Cape cart procession of judge and advocate through the countryside. 1969 J.R. GRINDLEY *Riches of Sea* 68 A few Malay fish hawkers with Cape carts survive. They still use the strange bleating call of the fish horn to advertise their wares. 1972 *Evening Post* 19 Feb. 13 An old Dutch Cape Cart, which has been in the bridegroom's family for more than 150 years, was used in place of a bridal car. 1989 *Weekend Argus* 25 Nov. (Suppl.) 2 The 18c stamp features the Cape cart, a typical South African vehicle; the 30c stamp the jubilee spider, which resembles the English surrey. 1989 J. CRWYS-WILLIAMS *S. Afr. Despatches* 193 He bought the correspondent's standard equipment: a horse, a Cape cart drawn by mules, clothes, camera, bedding, and a servant. 1991 *Best of S. Afr. Short Stories* (Reader's Digest Assoc.) 179 Two-wheeled, hooded carts were described at the Cape in 1829, and were probably in use well before that date. To distinguish the hooded cart from the hoodless varieties, it was called a *kapkar* — a 'cart with a hood'. Faulty translation by English-speakers soon rendered this as 'Cape cart' and towards the end of the 19th century the term had become so well established that it was used even by cart-makers.

Hence (*nonce*) **Cape-cart** *v.*, to travel in a Cape cart.

1920 R.Y. STORMBERG *Mrs Pieter de Bruyn* 44, I Cape-carted it over to the outspan winkel. *Ibid.* 63 We're having a last little indaba all together, and then Gwenno Cape-carts it back home.

Cape Clouds *n. phr. Obs. exc. hist. Astronomy.* [Named for the *Cape of Good Hope.*] The Magellanic clouds, two satellite galaxies of the Milky Way consisting of luminous clouds formed by vast numbers of nebulae and star clusters and visible in the southern hemisphere. See also MONS MENSAE.

1795 C.R. HOPSON tr. *C.P. Thunberg's Trav.* II. 208 Charles' wain .. was here sunk below the horizon, and the Cape clouds, as two dark spots in the firmament are called, seemed to be a similar token to the inhabitants here. 1815 J. CAMPBELL *Trav. in S. Afr.* 41 One of the three perpetual clouds called by seamen The Cape Clouds, appeared black, but I was satisfied that it is only a part of the Via Lactea, or Milky Way. 1880 A. GIBERNE *Sun, Moon & South* 269 The famous Magellanic Clouds in the southern heavens. Sometimes they are called the Cape Clouds. 1921 H.J. MANDELBROTE tr. *O.F. Mentzel's Descr. of Cape of G.H.* I. 17 His object was merely to observe the two so-called Cape clouds above the Table Mountain .. two small stars which, like the Milky Way, appeared to be made up of numerous nebulous stars. 1948 H.V. MORTON *In Search of S. Afr.* 69 'What a number of words the Cape has prefixed ... How many do you think there are?' ... 'Cape Clouds,' said the Doctor firmly. 'Yes,' said Professor B., 'the Magellan Clouds'. 1986 J. & I. RUDNER (tr.) in V.S. Forbes *Carl Peter Thunberg 1772–5* 326 The Magellanic Clouds, though these are not dark but luminous ... They figure as Le Grand Nuage and Le Petit Nuage in the star map in Le Caille 1763. Three Cape Clouds, one of them black [Coalsack] are mentioned by Campbell.

Cape Coloured *ppl adj. phr.* and *n. phr.* [CAPE + COLOURED.]

During the apartheid era, 'Cape Coloured' was an official ethnic designation for race-classification purposes, being one of the sub-groups of the 'Coloured' group.

A. *ppl adj. phr.* Of or pertaining to people of mixed ethnic descent, speaking Afrikaans or English as home language, and (usu.) resident in the Western Cape; particularly, those who are not followers of Islam. Cf. CAPE MALAY *adj. phr.* See also COLOURED *ppl adj.*

1897 LORD A. MILNER in C. Headlam *Milner Papers* (1931) 89 The better treatment of Cape Coloured people. 1915 D. FAIRBRIDGE *Torch Bearer* 231 Sabina .. had begged to be retained as hospital maid, and had displayed all the versatile dexterity and quickness of the Cape coloured girl. 1928 E.A. WALKER *Hist. of S. Afr.* 45 Soon three fourths of such slave children as there were, were half-breeds. The Cape Coloured folk had emerged. 1941 C.W. DE KIEWIET *Hist. of S. Afr.* 44 In the veins of the Cape coloured folk .. ran the blood of Hottentots, Malays, negro slaves, and white men. a1951 H.C. BOSMAN *Willemsdorp* (1977) 58 His skin was a light copper colour. He might have been Cape Coloured, with a strong strain of European blood in his veins. 1953 DU PLESSIS & LÜCKHOFF *Malay Quarter* 43 The Malays, as indeed the Cape Coloured community as a whole, are not only partial to music, but display a marked aptitude therein. 1971 [see CLASSIFICATION]. 1977 *E. Prov. Herald* 4 May 18 The language is there too; that extraordinary patois of English and Afrikaans which is the hallmark of a section of the urbanised Cape Coloured community. 1989 [see sense B]. 1990 R. GOOL *Cape Town Coolie* 8 Because it is a holiday, there will be no early hawkers in the Cape Coloured and Malay Quarter of District Six.

B. *n. phr.* Pl. unchanged, or -s. A person of mixed ethnic descent, speaking Afrikaans or English as home language, and (usu.) resident in the Western Cape; particularly, one who is not a follower of Islam; CAPEY sense 1 a; MALAY *n.* sense 2. See also COLOURED *n.*

See note at CAPE MALAY *n. phr.*

1936 *Cambridge Hist. of Brit. Empire* VIII. 294 The successors of slaves and Hottentots, known as 'Cape Coloured', rank to-day as a civilised people. 1946 S. CLOETE *Afr. Portraits* 15 There was a special man-made race — the Cape Coloured, a bastard mixture of Malay, Hottentot, Bantu and European. 1949 J. MOCKFORD *Golden Land* 37 The Malays are often tailors, carpenters and masons, while the Cape Coloureds are fishermen, farm hands and factory workers. 1954 P. ABRAHAMS *Tell Freedom* 279 This year, 1938, was the year the South African Government made its first moves to deprive the Cape Coloureds of their right to vote on the same roll as the whites. 1966 VAN HEYNINGEN & BERTHOUD *Uys Krige* 114 The Cape Coloureds are nearly all Afrikaans-speaking, but for the mass of them it is .. an Afrikaans with English words and corruptions of English words freely mixed in, as well as a sort of slang of the slums, where large numbers of the 'Coloureds' live. 1971 *Post* 7 Mar. 5 Can any reader tell me what is the difference between a Cape Malay, Griqua, Baster, Cape Coloured, Other Coloured, and Mixed? 1987 [see HOTNOT sense 2]. 1989 *Frontline* Apr. 32 In my family there were brothers classified 'Cape Coloured' and others classified 'Other Coloured', which caused a problem because the 'Cape Coloureds' were supposed to be the real thing.

Cape Doctor *n. phr.* [CAPE + Eng. *doctor*; see quot. 1890.] *The Cape Doctor*: A nickname given in the Western Cape to the prevailing south-east wind which blows strongly esp. during the summer months; *the Doctor*, see DOCTOR sense 2. Cf. BLACK SOUTH-EASTER.

1861 LADY DUFF-GORDON *Lett. from Cape* (1925) 31 It portends a 'south-easter', i.e. a hurricane, and Cape Town disappears in impenetrable clouds of dust. But this wind .. is the Cape doctor, and keeps away cholera, fever of every sort, and all malignant or infectious diseases. 1882 C. DU VAL *With Show through Sn Afr.* I. 50 The 'Cape Doctor' .. does for Cape Town what its Town Council and Urban Authorities appear unable or unwilling to do — viz., drives out the contagion, low fever, etc., generated by the insufficient drainage and want of care .. in .. its sanitary requirements. 1890 A. MARTIN *Home Life* 15 That rough but benevolent south-east wind, which, owing to its kindly property of sweeping away the germs of disease, is called 'the Cape doctor'. 1913 H. TUCKER *Our Beautiful Peninsula* 2 Even the worst enemy of our comfort, the impetuous south-east wind, bears 'healing on its wings,' as its popular title, 'the Cape Doctor,' signifies. 1948 H.V. MORTON *In Search of S. Afr.* 46 The 'Cape Doctor' is the name of Cape Town's private and personal monsoon, the South-Easter .. because it always blows seaward and is said to carry away all the germs with it. 1966 *Listener* (U.K.) 18 Aug. 237 The Cape south-easter was blowing — the wind they call the Cape doctor because it blows the rubbish from the streets. 1973 *Cape Times* 27 Jan. (Weekend Mag.) 10 It is a little like the air pollution question in Cape Town ... Just when the .. media make the public aware of the extent of the problem .. the old Cape Doctor comes along and the problem seems to have solved itself. 1976 W. HÉFER in *Optima* Vol.26 No.2, 46 It used to be said that this wind, known as the Cape doctor, helped the fruit farmer by blowing away various diseases. 1983 *Sunday Times*

14 Aug. 16 The 'miracle Cape Doctor' — the south-easterly wind — has saved the rich, beautiful West Coast from oil pollution. **1987** KIRKBY & HOUWING in *Weekend Argus* 26 Sept. 1 The eight sailing ships of the Australian Bicentennial First Fleet were pinned down in Table Bay Harbour by a raging south-easterly gale ... The Cape Doctor, gusting to more than 50 knots, prevented the fleet from leaving Table Bay. **1993** A. JARDINE in *Ibid.* 9 Jan. 18 The Cape Doctor took centre stage .. as the [golf] tournament entered .. the 'championship round'. An uncharitable south-easter played havoc with the pack yesterday and swept hats, golf balls and aspirations away.

Cape Dutch *n. phr.* and *adj. phr.* [CAPE + Eng. *Dutch* (a person) originating from Holland.]
A. *n. phr. Obs.* exc. *hist.*
1. *The Cape Dutch* (*pl.*): The early Dutch-speaking colonists at the Cape. Cf. *the Dutch* (see DUTCH *n.* sense 1), *the South African Dutch* (see SOUTH AFRICAN DUTCH *n. phr.* sense 2).

1822 W.W. BIRD in J.C. Chase *Cape of G.H.* (1843) 258 Ambition and politics, two of the grand tormentors of human life, have no field in South Africa large enough for an Englishman, and the Cape Dutch know them not, for they are content to be quiet and to obey. **1826** *New Monthly Mag.* II. 488 The Cape Dutch .. possess many estimable qualities. **1921** W.C. SCULLY *Harrow* 44 The proper policy was to try and make the Cape Dutch rise while the troops were in the country and — as they said — finish the business once and for all. **1936** *Cambridge Hist. of Brit. Empire* VIII. 511 Rhodes soon realised that he could not pursue his policy without the support of the Cape Dutch. **1948** H.E. HOCKLY *Story of Brit. Settlers of 1820* 6 The European colonists .. gradually developed their own distinctive characteristics and outlook, becoming known to the outside world through travellers and writers of those days as the Cape Dutch, to distinguish them from the parent stock in the Netherlands. **1977** *S. Afr. Panorama* May 9 The early settlers took root, and by the beginning of the 18th century the Cape Dutch, strengthened by a modest influx of French Huguenots and German employees of the company, were already evolving a subnationality of their own. **1981** A. PATON in *Optima* Vol.30 No.2, 89 One can of course stress too far the differences between the Cape Dutch and those who had trekked into the interior, but differences there were.

2. The form of Dutch spoken by the early settlers at the Cape. Cf. DUTCH *n.* sense 2 a.

1835 J.W.D. MOODIE *Ten Yrs* II. 256 Not being able to produce interpreters who understand English, the preacher is obliged to deliver his sermons in Cape Dutch. **1873** F. BOYLE *To Cape for Diamonds* 169 A Dutchman — a boer, that is — climbed up and attempted to address the meeting in Cape Dutch. **1882** C. DU VAL *With Show through Sn Afr.* I. 43 Amongst these various races the language principally used is Cape Dutch — a somewhat hybrid and very consonantal one, and being gutteral, is more or less useful for clearing the throat. **1900** B.M. HICKS *Cape as I Found It* 16 The Coloured people seemed to be everywhere, jabbering away to each other in Cape Dutch. **1903** J.C. EVERETT *Easy Anglo-Afrikander Taal Guide* 7 Cape Dutch, or the Taal, as it is now usually designated, is a simplified form of the Netherlands, or Hollander language. **1924** L.H. BRINKMAN *Glory of Backveld* 144 The moment our churches adopt Cape Dutch as a medium of worship, it will be farewell to High Dutch. **1973** J. MEINTJES *Voortrekkers* 19 Speech was conditioned by environment to such an extent that a new language began to evolve, then simply called the Taal (the language), or Cape Dutch, and much later Afrikaans. **1988** D. DANNHAUSER in *S. Afr. Panorama* Feb. 20 Around 1869, farmers spoke a kind of Cape Dutch at home which had no fixed form because it wasn't the written language and differed from the written language, High Dutch, used in church and at formal gatherings.

B. *adj. phr.*
1. *hist.* Of or pertaining to the Dutch-speaking colonists at the Cape. See also DUTCH *adj.* sense 1.

1827 G. THOMPSON *Trav.* II. 207 He would find it useful to avail himself, in all ordinary affairs, of the experience of the Cape Dutch colonists in his vicinity — a class of men not deficient in shrewdness. **1847** 'A BENGALI' *Notes on Cape of G.H.* 16 The Cape Dutch farmers are a remarkably fine, handsome, almost gigantic race. **1891** H.J. DUCKITT *Hilda's 'Where Is It?'* 55 In most Cape Dutch houses this dish [*sc.* rice dumplings] is eaten with meat. **1920** R. JUTA *Tavern* 22 Literal translation of a Cape Dutch proverb. **1946** T. MACDONALD *Ouma Smuts* 25 Jan Hofmeyr of the Cape Dutch Bond suggested he should go to Kimberley to make a political speech. *c*1964 'KWELA' in *New S. Afr. Writing* 158 'But she is not ordinary Dutch' Anna had added. 'She is Cape Dutch, which is a people almost as good as the English.' **1975** *S. Afr. Panorama* Dec. 1 Pannevis, concerned about the Coloured people at the Cape who only spoke the 'Cape Dutch' dialect strove for the translation of the Bible into this medium. **1988** A. SHER *Middlepost* 200 Doctor Kiesow's Specific Nerve-Pain Remedy . . . Cape Dutch Remedies — best in the world. **1991** *Flying Springbok* May 167 The only truly indigenous South African cuisine is the Cape Dutch repertoire with its amalgams of savoury and sweet, its Malay-influenced stews and kebabs, its heavy, rich, wonderful desserts.

2.a. *Archit.* Of, pertaining to, or designating the gabled, whitewashed style of early Cape architecture.

[**1835** G. CHAMPION *Jrnl* (1968) 10 On either side of the street stand the neatly thatched & white-washed Dutch houses, each with a stoup in front.] **1913** H. TUCKER *Our Beautiful Peninsula* 32 The famous mansion — restored and enlarged by its owner with a sympathetic adherence to the distinctive old Cape Dutch style of architecture. *c*1937 *Our Land* (United Tobacco Co.) 4 *Groote Schuur, C.P.*, Built in the style of the best Cape-Dutch architecture this house was bequeathed to the nation as the official residence of the Premier of the Union. **1943** 'J. BURGER' *Black Man's Burden* 16 These gentlemen farmers built the beautiful old Cape Dutch houses that stand to this day, and lived the leisurely lives of slave-owners. **1965** FRANSEN & COOK *Old Houses of Cape* p.vi, In the relatively short space of 300 years, South Africa has made two original and significant contributions to world culture — Cape Dutch architecture and the Afrikaans language. **1972** *Cape Argus* 16 Sept. 13 The homes range in style from old Cape Dutch to modern Spanish and A-frame dwellings. **1978** *Signature* June, There are several fine examples of the architecture which has come to be known as Cape Dutch. **1987** G. VINEY *Col. Houses* 171 The two jutting wings .. now boasted curvy, Cape Dutch-ish gables of his own invention. **1988** C. MARAIS in *Personality* 19 Dec. 34 In the old days a Cape Dutch house was considered second grade, and dubbed 'The Hottentot Style'. Nowadays, however, Cape Dutch is most definitely 'in'.

b. Of, pertaining to, or designating traditional Cape furniture styles. See also *Cape furniture* (CAPE sense 2 b).

1959 L.E. VAN ONSELEN *Cape Antique Furn.* 8 At the Cape, these ideas came into conflict with Dutch conservatism. This led Huguenot craftsmen to adopt the better features of Cape Dutch styles and to implement them with their own revolutionary ideas. **1972** *Farmer's Weekly* 21 Apr. 84 Antiques. Cape Dutch and English (B.A.D.A.) Rusbank Gallery, 41 High St. Worcester. **1978** P.-D. UYS in S. Gray *Theatre Two* (1981) 125 The furniture is antique Cape-Dutch, a large dinnertable with six chairs. **1985** *Style* Oct. 129 There are examples of fine Cape Dutch furniture, art deco, Victorian glass, books, porcelain, paintings. **1990** *Weekly Mail* 28 Sept. 3 Whether you prefer Cape Dutch or Japanese, Antique or Modern .. we will suit your style and budget . . . Domestic and commercial interior decorators.

Cape Flats *n. phr.* [Calqued on S. Afr. Du. *Kaapsche Vlakte* 'Cape Plains'; perh. influenced by Eng. *flat* 'piece of level ground'.] *The Cape Flats*: The stretch of flat, sandy country lying between Cape Town and Somerset West and linking the Cape Peninsula to the hinterland; *the flats*, see FLATS sense a. Also *attrib.*

1822 W.J. BURCHELL *Trav.* I. 58 The Dutch denominate one part, the *Kaapsche Duinen* (Cape Downs), and another, the *Kaapsche Vlakte* (Cape Flats). **1835** G. CHAMPION *Jrnl* (1968) 8 We crossed what are styled the 'Cape Flats' being the perfect level ground which lies between Table & False Bays ... Nothing but Sand, Sand, Sand. **1836** A.F. GARDINER *Journey to Zoolu Country* 397 Having ridden eighty-four miles, the latter part of which, over the Cape Flats, being loose sand, is the most tedious. **1841** B. SHAW *Memorials* 220 Reached the house of *Diana*, a woman of colour, who resides upon the Cape Flats, a little after sunset. **1881** *Cape Monthly Mag.* IV. Mar. 137 At Captain Kuiper's kraal across the Cape Flats they found one of Gonnema's people, whom they compelled under threat of death to act as guide. **1913** H. TUCKER *Our Beautiful Peninsula* 70 The designation of the 'Cape Flats' is given to all the low-lying plain which extends beyond the succession of suburban townships strung on the thread of the railway line. **1949** J. MOCKFORD *Golden Land* 34 From these townships on the Cape Flats fast and frequent trains transport the Coloureds to their places of work in and around Cape Town. **1953** *Drum* Oct. 45 The proposals of the Land Tenure Advisory Board .. envisage the non-Europeans in small pockets in the Cape Flats while the best and most desirable areas are reserved for European ownership and occupation. **1973** *Sunday Times* 9 Dec., Many Coloureds .. trekked to .. the Cape Flats, but unlike other trekkers before them there was no promised land. **1986** *Weekly Mail* 18 Apr. 4 The rents boycott in the Cape Flats townships, already entering its sixth month, took a new turn this week. **1990** R. GOOL *Cape Town Coolie* 147 The entire population of District Six would be evacuated to the Cape Flats ... The Cape Flats could be turned into a Coloured and Malay dormitory. **1991** [see GHOMMA sense 2].

Cape Floral Kingdom *n. phr.* [CAPE + Eng. *floral kingdom*.] The smallest of the world's six plant kingdoms or biomes, stretching from the Western Cape to the Eastern Cape and characterized by flora known as FYNBOS.

1960 C. LIGHTON (title) *Cape Floral Kingdom*. **1983** *Grocott's Mail* 8 Nov. 4 The calendar .. is also intended to alert the public to the dangers threatening the Cape floral kingdom. **1986** C.J. ESTERHUYSE *Protea Species* 12 Sixty-nine protea varieties occur in this fynbos plant community or Cape Floral Kingdom. **1987** T.F.J. VAN RENSBURG *Intro. to Fynbos* 2 The Cape Floral Kingdom (also called the South African Kingdom or the Fynbos Biome) .. covers only approximately 0,04% of the total land surface of the earth and is situated at the southern tip of Africa. **1988** H. DUGMORE in *Personality* 27 June 64 The Cape Floral Kingdom contains about 9 000 species, which is the highest number of species in any of the world's floral kingdoms. **1989** *Motorist* 3rd Quarter 21 The renowned Cape Floral Kingdom occupies a glorious region of forests, mountains, rivers and vast heath lands.

Cape foot *n. phr.* [CAPE + Eng. *foot*.]
1. *Obs.* exc. *hist.* A unit of land measurement: see quot. 1974. See also CAPE ROOD.

1861 *E. Prov. Yr Bk & Annual Register* 61 Since 12 Cape feet are equal to 1 Cape rood, 1 English mile is equal to nearly 425.944 Cape roods. **1866** *Cape Town Dir.* 119 *Land Measure*, The ratio of the Cape land-measure foot to the British Imperial foot was investigated by the Land-measure Commissioners ... They ascertained that 1,000 Cape feet are equal to 1,033 British Imperial feet. **1893** *Brown's S. Afr.* 15, 12 Cape feet = 1 Cape Rood = 12.396 Eng. ft. **1926** M. NATHAN *S. Afr. from Within* 310 The English denominations of coinage and weights and measures, prevail throughout the Union, except that, .. the 'Cape' foot differs in length from the English foot, being .3148 of a metre (a metre being equal to 1.0936 yards). **1931** G. BEET *Grand Old Days* 94 The area of the mine is equal to 3,482 claims, or 900 Cape square feet. In English measurement, this represents 78 acres. **1934, 1942** [see CAPE ROOD]. **1951** H.C. BOSMAN in L. Abrahams *Unto Dust* (1963)

178 By that time the sun was sitting not more than about two Cape feet above a tall koppie on the horizon. **1974** McGraw-Hill *Dict. of Scientific & Technical Terms* 219 *Cape foot*, .. A unit of length equal to 1.033 feet or to 0.3148584 meter.

2. In Cape Dutch furniture: the tapering foot of a turned table- or chair-leg, having a broader ring or 'bracelet' just above it. See also CAPE DUTCH *adj. phr.* sense 2 b.

1959 L.E. VAN ONSELEN *Cape Antique Furn.* 20 The foot which raises it [*sc.* the armoire] from the floor is a turned foot of stinkwood. This foot is often found supporting Cape furniture and as it does not resemble any foot of overseas origin it is perhaps practical to term it a distinctive Cape foot. **1965** M.G. ATMORE *Cape Furn.* 73 The circular fluted leg terminating in a 'Cape' foot was used in a slender form by Sheraton in about 1800. **1971** [see Baraitser & Obholzer quot. at JONKMANSKAS].

Cape gilder var. CAPE GUILDER.

Cape gooseberry *n. phr.* [Etym. dubious: either CAPE + Eng. *gooseberry*; or Eng. *cape* cloak, referring to the papery sheath round the berry.] The fruit of the naturalized plant *Physalis peruviana* of the Solanaceae, a smooth, yellow berry enclosed in a papery sheath; the plant itself; APPEL-DER-LIEFDE. Also *attrib.*

1821 E.S. PIGOT *Journal.* 75 Kate came in with her Apron full of Cape Gooseberries. **1843**, **1856** [see APPEL-DER-LIEFDE]. **1870** C. HAMILTON *Life & Sport in S.-E. Afr.* 67 We made a hearty supper of venison and Cape gooseberry-pudding. **1890** A. MARTIN *Home Life* 231 Very good home-made jams can be obtained from the Cape gooseberry — a kind of small tomato, enclosed in a loose, crackling bag much too large for it. **1891** H.J. DUCKITT *Hilda's 'Where Is It?'* 123 Jam (Separi or Cape Gooseberry). One pound of 'gooseberries' to three-quarters of a pound of sugar. **1907** T.R. SIM *Forests & Forest Flora* 44 A copious growth of Ferns, Solanums, Physalis (Cape Gooseberry) .. had taken possession. **1917** R. MARLOTH *Common Names* 33 Gooseberry, Cape, Physalis peruviana. The plant is not a gooseberry nor a native of the Cape. *c*1936 *S. & E. Afr. Yr Bk & Guide* 298 Special attention has been given .. to the manufacture of preserves from the Cape Gooseberry, which has already established a demand in the European markets. **1941** *Bantu World* 25 Jan. 8 She .. tells you how to make jam from mulberries, Cape gooseberries, tomatoes and other fruits. **1950** H. GERBER *Cape Cookery* 133 Gooseberry Pancakes ... Pour hot stewed Cape Gooseberries over the pancake mound just before serving. **1979** HEARD & FAULL *Our Best Trad. Recipes* 104 Actually the Cape gooseberry is not advertising the Cape Province. The 'cape' derives from the shawl or cape which cocoons the fruit. **1990** *Style* May 18 Splash out on the theatrical choux-pastry swan filled with sweet Cape gooseberries and custard. **1994** L. DAVIDSON in D. McCormack *Perm Bk of 'Test the Team'* 60 The name of the fruit the Cape gooseberry has nothing to do with the Cape of Good Hope. *Ibid.* 167 The plant was introduced into South Africa from South America via Holland before 1800. 'Cape' refers to the papery covering round the berry.

Cape guilder *n. phr. Obs. exc. hist.* Also **Cape gilder**, **Cape gulden**. Pl. -s, or unchanged. [CAPE + Eng. *guilder*, fr. Du. *gulden* a silver or gold coin.] A unit of currency used during the early years of the Cape settlement. See also RIX-DOLLAR.

*c*1795 *Revenue Returns* in G.M. Theal *Rec. of Cape Col.* (1897) I. 135 Three Cape Guilders are equal to a Cape Rixdollar, two Silver Guilders of Holland equal to do [*sc.* ditto]. **1798** S.H. WILCOCKE tr. *J.S. Stavorinus's Voy. to E. Indies 1768–71* I. 569 At public sales, and likewise in retail, the prices are taken at Cape gilders of sixteen stivers each. **1827** *S. Afr. Almanack & Dir.* 100 The relative value of the paper currency with British money is as follows: .. 1 Rix dollar equal to one shilling and six pence. 1 Cape Guilder equal to six pence. Cape of Good Hope 15th June 1825. By His Excellency's Command. **1919** M. GREENLEES tr. *O.F. Mentzel's Life at Cape in Mid-18th C.* 153 The East India Company takes all the grain that the farmers can sell to it at a fixed price of eight Cape gulden the muid. **1925** H.J. MANDELBROTE tr. *O.F. Mentzel's Descr. of Cape of G.H.* II. 137 Some people argue that the intrinsic value of all coins in the Dutch possessions is lower than in Holland, and quote the Cape gulden as a unit of 16 stuivers. **1964** L.G. GREEN *Old Men Say* 96 He was suspected of plundering a wreck but this crime .. was never pinned on him. Meyboom left eighty thousand Cape gulden.

Cape gun *n. phr. Hist.* [CAPE + Eng. *gun*.] A type of double-barrelled firearm, usu. with one barrel smooth-bored and the other rifled; CAPE RIFLE. Also occas. **Cape gun-and-rifle**.

[**1843** *Cape of G.H. Almanac & Annual Register*, All the necessary Gun apparatus, Guns, *Cape Pattern*, with hair Triggers.] **1877** *Field* 13 Oct. (Jeffreys), The 'Cape Gun,' a rifle and shot gun combined. The right barrel, being for shot, is a 12-cylinder bore; the left is 577.450 with Henry rifling, using the government Boxer cartridge. **1893** 'HARLEY' in *Cape Illust. Mag.* June 379 The approved sporting Cape weapon of offence or defence, being one barrel smooth bore and the other rifled, the favourite weapon with the colonist even in war, the smooth bore being found handy when loaded with buck shot at close quarters ... The best of all weapons — the Cape gun-and-rifle, as it is called. **1971** F.V. LATEGAN in *Std Encycl. of Sn Afr.* IV. 525 The 'Cape gun', a double-barrelled smooth-bored weapon of .75-inch calibre, made for the Cape Mounted Riflemen in 1845 and for the Cape Volunteer Corps in 1857. **1990** *Caption, 1820 Settlers' Memorial Museum (Grahamstown)* It is thought that Weakley designed the original ... Double-barrelled 'Cape' gun, percussion cap 12 bore/.577".

Cape-jie var. CAPEY.

Cape lady *n. phr.* [CAPE + Eng. *lady*.] Any of several marine and freshwater fishes:

1. The FRANSMADAM, *Boopsoidea inornata*.

1949 J.L.B. SMITH *Sea Fishes* 274 *Boopsoidea inornata* Castlenau ... Frans Madame or Jacopever (Cape) .. Cape Lady (Transkei).

2. The PAMPELMOESIE, *Stromateus fiatola*.

1949 J.L.B. SMITH *Sea Fishes* 303 *Stromateus fiatola* Linnaeus. [*Stromateus Capensis* Pappe.] Butterfish. Cape Lady. Pampelmoes. Bluefish ... Attains 18 ins. An Atlantic species. **1971** L.G. GREEN *Taste of S.-Easter* 187 A comparative rarity known as the butterfish ... Others referred to the Cape Lady or steenklipvis. **1979** SNYMAN & KLARIE *Free from Sea* 26 Butter Fish, Cape Lady, Pampelmoes, Bluefish.

3. The MOONFISH (sense 1 a), *Monodactylus falciformis*.

1949 J.L.B. SMITH *Sea Fishes* 233 *Monodactylus falciformis* Lacepede ... Cape Lady (Knysna). Moon-fish. Moony. Kite-fish. Seakite (Eastern Cape and Natal) ... Brilliant silvery with iridescence. **1967** R.A. JUBB *Freshwater Fishes* 192 *Monodactylus falciformis* .. Cape lady or Moony ... *Monodactylus argenteus* .. Moon-fish.

Cape Malay *n. phr.* and *adj. phr.* Also **Cape Malayan**. [CAPE + MALAY.]

A. *n. phr.* A member of a predominantly Afrikaans-speaking and Muslim group being partly descended from slaves or political exiles sent to the Cape in the 17th and 18th centuries from Indonesia, India, Ceylon (Sri Lanka), Malaysia, and Madagascar; CAPE MUSLIM *n. phr.*; MALAY *n.* sense 1.

Perh. used by some in a broader sense, designating a CAPE COLOURED. During the apartheid era, 'Cape Malay' was an official ethnic designation for race-classification purposes, being one of the sub-groups of the 'Coloured' group.

Members of this group live mainly in the Western Cape, but there are also well-established Cape Malay communities in other (esp. large urban) areas.

1861 J.S. MAYSON *Malays of Capetown* 17 The Cape Malays are of the orthodox sect of the Sonnites. **1883** 'A CAPE COLONIST' *Cape Malays* 6 In consequence of the various changes that have taken place, and their being mixed with the Malagasey, Angola and other slaves, and also with the European race, the Cape Malays are presented now in somewhat a different aspect. **1923** [see COLOURED *ppl adj.* sense a]. **1944** I.D. DU PLESSIS *Cape Malays* 1 The local Muslims .. can roughly be divided into two groups: the Cape Malays (about 35,000), whose home language is Afrikaans, and the Indians (about 5,000), who speak their own languages as well as English. **1952** *Drum* July 21 The Cape Malays have preserved many excellent customs from the East. **1961** *Off. Yr Bk of Union 1960* (Bureau of Census & Statistics) 566 *Cape Malays*. Persons who in fact are, or who are generally accepted as members of the race or class known as the Cape Malays ... .Although the Cape Malays are a separate group, they only numbered 62,807 at the 1951 census, and they are generally not shown separately for statistical purposes, but included in the Coloured group. **1963** A.M. LOUW *20 Days* 74 Her eldest daughter had married a Cape Malay. That was the reason for the curry dish. **1971** [see MELKTERT]. **1971** [see CLASSIFICATION]. **1985** S. Afr. Panorama Jan. 22 One of the most spectacular customs of the Cape Malays is the *kalifa*. **1985** *Ibid.* Jan. 20 The Cape Malayan traditionally believes that he must live among the kramats to protect himself from fire, hunger, disease and earthquake. **1988** F. WILLIAMS *Cape Malay Cookbk* 95 Cape Malays adhere strictly to Islamic religious customs on feast days and holy days so that we find certain foods are served on special occasions.

B. *adj. phr.* Of or pertaining to the Cape Malay group; CAPE MUSLIM *adj. phr.*; MALAY *adj.* Cf. CAPE COLOURED *ppl adj. phr.*

1913 *Indian Opinion* 7 June 133 A very old established section of the Cape community, and a large one in point of numbers, viz., the Cape Malay Community, has always followed the Mahomedan faith. **1920** R. JUTA *Tavern* 100 Cape-Malay women, exquisitely-made, dainty creatures, with lustrous dark eyes blackened, henna-stained finger nails, yellow or green silk head handkerchief drawn low and square over the brow. **1953** *Drum* May 44 Those who feel like praising the Cape Malay community usually think of only one description for them — 'The most law-abiding section of the Coloured community'. **1960** J.J.L. SISSON *S. Afr. Judicial Dict.* 88 A woman who was born in India of a Cape Malay mother and Asiatic father and who lived as a member of a Cape Malay community. **1971** on Radio South Africa 2 Feb., As the older members of the Cape Malay people pass on so the old songs vanish. **1981** *S. Afr. Panorama* July 34 It is in the field of folk singing that the Cape Malayan community has made its most significant contribution to South African cultural life. **1987** *Ibid.* May 49 This band, that must have taken some tips from a Cape Malay band, performs over weekends at the centre. **1988** E. PLATTER in *Sunday Times* 24 July 25 All the delicacies which for years have been described as Cape Malay. **1988** *Daily Dispatch* 23 Feb. 17 Mr Essop said he was classified Cape Malay. **1990** *Drum* Dec. 49 He was impressed with their unique rap style mixed with Geema African, Cape Malay, Boeremusiek and the mbaqanga township-street-beat.

Cape Muslim *n. phr.* and *adj. phr.* [CAPE + Eng. *Muslim* an adherent of Islam, of or pertaining to Islam.]

A. *n. phr.* CAPE MALAY *n. phr.*

1944 I.D. DU PLESSIS *Cape Malays* 13 The Sultan of Turkey showed his interest in the Cape *Muslims* by allowing A' Ali Pasha, his minister of Foreign Affairs, to help the local community in connection with the *Chalifah* controversy. **1979** 'J.C.' in *Natal Witness* 2 Feb. 11 A pioneering attempt to establish the numbers and geographical origin of the early Cape Muslims, formerly known as the Cape Malays. **1979** W.S. ROBERTSON in *Sunday Times* 11 Feb. 4 The people we should more properly call the Cape Muslims. **1985** *S. Afr. Cookbk* (Reader's Digest Assoc.) 94 The bredie, a subtly flavoured meat and vegetable stew, was introduced to South African cuisine by the Cape Muslims, who eat particular bredies at religious and social occasions. **1989** T. BOTHA in *Style* Dec.-Jan. 158 The real Malay Quarter isn't really a quarter. It's not even an eighth. Of the Bo-Kaap, that is ... The Bo-Kaap, home to some 6000 Cape Muslims.

B. *adj. phr.* CAPE MALAY *adj. phr.*

1978 A. DAVIDS in Bradlow & Cairns *Early Cape Muslims* 1 The individualistic culture of the Cape Muslim community could not have grown and developed as it did by the mere importation of slaves and their emancipation; or by the banishment of political exiles and convicts to the Cape. *Ibid.* 2 Cape Muslim history is transmitted almost exclusively by word of mouth. **1979** 'J.C.' in *Natal Witness* 2 Feb. 11 An immense amount of research has been done .. among the Cape Muslim community.

Capenaar var. KAAPENAAR.

Caper /ˈkeɪpə/ *n. Obs.* exc. *hist.* [CAPE + Eng. suffix *-er*, expressing the sense 'a native of', 'a resident in'.]

1. KAAPENAAR sense 1.

1829 C. ROSE *Four Yrs in Sn Afr.* 13, I have now discussed the Races, the South-easter, the arrival of a Mail, and the Masquerade; and I will defy the most hackneyed Caper to name another thing that 'Breaks the tedium of fantastic idleness' in the capital of Southern Africa. **1888** *Cape Punch* 1 Aug. 47, I read it in the paper, It is so strange, so queer, To me a simple Caper At whom Uitlanders sneer. **1913** F.H. ROSE *Caper on Continent* (title-page), *Caper*, A native of the Cape.

2. In full *Caper tea*: a coarse tea mixed in China during the 19th century esp. for the Cape market.

1847 *Graham's Town Jrnl* 2 Jan. 1 (*advt*) At reduced prices, for sale, at the stores of Edward Herron, & Co. Rio coffee, Mauritius sugar, .. Caper Tea. **1855** J.W. COLENSO *Ten Weeks in Natal* 86 The latter [tea] was of a kind manufactured expressly for the Cape Colony, and called *Caper* tea. **1857** *Cape Monthly Mag.* II. Sept. 187 Articles of import may be quoted thus: .. Caper tea, direct, 32s. p 10 catty box. **1883** *Daily News* 27 July 6 Tea .. scented Caper 5d. to 1s. 01/4d. *c*1963 B.C. TAIT *Durban Story* 56 For beverage, the housewife refreshed her family with the rather coarse 'Caper' tea from China mixed especially for the Cape market. **1976** D.M.B. PRESTON *Story of Frontier Town* 58 Tea was rough and coarse and made by 'John Chinaman' especially for the Cape market, and known as 'Caper'. It was sold universally in 10 catty boxes (about 12 lbs) a package.

Cape rifle *n. phr. Hist.* [CAPE + Eng. *rifle*.] CAPE GUN.

1887 W.S.S. TYRWHITT *New Chum in Queensland Bush* 147, I have found the Cape rifle .. a very useful gun for Queensland work [i.e. kangaroo shooting]. [**1893** see CAPE GUN.] **1957** G. TYLDEN in *Africana Notes & News* Vol.12 No.6, 209 Although the so-called 'Cape Rifle' had been made in various bores to take different bullets for some years, it was the Enfield ammunition that made it so popular and so widely used. *Ibid.* 216 Octavius Bowker .. fought in all the wars on the Eastern and Basuto borders from 1835 to 1881 ... and had much to do with popularising the Cape Rifle. **1971** F.V. LATEGAN in *Std Encycl. of Sn Afr.* IV. 526 In 1854 the Cape rifle was also provided with Minié rifling ... The lighter .577 Enfield bullet, together with 2½ drams of powder in a greased paper cartridge, made the Cape rifle particularly popular ... This rifle, usually with one barrel rifled, was supplied in .45 and .50 inch by the Grahamstown gunsmith Hayton, among others.

Cape rood *n. phr. Hist.* [CAPE + Eng. *rood* land measure, prob. influenced by Du. *roe(de)* measure.] A unit of land measurement equivalent to 3,78 metres or 12,396 English feet. See also CAPE FOOT sense 1.

1861 *E. Prov. Yr Bk & Annual Register* 61 Since 12 Cape feet are equal to 1 Cape rood, 1 English mile is equal to nearly 425.944 Cape roods. **1893** *Brown's S. Afr.* 15, 12 Cape feet = 1 Cape Rood = 12.396 Eng. ft. **1926** M. NATHAN *S. Afr. from Within* 310 For area, the Cape rood is taken as the basis of measurement. **1934** C.P. SWART Supplement to Pettman. 29 *Cape Rood*, The unit of length in Cape land measure, 12 Cape feet in length or 12,396 British feet. It is not to be confused with the British rood, which is a measure of area and is one-fourth of an acre. **1942** *Off. Yrbk of Union 1941* (Union Office of Census & Statistics) 982 Denominations which are permitted for Expressing Trade Contracts ... *Length* The Cape foot = 0.3148581 metre. The Cape rood. **1957** *Handbk for Farmers* (Dept of Agric.) I. 345 Table of Measures, Weights, Etc ... *Areas* .. 1 Morgen = 600 square Cape Roods.

Cape salmon *n. phr.* [CAPE + Eng. *salmon*.] Any of several species of marine fish.

1. Either of two species of KOB (family Sciaenidae):

a. In the Western Cape: the GEELBEK (sense 1 a), *Atractoscion aequidens*. **b.** In KwaZulu-Natal: the KABELJOU, *Argyrosomus hololepidotus*. In these senses also called SALMON.

1846 H.H. METHUEN *Life in Wilderness* 17 The cape salmon, a heavy fish, in size and in external aspect somewhat resembling its British namesake. **1856** *Cape of G.H. Almanac & Annual Register* 283 Fish abound in the rivers .. and in the bay. The mullet, rock cod, and Cape Salmon, are most esteemed. **1865** *Hardwicke's Science Gossip* 64 *Cape Salmon*, Under this name the 'Geelbek' .. has been eulogized ... Why call it Cape Salmon? **1905** H.E.B. BROOKING in *E. London Dispatch* 14 Aug. 7 The kabeljaauw (sciaena aquila) is sometimes called Cape salmon by the deep sea fishermen. **1910** J. RUNCIE *Idylls by Two Oceans* 31 Rachel varied the diet of her bairns with things from the dust bin. The head of a snoek or harder or Cape salmon she would bring along in her mouth. **1936** M. HIGHAM *Hsehold Cookery* (1939) 26 Certain large fish, notably Kabeljouw, Cape Salmon and Stockfish are in season during the summer. **1950** H. GERBER *Cape Cookery* 74 For this old Cape favourite choose any firm fish, such as snoek, Cape salmon, kabeljou, albacore, etc. **1973** *Farmer's Weekly* 13 June 101 The species being tagged include grunter and white steenbras, elf (shad), kob (Kabeljauw or Cape Salmon in Natal) haarder (mullet) and leervis (garrick). **1979** *Weekend Argus* 10 Mar., Various fish dishes such as sea food soup, rollmops in mustard cream, fresh grilled crayfish, perlemoen, .. kingklip in parsley sauce and Cape salmon. **1989** E. PLATTER in *Style* Dec. 18 At lunch your straight-from-the-line red roman, red steenbras, kob, Cape salmon and yellowtail .. is simply grilled or batterfried.

2. Esp. in the Eastern Cape: the SPRINGER (sense 2 a), *Elops machnata*.

1905 *E. London Dispatch* 14 Aug. (Pettman), Our *Cape salmon* (*Elops saurus*) must not be confounded with the geelbek or yellow-mouth (*Otolithus aequidens*). **1913** C. PETTMAN *Africanderisms* 114 *Cape salmon*, .. (2) On the east coast — Port Elizabeth, East London, etc. *Elops saurus* is thus designated. **1949** J.L.B. SMITH *Sea Fishes* 86 *Elops Saurus* Linnaeus .. *Wildevis* (Mossel Bay — Knysna). *Cape salmon* (Knysna — East London). *Skipjack* (Transkei) .. *Springer* (Natal). **1972** *Grocott's Mail* 28 Jan. 3 One [catch] was a skipjack (Elops Saurus, .. also called Cape salmon, Springer, or wildevis), weighing 3,600 kg, caught in the surf from a high rock.

capeskin *n. obsolescent.* Also **Cape skin**. [CAPE + Eng. *skin* hide or pelt.] Originally, a soft gloving or clothing leather made from South African hair sheepskin; a sheepskin so used; later, any such leather; *Cape leather*, see CAPE sense 3. Also *attrib.*

1911 *Farmer's Weekly* 4 Oct. 122 East London and Capetown brokers fear that sheepskins may come down in sympathy with the wool market. The Bay quotations are as follows: .. Capeskins 26— Capeskins, damaged 06 — 07. **1937** *Handbk for Farmers* (Dept of Agric. & Forestry) 277 Very often prime Blackhead Persian and Cape skins have attached to them a thick fatty layer which it is impossible to remove entirely without resorting to the knife. **1938** *Times* (U.K.) 11 Mar. 19 The Gay Nineties type of flat crown .... Of particular interest are those of patent leather or capeskin. **1959** *Observer* (U.K.) 5 Apr. 13 The supplest and lightest weight of capeskin leathers, silky to the touch, printed in delicate marbled designs.

Cape smoke *n. phr. Obs.* exc. *hist.* [Etym. unkn.; perh. fr. Du. *Kaap* Cape + *smaak* taste; or CAPE + Eng. *smoke*, alluding to the spirit's cloudy colour. Cf. U.S. slang, *smoke* 'cheap (home-made) liquor' (early 1900s).] A rough brandy made during the 19th century of either peaches or grapes; *Kaapse smaak*, see KAAPSE sense 3. See also CAPE BRANDY.

[**1821** T. PRINGLE Letter. 12 June, The best [wine] produced on the frontier at present I fear could not appear on his board. It is all deeply tainted with the vile *Kaap smaak*. **1834** — *Afr. Sketches* 515 Some of the lighter Cape wines are occasionally found of good quality and agreeable flavour, though seldom *altogether* free of the earthy taste, or *Kaap smaak*, which seem peculiar to the soil or climate.] **1846** H.H. METHUEN *Life in Wilderness* 232 Already in imagination were they revelling in the luxuries of *Cape smoke*, or brandy, and sheep-tail fat. **1850** J.D. LEWINS Diary. 16 Oct., Feel slightly seedy from the glasses of Cape brandy I drank yesterday at Whitehead's. Cape Smoke does not agree with me. It is wretched stuff, .. & sickens both head and stomach. *a*1858 J. GOLDSWAIN *Chron.* (1946) I. 36, I did not stop at this place Long for thear was to much Cape Smoke. **1862** LADY DUFF-GORDON *Lett. from Cape* (1925) 117 'Cape Smoke' (brandy, like vitriol) ninepence a bottle. **1878** T.J. LUCAS *Camp Life & Sport* 36 In the way of spirit, there is Cape smoke, a coarse kind of peach brandy with something of the character of gin, with a raisin'y flavour, a very rank spirit. **1892** J.E. RITCHIE *Brighter S. Afr.* 53 The following recipe for the manufacture of 'Cape Smoke' .. is not an exaggeration, but carefully followed by some of the most enterprising brandy traders in the colony: Quarter of a pound vitriol, two ounces of Cayenne pepper, half a roll of Boer Tobacco, water ad libitum, and flavoured to taste. **1900** H.C. HILLEGAS *Oom Paul's People* 297 Cape Smoke, the name given to a liquor made in Cape Colony, is credited with the ability to kill a man before he has taken the glass from his lips. **1900** *Daily News* (U.K.) 11 Apr. 3 The poisonous 'Cape Smoke', or 'tanglefoot', which they [sc. soldiers] get in too great abundance out here. **1924** [see DOP *n.* sense 2 a]. **1936** C. BIRKBY *Thirstland Treks* 172 A glass of 'Cape smoke' — the fiercest brandy that ever came from a still. **1968** L.G. GREEN *Full Many Glorious Morning* 223, I made inquiries about 'Cape smoke' and found .. that it was enshrined in South African literature. Hans Sauer described it as 'the most pernicious drink on earth'. **1976** B. ROBERTS *Kimberley* 85 Down-at-heel diggers could be seen reeling out of them [*sc.* canteens] at all hours of the day, blind drunk of a vicious cheap brandy known as 'Cape Smoke'. **1983** D. HUGHES et al. *Complete Bk of S. Afr. Wine* 93 Cape Smoke was made from the wet mash of husks, pips and stalks which remained after the fermented must of the grapes had been run off in the traditional process of wine making. **1991** *Flying Springbok* May 105 The rough 'fire water' which passed as brandy, also referred to in those days as Cape Smoke, was good enough for soldier, sailor, worker and servant.

Capetonian /ˌkeɪpˈtəʊnɪən/ *n.* Also occas. **Capetownian**. [*Cape Town* name of the city + Eng. n.- and adj.-forming suffix *-ian*.] A resident of Cape Town (see MOTHER CITY); also called CAPEY (sense 2). Also *attrib.*

1904 *Argus Christmas Annual* (Cape Colony Sect.) 23 A Capetonian .. states that it would take days to explore them [*sc.* the Cango Caves]. **1927** *Outspan* 4 Mar. 82 A breathing space has been reached for the large body of Capetonians whose duty it has been to make sure that the attractions of the Peninsula are on everybody's tongue at home and abroad. **1950** H. GIBBS *Twilight* 33 We arrived in a flourish of American cars and anticipation, and were soon attacking one of those five-course lunches which Cape-townians dismiss as a 'simple snack'. **1976** [see VAALIE]. **1979** *Cape Times* 2 July 1 Capetonians can draw comfort from the fact that in 200 years of meteorite strikes only six injuries, and no deaths, are recorded. **1987** C.

HOPE *Hottentot Room* 121 The heart, remember, Looper repeated to himself in passable imitation of the flat Capetownian vowels of Christiaan Barnard – is only a pump. **1989** S. SOLE in *Sunday Tribune* 1 Jan. 2 Capetonians have more words for foreigners (anyone from North of the Huguenot tunnel) than Free State farmers have to describe their sheep, none of them as complimentary. **1989** [see VAALIE]. **1990** J. MICHELL in *Style* Nov. 62 Durbanites eat for enjoyment and energy rather than to impress their clients; and, unlike Capetonians, they aren't prepared to spend hours fussing over prissy little plates of nouvelle cuisine.

Cape Triangular *n. phr. Hist.* [CAPE + Eng. *triangular* having the form of a triangle.] Any of several rare triangular stamps issued at the Cape from 1853 to 1900. Also *attrib.*

1949 L.G. GREEN *In Land of Afternoon* 82 A complete copy of Ritter's almanac .. would be worth as much as any Cape Triangular. [**1953** U. KRIGE *Dream & Desert* 57 For a long time they had stood motionless, gaping at a whole page full of large blue, green and red Cape of Good Hope triangular stamps- .. the faint figure of Hope sadly reclining against her anchor.] **1975** *S. Afr. Panorama* Jan. 30 The Cape triangulars, together with the early stamps of Britain, Europe and the U.S.A., are regarded as the corner-stones of the classic heritage of philately. **1982** *Ibid.* Apr. 35 Charles Davidson Bell (1813–1882) .. is world-famous as the designer of the rare and valuable Cape triangular stamp first issued in 1853. **1990** *Weekend Post* 5 May (Leisure) 7 Charles Bell, Surveyor-General of the Cape of Good Hope, drew her [*sc.* 'Hope'] seated (semi-reclining) on the old Cape Triangular.

Cape wine *n. phr.* [CAPE + Eng. *wine.*] Wine made at the Cape of Good Hope: in early times referring to CONSTANTIA, but subsequently to South African wines in general.

See also *Cape Madeira* (CAPE sense 2 b), FRONTIGNAC, HANEPOOT sense 2, JEREPIGO, METHODE CAP CLASSIQUE, PINOTAGE sense 2, PONTAC sense 1, PREMIER GRAND CRU, RIESLING, STEEN sense 1, STEIN sense 1.

[**1731** G. MEDLEY tr. *P. Kolb's Present State of Cape of G.H.* II. 80, I have drank, at the Governour's, *Capian* Wine which was Six Years old; and which sparkled like old Hock, and was as racy as the noblest Canary.] **1773** J. BYRON in J. Hawkesworth *Acct of Voy.* 137, I gave all the people leave to go on shore by turns, and they always contrived to get very drunk with Cape wine before they came back. **1795** C.R. HOPSON tr. *C.P. Thunberg's Trav.* I. 280 *Constantia*, consisting of two farms, called *great* and *little Constantia* .. is celebrated for its highly delicious wine, known by the name of *Constantia* or *Cape Wine*, which is sold in Europe at so high a price. **1797** T. HOLCROFT *Stolberg's Trav. through Germany, Switzerland, Italy & Sicily* III. 351 Red Cape wine .. of the best kind, called Constantia. **1805** R. SEMPLE *Walks & Sketches* 101 His invitation came too seasonably to be refused, and our dinner and some good Cape wine restored our spirits. **1838** J.E. ALEXANDER *Exped. into Int.* II. 296 Unless some great improvement speedily takes place in the quality of Cape wines, and which is quite possible with care, the Cape must look to Australia as the place for the chief reception of its vinous produce. **1844** W.N. IRWIN *Echoes of Past* (1927) 230 Best Cape wine from 8d. to 1s. a bottle. **1857** *Cape Monthly Mag.* II. Sept. 188 We are satisfied that good Cape wine will realize good prices, and that the exporter of a genuine article will benefit by the care taken in its preparation. **1886** A. VON BABO in C. Cowen *S. Afr. Exhibition* 195 The name 'Cape Wine' should have some legal protection, and it should be a punishable offence if such concoctions are sold under the name of 'Cape Wine'. **1896** [see DOP *n.* sense 2]. **1900** O. OSBORNE *In Land of Boers* 58 For one New Year's picnic we went to a wine farm at Constantia, a place close to Cape Town, from whence the best Cape wine derives its name. **1926** P.W. LAIDLER *Tavern of Ocean* 170 As the century aged, Cape wines came into great repute. Cape champagne was voted equal, if not superior, to the best continental. **1936** *Cambridge Hist. of Brit. Empire* VIII. 229 The colony possessed three chief sources of income: the British garrison, the entertainment of invalids from India, and the export of Cape wine. **1950** H. GIBBS *Twilight* 81 Cape wines and brandies are exported on an ever-increasing scale as shipping refrigeration increases. **1965** A. GORDON-BROWN *S. Afr. Heritage* IV. 19 There were clean tablecloths and tidy waitresses, and the meal, which consisted of 'kerrie' (mulligatawny), two sosaties and boiled rice, and half a pint of Cape wine, cost a quart of a rix-doller (4 cents). **1976** *U.C.T.* (Univ. of Cape Town) Vol.6, 24 Wines other than those from Constantia were known as *common Cape wines* ... The Cape wines sent to Batavia and Amsterdam by the Company between 1740 and 1780 varied considerably in quality and were received with mixed feelings by brokers. **1990** J. PLATTER in *Sunday Times* 16 Dec. 21 Shut out from the major supermarket chains of Europe and generally ostracised and ignored along with most things South African, Cape wine has had to sneak in through backdoors.

Capey /ˈkeɪpi/ *n. colloq.* Also **Ca(a)pie, Cape-jie.** [Prob. formed on Afk. *Kaapie, Kaap* Cape + -IE.]
1.a. CAPE COLOURED *n. phr.* Also *attrib.*

1940 V. POHL *Bushveld Adventures* 188 Our oarsman, a 'Capie' named Willem, a short but extremely powerfully built fellow, placed a shot-gun in the boat as we were about to depart. **1949** O. WALKER *Wanton City* 171 'E's a bad ole bastard, eh?' said the driver. 'Always muckin' around with the Capies.' **1959** J. MEIRING *Candle in Wind* 139 'He *must* be white. What is he doing with a Capie?' said the first girl, crossly. **1963** A. FUGARD *Blood Knot* (1968) 131 Just a little bit black, And a little bit white, He's a Capie through and through. **1965** K. THOMPSON *Richard's Way* 45 The little miss is married – did you know? and lives at Tokai over the-e-e-re. The long drawn Capey vowel indicated great, very great distance. **1974** D. ROOKE *Margaretha de la Porte* 48 She learned new songs from the Capies at their fires: 'Polly we are going to Paarl' and 'Here comes the *Alabama*'. **1981** [see *Kleurling-Afrikaans* (KLEURLING sense 2)]. **1990** R. GOOL *Cape Town Coolie* 59, I 'eard it you living in the Cape now ... You looking like a Cape-jie already.

b. In full *Capeytaal* /-tɑːl/ [Afk. *taal* language]: the argot spoken by some 'coloured' people, consisting of a mixture of languages, esp. Afrikaans, English, and Xhosa; *gammat-taal* (often *derog.* and *offensive*), see GAMMAT sense 2.

1979 C. VAN DER MERWE in *Frontline* Dec. 17 Flytaal .. embraces Capeytaal and a large chunk of fanakalo. **1981** V.A. FEBRUARY *Mind your Colour* 95 Kaaps .. is not what some Englishman in South Africa refers to as 'Capey', .. not what some Afrikaans-speaking persons refer to as Gamat-taal.

2. An inhabitant of the Western Cape, or of the city of Cape Town; cf. KAAPENAAR sense 1. See also CAPETONIAN.

1970 *Drum* Nov. 15 If there ever has to be a roll call of Capeys in Durban it'll have to be on a scroll to contain all the names. **1974** A.P. BRINK *Looking on Darkness* 226 'You know mos the old story, hey, Capey? ' .. And it was with conscious irony that he called me 'Capey', for he was as much a Capetonian as myself, and much darker too. **1979** [see UDI]. **1979** *Capetonian* July 4 Having just read why Capeys are different from Transvalers, I guffawed so loudly it was heard by everybody in this building. **1981** C. BARNARD in *Daily Dispatch* 16 Nov. 8 In the good old days of the Cape, which most middle-aged Capies can remember clearly, the local fishermen would travel around town on a cart announcing themselves with a blast on a long tube of dried seaweed. **1989** S. HOBBS in *Style* Dec. 6 You Caapies seem to think yours is the only town with some sort of scenic beauty. [**1994** 'T. COBBLEIGH' in *Sunday Times* 2 Jan. 19 Johannesburg! .. the city so scorned by Kaapies and Banana-boys.]

capitein var. KAPTEIN.

capoc var. KAPOK.

Capoid /keɪpɔɪd/ *adj.* and *n.* [CAPE + Eng. adj.- and n.-forming suffix *-oid* having the form or nature of, resembling (*OED*).]

A. *adj.* Of or belonging to a purportedly distinct racial group comprising the Khoikhoi, Korana, San, and the Sandawe of Tanzania. See also *Khoisanoid* (KHOISAN).

The Capoid group is believed by some to be one of the major groups into which *Homo sapiens* may be divided.

1963 S.C. COON *Origin of Races* 3, I am using a conservative and tentative classification of the living peoples of the world into five basically geographical groups: The Caucasoid, Mongoloid, Australoid, Congoid, and Capoid. **1983** D. HUGHES et al. *Complete Bk of S. Afr. Wine* 16 Bands of Hottentots (Xhoisan, or Capoid, people), the only indigenous population here .. had no settled community or agriculture, living meagrely off shellfish and fruit. **1991** J. COULTER in *Weekend Post* 4 May (Leisure) 3 These unique African people [*sc.* the San] are the descendants of the ancient Capoid or Khoisanoid division of man.

B. *n.* Always in *pl.*: A collective name for members of this group. See also KHOISAN sense 1.

1963 S.C. COON *Origin of Races* 636 The Capoids, named by Broom after the Cape of Good Hope, constitute one of the five subspecies of modern man. They include the living Bushmen, the living Hottentots and that branch of the Hottentots known as the Korana, a few beachcombing remnants of an earlier coastal Bushman population known as Strandlopers, and certain relict populations in Tanganyika and possibly farther north. **1971** P.V. TOBIAS in *Std Encycl. of Sn Afr.* III. 95 The Capoids comprise the Bushman and, in a mixed state, the Hottentots, Korana and Sandawe of Tanganyika. Thus the term covers the congeries of people commonly grouped as the Khoisanoid or Khoisaniform race or complex of races. The Capoids or Khoisanoids were formerly regarded as one of the five major subdivisions of living mankind. Subsequently genetical research indicated that they had many affinities with the Negroid peoples of Africa.

capp(e)y, cappie, cappje varr. KAPPIE.

captain *n. hist.* [Special sense of general Eng. *captain* a leader or chief; influenced by (or tr. of) S. Afr. Du. *kaptein*, see KAPTEIN.] KAPTEIN sense 1.

During the 1970s, this obsolescent title was briefly revived by the government as a substitute for 'chief'.

1688 G. TACHARD *Voy. to Siam* II. 68 Every one of these Nations have their Head or Captain whom they obey, that Office is Hereditary, and goes from Father to Son. **1731** G. MEDLEY tr. *P. Kolb's Present State of Cape of G.H.* I. 85 The Captain of a *Kraal*, or Village, looks to the Preservation of the Peace and the Administration of Justice in His Jurisdiction. **1786** G. FORSTER tr. *A. Sparrman's Voy. to Cape of G.H.* I. 240 Captain, says he, is merely an empty title, formerly bestowed by the regency at the Cape on some princes and patriarchs of the Hottentots. **1798** S.H. WILCOCKE tr. *J.S. Stavorinus's Voy. to E. Indies 1768–71* I. 547 [Hottentots] .. dwell together in villages, called *kraals*, and under a chief, whom they elect themselves, and who has the title of captain. **1801** [see TIGER sense 1]. **1804** R. PERCIVAL *Acct of Cape of G.H.* 81 The Dutch have paid some marks of respect to the chiefs or heads of those tribes; and have publicly nominated them captains over the next. **1819** G. BARKER Journal. 28 Sept., Linx, or Makana, the Caffre Captain passed this to Algoa Bay, to go on board a man of war in order to be sent to The Cape. **1827** G. THOMPSON *Trav.* II. 30 A chief or captain presides over each clan or kraal, being usually the person of greatest property; but his authority is extremely limited, and only obeyed so far as it meets the general approbation. **1838** *Graham's Town Jrnl* (26 Apr.) in J. Green *Kat River Settlement in 1851* (1853) 48 Meyers told me that .. all the Kaffir Captains, with the exception on Tyalie, Macomo, and Pato, were ready to make war against the English. **1839** W.C. HARRIS *Wild Sports* 41 When near Danielskuil – a kraal of Griquas, or mulatto Hottentots, we met their Chief, Captain Down. **1857** H.F. FYNN Letters to Secretary of Native Affairs. 5 June, I must add that not only Ketchwiya, but Panda himself, and the captains also, urgently expressed their wish that the Natal Government would send an officer to reside amongst them in whom they could place confidence. **1861** P.B. BORCHERDS *Auto-Biog. Mem.* 157 In 1781 a report was received .. that several Kaffir captains and Kaffirs had, contrary to treaty, occupied land on this side of Great Visch River. **1930** A. ELLIOTT *S. Afr. through Centuries* 860 (*caption*) Captain B. Plaatjes. Captain of a Bushman tribe at Harlam ... He is shown wearing his badge and staff of office ... circa 1806. *c***1936** *S. & E. Afr. Yr Bk & Guide* 176 The Hottentots were originally divided into 10 tribes or clans, at the head of each of which was a captain who was assisted by councillors appointed by the male population. **1958** A. JACKSON *Trader on Veld* 56 At least one famous man came to my store at Rietfontein. He was Hendrik Witbooi, 'Captain' or Chief of the Witbooi tribe of Hottentots, who wore white bands round their hats. **1961** L.E. VAN ONSELEN *Trekboer* 112 These Koranna Hottentots were a fierce clan led by a succession of halfbreed captains. **1970** *S. Afr. Panorama* Sept. 14 (*caption*) Senator J.J. Boshoff with the chairman of the Zulu Territorial Authority and members of the Executive Council. Third from the right is Captain Gatsha Buthelezi. **1973** *Ibid.* July 46 There are 1766 schools in KwaZulu ... One of these schools, the Bhekuzulu captains' sons' school, trains captains' sons for the leadership and responsibility which they will have to assume in their various tribes. **1987** C. HOPE *Hottentot Room* 157 It's historically valuable, you see. It's the cane colonial governors gave to the Hottentot captains. **1994** M. ROBERTS tr. *J.A. Wahlberg's Trav. Jrnls 1838–56* 34 Zambus, Dingaan's greatest Captain, arrives at Peter Maritzburg.

Hence **captaincy** *n.*, a political system in which a 'captain' presides over a district or people.

1976 R. Ross *Adam Kok's Griquas* If there had been a division between black and white inherent from the beginning of South Africa, then the anomaly of a free, independent, 'coloured' polity, such as the Griqua Captaincies, would not have come into existence.

carabenatje var. KARBONATJIE.

carass var. KAROSS.

carbonaadtje, carbo-naatje, carbona(a)tjie, carbonadj(i)e, carbona(i)tje, carbonardjie varr. KARBONATJIE.

cardell var. KATEL.

care var. KIERIE.

caree var. KAREE *n.*²

carl var. KAAL.

carle var. KÊREL.

carom var. KEREM.

Caro(o), Carouw varr. KAROO.

caross(e) var. KAROSS.

carparter var. KAPATER.

carpenter *n.* Also **karpenter**. Pl. unchanged, or **-s**. [Prob. ad. S. Afr. Du. *kaapenaar* one from the Cape.] The small seabream *Argyrozona argyroxona* of the Sparidae; KAAPENAAR sense 2; SILVER-FISH sense 1 a. See also DOPPIE sense 2.

A fish of some commercial importance. The name 'carpenter' is used for this species in Smith and Heemstra's *Smiths' Sea Fishes* (1986).

1913 C. PETTMAN *Africanderisms* 116 Carpenter, This word seems to be a corruption of Kaapenaar; *Dentex argyroxona* is so called in East London. **1949** J.L.B. SMITH *Sea Fishes* 278 *Argyrozona Argyrozona* .. [*Dentex* or *Ploysteganus argyrozona*] Silvervis. Silver. Fish. Doppie (Cape). Rooitjie (Knysna). Karp (Port Elizabeth) Karpenter or Kaapenaar (East London to Natal). **1976** *E. Prov. Herald* 14 Oct. 21 How does one stop these fish being caught? They were in an area where we were having excellent fishing for daggerhead, roman, carpenter and fairly large steenbras. **1981** *Ibid.* 23 Apr. 11 The original name of the carpenter, a common reef fish, was kaapenaar indicating that it was caught in Cape waters and this became anglicised to carpenter. However, it is still known in Afrikaans by its original name. **1988** G. WINCH in *Ski-Boat* Nov.-Dec. 9 They [*sc.* foreign vessels] are .. limited to catch no more than 15% of other species (carpenter, panga, steenbras) as a by-catch when trawling for hake or maasbanker. **1993** R. VAN DER ELST *Guide to Common Sea Fishes* 336 The flesh of the carpenter is excellent, and significant commercial catches are still made by line-boats and trawlers.

carper var. KARPER.

carrie var. KIERIE.

Carro(o), Carrow varr. KAROO.

carross var. KAROSS.

cartel(l), cartle varr. KATEL.

cary var. KIERIE.

cased /keɪst/ *ppl adj. Obsolescent. slang.* Also **kysed**. [ad. general Eng. *case* an infatuation, a love-affair (cf. U.S. slang *to have a case on* to be infatuated with). The spelling *kysed* results from a misconception that the word is Afk. in origin.] In the language of schoolchildren: *to be cased*, to be going steady (with someone).

1958 D.A. STEWART in *Pietersburg Eng. Medium School Mag.* 72 Though now I know the ways of girls, I have not found my taste. The one I loved is in my mind But she, alas, is cased. **1963** A.M. LOUW *20 Days* 32 'All the girls in my class are cased,' said Ingrid. 'They say I am a square, that's why the boys don't ask me.' **1970** K. NICOL *Informant*, Durban John and Jane are kysed (going steady). **1977** C. HOPE in S. Gray *Theatre Two* (1981) 43 Jimmie (he has taken out his comb and begins to groom his hair): I'm not chaffing you. Tell me. I wanna ask you. You cased or anything? Going steady?

Casspir /'kæspə/ *n.* Also **Caspir**, and with small initial. [Anagram of *SAP* (see SAP *n.*²) + *CSIR* (see CSIR).] An armoured troop-carrying vehicle used by the police and the defence forces. Also *attrib.*, and *fig.* See also BUFFEL sense 2.

1981 S. WROTTESLEY in *E. Prov. Herald* 30 Nov. 3 A police unit almost entirely composed of Ovambos is operating against Swapo insurgents in close cooperation with the Defence Force ... The unit .. uses its own specially designed transport vehicles — the Casspir. **1985** *Rand Daily Mail* 16 Apr. 3 When policemen in two Casspirs blocking the road ahead of the procession opened fire on the crowd, police in a third Casspir patrol vehicle parked behind the crowd, fired on fleeing people. **1986** *Rhodeo* (Rhodes Univ.) May 8 Hey bra! Did you know that the word 'caspir' is an anagram for the SAP and CSIR (Council for Scientific and Industrial Research), who designed the vehicle. **1987** G. THOMAS in *Best of S. Afr. Short Stories* (1991) 407 Clumsy-looking troop carriers called Casspirs. **1988** BUNN & TAYLOR *From S. Afr.* 28 'Casspir' .. is this armored, troop-transporting combat vehicle, with its characteristically hunched, high-gaited step (designed to withstand land-mine blasts). **1990** R. MALAN in *Cosmopolitan* Apr. 169 Making the language [*sc.* Afrikaans] kosher again — taking it from being a Casspir language to a language of the people where it belongs. Where it's OK to speak it and not be a fascist. **1991** *Weekly Mail* 24 May 14 The distinguished voice of .. Tony Heard has been added to those criticising the press for allegedly subjecting Winnie Mandela to 'trial by media'. He accuses newspapers of 'driving a squadron of casspirs through the *sub judice* and contempt rules'. **1992** B. KELLER in *Scope* 13 Nov. 95 Within the precincts of the hostels the South African Police rarely dismount from their high-riding, mine-proof armoured patrol vehicles — the Casspirs. **1993** [see BUFFEL sense 2].

Castle *n.* [tr. Du. *kasteel.*] *The Castle*: The star-shaped fort erected at the Cape of Good Hope by the Dutch East India Company. Also *attrib.*

Built between 1665 and 1679, the Castle is now the headquarters of the South African National Defence Force in the Western Cape.

1688 G. TACHARD *Voy. to Siam* 65 The Lieutenant of the Castle .. told me that the Rhinoceros being in rage runs his greatest Horn into the Ground and continues to run a kind of furrow with it, till he comes up with him that has smitten him. **1796** *Van Ryneveld vs. Brown & Spooner.* 3 The said 18 bales of Callicoes being sold .. to *Josias Brink*, a Burgher .. from whom the same were recovered after the Discovery was made and conveyed to the Castle. **1868** W.R. THOMSON *Poems, Essays & Sketches* 211 After the execution, the whole Senate, escorted by the guard in the order before-mentioned, returned to the Castle and to the Governor's house. **1920** K.M. JEFFREYS tr. *Memorandum of Commissary J.A. de Mist* 176 Every wagon had to pass the military guard at the Castle before it was allowed to enter the town, and the amount [*sc.* the tithe] to be paid to the Company was estimated on the supposed value of the load. **1941** N. DEVITT *Celebrated S. Afr. Crimes* 5 He was captured in a distant part of the country, taken to Cape Town under a strong escort of burghers and lodged in the Castle. **1969** I. VAUGHAN *Last of Sunlit Yrs* 49 The Castle, my first and best love, was the oldest building in the country. **1980** D.B. COPLAN *Urbanization of African Performing Arts.* 48 Bell attended a European dance at the Castle in Cape Town in 1834, where music was provided by Black men dressed in British uniforms and playing Western instruments. **1991** B.J. BARKER *Fairest Cape* 13 The visitor to the Castle can .. admire the elegance of its cool museums and ballrooms, all contained within massive stone walls that .. were never called upon to resist an enemy attack.

catch-peeren var. KATJIEPIERING.

CATE /keɪt/ *n. hist.* Acronym formed on the initial letters of *College for Advanced Technical Education*, an earlier name for TECHNIKON.

*c***1977** *S. Afr. 1976: Off. Yrbk* (Dept of Info.) 682 Colleges for advanced technical education (CATEs), technical colleges and technical institutes have various systems of training. *Ibid.* 683 Colleges, especially CATEs, also offer courses of their own not controlled by the department, .. some of which are classified under 'adult education'. **1983** *S. Afr. 1983: Off. Yrbk* (Dept of Foreign Affairs & Info.) 686 In terms of the Advanced Technical Education Act 1967 (Act 40 of 1967), the status of four existing technical colleges was advanced, and from 1968 they were designated CATEs, now known as technikons.

catel var. KATEL.

catfish *n.* [Transf. use of Eng. *catfish* a name given to various fishes.]

1. An octopus of the species *Octopus bimaculatus, O. dofleini,* or *O. vulgaris*, belonging to the order Octopoda; SEA-CAT; SEEKAT. Also *attrib.*

1862 'A LADY' *Life at Cape* (1963) 77 A most horrible creature called a 'catfish', but which ought more properly to have been named 'a sea devil' .. as it was all arms and legs and huge goggle-eyed head. **1913** C. PETTMAN *Africanderisms* 117 Catfish, In the neighbourhood of the Cape *Octopus vulgaris* is thus designated. **1945** H. GERBER *Fish Fare* 51 Octopus or catfish .. is not very often eaten in South Africa ... Its meat, when suitably cooked, has much similarity to sweetbread or brains. **1961** *Red Wing* (St Andrew's College, Grahamstown) 12 Octopi, commonly known as cat fish, are as abundant as anywhere along the coast and are a favourite of many fishermen, being tough and thus difficult to be nibbled off the hook. **1972** *Grocott's Mail* 11 Feb. 3 He caught a massive white steenbras of 9,6 kg on cat-fish bait, fishing on the breakwater wall at Port Elizabeth.

2. BARBEL sense 3.

1864 T. BAINES *Explor. in S.-W. Afr.* 4 Beyond was a broad flat, covered with cat, dog and other mud-frequenting fish. **1897** PARKER & HASWELL *Text-Bk of Zool.* II. 212 The Cat-fishes (*Siluridae*). **1900** H.A. BRYDEN *Animals of Afr.* 196 There is another strange, mud-loving fish which swarms in many of the larger South African rivers. I mean the Cat-fish, one of a class of fish known to naturalists as Siluroids. **1906** STARK & SCLATER *Birds of S. Afr.* IV. 57 Ayres found a two-pound Catfish (*Clarias*) in the stomach of one individual.

1967 [see BARBEL sense 3]. **1986** *Motorist* 2nd Quarter 35 Yellowfish, young catfish, carp and bass are among those suitable for drying. Catfish over about 10kg and some other fatty fish are not suitable. **1988** [see BARBEL sense 3].

3. BARBEL sense 2.

1949 J.L.B. SMITH *Sea Fishes* 109 *Tachysurus Feliceps ... Barbel. Barber. Sea Barbel. Catfish. Bagger* ... Found only in South Africa right round our coasts, common in estuaries. **1975** M.M. SMITH in Smith & Jackson *Common & Scientific Names of Fishes* 20 *Order Siluriformes*, .. Plotsidae — eel — catfishes ... Ariidae (Tachysuridae) — Sea-catfishes.

catjepiring var. KATJIEPIERING.

cat's tail *n. phr.* Also **catstail, cat tail.** [Transf. use of general Eng. *cat's tail* a name applied to various plants (some of which also occur in S. Afr.); so named from a supposed resemblance of parts of the plant to the tail of a cat.]

1. In full ***cat's tail grass***: either of two grasses of the Poaceae, *Sporobolus pyrimidalis* (subfamily Chloridoideae) or *Imperata cylindrica* (subfamily Panicoideae).

1955 A.W. BAYER in D. Meredith *Grasses & Pastures* 549 *Eragrostis-Sporobolus* grassland is now widespread, especially in the savanna country ... The dominant species are *Sporobolus pyramidalis* (Catstail Grass), [etc.]. **1955** J.D. SCOTT et al. in *Ibid.* 604 *Sour Veld ...* Fallow Lands: .. *Sporobolus pyramidalis* Catstail. **1982** FOX & NORWOOD YOUNG *Food from Veld* 296 *Imperata cylindrica*, .. *Common names*: English — *bedding grass, cat tail, cottonwool grass, silver speka*. **1991** G.E. GIBBS RUSSELL et al. *Grasses of Sn Afr.* 311 *Sporobolus pyramidalis* .. Catstail grass.

2. Any of several shrubs of the Selaginaceae, esp. the dune shrublet *Hebenstreitia integrifolia*.

1966 C.A. SMITH *Common Names* 190 *Cat's tail*, Several species of *Hebenstreitia* (Nat), .. *Setaria verticillata* (Cape), .. *Typha capensis* (Nat) ... The vernacular name is derived from the appearance of the elongated cylindrical inflorescences. **1982** A. MORIARTY *Outeniqua Tsitsikamma* 166 *Hebenstreitia integrifolia Cat-Tail*, .. A compact much branched plant up to 600mm high ... Numerous terminal spikes of small white flowers, each with an orange splash on the lower petal, make this a pleasing shrublet of the dune veld, from Herold's Bay to Humansdorp and in the grassveld of the Langkloof.

3. Any of several species of *Bulbinella* of the Liliaceae, esp. *B. latifolia*.

1985 *Fair Lady* 3 Apr. 139 Bulbinella or Catstail — these brilliant little yellow torches bloom in late winter. [**1988** LE ROUX & SCHELPE *Namaqualand* 36 *Bulbinella latifolia*, .. This plant name has changed from *Bulbinella floribunda* ... There are about 16 species of Bulbinella in southern Africa.] **1991** *S. Afr. Panorama* Jan.-Feb. 39 The descriptive flower names are like music to the ear. There are button flowers, Hottentot's cabbage, .. cat's tail, desert rose and many more ... Orange cat's tail (*Bulbinella floribunda*) colour the hills at Nieuwoudtville. Yellow cat's tail also grow in the area while white and pink ones occur in the Biedouw Valley. **1992** C. CURZON in *Motorist* Aug. 6 *(caption)* Cat's-tail (*Bulbinella*) on the bank of a dam.

cat-thorn *n.* Also **cat's thorn.** [tr. S. Afr. Du. *katdoorn*, see KATDORING.] Any of several plant species with hooked thorns. In all senses also called WAG-'N-BIETJIE.

1. Any of several species of wild asparagus of the genus *Protasparagus* (family Liliaceae); KATDORING sense 3.

1821 C.I. LATROBE *Jrnl of Visit* 141 A table, covered with a white cloth, and decorated with festoons of cat's-thorn and field-flowers. **1917** R. MARLOTH *Common Names* 18 *Cat thorn, Asparagus stipulaceus* of the drier regions. Forming an entangled mass full of sharp recurved spines. **1979** *Sunday Times* 15 July (Mag. Sect.) 5 The root of the cat-thorn, a species of wild asparagus, is used against tuberculosis.

2. Either of two trees of the Rhamnaceae:

a. *Scutia myrtina*; DROOG-MY-KEEL sense 2; KATDORING sense 1.

1972 PALMER & PITMAN *Trees of Sn Afr.* II. 1401 *Scutia myrtina*, .. The specific name means 'myrtle-like'. The common names 'cat-thorn' and 'katdoring' refer to the sharp, hooked thorns. **1982** FOX & NORWOOD YOUNG *Food from Veld* 314 *Scutia myrtina*, .. *Common names*: English — *cat thorn, dry throat*. **1987** F. VON BREITENBACH *Nat. List of Indigenous Trees* 123 *Scutia myrtina*, .. *Cat-thorn*.

b. Less commonly, the *buffalo thorn* (see BUFFALO sense 2), *Ziziphus mucronata* subsp. *mucronata*.

1987 F. VON BREITENBACH *Nat. List of Indigenous Trees* 122 *Ziziphus mucronata*, .. *Buffalo-thorn*, Cat-thorn, Bogwood.

3. The tree *Acacia caffra* of the Fabaceae; KATDORING sense 2.

1982 FOX & NORWOOD YOUNG *Food from Veld* 199 *Acacia caffra*, .. *Common names*: English — *cat thorn, common hook thorn, kaffir thorn, water thorn*.

cattle-killing *n. hist.* Also with initial capitals. ***The cattle-killing***: The systematic destruction of cattle by the Xhosa during 1857, following the visions and prophecies of a young girl, Nongqawuse, in the belief that their ancestors would arise and a new millenium would dawn; NATIONAL SUICIDE. Also *attrib.*

1858 in J.B. Peires *Dead Will Arise* (1989) 234 The cattle-killing was got up to deprive the people of property that required so many to look after, the people would go more free to fight. **1867** C. BROWNLEE in *Ibid.* 212, I freely admit that during the disorders and excitement attending the cattle killing we did many things which would not be justifiable under ordinary circumstances. **1877** J. NOBLE *S. Afr.* 217 Unexpected events: — the Cattle-Killing Delusion. **1909** C.D. HOPE *Our Place in Hist.* 163 The real power of the clan system was broken by the failure of the cattle killing in 1857. **1916** C. BROWNLEE in J.B. Peires *Dead Will Arise* (1989) 156, I came to save Sandile, and those who had gone into the cattle-killing movement. I have failed. *c*1935 M. ANDREWS *Story of S. Afr.* 36 As the natives recovered from the cattle-killing tragedy and their numbers increased, they needed more land. **1971** J. MEINTJES *Sandile* 245 This then was the beginning of the great cattle-killing delusion, the most fantastic occurrence during the reign of Sir George Grey .. and also the strangest in South African history. **1980** D.B. COPLAN Urbanization of African Performing Arts. 77 Successive Xhosa defeats and mounting land pressure from European encroachment led to a nativistic movement .. in which thousands of traditional pastoralists slaughtered their cattle and planted no crops in expectation that their ancestors could be moved to drive the Whites from their country. When this 'cattle killing' led to famine instead, the power of traditional political authorities disintegrated. **1989** J.B. PEIRES *Dead Will Arise* 138 The Xhosa Cattle-Killing movement, suggested in the first instance by the lungsickness epidemic of 1853, tapped a deep-seated emotional and spiritual malaise resulting from material deprivation and military defeat. **1989** B. MACLENNAN in *ADA* No.7, 57 Peires effectively destroys the myths that the Cattle Killing was a plot by the Chiefs to bring about war with the colony, or was directly initiated by Grey in order to destroy the Xhosa nation.

cattle place see PLACE *n.*[1] sense 2.

catty *n. colloq.* Also **caddie, cattie, kattie, katty, kettie.** [Formed on Eng. *catapult* + (informal) n.-forming suffix *-y* (or *-ie*). The *k-* spelling-forms are influenced by Afk.] Esp. in the language of children: a catapult. Also *attrib.*

1970 J. TAYLOR *Informant, Salisbury (Harare, Zimbabwe)* Caddie. A catapult. When a schoolgirl .. was asked in a quiz show .. how David killed Goliath her reply was: 'Oh with a caddie.' **1970** Y. HOLLOWAY *Informant, Durban* I'm going to take my kettie and see if I can hit that tree over there. **1970** B.C. MARITZ *Informant, Port Elizabeth* Use your fly-kattie for shooting orange peels with. **1973** BRINK & HEWITT ad. Aristophanes's The Birds. 11 You're threatened, laughed at, hunted, trapped. Children throw stones at you and shoot at you with catties. **1977** *E. Prov. Herald* 30 Apr. 1 For a few cents you can arm yourself with a modern and highly sophisticated 'catty' (not just a twig-fork plucked at random from a tree and a strip of inner tube; these are made of plastic) and load up with lead shot. **1981** *Daily Dispatch* 18 Feb. 8 Modern, factory-produced catapults with metal frames .. are mere assembly line trash, upstarts .. compared to the classic 'blougom en tjoob' of the pukka kettie. **1986** *Crux* Aug. 43 When Goliath spots this little ou, he only mocks him and tunes him, 'Sonny, get lost!' But David .. pulls out his slingshot (a catty-like boulder-holder), grafts one stone in and aims at Goliath. **1987** S. GOUVELIS in *Eng. Alive '86* 35 Our field-gun, an over-sized catty, is cached away in the 'fort'. **1991** A.C. EIDELMAN *Informant, Johannesburg* Katty. A sling, home-made from the y-shaped branch of a tree — with 2 pieces of rubber and a centre-piece of leather or what have you. **1992** C.M. KNOX tr. *E. Van Heerden's Mad Dog* 138 'Have a go with my cattie, Josh,' Knackers offered. 'I cut a new piece of car-tube for it on Saturday.' We chatted all the way to school, .. taking pot-shots at the dogs with the cattie.

CCB *n. hist.* Initial letters of *Civil Co-operation Bureau*, a secret unit of the South African Defence Force, for a time carrying out covert operations against selected opposition targets. Also *attrib.*

1990 *Weekend Post* 10 Feb. 1 Allegations have been made in the court case about a secret organisation connected to the Defence force. The spokesman said the CCB was a covert organisation of special forces in the Defence Force. **1990** *Sunday Times* 11 Feb. 6 The CCB .. was composed of former policemen and Defence Force members who carried out surveillance of 'aggressive activists'. **1990** *Armed Forces* Nov. 27, CCB agents might have operated in certain instances without the knowledge of their superiors. **1991** *Sunday Times* 10 Mar. 22 At the heart of the CCB affair lies a question of murder: did rogue elements of the SADF — or a rogue force created, funded and protected by the SADF — carry out the assassination of .. David Webster? **1991** J. PAUW *In Heart of Whore* 136 The Star revealed that the CCB was a section of the SADF's Special Forces, was commanded by a general, had at least 16 cells across the country and used prominent companies as fronts for its activities. *Ibid.* 147 The CCB became a sinister monster, the creation of securocrats obsessed with retaining power and blinded by the delusion of a communist plot to expel the white man from South Africa. **1992** *Natal Mercury* 3 Nov. 4 Certain CCB projects had to be wrapped up before former CCB members could have their pensions paid out.

cedar see CLANWILLIAM CEDAR and SOUTH AFRICAN CEDAR.

Ceded Territory *n. phr. Hist.* Also with small initials. A name given by the British Colonial Office during the 19th century to the region bounded by the Kat River hills and the Tyhumie, Keiskamma, and Fish rivers; NEUTRAL TERRITORY.

1819 *Cape Gaz.* in G.M. Theal *Rec. of Cape Col.* (1902) XII. 344 Strong Military Posts shall be established between the Keiskamma and the Fish River, to prevent the future occupation of the Ceded Territory by any petty Chieftain. **1851** GODLONTON & IRVING *Narr. of Kaffir War 1850–1* 6 Sir Andreas Stockenstrom restored to the Kaffirs that portion of the country which they had lost in the war of 1834, lying between the Great Fish and Keiskamma Rivers, which now took the name of the Ceded Territory. **1853** F.P. FLEMING *Kaffraria* 20 The fourth article [of the treaty of 5th December 1836] provided that this territory .. was to be held by the Kaffirs as a *loan* ... This territory then and thenceforth was styled the 'ceded territory' .. no occupation of the land by Europeans being permitted. **1877** J. NOBLE *S. Afr.* 48 The intervening ceded territory was styled 'neutral ground,' and for some time remained unoccupied. **1963** W.M. MACMILLAN

Bantu, Boer & Briton 130 Pato had .. been for years in peaceable occupation of the lower and less attractive part of the Ceded Territory, in Peddie. **1968** E.A. WALKER *Hist. of Sn Afr.* 186 D'Urban still proposed .. to give out all the Ceded Territory in farms. **1981** J.B. PEIRES *House of Phalo* 131 Originally D'Urban had planned to settle the Mfengu in the Ceded Territory as a human buffer against the Xhosa.

censure *v. trans.* [Calque formed on Afk. *sensureer* to subject to church discipline.] In the Dutch Reformed churches: to place (a member) under discipline for misconduct. Often *passive*.

1937 C.R. PRANCE *Tante Rebella's Saga* 60 Both the brothers with half the jurymen were censured publicly in the kerk for speaking scandal about a Predikant. **1974** *Daily Dispatch* 3 Aug. 1 The church wrote .. telling him that he had been censured and that unless he showed regret for calling the dominee a liar he would remain censured for a period of six months. **1985** *Sunday Times* 3 Feb. 17 Although the church doesn't censure ordinary church members for extra-marital affairs or divorce, it is unacceptable in the case of a dominee ... 'I have been censured and since my resignation, not been allowed to administer a congregation.'

certificate *n. obs.* In full *registration certificate*:
1. PASS sense 1.

1899 W.J.K. LITTLE *Sketches & Studies* II. 127 It was required that he [*sc.* a Khoikhoi] should have .. a 'pass' or certificate when moving from place to place, and should be fined or punished as a vagrant if unable, when required, to produce this pass. **1941** C.W. DE KIEWIET *Hist. of S. Afr.* 45 They were naturally inclined to arrest the Hottentot as a vagabond and compel him to take service or achieve the same result by refusing him the pass or certificate without which he could not move from one district to another.

2. PASS sense 2.

1902 in *Stat. Law of Tvl 1839–1910* (1910) II. 871 Any native found in any street public place or thoroughfare .. between the hours of nine pm. and four am. without a written pass or certificate .. shall be liable to a fine. **c1928** R.R.R. DHLOMO *Afr. Tragedy* 14 He had forgotten his certificate – therefore was not qualified to be out at that hour. *Ibid.* 20 As he undressed he saw his Registration Certificate lying on the dressing table where he had forgotten it. **c1948** H. TRACEY *Lalela Zulu* 55 The police .. may demand on sight that any male native shall produce his registration certificate, usually called the 'pass'.

cess var. SIS *int.*

Ceuta var. SOTHO.

Ceylon rose *n. phr.* [tr. S. Afr. Du. *selonsroos* (see SELONS); see quot. 1731.] Any of several poisonous flowering shrubs of the Apocynaceae, esp. the common oleander, *Nerium oleander*; SELONS.

1731 G. MEDLEY tr. *P. Kolb's Present State of Cape of G.H.* II. 281 There are .. Roses of the Ceylon Kind, being first brought to the *Cape* from *Ceylon*. The Cape-Europeans call 'em *Ceylon Roses*. **1829** C. ROSE *Four Yrs in Sn Afr.* 22 How beautiful .. that high hedge covered with the blossoms of the Ceylon rose! **1842** R. GODLONTON *Sketches of E. Districts* 67 Lemon trees, interspersed with the acacia and Ceylon rose. **1850** J.D. LEWINS *Diary.* 9 Aug., To put in tomorrow oaks, currants, mulberries & the 2 Ceylon Roses. **1858** W. IRONS *Settler's Guide to Cape of G.H. & Natal* 96 Lemon trees, interspersed with acacia, and oleander or the Ceylon rose. **1868** J. CHAPMAN *Trav.* II. 15 The Ceylon rose .. is .. the other poison with which the Damaras tip their arrows in war. **1919** T.R. SIM *Flowering Trees & Shrubs for Use in S. Afr.* 116 N. Oleander, known as The Oleander, and as the Ceylon Rose, has the coronasegments pointed or tripod. **1966** C.A. SMITH *Common Names* 190 Ceylon(s) .. rose, *Nerium odorum*, a plant similar to the *Oleander*. A native of Asia Minor and India and introduced at the Cape during very early days as an ornamental plant. **1988** J. MUNDAY *Poisonous Plants in S. Afr. Gardens & Parks* 23 *Nerium oleander*, .. Ceylon rose, Oleander, Rose bay.

chaar ou var. CHAR OU.

chabba var. GABBA.

chacma /ˈtʃækmə/ *n.* Also with initial capital. Pl. **-s**, or unchanged. [ad. Khoikhoi *chŏachamma, choa kamma, chŏakkamma, t'chackamma*.] In full *chacma baboon*: a southern African species of baboon, *Papio ursinus* of the Cercopithecidae; BAVIAAN sense 1 a; BOBBEJAAN sense 1 a.

[**1731** G. MEDLEY tr. *P. Kolb's Present State of Cape of G.H.* I. 33 *A Collection of Hottentot Words, with their Interpretation. Ibid.* 35 *Chŏakãmma*, A Baboon.] **1835** *Penny Cyclopaedia* III. 229 The Chacma, so called from the Hottentot word T'Chackamma, the aboriginal name of this baboon in South Africa .. when full grown, is equal in size, and much superior in strength, to a common English mastiff. **1855** M. REID *Bush Boys* 447 Totty dispersing the Chacmas. **1866** J. LEYLAND *Adventures* 89 Baboons or Chacma, (Cynocephalus Porcarius,) are very abundant in the mountain districts of the Colony. **1900** W.L. SCLATER *Mammals of S. Afr.* I. 15 The chacma is an inhabitant of the steep and rocky krantzes which abound in all parts of Africa. **1932** S. ZUCKERMAN *Soc. Life Monkeys & Apes* 200 The barks of the Chacma are almost indistinguishable from those of the Hamadryas baboon. **1934** *Outspan* 13 July 22 On the face of the kranz were many clefts and crannies .. accessible only to the Chacma baboons. *a***1936** E.N. MARAIS *Soul of Ape* (1969) 64 The mental processes of the chacmas are generally so human-like that it proved impossible to submit them to a critical examination without accepting as a standard our common human experience. **1951** A. ROBERTS *Mammals* 9 It has even been necessary to organize commandos of farmers armed with firearms and often supported by dogs, to surround and exterminate these Chacma Baboons. **1988** A. HALL-MARTIN et al. *Kaokoveld* 30 The Chacma baboon is the most widespread of the primates and is found scattered throughout the Kaokoveld except for the waterless regions. **1990** *Sunday Times* 18 Nov. (Mag. Sect.) 14 A Chacma Baboon became a railroad signalman near Uitenhage, South Africa, earning twenty cents a day and half a bottle of beer on Saturdays.

chaff /tʃɑːf/ *v. trans. Slang.* Also **charf, tjaaf**. [Special senses of general Eng. *chaff* to banter, tease.]
1. *rare.* To give (someone something).

1963 L.F. FREED *Crime in S. Afr.* 104 'Mossie' .. had been a professional boxer who .. never went into the ring without a shot of dagga ... His friends used to invite him to 'scale a jam' (steal a car) and he would 'chaff them a shot', and be with them.

2.a. To say (something). Cf. TUNE sense 2 d.

1966 J. TAYLOR 'Mommy, I'd Like to Be'. (lyrics) Sussie I chaff I'll win, Win my bet to make you grin, With a blade of grass I'll tickle your chin, Sussie I chaff I'll win. **1990** R. MALAN *My Traitor's Heart* 53 Black dope dealers were suspicious of whites, so you had to .. gooi (give) the double-horned devil's hand sign and charf (say), 'Level with the gravel, ek sê'.

b. To tell (someone something). Cf. TUNE sense 2 b.

1970 J.F. PRINSLOO *Informant*, Lüderitz (Namibia), I have .. heard people say: 'Don't chaff me half', meaning: 'Don't talk nonsense to me.' **1988** S.A. BOTHA in *Frontline* Apr.-May 24 'I tjaaf you, the peckies are getting white these days,' said Don. **1991** B. CARLYON *Informant, Johannesburg* Chaff. Tell. I chaffed him that we had to go to the dentist, so he said we could go early.

3. To 'chat (someone) up', make a pass at (someone), flirt with (someone); TUNE sense 2 e. Also in the phr. **chaff up**.

1970 J.F. PRINSLOO *Informant*, Lüderitz (Namibia) 'Man, I smaak that goosie, I think I'll chaff her'. (This word in S.A ... seems to have taken the meaning of 'making a pass at a girl') **1970** K.M. BRAND *Informant, East London* He's been chaffing the babe for months now with no success! (trying to get off with a girl) **1977** [see CASED.] **1984** *Sunday Times* 29 Jan. 13 On the way the passenger tried to 'chaff' her when Mr Grundlingh stopped the car to make a telephone call to his mother. **1984** [see GOOSIE sense 2]. **1985** P. SLABOLEPSZY *Sat. Night at Palace* 27 Vince: .. Should have swallowed my pride and gone home with that chick. Forsie: So, why didn't you? Vince: Fear of rape. Didn't want to risk it. Forsie: Please! You just couldn't chaff her, that's all. **1986** L. SAMPSON in *Style* May 100, I remember you, your name is Clive and you used to chaff my sister. **1988** S. SOLE in *Ibid.* Apr. 49 Anyway, these two ous didn't go to work, got drunk, and then they wanted to charf her, so she swore them blind. **1991** H.C. WATTS *Informant, Cape Town* That's a lekker looking girl — I'll go and charf her and make a date. **1991** B. CARLYON *Informant, Johannesburg* Hey! Look at that stukkie. I'm going to sommer chaff her up.

4. To ask (someone something).

1988 *Sunday Times* 25 June 19 When the Adj went to chaff the 2 IB about next week's rock festival he got a storing.

chaile var. TJAILE *n.*

chains *pl. n. Hist.* Freq. with initial capital. [Named for the chains at each end of Simmonds Street which formerly closed the area to traffic.]
1. In the phr. *between the chains*.
a. As adv. phr.: In the chained-off portion of Simmonds Street, Johannesburg (alluding to stock dealing).

1888 in *Story of Jhb. Stock Exchange* (Comm. of Jhb. Stock Exchange) (1948) 20 One of the sights in the afternoon is that to be witnessed 'between the chains' ... It is between the chains, too, that the larger part of landed property for sale in the town is put up for auction. **1940** F.B. YOUNG *City of Gold* 417 When the stock-exchange was closed, excited brokers gathered 'between the chains' still buying and selling. *Ibid.* 58 Dealing 'between the chains' and street dealing elsewhere was finally prohibited in May, 1902. **1967** E. ROSENTHAL *Encycl. of Sn Afr.* 56 'Between the Chains' came to an end about the time of the Boer War, and was never revived, because of the new Stock Exchange built in 1903. **1983** J.A. BROWN *White Locusts* 70 The crowd between the chains was shouting the odds of shares when he drove up and dismounted.

b. As n. phr.: The Johannesburg Stock Exchange (see JSE). Also *attrib.*

Used as a name for the Johannesburg Stock Exchange from 1887 to 1902. See note at JSE.

1958 A. JACKSON *Trader on Veld* 50 The old 'Corner House', a three-storey building with a wooden verandah opposite the famous 'Between the Chains' Exchange. **1972** *Sunday Times* 23 Apr. 4 Another attraction was the Stock Exchange, known as 'Between the Chains' — the stretch of Simmonds Street between Market Street and Commissioner Street, which was cordoned off at both ends by chains and thus closed to vehicular traffic. **1990** C. LAFFEATY *Far Forbidden Plains* 28 Because of the special chained-off portion in the street the Exchange is often spoken of as 'Between the Chains'.

2. *The chains*: That portion of Simmonds Street where the Johannesburg Stock Exchange was at one time situated. Also *attrib.*

1900 H.C. HILLEGAS *Oom Paul's People* 296 The popular gathering place in the city is the street in front of one of the stock exchanges known as 'The Chains.' **1913** C. PETTMAN *Africanderisms* 119 Chains, The, That portion of Simmonds Street, Johannesburg, which is closed to vehicular traffic, and reserved for the operations of stock and mining speculations.

chakka var. CHOKKA.

chali var. TSHWALA.

chalifah var. KHALIFA.

chalkdown *n.* Also **chalks down**. [By analogy with general Eng. *down tools* to strike.] A teachers' strike. Also *attrib.*

1990 *Weekly Mail* 8 June 5 In Lethlabile, the suspension of 13 teachers .. had sparked a three-week-old 'chalks down' strike. **1991** A. JEFFERY in *Spotlight* (S.A.I.R.R.) Mar. 3 School boycotts and chalk-downs (strikes by teachers). **1993** *Weekend Post* 22 May 1 There had been threats that as many as 80 000 teachers would hold a 'chalk-down' strike. **1993** *Weekend Argus* 14 Aug. 3 The .. South African Democratic Teachers' Union .. has opted for a chalkdown over demands for a 20 percent pay increase. **1994** *Sunday Times* 18 Sept. 22 Vocal minorities in both the teaching and pupil corps are ever ready to instigate demonstrations, protests, boycotts and chalk-downs for short-term gains.

Hence **chalkdown** *v. intrans.*, to participate in a teachers' strike.

[**1993** *Cape Times* 10 Aug. 5 (*caption*) Teachers to down chalk.] **1993** *Weekend Argus* 14 Aug. 3 More than 70 000 Sadtu members are due to chalkdown from Monday.

chaloa var. TSHWALA.

Chamber of Mines *n. phr.* A central co-operative organization of gold-, coal-, and uranium-producing companies, acting on behalf of its members in matters of common concern. Also *attrib.*

1893 *Poster, Witwatersrand Mine Employees & Mechanics Union* Feb., A mass meeting .. will be held .. to protest against the Gold Thefts Bill proposed by the Chamber of Mines. The chair will not be taken by Lionel Phillips .. (Chairman of the Chamber of Mines). **1898** G. ALBU in T. Froes *Kruger & Co.* (1900) 5 The thieving of amalgam and gold has been brought to a veritable science. We cannot rely upon the Detective Department alone, but must ourselves, through 'the Chamber of Mines,' the representative body of the Industry, devise some plan by which the evil can be lessened. **1900** H.C. HILLEGAS *Oom Paul's People* 72 The Second Volksraad was created, .. and many reforms, which at the time were warmly approved by the Johannesburg Chamber of Mines, representing the mining population, were instituted. **1916** *Rand Daily Mail* 1 Nov. 3 The Rest Room for Soldiers .. is situated .. in the block of buildings owned by the Chamber of Mines. **1936** *Cambridge Hist. of Brit. Empire* VIII. 783 By 1889, when the first Chamber of Mines was established, confidence had been severely damaged. **1968** COLE & FLAHERTY *House of Bondage* 22 We were picked up by a Chamber of Mines official and driven to the WNLA depot. **1987** *Learn & Teach* No.5, 8 The strike was a big achievement. 'We took on the Chamber of Mines — the organisation behind the pass laws, the migrant labour system and the hostels'. **1991** *S. Afr. Panorama* Jan.-Feb. 32 The Chamber of Mines, members of which are the six mining giants, Anglo American, Rand Mines, Gold Fields, Johannesburg Consolidated Investments, Genmin and Anglo-vaal, accounts for most of the gold, uranium, coal, platinum and diamonds produced.

Chamber of Seventeen see SEVENTEEN.

chamboc(k) var. SJAMBOK *n.*

chamois *n. obsolescent.* [Transf. use of general Eng. *chamois* the European antelope *Rupicapra tragus*.] The KLIPSPRINGER, *Oreotragus oreotragus*.

1885 *Macmillan's Mag.* (U.K.) Feb. 280 The klipspringer, the little chamois that is so clever at eluding dogs and men. **1890** A. MARTIN *Home Life* 223 Rarest among the antelopes is the klipspringer, which is called the chamois of South Africa, and which, both in appearance and habits, closely resembles the Alpine animal. **1898** G. NICHOLSON *50 Yrs* 35 Higher up among the precipitous rocks near the summits the African Chamois (klipspringer) is always to be found. **c1936** *S. & E. Afr. Yr Bk & Guide* 1086 The *Klipspringer*, .. sometimes spoken of as the 'chamois of South Africa.' **1936** R. CAMPBELL *Mithraic Emblems* 68, I always thought to be A klipspringer or chamois. **1966** J. FARRANT *Mashonaland Martyr* 120 Were they attracted by the klipspringers? Were they curious about the man who could tame these fleet and nimble little antelopes, the 'rock chamois' of southern Africa?

Chamtouers var. GAMTOUERS.

chandelier *n. obsolescent.* Also **chandalier**, and with initial capital. [Special senses of Eng.; named for the shape of the plant or its inflorescence.] Usu. *attrib.*, in the following senses (in all senses occas. called ***chandelier plant***):

1. ***chandelier lily*** (also simply *chandelier*): the plant *Brunsvigia orientalis* of the Amaryllidaceae; also called CANDELABRA (sense 1).

1818 C.I. LATROBE *Jrnl of Visit* 165 We noticed here a gigantic species of a plant, from its singular form .. called the chandelier. **1835** A. STEEDMAN *Wanderings* I. 328 The surface of this part of the country was thickly covered with a variety of elegant bulbous plants, particularly a species called by the natives the chandelier. It has a vast number of shoots proceeding from one high stem in the centre, and branching out with beautiful scarlet flowers at each extremity. **1839** W.C. HARRIS *Wild Sports* 304 The chandelier plant, and purple amaryllis, with many other splendid bulbs, grow wild in profusion. **1856** R.E.E. WILMOT *Diary* (1984) 78 For miles along the open Veld, huge heads of rich roseate chandelier lily reared themselves in beauty. **1871** *Cape Monthly Mag.* III. Aug. 122 A grand family of plants — the *Amaryllidaceæ* — of which our 'Chandelier lily,' (*Brunsvigia Josephinæ*) is an example. **1966** C.A. SMITH *Common Names* 191 *Chandelier lily, Brunsvigia orientalis* ... The vernacular name was recorded as far back as 1818 and refers to the candelabra-like nature of the massive inflorescence.

2. ***chandelier aloe***: CANDELABRA sense 3.

1827 T. PHILIPPS *Scenes & Occurrences* 4 We .. crossed a tract of land covered with aloes, called likewise the chandelier plant. *Ibid.* 49 On the craggy hills the chandelier aloe expands its radiant branches.

3. ***chandelier euphorbia, -tree***: a tree of the species *Euphorbia ingens, E. triangularis*, or *E. grandidens* (family Euphorbiaceae). Also *attrib.* See also CANDELABRA sense 2, NABOOM.

1844 J. BACKHOUSE *Narr. of Visit* 151 The Chandalier Euphorbia, *Euphorbia grandidens*, a singular tree, with erect, angular, leafless branches .. forms a remarkable feature in the woods of the eastern part of the Cape Colony, and adjacent portions of Caffraria. **1966** C.A. SMITH *Common Names* 191 *Chandelier plant (-tree), Euphorbia triangularis* and *E. grandidens* ... The vernacular name for these two species .. refers to the candelabra-like disposition of the branches.

Changana var. SHANGAAN.

channa *n.*[1] var. GANNA.

channa *n.*[2] var. KANNA *n.*[2]

chara var. CHARRA.

charf var. CHAFF.

Chariguriqua /ˌtʃarɪgʊˈrɪkwa/ *pl. n. Obs.* exc. *hist.* Also **Chariguriquas, Cherigriquois, Chirigriquas**. [See GRIQUA.] GRIGRIQUA.

1731 G. MEDLEY tr. *P. Kolb's Present State of Cape of G.H.* I. 65 The Nation of the *Chirigriquas* is next, running along by the Bay of *St. Hellens*. They are a numerous People, .. and have the Vogue, above all the other *Hottentot* Nations, for Strength and Dexterity in Throwing the *Hassagaye*. **1795** C.R. HOPSON tr. *C.P. Thunberg's Trav.* I. 307 The next neighbours .. are the *Chirigriquas*, a more populous and wealthy nation. **1838** D. MOODIE *Record* I. 247 *Little Chariguriquas*, a people about as numerous as the Goringhaiquas, .. subject to Oedasoa, though they have rebelled against him; they were accustomed to be his stock keepers, but appropriated his cattle to their own use. *Ibid.* 248 *Namaquas*, with whom the great Chariguriquas have sought and formed an alliance. **1846** J.C. BROWN tr. *T. Arbousset's Narr. of Explor. Tour to N.-E. of Col.* 21 The word *Griqua* appears to be an abbreviation of Cherigriquois, the name of a tribe living to the south of the Little Namaquas. **1905** G.W. STOW *Native Races of S. Afr.* 316 Among the old Hottentot tribes .. was a clan .. variously called Chariguriqua and Grigriqua ... From this tribe the modern Griquas derived their name. **1928** [see GRIQUA sense 1]. **1976** R. ROSS *Adam Kok's Griquas* 12 The term [Griqua] referred to a Khoikhoin tribe, the Chariguriqua, which had lived about a hundred miles north of Cape Town.

char ou /ˈtʃɑːrəʊ/ *n.* Also **chaar ou, char(r)o**. [Etym. dubious: prob. a blend of ATJAR and OU, see Green quot. 1983; cf. CHARRA.] In the South African Indian community: a person of Indian descent; INDIAN *n.* sense 2 a. Occas. used derogatorily: CHARRA. See also OU *n.* sense 2 b, *roti ou* (ROTI sense 2).

1978 [see ROTI sense 2]. **1978** A. AKHALWAYA in *Rand Daily Mail* 10 July 7 Our main ou, who is also a 'chaar ou' (Indian), has friends of all races. **1980** R. GOVENDER *Lahnee's Pleasure* 38 Char ous were working there for years — longer than some of the wit ous, but they weren't earning more than even the lightie wit ous. **1982** *Daily News* 15 June 1 At the end of the meeting .. Mr — clashed once again with the mayor after he had referred to Indian people as 'charos'. **c1983** R. MESTHRIE Lexicon of South African Indian English. 75 *Char-ou*, .. An Indian. Not usually derogatory, except perhaps when used by some Whites. Often jocular in SAI[ndian]E[nglish]. **1983** M. GREEN *Informant, Durban* A member of the Indian community has given me an interesting explanation of 'charra'. He says the word originated from the fact that spiced pickles became very popular with South African whites. These were sold mainly by Indian storekeepers and the word (which is Hindi) for them was 'achaar'. White parents would send their children to the 'chaar ou' ('ou' being Afrikaans for person) to buy spiced pickles and the term chaar ou, shortened to charra, eventually came to be applied to all Indians and later took on its present derogatory implication. **1986** L.A. BARNES in *Eng. Usage in Sn Afr.* Vol.17 No.2, 4 Different ethnic groups are referred to by terms such as *char ou's*, 'Indians', *gora*, 'White man', and *roti ou* 'Hindi speaking person'. **1993** W. JUNGE *Informant, Pietermaritzburg* She said to me, 'Could you identify this man?' and I said, 'Yes, he was a charro, a coolie.'

charra /ˈtʃara/ *n. Derog.* and *offensive*. Also **chara, churra, tjarra**. [Prob. ad. CHAR OU.] An insulting name for a person of Indian descent. Also *attrib.* Cf. CHAR OU.

1970 B. KIRK-COHEN *Informant, Bloemfontein* Charra. Indian. **1971** J. MCCLURE *Steam Pig* (1973) 201 Ach, it was real churra talk — maybe it was a tip-off. I don't think so. **1973** *Sunday Tribune* 1 Apr. 20 We have told them that all men are created in the image of God, but have called them 'kaffirs', 'black savages' and 'charas'. **1974** J. MCCLURE *Gooseberry Fool* (1976) 87 All the shops had shut so he would have to go down to the Indian quarter for the present. 'Trust the bloody *churras* to be Mohommedan,' Scott grunted. 'Do anything to keep their shops open.' **1975** L. HOGG *Informant, Pietermaritzburg* Tjarra. Common Natal expression for the Indian population. (Also chilli cracker and curry-muncher). **1983** [see Green quot. at CHAR OU]. **1984** 'DAN' in *Frontline* Feb. 26 Maybe with a name like that B. Nanabhai isn't so much a bushy anyhow, more like a chara ... Maybe they sent him to Durbs, .. where he had to live among other charas ... Charas are tailors, unless they're waiters. **1989** D. MULLANY in *Scope* 21 Apr. 4 The crafty 'charra' in his fur-dash, rust-crusted Cortina; the hunkheaded Transvaal 'kaydaar' in his Datsun Laurel, Toyota Cressida, or gold-wheeled Sierra. **1990** J. NAIDOO *Coolie Location* 47 She didn't want to touch my hand when paying for the fruit or vegetables she had just bought; and more than once I was carelessly called *'Sam'* or *coolie* or *Charra*.

charro var. CHAR OU.

Charter *n.* Also with small initial. ***The Charter***: Ellipt. for *The Freedom Charter*, see FREEDOM CHARTER sense 1.

1963 M. BENSON *Afr. Patriots* 214 Throughout that day .. delegates listened intently to a Freedom Charter read in English, Sesotho and Xhosa ... Luthuli had sent a message: he saw the Charter as 'a torchlight in whatever dark skies may overcast the path to freedom.' **1981** A. AKHALWAYA in *Rand Daily Mail* 16 June 5 The charter .. is regarded by many as one of the most significant documents in South African black political history. **1985** *Weekly Mail* 23 June 13 The Charter .. was the central document in the famous 1956 Treason trial ... The State regarded the Charter as a treasonous document. **1986** P. MAYLAM *Hist. of Afr. People* 188 To some liberals the Charter looked like a socialist programme; for some Marxists the Charter represented ideals of bourgeois democracy; and for Africanists the Charter made dangerous concessions to multi-racialism. **1990** *E. Prov. Herald* 9 Feb. 5 The mood of the charter should be encapsulated in the slogan 'The people shall govern'.

Hence **Charterism** *n.*, adherence to the principles of the Freedom Charter.

1990 R. MALAN *My Traitor's Heart* 133 Black Consciousness organizations did not accept white members. All that remained for a white man's salvation was the broad faith of Charterism.

Charterist *n.* and *adj.* [CHARTER + Eng. suffix *-ist* designating a follower or adherent of (a philosophy).]

A. *n.* One who supports the principles of the FREEDOM CHARTER (sense 1); esp., a member of the African National Congress. See also UDF *n.*[2]

1958 A. SAMPSON *Treason Cage* 112 The Charterists – as the Congress leaders were now called – eventually won the day, and the Freedom Charter was officially adopted by Congress at Easter, 1956. **1986** *Sunday Star* 8 June (Review) 18 The Charterists believe the struggle is a popular movement for all races. **1989** *Sunday Tribune* 17 Dec. 6 Between the Africanists and the Charterists (those who adhere to the ANC's Freedom Charter) lies a wide chasm. **1990** *Sunday Times* 28 Oct. 26 The foment inside the ANC did not stop there. The main issue was the differences between liberals (called Charterists after the Freedom Charter was adopted in 1955) and Africanists. **1991** G. MOKAE in *Frontline* May 17 One could go on and on .. annotating incidents where 'liberal' universities .. are guilty of complicity in stalinistic censorship against non-Charterists.

B. *adj.* Of or pertaining to supporters of the FREEDOM CHARTER (sense 1).

1986 *Sunday Star* 8 June (Review) 18 The ANC in exile was galvanised into action because it had largely been on the sidelines in 1976 and 1977. It then supported the rise of new Charterist popular fronts in the country. **1987** 'A. AMAPHIXIPHIXI' in *Frontline* Oct. 21 It is an accepted fact that funding .. goes only to those with charterist leanings. **1989** C. PERKINS in *Sunday Times* 20 Aug. 2 It is the first time that different ideological camps – black consciousness and those following the 'charterist' tradition – have set aside their hostilities. **1990** T. SEBUSI in *Frontline* Dec. 22 These basics cut across ideological boundaries, engendering .. a 'sophisticated' analysis from the Charterist aligned youths.

Chateau Cardboard *n. phr.* [Pseudo-Fr. formation, a play on names typically given to wines.] A nickname given to wines sold in 2-litre or 5-litre bag-in-a-box packages. Also *attrib.* See also HAPPY BOX.

1988 D. HUGHES et al. *Complete Bk of S. Afr. Wine* 81 'Chateau Cardboard' swept the country in the early eighties, with sales of almost nine million boxes annually .. , about 30 per cent of all wine made in South Africa. **1993** A. WHITLOCK in *Weekend Post* 10 Apr. 3 Basil Rothner could not figure out why his favourite wine, packed in the convenient 5 litre box, was vanishing so quickly ... Last weekend .. Mr Rothner solved the problem which has baffled many Port Elizabeth chateau cardboard lovers. **1994** 'T. COBBLEIGH' in *Sunday Times* 24 July 17, I can drink Chateau Cardboard and orange juice and listen to operamaniacs arguing in the foyer.

chattes var. GATTES.

chawb var. CHORB.

‖**checha** /ˈtʃetʃa/ *int.* Also **chêchê, chercher.** [ad. Fanakalo *tshetsha*, fr. Zulu *shesha* hurry, move quickly.] Hurry; be quick.

1908 D. BLACKBURN *Leaven* 13 Pick that up. Chercher! Be quick, that means in your infernal lingo. **1911** P. GIBBON *Margaret Harding* 118 'Voetzaak,' she ordered shrilly. 'Hamba wena – ch'che! Skellum! Injah! Voetzaak.' *c*1957 D. SWANSON *Highveld, Lowveld & Jungle* 46 The Major shouted to a Native servant passing on the verandah: 'Boy! Bring coffee for four. Checha!' 'Ja, Baas.' The boy hurried off. **1970** S.E. NATHAM *Informant, Cape Town* Chêchê. Quickly. **1974** J. MCCLURE *Gooseberry Fool* (1976) 162 'Your superior will come for you.' 'He said this?' 'To myself, personally.' 'Then ring him – *checha!*' Mtembu hurried all right. **1975** —— *Snake* (1981) 162 Go quickly and ask him to give the button to you – go on. And bring it here, *checha.*'

check *v. slang.* [U.S. slang.]

1.a. *intrans.* In the imperative phr. ***check at (someone or something)***: look at (someone or something).

1970 J. GREENWOOD *Informant, Johannesburg* Check at that new car. **1985** P. SLABOLEPSZY *Sat. Night at Palace* 36, I mean check at the shape .. I mean, this isn't just sommer a chip any more – it's a bladdy twentieth-century work of art! I mean check at it!

b. *trans.* In the phr. ***to check (someone or something) skeef*** [see SKEEF *adv.*], to give (someone or something) a dirty look, to look askance at (someone or something).

1977 C. HOPE in S. Gray *Theatre Two* (1981) 56 Should have seen the way she was checking me skeef when I asked her for more beer. **1989** D. BRISTOW in *Weekly Mail* 21 Apr. 29 The men in Port Nolloth drink a lot. There are not many women here, and those that there are – make sure you don't check them too *skeef.* **1993** A. GOLDSTUCK in *Rhodent* (Rhodes Univ.) 28 Pastimes include .. donnering the bliksem out of anyone who checks him skeef.

c. *trans.* To look at (someone or something); to watch (someone or something).

1980 E. PATEL *They Came at Dawn* 48 Sommer Haanetjie is checking the scene like the especial branch do.

2.a. *trans.* and *intrans.* To see (someone or something).

1980 R. GOVENDER *Lahnee's Pleasure* 16 While I'm filling away I checked these two ous behind nother one tree. **1987** [see SUN CITY]. **1991** D. GALGUT in *Cosmopolitan* Aug. 163 'Y'check?' he inquired, gesturing toward me with his hand ... 'Y'check what a baby you are?'

b. *trans.* In the interjectional phr. ***check you***, 'see you', goodbye.

1987 L. BEAKE *Strollers* 6 'I'm *really* going.' Nothing. 'Well, check you man!' Nonchalantly Abel left. **1989** J. HOBBS *Thoughts in Makeshift Mortuary* 177 For a moment she thought .. that he would leave in a huff and not speak to her again. But he said 'Check you, OK?' and went out.

checkers *n.* Also **checkas**. Pl. unchanged. [fr. *Checkers*, the proprietory name of a national supermarket chain.] In urban (esp. township) English: any plastic supermarket packet with handles.

1982 A. JACOT-GUILLARMOD *Informant, Grahamstown* A checkers. A plastic bag, preferably with handles. Such a bag may have OK writ large, but is still a 'checkers' ... Word commonly used by non-whites throughout South Africa. **1987** *Informant, Grahamstown* Please, sisi, have you got a checkers for my peaches? **1988** *Weekend Argus* 19 Mar., Next to him was a vase of colourful flowers mostly made from 'checkas' – yellow plastic shopping bags. **1990** *Informant, Grahamstown* Ma'am can I have a nice checkers please?

cheeky *adj. offensive.* [Special sense of general Eng. *cheeky* impertinent (this sense also being used in S. Afr. Eng.).] Uppity; acting above one's station; PARMANTIG sense a.

The term has racist overtones, being used by whites of or to blacks who are thought not to 'know their place': cf. WHITE *adj.* sense 1 b.

1863 LADY DUFF-GORDON in F. Galton *Vacation Tourists* (1864) III. 178 'You see it makes the d . . . .d niggers cheeky' to have homes of their own – and the girls are said to be immoral. **1924** G. BAUMANN in Baumann & Bright *Lost Republic* (1940) 138 'Don't you remember me, Baas? I neglected my duty' (or 'I was cheeky to my Baas', or something or other) 'and you gave me a flogging'. **1949** L. HUNTER *Afr. Dawn* 111 There was the one *Nkosikazi* who could not speak Xhosa. She had been very angry, however, when he had spoken to her in English. Telling him he was 'cheeky' she had sent him off. **1956** T. HUDDLESTONE *Naught for your Comfort* 80 Their venom is directed at the 'educated kaffir', the 'cheeky nigger', the 'smart skellum'. **1960** Z.K. MATTHEWS in H. Spottiswoode *S. Afr.: Rd Ahead* 173 [African education was], according to other white people, deserving the highest condemnation because it taught Africans some 'book-learning' and made them 'cheeky'. **1963** B. MODISANE *Blame Me on Hist.* (1986) 94 There is a resentment against the educated African, not so much because he is allegedly cheeky, but that he fails to conform to the stereotype image of the black man. **1978** A.P. BRINK *Rumours of Rain* 247 We always got along very well with the Kaffirs. I mean, they were noisy and all that, but they knew their place. Nowadays they're so cheeky, one doesn't know what to do any more. **1985** P. SLABOLEPSZY *Sat. Night at Palace* 50 All you see is black faces. Bus drivers, bank tellers, bloody three-piece suits, man! And cheeky! **1990** R. MALAN *My Traitor's Heart* 32 Mathibes was said to be 'cheeky', but he was very clever with his hands, knew welding and soldering .. , so he was put up with – respected even.

Hence **cheekiness** *n.*

1976 *Weekend World* 26 Sept. 33 B– worked as a clerk for the Department of Native Affairs for two years – and had his ups and downs for 'cheekiness'. **1980** J. COCK *Maids & Madams* 97 Several colonial twentieth century societies made provision for the physical chastisement of domestic servants for 'cheekiness' and other wrongdoing.

cheesa /ˈtʃiːzə/ *vbl n. Mining.* Also **chessa, chisa, tshisa.** [ad. Fanakalo *tshisa*, fr. Zulu *shisa* make hot, burn, set alight.] Heating, burning, blasting; used *attrib.* and in *comb.*, esp. in mining terms adapted from Fanakalo, as ***cheesa-boy***, a man who ignites the fuses during blasting operations, and ***cheesa-stick***, a hand-held fuse-igniter.

1915 A. MARSHALL *Explosives* 441 In South Africa 'Cheesa sticks' are used, which consist of sticks of cordite with ammonium oxalate and shellac. **1956** K. COURLANDER *I Speak of Afr.* 164 The rock-breaker would fill these apertures with explosives and the 'cheesa boy' .. would come along with a slow-burning fuse. **1957** *As a Matter of Fact* (P.R.D. Series, No.56) 15 *Cheesa-stick*, a slow-burning fuse igniter consisting of a hard cardboard tube filled with an inflammable mixture. [**1958** A. SAMPSON *Treason Cage* 35 Letters connected with the African National Congress had been written from a so-called *'Cheesa-Cheesa Army'*, calling on people to burn down Afrikaner houses and churches.] **1960** *Star* 9 Nov., Muthuso, a Bechuana 'cheesa boy', or fuse lighter, was lighting fuses under the direction of the European ganger. **1970** B.C. MARITZ *Informant, Port Elizabeth* Pass me the cheesa pipe to cut this metal (cutting torch). **1971** P.J. SILVA *Informant, Coalbrook (OFS)* Cheesa stick. A stick more or less 2'6" long used to light the fuse to the dynamite in a coal mine. **1983** *Mining Dict.* (Terminology Bureau) 44 *Cheesa stick.* **1988** J. MATLOU in *Staffrider* Vol.7 No.3, 52 Before the blasting, small holes were drilled in the walls and a man referred to as *chessaboy* put explosives into them. **1988** M.A. WILSON *Informant, Johannesburg* Chesa-stick (pron. cheeza). The usage is common in the mining industry and is: 'The hand-held, and long-burning stick used to light fuses.' **1989** B. COURTENAY *Power of One* 481 Back at the grizzly level you connect the cordtex to a fuse, signal the African to blow the warning hooter, light the fuse with a cheesa stick, a flare the size of a thick pencil which, once lit, cannot be extinguished. *Ibid.* 488 In my dream I held the lighted cheesa stick to the fuse,

cheese-kop /ˈtʃiːzkɔp/ *adj.* and *n. Slang.* [Part. tr. Afk. *kaaskop* closely shaven head, *kaas* cheese + *kop* head.]
A. *adj.* With closely-cropped hair, or a shaven head.
  1970 *Drum* Apr. 11 He had only a little topping of hair on his head, but they told me to go and get him cheesekop (close-crop). They always wanted to see him cheesekop. **1982** *Voice* 31 Jan. 13, I didn't see the one who throttled me, Ntate, only the cheesekop one who asked for matches!
B. *n.* Closely-cropped hair, or a shaven head.
  1985 J. Khumalo in *Pace* Sept. 19 The Pantsula of old, complete with cheese-kop, muscles and flick-knife, is fast becoming extinct ... If you turn out for an interview sporting a cheese-kop and in baggy pants .. the prospective employer will take one look at your cheese-kop and suddenly he will have visions of an ex-convict.

Cheetah *n. Military.* [Special sense of general Eng. *cheetah* hunting leopard.] A supersonic fighter aircraft, re-designed in South Africa from the French Mirage III-R2Z fighter bomber. Also *attrib.*
  1986 *Financial Mail* 25 July 6 The SAAF takes the wraps off a fighter aircraft called the Cheetah, re-developed from the French Mirage III. **1987** *S. Afr. Digest* 10 July 9 The Cheetah fighter aircraft is equipped with the latest navigational aids and weapons systems. **1988** *Cape Times* 17 Nov., The Cheetah, locally rebuilt and updated Mirage IIIs which now form the South African Air Force's most potent ground attack capability. **1989** S. Johnson in *Weekly Mail* 3 Mar. 13 Many hold that the superiority of Angola's MiGs over South African Cheetahs (refurbished Mirages) was the spur to the recently achieved peace accord in that region.

cheld var. GELD.

cheque-book *n. colloq.* Used *attrib.* or as *quasi-adj.*, esp. in the phr. ***cheque-book farmer***, one with capital at his disposal and therefore removed from active participation in farming, or freed from dependence on farming income. Cf. *stoep-farmer* (see STOEP sense 2).
  1926 M. Nathan *S. Afr. from Within* 289 Many born South Africans, even those with plenty of capital at their command (known colloquially as 'cheque-book farmers') have not succeeded. **1937** C. Birkby *Zulu Journey* 130 He came to South Africa as a cheque-book settler, farmed through half a dozen plagues and then realised with the setting of one droughty sun that he was penniless. **1976** S. Cloete *Chetoko* 173 He looked at Frank Metz's shiny new car disappearing down the farm road and wished he was a cheque-book farmer too.

chercher var. CHECHA.

Cherigriquois var. CHARIGURIQUA.

cherry *n. slang.* Also **cher(r)ie**, **tcherrie**, **tjerrie**. [fr. Isicamtho *amacherry* (prob. ad. U.S. slang *cherry* virgin, see quot. 1978); see also AMA-.] A girl or woman; a girlfriend.
  1962 J. Taylor 'Hennie van Saracen'. (*lyrics*) The hardest thing of all was saying goodbye to my chick, 'Cause she's a lekker cherry And I digs her kind of kick. **1965** K.M.C. Motsisi in *Post* 11 Dec. (*Drum*) 11, I had to invite that most fascinating cherie in this man's town, Sis Sharon with goo-goo eyes. **1975** 'Blossom' in *Darling* 29 Jan. 103 Howzit, cherries and okes. **1975** S. Roberts *Outside Life's Feast* 85 When I was with the vice-squad we had a lekker time some nights you catch these young ous with their cherries in the back seats and you frighten the hell out of them. [**1978** B. Maclennan in *E. Prov. Herald* 1 May 3 The word 'imoli' for girl, after the American gangster moll. This word with 'amacherry' was popular in the 50s but both had given way to 'ichick' and 'ipunki' which meant .. 'a delectable young girl'.] **1982** [see MSHOZA]. [**1986**

see OU *n.* sense 4.] **1987** H. Hamann in *Frontline* Apr. 20 In the old days we used to take the cherries to a session. **1990** J. Naidoo *Coolie Location* 153 This guy he meets this cherrie. And she's really lekker and all that .. she's really a civilized chick.

Cherupiga var. JEREPIGO.

chesanyama /ˈtʃiːzɑˌnjamɑ/ *n.* Also **chisa nyama**, **tshisa-nyama**. [Fanakalo, lit. 'hot meat', fr. Zulu *shisa* to be hot, to make hot + *inyama* meat.] In urban (mainly township) English: an eating house at which cheap meals are sold. Also *attrib.*
  1975 K.M.C. Motsisi in *Drum* 8 Mar. 56, I don't mind seeing as I take a curtain-raiser at the Tshong's chesa nyama's shop on my way to this place of Aunt Peggy. **1980** M. Matshoba in M. Mutloatse *Forced Landing* 124 Fridays they did not dine together. Everyone ate an almost substantial meal in one of the city '*chesanyamas*' and returned to the hostel replete. **1981** *Pace* Sept. 81 We went to the pass office and several 'Chisa nyama' restaurants to put our play together. **1982** D. Mqhaba in Chapman & Dangor *Voices from Within* 174 The plates must be of aluminium, The spoons, big, round and rusty ... Let a Bantu man call it Tshisanyama ... It is a restaurant solely for Bantus. **1986** *Learn & Teach* No.2, 31, I have no-one to cook for me, so I come to the chisanyama to buy myself food ... The other reason is that I meet most of my friends right here .. the only place we meet is here at chisanyama. **1993** B. Khumalo in *Weekly Mail* 10 Dec. 45 A *tshisanyama* is a feature of South African society that is found in industrial areas. These are .. owned mostly by immigrants ... The clientele in these establishments is mostly black. These shops tend to be filthy and customers have to shout at the top of their lungs when they buy.

chessa var. CHEESA.

Chevril /ˈʃɛvrɪl/ *n. hist.* Also **Cheveril**, and with small initial. [Blend formed on Fr. *cheval* horse and Eng. trade name *Bovril*.] An extract of horsemeat made during the siege of Ladysmith in 1900.
  1900 H.H.S. Pearse *Four Months Besieged* 217 Colonel Ward has set up a factory .. for the conversion of horseflesh into extract of meat under the inviting name of Chevril. This is intended for use in hospitals ... It is also ordered that a pint of soup made from this Chevril shall be issued daily to each man. **1900** R.G. Archibald in R.E. Gordon *Honour Without Riches* (1978) 275 The Authorities are now issuing a concoction of flesh boiled down into a kind of 'Bovril' — it is called 'Cheveril', but the stuff does not take on at all and the smell of it in a few hours time is just awfully too-too — it's unfit for food. **1900** G.C. Musgrave *In S. Afr. with Buller* 334 After many experiments pure essence of horse was concocted, the locomotive house being improvised as a factory. The animals were shot at one end, emerging from the front door in jars and bottles labelled *chevril*. This horse-extract, trade-marked 'Resurgam' .. provided a nourishing liquid food for the besieged. **1972** *Std Encycl. of Sn Afr.* VI. 519 Soon bread was reduced to a daily 230 grams, .. the most sustaining item of diet being a pint of chevril (extract of horse). **1979** E. Drummond *Burning Land* 312 A young inventive lieutenant had constructed an apparatus in one of the rail sheds that compounded horse-flesh into a tasty and sustaining essence immediately patented as 'Chevril'.

chiaten var. KIAAT.

chick *n. Ostrich-farming.* [Shortened form of CHICKEN FEATHER.] A body feather taken from an immature ostrich; CHICKEN FEATHER. Also *attrib.* See also FEATHER sense a, JUVENAL, SPADONA.
  1896 R. Wallace *Farming Indust. of Cape Col.* 233 All kinds of ostrich feathers, including 'Dark Chicks,' worth 2s. per lb., and 'Prime Whites,' worth many pounds sterling per lb., are included. **1902** *Agric. Jrnl of Cape of G.H.* XX. 721 Chicks £0.1.0 – £0.1.6. **1909** J.E.

Duerden in *Ibid.* XXXIV. 519 With the fourth plumage, 'second-after-chicks,' the valuable wingquills of both the cock and the hen have reached their full size and show their best characteristics ... With the high feeding now largely followed the .. first-after-chicks show almost mature characteristics. **1930** [see JUVENAL]. **1955** G. Aschman in *Saron & Hotz Jews in S. Afr.* 130 The different types of feathers that the ostrich produces – chicks, wings, bodies. **1973** D.J. Maree in *Std Encycl. of Sn Afr.* VIII. 398 The first feathers are taken .. at the age of six to eight months – the wings are known in the trade as 'spadonas' and the body feathers as 'chicks'.

chicken feather *n. phr. Obs. Ostrich-farming.* CHICK.
  c**1881** A. Douglass *Ostrich Farming* 92 (*fold-out*) Chicken feathers, being the first crop from the wings of the young bird. **1890** A. Martin *Home Life* 105 A young ostrich's rough, bristly, untidy-looking 'chicken feathers' are plucked for the first time when he is nine months old; they are stiff and narrow, with very pointed tips, and their ugly appearance gives no promise of future beauty.

chicken run *n. phr. Colloq.* Also with initial capitals. [fr. Eng. slang *chicken* cowardly + *run*, with a play on the meanings 'an act of running' and 'a coop'.] *The chicken run:* The exodus of people from South Africa because of fear for their future. Also *attrib.*
  The term was first used in Rhodesia (now Zimbabwe).
  1977 *Daily Dispatch* 14 Dec. 12 'There's no point in staying and watching rot set in when the blacks take over,' a British-born engineer said .. explaining why he is joining what has become known derisively as 'The Chicken Run'. **1978** *Sunday Times* 5 Mar. 17 'I've decided to emigrate,' he confessed, .. 'I've had enough.' 'Not you too!' I gasped. 'Not the chicken run.' **1978** *Daily Dispatch* 19 May 5 Many people leaving South Africa on the 'chicken run' and he had no sympathy for them, Mr Brian Page .. said in the Immigration Vote yesterday. **1985** B. Ronge in *Fair Lady* 27 Nov. 26 Today's times are not happy ones, and perhaps like mine, your mind is bent on escape. I don't intend going on the chicken run, of course. **1987** M. Spring in *Star* 3 June 14 Every few years there is an outbreak of chicken-run fever that sends thousands of South Africa's brightest and best overseas to escape the 'coming racial violence'. **1988** *Fair Lady* 3 Feb. 7 (*letter*) Whenever I hear emigration referred to as 'the chicken run' I want to scream. **1993** T. Betty in *Sunday Times* 25 Apr. 2 Chicken run is a boon for business. The white flight from South Africa has boosted business for a local moving firm, making it the eighth largest international mover in the world.

Hence **chicken-runner** *n.*
  1986 G. McDougall in *Style* Nov. 8 Your chicken-runners remind me of people I once saw come down to a beautiful, spotless beach. They littered it .. then moved off to sit on a fresh, clean space. **1987** *Frontline* May 24 A good percentage of South African immigrants are so-called Coloured and Indian folk ... Even now, when they are apparently being elbowed aside by white chicken-runners, they still comprise between 10% and 20% of the Australian intake. **1989** H.P. Toffoli in *Style* Feb. 36 One of those .. not-to-be-taken-too-seriously-but-at-least-we-all-know-exactly-what-we're-talking-about terms: like yuppie, kugel, .. chicken runner and so on. **1994** *Style* Oct. 12 Hypocritical outpourings from chicken-runners who decide to spend a short time in South Africa.

chief *n. colloq.* [Perh. fr. U.S. Eng. *chief* an informal term for a leader or boss.] A form of address:
1. Used esp. in the townships, when the person addressed is a stranger: 'pal', 'mate'.
  1980 C. Hope *A Separate Development* (1983) 65 Hop in Chief, before the cops lumber you for loitering. **1987** *Drum* July 10, I have always noted a tinge of cynicism in anybody calling a traditional leader a

kaptein. There is also a note of irreverence when a township slicker calls you Chief.

2. *offensive.* Used by some whites as a (condescending) form of address to a black man, particularly one whose name is not known.

1982 *E. Prov. Herald* 20 Sept. 8 At the next table was a man who kept calling the head waiter 'chief'. 1985 P. SLABOLEPSZY *Sat. Night at Palace* 14 Vince: Don't talk to me. You must get it fixed. You got some change? Hey, chief, I'm talking to you. September (*going back inside*): Aikona. (*He mumbles in Zulu.*) 1987 N. MATHIANE in *Frontline* Feb. 21, I tried to make him feel better by saying in Durban they say 'good morning, sir' to a white person and 'good morning, chief' to a black. He was not impressed. 1994 on CCV TV 20 Aug., (*advt*) Hey chief, park it as close to the fountain as possible, lapa side.

Chief Minister *n. phr. Hist.* [Prob. tr. Afk. *hoofminister.*]

1. The executive head of a SELF-GOVERNING state; also used as a form of address.

1968 J. LELYVELD in Cole & Flaherty *House of Bondage* 10 Kaiser Matanzima, chief minister of the Transkei, the first of the 'Bantu homelands', or states within the state, which the Government is establishing. 1973 M. HORRELL *Afr. Homelands* 45 The Chief Minister, (who is also Minister of Finance), is elected by secret ballot by the members of the assembly. 1980 *E. Prov. Herald* 8 Aug. 1 The Chief Ministers of South Africa's partially self-governing homelands meet the Prime Minister, Mr P W Botha, today for talks. 1985 C. SAUNDERS on TV1, 3 Mar. (News Focus), Chief Minister, how do you view the consequences of disinvestment? 1986 P. MAYLAM *Hist. of Afr. People* 169 At the first session of the Legislative Assembly Mangope was elected as chief minister by an overwhelming majority. And it was he who was to become president of Bophuthatswana when it too received its quasi-independence in 1977. 1990 *New African* 16 July 6 Chiefs have been told by the KwaZulu Chief Minister Gatsha Buthelezi that Contralesa wanted to take away their chieftainship.

2. *rare.* The chairman of one of the three houses of the TRICAMERAL parliament.

1986 *E. Prov. Herald* 26 Aug. 1 The Chief Minister in the House of Delegates, Mr Amichand R—, will receive a 'golden handshake' of twice his annual salary.

chiela *n.* var. TJAILE *n.*

chiela *v.* var. TJAILE *v.*

chihele var. TJAILE *n.*

chila var. TJAILE *v.*

children *pl. n.* ***The children***: Young black activists. Cf. *the comrades* (see COMRADE).

1978 *Time* 26 June 21 'The Children,' as they had come to be called, decreed a two-day general strike .. so that Sowetans could gather in churches to honor the dead with hymns extolling black power. 1980 E. JOUBERT *Poppie Nongena* 314 The children didn't stop with burning down schools and administration buildings and beer halls. They got bolder. The older ones called themselves the Comrades and told the adults: Your time is past: When we speak, you must listen. 1986 *Cape Times* 6 Mar., O'Brien predicts deepening anarchy as the necklace-loving 'children' of the township seek to destroy every person and institution that stands between them and the revolutionary millenium. 1987 L. BEAKE *Strollers* 63 The windows were still broken where the children had thrown stones during the strikes. 1987 *Learn & Teach* No.5, 15 In my day the bosses and their friends were stronger than us ... The children today are strong. They are making history like we did.

chilli-bite /ˈtʃɪlibaɪt/ *n.* Also **chili-bite, chilliebite**. A savoury fritter of pea-flour containing chillies, onion, and other vegetables; BHAJIA. Also *attrib.*

1968 *Instructions on packet, Pakco (Pty) Ltd* Chilli-bite Mix ... Make a stiff batter; then add one of the following to the batter, chopped onions, coarsely chopped lettuce, water cress or chopped spinach. For a stronger flavour add cayenne pepper or green chillies. 1977 *Sunday Times* 1 May (Mag. Sect.) 9 Down on the corner of Diagonal and President, chili-bites are being offered for sale — still warm from the pan — at 20 cents a packet. 1982 Z. MAYAT *Indian Delights* 228 Bhajias (chilli bites). Basic recipe. 1 cup pea or chana flour, .. 2 tsp coarsely crushed dhunia, 3 green chillies pounded fine. 1992 R. MESTHRIE *Lexicon of S. Afr. Indian Eng.* 5 *Bhajia/Bajia*, .. A small, spicy snack fried with onion, chilli etc. Same as *chilli-bites.*

China snoek see SNOEK sense 4.

chincherinchee /ˌtʃɪntʃərɪnˈtʃiː/ *n.* Forms: α. **tinterintie, tintirintie**; β. **chinkeri(n)chee, chinkering ching, tjienkerientjee**; γ. **chincherinchee, chincher-and-ching.** [Englished form of S. Afr. Du. *tintirintie, tjienkerintjie*, perh. a blend of Du. *tjienken* to produce a short ringing sound and *uintjie* bulb; see quot. 1924.] Any of several bulbous plants of the genus *Ornithogalum* of the Liliaceae, esp. *O. thyrsoides*, with showy, long-lasting flowers; CHINK. See also VIOOLTJIE.

α. 1793 tr. *C.P. Thunberg's Trav.* I. 153 *Tintirinties* is a name given to a species of *Ornithogalum*, with a white flower, from the sound produced, when two stalks of it were rubbed against each other. 1809 J. MACKRILL Diary. 61 Tintirinties, species of Ornithogalum, so called, from the sound produced, by rubbing two stalks together, it has a white flower.

β. 1904 *Cape of G.H. Agric. Jrnl* July 6 (Pettman), The *Chinkerinchee, Chincher-and-ching*, 'Viooltjes', as that beautiful white flowering bulb, the *Ornithogalum thyrsoides*, is variously called in South Africa, occurs over a wide area. The flower heads are now known to be a deadly poison when eaten by horses. 1916 S. BLACK in S. Gray *Three Plays* (1984) 214 I'll have a bouquet in my hand — how about chinkerinchees? — No, not ginger and cheese — chinkerinchees, a South African flower. 1932 *Grocott's Daily Mail* 9 Jan. 3 The flowers which form the subjects of these delightful fantasies are .. Chinkenchee, Blaauw Bloem and Wild Dagga. 1957 L.G. GREEN *Beyond City Lights* 18 White sheets of tjienkerientjees. 1973 P.A. WHITNEY *Blue Fire* 145 A bunch of green chinkerichees for herself. She had loved these South African 'chinks' as a child with their green buds that climbed a long stalk and would open later into long-lasting white flowers. 1984 J. ONDERSTALL *Tvl Lowveld & Escarpment* 46 *Ornithogalum saundersii, Transvaal Chinkerinchee.* 1986 N. CHARTON *Informant, Grahamstown* The white chinkerinchees are budding along the roads, and there are fields of yellow daisies.

γ. 1904 [see above]. 1905 D. HUTCHEON in Flint & Gilchrist *Science in S. Afr.* 355 *'Chincher-and-Ching'* or *'Chinkerinchee'* ... This well-known and popular flowering plant grows .. in moist lands and vleis. 1910 D. FAIRBRIDGE *That Which Hath Been* (1913) 105 Flowers bloomed everywhere in the warm sunshine .. from the crimson kalkoentje to the pure white chincherinchees. 1924 —— *Gardens of S. Afr.* 124 The local name — *Chincherinchee* (originally *Chincher uintjie*) is not American-Indian or Sesuto ... It owes its origin to the noise made by the stems when they are rubbed together. 1930 [see GIFBLAAR]. 1939 *Outspan* 13 Oct. 85 Chincherinchees for friends overseas ... We are now shipping these beautiful flowers. Delivered in England and Scotland 7/6 and 12/6 per box. 1969 *Personality* 5 June, The most yahoo touch I have ever seen is dyed chincherinchees. 1976 J. BECKER in *Quarry '76* 72 Vacuum, our Coloured gardener, picked the strelitzia and protea and chincherinchees (which he called chinkery-cheese). 1983 [see NAMAQUALAND DAISY]. 1989 *Gardening Questions Answered* (Reader's Digest Assoc.) 329 *Ornithogalum thyrsoides*, (Chincherinchee) Indigenous, spring flowering bulb ... *Origin*: South-western Cape.

Chinese *n. Obs.* exc. *hist.* [tr. S. Afr. Du.; so named for a supposed resemblance to Chinese people in skin-colour and eye shape.] CHINESE HOTTENTOT.

1786 G. FORSTER tr. *A. Sparrman's Voy. to Cape of G.H.* I. 227 The Chinese, or *Snese-Hottentots*, so called from their complexion, which is yellower than that of the other Hottentot nations. 1795 C.R. HOPSON tr. *C.P. Thunberg's Trav.* II. 95 Eastward of the Snow-mountains .. a people that are whiter than the Hottentots, with curling hair .. are called Little Chinese. 1988 P.E. RAPER tr. *R.J. Gordon's Cape Trav. 1777–86* I. 79 The real Hottentots who call themselves 'Oesjswand' or also 'Saana' .. are called 'Bushmen' or 'Chinese' by us.

Chinese Hottentot *n. phr. Obs.* exc. *hist.* Pl. **-s**, or unchanged. [See prec. + HOTTENTOT.] Usu. in *pl.*: A name given to certain KHOISAN peoples (particularly the NAMA); CHINESE.

1790 tr. *F. Le Vaillant's Trav.* II. 346 In some cantons they are called Chinese Hottentot. Chinese Hottentots, because their colour approaches near to that of the Chinese found at the Cape. [1838 see NAMAQUA.] 1847 J. BARROW *Reflect.* 174 The flat nose, high cheekbones, prominent chin and concave visage, partake much of the apish character, which their keen eye, always in motion, does not tend to diminish. The upper lid of this organ .. is rounded into the lower on the side next the nose. They are known .. by the name of Chinese Hottentots. 1914 C. PETTMAN *Notes on S. Afr. Place Names* 17 The Sneeze Flats, to the north of the Fish River .. were at one time occupied by a tribe of Bushmen or Hottentots whose bright yellow complexions so resembled those of the Chinese seen at the Cape that the Voortrekkers .. designated them Sinese (or Chinese) Hottentots. 1946 L.G. GREEN *So Few Are Free* 145 The Namaquas, known to the early Dutch settlers as the 'Chinese hottentots' .. have yellowish complexions and narrow eyes.

Chinese lantern *n. phr.* [Transf. use of Eng. *Chinese lantern* a name for the plant *Physalis alkekengi*; so called fr. shape and arrangement of flowers or fruits (see quots 1966 and 1984).] Freq. also **Chinese lanterns** used with singular force.

1. The plant *Sandersonia aurantiaca* of the Liliaceae. Occas. in the phr. ***Chinese lantern lily.***

1917 R. MARLOTH *Common Names* 19 *Chinese lantern lily, Sandersonia aurantiaca.* Eastern district. *c*1968 S. CANDY *Natal Coast Gardening* 73 *Sandersonia aurantiaca*, .. 'Chinese Lanterns' ... The lovely, hanging, 1-inch golden bells are constricted at the mouth to give the 'lantern' shape. 1975 J.M. GIBSON *Wild Flowers of Natal* 5 *Sandersonia aurantiaca Hook*, (Chinese Lantern) ... This flower has become so rare because Africans used to pick it for sale, as it lasted for so long.

2.a. Occas. in the phr. ***Chinese lantern tree***:

i. The *klapperbos* (see KLAPPER *n.*[2] sense 2), *Nymania capensis* of the Meliaceae. See also sense 2 b.

1917 R. MARLOTH *Common Names* 19 *Chinese lantern, Nymania capensis.* The inflated capsules generally red. 1931 *Nat. Geog. Mag.* Apr. 408 Our road thither led us past avenues of mammoth cactus and through rocky remotenesses where bloomed the klapperbos, or Chinese lantern tree. 1961 PALMER & PITMAN *Trees of S. Afr.* 279 Passing through the Karroo in spring, travellers often pause in astonishment at splashes of pure and vivid colour ... This is the famous klapper or Chinese lanterns, *Nymania Capensis* ... The flowers .. develop into inflated fruits with a papery covering like that of a large gooseberry ... These fruits give the tree its common names of klapper and Chinese lanterns. 1971 M.R. LEVYNS in *Std Encycl. of Sn Afr.* III. 198 *Chinese Lanterns*, .. The decorative pink fruits resemble papery lanterns. 1989 *Conserva* Vol.4 No.4, 22 *Nymania capensis, Chinese Lanterns*, The seed must not be removed until the balloon-like capsule commences disintegrating.

ii. The tree *Dichrostachys cinerea* of the Mimosaceae.

1966 C.A. SMITH *Common Names* 191 *Chinese lantern tree, Dichrostachys cinerea* ... When in full bloom the showy inflorescences resemble Chinese lanterns. 1984 J. ONDERSTALL *Tvl Lowveld & Escarpment* 102 *Dichrostachys cinerea* subp. *nyassana* Large-leaved Sickle Bush, Chinese Lantern Tree, .. The charming pendent inflorescences .. are like little Chinese Lanterns. 1987 F. VON BREITENBACH *Nat. List of Indigenous Trees* 61

Dichrostachys cinerea, ... Sickle Bush, .. Chinese Lanterns.
b. *rare*. The lantern-like fruit of the Chinese lantern tree, *Nymania capensis* (see sense 2 a i above).

1966 C.A. SMITH *Common Names* 191 Chinese Lanterns, The fruits of *Nymania capensis* ... The vernacular name is derived from the shape of the pendulous bladdery fruits, which are flushed pinkish-red when ripe.

chink *n. colloq.* Short for *chinkerinchee*, see CHINCHERINCHEE.
Common in speech.

1949 L.G. GREEN *In Land of Afternoon* 73 'Chinks' grow only in the Western Province. *Ibid.* 74 New York flower shops sell 'chinks' at the equivalent of eight pence each. **1960** C. LIGHTON *Cape Floral Kingdom* 117 The 'chinks' have always been welcome in Britain as a change from the usual run of early winter flowers. **1973** [see CHINCHERINCHEE]. **1982** A. MORIARTY *Outeniqua Tsitsikamma* 34 *Ornithogalum dubium*, Yellow Chink ... The flowers are a deep orange-yellow with a dark green ovary.

chinkeri(n)chee, **chinkering ching** varr. CHINCHERINCHEE.

Chirigriquas var. CHARIGURIQUA.

chirp *v. slang.* [Transf. use of general Eng. *chirp* 'to talk in sprightly and lively tones', or 'to utter the short sharp thin sound proper to some small birds and certain insects' (*OED*).]
a. *trans.* To taunt (someone); to cheek (someone).

1991 T. BARON in *Sunday Times* 22 Sept. 34, I chirped him that, maybe, I had more right to be tired after going for my first jog in three weeks when all he'd done was win the IBF junior lightweight title. **1994** J. DEWES in *E. Prov. Herald* 25 Mar., Law student B—W— 'chirped' (taunted) two policemen at the 1992 Woodridge Country Fair minutes before he was arrested for being drunk in public ... 'I was arrested because I chirped them'.
b. *intrans.* To complain.

1993 J. SMALL in *Weekend Post* 14 Aug. 1 'A penalty was given, somebody chirped and the referee advanced the penalty 10m towards our goalline,' he said. **1994** on TV1, 5 Mar., Batsmen don't usually chirp about it.
Hence **chirp** *n.*, a taunt, a complaint; **chirping** *vbl n.*, taunting, complaining.

1993 J. SMALL in *Weekend Post* 14 Aug. 1 There was some more chirping, again he moaned about this time he walked inwards to the goalposts instead of straight forward to the tryline. **1994** on TV1, 5 Mar., Another chirp going on there between the two of them. **1994** *Ibid.* 8 Mar. (News), Some of the players were upset by the constant chirping of the crowd. **1994** J. DEWES in *E. Prov. Herald* 25 Mar., Student 'was arrested for chirping'.

chisa var. CHEESA.

chisa nyama var. CHESANYAMA.

Chivenda var. VENDA *n.* sense 2.

chlorodyne /ˈklɒrədaɪn/ *n.* Freq. with initial capital. [Blend of *chloroform* and *anodyne*; a name coined by its South African inventor, Collis Browne.] The proprietary name of a patent medicine used (world-wide) as a narcotic and anodyne, and containing chloroform, morphia, tincture of Indian hemp, prussic acid, and other substances.
Previously widely used as a home remedy, chlorodyne is now obtainable only on prescription.

1863 MRS CARLYLE *Lett.* III. 158 I .. have been thinking of realising some chlorodyne. **1872** C.A. PAYTON *Diamond Diggings* 36 Quinine and Collis Browne's Chlorodyne are good medicines to take up. **1878** T.J. LUCAS *Camp Life & Sport* 32 Dr. Collis Browne, now well-known as the inventor of chlorodyne, that universal soother of miseries, a valuable medicine, which has indeed won him a European reputation. **1911** L. COHEN *Reminisc. of Kimberley* 433 More I could not do, but as he was suffering from colic, left the waggon to procure chlorodyne. **1914** *Farmer's Annual* 175 Chlorodyne is a remedy much used in the home for many of the ills that human flesh is heir to, and it can equally well be used for the animals on the farm. **1919** *Dunell, Ebden & Co.'s Price List* Aug. 35 Brown's Chlorodyne. **1972** W. MARTINDALE *Extra Pharmacopoeia*, Chlorodyne: The formula of the B.P. 1885 included 6.25% volume per volume of hydrocyanic acid. This ingredient has been omitted from the formula of the B.P.C. The synonym Tinct. Chlorof. et morph. BP85 has been retained. **1976** S. CLOETE *Chetoko* 151 He's a bit of a doctor. 'You can do a lot with some aspirins, Epsom salts, Chlorodyne and carbolic acid.' **1978** A.P. BRINK *Rumours of Rain* 245 All the thin bottles familiar from Ma's dispensary: red and white dulcis and Haarlem drops, chlorodyne, wonder essence, Jamaica ginger, chest drops, cascara.

Choana var. CHUANA.

Chochaqua var. COCHOQUA.

chocka var. CHOKKA.

chocolate *n. slang.* [Named for the brown colour of the banknote.] In urban (esp. township) English: a twenty-rand banknote. Also *attrib.*

1984 M. MTHETHWA in *Frontline* July 28 Their pockets and wallets and purses are thickly lined with stacks of 'cabbages' and 'chocolates' – ten and twenty-rand banknotes. **1991** C. VAN ULMENSTEIN in *Weekend Argus* 12 Jan. (Suppl.) 5 Other denominations of money also have their own names: R100 is known as a clipper, .. R20 as a chocolate. **1992** [see CABBAGE]. **1994** WILHELM & NAIDOO in *Sunday Times* 1 May 15 Notes all have different names: .. the brown R20 note is a *chocolate* note.

chokka /ˈtʃɒkə/ *n.* Also **chakka**, **chocka**, **chokker**, and (formerly) **ts(c)hokka**. [ad. Afk. *tjokka*, perh. ad. Pg. *choco* a species of cuttlefish; but see quot. 1902.] Any of several shallow-water species of squid (*Loliginidae* spp.) of the Loliginidae widely used as bait (but see quot. 1982); by extension, any of several species of cuttlefish (*Sepia* spp.) of the Sepiidae. Also *attrib.*

1902 J.D.F. GILCHRIST in *Trans. of S. Afr. Phil. Soc.* XI. 224 (Pettman), Though not a fish the 'Tschokka' may be mentioned ... [The name] is applied to the Cuttlefish, or Squid, on account of the peculiar noise it makes when landed. **1913** C. PETTMAN *Africanderisms* 517 *Tshokka*, An onomatopoeic name given to the cuttlefish; it refers to the peculiar sound it makes when taken out of the water. **1923** *S. Afr.: Land of Outdoor Life* (S.A.R. & H.) 234 The sea cat or smaller varieties of octopus, the chakka or squid, and the crawfish, are also good summer baits. **1930** C.L. BIDEN *Sea-Angling Fishes* 42 A species of cuttlefish .. locally called 'chokker' and .. classified as *Loligo indica* ... Elf and albacore feed on immature 'chokker' of two or three inches long. **1951** L.G. GREEN *Grow Lovely* 57 Octopus makes an appetizing soup, and the Golden Dragon sometimes serves the local chokka (squid) as a tender fried dish. **1955** C. HORNE *Fisherman's Eldorado* 49 Bait runs low, prices rising as demand increases. Under these circumstances a single chokka frequently commands a price as high as £1. **1971** *Het Suid-Western* 17 May, The menu will include Danish mussels, oysters, chokka, crayfish thermidor, nasi goreng and arikreukel, a delicacy much favoured by gourmets. **1979** *E. Prov. Herald* 15 Nov. 23, I was out with two of my sons and one of them .. put down a chokka dolley. He did not get any chokka but he had a tremendous take on the dolley. **1982** KILBURN & RIPPEY *Sea Shells* 141 Squid is consumed in Southern Africa as 'calamari' and is used as bait under the name 'chokka'. **1990** L. RICHFIELD in *Flying Springbok* June 133 They're the arch-conservatives in their food tastes ... They're known sometimes to order deep-fried calamari as a starter — but if you call it chokka, they choke.

chommie /ˈtʃɔmi/ *n. slang.* Also **tjommie**. [Englished form of Afk. *tjommie* ad. Eng. *chummy* friend.] 'Pal', 'mate'; also used as a form of address.

1946 *Cape Times* in E. Partridge *Dict. of Underworld* (1950) 28 Cronies (variously known as chommies, pallie-blues, or beaus). [**1959** L. LONGMORE *Dispossessed* 190 The leader of a tsotsi gang is known as the 'big shot', .. and the rank and file are variously known as 'the brigade', 'men', 'tjommies', 'morongas', 'u-majikas'.] **1970** S.E. NATHAN *Informant, Cape Town* Tjommies. Pals. **1974** J. MATTHEWS *Park* (1983) 22 We get more dagga at de Alabama. De burgie who puss issa ou chommie. We do six months without moer. **1977** C. HOPE in S. Gray *Theatre Two* (1981) 40 Jimmie: ... We can't get that sort of knife here in Pretoria, man, where the blade comes out the front. Howellsie (knowingly): My broer's chommie's got one. **1978** S. ROBERTS in *New Classic* No.5, 24, I won't stick my neck out for nothing .. maybe for a tjommie but not for any idea. **1979** *Sunday Times* 26 Aug. 18 What title does he confer on himself ... 'It depends on the girl. If she's literate, it's "poet". Otherwise it's "tjommie" or "china"'. **1981** M. MUTLOATSE in *Staffrider* Vol.3 No.4, 40 Well, if this bugger gets up he's going to moer us again; or his chommies will get here and bliksem us to pieces. **1988** A. SHER *Middlepost* 84 Hey, don't look so sad, mad and bad, chommie. You're going to get your heart's desire. **1990** J. ROSENTHAL *Wake Up Singing* 18 Each was there with all his chommies from school in Soweto.

Chonacqua var. GONAQUA.

chongololo var. SONGOLOLO.

choon var. TUNE.

chorb /tʃɔːb/ *n. colloq.* Also **chawb**, **chorbe**. [Unkn.; perh. fr. a Sintu-language (or Bantu-language) word rel. to seTswana (*se*)*tshubaba*, see CHUBABA.] Esp. in the language of schoolchildren: a pimple.

1970 J. GREENWOOD *Informant, Johannesburg* You have terrible chorbes. **1970** G.E.Q. ABSOLOM *Informant, Germiston* She had a nasty chawb on her chin (pimple). **1978** 'BLOSSOM' in *Darling* (Branford 4th ed.), My boet is a skinny ou of fifteen with sticking-out ears and chorbs. **1983** *Sunday Times* 8 May 29 'You use it when you have *chorbs*, Woesie,' Lynn says ... 'It's a pimple cream!' shouts Woesie triumphantly. **1991** DAWSON *Informant, Moseley* (Natal) The teenager was worried when her face started breaking out in chorbes.

chorrie var. TJORRIE.

chraal var. KRAAL *n.*

‖**Christenmensch** /ˈxrəst(ə)n,mens, -mēs/ *n. Obs. exc. hist.* Pl. usu. **-en**. Forms: *sing.* Christemens, Christ(en)mensch; *pl.* Christen menschen, Christen mense, Christi mensche, Criste menchen, Kriste-mensch. [S. Afr. Du., *Christen* Christian + *mens(ch)* person.] **a.** A Christian. **b.** A white person. **c.** An Afrikaner (see AFRIKANER *n.* sense 2 a). In all senses also CHRISTIAN. Cf. MENS *n.* sense 1.

1806 J. BARROW *Trav.* I. 398 Bursts of rage and resentment on being put on a level with one, as the boors call them, of the *Zwarte Natie*, between whom and the *Christian Mensch* they conceive the difference to be fully as great as between themselves and their cattle. **1822** *Missionary Notices* 327 The fact is, in this country they consider it an honour to be baptised, and are always wishful to get the name of Criste Menchen (or Christians) whether God has begun a work of grace upon their hearts or not. **1822** W.J. BURCHELL *Trav.* I. 221 They think that a Christenmensch (a Christian), so they term all white men, should never be passed without salutation. **1824** *Ibid.* II. 467 He often assumed over the other Hottentots, an insolent command which he supposed to belong to him in right of his being a 'Christmensch'. **1832** *Graham's Town Jrnl* 2 Mar. 39 All the parsens speetchified and preetchified so long about drunkenness, and blackened the *Cristemens* and whitewashed the Ottentots so much as you never seed in your born days. [**1834** T. PRINGLE *Afr. Sketches* 527 Christian men (Christen menschen) is the term always used by the Boors to distinguish themselves from the coloured races.] **1846** R. MOFFAT *Missionary Labours* 9 Whenever they saw him .. go into the bush for prayer or meditation, one of other or the *Christi mensche* (Christians) immediately ran into his tent to steal. **1863** LADY DUFF-GORDON in F. Galton *Vacation Tourists* (1864) III. 187 The Dutch pastors still remember the distinction between 'Christenmenschen' and 'Hottentoten'. **1871** J. MACKENZIE *Ten Yrs* (1971) 35 While no one had any reason to fear personal violence at the hands of the Dutchmen, the spoliation of Dr. Livingstone's station at Kolobeng taught us all that our equipment .. would probably be regarded as a fair prize .. by the 'Christen menschen' of the Transvaal. **1885** L.H. MEURANT *60 Yrs Ago* 81 Drie monts Krediet for de Christemens — no Krediet for de Settlaar. **1896** M.A. CAREY-HOBSON *At Home in Tvl* 495 Surely, whatever they did as regarded blacks, they would not leave Christenmenschen (Christians) to be devoured by vultures! **1913** A.B. MARCHAND *Dirk, S. African* 7 (Swart), We're plain folks, but not so rough as that we haven't a bed and a bite for another *Christenmensch* that has come so far. **1968** E.A. WALKER *Hist. of Sn Afr.* 275 The Boers had held even more strongly than the townsmen .. that the natives were children of Ham, definitely inferior to *Christen mense*, divinely appointed hewers of wood and drawers of water.

Christian *n. obs.* [Special sense of general Eng., influenced by S. Afr. Du. *Christenmensch* (see prec.).] CHRISTENMENSCH. Also *attrib.*

1786 G. FORSTER tr. *A. Sparrman's Voy. to Cape of G.H.* I. 207 The Boshies-men have been a long time in a savage state, and now, since the Christians have invaded their country, .. many of them are brought into a still more miserable situation. **1798** S.H. WILCOCKE tr. *J.S. Stavorinus's Voy. to E. Indies 1768–71* II. 56 The more distant farmers .. both in their manners and appearance, more resembled Hottentots than Christians. **1827** G. THOMPSON *Trav.* II. 341 On the frontier .. mutual hostility and depredation continued to subsist between the Caffers and the Christians. **1835** G. CHAMPION *Jrnl* (1968) 14 To call a slave a Christian is in their [*sc.* the Dutch's] eyes synon. with making him a white man, for the term has that meaning in this country. *a***1838** A. SMITH *Jrnl* (1975) 50 The Christians — as the whites of South Africa designated themselves in contradistinction to the blacks. **1882** C. DU VAL *With Show through Sn Afr.* I. 259 Snap went the chain, leaving half the Christian and all the Kaffir muscularity sprawling on the bank. **1898** (tr. W.S. van Ryneveld) in G.M. Theal *Rec. of Cape Col.* III. 242 The Landdrost has endeavoured to instigate the Caffers against the Christians, .. but .. the honest protector of our native Country Coenraad de Buys has prevented it. *c***1963** *Stellenbosch: Oldest Village in S. Afr.* (brochure) 8 The well-known D.R. Minister Meent Borcherds included in his memoirs a detailed description of the village as he knew it in 1825 .. the population .. consisting of 774 Christians, 144 Hottentots, 852 slaves, 22 prize negroes and 64 free blacks.

Christian-National *adj.* Also **Christian-Nationalist**. [tr. Afk. *Christelik-Nasionaal*.]

1. Special collocation: **Christian National Education** [tr. Afk. *Christelik-Nasionale Onderwys*, see C.N.O.], an educational philosophy grounded upon, and promoting, the religious and cultural beliefs of the Afrikaner people; C.N.E.; C.N.O. Also *attrib.*

Initiated in the 1870s in response to Lord Alfred Milner's policy of anglicization after the Boer War; re-introduced by the National Party government in the 1950s.

1941 C.W. DE KIEWIET *Hist. of S. Afr.* 147 Against the superior teachers, the better equipment, and the financial strength of the government schools the Dutch 'Christian National Education' schools could not prevail. **1950** H. GIBBS *Twilight* 78 Nationalist-Calvinist-Afrikaners .. believe, as shown in their policy of Christian-National Education .. , that since the fall of Man all children are born in a state of sin. Particularly Natives. **1956** M. ROGERS *Black Sash* 230 Nationalist organisers were forming a committee which produced a Christian Nationalist Education policy. **1966** [see C.N.E.]. **1971** *Rand Daily Mail* 28 Aug. 10 They recoil, too, when Nationalist jingoism asserts itself .. when it forces Black children and English children and Coloured children to be educated according to the principles of Christian National Education. **1986** B. NASSON in Burman & Reynolds *Growing Up* 95 South Africa's segregated schooling networks (Bantu Education, Christian National Education, Coloured Teaching and Education). **1990** *Sash* Vol.33 No.1, 31 The Home and School Council .. , an amalgamation of Parent Teacher Associations in Johannesburg, arose out of a concern with the enforcement of Christian National Education and its witch hunts to ensure that Afrikaans children were not attending English language medium schools and vice versa.

2. Of or pertaining to an ideology or world view based on (the pre-eminence of) the religion, culture, and language of the Afrikaner people.

*c***1949** CURREY & SNELL *Threat to Freedom* (Standing Committee of Assoc. Church Schools of S. Afr.) 5 For all children having Afrikaans as their mother-tongue, and for all Coloured and Native schools, it is explicitly laid down that the education supplied must be based on a Christian-National foundation. **1952** B. DAVIDSON *Report on Sn Afr.* 158 The 'Afrikanerization' of public life and education 'in the Christian National sense'. **1956** M. ROGERS *Black Sash* 140 Christian-National Republicanism .. [was] set out by Dr Otto du Plessis of the State Information Office, in 1940. **1972** *Sunday Times* 24 Sept. 17 Some Broederbond members wanted a 'Christian-national' republic in which Afrikaners would be the avowed elite. **1973** *E. Prov. Herald* 6 July 7 The establishment of a prize for publication with Christian national principles as basic themes. **1985** PLATZKY & WALKER *Surplus People* 95 When they took office, the apartheid manifesto of the Nationalists consisted of little more than a broad set of principles: white supremacy, racial segregation, a Christian National state. **1989** J. HOBBS *Thoughts in Makeshift Mortuary* 207 They were equally submissive in school, never questioning the word of authority which came tightly laced in Christian National corsets. **1994** *Noseweek* No.10, 10 Apparently, that is all regarded as acceptable banking and accounting practice in Christian Nationalist circles.

Christian-Nationalism *n.* [ad. Afk. *Christelik-Nasionaal.*] An ideology grounded in the religious, cultural, and ethnic beliefs of the Afrikaner people. Also *attrib.*

1931 W.A. COTTON *Racial Segregation* 11 What I have advocated is segregation ... What I have advocated is Christian nationalism as a better social scheme than the system of Asiatic caste separations. **1948** *Press Digest* No.5, 38 The Jew whose co-operation we are looking for must be able to subscribe to the principle of Christian-Nationalism without any reservation. *c***1948** *Nationalist Party's Great Christian Nationalism Political Fraud* (United Party) 10 You might say that this policy may be Nationalism, but that it is not *Christian* Nationalism to separate a man from his family. **1984** R. DAVIES et al. *Struggle for S. Afr.* II. 268 The emerging *Broederbond* ideology of 'Christian Nationalism' embodied a rigid ethnic exclusivism, an anti-British republicanism and a growing concern with developing the principles of 'apartheid'. **1990** R. MALAN *My Traitor's Heart* 39 Later, we were taught that history began in 1488, when a Portuguese navigator first rounded the Cape. We were likely to point to such things as proof that the rockspiders were giving us lies for truth and trying to wash our brains with 'Christian nationalism'.

Christi mensche *pl.* form of CHRISTENMENSCH.

Christmas *n.* Special Comb. (some of which occur in general Eng. in different senses): **Christmas bee** or **-beetle**, any of several species of cicada (family Cicadidae), the males of which produce a shrill mating song during summer; **Christmas box** [extension of Brit. Eng. *Christmas box* a gratuity given at Christmas time to delivery men, servants and roundsmen, for services rendered], any special gift, usu. given at Christmas time; also *fig.*; **Christmas bush**, the shrub *Pavetta lanceolata* of the Rubiaceae, which bears masses of white flowers at Christmas time; **Christmas flower** or **- rose**, any of several species of flowering shrub of the genus *Hydrangea* of the Saxifragaceae, with pink, white or blue flower-clusters which bloom in December; **Christmas Tree**, (*a*) the *klapperbos* (see KLAPPER $n.^2$ sense 2), *Nymania capensis*; (*b*) *Christmas bush*, see above; (*c*) the name given to a party held at Christmas time, esp. one for (underprivileged) children which is organized by a school, company, or welfare organization; **Christmas worm** [tr. Afk. *Krismiswurm*], a nickname for the concertina.

1912 *E. London Dispatch* 16 Feb. 7 (Pettman), The **Christmas bee** or cicada is another familiar insect of which only the male has the power of 'song'; and it must be confessed he is exceedingly persistent in the exhibition of his accomplishment, for a noisier insect it would be hard to find. **1920** R.Y. STORMBERG *Mrs Pieter de Bruyn* 93 At night, the Christmas bees made the longest winded chorus I've ever heard. **1968** K. MCMAGH *Dinner of Herbs* 153 The steep narrow valley where the Christmas bees shrilled in the blue gum trees. **1882** *Meteor* 27 Nov. 4 **Christmas Beetles** commenced their monotonous song on Tuesday, November 12. **1913** C. PETTMAN *Africanderisms* 121 *Christmas bee* or *beetle*, The various *Cicadae*, which fill the air with deafening shrillness about Christmas time, are so called in some localities. **1937** M. ALSTON *Wanderings* 158 At last the 'Christmas beetles' (cicadas) had competitors in the field .. and what with the Christmas beetles and frogs I was glad to retreat. **1950** D. REED *Somewhere S. of Suez* 147 The lights of Port Elizabeth sprang out, the Christmas beetle began to harp on its one shrill note, darkness came down, and still I sat. **1966** 'RAYMOND' in K.M. Durham *New Voices*, I recalled .. The electric buzz of Christmas beetles. **1971** J. MCCLURE *Steam Pig* (1973) 70 Under the blue gums by a slow brown river, with Christmas beetles shrilling in the bush beyond. **1981** *Sunday Times* 22 Feb., I too have been suffering from a loud singing noise in my ears — like the sound made by a cicada or a Christmas beetle — for the past five years. **1993** P. LEEMAN in *Natal Mercury* 30 Dec. 7 He has also — through electronics — replicated the sounds of the tropics and sub-tropics such as those of cicadas or Christmas beetles. **1897** J.P. FITZPATRICK *Outspan* 221 Why, you are a **Christmas-box** yourself. Remember, I have taken possession of you, and mean to present you to father to-morrow morning as my Christmas-box. **1963** L.F. FREED *Crime in S. Afr.* 125 On Christmas morning .. the streets swarm with merrymakers ... The girls .. with scarlet on their cheeks shout 'Happy' to the sex-hungry men; and the meanest of men may ask for a Christmas box and get kissed. **1972** F.G. BUTLER *Informant, Grahamstown* 'C.M.R. Beetle.' I've just heard that this is from 'Cape Mounted Rifles', whose colours were also yellow and black (?). My Xmas box for the Dictionary. **1980** *Daily Dispatch* 21 Apr. 9 Mr Nujoma said his forces were fighting to 'liberate' every inch of SWA and that included Walvis Bay, which was 'given to the Boers as a Christmas box by the British'. **1989** 'HOGARTH' in *Sunday Times* 3 Dec. 26 Christmas box ... Let's hope he [*sc.* F.W. de Klerk] doesn't forget about the media regulations. Removing them would be a worthy present for all South Africans this Christmas. **1913** C. PETTMAN *Africanderisms* 121 **Christmas bush**, *Pavetta caffra* is known by this name. **1951** N.L. KING *Tree-Planting* 69 *Pavetta lanceolata* (Christmas bush), A beautiful shrub which occurs in open forests and along the edge of forests in eastern Cape, Natal and Zululand ... Makes an excellent hedge. **1913** H. TUCKER *Our Beautiful Peninsula* 33 A delightful garden .. leads on to terraces of red and yellow cannas and slopes of blue hydrangeas. **'Christmas flowers,'** some call the latter. **1924** D. FAIRBRIDGE *Gardens of S. Afr.* 193 *Hydrangea hortensis*, The Christmas Flower of the Cape. **1951** S. ELIOVSON *Flowering Shrubs & Trees* 88 Hydrangeas are probably the most popular shrubs in South Africa, where they are also called Christmas flowers ... They come from Asia and grow into well-rounded bushes up to six feet in height. **1954** U. VAN DER SPUY *Ornamental Shrubs & Trees* 139 *Hydrangea macrophylla*, Hydrangea or Christmas Flower ... Bears large flattish rounded heads of tiny florets. Flowers are white, pink or blue but are apt to change colour according to the nature of the soil in which they grow. **1977** I. MARGO in *Quarry '77* 153 The garden is long, lawns on two different levels, one terrace of pink and blue Christmas flowers and geraniums with leaves of soft fur. **1993** *Weekend Post* 18 Dec. (Leisure) 7 Most commonly known as Christmas flowers, hydrangeas will grow and flower happily in the same container for many years. **1906** B. STONEMAN *Plants & their Ways* 117 In the **'Christmas rose,'** leaves and leaflets take the place of ovaries and ovules. **1992** *S. Afr. Garden & Home* Dec. 92 Hydrangeas, or Christmas Roses as many gardeners call them, will grow under the most unlikely conditions. *Ibid.* 94 Few gardeners know there is also a double form of Christmas rose. **1906** B. STONEMAN *Plants & their Ways* 231 *Aitonia.* Dear to the children's hearts is the **'Christmas Tree'** of Oudtshoorn, Uitenhage, and Albany districts. **1913** C. PETTMAN *Africanderisms* 121 *Christmas tree, Pavetta lanceolata, Eck.* .. This shrub blooms in pure white about Christmas time. **1959** C.F.P. HERSELMAN in *Pietersburg Eng. Medium School Mag.* 16 A fancy dress parade .. will .. add extra colour to the usual Xmas Tree. **1974** J. MCCLURE *Gooseberry Fool* (1976) 166 They showed him the unwanted books which white youngsters had donated to their school's Christmas tree. **1991** M. HOFFMAN in *Iscor Management Ladies Club Newsletter* 1 This year we are planning a Christmas Tree for the children of Black Iscor employees. **1991** *S. Afr. Panorama* May-June 20 When one thinks about boeremusiek, the concertina (alias the **Christmas worm**, wailing worm or donkey's lung) is the first instrument that comes to mind.

chuala, chuallah varr. TSHWALA.

Chuana *n. obs.* Also **Choana, Chwana**. [English form of seTswana *Tswana* (see MOTSWANA), or perh. representing obs. seTswana pronunciation of an earlier form of the word.] Also *attrib.*, passing into *adj.*

1.a. BECHUANA sense 1 a. **b.** TSWANA sense 2 a.

*a*1864 L. GROUT *Zulu-Land* 60 The numerous tribes which occupy this broad section of southern and central Africa .. form a single group ... For this group no name has yet been definitely adopted ... Some would call it *Kafir* ... The term *Chuana*, the root of *Bechuana* and *Sechuana*, is .. less objectionable and has already been used to some extent by able writers. **1930** S.T. PLAATJE *Mhudi* (1975) 35 This Matabele speared his comrade for allowing a dog of a Chuana woman to curse his king's armies.

2. SETSWANA.

1928 [see SOTHO sense 2 a]. **1932** D. JONES *Outline of Eng. Phonetics* 227 Strong stress without accompanying loudness is a common feature of the Chwana language of South Africa. **1952** *Drum* Jan. 27 He became the author of many Chuana books and established bursaries for the children to get higher education.

chubaba /tʃu'baba/ *n.* Pl. **-s**, or unchanged. [fr. seTswana *(se)tshubaba* a birthmark, a mark (on the skin) of any colour but white (pl. *ditshubaba*). Cf. CHORB.] Among speakers of the Sintu (Bantu) languages: a dark patch or blemish on the skin, caused by using skin-lighteners.

Usu. in *pl.*

1982 *Voice* 10 Jan. 7 Major skin problems reported among Black people are hydroquinone burns (chubaba), pimples [etc.]. **1989** *Drum* Apr. 64 *(advt)* Supreme 21 helps lift off Chubabas, Dark Patches of Burnt Skin (from skin lighteners). **1990** *Pace* Apr. (Queen) 5 A new range of scientifically-proved skin care treatments that are very effective in removing chubabas and making old, blemished skin young and clear again. **1991** *Drum* Dec.-Jan. 120 *(advt)* If you have Chubabas or oily, problem skin I recommend Cosmo Gold your skin's friend for life.

chullah var. TSHWALA.

chune var. TUNE.

church house *n. phr. Obs.* [tr. Afk. *kerkhuis*, see KERK sense 2.] SUNDAY HOUSE.

1913 A.B. MARCHAND *Dirk, S. African* 45 (Swart), All heaved a sigh of relief as they mounted into the shade of the church house's stoep. **1914** L.H. BRINKMAN *Breath of Karroo* 57 Tante Let possessed a little house in town, known as a church house — being only occupied on church occasions. **1934** M.E. MCKERRON *Hist. of Educ.* 60 (Swart), At a later date the well-to-do farmer often owned a 'church house' in the nearest village.

churra var. CHARRA.

chwala var. TSHWALA.

Chwana var. CHUANA.

ciphy var. SIFFIE.

circuit court *n. phr.* Also with initial capitals. [Transf. use of Eng. *circuit court* a court held periodically in the principal towns of Scotland.] A court which periodically travels to country towns and in which a Supreme Court judge hears criminal cases which are beyond the jurisdiction of the magistrates' and regional courts.

Cf. *Brit. Eng.* 'assizes'.

1832 *Graham's Town Jrnl* 16 Feb. 31 The Circuit Court will be held at Uitenhage on the 9th April; Graham's Town on the 18th. **1843** *Cape of G.H. Almanac & Annual Register, (advt)* In the Supreme Court of the Colony of the Cape of Good Hope, It is ordered that Pieter Fredrik Johannes Korsten, Esq. of Stellenbosch, Notary Public, be admitted to act as an Attorney in any circuit court within this Colony. **1887** *S.W. Silver & Co.'s Handbk to S. Afr.* 27 In 1811 Circuit Courts were established, presided over by two members of the Supreme Court, who visited each district in rotation once a year. **1904** H.A. BRYDEN *Hist. of S. Afr.* 41 The Earl of Caledon, who governed at the Cape from 1807 to 1811, .. established Circuit Courts for the administration of justice among all classes of the community. **1911** *E. Prov. Herald* 3 Oct., John Msizi, the native who was condemned to death at the Circuit Court for the Cleveland Road outrage, was removed to Bloemfontein under escort. **1930** *Friend* 25 Aug. 14 Circuit Courts will be held in the Free State on the dates and places shown: Fauresmith, Wednesday, September 3. **1961** H.F. SAMPSON *White-Faced Huts* 1 Murder cases are tried in a periodical Circuit Court, in which a judge of the Supreme Court sits with a jury or, as a rule, with two magistrates or advocates. **1965** C. VAN HEYNINGEN *Orange Days* 45 When the circuit court came to Winburg, we often had a dinner party for the Judge and his entourage. **1972** A. SCHOLEFIELD *Wild Dog Running* 228 The handcuffs bruising my wrists and the weeks in the *tronk* awaiting the arrival of the circuit court. **1987** *Weekly Mail* 7 Aug. 7 The trial of the 19 men resumed on Monday after a month-long winter recess, switching from the circuit court in Delmas to Court C in Pretoria's Palace of Justice.

circumcision *n.* Also with initial capital. [Special senses of general Eng. *circumcision* the act or rite of circumcising.] According to traditional custom among some African peoples:

1. The period of isolation and initiation, during which circumcision is also performed, after which the status of manhood is conferred upon initiates. Often *attrib.* See also ABAKWETHA sense 2, BOGUERA.

[**1803** J.T. VAN DER KEMP in *Trans. of Missionary Soc.* I. 439 Circumcision is performed on boys of about twelve or fourteen years old, and is accompanied with ceremonies, which seem to be emblems of a total renewal of the person. After he is painted white all over the body, he is driven into a river, and there washed clean; his old garments, &c. are thrown away, and new ones given him.] **1953** LANHAM & MOPELI-PAULUS *Blanket Boy's Moon* 91 Libe came back from Circumcision, and a great feast was arranged for all those who had passed through the school. **1971** [see STICK-FIGHT]. **1973** *Daily Dispatch* 8 May 2 The case is a sequel to the death of M— M—, 15, who was hacked to death with an axe .. at a circumcision dance. **1977** P.C. VENTER *Soweto* 44 Simon .. rejects the tribal ways. Educated as a Christian, he has never been inside a circumcision hut and scoffs at initiation rites. **1982** C. VAN WYK *Message in Wind* 14 Eventually the two tribes grew so close that the boys from both tribes even attended circumcision rites together. **1990** *Daily Dispatch* 19 July 8 He had met the men on his way to attend a circumcision concert at Kubusie. **1990** *Weekend Post* 8 Dec. 3 The Stellenbosch master's student who made headlines .. when he submitted to Xhosa circumcision rites, is a former headboy and A student.

2. *comb.* **circumcision school**, an institution in which initiates are isolated, taught, and circumcised according to custom; the group of young men undergoing this instruction; INITIATION SCHOOL. See also *to go to the bush* (BUSH *n.*[1] sense 4).

1949 C. BULLOCK *Rina* 117 They came out in scores, stark naked and painted a ghastly white ... 'What are they?' I asked ... 'A circumcision school, our carriers say ... They are WaRemba and have the right to kill us according to their ideas.' **1952** H. KLEIN *Land of Silver Mist* 47 From the hills opposite the store, there came the dirge of tribal song and smoke rose from a lonely hut. 'Sutu lodge,' Land explained. 'There's a circumcision school up there.' **1965** E. MPHAHLELE *Down Second Ave* 16 Often, if a Christian chanced to meet a circumcision school, the initiates gave chase and beat him up, swearing at him and all his ancestry in the process. **1972** *Drum* 8 Apr. 4, I passed my standard six in 1966 ... Now I've just come from my circumcision school ... will they admit me back into the high school? **1982** *Ibid.* July 20 The civil servant .. asked for protection, saying he was been dragged off to the circumcision school against his will ... 'I come from a Christian family. We're totally opposed to circumcision schools.' **1986** P. MAYLAM *Hist. of Afr. People* 29 Dingiswayo is said to have abolished the circumcision schools and developed the age-regiments, while Shaka is thought to have introduced full-time military service. **1988** M. SALISO in *E. Prov. Herald* 13 Feb. 3 He had been fetched from his customary circumcision school in the bush by the police to give evidence for the State at the trial. **1989** L.S. BALEKA in *Weekend Post* 23 Dec. 4 Our younger brothers and sons will have little respect for their own circumcision schools as they will know in advance what to expect. African men keep what happens at the school strictly secret. **1993** S. DIKENI in *House & Leisure* Nov. 42 We used to walk home from circumcision school in the secret of the night.

Ciskeian /sɪs'kaɪən/ *adj.* and *n.* [*Ciskei* (fr. L. *cis* on this side + *Kei* name of river) + Eng. n.- and adj.-forming suffix *-an*.]

A. *adj.* Of or pertaining to that region of the Eastern Cape occupied predominantly by Xhosa-speaking people and situated to the south-west of the Kei River; *hist.*, of or pertaining to the Republic of Ciskei (1981–1994).

1848 H.G. SMITH in *Imp. Blue Bks* Command Paper 969-1848, 24 I this day reached King William's Town, and having previously directed an assembly of all the Cis-Keian Chiefs, their 'Amapakati,' or councellors, and many of their people, I .. read and fully explained to them my proclamation of the the 17th instant. **1928** R.L. BUELL *Native Problem in Afr.* V. 76 Report of Commission of Inquiry (Ciskeian Section) into the social and Economic conditions of the Native Peoples. *c*1939 *Off. Yrbk of Union 1938* (Union Office of Census & Statistics) 19 The Ciskeian General Council was established under Proclamation no 34 of 1934, with effect from 1st April, 1934. **1953** E.P. DVORIN *Racial Separation* V. 133 The Nationalist Government in the implementation of apartheid is looking to the Ciskeian and Transkeian councils as examples which might well be followed in the other Native areas of the Union. **1978** *Daily Dispatch* 10 Mar. (Indaba), (*advt*) A senior position for a Professional Control Training Officer (Ciskeian citizen). **1987** *Flying Springbok* Nov. 47 Many Ciskeian schools include university graduates in their faculties.

B. *n.* An inhabitant of the Ciskeian region; *hist.*, a citizen of the Republic of Ciskei (1981–1994).

1976 S. ZONDANI in *E. Prov. Herald* 24 Nov. 13 If you want me to be happy, call me an African, not a Ciskeian. I believe in one unfragmented South Africa. **1978** D. MICKLEBURGH in *Bona* Oct. 81 All he wants is for every Ciskeian to pull his weight and put his shoulder to the wheel. **1980** C. FREIMOND in *Rand Daily Mail* 18 Dec. 1 In the first referendum of its type, Ciskeians have voted overwhelmingly in favour of independence from South Africa. **1983** J. PARFITT in *E. Prov. Herald* 14 May 1 The original charge sheets made no mention of the accused being Xhosa or Ciskeian. **1987** *New Nation* 23 Apr. 5 'As patriots, we should give generously,' he said. 'It is essential for Ciskeians to sacrifice in order to promote national interests.' **1990** *E. Prov. Herald* 19 Jan. 3 He said Ciskeians had voted for independence in a referendum and would go into negotiations over the constitutional future of southern Africa as a nation. **1992** S. BRYANT in *Guardian Weekly* 2 Oct. 2 Would the Ciskeians, having democratically elected to end their rule by dictatorship, be willing to return to non-voting status as non-white citizens of South Africa?

ciss var. SIS *int.*

cis toch var. SIESTOG.

citistate var. CITY STATE.

Citizen Force *n. phr.*

1. *hist.* A division of the Union Defence Forces, comprised of trained, demobilized soldiers who were liable to be called upon during times of war. Also *attrib.* See also ACTIVE CITIZEN FORCE sense 1.

1912 *Act 13* in *Stat. of Union* 198 The Citizen Force shall consist of all persons liable to render personal service in time of war, who are not members of the Permanent Force. **1936** H.F. TREW *Botha Treks* 15 On his right flank, General Maritz was commanding a column of Citizen Force which was to support him in his invasion of German territory. **1942** *Off. Yr Bk of Union 1941* (Union Office of Census & Statistics) 394 The Citizen Force .. comprises three divisions, viz., the Active Citizen Force, the Citizen Force Reserve, and the National Reserve.

2. The reserve force of the South African Defence Force, comprised of civilians who, having completed a period of national service, have to serve additional short periods annually for several years. Also *attrib.* See also ACTIVE CITIZEN FORCE sense 2.

1957 R.B. DURRANT in *Hansard* 27 Feb. 1834 The Citizen Force soldier is trained as a full-time soldier to play a full-time part in the event of immediate mobilization. **1957** *Act 44* in *Stat. of Union* 530 *Composition and Organization of the South African Defence Force and Reserve* The South African Defence Force shall consist of: (a) The Permanent Force; (b) The Citizen Force; and (c) Commandos. **1963** *Rand Daily Mail* 3 May 2 Members of both the Permanent Force and the Citizen Force were trained as military police. **1963** M. BENSON *Afr. Patriots* 287 In May 1961 Mandela called the three-day strike. Whereupon the Government called out the police, army, commandos, citizen forces and Saracen armoured cars. **1971** *Std Encycl. of Sn Afr.* III. 614 As far as legislation is concerned, the Defence Act of 1957 .. warrants special mention ... Among the changes of note are .. the clear definition of the functions of the Permanent Force (formerly the South African Permanent Force), the Citizen Force (formerly the Active Citizen Force) and the Commandos. **1977** B. MARKS *Our S. Afr. Army* 13 South African Army members, Permanent Force, Citizen Force, Commando Force and National Servicemen. **1981** *Cape Times* 2 Dec. 1 One of his colleagues was a Citizen Force sergeant with a healthy distrust of things that go bang. **1983** J. KEEGAN *World Armies* 530 Citizen Force units are fed by national servicemen but in recent years have been under strength ... Since the South African army has few permanent operational units except those under training as national servicemen, the Citizen Force is the mainstay of the conventional forces. **1987** *Uniform* 7 Apr. 1 The closing date for applications from young ladies wishing to do a year's voluntary Citizen Force military training in 1988, at the South African Women's College in George, is 31 May 1987. **1990** [see ACTIVE CITIZEN FORCE sense 1].

City of Gold *n. phr.* Also with small initials. GOLDEN CITY.

1924 L. COHEN *Reminisc. of Jhb.* 31 The City of Gold — more or less — does not pride itself on his matured glories. **1937** H. KLEIN *Stage Coach Dust* p.xi, Present-day Johannesburg, the great City of Gold. **1940** F.B. YOUNG (*title*) City of Gold. **1950** H. GIBBS *Twilight* 167 They and a few who have joined them seek a new locality close by and lay it out as a new township .. to house only a few prospecting families: the founders and site of Johannesburg, city of gold. **1959** L. LONGMORE *Dispossessed* 200 Johannesburg's half million Africans, upon whose cheap labour her economy rests, call her Igoli — City of Gold. **1964** [see EGOLI]. **1987** E. KEYLER in *S. Afr. Panorama* Oct. 26 Johannesburg, well-known as South Africa's city of gold, is built on one of the richest gold reefs in the world. **1990** C. SHERLOCK *Hyena Dawn* 92 Egoli, the city of gold. I went there when I was young .. to seek my fortune in the gold mines. **1991** M. MTHETHWA in *Pace* Feb. 52 'I packed my belongings and headed for the city of gold,' recalls Elizabeth. Liza left her home in 1982 to seek fame in Johannesburg.

City of Saints *n. phr.* Also **City of the Saints**. [See quots c1970 and 1978.] A name given to Grahamstown, a town in the Eastern Cape. See also SAINT.

1871 'A LADY' in *Cape Monthly Mag.* III. Aug. 88, I hope we may find more catholicity of sentiment prevailing than what I have been led to expect in this so-called 'City of the Saints'. **1896** 'S. CUMBERLAND' *What I Think of S. Afr.* 196 Grahamstown .. is called the City of Saints, and I am inclined to believe that the exceedingly pious folk thereof think the description not at all inaccurate. **1913** C. PETTMAN *Africanderisms* 121 City of the Saints, A nickname given in early days to Grahamstown. **1947** [see Settlers' City (SETTLER sense 2 b)]. **1955** A. DELIUS *Young Trav.* 127 'The old City of Saints!' said Mr Johnson affectionately. 'They've got as many churches here as they've got schools, and that's a fair number.' c**1970** *Grahamstown, Cape Province* (Grahamstown Publicity Assoc.) 20 The City Of Saints. The most popular version of how Grahamstown earned this nickname has it that, during the early Frontier days, an outlying fort sent to town to fetch a vice. After calling at the various trading stores, the trooper returned to his outpost and reported, 'There is no vice in Grahamstown.' **1978** *Reader's Digest Illust. Guide to Sn Afr.* 144 The city of Grahamstown has been given many picturesque names: the 'City of Saints' because there are more than 40 places of worship here. **1991** F.G. BUTLER *Local Habitation* 124 What weather in the world can beat the autumnal glow of much of May and early June in the City of the Saints?

city state *n. phr. Hist.* Also **citistate**. [Special sense of general Eng. *city-state* a state consisting of an autonomous city.] Any of several autonomous black cities, proposed as part of the apartheid policy, to be created near major white metropolitan areas but linked politically to ethnic 'homelands'. See also HOMELAND sense 1.

1978 [see GREY]. **1979** *Survey of Race Rel. 1978* (S.A.I.R.R.) 320 Each 'city state' would cater for an ethnic group related to the group occupying the adjacent homeland. The new cities would be incorporated as far as possible into the homelands by the moving of boundaries. Where cities fell outside homelands they would nevertheless be regarded as part of the land area of the contiguous homeland and the population would exercise rights within the homeland. **1986** *Sowetan* 13 Aug. 1 Black leaders would have to emerge from self-governing and autonomous black citistates just as they had done in the self-governing states, Mr Botha said. **1987** P. VAN NIEKERK in *New Statesman* (U.K.) 20 Feb. 14 A rambling and largely incoherent speech in which Botha once again resurrected the discredited concept of 'city states' as his way of accommodating black political rights. **1987** *E. Prov. Herald* 18 May 2 President P W Botha's proposed 'city states' for blacks were rejected by the Kwazulu Chief Minister, Chief Mangosuthu Buthelezi, as a move by the Government to make blacks sell their birthright and forgo their rightful place in South Africa .. by agreeing to seek political rights in a city state in which they were allowed to run their own affairs.

civic *n. colloq.* [Short for *civic association*.] An elected, community-based body concerned with local government in a black township. Also *attrib*. See also STREET COMMITTEE.

Civics were first instituted under the aegis of the Soweto COMMITTEE OF TEN, and were intended to replace the government-instituted, and usually discredited, community councils (see COMMUNITY COUNCIL).

[**1985** *Weekly Mail* 9 Aug. 4 Organisations whose members have been held: Civic Associations (Port Elizabeth CA, Soweto CA, Graaff Reinet CA, East Rand Peoples Organisation).] **1990** M. KENTRIDGE *Unofficial War* 7 Youth organisations, township civics, educational, student, women's, cultural and sporting organisations and associations are all represented within the structures of the UDF. **1990** P. GOODENOUGH in *New African* 18 June 2 'The Civic Organisation has successfully forced the House of Representatives to unconditionally recommend and accept the candidatures,' said civic chairperson Abie October. **1990** S. FRIEDMAN in *Weekly Mail* 27 July 6 The 'civic' movement emerged during the 1980s: its job was to mobilise people around their immediate problems — housing, rents, living conditions and services. In many ares, 'civics' played a major role in pressuring township councils. **1991** *Spotlight* (S.A.I.R.R.) Mar. 6 It is not correct to regard every civic as a proxy ... The ANC does not control the civics. **1991** J. COLLINGE in *Daily News* 17 Dec. 21 The Metro Chamber experience .. has drawn the Soweto Civic Association and other civics from around Johannesburg into close bargaining with four white municipalities, three black town councils and the Transvaal Provincial Administration. **1992** D. NINA in *Focus on Afr.* Apr.-June 34 Mama Irene finally started to look more relaxed. One of the civic comrades had helped her in dealing with her yard neighbours. **1992** *Weekly Mail* 5 June 23 Now civics have entered into the process of negotiating with state institutions for the future. Once a legitimate local government is in place, the civic will no longer need to claim to represent everybody. Instead of two functions, it will have one: to represent the interests, demands and policies of its constituency. Civics are concerned with urban development issues, and in the future will continue to be ... Coovadia sees civics in a post-apartheid South Africa as filling two roles. First, they should be 'independent, non-party political, mass-based structures' able to intercede in local government on behalf of constituents ... At the same time, he views civics as pressure groups — 'to ensure that local government is accountable'. **1993** D. SANDI in *Grocott's Mail* 25 June 7 Civics should be grassroot residents and voters organisations. **1993** B. NZIMANDE in *Sash Newsletter* (Black Sash) 29 June 2 People tend to say civics will act as watchdogs on the state, but I believe they are more than that. The better approach is the original conceptualisation of a civic: organs of people's power. **1993** S. COLLINS in *Democracy in Action* 31 Aug. 27 At the request of the community, who

civilized labour *n. phr. Obs. exc. hist. Offensive.*
1. Labour perceived to conform to Western (or white) standards; white labour. Cf. UNCIVILIZED LABOUR.

1924 *Prime Minister's Circular No.5* in E. Hellmann *Handbk on Race Rel.* (1949) 152 Civilized labour .. [is] the labour rendered by persons whose standard of living conforms to the standard generally recognized as tolerable from the usual European standpoint. **1924** L.D. GILSON in *Hansard* 31 July 118 The Minister in defining 'civilized labour' in this country, said he regarded as civilized labour those white and coloured workers who lived on the higher standards ... That is going to create a very bad impression on the natives of this country ... I do hope that .. if he is going to include the coloured worker, he will say civilized labour is the labour of any man who lives on a higher plane and not of the coloured man only. **1943** 'J. BURGER' *Black Man's Burden* 29 When South Africans speak about the 'Labour Movement' they refer to European, or as it is sometimes delightfully called, 'civilized' labour. *c*1949 *Survey of Race Rel. 1948–9* (S.A.I.R.R.) 32 In all Government Departments, except Native Affairs and the Railways and Harbours, 'civilized' labour is to be substituted for that which might be regarded as 'uncivilized'.

2. In the phr. *civilized labour policy*, the official labour policy introduced in 1924 which protected the white (and 'coloured') workers by excluding black workers from many jobs. See also JOB RESERVATION.

1936 *Cambridge Hist. of Brit. Empire* VIII. 805 Government authorities responded to public insistence that government enterprises such as the railways should adopt a 'civilised labour' policy which implies the payment of higher wages to Europeans than their coloured and native competitors would have been glad to accept for the work. **1943** 'J. BURGER' *Black Man's Burden* 38 The first Nationalist Government .. inaugurated the 'civilized labour' policy of subsidising European unskilled labour. *c*1949 *Survey of Race Rel. 1948–9* 12 In May 1949, a circular was issued by the Prime Minister's Department, re-affirming the 'civilized labour' policy of 1924. **1969** A. HEPPLE *S. Afr.: Workers under Apartheid* 45 The so-called 'civilised labour' policy .. was first applied .. when the Nationalist-Labour government of the day instructed state departments and provincial authorities to employ 'civilised' labour insted of 'uncivilised' labour, i.e. to employ white and not Africans in unskilled jobs. **1986** P. MAYLAM *Hist. of Afr. People* 159 Mission-trained craftsmen, small-scale producers and property-holders .. were becoming increasingly proletarianised as a result of the Pact government's civilised labour policy and its assault on the position of the African middle class. **1989** *Reader's Digest Illust. Hist.* 333 The state tried to protect white workers by introducing what it termed a 'civilized labour' policy — in other words, a system that guaranteed work for whites at the expense of blacks.

clack *n. Obs. exc. hist.* [Eng.; echoic, perh. a back-formation fr. CLACKING.] CLICK. Also *attrib.*

1786 G. FORSTER tr. *A. Sparrman's Voy. to Cape of G.H.* I. 227 What cannot but render this language still more difficult for strangers, is, that these clacks are said to be performed, according to different circumstances, in three different ways, viz. more or less forward or backward on the palate. **1800** W. SOMERVILLE *Narr. of E. Cape Frontier* (1979) 28 In their language, both have the peculiar clack of the tongue in uttering their words, but it much more frequently occurs in the Bosjesmans than in the Hottentots language. **1989** [see KHOI sense 2].

clacking *vbl n. Obs.* [Special sense of general Eng. *clacking* 'the making of a sharp, hard noise; chatter of tongues' (*OED*).] The action of producing a speech sound known as a CLICK; CLAPPING; *clocking*, see CLOCK.

1601 J. LANCASTER in R. Raven-Hart *Before Van Riebeeck* (1967) 24 Their language is very hard to be pronounced, by reason of a kinde of clacking with the tongue; so that we could not learne one worde of their language. **1795** C.R. HOPSON tr. *C.P. Thunberg's Trav.* II. 72 The Hottentot language is not every where the same, but has very different dialects; all of them, however, are pronounced with a kind of smack, or clacking of the organs of speech ... These clackings are the more difficult to perform, as they must be made at the very instant of uttering the word, and not before nor after. [**1841** B. SHAW *Memorials* 19 Almost all their monosyllables, and the leading syllables in compound words are thrown out of the mouth with a sudden retraction of the tongue from the teeth or palate, and sound not unlike the clacking of a hen with her chickens.]

Clanwilliam cedar *n. phr.* [Named for the town of *Clanwilliam*, in the Western Cape; see quot. 1971.] The indigenous evergreen tree *Widdringtonia cedarbergensis* of the Cupressaceae, much prized for its timber; *Cape cedar*, see CAPE sense 2 a.

[**1868** W.H. HARVEY *Genera of S. Afr. Plants* 353 *Widdringtonia*, Endl., .. South African trees, the 'Cedars' of the Cedarberg Mountains.] **1894** R. MARLOTH in *Trans. of S. Afr. Phil. Soc.* p.lxxxvi, The Clanwilliam cedar (*Callitris arborea*). **1905** D.E. HUTCHINS in Flint & Gilchrist *Science in S. Afr.* 392 The Clanwilliam Cedar is an exception to the difficult propagation, the slow growth, and delicate constitution of the indigenous trees generally. Unfortunately, that tree will not thrive away from its home in the rugged Cedarberg country — an area of 150 to 200 square miles. **1917** R. MARLOTH *Common Names* 18 Cedar, Clanwilliam, .. *Widdringtonia juniperoides* ... Growing on the Cedar mountains at and above the 3000 feet level. *c*1936 S. & E. Afr. Yr Bk & Guide 320 In the Cedarberg mountains, north of Capetown, a distinct type of forest occurs, that of the Clanwilliam Cedar (*Widdringtonia juniperoides*). **1957** L.G. GREEN *Beyond City Lights* 186 Clanwilliam cedars are pyramidal conifers, growing like Christmas trees at first, then branching out. **1961** PALMER & PITMAN *Trees of S. Afr.* 127 The Clanwilliam cedar is one of our most valuable timber trees. **1971** J.A. MARSH in *Std Encycl. of Sn Afr.* III. 134 Cedar, Clanwilliam, .. This coniferous tree is a member of the family Cupressaceae. The last remnants of this nearly extinct species are found on rocky outcrops at altitudes above 3,000 ft .. in the Cedarberg Range in the Clanwilliam district of the South-Western Cape. **1990** *Afr. Wildlife* Vol.44 No.5, 278 Like the true cedars .. the Clanwilliam cedar also produces a beautiful, aromatic timber which is easily worked and takes a fine polish.

clap *n.*[1] var. KLAP *n.*[1]

clap *n.*[2] var. KLAP *n.*[2]

clap *n.*[3] *obs.* [Special senses of general Eng.; echoic.]

1. [Perh. a back-formation fr. CLAPPING.] CLICK.

1822 W.J. BURCHELL *Trav.* I. 192 The Hottentots call this shrub 'Num'num (or Noomnoom, agreeably to English orthography), each syllable preceded by a guttural clap of the tongue. **1824** *Ibid.* II. 251 This dialect .. has a greater affinity to that of the Hottentots proper, than of the Bushmen; and though requiring a more frequent use of the different claps of the tongue than the former, yet it does not employ them so often as the latter. **1835** A. SMITH *Diary* (1940) II. 187 They spoke a language which consisted almost entirely of claps and quite unintelligible to them.

2.a. The crack of a whip.

1822 [see LOOP sense 1 a]. **1939** S. CLOETE *Watch for Dawn* 33 Clap and echo sounded into the mountains; birds rose from the trees; and the peace of the valley was broken.

b. With qualifying word: **back-clap**, the crack of a whip behind one's head.

*c*1963 B.C. TAIT *Durban Story* 2 The fellow who could in one and the same swing, reverse the whip and achieve a back-clap, was the show-off of the street.

clap *v.*[1] var. KLAP *v.*

clap /klæp/ *v.*[2] *obsolescent.* [Eng., influenced by Du. *klappen* to make an explosive sound.]
1. *trans.* To crack (a whip).

1822 W.J. BURCHELL *Trav.* I. 421 As the guide assured us that Speelman could not be beyond hearing, we clapped the whip with all our might, in hopes of calling him to our assistance. **1887** S.W. Silver & Co.'s *Handbk to S. Afr.* 227 As the drivers 'clap' their long whips, and the teams, eight pairs of oxen labouring at each wain, move briskly over the way, all eyes are upon them. **1958** S. CLOETE *Mask* 25 One who must have spent much time in the country to be able to clap a great sixteen-foot driving whip the way he did.

2. *intrans.* Of a whip: to make a sharp cracking sound.

*a*1858 J. GOLDSWAIN *Chron.* (1949) II. 114, I soon heard a wip clap and knew that thear was wagons coming. **1939** S. CLOETE *Watch for Dawn* 33 The drivers .. ran beside their spans, their long whipsticks bent like bows under the weight of the clapping thongs.

clapper *n.*[1] var. KLAPPER *n.*[1]

clapper *n.*[2] var. KLAPPER *n.*[2]

clapping *vbl n. Obs.* [Special sense of general Eng. *clapping* 'striking, noise as of striking' (*OED*).] CLACKING.

1790 tr. *Le Vaillant's Trav.* II. 236 The Hottentots name this antelope *nou*, preceded by that .. clapping which I have already mentioned. It was probably this clapping which induced Colonel Gordon to add a *g* to the proper name, which renders the pronunciation of it almost the same. **1841** B. SHAW *Memorials* 23 The Namacqua *language*, though in some respects different, is evidently of the same origin with the Hottentot; and abounds with the peculiar clapping of the tongue.

classification *n.* [Special sense of general Eng.] Usu. in the phr. *race classification*: the official registration of a person as a member of a particular racial group, as defined by the POPULATION REGISTRATION ACT of 1950. Also *attrib.* See also *re-classification* (RE-CLASSIFY).

1950 *Act 30* in *Stat. of Union* 279 If at any time it appears to the Director that the classification of a person in terms of sub-section (1) is incorrect, he may .. alter the classification of that person in the register. **1956** M. ROGERS *Black Sash* 5 Still more startling was the Race Classification programme where African, Indian and Coloured families were torn asunder and separated on racial grounds. **1956** A. SAMPSON *Drum* 209 To the Nationalist Government, this merging of the races was a nightmare ... They have embarked on a great scheme of classification, and subjected people to every kind of humiliation to discover their race. **1961** *Off. Yrbk of Union 1960* (Bureau of Census & Statistics) 580 A further development is the establishment of Regional Offices under the control of Representatives of the Population Registrar at Johannesburg, Cape Town, Port Elizabeth and Durban, whose functions will be the local investigation and classification of doubtful racial cases, and the issue of identity cards. **1963** A.M. LOUW *20 Days* 122 The rest of the people, awaiting classification, occupied self-built shanties on plots let to them at a minimum monthly charge. **1971** *Rand Daily Mail* 29 Jan., There are seven race classification categories used on personal identity cards relating to South Africans who are not Asian, Chinese, Bantu or White. These are 'Cape Malay', 'Griqua', 'Baster', 'Cape Coloured', 'Coloured', 'other Coloured', and 'Mixed'. **1977** J. SIKAKANE *Window on Soweto* 22 Those whose fair complexion and straight hair made them look 'white', but suspected otherwise by the race classification board, had blood tests taken and were examined for mongolian blue spots. **1988** *Staffrider* Vol.7 No.1, 87 The grimness of the narrative involving the destruction of Sophiatown, the insult of racial classification and a descent into the horrors of gang warfare. **1991** A. MAIMANE in *Weekly Mail* 15 Feb. 17 That other apartheid device, race classification, will bite the dust this parliamentary session as De Klerk continues his reforms.

classify *v. trans.* [Special sense of general Eng.] To assign (someone, or, less frequently, something) to a racial group, as defined by apartheid legislation. Usu. *passive*. See also RE-CLASSIFY.

1950 *Act 30* in *Stat. of Union* 279 Every person whose name is included in the register shall be classified by the Director as a white person, a coloured person or a native, as the case may be, and every coloured person and every native whose name is so included shall be classified by the Director according to the ethnic or other group to which he belongs. **1966** *Survey of Race Rel. 1965* (S.A.I.R.R.) 112 The two youngest children attended a school that was at one time 'mixed': they chose to stay on there when the school was later classified 'Coloured'. **1967** *Govt Gaz. Extraordinary* Vol.24 No.1753, 1 Definition Of Coloured Groups In Terms Of Section *Five* Of The Population Registration Act, 1950 ... With effect from the seventh day of July, 1950, the following groups shall be the groups into which coloured persons shall be classified. **1970** *E. Prov. Herald* 4 Sept., No one is just a person in South Africa. Every living soul — or dead one, for that matter — is officially classified by race. **1973** P. LAURENCE in *Star* 16 June 5 The Coloured man whose daughter was classified as an African and who had to employ her as a servant to legalise her presence in his home is a recent victim. **1978** *Drum* June 79, I would like to know what the offspring of a coloured guy and a black girl would be classified as. I know that a child resulting from a white guy and a black girl would be coloured. **1988** *Daily Dispatch* 23 Feb. 17 Where a father was classified black — this included Indian, coloured or African — the child was also classified black. However, when the father was white and the mother was not, then the child took the same racial classification as the mother. **1990** *City Press* 4 Mar. 12 The government decreed that everyone had to be racially classified and that it was a crime for people of different races to live in the same suburb, marry or have sexual contact.

clawsickness *n. Pathology. rare.* [tr. S. Afr. Du. *klauwziekte*.] KLAUWZIEKTE.

1973 O.H. SPOHR tr. *F. Krauss's Trav. Jrnl* 28 The clawsickness of cattle could be foot-and-mouth disease.

clear *v. intrans. Army slang.* In the phr. ***to clear out*** [tr. Afk. *uitklaar, klaar uit* see KLAAR *v.* sense 1], *to klaar out* (see KLAAR *v.* sense 1). Hence **clearing out** *vbl n. phr., klaaring out* (see KLAAR *v.* sense 1); also *attrib.*

1980 *Sunday Times* 12 Oct. 9 The attitude of the defence force now was to encourage and motivate national servicemen to study from the time they received their call-up papers to the time they clear out. **1988** *E. Prov. Herald* 27 May 3 SADF: Clearing out dates to be spread ... National servicemen would be advised individually by their units when they would clear out in order to enable them to make the necessary arrangements with their parents.

cleavage *n. Diamond-trade.* [Special sense of general Eng. *cleavage* tendency of crystals to split along definite planes.] Small broken diamonds of more than one carat in weight. See also MELEE, STONE.

1913 J.B. MANNIX *Mines & their Story* 149 Rough diamonds direct from the mines are, for gem-cutting purposes, divided into two classes, 'close' and 'cleavage' ... 'Cleavages' are crystals of a shape unsuitable for cutting as they stand. They are split before passing into the cutter's hands. **1969** J.M. WHITE *Land God Made in Anger* 279 There are also special terms for diamonds classified by weight, 142 carats being reckoned to the ounce. Small diamonds of less than a carat are known as 'melée', while broken stones are described as 'chips' if of melée size, and 'cleavages' if larger. **1971** *Std Encycl. of Sn Afr.* IV. 19 There are six major cutting centres in the world: .. Each centre has gradually, over the years, come to specialise in cutting diamonds of a particular quality. Cleavages and chips are, in the main, worked in Antwerp: stones and shapes in U.S.A.; melee in Amsterdam, Israel and Western Germany.

cleugh var. KLOOF.

clever /ˈklevə/ *n. slang.* Also **cleva(h)**, **uclever** /ʊˈklevə/. Pl. **-s**, or (occas.) **ooclever** /ʊːˈklevə/. [ad. Isicamtho *uclever*, Sintu-language (Bantu-language) n. prefix *u-* + Eng. *clever*.] In urban (esp. township) English: a 'city slicker'; a young street-wise male. Cf. TSOTSI sense 1.

1963 WILSON & MAFEJE *Langa* 22 The *townees* or *tsotsis* are also called *'location boys', ooclever, bright boys* and *spoilers*. *Ibid.* 35 The Xhosa are spoken of as 'a very hard people', 'ooclever', precocious. **1978** [see HA-JA sense b]. **1979** F. DIKE *First S. African* 4 That's a small time clever. He thinks he's going to jive me. **1979** S. SILLIE *Informant* This clever man (uclever) — is a person who is town-rooted — he can either be a tsotsi himself or may not be. He knows the liquor outlets and the dagga smugglers. **1982** M.O. MTSHALI in Chapman & Dangor *Voices from Within* 75 He's a 'clever' not a 'moegie'; he never says baas to no bloody white man. **1983** *Drum* June 38 Today Masekela cuts an image of the 'clevers of the 50s and 60s'. His manner of talking, walking and dancing is that of those hectic-dizzy yester-years. **1984** M. MTHETHWA in *Frontline* July 29 Dumani belongs to the township clevers — the Pantsulas and their girlfriends, the Mshozas. **1988** J. KHUMALO in *Pace* Oct. 60 Places like Sophiatown and Alex .. were famous for the city slickers — known as 'clevers' and carbon copies of their American movie heroes. **1990** J. NAIDOO *Coolie Location* 130 From his speech, tone and general manner it was evident that he was one of those smooth-talking smart ones, a *cleva*, a sophisticated *tsotsi*. I detected a mocking wily glint in his eyes.

click *n.* Also (rarely) **klick**. [Special sense of general Eng. *click* 'a slight, sharp, hard, non-ringing sound of concussion' (*OED*).] Any of a group of speech sounds of the Khoisan languages (and some of the Nguni languages, particularly Xhosa) formed on an ingressive air stream and caused by the sudden withdrawal of the tongue from the part of the mouth with which it is in contact; CLACK; CLAP *n.*[3] sense 1; CLUCK. Also *attrib.* See also CLACKING, CLOCK.

1829 C. ROSE *Four Yrs in Sn Afr.* 164 After repeated attempts, we failed in giving the true pronunciation to their names; which was, in truth, no easy thing, many of their words commencing with a click, a kind of sound in the throat, that mingles with the syllable. **1836** A.F. GARDINER *Journey to Zoolu Country* 102 In the Zoolu, the clicks are far less frequent ... It is considered by those competent to judge, as at least a purer language than the Kafir, if not that from which it was originally derived. **1838** J.E. ALEXANDER *Exped. into Int.* I. 193 The Great Namaquas use the very same clicking dialects as the Little Namaquas do. Almost every word has an initial click, or has one in the middle of it, and some words have two clicks. The clicks are of three kinds. **1846** R. MOFFAT *Missionary Labours* 2 Their language .. has, in addition to the klick of the Hottentot, a croaking in the throat. **1853** F.P. FLEMING *Kaffraria* 94 Speaking of their language .. it is soft and melodious in its sound, which is only marred by what are called *'the Clicks.'* These are peculiar sounds given to the pronunciation of the three letters, c, q, and x, whenever they occur. **1862** LADY DUFF-GORDON *Lett. from Cape* (1925) 103 They had just printed their first book in the Kafir language .. a beautiful language, like Spanish in tone, but with a queer 'click' in it. **1871** J. MACKENZIE *Ten Yrs* (1971) 492 What Europeans know as 'clicks', are to be found in all the languages of the Hottentot family. Three-fourths of the syllabic elements of the Hottentot language are said to begin with clicks. **1889** F. GALTON *Trav. in S. Afr.* 11 The 'Nara, with long runners, covered numerous sand hillocks. [*Note*] The comma before N means that the letter is preceded by a Hottentot click. **1906** J. STEWART *Outlines of Kaffir Grammar* 1 Three letters known in Kaffir as *Clicks* are *c, q*, and *x*; while *r* is a guttural. **1914** L.H. BRINKMAN *Breath of Karroo* 153 He knew several Bushman caves in the surrounding hills, and could speak their language, with its peculiar clicks, fluently. **1937** H. SAUER *Ex Afr.* 4 The language spoken by these little yellow men consisted of a series of 'clicks' in different intonations, quite impossible to imitate and still more impossible to reduce to writing. **1948** O. WALKER *Kaffirs Are Lively* 113 How explosive sounded the Xhosa clicks as I stood for the opening of Bunga. **1968** *New Scientist* 29 Feb. 456 The click-speaking Bushmen and Hottentots. **1971** *S. Afr. Panorama* Dec. 1 The complicated click-studded language of South Africa's oldest and longest surviving primeval inhabitants, the Bushmen. **1981** J.B. PEIRES *House of Phalo* 24 One sixth of all Xhosa words contain clicks. Very few of these have Zulu cognates, which suggests that most of the linguistic changes took place after the Nguni settlement of the coastal region. **1990** *New African* 18 June 12 Makeba won the hearts of Americans through her dance tune 'Pata Pata' ... Her version of the 'click song' also became an international hit. **1992** V. MAYEKISO in *Focus on Afr.* Apr.-June 51 The Xhosa language has almost 2500 words that have clicks, a sixth of the language; the Zulu language, whose nation abuts the land of the Xhosas, has 400 words that use clicks. The Sothos also have clicks whose frequency diminishes in direct proportion to the increase in distance.

clicking *ppl adj. Obs.* [fr. *click*, a v. as yet undocumented, deriving fr. the n. (see CLICK).] **a.** Of a person: speaking with clicks (see prec.). **b.** Of a language or set of sounds: including clicks.

1838 [see CLICK]. **1853** F. GALTON *Narr. of Explorer in Tropical S. Afr.* 42 When I say Oerlam, Hottentot or Bushman, the identically same yellow, flat-nosed, woolly-haired, clicking individual must be conjured up. **1871** W.G. ATHERSTONE in A.M.L. Robinson *Sel. Articles from Cape Monthly Mag.* (1978) 161 What is this peculiar noise — these low chattering, clicking sounds that are gradually approaching us? .. The truth flashes across our wondering brain — a troop of Korannas speaking their own wild language.

clipfish var. KLIPFISH.

clipper *n. slang.* Pl. unchanged. [Etym. dubious: see quot. 1994, or perh. an Englished form of Afk. *klippe* diamonds, a theory reinforced by the unmarked pl. form.] One hundred rand; KLIP *n.* sense 5.

1991 C. VAN ULMENSTEIN in *Weekend Argus* 12 Jan. (Suppl.) 5 As South Africa moves towards a 'new' South Africa, so too its language is evolving ... Denominations of money also have their own names: R100 is known as a clipper. **1991** *Informant, Bellville* Our registration fee was raised from R75 to a clipper (R100). **1992** A. BRIDGE et al. *Informant, Soweto* Clipper: R100. Three clipper: R300. **1993** *Weekly Mail & Guardian* 23 Dec. 11 The following is a guide to street words of 1993: .. *Clipper*: R100. **1994** *Sunday Times* 1 May 15 A *clipper* is R100 of R10 notes — because you needed a paper clip to keep it together.

clock *v. intrans. Obs.* Also **clocke**. [Scottish and northern dialectal *clock* to cluck.] To produce a CLICK, a speech sound found in the Khoisan and some of the Nguni languages. So **clocking** *vbl n.*, CLACKING.

1598 J. DAVYS in R. Raven-Hart *Before Van Riebeeck* (1967) 20 Their words are for the most part in-articulate, and, in speaking, they clocke with the Tongue like a brood Hen, which clocking and the words are both pronounced together, verie strangely. **1601** J. LANCASTER in *Ibid.* 23 Their speech is wholly uttered through the throate, and they clocke with their tongues in such sort, that in seven weeks which wee remained heere in this place, the sharpest wit among us could not learne one word of their language.

clo(e)f, cloff(e) varr. KLOOF.

clomp var. CLUMP.

clompie, clompje varr. KLOMPIE.

cloof var. KLOOF.

closed ppl adj. Hist. rare. [Special sense of general Eng. *closed* confined to a few people; limited by certain conditions.] Of (educational) institutions, public facilities, and residential areas, under apartheid legislation: reserved for white people only. Cf. OPEN adj.

1957 *Open Universities in S. Afr.* (Council of Universities of Cape Town & Witwatersrand) 3 These four universities do not admit any non-whites. They are segregated universities for white students, and may be called 'closed' universities. 1989 M. AMBLER in *Sunday Times* 8 Oct. 7 Durban used to be up front in desegregation and now we are sitting with closed beaches while every city is moving ahead. 1989 *Sunday Times* 8 Oct. 7 Discriminatory signs on 'closed' beaches .. had been erected in terms of existing legislation.

closer settlement n. phr.
1. hist. A government-assisted scheme whereby farmers (often immigrants) were settled on irrigated farms of relatively small size, which were concentrated in a particular area and held either by freehold or on long lease; a group of such farms. Also attrib.

1908 J.W. JAGGER in *Cape of G.H. Parl. Debates* 423 A judicious and well-considered scheme of closer settlement .. would materially tend to promote the best interests of the agricultural industry of the Colony. c1936 *S. & E. Afr. Yr Bk & Guide* 577 The Kendrew Directed Closer Settlement, now in course of development .. presents a pleasant prospect of orchards and green fields, some 7,000 acres are under fruit and lucerne. 1984 A.J. CHRISTOPHER *Crown Laws of British S. Afr.* 115 In the final phase of Natal's separate land policy, the Government embarked upon a land purchasing spree in which some 121,990 acres were purchased between 1908 and 1912 for nine closer settlement schemes.

2. See quot. 1985.

1967 in C. Desmond *Discarded People* (c1970) 228 The people belonging to a specific Church will be removed as a Community. Released Area 53 (Bantu Homelands) has been divided into five Chief's Wards. In every ward a small township or as it is being called a 'closer settlement' with rudimentary services will be laid out. c1970 C. DESMOND *Discarded People* 128 The facilities, or lack of them, are those of a closer settlement: no houses provided, no sanitation, no running water, no clinic. But the people [of Dientje] have cattle, which is not a feature of either a township or a closer settlement. 1985 PLATZKY & WALKER *Surplus People* p.xii, Closer settlement, The official term used to describe a type of settlement established for African people on reserve or Trust land that is for residential purposes only — no agricultural land is attached — and far more rudimentary in the type of facilities it has than a township. People who are removed off black spots and white farms are generally relocated to these settlements. They are provided with temporary accommodation and are expected to build their own permanent houses. Facilities vary but generally (not always) include pit latrines and one or more communal water supply points.

clough var. KLOOF.

cluck n. obs. [Special sense of general Eng.] CLICK. Also attrib.

1828 J. PHILIP *Researches* I. 15 Words of more than one syllable are accompanied or divided and rendered special and emphatic in their application by two clucks. 1840 T. PRINGLE *Narr. of Res.* 93 The dialect now spoken by the frontier Caffers partakes to a certain extent of the Hottentot *cluck*, a peculiarity not to be found among the tribes farther back.

clufe, cluff, clugh varr. KLOOF.

clump n. rare. Also **clomp**. [Calque formed on Afk. *klomp* 'lump', 'crowd', 'lot', 'bunch', 'heap'.]

In general Eng. usage, the common Eng. senses of *clump* 'a cluster of trees', 'a compact mass or patch of any growing plant' (*OED*), in use since the late 16th century, are rarely extended to people, animals, etc.] KLOMPIE n.¹

1871 'JNO' in A.M.L. Robinson *Sel. Articles from Cape Monthly Mag.* (1978) 131 A native attending on one of the wagons at a neighbouring outspan had been struck dead by lightning, and .. a clump of sheep had shared the same fate. 1886 [see MANNETJIE sense 1]. 1911 *Farmer's Weekly* 29 Mar. 11 If a clump of sheep got away there was no telling how far they would wander before they were found, if they were found at all. 1970 J. MCINTOSH *Stonefish* 271 They gathered together outside the door, on the crumbling steps, and stood close together, in a clump, as if for protection. 1970 C. TUCKETT *Informant, Bloemfontein* Kraal. A clomp of natives' huts, usually many huts built in a circle.

clumpjie, clumpy varr. KLOMPIE.

clup var. KLAP v.

clyne, clynie varr. KLEIN, KLEINTJIE.

CMR n. hist. Also **C.M.R.** [Initial letters of *Cape Mounted Rifles, — Riflemen.*]
1. An imperial cavalry unit formed out of the Cape Regiment in 1827.

Orig. made up of Khoikhoi soldiers serving under seconded British officers, and later consisting of both white and Khoikhoi soldiers, this unit was disbanded in 1870.

1844 E.L. KIFT Letter. 12 June, Forty men & Lt. Campbell of the C.M.R. are to proceed to Natal via Port Elizabeth in a few days. 1971 N. ORPEN in *Std Encycl. of Sn Afr.* III. 33 For reasons of economy the Imperial C.M.R. had been recalled to England in 1870, with only ten Coloured members left, all the rest being White volunteers, who were disbanded ... The Colonial C.M.R. were organized with the Government only supplying arms and ammunition initially.

2. A colonial regiment, formed in 1878 out of the Frontier Armed and Mounted Police, and functioning as both a military and a police force; members of this unit, collectively.

This regiment merged into the South African Mounted Riflemen in 1913.

1880 *Alice Times* 30 Jan., The Artillery Troop of the CMR are to be stationed here. c1880 F.W. DAMANT in *Looking Back* (Hist. Soc. of Port Elizabeth, Apr. 1984) 21 Poor Capt Nettleton cried when he found that all but 3 men out his troop of 60, mostly all Grahamstown were killed. The C.M.R. and infantry had to fight to get the bodies of our killed and wounded. 1882 C. DU VAL *With Show through Sn Afr.* I. 170 At King Williamstown, which we reached after nightfall, we met a wing of the Cape Mounted Rifles, or C.M.R. as they are more familiarly called. 1891 T.R. BEATTIE *Ride through Transkei* 14 The C.M.R. do police duty here, but the general complaint of Europeans is that there is not a sufficient number of men to deal with such an extensive district. 1897 *E. Prov. Herald* 19 Feb., Captain Woon, with a small patrol of 80 C.M.R. and some police, have succeeded in locating Galishwe in the Langberg. 1900 E.E.K. LOWNDES *Every-Day Life* 82 About once a week the C.M.R. (Cape Mounted Rifles) ride around their district to see if the farmers have had any cases of sheep-stealing or other trouble with the natives. 1913 *Nongqai* 12 Nov. 16 The Cape Mounted Riflemen, better known as the C.M.R., held the distinction of being the oldest permanent Colonial Force in the Empire ... Under the title of the Armed and Mounted Police, then as the F.A.M.P., and finally as the C.M.R., the regiment has had over half a century's fighting. 1947 C.R. PRANCE *Antic Mem.* 3 The troop had only one officer as yet, a bright young scallywag from the old C.M.R. of gallant memory, and the job would have been tough for a larger force of Regular infantry. 1969 I. VAUGHAN *Last of Sunlit Yrs* 48 The three drums .. had once been the proud possession of the old Cape Mounted Rifles, disbanded at Union ... I thought of their past in the military barracks in King William's Town — once the headquarters of the old C.M.R. 1989 B. GODBOLD *Autobiography.* 13 Small garrisons of Cape Mounted Riflemen (the renowned C.M.R.) .. were stationed at villages to police the districts.

3. Special Comb. **CMR beetle** [see quot. 1961], the garden pest *Mylabris oculata* of the Meloidae.

1949 L. HUNTER *Afr. Dawn* 191 Then there were the thousands of 'C.M.R.' beetles that settled on the plants and devoured the leaves and flowers. 1955 J.B. SHEPHARD *Land of Tikoloshe* 104 The brightly coloured insect known as the C.M.R. beetle — so called because it colours correspond to those of a famous corps, the Cape Mounted Rifles. 1961 D. BEE *Children of Yesterday* 9 The insects were of the same species, black-and-yellow, and were called C.M.R. beetles after the Cape Mounted Riflemen of long ago who had borne those colours. 1963 S.H. SKAIFE *Naturalist Remembers* 23 C.M.R., or blister beetles, are poisonous — they contain a virulent poison called cantharadin. 1972 [see *Christmas box* at CHRISTMAS]. 1985 F.C. DE MOOR in Scholtz & Holm *Insects* 260 The blister, oil and CMR beetles, as they are commonly known, are small to medium-sized beetles. Ibid. 262 Members of the Mylabrini (e.g. *Mylabris oculata*, the CMR beetle), which feed on the petals of flowers, are considered pests in ornamental gardens. 1994 *S. Afr. Garden & Home* Sept. 119 Nothing seems to put an end to those CMR beetles that love the roses.

C.N.E. n. Also **CNE**. Initial letters of *Christian National Education*, see CHRISTIAN-NATIONAL sense 1. Also attrib.

1966 *Cape Argus* 27 Sept. 19 There was a considerable movement afoot to have the national education policy based on the principles of the 'so-called Christian National Education'. He wanted to know to what extent the national policy was going to be aligned with C.N.E. 1971 J.C. COETZEE in *Std Encycl. of Sn Afr.* III. 215 After the Second Anglo-Boer War (1899-1902) .. especially in the Transvaal and the Orange River Colony a powerful C.N.E. system with its own private schools developed. C.N.E. is an education wholly Christian in its basis, character, aim and spirit ... C.N.E. is to the Afrikaner an education completely national in its foundation, character, aim and spirit. 1987 *Pretoria News* 15 June 4 CNE entrenches the notion of discrimination superiority and inferiority and presents a singularly inaccurate and distorted view of history. 1991 F.G. BUTLER *Local Habitation* 101, I found myself .. dashing about to address anti-C.N.E. meetings as far as Tweespruit in the Free State.

C.N.O. n. [Initial letters of Afk. *Christelik-Nasionale Onderwys* (earlier *Christelijk Nationaal Onderwijs*).] *Christian National Education*, see CHRISTIAN-NATIONAL sense 1. Also attrib.

1926 M. NATHAN *S. Afr. from Within* 108 Dissatisfied with the State schools, they set up their own educational system, known as the C.N.O ... where, they considered, they could give their children proper instruction in Dutch. 1934 C.P. SWART *Supplement to Pettman.* 31 *C.N.O.*, Christelike Nationaal Onderwys — Christian National Instruction. The name given to schools founded in the Free State and Transvaal for the purpose of upholding Afrikaner ideals and the Dutch language, which, it was feared would be suppressed under the new regime after the Anglo-Boer War. 1949 *Blueprint for Blackout* (Educ. League) (pamphlet) 16 The present C.N.O. policy .. originated as a political measure. The early Christian-National schools of the beginning of the century were founded to resist the attempt, by Lord Milner .. to anglicise Afrikaans children after the Boer War. 1960 L.M. THOMPSON *Unification of S. Afr.* 1902-10 19 They contended that article 5 of the Treaty of Vereeniging meant that Dutch was to be used as the medium of instruction .. in government schools where the parents desired it, and when that argument had been rejected they founded private schools for *Christelijk-Nationaal Onderwijs* (Christian National Education). In these C.N.O. schools the Calvinist tradition was emphasized. 1970 J. DU P. SCHOLTZ in *Std Encycl. of Sn Afr.* I. 72 Under the leadership of the church C.N.O. (Christian National Education) schools were established.

coal n. [Influenced by Afk. *kole* wood embers. In general Eng. this sense is unusual.] Usu. in *pl.*: The glowing embers of a wood or charcoal fire.

1891 W. SELWYN *Cape Carols* 3 *Carbonaitje*, The Colonial designation of a piece of mutton roasted on a forked stick or live coals, in the absence of the more civilized gridiron. **1891** H.J. DUCKITT *Hilda's 'Where Is It?'* p.ix, Anyone who has travelled in South Africa will remember how good was the 'Sasatie' (Kabob) or 'Carbonatje' (Mutton Chop), steaming hot from the gridiron on wood coals, or two-pronged fork held against the coals. **1900** B.M. HICKS *Cape as I Found It* 170 The coffee is the most delicious you ever tasted in your life — the roestekoeks, too, that have been roasting on the 'coals'. **1913** C. PETTMAN *Africanderisms* 124 *Coal*, The word is commonly used in the Colony in the Bible sense; 'having a live coal in his hand', Is. vi. 6. A glowing wood cinder; a meaning which has become archaic in the English of the homeland. **1935** [see RIBBETJIE]. **1968** K. MCMAGH *Dinner of Herbs* 83 The men made the fires that would die down to give the 'coals' on which to grill chops of mountain lamb, home-made sausages and skewered sasaaties. **1978** *Darling* 1 Feb., Come for a braai ... Baste the chicken on the coals ... Bake them directly on the hot coals ... Put the fish on ... over medium coals. **1980** *Argus* 28 Aug. 12 Traditionally the pot-brood was made while people had a campfire going so that there was a stock of glowing coals on hand. **1982** *Cape Times* 8 Sept. 10 Just then a party left, their fire-place still aglow with coals. **1991** *Shell advertising pamphlet* (Special Springtime ed.), Long-burning Camelthorn charcoal .. gives you perfect coals for perfect steaks.

coat *n. colloq.* Ellipt. for BLUE-COAT sense 2.

1949 H.C. BOSMAN *Cold Stone Jug* (1969) 37, I been brought up on a farm. And I smoke dagga. And I been twice warned for the coat. And if I was brought up in a city, where would I be to-day, I'd like to know? And the Bombardier says I would be a criminal, most likely. **1974** [see BAADJIE sense 2].

cob *n.*[1] [Anglicized form of *kob.*] KOB sense a. See also KABELJOU.

1906 [see KOB]. **1913** W.W. THOMPSON *Sea Fisheries of Cape Col.* 155 Kabeljaauw, .. Cob or Kob (East London). **1947** K.H. BARNARD *Pict. Guide to S. Afr. Fishes* 121 A large family of warm water fishes, mostly of large size, and of great economic importance ... *Kabeljou; Cob; Salmon-bass (Sciaena hololepidota).* **1960** J. COPE *Tame Ox* 40 The trawlers came in from the deep sea loaded down to the gunwales with stock-fish, not to mention soles, silver, gurnet, kingklip, cob .. and tunny. **1971** *Grocott's Mail* 11 May 2 The man, an experienced Kowie River fisherman, said it was normal for cob to enter the estuary during the summer months. **1982** *S. Afr. Fishing* Apr.-May 10 Rock and surf fishing along the East London coast is still rather poor with only the odd day producing good bags of cob and pignose grunter. **1989** B. KURTEN in *Evening Post* 25 Jan. 18 The best fish from this area was a big cob of 44kg caught by young Gerhard Güse. **1991** *E. Prov. Herald* 24 May 29 In last weekend's programme Pieterse dealt with cob or kabeljou as West Coast folk call them.

cob *n.*[2] *slang.* [Unkn.; perh. fr. a supposed resemblance of the marijuana package to a maize cob (maize-leaves are also freq. used as packaging material).] Among drug users: a quantity of marijuana (see DAGGA *n.*[2] sense 1). Cf. ARM.

1970 G. HUGO in *Forum* Vol.6 No.2, 19 'Remember that cob of Malawi we had just after the vac.' *Ibid.* 20 'It was tremendous. How's the pipe?' I tend to miss every joint, pipe, roach, cookie, roller, twist, cob, stick, grass-thing that's around. **1972** *Daily Dispatch* 22 Mar. 4 He said the five cobs of dagga were his sole responsibility and his friends were not involved. **1982** *Sunday Times* 18 July 11 Last month, the customs official found a 'cob' of Malawi dagga in her luggage.

cobblejaw var. KABELJOU.

Cochoqua /kəˈtʃɒkwə/ *n. Obs.* exc. *hist.* Also **Chochaqua, Kochaqua, Kokoqua.** Pl. **-s**, or unchanged. [Khoikhoi.] A member of a Khoikhoi people who lived near present-day Riebeeck-Kasteel, Western Cape, during the 17th and 18th centuries. Also *attrib.*

Early Dutch settlers considered the Cochoqua to be a powerful people (see quots 1952 and 1968).

1670 J. OGILBY *Africa* 576 The chiefest people hitherto discover'd in this Southerly part of Africa, are the Gorachouqua's, Goringhaiqua's, Goringhaikona's, Kochoqua's, .. Namaqua's, Heusaqua's, Brigoudins, and Hankumqua's. **1731** G. MEDLEY tr. *P. Kolb's Present State of Cape of G.H.* I. 62 The *Kochaqua's*, as do other nations of the *Hottentots*, remove with their Cots and Cattle, from one Part to another of their Territories for the Convenience of Pasturage. **1795** C.R. HOPSON tr. *C.P. Thunberg's Trav.* I. 305 The *Kokoquas nation* inhabited the country that bordered upon the Cape on the northern side in the environs of *Groene Kloof.* **1880** *Cape Monthly Mag.* II. 140 A few descendants of the Cochoqua are still in existence at Bethany, Great Namaqualand, calling themselves by that tribal name. **1905** G.W. STOW *Native Races of S. Afr.* 242 The Cochoqua were the people who sold the Cape peninsula to the Dutch in 1672. The first hostilities between the Dutch and these Hottentots broke out the following year. **1914** C. PETTMAN *Notes on S. Afr. Place Names* 13 Gonnema, chief of the largest division of the Cochoquas. **1952** H.B. THOM tr. *J. Van Riebeeck's Jrnl* I. 370 The Kaapmans and the tribe of the Black Captain .. were encamped in the midst of them all. [*Note*] The Black Captain was Gonnema, chief of the Cochoquas. He was so called because he smeared his body with soot. *Ibid.* II. 189 The Cochoquas .. are rich in cattle and are the most powerful of all the real Saldanhars. **1968** E.A. WALKER *Hist. of Sn Afr.* 36 Explorers and visitors soon taught him [*sc.* Van Riebeeck] of the existence of other clans: .. two groups of Chochaquas, the strongest of all the local clans, under Gounema and Oedosos in the neighbourhood of Saldanha Bay. **1972** J.J. OBERHOLSTER in *Std Encycl. of Sn Afr.* V. 267 *Gonnema*, .. Cochoqua chief. During the first ten years of the European settlement at the Cape, this Hottentot chief lived in the vicinity of the present Riebeek-Kasteel and Twenty-four Rivers. **1972** *Std Encycl. of Sn Afr.* VII. 164 The neighbouring area [*sc.* in the Malmesbury district] was reserved for the remnants of Hottentot tribes, the Cochoquas, [etc.].

Cockney *n.* Also **Kokney**. [Anglicized form of *Kokani*, see KOKANI.] A South African of Indian descent who belongs to the Muslim faith and originates from Konkan (southern Maharashtra), a coastal region of western India; the language spoken by such a person. Also *attrib.*

1968 *Post* 11 Feb. 7 Who the devil does Koos think he is insulting the Cockney community of Vryburg so uncouthly. He says Cockneys swear in Ramadaan. Hasn't he ever heard anyone else swear in Ramadaan? **1971** *Ibid.* 24 Oct. 2 Enraged members of the Kokneys clan to which Ahmed belonged set upon members of the rival Alipuris. *c*1983 [see KOKANI].

cock-o-veet, cock-o-viek varr. KOKKEWIET.

cocopan /ˈkʊkʊpæn, ˈkəʊkə-/ *n.* Also **kokopan**. [ad. Zulu *i-ngqukumbana, -bane* lit. 'stumpy wagon'.] A small v-shaped tip-truck, usu. on rails, used esp. in mines for transporting ore. Also *attrib.*

1914 *Minutes of Proceedings of S. Afr. Soc. of Civil Engin.*, The pick, shovel, wheelbarrow and coco pan suited to the low-waged native labourer. **1937** H. KLEIN *Stage Coach Dust* 107 Various duties were assigned to the gangs; some loaded the pulverized blue ground into trucks for transporting to the washing machines. Others tipped 'cocopans' (little half-ton trucks) containing the 'maiden blue' just out of the mines. **1949** H.C. BOSMAN *Cold Stone Jug* (1969) 83 We moved thousands of tons of earth and stone by wheel-barrow and by hand and by coco-pan. **1951** G. VAN DELDEN *I Have a Plan* 102 Several kokopans, such as are used for transporting sugar-cane. **1967** W.A. DE KLERK *White Wines* 59 Above cement fermentation pits stood a formidable line of cocopan-like receptacles, compartmented, so as to receive the fresh must. **1968** *Farmer's Weekly* 3 Jan. 93 (*advt*) Railway fencing poles. Made from used railway and cocopan rails. **1977** F.G. BUTLER *Karoo Morning* 65 The loose stones, previously blasted from the rock face, were loaded by big black men into coco pans, and pushed on little railway lines to a ramp, where they were tipped, and stacked. **1982** M. DIKOBE in *Voice* 20 June 10 The dancers swayed from side to side like mealie stalks ... Martha moved like a cocopan full of minesand turning at an intersection. **1990** M. ESPIN in *Staffrider* Vol.9 No.1, 70 The cocopans roll along the rails pushed by men with wet bandannas on their heads.

code *n. colloq.* [Special sense of general Eng. *code* a variety within a sport (e.g. Australian rugby is a 'code' of rugby).] A particular sport, e.g. hockey, soccer, swimming, etc.

1991 Report. (S.A. Universities Sports Council), It is grossly unfair that the 'cinderella codes' should battle to gain official SAU status ... In a sport like yachting, many universities are excluded because they simply don't have the natural resources and sometimes not the will to offer the code. **1992** B. CHETTY on Radio Algoa 29 May, Soccer is the biggest code of sport in South Africa, and in Port Elizabeth. **1993** P. DU TOIT in *Weekend Post* 22 May 6 Other World Games sports codes which could use the building are gymnastics, karate, tumbling and trampolining. **1994** on Radio South Africa 7 June, What made you choose basketball out of all the codes?

Codesa /kəˈdesə/ *n. hist.* Also **CODESA**. [Acronym formed on *Convention for a Democratic South Africa*.]

1. Either of two successive all-party conventions held between 1991 and 1993 to determine guidelines for a new constitution and a democratic franchise for a multi-party government of transition; occas. with a distinguishing numeral, as **Codesa I, Codesa II**; *rare*, a collective name for the delegates attending either convention. Also *attrib.*

1991 J. MACLENNAN in *Sunday Tribune* 15 Dec. 1 The issue .. could surface again with divisive results at this week's inaugural meeting of the Convention for a Democratic South Africa (Codesa). **1991** C. WHITFIELD in *Natal Mercury* 23 Dec. 1 Codesa ushered in a new dawn for South Africa at the weekend. **1992** Q. WILSON in *South* 27 Feb. 16 When .. Mrs Helen Suzman proposed that there should be at least one woman active in each of the five working groups, Codesa 1 thundered in hefty applause. **1992** *Academic Standard* Apr. 3 Because of recent negotiated settlements in Angola, .. and the CODESA process in South Africa, the Southern African region can look towards the future with hope. **1992** D. FRIEDMAN in *Weekly Mail* 15 May 25 If Codesa II does agree on interim government, will we really be on the road to a democracy? **1993** *Sash Newsletter* (Black Sash) 29 June 4 [The National Party] intends to remain in charge by constitutional manoevering, a tight hold on economic power, management of the process of transition, and the discrediting of its political opposition. This was clearly demonstrated in the demands which led to the breakdown of CODESA II. **1994** M. EDMONDS on Radio South Africa, 6 May, Codesa, I can imagine, must have been a low point for many people because of its horrible failure.

2. *transf.* Any discussion between interest groups or parties holding widely divergent views.

1992 *Cape Times* 20 May 8 Economic Codesa. The establishment of a virtual economic Codesa at a meeting in the city this week is arguably the biggest breakthrough in weeks in the negotiations for a new order in South Africa. That the meeting between government, business and labour could take place at all is encouraging.

3. See quot.

1994 WILHELM & NAIDOO in *Sunday Times* 1 May 15 Codesa, however, is enjoying a much longer life. It is now a township jive dance.

Codesa-desa /kədesəˈdesə/ *v. trans. Slang.* [Formed on CODESA.] To negotiate (something).

1992 G. ANSTEY in *Cue* 6 July 1 *Mooi Street Blues* is masterly in its use of language, and to borrow some street lingo from the play, I'm now going to 'codesa, desa' a ticket to Slabolepszy's other play at the fest. **1994** P. SLABOLEPSZY *Mooi Str. & Other Moves* 271, I can organise. We Codesa-desa the price. Jus' say the word ... I'm offering you a good deal here. *Ibid.* 335 *Codesa-desa*, negotiate.

coedoe var. KUDU.

coerhen var. CORE-HEN.

coffee-kettle *n. Obs.* exc. *hist.* [Calque formed on Afk. *koffie-ketel.*] A coffee pot.

1857 R. GRAY in *Jrnl of Visitation to Diocese of Grahamstown* 60, I have also given him a coffee-kettle, and the Winklers say that coffee is in demand at Kreli's kraal. **a1858** J. GOLDSWAIN *Chron.* (1949) II. 65 We had three days rashons to carrey: our coffe Kittle: our Kanteen for water or git not one drop for twentey four hours. **a1867** C.J. ANDERSSON *Notes of Trav.* (1875) 17 He next demanded our coffee-kettle, dresses for his women, the waggon-chests, &c., indeed I verily believe everything he *saw.* **a1878** J. MONTGOMERY *Reminisc.* (1981) 99, I found them seated at their camptable with their coffee-kettle — a cup of contents of which was very acceptable to me after such a disturbed night. **1896** H.A. BRYDEN *Tales of S. Afr.* 66 Supper at length over, the coffee-kettle was banished to obscurity and the whiskey produced. **1968** K. MCMAGH *Dinner of Herbs* 83 The coffee maker had his own fire burning, his flat bottomed enamel coffee kettles, their flannel coffee-bags bulging, all ready and bubbling for any who fancied a cup.

cogolomander var. KOGGELMANDER.

Coin *n. hist.* Also **COIN**. [Blend of Eng. *counter* and *insurgency.*] A short name given to the counter-insurgency units of the South African Defence Force and police force. Freq. *attrib.*

1983 W. STEENKAMP in *Leadership* Vol.2 No.4, 56 The Army is divided into two legs, the conventional force and the counter-insurgency (COIN) force ... The COIN force, is charged with maintaining internal security 'in support of the civil power'. **1986** *Paratus* July 18, 32 Battalion has since been utilized in conventional, semi-conventional, COIN and guerilla roles. **1987** *Informant, Port Elizabeth* Ja, good news. Coin Ops [have been] reduced to only 2 weeks. Means two weeks less of sitting in a casspir in the townships. **1987** J. SUTHERLAND in *Weekly Mail* 3 Apr. 3 SWA police headquarters said their special counter-insurgency unit, Coin, had tracked down and killed five guerillas after the infiltrators destroyed four telephone poles on a farm in the area.

cokey *n.*[1] var. KOEKIE.

cokey *n.*[2] var. KOKI.

cokimakranki var. KUKUMAKRANKA.

Colenso /kəˈlenzəʊ/ *n. hist.* [Surname of *J.W. Colenso*, Bishop of Natal 1853–64.] Used *attrib.*, alluding to the ecclesiastical controversy and schism following upon Colenso's deposition as Bishop in 1864.

1865 'A LADY' *Life at Natal* (1972) 115 The 'Colenso difficulty,' as it is called, gets more and more complicated .. and great is the consternation among the Orthodox. **1955** B.B. BURNETT *Anglicans in Natal* 67 When the Colonies received a measure of self-government the relationship between Church and State needed defining afresh. In this the Church of the Province led the way, and the painful road by which it arrived at its goal was the Colenso controversy. **1963** P. HINCHLIFF *Anglican Church* 1 Within a short time of Baines's consecration all but one of the Colenso churches had come into the Province ... The last remaining 'Colenso Church' became a part of the province under the special terms a few years ago and the Colenso schism is at an end. **1965** BROOKES & WEBB *Hist. of Natal* (1979) 110 The intricate constitutional and legal issues arising out of the Colenso controversy really made the Anglican Communion what it is today — a group of independent national Churches, in no way subject to the Church of England. *Ibid.* 110 Nearly all the 'Colenso' congregations gradually came into the Church of the Province. **1982** J. & A. VERBEEK *Victorian & Edwardian Natal* 1 These years [*sc.* the 1860s] .. saw the beginnings of the Colenso controversy which was to affect the Church of England throughout South Africa and to cause much bitterness in Natal.

Hence **Colensoite** *n.*, a supporter of Bishop Colenso's cause.

1965 BROOKES & WEBB *Hist. of Natal* (1979) 110 When .. the Bishop of the Orange Free State .. offered to hold a Confirmation Service in the Cathedral, he found the Church being washed by the Colensoites and the nave deep in water.

coll(e)y var. COLY.

Colonial *adj.* and *n. Hist.* Also with small initial. [Eng.]

Used also in the general Eng. senses, but primarily with the following meanings.

A. *adj.* Of or pertaining to the Cape Colony. See also COLONY.

1824 W.J. BURCHELL *Trav.* II. 97 Bidding me farewell in the colonial manner, by repeating the word *dag*, they hasted away to their Kraal. **1824** *S. Afr. Jrnl* I. 84 There are now on the books of the two Free Schools maintained by the Colonial Government in Cape Town, the names of five-hundred-and-twenty children. **1831** *S. Afr. Dir. & Advertiser* 100 Total estimated value of Colonial Produce and manufactures exported during the year 1829 £285,247 15 $10\frac{1}{4}$. **1836** A.F. GARDINER *Journey to Zoolu Country* 256, I should probably reach the colonial frontier in the course of a very few days. **1861** [see *burghership* at BURGHER]. **1873** F. BOYLE *To Cape for Diamonds* 297 There are hundreds of diggers, both boer and colonial, who have gone to the fields with the resolve of earning some definite sum, large or small. **1888** *Cape Punch* 28 Mar. 182 Mr *Cape-Punch* hears there is some likelihood of a Colonial Cricket Team visiting England to try conclusions with the old country. **1891** H.J. DUCKITT *Hilda's 'Where Is It?'* p.vii, To my country cousins and far-off friends in South Africa .. this collection may prove useful. Few Colonial cooks of the present day understand the *art* of cooking. **1899** *Volkstem* 5 Oct. 1 Emissaries of the Transvaal have been at work among the Colonial country-folks. Arms have been distributed on behalf of the Transvaal Government, and Colonial disaffection is reckoned on as a factor of considerable importance. **1901** *George & Knysna Herald* 30 Oct. 3 Seven Colonial Dutch farmers suspected of having given information to the Boers respecting the movements of British troops, have been apprehended, and brought into town from the Albany District. **1902** H.J. DUCKITT in M. Kuttel *Quadrilles & Konfyt* (1954) 16 Buck Bay — a cattle-farm belonging to my eldest brother, with a picturesque old Colonial house. **1903** D. BLACKBURN *Burgher Quixote* 65 Riding on the level ground right below us were eight khakis, whom we knew not to be Colonial volunteers by the way they rode — with a long stirrup and straight up in the saddle. **1923** D.F. BLEEK *Mantis & his Friends* Intro., Their narrators were all Colonial Bushmen, who lived on the rolling plains south of the Orange River. **1971** *Grocott's Mail* 24 Aug. 3 It is, as its title page states, a 'Picture Record of the Movements of the British, Colonial and Boer Forces engaged in the Conflict'.

B. *n.* An inhabitant of the Cape Colony; one born there.

1917 A.W. CARTER *Informant, Ladybrand* 20 Aug., The Administrator — Gorges — is a Colonial and not imposing but was very affable and has just let me know that he is arranging a visit to the Govt. Farm. **1987** W. STEENKAMP *Blockhouse* 22 If your horse gave in, that was the end of you, especially if the English got you and you were a rebel colonial. Then it was a short trial and a fast hanging.

Colony *n. hist.* Also with small initial. ***The Colony***: The Cape Colony; *the Cape*, see CAPE sense 1 b; KOLONIE. Also with qualifying word, **The Old Colony**.

1796 Van Ryneveld vs Brown & Spooner. 24 The Benefit as well for the Colony in general as for each Individual in particular, that the Administration of Justice should be conferred on and remain [in] the Hands of those who have hitherto performed that weighty function. **1806** in G.M. Theal *Rec. of Cape Col.* (1899) V. 301 The Inhabitants of the Colony who are comprehended in the Capitulation are to enjoy the same rights and privileges as have been granted to those in Cape Town. **1810** G. BARRINGTON *Acct of Voy.* 333 The Sneuwberg .. is the best nursery for sheep in the whole Colony. **1838** F. OWEN Letter to Church Missionary Society. (Killie Campbell Africana Library KCM53500) 19 Apr., I now avail myself of an opportunity which offers of sending letters overland to the Colony to write again, to give you some notion of our present condition. **1847** 'A BENGALI' *Notes on Cape of G.H.* 6 In 1814 the Colony was finally and formally ceded to Great Britain at the Treaty of Vienna. **1849** [see NACHTSLANG]. **1851** H. WARD *Cape & Kaffirs* 8 There is no prospect of filling up any portion of it with Boers, and little by any removals from the old Colony; the only effective remedy .. appears to us to consist in an extensive emigration from the United Kingdom. **1851** J.F. CHURCHILL Diary. (Killie Campbell Africana Library MS37) 18 June, Bad news from the Old Colony nearly all the Hottentots disaffected & Settlers in doubt whom to trust. **1852** R.B. STRUTHERS *Hunting Jrnl* (1991) 15 Dr M(orris) is a very agreeable young man — is from the old colony and has been in the late Kaffir wars. **1852** C. BARTER *Dorp & Veld* 15 (Pettman), The greatest drag to the commerce of Natal is its intimate connexion with, and almost entire dependence on, the *old Colony.* **1862** [see HICCUP-NUT]. **1864** 'A LADY' *Life at Natal* (1972) 44 Here, as in the 'old colony', I find that Christian Kafirs are held to be no improvement upon the 'pure and simple' savage. **1882** O.E.A. SCHREINER Diamond Fields. 152 Perhaps you have seen such houses here, because you go about, but I haven't. It's just like the Colony. **1883** J. EDWARDS *Reminisc.* 81 (Pettman), We were now in the *old Colony*, where we felt ourselves more at home. **1887** J.C. BROWN *Crown Forests* 122 Can you inform the Committee to what extent the Crown forest lands were sold when the licenses were withheld? — No; that was before I came to the Colony. **1913** C. PETTMAN *Africanderisms* 346 *Old Colony, The*, The Cape Colony is frequently so designated to distinguish it from those Colonies and States of South Africa of more recent origin. **1927** *Outspan* 18 Mar. 45 Let us beg the Johannesburg people not to refer to the Cape Province as 'The Colony'. **1928** E.A. WALKER *Hist. of S. Afr.* 515 The Afrikaner Volk proceeded to find itself along cultural and then along political lines. The Old Colony led the way. **c1936** *S. & E. Afr. Yr Bk & Guide* 97 Other causes have been overstocking, veld burning and the goat. In some areas, particularly the Native Reserves in the old Colony .. the damage done may prove irretrievable. *Ibid.* 225 In the old colony numbers have sunk to the 'poor white' level from losses incurred through drought and from the gradual deterioration of lands. **1964** L.G. GREEN *Old Men Say* 255 A Mr. George Tuistle complained in 1801 that Rex had been presented with one of the best posts in the colony simply because he was a son of George III. **1977** [see GUN WAR]. **1985** W.T. POWELL in M. Fraser *Jhb. Pioneer Jrnls 1888–1909* 211 He was thinking of making a trip home. As I knew he was born down in Cape Colony I asked him what part of the Colony he was going to. 'I am not going to the Colony. I am going to London.'

colored var. COLOURED.

colour *n.* [Special senses of general Eng.]

1. *Obs.* exc. *hist.* In the phr. ***free person of colour***, a KHOIKHOI; any person of mixed ethnic descent who was not a slave.

1822 in G.W. Eybers *Sel. Constit. Doc.* (1918) 26 Hottentots and other free persons of colour have been subjected to certain restraints as to their residence, mode of life, and employment. **1828** in DAVENPORT & HUNT *Right to Land* (1974) 12 Ordinance 50 .. Whereas doubts have arisen as to the competency of Hottentots and other free Persons of colour to purchase or possess Land in this Colony: Be it therefore enacted and declared, That all Grants, Purchases and Transfers of Land or other Property whatsoever, heretofore made to, or by any Hottentot or other free Person of colour, are and shall be, and the same are hereby declared to be of full force and effect. **1832** *Graham's Town Jrnl* 8 June 94 The propriety of a concentrated population was equally apparent, and hence it was offered exclusively to Hottentots and other free persons of color, as being the most suitable class of the community to answer the end proposed by its colonization. **1833** *S. Afr. Almanac & Dir.* 204 Abbreviations. — E.R. European Race .. C. Caffer. F.C. Free person of Color. S. Slave. **1989** *Reader's Digest Illust. Hist.* 97 Ordinance 50 of 1828 .. guaranteed to all 'Hottentots and other free persons of colour' residing in the Cape the same freedom and protection as enjoyed by whites.

2. *obs.* In the phr. ***person of colour***, COLOURED *n*. sense a.

1833 *Graham's Town Jrnl* 10 Jan. 3 Jephta, a person of colour, who deposed — That he is the defendant's slave. **1836** *Albany Settlers 1824–36* (Soc. for Relief of Distressed Settlers) 16 Two persons of colour, named Willem Willems and Jager Jantjes, appeared next. They were wagon-drivers in the employment of Messrs. Simpson & Ford, Caffer traders. **1836** R. GODLONTON *Introductory Remarks to Narr. of Irruption* 12 To prevent the possibility of his return, the country was subsequently occupied by Hottentots and people of colour, and now forms the Kat River Settlement. **1837** *Moderator* 10 Jan. 3 Hendrik Rygaard, a person of color, residing in the Cape District, was charged before the Magistrate. **1841** B. SHAW *Memorials* 16 Perhaps more than half the population of the Cape districts are *persons of colour*, who are generally either heathens or Mahommedans.

colour bar *n. phr. Hist.* Also with initial capitals. [Special sense of U.S. Eng. *colour bar* the legal, social and political distinction between white and black people.] The practice or policy of excluding black people from skilled jobs, first entrenched in the Mines and Works Act, No.12 of 1911. Cf. JOB RESERVATION. Also *attrib.*

Used also in the general Eng. sense.

1926 M. NATHAN *S. Afr. from Within* 183 The mines now employed coloured men on engine-driving, which was one of the occupations forbidden by the colour-bar regulation. **1936** F.S. MALAN in *Cambridge Hist. of Brit. Empire* VIII. 659 The expression 'colour bar' as used in the Union means the exclusion of the natives from any skilled or semi-skilled work. **1941** 'R. ROAMER ESQ.' in *Bantu World* 25 Jan. 4 In Xhosa and Sutho it urged us to 'come in our thousands and fight the Pass and Tax Laws, Pick-up vans, Colour Bar, Low wages and discriminating laws'. **1955** A. DELIUS *Young Trav.* 52 You must remember that the Bantu workers don't get much in the way of wages and there are many kinds of work which they are not allowed to do, mainly the higher-paid jobs. That is part of what is known as the 'Colour Bar'. **1960** *Cape Times* 1 Aug. 24 The sedulous deference to victims of economic and social inadequacy has brought about the whole apparatus of the industrial colour-bar and job reservation. **1964** O.D. SCHREINER *Nettle* 37 A major effect of the colour bar is to keep the wages of Non-whites depressed. **1971** *Rand Daily Mail* 31 May 12 The industrial colour bar puts a brake on industry and affects the prosperity of all races in the republic. **1986** KALLAWAY & PEARSON *Johannesburg* 90 Workers were .. in conflict with owners regarding their rightful share to profits, but because the situation was 'colonial' — and therefore racially divided — workers were equally in conflict with one another over the issue and nature of the 'colour bar' in industry. **1989** *Reader's Digest Illust. Hist.* 306 The colour bar itself operated on three tiers. The first was the legal tier established by the Mines and Works Act of 1911. **1992** V.L. ALLEN in *Guardian Weekly* 10 July 2 To the outside world, de Klerk's reforms were breathtaking but to blacks they were merely legal acknowledgements of changes already present. The legal colour bar had been abolished in 1988, the pass laws to prevent the urbanisation of blacks were a dead letter.

coloured *ppl adj.* and *n.* Also (freq.) with initial capital, and (formerly) **colored**. [Special senses of general Eng. *coloured* (of or pertaining to) a dark-skinned person entirely or partially of black African descent, a meaning no longer current in S. Afr. Eng.]

Since the late 1970s used often in inverted commas, or in the phr. *so-called coloured*, indicating the speaker or writer's disapproval of ethnic CLASSIFICATION.

A. *ppl adj.* Of a person or group.

a. Of mixed ethnic origin, including Khoisan, African slave, Malay, Chinese, white, and other descent; of or pertaining to such a person or group; BROWN *adj.* sense 2; EURAFRICAN *adj.*

The word has been used for over one and a half centuries, and numerous Acts have entrenched its use. However the POPULATION REGISTRATION ACT of 1950 made this term an official ethnic label in terms of the law (see next sense).

1829 W. SHAW *Diary.* 20 Sept., I was much gratified with every part of the arrangements, excepting that the poor black and coloured children appeared to me, to be too lightly esteemed, though forming an interesting and important part of the Institution. **1833** —— in B. Shaw *Memorials* (1841) 233 The original chapel .. is now used as a school-house, and also as a place of worship for the black and coloured population, for whose benefit it is requisite to hold separate services, as they do not generally understand the English language. **1844** J. MACGILCHRIST *Cape of G.H.* 20 The native population of the colony is generally called Hottentot, or bastard Hottentot, most of the coloured people approaching pretty nearly to the Hottentot formation, and some presenting a greater or smaller mixture of other, principally European blood. **1859** *Cape Town Weekly Mag.* 21 Jan. 14 During a severe storm experienced on Friday afternoon, in the neighbourhood of Burghersdorp, a coloured man, by name of Jan Hopely, was struck dead by lightening. **1871** J. MCKAY *Reminisc.* 291 Our Kafir and coloured populations stand in the ratio of three to every one white (Dutch and British) and it therefore becomes us to legislate on our coloured population by procuring work for them, and thereby enriching the colony. **1892** *The Jrnl* 14 Jan. 2 The criminals are for the most part Coloured or Native men. [**1898** *Cape Argus* (Weekly Ed.) 2 Feb. 40 The 'cullud' lady .. had a dispute with a former mistress.] **1909** R.H. BRAND *Union of S. Afr.* 97 A 'Coloured Man' is not a Kafir. He is a person of mixed white and black blood. **1923** *Act 21* in *Stat. of Union* 140 *Act* to provide .. for the exemption of coloured persons from the operation of pass laws. *Ibid.* 189 'Coloured person' means any person of mixed European and native descent and shall include all persons belonging to the class called Cape Malays. **1934** A.J. BARNOUW *Lang. & Race Problems* 28 By 'colored people' the South African means half-castes. They form 48 per cent of the population of Capetown, and their native language is Afrikaans. **1949** E. HELLMANN *Handbk on Race Rel.* 348 The commission on the Cape Coloured population of the Union offered the following definition of a Coloured person: 'a person living in the Union of South Africa who does not belong to one of its aboriginal races, but in whom the presence of Coloured blood (especially due to descent from Non-Europeans brought to the Cape in the seventeenth and eighteenth centuries or from aboriginal Hottentot stock, and with or without an admixture of white or Bantu blood), can be established.' **1956** N. GORDIMER in D. Wright *S. Afr. Stories* (1960) 71 He had accompanied Jake to a shebeen in a coloured location. **1980** C. HERMER *Diary of Maria Tholo* 198 The official designation of the Western Cape as a 'coloured' preference area persists. **1990** R. GOOL *Cape Town Coolie* 90 The very last franchise is the Coloured Vote and the Cape Municipal Franchise. **1990** *Sash* Vol.33 No.1, May 21 Gang warfare in the so-called 'coloured' areas has become an uncontrollable problem in East London. **1990** J. MCCLURG in *Star* 11 Sept. 11 'Coloured' now tends to be avoided as a designation for those of mixed blood, yet no satisfactory substitute has been found for it. And, praiseworthy though the effort to get rid of racial designations is, we have to resort to them sometimes for the sake of clarity. **1992** J. PEARCE in *South* 27 Feb. 4 A new organisation aims to keep the coloured flag flying because it believes the coloureds are being marginalised.

b. *hist.* During the apartheid era: classified as a 'coloured' according to the provisions of the Population Registration Act; of or pertaining to such a person or group. See also CAPE COLOURED *ppl adj. phr.*, CLASSIFY, OTHER COLOURED *ppl adj. phr.*

1950 *Act 30* in *Stat. of Union* 277 'Coloured person' means a person who is not a white person or a native. **1952** P. ABRAHAMS in *Drum* July 11 He had known a Coloured man who had been white nearly all his life, who had fought in the last war as a white officer, who had had a world of white friends — and then became a Coloured man quite suddenly. **1953** *Off. Yrbk of Union 1950* (Bureau of Census & Statistics) 1157 The population is divided for census purposes into four racial groups as follows: .. (4) Mixed and other coloured — this group consists chiefly of Cape coloured, but includes also Cape Malays, Bushmen, Hottentots, and all persons of mixed race. For consideration of space the name of this group is usually concentrated to 'coloured'. **1968** J. LELYVELD in Cole & Flaherty *House of Bondage* 18, I once met a man who carried both an African reference book and a Colored identity card so he could be African or Colored as the mood took him. **1970** A. SPARKS in *Daily Dispatch* 10 Dec. 16 The Coloured group, as defined in our Population Registration Act, is a pretty variegated community. In fact it includes everybody who is neither White nor African. **1971** [see CLASSIFICATION]. **1979** *Cape Times* 20 Dec. 12 [He] was an outstanding representative of the generation of intellectual and political leaders of the so-called coloured community. **1982** *Reader's Digest Family Guide to Law* 744 The State President has not declared any group of blacks to be a separate declared group, but has separated Indian, Chinese and Malay groups from the coloured group. **1983** R. RIVE in *Best of S. Afr. Short Stories* (1991) 315 To get in [*sc.* into the club] you mustn't only be so-called coloured, you must also be not too so-called coloured. You must have the right complexion, the right sort of hair, the right address and speak the right sort of Walmer Estate or Wynberg English. **1990** R. GOOL *Cape Town Coolie* 31 Her arms were plump and peach-coloured — was she European? .. Broad cheekbones distinguished her as Coloured. **1990** S. MAKGABOTLANE in *Tribute* 120 When Stella's birth certificate arrives, she discovers she has been classified 'coloured' (an offspring of mixed heritage), although her mother was 'white'. **1990** S. GRAY in *Staffrider* Vol.9 No.1, 50, I said I would not phone the Harbour Cafe, the famous tourist restaurant on the Cape Town waterfront, either to make a booking or confirm if I could bring my so-called coloured friend along.

B. *n.* Pl. **-s**, or unchanged. **a.** A person of mixed black (or brown) and white descent who speaks either English or Afrikaans as home language; AFRIKANDER *n.* sense 2; BROWN *n.* sense 1; EURAFRICAN *n.*; HOTTENTOT *n.* sense 4 a; KLEURLING *n.* sense 1 (often *derog.*); *person of colour*, see COLOUR sense 2. See also BASTARD *n.* sense 1. **b.** *hist.* One 'classified' as coloured in terms of the Population Registration Act. See also CAPE COLOURED *n. phr.*, OTHER COLOURED *n. phr.*

1949 J.S. FRANKLIN *This Union* 196 There are nearly a million Coloureds in the Union, and but for the European they would not be there. **1953** *Drum* Oct. 45 Athlone and Elsies River, which are earmarked for Coloureds are .. too small to absorb the present Coloured population of the Peninsula. **1968** J. LELYVELD in Cole & Flaherty *House of Bondage* 18 At one end of this spectrum many Coloreds pass as whites. At the other many Africans pass as Coloreds. **1970** E. *Prov. Herald* 4 Sept., Coloureds — those residents (two million officially, but perhaps three million in fact) who have White-Black parentage somewhere on the family tree, the mixture generally dating back to an illicit liaison between a White farm owner and his Black female serfs. **1979** *Sunday Post* 3 July 7 According to an announcement in Parliament this week, 150 'coloureds' became 'white' in 1978. Seems a bit of a desperate way to get back on the voters' roll. **1980** [see GROUP AREA *adj. phr.*]. **1986** A. KLAASTE in *Frontline* June 5 Many is the black person, endowed with a lightish complexion, who declared himself or herself a 'coloured' and went for the precious coloured identity document. **1988** *Daily Dispatch* 23 Feb. 17 He said that in 1984 alone, 795 South Africans were reclassified. Whites became Chinese, Africans became coloureds, and coloureds became whites. 'In this House we have a pure Egyptian classified coloured'. **1990** R. STENGEL *January Sun* 40 Since 'light-skinned' Coloured were virtually impossible to differentiate from Afrikaners, the Population Registration Act of 1950 emphasized association and ancestry as the principal ways of establishing who was white. **1991** F.G. BUTLER *Local Habitation* 199 Until Fugard's *Blood Knot* (1969) actors and producers could present so-called coloureds only as comic carnival coons or parodies of whites, not as people. **1992** J. CONTRERAS in *Newsweek* 20 July 33 The movement [*sc.* the ANC] was not 'making much progress' among whites or the country's other two minorities, Indians and mixed-race Coloreds.

Colouredstan see -STAN.

coly /ˈkəʊli/ *n.* Also **coll(e)y**. [Prob. fr. Modern L. generic name *colius* fr. Gk *kolios* a kind of woodpecker; but see also quot. 1913.] MOUSEBIRD.

[**1801** J. BARROW *Trav.* I. 232 The modest garb of the *colii*, of which I met with three species, formed a striking contrast with the gaudy plumage of the others.] *c*1808 [see MOUSEBIRD]. **1838** J.E. ALEXANDER *Exped. into Int.* I. 182 We got here plenty of birds, as .. collys with blueish plumage, crests, and long tails. *a*1867 C.J. ANDERSSON *Notes on Birds of Damara Land* (1872) 204 (Pettman), It is not unlike a gigantic *Coly*; it also climbs and flies like the colies, which it strongly resembles in its general habits. **1910** A.B. LAMONT *Rural Reader* 32 Colies (muisvogels) devour great quantities of strawberries. **1913** C. PETTMAN *Africanderisms* 125 *Colley*, This name, which in England (Somerset) is given to the blackbird, is occasionally used in South Africa of the Muis-vogel. **1923** HAAGNER & IVY *Sketches* 87 The Mousebirds, or Colies (Family Coliidae), are as bad at fruit-thieving as the Bulbuls, if not more so, and devour large quantities of apricots, plums, peaches, etc. **1937** M. ALSTON *Wanderings* 97 Most numerous of all were the mouse-birds or colies, those long-tailed, grey, parrot-like birds peculiar to South Africa. **1953** J.M. WINTERBOTTOM *Common Birds of S.-E.* 19 The Red-faced Coly is found wherever there are trees and bushes .. This Coly has been reported as a host of the Black-and-Grey Cuckoo. **1970** O.P.M. PROZESKY *Field Guide to Birds* 168 Mousebirds or colies are smallish long-tailed birds peculiar to Africa. **1985** G.L. MACLEAN *Roberts' Birds of Sn Afr.* 369 Family 51 Coliidae — Mousebirds (Colies).

comage var. KOMMETJIE.

comando var. COMMANDO.

comberse var. KOMBERS.

combi(e) see KOMBI.

combuys var. KOMBUIS.

come *v. intrans.* In the phr. *to come right* [calqued on Afk. *regkom* end well, straighten out]:

1. To end well; to turn out well; to return to normal; often more fully as ***all* -, *everything will come right*** [tr. Afk. *alles sal regkom*, see ALLES SAL REGKOM].

Also found in other varieties of English, but particularly common in *S. Afr. Eng.* due to the influence of Afrikaans.

1870 A.W. COLE in A.M.L. Robinson *Sel. Articles from Cape Monthly Mag.* (1978) 9 Having full confidence in coachee's skilful assurance that '*Alles zal wel recht kom, mynheer; klim maar op!*' (all will come right by-and-by, sir; jump up!) the perilous ascent is made accordingly. **1882** C. DU VAL *With Show through Sn Afr.* I. 107 His motto, '*Alles zal recht kommen*' ('All will come right'), as the best index to a character in which calmness and a firm regard for justice seem equally blended. **1900** T. FROES *Kruger & Co.* 14 The promise .. that all would come right. **1911** A.H. FROST in *Farmer's Weekly* 4 Oct. 134 Some farmers think that by buying good rams everything will come right. **1916** *Farmer's Weekly* 27 Dec. 1585 Alles zal reg kom if .. the crops come bumpers. Unfortunately they do not as a rule 'come right'. **1939** [see ALLES SAL REGKOM]. **1961** D. BEE *Children of Yesterday* 275 Eventually the radio 'came right'. **1972** *S. Afr. Panorama* Mar. 31 No one could gaze on the calm, unruffled features of Andries Pretorius without feeling that all would come right. **1982** D. KRAMER *Short Back & Sides* 57, I dreamt I'd been reclassified Non-white And when I told my wife she started crying I said 'Don't worry, Skattie, I'm sure it'll come right.' **1985** C. RYAN in *Frontline* Aug. 35 Zimbabwe is coming right despite its government. **1990** [see SHARPEVILLE sense 1].

2. To succeed in an endeavour; to manage to do something (esp. something difficult).

1872 *Cape Argus* 11 May 3 He was young to the work, but with the advice of his experienced colleague .. he had no doubt he would come right. **1985** P. SLABOLEPSZY *Sat. Night at Palace* 27 You must come right with the chicks, man. *Ibid.* 67 You play ball they kick you out. You come right, they knock you down. **1989** E. BURSIK in *Ski-Boat* Jan.-Feb. 24 A trick to catch these fish .. is to drift with fillets. We did not come right, but some good fish were taken this way.

come down see DOWN sense a.

cometj(i)e var. KOMMETJIE.

cómfáát, comfyt varr. KONFYT.

comiche var. KOMMETJIE.

comma *n.* [Special sense of general Eng.] A mark (,) representing the decimal point. So called in both written and spoken contexts, although in writing the mark is more commonly used than the word.

Introduced in terms of the Measuring Units and National Measuring Standards Act (Act 76 of 1973).

1974 *Sunday Times* 15 Sept. 12 It is the same with the new practice of talking about 'comma' instead of 'point' in decimal numbers ... Why .. should we now be required to talk about a 'comma' when 'point' serves the purpose far better? **1975** *Het Suid-Western* 30 Jan., A miss is as good as one comma six one kilometers. **1981** N. AIYER in *Staffrider* Vol.3 No.4, 1 The Chairman of the Board reports a net profit, after tax of two comma five. **1985** on TV1, 14 Mar. (News), The consumer will have to pay about twelve comma five percent more for sugar. **1992** *Weekend Post* 15 Aug. (Business) 6 We will .. sell by public auction the following property: Remainder of portion 11 ... In Extent: seventy five comma five nine six eight (75,5968) hectares.

commandant /kɒmənˈdant, -ˈdɑːnt, -ˈdænt/ *n.* Also with initial capital. [Du. *commandant*, *kommandant* commanding officer of a fort, town or district.]

1. *hist.* During the 19th (and late 18th) century, and esp. among the Boer forces during the Anglo-Boer wars: the chief military officer of a district; the leader of a commando; also used as a title; FIELD COMMANDANT; KOMMANDANT sense 1; VELD COMMANDANT.

1791 G. CARTER *Loss of Grosvenor* 149 Hynes thinks that Quin was a kind of commandant. **1812** A. PLUMPTRE tr. J. Lichtenstein's *Trav. in Sn Afr.* (1928) I. 101 A party .. had been sent in pursuit of them by the commandant of the district. **1838** F. OWEN *Diary* (1926) 125 The commandant thanked me for speaking my sentiments openly to *them*, rather than to the natives. **1846** J.M. BOWKER *Speeches & Sel.* (1864) 225 If I can get horses, I intend to join the Commandant of the Burgher force. **1852** M.B. HUDSON *S. Afr. Frontier Life* 225 Commandant Joubert, who has thrice brought a body of Burghers into the field this war against 'the Tambookies,' was one of the Commandants during the time of the old Commando System. **1877** C. ANDREWS *Reminiscences of Kafir War 1834–5.* 11 The Colonel had to dinner the noble old Dutch commandant of the Swellendam Burghers, Linde. **1880** E.L. PRICE *Jrnls* (1956) 397, I ought to have told you of Commandant Fereira's adventure ... He is .. a Commander of an army. **1900** H.C. HILLEGAS *Oom Paul's People* 206 Second in authority to the commandant-general are the commandants, permanent officials who have charge of the military affairs of the seventeen districts of the republic. **1913** J. BRANDT *Petticoat Commando* 27 The many armed burghers passing through the town would only obey orders of their own respective Commandants and Field-Cornets. **1924** D. FAIRBRIDGE *Lady Anne Barnard* 127 The Commando system .. was instituted .., Adriaan van Jaarsveld being appointed Commandant. *a*1930 G. BAUMANN in Baumann & Bright *Lost Republic* (1940) 167 When war was declared and the commandos called up for field service, the old elected Commandants took command of their different districts. [**1947** E.R. SEARY *S. Afr. Short Stories* 228 Commandant (Afrikaans): chief officer of a commando, i.e. of a troop of burgher soldiers raised in one district.] **1971** *Personality* 11 June 37 He was the commandant of a *burgher* commando of the Camdebo, engaged in the frustrating task of chasing elusive Bushmen.

2. The commanding officer of a unit of the police force; KOMMANDANT sense 2. Also used as a title.

1866 E. WILSON *Reminisc.* 41, I received instructions from the Commandant, to prosecute enquiries into the .. robbery. **1933** W.H.S. BELL *Bygone Days* 73 Appointed to the command of the Frontier Armed and Mounted Police in the place of Commandant James Henry Bowker. **1947** C.R. PRANCE *Antic Mem.* 135 Though he never mastered six words of the world's worst Afrikaans as spoken by His Majesty's South African Constabulary, his horsemanship and his simple friendliness quickly endeared him to his Brother Boer. He would ride day-long, farm-visiting with the Commandant. **1960** J. COPE *Tame Ox* 65 The squad car arrived at the wayside station with the commandant of the district police in uniform. **1969** M. BENSON *At Still Point* (1988) 115 Matthew .. told him he would at once telephone the Commandant. **1971** H. ZEEDERBERG *Veld Express* 155 Commandant Tjaardt Kruger, the chief of the Republic's Intelligence Service .. told Pieter Zeederberg, then Hoofd Kommandant of Pretoria, that Jameson's original plan was to use the coaches for the 'invasion' of the Transvaal.

3. An officer commanding a commando unit in the Union Defence Forces; subsequently, one commanding a reserve defence unit of the South African Defence Force; also used as a title. See also COMMANDO sense 5.

1922 *Rand Daily Mail* in J. Crwys-Williams *S. Afr. Despatches* (1989) 236 Commandants walked calmly about signalling instructions. **1957** R.B. DURRANT in *Hansard* 27 Feb. 1834 More than half the commandants of the commandos had not had military training. **1973** *E. Prov. Herald* 10 May 4 The Officer Commanding the Graaff-Reinet Commando, Commandant Piet Hugo, has been appointed acting OC of Group 5. **1988** *Cape Times* 29 Dec. 6 The departure from the Defence Force this week of Commandant Andre Malan, former OC Outeniqua Commando.

4. An officer in the South African Army or Air Force; also used as a title.

Previously the rank of Lieutenant-Colonel, and ranking between Major and Colonel.

1950 D. REED *Somewhere S. of Suez* 187 The Nationalist Afrikaner Minister of Defence, in 1948, announced that it [*sc.* the Defence Force] would be reorganized ... The British military model and nomenclature were done away with and the Boer Commmandos revived, with their ranks from Field Cornet to Commandant. **1977** *Joint Operational Dict.* 95 *Commandant,* .. Person holding this rank; equivalent rank in the SA Navy: Commander. **1979** *Cape Times* 2

July 5 Kilted soldiers of the Cape Town Highlanders said goodbye .. to Commandant C 'Bud' O'Brien, their commanding officer during two tours of active service. **1983** *Pretoria News* 24 May 1 The transport pilot who had the most flying hours in the South African Air Force, Commandant Izak Jacobus Henning.

5. *hist.* With qualifying word: **Chief Commandant** [tr. Du. *Hoofd-Kommandant*], the senior commandant of two or more commandos acting jointly.

[1971 see sense 2.] **1971** D.W. KRÜGER in *Std Encycl. of Sn Afr.* III. 345 In the Orange Free State the designation of **Chief Commandant** was revived during the Second Anglo-Boer War, when it was conferred upon the senior commandant of two or more commandos acting jointly ... A rank of Chief Commandant was created in the South African Defence Force in May 1969. It indicates the grouping of a number of local commandos under a superior officer with the new designation.

6. The leader of a 'commando' of Voortrekkers, an Afrikaans youth movement similar to the Boy Scouts and Girl Guides; also used as a title; KOMMANDANT sense 3. See also VOORTREKKER *n.* sense 2 b.

1975 J.F.P. BADENHORST in *Std Encycl. of Sn Afr.* XI. 288 Membership is open to White boys and girls, officers ('field-cornets' and 'commandants'), executive members and 'lay members'. **1990** *Sunday Times* 30 Sept. 13 The commandant of the Maritzburg based Gerrit Maritz Voortrekker Commando .. said the movement was 'definitely not right-wing'.

7. An officer in the military- or paramilitary wing of a right-wing political organization.

1991 H. JANSEN in *Sunday Times* 14 July 4 He had bought the farm Witklipbank from former Delmas AWB commandant Bill R—.

commandant-general *n. hist.* Also with initial capitals. [tr. Du. *commandant -, kommandant generaal.*]

1. The commander-in-chief of a number of commandos of the defence forces of the Boer republics; also used as a title. See also COMMANDO sense 4.

1877 F. JEPPE *Tvl Bk Almanac & Dir.* (1976) 36 A commandant-General is chosen by the whole laager. **1880** G.F. AUSTEN *Diary* (1981) 6 They were acting under the orders of the Commandant General, PA Cronje. **1893** J.F. INGRAM *Story of Gold Concession* 236 He .. was .. appointed commandant-general of the then struggling and almost penniless republic. **1899** *Volkstem* 12 Oct. 1 Commandant-General Joubert left camp last night with his forces. **1900** H.C. HILLEGAS *Oom Paul's People* 51 A single republic, with Marthinus Wessel Pretorius as President, and Paul Kruger as commandant-general of the army. **1900** [see FIELD CORNET sense 1]. *a*1930 G. BAUMANN in Baumann & Bright *Lost Republic* (1940) 162 The proposals were .. to allow new citizens, like old citizens, to vote for a State President and Commandant General. **1946** S. CLOETE *Afr. Portraits* 48 In 1852, he was made a full field cornet and accompanied the old Commandant-General Pretorius to the Sand River. **1950** [see *Dopper Church* (DOPPER *n.*¹ sense b)]. **1974** K. GRIFFITH *Thank God We Kept Flag Flying* 30 Joubert, the Transvaal commandant-general, had crossed the northern Natal border with his army on 12 October 1899. **1989** *Reader's Digest Illust. Hist.* 245 This dependence on part-time soldiers extended all the way to the top — and only the SAR had a full-time professional soldier, and elected Commandant-General.

2. The commander-in-chief of the defence forces of the Union of South Africa, and subsequently of the Republic of South Africa.

Now called 'Chief of the Defence Force'.

1915 J.K. O'CONNOR *Afrikander Rebellion* 66 He was appointed to a non-political position, that of Commandant-General of the Defence Force. **1933** W.H.S. BELL *Bygone Days* 333 General Christian Frederick Beyers was Commandant-General of the Union Defence Force. **1971** *Std Encycl. of Sn Afr.* III. 614 The designation of the more senior posts have .. undergone a complete change ... The old title of Commandant-General was reinstated and superseded that of Chief of the General Staff. *Ibid.* 617 The Commandant-General of the South African Defence Force is, since 17 Oct. 1966, simultaneously the commander-in-chief of the armed forces of the Republic of South Africa and the chief accounting officer of the Department of Defence. **1977** *Joint Operational Dict.* 95 *Commandant-general*, Former post designation of the General Officer (General) who was Chief of the SADF. Present title Chief of the Defence Force.

commandeer *v.* Formerly also **kommandeer**. [ad. Du. *commanderen, kommanderen* to press or requisition.]

Now in general Eng. usage.

1. To seize (goods, domestic animals, vehicles, buildings, etc.) for military use.

a. *trans.*

1810 J.G. CUYLER in G.C. Cory *Rise of S. Afr.* (1910) I. 223 Horses of course will have to be commandeered. *a*1875 [see sense 2]. **1880** G.F. AUSTEN *Diary* (1981) 17 Commandeering goods, liquors &c. going on as before — but more so. **1885** LADY BELLAIRS *Tvl at War* 206 Many attempts at evasion were practised to avoid handing over stores or horses *commandeered*. **1900** S.T. PLAATJE *Boer War Diary* (1973) 67 All grain belonging to storekeepers was commandeered. *c*1936 *S. & E. Afr. Yr Bk & Guide* 73 A large quantity of bullion was commandeered from the mines. **1937** H. KLEIN *Stage Coach Dust* 196 When supplies gave out he was empowered to forage round the farms in the vicinity and commandeer whatever he wanted: oxen, sheep, cows, poultry. **1941** C. BIRKBY *Springbok Victory* 153 He commandeered a donkey and trekked back through the bush. **1958** A. JACKSON *Trader on Veld* 71 The Government warned business people in the country districts to take stock of their belongings and deposit stock sheets with their respective magistrates, in order to establish any claims for goods that might be commandeered. **1987** J. SILVER in *Personality* 7 Oct. 12 Like all other plane owners in that year, he'd had his aircraft commandeered by the Defence Force. **1990** [see COMMANDO sense 4].

b. *intrans.*

1881 *Times* (U.K.) 25 Jan. 5 The Boers are in Lydenburg commandeering from the stores. **1882** *Standard* (U.K.) 12 Dec. 5 The action of the Government in commandeering so extensively.

2.a. *trans.* Usu. *passive.* To force (someone) into military service; *commando v.*, see COMMANDO *n.*

1859 *Cape Town Weekly Mag.* 28 Jan. 27 A large commando will again go out against .. Bechuana tribes ... The burghers have already been commandeered, and are preparing to turn out. **1871** J. MACKENZIE *Ten Yrs* (1971) 37 The men who had been 'commandeered,' or called out, had been again disbanded. *a*1875 T. BAINES *Jrnl of Res.* (1964) II. 84 The old Field-Cornet Cronjee .. 'kommandeered' Piet, Christian and Baart Harmse, as well as a horse, with saddle and bridle. **1881** G.F. AUSTEN *Diary* (1981) 37 Most of the inhabitants of the town have been today commandeered to do personal service on Monday next or to pay fines from £10 upwards. **1897** F.R. STATHAM *S. Afr. as It Is* 285 A considerable number of British subjects resident in the Transvaal were 'commandeered' for service in the field against one Malaboch, a recusant native chief. **1900** W.S. CHURCHILL *London to Ladysmith* 141 'So now you fight against your country?' 'I can't help it,' he repeated sullenly, 'you must go when you're commandeered.' **1905** *Star* 2 Oct. 7 Every civil servant, and indeed every burgher who was capable of carrying arms, .. was liable upon the outbreak of war to be commandeered to do military duty. *a*1930 G. BAUMANN in Baumann & Bright *Lost Republic* (1940) 183 There was no discrimination, when commandeering Free State Burghers, as to whether their origin was English, German or any other nationality. **1940** F.B. YOUNG *City of Gold* 178 The general wants wagons, so now you are commandeered. Report yourself to headquarters. **1963** M. BENSON *Afr. Patriots* 48 Thema .. as a child during the Anglo-Boer War had been commandeered by the Boers to be at one time or another a kitchen-boy, cook, batman, waiter and labourer. **1982** *Sunday Times* 16 May, *(caption)* Helgard Prinsloo ... commandeered at 15.

b. *intrans.*

1977 R.J. HAINES in R.J. Bouch *Infantry in S. Afr. 1652–1976* 3 In order to avoid inflicting too great hardships on the border dwellers a system of commandeering in rotation was introduced so that the burgers of Swellendam and Tulbagh were also compelled to enter occasional service.

3. *transf.* To take arbitrary possession of (something). Also *fig.*

a. *trans.*

1901 R. KIPLING in *War's Brighter Side* 135 We never use such words as steal, or 'collar', 'pinch' or 'shake'. The fashion is to say he 'commandeers' it. **1901** *Grocott's Penny Mail* 3 Jan. 2 The Boers .. professed to have 'commandeered the Almighty ..'. **1910** D. FAIRBRIDGE *That Which Hath Been* (1913) 172 The laws with regard to cattle-barter with the Hottentots had been joyfully defied and raids organised in which, under pretext of barter, natives had been killed and the cattle commandeered. **1925** D. KIDD *Essential Kafir* 17 As the children grow older they annex or 'commandeer' some rudiments of dress. **1972** *Argus* 9 Dec. 17 Their car wouldn't start. They commandeered another and took the man to hospital. **1978** A.P. BRINK *Rumours of Rain* 211 His wagon was among those commandeered to convey the immigrants to their farms in the interior.

b. *intrans.*

1937 C.R. PRANCE *Tante Rebella's Saga* 113 Orders are orders and Blinkers was up against the necessity to 'commandeer' unscrupulously with no other course available.

Hence (senses 1 and 2) **commandeered** *ppl adj.*, pressed into or appropriated for military service or use; *absol.*, the people so commandeered; **commandeering** *vbl n.*, the action or system of pressing or requisitioning for military purposes; also *attrib.*

1880 G.F. AUSTEN *Diary* (1981) 7 The officers .. on this day commenced ordering liquors and other refreshments to be supplied for their use, in some cases giving no acknowledgement, in others a commandeering order — as they term it — compelling its delivery by their force. [**1881** *Ibid.* 43 A number of the English inhabitants have to day received commandeer orders to serve personally — to appear tomorrow.] **1882** C. DU VAL *With Show through Sn Afr.* II. 9 'Commandeering' is a South African term which refers to the taking over, or otherwise seizing, in the name of the governing body, any and every article deemed necessary to the successful carrying on of warfare, with or without payment or acknowledgement. **1885** LADY BELLAIRS *Tvl at War* 105 Fatigue-parties were engaged everywhere, loading up the *commandeered* supplies. **1887** A.A. ANDERSON *25 Yrs in Waggon* II. 45, I found myself among the commandeered. **1894** *Westminster Gaz.* (U.K.) 23 June 6 A number of commandeered settlers. **1898** A. MILNER in C. Headlam *Milner Papers* (1931) I. 197 Commandeering. If need be, we must face a big row about this. **1899** *Daily News* 13 June 4 Each commandeered burgher. **1900** A.W. CARTER *Informant, Ladybrand* 24 Jan. 1 There is nothing about the new commandeering — I would like to know who they got out of L[ady] B[rand]. **1913** M.M. CLEAVER *Young S. Afr.* 98 The commandeering official knocked at the door and demanded Ou Baas. **1921** W.C. SCULLY *Harrow* 154 The commandeering of cattle, .. and of wagons proceeded apace. The effect was absolutely ruinous ... Commandeering came in the case of the suspect to spell confiscation ... Without such receipts payment for the commandeered items could not be claimed. **1936** H.F. TREW *Botha Treks* 43, I was shown a commandeering note he had given to the hotel-keeper at Pienaars River. **1937** H. KLEIN *Stage Coach Dust* 196 As payment for the commandeered stock he gave the farmer a voucher, equivalent to the value taken. **1944** 'TWEDE IN BEVEL' *Piet Kolonel* 62 Whenever we moved, the most colossal crates would necessitate the commandeering of all available transport.

commando /kəˈmɑːndəʊ/ *n.* Also **comando**, and with initial capital. Pl. **-s**, less freq. **-es**. [S. Afr. Du. *commando, kommando* armed party, fr. Pg. *commando* command, party commanded.] A small fighting force. See also COMMANDANT.

1. *hist.*

a. An armed and usu. mounted party of men, usu. civilians, mustered esp. against indigenous peoples for forays, reprisals, and the recovery of stolen cattle; an expedition undertaken by such a party. Also *attrib.* See also BURGHER sense 3 a.

1790 tr. *F. Le Vaillant's Trav.* I. 319 A planter .. complains to the governor that the Caffres have carried away all his cattle; and he requests a *commando*, that is to say, permission to go and recover his property with the assistance of his neighbours. **1801** W.S. VAN RYNEVELD in G.M. Theal *Rec. of Cape Col.* (1899) IV. 92 Their chief business is to form bodies of armed men (commandos) against Bosjesmen and other Vagabonds, who disturb the Country and rob the farmers of their Cattle. **1818** G. BARKER Journal. 5 Jan., 25 of our people and pack oxen went to join the comando against the Caffres. **1829** C. ROSE *Four Yrs in Sn Afr.* 75 The crimes were individual, but the punishment was general: the duty of the Commando was to destroy, to burn the habitations, and to seize the cattle. **1833** *Graham's Town Jrnl* 21 Mar. 3 Colonel Frayer immediately called together an Army, or Commando, consisting of Boers, Soldiers, and Hottentots from the missionary institution Theopolis. **1835** G. CHAMPION *Jrnl* (1968) 4 The ghosts of Hottentots & Bushmen & Caffers that have been murdered by commandoes in S. Africa in past years. **1844** J.C. CHASE in R. Godlonton *Mem. of Brit. Settlers* 58 We were denounced as having been *often* engaged in Commandoes, or semi-military Expeditions against the aborigines. **1863** J.S. DOBIE *S. Afr. Jrnl* (1945) 64 'Commando' means a calling out by authority, volunteers who place themselves under a magistrate or other officer .. with the object of punishing some raid or turbulent conduct of Kafirs or Bushmen. **1875** C.B. BISSET *Sport & War* 107 A strong party of Dutch — part of the field force called a commando — had been attacked by an ambush of Kafirs only a few days before. **1882** C.L. NORRIS-NEWMAN *With Boers in Tvl* 14 After 1831 the Commissioner-General for Frontier Affairs .. set himself against these border raids and 'commandoes', as being both injurious to the colonists and unsettling to the natives. **1919** M. GREENLEES tr. *O.F. Mentzel's Life at Cape in Mid-18th C.* 41 An ensign of the Cape Garrison, Rhenius by name, had been sent with a commando of about forty soldiers. **1950** H. GIBBS *Twilight* 144 Commandos of Boer burghers penetrated Basuto territory to get back their cattle, burning down huts and carrying off prisoners. **1956** F.C. METROWICH *Valiant but Once* 13 The Hottentot chief adopted so threatening an attitude, that the commando, completely outnumbered, thought it advisable to withdraw. **1977** R.J. HAINES in R.J. Bouch *Infantry in S. Afr. 1652–1976* 1 The commando of these years was a mixed group of regular soldiers, burgers and Coloureds. **1979** C. ENDFIELD *Zulu Dawn* 82 The War Office .. had failed to furnish Chelmsford with cavalry. Some of these needs were being supplied by local white volunteers formed into irregular commando groups.

b. Occas. with defining word: **straf-commando** /ˈstraf-/ *n.* [Afk., *straf* punishment], a punitive expedition.

1928 E.A. WALKER *Hist. of S. Afr.* 73 The company supplied the ammunition; those who took part in each *straf-commando* reported the result to the Castle.

c. *comb.* **commando beskuit** *rare* [Afk. *beskuit*, see BESKUIT], rusks taken as provisions on commando; **commando law**, a law allowing the pressing of civilians into military service; **commando tax**, a tax levied at the Cape from 1812 to supply funds for maintaining commandos.

1899 M. MARQUARD *Lett. from Boer Parsonage* (1967) 40 We have begun tackling our second muid of meal for **commandobiskuit** today. **1908** J.M. ORPEN *Reminisc.* (1964) 203 After the Constitution was completed, I drew up and proposed the **Commando Law**, which was adopted as proposed by me and continued fundamentally unchanged, while the Free State remained a Republic. **1926** M. NATHAN *S. Afr. from Within* 72 The field-cornet at Pretoria, purporting to act under commando law, impressed five uitlanders, all British subjects, into service. **1827** *Reports of Commissioners upon Finances at Cape of G.H.* II. 60 Since the year 1812 another tax has been assessed, upon the principle of the 'opgaaf,' denominated the '**commando tax**'. **1833** *Cape of G.H. Lit. Gaz.* III. 181 (Pettman), The pay of the military body, an expense which the whole Colony had to meet in the shape of a *Commando Tax*, without any return whatever. **1913** C. PETTMAN *Africanderisms* 127 *Commando Tax*, A tax established in the Cape Colony by Government Proclamation, 4 December, 1812, 'for the maintenance of a corps for the defence of the frontier'.

2. *hist.* In the phr. ***on commando***, on a military expedition; engaged in military service.

1800 J. BACKSTROM (tr. J.A. Truter) in G.M. Theal *Rec. of Cape Col.* (1898) III. 278, 30 lbs. of Powder & 60 lbs. of Lead were added .. that the .. Veld Commandant might make use of it in case he had occasion to send a party on commando. **1835** A. SMITH *Diary* (1940) II. 174 The Matabeli, when they go on commando, advance during the night .. with great rapidity. **1861** P.B. BORCHERDS *Auto-Biog. Mem.* 56 This service was known under the appellation of 'commando gaan' — to go on commando — the term for an armed body of inhabitants dispatched on active service. **1887** J.C. BROWN *Crown Forests* 12 A person I had once engaged was prevented by his attendance being required on commando. **1900** G.H.M. RITCHIE in E. Hobhouse *Brunt of War* (1902) 15 Unless the men at present on commando .. surrender themselves and hand in their arms to the Imperial authorities .. the whole of their property will be confiscated and their families turned out destitute and homeless. **1915** J.K. O'CONNOR *Afrikander Rebellion* 12 'On Commando' to them is a term meaning a happy time of riding on horseback from town to town, living on the country as they proceed and doing no work. *c***1936** *S. & E. Afr. Yr Bk & Guide* 73 Some 20,000 Boers were still on commando but, outside of these, nearly the whole nation was being maintained by Great Britain. **1946** S. CLOETE *Afr. Portraits* 359 His force of mounted burghers were dependent on grass to feed .. the driven cattle which they used for food when on commando. **1963** R. LEWCOCK *Early 19th C. Archit.* 242 Matters were not improved by the unavoidable absence, from August 1822, of Retief on commando against Macomo. **1973** J. MEINTJES *Voortrekkers* 95 Virtually everybody was known to everybody else due to their migrations and hunting trips, .. and service on commando. **1983** F.E. O'B. GELDENHUYS in *Optima* Vol.31 No.3, 154 The burghers on commando .. came back to farms destroyed and burned down by the English.

3. *hist.* During the 19th century: an armed group, or regiment, of black soldiers; an expedition undertaken by such a group. See also IMPI sense 1 a.

1835 W.B. BOYCE in A. Steedman *Wanderings* II. 269 The Ficani Chief .. has been driven thence, by a commando from Dingaan, the Zulu Chief. **1839** W.C. HARRIS *Wild Sports* 111 We saw comparatively few men, the larger proportion of the able-bodied being absent with Kalipi on the commando against the emigrant farmers. **1846** J.M. BOWKER *Speeches & Sel.* (1864) 223 The commando of the Kafirs were round us all day. **1881** E.L. PRICE *Jrnls* (1956) 451 Do you remember .. hearing of our Bakwena fighting with another tribe close by ... They have set out today in what we call 'a *commando*' in this country — wh. is, in fact, an *army*. **1905** G.W. STOW *Native Races of S. Afr.* 311 Moselekatze .. sent a large commando in pursuit, with orders to overtake the marauders .. and recover the cattle which had been seized.

4. *hist.* A unit of the Boer forces during the Anglo-Boer wars of 1880–81 and 1899–1902, usu. mustered from a particular town or farming district; KOMMANDO sense 1 a. Also *attrib.* See also BURGHER sense 3 a.

1899 *Westminster Gaz.* (U.K.) 11 Nov. 8 The President .. has the right of declaring war and calling up one or more commandos. **1900** J.B. ATKINS *Relief of Ladysmith* 87 A commando of Boers was within half a mile of our picket. **1902** *Encycl. Brit.* XXXIII. 438 Each field-cornet .. was responsible for the arms, equipment and attendance of his commando — the commando being the tactical as well as the administrative unit. **1929** D. REITZ *Commando* 26 It was magnificent to see commando after commando file past the Commandant-General each man brandishing hat or rifle according to his individual idea of a military salute. **1937** C.R. PRANCE *Tante Rebella's Saga* 152 The waterless 'hinterland', .. too hopeless as farm-land even to be palmed-off on simple burghers as reward for their commando-service. **1957** D. GRINNELL-MILNE *Baden-Powell at Mafeking* 27 Were there not brave men in the *commandos*, resourceful, inured to hardship, every man accustomed to long hours in the saddle .. ? [*Note*] The units of the Republican militia, each designated by the district in which it was raised. **1971** *Daily Dispatch* 16 Dec. 10 The commando which took the field was a well-organised and fully equipped fighting machine. It consisted of 464 mounted men, each with a spare horse. **1987** *S. Afr. Panorama* Sept. 35 Willem Smits, called up for commando service with the Boers, found himself at war with his own chairman, Lord Harris. **1990** *Weekend Argus* 29 Sept. 13 Operating over a 275 000 sq km area, the commandos were highly mobile. They were self-contained units, either buying, commandeering or capturing supplies from the enemy.

5. An area protection force, initially under the control of the Union Defence Force, subsequently of the South African Defence Force, consisting of civilian personnel who, having completed an initial period of national service, must regularly report for shorter periods of service or training; KOMMANDO sense 1 a. In *pl.*, a collective term for the members of such a force. Also *attrib.*

1912 *Act 13* in *Stat. of Union* 200 The Citizen Force Reserve shall be divided into two classes, A and B ... Class B shall be organised as far as may be practicable so that members therof .. shall form territorial corps or commandos with sub-divisions corresponding as far as possible with the arrangement of Rifle Associations in each district. **1922** *Rand Daily Mail* in J. Crwys-Williams *S. Afr. Despatches* (1989) 231 A striker carried the news to a commando at the Town Hall that there was a 'scrap going on with coolies and Chinese,' and immediately the commando broke up and raced down on foot and on bicycles to the .. lower end of Market Street. **1936** E. ROSENTHAL *Old-Time Survivals* 26 Commandos rode against the Germans in South-West Africa during the Great War .. along-side the regimental units from the South African cities. **1957** *Act 44* in *Stat. of Union* 544 There shall be established under such designations as the Minister may determine, a system of commandos so as to ensure that citizens liable to render service in defence of the Union .. shall as far as possible be proficient in the use of military weapons. **1971** *Std Encycl. of Sn Afr.* III. 603 As the commando exists today it is intended to defend its own defined territory in times of emergency. War equipment, ammunition and uniforms are issued to members of the commandos. At the conclusion of a period of service in the commandos the members are posted to the Commando Reserve. **1977** B. MARKS *Our S. Afr. Army* 11 The Commando organization dates back to the Vryburgers in 1657. Since its inception it has been a volunteer force aimed primarily at territorial defence. It is the largest of the three components of the SA Army and despite its territorial context, it can operate in any operational area. Its members are trained as Infantrymen with the emphasis on counter-insurgency operations, both rural and urban. **1982** *Uniform* Sept. 9 *Country commandos* will be applied to protect their own districts. Other responsibilities are the protection of national key points, collecting information and area studies, anti-terrorist action and the promotion of Civic Service ... *Urban commandos* are usually composed of members who are not area-bound. Their main task will be to assist the SAP with crowd control, cordons, road blocks and curfews. **1983** J. KEEGAN *World Armies* 530 The Commandos were reorganised in June 1982 as a result of a shortfall in manpower of some 37% ... Essentially Commandos will be locally-based militia who are tasked with the protection of their own locality. **1985** H.R. HEITMAN in *Frontline* Dec. 16 At present the SADF has a standing force of around 80000 .. backed up by some 320 000 members of the Citizen Force and Commandos. **1988** *Personality* 25 July 5 For the first time ever (and at 42 years of age) my husband received a call-up from our local Commandos for a week's camp and intensive training. **1990** 'HOGARTH' in *Sunday Times* 12 Aug. 16 The SADF's plan to provide commando and citizen force members with automatic rifles and radios in their homes raises some thorny questions.

6. An army unit trained to carry out lightning military raids and to engage in guerilla warfare; a member of such a unit. Also *attrib.*

This sense of the word is also in general Eng. usage.

1940 W.S. CHURCHILL *Second World War* (1949) II. 566 Plans should be studied to land secretly by night on the islands and kill or capture the invaders. This is exactly one of the exploits for which the Commandoes would be suited. **1941** C. BIRKBY *Springbok Victory* 244 Jews and Arabs, hereditary enemies, fought side by side .. in a Middle East 'Commando,' one of those new units of shock-troops, which were a secret at that time. These commandos are composed of tough, specially-selected men, young, athletic, armed with powerful light weapons ... Commandos .. are highly mobile, hard-striking and elusive. **1959** L. LONGMORE *Dispossessed* 185 The railway police .. are not proficient in boarding trains in motion, because they have not been trained in 'commando' tactics. **1971** *Encycl. Brit.* VI. 141 The distinctive commando symbol later came to be the green beret. Popular usage to the contrary, a commando was not an individual, but a unit roughly equivalent to an infantry battalion. In the beginning commandos were formed of volunteers from army units; from 1942 onwards they were also formed from Royal Marines. **1972** *Sunday Times* 3 Dec. (Mag. Sect.) 1 South African servicemen sent for commando training learnt their battle technique at the Danie Theron Combat School. **1972** W.H. GARDNER in A. Lennox-Short *English & S. Afr.* 21 An old injury to his left hip developed into chronic osteo-arthritis, which prevented him from achieving his dearest ambition — to fight as a commando. **1985** *Time* 1 July 27 In late May, South African commandos made a foray into Angola. **1991** G. NEVILL in *Sunday Times* 3 Mar. (Extra) 3 Mr Ebrahim admitted that the Umkhonto we Sizwe 'regional commando' under his leadership in 1961 became the first ANC section to take up arms against the government.

7. The military or paramilitary wing of any of several (usu. right-wing) political organizations; a member of such a group. Also *attrib.* See also *boerekommando* and *wenkommando* (KOMMANDO sense 1 b).

1948 *Press Digest* No.10, 67 A Rand leader of the Ossewa Brandwag answered that in the past few months more than two hundred guerilla commandos had been formed in mines, factories and other places of work. **1972** *Sunday Times* 24 Sept. 7 The Nazi-type movement planned a special commando and 'the take-over of the present democratic state and the appointment of a National-Socialist state.' **1986** B. ROOS in *Cape Times* 4 Dec. 12 The cause of the vandalism .. is not the cricket tour at all. It is the destructive, violent laws of apartheid ... Those who wish to condemn the 'commandoes' should not forget that it is not cricket they are opposed to but apartheid. **1991** *Sunday Times* 7 Apr. 11 The time the team filmed an AWB Kruger Day rally, Mr Terre Blanche was enraged. Only 400 commandos arrived with their wives and children. **1992** S. MACLEOD in *Time* 9 Mar. 27 With the police on his tail, he disappeared underground for six months and tried to organize commando cells.

8. *Fig.*, and *transf.*

1955 D.L. HOBMAN *Olive Schreiner* 140 They fought the battle of their sex, in which the spectacular commandos of the militant suffragettes were less effective than the patient engineering of the pioneers of mental work. **1956** M. ROGERS *Black Sash* 167 The Transvaal 'commandos' of this great mass protest crossed the Vaal .. into the Free State. **1972** tr. *E.N. Marais's Rd to Waterberg* 95 In the big real black-ant commandos which battle with termites .. there is a preservation of unity in both the swarm and its behaviour.

9. A unit in the Voortrekker movement, the Afrikaans scouting organization; KOMMANDO sense 2. See also VOORTREKKER *n.* sense 2 b.

1966 *Cape Argus* 8 Mar. 5 The annual fund-raising campaign of the Riversdale Voortrekker Commando. **1975** *E. Prov. Herald* 7 Apr. 4 Eleven George Voortrekkers have raised R2 000 for their commando. **1975** J.F.P. BADENHORST in *Std Encycl. of Sn Afr.* XI. 288 The Penkoppe, Drawwertjies and Verkenners are grouped into field-cornetcies for boys and for girls, and two or more field-cornetcies form a commando. **1990** [see COMMANDANT sense 6].

Hence **commando** *v. trans. nonce*, COMMANDEER sense 2 a.

1880 *Grocott's Penny Mail* 28 Dec. 3 A party of Boers came to Mooi River, near Stormfontein, giving notice to the English residents that they would commando them on the following day, under the Grondwit [*sic*].

commando system *n. phr.* Also with initial capitals. [fr. prec.]

1. *hist.* During the 18th and 19th century at the Cape: the system of reprisal raids for the recovery of stolen cattle; the regulations governing this system. See also COMMANDO sense 1 a.

Also occas. called *reprisal system.*

1828 T. PRINGLE *Ephemerides* 202 The Commando system .. was prosecuted with great vigour under the recent administration of the Cape. **1834** — *Afr. Sketches* 373 The frontier colonists, be they Dutch or British, must of necessity continue to be semi-barbarians, so long as the *commando system* — the system of hostile reprisals — shall be encouraged or connived at. **1852** A.W. COLE *Cape & Kafirs* 129 Another subject of complaint among the boers was, the abolition of the Commando system against the Kafirs. **1955** L. MARQUARD *Story of S. Afr.* 71 Under the commando system every male burgher between sixteen and sixty was liable for military service and could be called on to defend the colony alongside regular soldiers. **1977** R.J. HAINES in R.J. Bouch *Infantry in S. Afr. 1652–1976* 23 For the early years the Republics depended on the commando system for defence purposes and no regular forces were established.

2. *hist.* A system of military organization in which an army was divided into units drawing soldiers from the region in which they were based and in which they mainly operated, esp. as used by the Boers during the Anglo-Boer War. See also COMMANDO sense 4.

The flexibility and mobility of units organized under this system proved particularly well-suited to guerilla warfare.

1920 F.C. CORNELL *Glamour of Prospecting* 318 The days of the old easy-going commando system of their fathers was a thing of the past, and .. rigid discipline had come in place of it. **1937** G.F. GIBSON *Story of Imp. Light Horse* 59 The inherent weakness of the Commando system, where every man was, to some extent, a law unto himself and his own General, with a resultant lack of discipline. **1974** A.P. CARTWRIGHT *By Waters of Letaba*, When Pretorius called for a commando of 1 000 men there might be a muster of 300 or even fewer ... The commando system .. was in danger of breaking down. **1989** *Reader's Digest Illust. Hist.* 244 It was a people's army wearing civilian clothes and based on the traditional commando system: the able-bodied men of each district called up under an elected Commandant assisted by field-cornets, one from each ward of the district.

3. A system of regional military service, part of the civil defence system of the South African Defence Force. See also COMMANDO sense 5.

1982 *Uniform* 13 Nov. 8 Advantages of the commando system are clearly evident, none more so than the sense of cameraderie through the experiences shared by the men. **1983** J. KEEGAN *World Armies* 530 Whilst in the past the Commando system was voluntary and very much based on traditions derived from the Afrikaner past it will now become largely a conscript organisation. **1993** *Sunday Times* 31 Oct. 31 The weapons are courtesy of the SADF commando system, which .. continues to do them proud.

commatje var. KOMMETJIE.

commercial rand see RAND sense 3 b.

commigee var. KOMMETJIE.

Commissary General *n. phr. Obs.* [Eng., or tr. Du. *commissaris-generaal* an official of the Dutch East India Company (see COMMISSIONER-GENERAL sense 2).] COMMISSIONER-GENERAL sense 2.

1688 G. TACHARD *Voy. to Siam* II. 46 Having informed himself that we were come to pay a Visit to the Commissary General and Governor, he commanded us to be let in. **1797** EARL MACARTNEY in G.M. Theal *Rec. of Cape Col.* (1898) II. 140 Soon after the surrender of this Colony, Mr Sluysken, the former Governor or Commissary General, delivered to Sir George Elphinstone and Generals Clarke and Craig a detailed account of the debts and credits of the Dutch East India Company at this place. **1812** A. PLUMPTRE tr. *H. Lichtenstein's Trav. in Sn Afr.* I. 108 At the place where we now were we found numbers of these kind of dissentions, the parties concerned in which were very eager to lay their grievances before the Commissary-general.

commissie trek, ‖**kommissie trek** /kəˈmɪsi ˌtrek, kɔˈmisi-/ *n. phr. Hist.* Pl. **-s**, ‖**-ke** /-kə/. [Afk. *kommissietrek* (fr. S. Afr. Du. *kommissie* -, *commissie trek*) fr. Du. *commissie* commission, committee + *trek* party of trekkers (see TREK *n.* sense 6).] A name given to any of three reconnaissance parties sent on ahead of the GREAT TREK.

1928 E.A. WALKER *Hist. of S. Afr.* 187 Three *commissie treks* went forth to spy out the land: one to the dry and thirsty *Dorsteland* in the present South-West Africa, another to the Zoutpansberg, the third and best known .. through Kaffirland to Natal. **1934** C.P. SWART Supplement to Pettman. 33 As a preliminary step they sent three reconnoitring parties, one to Natal .., one to the Transvaal and one to Damaraland. These were the so-called 'Commissie treks'. **1936** *Cambridge Hist. of Brit. Empire* VIII. 321 Exploring parties rode out to South-West Africa, to the north-eastern Transvaal, and along the coast belt to Natal. These *kommissie trekke* reported early in 1835. **1948** A. KEPPEL-JONES *S. Afr.: Short Hist.* 68 While the War of 1835 was being fought some scouting parties, *commissie treks*, were spying out the land in various directions. **1955** B.B. BURNETT *Anglicans in Natal* 12 Piet Uys of Uitenhage had led a *Kommissie trek* in 1834 to see if there lay a land worth colonising beyond the turbulent Cape Eastern frontier, free of the irksome restraint and ineffectual policies of the British administration. **1963** W.M. MACMILLAN *Bantu, Boer & Briton* 200 Land-hunger was .. at least one motive inspiring the so-called *commissie* treks. **1973** J. MEINTJES *Voortrekkers* 99 Piet Uys .. has been mentioned before, having gone on the early 'Commissie trek' to Natal to explore the territory and to come to an agreement with Dingane. **1978** T.R.H. DAVENPORT *S. Afr.: Mod. Hist.* 38 An overland *kommissie-trek* under Piet Uys set off .. to examine .. the prospects for hunting and for trading with the Africans. **1989** *Reader's Digest Illust. Hist.* 113 In 1834 .. kommissie treks (scouting parties) were secretly dispatched into the interior.

Commissioner-General *n. hist.* Also with small initials. [Eng.; in sense 2, prob. tr. Du.

commissaris-generaal; in sense 3, prob. tr. Afk. *kommissaris-generaal*.]

1. [Eng.] An officer of the imperial British government appointed to regulate and expedite legal and military procedures in the outlying frontier regions of the Cape Colony.

Created in 1828, the office was abolished again in 1834.

a1864 A. STOCKENSTROM in C.W. Hutton *Autobiog. of Late Sir Andries Stockenstrom* (1887) I. 431, I had been .. Commissioner-General of the Eastern Province. **1882** [see COMMANDO sense 1]. **1891** G.M. THEAL *Hist. of S. Afr.* 333 For the eastern province a commissioner-general was appointed, to control the proceedings of the inferior officers in cases where the delay of a reference to Capetown would be prejudicial to the public interests, and under the governor's direction to exercise special superintendence over the affairs of the border. **1989** *Reader's Digest Illust. Hist.* 106 Andries Stockenström, a former *landdrost* of Graaff-Reinet and Commissioner-General for the Eastern Districts.

2. An officer appointed by the Dutch East India Company during the Dutch rule at the Cape of Good Hope to report on agricultural and social conditions and administrative and revenue matters; COMMISSARY GENERAL.

1920 K.M. JEFFREYS tr. *Memorandum of Commissary J.A. de Mist* 161 The Indian Government in Holland has remained ignorant of the good effects which have resulted from the various reforms which the Commissioners-General brought into operation at the Cape. **1941** C.W. DE KIEWIET *Hist. of S. Afr.* 277 Commissioner-General (under Batavian Republic): J.H. de Mist, Feb. 21, 1803 – Sept. 25, 1805. **1971** A.J. BÖESEKEN in *Std Encycl. of Sn Afr.* III. 351 *Commissioner-General*, Office created by the Dutch East India Company, in rank lower than that of ordinary Councillors of India, but higher than that of Governors ... The Commissioners-General S.C. Nederburgh and S.H. Frijkenius were commissioned by the States General to improve the administration at the Cape, to cut expenses and increase revenue. **1975** C.G. HENNING *Graaff-Reinet* 20 On the 21 February 1803, the British Administration handed over control of the Cape Colony to the Batavian Republic, with J.A. de Mist as Commissioner-General until the 25th September 1804 and Lieutenant-General J.W. Jansens as Governor.

3. An official appointed by the South African government in terms of the Promotion of Bantu Self-Government Act of 1959 to head the administration of a black 'homeland' in the period leading up to independence.

1959 *Act 46* in *Stat. of Union* 516 A commissioner-general shall represent the Government with the national unit .. and shall in relation to that unit – (a) furnish guidance and advice in respect of all matters affecting administrative development and the social, educational, economic and general progress of the population; (b) promote the development of the administration of justice and of courts of law. **1970** E. KAHN in *Std Encycl. of Sn Afr.* I. 481 The offices of Commissioners-General, White Government representatives to guide and control the eight prospective Bantu national units, through 'creative self-withdrawal' by the 'European guardians', to self-government. **1973** *Sunday Times* 7 Oct. 4 If it is good enough for Hans A— to be Commissioner-General of a Bantustan, what is wrong with having a film censor who is deaf? **1986** P. MAYLAM *Hist. of Afr. People* 167 The Promotion of Bantu Self-Government Act .. proclaimed the existence of eight African 'national units' ... A white commissioner-general was to be appointed to each unit as the South African government's official representatives.

Hence (sense 3) **Commissioner-Generalship** *n.*, the office of Commissioner-General.

1970 *News/Check* 29 May 4 The appointment of Natal NP leader *Henry Torlage* to the commissioner-generalship of the Zulus.

commissioner's court *n. phr. Hist.* Also with initial capitals. Often in the phrr. **Bantu -**, **Native commissioner's court**. A special court dealing with civil, criminal, and administrative matters affecting black people only.

Instituted by the Native Administration Act of 1927, these courts were abolished in April 1986.

1927 *Act 38* in *Stat. of Union* 322 The Governor-General may .. constitute courts of native commissioners for the hearing of all civil causes and matters between Native and Native only: Provided that a native commissioner's court shall have no jurisdiction in matters which (a) the status of a person in respect of mental capacity is sought to be affected. **1937** *Star* 4 Aug. 12 A legal machinery that worked at such remorseless speed and achieved results by methods as summary as those that the exigencies of the Native Commissioner's Court seem to demand. **1948** E. HELLMANN *Rooiyard* 79 Many Natives are handicapped by their ignorance of legal procedure and have no knowledge of the approach to the Native Commissioner's Court where they could obtain redress for their wrongs. **1964** *Black Sash* Vol.8 Nos 1/2, 51 They have made investigations into .. the operation of the Native Commissioners' Courts. **1970** [see AID CENTRE]. c**1980** *S. Afr. 1979: Off. Yrbk* (Info. Service) 305 The presiding officer in the Commissioner's Court is an official of the Department of Co-operation and Development. He must be in possession of the same minimum legal qualifications as a magistrate. **1980** *Rand Daily Mail* 29 Nov. 1 Instead of blacks appearing in the commissioners' courts and whites in the magistrates' courts, everyone will go before the commissioners. **1984** *Frontline* Feb. 13 The Commissioners' Courts, intended to create a simple, inexpensive way of settling disputes between blacks, comprehensible to the litigants and run by experts in indigenous law and custom, hardly seem to have lived up to expectations. **1987** *Race Rel. Survey 1986* (S.A.I.R.R.) I. 338 The Special Courts for Blacks Abolition Bill .. provided for the scrapping of special courts for Africans ... Commissioners' courts .. were abolished.

commitj(i)e var. KOMMETJIE.

Committee of Ten *n. phr. Hist.* Also with small initials. A civic body in Soweto, first elected in 1977 in opposition to the government-appointed COMMUNITY COUNCIL. Also *attrib*. See also CIVIC.

The first of many community-based associations formed in opposition to community councils around the country, the Committee was replaced in 1984 with a new executive committee.

1977 *World* 23 Sept. 6 Speak to the Committee of Ten and get meaningful elections off the ground in Soweto now, is the appeal from Beeld, the Afrikaans morning newspaper, to the Government. **1978** *Survey of Race Rel.* (S.A.I.R.R.) 35 Following the collapse of the Soweto Urban Bantu Council, it was suggested .. that prominent people in Soweto should establish a civic body to run the affairs of the area. *Ibid.* 403 A resolution .. stated that Government-created institutions should be rejected and that the interim committee of ten should be elected to research how affairs in Soweto should be run. **1982** M. MZAMANE *Children of Soweto* 241 A people's interim government of Soweto, the Committee of Ten. **1983** H. MASHABELA in *Frontline* May 45 When civic associations, under the umbrella of the Soweto Committee of Ten, mushroomed .. some of us believed the organisational ills ravaging the body of the community would be tackled and overcome. **1985** *Race Rel. Survey 1984* (S.A.I.R.R.) 177 The Soweto civic association claimed to have 13 registered branches ... The Soweto committee of ten which is the executive committee of the association, .. was disbanded and a new executive of eight members who had 'greater ties with the grassroots' elected. **1989** *Reader's Digest Illust. Hist.* 455 The Port Elizabeth Black Civic Association .. , formed as an expression of popular opposition to the government-sponsored community council in much the same way as Soweto's Committee of Ten.

commonage *n.* [Brit. Eng. (now *obs.* in this sense).] The usual term for common land, a common; OUTSPAN *n.* sense 1 b. Also *attrib*.

1880 G.F. AUSTEN *Diary* (1981) 5 The draught oxen .. and 3 spans of mules grazing in the commonage were seized and carried off by the Boers. **1884** *Meteor* Feb. 1 Seven a.m., (April 20,) outspanned on the commonage just outside the rising town of Bedford. This outspan was a charming spot. **1896** R. WALLACE *Farming Indust. of Cape Col.* 267 In such a place as Worcester it was interesting to see the commonage herd, .. brought home at five o'clock. **1900** *Daily News* 24 Apr. 5 Two young Dutchmen acting as spies .. were found hidden in a Kaffir hut on Barkly Commonage. **1910** [see OUTSPAN *n.* sense 1]. **1916** *Act 40* in *Stat. of Union* 780 A commonage for the use of owners of erven in the township of Roos Senekal. **1926** [see ISRAELITE]. c**1936** [see CAMP *n.*[1] sense 4]. **1948** O. WALKER *Kaffirs Are Lively* 175 Old people .. lying on the commonage of another platteland .. town with nowhere to go. **1971** *Grocott's Mail* 27 Apr. 1 Portion 23 of Salem Commonage, .. situated in the Division of Albany. **1977** [see TRANSPORT-RIDER]. **1984** A.J. CHRISTOPHER *Crown Laws of British S. Afr.* 166 Extra grazing for a commonage was acquired and the scheme appeared to be set to play its part in settling poor whites. **1986** [see ISRAELITE]. **1994** *Grocott's Mail* 29 Mar. 7 Proposed lease of portion of the Bathurst Commonage ... It is the intention of the Bathurst Municipal Council to lease .. the four most westerly camps of the Bathurst Commonage.

community council *n. phr. Hist.* Also with initial capitals. The local authority of an urban black township, established by the government in terms of the Community Councils Act of 1977. Also *attrib*. See also UBC.

Many communities did not accept the system of local government by community councils, and set up other bodies in opposition to them: see CIVIC. See *Weekly Mail* quot. 1986.

1977 *World* 19 Sept. 3 The community councils are part and parcel of the homelands' set-up. The community councils are just a reversed version of the defunct UBC. **1978** *Survey of Race Rel.* (S.A.I.R.R.) 5 In terms of the Community Councils Act of 1977, community councils, elected on a non-ethnic basis, are planned to replace urban Bantu councils in urban African townships. c**1980** *S. Afr. 1979: Off. Yrbk* (Info. Service) 227 The *Community Councils Act* .. will provide urban Black communities with certain rights to self-government in that certain functions will be taken over from the administration boards ... Up to June 1978 some 100 community councils had been established. **1982** *Pace* Nov. 164 Azapo's comment was: 'A vote for the Community Council or any Government-instituted body is a betrayal to the black cause'. **1983** *Survey of Race Rel. 1982* (S.A.I.R.R.) 297 The Community Council system was perceived as an unacceptable extension of the administration boards and apartheid system. **1986** *Weekly Mail* 29 Aug. 2 With the demise of the development boards on July 1, all remaining community councils have been transformed into fully-fledged local authorities. **1987** *Race Rel. Survey 1986* (S.A.I.R.R.) I. 119 The chairman of the Duncan Village (East London) community council .. claimed .. that the council had the support of the 'vast majority' of residents and challenged anyone to prove otherwise.

Hence **community councillor** *n. phr.*

1983 *E. Prov. Herald* 28 Apr. 1 These events follow the assassination earlier this week of Mr Harrison Dube, a local community councillor. **1986** [see FATHERS]. **1987** *Cape Times* 10 July 2 The 'political killings', including necklace murders and the killing of community councillors, must be seen in the context of ongoing violence. **1988** THORNTON & RAMPHELE in Boonzaier & Sharp *S. Afr. Keywords* 32 Some community councillors were elected with percentage polls as low as one per cent.

community of property *n. phr. Law.* A marriage contract in which the possessions of the partners are merged in a joint estate, and disposed of by means of a joint will. Cf. ANTE-NUPTIAL CONTRACT.

[1810 G. BARRINGTON *Acct of Voy.* 165 By law also, a community of all property, both real and personal, is supposed to take place on the marriage of two persons, unless the contrary should be particularly provided against by solemn contract previously made. **1843** see ANTENUPTIAL CONTRACT.] **1861** W.A. NEWMAN in J.S. Mayson *Malays of Capetown* 25 The Cape colonial law, with regard to the disposal of property, differs greatly from the laws which obtain elsewhere; *e.g.*, a man (whether Dutch or English, Malay or South African) marrying in the colony, without an *ante-nuptial contract*, immediately creates a partnership between himself and his wife. According to the colonial law he marries in 'community of property,' and one clear half of his estate becomes the property of his wife and her heirs. *Ibid.* 26 A is married according to the colonial law ... His wife dies, leaving a number of children *who are of age*. They are entitled *immediately* to demand their maternal inheritance. **1887** *S.W. Silver & Co.'s Handbk to S. Afr.* 328 'Community of property' .. is .. a partnership in equal shares in all the property belonging to the spouses, or either of them, before the marriage, or which shall be acquired during its subsistence. **1909** J.F. SOLLY in *State* Aug. 190 If married in community of property she has the protection of the joint will. **1927** *Act 38* in *Stat. of Union* 332 A marriage between Natives, contracted after the commencement of this Act, shall not produce the legal consequences of marriage in community of property between the spouses. **1930** *Outspan* 25 July, There are two ways of getting married in South Africa as far as concerns the respective rights of the contracting parties in regard to their property ... *In Community of Property* or *Out of Community*, and the latter method involves the entering upon and completing a document called an Ante-Nuptial Contract, in which the *Community of Property* is specially excluded. **1947** E.R. SEARY *S. Afr. Short Stories* 229 By antenuptial contract the husband and wife retain control of their own property, but in community of property, as the name implies, their possessions are merged in one estate. **1973** *Weekend Post* 7 July 6 As he is joining me as a partner in our family business I think he should be married without community of property. **1986** *Reader's Digest Family Guide to Law* 239 Whereas marriage without an antenuptial contract used to give rise to community of property and the marital power, it now gives rise to community of property and joint administration. **1990** C. LAFFEATY *Far Forbidden Plains* 597 Hester and I were married in Community of Property ... It means that everything I own belongs jointly to Hester, and if there were a divorce I'd have to split everything down the middle with her.

Company *n. hist.* ***The Company***: Ellipt. for (*the*) *Dutch East India Company*; VOC sense 2; informally called JAN COMPAGNIE, JOHN COMPANY. Also *attrib.* See also SEVENTEEN.

Established as a trading company in 1602, the Dutch East India Company was responsible for the first permanent white settlement at the Cape of Good Hope.

1685 J. TYRELL in R. Raven-Hart *Cape G.H. 1652–1702* (1971) II. 255 They have wine that they make there at 9d a quart the Nearst prise and frute as Quinces plenty and aples Sum Small Quantity in the Companyes Garden, and other frutes. **1696** W. ERLE in *Ibid.* 423 Severall of the Inhabitants have very pretty Gardens, and the Company, a large Town. **1731** G. MEDLEY tr. *P. Kolb's Present State of Cape of G.H.* I. 4, I obtain'd of the said Directors the Favours compriz'd in the following Articles. 1. To pass to the *Cape of Good Hope* in one of the Company's ships. **1773** J. BYRON in J. Hawkesworth *Acct of Voy.* 137 The Company's garden is a delightful spot, and at the end of it there is a paddock belonging to the Governor, in which are kept a great number of rare and curious animals. **1798** S.H. WILCOCKE tr. *J.S. Stavorinus's Voy. to E. Indies 1768–71* I. 558 Zebras are sometimes caught alive, brought to the Cape, and tamed. I saw one in the Company's menagery. **1810** G. BARRINGTON *Acct of Voy.* 167 Nothing can be so mean and cringing as the conduct of the first description of planters, when they have anything to transact with the principal officers of the Company. **1857** *Cape Monthly Mag.* II. Sept. 153 The empire of 'the Company' knew only colonial tyrants and the mass upon whom these tyrants trampled. **1911** H.H. JOHNSTON *Opening Up of Africa* 185 In 1770 the total European population in Dutch South Africa .. was nearly ten thousand in number, of whom eight thousand were free colonists, and the remainder the servants or *employés* of the Company. **1941** C.W. DE KIEWIET *Hist. of S. Afr.* 8 When the days of the Company were over, there was no legend amongst the Boers of oppression. **1971** *S. Afr. Panorama* May 9 The Company felt that the establishment of an independent farming community close to the settlement would save the V.O.C. a considerable sum of money. **1983** M. DU PLESSIS *State of Fear* 102 The Company's garden was designed .. to save the sailors from scurvy and to tame a metaphysical wilderness. **1987** G. VINEY *Col. Houses* 59 In the last days of Company rule official corruption reached a perfectly disgraceful level.

compound *n.* [Special sense of general Eng. *compound* 'the enclosure within which a residence or factory (of Europeans) stands, in India, China, and the East generally' (*OED*). The ultimate etym. is disputed: orig. Indian Eng., prob. ad. Malay *kampong, kampung* enclosure, village (Du. orthography *kampoeng*). Earlier theories were that the word was an ad. of Pg. *campanha* or Fr. *campagne* country, or of Pg. *campo* field, camp.]

1. A (fenced or walled area enclosing) single-sex living quarters in which migrant labourers, usu. miners, live for the duration of their contracts. Cf. HOSTEL sense 1 b. Also *attrib.*

1886 G.A. FARINI *Through Kalahari Desert* 28 He .. goes to seek for some Kaffir friends of his at the mines, and finds his way into a compound. Arrested for being there without permission, .. he .. eventually gravitates to the prison. **1892** *The Jrnl* 15 Sept. 2 A large new compound, built by the Nigel G.M. Company, .. is a good solid structure built of stone and is capable of housing over 800 kafirs. **1895** A.B. BALFOUR *1200 Miles in Waggon* 67 The Kaffirs who work in the mines are kept in compounds during the whole time they engage to work in the mines, never being allowed to go outside, for fear of diamond stealing. **1903** *Ilanga* 10 Apr. 3, I went over to the kafir store in the compound of the City and Suburban Mine, Johannesburg. **1910** J. RUNCIE *Idylls by Two Oceans* 38 He went to the Falls, saw the Chinese compounds, saw how they washed diamonds. **1918** H. MOORE *Land of Good Hope* 18 The native workers, at this and all South African mines, live in 'compounds': huge enclosures surrounded by high walls. **1926** M. NATHAN *S. Afr. from Within* 298 Inspection of a mine 'compound' enables one to compare the life of the natives under a system of control with that led by them in the freedom of their kraals. **1936** WILLIAMS & MAY *I Am Black* 120 The compound was a large square around which were the sleeping houses of the black miners, arranged in long, low dormitories in which twenty or thirty men had their sleeping bunks. **1949** J.S. FRANKLIN *This Union* 184 The work on our farms and in our gold mines and in our industries would come to a complete standstill without the Native. And so he is to come in for a period or periods unaccompanied by his women-folk and his family, and he is to be herded in compounds. **1952** *Drum* Mar. 7 We were led into a compound surrounded by a high stone wall, given a blanket each and told to sleep in one of the low, dirty, mud-walled, long rooms by a black foreman. **1974** A. FUGARD *Dimetos & Two Early Plays* (1977) 93 There's no women in those compounds and they don't let you out. **1977** J. SIKAKANE *Window on Soweto* 12 Compound shops were also provided for African miners to buy food and clothing thus further restricting their movement to the mining premises only. **1980** M. LIPTON in *Optima* Vol.29 No.2, 99 Housing men in barracks or compounds, under close surveillance, for the duration of their contracts, originated in the 1880s on the diamond mines at Kimberley. **1989** L. VOGELMAN in *Weekly Mail* 20 Jan. 18 Compound living deprived them of their privacy, adequate food, comfortable sleeping conditions, appropriate living space, and heterosocial and heterosexual relationships. **1991** *Sunday Times* 10 Nov. 28 We tend to prefer the pleasure of word games to the pain of acknowledging what a century of neglect has done to our urban African population, the same conniving mentality that transforms locations into 'townships', compounds into 'hostels', and shebeens into 'taverns'.

2. *comb. Mining.* **compound manager**, the official supervisor of a mine compound; **compound system**, the system of housing and controlling migrant labourers in especially constructed, enclosed living quarters.

1892 J.E. RITCHIE *Brighter S. Afr.* 209 He commenced a new career as **compound-manager** for the great diamond company at Kimberley known as De Beers. **1908** D. BLACKBURN *Leaven* 205 Sidney Dane, Compound Manager of the New Yankee Gold Mining Company, Limited was .. a Natalian. **1911** T.L. CARTER in *Best of S. Afr. Short Stories* (1991) 64 Bacon Sothern, the compound manager, .. passed as an expert in the Chinese language, and .. had been engaged to superintend the yellow men at this mine. **1946** *Tribal Natives & Trade Unionism* (Tvl Chamber of Mines) 6 All matters affecting Native employees as mine residents are under the administration of the compound manager of each mine. **1968** L.G. GREEN *Full Many Glorious Morning* 26 Two hundred mine natives were in danger of starvation. The resourceful compound manager sent them out into the veld to collect locusts. **1986** P. MAYLAM *Hist. of Afr. People* 147 The compounds were tightly controlled. Each fell under the authority of a white compound manager who maintained discipline and kept pressure on workers to carry out their shifts. **1887** J.W. MATTHEWS *Incwadi Yami* 218 The enormous cost of the searching and detective departments will to my mind be done away with if the '**compound system**' inaugurated by the Central Co. in the Kimberley mine can be carried out by other companies. **1891** R. SMITH *Great Gold Lands* 77 This searching system appears to have been ineffectual. For what is called the 'Compound System' was adopted in preference to the other by the great mining companies. **1913** C. PETTMAN *Africanderisms* 128 *Compound system*, The requirements of the labourers confined in the compounds are met within the compound, provisions being made for the supply of all necessaries, even to hospital and church accommodation. **1936** *Cambridge Hist. of Brit. Empire* VIII. 778 Great temptations were offered to the natives by illicit diamond buyers to steal and sell part of the stones found, the losses being estimated at from £500,000 to £1,000,00 each year before the introduction of the compound system by De Beers in the 'eighties. **1948** A. PATON *Cry, Beloved Country* 80 The compound system .. brings men to the towns without their wives and children, and breaks up the tribe and the house and the man. **1952** *Drum* Mar. 4 It is impossible to prevent abuses of the employment of contract labour with the accompanying compound system. **1986** *Frontline* June 20 Out of the needs of the mines sprang the mine compound system, rigidly controlled migrant labour, and all the rest of it. **1989** *Reader's Digest Illust. Hist.* 357 The AMWU called for regular wage increases .. and the total abolition of the compound system.

Hence **compound** *v. trans. rare*, to confine to a compound; **compounded** *ppl adj.*; **compounding** *vbl n.*

1892 *The Jrnl* 6 Sept. 2 We suppose .. that nothing short of compounding the natives will prevent the drunkenness and violence that are now so scandalously rife. **1897** H. RAYMOND *B.I. Barnato* 83, I would like to say a word about .. the compounding of natives. The compound system .. has been a very good thing for the moral and social well-being of Kimberley. **1989** *Reader's Digest Illust. Hist.* 175 The 'solution' they hit upon was to house Africans in barracks, or closed compounds ... Many shopkeepers objected, saying that this deprived them of legitimate custom.

Rhodes .. pressed on, placating the Chamber of Commerce with assurances that the mining companies would buy all that they required for the compounded Africans from the Griqualand West dealers only.

comrade *n.* Also with initial capital. [Special sense of general Eng. *comrade*, a designation used by socialists or communists for a fellow socialist or communist.] Usu. in *pl.* as a collective term, *the comrades*: young, usu. left-wing activists, particularly militant supporters of the African National Congress; *amaqabane*, see IQABANE; cf. IBUTHO sense 2 b. Also *attrib.* Cf. *the children* (see CHILDREN), SIYAYINYOVA *n.* See also VIGILANTE.

1976 M. THOLO in C. Hermer *Diary of Maria Tholo* (1980) 101 The comrades have stopped the children entering the schools even if there are no lessons. *Ibid.* 175 Tonight the comrades came. Where these youths came from or where they collected I don't know ... They had come to take over from the men. 1980 [see CHILDREN]. 1986 *Evening Post* 21 Mar. 4 Seven bodies were found after 'Comrades' and 'Fathers' apparently set out to settle differences. 1986 *City Press* 13 July 5 On the first two days of her detention she was beaten severely, and asked if she was 'a comrade member'. 1987 N. MATHIANE in *Frontline* Aug.-Sept. 11 Came 1985, there was chaos in the country ... Comrades and com-tsotsis emerged. Cars were forcefully taken away from owners, people were necklaced. 1988 J. SIKHAKHANE in *Pace* Nov. 61 Vigilantes and comrades have especially made life miserable for residents and villagers around Durban and Pietermaritzburg .. as a result of the conflict between Inkatha and the UDF. 1989 L. VENTER in *Sunday Times* 3 Dec. 24 'Comrades' tried to make townships ungovernable because bungling civilian officials had made them virtually uninhabitable. 1991 A. GOLDSTUCK in *Weekly Mail* 20 Dec. (Suppl.) 42 The bitter East Rand warfare between mainly-Xhosa township residents, the 'comrade' side, and mainly-Zulu hostel dwellers, the impi side. 1993 [see FATHERS].

Comrades *n.* [Ellipt. for *Comrades Marathon*; the 'League of Comrades' granted permission for this name to be used for a race commemorating soldiers who had died in World War I.] *The Comrades*: An ultra-marathon run annually between the cities of Durban and Pietermaritzburg. Also *attrib.*

First run in 1921, this race is usu. run in May.

[1921 *Natal Mercury* 18 May 12 Comrades' Marathon. Empire Day attraction. Race from City to Durban. The race will be started by the Mayor of Maritzburg at 7 a.m. on Tuesday, May 21 from the Town Hall.] 1955 *Rand Daily Mail* 1 June 18 Gerald Walsh .. won the 54 mile Comrades Marathon from Maritzburg to Durban today ... Walsh gave credit to his helper, Allan Boyce, winner of the 1940 Comrades, who coached him all the way down. 1979 *Daily Dispatch* 1 June 20 Vorster .. threaded his way through hundreds of applauding spectators to notch his first Comrades win. 1987 M. TINDALL in *Style* Feb. 45 With eleven thousand people taking part, the Comrades has lost a lot of its comraderie. 1989 *Personality* 29 May 67 The 80-year-old Wally Hayward has just run into the stadium, well within Comrades qualifying time. 1990 A. KENNY in *Frontline* Dec. 13 It is said that we remember the joy and forget the pain. This might be true of mothers looking back on childbirth or runners looking back on the Comrades.

comtsotsi /kɒmˈtsɔ(ː)tsɪ/ *n.* Also with initial capital. [Blend of COMRADE and TSOTSI.] A criminal operating under the cloak of left-wing political activism in a black township. Cf. COMRADE, TSOTSI sense 1.

1986 *City Press* 8 June 1 B— and N— were accused of having hired 'comtsotsis' to burn other shops so their business could prosper. 1990 *Sunday Times* 1 Apr. 20 The amabutho (Inkatha vigilantes), warlords (shackland leaders) and 'comtsotsis' (dissident comrades) run protection rackets in their private fiefdoms and undertake looting sprees into rival territories. 1991 S. MATTHEWSON in *Natal Mercury* 1 Apr. 7 Reports of comrades — or at least a sinister criminal sub-group referred to as 'comtsotsis' — trying to rape a woman. 1993 *Africa S. & E.* May 14 He was surprised by Radebe's honesty in conceding that criminal elements — the 'comtsotsis' — had infiltrated ANC ranks.

concentration camp *n. phr. Hist.* Also with initial capitals. [Eng. *concentration*, here prob. fr. Eng. *reconcentration*, formed on *reconcentrate* tr. Sp. *reconcentrar* to detain together in one place, used in the context of the system of detention instituted by the Spanish military in Cuba in 1895 + *camp* encampment.] A camp in which non-combatants were detained by the British during the Anglo-Boer War of 1899–1902; *burgher camp*, see BURGHER sense 3 b; CAMP *n.*[1] sense 2; REFUGEE CAMP.

Now in international use, designating a camp for the internment of aliens, political prisoners, or prisoners of war.

1901 J. CHAMBERLAIN in C. Headlam *Milner Papers* (1933) II. 228 The mortality in the concentration camps has undoubtedly roused deep feeling among people who cannot be classed with the pro-Boers. 1911 *E. Prov. Herald* 25 Oct., Mr Botha gave it as his opinion that the death rate in the concentration camps in the first place was due to 'an entire want of proper accommodation' and 'want of proper food'. 1926 M. NATHAN *S. Afr. from Within* 102 Kitchener .. brought all the Boer women and children into concentration camps, where .. there was terrible mortality. 1936 [see NATIONAL SCOUT]. 1946 V. POHL *Adventures of Boer Family* 158 Most people left on farms during the latter half of the Boer War either were put into concentration camps by the British or, to avoid that fate, they followed in the wake of the commandoes. 1955 D.L. HOBMAN *Olive Schreiner* 117 Concentration camps .. originated in the Boer War, a fact which, without the necessary qualifications, was of the greatest value to the late Dr Goebbels, both as a stimulus to anti-British feeling and as an apologia for Nazi policy. 1965 C. VAN HEYNINGEN *Orange Days* 73 All the women and children and old and ill men were taken to large camps and had to live in tents with very little comfort or food ... These camps were called 'concentration' camps, but they were really prison camps. 1979 T. PAKENHAM *Boer War* (1982) 495 Today, Kitchener is not remembered in South Africa for his military victories. His monument is the camp — 'concentration camp', as it came to be called. 1983 [see ENGELSMAN sense 1]. 1990 *Sunday Times* 8 July 18 More than 14 000 blacks died in British concentration camps, as did 28 000 Boer women and children.

concertina *n.* Ellipt. for CONCERTINA GATE.

1975 W. STEENKAMP *Land of Thirst King* 157 It is an easy gate this ... I do believe that if it had been a wire concertina of the type they call a 'smoelneuker' (nose-basher), my shaking hands would not have got it undone. 1989 F.G. BUTLER *Tales from Old Karoo* 21 This kind of gate bears the charming name concertina .. because it folds upon itself and stretches out like a concertina, and has no spine.

concertina gate *n. phr.* [See quot. 1989.] A farm gate made of wire strands and poles, having no rigid frame but being held erect by tension; CONCERTINA.

1928 N. STEVENSON *Afr. Harvest* 121 She soon reached the concertina gate. 1934 C.P. SWART *Supplement to Pettman.* 33 *Concertina Gate*, The name given to certain farm gates, made of barbed wire strands and parallel wooden poles, the frame of which resembles a concertina. Like this instrument they can also expand and contract. Also known as stomach-hitter. 1944 C.R. PRANCE *Under Blue Roof* 151 With the Bart. in the front seat, handy to jump out and push behind through a sand-patch or to open 'concertina' (collapsible barb-wire) gates .. they roared and boiled all afternoon at 15 m.p.h. maximum. 1958 R.E. LEIGHTON *Out of Strong* 142 They were approaching a 'concertina' wire gate. 1989 F.G. BUTLER *Tales from Old Karoo* 21 A concertina gate is .. merely a bit of fence, but without any frame. It is held erect entirely by tension.

concord *n. Grammar.* Also with initial capital. [Eng.; first used in relation to the Sintu-language (Bantu-language) prefix system by William B. Boyce (1803–1889) referring to Xhosa (see quot. 1833).

Boyce's grammar was first published in 1834, and Kay (see quot. 1833) does not indicate his source.]

1. With defining words, *alliteral concord* (see ALLITERAL), *alliterative concord, euphonic concord*: in Sintu (Bantu) languages, grammatical agreement between a noun or pronoun and another word, produced by attaching a prefix to the other word or to its stem, most such prefixes being similar in sound to the pronouns or noun prefixes with which they are associated, so that alliterative or assonant effects may be produced.

1833 S. KAY *Trav. & Researches* 280 There is .. one remarkable peculiarity in the language, which renders it difficult of acquirement by Europeans; and which, as my worthy brother Missionary Mr. Boyce observes, may be termed 'the *euphonic* or *alliteral concord*. One principal word in a sentence governs the initial letters or syllables of the other words ... Changes must be made in the initial letters or syllables of the word which is governed by this euphonic concord.' 1860 W. SHAW *Story of my Mission* 545 The euphonic concord, as Mr. Boyce aptly designated it, runs through and regulates almost the entire grammatical structure of the Kaffir language. 1906 J. STEWART *Outlines of Kaffir Grammar* 10 There is a peculiarity of the Kaffir language called *Alliteration* ... It is of constant use in Kaffir, and is known generally in Grammars as Euphonic Concord. 1928 E. JACOTTET *Practical Method to Learn Sesuto* 4 All the grammatical concord of Sesuto (called by some Grammarians the Euphonic Concord) is based upon the structure of the Nouns.

2. A prefix so used. Often with defining word indicating some function of the prefix, as *adjectival -, possessive -, relative -, subjectival concord*, etc. Hence **concordial** *adj.*, making use of such prefixes.

1926 C.M. DOKE *Phonetics of Zulu Language* 283 A relative .. qualifies a substantive, and is brought into concordial agreement therewith by the relative concord. *Ibid.* 286 Formatives in Zulu may be divided roughly into, Stems or Roots, Prefixes, Concords, Suffixes, Verbal Auxiliaries, and Prefixal Formatives ... Concords .. are of five types, adjectival, relative, possessive, subjectival-verb, and objectival-verb. They must be kept distinct from the pronouns. 1938 G.P. LESTRADE in *Bantu Studies* Vol.38, 36 Sotho possesses a number of words which by their form, concords or both are identifiable as locative-class nouns, defining the latter .. as words which employ locative-class prefixes and/or concords. *Ibid.* 41 Two instances of Adjectival Concord occur in Sotho. 1992 DU PLESSIS & VISSER *Xhosa Syntax* 88 The infinitive is associated with concordial agreement elements, such as a subjectival, objectival, and adjectival concord.

confeit var. KONFYT.

confetti bush *n. phr.* [See quot. 1974.] Any of several species of *Coleonema* of the Rutaceae, esp. *C. pulchrum*, bearing tiny pink flowers.

1971 *Horticultural Terms* (Dept of Nat. Educ.) 46 *Coleonema pulchrum* Hook, (confetti bush). 1974 *Reader's Digest Complete Guide to Gardening* II. 646 *C. pulchrum*, (confetti bush) ... The numerous, bright pink flowers of this species resemble confetti. The leaves are pale to mid-green. 1986 M. TWEEHUIZEN tr. T. Engelbrecht's *Boys of Summer* 34 There was nothing left over; just an empty beach. All the confetti bushes, the sand violets and koekemakranka had vanished. 1989 *Gardening Questions Answered* (Reader's Digest Assoc.) 330 *Confetti Bush*, .. Rounded, indigenous, evergreen shrubs with slender branches and fine, aromatic, green or yellow-green foliage. Small pink or white flowers from autumn to spring.

conf(e)yt, confijt varr. KONFYT.

Congress *n. colloq.* Also with small initial. **1.** A shortened form of the name of any of several parties or organizations, particularly the *African National Congress* (see ANC *n.*[1]), but also the *Congress of Democrats*, the *South African Congress of Trade Unions* (see SACTU), and the (*Natal -, Transvaal -, South African -*) *Indian Congress*. Also *attrib.* See also NIC, TIC.

*c*1914 R.W. MSIMANG *Natives Land Act 1913: Specific Cases of Evictions & Hardships*, The President of the Congress .. made strong allegations of people being turned out from their homes and their ancient residences. **1941** R.G. BALOYI in *Bantu World* 25 Jan. 4 The question of leadership today occupies the first and foremost place in the minds of all followers of Congress. **1950** H. GIBBS *Twilight* 114 The Congress states that it was founded by Mahatma Gandhi in 1894. It would be more accurate to say that the Mahatma helped to found it. **1952** in *Drum* July 10 Desai, (editor of The Spark, a Transvaal Indian Youth Paper): Congress educates people through the day to day struggle. **1953** *Ibid.* May 10 Can Congress claim to be truly representative? [A. Luthuli:] Yes. We genuinely represent organised African opinion in this country. **1956** A. SAMPSON *Drum* 131 Mayibuye Afrika – that means 'Come back, Africa' ... It's one of the slogans of Congress; it means back to the old days of freedom before the white man came. **1958** — *Treason Cage* 4 By assembling all the leaders of the Congresses in one place and keeping them there day after day in confinement, the Government were not only trying the opposition, they were creating it. **1959** *Contact* 21 Feb. 3 When Africanists began singing 'Nkosi Sikele' Congress supporters had first stood up instinctively then when called on to do so by leaders, sat down. **1963** K. MACKENZIE *Dragon to Kill* 137 They are going to start singing the congress songs just now. You really should be here for that. **1966** *Survey of Race Rel. 1965* (S.A.I.R.R.) 238 The left-wing S.A. Congress of Trade Unions (Sactu) has, in the past, allied itself with the A.N.C. and other members of the (political) Congress Group. **1982** [see MAYIBUYE]. **1990** G. SLOVO *Ties of Blood* 254 There's a new mood inside Congress – a new militancy.

2. *hist.* In the phr. ***Congress of the People***, a gathering organized by the Congress Alliance at Kliptown near Johannesburg in June 1955, at which the FREEDOM CHARTER (sense 1) was adopted.

1953 [see FREEDOM CHARTER sense 1]. **1958** A. SAMPSON *Treason Cage* 37 Chief Albert Luthuli and Oliver Tambo .. had been deeply implicated in .. the Congress of the People. *Ibid.* 106 The Congress of the People was held on a private football field at the African township of Kliptown, fifteen miles from Johannesburg. **1963** M. BENSON *Afr. Patriots* 211 The Congress of the People .. was about to take place ... The A.N.C., forming an Alliance with the S.A. Indian Congress, the C.O.D., the S.A. Coloured People's Organization, and the S.A. Congress of Trade Unions, had invited not only other non-white organizations but a wide range of white parties to take part. **1972** *Std Encycl. of Sn Afr.* V. 33 *Freedom Charter*, Socialist propaganda manifesto adopted by the African National Congress and the Congress of Democrats at a congress convened by the 'Congress of the People' .. in June 1955. **1979** [see MOLIMO]. **1983** *Educating for Change* (Nusas) (*pamphlet*) 13 The most significant campaign was the organisation of the Congress of the People .., where 3000 delegates from organisations around the country accepted the Freedom Charter. **1990** *New African* 25 June 5 When the Congress of the People was convened in 1955, it provided a forum for all strata of the racially oppressed – workers, professional artisans, and business people alike.

3. *comb. hist.* **Congress Alliance**, see quots. 1983 and 1989; **Congressman**, a member of the African National Congress, or of any other organization belonging to the Congress movement; **Congress movement**, a collective name for the organizations which adhered to the FREEDOM CHARTER (sense 1); **Congress salute**, a thumbs-up gesture formerly used by members of these organizations as a salute.

1981 E. WEINBERG *Portrait of a People* 126 The preparations for the Congress [of the People] were planned by the '**Congress Alliance**', headed by the African National Congress. Other members of the Alliance were the South African Indian Congress, the South African Congress of Trade Unions, the Coloured People's Congress and the Congress of Democrats (an organisation of white supporters of the ANC). **1983** *Educating for Change* (Nusas) (*pamphlet*) 12 It was only in the fifties that SA saw the emergence of a popular mass movement for democratic change, led by the ANC. This movement included the SA Indian Congress, the Congress of Democrats, the SA Coloured People's Congress, and the SA Congress of Trade Unions (SACTU). These organisations together formed the Congress Alliance. **1989** *Reader's Digest Illust. Hist.* 487 *Congress Alliance*, Agreement in 1953 between the ANC, CAIC, Coloured People's Congress and South African Congress of Trade Unions following the Defiance Campaign to work towards the congress of the People .. and the adoption of the Freedom Charter. **1952** H. NXUMALO in *Drum* Dec. 12 **Congressmen** as a body seldom know what line to follow until they are influenced by lobbying at conference and then vie with the popular vote. **1958** A. SAMPSON *Treason Cage* 41 There are times of sudden indignation in the locations when nearly everyone claims to be a Congressman, others when congress appears to consist of only a hard core of enthusiasts. **1956** M. ROGERS *Black Sash* 154 An eleventh group .. was the **Congress movement**, composed of the African National Congress, the Indian Congress, and the Congress of Democrats, linked with the Congress of Trade Unions. Its aim was, and is, perfectly straightforward and based on the United Nations Charter of Human Rights – in one word, equality. **1959** B. BUNTING *Story behind Non-White Press* 9 The only newspaper with a large national circulation .. stands four-square with the Congress movement in the struggle for liberation. **1990** *Sunday Times* 1 Apr. 20 The national symbols of the congress movement and the homeland symbols of Inkatha. **1952** *Bantu World* 27 June 1 There was loud and prolonged cheering, singing and cries of 'Afrika' while the **Congress salute** was also given. **1963** M. BENSON *Afr. Patriots* 215 The whole crowd rose to their feet, hands raised in the Congress salute, thumbs pointing at the police, and burst into singing 'Mayibuye' to its gay tune of 'Clementine'.

Conquered Territory *n. phr. Hist.* An area of the eastern Orange Free State bordering on the Kingdom of Lesotho, formerly the grazing and agricultural lands of the Basotho, but ceded to the Orange Free State by the treaty of Thaba Bosiu (1866). Also occas. in *pl.*

1909 G.Y. LAGDEN *Basutos* II. 450 President Brand on January 13, 1869, summoned his Volksraad ... Raiding was prevalent in the conquered territory; they were precluded from pursuing delinquents into British territory. **1924** G. BAUMANN in Baumann & Bright *Lost Republic* (1940) 103 After the Basuto were defeated in 1865, part of Basutoland was ceded to the Free State (the Conquered Territory). *c*1936 *S. & E. Afr. Yr Bk & Guide* 605 The Conquered Territory, about 30 miles broad, of which Ficksburg is the centre, runs along the Western slopes of the Maluti Mountains for a distance of about 100 miles, .. and has been alluded to as 'the Granary of South Africa'. **1948** E. ROSENTHAL *Afr. Switzerland* 62 'The Conquered Territory' is the name .. still given by South Africans to that wide strip of fertile country abutting on the eastern side of the Orange Free State ... Among the Basuto it is regarded .. as still forming a portion of their homeland. **1975** [see VRYSTAAT *n.*]. **1987** G. VINEY *Col. Houses* 208 The lush eastern crescent in the foothills of the Basutoland mountains – the so-called Conquered Territories. **1989** *Reader's Digest Illust. Hist.* 161 In terms of the treaty, the OFS claimed a large slice of Basotho land, which became known as the Conquered Territory.

Constantia /kɒnˈstænʃ(ɪ)ə, kən-/ *n. hist.* [The name of the district in the Western Cape where this wine is produced; orig. the name of a farm granted to Simon van der Stel in 1685.] In full ***Constantia wine***: Any of several sweet, heavy dessert wines produced on one of the wine estates in the Constantia valley; any similar Cape dessert wine. See also CAPE WINE. Also *attrib.*

[**1772** J.R. FORSTER tr. *L.A. De Bougainville's Voy. around World* 464 The district of Constantia .. produces the famous wine of that name. This vineyard .. is distinguished into High and Little Constantia ... The wine which is made there is nearly alike in quality, though each of the two Constantia's has its partisans.] **1777** W. HICKEY *Memoirs* (1918) 19 July, They gave me some stuff under the name of Constantia, which to my palate was more like treacle-and-water than a rich and generous wine. *c*1795 D. CAMPBELL in G.M. Theal *Rec. of Cape Col.* (1897) I. 137 The most esteemed and best calculated for the European markets is the Constantia, a sweet wine, of which there are two kinds, red and white. **1807** *Afr. Court Calendar*, A sweet luscious wine, well known in England by the name of Constantia, the produce of two farms lying close under the mountains. **1811** J. AUSTEN in D.J. Opperman *Spirit of Vine* (1968) 292, I have some of the finest old Constantia wine in the house, that ever was tasted. **1843** *Cape of G.H. Almanac & Annual Register*, (*advt*) Constantia wines of the following description, and of the first quality, viz. Frontignac Constantia, Pontac do. Red. do. White do. **1862** LADY DUFF-GORDON in F. Galton *Vacation Tourists* (1864) III. 151 The sweet Constantia is also very good indeed; not the expensive sort, which is made from grapes half dried, and is a liqueur, but a light, sweet, straw-coloured wine, which even I liked. **1880** E.F. SANDEMAN *Eight Months in Ox-Waggon* 14 The wine known by the name of Constantia is too sweet and strong for anything but a liqueur and in that capacity, it is very pleasant to the taste. **1897** 'F. MACNAB' *On Veldt & Farm* 158 Even in this country persons may be living who remember the old Constantia – a pipe of which it was customary to ship every year for the use of our Sovereign. **1926** P.W. LAIDLER *Tavern of Ocean* 170 Sheridan, drinking Constantia wine at dinner in London, tried to cause the production of more bottles, so much did he enjoy it. *c*1936 *S. & E. Afr. Yr Bk & Guide* 304 A bottle of Constantia, 125 years old, was opened in 1925 and found to be in perfect condition. **1968** D.J. OPPERMAN *Spirit of Vine* 292 Constantia might very well at a later stage, have come to mean any dessert wine from the Cape. **1980** *Daily Dispatch* 10 Mar. 7 A half bottle of Constantia white dating back to 1791 was bought for R2 500. **1983** [see DOPPEN BEER]. **1988** D. HUGHES et al. *Complete Bk of S. Afr. Wine* 35, *1761/2* The first notable exports of red and white Constantia wine take place *1778* Groot Constantia is acquired by the Cloete family. The following decades see the sweet Constantia wine winning acclaim throughout Europe. **1990** J. PLATTER in *Sunday Times* 16 Dec. 21 The glories of Cape Constantia sipped – or more probably glugged, such was its appeal.

constructive engagement *n. phr. Hist.* [Coined by Chester Crocker, a former United States Assistant Secretary of State for Africa.] A policy by which the United States administration (under President Ronald Reagan) regulated its relations with South Africa during the 1980s, favouring the maintenance of ties with the government in the hope of influencing developments towards the creation of a democratic society.

1983 *Financial Mail* 29 July 58 Despite the Ronald Reagan administration's policy of constructive engagement with SA, the deep anti-apartheid sentiment in the US is surging to a crest in Congress this summer. **1985** J. MCMAHAN *Reagan & the World* 100 Sentimental moralizing about the rights of the black majority in South Africa would have to be subordinated to a healthy sense of American self-interest, and the administration soon announced that its policy toward South Africa would be one of 'constructive engagement' rather than 'confrontation'. **1989** *Daily*

Dispatch 31 Jan. 12 A former university professor who has been an Africa specialist for 30 years, he [*sc.* Crocker] first came to former President Reagan's attention through his 'constructive engagement' theory advocating co-operation rather than confrontation with Pretoria. **1991** *Sunday Times* 7 Apr. (Metro) 21 More than a decade ago he authored America's policy of constructive engagement towards South Africa.

contact *n. Military.* [Eng.; in this sense, prob. first used by government forces of Rhodesia (Zimbabwe) during the war of the 1970s.] An encounter with an enemy force; a patrol or expedition intended to lead to such an encounter. Also *attrib.*

Not exclusively *S. Afr. Eng.*

1977 *Joint Operational Dict.* 104 *Contact*, Any form of encounter between the security forces and terrorists other than a mere sighting. **1978** [see FLOPPY]. **1979** *S. Afr. Digest* 5 Oct. 3 The terrorists had been killed in nine contacts. The contacts had been made on the initiative of the security forces. **1980** *Fair Lady* 3 Dec. 63 'I wasn't thinking about anything in particular when we left on this contact. We drove through the night ...' ... I didn't ask him about the contact because he is not allowed to divulge details. **1983** *Sunday Times* 4 Sept. (Lifestyle) 1 Danny .. used to lie in ambush with his fellow trainees, hoping there wouldn't be a contact. **1985** *Frontline* Aug. 54 Some ous would get morphine from the medics, but most of us were just on dagga. We'd smoke before contact. You get scared in contact, you know. **1989** *Sunday Times* 9 Apr. 2 'There's a contact with Swapo close by,' he said.

Contralesa /ˌkɒntrəˈleːsə, -ˈliːsə, -zə/ *n.* Also **CONTRALESA**, and (formerly) **COTRALESA**. [Acronym formed on *Congress of Traditional Leaders of South Africa*.] A political organization founded in (the former 'homeland' of) KwaNdebele in 1987 and composed of chiefs and headmen opposed to the 'homeland' system and sympathetic to the African National Congress (see ANC *n.*[1]), the Mass Democratic Movement (see MDM), and the United Democratic Front (see UDF *n.*[2]). Also *attrib.*

1988 *Race Rel. Survey 1987–8* (S.A.I.R.R.) 922 On 23 September [1987] the formation of a new organisation, the Congress of Traditional Leaders of South Africa (COTRALESA), was announced ... It had been formed by chiefs in KwaNdebele and Moutse with the specific aim of challenging the homeland system ... Cotralesa already had members in Bophuthatswana and Venda. **1990** *Weekly Mail* 2 Mar. 5 The homeland governments .. have retained their traditional political structures despite the marginalisation of the chiefs' role through the rise of organisations such as the Congress of Traditional Leaders (Contralesa), which is sympathetic to the ANC. **1990** S. KHUMALO in *New African* 16 July 6 Contralesa's stategy for rural areas is to set up village committees to popularise the activities of the mass democratic movement. **1990** M. KENTRIDGE *Unofficial War* 224 Within CONTRALESA the Zulu chiefs and their headmen are no longer seen as stooges of the South African state through the proxy of the KwaZulu government: they have been rehabilitated as important traditional leaders with a part to play in the struggle for liberation from apartheid.

convyt var. KONFYT.

coodoo var. KUDU.

cook *v. trans. Obs.* In the colloquial phr. ***to cook the kettle*** [calqued on Afk. *om ketel te kook*], 'to boil the kettle', to boil water (for tea).

1900 B.M. HICKS *Cape as I Found It* 71 (Pettman), As soon as we got to the top we outspanned, and .. made a fire, and began cooking the kettle. **1900** M. MARQUARD *Lett. from Boer Parsonage* (1967) 56 His pathetic stories of the faithful old 'achterrijder' Valentyn cooking his *keteltje*. **1913** C. PETTMAN *Africanderisms* 258 *Kettle, To cook the*, A colloquialism common in South Africa for making the water in the kettle to boil. **1938** F.C. SLATER *Trek* 17 Rouse ye, rouse ye, men of mettle! Kindle fires and cook each kettle. [*Note*] Afrikanderism for 'boil'. **1949** [see KOMMETJIE sense 1].

cookie *n. ?obs.* [ad. Du. *koekje* little cake; cf. Scottish and U.S. Eng. *cookie*.] A flat cake or bread roll baked in hot embers on an open fire, or on a grid-iron over a fire. Cf. ASKOEK sense 1, ROOSTERKOEK sense a. See also KOEKIE sense 1.

Now more commonly used in the general English sense of 'biscuit'.

1852 C. BARTER *Dorp & Veld* 107 Cookies, or unleavened cakes of coarse meal, baked on the grid-iron. **1897** E. GLANVILLE *Tales from Veld* 51, I sat down to his simple fare after raking the 'cookie' from the fire-place, whence it came baking hot, with wood cinders embedded in its steaming crust. **1913** C. PETTMAN *Africanderisms* 129 *Cookies*, (D. *koek*, a cake, gingerbread.) A common name applied to comestibles as varied as the lightest and sweetest production of the professional pastry-cook and the dough cake roasted on the coals of a wood fire at the wayside outspan.

cooldrink /ˈkuːldrɪŋk/ *n.* [Prob. tr. Afk. *koeldrank* soft drink; however the Afk. may be influenced by Eng. The term has been used in Jamaican and Bahamian Eng. since the 1700s.] A soft drink, whether carbonated, powdered, made from a concentrate, or home-made; a bottle, glass, can, or other container of such a drink. Also *attrib.*

1930 M. RAUBENHEIMER *Tested S. Afr. Recipes* 93 *Lemon syrup*, .. Will make six bottles of syrup. Use with water as a cool drink. **1940** M.G. GILBERT *Informant, Cape Town* It was too hot for lunch, so we only had a cool drink. **1953** D. JACOBSON *Long Way from London* 53 We found the Africans sitting on the pavement in the sun, .. eating bread and drinking bottles of cooldrinks. **1969** A. FUGARD *People Are Living There* 49 Get us a cake ... Cooldrinks, peanuts and raisins. *Ibid.* 54 We can't toast you with cooldrink. **1974** *Bona* Mar. 56 Richard went to the kitchen and brought from the refrigerator a litre of cooldrink. Michael .. held the glass of cool-drink firmly between his hands. **1982** *Sunday Times* 19 Sept. (Mag. Sect.) 25 Just sit and watch the fun with a vetkoek in one hand and a fizzy mamba-green cooldrink in the other. **1984** *Rand Daily Mail* 17 Jan. 3 A police spokesman said yesterday a bomb had ripped through a cool-drink factory early on Sunday morning. **1987** [see JA *adv.* sense 4]. **1990** M.M. HACKSLEY (tr. E. van Heerden) in *Lynx* 203 He squirted the cold soda into plastic glasses, Ma added Oros and we all sat staring into the night with the fizzy cooldrink in our cheeks. **1993** *Pace* July 2 We darkies are fond of expensive funerals .. our bills include buying of beasts, cakes, cooldrinks, caskets and hiring of expensive cars to ferry mourners.

coolie *n. Offensive* and *derog.* Also with initial capital. [Special senses of general Eng. *coolie, cooly* 'hired labourer', fr. Indian Eng. ad. of a word found in various forms in Indian languages, as Tamil and Telegu *kūli*.]

1. An insulting term for one of Indian descent. Also *attrib.*

1873 F. BOYLE *To Cape for Diamonds* 285 A coolie cook, clad in tunic and turban, pursues the study of his art, with Kaffir assistance, in the tent near by. **1878** H.A. ROCHE *On Trek in Tvl* 21 Jim the Kafir, Sam the Coolie, or Tom the little Oomfan, – all equally 'Boys,' – required a little touching up to hasten their movements. **1894** E.N. THOMAS *How Thankful We Should Be* 6 Rickshas .. are drawn by Kafir runners, who are called 'boys,' in distinction to the Indians who are always called 'coolies.' **1896** *Star* in J. Crwys-Williams *S. Afr. Despatches* (1989) 105 The majority are coloured people, while the rest are made up of the poor Dutch class .. , and Coolies and Chinamen. **1916** S. BLACK in S. Gray *Three Plays* (1984) 235 You ought to give me the D.S.O. for dondering that coolie op. **1922** [see COMMANDO sense 5]. *c*1936 *S. & E. Afr. Yr Bk & Guide* 297 The business, in Natal, is unfortunately largely in the hands of Coolies, with whom whites can hardly compete. **1943** L. SOWDEN *Union of S. Afr.* 203 The White man's attitude to the Indian in South Africa is complicated by the first impression which he received from the early indentured labourers or coolies, for since then the Indian has been to the average South African the 'coolie,' or, at best, if he happens to be selling vegetables at the door, he is the 'Sammy.' **1955** A. DELIUS *Young Trav.* 144 Just because we won't let these coolies buy land anywhere they start passive resistance movements. **1957** M. DESAI tr. *M.K. Gandhi's Autobiog.* 107, I was hence known as a 'coolie barrister'. The merchants were known as 'coolie merchants'. The original meaning of the word 'coolie' was thus forgotten, and it became common appellation for all Indians. **1967** *Guardian* (U.K.) 4 Oct. 13 In South Africa the word 'coolie' is used by some whites to describe Asians, and is as bitterly resented by them as the word 'Kaffir' is resented by Africans. **1971** *Rand Daily Mail* 26 Feb. 14 To say that a coolie is a 'South African Indian' is an insult to the Indian and the greatest travesty of words. **1987** L. NKOSI *Mating Birds* 92 This is a cutthroat world ... Coolies! Kaffirs! Boesmans! **1990** J. NAIDOO *Coolie Location* 120 'It's always the same with you Coolies: impossible to pick one of you up without having the entire family troop down to the police station ...' It wasn't the observation of Indian clannishness .. that struck me, it was the word 'Coolie', and the careless and cocksure way it was used. **1993** [see CHAR OU].

2. *comb.* (All *offensive* and *derog.*) **Coolie Christmas**, an insulting name for the Islamic festival of Moharram and the Hindu festival of Diwali (see DEEPAVALI); also *transf.*; **coolie creeper**, in the game of cricket, a ball which stays low after having been bowled (elsewhere called a 'creeper'); **coolie pink**, shocking pink or magenta; *tottie pink*, see TOTTIE sense 2 b; **coolie shop**, **- store**, a small shop owned or managed by a person of Indian origin.

1902 *Graaff-Reinet Advertiser* 2 May (Pettman), The **Coolie Christmas** celebration at Umgeni (Natal) last Monday ended in a serious riot. **1905** *E. London Dispatch* 18 Mar., The festivities in connection with the Hindoo's festival Mohorrum, known locally as the Coolie Christmas, commences to-night. **1911** BLACKBURN & CADDELL *Secret Service* 80 Within a month he either owned or had a lien on .. enough paraffin lamps to supply a coolie temple with illumination on the Coolie Christmas. **1967** E. ROSENTHAL *Encycl. of Sn Afr.* 125 *Coolie Christmas*, Old-fashioned name applied in Natal to Muharram .. and .. Diwali. **1974** *Informant, Grahamstown* He's all togged up like a coolie Christmas. **1989** J. HOBBS *Thoughts in Makeshift Mortuary* 346 He was wearing a short-sleeved shirt in loud stripes, maroon trousers, a mock leopard-skin belt ... 'Jake! You look like a –' she stopped herself just in time from saying 'coolie Christmas' and said, '– Christmas tree'. *c*1978 CILLIE & JORDAAN *Krieketterme* 9 **Coolie creeper** (*creeper*), kruipbal. **1970** [**coolie pink**: see TOTTIE sense 2 b]. **1975** *Dict. of Eng. Usage in Sn Afr.* 53 *Coolie pink*, .. Violent pink colour. **1906** *Star* 2 July 6 A native, sentenced .. for stealing a bag of fruit and vegetables from B.J. Smith, in a **coolie shop**, at the corner of Sixth and Kafir streets. **1946** V. POHL *Adventures of Boer Family* 11 One of their men returned from a coolie shop laden with streamers. **1969** A. FUGARD *People Are Living There* 13 Ask some old coolie shop for beetroot leaves? On a Saturday night? Are you mad? **1985** PLATZKY & WALKER *Surplus People* 102 They were pushed out to segregated shopping centres in their own group areas – the .. 'Oriental Plazas' of the big centres and the 'coolie shops' of the small towns. **1937** C.R. PRANCE *Tante Rebella's Saga* 125 Debtors .. on their way to the dorp to spend .. perhaps £20 in cash at a **'Coolie' store**. **1990** M. NICOL *Powers that Be* 81 No more loitering .. outside the coolie store.

coon *n.* Also with initial capital. [U.S. Eng., a performer wearing blackface in a minstrel show; see quots 1980 and 1983.]

1. A member of one of the troupes which parade annually in the *Coon Carnival* (see sense 2), wearing costume and made up in black-face, with white-ringed eyes and mouth. Also *attrib.* See also KLOPSE sense 1.

The offensive general Eng. use of the word as a derogatory term for a black person also occurs in S. Afr. Eng.

1924 *Cape Argus* 3 Jan. 8 The quiet streets of Cape Town were enlivened by the marching of troupes of coloured youths, gay in coon costumes ... A storm of applause goes up as the coons approach. **1944** I.D. DU PLESSIS *Cape Malays* 60 Malay choirs .. must not be confused with the coons who parade the streets on New Year's Day. **1947** L.G. GREEN *Tavern of Seas* 14 The Coons of Cape Town, the carnival troupes ... , are said to have sprung from the thanksgiving celebrations when the slaves were liberated one hundred and thirteen years ago. **1951** [see LIEDJIE]. **1959** R.E. VAN DER ROSS in Hattingh & Bredekamp *Coloured Viewpoint* (1984) 33 The coons are essentially democratic, and they have Coloured, Malay, African and even White members. Yes, there are some White coons who blacken their faces and don costume with the others. **1964** L.G. GREEN *Old Men Say* 58 One of my wise old men told me that the pioneer coons had modelled their dress and performances on a band of Christy Minstrels who played in Cape Town during the eighteen sixties. **1971** *Sunday Times* 7 Nov. (Mag. Sect.) 5 New Year's Day is a memory of a river of colours as the 'Coons' danced by with their unique double shuffle and sequined cloaks and hats. **1980** D.B. COPLAN *Urbanization of African Performing Arts.* 431 Coon ... In South Africa, American-derived popular African ragtime songs and performers of the early 20th century, popular with African students. Better known from the Coon Carnival a New Year street parade in Cape Town of Coloured men's performances clubs in American minstrel costume and blackface, performing Afrikaans and American minstrel and jazz music. **1981** *S. Afr. Panorama* July 34 The Coons wear multi-coloured glossy satin uniforms, with top hat and frock coat, blacken their faces and cavort along the streets en route to venues .. where they hold singing competitions. **1983** *Flying Springbok* Dec. 19 The word coon is derived from that furry, nocturnal animal, the raccoon, with its large eyes set in equally large white rings on a black face. And the carnival dancer models his black-painted face and white-painted lips on the raccoon. **1991** [see COLOURED n.].

2. *comb.* **Coon Carnival**, occas. also **Coons -, Coon's Carnival**, and with small initials: the parades by, and the competitions between gaily costumed troupes of singing and dancing performers, held in Cape Town on the 1st and 2nd of January each year; any similar entertainment. Also *attrib.*

1936 E. ROSENTHAL *Old-Time Survivals* 36 Still more resplendent is the turn-out at the 'Coon's Carnival' at the Cape, celebrated on January 1, 2, 3 ... Hundreds of coloured men and women turn up with their banjoes, .. giving the New Year an uproarious, but quite harmless welcome. **1937** *S. Afr. Dancing Times* Feb. 8 An effective group which participated in the Capetown Coloured Coons Carnival, held at the Peninsular on New Year's Day. **1952** T. MATSHIKIZA in *Drum* July 38 In and around Johannesburg on a Saturday you might come across .. a bunch of ten-year-olds staging a coon carnival. **1963** K. MACKENZIE *Dragon to Kill* 140 We need to be angry — not laughing 'happy Natives' in the streets, smiling, Coon carnival, *kwela* — but angry. **1973** *Cape Times* 13 Jan. (Weekend Mag.) 4 Green Point Track .. was the home of organized coon carnivals since 1906. **1977** *Argus* 30 Dec. 3 The Cape's traditional extravaganza of colour and music, the annual Coon Carnival, gets under way early in the New Year. **1988** *Cape Times* 4 Jan. 1 (*caption*) This member of one of the Coon Carnival troupes parading through the streets of Cape Town on Saturday was obviously enjoying his 'Tweede Nuwe Jaar'.

Hence **coonery** *n.*, participation in the Coon Carnival.

1990 M.C. D'ARCY in *Staffrider* Vol.9 No.1, 11 The immediate eradication of coonery to restore the dignity and worth of the coloured was vital to the cause. *Ibid.* 15 He did not agree with all the aspects of the institution of coonery but it was his living.

Co-operation and Development *n. phr. Hist.* A name for the government department chiefly responsible for the administration of the affairs of black people, particularly with regard to urbanization and the administration and development of the 'homelands'. Also *attrib.*

The name 'Bantu Administration and Development' (see BAD) replaced the name *Native Affairs* (see NATIVE *n.* sense 1 c) in the 1950s, and was current until 1978, when 'Plural Relations and Development' briefly replaced it; the name 'Co-operation and Development' was current from 1979 until 1985.

The 'reallocation of functions' (quot. 1986) preceded the abolition of INFLUX CONTROL in 1986.

1979 M. MOHLOMI in *Sunday Post* 8 July 9 The Minister of Co-operation and Development .. predicted that by 1982 the black businessman will be a free entrepreneur, able to operate in areas of his choice. **1981** *Optima* Vol.30 No.3, 160 He denounced the three 'Koornhof bills' (respectively on black community development, local government and 'co-operation and development'). **1983** *S. Afr. 1983: Off. Yrbk* (Dept of Foreign Affairs & Info.) 148 *Department of Co-operation and Development*, .. Aim. To administer matters pertaining to Black people in the White area and to promote the development of the various Black national units towards self-determination. *Ibid.* 224 The Minister of Co-operation and Development said .. one [specialist committee] .. would be mainly concerned with the general circumstances of urban Blacks — employment opportunities, the planning and development of residential areas, the promotion of orderly urbanization and the development of local authorities. The Committee would also examine the constitutional position of urban Blacks. **1985** PLATZKY & WALKER *Surplus People* 414 Cooperation and Development Department (Native Affairs 1910–1959, Bantu Administration and Development 1959–1978, Plural Relations 1978–1979, present title since 1979). **1986** *Race Rel. Survey 1985* (S.A.I.R.R.) 259 On 1 September the department of co-operation and development was replaced by a department of development aid in accordance with a reallocation of functions, mainly to the department of constitutional development and planning.

copjie var. KOPPIE.

copper *n.* Ellipt. for *copper steenbras*, see STEENBRAS sense b.

1983 *Daily Dispatch* 12 Apr. 12 What does Bird Island usually offer? 'Coppers, yellow tail, black steenbras,' said Edsel. **1989** A. SPARG in *Ski-Boat* Jan.-Feb. 35 Most of the teams went out into deeper water in search of coppers (red steenbras or *Petrus rupestris*). **1989** *Stanger Mail* 19 May 11 In a competition held .. in the Transkei boaters caught some big red steenbras ... The biggest fish caught was a 'copper' (red steenbras) of 47 kg.

copper bream *n. phr.* [Named for its colouring, see quot. 1949.] BRONZE BREAM.

1949 J.L.B. SMITH *Sea Fishes* 276 *Pachymetopon aeneum* ... Hottentot. Bluefish. Copper Bream ... Fresh from the water of great beauty, with cobalt blue head and blue-streaked bronzy yellow body. [**1971** see BRONZE BREAM]. **1989** *Stanger Mail* 19 May 11 Second prize (R40) was won by S Thulsi with a copper bream of 1, 8kg.

coppie, coppje, coppy varr. KOPPIE.

Cora var. KORA.

coraal var. KRAAL *n.*

corallodendron *n. obs.* Also **cora(l)lodendrum**. [Previous generic or specific name, fr. Gk *corallion* coral + *dendron* tree.] The coral tree or (*offensive*) KAFFIRBOOM.

Although the scientific name was changed to *Erythrina caffra* as early as 1827, 'corallodendron' continued as a common name for a time.

1809 J. MACKRILL *Diary.* 55 Corallodendron, The Coral Tree, appears to be what the French call Bois immortel ... Grows in strand street — a diadelphous flower. **1827** T. PHILIPPS *Scenes & Occurrences* 91 The beautiful coralodendrum grows tall and stately ... This tree at the approach of spring throws out large clusters of deep scarlet flowers. **1840** T. PRINGLE *Narr. of Res.* 36, I frequently noticed the *erythrina cafra* or *corallodendrum* (called by the colonist *Cafferboom*). **1870** C. HAMILTON *Life & Sport in S.-E. Afr.* 15 Here I first saw a beautiful plant, called the coralodendrum, or Kaffir boom.

Coran *n.*[1], **Coran(n)a** varr. KORANNA.

coran *n.*[2], **coranne** varr. KORHAAN.

core-hen *n. obs.* Also **coerhen, cor-hen, courhen.** [Calqued on S. Afr. Du. *korhaan*.] KORHAAN sense 1 a.

1798 LADY A. BARNARD *Lett. to Henry Dundas* (1973) 127 Two core-hens and certain partridges and curlews .. fell victim to his gun. **1835** E.A. KENDALL *Eng. Boy at Cape* III. 257 The Cape bustards (pows, and corhaans or cor-hens) .. were also numerous. **1860** T. SHONE *Diary.* 23 June, Food as usual, a coerhen for dinner. **1861** *Ibid.* 12 Jan., Some Courhen for dinner.

corha(a)n var. KORHAAN.

Corner House *n. phr. Hist.* [The name given to the original corporate headquarters, see quot. 1973.] The popular name for the Central Mining and Rand Mines group of companies; the leaders of this group. Also *attrib.*

[**1902** *Star* 14 Aug., The pulling down of the 'Corner House', one of the most historic centres of finance associated with Johannesburg, has been proceeding rapidly.] **1921** W.C. SCULLY *Harrow* 7 There are wheels within wheels. When one gets a hint from the 'Corner House', you know, it hardly does to stand out. **1944** C.R. PRANCE *Under Blue Roof* 169 The prospector was always the original and only genuine discoverer of De Beers and the Rand, diddled out of his rights by minions in the pay of 'Corner House'. **1967** E. ROSENTHAL *Encycl. of Sn Afr.* 126 The Corner House group is one of the largest on the Rand, with over 100,000 employees and, besides gold, has important interests including coal, lime, cement, timber, diamonds, base metals, etc. **1973** S. ORPEN in *Std Encycl. of Sn Afr.* IX. 241 Rand Mines was an important component in the Central Mining-Anglo American sphere ... Known in the early mining days as the 'Corner House' — because of the corner situation of its premises .. - the group later moved four times, taking the 'corner house' tag with it. **1979** J. GRATUS *Jo'burgers* 59 Companies .. were speedily becoming famous through-out the financial world. Corner House, Consolidated Gold Fields, Anglo-French, Lewis and Marks, General Mining, Barnato Brothers. **1982** *S. Afr. Panorama* Mar. 25 Florence Philips, wife of Corner House (Rand Mines) company chairman Sir Lionel Philips, rode out of the dust and dirt of the mining camp of Johannesburg. **1986** *Frontline* June 20 In the decade before Anglo-American, the Corner House was 'the fifth province' of the new Union, with a turnover in diamonds, gold and land greater than the budgets of the Free State or Natal and enormous political influence.

cornet *n. hist.* [Englished form of Du. *kornet* a military rank, perh. influenced by Eng. *cornet* cavalry officer.] FIELD CORNET sense 1.

1795 G.D. GEROTZ et al. in G.M. Theal *Rec. of Cape Col.* (1897) I. 211 Your Excellency's most obedient servants, [*signed*] Carel David Gerotz, provisional Landdrost, A. van Jaarsveld, Captain, Andries Adriaan Smit, Cornet. **1843** J. COLLETT *Diary.* II. 2 Mar., Saw the Cornet this Evg. for the first time. **1878** T.J. LUCAS *Camp Life & Sport* 161 One of my fellow cornets .. asks me to dine with him. **1955** V.M. FITZROY *Dark Bright Land* 30 He is grown a likely young Man, and being now a Cornet .. is sure that fame and glory await him. **1971** J. PLOEGER in *Std Encycl. of Sn Afr.* III. 342

Increasing friction with the Bushmen led to the decision in 1774 to reorganise the defence .. by instituting the office of 'veldcommandant'. These .. office-bearers were invested with the rank of 'cornet' and were placed in charge of thirteen field-corporals. **1972** D.W. KRÜGER in *Ibid.* VII. 397 In the mounted units [of the Burgher Militia] there were the following ranks: a 'ritmeester', a lieutenant, a cornet, .. and one adjutant to every company of dragoons.

Hence **cornetcy** *n.*; **cornetship** *n. Joc. nonce.*

1800 G. YONGE in G.M. Theal *Rec. of Cape Col.* (1898) III. 360 There were only two Cases out of the succession one a Son of B. Gen. Fraser's to a vacant Cornetcy. **1809** R. COLLINS in *Ibid.* VII. (1900) 20 The veld cornets might warn one of their inhabitants to proceed to the drostdy once a week .. to receive the Courant and whatever letters there may be for his cornetship.

Corporaal /ˌkɔ(r)pɔˈrɑːl/ *n.* Also **Korporaal**. [Du. (later Afk.) *korporaal* corporal.] Among the Khoikhoi: a title given to a headman or other leader.

1821 G. BARKER *Journal.* 10 May, Could not hold school to day, on account of a complaint in hand among the Corporaals. [**1822** W.J. BURCHELL *Trav.* I. 516 Our expectation of having Hendrik Abra with us, had been counteracted by an order from the Klaarwater captain, appointing him to the duty of superintendant, or, as they call it, corporal, of one of the out-posts.] **1823** G. BARKER *Journal.* 6 Jan., Was busy all day with the temporal affairs of the Station, electing new Corporaals &c. **1975** *Sunday Times* 12 Oct. (Mag. Sect.) 3 On arrival at the shack I met the headman or *Korporaal*, as he is called by the Koebus Nama Hottentots.

Corran(n)a var. KORANNA.

corrass, **corrose** varr. KAROSS.

Corunna var. KORANNA.

cos var. KOS.

Cosas /ˈkəʊsæs/ *n.* Acronym formed on the initial letters of *Congress of South African Students*, a national student organization formed in 1979, and involved in liberation politics. Also *attrib.*

Cosas was banned by the government from August 1985 to February 1990. Cf. SANSCO.

1979 *Sunday Post* 7 June 1 In a major breakthrough in student politics, more than 80 students from several centres met in Roodepoort at the week-end to form a national body, the Congress of South African Students (Cosas). **1980** *Survey of Race Rel. 1979* (S.A.I.R.R.) 500 The aims of Cosas are to normalise relationships between students and teachers; .. strive for an education for all that is dynamic, free and compulsory for the betterment of society. **1982** *Drum* Nov. 12 Both Cosas and Azaso also work closely with non-student organisations — trade unions and community groups — as part of a broader movement towards the society they envisage for South Africa. **1985** *Probe* Oct. 11 Instead of talking to the people who matter, he bans Cosas. He should have banned his Department of Education and Training (DET) first. **1990** *New African* 11 June 11 The relaunch of the Congress of South African Students (Cosas) in Johannesburg. Cosas was banned by the government in the early 1980s and was unbanned in February.

Cosatu /kəˈsɑːtuː/ *n.* Also **COSATU**. Acronym formed on initial letters of *Congress of South African Trade Unions*, a labour federation formed in 1985, with an initial affiliation of over thirty trade unions. Also *attrib.* See also FOSATU, SACTU, TRIPARTITE ALLIANCE.

Cosatu is the largest labour federation in South Africa.

1985 VAN NIEKERK & STREEK in *Cape Times* 2 Dec. 1 The Congress of South African Trade Unions (Cosatu), representing more than half-a-million mainly black workers, adopted a tough political stance which could lead to imminent confrontation with the government. **1987** *New Nation* 5 Mar. 1 The country's biggest and most powerful trade union federation, the 700 000-strong Congress of SA Trade Unions (Cosatu) has come out in open support of the call. **1987** [see FFF]. **1987** *Star* 2 Sept. 14 Cosatu is .. an active opponent of the Government, politicising labour as a weapon against apartheid. **1991** M. RAY in *Natal Witness* 28 Mar. (Echo) 10 Cosatu's apparent failure to reach agreement among affiliates on a definite national minimum wage .. weakened the potential force of the campaign. **1992** J. CONTRERAS in *Newsweek* 20 July 30 The Congress of South African Trade Unions (Cosatu), the country's largest trade-union federation, sulked over its exclusion from the constitutional talks.

cose var. INKOSI *n.*

cost var. KOS.

cotch /kɒtʃ/ *v. intrans.* Slang. Also **kotch**. [Englished form of Afk. *kots*.] To vomit.

1970 *Informant, Grahamstown* The cat cotched on the carpet. [**1970** T. KRIGE *Informant, Bloemfontein*, I shall kots in the car if you don't stop now.] **1992** P. DOBSON *Informant, Cape Town* Cotch. Vomit.

Hence **cotch** *n.*, vomit; also *attrib.*; **cotch** *adj.*, unpleasant.

1983 *Grocott's Mail* 18 Feb. 13 *Kotch Creek*, Scenic brook with algae of undisclosed origin. **1989** T. BOTHA in *Style* June 112 The Radnor Hotel in Hopetown looks inviting, much better than the kotch-green one back in Strydenburg. **1991** C.E. HILL *Informant, Johannesburg* Cotch (*adj.*). Unpleasant. It was a cotch job I had to do.

cotla var. KGOTLA.

coudou var. KUDU.

Council of Seventeen see SEVENTEEN.

council police *n. phr.* A municipal police force, employed by a local authority to police black urban areas. Also *attrib.* Hence **council policeman** *n. phr.*

1986 *Weekly Mail* 29 Aug. 1 A group of chanting youths .. moved in a horn-shaped formation towards the council police vans. **1987** *City Press* 5 Apr. 1 Lawyers .. were instructed to institute civil claims against the council and 12 council policemen. **1987** *New Nation* 2 Apr. 1 In New Brighton, two residents have laid charges of assault against the town-ship's council police, known as the 'Amatshaka'.

coupé /kuˈpeɪ/ *n.* [Brit. Eng. (1850s; now obs.?).] An end compartment in a railway carriage, with seats (or beds) on one side only.

1920 R.H. LINDSEY-RENTON *Diary* (1979) 73 Caught the 8.45 a.m. train to Johannesburg in a reserved *coupé* to myself. **1931** K. LINDSAY *'Neath Sn Cross* 24 The train was by no means full and he was lucky enough to secure a first-class coupé to himself, and so passed a very comfortable night. **1977** [see THIRD-CLASS]. **1990** *Style* May 80 Back to cognac at the piano-shaped mahogany bar tucked at one end of the observation car before tottering off to my coupé and bed. **1992** J. ROPER in *E. Prov. Herald* 18 May 4 (*letter*) We had a coupé (first class) which cost us R350 each. **1994** A. GREAVES on Radio South Africa 18 Sept. (Sunday at Home), We had a coupé as we call it in this country — one upstairs bunk, one downstairs bunk.

courhen var. CORE-HEN.

Covenant, **Day of the** see DAY OF THE COVENANT.

coyatta var. KIAAT.

coyatte hout var. KAJATENHOUT.

CP *n.* [Initial letters of *Conservative Party*.] A right-wing white party which broke away from the governing National Party in 1982, and which advocates apartheid and the partitioning of South Africa into racially homogeneous territories; a member of this party; colloquially, KAAPEE. Also *attrib.*

1982 *Sunday Times* 25 July 28 The CP finally came up this week with what it laughingly calls a race policy. As far as it can be understood at all, it sounds like apartheid circa 1949. **1983** J.D. GROBLER in *Hansard* 28 Feb. 1922 Here in this House we asked the hon. member to dissociate himself from the AWB; to repudiate the AWB. But to this day not a single member of the CP has reacted to this! **1983** *Survey of Race Rel. 1982* (S.A.I.R.R.) 12 The CP's success was due to the fact that it had become the genuine representative of the Afrikaner working and lower middle class — in particular the blue collar workers, lower paid civil servants and marginal farmers. **1987** *S. Afr. Digest* 8 May 5 The CP's policy of partition .. leads to a system where each nation governs itself and eradicates any problems of how to negotiate with Blacks. **1989** [see FAIREST CAPE]. **1990** R. STENGEL *January Sun* 184 In Brits, the CP people .. put up signs in their restaurants that say, For Whites Only. **1990** *Sunday Times* 12 Aug. 17 An NP/ANC coalition will usurp all power and suppress the living daylights out of AWBs, PACs, CPs, Azapos, Democrats and anyone else who dares express a dissenting view.

CPSA *n.*[1] Also **C.P.S.A.** [Initial letters of *Church of the Province of South(ern) Africa*, *Province* being a general Eng. ecclesiastical term for a district within the jurisdiction of an archbishop.] The Anglican (Episcopal) Church in southern Africa, comprising dioceses in South Africa, Namibia, Lesotho, Swaziland, Mozambique, and the islands of St Helena, Ascension, and Tristan da Cunha. Also *attrib.* See also ORDER OF ETHIOPIA.

[**1870** *Declaration of Fundamental Principles* in C. Gray *Life of Robert Gray* (1876) 488 We, being by representation the Church of the Province of South Africa, do declare that we receive and maintain the Faith of our Lord Jesus Christ as taught in the Holy Scriptures, held by the Primitive Church, summed up in the Creeds, and affirmed by the undisputed General Councils. **1891** C.R. GOODLATTE *Church of Province of S. Afr.* 8 In 1870 .. the first Provincial Synod .. framed the Constitution and Canons of the Church of the Province of South Africa.] **1898** in M. Nuttall *Making of Tradition* (1970) 13 (*title*) Journal of the Fifth Synod of the C.P.S.A. **1970** in *Ibid.* 2 [This book was] first published in 1970 by CPSA/SPCK, Johannesburg. **1984** D. TUTU in *Seek* Jan. 1 Our own CPSA bishops held one of their 1983 sessions of episcopal synod in Namibia to express solidarity with their fellow Anglicans and fellow Christians in Namibia. **1986** *Evening Post* 15 Apr. 5 A source in the CPSA said it was 'quite remarkable' the election had been dealt with in one day ... Bishop Tutu's election was an 'encouraging sign of unity' between blacks and whites in the church. [**1988** J. ALLEN in *Inside S. Afr.* Feb. 3 Archbishop Desmond Tutu is not .. the primate of the Church of England in South Africa. He is primate of the Church of the Province of South Africa.]

CPSA *n.*[2] *hist.* Also **C.P.S.A.** Initial letters of *Communist Party of South Africa*, established in 1921, banned in 1950, and reorganized (illegally) in 1953 as the South African Communist Party (see SACP).

[**1921** *Manifesto of Communist Party of S. Afr.* in A. Lerumo *50 Fighting Years* (1987) 105 The Communist Party of South Africa, which .. expects shortly to be affiliated to the World Communist International, makes its appeal to all South African workers, organised and unorganised, white and black, to join in promoting the *overthrow of the capitalist system*.] **1956** H.M. BATE *S. Afr. without Prejudice* 81 When it became known how strong a footing the Communists were getting .. , the Communist Party of South Africa (C.P.S.A.) was declared illegal ... In anticipation .. the C.P.S.A ... issued a statement that the Party had 'dissolved'. **1961** *Story of Communist Party* in A. Lerumo *50 Fighting Years* (1987) 137 In 1950 they passed the 'Suppression of Communism Act', which declared the Communist Party unlawful. They listed every member or supporter of the CPSA they knew. **1989** *Reader's Digest Illust. Hist.* 325 The Communist Party of South Africa (CPSA) .. was pushing ahead with its plans for a new South Africa — adopting, in 1928, a plan for a 'native republic' based on a programme of mobilising rural Africans. **1990** *New African* 25 June 6

The new SACP .. took over the tasks and banners of the former CPSA.

craal var. KRAAL *n.*

cracker *n.* Also **'cracker**. Pl. **-s**, or unchanged. [Ellipt. for MUSSELCRACKER.] The *white mussel-cracker* (see MUSSELCRACKER sense 2), *Sparodon durbanensis*. Also *attrib.*

1971 *Grocott's Mail* 25 May 3 Roger Amos came along with a fine 'cracker (silver steenbras.) **1982** *S. Afr. Fishing* Apr.-May 10 Cracker, hottentot and out of season galjoen are being caught by rock anglers. **1989** *E. Prov. Herald* 20 Oct. 21 *(caption)* Eastern Province 'cracker twins' Diddi Damm .. and Hein vd Walt living up to their reputations as two of the top spearfishermen in the country ... They accounted for five musselcrackers each, the legal limit. **1990** *Ibid.* 14 Sept. 18 We often caught cracker from the breakwater .. but the breakwater crackers were seldom over 25lb (11,32kg) ... My heaviest cracker still stands at 38lb (17,21kg).

crackers *pl. n. Obs.* exc. *hist.* [See quot. 1879.] Poorly tanned sheepskin or leather trousers as worn during the 19th century. Cf. VEL-BROEKS.

1833 *Cape of G.H. Lit. Gaz.* 2 Sept. 238 (Pettman), Old *Crackers alias* leather breeches. **1837** 'N. POLSON' *Subaltern's Sick Leave* 100 Plain in person .., clothed in .. a pair of tanned sheep-skin oh-no-we-never-mention-ems, commonly called crackers. **1838** T. SHONE Diary. 15 Nov., Finished a pr of crackers for Henry. **1847** 'A BENGALI' *Notes on Cape of G.H.* 19 The Dutch farmer's dress is very uniform; leather trowsers, called 'crackers', a straw hat with a green veil. **1852** A.W. COLE *Cape & Kafirs* 90 The Hottentot .. wore leather 'crackers', as the nether garments are termed in South Africa. **1879** T.J. LUCAS *Zulus & Brit. Frontiers* 88 Leather pantaloons. These were euphoniously termed 'crackers' from the peculiar noise which they made when in motion. **1883** M.A. CAREY-HOBSON *Farm in Karoo* 196 'Fancy being caught in a shower with leather trousers on.' 'Yes, and then the hot sun coming out and drying them on you, causing them to crackle up in all sorts of sharp angles; they might well call them crackers, which was the name they gave them.' **1896** [see BAADJIE]. **1911** D.B. HOOK *'Tis but Yesterday* 20 They all wore 'leather-crackers', and wild cat skins, extending from the waist to the knee. *Ibid.* The little swordsman in leather 'crackers,' who rode at him like the very devil! **1913** C. PETTMAN *Africanderisms* 530 Leather or skin trousers were much worn in the earlier days of the Colony, and were known among the settlers of 1820 and their descendants as 'Crackers'. **1949** L.G. GREEN *In Land of Afternoon* 15 The inhabitants were supposed to be all Boers, dressed in leather crackers and batjes and shod with veldchoons. **1975** D.H. STRUTT *Clothing Fashions* 169 The prepared sheepskin trousers worn by some of the early settlers were known as *crackers* from the noise they made with the slightest movement of the wearer. **1975** *Ibid.* [see KLAPBROEK].

crael var. KRAAL *n.*

crance var. KRANTZ.

crane flower *n. phr.* [See quot. 1966.] The plant *Strelitzia reginae* of the Strelitziaceae; its flower; also called STRELITZIA.

1946 *Farmer's Weekly* 30 Oct. 49 A grower in California showed me hundreds of Strelitzias (crane flowers) telling me that he got a dollar per bloom for them from the Hollywood stars. **1951** S. ELIOVSON *Flowering Shrubs & Trees* 132 The crane-flower should be planted in full sun and grows best in warm climates. **1965** —— *S. Afr. Wild Flowers for Garden* 271 *S. reginae* is called crane flower in South Africa, but is given the more glamorous name of bird-of-paradise in other countries, where it is highly prized as a cut flower. **1966** C.A. SMITH *Common Names* 195 *Crane flower('s bill)*, .. The vernacular name is derived from the rather striking resemblance of the flower to a crane's head, particularly of an enraged crane. **1975** *S. Afr. Panorama* Jan. 11 Thirty dozen Strelitzias — the exotic crane flower which occurs in KwaZulu .. decorated the marble hall and exhibition venue.

crawfish *n. obsolescent.* [Transf. use of Brit. *crawfish* a name applied esp. to the langouste *Palinurus vulgaris* (fr. Fr. *crevice, crevis* freshwater crustacean); cf. CRAYFISH.] CRAYFISH. Also *attrib.*

1853 L. PAPPE *Synopsis of Edible Fishes* 11 This crawfish [*sc.* the Cape lobster, *Palinurus lalandii*], peculiar only to the West Coast, and common to Table Bay, is easily caught. **1877** S. TURNER in D. Child *Portrait of Pioneer* (1980) 89 The Captain and another man went to look for crawfish. **1913** W.W. THOMPSON *Sea Fisheries of Cape Col.* 50 The crawfish (Palinurus) (Jasus lalandii) is found in very great numbers on the west coast, from Walwich Bay to Cape Point, but does not seem to flourish in any appreciable extent eastwards of that headland. **1940** *Act 9* in *Stat. of Union* 38 In this Act, unless inconsistent with the context — 'crawfish' means any crawfish, or any part of any crawfish, whether it has been treated or not. **1953** [see ROCK LOBSTER]. **1954** K.H. BARNARD *S. Afr. Shore-Life* 27 Farther east, instead of the Cape Crawfish, other species are found which are called *stridentes* or noisy Crawfishes ... Gilchrist's Crawfish from the Agulhas Bank has the two short whips on each of the shorter feelers ... The Port Elizabeth Crawfish .. is a squat form. **1961** *Cape Times* 21 July 11 Our *kreef* which still appears as crayfish or crawfish on Cape restaurant menus, is the *langouste.* We changed our *kreef* from crawfish to rock lobster to please American taste. It seems they despise the small, river crawfish with which they are familiar. **1964** L.G. GREEN *Old Men Say* 121 Fish soups are served occasionally at the Cape, a very good crawfish soup and a so-called Bisque Blaauwberg which is a puree of mussels. **1973** L. DICKSON in *Cape Times* 2 July 5 The Cape Times helpfully explained the difference between crayfish, crawfish, kreef, rock lobster and langouste ... It leaves me as confused as ever.

crawl *n. obs.* [Anglicized pronunciation-spelling of *kraal*, see KRAAL *n.*]

Found elsewhere with related meanings, e.g. in *Jamaican Eng.* meaning 'sty'.

a. KRAAL *n.* sense 1 a.

1771 J. BANKS *Jrnl* (1896) They [*sc.* the Khoikhoi] train up bulls which they place round their crawls or towns in the night. **1792** W. BLIGH *Voy. to S. Seas* 39 A reputable farmer .. had information from some Caffre Hottentots that at a crawl, or village, in their country, there were white men and women.

b. KRAAL *n.* sense 3 a.

*a***1862** J. AYLIFF *Jrnl of 'Harry Hastings'* (1963) 70 The fold (but I find the proper name is 'crawl', not fold) was made of posts and rails.

crayfish *n.* [Transf. use of Brit. *crayfish* a name applied esp. to the langouste *Palinurus vulgaris* (fr. Fr. *crevice, crevis* freshwater crustacean); cf. CRAWFISH.] Any of several species of spiny lobster of the Palinuridae, esp. the Cape or South African spiny rock lobster *Jasus lalandii* (see KREEF), but also *Palinurus delagoae* and *P. gilchristi*, and the langouste, *P. vulgaris; Cape lobster*, see CAPE sense 2 a; CRAWFISH; ROCK LOBSTER. Also *attrib.*

Confined in its distribution to the west coast of southern Africa, *Jasus lalandii* is commercially the most important of the rock lobsters.

1831 *S. Afr. Almanac & Dir.* Jan., Fish in Season. Hottentot, red and white Stumpnose, Harder, Roman, red Steenbrassem, Mackarel, Gurnet, Oyster, Crayfish, Shrimp, Mussles, Klip Fish, Smelt, Sole, &c. **1844** J. BACKHOUSE *Narr. of Visit* 82 There were some curious beetles, and one of vivid green was feeding indiscriminately on the remains of *Crayfish* cast up on the shore. **1860** A.W. DRAYSON *Sporting Scenes* 14 A delay of a few hours enabled me to haul on board a good dish of grotesque-looking fish, and some crayfish: the latter were excellent eating. **1902** [see *Cape lobster* (CAPE sense 2 a)]. **1915** D. FAIRBRIDGE *Torch Bearer* 148 It didn't matter what you called it — crayfish was crayfish, and — while everyone in the audience was familiar with the delicate small kreef in mayonnaise or dressed in other ways — who would dream of eating the large ones except Malays? **1925** H.J. MANDELBROTE tr. *O.F. Mentzel's Descr. of Cape of G.H.* II. 89 Local crayfish are not lobsters as Kolbe states. I have never seen a true lobster at the Cape. The crayfish are of the very large variety ... They have small claws and spikes on their backs, and require care in handling. They are not very nice to eat and cannot be enjoyed without vinegar. *c***1936** *S. & E. Afr. Yr Bk & Guide* 347 The canning of crayfish as an industry commenced about 1890. **1955** A. DELIUS *Young Trav.* 86 Dick .. chose .. 'Crayfish Cardinale'. Crayfish, Mr. Sharp explained, was the Cape Lobster. **1967** W.A. DE KLERK *White Wines* 34 The 'Crayfish Agreement' of 1935 — a treaty whereby France undertook to buy Cape crayfish on condition that South Africa would refrain from using a number of French wine names .. such as .. 'Champagne', 'Burgundy' and 'Cognac'. **1973** [see ALIKREUKEL]. **1978** [see KREEF]. **1988** *Style* Feb. 18 What is the difference between crayfish and lobster? 'None at all ... The crayfish is one of the few sea creatures to have its name changed by law. We couldn't sell crayfish in the States so we changed its name to lobster.'

CRC *n. hist.* Also **C.R.C.** [Initial letters of *Coloured (Persons') Representative Council.*] A legislative body of elected and nominated 'coloured' representatives, established in 1969 to deal with community affairs, education, and finance. Also *attrib.*

This body was dissolved in 1980.

[**1969** *Govt Gaz.* Vol.46 No.2347, 1 Under the powers vested in me by section 1 (1) of the Coloured Persons Representative Council Act, 1964 .., I hereby determine the 1 July 1969, as the date on which the Coloured Persons Representative Council .. is established.] **1970** *Argus* 3 Oct. 3 The political future of the Coloured people is going to be debated ... The uncertainty of our future and the ineffectiveness of the C.R.C. is expected to be hotly debated. **1973** *Black Review 1972* 92 Objections to the creation of and participation in the C.R.C. is that the C.R.C., like other government-created platforms, is .. a 'toy telephone' designed for 'window dressing' for the international scene and to divide blacks. **1976** *Argus* 20 Sept. 3 The Coloured Representative Council is expected to receive a full report .. about tomorrow's CRC talks with the Prime Minister, Mr B.J. Vorster, on the present unrest and detentions. **1981** *Survey of Race Rel. 1980* (S.A.I.R.R.) 25 From the date of the proclamation dissolving the CRC, that is from April 1, 1980, until a date determined by the State President the CRC would not be constituted. **1984** R. DAVIES et al. *Struggle for S. Afr.* II. 397 Labour managed to secure the adoption by the CRC of a motion calling for the abolition of all the institutions of apartheid, including the CRC itself.

Creaky var. GRIETJIE.

cream of tartar *n. phr.* [Special sense of general Eng., prob. fr. taste of fruit pulp (see quot. 1966); or perh. tr. Afk. *kremetart*, see KREMETART.] In full ***cream of tartar tree***: the baobab tree *Adansonia digitata*, the sole species of the Bombacaceae; KREMETART sense 1.

1860 [see KREMETART sense 1]. *a***1875** T. BAINES *Jrnl of Res.* (1964) II. 141 The nut of the 'Cream of Tartar' tree, a species of Baobab, hung in a bag inside ... Inside were .. hard, brown seeds .. in compartments filled with a powder slightly acid to the taste and exactly resembling that from which it derives its name. **1878** P. GILLMORE *Great Thirst Land* 406 It is frequently called the cream of tartar tree, because between the seeds there is a pulpy, crystallised substance, which when soaked in water makes an extremely pleasant acid drink. **1894** W.C. BALDWIN *Afr. Hunting* 295 We measured a tree called Cream of Tartar sixty-one feet round the bole; but there are many very much larger. **1913** C. PETTMAN *Africanderisms* 132 *Cream of tartar tree, Adansonia digitata.* This tree is sometimes called the 'Monkey bread tree' and the 'Calabash baobab tree'. **1917** R. MARLOTH *Common Names* 21 *Cream-of-tartar tree* v. *Baobab*, The fruit contains a whitish acidulous powder, but not any tartar, the acidity being due to citric acid. **1936** [see KREMETART sense 1]. **1949** C. BULLOCK *Rina* 40 The great unnatural boles and misshapen branches of the cream-of-tartar. **1966** C.A. SMITH *Common Names* 195 *Cream-of-tartar tree*, .. The juice of the pulpy fruit contains citric acid, and produces a refreshing beverage having the taste of a tartaric solution, whence the vernacular name. *Ibid.* 311 The vernacular name [*sc.* 'kremetartboom'] is a part corruption of cream-of-tartar tree. **1990** *Weekend Post* 6 Oct. (Leisure) 4 The fat and bulbous baobab .. is also known as the cream of tartar tree and the 'sherbet' in the seed pod is a delight to monkeys and small boys.

Creeche, Creechy, Creeky, Creetje varr. GRIETJIE.

crimen injuria /ˌkraɪmən ɪnˈdʒuːrɪə, ˈkriːmən ɪnˈjuːrɪa/ *n. phr. Law.* [Eng., fr. L. *crimen* charge, accusation + *injuria* indignity.] A wilful injury to the dignity of another, caused by e.g. the use of obscene language or gestures, or racial insults.

[**1912** *S. Afr. Law Reports: TPD* 1106 The accused was charged .. with the crime of criminal *injuria* by wilfully and unlawfully exposing his private parts in the presence of certain persons with an .. intent to injure and insult them.] **1958** B. BENNETT *This Was a Man* 119 A man was charged with defamatory libel on the Master of the Cape Supreme Court by publishing a scurrilous letter about him ... An alternative charge of *crimen injuria* was framed on the ground that the letter was sent to the Master 'with intent to injure and insult.' **1971** E.M. BURCHELL in *Std Encycl. of Sn Afr.* III. 496 *Criminal injuria* or *crimen injuria* is a wilful aggression upon the dignity or honour of another. On account of the immoral nature of this crime an accused will only be found guilty if, in the opinion of the court, his conduct was of a sufficiently reprehensible character to warrant punishment judged by present-day moral standards. [**1984** *Cape Times* 18 Jan. 23 A Man who called a Brooklyn woman a 'f— jintoo' (whore) was yesterday fined R250 (or 100 days) after being convicted in the Magistrate's Court of criminal injuria.] **1987** B. KRIGE in *Frontline* Feb. 13 [They] were charged with crimen injuria for alleging they had smelt liquor on the breath of the officer in charge. **1987** G. SILBER in *Ibid.* Mar. 9 In the seventies Van Tonder's fame centred on his crusade for the right to be served in Afrikaans wherever he chose to take his custom: 'If you want to speak Afrikaans, speak to the kaffir,' one shop owner told him. He took her to court, where she was fined R50 for crimen injuria. **1987** *Pace* Nov. 4 They had some sort of altercation .. which ended with the Scotsman calling the driver a silly —. The driver was .. most offended and took the wee Scots fellow to court for using racially offensive language, crimen injuria – you name it he threw the book at him.

cripple-wood *n. obs.* [tr. S. Afr. Du. *kreupelhout*, see KREUPELHOUT.] The KREUPELBOOM (sense a), *Leucospermun conocarpodendron.*

1731 G. MEDLEY tr. *P. Kolb's Present State of Cape of G.H.* II. 185 At the *Cape* there are but very few Wood-Lice; and they are only seen upon the Cripple-Wood. *Ibid.* 259 Another sort of Trees [*sic*] at the *Cape* .. is what the *Cape-Europeans* call *Cripple-*Wood. These are Dwarf-Trees, with very crooked knotted Branches.

crissy /krɪsi/ *adj.* Also **crizzy, krissy.** [Englished form of Afk. *kroes* frizzy + Eng. adj.-forming suffix *-y.*] KROES sense 1.

1980 C. HOPE *A Separate Development* (1983) 56 With your complexion, *crissy* hair and all, next to you even my kaffir girl's good looking. **1984** *Darling* 24 Oct. 90, I cut my hair short so that it can be easier to manage but it still looks a mess ... It goes 'krissy' in cold or hot weather. **1989** J. HOBBS *Thoughts in Makeshift Mortuary* 313 Do you really want babies with dark skins and krissy hair? **1990** M. GEVISSER in *Weekly Mail* 8 Feb. 10 She was the little girl, born of white parents in Piet Retief, who was forcibly removed from her school after the principal notified the police that her skin was turning dark and her hair was becoming 'crizzy'.

Criste menchen pl. form of CHRISTENMENSCH.

crocodile *n. colloq.* Often in the n. phrr. ***the Big Crocodile, the Great Crocodile*** [tr. Afk. *groot krokodil*]. *The Groot Krokodil,* see GROOT KROKODIL sense a.

1989 *Newsweek* 13 Feb. 13 He has long been the glowering face of white South African defiance. But even members of President P.W. Botha's inner circle were caught off guard last week when the 73-year old 'Great Crocodile' .. took a step toward retirement. **1990** *Sunday Times* 18 Mar. 22 Somewhere in the Wilderness, The Big Crocodile stirs ... Ex-president P W Botha is planning .. an attempt to have his voice heard in political affairs once again. **1992** *Financial Mail* 13 Mar. 25 The Big Crocodile has been biding his time in his retirement lair at the Wilderness. **1994** R. MALAN in *Style* May 35, I last felt truly optimistic in the southern summer of 1989, in the interlude between the downfall of Botha the Crocodile and the Great Leap Forward of February, 1990. **1994** P. LEE in *Ibid.* 58 Go back to the blank columns in the newspapers .. excised by a power-crazed Minister. Go back to the thrashing tail of the crocodile haphazardly scything tender advances off at the knees. Go back further to mass telephone tapping, .. young men going off to fight phantoms in Angola.

crombec /ˈkrɒmbek, ˈkrɔmbek/ *n.* Also **krombek,** and (formerly) **kromebec.** [Englished form of Afk. *krombek*, fr. Du. *krom* crooked + *bek* beak. The earliest occurrence of the name is in F. le Vaillant's *Histoire Naturelle des Oiseaux d'Espagne*, 1802.] The bird *Sylvietta refuscens* of the Sylviidae, with a long, curved beak and short tail; STUMPTAIL.

In G.L. Maclean's *Roberts' Birds of Sn Afr.* (1993), the name 'longbilled crombec' is used for this species. Although *S. refuscens* is the only crombec which occurs in South Africa, the name 'crombec' is given in general Eng. to all birds of this genus.

*c*1808 C. VON LINNÉ *System of Natural Hist.* VIII. 466 *The curved-bill Fig-eater,* This species is plentiful about the Elephant-river, where it is called *kromebec,* which in Dutch signifies a curved bill. **1884** LAYARD & SHARPE *Birds of S. Afr.* 303 Sylvietta rufescens ... The 'Stomp-stertje' of the Dutch colonists, and the 'Crombec' of Le Vaillant. **1901** STARK & SCLATER *Birds of S. Afr.* II. 115 *Sylvietta refuscens*, The Crombec ... 'Stomp-Stertjie' (Stump-tail) of Dutch Colonists. **1908** [see STUMPTAIL]. **1937** M. ALSTON *Wanderings* 38 In this aloe hedge .. were mouse-birds and wren-warblers and that funny-looking little warbler known as the crombec or stumptail, which has no tail to speak of. **1955** [see STUMPTAIL]. **1962** W.R. SIEGFRIED *Some Protected Birds* Pl.130, *Crombec, Long-billed Crombec, Stumptail, Sylvietta refuscens.* A very distinctive little bird which in the field appears to have no tail. Found in a wide variety of bush and shrub habitats. **1970** [see STUMPTAIL]. **1978** MCLACHLAN & LIVERSIDGE *Roberts Birds of S. Afr.* 437 *Crombec ... Sylvietta refuscens ... Voice*: A pretty, shrill call, 'peep-peep-peep'. The phrase used for another species of crombec is equally good for this species. **1993** G.L. MACLEAN *Roberts' Birds of Sn Afr.* 563 *Longbilled Crombec* ... Bill long (much longer than that of Redfaced Crombec).

cross var. KAROSS.

cross-berry *n.* [tr. Afk. *kruisbessie.*] The KRUISBESSIE (sense b), *Grewia occidentalis.*

1976 A.P. BRINK *Instant in Wind* 56 White-thorn and tanglewood, .. kiepersol, and karee and cross-berries, assegai wood, the pale blue of plumbago. **1982** FOX & NORWOOD YOUNG *Food from Veld* 355 *Grewia occidentalis L., Common names*: English – *cross-berry* .. The ripe purplish fruit is quite pleasant to eat. **1987** F. VON BREITENBACH *Nat. List of Indigenous Trees* 129 *Grewia occidentalis L.,* .. Cross-berry, Dew-berry, Bow-wood, Assegaiwood, Four-corners, Button-wood. **1987** [see NUM-NUM]. **1990** [see KRUISBESSIE]. **1990** T. VAN RENSBURG in *Conserva* Vol.5 No.3, 21 My brother and I became acquainted with all the Bushveld fruit-trees – maroela, crossberry, moepel and stamvrug. **1991** *Dict. of Horticult.* (Dept of Nat. Educ.) 451 *Kruisbessie, (Grewia occidentalis,* ..): cross-berry, dew-berry. **1992** [see KRUISBESSIE]. **1994** *Weekend Post* 22 Oct. (Leisure) 7 *Grewia occidentalis* (cross berry) is another good standby in an indigenous garden. It bears pretty pink-mauve flowers in spring and early summer and these are followed by the berries which give the shrub its common name.

crow *v. trans.* and *intrans. Obs.* [Englished pronunciation-spelling of dialectal Afk. *gra(a)u, grou* fr. *grawe* (Du. *graven*); Pettman's theory (see quot. 1913) seems unlikely.] To dig (a hole, the ground, or something buried under the ground). Also *comb.* **crow-water,** see quot. 1853.

1853 F. GALTON *Narr. of Explorer in Tropical S. Afr.* 79 This method of digging is called in Dutch patois 'crowing' the ground; thus, 'crow-water', means water that you have to crow for, and not an open well, or spring. *c*1870 J.G. WOOD *Natural Hist. of Man* I. 343 The Damaras .. will sometimes 'crow' holes eighteen inches .. in depth. **1879** — *Uncivilized Races* I. 313 The Damara wife costs her husband nothing for her keep, because she 'crows' her own ground-nuts. **1896** H.A. BRYDEN *Tales of S. Afr.* 47 With this last implement she can the more easily crow up their dinner. **1913** C. PETTMAN *Africanderisms* 133 *Crow, To,* (Hot. *gora,* to dig.) A corruption of the Hottentot word. It refers to the mode of digging holes employed by the Damaras. They take a pointed stick in their right hand, pierce the ground with it, clearing away the broken soil with their left hand, and having to 'crow' holes for house-building, for water, roots, etc., in this primitive fashion, they became very expert at it.

crunchie *n. slang.* [Perh. formed on *mealie cruncher* + Eng. (informal) n.-forming suffix *-ie*, or ad. *kransie* fr. slang *krantz-athlete* a baboon (see Gouws quot. 1970).] A derogatory and offensive name for an Afrikaner. Also shortened form **crunch.**

1970 V.R. VINK *Informant, Florida* The litter at the picnic spot was caused by a bunch of crunchies. **1970** T. RAY *Informant, Cedara (Kwa-Zulu Natal)* If an ou is coarse, you call him a crunchie or a rock. But don't say it to his face or he'll bop you. **1970** J. GOUWS *Informant, Oudtshoorn* In the Oudtshoorn military camp, krantz-athlete shortened to krantzie – crunchie for English-speakers. **1973** *Cape Times* 13 Apr. 3 Prof. G.R. Bozzoli, Principal of the University of the Witwatersrand, referred to the use of the words, 'crunch', 'Hairyback' and 'rock spider' in the latest issue of *Wits Student.* **1981** D. KRAMER in *Frontline* May 14 Call me a crunchie And I'll take you outside I'll show you just how The crunch is applied Then you'll keep ... tjoepstil. **1982** *Fair Lady* 24 Feb. 97 Back in South Africa, David was writing songs with a political edge. He had a go at the 'crunchie' with green fluff on his dashboard, the woman who sleeps with a gun under her pillow, the limp liberal who runs overseas when things get tough. **1989** C. PERKINS in *Sunday Times* 19 Mar. 5 From now on, any student or staff member who insults people by calling them 'coolies', 'crunchies', 'kaffirs' or 'spics' will have to be careful what he or she says. **1991** I. & F. DE MOOR *Informants, Grahamstown* Hairyback, Dutchman, Dutchie, rock-spider, rocky, crunchy – all derogatory terms for an Afrikaner. **1994** [see ROCK *n.*].

CSIR *n.* Also **C.S.I.R.** [Initial letters of *Council for Scientific and Industrial Research.*] A statutory body founded in 1945 and consisting of a number of institutes for research in science and technology. Also *attrib.*

[**1945** *Act 33* in *Stat. of Union* 298 As from a date to be fixed by the Governor-General .. there shall be established a council to be known as the Council for Scientific and Industrial Research which shall be a body corporate.] **1961** *Off. Yrbk of Union 1960* (Bureau of Census & Statistics) 272 *C.S.I.R. Information* – a monthly list of library accessions. **1971** *Std Encycl. of Sn Afr.* III. 457 The C.S.I.R.'s terms of reference, which cover the promotion of scientific research in general, are extremely broad, but do not include research into agriculture, medicine and the social sciences. **1977** NAUDÉ & BROWN in A.C. Brown *Hist. of Scientific Endeavour* 81 By 1961 .. the CSIR had grown into a large research organization, with nine national laboratories and institutes covering virtually the whole scientific and industrial field. *c*1990 *S. Afr. 1989–90* (Bureau for Info.) 560 By the early 1980s CSIR had begun to reassess its role in research ... CSIR was restructured to become a more market-orientated research, development and implementation organisation and entered the market in April 1988 as a technology partner to its clients in the private and public sectors of the economy.

cubbyhole *n.* [Eng., a small room, a cosy space.] The glove-compartment of a motor vehicle. Also shortened form **cubby**, and *attrib.*

1970 J. MCINTOSH *Stonefish*, He remembered the handbag; and he hurried back to the car, .. and got it out of the cubbyhole. 1986 J. ARMSTRONG in *Eng. Alive '86* 30 They stopped the car ... One of them took a small black book out of the cubbyhole. 1989 M.M. HACKSLEY tr. E. *Van Heerden's Ancestral Voices* 50 The magistrate stuck his hand through the open window of the car to take .. his .. cigars from the cubby-hole. 1991 C. NIXON in *E. Prov. Herald* 5 Mar. 1 When she took the wallet from the car's cubby to pay the man, he snatched it from her hands and fled. 1991 *Leisure Bks Catalogue* Apr.-June 11 *A Guide to Exploring the Western Cape*, Here is a value-for-money guide in a cubbyhole format that will provide you with comprehensive information on this .. region. 1991 J. WARDEN in *Sunday Times* 28 July (Motoring) 3 Being a 1300 it is .. not too fast ... , otherwise I would probably have a bunch of speeding fines in my cubbyhole.

cuca-shop /ˈkʊkə ˌʃɒp/ *n. Military slang.* Also **kuca shop.** [fr. *Cuca* the trade name of an Angolan beer + Eng. *shop.*] A trading store, often a liquor outlet, in the northern border area of Namibia.

Introduced into *S. Afr. Eng.* by soldiers sent on military service to Namibia.

1977 *Informant (army song)* Ag pleez Major won't you take us to the Cuca Shop, That's the right place if you want a dop. 1980 S. COLLETT in *Optima* Vol.28 No.4, 203 The *cuca* shops of Owambo, so-called because they originally sold Angolan beer of that name, are an important .. part of the distribution channel; there are an estimated 5 000 spread through Owambo, each catering for an average of about 80 people or 13 households. 1982 *Evening Post* 17 Aug. 1 Nine civilians died when a cuca shop (country general store) owned by a member of the Special Police in SWA/Namibia came under Swapo mortar fire. 1989 S. JOHNSON in *Weekly Mail* 10 Feb. 13 The *Cuca*-shop is an allegory of Owamboland's uncomplaining, almost impish approach to suffering ... These unique Namibian shebeens have been social rallying-points for a shattered community. 1995 *BBC Focus on Africa* Apr.-June 33 Ovamboland doesn't have bars, it has Cuka shops, named after the cheap Angolan beer they used to sell. The regions have literally thousands of Cuka shops.

cuddu var. KUDU.

cuka shop var. CUCA-SHOP.

culpable homicide *n. phr. Law.* [Eng. *culpable* deserving blame or censure + *homicide* the action, by a human being, of killing a human being.] The unlawful but unpremeditated killing of a person.

Used also in *Scot. Eng.* Cf. *Brit. Eng.* 'manslaughter'.

1832 *Graham's Town Jrnl* 20 Apr. 68 Hermanus Terblantz, Hottentot, was indicted for Culpable Homicide, in having caused the death of Katreyn, his wife, by blows of an *achter os sambok*, and other injuries. 1889 *Cape Law Jrnl* VI. 110 Topsy v. The State ... On an indictment for the culpable homicide .. of her new born infant, *Held*, that the prisoner could not be found guilty of concealment of birth. 1904 C.H. TREDGOLD *Handbk of Col. Criminal Law* 119 Killing, which would otherwise be murder, is culpable homicide if the act causing death is done in the heat of passion, caused by provocation. 1949 E. HELLMANN *Rooiyard* 93 A Native, in a state of extreme intoxication, had stabbed a Rooiyard Native fatally. The offender was found guilty of culpable homicide and sentenced to lashes and a lengthy term of imprisonment. 1955 *Act* 56 in *Stat. of Union* 1160 Any person charged with murder in regard to whom it is proved that he wrongfully caused the death of the deceased, but without intent, may be found guilty of culpable homicide. 1960 HAHLO & KAHN *Union of S. Afr.* 312 Culpable homicide differs from murder in that the unlawful killing is not accompanied by intention to kill, some lesser but nevertheless blameworthy state of mind being sufficient. 1979 W. EBERSOHN *Lonely Place* 178 To kill an Afrikaner was murder. To kill a Jew might be no more than culpable homicide. But N'Kosana was black. Killing him would not be a crime of any description. 1986 *Reader's Digest Family Guide to Law* 101 Murder and culpable homicide are both forms of unlawful killing, but the crucial difference is that if a man kills intentionally it is murder, whereas if he kills negligently it is culpable homicide. 1991 *E. Prov. Herald* 14 Mar. 3 A stern warning was given to reckless motorists yesterday, when a Johannesburg magistrate .. sentenced a 19-year-old woman to an effective 18 months' imprisonment for culpable homicide.

cumbess var. KOMBERS.

Currie Cup *n. phr.* [Named for its donor, *Donald Currie.*] A sporting trophy awarded annually, orig. for inter-provincial rugby, swimming, soccer, and cricket. Also *attrib.*

Since the unification of ethnically separate sports associations in the early 1990s, the 'Currie Cup' has not been awarded in cricket and soccer.

1897 G.A. PARKER *S. Afr. Sports* 22 The Currie Cup match in Johannesburg, played in April 1891 between .. Griqualand West and Transvaal, furnished the most interesting and exciting event. 1910 *S. Afr. 'Inquire Within'* (Cape Times) 134 *Cricket*, ... The Currie Cup Tournament takes place every year, Western Province being the present holders. 1927 M. LIEBSON in *Outspan* 1 Apr. 47 In the various Currie Cup tournaments, the four or five entries of a generation ago have now grown to eight or nine. 1939 L. BROWN in *Ibid.* 13 Oct. 47 Old Currie Cup rivalries will be renewed. 1971 M. MURRAY in *Std Encycl. of Sn Afr.* III. 529 The name of Currie is a household word in South Africa by the annual award of sporting cups for cricket, rugby, soccer and swimming, the first of the these 'Currie' cups (for cricket) dating from 1888. 1986 *Personality* 1 Sept. 32 There's a needle to the Currie Cup matches .. which promises great things .. for our rugby. 1990 *Femina* June 50 Spurned by the rest of the world, South African rugby teams have been unable to prove themselves against international competition (the Currie Cup is a poor substitute for the world crown).

CUSA /ˈkjuːsə, ˈkuːsə/ *n. hist.* Also **Cusa.** Acronym formed on initial letters of *Council of Unions of South Africa*, a federation of black trade unions formed in 1980. Also *attrib.*

Absorbed into NACTU in 1986.

1980 S. FRIEDMAN in *Rand Daily Mail* 15 Sept. 2 The presence of a wide range of black organisations was 'a tribute to Cusa's ability to draw support from the black community, regardless of ideological affiliations'. 1982 *Reader* Dec. 16 One trade union group, the Council of Unions of South Africa (Cusa) has nearly twice as many members now. 1988 E. JAYIYA in *Pace* Oct. 14 Cyril [sc. Ramaphosa] wanted Cusa (Council of Unions of South Africa) to join Cosatu. 1989 *Race Rel. Survey 1988–9* (S.A.I.R.R.) 455 At the formation of COSATU in 1985, the Council of Unions of South Africa (Cusa) had failed to become part of the new federation, because of fundamental differences of principle.

customary *adj.* Usu. in the collocations *customary law, customary union.* Of or pertaining to black African traditional custom or law. See also *Native Law* (NATIVE *n.* sense 1 c).

1927 *Act* 38 in *Stat. of Union* 332 No male Native shall, during the subsistence of any customary union between him and any woman, contract a marriage with any other woman. 1929 *Act* 9 in *Ibid.* 42 'Customary union' means the association of a man and a woman in a conjugal relationship according to native law and custom, where neither the man nor the woman is party to a subsisting marriage. 1953 S.M. SEYMOUR *Native Law* 68 A grown-up girl is not capable of contracting a customary union by herself. The contracting parties are the bride's guardian and the bridegroom. 1971 *Daily Dispatch* 2 June 1 The Transkeian Customary Unions Bill is a move to force those married under tribal customs to register their marriage. 1986 D. WELSH in P. Maylam *Hist. of Afr. People* 84 Customary law and the judicial powers of chiefs was recognised in the reserves in cases involving Africans, and in civil cases between Africans outside the reserves. 1986 *Reader's Digest Family Guide to Law* 237 A woman married by customary rites has certain claims to inherit from her husband on his death. *Ibid.* 260 When blacks marry they can choose whether they wish to be married according to black customary law or according to the ordinary law of the land. The first type of marriage is usually .. referred to .. as a customary union. 1992 E. JAYIYA in *Pace* Sept. 15 Another pretty woman has become the fifth wife in the kraal of King Goodwill Zwelithini ... Despite being a customary union, the bride was clad in an expensive white gown. 1993 D. WILLERS in *Natal Witness* 6 Jan. 12 The constitution recognises and protects the right of those who identify with traditional and customary law to live by their own set of rules, and respects the role of traditional leaders and court systems to create and administer such law. 1993 R. MCNEILL in *Sunday Times* 20 June 16 Race may finally have been abolished as a determining factor in law in South Africa, but we still have customary union and indigenous courts, and neither apply to whites. 1994 J. RAPHAELY in *Femina* Jan. 6 One of the direct results was the throwing out of a proposal by traditional leaders that customary law should take precedence over the principle of equality in the Bill of Rights.

cut *v. trans.* [See LINE]. In the slang phr. *to cut a line*: LINE.

1990 R. GOOL *Cape Town Coolie* 59, I 'ave to cut a line now. I'll give you a look-up when I hit the Cape.

cut-throat lark *n. phr. Obs.* [So named for the orange throat-patch.] The KALKOENTJIE (sense 1), *Macronyx capensis.*

1884 LAYARD & SHARPE *Birds of S. Afr.* 530 This handsome pipit, which is called the 'Cut-throat lark' by the English colonists, *Kalkoentje* by the Dutch, is common throughout all the open country of the Colony. 1908 [see KALKOENTJIE sense 1]. 1913 C. PETTMAN *Africanderisms* 245 *Macronyx capensis* .. is also called the Cut-throat lark. 1923 HAAGNER & IVY *Sketches* 201 The Orange-throated Longclaw .. is known as the Cut-throat Lark or kalkoentjie (little Turkey). 1931 *Guide to Vertebrate Fauna of E. Cape Prov.* (Albany Museum) I. 87 *Macronyx Capensis* Linn. Cape Longclaw .. Cut-throat Lark or Skylark.

cuytge var. GEITJIE.

D

daag var. DAG.

daaga var. DAGGA n.[2]

daar doer see DOER.

daarem var. DAREM.

daba grass /ˈdaba grɑːs/ n. phr. Also **dob(b)o grass**. [Xhosa *idobo* any very coarse long grass + Eng. *grass*.] The coarse grass *Miscanthus capensis* of the Poaceae (sub-family Panicoideae), often used for thatching.

    1904 *E. London Dispatch* 23 Aug. 6 What about those brave fellows who fell at Gwadana and .. Fort Bowker? They have lain there for the last quarter of a century, friendless and uncared for, with the rank daba grass flourishing over them. **1912** *Ibid.* 18 Oct. 6 (Pettman), There doubtless rang out the familiar call that brought the family once more together to sleep, perhaps, amongst the rustling *dobbo* grass. **1913** C. PETTMAN *Africanderisms* 135 Daba grass, .. In the native territories the tough, flag-like grass used by the natives as thatch for their huts is so called. **1966** C.A. SMITH *Common Names* 196 Dabagras (-grass), *Miscanthidium capense* ... The name has been derived by phonetic abrasion from the original Xhosa 'i-dobo,' a general name for coarse tall-growing grasses .. used by the Bantu in the eastern territories for thatching their 'indaba' huts. **1980** *Daily Dispatch* 12 Sept. 10, I have a lot of 'dobo' (reed) grass on the farm. **1983** *Ibid.* 10 June 14 Large areas of dobbo grass have remained untouched. **1991** G.E. GIBBS RUSSELL et al. *Grasses of Sn Afr.* 221 *Miscanthus capensis* .. dabagrass ... All three broad-leaved species formerly recognized in *Miscanthidium*, .. are combined here because of great variability in the characters upon which separation has been attempted.

dabbies v. trans. [Etym. unknown.] In the language of children: a word which claims an object or privilege for the speaker.

    Although seldom recorded, the word has been in colloquial use since before 1940, and is remembered in use in Port Elizabeth c1955.

    1994 P. HAYES in *Daily Dispatch* 27 Oct. 20 Dabbies — meaning 'I want something' — was in common use at that time [sc. the 1930s].

dabby /ˈdabi, ˈdæbi/ n. Forms: α. **dabb(i)e, dabby, dubbee**; β. **davib, daweb, dawee(p), dawib, dawip**. [fr. Afk. *dabbie*, ad. Nama *dawe-b*, or Khoi *daba-hei-s* tamarisk; or see quot. 1989.] In full **dabby boom** /-buəm/ [Afk. *boom* tree], - **tree**, - **bush**: the wild tamarisk *Tamarix usneoides* of the Tamaricaceae. Also *attrib.*

    α. **1838** J.E. ALEXANDER *Exped. into Int.* I. 92 Mimosa and dubbee, or tamarisk trees .. lined its banks. *Ibid.* II. 62 The dubbee boom, or tamarisk tree, apparently the type of this part of Africa, and which I had constantly seen from the Kousie to the Kuisip, was now covered with white bloom. **1844** J. BACKHOUSE *Narr. of Visit* 549 In many places, *Tamarix orientalis*, was mixed with the Dabby-tree; both are confounded under the name of Abiquas-geelhout, which belongs however to the latter. **1859** 'A.B.C.' in *Cape Monthly Mag.* VI. Oct. 223 The north bank of the Swakop River .. is fringed by noble trees .. , and that termed Dabbe in southern parts of the colony. **1870** R. RIDGILL in A.M.L. Robinson *Sel. Articles from Cape Monthly Mag.* (1978) 37 A few stunted dabby bushes in the dry bed of the 'Hooms. **1889** F. GALTON *Trav. in S. Afr.* 11 Bushes (Dabby bushes I have always heard them called) not unlike fennel, but from eight to twelve feet high, grew plentifully. **1913** C. PETTMAN *Africanderisms* 135 Dabby bushes, .. *Tamarix articulata*. **1914** — *Notes on S. Afr. Place Names* 32 The Dabby tree (Tamarisk) has given its name to one or two places in Namaqualand: eg. Daweros and Daweras (Daweb, tamarisk). **1966** C.A. SMITH *Common Names* 196 Dabbie (dabees), *Tamarix usneoides* ... The vernacular name is a corruption from the Nama Hottentot name for the plants. [**1983** P.S. RABIE tr. *Nienaber & Raper's Hottentot Place Names* 92 Dabbe(draai), .. named after the *Tamarix usneoides* or 'tamarisk tree' ... *Dabbe, dabbie, dabby, dabe, dabi, dawe, dawi* are various spellings of the name as it appears in many .. place names.]

    β. [**1837** ECKLON & ZEYHER *Enumeratio Plantarum Africae* 330 *Tamarix orientalis*, ... Ab Hottentottis 'Daweep'.] **1917** R. MARLOTH *Common Names* 22 Davib or Dawee, *Tamarix articulata*. A small tree on the banks of rivers in the drier districts. **1935** A.W. VAN DER HORST (tr.) in E.E. Mossop *Jrnl of Hendrik Jacob Wikar* 53 When the children are six or eight years old, sharp sticks are cut for them and shaped after the fashion of an assegaai, from 'dawee' or 'saprey' wood. **1966** C.A. SMITH *Common Names* 197 Dawe (daweb) (daweep), *Tamarix usneoides* ... The vernacular name in all the variations of the original Hottentot name 'dabee'. *Ibid.* 198 Dawib (dawip), .. See dawee. **1977** E. PALMER *Field Guide to Trees* 222 *Tamarix usneoides* ... Sometimes known as dawee, a corruption of the original Hottentot name. [**1983** see above.]

dacca, dacha varr. DAGGA n.[2]

dachbreaker see DAGBREKER.

dacka var. DAGGA n.[2]

Dad's Army n. phr. Colloq. Also with small initials. [Transf. use of a Brit. Eng. nickname for the Home Guard in the U.K. during World War II, subsequently used during the Rhodesian war: 'The fourth category was "Dad's Army", who are the older whites of over 38 years ... After a long period of semi-obscurity, the Protection Units and Dad's Army have finally found their own identity in the Rhodesia Defence Regiment, with their own insignia and embellishments.' (*Fighting Forces of Rhodesia* No.5, c1978, p.73).] A jocular name for the system of compulsory local military duty for older men, introduced in 1983; (any one of) the military units established under this system. Also *attrib.* See also COMMANDO sense 5.

    1982 *Sunday Times* 28 Mar. 27 The Bill to create a South African 'Dad's Army' is being referred to a Select Committee ... Beneath the joshing about dads' armies .. is a profound unease about what it really means, this business of 60-year-olds being soldiers again. **1982** *Daily Dispatch* 3 Apr. 5 'Dad's Army', or 'Salusa Scouts', as we oldies seem destined to be called. **1983** *Ibid.* 3 May 2 The country's first 'dad's army' .. was formed at the beginning of last month. **1991** *Sunday Times* 13 Jan. 16 Graham M— is a former MP and was court martialled in 1987 for refusing to report for a 'dad's army' call-up.

daeraad var. DAGERAAD.

‖**dag** /dax/ int. Also **daag**. [Afk., earlier S. Afr. Du., ellipt. form of *goeie dag*, formerly *goeden dag* (see GOEDEN DAG).] 'Good day'; 'good-bye'; GOEDEN DAG.

    Usu. in contexts reporting speech which is *S. Afr. Du.* or Afrikaans.

    1822 W.J. BURCHELL *Trav.* I. 113 The Hottentots .. in a good-natured, respectful manner, accosted each of us with 'Dag, Mynheer!' meaning, 'Good day, Sir!' **1824** *Ibid.* II. 97 Bidding me farewell in the colonial manner, by repeating the word *dag*, they hasted away to their Kraal. **1837** J.E. ALEXANDER *Narr. of Voy.* II. 318 We had often three generations with us. First; the grandfather .. jogging silently on, Dutch-like, after a gruff 'daag, mynheer'. **1868** W.R. THOMSON *Poems, Essays & Sketches* 167 You go up without introduction, hold out your hand, and say 'Dag!' She holds out her hand, and says 'Dag!' **1900** B. MITFORD *Aletta* 47 'Daag, Oom Sarel!' called out the two in the buggy. But the old man met this amenity with a torrent of abuse. **1912** F. BANCROFT *Veldt Dwellers* 38 The young boer put forth a limp hand, and with a single word '*dag*' went the round of the company. **1920** S. BLACK *Dorp* 229 At length Mijnheer wiped his mouth, got up and said '*dag*' ... And he went carefully down the steps. **1937** H. SAUER *Ex Afr.* 19 On entering he walked slowly round the room, shaking hands with everyone and uttering the one word *Daag*, which means 'Good day'. **1975** W. STEENKAMP *Land of Thirst King* 22 'Hello, Oupa!' I shout, and he grins and says .. '*Dag, jong,*' and I know that I am home. **1976** [see OUSIE sense 1]. **1987** L. BEAKE *Strollers* 91 He nodded in an impertinent way towards Abraham. 'Dag, Spider Man.' 'Mr Xhashan, you say,' Abraham said with dignity. **1990** D. BECKETT in *Frontline* Mar.-Apr. 20 'Dag,' I say. 'Dag,' he nods. They wheel-spin off.

Hence **dag** v. trans. nonce, to offer (a greeting of '*dag*').

    1920 R. JUTA *Tavern* 218 Vague shadowy humanity .. 'Daaged' a late day greeting to them from out of the shadow.

daga n.[1] var. DAGGA n.[2]

daga n.[2] var. DAGHA n.

dagbestuur see BESTUUR sense 2.

‖**dagboek** /ˈdaxbʊk/ n. Pl. -e /-ə/. [Afk., diary (lit. 'day book').] An Afrikaans journal, diary, or logbook.

    a**1928** C. FULLER *Trigardt's Trek* (1932) 75 The Sikoroso speak almost as if they had quite familiarised themselves with the contents of the *Dagboek*. **1934** P.R. KIRBY *Musical Instruments of Native Races* (1965) 155 The earliest mention of an ensemble of this kind occurs in the *dagboek*, or journal, of Louis Trigardt (1836), the voortrekker. **1949** J. MOCKFORD *Golden Land* 233 In all Afrikaans literature perhaps nothing is so poignant as the last entries in Trigardt's dagboek, his diary, wherein, before he himself died in exile, he records his wife's death. **1951** L.G. GREEN *Grow Lovely* 94 'Van Riebeeck could not have chosen a better site', Mr van den Houten told me. 'I still find his dagboek and garden almanac of value.'

dagbreker /ˈdaxbrɪəkə(r)/ *n.* Also **dachbreaker**, **dakbreeker**. [Afk., *dagbreek* dawn, *dag* day + *breek* break, + agential suffix *-er*.] Any of three species of chats of the family Turdidae: *Ceromela familiaris* (see SPEKVRETER), *C. sinuata*, or *Saxicola torquata*. Also in dim. form **dagbrekertjie** /-ki/, and part. tr. **dachbreaker**.

In G.L. Maclean's *Roberts' Birds of Sn Afr.* (1984), the name 'familiar chat' is used for *C. familiaris*, 'sickle-winged chat' for *C. sinuata*, and 'stonechat' for *S. torquata*.

1892 S. SCHONLAND in *The Jrnl* 12 Jan. 3 Albany Museum. During the months of November and December, 1891, the following donations have been received ... *Dachbreaker*, (Saxicola galtoni), [etc.]. **1908** HAAGNER & IVY *Sketches* 20 This bird is called the 'Dagbreker' by the Boers (meaning daybreaker), a name which is, however, also applied to the Familiar chat in some districts. *c***1923** *Ibid.* 29 At Springfontein, .. the local name for both this bird [*sc.* the Sicklewinged Chat] and the Familiar Chat is the 'Dagbreker'. **1956** A.G. MCRAE *Hill Called Grazing* 38 The ravages of time and the little *dakbreeker* birds had made great, gaping holes in this cover. **1973** J. COPE *Alley Cat* 76 The *dagbreekertjie*, the little flycatcher, is making its whistling song for the coming day.

dageraad /ˈdɑːxərɑːt, ˈdæɡərɑːd/ *n.* Also **daeraad**. [S. Afr. Du., prob. fr. Fr. *daurade* seabream or 'gilthead', influenced by Du. *dageraad* dawn, daybreak (see quots. 1913 and 1949).] Any of three species of seabream of the Sparidae: **a.** *Chrysoblephus cristiceps*, known for the impressive changes of colour it undergoes when close to death; ROMAN sense 1 b. **b.** The ROMAN (sense 1 a), *C. laticeps*. **c.** The PANGA (*n.*[1] sense a), *Pterogymnus laniarus*. In all senses also called DAGGERHEAD.

In Smith and Heemstra's *Smiths' Sea Fishes* (1986), the name 'dageraad' is used for *C. cristiceps*.

1843 J.C. CHASE *Cape of G.H.* 168 Dageraad — one of the choicest of fishes. **1853** L. PAPPE *Synopsis of Edible Fishes* 20 *Pagrus laniarius* .. (*Dageraad*) .. Strong conical teeth in the upper jaw, which .. project from the mouth ... The whole fish is of a dark rose-colour, with a black spot at the insertion of the pectorals. **1887** *S.W. Silver & Co.'s Handbk to S. Afr.* 182 *Dageraad*, Highly prized. Not caught in Table Bay but in the waters east and south of Cape Town. **1893** [see PAMPELMOESIE]. **1913** C. PETTMAN *Africanderisms* 135 *Dageraad*, .. The striking colours exhibited by this fish seem to have evoked a flash of poetic imagination ... This word is sometimes corrupted into Daggerhead, Daggerheart, etc. **1949** J.L.B. SMITH *Sea Fishes* 271 *Chrysoblephus cristiceps* ... *Dageraad* (Cape). *Redfish. Daggerhead* (Natal) ... Adults at death one of the most beautiful of all creatures as waves of different colours pass over the body, hence the early Dutch name of Dageraad, i.e. Dawn. **1958** L.G. GREEN *S. Afr. Beachcomber* 112 Dageraad is a corruption of the Portuguese word dorado, the fish that shines like gold. Cape fishermen do not use the word dageraad for dawn, they say dagbreek or daglumier. **1966** VAN HEYNINGEN & BERTHOUD *Uys Krige* 144 *Daeraad* is a lovely word for a lovely fish. **1984** *Daily Dispatch* 6 Nov. 13 Sustained catches of these fish had resulted in serious depletion of the stocks of species such as galjoen, .. dageraad and seventy four. **1991** *Weekend Post* 6 Apr. 4 Some of the species that new legislation aims to protect are santer .. , dageraad, .. and red roman.

dagga *n.*[1] var. DAGHA *n.*

dagga /ˈdaxa, -xə/ *n.*[2] Also **da(a)ga**, **dacca**, **dacha**, **dacka**, **dak(h)a**, **dakka**, **docha**, **doka**, **tagga**. [Afk., earlier S. Afr. Du. ad. Khoikhoi *dachab*.]

1. The marijuana or Indian hemp plant *Cannabis sativa* of the Cannabaceae; (esp.) the dried leaves of this plant, used as a narcotic; BOOM *n.* sense 1; *hoenderpoot*, see HOENDER sense 1; INSANGU; MATEKWANE; PARCEL sense 2; STOP sense 2; TREE OF KNOWLEDGE; ZOL *n.* sense 2. Also *attrib.* See also *Durban poison* (DURBAN), MAJAT.

Quantities of dagga are variously referred to as ARM, COB *n.*[2], STOP (sense 1), ZOL (sense 1 b).

1670 J. OGILBY *Africa* 583 A powerful Root, which they call *Dacha*; sometimes eating it, other-whiles mingling it with Water to drink; either of which ways taken, causeth Ebriety. **1731** G. MEDLEY tr. *P. Kolb's Present State of Cape of G.H.* I. 210 *Dacha*, is a Thing, of which the *Hottentots* are .. mighty fond. It banishes Care and Anxiety, say they, like Wine or Brandy, and inspires them with a Million of delightful Fancies .. this I know, that it often intoxicates 'em to downright Madness .. They often mix *Dacha* and Tobacco together. **1796** tr. *Le Vaillant's New Trav.* III. 267 The people wished for tobacco and dacca (the leaves of hemp). **1821** C.I. LATROBE *Jrnl of Visit* 471 There is in this country a plant, called by the Hottentots, Dacha, a species of wild hemp (cicuta). Some of them smoke it like tobacco, or mix it with the latter herb, and are exceedingly fond of it. **1822** W.J. BURCHELL *Trav.* I. 366 The common hemp, called dakka, was here raised for the purpose of being given as presents to the Bushmen, who smoke it instead of tobacco; as do also many of the Hottentots; but it is considered more deleterious and inebriating. **1836** A.F. GARDINER *Journey to Zoolu Country* 106 Tobacco composed of the dried leaf of the wild hemp, here called Dacca, is in general use, and has a very stupifying effect, frequently intoxicating. **1852** in GODLONTON & IRVING *Narr. of Kaffir War of 1850–51–52* 306 A shot from a lurking Kaffir passed through his dacha sack at the saddle bow. **1860** W. SHAW *Story of my Mission* 507 By means of a long tube they contrived to draw the smoke from a long wooden pipe filled with burning *dacha*, or wild hemp. **1878** T.J. LUCAS *Camp Life & Sport* 94 They are .. much addicted to smoking the wild hemp called 'dacca,' which they cultivate for the purpose. The smaller leaves of this plant are dried in the sun, and being ground fine, the fumes are inhaled through a pipe, exciting the nervous system frightfully. **1879** [see GWAAI sense a]. **1886** G.A. FARINI *Through Kalahari Desert* 125 We gave our visitors some docha, a kind of wild hemp used by them as tobacco, and when they became excited under its influence they treated us to the spectacle of a dance. **1897** F.W. SYKES *With Plumer in Matabeleland* 101 Daaga, a compound smoked by the natives in the same way that the Chinese smoke opium. **1902** G.M. THEAL *Beginning of S. Afr. Hist.* 21 Another powerful intoxicant with which they were acquainted was dacha, a species of wild hemp, and whenever this was procurable they smoked it with a pipe made of the horn of an antelope. **1926** *E. Prov. Herald* 9 Jan. 9 Two months hard labour was the sentence passed on Macdonald Plaatjies, a native, .. when charged with being in possession of dagga. **1950** E. PARTRIDGE *Dict. of Underworld Slang* 175 *Dagga* is not c[ant] but the Standard South African name for *Cannabis indica* (hashish, marijuana). **1952** 'MR DRUM' in *Drum* Sept. 12 The colossal figure of £750,000 is spent on dagga annually on over 300,000 pounds of this deadly drug ... Two million people smoke and peddle the weed ... The ages of dagga addicts ranges [*sic*] from 11 years upwards. **1954** *Star* in L.F. Freed *Crime in S. Afr.* (1963) 79 These young men were the White tsotsis of Johannesburg ... They were hardly out of school before they became members of liquor and dagga gangs operating in the heart of the city. **1966**, **1971** [see INSANGU]. **1977** D. MULLER *Whitey* 16 The dagga zol was a three-out zol, and he drew it quick and long into his body. **1978** C.M. RIP *Contemp. Social Pathology* 87 Whereas dagga, marihuana or Indian hemp are the top leaves of the plant, Hashish is the resin. **1984** D. PINNOCK *Brotherhoods* 11 Dagga (the local name for marijuana) has a usage in South Africa long predating European colonisation. In our time, however, sale, possession or use is prohibited under the Abuse of Dependence-producing Substances and Rehabilitation Centres Act of 1971. **1989** *Reader's Digest Illust. Hist.* 25 *Dagga* (*Cannabis sativa*) ... The actual smoking of dagga by the Khoikhoi and black people of Southern Africa only began after the introduction of the smoking pipe by whites. Prior to this, dagga was chewed, or boiled in an infusion and drunk. **1992** *South* 27 Feb. 6 There is considerable debate over the effects of dagga. While most heavy drug users began with dagga, there is no evidence to prove that dagga creates a dependency on hard drugs.

2. Usu. with distinguishing epithet, as **klip-dagga** /klәp-/ [Afk., *klip* rock], **red dagga**, **wild -** or **wilde dagga** /vəldə-/ [Afk. (earlier S. Afr. Du.), *wilde* wild]: any of several species of plant of the genus *Leonotis* of the Lamiaceae, esp. the flowering plant *Leonotis leonurus*, noted for its medicinal properties, and traditionally smoked for its intoxicating effect.

1786 G. FORSTER tr. *A. Sparrman's Voy. to Cape of G.H.* I. 145 *Bucku* (*diosma*) and wild *dacka* (*phlomis leonurus*) .. are known both by the colonists and the Hottentots to be as efficacious as they are common. **1796** C.R. HOPSON tr. *C.P. Thunberg's Trav.* II. 191 They .. take delight in smoking tobacco, either pure, or mixed with hemp, and, when they cannot procure these, wild Dakka (*Phlolmis*). **1815** J. MACKRILL *Diary.* 96 The Wilde Dakka or Phlomis Leon. is applied .. in the Cure of venereal Complaints, which it readily eradicates. **1835** J.W.D. MOODIE *Ten Yrs* II. 169 My father took two or three handfuls of 'wilde dacha,' (a kind of wild hemp which grows in rich ground near the coast), and boiled it in a pan, and made the slave drink a cupful every day for two or three weeks; and he made him as well again as he ever was in his life. **1847** 'A BENGALI' *Notes on Cape of G.H.* 23 They [*sc.* the San people] are ardent smokers of the 'dacha', a kind of hemp, for which the botanical name is, I believe, 'Plomis leonurus', which speedily intoxicates, and must be something like our Indian 'bang'. **1912** *E. London Dispatch* 28 June 9 The red Dagga, or 'Mfincafincane', of the Kaffirs. **1932** [see CHINCHERINCHEE]. **1953** J. HOYLE *Some Flowers* 15 Wild Dagga belongs to the same family as the Blue Salvia, and flowers at the same time. **1955** J.B. SHEPHARD *Land of Tikoloshe* 8 'There are doubtless herbs in the bush which are good for snake bites.' One of these .. is Red Dagga (*Leonotis Leonarius*), of which the root only is used .. while the leaves of Klip Dagga (*Leonotis ovata*) are said to cure viper bites. **1974** *Daily Dispatch* 29 June 4, I wonder how it came to be called Wild Dagga. No relation at all to the drug plant. **1983** P.S. RABIE tr. *Nienaber & Raper's Hottentot Place Names* 93 *Dagga(fontein)* .. , *Dagga(kraal)* .. , *Dagga(rand)* .. , farms, post office, station, etc. The component *dagga* (in English *dagga* and *dacha*) is the name of the *Leonotis leonurus*, a species of wild hemp. **1992** H. HUTCHINGS in *Weekend Post* 22 Aug. (Leisure) 7 *Leonotis leonurus*, commonly known as wild dagga, is an attractive large shrub.

3. *comb.*

a. Objective: **dagga-smoking** *vbl n.*, also *attrib.*

1894 C.H.W. DONOVAN *With Wilson in Matabeleland* 40 It is exceedingly entertaining to watch these boys 'dakha-smoking'. **1924** S.G. MILLIN *God's Step-Children* 13 The Rev. Andrew had not been warned about dagga-smoking. **1946** [see BOOM *n.* sense 1]. *a***1951** H.C. BOSMAN *Willemsdorp* (1977) 38 I've been getting a good number of complaints lately about dagga smoking ... It's supposed to be not only kafirs smoking it today, but white men also. **1971** *Daily Dispatch* 10 Sept. 13 Dr. Louria said .. the main drug abuse problem in the city was dagga smoking. **1979** *Drum* Mar. 28, I took part in a dagga smoking spree and drank a lot of alcohol. **1990** J. NAIDOO *Coolie Location* 95 James Karia Kollapen, the tough, dagga-smoking Delfos centre half and star .. dashed on to the field.

b. Special Comb. **dagga pipe**, (*a*) a pipe (made and) used for smoking dagga; cf. BOTTLENECK sense b; (*b*) PIPE sense 2 a; **dagga-run**, a name given to the most common routes taken by smugglers of dagga from the Transkei into the rest of South Africa; **dagga-runner**, one who smuggles dagga; **dagga-running**, the smuggling of dagga; **dagga smoker**, DAGGA-ROOKER.

[1860, 1902 dagga pipe: see quots at sense 1 above.] 1949 H.C. BOSMAN in L. Abrahams *Unto Dust* (1963) 131 The chief used to lie .. in front of his hut, smoking his long dagga-pipe. 1966 I. VAUGHAN *These Were my Yesterdays* 67 Old Andries our Bushman groom .. got so upset, rushed to smoke a dagga pipe behind the cart house and got quite drunk. 1977 *Sunday Times* 1 May 7 All are proficient at making dagga pipes from bottlenecks, match boxes, toilet rolls and so on. 1987 *Scope* 20 Nov. 40 Wollies was loading up the dagga pipe. 1977 *E. Prov. Herald* 10 June (Indaba) 1 A 30-year-old expert driver making big money on the **dagga run** from Transkei crashed to his death while taking a bend at speed. 1980 *Ibid.* 10 Oct. 1 The Dordrecht-Molteno route is becoming known as the dagga run. There is an increasing use of the round route by smugglers from Transkei. 1963 A. DELIUS *Day Natal Took Off* 9 The **dagga-runner** had delivered his load, he was returning with an empty car, and all his papers were in order. 1963 *Ibid.* [see NATIONAL ROAD]. 1971 *Sunday Times* 21 Mar. 5 Informed sources believe that the South African 'dagga runners,' who appear to some extent to have become the slaves of big-time racketeers in London, are responsible for much of the alarming increase in hard drug-taking in the Republic. 1977 *E. Prov. Herald* 10 June (Indaba) 1 Dagga runner killed. 1972 *Drum* 8 Aug. 20 In our games there will also be an event for dagga-runners. What with the many roadblocks they have to hurdle, **dagga-running** could be an exciting event. 1910 J. BUCHAN *Prester John* (1961) 73 He must have been a **dacha smoker**, for he coughed hideously. 1944 I.D. DU PLESSIS *Cape Malays* 81 Dagga smokers make the Quarter unsafe. 1954 *Off. Yrbk of Union 1952–3* (Bureau of Census & Statistics) 1096 The undesirable class which comprises the 'skollies', the habitual convicts and ex-convicts, the drunkards, the dagga-smokers, and the habitual smokers. 1971 *Post* 30 May 23 As he throws back his head and breathes out the dense smoke a chuckle breaks from his throat. It rises, becomes a bubbly laugh — the laugh of the dagga smoker. 1988 E. POPLE in *You* Jan. 17 Most parents do not even know how to recognise the symptoms of a dagga smoker: red eyes, loss of appetite, bottle-necks in evidence, foreign-looking pipes, pieces of neatly rolled up paper, .. a nagging cough, headaches. 1990 S. MCHUNU in *New African* 3 Sept. 9 When we teamed up with Johnny to form Juluka, the police didn't want to see us together. Some thought we were dagga smokers or dealers. 1963 L.F. FREED *Crime in S. Afr.* 102 Dagga-smoking was so rife in Jeppe that the suburb had earned the nick-name of the '**Dagga Town**'.

dagga v. var. DAGHA v.

dagga-rooker /ˈdaxaˌrʊəkə(r)/ n. Also **dagga-roker**. [S. Afr. Du., *dagga* (see DAGGA n.²) + *rooker* (later Afk. *roker*) smoker, *rook* to smoke + agential suffix *-er*.] One who habitually smokes dagga; *boom boy*, see BOOM n. sense 2; *dagga smoker*, see DAGGA n.² sense 3 b; ROOKER.

1835 J.W.D. MOODIE *Ten Yrs* I. 41 The 'dacha rookers' are held in great contempt by the tobacco smokers of their [*sc.* the 'Hottentot'] nation. 1838 J.E. ALEXANDER *Exped. into Int.* II. 237 In the garden at Bethany the 'Dakka rookers,' or smokers of the intoxicating and deleterious leaves of hemp, had an opportunity of filling their pouches with what they preferred far above tobacco even, from the pleasant visions which dakka (like opium) inspires. 1949 H.C. BOSMAN *Cold Stone Jug* (1969) 53 Gradually, because so many of the people who committed crimes turned out to be dagga-rookers, dagga got into disrepute with the authorities and somebody brought in a law about it. 1971 E. HIGGINS *Informant, Grahamstown* Social mechanisms that draw people together are the same among Boy Scouts as they are among daggarokers. 1987 S.A. BOTHA in *Frontline* Oct.-Nov. 14 Tattoed [sic] around his neck will be a bowtie, around his ankles chains, and in the outer edges of his eyes Cleopatra-like lines, or flies on his neck, and saints and dots on his hands to identify him as a dagga-roker. 1990 J. NAIDOO *Coolie Location* 106 Sometimes I wondered if Sam wasn't a *dagga-rooker*, for his temerity was second to none.

daggerhead n. Pl. unchanged. [Calque formed on S. Afr. Du. *dageraad*.] DAGERAAD.

1906 *E. London Dispatch* 3 July 3 This fish was probably what is known as 'daggerhead' (pagrus laniarius). 1906 *Natal Mercury Pictorial* 719 (Pettman), While their catches include no very large fish, they got a fine variety. Among other sorts I noticed .. *Danes*, Daggerheads. 1913, 1949 [see DAGERAAD]. 1957 S. SCHOEMAN *Strike!* 40 The dageraad is also called daggerhead along the Pondoland and Natal coast. 1966 VAN HEYNINGEN & BERTHOUD *Uys Krige* 144 Daggerhead .. is, of course, a corruption of *dageraad*. 1976 *E. Prov. Herald* 14 Oct. 21, I have heard it said that the small red fish, like daggerhead and roman, are all of one sex. 1982 D. BICKELL in *Ibid.* 14 Dec. 19 Some of the most popular table fish .. include red steenbras, red roman, daggerhead, [etc.]. 1992 *Weekend Post* 13 June 10 The reef fish (like daggerhead and red roman) have largely disappeared because trawlers, local and foreign, have 'dragged' the reefs.

dagha /ˈdɑːɡə, ˈdaɡə/ n. Also **daager**, **dag(g)a**, **dagher**, **daka**, **dargha**, **dargher**, **dugga**. [Afk., ad. Zulu and Xhosa *udaka* mud, clay, mortar.]
a. Building mortar, used for laying bricks and for plastering walls and floors, previously made chiefly of mud or ant-hill soil and sometimes mixed with cow-dung and/or blood; now often a mixture of soil, sand, and lime. Also *attrib.* See also *dagha-boy* (BOY sense 1 b). Cf. *misvloer* (see MIS sense 3).

1879 R.J. ATCHERLEY *Trip to Boerland* 215 This daager is a great South African institution; it consists of a mixture of blood and cow-dung, which is smeared daily upon the floor, and is the only means by which the fleas can be kept under. 1880 H.M. PRICHARD *Friends & Foes* 282 Kafir women are now summoned, who smear the walls and floor with 'dargha' (dried manure), and work up the surface with crushed ant-heap. c1881 A. DOUGLASS *Ostrich Farming* 230 Mortar dagga (that is, clay worked up the same as for making bricks). 1896 H.L. TANGYE *In New S. Afr.* 326 The inhabitants adapted themselves .. to the practice of the country, and lived in dagher huts. 1899 *Natal Agric. Jrnl* 31 Mar. 4 'Daga,' the mud which is used for mortar is a well-known word wherever buildings are being erected. 1903 D. BLACKBURN *Burgher Quixote* 229 The floor, .. as in all old Boer houses, was of dagga or ant-hill earth, made black, hard, and shiny with bullock's blood. 1918 C. GARSTIN *Sunshine Settlers* 136 You put up a good stout house of dagga plastered on a heavy skeleton of planted poles, thatched it over with the best season's river-grass. 1931 F.C. SLATER *Secret Veld* 153 His two assistants were hard pressed to keep him supplied with stones and dagga. 1937 S. CLOETE *Turning Wheels* 166 Earth was mixed with water, the Kaffirs turning it with their shovels and finally tramping it with bare feet till it reached the consistency of thick whipped cream. This dagga they flung against the rough wood poles, filling in the spaces between them, and finally plastering the whole, inside and out. The floor was also made of dagga and finished off with a layer of cow dung mixed with blood. 1963 R. LEWCOCK *Early 19th C. Archit.* 378 For many years it was disputed whether lime mortar or 'dagga' (clay mortar) was the more resistant to moisture. 1977 [see SKEP sense 1 a]. 1984 D. BECKETT in *Frontline* Mar. 29 First stop was Motlana's birthplace. The house then, he said, had been a humble cottage with dagga walls and thatched roof ('the best kind, cool in summer and warm in winter'). 1992 A. BODENSTEIN in *Grocott's Mail* 21 July 1 It was a daga structure with wood and iron roof.

b. In the phrr. **dagha-and-pole**, **pole-and-dagha**, usu. *attrib.*, descriptive of a method of construction using a framework of poles, and sometimes wire-netting, to support dagha walls, which are then plastered.

1936 P.M. CLARK *Autobiog. of Old Drifter* 113 They were used to the building of huts made of wood, with thatched roofs — a mode of construction giving huts that are cool to live in. 1967 E.M. SLATTER *My Leaves Are Green* 58 John Lodick's partner was lying in the small pole-and-dagga hospital on the ridge. 1974 *E. Prov. Herald* 25 May, A house made out of flattened and rusted paraffin tins, beaten flat and laid .. over pole-and-dagga walls.

dagha /ˈdɑːɡə, ˈdaɡə/ v. trans. Also **daager**, **dagga**, **dagher**. [See prec.] To smear (floors or walls) with dagha.

1855 R.J. MULLINS *Diary.* 17 June, I will have a new floor put in my room when I come back from Grahamstown. Meanwhile I am going to dagga some damaged patches. 1878 H.A. ROCHE *On Trek in Tvl* 251 A Kafir came to 'daager' or smear our floors. 1913 C. PETTMAN *Africanderisms* 137 *Dagher, To*, To apply dagher to floors or walls.
Hence **daghaed** ppl adj., **daghaing** vbl n.

1879 R.J. ATCHERLEY *Trip to Boerland* 215 We all three tried to sleep, in one bed . . . I preferred the daagered floor, which was comparatively flea-free. 1893 BLENNERHASSETT & SLEEMAN *Adventures in Mashonaland* 32 We had heard .. that 'daghering' and 'smearing' would be essential parts of our work. 1918 C. GARSTIN *Sunshine Settlers* 141 Eventually we got the poles tarred, planted in position, and wired together. Then came the daggaing. The earth was shovelled out of an abandoned ant-heap, mixed with water and cow-dung, and trodden into a paste by the feet of my boys, very much as grapes are trodden in Provencal winepresses.

dahl var. DHAL.

daka n.¹ var. DAGGA n.²

daka n.² var. DAGHA n.

dakbreeker var. DAGBREKER.

dakha, dakka var. DAGGA n.²

dakha bono var. DAKUBONA.

dakkamer /ˈdakˌkɑːmə(r)/ n. Archit. Also with initial capital. [Afk., *dak* roof + *kamer* room.] A small room built on the flat roof of a Cape house at the centre of the facade, and incorporated into it by means of a pseudo-gable. Also *attrib.*

1951 L.G. GREEN *Grow Lovely* 33 What was the purpose of the dak kamer? — the solitary room on the roof? Early writers on Cape architecture put forward the theory that the dak kamer was built so that the owner could watch the shipping .. Dak kamer gables are different from all the other types. 1952 J. WALTON *Homesteads & Villages* 19 Dr. Cook has suggested that they were introduced from Amsterdam where, in the combined dwelling-warehouses, the *Dak-kamer* housed the gear for hoisting goods to the storerooms on the upper floors. The *Dak-kamer* gables are of the Cape-Flemish style, having a triangular pediment with flanking scrolls. 1960 M. MULLER *Art Past & Present* 109 They built single rooms on the roof as vantage-points — the Dak Kamer. A gable was then built round the window of the Dak Kamer. 1972 *Std Encycl. of Sn Afr.* VII. 75 Martin Melck House, This former parsonage of the Lutheran church .. is the typical 18th-century Cape dwelling-house with an attic. This 'dak-kamer' or belvedere (of which this is the only surviving example) was sometimes used to look out for ships. 1985 A.M. OBHOLZER et al. *Cape House & its Interior* 85 The Lutheran Parsonage .. 15. Gabled 'dak-kamer'.

dakriet var. DEKRIET.

dakubona int. and n. Obs. Also **dakha bono**. [Perh. an obs. variant of the Zulu greeting *sawubona* 'we see you' (see SAWUBONA); or the Xhosa salutation *ndakubona* 'I will see you', spoken on parting, mistakenly used in a Zulu context by the Eng.-speaking writers.] SAWUBONA int. and n.

1837 F. OWEN *Diary* (1926) 28 The natives saluted us in their usual style 'Dakubona wena' I see you, to which the proper reply is 'yearbo,' = yes. *Ibid.* 29 At length he saluted us in the usual style with a good humoured tone 'Dakubona' I see you. 1839 W.C.

HARRIS *Wild Sports* 181 They all saluted us with 'Dakha bono!' 'I see you: give me some snuff!'

dâl var. DHAL.

dam /dæ(:)m/ *n.* [Brit. Eng. dialect, but standard in S. Afr. Eng., Austral. Eng., and N.Z. Eng.; reinforced in S. Afr. Eng. by Afk. *dam*, in this sense.] A man-made pond or reservoir where rain- or springwater is collected for storage. Also *attrib.*

Used primarily of the reservoir and its contents: in *S. Afr. Eng.*, the wall is seldom called the 'dam', but rather the 'dam wall' (see quot. 1912).

1826 G. BARKER Journal. 12 Dec., Visited the Dam &c & was delighted with the quantity & quality of the water. **1836** J. COLLETT Diary. I. 23 Feb., *Rain most excessive* Dams running over in Torrents but no great damage. **1840** *Ibid.* II. 12 May, Dams & Rivers full & Land springs all running. **1843** J.C. CHASE *Cape of G.H.* 155 On his estate .. there are now three dams, each capable of floating a considerable sized vessel. **1859** *Queenstown Free Press* 1 June (Pettman), The remedy for this is not the excavation of *dams*, the digging of wells, or the formation of tanks, but the construction of a railway. **1878** A. AYLWARD *Tvl of Today* 156 The word 'dam' in Africa means *reservoir*, and not 'containing wall', as it does here. **1890** A. MARTIN *Home Life* 82 Every Karroo house has a dam near it, and on a large farm there are generally three or four more of these reservoirs in different parts of the land. **1909** LADY S. WILSON *S. Afr. Mem.* 85 In the distance we could see the glimmering blue waters of a huge dam. **1912** *Northern News* 30 Aug. (Pettman), *Dam* and dam which in Holland and England are embankments, here denote a pool or reservoir, and 'wal' takes the place of the Dutch 'dam'. **1931** F.C. SLATER *Secret Veld* 42, I came upon a large dam, fringed with weeping willows ... Two Kaffirs, with the aid of two oxen and a dam-scraper, were engaged in dredging the dam. **1948** H. WOLHUTER *Mem. of Game Ranger* 4 We used to spend the whole day swimming and boating in the dam. **1960** J. COPE *Tame Ox* 133 Making money was easy as falling in a dam. **1971** *Daily Dispatch* 4 June (Queenstown Suppl.) 6 Water? We've a dam full to spare ... The dam, situated between beautiful rolling hills, has numerous picnic sites around it and the dam itself is stocked with black bass and bluegill. **1979** J. GRATUS *Jo'burgers* 116 The farm dam had been greatly enlarged and was now filled with the inky water. **1989** [see *safari suit* (see SAFARI)]. **1991** F.G. BUTLER *Local Habitation* 52 The success of his still incomplete dam had been in doubt ... Now the dam was full of water.

Damara /ˈdæmərə/ *n.* Also **Dammara**, and (rarely) in shortened form **Dama**. [ad. of the feminine pl. form of Nama *damap* black people.] The name of a black African people of Namibia, used *attrib.* and in Special Comb. **Damara(land) Cattle**, a breed of indigenous cattle, now extinct; **Damara(land) dik-dik**, the tiny antelope *Madoqua kirkii* of the Bovidae, found in parts of Namibia and southern Angola; **Damara('s) mother (tree)**, HARDEKOOL; **Damara tern**, the small migratory seabird *Sterna balaenarum* of the Laridae.

1856 C.J. ANDERSSON *Lake Ngami* 319 From their quick step, good feet, and enduring powers, the **Damara cattle** are much prized by the farmer of the Cape-Colony. **1896** R. WALLACE *Farming Indust. of Cape Col.* 256 *Damaraland cattle* are the best of animals for light bullock traffic. **1906** F. BLERSCH *Handbk of Agric.* 313 *South African cattle*,.. It is very probable that, with the exception of Damaraland, Pondo, and Zulu cattle, few of the indigenous breeds are now found. **1934** C.P. SWART Supplement to Pettman. 38 *Damaraland Cattle*, The most common characteristic of this breed .. is their colour which is black and tan, with a tan muzzle. **1971** G. SWANEPOEL in *Std Encycl. of Sn Afr.* III. 553 During the first years of the 20th century purebred Damara cattle became extinct owing to the infusion of Afrikander bulls. **1900** W.L. SCLATER *Mammals of S. Afr.* I. 182 The **Damaraland dik-dik** ... Nothing regarding the habits of this antelope is recorded except that it inhabits rocky and barren hills near the sea coast, and is difficult to procure owing to its great agility. [*c*1936 *S. & E. Afr. Yr Bk & Guide* 1087 The *Damaran Dik-Dik* or *Damaraland Antelope* ... The largest of the dik-diks.] **1952** L.G. GREEN *Lords of Last Frontier* 48 The Damara dik dik is a much finer dish. Dik dik occurs in and around the Kaokoveld and again in northern Tanganyika. **1961** O. LEVINSON *Ageless Land* 136 One may startle a little Damara dikdik, smallest of all the antelope, and not much bigger than a hare. **1971** C.M. VAN DER WESTHUIZEN in *Std Encycl. of Sn Afr.* IV. 39 The Damara dik-dik (*M. kirki damarensis*) .. inhabits the dry western region and ranges from Damaraland to Southern Angola. **1988** M. SPENCE in *Motorist* 4th Quarter 4 What impresses most about Etosha is the number and variety of game .. from the tiny Damaraland dik-dik to long-necked giraffes. **1864** T. BAINES *Explor. in S.-W. Afr.* 147 Then there is the Motjeerie, or **Damara's mother**, with its rough cruciform points. *Ibid.* 187 The 'Damara mother' .. is really beautiful with her drooping seed, clusters of rich brown yellow, supported by the green of the young leaves and the angularities of her stem softened and half-veiled by them. **1902** G.M. THEAL *Beginning of S. Afr. Hist.* 50 The Ovaherero on the western coast believe that human beings and every kind of animal sprang from a particular kind of large tree in their country ... For this reason it is now commonly called by the Europeans .. the Damara mother tree, Damup, corrupted by the Dutch colonists into Damara, being the Hottentot name of the black people living north of Walfish Bay. **1978** FROST & JOHNSON in *Optima* Vol.27 No.4, 106 The **Damara Tern** (*Sterna balaenarum*), a small seabird endemic to Southern Africa which nests in colonies widely scattered along the coast and feeds on tiny fish or crustaceans captured in sheltered inshore waters, is in danger of extinction. **1983** D. BICKELL in *E. Prov. Herald* 19 Dec. 11 The damara tern is another endangered bird species which breeds in the dunes there. **1986** *Weekend Argus* 9 Aug. (Suppl.) 4 The rare Damara terns nest in the dune system.

damba /ˈdæmbə, ˈdamba/ *n.* Also with initial capital. Pl. usu. unchanged; occas. **-s**. [fr. Xhosa *idamba*.] In the Eastern Cape: **a.** The GALJOEN (sense 1), *Coracinus capensis*. **b.** The *banded* - or *bastard galjoen* (sense (*a*), see GALJOEN sense 2), *C. multifasciatus*.

1906 H.E.B. BROOKING in *E. London Dispatch* 6 Feb. 6 The fish, with the exception of a nice black-tail or two, were all 'dambas'. **1913** C. PETTMAN *Africanderisms* 138 *Damba*, The fish known at East London and elsewhere as the Galjoen .. is known on the Transkei coast by this name. **1949** J.L.B. SMITH *Sea Fishes* 248 *Coracinus capensis* ... *Galjoen* (Cape, general). *Highwater* or *Damba* (Eastern Cape). *Blackfish* or *Black Bream* (Natal). *Ibid.* 249 *Coracinus multifasciatus* ... *Banded Galjoen* or *Bastard Galjoen*, or *Damba* (Eastern Cape — Natal). **1955** [see BLACK BREAM]. **1971** *E. Prov. Herald* 15 July 16 Galjoen is by far the most popular name for the fish, but as we go up the coast from Port Elizabeth, it becomes Highwater, Damba, and then Blackfish in Natal. **1985** T. BARON in *Frontline* Feb. 30 Galjoen changes his name as he swims round the country, going by names like damba and highwater and blackbream. **1985** [see GALJOEN sense 1]. **1987** *E. Prov. Herald* 28 Mar. 6 In the East London area at least one tribal name is used and that is damba for the galjoen. **1993** R. VAN DER ELST *Guide to Common Sea Fishes* 186 *Coracinus capensis* ... *Common names* galjoen, damba and many others.

Dammara var. DAMARA.

danebol, danepit varr. DENNEBOL, DENNEPIT.

‖**dankie** /ˈdaŋki/ *int.* Also **danke(n)**, **danki**, **dank u**, **tankee**. [Afk., fr. Du. *dank u* thank you.]

Usu. used to suggest Afrikaans dialogue.

1.a. Thank you, thanks. Hence as *n.*, an utterance of the word 'dankie'.

1799 LADY A. BARNARD *S. Afr. Century Ago* (1925) 87 He .. placed all once more in the hat .., and with a deep sigh and a consoled '*Tankee*,' went off. **1901** E. WALLACE *Unofficial Despatches* 214 If we surrender to the British, what will become of 'onze taal'? .. If we surrender we shall have to say to our Kaffirs, 'As u belieft, Jan!' (Please, John) and 'Danke, Jan!' (Thanks, John). **1913** D. FAIRBRIDGE *Piet of Italy* 166 A skinny hand shot out from his rags and grasped the half-crown ... 'Danke, missy, danke.' **1949** C. BULLOCK *Rina* 9 She looked quickly at me .., then with a mumbled 'Dankie' hurried to a seat further along the coach. **1955** W. ILLSLEY *Wagon on Fire* 68 'You may close up when you've finished ...' 'Dankie, baas,' he answered. **1963** A.M. LOUW *20 Days* 30 'Dankie, oubaas,' said the policeman smiling. 'Thank you, old master.' **1972** *Cape Times* 25 Aug. 7 We thought that with this council we would be better treated ... Instead we are always required to say '*dankie baas*'. **1976** J. MCCLURE *Rogue Eagle* 61 I .. was asking his name .., when he rang off with a quick *dankie*. **1987** L. BEAKE *Strollers* 10 Johnny put a two cent piece into the cupped hands. 'Dankie, Madam,' the standard response. **1990** O. MUSI in *City Press* 17 June 9 They must say dankie that the old days have passed.

b. In the int. phrr. ***baie dankie*** or (*joc.*) ***baie donkey*** [Afk. *baie* see BAIE], 'thank you very much'. Hence as *n. phr.*, an utterance of the phr. 'baie dankie'.

1963 B. MODISANE *Blame Me on Hist.* (1986) 59 'Baie dankie, baasie,' I said, bowing my head several times, 'thank you very much, my baasie.' **1968** G. CROUDACE *Black Rose* 19 'Baie dankie, mynheer', he said at last; 'but we've food and coffee in our saddle-bags.' **1977** A. SHAW in *The 1820* Vol.50 No.12, 12 Many thanks .. for a most memorable day. *Baie dankie.* **1977** *Sunday Times* 27 Nov. 18 Not a word of Afrikaans, which is just as well since I never go beyond 'baie donkey'. **1980** A.J. BLIGNAUT *Dead End Rd* 71 They both thanked him and Dolf wrapped his 'Baie dankie' in a kind thought. **1988** M. MTHETHWA in *Pace* Nov. 39 He is what he is today because of me, but look at the 'baie dankie' he is giving me.

2. *obs.* [Afk., fr. Du. *bedanken* or *danken* to decline with thanks.] 'No thank you', a polite refusal; THANK YOU. So as *n.*, an utterance of the word 'dankie', used in declining an offer.

1833 *S. Afr. Almanac & Dir.* 92 Never, when invited to eat, reply with a genteel thank ye, (dank u) as that piece of politeness is understood throughout the colony as a negative ... 'Ja, Mynheer' will be thought quite polished enough. **1857** C.J. ANDERSSON *Lake Ngami* 264 (Pettman), In the Dutch language *danken* signifies a direct refusal, but not being aware of this, I interpreted it in the very reverse sense, as meaning 'If you please'. As often, therefore, as I repeated the ominous words so often had I the mortification of seeing the smoking dishes pass by me. **1913** C. PETTMAN *Africanderisms* 139 *Danki*, .. This word is used in declining an offer, as 'Asseblief' is employed when accepting.

dannebal var. DUNNEBALL.

dannepit var. DENNEPIT.

Dan's cabbage *n. phr.* [Etym. unkn.] Any of several species of plant of the genus *Senecio* (family Asteraceae), esp. *S. isatideus*, suspected of causing (or known to cause) poisoning in livestock. See also *Molteno disease plant* (MOLTENO sense b).

The disease associated with this poisoning is called DUNSIEKTE (sense 1 b) or *Molteno disease* (see MOLTENO sense a).

1912 *S. Afr. Agric. Jrnl* July 3 (Pettman), The plant commonly known as the ragwort (or, in Natal, as *Dan's cabbage*) *Senecio latifolia*. **1934** [see *Molteno disease plant* (MOLTENO sense b)]. **1966** C.A. SMITH *Common Names* 197 *Dan's cabbage, Senecio isatideus* ... The species has been found to be toxic to stock and is thought to figure in the disease dunsiekte in horses. The name is sometimes, though erroneously, applied to *S. othonnaeflorus*. **1976** MÖNNIG & VELDMAN *Handbk on Stock Diseases* 213 Many species of Senecio occur in the Republic ... These plants are known in different regions as ragwort, groundsel, Dan's cabbage and

Molteno disease plant. **1981** J. VAHRMEIJER *Poisonous Plants of Sn Afr.* 158 Other *Senecio* species which .. have frequently been suspected of causing poisoning, are *S. isatideus* (known as Dan's cabbage, or Inkanga) and *S. burchellii* (geelgifbossie or Molteno disease plant).

daou var. DAUW.

darem /'darəm/ *adv. colloq.* Also **daarem, darema.** [Afk., 'all the same', 'though', 'however' fr. *daarom* therefore, hence.] Used for emphasis: a rough equivalent of 'after all', 'at least', 'really', 'though'. Cf. MAAR *adv.* sense 2.

1920 R.Y. STORMBERG *Mrs Pieter de Bruyn* 60 That was daarem not so bad, but (sarcastically) don't you think it a shame to sack the pantry so? *c***1966** M. JABOUR in *New S. Afr. Writing* 92 We darema had that bit of rain last month. **1968** F.G. BUTLER *Cape Charade* 11, I never saw a man kick in his night shirt before ... That was darem .. the funniest thing of the whole New Year. **1972** L. VAN DER POST *Story like Wind* 143 *Darem* is even more difficult to explain, suggesting an apprehension of reality independent of all possible qualification of adjective or adverb, a word for which one has encountered no equivalent in any other language ... It would mean something to the effect that 'in the meantime, notwithstanding, however.' **1972** *Ibid.* [see JA-NEE sense 3]. **1973** Y. BURGESS *Life to Live* 97 Susan leaned over to whisper triumphantly: 'You see? Freek darem isin' as bad as that.' **1981** *Daily Dispatch* 27 Oct. 14 'A man has a responsibility to his volk,' he explained, 'But the government darem makes it difficult for a person these days.' **1984** 'DAN' in *Frontline* May 39 Maybe its the cost of living in the modern world, Koos, but it's darem sad.

Dark City *n. phr.* A nickname for the township of Alexandra, near Johannesburg.

1955 W.M. MANQUPU in *Drum* 40 A velvet pall .. hung over Alexandra Township ... In this evening frock, the 'Dark City,' as it is called, could compete for loveliness with any other town and hold its own. **1963** L.F. FREED *Crime in S. Afr.* 109 Alexandra Township. This township, known as 'the Dark City', is notorious as a crimogenic area ... The township lies outside the Johannesburg municipal area, and is situated approximately eight miles from the centre of the city. **1982** D. BIKITSHA in *Rand Daily Mail* 14 Oct. (Eve) 5 Former famous black residential areas like Sophiatown, Western Native Township and Alexandra went under quaint names like 'Kofifi' 'Casbah' and 'Dark City'.

darsee var. DASSIE.

das /das/ *n.* Also **dass.** Pl. **dasses, dassen.** [S. Afr. Du., fr. Du., 'badger'.]

1. *obs.*

a. DASSIE sense 1. Also *attrib.*

[**1652** J. VAN RIEBEECK *Daghregister* 14. Nov., .. 5 dode ende 5 lewendige dassen.] **1786** G. FORSTER tr. *A. Sparrman's Voy. to Cape of G.H.* I. 309 Those little animals which .. by the colonists are called *dasses*, or badgers. **1795** C.R. HOPSON tr. *C.P. Thunberg's Trav.* I. 284 In my various excursions to Table Mountain, I observed in its crevices both *Dasses* and *Baboons.* **1798** S.H. WILCOCKE tr. *J.S. Stavorinus's Voy. to E. Indies 1768–71* I. 35 *Dassen*, or *Badger* Island .. is improperly called Coney Island .. : it has its name from the quantities of a species of Guinea-rat, or the *cavia capensis*, .. which are wrongfully called *dassen* or *badgers*, by the people of the Cape. **1801** J. BARROW *Trav.* I. 27 In the caverns of Table Mountain .. is found in considerable numbers a small dusky-coloured animal .. called here the Das .. and by Pennant .. [the] Cape Cavy. **1812** A. PLUMPTRE tr. *H. Lichtenstein's Trav. in Sn Afr.* (1928) I. 88 The das or *hyrax capensis* of Linnaeus, is a small dusky coloured animal, about the size of a rabbit, with short ears and no tail, which inhabits many of the mountains in the colony. **1822** [see DASSIE sense 1]. **1841** B. SHAW *Memorials* 305 *Vaillant* .. , when on his journey to Namacqua-land .. engaged in hunting the dassen of the mountains. **1884** WOOD in *Sunday Mag.* Nov. 719 The most successful Das hunter.

b. *comb.* **das-adder,** a mythical animal with the head of a hyrax and the body and tail of a snake; *dassie-adder* or *-serpent*, see DASSIE sense 3.

Associated by some with the rock monitor *Varanus exanthematicus* subsp. *albigularis*. See also LEGUAAN.

1849 A. SMITH *Illust. of Zoo. of S. Afr.: Reptilia* Pl.2, *Varanus Albigularis* ... The animal which is called the *Das adder* by the colonists, and which is so much dreaded under an idea of its being extremely venomous. *a***1875** T. BAINES *Jrnl of Res.* (1964) II. 77, I had repeatedly heard accounts of an animal called the dass-adder, a union of the form of the dassie – Hyrax Capensis – and the snake, but had doubted its existence. **1934** C.P. SWART Supplement to Pettman. 38 The Research Bureau of The Argus 5/5/34 states: the das adder is a purely fabulous animal and its existence only as real as a purely fallacious belief can make it. It is interesting as an essentially South African belief. The beast is said to exist in mountainous regions and to have the head of a 'dassie' or rock rabbit, and the body of a snake. **1951** L.G. GREEN *Grow Lovely* 138 The mystery of the das-adder – a fabulous monster with the head of a dassie and the body of a snake .. the 'das-adder' legend persists in the Cape, and some people in the country cannot be shaken in their belief.

2. *rare.* Either of two species of seabream of the Sparidae: **a.** The BLACKTAIL, *Diplodus sargus capensis*. **b.** The BRONZE BREAM (sense b), *Pachymetopon grande*.

1902 J.D.F. GILCHRIST in *Trans. of S. Afr. Philological Soc.* XI. 227 Dasje, Das (Knysna)? .. Sargus rondelletii. **1972** *Daily Dispatch* 20 June 17 Our favourite fish, the jan bruin, is elsewhere a Hottentot, a das, a fatfish, butterfish, bluefish, or bronze bream, to mention some of its various names. **1979** SNYMAN & KLARIE *Free from Sea* 25 Blue Hottentot, .. das.

dasja, -je varr. DASSIE.

dasjespis, dassenpis varr. DASSIEPIS.

dasses piss *n. phr. Obs.* Also **dassen piss.** [Part. tr. S. Afr. Du. *dassenpis* or *dasjespis, dassen* or *dasjes* (see DAS and DASSIE) + *pis* urine.] HYRACEUM.

1785 G. FORSTER tr. *A. Sparrman's Voy. to Cape of G.H.* I. 309 On those places in the mountains, where these creatures dwell, there is found a substance called here *Dassen-piss* .. used by some people for medical purposes. **1795** C.R. HOPSON tr. *C.P. Thunberg's Trav.* I. 166 A kind of *bitumen*, which the country people were pleased to call *dasses p—*; supposing it to be the inspissated urine of the great mountain rat (*cavia capensis*) that is found there. **1810** J. MACKRILL Diary. 88 What the Country people ridiculously call Dasses Piss, Cavia Capensis or great Mountain Rat is a Bitumen found in the Crevices of Rocks & used in Fractures.

dassie /'dasi/ *n.* Also **darsee, dasja, dasje, dasse(e), dassé, dassi, dassy, dossi.** [Afk., earlier S. Afr. Du. *dasje*, dim. form of Du. *das* badger (see -IE).]

1. Any of three species of hyrax of the Procaviidae: **a.** *Procavia capensis*; also with distinguishing epithet, **klipdassie** [Afk., *klip* rock], **rock dassie**; KLIPDAS sense a; **b.** *Heterohyrax brucei*; now often with distinguishing epithet **yellow-spotted (rock) dassie**; KLIPDAS sense b; **c.** *Dendrohyrax arboreus*; also with distinguishing epithet, **tree dassie** (formerly also **boom -** /bʊəm-/ [Afk., *boom* tree], **bosch -** [Du., *bosch* see BOSCH], or **bush dassie**). In these senses, formerly also called DAS (sense 1 a). Also *attrib.*

1809 J. MACKRILL Diary. 56 Esculent & fit for Food, viz. Cavia capensis – or Darsee, Hystrix the porcupine. **1810** *Ibid.* 89 Cavia capensis, Dassee or great mountain Rat. **1822** W.J. BURCHELL *Trav.* I. 265 Here I procured for the first time, the Das or Dasje. This is of a brown color, and has much the appearance of a Rabbit: it is found in rocky places, where it takes shelter in the crevices. Its flesh is eatable; but the animal is exceedingly wary and difficult to get. **1835** J.W.D. MOODIE *Ten Yrs* II. 192 There is another curious animal found in this part of the country, called the 'bosch dassie,' or wood rabbit. **1835** A. SMITH *Diary* (1940) II. 106 The dassie chews the cud. Two more obtained today, both with the black mark on the back. **1838** [see KLIP-SALAMANDER]. **1838** W.H.R. READ in *Penny Cycl.* XII. 419 Its [*sc.* the hyrax's] name at the Cape is the Dasse, which is, I believe, the Dutch for a badger. **1866** J. LEYLAND *Adventures* 7 Looking up, I saw an eagle with a Dasse in its claw. **1878** T.J. LUCAS *Camp Life & Sport* 129 These stony kloofs afforded shelter to innumerable 'dassies', or rock rabbits; singular little creatures between a rat and a rabbit, of a dark-brown colour, destitute of tail, whose feet, denuded of fur, and covered with black leather cuticle, proclaim it as belonging to the order of pachydermata. **1882** S. HECKFORD *Lady Trader in Tvl* 106 A dassy, or rock rabbit, a round furry little beast, guiltless of a tail, and with the brightest eyes, and the sharpest of white teeth, which it was not slow to use. **1900** W.L. SCLATER *Mammals of S. Afr.* I. 313 The dassie or more correctly dasje (this name is really only the Dutch diminutive for badger, with which of course the present animal has no relationship at all), is found in the rocky cliffs and stony hills which abound all over South Africa. **1908** *E. Prov. Herald* 18 Nov. (Pettman), The tree dassie .. lives in trees and feeds upon the leaves. Colonists know this dassie as the boom or bosch dassie. **1911** *E. London Dispatch* 20 Dec. 5 (Pettman), Bush dassie,.This little creature makes its home in a hollow tree. He feeds and gets about his business at night. **1913** C. PETTMAN *Africanderisms* 79 *Boom dassie*, .. *Procavia arborea*, called also *Bosch dassie. Ibid.* 140 *Dassie*, .. These animals are near relations of the 'conies' of the Old Testament Scriptures. **1926** P.W. LAIDLER *Tavern of Ocean* 32 Salted dassies, or rock rabbits, were much in demand and Van Riebeeck pronounced them better-flavoured than their European cousins. **1931** *Guide to Vertebrate Fauna of E. Cape Prov.* (Albany Museum) I. 53 *Dendrohyrax arborea* ... Bush-dassie. **1937** [see SLIM sense 1]. **1951** R. GRIFFITHS *Grey about Flame* 141 Nyoka learned to spear the dassies that were so valuable for their warm brown fur. **1955** L.G. GREEN *Karoo* 174 At one time all dassies lived in the trees, and there is still a tree dassie .. found in the eastern Cape Province and far to the north. **1967** E. ROSENTHAL *Encycl. of Sn Afr.* 139 There are two types: the Rock Dassie (*Procavia capensis*) of mountainous country and cliffs, and the Tree Dassie (*Procavia arborea*) which prefers forested country ... The Rock Dassie lives in crevices among stones but does not dig itself in. **1973** J. COWDEN *For Love* 39 Black eagles live mainly on dassies (hyrax), and their domain includes several rocky stretches inhabited by these little mammals. **1973** O.H. SPOHR tr. *F. Krauss's Trav. Jrnl* 30 On the limestone hills nearby live lots of klipdassies, hyrax capensis. **1976** J. HANKS *Mammals* 76 The three species are very difficult to distinguish in the field. The photograph is of the yellow-spotted dassie. **1984** G.L. MACLEAN *Roberts' Birds of Sn Afr.* 117 Food [*sc.* of the Black Eagle]: About 90% dassies (Rock and Yellowspotted Dassies in equal proportions in Zimbabwe). **1987** B. MUNITICH *Ben's Buddy* 5 He could even call certain animals, like the little rock dassies, who came scampering and bounding from rock crevices and caves when he imitated their highpitched 'whit-she, whit-she' call. **1989** P. CANNAN in *E. Prov. Herald* 21 Feb. 6 Tree dassies look similar to the ordinary rock dassie .. , but differ in their habits and habitat. They are mainly active at night, usually solitary and live in trees in forested areas. **1990** SKINNER & SMITHERS *Mammals of Sn Afr. Subregion* 553 There is ample evidence to show that extant dassies are related most closely to the dugongs and the elephants. *Ibid.* 561 The yellow-spotted rock dassie occupies similar habitat to the rock dassie and in many parts of their distributional range the two species live on the same rocks.

2. [See quot. 1930.] Any of three species of seabream of the Sparidae: **a.** The BLACKTAIL, *Diplodus sargus capensis*. **b.** *obs. rare.* The STEENTJIE (sense 1 a), *Spondyliosoma emarginatum*. **c.** *obs. rare.* The ZEBRA, *Diplodus cervinus hottentotus*.

1853 L. PAPPE *Edible Fishes of Cape of G.H.* 22 *Cantharus Emarginatus* .. Dasje ... Rare in Table Bay but more frequently caught in the several bays to the East of the Cape. **1887** *S.W. Silver & Co.'s Handbk to S. Afr.* 183 *Dasje*, Rare in Table Bay, but common in the bays east of the Cape. Highly esteemed. **1902** *Trans. of S. Afr. Philological Soc.* XI. 220 The Dasje might also with a little stretch of the imagination be likened to the rabbit or dassie from its general shape, and this is the name by which it is known in Cape Town, Hout Bay, and Kalk Bay. **1906** [see BLACKTAIL]. **1930** C.L. BIDEN *Sea-Angling Fishes* 198 The name Dassie is stated to have been given by the early Dutch colonists, who saw something in the fish's character similar to that of the rock rabbit. Whether it referred to the fish's habit of frequenting the rocks, or to its short high and somewhat rounded body .. or to its shy and timid nature, will never be known. **1945** H. GERBER *Fish Fare* 38 Dassie is a small fish which is recognisable by the black spot on its tail ... Its meat is similar to that of white stompneus. **1954** K.H. BARNARD *S. Afr. Shore-Life* 58 The Biskop or 'Brusher' of Natal, the White Stumpnose, Dasje and Wilde Paard have chisel-like front teeth .. with which to wrench mollusc shells off the rocks, and strong back molars to grind them up. **1955** C. HORNE *Fisherman's Eldorado* 16 Galjoen and dassies often provide good catches. The dassie, when he travels eastwards, becomes the blacktail in both Natal and the Eastern Province. **1973** *Farmer's Weekly* 18 Apr. 102 The hottentot responds to all the usual methods of cooking and the same may be said of the dassie – a silvery fish with a black stripe across its tail. **1987** *E. Prov. Herald* 28 Mar. 6 A small fish which is often overlooked for its fighting qualities and which light tackle anglers will go for this coming winter is the blacktail – also known as dassie. **1992** YELD & GUBB in *Afr. Wildlife* Vol.46 No.2, 201 They [*sc.* the trek-fishermen] are entitled to take .. unlimited quantities of 'angling' species such as white steenbras, yellowtail, elf, kob, white stumpnose, dassie and belman during a season.

3. *comb.* (sense 1) **dassie-adder** *obs.*, *das-adder* (see DAS sense 1 b); **dassiebos**, either of two species of shrub, *Stachys linearis* or *Salvia disermas* of the Lamiaceae; **dassie rat**, the small mammal *Petromys typicus* of the Petromuridae; **dassie serpent** *obs.*, *das-adder* (see DAS sense 1 b).

1890 A. MARTIN *Home Life* 257 An object of even more superstitious dread is that mysterious and deadly creature – half quadruped, half reptile, and certainly altogether fabulous – the so-called **dassie-adder**. **1898** M.E. BARBER *Erythrina Tree* 56 In a conflict with the Dassie adder, if either of the contending parties is injured, both at once rush off to the nearest stream, to take a plunge into its healing waters, the winner in the race being the survivor, while the loser dies. **1932** F.W. FITZSIMONS *Snakes* 139 Periodically the old myth of the existence of a Dassie Adder is revived ... It is alleged an adder of unusually large size exists in South Africa which feeds almost exclusively on Klip Dassie (Coney), and that its bite is certain death. **1917** R. MARLOTH *Common Names* 22 **Dassiebos**, *Stachys rugosa*. Strongly scented half-shrub of the mountains in the central and northern districts. **1965** S. ELIOVSON *S. Afr. Wild Flowers for Garden* 192 *S[alvia] rugosa, Dassiebos* This evergreen, hardy perennial has large tapering leaves with a dull, wrinkled surface. **1976** A.P. BRINK *Instant in Wind* 153 That first night, she thinks, watching him roast some dried meat and boiling *dassiebos* for tea: that first night she sat looking at him like this. **1986** *S. Afr. Panorama* June 30 The **dassie-rat**, a squirrel-like animal, lives in the rocky areas of Namaqualand and Namibia, and its behaviour is similar to that of its unrelated namesake, the dassie or rock hyrax. **1988** C. & T. STUART *Field Guide to Mammals* 98 Like the dassies the Dassie Rat urinates at specific sites which become stained yellowish-white. **1990** SKINNER & SMITHERS *Mammals of Sn Afr. Subregion* 233 Dassie rats have acquired their colloquial name because, like dassies of the Family Procavidae, they are closely confined to a rocky habitat and have habits that are reminiscent of dassies. **1903** D. BLACKBURN *Burgher Quixote* 5 The **Dassie serpent** – that great snake with the head of a rabbit and body of a reptile, only seen about the season of Nachtmaal.

‖**dassiepis** /ˈdasipəs/ *n.* Also **dassi(es)pis**, and (formerly) **dasjespis**, **dassenpis**. [Afk. (earlier S. Afr. Du. *dasjespis*), *dassie* see DASSIE + *pis* urine.] HYRACEUM.

[**1731** G. MEDLEY tr. *P. Kolb's Present State of Cape of G.H.* II. 313 In the Niches of the Rocks are found several bituminous Substances ... There is a Sort which .. the *Hottentots* .. affirm, that 'tis the urine of *Ermins* mixed with very fine Dust.] **1868** L. PAPPE *Florae Capensis* 46 A remedy derived from the *animal Kingdom* .. *Hyraceum*, much valued by many farmers, and well known amongst them by the rather harsh name of *Dasjespis*. *Ibid.* 47 Amongst the farmers, a solution of this substance is highly spoken of as an antispasmodic in hysterics, epilepsy, convulsions of children, St. Vitus's dance, in short in spasmodic affections of every kind. **1942** S. CLOETE *Hill of Doves* 119 'This is dassiepis' – she held up a small lump of something that looked like gum or bitumen. **1955** L.G. GREEN *Karoo* 176 Early travellers in the Cape .. were puzzled by a peculiar substance they found in some caves, black masses like pitch. Thunberg thought it was bitumen. But the Bushmen and Hottentots knew better, and so did many farmers. They call the substance *klipsweet* or *dassipis*. In the Cape Pharmacopoeia it is listed more delicately as hyracium. **1988** P.E. RAPER tr. *R.J. Gordon's Cape Trav. 1777–86* I. 222, I found a large piece of *dassenpis* which was positioned in such a way I do not think it was urine. **1991** H. BRADFORD in *Cosmopolitan* Aug. 127 A reputedly excellent abortifacient spread from the Khoisan to white settlers ... It acquired an earthy Afrikaans name appropriate to its derivation from rock-rabbit urine. It was .. mingled with more palatable ingredients: by mid-20th century, an Afrikaner folk recipe for abortion contained not only *dassiespis*, but also valerian roots, wild sage and the tips of a wild olive tree.

dassievanger /ˈdasiˌfaŋə(r)/ *n.* [S. Afr. Du., *dassie* see DASSIE + *vanger* catcher (see quot. 1867).] The BLACK EAGLE, *Aquila verreauxii*.

This name has also been associated, perhaps mistakenly, with the bateleur, *Terathopius ecaudatus*: see BERGHAAN sense 2.

1867 E.L. LAYARD *Birds of S. Afr.* 11 *Aquila Verreauxii* ... *Dassie Vanger* and *Berghaan* of Colonists ... It is called '*Dassie Vanger*' (coney-eater) and '*Berghaan*' (mountain cock) by the Colonists .. from feeding principally on the coney, or rock-rabbit. **1889** [see BERGHAAN sense 1]. **1908** [see BLACK EAGLE]. **1918** S.H. SKAIFE *Animal Life* 237 The black eagle, or dassie-vanger, .. is said to be very fond of dassies, .. but it will often attack small buck and even sheep and lambs. **1920** F.C. CORNELL *Glamour of Prospecting* 124 An absolute silence, unbroken except the occasional scream of a dassie vanger, as the big eagles are called that sweep round the slopes of the peaks in search of an unwary rock-rabbit. **1955** L.G. GREEN *Karoo* 101 The dassie colonies are often menaced from the sky when a Verreaux's eagle (known as the dassievanger) swoops down on a fat, sun-loving dassie. **1964** [see BLACK EAGLE]. **1973** J. COWDEN *For Love* 39 Aquila verreauxi is known in South Africa as the Black Eagle, Witkruis arend .., Dassie-vanger (dassie catcher) and, by the Zulus, as uKozi.

dassy var. DASSIE.

da-t'kai var. GATAGAY.

dauw *n. obs.* Also **da(o)u**, **douw**. [S. Afr. Du., fr. Khoikhoi *daou* or San *dou*, current in Xhosa as *dawuwa, dauwa*.] The *mountain zebra* (sense (*a*), see MOUNTAIN), *Equus zebra zebra*.

1802 *Sporting Mag.* XX. 140 Two sorts of wild horses, the Dau and the Kwagga. **1810** G. BARRINGTON *Acct of Voy.* 273 There are no tame horses in Caffreland .. but there are two sorts of wild horses, the *dau* and the *kwagga* or *quacha*: the former is more beautifully streaked than the latter. **1822** W.J. BURCHELL *Trav.* I. 139 The *Wilde Paard*, named *Dauw* by the Hottentots and a much scarcer animal than the other two, was never suspected to be a different species. [*Note*] Pronounced *Dow*, as in the English word *dower*. *Ibid.* 265 At this place my Hottentots went out every day hunting, but without success: their object was that beautiful animal the Mountain-horse or Dauw. [*Note*] *Equus montanus*. **1835** A. STEEDMAN *Wanderings* II. 92 Three different and beautifully-marked species of the horse genus, the zebra, the dauw, and the quagga, likewise inhabit the plains and karroos of Southern and Central Africa. **1847** *Natural Encycl.* I. 265 The indigenous Pachydermata are .. the zebra, the dauw, the quagga.

davib var. DABBY.

Davidj(i)es, Davitjes varr. DAWIDJIES.

daweb, dawee(p), dawib varr. DABBY.

Dawidjies /ˈdɑːvəkis, -kiːz, -cis/ *n.* Also **Davidj(i)es, Davitjes, Dawedjies.** Pl. unchanged. [Afk., etym. unknown; perh. fr. the Biblical name *David*, or (less probably) rel. to Nama *dawee* tamarisk (see DABBY), + dim. suffix -IE + pl. -*s* (but usu. used with sing. force).] Any of several shrubby climbing plants or (*pl.*) their roots, formerly used medicinally, the roots as an emetic and purgative, and the toxic leaves as a paste for boils and snake bites.

1. In full ***Dawidjieswortel*** /-ˌvɔ(r)təl/ [Afk. *wortel* root]: **a.** *Zehneria scabra* of the Cucurbitaceae; **b.** *Kedrostis africana* of the Cucurbitaceae; **c.** *rare. Cissampelos capensis, C. torulosa*, and *C. mucronata* of the Menispermaceae. Also occas. **Dawidsworteltjie** /ˈdɑːvətsˌvɔrtəlki/ [see -IE].

1809 J. MACKRILL Diary. 56 Bryonia africana, Davitjes, Emetic & purge. **1868** L. PAPPE *Florae Capensis* 2 *Cissampelos capensis* ... This shrub is found in almost every mountainous part of the Colony. The roots are used as an emetic and purgative by the Boers, and go by the name of *Davidjes*. *Ibid.* 13 *Pilogyne Ecklonii* ... *Root* tuberous; *stem* climbing ... The porous resinous root of this old Hottentot remedy is nauseous in taste. In the form of decoction, it acts simultaneously as an emetic, cathartic, and diuretic. The natives call it *Davidjes-wortel*, and use it in cutaneous affections, dropsy, and syphilis ... This plant, the *Bryonia Africana* of former botanists, grows upon the slopes of Table Mountain, amongst bushes. **1913** C. PETTMAN *Africanderisms* 141 *Davidjes, Cissampelos capensis* ... A decoction of the roots of this plant is used by Kaffir herb-doctors and also by the Dutch as an emetic and purgative in cases of snake-bite, while a paste of the leaves is applied to the wound. *Ibid. Davidjes wortel*, .. *Zehneria scabra* ... The resinous root of this plant is an old Hottentot remedy for skin diseases, etc. **1917** R. MARLOTH *Common Names* 22 *Davidjes, Antizoma capensis* (*Cissampelos capensis*). The roots employed like sarsaparilla. The foliage poisonous. **1927** C.G. BOTHA *Social Life in Cape Col.* 103 An old Hottentot remedy was the use of the Davidsworteltje which in the form of a decoction acted simultaneously as an emetic, cathartic and diuretic, and the tincture or infusion of the root in wine or brandy was a powerful emetic and purgative. **1932** WATT & BREYER-BRANDWIJK *Medicinal & Poisonous Plants* 54 A dilute decoction of the root of *Cissampelos capensis* .. , Dawidjies, is taken as a 'blood purifier' in boils and syphilis ... The Zulus apply a poultice of the leaf of *Cissampelos torulosa* .. , Dawidjies .. to 'scrofulous swellings'. *Ibid.* 178 *Melothria punctata* ... Dawidjieswortel, Dawidjies, is suspected of being poisonous. **1947** L.G. GREEN *Tavern of Seas* 199 The roots of the plant called Dawidjies, forming a strong emetic and purgative, but entirely useless in snake-bite cases. **1966** C.A. SMITH *Common Names* 197 *Dawedjies(wortel), Antizoma (Cissampelos) capensis* ... A shrubby dioecious climber ... The root is used medicinally like sarsaparilla as an emetic and a purgative and as a blood purifier. *Ibid.* 198 *Dawidjieswortel, Melothria cordata* ... Thunberg .. noted that, in infusions of wine or brandy, the root was used as an emetic and purgative. As far back as 1897, the species was regarded as poisonous ... *Kedrostis crassirostrata* ... The tuber used as in *Melothria cordata*. *c***1969** E. GLEDHILL *E. Cape Veld Flowers* 170 *Melothria punctata* .. *Dawetjieswortel* ... Climber with slightly rough stems and leaves ... Very common on margins of forest and shrub and as a weed of hedges.

2. *rare*. The plant *Cynanchum africanum* of the Asclepiadaceae; also called KLIMOP (sense 2), and MONKEY-ROPE.

1932 WATT & BREYER-BRANDWIJK *Medicinal & Poisonous Plants* 150 *Cynanchum africanum* .., Excelsior, Klimop, Bobbejaanstou, Dawidjies, is also toxic, and causes loss of stock. [1989 B. COURTENAY *Power of One* 155 Monkey rope strung from tall trees .. was given names such as: traveller's joy, lemon capers, climbing saffron, milk rope and David's roots.]

dawip var. DABBY.

Day of Goodwill *n. phr.* The 26th of December, observed as a public holiday. Occas. also called **Goodwill Day**.

Also known as 'Boxing Day', as in Britain.

1980 *Act* 72 in *Govt Gaz.* Vol.180 No.7060, 3 To amend the Public Holidays Act, 1952 .. 2 .. (e) by the substitution for the words 'Boxing Day' of the words 'Day of Goodwill'. 1981 *Cape Times* 22 Dec. 1 The Cape Times will be published as usual on Friday, December 25 (Christmas Day) but not on Saturday, December 26, Day of Goodwill (Boxing Day). 1982 *Grocott's Mail* 23 Dec. 12 Sport certainly takes a backseat this weekend, with .. the Day of Goodwill not likely to see much sport as locals either head for the coast or spend a restful day with the family. 1984 *Sunday Times* 1 Jan. 9 An outing on the Day of Goodwill turned sour when a picnicking group were chased from a North Coast beach. c1992 *S. Afr. 1992: Off. Yrbk* (Bureau for Info.) 206 Public holidays. The following are at present public holidays in the Republic of South Africa, Prince Edward Island and Marion Island: New Year's Day (1 January), .. Christmas Day (25 December) and Day of Goodwill (26 December). 1994 *E. Prov. Herald* 8 Sept. 1 The Cabinet agreed that New Year's Day on January 1 would be retained, along with Goodwill Day (December 26) [etc.].

Day of Reconciliation *n. phr.* The 16th of December, a public holiday instituted in 1995.

See note at DAY OF THE VOW.

1994 *E. Prov. Herald* 8 Sept. 1 The Day of Reconciliation, falling on the old Day of the Vow, would be on December 16. 1994 *Ibid.* 8 Dec. 2 The confusion that has existed over the past few months regarding the public holidays for 1995 ended today, by the publication of the Public Holiday Act 1994 in the Government Gazette ... The full list of public holidays is as follows: .. December 16 Day of Reconciliation, [etc.].

Day of the Covenant *n. phr.* [Prob. tr. Afk. *Geloftedag, gelofte* vow, covenant + *dag* day.] DAY OF THE VOW. Also *attrib.*

See note at DAY OF THE VOW. Although officially renamed in 1980, the name 'Day of the Covenant' remained in popular use throughout the 1980s.

1952 *Act* 5 in *Stat. of Union* 39 Section *one hundred and seventy-five* of the Liquor Act, 1928, is hereby amended by the insertion .. of the following paragraph: (d) .. Day of the Covenant (sixteenth day of December). 1964 H.H.W. DE VILLIERS *Rivonia* 74 The 16th December is a National Day in the Republic. It is called 'The Day of the Covenant'. 1965 [see DINGAAN'S DAY]. 1971 *Daily Dispatch* 16 Dec. 10 The main theme of the Day of the Covenant should surely be reconciliation as an expression of positive gratitude. 1980 A. PATON *Towards Mountain* 52 Before the battle the Boers swore a covenant to keep the day holy forever should God give them the victory. It was called Dingane's Day for more than a hundred years, but was then called more appropriately the Day of the Covenant. It is by law observed as a Sunday, and no cinema or theatre or race meeting or public sports event may be held on that day. [Note] In 1980 it was renamed the Day of the Vow. 1983 S. ROBERTSON in *Optima* Vol.31 No.3, 147 An overtly religious occasion, such as the Day of the Covenant service, can be used to remind the people of their wrongs and of their heritage. 1986 P. LE ROUX in Burman & Reynolds *Growing Up* 191 The *volksfeeste* (folk festivals) — Republic Day, Kruger Day, and Day of the Covenant — interspersed with National Party *stryddae* (fêtes), attracted fewer participants every year. 1991 A. VAN WYK *Birth of New Afrikaner* 47 December 16 has come to be celebrated by Afrikaners as an extra Sunday — with religion and politics blended for the grown-ups, and in between much romping about for the children. Known as Dingane's Day in those years, its name was changed by the National Party Government to the Day of the Covenant in 1952.

Day of the Vow *n. phr.* The 16th of December, a public holiday commemorating the vow made by a Voortrekker group to keep the day holy should they defeat the Zulu army at the Battle of Blood River on that day in 1838. Also *attrib.*

Formerly called DINGAAN'S DAY (sense 2), it was officially named DAY OF THE COVENANT in 1952 and renamed 'Day of the Vow' in 1980. Replaced by the DAY OF RECONCILIATION in 1995. See also HEROES' DAY sense 2.

1980 *Act* 72 in *Govt Gaz.* Vol.180 No.7060, 3 Act to amend the Public Holidays Act, 1952 ... (d) by the substitution for the words 'Day of the Covenant' of the words 'Day of the Vow'. 1980 [see DAY OF THE COVENANT]. 1983 *Educating for Change* (Nusas) (pamphlet) 5 The difference between the official interpretation of SA's history and the way it is interpreted and understood by many South Africans, is reflected in the different commemorations held on December 16. For the Afrikaner nation, it is the Day of the Vow, a commemoration of the final victory over black South Africans; in the townships, it is known as Heroes Day, and tribute is paid to those who have died or suffered through their commitment to overthrowing apartheid. 1986 S. COOPER in *City Press* 8 June 1 We believe the people have the right to commemorate June 16 — more than the Afrikaners have the right to commemorate the Day of the Vow. 1992 *Natal Witness* 30 Dec. 9 Holidays such as the Day of the Vow and Kruger Day should not have the status of 'national' holidays. 1994 [see DAY OF RECONCILIATION].

DC *n.*[1] *hist.* Initial letters of DIVISIONAL COUNCIL. Also *attrib.*

1948 *George & Knysna Herald* 21 May 8 D.C. Elections. The local Council had been notified that the next divisional council elections will be held in November 1949. 1986 J.B. HOBSON in *Grocott's Mail* 7 Oct. 9 Port Elizabeth provides a substantial source of revenue as is evidenced by the services provided by Dias DC. Therefore we farmers .. elected to remain in the existing DC area.

DC *n.*[2] [Initial letters of DISCIPLINARY COMMITTEE.] PEOPLE'S COURT sense 3. Also *attrib.*

1990 M. NDWANDWE in *Tribute* Sept. 64 People's courts, or 'disciplinary committees' (DCs) were a phenomenon of life in the townships in the eighties. *Ibid.* 65 Youths who participated eagerly in the DC hearings and who were the 'shock troops' of the people's courts.

dead still *adv. phr.* [Eng., influenced by Du. (later Afk.) *doodstil* completely silent, *dood* dead + *stil* silent.] Completely motionless.

Although recorded in general English usage, 'dead still' is particularly common in *S. Afr. Eng.* because of the influence of the Afrikaans word.

1835 J.W.D. MOODIE *Ten Yrs* II. 177 We .. remained 'dead still' till they came within shot, when we fired all together and killed them on the spot. 1953 U. KRIGE *Dream & Desert* 68 He was looking into a dark pool but looking into it as if he stood level with its floor — its waters deadstill as if frozen solid. 1983 *E. Prov. Herald* 28 Apr. 1 He kept dead still and waited. The reptile moved away instead of towards him. 1991 *Natal Witness* 28 Dec. 2 The burglar dived through it [sc. the window] into the garden. The man tried to get up, then flopped forward and 'lay dead still'.

debris *n. Obsolescent. Mining.* Also **débris, dêbris**. [fr. Fr.] The muddy waste discarded after gold or diamonds have been extracted from metal-bearing or diamondiferous ore. Also *attrib.*, and *comb.* (objective), **debris washer**, **debris washing** *n. phrr.*

Not exclusively *S. Afr. Eng.*, but apparently first used in this sense in South Africa.

1871 J. SHAW in *Cape Monthly Mag.* II. June 358 In the paucity of materials in the *débris* of pans worked for diamonds, I would have less difficulty in finding traces of these rocks. 1887 J.W. MATTHEWS *Incwadi Yami* 373 The mountains, with the grassy plains rolling between, to one who for years had seen nothing but heaps of diamond debris and tailings from washing machines seemed inexpressibly and overpoweringly grand. 1891 R. SMITH *Great Gold Lands* 74 The smaller diggers find in *debris* washing more profit than in mining in maiden ground. There is no excavation to be done, and the very imperfect washing and sorting of the early days has left plenty of diamonds still amongst the pebbles. 1899 O.E.A. SCHREINER *Eng.-South African's View of Situation* 63 One stands looking .. at the great mining camp of Johannesburg .. with its heaps of white sand and debris mountain high. 1902 D. WARD *Digest of Criminal Cases Decided in Superior Courts* 5 The accused, an employé, not of De Beers, but of a *débris* washer. 1911 L. COHEN *Reminisc. of Kimberley* 24, I betook myself to the different mounds of debris, on the top of which were claim holders, seated each in front of a rough table, piled with carbonaceous earth, brought from the mine to them by Kaffirs ... A number of men made their living, and sometimes more, by débris washing. 1920 F.C. CORNELL *Glamour of Prospecting* 23 This mile-long beach looked like a vast débris heap of all the fancy pebbles the 'new-chum' digger usually collects during his first month or so on the River Diggings. 1949 C. BULLOCK *Rina* 112 We plugged away, getting out the infall of débris which always masks old workings.

Deepavali /ˌdiːˈpɑːvəlɪ, ˌdiːpəˈvɑːlɪ/ *n.* Also **Deepavalli, Depawali**. [Tamil, fr. Skr. *dipa* lamp, light + *avali* a row, line.] The 'Festival of Lights', the major religious festival of the Hindu year, celebrated in October or November. Also *attrib.*

Familiar esp. in KwaZulu-Natal and Gauteng, 'Deepavali' is used as well as the Hindi word 'Diwali' (which appears to be the usual form in world English).

1937 C. BIRKBY *Zulu Journey* 31 The great day of their year is Deepavali, the Day of Lights, when they celebrate Vishnu's reincarnation and victory over a particularly troublesome enemy. No matter how poor they may be, every Hindu family celebrates the Deepavali about a month before we celebrate Christmas. 1978 J.N. REDDY in *Fiat Lux* Oct. 34 On behalf of the South African Indian Council I wish to extend a message of goodwill to the Hindu community on the occasion of the Deepavali celebrations. 1980 *Rand Daily Mail* 6 Nov. 2 The Rand Daily Mail wishes its Hindu readers a happy Deepavali today. Deepavali is the main traditional ceremony celebrated by all Hindus. 1990 S. PADAYACHEE in *Sunday Times* 14 Oct. (Extra) 6 Deepavalli literally means 'row of lamps'. 1992 *Ibid.* 25 Oct. (Extra) 6 (*advt*) Oriental Plaza .. Fordsburg, Johannesburg. The management and staff wish all our valued Hindu clients and friends a Happy Deepavali.

deepie var. DP *n.*[1]

Defence Force *n. phr.* Also with small initials. [Shortened form of *Union Defence Forces* or (later) *South African Defence Force.*] The armed services, presently consisting of the Army, Navy, Air Force, and Medical Service. Also *attrib.*

Formerly known as the *Union Defence Forces* (see U.D.F. *n.*[1]), the name was officially changed to *South African Defence Force* (see SADF) in 1957, and to *South African National Defence Force* (see SANDF) in 1994.

1914 *Rand Daily Mail* 19 Dec., Fourie said that he was sorry he had shot so many of the Defence Force at Nooitgedacht; he would prefer to have shot the S.A.P. or the S.A.M.R. 1936 H.F. TREW *Botha Treks* 54 He and Maritz were the only two leaders who, being members of the Defence Force, came up for service when called on and then deserted in uniform to join in war against the Government. 1980 *Rand Daily Mail* 21 Nov. 3 Another DF rifle kills a civilian ... It was the second incident in the Western Transvaal this month in which a firearm belonging to the Defence Force was involved. **1984** *Daily Dispatch* 9 Oct. 1 Defence Force troops were called in at the weekend to join police patrolling the townships after youths stoned a police vehicle. **1986** *Rhodes University Diary* (Grahamstown) 144 Every year between three and four thousand South Africans refuse to enter the defence force. **1991** *Race Rel. News* (S.A.I.R.R.) Vol.53 No.1, 15 Black township residents were reported to have cheered when defence force trucks carrying white troops moved into a Natal village near Pietermaritzburg.

Defiance Campaign *n. phr. Hist.* Shortened form of *Defiance of Unjust Laws Campaign*, a nation-wide campaign of non-violent civil disobedience, initiated in 1952 in resistance to certain apartheid laws; a similar campaign organized in 1989. Also *attrib.*, and *transf.* See also FREEDOM DAY sense 1.

[**1952** N. MANDELA in *Drum* Aug. 35 Our Defiance of Unjust Laws Campaign began on the 26th of June.] **1952** H. NXUMALO in *Drum* Dec. 11 Moroka has found himself in the forefront of the 'Defiance' campaign, and soon he and 19 of his associates will face the Supreme Court. **1963** M. BENSON *Afr. Patriots* 183 Moroka, Sisulu, Mandela, together with Dadoo, the Cachalias, Marks, Bopape and several others . . appeared for the preparatory examination in a court crowded out and surrounded by people singing Defiance Campaign songs. **1978** T.R.H. DAVENPORT *S. Afr.: Mod. Hist.* 263 The African and Indian congresses began to work cautiously together on a basis of non-violent non-cooperation with the authorities, towards the partnership which led in 1952 to the launching of a joint Defiance Campaign. **1984** BHANA & PACHAI *Doc. Hist. of Indian S. Africans* 225 The *Defiance Campaign*: (a) revolutionised the outlook of the non-white people on a mass scale and instilled the spirit of defiance in them; (b) established the African & Indian Congresses as the true spokesmen of the aims of the majority of the people of South Africa. **1986** P. MAYLAM *Hist. of Afr. People* 185 The main defiance campaign . . began on 26 June 1952. The campaign centred on the defiance of apartheid regulations — using facilities reserved for whites, and disobeying the pass laws and municipal curfews. **1990** P. KEARNEY in *Weekly Mail* 27 Apr. (Suppl.) 7 In the long history of resistance to apartheid the defiance campaigns of 1952 and 1989 stand out as times of intense non-violent action to bring about change. **1990** *Sunday Times* 4 Mar. 17 Maponya likes to describe himself as a squatter. And while he may be the world's first diamond-encrusted squatter, his small but tenacious defiance campaign has undoubtedly created waves. **1990** *Race Rel. Survey 1989–90* (S.A.I.R.R.) 346 In August 1989 the Mass Democratic Movement (MDM), . . launched a defiance campaign against the government's policies of apartheid. The campaign was . . in support of the demands . . for . . the lifting of the banning orders on leaders and organisations, the release of all political prisoners, the ending of the state of emergency and the withdrawal of troops from the townships.

||**dekgras** /ˈdekxras, ˈdɛk-/ *n.* [Afk., *dek* to cover + *gras* grass.] Any of several species of grass of the Poaceae (subfamily Panicoidae) used for thatching. See also TAMBOOKIE *n.* sense 2.

1931 E.P. PHILLIPS *S. Afr. Grasses* 76 Dekgras . . *Schizachyrium semiberbe* (Waterberg). **1934** C.P. SWART Supplement to Pettman. 40 *Dekgras*, . . The popular name of the Schizachyrium semiberbe, a common and useful thatching grass in the Waterberg district. **1966** C.A. SMITH *Common Names* 198 *Dekgras, Schizachyrium semiberbe* . . a tall, tufted, perennial grass, used by farmers and natives for thatching . . huts and kraals. **1991** G.E. GIBBS RUSSELL et al. *Grasses of Sn Afr.* 293 *Sehima galpinii* . . Dekgras.

dekker var. DUIKER.

dekriet /ˈdekrit, ˈdɛk-/ *n.* Also **dakriet**. [S. Afr. Du., *dek* to roof or cover (or *dak* roof) + *riet* reed.] Any of several species of grass-like reed of the Restionaceae, used for thatching. See also TAMBOOKIE *n.* sense 2.

[**1656** J. VAN RIEBEECK *Daghregister* 4 July, 450 bossen deckriet.] **1822** W.J. BURCHELL *Trav.* I. 26 It is thatched with a very durable species of rush, peculiar to this part of the world, and which the Dutch call 'Dak-riet' (Restio tectorum). **1856** L. PAPPE in *Cape of G.H. Almanac & Annual Register* 342 *Elegia nuda*, . . This useful reed (Thatching-reed, Dakriet), covers the sandy tracts of a great portion of the colony. Not only does it fix the otherwise shifting sand, but supplies the farmers with a most excellent material for roofing their houses. **1917** R. MARLOTH *Common Names* 22 *Dakriet, Dovea tectorum* . . . Other Restiaceae also employed for thatching are *Thamnochortus spicigerus* and *Restio giganteus*. **1951** L.G. GREEN *Grow Lovely* 164 Most of the Cape Peninsula's thatch is the pale yellow dekriet from the Riversdale and Albertinia dunes. Once looked upon as a dangerous weed, the dek-riet is now carefully preserved. **1966** C.A. SMITH *Common Names* 196 *Dakriet*, Various species of Restionaceae which are used for thatching . . . *Dekriet, Chondropetalum tectorum* . . . If properly thatched, a roof may last for more than twenty-five years. Several of the above species are also used for making yard and/or stable brooms. **1968** *Farmer's Weekly* 3 Jan. 94 Thatching Reed (Kaapse Dekriet) — For your roof order direct from producers. Small and large quantities. **1977** *Evening Post* 26 Mar. 3 There are occasional patches of 'dekriet', the reed used for thatching. **1979** *Farmer's Weekly* 11 Apr. 120 *Cape Dekriet* (Thatching Reed) in full truck loads. **1985** B. JOHNSON-BARKER in *Wynboer* June 72 He remembered building it . . : cutting the *dekriet* near to where three men now lay in the shade and circulated wine and wisdom.

dendengvleis var. DENNINGVLEIS.

deng sik var. DUNSIEKTE sense a.

dennebol /ˈdenəbɔl, ˈdɛn-/ *n.* Also **danebol**. Pl. **-s, -le** /-lə/. [Afk., *denne* combining form of *den* pine tree + *bol* ball, cone (pl. *-bolle*).] Esp. in the Western Cape: a pine cone or fir cone; DUNNEBALL. Also *attrib.*

1909 *The State* II. 768 (Pettman), She . . began to break up a dennebol between two stones. **1947** L.G. GREEN *Tavern of Seas* 65 Tameletjies, the sweets made of sugar, water, eggs, naartjie peel and dennebol pits — sweets that were typical of an earlier Cape Town. **1948** [see DENNEPIT]. **1953** *Cape Times* 31 Mar. 16 Dennebols for your fires only sixpence for 50. **1966** C.A. SMITH *Common Names* 198 *Dennebol(le)*, The cones of several species of *Pinus*, chiefly those of *P. pinea* and *P. pinaster*, which are used for firing boilers, geysers, etc., though the tarry accumulation on the pipes militates against their continued use. **1974** D.K. VRIJZEE in *Cape Times* 12 Jan. (Weekend Mag.) 7 A reference to dennebol pips brought back memories of the walks by us children from our home to Raapenberg where we searched among the pine needles for pips and collected cones.

dennepit /ˈdenəpət, ˈdɛn-/ *n.* Also **dan(n)epit, donnepit**. Pl. **-s, -pitte**. [Afk., *denne* combining form of *den* pine tree + *pit* seed, pip (pl. *pitte*).] Esp. in the Western Cape: an edible pine kernel from the cone of *Pinus pinea* (the stone or 'umbrella' pine), or other species. Also in dim. form **dennepitjie** [see -IE]. Also called PIT.

1948 V.M. FITZROY *Cabbages & Cream* 207 'Umbrella pines. Think how the children will love having their own *danepits*.' It ends in my collecting as many *danebols* as I can carry to take home to the children and they leave sticky streaks of resin in the back of the car. **1950** H. GERBER *Cape Cookery* 92 Coat with mayonnaise . . to which you could add some finely chopped pistachio nuts (dannepits will do). **1960** G. LISTER *Reminisc.* 48 On these ['monkey ropes'] the baboons used to swing when they came down from the rocky cliffs of Devil's Peak above to eat dannapitjies (fir nuts). **1971** L.G. GREEN *Taste of S.-Easter* 159 Some makers use dried peas as a substitute for the dennepit; not the same thing at all. **1972** N. HENSHILWOOD *Cape Childhood* 49 In winter the storms lashed their branches with fury and at times a sudden crash would scatter the cones, throwing far across the garden the 'donnepits' as we called the seeds (anglicising the Afrikaans word *dennepitte*). **1973** *Cape Times* 13 Oct. 12 The current price of dennepits, when available, has risen higher than pine trees. **1973** *Drum* 8 Nov. 26 Here is a traditional South African recipe to add to the variety of your sweets . . . While boiling briskly, add dennepitte (pine kernels) or almonds, grated lemon, naartjie peel or petals of orange blossoms.

||**denningvleis** /ˈdenəŋˌfleɪs, ˈdɛn-/ *n.* Also **dendengvleis**. [Afk., *denning* (ad. Malay *dendeng* strips of spiced dried meat) + *vleis* meat.] A traditional Cape Malay dish made with lamb or mutton in a spicy sauce.

1944 I.D. DU PLESSIS *Cape Malays* 43 *Denningvleis* (*dendengvleis*) is meat flavoured with bay leaves and tamarind. **1950** H. GERBER *Cape Cookery* 87 Denningvleis (Malay): Malay dish with mutton and garlic. **1953** DU PLESSIS & LÜCKHOFF *Malay Quarter* 15 Of the less well known dishes partaken of by the Malays, the following may be mentioned: *denningvleis* or *dengdengvleis*, a meat dish flavoured with tamarind and bay leaves. **1983** M. LORENTZ in *Rand Daily Mail* 3 Apr. 10 The denningvleis was excellent. This is a fricassee of lamb . . gently casseroled in a cluster of spices: bay leaf, cinnamon stick, mace, clove with a touch of nutmeg. **1988** F. WILLIAMS *Cape Malay Cookbk* 33 *Denningvleis*, There is no other name in any language for this popular Malay dish. At first glance it looks like lamb stew, but when eaten it has a lingering, spicy undertone.

departheid see APARTHEID.

Depawali var. DEEPAVALI.

deproclaim *v. trans. Hist.* [Eng. prefix *de-* undoing or reversing the action of the verb + PROCLAIM.] To declare (an area) free of an existing proclamation which restricts occupation or use thereof to the members of one particular racial group under the Group Areas Act. Usu. *passive*. Cf. PROCLAIM.

1970 *Daily News* 16 Jan. 1 The area had been deproclaimed earlier this year and . . no decision had yet been made about where the displaced Zulus were to be moved. **1985** PLATSKY & WALKER *Surplus People* 33 Where a town was within commuting distance (up to 75 kilometres) of a bantustan, the African township was deproclaimed and the residents moved. *Ibid.* 132 In the case of a township being deproclaimed or a group area being proclaimed, the notice appears in the Government Gazette.

Hence **deproclamation** *n.*

1971 *Fiat Lux* Vol.6 No.2, 2 Referring to the deproclamation of the Forbes Street Indian group area at Ladysmith, the Council welcomed the assurance given by the Ministers. **1980** J. JOUBERT in *E. Prov. Herald* 10 Oct. 5 Grahamstown's coloured community, who have always opposed the alienation of the historic Fingo Village from Africans, yesterday officially endorsed their views by hailing its deproclamation in favour of Africans. **1985** PLATSKY & WALKER *Surplus People* 33 In the 1960s there was massive relocation particularly in the Transvaal and OFS as a result of deproclamation of townships.

||**derde mannetjie** /ˌdɛrdə ˈmanəki, -ci/ *n. phr.* Also **derde manetje**. [Afk., *derde* third + *man* man + -IE.] 'Twos and threes', a chasing game in which players stand in a ring in pairs, one player of each pair behind the other, except for two players who act as the chaser and the chased. In order to escape, the player being chased stands in front of one of the pairs in the circle, thus displacing the player at the back, who then becomes the new target of the chaser.

1868 W.R. THOMSON *Poems, Essays & Sketches* 179 There will be plenty of time after dinner for *Derde Manetje*, and other good old South African frolicsome picnic games. **1920** R.Y. STORMBERG *Mrs Pieter de Bruyn* 94 There was roaming and bathing and derde mannetjie throughout the morning. **1953** B. FULLER *Call*

Back Yesterday 218 The men played cricket, the women croquet, while the children romped in such games as 'Derde mannetjie,' or perhaps, 'Rise Sally Waters for a nice young man'. **1964** J. MEINTJES *Manor House* 35 Berta and I played with the dusky children of the *volkies*, went riding with them, held 'funeral' and 'church', and engaged in games of *sop-sop, kennetjie, derdemannetjie, blindemol* and others. **1971** V. DE KOCK in *Std Encycl. of Sn Afr.* III. 190 Other writers mention rounders, 'derde mannetjie' (twos and threes), [etc.].

derm /'dɛrəm, 'de-/ *n.* Also **derem, dêrem.** [Afk.] **a.** *slang.* Usu. in *pl.*: Intestines, 'guts'. Also *transf.*, and *fig.*

[**1886** G.A. FARINI *Through Kalahari Desert* 295 It is the *laste derms* (last gut). We did not tell you, as most white people will not eat it if they know what it is; and we did so wish you to taste it.] **1970** S.E. NATHAM *Informant, Cape Town* Dêrems. Innards. **1978** 'BLOSSOM' in *Darling* 30 Aug. 123 I'm sommer building up the suspense, see? .. Keep yore readers dangeling .., then zap them in the derems with yore punch-line. **1979** A. FOXCROFT in *Quarry '78–9* 147 'Now you watch Johannes take their derms out.' Blunt knife saws through the tough skin between their pointing legs. **1985** *Daily News* 29 Jan. 25, I just loved your idea about removing the engine and using the starter motor of the car. It made me wonder what other derms could be removed from my car. **1988** *Femina* Mar. 89 Together we would crouch over the coals and watch as the thick, fat *derms* crisped and crackled and dripped into the embers.

‖**b.** With qualifying word denoting a specific part of an animal's intestine, eaten as a delicacy: **nersderm** /'nɛrs-/ [Afk., *ners* anus], the rectum; **vetderm** /'fet-/ [Afk., *vet* fat], the colon or rectum.

1973 Y. BURGESS *Life to Live* 41 The family lived on 'psalmpensies' and '**nersderms**', the once-despised offal of offal. **1955** L.G. GREEN *Karoo* 100 A dish seldom tasted outside the North West Cape is *suurlewer*, composed of squares of sheep's liver, flour, vinegar, salt and part of the sheep's intestines known as the **vet-derm**. **1984** P. SCHWARTZ in *Rand Daily Mail* 2 Feb. (Eve) 12 Liver was sometimes cut up and mixed with finely cut meat from the rest of the carcass. The chitterling (vetderm) of the animal is stuffed with this mixture and fried over the coals.

‖**Dertiger** /'dɛ:(r)təxə(r)/ *n.* Also with small initial. [Afk., *dertig* thirty + agential suffix *-er.*] A member of an innovative group of Afrikaans poets of the 1930s, characterized by the confessional nature of their poetry and their consciousness of (and accent on) form. Cf. SESTIGER.

[**1962** GROVÉ & HARVEY *Afk. Poems with Eng. Translations* p.xv, The generation of 1930, a group that .. brought Afrikaans poetry to its maturity ... Van Wyk Louw, the spokesman and pacemaker of Dertig (the generation of the thirties).] **1966** VAN HEYNINGEN & BERTHOUD *Uys Krige* 42 'The critics have called me a "dertiger",' he [*sc.* Uys Krige] says, referring to the literary movement of the 1930's in which he has sometimes been pigeon-holed. **1970** D.J. OPPERMAN in *Std Encycl. of Sn Afr.* I. 146 Previously a work of art in Afrikaans was dedicated to the national effort and the struggle for language rights ... While the earlier writers had to teach themselves to write Afrikaans, the Dertigers belonged to the first and second generation of those who had already learnt Afrikaans at school or the university. **1976** V. ROSENBERG *Sunflower* 167 There was the soaring renewal in Afrikaans literature, particularly the poetry of the 'Dertigers' (the generation of the 'thirties'), notably N.P. van Wyk Louw, W.E.G. Louw, Uys Krige and others. **1983** M. DU PLESSIS *State of Fear* 41 Then, there was a group called the Dertigers. Poetry becoming private.

desselboom var. DISSELBOOM.

DET /di: i: 'ti:/ *n. hist.* Also (rarely) **Det.** [Initial letters of *Department of Education and Training.*] A name given to the government department administering the education of black schoolchildren during the apartheid era. Also *attrib.*

Called the *Department of Bantu Education* until 1978: see note at BANTU EDUCATION.

1981 *Pretoria News* 26 Nov. 13 The Joint Matriculation Board is still waiting for a full report from the Department of Education and Training ... A full report from the Det was submitted. **1983** E. JAYIYA in *Afr. Today* 8 Apr. 8 Main target of the DET plan is the problem of under-qualified teachers. **1985** *Probe* Oct. 11 Authorities in the DET told us that they were working towards one educational system. **1988** *Star* 26 Apr. 4 Fewer DET teachers have no matric. **1990** M. KENTRIDGE *Unofficial War* 104 In Natal .. the Department of Education and Training (DET) of the South African government .. administers schools in black areas not incorporated into KwaZulu. **1993** *Natal Witness* 2 Jan. 3 The 43,8% of black matrics who passed the DET exams stands in stark contrast to the 97,9% pass rate posted by white matrics in the Transvaal in 1992.

deurmekaar /ˌdiœ(r)mə'kɑ:(r)/ *adj. colloq.* Also **deurmeka, doormakar, doormekaar.** [Afk., ad. Du. *door malkaar, door malkander* (*door* through + *malkaar, malkander* one another), dialect variants of *door elkaar* confused, disordered.]

1. Confused, muddled; disorganized. See also MEKAAR.

1871 W.G. ATHERSTONE in T. Gutsche *No Ordinary Woman* (1966) 24 View of de Beers .. groups of diggers at work in quaint dresses .. tents of every conceivable shape & size .. ladies and children and blacks all 'deur makaar'. **1901** A.R.R. TURNBULL *Tales from Natal* 121, I shall then have a day of reckoning with Jass, Pen and Mess, if not before, for leaving us in this door-makaar strait. **1913** C. PETTMAN *Africanderisms* 150 *Doormekaar*, (C[ape] D[utch] mixed, confused, topsy-turvey.) In common use. **1972** *Cape Times* 8 Nov. 1 He would not have minded, he said, if they had put his name to the colour brochure .., but this pamphlet was too deurmekaar and smudgy. **1975** *Evening Post* 25 Jan., The woman's brother said that she suffered from hardening of the arteries and was sometimes 'deurmekaar'. **1980** *Fair Lady* 19 Nov. 384 We turned and burned, dreaming in Afrikaans, mumbling in French, Yiddish, or German and totally *deurmekaar.* **1983** J. SCOTT in *Daily Dispatch* 9 Sept. 9 Mr F.W. de Klerk couldn't understand .. how two Afrikaners .. could study the new constitutional document and come to two completely contradictory opinions ... 'It shows you how deurmekaar the document is,' replied Mr S— B—. **1991** M. O'SHEA *Informant, Kokstad* Confused? I'm afraid he's completely deurmekaar. **1991** E. WILLIAMS *Informant, Cape Town* I'm not ever having tenants again, they left the house so deurmekaar, I'll never get it straight. **1992** T.M. PEARSON *Informant, Knysna* 'Deurmekaar' is becoming popular with English speakers, as is 'khokos' for insects .. (also, in Natal, 'Nunus').

2. *comb.* **deurmekaarbos** /-ˌbɔs/, pl. **-bosse** /-ˌbɔsə/, [Afk., *bos* bush; see quot. 1966], the shrub *Ehretia rigida* of the Boraginaceae (forget-me-not family); *Cape lilac* sense (b), see CAPE sense 2 a; PUZZLE BUSH.

1932 C.R. VAN DER MERWE in *Farming in S. Afr.* Mar. 495 The locality is covered with a fairly dense growth of shrubs, such as 'noorsdoring', 'deurmekaarbos', .. etc. **1966** C.A. SMITH *Common Names* 198 *Deurmekaarbos, Ehretia rigida* ... The vernacular name is derived from the somewhat interlaced nature of the decurving branches, thus giving the plants an unkempt and untidy (Afk.: deurmekaar) appearance. **1971** A.A. MAUVE in *Std Encycl. of Sn Afr.* IV. 643 Several indigenous species [of the Forget-Me-Not family], e.g. deurmekaarbos (Ehretia rigida), douwurmbos .. are used in Bantu medicines. **1972** PALMER & PITMAN *Trees of Sn Afr.* III. 1945 The specific name means 'rigid', and is a good description of the tree. So is the most widely used of its common names, 'deurmekaarbos' or 'tangled bush'.

Hence **deurmekaar** *n. ?nonce*, a commotion, a mishap.

1990 J. NAIDOO *Coolie Location* 33 And you man, how did you get yourself into such a deurmekaar?

development board *n. phr. Hist.* Also with initial capitals. The regional government body which assumed the functions of an ADMINISTRATION BOARD from 1984 to 1986. Also *attrib.*

See note at ADMINISTRATION BOARD. Often combined with the name of the region served, e.g. *East Cape Development Board.*

Although sources report that the name was changed in 1982, the Black Communities Act (No.4 of 1984) was signed only on 22 February 1984, and published in the Government Gazette on 2 March 1984.

1984 *Survey of Race Rel. 1983* (S.A.I.R.R.) 254 Under the Black Communities Development Bill, published in 1982 and then referred for re-examination by a parliamentary select committee, the administration boards are to become development boards but will remain subject to the external control and direction of the Department of Co-operation and Development. **1984** *Govt Gaz.* Vol.225 No.9080, 11 Any reference in any law or document to such administration area or to such administration board shall be construed as a reference to the development board area or the development board concerned. **1985** PLATZKY & WALKER *Surplus People* p.xxix, Administration Boards became known as Development Boards. (The name was changed in 1982.) **1986** *E. Prov. Herald* 20 June 4 A total of 1 204 development board inspectors had been given new jobs because of the abolition of influx control. **1988** [see DIVISIONAL COUNCIL]. **1988** R. RIORDAN in *Monitor* June 71 The East Cape Development Board, and the Ibhayi Town council, are the government authorities who run PE's townships.

devil's thorn *n. phr.* Also **devil thorn**, and with initial capital. [Formed on Afk. name *duiweltjie*, see DUBBELTJIE *n.*^{2}] DUBBELTJIE *n.*^{2}

1906 J.M. WOOD *Natal Plants* VI. Pl.360, *Emex australis* ... A troublesome weed known to the young people as 'Devil's thorn'. As the seed vessels lie on the ground one of the thorns is always erect or nearly so, and therefore likely to inflict painful wounds. **1953** D. ROOKE *S. Afr. Twins* 45 Uncle Tys Swanepoel .. thinking he was pursued by a ghost had leapt through a window on to a patch of devil-thorn. **1955** E.A. RITTER *Shaka Zulu* 67 He instructed the Fasimba regiment to collect many basketsful of inkunzanas, the three-pronged 'devil thorns' which always have one prong pointing upwards. **1971** *Golden Fleece* (S. Afr. Wool Board) June 8 Other pioneers that are found generally are weeds such as Devil's thorn (Tribulus terrestris). **1978** A. ELLIOTT *Sons of Zulu* 34 Shaka .. ordered an assembly and covered his parade ground with triple-spiked 'devil-thorns'. These formidable little creations are known in Afrikaans as 'duiweltjies' (little devils) and in Zulu as 'nkunzana' (little bulls) but no matter what their name they are one of nature's most devastating devices to walk on. **1982** FOX & NORWOOD YOUNG *Food from Veld* 304 *Emex australis ... Common names English — cat's head, devil's thorn, spiny emex.* **1982** A. MORIARTY *Outeniqua Tsitsikamma* 124 *Tribulus terrestris* ... The fruit is well named 'devil's thorn' as it has 2–8 wicked thorns. **1987** B. MUNITICH *Ben's Buddy* 23 He sat down to examine his bare foot and found a small, round hole in his heel. 'A devil thorn,' he said to John, poking at the spot.

dew-berry *n.* The KRUISBESSIE (sense b), *Grewia occidentalis.*

1987 [see CROSS-BERRY]. **1991** *Dict. of Horticult.* (Dept of National Educ.) 307 *Dew-berry, (Grewia occidentalis,* cross-berry): Kruisbessie, booghout, assegaibos.

dhal, dholl /dal, dɔl, dɑ:l/ *n.* Also **dahl, dâl, dhall.** [ad. Hindi *dāl* split pea.] Esp. among those of Indian descent: a name used for various lentils and pulses; a sauce made from lentils and served esp. with breyani. Also *attrib.*

Not exclusively *S. Afr. Eng.*, but in common use esp. in KwaZulu-Natal and the provinces of the Transvaal. Naturalized in *Brit. Eng.* among Eng.-speaking people of Asian origin.

1906 *Indian Opinion* 15 Sept. 1, B. Ebrahim Ismail & Co Wholesale Merchants and Direct Importers have always on stock: Rice, Dholl, Oils, Ghee, Spices, Fish. **1917** R. MARLOTH *Common Names* 23 *Dhal, Cajanus indicus*. Seeds used like peas by the Indians in the Tr[ansvaal]. **1958** *Act 13* in *Stat. of Union* 85 Permissible weights per bag or other measure or container used in trade, of barley, bran, beans, buckwheat, cement, corn, dholl, .. samp .. and other dry commodities. **1971** *Drum* Mar. 22 She remembered giving him rice, dholl and herbs for lunch in a white billy can. **1982** Z. MAYAT *Indian Delights* 71 Wash moong dhal ... Drain off water. Put dhal in pot with .. onions .. masalas [etc.] .. and cook very slowly while dhal is softening. *Ibid.* 72 1 litre of left over dhal curry. **1988** *Stanger Mail* 2 Dec. 21 (*advt*) 1 kg pea dhall ... R1.68. **1990** E. GRIEVE in *E. Prov. Herald* 7 May (La Femme), Dhal: White lentils, covered with water and simmered ... Sauce texture should be thickish. **1990** *Weekly Mail* 8 Feb. 20 The lentil burger. The easiest way to make it is to cook some dahl (with red lentils, so they fall apart) ... If you're not into dahl making, you can use leftover lentils from lentil stew.

dhania, **dhanya** varr. DHUNIA.

Dhlambi var. NDLAMBE.

dholl var. DHAL.

dhomba var. DOMBA.

dhukkum var. DOEKUM.

dhunia /ˈdʌnja, -jə/ *n.* Also **dhania, dhanya, dunya.** [Hindi and Urdu *dhaniyā*, Telegu *dhaniyālu*.] The seeds or leaves of the aromatic plant coriander (*Coriandrum sativum*), used esp. in Indian cookery.

1977 *Fair Lady* 8 June (Suppl.) 33, 1 teaspoon dhunia/jeero (coriander leaves crushed with cumin seed, both are finely ground and combined). **1978** *Sunday Times* 26 Mar. (Mag. Sect.) 6 Marinate in a special Indonesian sauce made of jeero, dhanya (bought from an Indian food shop). **1988** R. LOUW in *Personality* 27 June 68 Sprinkle with 5ml garam masala, chopped dhunia and shallot. **1990** *Stanger Mail* 27 Apr. 7 Liquidise the garlic and ginger, chillies, onions and dhania. **1992** R. MESTHRIE *Lexicon of S. Afr. Indian Eng.* 14 *Dhania*, .. Coriander, .. fresh green leaves of coriander used to flavour curries. Sometimes referred to as *Indian parsley*.

Diagonal Street *n. phr.* [The name of the street in which the Johannesburg Stock Exchange is situated.] Used allusively to refer to the Johannesburg Stock Exchange (see JSE).

1983 *Frontline* June 39 (*advt*) It's the South African bank that can help you find your way between Diagonal Street and Wall Street. **1988** A. HOGG in *Style* June 24 The merely wealthy .. collectively spent a quarter less in inflation-adjusted terms than they did the year before ... Makes one wonder about the unfortunates who sell Porsches or peddle shares down Diagonal Street way. **1991** A. GILL in *Weekend Post* 30 Mar. 10 A year from March 28, 1990, Diagonal Street has taken on a look markedly different, with some shares looking decidedly weaker and some surprisingly stronger.

diaken /diˈɑːkən/ *n.* Pl. **-s**, ‖**-en.** [Afk., fr. Du.] A deacon in the DUTCH REFORMED church.

[**1877** F. JEPPE *Tvl Bk Almanac & Dir.* (1976) 38 The Church is ruled by a General Church Meeting (Algemeene Kerk Vergadering) consisting of the clergy, the half of the serving Churchwardens (Dienst doende Ouderlingen) and two Deacons (Diakenen) from each congregation.] **1931** H.C. BOSMAN in V. Rosenberg *Almost Forgotten Stories* (1979) 33 The ouderling and diakens in the church council said that perhaps they could permit a minister to look underneath his lids while he was praying, but it was only right that his eyes be shut all the time when he pronounced the blessing. **1955** L.G. GREEN *Karoo* 81 Many familiar scenes .. black suits of *ouderlinge* and *diakens* in the Sunday walk to Church. **1958** A. JACKSON *Trader on Veld* 34 As for Meneer die Predikant, he travelled in style about the district by cart and horses of his own, or was taken by one of his diakens (deacons) to make huisbesoeke (house visits). **1973** M. VAN BILJON in *Star* 25 Aug. 6 A newly elected diaken of the church came on his visit the other evening. **1979** *Daily Dispatch* 19 Oct. 13 Tier upon tier within the magnificent, wall-to-wall carpeted synod chamber in Orange Street they sit, dominees, ouderlings and diakens, in black suits and white ties. **1989** F.G. BUTLER *Tales from Old Karoo* 28 'You see his hands?' said my Uncle '— clasped behind his back like a *diaken* with a big moral problem on his mind?'

Diamond *n.* An element in various nicknames given to the city of Kimberley in the Northern Cape, the headquarters of the diamond industry, as ***Diamond City, Diamondia, Diamondopolis, Diamond Town.***

1924 L. COHEN *Reminisc. of Jhb.* 88 A good tale is told of Couper during the time he kept a boxing school in Diamondopolis. **1928** L.P. GREENE *Adventure Omnibus* 459 In order to bring that affair to a successful conclusion the Major had been obliged to move to the Diamond Town. **1931** G. BEET *Grand Old Days* 138 J.B. Robinson Diamond Merchant, of Diamondia, Begs to announce to the Diggers that he has removed to the New Rush, De Beers, where he will continue to buy Diamonds at the highest market prices. **1966** *Std Bank Pocket Guide to S. Afr.* 14 *The Big Hole* is 3,601 feet deep, 1,520 feet across and almost a mile in circumference. It is situated at Kimberley, South Africa's 'Diamond City'. **1971** *Daily Dispatch* 10 July (Suppl.), Diamond City Celebrates. **1989** *Personality* 13 Mar. 38 Then came the South African War and the siege of Kimberley, with the Boers at the gates of Diamond City. **1992** *E. Prov. Herald* 30 Jan. 2 At a historic conference held in Kimberley yesterday, the majority of delegates from 30 organisations decided in principle on a multi-racial council for the Diamond City.

diamond fields *pl. n. phr. Hist.* Formerly with initial capitals. ***The diamond fields***: The area near the confluence of the Vaal and Orange rivers, within the region previously known as Griqualand West, where diamonds were first discovered in 1866; *the Fields*, see FIELD sense 2 a. Also *attrib.*

1871 *The Jrnl* 9 Jan., The Diamond-fields are, it is to be inferred, made British. **1873** *Standard & Mail* 4 Rostoll's Pont is now the best on the Orange River. It is nearest to Hope Town and the most Direct Road to the Diamond-Fields and the Transvaal. **1882** J. NIXON *Among Boers* 106 The Free State has been better off by being deprived of the right of sovereignty. It could never have dealt with the unruly population at the Diamond Fields. **1896** PURVIS & BIGGS *S. Afr.* 143 The 'dry' diggings were discovered, and the foundations of what have since become widely known as 'The Diamond Fields' were definitely laid. **1911** L. COHEN *Reminisc. of Kimberley* 17, I caught .. my first sight of the Diamond Fields. **1915** [see ENGELS *n.* sense 1]. **1933** W.H.S. BELL *Bygone Days* 83 The discovery of the Diamond Fields in Griqualand West in 1870 and their marvellous richness had made a vast difference in the prospects of the Colony. **1958** A. JACKSON *Trader on Veld* 13 The intimate link between 'The Bay' and the Diamond Fields, in the opening of which Port Elizabeth had led the way. **1973** *S. Afr. Panorama* Aug. 27 The railway between Cape Town and the diamond fields was completed in 1885 and extended to the Witwatersrand in 1895. **1989** *Personality* 13 Mar. 38 His brother had left for the diamond fields and he followed, full of hope for the future.

Hence **diamond fielder** *n. phr.*, one living and working on the diamond fields.

1911 L. COHEN *Reminisc. of Kimberley* 231 In these early times Diamond Fielders, no matter their social position, were very independent and all white men on an equality.

diccop, dick-kop, dickop varr. DIKKOP.

didric var. DIEDERIK.

die Baai see BAAI.

diederik /ˈdid(ə)rək, ˈdɪd-/ *n.* Also **didric, diederick, diedric(k), diedrik**, and with initial capital. [S. Afr. Du. ad. of F. le Vaillant's onomatopoeic name for the bird, *didric*.] In full ***diederik cuckoo***, occas. also ***diederiks cuckoo***: the metallic green cuckoo *Chrysococcyx caprius* of the Cuculidae.

1790 tr. *F. Le Vaillant's Trav.* I. 347 The *green-golden cuckoo* of the Cape .. continually repeats, and with a varied modulation, these syllables, *di, di, didric*, as distinctly as I have written them; for this reason I have named it the *didric*. *c***1808** F. LE VAILLANT in C. von Linné *System of Natural Hist.* VIII. 237 Means of studying the didric cuckoo have not been wanting to me. **1853** *Edin. New Philos. Jrnl* (U.K.) IV. 82 The pretty notes of the .. *diedrick* further enliven the growing day. **1867** E.L. LAYARD *Birds of S. Afr.* 250 This beautiful little cuckoo, known by the name of '*Didric*', .. is extremely abundant throughout the Karroo. **1908** HAAGNER & IVY *Sketches* 169 The Didric .. is metallic-green with coppery reflections above. **1923** *Ibid.*, The Diedric .. derives its trivial name from its loud plaintive cry. **1939** S. CLOETE *Watch for Dawn* 114 He loved the hot .. silence of the day that was broken only by the intermittent calls of michi and diedrik. **1948** A.C. WHITE *Call of Bushveld* 259 The Diederik is commonly spoken of as the bronze cuckoo. It is, of course, a migratory bird. **1977** F.G. BUTLER *Karoo Morning* 248 The diederick is a cuckoo. It hatches among sparrows. Its foster parents do their best for it, but .. inevitably they lose patience and drive it from their nest. **1982** *S. Afr. Panorama* Sept. 48 The iridescent, green Diederiks cuckoo is a particularly brilliant Bushveld bird.

‖**diener** /ˈdinə(r)/ *n.* Also **diender**, and (formerly) **dienaar.** Pl. **dien(d)ers**, formerly **dienaaren.** [Afk. (lit. 'one who serves'), conflation of Du. *dienaar* servant and *diender* policeman, bailiff.] Esp. in the Western Cape: a policeman; occas., any officer of the state.

Historically an official rank, 'diener' has now become slang for 'policeman'.

[*c***1795** W.S. VAN RYNEVELD in G.M. Theal *Rec. of Cape Col.* (1897) I. 244 The Fiscal had in his employ three Sergeants of Police, .. ten constables, or Gerechts-dienaaren.] **1827** G. THOMPSON *Trav.* I. 285 Being supplied by the Landdrost, Mr. Ryneveld, with fresh horses, and a *dienaar* (police man) to accompany me, I arrived, in a few hours, at Rondebosch. **1838** J.E. ALEXANDER *Exped. into Int.* I. 68 He, the field-cornet, being a government dienaar (officer), can do what he likes with the land. *a***1878** J. MONTGOMERY *Reminisc.* (1981) 51, I remained where I was .., when up came three dienaars (constables) and took me in charge. I was taken before Mr B ... He then called a dienaar or constable. **1926** P.W. LAIDLER *Tavern of Ocean* 160 Constables received poor pay ... The service was therefore disliked, and looked down upon as a degradation. The *dienaars*, dissatisfied with their lot, became drunken. **1934** *Cape Argus* 3 Mar. (Swart), These 'Dienaaren' or police officers, are specially instructed to see that the streets were kept in clean and good repair by the inhabitants. **1946** [see GOOI sense 2]. **1960** J. COPE *Tame Ox* 74 'You tell the dieners once, not twice.' 'You lie! I never told the police nothing.' **1963** A.M. LOUW *20 Days* 86 The 'Kaffers' had been to the charge office to ask the 'dienders' to arrest them for not carrying their passes. **1982** [see GAMMAT sense 2].

‖**die stryd duur voort** /di ˌstreɪt dyːr ˈfʊə(r)t/. [Afk., *die* the + *stryd* struggle + *duur* continues + *voort* ahead.] A political slogan. Cf. A LUTA CONTINUA.

1979 *Voice* 30 Sept. 2 As Bokassa is coup'd, Idi Amin ousted, Paramount Chief Sabata detained, Lt Rawlings takes over power and Chief Mpephu assumes uhuru at Thohoyandou, 'die stryd duur voort'! Amandla! **1988** L. BRYER (tr. W. Odendaal) in Bunn & Taylor *From S. Afr.* 116 Mrs Fitzgerald .. speaks out with hoarse fervour: 'Don't turn back, workers ... Stand firm in the struggle ... *Die stryd duur voort*, yes, the struggle continues.' **1990** *Weekend Argus* 17 Feb. 12 We have need of at least some whites to shout apartheid, ban the lot and *die stryd duur voort*, if only .. to help us maintain a measure of historical perspective.

difaqane /ˌdifəˈkɑːne, -ˈgɑːne, ˌdifaˈɬaːne/ *n. hist.* Also **lifaqane**, and with initial capital. Pl. unchanged. [S. Sotho *difaqane, lifaqane* (both being pronounced /di-/, the initial *di-* and *li-* reflecting the orthographic systems of South Africa and Lesotho respectively), migratory troop of warriors; period of disaster caused by war.] MFECANE. Also *attrib.*

[1846 J.C. BROWN tr. *T. Arbousset's Narr. of Explor. Tour to N.-E. of Col.* 134 The Bechuanas more generally call them [*sc.* the Zulu] *Bakoni*, and sometimes they give them the nickname of *Lifakani*, that is to say, *those who hew down*, or cut their enemies in pieces with the *chake*, their formidable battle axe.] *c*1905 J.C. MACGREGOR *Basuto Traditions* 16 The wars of Difakane .. were .. an important factor in cementing together the agglomeration of tribes now called the Basuto, under Moshesh. **1912** *Ibid.* tr. *D.F. Ellenberger's Hist. of Basuto* 117 The word Lifaqane is of Setebele origin, and denotes a state of migration. It is used here as describing the struggles of wandering tribes accompanied by their families, flocks, and herds, as distinct from the ordinary expeditions of inter-tribal warfare in which as a rule only the fighting men took part. **1933** G.P. LESTRADE in A.M. Duggan-Cronin *Bantu Tribes* II. iii 64 The raids of the Zulus or their offshoots .. caused a great amount of ethnic pressure, and .. a great increase in the number and severity of inter-tribal wars ... The *Lifaqane*, as these wars are called in Southern Sotho, are still remembered as constituting the darkest and most despairing chapter in the history of the people ... When the *Lifaqane* were over, Moshoeshoe had under him a united Sotho nation. **1972** J.P. VAN S. BRUWER in *Std Encycl. of Sn Afr.* VII. 544 During the period of strife caused by the wars of Shaka and known as the lifaqane (1813–30), he [*sc.* Moshoeshoe] collected refugees from numerous tribes and welded them into the Basuto nation. **1980** LYE & MURRAY *Transformations* 31 The refugees who escaped .. burst upon their unsuspecting neighbours to precipitate a holocaust in every direction. Such was the *Difaqane*, as the Sotho victims named the wars, 'the Scattering'. **1982** M. MZAMANE *Children of Soweto* 85 He .. unleashed a spate of atrocities such as the township had never seen before and probably the whole of black Africa since the lifaqane wars. **1989** *Reader's Digest Illust. Hist.* 77 The ripple effects of his [*sc.* Shaka's] conquests spread far beyond the immediate area of Zulu influence ... The Nguni people called this the *Mfecane*, the Sotho people whom it affected called it the *Difaqane*. **1990** R. STENGEL *January Sun* 38 In the nineteenth century, the Tswana were buffeted by the *Difaqane*, .. a series of bloody conflicts among the black tribes in central South Africa.

dik /dək/ *adj. slang.* [Afk., 'thick'; 'full'.]
1.a. Full, replete, sated.

1970 A. VAN DER BERG *Informant, Pretoria*, I feel so dik from all that lovely food. **1970** K. NICOL *Informant, Durban* We just had a dik graze. (Filling, big — denotes approval). **1970** V. JAQUES *Informant, Pietersburg* I'm dik — I've had enough to eat. **1977** F.G. BUTLER *Karoo Morning* 42 She offered me a slice of cake. I shook my head and declined: 'Uh-uh. Dik.' **1980** *Weekend Post* 13 Sept. 2 Fat 'tannies' who ate themselves 'dik'. **1986** *Informant, East London* I've eaten myself dik. **1991** B. CARLYON *Informant, Johannesburg* I've eaten so much I feel really dik.

b. In the expression *to be dik of*, to have tired of someone or something.

1986 L.A. BARNES in *Eng. Usage in Sn Afr.* Vol.17 No.2, 2 *I'm dik of your praatjies* 'I'm tired of your nonsense.'

2. Stupid, dense, 'thick'. Also *absol.* Cf. DOM sense a. See also DIKKOP sense 4.

1970 K. NICOL *Informant, Durban* Only a dik ou could plug that exam. **1971** I. WILSON *Informant, Grahamstown* Surely John couldn't be so dik as to have taken that film away with him. **1977** C. HOPE in S. Gray *Theatre Two* (1981) 49 You know why, Howellsie? 'Cause they got dik guys like you who don't know no better working their guts out for 'em. **1991** S. PAM in *Fair Lady* 6 Nov. 88 Let's burn the three D's — the dom, dik and difficult, and every flat-footed son of a footballer!

3. Fat, large.

1970 K. NICOL *Informant, Durban* Cassius Clay is a dik ou. (Hefty, big). **1982** D. KRAMER *Short Back & Sides* 11 The bridesmaids wear turquoise and lemon yellow, .. and he is confronted by some dik tannie who says: 'Ag Boetie, wil jy nie kom dans nie?' **1982** J. SCOTT in *Daily Dispatch* 2 Apr. 5 Mr Coetzer .. suggested that the NRP 'stand nearer to the National Party'. 'You and the NRP are vrying mekaar dik,' cried Mr Tian van der Merwe .. disgustedly. And a Nationalist .. asked: 'What do you say, V—?' Mr V— R— probably felt he was 'dik' enough. **1994** *Sunday Times* 23 Jan. 28 (*advt*) Watching rugby without a dik stick of biltong and a Joe Rogers knife in front of you would be like playing rugby without a ball.

dikbek /ˈdəkbek/ *n.* and *adj. Slang.* [Afk., *dik* thick + *bek* beak, muzzle.]
A. *n.* Pl. **-bekke** /-bekə/. A sour-faced, sulky, or surly person.

1970 C.B. WOOD *Informant, Johannesburg* My servant was efficient but a real 'dik-bek'. (Sour face). **1991** R. MCNEILL in *Sunday Times* 17 Mar. 24 At the end of the programme Terre Blanche thanked John Bishop for interviewing him — something, he averred, that his Afrikaans colleagues didn't have the guts to do. I wonder how many *dikbekke* that produced in the newsroom.

B. *adj.* Angry, furious, peeved.

[**1979** *Sunday Times* 9 Sept. (Mag. Sect.) 5 Do you remember how cold the wind was? .. We called it the dikbekwind, the angry wind.] **1986** J. ALLAN in *Ibid.* 2 Jan., Going home Tannie .. is dikbek .. Kev won't let her come with us for a dop and insists on taking her straight home. **1991** L. KENT *Informant, Krugersdorp* He felt angry when he was picked out so now he is dikbek. **1991** G. DE BEER *Informant, Port Nolloth (N. Cape)* Dikbek (Surly/sulky). She was so dikbek all day, because she'd been excluded. **1992** C. VAN REENEN *Informant, Grahamstown* The one teacher was quite dikbek about having to share a taxi.

dikbekkie /ˈdəkˌbeki/ *n.* [Afk., *dik* thick + *bek* beak, mouth + dim. suffix -IE, prob. fr. *dikbek panga*, see quot. 1947.] Either of two species of marine fish: **a.** *rare.* The DIKKOP (sense 3), *Caffrogobius nudiceps.* **b.** The PANGA (*n.*[1] sense a), *Pterogymnus laniarius.*

It appears likely that Pettman (quot. 1913) is mistaken: the common name for *Gobius nudiceps* is 'dikkop' (see DIKKOP sense 3).

[**1913** C. PETTMAN *Africanderisms* 144 *Dikbekje*, .. A species of *Gobius.* **1947** K.H. BARNARD *Pict. Guide to S. Afr. Fishes* 149 Panga (*Pterogymnus laniarus*) ... A well-known Cape table-fish. A curious pugnosed deformity is occasionally captured, called by the fishermen a Dik-bek Panga.] **1949** J.L.B. SMITH *Sea Fishes* 270 *Pterogymnus laniarius* ... Panga (Cape). *Dikbekkie.* Reds (Eastern Cape) ... Lips villose, almost furry. **1975** *Dict. of Eng. Usage in Sn Afr.* 132 *Panga*, .. (*Pterogymnus laniarius*) alt.: dikbekkie, reds (E[a]st Cape) very common sparid fish in S. Afr; .. easily recognised by its furry lips. **1977** *E. Prov. Herald* 13 Oct. 15 A digbekkie came all the way from the bottom to take the jig. Maybe the slight swell and the drift of the boat made the jig look edible to the fish on the bottom.

diker-buck *n. obs.* Also **duyker buck**. [Englished form of DUIKERBOK.] DUIKER sense 1 a.

1823 T. PHILIPPS *Lett.* (1960) 198 Our Sportsmen .. had met with tolerable success, .. 1 Spring Buck, 1 Duyker Buck, 1 Hare. **1861** T. SHONE Diary. 7 Sept., Henry, Bowles and Venables went a fishing, they caught some little fish, and shot a Diker buck. **1881** P. GILLMORE *Land of Boer* 191 In these little covers the stein-buck and diker-buck find a shelter.

dikkop /ˈdəkɔp/ *n.* Also **diccop, dickop, dick-kop, dyk kop**, and with initial capital. [S. Afr. Du., fr. Du. *dik* thick + *kop* head.]
1.a. Pl. unchanged, **-s**, or **-koppe** /-kɔpə/. Either of two species of nocturnal or twilight birds of the Burhinidae: **i.** *Burhinus capensis*, now usu. called **spotted dikkop**, but freq. also **Cape dikkop**; formerly called **bush-** or **veld dikkop**; **ii.** *B. vermiculatus*, usu. called **water dikkop**. Also *attrib.*

Species of this family are elsewhere generally known as 'thick-knees' or 'stone curlews'.

1853 *Edin. New Philos. Jrnl* (U.K.) IV. 83 The *dickop* .. seem to emerge from their daylight concealment. **1856** R.E.E. WILMOT *Diary* (1984) 131 The noisy dickop or little bustard (nearly identical to our stone curlew). **1860** A.W. DRAYSON *Sporting Scenes* 17 One or two of the bustard tribe are also found here, and are called the diccop, coran, and pouw. **1867** E.L. LAYARD *Birds of S. Afr.* 288 *Dikkop* of Colonists .. feeds on seeds, insects, and small reptiles. **1873** 'F.R.' in A.M.L. Robinson *Sel. Articles from Cape Monthly Mag.* (1978) 105 That birds and animals assume the colour of the soil in which they are found is well exemplified in the Karoo, where .. the kieviet, the dik-kop, and the pauw .. all differ in the same manner from those found near the sea-board. **1894** E. GLANVILLE *Fair Colonist* 76 The whistle of the dik-kop, plaintive as the cry of the plover. **1900** *Grocott's Penny Mail* 24 Oct. 5 At the close of the day the 'bag' was found to consist of 227 quail, two dikkops, 13 woodpigeons. **1908** HAAGNER & IVY *Sketches* 131 The Bush Dikkop .. inhabits the open thorn scrub, .. seldom wandering far from the 'bush' localities. *Ibid.* 132 The Water Dikkop (*Œ. vermiculatus*) is slightly smaller than the Bush Dikkop. **1913** J.J. DOKE *Secret City* 272 The cry of a bird, a dikkop, was repeated from bush to bush until it died away down by the river. **1931** R.C. BOLSTER *Land & Sea Birds* 109 The Veld Dikkop is popularly called the Bush Dikkop to distinguish him from a close relation, the Water Dikkop. **1937** M. ALSTON *Wanderings* 100 The dikkops (thick heads) are also known in South Africa as thick knees ... They are odd birds with their big round heads and yellow eyes, unusually large, and long legs. **1947** J. STEVENSON-HAMILTON *Wild Life in S. Afr.* 270 The dikkops or stone curlews. Two species of these are described in South Africa, the Cape Dikkop (*Burhinus capensis*) and the Water Dikkop (*Burhinus verniculator*). **1948** J. MEIRING in *Contrast 48* 10 A dikkop cried its lonely penetrating call into the night. **1971** K.B. NEWMAN *Birdlife in Sn Afr.* (1979) The plovers, wagtails and Water Dikkop, pick the food up from the mud or water along the shoreline. **1978** K. SUTTON in *E. Prov. Herald* 14 Dec. 15 A pair of Cape dikkop (*Burhinus capensis*) .. have taken over their extensive back garden ... Dikkop, though common in rural and semi rural areas, are not usually seen in built up suburbs. **1980** J.O. OLIVER *Beginner's Guide to our Birds* 68 The Cape Dikkop .. is found in the dry parts of the country among the scrub and bush ... Its weird, whistling call can be heard on moonlight nights ... The *Water Dikkop* .. has a pale, whitish wing-bar and its legs are greenish, not bright yellow. **1985** G.L. MACLEAN *Roberts' Birds of Sn Afr.* 263 Spotted Dikkop (Cape Dikkop) ... *Burhinus capensis.* **1986** J. CLARK in *Sunday Star* 23 Nov. (Review) 12 We also have, for the fifth summer in succession, a pair of dikkops who have nested on the same dusty patch. What a hideous name — thick-heads! **1990** *Weekend Post* 24 Mar. 3 Among her menagerie are two spotted eagle owls, two dikkoppe, .. and geese.

b. [See quot. 1903.] ***to play dikkop***: to deceive, to feign injury.

1903 E. GLANVILLE *Diamond Seekers* 116 They're playing dik-kop ... The dikkop drops his wing and shams hurt to lead you off. **1913** C. PETTMAN *Africanderisms* 144 *Dikkop, To play*, To try to deceive as the plovers do by feigning to have a broken wing, when one approaches their eggs or young.

2. *noncount. Pathology.* A disease of livestock.
a. In full ***dikkopziekte, -siekte*** [S. Afr. Du., *ziekte* (later Afk. *siekte*) sickness]: a form of HORSE-SICKNESS affecting the heart and causing swelling of the head, neck and tongue; BLUE TONGUE sense b. Also *attrib.* Cf. DUNKOP.

1871 T. BAINES *Diary* (1946) III. 762 One of whose horses was standing apart, suffering from the 'dikkop' form of horse sickness. **1878** A. AYLWARD *Tvl* *of Today* 333 The symptoms .. had hitherto been noticed only in horse-sickness of the Dyk Kop, or swollen head and staggering type, as distinguished from the pleuritic type common in the Free State and Natal. **1882** S. HECKFORD *Lady Trader in Tvl* 88 There are two species of disease called 'horse-sickness', one of them is also called 'Dick-kop,' or 'thick-head' sickness. **1893** [see DUNSIEKTE sense 1]. **1897** J.P. FITZPATRICK *Outspan* 128, I had left my horse dying of Dikkop sickness just this side of Kilo 26. **1929** [see DUNKOP]. **1937** J. STEVENSON-HAMILTON *S. Afr. Eden* 38 On the evening of my arrival my roan pony Charlie developed indications of the *dikkop* form of horse-sickness. [**1957** see DUNKOP]. **1967** [see BLUE TONGUE]. **1976** MÖNNIG & VELDMAN *Handbk on Stock Diseases* 72 Dikkop shows the following lesions: Swelling of the hollows above the eyes, eyelids, etc., excessive fluid in the heart-sac and haemorrhages on the heart. **1980** P. SCHIRMER *Concise Illust. S. Afr. Encycl.* 12 *Dikkop (African horse sickness)*, This acute infectious disease of horses, mules, and, sometimes, donkeys, has been almost eliminated.

b. Ellipt. for GEELDIKKOP.

*c*1913 W. VAN HEUSDEN *Treatment of Horses, Cattle, Sheep & Poultry* 144 *Sheep and goats — Dikkop (Geel Dik Kop)*. This disease causes tremendous swelling of the sheep's ears, lips, eyelids, etc. **1937** *Handbk for Farmers* (Dept of Agric. & Forestry) 458 The finely bred Merino sheep and Angora goat .. are more susceptible to the disease ... Outbreaks of dikkop may .. remain undetected for several days. **1959** *Cape Times* 28 Jan. 2 Dikkop, the dreaded sheep-killing disease, is raging at Murraysburg.

3. Pl. **-s**. The marine fish *Caffrogobius nudiceps* of the Gobidae (goby family); DIKBEKKIE sense a.

1913 C. PETTMAN *Africanderisms* 144 *Dikkopje*, A species of *Gobius*. **1913** D. FAIRBRIDGE *Piet of Italy* 6 The black and white zebra-fish .. frisk in the company of dikkops, striped bamboo-fish and baby maasbankers. **1949** J.L.B. SMITH *Sea Fishes* 336 *Gobius nudiceps* Cuvier .. *Dikkop. Bully. Goby* ... The most abundant Goby of our South coast, in all rock pools, not timid. **1966** — *Fishes of Tsitsikamma Coastal National Park* 104 *Dikkop*, .. Found in almost every rocky tide pool it is a bold and greedy fish, taking any small bait. **1973** BEETON & DORNER in *Eng. Usage in Sn Afr.* Vol.4 No.1, 33 *Dikkop*, alt: bully, goby; small marine fish, the most common goby of the s coast; found fr the w coast to Natal in rock pools & estuaries.

‖**4.** *colloq.* 'Blockhead', 'idiot'. See also DIK sense 2.

1913 C. PETTMAN *Africanderisms* 144 *Dikkop*, A term of reproach meaning numskull, blockhead. **1916** S. BLACK in S. Gray *Three Plays* (1984) 225 Peace: Look here, don't you come it with me. Van K: Well, what do you think of this old dikkop! **1970** BEETON & DORNER in *Eng. Usage in Sn Afr.* Vol.1 No.1, 36 *Dikkop*, .. Afk equiv of 'blockhead, numbskull'.

‖**ding** /dəŋ/ *n.* Pl. **-e** /-ə/, occas. **-ers** /-ərs/. [Afk., fr. Du.]

a. A thing, object, or matter. Cf. DINGES.

1841 B. SHAW *Memorials* 83, I had often seen men engaged in making ploughs, and .. I resolved to make the attempt. The people flocked around me, enquiring, 'What sort of a ding (thing) will that be?' **1986** *E. Prov. Herald* 5 May 1 Satirist Pieter-Dirk Uys .. set up his 'lights and dinge' in the Opera House for tonight's opening of his new one-man show. **1986** S. SEPAMLA *Third Generation* 74 And when the *dingers*, I mean things, go wrong, who is in trouble? You!

b. In the phr. *ou ding(etjie)* [Afk., *ou* old + *ding* (+ -IE)], a term of endearment.

1969 A. FUGARD *Boesman & Lena* 3 Don't look at me *ou ding*. Blame the white man. **1977** S. ROBERTS in E. Pereira *Contemp. S. Afr. Plays* 235 It might be noisy round your place, ou dingetjie, but boy, there's a bit of life there at least. **1987** — *Jacks in Corners* 118 Ag tog, why must you disturb me, *Dingetjie*.

Dingaan's apricot /ˌdɪŋgɑːnz ˈeɪprɪkɒt/ *n. phr.* Also **Dingaan apricot, Dingan's apricot**. [Named for *Dingane*, a Zulu king who reigned from 1829 to 1840.] *Kei apple*, see KEI sense 1. Also *attrib.*

1853, 1876 [see *Kei apple* (KEI sense 1)]. **1891** R. RUSSELL *Natal* 31 The Dingaan apricot, or Kaw apple is the fruit of a species of ebony tree. **1897** J.P. FITZPATRICK *Outspan* 106 Heron had decided to outspan .. under a big Dingaan apricot-tree. **1921** — Letter. (Fitzpatrick Papers, N.E.L.M.), I wrote to ask if you could identify and get the seed of a wild fruit which you used to call 'Dingaan's Apricot' ... It was by far the best wild fruit I have ever found in the country. **1966** C.A. SMITH *Common Names* 199 *Dingaan's apricot, Dovyalis caffra* ... The vernacular name is derived from the resemblance of the fruit to that of an apricot. **1972** M.R. LEVYNS in *Std Encycl. of Sn Afr.* VI. 320 The almost round, bright yellow fruit (in Natal sometimes called 'Dingaan's apricot') is about 25mm in diameter and may be eaten fresh or used for making jam or jelly. **1987** [see *wild apricot* (WILD sense a)].

Dingaan's Day /ˈdɪŋgɑːnz ˌdeɪ/ *n. phr.* Also **Dingane's Day**. [See prec.]

1. *obs.* The 16th of December 1838, the day of the Battle of Blood River.

1881 F.R. STATHAM *Blacks, Boers & Brit.* 106 It was owing to that defeat of the Zulus on 'Dingaan's Day' that Natal only became colonisable. **1889** F. JEPPE *Tvl Almanac & Dir.* 28, December 31 days .. Dec. 16 Dingaan's Day, 1838 Holiday. **1893** J.F. INGRAM *Story of Gold Concession* 237 'Ah! yes,' the president says, 'I remember Dingaan's Day well. I was then but a boy of about twelve years of age, but every incident .. is still engraved in my memory.' **1913** V.R. MARKHAM *S. Afr. Scene* 82 This was the period of Weenen, of Dingaan's Day, of those fierce struggles in the remote interior of the itinerant Boers with the Zulu hosts.

2. *Obs.* exc. *hist.* DAY OF THE VOW. Also *attrib.*

So named by Act 3 of 1910 (although in use before this). Officially renamed DAY OF THE COVENANT in 1952: see note at DAY OF THE VOW.

1885 LADY BELLAIRS *Tvl at War* 246 About the 12th of December .. the Boers had announced their intention of retaking their old capital and hoisting their flag on the 16th December, this day being conspicious to them as the anniversary of their victory over the Zulu King Dingaan, and commonly known as 'Dingaan's Day'. **1897** F.R. STATHAM *S. Afr. as It Is* 92 The anniversary of this famous battle — the 16th of December, known as 'Dingaan's Day' — is regarded by the descendants of the emigrant farmers as a national festival. **1899** *Mafeking Mail* 15 Dec., To-morrow, Saturday, the 16th of December, will be 'Dingaan's Day,' the anniversary of the day on which the Boers .. made .. a sucessful stand against about 10,000 Kafirs under Dingaan. **1900** P.J. DU TOIT *Diary* (1974) 20, 16.12.1900 Dingaansday! Independence day! Where are they now? Poor Transvaal! **1911** *E. Prov. Herald* 18 Dec., The celebrations of Dingaan's Day brought some 3,000 people from many miles around to Vryheid, the festivities being spread over three days. **1936** E. ROSENTHAL *Old-Time Survivals* 30 From Dingaan's Day, December 16th, until after New Year, the villages virtually suspend business .. and everybody concentrates on holidaying. **1946** T. MACDONALD *Ouma Smuts* 37 The Boers were outnumbered by thousands, but their weapons mowed down the attacking Zulus in a massacre which made the river run red. Dingaan's Day came into the South African calendar as a holy day. **1955** W. ILLSLEY *Wagon on Fire* 207 December the sixteenth has for many years been observed as Dingaan's Day, in commemoration of the defeat inflicted on the Zulu chief by a party of Voortrekkers under Andries Pretorius in 1838. **1963** M. BENSON *Afr. Patriots* 79 On December 16, Dingaan's Day, 1935, the All-African Convention met in Bloemfontein location. *c*1965 *State of S. Afr. 1965* 107 Day of the Covenant (December 16, formerly known as Dingaan's Day). **1970** M. DIKOBE Marabi Dance. 67 December 16, Ja, it's Dingaan's Day. Ja, it will be his day off. **1976** M. THOLO in C. Hermer *Diary of Maria Tholo* (1980) 157 The youths have declared that December 16 is to be our black Christmas. December 25 is for whites only. Ours must be what used to be called Dingaan's Day because Boer blood was shed on that day. **1980** [see DAY OF THE COVENANT]. **1986** P. MAYLAM *Hist. of Afr. People* 160 The following year [*sc.* 1930] the leader of the Communist Party in Durban, Johannes Nkosi, organised a Dingane's Day pass-burning campaign. **1991** A. VAN WYK *Birth of New Afrikaner* 44 School and church served as centres for public functions, except for the annual Dingane's Day festival, which was chiefly observed elsewhere.

dingaka pl. form of NGAKA.

Dingan's apricot var. DINGAAN'S APRICOT.

dinges, dingus /ˈdəŋəs, ˈdɪŋəs/ *n. colloq.* [Afk. *dinges*; perh. some quots reflect the general Eng. *dingus*.] 'Thing-um-a-bob', 'what-do-you-call-it', 'what's-his-name'; used where the name of a person or object is unknown or cannot be recalled, or in place of a word which is considered indecent. Cf. DING sense a.

Current in other parts of the English-speaking world as 'dingus', but used only of inanimate objects.

1898 'FOSSICKER' in *Empire* 27 Aug. (Pettman), 'Lord! you don't say so? Where d'ye find the animile?' 'Animal, Mr Pike?' 'The *dingus* — the gentleman who lumbers round in space.' **1913** C. PETTMAN *Africanderisms* 145 Things animate and inanimate in Dutch-speaking districts are all of them *dingus* if the speaker fails to recall their names. **1916** S. BLACK in S. Gray *Three Plays* (1984) 214 Van K: Have you got the telephone laid on? Where's the dingus? Halford: The what? Van K: The dingus — what you talk in. **1930** N. STEVENSON *Farmers of Lekkerbat* 22 The Westhuizens, or the *dinges*, as they were called contemptuously as a family of tarnished origin and of no importance. [*Note*] What's-his-name. **1973** *E. Prov. Herald* 12 June 9 There were still a few [old engines] going strong in the district like old Dingus's and that one of ou Green's. **1973** L. DICKSON in *Cape Times* 2 July 5 South Africans are lucky — they need never be at a loss for a word. In an emergency absolutely anything can be described as a 'dingus': 'Pass me that "dingus", nurse, ' or 'It's that "dingus" in the differential again,' or even 'No it's not that "dingus" — it's the other "dingus".' **1976** J. MCCLURE *Rogue Eagle* 91 He's lucky I've got a lighting plant, or that enlarger *dinges* wouldn't work. **1987** L. NKOSI *Mating Birds* 167, I remember .. an English-speaking white man bellowing at the top of his voice across the vast silent courtroom, 'Bloody rapist kaffir bastard! Why not cut off his filthy black dingus .. !' **1990** P. MYNHARDT on TV1, 15 Nov., I sat in the front row, I was so close to the stage that the helicopter almost landed on my dinges.

din sikte var. DUNSIEKTE sense 1.

dinziekte var. DUNSIEKTE sense 1.

‖**diretlo** /diˈretlɔ/ *n.* Also **diretlô, liretla, liretlo**. [S. Sotho *diretlo, liretlo* (both spelling-forms being pronounced /di-/, the initial *di-* and *li-* reflecting the orthographic systems of South Africa and Lesotho respectively), fr. *retla* to cut up small pieces of meat.] Among Sotho-speakers: **a.** *ritual killing*, see RITUAL; **b.** pieces of human flesh used for medicinal purposes or in witchcraft. Also *attrib.*

1952 B. DAVIDSON *Report on Sn Afr.* 220 The outbreak in 1947 and 1948 of a wave of *diretlo* or 'medicine murders' in Basutoland. Such murders have been neither peculiar to Basutoland nor recent in origin. **1952** [see RITUAL]. **1953** LANHAM & MOPELI-PAULUS *Blanket Boy's Moon* 130 Libe knew little of *liretlo*, he was not of the *pitso* ... The police of Lesotho would discover that it was an impi from Lomontsa that had committed the Ritual Murder. **1957** A.A. MURRAY *Blanket* 123 A man who killed his own brother. A liretla murder, too. That is an ugly thing, now. **1968** A. FULTON *Dark Side of Mercy* 28 The Moruti, the priest who had baptised him .. denounced all killing as evil, and Liretlo, the ritual killing, as the greatest evil of all. *Ibid.* 224 The clever lawyer .. had surely made plain to the court that Liretlo was not murder as was any other killing where men took life for some petty personal motive such as gain, greed, revenge or lust for power. That which had been done had been done

DISA

for the good of all Lesotho ... The crops were good and the land fertile. **1970** J.P. VAN S. BRUWER in *Std Encycl. of Sn Afr.* II. 119 The most widely known use of parts of the human body has been in 'medicine murders' in Lesotho ... These parts, known .. as *diretlô*, are used to prepare a salve. **1972** B. BENNETT in *Ibid.* VII. 652 From a victim's body are cut strips of flesh or particular organs falling under the general term 'diretlo' and used to make magic compounds or 'protective medicines'. c**1976** H. FLATHER *Thaba Rau* 51 'There .. is *diretlo* — that's what we are going to discuss.' ... 'Body-snatching, that's what he's talking about ... They slice choice bits off your anatomy and use them for medicine.' **1980** LYE & MURRAY *Transformations* 67 *Diretlo*, or ritual murder, persisted in Lesotho.

disa /'daɪsə, -zə/ n. [Modern L., named by Swedish botanist P.J. Bergius in his thesis *Descriptiones Plantarum ex Capite Bonae Spei* (1767); etym. obscure, perh. L. *dis* rich; or Gk *disa* goddess; or named for the *dísir*, female deities in Norse mythology.]

a. Any of several species of orchid of the genera *Disa* and *Herschelia* of the Orchidaceae, esp. the PRIDE OF TABLE MOUNTAIN, *D. uniflora*. Also *attrib.*

1795 C.R. HOPSON tr. *C.P. Thunberg's Trav.* I. 220 Among these the *Orchis grandiflora*, or Disa uniflora .. was conspicuous by its beautiful flowers. **1844** *Curtis's Bot. Mag. 1787–1844* LXX. 4091 *(heading)* Horned-flowered Disa. **1890** WATSON & BEAN *Orchids* 235 A position in a house which suits cool Odontoglossums will be found agreeable to Disas. **1910** [see MOEDERKAPPIE]. **1913** H. TUCKER *Our Beautiful Peninsula* 93 None of them can vie in splendour with the pride of Table Mountain which the summer season brings — the great scarlet disa, whose regal blossoms: 'Hover like moths on broad and crimson wings' over the streams that cleave the deep gorges on the mountain summit. **1953** M.L. WICHT in *Jrnl of Botanical Soc.* XXXIX. *Disa uniflora*, the most famous of the disas, lines the stream-banks, and it was with great joy that we beheld a cluster of these bright orchids casting their red reflections on the surface of a clear, calm pool. **1970** [see PRIDE OF TABLE MOUNTAIN]. **1981** *Flying Springbok* Sept. 17 Amongst the orchids will be *Disa uniflora*, the Pride of Table Mountain, Flower of the Gods, first described in 1767 ... Of the 434 indigenous species of orchids found in South Africa at least 100 of them are Disa species, ranging in colour from pinkish red, bright scarlet, deep crimson, orange, white, blue and yellow. **1988** A. PILLANS in *S. Afr. Panorama* Oct. 22 The disa was given its name by the Swedish botanist, Pêter Jonas Bergius (1730–1790). He never explained why he chose the name when he established it in his thesis *Descriptiones Plantarum ex Capite Bonae Spei*.

b. With distinguishing epithet, denoting a particular species of orchid of the genera *Disa* and *Herschelia*, as **blue disa**, *H. graminifolia*; **drip disa** [see quots c1951 and 1983], also called **mauve disa**, *D. longicornis*; **red disa**, the PRIDE OF TABLE MOUNTAIN, *D. uniflora*.

References to other species such as the **cluster -, early blue -, green-bearded -, lilac -, vlei -,** and **yellow disa** are found mainly in specialist publications.

1917 R. MARLOTH *Common Names* 23 *D. graminifolia*, the **Blue Disa.** c**1933** J. JUTA in A.C. Partridge *Lives, Lett. & Diaries* (1971) 163 The beautifully formed blue disa is found among reeds both on mountains and flats, where there is a good rainfall. **1967** *Some Protected Wild Flowers* (Cape Prov. Admin.) Pl.181, *Herschelia graminifolia*. Blue Disa ... Summer ... Western and South-western Cape. **1985** A. TREDGOLD *Bay between Mountains* 181 The blue disas growing erect out of the sand, white everlastings in great clumps. **1913** C. PETTMAN *Africanderisms* 154 **Drip disa**, The popular name of *Disa longicornu*. c**1951** RICE & COMPTON *Wild Flowers of Cape of G.H.* Pl.171, *Disa longicornu*. Drip Disa, Mauve Disa ... Growing out horizontally from moist rocky faces in the mountain cloud-belt, ... rare. **1967** *Some Protected Wild Flowers* (Cape Prov. Admin.) Pl.175, *Drip disa, Mauve Disa* ... Summer .. Western Cape. **1989** *Motorist* Aug. 21 The summit of Table Mountain alone supports over 1 000 species of flowering plants, including an orchid found no-where else on earth — the fragile blue drip disa. **1917** R. MARLOTH *Common Names* 23 *D. longicornu*, the **Mauve** or *Drip* [disa]. **1983** M.M. KIDD *Cape Peninsula* 40 *Disa longicornis. Mauve Disa, Drip Disa* .. local on wet shaded rocky cliffs on Table Mountain and Constantiaberg. **1917** R. MARLOTH *Common Names* 23 *Disa*, A large genus of S.A. orchids. The best known species are: *D. uniflora*, the Large **red** - (Pride of T. Mt.); *D. graminifolia*, [etc.]. **1951** L.G. GREEN *Grow Lovely* 19 Twenty years later Thunberg admired the red disa on Table Mountain. **1968** M. MULLER *Green Peaches Ripen* 16 The mossy rocks were bejewelled with hundreds of red disas — the most beautiful and opulent of South African orchids. **1984** A. WANNENBURGH *Natural Wonder of Sn Afr.* 80 The red disa, pride of Table Mountain, is a ground orchid which grows in wet clefts in the rock and on the banks of mountain streams. **1992** S. JOHNSON in *Afr. Wildlife* Vol.46 No.4, 177 Marloth's most celebrated discovery was that the magnificent red disa (*Disa uniflora*), widely known as the emblem of the Mountain Club of South Africa and the Western Province Rugby Union, is pollinated by [the butterfly] *Meneris*.

disciplinary committee *n. phr.* **a.** A committee in a black township to which 'people's courts' are answerable. **b.** PEOPLE'S COURT sense 3. Also *attrib.*

1987 *Weekly Mail* 17 July 4 It is .. alleged that they .. formed 'alternative judicial organs, namely the "People's Court" which was answerable to the "disciplinary committee".' **1990** M. NDWANDWE in *Tribute* Sept. 64 People's courts, or 'disciplinary committees' (DCs) were a phenomenon of life in the townships in the eighties.

‖**dispens** /dəs'pens/ *n.* [S. Afr. Du., perh. introduced by seamen fr. Pg. *despensa* pantry; or fr. Old Fr. *despense* (cf. L. *dispendere* to distribute).] A larder, pantry, or storeroom for provisions.

The shortened form 'spens' is now current in Afrikaans.

1913 C. PETTMAN *Africanderisms* 145 *Dispens* or *Spens*, (L. *dispendere* to distribute.) The cupboard or pantry in which the household stores are kept and from which they are dispensed ... Compare Chaucer's 'All vinolent as botel in the *spence*' (Somner's Tale). **1927** C.G. BOTHA *Social Life in Cape Col.* 31 Rooms led off from the dining-room to bed-rooms, also to the 'dispens' or provision room now called a pantry, which was the pride of the housewife who kept on the shelves many bottles of confitures and fruit. **1969** D. CHILD *Yesterday's Children* 27 At the back the two wings of the dwelling partially enclosed a paved courtyard. One wing contained the nurseries, and the other the *dispens* (pantry) and the *kombuis* (kitchen). **1980** *Cape Times* 30 Aug., *(advt)* Authentic Victorian charm in select oak lined avenue ... Large kitchen, spens and breakfast room.

disselboom /'dəs(ə)lbʊəm, 'dɪs-/ *n. Wagon-making*. Formerly also **desselboom, diselboom, dusselboom, düsselboom, thisthelboon, thistleboom, tisselboom.** [Du., *dissel* shaft, pole + *boom* beam.] The pole or single shaft of an ox-wagon or horse-drawn cart. Also *fig.*

1822 W.J. BURCHELL *Trav.* I. 150 The pole (disselboom) is ten feet long, having at the end a strong iron staple. **1839** W.C. HARRIS *Wild Sports* 354 They drew up their fifty waggons in a compact circle, closing the apertures between and beneath them with thorn-bushes, which they firmly lashed with leathern thongs to the wheels and *dissel-booms*. [*Note*] Waggonpoles. **1850** J.E. METHLEY *New Col. of Port Natal* 22 A span of twelve or fourteen oxen .. attached by yokes fastened on the neck to a long chain .. which is made fast to the dissel-boom or pole of the waggon, to which the hind oxen are yoked, and depended upon for guidance. **1861** T. SHONE *Diary.* 27 Mar., Henry made a thisthelboon for his new waggon, and loaded the Waggon with forage for Market. **1864** [see FORESTELL]. **1873** F. BOYLE *To Cape for Diamonds* 258 One of the two iron braces holding the dussel-boom split in two places. We bound it up with a second halter, and proceeded miserably. **1875** 'P.' in A.M.L. Robinson *Sel. Articles from Cape Monthly Mag.* (1978) 193 It appeared a miracle that the whole wagon and its contents were not turned bodily over upon the oxen yoked to the disselboom. **1876** T. STUBBS *Reminiscences.* I. 81 Pike was sitting on the diselboom of the waggon .. lighting his pipe. **1879** R.J. ATCHERLEY *Trip to Boerland* 46 The wood employed is chosen with great care, stink or assegai wood being used for the 'dissel-boom' or pole. **1882** C. DU VAL *With Show through Sn Afr.* I. 235 The horses were tied to the pole, or, as the colonials call it, disselboom, of my waggon. **1895** A.B. BALFOUR *1200 Miles in Waggon* 72 The harness is of the most elementary kind, consisting of a trek-chain fastened to the end of the düsselboom (pole), and having yokes attached to it at intervals of about eight to ten feet. **1899** G.H. RUSSELL *Under Sjambok* 129 Now that the dessel-boom .. was lying on the ground, the seat .. was at an angle of fortyfive degrees. **1909** N. PAUL *Child in Midst* 11 The two best-trained oxen in the team are always inspanned in the front, and the two strongest beside the disselboom. **1914** S.P. HYATT *Old Transport Rd* 263 The only tools used by the transport-rider .. in getting düsselbooms or 'lang-wagons' were an auger and a side-axe. **1930** R. CAMPBELL *Adamastor* 65 In my last trek be thou the Star To whom I hitch my disselboom. **1944** J. MOCKFORD *Here Are S. Africans* 65 The wagon's front wheels pivoted freely as the single, short shaft, the *disselboom*, swung to the left or right with the turning span of plodding oxen. **1958** A. JACKSON *Trader on Veld* 37 The little open buggy, £25 (no hood), exposed you to all weathers, but was a light vehicle. It was built with two shafts for one horse, or a disselboom (one shaft) for two horses. **1967** E.M. SLATTER *My Leaves Are Green* 121 Above the screams and yells of the driver I heard the disselboom snap. The wagon slid down the slope, leaving a tangled mass of chains and oxen on the track. **1977** F.G. BUTLER *Karoo Morning* 91 A particular ox who worked well on the left of the disselboom might be useless on the right.

District Six *n. phr.* Also with small initials. [The name of the sixth of six municipal districts into which Cape Town was divided in 1867.] Used allusively, symbolizing any urban area from which the inhabitants are forcibly removed as a result of the area being declared 'white' in terms of the Group Areas Act.

Occupied mainly by 'coloured' people, District Six was cleared of its inhabitants between 1968 and 1982.

1971 *Evening Post* 25 Sept. 1 She also shouted: 'You call yourself a South African. You will turn this place into a district six. One day there will be another Blood River here.' **1990** *Weekly Mail* 27 July 6 The country is littered with District Sixes, less visible but equally painful for those who were forcibly moved.

Hence **District Sixer** *n. phr.*, an inhabitant of District Six; SIXER.

1972 *Drum* 1 Jan. 20 Hardened District Sixers, to whom gang wars are common-place, still shudder at the vicious violence that spilled blood across the street.

district surgeon *n. phr.* Also with initial capitals. A medical doctor appointed by the government to serve a particular district in supervising vaccinations, post-mortems, and the general health-care of people for whose welfare the state is responsible.

Orig. privately contracted by the magistrate of a district, district surgeons were first appointed by the Cape colonial government in the 1820s.

1831 *S. Afr. Almanac & Dir.* 64 Instructions for District Surgeons. Colonial Office Cape of Good Hope 29th July 1829 ... He must visit the Prison daily. *Ibid.* 66 The district surgeon shall be obliged to Vaccinate in his District, gratis. **1882** J. NIXON *Among Boers* 69 He had been district surgeon for six years, and said that he had only seen one case of phthisis among the whole population during that period. **1921** W.C.

SCULLY *Harrow* 35 Dr. Terence Ryan, the district surgeon .. had brought his kind heart, his irascible temper and his brogue from the south of Ireland some thirty years previously. **1922** S.G. MILLIN *Adam's Rest* 69 There was a District Surgeon in Adam's Rest, but he was old and lazy and generally a little drunk. **1958** E.H. BURROWS *Hist. of Medicine* 87 Dr. Barry modified this situation by having promulgated in 1823 'Regulations for the Guidance of the Respective District Surgeons' ... The district surgeon, 'being also considered as District Apothecary', was to sell all medicines .. to anyone demanding them ... Apart from this, he received free medicines for his attendance upon police officers, prisoners, convicts and paupers. **1982** *E. Prov. Herald* 8 June 1 Dr Neil Aggett might be alive today if he had seen a district surgeon while in detention ... In terms of the Prisons Act and Public Health Act, district surgeons did not need police permission to see detainees. **1986** *Reader's Digest Family Guide to Law* 64 Anyone assaulted by the police should see a doctor as soon as possible. If he is in custody he should ask for a district surgeon. **1989** C. RICKARD in *Weekly Mail* 23 Feb. 5 He said when lawyers heard allegations of torture in detention, they should speak to doctors about the claim as district surgeons had a duty to intervene in such a case.

Hence **district surgeoncy** *n phr.*, the office of district surgeon.

1870 *E. Prov. Herald* 15 Aug., The district surgeoncy of Stockenstroom was lately offered to Dr. Bird, of Dordrecht, but declined by that gentleman. **1958** E.H. BURROWS *Hist. of Medicine* 213 Coolies were imported in the 1860's and one of the clauses of the agreement reached with the Indian Government insisted upon regular medical attention for them. This provision led to the appointment of Indian Medical Officers to 'Circles' of territory corresponding roughly to the various district surgeoncies.

diver *n. obs.* Also **dyver.**
1. [The first quot. reflects a special sense of general Eng. *diver* one who dives; subsequent quots are often tr. S. Afr. Du. *duiker*.] DUIKER sense 2 a.

1607 W. KEELING in R. Raven-Hart *Before Van Riebeeck* (1967) 35 This forenoone wee sawe many seals velvett sleeves and dyvers alsoe sea fowles and trombos. **1878** T.J. LUCAS *Camp Life & Sport* 29 The harbour presents altogether a bustling scene, with its numerous craft, swarms of divers and ducks of various kinds streaming restlessly to and fro. **1906** *Natal Mercury Pictorial* 703 (Pettman), I notice a number of those ugly, useless, and predaceous birds known as *divers* in the Bay. **1913** C. PETTMAN *Africanderisms* 146 Divers, The cormorant is so called in Natal. [**1946** L.G. GREEN *So Few Are Free* 70 Cormorants inhabit the outer rocks of Dassen Island in vast numbers. This voracious fisheater is known in South Africa as the duiker (diver).]

2. [tr. S. Afr. Du. *duiker*.] DUIKER sense 1 a.
1810 G. BARRINGTON *Acct of Voy.* 157 Another animal is called the Düiker or Diver, from the manner of its plunging and concealing itself among the bushes. **1812** A. PLUMPTRE tr. *H. Lichtenstein's Trav. in Sn Afr.* (1928) I. The duiker or diver .. will every now and then raise its head up to look at passing objects, and then immediately plunge down again. **1822** [see DUIKER sense 1 a]. **1834** T. PRINGLE *Afr. Sketches* 510 The Duiker, or Diver, .. is so named on account of its peculiar mode of plunging among the brushwood when startled or pursued. **1847** [see DUIKER sense 1 a].

diving goat *n. phr. Obs.* [Calqued on S. Afr. Du. *duikerbok* (see DUIKERBOK).] DUIKER sense 1 a.
1731 G. MEDLEY tr. *P. Kolb's Present State of Cape of G.H.* II. 116 The Diving Goat at the *Cape* is near as large as an ordinary tame one, and much of the same Colour. [**1777** see DUIKER sense 1 a]. **1786** [see DUIKERBOK]. **1795** C.R. HOPSON tr. *C.P. Thunberg's Trav.* II. The wild goats (Steenbocks), and particularly the diving goats (Duykers) damaged the gardens greatly. **1900** W.L. SCLATER *Mammals of S. Afr.* I. 158 Duiker or Duikerbok (i.e., Diving Goat) of the Colonists. **1931** *Guide to Vertebrate Fauna of E. Cape Prov.* (Albany Museum) I. 46 *Sylvicapra grimmi* ... The Duiker ('Diving Goat').

Divisional Council *n. phr. Hist.* Also with small initials. In the Cape Colony and later the Cape Province: a local government body consisting of a council of elected members responsible for the provision of services outside municipal boundaries; DC *n.*¹ Also *attrib.*

Introduced in 1855, divisional councils were superseded by regional services councils (see RSC) in the late 1980s.

1855 *Act 5* in G.W. Eybers *Sel. Constit. Doc.* (1918) 83 Every such district shall elect one person to be a member of the Divisional Council of such division. *Ibid.* 71 V. All persons .. registered as voters .. shall be entitled to vote for the members of the divisional council. **1864** *Act 27* in *Stat. of Cape of G.H.* (1868) 113 It shall be lawful for the divisional council of any division .. to employ .. labourers to eradicate and burn the said weed. **1871** J. MCKAY *Reminisc.* 277 Why should not Divisional Councils expend a little money for the extirpation of ignorance, as well as the burrweed. c**1881** A. DOUGLASS *Ostrich Farming* 234 The Divisional Council valuations can always be obtained by inquiring at the Divisional Council office, which is in the town where the district magistrate resides. **1915** D. FAIRBRIDGE *Torch Bearer* 304 What state are the roads in then, that one of the horses should have come down .. ? I will tell Johannes to write to the Divisional Council. **1926** M. NATHAN *S. Afr. from Within* 254 The Cape rural districts are governed by divisional councils, which are mainly concerned with roads and bridges, and have the power to raise rates for carrying out their objects. **1942** *Off. Yrbk of Union 1941* (Union Office of Census & Statistics) 93 *Divisional Councils*, The powers and functions of divisional councils .. relate to the maintenance of roads, bridges, pontoons and ferries, and the control of outspans and trekpaths; local rating; vehicle taxation; and public health. **1948** [see DC *n.*¹]. **1951** L.G. GREEN *Grow Lovely* 144 Trapping of game on the mountain slopes was discussed by a special meeting of the Divisional Council in 1910. **1978** *Rhodeo* (Rhodes Univ.) 28 July 5 In February 1975 the Cape Divisional Council rounded up squatters in the peninsula and resettled them at Crossroads. **1988** *Race Rel. Survey 1987-8* (S.A.I.R.R.) 122 As a result of the establishment of RSCs a number of bodies were abolished, including the 13 development boards, the Transvaal Board of Peri-Urban Areas and 38 divisional councils in the Cape.

Hence **divisional councillor** *n. phr.*, a member of a divisional council.

1980 *Grocott's Mail* 30 Sept. 5 Dias Divisional Councillor Mr J— L— was acquitted last Wednesday on a speeding charge after a speed trap ... was described .. as 'highly irregular and illegal' by a Grahamstown magistrate. **1982** *E. Prov. Herald* 18 June 2 The committee would resume its hearing on Tuesday when it would start concentrating on getting evidence from divisional councillors.

diwilkie *var.* DUIWELTJIE.

djentoe *var.* GENTOO.

dobbeltjiedoorn *var.* DUBBELTJEDOORN.

doblejie *var.* DUBBELTJIE *n.*²

dobo grass *var.* DABA GRASS.

docha *var.* DAGGA *n.*²

doctor *n.* [Special senses of general Eng. *doctor.*]
1.a. A traditional African healer. Cf. WITCHDOCTOR.

1731 G. MEDLEY tr. *P. Kolb's Present State of Cape of G.H.* I. 173 The Doctor of the *Kraal* is call'd with his Amulet to remove it; which tho' he cannot do, 'tis still Witchcraft, and is so call'd to the End of the Chapter. **1829** W. SHAW *Diary.* 23 Jan., The petty Chief, was reputed a doctor and a Wise man; .. he .. gave them a basket of Milk to drink, in [which] he had mixed certain herbs which were to operate as a charm, both for the success of their enterprize, and to ensure their safety. **1835** W.B. BOYCE in A. Steedman *Wanderings* II. 273 She was sent to a female doctor for her education, as she was intended by her parents for a doctor. In going through the initiatory dancings and singings she probably caught a severe cold. **1849** [see BONE sense 1]. **1870** [see ISIBONGO sense 1]. **1871** [see MOLOI]. **1893** B.M. ATHELING in *Cape Illust. Mag.* Jan. 158 Considering it a case of witchcraft, he wishes to go to a Doctor and find out who it is who is acting under his rival's instructions and causing him so much trouble. **1948** O. WALKER *Kaffirs Are Lively* 63 There was, he said, a good deal of 'competition' from Native doctors, usually and erroneously referred to as witchdoctors. **1959** L. LONGMORE *Dispossessed* 232 There are two principal types of doctors, namely a doctor and a diviner, the so-called 'witch-doctor'. A doctor is one who has been called to this profession by his gods through the spirits. To him it is a commitment, a responsibility, a service to humanity, a service to members in and outside his community. **1959** *Ibid.* [see INYANGA sense 1]. **1980** [see SMELL].

b. With distinguishing epithet denoting a healer's particular field of expertise: **lightning (and hail) doctor; medicine doctor; poison doctor; rain doctor; smelling doctor,** ISANUSI; **war doctor.**

1887 J.W. MATTHEWS *Incwadi Yami* 40 It may not be out of the way here for me to mention the different recognized kinds of doctors (*izinyanga*): 1st, the wizard or diviner (*inyanga yokubula*); 2nd, the rain doctor; 3rd, the **lightning and hail doctor**; 4th, the medicine doctor (*inyanga yokwelapa*). **1913** W.C. SCULLY *Further Reminisc.* 302 The important position held by the 'lightning doctor' among the Natives who still adhere to their tribal customs. **1941** N. DEVITT *Celebrated S. Afr. Crimes* 128 Mjila got back and was met by the witch-doctor. The latter told him he was a man of repute, a lightning doctor, a rainmaker. **1955** J.B. SHEPHARD *Land of Tikoloshe* 11 The wise man calls in the lightning-doctor to give his huts, his family and his stock preventive treatment which he firmly believes will insure him against the attacks of the Umpundulu bird. **1887** [**medicine doctor**: see quot. at *lightning and hail doctor* above]. **1821** C.I. LATROBE *Jrnl of Visit* 124 The bite of the Nachtschlange, or night-serpent, is said by the Hottentot **poison-doctors**, to be incurable. **1887** [**rain doctor**: see quot. at *lightning and hail doctor* above]. **1836** C.L. STRETCH *Journal.* 254 If any one in a kraal becomes sick, the **Smelling Doctor** is sent for to find out if the person has been affected by the charm of a witch. **1851** R.J. GARDEN *Diary.* I. (Killie Campbell Africana Library MS29081) 30 June It is the custom of every known Caffir tribe for the Chief to have a **War-Doctor** ... Those Doctors profess to strengthen the Chief by giving him superior power over his enemies. He is consulted prior to any approaching war and uses various plants from which he composes decoctions with which the Chief washes his body. **1907** W.C. SCULLY *By Veldt & Kopje* 62 He aimed a glance of scathing contempt at the war-doctor, with whom he had been bickering considerably throughout the meeting. **1931** J.H. SOGA *Ama-Xosa* 66 The tola or war-doctor is the central figure in this special duty. His office is usually, though not always, hereditary. **1961** T.V. BULPIN *White Whirlwind* 112 The ritual war-doctor appeared before the army carrying a blazing torch of grass prepared with the fats of certain animals known to be fierce and powerful fighters of the wilds. **1985** J.B. PEIRES in *Staffrider* Vol.6, No.2, 29 The best-known of Robben Island's early prisoners was the giant prophet and wardoctor Nxele (Makana), who attacked Grahamstown in 1819.

2. *fig. obs.* **The Doctor:** Ellipt. for *the Cape Doctor*, see CAPE DOCTOR.

Used also in the W. Indies and Australia of similar winds.

1843 J.C. CHASE *Cape of G.H.* 22 At the Cape .. the south-east wind is proverbially designated 'the Doctor', and no doubt by driving off the miasmatic exhalations, .. it converts what might constitute *malaria*, into *the most salubrious atmosphere in the world.* **1856** F.P. FLEMING *Sn Afr.* 62 The South-Easter, from blowing all pestilential vapours and effluvia out to sea .. has obtained the local epithet of 'the Doctor'.

Hence (sense 1) **doctor** *v. trans.*, **doctoress** *n.*, **doctoring** *vbl n.*

1890 J. MACDONALD *Light in Afr.* 178 After this the army is assembled, and war dances are held at intervals while the process of 'doctoring' proceeds. **1893** B.M. ATHELING in *Cape Illust. Mag.* Jan. 159 The Doctoress looked at us for a moment in silence, and then sank down in a sitting posture on her heels. **1923** [see HUT TAX]. **1941** N. DEVITT *Celebrated S. Afr. Crimes* 128 Sotwana proceeded to doctor the chief. **1949** O. WALKER *Proud Zulu* (1951) 143 John was not present .. at the anointing of the king with special medicines. He saw Cetewayo only after he had been doctored.

dodai, do-die varr. DOH-DIE.

doedoe /ˈdudu/ *v. intrans. Colloq.* Also **do-do(o)**. [Nursery word, in Afk. as *doedoe*, but of many possible origins: Zulu *duduza* to lull (a baby) to sleep, or Du. *dodijnen* to rock (a child) to sleep, or Malay *dodoi* a lullaby.] In children's language: to (go to) sleep. Also (freq. with **-s**) used with adverbial or adjectival force in the phrr. ***to go doedoe(s)***, or (by analogy with 'beddy-byes') ***to go doedoebye(s)***, to go to sleep, to go to bed. Cf. LALA.

[**1934** C.P. SWART Supplement to Pettman. 42 *Doedoe*, An onomatopoeic word used by Afrikaans-speaking mothers when children are lulled to sleep. The term is also used as a verb signifying to sleep.] **1970** J. LENTON *Informant, Orkney* Do-doo. Sleep (slang). **1972** on Radio South Africa 17 Oct. (Children's Programme), Doe-doe my baby, Doe-doe my darling, Sleep, little sleepy-head. **1989** M. CEH *Informant, Johannesburg*, I must actually go doedoes now; I'm very tired, only got back after 12 last night. **1990** *Informant, Grahamstown* Time to go *doedoebyes*, my baby.

Hence **doedoe** *n.*, a sleep, a nap.

1991 V. WARREN *Informant, Alberton* Don't make a noise, the baby is having a doedoe.

doek /dʊk, duk/ *n.* Also **dook, douk**. [S. Afr. Du., fr. Du. *doek* cloth.]

1. *obs.* A cloth or handkerchief.

1798 LADY A. BARNARD *Lett. to Henry Dundas* (1973) 145, I offered her four schellings or a dook, viz. a handkerchief; she preferred the last. **1899** *Natal Agric. Jrnl* 31 Mar. 4 English colonists .. often use such words as 'lepel,' spoon; .. 'doek,' cloth; and 'roer' .. for firearms of all descriptions. **1912** W. WESTRUP *Land of To-Morrow* 100 'Stringy old fowl. It's probably one he swopped a dook for.' 'A dook?' 'A sixpenny handkerchief.' **1913** C. PETTMAN *Africanderisms* 147 *Doek*, .. A dish-clout. **1947** H. KUPER in *Vandag* Vol.1 No.8, 2 The tears stopped, and from her canvas bag she took a large new yellow doek with which she blew her nose.

2. A headscarf or kerchief, tied about the head in any of several ways; DOEKIE; KOPDOEK.

1852 H. WARD *Jasper Lyle* 12 To the family party were now added three or four Hottentot servant-girls, their woolly locks concealed beneath bright-coloured *douks* (head-kerchiefs). **1894** E. GLANVILLE *Fair Colonist* 89 A fat, black cook, with a coloured dook about her head, made a sudden swoop upon the dog with a shrill cry of 'voetsack'. **1927** D. FAIRBRIDGE *Lett. from Cape by Lady Duff-Gordon* 50 They were scandalized at the uncovered head of the pretty, graceful Malay girls, and .. they sailed away leaving every woman's head covered with a 'dook' — a brilliant silk handkerchief, preferably orange or magenta, folded with consummate care over a framework which rests on the head. **1941** M.G. GILBERT *Informant, Cape Town* 2 Dec. 4, I washed my hair after breakfast .. so I had to put a doek on, & went like that. **1948** O. WALKER *Kaffirs Are Lively* 76 Several tall Herero women of fine bearing .. distinguished by their bright yellow-and-red silk turbans, or *doeks*. **1954** P. ABRAHAMS *Tell Freedom* 59 Common to all the women, African and Coloured, was the *doek*. This was the kerchief they wore over their heads. It was an institution ... It was usually white, and always spotlessly clean. It was tied so that it covered all the hair. **1962** M. BRANDEL-SYRIER *Black Woman* 27 It is these women, the full-bosomed, aproned matrons of our townships with their *doeks* tightly framing their strong-boned faces, who come together every Thursday in their *Manyanos*. **1971** *Post* 24 Oct. 33 (*advt*) Plain doeks R2.40 a doz. Plain Nylon doeks Extra large R2.70 a doz. And printed Rayon doeks R3.25 a doz. **1973** P.A. WHITNEY *Blue Fire* 53 The cook, a small, brown-skinned woman with a doek about her head — the white kerchief draped in the special manner of South Africa — came in to ask about lunch. **1985** M. TLALI in *Fair Lady* 26 June 105 Those who had spare *doeks* passed them over to her to make slings to support broken or swollen arms. **1990** J. NAIDOO *Coolie Location* 91 A hardy African woman, with her doek-covered head, looking dashed and defiant. **1992** S. GUTKNECHT in *Sunday Times* 19 Apr. (Mag. Sect.) 28 That scarf-thing women wear over the heads, the doek.

3. *comb.* **doek-pudding**, ‖**doek-poeding** /-ˌpudəŋ/ [Afk., *poeding* pudding], a steamed pudding, boiled in a cloth.

1964 L.G. GREEN *Old Men Say* 133 They carry the old Cape cuisine in their heads, from *frikkadel* and *sosaties* to *geelrys* and *doekpudding*. [**1969** *Sunday Times* 23 Nov. (Advt Suppl.), Outydse Doekpoeding (Steamed Pudding) ... Pour mixture onto greased muslin cloth ... Tie ends tightly with string leaving about 3" space to rise.] **1978** M. VAN BILJON in *Ibid.* 24 Dec. (Branford), Our cook Ai Nettie Pekeur's stupendous 'doekpoeding' made with grated carrots.

doekie /ˈdʊki, ˈduki/ *n.* [Afk., *doek* see DOEK + dim. suffix -IE.] DOEK sense 2.

1953 *Drum* Sept. 3 Doekies off — smart hats on — that's the spring motto of modern women. **1963** B. MODISANE *Blame Me on Hist.* (1986) 29 Young girls .. wearing black shawls or wrapped in blankets, wearing black doekies, head scarves or black berets. **1979** *Het Suid-Western* 12 Sept., Everything about the baking of those cakes is immaculately hygienic — from the doekie Mrs Wilma wears around her hair to the sterilising of all the implements used. **1985** A. TREDGOLD *Bay between Mountains* 80 The women in bright skirts .. topped by a pretty blouse and an embroidered 'doekie'. **1990** G. SLOVO *Ties of Blood* 279 Moses could see the heads of the people ... , the women's *doekies* bobbing up and down as they gossiped.

doekom var. DOEKUM.

doeksteen *n. Obs. Mineralogy.* [S. Afr. Du., 'asbestos', fr. Du. *doek* cloth + *steen* stone.] Blue asbestos, a fibrous variety of riebeckite mined as a source of asbestos. Cf. HAWK'S-EYE.

[**1815** J. CAMPBELL *Trav. in S. Afr.* 272 We had a little boy, named Dookstens, (or Asbestos,) travelling with us.] **1822** W.J. BURCHELL *Trav.* I. 333 A production of these mountains, which, observing to have the singular property of becoming, on being rubbed between the fingers, a soft cotton-like substance, resembling that which they made from their old handkerchiefs for the purpose of tinder, they have named Doeksteen. (Handkerchief-stone, or Cloth-stone) ... The Doeksteen is a kind of Asbestos, of a blue color ... I made a drawing of the remarkable laminated rocks, between the thin horizontal layers of which it is found. **1912** *E. London Dispatch* 17 May 6 (Pettman), The blue asbestos mountains (*Doeksteen* of the Hottentots) just opposite Prieska. **1913** C. PETTMAN *Africanderisms* 147 *Doeksteen*, .. The by no means inappropriate Dutch name for the Blue crocidolite.

‖**doekum** /ˈdʊk(ə)m, ˈduk-/ *n.* Also **dhukkum, doekom, dukum, dukun**. [ad. Afk. *doekoem, doekom* (Du. *doekoen*), fr. Malay *dukun* traditional doctor, midwife.] In the Cape Malay community: a traditional healer or medicine man; cf. SLAMAAIER sense 2.

1963 K. MACKENZIE *Dragon to Kill* 246 Maria .. insisted on putting some small pieces of rag under Tony's mattress which she had got from her *doekum* and which always had a miraculous effect on boils. **1964** *Drum* Nov. 21 At the time of the murder, .. fortune tellers had read their cards, doekums had burned their incense and witchdoctors had thrown their bones. **1966** I.D. DU PLESSIS *Poltergeists* 46 The potential *dukun* (medicine man) must walk round the grave three times, calling on the murdered man by name and repeating a certain Malay formula. **1971** L.G. GREEN *Taste of S.-Easter* 146 A dukun buried egg-shells with magic words under the wicket before a cricket match to ensure victory for the team of his choice. **1979** P. MILLER *Myths & Legends* 72 Some dukuns become very proficient in their trade ... They are often called to exorcise the many stone-throwing poltergeists which seem to pester the Malays. **1980** *Cape Times* 12 Sept. 4 'Doekoms' (witchdoctors) were often consulted either to make a court sentence less severe or to make a job easier ... When I was out on bail, the 'doekom' gave me a small thing ... He told me I must rub it with my fingers every time the magistrate talked to me. **1986** A. ADAM in *Cape Herald* 25 Jan. 4 They have shown a peculiar blindness to problems which should concern them most, such as .. superstitious beliefs such as 'dukums' (many Imams are 'dukums' themselves).

‖**doemela-klontjie** /ˈduməlaˌklɔɪŋki, ˈdʊ-, -ci/ *n.* Also **dumily-klontje, duminy klontjie**. [Afk., *doemela* (unkn.) + *klontjie* a small lump (of sugar).] A traditional boiled sweet, flavoured with aniseed. Also *ellipt.* **doemela**.

1947 L.G. GREEN *Tavern of Seas* 72 There were burnt almonds, bossuiker (a sort of sugar-stick), the aniseed flavoured dumily-klontjes and almond rock. **1968** K. MCMAGH *Dinner of Herbs* 4 There were duminy klontjies, there were sugar sticks. **1971** B. TAUTE in *Std Encycl. of Sn. Afr.* IV. 615 The culinary heritage includes sweets such as 'doemela-klontjies' (boiled, pulled, crisp sweets delicately flavoured and coloured). **1973** *Fair Lady* 26 Dec. 120 The old *wakis* was filled to the brim with *soet-* and *rooi-bolus koekies*; and there were *doemalas* — delicious, pepperminty home-made sugar sticks.

doepa /ˈdupa, -pə/ *n.* Also **dupa**. Pl. unchanged, or **-s**. [Afk., fr. Malay *dupa* incense.]

1. A love potion or magic potion, either taken by mouth or worn as an amulet, and believed to give the user luck and power.

Orig. used of gum benzoin (see sense 2 below), the word now applies to a variety of herbs and balsams.

1857 'KU'EEP' in *Cape Monthly Mag.* I. June 369 There is .. a belief among them that any one who is in possession of 'Doepa,' or Gum Benzoin, can work with and tame the best oxen. **1864** T. BAINES *Explor. in S.-W. Afr.* 425 His chief object .. at present was to get us to make him dupas, or pastilles, Snyman having told him the tales current among the Malays at the Cape respecting their efficacy as love charms or other surgical properties. **1934** C.P. SWART Supplement to Pettman. 42 *Doepa*, (Malay doepa, incense). A Malay love potion. **1948** E. HELLMANN *Rooiyard* 64 Zulu mothers, in their fear of the .. '*Basotho* sickness' take the most elaborate precautions to ensure the well-being of their babies ... A herb, *dupa*, is sewn into a braid and put around his neck. **1966** I.D. DU PLESSIS *Poltergeists* 53 The use of *dupa* for the same purpose [*sc.* of attracting a girl] is another popular belief. *Dupa* is a Malay word for incense; but in this connection it is used for a love potion which is given to the desired one. **1970** J.F. PRINSLOO *Informant, Lüderitz (Namibia)* Doepa. A mixture of so-called magic power placing the user under a spell. Also a formula used by anglers in their bait to attract the fish. **1978** A.P. BRINK *Rumours of Rain* 235 Next week I'm rounding up all the women again for injections. No use giving them the pill, they just throw it away or carry it in a bag round their necks for doepa. **1989** *Sunday Times* 29 Oct. 3 Mr J— accused Mr B— of giving Miss J— a magic potion (doepa) to make her besotted with him, and threatened to get a Malay diviner to lift the spell on his daughter.

2.a. Gum benzoin, a patent medicine used, either as a powder or in small pieces, for colic and flatulence. See also *(old) Dutch medicine* (DUTCH *adj.* sense 2).

1919 *Dunell, Ebden & Co.'s Price List* Oct. 20 Doepa 3/6. **a1970** *Lennon's Dutch Medicine Handbk*, *Doepa*, This preparation gives relief in cases of wind, flatulence and colic and can be taken for minor kidney and bladder complaints. **1972** [see sense b]. **1988** S. VOLLENHOVEN in *Frontline* Apr. 11 She never takes modern medicine. The chest of drawers is decorated with Duiwel's Drek, Doepa and many other little Heynes Mathew bottles. **1989** D. SMUTS *Folk Remedies* 25 Colic: Crush doepa finely: 1/4 teaspoon taken 3 times a day.

b. *comb.* **doepa-olie** /-ˌʊəlɪ/ *n.* [Afk., *olie* oil], gum benzoin or balsam of Peru, used for chest ailments and as an ointment for the treatment of wounds.

1919 *Dunell, Ebden & Co.'s Price List* Oct. 20 Doepa Olie, 2 dram 5/-. **a1970** *Lennon's Dutch Medicine Handbk*, *Doepa-olie*, A useful remedy for coughs, croup and bronchitis ... Externally, mixed with lard, it is a useful antiseptic ointment. **1972** N. SAPEIKA in *Std Encycl. of Sn Afr.* VII. 302 A list of .. traditional remedies .. includes bloedstillende druppels (tincture of ferric perchloride), boegoe-essens (tincture of buchu), doepa (benzoin), doepa-olie (balsam of Peru), [etc.].

doer /duːr/ *adv.* [Afk., yonder, far away.] In the adv. phrr. ***daar doer*** /dɑː(r)'duːr/ [Afk., *daar* there], ***doer and gone*** (*slang*), also ***doer 'n gone***, [by analogy with Eng. *hell and gone*]: very far away. See also *moer and gone* (MOER *n.*² sense 2).

1972 *Informant* It's doer and gone over there – we'll never get there in time. **1975** *Sunday Times* 3 Aug. 18 Daar doer in the Cape the Taalfees .. is once again racked by a row over who shall sit with whom at the opening of the R1-million Taal monument at Paarl. *Ibid.* 21 Sept. 20 Daar doer in the Free State this week, for example, was Senator van der S— .. reassuring the political flat-earthers. **1981** *Rand Daily Mail* 28 Apr. 14 A couple of years ago I had the privilege of being a witness to South Africa's first atom bomb experiment *daar doer* in the Kalahari. **1987** *Informant, Grahamstown*, I walked doerandgone up the hill and then back into town. **1993** A. HESS *Informant, Alberton* We came over the ridge and there doer-and-gone in the valley were the 'professional hikers' – they had lost their way. **1993** P.S. WALTERS *Informant, Grahamstown* The college was doer and gone over the hill.

Hence **doer and gone** *n. phr.*, a great distance.

1985 T. BARON in *Frontline* Feb. 30 Port Nolloth is to doer and gone and cold and wet and windy and there are sullen fishermen who have named their boats P.A.Y.E. [**1993** D. KRAMER on M-Net TV, (*advt*) A farm called Doer-and-Gone.] **1994** *Informant, Grahamstown* 'Is he a local guy?' 'No, he's from doer 'n gone.'

dof /dɔf/ *adj. colloq.* [Afk.] Stupid, dull, 'dim'; uninformed. See also SIMPEL.

1979 M. ANDERSON in *Sunday Times* 21 Oct. (Mag. Sect.) 1 *Dof* is being out of it. **1985** *Woman's Value* Mar., I think Popshop is pretty dof in its whole approach, from a totally bloodless mode of presentation .. to the sometimes dubious choice of canned 'popular' music. **1986** *Informant, Durban* Don't be dof, can't you see what he's going for? **1987** *Fair Lady* 21 Jan. 144 'Where've you been for the last 15 years?' said the exasperated one. 'You're just *dof*.' **1989** A. DONALDSON in *Style* Feb. 125 Good ideas for parties are .. black tie swing era things where everybody gets very bored very quickly with the *dof* selection of taped Glenn Miller standards. **1991** C.L. WARD *Informant, Cape Town* Dof (adj.), dim (applied to intellect). It's dof to boil an egg for 30 seconds and think that it'll be hard-boiled. **1992** J. KHUMALO in *Pace* Sept. 19 Mention the name Joseph Shabalala and Black Mambazo to some *dof*, not-so-clued-up foreigners and suddenly images spring to their minds. **1993** *Sunday Times* 4 Apr. 21 After two years .. , researchers at Cardiff University have come to the conclusion that parrots are no smarter than pigeons ... Polly may be pretty, but he's also pretty *dof*.

Hence **dof** *n.*, DOFFIE.

1991 *Informant, Durban* That girl is so thick, she doesn't have a brain in her head. What a dof! **1991** [see DOFFIE].

doffie /'dɔfi/ *n. colloq.* [DOF + Eng. (informal) n.-forming suffix *-ie*.] A dim-witted person, an idiot.

1991 H.C. WATTS *Informant, Cape Town* If you can't put 2 and 2 together and make 4 you must be an utter dof/doffie/nerd. **1991** C.L. WARD *Informant, Cape Town* You're a doffie if you boil an egg for thirty seconds and think it'll be hard-boiled.

dog's meat *n. phr.* [See quot. 1963.] In urban (esp. township) English: an ironic name given to inferior meat of the cheapest cut, as bought for servants by employers; cf. the offensive expression *boy's meat* (see BOY sense 1 c). Also *attrib.*

1963 B. MODISANE *Blame Me on Hist.* (1986) 56 It was the luxury we called 'dog's meat', from the stories told around the locations that kitchen girls served their boy friends dishes prepared from the rations for the dogs, which were fed more nutritiously than the children of the locations. [**1980** J. COCK *Maids & Madams* 71 Domestic workers are also called inyama yezinja, 'dog's meat', by workers in other occupational roles, for it is said that employers tend to buy them inexpensive and 'horrid' meat, and/or because they receive insufficient food and meat.] **1985** J. MAKUNGA in *Staffrider* Vol.6 No.2, 36 He crept towards Tsidi's 'dog's-meat' home, so-called because when the maddie went shopping, part of the meat she bought was allotted the servant. 'These fucking dogs live and eat better than we do.' **1988** E. MPHAHLELE *Renewal Time* 187 A boy who had a girl-friend in the kitchens, .. always told his friends that he was coming for dog's meat when he meant he was visiting his girl. This was because we gave our boy-friends part of the meat the white people bought for the dogs and us.

‖**doh-die** /'dəʊdaɪ/ *n.* Also **dodai**, **do-die**, and with initial capital. [Etym. unkn.] The winning number in a game of FAH-FEE.

1956 L. LONGMORE in *S. Afr. Jrnl of Science* Vol.52 No.12, 277 There are 36 numbers in all, 3 of which are called 'stops' or Dodais ... This is Saturday, so the numbers which came on Wednesday, Thursday and Friday are the 'stops'. Thursday and Friday numbers cannot come; Wednesday's may be the remote possibility. **1973** M. PHILLIPS *Catchee Chinaman*, Thirty-six numbers – each of them .. a possible Do-Die or winning number – The Do-die is written on a tiny slip of paper which is taken from the red lacquer box each evening by the Fah Fee King – or Die China who is the banker. **1980** R. GOVENDER *Lahnee's Pleasure* 28 Sunny: .. What's doh-die today? Johnny: Thirty-six.

doka var. DAGGA *n.*²

dolf /dɔlf, dɒlf/ *n.* Also **dolph**, and with initial capital. [Named for a 19th century cabinet-maker, *Dolf Labuschagne*.] Esp. in Namibia: KIAAT. Also *attrib.*

1975 *S. Afr. Panorama* June 22 These artists can chop the wood for their work literally at their doorstep ... Their favourite is red Dolph wood which is ideal for carving purposes. **1976** O. LEVINSON *Story of Namibia* 64 Kavango was the most fortunate of the homelands as far as water was concerned ... Timber is a promising industry with the beautiful 'dolf' and 'usivi' (chivi) trees. **1979** *S. Afr. Digest* 16 Nov. 3 A sawmill at Rundu, built to help conserve indigenous trees and supply wood to the local carving industry ... Only Dolf wood, .. Rhodesian teak and usivi (*guibortia coleosperma*) are used. **1984** R.J. POYNTON *Characteristics & Uses of Sel. Trees* 127 Dolf, *Pterocarpus angolensis*.

dollar *n. obs.* A monetary unit formerly in use at the Cape: **a.** Ellipt. for RIX-DOLLAR. **b.** *transf.* An amount of 1s. 6d. (one shilling and sixpence), the value of the rixdollar during the 1840s when it was withdrawn from circulation. See also RIJKSDAALDER.

1772 G. FORSTER *Voy. round World* I. 71 The company allows the sum of forty dollars for each leagre, of which the farmer receives but twenty-four. **1786** [see SCHELLING]. **1795** J.H. CRAIG in G.M. Theal *Rec. of Cape Col.* (1897) I. 271, I have .. given him 500 Rixdollars ... A dollar is about four shillings. **1801** [see BAAKEN sense 1]. **1809** [see ERFPACHT]. **1809** 'G. VALENTIA' *Voy. & Trav.* I. 32 Our host profitably refused to make any charge for us or our horses; .. we gave him fifteen dollars for the party. **1819** H. GOSLING in G.M. Theal *Rec. of Cape Col.* (1902) XII. 303, I have paid him a dollar when I could get them elsewhere for 4 skillings. **1820** J. HANCOCK Diary. 24 June, Mr Sephton owes me for stores 38 Dollars. **1832** *Graham's Town Jrnl* 16 Feb. 31 The wagon, oxen, two asses, (that Mr D. had just purchased for 400 dollars) .. were immediately carried away .. by the stream. **1847** 'A BENGALI' *Notes on Cape of G.H.* 65 The Hotels are expensive ... Formerly the best resident families took in strangers at a dollar a day. **1866** J. LEYLAND *Adventures* 3 At this time there was a fine of forty to fifty dollars inflicted on any persons known to destroy one of these birds. **1882** C. DU VAL *With Show through Sn Afr.* I. 84 The ordinary price of a cabbage is from 1s to 1s. 6d, or a 'dollar', as the latter amount is colonially called. **1893** *Brown's S. Afr.* 15 The local terms 'tikkie' and 'dollar' frequently heard, represent respectively 3d. and 1s 6d. **1910** R. JUTA *Cape Peninsula* 27 When slaves landed at the Cape, they cost from a hundred and twenty to a hundred and fifty dollars (i.e., rixdollars) each, that being about £22.10s to £27.10s. **1913** C. PETTMAN *Africanderisms* 148 *Dollar*, A term often used in South Africa for one shilling and sixpence. **1914** [see RIJKSDAALDER]. **1949** L.G. GREEN *In Land of Afternoon* 102 You still hear one and sixpence referred to as a dollar at the Cape. This may be traced back to a government notice of 1825 in which the people of the Cape were informed that they could exchange British silver money for the new paper rix-dollars at the rate of one shilling and sixpence for each rix-dollar.

dollas var. DOLOS.

dollie /'dɒli/ *n.* Also **doll(e)y**. [Etym. unkn.] A fishing lure, used usu. for catching snoek.

1930 C.L. BIDEN *Sea-Angling Fishes* 136 A few strands of strong flexible wire, 2 or 3 feet long, connect the line by a swivel to a cigar-shaped lead, to which is attached a barbless steel hook of 10/0 size. Three or four thin strips of shark leather (shark skin) or ribbon are tied to the shank, thus completing the lure or 'dolly' as the fishermen term it. **1934** *Cape Argus* 19 May (Swart), This 'dollie' or 'bokspan' is fixed on to a short length of flexible copper wire, the end of which is attached to a stout line. **1957** S. SCHOEMAN *Strike!* 117 Professional fishermen catch thousands [of snoek] on 'dollies', which are cigar-shaped pieces of lead .. with a large barbless hook attached. A few thin strips of shark skin or pork rind or even a piece of red rag or silver paper is tied to the shank of the hook. **1979** *E. Prov. Herald* 15 Nov. 23 One of them, whose skiboat we were fishing from, put down a chokka dolley. He did not get any chokka but he had a tremendous take on the dolley.

dolloss var. DOLOS.

dolly var. DOLLIE.

dolos /'dɔlɔs/ *n.* Also **dollas**, **doll oss**. Pl. unchanged, or **-se** /-sə/, **-ses**, and formerly **-sen**. [Etym. unknown; recorded in 19th century Afk. (1880) as *dollossie* knuckle-bone, perh. ad. of *dobbelos* (fr. Du. *dobbel* to gamble + *os* ox); or fr. *dol* mad, wild, or *dollen* to romp about + *os* ox; or perh. ad. of medical term *talus* knuckle-bone. Found in modern Xhosa as *dolosi* dice, divining bones (cf. older Xhosa *indawule* divining bones).] **1.** One of a set of carved divining dice, knuckle-bones of various animals, and other objects used by a traditional healer in divination; BONE sense 1; DOLOSSIE sense 2. Also *attrib.* See also *to throw (the) bones* (THROW sense 2).

[**1860** J. SANDERSON in *Jrnl of Royal Geog. Soc.* XXX. 243, I had here a specimen of native divination, performed by casting on the ground four pieces of bone, or horn, of several shapes .. called altogether 'daula.'] **1873** *Queenstown Free Press* 9 Sept., A Kafir Doctor gave a lecture to an admiring audience ... The subject .. was .. the merits of two 'dol ossen,' two shank bones of a sheep and sundry paraphernalia which lay spread out before him. **1897** J.P. FITZPATRICK *Outspan* 98 An old fellow, a witch-doctor, brought the pocket-book. He said he found it by divination – casting the dollas. **1901** D.M. WILSON *Behind Scenes in Tvl* 85 No reference to Kaffir lore would be complete without an allusion to the doll oss, or fetish used by the witch doctors in the practice of divination. Throwing the doll oss is the Kaffir equivalent to consulting the cards. **1905** *Native Tribes of Tvl* 126 The most familiar 'properties' of the witch-doctors are the 'knuckle-bones', known to the natives as 'daula' and to the Boers as 'dolos'. They may consist of pieces of bone, or wood or stones or almost any substance. They are much in evidence whenever a witch-doctor is consulted, as from the manner in which the bones fall when thrown, he decides the answer to the question asked him. **1937** C.R. PRANCE *Tante Rebella's Saga* 186 Each night the Kafir had said that the spirits would not let his 'doloss' talk to him tonight, so that they had to pay again every night. **1941** N. DEVITT *Celebrated S. Afr. Crimes* 161 At the woman's request he had given her a love potion ... He had also thrown cards and dolossen, in order to discover if he did love her. **1947** F.C. SLATER *Sel. Poems* 30 The Rain-maker manipulated His dry dolosses in vain. **1958** S. CLOETE *Mask* 89 He turned out his bones, his *dolos* as they are called ... Most of them were the *astragalis* or the knuckle-bones of various animals ... But there were also cowrie shells, two ancient ceramic beads, an oblong of ivory, a double marula pip, the pyramid points of ox hoofs, stones from the stomach of the crocodile, hair balls from calves and the beak of a vulture. **1974** A.P. BRINK *Looking on Darkness* 230 He opened his grey-striped bag of wildcat skin, and shook out his smelly *dolos*-bones to read our fortunes. **1982** *Drum* Mar. 38 Turf history has no record of all punters backing the winner. Could all these pluralstanians have been to the same inyanga whose dol osse had predicted the winner? **1985** J. MASON in *Cosmopolitan* May 154 My consultation had begun. The child .. gave me a greasy leather pouch containing the bones. 'You are to blow your spirit into the bag, then throw the *dolos* on to the grass mat,' I was instructed. **1994** G. PRETORIUS in *Weekend Post* 14 May 5 We throw the *dolosse* (a bag containing an assortment of bones, shells, domino pieces and coins) and then tell them what the problem is.

2.a. The knuckle-bones (or vertebrae) of sheep or goats, formerly used by children as imaginary oxen and in other games; any other bones used similarly; DOLOSSIE sense 1 a. Also *attrib.*

[**1900** B.M. HICKS *Cape as I Found It* 151 Out of his [*sc.* the traditional doctor's] bag he took his *doll-oxen* as the bones are called that the children play with.] **1965** C. VAN HEYNINGEN *Orange Days* 14 We put empty cotton reels on sardine tins .. and we inspanned 'dolosse' (sheep vertebrae) .. and we spent many happy hours carting sand and stones in them to build little houses. **1977** *Weekend Post* 23 Apr. (Suppl.) 5 Made of an ox jawbone, it has 'dolosse' (knuckle joints) to serve as oxen with each ox named for his place in the team. **1989** D. BRISCOE in *Motorist* Nov. 4 Whether it's the massive sombre hearse of bygone days or a bar of homemade soap or a child's 'dolosse' wagon, there's a story to be told.

b. Any of several games formerly played by children, using the knuckle-bones of sheep or goats; DOLOSSIE sense 1 b.

1974 J.M. COETZEE *Dusklands* 122 The farmer's son and the servant's son playing *dolosse* together in the yard graduating with adulthood into the more austere relation of master and servant.

3. *Engineering.* [So called fr. its resemblance to a knuckle- or ankle-bone (see quots 1970 and 1976).] A large concrete anchor block which, when interlocked with other identical blocks, prevents erosion of the coastline and of harbour walls.

1970 E. MERRIFIELD in *Daily Dispatch* 25 Mar. 29, I wanted a name for the interlocking blocks that would always identify them with South Africa. I chose the name dolosse myself because the shape I designed reminded me of those little bones taken from the ankles of animals that Voortrekker children used to play with, pretending they were oxen (hence the name) and which are still used today by African witchdoctors when they 'throw the bones.' **1970** *Ibid.* 9 Oct. 13 Mr Merrifield produced the first prototype dolos seven years ago. The block has since proved to be five to six times more stable than any other block in use in the world and also 40 percent cheaper to manufacture and handle. **1976** *Illust. London News* (U.K.) Nov. 24 The outer wall of the eastern coffer dam faces the South China Sea, which stretches unbroken for thousands of miles to South America. Huge concrete *dolosse* protect the dam, absorbing the force of the breakers .. each weighing 25 tons and shaped like a giant letter H with one arm twisted through 90°. **1982** *E. Prov. Herald* 1 June 4 (*caption*) This young fishing party took advantage of mild winter weather for a spot of angling from Port Elizabeth's artificial rocks, the dolosse. **1989** *Stanger Mail* 7 July 8 Another freak accident happened at the Dolosses at Richards Bay recently. An angler was casting when an onlooker popped his head from behind one of the dolosses. **1990** *E. Prov. Herald* 16 Oct. 4 Van Greunen .. was fishing from the 'dolosse' at 3.30pm.

dolossie /ˈdɔlɔsi/ *n.* Also **dol' ossi**. [Afk., *dolos* see DOLOS + dim. suffix -IE.]

1.a. DOLOS sense 2 a.

1912 F. BANCROFT *Veldt Dwellers* 2 Upon their skill as marksmen the number of *dol'ossi* — which to farm children in South Africa represent cattle, *i.e.* wealth — depended. The fundamental rule of the game was that each marksman should aim at the coveted toy *with closed eyes*. If successful in hitting the *dol'ossi* .., the treasured ivory-joint became his. **1955** V. DE KOCK *Fun They Had* 65 Using the metatarsal and metacarpal bones of sheep and goats as their dolossies or oxen, the little boys pulled their tiny wagons over hurriedly-made hills and along dangerous precipices. **1969** D. CHILD *Yesterday's Children* 40 A whole team of these oxen would be 'inspanned' to a toy wagon made of sticks and reeds. The metatarsal and metacarpal bones of sheep and goats were also used as *dolossies* or miniature oxen.

b. DOLOS sense 2 b.

1913 C. PETTMAN *Africanderisms* 148 *Dollossi*, A game played by children with the small sheep or goat bones above mentioned. **1955** V. DE KOCK *Fun They Had* 65 Many of the early visitors to South Africa have remarked on the game played with such obvious enjoyment by farm children, and called by them *dolossies*.

2. DOLOS sense 1.

1967 O. WALKER *Hippo Poacher* 72 You should find out what your *dolossies* (bones) say to free him of the spells of witchcraft that beset him here.

dolph var. DOLF.

dom /dɔm/ *adj. colloq.* [Afk.]

a. Stupid, foolish. So comparative form **dommer**, superlative form **domste** /ˈdɔmstə/ [Afk.], or **dommest**. See also DOMKOP, SIMPEL.

[*a***1878** J. MONTGOMERY *Reminisc.* (1981) 88 The people had to help me off the wagon. They were very kind and did all they could to relieve the pain, although they called me a domme Engelsman (a stupid Engelsman).] **1942** S. CLOETE *Hill of Doves* 635 *Dom*, Foolish. **1949** C. BULLOCK *Rina* 35, I would gladly apologise if I had been too forward in any way ... I consulted Piet .., but he rudely said that it was just that I was dom. **1968** F.G. BUTLER *Cape Charade* 66 Andrew Geddes Bain Was very very dom To think he could placate his wife With sommer a botterblom. **1973** D.A.C. MACLENNAN in *Bolt* No.7, 20 George is just as dom as the rest of us. We all bloody dom. **1980** J. SCOTT in *Daily Dispatch* 27 Feb. 13 He accused Dr S— of being much dommer than Mr Colin E—, of being, in fact, the domste Leader of the Opposition. The Speaker asked Mr P— to stop repeating his allegation that the Leader of the Opposition was dom. *Ibid.* 17 Oct. 10 You're a bit dom this afternoon, if you don't mind my saying so. **1987** C. GUTUZA in *South* 9 July 3 When I asked him why he was beating my wife, he replied: 'Keep quiet, you dom Kaffir.' **1989** *E. Prov. Herald* 17 Feb. 1 One of the white policemen told them, 'Don't be dom, there is money for you. We must finish the UDF.' **1990** A. MAIMANE in *Weekly Mail* 8 Feb. 11 His manner was that of a lecturer instructing *dom* — dim — students. **1991** [see DIK sense 2]. **1994** *Informant, Grahamstown* He's the dommest boy in our class.

‖**b.** In the phr. ***dom astrant*** /ˌdɔm aˈstrant/ [Afk., *astrant* bold, impudent], deliberately uncooperative. So **dom astrantheid** /-heɪt/ [Afk., n.-forming suffix *-heid* -hood], cussedness, perversity.

1978 *Sunday Times* 9 Apr. 16 Did the arrogance and self-centred righteousness of the Fifties and Sixties last too long? Can the tide of international hostility aroused by a generation of dom-astrantheid still be stemmed? **1982** *Sunday Times* 25 Apr. 26 As Willem de Klerk says: 'It is reckless, dom astrant, incredulous, unpatriotic, even criminal, to pretend in the face of such irrefutable facts that South Africa can simply continue as in the past.'

domba /ˈdɔmba/ *n.* Also **dhomba**, and with initial capital. [Venda.]

1. The period of initiation of young Venda girls into womanhood; the rites associated with this initiation; the dance performed during these rites (see sense 2 below). Also *attrib.* See also BOYALE.

1931 H.A. STAYT *BaVenda* 309 The python dance of the *domba*, which has been described as a probable fertility rite, is made clearer when the beliefs concerning drought are understood. **1932** N.J. VAN WARMELO *Contribution towards Venda Hist.* (Dept of Native Affairs) 52 The *Domba* is held only at the kraals of chiefs. At intervals of about three or four years all girls who have attained the age of puberty must be brought thither, and remain there to dance the *Domba* ... Boys are also required to join in the dancing but are bullied less, and the *Domba* appears primarily a rite for females. **1964** B. TYRRELL in *Natal Mercury* 1 Oct., Domba is initiation for marriage of Venda girlhood. **1976** WEST & MORRIS *Abantu* 96 (*caption*) Most famous of Venda rituals is the *domba*, or girls' initiation rite. This can last three months or more during which time the girls live in special villages and use words secret to the *domba*. **1976** [see PYTHON DANCE]. **1982** *Pace* Feb. 110 The unending months of the *domba*, the initiation rites which today are still a general preparation for womanhood and marriage for some Venda women ... The girls .. would be divided into work parties to work the fields of the chief. Thus the *domba* was a valuable source of labour as well. **1987** J. QUEST *Burning River* 36 'You do not know the *domba*?' Dirk shook his head. Takalani looked surprised. 'Nor the python dance, then, I suppose. It comes after the *vhusha*, the girls' first initiation. The *domba* comes later on when they are ready for marriage. Every day they do the python dance in the honour of the ancestors and to obtain their favour ... When the time of the *domba* is over, they are women, ready to be married.' **1989** *Flying Springbok* Oct. 166 *Domba* figures made by Nelson Mukhuba (used ritually as teaching aids in girls' initiation ceremonies).

2. *comb.* **domba dance**, PYTHON DANCE.

1932 N.J. VAN WARMELO *Contribution towards Venda Hist.* (Dept of Native Affairs) 63 To the accompaniment of several drums, .. they begin to dance the peculiar *Domba* dance, moving slowly forward step by step and swaying from side to side. **1948** O. WALKER *Kaffirs Are Lively* 80 The *dhomba* dances are one of the real heathen spectacles of Vendaland ... and are really initiation dances for girls crossing over from puberty to womanhood. **1964** B. TYRRELL in *Natal Mercury* 1 Oct., To the python is dedicated the mysterious Domba dance, performed by a slow-moving line of chanting initiates. **1979** P. MILLER *Myths & Legends* 135 The ritual python, or *domba*, dance performed by girls preparing for marriage.

domboek /ˈdɔmbʊk, -buk/ *n. Hist. colloq.* [Afk., *dom* stupid + *boek* book.] DOMBOOK. Also *attrib.*

1971 *Informant, Grahamstown* That master said I must come again tomorrow and bring my mother's domboek. **1973** W.R.G. BRANFORD in *E. Prov. Herald* 6 Aug. 6 A man with no domboek is not a man. **1975** *Sunday Times* 25 May 9 Look. The reference book is mine. It's my name, my picture. That 'domboek' is part of me. **1979** [see STINKER].

dombook /ˈdɔmbʊk/ *n. Hist. Colloq.* [Part. tr. of Afk. *domboek*, see prec.] A contemptuous name for a PASS (sense 3). Also *attrib.*

1966 K.M.C. MOTSISI in *Post* 30 Jan. (Drum) 18 Dompass or dom-book is the contemptuous term used by Africans in the Republic of South Africa, for an identity and job pass they are required to carry, and which is euphemistically called a Reference Book by the authorities. **1975** *Daily Dispatch* 22 Apr. 12 We will not cause them to carry dombooks, or do to them any inhuman things done to us since 1652. **1978** A.P. BRINK *Rumours of Rain* 427, I was just in time to grab my *dombook* before the water took it away. **1981** M. MUTLOATSE in *Staffrider* Vol.3 No.4, 40 Naked fright was conspicuously sculptured in his face. He was a man on the run – from the dombook police.

domela var. DUMELA.

dominee /ˈduəməni, ˈdʊə-/ *n.* Also **domin(i)e**, **dominy**, **duminy**, and with initial capital. [Du., 'clergyman', 'minister', fr. L., being the voc. case of *dominus* lord. In the earlier quots, the form 'dominie' is perh. the (chiefly Scottish) Eng. *dominie* teacher, and 'domine' the Brit. Eng. *domine* clergyman.]

Used also in *U.S. Eng.* (as 'dominie').

1. *obs.* A parish clerk, catechist, or other minor cleric in the DUTCH REFORMED churches; VOORLEZER. See also SIEKETROOSTER.

1846 J. SUTHERLAND *Memoir* II. 62 Sacrament was performed to the sick of the ship *Bull* by the domine. **1861** P.B. BORCHERDS *Auto-Biog. Mem.* 18 At the age of seven years, I was sent to a Dutch school under the Master George Knoop, the parish clerk, commonly called the Dominie. *Ibid.* 179 Previously to the minister ascending the pulpit .. the Dominie, or parish clerk, read chapters out of the Bible. **1925** H.J. MANDELBROTE tr. *O.F. Mentzel's Descr. of Cape of G.H.* II. 17 These posts include .. the upper surgeon, who .. has to have a knowledge of both medicine and surgery; the dominie or sick-comforter; and the commander of troops.

2.a. PREDIKANT sense a.

1883 M.A. CAREY-HOBSON *Farm in Karoo* 231 Look at this one [*sc.* feather], would it not make a splendid exaggeration of a quill pen for an old dominie in a charade? [**1913** C. PETTMAN *Africanderisms* 149 *Domine*, Occasionally this word is used in Cape Dutch for clergyman, minister, but most commonly he is now spoken of as the 'Predikant,' and in direct address, 'Mijnheer'.] **1948** H.C. BOSMAN in L. Abrahams *Unto Dust* (1963) 33 'I was expecting a Catholic priest,' Gertruida said ... 'But if the Lord has sent the dominie and his ouderling, instead, I am sure it will be well, also.' **1950** [see *Dopper Church* (DOPPER *n.*[1] sense b)]. **1953** A. PATON *Phalarope* (1963) 69 Before the young dominee preached, old Dominee Stander said a few words about him. **1965** C. VAN HEYNINGEN *Orange Days* 30 In those days .. they were 'predikante' and not 'dominees'. **1973** Y. BURGESS *Life to Live* 28 The Volkspele, or folk dancing, .. had been declared innocuous, even patriotic, by the dominee himself. **1980** *Sunday Times* 31 Aug. (Extra) 3 A dominee-type gentleman is there with a fixed smile. **1989** *Style* Feb. 45 Helet's father, a dominee in the N G Mission Church .. has participated in a march on Parliament. **1991** A. VAN WYK *Birth of New Afrikaner* 52 The regular communion service was conducted by our white minister ... The white *dominee* always invited some of the members of his own congregation to attend.

b. 'Minister', used: **i.** As a term of address. **ii.** With a name, as a title; Ds; PREDIKANT sense b.

1948 H.C. BOSMAN in L. Abrahams *Unto Dust* (1963) 34 We noticed that Gertruida called the predikant 'Father' now, and not 'Dominie'. **1953** [see sense a]. **1960** U. KRIGE (tr. J. van Melle) in D. Wright *S. Afr. Stories* 129 My time is up, Dominee. All I can do now is to prepare for the end. **1964** J. BENNETT *Mr Fisherman* (1967) 43 Tomorrow, if they were not home, Dominee Uys would hold a special service for the fishermen. **1979** A.P. BRINK *Dry White Season* 142 Dominee, tonight I'm coming to you like Nicodemus. I've got to talk to you. **1982** *Drum* Oct. 104 Dominee Nico Smit took a sharp left turn away from the Broederbond and Nationalist circles into the arms of a black congregation because he could find no moral justification for apartheid. **1991** *E. Prov. Herald* 22 May 1 Haven director Dominee Willie van der Merwe said .. the children would cherish the day for the rest of their lives.

domkop /ˈdɔmkɔp/ *n.* Also with initial capital. Pl. **-koppe** /-kɔpə/, formerly **-koppen**. [Afk., *dom* stupid, foolish + *kop* head.]

a. A fool, dunce. Also *attrib.*

1910 D. FAIRBRIDGE *That Which Hath Been* (1913) 134 If these *domkoppen* could but see it, they stand to make more by following his Excellency's advice than by ignoring it. **1915** —— *Torch Bearer* 204 My, but that was a close shave! .. Did you mean your domkop driver to go off without you? **1920** [see BLERRY *adj.*]. **1970** C.B. WOOD *Informant, Johannesburg* He's a real 'domkop' (stupid). **1987** *Drum* June 60 Although he is a school dropout there is no proof that he is a domkop. **1989** B. COURTENAY *Power of One* 219 Bronkhorst, you are a domkop.

b. Used as a term of address.

[**1947** C.R. PRANCE *Antic Mem.* 72 Stripped to the waist at last, Oom Jurie bobbed out to try protest again, 'Maar, Majoor, ek ...', only to be called 'domkop' or dunderhead and ordered back to take off his boots and trousers.] **1953** U. KRIGE *Dream & Desert* 87 'Must be a mad horse to stand up on its hind legs like that!' 'Not mad, *domkop*, just proud .. !' **1965** K. MACKENZIE *Deserter* 139 You told him? Oh Japie, you fool! You *domkop*! **1974** *Drum* 22 July, He had written Bantu. The official must have reached the end of his tether, because he screamed 'domkop', scratched it all out and then scribbled 'South African'. **1978** *Sunday Times* 9 Apr. (Extra) 3 You domkop. Some of the floating things have eyes and big mouths – and they are called crocodiles. **1980** C. HOPE *A Separate Development* (1983) 99 She nodded contentedly and stuck up eight fingers. *Domkop*! You tell Mama nothing. **1989** B. COURTENAY *Power of One* 36 Domkop! Don't you even know your left from your right?

dompas /ˈdɔmpas/ *n. Hist. colloq.* Also with initial capital. [Afk., *dom* stupid + *pas* pass.]

1. A contemptuous name for a PASS (sense 3). Also *attrib.*, and *transf.* See also *hamba dompas* (HAMBA sense 5).

1961 M.A. WALL (*title*) The Dominee and the Dom-Pas or, The Padre and the Passes. **1970** M.P. GWALA in *Ophir* 11 Apr. 2 Dompas! I looked back. Dompas! I went through my pockets. Not there. **1974** *Daily Dispatch* 20 July 8 The dompas, or pass, or reference book, has long been the most resented example of racial discrimination. **1982** *E. Prov. Herald* 9 Aug. 9 On August 9, 1956, a huge, silent crowd came to protest against the Government's intention of extending the hated 'dompas' to black women. **1985** *Probe* Oct. 8 The card could .. give officials instant computerised access to information about all South African residents. In this way, the pass law system could go and the plastic Dompas for all may well come in. **1986** *Drum* Aug. 55 Now that the euphoria about the death of the old dompas has waned and in its wake comes the new Book of Life .. I pay a silent requiem and give a mighty voertsek to a document known in the Pretoria files as NIN 1890222. **1989** *New Nation* 15 June 8 Imagine a dompas in the form of a magnetically-coded plastic ID card, that the police could put into a computer to find out what records they have on you. **1990** K. MKHIZE *Natal Witness* 12 Apr. (Echo) 7 It is a fight to restore apartheid and postpone .. our liberation and freedom from the *dompas* syndrome. **1993** H. TYLER in *Weekly Mail & Guardian* 9 July 29 One huge exhibit consists of a dozen or more old 'reference' books, the obligatory *dompas* Africans once had to carry at all times.

2. *comb.* **dompas system**, the system of controlling the rights of black people through the use of the dompas; cf. *pass system* (see PASS sense 4).

1979 *Daily Dispatch* 8 May 1 The Minister .. said last night he intensely disliked the 'dompas' system for blacks and that his department felt the same. **1981** *Rand Daily Mail* 24 June 1 The recommendations could include ... Doing away with the 'dompas' system by which blacks are stopped on the street and asked for their reference books. **1985** *Probe* Oct. 8 The controversial Dompas system which has resulted in the arrest of about 18 million black people since 1916, and the equally controversial section 10 practice which has kept black people out of South Africa's cities, seem to be on the way out. **1988** F. KHASHANE in *Pace* June 86 Huge sums of money were lost in running the old dompas system, revoking it and processing the so-called 'new ID for all'.

dompass /ˈdɔmpɑːs/ *n. Hist. colloq.* Also with initial capital. Pl. **-es**. [Part. tr. Afk. *dompas*, see prec.] DOMPAS sense 1.

*a*1958 K.M.C. MOTSISI in M. Mutloatse *Casey & Co.* (1978) 10 No mother's son or daughter of a bug is going to hitchhike to town in my new New Year's suit when I go to work. At least not until my 'dom pass' has worn out my inside coat pocket. **1963** M. BENSON *Afr. Patriots* 217 The Government had announced that from 1956 African women must carry passes, the 'verdomde' – accursed – 'dompass' that more than any other law in South Africa tormented Africans. **1966** [see DOMBOOK]. **1973** M.G. BUTHELEZI in *E. Prov. Herald* 15 Oct. 11 There are instances where Zulu-speaking Africans get their 'dom-passes' stamped under the influx control regulations and are told: 'Go to Gatsha, he must give you work.' **1976** *Drum* 15 May 49, I rush back home to collect my 'dom' pass. **1977** J. SIKAKANE *Window on Soweto* 25 One of the inmates will stumble around the room in search of a matchbox to light a candle and find the 'dompasses' to prove to the policemen that they are registered workers. **1980** *Cape Times* 10 July 3, 200 000 blacks had been arrested under the pass laws, despite Dr Piet Koornhof's declaration of war on the 'dompass'. **1982** *Voice* 1 Aug. 5 People who have Section 10 qualification in their dompasses will be able to work wherever they want to. They will be able to rent or buy houses and can have their wives, children and aged parents live with them. **1985** *Rand Daily Mail* 16 Apr. 5 PW Botha .. equates the identity document issued to whites, coloureds and Indians with the 'dompass' which has always to be produced by blacks on demand. **1991** *Drum* Dec. (Then & Now) 20 In 1955, women marched from Johannesburg to the Union Buildings in Pretoria to protest against having to carry dompasses.

Dom Pedro /ˌdɒm ˈpedrəʊ/ *n. phr.* Also **Don Pedro**. [Pg., *Dom* (or Sp. *Don*) sire, lord (in modern usage, mister) + *Pedro* Peter. The source of this name is uncertain: perh. named for the U.S. card-game of this name; or perh. named for the Brazilian emperor Dom Pedro II.] A drink made by blending ice cream (and sometimes cream) with whisky or a whisky liqueur; served esp. as a dessert or after-dinner drink in restaurants.

1985 *Fair Lady* 30 Oct. 142 (*advt*) Blend 2 tots Cape Velvet and 1 glass ice-cream. An indescribably smooth Don Pedro. **1986** *Grocott's Mail* 23 Dec. 2 Special desserts include Irish or Kahlua coffee, Dom Pedro or ice creams with liqueur flavourings. **1988** H. PRENDINI in *Style* June 104 The pudding will be Sal's idea of a stylish dessert, a Dom Pedro ... (Anything to which whisky is added becomes stylish.)

domsiekte /ˈdɔmsiktə/ *n. Pathology.* [Afk., *dom* stupid + *siekte* sickness; see quot. 1934.] Either of two ailments of sheep:

a. Twin pregnancy disease (see quot. 1976).

1927 *Farming in S. Afr.* Dec. 490 (Swart), There appears to be a correlation between domsiekte and droughty conditions. **1932** M.W. HENNING *Animal Diseases* 871 (Swart), Domsiekte is a disease of pregnant ewes occurring during the last few weeks of gestation, usually within a few days before lambing. **1934** C.P. SWART Supplement to Pettman. 43 *Domsiekte*, .. A new disease in pregnant ewes the cause of which is at present unknown, but it appears to be connected with the severe drought conditions that have prevailed during the last few years. Affected animals quite suddenly stop feeding, become dull and dejected, .. and may stand on one spot for hours ... A very stupid appearance is characteristic of the disease, hence the designation. **1937** *Handbk for Farmers* (Dept of Agric. & Forestry) 153 September ... Take precautions against domsiekte. **1957** *Ibid.* (Dept of Agric.) III. 463 The cause of the disease has long been a mystery, but it has been shown at Onderstepoort that if fat, heavily pregnant ewes are suddenly put on to a poor diet of dry hay they contract domsiekte within a few days. **1957** *Ibid.* [see quot. at *sprinkaanbos* (SPRINKAAN sense 2)]. **1976** MÖNNIG & VELDMAN *Handbk on Stock Diseases* 257 Twin Pregnancy Disease (Domsiekte, Pregnancy Disease) .. is caused by a sudden shortage of easily combustible carbohydrate in the body of the sheep.

b. *nonce.* Seneciosis: see DUNSIEKTE sense 1 b. Cf. MALKOP *n.* sense 1.

1990 J. GLEN-LEARY in *Farmer's Weekly* 4 May 65 The alkaloid poisons cause seneciosis (the staggers, or *domsiekte*).

donder /ˈdɔnə(r)/ *int.* and *n. Slang.* Also **don'er**, **donner**. [Afk., 'wretch'.] Not in polite use.

A. *int.* Often in the phr. *donder and bliksem* [Afk. *donder en bliksem* lit. 'thunder and lightning']: an expression of frustration or anger, equivalent to 'confound it', 'blast'. See also BLIKSEM *int.*

1863 LADY DUFF-GORDON in F. Galton *Vacation Tourists* (1864) III. 182 The hardest blows are those given with the tongue ... 'Verdomde Schmeerlap!' — 'Donder and Bliksem! am I a verdomde Schmeerlap?' **c1966** M. JABOUR in *New S. Afr. Writing* 91 Donder, now what's the matter with the thing, hey? Cohen said it was in perfect condition. **1985** *Fair Lady* 1 May 20 The vullis spread by our nation's enemies must be stood on. Donner and bliksem! **1987** S. ROBERTS *Jacks in Corners* 76 Why the *donder* must he come and visit today?

B. *n.*
1. An abusive term; a 'blighter' or 'bastard'.
a. BLIKSEM *n.* sense a.

1872 *Cape Argus* 29 Oct. 4, I told prisoner to leave off beating her, and he said he would give it me on my *donder* if I interfered. **1961** D. BEE *Children of Yesterday* 71 He said to me 'bloody bastard' then I asked him to fight but he was afraid. He was a big donder but he knew I would have thrashed him. **1969** A. FUGARD *Boesman & Lena* 36 The *pondoks* falling. The men standing, looking, as the yellow *donner* [*sc.* bulldozer] pushed them over. **1970** S. ROBERTS in *Ophir* 12 Sept. 12, I skel him out i threaten to fire the donder i must get another boy. **1973** [see GATS]. **1977** A. ROSCOE *Uhuru's Fire* 227, I will shoot whatever hotnot or kaffir I desire, and see me get into trouble over it. I demand respect from these donders. **1979** W. EBERSOHN *Lonely Place* 37 Old-boss Marthinus not hit me, I don't want the mad don'er must hit me. **1988** *E. Prov. Herald* 19 Mar. 2 Why didn't you give the donder (blighter) another shot while he was down?

b. BLIKSEM *n.* sense b.

1920 F.C. CORNELL *Glamour of Prospecting* 21 'You donder!' I heard Du Toit snort (I found later his nose was badly bashed by a bucket). 'I knew you didn't tie the verdomte touw properly.' **1954** J. WILES *Moon to Play With* 22 '*Donners*!' shouted the old woman .. '*Voetsek*!' But the children treated that as a joke. **1960** J. COPE *Tame Ox* 183 'No boat is worth a man's life,' he said, helping Stonewall up. 'Remember that, you black donner.' [**1965** E. MPHAHLELE *Down Second Ave* 43 The Black man pulled me away with a jerk that sent pain shooting through my side. 'Are you going to tell the truth, "jou donder"?' I didn't care now.] **1985** *Cape Times* 6 Nov. 2 A navy blue police van came past and someone shouted 'you are going to die you donders', and then the police opened fire. **1986** S. SEPAMLA *Third Generation* 129 The major .. towered over Solly and, screwing his mouth said: 'Stand up! Stand up, donner!'

2. In the adj. phrr. *the donder in, die donder in* [Afk., *die* the, *in* in], *the hell in* (see HELL sense 2).

1978 *Speak* Vol.1 No.2, 55 We get a theatre in Pretoria ... Mother and Father Grundy were however alive and well and Die Donner in! **1978** S. ROBERTS in *New Classic* No.5, 24, I felt the donder-in for my old friend ... Ol' Chris always used to be so full of loyalty for his language and his country.

donder *v.* var. DONNER *v.*

donder padda *n. phr. Obs.* Also **donder paade**, **donder padde**. [S. Afr. Du., fr. Du. *donder* thunder + *padde* (obs. dial. form of *pad*) frog, toad; see quot. 1937.] Either of two species of frog.

a. The bullfrog *Pyxicephalus adspersus* of the Ranidae. See also BLAASOP sense 3. Also *fig.*

1856 F.P. FLEMING *Sn Afr.* 409 The 'Monster Toad of Kaffraria', called by the Dutch the '*Donder paade*'. This is a large ugly-looking monster, about eleven inches or a foot in length. *Ibid.* 411 The head [of the wine cask] was immediately stove in when an immense '*Donderpaade*,' or Monster Toad, was found in it. **1870** C. HAMILTON *Life & Sport in S.-E. Afr.* 213 The peaceful twilight is soon disturbed by .. the incessant and discordant croaking of the 'donder-paade', or monster toad, whose voice was predominant amid the splashing of the large game in the water. **1913** C. PETTMAN *Africanderisms* 149 Donder padde, (D. donder, thunder; pad, toad.) (1) The Dutch name for the Bullpodder .., which all animals seem to dread. (2) The expression is also applied to a passionate man, a bully, a boaster.

b. *Breviceps parvus* of the Microhylidae; *reenpadda*, see PADDA sense 1 c; also called RAIN FROG.

1937 *Guide to Vertebrate Fauna of E. Cape Prov.* (Albany Mus.) 116 Breviceps parvus, Donder Padda, Jan Blom. At once recognised by the swollen body, very short limbs, very short snout with narrow mouth ... Vocalising is at the maximum during the afternoon, specially after storm showers.

donderse var. DONNERSE.

don'er var. DONDER *int.* and *n.*

donga /ˈdɒŋɡə, ˈdɔŋɡə/ *n.* [Xhosa and Zulu *udonga*.] An eroded gully or watercourse formed by the action of running water, but usu. dry and with steep, bare sides; cf. SLOOT sense 2. Also *attrib.*

1879 R.J. ATCHERLEY *Trip to Boerland* 134 The dongas which debouched into the creek became so deeply cut in the earth that, in order to avoid the repeated difficulties we encountered in crossing them, we had to shape our course higher up on the brow of the hill. **1881** *E. London Dispatch & Frontier Advertiser* 26 Jan. 3 As the enemy seemed to appear and disappear very quickly in that direction there must be some large body hidden in a donga, or deep declivity, who might be massing for an attack. **1884** LAYARD & SHARPE *Birds of S. Afr.* 547 Nests were found .. built on the banks of streams or dry 'dongas'. **1896** W.C. SCULLY in A.D. Dodd *Anthology of Short Stories* (1958) 30 'Incinci', the honey-bird, .. often led them to where the bees had stored their treasure in hollow trees and holes in the donga-banks. **1899** *Natal Agric. Jrnl* 31 Mar. 4 'Donga' a dry water course, and equivalent to the Indian 'nullah' is a useful word for South Africa. **1907** W.C. SCULLY *By Veldt & Kopje* 75 With lightnings and thunderings the long-sealed fountains of the sky burst open, and every kloof and donga became a roaring river. **1911** *Farmer's Weekly* 4 Oct. 117 The rain that falls on the bared mountain side rushes off in silt-laden torrents which cut deep dongas through the agricultural lands below .. to convert a fruitful country into an arid desert. **1922** J.P. FITZPATRICK Letter. (A/LC 11 1048/72, N.E.L.M.), You have yourself seen how roads are turned into dongas and how costly and almost impossible it is to drain them once they have worn down. **1931** G. BEET *Grand Old Days* 91 A stream from the neighbouring hills trickled through the valley in the rainy season, though for many months in the year it was only a dry donga. **1948** H.V. MORTON *In Search of S. Afr.* 174 Thousands of miserable cattle and goats roamed everywhere, making tracks that would some day form cracks which successive rains would open into gullies and dongas. **1968** *Post* 4 Feb. 12 There are no latrines in this place and we have to go to the dongas or the veld. **1976** J. MCCLURE *Rogue Eagle* 69 The lowlands were everywhere striated by the deep, sharp-edged gullies called *dongas*. **1986** J. DEACON in *S. Afr. Panorama* Sept. 9 Here, in Ciskei, gabions (stones in wire baskets,) have been used to dam a donga. The result: water and soil accumulates, grass grows. **1993** *Weekend Post* 31 July (Leisure) 1 Through dongas, up mountain passes, across grasslands, through mud, tornadoes and any other natural disaster, his vehicle has gone places.

Hence **donga-ed** *adj. nonce*, scarred by dongas.

1990 T. HULL in *Personality* 18 June 30 The rest of the time you're scrabbling in low ratio four-wheel-drive up and down rocky donga-ed slopes that bounce you around like puppets.

Donkey Church *n. phr.* [See quots 1943 and 1965.] A nickname for the Methodist Church in Africa, which seceded from the Methodist Church in 1933.

Orig. known as the Bantu Methodist Church of South Africa, this church was renamed the Methodist Church in Africa in 1979.

1943 L. SOWDEN *Union of S. Afr.* 194 There is, or was a short time ago, a Donkey Church in the southern part of the Orange Free State, so called by observers because a heavily draped donkey was used in all the ceremonies. **1961** B.G.M. SUNDKLER *Bantu Prophets* 172 H. with a great deal of flair for stage management — *inter alia* using a donkey as a symbol of the Church, hence the nickname 'Donkey Church' — led the masses until, more than a year later, R. gave the hint that he was available. **1963** WILSON & MAFEJE *Langa* 97 The Bantu Methodist Church of South Africa is an offshoot of the Methodist Church; it broke away in 1933, after a dispute .. over church dues ... People felt that they were being exploited to provide their superiors with cars, and yet Jesus Christ himself used a donkey ... 'The Donkey Church', as it is popularly called, 'is becoming more and more respectable and one wonders if its leaders are still strong believers in donkey riding.' **1965** E. MPHAHLELE *Down Second Ave* 92 Pastor M'Kondo .. had broken away from the Methodist Church of South Africa. He was said to be a branch of what was commonly known as the Donkey Church. Its emblem was a picture of Christ entering Jerusalem on a donkey. **1973** *Informant, Grahamstown* 'He belongs to the African Methodist Episcopal Church.' 'That isn't the same as the Donkey Church is it?' **1987** M. MELAMU *Children of Twilight* 110 Those were the days following the historic secession from the Methodist Church to what came to be known as the 'Bantu Methodist' or 'Donkey' Church. **1989** L.W.M. XOZWA *Methodist Church in Afr.: Hist.* 56 In the 1979 Conference .. we agreed on a new name which is *Methodist Church in Africa* ... We have slightly changed the name. We have not changed our nickname, which is *Donkey Church*.

donnepit var. DENNEPIT.

donner *int.* and *n.* var. DONDER *int.* and *n.*

donner /ˈdɔnə(r)/ *v. trans. Colloq.* Also **donder**. [Afk., to thrash, strike with force.] Not in polite use.

1. Often in the phrr. *to donner (someone) up* or (less commonly) *to donner (someone) op* [prob. influenced by both Eng. *beat up* and Afk. *opdonder*]. To beat up, thrash, hit; MOER *v.* sense 1; NEUK sense 1.

1916 S. BLACK in S. Gray *Three Plays* (1984) 237 Van K: I come from Cape Town — I want a commission in the army, man — I'm related to a British general — I dondered an old coolie op. **1949** H.C. BOSMAN *Cold Stone Jug* (1969) 123 'Yah! He's yellow,' a young convict, an ex-reformatory boy, exclaimed, 'Donner him.' **1960** J. TAYLOR 'Ballad of the Southern Suburbs'.

(*lyrics*) Won't you take us to the wrestling, We wanna see an ou called Sky-High Lee. When he fights Willie Liebenberg there's gonna be a murder, 'Cause Willie's gonna donder that blerrie Yankee. **1960** C. HOOPER *Brief Authority* 60 'These boys were chasing us.' 'Why? ' One of the European boys spoke up: 'The policeman told us to donner them.' **1963** L.F. FREED *Crime in S. Afr.* 98 The gangsters were urged on by ducktail girls, shouting: 'Smash them! Donder them!' **1969** A. FUGARD *Boesman & Lena* 23 It's *mos* funny, Me! *Ou meid* being *donnered*! **1975** 'BLOSSOM' in *Darling* 26 Feb. 111, I doesn't see what's so scientific about two ou's dondering each other up, but never mind. **1977** F.G. BUTLER *Karoo Morning* 100, I told Bul if he said that again, I'd be happy to donner him up 'into a raw sosatie.' **1980** M. LIPTON in *Optima* Vol.29 No.2, 112 Before if he (a Black miner) didn't do what you said, you'd *donder* (hit) him. Now if you just touch him, man .. they pull you up before a board. **1989** *Cape Times* 4 Sept. 6 If I meet a cop armed with revolver, truncheon, quirt, tear-gas, rubber bullets and a gun full of birdshot, and he tells me to disperse or he'll *donner* me, I don't argue with him. **1990** J.G. DAVIS *Land God Made in Anger* 239 Then they start beating up Jakob. They *donnered* him something terrible, cracking his ribs, and they burned him with cigarettes. **1993** [see BLIKSEM *n.* sense d].

2. *fig.* To beat, overcome, defeat (someone or something).

1965 K. MACKENZIE *Deserter* 79 You are mad, Japie. How can you have a war without shooting Englishmen? And they will *donner* you eventually. **1976** *Sunday Times* 1 Aug. 14 The time has come to 'donner' the 'HNP' and everything else that stands for stagnation and reaction in South African politics. **1980** M. MUTLOATSE *Forced Landing* 5 We will have to *donder* conventional literature: old-fashioned critic and reader alike ... We are going to experiment and probe and not give a damn what the critics have to say. **1987** F. VAN ZYL SLABBERT in *South* 9 July 15 Those who rule wish to save us from the totalitarianism of the left by imposing on us totalitarianism from the right. For most of us the difference is academic. We get 'donnered' either way. **1990** *Sunday Times* 25 Mar. 5 We are busy *dondering* you around but you can do nothing about it because we don't want to do business with you.

Hence **donnering** *vbl n.*

1976 S.A. MATTHEWS in *E. Prov. Herald* 26 Oct. 2 Security has come to mean 'dondering' of any opposition that offers a serious challenge.

‖**donnerse** /ˈdɔnə(r)sə/ *adj.* Also **donderse**. [Afk., pronunciation-spelling of *donderse, donder* (see DONDER *n.*) + adj.-forming suffix *-se*.] Not in polite use. Damned, 'bloody'; huge, tremendous. So **donners** *adv.*, very, 'bloody'.

1959 A. DELIUS *Last Division* 75 It was like there'd been a donderse battle With Loch Ness Monsters and people and cattle and spooks and goggas and in-betweens. **1973** *Star* 3 Nov., A great many Afrikaners I know think 'Kaffer' is an o.k. word and that 'Hotnot' won't give offence even when its applied to a university lecturer. But call that same Afrikaner a 'donnerse boer' and he's yelling for the referee. **1979** D. SMUTS (tr. *E. Joubert's Swerfjare van Poppie Nongena*) in *Fair Lady* 9 May 112 Buti Plank was drunk and scolded her: Always Mdantsane, the donnerse Mdantsane. **1979** W. EBERSOHN *Lonely Place* 103 Its don'ers funny that Freek Jordaan should 'phone me about you coming out here. **1985** D. KRAMER in *Cosmopolitan* May 102 The bloody motor would shudder into life sounding like a donnerse diesel tractor starting up in the house.

Don Pedro var. DOM PEDRO.

DONS /dɒnz, diː əʊ en ˈes/ *n. hist.* Also **Dons**. Acronym formed on initial letters of *Department of National Security*. Also *attrib.*

See note at BOSS.

1979 *Daily Dispatch* 25 Oct. 11 The Department of National Security (Dons), formerly the Bureau for State Security (Boss), has started advertising for staff. **1980** *Rand Daily Mail* 7 Jan. 1 He claimed yesterday DONS also had files on top mining company directors .. and on leading writers. **1984** R. DAVIES et al. *Struggle for S. Afr.* I. 196 The 'information scandal' profoundly affected the whole of the BOSS organisation. Following the resignation of van den Bergh in .. 1978, its name was changed to the Department of National Security (DONS). [**1987** S. ROBERTS *Jacks in Corners* 156 She wondered briefly how the South African secret police, BOSS, DNS, etc., managed to earn such a good name for efficiency if they employed people like William.]

doodgooi /ˈduətxɔɪ, ˈdʊət-/ *n. colloq.* [Afk. *doodgooi(er)* a dumpling, *dood* dead + *gooi* throw (+ agential suffix *-er*).] A jocular name for dumplings, or for heavy bread or cake which has failed to rise.

1913 C. PETTMAN *Africanderisms* 150 *Doodgooi*, .. A jocular name for a dumpling. It has been taken over by the Kaffirs in the form *i Dodroyi*, the r being gutteral. **1973** C. DAVENPORT *Informant, Grahamstown*, I never bake cakes when Marion's at home; mine are just doodgooi beside hers. **1975** M.J. MCCOY *Informant, Port Elizabeth* Sorry, but we're only getting doodgooi for eats tonight. **1977** F.G. BUTLER *Karoo Morning* 91 She did not take the trouble to mix yeast into her batch of dough the evening before, with the result that her baking was sad — real doodgooi. *Ibid.* 142 Sandstone is like white bread samidges. Comes in layers, you see ... But ironstone is like 'doodgooi': solid and same all through.

dook var. DOEK.

dooren-boom, **dooringboom**, **doornboom** varr. DORINGBOOM.

doormakar, **-mekaar** varr. DEURMEKAAR.

doornhout var. DORINGHOUT.

Doorst-land var. DORSLAND.

dop /dɔp/ *n.* Also with initial capital. Pl. **-s**, **-pe** /-pə/. [S. Afr. Du., fr. Du. *dop* husk, shell.]

1. A container or lid.

a. Any more-or-less bowl-shaped or spherical object, as a bowl, husk, shell, skull, etc. Cf. DOPPIE sense 1 c.

1841 B. SHAW *Memorials* 144, I here engage, before God and his people, that the dop (part of a calabash which serves as a cup) shall no more pass my lips. **1920** *Chambers's Jrnl* (U.K.) Aug. 482 The vessel or 'dop' is then lifted off and the full effect of the operation [*sc.* cutting hair] is disclosed. [**1946** S. CLOETE *Afr. Portraits* 65 Kruger belonged to the Christelijk-Gereformeerde Church .. called the 'Dopper' or canting church, the word 'dop' deriving from a dop, a damper, or extinguisher used for putting out candles, the idea being that the Doppers were against all new ideas and put them out 'as a dop put out a candle.'] **1970** *Informant, Grahamstown*, I wish I could get this Latin into my dop (brain, head). **1978** J. HOBBS *Darling Blossom* 57 Another thing about Dumbo, he scorns to wear a crash helmet (what he calls a dop) ... He reckons nobody's gonna catch him looking like a .. pampoen.

b. Usu. in *pl.*: Grape-skins, the residue which is left after grapes have been pressed for wine-making; DOPPIE sense 1 b.

1909 *E. London Dispatch* 18 May 5 It is a fair assumption that 'Dops' are at present responsible for an output of from 500,000 to 600,000 gallons per annum. **1913** C. PETTMAN *Africanderisms* 151 The skins of the grapes are called *dops*. **1979** M. PARKES *Wheatlands* 26 Parkes' Brandy became a legend ... It is said that the secret lay in the distilling from 'most', instead of from the 'dops' or skins or refuse. **1988** J. TAYLOR in *Inside S. Afr.* July 31 Now you must work fast and take off the skins. This is where a press would come in handy. If you haven't got one then you will have to resort .. to wringing the *doppe* out in sacking with your bare hands.

2. *noncount.*

a. In full ***dop brandy***: **i.** *hist.* A brandy distilled from the grape-husks left after grapes have been pressed for wine-making, and usu. aged in wood; *Cape dop* (see sense c below); cf. WITBLITS sense b. **ii.** *transf.* Any brandy; see also CAPE BRANDY. **b.** *transf.* Any spirituous drink. Also *attrib.*

1870 *E. Prov. Herald* 13 Sept., 250 hogsheads White Dop Brandy, .. 40 hogsheads Fine Old Boer Brandy, 10 hogsheads Cango Brandy. **1881** *E. London Dispatch & Frontier Advertiser* 2 Feb. 4 Ex various steamers: Cape Meal, 1st and 2nd., Dop Brandy, Superior Cango Brandy. **1888** *Cape Punch* 25 Jan. 35 The Sabbath Day it is the Lord's, And cursed be all who break it (The deadly Dop it is the Boer's, And blest are they who make it). **1895** W.C. SCULLY *Kaffir Stories* 18 Jim .. got his daily number of tots of poisonous 'dop' brandy. **1896** R. WALLACE *Farming Indust. of Cape Col.* 159 *Brandy*, dop or Cape smoke, is a product derived from Cape wines, in the making of which the grape stalks are removed. **1900** O. OSBORNE *In Land of Boers* 68 From the residue of skins, stalks, and jimmy-jam which remains in the vats, dop brandy was afterwards distilled, and a very excellent and pure spirit it rendered. **1903** R. KIPLING *Five Nations* 201 Ah there, Piet! — be'ind 'is stony kop, With 'is Boer bread an' biltong, an' 'is flask of awful Dop. **1910** 'R. DEHAN' *Dop Doctor* 98 'Dop,' being the native name for the cheapest and most villainous of Cape brandies, has come to signify alcoholic drinks in general. **1924** L. COHEN *Reminisc. of Jhb.* 28 There was floating about any amount of Cape smoke, square face, dop brandy, and a horrible local liquid preparation made of raw potato spirit, tobacco juice and pepper. **1931** F.C. SLATER *Secret Veld* 116, I think you must have had a flask of dop with you this afternoon. You must take more water with it in future! **1942** S. CLOETE *Hill of Doves* 31 It would be safer to take a barrel of dop from a wedding than a single mealie cob from you. **1950** L.G. GREEN *At Daybreak for Isles* 4 Dop brandy was to be had for sixpence a bottle. **1960** *Our First Half Century 1910–1960* 445 'Dop brandy' distilled from husks, has long been taxed out of existence by a prohibitive excise duty and there are few other countries where the distillation of husks is so firmly suppressed as in the Union. **1969** I. VAUGHAN *Last of Sunlit Yrs* 11 He never explained how he fell from his high estate to his present lowly one, .. but I am almost certain it was due to his failing with the dop bottle, for he was drunk every weekend. **1977** C. CLAYTON in *Contrast 43* Vol.11 No.3, 23 Too bladdy drunk, old Alice, too bladdy drunk. But they mustn't ask me to give up my dop. Life's too short for that. **1983** D. HUGHES et al. *Complete Bk of S. Afr. Wine* 93 Brandy .. has a strong, separate tradition .. in South Africa. 'Dop', 'Witblits', .. 'Boerblits', and 'Cape Smoke' were some of the names by which local brandy was known in earlier years. **1985** D. BASKIN in *Frontline* Dec. 10 Mrs Potgieter's liquor licence .. prevents the sale of white dop to Blacks, coloureds or Indians unless they are staying at the hotel. **1990** R. GOOL *Cape Town Coolie* 15 When I think of all that *dop* brandy in the cellar! **1991** *Best of S. Afr. Short Stories* (Reader's Digest Assoc.) 92 Used as a general term for a tot or a drink, especially of spirits, 'dop' more specifically refers to brandy.

c. *hist.* With defining word, **Cape dop**: *dop brandy*, see sense 2 a i. Also *attrib.*

1896 *Johannesburg Weekly Times* 8 Aug. 8 Several samples of whiskies, Cape dop, and Cape brandy were examined. **1921** *Chambers's Jrnl* (U.K.) 647 The Cape 'dop' bottle brought oblivion to his tortured mind. **1935** H.C. BOSMAN in S. Gray *Makapan's Caves* (1987) 89 The predikant .. was quite overpowered at the thought that a member of his church was going into the bar, during Nagmaal, to drink cheap Cape dop. **1937** H. SAUER *Ex Afr.* 29 After supper tobacco pouches were again exchanged, and the master of the house produced a bottle of peach brandy or Cape dop. **1968** L.G. GREEN *Full Many Glorious Morning* 173 Among the sweets was a dop flame pudding; you cut up a tinned sponge cake saturate it with 'good Cape dop', set it alight and serve it blazing. **1972** *Sunday Times* 23 Apr. (Mag. Sect.) 4 The canteens carried a surprisingly large range of goods — from Cape 'dop' and 'mampoer' to imported liquors.

3.a. *colloq.* A drink; a quantity of alcohol; a 'tot' of spirits; DOPPIE sense 3. Cf. SOPIE.

1950 *Cape Times* 17 June (Weekend Mag.) 5 The pay of the *mailer* is good ... Added to this, there is an occasional *dop* from both shebeener and customer. **1961** *Cape Argus* 8 Aug. 2 He wanted to buy a 'dop'. **1963** A. FUGARD *Blood Knot* (1968) 113 Some of them used to come back six times and try, with a dop in between to give them hope. **1969** — *Boesman & Lena* 42 Few *dops* and a guitar and its *voetsek* yesterday and to hell with tomorrow. **1970** *Post* 15 Mar. 9 I'm thinking of those farmers in the vineyards of the Cape who pay their labourers with a dop of wine. **1981** *Fair Lady* 9 Sept. 250 They are addicted to pinball machines, motor bikes, racing and having a dop — not necessarily in that order. **1985** *Sunday Times* 8 Sept. (Lifestyle) 2 He .. enjoyed a couple of *dops* of his favourite tipple. **1988** SMUTS & ALBERTS *Forgotten Highway* 184 You put a quid in your cheek — just now you're like a man who's had a good few *dops* of wine; after a while you feel nothing. **1990** R. MALAN *My Traitor's Heart* 242 So I said to Andries, 'Call your boy to the door, man, and I'll give him a dop (a shot of spirits), too'. **1993** S. GRAY in *Weekly Mail & Guardian* 5 Nov. 48 As a newcomer I was stood my first complimentary dop of the local mampoer — 75 percent proof, not a degree less.

b. With defining word: **overdop**, an extra quantity of wine given to workers under the *tot system* (see TOT *n.*[2] sense 2).

1952 'MR DRUM' in *Drum* June 8 When there is extra work or they have to work at week-ends, they are given an extra tot or 'overdop' as an incentive.

c. *comb.* **dop system**, *tot system* (see TOT *n.*[2] sense 2).

1987 *Cape Times* 17 Apr. 4 The outdated and obviously wrong practices such as the dop system have been discarded by most farmers a long time ago. **1987** G. HILL in *South* 2 July 6 Wages are still low and he and his fellow workers are still on the 'dop' system. **1989** M. FRIDJHON in *Financial Mail* 10 Nov. 157 The use of prison labour and application of the *dop* system (part payment of wages in alcohol) provide an emotional rallying point. **1991** *Weekend Argus* 26 Jan. 10 The central theme this year is to combat alcohol abuse and the infamous 'dop system' — in which farmers 'pay' workers with alcohol. **1991** J. PLATTER in *Sunday Tribune* 19 May 18 Important wine authors in Britain .. always included the Dop system among specific anti-apartheid aversions. Let's hope the Dop will be history soon.

4. In the n. phr. ***dop en dam***, also ***dop and dam, dop-en-dum, dop-'n-dam*** /ˌdɔpən'dam/ [Afk., *dop* brandy + *en* and + *dam* 'dam' i.e. water], (a drink of) brandy and water.

1964 D. MARAIS *I Like it Here, (cartoon caption)* Take that filthy stuff [*sc.* whisky] away and bring me a good, honest dop-en-dam. **1965** J. BENNETT *Hawk Alone* 72 'Dop-'n-dam, please,' he said. He liked to make a joke of his drinking. The barman poured him a brandy and water. **1973** S. STANDER tr. *A.P. Brink's Brandy in S. Afr.* 3 Tap-water. Pure tap-water. Now it's 'dop-en-dam' ... Brandy and water, precisely half and half. **1974** *To the Point* 7 June 44 It was dop and dam and a willing girl when we were young and green. **1974** G. JENKINS *Bridge of Magpies* (1977) 45 He fiddled at a small mahogany bar. 'Something to keep out the cold — a dop-en-dum (brandy and water)?' **1980** K.W. KÜHNE *Informant, Bloemfontein* College is veiled in a nostalgic sort of 'I remember, I remember ..', not least the dop-en-dam and fine discussions we had. [**1985** see MAN *n.*[2] sense 1 b.] **1989** F.G. BUTLER *Tales from Old Karoo* 30 The farmer would have to .. fetch them home for a couple of identical *dop-en-dams*. **1990** *Personality* 27 Aug. 12 If a man walks into a pub now and asks for a dop and dam, they look at you as if you're mad. You have to spell it out: 'Brandy and water, you fool?'

dop /dɔp/ *v.*[1] *colloq.* [Afk.]

a. *intrans.* To fail.

1955 E. BOLD in *Pietersburg Eng. Medium School Mag.* Nov. 35 As we finished the sentence on Atilla the Hun Most of us were sure of 'dopping'. **1970** *Informant, Krugersdorp* Dop. To fail at school. **1970** [see BANG]. **1971** *Informant, Grahamstown* He said he has no doubts about my dopping at the end of the year — sorry, I mean my passing! **1974** *Eng. Usage in Sn Afr.* Vol.1 No.5, 17 'I'm going to dop.' Going to fail (an examination).

b. *trans.* To fail (something).

1970 M. GORBEL *Informant, Bloemfontein* He dopped standard six. **1974** *Informant, Grahamstown (student essay)* You hear children saying 'I dopped that exam'.

dop /dɔp/ *v.*[2] *colloq.* [Afk., fr. *dop* a drink, see DOP *n.*]

a. *intrans.* To drink.

1977 *Sunday Times* 1 May 7 It is a society with a language of its own. You 'dop' too much, become 'gerooked' and have 'babelaas' next morning. **1983** G. SILBER in *Sunday Times* 28 Aug. (Mag. Sect.) 18 People come to Bapsies to braai and sit on blankets and dop ... Sometimes the okes dop a little too hard and .. fall into the pool. **1985** [see Vula quot. at JOL *n.* sense 1]. **1991** D. ASHMAN *Informant, Cape Town* Doppie (n.): A person who dops.

b. *trans.* To drink (alcohol).

1981 *Cape Times* 28 Dec. 9 These holiday jollers .. gooi a line without any bait in our muddy waters after dopping a cellar cask.

Hence **dopped up** *ppl adj. phr.*, drunk.

1989 D. KRAMER in *ADA* No.7, 8 When they got to the braai the guys who had invited them had already had a braai. So they were quite 'dopped' up.

doppen beer /'dɔpənbɪə/ *n. phr. Obs.* exc. *hist.* [Du. *doppen* husks + Eng. *beer.*] A light, inferior wine made by fermenting the husks of pressed grapes in water.

Formerly used as a wine for labourers.

1862 *Abstracts* in *Stat. Law of Cape of G.H.* p.xxvii, Confiscation of tobacco privately imported. Against making doppen beer. Against making spruce beer. **1983** *Flying Springbok* Apr. 27 C. de Bosdari, in his *Wines of the Cape* describes the trouble taken by Hendrick Cloete in preparing new barrels — a process that took a couple of months of washing, sulphuring, steaming and seasoning with 'doppen beer' and pure Constantia wine.

Dopper /'dɔpə(r)/ *n.*[1] and *adj.* Also **Dorper**, and with small initial. [Etym. obscure:

'The late Paul Kruger — a great pillar of that church — used to say that the word came from the Dutch "Domper", meaning extinguisher, because the Reformed Church objected to the "new lights" introduced by other churches into their worship, .. for which reason the name "domper" (degenerated into "dopper") was given to the church. Another good authority stated that the word "dopper" is derived from "dorper", meaning villager, a term used to distinguish the countryman from the townsman; while the oldest derivation is from "dop", a shell, from the way in which the old people used to cut their hair so as to resemble an inverted calabash shell on their heads.' (L.H. Brinkman *Glory of Backveld*, 1924, p.58.) See also quot. 1990.]

A. *n.*

a. A nickname for a member of the strictly calvinist *Gereformeerde Kerk in Suid-Afrika* (see GEREFORMEERDE); sometimes *derog.*

1850 N.J. MERRIMAN *Cape Jrnls* (1957) 142 These Doppers are a sort of Dutch Church Puritans, their principal characteristics being a Quakerish costume in dress, a disinclination to sing hymns in the church, [etc.]. **1856** R.E.E. WILMOT *Diary* (1984) 51 *Doppers* .. are a species of Dutch Boer happily confined to the Eastern Province and sovereignty, whose religious tenets differ from the Dutch Reformed Church. **1878** P. GILLMORE *Great Thirst Land* 275 The Boers I am surrounded by all belong to a religious sect called 'Doppers.' Their dress is a short single-breasted coat, trousers very loose, and peculiar-shaped broad-brimmed hats. **1881** G.F. AUSTEN *Diary* (1981) 27 Committed to the care of the Revd. Maury — (Dopper). **1887** J.W. MATTHEWS *Incwadi Yami* 401 These 'doppers', relics of the past, .. do not differ essentially from the members of the Dutch Reformed Church in doctrine; they are simply more conservative in feeling, less liberal in action, very jealous of innovation and entirely unprogressive in ideas. **1892** W.L. DISTANT *Naturalist in Tvl* 27 The Doppers are the Quakers and Plymouth Bretheren of the Dutch Church in the Transvaal. As a rule no instrumental music is used in their services, and no hymns are allowed, the Psalms of the Old Testament alone being sung. **1899** [see TAKHAAR]. **1924** L.H. BRINKMAN *Glory of Backveld* 58 Grobler was a strictly orthodox man, belonging to the Reformed Church — a sect commonly referred to as 'Doppers'. **1946** [see DOP *n.* sense 1 a]. *c***1949** M.C. BOTHA in *20th C. Inquisition* (Education League) *(pamphlet)*, I have no objection to the doctrine of the Gereformeerde Church and it has always seemed very possible to me for Doppers and members of the Dutch Reformed Church to live together as Afrikaners in love and peace. **1959** L.G. GREEN *These Wonders* 148 Religious arguments arose, and the Doppers moved off and founded a settlement of their own. **1984** *Cosmopolitan* Mar. 44, I am a Dopper, which in Afrikaans religious circles means something of a maverick. So you will excuse me, please, for not hesitating to speak out. **1990** R. MALAN *My Traitor's Heart* 17 Many Afrikaners were calling themselves Doppers, after the little metal caps with which they snuffed out candles. They called themselves Doppers because they were deliberately and consciously extinguishing the light of Enlightenment. **1991** A. VAN WYK *Birth of New Afrikaner* 109 They are known as *Doppers* and, although orthodox in Calvinist/Protestant doctrine, they have for years been more enlightened in their political way of thinking than their DRC brethren ... I respect FW as a good *Dopper.*

b. *comb.* **Dopper Church**, ‖**Dopper Kerk** [Afk., *kerk* church], the *Gereformeerde Kerk in Suid-Afrika* (see GEREFORMEERDE), one of the family of Afrikaans Calvinist churches; the church building used by members of this church.

See note at DUTCH REFORMED.

1877 [**Dopper Church**: see NED GEREF]. **1893** *Brown's S. Afr.* 218 Other Churches are the Dopper Church where the President occasionally preaches and the Wesleyan Church in Church Street; the German, Baptist, Kaffir Church &c. **1903** D. BLACKBURN *Burgher Quixote* 2, I hold that .. no man has a right to preach unless he be a qualified predikant — by which it will be seen that I have no part or lot in the Dopper Church. **1929** D. REITZ *Commando* 20 On Sundays he preached in the queer little Dopper church. **1949** J. MOCKFORD *Golden Land* 249 The spire of the 'Dopper' Church across the street where President Kruger worshipped is one of the landmarks of the city. **1950** H.C. BOSMAN in S. Gray *Makapan's Caves* (1987) 141 The commandant-general and the dominee had words about whether the *plein* in the middle of the dorp should be for the Dopper Church, with a *pastorie* next to it. **1963** S. CLOETE *Rags of Glory* 22 The little Dopper Church, where he preached every Sunday and waited for those who wished to see him. **1975** *E. Prov. Herald* 27 May 37 Two churches, the Nederduitse Gereformeerde Kerk and the Gereformeerde (**Dopper**) **Kerk**, were the foundations on which the town grew.

B. *adj.*

a. Of or pertaining to the Doppers, or descriptive of their former conservative, old-fashioned dress and hairstyle.

1881 P. GILLMORE *Land of Boer* 111 A stalwart Boer from the Transvaal, and dressed in the Dopper costume. **1882** C. DU VAL *With Show through Sn Afr.* I. 289 His head, surmounted by what is known as a Dopper hat — namely, a black cloth steeple-crowned edifice, with a brim not less than seven inches deep and turned up with green. **1899** R. DEVEREUX *Side Lights on S. Afr.* 76 One of the farms I visited belonged to one Erasmus, not the rich Erasmus who recently married into the Kruger family, but a fair average specimen of the 'Dopper' Boer class. **1908** J.M. ORPEN *Reminisc.* (1964) 240 When he left the Raad he was dressed in the dopper fashion with a jacket reaching to the top of his hips and a broad-rimmed, hard felt hat. **1936** [see HOLLANDER]. **1946** S. CLOETE *Afr. Portraits* 379 This remarkable man stands for the future of South Africa as clearly as the Dopper Boer stands for its past. **1949** L.G. GREEN *In Land of Afternoon* 165 There was a 'Dopper' style of hair-cut, and for a period the word 'Dopper' was used derisively. *a***1951** H.C. BOSMAN *Willemsdorp* (1977) 94 The cut had been fashionable a century ago: those 'dopper' suits with embroidered jackets were worn in homage to the Voortrekkers and the Transvaal's historic past. **1971** L.G. GREEN *Taste of S.-Easter* 179 He had watched a Cape Flats housewife giving her son a dopper haircut using half a pumpkin to guide her scissors. **1989** *Reader's Digest Illust. Hist.* 114 The trekkers, dressed in traditional *dopper* coats (short coats buttoned from top to bottom), *kappies* (bonnets) and hand-made *riempieskoene* (leather thong shoes).

b. *nonce.* Of or pertaining to unsophisticated, rural people.

1900 *Daily News* 13 Feb. 7 The burghers being chiefly of the 'dopper' or back-country class.

Hence (*nonce*) **Dopperdom** *n.*, the 'Doppers' collectively; **doppered** *adj. joc.*, dominated by 'Doppers'; **doppery** *adj.*, see quot. 1901.

1888 *Cape Punch* 28 Mar. 184 Australia: .. Perhaps old mama Britannia adopted you. Cape: Yes, I'm an adopted son, although mamma sometimes says I'm a doppered son. **1898** W. HARCOURT in A.G. Gardiner *Life of W.H.* (1923) II. 461 It is with a view to this that A.M. [*sc.* Alfred Milner] wants a display of more force .. to 'convince Dopperdom that *England means war*', if Kruger does not do our bidding. **1901** W.S. SUTHERLAND *S. Afr. Sketches* 86 The calibre of people comes out in a camp as it does in a big city ... 'East-end' hails from Zastron, and is somewhat 'doppery'.

dopper /ˈdɔpə(r)/ *n.*² *slang.* [DOP *v.*² + Eng. agential suffix *-er.*] A drinker.

1990 *Personality* 3 Dec. 22 Let's first look at Durban, where 'the fun never sets' and where, it appears, there are many dedicated and devoted doppers.

doppie /ˈdɔpi/ *n.* [Afk., *dop* (see DOP *n.*) + -IE.]

1. A container.

a. A common term for a cartridge case; a percussion cap.

1897 H.A. BRYDEN *Nature & Sport* 19 Some natives from the cattle-post here (Seruey) brought a quantity of new milk in the great Bechuana pitcher-like wooden vessels. They only required a few percussion-caps ('doppies') in exchange. **1958** A. JACKSON *Trader on Veld* 39 My first weapon was a single 12-bore muzzle-loading shotgun, complete with powder flask — the container for shot and percussion caps (doppies). **1961** D. BEE *Children of Yesterday* 16 He had a collection of *doppies* (cartridge cases) ... There were bright silver- and copper-coloured .22 *doppies* ... Others were .303 and shotgun cartridge cases. **1972** *Informant, Grahamstown* Justin always smells the doppie the minute he clears the breach. He likes the way the gunpowder smell smokes into his nose. **1977** F.G. BUTLER *Karoo Morning* 223 Taking an old .303 cartridge case or 'doppie', I filled it with the mixture. **1977** *Fair Lady* 16 Mar. 69 One was wearing a camouflage cap and the other had a packet of doppies (cartridge cases) and they were playing with them. **1988** T.J. LINDSAY *Shadow* (1990) 94 He studied the expended cartridge cases scattered about the bodies. 'These *doppies* were not fired here' he said at last. **1989** *Reader's Digest Illust. Hist.* 488 *Doppie*, Small shell or percussion cap; bullet casing. **1992** *Weekly Mail* 24 Apr. 3 Two little boys also lay dead ... 'There were many *doppies* (spent shotgun cartridges),' said Mathonsi.

b. DOP *n.* sense 1 b. Also *attrib.*

1948 *Cape Times* 24 Jan. (Weekend Mag.) 12 (*advt*) A Grape Crusher and two Wine and Doppies Pumps manufactured by Consani's for the Wine Industry. **1955** J. PACKER *Valley of Vines* 13 If you fell into a tank among the *doppies* — the skins — and the wine, you died. **1963** —— *Home from Sea* 24 The white wine was made in closed tanks without the 'doppies' — the skins.

c. *colloq.* Any container, shell, etc. Cf. DOP *n.* sense 1 a.

1949 H.C. BOSMAN *Cold Stone Jug* (1969) 76 A half-ounce ration of tobacco was divided into twenty 'doppies', each about the size of a smoke. And for five doppies I could get a small tin of hard fat smuggled in to me from the kitchen. **1972** *Notice, Hout Bay (Western Cape)* Rock Lobster doppies for sale. **1990** *Informant, Grahamstown* Please may I have the doppies from my pens in case they drop onto the floor and the dog chews them.

2. In the Western Cape: the CARPENTER, *Argyrozona argyrozona.*

Perh. applied esp. to the juvenile of the species.

1949 J.L.B. SMITH *Sea Fishes* 278 *Argyrozona argyrozona* ... *Silvervis. Silver Fish. Doppie* (Cape) ... At the Cape juveniles known as 'Doppies' are captured in large numbers and are believed by many to be a distinct species. **1958** L.G. GREEN *S. Afr. Beachcomber* 114 Grain farmers gave their labourers fish for breakfast at harvest time, and doppies or hottentot and silver fish (sold in bunches of ten) served the purpose very well. **1960** [see STELLASIE]. **1970** [see BOKKEM]. **1972** L.G. GREEN *When Journey's Over* 148 Agmat made his own *bokkems* in the yard from the little silver fish known as *doppies*, from *harders*, *marsbankers* and *elf*. **1979** SNYMAN & KLARIE *Free from Sea* 50 Silver Fish, Doppie. **1986** SMITH & HEEMSTRA *Smith's Sea Fishes* 582 At the Cape, juveniles known as 'Doppies' are believed by many to be a distinct species. **1993** R. VAN DER ELST *Guide to Common Sea Fishes* 336 A few decades ago, bunches of these fish [*sc.* carpenter], known as 'doppies', were sold directly from the wharfside.

3. DOP *n.* sense 3 a.

1950 E. PARTRIDGE *Dict. of Underworld Slang* 199 *Doppie*, A drink: South Africa (esp. and orig. Afrikaans-speakers). *c***1957** D. SWANSON *Highveld, Lowveld & Jungle* 86 Either we'll get rain and live another year or we'll all be damn-well finished. Let's have another doppie. **1970** C.B. WOOD *Informant, Johannesburg* He gave me a 'doppie' (tot). **1971** *Drum* Mar. 16 One Saturday night Klaas .. felt like celebrating, and had a few extra doppies of his own. **1973** J. COPE *Alley Cat* 99 A cup of coffee and a doppie brandy in it maybe, just a small one, to put heart into you. **1976** *Farmer's Weekly* 28 Jan. 93 Can't a man sommer enjoy a little doppie at a braaivleis! I know how to take my drink. **1988** ADAMS & SUTTNER *William Str.* 49 Ruby takes her doppie brandy, all her brothers come with and they all drunk .. too.

doringboom /ˈduərəŋbuəm, ˈduə-/ *n.* Forms: α. **door(e)n-boom, dorn boom**; β. **do(o)ringboom.** Also with initial capital. Pl. **-bo(o)me** /-buəmə/. [Afk. (earlier S. Afr. Du. *doornboom*), fr. Du. *doorn* thorn (pl. *doren*) + *boom* tree.] Any of several thorny trees, usu. of the genus *Acacia* of the Fabaceae, esp. *A. karroo*, which has long, conspicuous white spines; THORN; THORN-TREE. See also *eina tree* (EINA *n.* sense 2), SWEET THORN.

α. **1786** G. FORSTER tr. *A. Sparrman's Voy. to Cape of G.H.* I. 243 At *Duyvenhoeks-rivier* we first saw the *dorn boom*, or tree called *mimosa nilotica*, which produces the *gum arabic*. **1790** tr. *F. Le Vaillant's Trav.* II. 305 The plain was covered with the mimosa, which the planters name *dooren-boom*. *a***1827** D. CARMICHAEL in W.J. Hooker *Botanical Misc.* (1831) II. 281 The *Doorn boom*, a species of *Mimosa*, .. never grows to any considerable height in the open plain, but spreads out like a parasol. **1844** J. BACKHOUSE *Narr. of Visit* 199 The country became drier, the grass was short and brown, and many of the hills were besprinkled with Doornboom. **1847** J. BARROW *Reflect.* 148 We met with a thicket of *doornboom*, or thorn-tree, a species of mimosa, armed from its summit to the ground with enormous double thorns. **1868** L. PAPPE *Florae Capensis* 11 *Acacia horrida* ... The demulcent derived from the *Doornboom* is well known as an article of commerce. **1906** F. BLERSCH *Handbk of Agric.* 258 The *doornboom*, karoo thorn, or mimosa (*Acacia horrida*), become injurious by their getting into and spoiling wool and hair. **1913** C. PETTMAN *Africanderisms* 150 *Doornboom, Acacia horrida.* A widely distributed tree, covered with large white thorns, growing in large numbers along the banks of Karoo rivers, as well as in the open veld. Though generally spoken of as a mimosa, it is not a true mimosa.

β. [**1936** C. BIRKBY *Thirstland Treks* 67 Dry rivers seam the way occasionally, lined with the *acacia horrida*, which the Afrikaner calls the *doringboom.*] **1971** BARAITSER & OBHOLZER *Cape Country Furn.* 270 Most furniture consists of crude chairs made from local shrubs and trees, particularly Karee and doringboom. **1973** O.H. SPOHR tr. *F. Krauss's Trav. Jrnl* 75 Again there were many dooring boome, mimosa horrida. **1983** T. BARON in *Frontline* June 29 Acacia is your .. common or garden doringboom .. various species .. abound .. the eina tree, wag-n-bietjie, gomdoring .. haak-en-steek, katdoring, papierdoring, soetdoring, rooi-doring, blinkhaakdoring, drievingerdoring and horingdoring .. to name a few. **1988** G. SILBER in *Style* July 31 Here is a man who is equally at ease in the company of Oliver Tambo under a *doringboom* in Lusaka, as he is in the company of Magnus Malan around a campfire in a northern Transvaal hunting lodge.

‖**doringdraad** /ˈduərəŋdrɑːt/ *n.* [Afk.] Barbed wire. Also *attrib.*

1961 L.E. VAN ONSELEN *Trekboer* 59 'Come, you and me fetch the "doring draad"' he said in a conspiratorial whisper. 'Doring draad' means 'barbed wire'. **1988** M. WILLIAMSON in *Argus* 31 May 7 Perhaps it was the hot water, or perhaps it was the zest. Whatever, the baby revived, and survived, and today at 87 she is proud of being 'as tough as *doringdraad*'. **1988** O. OBERHOLZER *Ariesfontein to Zuurfontein*, From here one could see bossies and stones scattered amongst open patches of ground. Just the occasional 'doringdraad' fences cut their loneliness.

‖**doringhout** /ˈduərəŋhəʊt, ˈduə-/ *n.* Forms: α. **do(o)rnhout**; β. **doringhout.** [Afk. (earlier S. Afr. Du. *doornhout*), *doring* thorn + *hout* wood.] The SWEET THORN, *Acacia karroo*; the wood of this tree; also called THORNWOOD.

α. **1796** C.R. HOPSON tr. *C.P. Thunberg's Trav.* II. 111 Dorn-hout (*Mimosa nilotica*) is used for Lock-shoes, to put under waggon wheels. **1798** S.H. WILCOCKE tr. *J.S. Stavorinus's Voy. to E. Indies 1768–71* II. 79 *Buckuhout* .. ; *roode else*, or red alder .. ; the *keureboom* .. ; *zwarte yzerhout*, or black ironwood .. ; *zwartbast* .. ; and *doornhout*, or thornwood (*mimosa nilotica*) .. are all used in the construction of waggons and their appurtenances.

β. **1971** BARAITSER & OBHOLZER *Cape Country Furn.* 279 *Doringhout, Acacia karroo* ... Also known as the Cape thorn tree, the sweet thorn and the mimosa thorn ... Widely distributed throughout South Africa .. It was used to make kraals for stock; and the wood makes an excellent fuel. **1979** *E. Prov. Herald* 19 Feb. 8 It is imperative to have a hard wood fire to give constant steady heat. We used 'doringhout'.

Dormer /ˈdɔːmə/ *n.* [Blend of *Dorset Horn* and *Merino.*] A local sheep breed, a cross between Dorset Horn and German Merino, bred primarily for slaughter-lambs. Also *attrib.*

1957 *Handbk for Farmers* (Dept of Agric.) III. 210 A commencement was made in 1940 with the development of the Dormer .. as a slaughter-lamb breed. This was done because the German Merino mutton sheep is resistant to *Muellerius* [*sc.* lungworm]. **1970** *Farmer's Weekly* 21 Apr. 70 (*advt*) Dormer 4 tooth ewes with 22 lambs. **1971** W.J. HUGO in *Std Encycl. of Sn Afr.* IV. 71 *Dormer*, Sheep of the mutton-wool type, developed since 1940 by crossing the Dorset Horn with German Merino ewes and interbreeding the half-bred progeny ... The Dormer had been developed chiefly as a fat-lamb breed for the winter-rainfall region. **1973** *Farmer's Weekly* 4 July 13 He has great faith in the Dormer breed, and says although essentially a mutton breed, they also give enough wool to substantially contribute towards their keep. *c***1977** *S. Afr. 1976: Off. Yrbk* (Dept of Info.) 612 The locally developed Dorper (a non-woolled mutton breed well adapted to arid conditions) and Dormer (a wool-mutton breed for the more temperate regions) now account for the bulk of all non-Merino sheep. **1982** [see AFRINO]. **1990** *Farmer's Weekly* 8 June 94 (*advt*) Dormer, the sheep bred in South-Africa for South-African conditions.

dorn-boom, dornhout varr. DORINGBOOM, DORINGHOUT.

dorp /dɔːp, dɔrp/ *n.* Also with initial capital. [Du.]

a. A country town or village; sometimes *derog.*, denoting a backward or unprogressive place; DORPIE. Also *attrib.*, and *fig.*

1802 TRUTER & SOMERVILLE in G.M. Theal *Rec. of Cape Col.* (1899) IV. 404 He had been with the well known Cornelis Kok on a journey through the dorp Patania and Litakoe to the Barrolow nation. **1835** A. STEEDMAN *Wanderings* I. 103 Beaufort .. generally presents a scene of activity, arising from the number of farmers, who on various accounts have frequent occasion to visit the *Dorp*. **1852** [see MARITZBURG]. **1853** *Friend* 17 Sept., New dorp — Van Wyk's Vley. The sale of Erven formerly advertised will positively be held on 19th October 1853 at Van Wyk's Vley. **1878** H.A. ROCHE *On Trek in Tvl* We will fancy the 'Dorp,' or town where the ceremony is to be performed by their Dutch minister, or Predikant, to be Pretoria. **1898** J.F. INGRAM *Story of Afr. City* 49 By degrees the straggling Dorp began to assume shape, and the long open spaces of veldt .. were built up or fenced off yard by yard. **1911** P. GIBBON *Margaret Harding* 134 It was a small, stagnant veld dorp, in fact, one of hundreds that are littered over the face of the Colony, and have for their districts a more than metropolitan importance. **1920** *Contemp. Rev.* (U.K.) Feb. 197 In the dorps and the backveld, society, business, religion and politics are closely interwoven. **1938** *Rand Daily Mail* 27 June 3 If the chemists had not discovered how to extract low-grade ore cheaply .. Johannesburg, instead of being a great vital city, would have been a dying, derelict dorp. **1948** H.V. MORTON *In Search of S. Afr.* 248 If you want to find out what pettymindedness is, .. just come and live in a dorp like this. **1950** [see *Dopper church* (DOPPER *n.*[1] sense b)]. **1960** C. HOOPER *Brief Authority* 25 For most of my life I had dreaded the vacuous, depopulated, waste regions of South Africa, with their dreary little dorps, their occasional windmills, their dusty aridity, their ox-wagon mentality. **1966** I. VAUGHAN *These Were my Yesterdays* 92 If you go on living in a small country dorp your girls will grow up like pumpkins with no advantages. **1973** *Weekend Argus* 21 Apr. 5, I was depressed by the desperate ordinariness .. of the average South African town or village. They really are just 'dorps' with everything the word connotes — one uninspiring main street in which filling station, hotel, church .. intermingle with stereotyped shops and 'kafees'. **1984** L. SIMPSON in *Style* July 109 In South Africa the small hotels, the Centrals and Royals have always formed part of .. dorp living. **1986** R. BALLEN *Dorps* 1 What distinguishes these dorps from American or European villages is the sense of Africa and the presence of black people in these villages. **1991** F.G. BUTLER *Local Habitation* 170 As Professor Geoff Durrant remarked .. : 'White South Africans all know each other, or of each other. It's an intellectual dorp.' **1992** E. DE WAAL in *Church Times* 13 Mar. 8 We stop off at small dorps, towns where there may be no more than two or three streets dominated by a huge, white-painted Dutch Reformed Church.

b. With distinguishing epithet: ||**onderdorp** [Afk., *onder* lower], BLIKKIESDORP sense 2; **outdorp** *nonce*, a small satellite village.

1970 E. STUART *Informant, Pinetown* The children from the **onderdorp** were a poorly dressed, ill-fed group, yet they seemed cheerful enough. **1914** L.H. BRINKMAN *Breath of Karroo* 264 The mournful aspect that the little town of Victoria West presented for days after the flood still survives in the memories of the inhabitants ... Almost every minister in the vicinity of each **outdorp** desired to take part in the funeral service.

Hence **dorpdom** *n.*, the state of being a dorp; **dorpenaar** *n.* /ˈdɔːpənɑː, ˈdɔrpənɑːr/ [Afk., *-enaar* suffix denoting 'an inhabitant of (a place)'], an inhabitant of a country village.

1928 J.S. FRANKLIN *This Union* (1949) 121 It is within the power of the ratepayers to decide and determine whether Bloemfontein is to go back to the humdrum existence of 'dorpdom' or .. play a big and important part in the development of .. this great sub-continent of ours. **1955** L.G. GREEN *Karoo* 81 They still share many familiar scenes ... Sheep in the market square .. above all, the streams of *dorpenaars* seeking relief in the streets at night from the heat. **1982** J. KRIGE in *Staffrider* Vol.5 No.2, 20 If you slide your feet like this then you can't stand on top of one, you dumb dorpenaar, and they all laughed.

Dorper *n.*[1] var. DOPPER *n.*[1]

Dorper /ˈdɔːpə/ *n.*[2] Also with small initial. [Blend of *Dorset Horn* and *Persian* (see PERSIAN).] (One of) a hardy local breed of non-woolled mutton sheep, a cross between the Dorset Horn and the blackhead Persian breeds (see *Blackhead Persian*, BLACKHEAD sense 2). Also *attrib.*

1953 [see FAT-TAILED sense b]. **1957** *Handbk for Farmers* (Dept of Agric.) III. 227 The Dorper has been developed by further breeding and selection from the Dorset Horn X Blackhead Persian half-bred ... Bred particularly for those regions which are unsuitable for Merinos, .. experience has shown that it adapts itself very well to the more arid regions. **1968** *Farmer's Weekly* 3 Jan. 31 A large portion of the rest of the farm is bushland being utilised by 2,000 Angoras, 1,000 Dorpers and 50 head of beef cattle. **1971** W.J. HUGO in *Std Encycl. of Sn Afr.* IV. 72 A meeting .. held on 19 July 1950 at the Grootfontein College of Agriculture, decided that the new breed they sought to develop would from then on be known as the Dorper. *c*1977 [see DORMER]. **1981** *Sunday Times* 14 June (Mag. Sect.) 12 His only hobby is farming. He has two farms .. where he keeps dorper sheep. **1988** P. KINGWILL *Message of Black Eagle* 77 They could hear her instructing someone to check the earmarks of every load of Dorper lambs delivered in the next twenty-four hours. **1991** *Philatelic Services Bulletin* No.8075, The Dorper is a truly South African sheep breed which was developed locally because a need existed for a breed specially adapted to arid regions and able to raise slaughter-lambs on the veld.

dorpie /ˈdɔːpi, ˈdɔrpi/ *n.* [Afk., *dorp* a country town or village + dim. suffix -IE.] Diminutive form of DORP (sense a).

1943 J.Y.T. GREIG *Language at Work* 106 Political discussions .. take place on the stoep or in the bar-parlour of a hotel in some dorpie of the platteland. **1955** A. DELIUS *Young Trav.* 109 The prominent buildings of the village, or *dorpie*, of Koringberg, was that of the Wheat Growers Cooperative. **1973** E. LE ROUX in S. Gray *Writers' Territory* 144 The dorpies are not big, yet they are easily visible as you charge by at eighty miles per hour on the straight tarred roads. **1985** *Sunday Times* 24 Nov. 11 This is a platteland dorpie. It is not feasible to hold mixed sports here .. no way in the platteland. **1986** S. SEPAMLA *Third Generation* 23 Like the other Free State *dorpies* the skyline of Parys is dominated by the sweeping wings of the *Nederduitse Gereformeerde Kerk* and the town hall. **1987** [see PLATTELAND *n.* sense a]. **1993** *Weekend Post* 14 Aug. (Leisure) 4 Even the church clock is an hour slow in the Eastern Cape dorpie which found itself on the tourist map with the screening of *A Road to Mecca* just over two years ago.

Dorsland /ˈdɔrslant, ˈdɔːslænd/ *n. hist.* Formerly also **Doorst Land, Dorst(e)land, Durstland,** and with small initial. [Afk., a name given to the arid region of the Kalahari desert or to a similarly arid, waterless region; *dors* (earlier *dorst*) thirst + *land* land.] *Comb.*: **Dorsland Trek** [see TREK *n.*], the migration, from 1874 to 1880, of Boer families from the Transvaal (or South African Republic) north-westward through present-day Botswana and Namibia into south-western Angola; *Thirstland Trek*, see THIRSTLAND sense 2; see also TREK *n.* sense 4; **Dorsland trekker** [see TREKKER], a member of the party of Boers who embarked on this journey; *Thirstland Boer* (see THIRSTLAND sense 2). Also *fig.*, and *attrib.* See also ANGOLA BOER.

*a*1951 H.C. BOSMAN in L. Abrahams *Bosman at his Best* (1965) 47 'The Great Dorstland Trek', Koos Steyn shouted as we got ready to move off. 'Anyway, we won't fare as badly as the Dorstland Trekkers. We'll lose less cattle than they did because we've got less to lose.' **1972** *Evening Post* 2 Sept. 10 He [*sc.* Sir de Villiers Graaff] has also performed a considerable task of leadership in holding the party together through its *dorslandtrek* in opposition. **1974** [see THIRSTLAND sense 2]. **1975** *E. Prov. Herald* 7 Aug. 1 An Afrikaans-speaking farmer from Sa da Bandeira, whose parents were members of the 'Dorsland Trek' from South West Africa to Angola at the turn of the century. **1977** [see ANGOLA BOER]. **1979** *Scope* July 25 The Van der Merwe's are the descendants of South West Africa's black Voortrekkers. They are the offspring of the .. black servants, who, towards the end of the 1870s accompanied the legendary white Dorsland Trekkers. **1988** A. HALL-MARTIN et al. *Kaokoveld* 24 The Dorsland trekkers, who had left the Transvaal and settled at Humpata in southern Angola, used the Kaokoveld as their annual hunting ground from about 1880 to 1908.

dossie var. DASSIE.

doublejee /ˈdʌbldʒi/ *n.* Also **doubeljee, doublegee.** [Englished form of Du. *dubbeltje.*]

1. [See DUBBELTJE *n.*[2]] *obs.* DUBBELTJE *n.*[2] sense 2.

1816 R.B. FISHER *Importance of Cape of G.H.* 52 There is, indeed, a large quantity of the old English penny-pieces coined by Mr. Boulton, now in circulation, under the name of double gees, or twopence, for which they pass current. **1889** *Blackwood's Mag.* (U.K.) Aug. 183 We had to put a doublejee or so into the wooden shoe.

2. [See DUBBELTJIE *n.*[2]] DUBBELTJIE *n.*[2]

No longer common in *S. Afr. Eng.*; used in *Austral. Eng.* (as 'double-gee') since 1872.

1823 T. PHILIPPS *Lett.* (1960) Our Dogs were soon disabled by a prickly seed which gets into their feet; it .. presents a thorn in every way it lies ... Called a 'doublejee' .. , but for what reason I cannot conjecture. **1833** *Graham's Town Jrnl* 21 Feb. 2 The next morning her mistress collected a quantity of 'doubeljees' (the prickly seed of a small plant) and strewed them under her. **1878** T.J. LUCAS *Camp Life & Sport* 86 There is a nasty thorn called the doublegee, which forms a triangle, and presents a point upwards whichever way it falls. **1980** J. COCK *Maids & Madams* 196 She was returned to her mistress who punished her by placing her in the stocks so as to cause extreme discomfort and a wound on her spine. At times she was made to sit on 'doublejees' (small thorns). [**1991** A. MALAN in *You* 7 Feb., The doublegee is a thorny weed that destroys pasture and maims lambs ... Accidentally introduced from South Africa in Western Australia's early farming days, the doublegee has thrived in the local conditions.]

douk var. DOEK.

douw var. DAUW.

down *adv.* [In sense a, prob. calqued on S. Afr. Du. (later Afk.) *af* in *die rivier kom af*; sense b prob. developed fr. sense a.] Of a (periodically dry) river:

a. In the intrans. v. phr. ***to come down***: to swell, to rise. Hence **coming down** *vbl n. phr.*, a flooding.

Also found in *Austral.* and *N.Z. Eng.* from the 1860s.

1854 R.B. STRUTHERS St. Lucia Hunting Diary. (Killie Campbell Africana Library KCM55079) 53 The river began to rise rapidly & we had just time to get the oxen back again, when the stream came down with overwhelming force. **1882** J. NIXON *Among Boers* 135 There was a man with an ox waggon outspanned on the bank, who told us that he had crossed that morning at eleven. He had some other waggons on the opposite side, but before he could get a second one over, the water came 'down' and cut him off from them. **1892** W.L. DISTANT *Naturalist in Tvl* 60 Three Dutch anglers who were sleeping .. on the banks of the Pienaar's River .. were swept away by a sudden flood or 'coming down' of the stream. **1897** J.P. FITZPATRICK *Outspan* 111 The next drift would be worse still. The river was coming down. *c*1904 E.L. PRICE

Jrnls (1956) 58 The danger .. kept my father & mother waking every now & again to listen whether the great river might not come down in the night – a great Swollen torrent – & sweep wagons & everything away with it. **1919** M.M. STEYN *Diary* 275 When we reached the Modder River .. we were stuck there because the river had come down and we were unable to cross. **1937** J. STEVENSON-HAMILTON *S. Afr. Eden* 94 During the night the river had come down in partial flood, and some rather urgently required belongings were marooned on the opposite bank. **1943** F.H. ROSE *Kruger's Wagon* 217 These particular reptiles .. had been swept into the pool on some occasion of the river 'coming down', as the African river floods are called. **1965** J. BENNETT *Hawk Alone* 153 Stuart had waded out neck-high one day with the surf dirty from the river coming down, got in a good cast, and turned shorewards to see two big yellow-belly sharks. **1981** *Daily Dispatch* 16 Feb. 9 The Buffels River came down in two peaks. The first was a normal flood level and receded reasonably significantly, but then the second peak came. **1990** R. MALAN *My Traitor's Heart* 318 The drought dragged on until 1982, only to break in a raging cloudburst ... The river came down in spate and crippled Neil's beloved waterwheel.

b. In the intrans. v. phr. ***to be down***: to be in flood, to be high, to be in spate.

1867 *Queenstown Free Press* 18 Jan., The rivers in this neighbourhood have been frequently 'down' during the last month. **1882** C. DU VAL *With Show through Sn Afr.* I. 103 We came to the Modder River, which was what is called, colonially, 'down', but which to the raw Briton would appear very considerably 'up'. **1897** E. GLANVILLE *Tales from Veld* 88 The Fish River was 'down'. It generally was down, in the sense of being low, but colonial rivers run by contraries – when they are down they are up. **1913** C. PETTMAN *Africanderisms* 152 *Down*, A river is said to be 'down' when the waters, increased by a heavy fall of rain higher up, rise in their channel.

DP *n.*[1] Also **deepie**. Initial letters of *Durban poison*, see DURBAN.

1978 *Rhodeo* (Rhodes Univ.) 13 Oct. 15 Dope is the most important thing in their lives and they pay exorbitant rates for DP, and stuff from the Transkei, Lesotho and Swaziland. **1978** *Darling* 8 Nov. 66 Ask someone from overseas why South Africa is famous and .. a few, a very small minority, will grin and say: 'Durban Poison, man.' Why? Because DP, dagga, is just about the best high in the world, fit to rank .. in the dope smoker's list of all-time greats. **1979** *Sunday Times* 2 Sept. 3 The transcript read: ' .. I am going to send you such a small amount you know, so it's undetectable in the letter, of this "deepie"' (slang term for a type of dagga).

DP *n.*[2] Initial letters of *Democratic Party*, a political party supporting the principles of western democracy and free enterprise, and in the past opposing apartheid; a member of this party. Also *attrib.* See also PROG.

Formed in 1989 by the amalgamation of the Independent Party (see IP), the National Democratic Movement (see NDM), and the Progressive Federal Party (see PFP).

1989 Z. DE BEER in *Progress* Mar. 1 The inner convictions of all who are engaged in forming the DP are such that we clearly belong together. We all stand committed for [*sic*] fundamental civil liberties. **1989** *Race Rel. Survey 1988–9* (S.A.I.R.R.) 659 *The Democratic Party* (DP) was launched in April 1989 following negotiations between three parties, the Progressive Federal Party (PFP) the Independent Party (IP) and the National Democratic Movement (NDM) to form a single party. **1990** B. STEVENSON in *Sunday Times* 23 Dec. 11 A large percentage of the DP support base lies among the business and professional communities ... Our DPs have a high profile and tackle local issues such as schools, environment, hospitals and tourism. **1991** A. VAN WYK *Birth of New Afrikaner* 110 A vision of myself in a vast crowd. It is a gathering of whites: former Nats and Saps, Progressives, DPs and perhaps a few CPs, too. **1993** L. KAUNDA in *Natal Witness* 13 Apr. 7 The task on the political front is to transform the DP into a provincial structure with five regions. Another challenge is to attract non-traditional members.

DPSC *n. hist.* Initial letters of *Detainees' Parents Support Committee*, an organization helping parents whose children have been detained as result of their political activities.

This committee was formed in 1981. Its activities included monitoring the numbers of people detained, helping parents to locate their children, and providing legal assistance to secure their release from prison.

1983 *Rand Daily Mail* 4 Feb. 5 Mr Le Grange said that an analysis of the DPSC had led him to the conclusion that it was a 'pressure group' serving the interests of the enemies of South Africa. **1987** D. FOSTER *Detention & Torture* 83 In 1982 the Detainees' Parents Support Committee (DPSC) collected 70 statements and affidavits from South African detainees claiming that systematic and widespread torture was used by the security police. **1988** *New Nation* 10 Mar. 6 Repression has taken on unprecedented proportions, detentions have reached new peaks and the Detainees' Parents Support Committee (DPSC) .. is now a banned organisation. **1988** BRITTAIN & MINTY *Children of Resistance* 72 In 1982, one year after the DPSC was started, 8 people under the age of 18 were detained under security legislation. During the 1986 State of Emergency of the 22,000 detainees, 8,800 were children under 18. **1990** J. ROSENTHAL *Wake Up Singing* 66 The support group, the DPSC, has been in touch with Mrs Xaba. Given her some advice on what she can do ... We may be able to take a parcel of stuff to Zach tomorrow.

DR /diːˈɑː(r)/ *adj. colloq.* Initial letters of DUTCH REFORMED.

1920 R.Y. STORMBERG *Mrs Pieter de Bruyn* 61 To-day we had the honour of a visit from the D.R. minister, his wife, and a deacon. *c*1936 *S. & E. Afr. Yr Bk & Guide* 473 The parsonage of the D.R. Church at Kruis Vallei was burned. **1963** [see CHRISTIAN]. **1965** A. GORDON-BROWN *S. Afr. Heritage* I. 18 The Dutch Reformed Church (Groote Kerk), Adderley Street, begun in 1699, is the oldest and largest D.R. church in South Africa.

‖**draadsitter** /ˈdrɑːtsətə(r)/ *n.* [Afk., *draad* wire, fence + *sitter* sitter; prob. tr. Eng. *fence-sitter.*] A fence-sitter, esp. in the context of politics. Also *attrib.*

1970 C. KINSLEY *Informant, Koegasbrug (N. Cape)* Draadsitter. A person of no strong political views. **1979** *Het Suid-Western* 3 Oct., He played the role of a draadsitter during the town council's debate on Sunday sport. Mr Joubert abstained from voting on the issue. **1979** *Sunday Times* 9 Dec. (Mag. Sect.) 1 After all the vacillating, draadsitter Vorster years, our country at last has a leader. **1987** P. LAURENCE in *Weekly Mail* 13 Mar. 5 Their high-sounding manifesto invites their categorisation as prevaricating *draadsitters* more that it commends them as intrepid innovators. **1992** K. OWEN in *Sunday Times* 8 Mar. 22 The wavering voters, even the draadsitters, await a leader who will .. tell them where we are going, and how we can make it work when we get there.

‖**draai** /draɪ/ *n.* Formerly also **draij**. [Afk., fr. Du.]

1.a. An avoidance or circumlocution.

1786 G. FORSTER tr. *A. Sparrman's Voy. to Cape of G.H.* II. 96 When .. any thing remarkable happens, a Hottentot endeavours to avoid, if he can, mentioning it for some days, and when at length he does speak of it, it is with a kind of circumlocution, or, as the colonists call it, with a *draij*, a sort of twist or winding.

b. A twist or turn.

1870 in A.M.L. Robinson *Sel. Articles from Cape Monthly Mag.* (1978) 120 The road was travelled and worn, until nothing seemed left but an axle-breaking track of sand and boulders. Adventurous people had made 'draais' amongst the grass and bushes. **1900** B. MITFORD *Aletta* 114 *Maagtig*, but he is fond of shooting birds. One *klompie* down on the *draai* by the white rock had nearly sixty birds in it, and now there are nine. **1970** C.B. WOOD *Informant, Johannesburg* Let's take a 'draai' (turn) around the block.

c. *fig.* In the intrans. v. phr. ***to make a draai***, to pay a visit, to drop in. Also in dim. form **draaitjie** [see -IE].

1970 *Informant, Pietersburg* Let's go make a draaitjie at Erna's house – visit. **1993** H. THOMPSON *Informant, Grahamstown* I've just finished your VAT [return] – can you please make a draai and come and sign it?

2. Ellipt. for TICKEY-DRAAI sense 2.

1941 [see OPSKUD *n.*].

draaibossie /ˈdraɪˌbɔsi/ *n.* Formerly also **draaibos(ch)je**. [Afk., *draai* twist, turn + *bossie* (earlier *bosje*, *boschje*, see BOSCHJE) bush; so called because of the spiral twist of the stem and older branches.] The small shrub *Felicia filifolia* of the Asteraceae. Occas. without dim. suffix, **draaibos**.

1896 R. WALLACE *Farming Indust. of Cape Col.* 86 *Diplopappus*, the 'draai-bosje,' takes its place on thin stony ridges or hill-sides, and grows best on a southern exposure. **1906** F. BLERSCH *Handbk of Agric.* 256 Other species of plants of considerable feeding value are *Atriplex capensis*, the Vaal boschje .. ; *Portulacaria afra*, the spek boom; *Diplopappus filifolius*, the draai boschje. **1910** A.B. LAMONT *Rural Reader* 257 The draaibos is another small bush, and takes the place of good karoo on poor soils and on rocky hillsides. **1917** R. MARLOTH *Common Names* 24 *Draai'bossie*, *Aster filifolius*. A valuable fodder-bush of the Karoo. **1966** C.A. SMITH *Common Names* 202 *Draaibos(sie)*, *Aster* sp ... Bushy, rigid, perennial shrubs up to 4 ft high ... The species are regarded as excellent fodder bushes. **1981** J. VAHRMEIJER *Poisonous Plants of Sn Afr.* 60 The following species are often host plants to the poison bush: *Felicia muricata* .., *Felicia filifolia* (draaibos), *Chrysocoma tenuifolia*.

drab *n. Ostrich-farming.* [Named for its dull grey-brown colour.] A long feather from a hen ostrich, taken from the place where the wing joins the body. See also ONDERBAATJIE. Also *attrib.*

*c*1881 A. DOUGLASS *Ostrich Farming* 82 The various heaps of blacks and drabs should be tied into bunches .. the long blacks and drabs are better in small bunches. *Ibid.* 92 (*fold-out*) Black and drab, being the inner rows of the wing, the Black coming from the Male, the Drab from the Female. **1896** R. WALLACE *Farming Indust. of Cape Col.* 235 Drab, long, and medium were about 10s. per lb. lower. **1896** [see BLACK *n.* sense 2]. **1909** J.E. DUERDEN in *Agric. Jrnl of Cape of G.H.* XXXIV. 523 Drabs .. the covert rows in the hen .. are always greyish, not black. They are classed as *long*, *medium*, and *short*. **1910** A.B. LAMONT *Rural Reader* 144 Two rows of blacks (in the cock) or drabs (in the hen) are also removed from the upper side of the wings, and some from the lower side or 'onderbaatje'. **1968** F. GOLDIE *Ostrich Country* 64 All her feathers were pure white with the exception of a row of drab feathers overlaying the upper portion of her wing feathers.

drachie var. DROGIE.

drag-mij-kell var. DROOG-MY-KEEL.

draij var. DRAAI.

Drakensberger /ˈdrɑːkənsˌbɜːgə, ˈdrɑːkənz-/ *n.* [*Drakensberg* name of region where breed was developed + Eng. n.-forming suffix *-er.*] (One of) a hardy local breed of beef cattle, suited to higher, colder regions: see quot. 1971. Also *attrib.*

*c*1951 *Off. Yrbk of Union 1949* (Union Office of Census & Statistics) 803 Another indigenous breed, the *Drakensberger*, was officially recognised in 1947. It is a dual purpose type specially adapted to higher and colder regions. **1971** J. VAN MARLE in *Std Encycl. of Sn Afr.* IV. 82 An indigenous, black, large-framed beef breed of cattle ... They have been known as Drakensbergers since 1947 when the South African Drakensberger Cattle-Breeder's Society was established.

The name includes three types – Uys cattle, Kemp cattle and Tritern Blacks – which were developed in the Drakensberg region of Natal. **1981** *S. Afr. Panorama* Nov. 27 The country's 250 Drakensberger stud breeders .. claim that their favourite is particularly resistant to disease and drought and able to live largely off the veld. *c***1988** *S. Afr. 1987–8: Off. Yrbk* (Bureau for Info.) 352 The indigenous Afrikaner, Bonsmara and Drakensberger are popular beef breeds. **1993** *Natal Witness* 31 Dec. 15 (*advt*) Farmers' Association sale Week: ... Special entry on behalf of Mr M. Liebenberg: 50 Drakensberger heifers 18–24 months old.

DRC *n.* Also **D.R.C.** Initial letters of *Dutch Reformed Church*: see note at DUTCH REFORMED. Also *attrib.*

1971 *Daily Dispatch* 20 May 8 Those DRC ministers who refused to pray for those men who were fighting for their country in the Second World War. **1982** *Reader* Dec. 9 This year there was a conference in Canada of all DRC churches in the world ... The Sendingskerk asked all the churches of the world not to talk to or mix with the white DRC of South Africa. They said the white DRC supported apartheid. **1983** F.E.O'B. GELDENHUYS in *Optima* Vol.31 No.3, 149 One must start by dispelling the myth that the DRC is the official state church in South Africa. **1991** A. VAN WYK *Birth of New Afrikaner* 88 The confession of the sins of apartheid by the session of the DRC Synod at Bloemfontein in October 1990 should be seen as a spiritual watershed. **1994** G. DOMINY in *Natal Witness* 8 Jan. 4 The young English-speaker .. attended the Dutch Reformed Church on a fairly regular basis and .. was asked to become an 'ouderling'. After much soul-searching he went to the chief ouderling and tried to decline the honour on the grounds he was not a member of the DRC, was too busy, granny was unwell, etc.

dressed *ppl adj. Obs.* exc. *hist.* [Special sense of general Eng.; alluding to the wearing of Western-style clothing (rather than traditional African dress).] Of urban African people: westernized in dress, manner, and language, but without a full school education. Cf. BLANKET, SCHOOL *adj.*

1943 'J. BURGER' *Black Man's Burden* 55 The older Natives now distinguish between 'dressed' and 'blanket' Natives. **1949** L. HUNTER *Afr. Dawn* 159 He had bought a second class ticket so that he would be in a section of the vehicle where his fellow travellers would almost certainly be 'dressed' Natives. **1980** D.B. COPLAN Urbanization of African Performing Arts. 57 As distinct from the highly Westernized African graduates of Cape mission schools, they were called 'dressed people' inferring their superficial adoption of European culture in the form of clothing, a limited fluency in Afrikaans or English, and an individualized, opportunistic social outlook ... The 'dressed people,' also called *abaphakathi* ('those in the middle'), occupied an insecure position between mission-school Africans and non-Christian traditionalists in African society as a whole.

driedoring /ˈdri ˌduərəŋ, -ˌduərəŋ/ *n.* Also **driedoorn** /-dʊə(r)n/, and with initial capital. [Afk. (earlier S. Afr. Du.), *drie* three + *doring* thorn.] Any of several thorny shrubs of the genus *Rhigozum* of the Bignoniaceae (thorny pomegranates), esp. *R. trichotomum*; THREETHORN. Also *attrib.*

1822 W.J. BURCHELL *Trav.* I. 299 Bushes, three or four feet high, of that singular shrub *Rhigozum trichotomum*, whose stiff branches, constantly dividing and subdividing, in a most regular manner, into threes, present a very rare and curious ramification, and have obtained for it the name of *Driedoorn* (Three-thorn). **1900** [see HAAK-EN-STEEK]. **1917** R. MARLOTH *Common Names* 24 *Driedoorn, Rhigozum trichotomum* and *R. obovatum*. Shrubs of the Karoo generally branching trichotomously. **1933** *Cape Argus* 27 July (Swart), Experiments are also being carried out with the grinding of the Drie Doring Bush, and it is stated that the feeding value of this meal is even greater than that of the Karoo bush. **1936** [see SOUTBOS]. **1955** L.G. GREEN *Karoo* 132 In sandy soil, the widespread *driedoring* is the dominant bush, and this produces a dense covering of white flowers when the drought breaks. There is another *driedoring* species, the *wilde granaat*; which prefers the koppies and gives out brilliant yellow flowers. **1972** PALMER & PITMAN *Trees of Sn Afr.* III. 2002 *Rhigozum*, .. Burchell founded this genus on the driedoring, *Rhigozum trichotomum*, the shrub whose spiky form .. is so typical a sight in the arid northern Cape and parts of the western Orange Free State. **1973** [see BRAKBOS]. **1983** K.C. PALGRAVE *Trees of Sn Afr.* 829 A shrub, *R. trichotomum* .. , the *driedoring*, with its branches characteristically arising in threes.

‖**drievoet** /ˈdrifʊt/ *n.* and *adj.* [Afk., *drie* three + *voet* foot.]

A. *n.* A trivet.

1970 E. MUNDELL *Informant, Pearston (E. Cape)* The kaffirpot stands on a drievoet. **1988** L.S. DIXON in C. Pedersen *Down Memory Lane at Riet River* 51 Cooking was done on an open fire, much of it in the cast-iron bakepot. All the pots stood on the 'drievoet' or a metal frame known as a trivet. **1994** G. JEZI *Informant, Grahamstown* You put the whole smiley on a drievoet and burn off all the hair, you wash it with a stone and hot water until it's clean, clean.

B. *adj. rare.* Having three legs: see also THREE-LEGGED.

1988 M. TLALI in *Staffrider* Vol.7 No.3, 360, I could see her stoking fire below a big 'drievoet' iron pot.

drift /drɪft/ *n.* Also (rarely) **drif.** [S. Afr. Du., fr. Du. *drift* point at which one can wade through a stream.]

1.a. A shallow point in a river where it may be safely crossed; a ford; now usu. a causeway, constructed where a river crosses a road. Also with qualifying word, **wagon drift** (*obs.*).

1786 [see sense b below]. **1795** C.R. HOPSON tr. *C.P. Thunberg's Trav.* II. p.xii, A *Drift* is that part of a river, where the water is shallowest, and, consequently, where it can be crossed in a carriage. **1826** G. BARKER Journal. 7 Dec., When crossing the Keiskama at a very bad drift, I slipped off a large stone into the river, nearly lost my hat with the stream. **1837** J.M. BOWKER *Speeches & Sel.* (1864) 54 Twenty-five oxen and eight cows .. have been stolen this week; the spoor was traced close past Trompeter's Drift Post, and through the upper waggon drift. **1843** *Cape of G.H. Almanac & Annual Register* 451 This river [*sc.* the Orange] .. is easily forded, the water at the usual drift, being shallow, and the banks of the river presenting an easy slope to the water's edge. **1850** R.G.G. CUMMING *Hunter's Life* II. 284 We held thither at a sharp trot, holding for the old waggon drift to avoid having to pass through dense reeds. **1853** F.P. FLEMING *Kaffraria* 46 Where the road crosses a river, what is called a *drift* is made – which is done by clearing the bed of the river of large stones, and cutting a sloping roadway through the banks on either side. *a***1858** J. GOLDSWAIN *Chron.* (1946) I. 73 They all went out and saw they Kaffer coming up they Wagon drift close to the House. **1863** LADY DUFF-GORDON in F. Galton *Vacation Tourists* (1864) III. 194 On we went, straight along the valley, crossing drift after drift; – a drift is the bed of a stream more or less dry; in which sometimes you are drowned, sometimes only pounded, as was our hap. **1872** [see PONT sense 1]. **1899** D.S.F.A. PHILLIPS *S. Afr. Recollections* 60 On most of the South African rivers there are certain places called 'drifts' (fords), which can be crossed by waggons. In cases where that is impossible there are ponts or bridges. *a***1912** [see INKRUIP PLAAS]. **1936** E. ROSENTHAL *Old-Time Survivals* 9 You can find wagons outspanned for the sultry hours of the day near river banks, or waiting to be taken across 'drifts' or fords by pont, which is the South African word for pontoon. **1953** U. KRIGE *Dream & Desert* 185 Against the ridge above the drif he conducted the service. **1974** *E. Prov. Herald* 6 Sept. 6 Farmers .. were able to cross low level bridges and drifts late on Wednesday for the first time since the rains. **1986** *Motorist* 3rd Quarter 29 The rains regularly washed away the drifts over the stream and a section of the road on either side of them. **1994** M. ROBERTS tr. *J.A. Wahlberg's Trav. Jrnls 1838–56* 58 The drift goes pretty obliquely through the stream, and is full of boulders.

b. Freq. with initial capital. As an element in place names: see quots.

1786 G. FORSTER tr. *A. Sparrman's Voy. to Cape of G.H.* II. 20 We arrived at *Zondags-rivier's drift*. **1835** J.W.D. MOODIE *Ten Yrs* II. 131 We pursued our journey along a high, level tract of country, towards 'Jagers Drift' or Hunter's Ford. **1837** [see sense a]. **1914** C. PETTMAN *Notes on S. Afr. Place Names* 30 The huge saurian, the crocodile, has its Crocodile River and Crocodile Drift. **1972** *Evening Post* 11 Mar. 2 The Addo Drift is often impassable. A causeway is to be constructed.

2. Always in *pl.* (usu. with initial capital) in the Special Comb. **Drifts crisis, Drifts question** *hist.*, the closure in 1895 of the fords on the Vaal river by president Paul Kruger of the South African Republic, as a result of a rail tariff dispute; the political consequences of this closure.

1928 E.A. WALKER *Hist. of S. Afr.* 453 During the **Drifts crisis** four of the Johannesburg Reformers .. had arranged with him [*sc.* Cecil Rhodes] that Jameson should come in from the western border. **1968** — *Hist. of Sn Afr.* 449 While the Drifts crisis was .. rising to its climax, Chamberlain settled the fate of the Bechuanaland Protectorate. **1917** BLELOCH & O'FLAHERTY *1000 Million Pounds* 108 Kruger had shrunk from a war on the **Drifts Question** prepared for him by the German control of the Railway Company. **1933** W.H.S. BELL *Bygone Days* 183 In the latter part of 1895 there had very nearly been a war with the Cape Colony over the 'drifts' question.

drift-sand *n.* [Eng. *drift* the action of drifting + *sand*.

In sense b found earlier, but only rarely, in Brit. and Austral. Eng.]

a. Usu. in *pl.*: Areas (usu. on the coast) where wind-blown sand is deposited as mounds, banks, or dunes.

1896 R. WALLACE *Farming Indust. of Cape Col.* 69 *Drift sands* occur on the *Cape Flats*, and at certain places along the south coast of Cape Colony, but most conspicuously and extensively on the peninsular area to the west of *Port Elizabeth* ... Drift sands occur when very fine sand lacking cohesion is cast up on the shore, and dried and blown inland by strong winds. **1971** E.K. LORIMER *Panorama of Port Elizabeth* 101 The Governor, Sir Bartle Frere, .. came in 1877 to the Bushy Park area and was taken .. to a high point from which a good view of the driftsands could be obtained. *Ibid.* 104 The driftsands were gradually planted with tiny seedlings of Port Jackson willow, imported from Australia. **1973** J.W. STEYN in *Std Encycl. of Sn Afr.* IX. 486 Extensive parts of the western and south-western coastal region of the Cape Province .. are exposed to drift-sands which .. can devastate large tracts of fertile grazing and cultivated land. **1988** LUBKE & VAN WIJK in R.A. Lubke et al. *Field Guide to E. Cape Coast* 172 Some attractive herbs occur in open drift sands, for example *Senecio elegans*.

b. *noncount.* Wind-blown sand. Also *attrib.*

1913 C. PETTMAN *Africanderisms* 153 *Drift-sand*, Sand driven, as it is in some localities, into enormous banks by the wind. **1951** N.L. KING *Tree-Planting* 37 (*caption*) Township on reclaimed drift sand, Port Elizabeth. **1973** J.W. STEYN in *Std Encycl. of Sn Afr.* IX. 486 Afforestation is one of the most successful methods of checking the drift-sand and reclaiming the soil. **1985** K.L. TINLEY *Coastal Dunes* 270 (*caption*) Slat-fence erected at Stilbaai to protect beach houses from becoming smothered by drift sand. **1992** E. VAN WIJK in *S. Afr. Panorama* Mar.-Apr. 49 This division manages 130 conservation areas including forests, nature reserves, wilderness areas, drift-sand areas, [etc.].

drilvis /ˈdrəlfəs/ *n.* Also **dril(l)visch, tril(l) visch,** and with initial capital. [Afk. (earlier S. Afr. Du. *drilvisch*), *dril* or *tril* shiver, vibrate, tremble + *vis* fish.]

1. Any of several species of fish belonging to **a.** the numbfish (family Narkidae); or **b.** the electric rays (family Torpedinidae).

1795 C.R. HOPSON tr. *C.P. Thunberg's Trav.* I. 295 The *Raja torpedo* too (called here *Trill visch*) was sometimes caught in the harbour, but not brought to table. **1913** C. PETTMAN *Africanderisms* 153 *Drill-visch*, .. *Astrape capensis*, sometimes called the Electric fish; both names have reference to the power which this fish possesses of giving an electric or benumbing shock when touched. **1949** J.L.B. SMITH *Sea Fishes* 73 *Torpedinidae, Electric Rays. Drilvis.* **1968** —— *High Tide* 35 Kolb's most entertaining account is that of the Drilvisch (electric ray). If a person touched or held this mysterious fish, he reports, he suffered terrible agony in all his limbs, especially in that holding the fish. **1971** R. RAVEN-HART *Cape G.H. 1652–1702* 500 *Drilvis, Narke capensis, Torpedo marmorata* .. ('Trillvis').

2. *obs.* A jellyfish.

1913 C. PETTMAN *Africanderisms* 515 *Tril Visch*, .. Jelly fish are known by this name in the Western Province Districts.

drink-gras var. DRONKGRAS.

droastdy var. DROSTDY.

droë-geilsiekte see GEILSIEKTE sense 2.

droëwors /ˈdruəvɔrs, ˈdrʊə- , -vɔːs/ *n.* Also **droe-wors**. [Afk., *droë* attrib. form of *droog* dry + *wors* sausage.] Air-dried sausage, salted and spiced. See also WORS sense 1.

1981 *Fair Lady* 9 Sept. 178 A hamper of biltong, droëwors and other treats. **1982** *Meat Board Focus* Mar. 21 (*advt*) Make money out of making biltong & droëwors! **1991** *Leisure Books Catal.* Apr.-June 19 Step-by-step instructions on how to master the traditional methods for making your own biltong, droëwors and sausages.

drogie /ˈdruəxi, ˈdrʊəxi/ *n.* Also **drachie, droggie, droogje**. [Afk., *droog* short for *droog-my-keel* + dim. suffix -IE.] DROOG-MY-KEEL, esp. the fruit.

1913 C. PETTMAN *Africanderisms* 155 *Dry-my-throat-bush*, .. The name conveys an idea of the peculiar effect produced upon the throat and tongue by the berries (*droogjes*) of this bush. **1917** R. MARLOTH *Common Names* 24 *Drachies, Scutia Commersonii.* See also Droog-mijn-keel. **1970** M. VAN RENSBURG *Informant, Port Elizabeth* Droggies. A berry, from the word 'Droogmykeel'. **1972** PALMER & PITMAN *Trees of Sn Afr.* II. 1401 These fruits are the 'drogies' — the little dry ones — of children and beloved by them. **1991** M. SLAUGHTER *Informant, Grahamstown* They're over there, collecting drogies.

‖**drol** /drɔl/ *n. slang.* Also **drôl**. Pl. **-le** /-lə/. [Afk., human or animal excrement.] Excrement; usu. *fig.*, as an abusive term of address or reference. Also in dim. form **drolletjie** [see -IE]. See also BOKDROL sense 2.

1969 A. FUGARD *Boesman & Lena* 3 Lena: Rubbish? Boesman: That long *drol* of nonsense that comes out when you open your mouth! *Ibid.* 31 Boesman (*to the old man*): You're an expensive *ou drol.* Two bottles of wine! *Ek sê.* **1982** *Rhodeo* (Rhodes Univ.) 6 Apr. 11 That's been the weakness of past 'satires' in South Africa — they were done by English speaking people who made jokes of the Afrikaners. They put on a heavy accent and say — sis, shame, poep, drôl — and then that's supposed to be very funny. **1990** Z. MATTHEWS in *Personality* 28 May 24 The *Publieke Telefoon* stands innocently on a square of *drolletjie*-infested grass surrounded by barbed-wire fencing.

dronk /drɔŋk/ *adj. colloq.* [Afk.] Drunk.

1983 M. DU PLESSIS *State of Fear* 135, I suppose I'm talking nonsense really, I'm a *bietjie dronk*, you see. **1986** *Informant, East London* You should have seen how dronk he was last night. **1987** L. BEAKE *Strollers* 10 A man was taking photographs with a polaroid camera. Shy teenage girls giggled at him from behind their hands and a dronk bergie shouted comments. **1990** *Weekend Post* 19 May 5 Arrogant, racist, skelm or dronk? White, coloured and black postgraduate students .. listed these opinions about each other at the stereotype reduction course ... *Coloureds: skelm, dronk*, unreliable, hostile, crude, jolly, outgoing, in an unfortunate position, funny.

dronkgras /ˈdrɔŋkxras/ *n.* Also **drink-gras**. [Afk., *dronk* drunk + *gras* grass.] Any of several plants which are poisonous to livestock: **a.** Any of several species of grass of the Poaceae, esp. *Melica decumbens* (sub-family Pooideae), but also the rye grass *Lolium temulentum* (sub-family Pooideae), and *Paspalum scrobiculatum* (sub-family Panicoidae). **b.** The horse-tail fern *Equisetum ramosissimum* of the Equisetaceae. **c.** The *styfsiektebossie* (see STYFSIEKTE sense 2), *Crotalaria burkeana*. Also part. tr. **dronk grass**. See also DRONKSIEKTE.

1896 E. CLAIRMONTE *Africander* 159 Another curious sickness which attacks cattle is the *dronk siekta*. It is caused by eating a kind of grass called *dronk* gras. **1896** R. WALLACE *Farming Indust. of Cape Col.* 95 A somewhat similar condition of helplessness from intoxication, or semi-paralysis, results when cattle feed upon *dronk grass, Melica dendroides. Ibid.* 100 It would appear that the giddiness and intoxication, described by one farmer as a 'wild delirium', from which animals suffer after eating dronk-gras, is similar to the effects produced after the seeds of darnel rye-grass .. have been consumed. **1906** F. BLERSCH *Handbk of Agric.* 257 The following are some weeds of a poisonous character found on pastures: Dronk gras (*Melica dendroides*), [etc.]. **1910** A.B. LAMONT *Rural Reader* 257 *Dronk grass* is one of the poisonous plants, and makes stock stupid when they eat it. **1913** [see BITTER KAROO]. **1932** WATT & BREYER-BRANDWIJK *Medicinal & Poisonous Plants* 117 *Malva parviflora* .. is said to produce symptoms similar to 'Dronkgras' intoxication (*cf.* Equisetum ramosissimum). **1991** G.E. GIBBS RUSSELL et al. *Grasses of Sn Afr.* 209 *Melica decumbens* .. Dronkgras ... Poisonous (to horses, cattle and donkeys). *Ibid.* 246 *Paspalum scrobiculatum* .. Creeping paspalum, dronkgras.

dronkie /ˈdrɔŋki/ *n. colloq.* [Afk., *dronk* drunk + -IE.] A drunkard; DRONKLAP. Also *attrib.*

1940 M.G. GILBERT *Informant, Cape Town* 16 June 4 The feeling that so many of them are going away soon, rather cast a shadow on everyone — except the dronkies! **1969** A. FUGARD *Boesman & Lena* 35 Crawling out of your holes. Like worms. *Babalas* as the day you were born. That piece of ground was rotten with *dronkies*. **1979** *Voice* 2 Sept. 5 Hee ... Heee ... Heeee! Boy, the dronkie Stinking old man, Come for a wash on my mamma's lap. **1979** *Sunday Times* 23 Sept. (Mag. Sect.) 8 His leading lady turns out to be a dronkie, so he calls in a last-minute replacement, a pretty ingenue who knows all the numbers. **1987** L. BEAKE *Strollers* 70 Woollen-capped dronkies down from the berg danced with their eyes closed until they fell over or were taken away. **1990** A. MAIMANE in *Weekly Mail* 22 June (Weekend Mail) 2 These figures suggested whites were the world's greatest *dronkies*, even if the average intake was diluted by applying the total census figures, thus including babies.

dronklap /ˈdrɔŋk lap/ *n. colloq.* [Afk., *dronk* drunk + *lap* rag.] DRONKIE.

1959 J. MEIRING *Candle in Wind* 7 Only three little drinks today and he had called her a drunkard, a dronk-lap! **1975** S. ROBERTS *Outside Life's Feast* 10 Their father is also a dronklap who makes the A.C.F. outjies laugh by carrying a brandy cork around in his pocket and taking it for sniffs. **1977** FUGARD & DEVENISH *Guest* 46 Those bloody pills aren't medicine. It's drugs he's taking. He's worse than a dronklap. **1977** D. MULLER *Whitey* 46 'So you're a dronklap from East London,' he said sourly. 'Perhaps you'd better go back that way, mister. We have enough hoboes down here.' **1979** A. HOUSE in *Staffrider* Vol.2 No.1, 10 Come from the library? Where's your books? Only a bottle of wine. *Dronklap*, drunkard. **1980** A. DANGOR in M. Mutloatse *Forced Landing* 165 'Hey you *fokken dronklap*!' A man obviously disturbed by Samad's raving stood at the railing of his balcony ... 'A man can't even get a decent night's sleep here.'

dronksiekte /ˈdrɔŋksiktə/ *n. Pathology.* Formerly also **dronk siekta, dronkziekte**. [Afk. (earlier S. Afr. Du. *dronkziekte*), *dronk* drunk + *siekte* disease, sickness.] An illness of livestock caused by the ingestion of any of several poisonous plants, and characterized by loss of coordination, staggering, and shivering. See also DRONKGRAS.

1896 [see DRONKGRAS]. **1913** C. PETTMAN *Africanderisms* 154 *Dronkziekte*, .. A sickness supposed to be produced by eating Dronk-gras. It is similar to that produced by eating the seeds of *Lolium temulatum*, L. known in the north of England as 'drunk'. **1914** *Farmer's Annual* 237 'Dronk-ziekte' a disease recognised at the Cape, but the cause of which is unknown, or a matter of dispute. **1937** *Handbk for Farmers* (Dept of Agric. & Forestry) 466 *Shivers, Dronksiekte or Horsetail Poisoning, (Equisetaceae)* ... When animals which have eaten the plant are driven they become exhausted easily, stagger about, fall down, and are unable to rise. **1972** W.J. LUTJEHARMS in *Std Encycl. of Sn Afr.* V. 596 The plant [*sc.* Horse-tail fern] is poisonous to stock ... The animals show symptoms making them look 'drunk and stupid' ('dronksiekte', *equisetosis*). **1981** J. VAHRMEIJER *Poisonous Plants of Sn Afr.* 26 *Equisetum* usually occurs in damp places, near water ... Poisoning, especially in mules and horses, is known variously as bewerasiesiekte, drilsiekte, dronksiekte or shivers.

droogje var. DROGIE.

droog-my-keel /ˌdruəx meɪ ˈkɪəl, ˌdrʊəx-/ *n.* Formerly also **drag-mij-kell, droog-m'-keel, droog-mij(n)-keel**. [Afk. (earlier S. Afr. Du.), lit. 'dry-my-throat', *droog* dry + *my* my + *keel* throat.] Any of several plant species which bear astringent fruits: **1.** Either of two species of Vitaceae (grape-vine family): **a.** *Rhoicissus tridentata*; also called WILD GRAPE (sense 1 a); **b.** the WILD GRAPE (sense 1 c), *Cyphostemma cirrhosum*. **2.** The CAT-THORN (sense 2 a), *Scutia myrtina*. In all senses also called DROGIE, DRY-MY-THROAT. Also *attrib.*

Used medicinally by early colonists, esp. for the treatment of throat infections.

1898 E. GLANVILLE in *Empire* 8 Oct. (Pettman), He marched off to a clump of *drag-mij-kell* bush about a hundred yards off. **1917** R. MARLOTH *Common Names* 24 *Droog-mijn-keel, Cissus cirrhosa.* Nearly allied to our wild grape, but the fruit contains such a powerful irritant that a single berry, if chewed, will cause great pain, hence the vernacular name. The same name applied to *Scutia Commersonii.* **1932** WATT & BREYER-BRANDWIJK *Medicinal & Poisonous Plants* 116 The Mapulanas use the juice of the bulbous root of *Cissus cirrhosa* .., Droog-my-keel, with water as a gargle, as an internal remedy, and as an application to glandular swellings and creeping sores. *c*1955 M. HUME *Sawdust Heaven* 45 Her throat was dry, as though she had been eating the blue-black berries of the droog-my-keel. **1965** J. BENNETT *Hawk Alone* 76 The land fell away towards the river in a broad sweep of prickly pear and droog-m'-keel and mimosa. **1971** *Std Encycl. of Sn Afr.* IV. 89 *Droog-my-keel*, This name, sometimes in the form droog-my-keelbos(sie), is used in a very wide sense, being applied in various localities to several indigenous plants whose fruits when eaten or tasted cause a drying of the throat due to astringency. **1972** A. SCHOLEFIELD *Wild Dog Running* 126 The little valleys were heavy with mimosa and kei-apple, wild olive and sneeze-wood, Caffre thorn and *boerboons* and *droog-mij-keel* bushes.

droosty var. DROSTDY.

droppels var. DRUPPELS.

dropper *n.* [Prob. orig. N.Z. Eng.] A light wooden, iron, or wire upright, placed between the planted posts of a fence to keep the wires taut and in a parallel position.

Also *N.Z.* and *Austral. Eng.*

1897 *E. Prov. Herald* 9 Apr., (*advt*) Sole agents for 'Lochrin' Patent Fencing, Standards, Droppers, Straining Pillars, Farm Gates, etc. **1914** *Farmer's Annual* p.xli, (*advt*) Barbed and Plain Wires, all gauges, English and American Fencing Standards and Droppers, .. Jackal netting. *c*1936 *S. & E. Afr. Yr Bk & Guide* 269 The 'ordinary' fence .. consists of five barbed or six plain wires, standards of iron or wood, not more than 15 or 20 yards apart, with four droppers in between. **1951** H.C. BOSMAN in L. Abrahams *Bekkersdal Marathon* (1971) 149 What kind of fence is it that they are going to put up? .. Will it have standards that you pull out and bend the fence down by the droppers for the cattle to walk over on bucksails? **1968** *Farmer's Weekly* 3 Jan. 93 (*advt*) Poles and droppers. Selected round pine, any lengths and widths, for rough building purposes and fencing. **1972** *Ibid.* 21 Apr. 79 Creosoted non-bending wattle droppers. Standard length about 5cm thick. **1989** J. DU P. BOTHMA *Game Ranch Management* 50 Types of material used for droppers: Wooden droppers: SABS creosote or tanalith-treated blue-gum (not pine) droppers. Iscor ridgeback iron droppers. Cable droppers — single old mine cables. Binding wire. **1990** M.M. HACKSLEY (tr. E. van Heerden) in *Lynx* 217 We hauled out the cross that we had nailed together out of old fence-droppers and a cut down telephone pole.

dros(dt)dy var. DROSTDY.

drosser var. DROSTER.

drost *n. obs.* Shortened form of LANDDROST.

1786 G. FORSTER tr. *A. Sparrman's Voy. to Cape of G.H.* I. 222 The *drost* gave us a good reception, and a bed at night. **1798** S.H. WILCOCKE tr. *J.S. Stavorinus's Voy. to E. Indies 1768–71* I. 571 Officers are appointed in the interior parts of the colony, called *drosts*, or sheriffs, who arrest criminals, but have no power of trying or judging them; they must be sent up to the council of justice, to be examined and punished.

drostdy /ˈdrɒstɪ, drɔsˈdeɪ/ *n.* Also **droastdy, dro(o)sty, dros(dt)dy,** and with initial capital. Pl. **drostdies.** [S. Afr. Du., fr. Du. *drost* bailiff + -(*d*)*ij*, suffix forming an abstract n. indicating function or sphere of influence.

'In none of the scientific dictionaries of our language [*sc.* Dutch] have we found the form *drostdy.* Still the etymology is very clear: < *drost* + allomorph suffix *-dji* (< *ij*). The meaning should be "office, rank, dignity of drost", "residence of a drost". Analogical formations in modern Dutch are *makelaardij* "brokerage", "agency" and *proosdij* "deanery".' (P.G.J. van Sterkenburgh, Stichting Instituut voor Nederlandse Lexicologie).]

1. *hist.* During the 17th, 18th, and early 19th centuries, a magisterial and administrative district at the Cape over which a LANDDROST had jurisdiction. Also *attrib.* See also SUB-DROSTDY.

1796 *Statement of Expenditure* in G.M. Theal *Rec. of Cape Col.* (1897) I. 351 Sundry officers of the Drostdy of Stellenbosch ... Rds 890. **1809** R. COLLINS in *Ibid.* (1900) VII. 20 This affords the advantage of a direct and regular communication between the two drosdies, and enables the Postholders to receive three dollars for each hour's distance. **1811** *Cape Town Gaz. & Afr. Advertiser* Vol.6 No.276, 1 A new Drostdy shall be formed from that part of the Drostdy of Zwellendam which lies to the Eastward of the Ghanka or Gauritz River. **1823** W.W. BIRD *State of Cape of G.H.* 22 The Landdrost, who is the chief officer of the district, or Drostdy, holds, together with six heemraden, as accessors, a court for petty cases. **1827** *Reports of Commissioners upon Finances at Cape of G.H.* I. 40 It were to be wished that the districts now called drostdies, but to which in future we propose to give the designation of 'counties', should be multiplied, and their dimensions reduced. **1831** *S. Afr. Almanac & Dir.* 152 This District [of Worcester] .. was separated from the Stellenbosch district and was erected into a Drosdy in 1803. **1843** J.C. CHASE *Cape of G.H.* 54 Instead of the late absurd changes these sections of the colony have undergone from the name of drostdy to district, and from district to division, we shall have it permanently called by the good old English designation of the shire or county of Utenhay, &c. **1877** J. NOBLE *S. Afr.* 24 He divided the country into five districts or 'drostdies' — Stellenbosch, Swellendam, Graaf Reinet, Uitenhage and Tulbagh. **1936** *Cambridge Hist. of Brit. Empire* VIII. 834 The district over which the Landdrost had jurisdiction was known as the *Drostdy*, but the meaning of this word changed, and in later years it was only used to denote his official residence. **1963** R. LEWCOCK *Early 19th C. Archit.* 237 In October 1820 Col. John Graham was appointed Landdrost for Albany with the seat of his Drostdy at Bathurst. **1974** *Cape Times* 28 Sept. (Suppl.) 1 The tree is as old as George itself and George was founded in 1811 — the second Drostdy to be established after the British occupation.

2. *hist.* The offices and residence of a landdrost. Also *attrib.*

1797 EARL MACARTNEY in G.M. Theal *Rec. of Cape Col.* (1898) II. 101 The said Landdrost is there not only to examine the Spot where the Drosty with the best propriety and Convenience could be erected if Government at any Time should resolve to do so; but also what Materials for the Building thereof are to be found in its Vicinity. **1810** G. BARRINGTON *Acct of Voy.* 336 The Sunday river, in its passage from the snowy mountains, winds round the small plain on which the Drosdy is placed, and furnishes it with a copious supply of water. **1812** A. PLUMPTRE tr. *H. Lichtenstein's Trav. in Sn Afr.* I. 172 The Drosty at Zwellendam was built of like materials. **1821** C.I. LATROBE *Jrnl of Visit* 177 The drosty is a substantial, spacious, well-furnished mansion, and the premises much improved by the present landrost. **1822** W.J. BURCHELL *Trav.* I. 128 At the distance of half an hour's walk northwards from the village, is the Drostdy, or official residence of the landdrost. **1832** *Graham's Town Jrnl* 1 June 90 Entering Graham's Town from Algoa Bay road, it is lamentable to see the Drostdy House in so miserable a state of decay, and more particularly when we reflect that this building has cost upwards of *Fifty Thousand* Rix-dollars for its erection. **1861** P.B. BORCHERDS *Auto-Biog. Mem.* 28 One day .. we were invited by the landdrost to call at the drostdy. **1883** [see STADTHUIS]. **1910** D. FAIRBRIDGE *That Which Hath Been* (1913) 237 At the head of the street was the Drostdy in which he slept, stately and beautiful in its simple dignity. **1927** C.G. BOTHA *Social Life in Cape Col.* 69 The principal buildings in a village were the drostdy, the parsonage and the church. The first comprised the residence of the Landdrost or Magistrate, with his court-room, offices and other accommodation to carry out the administrative duties of his district. **1936** [see sense 1]. **1948** H.E. HOCKLY *Story of Brit. Settlers of 1820* 73 It was Donkin's intention to move the entire civil administration of the newly constituted district of Albany from Grahamstown to Bathurst on the completion of the drostdy at the latter place. **1969** D. CHILD *Yesterday's Children* 36 Next to the church stood the parsonage, and the only other buildings of note were the *drosty* — residence of the *landdrost* or magistrate — and his courtroom and offices. **1983** *S. Afr. Panorama* Jan. 24 Swellendam, with its numerous historical buildings, prides itself on one of the few remaining *drostdy* (magistrates) buildings in the country. **1988** D. HUGHES et al. *Complete Bk of S. Afr. Wine* 266 Slight damage to the old Drostdy during a storm in 1822 prompted the Governor to transfer the magistrate to new quarters.

3. *obs.* The capital town of a magisterial district.

*a*1823 J. EWART *Jrnl* (1970) 411 This Court .. is always held in the principal village of the district from that circumstance called the drosdy or seat of the landrost. **1833** *Graham's Town Jrnl* 2 May 2 This spot ought unquestionably to have been fixed on for the capital or drostdy of the extensive district of Somerset. **1834** T. PRINGLE *Afr. Sketches* 133 She had come from the drostdy, or district town, of Uitenhage. *Ibid.* 296 The source of the Ghamka, where the drostdy, or district village of Beaufort had been recently erected. **1842** R. GODLONTON *Sketches of E. Districts* 51 This duty discharged, a visit to the 'Drostdy', or market town, affords them an opportunity for laying in a supply of household necessaries.

droster /ˈdrɒstə, ˈdrɔstə(r)/ *n. Obs.* exc. *hist.* Also **drosser.** [S. Afr. Du., fr. Du. *drossen* to run away + agential suffix *-er.*] A runaway, usu. a slave or (subsequently) a servant; an outlaw.

1824 W.J. BURCHELL *Trav.* II. 158 Such Hottentots or slaves as are found, improperly or illegally wandering about the country, without a passport, or unable to give a credible account of themselves .. are commonly called by the colonial term of *drossers* or *gedrost Hottentotten* (runaways). **1913** C. PETTMAN *Africanderisms* 154 *Drossers* or *Drosters*, In the old slave days such slaves or Hottentots as were found wandering about the country without a 'Pass' .. or unable to give a good account of themselves. **1949** L.G. GREEN *In Land of Afternoon* 23 The same climber told me about the drosters' nests in the Cape mountains. Nowadays this expressive Afrikaans word means a disreputable wanderer; but the first drosters were men of all colours who fled from the old Cape settlement and became outlaws ... Often the drosters were runaway slaves. **1964** — *Old Men Say* 181 In the eighteenth century, bands of runaway slaves known as *drosters* were able to live in the Table Mountain caves and other remote hiding-places on the Cape Flats with a fair prospect of safety. **1975** *Weekend Post* 25 Oct. (TV Post) 10 What was a droster? (a) Runaway slave; (b) Type of wagon; (c) Cape Dutch house. **1983** R. ROSS *Cape of Torments* p.x, *Drossen*, To run away, desert, hence drosser, runaway, gedrost, ran away.

drosty var. DROSTDY.

drummie /ˈdrʌmi/ *n. colloq.* [Formed on Eng. *drum majorette* + (informal) n.-forming suffix *-ie.*] A drum majorette. Also *attrib.*

1972 *Rhodeo* (Rhodes Univ.) 2 Mar. 3 Welcome to Rhodes ... What with Inky Social, Drummies and the weather, these poor Inkettes have had a hard time. **1980** *Ibid.* 15 Mar. 2 Just think what Rag would be like without drummies? **1984** *Daily Dispatch* 14 May 5 The drummies not only marched well but walked about holding their trim young bodies erect and proud. **1986** *Pretoria News* 24 Sept. 1 The competition has 12 high school and four primary school drummie squads competing for the R2 500 prize money. **1990** *Sunday Times* 11 Feb. 3 A former 'drummie' and a reigning West Rand beauty queen are two of the contenders for the 1990 Miss South Africa crown ... Karen Wynne, 20, is a 'graduate' of St Dominics drum majorette squad. **1993** *E. Prov. Herald* 10 Mar. (La Femme) 8 Help our drummies. If sponsorship can be raised, drum majorettes from East London's Stirling High School could be marching in the World Drill Championships in Japan.

druppels /ˈdrəp(ə)lz, ˈdrœp(ə)ls/ *pl. n.* Also **droppels.** [Afk.]

a. 'Drops': liquid medicines, esp. patent household remedies, taken in small quantities. See also (*old*) *Dutch medicine* (DUTCH *adj.* sense 2).

1902 *Report upon Concentration Camps* in W.H.S. Bell *Bygone Days* (1933) 364 Some of what are known generally as 'Dutch medicines' or 'droppels' contain laudanum ... Besides the pernicious 'droppels', the Boer women resort to other and even more dangerous methods of treatment. **1906** *Rand Daily Mail* 1 Mar. 6 The large supply of medicines — mysterious things called 'droppels' that invariably occupy so much shelf-room in the country store. At some time or other a necessity for each particular droppel has arisen and a box of the little bottles has been purchased. **1949** C. BULLOCK *Rina* 33 The main items were two bucksails for shelter and waterproof packing ... and lastly the druppels in a little medicine chest with a few other simple remedies and disinfectants. **1959** [see ROOILAVENTEL]. **1984** B. JOHNSON-BARKER in *Wynboer* Feb. 62 In due course there appeared in the cities .. bottles of druppels which had on the label a picture of the face of Doctor Brown. **1991** [see quot. at *krampdruppels* below].

b. With distinguishing epithet, designating a particular type of druppels according to:

i. The application of the remedy: **benoudhijds druppels** /bəˈnəʊtheɪts -/ [S. Afr. Du., combining form of *benoudhijd* tightness of the chest (Afk. *benoudheid*)], drops for the relief of breathing complaints, croup, or asthma; see also BENAUWDHEID; **bloedstillende druppels** /ˈblʊt ˈstələndə -, ˈblut -/ [Afk., *bloedstillend(e)* having styptic properties], a styptic, tincture of ferric perchloride; **borsdruppels**, see as a main entry; **entrance druppels**, or **entress druppels**, see quot. 1959; **hoes druppels** /ˈhʊs -, ˈhʊs -/ [Afk., *hoes* cough], drops for the relief of coughs; **hoofdpijn druppels** /ˈhʊəftpeɪn-/ [S. Afr. Du., *hoofdpijn* headache (Afk. *hoofpyn*)], drops for the treatment of headaches; **koors druppels** /kʊə(r)s-/, also **koortsdruppels**, [Afk., *koors* fever], drops for the relief of fever; **krampdruppels** /kramp-/ [Afk., *kramp* cramp], drops for the relief of convulsions and stomach cramps; **pynstillende druppels** /ˈpeɪnˌstələndə -/ [Afk., *pynstillend(e)* soothing, pain-killing], drops for the relief of pain; **sleep druppels** [Eng. *sleep*], drops inducing sleep; **versterkdruppels**, see as a main entry; **zinkingsdruppels** /səŋkəŋs-/ [S. Afr. Du., *zinkings* neuralgia (Afk. *sinkings*)], drops for the relief of pain.

 1919 *Dunell, Ebden & Co.'s Price List* Oct. 20 **Benaauwdheid Druppels** 3/6. 1958 A. JACKSON *Trader on Veld* 30 Remedies of every description formed no small proportion of a country store's goods, especially the old 'Dutch' medicines... To mention just a few of the favourites: Versterkende Druppels, Roode Lavendel, Peppermint Druppels, Harlemensis, Witte Dulcis, Benoudhijds Druppels, Paragoric, Hoofdpijn Druppels, Arnica, Anijs Druppels. 1919 *Dunell, Ebden & Co.'s Price List* Oct. 20 **Bloedstillende Druppels** 3/6. 1949 L.G. GREEN *In Land of Afternoon* 45 Bloedstillende druppels, Cajoputi oil for pain in the limbs, buchu *azyn*, Groene Amara for stomach ache and Hoffman's druppels for headache. 1972 [see DOEPA sense 2 b]. 1919 *Dunell, Ebden & Co.'s Price List* Oct. 20 **Entress Druppels** 3/6. 1959 [see ROOILAVENTEL]. 1943 D. REITZ *No Outspan* 83 He heard an old burgher say to President Kruger, 'Chamberlain's politics are damn rotten, but we must admit that his cough mixture (**hoes druppels**) is very good.' 1958 [**hoofdpijn druppels**: see quot. at *benoudhijds druppels* above]. 1949 **koorsdruppels**: see quot. at *pynstillende druppels* below]. 1958 E.H. BURROWS *Hist. of Medicine* 191 **Koors druppels** (lit. Fever Drops): used for fever in children. 1884 B.G. Lennon & Co.'s Catal. 1884 65 **Kramp Druppels**. 1919 *Dunell, Ebden & Co.'s Price List* Oct. 20 Kramp Druppels 3/6. 1934 [see Sunday Times quot. at LEWENSESSENS]. 1989 D. SMUTS *Folk Remedies* 84 Stomach ache, 2 drops rooilaventel, 3 drops krampdruppels .. in a little luke-warm water with a little sugar. 1991 *Best of S. Afr. Short Stories* (Reader's Digest Assoc.) 112 Among a bewildering variety of *druppels* or drops were *kramp* (cramp) *druppels* and *versterk* (strengthening) *druppels* as well as *Hoffmansdruppels* and *Haarlemmerdruppels*. 1884 B.G. Lennon & Co.'s Catal. 1884 65 **Pynstillende Druppels**, doz. 5s.0d. 1919 *Dunell, Ebden & Co.'s Price List* Oct. 20 Pynstillende Druppels 3/6. 1949 L.G. GREEN *In Land of Afternoon* 45 Pynstillende druppels, zinkingsdruppels (own recipe), koorts druppels, oogwater all speak for themselves. 1958 E.H. BURROWS *Hist. of Medicine* 191 Pynstillende droppels (lit., Pain-stilling Drops): used for relieving all kinds of pain, cramp and for vomiting, especially in women. 1884 B.G. Lennon & Co.'s Catal. 1884 67 **Zinkings Druppels**, doz. 5s.0d. 1919 *Dunell, Ebden & Co.'s Price List* Oct. 20 Zinkings Droppels 3/6. 1949 [see *pynstillende druppels* above]. 1937 C.R. PRANCE *Tante Rebella's Saga* 182 Three times already she had got out of bed to take **sleep-droppels** from her Home-Medicine chest, and now the bottle was empty she felt more wakeful than before, though she said all her prayers again each time to help the sleep-drops.

ii. The source from which the drops are derived, or an attribute of the drops: **anijs druppels** /aˈneɪs -/ [S. Afr. Du., *anijs* aniseed (Afk. *anys*)], drops containing aniseed; **duiwelsdrekdruppels**, see DUIWELSDREK sense b; **harmans druppels** /ˈharməns -/, also occas. shortened form **harmansdrup**, [Afk., *harman* ad. Haarlem (see HAARLEMMER)], HARLEMENSIS; **Hoffmansdruppels**, see as a main entry; **peppermint druppels**, drops containing peppermint; **staaldruppels** /ˈstɑːl-/ [Afk., ?staal steel], see quot.; **wonderdruppels** /ˈvɒn(d)ə(r)-/ [Afk., *wonder* miracle], drops for the relief of pain.

 [1884 B.G. Lennon & Co.'s Catal. 1884 63 Anÿs Olie, 2 dram vials. 1919 *Dunell, Ebden & Co.'s Price List* Oct. 20 Anijs Olie, 2 dram vials, 6/-.] 1958 [**anijs druppels**: see quot. at *benoudhijds druppels* above]. 1958 E.H. BURROWS *Hist. of Medicine* 191 **Harmans druppels**: used for bladder disturbances. 1989 D. SMUTS *Folk Remedies* 22 Chest with phlegm, 2 large tablespoons honey, 2 tablespoons coconut oil, 1 teaspoon borsdruppels, 1 bottle raw linseed oil, 1 bottle harmansdrup. 1919 *Dunell, Ebden & Co.'s Price List* Oct. **Peppermint Droppels** 3/6. 1958 [see *benoudhijds druppels* above]. 1884 B.G. Lennon & Co.'s Catal. 1884 66 **Staal Druppels**. 1919 *Dunell, Ebden & Co.'s Price List* Oct. 20 Staal Droppels (stoppered bottles) 3/6. 1989 D. SMUTS *Folk Remedies* 22 Childlessness, 1/2 bottle staaldruppels. 1970 S. DE WET in J.W. Loubser *Africana Short Stories* 93 Then my mother took the **wonderdruppels** that she had for her pain in her side, and she began to give them to Dirk. And he didn't get worse.

dry digging *vbl n. phr. Hist.* Diamond-mining. [Transf. use of U.S. Eng. *dry-digging*, a gold-mining term.] Usu. in *pl.*: **a.** A mining operation in which diamonds were extracted from weathered ground. **b.** The locality or mining camp associated with such a mining operation. Cf. RIVER-DIGGING.

 1872 C.A. PAYTON *Diamond Diggings* 7 The 'dry diggings', lying about twenty-five miles away from the Vaal River, have been found, during the year 1871, to be so much more *uniformly* remunerative than those on the banks of the river. 1872 J.L. BABE *S. Afr. Diamond Fields* 69 The manner of mining at the dry diggings is as follows... It takes the four natives all their time to dig and sift out enough dirt to keep the two white men sorting. 1887 J.W. MATTHEWS *Incwadi Yami* 266 The rush from the river to what were called 'the dry diggings' was one of the most remarkable ever recorded. 1896 PURVIS & BIGGS *S. Afr.* 143 At first it was thought that any diamonds found would be obtained from the river ... But at length the 'dry' diggings were discovered, and the foundations of what have since become widely known as 'The Diamond Fields' were definitely laid. 1899 G. LACY *Pictures of Trav., Sport & Adventure* 173 The 'dry diggings' are thirty miles to the south-east of Pniel. They are so called because the gems are not found in river-wash, but in dry tufa, which has apparently never been in contact with water. 1904 H.A. BRYDEN *Hist. of S. Afr.* 131 Presently, upon certain Boer farms, the 'dry diggings', as they were called, were discovered, and the mines of Kimberley, Dutoit's Pan and De Beers sprang into existence. 1904 [see river digger (RIVER-DIGGING)]. 1936 *Cambridge Hist. of Brit. Empire* VIII. 450 In 1870, to the 'river diggings' along the courses of the Vaal and Orange were added the 'dry diggings' in the long hill between the Vaal and Modder Rivers. 1963 O. DOUGHTY *Early Diamond Days* 46 The Dry Diggings .. was in all a tract of some sixty square miles of chiefly arid, barren country. 1983 D.E. SCHAEFER in *Optima* Vol.31 No.2, 81 A centrifugal washing machine .. required much less water and was therefore particularly popular for working the diamondiferous volcanic pipes (known as the 'Dry Diggings' as opposed to the 'River Diggings'). 1985 A.J.A. JANSE in Glover & Harris *Kimberlite Occurrence & Origin* 22 Diamonds were plentiful in this dry digging, so it caused a rush, and the digging was called De Beers Rush. 1987 *S. Afr. Holidays Guide* (brochure) 46 In 1869, a rich deposit of diamonds was found on a Griqualand West farm, Bultfontein, far from the nearest river. Diggers rushed to the farm and soon established 'dry' diggings there.

Hence **dry dig** *v. intrans.* ?nonce, to extract diamonds from weathered material.

 1968 J.T. McNISH *Rd to Eldorado* 200 His first attempt, late in 1869, at what was to become known as 'dry digging' as against 'river digging' was where the Du Toits Pan and Bultfontein diggings later emerged.

dry-my-throat *n.* [tr. Afk. (earlier S. Afr. Du.) *droog-my-keel*.] DROOG-MY-KEEL. Also *attrib.*

 1897 E. GLANVILLE *Tales from Veld* 136, I got under a thick 'dry-my-throat' bush where I hid. 1913 C. PETTMAN *Africanderisms* 155 Dry-my-throat bush, Scutia Commersoni .. This is a literal rendering of the Dutch name *Droog-mij-keel bosje*. 1972 PALMER & PITMAN *Trees of Sn Afr.* II. 1401 These fruits .. dry the throat very noticeably, hence the most widely used common name 'droog-my-keel' or 'dry-my-throat'. 1976 [see NUM-NUM].

dry-sort see SORT *v.*

dry-sorting see SORTING sense 1 c.

Ds *n.* Also **Ds.**, **DS**, and with small initial. [Afk.] The written abbreviation of *dominee* (see DOMINEE sense 2 b ii).

 1901 'DR BROWNE' in R. Raven-Hart *Cape G.H.* 1652–1702 (1971) II. 388 They value noe monie except it bee a skilling or a duleke with which they buy brandie or tobacco from the Dutch. 1731 G. MEDLEY tr. *P. Kolb's Present State of Cape of G.H.* I. 168 They [sc. the Hottentots] have now and then in the Service of an European a Dubbletie given 'em, a two Penny Piece of Dutch money. 1795 C.R. HOPSON tr. *C.P. Thunberg's Trav.* I. 231 Two-pences (dubbeltjes) and single pence (or stivers) are scarce, as also are ducats, and the gold coin called riders (goude reijers). 1861 P.B. BORCHERDS *Auto-Biog. Mem.* 21 With the schoolmistress I was also on the best of terms. The little silver dubbeltje (a Dutch coin), which was my Sunday allowance, was always

dubbee var. DABBY.

dubbeltje *n.*[1] var. DUBBELTJIE *n.*[2]

dubbeltje /ˈdəbəlki/ *n.*[2] *hist.* Also **dubbeltjie**, **dubbletie**, **dublejee**, **dubleke**, **duppeltje**. [Du., lit. 'little double one'.] Either of two coins used at the Cape of Good Hope at various times:

1. The two-stuiver piece used during the rule of the Dutch East India Company, and worth about twopence. See also STIVER.

 The Zulu word for 'penny' is *indibilshi*, an adaptation of 'dubbeltje'.

 1691 'DR BROWNE' in R. Raven-Hart *Cape G.H.* 1652–1702 (1971) II. 388 They value noe monie except it bee a skilling or a duleke with which they buy brandie or tobacco from the Dutch. 1731 G. MEDLEY tr. *P. Kolb's Present State of Cape of G.H.* I. 168 They [sc. the Hottentots] have now and then in the Service of an European a Dubbletie given 'em, a two Penny Piece of Dutch money. 1795 C.R. HOPSON tr. *C.P. Thunberg's Trav.* I. 231 Two-pences (dubbeltjes) and single pence (or stivers) are scarce, as also are ducats, and the gold coin called riders (goude reijers). 1861 P.B. BORCHERDS *Auto-Biog. Mem.* 21 With the schoolmistress I was also on the best of terms. The little silver dubbeltje (a Dutch coin), which was my Sunday allowance, was always spent in the cakes which she so nicely baked. **1920** K.M. JEFFREYS tr. *Memorandum of Commissary J.A. de Mist* 279 The double stuiver, called the dubbeltje, was circulated at 36 for one ducaton or driegulden, and 12 for one gulden. **1925** H.J. MANDELBROTE tr. *O.F. Mentzel's Descr. of Cape of G.H.* II. 65 When barred at the gate by a group of men with drawn swords, they gave each a duppeltje, *i.e.*, 2 stuivers! The men had to hide their chagrin and let them pass.

2. The English penny piece, used in South Africa during the late 18th century and the 19th century, at a value of two stuivers, or twopence; DOUBLEJEE sense 1. Cf. OULAP *n.*

1821 C.I. LATROBE *Jrnl of Visit* 240, I presented him with a few doppelgens (penny-pieces). **1822** W.J. BURCHELL *Trav.* I. 78 The only current coin, are English pennypieces, which here pass for the value of two pence, and are called *dubbeltjes*. **1833** S. KAY *Trav. & Researches* 283 At last he had scarcely *dublejees* (pence) sufficient to carry him back to the colony. **1850** T. SMITH *S. Afr. Delineated* 161 One individual .. sent a note .. enclosing what he called his *dubbeltje* (penny), which proved, when the note was opened, to be a sovereign. **1926** P.W. LAIDLER *Tavern of Ocean* 143 The only coin in use was the English penny, and, as it passed for twopence, it was known as a 'dubbeltje'. To-day its name is an 'ou lap', a worthless old rag. **1949** L.G. GREEN *In Land of Afternoon* 102 The heavy 'cartwheel' penny pieces bearing the head of George III soon became known as 'dubbeltjes', as they were worth twopence. **1963** HEWSON & VAN DER RIET *Jrnl of 'Harry Hastings'* 25 The British penny piece was at that time in circulation at the Cape and was called a 'dubbeltje' being worth two stivers (stuivers), or a twenty-fourth part of a rixdollar. **1968** E.A. WALKER *Hist. of Sn Afr.* 128 Macartney tried to check the vagaries of the exchanges by importing silver Spanish dollars (4s.8d.) and copper *dubbeltjes*, pence which passed for twopence. **1972** *Daily Dispatch* 5 Apr. 12 With the first British occupation of the Cape in 1795 two coins were introduced to help relieve the shortage of small money. One was the 'Dubbeltjie' — the British twopenny piece, also known as the 'Cartwheel'. It got its name because it was declared current at two stuivers.

‖**dubbeltjedoorn** /ˈdœbəlkiˌduə(r)n/ *n.* Also **dobbeltjiedoorn.** [S. Afr. Du., *dubbeltje* see DUBBELTJIE *n.*² + *doorn* thorn.] DUBBELTJIE *n.*² sense a. Also *attrib.*

1905 D. HUTCHEON in Flint & Gilchrist *Science in S. Afr.* 347 A small plant called the 'Dubbeltje Doorn' — *Tribulus Terrestrus Lin.* — which springs up luxuriantly after rain, the time when the disease [*sc.* geeldikkop] becomes most prevalent. **1911** *Farmer's Weekly* 22 Mar. 11 The disease 'Geel-Dikkop' of sheep is prevalent at the moment ... It is .. said to be due to eating the creeping plant called 'dubbeltjedoorn' after rains during the hot weather. **1912** *E. London Dispatch* 13 Sept. 7 The ever-increasing spread of the 'Dubbeltje Doorn' weed. **1917** R. MARLOTH *Common Names* 24 *Dubbeltje* or *-doorn*, .. Several S. A. plants, decumbent or trailing on the ground, the fruits provided with sharp spines. *c*1929 *Diseases & Pests Affecting Sheep & Goats* (Cooper & Nephews) 86 It has now been definitely proved by feeding experiments that the disease [*sc.* geeldikkop] is caused by eating the 'dubbeltje doorn' (tribulus terrestris) when in a wilted condition. **1979** T. GUTSCHE *There Was a Man* 301 Hutcheon's men had later identified it with the Dobbeltjiedoorn (little double-thorn) or Tribulus terrestris.

dubbeltjie *n.*¹ var. DUBBELTJE *n.*²

dubbeltjie /ˈdəbəlki, ˈdœ-, -ci/ *n.*² Also **doblejie, dubbeljee, dubbeltje(e), dubbletje, dubeltie.** [Afk. (earlier S. Afr. Du. *dubbeltje*).

The ultimate origin is uncertain: prob. named for the two-four construction of the thorns (fr. Du. *dubbel* double); or perh. ad. Du. *duiveltje* 'little devil', from the supposed resemblance of the fruit, esp. that of *T. terrestris*, to a horned devil.]

A name given to the angular, spiny fruit of any of several indigenous herbaceous plants, and to the plants themselves: **a.** Any of several species of *Tribulus* of the Zygophyllaceae, esp. *T. terrestris*; DUBBELTJEDOORN. **b.** *Emex australis* of the Polygonaceae. In both senses also called DEVIL'S THORN, DOUBLEJEE (sense 2), DUIWELTJIE. Also *attrib.*

The sheep disease tribulosis (see GEELDIKKOP) is caused by the ingestion of any of several species of *Tribulus*.

1795 C.R. HOPSON tr. *C.P. Thunberg's Trav.* I. 148 Great complaints were made of the seed-vessels of the *rumex spinosus* (*dubelties*), which grew very common here, as the sharp prickles of them cut the feet of the slaves and others, who walked bare-footed. **1827** G. THOMPSON *Trav.* I. 125 The soil was also sprinkled with the seed of a plant covered with prickles, making it very unpleasant to sit or lie down. These seeds are jocularly called by the colonists *dubbeltjes*. **1833** *Graham's Town Jrnl* 25 Apr. 3 My mistress moved the stocks up and down, to make the *dubbeljees* come in contact with my person and give me more pain. **1860** J. SANDERSON in *Jrnl of Royal Geog. Soc.* XXX. 239, I here for the first time met with a low creeping plant, called by the Dutch 'dubbeltjes,' and producing a prickly seed-vessel like caltrops, exceedingly injurious to sheep from striking into their hoofs. **1868** T. STUBBS Men I Have Known. 50 The place was covered with thorns (doblejies). **1896** R. WALLACE *Farming Indust. of Cape Col.* 115 The *dubbletje, Emex centropodium* .. is excessively troublesome as a weed when once established. **1900** [see HAAK-EN-STEEK]. **1906** W.S. JOHNSON *Orangia* 14 Many other plants have spiny seeds, such as the dubbeltje, which often punctures the tyres of our bicyles. **1913** J.J. DOKE *Secret City* 51 Even when .. one .. had crept sleepy into bed only to find the pillows doctored with pepper or dibbeltjies at one's feet .. it was almost impossible to be cross. **1919** R.Y. STORMBERG *With Love from Gwenno* 44 'Dubbletjes' — says Gabriel — 'are a joint invention of South Effrica end the devil whichwith to mock cyclists.' **1936** C. BIRKBY *Thirstland Treks* 252, I saw erstwhile desert blooming with golden sheets of *dubbeltjie* flowers and the sheep all plump and prospering. **1943** D. REITZ *No Outspan* 69 A troublesome growth of spiked thorn (dubbeltjies) springs up, and if left undisturbed kills off the grass, and as ostriches eagerly graze the thorn they are used as animated weeding machines. **1956** P. BECKER *Sandy Tracks* 96 To the accompaniment of the cracking of whips and sjamboks they made Oom Tys dance among the 'dubbeltjies', the dreaded three-pronged 'devil thorns' of the South African veld. **1963** M. KAVANAGH *We Merry Peasants* 39 It was possible to invite a puncture that took time to mend, merely by deviating from the rough road and collecting thorns, '*dubbeltjies*', in our tyres. **1981** J. VAHRMEIJER *Poisonous Plants of Sn Afr.* 90 *Tribulus terrestris*, .. ('Dubbeltjie' family) ... The dubbeltjie is generally regarded by farmers in the Karoo as an essential and life-saving fodder plant ... It has, however, been proved that under certain weather conditions dubbeltjies are associated with 'geeldikkop' in sheep. **1986** *Farmer's Weekly* 25 July 14 Broad-leaved weeds, such as dubbeltjies (*Emex australis*) can be effectively eliminated in the grain by using a suitable herbicide.

dubbletie var. DUBBELTJE *n.*²

dubbletje, dubeltie varr. DUBBELTJIE *n.*²

dublejee, dubleke varr. DUBBELTJE *n.*²

ducker var. DUIKER.

duckie *n.*¹ *Obsolescent. colloq.* Also **ducky.** [Formed on DUCKTAIL + Eng. (informal) n.-forming suffix *-ie* (or *-y*).] **a.** The ducktail hairstyle. **b.** DUCKTAIL. Also *attrib.*

1962 J. TAYLOR 'Hennie van Saracen'. (*lyrics*) When they saw my ducky hairstyle .. in twenty seconds flat they shaved off all my hair. **1977** C. HOPE in S. Gray *Theatre Two* (1981) 35 Others aspired to the tone of voice but only the true duckie managed the proper accents and delivery without sounding phoney.

duckie *n.*² *colloq.* [Formed on Eng. *duck* ellipt. for RUBBER DUCK + suffix *-ie* forming nouns which are used informally.] RUBBER DUCK.

1989 G. ADDISON in *Motorist* 4th Quarter 45 Rubber rafts or 'duckies', are also used to drift down the Richtersveld stretch. **1989** *Weekend Post* 9 Dec. 1 It's not only going to be a turkey for John .. this Christmas — he's also got himself a real 'duckie'. Winner of the .. Win-a-Boat Competition. **1991** *Ibid.* 5 Jan. 2, PE beach manager Johan Crafford said the only area where duckies came close to swimmers was at Hobie Beach.

ducktail *n. Obs.* exc. *hist.* [Transf. use of U.S. Eng. *ducktail*, denoting a man's hairstyle.] During the 1950s and 1960s: a young white male (often a member of a gang) who sported a 'ducktail' hairstyle and adopted a characteristic style of dress, usu. a leather jacket, narrow trousers, and pointed shoes; DUCKIE *n.*¹ sense b. Also *attrib.*, and occas. *fig.* See also SHEILA sense 2. Cf. TSOTSI sense 1.

Regarded by many as equivalent to the British 'teddy-boy'.

1956 *Rand Daily Mail* 21 Dec. 6 A man who admitted picking up a police constable and throwing him to the ground, said in the .. Magistrate's Court .. that because he was a former ducktail, trying to reform, the world 'had it in for him'. **1957** B. FRASER *Sunshine & Lamplight* 168 The ducktail boys, as South Africans call their 'Teddy boys' are its [*sc.* dagga's] greatest white addicts. **1960** *Guardian* (U.K.) 28 Mar. 1 He [*sc.* Dr Verwoerd] described South Africa's overseas critics as 'the ducktails (Teddy boys) of the political world'. **1963** L.F. FREED *Crime in S. Afr.* 81 The ducktail girls are also known as 'quacktails', 'sheilahs', and 'ponytails'. **1963** *Ibid.* [see GOOI sense 1 a]. **1963** [see MENSETAAL]. **1964** H.W.D. MANSON *Pat Mulholland's Day* 73 Immediately after Mulholland enters the pub door, .. three young men, dressed in the ducktail fashion, enter from the left. **1973** *Cape Times* 13 Oct. 12 Also classifiable, perhaps, as 'fauna' is that now almost extinct species — the ducktail ... 'South African for a young hooligan or "Teddy Boy"'. **1977** P.C. VENTER *Soweto* 62 Tsotsis, those black fossils of the ducktail era who indulge in anything from petty larceny to grand theft to keep them from doing honest work. **1977** C. HOPE in S. Gray *Theatre Two* (1981) 61 *The ducktail accent and delivery*, A rapid, staccato delivery, sometimes accompanied by a nasal twang, achieved by using the front of the mouth, the area just behind the teeth. **1983** A. GOLDSTUCK in *Frontline* Oct. 58 The excitement — 'the vibe' — has gone out of Springs and the ducktail has turned 40 and drifted away. **1990** R. GOOL *Cape Town Coolie* 156 A firm of Afrikaner Nationalists .. were assembling an armed mob of *ducktails* or European hooligans to move in if any demonstration against rent increases occurred. **1991** *Sunday Times* 26 May (Mag. Sect.) 14 The café owners were terrorised by gangs of ducktails back then.

Hence **ducktailism** *n.*, ducktail behaviour or norms.

1983 A. GOLDSTUCK in *Frontline* Oct. 61 Ducktailism doesn't work anymore. Its midwives, Elvis Presley and James Dean, are dead. Its high priests, the Rolling Stones, are safe and acceptable today.

ducky var. DUCKIE *n.*¹

dug-out *n.* [Fig. use of general Eng. *dug-out* (in trench-warfare) a roofed shelter excavated in the trenches.] SHELLHOLE. Also *attrib.*

1929 *Star* 5 June 8 A very successful bridge drive was given by the Roodepoort Dugout M.O.T.H. in the Roodepoort Club, in aid of the Roodepoort hospital fund. **1972** J.D. ROBINSON in *Std Encycl. of Sn Afr.* VII. 328 At a meeting of twelve enthusiasts .. a constitution was drafted and a headquarters 'dug-out' was formed. Since then the organization [*sc.* the Moths] has spread throughout South Africa, Rhodesia, Zambia and Malawi. It embraces some 465 Shellholes and has a membership of about 35 000.

duiker /ˈdaɪkə, ˈdœikə, ˈdeɪkə/ *n.* Also **dekker, ducker, d(u)yker.** Pl. **-s,** or unchanged. [S. Afr. Du., transf. uses of Du. *duiker* diver (fr. *duiken* to dive).]

1. [Named in S. Afr. Du. for their characteristic behaviour, esp. when fleeing (see quot. 1896).] **a.** Any of several species of small antelope of the genera *Philantomba* and *Sylvicapra* of the Bovidae; DIKER-BUCK; DIVER sense 2; DIVING GOAT; DUIKERBOK. Also *attrib.*

1777 G. FORSTER *Voy. round World* I. 84 The duyker or diving antelope .. is not yet sufficiently known. **1790** tr. *F. Le Vaillant's Trav.* II. 110 They scarcely ever eat the flesh of the hare, or of the antelope called *duykers.* **1822** W.J. BURCHELL *Trav.* I. 187 The Duyker (Diver) is one of the smaller Antelopes, being not much above two feet in height; very light and elegantly made, like most of that tribe. *a*1827 [see RHENOSTERBOS sense 1]. **1847** J. BARROW *Reflect.* 145 Of the genus antelope we procured, within the Cape district, the *duyker,* the *griesbok,* and the *klipspringer* (the diver, the grizzled, and the rockleaper). **1860** A.W. DRAYSON *Sporting Scenes* 60 The duiker (*Cephalopus mergens*) most frequently found amongst bushes, or long grass; about two feet high, three feet eight inches long; horns four inches in length. **1866** E. WILSON *Reminisc.* 169 The medicines and charms are carried in a bag made of the skin of the dekker (a wild buck). *a*1867 C.J. ANDERSSON *Notes of Trav.* (1875) 227 Now and then a steinbok, a ducker, a hartebeest, and so forth, may be seen. **1872** C.A. PAYTON *Diamond Diggings* 81 Fred, the driver, shot a 'duiker' doe one rainy day; it is a pretty little antelope of a quiet dun-brown colour. **1896** R. WARD *Rec. of Big Game* 96 From the south of Cape Colony right away through Africa, there is to be seen the timid, crouching Duiker. The name Duiker, by the way, which, translated from the Dutch, means 'diver,' aptly illustrates the furtive, squatting, dodging habits of this small antelope. **1913** J.J. DOKE *Secret City* 125 A duiker passed like a shadow into the deeper shadow of the hedge, followed by her fawn. **1936** C. BIRKBY *Thirstland Treks* 298 Few other animals can live in the desert. The *springbok* is one, .. and the *duiker,* the dainty antelope which King Khama of Bechuanaland used as his crest. **1951** R. GRIFFITHS *Grey about Flame* 120 M'Busi leaped to the sleeping mats and threw a heavy duiker skin kaross over his son's head. **1973** *Cape Times* 13 Jan. (Weekend Mag.) 4 Duikers are divided mainly into two groups, the forest duikers and the bush duikers. The forest duikers frequent the mountainous areas and bush duikers the dense scrub country. **1979** [see ELAND sense 1 a]. **1988** M. NEL in *Personality* 25 Apr. 54 The duiker have become so cheeky they come into town and nibble the hedges around the hotel. **1991** H. HUTCHINGS in *Weekend Post* 30 Mar. (Leisure) 7 Mr and Mrs Beukes have regular visits from grysbok and dyker in their garden.

b. With distinguishing epithet, denoting a particular species of antelope: **blue duiker**, the smallest southern African antelope *Philantomba* (or *Cephalophus*) *monticola*; BLAUWBOK sense 2; BLOUBOKKIE; BLUEBOK; BLUE BUCK sense 1; IPITI; **common** - or **grey duiker**, the widely distributed antelope *Sylvicapra grimmia*; IMPUNZI; PUTI; **red duiker**, *Philantomba natalensis*, chestnut in colour.

1900 W.L. SCLATER *Mammals of S. Afr.* I. 164 The **blue duiker** was known to the travellers of the end of the last century. **1973** [see BLOUBOKKIE]. **1976** J. HANKS *Mammals* 20 The .. blue duiker is able to scurry under bushes and shrubs which the common duiker would jump over or go around. **1988** *Natura* No.15, 4 The *blue* duiker derives its name from the bluish sheen on its coat. **1992** E. COLLINS in *Weekend Post* 4 July (Leisure) 1 It [*sc.* the park] .. contains a number of blue duiker, an endangered antelope listed in the *Red Data Book.* **1951** A. ROBERTS *Mammals* 326 *Sylvicapra grimmia grimmia* .. **Common** or Grey **Duiker**. **1976** J. HANKS *Mammals* 21 The common duiker can be readily distinguished .. by the crest between the horns and its yellow to greyish-brown colour. **1990** SKINNER & SMITHERS *Mammals of Sn Afr. Subregion* 642 Common duikers are almost exclusively browsers, only very rarely eating grass. **1862** 'A LADY' *Life at Cape* (1963) 105 By the merest chance I came across the lovely **grey 'duiker'**. **1951** [see quot. at *common duiker* above]. **1971** *Sunday Times* 21 Mar. (Business Times) 4 The ticket on a safari included the shooting of .. warthog, grey duiker and 20 birds. **1988** A. HALL-MARTIN et al. *Kaokoveld* 35 Of the four dwarf antelope species of the Kaokoveld, the grey duiker is the most solitary. **1990** SKINNER & SMITHERS *Mammals of Sn Afr. Subregion* 638 They [*sc.* common duiker] may be referred to as the grey duiker but in some parts of their distributional range they vary from rufous to yellow in colour. **1900** W.L. SCLATER *Mammals of S. Afr.* I. 162 The **red duiker** is essentially a forest dweller .. inhabiting the thickest bush and kloofs where there is water. **1971** *Sunday Times* 24 Jan. (Mag. Sect.) 5 Red duiker — a species which, for many years, had been thought to be extinct. **1976** J. HANKS *Mammals* 20 The uniform chestnut colour should distinguish the red duiker from other species. **1990** CLINNING & FOURIE in *Fauna & Flora* No.47, 16 Red duikers are inhabitants of moist forests and coastal scrub, and occur from the southern Sudan southwards .. to as far south as Natal.

c. *comb.* **duikerwortel** /-vɔːtəl, -vɔrtəl/ [Afk., *wortel* root], any of several species of the plant *Grielum* of the Rosaceae, the rootstock of which is said to be favoured by duikers.

1966 C.A. SMITH *Common Names* 205 *Duikerwortel, Grielum marlothii* ... The plants are said to be a good and fattening stock feed. The succulent rootstock .. is a favourite food of the duiker buck. **1974** [see WEESKINDERTJIES]. **1975** *Argus* 17 Sept. 28 Here is the derivation of the other name of the plant, duikerwortel ... In the spring and summer months the duikers use their neat, pointed little hoofs to dig the roots up out of the sandy places in which they tend to grow. **1983** M.M. KIDD *Cape Peninsula* 134 *Grielum grandiflorum* ... *Duikerwortel.* Prostrate or straggling.

2.a. [Named for its characteristic feeding behaviour.] Any of several species of cormorant of the Phalacrocoracidae, occurring in both marine and inland waters; DIVER sense 1. See also sense 2 b.

1838 D. MOODIE (tr. *J. Van Riebeeck's Jrnl*) *Record* I. 13 The yacht returned from Robben Island, bringing about an hundred black birds, called *duikers,* (cormorants) of a good flavour. **1856** C.J. ANDERSSON *Lake Ngami* 16 The way in which the 'duikers' (cormorants and shags) obtain their food is not uninteresting. **1867** E.L. LAYARD *Birds of S. Afr.* 380 *Graculus Carbo* ... *Duiker* of Colonists ... Its chief haunt is the rocky, lonely shore at the base of Cape Point. **1910** D. FAIRBRIDGE *That Which Hath Been* (1913) 311 The white seabirds wheeled around his head, uttering shrill cries, the duikers plunged and dived in the dark water. **1931** R.C. BOLSTER *Land & Sea Birds* 175 The Duikers .. have bodies 'sharpened to a point for diving' ... [They] sun and dry themselves with wings outstretched. *c*1936 *S. & E. Afr. Yr Bk & Guide* 352 Guano is deposited by Malagas (or Gannets), Penguins and Duikers in the latter half of the year. **1969** *Personality* 5 June, There is also a shooting season of three months as these lakes are well known for their bleshoenders, duikers and certain types of wild duck. **1973** M. PHILIP *Caravan Caravel* 30 A *duiker* squawked as it flapped its wings in rapid flight and then dived into the sea in front of them. **1977** *Het Suid-Western* 31 Aug., Hundreds, perhaps thousands of black Cape cormorants (also known as duikers) have been dying all along the Southern Cape coast in the past two weeks. **1988** J.A. BROWN *Mousanzia* 1 'Keep your eyes peeled for duikers, Black Mo' ... Soon the dark-winged birds would be leaving their roosts on the rocky ledges of Seal Island.

b. With distinguishing epithet, denoting species of water bird:

i. Any of several species of cormorant: **bank duiker**, *Phalacrocorax neglectus*; **reed duiker**, *P. africanus*; **trek-duiker** [Afk., *trek,* see TREK *n.*], the *Cape cormorant* (see CAPE sense 2 a), *P. capensis*; **white-breasted duiker**, *P. carbo.*

1931 R.C. BOLSTER *Land & Sea Birds* 202 The .. **Bank Duiker**, which generally goes in small parties of three and four, frequents the fishing-banks. **1950** L.G. GREEN *At Daybreak for Isles* 129 Besides the trek duiker and the white-breasted duiker, there is a species on the island known as the bank duiker. **1906** STARK & SCLATER *Birds of S. Afr.* IV. 10 In South Africa the **Reed Duiker** is generally distributed throughout the country wherever there are suitable conditions. **1931** R.C. BOLSTER *Land & Sea Birds* 175 Both the Reed Duiker and the Snake Bird swim low in the water with little more than the head and neck showing. **1950** L.G. GREEN *At Daybreak for Isles* 129 The reed duiker .. also nests on the islands; but this is really a fresh-water bird. **1906** STARK & SCLATER *Birds of S. Afr.* 6 The **Trek Duiker** is found all along the coasts of Southern Africa as far north as the Congo on the west, but not beyond Durban on the east. **1918** S.H. SKAIFE *Animal Life* 235 The *duikers,* or cormorants, are well-known sea birds around our coasts. The *trek-duiker* is especially common on the south and west coasts. **1931** R.C. BOLSTER *Land & Sea Birds* 202 The Trek Duiker .. is so called because the birds, which are often in very large flocks, fly straight and low, with continuous flaps of the wings and periodical glides, in long lines to their fishing-grounds. **1946** L.G. GREEN *So Few Are Free* 70 Trek-duikers are by far the most common. **1906** STARK & SCLATER *Birds of S. Afr.* IV. 5 Though not nearly so common as the next species (*P. capensis*), the **White-breasted Duiker** cannot be called a scarce bird. **1908** HAAGNER & IVY *Sketches* 141 The White-breasted Duiker .. is found all along the South African coast. **1950** [see quot. at *bank duiker* above].

ii. **sweet-water duiker**, the darter *Anhinga melanogaster* of the Anhingidae.

1867 E.L. LAYARD *Birds of S. Afr.* 378 *Plotus congensis* .. **Sweet-water Duiker** ... The '*Anhinga,*' '*Snake-bird,*' or '*Darter,*' is not unfrequent in certain localities.

duikerbok /ˈdœɪkərˌbɔk, ˈdeɪkə-, ˈdaɪkə-/ *n. Obs.* exc. *hist.* Also **duiker-bock**, **duykerbok**, **duykers bock**. [S. Afr. Du., *duiker* (see DUIKER) + *bok* (see BOK).] DUIKER sense 1 a.

1786 G. FORSTER tr. *A. Sparrman's Voy. to Cape of G.H.* I. 44 *Duykerboks* or *diving-goats,* so called from a peculiar manner they have of leaping and of diving, as it were under the bushes. **1795** C.R. HOPSON tr. *C.P. Thunberg's Trav.* II. 26 The Spring buck .. does not reside .. in the thickets like the steenbock, or duykers bock. **1804** R. PERCIVAL *Acct of Cape of G.H.* 159 The duiker-bock .. is the size of the common deer, of a dirty brown colour with two long straight horns of a black hue. **1837** J.E. ALEXANDER *Narr. of Voy.* I. 339, I went out to shoot *duikerbok,* (a brown deer with small upright horns, and its height two feet). **1896** R. WARD *Rec. of Big Game* 96 The Duiker, or Duikerbok, of which there are several varieties to be found in various parts of the African Continent, is .. quite the most ubiquitous of all the antelope family. **1900** [see DIVING GOAT]. **1973** O.H. SPOHR tr. *F. Krauss's Trav. Jrnl* 44 The smaller types of antelope like .. duykerbok (A. mergent Blains) .. were found here.

duinebessie /ˈdeɪnəbesi, ˈdœinəbesi/ *n.* Also **duinbessie**, and (formerly) **dunnebesje**. [Afk. (earlier S. Afr. Du.), *duine* dunes + *bessie* berry.] The spiny shrub *Nylandtia spinosa* of the Polygalaceae, common on sand-dunes and sandy flats; its edible fruit; *skilpadbessie,* see SKILPAD sense b.

[**1843** J.C. CHASE *Cape of G.H.* 152 The wild fruits, indigenous to the country, are also incredibly numerous, .. quarri (*Euclea undulata*), num num, the Hottentot name, (*Ardunia Ferox*), duin berries (*Mundia spinosa*), with a great number of others.] **1913** C. PETTMAN *Africanderisms* 159 *Dunnebesjes,* .. Another name for the berries known as Skelpadbesjes. **1917** R. MARLOTH *Common Names* 25 *Duine'bessie, Mundtia spinosa.* A spiny shrublet of the Cape Flats and other sandy tracts, bearing large red berries, eagerly eaten by tortoises and children. **1934** C.P. SWART Supplement to Pettman. 46 *Duinebessie,* .. Mundtia spinosa is so called because the shrub is commonly found on the coastal dunes. **1964** L.G. GREEN *Old Men Say* 100 Aromatic berries known as *duinbessies* were brought to the market from Green Point Common and sold at a penny a pound. They made a grand fruit sauce which was served with meat dishes. **1980** D. BICKELL in *E. Prov. Herald* 23 June 7 One area which attracted us we called 'Tortoise Town' because of the number of these creatures we found there, particularly among the duinebessies in the sandy areas. **1983** *Ibid.* 16 May 11 In time, among the beautiful flora which will come home to the valley will be proteas, ericas, waxies, everlastings, gladioli, watsonias, duinebessies, .. and euphorbias.

duivelsdrek var. DUIWELSDREK.

duiveltj(i)e var. DUIWELTJIE.

‖**duiwel** /ˈdeɪvəl, ˈdœivəl/ *int.* and *n.* Formerly also **duivel, duyvel.** [Afk., fr. Du. *duivel* devil.]

A. *int.* ***De duiwel*** [Du., *de* the], ***the duiwel***: 'the devil'. Occas. ***der duiwel*** [Afk., *der* of the]: 'of the devil'.

1838 J.E. ALEXANDER *Exped. into Int.* I. 73 In the old times we could do what we liked with them, and no one meddled with us; now, with the government and the zendelings (missionaries), we can get nothing done – Der duivel! **1883** M.A. CAREY-HOBSON *Farm in Karoo* 190 In the middle of the night up jumps the farmer and screams out, 'A snake has bitten my nose! oh, de duivel! he has bitten my nose!' **1908** F.C. SLATER *Sunburnt South* 149 'Neef Koos,' I began, 'what the *duivel* do you mean by stealing my saddle?' **1980** A. DANGOR in M. Mutloatse *Forced Landing* 163 'Who's there?' 'Me.' 'Who the duiwel is me?' **1988** — in *Staffrider* Vol.7 No.3, 80 Pyp, are you ready with that wire? Pyp? Where the *duiwel* are you?

B. *n.*

1. Used as a term of reference or (occas.) address: a devil, the devil.

[**1786** G. FORSTER tr. *A. Sparrman's Voy. to Cape of G.H.* II. 64 The buffaloes belonged to certain supernatural beings, who in this manner marked them for their own cattle. In order to give a notion of these beings, they made use of the Dutch term *duyvel*, which signifies devil.] **1910** 'R. DEHAN' *Dop Doctor* 175, I tell you that man has the wickedness of the duyvel in him, and the cunning of an old baboon! **1910** D. FAIRBRIDGE *That Which Hath Been* (1913) 244 The son of the house is drawn towards the cause of liberty, but his mother is a *duivel*. **1912** F. BANCROFT *Veldt Dwellers* 83 *Duivels* they are, and care not for God nor man; they know how to play all our games, yet to trap them, so far, we cannot. **1920** R. JUTA *Tavern* 19 To the Duivel with these emigrants ... why man, dere is not corn enough for half of dem! **1939** S. CLOETE *Watch for Dawn* 33 Now he could distinguish the names of the oxen as his boys called to them .. Witkop .. Bles .. Bokveld .. Blauberg. Loop .. loo-oop, you duiwels! **1972** *Drum* 8 Dec. 9 We drove away. But my head was thumping ... 'Just who the hell let the duiwel loose?'

2. *Cooperage.* An s-shaped iron tool used to pull the bottom of a cask into the groove made to hold it.

1988 A. VAN WYK in *S. Afr. Panorama* Sept. 50 The bottoms at either end are fitted by making grooves on both ends on the inside of the cask. They are hammered right with a hook and a 'duiwel' (devil), long bent iron tubing. Finally, all the hoops are again driven tight to make the panels fit tightly.

duiwelsdrek /ˈdeɪvəlzdrek, ˈdœiv(ə)ls-, -drɛk/ *n.* Also **duivels drek.** [Afk., combining form *duiwels* devil's + *drek* excrement.]

a. A bitter-tasting plant resin derived from any of several Asian trees of the genus *Ferula*, used for the treatment of nervous tension and stomach upsets. Also *attrib.* See also (*old*) *Dutch medicine* (DUTCH *adj.* sense 2).

Variously known as 'asafoetida', 'devil's dirt', and 'devil's dung' elsewhere.

1919 *Dunell, Ebden & Co.'s Price List* Oct. 20 Duivels Drek. Per doz. 7/-. **1943** [see HOFFMANSDRUPPELS]. **1969** *Sunday Times* 4 May, He found eight bottles of satan's dung (duiwelsdrek) hidden in the roof of the manse. Three more bottles of the potion were unearthed in the church building. *c***1970** *Lennon's Dutch Medicine Handbk, Duiwelsdrek,* In cases of nervousness, hysteria, and sleeplessness, this preparation will be found to soothe and calm the nerves. It can also be recommended for flatulence and stomach pains. **1973** S. STANDER tr. *A.P. Brink's Brandy in S. Afr.* 172 Results could be attained by drawing a dessertspoon of 'duiwelsdrek' with a half-bottle of brandy and a pinch of salpetre. **1976** *E. Prov. Herald* 12 Feb. 5 He never regained consciousness after being fed the 'pill' made of curry powder, tumeric, garlic, pea powder, epsom salts and 'duiwelsdrek' during a ceremony at the .. men's hostel. **1988** [see DOEPA sense 2 a]. **1989** D. SMUTS *Folk Remedies* 5 *Asafoetida (duiwelsdrek)*: Duiwelsdrek is recommended for cases of nervousness, hysteria and sleeplessness.

b. *comb.* **duiwelsdrekdruppels** /-ˌdrəp(ə)lz, -ˌdrœp(ə)ls/ [Afk., *druppels* drops], **-drops**, drops containing duiwelsdrek.

*c***1970** *Lennon's Dutch Medicine Handbk*, **Duiwelsdrek-druppels**, These drops are intended for the same ailments as Duiwelsdrek. For nervousness, hysteria and sleeplessness take ten to fifteen drops. **1989** D. SMUTS *Folk Remedies* 39 *Fainting*, Duiwelsdrek drops (asafoetida drops), 20 to 30 drops on sugar or in half a small glass of water.

duiweltjie /ˈdœivəlki, ˈdev(ə)lki, ˈdəv(ə)lki, -ci/ *n.* Also **diwilkie, duiveltj(i)e, duwweltje, duwweltji(e).** [Afk., etym. dubious: see DUBBELTJIE *n.*[2]] DUBBELTJIE *n.*[2] Also *attrib.*

1894 R. MARLOTH in *Trans. of S. Afr. Phil. Soc.* 29 Aug. 9 (Pettman), The little nuts of *Tribulus terrestris* and *T. Zeyheri* are armed with strong, sharp spines ... The fruitlets of *Emex centropodium* are quite similar, both having deserved thereby the Dutch designation of 'Duiveltjes'. **1937** *Handbk for Farmers* (Dept of Agric. & Forestry) 458 The Karroo veld consists of the various types of Karroo bush and a secondary plant-growth .. , amongst which the few grass species and especially the .. widely-distributed duwweltjie (*Tribulus* sp.) can be included. **1948** A.C. WHITE *Call of Bushveld* 195 A pointer .. may get an occasional duiweltjie in his foot which a knowing dog will extract immediately and without assistance. **1948** V.M. FITZROY *Cabbages & Cream* 208 Those peculiarly devilish little thorn-bearing weeds known as duiveltjes. **1961** L.E. VAN ONSELEN *Trekboer* 27 The Trekboer learned to use a queer assortment of herbs and plants for their medicinal properties from the Hottentots and Bushmen. Leaves of the duiweltjie weed were used as plasters to heal an abscess. **1969** J.M. WHITE *Land God Made in Anger* 22 Water is sweeping around the bend .. drowning the thorny little *duwweltjes* .. that have somehow survived for eight parched years in the clefts of the baked boulders. *Ibid.* 230 The Bushman [*sic*] know how to compound ointments from insects and reptiles, and how to make poultices from the *duwweltjie* and other plants. **1970** B.C. MARITZ *Informant, Port Elizabeth*, I stepped onto a diwilkie and it's gone into my foot. **1973** M. PHILIP *Caravan Caravel* 67 'Phew,' said Peter, as he and Johan both examined their feet. '*Duiweltjies* in that grass.' **1982** J. KRIGE in *Staffrider* Vol.5 No.2, 20 'Eina bliksem,' I shouted, lifting one of my feet. I had walked into a patch of duiweltjies and the little prodded thorns were sitting like flies on the soles of my feet. **1991** D.M. MOORE *Garden Earth* 196 (*caption*) Duwweltji (*Tribulus terrestris*) grows along rivers and in lowlying areas, where its long taproot can draw on water deep in the ground.

dukum, dukun varr. DOEKUM.

dulsies /ˈdəlsis, ˈdœl-/ *pl. n.* Also **dulcis.** [Afk. (earlier *dulcis*, shortened form of (*spiritus*) *nitri dulcis* sweet nitre).] Usu. with distinguishing epithet, as **brown dulsies** or **bruindulsies** /ˈbreɪn-, ˈbrœɪn-/ [Afk.], **red dulsies, white dulsies** or (most commonly) **wit-** /ˈvət-/, or **witte dulsies** /ˈvətə-/ [Afk.]: a patent medicine used for the treatment of a variety of ailments, esp. colds and influenza. See also (*old*) *Dutch medicine* (DUTCH *adj.* sense 2).

1919 *Dunell, Ebden & Co.'s Price List* Oct. 20 Essence Dulcis 3/6. *Ibid.* Witte [*printed* Witie] Dulcis 3/6. **1931** H.C. BOSMAN in V. Rosenberg *Almost Forgotten Stories* (1979) 13 There was something the matter with her which rooi-laventel, wit dulsies and other Boer remedies could not cure. **1949** L.G. GREEN *In Land of Afternoon* 44 Halle medicines, advertised in the 'Cape Town Gazette' in 1817, included 'wonder essence, Dulcis, Amara, cramp drops and red powder.' **1958** [see GROENE AMARA]. **1958** E.H. BURROWS *Hist. of Medicine* 191 *Bruindulsies*: used for colds and wet weather ... *Witdulsies*: .. used as a tonic .. for heart complaints, fever, 'flu and head colds. **1971** *Evening Post* 6 Nov. 3 Mix together 4 drops white iodine, 3 drops wit dulsies (sweet nitre – an old Dutch remedy); 4 drops oil of cloves in a little milk, and drink morning and evening. **1978** A.P. BRINK *Rumours of Rain* 245 The place was crammed to capacity by wares ... Snuff and cigarettes, medicine (Vicks and Aspro and all the thin bottles familiar from Ma's dispensary: red and white dulcis and Haarlem drops, chlorodyne, wonder essence, Jamaica ginger, chest drops, cascara). **1984** B. JOHNSON-BARKER in *Wynboer* Feb. 64 Thys Denyssen, who had a compassionate nature, so far forgot his own advice as to recommend witdulsies – half a teaspoonful three times a day in a wine glass of water. **1989** D. SMUTS *Folk Remedies* 23 *Childlessness*, .. 1 small bottle bruindulsies (if the fault lies with the woman; if the fault lies with the man, leave out the bruindulsies and add witdulsies).

‖**dumela** /duˈmeːla/ *int.* Also **domela, dumella, lumela, ruměela, ruméla.** [SeSotho and seTswana. The form 'lumela' (also pron. /duˈmeːla/) represents the orthography of Lesotho.] 'Good day'; 'hello'; 'goodbye'.

The pl. form 'dumelang' (see quot. 1990) is used in seSotho and seTswana when more than one person is greeted.

1824 W.J. BURCHELL *Trav.* II. 431 On taking leave of me at night, his usual word was, *Rumēela*; a polite and friendly term of greeting, often used also at meeting. **1846** R. MOFFAT *Missionary Labours* 103 We passed many women, who were employed in their gardens, who, on seeing us, threw down their picks, and .. lifted up their hands, exclaiming 'Ruméla,' (their manner of salutation). **1878** P. GILLMORE *Great Thirst Land* 295 They are well formed, and although not pretty, look good-natured; and, above all, they are polite, for not one fails to greet the soil-stained travellers with their pretty expression of welcome, 'Dumela!' **1912** W. WESTRUP *Land of To-Morrow* 174 He dismounted before the two white men ... 'Lumela, Raphofoolo,' he said ... .'Lumela, Rufingwana.' Dangerfield took the extended hand. **1920** S.M. MOLEMA *Bantu Past & Present* 137 The Bechuana-Basotho people say Dumela, a word meaning hail, or hail to you. **1924** G. BAUMANN in Baumann & Bright *Lost Republic* (1940) 137 All the boys whom I had had occasion to flog saluted me with upraised arm: 'Domela Morena' (Sesuto – 'Hail, Master'). **1930** S.T. PLAATJE *Mhudi* (1975) 31 'Dumela (good day), my sister,' he said, 'I am Ra-Thaga, the son of Notto.' **1955** W. ILLSLEY *Wagon on Fire* 87 'Dumela, ntate,' he greeted the old man politely. 'Dumela, my child.' *c***1976** H. FLATHER *Thaba Rau* 215 He .. greeted Leach with a raised arm and then a double-handshake ... 'Dumela morena', he said. 'Welcome back.' **1986** *Star* 31 July 10 Dumela folks! **1990** *City Press* 1 July 15 Sipho had come to buy food for his family. 'Dumelang,' greeted Sipho. 'Ja, Josef, what do you want?' said Boetie arrogantly.

Hence (*nonce*) **dumela** *v. trans.*, to greet (someone) with the word 'dumela'.

1887 J.W. MATTHEWS *Incwadi Yami* 374 Hundreds met us on the banks of the river; the crowd, 'lumelaing' (saluting) us and singing and dancing their war dances.

dumily-klontje, duminy klontjie varr. DOEMELA-KLONTJIE.

duminy var. DOMINEE.

dump *n.* [Orig. *U.S. Eng.* (1865 in *OED*), fr. *dump* to deposit refuse. Cf. MINE DUMP.] MINE DUMP.

1919 R.Y. STORMBERG *With Love from Gwenno* 11 It [*sc.* Johannesburg] is quite the most volatile village in young Old Afriky. There are great white ice-bergs that float about the grey-green landscape: dumps they are called – the crushings of the white granite that contains the gold. **1920** R.H. LINDSEY-RENTON *Diary* (1979)

41 We passed several of the dumps that are the curse of Johannesburg. These dumps consist of the dust to what the rocks and earth are reduced after having been crushed and washed etc. during the gold extracting process. **1922** *Rand Daily Mail* in J. Crwys-Williams *S. Afr. Despatches* (1989) 234 One of the many fights centred around .. the Robinson Dump ... A body of police took up a position in the ditch beside the road, with others some little way up the dump itself. **1936** R.J.M. GOOLD-ADAMS *S. Afr. To-Day & To-Morrow* 159 Johannesburg sank .. into that curious dust-haze which is all its own, swept as it is from the dessicated sides of the dumps. **1936** A. LEZARD *Gold Blast* 260 These glistening dumps, these man-made mountains, present a permanent background to the town. They are silhouetted against every Johannesburg sky. **1941** C.W. DE KIEWIET *Hist. of S. Afr.* 176 The higher price for gold, which indefinitely extended the life of the industry, removed the fear of .. 'dumps' that would slowly be worn away by the keen August winds. **1950** D. REED *Somewhere S. of Suez* 46 Around the city are great dumps, the size of Durham slag-heaps but of different colour. **1972** *S. Afr. Panorama* May 29 Lush green vegetation is being established on dumps of virtually inert powdered quartz left by the gold mines of the Witwatersrand. **1988** G. SILBER in *Style* Apr. 38 The Klein Letaba Gold Mine, the richest gold producer in the northern Transvaal until a rock slide and rock bottom gold price forced it to seal its shafts in 1968 .. was just an old dump.

dumpy *n.* [Named for the stout appearance of the bottle.] A 340 ml non-returnable beer bottle. Also *attrib.*, and *transf.*

1966 *Daily News* 12 Sept. 2 The squat bottles popularly known as 'dumpies' .. are non-returnable, and deposits are not levied on them at times of purchase. **1973** *Evening Post* 19 May 1 Apart from the 30 men on the field at any one time, exuberant supporters packed the stands, a girl in one hand, a dumpy in the other. **1987** G. SILBER in *Weekly Mail* 12 June 24 There were generous glimpses of the First Lady, looking like a dumpy of tomato sauce in vivid red stretch crimplene, with matching twist-off cap. **1989** *E. Prov. Herald* 3 Nov. 1 Since yesterday, a shortage of pint bottles has been hitting bottle stores and bars, and drinkers will have to switch to dumpies for at least a week. **1993** *Sunday Times* 10 October 18 (*advt*) Our .. improvements are set to make drinking your favourite beer even more rewarding ... The all-new dumpy boasts a shape that's easier to handle and quicker to grab. **1994** B.N. STARKE *Informant, Johannesburg* We [*sc.* South African Breweries] introduced dumpy bottles to the South African beer market in *1962*. Our understanding is that the term derived from American usage (the Australian equivalent was 'stubby'). **1994** *E. Prov. Herald* 23 June 1 Beer — Up 6c a litre or about 2c a 340ml can or dumpy.

dung roller *n. phr.* Any of several species of dung beetle (family Scarabaeidae) which roll dung balls either for food or as nests for their larvae.

1853 W.R. KING *Campaigning in Kaffirland* 307 The supplies of dung for fuel were very materially interfered with by millions of black beetles, called 'dung rollers', a kind of scarabaeus, which swarmed day after day on every part of the plain. **1913** C. PETTMAN *Africanderisms* 159 *Dung rollers*, This name is given to several beetles of the *Scarabaeidae* Family. The nidus in which they deposit their egg is formed of dung, which they shape into a round ball; they roll this with great labour to a suitable locality and cover with loose soil. **1967** E. ROSENTHAL *Encycl. of Sn Afr.* 160 *Dung Roller*, Beetle so called on account of its habit of making balls of dung in which to deposit its eggs. **1970** C. KOCH in *Std Encycl. of Sn Afr.* II. 250 Dung-beetles .. live on dung and excrement. In the group of dung-rollers the female makes a ball of fresh dung round the egg, which is buried in the soil as a source of food for the larva.

dunkop /ˈdœnkɔp/ *n. Pathology.* [Afk., *dun* thin + *kop* head.] A form of HORSE-SICKNESS, a viral disease affecting the lungs; DUNSIEKTE sense 1 a. Also *attrib.* Cf. DIKKOP sense 2 a.

1929 *Handbk for Farmers* (Dept of Agric.) 243 In a second form, termed 'Dikkop', the heart is principally affected ... This form is not as fatal as the 'Dunkop' or lung form, which starts with high fever and general symptoms of illness. **1957** *Ibid.* III. 427 Sir Arnold Theiler distinguished four clinical forms of horsesickness, viz ... Horsesickness fever, .. the lung form (dunkop horsesickness), the heart form (dikkop horsesickness) and .. the mixed form. **1974** R. CLARK in *Std Encycl. of Sn Afr.* X. 301 In the 'dunkop' (thin-head) form there is massive effusion of fluid into the lungs. **1976** MÖNNIG & VELDMAN *Handbk on Stock Diseases* 71 *Dunkop*, This is the most dangerous form of the disease ... The lungs are attacked.

dunneball /ˈdʌnəˌbɔːl/ *n.* Also **dannebal**, **dunna-ball**. Englished form of DENNEBOL. Also *attrib.*

1913 D. FAIRBRIDGE *Piet of Italy* 74 Sitting by the blazing dannebal fire while the winter rains splashed and thundered on the tin roof. **1970** M.E. TAMLIN *Informant, Cape Town* Dunna-ball. Fir cone. **1982** J. SCOTT in *Cape Times* 8 Sept. 10, I got the fire going. 'Go and find me some dunneballs.'

dunnebesje var. DUINEBESSIE.

dunsiekte /ˈdœnsiktə/ *n.* Also **deng sik**, **din sikte**, **dinziekte**, **dunziekte**. [Afk. (earlier S. Afr. Du.), *dun* thin + *siekte* sickness.]

1. *Pathology.* Either of two diseases of livestock: **a.** DUNKOP. **b.** Seneciosis, chronic poisoning caused by the ingestion of any of several species of *Senecio* (family Asteraceae), affecting the liver of the animal; DOMSIEKTE sense b.

Called 'dunsiekte' esp. in horses, Seneciosis is more usually known as *Molteno disease* (see MOLTENO sense a) in cattle.

1893 F.C. SELOUS *Trav. & Adventure* 4 These two forms of horse sickness are known as 'din ziekte' and the 'dik-kop ziekte' (Thin sickness and thick head sickness). **1898** G. NICHOLSON *50 Yrs* 207 The horses sold as 'salted', or acclimatised, have perhaps survived an attack of the milder form of the disease, locally known as the 'din sikte'. **1899** *Natal Agric. Jrnl* 31 Mar. 4 Stock maladies are well known to the English pastoralist under their Dutch or South African Dutch names — 'dunziekte', literally thin-sickness in horses. *c*1913 W. VAN HEUSDEN *Treatment of Horses, Cattle, Sheep & Poultry* 144 Sheep and Goats. Dinziekte (Chronic Diarrhoea). **1916** *Farmer's Weekly* 20 Dec. 1537 Lately donkeys got what can best be described as 'dunziekte'. **1929** J. STEVENSON-HAMILTON *Low-Veld* 19 Horse sickness is of two types: deng sik, in which the lungs are primarily affected, and the animal is choked to death by masses of frothy mucus coughed up therefrom; secondly, dikkop, when the head swells up, and the horse dies of heart pressure. **1930** [see JAAGSIEKTE sense 1]. **1934** C.P. SWART Supplement to Pettman. 47 *Dunsiekte*, .. The common name of chronic Senecio poisoning. The horse, after having ingested large quantities of the Senecio plant, becomes listless, stands with closed eyes, breathes with difficulty, loses its appetite and becomes emaciated (hence the name) and succumbs in a subconscious state within from three to ten days. **1940** F.B. YOUNG *City of Gold* 195 Then horse sickness appeared in its most fatal form: the variety known as *deng sik*. **1966** [see DAN'S CABBAGE]. **1966** C.A. SMITH *Common Names* 207 The species [*sc. Senecio retrorsus*] is apparently one of the causes of *dunsiekte*, also called Stomach Staggers in horses, and Molteno Disease in cattle and sheep. **1972** N. SAPEIKA in *Std Encycl. of Sn Afr.* VII. 296 Ingestion of certain *Senecio* plants has long been known to cause liver damage, which may result in death in cattle and horses (Molteno sickness, dunsiekte). **1988** [see MOLTENO sense a].

2. *comb.* **dunsiektebossie** /-ˈbɔsi/ [Afk., *bossie* (*bos* bush + -IE)], *Molteno disease plant* (see MOLTENO sense b).

1973 F.J. VELDMAN in *Std Encycl. of Sn Afr.* VIII. 608 *Senecio retrorsus* (dunsiektebossie) — South-Eastern and Eastern Cape.

dunya var. DHUNIA.

dupa var. DOEPA.

duppeltje var. DUBBELTJE *n.*[2]

Durban /ˈdɜːbən/ *n.* The name of the largest city in KwaZulu-Natal, a port and holiday resort, used *attrib.* in special collocations: **Durban July**, [shortened form of *Durban July Handicap*], JULY sense 1; also *attrib.*; **Durban poison** *slang* [see KIF], a particularly potent type of dagga (marijuana) cultivated in KwaZulu-Natal; South African dagga generally; DP *n.*[1] See also DAGGA *n.*[2] sense 1, TEGWINI.

1927 J.T. WALLACE in *Outspan* 8 Apr. 17 Valuable stakes are the vogue — the Christmas Handicap of £6,000, the **Durban July** £5,000. **1948** H.C. BOSMAN in L. Abrahams *Cask of Jerepigo* (1972) 232 If you can pick the winner of the Durban July, then it doesn't matter so much if a couple of long-haired painters that you thought were Van Goghs turn out to be also-rans. **1970** [see INYANGA sense 1]. **1971** *Sunday Times* 4 July 1 Mazarin must now rank with some of the greats of the Durban July. **1989** F.G. BUTLER *Tales from Old Karoo* 54 Perhaps he'd been tempted to put too much money on the Durban July and lost it. **1990** *Grocott's Mail* 19 June 6 Lifestyle Promotions .. have come up with a sparkling idea for Durban July Day, July 7. **1994** G. WILLOUGHBY in *Weekly Mail & Guardian* 8 July 38 It's Durban July day, folks. *Ibid.* The Durban July is a fascinating cultural phenomenon. We have very few public rituals like it that catch the public imagination right across the land, from Cape Town to kwa-Mashu. **1971** *Daily Dispatch* 4 Sept. 6 Amounts and proportions of cannabinol and tetrahydrocannabinol determine the potency of the dagga. This varies considerably in different parts, .. but that from Zululand and Natal is generally acknowledged to be among the most potent in the world (**Durban poison**). **1973** *Rand Daily Mail* 27 Oct. 5 He bought a roll of 20 reefers of dagga known as 'Durban poison' from him for R5. **1978** A. AKHALWAYA in *Ibid.* 10 July 7 Be careful if you are offered 'Durban poison'. You could be arrested. For the 'poison' is another name for dagga. **1978** *Darling* 8 Nov. 66 Ask someone from overseas why South Africa is famous and .. a few, a very small minority, will grin and say: 'Durban Poison, man.' Why? Because DP, dagga, is just about the best high in the world, fit to rank .. in the dope smoker's list of all-time greats. **1986** *Style* Feb. 64 What is Durban's most lucrative alternative sport? Second to riding high on the surf is riding high on Durban Poison. **1990** [see MAJAT]. **1993** *Fair Lady* 21 Apr. 76 Dagga, commonly known as Durban poison, is one of South Africa's most sought-after exports in the international drug market.

So **Durbanite** *n.*, a resident of Durban.

1894 E.N. THOMAS *How Thankful We Should Be* 7 We amuse ourselves by watching the ordinary street life of Durban. We miss the hurry and bustle of Adderley-street; Durbanites take things 'sootjes'. **1927** *Outspan* 11 Mar. 13 Durbanites are very jealous and envious of Johannesburg — and what is more they tell us so frankly. **1934** B.I. BUCHANAN *Pioneer Days* 28 We can never forget the kindness of the Durbanites who had so very little for themselves. **1952** T. MATSHIKIZA in *Drum* Nov. 31 She's one of Durban City's favourite light sopranos .. Aren't Durbanites lucky? **1989** S. SOLE in *Sunday Tribune* 1 Jan. 2 Durbanites are *sooooooo* cliquey and keep to their own little social circle. Capetonians are ready to compromise. **1992** K. MKHIZE in *Natal Witness* 4 Jan. 5 Pietermaritzburg folks .. should rather be encouraging Durbanites to think big about the numbers which are stretching their resources and take heed of the fact that Durban is the second fastest growing city in the southern hemisphere.

Durbs /dɜːbz/ *n. colloq.* An affectionate or jocular name for the city of Durban; *Banana City*, see BANANA sense 2. Sometimes in the phr. ***Durbs-by-the-sea***.

1975 [see TRUE sense b]. **1975** S.K. SMITH in *Darling* 12 Mar. 4 Us chicks in 'Durbs' waits with bated breath for Bloss's latest spiel. **1976** [see 'Blossom' quot. at SLIP-SLOP]. **1979** *Darling* 7 Feb. 25 'What's it *like* up there?' I ask again. 'Like Durbs at Christmas time but without the sea,' someone answers. **1984** *Fair Lady* 30 May 176 South Africa's first multiracial feminist group started in sleepy old Durbs years ago when others were still rabbiting on about sharing the washing-up. **1987** *Ibid.* 13 May 87 *Complacency*: In Durbs by the Sea (with a little help from the state of emergency) the tragic cry of the beloved country is a soothing murmur in the background. **1990** W. HENNING in *Sunday Times* 2 Dec. (Mag. Sect.) 36 These holidays, head for Durbs-by-the-sea. You could catch far more than a tan. **1991** G. EICHORN in *Natal Mercury* 3 Apr. 22 Seems I'm not a Banana Boy ... I mean, I know we've only been in Durbs about 17 years .. and maybe I don't qualify for some obscure technical reason on that account.

Durstland var. DORSLAND.

Dusi, Duzi /ˈduːzi/ *n.* [Shortened form of Zulu name *Umzindusi*.] ***The Dusi***: An annual canoeing marathon on the Umzindusi river in KwaZulu-Natal. Also *attrib.*

1985 [see JOL *n.* sense 2]. **1989** G. ADDISON in *Motorist* 4th Quarter 45 The famous canoeing marathons like the Dusi and the Berg tend to attract only the toughest sporting types. **1990** *Weekend Post* 19 Jan. 9 Duzi 'king' Graeme Pope-Ellis. **1990** *Ibid.* (Leisure) 1 'The Duzi' is unique in world canoeing because it is a supreme test of physical fitness and stamina, presenting entrants with white water, opportunities for sprinting and, to pile agony on agony, portaging overland at selected points. Canoeists have to carry their canoes over some 48 km during the race ... In the early years of the Duzi, canoes were made of wood and canvas. **1990** *Sunday Times* 2 Dec. 27 Whiplash memories of a rolling microbus in hot pursuit of Duzi canoeists in the Valley of 1000 Hills. **1992** *Natal Mercury* 18 Dec. 19 The two short .. races are ideal last minute qualifiers for those Dusi hopefuls who have not yet had the chance to finish the four races needed to compete in the Dusi.

dussel-, düsselboom varr. DISSELBOOM.

dust-devil *n. rare.* [Extension of the general Eng. sense 'a miniature whirlwind'.] A dust storm or tornado.

1949 J. MOCKFORD *Golden Land* 69 The bigger dust-devils will even topple over jerry-built shacks and Native huts, and tear the roofs off houses; but as a rule these dust storms are uncomfortable rather than dangerous. **1955** H. KLEIN *Winged Courier* 46 The airmen experienced a new African flying hazard in the form of dust devils, some of which rose as high as 8, 000 ft. **1973** *Cape Times* 12 June 1 A Gigantic whirlwind 'dust devil', turning anti-clockwise at speeds up to 60 km/h and tunnelling high-pressure air to sea level at a point about 1 600 km east of Cape Town in the Indian Ocean, added choking grit to yesterday's heat and reduced visibility to 2000 metres.

Dutch *n.* and *adj.* [Special senses of Eng. *Dutch* of or originating from Holland.]

A. *n.*

1. *hist.* ***The Dutch*** (*pl.*): The white Dutch-speaking inhabitants of Cape Town, of the Cape Colony, and later of Natal, the Orange Free State, and the Transvaal; *the African Dutch* sense (*b*), see AFRICAN *adj.*[1] (sense 1 b ii). Cf. CAPE DUTCH *n. phr.* sense 1, SOUTH AFRICAN DUTCH *n. phr.* sense 2.

1685 J. TYRELL in R. Raven-Hart *Cape G.H. 1652–1702* (1971) II. 255 The duch was Very Sivill in thayer expression in promising to supply us with any thing that thayer place did afford. **1797** LADY A. BARNARD *Lett. to Henry Dundas* (1973) 38 The Dutch .. had fairly flattered them-selves till a governor came, that a governor never woud come, and that the place woud somehow, or another fall back into the old Hands. **1822** W.J. BURCHELL *Trav.* I. 21 Whenever mention is made of the Dutch in a more general sense, that part of the population of Cape Town, or of the colony, not English, is intended. **1837** 'N. POLSON' *Subaltern's Sick Leave* 100 The Dutch of Cape Town or Kapenaars, are a distinct race of themselves. **1897** 'F. MACNAB' *On Veldt & Farm* 15 In matters of commerce, the fault of the Dutch Is the giving too little, and asking too much. **1910** J. RUNCIE *Idylls by Two Oceans* 102 It is good to remember in this sunny home of Dutch and English and Kafir the wonderful green of Europe. **1933** S.G. MILLIN *Rhodes* (1936) 226 There was hardly anything Rhodes did in Parliament which had not as its object the favour of the Dutch. He wanted Union. **1940** J. BUCHAN *Memory* 109 The hope of breaking the racial barriers between town and country was always very dear to Milner's heart. He wanted to see the Dutch share in the urban industries, and men of British stock farming beside the Boers of the veld.

2.a. *hist.* The form of Dutch spoken by the early colonists at the Cape and their descendants, which gradually developed into a distinct language (see SOUTH AFRICAN DUTCH *n. phr.* sense 1). Cf. CAPE DUTCH *n. phr.* sense 2. **b.** A derogatory name for the Afrikaans language. Also *attrib.*

1731 G. MEDLEY tr. *P. Kolb's Present State of Cape of G.H.* I. 26 The People far up the Country, on the Appearance of Strangers, are us'd to say in *Dutch, wat Volk*, i.e. *What People?* **1800** *Cape Town Gaz.* 16 Aug. 2 Wanted, a Person who understands Dutch, and has a little English, to supervise the Housekeeping of a Gentleman. **1836** A.F. GARDINER *Journey to Zoolu Country* 326 And oh, what barbarous Dutch I've heard, Fit language for an ox's ear. **1861** *E. Prov. Yr Bk & Annual Register* 148 Minto Gaxa, Interpreter in the Kafir and Dutch languages and office keeper £55. **1872** *Wesleyan Missionary Reports* 74 Fifteen Missionaries and 20 Catechists, assisted by 240 Local Preachers, labour in the Circuits in the English, Dutch, Kaffir, and Sesuto languages. **1880** E.L. PRICE *Jrnls* (1956) 419 Poor lonely little family, they looked so sad and desolate without the Father! .. I wish I could speak Dutch to the poor woman, or she English. **1898** J.F. INGRAM *Story of Afr. City* p.xl, Mr. John M. Hershensohnn, Cape University, Sworn Translator of the English and Dutch Languages, 201, Burger Street, Maritzburg. **1901** E. HOBHOUSE *Report of Visit to Camps* 4 We cried together, and even laughed together, and chatted bad Dutch and bad English all the afternoon. **1915** J.K. O'CONNOR *Afrikander Rebellion* 88 Dutch was to be the official language, and no attempt would be made to suppress English, which would be allowed to be used in the law courts and would be taught in Schools, if so desired. **1919** R.Y. STORMBERG *With Love from Gwenno* 9 Let me introduce her: Mrs Malherbe — in English, Mal-herby, in Dutch, Mal-hair-ber. **1937** F.B. YOUNG *They Seek a Country* 223 'We were talking in Dutch when you lay there. You must have heard.' 'Dutch? But you are English, surely?' **1961** T.V. BULPIN *White Whirlwind* 187 If you can speak Dutch and English you will never starve here ... I'll get you a civil service appointment tomorrow if you want it. **1971** *Daily Dispatch* 11 May 10 The Postmaster looked at the telegram and handed it back saying 'I do not dispatch telegrams in dirty Dutch.' **1987** C. HOPE *Hottentot Room* 51 'That's right. Mock my accent. I simply cannot get my tongue around those Dutch words,' said English Rose.

c. With qualifying word: *African Dutch* (sense (*a*), AFRICAN *adj.*[1] sense 1 b ii), HIGH DUTCH.

B. *adj.*

1. Of or pertaining to Dutch-speaking (and later Afrikaans-speaking) South Africans; SOUTH AFRICAN DUTCH *adj. phr.* See also AFRIKANER *adj.*, CAPE DUTCH *adj. phr.* sense 1.

1697 W. DAMPIER in R. Raven-Hart *Cape G.H. 1652–1702* II. (1971) 381 At about 2 or 300 paces distance from thence, on the West side of the Fort, there is a small Dutch Town, in which I told about 50 or 60 Houses. **1700** 'S.L.' (tr. C. Schweitzer) in *Ibid.* 243, I lay at a Dutch Countryman's House under the Devil's Hill: he was forc'd to Keep several trusted *Hottentots*, and great Dogs, to secure his Vineyards. *c*1795 D. CAMPBELL in G.M. Theal *Rec. of Cape Col.* (1897) I. 139 The Colony is become very extensive; the Dutch farmers having penetrated very far in the interior, to the middle of what is called the Hottentot Country. **1834** T. PRINGLE *Afr. Sketches* 127 Tall Dutch-African boors, with broad-brimmed white hats, and huge tobacco pipes in their mouths, were bawling in Colonial-Dutch. **1845** J.N. REYNOLDS *Voy. of U.S. Frigate 'Potomac'* 86 About the close of 1831, rumours were industriously circulated, by persons unknown, among the Dutch African boors of the Eastern frontier, to the effect that the Hottentots of the Kat river were preparing to attack them on New-Year's day. **1851** J.F. CHURCHILL Diary. (Killie Campbell Africana Library MS37) 21 Oct., Learned a little more of the Dutch trade & mode of business. A few Dutch farmers & Traders came in whilst I was there bringing Ivory, Wool & Butter. **1855** J.W. COLENSO *Ten Weeks in Natal* p.vii, The present population of the district may be numbered at about 6,000 Europeans, of whom, perhaps, 1,000 are Dutch. **1861** J.S. MAYSON *Malays of Capetown* 13 Of the Dutch Malays, some of the present generation are the immediate offspring of female slaves and their Dutch masters. **1864** 'A LADY' *Life at Natal* (1972) 20 There are scarcely any Dutch families in Durban, although they abound 'up country'. Nor are there any 'colonial-born' families, except one or two that have been transplanted from the Cape Colony. **1881** *Volkstem* 23 Aug. 1 It is precisely by means of the Dutch language we would the better be enabled to reach that part of the community which stands most in need of newspaper literature. **1884** B. ADAMS *Narr.* (1941) 159 There was [*sic*] only three left in the hospital hut, namely myself, a blind man and a Dutch Burgher who had lost one arm. **1913** E.M. RITCHIE in *Nongqai* Vol.1 No.1, 12, I was shown into the beautiful Dutch-furnished drawing room of the authoress of 'The Petticoat Commando'. *c*1936 *S. & E. Afr. Yr Bk & Guide* 82 A Dutch rising which took place was suppressed by December 20th, 1914. **1941** J.C. COETZEE in *20th C. Inquisition* (Education League) (*pamphlet*), Our schools should train Dutch South African national citizens, men and women who love no other country, .. who have no other history, geography, culture but those of Dutch South Africa. **1955** D.L. HOBMAN *Olive Schreiner* 26 Her childhood attitude towards the Dutch people was also one of British superiority. **1963** A. DELIUS *Day Natal Took Off* 1 That puts the kibosh on everything! We're completely under Dutch Domination now! **1980** *E. Prov. Herald* 31 July 18 When we spoke earlier you mentioned the process of a Dutch family becoming an Afrikaner family. What is that process?

2. Special collocations. **Dutch Church**, the Dutch Reformed Church (see note at DUTCH REFORMED); **Dutch drops**, HARLEMENSIS; **(old) Dutch medicine, -remedy**, a patent household medicine, widely used esp. in country districts (for examples of such remedies see DOEPA sense 2 a, DUIWELSDREK, DULSIES, GROENE AMARA, HARLEMENSIS, LEWENSESSENS, *patat salf* (PATAT sense b), and ROOILAVENTEL); see also BOERERAAT, DRUPPELS; **Dutch Republic** *hist.*, BOER REPUBLIC.

1903 E.F. KNIGHT *S. Afr. after War* 55 When one of these little agricultural townships first springs up the **Dutch Church** forms the nucleus of it. **1926** W. PLOMER in *Voorslag* Vol.1 No.2, 48 Cormorant came round a corner to find himself right before the Dutch church, the glory and pride of Rooi Rivier. **1968** COLE & FLAHERTY *House of Bondage* 150 The Dutch Church teaches *apartheid* as an integral part of Christianity. **1958** E.H. BURROWS *Hist. of Medicine* 191 *Haarlemensis, Haarlemmer essens, Haarlemmer droppels* (**Dutch Drops**): world-famous with many uses. **1833** *Graham's Town Jrnl* 30 May 1 Just received, a supply of Dr Wrights's celebrated Pearl Ointment, Dalby's, **Dutch Medicines**, etc. etc. **1843** *Cape of G.H. Almanac & Annual Register*, Juritz, Carel Friedrich, apothecary, chemist, and druggist, depot of the patent Dutch medicines from the orphan house of Halle, 29 Loop Street. [**1866** *Cape Town Dir.*, Medical materials, of approved quality, at low rates, English & Dutch Patent Medicines.] **1902** [see DRUPPELS sense a]. **1911** [see HARLEMENSIS]. **1919** *Dunell, Ebden & Co.'s Price List* Oct. 20 Dutch and Household Medicines and Toilet Preparations. **1934** [see Sunday Times quot. at LEWENSESSENS]. **1945** L.G. GREEN *Where Men Still Dream* 129 A few of those marvellous mixtures known as 'old Dutch Medicines', and a still more powerful physique, make the trekboer independent of doctors. **1958** A. JACKSON *Trader on Veld* 28 Remedies of every description formed no small portion of a country stores's goods, especially the old 'Dutch' medicines. **1972** *Star* 10 Mar. 6 'Chemist and Druggist' says the inscription on the glass front of the shop and adds: 'Drugs, patent medicines, Dutch medicines.' **1972** [see LEWENSESSENS]. **1975** *E. Prov. Herald* 2 Apr. 18 Kopiva is an old Dutch remedy or patent medicine that is still sold in this age of wonder drugs, for the treatment of real or imaginary ills. **1983** *Pace* Oct. 168 (*advt*) There are over 30 different Lennon Dutch Remedies with which to treat most minor ailments at home. **1989** N. VON BLERK in D. Smuts *Folk Remedies* Preface, The old Dutch remedies with their wondrous names were part of the medicine 'trommel' on farms, and indeed are still popular in urban and rural areas. **1990** *You* 18 Oct. 34 The entire, natural GR Dutch medicine range. The tried and tested Cape Dutch remedies like Jamaica Ginger, Rooi Laventel and Essence of Life. **1893** *Brown's S. Afr.* 67 The **Dutch Republics** do not encourage immigration in any way. **1897** F.R. STATHAM *S. Afr. as It Is* 201 What was in the wind was a distinct design against the independence of the Dutch Republics in South Africa, the Transvaal especially. **1962** F.C. METROWICH *Scotty Smith* 16 As long as Scotty confined his activities to the two Dutch Republics, the Cape authorities .. did not interfere with his movements.

Dutchman *n.* Also with small initial. [Special senses of general Eng.]

1.a. *obsolescent.* AFRIKANER *n.* sense 2 a. Cf. HOLLANDER.

1797 LADY A. BARNARD *Lett. to Henry Dundas* (1973) 86 There was a large opening in the roof I begun to congratulate her on its being a trap door and that we should see half a dozen dutchmen swinging her up to the regions above before morning. **1797** [see STOEP]. **1820** W. SHAW Diary. 11 June, A journey over the rocks & hills of Africa, in a waggon drawn by oxen — and driven by Dutchmen, but Praise the Lord — not a bone is broken. **1827** G. THOMPSON *Trav.* II. 234 The same acts of rapacity and cruelty which marked the progress of the Spaniard in Mexico and Peru, and of the Englishman in North America, have merely been acted over again by the Dutchman in Southern Africa. **1838** F. OWEN Letter to Church Missionary Society. (Killie Campbell Africana Library KCM53500), Two Dutchmen who are here at present intend setting off for the Boers camp tomorrow. **1841** B. SHAW *Memorials* 96 You once told me that our names did not stand in the book, and that the gospel did not .. belong to us Namacquas. Will you now tell me master, whether the name of Dutchman or Englishman, is to be found in it? **1855** J.W. COLENSO *Ten Weeks in Natal* 195, I seemed to hear the sound .. of the driver's voice, lecturing and scolding his oxen .., of whom the worst is generally by the Dutchmen called *England*, and gets more than an ordinary share of abuse and beating. **1875** C.B. BISSET *Sport & War* 23 Hintza used to ride his own horse, .. presented to him .. by Piet Uys, a celebrated Dutchman. **1882** J. NIXON *Among Boers* 15 The Dutchmen who are seen in Capetown come from the western side of the Great Karroo and are better off and more civilised than their brethren further up country. **1908** M.C. BRUCE *New Tvl* 40 It sometimes happens that an English woman marries a Dutchman. **1920** R. JUTA *Tavern* 38 She had three daughters ... She regarded all as future nuns, as their father would never allow them to marry Cape Dutchmen. **1930** L. BARNES *Caliban in Afr.* 13 What the Dutchman trekked away from was always order and good government. **1937** M. ALSTON *Wanderings* 56 The old Dutchman, on whose land we were camping, came along to see how we were faring and was the very soul of kindly helpfulness. **1936** A. LEZARD *Gold Blast* 265 Both the Dutchman and the Englishman in South Africa is a fine man. Each has his patriotic emotions. **1949** C. BULLOCK *Rina* 26 The Afrikaner, or the Dutchman as we called him then, is your true *baanbreker.*

b. *slang.* A derogatory and offensive name for an Afrikaner, used of both men and women. Cf. DUTCHWOMAN sense b.

1943 I. FRACK *S. Afr. Doctor* 201 It would be preferable to hear this, than to listen to two youngsters calling each other a bloody Engelsman or a bloody Dutchman, as the case may be. **1946** *Forum* Nov. 32 Today only the prejudiced and the unenlightened persist in calling Afrikaners 'Dutchmen'. *a***1951** H.C. BOSMAN *Willemsdorp* (1977) 10 Going by his name I should say he's a bloody Dutchman, too. I got no time for that sort ... A boer working on an English newspaper. **1953** D. JACOBSON *Long Way from London* 29 No blows had been struck, and no one had called anyone a bloody Dutchman or a bloody Jew, so everything was as well as could be expected. **1956** A. SAMPSON *Drum* 85 The English just use long words and big talk, isn't it? Segregation — ah, democracy — ah, civilised men ... The dutchmen just say 'you blerry Kaffir, you, voetsak!' **1956** [see NAT *n.* sense a]. **1968** [see JAPIE sense 1]. **1975** *Informant, Grahamstown* Dutchman. (*Not* a Hollander). **1987** *E. Prov. Herald* 14 May 2 When he had to register for military service he had opposed it because he saw the SADF as 'the Dutchmen's' army. **1992** D. OPPERMAN on TV1, 27 May (Bishop's Beat), When I was at school — and that was only thirteen years ago — I was a Dutchman, a rock-spider, a plank — all the derogatory names that are given to an Afrikaner.

2. *?obs.* Quartz resembling uncut diamonds.

1913 C. PETTMAN *Africanderisms* 159 *Dutchman*, The name given by the diamond sorters to pieces of quartz, which somewhat resemble uncut diamonds. **1967** E. ROSENTHAL *Encycl. of Sn Afr.* 162 *Dutchman*, Name given by diamond diggers to a kind of quartz resembling uncut diamond. **1984** P. BEALE *E. Partridge's Dict. of Slang & Unconventional Eng.* 355 *Dutchman*, .. 2. A piece of quartz somewhat resembling an uncut diamond: S. African diamond-diggers'.

Dutch oven *n. phr.* [DUTCH *adj.* + Eng. *oven.*] BAKOOND sense 1.

1852 *Natal Mercury* 23 Dec., Clearance Sale ... 1 Dutch Oven. **1931** F.C. SLATER *Secret Veld* 155 He next concentrated his energies on burning bricks and building a Dutch oven .. about six feet high, six feet long and four feet wide. It had stone foundations and was otherwise constructed entirely of bricks — including an arched roof of brick-work. It had a small shelf or ledge at its front and an iron door about two feet square. **1958** [see BOEREBESKUIT]. **1965** C. VAN HEYNINGEN *Orange Days* 19 My sister's wedding cake was a huge success. It was baked in a Dutch oven we had. This oven was built outside the kitchen, of bricks, with a curved top and a door leading into the kitchen — a hole at the back of the oven let the smoke out. **1970** S. SPARKS *Informant, Fort Beaufort* Granny used to bake her bread in the bakoond outside (Dutch oven). **1987** B. MUNITICH *Ben's Buddy* 21 Emily was in the courtyard, busy removing loaves from the old Dutch oven ... Made out of clay bricks, it had baked bread for the Marshalls for over a hundred years. **1990** *Weekend Post* 17 Feb. (Leisure) 5 Another restoration project on the cards is the dutch oven in the garden at the back of the house.

Dutch Reformed *adj. phr.* Of or pertaining to the main-stream Afrikaans Calvinist churches; DR; REFORMED. See also *Dutch Church* (DUTCH *adj.* sense 2).

The family of Dutch Reformed churches consists of the *Nederduitse Gereformeerde Kerk* (see NGK sense 1) and its associated churches, the *Nederduitse Gereformeerde Sendingkerk* (Dutch Reformed Mission Church, see SENDINGKERK), the *Nederduitse Gereformeerde Kerk in Afrika* (Dutch Reformed Church in Africa, see NGK sense 2), and the Reformed Church of Africa (formerly the Indian Reformed Church), as well as the *Nederduitsch Hervormde Kerk in Afrika* (see HERVORMDE) and the *Gereformeerde Kerk in Suid-Afrika* (see GEREFORMEERDE). The term 'Dutch Reformed Church' is most often used to refer to the *Nederduitse Gereformeerde Kerk.* During 1994 the *Nederduitse Gereformeerde Sendingkerk* and the *Nederduitse Gereformeerde Kerk in Afrika* amalgamated to form the United Reform Church of Southern Africa. See also DRC.

1827 G. THOMPSON *Trav.* I. 75 Mr. Murray .. is of the Church of Scotland, which in doctrine and discipline corresponds almost entirely with the Dutch Reformed communion. **1847** 'A BENGALI' *Notes on Cape of G.H.* p.vii, The entrance to the Paarl valley is pretty. There are two churches, the London Mission, and the Dutch Reformed or Calvinistic. **1856** R.E.E. WILMOT *Diary* (1984) 126 Which of all the sects then will the Kaffirs choose? I imagine this Dutch Reformed, which never allows a member out of sight or ken. **1899** B. MITFORD *Weird of Deadly Hollow* 222 The doctor returned thanks and toasted the Dutch Reformed minister, whose flock being of Barabastadt was, he was sure, the most upright and liberal in the whole colony. **1926** P.W. LAIDLER *Tavern of Ocean* 25 No adherent of any religion other than the Dutch Reformed was to be admitted on any account, and any suspect was to be reported to the Fiscal immediately. **1964** J. MEINTJES *Manor House* 44 'For all the preaching you do at me,' Rina sniffed, 'you'll make an excellent Dutch Reformed minister.' **1973** J. COWDEN *For Love* 28 Potgieter, unable to persuade Dutch Reformed churchmen to accompany him over 'the formidable barrier', asked the Rev. Archbell to be his official chaplain. **1980** E. JOUBERT *Poppie Nongena* 48 Ouma sent us to the Dutch Reformed Mission school where the coloured children went. **1982** C. HOPE *Private Parts* 15 'What religion are you?' 'Dutch Reformed.' 'I'm glad.' **1988** J. DEACON in *S. Afr. Panorama* May 44 Dutch Reformed parsons would visit the Hell twice a year to conduct weddings and baptisms. **1988** K. BRYNARD in *Star* 28 May 11 There was .. an idyllic vision of a political solution (to the black problem) through separate development, morally boosted by the Dutch Reformed churches.

Dutch Reformed Moederkerk see MOEDERKERK.

Dutchwoman *n.* [Special senses of general Eng.]

a. *obsolescent.* An Afrikaner woman (see AFRIKANER *n.* sense 2 a).

1870 C. HAMILTON *Life & Sport in S.-E. Afr.* 8 The hostess .. was a Dutchwoman. **1920** R.Y. STORMBERG *Mrs Pieter de Bruyn* 51 His mother a Dutchwoman, he can carry so much of an Imperial air. **1965** W. PLOMER *Turbott Wolfe* 107 He had married a young Dutchwoman from the back of beyond.

b. *rare.* A derogatory and offensive name for an Afrikaner woman. Cf. DUTCHMAN sense 1 b.

1971 *Informant, Coalbrook (OFS)* To look at her, she's a real dour old Dutchwoman.

duur voor, die stryd see DIE STRYD DUUR VOORT.

duwweltje, -tji(e) varr. DUIWELTJIE.

duyker var. DUIKER.

duyker bok, duykers bock varr. DUIKERBOK.

duyker buck var. DIKER-BUCK.

duyvel var. DUIWEL.

Duzi var. DUSI.

dwaal /dwɑːl/ *n. colloq.* [Afk.]

a. In the adv. phr. ***in a dwaal*** [Afk. *in 'n dwaal* in a daze], dazed, absent-minded, distracted.

1963 K. MACKENZIE *Dragon to Kill* 51 He had an expression of vague surprise and annoyance as he picked his way through the Africans. In a *dwaal*, as usual, thought Tony. **1964** M.G. MCCOY *Informant, Port Elizabeth* When I got up at 6 a.m. on Monday morning I was standing in the kitchen in a bleary sort of dwaal. **1969** A. FUGARD *Boesman & Lena* 6 The roads are crooked enough without you also being in a *dwaal.* **1974** in *Eng. Usage in Sn Afr.* Vol.5 No.1, 15 'She's in a dwaal.' She is in a dreamlike state, distrait. **1978** *Sunday Times* 23 Apr. 18 Vaal in a dwaal ... Western Province thrashed the much-vaunted, new super-Vaalers 25–10. **1985** P. SLABOLEPSZY *Sat. Night at Palace* 15 Yassas — Carstens!! Wake up, man. You in a real dwaal tonight. **1985** H. PRENDINI in *Style* Oct. 39 Jislaaik ou pellie! You nearly came short with that bakkie! You're in a dwaal. **1992** C. SCOTT on TV1, 30 Dec. (Good

Morning South Africa), I was standing there in a kind of a dwaal, thinking about next week's lines.
‖**b.** See quot.
1970 A. FUGARD *Notebks* (1983) 185 Boesman and Lena load up their bundles and walk — suggestion of the 'dwaal' (confused wandering) in the back streets after the demolition — round and round the stage.

‖**dwaal** /dwɑːl/ *v. intrans.* [Afk., 'to lose one's way, to go astray'.] To wander aimlessly. Also *fig.*, to daydream.
1963 K. MACKENZIE *Dragon to Kill* 251 *Dwaal*, To wander or get lost. 1970 *Informant, Grahamstown* Don't dwaal all day. (Dream). 1970 BEETON & DORNER in *Eng. Usage in Sn Afr.* Vol.1 No.1, 41 'To *dwaal* around' = 'to wander about aimlessly'.

‖**dwadwa** /ˈdwadwa/ *n.* Also **isiDwadwa**. [Xhosa *isiDwadwa*.] The shrub or small tree *Leucosidea sericea* of the Rosaceae; OUHOUT sense c.
Used medicinally and as fuel.
In F. von Breitenbach's *Nat. List of Indigenous Trees* (1987), the name 'oldwood' is used for this species.
[1868 W.H. HARVEY *Genera of S. Afr. Plants* 95 *P. sericea* is a densely leafy shrub, the 'Dwa-dwa' of the natives, who use it as an astringent medicine.] 1913 C. PETTMAN *Africanderisms* 159 *Dwa dwa, Leucosidea sericea*... This plant is used by the natives as an astringent medicine. 1917 R. MARLOTH *Common Names* 25 *Dwadwa, Leucosidea sericea* (East). 1932 WATT & BREYER-BRANDWIJK *Medicinal & Poisonous Plants* 63 The Zulus apply a paste of the ground-up leaves of *Leucosidea sericea*.. Oubos, Ouhout, Dwadwa, Zulu *umTshitshi*.. to the eyeball, and inside and outside the lids, in ophthalmia. 1980 [see OUHOUT].

dwa-grass var. TWA-GRASS.

dwang /dwæŋ/ *n. slang.* [Afk., 'compulsion', 'coercion', 'constraint', fr. *dwing* to force.] In the (euphemistic) phr. *in the dwang*, in trouble, constrained.
1994 G. RALLS *Informant, Grahamstown* We can only afford to employ him for about a week each month, so if we hired a proper contractor we'd really be in the dwang. 1994 A. GOLDSTUCK *Informant, Johannesburg* In the dwang.. 'in shit' or, more politely, 'in deep trouble'... I used to hear it in the army (about 17 years ago) and then on campus and finally from the good ol' boy type. 1994 *E. Prov. Herald* 9 Sept. 7 *(caption)* In dwang... Thailand Commerce Minister Uthai Pimchaichon addresses a news conference after a man, disguised as a photographer, threw a bag of excrement at him. 1994 V. WILD *Informant, Grahamstown* You'd better not let your father know what you've done or you'll be in the dwang again.

Dwyka /ˈdwaɪkə/ *n. Geology.* [The name of a river in the Cape, fr. a Khoikhoi word meaning 'salty', 'brackish' (see Kokot quot. 1991).] Usu. *attrib.*, designating one of the geological groups which make up the lower beds of the Karoo System, or (in the phrr. *Dwyka conglomerate*, *-shale*, *-tillite*, etc.) any of the types of rock found in this group. See also ECCA, *Karoo System* (KAROO sense 3).
1896 R. WALLACE *Farming Indust. of Cape Col.* 55 In superposition to this is the *Dwyka* or *trap conglomerate*, a unique formation which has puzzled geologists. 1896 *Ibid.* [see ECCA]. 1897 'F. MACNAB' *On Veldt & Farm* 187 It is a deposit from the crumbling hills of boulder and rock of the Dwyka [printed *Duryka*] conglomerate. 1905 A.W. ROGERS in Flint & Gilchrist *Science in S. Afr.* 241 The area occupied by the Karroo formation is sharply defined by the outcrops of the Dwyka series, of which the well-known glacial conglomerate is the most important member. *Ibid.* 242 A thick band of shale and sandstone (the Lower Dwyka shales) intervenes between the conglomerate and the uppermost member of the Cape system. 1920 F.C. CORNELL *Glamour of Prospecting* 267 We found the pits.. sunk at the side of a dolerite dyke.. bisecting the Dwyka shale of the pan, and from which it takes its name. 1965 HAMILTON & COOKE *Geology for S. Afr. Students* 258 Two divisions of the Dwyka Series are distinguishable, but only the Dwyka Tillite is really extensive. 1971 D.F. KOKOT in *Std Encycl. of Sn Afr.* IV. 146 *Dwyka River*, C.P ... The name is derived form the Hottentot word 'dwinka', meaning salty... The river gives its name to the geological Dwyka Series, which extends over 800 miles of the south-central part of the sub-continent and forms the base of the Permo-Triassic Karoo System. 1971 T. STRATTEN in *Ibid.* 146 *Dwyka Series*, This geological series forms the lowermost subdivision of the Karoo System. It is subdivided into Dwyka tillite at the base, which is overlain, in the southern and western parts of the Karoo Basin, by the Upper Dwyka shales, which are in turn overlain by a conspicuous zone of black carbonaceous shales. These weather white on exposure and are accordingly known as the White Band.

dyker var. DUIKER.

dyk kop var. DIKKOP.

dyver var. DIVER.

E

earth-hog *n. obs.* [tr. S. Afr. Du. *aardvark.*] AARDVARK.

    1731 G. MEDLEY tr. *P. Kolb's Present State of Cape of G.H.* II. 118 The tongue of an Earth-Hog is long and pointed. When he is hungry, he looks for an Ant-Hill; and coming nigh the same, he lays him down, .. stretching out his long tongue .. the upper part of which being very clammy, the Ants are held thereon by the Legs. **1796** [see AARDVARK]. **1810** G. BARRINGTON *Acct of Voy.* 349 The *earth-hog* .. is covered with short hair, and being extremely fat, is esteemed very delicious food by the Planters and the Hottentots. **1843** J.C. CHASE *Cape of G.H.* 69, I beg also to bear testimony to other niceties of the native African cuisine ... The leg of an earth-hog (*Myrmecophega Capensis*) equal to the most delicate veal, with a goût only to be compared to its own. **1847** [see AARDVARK].

earth-pig *n. obs.* [tr. S. Afr. Du. *aardvark.*] AARDVARK.

    1786 [see AARDVARK]. **1809** J. MACKRILL *Diary.* 56 Fit for food, .. Myrmecophaga, Ant Eater alias Earth Pig. **1878** [see AARDVARK]. **1834** [see ANT-EATER].

earth-rose *n. obs.* [tr. S. Afr. Du. *aardroos.*] The plant parasite *Hyobanche sanguinea* of the Scrophulariaceae; also called AARDROOS (sense 1).

    1795 C.R. HOPSON tr. *C.P. Thunberg's Trav.* I. 287 The *Earth-rose* (Aard-roos) was the name by which the inhabitants both of the town and country distinguished the *Hyobanche sanguinea*, a plant with a low deep-red flower, which is scarcely of a finger's length, and has neither branches nor leaves. **1809** J. MACKRILL *Diary.* 68 The Hyobanche sanguinea, called by the Country people Earth Rose (Aard Roos).

East Coast Fever *n. phr. Pathology.* Also with small initials. [So named because endemic on the east coast of Africa.] An acute and often fatal disease of cattle, caused by the protozoan *Theileria parva* and transmitted by the BROWN EAR TICK; AFRICAN COAST FEVER. Also *attrib.*

    A notifiable disease.

    1904 A. THEILER in *Report of S. Afr. Assoc. for Advancement of Sci.* 211 East Coast Fever being a piroplasma disease, led investigators to believe that it must be carried by ticks. **1909** *Ilanga* 1 Jan. 4 The dispute .. in connection with cattle, which the Government has ordered to be destroyed, under the East Coast fever regulations. **1913** C. PETTMAN *Africanderisms* 500 The fact has been established that ticks are the medium by which the diseases known as redwater, heart-water, and east-coast fever are conveyed from one area to another. **1921** *E. Prov. Herald* 4 Feb., East Coast Fever has now become so serious that a series of meetings .. will be held .. in order to organise a campaign to stamp out this scourge. **1937** C. BIRKBY *Zulu Journey* 41 The rinderpest of 1897 wiped out cattle at a rate of 500 a week ... And then in 1904 we had the East Coast Fever. **1955** *Report of Commission for Socio-Economic Dev. of Bantu Areas* (UG61-1955) 80 Tick-borne diseases, and in particular East Coast Fever, constitute an ever present or potential menace. **1955** [see AFRICAN COAST FEVER]. **1966** C.A. SMITH *Common Names* 459 East Coast fever is said to be unknown in Mopani veld. **1974** A.P. CARTWRIGHT *By Waters of Letaba* 140 On account of the East Coast Fever epidemic we were not allowed to use oxen. **1986** P. MAYLAM *Hist. of Afr. People* 140, 1903 was a year of drought, and it was followed by the spread of east coast fever over the next few years. **1990** B. GODBOLD *Autobiography.* 104 Rinderpest and East Coast Fever had greatly reduced the number of cattle during the early years of this century.

Eastern Province *n. phr.*
1. An informal name given to: **a.** The eastern districts of the Cape Colony. **b.** The eastern districts of the Cape Province (from 1910). **c.** The western part of the Eastern Cape Province (from 1994). See also EP.

    During the 19th century there was a determined but unsuccessful attempt to separate the Eastern Province from the western part of the Cape Colony (the seat of government).

    1832 *Graham's Town Jrnl* 9 Mar. 42 Double the number of years may probably elapse before one farthing of 'our' contributions in taxes can be applied for the general benefit of the Eastern Province. **1840** [see QUITRENT sense 2 b]. **1843** J.C. CHASE *Cape of G.H.* 31 The Eastern Province of the colony of the Cape of Good Hope comprises the divisions or counties of – 1. Albany; 2. Utenhay; 3. Somerset; 4. Cradock; 5. Graf Reinet; 6. Colesberg. *Ibid.* 95 The Eastern Province .. is totally unrepresented in these [legislative and executive] councils, not a single member being returned by or connected with the frontier and country districts. **1877** J. NOBLE *S. Afr.* 253 Another subject which .. agitated the public mind was, that of separation, or local self-government for the Eastern province. [*Note*] It became habitual to talk of the Eastern Province, although except for the Election of Members for the Legislative Council, according to the Constitution Ordinance, no such designation occurred in any other legal enactment. **1893** H.B. SIDWELL *Story of S. Afr.* 108 It was the old often-repeated story of savage cruelty, of blazing homesteads and wasted hearts, .. of ruined lives and broken hearts, with which the Eastern Province is so sadly familiar. **1913** [see *vlei grass* (VLEI sense 2)]. **1955** [see WESTERN PROVINCE]. **1961** [see VLIER]. **1986** [see AVO]. **1994** Eastern Province Herald (*title*).

2. The name given to the provincial sports teams representing this area; EP.

    1897 G.A. PARKER *S. Afr. Sports* 63 The competing [rugby] teams were: Western Province (holders), Transvaal, Griqualand West, Eastern Province, Border, and Natal. **1990** *Weekend Post* 23 June 20 Eastern Province overran Free State .. in Bloemfontein on Saturday ... EP's win puts the coastal men back into the hunt for the coveted gold cup while the 'Blikore' are surely now also rans.

Hence (*nonce*) **Eastern Provincial** *n. phr.*, an inhabitant of the Eastern Province.

    1955 V.M. FITZROY *Dark Bright Land* 98 Lord Charles Somerset scoffed at it [*sc.* the Donkin pyramid], but here at least he could not interfere, and it remained. Eastern Provincials have an affection for its very ungainliness.

eat *v. trans.* In the phr. *to eat up obs. exc. hist.* [tr. Xhosa and Zulu *dla* eat, consume, impose a fine; the use of this phr. in S. Afr. Eng. seems to have arisen independently of the general Eng. use of a similar phr. which appeared long before this]: to punish (someone, esp. one accused of witchcraft) by taking possession of all his or her property and cattle; to exterminate (a people or group); to destroy (the crops or possessions of a people or group); to send a punitive expedition against (a people or group).

    1827 G. THOMPSON *Trav.* I. 202 They were coming to eat up the corn and cattle of the Bechuanas, and .. afterwards they would proceed against the Macooas (white people) in the south. **1832** *Graham's Town Jrnl* 6 July 109 We consider it quite indifferent to the cause of humanity whether Dingaan eats him up or he Dingaan, as both these Chiefs are conquerors in their way. **1835** T.H. BOWKER *Journal.* 22 Apr., Yesterday a fingoo complained that a Caffir Capt. had eat him up, Col Smith to[l]d him to go & eat him up in return. Upon which the fellow went away and returned again this morning with 18 head of cattle. **1848** H. WARD *Five Yrs in Kaffirland* I. 131 Umhala, a Kaffir Chief, was summoned by the Lieutenant-Governor, to show cause why he had threatened to 'eat up' Gasella, another Chief, his step-brother. **1852** R.J. GARDEN *Diary.* I. (Killie Campbell Africana Library MS29081) 21 Apr., The man denounced is forthwith eaten up by the tribe, that is robbed & plundered & reduced to beggary. In some cases death is the portion. **1855** J.W. COLENSO *Ten Weeks in Natal* 28 Moshesh has lately 'eaten up' Sinkoneyalla, one of our 'allies,' who has applied to us for redress, which he will not get. **1882** C.L. NORRIS-NEWMAN *With Boers in Tvl* 30 The history of Natal may thus fitly be summed up as having been for many years the home of a peaceful and primitive peaple, who were ruthlessly 'eaten up' by the Zulu hordes under Charka. **1895** J. WIDDICOMBE *In Lesuto* 181 The rebel party .. proceeded to eat them up with all speed, and with the utmost thoroughness. Their village was burnt, everything they possessed taken from them, and they themselves compelled to take refuge with us at 'the Camp.' **1913** C. PETTMAN *Africanderisms* 160 Eat up, To. Among the Zulus, the evil-doer, his wives and children, were all massacred, his property confiscated, and his name blotted out; he was said to be 'eaten up'. Among the Cape Kaffirs the man's property was seized and he was driven out to wander as an outcast ... The expression is also used to describe the result to the vanquished of a pitched battle of tribe against tribe. **1926** W.A. COTTON *Race Problem* 126 Basutoland, as part of the Union, would sorely tempt the cupidity of the Orange Free State men to cross the Caledon and 'eat it up'. **1937** B.H. DICKE *Bush Speaks* 30 He threatened to 'eat up' (destroy with anything he had) any native (and his family) who should infringe this order. **1949** O. WALKER *Proud Zulu* (1951) 70 No-one who leaves my district to pray for Cetewayo need think of returning to it; he who does can consider himself turned out and his family eaten up. **1951** T.V. BULPIN *Lost Trails of Low Veld* 137 The .. Basuto of Swaziland were rapidly eaten up by the voracious Sobuza. His tribe fattened on the captured warriors and women and its numbers and wealth doubled and doubled again. **1964** G. CAMPBELL *Old Dusty* 27 The people living in the valley were eaten up by an impi. **1972** A. SCHOLEFIELD *Wild Dog Running* 134 Far to the north-east of us Chaka, King of the Zulus, was 'eating up' the tribes that surrounded him.

Hence **eating up** *vbl n. phr.*, the appropriation by a chief or his people of the possessions of an individual, clan, or tribe in disfavour. Also *attrib.*

1836 A.G. BAIN *Jrnls* (1949) 185, I sent the prisoner to Fort Cox to Capt. Stretch requesting him, should there be any 'eating up' in this case, to give Makaluma a mouthful. **1844** J.M. BOWKER *Speeches & Sel.* (1864) 181 He is also dreadfully afraid of the eating-up-system, which, as a system of his own, he perfectly understands, and knows well that brother will join against brother when that's to be done. **1852** A.W. COLE *Cape & Kafirs* 191 'Eating-up' has a very awkward sound, when applied to their fellow-men by savages. The Kafir is very fond of the term, and the practice is very common among his people: but it simply means taking a man's cattle, his land, his corn, his property of every description, burning down his hut, and turning him out ... 'Eating-up' is practised by the Chiefs against refractory or obnoxious subjects, and is occasionally adopted to punish certain crimes. **1860** W. SHAW *Story of my Mission* 443 The Chief's cattle-folds are replenished from time to time by fines and occasional 'eating up' of delinquents, by which is meant the confiscation of the whole of their property, for alleged witchcraft, treason, or other great political crimes. **1885** H. RIDER HAGGARD *King Solomon's Mines* 192 The 'eating up' of your kraals shall cease; each one of you shall sleep secure in his own hut and fear not.

eBhayi var. IBHAYI.

ECC *n. hist.* Initial letters of *End Conscription Campaign*, an organization formed in 1983 with the aim of bringing conscription to an end, and in the interim of promoting acceptance by the government of constructive alternatives to military service for conscientious objectors. Also *attrib.*

1985 *Race Rel. Survey 1984* (S.A.I.R.R.) 748 A conscientious objectors' support group of the Black Sash took a decision in July 1983 to launch an 'end conscription campaign' (ECC). By January 1984 committees had been formed in Cape Town, Durban, and Johannesburg to take up the campaign, and in June and July 1984 the declaration of the ECC was formulated. **1986** *Rhodeo* (Rhodes Univ.) May 5 The SADF leaves no choice about conscription. ECC asks for voluntary help. **1987** R. SMITH in *Grocott's Mail* 5 May 6 The ECC seeks to serve South Africa by working for a just peace through negotiation rather than a shaky security through military action. **1987** *End Conscription Campaign in Perspective (pamphlet)*, The Nationalist Government .. perceive the ECC as being an attempt to discredit and undermine their system of compulsory military service which they view as vital for the survival of Nationalist rule. **1988** N. BORAIN in *Frontline* Feb. 27, I am sure there would not be a single ECC member who would not criticise the practice of necklacing. **1989** *Race Rel. Survey 1988–9* (S.A.I.R.R.) 519 The ECC was banned from carrying out its activities by the government on 24 August. **1993** C. DE VILLIERS in *Star* 21 July 13 The ECC .. proposes that our future defence force should comprise a relatively small permanent force, supplemented by short-service volunteers .. and a voluntary reserve. **1994** *E. Prov. Herald* 19 Aug. 3 The End Conscription Campaign (ECC) is to disband immediately, after Defence Minister Joe Modise announced a halt in prosecution of call-up offenders ... Organisers said ECC had planned to disband in 1993, but continued when the Defence Force continued call-ups.

Ecca /ˈekə/ *n. Geology.* [fr. *Ecca Pass*, on the road between Grahamstown and Fort Beaufort (Eastern Cape), named in 1858 by R.N. Rubidge after the Ecca River, a tributary of the Great Fish. 'The name is of Khoekhoen origin and probably means "salty" or "brackish river".' (P.E. Raper, *Dict. of S. Afr. Place Names*, 1987).] Usu. *attrib.*, esp. in the phrr. ***Ecca beds, -flora, -series***, etc., designating a geological group made up of shales and sandstones, and the plant fossils found therein.

The Ecca group is one of several groups which form the lower beds of the Karoo System. See also DWYKA, *Karoo System* (KAROO sense 3).

1896 R. WALLACE *Farming Indust. of Cape Col.* 55 The Lower Karoo beds are of great thickness, very old and distinctly unconformable to the Upper Karoo beds. It has consequently been necessary to distinguish them by different names ... The Lower Karoo beds are now familiarly known as the Ecca beds, and include the Dwyka conglomerates already referred to. **1905** H. BOLUS in Flint & Gilchrist *Science in S. Afr.* 224 Only on the southern and western margins do the Ecca and Dwyka series make their appearance. **1905** A.W. ROGERS in *Ibid.* 243 The youngest strata found to have been involved in the Zwartberg folding are the Ecca beds, which lie at high angles along the northern flanks of the northernmost ranges, and which occur on the downthrow (south) side of the Worcester fault in contact with the Malmesbury beds on the northern side. **1905** W. ANDERSON in *Ibid.* 268 It [*sc.* the Stormberg series] consists of shales and sandstones with occasional coal-seams, containing a fossil flora entirely distinct from the Ecca flora. **1951** *Archeology & Nat. Resources of Natal* (Natal Regional Survey) I. 36 Beds of the Dwyka, Ecca and Beaufort series crop out in normal succession and exercise control over the surface configuration. **1965** HAMILTON & COOKE *Geology for S. Afr. Students* 260 *Ecca Series*, This series follows the Dwyka conformably in Natal and the Cape Province and attains its maximum development of over 6,000 feet near the Cape Folded Belt. It thins out very considerably northwards and in the Transvaal is only some 600 or 700 feet thick. **1971** A.E. SCHOCH in *Std Encycl. of Sn Afr.* IV. 192 *Ecca Series*, In the Karoo of South Africa there is a huge basin-shaped occurrence of successive sedimentary rock strata, collectively known as the Karoo System or Karoo Supergroup ... Since the successive rocks are stacked upon one another as nearly horizontal strata to fill the basin, it is convenient to divide it into a number of Series or Groups. From the bottom upwards these are respectively named the Dwyka Series, the Ecca Series, the Beaufort Series and the Stormberg Series, each with its own peculiar characteristics. The Ecca Series is composed of successive and alternating beds of shales and sandstones ... The coal beds occur especially in the middle portion of the Coal Ecca, also coal, which originated from compressed plant remains. **1984** A. WANNENBURGH *Natural Wonder of Sn Afr.* 11 In these drab Ecca sediments the typical fossils are of plants — seed-ferns, which are intermediate between ferns and cycads, and tree-sized varieties of today's club-mosses — belonging to a distinct type of vegetation that evolved in the southern hemisphere after the Dwyka glaciation. **1994** N. HILLER *Informant, Grahamstown* Fossil plants in the Ecca belong to the *Glossopteris* flora.

echte var. EGTE.

eeland var. ELAND.

eendjie /ˈɪəŋki, -ci/ *n. obsolescent.* Also **eendje**. [Afk., 'duckling', *eend* duck + dim. suffix -IE.] Usu. in *pl.*: A name for the inflated pods of the plants *Sutherlandia frutescens* and *S. tomentosa* of the Fabaceae.

1913 C. PETTMAN *Africanderisms* 161 *Eendjes*, .. The name given by the Grahamstown boys to the pods of *Sutherlandia frutescens, R. Br.* which they break off and float in water. **1917** R. MARLOTH *Common Names* 25 *Eendje, Sutherlandia frutescens.* The pods form a toy for children .. (floating them on the water). **1966** C.A. SMITH *Common Names* 208 *Eendjies*, The inflated pods of *Sutherlandia Frutescens* .. and *S. Tomentosa* .. drift on water like ducks.

‖**Eendrag maak mag** /ˈɪəndrax ˈmɑːk ˈmax/ *phr.* Formerly also **Eendracht maakt macht, Eentracht maakt macht.** [Afk., fr. Du. *Eendracht maakt macht, eendracht* union, unity + *maakt* makes + *macht* power, might.

Eendracht maakt macht was the motto on the coat of arms of the Transvaal Republic. It was an adaptation of the Latin *Concordia res parvae crescunt* 'In unity weak things grow', the motto on the coat of arms of the Republic of the United Netherlands.]

The usual Afrikaans representation of the Latin phrase *Ex Unitate Vires* ('From unity (comes) strength'), the motto on the South African coat of arms.

1908 M.C. BRUCE *New Tvl* 17 *'Geduld en Moed'* (patience and courage) was the motto preached through the length and breadth of the Transvaal, in conjunction with the older one: *'Eentracht maakt Macht'* (l'union fait la force). **1913** J. BRANDT *Petticoat Commando* 167 In South Africa might is not right. Our motto, 'Eendracht maakt Macht,' means 'Unity is strength.' **1961** D. BEE *Children of Yesterday* 248 On the Union coat-of-arms is written *Ex Unitate Vires — Eendrag Maak Mag.* I see it spelt in the old way on farm documents in my desk — Eendracht Maakt Macht. And I think what a fine spirit there was when Union was made. **1974** *Sunday Times* 15 Sept. 12 Beeld and Dagbreek merged, both then vanished, and the resultant product was *Rapport*. Here certainly was a case which proved that *Eendrag maak mag.* **1985** *S. Afr. Panorama* May 23 It culminated in the Union of South Africa on May 31, 1910. The motto was *Eendracht maak macht* (Unity begets Strength). **1988** P. MAHLANGU in *New Nation* 14 Jan. 9 It is said that unity is strength (eendrag maak mag).

egeerha var. IGQWIRA.

egg-eater *n.* [tr. S. Afr. Du. *eiervreter*, Du. *eier* egg + *vreter* eater.] Any of several species of non-poisonous egg-eating snakes of the genus *Dasypeltis*, esp. *D. scabra scabra*; EIERVRETER.

1821 C.I. LATROBE *Jrnl of Visit* 497 Our good natured Hottentots, perceiving that I had begun to collect serpents, brought me several kinds, among which were the nacht-schlange (night serpent); earth-serpent, eyerfreter (egg-eater), schaapsteker (sheep stinger). **1887** *Encycl. Brit.* XXII. 194 A .. genus of snakes *Dasypeltis* ... In Cape Colony these snakes are well known under the name of 'eyer-vreter', i.e. 'egg-eaters'. **1911** *E. London Dispatch* 1 Sept. 7 (Pettman), The *Egg eater* lives almost entirely on eggs, which it eats in a curious fashion. **1913** C. PETTMAN *Africanderisms* 161 *Egg-eater*, A snake of the *Dasypeltidae* family .. furnished with a saw-like row of vertebral teeth in the gullet, by which the shells of eggs, which are almost its sole food, are pierced; the contents swallowed, the shell is ejected. **1950** W. ROSE *Reptiles & Amphibians* 260 The egg-eater does not hiss in the usual snake manner. **1967** J.A. PRINGLE in E. Rosenthal *Encycl. of Sn Afr.* 507 Some [snakes] are fastidious about their food: the Night Adder eats only frogs, the Egg-eater only eggs. **1975** J. MCCLURE *Snake* (1981) 103 Snakes do not chew their food, but swallow it whole. The nearest thing to mastication is found in the egg-eater, known hereabouts as *Daspeltis scaber.* **1992** *Afr. Wildlife* Vol.46 No.2, 221 The common egg-eater *Dasypeltis scabra* is a fairly common non-poisonous snake with an exclusive diet of eggs.

Egoli /eˈgɔːli, ɪˈgəʊlɪ/ *n.* Also **E Goli, eGoli, Goli, Igoli, iGoli.** [Zulu, 'place of gold', locative prefix *e-* + *-goli* (ad. Eng. *gold*).] GOLDEN CITY. Also *attrib.*

[**1925** D. KIDD *Essential Kafir* 26 If they have been to Johannesburg — 'Goldi' or 'Josaberg' is what they usually call it — they will probably have brought back with them a great variety of things.] *c*1948 H. TRACEY *Lalela Zulu* 24 This is a song .. about a man who is courting a girl whose original lover is away working in 'Goli' (Johannesburg). *Ibid.* 80 Beyond the banks of the Vaal, We come to the great city of Goli. **1951** *Drum* Oct. 6 In Britain, with forty times the population of the Reef, there is only one murder every three days. Egoli has a worse record than anywhere else in the civilised world. **1959** L. LONGMORE *Dispossessed* 16 *Igoli*, the Golden City, the dazzling magnet attracting Africans from all over the vast sub-continent of Africa, has provided the biggest problem that Africa has to face today, namely, the African projected into an urban, industrialized environment. **1964** H.H.W. DE VILLIERS *Rivonia* 43 The Bantu usually refers to Johannesburg as 'Goli' ('Goldie'). The Whites sometimes refer to Johannesburg as the 'City of Gold'. **1973** M. REINHART in *Sunday Times* 9 Dec. 5 Johannesburg in summer ... When .. the jacarandas are in bloom ... Egoli is as green as Natal and twice as exciting. **1989** O. MUSI in *Drum* Apr. 36 Goli children know nothing about livestock except that these become food as soon as they are slaughtered and taken to the butchery around the corner. **1991** P. SLABOLEPSZY *Braait Laaities*. 15 If you stay long-time in eGoli you get quick-quick very old. **1994** R. MALAN in *Sidelines* Dec. 31 Egoli's factories began to run at full capacity.

egqwira var. IGQWIRA.

‖**egte** /ˈɛxtə, ˈɛxtə/ *adj.* Formerly also **echte**. [Afk.] Real, genuine. Cf. REGTE.

1906 G.B. BEAK *Aftermath of War* 227 Finally, there are the 'echte vaderlanders' the Boers who fought to the bitter end. **1982** *Fair Lady* 6 Oct. 6 The result would still be *ersatz* French not *egte* South African. Our cuisine consists of careful copies or straightforward simplicity. **1987** L. BEDFORD-HALL in *Style* May 12 I've searched for a long time for a small eaterie in the country, serving *egte*, home-style Sunday dinner. **1994** [see BOEREKOS].

ehe /eˈheː/ *int.* [Zulu *ehhe* yes.] Esp. among Zulu-speakers: an exclamation indicating affirmation, assent, or approval. Cf. YEBO.

1909 N. PAUL *Child in Midst* 213 'Manzi, what can we do?' she cried. 'Can't you save us?' 'Ehe, inkosazan', me sav' you jus' now.' **1953** D.C. THEMBA in *Drum* Apr. 48 'Ehe! So you are a Letebele after all.' **1961** T. MATSHIKIZA *Choc. for my Wife* 77 'Ehe, but he's okay. He gets the booze if you ask him. He's okay.' **1989** *Daily News* 1 Dec. 7 Ehe! Alfred Qatonla, one of the foremost oral poets in Natal, in full cry.

ehlosé var. IDLOZI.

ehna var. EINA.

eh ta var. HEIT.

ehwe var. EWE.

Eid /iːd/ *n.* In full **Eid-ul-Fitr** [ad. Arabic *Id al-fitr* 'festival of charity', the festival of breaking the fast after Ramadan]: the Islamic festival celebrating the end of the month-long fast of Ramadan; LABARANG. Also *attrib*.

In general English use, written *Id-ul-fitr*.

There are in fact two 'Eids' during the Islamic year: 'Eid-ul-Fitr', and 'Eid-ul-Adha', the Festival of Sacrifice which corresponds with the pilgrimage to Mecca, the 'Hadj'.

1979 *Sunday Times* 26 Jan. (Extra) 1 Eid is the day on which Muslims celebrate the end of Ramadan, a holy month of fasting and prayer. **1980** *Voice* 13 Aug. 1 Happy Eid. The Editor and Staff wish all our Muslim Readers a Happy and Joyous Eid-Ul-Fitr. **1986** F. KARODIA *Daughters of Twilight* 53. I watched the progress of the identical taffeta skirts Ma was sewing for me and Yasmin. These were for Eid, the day of celebration following the new moon after Ramadan. **1988** *South* 21 July 1 South wishes all Muslims a Happy Eid.

‖**eiervreter** /ˈeɪə(r)ˌfriətə(r)/ *n.* Also **eyerfreter, eyer-vreter.** [S. Afr. Du. (later Afk.), *eier* egg + *vreter* eater.] EGG-EATER.

1821 [see EGG-EATER.] **1849** A. SMITH *Illust. of Zoo. of S. Afr.: Reptilia* Appendix 20 *Dasypeltis scaber,* .. Eyervreter of the Cape Colonists ... Consumes with avidity the eggs of birds. **1887** [see EGG-EATER]. **1970** H.M. MUSMECI *Informant, Port Elizabeth,* I don't think that eiervreter is poisonous. (An indigenous snake, *Dasypeltis scabra,* which lives on an exclusive diet of eggs.)

‖**eiesoortig** /ˌeɪəˈsʊərtəx/ *adj.* and *adv.* [Afk., *eie* own + *soort* kind + *adj.-* and *adv.*-forming suffix *-ig*.]

Used orig. and esp. with reference to the emphasis placed by proponents of apartheid on the cultural and racial identity of groups.

A. *adj.* Also *(attrib.)* **eiesoortige** [Afk. attrib. suffix *-e*]. Distinctive, unique, culturally specific.

1976 *Sunday Times* 1 Aug. 15 The old apartheid policy that was re-written in 1958 by Dr Verwoerd as eiesoortige (own identity) development failed shortly after it was proclaimed. **1979** *Evening Post* 3 July, There is nothing genuinely South African or *eiesoortig* about separate development ... A fresh start can only be made in consultation with all races. A National Convention for this purpose would be truly 'eiesoortig' and South African'. [**1988** A. FISCHER in Boonzaaier & Sharp *S. Afr. Keywords* 130 An important qualification was added to the notion of 'development': this was the idea of '*eiesoortige ontwikkeling*' (autogenous development).] **1990** S. DE WAAL in *Weekly Mail* 23 Feb. (Suppl.) 9 He does that language a great service in his vigorous defence of it as more than the preserve of a Nationalist clique. He also does it beautiful justice in his *eiesoortige* prose.

B. *adv.* Distinctively; in a manner intended to emphasise singularity.

1988 A. FISCHER in Boonzaaier & Sharp *S. Afr. Keywords* 130 Africans were to be developed '*eiesoortig*' under the guidance of the trustee, according to their particular character and capabilities.

So **eiesoortigheid** /-ˌheɪt/ *n.* [Afk., n.-forming suffix *-heid -*ness], uniqueness, esp. cultural distinctiveness.

1960 B. MARAIS in H. Spottiswoode *S. Afr.: Rd Ahead* 166 As far as the Christian Church is concerned this *eiesoortigheid*, this fact of a group being *sui generis*, is important and may not be ignored. It could constitute an argument for separate Churches for widely different linguistic or racial groups, but it could not be used as justification for forced segregation within any Christian Church.

eigendom /ˈeɪxəndɔm/ *n. Obs. exc. hist. Law.* Also (usu. in *attrib.* use) **eigendoms.** [Du., 'ownership (of property)'.] Freehold; freehold land held in perpetuity. Also *attrib.*, and *comb.* **eigendoms brief** /brif/ [see BRIEFIE], deed of ownership. See also LEENINGS EIGENDOM.

1795 J.H. CRAIG in G.M. Theal *Rec. of Cape Col.* (1897) I. 256 The Rents of Lands called Eigendoms Land or Property Land. These are Lands given in Property, but subject to the annual payment of about half a Rixdollar per Dutch acre. **1806** J. BARROW *Trav.* II. 56 Most of the grounds in or near the village are what they call Eigendoms or freeholds, though they are held by small recognizance to Government, but they are totally different to loan-farms which are the normal kind of tenure in the colony. **1809** LORD CALEDON in G.M. Theal *Rec. of Cape Col.* (1900) VII. 184 *Eigendoms Land or Land held in perpetuity* is the property conveyed to the party by a stamped deed bearing the Governor's Signature. **1811** J.A. TRUTER in G.M. Theal *Rec. of Cape Col.* (1901) VIII. 100 The sum of 24 Rds. is expressly said to be the annual tax *on each place*, which on the delivery of the eigendoms brief is measured and taken at 60 morgen. **1884** *Cape Law Jrnl* I. 319 A few grants were issued under certain 'resoluties' or Government Regulations of the years 1654 and 1657, .. on condition that at the expiration of three years so much land as had been cultivated to the full extent of the capability of the soil should be granted in eigendom or freehold. **1967** W.A. DE KLERK *White Wines* 91 As the Old Cape Freeholds state — Vogelvallei was given to Abraham in *eigendom*, 'because of his poverty and large family.' **1974** DAVENPORT & HUNT *Right to Land* p.v, Freehold (eigendom) *tenure*. Ownership under individual title of the land and of any structures built upon it. Dutch freehold tenure was often saddled with conditions, English was not.

eighthman *n.* In rugby: a number eight forward.

Positioning the number eight player at the back of the scrum apparently originated in South Africa around the time of the first World War, so it is possible that the name was introduced at that time.

1955 D.H. CRAVEN *Springbok Story 1949–1953* (2nd ed.) 10 *Eighth Men*: H. Muller, B.J. Kenyon, A. Hummel.

1992 D. RETIEF in *Sunday Times* 17 May 29 Eighthman Terence Stewart .. scored. **1993** E. GRANT in *Weekend Post* 13 Nov. 4 Thirty years down the line, a former .. rugby star still has a hard-working pack in front of him ... The 1960s eighthman does not actually hitch up and work alongside his mules.

eiland var. ELAND.

eina /ˈeɪnɑː, -nɑ/ *int., n.,* and *adj.* Formerly also **aina, ehna, enna, ijna.** [Afk.; perh. fr. Khoikhoi interjections /é/ (of pain) + ‖*ná* (of surprise), or fr. Nama interjection /ei, nasalised in pronunciation; or see quot. 1934.

According to H.C.V. Leibbrandt (*Het Kaapsche Hollandsch*, 1882), the words *aina, ina(na), einá,* and *einaná* all mean 'mother'.]

A. *int.* An exclamation of pain.

1913 C. PETTMAN *Africanderisms* 164 *Enna* or *Ijna,* (Hot. **e*! Interj. of pain; **ná*! Interj. of astonishment — each word has an initial click, the former the dental, the latter the lateral.) An exclamation of pain common in the Midlands. **1934** C.P. SWART Supplement to Pettman. 48 *Eina*, An exclamation of pain, very common in South Africa even among English-speaking children. According to Kroenlein it is derived from the Hottentot 'aisen' to become ill. **1959** J. MEIRING *Candle in Wind* 742 And now, ou Rosie, if the baby .. ag, eina! .. Ag, but the pains are terrible. **1963** A. FUGARD *Blood Knot* (1968) 163 My feet are killing me again. I've been on them today you know (*touching the toes*) Eina! Eina! **1971** *Fair Lady* 24 Nov. 27 Ouch! Eina! Ouff! Blow by blow we housewives are being beaten into despair by the ugly bogy — the cost of living. **1982** [see DUIWELTJIE]. **1982** *Drum* Oct. 88 Einaaa ... well, that's what happens when an impi .. surges forward to get a last glance of their king ... some just have to topple over. **1988** D. KENMUIR *Song of Surf* 27 'Eina!' The expression broke from his lips, but further exclamations of pain were smothered as an icy wave surged into the pool. **1990** A. WAGENAAR in *Personality* 21 May 23 You thought South African prices were going through the roof. R30 000 for a Toyota. Eina! R150 000 for a Merc. *Voertsek!* **1991** P. SLABOLEPSZY *Braait Laaities.* 20 Eina! Dammit! Look what you've done now — ! **1994** on M-Net TV 8 Sept. (Egoli), 'That little girl — eina!' 'You can say that again!'

B. *n.*

1. Pain; a wound.

1971 *Personality* 24 Sept., *(advt)* First aid for cuts — without the 'eina'. Sometimes treating your child causes more fuss than the actual wound. **1972** M. GREENBLO *Informant, Cape Town* 'What happened to Katherine's leg?' 'You've got an eina, haven't you, love?' **1991** T. BARON in *Sunday Times* 5 May 27, I had *einas* enough .. without wanting to listen to what was bothering him.

2. *comb.* **Eina-taal,** FANAKALO; **eina tree,** a species of Acacia; also called DORINGBOOM.

1972 P. BECKER in *Star* 17 Mar. B6, Some of the Fanakalo jargon is .. discordant to the philological ear ... I've even heard it called '**Eina-taal**'. **1983** [eina tree: see DORINGBOOM].

C. *adj.* Painful.

1982 *E. Prov. Herald* 25 Aug. 24 *(advt)* Eina!! (But what the heck!) Giddy's Eina Price R438,80. This Eina Week ends 4th September! **1989** *Sunday Times* 24 Dec. 11 If there's criticism of something I've written that I'm not so sure about .. bliksem! It's eina!

eintjie var. ENTJIE.

eis var. ACE.

eita var. HEIT.

ek sê /ekˈseː, ɛkˈsɛː/ *int. phr. Slang.* Also **ek se, ekse.** [Afk., 'I say', *ek* I + *sê* say; prob. a shortened form of *Ek sê vir jou* I'm telling you.] An exclamation:

a. Used to attract attention, or as a point of entry into a remark or a conversation.

1959 M.W. SPILHAUS *Under Bright Sky* 56 Ek sê, you look so down. Wat I come for, Mr Kone, I come to ask

Mr Kone has he got a secon'-han' settee he can sell me? **1969** A. FUGARD *Boesman & Lena* 4 *Ek sê!* His backside in the Swartkops mud, but Boesman's happy. **1975** *Drum* 8 Nov. 12 'Ek se,' he said. 'I havva been lookin for yer baby.' **1982** M. MZAMANE *Children of Soweto* 131 *Ekse*, has this attack been planned, *na*? **1987** *Learn & Teach* No.2, 48 Ekse mfo, dig that rich smell! **1990** J. NAIDOO *Coolie Location* 33 Ek sê, it's a pity you're not in the States; .. they would have had you fixed up in two weeks.

b. Used for emphasis, or to express surprise or admiration.

1969 A. FUGARD *Boesman & Lena* 31 Two bottles of wine! *Ek sê*. Boesman has a party tonight. **1977** *Sunday Times* 24 Apr. (Mag. Sect.) 1 The biggest agency in London — the Biggest ek se — is run by a cat from Durbs. **1978** 'BLOSSOM' in *Darling* 22 Nov. 84 If he doesn't give me the bucks I'll muck him up, ek sê. He mustn't tune me bull ... I gottim good, ek sê. **1982** R. BHENGU in *Voice* 16 May 5 There is a lot of work ahead of us, and we have to move sharp, *ek se*. **1988** W. MONDLANE in *Staffrider* Vol.7 No.1, 48 It's time to go ek sê my sizza. **1991** A. VAN WYK *Birth of New Afrikaner* 75 He brought us some encouragement in the form of a few cans of red jerepigo, *ek sê*. **1992** S. GUTKNECHT in *Sunday Times* 19 Apr. (Mag. Sect.) 28 Windgat? no, ek sê, David Kramer says bakgat is the most expressive word in the SA English Dictionary.

‖**ekskuus** /ek'skys, (k)'skis, ə'skis/ *int.* Also **a(a)skies, exkes, skies, 'skuus.** [Afk.] Among Afrikaans-speakers: 'I beg your pardon'.

[**1906** A.H. WATKINS *From Farm to Forum* 17 Oh *excuse*, I asked you if you would have coffee and I thought you said 'No'.] **1916** S. BLACK in S. Gray *Three Plays* (1984) 213 Halford: You diabolical conglomeration of unaspirated iniquity! .. Van H: Exkes? **1960** C. HOOPER *Brief Authority* 134 Soon we shall have to go to the Native Commissioner and ask, *'Skies-tog my baas*, please can I have a permit to conceive a child!' **1979** *Daily Dispatch* 19 Oct. 13 Delegates address one another as 'Broeder'. Even if a speaker coughs he says: 'Ekskuus, broeders.' **1982** M. MZAMANE *Children of Soweto* 170 'Micky, you still have a lot of explaining to do.' *'Aaskies?'* 'You heard me very well.' **1990** *City Press* 17 June 17 Eina! Askies my baas, It is not me. **1990** J. ROSENTHAL *Wake Up Singing* 16 ''Skuus, Baas,' said Zach. 'Ja, Oom — sorry, Oom,' said Em.

EL /iː 'el/ *n.* Also **E.L.** Initial letters of *East London*, a port city in the Border region of the Eastern Cape: usu. *attrib.*

Used esp. in newspaper headlines.

1978 *Daily Dispatch* 9 Sept. 3 EL landmark comes down ... Yet another old East London landmark is falling under the breaker's hammers — this time the tearoom at the harbour. **1979** *E. Prov. Herald* 1 June 1 EL man wins six jackpots. **1980** *Rand Daily Mail* 22 Oct. 1 EL poll crucial to both parties. East London North voters go to the polls today. **1987** *Daily Dispatch* 4 May 3 For years we have had an MP who has done nothing for E.L. North.

eland /'iːlənd, 'ɪəlant/ *n.* Also (rarely) **eeland, (e)iland, elland, ey(e)land.** Pl. unchanged, or **-s.** [S. Afr. Du., transf. use of Du. *eland* elk.]

1.a. The antelope *Taurotragus oryx* of the Bovidae, the largest of the African antelopes, several subspecies of which are found in southern and central Africa; IMPOFU; KANNA *n.*[3]; POFU. Also *attrib.*

1786 G. FORSTER tr. *A. Sparrman's Voy. to Cape of G.H.* II. 204 *Eland*, or *Kaapse Eland* .. is a name given by the colonists to a species of gazel which is somewhat larger and clumsier, though, upon the whole, handsomer than the *hartbeest*. **1790** W. PATERSON *Narr. of Four Journeys* 54 We saw several Elks, Eyelands, &c. **1824** W.J. BURCHELL *Trav.* II. 23 By the same misuse of names, the *Kanna* of the Cape Colony is called *Eland*, which is the proper name of the *Cervus Alces* or Elk. *a***1827** D. CARMICHAEL in W.J. Hooker *Botanical Misc.* (1831) II. 273 The larger animals such as the *Ox*, the *Eland*, the *Buffalo*, the *Hart-beest*, and even the *Ostrich*. **1837** 'N. POLSON' *Subaltern's Sick Leave* 138 The eiland, an animal as large as an ox; and the best eating of any of the genus. When thin, eilands gallop fast; but when fat, the old bulls may be easily ridden up to. **1841** B. SHAW *Memorials* 8 A number of rhinoceroses, eilands, antelopes, one troop of seven, and another of eight elephants. **1887** *S.W. Silver & Co.'s Handbk to S. Afr.* 170 The eland together with the koodoo, gemsbok, and springbok, are antelopes which can exist almost without water, as long as there is any sap in the herbage. **1897** H.A. BRYDEN *Nature & Sport* 217 The eland, from its great size and astonishing fatness, is the easiest of all game to be destroyed. **1937** H. SAUER *Ex Afr.* 51 The eland is the only African antelope that carries fat in his internal exonomy, a peculiarity which makes him a valuable prize in the hunting veld, where fat is scarce. **1951** A. ROBERTS *Mammals* 20 *Elands* ... The primitive Bushmen were evidently very partial to them, as they figured in their paintings more often than any other animals. **1979** HEARD & FAULL *Our Best Trad. Recipes* 53 Our own big game hunters favour the following for venison: eland, springbok, duiker .. and oribi. **1980** J. HANKS *Mammals* 33 *Eland, Taurotragus oryx*, Very large antelope with a slight hump at the shoulder, a prominent dewlap ... Although a very heavy animal, eland can easily clear a 250cm high fence from a standing start. **1990** *S. Afr. Panorama* July-Aug. 19 A remaining wilderness island where large numbers of the rare eland and gemsbok still roam undisturbed. **1994** M. ROBERTS tr. *J.A. Wahlberg's Trav. Jrnls 1838–56* 61 Bagged my first Eland, a cow.

b. *comb. obs.* **elandbok** [S. Afr. Du., *bok* antelope], the eland; **eland-vogel** [Du., *vogel* bird], some unknown bird.

1796 C.R. HOPSON tr. *C.P. Thunberg's Trav.* II. 58 **Elandboks** .. were sometimes to be met with and shot. **1838** J.E. ALEXANDER *Exped. into Int.* I. 115 Hares I found in plenty at the Orange river mouth; there is also the large **elandbok** to be found here. **1822** W.J. BURCHELL *Trav.* I. 245 The **Eland-vogel** which was procured here, is a handsome bird, and may easily be discovered by its remarkable clear and loud note.

2. *Military.* Usu. with initial capital. A small armoured reconnaissance vehicle developed by the South African army during the 1960s from the French Panhard. Also *attrib.* See also BUFFEL sense 2.

Often as *Eland 60* or *Eland 90*, these being the measurement, in millimetres, of the cannon with which these vehicles are armed.

1977 B. MARKS *Our S. Afr. Army* 29 The Eland 60 armoured car, with a turret mounted mortar and light machine-gun .. is an extremely manoeuvrable vehicle and has a very long operating range. **1979** *Paratus* Jan. 19 At the other end of the operational area the local population and the SA soldiers are guarded by members of 2 SS B with their Eland 90 armoured vehicles. **1983** *Jane's Armour & Artillery 1982–3* 202 Reconnaissance vehicles ... South Africa. Eland Light Armoured Car. **1988** *E. Prov. Herald* 11 Feb. 1 A black Mercedes-Benz with Bophuthatswana military officials .. was forced back by a SADF Eland.

elandsboontjie /'iːləndz'bʊɪŋki, 'ɪəlants-/ *n.* Formerly also **elands bo(o)ntje.** [Afk. (earlier S. Afr. Du. *elandsboontje*), *eland* see ELAND + linking phoneme *-s-* + *boontjie* bean; see quot. 1966.] The plant *Elephantorrhiza elephantinea* of the Fabaceae, having seeds which are used as a coffee substitute, roots as a source of dye, and underground stems as food for stock.

1868 W.H. HARVEY *Genera of S. Afr. Plants* 92 Glabrous undershrubs, with large fleshy roots (Elandsboontjes). **1905** GREEN *Richard Hartley, Prospector* 229 (Pettman), 'Have you seen any *Elandsboontje*?' Hartley went on, well knowing that the plant was very rare in that region. **1906** B. STONEMAN *Plants & their Ways* 225 *Elephantorhiza* (Eland's bontjes) is a small glabrous shrub with very large roots. **1916** *Farmer's Weekly* 20 Dec. 1504 Would any reader kindly let me know ... How to prepare the 'Elandsboontjie' for tanning purposes? **1917** R. MARLOTH *Common Names* 25 *Elands boontje, Elephantorrhiza Burchellii*. The popular name refers to the large size of the pods. A small deciduous perennial, the annual shoots a foot or two high, but the stout rootstock very big, weighing up to 10 pounds. This contains much tannin, hence its other name Looier's bossie. **1966** C.A. SMITH *Common Names* 209 *Elandsboontjie*, The plants have a thick, underground, rootlike stem ... Burchell reported that the underground stems were a favourite food of elephants. The pods are eaten by the eland antelope.

elephant *n.* Special Comb. **elephant fish** [see quot. 1867], the marine fish *Callorhinchus capensis* of the Callorhincidae (this name being used for the species in Smith and Heemstra's *Smiths' Sea Fishes*, 1986); JOSEPH; **elephant-gun** *hist.*, ROER sense a; **elephant rock** *Geology* [see quot. 1913], weathered dolomite; **elephant's ear**, also **elephant ear, elephants ears** [see quot. 1913; the name has been used elsewhere of other large-leafed plants], any of several plants with large leaves said to resemble elephants' ears, esp. *Grewia lasiocarpia* (Natal), *Eriospermum capense* (Eastern Cape), and two species of the Arum family, particularly *Arum esculentum*; **elephant's food**, also **elephants' food** [see quot. 1856], SPEKBOOM sense 1; also *attrib.*; **elephant's foot** [see quot. 1913; the name is used in general Eng. for other plants], the yam-like plant *Dioscorea elephantipes* of the Dioscoreaceae, having a large edible tuber growing partly above the ground; *Hottentot('s) bread* sense (*b*), see HOTTENTOT *n.* sense 6 a; also *attrib.*; **elephant shark**, *elephant fish* (see above); **elephant shrew** [see quot. 1918], any of several African shrews of the Macroscelididae, characterized by a flexible, trunk-like snout; **elephant's trunk** [see quot. 1913], the HALFMENS, *Pachypodium namaquanum*.

1790 J. COOK *Voy. of Disc.* (1908) IV. 1283 Fish .. known to seamen by the name of **elephant fish**. **1833** W.F.W. OWEN *Narr. of Voy.* II. 228 Two boats were sent to survey, while others were engaged fishing off Pelican Point, but they produced only a boat-load of young ground-sharks, elephant fish, and white bass. **1867** W.H. SMYTH *Sailor's Word-Bk*, *Elephant-fish*, the *Chimæra callorhynchus* named from the proboscis-like process on its nose. **1913** C. PETTMAN *Africanderisms* 162 *Elephant fish*, *Callorhyncus antarcticus*, is so called because of the proboscis-like process which it bears on the front of the head. **1949** J.L.B. SMITH *Sea Fishes* 77 *Callorhynchus capensis* ... *Doodskop. Josup. Josef. Monkeyfish. Elephant fish* ... Lives in shallower water than the other members of this order ... An object of curiosity whenever seen, but not rare. **1986** SMITH & HEEMSTRA *Smiths' Sea Fishes* 147 Elephantfish ... Flesh excellent especially when marinated. **1993** R. VAN DER ELST *Guide to Common Sea Fishes* 33 The elephantfish has no scales and its skin is exceptionally smooth ... Increasingly marketed as a substitute for kingklip fillets. **1877** R.M. BALLANTYNE *Settler & Savage* 174 George Rennie, who ultimately acquired the title of the Lion-hunter, came to the rendezvous with a large **elephant-gun** on his shoulder. **1897** R.S.S. BADEN-POWELL *Matabele Campaign* 152 The boom of the elephant gun roaring dully from inside a cave is answered by the sharp crack of a Martini-Henry. **1937** [see ROER sense a]. **1957** G. TYLDEN in *Africana Notes & News* Vol.12 No.6, 216 Frederick Courteney Selous, killed in action in Tanganyika at the age of 65 in 1916. In 1871 he trekked North with Viljoen using a 'Boer elephant gun.' **1971** F.V. LATEGAN in *Std Encycl. of Sn Afr.* IV. 518 In his description of the Battle of Blood River, Preller .. refers to the small arms used by the Boers during the fight as snaphaan and elephant-gun. *Ibid.* 520 The Voortrekkers .. had elephant-guns of 4, 6, 8 and 10 bore. [**1983** see ROER sense a. **1987** *Weekly Mail* 12 June 12, I borrowed one of Barney's white elephant guns and bought a pensioner's special on SAA.] **1896** R. WALLACE *Farming Indust. of Cape Col.* 54 *Dolomitic limestone* .. weathers into curious irregular shapes, which somewhat resemble the wrinkled hide of an elephant, hence the origin of one of its names, **Elephant Rock**, or in Dutch 'Oliphant Klip.' [**1905** H. KYNASTON in Flint & Gilchrist *Science in S. Afr.* 283 The rock is known as 'Olifants Klip' by the Boers.] **1913** C. PETTMAN *Africanderisms* 162 *Elephant rock*, A stratum comprised principally of dolomite limestone, when exposed to the weather it is worn into irregular corrugations, which are not unlike the wrinkles on the hide of an elephant – hence the name, which is a literal rendering of the Dutch 'Olifants Klip'. **1970** BEETON & DORNER in *Eng. Usage in Sn Afr.* Vol.1 No.1, 43 *Elephant rock*, .. Name for dolomite. **1913** C. PETTMAN *Africanderisms* 163 **Elephant's ear**, In Queenstown the boys give this name to *Eriospermum Bellindi, Sweet*; a liliaceous plant bearing a single cordate ovate leaf, resembling an ear. **1917** R. MARLOTH *Common Names* 26 *Elephant's ear, Eriospermum Bettendem* (Queenstown). Tuber and leaf the largest in the genus. *c***1968** S. CANDY *Natal Coast Gardening* 32 *Xanthosoma violaceum*, 'Elephant Ear'. An aroid with large, blue-grey, safittale leaves and deep blue, long leaf-stems. Grown in many Natal coast gardens. **1971** *Std Encycl. of Sn Afr.* IV. 288 *Elephant's-Ear, Olifantsoor*, Name applied to several plants belonging to different families, but probably most often to two species of the arum family (Araceae). **1976** S. CLOETE *Chetoko* 110 The plants on the veranda .. looked beautiful – elephant ears, ferns, begonias, caladiums and rubber plants. **1990** *Weekend Post* 26 May (Leisure) 7 The botanical name of the plant is *Colocasia esculenta* or *C. antiquarum* and many gardeners will know it as elephants ears. *Ibid.* 3 Dec. 7 *Strelitzia nicolai* and a giant alocasia (elephant's ear) add to the tropical atmosphere. [**1829 elephant's food**: C. ROSE *Four Yrs in Sn Afr.* 71 The speck boom, food for the elephant, almost hid by the ivy geraniums rising to its top.] **1856** F.P. FLEMING *Sn Afr.* 125 The Elephant was said to live upon it [*sc.* the spekboom], hence it has likewise been styled in Africa, 'Elephant's-food.' [*a***1884** E. WIGGILL in J.K. Larson, Talbots, Sweetnams & Wiggills. (1953) 17 A peculiar tree grows here in abundance, called 'speck-boom' by the Dutch, known in England as 'elephant's food.' The leaves are small, thick, and juicy, and very sour.] **1891** O.E.A. SCHREINER *Thoughts on S. Afr.* (1923) 36 You climb out and light a fire and gather from afar and near stumps of dried elephant's food and euphorbia, and throw them on the fire. **1917** R. MARLOTH *Common Names* 26 *Elephant's food*, = Spekboom. **1964** A. ROTHMANN *Elephant Shrew* 33 Miles and miles of bush, a dense, impenetrable mass of num-num, thorn bushes, 'taaibos', .. and above all elephant's food or 'spekboom'. **1966** C.A. SMITH *Common Names* 210 *Elephant's food, Portulacia afra* ... The species in earlier days was much browsed by elephants. Today the plants form the staple food of the elephants preserved in the Addo Bush. **1971** [see SPEKBOOM sense 1]. **1974** *Grocott's Mail* 3 Dec. 1 Elephant's food or spekboom contributes the most to the diet of goats. **1986** P. PIETERSE *Day of Giants* 38 Near the house he squatted beside the shiny, greyish pink bole of an elephants' food tree. **1790** W. PATERSON *Narr. of Four Journeys* 72 Found many curious plants, among which was one called **Elephant's Foot** ... It has a large solid bulb, which sprouts to the height of five or six feet, and afterwards shoots out into small climbing branches with roundish heart-shaped leaves. **1872** D. OLIVER *Lessons in Elementary Botany* II. 271 *Testudinaria elephantipes* .. From the appearance of the rhizome it is called 'Elephant's foot' at the Cape of Good Hope. **1883** M.A. CAREY-HOBSON *Farm in Karoo* 215 The 'elephant's foot,' wonderfully like a huge tortoise which had been fantastically decorated with the most delicate wreaths of pale-green leaves, added not a little to the novelty of the scene. **1887** *S.W. Silver & Co.'s Handbk to S. Afr.* 161 The Elephant's Foot, which is also called Hottentot's Bread, *Testudinaria Elephantipes* .. belongs to the same order as the Yam ... Varying in size from that of the bottom of a wineglass to that of a chair, succulent, tuberous, excrescent-like, perennial growths, divided into compartments like the back of a tortoise, whence the plant has received its generic name of *Testudinaria*. **1906** B. STONEMAN *Plants & their Ways* 276 *Testudinaria* (Elephant's foot). **1913** C. PETTMAN *Africanderisms* 163 *Elephant's foot, Testundinaria elephantipes*. The popular name of this curious member of the Yam family. It has a hard woody protuberance, sometimes of enormous size, partly embedded in the earth, which bears some slight resemblance to an elephant's foot. **1972** [see BUTTERTREE]. **1976** A.P. BRINK *Instant in Wind* 238 We have also found hidden jackal's food and *ngaap* and elephant's foot. **1988** *Personality* 17 Oct. 38 The biggest succulent ever found in the area was .. an 'Elephant's Foot' .. said to be more than 1 000 years old, 1,25 metres high and 2 metres in diameter! **1994** A. CRAIG in M. Roberts tr. *J.A. Wahlberg's Trav. Jrnls 1838–56* 7 Elephant's foot *Dioscorea elephantipes*, which has a large tuber partly above the ground, and produces a spray of greenish flowers in summer. **1947** [**elephant shark**: see JOSEPH]. **1868** J.G. WOOD *Homes without Hands* 15 The **Elephant Shrew** of Southern Africa (*Macroscelides typicus*) a thick-furred, long-snouted, short-eared burrower. **1905** *Science in S. Afr.* 135 The Elephant shrews (*Macroscelides*) are met with mostly among the rocky kopjes, and on the dry open karroo. **1913** C. PETTMAN *Africanderisms* 163 *Elephant shrew, Macroscelides typicus, Smith*. The name has reference to the proboscis-like snout, which is not unlike a diminutive elephant's trunk. **1918** S.H. SKAIFE *Animal Life* 253 The elephant shrew are so called, not because of their size, but because of their elongated snouts which slightly resemble short trunks. **1964** A. ROTHMAN (*title*) Elephant Shrew. **1971** D.J. POTGIETER et al. *Animal Life in Sn Afr.* 346 The elephant-shrews or jumping shrews (*Macroscelidea*) are insect-eaters, and the whole order is confined to Africa. **1986** R.H.N. SMITHERS *Land Mammals* 9 Family *Macroscelididae*, elephant shrews. The characteristic feature of members of this family is the elongated, trunk-like, exceedingly mobile snout. **1992** [see SPEKBOOM sense 1]. **1992** M. BRUORTON in *Afr. Wildlife* Vol.46 No.6, 272 Elephant-shrews are an important, but little known and largely unseen, component of our indigenous mammalian fauna ... All the elephant shrews belong to the family Macroscelididae ... In southern Africa the family is well represented by seven species belonging to three genera, *Petrodromus* (one species), *Elephantulus* (five species), and *Macroscelides* (one species). **1868** J. CHAPMAN *Trav.* II. 325 Isaac .. noticed a plant of the cactus or euphorbia tribe, known by the name of **elephant's trunk**. **1868** W.H. HARVEY *Genera of S. Afr. Plants* 247 A[denium] *Namaquanum*, Wyl. (the 'Elephant's Trunk') is a singular shrub of Namaqualand. **1887** *S.W. Silver & Co.'s Handbk to S. Afr.* 161 Still more remarkable for its appearance is the Elephant's Trunk, found in Namaqualand, the *Adenium Namaquanum* ... The Bushman name of this plant is *Hurip*, preceded by a click. **1913** C. PETTMAN *Africanderisms* 163 *Elephant's trunk*, .. A singular plant found in Namaqualand, having a thick, fleshy trunk some 5 or 6 feet high, not unlike an elephant's trunk in shape. **1973** BEETON & DORNER in *Eng. Usage in Sn Afr.* Vol.4 No.1, 41 *Elephant's trunk*, .. Spiny succulent found in Namaqualand; has stout cylindrical stems wh[ich] grow to a height of 2,5m. **1990** S. ROWLES in *Weekend Post* 16 June (Leisure) 1 Stopping at a *halfmens* tree (also called elephant's trunk) Kobus pointed out some of the features of the area. **1992** T. VAN RENSBURG in *S. Afr. Panorama* Mar.-Apr. 8 In the Richtersveld .. the quiver tree .. and the elephant's trunk (*Pachypodium namaquanum*) are the most typical [plants].

elf /elf/ *n.* Also (esp. formerly) **elft**. [Afk., earlier Du. *elft* shad.]

a. The marine fish *Pomatomus saltatrix* of the Pomatomidae, prized as a food; SHAD sense 1; SKIPJACK sense 3. Also *attrib.*

The name 'elf' is used for this species in Smith and Heemstra's *Smiths' Sea Fishes* (1986).

1731 G. MEDLEY tr. *P. Kolb's Present State of Cape of G.H.* II. 190 In the *Table*-Bay, and in Bay-Falzo, is caught a Sort of Fish the *Dutch* call *Elft*. The Elft is Three Quarters of a Yard long or more; and is scal'd much like a Herring. **1823** [see JACOB EVERTSON]. [**1893** see PAMPELMOESIE.] **1918** S.H. SKAIFE *Animal Life* 207 The elft is a large, silver-coloured relative of the *maasbanker*. It is fairly common around the coast, and is caught in numbers as it is highly esteemed as a food fish. **1930** C.L. BIDEN *Sea-Angling Fishes* 33 In South Africa the elf is seldom seen to display its natural habit of leaping from the water. **1955** C. HORNE *Fisherman's Eldorado* 24 Occasionally elf, or shad as these fish are known to Eastern Province and Natal anglers, run well in summer. **1959** [see LEERVIS]. **1964** J. BENNETT *Mr Fisherman* (1967) 25 'Plenty elft tonight, master,' said one of the fishermen. He pointed to the fish on the quay. **1970** *Argus* 30 Jan. 8 Bailey's Cottage keeps producing elf, but the good runs of the previous week, when the fish were going for spinner in this area, have not yet recurred. **1980** *E. Prov. Herald* 31 July 15, I have done this on evening elf trips to Roman Rock. While the rest of the crew fished in the conventional way for elf, I put out bass plugs on bass tackle and was well rewarded. **1980** [see SKIPJACK]. **1989** *E. Prov. Herald* 3 Nov. 25 The elf season is open but, remember, no matter how plentiful they are, only five each with a minimum size of 30cm. **1992** V. KABALIN in *Afr. Wildlife* Vol.46 No.2, 201 Sustainable stock in the Bay of yellowtail, kob, baartman, elf and steenbras.

b. With defining word designating an elf of a large size which has a distinctive colouration: **blueback elf, greenback elf**.

1982 *E. Prov. Herald* 10 June 8 Then throughout the winter, as now, we caught elf of all sizes. The real big ones were called **blueback elf** because of their colour. **1988** *Ibid.* 27 Feb. 8 Another favourite cool weather fish is the elf. Big ones, known as **greenback elf**, are caught then.

elland var. ELAND.

els /els/ *n.* Also **else**. [Afk., earlier Du. *else*.] Used *attrib.* to designate an alder tree. Usu. with distinguishing epithet: see ROOI-ELS, WIT ELS.

1829 C. ROSE *Four Yrs in Sn Afr.* 125 The rich foliage of the wild fig, the plum, and that of the gnarled and twisted else-wood. **1985** A. TREDGOLD *Bay between Mountains* 157 On its banks there used to grow many els trees.

Embo var. MBO.

emer var. EMMER.

Emergency *n.* Also with small initial. [Short for *state of emergency*.] A period during which the government, in order to contain or suppress political dissent or unrest, restricts freedom of speech, movement, and association, and limits the rule of law, by extending the powers of the executive and restricting the jurisdiction of the courts; also, the regulations governing conduct during such a period. Also *attrib.*

The first national state of emergency in South Africa was declared in 1960, and several were imposed during the 1980s. See also 90-DAY (under 'N'), 180-DAY (under 'H').

1962 A.J. LUTHULI *Let my People Go* 198 Arrests began on a large scale ... A few evaded the police net and sat out the Emergency in more hospitable places. *Ibid.* 199 The arrests were illegal since at that time the Emergency had not been gazetted. **1986** S. SEPAMLA *Third Generation* 105 Bra Joe .. reminded him of someone from the days of the Emergency ... He was hauled in with many other activists and .. bundled into the same cell. **1986** P. BROWNE in *Style* July 43 The government .. has decided to curb the presence of television .. equipment during unrest situations in emergency areas. **1987** *E. Prov. Herald* 14 May 4 'Free the children' T-shirts worn by two of the women contravened the emergency regulations. **1987** *New Nation* 11 June 6 This emergency is by far the most severe ... The last emergency was only partial, and the regulations were not as stringent and harsh. **1987** *Weekly Mail* 12 June 1 Important security trials were held up because Emergency detainees were not available as witnesses. **1987** *Pretoria News* 17 June 1 This newspaper is produced under emergency restrictions. Curtailment of certain reports may lead to an incomplete presentation of the events of the day. **1987** *Weekly Mail* 17 July 3 If the three Emergencies were aimed at silencing militant unions, all that massive strong-arm effort appears to have failed. **1990** G. SLOVO *Ties of Blood* 377 'They have banished me,' he said simply ... 'Ever since the Emergency.'

emigrant *adj.* and *n.* *Obs.* *exc.* *hist.* [Special sense of general Eng.]

A. *adj.* Usu. in the collocations *emigrant Boer* or *emigrant farmer*, VOORTREKKER *n.* sense 1.

1837 ANDERSON in D.J. Kotze *Lett. of American Missionaries* (1950) 165 A number of these Emigrant Boers .. were on Vaal River, a few miles above the hunters' camp, at the time it was attacked by Moselekatsi. 1837 *Reply to the Memorial of Several Brittish Subjects Resident at Port Natal* in *S. Afr. Archival Rec.: Natal* I. 407 Reporting the arrival of the Emigrant Farmers at Port Natal and the Public Expressions of their determination to occupy that place and the adjacent country, and praying for the Protection of the British government. 1839 [see COMMANDO sense 3]. 1841 G. NAPIER in *S. Afr. Archival Records: Natal* I. 378 Her Majesty has desired me to inform the Emigrant Farmers that she cannot acknowledge a portion of her own subjects as an independent Republic. 1847 'A BENGALI' *Notes on Cape of G.H.* 21 It will be recalled that these Emigrant Boers had already once defied the British Government at Natal in 1840. 1888 W. BIRD *Annals of Natal* I. 438 Journal of the Expedition of the Emigrant Farmers Under Their Chief Commandant A.W.J. Pretorius (Formerly of Graaf-Reinet) Against Dingaan, the King of the Zulus In the months of November and December 1838. 1897 [see GREAT TREK sense 1]. 1905 G.W. STOW *Native Races of S. Afr.* 219 Commandos, long before the emigrant farmers moved in a body across that stream, were sent to scour the country to the north of it and to destroy as many of the hordes as they could discover. 1973 J. MEINTJES *Voortrekkers* 13 The emigrants .. never referred to themselves as Voortrekkers — that came much later — but as emigrant farmers.

B. *n.* VOORTREKKER *n.* sense 1.

1838 ANDERSON in D.J. Kotze *Lett. of American Missionaries* (1950) 236 The latest accounts .. stated the effective force of the Emigrants at from 1,000 to 1,300 men ... The fire-arms and the prowess of the Emigrants are .. likely to make them masters of the country. 1839 H. JERVIS in *S. Afr. Archival Records: Natal* I. 314 Notwithstanding whatever Colonial Emigrants may think to the contrary, they cannot throw off their allegiance or cease to be considered as subjects of the Queen of England. *a*1875 T. BAINES *Jrnl of Res.* (1964) II. 161 A Boer who has been at the Dorp informs us that it is decided that no person residing within the Sovereignty shall be capable of holding land among the Emigrants. 1877 J. NOBLE *S. Afr.* 91 The condition of the emigrants for some time after this was miserable enough. 1973 [see sense A]. 1994 M. ROBERTS tr. *J.A. Wahlberg's Trav. Jrnls 1838–56* 58 Get on the wrong road and outspan by a spruit on the other side of the Modder laager (where the emigrants stayed for a long time).

Eminent Persons Group *n. phr. Hist.* Also **Eminent Persons' Group**. A group of Commonwealth politicians who visited South Africa in 1986 in an attempt to mediate between the government and the ANC, and to investigate ways of moving away from apartheid peacefully; EPG.

1986 *Guardian* (U.K.) 5 Feb. 7 Sir Geoffrey won the support for the Commonwealth Eminent Persons Group of the EEC-Frontline States meeting. 1986 *Times* (U.K.) 20 May 1 The Commonwealth Eminent Persons Groups (EPG), which is trying to mediate between Pretoria and the ANC, had left Lusaka .. for Cape Town. 1986 S. CRONJÉ in *New Statesman* (U.K.) 23 May 17 The Eminent Persons Group was formed after the Bahamas Commonwealth Prime Ministers' meeting last October ... , to promote a peaceful move away from apartheid. 1987 *E. Prov. Herald* 29 Apr. 13 Dr Denis Worrall has told a London newspaper that the Government's handling of the Eminent Persons' Group was one of the reasons why he decided to oppose the National Party. 1989 *Reader's Digest Illust. Hist.* 481 The Commonwealth Eminent Persons Group, a team of highly placed Commonwealth 'eminent persons' who had been charged by the October 1985 Commonwealth conference to try to seek a solution to the South African impasse. 1991 'HOGARTH' in *Sunday Times* 17 Mar. 22 Having suffered expulsion, trade embargoes, boycotts, the Eminent Persons Group and the Gleneagles agreement, South Africans have earned the right to insist that other Commonwealth countries live up to our standards — or suffer the same punishments.

emmer /ˈemə/ *n.* Also **emer**, **emir**. [Du., later Afk.] A bucket; *obs.*, a unit of measurement, esp. for farm produce. Occas. with defining word, **melkemmer** /ˈmelkˌemə/ [Afk., *melk* milk], a milking bucket.

1817 G. BARKER Journal. 20 June, Two emmers of barley were sown whilst I was at Grams-town. 1850 R.G.G. CUMMING *Hunter's Life* I. 161, I purchased eight 'emirs' or measures of wheat from one of the Griquas. 1860 J. SANDERSON in *Jrnl of Royal Geog. Soc.* XXX. 252 He had sold nearly all [the peaches] he had dried at 3s. per emmer, or 24s. per muid. 1866 E.L. PRICE *Jrnls* (1956) 190 Ma-Sebele & Sara Paul came down to see me — and a servant carrying an emer full of corn as a present fr. the former. 1913 C. PETTMAN *Africanderisms* 164 Emmer, .. In the early days of the Colony the bucket was often found to be a convenient measure when bartering. 1971 BARAITSER & OBHOLZER *Cape Country Furn.* 257 From the melkbalie milk was poured into a melkemmer (milking bucket), a wooden bucket with two or three metal hoops and a metal handle. 1979 M. MATSHOBA *Call Me Not a Man* 80 First rinsing the baby pail outside, she emptied the hot water into it, cooled it with two jugs from the *emmer* under the kitchen table and went back to her room.

Hence **emmerful** *n.* [+ Eng. *-ful*; or tr. Afk. *emmervol*], a bucketful.

1874 A. EDGAR in *Friend* 18 June, Mr Boshoff said they had stolen about an 'emmerful' of bojala or Kafir beer.

empofos var. IMPOFU.

encose, -cosi varr. ENKOSI *int.*

encossi var. INKOSI *n.*

en-daba var. INDABA.

endjie var. ENTJIE.

endorse *v. trans. Hist.* [See quot. 1962.] In the phr. *to endorse (someone) out*, to order (a black person) to leave an urban area because certain requirements of the Native Laws Amendment Act of 1952, or subsequent Acts, were not met by that person (see quot. 1963). Usu. *passive*. Also *transf.*

A person endorsed out of an urban area was expected to 'return' to the rural area or 'homeland' set aside for occupation by his or her ethnic group. See also HOMELAND sense 1, INFLUX CONTROL, PASS sense 3.

1959 M. HORRELL *Racialism & Trade Unions* 14 Dubbed an 'agitator', dismissed from his job, and, possibly, 'endorsed out' of the area concerned. 1962 B. WILKS in *Black Sash* June 27 Since January, 1956, twenty-six thousand .. Africans have been 'endorsed out' of the Western Cape under the Bantu Urban Areas Act, that is, an endorsement has been stamped in their Reference Books stating that they have no permit to remain in the area. 1963 WILSON & MAFEJE *Langa* 2 A man is 'endorsed out' if he is without employment, and has not lived in Cape Town for at least fifteen years, or been with one employer for at least ten years; a woman if she is neither employed nor the wife of a man 'exempted' because of the length of his employment in town. 1968 J. LELYVELD in Cole & Flaherty *House of Bondage* 12 If he is [unemployed], he can be 'endorsed out' for being what the law calls 'an idle Bantu'. 1972 *E. Prov. Herald* 10 Feb. 1 He did not believe that the White people in the areas the Transkei wanted should be 'endorsed out'. 1973 *Ibid.* 31 May 7 We have .. restricted the rights of those we regard as our inferiors. We endorse out of existence those who cannot defend themselves and relegate them .. to the cold and starvation of .. Dimbaza .. and Orangefontein. [1974 A. FUGARD *Statements 25 'Sizwe Bansi. Endorsed to King William's Town ...'* Takes your book, fetches that same stamp, and in it goes again.] 1976 R.L. PETENI *Hill of Fools* 136 There were many people, men and women, who were endorsed out of Port Elizabeth for one reason or another, though they had lived there for many years. 1976 M. THOLO in C. Hermer *Diary of Maria Tholo* (1980) 23 Another strike was supposed to start this week ... We Africans do not have permanence in Cape Town and the Government could use it as an excuse to endorse us out. 1981 *Pace* Sept. 16 By 1979, a further 500 000 blacks had been endorsed out of urban areas under the pass laws. 1982 A. BERRY in *Seek* Sept. 6 (*cartoon caption*) The Garden of Eden was declared a closed Group Area .. and the occupants were endorsed out. 1986 P. MAYLAM *Hist. of Afr. People* 180 'Those who because of old age, weak health, unfitness, or other reasons are no longer able to work' .. were the people who could be 'endorsed out' of urban areas for not possessing section 10 rights under the 1952 Native Laws Amendment Act. 1990 R. MALAN *My Traitor's Heart* 51 A black breadwinner had died, and his survivors were being evicted from their township house and 'endorsed out' to the homelands.

Hence **endorsement out** *n. phr.*; **endorse-out** *adj.* (*rare*, perh. *nonce*), see quot. 1972; **endorsing out** *vbl n. phr.*

1963 M. BENSON *Afr. Patriots* 265 'Endorsing out' was the Government's euphemism for driving out Africans from urban areas to reserves under the notorious Section 10 of the Urban Areas Act. 1971 *Daily Dispatch* 18 Aug. 11 The resettlement camps were bleeding wounds sapping out the life of the African people. To heal them would be to stop the flow first — removals and endorsements out of people in urban areas. 1972 *Drum* 8 Mar. 29 The endorse-out man who packed *his* bags ... He was boss of Johannesburg Non-European Affairs Department ... He was the man who did the endorsing out. 1973 *Weekend Post* 28 Apr. 11 Consider .. the constant fear of pass raids and prison or 'endorsement-out'. 1973 M. VAN BILJON in *Star* 30 June 6 Endorsing all the Black women and children out of White areas .. was a proposition that was carried almost unanimously.

‖**Engels** /ˈeŋ(ə)ls/ *adj.* and *n.* Formerly also **Engelsch**. [Afk., earlier Du. *Engelsch*.]

Usu. used ironically, or in Dutch or Afrikaans phrases.

A. *adj.* Also (*attrib.*) **Engels(ch)e**.

1. From or of England or Britain; of the English or British.

1822 W.J. BURCHELL *Trav.* I. 184 On my way back to the village, I met a Hottentot, who, asking me if I was not de engelsche heer (the English gentleman) presented a letter from my friend Poleman. 1837 'N. POLSON' *Subaltern's Sick Leave* 156 The Boers in the provinces .. had .. an inveterate prejudice against the 'Engelsch vark' (English pig!) as they styled the Saxon and Merino sheep. *c*1838 A.G. BAIN *Jrnls* (1949) 196 Then to an Engels settler fool We had ourselves contracted. 1862 LADY DUFF-GORDON in F. Galton *Vacation Tourists* (1864) III. 136 One may board in a Dutch farm-house very cheaply, and .. they will drive you about .. and tend your horses for nothing, if you are friendly, and don't treat them with *Engelsche hoogmoedigheid*. 1912 F. BANCROFT *Veldt Dwellers* 31 You've taken the oath of allegiance to Kruger, and though your blood is *Engelsch* — more's the pity — you can't go against that oath without being a traitor.

2. ENGLISH *adj.* sense 2.

1972 J. PACKER *Boomerang* 36 'They tease him.' 'What about?' 'Having 'n Engelse nooi.' 1985 *Vula* Oct. 10 The Afrikaaners are tired of taking a backseat to pretentious Engelse intellect né. 1990 *Sunday Times* 1 Apr. 19 Afrikaans drama has .. an unerring sense of place and identity ... None of the characters in .. the new six-part series .. on TV1 .. could possibly be *Engels*.

3. Special collocations. **Engelse Kerk** /-ˈkɛrk/ [Afk., *kerk* church], the 'Anglican' Church (Church of the Province of Southern Africa, see CPSA *n.*[1]); any English-language church; cf. ENGLISH *adj.* sense 1; **Engelse Oorlog** /-ˈʊə(r)lɔx/

[Afk., *oorlog* war], ANGLO-BOER WAR sense 1; **Engelse pers** /-pɛrs/ [Afk., *pers* press], *English Press* (see ENGLISH *adj.* sense 3).

1984 B. JOHNSON-BARKER in *Wynboer* June 72 Albert Hockley had no right .. to be going to the Pastorie, because he belonged to the **Engelse kerk**, as he .. delighted in saying when Dominee Kuys was rounding up the others. **1989** *Style* Feb. 36, I speak as one whose investigations .. have resulted in some minor skirmishes harking back to that war the English call the Boer War and the Afrikaners call the **Engelse Oorlog**. **1963** J. SINCLAIR in *Black Sash* Dec. 5 They hate all those in opposition groups; they hate the Africans, the Indians and the Coloureds; they hate the '**Engelse pers**'. **1971** *Sunday Times* 27 June 16 He wants nothing to do with the 'Engelse Pers'. When some Parliamentary correspondents of English-language newspapers invited him to lunch recently, he refused. **1979** *Daily Dispatch* 18 Apr. 3 You've got to pick up praise where you can find it, even if it's in the Engelse pers. **1983** *Frontline* Feb. 40 A well known critic of the press .. makes a number of observations which the Engelse Pers, in particular, is apt to consider hostile. **1984** J. SCOTT in *Cape Times* 31 Mar. 11 Would you believe .. Dr. Treurnicht, Dr. Mulder and old Oomie Tom Langley and all entertaining the dreaded *Engelse pers* to champagne and scrambled eggs? **1987** H. PRENDINI in *Style* Feb. 30 As a representative of the diabolical Engelse Pers .. shouldn't I be regarded with a little suspicion? **1993** [see NATIONALIST *adj.*].

B. *n.* Pl. **-e** /-ə/, occas. **-es** /-əs/.

1. Usu. in *pl.*: Persons of English or British origin. See also ENGELSMAN sense 1.

1913 D. FAIRBRIDGE *Piet of Italy* 149 Koos .. scouted the idea of a mishap. 'Him eat plenty aprikose, then him walk plenty. All Englese [*sic*] like that.' **1915** J.K. O'CONNOR *Afrikander Rebellion* 31 The acquisition of the Diamond Fields by Britain is another episode which in the hands of a 'patriotic' teacher lends itself to the exposure of the 'underhand methods' adopted by that 'lagere natie, de Engelse'. *a***1931** S. BLACK in S. Gray *Three Plays* (1984) 170 The vervlukste Engelse are all the same. **1944** 'TWEDE IN BEVEL' *Piet Kolonel* 36 The general attitude of the Afrikaner was one of good humoured surprise tinged with genuine affection for the idiosyncracies of the Engelse. **1992** G. ETHERINGTON in *Weekend Post* 9 May (Leisure) 4 The *Engelse* were encamped on a koppie overlooking Van Puttensvlei.

2.a. In *pl.*: ENGLISH *n.* sense a. See also ENGELSMAN sense 2, *mak Engelse* (MAK sense 2).

1973 *Cape Times* 2 June 8 His thinking rests on the historic fear of Afrikaner Nationalism that the *Engelse* will make common cause with Black political or economic power to 'plough the Afrikaner under'. **1976** *Daily Dispatch* 6 Feb. 14 The Engelse are only fully tolerable if they support the National Party, and only on the clear understanding that they can never be admitted to the innermost circle of the ruling class of Broeders. **1981** A. PATON in *Optima* Vol.30 No.2, 92 The descendants of the 1820 settlers of the Eastern Cape Province and of the 1850 settlers of Natal all became known as '*die Engelse*'. **1984** *Frontline* Mar. 46 Is there no end to the arrogance of certain Engelses? They're living in South Africa, they seem to forget, which is a multi-lingual country. **1986** *Style* Dec. 41 The only good bantus, commies, liberals and Engelse were dead ones ... The regte boere ruled with an iron fist. **1988** J. SCOTT in *E. Prov. Herald* 5 Mar. 6 We will be faced with what the Engelse call Hodgson's Choice, or something like that.

b. *comb.* **Engelsehaat** /-hɑːt/ [Afk., *haat* hatred; prob. formed by analogy with BOEREHAAT], hatred of English-speakers; cf. BOEREHAAT. See also HAAT *n.*

1972 *Evening Post* 27 May 11 (*letter*) One hears a lot about 'boerehaat', but what about 'Engelsehaat'. **1980** *Sunday Times* 12 Oct. 4 The English daily newspaper, the Windhoek Advertiser, lashed back, asking .. 'Does he perhaps think that the "Engelsman" is a hard-assed punk who has no feelings? .. The Joernaal is fanning the flames of bitterness and hate, "Engelsehaat".' **1981** *Ibid.* 25 Jan. (Mag. Sect.) 4 We English-speaking South Africans have been accused of boerehaat at election times, but 'The Settlers' is a vicious piece of 'Engelse haat'.

3.a. The English language.

1987 P. SCHIRMER in *Personality* 7 Mar. 81 He'll speak *Engels* one day when he goes to school, he assures me. **1990** *Cue* 30 June 3 A ware Suid-Afrikaanse band, their liedjies are in both Engels and Afrikaans. They even lapse into gibberish .. at times.

b. *comb.* **Engels-sprekende** /-ˈspriəkəndə/ [Afk., *sprekende* speaker], an English-speaking person (see ENGELSMAN sense 2); as *adj.* [Afk., *sprekende* speaking], English-speaking (see ENGLISH *adj.* sense 2 b).

1974 *Daily Dispatch* 21 Oct. 8 Die Engels-sprekende bloedsappe show that conservatism is alive and well and living in the official Opposition. **1977** *The 1820* Vol.50 No.12, 20 It was the British who brought rowing to South Africa and today Afrikaners and Engelsprekenders [*sic*] row in schools, universities and clubs all over the country. **1988** J. RAPHAELY in *Femina* May 152 He thought that it was all right 'as long as only the *Engels-sprekendes* saw it'.

‖**Engelsman** /ˈeŋ(ə)lsman, ˈəŋ(ə)ls-/ *n.* Pl. **-manne**. Also **Engelschman**, **Ingelsman**, **Ingilsman**. [Afk. (earlier Du. *Engelschman*), *Engels* English + *man* man, person.]

Usu. used by writers to indicate that the speaker's home language is Afrikaans.

1. One from England. Cf. ENGLANDER. See also ENGELS *n.* sense 1.

1837 'N. POLSON' *Subaltern's Sick Leave* 102 The conversation .. hangs heavy or lags if the traveller is a '*regt Engelschman*,' but if he has sufficient savoir faire to enter into the spirit of the thing .., he will get over the time pleasantly enough. **1899** B. MITFORD *Weird of Deadly Hollow* 97 Allamagtag! but the Engelschman can shoot! **1912** F. BANCROFT *Veldt Dwellers* 39, I hand over this *Engelschman* — taken in arms against the Republic — to your charge, Mynheer Brandon. **1920** F.C. CORNELL *Glamour of Prospecting* 57 He questioned me minutely .. and at each and all of my answers in broken Dutch he and his whole tribe laughed immoderately. He himself, as he proudly told me, had seen an Engelsman before, often, but not so his children. **1929** J.G. VAN ALPHEN *Jan Venter* 57 His cart .. off-loaded .. fresh milk for the camp. The message was the Engelsman (that's me) mustn't drink it all but give the new policeman some too. *a***1931** S. BLACK in S. Gray *Three Plays* (1984) 170 If they find gold in the moon, there will come an Engelsman by. **1983** M. DU PLESSIS *State of Fear* 25 My mother goes on and on about the concentration camps in the Boer War, still to this day she won't speak to an 'Ingelsman'. **1990** *Weekend Argus* 17 Feb. (Suppl.) 5 His English wife, whom he refers to fondly as the 'Ingilsman', has begun translating some of his .. works.

2. An English-speaking South African; *Engels-sprekende n.*, see ENGELS *n.* sense 3 b; ENGLISH *n.* sense b; ENGLISHMAN sense 2 a. See also ENGELS *n.* sense 2 a.

Usu. used of white persons.

1943 [see DUTCHMAN sense 1 b]. **1949** C. BULLOCK *Rina* 28 'You're only an Engelsman, and would not understand', he said scornfully ... English, or South African English, I might be, but I had a good knowledge of more than one Native tongue. **1980** *Sunday Times* 12 Oct. 4 The English daily newspaper, the Windhoek Advertiser, lashed back, asking .. : 'Does he perhaps think that the "Engelsman" is a hard-assed punk who has no feelings?' **1982** *E. Prov. Herald* 25 Feb. 25 Newspapers are a vital part of our English heritage. It seems that wherever two or three Engelsmanne are gathered together you'll find a mayor, a newspaper and a club. **1983** *Frontline* May 54 They do a lot to help perpetuate the common Afrikaner belief that actually the Engelsman is a kind of half-way, fair-weather, South African. **1990** F. BATES in *Style* Oct. 78 'Hey, Engelsman,' he said suddenly 'Have some of this.' And he held out a half-eaten koeksister as though offering a dog a scrap of food. **1991** A. VAN WYK *Birth of New Afrikaner* 63 Michael Young, the lone Sap in our midst whom we all called *Engelsman* and who had long accepted his nickname goodnaturedly.

Englander *n. Obs.* exc. *hist.* [A misrepresentation of Afk., prob. by confusion with G. *Engländer*, the source of this word as found in Brit. Eng.] A native of England; an Englishman. Cf. ENGELSMAN sense 1.

1852 A.W. COLE *Cape & Kafirs* 122 Though a peaceably-disposed set of men, they at all times entertain a considerable feeling of contempt for any diminutive 'Englander'. **1899** [see *salting vbl n.* at SALT *v.*]. **1903** D. BLACKBURN *Burgher Quixote* 3 It is a common reproach among Englanders that we Transvaal Boers are ignorant. *a***1936** R. KIPLING in C. Corrington *Rudyard Kipling* (1955) 316 It is only the little Englanders in London who say that the Transvaal is merely fighting for its independence, but over here both sides realize it is a question of which race is to run the country. **1937** [see HANDS-UPPER sense 1 b]. **1975** S. GRAY in *Bolt* No.12, 7 Jan Maat was there seen to undergo a final snapping of the moral fibre, which the Good Lord had doubtless designed to be of little holding-power amongst the Dutch Elect; we Englanders rather inclining to obstinacy .. which even the moderate application of liquor and subtropical solarity cannot tarnish, being the better man.

Englikaans var. ANGLIKAANS.

Englikaner see ANGLIKAANS.

English *adj.* and *n.* [Special senses of general Eng.]

A. *adj.*

1.a. Of or pertaining to the Anglican Church (officially, the Church of the Province of Southern Africa, see CPSA *n.*[1]); freq. *comb.* **English Church**. **b.** Of or pertaining to the English-language churches. Cf. *Engelse Kerk* (see ENGELS *adj.* sense 3).

1832 J. CAMERON in B. Shaw *Memorials* (1841) 201 Attended the service of the English Church. The *bishop of Calcutta* .. preached a truly evangelical sermon. **1913** H. TUCKER *Our Beautiful Peninsula* 37 With what equal astonishment would he have found it [*sc.* his rural retreat] rechristened 'Bishopscourt' and become the home of an Archbishop of the English Church. **1971** *Seek* June 1 Recent allegations in Parliament that the 'English Parsons' incited Port Elizabeth's Coloureds during recent bus riots. **1991** F.G. BUTLER *Local Habitation* 274 Members of a steadily-diminishing English-speaking community still worshipping in 'English' churches.

2.a. Of or pertaining to (white) English-speaking South Africans. **b.** English-speaking; *Engels-sprekende adj.*, see ENGELS *n.* sense 3 b. In both senses also called ENGELS *adj.* sense 2.

1893 'HARLEY' in *Cape Illust. Mag.* June 377 Dutch and English Colonial farmers and a few young Englishmen, who .. had come to South Africa to learn farming. *a***1930** G. BAUMANN in Baumann & Bright *Lost Republic* (1940) 163 The Remington Scouts, .. made up not only of Cape Colonials but, I am sorry to say, of a number of Free State-born English boys. **1949** C. BULLOCK *Rina* 34 'You *are* English, are you not, Mr Marston?' 'English South African,' I pointed out. **1956** M. ROGERS *Black Sash* p.xvi, The Afrikaner has an entirely different solution to the English South African in whom the traditional British colonial approach is still strong — occupation, education, emancipation. **1963** M.G. MCCOY *Informant, Port Elizabeth* The article .. is the same one we had published in the Evening Post, .. saying that the English South Africans are traitors to their political & moral traditions. **1970** *News/Check* 4 Sept. 5 It is sad that so many English South Africans today still persist in believing in the old time-caricature of A Monolithic Afrikanerdom, of one mind and one purpose. **1971** *Evening Post* 5 June (Mag. Sect.) 9 Many 'English' rugby fans who understand Afrikaans have got into the habit of listening to rugby commentaries in that language. **1990** *Sunday Times* 1 Apr. 22, I, and many other English-speaking, but bilingual, South Africans become intensely annoyed when referred to as English or British. **1993** L. HARRIS in *Daily News* 14 Jan. 13 It was traditional for Afrikaans schools to make extensive use of fund-raising ... 'English schools usually prefer to enforce higher school fees.'

3. Special collocation. **English Press**, the South African English-language press; *Engelse pers*, see ENGELS *adj.* sense 3.

1943 'J. BURGER' *Black Man's Burden* 246 The English Press in the Union is Pro-British, and attacks the republican and Afrikaans movement wherever possible. **1960** J.H. COETZEE in H. Spottiswoode *S. Afr.: Rd Ahead* 73 It is quite impossible to build up a better understanding as long as the English press sticks to its myth of the Afrikaner bully and suppressor of poor innocent Natives and Englishmen. **1963** A.M. LOUW *20 Days* 69 The United Party is blaming the Nationalists for the riots, and the Nationalists are putting the blame right back on the United Party and their English press. **1972** J. MERVIS in *Communications in Afr.* Vol.1 No.2, 2 It is the English Press .. the direct heirs and successor to Fairbairn and Pringle .. which more than any other section of the Press in South Africa, is maintaining the highest standards and traditions of newspaper independence and freedom. **1973** *Sunday Times* 27 May 12 On the instructions of Dr. Verwoerd, secret plans to take action against the English Press were prepared in 1964 and 1965 by a special Cabinet committee assisted behind the scenes by certain Transvaal judges. **1979** W. EBERSOHN *Lonely Place* 50 The whole thing is typical of the English press — get hold of a little thing and blow it up out of all proportion to discredit the Afrikaner. **1993** H. TYSON *Editors under Fire* 11 Every Nationalist speech from every political platform across the country devoted much of its content to the evils — and the dangers — of the *Engelse pers*, the English press.

B. *n.* Pl. unchanged. **a.** Usu. *pl.*: White English-speaking South Africans collectively; ENGELS *n.* sense 2 a. **b.** *sing. rare.* A white English-speaking South African: ENGELSMAN sense 2.

Occas. used as a sing. in place of 'Englishmen', but representing the English-speaking group as a whole (see quots 1966, 1971).

1952 B. DAVIDSON *Report on Sn Afr.* 153 Against the long slow crucifixion of the Africans in South Africa the battle of words and shaken fists between the 'English' and the Afrikaners of today can seem, to strangers, little better than a shoddy farce. **1956** M. ROGERS *Black Sash* p.xv, Here the second great national problem arises: large numbers of this section of the South African nation, the English, refuse to recognise this fact. **1960** J.H. COETZEE in H. Spottiswoode *S. Afr.: Rd Ahead* 74 The English in South Africa have to accept the real situation: they are South African, not Britishers. **1966** W. MAREE in *Argus* 8 Apr. 6 From now on, as far as a common loyalty to South Africa is concerned, Afrikaner and English will stand and work together. **1971** *Rand Daily Mail* 8 June 1 The Afrikaner .. had a tougher attitude towards the African whom he seemed to look on as a source of labour, while the English appeared to want a change over apartheid. **1973** *Sunday Times* 25 Feb. (Mag. Sect.) 10 It has been said that the South African English agree with the Progs, vote United Party, and thank God for the Nats. **1979** [see Alexander quot. at FORTY-PERCENTERS]. **1989** K. SUTTON in *E. Prov. Herald* 25 Feb. 4 We will not have foreigners criticising our Afrikaners — that's our job, we 'English' .. they're family. **1989** *Frontline* Nov. 36 The double-dealing of those post-colonial clones whom he describes as 'the English'. **1989** J. HOBBS *Thoughts in Makeshift Mortuary* 381 'We are fighting this war to the death for our country. You English are irrelevant — ' 'Don't call me English!'

Englishman *n.* [Special senses of general Eng.] **1.** Also with small initial. [See quot. 1951.] The large edible seabream *Chrysoblephus anglicus* of the Sparidae. Also *attrib.*

The name 'Englishman' is used for this species in Smith and Heemstra's *Smiths' Sea Fishes* (1986).

1913 C. PETTMAN *Africanderisms* 164 Englishman, *Chrysophrys Anglicus* is so named in Natal. **1949** J.L.B. SMITH *Sea Fishes* 272 *Chrysoblephus anglicus* ... *Englishman* (Natal) ... Found only on the East coast of Africa in deepish water ... Occasionally seen at East London, not uncommon in Natal waters. **1951** L.G. GREEN *Grow Lovely* 91 There is an Englishman fish in Natal waters, a regular John Bull of a fish with a ruddy complexion. **1984** *E. Prov. Herald* 3 Nov. 2 Fishermen would be restricted to a daily bag limit of five of the .. protected species ... The .. species are: .. elf, galjoen, .. englishman, .. dageraad.

2. [Influenced by Afk. *Engelsman*.] **a.** ENGELSMAN sense 2. **b.** Occas., an Afrikaner who usu. chooses to speak English rather than Afrikaans.

1936 A. LEZARD *Gold Blast* 265 Both the Dutchman and the Englishman in South Africa is a fine man. Each has his patriotic emotions. **1973** *Star* 8 June 13, I once heard an Englishman say: 'I've voted UP since 1948 and I've never had it so good in this country'. **1973** *Weekend Post* 15 May 1 'If you meet a tramp on the road he is either an Englishman or a Black alcoholic but not an Afrikaner,' he said. **1989** B. RONGE in *Sunday Times* 3 Dec. 30 These poor-white characters who live on a smallholding on the East Rand make pointed references to Englishmen, indicating that they are Afrikaans, yet they speak English. **1990** *Sunday Times* 11 Feb. (Mag. Sect.) 32 Perhaps in another century's time relationships between Englishmen and Afrikaners will be more relaxed. **1990** R. VAN TONDER in *Frontline* Sept. 27 Not a single Englishman ever became president or prime minister ... The so-called Afrikaners ruled the roost for the entire eight decades until now. **1991** A. VAN WYK *Birth of New Afrikaner* 20 The Natal Englishmen could fool themselves with a pretence of opposing apartheid, but they didn't fool me — nor the blacks on the receiving end.

||**enkosi** /(e)ŋˈkɔːs(i)/ *int.* Also **encose**, **encosi**, **e,nkosi**, **inkors**, **(in)kosi**, **nkosi**, **unkoes**. [Xhosa *enkosi*, *nkosi* fr. *inkosi* lord; see quots 1915 and 1976.] 'Thank you'.

Used chiefly among Xhosa-speakers. Cf. INKOSI.

1803 J.T. VAN DER KEMP in *Trans. of Missionary Soc.* I. 438 He cuts off his piece with his assagay, and divides it with some of the company, .. who on receiving it say *unkoes*! (I thank you!). **1835** T.H. BOWKER Journal. 6 June, With this they appeared to be pleased and cried out 'encose' thankyou. **1891** T.R. BEATTIE *Pambaniso* 170 The words *Imibulelo* and *Enkosi* mean thanks, and surely when a Kaffir makes use of these words when he receives anything from a white man, it shows that the gift or favour is appreciated. **1913** C. PETTMAN *Africanderisms* 226 A Kaffir will express his sense of indebtedness for a favour by saluting the person bestowing it as an 'Inkosi' or benefactor. The word has, however, in the form *enkosi* come to be regarded, and is often used by colonists, as being the equivalent of the English 'Thank you'. **1915** A. KROPF *Kafir-Eng. Dict.* 194 *Enkosi*! or the simple vocative *nkosi*! is used .. as the English 'thanks,' to express gratitude to a giver by saying *uyinkosi*, you are a lord. **1971** *Drum* July 57, I looked around .. and said to them: 'Well, now I'm glad you have had the sense not to let this unpleasantness spoil your party.' 'Nkosi!' they cried. **1976** WEST & MORRIS *Abantu* 22 The word for 'thank you' in Xhosa is *inkosi* (chief), the implication being that generosity is the mark of a chief. **1979** F. DIKE *First S. African* 1 Freda: Good morning bhuti ... Can you tell me where the superintendent's office is? ... Oh, that door ... Thank you very much. Enkosi kakhulu. **1987** D.J. GRANT in *Frontline* June 13 At the stops people clamber, still singing, towards the exit. 'Encosi driver!' 'Thank you driver!'

enkosi *n.* var. INKOSI *n.*

enna var. EINA.

'ensopper var. HENSOPPER.

enspan var. INSPAN.

||**entjie** /ˈeŋki, ˈeɪŋci, ˈeɪntʃi/ *n.* Also **eintjie**, **endjie**. [Afk. *end* end + dim. suffix -IE.]

a. STOMPIE sense 1 a.

1950 E. PARTRIDGE *Dict. of Underworld Slang* 222 *Entjie*, A cigarette-butt: South Africa; late C. 19–20. **1981** V.A. FEBRUARY *Mind your Colour* 158 He .. identifies the following slang expressions in the novel: juba (a chappie); endjie (a cigarette stub); blerrie (bloody); ching (money); rooker (gangster); bokkie (girl friend). **1986** K. MCCORMICK in Burman and Reynolds *Growing Up* 302 Amanda's got two teeth out and then the children shout at her '*entjie bek!*' ['cigarette mouth']. **1994** E. KELLEY-PATTERSON in *E. Prov. Herald* 6 Apr. (la Femme) 2 The porters .. loaded and unloaded trucks — always keeping a sharp look-out for any cigarette *entjies* — they knew this baas, he smoked forever.

b. STOMPIE sense 2.

1969 A. FUGARD *Boesman & Lena* 28 You asked me and now I've told you. Pain is a candle *entjie* and a donkey's face.

c. A small amount.

1970 K. NICOL *Informant, Durban* We only get an eintjie graze at the hostel.

entombie var. INTOMBI.

entuna var. INDUNA.

enyanga var. INYANGA.

EP *n. colloq.* Initial letters of EASTERN PROVINCE; a sports team representing this region. Often *attrib.*

1971 *E. Prov. Herald* 1 Jan. 12 Can E.P.'s top batsmen keep their form? .. Brenda Petersen (E.P.) hit her best form at the .. championships. **1983** *Grocott's Mail* 28 Jan. 20 Dolphin swims his way to EP records. **1984** *Daily Dispatch* 5 June 1 A former EP rugby player had been at the forefront of it all. **1990** [see BLIKOOR]. **1990** *Weekend Post* 20 Oct. 16 EP have been criticised severely and at times fairly for our poor pitches. **1993** *Weekend Post* 12 June 11 (*letter*) They [*sc.* people from the townships] don't care for EP so they don't attend its matches ... To paraphrase Donald Woods: the day EP drops apartheid in word and in deed, EP will be Currie Cup champions. **1993** C. ROBERTSON in *Sunday Times* 17 Oct. 25 EP regional police commissioner Major-General Daan Huggett .. concluded that several of the smaller stations in the corridor were superfluous.

EPG *n. hist.* Initial letters of EMINENT PERSONS GROUP. Also *attrib.*

1986 *Sunday Times* 16 Mar. 1 The members of the EPG are former Australian Prime Minister Malcolm Fraser, former British Chancellor of the Exchequer Lord Barber, former Nigerian Head of State General Olusegan Obasanjo, former Tanzanian Foreign Minister Mr John Malecela, Dame Nita Barrow of Barbados, Archbishop Edward Scott, Primate of Canada's Anglican Church, and former Indian Foreign Minister Mr Swaran Singh. **1986** *Rhodeo* (Rhodes Univ.) Aug. 11 When Margaret Thatcher sent her personal envoy to South Africa she devalued the earlier Commonwealth initiative on South Africa — the so-called EPG. **1987** *New Nation* 22 Oct. 7 The collapse of the EPG initiative after South Africa attacked the Frontline states .. must be seen in the context of PW Botha's demand that the ANC renounce violence, whereas the government's position during the EPG visit was that the ANC suspend violence.

epiti var. IPITI.

erdvark, -verk varr. AARDVARK.

erf /ɜːf/ *n.* Formerly also (*rare*) **hearf**. Pl. **erven**, **erfs**; formerly also (*rare*) **ervin**, **hervings**. [Du., in same sense, orig. 'inheritance'.]

a. A plot of land; cf. STAND sense 1 b. Also *attrib.*

The word 'erf' is used in both urban and rural contexts: although not a unit of measure, it is used only of relatively small plots, up to the size of smallholdings.

1811 J.A. TRUTER in G.M. Theal *Rec. of Cape Col.* (1901) VIII. 103 The Regulation on the granting of small pieces of ground (Erven) *to hold but a small number of cattle*. [**1812** A. Plumptre tr. *H. Lichtenstein's Trav. in Sn Afr.* (1928) I. 335 Instead of extensive farms, it should be divided into small parcels of land, or *erbes*.] **1821** C.I. Latrobe *Jrnl of Visit* 371 His industry put him in possession of this *erf*, a name given to a small lot of ground, not being a complete farm. **1827** G. Thompson *Trav.* II. 57 At the public sale of the *erven*, or lots of ground for houses and gardens, there was great competition. **1846** *Natal Witness* 10 Apr. 1 Mr B. will, on the same day, dispose of 100 or 150 feet of Ground of the Erf he is occupying. **1857** T. Shone Diary. 3 July, Henry was quarrying of stone, he Brought one load to his Ervin in Bathurst. *a***1858** J. Goldswain *Chron.* (1946) I. 50 They gave everey one that maid appelaction to them a hearf of ground to buld thear house on and to make a Garding: sum of the hervings were two acers but what was caled Mecanic Hearfs was onley half an acer. **1861** *E. Prov. Yr Bk & Annual Register* 156 The water .. is led out of the rivers and streams by furrows over the erven. **1892** W.L. Distant *Naturalist in Tvl* 95 Erven, or plots, that could have been purchased a few years earlier .. for £14, and now worth from £200 to £300. **1905** G. Baumann in Baumann & Bright *Lost Republic* (1940) 244 At Winburg, the Resident Magistrate .. in Transfer Deeds described the erven as being 'on or about' so many feet frontage. **1926** P.W. Laidler *Tavern of Ocean* 82 In 1785 a pottery was organised by P.J. Caude .., who asked the Company for an erf in Table Valley for that purpose. **1934** B.I. Buchanan *Pioneer Days* 1 An erf extended from one main street to the next, and its area was one and a half acres, affording space for garden and orchard. **1950** H.C. Bosman in S. Gray *Makapan's Caves* (1987) 141 Bekkersdal was proclaimed as a township, and the bush was cleared away and the surveyor measured out the streets and divided up the erfs. **1960** J.J.L. Sisson *S. Afr. Judicial Dict.* 253 According to the ordinary meaning of language *erf* (or at any rate an *erf* of a village) is a limited area of land measuring something like 100 feet by 200 feet, or, in the case of large *erven*, 200 feet by 200 feet. **1971** *Daily Dispatch* 25 Aug. 1 The Fingo village was given in trust to the Fingo people in 1857 ... Most erven are owned by African ratepayers. **1987** G. Viney *Col. Houses* 92 The erfs of Sidbury village were deductions off Bushy Park. **1990** *Grocott's Mail* 5 Apr. 3 Both these erven have business rights, but could be used for residential purposes as well. **1992** *Sunday Times* 20 Sept. 15 The configuration of outbuildings which frame the erf are among the finest in the country.

b. With defining word denoting a specific type of erf: **dry erf**, an erf with no access to water; **water erf** or (*obs.*) **wet erf**, an erf with water rights.

1833 *Graham's Town Jrnl* 20 June 3 The proclamation which established Graham's Town provided that the Erven should pay certain Water-Rates; and some of them denominated '**dry erven**' were to pay it even without receiving water. **1867** *Blue Bk for Col. 1866* JJ13, The dam will be of considerable benefit to the inhabitants by furnishing the dry erven with a permanent supply of water for domestic purposes. **1882** [see *wet erf* below]. **1977** *Family Radio & TV* 28 Apr. 47 We've got what we call dry erven where residents don't lead off water from the main street furrow, and water erven where they do. **1860** E.R. Murray in J. Murray *Young Mrs Murray* (1954) 27 Water was led from its Spring (or 'Fountain') in open furrows across a block of **water erven**, one of which was the Parsonage grounds. **1871** W.G. Atherstone in A.M.L. Robinson *Sel. Articles from Cape Monthly Mag.* (1978) 145 'Sannah's Poorte', through which a small streamlet languidly trickles, *threatening* to water some half dozen 'water erven' owned by the church, which sows not, reaps not, gardens not. **1914** [see sense c]. **1949** L.G. Green *In Land of Afternoon* 17 An erf is not a farm, but there are people who draw much of their support from a water-erf. **1958** I. Vaughan *Diary* 7 There are big houses with gardens they are calling them water erfs becos they are the only ones getting watter in a furrow from the big dam at top of the street. **1977** *Family Radio & TV* 28 Apr. 47 For the dry erven we charge 10c a year for all the water they can take out in buckets and for the water erven it's 20c a year. **1982** *Het Suid-Western* 29 Dec., Irrigation Water Fees: R18,50 per year per original water erf (100 per cent). **1882** J. Nixon *Among Boers* 124 The town is divided by the spruit into **wet** and dry '**erven**', that is to say, the 'erven', or blocks of property into which the town is cut up, are irrigated on one side of the spruit, but not on the other. The principal residential properties and gardens are on the wet erven.

c. *comb.* (objective) **erf-holder**, the owner of an erf; occas. with defining word (see quot. 1914).

1851 J.J. Freeman *Tour* 184 Burning commenced immediately, and no entreaties of erf-holders, tears of mothers and children availed. **1867** *Blue Bk for Col. 1866* JJ44, Many of the native erf-holders are too poor and others too lazy, to cultivate their erven. **1873** F. Boyle *To Cape for Diamonds* 318 It was the bit of ground on which his Kaffirs 'sorted' which was rightfully taken from him, on application of the erf-holder. **1896** M.A. Carey-Hobson *At Home in Tvl* 431 Pilfering continually going on in the gardens of the Pretorian erfholders. **1914** L.H. Brinkman *Breath of Karroo* 53 The monopoly of a small number of water-erf holders. **1924** G. Baumann in Baumann & Bright *Lost Republic* (1940) 86, I advised the Municipality to buy out the erf-holders to the south. **1977** *Grocott's Mail* 2 Sept. 1 Who draws the rent for the properties, including the shacks which at present are part of the erf-holder's income?

erfgrondbrief *n. Obs. Law.* [Du., *erf* plot of land, inheritance + *grond* ground + *brief* note, letter.] The first title-deed granted on a plot of land at the Cape: see quot. 1934.

1810 M.C. Gie in G.M. Theal *Rec. of Cape Col.* (1900) VII. 432, I can discover nothing further about the place .. than that the Erf Grond brief contains 52 morgens 120 roods measured land. **1811** J.A. Truter in *Ibid.* VIII. (1901) 100 It is only necessary to look into the Erfgrondbriefs, which are different from other Erfgrondbriefs only herein, that the land is expressed as having been formerly held on loan. **1813** J. Cradock in *Ibid.* IX. (1901) 207 The Title Deed (Erfgrondbrief) on such application shall be granted after the place shall have been surveyed. **1934** C.P. Swart Supplement to Pettman. 49 *Erfgrondbrief*, .. The first title-deed or original grant of land held on a tenure that formerly existed in Cape Colony, called 'loan freehold'. The term also applied to the first title-deed or grant of such land when under Sir John Cradock's Proclamation of 1813 the tenure was changed into 'perpetual quitrent'.

erfpacht /'ɛrfpaxt, 'ɜːf-/ *n. Obs.* exc. *hist. Law.* Also **erfpag**. [Du., 'hereditary tenure, long lease', *erf* tenure, inheritance + *pacht* lease.] QUITRENT sense 2 a. Also *attrib.*

1809 Lord Caledon in G.M. Theal *Rec. of Cape Col.* (1900) VII. 184 The Erfpacht or Quitrent. To hold under this tenure it is requisite that the land should be surveyed when the possessor receives a Title deed upon a 10 dollar Stamp and is subject to the Yearly rent of from 4 to 8 skillings per Morgen. **1928** E.A. Walker *Hist. of S. Afr.* 96 It doubled the rents of the loan farms and offered small farms adjoining them on *erfpacht* — that is, lease for fifteen years at a low rental with the promise of compensation for improvements on resumption. **1936** C. Birkby *Thirstland Treks* 213 A Nel of the old days was granted 54,000 *morgen* of arid land along the river on the *erfpag* system devised by the Cape colonial government, and now his sons have developed still further the fine farm he made of it. **1945** G. Wille *Principles of S. Afr. Law* 197 Quitrent is in all respects identical with the *erfpacht* or *emphytensis* of the Roman-Dutch law ... Erfpacht .. was a right to the use and enjoyment of another person's land subject to the payment of a yearly canon or vectigal. **1974** Davenport & Hunt *Right to Land* 4 The Field Cornet begins .. by laying down a middle point, and investigates whether, from this middlepoint, it is possible to cross the veld for half an hour in all directions without violating the *Eigendoms-*, *Erfpacht-*, or *Leenrecht* of surrounding farms, nor any Government Land. **1984** R.C. Fisher in Martin & Friedlaender *Hist. of Surveying & Land Tenure* I. 79 In Roman-Dutch law *erfpacht* or quitrent tenure was a grant of land for an indefinite or limited period subject to the payment of an annual rent.

Hence **erfpachter** *n.*, one who holds land on erfpacht.

1945 G. Wille *Principles of S. Afr. Law* 197 Erfpacht was a kind of perpetual tenure of land and approached very near to dominium though the *erfpachter* or *emphytenta* was not entitled to take the minerals from the land.

erven, **ervin** pl. forms of ERF.

eschenhout var. ESSENHOUT.

Escom var. ESKOM.

esebongo var. ISIBONGO.

||**esel** /'ɪəsəl/ *n.* Formerly also **ezel**. [Afk., earlier S. Afr. Du. *ezel* fr. Du. *ezel* donkey.]

1. *obs.*

a. A zebra; often with defining word, **streep-esel**, **wilde esel**.

1796 E. Helme tr. *F. Le Vaillant's Trav. into Int.* III. 34 At the Cape, the zebra is known under the name of *streep-ezel* (the striped ass). **1844** J. Backhouse *Narr. of Visit* 572 The Mountain Zebra, *Equus Zebra*, called Wilde Ezel or Wild Ass, is abundant here. **1959** A. Cattrick *Spoor of Blood* 23 Here is his description of what they saw in the area that is to-day Namaqualand: 'We saw on the plains great herds of divers species of game such as rhinosceri, giraffes, buffaloes, witte wilde paarden, ezels, [etc.].'

b. An ass or donkey; also *fig.*, a dunce or idiot (see also *eselkop* at sense 2).

1910 D. Fairbridge *That Which Hath Been* (1913) 92 If it had occurred to the verdoemde ezel .. to lean against the wall .. we should have found ourselves in a tight place. **1913** A.B. Marchand *Dirk, S. African* 144 (Swart), Hi, Fanie, You great ezel, wake up!

2. *comb. rare.* **eselbos** /-bɔs/ [Afk., *bos* bush] or **eselkos** /-kɔs/ [Afk., *kos* food; see quot. 1966], the succulent plant *Euphorbia meloformis*; **eselkop** /-kɔp/ [Afk., *kop* head], dunce, idiot (see also sense 1 b).

1933 *Farming in S. Afr.* May 190 (Swart), The '**eselbos**', closely resembling the springbok bos, is occasionally found. **1900** B. Mitford *Aletta* 69 Now, do you not see, you **eselkop**? **1966** C.A. Smith *Common Names* 211 **Eselkos**, .. The species is much eaten by donkeys, .. whence the vernacular name.

Esemkofu *n. obs.* Also **Esimkovu**. Pl. unchanged. [Prob. ad. Zulu *izimkhovu*, obs. pl. form of *umkhovu* an exhumed corpse brought back to life as the familiar of a witch or wizard. (The pl. is now usu. *imikhovu*.)] (Usu. *pl.*) Among Zulu-speakers: the familiar of a witch or wizard, said to be a corpse brought back to life by magic. See also WITCHDOCTOR.

1875 D. Leslie *Among Zulus* 120 'What are Esemkofu?' 'An Esemkofu is a person who has been dead, and has been raised again by witches, who cut off his tongue, and so prevent him from talking and telling secrets; he can only utter a wailing noise — "Maieh! maieh!"' **1895** H. Rider Haggard *Nada* 184 Many tales had been told to me of this Ghost Mountain, which all swore was haunted .. said some, by the *Esemkofu* — that is, by men who have died and who have been brought back again by magic. **1925** D. Kidd *Essential Kafir* 128 The Esimkovu are supposed to be people who have been dead and have been raised from the dead by witches.

esikoko var. ISICOCO.

Esimkovu var. ESEMKOFU.

Eskom /'eskəm/ *n.* Formerly also **Escom**. [Acronym formed on Eng. *Electricity Supply* + Afk. *Kommissie* commission. (Formerly called *Escom* in Eng. and *Evkom* in Afk., see quot. 1987.)] A statutory body established by the Electricity Act of 1922 to provide a national electricity grid. Also *attrib.*

Originally a convenient abbrev. of the full name, Eskom has been the official company name since 1987.

[c1937 *Our Land* (United Tobacco Co.) 29 'Escom House' .. the headquarters of the Electricity Supply Commission.] **1943** L. SOWDEN *Union of S. Afr.* 109 He was chairman of Iscor and of another great state undertaking, the Electricity Supply Commission – Escom for short – which had been established by the Smuts Government in 1923 to operate free of Parliamentary control on a non-profit-making basis. **1951** *Yr Bk & Guide to Sn Afr. 1951* 101 In the 25 years of its existence, Escom, the National Power Supply Authority, has been .. constantly extending its service to the Nation. **1960** *Star* in J. Crwys-Williams *S. Afr. Despatches* (1989) 330 Escom technicians were marking out the route the power line will take from the mine headquarters to the new shaft. **1978** *S. Afr. Digest* 27 Oct. 12 The Electricity Supply Commission (Escom) is to call tenders early next year to build a giant R1 200-million, 3 600 MW coal-fired power station in the Bethal-Ogies-Witbank area in the Transvaal. **1983** *E. Prov. Herald* 26 Feb. 1 The entire Cape Province was plunged into darkness early today by a massive power failure on Escom's main transmission line. **1987** *Daily Dispatch* 3 Nov. 11 The Electricity Supply Commission, alias Escom, alias Evkom, is no more ... Henceforth the name .. is simply Eskom ... The official name in terms of the Eskom Act No.40 of 1987 .. provides for a single spelling in both English and Afrikaans ... 'Eskom thus refers to a legal entity in its own right and is not an acronym for any other name.' **1990** *Flying Springbok* June 114 Eskom generates 97% of all electricity in South Africa ... Eskom's generation represents nearly 60% of the electricity used on the entire African continent. **1993** *Star* 21 July 15 Eskom, South Africa's giant utility parastatal, plays a critical role in the development of industry .. in southern Africa.

Essa /ˈesə/ *n.* Also **ESSA**. Acronym formed on *English-speaking South African*. See also SOUTH AFRICAN *adj. phr.* sense 4 b.

1974 *Rapport* 21 July 15 There's a newly conscious species around. It's called an Essa: English-speaking South African. **1974** F. WILSON in De Villiers *Eng. Speaking S. Afr. Today* (1976) 154 There is a fourth story which should perhaps be included lest some should leave this hall feeling that wide though the definition of ESSA's is, it appears to include only Whites. Far from it. **1978** tr. *Rapport* in *S. Afr. Digest* 14 July 20 The accent even fell on new political thought, something for which the Essas are not really known. For too long their political contribution was restricted to criticism of everything the Afrikaner came forward with. **1979** T. HAUPTFLEISCH in *HSRC Languages Survey: 1st Report*, It was found that the Afrikaner normally appears more willing than the ESSA to employ L2, but only in situations outside his family circle ... The Afrikaner reacts strongly – either positively or negatively – to being taken for an English speaker, whereas the ESSA is little concerned about this factor. **1987** [see Ndebele quot. at OWN AFFAIR sense 1]. **1988** D. CHRISTIE *Informant, Grahamstown*, I have no doubt that modifications [to English] will occur which might send us ESSAs reeling for the gin, but which are inevitable. **1991** F.G. BUTLER *Local Habitation* 168 The small group of mother-tongue speakers of English in my country – The English Speaking South Africans, or ESSAs.

Essbee see quot. 1977 at SB.

‖**essenhout** /ˈes(ə)nhəʊt/ *n.* Formerly also **eschenhout**. [S. Afr. Du., fr. Du. *eschenhout*, *esch(en)* ash + *hout* wood.] Either of two species of tree, esp. *Ekebergia capensis*: **a.** *Ekebergia capensis; Cape ash*, see CAPE sense 2 a. **b.** The *Natal mahogany* sense (*a*) (see NATAL sense b), *Trichilia emetica*; occas. with defining word, **rooi-essenhout** [Afk. *rooi* red], (see quot. 1984). In both senses also called ESSENWOOD.

[**1786** G. FORSTER tr. *A. Sparrman's Voy. to Cape of G.H.* I. 311 The name of *Essen-bosch* is given to a kind of woody tract along *Essen-rivier*, which, as well as the wood, has taken its name from the esse or ash-tree. **1789** W. PATERSON *Narr. of Four Journeys* 80 A tree very useful in making waggons, which the Dutch call Essen or ash.] **1798** S.H. WILCOCKE tr. *J.S. Stavorinus's Voy. to E. Indies 1768–71* II. 79 Among the various sorts of timber, either unknown, or extremely rare in Europe, the following abound here, viz ... *essenhout*, the ash (*ekebergia capensis*), which is hard and of a close texture, and is used for making of tools and implements of various kinds; [etc.]. **1843** J.C. CHASE *Cape of G.H.* 160 Ash (Essen Hout) .. Tough. **1860** HARVEY & SONDER *Flora Capensis* I. 525 The tree is called by the inhabitants 'Eschenhout;' the edible fruit, 'Zuurebesges.' **1887** *S.W. Silver & Co.'s Handbk to S. Afr.* 132 The tree of which there were fewest was the Essenhout. These and the Yellowwood were generally situated deep in the forest. **1950** *Cape Argus* 18 Mar. (Mag. Sect.) 7 The Cape ebony, white stinkwood, flatcrown, essenhout and umzimbiti, trees that yield beautiful timber for furniture-making, grow in profusion in every kloof. **1961** PALMER & PITMAN *Trees of S. Afr.* 277 The essenhout or dog plum is a medium sized tree found in most of the forests of the country. **1975** *Afr. Wildlife* Vol.29 No.1, An extensive forest of *Ekebergia capensis* (Essenhout) forms an ideal habitat for numerous birds, insects and other small forms of life. **1984** [see *Cape mahogany* (CAPE sense 2 a)].

essenwood /ˈes(ə)nwʊd/ *n.* [Part. tr. Afk. (earlier S. Afr. Du.) *essenhout*.] ESSENHOUT. Also *attrib.*

1891 R. SMITH *Great Gold Lands* 179 Essen-wood, the South African ash (Eckebergia capensis). **1910** J. BUCHAN *Prester John* (1961) 134 The wood was now getting like that which clothed the sides of the Berg. There were tall timber trees – yellowwood, sneezewood, essenwood, stinkwood. **1965** P. BARAGWANATH *Brave Remain* 3 He made for the dark-leaved essenwood tree where he knew he would have dense shade, no matter how hot the sun became.

estate *n.* [Special senses of general Eng. *estate* a (usu. large) property on which a crop is cultivated; a vineyard.]

1. *comb.* **estate wine**, wine produced (and sometimes bottled) on a vineyard from the grapes grown there; but see also quot. 1993.

Since 1972 this designation has been restricted by law to those wines produced on vineyards legally recognized as 'estates' (see sense 2 below).

1967 W.A. DE KLERK *White Wines* 73 There are those who would claim that the only true estate wine is one that is produced, matured, bottled on the farm, and marketed from it. Some would even go further and say that only grapes grown on the estate itself should be used. **1972** *Govt Gaz.* Vol.84 No.3569, 9 If the indication 'estate wine' is intended to be used .. state whether the estate wine is to be .. produced, made and bottled on the estate or .. produced and made on the estate and bottled elsewhere. **1975** C.J.G. NIEHAUS in *Std Encycl. of Sn Afr.* XI. 462 Legislation has been amended and extended to provide for the production and sale of 'estate wines' as well as wines of origin. **1981** J. DOXAT *Indispensable Drinks Bk* 52 'Estate' wines are .. specifically designated on the neck label, as well as having to conform to certain rules. **1982** M. BEAZLEY *Hugh Johnson's Pocket Wine Bk* 171 *Estate wine*, A strictly controlled term applying only to some 60 registered estates making wines made of grapes grown on the same property. *c***1993** J. PLATTER *S. Afr. Wine Guide* 17 'Estate' wine can also be made by one grower drawing grapes from two or more separate farms, provided they enjoy comparable climates and soils – a rather elastic condition.

2. A registered vineyard producing (and sometimes bottling) wines made exclusively from grapes grown within its boundaries. Often *attrib.* Cf. *wine farm* (see WINE FARMER).

1972 *Act 62* in *Govt Gaz.* Vol.84 No.3551, 7 The Minister may for the purpose of the sale or export of any wine or spirits .. define any estate or area ... Any person desiring an estate or area to be defined .. shall apply therefor to the Wine and Spirit Board .., furnishing such particulars in connection with his application as may be required. **1975** C.J.G. NIEHAUS in *Std Encycl. of Sn Afr.* XI. 462 The estate producers have organised themselves into a society. **1982** [see sense 1]. **1988** D. HUGHES et al. *Complete Bk of S. Afr. Wine* 113 Together with this provision went a number of others regarding cellar equipment and procedures, which had to be up to a rigorous standard before a farm could be granted Estate status. The regulations did not cover bottling or distribution, which many Estate farmers prefer to leave in the hands of a large wholesaler. *Ibid.* 290 He consolidated the two farms and registered Weltevrede as an Estate with the Wine and Spirit Board during 1974. *c***1993** J. PLATTER *S. Afr. Wine Guide* 17 *Estate Concept*, Fewer than 100 of South Africa's 4 900 grape growers make wine on their own premises and fewer still actually bottle their wines on the property in the purist, *mis en bouteille au chateau* manner ... However, a handful of estate growers do match the complete and true idea of chateau or domaine bottling.

Ethiopian *adj.* and *n.* [Transf. use of the name given to the first church of this type, after Psalm 68 v.31 (see quot. 1989 at sense A).]

A. *adj.* Of or pertaining to those black churches which, towards the end of the 19th century, broke away from white-dominated churches and formed separatist churches in a spirit of black nationalism. See also ORDER OF ETHIOPIA.

The Ethiopian Church of South Africa was founded in 1892 as a breakaway from the Anglican and Methodist Churches. Some of its members were later absorbed into the American Methodist Episcopal Church (see AME) and the Order of Ethiopia, while others remained independent.

1903 F.B. BRIDGMAN in *Ilanga* 17 July 4 In the seven years since the movement became prominent it has gained a membership of about 25,000. Compared with the slow, laborious growth of Mission Churches .., this large number is a doubtful compliment to the Ethiopian type of Christianity. **1903** E. NUTTALL Private Circular. (Wesleyan Methodist Church of S. Afr.), Transfer of Members to or from A.M.E. Church and Ethiopian Associations ... Consideration was given to the question, raised by the Native Synods, as to the attitude we are to assume towards the various movements known as African Episcopal and Ethiopian. **1906** *Question of Colour* 253 The Ethiopian Movement is a remarkable one, and has gained a great hold upon the natives of South Africa. The members believe that they are descendants of the Ethiopians. **1915** J. HASTINGS *Encycl. of Relig. & Ethics* VIII. 736 *S. Africa* ... The racial factor is especially in evidence in the 'Ethiopian Movement', composed of groups of congregations who in 1892 formally seceded from their missionary connections. **1921** *S. Afr.* 2 Nov. 195 Greytown, Natal, has been agitated recently by the *Ethiopian* movement. **1923** G.H. NICHOLLS *Bayete!* 52 God has guided me in all I have done, and the result is the establishment of the Ethiopian Church under the banner bearing the words – 'Africa for the Africans'. **1948** B.G.M SUNDKLER *Bantu Prophets* 53 We shall distinguish between two main types of independent Bantu Churches. I propose to call them the 'Ethiopian' type and the 'Zionist' type. **1963** P. HINCHLIFF *Anglican Church* 207 The natural nationalism which resulted made them regret the fact that most of the Churches were 'white' and were governed by white officials. The Ethiopian movement .. has produced literally thousands of purely African splinter sects. **1980** D.B. COPLAN Urbanization of African Performing Arts. 111 Whites were quick to accuse the 'Ethiopian preachers' of anti-White racialism, subversion, and responsibility for the political unrest among Africans in Natal. **1988** G. WILLOUGHBY in *Inside S. Afr.* Dec. 33 My father was a priest of the indigenous Ethiopian church and from him I learnt to trust to my ancestors. **1988** SPIEGEL & BOONZAIER in Boonzaier & Sharp *S. Afr. Keywords* 52 The 'Ethiopian' churches began as a breakaway from the established mission churches; they have an all-black leadership, but retain the basic Christian teachings. **1989** *Reader's Digest Illust. Hist.* 285 With 20 followers he founded the Ethiopian Church – so called because he interpreted the biblical prophecy, 'that Ethiopia shall soon stretch out her hands unto God', as referring [to] Africans. **1990** *S. Afr. Panorama* Nov.-Dec. 4 Present-day examples of Ethiopian churches are the African Methodist Episcopal Church, the Presbyterian Church of Africa, the Zulu Congregational Church and the Bantu Methodist Church.

B. *n.* **a.** A member of an Ethiopian church. **b.** A church belonging to the Ethiopian movement.

1903 F.B. BRIDGMAN in *Ilanga* 17 July 4 What shall be the attitude of mission churches to the Ethiopian; Shall they fellowship with him? **1911** *Encycl. Brit.* XVIII. 593 Each bishop [in South Africa] now deals with the Ethiopians in his own diocese. **1923** G.H. NICHOLLS *Bayete!* 93 Behind them walked a long line of surpliced Ethiopians ... The Ethiopians took up their station standing in the rear of the line of chairs, and in front of the altar. **1948** B.G.M. SUNDKLER *Bantu Prophets* 53 As Ethiopians I classify such independent Bantu Churches as have (*a*) seceded from White Mission Churches chiefly on racial grounds, or (*b*) other Bantu Churches seceding from the Bantu leaders classified under (*a*). *Ibid.* 56 To both Ethiopians and Zionists the name of the Church has a special significance. It contains the charter of the Church. **1962** M. BRANDEL-SYRIER *Black Woman* 235 Not so anti-European as the Ethiopians. **1976** WEST & MORRIS *Abantu* 170 These churches are without exception under African control, with an all-African membership, and they can be divided into two categories: the 'Ethiopians' and the 'Zionists'.

Hence **Ethiopianism** *n.*, see quot. 1980, **Ethiopianist** *adj.* and *n.*

1903 F.B. BRIDGMAN in *Ilanga* 17 July 4 The influence of Ethiopianism, with its divisive anti-missionary spirit, .. [can] be viewed only with grave foreboding. **1906** *Daily Chron.* (U.K.) 13 Feb. 5 The rising in Natal is now officially declared .. to be the result of the teaching of Ethiopianism, namely 'South Africa for the Black races'. **1910** J. BUCHAN *Prester John* (1961) 131 It is what they call 'Ethiopianism', and American negroes are the chief apostles. **1923** G.H. NICHOLLS *Bayete!* 153, I believe his Ethiopianism is political. **1936** *Times Lit. Suppl.* (U.K.) 28 Mar. 252 So-called Ethiopianism appears to have been started in South Africa by various disgruntled native ministers of the Gospel. **1968** P. HINCHLIFF *Anglican Church* 93 Ethiopianism seemed to be political because it stood for a rejection of white guidance and control. **1978** T.R.H. DAVENPORT *S. Afr.: Mod. Hist.* 154 Ethiopianism .. in Natal and the O.R.C ... became a synonym for irresponsible black nationalism in official eyes. **1980** D.B. COPLAN *Urbanization of African Performing Arts.* 182 Ethiopianist ideas appealed strongly to urban workers ... In Natal Ethiopianist preachers were accused of fomenting rebellion ... Middle-class separatists, called 'Ethiopianists', were in general too intent upon cultural Westernization .. to create a strong church-based opposition movement. **1980** *Ibid.* 432 Ethiopianism, In South Africa, a separatist or independent African Christian movement based on an ideology of pan-African Christian unity and political and religious independence. **1986** P. MAYLAM *Hist. of Afr. People* 161 Another form of African opposition that cannot easily be analysed in class terms was Ethiopianism. African independent churches in South Africa date back to the 1880s when the Thembu Church was founded in the Transkei.

Eurafrican *adj.* and *n.* ?*Obs.* [Blend formed on Eng. *European* + *African.*]

A. *adj.* COLOURED *ppl adj.* sense *a*.

1922 S.G. MILLIN *Adam's Rest* II. 156 Frances no longer looked as if she might be a beautiful Spaniard or Italian. She was obviously Eurafrican. **1970** *Drum* Feb. 18 He did his early schooling at Newtown Primary from where he proceeded to the Eurafrican Training College in Vrededorp.

B. *n.* COLOURED *n.* sense *a*.

1927 W.M. MACMILLAN *Cape Colour Question* 288 All recent restrictive legislation, designed for the 'segregation' of the Natives, classes the 'Eurafrican' with the Europeans. **1934** C.P. SWART *Supplement to Pettman.* 50 *Eurafrican*, A half-caste, one of whose parents is European, the other African or native. **1951** H. DAVIES *Great S. Afr. Christians* 16 His segregation policy was conceived in the interests of Eurafricans and Africans.

European *n.* and *adj.* *Obsolescent.* [Special senses of general Eng. *European* (one) from Europe.]

The word changed gradually from the usual Eng. meaning; in some citations, esp. early ones, it is difficult to tell which sense is intended. The term 'white' has now almost completely displaced 'European' in *S. Afr. Eng.*

A. *n.* A white person; for a period, the official term used for a white person. Cf. NON-EUROPEAN *n.*

1696 J. OVINGTON *Voy. to Suratt* 293 Three and Thirty, Slaves, besides *Europeans*, are daily imply'd in looking after it [*sc.* the Company's garden]. **1731** [see HARDER]. **1731** G. MEDLEY tr. *P. Kolb's Present State of Cape of G.H.* II. 353 The White of the Eyes of Numbers of *Europeans* and *Negroes* at the Cape take, in that Season, a very fiery Red. **1790** W. PATERSON *Narr. of Four Journeys* 90 About eight in the evening we met three Caffres who were much surprised at our appearance, as we were certainly the first Europeans they had ever seen. **1820** W. SHAW *Diary.* 25 Dec., Alas in Graham's Town there is no Minister not even for the Europeans, and both classes are generally speaking sunk very low in drunkenness, lewdness, and other deadly sins. **1832** [see ADVOCATE]. **1847** J. BARROW *Reflect.* 209 The Hottentot considers the lion his most formidable enemy, and is quite certain that he will single him out to be devoured in preference to an European. **1855** [see DUTCH *adj.* sense 1]. **1871** J. McKAY *Reminisc.* 209 It was native against native — Fingoe against Kafir; while we, the lords of the colony — the Europeans — sat perched on the rocky crags above, looking down at the dexterity of both sides. **1900** *Grocott's Penny Mail* 31 Oct. 1 (*advt*) Wanted. An Experienced Housemaid. European preferred. **1911** L. COHEN *Reminisc. of Kimberley* 419 Most of the sufferers were Cape boys, but some of them were white enough to be Europeans, which perhaps they were. **1925** D. KIDD *Essential Kafir* 151 All search proved fruitless: no native would give information of a black man to the Europeans. **1941** *Bantu World* 15 Feb. 9 Benoni Magistrate's court on January 31 was crowded to the doors with Europeans, Asiatics, Coloureds and Bantu. **1949** C. BULLOCK *Rina* 9 She was Coloured; and .. she would not attempt to associate on an equality with a South African European. **1950** *S. Afr. Law Reports* IV. 200 In South Africa a person is a European or white person when he is such by appearance and habits, and he is not proved by descent not to be predominantly of European blood. **1952** *Drum* Aug. 11 An American visitor's first dose of the apartheid pill is the startling discovery that in this country an American can also be a European. **1959** L. LONGMORE *Dispossessed* 317 All white people in South Africa, whether or not born in Europe, are referred to as Europeans. **1960** J.J.L. SISSON *S. Afr. Judicial Dict.* 258 A European is a person who is white as a racial quality, and from a racial point of view, that is, who belongs to a white race; .. a non-European, on the other hand, is a person who is not white from a racial point of view and as a racial quality; that is, he does not belong to a white race. **1960** *Rand Daily Mail* in J. Crwys-Williams *S. Afr. Despatches* (1989) 325 Five of the six Europeans entombed are married men, and are all South Africans. The other is a young Hungarian. **1964** N. NAKASA in *Ibid.* 345, I don't see that there is any justification in calling me a non-European ... That is as silly as this business of South African Whites who insist that they are Europeans. **1980** D.B. COPLAN *Urbanization of African Performing Arts.* p.xi, The term 'European,' a synonym for White in South African usage, appears only rarely to avoid confusion between South African Whites and present or past native inhabitants of the continent of Europe. **1990** *Sunday Times* 18 Feb. 12 Mr Mandela .. refers to 'Europeans' and 'Africans', the terminology in use when he was arrested and began his exile in August 1962. But he corrects himself immediately. **1990** O. MUSI in *City Press* 17 June 9 There are still some hospital administrations .. who think there are citizens of this country who are called 'Europeans' ... They stress 'European staff only please'. **1990** G. SLOVO *Ties of Blood* 287 One of the multi-faceted signals of apartheid: 'Europeans only' it said — 'slegs vir blankes'. **1990** [see LARNEY *n.* sense 1].

B. *adj.* Denoting a white person; of, pertaining to, or used by white people. Cf. NON-EUROPEAN *adj.*

1731 G. MEDLEY tr. *P. Kolb's Present State of Cape of G.H.* II. 335 The *European* women at the *Cape* suffer but little in Travail ... Women born in *Europe*, and brought to Bed at the *Cape*, have altogether as happy a Time as the Women born in the Settlements. **1818** G. BARKER *Journal.* 20 Sept., I preached at Grahamstown. In the morning in English to the European soldiers .. & in the afternoon to the Hottentot soldiers in Dutch. **1833** *Graham's Town Jrnl* 21 Mar. 3 To secure the Subscribers against the losses to which Breeders are at present exposed, from the recklessness of colored servants, it is proposed that .. none but European Shepherds will be employed by the Association. **1857** F.W. REITZ in *Cape Monthly Mag.* II. Oct. 194 Of the white or European population .. I think it would be possible to get perfectly accurate and reliable returns. **1882** *Tvl Advertiser* 14 Jan. 1 It shall be our endeavour to as far as possible abate the prejudices now existing between the European races. **1897** F.R. STATHAM *S. Afr. as It Is* 16 The doctrine was inculcated that, unless the European populations of South Africa could be bound together by some form of federated government, they were in danger of being obliterated by a general and combined rising of natives. **1936** R.J.M. GOOLD-ADAMS *S. Afr. To-Day & To-Morrow* 32 The often forgotten division of the black races into those who live in their own villages among their own people, .. and those, the other half, who live in European cities or on European farms. **1947** *Argus* in J. Crwys-Williams *S. Afr. Despatches* (1989) 291 The throng in Adderley-street .. represented all sections of South Africa's European and non-European community. **1952** B. DAVIDSON *Report on Sn Afr.* 59 This was my first glimpse of a Native Reserve. The good land round Zastron is of course 'European'. **1956** N. GORDIMER in D. Wright *S. Afr. Stories* (1960) 74, I can't remember, y'know, about buses. I keep getting put off European buses. **1963** L.F. FREED *Crime in S. Afr.* 73 The prevalence of crime in the European residential area of Johannesburg may .. be studied .. with reference to its distribution. **1985** *Cape Times* 7 Jan. (Jobfinder) 13 (*advt*) Accounts Clerk. Mature European lady, 35 to 45, with debtors, cash book, general office experience. **1990** R. GOOL *Cape Town Coolie* 63 The Smuts government .. made Indians owning property in European areas a bad thing — very, very bad. **1990** [see Musi quot. at sense A].

evening flower *n. phr.* [tr. S. Afr. Du. *avondbloem* (later Afk. *aandblom*) evening flower.] AANDBLOM.

[**1731** G. MEDLEY tr. *P. Kolb's Present State of Cape of G.H.* II. 238 The seven last Sorts [*sc. Geranium Africanum spp.*] afford, in the Night, a fragrant Smell ... The Cape-*Europeans* call all the Sorts Night-Flowers.] **1822, 1847** [see AANDBLOM]. **1855** E. RUTHERFORD in J. Murray *In Mid-Victorian Cape Town* (1953) 105 Those pretty little deep blue flowers, the yellow stars (Hypoxis), another blue flower like a forget me not, Evening flowers, night-scented Geraniums. **1925** M.R. BOYD in F.C. Slater *Centenary Bk of S. Afr. Verse* 24 The evening flower exhales its sweet content and offers incense on the quiet air. **1964** [see AANDBLOM]. **1970** M.R. LEVYNS in *Std Encycl. of Sn Afr.* I. 1 The name aandblom-(metjie) — 'evening flower' — applies to most species of *Hesperantha* (family *Iridaceae*), but these two are most commonly so called. **1993** *Programme, Rhodes University Chamber Choir, Aandblom is 'n wit blom* ... Evening flower is a white flower.

everlasting *n.* [Eng. *everlasting* long-lasting, as applied to plants; here transf. to local species.] In full **everlasting flower**: any of several species of *Helichrysum* and *Helipterum* (family Asteraceae), bearing highly-coloured papery blooms which retain their shape and colour for a considerable time; one of these flowers; *seven year(s') bloem*, see SEVEN YEAR; SEWEJAARTJIE.

Occas. also with distinguishing epithet, as **Cape -**, **pink -**, **strawberry -**, **white everlasting**, etc. Freq. in *pl.*, as **everlastings**.

[**1731** G. MEDLEY tr. *P. Kolb's Present State of Cape of G.H.* 232 Elichrysum Africanum ... Broad leaf'd stinking African Eternal flower, with yellow heads.] **1784** J. COOK *Voy. of Disc.* (1790) II. 391 The everlasting-flower .. when it is plucked it cannot be perceived to fade. **1797** LADY A. BARNARD *S. Afr. Century Ago* (1910) 120 On t'other side of the mountain there grew a profusion of what are called everlasting flowers ... The white remain for ever the same; the red ones are the most curious, being as bright as if made by red foils. **1804** R. PERCIVAL *Acct of Cape of G.H.* 146 The everlasting flower .. derives its name from appearing as fresh .. after being seven years pulled as the day when it was first torn from the stalk ... When first plucked it feels like an artificial flower of painted paper. **1815** A. PLUMPTRE tr. *H. Lichtenstein's Trav. in Sn Afr.* II. 121 While the English name, *everlastings*, and the French, *immortelles*, refer to the imperishable nature of their beauty, we Germans are pleased to call them *paper-flowers*, or *straw flowers*; to designate, in truly prosaic terms, the dryness which prevents their fading. **1847** J. BARROW *Reflect.* 170 Among the herbaceous plants, common to the colony, were the *xeranthemum* and *gnaphalium*, to the flowers of which the Dutch have given the name of *seben-yaars' bloom* — seven years' flowers, a duration which in England we have extended to *everlastings*. **1852** E. RUTHERFOORD in J. Murray *Young Mrs Murray* (1954) 25, I gathered large bunches of everlastings and tied them to the end of Mr Newton's gun. **1857** [see SEVEN YEAR]. **1861** 'A LADY' *Life at Cape* (1963) 32, I have never seen anything to equal the metallic lustre of the 'everlasting' flowers, which are hawked about in great bunches by the broom-cutters for a few pence. **1893** *Cape Illust. Mag.* Feb. 221 Beautiful masses of *everlastings* and heath. **1906** B. STONEMAN *Plants & their Ways* 111 A *capitulum* or flower head has a shortened axis and sessile flowers, as in the Everlasting family and *Protea*. **1907** T.R. SIM *Forests & Forest Flora* 247 *Helichrysum senecioideae*, .. Involucre sometimes shorter than the florets, sometimes longer, white, rosy brown or yellow, and then forming the ornamental and persistent 'flowers' popularly known as *Everlastings*. *c***1911** S. PLAYNE *Cape Col.* 49 'Everlasting flowers,' numerous in species, in some instances exhibit pure white bracts, but some with tinted bracts grow in rich profusion. **1917** R. MARLOTH *Common Names* 26 *Everlasting*, The commercial kind for export is *Helichrysum vestitum*. Several others often employed for floral ornaments. **1945**, **1949** [see SEWEJAARTJIE]. **1951** A. GORDON-BROWN *Yr Bk & Guide to Sn Afr.* 329 The exports of *Everlasting Flowers* normally amount to a few hundred pounds a year. **1960** G. LISTER *Reminisc.* 68 He had picked a remarkable everlasting flower which he brought home to me and which I still keep. It has the globe shape of the Swellendam 'strawberry' everlasting, but it is white with brown spots. **1971** *Cape Times* 15 May (Weekend Mag.) 5 Daniel Carse, of Stanford .. made a fortune exporting everlasting flowers to Germany where they were used for funerals. **1986** [see SEWEJAARTJIE]. **1987** *Flying Springbok* Jan. 31 Already the world-famous ericas and Cape everlastings are flowering. **1988** M. BRANCH *Explore Cape Flora* 17 The pink everlasting is a perennial with tiny leaves and a woody stem. The papery petals dry without losing their colour. **1989** J. HOBBS *Thoughts in Makeshift Mortuary* 251 A small handful of pale pink everlastings, the straw flowers that star the mountain grass in summer. **1990** *Weekend Argus* 10 Feb. 4 On the way we would pass a Malay kramat where there were always vases of everlastings, stone jars containing strange concoctions [etc.].

evertrever var. EWWATREWWA.

everything will come right see COME sense 1.

‖**ewe** /ˈeːwe, eˈweː/ *adv.* Also **ehwe**, **eweh**. [Xhosa.] Among Xhosa-speakers: 'Yes'.

a. An affirmative response to a question or statement; an affirmative exclamation.

1894 E. GLANVILLE *Fair Colonist* 89 'Do you wish to see me?' asked the first lady, inquiringly. 'Eweh, inkosikasi,' replied the man respectfully, in deep tones. **1913** J.J. DOKE *Secret City* 29 'Lumkile knows his kraal. He can find his way from hut to hut in the dark.' 'Ewe, Inkosana,' he answered. *a***1931** S. BLACK in S. Gray *Three Plays* (1984) 141 Abraham: And so the girl gets the farm? Jeremiah: Ewe, Miss Helena get the farm. **1937** C. BIRKBY *Zulu Journey* 232 'Ehwe, inkosi,' said the old man. 'In this krantz there was once a cave filled with ivory. It was the treasure-house of the Bushmen.' **1965** J. BENNETT *Hawk Alone* 131 'Have you got a knife?' Alias nodded ... 'Ewe, Baas Gord.' **1978** A.P. BRINK *Rumours of Rain* 203 Struggling to scrape together individual words from the bit of Xhosa I'd picked up through the years, I said: 'Is everything still all right on the farm?' 'Ewe.' **1981** *Job Mava* (Ikwezi Players) in *Staffrider* Dec. 29 Zizamele: Am I right? Mabandla: Ewe! The man who says all life is shit needs a good wash.

b. A greeting, or, more commonly, a response to a greeting.

1963 A.M. LOUW *20 Days* 118 'It is good day to you, father,' said Enog politely. 'Ewe,' said the old man laconically. **1987** M. POLAND *Train to Doringbult* 95 Petrus stopped and raised a hand in greeting. 'Ewe', he said. 'Ewe', replied the woman cautiously.

So **ewe** *n.*, an utterance of the word 'ewe'.

1890 *Cape Law Jrnl* VII. 233 According to our Gcaleka custom I assented to each sentence with a loud 'Ewe!' as we always do. No Gcaleka can go on talking to another person unless he receives some reply.

ewwatrewwa /ˈevəˈtrevə/ *n.* Also **evertrever**, **ewa-trewa**. [Etym. unkn., perh. onomatopoeic (see quot. 1966).] The terrestrial orchid *Satyrium coriifolium* of the Orchidaceae, with red to orange-red flowers, found in the western and eastern Cape.

1913 H. TUCKER *Our Beautiful Peninsula* 92 The many-tinted evertrevers, like fairy aloes, fringe the pine-woods. **1917** R. MARLOTH *Common Names* 26 *Ewa-trewa*, (pron: evertrevor). *Satyrium coriifolium*. Name? Perhaps from 'ou'ma-Trewa', as in use at Hermanus. **1950** M.M. KIDD *Wild Flowers* 172 *Satyrium coriifolium*. Orchidaceae. *Ewwatrewwa, Ouma-trewwa* .. occasional on flats and low mountain slopes .. July-Oct. **1966** C.A. SMITH *Common Names* 212 *Ewwa-trewwa*, A robust, tall-growing terrestrial orchid ... The vernacular name appears to be onomatopoeic and is derived from the sound produced when the stems are rubbed up against one another. The generic name is said to be derived from the two spurs which are suggestive of the horns of a satyr. **1967** *Some Protected Wild Flowers* (Cape Prov. Admin.) 194 *Ewwa Trewwa*, Spring .. Western, South-western and Eastern Cape.

excuse-me *n. Derog. slang.* Also **'scuse-me**, **scuse-me**. Pl. **-s**, **ooscuse-me**, **bo-excuse-me**. [See quot. 1982. The pl. forms *ooscuse-me* and *bo-excuse-me* are formed by the addition of the Xhosa pl. prefix *oo-* and the Sotho pl. prefix *bo-* (see BO-), respectively.] In the townships, a term of contempt for an educated person of the middle class. Also *attrib.* Cf. SITUATION.

1963 WILSON & MAFEJE *Langa* 15 The urbanized whose homes are in town ... 'Decent people', some of whom form an educated middle class — the ooscuse-me — and others the respectable lower class. *Ibid.* 26 The educated people are referred to by others, somewhat derogatorily, as *ooscuse-me*, and accused of being aloof and conceited ... *Ooscuse-me* include those in professional jobs — teachers, lawyers, doctors, ministers of religion, nurses, secretaries — as well as university students and others. **1977** J. SIKAKANE *Window on Soweto* 9 The ghetto dwellers generally refer to Dube Township as .. the place of 'excuse me's' because the African intelligentsia residing there prefer speaking English. **1979** S. SILLIE *Informant* Ooscuse-me used to include professional men .. teachers, clerks, lawyers, nurses etc. but is no longer like that because some people with a low standard of education who live decent lives, dress respectably and are gentle and polite in their manner are also called scuse-me. **1979** *Daily Dispatch* 12 Oct. (Indaba) 7 Those women who thought I was a 'scuse-me can now freely offer me their wine — I shall taste it. **1980** S. SEPAMLA in M. Mutloatse *Forced Landing* 83 In the backyards '*ugologo*', the drinking of kaffir-beer ... From the front door the excuse-me-people play music called jazz ... That was Sophiatown. **1982** M. MZAMANE *Children of Soweto* 35, I don't know why he should venerate teachers so much. Just because they wear ties and speak English ... I've no time at all for these excuse-me's. *Ibid.* 153 They were forever trying to situate themselves outside everyone else's social orbit; other people called them *Bo-Excuse-me* because they were always putting on dainty manners.

exit permit *n. phr.* [Special sense of general Eng.] A travel document granted to one whose passport has been withdrawn for political reasons, permitting departure from South Africa but denying the right to return.

1968 J. MAYET in *Drum* Sept. 8 Roughly thirty of my friends .. were forced to leave on exit permits, thus being deprived of the right to come back to the land of their birth and enjoy the kinship of their loved ones. **1969** A. PATON *Kontakion* 135 When his job was done, he was given an exit permit, a document which allows one to leave but never to return. **1970** *Survey of Race Rel.* (S.A.I.R.R.) 45 According to the Minister of the Interior, 69 'exit' (permanent departure) permits were issued in 1968, to 16 whites, 11 Coloured, 9 Asians, and 33 Africans. **1970** *Daily News* 10 June, Catherine .. will leave on an exit permit because the authorities have refused to renew her passport. **1988** E. ANDERSON in *Frontline* May 12 You can have an exit permit to somewhere far away — we suggest England — and you needn't come back. Ever. **1989** J. HOBBS *Thoughts in Makeshift Mortuary* 163 If I leave .. I'll have to go on an exit permit ... They've withdrawn my passport.

exkes var. EKSKUUS.

extension *n.* [Special sense of general Eng. *extension* enlargement in scope or operation.] Education and assistance in the agricultural sector. Usu. *attrib.*, or in Special Comb., as **extension officer**, an employee of the Department of Agricultural Technical Services who is retained to advise and assist farmers; cf. AGRICULTURAL DEMONSTRATOR; **extension services**, **-work**, the activities of such officers.

1918 *Off. Yrbk of Union 1910–16* (Union Office of Census & Statistics) 410 Extension Work. Considerable progress has been made in developing this class of work, and the extension lecturers have been well received by the farming community. **1937** *Handbk for Farmers* (Dept of Agric. & Forestry) 1126 The Extension Service. The extension officers serve the rural population. Each officer has one or more districts under his control, and his work consists in advising and assisting the farmers therein ... He addresses farmers' meetings on matters agricultural; assists in promoting farmers' organizations; carries out co-operative experiments and demonstrations in collaboration with farmers .. and, generally, assists in giving effect to Government schemes for the furtherance of farming etc. **1970** C. VAN H. DU PLESSIS in *Std Encycl. of Sn Afr.* I. 242 Research in the several faculties of agriculture is co-ordinated by the Department of Agricultural Technical Services. Graduates of these faculties are of great value to agriculture as research workers, extension officers, [etc.]. **1981** *E. Prov. Herald* 9 Apr. 3 In an interview yesterday from Queenstown, the chief extension officer for the central region of the Eastern Cape .. said veld in the area .. had responded well to recent rains.

eye *n.* [Obs. in Brit. Eng.: prob. retained in S. Afr. Eng. through the influence of Du. and subsequently Afk. *oog*, in this sense.] The source of a spring or river. See also FOUNTAIN.

1799 W. SOMERVILLE *Narr. of E. Cape Frontier* (1979) 43 In the Eye of the fountain a substance of metallic appearance is found resembling the ore of Lead. **1838**

J.E. Alexander *Exped. into Int.* I. 159 The water continually bubbled up from two or three 'eyes' and the heat was of the agreeable temperature for bathing of 103°. **1857** D. Livingstone *Missionary Trav.* 111 A hollow, which anciently must have been the eye of the fountain, but is now filled up with soft tufa. **1871** J. Mackenzie *Ten Yrs* (1971) 140 There are three separate wells or 'eyes' to this fountain. **1882** J. Nixon *Among Boers* 250 The so-called eye was a .. series of springs in a depression from which bubbled a clear, beautifully limpid water. **1886** G.A. Farini *Through Kalahari Desert* 61 Oh, that is the eye of the *fontein*, the place where the water from the spring bursts out! **1893** 'Africanus' in *Cape Illust. Mag.* July 416 The eye of the fountain is at the foot of a peak. **1933** W. Macdonald *Romance of Golden Rand* 124 The few isolated habitations of the .. Voortrekkers, each situated at the fountainheads, or '*eyes*', of the numerous sparkling streams which flowed north and south from the Rand. **1944** C. Rogers in *S. Afr. Geog. Jrnl* XXVI. 30 A number of 'eyes' or springs, south of the Pretoria Series .. form the sources of the Groot Marico River. **1952** L.G. Green *Lords of Last Frontier* 49 Only twenty-six miles away is Kaoko Otavi, the largest single 'eye' in the Kaokoveld, a magnificent spring with a huge pool below. **1963** S.H. Skaife *Naturalist Remembers* 109 All I had to do was open up the 'eye' of the spring and lead the crystal-clear water down to the house and garden by gravity. **1979** *S. Afr. Panorama* Aug. 25 A huge glass-roofed pool is situated above the 'eye' or source of the main healing spring which has a daily flow of 2 million gallons. **1985** J. Mitchell *Church Ablaze* 135 Sheets of iron covered this fountain eye to prevent the cattle trampling the mud and closing the eye. **1988** M.M. Hacksley tr. E. Van Heerden's *Ancestral Voices* 180 The Eye was bubbling up full of clear water.

eyeland var. ELAND.

eyerfreter, -vreter varr. EIERVRETER.

eyland var. ELAND.

eysterhout var. YZER HOUT.

ezel var. ESEL.

F

faatje, fachey varr. VAATJIE.

faction n. [Specific uses of general Eng. *faction* (derog.) a party or group having selfish aims, or using unscrupulous methods.]

Use of this term is now seen by many as simplistic or misleading, in that it attributes violence primarily to 'tribal' divisions rather than to social conditions such as poverty or urbanization (see quots 1986 and 1988). Cf. *black-on-black* (see BLACK n. sense 1 d).

A group or clan of (esp. rural) black people engaged in warfare with another group, often over a considerable period of time:
a. Almost invariably *attrib.*; esp. in the n. phrr. *faction fight* and *faction fighter*, and the vbl n. phr. *faction fighting*.

'Faction' and 'faction fight' have been used also of the conflict in Ireland.

1897 *E. Prov. Herald* 5 Mar., Four Kafir labourers, on the railway, were found guilty of causing the death of Scholtz Jacoba, in a faction fight at Graaff-Reinet. 1903 [see AMALAITA]. 1905 *Native Tribes of Tvl* 124 These orgies .. are not infrequently the cause of faction-fights between the circumcised and the uncircumcised portions of a tribe. 1908 D. BLACKBURN *Leaven* (1991) 29 His veritable *bête noire*, the sheep-stealing, faction-fight-provoking, drunken old representative of a once mighty line of warriors. 1913 V.R. MARKHAM *S. Afr. Scene* 52 Fierce faction fights .. break out from time to time in the compound. 1926 *E. Prov. Herald* 5 Jan. 9 Fatal faction fight on Rand. Four natives killed. 1930 S.T. PLAATJE *Mhudi* (1975) 93 A faction fight broke out .. between a number of young men of the rival teams. c1948 H. TRACEY *Lalela Zulu* p.viii, Faction fighting is not 'warfare' as we know it, but is to the Zulu a kind of national sport. 1963 B. MODISANE *Blame Me on Hist.* (1986) 105 At the model townships of Daveyton, Dube and Meadowlands .. Zulu impis clashed with Basuto factions in the bloodiest faction fights in South African history since the Tshaka wars. 1971 *Post* 22 Aug., Chris Molife is an enigmatic Zulu, having come down into Zululand after the so-called faction wars. 1971 *Daily Dispatch* 10 Sept., Police have made 63 arrests in a cleanup of the Mqanduli Kwaaiman area — the Transkei 'faction fight belt'. 1973 *E. Prov. Herald* 31 May 1 Police were forced to open fire .. during the last of a series of faction kraal-to-kraal raids. 1974 *Daily Dispatch* 29 May 2, 15 arrested for faction killing ... Four men were killed during a beer-drink when 30 members of one faction started fighting. 1976 R.L. PETENI *Hill of Fools* 78 The only occasion for contact between Hlubi boys and Thembu boys was a faction fight. a1977 [see RUSSIAN n. sense 1]. 1981 *Sunday Times* 25 Oct. 24 The homestead is in the heart of the faction-fighting area. 1982 *Pace* Feb. 150 Zulu men who had come from Msinga and elsewhere to form factions. 1982 *Sunday Times* 28 Nov. (Mag. Sect.) 16 In one room one might find a preacher, a drunkard and a faction fighter. When one prays, the other drinks 'mbamba' (skokiaan) and the other one fixes his weapon for slaughter. 1983 *City Press* 11 Sept. 3 Police fought a fierce gun battle .. following .. what appeared to be a faction feud between migrants from Msinga ... The shooting is a sequel to the Msinga faction fights. 1983 *Sowetan* 12 Sept. 2 Police are working on a new strategy to curb the rising number of 'faction' killings at Soweto's hostels .. after the killing of a 'faction' gunman who earlier shot two people. 1986 H. PRENDINI in *Style* July 65 A storm of dissent interrupts him. 'That's a fallacy, the tribal hatred.' 'Those faction fights take place because they're crammed like rats into those mine hostels.' 1988 P. SKALNIK in Boonzaier & Sharp *S. Afr. Keywords* 68 The general public in South Africa .. appear to assume that if virtually any outbreak of violence is labelled a 'tribal' or 'faction' fight, there is no need to seek for further explanation in contemporary circumstances. 1988 [see *black-on-black* (BLACK n. sense 1 d)]. 1993 *Daily News* 5 Jan. 4 Two men were killed in a faction fight involving members of two families in the Mid-Illovo district of the Natal midlands. 1993 *Natal Witness* 13 Apr. 2 Faction fighting broke out between the Sokhela and Mbatha tribes at Ngqongeni in the Msinga district.

b. ?nonce. A faction fight.

1979 M. MATSHOBA *Call Me Not a Man* 95 There have been stabbings, tragic 'factions', *inkunzi* (muggings) and rape. *Ibid.* 196 He had lived through the 'seventy-six hostel-location 'factions'.

Hence **factional** *adj.*

1986 *Sunday Times* 21 Dec. (Extra) 3 Men, women and children .. fled from their blazing shacks during the bitter factional fighting in the area in June this year.

fad(d)ock var. VADOEK.

Faderland var. VADERLAND.

fadje var. VAATJIE.

fafeh, fa-fi varr. FAH-FEE.

fagie var. VAATJIE.

fah-fee /ˈfɑːˈfiː/ n. Also fafeh, fa-fi, fah-fhee, and with initial capital(s). [Unkn., perh. Chinese.] An illegal but widely-played gambling game taking the form of a lottery with thirty-six numbers, the winning number being selected in advance by the banker and revealed to the bet-collector in exchange for the stakes collected and a list of the bets placed. Also *attrib.* See also DOH-DIE, PULL.

Fah-fee was apparently introduced by Chinese immigrants. The banker (usu. a person of Chinese descent) employs runners to collect bets. Superstition, dreams, and symbolism play important roles in the game, each number having a name, a symbol, and a part of the body associated with it.

1909 *Rand Daily Mail* 2 Oct. 7 'Fah Fee' is a game of chance beloved by 'the heathen Chinese' and has rapidly become an absorbing passion among the coloured servants, male and female, of the town [*sc.* Kimberley]. 1938 *Star* 3 May 9 Joseph Mareletsi, a Msutu labourer, and Lai Szi, a Chinese housewife pleaded guilty .. to having assisted in the management of a fah-fee lottery. 1946 *Cape Times* in E. Partridge *Dict. of Underworld* (1950) 589 Made a bit of money out of being a runner (contact man for a fah-fee game). 1956 L. LONGMORE in *S. Afr. Jrnl of Science* Vol.52 No.12, 275 Although Fah-Fee is illegal the Chinese bankers manage to get into the Townships .. each day ... They leave their cars parked some distance from the 'pulling house' in order to avoid arrest. 1963 B. MODISANE *Blame Me on Hist.* (1986) 49, I jumped into a bus .. a few yards from Nobeni's shebeen, across the street from the shop which was a front for Sophiatown's biggest Fah Fee, numbers game, pool. 1965 [see OOMPIE sense 2 a]. 1974 A.P. BRINK *Looking on Darkness* 120 Every few minutes a new visitor would arrive .. to deliver or fetch contraband and in small parcels, .. to collect fafeh bets, to borrow money without security, or simply to chat. 1977 *Sunday Times* 27 Mar. 19 It's impossible even to guess the number of Africans who regularly place bets with the fahfee runners, but in Soweto alone it must run into tens of thousands. 1977 [see *pull* n. at PULL v.]. 1979 [see FAT-KOEK]. 1980 C. HOPE *A Separate Development* (1983) 98 Look, the Chinaman's collecting the *fahfee* money. Let me take a ticket for you ... Tell me your dream and they'll give you a number. 1982 *Grocott's Mail* 30 Apr. 12 Bets are taken by 'Runners' — blacks who go around taking bets from a circle of clients whom they usually know personally ... Dreams and superstitions play an important role in Fah Fee. Each number is represented by a symbol or image and it is believed that dreams can foretell the winning numbers. 1987 *New Nation* 3 Dec. 13 To stay alive many women turned to illegal .. ways of making money. Some bet their pennies in the gambling game of fah-fee. 1993 *E. Prov. Herald* 23 Apr. 7 Fah-fee could have an annual turnover of R3bn to R5bn, the Howard Commission Report states ... The evidence supported the conclusion that Fah-fee probably attracted as much money as horse-racing.

fahl var. VAAL.

Fairest Cape n. phr. Also **fairest Cape**. [fr. an early description (see quot. 1589) often attributed to Sir Francis Drake, but probably written by someone accompanying Drake on his voyage around the world.] The Cape peninsula; Cape Town and its environs. See also CAPE.

[1589 in W.S.W. Vaux *World Encompassed by Sir Francis Drake* (1854) 251 From *Jaua Maior* we sailed for the cape of *Good Hope* ... This Cape is a most stately thing, and the fairest Cape we saw in the whole circumference of the earth, and we passed by it the 18. of June [1580].] 1987 *Cape Times* 28 Dec. 9 Please don't leave your empty, broken bottles on beaches — or anywhere else in scenic and picnic spots in our Fairest Cape. 1989 S. BILAC in *Personality* 10 Apr. 30 (caption) In 'the Fairest Cape' the CP holds no mandate over Pearly Beach — but the segregation signs still stand. 1991 *Weekend Post* 5 Jan. 7 Visiting Transvaal windsurfers .. say they have experienced little kindness and much abuse from the citizens of the fairest Cape. 1992 [see GARDEN sense 2]. 1994 *Weekly Mail & Guardian* 13 May 13 Fair fight for fairest Cape.

FAK /ef ɑː ˈkɑː/ n. Also **F.A.K.** [Initial letters of Afk. *Federasie van Afrikaanse Kultuurvereniginge*, 'Federation of Afrikaans Cultural Associations'.] An organisation established in 1929 by the Broederbond to guide and promote Afrikaans cultural activities. Also *attrib.* See also BROEDERBOND sense 1.

1948 *Press Digest* No.5, 37 F.A.K. to request legislation preventing buying up of farms by big capital. **1949** *Blueprint for Blackout* (Educ. League) 28 F.A.K.: *Federasie van Afrikaanse Kulturverenigings*: A very powerful body, with an influence in every Afrikaans social and cultural society, throughout the country; strongly Nationalist in sentiment. **1973** *Weekend Argus* 24 Feb. 7 Party-political indoctrination in schools by Sabra, the Rapportryers, the F.A.K. (Federasie van Afrikaanse Kultuurverenigings) and by slanted syllabi. **1979** *Scope* 20 July 32 The FAK, we discovered in due course, is the front organisation that co-ordinates the many organisations that are trying to keep the Afrikaners together. **1984** R. DAVIES et al. *Struggle for S. Afr.* 270 The leading and acknowledged 'public arm' of the secret *Afrikaner Broederbond* .., the FAK seeks to provide 'direction' and 'central guidance' to all Afrikaans cultural organisations. **1990** *Sunday Times* 3 June 4 They had microphones, backing musicians and shiny, shiny smiles. But the TV age has caught up with the FAK.

fall *v. intrans.* [Scot. and N.-country Eng., becoming increasingly common in colloq. Brit. usage. Prob. formed by analogy with *fall ill*; or perh. originating in religious notions of sexuality and the fall (cf. *fallen woman*).] Usu. in the phr. ***to fall pregnant***. To conceive a child, to become pregnant.

In S. Afr. Eng., the standard expression for many.

1959 L. LONGMORE *Dispossessed* 88 A number of my informants stated that girls fear sexual intercourse only because they are afraid of falling pregnant. **1972** *Evening Post* 4 Nov. 8 I'd hoped to fall for a baby as soon as we got married, but it's over six months now. **1973** *Drum* 22 Jan. 33 Your girlfriend is very young to start a sex life. She may be afraid of falling pregnant. **1977** *Sunday Times* 6 Nov. (Extra) 7 We have been in love since 1974. Last year when I was doing form II he paid lobola for me, but unfortunately during the December School Vacations I fell pregnant. **1980** C. HERMER *Diary of Maria Tholo* 1 In order to make her parents consent to the marriage she fell pregnant. **1987** *Fair Lady* 18 Feb. 146 Paulina had fallen pregnant with her fifth child and had gone home to have it. **1989** J. HOBBS *Thoughts in Makeshift Mortuary* 9 What do you call getting into a car with a boy and falling pregnant at eighteen, then? An act of genius? **1992** *Pace* Sept. 53 Sometimes, girls will even fall pregnant because they think this will make the boys marry them.

family *n. noncount.* [Calque formed on Afk. *familie* kin.] Used without an article or a pronoun: kinsfolk; blood relatives beyond the nuclear family. Also *attrib.*, and *fig.*

'Married-on family' (quot. 1990) is calqued on Afk. *aangetroude familie* ('in-laws').

1970 *Post* 15 Mar. 7 Now Britain and Rhodesia aren't even 'family' since the republic was declared, the chances are they never again will be. **1975** Z. Roos in *Darling* 1 Oct., Make sure your .. wine comes from some .. noble estate — preferably one run by your uncle. If you haven't got family in the trade try [brand X] or [Y]. **1975** *Friend* 2 Apr. 1 A 15-year-old White Bloemfontein schoolgirl was attacked .. at the weekend while on her way to visit family in West End. **1978** A. ELLIOTT *Sons of Zulu* 70 All the little girls act as nursemaids and help any mother, whether family or not, who has her hands full. **1984** *Sunday Times* 4 Mar. 5 She was visiting family in England. **1986** T. LURIE in *Eng. Alive '86* 52 Family had whispered of a nervous disease and cowardly shrunk from facing any responsibility or attachment. **1988** *You* 21 Jan. 102 South Africans are known for their aversion to staying in hotels — especially when they have family they can land themselves on. **1989** K. SUTTON in *E. Prov. Herald* 25 Feb. 4 We will not have foreigners criticising our Afrikaners — that's our job, we 'English' .. they're family. **1990** M. BODDY-EVANS *Informant, London* In March we spent a night on a married-on family farm in the Karoo. **1994** *Weekend Post* 22 Oct. 4 Nonki J— .. was with family who were visiting friends in First Avenue.

Family Day *n. phr.* The name of a public holiday.

1. *obs.* The second Monday in July. Also *attrib.*

Formerly known as the *Queen's Birthday*, this holiday was re-named in 1961 after the establishment of the Republic of South Africa. It was abolished altogether as a holiday in 1973.

1961 *Act 68* in *Stat. of Rep. of S. Afr.* 1046 The First Schedule to the principal Act is hereby amended by the substitution for the words 'Union Day' of the words 'Republic Day' and for the words 'Queen's Birthday' of the words 'Family Day'. **1962** D. MARAIS *I Got a Licence, (caption)* A great institution this Family Day holiday — a man can get away from the wife and kids for a while. **1964** A. GORDON-BROWN *Yr Bk & Guide to Sn Afr. 1965* 51 Public Holidays ... Family Day (2nd Mon. in July). **1973** *Govt Gaz.* Vol.95 No.3892, 2 The first Schedule to the Public Holidays Act, 1952, is hereby amended — (*a*) by the deletion of .. the words 'Family Day (second Monday in July)'.

2. After 1980: a name given to Easter Monday.

1980 *Govt Gaz.* Vol.180 No.7060, 3 The First Schedule to the principal Act is hereby amended - .. (*b*) by the substitution for the words 'Easter Monday' of the words 'Family Day (the Monday after Easter Sunday)'. **1981** *Sunday Times* 19 Apr. (Mag. Sect.) 1 Tomorrow is Family Day — a new name for what used to be called Easter Monday. **1982** *Registrar's Circular* (Rhodes Univ.) 18 Feb., This year the University will be closed from Good Friday .. to Family Day .. but mail will be available on Saturday. **1988** *E. Prov. Herald* 31 Mar. 1 The paper will be published on both public holidays next week — Family Day on Monday and Founders' Day on Wednesday.

famo /ˈfɑːmɔ/ *n.* Also with initial capital. [S. Sotho term for an indecent dance, fr. *famola* to dilate the nostrils, or (secondarily), to expose the (female) genitalia.] Among Sothos (esp. mine-workers) in townships on the Reef:

1. An erotic dance in which the body is exposed. Also *attrib.*

At first associated with the Russian gang, see RUSSIAN sense 1.

1952 *Drum* May 37 A type of dance called 'Famo,' in which the women dance gracefully, showing parts of their body. **1963** L.F. FREED *Crime in S. Afr.* 115 The mine workers, who are part of the gang, are easily tantalised by a type of dance called 'Famo', in which the woman dances with a seductive voluptuousness, revealing the more intimate parts of her body. *a***1968** D.C. THEMBA in E. Patel *World of Can Themba* (1985) 133 That is Famo, the famous sex dance of the Russians, Basotho gangsters on the Reef. **1980** D.B. COPLAN Urbanization of African Performing Arts. 214 According to Mpahlele and numerous other eyewitnesses, the *famo* (from *ho-re-famo*, to open nostrils; to raise garments, displaying the genitals) .. was a kind of striptease. Women made suggestive shaking and thrusting movements with their shoulders, hips and bosoms while lifting their flared skirts ... The dancers wore no underwear but instead 'had painted rings round the whole area of their sex, a ring they called "stoplight"'. **1990** M. MELAMU in *Lynx* 276 A kind of lewd sex dance .. was prevalent in areas of the Rand where there was a heavy concentration of Basotho. It was known as 'famo'. [**1991** E. LESORO *Informant, Grahamstown* Famo is an indecent game played very seriously by miners and their women ... The men and women line up, naked, and admire each other's private parts.]

2. A wild drinking- and dancing-party culminating in a sexual orgy. Also *attrib.*

1977 P.C. VENTER *Soweto* 94 A Famo usually ends in a chaos of coupling, with bodies making love everywhere; it is probably the most sensual and abandoned of all Soweto parties. **1980** D.B. COPLAN Urbanization of African Performing Arts. 432 *Famo*, An urban dance and dance occasion in which Basotho women perform primarily for the entertainment of men, to the accompaniment of neo-traditional focho music or syncretic marabi music. **1987** *New Nation* 16 July 10 An organist from the Eastern Cape .. played for 'famo' — a Sotho version of the stokvel. **1990** M. MELAMU in *Lynx* 280 On Friday evening, while some of the men were busy putting the final touches to the 'famo' tent, Hlalele and a group of other 'Russians' .. made their way .. across the railway line to Randfontein.

3. See quots.

1980 D.B. COPLAN Urbanization of African Performing Arts. 215 Apart from the dance, the term *famo* refers to a category of lengthy recitative songs performed by the women ... The women often addressed their *famo* songs to the men. *Ibid.* 432 *Famo*, .. A form of Basotho proletarian women's song performed at famo dances and recounting the singer's life experience.

fanakalo /ˌfanagaˈlɔ, ˈfanagalɔ/ *n.* Forms: α. **fanagalo, fana-galo, fanagolo, fanago-lo, sefanagalo**; β. **fanakalo, fana-ka-lo, fanakolo.** Also with initial capital. [Fanakalo, formed on the Nguni-language word *fana* be like + possessive particle *ka-* + *lo* this, an expression supposedly used often in Fanakalo when one person instructs another to do something 'like this', 'in this manner'.]A *lingua franca* developed and used by southern African mining companies, composed of (freq. corrupted) elements of the NGUNI languages, English, and Afrikaans; *eina-taal*, see EINA *n.* sense 2; *lapa language*, see LAPA *adv.* Also *attrib.*, and *fig.*

The name 'fanakalo' was adopted by mining authorities and other employers to avoid the offensive word 'kaffir' in the former names *kitchen kaffir* (see KITCHEN *n.* sense 1 b) and *mine kaffir* (see KAFFIR *n.* sense 3 d).

α. **1948** O. WALKER *Kaffirs Are Lively* 28 'Fanago-lo' .. evolved on the Rand goldmines as a *lingua franca* for the transmission of commands between the white mine-captains and boss-boys and the broad, heterogeneous mass of many-tongued African labourers. **1957** J.D. BOLD *Dict., Grammar & Phrase Bk of Fanagalo* 6 *Fanagalo* is a very much simplified form of Nguni (Zulu, Xhosa and related languages), with adaptations of modern terms from English and Dutch. It was probably evolved in the Eastern Cape and Natal during contacts between European settlers and native tribes ... The appellation 'Fanagalo' probably derives from 'kuluma fana ga lo', meaning to 'speak like this'. The language has also been called 'Kitchen Kaffir', and 'Mine Kaffir'. **1958** H. WICHT *Rd below Me* 78, I found some difficulty in communicating .. until a mine-boy came along ... In Fanagalo we had a language that we both understood. **1977** *Family Radio & TV* 29 Aug. 24 He conquered the strangeness of Fanagalo and could communicate with men from as far as South West Africa. **1982** D. BIKITSHA in *Rand Daily Mail* 14 Oct. (Eve) 5 This language unlike 'fanagalo' which is considered an affront and bastardisation of black languages, has a romantic and flamboyant history. Where fanagalo is gross, heavy and uncouth, tsotsi taal is smooth, facile and poetic to an extent. **1989** J. HOBBS *Thoughts in Makeshift Mortuary* 92 She did not use the pidgin Zulu once known as kitchen kaffir, but now that the word 'kaffir' was acknowledged as insulting, called Fanagalo. **1990** *Weekend Argus* 17 Feb. 12 The language .. might sound a bit like a Fanagalo of politics at times. But .. it is .. to be expected .. when strangers living in the same country suddenly find themselves thrown together in the same political workplace. **1991** *Advertising leaflet, Reader's Digest Assoc.*, Did you know that .. Blacks regard Fanagalo .. as an inferior and undignified means of communication. **1993** K. KGOSITSILE in *Sn Afr. Review of Bks* July-Aug. 21 Even when in despair I try to point out correctly that our languages are much older, much more expressive, poetically much richer than English, which is an admirably advanced *fanagalo* in spite of its imperialist, sexist, racist and class biases, my advice tends to remain suspect because: 'But, don't I say, Bra Willie writes in English himself mos, so how come then?' **1994** A. LEVIN in

Style Oct. 95 Rattling away in Fanagalo, he drags me through the crowd.

β. **1951** *Cape Argus* 19 Jan. 8 Most people with a reverence for their own mother-tongue will sympathise with Professor Jabavu's opinion of 'Fanakalo'. **1962** A.P. Cartwright *Gold Miners* 223 'Mompara' (the Fanakalo word for one who is dim-witted). **1972** P. Becker in *Star* 17 Mar. B6 Don't speak Fanakalo as long as you can converse in a vernacular language. But if you can't .. then .. resort to that droop-eared, scraggy-haired, communicating donkey called Fanakalo. **1972** S. Lynne *Glittering Gold* 46 Fana-ka-lo, the simple mine language .. taught to the Africans and white employees on their arrival at the mine. **1979** *Voice* 7 Oct. 2 Ari Paulus's fanakalo (miners) boys could beat the daylights out of him, anywhere, at any time. **1979** C. van der Merwe in *Frontline* Dec. 17 Flytaal .. embraces Capeytaal and a large chunk of fanakalo. **1984** *Sunday Times* 29 Jan. 11 Conservative followers .. reject what they call the 'fanakalo Mass' in favour of the original Latin Mass. **1986** *Thousand Ways to Die* (National Union of Mineworkers) 32 It is important for everybody underground to speak the same language. But .. most workers hate Fanakalo. They say that Fanakalo is insulting, or '*Fanakalo is the language of masters and slaves*.' **1988** J. Matlou in *Staffrider* Vol.7 No.3, 49 Mine people were .. singing .. in the mine language, 'sefanagalo'. **1989** T.C. Mbatha in *Natal Witness* 30 Mar. (Witness Echo) 19, I am totally against those semi-literate people who speak semi-English and fanakalo Zulu with whites and Indians ... This fanakalo language is theirs, not ours. **1990** *Natal Witness* 28 Dec. 5 South Africa's largest mining groups have begun phasing out the hybrid language of command ... 'Fanakalo is not a language in which you can share feelings, express grievances, share information. It is not the language for the style of management we want.'

fancy *n.* [fr. ellipt. use of general Eng. adj.: see earliest quots for each sense.]

1. *Ostrich-farming.* byock.

[*c*1881 A. Douglass *Ostrich Farming* 81 Sort first into heaps consisting of .. best fancy-coloured, and second fancy-coloured.] **1909** J.E. Duerden in *Agric. Jrnl of Cape of G.H.* XXXIV. 523 If the blacks show much admixture of white, they are placed among the fancies. **1930** M.F. Wormser Ostrich Industry. 11 Towards the end of the series of wing quills, 3 or 4 plumes of the cock, instead of being pure white, are a particolour of black and white; these are called fancies or byocks.

2. *Diamond-trade.* A diamond of gemstone quality, of a colour other than pure white or blue-white. Also *attrib.*

Not exclusively *S. Afr. Eng.*

[**1870** *E. Prov. Herald* 12 Aug., Diamonds are found every day ... By far the prettiest is of a greenish colour — a beautiful fancy gem. **1873** see off-colour *adj.* **1878** T.J. Lucas *Camp Life & Sport* 123 Many tinted stones are found, from the faintest tinge of yellow, green or bluish and but rarely rose, to the full coloured positive shades of orange, blue, green, and even brown (called fancy stones) and fetching a fancy price accordingly.] **1946** J.R. McCarthy *Fire in Earth* 210 In the diamond trade they are called 'fancies,' the rare stones of well-marked colours. They may be red, pea green, apple green, rose, violet-blue, pale sapphire blue, absinthe green, golden brown, orange, and every colour and combination of colours extant. **1969** J.M. White *Land God Made in Anger* 279 'Fancies' are coloured diamonds, produced by eccentric conditions of chemical content or of firing in the volcanic pipes ... Fancies are not favoured by the public, and are therefore not greatly sought after by the trade. **1973** A. Hocking *Diamonds* 19 Often a particular mine is noted for stones of a particular colour that it produces — and they are known in the trade as 'fancies'. **1977** *Weekend Post* 18 June (Suppl.) 2 Diamonds occur naturally in five different shapes and nine colours — four of white and five yellow (Cape) — as well as the fancies, like reds, greens and blues.

fandisi var. vendusie.

fanko *n. obs.* [Unkn.; prob. a trade-name.] See quot.

1908 M.C. Bruce *New Tvl* 77 Until recently, mealie meal, of which porridge is made, was the only variety of food-stuff made from this plant, but within the last couple of years the making of fanko at the factory of Messrs. Fleming in Johannesburg, has firmly established one more Transvaal industry. Fanko is in reality the grounding [*sic*] of the mealie seed into a delicate flake which can be used with eggs and milk to make the most delicious puddings and biscuits.

farm *n. colloq.* [Special sense of general Eng., by metonymy.] ***The farm***: The country; often alluding to a person's rural background, or to life in the rural areas. See also platteland *n.* sense a.

1966 L.G. Berger *Where's Madam* 185 Where had the wife been living until now? Oh, she'd just this minute come up from the farm. She'd never been to El Goli, the city of gold before. **1975** *Sunday Times* 20 Apr. 16 If he is a plattelander, his closest and best experience of his fellow (Black) South African was probably during games of kennetjie with Black children down on the farm. **1979** M. Matshoba *Call Me Not a Man* 80 You're so superstitious, my mother's child. One would think you were born on the farm. **1980** *Staffrider* Vol.3 No.1, 2 There are some signs that people use on the farm. If that bell rings and then stops, and then rings and then stops, oh, we know that there was somebody who had passed away. **1987** *Frontline* May 12 A smattering of boos and hisses breaks out. A black man, riskily conspicuous, yells loudly: 'Go back to the farm'.

farm *v. intrans.* In the phr. ***to farm with*** [Eng., influenced by Afk. *boer met*], to rear (livestock, etc.) or grow (a particular crop).

1916 L.D. Flemming *Fool on Veld* (1933) 60, I am a bee farmer, .. what a comedown this is to me after having farmed with big things like cows and sheep ... I tried farming with practically every other thing on the earth except elephants. **1972** *Farmer's Weekly* 21 Apr. 6 Apart from having a very big soft spot for this breed I find them extremely profitable to farm with. **1973** *Ibid.* 4 July 13 Mr Ross .. farmed with wine grapes in the Cape for six years. **1974** *S. Afr. Panorama* Mar. 3 Mr Le May has been farming with poultry for the past 27 years. *Ibid.* Apr. 15 In the town the people farm with fruit, sheep, vineyards and strawberries. **1974** *E. Prov. Herald* 25 May 4 Farming with game is a profitable business ... One of the main advantages of farming with buck in preference to livestock is that springbuck are the only buck affected by ticks. **1978** A.P. Brink *Rumours of Rain* 244 He tried to farm with angora goats, before they were all killed off by the cold one winter. **1980** *Grocott's Mail* 2 May 2 In an agricultural census some time ago there was a question 'Do you farm with: Merino sheep? Dorper sheep? Persian sheep?' **1984** *E. Prov. Herald* 21 July 8 He was full of his impending retirement and the prospect of farming with a few fruit trees on his smallholding. **1988** J. Le May in *Inside S. Afr.* May 12 His grandfather farmed with pigs near Pretoria.

farm school *n. phr.* A rural school providing (primary) education for the children of a district, and often situated on a farm; *plaasskool*, see plaas sense 1 c. Also *attrib.*

1903 E.F. Knight *S. Afr. after War* 255 Here the Government has established one of its farm schools, which is under the direction of an English lady. Close to it is a rival Dutch private school. **1905** J. Robinson in Flint & Gilchrist *Science in S. Afr.* 462 The first published Education Law of the South African Republic was Law No. 4 of 1874 ... Three classes of schools were recognized ... In practice the Ward School was described as a 'Farm' School and the District School as a 'Town' School. *c*1911 S. Playne *Cape Col.* 674 There are .. a large number of farm schools to meet the needs of the rural population. **1937** C. Birkby *Zulu Journey* 258 Between them, the Church and the farm school at Tsolo are more important to the black man of the Transkeian Territories than most of the black men know. *a*1951 H.C. Bosman *Willemsdorp* (1977) 17 There was that Kafir-path that he and his younger brother had walked along every afternoon back from the farm-school. **1958** E. Bold in *Pietersburg Eng. Medium School Mag.* 86 Another school with whom a spirit of co-operation and friendship has developed is the Kuschke Farm School. **1973** *E. Prov. Herald* 9 Nov. 17 Desks are scarce, as in most farm schools, so the floor is used instead. **1974** *Ibid.* 22 Apr. 13 The Department of Bantu Education threatened to close down the overcrowded and ramshackle .. farm school. **1974** A.P. Cartwright *By Waters of Letaba* 143 In 1917 .. the Administrator .. initiated a system of farm schools as part of his plan for providing an education, combined with agricultural training, for the children of the many poor white families in the platteland. **1986** *City Press* 23 Feb. 4 The unnamed teacher said the conditions in farm schools were 'precarious'. **1988** *E. Prov. Herald* 10 Mar. 7, 36% of all rural black children between the ages of 14 and 16 were not in school .. in spite of the commendable efforts of most farmers in supporting the farm school system, often at their own expense. **1988** Smuts & Alberts *Forgotten Highway* 152 Even in our century, people .. walked for hours to get to the nearest farm school — barefoot, carrying the only pair of shoes they possessed. **1992** *Weekly Mail* 16 Apr. 14 Before the school was built, the area's 20 000 children were expected to squeeze into a farm school, one .. which was already full and schools in Daveyton, eight kilometres away.

fat cake *n. phr.* [Brit. and Austral. Eng., reinforced by Afk. *vetkoek*.] vetkoek sense a.

Occas. *noncount.*

1883 O.E.A. Schreiner *Story of Afr. Farm* 134 Doss lay with his nose close to the covered saucer, and smelt that some one had made nice little fat cakes that afternoon. **1924** L.H. Brinkman *Glory of Backveld* 35 Indoors the women were .. busy making biscuits, bread, fat-cakes, yards and yards of sausages. **1954** P. Abrahams *Tell Freedom* 83 On the bench near the fire, heaped on a plate, were golden fatcakes. **1961** D. Rooke *Lover for Estelle* 105 Estelle had made fat cakes for the children and had given Ocky a piece of game biltong to teethe on, so they were quiet at least. **1976** B. Head in *Quarry '76* 17 I'd like to buy one bag of bread flour and cooking oil for fat cakes so that we can have a change of food. **1980** J. Matthews in M. Mutloatse *Forced Landing* 38 Mugs of coffee and still-hot fat cakes from the portable coffee stalls of the vendors. **1982** 'I.M.' in M.B. Mtshali *Give Us a Break* (1988) 28 Made tea and went to the shops to buy fat cakes. **1988** N. Mathiane in *Frontline* Nov. 34 The township children usually have lunches of fatcake and chips. **1990** *Sunday Times* 4 Mar. 17 He .. provides trays of fatcakes and crates of cold drinks to radical youths at street meetings. **1994** F. Ulana in *E. Prov. Herald* 26 Aug. 10, I was an ordinary peasant trying to make a living, selling paraffin and fatcakes from dawn to dusk ... Young criminals .. stole my wares when it got dark.

fat cook *n. phr.* [Calque formed on Afk. *vetkoek*.] vetkoek sense a. Also **fat cookie**.

1975 *Darling* 23 July 4 Passing a bakery shop one day, I noticed the following sign in the window: *Fat Cooks, 3c each*. This aroused such a delightful mental picture that I doubt whether I could have brought myself to eat one of those vetkoeks! **1977** *Sunday Times* 7 Aug. (Mag. Sect.) 3 Eat eggs, butter and chicken fat cookies like your mother used to make and your tubes get clogged by cholesterol. **1987** *Argus* 13 Jan., One item on the menu of a coffee bar in Parow says: 'Fat Cooks, R1,50.' I wonder whether they serve thin chefs for slimmers.

Fatherland *n. Obs.* exc. *hist.* [tr. Du. *Vaderland*.] Any of several breeds of imported livestock, esp. certain types of cattle first introduced from Holland in the late 18th century, including the Friesland; cf. Vaderland *adj.* Usu. *attrib.*

1827 T. Philipps *Scenes & Occurrences* 13 Several Devon bulls have been imported and some black from Holland; these are called as well as their produce, Vaderland, or Fatherland, and are certainly the best formed. **1831** *S. Afr. Almanac & Dir.* 160 Hardy Bastard Fatherland Cattle are bred here. **1836** *Albany*

Settlers 1824–36 (Soc. for the Relief of Distressed Settlers) 49 They had between 50 and 60 head of Fatherland cattle, and about 250 sheep: the cattle are all lost. **1852** *Durban Observer* 9 Jan. (Pettman), The Fatherland, as the name betokens, is the pure European breed, without cross or admixture. They are a large sized, small headed, light-necked, and well-made breed noted as furnishing the best milch cows in the Colony. **1870** C. HAMILTON *Life & Sport in S.-E. Afr.* 204 The Kaffir .. always declares that the Dutch were the first importers of it [*sc.* lungsickness], and with some truth, as it was said to have been unknown till brought out by an importation of Fatherland bulls. *a***1878** J. MONTGOMERY *Reminisc.* (1981) 110 The Fatherland rams would not keep company with the Cape ewes. **1955** L.G. GREEN *Karoo* 146 One writer noted: 'It was very remarkable that the wool of the Fatherland sheep, sent to the Cape, improved so perceptibly by the change of climate.' **1957** *Handbk for Farmers* (Dept of Agric.) III. 39 Van Rhyneveld .. in 1804 .. refers to a Friesland bull and cow which Governor Van Plettenberg had imported 20 to 25 years before. Earlier references to imported cattle simply made mention of fatherland stock. Some of these were probably also cattle of the Friesland, or black-and-white type. **1972** J. VAN MARLE in *Std Encycl. of Sn Afr.* V. 51 According to some, Governor Van Plettenberg imported the first Frieslands from the Netherlands during 1774 when they were called 'Fatherland cattle'.

fathers *pl. n.* In the Cape Town area: a collective name for WITDOEK vigilantes.

1986 *Argus* 2 Jan. 1 They claimed .. the 'fathers' travelled in a large group of between 200 and 300, wore white headbands and leg ties, and were led by certain community councillors. **1986** *Cape Times* 3 Jan. 2 The 'fathers' — conservative men, supportive of the community councillors, .. have been hunting militant 'maqabanes' (comrades) in a feud which began on Christmas Eve. *Ibid.* 9 A leader of the vigilante group of 'fathers' .. said yesterday the group had been assured police would not interfere with their operations. The 'fathers' were 'trying to get discipline into the township' ... If the 'maqabanes' would not listen to the 'fathers', then 'we want to catch them ... We will take them to the police, but if they fight with us we will kill them'. **1986** [*see Evening Post* quot. at COMRADE]. **1986** [see A-TEAM]. **1990** R. MALAN in *Cosmopolitan* Apr. 167 Conservative vigilantes known as Fathers were killing their comrade sons, and everyone was exterminating those they regarded as traitors. **1993** D. ELLES in *Democracy in Action* 31 Aug. 14 You know the famous story of the faction fight between the so-called 'conservative fathers' (later called witdoeke, because they wore white cloths tied round their heads or arms) and the youth of New Crossroads (comrades) ... To us the so-called fathers were vigilantes who wanted to impose an undemocratic tribal system in an urban set-up.

fatje var. VAATJIE.

fat-koek /'fætkʊk/ *n.* [Part. tr. Afk. *vetkoek.*] VETKOEK sense a.

1979 *Voice* 2 Sept. 5 The ever-talking aunties selling fat-koeks at the central bus stop; the gambling of fah fee; the uncountable shebeen queens; .. even red-clad Wesleyan Church aunties.

fat-tailed *adj.*

a. In the n. phr. ***fat-tailed sheep*** (occas. also ***fat-tailed ram***), an indigenous hairy sheep with a large tail of solid fat; *Cape sheep*, see CAPE sense 2 a. Occas. *ellipt.*, **fat-tail**. See also AFRIKANDER *n.* sense 7, SHEEP'S TAIL FAT.

The tails of these sheep, much prized for culinary purposes, were sometimes so heavy that they needed small wheeled carts or 'tail trucks' to support them (see quot. 1937).

[**1598** J. DAVYS in R. Raven-Hart *Before Van Riebeeck* (1967) 20 Their Sheepe have exceeding great tailes only of fat, weighing twelve or fourteene pounds: they have no wooll but a long shag haire. **1688** G. TACHARD *Voy. to Siam* 73 The Captain accepted our Presents, and in gratitude sent us two fatSheep each of whose Tails weighed above twenty pound weight. **1812** A. PLUMPTRE tr. *H. Lichtenstein's Trav. in Sn Afr.* (1928) I. 107 The sheep that bear the fine wool are separated from those with the fat tails.] **1858** G. GREY in *Corresp. between Colonial Office & Governor Sir George Grey Respecting his Recall from Cape of G.H.* (H.C.216–1860) 4 They [*sc.* the boers] would keep nothing but hairy fat-tailed sheep. **1871** W.G. ATHERSTONE in A.M.L. Robinson *Sel. Articles from Cape Monthly Mag.* (1978) 89 The fat-tailed sheep in these parts are considered full-grown and at maturity, are sold to the butcher, at twenty months old. **1888** *Castle Line Handbk & Emigrant's Guide* 55 The farmers generally were very slow to appreciate the advantages of the wool bearers over the old hairy fat-tailed sheep of the country. The fat-tails held their own for many years. **1898** W.C. SCULLY *Vendetta* 11 His flock of fat-tailed sheep were kraaled at an outpost which was in charge of a Hottentot herd. **1909** H.E.S. FREMANTLE *New Nation* 287 The Boers were so prejudiced, that they would keep nothing but hairy fat-tailed sheep. **1937** S. CLOETE *Turning Wheels* 178 The main thing that worried her was how Blesbock, her fat-tailed ram, had got on ... No one could fasten on the little cart — it was really a plank with two wheels — that carried his long, fat tail as securely, or as comfortably, as she. **1941** C.W. DE KIEWIET *Hist. of S. Afr.* 9 Wool failed, though the wiry-haired fat-tailed sheep did well. **1958** [see KAIINGS]. **1968** J.T. MCNISH *Rd to Eldorado* 109 Dry, stunted Karoo bushes upon which an occasional skinny goat or a fat-tailed sheep fed listlessly. **1974** *The 1820* Vol.47 No.9, 10 Before 1820 the Dutch farmers had concentrated on fat-tailed sheep, useful for the production of cooking fat, tallow and soap. **1989** *Reader's Digest Illust. Hist.* 21 The fat-tailed sheep that were acquired by the Khoikhoi were in fact known in the Middle East about 4000 years before, when they were tended by Semitic-speaking people.

b. Having a large tail of solid fat.

1953 *S. Afr. Stockbreeder & Farmer Ref. Bk* 230 The non-woolled sheep are mostly fat-tailed, e.g. the indigenous Namaqua and Ronderib Afrikaner, the Blackhead Persian and the van Rooy. Recently a non-woolled sheep without a fat tail, viz.: the Dorper, has been developed.

Feast of the Orange Leaves see ORANGE LEAVES.

feather *n. Ostrich-farming.* [Special senses of general Eng.]

a. As a commodity: an ostrich feather. Also *attrib.* See also BODY-FEATHER, CHICK, ONDERBAATJIE, PRIME, TAIL, WING.

Ostrich-feathers have been valuable articles of trade since the earliest European settlement at the Cape. They form the basis of an industry concentrated around the town of Oudtshoorn, and in parts of the Eastern Cape. See also OSTRICH.

[**1786** G. FORSTER tr. *A. Sparrman's Voy. to Cape of G.H.* I. 130 *Ostriches*, the birds whose feathers our luxury occasions to be brought from the remotest plains of Africa, I likewise saw today in their wild state, at the southernmost promontory of this quarter of the globe.] **1866** E.L. PRICE *Jrnls* (1956) 194 Sebele asked Roger to add up .. the price of the house in *feathers*, & other things. *Ibid.* 195 Instead of 300 pounds *sterling* (or 1,800 feathers) he had thought it was to be 300 feathers only. **1877** DE MOSENTHAL & HARTING *Ostriches & Ostrich Farming* 195 It is by no means uncommon to meet a .. Hottentot boy with three or four first-class feathers stuck jauntily through his ears, or fastened in his woolly head. *Ibid.* 198 The average length of a really good feather is about two feet, and eight to nine inches wide. **1880** *S.W. Silver & Co.'s Handbk to S. Afr.* 227 Before domestication was attempted .. the chief sources of the feather supply were .. in the far interior. **1886** W. BRUCE in C. Cowen *S. Afr. Exhibition 1886* 9 To some extent, like diamonds, articles of luxury, feathers have recently been in very limited demand in Europe. *c***1911** O. EVANS in S. Playne *Cape Col.* 53, I may here give details of the growth of the industry from returns of feather sales and exportations: *1865* 17,811 lbs — £65,426 .. *1905* 471,024 lbs — £1, 081,187. **1913** C. PETTMAN *Africanderisms* 167 Feathers vary in value according to the sex of the bird and the part of the body from which they are plucked; they are also named accordingly. **1920** *Dunell, Ebden & Co.'s Price List* May-June [Cover], Telephone Numbers: Counting House 850 ... Native Truck-Manchester 393 ... Feathers 549. **1930** M.F. WORMSER Ostrich Industry. 51 The outbreak of war brought the final collapse of the feather trade. *Ibid.* 67 The commoner feathers, a fair quantity of which was absorbed by the brush and broom factories, were sold for good prices. *c***1936** [see KGALAGADI]. **1955** G. ASCHMAN in Saron & Hotz *Jews in S. Afr.* 130 The immigrants themselves learnt to sort feathers just as they quickly learnt the names of all the different types of feathers. **1956** P.J. BOTHA in F. Goldie *Ostrich Country* (1968) 55 Palatial twenty bedroomed .. mansions built in the town and district of Oudtshoorn by many feather-rich farmers. **1968** F. GOLDIE *Ostrich Country* 50 Critics declared that tame feathers would not curl, and would be of little value in competition with wild feathers. *Ibid.* 53 The disastrous feather slump of 1914 brought many ostrich farmers and others dependent upon the sale of feathers to ruin. **1973** G.J. BROEKHUYSEN in *Std Encycl. of Sn Afr.* VIII. 396 Feathers are still required for dusters and for ornamental purposes. **1983** *Flying Springbok* Jan. 52 Ostrich farms were established in the late 19th century boom when zealous feather hunters threatened to wipe out South Africa's wild ostrich population. **1989** *Reader's Digest Illust. Hist.* 227 The new industry inevitably attracted great numbers of commercial operators, most of them reasonably honest, but some, especially among the itinerant feather-buyers, decidedly crooked.

b. *comb.* **feather bird**, see quot.; **feather boom**, the period of prosperity following the development of ostrich-farming during the nineteenth century; **Feather City**, the city of Oudtshoorn, in the south-eastern Cape; **feather market**, commerce in ostrich products; a place in which ostrich products are traded; **feather palace**, a name given to any of a number of large houses built in the Oudtshoorn district by ostrich farmers and dealers in ostrich products during the feather boom; *ostrich palace*, see OSTRICH.

*c***1881** A. DOUGLASS *Ostrich Farming* 67 From one to four years old, they are called .. **feather birds**. *Ibid.* 173 A nice 'feather bird' .. will give at least £12 a year in feathers. *c***1936** *S. & E. Afr. Yr Bk & Guide* 557 The fantastic figures due to the **feather boom** have gone. **1968** F. GOLDIE *Ostrich Country* 51 The feather boom .. always depended almost entirely on the vagaries of fashion. **1991** *Best of S. Afr. Short Stories* (Reader's Digest Assoc.) 103 In the 'feather boom' many Oudtshoorn farmers reaped rich rewards which they spent in erecting elaborate homesteads. **1983** *Frontline* Feb. 46 It had been a spanking hot, bright day when we set off from **Feather City** .. in the direction of Mossel Bay. *c***1881** A. DOUGLASS *Ostrich Farming* 4 Business men were always prognosticating that the **feather market** would collapse with the increase of the ostrich; but the reverse has been the case. **1968** F. GOLDIE *Ostrich Country* 53 The need for a local feather market was met when the .. Landboukoöperasie at Oudtshoorn initiated regular feather sales. **1968** C.J. ORFFER in D.J. Opperman *Spirit of Vine* 120 After the collapse of the feather market in 1913, the farmers went back to the tried ways and vineyards were again widely planted. **1988** D. HUGHES et al. *Complete Bk of S. Afr. Wine* 32 The advent of the motor-car made billowing plumage disconcerting and the feather market collapsed. **1968** F. GOLDIE *Ostrich Country* 4 Ornate Victorian mansions .. known as **feather palaces**, bear testimony to the boom years of the feather industry. **1978** *Argus* 7 Apr. 9 The old 'Feather Palace', the magnificent homestead on Greylands ostrich farm .. has been declared a national monument. **1980** *Het Suid-Western* 13 Feb., The Oliviers' magnificent 20-room feather palace .. became the centre of gracious living. **1993** *Sunday Times* 24 Jan. 5 Ostrich barons exhibited their wealth by building magnificent Victorian mansions which became known as 'feather palaces'.

Fecane var. FETCANI.

‖**fees** /fɪəs/ n. Pl. **feeste** /ˈfɪəstə/. [Afk.] A celebration or festival, esp. one taking place in the Afrikaans community and commemorating a particular (cultural) event. Also *attrib*.

 1971 *S. Western Herald* 16 July 2 It is .. disgusting that people .. on just about every public holiday or fees-day .. should see nothing wrong with littering their allegedly-beloved country with the evidence of their pestilential presence. 1975 *Sunday Times* 3 Aug. 18 Even farther to the right a group which seems determined to prove that Afrikaans is not the language of love will hold its own purified fees on Church Square — far from the mixed and madding throng which will gather to tell taal tales at the Voortrekker Monument. 1987 *E. Prov. Herald* 12 Apr. 32 Tale of two feeste. 1988 *Frontline* Jan. 3 Feeste for Africa. Klaas de Boer takes admiring note of all the cultural festivals coming up this year, and wonders why the spirit of 1938 has gone. 1988 'K. DE BOER' in *Ibid.* 28 Commemorations! Feeste! Feeste for Africa, if I may use the term ... All the feeste awaiting us in 1988. 1991 A. VAN WYK *Birth of New Afrikaner* 78 In 1971, when the newly completed laager of bronze wagons was dedicated at the site of the Battle of Blood River, I took Stompie to the *fees* (memorial gathering) there.

fei-bosch var. VYGEBOSCH.

feiky var. VAATJIE.

felchoon var. VELDSKOEN.

feld cornet var. VELD CORNET.

feldt var. VELD.

feldtchoen var. VELDSKOEN.

feldt comberse var. VELKOMBERS.

feldt cornet var. VELD CORNET.

feldtschoen var. VELDSKOEN.

feldwag(h)tmeester var. VELDWAGTMEESTER.

fellschoen, feltchoon, -scoon, -shoon varr. VELDSKOEN.

femina /ˈfemɪnə/ n. Ostrich-farming. Pl. unchanged, or -s. [L., 'woman'.] Usu. *pl.* The long greyish feathers taken from the wing-tip of a hen ostrich. Also *attrib.* See also WING.

 1877 DE MOSENTHAL & HARTING *Ostriches & Ostrich Farming* 226 Boos — Dark femina .. Spadones. White and Light femina. c1881 A. DOUGLASS *Ostrich Farming* 93 A process has been discovered by which the natural colouring of our femina and fancy-coloured feathers can be extracted. 1896 R. WALLACE *Farming Indust. of Cape Col.* 235 White and light Femina were very firm. Dark femina, 5s. and 10s. per lb. higher ... 'White' refers to the long pure wing feathers of the male bird, 'Femina' indicating the corresponding plumage of the female, hence the name. 1909 J.E. DUERDEN in *Agric. Jrnl of Cape of G.H.* XXXIV. 523 Feminas .. are the wing-quills of the hen bird which correspond with the whites of the cock ... Distinguished by having a .. greyish appearance .. they are classed according to the amount of pigment as *tipped, light* or *dark.* 1930 [see PRIME]. 1932 *Grocott's Daily Mail* 14 Jan. 3 Feminas: Superior, now offered; good average, 15/- to 20/-.

fencing stick n. phr. Obs. FIGHTING STICK sense 1.

 1833, 1835, 1860 [see INTONGA].

Fengu var. MFENGU.

fenkel var. VINKEL.

feodhook var. VADOEK.

ferneuk var. VERNEUK.

Festival of the Orange Leaves see ORANGE LEAVES.

Fetcani /fetˈkaːni, feˈlaːni, fəˈkaːni/ n. hist. Also **Fecane, Fetekane, Fikani, Fi(t)cani, Fitkanie**. Pl. unchanged. [Englished form of Xhosa *iimfecani* marauders (sing. *imfecane*), see MFECANE.]

1. *pl.* A name given to any of several groups, clans, or tribes (esp. the Ngwane), who, retreating southwards from present-day Kwa-Zulu-Natal during the wars of the early 19th century, overpowered many southern Nguni peoples in turn; these groups collectively; IMFECANE sense 1. Also *attrib.* See also MANTATEE.

 1827 W. SHAW Diary. 31 Aug., The tribe now approaching the Colony & Caffreland is called by the Caffres Fikani, and are .. intrepid in warfare, very numerous, and very cruel. 1835 W.B. BOYCE in A. Steedman *Wanderings* II. 269 Api, the Ficani Chief, who was last April living above Faku, near the sources of the Zimvooboo, has been driven thence, by a commando from Dingaan the Zulu Chief. 1841 B. SHAW *Memorials* 47 Other travellers have supposed them to be the same race of men as those known to the Kaffirs by the name of Ficani; for it is ascertained that Mantatees in the Bechuana language, and Ficani in the Kaffir, are synonymous terms, both signifying invaders. 1850 J.W. APPLEYARD *Kafir Lang.* 42 Fecane is the root of *imfecane*, the Kafir word for *desolater* or *marauder.* It must not be mistaken, therefore, for a tribal name, being simply a descriptive term by which the Kafirs designate an unknown and foreign invader. 1877 R.M. BALLANTYNE *Settler & Savage* 279 A wandering and warlike horde named the Fetcani had been for some time past driving all the other tribes before them, and were said at last to be approaching the Winterberg frontier of the colony. 1912 AYLIFF & WHITESIDE *Hist. of Abambo* 16 The name they gave the Amangwane was that of 'Fetcani', the Kaffir word for 'desolaters, marauders', and they described them as fiends in human shape. It is as Fetcani they are known in Colonial History. 1946 [see IMFECANE sense 1]. 1972 A. SCHOLEFIELD *Wild Dog Running* 134 A branch of the Mantatee horde called the Fetcani had driven south-west and, after savaging the land of the Tambookies, were now plundering the country of the Galekas. 1980 LYE & MURRAY *Transformations* 50 He used time and circumstances to consolidate his power. As his son, Nehemiah Moshoeshoe, observed, 'The paramountcy was created by the disturbances of the Fetcani', the wandering hordes.

2. *The Mfecane,* see MFECANE.

 1972 J.P. VAN S. BRUWER in *Std Encycl. of Sn Afr.* IX. 598 From these wars resulted the forced migration (termed *lifaqane, difaqane, fetcani* or *mfecane* by the Bantu) of many tribes between 1818 and the time of the Great Trek.

feusach, -sack varr. VOETSAK.

fever tree n. phr. [See quot. 1984.]

1. The tall tropical tree *Acacia xanthophloea* of the Leguminosae (sub-family Mimoseae), remarkable for its powdery yellowish-green bark.

 1893 BLENNERHASSETT & SLEEMAN *Adventures in Mashonaland* 99 These 'fever trees' are a species of mimosa, with pallid boles and livid green foliage, and the experienced explorer always avoids their neighbourhood. 1908 R. KIPLING *Just So Stories* (1937) 59 At last he [sc. the Elephant's Child] came to the banks of the great grey-green, greasy Limpopo River, all set about with fever trees. 1913 C. PETTMAN *Africanderisms* 168 Fever trees, .. This name is applied 'up country' to a species of mimosa (*Acacia xanthophloea*), because the trees are supposed to indicate that the locality in which they grow is unhealthy for Europeans. 1922 J. STEVENSON-HAMILTON *Low-Veld* 53 In some swampy land below the kopjes are growing a number of the curious so called 'fever trees' (Acacia xanthophloea) handsome in their peculiar way, and some of them quite fifty feet high. a1936 E.N. MARAIS *Rd to Waterberg* (1972) 89 The river-banks are thick with gigantic forest trees, some evergreen — like the sinister 'fever trees', with their ghastly yellow trunks, characteristic of Komatipoort and other malarial areas. 1937 C. BIRKBY *Zulu Journey* 115 No man who has ever seen fever trees will ever forget them ... Tall and gnarled, like some weird dead thing that is not yet dead ... Twisted, naked trunks tinted a vivid sulphurous-yellow, and their greenery-yallery branches are covered with a slimy bloom. 1958 H. WICHT *Rd below Me* 146 There are still groves of fever trees, yellow-barked and leprous. 1984 A. WANNENBURGH *Natural Wonder of Sn Afr.* 139 Fever trees .. were long thought to cause malaria ... However, the association stems from the fact that the trees grow well in swampy areas, the ideal breeding ground for the malarial mosquito. 1990 W.R. TARBOTON in *Fauna & Flora* No.47, 12 In many of the lower-lying ravines the spectacular, giant-leaved forest fever tree is found.

2. Any of several species of gum-tree (Eucalyptus), so called because of their antifebrile properties; but see also quot. 1917.

 1896 R. WALLACE *Farming Indust. of Cape Col.* 24 Millions of the Australian 'blue-gum' or 'fever tree,' *Eucalyptus globulus,* Labill., have been planted within a few miles of Johannesburg. 1917 R. MARLOTH *Common Names* 151 Frequently planted in South Africa are E[ucalyptus] *globulus,* the Blue gum, also called Fever-tree, because it has proved itself very effective for rendering swampy localities habitable by drying them up. 1970 BEETON & DORNER in *Eng. Usage in Sn Afr.* Vol.1 No.2, 2 'Fever tree' is also applied to various other trees, eg species of *Eucalyptus,* on account of their alleged anti-febrile medicinal properties.

FFF n. hist. Initial letters of *Five Freedoms Forum,* an organization established in the 1980s to monitor the abuse of civil rights. Also *attrib.*

 1987 *New Nation* 11 June 7 The last state of emergency was 'a year of despair' and the worst assault on democracy South Africa has faced, say the Five Freedoms Forum (FFF) ... The FFF singled out the campaign as the Congress of SA Trade Unions (Cosatu) as being particularly ominous. 1986 D. WEBSTER in *Star* 30 May 9 As part of its commitment to ending the nightmare, the FFF has undertaken two special projects which form part of its current campaign, '101 Ways to End Apartheid'. 1990 *Weekend Post* 29 Sept. 1 FFF members who were spied on served notices of intention to sue city council officials on the grounds of invasion of privacy.

Ficani var. FETCANI.

Fidas var. FIETAS.

field n. [Special senses of general Eng.]

1. *obs.* [Influenced by Du. *veld.*] VELD sense 2 a i. Also *attrib.*

 1812 A. PLUMPTRE tr. H. Lichtenstein's *Trav. in Sn Afr.* (1928) I. 30 The house was too small .. , so some of our tents were set up, and here we commenced sleeping in the field. 1827 G. THOMPSON *Trav.* II. 358 A man on the death of his wife is considered unclean ... He is not allowed to enter any kraal or dwelling, but must remain in the field .. until the period of separation is expired. 1838 J.E. ALEXANDER *Exped. into Int.* I. 49 In a sheltered nook among the hills were two large circular huts ... This was the field residence of Mynheer Nieuwoud. 1841 J. TINDALL *Jrnl* (1959) A host of wild dogs infested the field which rendered it necessary to drive our almost worn out cattle to the kraal in the evening. 1921 H.J. MANDELBROTE tr. O.F. Mentzel's *Descr. of Cape of G.H.* I. 57 Oxen .. damage the grain by soiling with fluid dung after .. being driven about in the field.

2. *hist.* Usu. with initial capital and in *pl.*, in the phr. *the Fields.*

a. Ellipt. for *the diamond fields* (see DIAMOND FIELDS).

 1871 *The Jrnl* 9 Jan., What can a British commissioner, or a special magistrate, under a queer Act of Parliament, do for the Fields? 1871 [see TICKEY sense 1 a]. 1873 [see OFF-COLOUR *adj.*]. 1879 E.L. PRICE *Jrnls* (1956) 340 We have to seek a new driver & leader here, as old Afrika only engaged to come as far as 'The Fields'. 1880 *Cape Monthly Mag.* II. 188 It took thirty days from Graham's Town to the Fields ... After helping my employer to load off and get out of the

Fields, we parted. *Ibid.* 190 The Fields — that El Dorado of the brave-hearted, energetic, and industrious. **1887** J.W. MATTHEWS *Incwadi Yami* 115 In the early days of the Fields the gambling spirit so infatuated many of the diggers, that .. they would prolong the accidents of fortune far into the night. **1895** *Jewish Chronicle* in Saron & Hotz *Jews in S. Afr.* (1955) 109 There was in those early days no local buying on the fields. All stones had to be sent to Cape Town. **1910** J. ANGOVE *In Early Days* 127 The opening of the telegraph line to Kimberley would be one of the red-letter days in the history of the Fields. **1931** G. BEET *Grand Old Days* 16 The Fields were .. found to consist of parched, hard soil and gravel, and big boulders, some weighing many tons, while the diamonds, instead of being placed .. conspicuously on the tops of the boulders .. were hidden well down under them. **1944** J. MOCKFORD *Here Are S. Africans* 92 Rhodes swept all the individual fortune-hunters into the co-operative of his monster joint-stock company which thereafter exploited the fields with a well-ordered and almost prosaic economy. **1965** D. ROOKE *Diamond Jo* 46 On the Fields you can get any price for blankets and clothes, flour too. **1972** A.A. TELFORD *Yesterday's Dress* 160 The discovery of diamonds in South Africa in 1866, brought fortune seekers from all over the world to the Fields. **1991** *Flying Springbok* May 122 He watched the diamond-hungry travellers making their way to the Kimberley fields.

b. *rare.* The gold fields of the Transvaal.

1890 C. & A.P. WILSON-MOORE *Diggers' Doggerel* 67 We talked together of things on the fields, And then he stood me a gin. **1893** 'JORUHTRA' in *Cape Illust. Mag.* Apr. 294, I .. came over this morning to have a look at the fields. **1897** J.P. FITZPATRICK *Outspan* 186 Two lucky diggers had passed through Newcastle from the fields, going home.

field commandant *n. phr. Obs.* exc. *hist.* [tr. S. Afr. Du. *veld commandant,* see VELD COMMANDANT.] COMMANDANT sense 1. Also used as a title.

1811 J.G. CUYLER in G.M. Theal *Rec. of Cape Col.* (1901) VIII. 28 Davel and a Hottentot were found dead by the Field Commandant Stoly. **1812** A. PLUMPTRE tr. *H. Lichtenstein's Trav. in Sn Afr.* (1928) I. 109 In every district there is a field-commandant, who has the supreme command of the parties which are occasionally sent out against the Bosjesmans, or against plundering-parties of fugitive slaves and Hottentots. **1835** C.L. STRETCH Journal. 4 Feb., Left Somerset .. to Spring buck flat where the Field Commandant Smit was bivouacked with 400 men. **1835** *Graham's Town Jrnl* in A. Steedman *Wanderings* II. 347 This party .. consisted of two hundred of the Swellendam Burghers, under the command of the veteran and gallant old Field-Commandant Linde. **1839** W.C. HARRIS *Wild Sports* 34 We were .. rather coolly welcomed by the Field Commandant, to whom we presented the Government letter. **1852** *Trial of Andries Botha* 103 The orders of the field-cornets and field-commandants were, that every man who ought to have been at Philipton, and was not there, was to be made a prisoner. **1875** C.B. BISSET *Sport & War* 189 We moved on to Queen's Town, being first met by the mounted Burghers of the District, drawn up under their field-cornets and field-commandants. **1971** J. PLOEGER in *Std Encycl. of Sn Afr.* III. 342 Increasing friction with the Bushmen led to the decision in 1774 to reorganise the defence of the northern frontier of the Colony by instituting the office of 'veldcommandant'. These new office-bearers .. were placed in charge of thirteen field-corporals with the rank of 'wagtmeester'. The .. field-commandants, who were subordinate to the landdrost, were chosen from among these 'wagtmeesters.' **1972** [see FIELD CORNET sense 1].

field cornet /ˈfiəld kɔːˈnet, -ˈkɔːnət/ *n. phr.* Also **field-cornett**, and with initial capitals. [tr. S. Afr. Du. *veld kornet,* see VELD-KORNET.]

1. *hist.* A civilian official invested with the rank and responsibilities of a military officer and with various judicial powers enabling him to act as a local administrator, magistrate, sheriff, and keeper of the peace in a ward; CORNET; VELD CORNET; VELD-KORNET sense 1. Also used as a title.

At the Cape, field cornets were appointed by the government but not directly remunerated for their services; in the Boer republics they were elected. Militarily subordinate to field commandants, in civil and judicial matters field cornets were responsible to landdrosts. They were replaced by justices of the peace in 1916.

1800 G. YONGE in G.M. Theal *Rec. of Cape Col.* (1898) III. 197 Correct Lists of all such Inhabitants as shall have taken out their regular License to kill Game, to be sent to the different Field Cornets in their Districts. **1811** EARL OF CALEDON in G.W. Eybers *Sel. Constit. Doc.* (1918) 104 The .. Publication shall be forthwith transmitted .. by the Landdrosts to the Heemraden, Field-Commandants, and Field-Cornets of their Districts, to be by them made known to the Inhabitants at large. **1812** A. PLUMPTRE tr. *H. Lichtenstein's Trav. in Sn Afr.* (1928) I. 67 Field-cornet is the title given to a magistrate who decides in the first instance little disputes that sometimes arise. **1835** J.W.D. MOODIE *Ten Yrs* II. 173 In the district of Uitenhage .. there were only inferior magistrates, called field-cornets, who were formerly empowered to inflict a certain degree of corporal punishment on refractory slaves or Hottentots at their own discretion, on complaint being made by the master. **1852** M.B. HUDSON *S. Afr. Frontier Life* 39 Every district throughout the colony has its Field-cornets or Constables. These officers have power to apprehend without warrant; as also to summons special constables. They are Coroners for their district, and the official organs of communication between the authorities and the inhabitants of their divisions. **1852, 1875** [see FIELD COMMANDANT]. **1877** J. NOBLE *S. Afr.* 29 One farmer told his Kafir servant, who had been with him for several years 'I have an instruction from the field-cornet to send you to your own country.' 'My own country? This is my own country.' **1880** E.F. SANDEMAN *Eight Months in Ox-Waggon* 94 On our first trek we met the field cornet, who combines in one the offices of magistrate, sheriff, chief constable, arbitrator, and executioner. **1900** H.C. HILLEGAS *Oom Paul's People* 206 As soon as the commandant-general issues an order for the mobilization of the volunteer army the commandants and their assistants, the field-cornets, speedily go from one house to another in their districts and summon the burghers from their homes. **1937** H.C. ARMSTRONG *Grey Steel* 171 Milner had dissolved the commando system, by which each ward was placed under a field-cornet and made responsible for its own police duties. **1972** J. BALL in *Std Encycl. of Sn Afr.* VII. 398 From service in the field, mostly against Bushmen, the titles of field-commandant and field-cornet .. arose so that these officers could be distinguished from those who remained at home ... As early as 1780 such officers are referred to. **1988** SMUTS & ALBERTS *Forgotten Highway* 122 He bought a farm .. in Piketberg, where he became a field cornet.

2. *hist.* A rank in the army, equivalent to that of Lieutenant; VELD-KORNET sense 2.

1950 D. REED *Somewhere S. of Suez* 187 The Nationalist Afrikaner Minister of Defence in 1948 announced that it [*sc.* the Defence Force] would be reorganized 'so that it would become independent of co-operation from sources outside the Union' ... In that spirit, apparently, the British military model and nomenclature were done away with and the Boer Commandos revived, with their ranks from Field Cornet to Commandant. **1971** F.A. VAN JAARSVELD in *Std Encycl. of Sn Afr.* IV. 488 The title of field-cornet disappeared finally as a civil office and was replaced by 'justice of the peace'. In 1960 the military rank was restored and took the place of lieutenant, to denote an officer of a particular rank in the South African army, but only in the land forces. The former second lieutenant now became assistant field-cornet.

3. A rank in the Voortrekkers (see VOORTREKKER *n.* sense 2 b), an Afrikaner youth organization.

1975 J.F.P. BADENHORST in *Std Encycl. of Sn Afr.* XI. 288 Membership [of the Voortrekker movement] is open to White boys and girls, officers ('field cornets' and 'commandants'), executive members and 'lay members'.

field cornetcy *n. phr.* Also **field kornetcy**, and with initial capital. [FIELD CORNET + Eng. abstract-n.-forming suffix *-cy.*]

1. *obs.* A subdivision or ward of a district, falling under the jurisdiction of a FIELD CORNET; VELD CORNETCY; VELD CORNETSHIP; VELDKORNETCY. Also *attrib.*

1828 *Ordinance for Regulating Manner of Proceeding in Criminal Cases* in *Stat. Law of Cape of G.H.* (1862) 44 In all cases the like duties, inspections, and examinations, shall and may be in like manner performed and conducted by any Field-cornet, each in his own particular Field-cornetcy. **1831** *S. Afr. Almanac & Dir.* 160 The actual extent of the Field-Cornetcy is not accurately known; but it will take a man on horseback three days to ride round it. **1847** 'A BENGALI' *Notes on Cape of G.H.* 7 The whole colony is divided into 'districts' and the districts sub-divided into 'Field-Cornetcies'. **1877** F. JEPPE *Tvl Bk Almanac & Dir.* (1976) 35 Each district is divided into several Field-cornetcies or Wards, superintended by a Fieldcornet, elected by each Ward. **1899** G.M. THEAL *Rec. of Cape Col.* V. 9 The farmers of the fieldcornetcies of Zwartkops River, the Zuurveld, and Bruintjes Hoogte remained faithful to the government they had established but the others were beginning to argue that it would be better to submit to the English than to be deprived of ammunition and of a market to buy and sell in. **1913** C. PETTMAN *Africanderisms* 169 *Field cornetcy,* The area over which a field cornet has jurisdiction.

2. *hist.* The office of field cornet.

1900 B. MITFORD *Aletta* 132 Then he came to the point. He wished to resign his field-cornetcy. **1946** E. ROSENTHAL *General De Wet* 26 So little was he concerned with their opinion that he did not even take into account the prestige value of his Field-Cornetcy. **1973** J. MEINTJES *Voortrekkers* 43 His son Carolus .. says that Louis was so busy with matters arising from his field-cornetcy that he as eldest son took over the supervision of their extensive farming activities.

3. *hist.* The militia unit commanded by a field cornet.

1929 D. REITZ *Commando* 24 A field-cornetcy was supposed to contain 150–200 men. **1940** F.B. YOUNG *City of Gold* 186 Each field-cornetcy had its own bivouac, and the triangular wall of wagon-tilts was flushed with the light of numerous fires. **1963** S. CLOETE *Rags of Glory* 41 A commando consisted of two field kornetcies, each of approximately two hundred men, which was again divided into eight corporalships of approximately 25 men each. **1987** W. STEENKAMP *Blockhouse* 6 In theory a commando was led by a commandant and consisted of a number of field-cornetcies, each commanded by a field-cornet. A field-cornetcy in turn was divided into a number of corporalships.

4. A division of the Afrikaner youth organization, the Voortrekkers (see VOORTREKKER *n.* sense 2 b).

1975 J.F.P. BADENHORST in *Std Encycl. of Sn Afr.* XI. 288 The Penkoppe, Drawwertjies and Verkenners are grouped into field-cornetcies for boys and for girls, and two or more field-cornetcies form a commando.

field pound *n. phr.* [tr. Afk. *veld pond.*] VELD POND.

1973 *Sunday Times* 27 May 6 They needed coins — so the State Mint-in-the-Field was established at Pilgrim's Rest, where 986 'field pounds' were produced. **1979** *S. Afr. Digest* 13 July 19 The highest bid was R2 800 for a rare *Veldpond* (field pound) in gold.

field shoe *n. phr. Obs.* [tr. Du. *veldschoen.*] VELDSKOEN *n.* sense 1.

1731 G. MEDLEY tr. *P. Kolb's Present State of Cape of G.H.* I. 204 The *Europeans* at the *Cape* have a Sort of Shoes they call Field-Shoes. These are cut out of the raw Hide of an Ox or Stag, and made, the hairy Side outward, in the Shape of a Half-Stocking, slit down in Front from the Ankle to the Toe. **1786** G. FORSTER tr. *A. Sparrman's Voy. to Cape of G.H.* I. 194 These field shoes, as they are called, made of almost raw leather, are much more durable. **1795** C.R. HOPSON tr. *C.P. Thunberg's Trav.* I. 195 They generally wear here what are called field-shoes, which the country people usually make themselves. **1838** J.E. ALEXANDER *Exped. into Int.* I. 8 Field shoes, or a sort of buskin, of untanned leather. **1882** S. HECKFORD *Lady Trader in Tvl* 139 His *feldt-schoons*, or field-shoes, made of untanned leather. **1896** H.A. BRYDEN *Tales of S. Afr.* 24, I had a pair of *velschoens* — Boer field-shoes, made of strong yet soft leather of home-tanned hide. These shoes were close-fitting, light, and pliable.

fies var. VIES.

Fietas /ˈfitas/ *n. slang.* Also **Fidas**, **Vietas**. [Prob. Afk. *fieta* + pl. *-s*, ad. *fiela* 'backward, slovenly person', cogn. with Du. *fielt* villain, scoundrel; or perh. ad. Zulu *i-vila* loafer, sluggard.] Esp. among its residents: Vrededorp (or Pageview), an area of Johannesburg from which residents were forcibly removed under the Group Areas Act.

1982 *Pace* May 158 They used to 'tune' it in the olden days around Vrededorp alias Fidas. **1982** *Star* 11 Nov. (Tonight) 4 'Die lingo' (language) whether it be in Soweto, District Six, Fietas (Vrededorp) or Durban is always vibrant, bubbling with clichés and anecdotes. **1984** *Frontline* Feb. 26 Fietas and Duries, which the newspapers .. call by hifalutin' names like Vrededorp (or even Pageview ..) and Doornfontein. **1986** *Star* 23 Apr. 19 Verses from the pre-war campfire song, 'This is the place Jo'burg' ... We've got some wonderful tramcars, Wot shakes like boxes of nails. They charge you a tickey by Fietas And a fourpence by the end of the rails. **1989** *Frontline* Mar. 28 Vrededorp — Vietas to its residents and Pageview to the map-makers — was Joburg's last indiscriminate area, and one of the last in the country to be laid low before the Group Areas Act ran out of steam. **1990** J. NAIDOO *Coolie Location* 209 My sister Ruby .. was then living in Fietas. **1993** [see GROUP AREA *n. phr.* sense 1].

fighting stick *n. phr.*

1. Either of the two short staves wielded in mock fights among young (rural) black men; FENCING STICK; INTONGA. See also STICK-FIGHT.

1985 *Cape Times* 30 Sept. 1 Chief Buthelezi .. arrived wearing a leopardskin headband and a necklace of lion claws and carrying a shield and fighting sticks. **1989** L. BEAKE *Cageful of Butterflies* 35 Mponyane would pick up the fighting sticks one more time and play the game again. They carried their sticks everywhere. **1991** *Sunday Times* 22 Sept. 29 He raises the fighting sticks he is carrying, adopts a combat position and yells an insult.

2. KIERIE.

1989 J. HOBBS *Thoughts in Makeshift Mortuary* 165 Each man carries a wooden fighting stick. *Ibid.* 166 Men on foot with assegais and fighting sticks are no match for men on horseback with guns. **1990** *Weekend Post* 31 Mar. 6 They .. kill each other, using pangas, fighting sticks and homemade guns, in horrifying acts.

Fikani var. FETCANI.

fikey var. VAATJIE.

financial rand see RAND sense 3 b.

fingerpohl, -pol, -pole, finger-poll varr. VINGERPOL.

finger-trek *n.* [Part. tr. Afk. *vingertrek*.] VINGERTREK. Also *fig.* (see quot. 1988).

1958 A. JACKSON *Trader on Veld* 45 A game called 'finger trek' (pulling the finger), was also popular with our farmers, and many a time .. I was challenged to hook my middle finger around that of a burly customer, only to find myself being pulled across bodily like a sack of flour in this unequal and rather painful tug-of-war. **1988** *Sunday Tribune* 31 Jan. (Today) 7 The already discredited tricameral system is coming further apart at the seams as the Great All-In-Non-Stop Arm-Wrestling Power-Play Finger-Trek, Name-Calling Rat-On-Your-Pals Extravanganza proceeds apace.

Fingo /ˈfɪŋɡəʊ/ *n.* Also **Fingoe**, **Fingoo**, **Phengoe**, and with small initial. Pl. unchanged, **-s**, or **-es**. [Englished form of Xhosa *amaMfengu* destitute wanderers seeking work and refuge, fr. *fenguza* seek service.]

a. MFENGU. Also *attrib.*

1827 W. SHAW Diary. 6 June, Had at night much interesting conversation on religious subjects with a Fingoo man who is the only person we found here, in charge of his Master's cattle. **1829** C. ROSE *Four Yrs in Sn Afr.* 193, I saw many fugitives, who are called Fingos, wanderers; and on my once mentioning Chaka before them, a woman exclaimed, 'that is the wolf that destroys us'. **1835** J. AYLIFF Journal. 15 May, A day full of interest to the Fingoe Nation, for on it they were put in possession of that land which was to become their home after years of wandering. **1835** [see EAT]. **1837** 'N. POLSON' *Subaltern's Sick Leave* 109 Some tribes of Mantatees [*printed* Mantalees] and Phengoes, nations of which small remnants took refuge in the Colony when their names as nations were destroyed by the kafirs in their gradual south-western movement. **1839** W.C. HARRIS *Wild Sports* 30 We resolved to halt for the night at a kraal of Fingoes or tame Kafirs. **1846** J.W. APPLEYARD *War of Axe* (1971) 62 The Board of Relief for distressed Fingoes met to-day for the purpose of seeing the applicants, and hearing their cases. **1846** J. HARE in *Imp. Blue Bks* Command Paper 786–1847, 89 The Fingoes are all well disposed and determined to stand by their best friends the Government, and recent events at Fort Peddie have strengthened their hatred of the Kafirs. **1852** M.B. HUDSON *S. Afr. Frontier Life* p.xi, The Fingoes .. whom, Sir Benjamin D'Urban finding in the war of 1835 as 'dogs' .. amongst the Kafirs .. admitted into the colony .. giving them grants of land. **1857** J. SHOOTER *Kafirs of Natal* p.iv, Their masters had denominated them Amafengu, 'destitute people in search of service' — a name which has been corrupted into Fingoes. **1871** J. MCKAY *Reminisc.* 4 At Grahamstown, we had the pleasure of seeing a company of H.M. Fingoe levies perform one of their war-dances, previous to their march to Kafirland. **1877** C. ANDREWS Reminiscences of Kafir War 1834–5. 2 The Galakas .. will, by their attack on the Fingoes, who are British subjects .. provoke a war with the Colony. **1882** C.L. NORRIS-NEWMAN *With Boers in Tvl* 15 Fingoes .. remnants of .. tribes dispersed by the conquests of Charka and Moselakatze .. and held in .. slavery by the Amascosa tribes. **1899** E. ROSS *Diary of Siege of Mafeking* (1980) 55 About 50 Fingoes went out last night for the purpose of worrying up the Boers, but they returned and did not do any damage. **1912** AYLIFF & WHITESIDE *Hist. of Abambo* 28 Fingos .. having fled into Hintsa's country, for refuge .. were converted into slaves, and held in the most degrading bondage, the Gcalekas .. regarding them in little higher estimation than beasts. **1943** D. REITZ *No Outspan* 51 A religious fanatic of the Fingo tribe .. collected a large following from among the natives in the Transkei territory. **1971** H. POTGIETER in *Std Encycl. of Sn Afr.* IV. 514 On their own initiative the Fingos collected funds .. for the large educational and training institution of Blytheswood .. opened in 1877. **1974** P. GIBBS *Right of Line* 20 Land promised by Rhodes to the Fingoes who had gone up to Rhodesia with the pioneer column — the origin of the present Fingoe Location near Bulawayo. **1979** *S. Afr. Panorama* July 31 The Ninth and last Frontier War .. broke out when colonial troops were used to protect the Fingoes against other Xhosa tribes. **1982** [see WHITE *adj.* sense 1 b]. **1987** *Daily Dispatch* 14 Feb. 1 He asked how Ciskei would be able to fit in with the present number of fragmented tribes in Transkei .. while Ciskei comprised Xhosa and Fingos and was not a 'torn blanket of nations'. **1990** *Weekly Mail* 8 Feb. 12 The 4 000 Mfengu (or Fingo) people of Humansdorp received a total of R200 000 in compensation for improvements to their land.

b. *comb.* **Fingo-Kafir**, also **Fingoe Kaffir**, a Fingo (see sense a); **Fingoland**, see quot. 1971.

1866 W.C. HOLDEN *Past & Future* 284 *Natal Kaffirs*, means those who reside in Natal; and **Fingoe Kaffirs**, those who reside on the frontier of the Cape Colony. These two are actually the same .. the former being those who remained in Natal .. the latter being those who were fully dispersed, and found their way into the old colony. **1872** *Wesleyan Missionary Reports* 73 There must be 25,000 or 30,000 Kafirs and Fingo-Kafirs in this Circuit, the great mass of whom are still heathen. **1902** *Encycl. Brit.* XXX. 3 The formerly degraded but now respected and civilized Fingos or Fengus, who gave their name to the district of **Fingoland**. *c*1911 S. PLAYNE *Cape Col.* 694 The Division of Peddie .. includes Fingoland, which has been occupied by the Fingoes since they were driven from their own country by the Zulus many years ago. **1937** B.J.F. LAUBSCHER *Sex, Custom & Psychopathology* 211 A small number of families of the mental patients who did not visit their children or relatives were visited wherever possible in .. Fingoland. **1971** H. POTGIETER in *Std Encycl. of Sn Afr.* IV. 514 *Fingoland*, C.P. Region in the Transkei, between the Great Kei and the Bashee Rivers, containing the villages of Butterworth, Nqamakwe, Tsomo, and Idutywa as well as parts of their districts.

finish(ed) and klaar see KLAAR sense 4.

fink /fɪŋk/ *n.* [Englished form of S. Afr. Du. *vink* finch.]

a. Any of several species of bird of the Ploceidae, including those of the genera *Euplectes* (commonly known as bishops and widows), *Ploceus* (weavers), and *Quelea*; VINK sense a.

*a*1823 J. EWART *Jrnl* (1970) 81 Wheat is very productive ... It has a great enemy in a small bird called the fink which perch upon it in flocks of several thousands. **1853** *Edin. New Philos. Jrnl* (U.K.) LV. 82 The yellow and green *finks* may be seen disporting in multitudes .. and entering every now and then into their grass-woven nests. **1867** E.L. LAYARD *Birds of S. Afr.* 185 On his being addressed as 'Fink,' he instantly replied, stretching his neck to the utmost, and uttering the most piercing, discordant shriek. **1894** E. GLANVILLE *Fair Colonist* 87 The pendant nests of the noisy finks hung like suspended flasks to the slender arms of the trailing willow. **1910** D. FAIRBRIDGE *That Which Hath Been* (1913) 119 Scarlet and black finks whirred through the clean air. **1913** —— *Piet of Italy* 136 Weeping-willows drooped over the water, and yellow finks swung on their pendulous nests, suspended from the frail branches, shrieking, twisting, gesticulating as only a yellow fink can. **1918** S.H. SKAIFE *Animal Life* 247 The weaver-birds, or *finks*, all build covered nests suspended from trees or reeds, thus differing from most finches. **1920** R.Y. STORMBERG *Mrs Pieter de Bruyn* 7 It has been vandalised by swarms of 'finks' and .. 'muisvogels' who snip off the blooms most viciously. **1942** S. CLOETE *Hill of Doves* 92 To his right, a fink twittered. **1947** E.R SEARY *S. Afr. Short Stories* Glossary, *Fink*, (Vink in Afrikaans): several species of weaver birds. **1951** R. GRIFFITHS *Grey about Flame* 30 In the reed beds the black and scarlet finks were shrill about their plaited nests. **1977** *S. Afr. Panorama* Oct. 27 Great nest-builders are the finks and weavers. [**1987** *Frontline* Mar. 22 When he should have been going to school he was herding cattle and chasing finke out of the wheat.]

b. *obsolescent.* With defining word: **blood -**, **kaffir -**, **red -**, or **scarlet fink**, the red bishop bird *Euplectes orix*; *red vink*, see VINK sense b.

1889 H.A. BRYDEN *Kloof & Karroo* 15 We saw and shot the red fink, sometimes called the red grenadier grosbeak (*Ploceus oryx*). **1896** A. PAGE *Afternoon Ride* 62 The Kafir fink swaying on the grass. **1899** R.B. & J.D.S. WOODWARD *Natal Birds* 70 It [*sc.* the Bishop bird, *Pyromelana oryx*] is popularly known as the 'Blood fink,' and .. the male bird has several little brown females. **1900** H.A. BRYDEN *Animals of Afr.* 160 One of the most beautiful of the many kinds of weaver-birds in Africa is the splendid Red Kaffir Finch, the Rooi fink of the Dutch colonists, sometimes also called the Red Bishop-bird. **1936** R. CAMPBELL *Mithraic Emblems* 34 The scarlet fink, the chook, the sprew, that seem to call me by my name.

finkel var. VINKEL.

finrand /ˈfɪnrænd/ *n.* Shortened form of *financial rand*, see RAND sense 3 b. Also *attrib.*

1980 S. WILLSON in *Rand Daily Mail* 28 Nov. 25 Finrand's days may be numbered. *Ibid.* 3 Dec. 16 The finrand bulls then turned sellers and brought the FR lower, dropping it to US 99.5c at one point. **1989** *E. Prov. Herald* 16 Mar. 10 Du Plessis against abolition of finrand. **1989** *Weekend Post* 23 Dec. 10 The finrand played havoc with gold shares and other market leaders .. which pulled down industrial leaders in their wake. **1992** *Business Day* 15 Dec. 3 The elimination of the finrand system at a time of low positive or negative real rates of return would probably .. precipitate a net outflow of foreign funds from the market. **1993** *Cape Times* 10 Aug. (Business Report) 8 The finrand's discount to the commercial rand widened to 29% from Friday's 27.7%.

fire lily *n. phr.* [See quot. 1985.] Any of several scarlet-flowered species of *Cyrtanthus* lilies (family Amaryllidaceae), esp. *C. contractus, C. sanguineus,* and *C. angustifolius*; BRANDLELIE. See also IFAFA LILY, *Kei lily* (KEI sense 1); KNYSNA LILY sense b.

1876 H. BROOKS *Natal* 169 The leading glory of the pastures at this time is a plant known to the Dutch under the expressive and most apt name of the 'fire-lily.' The pastures are frequently literally ablaze with its broadly spread carpet of scarlet. **1913** C. PETTMAN *Africanderisms* 171 *Fire lily, Cyrtanthus angustifolius* ... The brilliant flame colour of its flowers is rendered more conspicuous by the blackness of the hills after the annual grass burning. **1929** M. ALSTON *From Old Cape Homestead* 81 After a fire armies of fire-lilies burst out of the charred earth – little aristocrats for all their hanging heads, .. flaunting their brilliance in the midst of black desolation ... Their botanical name is Cyrtanthus sanguineus. **1965** S. ELIOVSON *S. Afr. Wild Flowers for Garden* 90 Cyrtanthus. *Fire-Lily* ... The common name *Fire-Lily* is given because some species which grow amongst grass appear profusely after veld fires ... There are nearly 50 species. **1975** J.M. GIBSON *Wild Flowers of Natal* 15 *Cyrtanthus contractus*, .. As children we used to make flutes out of the stems of this fire lily, and I don't think it grows unless there has been a veld fire. **1985** K. PIENAAR *Grow S. Afr. Plants* 41 Bulbs in this genus are commonly known as fire lilies because some species burst into bloom after veld fires, forming brilliant scarlet patches in the still-blackened veld. **1988** M. BRANCH *Explore Cape Flora* 38 The fire lilies .. will lie dormant for over 20 years if there is no fire. **1989** 'BABIANA' in *E. Prov. Herald* 18 Mar. 8 The George Lily is certainly the most beautiful of the whole group of red cyrtanthuses, all commonly known as fire lilies.

fiscal /ˈfɪskəl/ *n.* Formerly also **fiscaal, fiscall.** [Englished form of obs. Du. *fiscaal.*]

1. *hist.* Usu. with initial capital. The chief legal officer at the Cape of Good Hope under Dutch East India Company rule, performing the functions of attorney-general, public prosecutor, chief magistrate, customs officer, and chief of police. Also *attrib.*

The post was instituted at the Cape in 1689, and existed also in other Dutch possessions. Until 1785 the Fiscal was responsible only to the board of the Dutch East India Company. After the Cape became a British colony in 1806, the Fiscal's duties were gradually transferred to other officials.

1696 W. ERLE in R. Raven-Hart *Cape G.H. 1652–1702* (1971) II. 422 To day the Fiscall & the Governrs. Son dined with me. **1731** [see LANDDROST sense 1]. **1768** J. BANKS in J. Hawkesworth *Acct of Voy.* (1773) 442, I should very ill deserve the favours they bestowed, if I did not particularly mention the First and Second Governor, and the Fiscal. **1798** S.H. WILCOCKE tr. *J.S. Stavorinus's Voy. to E. Indies 1768–71* I. 570 The second in rank next to the governor, and the fiscal, who is independent of him, have the rank of senior merchants. **1806** *Gleanings in Afr.* (anon.) 251 The Chief magistrate at the Cape, is the fiscal ... His principal emolument arises from fines, which being a power vested in him as discretionary, is so much the more dangerous to the colonists. **1822** W.J. BURCHELL *Trav.* I. 78 The Fiscal, being the head of the police and the sitting Magistrate, a great variety of business is daily transacted at his office. **1858** *Cape Monthly Mag.* III. Mar. 150 The Governor .. presides over a Council consisting of the second or deputy Governor, the fiscal, the major (who commands the fort), the secretary, the treasurer, the comptroller of provisions, the comptroller of liquors, and the bookkeeper, each of which has a branch of the Company's service assigned to his care. **1887** *S.W. Silver & Co.'s Handbk to S. Afr.* 21 The Fiscal, who acted as Attorney General and secretary of this court, was supposed to possess legal knowledge. **1921** H.J. MANDELBROTE tr. *O.F. Mentzel's Descr. of Cape of G.H.* I. 141 Next to the Governor the Fiscal is the most lucrative post at the Cape. He derives heavy fees from judicial proceedings. **1936** *Cambridge Hist. of Brit. Empire* VIII. 249 Apprehensive as to the attitude of the *Commercial Advertiser*, the Fiscal sent for the printer, Greig, and .. demanded 10,000 rix-dollars as security. **1951** L.G. GREEN *Grow Lovely* 45 For nearly two centuries Cape Town's chief of police was an official with the title of Fiscal – a name which survives in the shape of Janfiskaal, Jacky Hangman or butcher-bird. That shows you how popular the fiscal was. **1976** A. DELIUS *Border* 142 The Fiscal asserted that he would censor all further issues of the Magazine.

2. *transf.* [See quot. 1913.] In full ***fiscal shrike*** (formerly also ***fiscal bird***): the butcher bird *Lanius collaris* of the Laniidae; CANARY-BITER; FISKAAL; JACK HANGER; JACKIE; JACKIE HANGMAN; JANFISKAAL; JOHNNY HANGMAN.

1795 C.R. HOPSON tr. *C.P. Thunberg's Trav.* I. 293 *Fiscal* and *Canary-byter* were the appellations given to a black and white bird (*Lanius collaris*) .. common in the town. **1801** J. BARROW *Trav.* I. 29 Turtle doves, a thrush called the Sprew, and the Fiscal bird .. frequent the gardens near the town. **1822** [see Latham quot. at CANARY-BITER]. **1824** W.J. BURCHELL *Trav.* II. 345 Several kinds of lanius .. are called *Fiscal-vogels* (Fiscal-birds) by the colonists. **1898** E. GLANVILLE in *Empire* 30 July (Pettman), The white-throated, black-headed, hook-billed fiscal made soft notes in imitation of the red-speckled breasted wrens, finishing up with a harsh screech which completely gave him away. **1913** C. PETTMAN *Africanderisms* 102 Other South African names [for the butcher bird] are Jack Hanger, Laksman, Kanariebijter, and Fiscal, all indicating its murderous propensities. *Ibid.* 171 *Fiscal*, .. This bird .. is as much feared among the smaller birds and animals, which it ruthlessly kills and impales, as the Fiscal of the old Dutch East India Company was by the earlier colonists. **1924** D. FAIRBRIDGE *Gardens of S. Afr.* 99 Birds which are among the gardener's friends are the Robin, the Bok-makerie, and even the maligned Fiscal, which all live on insects. **1931** *Guide to Vertebrate Fauna of E. Cape Prov.* (Albany Museum) I. 98 *Lanius collaris*, Linn. Fiscal Shrike, Butcher-Bird ... Chiefly found in and around the towns, villages and human habitations. Nests cup-shaped. **1967** *Some Protected Birds of Cape Prov.* (Dept of Nature Conservation) Pl.144, *Fiscal Shrike, Butcher Bird, Johnny Hangman*, The commonest true shrike found in South Africa. **1978** MCLACHLAN & LIVERSIDGE *Roberts Birds of S. Afr.* 503 The Fiscal does not tolerate other birds in its haunts and even carries its raids into neighbouring gardens and destroys anything that is too slow to avoid it. **1980** J.O. OLIVER *Beginner's Guide to our Birds* 84 The Fiscal is black and white with a long tail and a white V on its back.

Hence (sense 1) **fiscalship** *n. rare*, the office of fiscal.

1809 H. ALEXANDER in G.M. Theal *Rec. of Cape Col.* (1900) VI. 470 The Deputy Fiscalship there remains directly under the Superintendance, and as an immediate Branch of the Fiscal's Office in Cape Town.

fish-cart *n. hist.* A horse-drawn cart formerly used in the streets of Cape Town by fish-vendors. Also *attrib.* See also FISH HORN.

1895 A.B. BALFOUR *1200 Miles in Waggon* 15 A cadger's cart, in which fish is .. hawked along the streets .. with invariable accompaniment of a horn ... The number of these fish-carts is extraordinary. *c*1904 J.H. DE VILLIERS in L.G. Green *Old Men Say* (1964) 64 The fish carts cannot drive to every house, so the drivers must blow their horns. **1915** D. FAIRBRIDGE *Torch Bearer* 138 Mrs Neethling .. paused in blank amazement at .. her distinguished lodger in parley with Abdol of the fish-cart. *a*1920 O.E.A. SCHREINER in D.L. Hobman *Olive Schreiner* (1955) 46 In the streets were Malays; and fish carts blowing their horns. **1927** *Outspan* 18 Mar. 45 Capetown also has to suffer .. the long-drawn-out moan of the fish cart horn. **1949** J. MOCKFORD *Golden Land* 48 Through the streets a horse-drawn fish-cart rumbles, heralded by unmusical but far-travelling blasts from a horn blown by a Malay fishmonger. **1972** L.G. GREEN *When Journey's Over* 147 They have to be content with what may be dropped at their doors by those dreadful fish carts. **1974** A.P. BRINK *Looking on Darkness* 84 A fishcart .. with the glistening smooth bodies of snoek and geelbek, kabeljou and mackerel. **1979** *Voice* 4 Mar. 7 The fish-cart with its blaring horn summoning the people to buy cray-fish .. or snoek fresh from the boats. **1987** *Living* June 104 A Village Management Board .. was soon busy regulating such things as .. 'noisy hooting of fish cart drivers'.

fish eagle *n. phr.* The eagle *Haliaeetus vocifer* of the Accipitridae, which preys mainly on fish and is found over a wide area of sub-Saharan Africa; SEA-EAGLE.

[**1885** H.M. STANLEY *Congo* II. 6 That white-collared fish eagle out-spreading his wings for flight. **1890** — in *Pall Mall Gaz.* (U.K.) 28 June 2 Fish eagles. **1913** C. PETTMAN *Africanderisms* 200 The fishing eagle.] **1949** C. BULLOCK *Rina* 57 A fish-eagle flew over the river. **1959** M.W. SPILHAUS *Under Bright Sky* 148 We lay on our oars watching a great fish eagle make for his haystack of a nest in a tree at the waterside. **1968** R. GRIFFITHS *Man of River* 17 A fish-eagle rose up and swept out across the blue haze, climbing steadily on wide curved wings. **1971** *Personality* 5 Mar. 16 High in the riverine trees, the beautiful white-headed fish eagles sit proudly .. their calls echoing between the banks ... Swooping downwards, strong claws extended, they clutch a fish from beneath the surface. **1971** K.B. NEWMAN *Birdlife in Sn Afr.* (1979) 61 The Fish Eagle .. will fish in the sea where one of its favourite prey species is the .. 'harder'. **1982** *S. Afr. Panorama* Sept. 50 No film on the Bushveld is complete without the plaintive cry of the fish eagle; its sound is the very spirit of Africa. **1992** *S. Afr. Panorama* Mar.-Apr. 120 The fish eagle is monarch of this primitive kingdom ... He surveys his wild domain, then uttering a haunting cry .. swoops down .. to scoop up a fish.

fish horn *n. phr. Hist.* The small horn used in the past by Cape Town fish-vendors to cry their wares. Also *attrib.* See also FISH-CART.

1871 W.G. ATHERSTONE in A.M.L. Robinson *Sel. Articles from Cape Monthly Mag.* (1978) 80 What sound is that, like a cracked fish-horn with a very bad cold? *c*1904 J.H. DE VILLIERS in L.G. Green *Old Men Say* (1964) 64 The noise of the fish horn is not very musical and might affect the nerves of extremely sensitive people. **1910** *Rand Daily Mail* Nov. 8 Malay carts, bearing hideous fish-horn blowers .. monstrosities .. known a century ago. **1913** W.W. THOMPSON *Sea Fisheries of Cape Col.* 82 The tuneless reverberations of the archaic fish-horn are decidedly open to improvement. [**1927** see FISH-CART.] **1936** H.I. BRIMBLE in I.D. Du Plessis *Cape Malays* (1944) 47 The fish-horn, that 'pest of the Cape Town streets'. **1947** L.G. GREEN *Tavern of Seas* 15 A weird, bleating call, a banshee wail .. it is the fish horn. **1955** V. DE KOCK *Fun They Had* 163 The vendor would slowly wend his way through the streets .. lustily blowing his fish horn. **1964** L.G. GREEN *Old Men Say* 64 Cape Town's earliest fish-horns were hollow lengths of kelp. More durable horns were made later from paraffin tins. **1969** [see CAPE CART]. **1979** HEARD & FAULL *Our Best Trad. Recipes* 63 The sea bamboo .. whose hollow dried stalks were used as fish horns .. to herald the approach of the Cape fish carts. **1986** *Fair Lady* 16 Apr., As the sound of the fish horn came nearer, they rushed .. to the front gate to await the arrival of the little cart and horse.

fish oil *n. phr.* Vegetable oil (used for frying). Also *attrib.*

1950 H. GERBER *Cape Cookery* 126 Onion Atjar. Boil up 1 pint fish oil with a little pounded garlic, borrie, a few chillies and some curry powder. **1951** L.G. GREEN *Grow Lovely* 58 Fish oil plays an important part in the Chinese cuisine. **1976** *Cape Herald* 14 Sept. 17 (*advt*) Fish oil 750 ml 67 1/2c. **1984** *Drum* Sept. 77 [Ingredients:] 2 onions .. green chillies .. 150 ml fish oil, [etc.]. **1988** K. NGWENYA in *Drum* Mar. 92 He made his first 'blik' guitar – an old fish oil tin strung with nylon fishing gut.

‖**fiskaal** /fəsˈkɑːl/ *n.* Also **fiskal**. [Afk., see FISCAL.] The FISCAL (sense 2), *Lanius collaris.*

1888 *Cape Punch* 4 Apr. 203 All the fiskaals and rooibekkies That I always used to catch. **1910** A.B. LAMONT *Rural Reader* 99 The cunning little shrike (fiskaal) that hangs his prey on thorn bushes. **1923** HAAGNER & IVY *Sketches* 160 The commonest .. is the ordinary Fiskal .. whose shambles is a well-known sight to every South African. **1930** N. STEVENSON *Farmers of Lekkerbat* 155 The *fiskaal* was filling its large larder, it never had enough. **1936** E.L. GILL *First Guide to S. Afr. Birds* 46 The Fiskaal .. habitually sits on telegraph wires ... Noted for killing canaries in cages ... Commonly supposed to imitate small birds' songs and so lure them to their doom. **1945** N. DEVITT *People & Places* 145 Jacky Hangman is .. the Natal name for the butcher bird, known in the Cape as the fiskaal. **1973** O.H. SPOHR tr. *F. Krauss's Trav. Jrnl* 12 The cheerful fiskal .. found everywhere hunting insects.

Fitcani, -kani varr. FETCANI.

flaaitaal /ˈflaɪtɑːl/ *n.* Also **flytaal**, and with initial capital. [Eng. *fly* knowing, clever + Afk. *taal* language.] An urban (esp. township) argot made up of a mixture of Afrikaans and Sintu-language (Bantu-language) grammatical structures, and vocabulary drawn from many of the languages spoken in South Africa as well as new coinages; *die taal*, see TAAL sense 1 b; ISICAMTHO; ISIJITA; MENSETAAL; *tsotsi-taal*, see TSOTSI sense 2; formerly also called SHALAMBOMBO.

'Flaaitaal' is preferred by some to 'tsotsitaal', the latter being considered either outdated or insulting (as 'tsotsi' means 'thug' or 'gangster'). Others prefer the term 'isicamtho'.

1959 L. LONGMORE *Dispossessed* 250 *Tsotsis* have their own secret language known as *flaaitaal* or *tsotsi* slang, which is continually being improved on and added to. These *flaaitaals* differ from city to city and even in different parts of the cities themselves. **1978** B. MFENYANA in *E. Prov. Herald* 1 May 3, I would like to focus specifically on the modern language of the tsotsis the lower class young people, and 'fly taal', the language of 'hip' city slickers. **1979** C. VAN DER MERWE in *Frontline* Dec. 17 If you know what's good for you, you'd better not call it tsotsi-taal ... Not that Flytaal is all *that* different from tsotsi-taal .. but it's finding itself a new image. *Ibid.* 18 Nobody seems to know where the 'Fly' of Flytaal comes from. (... It might just as well be 'flie', 'vlei' or 'flaai'.) **1987** C.T. MSIMANG in *S. Afr. Jrnl of Afr. Langs* July 82 Tsotsitaal is also known as Flaaitaal. **1989** WILLEMSE & ZILLER in *Staffrider* Vol.8 No.1, 120 Makhadu's paper on *flaaitaal* was received with great scepticism from the floor. Makhadu pressed for the recognition of the existence and literary worth of *flaaitaal.*

Hence **flaaitaler** /-tɑːlə/ *n.*, one who speaks flaaitaal.

1979 C. VAN DER MERWE in *Frontline* Dec. 17 Flytalers declare that, give or take a few regional variations, they can make their way from Seshego to Manenberg on it ... True Flytalers react to the term tsotsi-taal in more or less the same way one might expect P.W. Botha to react if you told him his policy was Baasskap, or even Apartheid. It's out, gone, yesteryear's name, something to be lived down.

flaauw var. FLAUW.

flae(y) var. VLEI.

flam var. VLAM.

flank *n.* [Special sense of general English *flank* side.] In full ***flank forward***: (the player occupying) the position of wing forward in rugby. Also *attrib.*

[**1937** *Rand Daily Mail* 10 Apr. 18 Of the flank or back rankers Strachan cannot be left out.] **1937** *Ibid.* 25 June 22 Van der Berg will probably be one of the flank forwards. **1956** V. JENKINS *Lions Rampant* 19 Scotland's Greenwood, at flank-forward, saw to it that his country's honour was not besmirched. **1960** E.S. & W.J. HIGHAM *High Speed Rugby* p.xx, We have adopted the name 'flank' instead of the more common 'wing forward' as being less likely to cause confusion between wing forward and wing three-quarter. *Ibid.* 154 The Flanks (wing forwards): These are the open play specialists. **1994** E. VAN DEN BURGH in *E. Prov. Herald* 30 Aug. 1 While the EP [rugby] selectors keep choosing me as a lock, I still prefer playing flank. **1994** G. DOOLAN in *Grocott's Mail* 2 Sept. 19 Garth Wakeford played his heart out in the unfamiliar role of second-row lock. The guy definitely deserves a run at flank.

flap var. FLOP.

flap-trousers *pl. n.* Also **flapped trousers**. [tr. Afk. *klapbroek*.] KLAPBROEK.

1936 [see KLAPBROEK]. **1970** BEETON & DORNER in *Eng. Usage in Sn Afr.* Vol.1 No.2, 46 *Klapbroek*, .. lit 'flap trouser'. **1973** J. MEINTJES *Voortrekkers* 99 The Doppers could easily be recognized by their appearance and dress, by their short jackets and flap-trousers of blue or brown nankeen.

flat-crown *n.* [See quot. 1913.] Either of two species of thorn tree of the Fabaceae, *Albizia adianthifolia* or *A. gummifera*, with flat, spreading foliage. Also *attrib.*

1868 J. CHAPMAN *Trav.* II. 451 The umbrella-like Flat-crown, common in the Berea-bush near D'Urban. **1897** 'M. TWAIN' *More Tramps Abroad* 444 The 'flat-crown' .. half a dozen naked branches, full of elbows, slant upward like artificial supports, and fling a roof of delicate foliage out in a horizontal platform as flat as a floor. **1913** C. PETTMAN *Africanderisms* 172 *Flat-crown*, An indigenous Natal tree so named because of its very flat top, looking as though it had been recently and carefully trimmed. **1937** C. BIRKBY *Zulu Journey* 49, I yarned with him under the shade of a flat crown tree at Mangete. **1950** [see ESSENHOUT]. **1961** PALMER & PITMAN *Trees of S. Afr.* 168 The flatcrown is a common tree along the eastern coast .. its flat, wide-spread crown and horizontally growing leaves distinguishing it from surrounding trees. **1986** J. CONYNGHAM *Arrowing of Cane* 16 The huge flat-crown off the sitting room provides added shade from beyond the reach of its roots. **1993** *Grocott's Mail* 6 Aug. 9 Albizia adianthifolia. Flat Crown.

flats *pl. n.* Also with initial capital. [Calque formed on Du. *vlakte(s)* plains.]

a. ***The flats***: Short for *the Cape Flats*, see CAPE FLATS.

1834 W.H.B. WEBSTER *Narr. of Voy. to Sn Atlantic Ocean* 263 The first few miles of the road the travelling was excellent, till we turned out into a dreary and barren sandy country called the Flats, which in some degree resemble the barren heath tracts of England. **1835** [see MOZAMBIQUE]. **1847** 'A BENGALI' *Notes on Cape of G.H.* 67 The sand on the flats is in some places in high white ridges, .. and totally devoid of vegetation. *c*1933 J. JUTA in A.C. Partridge *Lives, Lett. & Diaries* (1971) 162 *The flats*, The sandy, shrub-covered area, separating the Cape peninsula from the hinterland. **1970** J. PACKER *Veronica* 16 My father has a nice little house – high up with a view of the Bay. The Government will take it from us and move us out to the Flats. **1980** E. JOUBERT *Poppie Nongena* 88 The winter was nearly over, but on the Flats the cold persisted. **1986** F. KARODIA *Daughters of Twilight* 57 They've proclaimed this a white area and they've opened an area for Indians up on the flats. **1987** L. BEAKE *Strollers* 35 The Spider Men! One of the worst gangs on the Flats! **1992** *Argus* 20 Feb. 15 That is all I can remember – getting out and away from the Flats and being poor. **1994** M. ROBERTS tr. *J.A. Wahlberg's Trav. Jrnls 1838–56* 9 Afternoon out with the Dreyers on horseback to the Flats, where I saw the Secretary Bird for the first time in a wild state.

b. An extensive plain; used as an element in place names.

1837 'N. POLSON' *Subaltern's Sick Leave* 128 North of the country of the Amakosa Kafirs is an immense extent of undulating downs styled the '*Bontibok Flats*, ' from the number of bonti or blesbok that are found there. **1852** T. SHONE Diary. 7 Jan., The news today is that they .. have cut the throats of an old man and a boy on Quaga Flats. **1914** C. PETTMAN *Notes on S. Afr. Place Names* 36 Zoetendal Vlei recalls the wreck of the galiot Zoetendal .. , as the Amsterdam Flats, near Port Elizabeth, does that of the Amsterdam in 1817. **1989** P.E. RAPER *Dict. of Sn Afr. Place Names* 102 *Committees Flats*, .. Between Breakfast Vlei and the Great Fish River.

flatty *n.* Also **flattie**. Esp. in the Eastern Cape:

1. [Named for the flattened appearance of the head.] *white stumpnose*, see STUMPNOSE sense 2.

[**1731** G. MEDLEY tr. *P. Kolb's Present State of Cape of G.H.* II. 204 There is another sort of *Stone Brassems* at the Cape ... The Cape-*Europeans* call These *Flat Noses*, on Account of the Flatness of the Fore-part of the Head.] **1949** J.L.B. SMITH *Sea Fishes* 268 *Rhabdosargus tricuspidens* ... *Blinkvis* (Witsand). *Stumpnose* or *Stompneus* (Knysna). *Flatty* (Eastern Cape). *Silvie* (East London). *Silver Bream* or *Bream* (Transkei – Natal). **1970** *Albany Mercury* 5 Feb. 14 She had positively identified the fish as a Natal silver bream .. , closely related to the prolific flatty – well known in our area. **1971** *Grocott's Mail* 3 Sept. 3 Some big flatties have been caught, up to 0,680 kg (1 1/2 lb). (Another name for the 'flatty' is stump-nose or silver bream.) **1972** *Daily Dispatch* 26 Apr. 27 Hartwell came home with .. a blacktail of 0,9kg and a flatty of the same weight. **1979** SNYMAN & KLARIE *Free from Sea* 54 *White Stumpnose, Blinkvis, Silvie, Flattie, Silver bream, Bream.*

2. [See quot. 1988.] Any of several common household or 'wall' spiders (*Anyphops* sp.) of the Selenopidae. Also *attrib.*

1987 *E. Prov. Herald* 11 Apr. 5 Meet fleet-footed flattie, a house guest credited with saving hosts from mosquitoes. Equipped with big eyes on swivelling stalks. **1988** *Afr. Wildlife* Vol.42 No.3, 93 The wall-spider (or flat spider – commonly known as the 'flatty'), an extremely fast-moving spider, which normally inhabits rocky terrain and which finds the walls of houses a suitable substitute. As the popular nickname 'flatty' implies, this type of spider is dorso-ventrally flattened to an extraordinary degree and it can insinuate itself into the narrowest of crevices and cracks. **1990** *Evening Post* 17 Mar. 8, I attributed our freedom from the mosquito nuisance to the presence of the flattie spiders. Their low profile, speed of movement and daylight hunting seemed to enable them to catch mosquitoes as they rested after their night shifts.

flauw *adj. obs.* Also **flow, flaauw**. [Du. (Afk. *flou*).] Faint, weak.

1834 T.H. BOWKER Journal. 19 Dec., While in Salem river find an Old Joker who had lost himself, his horse is *flow*. **1844** J. BACKHOUSE *Narr. of Visit* 513 One of our after oxen fell down from exhaustion, being what the Dutch call '*flaauw*', *faint*. **1913** C. PETTMAN *Africanderisms* 173 *Flauw*, Used of men and animals when exhausted by vigorous or long-sustained effort.

flay, flea varr. VLEI.

fleck /flek/ *v. trans.* Also **flek**. [Englished form of Afk. *vlek*.] VLEK.

1890 A.G. HEWITT *Cape Cookery* 11 Have the snoek cut into motjes, not flekked, put the pieces to drain. **1973** *Farmer's Weekly* 18 Apr. 101 The fish has a firm but a delicate flesh which rapidly goes soft and bad unless it is 'flecked', i.e. cut down the back and backbone and entrails removed, soon after it is caught.

Hence **flecked** *ppl adj.*; **flecking** *vbl n.*, the action or process of gutting or opening out (a fish or carcass); *vlekking*, see VLEK.

1960 [see STELLASIE]. **1977** S. STANDER *Flight from Hunter* 158 Mbanji was still hunched over the antbear carcass, skinning it out, using the flecked-out hide to keep the raw meat clean of sand. **1993** *Flying Springbok* Apr. 123 Flecking, salting and wind-drying ensure unsurpassed flavour and texture.

fleckvark var. VLAKVARK.

fleh var. VLEI.

flek var. FLECK.

fley var. VLEI.

‖**fliek** /flik/ *n.* [Afk., ad. Eng *flick.*] A film, particularly an Afrikaans film. Also *attrib.* See also BIOSCOPE sense 1 a.

1982 *Sunday Times* 11 Apr. (Mag. Sect.) 1 The happy-go-lucky barefoot kid .. staying at home for a braai and the *flieks* grew up into an international rugby player. **1985** *Ibid.* 10 Mar. (Lifestyle) 3 This is not Evita's first *fliek*. She starred in *Baggel en die Akkedis* in 1956. **1990** R. DANIEL in *Weekend Mail* 5 Oct. 13 *Agter Elke Man* 'die fliek' .. is but a pale shadow of its boxed-in predecessor.

floor *n. Hist. Diamond-mining.* [Special sense of general Eng. *floor* level space upon which some industry is carried out.] Usu. in *pl.*, often ***the floors***: flat surfaces in the open air upon which diamondiferous rock was spread, to be broken down over several years by natural weathering.

1886 G.A. FARINI *Through Kalahari Desert* 32 The hard, flinty clay .. is left exposed for a time to the atmosphere of the 'floors'. **1893** T. REUNERT *Diamonds & Gold* 55 For a time the blue ground remains on the floors without much manipulation. The heat of the sun and moisture soon have a wonderful effect upon it. **1899** R. DEVEREUX *Side Lights on S. Afr.* 147 An endless stretch of sad grey fields, surrounded by high walls of barbed wire, topped by huge electric light globes. These are the 'floors' over which the blue ground is spread, as soon as it is taken from the mine. **1937** H. SAUER *Ex Afr.* 47 The De Beers' Company had to buy the bulk of their own diamonds from the natives whom they employed on the 'floors'. **1946** S. CLOETE *Afr. Portraits* 129 The bluish indurated mud is .. spread out on floors, where it is allowed to rot for two or three years during which time it oxidises and disintegrates from exposure. **1956** L.G. GREEN *Secret Hid Away* 80 The diamond-bearing 'blue ground' .. was spread on 'floors' for a year so that the weather might break up the rock. **1973** A. HOCKING *Diamonds* 7 Great stretches of the nearby veld were cleared and levelled and the mined ground was spread over these 'floors'. **1989** P.E. RAPER *Dict. of Sn Afr. Place Names* 162 *Floors*, Suburb of Kimberley ... Established in 1948, it received its name from the old diamond 'floors' on which it was laid out.

Hence **flooring** *n.*, the process of breaking down diamondiferous rock on the floors; also *attrib.*

1931 G. BEET *Grand Old Days* 99 As the Kimberley mines became deeper the blue ground became harder and less amenable to the flooring treatment ... It was decided in 1920 to abandon flooring .. in favour of stage crushing and washing.

flop *n.* Also **flap**. [See quots 1899 and 1900.] Any of several birds of the genus *Euplectes* (family Ploceidae), esp. the redshouldered widow, *E. axillaris*. See also SAKABULA.

1899 R.B. & J.D.S. WOODWARD *Natal Birds* 69 (Pettman), The boys call it *flop*, no doubt from the way in which it suddenly stops in its flight and alights on the grass. **1900** STARK & SCLATER *Birds of S. Afr.* I. 134 *Urobrachya axillaris, Red-shouldered Widow Bird* ... 'Flop' of Natal Colonists ... In spring the handsome males .. may be seen flitting over the reeds or grass with a curious 'flopping' flight. **1913** C. PETTMAN *Africanderisms* 173 *Flop, The, Urobrachya axillaris* is so-called in Natal. **1978** MCLACHLAN & LIVERSIDGE *Roberts Birds of S. Afr.* 582 Males often fly about rather aimlessly just above the grass, bobbing up and down and suddenly twisting backwards and dropping down on to some conspicuous perch — hence the trivial name of 'flap'. [**1980** A.J. BLIGNAUT *Dead End Rd* 92 Wasn't the predikant funny — his beard bobbed up and down like a flap-finch's tail.] **1983** K.B. NEWMAN *Newman's Birds* 444 Popular bird names in general use ... Flop — Longtailed Widowbird.

floppy *n. Derog. offensive. slang.* [Prob. military slang used in the former Rhodesia.

'Unless one was with Ian Smith's conscripts during that last "Rhodesian War" .. one will have to read this book with a finger stuck .. in the glossary at the end ... "Floppies were people who flopped down dead when you switched your gat [*sc.* gun] to sing".' (*Weekly Mail & Guardian*, Feb. 1994, quoting Angus Shaw's *Another Time, Another Place*).]

An insulting term for a black person.

1978 E. DIBB in *Fair Lady* 25 Oct. 108 'Victor nine, Tango three. How did it go?' 'Positive. Small contact single floppy.' **1986** V. COOKE et al. in S. Gray *Market Plays* 34 Black people can do what they like. Murder old men and children, rape women, get drunk, smoke dagga, and they don't go to jail because they floppies. **1988** S. SOLE in *Style* Apr. 48 He tried to sell the gun to one of the floppies (blacks) at the hotel. **1991** G. MURRAY *Informant, Alberton* The floppies at the bus stop got a big fright when the car backfired — the trouble in the township has made them nervous.

Florisbad /ˈflɒrɪsbæd, ˈfluərəsbat/ *n.* The name of a small town near Bloemfontein, in the Orange Free State, applied *attrib.* to (the remains of) a primitive hominid discovered there. (*OED*).

1935 J.F. DREYER in *Proc. Sect. Sci. Kon. Akad. Wetensch. Amsterdam* XXXVIII. 124 Until .. the classification of the Hominidae is revised and modernised, the status of the Florisbad Man will be most suitably expressed by giving it the value of a sub-genus and calling it: Homo (Africanthropus) helmei. **1940** *Jrnl R. Anthrop. Inst.* 18 The Florisbad skull. **1959** J.D. CLARK *Prehist. of S. Afr.* 27 In 1932 Professor Dreyer found the Florisbad skull during excavations in the mineral spring there. *Ibid.* 87 At the time that Florisbad Man was living at the site the vegetation must have been very like that of the Karoo and Middleveld today. **1963** C.S. COON *Origin of Races* 636 Two principal theories have been advanced to explain the origin of the Capoids ... The second is that they evolved from local ancestors, including not only Saldanha Bay man and Broken Hill man, but also Florisbad. **1985** *S. Afr. Panorama* Sept. 2 Professor Sampson is holding .. Acheulian hand-axe, and Florisbad and Zeekoegat spear points. **1985** G.T. NURSE et al. *Peoples of Sn Afr.* 43 The Florisbad skull can also be seen as a link between 'large-headed Khoisan' and 'Rhodesian' man.

floss /flɒs/ *n. noncount. Ostrich-farming.* Also **flos**. [Special sense of general Eng. *floss* fine filaments, fluff.] The short, soft feathers from the underside of the wing of an ostrich. Also *attrib.* See also ONDERBAATJIE.

*c*1881 A. DOUGLASS *Ostrich Farming* 75 The floss feathers .. the row of light feathers next the leg .. are of little value and greatly help to keep the bird warm. *Ibid.* 82 The floss are the soft feathers that should not be plucked, but of which there are always some taken by accident. **1896** R. WALLACE *Farming Indust. of Cape Col.* 235 Floss is derived mostly from the under-wing coverts of the birds, both male and female, and is of a soft nature ... Floss in good demand, especially shorter lines, which advanced 5s. to 7s. 6d. per lb. **1930** M.F. WORMSER Ostrich Industry. 11 Floss grows on the underside of the wing. **1934** C.P. SWART Supplement to Pettman. 52 *Floss*, Downy ostrich feathers. **1955** G. ASCHMAN in Saron & Hotz *Jews in S. Afr.* 130 The immigrants themselves learnt to sort feathers .. long cuts, flos, broken tails.

flow var. FLAUW.

'Flu /fluː/ *n. Hist. Pathology.* Also **Flu**, and with small initial. [Shortened form of Eng. *influenza.*] ***The 'Flu***, also ***the Big 'Flu, the Great 'Flu***: the influenza epidemic which resulted in 140 000 deaths in South Africa during 1918 and 1919. Also *attrib.*

1964 J. MEINTJES *Manor House* 24 The doctor says it looks like a case of the great 'flu epidemic .. when people died like flies and many were buried *alive*. **1979** *E. Prov. Herald* 2 Apr. 6 In the old days, time .. was reckoned as being before or after the Drought, the 'Flu or the Rinderpest. **1980** *Daily Dispatch* 30 May 3 Mrs Booi was born on a farm near Alexandria 'before the 'flu', that is, before 1918. **1980** E. JOUBERT *Poppie Nongena* 12 He died in the Big 'Flu of 1918. The isibetho .. was the plague that the Lord sent us, the people were sick for three days and then they died. **1982** *E. Prov. Herald* 27 Sept. 13 It was certainly before the Great Flu of 1918–19, because I can remember how my father .. used to go around dosing the victims with brandy and paraffin.

‖**fluitjie** /ˈflœiki, ˈfleɪki, -ci/ *n.* Formerly also **fluitje, vlijtje**. [Afk., *fluit* flute, whistle + dim. suff. -IE.] A mouth-organ; MONDFLUITJIE.

1913 C. PETTMAN *Africanderisms* 174 *Fluitje*, .. The Dutch name for a mouth organ. **1920** R.Y. STORMBERG *Mrs Pieter de Bruyn* 93 Someone tuned up a guitar. Someone else worried a vlijtje (how do you spell a mouth-organ in Dutch?). **1927** M.E. DEECKER in *Outspan* 20 May 21 The 'band' .. consisted of three Cape boys with a violin — of sorts — a concertino [*sic*], and a 'fluitje'; but it was quite wonderful the music they managed to get out of these antiquated instruments. **1933** *Outspan* 4 Aug. (Swart), The 'fluitjie' is the music of the out-of-doors. Hear its nasal notes in any other part of the world and you are completely overcome by home-sickness for South Africa. **1972** N. HENSHILWOOD *Cape Childhood* 36 We raced to the gates to see them pass by our gardens, a medley of lilting music of banjos and fluitjies (mouth organs).

fly *n.* [Ellipt. for *tsetse-fly*, see TSETSE.]

1. TSETSE sense 1. Freq. *attrib.*, and *comb.* **fly-belt**, fly-infested country.

1835 A. SMITH *Diary* (1940) II. 165 He lost his cattle from .. 'the flies'. **1871** J. MACKENZIE *Ten Yrs* (1971) 176 The missionary's cattle had been bitten by the deadly fly. **1878** A. AYLWARD *Tvl of Today* 83 Of sixty horses .. a few had been stung by the fly .. — these had also died. **1881** P. GILLMORE *Land of Boer* 370 Into the fly country I went, game I found in the utmost abundance, particularly buffalo. **1890** F.C. SELOUS *Hunter's Wanderings* 131 The natives living in the 'fly' country possess both dogs and goats, I admit, but these .. have become acclimatised ... Even now, the natives told me, out of a litter of pups, born in the country and of acclimatised parents, some always die of 'fly' symptoms. **1896** PURVIS & BIGGS *S. Afr.* 237 The terrible fly-belt, where once the ubiquitous tsetse reigned supreme. **1935** H.N. HEMANS *Log of Native Commissioner* 53 The proximity or otherwise of 'Fly', should you be in a district where the dreaded Tsetse are found. **1940** F.B. YOUNG *City of Gold* 317 The widest fly-belts could be avoided. **1952** H. KLEIN *Land of Silver Mist* 137 The Nabatema lived out of the 'fly' belt and were rich in cattle. **1961** T.V. BULPIN *White Whirlwind* 55 At night the deadly fly was inclined to be less active ... They would have to make a very early start and get through the fly area before light. **1979** T. GUTSCHE *There Was a Man* 12 All was not as idyllic as it seemed. Some of the lovely country, rich in grazing, was verboten territory because of 'fly'. *Ibid.* 203 Animals should be protectively stabled during the fly season.

2. *transf.*

a. *Pathology.* NAGANA. Also *comb.* **fly-proof** *adj.*, immune to nagana.

1850 A. COQUI in T. Baines *Jrnl of Res.* (1964) II. 177 Some of the Kafirs caught the Tsetse, or fly, and .. we pushed on as speedily as possible to save our cattle from its deadly sting. **1907** J.P. FITZPATRICK *Jock of Bushveld* (1909) 414 It was clear that, not drought and poverty, but 'fly' was the cause of their weakness. **1937** J. STEVENSON-HAMILTON *S. Afr. Eden* 211 There are many places in Africa where fly exists without any game being available for its support, and conversely others where game exists without attendant fly. **1940** F.B. YOUNG *City of Gold* 356 When the last commando had been disbanded, Janse bought a new wagon and a fine team of fly-proof mules and went down to the Low Country again. **1968** E.A. WALKER *Hist. of Sn Afr.* 363 Fly and redwater fever were playing havoc with the transport cattle.

b. *obs.* TSETSE sense 2 b.

1868 J. CHAPMAN *Trav.* I. 163 At night, as the moon rose, we started to get through the fly, but, on entering it, our wagon struck against a large tree. **1895** A.B. BALFOUR *1200 Miles in Waggon* 222 From there to the coast you have to go through 'the fly' .. that is, the belt of land infested with the tsetse fly, whose bite is certain death to cattle, horses, and donkeys.

flytaal var. FLAAITAAL.

focho /ˈfɔː(t)ʃɔ/ *n. Music.* Also **foco**. [Etym. obscure: perh. rel. to S. Sotho *fôjho* intoxicating drink; or rel. to Tsonga ideophone *fòxò* of a crashing sound; or fr. N. and S. Sotho *phošo* mistake; see also quot. 1980.] A neo-traditional style of Sotho music, played usu. on a concertina (or accordion) and drum.

Focho evolved in the early 1900s, and was a forerunner of TSABA-TSABA.

1980 D.B. COPLAN *Urbanization of African Performing Arts.* 72 Sotho migrants produced neo-traditional music with the concertina, guitar, and voice .. within the structure of the Western 'three-chord' .. system. Older informants can recall this music, called *focho* ('disorder') being played in Johannesburg as early as the decades preceding the First World War. **1990** G. SLOVO *Ties of Blood* 109 The .. traditional sound of *foco* as a concertina and homemade drum joined together to create their own kind of disorder.

foefie slide /ˈfufiˌslaɪd/ *n. phr.* Also **foof(f)y -, foofy -, fuffie -, fuffy slide**. [Prob. Afk. *foefie* stunt, trick + Eng. *slide* a smooth or slippery surface for sliding on.] A slide formed of a rope or cable secured between two points (one higher than the other) enabling a rapid descent by one holding on to, and suspended beneath, an attached handle or pulley.

1970 J.F. PRINSLOO *Informant, Lüderitz (Namibia)* Foefieslide. A wire between two trees, at one end higher than the other. A short piece of pipe is then used by boys to hold on while they slide from the highest to the lower end. **1973** *Fair Lady* 31 Oct. 40 The foefie slide is a simple contraption ... A thick wire or rope secured to the highest point in the vicinity, usually a tree, and then slung down, sometimes over water, to an arm-high point where it's once again secured. A piece of iron pipe is threaded on to this rope or wire and you .. launch yourself into space hanging from the pipe. **1982** *Grocott's Mail* 13 Aug. 3 (caption) This foefie slide was one of the popular events at the Graeme College Fete. **1983** *Daily Dispatch* 6 Apr. 1 Foofie slide to freedom. Two young East Berliners escaped to the West by shooting and suspending a steel cable more than 25m above the Berlin Wall and, using a pulley, gliding across to freedom. **1987** *Fair Lady* 4 Mar. 95 The oak tree from which foefie slides have so often been intrepidly slung. **1989** E. REID *Motorist* Oct.-Dec. 18 New facilities at Water Wonderland include a 'foofie-slide' made for sliding along a rope into the water below.

Hence **foefie-sliding** *n.*, the riding of a foefie slide.

1974 *Personality* 29 Nov. 117 Foofy-sliding may be great fun for the André de Beers of this world. But what about their poor mothers?

foei /fui/ *int. obs.* Also **fooi**. [Afk.] An exclamation expressing disapproval, distress, or disgust: 'fie'; FOEITOG sense 2.

Often used by writers to suggest Afrikaans dialogue.

1906 A.H. WATKINS *From Farm to Forum* 36 'Foei, Mr. Baxter,' expostulated the Boer, 'it isn't right to "spot" at (make fun of) Bible things.' **1912** *State* July 84 The rheumatism — *foei*! it can pinch! **1920** R. JUTA *Tavern* 109 Is it true, then, Master Dirk — true all the stories told of Sana — Ooi! Fooi! Fooi! Ibid. 139 Fooi! How shamelessly I talk. **1942** S. CLOETE *Hill of Doves* Glossary, *Foei*, exclamation; fie.

foeitog /ˈfuitɔx, ˈfʊɪ-/ *int.* Also **foei toch, foi(e) toch, fooi(e) toch, fooi tog, fye toch**. [Afk., *foei* for shame + *tog* (earlier *toch*) all the same, nevertheless.]

See also TOG sense 1.

1. A phatic exclamation; an interjection expressing mild surprise.

1910 D. FAIRBRIDGE *That Which Hath Been* (1913) 268 'Foei toch,' said Mevrouw Bek, vaguely, feeling that something was expected of her. **1916** S. BLACK in S. Gray *Three Plays* (1984) 233 Sis black 'n' really mean anything at all. It's the same as foi toch. **1920** R. JUTA *Tavern* 207 Aletta tells me Mijnfrau exclaimed 'Allemacht! Fooi toch!' I am so relieved she kept to vague expressions. **1985** J. ALLAN in *Sunday Times* 10 Mar. (Lifestyle) 3 *Foeitog* a lesser person would find herself at the end of her dither.

2. FOEI.

1913 D. FAIRBRIDGE *Piet of Italy* 135 Mrs. Malherbe .., filled with anxious wrath, .. drove them indoors ... To think of their sitting out of doors — *fooie toch* — when there was a good paraffin-lamp burning in the voor-huis! **1968** G. CROUDACE *Silver Grass* 186 'I have such a fondness for you,' he said ... 'Foeitog!' she exclaimed. 'You're as bad as all the rest.'

3. Expressing sympathy or pity; sometimes used ironically. See also SHAME. Also *attrib.*

1913 A.B. MARCHAND *Dirk, S. African* 83 (Swart), Foei toch the poor soul, who could help pitying her? **1919** M.M. STEYN *Diary* 34 The sympathising old friend seemed quite concerned, and said, 'Foi toch!' (Oh, Fie!), .. 'Poor John's eldest son has gone off his head.' **1935** P. SMITH *Platkop's Children* 86 She looked in the .. throat to see what the matter was. But she couldn' see anythin'. But Ou-ma said, Fye toch! an came and tied a red flanney round it. **1965** D. ROOKE *Diamond Jo* 30 'Foei tog,' she muttered when she saw him: she gave him a double helping of mealie meal and meat. **1972** *Cape Times* 10 Nov. 8 Mr. Botha admitted the cost of living had also increased but, he asked defensively, didn't Mr. Streicher know that the increase was part of a world-wide phenomenon? 'Ag, foeitog!', he said. **1982** *Daily Dispatch* 3 Mar. 7 Mr Du Plessis: My 'legalese' is .. not so good but I can at least understand Afrikaans. Dr Treurnicht: Foeitog. Mr Du Plessis: It is not 'Foeitog,' it is the truth. **1985** [see NÊ].

4. Expressing affection or warmth towards something endearing (usu. a child). See also SHAME.

1970 V.R. VINK *Informant, Florida* Ag foeitog, isn't it a sweet baby! **1985** J. ALLEN in *Sunday Times* 10 Mar. (Lifestyle) 3 Even Thoko Ntshinga's little *piccanien* has a part. Ag *foeitog* his name is Mielie and you'll see him .. squirting the garden hose at the Cabinet Ministers.

5. Introducing an appeal or supplication: 'for pity's sake'.

1980 *Sunday Times* 9 Mar. (Extra) 3 For our ignorance, we apologise. But foeitog, have a heart, man. Right from the start we did play ball.

Hence **foeitog** *n.*, an utterance of the word 'foeitog'; also *(nonce)* as *adj.*

1974 *E. Prov. Herald* 9 May 32 We tended to put up the tattered black cowl and push it protectively, which earned us fond smiles and foeitogs. **1982** *Daily Dispatch* 3 Mar. 7 Afrikaans as I understand it is not a 'foeitog' Afrikaans.

foerlouper var. FORE-LOUPER.

foetsek var. VOETSAK.

Fofatusa /fəʊfəˈtuːzə, fɔ-, -sə/ *n. hist.* Also **FOFATUSA**. Acronym formed on *Federation of Free African Trade Unions* (1959–1966), a coordinating body established to protect the interests of smaller African trade unions excluded from affiliation to TUCSA. Also *attrib.*

1969 A. HEPPLE *S. Afr.: Workers under Apartheid* 68 A few small African trade unions which maintained some liaison with Tucsa unions, joined together to form the Federation of Free African Trade Unions (Fofatusa). *Ibid.* 73 Although claiming to be non-political, Fofatusa had strong ties with the Pan Africanist Congress ... Fofatusa was at no stage of its existence particularly active. **1973** *Black Review 1972* 105 More trade unions and coordinating bodies came and went, most important among them being the South African Congress of Trade Unions .. and the Federation of Free African Trade Unions (FOFATUSA) which has also gone out of existence. **1975** E. FEIT *Workers without Weapons* 141 On October 3, 1959 .. FOFATUSA was formally established ... The President of FOFATUSA, Mr. Nyaose, and other FOFATUSA officials, were members of the Pan Africanist Congress which had split off from the ANC and was now its rival. **1985** R.M. IMRIE *Wealth of People* 29 The Federation of Free African Trade Unions (Fofatusa) .. [catered] especially for those Black unions which were excluded from affiliation to Tucsa but which preferred to work closely with it rather than affiliate to the more politically orientated Left-wing South African Congress of Trade Unions.

foi(e) toch var. FOEITOG.

Fokeng pl. form of MOFOKENG.

folk *n. rare.* [Calque formed on Du. and Afk. *volk.*]

a. In pl.: VOLK sense 2.

1866 E.L. PRICE *Jrnls* (1956) 231 The storm is now quite hushed. The folks are merry and noisy, having crowded into my new little kitchen, & most of them are perched on the hearth.

b. *noncount.* VOLK sense 3 b. Also *attrib.*

1972 *Evening Post* 29 Apr. 1 The Afrikaner student must play a central role in breaking up the cult of Afrikanerdom and to free their universities from the 'Folk captivity' in which they operated.

Folksraad var. VOLKSRAAD.

fontein /fɔnˈteɪn/ *n.* Also **fonteyn**. Pl. **-s, -e**. [Du.]

‖ **1.**

a. FOUNTAIN. Also *attrib.*

[**1786** G. FORSTER tr. A. Sparrman's *Voy. to Cape of G.H.* I. 321 In a marshy place .. a place full of land-springs, (*fontein grond*) he had observed pretty distinct vestiges of elephants.] **1837** 'N. POLSON' *Subaltern's Sick Leave* 90 From the Braak River a good day's work with tired and thirsty oxen will bring the traveller to a small spring or '*fontein*', at the western end of a conical hill called the *Roode Berg*. **1849** R. GRAY *Jrnl of Bishop's Visitation* I. 80 Where there is a '*fontein*', there are patches of arable land covered with luxuriant crops. **1882** J. NIXON *Among Boers* 121 Not far from the house was a '*fontein*' of clear fresh water, which .. had never been known to fail in the severest drought ... This *fontein* .. had induced him to purchase the farm. **1904** H.A. BRYDEN *Hist. of S. Afr.* 108 The Boers .. planted fruit orchards, into which they led irrigation furrows from the nearest spring, or fontein. **1924** S.G. MILLIN *God's Step-Children* 70 When they came across a likely looking bit of ground .. beside a natural spring (which they called a *fontein*), they would outspan their oxen. **1937** C.R. PRANCE *Tante Rebella's Saga* 141 Suikerboswoestyn's 'fontein' was that year 'backwards in coming forward'. **1955** L.G. GREEN *Karoo* 82 The old Hottentot who lived there beside the *fontein* a century and a half ago was a certain Konstabel. **1968** K. MCMAGH *Dinner of Herbs* 48 The farm Platrug was the most unpromising of all for .. it had no water — no spring, no fontein. **1976** R. Ross *Adam Kok's Griquas* 43 Where possible, the *fonteins* were led out to allow cultivation, mainly of wheat.

b. An element in place names, signifying the (former) presence of a natural spring, e.g. *Bloemfontein, Fonteintjiesberg, Garsfontein, Matjiesfontein*.

[**1822** W.J. BURCHELL *Trav.* I. 259 In dry countries, any circumstance relating to water, is of sufficient importance to distinguish that place. Thus it is that the Dutch word Fontein is made such liberal use of in every part of the Colony: the Hottentot word Kamma (water), is not less frequently found in the composition of the aboriginal names.] **1916** L.D. FLEMMING *Fool on Veld* (1933) 1 Seventy-five percent of the farms are 'fonteins', with a prefix, generally denoting the number of 'fonteins' upon it ... There must have been a good many more fonteins in the old days than there are now. **1924** S.G. MILLIN *God's Step-Children* 70 They would call the place .. after themselves, 'Potgietersfontein'. **1987** K. BERMAN in *Weekly Mail* 19 June 19 Towns that are mere pinpricks on the map .. each one .. ending in the suffix 'fontein'. **1988** *Flying Springbok* June 22 South Africa has some 60 communities and railway sidings with names ending in 'fontein'. Most are remote, situated in the drier areas (and most of the actual springs have long since dried up). **1989** P.E. RAPER *Dict. of Sn Afr. Place Names* 515 *Sterkfontein Caves*, .. The first adult skull of *Australopithecus* was discovered there in 1936, and in 1948 Robert Broom found 'Mrs Ples', or Sterkfontein hominid 5, an almost perfect cranium. **1989** T. BOTHA in *Style* June 112 On my map I check the route for tomorrow ... Zevenfontein, at least two dozen other fonteins, Geluk and Paradys.

2. *comb.* **fonteinbos** /-bɔs/ [Afk. *bos* bush], either of two shrubby aromatic plants, *Psoralea aphylla* or *P. pinatta*, usu. found growing near running water or springs.

1963 S. CLOETE *Rags of Glory* 522 They splashed through a little river of brown water edged with lilies, the air sweet with the honey scent of fonteinbos. **1966** C.A. SMITH *Common Names* 217 *Fonteinbos, Psoralea aphylla* and *P. pinnata* ... Shrubs up to 12 ft high; leaves aromatic; flowers blue. Almost invariably found growing in the vicinity of running water and springheads.

foochie-foochie var. VOETJIE-VOETJIE.

fooffy -, foofie -, foofy slide varr. FOEFIE SLIDE.

fooi var. FOEI.

fooi(e) toch, fooi tog varr. FOEITOG.

footchy footchy var. VOETJIE-VOETJIE.

footganger *n. obs.* Also **foot gangher**. [Englished form of Afk. *voetganger*.]

1. VOETGANGER sense 1.

1873 F. BOYLE *To Cape for Diamonds* 300 We drove through a host of foot-gangers on the trek. These are the larvae of the locust, much more dreaded than the full-grown insect. They remain without wings for three years, moving about the country in the multitudes so often described. **1875** C.B. BISSET *Sport & War* 170 The unfledged locusts are also called the foot ganghers, or foot-soldiers, and nothing can impede their advance. **1877** R.M. BALLANTYNE *Settler & Savage* 249 The ground was alive with them. Armies, legions were there — not full-grown flying locusts, but young ones, styled foot-gangers, in other words crawlers, walkers, or hoppers.

2. VOETGANGER sense 2 a.

1901 P.J. DU TOIT *Diary* (1974) 43 A good many of Kemp's Footgangers and some Kamp-vreters were mostly caught. Two of the cannon taken were defect [ive].

footsack /ˈfʊtsæk/ *v. intrans.* Also **footseck, futsack**. [Englished form of Afk. *voetsek* (see quots 1899 and 1970).]

1. VOETSAK *v.* sense 1 a.

1855 G.H. MASON *Life with Zulus* 224 On our approach, several shaggy wolf-dogs made their appearance .. but on hearing the well-known 'Footsack, ainga' (Lie down, dog) from Jacob, they quickly came bounding about him. **1871** M.E. BARBER in *Cape Monthly Mag.* III. Dec. 332 Cries of 'foot-sek,' with the slashing of a whip and the yelping of a defeated cur. **1890** C. & A.P. WILSON-MOORE *Diggers' Doggerel* 22 'Bonzela Baas, Inkos!' He tell me 'Hamba, footsack!' **1899** *Natal Agric. Jrnl* 31 Mar. 4 'Voetsek,' according to Cape, or 'footsack,' according to Natal newspaper spelling, is an expression that soon attracts the attention of new-comers. It means 'forth say I,' an abbreviation of 'voort zeg ik,' and is exclusively applied to dogs. **1900** 'ONE WHO WAS IN IT' *Kruger's Secret Service* 158 He suddenly ejaculated 'Footsack' (I spell it like that, .. a low Dutch word, meaning 'Get out, you cur,' and generally applied to a dog ..). **1903** R. KIPLING *Five Nations* 165 Footsack you — M.I.! **1918** C. GARSTIN *Sunshine Settlers* 50 He learnt that when he heard the word 'Mike' he was wanted, and when he heard the word 'Footsack' he was not. **1970** *Daily Dispatch* 30 Jan. 14, I found it was pointless saying 'Voertsek!' to him, even when pronouncing it 'footsack!' in the local way. There was just no reaction. **1974** 'BLOSSOM' in *Darling* 9 Oct. 95, I trip over Bliksem what's sleeping there and shout 'Footsack!' and that ruins the atmosphere a bit.

2. VOETSAK *v.* sense 2 b.

1936 P.M. CLARK *Autobiog. of Old Drifter* 54 'Foot-sack to hell out of it,' was the obliging reply, 'or you'll get a load of buck-shot into you!' There was no use arguing. I simply foot-sacked!

footsie-footsie *n. colloq.* [ad. general Eng. *footy(-footy)*, prob. influenced by Afk. *voetjie-voetjie* (see VOETJIE-VOETJIE); *footsie* does however occur in general Eng. as a var. of *footy*.] VOETJIE-VOETJIE. Also *attrib.*, *fig.*, and in shortened form **footsie**.

1953 A. MOGALE in *Drum* Sept. 25 Maybe they're playing footsie in her boudoir. **1978** *Sunday Times* 10 Sept. 14 Surely we are in enough trouble in America — and don't need to be caught playing footsie with Mr Watergate. **1987** L. STAFFORD in *Style* Aug. 92 The best little Whorehouse in Jo'burg ... The price of a sojourn upstairs? A flat R130, whether you play footsie-footsie or swing from the chandeliers. **1989** *Viewpoint* Sept. 6 The director of information for the NP in Natal .. said that the DP was playing 'footsie-footsie' with the ANC. **1990** H. STRAUSS in *City Press* 25 Feb. 11 Let us not fall into the trap of 'footsie-footsie' politics because that will also put us back on the road to chaos. **1991** L.A. AUPIAIS in *Style* Nov. 133 We live in turbulent times what with Hussein going off half-cocked and Russia playing footsie-footsie left, right and centre.

for Africa *adv. phr. Colloq.* In huge numbers or quantities; a lot; galore.

1970 M. BRONSLOW *Informant, Cape Town* I've got homework for Africa! (a lot). **1970** *News/Check* 18 Sept. 4 (*advt*) We've got trucks for Africa. Big trucks. Tough trucks. Eager trucks. **1970** S. BAYMAN in *Cape Argus* 3 Oct. (Mag. Sect.) 13 There are still bottles for Africa around but in the not too distant future glass of any variety will be a thing of the past. **1975** *Darling* 12 Feb. 119 Not to mention .. having to lurk behind rocks .. covered in barnacles for Africa. **1980** C. HOPE *A Separate Development* (1983) 103 An entire museum of vintage stuff including .. Bentleys for Africa. **1985** *Fair Lady* 3 Apr. 137 Flowers for Africa .. in the razzle-dazzle of our indigenous spring — go to Namaqualand to see flowers in their millions. **1987** H. PRENDINI in *Style* Feb. 33 The whole Taiwanese trip was 'an experience and a privilege' and they came back with 'presents for Africa'. **1990** W. HAYWARD in *Personality* 13 Aug. 27 While 'slow Joe' toyi-toyied for Africa .. red flags flapped in the sunset. The South African Communist Party's first public rally in 40 years. **1990** *Sunday Times* 7 Oct. 15 Hippos for Africa .. by the Sand River in Londolozi. **1991** *Cosmopolitan* Aug. 60 Go ahead and indulge — there'll be juice for Africa! **1994** on TV1, 9 Aug., (*advt*) I know trouble when I see it, and here's trouble for Africa.

forced removal see REMOVAL.

forcet(s) var. VOERCHITZ.

fore-clap *n. obs.* [Calque formed on S. Afr. Du. *voorklap*, *voor* front + *klap* flap.] The canvas curtain hanging at the front of a covered wagon. Cf. AFTER-CLAP, KLAP *n.*[2]

1850 R.G.G. CUMMING *Hunter's Life* I. 23 'Fore-clap' and 'after-clap,' which is the colonial name for two broad canvas curtains, that form part and parcel of the sail, and hang in the front and rear of the waggon, reaching to within a few inches of the ground. **1897** H.A. BRYDEN *Nature & Sport* 208 From the fore-clap (curtain) of the buck-wagon the faces — none too clean — of two or three children peer forth.

forehause var. FORE HUIS.

forehouse *n. obs.* [Calque formed on Du. *voorhuis*.] VOORHUIS. Also *attrib.*

1816 G. BARKER Journal. 9 Aug., Made a window for the fore house. **1835** A. SMITH *Diary* (1939) I. 258 Titus, seeing this, levelled his gun at Pinnear and fired; he fell back into the forehouse dead. **1851** N.J. MERRIMAN *Cape Jrnls* (1957) 174 They all live (family, and to a great extent servants too) in the great 'fore house'. **1852** A.W. COLE *Cape & Kafirs* 301, I accepted the invitation, and took my seat in the 'fore-house,' or large centre room of the dwelling. **1866** E.L. PRICE *Jrnls* (1956) 219 He had large congregations & much work as usual — a short but disturbed midday nap on Sechele's forehouse sofa. After the evening service, had been invited with the traders to take tea with His Majesty in this same forehouse (or diningroom).

fore huis *n. phr. Obs.* Also **forehause**. [Part. tr. Du. *voorhuis*.] VOORHUIS.

*a*1873 J. BURROW *Trav. in Wilds* (1971) 12 Late in the evening we found Cotton .. waiting for us, having provided a dinner at the hotel, which we found smoking on the table in the *fore huis*. **1878** H.A. ROCHE *On Trek in Tvl* 134 The 'fore huis' or general room. **1900** H. BUTTERWORTH *Trav. Tales* 46 'May I go to the fore huis (front house)?' gasped the youth. **1935** P. SMITH *Platkop's Children* 77 We all went in to the forehause where dinner was ready for us.

fore-kamer see VOORKAMER.

fore-looping *vbl n. Obs.* [Back-formation from FORE-LOUPER.] The task or action of leading the foremost pair of a team of draught oxen.

1862 A.W. DRAYSON *Tales at Outspan* 19 It is the duty of the Fingoe to hold a line which is made fast to the heads of the leading oxen, and thus to guide them on the road they should go; this duty is called 'fore-looping.' **1878** H.A. ROCHE *On Trek in Tvl* 161 The boy did not understand forelooping well, and Carolus .. could not make up for his deficiencies.

fore-loup *v. intrans. Obs.* Also **fore-loop, fore-lope**. [Calque formed on Afk. *voorloop*.] VOORLOOP *v.*

1881 P. GILLMORE *Land of Boer* 134 Umganey, divested of every particle of clothing, foreloping. *Ibid.* 388 Next day Umganey and I trecked and foreloped. **1882** J. NIXON *Among Boers* 193 Swartboy .. sang for glee as he 'forelooped.' **1889** *Catholic Hsehold* 30 Nov. 7 Fr. Le Bihan .. 'fore-louping' because one of their boys had cut his foot.

fore-louper *n. .obs.* Also **foerlouper, forelo(o)per**. [Calque formed on S. Afr. Du. *voorloper*.] VOORLOPER sense 1.

1848 H. WARD *Five Yrs in Kaffirland* I. 135 Some society would probably be established for providing a dress for the fore-louper, .. and some species of comfortable leggings for the wagon-oxen. **1852** —— *Jasper Lyle* 102 Drivers, forelоupers (leaders of the draught cattle), guides and oxen .. drank thankfully of the slimy waters. **1860** A.W. DRAYSON *Sporting Scenes* 15 A .. Hottentot boy or Fingoe is employed to perform the part of leader: he is called 'forelouper', his duty being to hold a small rope that is fastened to the horns of the two front oxen, and to lead them in the right road. **1878** T.J. LUCAS *Camp Life & Sport* 43 The oxen are not guided by reins as in the mule waggons, but are led in different places by a 'foer louper,' or runner. **1880** E.F. SANDEMAN *Eight Months in Ox-Waggon* 46 We selected .. a strong, tall half-caste from the old colony, as driver at 50s a month; another half-caste at 20s. as forelouper or leader of the oxen. **1882** J. NIXON *Among Boers* 131 The patient oxen sitting or standing in long rows waiting the time for their master, .. while the black 'foreloopers' or 'forerunners' squatted with equal patience in the dust. **1887** A.A. ANDERSON *25 Yrs in Waggon* I. 9 The foreloper, one who leads the two front oxen in dangerous places .. was named Shilling. **1887** A.B. ELLIS *S. Afr. Sketches* 108 The Tottie 'fore-louper', or boy who leads the leading pair of oxen, .. was standing by the span, shivering with cold. **1911** L. COHEN *Reminisc. of Kimberley* 397

The Hottentot forelouper (or leader) guided the bullocks on their journey.

foreslock *n. obs.* [Englished form of S. Afr. Du. *voorslag.*] VOORSLAG sense 1.
  1850 R.G.G. CUMMING *Hunter's Life* I. 25 The '*foreslock*,' about which the waggon-drivers are very particular, is about a yard in length, and is formed of a strip of the supple skin of some particular variety of antelope. 1853 F.P. FLEMING *Kaffraria* 46 Long whips, made with bamboo handles, .. and tapering towards the end, where the 'foreslocks' or lashes .. are fastened. 1873 F. BOYLE *To Cape for Diamonds* 56 The butt is a pliant reed, twelve to fifteen feet long, and the lash, of bullock's hide plaited, measures sometimes twenty feet ... Such an instrument would cut a piece from a horse's back like a knife, but it is reduced to more moderate torture by appending a fore slock of antelope skin. [1894 E. GLANVILLE *Fair Colonist* 229 A piece of bush-buck hide .. looped over a big tow and stretched tight, while he swiftly drew a smalled loop up and down the thong, .. to serve as a terrible lash or *foreslag* for the long waggon-whip.]

forestell *n. Obs. Wagon-making.* [Englished form of S. Afr. Du. *voorstel.*] VOORSTEL.
  1850 R.G.G. CUMMING *Hunter's Life* II. 58 We outspanned, and, having unloaded the waggon, we put a support under it, and took out the forestell. 1864 T. BAINES *Explor. in S.-W. Afr.* 85 Our dissel boom had split where the bolt joins to the *fore stell* or carriage, and in a short time came completely out, the team running off at full speed without the wagon.

fore-tongue *n. Wagon-making.* Also **foretong**. [Calque formed on Afk. *voortang.*] VOORTANG.
  1919 Dunell, Ebden & Co.'s *Price List* Aug. 35 Foretongs, Wagon, 8in. 11/6 rough, 21/6 dressed. 1934 C.P. SWART Supplement to Pettman. 53 *Fore Tongue*, The anglicised form of voortang .. , a part of a wagon; sometimes also written foretong. *Ibid.* 187 *Voortang* .. is also called foretong or foretongue by manufacturers. 1973 E. PROV. HERALD 28 May 13 A typical wagon of the Great Trek period would have had .. disselboom, foretong, long wagon and other heavy carrying timbers, of black ironwood.

fore-tow *n. obs.* [Englished form of S. Afr. Du. *voortouw.*] VOORTOU.
  [1817 G. BARKER *Journal.* 20 May, My two fore Trektows were twisted today.] 1850 R.G.G. CUMMING *Hunter's Life* I. 30 The leader has made up his 'fore-tow' which is a long spare rheim attached round the horns of each of the fore or front oxen. 1887 [see FRONT OX].

fore-tracker, -trekker see VOORTREKKER.

forget *v. trans.* [Influenced by Afk. *vergeet* to leave behind.] To leave (something) behind (somewhere), unintentionally or through a lapse of memory.
  Also *U.S. Eng.*
  1916 S. BLACK in S. Gray *Three Plays* (1984) 218 Van K: Did you get them? Van Slaap: Good Lord, yes — I've forgotten them in the taxi. 1970 BEETON & DORNER in *Eng. Usage in Sn Afr.* Vol.1 No.2, 6 'I forgot my book at home' .. in the sense of 'I left my book at home'; .. prob Afk inf 'Ek het my boek by die huis vergeet'. 1973 *S. Afr. Panorama* Dec. 34 A friend borrowed them and forgot them outside on the lawn. They were stolen, of course, and the child's anguish knew no bounds. 1974 A.P. BRINK *Looking on Darkness* 92 That afternoon the whole yard was searched for the lost book. It would have been so easy to tell Willem: 'You forgot it outside, so I kept it for you.' But I remained silent. 1985 *Drum* July 25 My dad .. says his prayers every morning and every evening ... Even when he has experienced what it is like to sleep in a police cell. All because he forgot his passbook at home.

formal *adj.* [Special senses of general Eng. *formal* according to recognized forms or rules.]
1. Of economic and business activity:
a. Structured according to established (Western) standards and operating within conventional parameters (such as city by-laws, commercial regulations, and taxation). Cf. INFORMAL sense 1 b.
  1989 C. NAIDOO in *Sunday Times* 8 Oct. (Business Times) 3 The formal economy cannot provide work for everyone. Spazas will grow in the years ahead, even more as the economy is derestricted. 1991 *Bulletin* (Centre for Science Dev.) Mar. 6 The more successful informal operators had access to the formal wage of a family member.
b. In the special collocation **formal sector**, the conventional, established business sector. Cf. *informal sector*, see INFORMAL sense 1 a.
  1990 R. RUMNEY in *Weekly Mail* 2 Nov. 46 There are 66000 spaza shops in formal metropolitan areas – or one out of every 40 households accommodates a spaza ... A leading shoepolish manufacturer has come up with a Spaza Shop Pack in which up to three sizes of shoe polish tins are offered ... It shows how seriously the formal sector is beginning to take the informal sector.
2. Of buildings: solidly constructed, meeting conventional (Western) standards. Cf. INFORMAL sense 2 b.
  1989 *Optima* Vol.37 No.1, 19 The nature of their shack (corrugated iron, breeze-block, lean-to against a formal house) ... Throughout the country formal black residential areas are overcrowded and further population growth .. will have to be accommodated mainly in free standing informal settlements. 1994 [see INFORMAL sense 2 b].

forslat var. VOORSLAG.

Fortypercenters *pl. n.* Also with small initial. [Named for the approx. 40% of white South Africans who are English-speaking.] *The Fortypercenters*: An organization founded in 1978 with the aim of promoting the interests of the English-speaking sector of the white population of South Africa.
  1979 G. BARAGWANATH in *Sunday Times* 8 Apr. 9 It is high time the English start sticking up for themselves ... The 'Fortypercenters' is not anti-Afrikaans. We simply want .. a fair share ... English speakers hold only five per cent of the top jobs in the public service. 1979 D. ALEXANDER in *Ibid.* 15 Apr. 11 The forty-percenters .. operate quite openly as a watchdog and pressure group to push for a bigger say for the English in running South Africa. 1979 *Daily Dispatch* 14 June 2 The Fortypercenters .. 'oppose all attempts to put the overriding stamp of one section of the population on the character of the nation ... We object to the activities of the Broederbond, such as its attempts to Afrikanerise English-speaking schoolchildren'. 1981 *Sunday Times* 14 June 6 The reduced English-speaking support for the National Party .. was partly due .. to the sustained campaign by the anti-Broederbond group, the Fortypercenters. 1985 L. DU BUISSON in *Avenue* May 36 Alexander threw the full weight of his Forty Percenters behind an energetic letter-writing campaign, openly advocating secession as the only road to social justice for English speakers.

FOSATU /fə'sɑːtu/ *n. hist.* Also **Fosatu**. Acronym formed on *Federation of South African Trade Unions*, a labour organization formerly affiliated to the UDF. Also *attrib.*
  Fosatu was disbanded in 1985 on the formation of COSATU.
  1980 *Survey of Race Rel. 1979* (S.A.I.R.R.) 266 It .. rejected all party political alignment or support and pledged itself to resist any attempts by a party political organisation to control FOSATU. 1981 *Rand Daily Mail* 21 Feb. 1 Fosatu — by far the biggest predominantly black trade union organisation — is reconsidering its .. attitude towards registration. 1983 *Survey of Race Rel. 1982* (S.A.I.R.R.) 147 FOSATU was committed to wide-ranging political change and to a society in which workers 'control their own destiny'. 1985 *Learn & Teach* No.3, 19 An organiser for FOSATU told Learn and Teach ... 'After 1950 the workers became weak and .. stoppped celebrating May Day. But now we celebrate May Day .. because we are strong again.' 1986 *Race Rel. Survey 1985* (S.A.I.R.R.) 183 In November the Federation of South African Trade Unions (FOSATU) disbanded and its eight affiliates became members of the newly formed COSATU ... At the time FOSATU claimed 123 924 paid-up members.

Founders' Day *n. phr.* The 6th of April, a public holiday commemorating the contributions made by the founders of the various communities making up South African society, but particularly the landing at the Cape in 1652 of Jan van Riebeeck.
  Formerly called VAN RIEBEECK DAY. Scrapped as a public holiday at the end of 1994.
  1980 *Govt Gaz.* Vol.180 No.7060, 3 The First Schedule to the principal Act is hereby amended .. by the insertion immediately under the words 'New Year's Day' of the words 'Founders' Day (sixth day of April).' 1982 *Citizen* 31 Dec. 9 A long weekend created by Good Friday (April 1) and Family Day (April 4), could be stretched into a six day weekend simply by taking off April 5 and running the weekend into Founders' Day (April 6). 1985 *Argus* 6 Apr. 5 Jan van Riebeeck's arrival at the Cape in 1652 was commemorated at a Founder's Day ceremony at the Cape Town Civic Centre today. 1988 *E. Prov. Herald* 31 Mar. 1 The paper will be published on .. Founders' Day. 1994 *E. Prov. Herald* 8 Sept. 1 Also to be cut [as public holidays] are Founders' Day and Ascension Day.

fountain *n.* [Calque formed on Du. *fontein* spring. Formerly used in general Eng., but now archaic: the word's continued and habitual use in this sense in S. Afr. Eng. is reinforced by Afk. *fontein.*] A natural spring or water source; FONTEIN sense 1 a. Also *attrib.* See also EYE.
  1789 W. PATERSON *Narr. of Four Journeys* 55 The water, by standing a few hours in the rocks, became similar in its qualities to that of the fountain. *Ibid.* 59 In the evening we arrived at a small fountain where we had hardly water enough to suffice us and our cattle. 1798 S.H. WILCOCKE tr. *J.S. Stavorinus's Voy. to E. Indies 1768–71* I. 39 Refreshed ourselves with a draught of the clear *fountain-water*. 1802 W. SOMERVILLE *Narr. of E. Cape Frontier* (1979) 67 The partridge fountain (so called from the multitudes of Namaqua partridges that frequent it to drink the brine). 1824 W.J. BURCHELL *Trav.* II. 307 We passed a fountain of clear water, in which stood a few reeds. This *fountain* or spring, though not copious enough to produce a stream, formed a small pond which had the appearance of being constantly supplied with water. 1827 G. THOMPSON *Trav.* I. 118 Though somewhat disturbed by the wild animals assembling at the fountain to drink, we were left unmolested. 1834 E. COOK in B. Shaw *Memorials* (1841) 170 The spot on which we met was near to a fountain of water, and was shaded by a camel-thorn tree; two of the most important things which this barren country produces. 1841 B. SHAW *Memorials* 102 The Fountain appears to be of considerable strength: but the water is somewhat sweet, yet good for use. 1857 D. LIVINGSTONE *Missionary Trav.* 110 Mr Moffat .. made a dam .. and led out the stream for irrigation, where not a drop of fountain-water ever now flows. 1867 *Blue Bk for Col. 1866* JJ5, The scarcity of water on many farms is still felt; but the farmers are busy in making dams, and some fountains have been opened. 1882 J. NIXON *Among Boers* 139 The garden was irrigated from a fountain of beautiful water near the house. 1882 *Meteor* 31 Oct. 3 In spring, when the rains have replenished every fountain, innumerable tiny cascades are trickling from the picturesque hills. 1890 A. MARTIN *Home Life* 77 It would be necessary to choose a farm possessing a good fountain; thus a constant supply of vegetables could be kept up. 1916 *Farmer's Weekly* 20 Dec. 1455 (*advt*) Abundant water supply, consisting of a large dam, permanent fountain, and a spruit running through the farm. 1936 *Cambridge Hist. of Brit. Empire* VIII. 9 There is .. little doubt that the flow of the rivers has become more irregular, that many 'fountains' have dried up, and that the vegetation in different regions has deteriorated. 1958 [see LEAD]. 1961 T.V. BULPIN *White Whirlwind* 194 Mbuzimbili ..

lived close to an isolated fountain at which enormous flocks of guinea-fowl habitually came to drink. **1975** *Friend* 1 Aug. 1 The worst floods in the history of the .. Northern Cape have been caused by the eruption of natural fountains. **1987** *Style* July 104 He found a fountain just below .. the old post office tree ... The surroundings of the early fountain are being restored so that the water will flow into an informal pool. **1991** J. WINTER tr. *P. Pieterse's Shadow of Eagle* 66 Their best chance was to follow the dry river-bed in the hope of reaching an underground spring or fountain forced up through the rocky ground.

four corners *n. phr.* [See quot. 1970.] **a.** KRUISBESSIE sense b. **b.** KRUISBESSIE sense a. Also *attrib.*

1917 R. MARLOTH *Common Names* 29 *Four corners* = Kruisbessie. **1966** C.A. SMITH *Common Names* 216 *Four-corners*, The edible fruits of *Grewia occidentalis*. **1970** M.R. LEVYNS in *Std Encycl. of Sn Afr.* II. 633 *Buttonwood*, kruisbessie ... The fruit when fully developed consists of four small, somewhat fleshy drupes (hence sometimes called four-corners-berry). **1977** E. PALMER *Field Guide to Trees* 212 *Kruisbessie or Four Corners, Grewia occidentalis* L. Fruit: .. typically 4-lobed, somewhat bristly, brown to purple. **1987** [see CROSS-BERRY].

fowl tick *n. phr.* The TAMPAN (sense b), *Argas persicus*.

1914 *Farmer's Annual* 277 *Fowl Tick or Tampans*, These horrible insects .. are on the increase in South Africa, and if you are fortunate to have none it is advisable to take every precaution to keep them away. **1929** *Handbk for Farmers* (Dept of Agric.) 255 *The fowl tick*, often called 'tampan,' is an oval-shaped, slate-coloured tick with light-yellow legs and has its mouth-parts situated below the anterior end of the body. **1946** C.W. SMITH *S. Afr. Poultry Bk* 145 Fowl Ticks. These are frequently called tampans in South Africa, a name which really belongs to a closely allied species. *Ibid.* 146 In some parts of the country fowl ticks are so bad that poultry-keeping is only a doubtful proposition. **1974** [see TAMPAN].

fraai var. VRY.

fransmadam /ˌfrans-, ˌfrɑːnsmaˈdam/ *n.* Also **fransch madam, frans madame**, and with initial capital. [Afk., *Frans* (earlier Du. *Fransch*) French + *madam* fr. Fr. *madame* lady; see quot. 1947.] The seabream *Boopsoidea inornata* of the Sparidae; CAPE LADY sense 1; FRENCHIE; FRENCH MADAM; JACOB EVERTSON sense 2; JACOPEVER sense 2.

The name 'fransmadam' is used for this species in Smith and Heemstra's *Smiths' Sea Fishes* (1986).

1913 C. PETTMAN *Africanderisms* 177 *Fransch madam*, This curious appellation is given to the fish *Pagrus holubi*. **1945** H. GERBER *Fish Fare* 39 This attractive little fish with its large eyes .. is a good eating fish and any recipe for hottentot may be used for Frans Madam. **1947** K.H. BARNARD *Pict. Guide to S. Afr. Fishes* 150 *Fransch Madam*, .. Supposed to derive its name from a fancied resemblance of the dark coloration and large lustrous brown eyes to a typical French lady. **1949** J.L.B. SMITH *Sea Fishes* 274 *Boopsoidea inornata* ... *Frans Madame* or *Jacopever* (Cape). *Dikoog. Peuloog* or *Grootogie* (Knysna area). *Cape Lady* (Transkei) ... Attains 12 ins. Found only in South Africa from the Cape to Natal, chiefly in reasonably deep water in rocky areas. **1966** VAN HEYNINGEN & BERTHOUD *Uys Krige* 145 What anonymous fisherman had the pleasant fancy of calling that other dark and attractive little Cape fish with the large lustrous eyes by the charming name, *Frans Madam*? It certainly is a monument to his sense of humour. **1972** J.L.B. SMITH in *Std Encycl. of Sn Afr.* V. 28 Fransmadam .. is a large-eyed colourful small fish which is a pest to anglers, as it occurs in great shoals which soon tear bait to shreds. **1988** E. WITHERS in *Fair Lady* 22 June (Suppl.) 15 This collection of diverse and delectable dishes .. features just about every conceivable fish available locally – from favourites such as kingklip .. to more obscure catches like .. fransmadam. **1988** R. LUBKE et al. *Field Guide to E. Cape* 111 Fransmadam only grows to 30 cm and appears to be omnivorous, with small invertebrates dominating the diet.

frau(w) var. VROU.

fray var. VRY.

freck var. VREK.

free *adj. hist.* [Special sense of general Eng.] Of urban areas: in apartheid legislation (esp. in the phrr. ***free settlement area*** and ***free trade area***), open to all races for residential or trading purposes respectively. See also OPEN *adj.*

1978 *Report of Commiss. of Inquiry into Legislation Affecting Utilization of Manpower* (RP32–1979) 225 Free trade areas ... The Commission recommends that .. the restrictive provisions on acquisition, ownership or occupation by disqualified persons in specific demarcated areas in the central business centres of cities and towns not be applicable to buildings, land and premises in such areas which are used exclusively for trading, commercial or professional purposes. **1981** P. LANGE in *E. Prov. Herald* 27 May 1 The move was made because of the recommendation by the Riekert Commission that the Group Areas Act be amended to create free trade zones. **1988** *Daily Dispatch* 27 July 1 The Free Settlement Areas Bill is part of a trilogy of proposed Group Areas legislation announced last month. **1989** *Weekend Post* 28 Oct. 3 North End .. is now .. thriving ... The business revival was aided by turning it into a free trade area. **1989** *E. Prov. Herald* 29 Nov. 1 The Government is pushing for Lawaaikamp, a settlement near George and classified as a 'brown group area,' to be declared a Free Settlement Area. **1989** 'HOGARTH' in *Sunday Times* 3 Dec. 26 Rather than grizzle about the shortcomings of free settlement areas (and there are many), why not test the new procedure to the limit by flooding the board with applications? **1990** *Weekly Mail* 9 Mar. 12 Planning Minister Hernus Kriel's suggestion last week that entire cities should become Free Settlement Areas, free of the Group Areas Act, was well publicised.

free black *n. phr. Hist.* [Eng. *free* liberated + BLACK *n.* sense 1 a.] A black person not bound in slavery; usu., one released from servitude before slavery was abolished at the Cape in 1834.

1795 C.R. HOPSON tr. *C.P. Thunberg's Trav.* I. 140 The free blacks are not permitted to go upon the municipal guard. **1805** D. WOODRIFF in G.M. Theal *Rec. of Cape Col.* (1899) V. 230 Hottentots, free blacks, and Burghers of every description. **1819** LORD C. SOMERSET in *Ibid.* (1902) XII. 244 There is a particular burying ground set apart for the class of Free blacks or slaves who have embraced the Christian faith. **1827** *Reports of Commissioners upon Finances at Cape of G.H.* I. 49 The burgher senate .. have the superintendence and direction of .. 'free blacks', whose services they can gratuitously command. **1832** *Graham's Town Jrnl* 30 Mar. 55 As the population now is, it .. comprises English, Dutch, Malays, Slaves, Hottentots, Caffers, and other free blacks of various descriptions. **1949** E. HELLMANN *Handbk on Race Rel.* 349 Missionary enterprise among the slaves and the 'free blacks' (that is, freed slaves and Hottentots) flourished. *c*1968 *Stellenbosch: Oldest Village in S. Afr. (brochure)* 8 He states the population as consisting [in 1825] of 774 Christians, 144 Hottentots, 852 slaves, 22 prize negroes and 64 free blacks, in total 1855 inhabitants. **1979** W.S. ROBERTSON in *Sunday Times* 11 Feb. 4 It would appear to be reasonably certain that the Quwal mosque in Upper Dorp Street was the first and oldest mosque at the Cape, standing on property transferred as far back as 1794 to a 'free black', Coridon of Bengal. **1989** *Reader's Digest Illust. Hist.* 53 A free black .. was a former slave who had been released from slavery.

free burgher /ˈfriː ˌbɜːgə/ *n. phr. Hist.* Also **free burger**, and with initial capitals. [Part. tr. Du. *vrijburg(h)er*, *vrij* free + *burgher* citizen.] A former employee of the Dutch East India Company who had been freed from its control; any white male who was not a Company official; VRYBURGER. Also *attrib.* See also BURGHER sense 1 a.

1827 *Reports of Commissioners upon Finances at Cape of G.H.* II. 55 The privileges accorded to the free burghers of Cape Town, .. followed by an extension of these privileges to the European colonists. **1857** *Cape Monthly Mag.* II. Sept. 155 The nocturnal expedition .. and the Landdrost's spirited assault of the 'free burgher's' castle, were crowned with even greater success than had been anticipated. **1877** J. NOBLE *S. Afr.* 5 Officers and servants of the company, a few of whom, after landing, were released from their engagements, and permitted to become 'free burghers' or cultivators of the soil. **1919** M. GREENLEES tr. *O.F. Mentzel's Life at Cape in Mid-18th C.* 9 The right to provide the meat is farmed out, for from six to seven years, to those of the free burghers who will guarantee to supply it at the lowest price. **1941** C.W. DE KIEWIET *Hist. of S. Afr.* 5 At the suggestion of van Riebeeck nine of the Company's servants became 'free burghers' and landholders. **1953** DU PLESSIS & LÜCKHOFF *Malay Quarter* 52 Only the free burgers of Cape Town were allowed on the streets after nine o'clock at night. **1971** *S. Afr. Panorama* May 9 Between February 21 1657, and February 13, 1658, 14 Free Burgher families had already been established at the Cape, though tenure papers were apparently not issued to all of them. **1971** *Personality* 14 May 27 The free *burghers* possessed .. such rights as the company was prepared to allow them. **1975** D.H. STRUTT *Clothing Fashions* 30 There were several separate and distinct classes of people, namely: the Company officials, the servants of the Company in de Kaap itself, and the Free Burghers farming away from the Bay and its contact with the outer world. **1988** D. HUGHES et al. *Complete Bk of S. Afr. Wine* 33 The late eighteenth century saw the emergence of the Free Burgher wine farmers of the Cape to an unexpected prosperity.

Hence **free burghership** *n. phr.*, the status of free burgher.

1858 *Cape Monthly Mag.* III. Mar. 147 Requiring one Eksteen, who had received .. free burghership, to go back into the Company's service, at his wages of *nine guilders a month*.

Freedom Charter *n. phr.*

1. ***The Freedom Charter***: A document setting out guidelines for human rights and the duties of the state in a democratic South Africa, for many years the political manifesto of the African National Congress (see ANC *n.*[1]); *the Charter* (see CHARTER). Also *attrib.*, and *transf.* See also CHARTERIST.

The Freedom Charter, drawn up by the Congress Alliance following a survey of the wishes of South Africans, was endorsed by the Congress of the People at Kliptown on 26 June 1955. See also CONGRESS sense 2.

1953 Z.K. MATTHEWS in M. Benson *Afr. Patriots* (1963) 198, I wonder whether the time has not come for the A.N.C. to consider the question of convening a National Convention, a Congress of the People, representing all the people of this country, irrespective of race or colour, to draw up a Freedom Charter for the Democratic South Africa of the future. **1956** *Rand Daily Mail* 25 June 1 The Special Branch .. and .. armed European police constables ringed the first anniversary meeting of the Freedom Charter Movement at Kliptown. **1958** A. SAMPSON *Treason Cage* 38 The Freedom Charter .. aimed to substitute for the existing State a People's Democracy. **1962** A.J. LUTHULI *Let my People Go* 158 The Freedom Charter was read out and unanimously adopted. **1970** A.H. MURRAY in *Std Encycl. of Sn Afr.* I. 61 Before it [*sc.* the Congress of the People] was broken up by the Police on the second day of its sessions it had adopted the Freedom Charter. **1982** *Times* (U.K.) 20 Dec. 6 South Africa complained about the terrorist threat, but for the last 25 years the ANC had offered them the alternative of the Freedom Charter. **1986** *Paratus* July 35 The SACP described the Freedom Charter .. as 'broad popular guidelines which describe the main contents of the people's power in the immediate aftermath of the national democratic revolution'. **1986** J.V. LEATT in *Leadership* Vol.5 No.4, 38 The debate which led to the writing of the Freedom Charter .. was essentially .. about which economic policy would best serve black nationalist interests. **1987** *Star* 5 May 10 (*advt*) The Freedom Charter declares that South Africa belongs to all who live in it, black and white. **1990** *New African* 4 June 2 The Freedom Charter did not call for a socialist future, as was sometimes believed. **1991** *Sunday Times* 3 Feb. 22 The Freedom Charter, a document .. swathed now in myth, and elevated by constant propaganda to the status of 'the will of the people'. **1991** B. RONGE in *Ibid.* 14 July (Mag. Sect.) 19 Was the whole exercise merely an invitation to the artists to write their own freedom charter?

2. *comb.* **Freedom Charter Day,** FREEDOM DAY sense 1.

1956 *Star* 23 June 3 The parade .. was held to draw attention to 'Freedom Charter Day' which will be observed by a mass rally at Kliptown tomorrow. **1986** *Financial Mail* 13 June 36 Confrontation is probable because of the countrywide ban placed on meetings in June to commemorate Soweto Day and Freedom Charter Day.

Freedom Day *n. phr.*
1. The 26th of June, the anniversary of the first national work stoppage (1950), the launch of the DEFIANCE CAMPAIGN (1952), and the endorsement of the Freedom Charter by the Congress of the People (1955); *Freedom Charter Day,* see FREEDOM CHARTER sense 2. Also *attrib.*

1981 *Rand Daily Mail* 26 June 5 Today is 'Freedom Day', marking the 26th anniversary of the adoption of the Freedom Charter. **1984** *City Press* 1 July, Special services and rallies were held .. this week to commemorate Freedom Day on June 26 ... On that day 32 years ago, the African National Congress and the South African Indian Congress launched the Campaign for the Defiance of Unjust Laws. June 26 was again an important year [*sic*] in the campaign against apartheid in 1955 — on that day, about 3 000 delegates from organisations affiliated to the Congress Alliance came together in Kliptown near Johannesburg. They adopted the historic Freedom Charter. **1985** *Learn & Teach* No.3, 18 A day of mourning and protest was called on 26 June 1950 to remember those who died on May Day. June 26 was called Freedom Day. And since then, every year on June 26 people come together to remember those who have died in the struggle for freedom. **1987** *South* 2 July 9 Cape strugglers were given a preview of the kind of festivities they might expect on Freedom Day at the UDF cultural evening.

2. The 27th of April, a public holiday instituted in 1995 commemorating the first non-racial elections held in South Africa in 1994.

1994 *E. Prov. Herald* 8 Dec. 2 The confusion that has existed over the past few months regarding the public holidays for 1995 ended today, by the publication of the Public Holiday Act 1994 in the Government Gazette ... The full list of public holidays is as follows: .. April 27 Freedom Day, [etc.].

freedom song *n. phr.* A song or chant sung at protest gatherings and demonstrations, strongly political in content, and often in a formulaic call-and-response style.

1962 A. FUGARD *Notebks* (1983) 53 Between speeches the Africans were led in 'Freedom' songs by one of the men on the platform. **1976** M. THOLO in C. Hermer *Diary of Maria Tholo* (1980) 36 You are not supposed to sing freedom songs. But you find yourself joining in because even if they have changed the words you still know the tune. **1982** *Staffrider* Vol.4 No.4, 17 'Amandla!' Bra Terra screamed. 'Ngawethu!' they rejoined, took up another of the freedom songs of the last confrontation, and sang their hearts out. **1985** *E. Prov. Herald* 20 July 2 Soldiers in armoured vehicles watched as thousands of youths gathered near the main road, chanting freedom songs. **1987** *Learn & Teach* No.5, 33 'Mayibuye i Africa,' he sings, calling for the return of South Africa .. to its people. This .. is a freedom song that will be sung everywhere — from Soweto to Gugulethu. **1988** A. GUMEDE in *New Nation* 14 Jan. 3 When schoolchildren are attacked because they are singing freedom songs, you cannot say the attack is not political. **1990** R. MALAN *My Traitor's Heart* 138 There was some half-hearted singing of freedom songs, but they sounded a little silly in English, and lame in the throats of whites. *Ibid.* 229 We were singing freedom songs — 'Rolihlala Mandela, freedom is in your hands, show us the way to freedom, in our land in Africa'.

free person of colour see COLOUR.

free settlement area, - trade area see FREE.

freesia /ˈfriːzɪə, ˈfriːʒə/ *n.* Also **freezia, friezia,** and with initial capital. [Modern L., named for F.H.T. *Freese.*] Any of several sweetly-scented species of flowering plants of the genus *Freesia* of the Iridaceae, esp. *F. alba* and *F. refracta.*

Hybrids of the genus are now cultivated worldwide in a great variety of colours.

1882 *Garden* (U.K.) 4 Feb. 73 Freesias. **1895** *Horticulture: Guide to Amateurs* (Smith Bros.) 88 Dahlias, Freesias, Gladiolus. **1917** R. MARLOTH *Common Names* 141 *Freesia refracta,* .. Buttercup, freesia. **1964** [see BOBBEJAANTJIE]. **1971** *Evening Post* 5 June 5 Few realise that freesias are indigenous to the Cape, and were distributed for world-wide delight by early colonists. **1986** A. BATTEN *Flowers of Sn Afr.* 181 Because Freesias come into bloom early and because of their long-lasting quality as cut flowers, .. a great many modern hybrids .. are available. **1989** *Motorist* 3rd Quarter 23 Many flowers which today are cultivated in the hot-houses of the world far from their country of origin, among them pelargoniums, gladioli, strelitzia, arum lilies, freesias [etc.]. **1994** *E. Prov. Herald* 26 Mar. 9 Freesia: The fragrance is exquisite. **1994** M. WASSERFALL in *S. Afr. Garden & Home* Sept. 4 How wonderful are the Namaqua daisies, the freesias, sparaxis, *bobbejaantjies,* felicias and all the other colourful flowers that greet us at this time.

Free State *n. phr.* and *adj. phr.* [Short for *Orange Free State* tr. Du. *Oranje Vrijstaat* (fr. *vrijstaat* free state, republic).]

A. *n. phr.* From 1854 to 1901, an independent Boer republic; subsequently one of the four provinces of the Union (later Republic) of South Africa, and one of the nine provinces of South Africa from 1994; OFS; VRYSTAAT *n.* Also *attrib.* See also BOER REPUBLIC sense b.

1858 H. HALL in *Cape Monthly Mag.* III. May 301 The contest now raging between the Dutch farmers of the Free State and the Basutu chief Moshesh has naturally excited a considerable degree of interest. **1876** F. BOYLE *Savage Life* 164 Lying just within the border of the Free State, it .. became the refuge of all those for whom our diamond fields had become too hot. **1900** F.D. BAILLIE *Mafeking Diary* 113 The Transvaalers .. hope to get the Free State Boers to fight their battles further away from their own territory. **1911** A.W. BARLOW in *Farmer's Weekly* 11 Oct. 154 In the Free State the natives pay in direct taxation more than double the amount derived from the quit-rent on farms. **1916** S.T. PLAATJE *Native Life* (1982) 27 The object of the bill was to remove a hardship .. by which a 'Free' State native was by law debarred from inheriting landed property. **1929** [see *vermeersiektebossie* (VERMEERSIEKTE sense 2)]. **1955** PENCHARZ & SOWDEN in *Saron & Hotz Jews in S. Afr.* 320 One of those vague, straggling villages which dotted the Free State landscape. **1971** J. MCCLURE *Steam Pig* (1973) 72 Zondi was going it like a Free State farmer on his way to a Rugby international. **1988** C. LEGUM in *Afr. Contemp. Rec. 1986–7* B720, Since the days of the old Boer Republics in the 19th Century no Indian was allowed to remain in the Free State for longer than 24 hours. **1990** M. KENTRIDGE *Unofficial War* 29 'Zola' refers to the Free State athlete Zola Budd.

B. *adj. phr.*
1. Used facetiously, alluding to the province's predominantly agricultural nature: of or pertaining to anything regarded as rustic, primitive, or defective.

1871 W.G. ATHERSTONE in A.M.L. Robinson *Sel. Articles from Cape Monthly Mag.* (1978) 145 All day at 'Free State' speed (the adaged rate of an old Dutch plough), we furrowed the alluvial flats. **1955** W. HULLY *Wagon on Fire* 175 A huge black cloud .. swept the town, darkening the sky but yielding no moisture ... 'Free State rain,' commented Pieter ironically, as he spluttered and shook his clothes. **1978** J. BRANFORD *Dict. of S. Afr. Eng.* 72 *Free State bolt,* a piece of wire used for fastening a door; *Free State nails,* stones used to keep a roof or roof-patch in place. **1983** T. MCALLEN *Kyk Daar,* Haircut: Regulation Free State, clipped 50mm above each ear. **1991** M. LUYT *Informant,* Grahamstown A Free State sandwich? Two slices of *stywe pap* with soft porridge in between!

2. *comb.* **Free State coal** *colloq.,* dried dung, used as fuel where wood and coal are scarce; *Karoo coal,* see KAROO sense 3; *kraal fuel,* see KRAAL *n.* sense 3 d; also called MIS (sense 1).

[**1882** J. NIXON *Among Boers* 127 There was a fireplace in the sitting room, in which, during the winter, coal was burned — coal from the Free State!] **1886** R. JAMESON *Rough Notes of Trip to Tvl Gold-Fields* 1 (Pettman), Busied himself collecting the Free State coal, as the dried cow-dung is euphoniously called. **1913** C. PETTMAN *Africanderisms* 178 *Free State coal,* A euphemism for the dried Mist .. which is largely used for fuel in up-country homesteads. **1945** N. DEVITT *People & Places* 142 Free State Coal was .. the humorous name given by the early transport riders to the dried cow-dung from which the campfires of those days were made on the main transport roads. **1971** *Informant, Tvl* We burn cow-dung in our province, but only in the sticks. It's called 'Free State Coal'. **1986** M. HENRY in *Somerset Budget* 2 Oct., Free State coal is .. cow dung used for fuel where wood is scarce, but why the honour went to the Free State .. is a mystery. **1990** C. LAFFEATY *Far Forbidden Plains* 235 Her pails filled with dry dung which they had christened 'Free State Coal', she would cross the drift again and the bitter, desolate reality would stare her in the face.

Hence **Free Stater** *n. phr.,* an inhabitant of the Orange Free State.

1882 S. HECKFORD *Lady Trader in Tvl* 19 In the Orange Free State .. I heard much political talk, adverse to the English, from an old Free-Stater somewhat addicted to the bottle. **1903** D. BLACKBURN *Burgher Quixote* 100 The Free Staters are vain and look upon themselves as very superior to Transvaalers, because they can mostly read. **1915** J.K. O'CONNOR *Afrikander Rebellion* 83 The desire for a republic among the Boers has grown stronger during recent months .. whether they be Transvaalers, Free Staters, or Kaapenaars. **1931** W.A. COTTON *Racial Segregation* 115 Sir Thomas Watt is not a Dutchman, but a Britisher. He is not a Free Stater, but a Natal man. **1946** T. MACDONALD *Ouma Smuts* 13 They envied the Transvaalers and the Freestaters their absolute freedom, because the Cape was under the British Crown. **1974** *S. Afr. Panorama* Jan. 13 Alina Lekgetha is a Free Stater by birth — a member of the Barolong people of Thaba 'Nchu. **1989** F.G. BUTLER *Tales from Old Karoo* 10 Hobbits are really footloose Free Staters in disguise. **1992** *Financial Mail* 13 Mar. 6 Ian Palmer, the Free Stater who startled European golf by winning the Asian Classic in Bangkok.

freezia var. FREESIA.

French grape *n. phr.* [tr. Afk. *Fransdruif.*] A Spanish white wine grape, known elsewhere as Palomino; *White French,* see WHITE *adj.* sense 2.

1896 [see GROEN DRUIF]. **1962** *Entertaining with Wines of Cape* (K.W.V.) 11 The sherry of the Cape is produced from Palomino grapes (known locally as 'French' grapes) which are the principal base of Spanish sherries. **1966** H. BECK *Meet Cape Wines* 10 The French grape has .. been more or less relegated to the task of making wine for distillation. **1968** C.J. ORFFER in D.J. Opperman *Spirit of Vine* 87 Probably the Green or 'French' grape was used, but the latter's name is incorrect because it should be known rather as the 'Spanish' grape. **1981** [see GREEN GRAPE].

frenchie *n. colloq.* [Formed on FRENCH MADAM + Eng. (informal) n.-forming suffix *-ie*.] FRENCH MADAM.

1988 'IZAAK' in *E. Prov. Herald* 5 Mar. 8 Near the surface a french madam took the plug, .. a brave frenchie to come so high up .. where elf were running.

french madam *n. phr.* Also **french madame**, and with initial capitals. [tr. Afk. *fransmadam.*] FRANSMADAM.

1930 C.L. BIDEN *Sea-Angling Fishes* 233 The John Brown .. rapidly darting upon the worm, seizes the head firmly between the teeth ... French madame and other fishes .. feed in the same manner. **1971** *Daily Dispatch* 17 Aug. 15 A blacktail and a French Madame each of 0,68 kg (1 1/2 lb.). **1974** *E. Prov. Herald* 9 May 24 He would never have believed a french madam would take a spinner on the surface if he had not seen it done. **1976** *Ibid.* 1 July 21 Pilchard is good bait, but .. soft. So rather use a strip of .. French madam with a bit of sardine lashed to it. **1988** 'IZAAK' in *Ibid.* 5 Mar. 8 Caught a french madam with which he caught other bait fish ... Near the surface a french madam took the plug.

frey var. VRY.

fricadel(le) var. FRIKKADEL.

Friendly City *n. phr.* A nickname for the city of Port Elizabeth; PE. Also *attrib.*

1951 'MAN ON THE SPOT' in *Cape Times* 2 May, Port Elizabeth .. likes to be known as '*The Friendly City*'. **1990** W. KRIGE in *Sunday Times* 12 Aug. 2 Coloured townships in Port Elizabeth this weekend had all the hallmarks of Beirut ... The death toll in the 'Friendly City' and nearby Uitenhage .. 47 and rising. **1990** J. MCARTHUR in *Sunday Tribune* 21 Oct. (Today) 4 Service was brisk and the staff certainly lived up to the friendly city image. **1990** *Weekend Post* 10 Nov. 5 Thank you, people of Port Elizabeth, .. for showing .. the warm hospitality that has earned our Friendly City her name. **1994** R. SIMPSON on Radio Algoa 25 Oct., Port Elizabeth, the Friendly City, also cloudy tomorrow, I'm afraid.

Friesland /'friːzlənd/ *n.* Formerly also **Friezland.** [The name of a province in the Netherlands.] (One of) a breed of black-and-white dairy cattle; also called FATHERLAND. Freq. *attrib.*

In *U.S. Eng.* this breed is known as 'Holstein', and in *Brit. Eng.* as 'Friesian'.

*c*1881 A. DOUGLASS *Ostrich Farming* 207 The young farmer when commencing should .. always keep a moderately well-bred colonial-born bull, with a good dash of English or Friesland blood. **1897** 'F. MACNAB' *On Veldt & Farm* 55 The Count laid great stress on the importance of feeding the veldt in rotation: first with goats .. then with Afrikander sheep .. then with Kaffir cattle; lastly with Afrikander and Friesland. *c***1911** C.A. POPE in S. Playne *Cape Col.* 425 Taking the Province as a whole the Friesland type of cattle predominates. **1914** *Rand Daily Mail* 26 Dec., Breeders of Friesland cattle in South Africa .. will be interested to hear of the remarkable prices realised .. in England recently. **1916** L.D. FLEMMING *Fool on Veld* (1933) 18 Bulls' knees are being discussed, as of yore, and percentages of butter fat, Hackneys, Frieslands and robust wool, have innumerable advocates. *c***1936** *S. & E. Afr. Yr Bk & Guide* 1100 In 1932, an authentic eland-Friezland hybrid was bred at Westminster, O.F.S., by Capt. Holme. **1957** *Handbk for Farmers* (Dept of Agric.) III. 38 The South African Friesland is principally descended from the Black-and-white animals of the Netherlands ... Since most of the black-and white cattle imported .. came from Friesland, they received the name of Friesland in South Africa. *Ibid.* 39 [see FATHERLAND]. **1972** J. VAN MARLE in *Std Encycl. of Sn Afr.* V. 51 Round about 1780 Governor Tulbagh imported a Friesland bull and cow ... The South African Friesland Cattle-Breeders' Society was founded in 1921. **1988** *S. Afr. Panorama* Jan. 22 The Friesland has played an important part in South African dairy farming ... A Friesland bull and cow .. are registered in the first volume of the the SA Stud Book which appeared in 1906. **1990** D. MEDALIE in M. Leveson *Firetalk* 37 A Friesland cow, with distinctive black and white markings.

friezia var. FREESIA.

frikkadel /frɪkə'del, frək-/ *n.* Also **fricadel(le), frikadel(le), frikkadell(e), frikkedel.** Pl. **-s, frikkadelle** /-'delə/. [Afk., fr. Du. ad. Fr. *fricandeau* sliced meat fried or stewed and served with a sauce.] A meat-ball; occas., a fish-ball. Also *attrib.*, and occas. in dim. form **frikkadelletjie** [see -IE].

1870 'A LADY' in *Cape Monthly Mag.* I. Oct. 224 '*Babootie*' and '*frickadel*' and '*potato-pie*' are great improvements upon the minced meats of England. **1873** F. BOYLE *To Cape for Diamonds* 147 We had fricadels. This is the most ingenious dish I know ... The problem is, to cook together mutton, onions, spices, parsley, and the fat of a sheep's tail, in such a manner as to leave the taste of a dirty dish-cloth. **1889** 'A HOUSEWIFE OF THE COLONY' *Col. Hsehold Guide* 25 Frikadels .. are often prepared for breakfast, and when nicely made are very tasty. Any uncooked or cooked cold meat can be used. **1891** J.P. LEGG in *Cape Illust. Mag.* I. 96 'Frikkadelle' .. seems to have quite superseded the English or French equivalent 'rissoles.' **1891** H.J. DUCKITT *Hilda's 'Where Is It?'* 75 'Frickadels' ... First stew the Frickadel in a rich stock, in which a slice of browned onion has been put. **1910** D. FAIRBRIDGE *That Which Hath Been* (1913) 65 Your excellent wife .. was a famous hand at making *frikkadels* in the old days. **1913** C. PETTMAN *Africanderisms* 178 *Frikadels* or *Frikadeletjes*, .. Balls of minced meat and vegetables either fried or baked. **1930** M. RAUBENHEIMER *Tested S. Afr. Recipes* 108 Mix all the ingredients. Make into small round 'fricadelles.' **1944** I.D. DU PLESSIS *Cape Malays* 43 The large oven-baked frikkadel must be served with yellow rice and beetroot salad. **1951** S. VAN H. TULLEKEN *Prac. Cookery Bk* 134 Fricadelles .. must be juicy when cooked. **1954** [see *broodkluitjie* (KLUITJIE sense 1 b)]. **1968** F. GOLDIE *Ostrich Country* 33 Frikkadelletjies — the fresh flesh being boiled, minced, and then made into rissoles in the usual way — are also popular. **1977** N. OKES in *Quarry '77* 133 Turn this miserable piece of stockfish into frikkedels. That's the way to fill a man's stomach. **1982** *Fair Lady* 7 Apr. 264 The men go out and catch a bit of the environment, clean it and tenderise it and the women produce the most wonderful perlemoen frikkadels .. on the spot. **1985** *S. Afr. Cookbk* (Reader's Digest Assoc.) 381 *Frikkadels, fricadelles,* Meatballs made of minced meat, fresh breadcrumbs and seasonings, then poached in stock or shallow-fried. **1988** F. WILLIAMS *Cape Malay Cookbk* 29 Place about 30 ml frikkadel mixture in centre of each cabbage leaf and roll up into parcels. **1990** M. VAN BILJON in *Yr Family* Oct. 178 Our national food is neither waterblommetjiebredie nor braaivleis; it's tomato sandwiches or frikkadels.

Frontier *n. hist.* [Special senses of general Eng.] **a.** The eastern districts of the former Cape Colony; the boundary zone between the area under the control of Xhosa-speaking peoples and the area under colonial rule. Also *attrib.* See also *the Border* (BORDER sense 1).

1812 J. CRADOCK in G.M. Theal *Rec. of Cape Col.* (1901) VIII. 435 To .. permanently establish the tranquillity of these distant districts I am under the necessity for a time to station the Cape Regiment upon the frontier and to sustain them by a considerable detachment of Europeans. **1819** LORD C. SOMERSET in *Ibid.* (1902) XII. 193, I have received advices from Lt. Col. Willshire of the 38th Regt., who commands on the Frontier, stating that .. the Caffers, 10,000 at least in number, attempted to surprize Graham's Town, the principal position on the Frontier. **1827** *Reports of Commissioners upon Finances at Cape of G.H.* I. 21 A measure of this kind had become necessary, from the increased pressure of business and correspondence with the remoter districts on the Frontier, occasioned by the settlement of the English emigrants. **1828** T. PRINGLE *Ephemerides* 210 Within these few years, five missionary institutions have been planted among the frontier tribes. **1832** *Graham's Town Jrnl* 13 Apr. 62 This brief sketch of the Frontier Trade, will serve to shew that the traffic with the colored tribes beyond the Boundary is a pursuit from which a large portion of the inhabitants of Albany derive their subsistence. **1839** W.C. HARRIS *Wild Sports* 345 The insecure state of the eastern frontier, and the inadequate protection afforded by the English Government against the aggressions of their wily and restless Kafir neighbours .. are the inciting causes assigned by the emigrants for the unprecedented and hazardous step they have taken. **1846** *Natal Witness* 10 Apr. 1 With satisfaction, then, the operations of our Government may be viewed, when compared with Frontier affairs. **1847** 'A BENGALI' *Notes on Cape of G.H.* 20 The word 'frontier' being used by the Cape town people to denote the eastern districts. **1868** W.R. THOMSON *Poems, Essays & Sketches* p.xxv, There is something radically wrong with our colonial system; you must come to the Frontier to see that. **1875** C.B. BISSET *Sport & War* 11 Fort Wiltshire .. was the largest and one of the strongest outposts on the Frontier, and was under the command of Major Halifax. **1888** *Cape Punch* 29 Feb. 125 A frontier paper tells us that on a recent occasion the hangman was detained .. for a whole month waiting instructions from head quarters. **1897** G.A. PARKER *S. Afr. Sports* 73 The Transvaal, Griqualand West, Western Province, and the Frontier were the contesting Associations [in the soccer tournament]. **1911** *Farmer's Weekly* 15 Mar. 14 Kingwilliams town and East London ... Some of the cattle were considered the finest seen on the Frontier since the rinderpest. **1941** C.W. DE KIEWIET *Hist. of S. Afr.* 49 Encroachment .. resulted in a confused and overlapping settlement that made all the frontier clamorous with charges and countercharges of trespass and cattle lifting. **1943** 'J. BURGER' *Black Man's Burden* 18 From about 1834 a few frontier farmers .. began to trek round the Bantu areas, across the Orange River, and on to the High veld. **1955** L. MARQUARD *Story of S. Afr.* 79 When Governor van Plettenberg visited the eastern 'frontier' in 1778 he found that, in fact, no real frontier was recognised either by Europeans or by Xhosa; cattle trading, cattle raiding, and cattle grazing by black and white frontiersmen were taking place on both sides of the Great Fish River. **1979** [see HIGH DUTCH]. **1989** *Reader's Digest Illust. Hist.* 70 The frontier burghers .. were incensed at officialdom's inability to 'control' the Xhosa. **1990** *Weekly Mail* 29 June (Suppl.) 2 That fateful meeting point of history, the eastern frontier.

b. *comb.* **Frontier war**, any of nine wars fought in the eastern areas of the Cape Colony in the period 1779–1878, between Xhosa-speaking peoples (and at times Khoikhoi) on the one hand, and the Dutch or British authorities and colonial inhabitants on the other; formerly offensively called *Kaffir war* (sense (*a*) see KAFFIR *n.* sense 2 e). See also WAR OF THE AXE.

1893 *Brown's S. Afr.* 179 The Amatola Mountains and forests .. were the scenes of many conflicts with the natives during the frontier wars. **1968** F.G. BUTLER *Cape Charade* 22 When did you first meet Frederick Rex? In 1838, after the Sixth Frontier war, in Grahamstown. **1979** E. BRADLOW *Somerville's Narr. of E. Cape Frontier* 13 In April 1799 .. a combined Xhosa-Khoi (Hottentot) force fell upon the colonists in the south-eastern part of the Graaff-Reinet district, thus precipitating the 3rd Frontier War. **1981** A. PATON in *Optima* Vol.30 No.2, 91 Both Afrikaner and tribesman were cattle owners and they each required land. So began the series of conflicts .. called the Frontier Wars. **1989** *Reader's Digest Illust. Hist.* 70 Van Jaarsveld's blitz netted the colonists 5 330 cattle and led to the deaths of an unrecorded number of Xhosa. This came to be known as the First Frontier War. **1990** *Weekend Post* 31 Mar. 14 Early shows had a multitude of problems to deal with, such as Frontier Wars and endemic stock disease.

frontignac /ˌfrɒnti'njak, 'frɒntənæk/ *n.* Also **frontinac, frontiniac,** and with initial capital. [ad. *frontignan*, a term for both grape and wine, named for *Frontignan*, a town in S. France; now *obs.* in general Eng. usage.] A heavy, sweet table wine made from muscat-type grapes; the grape type from which this wine is made. Also *attrib.* See also CAPE WINE.

1821 C.I. LATROBE *Jrnl of Visit* 481 The old lady .. insisted upon our tasting all the different wines made on her property. Among them were Hahnen Pootgen, white and red; Frontiniac; Klipp-wine, and another, of a rough taste. **1829** *S. Afr. Almanack & Dir.* 148 There are five descriptions of Wines made at the Constantia, viz. 1, Red Constantia; 2, White Constantia;, 3, Frontignac; 4, Pontac Constantia; and 5, Steen Constantia. **1843** *Cape of G.H. Almanac & Annual Register,* (advt) He has always on sale .. sweet wines of very excellent quality and fine flavor, to wit: Pontac, Frontignac, Muscadel, etc. not to be equalled. **1845** *Ibid.*, (advt) Frontignac, White and Red Muscadel or Perle Constantia. **1856** *Ibid.* (Annual Advertiser) 68 Genuine Constantia wines consisting of Pontac, Frontignac, white, red, which may be had .. in bottle or cask. **1861** [see HANEPOOT sense 2]. **1880** *S.W. Silver & Co.'s Handbk to S. Afr.* 222 *The Muscadels* and *Frontignac* are, for the most part, used for *sweet wines*, such as are made at Constantia and the Paarl. These are said to resemble the sweet Muscat and Frontignan wines of the South of France. **1905** P.D. HAHN in Flint & Gilchrist *Science in S. Afr.* 415 The vines cultivated at the Cape .. [for red wines] were known as .. Pontac, Frontignac and Muscadel Grape. *c*1955 *Handbk on Wines* (K.W.V.) 25 Cape wine-growers still produce .. many excellent varieties of dessert wine ... Among them .. frontignac, pontac, muscatel, moscato, marsala and jerepigo. **1957** L.G. GREEN *Beyond City Lights* 126, I shall stick to the full-bodied wines, the Frontignac and Muscadel and Pontac which have made Worcester famous. **1966** H. BECK *Meet Cape Wines* 12 As far as I know the frontignac is used only for making dessert wines and the pontac was used for much the same purpose ... Neither the frontignac nor the pontac are very widely grown. **1974** A.P. BRINK *Dessert Wine* 61 It was .. a skilful blending of red and white muscadel, with some Frontignac, and with a strong hint of hanepoot in its bouquet. **1979** C. PAMA *Wine Estates of S. Afr.* 40 The two farms produced the famous red and white Constantia, natural, sweet, muscadel wines, blended with Frontignac and Pontac wines. **1980** J. PLATTER *Bk of S. Afr. Wines* 90 A .. lesser-known and little-grown Muscat Frontignan is also made into a dessert wine and often given the name Frontignac. *Ibid.* 102 Schanderl ... Made principally from a unique red clone of frontignac .. it has a .. light-bodied .. character. **1982** *S. Afr. Panorama* Jan. 21 These regions produce the sweeter, heavier dessert wines such as frontignac, pontac, hanepoot and the best muscadel. **1988** D. HUGHES et al. *Complete Bk of S. Afr. Wine* 118 Made from Red and White Muscadel together with some Frontignac, it was this wine to which the Governor gave the name of 'Constantia'.

frontline *adj.* Also with initial capital. [Special senses of general Eng. *frontline*, of or pertaining to the most advanced line or military unit of an army.]

1. In the phr. ***frontline state***: any African country sharing a border with South Africa; *hist.*, any African country actively supporting liberation movements in their struggle to bring majority rule to South Africa. Freq. in *pl.*, these states collectively.

Also in general English use. The frontline states include Tanzania, Zambia, Angola, Botswana, Mozambique, and Zimbabwe.

[**1964** J. NYERERE in *Freedom & Unity* (1967) 288 For Africa, Tanganyika is a 'border-state' ... We have many Freedom Fighters from Mozambique and South Africa organizing their affairs in this country.] **1976** K. KAUNDA in *Afr. Research Bulletin* (Political, Cultural & Social Series) 1 Apr. 4002 The strength of the front line states is paramount, and Africa must .. strengthen these states .. in the heroic struggle against racist oppression and exploitation. **1980** LYE & MURRAY *Transformations* 87 Though Botswana has remained dependent upon South Africa economically .. it has also taken an active role as a 'Front Line State' in the negotiations over the settlement of the Zimbabwe/Rhodesia and South West Africa/Namibia issues. **1984** *Daily Dispatch* 10 Mar. 1 Invitations to .. leaders of the other front line states .. have been issued by President Machel. **1986** *Star* 26 Sept. 2 Commonwealth Finance Ministers have ended a two-day meeting .. with a plea for R11,8 billion in international aid for the black African Frontline states hit by what they called South African aggression. **1987** *New Nation* 12 Dec. 8 Pretoria is trying to use every method in the book to destabilise the 'Frontline states'. **1988** *Leaflet* (Progressive Federal Party), The ANC has over 10 000 guerillas under arms in the front line states. **1988** WILLIAMS & HACKLAND *Dict. of Contemp. Politics of Sn Afr.* 99 The 'frontline' states .. regard themselves as in the 'frontline' of the struggle against apartheid and white minority rule. **1990** *Weekly Mail* 21 Dec. (Suppl.) 15 The mass slaughter of civilians continued despite negotiations on both Mozambique and Angola, and crossborder violence against other frontline states .. likewise heated up. **1990** S. SMITH *Front Line Afr.* p.vii, The 'Front Line States' .. have formed an alliance to fight apartheid and white minority rule in South Africa. They are formally constituted as a group led by one of the Presidents, and they meet regularly to coordinate their policies. **1994** M. ELLIOTT in *Newsweek* 7 Nov. 15 Nelson Mandela's government is determined to work with the former 'frontline states' on regional questions.

2. Of or pertaining to the frontline states.

1978 *Afr. Research Bulletin* (Political, Cultural & Social Series) 1 June 4900, SWAPO .. told a front-line Heads of State meeting .. that it would intensify armed struggle against South Africa's occupation of Namibia. *Ibid.* 4901 Two things are significant about the front-line presidents' statement. **1984** *E. Prov. Herald* 6 Apr. 1 Mr Ja Toivo .. held talks with frontline leaders in Kenya, Tanzania and Zambia. **1986** *Pretoria News* 25 Sept. 2 Schultz to meet Frontline officials ... The US Secretary of State .. will hold talks with Foreign Ministers of the six Frontline States. **1988** R. MCNEILL in *Sunday Times* 10 July 18 You will find no shortage of Frontline politicians to slang off South Africa. **1990** *Sunday Times* 14 Jan. 16 Robert Mugabe, still speaking in the anti-South African jargon of the 80s, is audibly out of step with his Frontline neighbours.

Hence **Frontliner** *n.*, a frontline state.

1986 *E. Prov. Herald* 24 Sept. 1 Beira plan no solution for Frontliners.

front ox *n. phr. Obs.* [tr. Du. *vooros*.] The foremost in a team of draught-oxen; VOOROS. Cf. AFTER-OX.

1833 *Graham's Town Jrnl* 30 May 3 One of them struck the front oxen with a stick: I asked them why they did it. **1850** [see FORE-TOW]. **1860** [see FORE-LOUPER]. *a*1867 C.J. ANDERSSON *Notes of Trav.* (1875) 193 The only real good front ox that we have the herd managed to lose last night. **1887** A.A. ANDERSON *25 Yrs in Waggon* I. 9 Each waggon had a fore-looper .. to take the foretow of the front oxen to keep them straight towards the opposite drift. **1907** J.P. FITZPATRICK *Jock of Bushveld* (1909) 229 The reputations of 'front oxen', in pairs or singly, are canvassed as earnestly as the importance of the subject warrants — for, 'the front oxen are half the span,' they say.

frot var. VROT.

frou var. VROU.

fuffie -, fuffy slide varr. FOEFIE SLIDE.

fufunyana, -yane varr. MAFUFUNYANA.

full *adj.* [Usage influenced by Afk. *vol* full, covered with; formerly used in Brit. Eng., but now obs.] In the phr. ***full of***, commonly used to mean 'covered with', 'covered in'.

1838 J.E. ALEXANDER *Exped. into Int.* I. 137 Jan's clothes were too full of blood to be of any use. **1905** P. GIBBON *Vrouw Grobelaar* 43 They went out and carried Fanie in with his clothes all draggled and his beard full of mud. **1921** W.C. SCULLY *Harrow* 73 They had .. been a long time in prison ... They were full of horrible vermin. **1925** L.D. FLEMMING *Crop of Chaff* 47 Cattle .. make a .. broad path along .. the fence which prevents your trousers and socks getting full of grass seed as you walk up and down mending .. wires. **1930** C.L. BIDEN *Sea-Angling Fishes* 287, I told my wife, 'just look at my hands, full of little itching blisters'. **1972** *Drum* 22 Feb. 42 My face is full of black spots .. and I want to get rid of them. **1976** *E. Prov. Herald* 11 Oct. 19 When the station closes the platforms are full of mice who come out of their hiding places. **1980** M. MELAMU in M. Mutloatse *Forced Landing* 52 Originally black, the tube is now full of red patches where it's been mended. **1987** P. SYDLE in *Personality* 18 May 31, I got him .. in a terrible condition ... He was full of ticks. **1988** E. POPLE in *You* 21 Jan. 15 (*caption*) The hands of a white pipe smoker .. stained yellow by the dagga and full of blisters from the searing heat of the bottle.

full place see PLACE *n.*[1] sense 2.

fundees var. UMFUNDISI.

fundi /ˈfʊndi/ *n.* [Perh. orig. Rhodesian (Zimbabwean) Eng., fr. Ndebele *umfundi* disciple, learner (pl. *abafundi*), fr. *funda* learn, read; or fr. *fundisa* teach, educate; or fr. the identical Xhosa and Zulu words. Cf. UMFUNDISI.]

1. *rare.* An academic; a learned person.

[**1937** C. BIRKBY *Zulu Journey* 281 Pondos will call the missionary or the farming lecturer or the doctor 'Umfundi' — the learned one.] **1971** P.J. SILVA *Informant, Grahamstown* He's not the teacher type — he doesn't strike one as being a great fundi.

2. An expert or authority on a particular subject. Also *attrib.*

[**1970** J. TAYLOR *Informant, Salisbury (Harare, Zimbabwe)* Fundi — an expert or specialist. Bessie is a fundi at gardening.] **1971** W.R.G. BRANFORD *Informant, Grahamstown* Mr A— is a fundi on Dr Johnson's Dictionary, so I'd like him to come in at this point. **1973** F. CHISHOLM in *Cape Times* 3 July 9 We have two problems for the language fundis. **1976** *Fair Lady* 13 Oct. 180 (*advt*) Actually I don't know anything about Hi-Fi terms .. but my friends think I'm a fundi. **1980** *Sunday Times* 3 Aug. (Mag. Sect.) 4 I'm fed up with food fundis telling me what to eat and what not to eat. **1983** *Star* 7 June 2 Oriental art fundis .. examine an 18th century .. tea jar. **1985** *Sunday Times* 13 Jan. (Business Times) 1 The slump in the stock market .. left some highly paid investment fundis with red faces. **1988** *Cape Times* 21 Nov. 15 Wine fundi Mr John Platter .. is to be called as an expert witness. **1988** R. SHER in *Sunday Times* 3 Apr. (Mag. Sect.) 44 I'm getting used to the pressure of being an Aids fundi. **1989** J. HOBBS *Thoughts in Makeshift Mortuary* 210 He's a Dickens fundi, you know? More interested in Victorian slums than the ones under his nose. **1990** *Weekend Post* 30 June 3 'He's a slippery prop,' says a rugby fundi. **1991** M. O'SHEA *Informant, Kokstad* Michael is a fundi on shell-collecting. **1991** M. HURT *Informant, Dorpspruit* Susan is a fundi at patchwork and John is quite a fundi with money, so .. she makes and he sells. **1992** *E. Prov. Herald* 3 July 22 Natal Parks Board director and turtle fundi, Dr George Hughes. **1994** *Sunday Times* 2 Oct. (Mag. Sect.) 10 They found themselves under the critical eye of fashion fundi Dion Chang.

3. One who shows enthusiasm for a particular subject or pastime, a 'buff'.

1977 *Fair Lady* 11 May 102 Indispensable items for fashion 'fundis'. **1978** *Sunday Times* 19 Feb. 5 Long grass holds all sorts of horrors for the sincere South African braai fundi. **1980** *Darling* 9 June 23 For the fitness fundis, Gloria provides yoga, modern dancing, acrobatics, antenatal classes and keep-fit lessons. **1983** *City Press* 6 Nov. 2 'Buick' as he was affectionately known to theatre fundis .. had amassed a huge business empire.

fundis var. UMFUNDISI.

funeral rice *n. phr.* [tr. Afk. *begrafnisrys* (see BEGRAFNISRYS).] *yellow rice*, see yellow sense c.

1927 C.G. BOTHA *Social Life in Cape Col.* 66 When a hot course of poultry or meat was given it was usual to serve 'yellow' rice with it. This was rice coloured by borrie with raisins added. Such a dish received the name of 'begrafenis rijs', or funeral rice. **1978** *Daily Dispatch* 2 Aug. 5 With the mock venison was served, all on one plate, waterblommetjie bredie .. funeral rice (rice with tumeric and raisins), .. sousboontjies .. , cinnamon pumpkin .. and slaphakskeentjies (onions in sauce). **1981** *Flying Springbok* Sept. 55 Typical South African dishes: the 'sosaties' or kebabs are usually eaten, with yellow rice ('begrafnisrys' in Afrikaans meaning 'funeral rice').

furrow *n.* [General Eng., now obs.; prob. influenced by Afk. (*water*)*voor* (water)furrow.] SLOOT sense 1. Also *attrib.*

1833 *Graham's Town Jrnl* 2 May 2 A part of the stream is directed into a furrow leading through the different streets, and plentifully irrigates the gardens and vineyards. **1849** J.D. LEWINS *Diary.* 5 Oct., Yankee & myself busy all day making furrows & leading water. **1882** J. NIXON *Among Boers* 230 Furrows of water intersected the streets .. but the water in them appeared to be applied to so many uses that we were very careful not to drink any of it. **1893** *Brown's S. Afr.* 196 The waste-water from the springs flows through the streets in paved furrows. **1900** E.E.K. LOWNDES *Every-Day Life* 86 A shallow ditch is dug, called a 'furrow', into which the water is turned. Other furrows branch from the principal one, which can be opened or closed at any time by means of a shovelful of earth. *c*1911 S. PLAYNE *Cape Col.* 323 The lucerne .. is irrigated by water from the Meirings Poort River, by means of weirs and furrows, the latter conducting the water direct on to the lands. **1932** *Grocott's Daily Mail* 12 Jan. 3 Lands were soon under cultivation, twenty-four miles of furrows to lead out water from the Kat River were made. **1940** F.B. YOUNG *City of Gold* 188 This whole farm is a network of furrows that follow the contours: he can lead water anywhere. **1965** C. VAN HEYNINGEN *Orange Days* 15 Many an hour was spent in making mud pies next to the furrow of water that ran near the house. **1972** *Farmer's Weekly* 21 Apr. 86 Lands with furrow irrigation are terraced and contoured. **1979** M. PARKES *Wheatlands* 9 The water from the weir was led down a furrow and a half a mile from the dam the furrow was stopped so that the water spread over the veld, finally running into a dam. **1985** *S. Afr. Panorama* Oct. 41 Supplied from natural springs .. these furrows watered vegetable gardens as well as orchards of quinces, peaches and pears. **1991** *Sunday Times* 9 June 7 Families .. were forced to collect water from ditches and furrows alongside the streets.

fuse *n. slang.* [Special sense of general Eng. *fuse* a tube filled with combustible material.] A cigarette.

1977 P.C. VENTER *Soweto* 44 They were always looking for some excuse to swing a stick. He couldn't even light a fuse there. And no booze on the premises, man. **1979** A.P. BRINK *Dry White Season* 178 He offered Ben his packet of Lucky Strike: 'Like a fuse?' [**1979** F. DIKE *First S. African* 38 'Het jy nie fus daar nie?' ... 'I've got cigarettes, but I won't bring them to you.']

Fusion *n. hist.* [Special sense of general Eng.] The political coalition formed by J.C. Smuts of the South African Party and J.H. Hofmeyr of the National Party, 1933–39; SAMESMELTING. Also *attrib.*, esp. in the phrr. ***Fusion cabinet, - ministry***, etc., of or pertaining to this coalition government.

This coalition preceded the formation of the United Party (see UP).

1934 J.C. SMUTS *Plans for Better World* (1942) 87 At this moment we are trying to lay the enduring basis of peace in our national life ... In our politics and our racial relations we are at present concluding the grand pact of union and of fusion. **1934** [see HOGGENHEIMER]. **1968** E.A. WALKER *Hist. of Sn Afr.* 636 Negotiations between Malan and Hertzog in which the former tried to entrench the right to conduct republican propaganda within the fold of the projected Fusion Party. *Ibid.* 637 At the close of this cheering Session the terms of Fusion were published. **1971** [see MALANITE]. **1977** T.R.H. DAVENPORT *S. Afr.: Mod. Hist.* 218 The Fusion Government was born of a common desire to settle the constitutional relationships with the Empire and to pull South Africa out of economic crisis ... Heaton Nicholls .. claimed that its [*sc.* the Joint Select Committee's] deliberations were inhibited by Fusion. **1983** C. SAUNDERS *Hist. Dict., Fusion* (*1934*), The merger of the National Party under Hertzog and the South African Party under Smuts to form the *United Party.* Fusion, flowing from coalition (1933), was born of a desire to pull the country out of its economic plight .. and to forge a new unity after the constitutional relationship with Britain had been adjusted. **1989** *Reader's Digest Illust. Hist.* 344 The 20-year political enmity of Jan Smuts .. and Barry Hertzog .. was buried with Fusion — a coalition of the National and South African parties in response to the crisis sparked by the Great Depression. *Ibid.* 345 At stake were the Fusion Government and five years of work by Smuts and Hertzog to bring about unity between English- and Afrikaans-speakers. *Ibid.* 347 The blossoming wartime industries created employment opportunities for thousands of blacks. But the war was fought by South Africa at the price of Fusion.

fusser see quot. *c*1868 at VOERCHITZ.

futsack var. FOOTSACK.

fye toch var. FOEITOG.

fynbos /ˈfeɪnbɔs, -bɒs/ *n.* Formerly also **fynbosch**. [See Moodie quot. 1987.] Cape macchia, a vegetation type of small, often heath-like trees and shrubs with fine, hard leaves, characteristic particularly of the Western Cape. Also *attrib.* See also CAPE FLORAL KINGDOM.

The term 'fynbos' is well established in specialized botanical and ecological writing.

1881 'W.H.P.G.' in *Cape Monthly Mag.* IV. June 375 If the elephants and buffels are all killed off, and the land is not opened up by the hand of man, there will be no getting through the forest and the fynbosch. **1918** J.W. BEWS *Grasses & Grasslands* 89 South-Western or Cape Region of Macchia or Fynbosch. **1925** — *Plant Forms & their Evolution* 11 The South African term Fynbosch should be maintained for it is equivalent more or less to the term Macchia. **1961** M. COLE *S. Afr.* 64 Proteas (Proteaceae) .. are characteristic of the Cape macchia (or *fynbos* as it is locally called). **1966** C.A. SMITH *Common Names* 217 Fynbos, .. The vernacular name has .. been employed to describe typical Cape vegetation with its high percentage of species with fine or ericoid leaves. **1976** S.C. SEAGRIEF *Reading Signs,* The *fynbos* is fire resistant and regenerates from perennial rootstocks. It is also extremely susceptible to invasion by exotic plants. **1977** *E. Prov. Herald* 4 May 19 The fynbos, the coastal vegetation type that starts with the Cape flora and extends to Port Elizabeth has been reduced to less than 40 per cent of its original size ... Consisting of about 11 000 species, it has an estimated 1 500 species classed as rare or endangered. *c*1980 *S. Afr. 1979: Off. Yrbk* (Dept of Info.) 17 A chaparral-like vegetation, variously known as sclerophyllous bush, 'fynbos', Cape scrub or Cape macchia, occurs in the winter rainfall area of the south western Cape and along parts of the south coast. **1981** *Afr. Wildlife* Vol.35 No.2, 13 The fynbos flora of the South-Western Cape justly draws tributes from botanists world-wide for its beauty and richness. **1983** SIEGFRIED & CROWE in F. Kruger et al. *Mediterranean-Type Ecosystems* 403 The Fynbos Biome .. is characterized by four indigenous vegetation types: Strandveld, coastal renosterveld, coastal fynbos and mountain fynbos. **1987** B. MOODIE in *Motorist* 2nd Quarter 14 Fynbos, meaning fine bush or small shrub in Afrikaans, popularly covers several shrub species which .. are able to conserve water during the hot summers. **1988** *Quagga* No.20–1, 21 The Cape fynbos is a unique plant kingdom which is understood by very few people. **1992** [see GEOMETRIC TORTOISE]. **1993** *Afr. Wildlife* Vol.47 No.2, 180 Researchers .. have recently discovered that smoke from fynbos fires stimulates the germination of seed of many fynbos species.

G

G *n.* The seventh letter of the alphabet, placed before numbers to designate locally-designed and manufactured howitzers, developed after an arms embargo came into effect in 1977.
a. *G5*: A 155 mm howitzer. Also *attrib.*

   1979 *Cape Times* 26 Apr. 1 Two brand-new South African weapons, the G5 artillery piece and the R4 service rifle, were yesterday taken out of wraps at a press conference in Cape Town. **1979** *Evening Post* 10 May 3 The development of the G5 was recently completed by Armscor as prescribed by the chief of the army. The G5 gun .. will be used in conventional and unconventional warfare. **1982** *Jane's Armour & Artillery 1982–3* 568 No specification or performance data on the G5 has been released but it is believed to be able to fire a HE projectile weighing 45.5 kg to a maximum range of 30 000 metres. **1987** *S. Afr. Digest* 10 July 9 The international arms boycott against South Africa .. led to the development of weapons such as the Ratel CV (infantry combat vehicle); 155 mm G5 field gun, .. 127 mm MRL (multiple rocket launcher); and the G6 HMSP (high mobility self-propelled) howitzer. **1989** [see sense b below]. **1991** G. EVANS et al. in *Weekly Mail* 1 Feb. 10 Military sources said yesterday it was very probable that some of the 200 G5 mobile howitzers bought from Armscor by Iraq have already been put to use in this week's land battles.

b. *G6*: A version of the G5, mounted on a self-propelled vehicle. Also *attrib.*

   1987 [see sense a]. **1989** *E. Prov. Herald* 9 Mar. 4 South Africa .. exhibited everything from riot control equipment to .. a G-6, the self-propelled armoured version of the G-5. **1991** G. EVANS et al. in *Weekly Mail* 1 Feb. 10 South Africa has now supplied both sides in the Gulf War, as it has recently sold G6 heavy artillery systems to the United Arab Emirates.

‖**ga** /xa/ *int.* Also **gha**. [Afk., fr. Khoikhoi *xā*; in Xhosa represented as *rhá*, in the same senses (but also an expression of (grudging) praise, or a threat).] An exclamation of strong distaste, disgust, or contempt; 'faugh', 'ugh'. Cf. SIS *int.*

   1913 C. PETTMAN *Africanderisms* 118 Ga, .. An interjection common throughout South Africa expressive of disgust; the G is guttural. **1913** J.J. DOKE *Secret City* 99 'Ga! Sis! he said contemptuously; 'witch-doctor! Lumkile is no witch-doctor. He is a clever man.' **1970** T. KRIGE *Informant, Bloemfontein* Ga! I just cannot take dust. **1971** D. ACTON in *Daily Dispatch* 21 July 10 Like the rest of your article, all that it boiled down to was a meaningless piece of invective, equivalent to saying 'Farmers, gha!' **1979** D. MQHABA in *Staffrider* Vol.2 No.1, 5 The food sold here is absolutely fire-smelling: Sies! I'll never eat that kind of junk! Ga!

‖**gaan** /xɑːn, xɑːn/ *v. intrans.* In the slang phr. *to gaan aan* /ˌxɑːnˈɑːn, ˌxɑːnˈɑːn/, occas. *to gaan on* [prob. fr. Afk. *aangaan* carry on, rave, storm at, itself perh. orig. formed on Eng. *go on*, as in 'don't go on like that']: to carry on; to complain, nag, or whine persistently.

   1985 H. PRENDINI in *Style* Oct. 39 The ou starts gaaning aan. I say 'What's your case? Don't aikona me, my china. Don't tune me grief.' **1986** P. BROWNE in *Ibid.* July 43 Danie Craven got a sock stuck in it when he started gaaning aan and getting all emotional about morals on the rugby field. **1989** B. HARRIS *Informant, Grahamstown*, I don't want people in my house who keep on gaaning aan about this and that. **1990** R. MALAN in L. Wright *Teaching Eng. Lit. in S. Afr.* 198, I know I am right in persisting ('gaaning on' is the current inelegant expression) in my belief that studying literature in the here-and-now gives a student an authority, a sure-footedness. **1991** G. DE BEER *Informant, Port Nolloth* (N. Cape) Gaan on (carry on, endlessly usually). She was gaaning on about her bill.

gaandereij /xɑːndəˈreɪ/ *n. Archit.* Also **gaanderij**, **gaandery**. [Afk., fr. Du. *gaanderij* long covered passage.] AGTERKAMER.

   1927 C.G. BOTHA *Social Life in Cape Col.* 31 The 'gaandery,' or large dining hall, led off from the 'voorhuis' from which it was separated by a screen of teak or some dark wood. **1984** *Style* Nov. 190 The gaandereij at Morgenstêr with the table set for luncheon. **1987** G. VINEY *Col. Houses* 52 A four-leaved, half-glazed screen separated the paved *voorkamer* from the *gaandereij*.

gaap var. GHAAP.

gaats var. GATS.

gaatvol var. *gatvol* (see GAT *n.* sense 1 b).

gabba /ˈxabə, -ba/ *n. colloq.* Also **chabba**, **gubba**. [ad. Yiddish *khaver*, fr. Hebrew *haver* comrade, friend (also found in Du. as *gabber*, and in the San languages as *gaba*).] A friend, pal.

   1970 G.E.Q. ABSOLOM *Informant, Germiston*, Gubba. Friend. **1971** P.J. SILVA *Informant, Grahamstown* Today they fight — tomorrow they'll be gabbas. **1974** T. DELL 'Heaven is my Motorbike'. (*lyrics*) And when I see it in the morning light, All chromy, chabba, it is pure delight. **1978** M. DARHE in *Sunday News* 8 Oct. (Mag. Sect.) 1 What he ignored were the products of mixed marriages. And that, my gabbans, is where there's the rub. **1987** *Scope* 6 Nov. 34 I've just come to visit the outside world for a while ... Just to tell my *gabbas* I'm still in circulation. **1992** H. HAMMAN in *Ibid.* 13 Nov. 36 A greaser from Queenstown ... He glanced at his mates, all *gabbas* .. and adjusted his leather jacket.

gabeen var. GAVINE.

gabeljouw var. KABELJOU.

gabowie *n. Obs. Music.* [Etym. obscure; perh. ad. Khoikhoi (Kora) *!gabu-s* musical bow.] A Khoikhoi musical instrument consisting of strings stretched over a body of wood.

   The construction of this instrument varied (see quots).

   1801 J. BARROW *Trav.* I. 98 They had different instruments; one was a kind of guittar with three strings stretched over a piece of hollow wood with a long handle; it was called in their language *gabowie*. **1804** R. PERCIVAL *Acct of Cape of G.H.* 91, I was highly entertained by seeing a number of Hottentots dance to an instrument played on by a young woman. It was a piece of deal board, three feet long and one broad; four or five strings of brass wire were stretched along it, and supported at each end by bridges or bits of upright wood, like those of our fiddles. In this rude sort of guitar which they called a *gabowie*, was inserted a piece of looking-glass ... The young woman who played .. kept touching the wires with a quill. *a*1823 J. EWART *Jrnl* (1970) 47 They are fond of dancing, which they perform to a few notes extracted from an instrument something like a guitar, form'd of three strings stretched along a piece of thick bamboo. This is called a Gabowie. **1934** P.R. KIRBY *Musical Instruments of Native Races* (1965) 252 The great width of the board, as estimated by Percival, would exclude the *gabowie* from the guitar class.

gaetye var. GEITJIE.

gahle, **gahlé** varr. GASHLE.

Gaika /ˈɡaɪkə/ *n. hist.* [Englished pronunciation-spelling of Xhosa *Ngqika*.] The colonial name for the NGQIKA (sense a). Also *attrib.*

   [**1800** F. DUNDAS in G.M. Theal *Rec. of Cape Col.* (**1898**) III. 55 Mr Maynier has .. been employed to strengthen and secure a good understanding with the Caffres and Boschesmen in general, and the great Caffre Nation in particular, having paid one visit to Guyka their King for that purpose.] **1844** E.L. KIFT *Letter.* 26 Sept., We are now awaiting to hear the result of the meeting of the Gov.ʳ with the Tambookie chiefs, after which he is to meet the Gaika chiefs — leaving the most troublesome for the last. **1845** J. MONTAGU Letter. (Cape Archives LG84, p.25) 12 Dec., If His Honn .. should be of opinion, that the Kafir Police employed with reference to the Gaikas, should be restored to the original number of twelve, His Excellency will have no objection to it. **1846** J. MACLEAN in *Imp. Blue Bks* Command Paper 786–1847, 110 He is a T'Slambi chief; how can he be a Gaika? if he wishes to be a Gaika, let him go. **1852** M.B. HUDSON *S. Afr. Frontier Life* p.x, In 1846, the Tambookie Chief, Mapassa, joined the Gaikas in war against the English. **1871** J. McKAY *Reminisc.* 31 Strongholds were then held by Sandilli, the Gaika chief, and his allies, the Kat-river Hottentots and Cape-corps deserters. **1878** *Eastern Star* in J. Crwys-Williams *S. Afr. Despatches* (1989) 38 Once at his back ten thousand men would have armed themselves to plunder and murder their hated conquerors: now not a single Gaika is near him. **1882** J. NIXON *Among Boers* 15, I came across a number of kaffirs belonging to the Gaika tribe. **1912** AYLIFF & WHITESIDE *Hist. of Abambo* 24 The Gaikas, another clan of the Ama-Xosa, were great cattle plunderers. **1931** [see RHARHABE]. **1931** J.H. SOGA *Ama-Xosa* 24 In 1835, Sir Benjamin D'Urban, who had been fighting the Ama-Rarabe (then called Gaikas or Ama-Ngqika) carried the war across the Kei against the neutral Gcaleka or royal house of the Xhosas. **1968** [see RHARHABE]. **1971** J. MEINTJES *Sandile* 1 In many ways this deformity was the key to the complexity of Chief Sandile, a prince of the House of Gaika (as Ngqika was known for many decades), Paramount Chief of the Gaikas or ama-Ngqika. **1989** J. CRWYS-WILLIAMS *S. Afr. Despatches* 34 The Ninth Frontier War (commonly known as the Gaika Rebellion). **1993** *Grocott's Mail* 20 July 9 The novel .. is to centre on the life of Sandile, Gaika paramount chief of the ama-Xhosa who were situated west of the Kei River.

gala /ˈɡɑːlə/ *n.* [Transf. use of general Eng. *gala* a festive occasion; also used in Brit. Eng.

(though less commonly) of a swimming contest.] Esp. with reference to schools: a swimming contest or meeting. Also *attrib.*

This is the primary sense of 'gala' in *S. Afr. Eng.*

1957 F.H. KEYSER in *Pietersburg Eng. Medium School Mag.* 44 As a result of having no swimming bath, it has been difficult to organise galas against other schools. **1960** *Capricorn High School Mag.* (Pietersburg) 34 The twenty-seven gala events took place without snag or difficulty, and the team events, particularly, produced a great deal of excitement. **1963** L.F. FREED *Crime in S. Afr.* 98 A group of 200 .. children, .. returning from a swimming gala at Ellis Park. **1974** J.J. REDGRAVE *Collegiate School for Girls, Port Elizabeth 1874–1974* 104 The Port Elizabeth Ladies Swimming Club was founded and held its first Swimming Gala in about 1910 ... At the next Gala the Collegiate carried off both the cups. **1984** *Diocesan School for Girls Mag.* (Grahamstown) 60 The swimming season started with a splash. We swam in 5 main galas in all ... Our School Gala was a mammoth 5 day event, the first attempt being rained out. The second attempt, the actual day of the gala, ended shortly after we had managed to swim back to our houses. **1992** *Argus* 20 Feb. 2 Queens College is to have an Olympic-sized swimming pool with facilities for galas, water polo and diving.

gala *v.* var. GALLA.

Galaka, Galeca, Galeka varr. GCALEKA.

galeon var. GALLEON.

galjoen /xalˈjun/ *n.* Pl. unchanged. [Afk. (earlier S. Afr. Du), fr. Du. *galjoen* galleon; see quot 1902.]

1. The marine fish *Coracinus capensis* of the Coracinidae; BLACK BREAM; BLACKFISH sense 1; DAMBA sense a; GALLEON; HIGHWATER. Also *attrib.*

The name 'galjoen' is used for this species in Smith and Heemstra's *Smiths' Sea Fishes* (1986).

1880 'C.W.' in *Cape Monthly Mag.* II. Mar. 157 A strong built dingy, .. two galjoen nets, .. a .. box of tackle. *Ibid.* 159 Murray's Bay .. is a famous place for the galjoen fish. **1890** A.G. HEWITT *Cape Cookery* 11 The Best Fish for Boiling. Stokvisch, geelbek, cabeljauw, galjoen, albacore, mackerel, elft, steenbrasem, hamburger, seventy-four. **1902** J.D.F. GILCHRIST in *Trans. of S. Afr. Philological Soc.* XI. iv. 221 The Galjoen .. can readily be supposed to have derived its name from its resemblance in shape to the high built three-decker of the fifteenth and sixteenth century called by the Spanish *galeon*, .. and by the Dutch 'Galjoen' or 'Galleon'. **1930** C.L. BIDEN *Sea-Angling Fishes* 208 The Cape coastal farmer .. synchronises haanepoot and galjoen, for at the time when his vines are sprouting the fish is at its best, fat and abundant. **1948** [see STOMPKOP]. **1949** [see DAMBA]. **1955** C. HORNE *Fisherman's Eldorado* 13 Galjoen .. are one of the most skilful and determined adversaries an angler can encounter. **1968** J.L.B. SMITH *High Tide* 53 The galjoen is almost our national fish, abundant and known from the earliest times. **1972** [see HIGHWATER]. **1985** B. GROBLER in *S.-Easter* Aug.-Sept. 45 The Cape galjoen occurs off vast stretches of our coastline, is a premier angling fish and is also known as black bream in the Eastern Cape and *damba* in Transkei. **1990** *You* 24 May 52 Galjoen is as difficult to find as the coelacanth. **1993** PROCHAZKA & GRIFFITHS in *Afr. Wildlife* Vol.47 No.1, 19 Information on the growth rates, movement patterns and population densities of galjoen have been obtained through a concerted tag and release programme ... To date some 10 000 galjoen have been caught and tagged.

2. With distinguishing epithet: **banded -, bastard galjoen**, *(a) Coracinus multifasciatus* of the Coracinidae; DAMBA sense b; *(b)* the PARROT FISH (sense 1), *Oplegnathus conwayi.*

The name 'banded galjoen' is used for *C. multifasciatus* in Smith and Heemstra's *Smiths' Sea Fishes* (1986).

1949 J.L.B. SMITH *Sea Fishes* 249 *Coracinus multifasciatus* ... **Banded Galjoen** or *Bastard Galjoen*, or *Damba* (Eastern Cape – Natal). **1913** C. PETTMAN *Africanderisms* 49 **Bastard galjeon**, Another name for the Parrot fish. **1949** J.L.B. SMITH *Sea Fishes* 201 *Oplegnathus conwayi ... Banded Galjoen. Bastard Galjoen. Beaked Galjoen. Pappegaaivis. Parrotfish. Golden Roman. Ibid.* 249 [see quot. at *banded galjoen*].

galla /ˈxala/ *v. intrans. Colloq.* Also **gala, gallah.** [Afk., ad. Xhosa *rhala* crave, long for, desire keenly; compare also Zulu *hala* 'to have a ravenous appetite, be very keen after' (Doke & Vilakazi *Zulu-Eng. Dict.* 1964).] Esp. in the Eastern Cape: to long (for), desire, crave, drool (over), stare longingly (at). Also in the phr. ***to galla for*** (something).

1970 B. HANSEN *Informant, Durban*, I was galaing for that ice cream. **1971** *Informant, Grahamstown* I'll eat my pork tonight and everyone else will sit and gala. **1973** P. HIGGINS *Informant, Grahamstown* We are going to go and galla at the shop windows. **1989** *Informant, Grahamstown* It's unfair of me to eat the chocolate if you sit there and gallah for a piece. **1991** K. SULLIVAN *Informant, Cape Town*, I am galaing for the kop and pootjie potjie that's on the go. **1991** I.E.G. COLLETT *Informant, Pilgrim's Rest* Galla-galla. Said usually about food, by someone who has something others might envy or crave.

Hence **galla** *n.*, a craving.

1987 D. RANDALL *Informant, Grahamstown*, I feel bad about eating these in front of George but we all have our little gallas, don't we?

gallamsiekte /ˌxalˈlamsiktə/ *n. Pathology.* Also **gal-lamziekte**, and with initial capital. [Afk. (earlier S. Afr. Du. *gal-lamziekte*), *gal* bile, gall + *lamsiekte*, see LAMSIEKTE.] LAMSIEKTE.

Formerly applied esp. when the symptoms of lamsiekte included splenic fever; however 'lamsiekte' and 'gallamsiekte' now usu. to refer to the same disease.

[**1911** J.F. PENTZ in *Farmer's Weekly* 11 Oct. 158 In treating lam-galziekte, we must not forget that there is no one living to-day who can tell you the real cause or seat of the disease, so as soon as cattle get sick it is put down as a case of lam-gal-ziekte ... It is very clear that no cattle can be 'salted' for lam-gall-ziekte.] **1911** *E. Prov. Herald* 10 Nov. 5 A deputation from the Farmer's Association has returned from a .. visit .. to investigate Mr. Meintjies' new cure for Gal-lamziekte. **1914** *Farmer's Annual* 214 Gal-lamziekte is often confused with gall-ziekte, the similarity of the names leading the reader astray ... The cause of gal-lamziekte is not yet known. **1935** H.C. BOSMAN *Mafeking Rd* (1969) 117 I .. knew a lot about blue-tongue in sheep, and about gallamsiekte and the haarwurm. *c***1936** *S. & E. Afr. Yr Bk & Guide* 355 *Gallam Siekte* is a form of ptomaine poisoning due to cattle eating putrefying bones and flesh found in the veld. **1957** *Handbk for Farmers* (Dept of Agric.) III. 345 The poison causes a paralysis which frequently proves fatal. It is the disease known as *'lamsiekte'* or *'gallamsiekte'* or *Botulism.* **1974** J.J. OBERHOLSTER in *Std Encycl. of Sn Afr.* X. 484 Theiler .. was faced with lamsiekte (or gallamsiekte) in cattle in the North-Western Cape. **1979** T. GUTSCHE *There Was a Man* 265 The increasing ravages of Gal-Lamziekte among the cattle of Bechuanaland.

galleon *n. obs.* Also **galeon, gallion**, and with initial capital. [Etym. obscure; either a special sense of Eng. *galleon*, or calqued on S. Afr. Du. *galjoen* (see GALJOEN).] In full ***galleon fish***: the GALJOEN (sense 1), *Coracinus capensis.*

*a***1827** [see GEELBEK sense 1 a]. **1843** J.C. CHASE *Cape of G.H.* 168 Galleon Fish ... The most delicate and delicious of Cape fishes, but more plentiful in the Western than Eastern waters. **1853** L. PAPPE *Synopsis of Edible Fishes* 23 *Dipterodon Capensis*, .. *(Galjoenvisch, Galleon-fish)* ... Highly esteemed as food. **1864** T. BAINES *Explor. in S.-W. Afr.* 19 Many times we could see the gallion or other smaller fish, leaping like salmon three or four yards out of the water. **1890** A.G. HEWITT *Cape Cookery* 14 Soused Galleon. Boil a medium-sized galleon fish. **1921** H.J. MANDELBROTE tr. *O.F. Mentzel's Descr. of Cape of G.H.* I. 81 Galleon has a finer flavour and is more tender than red fish, but its flesh is interwoven with many black veins that detract from its appetising appearance.

gallsick *n. Obs. Pathology.* [Ellipt. for GALLSICKNESS.]

a. GALLSICKNESS sense 1. Also *attrib.*

1903 D. BLACKBURN *Burgher Quixote* 9 He had a learned book from which he made medicine for gallsick for cattle. **1911** W.O. HART in *Farmer's Weekly* 11 Oct. 158 *(letter)* Several farmers in this district say that to feed dry straw to hungry animals causes Gall Sick. **1911** J.F. PENTZ in *Ibid.* 158, I have heard of a 'gallsick' microbe, but not of a 'lam-sick' microbe.

b. With qualifying word: **black gallsick**, *black-gallsickness* (see GALLSICKNESS sense 2).

1911 W.O. HART in *Ibid.* 11 Oct. 158 The gall was dark green and very thick, so there was no doubt that it was 'Black Gall Sick'.

gallsickness *n.* [tr. S. Afr. Du. *galziekte*, see GALSIEKTE.]

1. *Pathology.* Any of several diseases of livestock, and particularly of cattle: **a.** Anaplasmosis, a disease caused by the parasites *Anaplasma marginale* and *A. centrale* and transmitted by ticks (esp. the BLUE TICK); GALSIEKTE sense 1 a; also with defining word, **true gallsickness. b.** Any of several conditions of the digestive tract: see *dry gallsickness, impaction gallsickness, wet gallsickness*, all at sense 2 b below. In both senses also called GALLSICK (sense a). Also *attrib.*

In the past there existed some confusion as to the nature and causes of these disorders and diseases, but nowadays '(true) gallsickness' is used only of anaplasmosis; 'dry', 'impaction' or 'wet gallsickness' is used only of digestive tract disorders in ruminants.

1862 T. SHONE Diary. 29 June, A Goat died of gall sickness, belonging to T. Knight. **1875** J. NOBLE *Descrip. Handbk of Cape Col.* 259 The 'gal zeickte' or gall sickness is also a common disease, and the chief barrier to rearing and grazing of sheep in the Zuurveldt. *c***1881** A. DOUGLASS *Ostrich Farming* 205 Gall-sickness is .. purely a disease of the liver and of the digestive organs, and is .. in no way infectious. **1896** R. WALLACE *Farming Indust. of Cape Col.* 288 *Gall-sickness* is a term indiscriminately applied by farmers to derangements of the liver, brought about by many exciting causes – rich food, little exercise, and hot weather being three of the most common. [**1896** *Ibid.* 288 see *black-gallsickness* (sense 2 below).] **1911** *E. Prov. Herald* 10 Oct. One of the diseases which had been under notice for a long time, and which he had only been able to trace to ticks about a year ago, was also commonly known as gall sickness. **1914** *Farmer's Annual* 126 Gall-sickness, or Bovine Anaplasmosis, is a disease of the blood caused by the parasite known as Anaplasma Marginale. *Ibid.* 214 Gallsickness (anaplasmosis) is a tick-borne disease, and can be inoculated against. It almost always accompanies redwater, another tick-borne disease. **1916** *Farmer's Weekly* 20 Dec. 1451 *(advt)* Steven's Gallsickness Powders for Cattle and Sheep, 5s. per packet, post free. *c***1929** *Diseases & Pests Affecting Sheep & Goats* (Cooper & Nephews) 27 Indigestion (So-called 'Gall-Sickness'). This is a derangement or disease of the digestive organs of ruminants – from simple indigestion and constipation .. to acute congestion of the liver and other internal organs. **1953** *Off. Yr Bk of Union 1950* (Bureau of Census & Statistics) 914 *Anaplasma marginale*, the cause of gallsickness in cattle. **1970** *Vet. Products Handbk* (I.C.I. Pharmaceuticals) 5 Accurate diagnosis can only be made through the examination of a blood smear to differentiate between gallsickness and heartwater. *Ibid.* 42 True gallsickness, also referred to as Anaplasmosis, .. is transmitted by the same group of ticks as those causing redwater. **1976** MÖNNIG & VELDMAN *Handbk on Stock Diseases* 387 Gallsickness – True or Tick (see Anaplasmosis). **1978** *Daily Dispatch* 16 Aug. 15 Anaplasmosis or gallsickness, a tick-born disease which can be fatal to livestock has .. become a great threat to the livelihood of farmers. **1991** [see BLUE TICK].

2. *Pathology.* With distinguishing epithet, designating any of several disorders affecting the digestive tract of livestock: **black-gallsickness** *obs.*, any disorder or disease which leads to the discoloration of the bile of the affected animal, particularly the often fatal sickness caused by poisoning due to eating species of *Homeria* and *Moraea* (see TULP); GALLSICK sense b; **dry gallsickness** (also called *droë-geilsiekte*, see GEILSIEKTE sense 2), or **impaction gallsickness**, constipation or blockage in ruminants caused either by eating too much dry fodder, or by infectious diseases accompanied by fever which prevent digestion and may paralyze any of the stomachs; **wet gallsickness**, purging.

1896 R. WALLACE *Farming Indust. of Cape Col.* 288 *True or* **black gall-sickness** or biliary hepatitis in grazing cattle is comparatively rare. **1905** D. HUTCHEON in Flint & Gilchrist *Science in S. Afr.* 354 A large admixture of mucous and other cellular elements along with the bile .. causes the latter often to present the appearance and consistency of Stockholm tar, which has given rise to the name of 'Black-gallsickness'. **1913** C. PETTMAN *Africanderisms* 62 *Black-gallsickness*, A form of sickness among cattle induced by eating Tulp. **1957** *Handbk for Farmers* (Dept of Agric.) III. 460 The term '**dry gallsickness**' merely indicates a stoppage of the alimentary tract of cattle. **1970** *Vet. Products Handbk* (I.C.I. Pharmaceuticals) 42 Dry gallsickness, .. a nutritional disorder with the symptoms of chronic constipation. **1971** *Farmer's Weekly* 12 May 40 Treat cattle with *dry gallsickness* with *Agricura Gall-Sickness Remedy* and *Nupurgon*. **1976** MÖNNIG & VELDMAN *Handbk on Stock Diseases* 285 Should these [rumination] movements stop for some reason or other, a condition follows that can be described as and includes any of the following: dry gallsickness, **impaction gallsickness**, impaction or paralysis of the fore-stomachs. *Ibid.* 287 The following measures assist in preventing dry gallsickness: 1) Provide a liberal supply of drinking water. 2) Dry food, e.g. hay, can be moistened with diluted molasses. **1970** *Vet. Products Handbk* (I.C.I. Pharmaceuticals) 42 **Wet gallsickness** .. is actually gastro-enteritis caused through nutritional disorders, and must not be confused with parasitic gastro-enteritis. **1976** MÖNNIG & VELDMAN *Handbk on Stock Diseases* 287 The condition [*sc.* dry gallsickness] is sometimes accompanied by purging. Such cases are spoken of as wet gallsickness.

3. *comb.* **gallsickness veld** /-felt/ [Afk. *veld* open, undeveloped countryside], uncultivated pasture infested with ticks capable of transmitting anaplasmosis.

1971 *Evening Post* 27 Feb. 21 All the cattle are bred on Redwater and Gallsickness veld. **1973** *Farmer's Weekly* 18 May (Suppl.) 12 Cattle are recognised for their hardiness and immunity to Redwater and Gallsickness, because of having been bred on virulent Redwater and Gallsickness veld. **1974** *Ibid.* 27 Feb. 13 All these cattle are in superb veld condition and are running on severe Heartwater, Redwater and Gallsickness veld. **1993** *Natal Witness* 31 Dec. 15 (*advt*) Livestock for Sale ... Entire commercial Brangus type breeding herd ... Cattle running on Heartwater/Redwater/Gallsickness veld.

‖**galsiekte** /ˈxalsiktə/ *n.* Formerly also **gall-ziekte, gal zeickte, gal-ziekte**, and with initial capital. [Afk., *gal* gall + *siekte* (earlier S. Afr. Du. *ziekte*) disease.]

1. *Pathology.*

a. GALLSICKNESS sense 1 a.

[**1871** J. MACKENZIE *Ten Yrs* (1971) 261 The Dutch call it 'gall-ziekte;' the English, inflammation ... A horse which has recovered from this sickness never gets it again, and, according to the colonial phrase, he is .. a 'salted horse.'] **1875** [see GALLSICKNESS sense 1]. *c*1911 S. PLAYNE *Cape Col.* 731 Calves have to be carefully reared on account of the existence of galziekte. **1944** C.R. PRANCE *Under Blue Roof* 75 At times .. a farmer's life seems but a turgid grind of worry with .. ticks, tampans, locusts, army-worm, bag-worm and cut-worm; spons-siekte, gal-siekte, nieu-siekte, vuursiekte. **1987** J. BOURHILL in *Frontline* Mar. 22 He can diagnose Galsiekte and he can milk a cow.

b. With defining word: **dronkgalsiekte** /drɔŋk-/ [Afk., *dronk* drunk], HEARTWATER sense 1.

1973 *Cape Times* 1 June 5 There was the cattle farmer who was given a cure, an 'infallible' cure, for *dronkgalsiekte* plaguing his calfs [*sic*].

2. *comb.* **galsiektebos** /-bɔs/, also **galziekte bosch**, [Afk., *bos* (earlier *bosch*) bush], the naturalized Central American plant *Chenopodium ambrosiodes* of the Chenopodiaceae, a member of the goosefoot family, believed to be a cure for galsiekte.

1912 *Agric. Jrnl of Union* Aug. 177 A strong smelling weed, often sent to us under the name galziekte bosch, and considered by many farmers to be a cure for galziekte. **1917** R. MARLOTH *Common Names* 30 *Galziektebos*, .. A doubtful remedy.

gama(a)t var. GAMMAT.

gamadoelas see GRAMADOELAS.

Gamatjie var. GAMMATJIE.

game *n.* [Eng., wild animals or birds.] Special Comb. **game farming, -ranching** *vbl n. phrr.*, the raising and utilization of game animals and birds as a commercial enterprise; hence **game farm, -ranch** *ns*, a farm on which such game is raised; also *attrib.*; so **game farmer, -rancher** *ns*.

These terms are used also in other African countries.

1975 *S. Afr. Panorama* Sept. 42 **Game farming** has, within recent years, gained tremendous popularity in South Africa. **1982** *Flying Springbok* Sept. 88 Gamefarm. Most people might imagine that the days of the white hunter, leading clients on safari through the African bush in search of big game, are over ... Coenraad changed the nature of the farm with the times and established a game ranch about 10 years ago. **1984** *S. Afr. Panorama* Dec. 33 There are hunting farms, game farms, farms adjoining fishing resorts, farms where one can ride horses. **1986** *E. Prov. Herald* 27 Nov. 10 He urged game farmers to get themselves organised and keep informed on all developments in the industry. **1986** *E. Prov. Herald* 27 Nov. 10 Mr Halse said: 'Whatever we do we start with the environment, without [which] the game farming, professional hunting and local hunting do not exist.' **1988** A. VON WIETERSHEIM in *Afr. Wildlife* Vol.42 No.2, 69 In an ecologically balanced game-farming operation the full spectrum of animals such as rodents, mongooses and even predators should have their rightful place. **1992** C. NEL in *Farmer's Weekly* 14 Feb. 12 During the next three years, he phased out cotton, establishing pastures on the old cotton lands and converting his operation to a game farm. **1968** L.G. GREEN *Full Many Glorious Morning* 174 **Game ranching** provides Rhodesia and overseas markets with eland and other forms of venison. **1972** *Daily Dispatch* 4 Sept. 10 As the management of our antelope herds improves and game ranching becomes an economic activity, the eland will occupy a proud place in our new wealth of wildlife. **1974** *Farmer's Weekly* 27 Feb., Located in the heart of the Zululand game country .. a highly developed 1133ha game ranch. Fully stocked with over 4 000 head of game. **1982** [see quot. at *game farming* above]. **1987** [see LAPA *n.* sense 2]. **1988** *S. Afr. Panorama* May 16 More than 3000 game ranches in various parts of the country cover millions of hectares and represent a multi-million rand capital investment. **1988** D. RICHARDS in *Proc. of Internat. Symposium: National Parks, Nature Reserves & Neighbours* (Endangered Wildlife Trust) 34 Initiating game ranching in protected and neighbouring areas would produce a viable red-meat production scheme, coupled with the added by-products of curios from hides, horns and hooves. **1989** J. DU P. BOTHMA *Game Ranch Management* 2 With a healthy marketing system, professional game ranch management and cropping programmes, a combination of game and stock can .. convert a large number of uneconomical stock ranch units into economically viable units in many areas. **1989** J. DU P. BOTHMA *Game Ranch Management* 31 The potential game rancher must be acquainted with the different nature conservation regulations which require a minimum area for certain game species. **1992** C. NEL in *Farmer's Weekly* 14 Feb. 12 Game ranchers have saved a number of mammal species from extinction since the beginning of the century.

Gami-nun see BONDELSWART.

gammadoelas var. GRAMADOELAS.

gammat /ˈxamat/ *n. Derog.* and *offensive.* Also **gama(a)t, ghammat**, and with initial capital. [ad. of *Mohamed.*]

1.a. A man of Cape Malay descent; a 'coloured' man. **b.** A given name for a stereotypical Cape Malay folk-figure, often the subject of jokes. Also *attrib.* In both senses also called GAMMATJIE. Cf. MERAAI.

*a*1951 H.C. BOSMAN *Willemsdorp* (1977) 58 From his speech and mannerisms, and also, to some extent, from his name, Josias, you would be .. inclined to classify him as a Cape Gamat. **1955** A. DELIUS *Young Trav.* 99 Scattered about .. were smaller, flat-roofed, two-roomed dwellings .. which .. belonged to the Kleurlinge, Gamats or 'Hotnots', as the coloured farm labourers were variously known. **1961** [see *korrelkop* (KORREL *n.* sense 2)]. **1970** *Post* 10 May 15 Gammat, a lodger: 'What's the weather like outside?' Landlady: 'Rather like your bill.' Gammat: 'What do you mean.' Landlady: 'Unsettled.' **1971** J. MCCLURE *Steam Pig* (1973) 216 How come a brother murders his own sister. Even for a gamaat, that's pretty low. **1974** *Drum* 22 Mar. (*cartoon*) You think you got troubles, Gammat – they got me for doing 51 kmh, for storing 11 litres of petrol, for drunken driving, my wife's left me, and I got Meraai into trouble. **1974** G. JENKINS *Bridge of Magpies* (1977) 40 A point of light showed ... 'It burns all night, every night. No *gamat* would stay otherwise.' *Gamat* is an affectionate term for the fine half-caste Malay fishermen of the Cape. **1980** A. DANGOR in M. Mutloatse *Forced Landing* 161 People now live .. in homes with scraggy, sandy gardens that the ingenious white man had reclaimed from the sea. *Gamat! You have become Neptune's tenant.* Pay your rent or he'll stick his trident up your arse. **1986** V. COOKE et al. in S. Gray *Market Plays* 34 Who's this goffel? .. Born in Cape Town. He's a gamat ... Does he think he's American or something. He's a Hottentot, man.

‖**2.** In full ***gammat-taal*** /-ˌtɑːl/ [Afk. *taal* language]: CAPEY sense 1 b. Cf. GAMTAAL.

1974 *Informant, Grahamstown* The Cape Coloured hawker on the Grand Parade has an idiomatic language – 'gammat-taal'– of his own. **1977** J. SUZMAN in *Darling* 16 Mar. 89 One of the interesting things about this country is the extraordinary mixes of language ... When Pieter Dirk Uys uses *gamattaal*, he's legitimately using the language form which expresses the nature of the people he's writing about. [**1981** V.A. FEBRUARY *Mind your Colour* 95 Kaaps .. is not what some Englishman in South Africa refers to as 'Capey', .. not what some Afrikaans-speaking persons refer to as Gamat-taal.] **1982** P. MCMAGH in J. Branford *Dict. of S. Afr. Eng.* (1987) 83 The word *diener* .. it's currently the gamat for *policeman*.

3. [A play on the Afk. pronunciation of *GMA* (/xiː em ˈaː/).] A nickname for either of two Garratt steam locomotives, the GMA or its modified version, the GMAM.

1978 LEWIS & JORGENSEN *Great Steam Trek* 52 In 1958 the GEAs were supplanted as far as Riversdale by GMAs (nicknamed 'Gammats'). *Ibid.* 94 Four types of articulateds were used on the Cape Eastern system from 1875, and the GMAMs or 'Gammats' were the only really successful ones.

Gammatjie /ˈxamatʃi, ˈxamaki, -ci/ *n. offensive.* Also **Gamatjie**, and with small initial. [GAMMAT + Afk. dim. suffix *-ie*, see -IE.] GAMMAT sense 1. Also *attrib.*

1960 J. COPE *Tame Ox* 185 Take a Gamatjie – unless he has a bottle of drink and a guitar he can't grind out a squeak. **1970** *Post* 10 May 15 Laugh with Gammatjie. Send your jokes to: *Post's* Gammatjie Jokes Department. **1971** A. MENDELOW in *Convocation Commentary* (Univ. of Witwatersrand) Apr. 7 The plethora of .. Jewish jokes, Gammatjie jokes, jokes about policemen, jokes about Scots, and so forth. **1976** M.

MANUEL in *Cape Herald* 14 Sept. 6 One request .. is that they should publish Gammatjies jokes. Then Cape Herald is the paper for grandparents, parents and children. **1986** D. CASE *Love, David* 14 We sat for a while listening to David's and Oupa's jokes about Gammatjie and Abdoltjie and Van Der Merwe.

gammors var. GEMORS.

||**gamtaal** /ˈxamtɑːl/ *n.* [Contraction of *gammat-taal*, see GAMMAT sense 2.] The argot habitually used by 'coloured' gang members in the Western Cape.

1984 D. PINNOCK *Brotherhoods* 102 The argot of the gangs is *gamtaal*, a fast-spoken mixture of Afrikaans, English and Xhosa, with innumerable variations in different areas. **1988** R. THORNTON in Boonzaier & Sharp *S. Afr. Keywords* 25 Culture .. is whole assemblages of safari-suits and tee-shirts, Zulu dance and sakkie-sakkie, Afrikaans, English, gamtaal and slang. **1991** J. ANDERSON in *Focus on Afr.* July-Sept. 82 The Prophets of the City have done one track in Gamtaal – a street slang based on Afrikaans with English borrowings. It's the language of the gangsters.

Gamtouers /xamˈtəʊə(r)s, -ˈtʊəs/ *pl. n. Hist.* Also **Chamtouers, Gamtoos, Kamtours.** [Khoikhoi name.] Collectively, the members of a KHOIKHOI people formerly living in the south-eastern Cape, near present-day Port Elizabeth. Also *attrib.*

1731 G. MEDLEY tr. *P. Kolb's Present State of Cape of G.H.* I. 79 On the *Houteniquas* border the *Chamtouers*; who are possess'd of a fine flat Country, well grass'd and water'd. *Ibid.* 288 The *Chamtouers* and *Heykoms* never cease fighting while their Chief plays on a sort of Flagelet. **1795** C.R. HOPSON tr. *C.P. Thunberg's Trav.* I. 308 Still farther to the eastward, following the coast, one first finds the *Kamtours* nation, then the *Heycoms*, and lastly the Caffres. [**1920** C. PETTMAN in *S. Afr. Jrnl of Science* Vol.17 No.3, 352 One place-name that is generally regarded as of Hottentot origin is the name *Gamtoos*, a river which runs into St. Francis Bay ... The name appears in the 'Kaaps Dagregister' very early in the eighteenth century in the form '*Gamtouws*,' as the name of a Hottentot tribe.] **1989** P.E. RAPER *Dict. of Sn Afr. Place Names* 171 *Gamtoos River*, .. Of Khoekhoen origin, the name is probably derived from that of a tribe, the Gamtoos or Gamtouers etc.

Ganaqua var. GONAQUA.

ganna /ˈxana, -nə, ˈkana, -nə/ *n.* Also **c(h)anna, ghanna, go(u)na, kanna.** [Etym. obscure: perh. fr. Khoikhoi, cf. *!khan* (see KANNA *n.*³), koŋ (see KANNA *n.*²).

The variety of spelling forms arises from the pronunciation of the Afk. 'ganna' as /ˈkana, -nə/ by English-speakers.]

1. In full ***gannabos(sie)***, ***gannabush***, ***ganna-shrub***, formerly also ***gannabosch***, ***ganna-bosje*** [Afk., *bos(sie)* (earlier *bosch, bosje* see BOSCHJE) bush]: any of several plant species of the genus *Salsola* (family Chenopodiaceae), esp. *S. aphylla* (also called *brak -*, *lye -* or *seepganna*, see sense 2 below). Also *attrib.* See also BRAKBOS.

The ashes of this plant form a white caustic alkali, formerly used in soap-making. See also SOAP BUSH.

1786 G. FORSTER tr. *A. Sparrman's Voy. to Cape of G.H.* I. 296 There is another shrub frequently found in the *Carrow*, which .. is called Canna-bosch. *Ibid.* 297 Having examined this .. Canna-shrub I found .. it formed a new species of *salsola* ... The leaves have a bitter salt taste. **1795** C.R. HOPSON tr. *C.P. Thunberg's Trav.* I. 199 At this farm they made soap from a ley, prepared from the *Canna bush* (*Salsola aphylla*). **1806** J. BARROW *Trav.* I. 42 The plant alluded to was a species of salsola or salt-wort ... It is known to the country-people by the Hottentot name of Canna and is that plant from the ashes of which almost all the soap, that is used in the colony, is made. **1812** A. PLUMPTRE tr. *H. Lichtenstein's Trav. in Sn Afr.* (1928) I. 124 Children and slaves collect the young shoots of the *Channa* bushes. **1822** W.J. BURCHELL *Trav.* I. 267 The *Kannabosch* (written *Ganna* by the Dutch) may probably have been considered as the favourite food of the *Kanna* [*sc.* the eland]. *Ibid.* 419 In many places grew abundance of Kannabosch (Kanna-bush), which I had now learnt to consider as an indication of a good soil of some depth, though not always free from a brackish quality. **1824** *Ibid.* II. 113 Formerly the alkali necessary for this manufacture [*sc.* of soap], was obtained here from the *Ganna* (or *Kanna-*)*bosch*; but that being .. all consumed through a constant demand for it, another species of *Salsola* .. was taken as a substitute. **1834** T. PRINGLE *Afr. Sketches* 305 Along the course of the Ghamka there was .. a narrow fringe of mimosa trees, with occasional tracts of alluvial soil thickly covered with *ghanna*, a species of salsola, the ashes of which form a pure white caustic alkali, generally used by the colonists for making soap. [**1843** J.C. CHASE *Cape of G.H.* 319 The alkali is produced from a species of *Salsola* or saltwort, called by the Hottentots Canna.] **1844** J. BACKHOUSE *Narr. of Visit* 112 This country is called the Little Karroo, or Kanneland; from its producing a bush abounding with soda called Kannabosch, *Caroxylon Salsola*. **1861** P.B. BORCHERDS *Auto-Biog. Mem.* 52 The plants in this part of the country are commonly thorny, and among the heaths is the 'Kanna Bush,' the ashes of which are very serviceable in soap-boiling. **1868** J. CHAPMAN *Trav.* I. 375 The 'gona, or soap-bush,' from the ash of which .. the ley for soap boiling is made. **1887** [see ZUURVELD]. **1907** T.R. SIM *Forests & Forest Flora* 14 On the rich alluvial soil along the dry river beds there are .. occasional trees of mimosa .., Karreeboom .., Blaauwbosch .. ; where water occasionally runs these sometimes form thickets, thickened by Gannabush (Salsola). **1913** C. PETTMAN *Africanderisms* 191 *Gona*, This appears to be a corruption of Kanna ... I have heard the bush referred to spoken of by the same individual by both names almost in the same breath. **1926** [see ASBOS]. **1927** C.G. BOTHA *Social Life in Cape Col.* 101 For the manufacture of the soap a shrub called the gannabosch (salsola aphylla) was used by burning it to ash from which lye was boiled. **1948** H.V. MORTON *In Search of S. Afr.* 257 The ganna .. is loved by sheep. **1955** L.G. GREEN *Karoo* 133 The gannabos, with its rich green leaves, flourishes in the *brak* soil. Sheep and goats love it, and it supplies the ashes which help to make soap on the farm. **1968** K. MCMAGH *Dinner of Herbs* 30, I crack the bones and cook them up for the fat in them and of this I boil soap. There are plenty of ganna bossies in the veld to burn for lye. **1972** L.G. GREEN *When Journey's Over* 59 A tent wagon, a strong team of oxen, a legplek with plenty of grass in season, kannabos for soap-boiling and a sound flock of long-tailed sheep. **1974** *Farmer's Weekly* 2 Feb., Grazing consists of healthy Karoo bushes, brak, ganna. **1979** E. & F. BRADLOW (tr. P.B. Borcherds's letter) *Somerville's Narr. of E. Cape Frontier* 206 Vegetation is mostly thorny and of little use, except one thorntree, a certain shrub generally known as a *Kannabos* from which a clear, pure gum flows which is burnt and the ashes are used in the manufacture of soap. *Ibid.* 207 Plenty of Gannabosjes to continue his soap-making in winter. **1986** *Style* July 94 It is called the Swartland because of the charcoal-coloured bush, the kanna bush, that used to grow abundantly in these parts. **1987** M. POLAND *Train to Doringbult* 42 The *kannabos* on the rock cleft clenching the fissures with its roots. **1988** A. HALL-MARTIN et al. *Kaokoveld* 4 Plants such as .. the low-growing coastal ganna (*Salsola aphylla*) .. have an extensive root system. **1989** F.G. BUTLER *Tales from Old Karoo* 34 As he walked over the first stream the stick took no notice, but as he crossed the second it turned up and gave him such a violent clout right between the eyes that it laid him out cold among the ganna bossies.

2. With distinguishing epithet, designating a particular species of *Salsola* or *Psilocaulon* (family Mesembryanthemaceae): **blomkoolganna** /ˈblɔmkʊəl-/ [Afk., *blomkool* cauliflower], *S. zeyheri* or *S. tuberculatiformis*; **brak ganna** /ˈbrak-/ [Afk., *brak* salt, salty], *S. aphylla*; **cattle ganna**, *S. arborea*; **koolganna** *obs.* [Afk., *kool* cabbage], *S. zeyheri*; **lidjes ganna** *obs.* [Afk. *litjie, lidjie* joint, jointed, fr. *lit* joint + dim. suffix -IE], *P. absimile*; see also ASBOS; **lye ganna**, *S. aphylla*; **rivierganna** *obs.* [Afk., *rivier* river, stream], *S. glabrescens*; **rooi ganna** *obs.* [Afk., *rooi* red], *S. calluna*; **seepganna** /ˈsɪəp-/ [Afk., *seep* soap], *S. aphylla*; **swartganna** /ˈswart-/ [Afk., *swart* black], *S. calluna*; also *attrib.*

1917 R. MARLOTH *Common Names* 30 Ganna, (sometimes pronounced Kanna). Several species of *Salsola*. The most frequent kind in brackish soil, especially along rivers, is *S. aphylla* (the *Brak-*); *S. Calluna* is the *Rooi-*, and *S. Zeyheri*, the *Kool-* or **Blomkool-**, the latter a sweet and highly valued fodder-shrub of the central and north-western districts. **1981** J. VAHRMEIJER *Poisonous Plants of Sn Afr.* 62 *Salsola tuberculatiformis* ... In spite of its salty or slightly bitter taste the plant is relished by sheep and game ... In the past 'blomkoolganna' was regarded as a valuable pasture plant. **1917** [**brak ganna**: see quot. at *blomkoolganna*]. **1983** K.C. PALGRAVE *Trees of Sn Afr.* 161 *Salsola arborea* .. **Cattle ganna**. **1917** [**koolganna**: see quot. at *blomkoolganna*]. **1932** *Farming in S. Afr.* Sept. 245 (Swart), The 'Koolganna' (Salsola Zeyheri), in Bechuanaland, .. marks the farms where there is no pica. **1908** J.M. ORPEN *Reminisc.* 13 The lye water was made from the ashes of a bush called **lidjes ganna**, which grew on the farm. **1983** K.C. PALGRAVE *Trees of Sn Afr.* 161 *Salsola aphylla* .. **Lye ganna**. **1931** *Farming in S. Afr.* Nov. 319 (Swart) It was found that one morgen of **Rivierganna** (Salsola glabresceus) carried one sheep for eleven months. **1917** [**rooi ganna**: see quot. at *blomkoolganna*]. **1971** L.G. GREEN *Taste of S.-Easter* 162 Rawlins had gathered samples of other bitter honeys .. **seepganna** honey from a bush that was once used on the farms for soapmaking, and **swartganna** honey.

||**gaps** /xaps/ *v. trans. Colloq.* Also **gap.** [Afk., snatch, 'swipe'; pilfer, 'pinch'.] To bite (something or someone); to seize (something or someone) violently. Also *fig.*

1989 M. BRAND in *Fair Lady* 25 Oct. 92 Gap (pronounced gup) – bite. **1990** *Personality* 24 Dec. 20 Its dreadful purpose is simple and implacable – to *gaps* some poor victim. **1991** D. CAPEL in *Personality* 2 Sept. 18 Those were the dark old days of total onslaught, when die groot krokodil was just waiting to gaps you if you put a foot out of line – or into his Rubicon.

garam masala /ˈgarəm məˈsɑːlə/ *n. phr.* Also **g(h)arum -, ghurum masala.** [Hindi, *garam* hot + *masala* spices.] Esp. among people of Indian descent: a mix of curry spices and herbs.

Used also in *Brit. Eng.*

1961 Z. MAYAT *Indian Delights* 13 After curries are done they are 'pepped' up with a last minute addition of mixed spices. This blended spice is known as Ghurum Masala. **1976** *Darling* 29 Sept. 100 The owner advised me to buy all their curry spices as well as their *garam masala* separately, and mix them to taste when I made a curry. **1977** *Fair Lady* 8 June (Suppl.) 33 Jinga Curry (Shrimps or Prawns) ... 1 teaspoon dhunia/jeero .. 1/4 teaspoon gharum marsala. **1982** Z. MAYAT *Indian Delights* 53 *Gharum Masala*, .. Elachi powder .. dhunia powder (coriander) .. jeero powder (cumin) .. cloves [etc.]. Good chefs buy the spices whole, roast them in the oven and then pound them fine. **1988** W. COLLEY in *Personality* 16 May 56, 1 teaspoon ground turmeric 2 teaspoons Pakco Roasted masala 3 teapsoons garum masala. **1992** R. MESTHRIE *Lexicon of S. Afr. Indian Eng.* 19 *Garam masāla*, .. A mixture of pounded spices, comprising ginger, garlic, bay leaves etc. dark green in colour. Not as hot as *masāla* .. despite the name. Lacking hot chilli.

garden *n.* Also with small initial.

1. [See quot. 1913.] In the phrr. ***the Garden Colony***, ***-Province***, ***the Garden of South Africa***, etc.: **a.** the colony of Natal; **b.** the Province of KwaZulu-Natal (formerly called Natal); **c.** the southern part of KwaZulu-Natal.

1877 J. NOBLE *S. Afr.* 319 Natal, the garden colony of South Africa – covers an area of 20,212 square miles. **1896** PURVIS & BIGGS *S. Afr.* 231 The new Natal

Franchise Bill .. certainly does not give unqualified satisfaction in the Garden Colony so far as Press comment is any guide. **1904** O. THOMAS *Agric. & Pastoral Prospects of S. Afr.* 197 (Swart), Natal, commonly called 'The Garden of South Africa', with which Zululand now is incorporated. **1908** D. BLACKBURN *Leaven* 205 The mine compound is .. the preserve of the Natalian .. for the .. reason that the youth of the miscalled 'Garden Colony' are the only South Africans who learn native languages. **1913** C. PETTMAN *Africanderisms* 181 *Garden Colony, The,* This designation has been given to Natal on account of the variety and beauty of its flora. *c*1936 *S. & E. Afr. Yr Bk & Guide* 24 The scenery of Southern Natal, 'the Garden of South Africa,' .. is certainly as beautiful as any to be found in this part of the continent. **1937** C. BIRKBY *Zulu Journey* 26 The scene is ever green – a common-place for people who live in the 'Garden Colony', but a benison on the eyes of those who come from that greater part of Africa which is brown all over. **1953** D. ROOKE *S. Afr. Twins* 13 Natal is known as the Garden Colony of South Africa because of its beautiful vegetation. **1973** [see BERG sense 2]. **1973** A.F. HATTERSLEY in *Std Encycl. of Sn Afr.* VIII. 47 *Natal,* .. On account of its fertility it is known as the Garden Province.

2. [See quot. 1989.] In the phr. ***the Garden Route***: the major road and railway line between Cape Town and Port Elizabeth, esp. the section between Swellendam and Humansdorp, known for its scenic beauty; the coastal belt through which this route passes.

1934 *Star* 12 May (Swart), A mail-boat express between Cape Town and Port Elizabeth, via the Garden route, will start on June 4. **1936** *Cambridge Hist. of Brit. Empire* VIII. 793 Between 1902 and 1906 about eleven hundred miles of new lines were completed, opening up the old 'Garden' waggon route from Cape Town through Mossel Bay and Oudtshoorn to Port Elizabeth. **1950** H. GIBBS *Twilight* 128 He goes by car from Cape Town, along the aptly-named 'Garden Route', cutting across the top of False Bay to Somerset West, to Caledon and Riversdale and Mossel Bay, along the National Road. **1955** A. DELIUS *Young Trav.* 112 The next stage of the Wisleys' journey lay over the 'garden route', the six-hundred-odd-mile stretch of south coastal belt which lay between Cape Town on the west and Port Elizabeth on the east. **1969** I. VAUGHAN *Last of Sunlit Yrs* 47, I came into Cape Town through the Garden Route, .. which, by rail, as well as by road, has always proved an attractive and absorbing path across the southern peak of Africa. **1971** *Golden Fleece* (S. Afr. Wool Board) June, Plettenberg Bay, with its lovely unspoilt beaches, has grown from a tiny fishing hamlet into one of the fastest growing seaside resorts along the Garden Route. **1987** C. SAWYER in *Style* Feb. 84 Rediscover the Garden Route's idyllic beaches and holiday magic. **1989** P.E. RAPER *Dict. of Sn Afr. Place Names* 172 *Garden Route,* .. Named thus because of the beautiful scenery ... It has also been suggested .. that the name is derived from the surname *Gardiner,* an entrepreneur, engineer or railway official during the early stages of the New Cape Railway Company. **1992** *Living* Feb. 112 So on to the Fairest Cape ... They hired a car to travel along the Garden Route from Cape Town to Port Elizabeth.

garenboom var. GARINGBOOM.

Gariepine *adj. obs.* [Khoikhoi *Gariep* name for the Orange River + Eng. adj.-forming suffix *-ine.*] Of or pertaining to the KHOIKHOI or SAN; of these two peoples collectively. See also *Khoisanoid* (KHOISAN).

For a note on the Khoikhoi-San division, see KHOIKHOI.

1857 *Cape Monthly Mag.* II. Sept. 183 The Hottentot or Gariepine race was met by Europeans landing on the south-western promontory. These Gariepine people speak a tongue of a different order. *c*1863 L. GROUT in E.M. Bliss *Encycl. of Missions* (1904) 314 The Gariepine tongue of the southern extreme belongs to the same family as the old Egyptian and Coptic, the Berber, and Ethiopic. **1872** T.M. THOMAS *11 Yrs in Central S. Afr.* 149 The other great division of the South African tribes is called the Gariepine race, and is that which includes the Hottentot and the Bushman races. **1887** J. MACKENZIE *Austral Afr.* II. 458 Comparative philologists .. use the term 'Gariepine' to mean the yellow people living in South Africa.

garingboom /ˈxɑːrəŋbʊəm/ *n.* Formerly also **garenboom**. Pl. **-bome** /-bʊəmə/. [Afk., *garing* (earlier *garen*) thread + *boom* tree.] The century plant *Agave americana* of the Agavaceae, with a rosette of thick, spiny leaves and a tall inflorescence which is produced once only, after which the plant dies.

Introduced from Central America, the garingboom has occas. been used as a fodder-plant during times of drought, and as a hedge-plant.

1913 C. PETTMAN *Africanderisms* 181 *Garenboom,* .. The name given in the Riversdale district to *Agave americana.* **1917** R. MARLOTH *Common Names* 30 *Garenboom, Agave americana,* not a tree. The leaves yield a tough fibre. **1972** *Sunday Times* 10 Sept. 15 Many of the birds nest in the stump of a Mexican Aloe or garingboom. **1973** *Farmer's Weekly* 11 July 27 Proportionately, it probably has more American aloe (garingboom), and salt bush than any other farm in the country. **1987** M. POLAND *Train to Doringbult* 140 Well beyond the huts the workers' houses stood on the bare earth behind a barrier of *garingbome.*

garrick /ˈgærɪk/ *n.* [Etym. unkn., but see quot. 1993.] The marine fish *Lichia amia* of the Carangidae; LEERFISH; LEERVIS.

The name 'garrick' is used for this species in Smith and Heemstra's *Smiths' Sea Fishes* (1986).

1906 A.B. CLIFFORD in *E. London Dispatch* 3 Apr. 6 Managed to get one garrick weighing 5 lbs. **1913** C. PETTMAN *Africanderisms* 182 *Garrick,* The fish known in the Cape Colony as the Leervisch .. *Lichia amia,* is known in Natal and at Port St. John as the *Garrick.* **1913**, *c*1936 [see LEERVIS]. **1945** H. GERBER *Fish Fare* 42 Garrick or Leerfish. This fish is almost unknown on the fish markets but is very popular with anglers from the Cape to the Natal Coast. **1966** *Daily News* 12 Sept. 5 Feeding on the sardines are reported to have been large numbers of garrick and shad. **1970** *Sunday Times* 8 Feb. (Mag. Sect.) 5 Garrick of 30 lb landed in Cape ... Outstanding in this catch was a garrick, tipping the scales at 30 lb. — an accomplishment beaten only once in club competitions — 14 years ago. **1974** [see LEERVIS]. **1984** G. VERDAL in *Style* Nov. 154 A suspension bridge .. links the beach with a rocky island which is a favourite fishing spot for garrick .. and other fish. **1993** R. VAN DER ELST *Guide to Common Sea Fishes* 151 The garrick is of no major commercial significance, but is a popular sport fish ... *Name derivation*: .. Garrick, meaning obscure, possibly a corruption of an Indian or Mauritian name.

garshly var. GASHLE.

garter snake *n. phr.* Also with initial capitals. [Prob. fr. S. Afr. Du. *kouseband,* see KOUSEBAND.] Any of several species of snake of the Elapidae characterized by cross-band markings; KOUSEBAND; NACHTSLANG sense 2 a. Occas. with defining word designating a particular species, as **Sundevall's garter snake** (*Elapsoidea sundevallii*).

1789 W. PATERSON *Narr. of Four Journeys* 163 The Kouse Band, or Garter Snake, is another of the poisonous reptiles. **1819**, **1860** [see KOUSEBAND]. **1910** F.W. FITZSIMONS *Snakes of S. Afr.* 84 (*caption*) The two smaller snakes are Garter Snakes ... Sundervall's Garter Snake or Kousband Slang. **1929** W. ROSE *Veld & Vlei* 140 Front-fanged snakes ... Peninsula representatives of this group are the Cape Cobra .. ; the Ringhals .. ; the Coral Snake .. ; and the Garter Snake. **1937** *Guide to Vertebrate Fauna of E. Cape Prov.* (Albany Museum) II. 73 *Elaps lacteus,* .. Garter Snake ... *Aspidelaps lubricus,* .. Coral Snake .. (Garter Snake. Kous Band). **1947** J. STEVENSON-HAMILTON *Wild Life in S. Afr.* 328 The various species of garter snakes (*Elaphecis* and *Homorelaps*) likewise are akin to the true cobra. **1950** W. ROSE *Reptiles & Amphibians* 298 We have noticed the Garter Snake to have the curious habit when disturbed of wriggling violently, without progressing, in a manner well calculated to dazzle and bewilder an enemy. **1988** B. BRANCH *Field Guide to Snakes* 90 Garter snakes burrow in sandy or humic soils, coming to the surface at night.

garum masala var. GARAM MASALA.

garvie var. GAWIE.

gashle /ˈgɑːʃli, ‖gɑːɬe/ *adv. colloq.* Also **gahle, gahlé, garshly, kah(a)le.** [Englished form of Xhosa and Zulu *kahle* well, nicely, sweetly, gently, in peace, pleasantly, carefully.] Carefully, gently. Also in the v. phr. ***go gashle, hamba kahle*** (HAMBA sense 2 b).

1898 B. MITFORD *Induna's Wife* 230 As they were dragging him roughly over the ground Sifadu interposed. '*Gahlé,* brothers. Do not bruise him.' **1907** J.P. FITZPATRICK *Jock of Bushveld* (1909) Glossary, *Kahle,* (pro[nounced] kaa-shle, corrupted in kitchen Kaffir to 'gaashly') .. gently, carefully, pleasantly, well. **1948** O. WALKER *Kaffirs Are Lively* 94 '*Gahle!*' ('gently') hissed the official, and I braked the car until we were crawling. **1970** Y. WINTERS *Informant, Kimberley* He is getting old and will have to take it kahle now. Transvaalers pronounce it garshlie. **1970** E.G.B. HARDY *Informant, Cape Town* Go garshly. Be careful. From Zulu (?) Hamba Kahle – 'go well'. A normal form of leave-taking. **1971** L.G. GREEN *Taste of S.-Easter* 103 That happy period when everyone poured his own measure. The barman is gazing anxiously at the glass and saying: 'Gashle, colonel!' **1980** O. MUSI in M. Mutloatse *Forced Landing* 180 When they speak from their lofty heights our rulers get carried away. One utterance, an oft-repeated one, was that the law would go *kahle* on the pass laws. **1984** *Pretoria News* 4 Apr. 21 'We were shot. And Magogogo, he has died.' 'Kahle,' the women encourage him. 'Don't worry. Malembe's small bus comes soon.' **1991** B. FARGHER *Informant, Grahamstown* We need to go garshly and move slowly on this one.

gat *int.* var. GATS.

‖**gat** /xat/ *n.* [Afk. fr. Du., hole (pl. *gate*); (vulgar) vent, anus (pl. *gatte*).]

Often used by writers to suggest Afrikaans dialogue.

1. A hole.

a. *obs. rare.* A large pool in a river.

1806 J. BARROW *Trav.* I. 209 Some of the gats, or holes, of the Sea-Cow river were five or six miles in length, and deep enough to float a line-of-battle ship. **1847** —— *Reflect.* 179 We collected .. at the Sea-Cow River ... It is a chain of deep stagnant pools or *gats.*

b. *Obs.* except in place names: a depression in the ground, large enough to be considered a topographic feature.

1838 J.E. ALEXANDER *Exped. into Int.* I. 45, I crossed over, and with a guide, rode on in the dark, to the outspan of the waggon at Kalk gat, or lime hole, and found the people cooking and enjoying themselves. **1914** C. PETTMAN *Notes on S. Afr. Place Names* 14 As the colony grew and education decayed, the farming element was deteriorated by the addition of a lower class of burger, and we can trace a corresponding rudeness in the place names .. in almost every district we have a superabundance of Doorn Hoeks, Modder Gats, Haasfonteins, [etc.]. **1988** J. DEACON in *S. Afr. Panorama* May 44 The Hell, as Gamkaskloof is popularly termed – the Boers called it Gatkloof (hole ravine).

2. *slang.* Not in polite use. Anus, 'backside'.

a. Used in the obscene expletive interjections ***jou gat*** /jəʊ -/ [Afk., *jou* your], used to express rage, disgust, or contradiction; ***se gat*** /sə -/ [Afk., *se* possessive pronoun (his, her, their)], an expression of disbelief or contradiction; cf. SE VOET.

1968 M. DOYLE *Impala* 20 'Father-in-law, *se gat!*' Gideon choked over the obscenity. 'I suppose you'd like me to call him Pappy as well next?' **1978** M.J. MTSAKA *Not his Pride* 8 Make sure that it's mixed with words from other languages. Throw in a few words like 'jou gat', 'jou moer' and so on. They'll learn other languages quicker that way, neh? **1984** 'DAN' in *Frontline* Feb. 27 You've heard all that stuff about the 'liberal tradition' of the Cape, .. right? Well, forget it. Liberal se gat.

b. *comb.* **gat-creeper, gat-kruiper** /-ˌkrœipə(r)/ [Afk., *kruiper* creeper, fr. *kruip* to creep], 'ass-creeper', sycophant, toady; cf. SCHLOEP *n*.; so **gatkruip** *v.*, to be obsequious, to attempt to ingratiate oneself; cf. *schloep v.* (see SCHLOEP *n.*); also *attrib*.; **gatvol** /ˈxatfəl/ *adj.*, also (occas.) **gaatvol** [Afk., *vol* full], *absol.*, or in the phr. *gatvol of*, extremely tired (of), bored or disgusted (with), 'fed up (with)'.

1985 P. SLABOLEPSZY *Sat. Night at Palace* 12 If there's one thing I can't handle it's a **gat-creeper**. Bloody schloep. Up a ou's arse. **1987** M. MAARTENS *Ring around Moon* 86, I hate these cowardly traitors .. these joiners .. these **gatkruipers**. **1991** *Fair Lady* 8 May 63 *Gatkruiper*, teachers' pet. **1993** M. HEPBURN in *E. Prov. Herald* 18 Feb. 4, I had been called a 'gatkruiper' and was told I would be eliminated. **1989** 'A. LETOIT' in *Weekly Mail* 27 Jan. 23 An Afrikaffer is somebody who isn't afraid to throw a rasta out of his flat ... It's when you've got past the stage of **gatkruiping** blacks. **1990** R. MALAN *My Traitor's Heart* 211 A few months back, he was on gatkruip patrollie, meaning 'ass-creep patrol' .. Ass-creep patrol is the hearts and minds aspect of riot control in South Africa. [**1980** *Sunday Times* 14 Dec. (Mag. Sect.) 5 At Herold's Bay .. a defiant owner called his holiday home '**Gatvol**'. I wonder which members of an extended family drove him to that.] **1984** L. SHAW in *Style* Nov. 213 Peter S— managed to resurrect himself for a few dances — after having pronounced himself 'gatvol deluxe'. **1986** *Informant, Durban* We're gaatvol of all these hassles. **1989** M. BRAND in *Fair Lady* 25 Oct. 92 *Gatvol*, Feeling of having had more than enough, often experienced after reading yet another article on acid rain. **1992** *Financial Mail* 13 Mar. 25 These are doubtful voters who .. worry about crime, about a declining standard of living and schooling, about job security, about their property and pensions ... They are *gatvol* with De Klerk, the Nats, the communists, .. Model C schools and suburban hijack murders ... But the great flaw in the *gatvol* reasoning is that none of the things that are upsetting people will go away if De Klerk is ousted from power. **1993** 'T. COBBLEIGH' in *Sunday Times* 25 Apr. 21 The Independent newspaper in London told its readers this week that South Africa's whites were 'gatvol' over the recent violence. The word means 'bellyful', the paper explained helpfully. **1994** D. CAPEL in *Ibid*. 25 Dec. 15 Three years ago, Koos, then a staunch Conservative Party MP, was so 'gatvol' with the changes being introduced .. that he plotted the government's downfall.

gata /ˈxatə/ *n. slang*. Also **gatha, gatta, gatte**. Pl. -s, or (occas.) unchanged. [Perh. fr. Sotho slang *legata* (pl. *magata*) member of police force, fr. -(*k*)*gata* catch (a thief); or ad. vulgar Afk. *gatte* (see GAT sense 1); perh. ultimately fr. Yiddish *khates*, see Gold quot. 1983 at GATTES.] In urban (esp. township) English, usu. in *pl.*: the police. Also as *sing.* (*rare*), a prison warder.

1977 P.C. VENTER *Soweto* 153 A stranger to the tsotsi's dangerous world could still save his throat if he has some knowledge of basic words and phrases: ... Die Gattes — the police. [**1977** J. SIKAKANE *Window on Soweto* 26 The Sowetonians call the SAP's 'amakgathas' meaning 'the arseholes'.] **1979** A.P. BRINK *Dry White Season* 84 You got a taxi. You're the first to know when the gattes are coming on a raid, so you can warn your pals. **1983** H. MASHABELA in *Frontline* Feb. 38 'How do you know it's yours?' one of the three *gatas* (cops) asked me ... Even though there was no doubt this was my jersey, the *gatas* refused to search for the other articles .. The *gatas* told senior officers they couldn't trace the culprits. **1985** [see MARY DECKER]. **1987** *Learn & Teach* No.1, 50 Do you smell what's coming? Cops! A Raid! Police! Gats! **1987** S.A. BOTHA in *Frontline* Oct.-Nov. 15 Prison slang .. Gatta — warder.

gatagay *n. obs*. Also **da-t'kai, gategey**. [ad. Khoikhoi; according to Boshoff and Nienaber, perh. *tatsegate* never, for ever (*Afrikaanse Etimologieë*, 1967, p.636).

In Afk., the word is found as *tatgai, gat*(*a*)*ga*(*a*)*i*, and *katg*(*a*)*ai*.]

Any of several species of plant of the genus *Peucedanum* (family Apiaceae), with edible but unpalatable roots, found in the Malmesbury district of the Western Cape.

[**1786** G. FORSTER tr. *A. Sparrman's Voy. to Cape of G.H.* II. 27 [Bushpigs] are wont to grub after the root of a shrub of the mesembryanthemum kind, which they [*sc.* the Khoikhoi] call da-t'kai.] **1795** C.R. HOPSON tr. *C.P. Thunberg's Trav.* I. 149 The root of the *gatagay* is likewise roasted in the embers and eaten, but has a bad and disagreeable taste. **1809** J. MACKRILL *Diary*. 56 Anise Wortel & Gategey, Tentandria umbelliferous plants, the Dutch eat th' roots. *Ibid*. 60 Gategay is used to eat, but is not pleasant.

gatha var. GATA.

‖**Gatjieponder** /ˈxaɪciˌpɔn(d)ə(r)/ *n. colloq*. Formerly also **Gatjaponner** /ˈxatjaˌpɔnə(r)/, and occas. with small initial. [Afk., ad. of earlier *Gatjaponner*, fr. *gatjapon* frock-coat (*gat* see GAT + *japon* gown) + *-er* suffix denoting a member of (an organization, or group of believers).

Members of the Gereformeerde Kerk in Suid-Afrika (see GEREFORMEERDE) coined the derisive epithet *Gatjaponner* from the colloquial word for the frock-coats worn by members of the Nederduitse Gereformeerde Kerk.]

Sometimes *derog.*: a member of the Nederduitse Gereformeerde Kerk (see NGK); occas., a member of any Afrikaans church.

In quot. 1983 the writer, a black minister in the Dutch Reformed church, has misinterpreted the meaning of the word; or perh. this is an example of a new sense.

1959 L.G. GREEN *These Wonders* 148 A party of Voortrekkers, some Doppers .. , others Gatjaponners (Nederduits Gereformeerde Kerk) .. formed a *laerplek* on the present town site. Religious arguments arose, and the Doppers moved off ... The Gatjaponners named their home Edenburg, an earthly paradise after the departure of the Doppers. **1973** E. LEROUX in S. Gray *Writers' Territory* 145 Past churches and church halls (Doppers, Gatjieponders, Anglicans, The Star of Judah, the Catholics with their merry Brabantian priests). **1983** in *Fair Lady* 16 Nov. 170 People didn't trust me because of my association with Afrikaners ... In a crowd there was always someone who whispered just loud enough for me to hear: *Gatjieponder, gatjieponder* (stooge) ... And in 1962 I woke up one night to find my church in flames.

gats /xats/ *int. colloq*. Also **gaats, gat(tela), gits**. [Afk., euphemistic substitute for *God* /xɔt/ God.] An exclamation of dismay, disquiet, or annoyance, comparable to 'hell', 'good God'; GOTS.

1919 R.Y. STORMBERG *With Love from Gwenno* 57 She made quite a brilliant ass of herself at the piano .. , bawling away at some ballads which I couldn't recognise for the badness of their rendition. Martin burst in with 'Maar gits! you should just hear Miss Davis sing that song! Nobody can sing like wot she ken!' **1970** J. STODEL *Informant, Cape Town* Ooh gats it's going to rain. **1973** J. COPE in S. Gray *Writers' Territory* 115 The boy was yelling at him: 'Gaats! man, look at your line — die donner!' The cord jerked and whipped, running hot through his nerveless fingers. **1978** *Randlords & Rotgut* (Junction Ave Theatre Co.) in S. Gray *Theatre Two* (1981) 84 Uh, gat, you're so bloody ugly I don't want to touch you. **1982** *Sunday Times* 21 Mar. 44 He was not happy when the British arrived. 'Can a person be happy in such a time? Gats! We were in jail!' **1992** C. KNOX tr. *E. Van Heerden's Mad Dog* 68 A commotion broke out at the cage ... 'He's caught hold of Jock, oh **gattela**!' Tattie looked round guiltily — I'd heard him sneakily egging Jock on to bark at the monkey.

gatta, gatte varr. GATA.

gattela var. GATS.

‖**gattes** /ˈxatəs/ *n. derog*. Also **chattes, ghattis**. [Prob. ad. Yiddish *khates* a bad person; but claimed by some to be ad. vulgar Afk. *gatte* (pl. form of *gat*, see GAT sense 1).] In the Jewish community: a derogatory term for an AFRIKANER (*n.* sense 2 a).

1970 M. WEITZMAN *Informant, Johannesburg* Ghattis. Afrikaner. The word Ghattis is taken from the word *gat*, which is used continually by the Afrikaner. **1983** J.H. KAHN *Informant, London* (U.K.) Chattes .. seems to be a peculiarly SA term yet is taken by many Jews to be Yiddish. It is used by SA Jews as a derogatory term for Afrikaners. It even has a Hebrew-style plural — *chatteisim*. **1983** D. GOLD *Informant, Haifa* (Israel) Chattes .. is of Western Yiddish origin (and unknown in Northeastern Yiddish, as well as other varieties of Eastern Yiddish). The word is well known to me and it has been recorded in a general sense of 'bad person' (hence its pejorative application to Afrikaners) and in a narrow sense, 'policeman' (hence Afrikaans *gattes* 'police'). It has been recorded in works published in 1812, 1822, 1840, and 1862, all outside South Africa ... In Yiddish it is of Hebrew origin. **1983** L. REICH *Informant, Grahamstown* Gattes is an inelegant Yiddish word for an Afrikaner which I don't let anyone use in my presence.

gaukum var. GOCUM.

Gauriqua var. GRIQUA.

Gauteng /xaʊˈteŋ, xaʊətəŋ/ *n*. Also **Gouteng**. [Sotho, fr. N. Sotho *gauta*, S. Sotho *gauda*, ultimately an adaptation of Afk. *goud* /xəʊt/ gold + *teng* there, inside; see E. Prov. Herald quot. 1994.]

1. GOLDEN CITY.

[**1961** *Southern Sotho-English Dict.*, Gaudĕng, Johannesburg. **1975** *Comprehensive Northern Sotho Dict.* 302 Gautêng Witwatersrand, Johannesburg.] **1991** I.E.G. COLLETT *Informant, Pilgrim's Rest* Johannesburg: The Big Naartjie, Joey's, Gouteng, eGoli. **1994** WILHELM & NAIDOO in *Sunday Times* 1 May 15 Egoli may now be as familiar as Johannesburg but there are a string of other slang words for the city ... Gauteng (from the Sotho word Gauge [*sic*] which means gold).

2. The name of one of the nine provinces of South Africa (previously the PWV Province, see PWV sense b). Also *attrib*.

1994 P. SMYTHE on TV1, 8 Dec. (Agenda), From all of us in the studio here in Gauteng, goodnight. **1994** *E. Prov. Herald* 9 Dec. 2 PWV renamed Gauteng ... Gauteng, Sotho for 'Place of Gold', was adopted as the new name for the Pretoria-Witwatersrand-Vereeniging province by the legislature yesterday — but will become official only after it is changed by national parliament. **1994** *Sunday Times* 25 Dec. 1 Gauteng children will be showered with candies by the region's SAPS Air Wing.

‖**gavine** /ɡaˈviːn(i)/ *n*. Also **gabeen, gavini, govini**. [Zulu *ugavini* a liquor made from sugarcane, of obscure origin, perh. rel. to *gava* act or talk foolishly or unrestrainedly; or rel. to *isivina* (grape) vine, fr. Eng. *vine*; but see also quot. 1954.] Esp. in township slang: a potent spirit distilled from home-brewed liquor. Cf. SHIMIYANA.

1954 F.J. EDMONSTONE *Thorny Harvest* 85 Saku poured a little of the spirit on the concrete floor, then taking a lighted match to it, immediately the *govini* burst into a blue flame. *Ibid*. 139 Govini, A prostituted word, coined to mean 'the government is against it'. Distilled from shimiyana. Extremely potent. **1959** *Drum* Jan. 27 (caption) Gavini: Distilled from Skokiaan, with a seasoning of wild fruits, especially Marula. Looks like milky gin. Half-a-jack has put men out for 18 hours. **1963** [see SHIMIYANA]. **1980** 'MRS M.' in *Staffrider* Vol.3 No.1, 2 People, as I say, were brewing gavine, shimiyana, everything.

gawie /ˈxaːvi/ *n. derog.* Also **garvie**, **ghawi**. [Afk., prob. fr. nickname *Gawie*, fr. *Gabriel*.] JAPIE sense 3. Also *attrib.*

1963 D. WRIGHT Letter. 16 Apr. (Pringle Coll. 462/47, N.E.L.M.), Censorship as proposed will make idiots of their children, make real garvies of them, unable to hold enlightened conversation with anyone in the outside world. **1964** J. MEINTJES *Manor House* 119 They referred to the backvelders as *duine-molle, japies, takhare, gawies* and so on. **1970** M.C. DICKERSON *Informant, East London* Gawie. A roughneck, someone without polish. **1970** J. STODEL *Informant, Cape Town* I can hear by your ghawi-accent that you're from 'South Africa.' A ghawi accent is a mixture between an Afrikaans and English accent. **1970** M. VAN RENSBURG *Informant, Port Elizabeth* Gawie. A countryman or peasant not versed in town manners. **1991** S.C. SCHOLTEN *Informant, Durban* Gawie. (Uncomplimentary) .. Afrikaans local boy. **1992** P. DOBSON *Informant, Cape Town* Jaap; Gawie; Crunchie; Hairyback; Rockspider; Rock, Dutchman: an Afrikaner.

gazaat /gəˈzat/ *v. slang.* Also **gazzat**, **gezat**. [Etym. unknown, perh. rel. to Sotho *gasa tshelete* give money for general development; or perh. (though less likely) Isicamtho ad. Arabic *zakaat* obligatory payment Muslims have to make to charity in terms of Islamic law.] In township slang: to contribute (money); to pool resources. Cf. LAS.

a. *trans.*

1978 M. MUTLOATSE *Casey & Co.* 133 Empties the cokes a bit then pours the mahog in the bottles and seals then ... This goes on, on and on as long as we have enough mazuma to gazzat. Once I overheard Mr Editor remark such-wise – 'Those two are the only people I know who can get drunk on coke.'

b. *intrans.*

1980 M. MZAMANE in M. Mutloatse *Forced Landing* 24 Take the bottle we're going to drink, for instance. Didn't Mazibuko and I gazaat when we met during lunch time? Anyway, I'm not too keen to broadcast the fact .. that I contributed half the amount that went to buying that bottle. [**1990** M.J.F. MFUSI Soweto Zulu Slang. Appendix A, *Ukugazatha*, to throw money into common fund for a specific purpose.]

So **gazaat** *n.*, a contribution, a collection (of money).

1974 A.P. BRINK *Looking on Darkness* 112 Save it up, I tole you. I made *gezat* fo' you.

gazania /gəˈzeɪnɪə/ *n.* [Modern L. *Gazania* (G. Gaertner *De Fructibus Plantarum*, 1791, II. p.451), fr. the name of *Theodorus Gaza* (1398–1478), a Greek scholar.]

a. Any of several herbs of the genus so named (family Asteraceae), having showy yellow, orange, or pink flowers; also called BOTTERBLOM, GOUSBLOM.

1813 W.T. AITON *Hortus Kewensis* V. 140 Great-flower'd Gazania. **1913** [see NEMESIA]. **1924** D. FAIRBRIDGE *Gardens of S. Afr.* 107, I have seen the shores of Saldanha Bay so thickly set with orange Gazanias that it hurts the eye to look at them ... There are so many shades amongst the orange and yellow varieties; there are also white and creamy Gazanias with glaucous foliage, and in some districts there are fine claret and purple varieties. **1921** G. JEKYLL *Colour Schemes* 63 A few belated Orange Lilies have their colour nearly repeated by the Gazanias next to the path. **1966** E. PALMER *Plains of Camdeboo* 280 There are Nemesias and Gazanias. **1972** M.R. LEVYNS in *Std Encycl. of Sn Afr.* V. 279 The genus *Gazania* stands rather by itself among the gousblom since is has a different type of involucre ... The name botterblom is also given to this species [*sc. Gazania krebsiana*]. **1976** U. VAN DER SPUY *Wild Flowers of S. Afr. for Garden* 102 Gazanias flourish in hot, dry places. **1986** L.B. HALL in *Style* July 97 Here is a blazing and brilliant Eden. Arctosis, .. gazanias. **1990** *Weekend Mail* 14 Sept. 6 I'm also fond of my gazanias. I have pink, orange and yellow ones which produce enormous blooms through most of the year without any attention. **1991** [see PIETSNOT]. **1993** I. VLADISLAVIĆ *Polly* 16 She .. pushed open the window and scattered the grains into the bed of gazanias below.

b. With qualifying word: **Peacock Gazania** *obs.*, *Gazania krebsiana subsp. arctotoides*, with large orange-coloured flower-heads.

1844 J.W. LOUDON *Ladies' Flower-Garden Ornamental Perennials* II. 29 The **Peacock Gazania** .. only expands its flowers in broad daylight.

gazzat var. GAZAAT.

Gcaleka /gaˈleːka, ǀaˈleːka, -ga/ *n.* Also **Galaka**, **Galeca**, **Galeka**. Pl. **-s**, **ama-**, or unchanged; occas. **Amacaleka(s)**, **Amagcalekas**. [Name of the Xhosa chief *Gcaleka* (*c*1730–1778); for an explanation of pl. forms, see AMA-.]

1. A member of a people forming one of the major divisions of the Xhosa. Also *attrib.* See also XHOSA *n.* sense 1 a. Cf. RHARHABE sense a.

See note at RHARHABE.

1809 R. COLLINS in G.M. Theal *Rec. of Cape Col.* (1900) VII. 20 There people are called Mandankees from the name of their founder. Hinsa's subjects are, .. from the same reason, called Galekas. **1846** *Natal Witness* 12 June, A party of the Amacaleka (Hintza's people) .. have sustained severe loss, and we hear the Amacalekas are fleeing. **1846** I. REID in *Imp. Blue Bks* Command Paper 786-1847, 88 I received letters from my son .. at Luponda, .. informing me of the commencement of hostilities between the Tambookies and Galakas. **1852** M.B. HUDSON *S. Afr. Frontier Life* p.xii, Passing over British Kaffraria, we come to the River Kei, beyond which is the territory of the Amagalekas. **1853** F.P. FLEMING *Kaffraria* 92 The nose also varies in form – in the T'Slambie tribes, being broader and more of the Negro shape, than in the Gaikas or Galekas. **1860** W. SHAW *Story of my Mission* 491 These strangers .. had .. attacked some of the more advanced Amagcaleka. **1866** [see NGQIKA]. **1879** G.C. CATO Letter. (Killie Campbell Africana Library MS1602b) 2 Feb., Zulu spies and messengers have gone along the foot of the Drakensberg to try and get Basutos, Pondos, and Galekas to rise. **1880** *Encycl. Brit.* XIII. 819 The Gcaleka chief, who is lord paramount of all the Ama-Xosa tribes, always takes his first or 'great wife' from the Ama-Tembu royal family, and her issue alone have any claim to the succession. **1882** J. NIXON *Among Boers* 58 The Galekas were 'up', and burgher law had been proclaimed. **1887** *S.W. Silver & Co.'s Handbk to S. Afr.* 380 The Gcalekas are the most warlike of the natives within or about the Cape. **1891** T.R. BEATTIE *Ride through Transkei* 5 Kreli, the Great Gcaleka Chief, is still endeavouring .. to regain his country from the Kei River to the Bashee. **1906** G. CALLAWAY in *E. & W. Mag.* (India) 424 The Gcalekas – the aristocratic tribe of the Amaxosa. **1912** [see *witch doctress* at WITCHDOCTOR]. **1920** S.M. MOLEMA *Bantu Past & Present* 73 The Gcaleka chief was recognised as taking the first place in all matters social and political, and especially the latter. **1926** M. NATHAN *S. Afr. from Within* 34 The Galekas and Gaikas rose in 1877, this resulting in what was known as the Ninth Kaffir War. **1937** B.J.F. LAUBSCHER *Sex, Custom & Psychopathology* 210 At one time the Tembus obtained their wives from among the Galekas. **1939** N.J. VAN WARMELO in A.M. Duggan-Cronin *Bantu Tribes* III. i. 25 Generations after the death of their common ancestor, Phalo, the chiefs of the Rarabe section continue to report to, and consult with, the Gcaleka chiefs concerning all the matters of first importance. **1972** [see FETCANI sense 1]. **1975** A.O. JACKSON *Ethnic Comp. of Ciskei & Transkei* 6 Phalo's great son was Gcaleka and his right-hand son was Rarabe. The most important division of the Xhosa was between these two brothers ... The Gcaleka tribes all live in the Transkei. **1981** J.B. PEIRES *House of Phalo* 31 The great split which occurred after Rharhabe crossed the Kei did not entirely divide the Xhosa nation, for .. the Gcaleka kings continued to assert their superiority over all the Xhosa chiefs. **1986** P. MAYLAM *Hist. of Afr. People* 96 The Thembu .. had fallen out with the Gcaleka over the division of the spoils after the defeat of Matiwane in 1828.

‖**2.** In the Eastern Cape: a derogatory name for a rural person from the (former) Transkei.

1979 *Daily Dispatch* 24 Aug. (Indaba) 2 The term 'Gcaleka' was in most cases used in an offensive manner. It is commonly heard in buses .. 'Most of the bus drivers are from the Transkei and you'll hear a commuter saying: "You Gcaleka, drive this bus carefully – do you think this is Transkei, stupid."'

GCM *int. slang.* [Unkn.: prob. ad. *Jesus*; but see also Slabolepszy quot. 1985.] An exclamation expressing a variety of feelings, as irritation, frustration, and approving or disapproving wonder.

1984 'DAN' in *Frontline* Feb. 24 I'll admit that there's not much as beautiful as the Cape on a good day ... You figure: 'GCM, God must have been in a hang of a good mood when he made this joint'. **1985** H. PRENDINI in *Style* Oct. 39 Southern Suburbs joller: No ways my china! No ways I work under a black! GCM! **1985** P. SLABOLEPSZY *Sat. Night at Palace* 15 Aah come on Vince man!! G.C.M.! A person can't get anything done with you around. *Ibid.* 77 *G.C.M.*, God, Christ and Moses (as in Jesus, Mary and Joseph).

gé /xeɪ/ *n. slang.* Also **ge**. [Etym. unknown.]

1. Friend.

1970 *Informant, Grahamstown* Everyone is a ge nowadays (in-crowd fellow). **1970** S.E. NATHAM *Informant, Cape Town* Ge. Friend. **1972** M. DEVELIN on Radio South Africa 25 Jan., Like my china's my gé (a friend in need is a friend indeed).

2. *derog.* SKATE.

1981 J. BATTERSBY in *Frontline* May 14 The stereotype *ge* making it with a supermarket cashier. **1982** D. KRAMER *Short Back & Sides* 22 You call me a rock spider You call me a gé You like to mock The things that I say. **1982** *Star* 31 Mar., Gé – a scruffy person, usually quite rough, who tends to drive a car with fur on the dash and an orange on the aerial.

Gebied *n.*[1] var. GEBIET.

‖**gebied** /xəˈbit/ *n.*[2] [Afk., territory, district.] A district or area, particularly an area demarcated by apartheid legislation. See also GROUP AREA *n. phr.* sense 1.

1971 J.A. BROWN *Return* 54 They made it difficult for him to settle down in any of the coloured *gebied*; and the women had heard too much talk about his wife. **1980** *Sunday Times* 31 Aug. (Extra) 3 He invites me to join his Karroo-cruising crew on a one-night gig in a one-horse, up-country gebied. **1981** *Voice* 8 July 2 Group Areas decreed his parents move from a district of Benoni called Brentwood Park to Actonville because it was what the system called 'a Blanke gebied'. **1982** *Pace* May 8 Where is justice and Christian feeling when blacks are wished away and balkanised in some obscure 'bantu gebied' without their consultation or their agreement?

Gebiet /xəˈbit, gə-/ *n.* Also **Gebied**. [G. *Gebiet* territory; the alternative spelling is Afk. *gebied* (with the same meaning).] Usu. in the n. phrr. ***Bastard Gebiet***, ***Baster Gebiet***, ***Rehoboth*** (***Baster***) ***Gebiet***. The territory (later an official district) inhabited by the Rehoboth Baster people (see REHOBOTH), south of Windhoek, Namibia.

1926 *Report of Rehoboth Commission* (UG41–1926) 3 The community known as the Rehoboth *Basters*, in the Mandated Territory of South-West Africa, and the area, commonly known as the *Gebiet*, occupied by them. **1936** L.G. GREEN *Secret Afr.* 75, I drove through the 'Gebied,' with its long grass and good trees, and found it almost unstocked. **1944** [see BASTARD sense 2]. **1952** L.G. GREEN *Lords of Last Frontier* 202 They have a reserve (known as the Baster Gebied) of about five thousand square miles of the finest cattle and karakul country in the whole territory. **1969** *Survey of Race Rel.* (S.A.I.R.R.) 260 The Rehobothers at present number approximately 14,000. Their Gebiet, to the south of Windhoek, at present measures about 5,066 square miles. **1969** J.M. WHITE *Land God Made in Anger* 196 Their Gebiet or District has enjoyed virtual independence from the beginning. **1971** *Daily Dispatch* 6 July 1 The Baster Advisory Council of the Rehoboth Gebiet is asking the United Nations Security Council to intervene in South West Africa. **1976** O. LEVINSON *Story of Namibia* 32 The Rehoboth Baster Gebiet is approximately 13 000 square kilometres of excellent pastoral country with a population of about 220000 people. **1984** *Sunday Times* 23 Sept. 11 Even Swapo recognizes the unique nature of the Rehoboth Gebiet, and has promised it will retain self-government after independence. **1990** *Ibid.* 11 Feb. 2 The Rehoboth Gebied — 14 000 sq kilometres of ranchland with the town of Rehoboth as its centre. **1992** *Pretoria News* 4 Aug. 6 His mother-in-law lives near Kalkrand, just south of the Rehoboth Gebied.

gebroken veld /xə'brʊəkənfeld, -fɛlt/ *n. phr.* [S. Afr. Du., *gebroken* 'broken', mixed + *veld* uncultivated vegetation (used as pasture).] MIXED VELD. Also occas. part. tr. **broken veld**.

1856 *Cape of G.H. Almanac & Annual Register* 291 Orange Free State... The pasturage of these plains .. is principally what is termed in the colony 'gebroken veld,' or a mixture of sour and sweet grass. **1896** R. WALLACE *Farming Indust. of Cape Col.* 81 The veld is familiarly classified into *sweet* .. , *sour* .. , and half and half (*gebroken*) veld, occupying an intermediate position in the matter of quality. **1896** *Ibid.* [see NENTA sense 1]. **1913** C. PETTMAN *Africanderisms* 182 *Gebroken veld*, .. Veld in which there is a mixture of sour and sweet grass, or of grass and Karoo herbage. **1975** W.J. HUGO in *Std Encycl. of Sn Afr.* XI. 171 The Van Rooy sheep is found chiefly in the North-Western Cape, particularly in broken veld on the Orange River. **1986** [see NAMAQUALAND DAISY]. **1988** P.E. RAPER tr. *R.J. Gordon's Cape Trav. 1777–86* I. 114 The landscape [consists of] gebroken veld, friable, reddish clayey soil, generally a slightly inclining slope, many mouse-holes, ganna bushes, thorn bushes and mesembryanthemums.

gedaan /xə'daːn, -dɑːn/ *adj.* Also **gedan**. [Afk. (earlier S. Afr. Du.), finished, exhausted.]

‖**1.** Exhausted; 'done for'. Cf. KLAAR *adj.* sense 3.

1841 B. SHAW *Memorials* 124 My boy William, though an African born, was gedaan, (done) and lingered far behind. **1886** G.A. FARINI *Through Kalahari Desert* 294 Dirk was unsaddling Lady Anna. 'She is *gedan* (done up),' he remarked. 'Two more giraffes like that and her bones will be picked up by the *aasvogels*.' **1971** *Informant* She should be operated on, but is, I gather, too old and gedaan.

2. *obs.* KLAAR *adj.* sense 1.

1915 D. FAIRBRIDGE *Torch Bearer* 39 A short, stout, dark-haired man of about forty-five came into the room. 'Gedaan, Mevrouw Neethling,' Then he stood in an attitude of expectation.

gedoente /xə'dʊntə/ *n. colloq.* [Afk.]
1. A fuss; a complicated matter.

1970 E. MUNDELL *Informant, Pearston* (E. Cape) Now that was a big gedoente loading the cow onto the little lorry. **1971** *Informant, Grahamstown* Jean says the builders are rampant in her house, and it's such a gedoente. **1993** M-A. FINNEMORE *Informant, Grahamstown* There was a whole gedoente about it.

2. A thing; a creation.

1972 B. MILLS *Informant, Grahamstown* Its a chair that's also a ladder — one of those gedoentes. **1982** *Rhodeo* (Rhodes Univ.) 6 Apr. 13 Woman's lib can be just as boring. But everybody must do their little gedoente. **1993** S. DIKENI in *Bua* Dec. 32 Marilyn Martin .. just went on in Xhosa as if it was one of those things. And the occasion was not a hierjy gedoente nie, it was some important whatchacallit in the Grahamstown festival.

geelbek /'xɪəlbɛk/ *n.* Also **geelbec(k)**, **kiel-back**. [S. Afr. Du., *geel* yellow + *bek* mouth, beak.]
1.a. The marine fish *Atractoscion aequidens* of the Sciaenidae, so named for the bright yellow edges to its jaws and gill covers; CAPE SALMON sense 1 a; also called KOB. Also *attrib.*

The name 'geelbek' is used for this species in Smith and Heemstra's *Smiths' Sea Fishes* (1986).

a**1827** D. CARMICHAEL in W.J. Hooker *Botanical Misc.* (1831) II. 267 The *Galeon* fish, the *Geelbek*, and *Cabillau*, were invariably found together. **1831** *S. Afr. Almanac & Dir.*, May: Fish in Season .. Snoek, Geelbek, Silverfish, Roman, Kabeljau. **1860** A.W. DRAYSON *Sporting Scenes* 302 The shooting amusement at Natal could be changed sometimes, as the fishing in the bay was excellent ... A large number of fish of different kinds were often caught — rock-cod .. and a fish there called a kiel-back. **1880** 'C.W.' in *Cape Monthly Mag.* II. Mar. 162, I kept a large line overboard baited with half a harder for geelbeck .. or indeed anything really big. **1890** [see INGELEGDE VIS]. **1891** H.J. DUCKITT *Hilda's 'Where Is It?'* 79 At the Cape the best fish for pickling are 'Kabeljou,' [printed Kabeljon] 'Geelbeck,' 'Roman,' etc. **1902** J.D.F. GILCHRIST in *Trans. of S. Afr. Philological Soc.* 216 (Pettman), The name Cape Salmon .. is now appropriated almost exclusively by the *Geelbek*, a fish which, seen fresh from its native element, certainly does call to mind the brilliance and majestic proportions of its European namesake. **1931** *Times Lit. Suppl.* (U.K.) 16 Apr. 301 Like so many of the Cape fish, .. the geelbek .. gets his name from the original Dutch settlers. **1949** J.L.B. SMITH *Sea Fishes* 227 *Atractoscion aequidens* ... Salmon. Cape Salmon. Geelbek. Teraglin (Australia) ... South coast of Africa and Australia. In our area known from the Cape to Natal. **1955** C. HORNE *Fisherman's Eldorado* 34 Geelbek have a habit which results in many fish being lost. While waiting ,for the gaff they resort to violent head shaking. **1964** J. BENNETT *Mr Fisherman* (1967) 104 They were going up the coast to the *geelbek* grounds at dawn and the mackerel were biting well. **1986** M. VAN WYK *Cooking the S. Afr. Way* 24 Whole baked geelbek, 1 whole geelbek, entrails removed. **1993** R. VAN DER ELST *Guide to Common Sea Fishes* 290 Whereas it is a rare catch for rock and surf anglers, the geelbek is frequently landed by ski- and line-boat fishermen.

‖**b.** *comb.* **geelbek toutjie** [Afk., *toutjie* a thin strip of dried meat], a strip of dried fish.

1979 SNYMAN & KLARIE *Free from Sea* 26 Cape Salmon is easy to cure and this has resulted in our unique Cape delicacy, 'Geelbek Toutjies'. *Ibid.* 83 Geelbek Toutjies ... A toothsome fish biltong which can be eaten raw or baked ... After a week or so your Geelbek Toutjies are ready to be eaten.

2. The duck *Anas undulata* of the Anatidae; yellow-bill, see YELLOW sense a. Also *attrib.*

1867 E.L. LAYARD *Birds of S. Afr.* 352 A[nas] *Xanthorhyncha* ... *Geelbec* of Colonists and Sportsmen. [**1893** H.A. BRYDEN *Gun & Camera* 404 This is a light-brown duck, and is easily identified by the bright yellow bill from which it takes its Boer name — 'geelbec.'] **1901** W.T. BLACK *Fish River Bush* 21 An occasional shot may be got at a Geelbec duck (*Anas*) as it flies low along the bush lining the river banks. **1906** STARK & SCLATER *Birds of S. Afr.* IV. 135 The Geelbec keeps as a rule to marshes, lakes and stagnant water, and avoids running streams. **1957** L.G. GREEN *Beyond City Lights* 224 On the vleis are wild geese, the wild duck called *geelbek*, and flamingoes. **1967** E. ROSENTHAL *Encycl. of Sn Afr.* 201 Geelbec, .. (*Anas undulata*). The best-known and most generally distributed duck in South Africa. Also known as Yellow-bill. **1972** G.J. BROEKHUYSEN in *Std Encycl. of Sn Afr.* V. 133 Common species of duck are the Cape shoveller .., the black duck .. , the geelbek or yellow-bill [etc.]. **1994** M. ROBERTS tr. *J.A. Wahlberg's Trav. Jrnls 1838–56* 56 Numerous flocks of ducks (Geelbecks Ent and Swart Ent): shot at them in vain.

3. *obs.* An insulting term for a 'coloured' person (see COLOURED *n.*).

1913 C. PETTMAN *Africanderisms* 183 Geelbek, .. The term is .. applied abusively to a coloured person. **1934** C.P. SWART *Supplement to Pettman.* 54 Geelbek, .. Coloured persons are so called in the Western Province on account of their yellowish colour. [**1943** *Weekend News & Sunday Mag.* 20 Mar., Stompie Geelbek and Pals celebrate Oubaas's Visit. 'Tank youse, Misser Geelbek,' ses Plaatjes. 'At least jou is sort de instinks ord er yennelman if jou is nort one!']

geeldikkop /'xɪəl ˌdəkəp/ *n. Pathology.* Formerly also **gheel dikop**. [Afk., *geel* yellow + *dikkop* see DIKKOP.] Tribulosis, a disease of sheep caused by the ingestion of any of several species of *Tribulus* of the Zygophyllaceae (particularly *T. terrestris*, see DUBBELTJIE *n.*^{2} sense a) in a wilted state, and which is characterized by intense jaundice, and swelling of the head and face; DIKKOP sense 2 b. Also *attrib.*

1897 'F. MACNAB' *On Veldt & Farm* 231 There is another complaint which is very deadly among sheep, called Gheel Dikop. It commences with large swellings about the head, and the animal generally dies at last of suffocation. **1905** D. HUTCHEON in Flint & Gilchrist *Science in S. Afr.* 347 Geel Dikkop, or Yellow Thick Head. This is a peculiar disease affecting sheep and goats. **1911** [see DUBBELTJEDOORN]. **1914** *Farmer's Annual* 220 'Geel Dikkop' in sheep seems to be due to some plants growing on the veld at certain times, and the first thing to do is to change the sheep on to new pastures. **1930** [see JAAGSIEKTE sense 2]. **1957** *Handbk for Farmers* (Dept of Agric.) III. 339 The 'vermeersiektebossie', *Geigeria* spp., and 'geeldikkop', *Tribulus terrestris*, poisoning, cause heavy losses in sheep in the drier parts of South Africa. **1966** HENDERSON & ANDERSON *Common Weeds* [The common dubbeltjie] is best known in connection with the disease 'geeldikkop' in sheep. **1979** T. GUTSCHE *There Was a Man* 301 In December 1915, 'Geel Dikkop' (Yellow Thick Head) in sheep .. suddenly became epizootic and threatened the whole mutton, wool and hide industry. **1981** [see DUBBELTJIE *n.*^{2}].

geele pisang see PISANG sense 2 b.

‖**geelhout** /'xɪəlhəʊt/ *n.* Also **geele-houtt**, **geel kout**. [S. Afr. Du., fr. Du. *geel* yellow + *hout* wood.] YELLOWWOOD.

1790 [see YELLOWWOOD sense 1]. **1795** C.R. HOPSON tr. *C.P. Thunberg's Trav.* I. 169 *Geel-hout*, or yellow wood (*ilex crocea*) is a large tree, the wood of which is very heavy .. and is used for making tables. **1801** J. BARROW *Trav.* I. 133 Trees of various kinds and dimensions; the most common was the *geel hout* or yellow wood, (*taxus elongatus*) erroneously called by Thunberg the *ilex crocea*. **1804** R. PERCIVAL *Acct of Cape of G.H.* 148 Of the species peculiar to this country I have observed the geel hout: it grows to a very large size ... The wood is of a bright yellow colour, and much used for furniture. **1824** W.J. BURCHELL *Trav.* II. 114 Doors and tables, and the larger beams, were here observed to be all of *Geelhout* (Yellow-wood). **1831** *S. Afr. Almanac & Dir.* 187 The Geel Hout (Taxus elongatus) or Yellow Wood .. is used for all the purposes of house building. It is however greatly affected by the variations of the atmosphere, and by no means durable. **1834** T. PRINGLE *Afr. Sketches* 219 The most common species was a tree greatly resembling the cedar in its external aspect, but belonging to a quite different genus, termed by the colonists geelhout, or yellow-wood (taxus elongata). **1953** *Cape Argus* 25 Feb. 9 Eighty trees, including jakkals-bessie, geelhout, wild fig, .. have been planted along Table Bay boulevard. **1981** *S. Afr. Panorama* July 48 The bulk of the furniture is made of geelhout (yellowwood), one of South Africa's most attractive woods with a satiny sheen and smooth grain.

‖**geelrys** /'xɪəlreɪs/ *n.* [Afk., *geel* yellow + *rys* rice.] yellow rice, see YELLOW sense c.

1939 S. CLOETE *Watch for Dawn* 284 She thought of geel rys, of klapper tert, of sourkleuitjes, of curries, of preserves and konfyts. **1964** [see AYAH sense 1]. **1972** [see HOENDER sense 2 b]. **1973** *Sunday Times* 18 Feb. (Mag. Sect.) 31 The meat dishes — chicken, mutton, geelrys (yellow rice flavoured with saffron and condiments and coloured with turmeric). **1983** M. DU PLESSIS *State of Fear* 123 There will be roast chicken, .. crisp new potatoes, beetroot salad, *sousboontjies*, onion sauce, geelrys, baked tomatoes — all of it in potential hospitality towards unexpected guests.

geelsiekte var. GEILSIEKTE.

‖**geelvis** /'xɪəlfəs/ *n.* Formerly also **geelvisch**. [Afk., (earlier S. Afr. Du. *geelvisch*) *geel* yellow + *vis* fish.] YELLOWFISH sense a.

Used esp. of the *Clanwilliam yellowfish* (see YELLOWFISH sense b), *Barbus capensis*.

1822 W.J. BURCHELL *Trav.* I. 280 In the deepest of its [*sc.* the *Zak-rivier's*] pools I found a beautiful kind of carp, entirely of a yellow-green with a brazen lustre. The largest .. was at least two feet long ... It was known by the name of *Geel-visch* (Yellow-fish). [*Note*] *Cyprinus aëneus.* **1937** *Guide to Vertebrate Fauna of E. Cape Prov.* (Albany Museum) II. 123 Genus *Barbus* ... The species are numerous and usually abundant in the fresh waters of Africa and Asia. Most are small, but some *e.g.* the 'Mahaseer' of India and our own 'Geel-vis,' attain a large size, and are angling fishes of the first rank. **1947** K.H. BARNARD *Pict. Guide to S. Afr. Fishes* 56 In the Cape the *Clanwilliam Yellow-fish, Geelvis* (*Barbus capensis*) .. is also a good sporting fish. **1973** *S. Afr. Panorama* Oct., At the Molopo Oog, .. kurpers, geelvis, carp and black bass are bred on a large scale.

geikje var. GEITJIE.

‖**geilsiekte** /ˈxeɪlsiktə, xɪəl-/ *n. Pathology.* Also **geel-**, **gielsiekte**, and (formerly) **-ziekte**, **gielzickte**. [Afk. (earlier S. Afr. Du.), *geil* rank, lush (of plant growth) or, due to confusion over spelling and pronunciation, *geel* yellow + *siekte* sickness.

In modern Afk. 'geilsiekte' is used exclusively for prussic acid poisoning, while 'geelsiekte' is used exclusively for enzootic icterus (sheep jaundice) caused by selenium poisoning.]

1. An often fatal disease of livestock (esp. sheep), resulting from the ingestion of plants containing dangerous quantities of prussic acid, and characterized by rapid breathing, bloating, and the discoloration of mucous membranes; KEIL SICK(NESS).

1852 M.B. HUDSON *S. Afr. Frontier Life* 17 As a proof of the pasture on which they had fed, One sheep was already of Giel Siekte dead. **1867** *Blue Bk for Col. 1866* JJ30, The loss of sheep has been great, and still further losses have been suffered after the first rains by 'geil-ziekte'. **1876** J.S. PARKES in M. Parkes *Wheatlands* (1979) 23 Gielzickte I pass over, for altho it is bad and perhaps worse than formerly, it is sometimes to be prevented by a little management. [**1899** *Natal Agric. Jrnl* 31 Mar. 4 Stock maladies are well known to the English pastoralist under their Dutch or South African Dutch names — ... 'geelsiekte,' gall.] **1905** D. HUTCHEON in Flint & Gilchrist *Science in S. Afr.* 358 Several opinions are entertained with respect to the nature and cause of 'Geilziekte,' but the one most generally accepted is, that it is due to the direct action of a chemical poison which is produced in certain succulent plants by the action of the scorching heat of the sun. **1913** W.M. MCKEE *S. Afr. Sheep & Wool* 458 Tympanitis is very frequently confounded with the disease known as Gielziekte, but it is .. perfectly distinct. **1925** L.D. FLEMMING *Crop of Chaff* 18 With consummate tact he says nothing about the price of cattle, gielziekte, the khaki bush, and the filing of the Agricultural Census Form A.F. No. 33. **1937** *Handbk for Farmers* (Dept of Agric. & Forestry) 449 The term 'geilsiekte' as used by farmers does not signify a definite disease, but is a collective name for different ailments most of which are caused by plant poisoning. By far the most cases .. are due to hydrocyanic acid (prussic acid) poisoning caused through the ingestion of wilted green grass. **1971** BEETON & DORNER in *Eng. Usage in Sn Afr.* Vol.2 No.2, 29 Under certain conditions the wilting leaves are said to cause geilsiekte or bloating in sheep. **1981** J. VAHRMEIJER *Poisonous Plants of Sn Afr.* 78 The paper-bark thorn is one of a number of *Acacia* species which cause prussic acid poisoning (geilsiekte). **1988** T.S. KELLERMAN et al. *Plant Poisonings & Mycotoxicosis of Livestock* 197 Geilsiekte still ranks as one of the important plant poisonings of livestock in southern Africa.

2. With distinguishing epithet, designating a particular ailment, **droë-geilsiekte** [Afk. *droë* (earlier Du. *droge*), attrib. form of *droog* dry], or **dry geilsiekte**, *dry gallsickness* (see GALLSICKNESS sense 2); **opblaas geilsiekte** [Afk., *opblaas* (fr. Du. *opblazen*) blow up, become bloated], tympany.

1913 W.M. MCKEE *S. Afr. Sheep & Wool* 460 Impaction of the Third or Leaf Stomach. This condition is often called '**Drooge Geilziekte**,' but it is perfectly distinct from that disease. Almost all forms of derangement of the digestive organs .. give rise to a dry and impacted condition of the third or leaf stomach. **1927** *Farming in S. Afr.* Oct. 333 (Swart), First of all there is the term 'droë-geilsiekte' which is sometimes used by farmers. **1934** C.P. SWART Supplement to Pettman. 44 *Droë-Geilsiekte*, .. A digestive disturbance in sheep, also known by the vague name of gallsickness. The disease is brought about by something that is present in the pasture during certain climatic conditions. **1914** *Farmer's Annual* 221, I am sorry the enquirer did not say what kind of 'geilziekte' as there are several kinds. We here have got '**dry geilziekte**' and '**opblaas geilziekte**'. **1932** *Farming in S. Afr.* Apr. 38 (Swart), Sometimes there is slime in the wind-pipe; in many instances the rumen will be bloated ('opblaas geilsiekte'). **1934** C.P. SWART Supplement to Pettman. 128 *Opblaas-Geilsiekte*, .. Hoven and Tympany.

‖**geitjie** /ˈxeɪki, -ci/ *n.* Also **cuytge**, **gaetye**, **geikje**, **geitje**, **geittjie**, **heiki**, **jieke**, **t'geitje**. [S. Afr. Du., of unknown origin: perh. fr. San !haĭ: /!haĭ:/ gecko + Du. dim. suff. -*(t)je* (see -IE); or onomatopoeic, fr. unrecorded San or Malay word imitating the clicking sound made by a gecko.] Any of several species of gecko of the Gekkonidae.

None of the southern African species of gecko is poisonous, although some were formerly thought to be so.

1786 G. FORSTER tr. *A. Sparrman's Voy. to Cape of G.H.* II. 333 *Aloven Smidt* .. had caught a dreadfully venomous lizard, called *t'geitje. Ibid.* 334 It is a fortunate circumstance, that the *geitje* is slow in its motions, and not of a very irritable disposition. **1815** A. PLUMPTRE tr. *H. Lichtenstein's Trav. in Sn Afr.* (1930) II. Poisonous lizards abound in old walls and forsaken houses. They are known by the name of geitjes. **1838** J.E. ALEXANDER *Exped. into Int.* II. 268 A small lizard, with blunt toes, .. said to be so poisonous that its bite occasions death within an hour .. inhabits Namaqua land, where it is called Geitjie. **1870** *E. Prov. Herald* 15 Mar., The dreaded 'jieke' (properly gecko) is a most *harmless, useful* lizard. **1877** J. NOBLE *S. Afr.* 80 (Pettman), Scant mercy is extended to the harmless *gaetye*, because of their imaginary venomous character. **1886** G.A. FARINI *Through Kalahari Desert* 301 The chirping *heiki* crawled forth in search of a dainty supper of sleeping flies and beetles. **1910** D. FAIRBRIDGE *That Which Hath Been* (1913) 139 Only the *geitjes*, as the little rock lizards are called at the Cape, ran actively from one hot stone to another. **1913** C. PETTMAN *Africanderisms* 185 *Geitje*, (Hot. *geip*, a lizard; the word has an initial click.) ... A small lizard erroneously credited by the natives with being exceedingly poisonous ... The present form of the name appears to be a corruption of the Hottentot name due to a striving after meaning. *c*1939 S.H. SKAIFE *S. Afr. Nature Notes* 132 The popular name, gecko or *geittjie*, is said to come from a Malay name given to these little lizards in imitation of the clicking cry some of them utter. **1957** L.G. GREEN *Beyond City Lights* 80 A small, toothless and inoffensive lizard known as the *geitjie* is also regarded as a killer. **1965** S. DEDERICK *Tickey* 13 The locusts and the geitjies, the scorpions and the toktokkies, and the singing cicadas hold their banquets on the top of that mountain. **1970** C. KINSLEY *Informant, Koegasbrug (N. Cape)* Geitjie. Gecko.

‖**gek** /xek, xɛk/ *adj.* Also (*attrib.*) **gekke** /ˈxɛkə/. [Afk., fr. Du. *gek* crazy; a fool.] Stupid; crazy; insane.

*c*1838 A.G. BAIN *Jrnls* (1949) 196, I learned een kleine beetjie But left, with wisdom just as full As gekke tanta Mietjie. **1868** W.R. THOMSON *Poems, Essays & Sketches* 152 Booy gradually dropped to the rear, and voting his master 'gek,' he kept up a running conversation in broken English and Dutch. **1913** D. FAIRBRIDGE *Piet of Italy* 116 The master he baing *gek*. He say, 'What for I not go the Club?' **1943** *Weekend News & Sunday Mag.* 20 Mar. 4 'Dorn't be blerry gek!' ses Sofie. **1970** S. MOORE *Informant, Port Elizabeth* Gladys really is gek, she acts so foolishly. **1987** G. VINEY *Col. Houses* 131 Dickie was deformed and Martha cheerfully acknowledged to be a 'bietjie gek'. [*Note*] Kitchen-Dutch for not quite like other people, 'dotty'.

‖**geld** /xelt, xɛlt/ *n. colloq.* Also **cheld**, **gelt**. [Afk. (fr. Du.), 'money, cash'.]

a. Money, cash; occas., gold when used as currency.

*a*1878 [see sense b]. **1882** C. DU VAL *With Show through Sn Afr.* I. 165 They arrive, and they won't give a hand without receiving *geld* — money. **1896** M.A. CAREY-HOBSON *At Home in Tvl* 501 They were not at all anxious to return to the time of 'Bluebacks,' which, without the Englishman's 'geld' they knew they must do, in a year or two at the farthest. **1899** *Mafeking Mail* 21 Nov., No more 'geld' for the arme Boer. The Standard Bank at Capetown have, and will retain, possession of gold to the tune of £150,000, shipped .. for the Transvaal Government. **1908** F.C. SLATER *Sunburnt South* 18 'Never mind that,' I said, 'I want it now, here is the hundred pounds.' So I gave him the *geld* and he gave me the bill and I rode home well pleased with myself. **1910** J. RUNCIE *Idylls by Two Oceans* 50 He had the 'geld' always ready in a big canvas sack, and 'geld' is a fact, and possibly the most convincing of facts. **1911** L. COHEN *Reminisc. of Kimberley* 37 'Now, here you are, your diamond or the gold — which will you have?' ... He simply stretched forth his hand, and said, 'Give me the gelt.' I paid him. **1916** S. BLACK in S. Gray *Three Plays* (1984) 186 Oright, but I want my wash geld! I go wait in the yard. **1966** I. VAUGHAN *These Were my Yesterdays* 19 He is always sending more 'geld' and not caring how hard he has it here sleeping and eating in one small tin shanty .. and very cold in winter ... He has a son Louis and he sends money every month. **1979** J. GRATUS *Jo'burgers* 221 As the gents with the geld drifted off so did their girls, leaving behind the echo of their raucous laughter and the faint smell of cheap cigars and perfume. **1985** H. PRENDINI in *Style* Oct. 39 The numerous .. terms for money .. include bread, .. gelt .. and frogskins. **1994** C.J. DRIVER *In Water-margins* 20 When Silence needs A bit of '*geld*', he cleans my car, then says 'I cleaned your car because it needed me'.

b. *obs.* With qualifying word: **hardegeld** [Du., *harde* attrib. form of *hard* hard], hard cash; **kostgelt** [Du., *kost* food], a ration allowance; **subsidiengeld** [Du., *subsidiën* pl. of *subsidie* subsidy, supplementary payment], a supplementary allowance.

*a*1878 J. MONTGOMERY *Reminisc.* (1981) 159 The country is most parklike and beautiful, but we could procure no food anywhere, not even for **harde geld**. **1924** L. COHEN *Reminisc. of Jhb.* 48 When a certain full-fledged financier heard of the negotiations, he, with his lawyer, drove a spanking Cape cart turn-out to the Dutchman's place, and offered him £100,000 in gold, *haardegelt*, as they say, for the property. **1919** M. GREENLEES tr. *O.F. Mentzel's Life at Cape in Mid-18th C.* 45 Herr Allemann's pay was fourteen gulden a month together with eighty-four stuivers **kostgeld**. Moreover, since he no longer required the **subsidiengeld**, that two gulden monthly ceased to be deducted from his pay.

‖**gelykstelling** /xəˈleɪksteləŋ/ *n. hist.* Formerly also **gelijkstelling**. [Afk. (earlier Du. *gelijkstelling*), fr. *gelykstel* to put on a level with, fr. *gelyk* alike + *stel* to set, put, place.] Equality brought about by the abolition of racial discrimination.

1936 *Cambridge Hist. of Brit. Empire* VIII. 293 Hottentot emancipation was a prime factor in creating that dread of *gelijkstelling* (equality) which modern writers are agreed was a prime cause of the Great Trek itself. [**1939** R.F.A. HOERNLÉ *S. Afr. Native Policy* 161 Afrikaans .. has two words for the single English 'equality,' viz. gelykstelling, which is rejected as implying the abolition of racial barriers; and gelykheid, which is accepted as compatible with the recognition of racial differences.] **1968** W.K. HANCOCK *Smuts* II. 218 The country was in danger because Smuts stood for *gelykstelling*, the equality of black and white. **1975** P.G.J. MEIRING in T. Sundermeier *Church & Nationalism* 64 The missionary efforts in the Hervormde and Gereformeerde Kerke were largely paralysed by the people's fear of 'gelykstelling' (equalisation).

gem *n.* [Special senses of general Eng. *gem* something small and precious.]

1. Freq. in the phrr. ***Gem of the Karoo***, or (formerly) ***Gem of the Desert***. A nick-name given to the town of Graaff-Reinet, in the Karoo.

[**1843** J.C. CHASE *Cape of G.H.* 73 The discouraging appearance of this district .. acts as a foil to the beautiful and extensive town .. , also named Graf Reinet, the capital of the county. The vast contrast .. has caused it to be called, in the homely diction of the inhabitants, 'the pearl upon a dunghill.'] **1854** 'FRANK' in *Graaff-Reinet Herald* 15 Feb., He who quits his dear home, to settle elsewhere, Enjoyment or a fortune to get, Both may readily find, with truth I declare, In the desert's bright gem – Graaff-Reinet. **1887** *Uitenhage Times* in C.G. Henning *Graaff-Reinet* (1975) 107 *The Gem* of the Midland Districts, lying in the warmest of warm corners of the oddly shaped hills ... We are constrained to say that it [*sc.* the Wesleyan Church, Cape Town] is completely eclipsed by the beautiful Church in the 'Gem of the Desert'. **1934** C.P. SWART Supplement to Pettman. 56 *Gem of the Karroo,* The sobriquet of Graaf-Reinet, the prettiest town in the Karroo. *c***1936** *S. & E. Afr. Yr Bk & Guide* 576 Graaf Reinet, 'The Gem of the Karroo', the oldest and largest town in the midlands districts, was founded in 1786 on the Sundays River, which rises among the Sneeuberg Mountains to the North of the town. **1951** H. DAVIES *Great S. Afr. Christians* 61 They were glad to .. share the copious meals at the *Pastorie* in Graaff-Reinet. Casalis had the unfortunate experience, through breaking his spectacles, of mistaking a gnu for a lion a few miles from the 'gem of the Karroo'. **1972** *E. Prov. Herald* 12 Sept. 11 My weekend in the historic and equally hospitable place Graaff-Reinet, the 'Gem of the Karoo'. **1975** C.G. HENNING *Graaff-Reinet* 170 There is a jaunty air of triumph over adversity that says much for the spirit of those who made Graaff-Reinet *The Gem of the Desert* – or, to apply a more recent designation, *The Gem of the Karroo.*

2. Usu. in the phr. ***gem squash***. A small, round variety of pumpkin, *Cucurbita pepo* of the Cucurbitaceae, about the size of an orange, with a hard green shell and soft yellow flesh.

1952 H.M. SLADE *S. Afr. Cookery Bk* 202 Boil gem marrows in salted boiling water .. , then drain, cut into halves, and serve with a dab of butter on top of each. These little marrows are most delicate and delicious ... If liked, .. remove seeds and fill with cooked young green peas. **1971** E. STRYDOM in *Std Encycl. of Sn Afr.* III. 519 *Cucurbita pepo*, Little Gem, a runner type producing spherical green fruits of the size of an orange, which are used unripe. **1972** *Farmer's Weekly* 21 Apr. 56 Gems, well supplied, demand moderate 30 to 50. **1975** *Sunday Times* 7 Sept. 4 Unfortunately the gems are not diamonds, but gem squashes. **1977** *The 1820* Vol.53 No.12, 15 But I'll read on, yes every word About gem squash and butternut too And braai instead of barbecue. **1987** M. MAARTENS *Ring around Moon* 19 He had trouble finding the Afrikaans word for squash and she teased him a little with Hubbard squash and gem squash until he said, 'You think I'm a pumpkin, young lady!' **1988** E. CROMPTON-LOMAX *S. Afr. Menu & Kitchen Dict.* 73 *Squash*, a vegetable of the gourd family such as gem squash, pumpkin and butternut.

gembuck var. GEMSBUCK.

gemeente /xə'mɪəntə/ *n.* [Afk.] The congregation or parish of a Dutch Reformed church.

1949 L.G. GREEN *In Land of Afternoon* 18 The ministers of this Dutch Reformed Church liked the place so much that from that day [*sc.* 1825] to this, only one has been called away. First in this pleasant *gemeente* was the Rev. J.J. Beck. **1955** A. DELIUS *Young Trav.* 103 'The Government has got nothing to do with the churches in this country', said Oom Thys. 'The *gemeente* – the congregation – pays him.' **1965** C. VAN HEYNINGEN *Orange Days* 10 The Boers had large farms and some of the 'gemeente' lived some distance from the dorp and had to be visited by the predikant. **1976** *Sunday Times* 1 Aug. 14 The saga of the Kameeldrif gemeente is yet another frightening sign of the Government's Canute-like stand in the face of rising Black disaffection. **1988** DARBY & MAXWELL in Laband & Haswell *Pietermaritzburg 1838–1988* 169 Expansion of the Dutch Reformed church has been noticeable since the war years ... In more recent years *gemeentes* have been established in Prestbury, Napierville .. and Hayfields.

gemors /xəmɔ(r)s/ *n. slang*. Also **gammors, gemos**. Pl. **-ses**. [Afk.]

a. A mess, muddle, or state of confusion; a disaster.

1970 C. LIVINGSTONE *Informant, Bloemfontein* The children made such a gemors of the house, I spent three days cleaning up after them. **1970** C. AMM *Informant, Bloemfontein* That work is a gemors and it must be done over tidily. **1971** *Informant, Grahamstown* What a gemors it was in P.E. – we had two blowouts on the way and had to buy new tyres on a public holiday. **1973** R. RODWELL in *Farmer's Weekly* 25 Apr. 45 The walls are so tremendously thick, being made of large rough boulders, lime and sand, that the damage was mostly internal and, said Mr. Duckitt, some walls were a real *gemors*. **1980** *Capetonian* Jan. 26 'Jus-like,' I says, 'we got to go haastig down to where die gemors comes out die skool in die basement en get dem blerry teef back!' **1984** *Frontline* Feb. 26 Apartheid in CA [*sc.* Cape Town] is even more of a gemors and a generally lost cause than in Joeys. **1985** on TV1, 28 Mar., You know the gemors we're in, it's HP up to the roof. **1987** *Style* Dec. 124 An outside perspective is the only way to make sense of our national *gemors*. **1990** 'NATANIEL' in *Ibid.* July 64 Pretoria to me is the epitome or concentration of everything that I hate about this country. The whole gemors starts there. **1990** 'A. LE TOIT' in *Ibid.* 81 This female and male role-playing is the basis for all the *gemors* between the sexes. **1991** E. FITZGERALD *Informant, Cape Town* She couldn't remember how many people were coming. She got the time of arrival wrong. What a gemors!

b. An insulting form of address or reference.

1981 *Sunday Times* 8 Mar. (Extra) 1 The Chairman of the Graaff-Reinet Community Council .. has threatened to lay a charge against a shop assistant who called him ''n gemors' (a rubbish), unless she apologises. **1981** *Voice* 29 Apr., A batch of 'gammorses', misguided .. barries, moegoes, dzaus and what have you.

gemsbok /'xemzbɔk, 'xems-/ *n.* Also **gemsboc(k), gemsboke, gemse-bok, gensbok, ghemsbok, hemps-bôk, jems bok**. Pl. unchanged, **-s**, or (rare) **-(k)e** /-ə/. [S. Afr. Du., transf. use of Du. *gems* chamois + *bok* (see BOK).]

1. The large, strikingly-patterned antelope *Oryx gazella* of the Bovidae, with long, straight, very sharp horns that incline slightly backwards; GEMSBUCK; KUKAMA. Also *attrib.* Cf. BASTARD GEMSBOK.

1777 G. FORSTER *Voy. round World* I. 84 The Egyptian antelope .. is here [*sc.* at the Cape] called gems-bock or chamois. **1786** —— tr. *A. Sparrman's Voy. to Cape of G.H.* II. 217 Another kind of gazel at the Cape, is known by the name of *gemse-bok*, or *chamois*. **1790** W. PATERSON *Narr. of Four Journeys* 53 This day we shot at several of a species of Antelope, with long sharp strait horns, called Gems Bock. **1824** W.J. BURCHELL *Trav.* II. 23 A herd of antelopes of the species known among the boors by the misapplied name of *Gemsbok* was observed at a distance. *Ibid.* 99 Here our dogs caught .. a young *gemsbok* (ghemsbok): the latter was not bigger than a domestic goat. **1827** G. THOMPSON *Trav.* I. 254, I observed several gemsboks. This is a beautiful and noble-looking antelope. His long, straight, sharp horns incline a little backward, and .. the animal can use them with formidable effect in self-defence. **1838** J.E. ALEXANDER *Exped. into Int.* I. 278 A troop of gemsboks appeared, the antagonists of lions, with their long straight horns, like that of the fabled unicorn. **1852** [see KUKAMA]. **1887** A.A. ANDERSON *25 Yrs in Waggon* I. 234 Gemsbok .. are pretty animals, rather larger than a zebra, nearly the colour of a donkey, with black marks down the back and along the flanks, whitish legs marked with black band, light face with black down the front. **1896** R. WALLACE *Farming Indust. of Cape Col.* 244 The gemsbok antelope, *Oryx gazella*, belongs almost exclusively to the deserts of South West Africa. **1914** W.C. SCULLY *Lodges in Wilderness* 230 Take .. the term 'gemsbok', as applied to the oryx; what could be more inappropriate? 'Gemsbok' means 'Chamois' – and we have in South Africa an antelope which is a chamois to all intents and purposes, but which is called a 'klipspringer.' **1936** C. BIRKBY *Thirstland Treks* 268 Through the long months of drought the gemsbok had followed their noses north, seeking tsamma melons and springs that had not dried to mud. **1977** K.F.R. BUDACK in A. Traill *Khoisan Ling. Studies 3* 19 The Topnaar, apart from an 'assegai', also used a gemsbok horn for the spearing of fish. **1988** A. HALL-MARTIN et al. *Kaokoveld* 38 Gemsbok behaviour and physiology is well adapted to survival in harsh desert areas. **1991** *Personality* 5 Aug. 27 Half-starved gemsbok, their skin hanging over their ribs, because they've been unable to adapt to feeding in captivity.

2. *comb.* **gemsbok cucumber, -komkommer** /kɔm'kɔmə(r)/ [Afk., *komkommer* cucumber; see quot. 1991], the plant *Acanthosicyos naudinianus* of the Cucurbitacea; its fruit; **gemsbok grass**, either of two species of grass of the Poaceae, *Stipagrostis uniplumis* (subfamily Arundinoideae) or *Eragrostis pallens* (subfamily Chloridoideae); **gemsbok tail grass**, *Stipagrostis hochstetterana*.

*a***1936** E.N. MARAIS *Rd to Waterberg* (1972) 89 The green and yellow prickly **gemsbok cucumber** – singular in its absence from South African fruit markets and a distinct loss to our palates. **1970** P.V. TOBIAS in *Std Encycl. of Sn Afr.* II. 618 Prominent among the water-rich plants are the *tsamma* melon .. , and the gemsbok cucumber. **1991** D.M.C. FOURIE in *Philatelic Services Bulletin*, Gemsbok cucumber .. grows in deep sandy soil and can be eaten raw, but is usually roasted in hot ashes for several hours ... The fruits are relished by many animals and in areas where gemsbok occur, they form an important part of that antelope's diet. **1992** *Getaway* Apr. 41 Other important water-carrying plants are the gemsbok cucumber (*Acanthosicyos naudinianus*), [etc.]. **1970** B. MAGUIRE in *Std Encycl. of Sn Afr.* II. 610 The yellowish oval melons of *Citrullus naudianus* (the so-called wild cucumber or **gemsbok-komkommer**), .. are covered with short, conical protuberances. **1986** *Motorist* 1st Quarter 36 The gemsbok komkommer .. [is a] main source of water for all the animals of the area as, even when it rains, the few millimetres of standing water in the pans usually evaporates within a week. **1973** J. COPE *Alley Cat* 57 It had rained weeks before and there were patches of red-dark **gemsbokgrass** in full seed like blood blots against the ash-grey dust. **1989** J. DU P. BOTHMA *Game Ranch Management* 602 Plant species of the late successional stages ... *Eragrostis pallens* (gemsbok grass). **1988** A. HALL-MARTIN et al. *Kaokoveld* 7 The ephemeral grasses of the plains .. dominate a sparse wispy grassland ... A few perennials like the **gemsbok tail grass** (*Stipagrostis hochstetterana*) .. also occur.

gemsbuck /'xemzbʌk/ *n.* Also **gembuck**. Pl. unchanged, or **-s**. [Part. tr. S. Afr. Du. *gemsbok*.] The GEMSBOK (sense 1), *Oryx gazella*. Also *attrib.*

1815 J. MACKRILL Diary. 91 Gems Buck is the Pasan of Buffon the Egyptian Antelope of Pinnant and the Capra Oryx of the Systema Naturae. **1856** *Cape of G.H. Almanac & Annual Register* 73 Koodoo, Gems Buck, Gnoo, Eland, Buffalo and other horns. **1871** J. MACKENZIE *Ten Yrs* (1971) 260 Mr. Price killed two giraffes, and I an oryx or gemsbuck, .. said to be the fleetest of the antelopes. **1883** [see KUKAMA]. **1898** G. NICHOLSON *50 Yrs* 108 The gemsbuck is about the size and weight of a large donkey ... The straight horns are often fifty-two inches or more long, and, sharp as a rapier, are splendid trophies. **1902** D. HUTCHEON

Rinderpest 3 The following antelopes are reported to have suffered most from Rinderpest. In the Northern Protectorate the eland, buffalo, gemsbuck, and rietbuck. **1961** L.E. VAN ONSELEN *Trekboer* 83 Here for many years, gemsbuck, springbok and wild ostriches roamed over these flats in great numbers. **1988** *S. Afr. Panorama* May 15 (*caption*) Gemsbuck on an extensive game and hunting ranch in the Soutpansberg territory.

Genequois var. GONAQUA.

general affair *n. phr. Hist.* In terms of the old Republic of South Africa Constitution Act of 1983: a parliamentary or administrative matter considered to affect the whole population of South Africa; usu. in *pl.* Also *attrib.*, and *transf.* Cf. OWN AFFAIR.

In terms of this Act, 'general affairs' (e.g. defence and foreign affairs matters) had to be debated by all three houses of the TRICAMERAL parliament, and administered by a single ministry.

1983 D.W. WATTERSON in *Hansard* 17 May 7225 There should be affairs that are general affairs right from the word go in the constitution, for example foreign affairs, defence, strategic planning, justice, police, prisons, industrial development and so forth. **1983** *Act 110* in *Govt Gaz.* Vol.219 No.8914, 12 Matters which are not own affairs of a population group .. are general affairs. **1984** *Survey of Race Rel. 1983* (S.A.I.R.R.) 71 With regard to 'general affairs' .. he [*sc.* the State President] acts in consultation with his cabinet, over which he presides. **1986** *Race Rel. Survey 1985* (S.A.I.R.R.) 68 The major general affairs portfolios handled by the provinces during 1985 were roads and traffic, and horse racing. **1987** [see S. Afr. Digest quot. at OWN AFFAIR sense 1]. **1987** *E. Prov. Herald* 22 Aug. 4 Whatever tourists do abroad will no longer be an own affair but a general affair. **1987** *Weekly Mail* 23 Aug. 10 The racially separate local authorities will each control their 'own affairs', while the multi-racial RSCs will exercise joint control of 'general affairs'. **1989** *Grocott's Mail* 27 Jan. 5 Strategies to .. improve skills training in technical fields ... Options .. : The transfer of tertiary institutions such as technikons and universities to the department of national education, whereby they would become a 'general affair'. **1990** *Weekend Post* 10 Mar. 1 The first crack in the wall of own and general affairs could come this session with a commitment in principle to scrap 'own' and 'general' health and have one overall department. **1993** W. HARTLEY in *Ibid.* 12 June 8 F W de Klerk announced that many own affairs functions, administered racially, would become general affairs.

general dealer *n. phr.* Also with initial capitals. [Now obs. in general Eng.]

1.a. A merchant, often the owner of a rural, village, or township store, who carries a varied stock to meet the general needs of a community; *negotie winkeler*, see NEGOTIE sense 3. **b.** Such a store; *negotie winkel*, see NEGOTIE sense 3; WINKEL sense a. In both senses also called ALGEMENE HANDELAAR. Also *attrib.* See also *Indian shop* (INDIAN *adj.* sense 2).

1832 *Graham's Town Jrnl* 6 Apr. 58 The Storekeeper is in the most extensive meaning of the term a general dealer; most of them, however, conduct their multifarious occupations in a business-like and creditable manner. **1843** *Cape of G.H. Almanac & Annual Register*, Stiglingh, Andries, general dealer, 40 roze-street ... Clark, John, general dealer, 123 long-street ... Clarence, Ralph, general dealer 60, (late 8) waterkant. **1870** *George Advertiser* 14 Apr. 4, J.C. Truter, General Dealer Meade Street, George Town. Has always on hand, a well assorted stock of Staple and Fancy Goods. **1887** *Act 38* in *Stat. of Cape of G.H.* (1906) 2506 'General dealer' means any person who carries on the trade or business of selling, or offering or exposing for sale, barter or exchange any goods, wares or merchandise, not being the growth, produce, or manufacture of South Africa. **1913** C. PETTMAN *Africanderisms* 481 This word [*sc.* store] is in general use throughout South Africa, and is applied to the small shop of the general dealer as well as to the more pretentious buildings of the large wholesale firms. **1932** *Grocott's Daily Mail* 12 Jan. 2 Rudolf van der Meulen Mentz, general dealer, of Committees district. **1944** C.R. PRANCE *Under Blue Roof* 135 The General Dealer, either in the dorp or on the outlying farm, sold tin candle-moulds, six in a block. **1955** *Report of Commission for Socio-Economic Dev. of Bantu Areas* (UG61–1955) 90 The type of business undertaken by traders in the Bantu Areas is that of a typical general dealer's store in a rural area, which stocks something of everything. **1966** L.G. BERGER *Where's Madam* 82 As I passed the usual tumbledown general dealer's store, I glimpsed a sign reading, 'Self-helping Funeral Parlour', with the window piled with a tumble of coffins. **1973** Y. BURGESS *Life to Live* 38 Oom Fred, whose shop was typical of General Dealers in that part of the world carried a wide range of goods: guns and grain, floral prints for Whites and tribal prints for the 'kaffirs', blankets and brooches, saucepans and saws, gadgets and groceries. **1974** H.J.J. REYNDERS in *Std Encycl. of Sn Afr.* X. 546 The general dealer's store, offering various commodities (clothing, groceries, hardware and many more) and found particularly in the rural districts and in the suburbs of cities. **1982** *Reader's Digest Family Guide to Law* 498 Mr Kara carried on a tearoom business in one room and a general dealer's business in an adjoining room ... There were two doors leading directly between the tearoom and the general dealer shop. **1992** *Sunday Times* 14 June (Business Times) 3 GST was difficult to enforce among general dealers in rural areas. **1994** *House & Leisure* Jan. 20 In the small-town tradition of general dealers, owners Tania and Marty Reddering sell fashion, decor and lifestyle accessories.

2. Special collocation: **general dealer's licence** *hist.*, a licence required by a merchant operating a general dealer's store.

1887 *Act 38* in *Stat. of Cape of G.H.* (1906) 2506 Sale of tonic bitters containing spirits under a general dealer's or importer's licence forbidden. **1925** *E. Prov. Herald* 22 July 7 It was suggested that the minimum for the General Dealer's licence should be reduced but objection to this was raised by the Cape and Free State. **1957** D. JACOBSON *Price of Diamonds* 76 He knew perfectly well who was going around spreading such stories about a man who had never had his general dealer's licence revoked for any cause whatsoever. **1984** *Farmer's Weekly* 13 Jan. 122 (*advt*) Café/Restaurant. Takeaway with General Dealers Licence for sale. **1987** *Frontline* Mar. 12 Other licence problems emerge – operating a restaurant on a general dealer's licence.

Hence **general dealership** *n. phr.*, the business (or establishment) of a trader.

1993 *Weekend Post* 14 Aug. (Leisure) 4 The general dealership, one of just two shops in the village, has been run by the same family for most of that time.

gensbok var. GEMSBOK.

gentoo /ˈdʒentuː, dʒɪn-/ *n. Derog. slang.* Also **djentoe, jentoe, jintoe, jintoo**, and with initial capital. [Named for the *Gentoo*, a ship which arrived at Cape Town in the mid-19th century with a group of women passengers who became prostitutes; the countries of origin of the women and the ship, and the circumstances of their arrival at the Cape, are obscure and in dispute (see quots).] Not in polite use. In Cape Town: a prostitute; a woman of loose morals. Also *attrib.*

1934 G.G. MUNNIK *Mem. of Senator* 20 The British authorities .. engaged about forty-six young girls [as servants] .. and sent them out to the Cape in an East Indiaman named the *Gentoo*. On arrival .. these girls were hired .. in the fashionable suburbs ... They .. drifted into Cape Town, and there practised the oldest profession in the world ... Even now girls who practise the same profession are still known in Cape Town amongst the Malays and coloured people as 'Gentoos', and the places where they live are called Gentoo houses. **1946** C.P. WITTSTOCK in E. Partridge *Dict. of Underworld* (1950) 366 Jintoe, probably from a French ship carrying women, which put in at the Cape many years ago. **1946** [see LIGHTY sense 1]. **1952** *Drum* Nov. 10 The word 'gentoo' is not one that you will hear used in polite company ... In 1846 an American ship called the '*Gentoo*' was wrecked near Struys Bay. Some of the female survivors trekked to Cape Town and later .. followed the world's oldest profession ... It is still the practice to call ladies of easy virtue 'Gentoos' after that ill-fated ship's women-folk. **1958** L.G. GREEN *S. Afr. Beachcomber* 80 Among the survivors were a number of young servant girls who .. soon drifted out of respectable employment ... They set up places which became known as 'Gentoo houses', with Malay orchestras to provide dance music. To this day a loose girl is called a 'Gentoo' by the Cape Malays. **1974** J. MATTHEWS in S. Gray *On Edge of World* 102 'Hey Maria. You old jentoe!' ... Maria, not put out by the slur cast on her character, waved back gaily. **1977** D. MULLER *Whitey* 83 A pair of gentoos sat playing a waiting game .., displaying their nylon-clad thighs and frilly slips. One .. smiled at him as he passed by. **1983** *Informant, Cape Town* That one on the left of the photo – pretty but she's a bit of a jintoe. **1984** *Cape Times* 18 Jan. 23 A man who called a Brooklyn woman a 'f ... jintoo' (whore) was yesterday fined R250 (or 100 days). **1988** M. TURNER *Shipwrecks & Salvage* 174 *Gentoo*, American ship ... Wrecked on Northumberland Point, Struis Bay .. on 29 April 1846 while on a voyage from Calcutta to Boston with a cargo of indigo, shellac, saltpetre and hides ... Among the survivors were a number of servant girls who had been engaged by wealthy Cape Town citizens. They soon drifted into prostitution, and to this day prostitutes are called 'gentoos' by the Cape Malays. [**1992** *Sn Afr.-Irish Studies* 2 271 In November 1850 the association for the promotion of female emigration sent 46 single Irish women to the Cape on the *Gentoo*. Their arrival .. was followed by a great storm of moral indignation when it was discovered that .. the girls had been allowed to mix freely with the men on board and 'gross improprieties' had taken place.]

geometric tortoise *n. phr.* [Named for the geometric patterns on its shell.] The land tortoise *Psammobates geometricus* of the Testudinidae, an endangered species found only in the Western Cape; formerly, any of several related species; STERRETJIE sense 3; SUURPOOTJIE. Also *attrib.*

[**1880** *Cassell's Nat. Hist.* IV. 252 The Ethiopian region of natural history has the greatest number of species of Tortoises, .. the Leopard Tortoise .. and the little Geometric Tortoise are familiar examples.] **1929** W. ROSE *Veld & Vlei* 189 A very striking appearance is presented by the members of .. the Geometric Group, in which the dorsal shields are raised into conical eminences, from the summits of which radiate brilliant streaks of black and yellow ... Geometric Tortoises may be considered typical of the more arid areas of the Western Cape Province, Namaqualand, Bechuanaland and South West Africa. **1977** [see SUURPOOTJIE]. **1985** *S. Afr. Panorama* Mar. 49 The geometric tortoise attains a length of 120–150mm and has an attractive black and yellow striped shell. No two tortoises possess the same stripe pattern. **1987** T.F.J. VAN RENSBURG *Intro. to Fynbos* 49 The following species are listed as endangered species: Geometric tortoise, [etc.]. **1989** E. BAARD in *Afr. Wildlife* Vol.43 No.4, 83 Another of the few surviving geometric tortoise populations in the south-west Cape is conserved. **1989** [see STERRETJIE sense 3]. **1992** T. VAN RENSBURG in *S. Afr. Panorama* Mar.-Apr. 14 The grysbuck, the geometric tortoise, the Cape sugar-bird and protea seed-eater are .. endemic to the fynbos biome.

George lily *n. phr.* [Named after *George*, a town in the Western Cape province, which was in turn named for George III of England.] The KNYSNA LILY (sense b), *Cyrtanthus purpureus*.

1913 C. PETTMAN *Africanderisms* 186 *George lily*, .. Chiefly found near the town of George on the Post Berg. **1917** R. MARLOTH *Common Names* 31 *George lily, Vallota purpurea*. Fairly frequent on the mountains from George to Humansdorp, locally called Berglelie, but more widely known as Knysna lily. **1932** [see

KNYSNA LILY sense b]. **1946** K.C. STANFORD in *Farmer's Weekly* 30 Oct. 49 George Lily .. is becoming scarce. An enterprising grower in that district could do well with it. **1966** C.A. SMITH *Common Names* 226 *George lily*, .. Bulbs have .. proved toxic to calves, rabbits and sheep. **1973** BEETON & DORNER in *Eng. Usage in Sn Afr.* Vol.4 No.2, 18 *George lily*, .. orig. found in the kloof near George in 1774 .. is now a popular garden flower. **1982** A. MORIARTY *Outeniqua Tsitsikamma* 46 George Lily, Knysna Lily .. can still be seen in the indigenous forests and along mountain streams in the Outeniqua and Tsitsikamma mountains and in the perennially moist kloofs off the Langkloof. **1985** K. PIENAAR *Grow S. Afr. Plants* 41 George lily ... A bulb with beautiful trumpet-shaped, scarlet flowers in spring. **1989** [see FIRE LILY].

geranium /dʒəˈreɪnɪəm/ *n.* [Transf. use of general Eng. *Geranium* a genus of herbaceous plants or undershrubs growing wild in temperate regions (in which sense the word is also used in S. Afr. Eng.).] A name commonly given to the PELARGONIUM.

Used also in *Brit. Eng.* in this sense.

[**1760** W. SHENSTONE *Works & Lett.* III. 315 An antique vase is introduced with a flower and two or three leaves of the scarlet Geranium.] **1790** W. PATERSON *Narr. of Four Journeys* 7 The mountains afforded me many beautiful plants, particularly Xheranthimums, Geraniums, Gladioluses, and many others quite new to me. **1809** 'G. VALENTIA' *Voy. & Trav.* I. 29 I .. could scarcely at first refrain from stopping to observe more closely many .. Geraniums, and other plants which I had with care cultivated in England, growing neglected in such immense profusion. *a*1827 D. CARMICHAEL in W.J. Hooker *Botanical Misc.* (1831) II. 19 The only individuals of them that are natives of the country, are the *Protea*, the *Geranium*, (or rather *Pelargonium*), [etc.]. **1924** D. FAIRBRIDGE *Gardens of S. Afr.* 199 January ... Cuttings may be put in of Coleus and Geraniums, letting the latter dry off for a few hours before planting in a mixture of sand and leaf-mould. **1976** U. VAN DER SPUY *Wild Flowers of S. Afr. for Garden* 105 Most gardeners the world over refer to both geraniums and pelargoniums as 'geraniums', a term which should be applied to very few of the plants commonly called by this name. Most of the plants called 'geraniums' .. are, in fact, pelargoniums. **1989** *Gardening Questions Answered* (Reader's Digest Assoc.) 337 *Geranium*, Pelargonium (Geranium). Large genus of easy-to-grow, bushy or trailing plants.

‖**Gereformeerde** /xəˌrefɔ(r)ˈmɪə(r)də/ *adj.* [Afk., 'reformed'.] Of or pertaining to the *Gereformeerde Kerk in Suid-Afrika* (Reformed Church in South Africa), one of the family of Dutch Reformed churches. See also DOPPER *n.*[1]

See note at DUTCH REFORMED. Hillegas is inaccurate in his labelling of the Doppers as 'Hervormde'.

1900 H.C. HILLEGAS *Oom Paul's People* 100 The Hervormde Dopper branch of the Dutch Reformed Church is the result of a disagreement in 1883 with the Gereformeerde branch on the singing of hymns during religious service. *c*1949 [see DOPPER *n.*[1] sense a]. **1975** P.G.J. MEIRING in T. Sundermeier *Church & Nationalism* 65 When the Gereformeerde Paul Kruger was taking the oath for the last time as president of the Z.A.R., he deemed it fit to call upon the Transvaal churches to recognise a higher loyalty than their loyalties to either state or people.

German *adj.* In the Special collocations ***German print***, or (occas.) ***German chintz*** [so called because introduced by German immigrants; see Bowie quot. 1994], a cheap cotton dress-material with white floral or geometrical designs, usu. on a dark blue or chocolate-brown background; *African print*, see AFRICAN *adj.*[1] sense 2 b; SIS *n.*[1] sense 2. Also *attrib.* See also VOERCHITZ.

1956 J. CHATTERTON *Return of Drums* 27 He paused and looked at the little girl dressed in the German print frock. **1965** E. MPHAHLELE *Down Second Ave* 60 You have to work, work, work, and stinge yourself rice and stew, and wear rough German print. *a*1968 D.C. THEMBA in E. Patel *World of Can Themba* (1985) 90 The dress she wore brought out all the girlishness of her, hidden so long beneath German print. **1968** K. MCMAGH *Dinner of Herbs* 115 There were bolts of german print, the sprigged navy blue cotton stuff from which the dresses and aprons of the house servants were made. **1970** [see MAKOTI sense 1]. **1978** A.P. BRINK *Rumours of Rain* 245 The place was .. crammed to capacity ... Rolls of German chintz, bags of dried beans, samp, rolled tobacco, bicycles, transistor radios, coffee. **1979** *Bona* June 147 Success in selling ethnic German-print clothes not only in the townships, but also in several Johannesburg shops. Their best sellers are simple dramatic caftans, wrap-over skirts. **1980** E. JOUBERT *Poppie Nongena* 108 She was a big woman, stouter and taller than Poppie, dressed in a long dress and pinafore of German print. **1994** B. BOWIE in *Weekend Post* 9 Apr. (Leisure) 3 Women wearing *blaudruck* (blue-printed) cotton cloth came to East London .. in 1858. They were hard-working German peasants who started a fashion which has remained to this day among the Xhosa people of the region. The long-lasting cotton was known as German print or 'sis'. It has a white design on a background of indigo (navy blue), chocolate-brown or red ... It is thought that the cloth originated in 19th-century Bohemia-Moravia, to be sold in Germany. **1994** *Weekly Mail & Guardian* 13 May 8 To mark 'Independence Day' .. township revellers donned ethnic costume: old fashioned Sotho *seseshwe*, of German print cloth.

‖**gerook** /xəˈrʊək/ *ppl adj. Slang.* Also **gerooked**. [Afk., smoked, cured.] Intoxicated (by drugs or alcohol); 'high', 'stoned'. See also BLUE *adj.* sense 2.

1970 K.M. BRAND *Informant, East London* Gerook. Drunk, intoxicated, e.g. He's nicely gerook after all the Brandy. **1974** *Eng. Usage in Sn Afr.* Vol.5 No.1, 11 A *roker* after a good *fix* becomes *happy*, he's *flying high*, all dillied up — simply *gerook*. **1977** *Sunday Times* 1 May 6 It is a society with a language of its own. You 'dop' too much, become 'gerooked' and have 'babelaas'. **1977** D. MULLER *Whitey* 62 If the police haven't got him he'll be so *gerook* by this time that he probably won't even recognise you. [**1980** D. COHEN in *Cape Times* 12 Sept. 4 The gang smoked dagga and tobacco combined, often taken together with liquor. 'When you are "gerook en gedronk" you do not really know what you are doing.'] **1988** 'J. KERKORREL' in *Weekly Mail* 9 Dec. 32 We get a lot of flak from most of the Afrikaans press. They say we're unpractised, *dik gerook* (stoned) and that the lyrics are naive.

gesang /xəˈsaŋ/ *n.* Also formerly **gezang**. Pl. **-e** /-ə/, formerly **-en**. [Afk. (earlier Du. *gezang*), hymn.] In the Dutch Reformed churches:
1. *obs.* A hymn. Freq. in *pl.*

1810 G. BARRINGTON *Acct of Voy.* 183 Excepting the Bible and William Sluiter's Gesangen, or songs out of the Bible done into verse by the Sternhold and Hopkins [*sic*] of Holland, a book of any kind is very seldom to be seen in any of their houses. **1868** W.R. THOMSON *Poems, Essays & Sketches* 170 He meets his lady-love at the '*Katechisatie*;' and week after week he and she keep up a silent telegraphic communication with their eyes, instead of attending to their *vrageboekje*, and their *psalmen* and *gezangen*. **1913** A.B. MARCHAND *Dirk, S. African* 34 (Swart), I'll never get over it — to step up the aisle while the minister is giving out the gesang or reading the intimations. **1934** C.P. SWART Supplement to Pettman. 56 Gesang, .. Some of the songs in the hymn-book of the Dutch Reformed Church are so termed.

‖**2.** *comb.* **gesang boek** /- bukə/, pl. **-boeke** /- bukə/, formerly **-boeken**, [Afk., *boek* book], a hymn book.

1896 M.A. CAREY-HOBSON *At Home in Tvl* 358 His wares comprised all the various articles they were likely to require between the times of visiting the town, such as calicoes, prints, dress goods and moleskins; .. crockery ware, Gesang-boeken, looking-glasses and clasp-knives. **1968** K. MCMAGH *Dinner of Herbs* 14 It had been the custom for elderly folk to have a couple of slaves precede them to church .. whilst another would bear the family's tooled leather 'gesang boeke' and Bibles, with their heavy brass clasps.

gesondheid /xəˈsɔnt(h)eɪt/ *int. colloq.* Formerly also **gezondheid, santheit**. [Afk., earlier S. Afr. Du. *gezondheid* (int.), fr. Du. *gezondheid* (n.), a toast.] 'To your health', 'here's to you'. So as *n.*, an utterance of 'gesondheid'.

1875 'M.' in *Cape Monthly Mag.* XI. July 30 The rising sun was greeted by a *gezondheid* from several lips as we quaffed a morning *soupie*. **1896** H.A. BRYDEN *Tales of S. Afr.* 183 Well, here's success to the Tapinyani concession! Santeit! and another thousand a year to us all! **1900** H. BLORE *Imp. Light Horseman* 194 *Gezondheid*, and all the pretty girls in their bloom to you. **1908** [see CAPE BRANDY]. **1937** C.R. PRANCE *Tante Rebella's Saga* 50 The doctor only nodded saying 'Cheerio' and kept on counting pills, till Gideon said 'Gesondheid', and drank off his tot. **1961** T. MATSHIKIZA *Choc. for my Wife* 60 She said, 'Heil,' each time she raised her glass then she sipped slowly ... 'Heil, Gesondheid, Mayibuye.' **1968** A. FULTON *Dark Side of Mercy* 13 'Gesondheid.' He grinned at Michael and downed the drink in a single gulp. **1971** L.G. GREEN *Taste of S.-Easter* 22 He had heard the same toasts .. year after year. 'Here's how!' 'Hope you choke!' 'Over the river!' 'Looking at you!' 'Gesondheid!' *c*1976 H. FLATHER *Thaba Rau* 179 She handed him his glass and raised her own: '*Gesondheid!*', she said and watched him with amusement over the rim of her glass.

gesuip /xəˈsœɪp, xəˈseɪp/ *adj. slang.* [Afk., past pple of *suip* (see SUIP).] Drunk. See also SUIP.

[**1980** *Cape Times* 12 Sept. 4 Sometimes .. you drink a lot 'en jy is dik gesuip'.] **1984** D. PINNOCK *Brotherhoods* 26 There were only a few who smoked pot and really got *gesuip* [drunk], but never the top dogs ... They always tried to do things that wouldn't bring a scratch to their good family name. **1984** *E. Prov. Herald* 10 May 17 It was a relief to go to work. There were no kids fighting; no ouma screaming at them and the old man getting *gesuip*.

‖**gevaar** /xəˈfɑː(r)/ *n.* [Afk.; derived from SWART GEVAAR.] A threat, a danger. Also *attrib.* See also ROOI GEVAAR, ROOMSE GEVAAR, SWART GEVAAR.

1973 *E. Prov. Herald* 27 Aug. 11 The greatest threat is the Swarthaak thorn bush, commonly known as the Swarthaak gevaar. The Swarthaak is a sort of galloping consumption of the veld. **1975** *Sunday Times* 23 Nov. (Mag. Sect.) 17 (*letter*) I should like to say: We're not a gevaar. **1981** [see PROG]. **1984** *Rand Daily Mail* 19 Oct. (Funfinder) 1 Evita-gevaar for the capital. Well wrapped up against the Total Onslaught, Evita Bezuidenhout will descend upon Pretoria .. for the first of a week's farewell performances of Pieter-Dirk Uys's 'Total Onslaught 1984 — Yes-No-Orwell-Fine'. **1986** J. CRONIN in *Frontline* Mar. 40 What political outlook underwrites the advocacy of a National Convention Alliance and the evocation of a 'majority gevaar'? **1987** *Daily Dispatch* 6 May 5 After hitting out at alleged National Party .. 'gevaar' politics, Mr Edlmann .. said: 'Instead of sowing fear, let us start spreading trust, respect for one another and goodwill'.

‖**gevalt** /gəˈvalt, xəˈvalt/ *n. colloq.* Also **gevolt, gewalt, gewolt**. [Yiddish, out-cry, protest. The -*w*- spelling and the pronunciation /xəˈvalt/ are a result of Afk. influence.] A row, noisy quarrel, rumpus.

*a*1931 S. BLACK in S. Gray *Three Plays* (1984) 160 Rebecca: Don't talk like that, Abie. It's so horrible vulgar, them Jewish expressions. Abraham: Vell, don't make a gewalt about it. **1949** H.C. BOSMAN *Cold Stone Jug* (1969) 35 'Wait till I finish, and I'll run with you, ' he says, 'What's the gevolt?' **1959** [see HELSE *adj.*]. **1971** B. SACHS *Herman Charles Bosman* 49 It wasn't a bust-up; it wasn't a rumpus; and it wasn't a gevalt — it was an altercation. **1978** S. ROBERTS in *New Classic* No.5, 20 He and his mates used to be wild ous when we were all at the tech. It was one gewolt after the other. **1983** J. ALLAN in *Sunday Times* 21 Jan., There was only a gevalt .. the night Tannie M— found E— in Miriam's kia.

gevlekte see quot. 1976 at VLEK.

gevolt, -walt, -wolt varr. GEVALT.

geyser *n.* [This sense is now obs. in general Eng.] A hot water storage tank, with an electric heating element.
 1993 on *Radio South Africa* 6 Mar. (Help Yourself), If you are the kind of person who has a bath or shower every day, the geyser will come into use. 1993 N. MUIRHEAD *Informant, Cape Town* Geyser. Hot Water Unit. 1994 B. FINDLAY in *House & Leisure* Feb. 84 The geyser burst and .. the resulting water damage revealed that the 'wall' dividing the two rooms was really just thick cardboard.

gezang var. GESANG.

gezat var. GAZAAT.

gezondheid var. GESONDHEID.

GG *adj.* and *n.* Also G.G. [Formerly the first two letters on the vehicle registration plate of all government vehicles; said to represent the initial letters of *Government Garage*.]
A. *adj.* Of or pertaining to the government, esp. the National Party government (1948–94).
 1956 *New Age* 5 July 5 The people of Albertynsville have been given a flat ultimatum: those working in Johannesburg must move to site and service plots; and the others must 'go back to where they were born' ... Official investigators — the 'G.G. cars,' the people call them, are daily at work in the camp. c1970 C. DESMOND *Discarded People* 222 One man asked and was given permission to leave his belongings in his old house until he had re-built elsewhere. But G.G. workers arrived and bulldozed his house. 1971 *Cape Times* 3 July 10 A level crossing in the Victoria Dock yesterday produced one of its periodical botsings between train and car, and the affair was a strictly inter-departmental one ... A shunting train had collected a GG car and chewed the after end slightly. 1972 *Sunday Times* 5 Nov. 16 If there is nothing wrong in Ministers using these Government cars on private business, why was somebody or other apparently ashamed to see Ministers in GG cars? 1974 J. McCLURE *Gooseberry Fool* (1976) 78 'GG spy!' she hissed ... Zondi .. poked her hard in the voicebox with one finger ... He grabbed her arms and dragged her into her tent ... 'You say GG one more time and I'll kill you, my sister.' 1983 *Sunday Times* 12 June 14 The GG trucks, the rows of latrines, the crude temporary huts .. are central features of South Africa under apartheid. 1985 PLATZKY & WALKER *Surplus People* p.xxx, The people had been told to leave the farm before the end of the year, but one month before the deadline they were taken by surprise and moved by GG trucks. *Ibid.* 385 The government is 'motivating people to move voluntarily'. But if, as the Bakwena of Mogopa were told, they refuse to move voluntarily, they will be moved by GG trucks. 1989 J. HOBBS *Thoughts in Makeshift Mortuary* 175, I remember .. mobs of shouting men with sticks marching up Gold Street, and the GG cars that went up and down.
B. *n.* Pl. usu. unchanged, occas. -s. Usu. *pl.*: Government officials; the government.
 1969 *Rand Daily Mail* in C. Desmond *Discarded People* (c1970) 250 'We were told to build, but only if we bought bricks from them.' 'Them' is of course 'GG,' the Government, the authorities, or their nominees. c1970 C. DESMOND *Discarded People* 18 In every settlement I visited, every person I spoke to .. said that they had not wanted to move. But 'We had no choice.' 'There was nothing we could do.' They were told by the 'G.G.' (Government officials) that they had to move. 1981 *Sunday Times* 12 July 20 People did not want to move, 'but when the "GG" (as government officials are referred to) say you must move, then you must move.' 1984 *Frontline* Mar. 30 When we asked how and why they had come, the answers were all the same. 'The GGs made us come.' Government vehicles long ago changed their GG — Government Garage — registration to 'R', which is usually assumed to stand for 'Regering' but officially is for Republiek/Republic. But the old name is dying hard. 'GG' is still the all-purpose term of reference to any branch of officialdom. 1989 J. LELYVELD in *Reader's Digest Illust. Hist.* 432 GG is as predictable as a natural calamity. GG scoops you up when you least expect it and drops you somewhere you have never been, leaving it to you to patch together the torn and ragged pattern of a life.

gha var. GA.

‖**ghaap** /gɑːp/ *n.* Also ghab, ghap, g(u)aap, ngaap. [Nama *ghoub, gnaap, ngaap*.] Any of several edible plants of the carrion flower family (Asclepiadaceae) esp. *Trichocaulon* spp., *Stapelia* spp., and *Pectinaria* spp.
 [1819 *Rees Cycl.* XXXIII. (s.v. *Stapelia pilifera*), The Hottentots are said to eat it, knowing it by the name of *Guaap*. 1822 W.J. BURCHELL *Trav.* I. 243 A short fleshy plant, well known to the Hottentots by the name of Guaap .. It has an insipid, yet cool and watery, taste, and is much used by them for the purpose of quenching thirst. 1856 L. PAPPE in *Cape of G.H. Almanac & Annual Register* 345 *Stapelia pilifera* Lin. (Asclepiadae), The stem of this plant which grows in the dreary wastes of the Karoo, is fleshy and of the size and form of a cucumber ... The natives .. call it *Guaap*.] 1878 *Trans. of S. Afr. Phil. Soc.* I. i. 24 (Pettman), Here we find stunted Mesembryanthemums, numerous kinds of Euphorbias, the peculiar *Ghap* (Stapelia) in at least a half dozen varieties. 1913 C. PETTMAN *Africanderisms* 186 Ghab, .. *Stapelia pilifera* (as well as others of these Carrion-flowers as they are called), is known by this name in the Karoo. 1924 L.H. BRINKMAN *Glory of Backveld* 53 The gaap belongs to the cactus family, and grows above the ground; it has the peculiarity of being extremely bitter when first put into one's mouth, but the saliva, acting on its juice, turns it into such saccharine sweetness that it becomes almost nauseating. [1932 WATT & BREYER-BRANDWIJK *Medicinal & Poisonous Plants* 151 Natives formerly ate the stem of *Stapelia pilifera* L., Nama *guaap*, as a thirst quencher. The Namas still use it for this purpose.] 1962 *Ibid.* 138 The Trichocaulons, known generically to the Hottentots as *ngaap* (the spiny-stemmed species) are mostly edible in the raw state. 1970 E. SCHEARKOGEL *Informant, Hennenman* (OFS) Ghaap .. has thorns and a soury taste, rather salty. 1988 J. MULLER in Smuts & Alberts *Forgotten Highway* 184 *Karona* is a *ghaap* (ghape) ... When you're thirsty you can only eat one at a time. It's slightly bitter, but after you've eaten it, your mouth is as sweet as honey! And then another *ghaap* is *Kopseer* ... If its crown is white, then you must know, you should leave it, it's got a headache.

ghammat var. GAMMAT.

ghanna var. GANNA.

ghap var. GHAAP.

gharum masala var. GARAM MASALA.

ghattis var. GATTES.

ghaukum var. GOCUM.

ghawi var. GAWIE.

gheel dikop var. GEELDIKKOP.

ghemsbok var. GEMSBOK.

ghocum var. GOCUM.

ghoef var. GOEF *v.*

ghoema var. GHOMMA.

ghoen /gʊn/ *n.* Also ghoon, goen. [Afk., prob. ad. Malay *gundu* marble.] In the language of children: **a.** A taw, the larger and more highly prized marble with which one shoots in a game of marbles. Cf. IRONIE. See also ARLIE. **b.** The stone which one throws in hopscotch. **c.** The stone or marble used in the game of GIFFIE.
 1913 C. PETTMAN *Africanderisms* 187 Ghoen, .. The stone with which hop-scotch is played; the marble with which a boy shoots. 1958 R.E. LIGHTON *Out of Strong* 78 The younger boys rode donkeys, played a quoit-like game with wagon washers, or pitched metal balls they called ghoens. 1958 I. VAUGHAN *Diary* 43 We also play a lot of skipping and rounders and hop scotch ... Many times we take off shoes and play with bare feet, which is easy for picking up the goen with your toes. 1970 F.G. BUTLER *Informant, Grahamstown* Goen. A large marble, frequently a large steel ball bearing used for rolling yakkies out of court; or, in certain other games, a stone, or flat piece of metal, used for throwing at counters. 1973 *Daily Dispatch* 6 Nov. 7 (advt) Marbles for Africa 49c per bag (100 + 1 Goen). 1975 D. WOODS in *Cape Times* 7 Feb. 12 The illustrations .. are most artistic. One showing a little girl hopping on to a square after her 'ghoen' has her hair tossing realistically. 1977 E. *Prov. Herald* 10 Feb. 1 'Five goes' gives the shooter five throws, each with a small marble ... A hit wins the goen or a substitute number of small marbles. 1982 T. BARON in *Frontline* Nov. 45 All you needed was a flat stone for a ghoon and three holes in the ground. You threw your ghoon, first into the middle hole, then into the far hole and back again. Now you were *giffie* and you threw your ghoon .. at your opponent's ghoon. 1988 [see ARLIE]. 1991 V. WARREN *Informant, Alberton* Goon & allies. A large marble and small marbles ... My goon hit six of his allies so I beat him.

ghoera var. GORAH.

gho-gho var. GOGGA.

ghôghôm, ghokum varr. GOCUM.

ghomma, goema /ˈgɔmə, ˈgʊ- ˈgʊ-, ˈgu-/ *n.* *Music.* Also **ghoema, g(h)ooma, gomma, guma**, and with initial capital. [Afk. *ghomma, ghoema* prob. fr. a dial. Malay word vel. to *gong gong* (see quot. 1953); cf. Eng. *gum-gum* iron bowl used as a drum. The word's similarity to Xhosa and Zulu *ingoma* (see quot. 1939) is prob. coincidental.]
1. A single-headed drum much used in the traditional music of the Cape Malay people. Also *attrib.*, and *comb.* (objective) **gomma-player** (see quot. 1944). See also GHOMMALIEDJIE.
 1934 C.P. SWART *Supplement to Pettman.* 60 One of the .. accompanying instruments .. is a gomma or small drum. 1939 P.R. KIRBY in *S. Afr. Jrnl of Science* XXXVI. 477 The *ghomma* .. was made from a small cask with a skin nailed over one of the two open ends. The instrument was held .. under the left arm and .. struck alternately by the right and left palms. *Ibid.* 480 The name *ghomma*, by which the Cape Malays call their drum, appears to be related to the Bantu word *ngoma*, .. applied to some types of drum from the south to the north of Africa, and .. to various dances involving the use of drums on the East coast of Africa. 1944 I.D. DU PLESSIS *Cape Malays* 59 At a Malay picnic the participants form a circle, join hands, and walk round slowly, singing a verse of a Dutch folk song. This is followed by a *ghommaliedjie*, led by a *ghomma*-player seated in the centre. 1949 E. HELLMANN *Handbk on Race Rel.* 593 The dancing is accompanied by the beating of Ghommas, a type of flat, tight, skin hand-drum. [1953 DU PLESSIS & LÜCKHOFF *Malay Quarter* 46 There is much uncertainty regarding the origin of the word. The Javanese use the word *ghom* for a gong when speaking Nederlands, and .. this may be its origin.] 1965 K. THOMPSON *Richard's Way* 79 A ghomma drum was patting out Eastern rhythms while the voice of a child keened out the nasal words of a Western song. 1970 *Cape Times* 6 June (Weekend Mag.) 2 To the throbbing beat of small hand-drums or *ghommas*, and monotonous chanting, the performers .. present solo acts of apparent painless self-mutilation ... Cape Town residents complained that the noise of booming *ghommas* and .. chanting .. in District Six and Malay Quarter houses was a disturbance. 1981 *Ibid.* 10 Jan. 12 Rowdy groups chose paraffin tins as their 'gommas' (drums). These they banged to their hearts content, much to the annoyance of superstitious adults who believed that

the striking of tins was an ill omen. **1988** ADAMS & SUTTNER *William Str.* 7 Hettie Adams begins her story .. with the sound of the 'goema' (pronounced 'gooma' as spelled in the text). **1989** *Personality* 26 June 77 District Six gave rise to a new kind of .. music. It had its roots in the beating of the *goema* drum on the slave ships sailing to Table Bay. **1993** D. KEEN in *Weekend Argus* 2 Jan. 1 It's carnival time in Cape Town! The city is reverberating to the beat of Ghoema drums.

2. *transf.* Also **goema-goema**. KLOPSE sense 2; latterly, a musical style blending klopse with jazz and rock music. Also *attrib.*

The more recent style of 'goema' was popularized in the 1980s by 'The Genuines' and is exemplified in this group's early songs and performances.

1980 D.B. COPLAN Urbanization of African Performing Arts. 290 Early Coloured dance bands in Johannesburg varied greatly in background and formal training ... For Coloured-African *stokfel* parties and public dances, they performed music of Cape Coloured social dances, for example, *vastrap, tickey draai*, set-part, *guma*, and squares. **1987** *New Nation* 30 July 12 Mr Mac has led many processions from goema 'Nag Troupe' to ballroom bands. **1987** *Ibid.* 3 Dec. 11 The Genuines have chucked out Goema's ja-baas connotations but have emphasized its humour, anger, sensuality and subversiveness ... Goema is an authentic original South African sound. **1991** G. SILBER in *Sunday Times* 20 Jan. (Mag. Sect.) 10 Between the hardcore Rap rhythms and the Goema-Goema jive of the Cape Flats, lies the sound of *Prophets of the City*. **1992** *Pace* Sept. 154 The group [*sc.* The Genuines] created a minor storm .. in the mid-Eighties with their complex fusion of traditional Cape ghoema music and jazz. **1993** *Business Day* 15 June 8 From traditional Zulu lullabies to Sarie Marais, from the '50s hit musical King Kong to Cape Malay goema, .. rhythms and melodies that have shaped this country's immensely rich cultural heritage.

ghommaliedjie /'gɔmaˌliki, 'gɔmə-, -'lici/ *n. Music.* [Afk., *ghomma* (see GHOMMA) + *liedjie* (see LIEDJIE).] A traditional song of the Cape Muslims, orig. accompanied on a ghomma, now also played on other instruments. See also LIEDJIE.

1934 *Cape Argus* 9 May (Swart), The gomma liedjies are sung in Afrikaans and are lively jig melodies with very simple music. **1934** C.P. SWART Supplement to Pettman. 60 *Gomma Liedjies*, .. The folk-songs of the Cape Malays .. are a traditional form of entertainment .. and have been faithfully handed down since 1750 by word of mouth. **1944** I.D. DU PLESSIS *Cape Malays* 58 In one way .. the indigenous *Ghommaliedjie* resembles the Malay *pantun*: there is no connection, or very little, between the first part of the song and the second; .. this is .. to be ascribed to the nature of this type of picnic or street song, which is often disjointed because fragments are added by individual singers according to their needs. **1944** [see GHOMMA sense 1]. **1946** L.G. GREEN *So Few Are Free* 14 The songs .. peculiar to the Cape Malays .. are called *gommaliedjies*. Some .. were known in Holland centuries ago; .. they are kept alive by Malays whose ancestors heard Dutch sailors singing them. **1953** DU PLESSIS & LÜCKHOFF *Malay Quarter* 46 *The ghommaliedjie* or picnic song is invariably accompanied upon a single-headed drum. **1962** *Coloured People of S. Afr.* (Dept of Info. & Dept of Coloured Affairs) 45 A long-playing record entitled *Malay Quarter — Songs of the Cape Malays* .. was made available .. during .. 1960. The 14 songs include wedding songs, comic moppies, picnic songs (Ghommaliedjies) and Dutch folk songs. **1973** *E. Prov. Herald* 24 Jan. 16 Distinctive old houses, pastel mosques with their decorative minarets and chanting muezzins, elaborate wedding ceremonies, folk tales and ghommaliedjies, are all part of the fascination of Cape Town's Islamic Malay quarter. **1973** F. CHISHOLM in *Cape Times* 4 Apr. 5 The sounds of beautifully harmonized singing of *gomma liedjies*, those favourite Malay folk songs, from a group of spectators. **1981** *Weekend Post* 28 Feb. (Family Post) 3 A selection of 'Gommaliedjies' from the Cape underline their back-grounds. **1988** J. KHUMALO in *Pace* May 32 When the .. 'District Six' musical hit Jo'burg .. it brought a whiff of the good old Cape Town with its banjos and ghoemaliedjies. **1989** D. KRAMER in *ADA* No.7, 8 Looking at Western Cape music, .. with the 'Moppies' and the 'goema liedjies' .. , was very important. **1992** *Summer School Brochure* (Univ. of Cape Town) 28 Working class versions of life in Cape Town, through the 'ghommaliedjies' of the Cape Muslims and the poems of the /xam will .. be discussed.

Ghona var. GONA n.²

Ghonaqua, Ghonoqua varr. GONAQUA.

Ghoninghayquaas var. GORINGHAIQUA.

ghonya /'gɒnjə, 'gɔn-, 'xɔn-/ *n.* Also **ghoonya, gonya, khonia**. [ad. Xhosa and Zulu *umkhonyo, umkhonya* a bladder grasshopper, fr. *khonya* (of a bladder grasshopper) make a shrill noise.] Esp. in the Eastern Cape: BLAASOP sense 1. Also *attrib.*

1869 W.G. ATHERSTONE in R. Noble *Cape & its People* 367 The 'Ghonya' — one of the pneumora — is that extraordinary inflated ghost of a green grasshopper ... His colonized name is derived from his cry — 'Ghonya-ghonya,' often heard on moonlight nights. **1893** *Trans. of S. Afr. Phil. Soc.* VIII. i. p.xxii, (Pettman), The male is familiar to residents in the Eastern Districts by the Kaffir name of *ghonya* as well as by the very loud and prolonged noise which he makes at night. **1897** E. GLANVILLE *Tales from Veld* 129 The ghonya from the darkness called again, as if the sorrows of the world were in the cry. **1909** 'SOMGXADA' in *E. London Dispatch* 8 Jan. 5 A large kind of grasshopper, called by the natives 'umkonya,' a name which is intended to represent its call. The same name, though with an introductory guttural, — 'ghonya' — is used by the Colonists also. **1914** W.C. SCULLY *Lodges in Wilderness* 219 The strangers .. set offerings before me. These consisted of ghoonyas, and nothing else. What did these people take me for; did they suppose I lived on a ghoonya diet — that I fed my caravan on ghoonya soup? **1974** on Radio South Africa 29 Oct. (Talking of Nature), Ghonya is the name given to them in the Eastern Cape — I think it's from the Xhosa. The Afrikaans word is blaasop. **1975** *Afr. Wildlife* Vol.29 No.1 (Toktokkie), In South Africa we have some very strange grasshoppers called 'Bulla — or Bladder-Locusts' or 'Khonias' known to scientists as pneumorids. The abdomen of the male is thin and filled with air .. and on each side there is a row of ridges. These .. are rubbed by small points or ridges on the inside of the hind legs to make sounds which are magnified by the inflated abdomen.

ghooma var. GHOMMA.

ghoon var. GHOEN.

ghoonya var. GHONYA.

Ghost Squad *n. phr. Hist.* Also with small initials. [Perh. so called because members would sometimes operate in plain clothes, thus being, metaphorically, invisible beings which became policemen when necessary.] A name for that branch of the police whose duty it was to check whether black people were carrying passes. Also *attrib.* See also PASS sense 3.

1963 L.F. FREED *Crime in S. Afr.* 81 Ghost Squad police who had attended the session in plain clothes called out the flying squad. **1971** *Post* 1 Aug., His blue-eyed soul brother .. is a member of the 'ghost squad' — the chaps who trudge Johannesburg streets demanding passes. **1986** *Drum* Aug. 55 The interview .. had to do with the increasing raids on blacks who happened to get caught by the so-called Ghost Squad in the city for failing to produce reference books. **1993** O. MUSI in *City Press* 12 Dec. 23 Remember the past brainwave of the 'Ghost Squad' whose job was to stop us for pass offences .. until they started getting into trouble because some tsotsis would pose as cops and harass law-abiding citizens.

ghurkum var. GOCUM.

ghurum masala var. GARAM MASALA.

ghwarrie var. GUARRI.

gielsiekte var. GEILSIEKTE.

||**gifappel** /'xəfap(ə)l/ *n.* Also **giftappel**. [Afk., *gif* (earlier *gift*) poison + *appel* apple.]

1. Either of two poisonous wild cucumber species of the Cucurbitaceae, *Cucumis myriocarpus* or *C. zeyheri*.

1822 W.J. BURCHELL *Trav.* (1953) I. 104 A kind of wild cucumber spreads itself over the bushes and along the ground, bearing a small yellow oval fruit hardly an inch long, covered with soft prickles, and called *Gift-Appel* (Poison-apple) on account of its extreme bitterness. [*Note*] Cucumis prophetarum. **1929** *Farming in S. Afr.* Sept. 280 'Bitter apples,' 'Wild cucumbers' and 'Gifappels', are names commonly employed by the farmer to describe a small cucumber-plant variety (*Cucumis myriocarpus*) which is frequently found in old maize-fields, is widely distributed throughout the Union, and is the cause of poisoning of sheep.

2. BITTER APPLE sense 2.

1970 [see BITTER APPLE sense 2]. **1975** *Dict. of Eng. Usage in Sn Afr.* 21 *Bitter apple*, .. (*Solanum oculeastrum, S. sodomaeum*), alt: apple of Sodom, giftappel, the vernacular names apply to both species. **1983** [see BITTER APPLE sense 2].

gifblaar /'xəfblɑː(r)/ *n.* Formerly also **gift-blaar**. [Afk., *gif* (earlier *gift*) poison + *blaar* leaf.] The dwarf herb *Dichapetalum cymosum* of the Dichapetalaceae, with leaves which are poisonous to livestock. Also *attrib.*

1910 *Tvl Agric. Jrnl* July 626 (Pettman), The following report on analysis and physiological tests of *Chailletia* or *Gift-blaar* (*Dichapetalum cymosum*, here also called *Chailletia cymosa*) .. has been received from the Director of the Imperial Institute. **1930** *Outspan* 31 Oct. 69 'Chincherinchee', which often finds its way into forage, 'gifblaar,' the various 'tulps' and 'slangkops,' are all responsible at different seasons and in different areas for considerable mortality among stock. *a***1936** E.N. MARAIS *Soul of Ape* (1973) 75 The fruit of the gifblaar is bright red in colour and very tempting in appearance — but the plant secretes a strictuous poison of extreme virulence and the fruit is especially rich in the deadly substance. **1936** [see SLANGKOP]. **1937** C.R. PRANCE *Tante Rebella's Saga* 145 This picturesque paradise was rotten with 'gif-blaar', the dreadful poison-plant which renders valueless so much of that land which looks dirt-cheap at 1-s. an acre. **1957** *Handbk for Farmers* (Dept of Agric.) II. 425 Gifblaar undoubtedly is one of the most poisonous plants the stock farmer has to contend with. Even a few leaves are fatal to sheep. **1970** BEETON & DORNER in *Eng. Usage in Sn Afr.* Vol.1 No.2, 12 *Gifblaar*, .. highly toxic plant with subterranean root system going down to 12m; only a small cluster of leaves sprouts on the surface of the soil in early spring before other grazing is available, so that it attracts animals to which it is fatal. **1988** T.S. KELLERMAN et al. *Plant Poisonings & Mycotoxicosis of Livestock* 108 Near Pretoria a gifblaar plant was reportedly excavated for 30 m to a depth of 12 m. **1989** J. DU P. BOTHMA *Game Ranch Management* 189 It appears that animals living in areas where certain toxic plants occur, learn not to eat them. Eland will not eat gifblaar, even if they are the only green plants remaining in a camp.

||**gifbol** /'xɪfbɔl/ *n.* Also **gift-bol, giftboll, gyfbol**. Pl. **-bolle**. [Afk. (earlier S. Afr. Du. *giftbol*), *gif* poison + *bol* bulb.] Any of several species of plant of the family Amaryllidaceae with highly toxic bulbs and leaves, esp. *Boophane disticha* (see SORE-EYE FLOWER sense b); occas., the poison derived from this plant. See also SLANGKOP.

[**1776** F. MASSON in *Phil. Trans. of Royal Soc.* LXVI. 277 A large bulbous root, growing on dry precipices, which the Dutch call *vergift-boll*, poison bulb; the juice of which, they say, the Hottentots use as an ingredient to poison their arrows. We found it to be a species of *amaryllis*.] **1796** C.R. HOPSON tr. *C.P. Thunberg's Trav.* II. 163 Poisonous bulbous plants (*Giftbolles, Amaryllis disticha*) grow in several places common, with their beautiful clusters of flowers. **1822** W.J. BURCHELL *Trav.* I. 539 This plant is well known to the Bushmen, on account of the virulent poison contained in its bulb. It is also known to the Colonists and Hottentots, by the name of *Gift-bol* (Poison bulb). [**1828** T. PRINGLE *Ephemerides* 174 Powerful vegetable and mineral poisons; the former being generally the juice of the root of a species of amaryllis, called by the boors .. the *gift-bol*, or poison bulb.] **1839** W.C. HARRIS *Wild Sports* 312 The due admixture of powerful vegetable and mineral poisons; the former being generally obtained from the root of a species of amaryllis, called by the colonists the gift-bol. *a***1875** T. BAINES *Jrnl of Res.* (1964) II. 32, I found a beautiful flower, or rather a crown of crimson bell flowers ... Jan called it *gyf bol*, or poison bulb, or headache flower. **1911** J.F. PENTZ in *Farmer's Weekly* 11 Oct. 158 (*letter*) We have a bulb here called 'gif-bol' or 'slangkop,' and we have sometimes wondered whether that plant was not the cause of the trouble [*sc.* livestock disease], but .. we decided against that plant as the likely cause of the disease. **1921** R. MARLOTH in B. Van der Riet, Letters. (Cory Library) 2 Feb., There grows also Buphane disticha in those parts, the giftbol. That has mostly a thick padding of old skins (an inch or more thick) and may be up to 10 inch[es] in diam. **1974** J.M. COETZEE *Dusklands* 99, I cut myself a willow bow and with arrows tipped in *giftbol* spent the mornings lying in wait for animals coming to drink.

‖**gifboom** /ˈxəfbʊəm/ *n.* Formerly also **giftboom.** [Afk. (earlier S. Afr. Du. *giftboom*), *gif* poison + *boom* tree.] Any of several toxic species of tree or shrub harmful to both people and animals: **a.** *Hyaenanchae globosa* of the Euphorbiaceae. **b.** *Acokanthera oppositifolia* and *A. oblongifolia* of the Apocynaceae; also called BUSHMAN'S POISON.

1795 C.R. HOPSON tr. *C.P. Thunberg's Trav.* I. 156 With the poison of serpents, and the juice of the *sideroxylum toxiferum* (*gift-boom*, or poison tree) the Hottentots poison their arrows. **1809** J. MACKRILL Diary. 62 Sideroxylon toxiferum (Gift boom or poison tree) used by the Natives to poison their arrows. **1886** G.A. FARINI *Through Kalahari Desert* 338 The colony Bushmen that I was brought up amongst .. use the milk of the *gift boom* (poison-tree) that grows on the mountains along the Orange River. **1937** *Handbk for Farmers* (Dept of Agric. & Forestry) 470 *Gifboom, Poison Bush, Poison Tree, (Apocynaceae) Acokanthera spectabilis* .. *Acokanthera venenata* .. The fruit is about 4 times less toxic than the leaves. **1973** *E. Prov. Herald* 28 Feb. 4 In the dry sub-tropical route was found migration of the gifboom, melkbos (or spurge), honey locust, blackthorn and skilpadbos (or vygie). **1976** [see BUSHMAN'S POISON]. **1992** P. CULLINAN *Robert Jacob Gordon* 122 (*caption*) The gifboom or 'poison tree' (*Euphorbia virosa*).

giffie /ˈxəfi/ *n. colloq.* [Afk., lit. 'the deadly one', prob. fr. *gif* poison + -IE.] Among children: a game in which the object is to shoot a stone or marble (see GHOEN sense c) into three holes in a particular sequence, the first player having achieved this then attempting to hit an opponent's stone or marble, thereby 'killing' him; a name given to the player who is allowed to 'kill' opponents.

1982 T. BARON in *Frontline* Nov. 45 *Giffie* was one of them. All you needed was a flat stone for a ghoon and three holes in the ground. You threw your ghoon, first into the middle hole, then into the far hole and back again. Now you were *giffie* and you threw your ghoon .. at your opponent's ghoon. **1983** R. DUTTON in *Daily Dispatch* 11 Mar. 16 One of the games we boys played some 30 years ago in the Pretoria district was giffie ... Three holes, into which the stones could fall, were dug about five yards apart and in a straight line. The object was to throw one's stone into each of the holes in turn in the fewest number of throws. The first player to complete the circuit .. was 'Giffie' and could then systematically 'kill' the other players. **1990** J. BERKS in *Sunday Times* 11 Feb. 9 Casual games of hasie, giffie, and slangetjie.

giftappel var. GIFAPPEL.

gift-blaar var. GIFBLAAR.

gift-bol, giftboll varr. GIFBOL.

giftboom var. GIFBOOM.

giraffe *n. obs.* Special Comb. ***giraffe acacia, -thorn,*** and ***-tree*** [so called because browsed by giraffes]: CAMEL-THORN.

1815 A. PLUMPTRE tr. *H. Lichtenstein's Trav. in Sn Afr.* (1930) II. 288 A tall and wide spreading giraffe tree, the *acacia giraffae*. **1856** C.J. ANDERSSON *Lake Ngami* 27 The principal trees thereabouts are the ana and the giraffe-thorn (*acacia giraffæ*). **1886** G.A. FARINI *Through Kalahari Desert* 195 The k'gung tree .. is very similar to the giraffe-tree. **1896** H.A. BRYDEN *Tales of S. Afr.* 44 Groves of giraffe acacia (*kameel doorn*).

girdle *n.* In the obsolete phrr. ***girdle of famine, girdle of hunger***: a leathern strap or thong tied tightly round the stomach to deaden hunger pangs; HUNGER-BELT; *lambile strap*, see LAMBILE.

1827 G. THOMPSON *Trav.* (ed.1) 255 The pangs of hunger pressed sore upon us, and our only relief was to draw our 'girdles of famine' still tighter round our bodies. **1829** C. ROSE *Four Yrs in Sn Afr.* 100 He [*sc.* the Khoikhoi] is capable of undergoing great privation; .. he can abstain from food for days, diminishing the gnawing pain of hunger by tightening the *girdle of famine* around him. **1834** T. PRINGLE *Afr. Sketches* 505 In seasons of long continued drought, the Corannas are .. forced, like the Bushmen, to subsist on wild roots, ants and locusts. On such occasions, they are accustomed to wear a leathern band bound tightly round their middle, which they term 'the girdle of famine'. **1837** J.E. ALEXANDER *Narr. of Voy.* I. 387 Round his loins is a double thong, also thickly set with brass rings. This is regarded as a great ornament in South Africa; and it also serves as a girdle of famine to confine the stomach, if on a journey food runs short. **1839** W.C. HARRIS *Wild Sports* 293 Dying of hunger, and my 'girdle of famine' tightened to the last hole, I felt strangely tempted to devour my Christmas repast uncooked. **1841** B. SHAW *Memorials* 80 The chief said, that .. some had nothing to eat, and were wearing their *girdles of hunger*. **1849** E.D.H.E. NAPIER *Excursions in Sn Afr.* I. 117 This said 'girdle of famine' is a leather belt, worn round the waist by most of the natives of Southern Africa. It is gradually tightened when hunger is felt, without the means of satisfying the same.

girl *n. offensive.* [Transf. use of general Eng. *girl* a female servant.]

a. An insulting term for a black African woman, used irrespective of her age, social position, or occupation; *Native girl*, see NATIVE *n.* sense 1 c. Cf. BOY sense 1 a.

1859 T. SHONE Diary. 5 Nov., He flogged Guika the girl. **1908** J.H. DRUMMOND Diary. 15 Sept., Our girl, Jerry, is as nervous as she is black. *a***1931** S. BLACK in S. Gray *Three Plays* (1984) 164 The girl will bring you some coffee. But perhaps you rader prefer tea. **1953** D. JACOBSON *Long Way from London* 52 Lunch was served by Ben, the African houseboy, for the girl, Betty, had gone to the location to make sure that her son .. was not among those injured. **1960** C. HOOPER *Brief Authority* 37 If wives go, they go usually to seek domestic service, to live on the premises of a white 'missus' who does not want 'boys' hanging around her 'girl'. **1968** COLE & FLAHERTY *House of Bondage* 73 Children watch how their parents treat the black 'boys' and 'girls' and soon the youngsters realize that they can get away with the same conduct. **1970** E. MUNDELL *Informant, Pearston (E. Cape)* The old girl will make us some tea. (Kitchen maid). **1970** BEETON & DORNER in *Eng. Usage in Sn Afr.* Vol.1 No.2, 12 *Girl*, .. Non-White female domestic servant, employee in business & industrial concerns. **1972** D.E. NTAMBULE in *Daily Dispatch* 29 Apr. 10 Mr. G. Qumza had criticised the words 'boy' and 'girl' used by whites when referring to blacks ... Whites, coloureds and Indians are never called 'boy' or 'girl'. Why? **1973** *Argus* 19 Apr. 8, I thank heaven for five sensible teenagers in the house, .. and also for a 'girl' (I wish someone would call me by that name) of some many years of faithful and willing service. **1973** *Drum* 8 Sept. 10 We are no longer a nation of 'boys and girls' as some people tend to think. We Blacks are men and women. **1980** J. COCK *Maids & Madams* 60 Servants .. are generally addressed in terms reserved for children and inferiors. The domestic worker is usually a 'girl' and the gardener a 'boy'. **1980** C. HOPE *A Separate Development* (1983) 30 Our girl, Charity, sat rocking in her chair at the door. I say girl, as a manner of speaking. She was sharp boned, surly, somewhere between thirty and menopause. **1986** [see AF sense 1]. **1987** [see INKOSAZANA]. **1990** R. MALAN *My Traitor's Heart* 30 Natives .. ate on enamel plates and drank out of chipped cups with no handles, which were known as the boy's cup or girl's cup and kept separate from the rest of our china. **1990** [see Malan quot. at MIESIES sense 1]. **1990** J. NAIDOO *Coolie Location* 5 Lena, my Aunt Kootie's African 'girl', spoke Tamil, when she wanted to, better even than I did.

b. With distinguishing epithet, specifying a particular occupation: **cook-girl, kitchen girl, nurse-girl, tea girl, wash(ing) girl.**

1957 D. JACOBSON *Price of Diamonds* 27 It was about Sylvia, the native **cook-girl**, and Sylvia's son Arthur. **1968** COLE & FLAHERTY *House of Bondage* 70 Families who would be lucky to afford part-time help .. if they lived in New York or London, have staffs of five or six full-time servants in South Africa. There is an African for every job – cook-girl or cook-boy, washing-girl and nannie, chauffeur, floor-boy, and garden boy. **1975** J. MCCLURE *Snake* (1981) 148 You say he went out to the cook girl's kia to get the clock and tell her about the morning – why didn't he shout for her? Is he a liberal? **1987** J. MATLOU in *Staffrider* Vol.6 No.4, 38 Matlou was a hard-working man and 'good boy' ... His wife was a '**kitchen girl**' with a good old reputation. **1958** F.G. BUTLER in R.M. Macnab *Poets in S. Afr.* 6 His ageing Xosa **nurse-girl** stands, head bent Unconsciously above her harbouring arms Where once his white resilience lay pent. **1974** *E. Prov. Herald* 24 Oct. 35 We should not talk about garden-boys or **teagirls** when we refer to grown up people – call them gardeners, tea-maids, messengers and pool attendants. **1988** 'SHINER' in *Personality* 30 Mar. 4 The only real sympathy I got was from the African tea girl – no wisecracks from her, just kindness. **1966** L.G. BERGER *Where's Madam* 45 'Seep-y,' I sounded it after him, puzzled. 'Soap' he explained. 'Oh, the Afrikaans word for soap. I see. What a peculiar name to give a baby. Why did you call it that?' 'Elizabeth she call it. She **washgirl**.' **1968** [see *cook-girl* above]. **1977** *Sunday Times* 27 Nov. 18, I remember telling old Lucy, my wash girl, how lucky she was not to have the vote in the circumstances. **1989** [see *cook boy* (BOY sense 1 b)].

gits var. GATS.

giya /ˈgiːjə, ˈgiːja/ *n.* Also **ukugiya**, and with initial capital. Pl. unchanged. [Zulu *giya* perform a war-like dance.] A Zulu dance (often performed at weddings) which celebrates conquests in battle, and in which exaggerated acts of aggression are mimed. Also *attrib.*

1905 R. PLANT *Zulu in Three Tenses* 39 Together with the bride's brothers, he begins a frantic leaping and jumping performance called *uku giya*. **1923** G.H. NICHOLLS *Bayete!* 25 None but those who had been often in battle could perform the giya ... It now remained for him to show by the giya that he was worthy of such warriors. **1943** D. REITZ *No Outspan* 65 Many of them were indulging in the provocative custom of giya whereby a man would break rank and rush forward, leaping and stamping, his shield and stabbing spear held threateningly aloft, while he boasted of his prowess in battle and his victories. **1955** E.A. RITTER *Shaka Zulu* 23 Shaka's commander, Buza, and in fact the whole regiment, did not fail to note the prowess of the young warrior; he was allowed to lead the giya or victory dance. **1960** J. COPE *Tame Ox* 20 As a thousand hands clapped a rhythm, he whirled into the *giya* dance with a stupendous leap, the war-dance of the Zulus. **1961** T.V. BULPIN *White Whirlwind* 97 He watched with humour and admiration as renowned warriors singled themselves out in the vain-gloriously exciting custom of *Giya* .. ; leaping into the air with shield and spear; running in front of the dancers with long, exaggerated strides; brandishing their skins and sticks; and shouting out the praises and glorious deeds of themselves, their regiments and chief. **1979** C. Endfield *Zulu Dawn* 150 Earlier on that same day he had participated in the *giya*, the exaggerated dance-mime performed by the regiment before the King, wherein was enacted the fantasy of how the shields they were begging would be used in engagement against the enemy. But the *giya* of some of the warriors were not fictions. They were accounts of true feats in battle, or in the hunt. **1991** J. Clegg on M-Net TV Feb., The Zulu male body is wired up to perform certain symbolic acts .. which include .. a thing called the giya which is like shadow-boxing but with your weapons, to show off your skill.

giya /ˈgiːjə, ˈgiːja/ *v. intrans.* [Zulu, see prec.] To perform a dance mimicking war antics.

1923 G.H. Nicholls *Bayete!* 25 The king ought, by custom, to giya in his turn to the music of the shields. **1949** O. Walker *Wanton City* 191 The yelling only became more frenzied, and several natives began 'giya-ing', made feinting rushes towards him, baring their teeth like dogs, and brandishing their sticks. **1950** C. Bullock *Mashona & Matabele* 184 The men suddenly rush to a corner of the kraal, and 'giya' — leap and gesticulate — pointing with their sticks at something outside in the veld. **1955** E.A. Ritter *Shaka Zulu* 85 There follows a prayer that the bride may be fruitful and then the father runs into the open and giyas, that is, he goes through the motions of fighting an imaginary foe. **1974** C.T. Binns *Warrior People* 210 They .. arrange themselves in a large semi-circle facing the bridal party, the groom himself being the centre. The moment all are settled he springs forward and commences to *Giya*, leaping wildly hither and thither, brandishing shield and assegai, stabbing at imaginary foes with even greater intensity and abandon than his bride had done earlier.

gladiolus /ˌglædɪˈəʊləs/ *n.* Pl. **gladioli, gladioluses**, or unchanged. [Transf. use of general Eng. *gladiolus* wild iris or gladdon (now obs.), fr. L., dim. of *gladius* sword.] Any plant of the genus *Gladiolus* of the Iridaceae, having sword-shaped leaves, and spikes of brilliant flowers; also called PYPIE. See also AANDBLOM, AFRIKANER *n.* sense 1, PAINTED LADY. Also *attrib.*

Although members of the genus were known in Europe during the Middle Ages, the plants now cultivated worldwide are usu. South African species.

1775 F. Masson in *Phil. Trans. of Royal Soc.* LXVI. 279 We collected a great number of beautiful plants, particularly ixiae, irides, and gladioli. **1790** [see GERANIUM]. **1796** tr. *Thunberg's Cape of G.H.* in Pinkerton *Voy.* (1814) XVI. 65 It [*sc.* a mole] feeds on several sorts of bulbous roots .. especially Gladioluses, Ixias, Antholyas, and Irises. **1801** [see AFRIKANER *n.* sense 1]. **1809** 'G. Valentia' *Voy. & Trav.* I. 31 The heaths were not in bloom, but the Ixiae, Gladioli, and smaller bulbous Geraniums were, and we could not have been at the Cape in a better season for collecting them. **1847** J. Barrow *Reflect.* 217 A walk by the foot of the Table Mountain will delight the admirer of the bulbous-rooted and liliaceous tribes of plants, flourishing in their native soil — the various species of amaryllis, the gladiolus, antholiza, iris, [etc.]. **1856** R.E.E. Wilmot *Diary* (1984) 47 Found a pretty rose coloured gladiolus of small size in the veld, and brought it home. **1906** B. Stoneman *Plants & their Ways* 198 *Gladiolus*, A great variety of colours is found in the flowers ... Eighty-one species of this large genus are found in South Africa. **1910** *S. Afr. 'Inquire Within'* (Cape Times) 89 *April*, .. Ranunculus, hyacinth, .. anemone, and gladiolus bulbs must now be planted. **1917** [see PAINTED LADY]. **1928** J.W. Mathews in *Jrnl of Botanical Soc.* XIV. 11 Like various other typical South African genera with a large number of species, the distribution of Gladiolus is spread throughout all the Provinces of the Union. **1933** [see PAINTED LADY]. **1937** L.B. Creasey in *Ibid.* XXIII. 10 In her flora, South Africa has paid a worthy contribution to the gardens of the world and, among our indigenous plants brought to horticultural perfection by hybridists, the Gladiolus stands supreme. **1949** [see NEMESIA]. *c*1968 S. Candy *Natal Coast Gardening* 24 Most Gladiolus flower approximately 90 days after planting ... Corms should be planted 3–4 inches deep. **1969** [see PAINTED LADY]. **1988** T.J. Lindsay *Shadow* (1990) 4 Grass and creepers concealed bunkers that pushed up out of the ground where once there had been beds of gladioli.

gli /gli(ː)/ *n.* [Khoikhoi.] The tuberous plant *Peucedanum gummiferum* of the Apiaceae; MOER *n.*[1] sense 1 a. Also *attrib.*

1796 C.R. Hopson tr. *C.P. Thunberg's Trav.* II. 31 *Gli* is, in the Hottentot language, the name of an umbelliferous plant, the root of which, dried and reduced to powder, they mix with cold water and honey in a trough, and after letting it ferment for the space of one night, obtain a species of Mead. **1868** W.H. Harvey *Genera of S. Afr. Plants* 141 *G[lia] gummifera*, .. the only species, grows in many places in the Western districts; it is the *gli* of the Hottentots, who prepare from its roots an inebriating drink. **1913** C. Pettman *Africanderisms* 189 *Gli*, .. *Glia gummifera*. From the roots of this plant the Hottentots prepare an intoxicating drink. **1966** C.A. Smith *Common Names* 230 *Gli(wortel), Glia gummifera* ... Rootstock an elongated tuber. **1976** A.P. Brink *Instant in Wind* 74 There were no fires as before, no noise of homing cattle, children screaming, the shrill voices of women, the darker merriment of the men gathered round the gli-root calabashes.

gnaarboom var. NABOOM.

gnu /nuː/ *n.*[1] Also **gneu, gnoe, gnoo, gnou, knoo, n'gou, nhoo**, and with initial capital. Pl. unchanged, or **-s**. [Khoikhoi and San, perh. onomatopoeic, imitating the snort of the animal when alarmed; variously written *gnu, !nu, !no:*, representing the pronunciations /ǂuː, -ʊ, -ɔ(ː)/; prob. orig. rel. to Khoikhoi and San *≠nu* black. It appears that the Khoikhoi and San distinguished between *!nu*, etc. black wildebeest, and San */gaob*, Khoikhoi */goab* blue wildebeest.]
a. WILDEBEEST sense a.

[**1777** G. Forster *Voy. round World* I. 83 There is another species of wild ox, called by the natives gnoo.] **1786** G. Forster tr. *A. Sparrman's Voy. to Cape of G.H.* II. 131 A *gnu* .. had been seen ranging by itself about this part of the country. *T'Gnu* is the Hottentot name for a singular animal, which, with respect to its form, is between the horse and the ox. [**1790** tr. *Le Vaillant's Trav.* II. 236 The Hottentots name this antelope *nou*, preceded by that .. clapping which I have already mentioned. It was probably this clapping which induced Colonel Gordon to add a g to the proper name, which renders the pronunciation of it almost the same.] *Ibid.* 283 One of my men was bringing in a kind of gazell, called a *Gnou*. **1802** Truter & Somerville in G.M. Theal *Rec. of Cape Col.* (1899) IV. 378 We saw .. many herds of quaggas and Gnoes. **1806** J. Barrow *Trav.* I. On every side was grazing a multitude of wild animals, as gnoos, [etc.]. **1821** T. Pringle Letter to Scott. (N.E.L.M. collection), 12 June, The hills are high .. but with .. grassy flats among them .. frequented by numerous .. quaggas, hartebeests, Wildebeests (or Nhoos) [etc.]. **1822** J. Campbell *Trav. in S. Afr. Second Journey* I. 152 Many quachas and knoos were seen. **1827** G. Thompson *Trav.* I. 120 The gnoo here was .. different from that on the other side of the Cradock, being of a dark blue colour, and having a black bushy tail, instead of a white one. **1836** A.F. Gardiner *Journey to Zoolu Country* 329 Here the first gneu was seen. **1837** 'N. Polson' *Subaltern's Sick Leave* 131 The skin of the *wildebeest* or gnu when brayed, is used for *reims* or thongs to harness the oxen. **1850** N.J. Merriman *Cape Jrnls* (1957) 141 A troop of these snorting gnus .. dashed into the vley to drink. **1878** H.A. Roche *On Trek in Tvl* 271 The wilder-beest or gnu is more clumsy, and has a far more formidable look than any other of its species. **1913** C. Pettman *Africanderisms* 189 *Gnu*, .. This animal is .. now only found on a few farms, where it is carefully preserved, in the Orange River Colony. **1930** S.T. Plaatje *Mhudi* (1975) 37 A frisky troop of gnu among the distant trees. **1945** F.C. Slater *New Centenary Bk of S. Afr. Verse* 227 An ungainly antelope .. termed Gnu from its loud bellowing snort. **1951** T.V. Bulpin *Lost Trails of Low Veld* 263 His proper English name, the gnu, is surely the only word of Bushman ever to have found a place in the composite English language. **1982** *E. Prov. Herald* 23 July 9 Why not a gnuburger .. ? **1985** C. Walker *Signs of Wild* (1987) 189 The name Gnu is derived from the Hottentot word referring to the sound it makes.

b. With distinguishing epithet: **black gnu**, *black wildebeest* (see WILDEBEEST sense b); **brindled gnu**, *blue wildebeest* (see WILDEBEEST sense b); **white-tailed gnu**, *black wildebeest* (see WILDEBEEST sense b).

1866 J. Leyland *Adventures* 75 A troop of Veldebeests, or **Black Gnoos**, came .. past. **1898** G. Nicholson *50 Yrs* 21 Black gnus and springbuck grazed. *a*1936 E.N. Marais *Soul of Ape* (1973) 82 Vast herds of .. black gnu (*Connochaetes gnou*) .. at one time covered the great inland plains. **1838** J.E. Alexander *Exped. into Int.* II. 144 These were the parts of a Kaop (master) buck or **brindled gnu**. **1863** J.H. Speke *Jrnl of Disc. of Nile* 36 'The bags' we made counted two brindled gnŭ, [etc.]. **1897** [see *blue wildebeest* (WILDEBEEST sense b)]. **1983** *Nat. Geog. Mag.* Mar. 355 Blue wildebeests, also known as brindled gnus. **1990** Skinner & Smithers *Mammals of Sn Afr. Subregion* 614 The blue wildebeest is also referred to as the brindled gnu, a name which has now largely fallen out of use. **1889** *Cent. Dict.*, *Gnu*, .. Common or **White-tailed Gnu**. **1896** R. Ward *Rec. of Big Game* 92 The White-tailed Gnu, or .. Black Wildbeeste, is assuredly one of the most extravagant of nature's creations ... Its extraordinary activity .. and .. mad pranks .. render it easily distinguishable form its cousin, the brindled gnu. **1972** *Grocott's Mail* 12 May 3 The .. white-tailed gnu .. have come from .. the Free State. **1990** Skinner & Smithers *Mammals of Sn Afr. Subregion* 612 The characteristic and most obvious feature of black wildebeest is their white tails and often they are referred to as white-tailed wildebeest or white-tailed gnu.

GNU /dʒiː en ˈjuː/ *n.*[2] Initial letters of *Government of National Unity*, the government formed after South Africa's first democratic election in April, 1994.

1994 R. Malan in *Style* May 46 Blacks will party, whites will sulk, and when the hangover wears off, our Government of National Unity will convene and attempt to impose order on chaos. It will be a curious animal, this GNU, a forced coalition of ancient enemies induced to compromise only by their inability to vanquish each other. **1994** P. Cull in *E. Prov. Herald* 19 Aug. 1 Angry National Party leader FW de Klerk warned yesterday that the 'red lights are flashing' for the Government of National Unity (GNU) following a flaming row over the appointments of chairmen of key parliamentary committees.

gnush var. MNGQUSH(O).

go-away *n.* Also **go-way, go'way**, and with initial capitals. [Echoic, see quots 1897 and 1984.]
1. In full ***go-away bird***: the grey loerie (see LOERIE sense 1 b), *Corythaixoides concolor.*

1881 E.E. Frewer tr. *E. Holub's Seven Yrs in S. Afr.* I. 289, I shot a great grey lory, that from its cry is called the 'go-away' by the English, whilst by the Boers it is known as the 'grote Mausevogel'. **1897** J.P. Fitzpatrick *Outspan* 55 There is a sort of bastard cockatoo in those parts which is commonly known as the 'Go way' bird, on account of its cry, which closely resembles these words, and of a habit it is supposed to have of warning game of the approach of man. **1906** *Chambers's Jrnl* (U.K.) Mar. 214 A pair of rare crested parrots, or 'go-away birds', as they are called. **1914** S.P. Hyatt *Old Transport Rd* 179 The Go-away bird warning the game of your approach. **1929** J. Stevenson-Hamilton *Low-Veld* 96 The grey lourie or 'go-away' bird, which, with its long tail jerking up and down with the effort, shouts out his warning of approaching danger to all and sundry. [**1933** see *grey loerie* (LOERIE sense 1 b).] **1940** V. POHL *Bushveld Adventures* 155 Later, when I questioned him about the popular belief that the 'Go-away' or 'Alarm birds' scare off game, he repled: 'Go-away bird him talk too much!' **1958** M. SPARK *Go-Away Bird* 74 All over the Colony it was possible to hear the subtle voice of the grey-crested lourie, commonly known as the go-away bird by its call, 'go 'way, go 'way'. **1967** [see *grey loerie* (LOERIE sense 1 b)]. **1984** G.L. MACLEAN *Roberts' Birds of Sn Afr.* 325 *Grey Lourie*, ... *Voice*: Loud drawn-out nasal *go-'way* (hence called Goaway Bird) or *kwê*.

2. The cry of this bird.

1933 J. JUTA *Look Out for Ostriches* 154 From the denser thickets .. the Grey Lourie kept uttering its cry of 'Go away, go away.' **1951** [see *grey loerie* (LOERIE sense 1 b)]. **1958** M. SPARK *Go-Away Bird* 74 All over the Colony it was possible to hear the subtle voice of the grey-crested lourie, commonly known as the go-away bird by its call, 'go 'way, go 'way'. **1968** G. CROUDACE *Black Rose* 88 'Go'way, go'way.' The sudden alarm call of the lourie startled her. **1971** *Argus* 10 Mar., Hunters call the Grey Loerie the go way bird because just after you creep up to your quarry after perhaps hours of spooring, this bird calls out from a tree-top in a coffee grinder voice 'go way'! **1984** [see sense 1].

go bush see BUSH *adj.* sense 2.

gocum /ˈɡəʊkəm/ *n.* Also **g(h)aukum, ghocum, ghôghôm, ghokum, ghurkum, goukom, t'gokum**, and with initial capital. [ad. Afk. *ghôkum, ghôkom*, perh. rel. to Nama ǁ*gũ* juicy, full of seeds.] *Hottentot('s) fig*, see HOTTENTOT *n.* sense 6 a. Also *attrib.*

1883 M.A. CAREY-HOBSON *Farm in Karoo* 42 'Master likes Gocums?' said the boy. 'Hottentot figs very good.' 'It is the fruit of the figbearing Mysembryanthemum, and many people are very fond of it. You had better let him show you how to peel them, for if you get any of the very saline outer covering, you will find it extremely disagreeable.' **1890** J.F. SEWELL *Private Diary* (1983) 119, I have not taken any more medicine for some days but I have been eating Goukoms which are a good blood purifier. **1894** E. GLANVILLE *Fair Colonist* 224 On the shoreward slopes there was a covering of soft-wooded trees, shrubs and flesh-leaved ghocums, forming a thick carpet. **1901** E. EMSLIE Diary. 25 Dec., Home Xmas day a nice day went to sleep after dinner & then went for Ghocums. *Ibid.* 26 Dec., Am busy making Ghocum jam for Charlotte. **1902** H.J. DUCKITT *Hilda's Diary of Cape Hsekeeper* 283 The leaves of ghokum or 'Hottentot fig' .. bruised and strained, are excellent as a gargle. **1912** *E. London Dispatch* 28 Sept. 12 (Pettman), We roamed the veld and bush in search of wild fruits — myrtle apples, 't'gokums,' 'gwenyas,' etc. — which I presume are still to be found by the enterprising East London youth. **1924** *Cape Argus* 1 Feb. 7 Crystallised ghurkums and naartjies are novel delicacies which she expects to put on the market. **1949** J. ALLEN Memoirs. 48 There were many wild fruits growing in the bush, such as zuurberries, gocums, sour figs and others. **1970** *Evening Post* 10 Oct. (Mag. Sect.) 3 *Gocums* .. are usually ready to be picked for jam in December and January. *Gocum Jam.* Peel the gocums and wash them well. Add one pound of sugar to every one pound of gocums. **1976** A.P. BRINK *Instant in Wind* 153 He brings her a concoction of *ghaukum* leaves picked far below the snowline that afternoon.

God, as true as see TRUE sense a.

ǁ**goduka** /ɡɔˈdʊɡa, -ˈduːkə/ *n.* Pl. **(a)magoduka, godukas**. [Xhosa and Zulu *igoduka* (pl. *amagoduka*), fr. *goduka* return home. For a note on pl. forms, see AMA- and MA- *pref.*[3]] Among speakers of Sintu (Bantu) languages: a migrant worker, esp. a mine worker; *migrant labourer*, see MIGRANT LABOUR.

[**1860** A.W. DRAYSON *Sporting Scenes* 42 They appeared to be in high spirits, and, in answer to my 'Uya pina?' (Where are you going?) shouted with exultation, 'Goduka' (Going home).] **1963** WILSON & MAFEJE *Langa* 17 The migrants, the *amagoduka*, are often referred to by townspeople as *amaqaba* .. i.e. pagans, but in fact a great many of them .. are 'school people' (amagqoboka). **1973** *E. Prov. Herald* 26 Mar. 1 Hundreds of Amagoduka — migrant labourers — went on the rampage in Langa on Saturday night. **1978** M. MATSHOBA in *Staffrider* Vol.1 No.3, 18 A 'goduka' (migrant labourer) on his way home to his family after many months of work in the city. **1979** — *Call Me Not a Man* 95, I felt like a *goduka* going to the Golden City for the first time in his life. *Ibid.* 144 The baggage of the *godukas*, all *godukas*, consists of their sweat and blood in the migrant labour system. **1983** G. MVUBELO in *Frontline* Feb. 25 The hostels .. are the only places which offer accommodation to the immigrant workers (Magoduka). **1985** M. TLALI in *Fair Lady* 26 June 105 What does he know about Soweto when he is a mere *goduka* (one who is passing).

goe dag, goeddag varr. GOEDEN DAG.

goede morgen var. GOEIE MÔRE.

goeden dag *phr. obs.* Also **goe dag, goeddag, goen daag**. [Du., *goeden* (attrib. form of *goed*) good + *dag* day.] DAG.

1802 TRUTER & SOMERVILLE in G.M. Theal *Rec. of Cape Col.* (1899) IV. 386 We left Litakoe at 8 o'clock, .. followed by many hundreds, who bade us adieu in pronouncing in bad Dutch Goe Dag Heeren. **1829** C. ROSE *Four Yrs in Sn Afr.* 82 A Kaffer, rising from the group, .. held out his hand, and repeated the salutation of good-will — Goedendag. **1837** 'N. POLSON' *Subaltern's Sick Leave* 101 Traveller — 'Goeden dag, Mynheer' ('Good day, Sir'). **1861** P.B. BORCHERDS *Auto-Biog. Mem.* 86 Hundreds followed us and we heard them calling out in broken Dutch, 'goeddag, goeddag, Heeren.' **1871** W.G. ATHERSTONE in A.M.L. Robinson *Sel. Articles from Cape Monthly Mag.* (1978) 95 '*Daars hy!*' ('There he is!') said he (by way of a welcome and the conventional 'goen daag',) with a knowing half wink. **1877** R.M. BALLANTYNE *Settler & Savage* 88 Then the Dutchman said 'goeden-dag,' or farewell, shook hands all round, cracked his long whip, and went off into the unknown wilderness. **1933** W.H.S. BELL *Bygone Days* 12 We took our boxes out of the wagon and placed them on the ground; he bade us 'goeden dag', cracked his whip and drove away, leaving us to our reflections.

goef /ɡʊf/ *n. slang.* Also **goof**. [As next.] A swim. See also GOOFIES.

1970 K.M. BRAND *Informant, East London* I'm going for a quick goof to cool down (swim). **1971** F.G. BUTLER *Informant, Grahamstown* Goef. A swim. **1975** 'BLOSSOM' in *Darling* 12 Feb. 119 'Ag, not *now*, man, Vern,' I groan. 'It's too bleksy hot for smooching, let's rather jis go catch a goef hey?' **1976** *Ibid.* 14 Apr. 115 Yesterday arvey we went for a goef .. and Dumbo nearly stood on a crocodile. **1991** M. HURT *Informant, Dorpspruit* I'll get my cozzie and go to the pool for a goef. I hope there aren't too many muggies there. **1991** Y. MAAKENSCHYN *Informant, Johannesburg* Bring your own sarmies and your cossie and we'll go for a goef.

goef /ɡʊf/ *v. intrans. Slang.* Also **ghoef, goof**. [ad. colloq. Afk. *ghoef* to swim (perh. echoic).] Esp. in the language of school-children: to swim.

1970 *Informant, Pietersburg* Let's go goeffing at Hillcrest this afternoon. **1970** T. RAY *Informant, Cedara (Kwa-Zulu Natal)* Some of us ous went goofing at Dick's cabin. After this we were so hungry, that we polished off all the graze in the joint. **1970** M.C. DUFFY *Informant, Durban* Ghoef. To swim. **1970** BEETON & DORNER in *Eng. Usage in Sn Afr.* Vol.1 No.2, 11 *Ghoef*, .. schoolboyism for 'swim' or 'go swimming'. **1974** *Daily Dispatch* 30 Oct. 1 'Bread' is money .. and 'tackies' is used not to describe tennis shoes but car tyres. 'Goef' is to swim. **1975** 'BLOSSOM' in *Darling* 12 Feb. 119 'Aren't we gonna goef?' I screech. 'In this heat?' ... 'Shore, we gonna goef. I jis said, no cozzie.' **1987** *Fair Lady* 21 Jan. 144 Surely there are no longer 14 year olds talking of .. *goeffing* in the Linden Municipal Baths.

goei var. GOOI.

ǁ**goeie môre** /xuiə ˈmɔːrə/ *phr.* Formerly also **goede morgen, gut morgen**. [Afk., ad. Du. *goeden* (attrib. form of *goed*) good + *morgen* morning.] A greeting, 'good morning'; MÔRE sense 1. Also *attrib.*

1841 B. SHAW *Memorials* 64 He smiled as I saluted him, 'goede morgen Mynheer,' (good morning, sir). **1876** F. BOYLE *Savage Life* 169 First came a fat man, all whiskers and paunch, rigged like a Dutch Falstaff, in straw hat and veldt schoen. 'Goede morgen baas,' I said, and 'Goede morgen,' he muttered. **1882** J. NIXON *Among Boers* 84 The farmer generally came to wish us 'gut morgen', and if we understood Dutch I have no doubt we should have been invited inside the house in most cases. **1920** R.Y. STORMBERG *Mrs Pieter de Bruyn* 40 He walked briskly up to a pile of linen in a darkened corner, trying vaguely to shake hands with it and saying cheerily, 'Goei'e more, Mrs. Marais!' **1973** Y. BURGESS *Life to Live* 9 She .. seemed to be looking up at him as she pointed to the notice and said 'Goeie more', which is to say, good morning. **1973** F. CHISHOLM in *Cape Times* 4 Aug. 8 We've had quite a bit lately about the long-winded 'Joe Soap and Co., good morning, *goeie môre*' greeting. Now let's hear what the busy telephonist has to say. **1988** A. KENNY in *Frontline* Apr. 21 There is a conspicuous lack of Platteland courtesy ... When you answer a phone and say, 'Goeie môre', the invariable response is 'Wie praat!' (who's speaking!).

ǁ**goëlery** /ˈxʊələreɪ/ *n.* Also **goelery, goolery**. [Afk., 'sorcery' (ad. Du. *goochelarij* conjuring, prestidigitation).] Sorcery, esp. *Malay magic* (see MALAY *n.* sense 3). See also SLAMAAIER sense 2.

1944 I.D. DU PLESSIS *Cape Malays* 76 The average Malay, while sometimes believing in and fearing 'Malay tricks', is as ignorant of these practices as the European; .. while tales of 'goelery' abound, the exact methods adopted remain a closely guarded secret, known only to the initiated few. **1957** L.G. GREEN *Beyond City Lights* 79 *Toordery*, and *goëlery*, the old magic of the Hottentots and Malays, has not vanished from the Western Province. **1970** *Cape Times* 6 June (Weekend Mag.) 2 'Malay trickery' and 'goëlery' are now widely accepted and firmly believed terms to many of the Cape's whites and non-whites. The traditional old Cape Malay khalifa is mainly responsible for the perpetuation of the popular Malay magic myth. **1972** L. VAN DER POST *Story like Wind* 229 The wagon master, .. perhaps because he also shared something of their submerged belief in 'goolery', settled the matter by announcing that .. he would agree to follow Francois. **1993** D. BERRY on TV1, 23 Feb. (Good Morning South Africa), It's enough to make you think of goëlery.

goema see GHOMMA.

goen var. GHOEN.

goen daag var. GOEDEN DAG.

ǁ**goeters** /ˈxʊtə(r)s, ˈxʊtəz/ *pl. n. Colloq.* Also **goeties**. [Afk., colloq. pl. form of *goed* 'things', chattels, belongings.] 'Things', personal belongings, trivia.

1970 J.A. BALDIE *Informant, Uniondale* Where are my 'goeters' (my things)? **1972** P. FREEDMAN on Radio South Africa 28 Mar., (*lyrics*) I've counted all the cutlery, So don't you drive away With the goeters from the drive-in caff. **1978** S. ROBERTS in *New Classic* No.5, 23 There's the wip-neus upper-class Afrikaner who only cares for money and all the goeters it can buy. **1983** J. CRONIN *Inside* 5 In the prison workshop, with John Matthews making contraband goeters, boxes, ashtrays. **1987** *Style* June 9 This scenario does not include piling *goeties* into the bottom drawer for a dowry. **1991** D. KRAMER on M-Net TV 3 Apr., It had lights and goeters and orange dashboard fluff.

goffel /ˈɡɔf(ə)l, ˈɡɒ-/ *n. Derog.* and *offensive. slang.* [Unknown.] An insulting term for a 'coloured' person. Also *attrib.*

1970 J. Ossher *Informant, Grahamstown* Tell me .. do you know the word goffel meaning a coloured person? **1977** D. Muller *Whitey* 108 'Who are these people?' 'Outies, goffels, rookers. Old ones who have no place ... This one here's a goffel.' Boon jerked the blanket from the inert form close to hand to reveal a dishevelled, tattered female. **1981** L. & P. Robertson-Hotz in *Bloody Horse* No.3, 38 When I'd finished explaining, he didn't laugh, didn't make a joke out of it like any of my goffel buddies would've. [*Note*] Goffel — 'coloured'. **1986** [see gammat sense 1].

gogga, goggo /ˈxɔxə, ˈxɔxɔ/ *n. colloq.* Also **ghogho, gogo, khoko.** [Afk., fr. Khoikhoi *xo-xon* collective term for creeping and slithering creatures.]

1. An insect, a 'creepy-crawly'; goggatjie; nunu sense 2. Also *attrib.*

1905 J. Du Plessis *1000 Miles in Heart of Afr.* 54 This country ought to be called *Gogoland*: it simply swarms with insects. **1909** 'Somgxada' in *E. London Dispatch* 8 Jan. 5 We have heard South Africa described as a land of goggas, and though in certain portions of the tropics a greater number of insects may be found, our country undoubtedly does contain a very considerable quantity. **1927** W. Plomer *I Speak of Afr.* 243 Mrs White: Another huge black beast! What is it? White: It looks like a gogga. **1934** G.G. Munnik *Mem. of Senator* 210 A brand-new plague has suddenly come upon us in the shape of a tiny little 'gogga' ... Our new friend drops out of the thatch in his hundreds and he is as quick as lightning. **1941** M.R. Drennan *Gogga Brown* 1 Of these borrowed words none suits its purpose better or has a greater wealth of meaning than 'gogga' ... It stands alone to signify the millions of creatures that crawl and creep and sometimes fly, and it even includes that low grade of living thing called vermin. **1955** C. Pagewood *Informant, Umkomaas (Kwa-Zulu Natal)* Mr. Ayres was a keen naturalist as well as a hunter and had a wonderful collection of trophies, stuffed birds, butterflies and all kinds of 'goggas'. **1958** A. Jackson *Trader on Veld* 65, I had to get rid of this collection .. because of the constant care it required to keep out moths, worms and other goggas. **1970** J. McIntosh *Stonefish* 155 Nel had chosen the fever tree because the ground there was hard and without grass, and there wouldn't be trouble from 'goggas' .. ants and furry caterpillars and so on. **1973** [see perlé]. **1977** F.G. Butler *Karoo Morning* 144 A muddy pool about six foot across, thick with padda-slime and alive with mosquito larvae, tadpoles, red wriggly worms, and other goggas. **1981** *Sunday Times* 15 Mar. (Extra) 3 Inside the shanties I was shocked and frightened out of my wits by the goggas and crawling little lizards. **1990** R. Rowlands *Informant, Grahamstown* The gogga boxes are so useful because the children may use them to look closely at the insect without hurting it. **1992** D. Berry on TV1, 29 Jan. (Good Morning South Africa), What about the goggos and creatures that live in the dunes? **1992** C. De Beer in *Getaway* Dec. 8 (*letter*) I was bitten, presumably by a spider, on my arm and because I am allergic to all *gogga* bites, a swelling the size of a R1-coin developed.

2. *fig.* and *transf.* Something menacing, frightening, or unwanted.

a. In politics, esp. of policies or election-tactics: a bogy, a monstrous creation. See also spook sense 1.

1934 *Friend* 14 Feb. (Swart), Has the gogga triumphed again, or has the Prime Minister converted his old racialist colleague to a saner and broader South Africanism. **1939** [see spook *n.* sense 1]. **1943** I. Frack *S. Afr. Doctor* 155 This gentleman returned to South Africa with his brand-new imported political 'gogga.' **1947** J.S. Franklin *This Union* (1949) 159 Senator van Zyl is raising another electioneering gogga, and this is another nightmare he himself has raised in order to create a certain amount of misgiving in the minds of the public outside. **1970** D. Prosser in *E. Prov. Herald* 15 Feb., A perfect 'gogga,' in the form of the so-called secret document, has been provided by the reconstituted (Hertzog) Nationalists to be used against them by the Vorster Nationalists in the coming General Election. **1975** *E. Prov. Herald* 5 Sept. 13 The 'goggas' the Government had created (the separate development legislative assemblies and other bodies) were now beginning to bite them. **1976** *Het Suid-Western* 1 Sept., In spite of all the rubbish .. that has been written .. there have been no rondloop goggas and factions on this town council. **1986** *Drum* Apr. 36 PW told the whole world that apartheid was a gogga that had outstayed its welcome, if it ever was welcomed. Unfortunately we see this snarling gogga daily.

b. A dangerous person or thing.

1983 *Drum* Apr. 11 The picture one conjures [up] of the 'General' from the evidence led in court is that of a behorned gogga with a tail and fangs. **1985** T. Walters in *E. Prov. Herald* 19 June 7 As .. chairman of the English Association of South Africa I have launched a campaign to eliminate five pestilences (taal goggas) from South African English. **1986** S. Sepamla *Third Generation* 75 She had heard the man curse and blabber about communists for so long that it was time she got to know more about these unforgivable goggas. **1991** on M-Net TV 5 May (Carte Blanche), If you are going to open up Pandora's box and goggas are going to jump out, you are going to have to be qualified to deal with those goggas. **1994** D.S. Henderson in *Financial Mail* 16 Sept. (Rhodes Univ. Suppl.) 5 You can only work with the resources at your disposal. Every stone will have a *gogga* under it, if you insist on looking — but some of the *goggas* can only receive attention next year.

c. A germ or 'bug', a disease.

1963 A. Fugard *Blood Knot* (1968) 111 Zach: I don't read notices. Morris: They're warnings. It's unfit for human consumption being full of goggas that begin with a B. I can never remember. **1978** A. Parnell in *Andrean* (St. Andrew's College, Grahamstown) 7 July 118 Shortly after his last official appearance as M.O. at last years Feast, as you all probably know, Dr. Wylde was struck down by a particularly vicious gogga, and spent the next four months in a recumbent position in the P.E. provincial hospital. **1987** *Pace* Mar. 4 It is alleged by reputable sources that prostitutes of the world have united for they are about to lose their livelihood because of the dreaded gogga that is causing the medical world sleepless nights.

d. Among anglers: an inedible fish.

1973 *Grocott's Mail* 11 May 3 A small shark caught by Dave van der Riet won the prize for the heaviest 'gogga' (non-edible fish).

goggatjie /ˈxɔxəki/ *n.* Formerly also **gogotje.** [Afk., *gogga* (see prec.) + -ie.] gogga sense 1. Also *fig.*, as a term of endearment.

1911 *E. London Dispatch* 27 Nov. 6 Another old, well-grown tree .. is infested with those abominable *gogotjes* which have already done considerable damage to it. **1972** B. Misheiker on Radio South Africa 30 May, Well, children, it's time to say goodbye to all you little goggatjies.

goggo var. gogga.

goggog var. gogog.

gogo /ˈgɔgɔ/ *n.*[1] *obs.* Pl. **amagogo.** [Xhosa *igogo* (pl. *amagogo*).] A prophet or seer. See also witch-doctor.

1856 R. Birt in *Imp. Blue Bks* Command Paper 2352–1857, 35 A child of a man, professing to be and regarded as a gogo or prophet, not many miles from this in the Xroon, has died of want. **1891** [see itola]. **1891** T.R. Beattie *Pambaniso* 19 The Amagogo assume to be the prophets or seers.

‖**gogo** /ˈgɔgɔ/ *n.*[2] [Zulu, vocative form of *ugogo*, an elderly person, a grandparent.] A term of respect for an elderly person; also used as a title. Cf. magogo.

1980 E. Joubert *Poppie Nongena* 79 And then there was oupa Melani, my father-in law's father's youngest brother .. and my father-in law's stepmother, and old ouma whom they called gogo Nomthinjana. **1982** B. Maseko in *Staffrider* Vol.5 No.1, 26 A young, dark, pretty woman approached her. 'Greetings, gogo,' said the young woman ... 'Greetings, my child,' answered the old lady looking carefully at this young pretty woman who was a symbol of a respectable makoti. **1987** *Informant, Grahamstown* Oh, look at her. She's the absolute apple of her gogo's eye. **1992** C. Greene in *True Love* Nov. 60 The traditional picture of an old *gogo* sitting in front of the fire with the children, telling them stories and teaching them the names of trees and animals, isn't quite so accurate any more. **1994** *Weekly Mail & Guardian* 13 May 8 Seventy-year-old Thelma Mabuso .. burst into a hymn, .. and she was immediately joined by the other *gogos* (grannies).

gogo *n.*[3] var. gogga.

gogog /ˈgɔgɔg, gɔˈgɔg/ *n.* Also **goggog, gogogo, gogok, gokok, igogog, kokok.** Pl. **-s,** or **amagogog.** [fr. n. stem *-gogogo* paraffin tin, common to several Nguni languages (rel. to Zulu *gogoza* rumble or bang, as of empty tins); perh. orig. echoic. For an explanation of the prefix in the plural form, see ama-.] A paraffin tin; a measure of roughly two buckets.

1961 D. Rooke *Lover for Estelle* 67 Across the plain three separate parties of women with kokoks on their heads were wending their way to buy sugar or blankets or mealies. **1968** R. Griffiths *Man of River* 18 When a woman carries water in a gog-gog on her head she puts leaves in the bucket to stop the water splashing when she walks. **1970** S. Sparks *Informant, Fort Beaufort* The African maid carried a 'gogog' of water on her head (4 gallon paraffin tin). **1971** M. Knowling *Informant, Grahamstown* An igogog is a paraffin tin, so called from the noise it makes when being emptied. **1978** M. King *Informant, Grahamstown* We get four gogoks of milk a day. **1982** M. wa Mmutle in Chapman & Dangor *Voices from Within* 167 My mother died a servant ... On a plank bed she slept Supported by four Gokoks. **1986** 'MvB' in *Cape Times* 19 Feb., During the Depression (and after) road workers slung a bit of gristly meat into an empty gogog, poured water over it, boiled it on an open fire and voila! potjiekos. **1987** O. Musi in *Drum* Apr. 61 A little boy .. was caught stealing fruit and angry villagers poured a whole gogogo of paraffin — that's a 25-litre tinful — on his hands and set them alight. **1989** F.G. Butler *Tales from Old Karoo* 114 A black child started beating out the time on an empty *gogog.* **1994** D. Bikitsha in *Sunday Times* 2 Jan. 13 Our new year celebrations are a combination of Guy Fawkes, Halloween and Rio's annual carnival ... Bonfires from car tyres erupt like a swarm of fireflies. The din from tin drums or *amagogogo*, church bells, sirens .. is deafening.

gogotje var. goggatjie.

goha(r) var. gorah.

gokok var. gogog.

Golden City *n. phr.* Also with small initials. [Named for its gold-mines.] ***The Golden City***: The city of Johannesburg; City of Gold; Egoli; Gauteng sense 1. See also Jo'burg.

1892 *The Jrnl* 14 July 3 Some days ago, at the Golden City, a well-known Secretary was catechising a youthful aspirant for the honoured post of office-boy. **1896** Purvis & Biggs *S. Afr.* 124 The evil influence of the concentration of power in the hands of the few magnates of the Golden City must be borne strongly in mind by all who desire to grasp the significance of certain South African problems. **1909** Lady S. Wilson *S. Afr. Mem.* 288 The Golden City itself was, to all outward appearances, as thriving as ever, with its busy population, its crowded and excellent shops, and its general evidences of opulence, which appeared to overbalance — or, in any case, wish to conceal — any existing poverty or distress. **1913** J. Brandt *Petticoat Commando* 15, I must ask my reader to turn his attention for a few moments to that great mining centre, Johannesburg, 'The Golden City' of South Africa. **1928** V.G. Desai tr. *M.K. Gandhi's Satyagraha in S. Afr.* 12 Johannesburg, the golden city of South Africa.

1936 R.J.M. Goold-Adams *S. Afr. To-Day & To-Morrow* 158 Below and in front of us was the Golden City. It was smaller and more delicate in appearance than I had expected, even in the distance. **1959** [see Egoli]. **1979** M. Matshoba *Call Me Not a Man* 95, I felt like a *goduka* going to the Golden City for the first time in his life, afraid it may swallow him, afraid he may not return from the dark earth's entrails of gold. **1987** N. Mkhonze in *True Love* Mar. 46 As the government was against blacks from other towns working in the Golden City, I was told that I did not qualify to register as a worker in Johannesburg. **1990** *Sunday Times* 25 Feb. 20 When Russian immigrants K & L first set up their business in the Golden City in 1895, their first pile came from syringes they made to inoculate cattle against the rinderpest. **1993** E. Khumalo in *Pace* July 77 In Plein Street we found a young man .. who came to Jo'burg two years ago ... 'I'm dying to go back home. I don't want to die in this filthy concrete jungle called the Golden City.'

golden eagle *n. phr.* An obsolescent name for the tawny eagle, *Aquila rapax* of the Accipitridae; also called lammervanger.

1846 J.C. Brown tr. *T. Arbousset's Narr. of Explor. Tour to N.-E. of Col.* 220 The English of the Cape call it the *golden eagle* .., and the Dutch farmers, *lamvanger*, or *lamb seizer*, because it is accustomed to seize, and carry off to its aerie, a lamb or kid. **1864** [see lammervanger]. **1970** *Daily News* 4 June 21 A 13-year old White youth captured a long taloned golden eagle (lammervanger) with his bare hands.

golden mole *n. phr.* [Named for the metallic gleam of its fur.]
a. Any of several species of insectivorous mole-like mammals of the family Chrysochloridae, with no visible eyes and no external ears or tails. Cf. blesmol.

1855 W.S. Dallas in *Syst. Nat. Hist.* II. 490 The peculiar metallic lustre of their coats, which has given rise to the name of Golden Mole (*Chrysochloris aurea*). **1905** W.L. Sclater in Flint & Gilchrist *Science in S. Afr.* 135 The *Chrysochloridae* (Golden Moles) and the *Macroscelidae* (Elephant Shrews), though not confined to South Africa, are restricted to the Continent, and apparently have their headquarters in the south. **1912** *State* Sept. 229 (Pettman), The *golden mole* is tailless, whereas the blesmol, mole rat and sand mole have short tails. In the *golden mole* the fur has a metallic sheen. *c*1939 S.H. Skaife *S. Afr. Nature Notes* 163 We have two distinct types of moles in South Africa – the little golden moles .. which are insectivorous, and the sand moles, or mole rats, which are vegetarians ... The golden moles are peculiar to Africa. **1972** *Cape Times* 13 Mar. 10 A sequence on the Golden Mole – first discovered near Gobabeb in 1963 – shows a blind animal .. evolved to live under the baking sands of the Namib. **1978** *Darling* 22 Nov. 33 Hidden in the sand dunes safe from the fierce heat and predators there are shovel-nosed lizards, the translucent palmeto gecko, the golden mole and the sidewinder rattlesnake. **1988** C. & T. Stuart *Field Guide to Mammals* 32 With the exception of a few species the golden moles do not push up heaps or mounds like the molerats, but long, meandering ridges just under the surface. **1990** J. Huntly *Afr. Wildlife Sketches* 88 To glimpse an African Golden Mole in the open above ground would be a rare event ... My only contact with a Golden Mole was over before it began, for my dog had caught and killed it before I could rescue it.

b. With distinguishing epithet: **Cape golden mole**, *Chrysochloris asiatica*; **giant golden mole**, *Chrysospalax trevelyani*; **Grant's golden mole**, *Eremitalpa granti*; **Visagie's golden mole**, *Chrysochloris visagiei*.

1901 W.L. Sclater *Mammals of S. Afr.* II. 170 *Chrysochloris aurea*, The **Cape Golden Mole**. **1988** M. Branch *Explore Cape Flora* 25 The small Cape golden mole is common in our gardens ... It makes runs just below the surface of the soil and gobbles up its own weight of insects and earthworms every day. **1901** W.L. Sclater *Mammals of S. Afr.* II. 173 *Chrysochloris trevelyani*, The **Giant Golden Mole**. **1993** Pringle & McMaster in *Afr. Wildlife* Vol.47 No.3, 124 The rare giant golden mole, *Chrysospalax trevelyani*, is known only from approximately 100 specimens in the Pirie Forest near King William's Town. **1987** T.F.J. Van Rensburg *Intro. to Fynbos* 52 As far as small mammals are concerned, there are quite a few endangered and endemic species in the fynbos. The following endangered species occur: **Visagie's golden mole** (Calvinia) **Grant's golden desert mole** (Lambert's Bay).

Goli var. Egoli.

‖**gologo** /ˈgɔlɔgɔ/ *n.* Also **ugologo**. [Zulu *ugologo* spirituous liquor, ad. Eng. *grog*.] In urban (esp. township) Eng.: strong alcoholic liquor.

1899 A. Werner *Captain of Locusts* 193 'You hold your tongue!' said MacVicar sharply. 'Now, Luzipo, what's this?' ''Kos'!' said Luzipo, 'this Umlungu has been drinking ugologo; therefore he knows not what he says or does.' [*Note*] grog. **1961** T. Matshikiza *Choc. for my Wife* 65 'Have a double brandy. The liquor here is much weaker than what we drink back home.' He knocked that off without wincing. 'Aha. We call it gologo from grog.' **1980** [see Sepamla quot. at excuse-me].

gom /xɔm/ *n. Derog. slang.* Shortened form of gomtor.

1970 A. Van der Berg *Informant, Pretoria* That man lying on the pavement is a real gom. **1973** *Informant* That green pork-pie of his looks a proper gom's hat. **1989** *Informant, Grahamstown* These Afrikaans goms are really .. gommie. **1990** R. Malan *My Traitor's Heart* 35 They were all goms, or rednecks – common, in my mother's prim Victorian estimation. On Friday nights they'd get drunk, and there'd be cars with twin-cam engines and furry dashboards revving up in the road, women screaming, men cursing and once, guns going off in the air.

gomassie var. kamassi.

gom-gom /ˈgɔmgɔm/ *n. Hist.* [Unkn., perh. rel. to ghomma; cf. *gum-gum*, recorded in the *OED* from 1700, fr. Malay, 'a hollow iron bowl, struck with an iron or wooden stick'.] **a.** gorah. **b.** A musical bow similar to the gorah, but designed to produce a more resonant sound.

1731 G. Medley tr. *P. Kolb's Present State of Cape of G.H.* I. 271 One of the *Hottentot* Instruments of Musick .. is call'd, both by *Negroes* and *Hottentots*, *Gom Gom* ... The *Gom Gom* is a bow. *Ibid.* 272 The Grand *Gom Gom* is made by putting on the String .. a Cocoa-Nut Shell, about a third part saw'd off, so that it hangs like a Cup. **1931** P.R. Kirby in *S. Afr. Jrnl of Science* XXVIII. Nov. 523 His description of what the English translator quaintly (and without authority) styled the 'Grand Gom-gom' introduces a problem. **1934** — *Musical Instruments of Native Races* (1965) 172 Kolbe .. was responsible for the next account of the *gora*, which he named the *gom-gom* ... He .. found it played by the Hottentots, though he was by no means sure that they had not derived it from the 'slaves' who also played upon it ... He complicated matters by adding .. the description of what he called a 'full-sounding' *gom-gom* ... He gave an illustration of the latter instrument, which I fear was purely imaginary. **1982** E. Mugglestone in *Afr. Music* VI. ii. 94 Kolb's text indicates that two types of musical bow were observed, to both of which he applied the name *gom-gom* ... As the 'lesser' *gom-gom* is in fact the *gora*, the two types of bow may be distinguished conveniently by referring to them as the *gora* and the *'grand' gom-gom* respectively.

gomma var. ghomma.

gommie /ˈxɔmi/ *adj. Derog. slang.* [fr. gom.] Common, low-class.

1970 C.S. Hendry *Informant, Somerset West* She's a gommie person (lives in a gommie part of town). **1970** J. Cloete *Informant, Pietersburg* Gommy (boorish). **1988** *Informant, Grahamstown* But he doesn't sound gommie and he's married to *that* woman! **1989** [see gom]. **1989** *Sunday Times* 1 Oct. 17 Swopping the languid tones of the Queen's English for *gommie* glottal stops and short nasal vowels. **1991** V. Warren *Informant, Alberton* Gommie. Lacks a touch a class. Those plastic flowers are really gommie.

‖**gompou** /ˈxɔmpəʊ/ *n.* Formerly also **gompaauw, gom pau, gompauw**. Pl. unchanged. [Afk. (earlier S. Afr. Du. *gompaauw*), *gom* gum + *pou* (fr. Du. *pauw*) peacock; see quot. 1936.] The kori, *Ardeotis kori*.

1867 E.L. Layard *Birds of S. Afr.* 283 The 'Gom-Paauw' .. is a noble bird, and when seen stalking about in its proper haunts, affords a sight to a hunter's eyes never to be forgotten. **1887** *S.W. Silver & Co.'s Handbk to S. Afr.* 176 The largest of these is the Kori Bustard or 'Gom Paauw' (*Eupodotis cristata*, Scop.) the adult male of which often weighs from 30 to 35 lbs. **1905** W.L. Sclater in Flint & Gilchrist *Science in S. Afr.* 143 The Bustards (*Otidae*) are represented by .. twelve species, ranging from the large Gom Pauw (*Otis kori*), the male of which sometimes weighs as much as 40 lbs. to the smaller Knorhaan (*Otis afra*). **1920** F.C. Cornell *Glamour of Prospecting* 79 The larger variety, known as the gom paauw, often weighs from 30 to 40 lb., and has been recorded up to 50 lb or more. **1936** E.L. Gill *First Guide to S. Afr. Birds* 150 The name Gom Pou reflects the general belief that this Bustard is particularly fond of the gum that exudes from certain thorn trees. **1948** A.C. White *Call of Bushveld* 236 Kori bustards, better recognised by their South African name, gom pau, are magnificent game birds. **1964** L.G. Green *Old Men Say* 100 Quaggas and the huge gamebirds called *gompou* were sometimes available but were never common. **1974** J.M. Coetzee *Dusklands* 127 A bustard (*gompou, Otis kori*) .. perished in a hail of smallshot and pebbles from Klawer's piece. This bustard is alas nearly extinct. **1981** *Zimbabwe Wildlife* June, One can still find old 'Boere' recipes for preparation of the 'Gom Paauw'. **1991** [see kori].

‖**gomtor** /ˈǁɔmtɔr/ *n. Derog. slang.* Also **gomtorrel**. [Afk., lout.] An uncouth or common person; gom; gopse sense 2.

1970 E.J. Le Roux *Informant, Bellville* Gomtor. Common people, just rubbish. **1970** V.R. Fink *Informant, Johannesburg* The litter at the picnic spot was caused by a bunch of gomtors (a derogatory term describing an ignorant, common type of Afrikaner). **1990** *Frontline* Mar.-Apr. 16 The throng is 90% decent people waiting with the patience of the rock of ages, and 10% loud drunken low-grade gomtorrels who swill liquor and use the floor as a dustbin.

gona *n.*[1] var. ganna.

Gona /ˈgɔnə, gəʊnə/ *n.*[2] *Obs.* exc. *hist.* Also **Ghona, Gonah, Gonna, Goonaa**, and with small initial. Pl. **-s**, or unchanged. [See Gonaqua.] Shortened form of Gonaqua (sense 1). Also *attrib.*

1809 R. Collins in G.M. Theal *Rec. of Cape Col.* (1900) VII. 20 The poor Gona pleaded with all the gestures of theatrical representation to be exempted from the prohibition against intruders into the colony. **1818** [see Briqua]. **1824** J. Ayliff Journal. 31 Two Goonaa Men (these being a race between the Caffres and Hottentots and [who] speak the Caffre Language). **1833** W. Shaw in B. Shaw *Memorials* (1841) 231 About fifty years ago this country was occupied by several powerful clans of Hottentots, especially the Gonakwas or Gonna Tribe. **1853** F.P. Fleming *Kaffraria* 8 There is .. a .. tribe on the Eastern frontier of the present colony, called Gonaquas, or Gona Hottentots, who are of intermingled Kaffir and Hottentot extraction. **1853** J. Green *Kat River Settlement in 1851* 70 The Kaffirs, Gonahs, and Hottentots immediately started off in pursuit in the most furious manner. *a*1858 J. Goldswain *Chron.* (1949) II. 134 Gonah .. (basterd betwen a Kaffer and Hottentot). **1957** Varley & Matthew *Cape Jrnls of N.J. Merriman* 119 The term Gona was frequently used in the Eastern Colony to designate a Xosa whose colour and general appearance approached those of the Hottentots. **1981** J.B. Peires *House of Phalo* 24 According to one report, there were more San than Gona Khoi living among the Gcaleka.

Gonakwebu var. GQUNUKHWEBE.

Gonaqua /gɔˈnakwa, gə-/ *n. Obs. exc. hist.* Also **Chonacqua, Ganaqua, Genequois, Ghonaqua, Ghonoqua, Gonaaqua, Gonagua, Gonakwa, Guanaqua, Gunaqua.** Pl. **-s**, or unchanged. [Khoikhoi, *gona* etym. unknown (perh. rel. to *gonna*, see GONNA *n.*[3]) + *-qua* pl. male suffix, 'man', 'people'.]

1. A member of a Khoikhoi people of what is now the Eastern Cape, absorbed by the end of the 18th century into the Xhosa polity; a member of a people of mixed Khoikhoi and Xhosa descent; GONA *n.*[2] Also *attrib.* See also GQUNUKHWEBE.

1776 F. MASSON in *Phil. Trans. of Royal Soc.* LXVI. 296 These Hottentots are called Gunaquas, but were mixed with another people whom the Dutch call Caffers, who border upon Terra de Natal. 1790 tr. F. Le Vaillant's *Trav.* II. 2 These hordes of Gonaquas, who equally resemble the Caffres and the Hottentots, must be a mixed breed produced by these two nations. 1798 [see OUTENIQUA sense 1]. 1799 LADY A. BARNARD *S. Afr. Century Ago* (1910) 213 The Gonagua man took great pains to tell Mynheer Barnard what pretty girls there are in that country. 1810 G. BARRINGTON *Acct of Voy.* 222 The Ghonoquas .. once considerable in their numbers .. are now reduced to so very small a number as to border upon a total extermination of the tribe. 1812 [see TIXO]. 1827 G. THOMPSON *Trav.* I. 51 This once numerous tribe, like many other Hottentot clans mentioned by early travellers, is now entirely extinct. The residue of the Gonaquas sought refuge among Caffers a few years ago, and they are now fully incorporated with that people. 1833 *Graham's Town Jrnl* 20 June 2 Gezwint Baartman, Goliat, Gonaqua Hottentots. 1860 W. SHAW *Story of my Mission* 318 Ghonaquas, a border tribe of Hottentots who had mingled much with the Kaffirs during one or two generations, and many of whom consequently could speak the Kaffir language. 1871 J. MACKENZIE *Ten Yrs* (1971) 517 In 1737 there was still a considerable tract of country between the Dutch settlers and the Kaffirs, which was inhabited by the Gonaqua Hottentots. 1930 I. SCHAPERA *KhoiSan Peoples* 46 The *Gonaqua*, at first apparently an insignificant tribe .. by the middle of the eighteenth century had become the most powerful group of Hottentots in the east. 1979 *Daily Dispatch* 11 May 5 Mr Ncapayi claims to be heir apparent to the tribe's paramountcy as a direct descendant of Paramount Chief Hoho who was head, in the 7th century, of the Ciskei Gonaqua Hottentots, who were also known as the Khoikois. 1986 B. MACLENNAN *Proper Degree of Terror* 60 At least one family of Ghonaqua Khoikhoi .. who certainly had no base in Xhosaland, were unceremoniously bundled across the border.

2. *rare.* PONDO sense 1 a.

1812 A. PLUMPTRE tr. H. Lichtenstein's *Trav. in Sn Afr.* (1928) I. 298 Proceeding along the coast [*sc.* after crossing the Bashee river], the next tribe to the Koossas is one which is called by many different names; that by which it is most generally known is the Gonaaquas, but by the colonists they are usually called Mambuckis; the Koossas call them the Imbos, and in Van Reenen's Journey they are called the people of Hambona.

gonie /ˈgɔːni, ˈgəʊnɪ, ˈgɒnɪ/ *n. slang.* Also **goney, gonnie.** [Isicamtho, origin unkn. (but see quot. 1962).] A knife.

[1962 W.S. MANQUPU in *Star* 22 Feb. 14 Other languages have also been drawn on for the tsotsis' *lingua franca,* Chinese, Latin, French, Indian and Central African. For example, as a group of Central African tribesmen are addicted to the use of the knife, the tsotsis now have the verb 'goni,' which means to stab. The word comes from the Angoni tribe of Nyasaland.] 1978 A. AKHALWAYA in *Rand Daily Mail* 10 July 7 'There's spans of ous vying around with gonies ...' Natal Indian slang is a language on its own. 1979 A.P. BRINK *Dry White Season* 80 'My wife keeps on nagging me to stop before someone tries to pasa me with a gonnie' — making a stabbing gesture with his left hand to clarify the tsotsi expressions he seemed to relish. 1985 J. MAKUNGA in *Staffrider* Vol.6 No.2, 36 Vuyo had the blade of his gonie on Tsidi's neck. 1987 S.A. BOTHA in *Frontline* Oct.-Nov. 15 Prison slang ... Goney. knife.

goniva *n. obs.* Also **gonivah.** [ad. Yiddish *g(e)neyve,* fr. Hebrew *geneva,* fr. *ganav* steal.] A stolen diamond. Also *attrib.*

1887 J.W. MATTHEWS *Incwadi Yami* 189 He had caught and thrashed a nigger who had had, as he said, 'the imperence [*sic*] to fancy that a respectable man like him would buy a "goniva".' 1887 'W.T.E.' *I.D.B.* 234 Say, stranger, have you struck the original I.D.B. cemetery; or how is it that you find such a thunderin' heap of gonivas [*printed* gouivas] in your ground? 1899 G.C. GRIFFITH *Knaves of Diamonds* 65 If you've got the gonivahs, why don't you plant 'em somewhere safe and run 'em down when you get a chance like the others do? 1911 L. COHEN *Reminisc. of Kimberley* 154 It was the habit of 'the boys' to lay in wait for him and relieve him of the superfluous cash, for this prime 'goniva' [*Anglicé* —I.D.B.] was a great gambler. Ibid. 216 These wholesale robberies .. formed one of the principal foundations of the immense fortune these men acquired. It was .. a rapid method of getting rich — to buy gonivas and sell them thus. 1924 — *Reminisc. of Jhb.* 248 Goniva, my poor innocents, is the polite term used amongst the learned professors of the game to denote a stolen diamond. 1950 E. PARTRIDGE *Dict. of Underworld Slang* 298 Goniva, A stolen diamond: South African (and illicit diamond men's) .. ex South African s[lang] *goniv*, 'an illicit diamond-buyer'.

gonna /ˈxɔna, -nə/ *int. colloq.* Also **gonnas.** [Afk., origin obscure; perh. fr. Khoikhoi, or ad. Afk. *gotta* a euphemistic substitute for *God* /xɔt/ God.] An exclamation of surprise or consternation.

1970 K. NICOL *Informant, Durban* Gonnas! I didn't expect to see you here! 1975 *Dict. of Eng. Usage in Sn Afr.* 76 Gonna, .. exclamation of surprise, the equiv. of 'oh dear!', 'good gracious!' 1988 A. SHER *Middlepost* 238 He will return, of that I have no doubt — oo gonna! — and when he does it will be with an army riding under the crown of England. 1989 *Personality* 11 Sept. 71 Names that roll easily off the tongues of people who say *gonnas* instead of 'I Say!' 1991 V. WARREN *Informant, Alberton* Oh gonna, I forgot to tell her about the meeting.

gonna *n.*[1] var. KANNA *n.*[2]

Gonna *n.*[2] var. GONA *n.*[2]

‖**gonna** /ˈxɔnə, gɒnə/ *n.*[3] Also **goonah.** [Afk., fr. Khoikhoi.] Any of several small shrubs of the Thymelaeaceae, including species of *Gnidia, Passerina,* and *Struthiola.* Occas. with distinguishing epithet, as **Outeniqua gonna** (*P. falcifolia*). Also *attrib.,* and *comb.* **gonnabos** /-bɔs/ (Afk., *bos* bush].

1913 A. GLOSSOP *Barnes's S. Afr. Hsehold Guide* 238 A splendid gargle .. is prepared from the 'Goonah' plant, which trails wild along the ground freely in country parts. 1966 C.A. SMITH *Common Names* 232 *Gonna*, A collective name, used by the Hottentots for several species of Thymeleaceae. 1983 M.M. KIDD *Cape Peninsula* 194 *Passerina vulgaris.* Thymelaeceae. *Gonnabos.* Shrub; 1-3,5m; very common; .. flowers vary from yellow to dull red. 1987 T.F.J. VAN RENSBURG *Intro. to Fynbos* 16 The Outeniqua gonna (*Passerina falcifolia*) with its rope-like, drooping branches and small leaves, .. [is] often found along streams.

gonnie var. GONIE.

Gonokwabie, -kwebie varr. GQUNUKHWEBE.

gonya var. GHONYA.

good-for *n. hist.* Pl. **-s**, occas. unchanged. [fr. Eng. *good for* drawn and valid for (of a promissory note).] An IOU, a promissory note. Also *attrib.*

1821 G. BARKER *Journal.* 29 Nov., Spent the whole morning collecting money, got all the good fors cashed. 1822 *Prohibition of Promissory Notes under Fifty Rixdollars* in *Stat. Law of Cape of G.H.* (1862) 64 Various notes, bills of exchange, and drafts for money, for very small sums, under the appellation of 'good-fors,' have been .. circulated and negotiated in the frontier districts of this settlement. 1832 *Graham's Town Jrnl* 4 May 75 The Messenger proved that he had told defendant, that his *Good For* was ceded, and had shown him the words 'pay to bearer' written on the back. a1862 J. AYLIFF *Jrnl of 'Harry Hastings'* (1963) 82 All was barter, or to receive what were called goodfors, a kind of paper money which the merchants had the power of issuing. 1866 *Cape Town Dir.* 86 No 'good for,' 'IOU,' or other acknowledgement of debt, not being a promissory note, shall require to be stamped, so long as it shall be retained by the creditor to whom it was first delivered, and it may be paid by the debtor to such creditor without being stamped. 1879 R.J. ATCHERLEY *Trip to Boerland* 232 These 'good fors', which answer to an English IOU, are common enough in South Africa, and, if backed by good names, circulate pretty freely. 1882 H. RIDER HAGGARD *Cetywayo* 133 As there was no cash in the country this was done by issuing Government promissory notes, known as 'goodfors'. 1897 J.P. FITZPATRICK *Outspan* 77 The Pretoria tradesmen .. would no longer accept 'good-fors' of even a few shillings value. 1903 D. BLACKBURN *Burgher Quixote* 152 Those that have no money to pay have given 'good-fors'. 1937 [see PAPBROEK]. 1940 F.B. YOUNG *City of Gold* 180 He drove his wagon to Headquarters .. and received a written acknowledgment, one of those 'good-fors' which had lately become the chief currency of the Transvaal Government. 1960 J.J.L. SISSON *S. Afr. Judicial Dict.* 326 *Good for,* a popular and brief form of acknowledgement of debt. It is not normally a negotiable instrument. 1972 A. SCHOLEFIELD *Wild Dog Running* 100 Normally the watch would have gone in straight barter for goods or for a kind of paper money which the merchants issued, called 'good-fors'. 1983 *S. Afr. Panorama* May 25 In January and February, 1900, 'good-for' vouchers with face values of one shilling, two shillings, and three shillings, were released for circulation in the besieged town. 1989 *Reader's Digest Illust. Hist.* 149 In 1865, in a new bid to bail the republic out of its financial difficulties, the government decided to print paper money ... But the currency was so worthless that it was rejected even by state officials, who .. chose rather to pay with credit notes called 'good-fors'.

Goodwill Day see DAY OF GOODWILL.

goof *n.* var. GOEF *n.*

goof *v.* var. GOEF *v.*

goofies /ˈgʊfiːz/ *n. slang.* Pl. unchanged. [Englished form of GOEF *n.* or *v.* + Eng. (informal) n.-forming suffix *-ie* + pl. *-s*.] Among schoolchildren: a public swimming bath.

1970 J. GREENWOOD *Informant, Johannesburg* Let's go to the Goofies today (swimming baths). 1970 G. FERREIRA *Informant, Pietersburg* Let's go to the goofies. 1992 T. BARON in *Style* Oct. 110 The big games were on Saturday morning. Huge crowds turned up at the public park next to the Yeoville goofies, Raleigh Street shut up shop so everybody could go cheer for the kids.

gooi /xɔɪ, xuɪ/ *v. trans. Slang.* Also **goei.** [Afk., throw, fling.] Used loosely with a range of meanings.

1.a. To give (someone something).

1946 [see sense 2]. 1963 L.F. FREED *Crime in S. Afr.* 105 When a ducktail or a 'joller' .. asks you to 'gooi a man 'n skyfie' he wants you to give him a cigarette. 1970 [see LAS]. 1974 B. SIMON *Joburg, Sis!* 129 Ag please ou china gooi me sommer five cents please. Ibid. 131 Ja, you know you walk three feet one yard in the bladdy street and there's somebody there gooi us a start assebliet ou china. 1979 *Sunday Times* 8 July (Mag. Sect.) 3 'Gooi me a zero,' chirped the robin and my own good buddy went bug-eyed. 1983 *Sunday Times* 18 Dec. (Mag. Sect.) 10 When the .. sun slips from the

.. sky over a base camp somewhere in the Operational Area, there really is nothing much you need to say. Except maybe: 'Gooi me a light' or 'Go buy your own Castle Lager.' ... This is what they [*sc.* the army] are gonna gooi us. **1985** H. PRENDINI in *Style* Oct. 39 Southern Suburbs Joller: .. I asked the hout on the site to gooi me some start so we could get some graze. **1990** [see CHAFF sense 2]. **1991** I.E.G. COLLETT *Informant, Pilgrim's Rest* Goei me a wettie. Give me a sip. **1994** G. WILLOUGHBY in *Weekly Mail & Guardian* 17 June 42 Goodday, *meneer*, what can I *gooi* you? .. The granadilla's a good choice.

b. To cause (something) to move: to throw or toss (something); to drop (something); to put (something) together; to use (something). Freq. in *imp.* Also *transf.*

1970 M.E. TAMLIN *Informant, Cape Town* Gooi that ball here. **1970** G. FERREIRA *Informant, Pietersburg* Gooi that paper away. **1977** C. HOPE in S. Gray *Theatre Two* (1981) 40 Sometimes I think those weights you gooi give you muscles in your head. **1981** *Cape Times* 28 Dec. 9 These holiday jollers .. gooi a line without any bait in our muddy waters after dopping a cellar cask. **1985** P. SLABOLEPSZY *Sat. Night at Palace* 33 He goes behind this rock, pulls out a stick of dynamite — lights it with his cheroot and he goois it at these ous. **1988** H. PRENDINI in *Style* June 104 Gooi some more wors on the fire, bokkie. **1990** P. O'BYRNE on Radio South Africa, So how many songs did you get? .. Well, gooi in your entries anyway. **1993** S. DIKENI in *Bua* Dec. 32 Then I gooi my Afrikaans ear and sowaar I got them. **1994** *Sunday Times* 23 Jan. 28 (*advt*) Let's .. get us a packet of slap chips ... And let's don't be shy with the salt and vinegar, just gooi it on and dig in. **1994** M. CORAZZA in *Weekly Mail & Guardian* 17 June 42 When the snow hits the Berg, .. it's time to fish out .. your well-worn slow cooker and *gooi* some old fashioned traditional bredie to warm the cockles of all and sundry.

2. In the phrr. ***to gooi a canary***, to whistle a warning; ***to gooi a spasm***, to react with joy or enthusiasm; to 'freak out'; ***gooi a U-ey***, make a rapid (often illegal) u-turn; ***to gooi on anchors***, to stop rapidly; ***to gooi (someone) grief***, to cause trouble; ***to gooi pomp*** [Afk. slang *pomp* (not used in polite speech)], to have sexual intercourse; ***to gooi strop*** [Afk. *strop* strap; or STROP *n.*[2]], to make trouble.

1946 *Cape Times* in E. Partridge *Dict. of Underworld* (1950) 299 When the gang is on a job there is always a lookout, .. who will 'gooi a canary' (whistle) if he should sight a diener or 'Transvaler'. **1985** H. PRENDINI in *Style* Oct. 39 They 'swaai a zephyr', or get 'goofed' on a 'skyf' (smoke dagga) before 'gooing pomp' (making love) and then 'zonking out' (going to sleep). **1985** P. SLABOLEPSZY *Sat. Night at Palace* 36 Vince: .. I'll tell you what. You make with a couple of Rocco Burgers — I'll forget about the five cents you owe me, OK? September: You are mad ... Forsie: Vince, stop gooing strop now, man. **1991** G. LEVIN *Informant, Johannesburg* The outcrop of rock was so spectacular that I gooied a spasm when I saw it. **1991** A.E. STEWART *Informant, Johannesburg* Gooi a U-ie: Do a U-turn. **1991** D. KRAMER on M-Net TV 3 Apr., I gooied on anchors, but it's all in vain. **1991** D. BOSWELL *Informant, Giyani (N. Tvl)* I'm warning you. Don't gooi me grief because I'm not in the mood ... I'll bliksem you. **1992** J. THOM *Informant, Springs* Gooi a U-ey means to do a quick U-turn.

goolery var. GOËLERY.

gooma var. GHOMMA.

Goonaa var. GONA *n.*[2]

goonah var. GONNA *n.*[3]

goorah var. GORAH.

goosie *n. slang.* Also **goose**. [Transf. use of Eng. *goose* 'a woman; hence, the sexual favour; low: from ca. 1870' (E. Partridge *Dictionary of Slang* ed. by P. Beale, 1984, p.489) + (informal) suffix *-ie*; or Afk. suffix -IE.]

1. *Prison slang.* The 'female' partner in a homosexual relationship. Cf. LIGHTY sense 2.

1965 R.H.L. STRACHAN in *Rand Daily Mail* 1 July 4 In Pretoria Central there were certain big cells containing about five prisoners and these were known as 'married quarters'. A number of long-term prisoners had their 'goosie' and these were open relationships.

2. A girl; a girlfriend.

1974 J. MATTHEWS *Park* 23 'No dice, Sly ou pellie,' Jammie said. 'No gang-bang dis time. I doan wanna scare de goosies.' **1982** *Sunday Times* 16 May 16 The boys talk (oh, but *what* talk; of gooses and graze!), and they bully September into making them some kos. **1984** 'DAN' in *Frontline* May 39 The old lekker plekke where an ou could sit on the grass and chaff his goosie are full of security fences now. **1985** P. SLABOLEPSZY *Sat. Night at Palace* 78 *Goose*, chick, bird, doll. **1990** R. GOOL *Cape Town Coolie* 59, I 'eard it you living in the Cape now ... Ow's all those Coloured *bokkies*? ... You could fix me up with some Malay *goosie*?

‖**gopse** /ˈxɔpsə/ *n. Derog. colloq.* Also **gops**. [Afk. *gops* (+ pl. *-e*); ultimate origin unkn.]

1.a. BACKVELD *n.* sense a. **b.** BUNDU sense 1.

1970 J.F. PRINSLOO *Informant, Lüderitz (Namibia)* Gopse. A backward area or otherwise the same as 'bundus'. **1970** BEETON & DORNER in *Eng. Usage in Sn Afr.* Vol.1 No.2, 14 *Gopse*, .. Inferior locality, place. **1989** F.G. BUTLER *Tales from Old Karoo* 34 Horrelpoot: What sort of a doctor are you, to leave my gate open? Doctor: Do you call that a gate? Horrelpoot: Where were you educated, man? In the *gops*?

2. *rare*, perh. *obs.* GOMTOR.

1970 BEETON & DORNER in *Eng. Usage in Sn Afr.* Vol.1 No.2, 14 'Gops', a low-class person.

Gorachouqua /ˌgɔrəˈtʃʊkwa/ *pl. n. Obs.* exc. *hist.* Also **Gorachouqua's, Gorachouquas, Korachoqua**. [Khoikhoi, see quot. 1933.] Collectively, the members of a Khoikhoi people of the south-western Cape believed to be the ancestors of the modern Kora peoples (see KORA sense 1). Also *attrib.* See also SALDANHA sense 1 a.

As is the case with many names of peoples and groups in *S. Afr. Eng.*, this word has been found only in plural uses; however, it may be that it has also been used in unrecorded singular forms.

1670 [see COCHOQUA]. **1880** [see GORINGHAIKONA]. **1928** [see KORAQUA sense 1]. **1930** I. SCHAPERA *KhoiSan Peoples* 47 The *Korana* or *!Kora* are .. traditionally the descendants of the Kora or Gorachouqua, who, originally resident in the Cape Peninsula, began to draw away inland from the Dutch settlement towards the end of the seventeenth century. [**1933** — *Early Cape Hottentots* 9 Also referred to in the early records as Chorachouquas, Ghorachouquas, Goerachouqua, Gorachouna, etc. They are generally held to have been the ancestors of the modern Korana .. and to have been named after their first chief !Kora .. ; their tribal name as given in the records would therefore mean 'men of !Kora'.] **1968** J.T. MCNISH *Rd to Eldorado* 3 One tribe at the Cape, the Korachoqua, from which the Korana finally emerged as a tribe living along the Vaal River, were living at Tigerberg in 1657. **1968** [see GORINGHAIKONA]. **1975** [see Std Encycl. quot. at KORANNA sense 1]. **1989** *Reader's Digest Illust. Hist.* 42 This hardening of the cattle price owed a lot to the efforts of a Gorachouqua Khoikhoi named Goree, who in 1613 was kidnapped and taken .. to London where he soon learned the real value of money and trade. *Ibid.* 44 Also living on or near the Cape Peninsula were the Gorachouqua and the Goringhaiqua.

gorah /ˈgɔrə/ *n. Music.* Also **ghoera, goha(r), goorah, gora, gôrah, goráh, gorra(h), goura, !goura, gowra, gura(h), korà, t'goerra**. [Prob. Khoikhoi *Xkora, Xgora*, or *qgora*.] A bow-like musical instrument having a flattened piece of quill or reed interposed between one end of the string (or strings) and its attachment to the bow, the player's blowing upon the quill or reed causing vibrations in the strings; GOM-GOM sense a. Cf. RAMKIE.

1786 G. FORSTER tr. *A. Sparrman's Voy. to Cape of G.H.* I. 229 The instrument is played on in the following manner: the musician, applying his mouth to the quill, draws in his breath very hard, so as to put it into a quivering motion, which produces a grating sound. This instrument is called a *t'Goerra*, a name .. tolerably expressive of the sound of the instrument. **1790** tr. *F. Le Vaillant's Trav.* II. 104 The *goura* is shaped like the bow of a savage Hottentot ... When several *gouras* play together, they are never in unison. **1796** C.R. HOPSON tr. *C.P. Thunberg's Trav.* II. 78 A kind of instrument called Korà. It resembled at first sight a fiddlestick, and was made of a wooden stick, over which was extended a string. At the end of this was fastened the tip of a quill, and upon this they played with their lips; blowing as if it were a wind instrument, so as to make it produce a jarring sound. **1801** J. BARROW *Trav.* I. 149 This instrument was called the gowra. **1804** R. PERCIVAL *Acct of Cape of G.H.* 91 A goura .. is formed by strings of dried gut, or sinews of deer, twisted into a cord and fastened to a hollow stick, about three feet in length, by a peg which on being turned round brings the cord to a proper degree of tension. At the other end the cord is placed on quills: played on by applying the mouth to the quills .. produce a faint noise like an aeolian harp. **1822** W.J. BURCHELL *Trav.* I. 458 The *Goráh* .. may be more aptly compared to the bow of a violin, than to any other thing; but, in its principle and use, it is quite different; being, in fact, that of a stringed, and a wind instrument combined: and thus it agrees with the Æolian harp. **1834** T. PRINGLE *Afr. Sketches* 17 Soothed by the gorrah's humming reed. **1835** J.W.D. MOODIE *Ten Yrs* I. 224, I have often listened with great pleasure to the wild and melancholy notes of the 'gorah' and 'ramkee'. **1834** W.H.B. WEBSTER *Narr. of Voy. to Sn Atlantic Ocean* 274 The whole of the slaves were assembled in the hall, .. accompanied by their musician, who soon seated himself on the earthen floor and commenced tuning his gorah. The gorah is an instrument well known in Africa. **1846** R. MOFFAT *Missionary Labours* 15 His gorah soothes some solitary hours, although its sounds are often responded to by the lion's roar or the hyena's howl. **1881** NOBLE in *Encycl. Brit.* XII. 311 The 'gorah' was formed by stretching a piece of the twisted entrails of a sheep along a thin hollow stick ... At one end there was a piece of quill fixed into the stick, to which the mouth was applied. **1902** H. BALFOUR in *Jrnl of Anthropol. Inst.* Vol. 32, 156 The *goura*, a stringed-wind musical instrument of the Bushmen and Hottentots. **1925** D. KIDD *Essential Kafir* 333, I have seen the instrument used in Pondoland; but the music was very rude, and it required an immense amount of energy to bring it forth at all. The Bushmen called it a Gorah, but the Pondos an Ugwali. **1934** P.R. KIRBY *Musical Instruments of Native Races* (1965) 178 That the *goráh* was a Hottentot instrument, though played by a Bushman, has been regularly neglected by those who have referred to Burchell's description. *Ibid.* 186 As the *gora* was first noticed in 1668, it would seem that its invention took place at some time between 1598 and that date. In its earliest form, the *gora* was simply a slender reproduction of the curved shooting bow. **1955** V. DE KOCK *Fun They Had* 35 We every night heard some old Hottentot in the servant's hut near the house playing on the *gorah*, the sound of which resembled the distant notes of the bugle. **1989** F.G. BUTLER *Tales from Old Karoo* 111 He filled his time by composing strange pieces, using local instruments like kudu horns, *gorahs* and heaven knows what. **1993** A.P. BRINK *First Life of Adamastor* 105 In a large circle the men sat .. tugging at the string of the *gurah*, while the women clapped their hands and danced around us.

Goraqua var. KORAQUA.

Goringhaikona /ˌgɔrɪŋhaɪˈkɔŋə, -na/ *n. hist.* Also **Goringaycona, Goringhaicona**. Pl. unchanged, or **-s**. [Khoikhoi; see quot. 1880.] STRANDLOPER sense 2 a.

The Goringhaikona were occas. confused with the GORINGHAIQUA.

1670 [see COCHOQUA]. **1880** *Cape Monthly Mag.* II. 141 Goringhaikona meant simply 'the small tribe living by the water;' Gorachouqua, the people whose chief was Gora or Chora. **1912** (tr. *J. Van Riebeeck's Jrnl*) in I.D. Colvin *Cape of Adventure* 221 'Goringaycona,' Caapmen. **1967** R. RAVEN-HART *Before Van Riebeeck* 199 Watermen ... They were the 'Strandlopers' of the Dutch period, or 'Goringhaiconas', with 'Herry' (Hadah) as their Chief. **1968** E.A. WALKER *Hist. of Sn Afr.* 36 Van Riebeeck found three clans wandering with their sheep and cattle in and about the Cape Peninsula: Herry's Strandloopers or, to give them their full title, Goringhaikonas, a mere eighteen strong; the Kaapmen or Goringhaikuas, some 600 warriors in all, and the Koras, Gorachouquas or tobacco-thieves, 300 fighting men all told. **1977** [see STRANDLOPER sense 2 a]. **1989** *Reader's Digest Illust. Hist.* 44 The first Khoikhoi whom the new settlers encountered were the Goringhaicona – the Strandlopers. Also living on or near the Cape Peninsula were the Gorachouqua and the Goringhaiqua.

Goringhaiqua /ˌɡɔrɪŋˈhaɪkwə/ *n. hist.* Also **Ghoninghayquaas, Goringhaikua(s), Goringhaiquas.** [Khoikhoi.] SALDANHA sense 1 a.

The Goringhaiqua were occas. confused with the GORINGHAIKONA.

1670 [see COCHOQUA]. **1833** *S. Afr. Almanac & Dir.* 204 In consequence of J. van Riebeeck distributing ground to the Dutch Settlers, the Ghoninghayquaas, a Hottentot tribe, commenced war against the Dutch. **1838** [see KAAPMANS]. **1952** H.B. THOM *Jrnl of Jan van Riebeeck* I. 25 'Those from Saldania' – the Hottentot tribe known as *Goringhaiquas* and also alluded to in the Journal as *Saldanhamen, Saldanhars, Saldiniers*, or *Kaapmans*. **1955** [see KORA sense 1]. **1968** [see GORINGHAIKONA]. **1977** [see STRANDLOPER sense 2 a]. **1989** [see GORINGHAIKONA].

Gorona var. KORANNA.

gorra(h) var. GORAH.

go to the bush see BUSH *n.*[1] sense 4.

‖**gots** /xɔts/ *int. colloq.* [Afk. *gods, gots*, euphemistic substitute for *God* /xɔt/ God.] GATS.

1975 S. SEPAMLA in *New Classic* No.1, 12, I asked, what about my pass-book? Joe shook his head as if he really pitied me ... Gots! There's so much of the yes-baas in you. **1986** —— *Third Generation* 46 *Gots!* The struggle was hard. *Ibid.* 53 Gots, *Kaffermeid*, don't give me that bull.

goudsbloem var. GOUSBLOM.

goukom var. GOCUM.

gouna var. GANNA.

goura, !goura varr. GORAH.

gousblom /ˈxəʊsblɔm/ *n.* Formerly also **goudsbloem, gousbloom.** Pl. **-blomme** /-blɔmə/. [Afk., transf. use of Du. *goudsbloem* marigold.] Any of several plant species of the Asteraceae with daisy-like flowers, esp. those of the genera *Arctotis* and *Gazania*; also called BOTTERBLOM. See also GAZANIA.

1822 W.J. BURCHELL *Trav.* I. 229 The term *Goudsbloem*, like too many of the colonial names, is applied gratuitously to various plants, fancied to have a resemblance to the *Marygold*. Different species of *Arctotis* have generally been pointed out to me for it, and sometimes a kind of *Cotula*. **1902** H.J. DUCKITT *Hilda's Diary of Cape Hsekeeper* 190 In September the ground is literally carpeted with endless varieties of gazanias – local name, Gousbloom. **1915** D. FAIRBRIDGE *Torch Bearer* 36, I went into a field behind the house, and I counted seventeen varieties without moving from one spot ... 'Big orange stars. I have seen them in gardens in England –' 'Gousbloom – gazanias, I mean –.' **1940** M.G. GILBERT *Informant, Cape Town* 6 Aug. 3 It is too lovely for words, with masses of 'gousblom' and various daisies. **1950** *Cape Argus* 5 Aug. 7 Namaqualand's most famous flower is the large, brilliant yellow gousblom ... Smaller varieties of gousblom are seen in many colours. The arctotis, for example, is a more delicate flower. **1957** *Cape Times* 31 July 1 Every piece of uncultivated ground splashed with orange, white and yellow of the gousblomme. **1971** *Ibid.* 28 Aug. 1 The display of cinerarias, forget-me-nots, daisies, vygies, gousblomme and kalkoentjies would not be a mass of colour till mid-September. **1973** [see BIETOU]. **1977** [see KALKOENTJIE sense 2]. **1981** *S. Afr. Panorama* Nov. 49 Over the next stony ridge you come upon a field of jubilant *gousblomme* (*galardias*). **1988** LUBKE & LA COCK *Vegetation & Ecology of Kwaaihoek: Site of Dias Cross (pamphlet)*, The species found in this community in decreasing order of importance are: *Gazania rigens* var. *uniflora* (dune gazania, gousblom). **1989** *Gardening Questions Answered* (Reader's Digest Assoc.) 322 *Arctotis*, Indigenous, bushy annuals and spreading perennials ... They produce large, daisy-like flowers in shades of red, orange, pink and white ... Also known as gousblom.

‖**gousiekte** /ˈxəʊsiktə/ *n.* Also **gouwziekte.** [Afk., *gou* quick + *siekte* disease; see quot. 1932.] **1.** *Pathology.* A disease of livestock resulting in sudden death and caused by the ingestion of any of several poisonous plants of the Rubiaceae.

1926 *Farming in S. Afr.* Apr. 3 In the past gousiekte has been most troublesome in sheep, but this year heavy losses have also recurred in cattle. **1930** [see JAAGSIEKTE sense 1]. **1932** WATT & BREYER-BRANDWIJK *Medicinal & Poisonous Plants* 175 It is called gousiekte from the fact that death is often very rapid and unexpected. **1954** MÖNNIG & VELDMAN *Handbk on Stock Diseases* 243 During 1954 it was proved that the plant *Pavetta harborii* is toxic to cattle and that it is responsible for a disease very similar to 'quick-sickness' or gousiekte. **1972** B. DE WINTER in *Std Encycl. of Sn Afr.* V. 120 The species which cause gousiekte are *Pachystigma pygmaeum* (gousiektebossie), *P. thamnus* (Natal gousiektebossie), *Fadogia monticola* (etc.). **1979** T. GUTSCHE *There Was a Man* 231 He had to .. investigate .. another mysterious disease – Gouwziekte causing sheep grazing normally suddenly to jump convulsively and drop dead. **1981** J. VAHRMEIJER *Poisonous Plants of Sn Afr.* 18 Five plant species all belonging to the family *Rubiaceae* or Gardenia family, cause gousiekte in ruminants. **1988** T.S. KELLERMAN et al. *Plant Poisonings & Mycotoxicosis of Livestock* 114 Gousiekte is a disease of domestic ruminants characterized by acute heart failure.

2. *comb.* **gousiektebossie** /-bɔsi/ [Afk., *bossie* (*bos* bush + -IE)] or **gousiekte bush**, either of two poisonous shrubs which cause gousiekte, *Pachystigma pygmaeum* or *P. thamnus*; occas. with distinguishing epithet, as **hairy gousiektebossie, Natal gousiektebossie; gousiekte tree**, the shrub or small tree *Pavetta schumanniana*, the ingestion of which results in gousiekte.

1927 D.J. STEYN in *Farming in S. Afr.* Aug. 247 A curious characteristic of the **Gousiektebossie** is that it is not always poisonous to the same degree. The nature of the soil and the climatic conditions determine this to a large extent. **1934** C.P. SWART Supplement to Pettman. 60 *Gousiekte*, .. A well-known South African disease caused by the ingestion of a poisonous plant, the gousiektebossie or V. pygmese. **1957** *Handbk for Farmers* (Dept of Agric.) III. 339 Poisonous plants such as tulp, .. gousiektebossie (Pachystigma pygmaeum), .. are still the main causes of plant poisoning in cattle. **1972** [see sense 1]. **1981** J. VAHRMEIJER *Poisonous Plants of Sn Afr.* 134 The gousiektebossie is usually one of the first plants to appear in the spring. **1988** T.S. KELLERMAN et al. *Plant Poisonings & Mycotoxicosis of Livestock* 114 *Pachystigma pygmaeum*, .. Hairy gousiektebossie ... *Pachystigma thamnus*, .. Natal gousiektebossie, smooth gousiektebossie. **1980** *Het Suid-Western* 19 Aug. (Suppl.) 4 On certain veld types .. game would probably fare considerably better than livestock, for example, in parts where poisonous plants like **gousiekte bush** and poison leaf occurred. **1981** J. VAHRMEIJER *Poisonous Plants of Sn Afr.* 140 *Pavetta schumanniana*, .. **Gousiekte tree** .. is the only member of the group of plants causing gousiekte which is a large shrub or tree and does not have a subterranean stem system.

Gouteng var. GAUTENG.

govini var. GAVINE.

go-way bird, go'way bird varr. GO-AWAY.

go well *int. phr.* [tr. Zulu *hamba kahle*, Xhosa *hamba kakuhle*, see HAMBA sense 2; phrases with similar meanings are also found in S. Sotho and seTswana.] An expression of good wishes spoken upon parting by one staying behind to one leaving; *hamba kahle*, see HAMBA sense 2 a. See also STAY WELL.

Orig. almost exclusively used by writers to suggest Xhosa or Zulu dialogue, but now in common use among English-speakers.

1948 A. PATON *Cry, Beloved Country* 222 'Go well, umfundisi.' 'Stay well, inkosi.' **1951** P. ABRAHAMS *Wild Conquest* 298 'Where do you journey?' 'To the land of the Basuto.' 'Go well, my friend.' 'Go well, white man.' **1960** R. BYRON in D. Wright *S. Afr. Stories* 32 'Send a man down to my house. In about an hour's time. Good. So, go well!' He replaced the receiver. **1961** H. STANTON *Go Well Stay Well* 5 'Go well.' 'Stay well.' Sesuto: 'Tsamea pila.' 'Sala pila.' These words constitute the customary expressions of good-will when African friends are parting. The friend who stays says to the friend who goes, 'Go well,' conveying the thought, 'May God protect you on your journey.' **1979** Y. BURGESS *Say Little Mantra* 2 'Another summer,' she said. 'Go well then. And say a little mantra for me.' **1979** M. MATSHOBA *Call Me Not a Man* 134 '*Awu*, they are going aboard already. So long, people.' 'Go well, Thandi.' **1982** M. MZAMANE *Children of Soweto* 114 'And now we must be off. Remain well, granny.' 'Go well, my children.' **1989** J. HOBBS *Thoughts in Makeshift Mortuary* 197 'Go well, Mr Kimber,' he says formally in Zulu. 'Stay well, Mgwetshana Tshabalala.'

gowra var. GORAH.

gqir(h)a var. IGQIRA *n.*[2]

Gqunukhwebe /ˌɡʊnʊˈkwe(ː)bi, -be/ *pl. n. Hist.* Also **Amagonakwaybie, Amagonakwebi, Amagqunukwebe, Amagqunukwebi, Amagunuquabi, Amakunugubi, Gonakwebu, Gonokwabie, Gonokwebie, Gunukwebe, Gunukwebi.** [Xhosa, (pl. prefix AMA- +) n. stem *-Gqunukhwebe*, ad. Khoikhoi *Gonaqua* (see GONAQUA).] Collectively, the members of a people of mixed Khoikhoi and Xhosa descent, living during the 19th century in what is now the Eastern Cape; also called *Gonaqua(s)*, see GONAQUA sense 1. Also *attrib.* or as *adj.*

As is the case with many names of peoples and groups in *S. Afr. Eng.*, this word has been found only in plural uses; however, it may be that it has also been used in unrecorded singular forms.

1829 W. SHAW Diary. 6 Oct., The Governor held a Meeting with the Chiefs .. Pato, Kama and Congo of the Amagonakwaybie Tribe .. this morning. **1836** J.M. BOWKER *Speeches & Sel.* (1864) 20 The Gonokwebie and Fingo chiefs. *Ibid.* 23, I am happy to report that no thefts of colonial cattle have been traced to either the Gonokwabies, or the Fingoes. *c*1847 H.H. DUGMORE in J. Maclean *Compendium of Kafir Laws* (1906) 7 The Amagqunukwebi extend along the sea-coast from the mouth of the Fish River nearly to that of the Buffalo, reaching between the Fish River and the Keiskamma, to the sources of the Beka. **1852** M.B. HUDSON *S. Afr. Frontier Life* p.xi, On the other side of the boundary line were, firstly, the Amakunugubi: a small tribe, of which Pato is chief ... The port of the Buffalo (East London) is situated in his location. **1920** S.M. MOLEMA *Bantu Past & Present* 33 The Ama-Gqunukwebe of Kwane were also half Hottentots, and half Xosa in descent. *c*1960 J.M. DONALD in J.B. Bullock *Peddie* 60 Theophilus Shepstone, .. then the Resident Agent for the Fingoes and the Gunukwebis .. stationed at Fort Peddie. **1970** M.F. KATZEN in *Std Encycl. of Sn Afr.* V. 56 The Xhosa had intermarried with Hottentot tribes (to produce the Gunukwebe clans) and were living in the Gamtoos River area until 1778 when they moved back to the Fish. **1986** P. MAYLAM *Hist. of Afr. People*

98 At one time the Gqunukhwebe threatened Port Elizabeth ... Phato, the Gqunukhwebe chief .. continued an intermittent, harassing style of resistance into 1847. **1989** J.B. PEIRES *Dead Will Arise* p.xii, The most important of the minor chiefdoms was that of the *Gqunukhwebe* Xhosa, led by Phatho and his junior brother Kama.

grace buck var. GRYSBUCK.

gracht /xraxt/ *n.* [Du., canal; ditch, moat.] In Cape Town: **a.** *Obs.* exc. *hist.* A canal. **b.** An element in street names. Also *attrib.*

1823 W.W. BIRD *State of Cape of G.H.* 149 Leaving the commercial Exchange, the heeregracht (Anglicè the gentlemen's ditch) presents itself, leading towards the public offices and the government gardens. **1910** D. FAIRBRIDGE *That Which Hath Been* (1913) 12 The streets lay almost due north and south, east and west, at as regular intervals as though scored with a ruler: the Heerengracht, Keisersgracht, Tuin Straat, .. with their comfortable, roomy dwellings and hospitable high stoeps. **1926** P.W. LAIDLER *Tavern of Ocean* 99 Cape Town — beautiful when seen from the sea, but ashore — behold, .. grachts stagnant and stinking, full of household refuse .. along which at intervals a great part of the town sewage flowed to the sea ... The grachts were the towns' only drainage scheme. *Ibid.* 183 The road nearest to the jetty and the Castle naturally became the most important, and the name Heeren was transferred to it; and, as was the habit in Holland, where more prominence was given to the canal, than to the street alongside, the suffix *gracht* was added, and it became the Heerengracht. **1965** A. GORDON-BROWN *S. Afr. Heritage* I. 13 'The Cape' had now become 'Cape Town'; and a pleasant town it was with oak-lined streets and rivulets — 'grachts' — running along them. **1969** D. CHILD *Yesterday's Children* 34 Fire-wardens and citizens ran to help put out the flames, using buckets of water from the *grachts* or open water channels along the sides or down the middle of the streets. **1975** *S. Afr. Panorama* Nov. 25 Museum staff .. saw an old gracht (water canal) wall and later sluice gates. These date back to 1661. **1979** *Cape Times* 20 Dec. 7 Relics of the Dutch occupation, when Cape Town was criss-crossed by a network of canals, or grachts, are to be incorporated in a .. City Council plan.

gramadoelas, gamadoelas /ˌx(r)ama'dʊləz, -'dʊlas/ *pl. n. Colloq.* Also **g(r)ammadoelas**, and with initial capital. [Afk., ultimate etym. unknown; perh. rel. to Zulu and Xhosa *induli* (pl. *amaduli*) hillock, summit of a small hill.] BUNDU sense 1. Also *attrib.*, and *transf.*

[**1948** L.G. GREEN *To River's End* 132 Northwards stretches the road, ever northwards to the remote country that is so well described by the Afrikaans word 'gramadoelas'.] **1950** H.C. BOSMAN in L. Abrahams *Jurie Steyn's Post Office* (1971) 32 She was a little girl staying in the lonely African wilds. *Gramadoelas* was the word that Aunt Susan used ... It was loose talk about wilds and gramadoelas and tropics that gave the Marico a bad name, we said. **1970** R.M. ANDERSON *Informant, Port Elizabeth* He's now living somewhere in the gamadoelas. (In the bush or veld.) **1978** *Cape Times* 1 Feb. 11 In that harsh part of the world .. they were stuck in the parched *gamadoelas* in the midday heat, kilometres from anywhere. **1979** *Sunday Times* 8 July 17 The gramadoelas await those who do not collaborate in the process of removing race discrimination and recognising the claims of black, as well as white, to basic human rights. **1982** *Flying Springbok* Nov. 26 Whoever first irreverently used the word *gramadoelas* to describe a panorama of wild and brutal desolation might have been standing, as we now are, .. looking down over the canyon. **1989** *Personality* 10 Apr. 40 The man from the *gamadoelas* of the world was suddenly rubbing shoulders with the likes of George Benson and Al Jarreau. **1990** A. RICE in *Frontline* Dec. 15 Just one passing reference to the gramadoelas and this Londoner is there, back in the bundu. **1993** M. OETTLE in *Weekend Post* 17 July (Leisure) 7 *85c* [stamp] .. : '*moon landscape*'. The deeply eroded *gramadoela* country to the north of the Kuiseb River.

grammat see quot. 1833 at KRAMAT.

grand apartheid /ˌgrænd ə'pɑːtheɪt, -ə'parthɛɪt/ *n. phr. Hist.* Also with initial capitals. [Either fr. Eng. *grand* (planned) on a large scale + Afk. *apartheid* 'separateness'; or an interpretation of Afk. *algehele apartheid* or *grootapartheid* (*algehele* total, comprehensive, or *groot* big).] Particularly during the 1960s and 1970s: a political ideology and policy which involved comprehensive racial segregation, and massive social engineering, such as the removal of black people from 'white' areas and the creation of separate ethnic 'homelands' in which blacks were expected to satisfy their political aspirations; *big apartheid, grootapartheid*, see APARTHEID sense 1 b. Also *attrib.* Cf. PETTY APARTHEID, SEPARATE DEVELOPMENT. See also HOMELAND, VERWOERDIAN.

1972 *Daily Dispatch* 2 Feb. 1 As for so-called grand apartheid, after all the talk two-thirds of the country's blacks still lived outside their homelands. **1983** *Drum* Jan. 20 The world's biggest ever social and racial engineering plan — grand apartheid — may only be half way. Already between 2,5-million and 3-million people, nearly all blacks, have been shifted in fulfilment of the Nationalist dream of ethnic purity in South Africa. *Ibid.* 24 The basic aim of the grand apartheid plan is white majority rule in South Africa outside the homelands. *c***1988** *Alternative* (Moderate Student Organisation) Vol.5, 5 To a large extent this shortage [of housing] is the consequence of the now abandoned scheme of 'Grand Apartheid' in which Blacks would not have lived in 'White South Africa' and consequently would not have needed housing. As a result the government failed to provide any new houses for Blacks from 1972 to 1981. **1989** [see HOMELAND sense 1]. **1990** *Sunday Times* 20 May 14 Consider .. the events of the past seven days. We have had a Government Minister announcing that grand apartheid had come to a dead stop. Homeland independence would be taken no further. **1991** [see WHITE *adj.* sense 1 c i]. **1991** A. VAN WYK *Birth of New Afrikaner* 81 Grand apartheid .. denied blacks any say in the affairs of whites, provided the broad structure for their 'separate development' in their own rural states-in-the-making, and urban group areas with their own schools, churches, universities, sporting facilities, political institutions, etc. **1993** A. NKABINDE in *Daily News* 14 Jan. 4 Those were the days of Grand Apartheid with separate tearooms for black and white staff members, a white council and a toothless black 'advisory' council.

grand cru /grɑːn(d) 'cruː, grɑ̃ -/ *n. phr.* Shortened form of PREMIER GRAND CRU.

1981 *Time* 7 Dec. (Suppl.), Crack a bottle of ice-cold Grand Cru or Riesling. **1982** M. BEAZLEY *Hugh Johnson's Pocket Wine Bk* 171 *Grand Cru* (*or Premier Grand Cru*), Term for a totally dry white, with no quality implications. **1987** *Guide to Stellenbosch Wine Route* 9 (*pamphlet*) The following wines are made and offered to the public: .. Dry White, Grand Cru, Cape Riesling. *c***1993** J. PLATTER *S. Afr. Wine Guide* 14 *Grand Cru*, Literally 'great growth' but denoting, in South Africa at least, the producer's own subjective rating of a wine. Not an official rating.

grantee *n. hist.* [Special sense of Eng. *grantee* one to whom a grant or conveyance is made.] A colonist to whom farming land (esp. conquered Xhosa territory in the eastern Cape Colony, during the 19th century) was given for a nominal rent, on the conditions of personal occupation and certain military duties. Also *attrib.*

[**1859** T. SHONE Diary. 12 Sept., We left Mandy's farm about 3 o'clock in the afternoon, for the Grant in Kafferaira.] **1862** *Ibid.* 20 June, Henry and John went to the Buffaloe, to the Shooting match, The Grantees won, by three shots. **1867** *Blue Bk for Col. 1866* JJ42, East London. There are stated to be in this division 200 resident farmers, grantees under the Cathcart system. *c***1960** J.M. DONALD in J.B. Bullock *Peddie* 45 Farms were granted at a moderate quitrent on condition of personal occupation, and the performance of certain burgher military duties ... It is appropriate that, under this 'Grantee System', a number of 1820 Settlers and their descendants .. should have taken advantage of the opportunity of settling in the territory. **1992** P.M. SILVA *Albany Jrnls of Thomas Shone* 239 The list of successful applicants for land in the Kat River had been published .. , but several grantees turned down their grants, and new applications were thus submitted to the government. **1993** *Sunday Times* 17 Oct. 25 Almost every piece of rolling veld has been owned by a grantee settler family since the 1850s, when Sir George Cathcart shared it among men who had helped fight the sixth, seventh and eighth Frontier Wars.

grapple-plant *n.* [See quot. 1966.] The plant *Harpagophytum procumbens* of the Pedaliaceae, with sharp, recurving thorns on its seed-capsules; HAAKDORING sense 2. Also *attrib.*

1822 W.J. BURCHELL *Trav.* I. 536 The beautiful *Uncaria procumbens* (or, Grapple Plant) was not less abundant. **1868** W.H. HARVEY *Genera of S. Afr. Plants* 278 The famous 'Grapple-plant' of Burchell, found in and beyond the Northern frontier, is *U*[*ncaria*] *procumbens*. **1893** J.T. BENT *Ruined Cities of Mashonaland* 17 Lurking in the grass is the Grapple plant, the *Harpagophytum procumbens*. **1898** P. MACOWAN in *Cape of G.H. Agric. Jrnl* 406 (Pettman), The Grapple-plant capsule is a thin oval affair of singular toughness and elasticity, with four or five curving marginal arms, reaching out and up. They are furnished with several formidable hooks at the tip, .. recurved, pointing downwards, and very sharp. **1917** R. MARLOTH *Common Names* 33 *Grapple plant*, The seed-vessel provided with numerous curved claws. **1966** C.A. SMITH *Common Names* 234 *Grapple plant*, .. name .. first assigned to the species by Burchell in 1811 ... Each of the long horns of the fruit bears 3 to 4 sharp recurved spines which recall the grappling irons used in early naval warfare. **1972** M.R. LEVYNS in *Std Encycl. of Sn Afr.* V. 317 The grapple-plant occurs in grass-land, mostly north of the Orange River.

grassveld /'grɑːsfelt, -fɛlt/ *n.* Formerly also **grassveldt**. [Part. tr. Afk. *grasveld* grassland, prairie.] Uncultivated land on which the dominant vegetation type is indigenous grass. Also *attrib.* See also VELD sense 3 c.

[**1844** J. BACKHOUSE *Narr. of Visit* 105 It is situated in the part of the colony, called the Gras Veld, *Grass Field*, which is hilly and verdant, and lies between the Langebergen, *Long Mountains*, and the coast.] **1882** O.E.A. SCHREINER Diamond Fields. 81 Think of some places in the old Colony, not up-country, in the Karroo and grass 'veldt', but down in the bush world. **1897** H. RAYMOND *B.I. Barnato* 95 Even the farmers of the open grass veld, the barren karoo, and the richly fertile kloofs, began to feel some excitement. **1910** A.B. LAMONT *Rural Reader* 252 Grass veld corresponds more or less to pasture. **1931** F.C. SLATER *Secret Veld* 10 As for grass-veld, we have the undulating hills of the Eastern Province .. ; the low, billowy, grass-clad hills of Pondoland .. ; and we have the long, even, monotonous grass-covered plains of the Orange Free State. **1934** *Friend* 16 Apr. (Swart), It was declared that the Free State union did not properly represent the interests of the 'grassveld' farmers. **1946** E. ROUX *Veld & Future* 15 Travelling east we come down off the Drakensberg into Natal. Here the rainfall may be 35 inches or more and we find a specially rich sort of grassveld, with very tall grasses. **1957** D. JACOBSON *Price of Diamonds* 40 Across the dry, flat veld, southwards into the Karroo, or north, east, west of the town, into the pale grassveld, Gottlieb's or Fink's car would tear. **1968** *Farmer's Weekly* 3 Jan. 86 Ewes also available. Acclimatised and bred on grassveld and therefore no risk for Transvaal, Natal and Northern Free State farmers. **1971** [see BITTER KAROO]. **1989** [see BUSHVELD sense 2]. **1993** F. VAN RENSBURG in *Getaway* Nov. 93 The end of March was too late to see the variety of bulbous grassveld plants in flower, but here and there some red-hot pokers .. were still to be seen.

graze *n. slang.* [Transf. use of Eng. *graze* to eat (something), usu. of animals but also (slang) of people.] Food.

1970 K. NICOL *Informant, Durban* We only got an eintjie graze at the hostel. **1976** 'BLOSSOM' in *Darling* 7 Jan. 87 You wouldn't believe the mince pies .. and other graze .. over the festive season by our house. Enough wors to stretch to Brits and back. **1977** C. HOPE in S. Gray *Theatre Two* (1981) 51 Jimmie: .. (*He moves over to the food table*) Hey, hey, lekker graze. **1978** [see LARNEY *adj.*]. **1979** M. ANDERSON in *Sunday Times* 21 Oct. (Mag. Sect.) 1 Listen, China — I gotta duck so I can catch a graze .. check you later. **1982** [see GOOSIE sense 2]. **1985** H. PRENDINI in *Style* Oct. 40 In the army, food is 'graze', 'chow', or 'munchies'. **1994** *Sunday Times* 23 Jan. 28 (*advt*) Let's zip down to [the] cafe and get us a packet of slap chips. The greasier the better ... Ay chinas, now that's good graze.

grease table *n. phr. Diamond-mining.* [See quot. 1931.] A sorting device in which a greased surface is used to retain the diamonds. See also *sorting table* (SORTING sense 1 b).

1931 G. BEET *Grand Old Days* 99 After a process of jigging, the final concentrates are made to pass over shaking grease-tables to which the diamonds adhere, while the other minerals are automatically washed away, the separation being based on the well-known affinity of the diamond for grease (petroleum jelly). **1946** S. CLOETE *Afr. Portraits* 129 A careless overseer .. spilt some grease on a table and it was found that diamonds stuck to the grease, allowing other pebbles to be washed past irrespective of their specific gravity. **1967** E. ROSENTHAL *Encycl. of Sn Afr.* 222 *Grease Tables*, .. The apparatus was built by George Labram .. and F.B. Kirsten at Kimberley and patented in 1897. De Beers Consolidated Mines used it under royalty, but ultimately bought it outright. **1973** A. HOCKING *Diamonds* 15 The concentrate less than 3 mm across goes over electro-magnetic vibrating screens which remove all water, then gravitate down to the grease tables. These have sloping, three-stepped decks which are vibrated as the concentrate steadily passes over them. **1977** *S. Afr. Panorama* Aug. 16 Syndicates began to be formed so that diggers could pool their resources and buy wims and traction engines, crushers and grease tables. **1978** E.L. WILLIAMS in *Optima* Vol.27 No.4, 103 The long process is completed with concentrates from the desert plants arriving .. for final concentration and the harvest of diamonds, up to 5000 carats a day, by X-ray separator, a technique now used .. in place of the historic grease tables and belts employed for so many years. **1990** B. STEYN in *S. Afr. Panorama* Jan.-Feb. 71 (*caption*) The grease tables where the final recovery of the precious gems takes place.

great *adj.* Also with initial capital. [tr. adj. stem *-khulu* big, large, great, important, found in the Nguni languages; in this context applied esp. to the possessions or relatives of an African chief or king, or to the (principal) wife of a common man, and her offspring or homestead.

Some of the combinations listed below are S. Afr. Eng. formations which have no standard equivalents in the Nguni languages.]

Special collocations. **great councillor**, a councillor advising an African chief or king; *great man* (see below); GROOTMAN sense 1; **great house** [tr. Zulu *indlunkulu*, see INDLUNKULU], (*a*) the family of an hereditary chief or king; the royal family; (*b*) *great hut*; **great hut**, (*a*) the largest hut in a royal homestead; (*b*) the main hut shared by a man and his (principal) wife in a traditional African homestead; in both senses also INDLUNKULU; **great kraal**, *great place* (see below); **great man**, *great councillor* (see above); **great place**, the official residence of an African chief or king; the capital town of an African people; HOOFSTAD *n.*[1]; cf. *royal kraal* (see KRAAL *n.* sense 2 c); **great son**, the eldest son of an African chief or king and his (principal) wife; the heir-apparent to the chieftainship; **great wife**, (*a*) INKOSIKAZI sense 1 a; (*b*) INKOSIKAZI sense 1 c; see also RIGHT HAND.

1981 J.B. PEIRES *House of Phalo* 30 The military preponderance of the king was due to the fact that .. he alone commanded the allegiance of the **Great Councillors**. **1836** R. GODLONTON *Introductory Remarks to Narr. of Irruption* 218 From this decision there is no appeal, except the party concerned be a member of the '**great house**,' or family of the hereditary chieftains. **1837** F. OWEN *Diary* (1926) 79 The king had sent a servant girl .. who is in some way or other connected with the 'great house,' having the care of some younger girls .. who are to be brought up in some capacity for the king. **1857** D. LIVINGSTONE *Missionary Trav.* 185 An uncle of Sekeletu, being a younger brother of Sebituane, got that chieftain's head-wife, or queen ... Her hut is called the great house, and her children inherit the chieftainship. **1860** W. SHAW *Story of my Mission* 435 The ruling Chief in Council, with his principal advisers, usually determines which of his wives shall be the mother of the great house of the clan, tribe, or nation. **1866** W.C. HOLDEN *Past & Future* 332 The other sons of the paramount chief take rank according to certain established usages, .. thus — after the 'Great House,' there is the 'Right Hand House,' etc. **1907** W.C. SCULLY *By Veldt & Kopje* 5 Makanda was a rich man, and, as the greater portion of his riches belonged to his 'great house,' such would, consequently, fall to Mangèlè. **1955** J.B. SHEPHARD *Land of Tikoloshe* 18 Mafuto's first wife came out of the Great House — the largest hut in the row. **1960** [see INDLUNKULU]. **1962** W.D. HAMMOND-TOOKE *Bhaca Soc.* 36 The Bhaca are unique among Transkeian tribes in that there is no segmentation of the polygynous family into two main sections (the great house and righthand house). **1976** WEST & MORRIS *Abantu* 14 Among the Pondo the central hut was that of the 'great house' — the house of the senior wife who would normally produce an heir for the head of the homestead. The 'great house' stood directly opposite the opening of the cattle kraal which was the focus of ritual importance. **1978** A. ELLIOTT *Sons of Zulu* 175 The main hut in a kraal is always bigger than any other .. and it is the 'Great House' of the man and his nkosikazi. **1989** J. CRWYS-WILLIAMS *S. Afr. Despatches* 34 Born in 1820, a son of the Great House of Gaika or Ngqika, Sandile commanded the territory between the Kei and Keiskamma Rivers. **1857** R. GRAY *Jrnl of Visitation to Diocese of Grahamstown* 44 Not liking the atmosphere of the **great hut**, in which there was a charcoal fire, and where all were smoking, I told Sandilli I must return to the Mission. **1895** H. RIDER HAGGARD *Nada* 78 They took me and led me to the royal house, and pushed me through the doorway of the great hut. **1962** [see INDLUNKULU]. **1967** J.A. BROSTER *Red Blanket Valley* 128 Each kraal .. has contributed a supply of beer and soon the older people adjourn to the great hut and the young people and the initiates to the smaller side hut. **1973** A.C. JORDAN in *Best of S. Afr. Short Stories* (1991) 36 Mother and children were in the cooking hut when he arrived home. He called out to his wife .. 'No-mawele, *phothula!* (grind some boiled millet),' and he hurried on to the great hut ... When she had produced enough for the family, she brought the *mphothulo* to the great hut. **1976** WEST & MORRIS *Abantu* 38 The great wife lived in the great hut, the *indlunkulu*, and the second wife, the *ikhohlwa*, was on the left. *Ibid.* 77 The basic layout common to most African peoples of South Africa; a central cattle kraal surrounded by huts with the great hut opposite the entrance to the enclosure and the huts of lesser wives ranked on either side. **1978** A. ELLIOTT *Sons of Zulu* 175 He builds his 'great hut' or ndlunkulu, with its doorway facing eastwards to get the morning sun and with a forward slope away in front. **1855** N.J. MERRIMAN *Cape Jrnls* (1957) 224 His former **Great Kraal** .. had been burnt by Sir G. Cathcart. **1885** H. RIDER HAGGARD *King Solomon's Mines* (1972) 159 The great kraal, where we had that morning been interviewed by the king. **1937** C. BIRKBY *Zulu Journey* 38 Chaka moved like an impatient vulture from one great kraal to another. He left his old 'great place' near Port Durnford and built a city at 'Ungungundhlovu'. **1968** [see PRAISER]. **1827** W. SHAW Diary. 2 June, We have had several Messages from Hintsa .. but two of his **great men** privately advised us, to commence building. **1827** *Ibid.* Apr., He [*sc.* Ngqika] was gone to his mothers Kraal, which is according to Caffre custom, considered the true **great place**, or Court of the tribe. **1857** J. SHOOTER *Kafirs of Natal* 99 The Great Place (as the chief's residence is termed) is the resort of all the principal men of the tribe. **1866** [see UMPAKATI]. **1898** B. MITFORD *Induna's Wife* 140 We would sit in the shade in or about the Great Place, watching the reviewing of young regiments put through their practice by their chiefs. **1907** [see IN-KUNDLA sense 2]. **1933** W.H.S. BELL *Bygone Days* 75 Colonel Griffith surprised and burned Kreli's Great Place and many other kraals on the 9th October. **1967** J.A. BROSTER *Red Blanket Valley* 68 The present First Minister of the Transkei, the Honourable Kaizer Matanzima, has his 'Great Place' at Qamata Poort. **1967** O. WALKER *Hippo Poacher* 113 In theory, the 'great place,' the kraal of the paramount chief, was the centre of the tribal state; around it were grouped the lesser kraals. **1974** *E. Prov. Herald* 22 Apr. 13 Thousands of people of all races gathered at the Nyandeni Great Place .. to pay their last respects to Paramount Chief Victor Poto. **1987** M. DE PARAVICINI in *Sunday Times* 23 Aug. 10 At his office in Qamata's Great Place, this tribal father of 200000 people, who has at least 18 chiefs and 108 headmen beneath him, receives a steady stream of visitors. **1989** J.B. PEIRES *Dead Will Arise* 150 The king was downcast, humiliated and unable to answer or evade the furious questions of the angry crowd ... Along the long lonely road back to his Great Place .. he tried to kill himself. **1835** C.L. STRETCH Journal. 24 Sept., Macomo's Sons are Maamba — 7 years old .. Konaa, **great son**, 17 years old. *c*1847 H.H. DUGMORE in J. Maclean *Compendium of Kafir Laws* (1906) 26 The mother of him who is to be the 'great son' may .. be the last wife the chief has taken. **1882** C.L. NORRIS-NEWMAN *With Boers in Tvl* 13 The old chief, Ngaika, died, leaving his 'great son', Sandilli, a minor, under the regency of Macomo, who was only the 'right-hand son.' **1907** W.C. SCULLY *By Veldt & Kopje* 254 The Chief's 'Great Son' was to be made a man at the time, and my father wanted me to be one of his blood-brothers. **1912** AYLIFF & WHITESIDE *Hist. of Abambo* 12 A small section of the Amahlubi adhered to Sidinane, the great son of Mpangazita. **1975** [see GCALEKA sense 1]. **1981** J.B. PEIRES *House of Phalo* 29 The heir to the chieftainship, known as the Great Son, was the son of the Great Wife, who was usually the Thembu. **1989** — *Dead Will Arise* 194 No matter how much Mhala may have wanted to believe in the Cattle-Killing, he had to proceed carefully. Makinana, his Great Son, said that he 'would believe the reports when he saw his grandfather H'lambie and not till then.' *c*1847 H.H. DUGMORE in J. Maclean *Compendium of Kafir Laws* (1906) 11 The eldest son of the '**great**' **wife** is presumptive heir to his father's dignity. **1856** R.E.E. WILMOT *Diary* (1984) 55 Gained a sight of Sandilli's great wife, that is the wife selected from some influential tribe for state purposes, and whose son succeeds to the family honours. **1880** [see GCALEKA sense 1]. **1891** T.R. BEATTIE *Ride through Transkei* 42 Nomacapayi, the great wife of the chief, lives here, and as soon as I entered the large hut my guide pointed her out to me. **1897** 'F. MACNAB' *On Veldt & Farm* 267 The land assigned to a Kaffir can only pass to the eldest son of his great-wife. **1907** W.C. SCULLY *By Veldt & Kopje* 5 [He] had many half-brothers who were older than himself, but, his mother having been the 'great wife,' he took precedence of the rest of the family. **1925** D. KIDD *Essential Kafir* 13 The hut facing the cattle kraal belongs to the chief or 'great' wife. **1949** O. WALKER *Proud Zulu* (1951) 68 A Great Wife requires younger wives to do her work. A husband needs other wives to clean his wooden spoons when his favourite is with child. **1961** H.F. SAMPSON *White-Faced Huts* 5 The first or great wife, when giving evidence, tried to deny knowledge of this fact. **1962** W.D. HAMMOND-TOOKE *Bhaca Soc.* 36 Among commoners the first wife married ranks as the great wife. **1968** F.C. METROWICH *Frontier Flames* 2 When he [*sc.* the chief] was getting on in years he was expected to contract a political union ... His newest acquisition became his great wife and their first male child became the heir to the throne. **1975** *Daily Dispatch* 4 Oct. 7 Great festivities are planned for a royal wedding in the Transkei next Friday when Paramount Chief Sabata Dalindyebo of the Tembus formally takes his great wife. Chief Sabata, 47, has two wives, but neither has been named by his people as the one who is to produce his heir. **1981** J.B. PEIRES *House of Phalo* 29 The bridewealth of the Great Wife was paid by all the people and her status was publicly proclaimed. **1989** *Reader's Digest Illust. Hist.* 64 The Great Wife, who often married the chief late in his life, produced the heir, whose oldest half-brother, by the first-married wife of the right-hand house, sometimes resented this line of succession.

Great Flu see 'FLU.

Great Trek *n. phr.* Also with small initials. [Eng. *great* + TREK n.; or perh. part. tr. Afk. *groot trek*.] Usu. *the Great Trek*:
1. *hist.* The voluntary exodus, from 1836, of Dutch-speaking families from the Cape Colony to the interior; TREK n. sense 11; VOORTREK. Also *attrib.* See also VOORTREKKER sense 1.

[**1877** J. NOBLE *S. Afr.* 73 The Voor-trekkers ... The Great Exodus.] **1882** J. NIXON *Among Boers* 91 The 'great trek' was a great emigration, or movement of Boers from the Cape Colony to the unsettled regions north of the Orange River, which took place in 1833 and the following years. **1896** PURVIS & BIGGS *S. Afr.* 42 Whatever else the Great Trek did, or was hoped to do, it proved the turning point in South African history: the parting of the Dutch and English ways, which have never since been fully reunited. **1897** J. BRYCE *Impressions of S. Afr.* (1969) 294 The emigrant Boers .. left Cape Colony in the Great Trek of 1836. **1900** H. BUTTERWORTH *Trav. Tales* 70 In 1836 began a general exodus of the Dutch out of Cape Town and the regions near the Cape Colony, under the name of the Great Trek. **1936** *Cambridge Hist. of Brit. Empire* VIII. 273 Slave emancipation had an important influence on the Great Trek, but the actual loss of property in slaves was not the determining factor among the motives which produced the emigration. **1944** J. MOCKFORD *Here Are S. Africans* Foreword, The strange exodus known as the Great Trek when thousands upon thousands of Dutch Boers, as they were called, abandoned their farms and, with their wives and children, their flocks and their herds, made for the unchartered wilds of the north in order to shake the dust of British governance from their feet. **1952** B. DAVIDSON *Report on Sn Afr.* 156 In 1938 .. the Broederbond developed a strong-arm branch in the shape of the Ossewa Brandwag .. at the moment, appropriately enough, of the centennial celebrations of the Great Trek. **1965** C. VAN HEYNINGEN *Orange Days* 1 The Great Trek had vastly extended the area of White settlement, but had left South Africa politically fragmented. **1973** *E. Prov. Herald* 28 May 13 A typical wagon of the Great Trek period. **1983** F.E.O'B. GELDENHUYS in *Optima* Vol.31 No.3, 151 The settlers saw in their Great Trek a parallel with Israel's exodus from Egypt on the way to the promised land. **1989** *Reader's Digest Illust. Hist.* 114 The Great Trek was a landmark in an era of expansionism and bloodshed, of land seizure and labour coercion. **1990** R. GOOL *Cape Town Coolie* 19, I come from the Cape Town branch of *Stellenbosch Van der Merwes* who .. had more than a hand in the beginnings of the Great Trek.

2. *Transf.* and *fig.* Any long and arduous journey or exodus to another place, esp. one undertaken by a large number of people; a difficult or noteworthy change of attitude, opinion, or belief; GROOT TREK.

1892 *The Jrnl* 10 Sept. 2 Many of the Transvaal farmers are thoroughly disgusted with the recent course of events in that republic, and .. a great trek — composed of nearly a thousand families — is being quietly organised. **1950** H. GIBBS *Twilight* 41 During and after the war many thousands of Natives did their own Great Trek to the cities to find work and more money than they could find in the reserves. **1973** *E. Prov. Herald* 26 Mar. 1 The Springboks' 'great trek' is expected to take them from South Africa to Los Angeles via South America. **1975** *E. Prov. Herald* 6 Aug. 1 The great trek to safety being made by a convoy of an estimated 1 500 vehicles might have been stopped along the way by armed guerillas. **1978** *Sunday Times* 20 Aug. 15 The Afrikaners' Great Trek to economic power has been accomplished. Will it be the turn of the black man next? **1986** M. PICARDIE in S. Gray *Market Plays* 92 (*Veldsman .. takes a small drum and begins to beat softly to help induce a trance*): It'll be difficult ... You've never done this sort of thing before. It's a journey into a new country for you. A sort of trek, yes, even a Great Trek, but in another direction. **1991** *Sunday Times* 10 Nov. (Motoring) 5 It's almost December. The season of goodwill and getting ready for the modern version of the Great Trek down to the coast. **1993** W. VERWOERD in *Leadership* Vol.12 No.3, 18, I can speak as an individual who's had a little Great Trek from being a member of the Voortrekkers, a junior Broederbonder and of anything else you can think of in the Afrikaans set-up, to becoming an ANC comrade. **1994** P. DICKSON in *E. Prov. Herald* 26 Aug. 10 They arrive in their dozens every month from the bleak droughtlands of the Eastern Cape in a modern great trek of hope to seek jobs and a future for their children in the big city.

Hence **Great Trekker** *n. phr.* (*rare*), VOORTREKKER sense 1.

1975 *Sunday Times* 23 Feb. 16 We thank God for our country's early pioneers — 1820 Settlers, Great Trekkers and many others.

Greek *n.* and *adj.* [See quot. 1977.]
A. *n.* [Ellipt. for the collocations *Greek café*, *Greek caffie*, etc., see sense B below.] CAFÉ. Also **Greeks**, **Greek's**.

1916 L.D. FLEMMING *Fool on Veld* (1933) 4 A tourist who expects to glide idly in a boat down the Orange River, plucking oranges on the way, will be disappointed. Orange, in this case, merely means the colour of the water. Oranges, however, can be bought from the Greeks. **1948** V.M. FITZROY *Cabbages & Cream* 182 You can get anything in the way of fruit and vegetables at the Greek's including those kinds which are out of season locally. **1985** P. SLABOLEPSZY *Sat. Night at Palace* 66 Scaling tins of baked beans from the corner Greek.

B. *adj.* In the collocations **Greek café**, **-caffie**, ||**kafee**, **-shop**, etc.: CAFÉ.

*c*1929 S. BLACK in S. Gray *Three Plays* (1984) 66 Van K: .. A bi-cycle. I left it round at the Greek shop. **1948** V.M. FITZROY *Cabbages & Cream* 183 The Greek shops in Town may be supplying cauliflowers and peas and brinjals all together, but with you it's potatoes and pumpkin and nothing else. **1949** J. MOCKFORD *Golden Land* 238 A Greek shop where they sell fruit and sweets and serve tea and meals. **1965** S. DEDERICK *Tickey* 21 The whole dorp wore a forsaken and desolate air. Even the Greek café was closed. **1968** M. DOYLE *Impala* 122 She kept a pile of Superman and Captain Marvel and Batman in her bedroom cupboard. Gideon laughed, but he wasn't beyond sneaking a quick look in the lavatory when she bought a new one at the Greek shop in Stoneview. **1970** J. McINTOSH *Stonefish* 185 He had got hold of a photograph, bought from under the counter at the Greek café near the railway station. **1972** [see TEAROOM sense 1]. **1977** *Sunday Times* 24 July (Business Times) 5 Not a cafe at all, but a neighbourhood convenience store, this type of business is so dominated by the country's 80000-strong Greek community that it is also widely known as the 'Greek shop'. **1983** [see NIGGERBALL]. **1987** N. MATHIANE in *Frontline* Oct.-Nov. 34, I have seen a Greek shop swept clean by school kids on an excursion. As they enter the shop, the girls flock to the counter and confuse the one at the counter. **1990** [see KAFEE].

green and gold *n. phr.* and *adj. phr.*
A. *n. phr.* **The green and gold**: **a.** Colours awarded to, and worn by, sportsmen and sportswomen selected to represent South Africa. **b.** By metonymy: A South African sports team; cf. *the Springboks* (see SPRINGBOK sense 2 a).

1977 *S. Afr. Panorama* Nov. 1 A festival match between a World XV .. and the green and gold, South Africa's Springbok team. **1986** *Daily Dispatch* 21 May 1 'Hey buddy you're a Springbok' .. the news was broken to him that he had finally earned the green and gold. **1986** *Weekly Mail* 28 June 15 'If .. a 34-year old coloured Caledon bricklayer, can play flyhalf for the Springboks .. and score a try *nogal*,' they said, 'then anyone can play in the green and gold'. **1986** *Personality* 6 Oct. 30 The Olympic Gold is one glory that still eludes her. Another is the green-and-gold. Although she has lived and ridden in South Africa for 15 years, she has never been awarded Springbok colours for show-jumping. **1989** [see AG]. **1990** *Sunday Times* 23 Sept. 9 Annatjie .. won the coveted green-and-gold in 1985 for korfbal — a game similar to netball. **1990** *Flying Springbok* July 24 He captained the Springboks 22 out of the 25 times he wore the coveted green and gold. **1992** *Sunday Times* 12 June 26 Pienaar's pride in the green and gold. **1992** E. GRIFFITHS in *Sunday Times* 16 Aug. 30 The spectacle of the green and gold will have brought tears to many eyes, inspiring boyish dreams and advancing the legend of years gone by: of Craven and Louw, of Du Preez and Muller, of heroes. **1994** G. HOFFMAN on Radio Algoa 30 Aug., In come eleven players who've not worn the green and gold before.

B. *adj. phr.* Of or pertaining to national colours for sport; belonging to a South African national team.

1985 *Sunday Times* 15 Sept. 29 Select band of green and gold heroes. **1989** *Ski-Boat* Jan.-Feb. 28 Springboks one and all! Twenty-two past and present green-and-gold anglers competed in the Billfish 15 000. **1990** *Femina* June 50 The ultimate sporting achievement was a Springbok cap ... He won more than just a green and gold jersey: doors magically opened, top jobs came his way. **1991** A. CLOETE in *Weekend Post* 5 Oct. 8 The kick-off to the symbols debate is often led by black sportsmen rejecting the Springbok emblem and green-and-gold colours worn by white South African athletes.

green bean *n. phr. Slang.* Also with initial capitals. [So named for the colour of their uniforms.] A derisive name for a township municipal policeman; GREENFLY. Also *attrib.* See also COUNCIL POLICE.

1987 M. BADELA in *Weekly Mail* 5 June 1 Flanked by 'green bean' council police, State President PW Botha enters Sebokeng ... State President PW Botha yesterday delivered his first direct invitation to black South Africans to participate in national government — behind the massed guns of several hundred soldiers, police and township 'green bean' police. **1987** [see BLACK JACK sense 2 a]. **1989** M. TYALA in *Sunday Times* 29 Jan. 7 Kitskonstabels and municipal policemen (known in the townships as blackjacks or green beans) have been criticised from various quarters since their introduction a few years ago. **1989** S. TEMA in *City Press* 19 Feb. 1 Residents said Stompie together with his best friend .. were always at odds with the 'Green Beans' — the township's municipal police. **1990** *Weekly Mail* 2 Mar. 7 Many said they saw 'green beans' (municipal police) gathering next to a house near the Constantia shopping centre where the march was to begin. **1990** R. MALAN *My Traitor's Heart* 217 'Blackjacks' or 'greenbeans' — young black men who were given guns, uniforms, and three weeks' police training and sent in to shore up the collapsing structures of state.

greenfly *n. slang.* [As prec.] GREEN BEAN. Also *attrib.*

1987 N. NTAMNANI in *Weekly Mail* 8 May 6 Duncan Village residents have accused the 'greenflies' (municipal police) of going on a rampage of revenge after one of their number .. was murdered last Saturday. **1987** *South* 18 June, The 'greenfly' .. asked him where the comrades were. When Zola said he knew nothing about comrades, the 'greenfly' picked up a brick and hit him on the forehead. **1987** F. KRÜGER in *Weekly Mail* 19 June 6 Key phrases and sentences had been altered to make it appear the complaints against the 'greenflies' were actually against the comrades, referred to in the pamphlet as 'Mandela's soldiers'. **1988** *Now Everyone Is Afraid* (Catholic Inst. for Internat. Rel.) 61 The outrage felt by ZR's family was enough to overcome the reluctance by township residents to seek legal recourse from 'greenfly' harassment.

Green Grape *n. phr.* Freq. with small initials. [tr. Afk. *groendruif, groen* green + *druif* grape; see second quot., 1988.] A local name for the white grape variety known in France as 'Sémillon'; GROEN DRUIF.

1880 *S.W. Silver & Co.'s Handbk to S. Afr.* 222 The most common vines, from which .. ninety-nine per cent of the Cape wine is manufactured, are .. *Green grape (both black and white), Steen grape,* [etc.]. *Ibid.* 223 *The Red Wine* called *Pontac* receives its colour and flavour from the grape. At Constantia this wine is never made till the grape has so far shrivelled up that it contains very little juice. This is supplied, in the best kinds of wine, by the addition of red Muscadel; but in the vineyards .. where the bulk of the Pontac is made, the green grape is used to supply the deficiency, and the result is a wine of inferior quality. **1887** [see STEEN sense 2]. **1905** [see PONTAC sense 2]. **c1911** [see HERMITAGE]. **1952** [see STEIN sense 2]. **1966** H. BECK *Meet Cape Wines* 10 When I first took an interest in our vineyards many years ago they were planted in the table wine areas mainly with French grape, green grape and hermitage. *Ibid.* 11 The green grape, on a process of selection from the vineyard and development in the winery, is today producing some wine of quality and character and making a valuable contribution to blends of other wines. **1980** [see GROEN DRUIF]. **1981** J. DOXAT *Indispensable Drinks Bk* 53 Another widely planted white wine grape is, curiously, the Palomino of Jerez, known here, even more curiously, as 'the French grape'. Semillon is known as 'the green grape', rather more logically. **1988** D. HUGHES et al. *Complete Bk of S. Afr. Wine* 47 Certain local cultivars are the same as the European varieties: for example, Steen has been identified as Chenin Blanc, Hanepoot as Muscat d'Alexandrie, White French as Palomino, and Green Grape as Sémillon, while the red wine grape Hermitage was found to be the same grape as Cinsaut (in France *Cinsault*). *Ibid.* 99 The leaves of the Green Grape .. are in the early growing season much lighter than those of most other vines.

greet *v.* [Calque formed on Afk. *groet* to make oneself known, to say hello; to bid (someone) farewell.]

1. *intrans.* To make oneself known; to say hello.

1880 E.L. PRICE *Jrnls* (1956) 439 They met your Father going up, & told him they were going to spend a day down here. They came & greeted and hoped, I think, that I wd. entertain them to dinner &c. **1985** B. JOHNSON-BARKER in *Wynboer* June 72 He watched as others came, and built small houses, and planted mielies. They would come to greet, but, because he had nothing to say, they too, found they had nothing to say, and so they didn't come again. **1989** 'BILINGUAL' in *E. Prov. Herald* 17 Jan. 6 The phone has been answered only in Afrikaans, despite my greeting in English ... On going into the charge office to report an incident, I always greet in English, but am answered in Afrikaans. **1990** *Frontline* Mar.-Apr. 20 On to De Rust, whose single street is a promenade. Pedestrians are strolling and greeting, drifting through the speckled streetlight, calling out to householders on stoeps.

2. *trans.* To bid (someone) farewell.

a1989 'ANGUS' *Informant, Pietermaritzburg* Jim van Zyl on the SABC programme 'Calling all Farmers' (6 – 6.30 am Mondays – Fridays) often signs off with 'And so we greet you until 6 o'clock on Monday morning.'

Gregory *n. Obs.* exc. *hist.* [See quot. 1976.] A tall story; a mis-statement; a blunder.

1946 S. CLOETE *Afr. Portraits* 109 Gregory, an expert, considered the diamond to be a geological accident, since there was no diamondiferous ground in Africa. His mistake caused blunders to be known as 'Gregories'. **1948** H.V. MORTON *In Search of S. Afr.* 168 In South Africa to this day any tall story is still 'a Gregory'. **1976** B. ROBERTS *Kimberley* 12 James Gregory's report to the Geological Magazine was soon discounted. His name, however, lived on. For a long time any misstatement or lie about diamonds was to be laughingly dismissed as a 'Gregory'. **1983** D.E. SCHAEFER in *Optima* Vol.31 No.2, 77 'Mr Gregory .. returned to his employers with the assertion that Cape diamonds were a myth, a delusion and a snare!' .. The Star of South Africa .. thoroughly discredited Gregory. The witticism of the hour ran: 'If you desired to tell a man that he had uttered a falsehood, (the euphemism) was that he had told a Gregory!'

greisbo(c)k, greiseboke varr. GRYSBOK.

Greitje var. GRIETJIE.

grey *adj.* [Special use of Eng. *grey* intermediate in character, here influenced by the frequent use of 'black' and 'white' to designate areas.] Of or pertaining to a residential area in which people of differing ethnic backgrounds live as neighbours, formerly often illegally but by common consent; often in the collocation ***grey area***. See also OPEN *adj.*

1978 *Sunday Times* 29 Oct. 16 The solutions offered are as diverse as the contributors, ranging from city states to 'grey areas' and NRP-type consociational democracy ... Prof Marais's solution is the establishment of large black cities in the homelands or on their borders. 'Alongside these cities – but in white areas – there should be black cities where provision is made for the blacks who do not come from the nearby homelands, as well as for blacks where ethnic differences do not play such an important role – the "grey cities".' **1985** *Argus* 31 Aug., (*advt*) Woodstock, Grey Area, 52 Dublin Street (off Victoria Road). This family residence consists [of]: Lounge, three bedrooms [etc.]. **1985** S. VOLLENHOVEN in *S.-Easter* Aug.-Sept. 5 Woodstock became a 'grey area', an apartheid misnomer for one of the few suburbs left in South Africa where history and variety have been left fairly intact. **1986** *Sunday Times* 20 July 28 Hopeful hints are emerging that .. the NP will come up with at least one piece of good news: approval of an amendment to the Group Areas Act to permit the creation of 'grey areas', to be decided upon as a local option by individual communities. **1986** *E. Prov. Herald* 14 Nov. 6 Three inner-city areas of Johannesburg have gone 'grey'. For every three or four whites living there, there is also one person of colour. **1987** *New Nation* 21 May 7 Rand Afrikaans University researchers have listed 13 'grey' suburbs in cities across SA. Johannesburg alone has an estimated 45 000 'illegals'. **1990** *Evening Post* 2 Feb. 8 Speaking on 'grey area' flat-block problems in general, Mr Kubheka said: 'Tenants are being manipulated and exploited not only by greedy lessors but also by the very people who purport to act in their interests.' **1990** [see OU *adj.* sense 1 b]. **1990** *Sunday Times* 18 Nov. 11 After moving house five times to escape racist attention, the two found a haven in Woodstock, a 'grey' Cape Town suburb. **1993** A. RALPHS in *Weekly Mail* 8 Apr. (Suppl.) 4 A .. caretaker of a local church in one of the 'grey areas' of Johannesburg had his grandchildren refused entry into the local Model C school ... He now has to .. transport them to schools in Soweto. **1993** C. ENGELBRECHT in *Weekly Mail & Guardian* 5 Nov. 18 'Red-lining' – the banks' refusal to lend in areas which are going 'grey' – will be one of the most critical problems facing a new government after April next year.

Hence **grey** *n. nonce*, one living in a grey area; **greying** *vbl n.*, desegregating (of a residential, or, less commonly, business area), whether legal or illegal.

1987 N. KUTUMELA in *Frontline* May 16 Let me and my fellow 'greys' continue to live our colourless existence. Let the government arrest the political stuntmen who are inciting conflict and disturbance in Hillbrow, instead of arresting us peaceful citizens who are revelling in the rich and full life which Hillbrow gives us. **1989** *Weekly Mail* 3 Nov. 6 The 'greying' of Johannesburg has seen an influx of blacks, coloureds and Indians into the city, but there are not enough schools to accommodate their children. **1990** *Ibid.* (Suppl.) 5 The period under review .. saw the opening up of free trade areas in the city centres, the desegregation of certain amenities, the 'greying' of certain city centres. **1992** P. BOND in *Ibid.* 16 Apr. 17 Whether you're a home-owner in Bloubosrand or a tenant in Hillbrow, you have a common problem: banks can switch off access to credit .. at a moments notice ... The catalyst might be .. a critical mass of residential 'greying'.

greysbok, greysbuck varr. GRYSBOK, GRYSBUCK.

Greyshirt *n. hist.* [Named for the colour of the shirts worn by the organization's uniformed security personnel.] A member of the South African National Party (1933–48), a national-socialist movement noted for its advocacy of anti-semitism and white supremacy, and its sympathy with the Nazi movement in Germany. Usu. in *pl.*, used collectively. Also *attrib.*

The South African National Party was subsequently renamed the White Workers' Party, and formed part of the coalition which brought the National Party to power in 1948, after which it disbanded.

1943 'J. BURGER' *Black Man's Burden* 33 The Purified Nationalists .. have now added Semitism, liberalism, and communism to the list of -isms that they abhor. In 1939 they received a slight accession of strength in the shape of the Grey Shirt, or South African Nazi, movement. **1950** H. GIBBS *Twilight* 179 New parties of Nazi sympathy .. moved into the field, attracting considerable support among young Afrikaners to whom they represented Germany's war with Britain as their own issue. Among these was the *Handhawersbond* ... Another group was Louis Weichardt's Greyshirts. **1963** M. BENSON *Afr. Patriots* 76 Anti-semitism surfaced in the Greyshirts and Blackshirts. **1972** *Std Encycl. of Sn Afr.* V. 348 *Greyshirts*, A national-socialistic movement initiated at Cape Town by Louis Theodor Weichardt on 26 Oct. 1933 ... The Greyshirts were schooled in the principles of race, the struggle against Communism, responsible leadership, and the ideal of a White state which would seek close association with a united Europe. The fourfold policy of self-determination for Whites, Bantu, Indians and Coloureds was propagated from the start. **1972** L.E. NEAME in *Ibid.* VII. 131 Oswald Pirow had launched his New Order and was appealing to Afrikaners with a brand of National socialism reminiscent of that advocated by Hitler; and the anti-semitic Greyshirts .. were putting forward similar ideas. **1990** G. SLOVO *Ties of Blood* 193 'Who are those funny-looking people?' Sarah asked. 'Greyshirts,' said Mrs Lewis. **1991** A. VAN WYK *Birth of New Afrikaner* 61 There were various contenders for the soul of Afrikanerdom – the anti-semitic Grey Shirt movement, [etc.] ... The Grey Shirts .. were small fry, with the real fight .. fought between the NP and OB. [**1993** S. BRANCA in *Sunday Times* 11 July 17 A woman agent who .. spent her spare time making uniforms for the OB's Greyshirts.]

griesbo(c)k, gries buck varr. GRYSBOK, GRYSBUCK.

Grietjie /ˈxriki, -ci/ *n. hist.* Also **Creaky, Creeche, Creechy, Creeky, Creetje, Greitje, Grietje, Gritje, Krechie.** [See OU GRIETJIE.] OU GRIETJIE. Also *attrib.*

1881 G.F. AUSTEN *Diary* (1981) 21 An attempt was made by the Boers to use an old cannon against the Fort, but .. it was soon given up, each erratic and mis-directed shot making old Greitje (as the cannon was named) cant over backwards and giving cause at each discharge for loud ironical cheers and laughter from the garrison at the Fort. *Ibid.* 41 Firing has continued at intervals during the day, though Greitje has not spoken since this morning. **1899** E. ROSS *Diary of Siege of Mafeking* (1980) 39 As a rule the enemy's big gun Creetje (as we have called her) has given us a good-night shell and we have generally waited for it, but tonight they have let us off. **1899** *Mafeking Mail* 13 Nov. 3 The devotional Boer laying aside his Mauser and giving old 'Creeche' a rest. **1900** *Ibid.* 16 Feb., The

Boers .. rigged a derrick over 'Greitje' preparatory to removal, some of the more hopeful took it as a sign that the damned old blunderbuss was wanted at Pretoria. **1900** S.T. PLAATJE *Boer War Diary* (1973) 63, I tried to go to town but 'Au Sanna', going strong, caused me to come back and take shelter. I wonder why some people call her 'Grietje', as 'Griet' for a thing of her potency, would be nearer the mark. **1934** *Sunday Times* 29 Apr. (Swart), My old father-in-law, Barend Pelser, the man that founded the Staats Artillerie and worked the cannon 'Grietjie' at Platrand, brought the last load away from the Capital just as the lancers were galloping in. **1957** D. GRINNELL-MILNE *Baden-Powell at Mafeking* 77 A big gun, no doubt of it, but not the nightmare monster of Kaffir imagination. The Boers had a pet name for it: *'Gritje'*, diminutive of Margrit. Sounded odd to English ears; when troops first heard it from enemy patrols during the Sunday truce they had written it down as 'Creechy' — made them laugh. **1972** *Std Encycl. of Sn Afr.* V. 396 Next in chronological order came the small field-pieces of the 'Grietje' type used by the Voortrekkers against the Zulus at Blood River and against the British at Congella. **1973** J. COMAROFF *Boer War Diary of Sol T. Plaatje* 142 This is one of the several names given to the Creusot siege-gun. The Boers termed it 'Gritje'. The British, who found this difficult to pronounce, called it 'Creechy' — which later developed into 'Creaky'. **1974** J. PLOEGER in *Std Encycl. of Sn Afr.* X. 249 In the early 1850s the Transvaal had two small cannon, nicknamed Grietjie and Weeskind, which had been used in the Battle of Blood River. **1980** B.P. WILLAN *Diary of Siege of Mafeking* 39 'Creetje' was .. further corrupted to 'Creeky'. An alternative version of the origin of the term .. has 'Creechy' as an abbreviation of 'Marguerite', after the gun's French origin. Other names for the gun .. amongst the defenders of Mafeking were 'Big Ben', 'Aunt Sally', 'Black Maria', and 'Her Ladyship'.

Grigriqua /grɪˈgrɪkwə/ *pl. n. Obs.* exc. *hist.* Also **Grigriquas**. [See GRIQUA.] Collectively, the members of a Khoikhoi people believed to have been the ancestors of the GRIQUA people; at first called CHARIGURIQUA.

As is the case with many names of peoples and groups in *S. Afr. Eng.*, this word has been found only in plural uses; however, it may be that it has also been used in unrecorded singular forms.

1862 *Abstracts in Stat. Law of Cape of G.H.* p.xviii, July 20, 1693 ... Mention of the Soosequas, Heesequas, Ubiquas, Grigriquas, and Namaquas. **1905** [see CHARIGURIQUA]. **1928** [see GRIQUA sense 1]. **1930** I. SCHAPERA *KhoiSan Peoples* 46 Another group, the Grigriqua or Chariguriqua, after receiving a considerable infiltration of white blood, moved away to the north about the middle of the eighteenth century ... Here it was gradually joined by other half-breed Hottentots, or 'Bastards', a name by which these people now began to call themselves. The missionary John Campbell .. induced them to resume their old but almost forgotten and now mutilated name of *Griqua*. **1957** L.G. GREEN *Beyond City Lights* 177 Originally there was a pure Hottentot tribe, the Grigriqua, and these people seem to have become a mixed group as a result of early contact with .. Germans and others in the service of the Dutch East India Company at the Cape. **1968** E.A. WALKER *Hist. of Sn Afr.* 36 Explorers and visitors soon taught him [*sc.* Van Riebeeck] of the existence of other clans: .. Little Grigriquas on this side of the Olifant's river, and Great Grigriquas and Namaquas beyond. **1986** [see GRIQUA sense 1].

grijsbok var. GRYSBOK.

Grikwa var. GRIQUA.

gril /xrəl/ *n. colloq.* Also **grill**. [Afk.] A shudder, esp. as a reaction to something weird or gruesome. Freq. in *pl.*, ***the grils***, 'the shivers'.

1973 *Cape Times* 21 June 7 This wall chart, attractive (if you don't mind the *grrrils* up and down your back) and *tweetalig nogal*, is to be distributed to all hospitals. **1982** *Rhodeo* (Rhodes Univ.) 6 Apr. 11 I decided to take all the spooks out of the dark corners. All the things that gee me a gril. **1984** *Informant, Grahamstown* It gives me the grils just to think of it. **1991** E. BRUWER *Informant, Cape Town* She gives me the grills.

Griqua /ˈgrɪkwə, ˈgri-/ *n.* Also **G(a)uriqua, Grikwa, Griquaa, Griquer**. Pl. **-s**, or unchanged. [Etym. obscure: perh. ad. Khoikhoi *!ke //kwa* people; or ad. *Chariguriqua*, later *Grigriqua* (see quot. 1986), fr. Nama *≠Karihuriqua* ('the small tribe which lives at the sea'), a Khoikoi people living north of the Cape settlement in the 17th century; or fr. name of a clan ancestor, *Xiri*.]
1. A member of a people of mixed Khoikhoi (prob. GRIGRIQUA), white, and black African origin, now living mainly in East Griqualand (in the province of KwaZulu-Natal) and Griqualand West (in the Northern Cape Province); also called BASTARD HOTTENTOT. Also *attrib.* See also BASTARD *n.* sense 1, CHARIGURIQUA.

1731 G. MEDLEY tr. *P. Kolb's Present State of Cape of G.H.* I. 78 Next to the Damaquas, lie the Gauros or Gauriquas. **1795** C.R. HOPSON tr. *C.P. Thunberg's Trav.* I. 308 *Gauriquas* land extends more to the north-eastward: this is very fine country, and abounds in grass. **1815** J. CAMPBELL *Trav. in S. Afr.* 349 The people in this part, being a mixed race, went by the name of Bastards; but .. they resolved to assume some other name ... They found the majority were descended from a person of the name of Griqua, and they resolved hereafter to be called Griquaas. **1827** A.J. JARDINE *Fragment of Church Hist.* 55 Among the Griquas there seems at present to be much commotion; and recently blood [h]as been shed. **1835** G. CHAMPION *Jrnl* (1968) 21 Have seen a chief of the Griqua nation (Kok) ... The Griquas are a nation on the northern border of the colony. They are properly Bastard Hottentots. **1843** M.H. OBERHOLZER et al. in G.W. Eybers *Sel. Constit. Doc.* (1918) 261 It is not our intention (or desire) to drive the colored people, either Griquas or Bastards, from their possessions or dwellings. **1857** D. LIVINGSTONE *Missionary Trav.* 104 By Griquas is meant any mixed race sprung from native and European. Those in question were of Dutch extraction, through association with Hottentot and Bushmen. **1870** C. HAMILTON *Life & Sport in S.-E. Afr.* 205 Several Griquas — that is to say, the descendants of Hottentots, allied with the lowest class of Dutch settlers, and adopting the nomadic customs of the former — came up in their waggons from nomans-land. *a*1892 G. MCKIERNAN *Narr. & Jrnl* (1954) 64 We heard that there was a Griqua Baastard hunter named Kruger, some days to the eastward, who had killed a lot of ivory. **1905** [see CHARIGURIQUA]. **1928** H. VEDDER in *Native Tribes of S.W. Afr.* 114 Chariguriqua in the neighbourhood of St. Helena Bay. Obviously it is the same tribe elsewhere called the Gouriqua, from which the word Grigriqua is formed. The real name of the tribe was ≠Karihuriqua =*i.e.*, the small (=≠Kari-) tribe which lives at the sea (-hurib=sea). This tribe was afterwards known under the name Griqua ... By then [*sc.* the first half of the 18th century] they had European blood in them. **1943** D. REITZ *No Outspan* 206 The Griquas were a yellow-skinned race, a cross between the bushmen and the Hottentots and originally they lived along the coastal belt of Malmesbury in the Western Province of the Cape. **1971** [see CLASSIFICATION]. **1975** W.F. LYE *Andrew Smith's Jrnl 1834–6* 311 *Griqua*, Part Hottentot people organised and settled beyond the Orange River by Adam Kok I and Cornelius Kok I. The name derived from the clan name of their chief (Xiri) and was adopted in 1813. **1976** R. ROSS *Adam Kok's Griquas* 1 The Griquas were descendants of early Boer frontiersmen; of the remnants of Khoisan tribes ..; of escaped slaves from the wine and wheat farms of the south-west Cape; of free blacks from the colony who could find no acceptable place for themselves in it; and of African tribesmen. **1977** R. ELPHICK *Kraal & Castle* 135 The original *Guriqua* may have been a Strandloper group which acquired livestock: this theory would explain their name (Sea People) .. and the fact that other Khoikhoi occasionally identified them as 'San'. **1980** [see Lye & Murray quot. at KHOI sense 1]. **1986** A. HENDRY in Cameron & Spies *Illust. Hist. of S. Afr.* 144 John Campbell .. persuaded the Bastards to adopt the name of Griquas in 1813. This name harked back to the Grigriqua, the original Khoikhoi group from which Adam Kok's people were descended. **1989** [see NO MAN'S LAND sense 1].

2. *comb.* **Griqualand**, a name given to those areas (once) inhabited by Griquas, esp. Griqualand West (see quot. 1989) and East Griqualand (or Griqualand East), the area round Kokstad; hence **Griqualander** *n.*, an inhabitant of either area. See also NO MAN'S LAND sense 1.

1840 C.A. KINLOCH in *Echo* 26 Oct. 2 This noble stream [*sc.* the Orange River] .. divides the district of Colesberg from Griqualand, a wide tract of land inhabited by the Bastards. **1897** A.J. BUTLER tr. *Ratzel's Hist. Mankind* II. iii. 295 The term 'Griqualanders' .. has become usual since the Griquas have .. had a country of their own allotted them. **1900** A.W. CARTER *Informant, Ladybrand* 8 Feb., Some Griqualanders had reported that the English were making a move down the river. **1989** P.E. RAPER *Dict. of Sn Afr. Place Names* 190 *Griqualand*, .. Region comprising the Hay district and the western part of Barkly West. So called because it was the home of the Griqua Khoekhoen. **1994** *Weekend Post* 22 Oct. 4 Hands off Kokstad, say Griqualanders.

griquaite /ˈgrɪkwəaɪt/ *n. Mineralogy.* [Named for its locality, Griqualand West.] An intergrowth of various minerals found in BLUE GROUND.

1974 *McGraw-Hill Dict. of Scientific & Technical Terms* 643 *Griquaite*, .. A hypabyssal rock that contains garnet and diopside, and sometimes olivine or phlogopite, and is found in kimberlite pipes and dikes. **1993** A.M. CLARK *Hey's Mineral Index* 271 *Griquaite*, intergrowth of augite and garnet.

griqualandite /ˈgrɪkwəˌlændaɪt/ *n. Mineralogy. rare.* [Named by G.G. Hepburn in 1887, from its locality, Griqualand West.] See quot. 1887.

1887 *Chem. News* LV. 240 *Griqualandite*, a pseudomorph of crocidolite. **1976** C.B. COETZEE et al. in *Mineral Resources of Republic of S. Afr.* (Dept. of Mines), 266 In the vicinity of Prieska the asbestos can be recovered from the weathered zone, but to the north the asbestos is altered to tiger's-eye or griqualandite at many places. **1993** A.M. CLARK *Hey's Mineral Index* 271 *Griqualandite*, syn. of crocidolite .. ; an unnecessary name .. for a pseudomorph after crocidolite ... Griqualand West, South Africa.

Griquastan see -STAN.

Gritje var. GRIETJIE.

groaner *n. Music.* One who sings in the style known as GROANING.

1971 *Post* 4 Apr. 11 The great mbaqanga singer Ndoda Mahlathi made his first appearance at the Rio cinema this week ... Some even dashed to the stage and threw coins to the Groaner. **1978** *Pace* Dec. 44 The name Simon Mahlathini Nkabinde dropped from every mouth, and the man led the 'groaners' brigade.

groaning *vbl n. Music.* [Special sense of general Eng.] A style of singing, traditional among Nguni men, featuring a rasping, deeply resonant vocal tone, and now featured in popular music, esp. in SIMANJE-MANJE.

Epitomized in the singing of 'Mahlathini' (Simon Nkabinde), of the group 'Mahlathini and the Mahotella Queens'.

1980 D.B. COPLAN Urbanization of African Performing Arts. 379 Bopape discovered some performers of outstanding ability whose neo-traditional music could be processed into the new style. These included Simon 'Mahlathini' Nkabinde ... He used a rasping bass, 'goat voice' vocal quality traditional among rural Nguni men and sang songs praising traditional social values. This 'groaning' style, as it was known in the urban areas, became the trademark of male *mbaqanga* or *simanje-manje* solo singing. **1990** [see MGQASHIYO].

Groen Druif /ˈxrun dreɪf, -drœif/ *n. phr.* [Afk.] GREEN GRAPE. Also (occas.) part. tr. **Groen grape**.

1896 R. WALLACE *Farming Indust. of Cape Col.* 134 'Steen' and 'Groen Druif', or Green Grape, besides several Chasselas varieties, the commonest of which is known as 'French Grape,' were among the earliest introductions. *Ibid.* 155 From *Riesling* hock is obtained; and light white wine from the Green Grape, or 'Groen Druif,' a sort of *Chasselas*. **1980** J. PLATTER *Bk of S. Afr. Wines* 89 *Semillon*, A soft grape .. not yet common in South African whites ... However, several wines are called semillon when the grapes, often known locally as Groen or Green, obviously are from vines that have undergone debilitating mutations.

groene amara /ˌxrunə əˈmɑːrə, -aˈmɑːra/ *n. phr.* Also **groen amara**, **groenamare**, and with initial capitals. [Afk., *groene* combining form of *groen* green + *amara* bitter medicine.] A patent medicine made from a variety of herbs and taken for the relief of stomach and chest complaints. See also (*old*) *Dutch medicine* (DUTCH *adj.* sense 2).

1949 L.G. GREEN *In Land of Afternoon* 45 Buchu *azyn*, Groene Amara for stomach ache. **1958** E.H. BURROWS *Hist. of Medicine* 187 We had our own *boere-rate*: white and brown *dulsies*, Hoffmann's *droppels*, *groene amara*, *versterk droppels*, red powder, [etc.]. **1974** [see VERSTERKDRUPPELS]. **1989** D. SMUTS *Folk Remedies* 22 *Chest with phlegm*, 2 large tablespoons honey, .. 1 bottle groen amara.

‖**Grondwet** /ˈxrɔntvet, -vɛt/ *n. Hist. Law.* Also with small initial. [Afk., *grond* foundation, ground + *wet* law.] The constitution of any of the republics proclaimed by Boers during the nineteenth century. See also WET.

The constitution of the Republic of Natal was first promulgated in 1838, that of the Orange Free State in 1854, and that of the Transvaal in 1858.

1873 *Volkstem* 27 Aug., According to our Constitution, the Grondwet, a bill, before coming on for consideration in the Volksraad, must be published for three months in the Staatscourant. **1877** F. JEPPE *Tvl Bk Almanac & Dir.* (1976) 37 The administration of law is regulated by the so-called Grondwet or Fundamental Law proclaimed in 1858, sundry Ordinances and Regulations passed from time to time .. and, further according to Roman Dutch Law. **1897** *E. Prov. Herald* 24 Feb., The sovereignty of the Republic must be maintained as the Convention would be broken if judgement were given in conflict with the Grondwet, and war would then ensue. **1899** A. MILNER in C. Headlam *Milner Papers* (1931) I. 350 The principle embodied in the new draft Grondwet that any Resolution of the Volksraad is equivalent to a law. **1904** H.A. BRYDEN *Hist. of S. Afr.* 110 The village of Pretoria was laid out, and in 1858 a Grondwet or Fundamental Law was agreed upon by the Volksraad assembled at Rustenberg. **1926** M. NATHAN *S. Afr. from Within* 88 Tested by the Grondwet or Constitution of the Country, a mere resolution of the Volksraad had no legal force, and could not repeal or override another law which had been duly passed. **1949** E. HELLMANN *Handbk on Race Rel.* 278 The *Grondwet* of the South African Republic (1858) made it clear that no equality between black and white would be tolerated. **1955** W. ILLSLEY *Wagon on Fire* 124 By this process of reasoning he could heartily subscribe to the Grondwet of the Republic when it declared that 'there shall be no equality in Church or State between black and white in this land'. **1976** A.R. WILLCOX *Sn Land* 200 Before resuming the Trek the combined parties hammered out a *grondwet* (constitution) for their proposed republic.

grootapartheid see APARTHEID sense 1 b.

groot baas /ˈxrʊətbɑːs/ *n. phr.* Also **groote baas**, and with initial capitals. [S. Afr. Du., *groot* great + *baas* master (see BAAS).]

1. A respectful form of address to an influential person, usu. the ultimate authority in a hierarchy; occas. also used as a common noun. See also BAAS.

1812 A. PLUMPTRE tr. *H. Lichtenstein's Trav. in Sn Afr.* (1928) I. 118 He often introduced the words Groot Baas, (Great Master), by which he meant to signify our chief. The Hottentots commonly call the masters they serve *Baas*, and the governor of the colony had ever since its establishment been always called both by them and their wild fellow-countrymen *Groot Baas*. **1833** *Graham's Town Jrnl* 3 Jan. 3 The skeleton was then taken .. to the *groot baas*, who ordered the whole to be salted and buried. **1899** G.H. RUSSELL *Under Sjambok* 60 'The groote Baas can get up if he likes,' he said, 'but I must first put down the waggon-sail and if he hears any one coming he must lie down again.' **1899** *Grocott's Daily Mail* 10 July 3 He would consider it more dignified to deal direct if possible with the 'groot baas' or head of affairs. **1959** M.W. SPILHAUS *Under Bright Sky* 62 'Address the *groot baas*,' the constable in charge of a case would order some sulky young rascal. **1972** *Cape Times* 10 Mar. 1 'The Groot Baas said he would help us,' Geelbooi was reported as saying. **1976** S. CLOETE *Chetoko* 23 At Graskop he was the centre of all things, the master, the *groot Baas*.

2. *Fig.*, and *transf.*

a. God.

1828 T. PRINGLE *Ephemerides* 214 Has not the Groot Baas (the Great Master) given plenty of grass, roots, and berries, and grasshoppers for our use?

b. The government.

*a*1875 T. BAINES *Jrnl of Res.* (1964) II. 99 The extension of British Government here would be a day of great rejoicing among the oppressed natives, who are now eagerly asking every Englishman when the *Groot Baas*, or Government is coming.

grootbek /ˈxrʊətbek, -bɛk/ *n. colloq.* [Afk., *groot* great, big + *bek* beak, mouth (usu. of an animal).] Freq. used as a title or form of address: a braggart or 'big mouth'; one who talks too much. Also *attrib.*

1942 U. KRIGE *Dream & Desert* (1953) 128 He recognised the face on the photograph. It was that of Mussolini, heavy-jowled, at his most confident and aggressive. 'Look at him ...' Mostert muttered, his voice rising. 'Just look at him, grootbek Caesar!' **1959** J. MEIRING *Candle in Wind* 186 Come tell us, Henry September, old grootbek, where is the City Hall you promised us? **1975** *E. Prov. Herald* 28 Nov. 17 The PRP was born in an atmosphere of deceit and dishonesty with a 'groot bek'. **1987** *Sunday Times* 1 Mar. 17 Marie Pentz repeats her role as the inimitable *grootbek* Mietie.

Groot Krokodil /ˌxrʊət krɔkəˈdəl/ *n. phr. Colloq.* Also with small initials. [Afk., *groot* great + *krokodil* crocodile (see quot. 1990), a parody on traditional African honorific titles given to leaders of stature.] **a.** *The Groot Krokodil*: A nickname given to P.W. Botha, dating from the term of his state presidency; CROCODILE. **b.** *transf.* (pl. *krokodille*), used of anyone perceived to be acting ferociously or relentlessly.

1989 S. JOHNSON in *Weekly Mail* 3 Mar. 23 For a man who gives a platform to people who'd have the *Groot Krokodil* grabbing for his hotline to Auckland Park .. he's no revolutionary. **1989** *E. Prov. Herald* 4 Mar. 5 Sometimes there are so many [red-billed queleas] on a tree that they fall off and are eaten by waiting crocodiles. This had .. a political connotation with the 'groot krokodil' – Mr PW Botha – waiting for his opponents to fall into his mouth like 'parliamentary gravy'. **1990** *Sunday Times* 11 Mar. 1 Suggestions that the Groot Krokodil – the nickname given Mr Botha because of his relentless pursuit of opponents – might make a comeback sent a shudder through National Party ranks. **1991** *Weekend Post* 9 Mar. 3 The 'groot krokodil' of Wilderness .. is alive, well and baring his teeth on the banks of the Touw River lagoon. **1991** [see TOTAL ONSLAUGHT]. **1992** 'HOGARTH' in *Sunday Times* 26 Apr. 24 President de Klerk's proposal for an elected council of '*Groot Krokodille*' to replace the state president is blatantly rigged. **1993** R. HARTLEY in *Business Day* 11 June 2 He said Sunday Times editor Ken Owen had subsequently accused him of imprisoning the 14 detainees in 'the black hole of Calcutta' and had described him as the 'groot krokodil' of Quibaxe. This had created the incorrect impression that he was 'some kind of authoritarian bully boy'. **1994** R. BARNES on Radio S. Afr. 1 Jan. (Woman's World), The groot krokodil being ousted from power, and F. W. de Klerk coming in.

grootman /ˈxrʊətman/ *n.* Pl. **-ne** /-nə/, **grootmen**. [Afk., *groot* big + *man* man.]

1. *obs. great councillor*, see GREAT.

1886 G.A. FARINI *Through Kalahari Desert* 282 Verlander, with the acquiescence of his *groot-men*, gave him a piece of land.

2. *slang.*

a. In urban (esp. township) English: a term of respect for an older man or a leader.

1980 E. JOUBERT *Poppie Nongena* 229 And always the men were standing round the house and not leaving them alone, clansmen, old ones, grootmanne, men in groups, waiting round the house. **1983** *Natal Mercury* 8 June, The youngsters don't speak the lingo properly any more, but they look up to a *grootman* who is a bra. **1992** A. KLAASTE in *Ibid.* 11 Nov. 6 The dinner was in memory of .. a former colleague .. and another 'grootman' I knew, Toto Dinalane. **1993** —— *Informant, Johannesburg* 'Grootman' is street language and means Big Brother. It is the sign of respect for age and the leadership qualities of the man so addressed.

b. An older brother.

1991 *Informant, Bellville* Grootman. Elder brother. My grootman resembles my father.

Groot Slang /ˌxrʊət ˈslaŋ/ *n. phr. Obs.* [Afk., *groot* great + *slang* snake.] A fabulous monster believed by some to inhabit the waters of the Orange River.

1920 F.C. CORNELL *Glamour of Prospecting* 143 So we made up some dynamite cartridges with fuse and detonator, and flung them out as far as we could, and stood by with the 'arsenal' handy in case the 'Groot Slang' was at home and objected. **1936** C. BIRKBY *Thirstland Treks* 64 The *Groot Slang*, which ravages the country when offended, is believed to be the guardian of all diamonds in the river. **1945** L.G. GREEN *Where Men Still Dream* 125 There is a legend that the 'Wonder Hole' or 'Bottomless Pit' is the source of the diamonds. You need a Hottentot guide to reach this mysterious hole ... They believe the deep, black cavern is the home of the 'Grootslang', the Great Snake of the Orange River.

‖**groot trek** /xrʊət ˈtrek, -ˈtrɛk/ *n. phr.* Also with initial capitals. [Afk.] GREAT TREK sense 2.

1988 'K. DE BOER' in *Frontline* Apr.-May 34 Looking back one day, the second half of the 1980's might well be a major baken on the groot trek of Afrikaans. **1988** G. SILBER in *Style* June 129 June, 1995: The groot trek to Jupiter reaches its climax. **1989** A. DONALDSON in *Ibid.* Dec. 8 The estimated 20 000-strong refrain has been with us ever since the alternative *Groot Trek* across the Limpopo and back.

Hence **groot trekker** *n. phr.*, VOORTREKKER sense 1.

1980 [see OSSEWA sense 2 b].

ground *n. noncount.* [Special sense of general Eng., influenced by Afk. *grond* land. In general Eng., *ground* usu. denotes a particular piece of land, and is almost invariably preceded by a name, or a possessive noun or pronoun (cf. quot. 1911), referring to its owner or occupier.] Land; real estate.

[*c*1911 E. GLANVILLE in S. Playne *Cape Col.* 661 He was also manuring his ground with kraal manure and it was possible for him to put down 1,000 acres of lucerne.] **1970** *Daily Dispatch* 16 Sept. 1 (*advt*) Your best investment today is ground .. it never depreciates. **1984** *Fair Lady* 30 May 86 This is the fifth and last article on the whys and wherefores of buying ground and building a house. **1988** C. MARAIS in *Personality* 19 Dec. 34, I can attract the small business man with cheap ground and plenty of unskilled labour.

group *n.* [Narrowed sense of general Eng., influenced by GROUP AREA.]

1. An ethnic group, as defined under the *Group Areas Act* (see GROUP AREA *n. phr.* sense 2 a). Also *attrib.*

1950 *Act 41* in *Stat. of Union* 415 The Governor-General may .. declare that .. the area defined in the proclamation shall be an area for occupation by members of the group specified therein. **1967** [see CLASSIFY]. **1983** [see E. Prov. Herald quot. at OWN AFFAIR sense 1]. **1985** *E. Prov. Herald* 16 Aug. 4 The Group Areas Act should not be applied to the advantage of any particular group, or to the detriment of any group. **1987** *Ibid.* 28 Mar. 2 Mr Botha told an audience .. that the devolution of power and the protection of minority groups were not possible without own residential areas and community lives for different groups. **1989** *Ibid.* 23 Aug. 3 Mr Nel said .. Mr De Klerk had vowed that the group principle was of the utmost importance for any political development in South Africa.

2. *comb.* **group rights**, the power of an ethnic group to determine its own future; used esp. with regard to the protection of the white minority. See also OWN AFFAIR sense 1.

1987 *E. Prov. Herald* 15 June 9 President PW Botha has .. drawn the line at the Constitutional Council's plans to scrap all references to 'group rights'. **1987** *Work in Progress* July 6 S- had strongly argued .. that the ANC should give the white population collective guarantees and group rights. **1990** *Weekly Mail* 4 May 12 Thabo Mbeki .. suggested there would only be two sides at the negotiations — the Nationalist Party and those who backed 'group rights', and the ANC and those who wanted non-racialism. **1991** R.W. JOHNSON in *Sunday Times* 10 Feb. 21 As soon as you hear someone talk about 'group rights' or 'the oppressor', you know which camp they're in.

group area *n. phr.* and *adj. phr. Hist.* Also with initial capitals. [Prob. tr. Afk. *groepsgebied*.]

A. *n. phr.*

1. In terms of apartheid legislation: a residential area demarcated by law for occupation by one official ethnic group, to the exclusion of all other groups. Also *fig.*, and *transf.* See also GEBIED *n.*[2]

1950 T.E. DÖNGES in *Hansard* 29 May 7433 The overriding principle of this Bill is to make provision for the establishment of group areas, that is, separate areas for the different racial groups, by compulsion, if necessary. **1952** [see sense 2 a]. **1958** D. MARAIS *Europeans Only* (1960), (*caption*) The Voortrekkers were a stern, upright, proud and courageous people who set out in search of their own group area. **1960** A.D. LAZARUS in H. Spottiswoode *S. Afr.: Rd Ahead* 92 After ten long and tortuous years, the Act has failed miserably to bring about the promised Utopia where the different races would live and develop to their fullest stature in their special Group Areas. *c*1970 C. DESMOND *Discarded People* 41 The Whites .. are regarded as one group, despite their differences of language and culture, and have .. 86.3% of the Republic. A small portion of this is set aside as 'Group Areas' for the approximately two million Asian and Coloured people. **1971** *Rand Daily Mail* 18 Feb., There were more than 300 Indian businesses in the Diagonal Street complex in Johannesburg when it was proclaimed a White group area last December. **1975** *Sunday Times* 23 Mar. (Extra) 4 Peace has returned to Sir Lowry's Pass valley .. after the announcement that part of the hamlet has been changed back from a White to a Coloured group area. **1978** A.P. BRINK *Rumours of Rain* 17 Newspaper reports about Indian shopkeepers removed by the Government to another group area, angry demonstrations and resistance, and forcible eviction. **1983** *Sunday Times* 8 May 1 Having opted for constitutional group areas by creating three chambers instead of one, the Government reduces coloured and Indians to the status of legislative *bywoners*. **1990** *Ibid.* 4 Mar. 1 Several Ministers have recently told private-sector lobbies working for the abolition of group areas that they want to hear as wide a range of practical proposals as possible. **1993** *Weekly Mail & Guardian* 29 Oct. 13 Kharsany and others insist that Fietas will not become another group area, only for Indians.

2.a. In the phr. ***Group Areas Act*** [short title of Act 41 of 1950], a law providing for the declaration of separate residential and other areas for each official ethnic group, and prohibiting occupation or ownership by members of any other group. Also *attrib.* See also GROUP sense 1, *pillar(s) of apartheid* (PILLAR), PROCLAIM.

One of the central laws of the apartheid system, this Act was first promulgated in 1950; consolidated in 1957 and 1966, it was repealed in June 1991.

1952 L. MARQUARD *Peoples & Policies* 152 In 1950 the Group Areas Act was passed empowering the Government to declare any area a group area for Coloured, European, African, or Asian. **1953** *Drum* Oct. 43 Of all legislative enactments affecting the residential and property rights of the non-Europeans of the Cape, the Group Areas Act is surely the most far-reaching. **1957** *Encycl. Brit.* XXII. 426 The Group Areas act of 1950 was one of a series of acts which sought to implement Smuts's Natives Land act of 1913, which checked the penetration of natives into European areas and vice versa. **1963** WILSON & MAFEJE *Langa* 47 Where would I be now with this mass removal under the Group Areas Act had I remained? **1968** COLE & FLAHERTY *House of Bondage* 52 The so-called Group Areas Act of 1950, a complicated piece of legislation, many times amended, whose purpose is to assure that each of the country's racial groups shall live in isolation from the others; that non-white businesses shall not operate in white urban centres; and that the few property rights of Africans in urban areas shall be withdrawn. **1975** *Drum* 22 Apr. 20 The Group Areas Act discriminates on the basis of race in land deals, housing sales or in the treatment of tenants, attendance at schools, hospitals, churches and membership of other social, sporting and cultural organisations. *a*1977 K.M.C. MOTSISI in M. Mutloatse *Casey & Co.* (1978) 103 Sophiatown is now on its deathbed, groaning its last, from an incurable disease, which has been diagnosed by a Government doctor as Group Areas Act. **1982** *E. Prov. Herald* 5 Mar. 4 Multiracial sport is to be freed from the restrictions of the Group Areas Act .. [which] prohibits people of one population group from using sports facilities in the group area of another race. **1985** *Ibid.* 26 Feb. 4 Whites comprised less than 2 per cent of the 126 176 families moved from their homes in terms of the Group Areas Act between 1966 and the end of August last year. **1987** [see POPULATION REGISTRATION ACT]. **1987** *New Nation* 21 May 5 The threat of a new Group Areas Act (GAA) clampdown may usher in a new phase of repression. **1988** M. MAPISA in *Pace* Mar. (Queen) 3 The Group Areas Act is an ugly story. Millions of South Africans are forced to live kilometres from their work place and from centres of entertainment. **1990** *Sunday Times* 3 June 18 One down and two to go as we tear down the three remaining props of the apartheid edifice. Left over are the Group Areas Act and the Population Registration Act. The former is also on its way out and merely awaits formal burial. **1990** A. AKHALWAYA in *Weekly Mail* 8 Feb. 14 The proposed scrapping of the Population Registration, Land and Group Areas Act signals the end of official apartheid, not of practical apartheid. **1994** *Race Rel. Survey 1993–4* (S.A.I.R.R.) 344 Despite the repeal in June 1991 of the Group Areas Act of 1966 it would be 'years' before significant desegregation of residential areas occurred.

b. Always in *pl.*, and with initial capitals: **Group Areas**, ellipt. for *Group Areas Act*, — *officials*, — *legislation*, etc.

1958 *Ikwezi Lomso* Sept. 7 A successful fight against Group Areas meant a fight against the whole of the oppressive laws of the country. **1970** J. PACKER *Veronica* 59 He'll be kept out of the best work by Job Reservation, the Immorality Act will see that he never marries a white girl and the Group Areas won't allow him to buy a house in a white district. **1972** *Drum* 22 Mar. 21 The Group Areas say he is in 'illegal occupation' of his parish house in the township. **1980** *Fair Lady* 5 Nov. 137 We lived in a big house — five rooms. Group Areas moved us here. There were no street lights, nothing. **1990** *Daily News* 20 Apr. 12 Immediate abolition of Group Areas would cause a chaotic tangle in legal and bureaucratic procedures which .. have become part of our system.

B. *adj. phr.* Of or pertaining to the Group Areas Act.

1950 *E. Prov. Herald* 26 May 1 In the assembly today, the Prime Minister .. gave notice that he would introduce a guillotine motion .. limiting the discussions on the Group Areas Bill to 52 hours. **1956** M. ROGERS *Black Sash* 6 The Group Areas Removal Scheme, despite its advantages of improved housing conditions, yet undermined the independence and pride of many owners of backyard homes. **1968** *Drum* Sept. 6 Indians who obtain Group Areas permits to employ Africans may not allow them to live on the premises. **1977** *Sunday Times* 14 Aug. 10 Mr Ivor Garb .. said it would be 'a tragedy' if the eight coloured families were moved under the Group Areas proclamation. **1980** *Fair Lady* 5 Nov. 137 By the time all projected Group Areas removals are completed in the Cape Province, 360 000 people — most of them 'coloureds' — from about 70000 families, will have been moved from one area to another. **1985** B. ADKINS in *E. Prov. Herald* 16 Nov. 1 Mixed U'hage newlyweds face Group Areas charge. **1987** *South* 3 July 1 Some Rondebosch East tenants, including a mixed couple, claim they have been visited by police investigating Group Areas contraventions. **1990** T. GQUBULE in *Natal Witness* 12 Apr. (Echo) 7 If the refugees were being evicted for a Group Areas violation, she should have been warned.

gruisbok var. GRYSBOK.

grysappel /ˈxreɪsap(ə)l/ *n.* Formerly also **grijsappel**. [Afk., *grys* grey + *appel* apple.] MOBOLA.

1913 C. PETTMAN *Africanderisms* 199 *Grijs appel, Parinarum mobola* .. is so called in the Transvaal. **1917**, **1929** [see MOBOLA]. **1932** M.W. HENNING *Animal Diseases* 746 (Swart), Grysappel (Parinarium capense) belongs to the family Rosaceae. *a*1936 E.N. MARAIS *Soul of Ape* (1973) 76 When it was eventually introduced to the two plants mentioned, its confidence had grown to such an extent that it plucked and ate a grysappel without hesitation. **1961**, **1972** [see MOBOLA]. **1973** F.J. VELDMAN in *Std Encycl. of Sn Afr.* VIII. 607 Gifblaar .. , grysappel (*Paranari capense*), gousiektebos .. and the goorappel .. are very similar and are sometimes confused.

grysbok /ˈxreɪsbɔk/ *n.* Also **greisbo(c)k, greiseboke, greysbok, griesbo(c)k, grijsbok, gruisbok, grysbock**. Pl. unchanged, **-s**, or **-bokke** /-bɔkə/. [S. Afr. Du., fr. Du. *grijs* grey, grizzled + *bok* (see BOK).] Either of two species of small antelope of the Bovidae, both reddish brown in colour with a sprinkling of white hairs, and with large ears and (in the male) straight pointed horns, esp. *Raphicerus melanotis* (now often with distinguishing epithet, **Cape grysbok**) but also *R. sharpei* (**Sharpe's grysbok**). Also *attrib.*, and in dim. form **grysbokkie** [see -IE]. In both senses also called GRYSBUCK.

1786 G. FORSTER tr. *A. Sparrman's Voy. to Cape of G.H.* II. 224 The *grys-bok* is of a greyish colour, with black ears, and a large black spot round the eyes, being probably the *A. Grimmia*. **1790** tr. *F. Le Vaillant's Trav.* I. 33 The most common .. are the *steenbock*, the *duyker*, the *reebock*, the *grysbock*, the *bontebock*, and all the different species of antelopes. **1804** R. PERCIVAL *Acct of Cape of G.H.* 159 The gries-bock is .. the size of a common deer, but bears a considerable resemblance to a goat: its colouring is greyish and the hair loose and frizzled. This species .. does a great deal of mischief to the gardens and vineyards in the nighttime. **1810** G. BARRINGTON *Acct of Voy.* 156 The Greisbok is of a grizzled or greyish colour, .. bright brown interspersed with silver hairs. **1837** 'N. POLSON' *Subaltern's Sick Leave* 123 On the coast side of the Langekloof the grysbok is the commonest species of small antelope. **1847** [see DUIKER sense 1 a]. **1859** WOOD *Nat. Hist.* I. 643 The Grys-bok .. is a native of Southern

Africa [etc.]. **1872** C.A. PAYTON *Diamond Diggings* 81 Last Sunday we bought from some Kafir boys a doe grysbok, rather bigger, reddish brown, with silvery hairs here and there, for 2s. **1885** W. GRESWELL in *Macmillan's Mag.* (U.K.) Feb. 280 The little greisbok that has continually been nibbling his vines. **1900** W.L. SCLATER *Mammals of S. Afr.* I. 178 The grysbok is also found in open country, but only where there is plenty of cover and shelter. **1938** F.C. SLATER *Trek* 25 In the grey And unrecording scrub the grysbok lies. **1958** L.G. GREEN *S. Afr. Beachcomber* 24 Oom Stoffel shot a grysbok on his first visit there. **1969** M.W. SPILHAUS *Doorstep-Baby* 141 A rare leopard still hid in the ravines hunting grysbok and duiker. **1975** *Sunday Times* 8 June (Mag. Sect.) 7, I tried to persuade dad to control the Grysbokke on our mountain slopes. **1976** *Farmer's Weekly* 28 Jan. 70 It would be impossible, without .. hunting hounds, to flush .. a gruisbokkie from the thick bush-clad areas. **1976** J. HANKS *Mammals* 23 Sharpe's Grysbok, *Raphicerus sharpei* ... White hairs in a background coat of rich rufous brown. *Ibid.* 24 Cape Grysbok, *Raphicerus melanotis*. Small antelope. **1982** *S. Afr. Digest* 8 Jan. 1 Mr .. Wright's Alsatian bitch .. has adopted this orphaned grysbokkie. **1983** *E. Prov. Herald* 3 June 1 A tiny, one kilogram Cape grysbok which he rescued from certain death. **1987** T.F.J. VAN RENSBURG *Intro. to Fynbos* 52 The grysbok is totally dependent on the fynbos for survival. **1990** *Weekend Post* 24 Mar. 3 The shy grysbok ram .. will also stay. **1990** CLINNING & FOURIE in *Fauna & Flora* No.47, 16 After emerging from a forest patch into an area of drier scrub one may encounter .. the Sharpe's grysbok, *Raphicerus sharpei*. **1992** J. FEELY in *Afr. Wildlife* Vol.46 No.4, 155 The Cape grysbok .. has traditionally been assumed to occur from the south-western Cape eastwards to the Komga district on the border with Transkei ... Sharpe's grysbok .. — sometimes called the tropical grysbok — is found from Tanzania southwards to Swaziland and the north-eastern Transvaal. *Ibid.* 157, I was .. most interested to see a shepherd carrying a knapsack made from grysbok skin in the Drakensberg foothills in the Maclear district.

grysbuck /ˈxreisbʌk/ *n.* Also **grace buck, greysbuck, gries buck**. [Part. tr. S. Afr. Du. *grysbok*, see prec.] GRYSBOK.

1827 T. PHILIPPS *Scenes & Occurrences* 87 We had destroyed .. gries bucks and several birds. **1884** 'E.V.C.' *Promised Land* 79 The Dutchmen called it 'the Roi grace buck'. **1897** *Encycl. Sport* I. 39 The Bushbucks .. Grysbuck (*Nanotragus melanotis*) are small antelopes. **1940** V. POHL *Bushveld Adventures* 185 These dogs never chased anything except a bushbuck ram ... Steenbuck, greysbuck and even bushbuck does they simply ignored. **1983** H. THESEN in *Outeniqualander/Herald* 21 Dec. 26 We came upon a grysbuck nibbling at a bush. **1992** [see GEOMETRIC TORTOISE].

GST *n. hist.* Also **gst**. Abbrev. of *General Sales Tax*, a tax applied at the point of sale to all items except basic foods and essential services. Also *attrib.*

Introduced in 1978; replaced by VAT in October, 1991.

1978 *Financial Mail* 7 Apr. 40 The voteless blacks in the 'white areas' of SA will be the hardest hit by the new 4% General Sales Tax (GST) on practically all goods and services. **1981** *Bona* Jan. 16 It [*sc.* soya mince] gives your family a tasty, nutritious meal at less than 15 cents a serving (G.S.T. excluded)! **1985** *Argus* 24 Jan. 1 The Government would be forced to increase taxation — most likely through GST — to bring in an additional R1 000-million to balance its books. **1989** *Spar Woman's Focus* 3 July 7 Your Spar guide to 13% GST tables. **1990** K. MKHIZE in M. Kentridge *Unofficial War* 117, I was at a funeral of an Edendale tycoon whose five and half grand casket (GST excluded) had to fly into the grave because time was expiring. **1992** [see GENERAL DEALER sense 1].

guaap var. GHAAP.

Guanaqua var. GONAQUA.

guarri, gwarrie /ˈgwari/ *n.* Also **ghwarrie, guárri, guarrie, guarry, guerri(e), gwarri, gwary, kwarrie, quarri.** [Khoikhoi *gwarri.*]
a. In full ***guarriboom*** /-buəm/ [Afk., *boom* tree], ***guarri bosch*** *obs.* [Du., *bosch* bush], ***guarri bush, guarri tree, guarriwood***: Any of several trees or shrubs of the genus *Euclea* of the Ebenaceae, esp. *E. undulata*. Also *attrib.* Occas. with distinguishing epithet, as **blue guarri** (*E. crispa*), **sea guarri** (*E. racemosa*), etc.

1790 W. PATERSON *Narr. of Four Journeys* 43 The ground is covered with shrubs about four feet high, called by the natives Guerrie, a species of Royena. **1795** C.R. HOPSON tr. *C.P. Thunberg's Trav.* I. 202 The berries of the *Guarri bush* (*Euclea undulata*) had a sweet taste, and were eaten by the Hottentots. Bruised and fermented, they yield a vinegar, like that made from Pontac. **1801** J. BARROW *Trav.* I. 149 The *guerrie bosch*, apparently a species of rhus. **1824** W.J. BURCHELL *Trav.* II. 588 Different species of *Euclea* are .. called *Guárri* by the Hottentots. **1887** [see sense b]. **1897** [see SWARTHAAK]. **1913** C. PETTMAN *Africanderisms* 202 *Guarri tea*, This is made by the Hottentots from the leaves of *Euclea lanceolata*. **1939** tr. *E.N. Marais'd My Friends the Baboons* 42 Near the sleeping-place there was, in a corner of the rocks, a large gwarrie-bush. **1961** PALMER & PITMAN *Trees of S. Afr.* 136 Gwarri trees of one kind or another are found in all the drier parts of the country, and often in the regions of higher rainfall as well. **1971** L.G. GREEN *Taste of S.-Easter* 161 There was .. a rare ghwarrie bush honey, pale and delicate. **1977** *E. Prov. Herald* 2 Mar. 1 Mutton chops, sosaties and a gwarrie wood fire are the basic ingredients for a braaivleis competition. **1980** *S. Afr. Digest* 17 Oct. 16 Blue Gwarri, also known as Bush Gwarri, Gwarri, and umNqandane (*Euclea crispa*) The most widespread of the Hottentot-named Gwarrie specie[s] ... The leaves, browsed by rhino, are also used medicinally by Blacks. **1987** T.F.J. VAN RENSBURG *Intro. to Fynbos* 20 Low bushes such as candlewood ... sea guarri (*Euclea racemosa*), glossy currant .. and coastal saffron .. often occur in patches. **1993** F. VAN RENSBURG in *Getaway* Nov. 93 On the way we encountered blue guarri *Euclea crispa*.

b. In full ***guarribessie*** /-ˌbesi/, formerly also **guarribesjie** [Afk., *bessie* (fr. Du. *besje*) berry], the succulent, edible fruit of any of several species of guarri.

1843 J.C. CHASE *Cape of G.H.* 152 The wild fruits, indigenous to the country, are also incredibly numerous .. among these are wild grape (*Vitis Capensis*), .. wild pomegranate (*Hamiltonia Capensis*), quarri (*Euclea undulata*). **1866** LINDLEY & MOORE *Treas. Bot.* s.v. *Euclea*, The fruit is globular, fleshy, and juicy, sometimes as large as a cherry. Those of many of the species, known by the colonists as Guarry, are eaten. **1887** *S.W. Silver & Co.'s Handbk to S. Afr.* 139 Guarribesjies, a well-known fruit, eaten by the natives as the fruit of the Guarriwood, *Euclea undulata*. **1966** C.A. SMITH *Common Names* 239 *Guarribessies*, The succulent and edible fruits of *Euclea undulata*. **1970** BEETON & DORNER in *Eng. Usage in Sn Afr.* Vol.1 No.2, 18 Edible small succulent fruits known as 'guarribessies' wh[ich] the Hott[entots] fermented to make a type of vinegar.

guava *n.*
1. *slang.* ***on*** (***one's***) ***guava***: on one's posterior.

1975 'BLOSSOM' in *Darling* 95 This oke sticks he's foot out .. so I trip over it and end up on my guava. **1976** *Ibid.* 18 Feb. 95 Hanging on to ribbons so's they doesn't fall by mistake on they guavas.

2. [Acronym formed on the initial letters of *grown* (or *growing*) *up and very ambitious*.] A term used of an upwardly mobile young adult. Cf. general Eng. 'yuppie'.

1989 *Style* Feb. 125 Guava: There seems to be some confusion about this demographic ugliness. Some say it stands for Growing Up and Very Ambitious, others say Grown Up And Very Ambitious and a third opinion exists that the little brutes are not Very Ambitious at all, but just Vaguely Ambitious ... There are a number of professions and careers to pursue which would give the aspirant Guava sufficient velocity to be catapulted into the limelight. **1989** M. BRAND in *Fair Lady* 25 Oct. 90 *Guava*, grown up and very ambitious; hippies going yuppie. **1991** *Style* Nov. 153 Exit the yuppie, enter the Guava — grown up and very ambitious. **1992** J. MICHELL in *Style* Feb. 53 R— F— is a bright-eyed, 23-year-old guava (Growing Up and Vaguely Ambitious) who remembers February 23, 1991 as a big day. **1992** 'IVAN JELLICLE' in *Scope* 13 Nov. 51 Besides being a Guava (Growing up and very ambitious) Wayne's also a bit of a daredevil.

gubba var. GABBA.

gubu var. UGUBU.

guerri(e) var. GUARRI.

guma var. GHOMMA.

gumba-gumba /ˌgʊmba ˈgʊmba/ *n. slang.* [Etym. unknown: perh. echoic.] Also in shortened form **gumba**. In urban (esp. township) Eng.:
1. A prolonged music and drinking session at which liquor is sold for profit. Also *attrib.*

1974 K.M.C. MOTSISI in *Drum* 22 Dec. 44 He tells me that Kid Bles is admitted to the Repair House (Bara Hospital) after he gets himself knifed at a gumba-gumba session way out in Naledi. **1977** [see STOKVEL sense 2]. **1979** N. MOTANA in *Staffrider* Vol.2 No.2, 47 Lesiba: .. Congrats man! Are you throwing a gumba? Fred: (*Mimics Lesiba*) 'Gumba, gumba,' that's what you know best. When we go uptown you think we go for wine ... 'Gumba, gumba,' that's what you are after, bloody sucker! **1981** *Voice* 25 Mar. 4 All-night parties at which ear-deafening disco-music is played have been banned. Commenting .., Major Mazibuko said he was referring to 'gumba-gumbas', and had asked the people of Soweto to immediately report to the police if these parties inconvenienced them. **1982** *Reader* Dec. 7 Crime is worse when there are gumba-gumba parties ... These gumba-gumbas .. go on for the whole weekend ... The trouble is started by the strangers ... People say they need the money from the gumba-gumbas. **1982** 'D.M.' in M.B. Mtshali *Give Us a Break* (1988) 40 Down across our street there was a gumbagumba — a wild party. Drunkards were going up and down shouting and making funny things. **1988** [see sense 2].

2. *transf.* High-fidelity sound equipment; an amplifier. Also *attrib.*

1988 J. MATLOU in *Staffrider* Vol.7 No.3, 49 People from the mines were playing records with their gumba-gumba. Bleskop was very quiet but gumba-gumba men were blasting records the whole night until 2.30 in the morning, when they boarded the Pretoria train. **1990** R. STENGEL *January Sun* 82 During the 1940's, Oukasie was considered a smart address. Parties were frequent. Someone would get a gramophone and some Gumba-Gumbas, as amplifiers were called. The music was jazz. **1991** E. KOCH in *Weekly Mail* 28 Mar. 8 One Monday a furniture truck arrived at Joseph X—'s village to take back the *gumba* (hi-fi set) he bought on hire purchase from a shop in Umtata during one of his trips back home.

gumboot dance *n. phr.* [U.S. Eng. *gumboot* Wellington boot + Eng. *dance*.] A lively dance developed by Bhaca mine-workers and performed in unison, mimicking military marching and springing to attention, the dancers wearing gumboots which are given resounding rhythmical slaps with the hands. So **gumboot dancer**, also **gumbooter**, a performer of such a dance; **gumboot dancing** *vbl n.* and *ppl adj.* See also MINE DANCE.

The gumboot dance is believed by some to be influenced by both Bhaca traditional dancing and by the German *Schuhplattler* (learned from German immigrants), and by others (see quot. 1980) to be rooted in the Zulu *isicathulo* ('shoe') dance. See also BHACA.

[**1953** DOKE & VILAKAZI *Zulu-Eng. Dict.* 103 *-cathulo* ... 1. shoe, boot, sandal ... 3. Kind of 'boot' dance, indulged in by boys since European contact.] **1963** B. MODISANE *Blame Me on Hist.* (1986) 281 We had gone round the location shooting scenes of penny-whistle troupes, gum-boot dancers, singing troupes, shooting hundreds of feet of film to be shown to the Department of the Interior. **1974** *S. Afr. Panorama* Sept. 26 The empty dustbins become drums, the lids become cymbals, grass brooms add to the syncopation and the gum boot dance is a natural and logical conclusion. **1974** P. VILAKAZI in *Unisa Eng. Studies* Vol.12 No.2, 147 Oh! exile means Never to see a Baca gumboot dance, never! **1980** D.B. COPLAN *Urbanization of African Performing Arts.* 179 Schools picked up new urban-influenced rural dances ... One such dance, *is'catulo* ('shoe') was adopted by students in Durban, whence it spread to dock laborers who obtained spectacular rhythmic effects by slapping and pounding their rubber Wellington boots in performance. Such effects made it popular with mine and municipal laborers elsewhere, especially Johannesburg. There it became the 'gumboot dance'. **1981** *Pace* Sept. 174 Are we going to be shown happy gumboot-dancing and singing miners from the protectorates, flexing muscles and charcoal-stained bodies, entertaining white tourists? **1982** [see BHACA]. **1982** *E. Prov. Herald* 14 Dec. 24 One of the most popular modern mine dances is the rousing gumboot dance — *isicathulo* — developed by the Bhaca. It bears some resemblance to Cossack and Schuhplattler dances in its body and leg-slapping rhythms. **1988** *New Nation* 11 Feb. 11 He hoped the evening would include .. gumbooters. **1990** *Sunday Times* 24 June 20 Here's a national leader who thinks nothing of gumboot dancing at his birthday party. **1990** J. MICHELL in *Style* Nov. 61 Choreography that includes anything from gumboot dancing to toyi-toying. **1994** [see ISICATHAMIYA].

gumpaauw *n. obs.* Also **gum pauw.** Pl. unchanged. [Part. tr. S. Afr. Du. *gompaauw*, see GOMPOU.] The KORI, *Ardeotis kori*.

1838 J.E. ALEXANDER *Exped. into Int.* II. 141 Here a gum pauw, or bustard, which subsists partly on gum, was shot, which measured eight feet and a half between the extremities of the wings. **1958** A. JACKSON *Trader on Veld* 64 Among the birds were the Namaqua partridge, .. a few 'gumpaauw' (bustard) [etc.].

Gunaqua var. GONAQUA.

gunpowder weed *n. phr.* [Named for its black seeds resembling gunpowder; either derived from or the source of Afk. *kruitbossie, kruit* gunpowder + *bossie* (small) bush.] The naturalized European herb *Silene gallica* of the Illecebraceae, with small white to red flowers, and fruit-capsules which produce many tiny black seeds.

1860 HARVEY & SONDER *Flora Capensis* I. 127 *Silene gallica* ... This is the 'Gunpowder-weed' of the colonists, its black seed resembling powder. **1897** EDMONDS & MARLOTH *Elementary Botany* 139 *Silene* ... Several species of Campion, also the so-called 'Gunpowder Weed' (*S. gallica*). **1903** G. HENSLOW *S. Afr. Flowering Plants* 103 A troublesome cornfield weed introduced from Europe is *S. gallica*, called 'Gunpowder weed' by the colonists. **1926** J.B. DAVY *Manual of Flowering Plants of Tvl* I. 149 *S. gallica* ... Gunpowder weed ... The black seeds resemble grains of gunpowder. **1946** M. WILMAN *Check List of Flowering Plants of Griqualand W.* 16 S[ilene] gallica .. an increasingly frequent weed; September. *Gunpowder weed*. **1966** C.A. SMITH *Common Names* 240 Gunpowder weed, *Silene gallica*. **1991** *Dict. of Horticulture* (Dept of Nat. Educ.) 262 *Silene gallica* (gunpowder weed).

Gunukwebe, -kwebi varr. GQUNUKHWEBE.

Gun War *n. phr. Hist.* Also with small initials. The war of 1880–81 which resulted from the Cape government's attempt to disarm the Basotho.

[**1893** H.B. SIDWELL *Story of S. Afr.* 118 The War of the Guns ... The Basutos .. felt as a bitter insult the demand of the Colonial Government to give up their guns, in 1880. They refused to obey, and war followed.] **1903** E.F. KNIGHT *S. Afr. after War* 67 The Basutos firmly believe .. that Mr. Sauer was their secret friend during 'the gun war,' and they are not ungrateful for his services. **1948** E. ROSENTHAL *Afr. Switzerland* 188 When the 'Gun War' began in 1880 more than 4 000 Basuto disappeared overnight and many workings came to a stop on this account. **1972** J.A. BENYON in *Dict. of S. Afr. Biog.* II. 699 The Gun War .. cost the colony £3 000 000 and eventually ended in the complete collapse of Cape authority in Basutoland. In 1884 the Cape was obliged to return the territory to the imperial government. **1977** F.G. BUTLER *Karoo Morning* 205 Chrissie .. came from north of the Orange River into the old Colony in search of safety, then food, then cash to buy cattle, then guns (until the 'Gun War'). **1980** C. MURRAY in *S. Afr. Labour Bulletin* 6 The Gun War .. in which the Basotho successfully resisted the Cape Government's attempt to disarm them. **1986** P. MAYLAM *Hist. of Afr. People* 117 The rebellion came to be called the Gun War because it was seemingly provoked by the Cape government's attempts to disarm the southern Basotho ... In military and political terms the Gun War represented one of the few successful acts of African resistance against colonial rule to occur in southern Africa. **1987** *New Nation* 6 Aug. 9 Ntoa ya Lithunya, the Gun War, was fought from September 1880 to April 1881. **1989** *Reader's Digest Illust. Hist.* 193 (caption) Cape troops march into Basutoland in a bid to disarm Basotho during the so-called 'Gun War' of 1880–81.

gura(h) var. GORAH.

Guriqua var. GRIQUA.

gut morgen var. GOEIE MÔRE.

gwaai /gwaɪ/ *n.* Also **gwy, (n)gwai.** [Zulu *ugwayi* tobacco, snuff.]

‖**a.** Tobacco; snuff. Also *attrib.*

1879 R.J. ATCHERLEY *Trip to Boerland* 68 While sitting at our noontide meal that day, a troop of Kafirs in warlike array bore down upon us, and commenced a grand lamentation in respect to the scarcity of *doka* (hemp) and *gwai* (tobacco). **1899** A. WERNER *Captain of Locusts* 196, I found that the saddle was all right; and then he told me to get myself ngwai, and behold, he put this into my hand. [*Note*] tobacco. *c*1929 L.P. BOWLER *Afr. Nights* 148 The impi followed the Botletle river, but at Kala Mabela and Makabel, found plenty of tobacco (*Gwai*) which Khoa had prepared for the death-smoke. [**1957** B. FRASER *Sunshine & Lamplight* 7, I turned to a heathen woman in her red clay topknot and gay but dirty blanket. She wanted 'ugwayi'. I passed her some tobacco for grinding into snuff and her change. **1967** O. WALKER *Hippo Poacher* 77 Tom, who signalled the old man to go on with his grinding of the home-grown tobacco and *ugwayi* leaves on a hot stone and mixing of aloe ashes in the old-fashioned way that went back to Chaka's time.] **1970** D. PROCTOR *Informant, Clarens (OFS)* Gwaai. Tobacco. **1970** *Evening Post* 14 Nov. (Mag. Sect.) 1 His handling of the 'gwaai' was as nothing compared with the old man's technique. **1990** D. CAPEL in *Personality* 27 Aug. 13 They have their own peculiar brand of bug, called 'chongololos,' which eat the tobacco crop, known as 'gwaai'.

b. *slang.* A cigarette.

[**1986** T. THOKA in *Eng. Usage in Sn Afr.* Vol.17 No.2, 18 'Hey man, howzabout stenge gwy 'sbema man?' (Hey man, buy some cigarettes and let's smoke).] **1991** L. COLBOURNE *Informant, Durban* Give me a gwaai/skyf, my bru ... (Please give me a cigarette, brother). **1991** C. SAMMY *Informant, Adelaide (E. Cape)* Gwaais. Cigarettes.

Gwamba var. MAGWAMBA.

gwarri(e), gwary varr. GUARRI.

gweva /ˈgweːva/ *n. slang.* [Transf. use of Xhosa *igweva* an illicit diamond-buyer.] In urban (esp. township) parlance: a bootlegger. See also MAILER.

1971 *Daily Dispatch* 2 Oct. 12 The 'gweva' (go-between) was the mainstay for supplies to shebeens and with the strict application of prohibition laws the existence of both gwevas and shebeens was understandable. *a*1977 [see MAIL *v.* sense 1]. **1993** M.K. HARVEY in *Weekly Mail* 23 Dec. 15 When the case is finished, it's back to the bottlestore or the local *gweva* (bootlegger) for the next one.

gwy var. GWAAI.

gxagxa pl. form of IGXAGXA.

gyfbol var. GIFBOL.

gyppo /ˈdʒɪpəʊ/ *n. Army slang.* Also **gypo.** [As next.] **a.** The act of shirking a duty, or the means by which this is achieved. **b.** A shirker. Also *attrib.*

1978 *Informant (Army)* It's a lekker gyppo if you're good at sport and you can play for the army — you get sent all over the place. **1978** *Sunday Times* 24 Sept. 11 After the completion of the 20-km training run he had ordered Gunner Bothma to run in circles round a tree at a distance of 70 m. While Gunner Bothma was running he had shouted to Gunners Cronje and De Vries to 'see to him' as he was a 'gyppo' (lazy person). **1982** A. ROBERTS *Informant, Grahamstown* Gypo. Shirker. **1989** *Stanger Mail* 3 Feb. 7 When your troopie comes home on his first weekend pass you will be asked to sew his gypo seams. These seams are sewn close to the edge at the front and back of his trousers where the crease is normally ironed. This will save him hours of ironing and ensure that he will pass inspection.

gyppo /ˈdʒɪpəʊ/ *v. Army slang.* [Perh. fr. U.S. army slang *gyp* to cheat, trick, swindle, fr. either *gipsy* or *Gyppo* Egyptian (World War II, N. Africa).]

a. *intrans.* To shirk duty; to contrive a way of avoiding something unpleasant.

1971 C. BRITZ *Informant, Namibia* There was a lawyer from East London. We couldn't handle him — he gyppo'd out of everything. **1979** *E. Prov. Herald* 17 May 9 If a soldier was 'gyppoing' — shirking his exercises — he should be given the benefit of the doubt as in a court case when a man was not guilty until he had been found guilty. **1979** *Daily Dispatch* 26 June 15 If some detainees know their mate is gypoing (malingering) and he's being given the opportunity to sit out, they might also start taking chances. **1980** *Sunday Times* 12 Oct. (Mag. Sect.) 5 'I got here by mistake,' said a young guy from Hillbrow. 'I tried to gyppo and got sent here. Best thing that ever happened to me.'

b. *trans.* To avoid (something).

1986 *Informant, Grahamstown* He never invoiced me because he wanted to gyppo the GST on the thing.

H

ha var. HAAR.

haai /haɪ/ *int*. Also **ha(a)yi, hai**. [fr. Xhosa *hayi* no.] 'No!': expressing fellow-feeling in conversation; an exclamation of surprise, disbelief, or disapproval. Cf. AI, AIKONA *int*.

 1941 'R. ROAMER' in *Bantu World* 8 Mar. 4 Hai, members, women's hearts have many doors, really. And these doors open so easily. **1949** L. HUNTER *Afr. Dawn* 19 *Hayi*, it was a waste of money sending girls to school, but boys could benefit by a good education and earn large salaries. **1959** A. DELIUS *Last Division* 76 Haai, Masters, this news was a terrible shock, And my heart was heavy like a concrete block. **1960** J. COPE *Tame Ox* 213 Haayi ... no more shouting, no swearing. **1969** A. FUGARD *Boesman & Lena* 49 *Outa* still worry you? *Haai* Boesman. He's dead. **1973** [see WRAGTIE]. **1973** M. VAN BILJON in *Star* 16 June 6 Haai shame, he could never have known how sensitive people are, down here in deepest civilisation. **1976** M. MELAMU in *New Classic* No.3, 3 This woman's language, *hayi*! **1989** L. BEAKE *Cageful of Butterflies* 11 Haai Maina! This child of yours will be a great warrior! **1991** P. SLABOLEPSZY *Braait Laaities*. 20 I am thinking — Police? Aikona! Hai sugga!

haakdoring /'hɑːkdʊərəŋ, -duərəŋ/ *n*. Formerly also **haakdoorn, haake(n) doorn**. [Afk. (earlier S. Afr. Du. *haakdoorn*), *haak* hook + *doring* thorn.]

1. Any of several species of thorn tree of the genus *Acacia* of the Fabaceae, esp. *A. mellifera* subsp. *detinens* (see BLACK THORN sense b); HACK-THORN; HOOK-THORN; SWARTHAAK; also called WAG-'N-BIETJIE. Also *attrib*.

 1822 W.J. BURCHELL *Trav*. I. 320, I halted .. to gather a beautiful parasitic plant, growing on the branches of a Haakdoorn. I approached the thorny bush with caution. **1827** G. THOMPSON *Trav*. I. 246 The country through which we passed was much encumbered with the accursed *Haak-doorn* or *Wagt een beetje*, (*Acacia detinens*,) from which I had formerly suffered so severely. **1880** *S.W. Silver & Co.'s Handbk to S. Afr.* 162 The colonists speak .. of the Doornboom, .. of the Haaken Doorn, and of the Haak en steek Doorn, having both hooked and straight thorns; and Dr. Kirk is said to have playfully classified the thorns .. as those which scratch the skin, those which tear the flesh, those which tear the clothes, and those which tear both clothes and flesh. **1907** T.R. SIM *Forests & Forest Flora* 15 In dry stony situations the scrubby Haakedoorn (Acacia detinens) and the Wild Olive .. were the prevailing trees or shrubs. **1917** S.T. PLAATJE *Native Life* 62 The flocks were feeding on the luscious buds of the haak-doorns. **1920** F.C. CORNELL *Glamour of Prospecting* 204 In one of the ravines where a thick bush known as haak doorn (hook thorn) abounded we found .. skeletons, firmly entangled in the thickest part of the bush. **1936** H.F. TREW *Botha Treks* 19 The corporal and a constable and I .. proceeded in the direction of the screams, to find our drunken visitor .. caught in a haakdoorn bush. **1948** H.C. BOSMAN in V. Rosenberg *Almost Forgotten Stories* (1979) 98 'In the morning, .. Jan Slabbert and Hendrik Buys would be outside, .. creeping through the wag-'n-bietjie thorns', Jurie Bekker said. 'The afternoons, of course, they keep free for creeping through the haak-doring thorns.' **1966** C.A. SMITH *Common Names* 240 *Haakdoring, Acacia mellifera* var. *detinens* ... A deciduous tree up to 25 ft high, armed with numerous pairs of recurved thorns. **1993** J. THOMAS in *House & Leisure* Nov. 50 The reality can be grim ... Mosquito larvae jack-knifing through your drinking water. Haakdorings and Puff adders.

2. *obsolescent*. The GRAPPLE-PLANT, *Harpagophytum procumbens*.

 1864 T. BAINES *Explor. in S.-W. Afr.* 147, I noticed a large hooked seed of the creeping plant, sometimes called Haak-doorn, but more properly the Grappler; the Haak-doorn .. being furnished .. with small but very strong and sharp hooked thorns, arranged in pairs, and tearing the flesh most cruelly whenever it catches. **1913** C. PETTMAN *Africanderisms* 203 *Haakdoorn*, .. Burchell gives this name to *Acacia detinens*, the Wacht-en-bitje ... It seems now to be more frequently applied, however, to *Harpagophyllum procumbens*. **1966** C.A. SMITH *Common Names* 240 *Haakdoring*, .. *Harpagophytum procumbens*.

haak-en-steek /,hɑːk(e)n'stɪək/ *n*. [Afk., *haak* hook + *en* and + *steek* stab.] **a.** The large, flat-topped deciduous thorn tree *Acacia tortilis* of the Fabaceae, bearing both curved and straight thorns; UMBRELLA THORN. Also *attrib*. **b.** A thorn from this tree. In both senses also called WAG-'N-BIETJIE.

 [**1880** see HAAKDORING sense 1.] **1900** F.R.M. CLEAVER in M.M. Cleaver *Young S. Afr.* (1913) 69 It may be .. that the thorn, on which he sits, is a dubbeltje, a haak-en-steek, a driedoorn-haak, a wacht-a-beetje, a krap-en-scheur, a duivel's jaap, or a klits-en-klauw. But to me such distinctions are trivial. **1905** J. DU PLESSIS *1000 Miles in Heart of Afr.* 139 The *haak-en-steek doorns* .. tear your garments and lacerate your skin, especially when you are in eager pursuit of game and unmindful of your pathway. **1948** O. WALKER *Kaffirs Are Lively* 76 We sighted his white tent-tops above the *haakensteek* — hook-and-stick — thorn bushes long before we reached him. **1951** H.C. BOSMAN in L. Abrahams *Bekkersdal Marathon* (1971) 123 I'll be glad to show you all over my farm where I'm not going to plant potatoes ... That is, among the haak-en-steek thorns. **1977** F.G. BUTLER *Karoo Morning* 40 The haak-en-steek presented a consistent friendly green. You had to walk into one to experience its camouflaged malice: not only did it have a straight thorn to prick your flesh, but a hooked thorn to grab you and not let you go. **1983** T. BARON in *Frontline* June 29 The Zulus say that this is the main reason for the bad temper of the black rhinoceros who has to start off each morning feeling prickly from last night's dinner of haak-en-steek. [**1993** *Getaway* Nov. 76 (caption) The spreading crowns of umbrella thorn trees *Acacia tortilis* ... Despite the fearsome combination of straight and hooked thorns that give them the Afrikaans name of *haak-en-steek*, the tiny leaves are well loved by all browsers.]

haanen-poot, haanepoot varr. HANEPOOT.

haar *n., int.,* and *adj*. *Obs*. Also **ha**. [Du.] 'Left'. Cf. HOT.

A. *n*. A cry of 'haar'.

 1786 [see HOT *n*.].

B. *int*. 'Turn left', a call to a draught-ox.

 1812, 1821, 1913, 1919 [see HOT *int*.].

C. *adj*. Of or pertaining to the left-hand position of an ox in a team of draught-oxen; the left-hand or 'near' side.

 1868, 1870, 1913, 1919 [see HOT *adj*.].

haardekool var. HARDEKOOL.

haarder var. HARDER.

haarlemensis var. HARLEMENSIS.

haarlemmer /'hɑː(r)ləmə(r)/ *n*. Also **harlemer**, and with initial capital. [Afk., named for *Haarlem* the Dutch town in which the medicine was first formulated in 1672 + *adj*.-forming suffix *-er*. Cf. general Eng. *Haarlem oil* (earliest quot. 1885).] Special Comb. **haarlemmer drops**, **-druppels** /-'drɔpəlz, -'drœpəls/ [Afk., *druppels* see DRUPPELS], **-essens** [Afk., *essens* essence], **-oil**, **-olie** /-,ʊəli, -,uəli/ [Afk., *olie* oil]: HARLEMENSIS.

 1937 S. CLOETE *Turning Wheels* 257 Medicines such as camphor, turpentine, senna beans, buchu, harlemer olie and jalap. **1958** [see HARLEMENSIS]. **1984** B. JOHNSON-BARKER in *Wynboer* Feb. 64 The doctor was holding up a small bottle, .. a bottle of druppels; Haarlemmer Olie, it looked like. **1989** D. SMUTS *Folk Remedies* 64 *Neuritis*, 1 bottle balsem vita, 1 bottle Haarlemmer drops, 2 teaspoons sweet olive oil. **1990** C. LAFFEATY *Far Forbidden Plains* 194 What, he wanted to know, would she prescribe for, say, pneumonia? A mixture of rue-water and haarlemmer oil, Mamma answered. **1991** [see *krampdruppels* (DRUPPELS sense b i)].

haarpis var. HARPUIS.

haarskeerder /'hɑː(r),skɪə(r)də(r)/ *n*. Formerly also **haar-scheerder**. [Afk. (earlier S. Afr. Du. *haarscheerder*), *haar* hair + *skeerder* cutter; see quots 1966 and 1970.] JAGSPINNEKOP.

 1905 [see ROMAN sense 2]. **1918, 1939** [see JAGSPINNEKOP]. **1966** E. PALMER *Plains of Camdeboo* 237 Our servants .. swear that at night they [sc. *Solifugae*] get into the hair of sleeping people and snip it off, and this is a very general belief for *haarskeerder*, or hair-clipper is one of their common names. **1970** C. KINSLEY *Informant, Koegasbrug* (N. Cape) Haarskeerder. A big red spider that is supposed to cut your hair while you sleep. Uses it to line his nest.

haartbeast var. HARTEBEAST *n*.

haartebeest var. HARTEBEEST *n*.

haas see HASIE sense 2.

haasbek /'hɑːsbek, -bɛk/ *n*. and *adj*. [Afk., 'rabbit's-mouth', *haas* rabbit, hare + *bek* beak, muzzle.]

A. *n*. Pl. **-bekke** /-bekə, -bɛkə/.

1. *rare*. See quot.

 1955 L.G. GREEN *Karoo* 227 Every man on the .. farms patrols the .. dam walls .. looking for the tell-tale gaps called *haasbekke* and the holes made by moles and rats.

2. *colloq*. A toothless or gap-toothed person.

1970 C. ROBERTS *Informant, Bloemfontein* The little boy is a haasbek (without some or all teeth). **1972** *Informant, Grahamstown* My mother had a most embarrassing time trying to entertain Mr —, a proper old haasbek — well, he had a few teeth, but they didn't meet anywhere, so he couldn't chew the food. **1973** BEETON & DORNER in *Eng. Usage in Sn Afr.* Vol.4 No.1, 57 *Haasbek,* .. lit.: rabbit's mouth, expression used when young children first lose their front teeth.

B. *adj. colloq.* Toothless; gap-toothed. Also *fig.*

1969 *Personality* 5 June, Walk around toothless for a few months. In South Africa this is called 'going haasbek'. **1980** *Weekend Post* 4 Oct. 14 Poor Ali — floating like an ostrich, stinging like a haasbek bee … And, .. at Madison Square Garden a year earlier, he was even then floating like an ostrich and stinging like a haasbek bee.

‖**haat** /hɑːt/ *n.* [Afk., 'hatred'; in S. Afr. Eng., prob. derived fr. *boerehaat* (see BOEREHAAT).] Hatred; rancour between South African groups, particularly between English- and Afrikaans-speakers. Often *attrib.* See also BOEREHAAT, *Engelsehaat* (ENGELS *n.* sense 2 b).

1972 *Sunday Times* 11 June (Mag. Sect.) 9 He felt both races were South Africans and it is sad to hear the 'haat' policy revived today. **1972** *Daily Dispatch* 12 May 10 The 'haat' tactic is like a childish game. Neither separate development nor 'haat' is the real issue, but the economy of the country. **1973** *Sunday Times* 4 Feb. (Mag. Sect.) 3 There would be no brain-washing of youth, no expedient cooking-up of haat campaigns.

‖**haat** /hɑːt/ *v.* [Afk., 'to hate'; see prec.]
1. *intrans.* To feel hatred.
1972 *Sunday Times* 30 Apr. 4 Because I am a dominee I am not permitted to haat.
2. *trans.* To hate (someone).
1972 *Daily Dispatch* 12 May 10 In 1948 there was the word 'apartheid' which caused whites to 'haat' Africans. **1974** *E. Prov. Herald* 1 Nov. 5 Nationalists do not haat the Engelse. It is liberal thought that is the target, regardless of language.

haau var. HAU.

haayi var. HAAI.

hackthorn *n. obs.* [Calque formed on S. Afr. Du. *haakdoorn.*] HAAKDORING sense 1.

1863 W.C. BALDWIN *Afr. Hunting* 173, I must have had nearly five miles through hack-thorns. **1871** J. MACKENZIE *Ten Yrs* (1971) 385 The hack-thorn (*acacia detinens*) is especially sacred; it would be a great offence to cut down a bough from this tree. **1936** E.C. LLEWELLYN *Influence of Low Dutch* 165 *Hackthorn,* .. a thorny shrub, so called from the hooked thorns.

hadeda, hadedah /ˈhɑːdidɑː, ˈhɑːdədɑː/ *n.* Also addada, hadada(h), hadadaw, haddada(u), haddidah, hadida(h), hah-de-dah, hardidah, oddida. Pl. usu. **-s,** occas. unchanged. [Onomatopoeic, see quots 1846 and 1899.] The large ibis *Bostrychia hagedash* of the Plataleidae, grey-brown in colour with metallic purple on the wings, and characterised by its loud, harsh call. Also *attrib.*

A common resident in built-up areas and cities, the hadeda is found in all but the drier regions of South Africa.

[**1786** G. FORSTER tr. *A. Sparrman's Voy. to Cape of G.H.* I. 280 Of the feathered tribe I found in *Houtniquas* a new species of *tantalus,* called by the colonists *hagedash,* and also *hadelde.* This latter name has, in some measure, the same sound as the bird's note.] **1801** J. BARROW *Trav.* I. 264 The Egyptian black *ibis* (*niger*), and another species of *tantalus,* called by the farmers the *haddadas,* were procured at this place. **1846** J.C. BROWN tr. *T. Arbousset's Narr. of Explor. Tour to N.-E. of Col.* 190 A large ibis, of a brown lustre, commonly called by onomatopy addada. **1861** T. SHONE *Diary.* 9 Mar., A hadadaw for dinner, food as usual. **1890** A. MARTIN *Home Life* 239 The grey ibis, now extinct in Egypt, but common enough in the Cape Colony, and .. irreverently and absurdly named by the colonials 'oddida'. **1899** R.B. & J.D.S. WOODWARD *Natal Birds* 191 This bird derives its popular name of 'Hadadah' from its peculiar cry of ha-ha-hada-dah. **1907** *Afr. Monthly* Oct. 445 Flocks of 'ha-di-da' grub silently and unconcernedly in close proximity to the camp. **1937** M. ALSTON *Wanderings* 100 We surprised two ha-da-dahs (ibises) feeding on some marshy ground by the river, .. handsome birds about thirty inches in length. **1956** P. BECKER *Sandy Tracks* 87 A flight of rowdy hadidah ibises passed overhead, to roost in the rocky slopes of the krantzes across the spruit. **1971** K.B. NEWMAN *Birdlife in Sn Afr.* (1979) 195 The Cattle Egret and the Hadeda Ibis are well-known examples of birds which have taken advantage of the changes caused by farming. **1989** H.P. TOFFOLI in *Style* Dec. 57 You have wildlife — hadedas or vervet monkeys depending on the location — on your front lawn. **1992** *S. Afr. Panorama* Mar.-Apr. 120 The mournful cries of hadedahs carry far on soft lake winds. **1993** A.P. BRINK *First Life of Adamastor* Glossary, *Hadeda,* race of ibis, apparently a harbinger of death. **1994** M. ROBERTS tr. *J.A. Wahlberg's Trav. Jrnls 1838–56* 20 Hadidas common in the woods. Wounded one antelope and one Hadida with small-shot.

haenapod(e), haen-pode varr. HANEPOOT.

haffie /ˈhɑːfi/ *n.* Urban slang for a HALF-JACK.

1979 *Voice* 30 Sept. 2 You'd sure find Bra Joe sharing a 'haffie' with the driver as the first stop Naledi was speeding through the townships.

hagurdis var. AKKEDIS.

Hahabee, -bi varr. RHARHABE.

hah-de-dah var. HADEDA.

hahnen pootgen, hahnepote varr. HANEPOOT.

hai var. HAAI.

haikhona, haikon(n)a varr. AIKONA.

hairyback *n. Derog. offensive. slang.* [Eng. *hairy* (derog.) suggesting ill-bred, primitive + *back.*] An insulting name for an Afrikaner. Also *attrib.*

1970 *Cape Times* 16 May, There should be a match arranged between the Springboks and an Invitation side from the hairiest hairy-back elements of the Universities of Cape Town and Stellenbosch. **1970** B. KIRK-COHEN *Informant, Pietersburg* Hairy backs. Afrikaners. **1973** [see CRUNCHIE]. **1973** [see *Cape Times* quot. at ROCKSPIDER]. **1975** G. MCINTOSH in *E. Prov. Herald* 11 Sept. 3 'Kaffir' is regarded as an insult in South Africa. It is in the same category as 'hairy back' 'dutchman' or 'coolies'. **1978** A.P. BRINK *Rumours of Rain* 405, I heard .. the red haired English lady shouting in a sudden outburst of quite uncontrolled hate: 'You bloody Boers, just a lot of hairybacks, that's what you are!' **1981** *Sunday Times* 15 Mar. 21 Would you like to be an Afrikaner and be plastered with 'Hairy back', 'Rock spider', 'Skaaps', 'Narrow', or be English and be plastered with 'Rooinek' and 'Kaffer-boetie'? **1990** J.G. DAVIS *Land God Made in Anger* 200 'No wonder you haven't got much time for the South African government.' 'Goddam Hairybacks.' **1990** [see Frontline quot. at AF sense 1]. **1993** [see AMABHUNU sense 1].

ha-ja /ˈhadʒɑː/ *n. slang.* Also **hajaa.** In urban (esp. township) Eng.:
a. HALF-JACK.
1966 K.M.C. MOTSISI in *Post* 16 Jan. (Drum) 19 Sleeping tablets in the form of a hajaa of mahog. **1973** — in *Drum* 8 Oct. 41, I prefer this brew myself when I find myself not in the financial position to patronise Aunt Peggy for a ha-ja of mahoga. **1978** *Staffrider* Vol.1 No.2, 54 Kid Casey old feller — We've loved your adventures of Hajas, Beeyahs, Die Hardes, Shake the Contents. **1980** B. SETUKE in M. Mutloatse *Forced Landing* 58 The amateur gangsters .. pay their way to and from the ghetto by bribing the barrier-attendants with a nip or 'ha-ja' of mahog as they pick the pockets of innocent passengers throughout the day in each and every train on the railway-line. **1987** O. MUSI in *Drum* Apr. 61 Hazardous pastimes in those parts include .. boozing. Yes, grog is taboo and if you are caught with a haja they first ask you which hand you used to pour and you tell them the left.
b. *transf.* MAHOG.
1975 K.M.C. MOTSISI in M. Mutloatse *Casey & Co.* (1978) 57 The haja he makes me as a curtain-raiser makes me feel that the more the merrier like any non-voter who has this healthy habit will tell you. **1978** S. MHLONGO in *Staffrider* Vol.1 No.2, 10 But my grimace (if you could see it) is actually the child of the 'bikinyana' from yesterday's booze supply, which those clevers and know-alls care to dub 'haja', or brandy to be formal.

half-cord /ˈhɑːfkɔːd/ *n.* [Calque formed on Du. *haalf-coord,* ad. Pg. *albacora* fr. Arabic *al* the + *bukr* (pl. *bakārat*) a young camel, a heifer.] The YELLOWTAIL (sense a), *Seriola lalandi.*

1856 F.P. FLEMING *Sn Afr.* 480 *Scomber Capensis, Cuv. and Val.* (*Halfcord.*) … A large fish measuring from two to three feet. **1887** *S.W. Silver & Co.'s Handbk to S. Afr.* 184 *Scomber Capensis.* Halfcord. Not much in request. Flesh deemed by some unwholesome. **1913** C. PETTMAN *Africanderisms* 26 Albacore, .. *Seriola lalandii.* This name, sometimes corrupted into albert-koord and half-cord, and at Somerset Strand into half-koot, is applied in South Africa to this species of mackerel; as employed .. by sea-faring men generally it refers to quite another fish. **1947** K.H. BARNARD *Pict. Guide to S. Afr. Fishes* 116 Yellowtail, Albacore (*Seriola lalandei*) … Albacore has become corrupted in the Cape fishermen's parlance to Half-cord. **1951** L.G. GREEN *Grow Lovely* 90 It is possible .. that such mysterious names as bafaro, sancord, halfcord, and kartonkel are really Malay names. **1954** E. ROSENTHAL *Encycl. of Sn Afr.* 630 *Yellowtail,* .. Albacore (corrupted to Half-cord). A highly esteemed food fish.

half-jack *n. colloq.* [Eng. *half* + *jack* a gill or quarter-pint measure.] A half-bottle (now 375 ml) of spirit, usu. sold in a flattened pocket-size bottle; a measure of spirit (esp. brandy) sold at a shebeen; HAFFIE, HA-JA sense a. Also *attrib.* See also NIPINYANA. Cf. STRAIGHT.

1953 LANHAM & MOPELI-PAULUS *Blanket Boy's Moon* 70 He took from his pocket a half-jack of white man's brandy. **1959** L. LONGMORE *Dispossessed* 222 African women who buy large quantitires of liquor .. may not sell a whole bottle of brandy or gin but measure out tots for 2s.6d, nips for 5s., half-jacks for 10s. **1967** O. WALKER *Hippo Poacher* 38 After a few pulls on a half-jack of brandy which one of the others carried, the old man perked up. [a**1968** D.C. THEMBA in E. Patel *World of Can Themba* (1985) 159 Our hostess waddled up to the cops. They ordered half-a-jack of brandy.] **1970** M. DIKOBE *Marabi Dance.* 9 The brandy drinkers ordered half-jack quantities, paid a pound and refused the change. **1975** 'BLOSSOM' in *Darling* 28 May 95 Biltong sarmies and other light refreshments such as, three demijohns of white malmsey and a half-jack medicinal brandy to keep the driver awake juring the wee small hours. **1982** *Fair Lady* 1 Dec. 183 A small garden table stacked with empty Coke bottles and 'nips' (the measure in which spirits are sold in shebeens — the equivalent of 250 ml or a half-jack). **1982** D. KRAMER *Short Back & Sides* 36 We got stoned on a half-jack of cane In the toilets of the school. **1987** O. MUSI in *Drum* June 58 Ngcobo was pleased at the reunion more especially as his new-found mate .. presented him with a half-jack as a 'thank-you' gift. **1993** I. VLADISLAVIĆ *Folly* 86 A half-jack of Johnny Walker and a nip of Drambuie .. now came to light. **1994** [see STRAIGHT].

half-man *n.* [Calque formed on Afk. *halfmens.*] The HALFMENS, *Pachypodium namaquanum.* Also *attrib.*

1911 *State* Nov. 487 (Pettman), The trunk is often almost the girth of a man at its thickest point, and the effect of these solitary erect figures against a background of rocks is such as to render their name of *half-men* very appropriate. **1986** *Motorist* 3rd Quarter 8 The well-known but comparatively rare *Pachypodium nama* ('half-man') .. always inclines its head

halfmens /ˈhalfmens, ˈhɑːf-/ n. Also **halvemens**, and (formerly) **halfmensch**. Pl. **-mense** /-mensə/. [Afk., *half* half + *mens* person.] The succulent plant or small tree *Pachypodium namaquanum* of the Apocynaceae, having a thick, tapering, spiny, and usu. branchless stem with a tuft of leaves at the top; *elephant's trunk*, see ELEPHANT; HALF-MAN. Also *attrib*.

Usu. 1,5m to 2,5m in height, the halfmens sometimes reaches *a height of* 5m.

[1911 *State* Nov. 487 (Pettman), The ravines and slopes were here dotted with the extraordinary column-like succulent *Pachypodium Namaquanum*, known to the Hottentots as *Half-mense*.] 1912 *E. London Dispatch* 17 May 6 (Pettman), Our north western divisions .. so empty of life that the inhabitants .. speak of a certain branchless, mopheaded, succulent plant growing there as *'n halve-mens*, that is its shape is half-man like as seen against the sky line! 1945 L.G. GREEN *Where Men Still Dream* 131 The *Pachypodium Namaquanum*, as the scientists call the 'half-mens', was discovered a century ago by the explorer Paterson. 1968 G. CROUDACE *Black Rose* 161 Jeremy knew the trees he was talking about. From a distance they looked like grotesque human beings. The Afrikaner trekkers had christened them *half-mens*. 1976 O. LEVINSON *Story of Namibia* 119 The weird desert tree 'halfmens' (*Pachypodium namaquanum*) said by the Namas to be their ancestors, who leaning towards the north from where they originated, were petrified. 1977 *Daily Dispatch* 26 Apr. 10 The halfmens is well represented in .. folklore and Nama legends .. Its Afrikaans vernacular name 'halfmens' .. is also generally used in English. 1987 I. CLAASSEN in *S. Afr. Panorama* Aug. 23 (*caption*) The *halfmens* (semi-human) plant, *Pachypodium namaquanum*, on Kodas Peak ... The head of each trunk of the plant is always turned in a northerly direction as if the lost souls are for ever trying to turn back to their fatherland. 1990 S. ROWLES in *Weekend Post* 16 June (Leisure) 5 (*caption*) This *halfmens* tree is estimated to be 300 years old. Examples of this rare plant as old as 1000 years are found in the Richtersveld. 1992 P. CULLINAN *Robert Jacob Gordon* 110 (*caption*) *Pachypodium namaquanarum* (a member of the Num-Num family) from the western banks of the Orange River. It is also known as the 'half-mens'.

half place see PLACE n.¹ sense 2.

ham var. AUM.

Hamaaqua see quot. 1801 at *Namaqua grouse* (NAMAQUA n. sense 2).

‖**hamba** /ˈha(ː)mba, ˈhʌmbə/ v. intrans. Also **amba, amber, humba**. [Xhosa and Zulu, 'go'.]
1. To go; freq. *imp*., 'go on', 'push off'. So also the emphatic **hambake** /ˈhambake/ also **hambarkai** [Zulu enclitic formative *-ke*], 'go immediately'. Cf. SUKA sense a, VOETSAK sense 1 a.

1827 G. THOMPSON *Trav.* I. 376 The Caffers .. say *hamba* for *get you gone*. 1829 [see LOOP sense 1 b]. 1855 G. BROWN *Personal Adventure* 105, I attempted to speak to him; but with a most emphatic 'hambake!' (go away now), he beckoned me off with his hand. 1857 R.J. MULLINS *Diary*. 31 May, Kafirs starving on all sides, and glad to pick up crumbs under your table, who six months ago would have told you to 'hamba' if you had proposed such a thing to them. 1878 H.A. ROCHE *On Trek in Tvl* 239 'Hamba! Hamba! Taaté,' a quick-march order which even a dog understands here. 1899 G.H. RUSSELL *Under Sjambok* 22 'Hambarkai!' (Go on) I shouted to my native driver and 'voorlooper.' 1920 R.Y. STORMBERG *Mrs Pieter de Bruyn* 30 She loops .. voetzaks – hamba's – i.e. gets the push, the end of this blissful month. a1931 S. BLACK in *S. Gray Three Plays* (1984) 143 Jeremiah: Two jobs and one hundred pound! Abraham: Yes, I promise. Go on, hamba! 1949 [see JA adv. sense 1]. 1963 A.M. LOUW *20 Days* 104 And what does the Black man get for his work? It is: .. Here, Kaffir, after your work is done, you no longer belong in this place, so hamba! 1979 F. DIKE *First S. African* 24 Sorry tata, I went to fetch my register from school, I forgot ... Hlazo: Hamba jou bloody fool. 1984 F. JAY in *Staffrider* Vol.6 No.1, 20 'Boy! *Umfaan*! *Get down* from there. *Hamba!* Can't you see the *nkosazaan* is swimming now.' .. '*Hamba!* Go and do your hedge-cutting somewhere else.' 1994 *Style* Oct. 30 Get Ahead has taken a three-year lease in the Cape .. and next? Hamba London-side.

2. In the phr. *hamba kahle* /ˌhʌmbəˈgɑːʃli, ˌhambaˈgɑːle/, also **hamba couthley, -ga(c)hle, -gahlé, -ga(s)hli, -gashly, -gathle, -gooshly, -gthlie, -kahale, -khole** [Zulu or (occas.) Xhosa form, see GASHLE (in Xhosa more commonly *hamba kakuhle*); when addressing more than one person, the form *hambani kahle* is used], used in the following ways:

a. As int. phr.: GO WELL. Cf. SALA KAHLE.

Now often used as a respectful farewell to a deceased person.

1836 A.F. GARDINER *Journey to Zoolu Country* 142 His last words were 'Amba couthley' (I wish you a pleasant journey). 1855 J.W. COLENSO *Ten Weeks in Natal* 45, I bade him come for a blanket to-morrow and then dismissed him with '*hamba kahle* – walk pleasantly,' to which he replied with '*tsala kahle* – sit pleasantly'. 1860 A.W. DRAYSON *Sporting Scenes* 223 All the women and children kept close in their kraals, they shouted to us 'Hambani gathle' (Go on well). 1870 [see SAWUBONA int.]. 1880 E.F. SANDEMAN *Eight Months in Ox-Waggon* 352 Their cheerful 'Amba gashly, amba gashly,' the usual mode of parting salutation meaning, 'Go gently or peaceably,' rang upon my ears. 1893 J.F. INGRAM *Story of Gold Concession* 127 I .. set out amidst a barking of dogs, a lowing of cattle, and a chorus of 'Hambanie gthlie, Myieesa!' ('Go in peace, Myieesa!') 1898 B. MITFORD *Induna's Wife* 160 Then the Amabuna rose and shook the King by the hand, and we, as they took leave of us, all called out, 'Hambani-gahli' with right good-will. [*Note*] 'Go ye in peace.' 1937 C. BIRKBY *Zulu Journey* 283 'Hamba gahle, ' I called to them in goodbye. 1941 A.G. BEE *Kalahari Camp Fires* (1943) 214 He shouted the Matabele word 'Salaniguthle,' meaning 'goodbye' and there came in chorus from our battered regiments the answer, 'Hamba gahle,' 'Go prosperously.' 1956 A. SAMPSON *Drum* 92 'Hamba Kahle' ('Go Well,' the African 'good-bye'). 1978 *Daily Dispatch* 1 Aug. 3 In a written message from the Lord Chief Justice .. it was said that .. Mr Titterton had brought lustre to the law in Transkei. 'Hamba kahle,' (go well) Mr Titterton was told in the message. [1982 M. MZAMANE *Children of Soweto* 216 As the coffin was being lowered into the grave, the church choir of St. Francis sang *'Hamba, hamba kahle'* (Farewell, farewell).] 1989 [see SALA KAHLE]. 1990 *Weekly Mail* 2 Feb. 26 Your spirit lives on – Hambe Kahle. Condolences to family and friends. 1990 *UDUSA News* Nov. 2 Obituary. S— T— N—, a founder member of the PAC, was brutally murdered on October 4th in Umtata, Transkei .. Our sympathies go to the family. *Hamba Kahle*. 1993 *Weekly Mail* 18 June 12 He is survived by his girlfriend and a kid. Hamba kahle Qawe.

b. As v. phr. (usu. *imp*.):

Sometimes partially translated, see *go gashle* (GASHLE).

i. Travel safely, 'go well'. Also *transf*., see quot. 1969.

1838 G. CHAMPION in J. Bird *Annals of Natal* (1888) I. 224 The king expected I would leave the country, and told me to 'Hamba gahli'. 1958 A. SAMPSON *Treason Cage* 55 Kadalie .. became persuaded by his European friends to drop the weapons of militancy and to keep to a policy of *Hamba Kahle* – hasten slowly – which amounted in effect to doing nothing. 1969 *Post* 7 Dec. 9 Mr M.C. Botha, Minister of Bantu Development, sees 1969 as the year of resettlement hamba kahle ... He is on record as saying: 'We have on occasions had to do a great deal of persuading to get them to move – but they are volunteers. The Bantu like moving.' 1970 J.V. WINTERS *Informant, Kimberley* Hamba Kahle. Zulu expression adopted by road safety and Springs Town City Council meaning Drive slowly. 1971 *Daily Dispatch* 15 Nov. 12 Paramount Chief Kaiser Matanzima .. intends to 'hamba kahle' still. He is well advised to take no chances.

ii. A warning: 'go carefully', 'watch out'.

1899 G.H. RUSSELL *Under Sjambok* 24 'Hamba gashli, Inkoss!' (Go easy, Sir) yelled Basket, my native driver. 1967 J.A. BROSTER *Red Blanket Valley* 185 Suddenly the children were shy, .. but the brave ones stepped resolutely forward, took my hand and with the tenderness of childhood said '*Hamba kahle*' (Go carefully). 1978 *Sunday Times* 23 Apr. (Mag. Sect.) 3 There's a Table Mountain guide .. and a map of the mountain can be obtained from the local publicity association. Hamba gahle.

3. In the phr. *hamba kaya* /ˌhʌmbəˈkaɪa/, also *hamba kyah* [see KAYA], go home. Also (*nonce*) as *adj*. See also KAYA sense 2.

1908 D. BLACKBURN *Leaven* 299, I should be only a kitchen boy, as I was in Maritzburg, with the police always waiting to catch me for being out after the 'hamba kyah' bell had rung. 1951 L.G. GREEN *Grow Lovely* 156 The plague frightened Cape Town and thousands of native labourers shouted 'Hamba Kya' and clamoured for passes so that they could return to their homes.

4. In the phr. *forever hamba* [esp. in early uses, a pun on the book title *Forever Amber*], used jokingly (as *n. phr.* and *v. phr.*) to allude to the forcible removal of people in terms of the policies of apartheid.

1952 'KAAPENAAR' in *Drum* Sept. 10 This is the story of the educated African who walked the streets of Johannesburg in search of a job ... And do you know what he has decided to call his masterpiece? .. 'Forever Hamba!' of course. 1964 *Drum* Nov. 45, 20,000 people removed after a century – the country cries Will we forever 'hamba'? 1974 *Ibid*. 8 Aug. 48 'The people are just not in a mood to start from scratch once more. They are sick and tired of being a nation of forever hambas,' he said pounding his fist into his palm. 1981 *Voice* 12 Aug. 2 So it's forever hamba. The removals of Blacks continue unabated. 1989 *Sunday Times* 19 Nov. 12 Another best-seller, Forever Hamba, also known as the Oshikati Exodus, is said to be a fascinating sequel to Good-bye Dolly Gray and is being fine-toothcombed by SA Intelligence.

5. In the imperative phr. *hamba dompas* /ˌhamba ˈdɔmpas/ [Afk. *dompas* see DOMPAS; see New Nation quot. 1987], 'push off, dompas', a slogan adopted by the National Party government to publicize the end of the law requiring black people to carry identity documents at all times. Also *attrib*. See also PASS sense 3.

1986 *Pace* Aug. 4 Anyhow, me too, I say Hamba Dompas (but no welcome to the new-one stinker either). 1987 *New Nation* 9 July 7 He rubbed shoulders with Peter Sepuma in a popular play, 'Hamba Dompas' ... The title of the play was later used by the South African government during the phasing out of 'stinka' or 'ndzangana' as the passbook is called. 1987 *Pace* Nov. 14 No amount of expense or 'positive' Hamba Dompas advertising could convince or coerce blacks into believing .. that they should flock in droves to apply for the new ID.

Hambona var. MBO.

hamburger n. *obs*. [Prob. ad. HANGBERGER.] HOTTENTOT n. sense 2 b.

1890 [see GALJOEN sense 1]. 1913 [see HANGBERGER sense 2].

hamel /ˈhaməl, ˈhɑːməl/ n. Also **hammal, hammel**. [Afk., fr. Du.] A wether, or castrated ram. Also *attrib*.

1831 J. COLLETT *Accounts*. I. 16 Jan., By 90 Ewe Bucks @ 1/4, 18 Hammels @ 2/6. 1835 A. SMITH *Diary* (1939) I. 376 If relatives rich, sometimes kill ten oxen and ten hamels. 1850 J.D. LEWINS *Diary*. 11 Jan., Is hammel & lambs wool generally packed by themselves? 1862 T. SHONE *Diary*. 11 Aug., Henry, Josiah and Bailey Cockcroft and another man, were sheering some hamels. 1870 H.H. DUGMORE *Reminisc. of Albany Settler*

13 A dozen of startled hamels, just separated from a large flock, would be likely to try a driver's legs, and lungs too. **1899** S.T. Plaatje *Boer War Diary* (1973) 29 Meko had slaughtered a fat hammel and the hard ox is not very desirable when palatable mutton is knocking about. **1923** W.C. Scully *Daniel Vananda* 150 Daniel went to a butcher and sold to him fifteen fat hamels (wethers) for ten shillings apiece. **1932** [see KIESIEBLAAR]. **1942** *Star* 30 Dec. 6 Average prices per lb. dressed weight .. : Merino hamels, prime 13d; medium 11d; inferior 9d. **1957** A.A. Murray *Blanket* 32 Tell Simpi to send me ten .. fine, fat hammals. **1973** *Farmer's Weekly* 18 Apr. 55 (advt) Merino hamel rams R21 to R25. **1977** F.G. Butler *Karoo Morning* 89 Uncle Norman and one of the old shepherds stand behind a table at the exit to the kraal. With a very sharp knife he cuts the tail off. He does something else to them, which I am told turns them into hamels. **1981** *Het Suid-Western* 18 Feb. 1 Australians receive R27 a head for export hamels and R18 a head for export ewes. We were always led to believe that old ewes and mature hamels were virtually valueless in Australia. **1988** P. Kingwill *Message of Black Eagle* 26 You're just in time to drive the hamels up to Langeberg.

hamerkop /ˈhɑːmə(r)kɔp/ *n.* Also **hamercop**. Pl. **-koppe** /-kɔpə/. [Afk. (earlier S. Afr. Du.) *hamerkop, hamer* hammer + *kop* head; see quot. 1937.] The HAMMERKOP, *Scopus umbretta*. Also *attrib.*

[**1937** B.J.F. Laubscher *Sex, Custom & Psychopathology* 14 The *Tekwane* (known in Afrikaans as *Hamerkop* on account of the peculiar hammer-like shape of its head) is another bird of ill-omen, and its presence near the kraal is taken to mean that someone is exercising witchcraft influences on a member of the kraal.] **1958** R. Collins *Impassioned Wind* 48 A large dark bird, probably a hamerkop, flared upwards. **1965** J. Bennett *Hawk Alone* 58 Down on the stones near a small pool a hamerkop bird was standing, watching something in the shallow water. **1966** E. Palmer *Plains of Camdeboo* 194 For many years a pair of *hamerkoppe* or hammerhead lived near a pool beyond the Cranemere gates ... Sometimes we would see them dancing together and would smile at their ungainliness, but at dusk nobody smiled at the hamerkops, for they were then always faintly sinister. **1980** J.O. Oliver *Beginner's Guide to our Birds* 43 The bird's strange appearance, its weird call and the wisdom it uses in nest building have caused Africans to look upon it with superstition, even moving their huts if a Hamerkop flies over them, calling as it goes. **1990** T. Van Rensburg in *Conserva* May 21 We scaled cliffs with home-made ropes .. to investigate the nest of a *hamerkop*. **1993** A.P. Brink *First Life of Adamastor* 72 *Hamerkop* birds perched at dusk in shallow water, treading the soft mud to stir up the spirits of the dead and foretell new deaths.

hammal, hammel varr. HAMEL.

hammerhead *n.* Pl. **-s**, or unchanged. [tr. Afk. *hamerkop*.] The HAMMERKOP, *Scopus umbretta*. Also *attrib.*

1881 E.E. Frewer tr. *E. Holub's Seven Yrs in S. Afr.* I. 112, I noticed an enormous nest, which at first I imagined must be an ape's; but I subsequently learnt that it belonged to the hammerhead (*Scopus umbretta*). **1889** [see HAMMERKOP]. **1923** Haagner & Ivy *Sketches* 139 The Hammerhead .. in its characteristic brown garb, crested head and long legs, .. is a familiar figure along the shores of water-courses, vleis and dams .. on the prowl for frogs and small fish. **1939** [see LIGHTNING BIRD]. **1966** [see HAMERKOP]. **1967** J.A. Broster *Red Blanket Valley* 54 In hushed voices they told me of a mysterious bird which feeds on frogs and tadpoles. It has great powers of magic, but if left alone is harmless. In Xhosa it is called *U-Thekwane*, in English, Hammerhead or Umber. **1980** *E. Prov. Herald* 11 Jan. 7 Peggy had been recounting the excitement with which a couple of hammerheads had discovered our old goldfish pond, and what a meal they made of the inhabitants. **1982** A.P. Brink *Chain of Voices* 84 The hammerhead was the most dire omen of all, whether you saw it peering into the water of the marsh and calling up the spirits of the dead, or flying past the setting sun, or uttering its three mournful cries over hut or house.

hammerkop /ˈhæməkɔp, -kɒp, ˈhɑː-/ *n.* Also **hammercop**. Pl. **-s**, or **-pe** /-pə/. [Englished form of Afk. *hamerkop*, see HAMERKOP.] The wading bird *Scopus umbretta*, the sole species represented in the family Scopidae, characterized by its brown colour, heavy crest, and large bill; HAMERKOP; HAMMERHEAD; PADDAVANGER; TEGWAAN. Also *attrib.*

Considered by some to be a bird of ill-omen: see IMPUNDULU.

*a*1827 D. Carmichael in W.J. Hooker *Botanical Misc.* (1831) II. 52 The Branaa valley .. is a tract of marshy ground .. harbouring .. hammerkops, sand-larks and pipers. **1834** A. Smith *Diary* (1939) I. 163 A Basuto said the hammerkop gives rain. **1867** E.L. Layard *Birds of S. Afr.* 312 The '*Hammerkop*' .. is a strange, weird bird ... At times, .. two or three .. feeding in the same pool .. will execute a singular dance, skipping round one another opening and closing their wings, and performing strange antics. **1889** H.A. Bryden *Kloof & Karroo* 7 A hammerkop (hammerhead) came down to the water. **1899** R.B. & J.D.S. Woodward *Natal Birds* 199 Hammerkop (*Scopus umbretta*). **1909** *The Cape* 23 Apr. 13 On a dizzy ledge above stood the eccentric nest of that eccentric bird the hammerkop — a paddavanger as it is sometimes called. **1918** S.H. Skaife *Animal Life* 233 The *hammerkop* is a quaint bird. **1949** C. Bullock *Rina* 49 Now came another prophet of evil in the shape of a dingy hammerkop squawking querulously over us. **1971** *Country Life* 28 Oct. 1127 Hammercops, curious bulky brown birds with crests and thick bills, flew about in pairs. **1988** T.J. Lindsay *Shadow* (1990) 312 Then he saw the hammerkop nest built of reeds, grass, twigs, and everything else obtained from close at hand.

hanapoot var. HANEPOOT.

hand see HANS.

handel *v. trans.* and *intrans. Obs.* Also **handle**. [Afk. *handel*, fr. Du. *handelen*.] To trade; to sell (something).

The *OED* provides examples of the word in this sense (used transitively) in *U.S. Eng.* from 1888.

1850 R.G.G. Cumming *Hunter's Life* p.i, The trader inquires of the Boer if he has any fat oxen to handle or barter. *a*1878 J. Montgomery *Reminisc.* (1981) 96 Before I had proceeded far I received a message from Karapan and Witvoet to visit their kraal, as they wished to handel (trade). **1887** A.A. Anderson *25 Yrs in Waggon* I. 40 The people at Wakkerstroom wanted to know what I was doing in the country, as I did not handel (trade).

So **handling** *vbl n.*, trading.

1850 R.G.G. Cumming *Hunter's Life* p.i, When 'handling' once begins, it often goes on briskly.

handlanger /ˈhantlaŋə(r)/ *n.* [Afk., *hand* hand + *lang(s)* alongside + agential suffix *-er*.] An assistant, esp. an unskilled worker who fetches and carries for a trained artisan; occas., an artisan.

1958 H. Wicht *Rd below Me* 9 To help me I had a .. bricklayer ... Then we had a disagreement and he left. After that, with only Willie as a *handlanger*, I did the rest. **1963** A.M. Louw *20 Days* 80 This rush job on at Fish Hoek and none of the Kaffir-handlangers — journey-men — coming to work. **1970** S. Sparks *Informant, Fort Beaufort* The mason has a handlanger to fetch and carry for him. **1975** *E. Prov. Herald* 14 Aug. 9 It was one of those films at which one felt extreme embarrassment — White people playing Black 'handlangers' with shoe-polished faces. **1977** *Evening Post* 26 May 10 Cheran is .. careful when choosing a bit for her electric drill ... 'As a kid, I was my father's "handlanger" — passer of tools.' **1980** *Service leaflet, St. Thomas's Church, (Rondebosch)* Carpenters! Handlangers! Helpers of all sorts — even those who don't know that a dovetail made on the Sabbath is a Sunday joint — are .. needed .. to help with the adjustments to the pews. **1986** *Spire* (Cathedral of St. Michael & St. George, Grahamstown) July 8 Merriman .. strode about his Parish .. with a faithful 'handlanger'. **1988** G. Croudace *Secret of Rock* 41 The other two started repairs to the canoe, Val accepting the role of handlanger to Jacques with no sign of resentment. **1991** F.G. Butler *Local Habitation* 184 Jane was a particularly eager *handlanger*. As soon as I picked up a hammer she regarded it as her responsibility to hand me something, anything for my free hand. **1992** J. Raphaely in *Femina* Apr. 6, I found a man with a lorry who said it would take one trip, two *handlangers*, and four hours to clear out the entire garden.

handle var. HANDEL.

handsapper var. HANDS-UPPER.

handsopper *n. obs.* [Part. tr. of Afk. *hensopper*, see HENSOPPER.]

1. HANDS-UPPER sense 1 a.

1903 E.F. Knight *S. Afr. after War* 60, I told them that .. we Transvaalers for our part had had our bellyful of war and wanted no more of it. They .. cursed me as a 'handsopper'. **1906** G.B. Beak *Aftermath of War* 63 The Repatriation Department could hardly expect to escape contact with the feud existing between the so-called 'handsoppers' and those who had fought to the finish. **1946** V. Pohl *Adventures of Boer Family* 173 Some of our men met a number of *handsoppers* who were employed by the British one way or another.

2. HANDS-UPPER sense 2.

1931 H.C. Bosman *Mafeking Rd* (1969) 148 The other farmers around there became annoyed on account of Koos Steyn's friendship with the rooinek. They said Koos was a handsopper and a traitor to his country. **1949** A. Keppel-Jones *When Smuts Goes* 202 The 'handsoppers' soon gained control of Johannesburg, whose city hall housed what was in effect a rebel government.

hands-up *v.* [See HENSOP.]

a. *intrans.* To surrender; *fig.*, to give up an unequal struggle. Cf. HENSOP.

1901 'Linesman' *Words by Eyewitness* 239 The refugee camps within the British lines wherein dwell the hundreds of Dutchmen who have surrendered or 'hands-upped'. **1901** P.J. Du Toit *Diary* (1974) 51 At Kleinplaats I met the scouts, 'hands-upped' and surrendered my arms to Captain Willows .. who took me to Colonel Higgy .. in command then at Witpoort. **1903** R. Kipling *Five Nations* 161, I am doin' my Sunday School best, .. To come in an' 'ands up an' be still, An' honestly work for my bread. **1935** H.C. Bosman *Mafeking Rd* (1969) 51 'I am turning back,' he said, 'I am going to hands-up to the English.' **1948** — in L. Abrahams *Unto Dust* (1963) 145 He had to resort to artificial aids to keep his hair and beard black .. in his hopeless struggle against the onslaughts of time ... In the end Gysbert Jonker had to hands-up of course. **1977** T.R.H. Davenport *S. Afr.: Mod. Hist.* 141 A.P. Cronje was the moving spirit behind the National Scouts, composed of Boers who had 'hands-upped' from conviction that their cause was hopeless and only surrender could bring relief. **1978** A.P. Brink *Rumours of Rain* 324 'Ja, the old useless,' commented Ma .. 'And Gert too. The whole lot of them handsupping just like that.'

b. *trans.* To cause or force (someone) to surrender.

1936 H.F. Trew *Botha Treks* 170 The man rode gaily along .. and so puffed into Grootfontein. To his alarm and astonishment he was promptly 'hands-upped' by a German picket. **1937** G.F. Gibson *Story of Imp. Light Horse* 220 Why on earth did you not 'hands-up' the old man and take him prisoner? **1946** V. Pohl *Adventures of Boer Family* 39 How on earth did you hands-up all these men by yourself? *a*1951 H.C. Bosman in L. Abrahams *Unto Dust* (1963) 160 My Mauser is very rusty. I'll have to hands-up or shoot one of the enemy and take his Lee-Metford off him.

Hence **hands up** *adj.*; **handup** *n.*, HANDS-UPPER sense 1 a; **hands-upping** *vbl n.*, surrendering.

1901 E. Hobhouse *Report of Visit to Camps* 3 There are nearly 2,000 people in this one camp, of which some few are men — they call them 'hands up' men and over 900 children. **1902** *Appleton's Ann. Cycl.* 629 The Boers who had accepted British sovereignty .. contemptuously called 'handups' by the others. **1975** W. STEENKAMP *Land of Thirst King* 78 Stories .. tell vividly of the cold ferocity with which the men of the three races struggled for the possession of Namaqualand. Hands-upping was a luxury they did not believe in much: You fought, and you won or died.

hands-upper *n.* Also **handsapper**. [Prob. fr. Afk. *hensopper*, see HENSOPPER.]
1. *hist.*
a. A derogatory term used by the Boers of those who surrendered to the British forces during the Anglo-Boer War; *handup*, see HANDS-UP; HANDSOPPER sense 1; HENSOPPER sense 1 a. Also *attrib.* Cf. BITTER-ENDER.

1901 in E. Hobhouse *Brunt of War* (1902) 268 The 'hands uppers' here in the camp, with the exception of three, have turned British subjects now by promising to take the oath of allegiance; I always bore an ill-feeling towards them, but now I simply loathe them. **1902** E. HOBHOUSE *Brunt of War* 38 The patriots .. felt and expressed contempt, often undeserved, for these neighbours, and nicknamed them 'hands uppers'. **1902** D. VAN WARMELO *On Commando* 40 The name of 'hands-upper' was earned by those burghers who of their own free will surrendered to the enemy. **1903** E.F. KNIGHT *S. Afr. after War* 171 It was with joy that the 'hands-upper' farmers read of Mr. Chamberlain's proper treatment of the impudent demands put forward by the irreconcilable section. *Ibid.* 210 It was the Boers in the field who in the first place treated the 'hands-uppers' as an enemy, and they have themselves to blame if some of these men under so great a provocation offered their services to us as National Scouts. **1913** J. BRANDT *Petticoat Commando* 148 There were three kinds of handsuppers; first, men who, through a mistaken sense of duty, surrendered themselves to the enemy, in order to bring the war to a speedy termination; .. second, the men who, wearied of the strife, became hopeless and despondent; .. and third, the men who, through their lust for gain, fell an easy prey to the temptations offered them. **1936** [see NATIONAL SCOUT]. **1941** G.H. GALPIN *There Are No S. Africans* 61 The burghers who yielded voluntarily before the end of the war, the handsappers, were treated to £2000000. **1963** A. KEPPEL-JONES *S. Afr.: Short Hist.* 138 Others who surrendered — 'hands-uppers' — thought the continued resistance madness and felt that the 'bitter-enders' would be responsible for the ruin of their country. **1965** K. MACKENZIE *Deserter* 100 'And so you are a hands-upper, I suppose, Japie?' 'No,' said Japie indignantly ... 'No, I wanted people to stop fighting because they did not like to kill each other and it wasn't doing any good.' **1974** J.P. BRITS *Diary of Nat. Scout* 3 The *hands-uppers* .. were burghers who voluntarily laid down their arms in obedience to Lord Robert's proclamation of 1 September 1900, and ceased to take any part in the war. **1987** W. STEENKAMP *Blockhouse* 47 'We aren't hands-uppers like some people.' 'No,' Van As agreed ... 'We're bitter-enders, that's what we are.'
b. JOINER sense 1.

1937 C.R. PRANCE *Tante Rebella's Saga* 35 By his breeches and leggings he must be a khaki-Englander; and when he remonstrated in Afrikaans she denounced him as a renegade and 'hands-upper' which is even worse. **1941** N. DEVITT *Concentration Camps* 24 National Scouts were burghers who, having surrendered to the British, took up arms against their own people at 5s. per day, rations and quarters. There were 5,000 of these men in the field ... They were called 'Hands-uppers' or 'Joiners'. **1944** [see JOINER sense 1]. **1979** [see Pakenham quot. at JOINER sense 1].

2. *Fig.* and *transf.* One who changes allegiance for questionable reasons; a fence-sitter; HANDSOPPER sense 2; HENSOPPER sense 2.

1941 J.C. SMUTS in C. Birkby *Springbok Victory* Introduction, A nation is never proud of its 'hands-uppers,' its fence-sitters, its players for safety. We South Africans reserve our respect and pride for the bitter-enders, for those who go all out.

hanepoot /ˈhɑːnəpʊət/ *n.* Formerly also **haanen-poot, haanepoot, haenapod(e), haenpode, hahnen pootgen, hahnepote, hanapoot, hanepod, hanepo(or)t, haneport, hanne poot**; occas. with initial capital. [S. Afr. Du., fr. Du., combining form of *haan* cock + *poot* claw; a euphemistic substitution for *hanekloot* (*kloot* testicle), in Du. a name given to the figwort *Ficaria verna*; see quots 1927 and 1944.]
1. A variety of muscat grape, Muscat d' Alexandrie, used as a dessert fruit, and for raisin- and wine-making; HONEYPOT. Also *attrib.*

1801 J. BARROW *Trav.* I. 65 A large white Persian grape, called here the haenapod. **1831** *S. Afr. Almanac & Dir.* 216 Persons .. willing to prolong the luxury of fresh grapes for the dessert, should select some bunches of the Haen-pode. **1872** 'Z.' in *Cape Monthly Mag.* V. Oct. 230 We will undertake never to turn sour at a dish of 'hahnepote'. **1891** H.J. DUCKITT *Hilda's 'Where Is It?'* 84 Take nice ripe Hanepot grapes, cut them with a piece of the stalk, prick with a steel pin; fill a jar. **1896** R. WALLACE *Farming Indust. of Cape Col.* 202 Of *grapes* the Haanepoot, a white variety, and the Barbarossa are considered the best for the British market. **1902** H.J. DUCKITT in M. Kuttel *Quadrilles & Konfyt* (1954) 13 In making 'Moss Bolletjies' .. substitute the fermented juice of the fresh 'Steen' grape, or 'Hanepoot', for the yeast made of raisins. *c*1911 [see HERMITAGE]. **1927** A.I. PEROLD *Treatise on Viticulture*, The Dutch name *Hanepoot* .. is an intentional corruption of Hanekloot, *i.e.* cock's testicle, which the berry of this variety resembles somewhat in shape and size. 'Hanepoot' has nothing to do with 'cock's foot'. **1944** MARAIS & HOGE (tr.) in H.J. Mandelbrote *O.F. Mentzel's Descr. of Cape of G.H.* III. 179 We shall .. describe the best types of grapes ... My favourite kind .. is not pressed, nor does it produce any wine. It is the 'Haanen-Kloote' (Cock's testicle), but called 'Haanen-poote' by the ladies of Africa. **1966** H. BECK *Meet Cape Wines* 11 Because of its fruitiness, the hanepoot, which was considered essentially a grape for dessert wine making, is sometimes used quite effectively in the making of natural wine. **1967** W.A. DE KLERK *White Wines* 10 White Hanepoot (Muscat d'Alexandrine), premier grape for good raisins and good fresh eating. **1968** W.E.G. LOUW in D.J. Opperman *Spirit of Vine* 323 Wines made chiefly from the muscadel or hanepoot grape, are usually somewhat paler. **1977** *Sunday Times* 6 Nov. (Mag. Sect.) 3 True withond is made from the purest of hanepoot grapes, not a drop of anything else and it's 90 per cent proof. **1985** J. GRIERSON in *S.-Easter* Aug.-Sept. 32 Muscat d'Alexandrie .. is .. the cultivar name for the hanepoot. **1986** M. LE CHAT in *Sunday Times* 20 July (Mag. Sect.) 32 The new music .. he's putting his aloe-bitter hanepoot-sweet voice to shows another side of David Kramer. **1988** [see GREEN GRAPE]. **1990** I. DU TOIT in *Fair Lady* 21 Nov. 216 An insolent pair of hanepoot-green eyes. **1992** P. DEVEREUX in *Sunday Times* 29 Mar. (Mag. Sect.) 6 Grapes like hanepoot, gewurztraminer, muscat and colombard frequently are overpoweringly floral. **1993** C. EDEN in *Food & Home* Aug. 138 There'd be no .. Table Mountain, no hanepoot grapes, no koeksusters.

2. Sweet wine made from these grapes, unfortified for table use, and fortified as a Muscatel dessert wine. Also *attrib.* See also CAPE WINE.

1804 R. PERCIVAL *Acct of Cape of G.H.* 188 The Hanepod made from a large white grape is very rich, but scarce and dear, and only used by the ladies at their parties. **1821** [see FRONTIGNAC]. **1861** 'A LADY' *Life at Cape* (1963) 61 Wine and desserts are so very cheap and varied here, .. 'hanepoot', pontac, frontignac, or sweet Constantia ports and sherries, at something less than two pence a glass! **1880** *S.W. Silver & Co.'s Handbk to S. Afr.* 223 The Hanepoot, which when young is a pale wine, frequently becomes with age as dark as the brownest of brown sherry. Really good old Hanepoot is, perhaps, the finest of Cape wines, and in taste resembles a very fair Madeira. **1952** C.L. LEIPOLDT *300 Yrs Cape Wine* 203 A .. common Hanepoot wine is a golden coloured, fairly sweet wine. **1975** *Daily Dispatch* 20 Sept. 5 More recently Hanepoot has found itself under the varietal name of Muscat d'Alexandrie as a premium table wine. **1982** *S. Afr. Panorama* Jan. 21 The sweeter, heavier dessert wines such as .. pontac, hanepoot and .. muscadel. **1990** *Excellence* Vol.6 No.2, Sydney Back makes an elegant hanepoot .. 'a truly great wine with complex aromas that include botrytis, raisins and ripe muscat scents', according to the judges. **1992** E. & C. LE ROUX in *Getaway* Dec. 7 A complimentary glass of sherry, muscadel or hanepoort.

hang /hæŋ/ *n.* and *int. Slang.* Also **heng**. [Euphemism for Eng. *hell*, fr. N.Z. Eng.; apparently obsolescent elsewhere.] Esp. in the language of children:
A. *n.* In the intensive phr. ***hang of*** (*a*):
a. *adj. phr.* Very big, great.

1960 J. TAYLOR 'Ballad of the Southern Suburbs'. (lyrics) Ag, sis, Deddy, if we can't graft to bioscope, or go off to Durban, life's a hang of a bore. **1970** M.J. MATULOVICH *Informant, KwaZulu-Natal* Those two jammies that we were dicing had a hang-of-a prang on the corner. **1974** 'BLOSSOM' in *Darling* 8 May 91 My boet gives a hang of a cackle. (He does it all the time now he's voice is starting to break ...) **1984** *Frontline* May 39 The SABC got a hang of a skrik from all the stories about how Bop was buying the best shows from abroad. **1991** D. BOSWELL *Informant, Giyani (N. Tvl)* We had a hang of a lot of homework.
b. *adv. phr.* Very, extremely. Cf. *hell of* (*a*), see HELL sense 1.

1970 V. JACQUES *Informant, Pietersburg* Hang of a. Very, eg. He's hang of a nice. **1988** A.M. SMITH in *SA in Poësie/SA in Poetry* 632 He's hang of a skraal and, His hair's only short, hey. **1991** D. BOSWELL *Informant, Giyani (N. Tvl)* We had to walk a hang of a long way. We had a hang of a lot of homework.

B. *int.* An exclamation expressing strong feeling, such as enthusiasm, frustration, resentment, or anger, equivalent to 'damn (it)'. Cf. JISLAAIK.

1965 S. DEDERICK *Tickey* 2 'Ag, come off it, man, Tickey,' said Ella. 'I knew you were there. Hang, but your hands are cold, hey?' *Ibid.* 3 Oh, hang — there's the bell. *Ibid.* 105 The first thing I saw was Table Mountain. Hang, but it's big! **1966** L.G. BERGER *Where's Madam* 182 'Heng ma,' he shuddered, 'I think you're bats staying out here in the bundu without even burglar bars.' **1974** 'BLOSSOM' in *Darling* 8 May 91 All this fuss they making in the papers about streaking — hang, you'd think it was something new. When meantime my ouma was already streaking 20 years ago. **1976** *Ibid.* [see WOES]. **1975** *Ibid.* [see OU *n.* sense 1 a]. **1989** J. HOBBS *Thoughts in Makeshift Mortuary* 173 Hang, but I loved those soldiers!

hangberger /ˈhæŋbɜːgə/ *n.* Formerly also **hangeberger**. [See quot. 1913.] Either of two marine fishes (formerly, in both senses, also called HAMBURGER):
1. *?obs.* The ZEBRA, *Diplodus cervinus hottentotus*.

1887 *S.W. Silver & Co.'s Handbk to S. Afr.* 182 *Sargus Hottentottus*, Hangeberger. Common in Table Bay. Much used for pickling.

2. HOTTENTOT *n.* sense 2 b.

1913 C. PETTMAN *Africanderisms* 207 *Hangberger*, A Cape Peninsula name for the Hottentot fish ..., sometimes corrupted to Hamburger. Fleming ascribes the name to the fact of the fish 'being chiefly taken in deep water; near a place called Hangberg (overhanging rock)'; others derive the name from the fish's habit of frequenting rocky ledges. **1949** J.L.B. SMITH *Sea Fishes* 276 *Pachymetopon blochii ... Hottentot. Hangberger* (Cape). **1970** BEETON & DORNER in *Eng. Usage in Sn Afr.* Vol.1 No.2, 25 *Hottentot (ii)*, .. (*Pachymetopon blochii*), alt: hangberger. **1979** SNYMAN & KLARIE *Free from Sea* 32 *Hangberger*, These dusty-faced fish have a most distinctive flavour — not to everyone's liking. **1994** [see HOTTENTOT *n.* sense 2].

hanne poot var. HANEPOOT.

hans /hans/ *adj.* Also occas. **hand**. [Afk., 'hand-fed', 'orphaned', prob. fr. unrecorded Afk. or Du. word *hands* by hand, hand-reared, formed on *hand* hand.] 'Hand-reared'; used *attrib.* with the names of various farm animals, esp. in the collocation **hanslam** /'hanslam/ [Afk., *lam* lamb], also **hanslamme(r)tjie** /'hans,lamə(r)ki/ [see -IE], or (Englished form) **hans lamb**: an orphaned or rejected lamb which is reared by hand.

[**1891** O.E.A. SCHREINER *Thoughts on S. Afr.* (1923) 166 The hand-lamb and a couple more fowls followed.] **1911** *Farmer's Weekly* 15 Mar. 19 Often the ewes will not have their lambs; in that case these 'hans' lambs are taken care of by the housewife, as pets or until they are old enough to graze with the flock. **1916** *Ibid.* 27 Dec. 1584 A week after the birth .. the mother was killed for the butcher's shop, and the little lambs either sold for 1s. 6d. as an hans-lamb or their throat cut. **1932** *Grocott's Daily Mail* 13 Jan. 1 (advt) 1 Filly, 3 years old. 4 Pigs. 3 Hans Sheep. **1958** A. JACKSON *Trader on Veld* 40 When ewes died after lambing, the offspring were taken into the homestead and brought up as the 'hanslam' (pets). The hanslam ran all over the place. **1963** M. KAVANAGH *We Merry Peasants* 40 No shearing, dipping, threshing to watch, hanslammertjie to feed (the little lamb that the ewe would not take). **1970** C. KINSLEY *Informant, Koegasbrug (N. Cape)* Hanslam. Lamb reared by farmer's wife, usually bottle fed. **1970** G. WESTWOOD *Bright Wilderness* 187 It will be a 'hans' lamb for you. Since you are going to bottle feed it, it will believe you are its mother. **1970** *Argus* 3 Oct. (Mag. Sect.) 13 No farmyard was ever complete without hans-lammetjies — orphaned lambs — and poultry. **1971** *Informant, George* He's a hans ossie — I wouldn't sell him. **1971** *Star* 18 Sept. 12 Snow followed by devastating cold wind and rain killed 2 000 sheep for some farmers ('everything but the hanslamb in the kitchen'). **1973** *Cape Times* 6 June 9 Whatever the .. link between no rains and big lamb crops, one tangible result is the tremendous number of *hanslammertjies* being hand-reared this year. **1974** A. SMALL in S. Gray *On Edge of World* 183 He grew up on this ground .. like a little *hansskaap* (motherless lamb). **1984** *Sunday Tribune* 16 Dec. (Today) 5 Field Marshal Pik Botha's 'handlammetjie', Generalissimo Riaan E—, is filled with righteous wrath about a statement by Chester Crocker. **1989** *Grocott's Mail* 4 Apr. 3 'Hans' lambs and 'Hans' kids, orphans all, .. were assiduously fed and cared for by enthusiastic youngsters while they awaited transport down to Bathurst to star in the miniature farmyard.

hansie /hansi/ *n.* and *adj.* Formerly also **hantjie**. [Afk., *hans* see HANS + -IE.]

A. *n.* An orphaned or rejected animal reared by hand.

1892 H.S. ELLERBECK in *Cape Illust. Mag.* Vol.3 No.4, 141 It was Mabel who always attended to the hantjies, the lambs whose mothers had died in giving them birth or refused to acknowledge their offspring. **1970** I. PALMER *Informant, Grahamstown* We feed the hansie three times a day. Means handreared (bottle fed) calf or lamb. **1973** *Cape Times* 6 June 9 They don't want to suckle their young ... The farmer, or his wife, has to bottle feed the neglected *hansies*.

B. *adj.* HANS.

1992 *Grocott's Mail* 31 Mar. (Suppl.) 3, I hope that we will have many cuddly lambs, bunnies and ducklings ... We are still looking for some 'Hansie' lambs and kids.

hao var. HAU.

hap /hap/ *n. colloq.* [Afk.] A bite, morsel, or mouthful. Also *fig.*, a chunk.

1970 C.S. HENDRY *Informant, Somerset West* Give me a hap of your apple. **1971** *Informant, Grahamstown* If you have a prospector's license, you can dig anywhere. Whatever you find, the government takes a hap out of it. **1971** B. REYNOLDS *Informant, Grahamstown* It's not dinner — just wine, dry bread, and a hap of cheese. [**1972** M.G. MCCOY *Informant, Port Elizabeth* Give me a hapsie of cheese, please.] **1984** *Frontline* Feb. 33 There had been a peach on the back seat .. One grabs it, takes a *hap*, and it quickly does the rounds. One bite each. **1988** *Informant, Grahamstown*, I ate mine. I didn't want anyone else to have a hap!

Hence **hap** *v. trans.*, to bite (something).

1977 *Het Suid-Western* 2 Mar. 1 Georgy Girl almost gave the impression that she was serving at the altar. I was afraid she might hap some of the bread out of the Dean's hand.

happy box *n. phr. Colloq.* A nickname given to 'bag-in-a-box' wine packaging. Also *attrib.* See also CHATEAU CARDBOARD.

1981 *Cape Times* 27 Oct. 5 First it was the 'happy box', the five-litre bag-in-box wine package that swept the wine trade some time ago, now its the instant refill. **1990** A. JERMIESON *Dealers' Daughters* 102 The usual cask .. was missing from the top of the piano ... 'Where's your happy box?' she asked. **1991** *Grocott's Mail* 24 May 9 You will be assured of a glass of wine, on the house nogal — a really good vintage happy box variety.

hapsie see HAP.

haraam /hə'rɑ:m, hə-/ *adj.* Also **haram**. [Arabic *haram, harīm*.] Unlawful according to Muslim law. Also *fig.*

1979 *S. Afr. Panorama* Dec. 25 Abattoir practice for Muslims is regulated in South Africa by the Muslim Butchers' Association ... Special slaughtering methods apply to cattle and chickens and halaal (lawful) and haraam (unlawful) carcasses may not make contact during storage and loading. **1980** A. DANGOR in M. Mutloatse *Forced Landing* 168 With a sudden movement Samad opened the bottle of wine and poured its contents over Leiman ... '*No! No!*' Leiman screamed, 'the wine is *haram*'. **1984** *E. Prov. Herald* 18 June 1 More than 3000 Moslems yesterday agreed to a resolution declaring participation and association with the Government's 'new dispensation' as 'haraam' (unlawful by religious law). **1985** A. DAVIDS in *Papers Presented at 5th Symposium on Ethnomusicology* (I.L.A.M.) 37 There still prevails a general misconception that music is *Haraam* or forbidden in Islam. **1987** *Frontline* May 6 The Mandela family .. the hallmark of the liberation struggle. What they think, say, do, is kosher. Any view to the contrary is haraam. **1987** G. DAVIS in *Weekly Mail* 17 July 5 It is *haraam* — forbidden — for a Muslim to serve in the South African Defence Force or the South West African Territorial Force ... 'No Muslim is allowed to participate in the apartheid army ... It is *haraam*.'

harbeest var. HARTEBEEST *adj.*

hard bank var. HARDEBANK.

‖**hardbieshuis** /'hartbis,hœɪs, 'hɑ:dbis,heɪs/ *n.* *Obsolescent* exc. *hist. Archit.* Also **hardbeeshuis**, **hardebies(ies)huis**. Pl. **-huise** /-hœɪsə, heɪsə/. [Afk., *hard* hard + *bies* reed + *huis* house; see quot. 1952.] *hartebeest house*, see HARTEBEEST *adj.* Occas. also **hardbieshuisie** [see -IE].

1952 J. WALTON *Homesteads & Villages* 92 *Hardbieshuise* .. were of such widespread occurrence in the early days of settlement across the Orange that they may be regarded as the typical house-type of the period. *Ibid.* 95 Backhouse's suggestion that the name 'Hartebeest' house derived from its resemblance to 'the species of buffalo' is not supported by the other early travellers nor by the Voortrekkers themselves, both of whom referred to it as a *hardbieshuis* or *hardbeeshuis*, from the hard reeds, or *harde biesies*, which were used in its construction. **1963** R. LEWCOCK *Early 19th C. Archit.* 133 Most of the settlers contented themselves for the time being with thatched shelters more or less after the native fashion, usually of a type then known on the frontier as 'hartebeest huts', 'hartbeeshuise' or 'hardbieshuisies' (or, correctly, 'hardebiesieshuise'). **1963** POLLOCK & AGNEW *Hist. Geog.* 61 The hartebeest hut .. was .. a long curved hut made with hard reeds or hardebiesies, covered with mud, and not from the skins of the buck. These huts should thus be termed hardebieshuise. **1969** D. CHILD *Yesterday's Children* 113 The first Voortrekker house had been the *hardbieshuis* in which stout reeds or *harde biesies* were used for covering a timber framework.

hardebank /'hɑ:dəbæŋk, 'hardəbaŋk/ *n. Geology. Diamond-mining.* Also **hard bank**, and (formerly) **hardibank**. [Afk., combining form of *hard* + *bank* ledge, shelf.] **a.** The hardest form of BLUE GROUND, unweathered because lying at considerable depths. **b.** *rare.* A mass of mineral matter, formed at a later stage than the blue ground and intruding into it (see quot. 1921). Also *attrib.*

1905 H. KYNASTON in Flint & Gilchrist *Science in S. Afr.* 300 The Schuller No. 1 pipe consists to a great extent of very hard blue-ground, resembling the Kimberley 'hardibank'. *c*1922 *Off. Yrbk of Union 1910–22* (Union Office of Census & Statistics) 603 There are also found imbedded .. larger fragments, moderate boulders and even greater masses of rock, which have come to be known under the name of 'floating reef'. Where these inclusions have been found to be true kimberlite .. they have been commonly alluded to in mining parlance as 'Hardebank'; but, owing to a similarity in appearance, this term was equally applied to the material derived from certain intrusive dykes of later age that are found sometimes traversing the ordinary pipe rock. **1965** HAMILTON & COOKE *Geology for S. Afr. Students* 275 Below the limits of oxidation, the same rocks [*sc.* tuff-like and brecciated kimberlite material] form the familiar blue ground, and the more solid and better preserved material at depth is known as hardebank. **1971** A.E. SCHOCH in *Std Encycl. of Sn Afr.* IV. 31 It is also more difficult to recover diamonds from the deep-seated, un-weathered kimberlite (the 'blue ground' and 'hard bank'). **1971** P.A. WAGNER *Diamond Fields* 27 In the soft blue ground occupying the upper levels of the pipes there are occasionally found rounded masses of comparatively well-preserved kimberlite up to five feet in diameter which generally go by the name of 'Hardebank boulders' ... As greater depths are attained in the mines the products .. are replaced in increasing measure by 'hardebank' or kimberlite, the parent rock, to the trituration and decomposition of which they owe their origin.

‖**harde beskuit** /'hɑ:də bəs,kœit, 'hardə-/ *n. phr. noncount.* [Afk., combining form of *hard* hard + *beskuit* rusk.] Hard rusk. See also BESKUIT.

1930 H.C. BOSMAN *Mafeking Rd* (1969) 63 My mother and sisters baked a great deal of harde beskuit. **1980** A.J. BLIGNAUT *Dead End Rd* 20 She could bake good harde beskuit, the stuff on which the Boers, with a little help from biltong and a Mauser, fought well.

hardebies(ies)huis var. HARDBIESHUIS.

hardegat /'hɑ:dəxat, hardə-/ *adj. slang.* [Afk., combining form of *hard* hard + *gat* (not in polite use) anus.] Stubborn, obstinate.

1950 E. PARTRIDGE *Dict. of Underworld Slang* 321 *Hardegat*, Stubborn. **1965** J. BENNETT *Hawk Alone* 205 He was independent then and hardegat and people did it his way or not at all. **1975** J.H. PICARD in *Eng. Usage in Sn Afr.* Vol.6 No.1, 37 The expression *hardegat* refers to a most stubborn person — this is of recent coinage. **1983** D. BECKETT in *Frontline* Feb. 33 The people who seek seriously to talk turkey about how to come to terms with a truly race-free South Africa, have no need to feel irrelevant. Let them consider the mess that the *hardegat* option wrought to the north of us; and be fortified. **1984** R. LEAVER in *Ibid.* Mar. 39 Those rare English Nats of the 50's and 60's were often peculiarly hardegat types, often bent on proving their belongingness by outRighting the Right. **1990** *Weekly Mail* 21 Dec. (Suppl.) 7 Once South Africa started to change .. its *hardegat* attitude to the outside world, .. a great deal more would follow.

Hence **hardegat** *n.*, pl. **-gatte** /-xatə/, an obstinate person.

1991 A. VAN WYK *Birth of New Afrikaner* 68, I was eventually crowned king of the *hardegatte* (tough cookies).

hardegeld see GELD sense b.

hardekool /'hɑ:də,kʊəl, 'hardə-/ *n.* Also **haardekool**, **hardekohl**, **hartekoal**. [Afk., combining form of *hard* hard + *kool* coal, charcoal, ember.] The tree *Combretum imberbe* of the Combretaceae, known for its hard, long-burning wood (occas. in full ***hardekool tree***); the wood of this tree; *Damara('s) mother (tree)*, see DAMARA; LEADWOOD. Also *attrib.*

1881 E.E. FREWER tr. *E. Holub's Seven Yrs in S. Afr.* II. 63, I had not reached the hardekool-tree before I heard a low whistle from Theunissen. **1928** E.H.L. SCHWARZ *Kalahari & its Native Races* 19 The motsweri, leadwood, or hardekohl is a fine tree that seems to prefer the dryer parts, for where there is a dense growth they become choked and die. **1944** C.R. PRANCE *Under Blue Roof* 91 Timber has been destroyed at the rate of ten square miles a year, leaving sparse Hardekool giants in a wilderness of stumps, to testify that it was matchless open forest till Progress took it in hand to supply charcoal to the mines. **1958** [see KAREE *n.*² sense 1 a ii]. **1966** C.A. SMITH *Common Names* 243 *Hardekool*, .. Before the introduction of steel hoes the natives of Portuguese East Africa used the hard wood for making hoes. **1972** *S. Afr. Garden & Home* Oct. 34 The birds are shown perched on the branches of a hardekool tree, which has an extremely tough wood and is often seen in the lowveld. **1976** *S. Afr. Panorama* Feb. 35 Meat .. grilled over burning maize cobs (Orange Free State and the Transvaal Highveld), wingerd stompies (vine cuttings — the Cape Province), cow dung, hardekool wood or pine cones (the Transvaal bushveld) or just plain charcoal.

hardepeer /ˈhardəpɪə(r), ˈhɑːdə-/ *n. obsolescent.* Formerly also **hardpeer.** [Afk. (earlier S. Afr. Du. *hardpeer*), combining form of *hard* hard + *peer* pear.] HARD PEAR sense a.

1801 J. BARROW *Trav.* I. 340 Hard peer ... Uses ... Sometimes in waggons. **1874** LINDLEY & MOORE *Treasury of Botany* (Suppl.), *Olinia*, The plant grows in rocky thickets and woods at the Cape, where it is known as Hardpeer. **1966** C.A. SMITH *Common Names* 243 *Hardepeer (hard pear), Olinia capensis* ... The wood is very hard, very compact, tough and heavy, being suitable for making musical instruments and general fancy work ... While this species is the original *hardepeer* of the early colonists, the vernacular name has been extended to other species of the genus.

harder /ˈhɑːdə, ˈhardər/ *n.* Also **haarder, harders, harter.** [Du., 'mullet'.] Any of several species of either marine or freshwater mullet of the Mugilidae, plentiful in Cape waters, esp. the marine mullet *Liza richardsonii*; SPRINGER sense 2 b. Also *attrib.* See also BOKKEM.

In Smith and Heemstra's *Smiths' Sea Fishes* (1986) the name 'southern mullet' is used for *Liza richardsonii.*

1731 G. MEDLEY tr. *P. Kolb's Present State of Cape of G.H.* II. 193 There is .. about the *Cape* a Sort of Herrings the Cape-*Europeans* call *Harters*. **1804** R. PERCIVAL *Acct of Cape of G.H.* 44 The harder, somewhat of the flavour and appearance of our herring, but thicker. *a*1823 J. EWART *Jrnl* (1970) 56 A small fish called harders, similar to mackrel, of which a quantity has been caught in one morning, valued at from two to three hundred rixdollars. **1831** *S. Afr. Almanac & Dir.*, January .. *Fish in Season*. Hottentot, red Stumpnose, Harder. **1838** [see SPRINGER sense 2]. **1861** 'A LADY' *Life at Cape* (1963) 2 Charles and Freddie .. catch 'harders' and 'klipfish' .. off the wharves and jetties running into Table Bay. **1880** [see GEELBEK sense 1 a]. **1891** H.J. DUCKITT *Hilda's 'Where Is It?'* p.ix, Some kinds of fish broiled are very good, such as the Cape 'Harder,' 'Hottentot Fish' or 'Snoek'. **1892** P.L. SIMMONDS *Commercial Dict. of Trade Products*, *Harder*, a kind of mullet .. caught near the coasts of the Cape Colony. **1910** J. RUNCIE *Idylls by Two Oceans* 31 The head of a snoek or harder .. she would bring along in her mouth. **1949** J.L.B. SMITH *Sea Fishes* 316 The *Mugilidae* feed mainly on minute plants, eggs, and .. young marine creatures ... Some of the species appear never to jump from the water save in small hops at any stage ... Those are termed 'Mullet' or 'Haarder'. Some species jump well from the earliest stages ... These are commonly termed 'Springers'. **1958** [see MAASBANKER]. **1960** J. COPE *Tame Ox* 157 He .. pointed off the bow. 'A shoal there, Mevrou, maasbankers or haarders.' **1973** *Farmer's Weekly* 18 Apr. 102 So fine is its flavour that the real harder-lover will always eat it simply grilled and served with lemon. **1985** A. TREDGOLD *Bay between Mountains* 143 Barrels were stacked in a shed on the beach and into these would be put as many as 10 000 harders for salting. **1993** *Flying Springbok* Apr. 126 Bokkems — harders salted and dried like biltong — are a popular snack.

hardibank var. HARDEBANK.

hardidah var. HADEDA.

hard pear *n. phr.* [tr. S. Afr. Du. *hardpeer*, see HARDEPEER.] Any of several species of tree: **a.** Any of several species of the genus *Olinia* of the Oliniaceae, esp. *O. ventosa*; the wood or fruit of this tree; HARDEPEER. **b.** *Pleurostylia capensis* of the Celastraceae. **c.** *Strychnos henningsii* of the Loganiaceae. Occas. with qualifying word designating a particular species, as **mountain hard pear** (*Olinia emarginata*).

1880 *S.W. Silver & Co.'s Handbk to S. Afr.* 127 In these kloofs grow .. the Hard Pear (*Olinia Capensis*), [etc.]. *Ibid.* 140 Hard Pear is the fruit of the *Olinia cymosa*. **1913** C. PETTMAN *Africanderisms* 207 *Hard Pear*, (1) In Natal this name is given to *Pleurostylia capensis*. (2) In the Cape Colony it is applied to *Strychnos Henningsii*. **1951** N.L. KING *Tree-Planting* 69 *Olinia emarginata (cymosa) (Hard Pear or Rooibessie)*, A nice umbrageous tree with pretty foliage. **1961** PALMER & PITMAN *Trees of S. Afr.* 252 The hard pear or rooibessie, *Olinia cymosa*, is found as a medium sized forest tree in the Knysna forests, as a many-branched, leafy, and often well-shaped tree in the open, and sometimes as a shrub on rocky hillsides. *Ibid.* 297 *Strychnos Henningsii. Hard pear*, .. This tree should not be confused with the 'hard pear' of the Knysna forests, which is *Olinia cymosa*, and which belongs to a different family. **1973** [see SAFFRAAN]. **1989** *Conserva* July 22 *Olinia emarginata* Mountain hard pear.

hardpeer var. HARDEPEER.

hardpuis var. HARPUIS.

hard veld /ˈhɑːd felt, ˈhart-, -fɛlt/ *n. phr.* [(Part.) tr. Afk. *hardeveld*.] Countryside consisting mainly of hard, unfertile soil. See also VELD sense 3 c.

[**1838** J.E. ALEXANDER *Exped. into Int.* I. 31 The Onder Bokkeveld, Bedouw, and Hantam, are considered the most fertile portions of Clanwilliam, whereas the Hardeveld is the most barren.] **1972** *Std Encycl. of Sn Afr.* V. 436 Its 'hard veld' is a shrill contrast to the sandy soils along the coast to the north and south. **1975** *Family of Man* Vol.3 Part 42, 1152 The Herero nation inhabited the northern plateau *hardveld* of what is today .. Namibia. **1975** *Farmer's Weekly* 21 Apr. 76 (advt) Farm For Sale ... Ideal for cattle, sheep or goat farming. Warm hard veld, consisting of sweetgrass and mixed bush. [**1986** *Personality* 3 Nov. 33 Some people call Namaqualand the 'Garden of the Gods'. It's a strange name for an arid region of *harde veld, sandveld,* and *klipkoppies*.]

harlemensis /ˌharləˈmensəs, ˌhɑː-/ *n.* Also **haarlemensis, harlemessens,** and with initial capital. [Afk., blend and ad. of Du. *haarlemmer essens*, see HAARLEMMER.] 'Haarlem oil': a patent medicine used for the treatment of kidney, bladder, and liver complaints; *Dutch drops*, see DUTCH *adj.* sense 2; *haarlemmer drops*, see HAARLEMMER; *harmans druppels*, see DRUPPELS sense b ii. Also *attrib.* See also *(old) Dutch medicine* (DUTCH *adj.* sense 2).

1911 *Farmer's Weekly* 11 Oct. 159, I tried a Dutch medicine called 'Harlemensis' which effected a cure within a short time ... About twenty per cent. of my lambs got affected with sore eyes, from which I cured them with one or two applications of this 'Harlemensis.' **1958** E.H. BURROWS *Hist. of Medicine* 191 *Haarlemensis, Haarlemmer essens, Haarlemmer droppels* (Dutch Drops): world-famous with many uses. **1973** S. STANDER tr. *A.P. Brink's Brandy in S. Afr.* 168 You could try 1 spoon of honey, five drops of 'harlemessens', 1 spoon camphor brandy, 1 dessert-spoon buchu vinegar and the yolk of an egg. **1989** D. SMUTS *Folk Remedies* 58 *Kidney problems*, 10 drops balsem sulphuris, 10 drops Haarlemensis oil, 1 wineglass of milk.

harlemer var. HAARLEMMER.

harmans drup(pels) see DRUPPELS sense b ii.

Harootzi(e) var. and pl. form of HURUTSHE.

harpuis /hɑːˈpeɪs, harˈpœɪs/ *n.* Perh. *obsolescent.* Also **arpuse, haarpis, hardpuis, harpuys.** [Afk., transf. use of Du. *harpuis* a mixture of pitch, resin, etc. used to smear ship's masts, etc. to protect against moisture and woodworm; but see also quot. 1966 at sense 1.]

1. Usu. *attrib.*, freq. in the *comb.* **harpuisbos(ch)** /-bɒs, -bɒʃ/ [Du. *bosch*, Afk. *bos* bush], **-bosje** /-bɔʃi/, or **-bossie** /-bɔsi/ [see BOSCHJE] (but also simply *harpuis*): any of several species of shrub of the genus *Euryops* (family Asteraceae) characterized by a resinous secretion.

1815 A. PLUMPTRE tr. *H. Lichtenstein's Trav. in Sn Afr.* II. 176 A shrub, which grows from two feet to three feet and a half high, called by the colonists *harpuisbosjes*, the rosin tree. **1822** W.J. BURCHELL *Trav.* I. 259 The inhabitants of this district, when in want of resin, use as a substitute, a gum which exudes from different species of shrubs; which they therefore call *Harpuis bosch* (Resin bush). **1846** H.H. METHUEN *Life in Wilderness* 112 A sea of flame raging on one side of the road, and consuming the resinous *arpuse* bushes with a roaring noise. **1861** P.B. BORCHERDS *Auto-Biog. Mem.* 54 Amongst the heaths .. I found one named the '*harpuis*' (rosin) bush, containing a juice of a gluey substance, having the scent of rosin. Of this herb the sheep are particularly fond, and it forms their chief nutriment. **1896** R. WALLACE *Farming Indust. of Cape Col.* 92 The harpuis (resin-pimple) plant is a species of *Euryops*, a showy composite with gay yellow blooms and a foliage not unlike that of a soft, rapidly grown, bushy young pine-tree. **1912** *Queenstown Daily Rep.* 9 Apr. 7 (Pettman), Many of the Camdeboo Mountain farms .. have had a large portion of their veld ruined by the spread of the rhenosterbosch and the *rosinbosch* (or haarpisbosch). **1917** R. MARLOTH *Common Names* 38 *Harpuisbos* (or simply *harpuis*). Several species of *Euryops* ... Twigs and leaves rich in resin hence inflammable even when green. *a*1920 O.E.A. SCHREINER *From Man to Man* (1926) 353 There was a pungent curious smell that seemed to burn her nostrils, something like when they burned harpuis (resin) bushes on the lands at home. **1966** C.A. SMITH *Common Names* 244 *Harpuisbos(sie)*, .. The name has an interesting origin, being derived from the Dutch word 'hars' (resin) and 'puisje' (a small pimple), referring to the resinous secretion extending from the stem and branches in the form of small pimply drops whence also the name Resin-Pimple bush.

2. The resin produced by these plants. Also *attrib.*

1951 S. VAN H. TULLEKEN *Prac. Cookery Bk* 274 Harpuis Soap. 26 lbs. fat, 2 1/2 galls. water, 3 1/2 lbs. caustic soda, 2 1/2 lbs. harpuis. Mix the water and soda, put it on the fire with the fat and harpuis. **1966** C.A. SMITH *Common Names* 243 *Harpuis*, The resin secreted from the stem and branches of practically all species of *Euryops* and greatly esteemed at one time by Hottentots and colonists for its alleged medicinal properties.

Harris buck *n. phr.* Also **Harris's buck**, and with small initial. [Named for *William Cornwallis Harris*, who first identified the species.] The sable antelope *Hippotragus niger* of the Bovidae; SWARTWITPENS.

[**1838** J.E. ALEXANDER *Exped. into Int.* II. 261, I brought home the first specimen which has appeared in Europe, of the *Aigoceros Niger* (Harris) or Sable Antelope.] **1863** W.C. BALDWIN *Afr. Hunting* 187, I saw this morning three beautiful harrisbucks. **1869** [see SWARTWITPENS]. **1876** E.E. FREWER tr. *J. Verne's Adventures of Three Englishmen & Three Russians* 71 They brought down a couple of harrisbucks. **1900** W.L. SCLATER *Mammals of S. Afr.* I. 221 *Hippotragus niger, The Sable Antelope* ... Vernacular Names: Sable or sometimes Harrisbuck of the English. Zwart-wit-pens .. of the Dutch speaking Colonists. **1913** C. PETTMAN *Africanderisms* 208 *Harris buck, Hippotragus niger.* So called after Major Cornwallis Harris who first obtained this antelope in the Magaliesberg near Pretoria. **1939** J.F. BENSE *Dict. of Low-Dutch Element in Eng. Vocab.* 615 Zwart-wit-pens .. is also known by the name of Harris buck. **1966** E. PALMER *Plains of Camdeboo* 71 His was the first description of this fine antelope, and for long it was known as the Harris buck. **1987** *S. Afr. Holidays Guide (brochure)* 3 The rare sable antelope called Harris's Buck has been reintroduced, and browses on the grassy summit plateau. **1990** J. HUNTLY *Afr. Wildlife Sketches* 73 J.G. Millais .. made some very realistic drawings and sepia paintings of the sable or Harris Buck, as it was called in those days.

Harry's Angels *n. phr.* [Named for *Harry F. Oppenheimer* of the Anglo American Corporation, who sponsored their operation; prob. formed by analogy with the name of the contemporary U.S. television series *Charlie's Angels.*] A nickname given to a team of medical specialists participating in a voluntary service, being flown from Johannesburg to work in Swaziland on a regular basis. Also *attrib.*

1971 *S. Afr. Panorama* Oct. 36 Dr. George Cohen, a radiologist of Johannesburg, who founded 'Harry's Angels', a medical specialist shuttle service operating between Johannesburg and Manzini, Mbabane and Hlatikulu in Swaziland. **1974** *Daily Dispatch* 17 July 1 Harry's Angels ... Mr Harry Oppenheimer had placed a company aircraft at the disposal of the team. He also gave financial assistance to the scheme – hence the term Harry's Angels. **1977** *E. Prov. Herald* 20 Oct. 5 The 10th anniversary of Harry's Angels, a voluntary specialist doctors flying service to Swaziland, will be celebrated on November 2. **1981** *Fair Lady* 23 Sept. 79 They were named the 'SA Flying Medical Specialists Service' – but it was 'Harry's Angels' that stuck ... Surgeons and anaesthetists in Harry's Angels' team often fit a week's work into one day in Swaziland.

hartbeast var. HARTEBEAST *n.*

hartbees(t) *n.* var. HARTEBEEST *n.*

hartbees(t) *adj.*, **hartbest** varr. HARTEBEEST *adj.*

hartebeast *n. obs.* Also **ha(a)rtbeast**. [Part. tr. S. Afr. Du. *hartebeest*, see HARTEBEEST *n.*]

a. HARTEBEEST *n.* sense a.

[**1731** G. MEDLEY tr. *P. Kolb's Present State of Cape of G.H.* II. 126 The Hart of the *Hottentot* Countries differs from the *European* Hart only in the Horns.] **1786** [see HARTEBEEST *n.* sense a]. **1796** C.R. HOPSON tr. *C.P. Thunberg's Trav.* II. The level country presented to our view .. a great number of *hart beasts (Capra Dorcas).* **1804** R. PERCIVAL *Acct of Cape of G.H.* 160 The bontebock and haart-beast are uncommonly large, and are chiefly found in the interior parts. **1835** A. SMITH *Diary* (1940) II. 34 Hartebeasts, springbok and quaggas appear to resort in great numbers to drink. **1887** A.A. ANDERSON *25 Yrs in Waggon* I. 210 Hartebeast, giraffes, and grysbok .. are all to be found.

b. With qualifying word: **bastard hartebeast** [see BASTARD *adj.*], the TSESSEBE, *Damaliscus lunatus.*

1835 A. SMITH *Diary* (1940) II. 42 A large troop of bastard hartebeast were seen close to where we halted last night.

hartebeast *adj.* var. HARTEBEEST *adj.*

hartebeest /ˈhɑːtəbiːst, -bɪəs, har-/ *n.* Also **haartebeest, hartbees(t), hartebees(te), hartibeest.** Pl. unchanged, **-s**, or **-beeste** /-bɪəstə/. [S. Afr. Du., fr. Du. *hart* (var. *hert*) hart + linking phoneme *-e-* + *beest* beast, animal; see quot. 1786.]

a. A name applied to any of several antelope of the genera *Damaliscus, Sigmoceros*, and *Alcephalus* of the Bovidae, esp. the *red hartebeest* and the *Lichtenstein's hartebeest* (see sense b below); HARTEBEAST sense a. Also *attrib.* See also TSESSEBE.

[**1786** G. FORSTER tr. *A. Sparrman's Voy. to Cape of G.H.* I. 129 The two largest sorts of *antilopa* or *gazels* .. are called by the Dutch, *hartbeest* and *Bunteboks*; the former name, which signifies *hart-beast*, was probably given to the former of these creatures on account of some resemblance they showed in colour to the harts of Europe. **1790** W. PATERSON *Narr. of Four Journeys* 81 A species of Antelope, called by the Dutch, Hartebeest, which is the Capra Dorcas of Linnaeus.] **1821** *S. Afr. Jrnl* (1824) I. i. 18 The countless herds of springboks, hartebeests .. and other large game, described by former travellers as .. adding so much life and beauty to the lonely landscape of Albany, have .. almost totally disappeared. *a*1827 [see ELAND sense 1 a]. **1846** T. PRINGLE in R. Moffat *Missionary Labours* 89 The hartebeest is one of the finest animals of the antelope family; it is fleet, and graceful in its gait. **1860** A.W. DRAYSON *Sporting Scenes* 62 The hartebeest .. : male five feet high, and nine in extreme length .. ; colour bright sienna, with a red shade, black stripes down the back of the neck, on the fore-leg and on the hind-leg. **1896** R. WALLACE *Farming Indust. of Cape Col.* 245 The hartebeest, *Alcelaphus caama*, is one of the fleetest and longest-winded of South African antelopes. **1914** W.C. SCULLY *Lodges in Wilderness* The ungainly hartebeest lumbered away .. at a pace which made pursuit hopeless. **1948** A.C. WHITE *Call of Bushveld* 149 The sessaby .. certainly is a branch of the hartebeest species – horns and head proclaim this fact. **1951** A. ROBERTS *Mammals* 277 The Hartebeests .. are not aggressive, attempting to get away rather than defend themselves, except as a last resort .. usually making-off in the so characteristic wavy lumbering gallop. **1970** *Life* 19 Jan. 49 The horns of the hartebeest ('hart' or 'stag' beast in South African Dutch) are unlike those of any other animal. **1976** D.M.B. PRESTON *Story of Frontier Town* 23 There are no hartebeest in this area today. Their beautiful red-brown pliable hides were much prized by the Xhosas and particularly by the Bechuanas for making soft cloaks, which fact contributed to their extermination. **1987** T.F.J. VAN RENSBURG *Intro. to Fynbos* 51 The hippo, black rhino and hartebeest .. disappeared a long time ago. **1991** *Personality* 5 Aug. 26 I've .. seen hartebeest lying dead in the pen while that lot was actually being auctioned.

b. With distinguishing epithet, designating a particular species of hartebeest: **bastard hartebeest** *obs.* exc. *hist.* [tr. of S. Afr. Du. *basterhartebeest*, prob. so called because the antelope was thought to be a hartebeest of impure stock; cf. BASTARD *adj.*], the TSESSEBE, *Damaliscus lunatus*; **Cape hartebeest**, see *red hartebeest* (below); **flat-horned hartebeest** [so called because its horns are flattened at the base], **Lichtenstein's hartebeest** /ˈlɪxtən,stəɪnz -/ [named for the German naturalist *M.H.K. Lichtenstein* (1780–1857)], or **mof(f)hartebeest** /ˈmɔf-/ [Afk., *mof* of impure breeding, prob. fr. Du. *mof, muf* lit. 'musty', an insult usu. applied to foreigners; cf. MOF *adj.*], the antelope *Sigmoceros lichtensteinii* (usu. referred to as 'Lichtenstein's hartebeest'), yellow-tawny in colour, and now found only in Zimbabwe and Mozambique, in small numbers; **red hartebeest**, any of several southern African subspecies of the antelope *Alcelaphus buselaphus*, esp. *A.b. caama*, reddish-brown to yellowish-fawn in colour, with pale rump; KAMA.

[**1801 bastard hartebeest**: see SASSABY.] **1839** W.C. HARRIS *Wild Sports* 378 *Acronotus Lunata.* The Sassayby. Bastard Hartebeest of the Cape Colonists. [**1896** see quot. at *Lichtenstein's hartebeest* below.] **1994** M. ROBERTS tr. *J.A. Wahlberg's Trav. Jrnls 1838–56* 111 Bring down 2 bastard hartebeest. **1989** D. DAY *Encycl. of Vanished Species* 194 Another Hartebeest, the Cape Red form .. was saved from extinction ... The **Cape Hartebeest** was abundant throughout South and South West Africa when the white settlers arrived. **1891** R. WARD *Sportsman's Handbk* 124 **Flat-horned Hartebeests**, found near the river Sabi, in south-eastern Mashunaland. **1896** —— *Rec. of Big Game* 65 The true Hartebeeste of South Africa – often called by the Boers the Rooi (red) Hartebeeste, to distinguish it from the Tsessebe (Bastard Hartebeeste or Zulu Hartebeeste of the Dutch hunters) and **Lichtenstein's Hartebeeste** – is still, thanks to its wariness, speed, and desert-loving habits, fairly abundant in many of its ancient haunts. **1900** W.L. SCLATER *Mammals of S. Afr.* I. 136 Lichtenstein's hartebeest is only found in the north-eastern part of South Africa. **1980** [see quot. at *red hartebeest* below]. **1987** *Weekend Argus* 5 Sept. (Suppl.) 5 Readers helped bring the Lichtenstein's hartebeest back to South Africa. **1900** W.L. SCLATER *Mammals of S. Afr.* I. 135 **Moff hartebeest**, See Lichtenstein's Hartebeest. **1985** *Breakfast cereal packaging, Kellogg Co. (Pty) Ltd* We have allowed the Mofhartebeest to disappear from under our very noses ... As little as 60 years ago some Mofhartebeest still graced our veld with their presence. Early hunters and explorers knew them well. **1900** W.L. SCLATER *Mammals of S. Afr.* I. **Red Hartebeest**, *Bubalis caama* ... Hartebeest of the Dutch and English Colonists. **1925** F.C. SLATER *Centenary Bk of S. Afr. Verse* 234 *Bubalis caama*, the Red Hartebeeste, is a large ungainly antelope once found throughout the country, but now restricted to the Kalahari region. **1964** G. CAMPBELL *Old Dusty* 132 The quagga are extinct, and the white rhino and red hartebeest are on the verge. **1974** *E. Prov. Herald* 7 Sept. 6 Only 1500 red hartebeest and 540 wildebeest remain – both .. enjoyed a far wider distribution in the past. **1980** J. HANKS *Mammals* 36 *Red Hartebeest, Alcelaphus buselaphus* ... Formerly occurred in Natal in high rainfall areas, but it is now restricted to arid parts of Southern Africa, where it is mainly a grazer ... *Lichtenstein's Hartebeest, Alcelaphus lichtensteini [sic]* Colour variable, usually a fairly bright rufous on the back. **1988** A. HALL-MARTIN et al. *Kaokoveld* 37 The red hartebeest is not normally regarded as a resident of the kaokoveld ... Their status is vulnerable.

hartebeest /ˈhɑːtəbɪəst, -biːst/ *adj.* Also **harbeest, hartbe(e)st, hartebeast, hart(e)bees, hartebeeste, hartebeests, hartebeest's.** [Calque formed on S. Afr. Du. *hardebies* 'hard reed' (see HARDBIESHUIS); but see also folk etymologies, quots 1835 and 1844.] Usu. in the collocations ***hartebeest house, -huis(ie)*** /-heɪs(i), -hœɪs(i)/, pl. **-huise** /-ə/, **-huisies** [Afk., *huis* house (+ -IE)], ***-hut***, but also *attrib.* (quot. 1871), and occas. *absol.* (quot. 1976): designating a house, hut, temporary shelter, etc., of simple construction, usu. consisting of an A-shaped thatched roof, sometimes with low reed or wattle-and-daub base walls; HARDBIESHUIS. See also KAPSTYLHUIS.

1815 A. PLUMPTRE tr. *H. Lichtenstein's Trav. in Sn Afr.* (1930) II. 95 Not far from this wretched cabin stood a somewhat more spacious, but very ruinous straw hut, of the sort which is here called *hartebeesthuisje.* **1820** T. PRINGLE in *Quarterly Bulletin of S. Afr. Library* (Dec. 1951) 54 Our *Hartebeest Huts* as they call them here (being entirely composed of willow trees covered with reeds without side walls) are both roomy and neat. **1821** C.I. LATROBE *Jrnl of Visit* 361 [A] hartebeest-house, being a roof put upon a wall about two feet in height. **1835** J.W.D. MOODIE *Ten Yrs* II. 138 In a few days we got our rude huts covered in ... These temporary habitations are called by the Dutch colonists 'harte-beest' huts, as they are in the habit of constructing them as a shelter when they are far from home, .. hunting the 'harte-beest' antelope. **1844** J. BACKHOUSE *Narr. of Visit* 357 The Hartebeest houses, are so called from an imaginary similarity in their figure, to the outline of .. the Hartebeest. *Ibid.* 437 Andres Van Wyk, a Bastaard, was the Field-cornet; he lived in a hartebeest-hut. **1871** J. MACKENZIE *Ten Yrs* (1971) 121 Though rough-looking .. it forms a delightful shelter from .. the sun ... It is 'hartebeest' shape. **1875** C.B. BISSET *Sport & War* 264 In those days these migratory farmers did not build houses, but .. erected what is called a hartebeast hut, made by a series of rafters sloping from the ground to where they meet above, with cross lathing and covered with long reeds or bulrushes, and plastered on one or both sides. **1896** H.A. Bryden *Tales of S. Afr.* 213 In the big wagon, or in some temporary hartebeest house of reeds and clay, had the family of this sturdy pair been reared around them. **1897** 'F. Macnab' *On Veldt & Farm* 125 One afternoon I took down my blankets to the Molopo, rigged up a hartebeest tent, and arrayed myself in costume suitable for bathing. **1911** D.B. Hook *'Tis but Yesterday* 45 The Hartebeest hut of grass and wattles in the shape of the tent of a Cape wagon was shady, and cool, and tidy. **1916** J.M. Orpen *Reminisc.* (1964) 304 We went to Joachim Prinsloo's 'hartebeest house'. **1927** C.G. Botha *Social Life in Cape Col.* 83 Those who moved from place to place built themselves a temporary dwelling .. a wattle and daub hut built after the fashion of the natives — a hartebeesthuis. The walls consisted of a palisade filled in with thatch and covered over inside and outside with mud. **1937** C.R. Prance *Tante Rebella's Saga* 152 The Police Sub-Inspector on his 800-mile round .. had Sarel's 'hartebeestehuis' marked on his time-table as the outspan for a day and night. **1945** C.J.J. Van Rensburg in *Outspan* 20 July 37 One evening I came to a little 'hartebeeste huisie' ... Together with the family of eight I slept in the one room of the house. The floor was smeared with cattle dung and we lay on goat-skins. **1946** E. Rosenthal *General De Wet* 7 Hartebeest-houses .. were the earliest kind of huts which the Boers .. put up in places where they halted their ox-wagons. Unable to secure bricks, they contented themselves with walls of reed, resting on roughly trimmed branches, and capped with a pitched roof of the same material. In the history of South Africa the Hartebeest-house plays the same part as does the Log Cabin in that of America. **1952** [see HARDBIESHUIS]. **1957** L.G. Green *Beyond City Lights* 124 There are white gables which show that the *hartbeeshuisies* of the cattle posts were abandoned early last century. **1962** F.C. Metrowich *Scotty Smith* 197 Not far from the town was a farm with a dilapidated hartebeeshuis on it. **1963** [see both quots at HARDBIESHUIS]. **1963** R. Lewcock *Early 19th C. Archit.* 218 These houses were only temporary shelters, many of them probably being 'hartebeeshuisies'. **1966** Van Heyningen & Berthoud *Uys Krige* 77 An old woman living alone, poor and forgotten, with her ancient servant Mina in a 'hartebeeshuisie' in the town of Pietermaritzburg. **1973** J. Cope *Alley Cat* 125 We reached the Koraqua stad, a tiny village of mud-brick and reed 'hartebees' houses and three or four boreholes with windpumps. **1976** B. Roberts *Kimberley* 16 Bultfontein consisted of 'a small mud cottage with two rooms, a hartebeeste (a little thatched outhouse) and a long upland flat sloping to a "pan" full of brak water'. **1977** F.G. Butler *Karoo Morning* 39 If you were lucky you lived in a hartebeeshuisie or rondavel rather than a bell tent. **1981** *Grocott's Mail* 7 Aug., The early trekboere .. moved eastwards from about 1745 and lived in humble 'hartbeeshuisie'. **1981** *Sunday Times* 13 Sept. 7 The couple moved unto the 'hartbees huisie' — made of mud bricks, and plastered with mud — in 1906. **1986** *S. Afr. Panorama* May 29 Contemplating the bustle of Pretoria today, it requires a considerable leap of the imagination to envisage the city as it was .. when the first Voortrekkers .. put up their wattle-and-daub *hartbeeshuisies*. *Ibid.* 31 The only remaining thatch-roofed Voortrekker house in the Transvaal is the Pioneer House in Silverton which .. is a more elaborate building than the true *hartebeest house*. **1989** F.G. Butler *Tales from Old Karoo* 38, I have all your pictures framed all round my *hartbeeshuisie* walls.

hartekoal var. HARDEKOOL.

harter var. HARDER.

hartibeest var. HARTEBEEST *n*.

Harutse, Harutsi varr. and pl. forms of HURUTSHE.

hasagaye var. ASSEGAI.

hash girl var. HESH GIRL.

hasie /ˈhɑːsi/ *n*. [Afk., *haas* hare + -IE.]
‖**1.** A hare.

Common in speech.

1948 A.C. White *Call of Bushveld* 201, I tried .. to persuade my friend that it was sure to be a stembuck and that .. he had better go to the spot where the dog was pointing. 'Never in the world', he exclaimed, 'it is only an old hasie .. !'.

2. *Prison slang*. Also **haas**. The 'female' partner in a homosexual relationship; RABBIT. Cf. HAWK.

1965 *Rand Daily Mail* 15 Oct. 4 Did you hear prisoners talking about sodomy? — Yes ... These people were called by various names? — Yes. Like 'hawk' and 'Haasie'? — That's correct. **1974** in *Eng. Usage in Sn Afr.* Vol.5 No.1, 10 The [prison] society produces its own lovers ... Here, 'gay' or 'camp' terms from outside are common (e.g. *moffie*) but specific distinction is drawn between *hawks* and *hasies* (sometimes *rabbits*). **1984** *Cape Times* 10 Aug. 1 'Do you know about "Moffies"? "Hasies" (rabbits)? Homosexuals?' he was asked ... 'My mother warned me against such things.' **1987** S.A. Botha in *Frontline* Oct.-Nov. 11 The Hawks were the masculine guys ... The Lighties, or Haase (rabbits) were the passive ones, mainly ignorant youngsters selling their orifices and smooth youthful skins for food, tobacco, drugs and protection.

3. In full *hasie-aboel* /-aˈbʊl/, or *hasie-ablou* /-aˈblɔʊ/, [Afk., ad. of an Eng. name for the game, *Castles are Blue*, which became *katsels-ablou, katsels-aboel*, then, by substitution of *hasie* for *kat* (cat), *hasie-aboel*]: a children's game in which the members of one team stand on the junctions of a grid of lines drawn on the ground, and the members of the other team try to run past them without being touched; a successful run-through; a player from the defending team who is allowed to run along the lines.

1971 *Std Encycl. of Sn Afr.* III. 190 The game of ablou — often called hasie-aboel — is played by two teams on a rectangular figure divided by cross-lines into blocks or 'rooms' ... The player who succeeds has made a 'hasie' (hare), and the team with the most 'hasies' is declared the winner. **1975** Levick & Mullins *'Prep' Story* 147 Playground games seem to be international ... It might be interesting to list the Prep crazes: Kennekie, Bok Bok, .. Hasie. **1982** T. Baron in *Frontline* Nov. 46 *Hasie* had a court scratched in the dirt, equivalent to the service lines in tennis ... The *Hasie*, alone, was allowed to run along the lines of the court. **1990** [see GIFFIE].

hassagai var. ASSEGAI.

hassagai hout *n. phr. Obs.* [S. Afr. Du., fr. Du. *hasegaij, hassegaai* (see ASSEGAI *n*.) + *hout* wood.] ASSEGAI WOOD.

1806 J. Barrow *Trav.* I. 83 Hassagai hout (the curtesia-faginea of the Hortus Kewensis) is a beautiful tree. **1810** G. Barrington *Acct of Voy.* 326 *Hassagai hout*, is a beautiful tree, .. and is used for naves, fellies, and spokes of waggon-wheels, and most implements of husbandry. The grain of this wood is somewhat closer and the colour darker than those of plain mahogany. **1815** J. Mackrill *Diary*. 91 Hassagai hout is the Curtisia faginea of the Hortus Kewensis. **1847** J. Barrow *Reflect.* 162 Next in size was the *yzer*, or ironwood (*sideroxylon*); *hassagai-hout* (*Curtisia faginea*). This beautiful tree is used for the naves and spokes of waggon-wheels.

hassagay(e), -guay, hassegai varr. ASSEGAI.

Hatten-tote var. HOTTENTOT.

hau /haʊ, hɑːʊ/ *int.* Also **haau, hao, hawu, hou**. [fr. Zulu *hawu*.] Esp. among Zulu-speakers: an exclamation expressing any of a range of feelings, from the mildest to the most forceful, encompassing surprise, wonder, admiration, amusement, pleasure, anger, disapproval, disappointment, distress, sympathy, resignation, shock, and fear; AU; AUK. Cf. MAWO, WAU.

1898 B. Mitford *Induna's Wife* 27, I see it all — the angry infuriated countenance of Umzilikazi, the dread anxiety on the faces of the other *izinduna*, which was as the shrinking before a great and terrible storm about to burst. *Hau!* **1907** W.C. Scully *By Veldt & Kopje* 9 'We of the Radebe,' shouted Mzondo .. 'hau — there are none like us ..'. **1923** G.H. Nicholls *Bayete!* 118 Hau! I'd like to strangle him. **1936** Williams & May *I Am Black* 60 Lapozo said 'Hau!' and put his hand to his mouth looking at Shabala with admiration. **1941** 'R. Roamer' in *Bantu World* 12 Apr. 4 Hawu! They lose their tempers as well? **1960** J. Cope *Tame Ox* 20 They say he is a tame ox. There he is, hau! hau! hau! a black maned lion among the herds! **1961** T. Matshikiza *Choc. for my Wife* 61 Hawu, Joe, you telling me to shut up when you wearing the best clothes from London's bespoke tailors? **1971** H. Stuart in *The 1820* Vol.43 No.12, 29, I couldn't translate R600 into Zulu so I told him 30 cattle. 'Hau!' he exclaimed. I can buy ten wives with that. **1975** S. Sepamla in *New Classic* No.1, 11 One day we heard we would be moved. Hawu! That was a shock to us. **1983** *Drum* Jan. 40, I can only mutter 'hau' and shake my woolly head ... Citizenship in South Africa is mlungu copyright. **1989** *Personality* 6 Mar. 34 The locals in the valley form an integral part of the race. We heard them cheering for .. one canoeist trying to surface after misjudging the weir at Duzi bridge — a loud 'Hawu shaaame!' **1989** J. Hobbs *Thoughts in Makeshift Mortuary* 4 Hawu, Missie Rose, but you wet, eh? **1994** D. Kandlovu in *Sidelines* Dec. 23 Hawu! That is our home. How can it be a no-go area? Hawu madoda!

Hence **hau** *n*., the exclamation 'hau'; as *v. trans.* (*nonce*), to exclaim 'hau'.

1941 'R. Roamer' in *Bantu World* 15 Feb. 5 It is no use 'hawu-ing' me, Mr Roamer. **1968** K. McMagh *Dinner of Herbs* 22 They loved the drum-major. He it was who called forth soft 'Haus' from the watching thousands.

haum var. AUM.

haus-vro(u)w var. HUISVROU.

HaVenda pl. form of VENDA.

hawk *n. Prison slang*. [Prob. transf. use of U.S. Eng. *hawk* one who procures young men and boys for homosexuals.] The dominant male in a homosexual relationship. Cf. HASIE sense 2.

1965, 1974 [see HASIE sense 2]. **1987** S.A. Botha in *Frontline* Oct.-Nov. 11 The Hawks were the masculine guys — usually doing a long stretch, sufficiently hungry for physical companionship not to care about whether the opposite sex provided it.

hawk's-eye *n. Mineralogy*. A blue or greenish variety of tiger's eye, a mineral formed by the natural alteration of crocidolite (blue asbestos) when the asbestos fibres are replaced by quartz; the semi-precious gemstone made from this mineral. Cf. DOEKSTEEN.

1946 L.J. Spencer *Key to Precious Stones* 199 Associated with it [sc. tiger's-eye] is found 'hawk's-eye' of a dark blue colour; here the blue crocidolite has been silicified without previous oxidation and decomposition. **1971** D.J.L. Visser in *Std Encycl. of Sn Afr.* III. 503 The fibrous colour depends on the degree of oxidation and hydration of the iron ... Colours vary from red (bull's-eye), golden brown (tiger's-eye), greyish yellow to blue (cat's-eye) and ash-greyish green (hawk's-eye). **1977** J.E. Arem *Color Encycl. of Gemstones* 99 Crocidolite (blue asbestos) may decompose and alter to quartz, retaining the fibrous structure. This can be further cemented by quartz and stained by iron oxides to yield a dense, siliceous, fibrous material called *tiger-eye* ... If the material is unstained by iron and therefore solid blue, it is called *hawks-eye*. Occurrence: South Africa. **1980** Bates & Jackson *Gloss. of Geology, Hawk's-eye*, .. a blue variety of tiger's-eye.

hawu var. HAU.

hayi var. HAAI.

hayik(h)ona var. AIKONA.

head-ring *n*. Esp. in traditional Zulu society: a ring of fibre, resin, and beeswax worked into the hair and worn as a mark of status by adult men; ISICOCO; RING *n.*[1]; RINGKOP sense b; RING-TOP sense b. See also RINGED.

1855 J.W. COLENSO *Ten Weeks in Natal* 175 On the way, Mr. Shepstone drew my attention to the singular stuff upon the Mimosa-thorn, which I have before mentioned as the material, out of which the Zulu-Kafirs construct their curious head rings. **1855** R.B. STRUTHERS *Hunting Jrnl* (1991) 93, I asked a native to procure me some 'Umgiane' the gummy matter used by the Zulus in making their 'isicoco' or headring. **1866** C. BARTER *Alone among Zulus* 51 When a Zulu soldier has attained a certain standing he receives the royal permission to marry, and adopt the head-ring as a mark of manhood. **1898** B. MITFORD *Induna's Wife* 45 His face was lined and his beard had grown grey; and his hair — which, being in some measure in disgrace, he had neglected to shave — seemed quite white against the blackness of his headring. **1905** *Native Tribes of Tvl* 67 The Shangaans .. approach more nearly to the Zulus in physique ... They alone wear an imitation of the Zulu head-ring, which with the Zulus denotes the proved warrior. **1907** [see KEHLA sense 1]. **1937** B.H. DICKE *Bush Speaks* 338 A tall magwamba who sported a head ring, like proved warriors of the Zulu tribes wear. **1946** S. CLOETE *Afr. Portraits* 215 Lobengula, the mountain of black flesh that had once been a Matabele warrior: a tall fat man naked but for his head ring, the feather of a parakeet in his hair, and a sporran of blue monkey skin about his loins. **1956** P. BECKER *Sandy Tracks* 129 Two old Swazi aristocrats .. were .. bent up with age; and smooth headrings, made of beeswax and roots, adorned their bald heads ... These old men .. were village heads, prominent tribesmen who had earned the privilege of wearing the distinctive headring. **1967** E.M. SLATTER *My Leaves Are Green* 21 When a Zulu was allowed by his king to wear a headring, he shaved his head except for a ring of hair on top which was wound round a circlet of fibre. This he waxed with black wax from a honeycomb, and finally polished with leaves. **1976** WEST & MORRIS *Abantu* 54 *(caption)* Around his head is the traditional head-ring of a married man ... Traditionally the head-ring was of wax into which the hair was woven .. but a rubber ring is the accepted modern alternative.

health committee *n. phr.* In the former provinces of Natal and the Transvaal: a local authority responsible for the management of small communities.

1942 *Off. Yrbk of Union 1941* (Union Office of Census & Statistics) 95 A form of local government by means of health committees is provided for, such committees to control matters of sanitation and public health. **1961** *Off. Yrbk of Union 1960* (Bureau of Census & Statistics) 119 The Administrator may, by proclamation, constitute a health committee for any area not being or forming part of a borough or township. *Ibid.* 120 Health committees may consist of persons appointed by the Administrator, or in certain instances they may be elected. **1972** W.E. VERSCHUUR in *Std Encycl. of Sn Afr.* VII. 15 Health committees .. constitute a simpler form of authority than village management boards. *c***1980** *S. Afr. 1979: Off. Yrbk* (Info. Service) 173 The health committees of Natal and the Transvaal comprise a limited number of local citizens appointed by the Administrators of the provinces concerned to supervise community services in villages too small to elect their own councils. **1989** P.E. RAPER *Dict. of Sn Afr. Place Names* 328 Mariannhill .. founded in 1882 as a Trappist monastery .. developed until in 1952 a health committee was established. **1991** *Newsletter* (Rhodes University) June 7 Pat has been chairman of the Everton Health Committee for the past five years.

hearf var. ERF.

heartwater *n.* [tr. Afk. *hartwater*, named for the characteristic accumulation of fluid in the pericardium.]

1. *Pathology.* A febrile disease of cattle, sheep, and goats (and also of antelope), caused by the virus *Rickettsia ruminantium*, transmitted usu. by the BONT TICK *Amblyomma hebraeum; dronkgalsiekte*, see GALSIEKTE sense 1 b. Also *attrib.*

1882 S. HECKFORD *Lady Trader in Tvl* 134 Investigation had proved that an ox had died of lung-sickness in the bush-veldt, but the fact had been hushed up by the Nel family, who swore that it died of what they call here 'heart-water', in order to save themselves trouble. **1896** R. WALLACE *Farming Indust. of Cape Col.* 380 Heart-water in sheep is another obscure disease of a specific nature, which seems to be unknown in other sheep countries. **1905** D. HUTCHEON in Flint & Gilchrist *Science in S. Afr.* 346 The characteristic lesion is an effusion of a clear buff-coloured sero-albuminous fluid into the thoracic cavity and pericardial sac, which coagulates into a firm jelly on exposure to the atmosphere. Hence its popular name, 'Heartwater'. **1914** *Farmer's Annual* 233 Heartwater is communicated by the 'bont-tick' (Amblyomma hebraeum), when the parasite has previously fed on another animal suffering from the disease. **1937** S. CLOETE *Turning Wheels* 58 When they were cut open their heart cavities were filled with a straw-coloured liquid. Having no name for it, the Boers called this new sickness heart-water. *a***1951** H.C. BOSMAN in L. Abrahams *Unto Dust* (1963) 139 I've never seen so much heart-water in Afrikaner herds. They should dip their cattle every seven days. **1972** *Star* 22 June 21 Springbok get heart-water in the north west Transvaal. **1981** *Meat Board Focus* May 33 The discovery of remedies for the treatment of heart-water, the discovery that sweating-sickness was caused by the variegated tick .. are but a few of the momentous breakthroughs resulting from their research. **1991** *Personality* 5 Aug. 30 One shipment of springbok all died of heartwater within three months. **1994** [see TOLLIE].

2. *comb.* **heartwater tick**, BONT TICK; **heartwater veld** [Afk. (earlier Du.) *veld* open, undeveloped countryside], grazing infested with the bont tick, and from which an immunity to heart-water may be acquired.

1937 *Handbk for Farmers* (Dept of Agric. & Forestry) 516 The bont, or **heartwater tick**, is very tough and not easily killed by dipping. *a***1951** H.C. BOSMAN in L. Abrahams *Unto Dust* (1963) 137 Even though he drives his cattle straight out on to the veld with the first frost, and he keeps to regular seven-day dipping, he just can't get rid of the heart-water ticks. **1974** B. SMIT in *Std Encycl. of Sn Afr.* X. 500 *Bont tick*, This variegated tick is well known as the notorious heart-water tick. **1972** *Farmer's Weekly* 21 Apr. 60 The animals are used to virulent **heartwater**, redwater and gallsickness **veld**. **1974** [see *gallsickness veld* (GALLSICKNESS sense 3)]. **1977** *Winterberg Nuus/News* 21 Sept. 11 The cattle being offered are of excellent quality and are in good condition, they have been reared on Heartwater and Gallsickness veld. **1993** [see *gallsickness veld* (GALLSICKNESS sense 3)].

heemraad /ˈhɪəmrɑːt, -rɑːd/ *n.* Also **heemrad**, **heimraad**, **hemra(a)d**, **humraad**, and with initial capital. Pl. **-ra(a)den**, **-raads**. [S. Afr. Du., fr. Du., 'dike-reeve', *heem* village, home + *raad* council.]

1. *hist.* One of a court of local officials appointed to assist a landdrost in the judicial and civil administration of the district under his control. See also LANDDROST sense 1.

Heemraden, of whom there were usu. six in each district, were chosen from among the most prominent members of the community, and were not remunerated. One of their most important functions was that of sitting as assessors in court cases presided over by a landdrost. The office was done away with when magistrates replaced landdrosts in December, 1827.

1795 in G.M. Theal *Rec. of Cape Col.* (1897) I. 209 The Burgher War Officer .. and two Heemraden named Hendrik Meyntjes van den Berg and Stephanus Naude have been dismissed on account of their sacrificing .. the general Welfare to the vain Friendship of the Landdrost, by agreeing always with the same. **1797** J.H. CRAIG in *Ibid.* (1898) II. 20, I have duly received by the hands of the Heemraad Nicolaas van der Walt and the Lieutenants .. your Letter ... They paid the necessary and due obedience to the Landdrost and Heemraden. **1806** [see OPGAAF sense 1]. **1811** J.A. TRUTER in *Ibid.* VIII. (1901) 105 In the judicial sentences of this Colony, and particularly in those of Landdrost and Heemraads, a deviation from that regularity may be met with. **1816** G. BARKER Journal. 21 Mar., The Landrost of Uitenhage & the Hemraads & Field-Cornets of the district. **1823** W.W. BIRD *State of Cape of G.H.* 23 An Englishman has been rarely called to the office of heemrad, except in the new drostdy of Albany, where the settlers are located. **1834** T. PRINGLE *Afr. Sketches* 525 A Heemraad was a provincial functionary somewhat analogous to a justice of the peace, and was a member of the landdrost's board. **1884** *Cape Law Jrnl* I. 84 The Court of Landdrost and Heemraden is composed of the Landdrost and two Heemraden or Assessors taken by rotation from the Heemraden for the district of whom there are six for each district elected by the Volksraad, and holding office for two years. **1909** G.M. THEAL *Hist. & Ethnography of Afr. S. of Zambesi* II. 258 A board of heemraden was established on the 30th of August, 1682. This court consisted of four of the leading inhabitants, who held office for two years, without receiving salaries for their services. **1927** C.G. BOTHA *Social Life in Cape Col.* 69 The Landdrost .. presided over a Board of Heemraden to try petty civil cases and adjust a variety of disputes between the inhabitants. **1943** 'J. BURGER' *Black Man's Burden* 18 The old Dutch local courts of *Landdrost* and *Heemraden* were abolished and paid magistrates appointed. **1957** L.G. GREEN *Beyond City Lights* 190 Stellenbosch soon became a place of importance, with Johannes Mulder as landdrost .., four heemraden, and a courthouse. **1972** *Std Encycl. of Sn Afr.* VI. 529 Heemraden existed at the Cape .. three years before the office of landdrost was instituted in 1682 ... At first not more than four heemraden were appointed to a district, but eventually the usual number was six, half of whom retired every year, whereupon the Governor appointed their successors. *Ibid.* 530 The voortrekkers took the office of landdrost with them to the Boer Republics, but not that of heemraad. **1989** *Reader's Digest Illust. Hist.* 100 In 1827, .. resident magistrates replaced *landdrosts* and *heemraden.*

2. *hist.* Also in *pl.*, but treated as *sing.*: the council or court made up of such officials.

1801 J. BARROW *Trav.* I. 12 The Cape of Good Hope .. is divided into four districts, over each of which is placed a civil magistrate called a *Landrost*, who, with his *Hemraaden*, or a council of country burghers, is vested with powers to regulate the police of his district, superintend the affairs of government, adjust litigations, and determine petty causes. **1806** D. BAIRD in G.M. Theal *Rec. of Cape Col.* (1899) V. 338 As soon after your arrival as possible you will assemble the Heemraaden or Council of the District to whom you will notify officially your appointment. **1861** P.B. BORCHERDS *Auto-Biog. Mem.* 150 He recommended the different members of the heemraad to honour and respect the landdrost as their president. **1913** D. FAIRBRIDGE *Piet of Italy* 57 The chief cashier of the Heemraad, Henricus Munkerus, looked up from beneath his heavy eyebrows as he asked the question. **1949** E. HELLMANN *Handbk on Race Rel.* 57 In country districts, the inferior courts consisted of the landdros, primarily an administrative officer, presiding over an appointed board of burghers known as the heemraad.

3. *obs. transf.* Among some colonists: UMPAKATI sense a.

1833 *Graham's Town Jrnl* 16 May 3 A trading station about 1 or 1 1/2 mile from the kraals of the robbers where the neighbouring Caffer Heemraden came to me, and where the cases were settled. **1835** J.W.D. MOODIE *Ten Yrs* II. 242 No important measure is ever undertaken without the advice and consent of their counsellors. These counsellors are all inferior or subordinate chieftains, who command the different subdivisions of the tribe, and are usually denominated 'Humraden' by the Dutch. **1835** C.L. STRETCH Journal. 16 Aug., During the day a son of Geanyaa Gaika's Hemraad arrived from Macomo with a message.

Heer /hɪə(r)/ *int.* and *n.* Also with small initial. [Du., found in all senses given below.]

A. *int.* 'Lord', 'God'; obsolescent form of HERE *int.*

1786 G. FORSTER tr. *A. Sparrman's Voy. to Cape of G.H.* II. 274 A sea-cow came out of the river, rushing upon us, with a hideous cry, .. at the same time, I heard the farmer call out, '*Heer Jesus*!' 1816 G. BARKER *Journal.* 3 Feb., I said Heer (naming his Lord) I cannot walk so fast as you. 1912 F. BANCROFT *Veldt Dwellers* 32 '*Heer*!' growled du Bruyn, removing his pipe .. , 'but they are coming, *neef.*' 1979 M. MATSHOBA *Call Me Not a Man* 43 *Heer*! You don't know how bad life can get for a black man in this godforsaken land, my friend.

B. *n. obs.*

1. Usu. designating a Dutch- or Afrikaans-speaker, and indicating that the man referred to is considered worthy of respect. See also MENEER.

a. In full *the Heer*: 'Mister', a respectful title used with a man's surname.

1800 LADY A. BARNARD in D. Fairbridge *Lady Anne Barnard* (1924) 185 Tomorrow the people embark, & the Heer Ross amongst the rest, who was in the Castle to-day with Mr Barnard. 1905 P. GIBBON *Vrouw Grobelaar* 109 The Heer van der Poel was always a quiet man, but there was nothing weak in him. [1919 M. GREENLEES tr. *O.F. Mentzel's Life at Cape in Mid-18th C.* 50 De Heer Gesagshebber, as he was called when he was Acting Governor.]

b. A man, a gentleman; sometimes used deferentially or respectfully as a term of address in the third person, instead of 'you' (see quot. 1822).

1800 LADY A. BARNARD in D. Fairbridge *Lady Anne Barnard* (1924) 250 Dr Tytler .. will be esteemed the Guardian Angel of the Cape by preserving the lives of the Heers & the beauty of the Vrouws. 1821 C.I. LATROBE *Jrnl of Visit* 85 Brother Bonatz adding, that I was De Heer, of whom he had told them, that he would come from Europe to see them. 1822 W.J. BURCHELL *Trav.* I. 194 At my declining her offer of a bedroom, the good lady expressed surprise that the Heer should think his waggon better than the house. [1824 *Ibid.* II. 107 My own Hottentots had given them to understand that I was not their inferior, and that, notwithstanding the weather-beaten appearance of my dress, I was an 'Engelsche Heer'.] 1833 in A. Gordon-Brown *Artist's Journey* (1965), Boy wanted me to stop — the heer in the veld bringing home the cattle — rode to meet him. [1910 D. FAIRBRIDGE *That Which Hath Been* (1913) 43 'What will d'oude Heer say?' he muttered in awestruck tones to Abdol. 1973 J. MEINTJES *Voortrekkers* 854 Hers was clearly not a happy marriage to a man more than twenty years her senior ... Yet, she was loyal to *den oude heer* (the old man).]

c. 'Sir', a respectful term of address.

1901 E. WALLACE *Unofficial Despatches* 62 You have sent word for me to bring in my cart and mules, and my horses, heer, but ach, what is the good of your asking?

2. In a religious sense: Lord; *obs.* form of HERE *n.*

1896 H.A. BRYDEN *Tales of S. Afr.* 217, I was always a merry one, and that, thank the Heer God, is the reason I have got so well through my troubles. 1906 H. RIDER HAGGARD *Benita* 77 One day Missee, he be a great man .. — if the Heer God Almighty let him.

Heere var. HERE.

heiki var. GEITJIE.

Heikum /ˈheɪkəm/ *n.* Also **Heikom, Heykom**. Pl. usu. unchanged, formerly -s. [fr. Khoikhoi *Hei-//om* 'bush-sleeper', fr. Nama *heib* bush + *//om* to sleep.] A member of a KHOISAN people originally living at the Cape, but long settled in Namibia. Also *attrib.* See also SAAN *n.*[2]

1731 G. MEDLEY tr. *P. Kolb's Present State of Cape of G.H.* I. 80 Bordering on the Chamtouers, North-Eastward, lies the Nation of the Heykoms. 1795 C.R. HOPSON tr. *C.P. Thunbergs Trav.* I. 308 Still farther to the eastward, following the coast, one finds the *Kamtours* nation, then the *Heykoms*, and lastly the Caffres. 1928 E.H.L. SCHWARZ *Kalahari & its Native Races* 167 The Heikum typically has strong Negro characteristics, shown in the large coarse features, tall stature, and black colour of the skin; many of them have mixed with the Qung and are dwarfs. 1930 I. SCHAPERA *KhoiSan Peoples* 34 To the west and south-west of the Kung in South-West Africa are the *Hei-//om* or *Heikum* ('tree dwellers'), who are scattered over a large extent of the country. 1956 A.G. MCRAE *Hill Called Grazing* 133 He grew into a tough little desert rat, able to .. hunt his food with a bow and arrow, like the ones the *Heikum* Bushmen use, but with no poison on the arrow tips. 1966 J.P. VAN S. BRUWER *S.W. Afr.: Disputed Land* 15 There are four distinct sections of Bushmen still living in the Territory ... The four sections are the !Khung, the Heikum, the Naron and the !Kgu or Mbarakwengo. 1969 J.M. WHITE *Land God Made in Anger* 225 Other groups in South West include the seldom-seen River Bushmen, who paddle their dug-out *makorros* on the Okavango, and the so-called Saan people. The latter are an ancient stock, taller and darker than the normal Bushman, who linger on in a small tribe called the Heikom. 1976 O. LEVINSON *Story of Namibia* 25 Only one tribe survived — the Hei//om (men who sleep in the bush) — generally incorrectly classed as Bushmen but who in fact are the last survivors of the Saan tribe. Possibly of mixed Bushman and Hottentot blood, these Hei//om, who are taller and blacker than the Bushmen, once lived on the Clayveld of the Etosha basin. [Note] Hei//om is commonly written Heikom. 1988 [see SAN sense 1].

heimraad var. HEEMRAAD.

heit, heita /ˈheɪt(a)/ *int. colloq.* Also **eh ta, eita, heitha, heito, het, heyitha, heyta, huit**. [Unkn.; perh. ad. Du. *het* (see Mfenyana quot. 1980); but see quot. 1964.]

a. In urban (esp. township) English: a greeting, 'hello'.

Latterly associated with particular political groupings: see quots 1989 and 1990.

1963 B. MODISANE *Blame Me on Hist.* (1986) 57 'Heit, bricade,' he said, 'this is my cheerie'. 1964 L.G. GREEN *Old Men Say* 61 'Het ou Pellie!' I suppose that is the most typical of the popular greetings that belong essentially to Cape Town; but the origin would be hard to trace. One expert thinks it falls into the Malay-Portuguese group. 1977 J. SIKAKANE *Window on Soweto* 26 When pouncing on his victim the policeman will say 'Hy'ta, pass jong' — meaning 'Hey, pass, man'. 1978 C. VAN WYK in *Staffrider* Vol.1 No.2, 26 Ebrahim: Ag that's ou Colin. But sommer call him Kop. Kiet: Heit, Kop. Bob: How's it Kop. 1980 B. MFENYANA in *Voice* 20 Aug. 14 About that classic greeting 'Heit!', he traces its parent-term to the Dutch article Het, as in 'het man — die man'. It must, he avers, have been but a short step from 'heit man', in view of African culture still [being] predominantly oral. 1982 M. MZAMANE *Children of Soweto* 94 Duke was the first to arrive. He was carrying a newspaper under his armpits. '*Heit!* majita. Hi! Bella,' he greeted. '*Heita*', we responded. 1986 T. THOKA in *Eng. Usage in Sn Afr.* Vol.17 No.2, 20 '*Heita*' is a popular greeting used by the Mapantsula. It simply means 'hello'. Of course, one can go further by saying 'Heita hoezet majita?' (Hello, how are you, friends?). 1988 [see IQABANE]. 1989 T. MKHWANAZI in *Weekly Mail* 1 Sept. 5 Cheers of '*Heita* Mandela, *heita* Sisulu' (hail Mandela, Sisulu). 1990 M. KENTRIDGE *Unofficial War* 24 At one point *Heytha*! was a standard way of hailing friends and acquaintances in the townships, but has now become so loaded with political implications that it is used with circumspection. *Ibid.* 92 '*Heythal*', the UDF greeting. 1990 L. KAUNDA in *Ibid.* 24 The *amaqabane* speak *tsotsi taal* (English, Afrikaans, some Zulu, some slang words from God knows where) and they greet each other with *Heytha*! 1993 C. RICKARD in *Sunday Times* 11 July 2 His wife was greeted .. '*Heyta*, comrade mama Marika de Klerk, *Heyta*!'

b. In the phr. *Heita daa(r)*, also *-daarso* /- dɑː(sɔ)/ [Afk. *daar(so)* there], 'hello there'.

1980 *Voice* 20 Aug. 14 We end up with heit, heito, heitadaa and various variations. 1986 M. MANAKA in S. Gray *Market Plays* 58 Jimi: Heitha daarso! Danny: Heitha Jimi. 1987 *Learn & Teach* No.1, 39 Heyta daar. See you next time. 1994 *Weekly Mail & Guardian* 13 May 9 'Eita Da' he yelled to the crowds; 'Eita Da-a-a-a-a' they responded.

hell *n. slang.*

1. In the adv. phr. **hell of (a)**, also **helluva** [special use of general Eng. *hell of a, helluva* used before a noun, e.g. 'a helluva job']: used as an intensifier, 'very', 'extremely'; HELSE *adv.* Cf. *hang of (a)* (see HANG *n.* sense b).

1956 D. JACOBSON *Dance in Sun* 15 They were going to start some sort of a home for sick people. A sanatorium, he said, remembering the word. 'This *dorp* is hell of a good for T.B. they say.' 1961 D. BEE *Children of Yesterday* 91 'Anyway Sam started to clout him around a bit. So all of a sudden bang! Bang! And Sammy's on the floor!' 'And then Claasens helps him up and says he's hell of sorry.' 1967 M.M. HACKSLEY *Informant, Grahamstown* She's hell-of brave, honestly — keeping going, .. with this dreadful fear of the worst always upon her. 1976 S. ROBERTS *Outside Life's Feast* 89, I tiptoed to the kitchen and it was helluva quiet. 1982 D. KRAMER in *Fair Lady* 24 Feb. 97 Our parents were helluva nice ... They never complained about driving us and our amazingly primitive equipment around. 1982 *Grocott's Mail* 9 Mar. 5 I've always come back from a season of Shakespeare or Sheridan helluva enriched and come back to Grahamstown and thought 'Oh God now I'm gonna die – again'. 1990 J. ROSENTHAL *Wake Up Singing* 63 I'm helluva sorry to wake you all up.

2. In the (predicative) adj. phr. *the hell in* [calqued on Afk. *die hel in*, lit. 'in hell'], furiously angry, enraged; *the donder in*, see DONDER *n.* sense 2; *the moer in*, see MOER *n.*[2] sense 2.

1966 L.G. BERGER *Where's Madam* 97 Sometimes when I get the hell-in with Silence, we have a fearful row which seems to clear the air. 1969 A. FUGARD *Notebks* (1983) 178 Boesman is the hell-in ... He works out his self-hatred on her. 1969 — *Boesman & Lena* 10 Where did I find him .. looking at the mud, the hell-in because we had lost all our things. 1971 *Informant, Grahamstown* She's always making a new will — whenever she gets the hell-in with someone she gets another done. 1981 *Sunday Times* 13 Sept. 23 If they install parking meters, everybody is going to be the hell in. 1989 *Style* Feb. 41 God's the hell's in with the Boere nation, who pray like Pharisees but never stop bickering.

hell se var. HELSE.

helper *n.* [Special sense of general Eng. *helper* one employed to assist in some kind of work.] HOUSEKEEPER.

1976 M. THOLO in C. Hermer *Diary of Maria Tholo* (1980) 55 Even for domestics it is worse to work for a black than a white madam in terms of kindness and time off. My neighbour is one example. She expects her helper to work seven days a week with no set time off and is always packing them off at a moment's notice when she is not satisfied. 1990 *Tribute* Apr. 29 People hired helpers for several reasons. Since both the wife and the husband had to toil to meet bond repayments, someone had to do the laundry and cooking ... White housewives don't trust their helpers ... I'm not saying helpers are bad people ... But any woman who has the nerve to bring a strange (and sometimes beautiful) woman into her house to clean, cook, wash and generally take care of the house is asking for trouble.

‖**helse** /ˈhelsə/ *adj.* and *adv. Slang.* Also **hell se**. [Afk., hellish, infernal.]

A. *adj.* Huge, 'bloody great'.

[1944 'TWEDE IN BEVEL' *Piet Kolonel* 110 And then he talked just the same Afrikaans as they did, with English words thrown in, and swore too and said great 'God(s) and 'Donners(s)' and 'Hell se (s).'] 1959 A. DELIUS *Last Division* 75, I was just coming from having a few When there's a helse gewolt in the Avenue And a Boere policeman up with his gun And knocks off a kaffir, and me the next one! **1985** *Sunday Times* 16 June (Mag. Sect.) 14 It's outstanding, darling: there's this huge garden with a swimming-pool slap in the middle; there's this *helse* patio with sliding glass doors.

B. *adv.* Extremely: *hell of (a)*, see HELL sense 1.

1988 *E. Prov. Herald* 27 Feb. 6 *Helse slim*, chief, if you don't mind my saying so.

hemps-bôk var. GEMSBOK.

hemra(a)d var. HEEMRAAD.

hendsop, hendsopper varr. HENSOP, HENSOPPER.

heng var. HANG.

Henkel yellowwood see YELLOWWOOD sense 2 b.

‖**hensop** /ˈhensɔp/ *v. intrans. Colloq.* Also **hendsop**. [Afk., ad. Eng. command *hands up*.] To surrender; *imp.*, 'hands up', 'surrender'. Cf. HANDS-UP sense a.

1947 C.R. PRANCE *Antic Mem.* 10 A gruff voice growled 'Hens-op' at point-blank range. **1980** *Cape Times* 29 Mar. 8 Nearly 2 percent of the total Boer forces of 54000 *hendsopped* (downed arms) in the first 10 months of conflict.

Hence **hensoppery** /ˈhensɔpəreɪ/ *vbl n.* [Afk., n.-forming suffix *-ery*], *fig.*, the abandonment of a struggle.

1972 *Sunday Times* 22 Oct. 16 The genuine Afrikaner .. does not indulge in this type of political hensoppery where, when you are criticised for your own alleged defects, you run for shelter behind the skirts of Afrikanderdom.

‖**hensopper** /ˈhensɔpə(r)/ *n. derog.* Also **'ensopper, hendsopper**. [Afk., *hensop* (see prec.) + agential suffix *-er*.]

1. *hist.*

a. HANDS-UPPER sense 1 a.

1960 [see BITTER-EINDER sense 1]. **1982** K. DAVIE in *Sunday Times* 21 Mar. 44, I ask if joiners are same as hensoppers (hands-uppers)? 'No they're not!' he says emphatically, 'the hensoppers gave up when the British came, the joiners joined the British and fought for them for five shillings a day.' **1987** in BUNN & TAYLOR *From S. Afr.* (1988) 110 *Hensoppers*, literally, 'handsuppers' — derogatory slang for Boers who surrendered to the British. **1990** [see JOINER sense 1]. **1990** *Sunday Times* 8 July 18 By the start of 1901 there were more Boer soldiers either back on their farms or on the English side as 'hensoppers' and 'joiners' than there were active on the battlefields of the Transvaal and the Free State.

b. JOINER sense 1.

1979 [see HANDS-UPPER sense 1 b]. **1989** *Reader's Digest Illust. Hist.* 257 Known contemptuously as 'joiners' or *hensoppers* (hands-uppers) they received scant sympathy from the Boers still in the field.

2. *fig.* and *transf.* HANDS-UPPER sense 2.

1974 *Sunday Times* 25 Aug. 15 If he had such a plan in mind, why did he recently denounce verligte Nationalists who have been urging a revision of race policy, as 'Hensoppers?' **1977** *Ibid.* 6 Feb. 10 For him there are two kinds: Real Afrikaners in the Kruger-Vorster mould following the Voortrekker road and 'hensoppers', rich intellectuals, found on university campuses, .. often pawns in the hands of Afrikaner enemies. **1980** *Weekend Post* 6 Sept. 5 The leader of the PFP .. was accused of 'blatant intimidation' of the electorate ... At times the PFP was described as 'spoilers' and 'hensoppers'. **1986** *E. Prov. Herald* 4 Mar. 10 If there are 'hensoppers', and he concedes there are, why do they have to wait until the UN has the place surrounded? **1986** *Cape Times* 6 Mar., The bittereinders might talk of nuking the UN, but the hensoppers would likely win the day, as they did at the end of the Boer War.

herald *n.* [See quot. 1988.] In full ***herald snake***: the common back-fanged garden snake *Crotaphopeltis hotamboeia* of the Colubridae, olive to olive-brown in colour (usu. with red or yellow lips), and having a poisonous but not fatal bite; *red-lipped herald*, see RED-LIPPED; also called NIGHT-ADDER (sense 2).

1910 F.W. FITZSIMONS *Snakes of S. Afr.* 57 The Red-lipped or Herald Snake .. is one of the best-known and most widespread snakes in Africa. **1937** [see NIGHT-ADDER]. **1947** J. STEVENSON-HAMILTON *Wild Life in S. Afr.* 330 The red-lipped or herald snake (*Leptodira hotamboeia*). This is distinguished by its upper lip being of bright red colour. c**1966** J. HOBBS in *New S. Afr. Writing* 157 We have had a cobra outside the kitchen that reared and spat .. , night-adders wriggling unobtrusively up the drains and behind storage bins, and harmless red-lipped herald snakes. **1967** [see RED-LIPPED]. **1970** V.F.M. FITZSIMONS *Field Guide to Snakes S. Afr.* 118 Herald or Red-lipped Snake ... According to the prevailing colour on the upper lips it is variously known as the white- or yellow-lipped snake. **1987** R. PATTERSON *Reptiles* 82 Herald Snake, .. Found in the moister southern and eastern half of southern Africa, the Herald is the garden snake of the region ... As a means of defence it adopts an adder-like position with the head flattened ... This pose has resulted in the humble Herald acquiring the erroneous title of Flame-mouth adder! **1988** B. BRANCH *Field Guide to Snakes* 85 Herald or Red-lipped Snake, .. The presence of this snake in South Africa was first noted in the Eastern Province Herald newspaper, hence its common name.

herbalist *n.* [Special sense of general Eng. *herbalist* 'one versed in the knowledge of herbs or plants; .. a botanist' (*OED*).] In African society: one who dispenses or deals in medicinal herbs and other traditional remedies for sickness or misfortune. Also *attrib.* See also *medicine man* (MEDICINE sense 2). Cf. BOSSIEDOKTER, WITCH-DOCTOR.

The role of diviner is sometimes erroneously attributed to the herbalist by writers.

[**1925** D. KIDD *Essential Kafir* 134 The diviner may send a patient to one of these people, saying that, as his illness is not caused by magic or by ancestral spirits, all that is needed is a course of medical treatment by a herb-doctor.] **1930** S.T. PLAATJE *Mhudi* (1975) 54 He remembered how, when people were ill, they consulted a herbalist and how the longana (wormwood) bush served as a tonic and cure for every ailment. **1949** C. BULLOCK *Rina* 84 The infusion of the bark of a certain tree and herbs of the field such as our herbalists knew of. **1950** D. REED *Somewhere S. of Suez* 227 The witch-doctor is always a herbalist when he is facing a white man; when he turns his face towards a tribesman he becomes a witch-doctor. **1962** W.D. HAMMOND-TOOKE *Bhaca Soc.*, Initially it is necessary to distinguish two types of 'doctor' viz. the herbalist (*inyanga* ..) and the diviner (*isangoma* ..). Both are practitioners in the art of healing .. The herbalist does not commune with the shades nor can he divine. **1977** N. XAYIMPI in *E. Prov. Herald* 11 Mar. 5 A Kwazakele trader, Mr. E Z Kabane, who started his business in a shack as a herbalist, has been chosen 1976 black businessman of the year in the Eastern Cape. **1984** E. MANTINI in *Sunday Times* 26 Feb. 7 The bills of inyangas and other traditional African healers will be tax-deductible ... Johannesburg's Receiver of Revenue .. adds: 'We will honour such receipts provided the inyangas are registered with a local herbalist association.' **1985** J. MASON in *Cosmopolitan* May 154 The herbalist .. has an intimate knowledge of the medicinal properties of herbs and powders, and .. sometimes divines with the use of bones. **1990** R. MALAN *My Traitor's Heart* 185 The classified sections of Soweto's newspapers carried ads in which 'traditional healers' or 'herbalists' offered to restore love to the lovelorn, seal homes against evil spirits, thwart the designs of enemies, and cure disease.

Hence **herbalism** *n.*, the art of a herbalist.

1972 *Scope* 8 Sept. 50 No one knows exactly how he made his money. It came from herbalism, from selling magic spells. **1981** *Pace* Sept. 64 Apart from this ancestral calling, she has completed a course in herbalism, for which she holds a diploma issued by the Dingaka Herbal Company. **1990** *Weekly Mail* 23 Mar. 11 It is the 'warriors' in Natal's civil war .. who have turned herbalism into big — but risky — business. No fighter goes into battle without *muti*.

Here /ˈhɪərə, ˈjɪərə/ *int.* and *n.* Also **Heere**. [Afk., a variant, used as an expletive or in religious contexts, of *Heer* lord.]

A. *int.* 'Lord', 'God': an exclamation expressing amazement, shock, annoyance, exasperation, anger, or fear; the modern form of HEER *int.* Cf. YIRRA. Sometimes in the phr. *my here* /ˌmeɪ-/, 'my God'.

1920 R.Y. STORMBERG *Mrs Pieter de Bruyn Glossary*, Heere! — Lord! **1965** J. BENNETT *Hawk Alone* 214 'You get out,' said Gord ... 'My Here,' he said, 'but your father'll hear about this'. **1975** S. SEPAMLA in *New Classic* No.1, 14 When I heard Africans were going to be moved from Stirtonville, I fell on one knee ... My first words were: Nkulunkulu! Here! You don't do it over the dead body of Fanyana? It is still over my living carcass? Hawu! **1979** [see MERREM sense 2 a]. **1982** *Rhodeo* (Rhodes Univ.) 6 Apr. 11 I thought, O Here, she went to the loo or she got lost, where is she now? **1990** J. NAIDOO *Coolie Location* 5 Ag, Heere Auntie! Gambling is no good.

‖**B.** *n.* In a religious sense: Lord; the modern form of HEER *n.* sense 2.

1986 D. CASE *Love, David* 89 'Here Jesus,' Oupa prayed, 'we give you the soul of our dear sister, Stumpy. Look after her well!'

‖**Herenigde** /hɛrˈɪənəxdə/ *adj. hist.* [Afk., 're-united', past participle of *herenig* re-unite.] In the n. phr. ***Herenigde (Nationalist) Party***: the 'Reunited National(ist) Party', a political party espousing Afrikaner nationalism, formed in 1939 by a merger of the *Gesuiwerde Nasionale Party* (Purified National Party) with a group of Afrikaners who had left the ruling United Party; HNP *n.*[1]

The Herenigde Nationalist Party, in coalition with the Afrikaner Party which had previously broken away from it, won the 1948 general election, and in 1951 the two merged to form the modern National Party (see NP sense 1).

1941 *Star* 1 Jan. 7 The Ossewa-Brandwag .. intends to drive those who break away from the Herenigde Party back 'with a sjambok'. **1947** *Cape Argus* 29 Mar. 6 Why then should he not be useful as a bell-wether ('voorbok') leading United Party sheep into the Herenigde kraal? **1947** G.A.L. GREEN *Editor Looks Back* 224 Steps are now to be taken to organise the Reunited (Herenigde) Nationalist Party or Volksparty. **1973** *Std Encycl. of Sn Afr.* VIII. 87 When Danial Malan's Herenigde (Reunited) National Party (HNP; NP after 1951) won the 1948 general election, about 48 000 coloured voters still retained a qualified franchise on the Cape electoral roll.

‖**hereniging** /hɛrˈɪənəxəŋ/ *n. hist.* Also **hereeniging**. [Afk., 'reunion', fr. *herenig* to reunite.] In politics: the reuniting of Afrikanerdom, particularly the reuniting of the Afrikaner members of the South African Party with the National Party. Also *attrib.* See also NP sense 1, SAP *n.*[1] sense 1.

1926 M. NATHAN *S. Afr. from Within* 173 An endeavour was made to reconcile the two opposing sections of the Dutch people ... The 'Hereeniging (Reunion) Conference' took place ... The Nationalists desired to retain republicanism in their party programme ... The members of the South African Party would not agree, and the conference broke down. **1934** *Star* 12 Feb. (Swart), Dr Van der Merwe .. said, that he was confident there would be no samesmelting, but hereniging. **1934** C.P. SWART *Supplement to Pettman.* 68 *Hereniging*, A re-union. Politically it means a re-union of the Nationalists with the Afrikaans-speaking members of the South African Party, leaving out the bulk of the English-speaking members. **1936** *Cambridge*

Hist. of Brit. Empire VIII. 645 A determined effort was made to attain the *hereeniging* or reunion of the South African Party, now led by General Smuts .., and the Nationalist Party under .. General Hertzog. **1950** H. GIBBS *Twilight* 177 The early 1939 bid for reunion among Afrikaner parties (*Hereniging*) did not materialize. **1968** W.K. HANCOCK *Smuts* II. 253 Malan was doing to Hertzog what Hertzog had done twenty years before to Botha ... In his view, Hertzog was pursuing vereniging, not hereniging — a political combination of incompatible elements, not Afrikaner reunion. **1977** T.R.H. DAVENPORT *S. Afr.: Mod. Hist.* 234 The occasion was used to celebrate the impending reunion (hereniging) of the Nationalists under Malan and Hertzog ... Hereniging was .. difficult .., however, for in five years the U.P. and the G.N.P. had drifted apart in sentiment and objectives; but it was achieved in December 1939.

Here Seventien /ˌhɪərə sɪəv(ə)n'tin, ɹɪərə -/ *n. phr. Hist.* Also **Here Sewentien, Here XVII**. [Du., *here* gentlemen, lords + *seventien* (a form of *zeventien*) or *sewentien* seventeen.] SEVENTEEN.

1973 [see VOC]. **1982** *S. Afr. Panorama* Jan. 21 Jan van Riebeeck .. pestered the *Here Sewentien* (Council of 17) for at least three years before eventually procuring stock vines from Germany, France, Spain, and elsewhere. **1987** W.A. DE KLERK in *Sunday Times* 25 Jan. 32 The Cape Patriots carried their *klagskrif* — indictment — to the *Here Seventien*, top structure of the VOC in Amsterdam. **1988** D. PAICE in *Femina* June 40 Even right at the beginning the government at the Cape was not a king but a commercial guild — the *Here XVII*.

Heritage Day *n. phr.* [See quot. 1994.] The 24th of September, celebrated as a public holiday from 1995.

1994 *E. Prov. Herald* 8 Sept. 1 Heritage Day, in which the various sectors of society could celebrate their cultures, would fall on September 24, which was also Shaka Day. **1994** *Ibid.* 8 Dec. 2 The confusion that has existed over the past few months regarding the public holidays for 1995 ended today, by the publication of the Public Holiday Act 1994 in the Government Gazette ... The full list of public holidays is as follows: .. September 24 Heritage Day, [etc.].

Hermitage *n. obsolescent.* [See quot. 1988.] A local name, esp. formerly, for the Cinsault (or Cinsaut) grape. See also PINOTAGE sense 1.

In the wine-making industry the name 'Cinsaut' has been used for this cultivar since 1973 (see quot. 1988).

*c*1911 S. PLAYNE *Cape Col.* 202 The vines .. are chiefly Muscatel, Haanepoort, and Pontac, Green Grape and Hermitage. **1915** [see STUKVAT]. **1964** [see PINOTAGE sense 1]. **1966** [see GREEN GRAPE]. **1972** A.G. BAGNALL *Wines of S. Afr.* 64 A 'Pinotage' grape which is nothing more or less than a cross between the Hermitage and the Pinot. **1977** [see PINOTAGE sense 1]. **1979** C. PAMA *Wine Estates of S. Afr.* p. xi, *Pinotage* (red, 2,9%) South Africa's own red wine, derived from a cross-pollination of a hybrid of the Pinôt Noir and the Hermitage (Cinsault). **1981** J. DOXAT *Indispensable Drinks Bk* 52 Pinotage is the most common red wine grape, a Cape speciality, a cross between Pinot Noir and the Cinsaut of the Rhône, sometimes confusingly known as Hermitage — hence the name. **1988** D. HUGHES et al. *Complete Bk of S. Afr. Wine* 106 The Cinsault cultivar (previously known in South Africa as Hermitage) originated in France, in the vineyards around the small town of Tain-l'Hermitage on the banks of the Rhône ... First introduced here in the 1850's, it was generally known within the industry as Hermitage ... Professor Perold .. identified Cinsaut and Hermitage as being one and the same ... Hermitage was used up to the introduction of the Wine of Origin legislation in 1973. **1992** P. DEVEREUX in *Sunday Times* 29 Mar. (Mag. Sect.) 6 Pinotage .. was invented here in 1925 by crossing two red grapes, Pinot Noir and Hermitage (Hermitage is today correctly called *Cinsaut*).

Hernhutter /'hɛrnhʊtə(r)/ *n. hist.* Also **Herneuter, Herrnhut(t)er, Herrnhütter**, and with small initial. [Either fr. *Herrnhuter* a member of the Moravian religious group, or named for a building at the mission station of Genadendal (see quot. 1986); both fr. G. *Herrnhut*, lit. 'the Lord's keeping', the name of the first Moravian settlement in Saxony + n.-forming suffix *-er*.] A particular type of sheath-knife formerly made at the Moravian mission station of Genadendal; BOSLEMMER. Also *attrib.* Cf. BUSHMAN'S FRIEND.

1916 J.M. ORPEN *Reminisc.* (1964) 306 Steenberg on my right loosed his right hand and seized his 'hernhutter' sheath knife from his pocket, saying he would rip me up. **1924** G. BAUMANN in Baumann & Bright *Lost Republic* (1940) 121 An argument ensued, during which E. drew his long hunting knife (*herrnhutter*) and stabbed young Koekemoer. **1937** F.B. YOUNG *They Seek a Country* 539 A sheath-knife with an eighteen-inch blade of the sort they called Herneuters. **1951** H. DAVIES *Great S. Afr. Christians* 5 The new missionaries built a station, a school, a mill and a cutlery. In the latter they made pruning knives which were in great demand by the fruit-farmers of the district who called them *herrnhuters*. **1972** [see BOSLEMMER]. **1973** J. MEINTJES *Voortrekkers* 107 Also part of every man's gear was his knife with a blade of from seven to eight inches in length and with handles from four to five inches long, known as a *Hernhutter*. Such a knife had a hundred uses — skinning game, cutting up the carcase, for eating, slicing biltong, as a weapon, and so on. **1986** *Motorist* 1st Quarter 13 The boys' hostel dates from before 1816 and is called Herrnhut, which gave its name to the Herrnhütter sheath-knives which were made there until well into the present century and which were prized possessions. **1990** on TV1, 28 Nov. (Antenna), Genadendal is the home of the famous Hernhutter knife.

Heroes' Day *n. phr.* Also **Heroes Day**.

1. The 21st of March, the date of the fatal shooting of 69 people in the township of Sharpeville in 1960, chosen (esp. by the PAC) to commemorate all those who have died in the struggle for racial equality; *Sharpeville Day*, see SHARPEVILLE sense 2. Also *attrib.*

1975 *Rand Daily Mail* 21 Mar. 2 The two Black unity organisations, the South African Students' Organization (SASO) and the Black People's Convention (BPC) are organising services all over the country today to observe 'Heroes Day' — the 15th anniversary of the Sharpeville shooting. **1981** *E. Prov. Herald* 23 Mar. 11 Speakers at the Heroes' Day commemoration meeting held in Lenasia, Johannesburg, at the week-end, sharply criticised people who participated in the two Government-created institutions. **1983** J. MATYU in *Weekend Post* 19 Mar. 4 A former Robben Island prisoner .. will be the main speaker at the annual commemoration service to mark the 23rd anniversary of the 'Heroes Day' — the Sharpeville shootings of pass book protesters. **1989** *Weekly Mail* 31 Mar. 29 Many 'young lions', who were once instrumental in enforcing consumer boycotts and the observance of people's holidays like June 16, May Day and Heroes Day, have now resorted to armchair activism. **1991** *Natal Witness* 28 Mar. (Echo) 8 A Heroes Day rally in Sharpeville township, outside Vereeniging, was washed out by torrential rain last Thursday.

2. The 16th of December, so named in memory of those who died or suffered in the struggle against apartheid.

See note at DAY OF THE VOW.

1983 [see DAY OF THE VOW]. **1990** S. VENTER in *Tribute* Sept. 46 The ideal symbolic return date bandied about in certain circles is 'by December 16' — Heroes' Day and the start of the first full-scale ANC conference in South Africa since the organisation was banned in 1960.

Herrnhut(t)er var. HERNHUTTER.

Herstigte /hɛr'stəxtə/ *n.* and *adj.* Also with small initial. [Afk., 'reconstituted', as used in the name *Herstigte Nasionale Party* 'Reconstituted National Party'.]

A. *n.* **a.** A member of the *Herstigte Nasionale Party* (see HNP *n.*[2]); HERTZOGITE *n.* sense 2. **b.** Loosely, one who holds extreme right-wing views.

1971 B.J. VORSTER in *Daily Dispatch* 7 Oct. 1, I refer to Dr. Albert Hertzog and the 'Herstigtes' who go out of their way to besmirch not only the Government but myself. **1975** *Daily Dispatch* 20 May 15 Delegates had changed suddenly into Progs in Nat clothing or closet Herstigtes. **1986** *E. Prov. Herald* 1 June 16 The country cannot afford to have an illiberal CP parading its racist views to the world, never mind the Herstigtes.

B. *adj.* Of or pertaining to the *Herstigte Nasionale Party* (see HNP *n.*[2]); HERTZOGITE *adj.* sense 1.

1975 *Sunday Times* 13 Apr. 4 Bring me .. a bottle of 1973 Scharzberg. You know, man, the kind we knock back .. at a Herstigte rally. **1986** *E. Prov. Herald* 20 June 8 The Herstigte and Conservative elements seem able to call the shots.

Hertzog Bills *pl. n. phr. Hist.* [Named for *J.B.M. Hertzog*, the Prime Minister at the time and a principal mover of the legislation.] ***The Hertzog Bills***: A collective name for two parliamentary bills, proposed and promulgated in 1936, which in effect created a legal framework for apartheid.

The Representation of Natives Bill proposed the removal of African voters from the ordinary electoral roll in the Cape Province and their placement on a separate roll; this became law as the Representation of Natives Act, No.12 of 1936. The Natives' Trust and Land Act Bill proposed the creation of the South African Native Trust; it became law as the Natives' Trust and Land Act, No.18 of 1936. See also LAND ACT sense b, TRUST.

1952 *Drum* Feb. 14 The Native Bills of 1936 (better known as the Hertzog Bills) attracted wide interest in the younger generation, but African moderates agreed upon a 'wait and see' policy. **1953** A.J. LUTHULI in *Ibid.* 11 Since the 1936 Hertzog bills the African peoples have lost faith in the good intentions of the Whites to improve their conditions. **1963** M. BENSON *Afr. Patriots* 86 The emergence of this rival organization, coming on top of the A.N.C.'s failure to lead the opposition to the Hertzog bills, shocked some of its members into a decision. **1989** *Reader's Digest Illust. Hist.* 339 Time had run out for the opponents of the Hertzog bills and on 6 April 1936, parliament approved the measures by an overwhelming 168 votes to 11.

Hertzogism /'hɜːtzɒgɪzm/ *n. hist.* [The name of the chief proponent of language equality, *J.B.M. Hertzog* + Eng. abstract n.-forming suffix *-ism*.] Among English-speakers: a pejorative name for the Afrikaner nationalist movement or philosophy which demanded that Dutch be afforded full equality with English in education.

1910 *E. Prov. Herald* 15 Apr., It will require the willing co-operation of like-minded men from end to end of South Africa who will only be fighting their own battles in grappling with Hertzogism. **1910** *Rand Daily Mail* 31 May 2 Mr. Sheffield said he would do his best to see that the Education laws were properly looked after. They did not want Hertzogism in the country. (Loud applause.) **1911** *Ibid.* 4 Dec., Well this stick of suspicion had been taken away from the clique but they got hold of another — the so-called Hertzogism. **1913** V.R. MARKHAM *S. Afr. Scene* 193 Hertzogism is an unfortunate manifestation, but through some such phase South Africa had doubtless to pass before the final adjustment between the races could take place. **1968** E.A. WALKER *Hist. of Sn Afr.* 542 'No Hertzogism' had been the rallying cry of the Free State British in the election of 1910. Hertzog was thus the bogey of the British and the idol of the Free State Afrikaners when Parliament essayed to guide the Provinces in the way they should go in the matter of language in the schools. **1973** F.J. DU T. SPIES in *Std Encycl. of Sn Afr.* VIII. 367 In 1908 Hertzog successfully introduced the so-called Hertzog Educational Bill in the Legislative Council, whereby school attendance was made

Hertzogite /ˈhɜːtzɒgaɪt/ n. and adj. [Named for J.B.M. Hertzog, one-time Prime Minister and founder of the Afrikaner Party (1941), or for his son, A. Hertzog, founder of the Herstigte Nasionale Party (1969) + Eng. n.- and adj.-forming suffix *-ite*.]

A. n.

1. hist. A supporter of J.B.M. Hertzog; a member of the Afrikaner Party, a small Orange Free State-based party founded by Hertzog in 1941 as a breakaway from the National Party.

The Afrikaner Party merged with the National Party in 1951.

1968 E.A. WALKER *Hist. of Sn Afr.* 546 Unluckily, the Hertzogites found fresh cause of offence in his [sc. Botha's] sympathetic references to Rhodes. 1977 T.R.H. DAVENPORT *S. Afr.: Mod. Hist.* 235 When the Hertzogites rallied .. and went on to form their breakaway Afrikaner Party in January 1941, only a small number of the H.N.P. supporters went with them. 1991 A. VAN WYK *Birth of New Afrikaner* 61 The Grey Shirts, New Orderites and Hertzogites were small fry, with the real fight, a bitter one, fought between the NP and OB.

2. HERSTIGTE n. sense a.

1969 S. UYS in J. Crwys-Williams *S. Afr. Despatches* (1989) 395 The Hertzogites simply don't want immigrants unless they can be assimilated immediately into Afrikanerdom and become card-carrying members of the H.N.P. 1973 *Star* 3 Nov. 6 Between what a Hertzogite regards as racial incitement and what a leftist-liberal working for a new United Party sees as such, there must surely be a vast gulf.

B. adj.

1. HERSTIGTE adj.

1970 *Argus* 30 Jan. 2 Hertzogite broadside misfires. The Herstigte Nasionale Party's first attempt to launch a wide-ranging parliamentary attack on the Nationalists, failed here today. 1972 *Weekend Post* 9 Sept. 1 He has been known as a near-verkrampte — in fact in the early days of the Hertzogite movement, he was an inner core member.

2. hist. Of or pertaining to supporters of J.B.M. Hertzog and his Afrikaner Party.

1991 A. VAN WYK *Birth of New Afrikaner* 61 There were various contenders for the soul of Afrikanerdom — the anti-Semitic Grey Shirt movement of L.T. Weichardt, .. the fascist New Order grouping of Oswald Pirow, .. ; the Afrikaner Party of N.C. Havenga and his Hertzogite supporters; [etc.].

hervings pl. form of ERF.

Hervormde /hɛrˈfɔrmdə, hɑːfɔːmdə/ adj. [Afk., 'reformed', ellipt. for *Nederduits Hervormde Kerk in Afrika* Dutch Reformed Church in Africa.] Of or pertaining to the *Nederduits Hervormde Kerk in Afrika* (Dutch Reformed Church in Africa), which was established in 1859, and is one of the family of Dutch Reformed churches; NED HERV. Usu. in the phrr. **Hervormde Church**, **-Kerk** /- ˈkɛrk/ [Afk., *kerk* church], a shortened name for this church; Ned Herv Kerk, see NED HERV.

See note at DUTCH REFORMED.

1931 H.C. BOSMAN in S. Gray *Makapan's Caves* (1987) 108 There were present members of both Dutch Churches, the Hervormde and the Gereformeerde, and the minister gave out only psalms, as he did not wish to antagonise the Doppers, who do not sing hymns. 1946 S. CLOETE *Afr. Portraits* 70 Many of the Hervormde Reformed Church had accused Kruger with meddling … Whoever was not a member of the Hervormde Church was not a fully qualified burgher, they said. 1974 *S. Afr. Panorama* Apr. 9 Only one denomination had a church there — the Hervormde Kerk in which the renowned Rev. Andrew Murray preached on more than one occasion. 1975 [see GELYKSTELLING]. 1982 C. FREIMOND in *E. Prov. Herald* 31 Aug. 2 The Hervormde Kerk was the least willing of the Afrikaans churches to admit blacks with only 8, 5 per cent of members willing to let them join and 17,7 per cent in favour of them as visitors. 1990 *Sunday Times* 21 Oct. 11 Three churches — the NG Kerk, Hervormde Kerk and the Afrikaanse Protestante Kerk — minister to the community's spiritual needs.

hesh girl /ˈhɛʃgɜːl/ n. phr. Slang. Also **hash girl**. [Prob. fr. Zulu *héshe* of swooping onto, or *heshe* hawk.] In urban (esp. township) Eng.: a prostitute who works in the lowest type of drinking establishment.

1973 P. BECKER in *The 1820* Vol.46 No.7, 32 The lowest class shebeens, known in some townships as Small Time Joints, are patronized by .. tsotsi gangs, fugitives from the law and the notorious 'hesh girls', or degenerate booze-soaked prostitutes who prey on youthful thugs and adult drunks. 1977 P.C. VENTER *Soweto* 124 Cheap shebeens, those Small Time Joints .. where the so-called hash girls promise sex and plunder your wallet without delivering. 1983 *Pace* Dec. 152 The 'small time joints', patronised by … tsotsi gangs .. and 'hesh girls'.

het var. HEIT.

Het Volk see VOLK sense 3 a.

‖**heuning** /ˈhiœnəŋ, ˈhɪənəŋ/ n. Formerly also honing. [Afk., earlier *honing* (fr. Du.) honey.] 'Honey', used attrib. in the names of plants, the leaves of which are used to make a fragrant herbal tea (see HONEY TEA sense b), as **heuning** (**-blom**)**bos** /-(blɔm)ˌbɔs/ [Afk., *blom* flower) *bos* bush], **heuning**(**blom**)**tee** /-(blɔm)tɪə/ [Afk., (*blom* flower) *tee* (earlier Du. *thee*) tea]: HONEY TEA sense a. Also attrib.

[1837 ECKLON & ZEYHER *Enumeratio Plantarum Africae* 153 Cyclopia genistoides … Sept.-Dec. — Incolis africanis: 'Honingthee' phthisi ab iis adhibita.] 1913 C. PETTMAN *Africanderisms* 215 Honingthee, .. Cyclopea genistoides Vent. An infusion of the leaves of this plant has a sweet, astringent taste, and is useful in colds and coughs. 1917 R. MARLOTH *Common Names* 40 Honing tee v. Bushtea. 1949 [see ROOIBOS sense 1 b]. 1950 M.M. KIDD *Wild Flowers* Pl.71, Cyclopia genistoides … Heuningtee. 1966 C.A. SMITH *Common Names* 247 Heuningtee, Cyclopia genistoides … The foliage and young flowers are used as a bush tea with an odour suggesting honey (Afr.: heuning) and free from stimulating alkaloids, having long (c.1830) been used as a restorative for coughs and colds. 1980 *Sunday Times* 19 Oct. 16 The secret to this farmer's success is a wild tea bush … All he does is harvest his crop, 'heuningblomtee' (honeyblossom tea), a wild bush, which grows wild in kloofs and ravines in the mostly deciduous fruit farming area of the Blackwood where he lives … The heuningblombos is a green bush with an attractive yellow flower when in season. 1982 *S. Afr. Panorama* May 38 The feast was rounded off with coffee, or else delicious heuningbos tea, served clear.

heuning-wyser var. HONING-WIJZER.

heuweltjie /ˈhiœvəlki/ n. Geology. Formerly also **heuvel(tje)**. [Afk., (earlier S. Afr. Du.), fr. Du. *heuveltje* hillock.] An ancient termite nest, manifesting as a fertile mound of earth.

1857 *Cape Monthly Mag.* 63 Can any of your scientific contributors inform me why the soil is richer on these so-called *heuvels*, and the probable cause of this curious formation of the earth's surface? 1903 *Cape of G.H. Agric. Jrnl* XXIII. 347 (Pettman), The incidence of the *heuveltje* in the cultivated lands, is an accepted phenomenon which offers food for reflection … These *heuveltjes* never need manuring and their originating cause is not as yet explained. 1905 E.A. NOBBS in Flint & Gilchrist *Science in S. Afr.* 381 A peculiar feature of many portions of the Colony .. is a spotted appearance of the land, with a more luxuriant growth of crop or natural herbage corresponding to these richer and often slightly raised patches, each a few yards in diameter. Sometimes they are close together, while again they may be found only every few hundred yards. Invariably the soil is deeper and richer on these 'heuveltjes' than elsewhere. 1910 C.F. JURITZ *Study of Agric. Soils of Cape Col.* 85 Attention was frequently directed by the local farmers to numerous slight elevations, from one to four feet in height, and twenty or more yards in diameter. The soil of these hillocks — called 'heuveltjies' by the farmers — was alleged to be extremely rich. 1991 MOORE & PICKER in *Oecologia* Vol.86, 424 Heuweltjies (earth mounds) in the Clanwilliam district, Cape Province, South Africa: 4000-year old termite nests.

hey /heɪ/ int. colloq. [Special senses of general Eng.]

Cf. HOOR.

1. Added to a statement or a question: a request for an utterance to be repeated; a request for confirmation of what has been said; used to turn a statement into a question, inviting agreement.

1900 H. BLORE *Imp. Light Horseman* 268 The sentry, evidently a young Boer who had been educated in the Cape Colony, replied, 'Well, ta-ta, pr'aps I see you again to-morrow night, hey?' c1929 S. BLACK in S. Gray *Three Plays* (1984) 66 He's quite an intellectual, hey? a1951 H.C. BOSMAN *Willemsdorp* (1977) 188 'You chain smokes, hey?' the detective remarked. 1961 T. MATSHIKIZA *Choc. for my Wife* 31 He only needs to direct people and the traffic with his hands, hey Daddy. Ibid. 51 'Isn't it a small world, hey?' 1969 A. FUGARD *Boesman & Lena* 3 It was funny hey Boesman! 1970 J. MCINTOSH *Stonefish* 257 'Julian,' she said, 'I renounce you.' 'Hey?' 'Not "Hey?" "What?" Or, "I beg your pardon?"' 1971 J. MCCLURE *Steam Pig* (1973) 97 'Not so busy you can't listen to serials on Springbok, hey?' The transistor set was poorly concealed. 1971 *Drum* May 42 But life's funny, hey? c1986 P. FIRTH in *Eng. Alive* '86 32 'You're in standard nine, hey?' 'Ja. You as well?' 1987 M. POLAND *Train to Doringbult* 190 Why don't we have a big party, hey Elsie? .. It's been so bladdy boring .. — don't you think?

2. Added to an instruction or a command to soften it, by implying that the assent of the one addressed is being sought.

1953 D. JACOBSON *Long Way from London* 63 You must drive slowly, hey, so that they can keep up, for your own good. 1963 M.G. MCCOY *Informant, Port Elizabeth*, I shall be longing to hear what you did .. , so don't delay, hey?! 1973 *Eng. Alive* 55 Bye Beauty, tell ma we'll write hey, okay? 1975 S. ROBERTS *Outside Life's Feast* 61 'Totsiens Tannie.' 'Ag goodbye my boy … come again hey!'

3. Added to a question to insist on an answer, or to indicate that the question refers to something which the one addressed ought to take note of, or pay attention to.

1956 D. JACOBSON *Dance in Sun* 24 What do you think of that — hey? 1961 T. MATSHIKIZA *Choc. for my Wife* 37 'Can you drink, jong, hey?' 'Yes, Baas Smitty.' 1964 M.G. MCCOY *Informant, Port Elizabeth*, I even know what a hootenanny is, so how's that for culture, hey? c1966 M. JABOUR in *New S. Afr. Writing* 91 Donder, now what's the matter with the thing, hey? Cohen said it was in perfect condition. 1975 'BLOSSOM' in *Darling* 26 Feb. 111 'So what happens when they come crashing down on top of us, hey?' I whisper in he's ear. 1988 D. SAMUELSON in *Fair Lady* 16 Mar. 133 Why did Oema have to do that, hey Oema, How long would it take, hey Oema? What is a borshin hey Oema?

4. Added to a statement to give it emphasis, or to retain the attention of the one addressed, through an implied request for a reply of some sort (when no reply is, in fact, required).

1975 J. MCCLURE *Snake* (1981) 162 'Do I make myself clear?' 'Yes, lady. I'm sorry, hey?' 1975 *Sunday Times* 23 Feb. 16 There, confronting me on the plate, were two completely white eggs … The white was white and the yolk was white. Yiss, it was only weird, hey. 1985 P. SLABOLEPSZY *Sat. Night at Palace* 33 Clint .. comes bashing through the door … He takes one look at ou Shirley — you know Clint hey — sommer in the bath, guns and all! It turns out, hey — turns out she's a prostitute — in disguise as a nun. **1986** B. SIMON in S. Gray *Market Plays* 113 You don't sukkel with anybody like that. I'm right hey. **1987** M. POLAND *Train to Doringbult* 128 'How many chaps do you want?' 'Five or six. Thanks hey.' **1993** *Informant, Grahamstown* 'Yissus, Bonnie!' 'I didn't say that!' 'That's lank rude, hey!'

heyitha, heyta varr. HEIT.

Heykom var. HEIKUM.

hiccup-nut *n.* Also **hiccough nut**, and with initial capital. [See quot. 1983.] The shrub or small tree *Combretum bracteosum* of the Combretaceae, bearing bright red blooms, and found mainly on the coasts of KwaZulu-Natal and the (former) Transkei.

1862 HARVEY & SONDER *Flora Capensis* II. 512 *P. bracteosum* ... Called 'Hiccup-nut' in the colony. **1868** J. CHAPMAN *Trav.* II. 447 The exquisite heads of scarlet flowers of the Hiccup-nut. **1899** WOOD & EVANS *Natal Plants* I. 63 The fruit is known locally as 'Hiccup Nut' and is palatable, but usually produces violent hiccough. **1951** *Dict. of Gardening* (Royal Horticult. Soc.) II. 531 C. bracteosum, Hiccup-nut. **1966** C.A. SMITH *Common Names* 247 *Hiccough-nut*, .. The vernacular name was .. apparently derived from the alleged use of the fruit to relieve hiccoughs. **1975** J.M. GIBSON *Wild Flowers of Natal* Pl.71, *Combretum bracteosum*, This sturdy shrub is 2 m or more in height ... The fruit .. has one seed inside, which produces violent hiccoughs. Hence it is known as the 'Hiccup Nut'. **1977** E. PALMER *Field Guide to Trees* 235 *Combretum bracteosum*, Hiccough Nut. **1983** K.C. PALGRAVE *Trees of Sn Afr.* 664 The source of the common name, hiccup-nut, is somewhat obscure; while Medley Wood said that the edible fruits produced hiccups, C.A. Smith held that they were used in treating the complaint. **1987** F. VON BREITENBACH *Nat. List of Indigenous Trees* 144 *Combretum bracteosum* ... Hiccup Nut, Hiccup Creeper.

||**hierjy** /'hirjeɪ/ *n. slang.* [Afk., fr. the exclamation *hier, jy* 'here, you', prob. because this is seen as a phrase typical of uncouth people.] A term of contempt for an uncouth person; a person scarcely worth mentioning. Also *attrib.*

[**1966** VAN HEYNINGEN & BERTHOUD *Uys Krige* 140 His characters use a great variety of words and images .. ; .. such contemptuous ones as 'twee hierjy's' (two here, you's) for two nonentities.] **1975** J. BUTLER *Informant, Grahamstown* Is she still having an affair with that terrible bloke who wore padded shoulders? — a real hierjy! **1993** S. DIKENI in *Bua* Dec. 32 The occasion was not a hierjy gedoente nie, it was some important whatchacallit in the Grahamstown Festival, ek whieties jou.

High Dutch *n. phr. Hist.* [tr. Du. *Hooghollands*, *hoog* high + *Hollands* Dutch (as contrasted to the altered forms of the language which developed in Netherlands dialects, and in South Africa).] The Dutch language in its standard form; cf. NEDERLANDS. Also *attrib.*

1880 *Cape Monthly Mag.* III. 38, I attempted to shew that so far from being an improvement upon High Dutch and a richer language than the latter, .. it [*sc.* Cape Dutch] is not only infinitely poorer on account of its defective vocabulary, but .. is no more than a Dutch dialect, or .. Dutch *patois.* **1899** LOGEMAN & VAN OORDT *How to Speak Dutch* 33 The main points of difference between so-called 'High Dutch' and Cape Dutch phonetics and spelling may be enumerated. **1903** H. ELFFERS *Englishman's Guide to Cape Dutch* 7 For a long time to come the public press and the public platform will keep up a similarity to the high Dutch, which 200 years of use have diminished but little. **1908** [see AFRIKAANS *n.*]. **1911** H.H. FYFE *S. Afr. To-Day* 96 High Dutch .. is not the language of the Dutch people in South Africa ... The 'taal' .. is the common speech. **1934** M.E. MCKERRON *Hist. of Educ.* 130 (Swart), In 1916 Afrikaans was accepted, together with High Dutch, as the offical language of the Dutch Reformed Church. **1936** HAARHOFF & VAN DEN HEEVER *Achievement of Afrikaans* 13 While we tried to write in High Dutch our thoughts were cast in rigid moulds; .. and the result was often secondhand rhetoric. **1946** T. MACDONALD *Ouma Smuts* 13 They wrote English and Nederlands (High Dutch) ... The language of the home .. was Afrikaans, the language of their own soil, with its roots in Dutch, German, French and even English. **1953** [see UPSADDLE sense 2]. **1958** L. VAN DER POST *Lost World of Kalahari* 60 In High Dutch I wrote: 'I have decided to-day.' **1966** J. FARRANT *Mashonaland Martyr* 117 Bernard [Miseki] was a most remarkable man ... He spoke English and High Dutch fluently, Portuguese and several native languages well, and had also a considerable knowledge of French, Latin and Greek. **1979** A. GORDON-BROWN *Settlers' Press* 11 This little publication is famous for Meurant's articles in early Afrikaans, which he included for the benefit of farmers on the frontier who were losing touch with the High Dutch language. **1984** [see OOMPIE sense 1].

highveld /'haɪfelt, -fɛlt/ *n.* Also with initial capital, and (formerly) **high veldt**. [Part. tr. Afk. *hoëveld*, fr. S. Afr. Du. *hoogeveld(t)*, see HOOGE VELD.] **a.** The inland plateau of southern Africa, lying mostly between 1 200m and 1 800m above sea-level; formerly called HOOGE VELD. See also LOWVELD, MIDDLEVELD. **b.** The grasslands of this region. **c.** Johannesburg and the area around it (the commercial and industrial centre of the region). Also *attrib.*

The highveld is one of the major physiographic regions of southern Africa. The South African highveld extends over the Gauteng Province, and includes parts of the Eastern Transvaal, the northern Orange Free State, the Northern Cape, and parts of the North-West Province; the boundaries of the region, based on vegetation, altitude, and prominent physical features, are not clearly defined.

1877 F. JEPPE *Tvl Bk Almanac & Dir.* (1976) 31 In the Southern Districts, and along the highveldt, the habit exists of burning off the grass during the dry winter season, in order to improve the pasturage. **1878** A. AYLWARD *Tvl of Today* 44 The farmers tracked out to what is known as the Highveld — the great, bare, but healthy and excellent pasturelands forming the plateau of the Transvaal proper. **1879** [see PLAAS sense 1 a]. **1882** C. DU VAL *With Show through Sn Afr.* I. 259 The fresh breeze of the rolling 'high Veld'. **1884** 'E.V.C.' *Promised Land* 14 Our trek was uninteresting enough until we reached the high veldt. **1898** G. NICHOLSON *50 Yrs* 161 The pasturage in the low-lying encircling bush veldt is generally of sweeter and better quality than that of the 'high veldt'. **1900** B. MITFORD *Aletta* 104 The sun flamed down from a blue and cloudless vault, but without much power, for it was about midwinter, and the atmosphere of the high veldt was clear and exhilarating. **1903** E.F. KNIGHT *S. Afr. after War* 286 We were still in the low veldt, but throughout this trek we ever saw ahead of us the dark, well-defined ridge that forms the edge of the healthier, cooler, but less fertile and drier high veldt, 1,000 feet above us. **1905** J.W. GREGORY in *Rep. Brit. Assoc.* 399 The old rocks that form the foundation of the present high veldt of Rhodesia. **1910** A.B. LAMONT *Rural Reader* 4 The High Veld stretches from the main watershed towards Griqualand West and into the Orange River Colony. **1919** M.C. BRUCE *Golden Vessel* 69 The bitterly cold evenings, which so often distinguish especially the High Veld winter. **1926** M. NATHAN *S. Afr. from Within* 209 In the Free State there is scattered bush, but, on the whole, the High Veld is grass country, with a monotonous landscape, except near Potchefstroom and on the Witwatersrand, where it is diversified by ranges of low hills. **1936** H.C. BOSMAN *Mafeking Rd* (1969) 7, I worked it all out once, when I had a pencil. That was on the Highveld, though. But from where we are now, in the Lowveld, the stars are further away. You can see that they look smaller, too. **1940** J. BUCHAN *Memory* 117 On the highveld you have grey-green plains, which carry the eye to an immense distance. **1955** A. DELIUS *Young Trav.* 54 Beyond the trees the Transvaal highveld rolled into the distance, covered, where the land wasn't ploughed, with the withering long grass. **1963** S. CLOETE *Rags of Glory* 283 In the Transvaal it would be cold now, rainless, clear, with occasional bitter winds sweeping across the high veld from the south. **1977** FUGARD & DEVENISH *Guest* 11 Highveld winter landscape. Wide and empty. **1979** W. EBERSOHN *Lonely Place* 43 Winter nights on the highveld are cold in a way that people who live in damp climates never experience. **1984** *Sunday Times* 23 Sept. (Lifestyle) 6 It was one of those unmatchable Highveld winter days with an unbroken blue sky. **1985** W. BOTHA in *Fair Lady* 20 Feb. 89 The Transvaal Highveld houses one of the most competitive, achievement-motivated societies in the world. **1988** N. RICHARDS in *Ibid.* Mar. 96 (*caption*) Divided neatly into four strips — the highveld, middleveld, lowveld and Lubombo range — the scenery in Swaziland appears to do something different around every corner. **1990** E. KOCH in *Weekly Mail* 27 Apr. 9 The air over the Highveld .. contains some of the world's highest concentrations of soot, noxious gases and acid rain ingredients. **1990** *Weekly Mail* 21 Dec. (Suppl.) 31 The Gereformeerde Blues Band .. gave the highveld alternative contingent something to buzz about. **1993** *Sunday Nation* 8 Aug. 7 Farmworkers on the Highveld.

Hence **highvelder** /'haɪfeldə/ *n.*, an inhabitant of the highveld.

1977 A. CRUICKSHANK in *The 1820* Vol.50 No.12, 19 Wine festivals and wine auctions are becoming frequent events ... The lucky people in the Cape are able to enjoy these occasions far more often than the Highvelders. **1988** LAMPERT & FOURIE in *You* 21 Jan. 102 Freeloading Highvelders are bankrupting their coastal cousins ... The holidays are over and happy Highvelders are bursting with seaside-induced health and vitality. Meanwhile the relatives with whom they stayed are talking to the bank about a personal loan. **1990** H.P. TOFFOLI in *Style* Nov. 56 Nine out of ten highvelders believe that Durban is a shoppers' absolute desert, darling.

highwater *n.* [Special use of general Eng. *highwater* high tide, see quot. 1949.] In full ***highwater fish***: on the east coast, a name for the GALJOEN (sense 1), *Coracinus capensis.* Also *attrib.*

1930 C.L. BIDEN *Sea-Angling Fishes* 208 General local name: Walvis-Natal — Galjoen. Additional names: East London — High water fish; Blackfish; i-Damba. **1949** J.L.B. SMITH *Sea Fishes* 248 Comes close inshore at high tide, hence the name 'Highwater'. A powerful swimmer, able to turn in a breaking wave. **1957** S. SCHOEMAN *Strike!* 24 From Walvis Bay to Port Elizabeth, the local name for galjoen is universally 'galjoen', but from East London to Durban it is known as 'highwater fish' or 'Damba'. **1971** [see DAMBA]. **1972** *Daily Dispatch* 20 June 17, I read an article recently on the confusion that exists over the popular names of our common fish. The galjoen, for example, is known as a high-water or a damba. **1979** [see BLACK BREAM].

||**hili** /'hi(:)li/ *n.* Also **uhili**, and with initial capital. Pl. unchanged. [Xhosa *uhili.*] Esp. among Xhosa-speakers: TOKOLOSHE sense 1.

1904 D. KIDD *Essential Kafir* 127 There is a wicked little dwarf called Tickoloshe or Hili. **1931** [see TOKOLOSHE sense 1]. **1933** A. WERNER *Myths & Legends* 289 Tikoloshe, or Hili, the water-sprite, who comes out to make unlawful love to women. **1950** A.W. BURTON *Sparks from Border Anvil* 177 The dwarfish river monster 'u-Tikoloshe' or 'hili,' half man and half baboon. **1974** *E. Prov. Herald* 23 Feb. 12 According to general belief, tokoloshe or uhili is formed after the pattern of a human being, is short and thickly covered with hair. [**1979** P. MILLER *Myths & Legends* 102 The ubiquitous *tokoloshe*, the water sprite, is probably the best known character in Xhosa folklore. They also call him *hili.*]

Hindoo /'hɪndu:/ *n.* and *adj. Obs.* exc. *hist.* [Transf. senses of general Eng. *Hindu* (formerly *Hindoo*) (one) from Hindustan (northern India), (one) of the Hindu faith, fr. Urdu *hindu* one who professes Hinduism.]

A. *n.* INDIAN *n.* sense 1.

1830 *Cape of G.H. Lit. Gaz.* 15 Sept. 43 As you seem surprised at finding any of the followers of Brahma in Africa, I must explain to you that *The Hindoos* is a sobriquet applied by the local residents to all visitors from India, – whether they be Koeehies from Calcutta, Mulls from Madras, or Ducks from Bombay. **1837** 'N. POLSON' *Subaltern's Sick Leave* 81 Should the Hindoo yearn for a little quiet 'gup', .. directly opposite the Commercial Hall stands invitingly open .. the shop of Mrs. Saunders the confectioner. *Ibid.* 83 '*Hindoo*' though I am, and in that title delight .. I shall never descend to libelling the beauties of the Cape. **1913** C. PETTMAN *Africanderisms* 211 *Hindoos*, A term applied in the earlier days of the Colony as a British possession to such Europeans as came from India to the Cape either to recruit their health or to take up their residence. **1926** P.W. LAIDLER *Tavern of Ocean* 172 Anglo-Indians .. were .. always known to Kapenaars as 'Hindoos'. **1957** L.G. GREEN *Beyond City Lights* 207 The colony of retired English people it [*sc.* the Cape] has attracted from India .. were nicknamed 'Hindoos'. **1972** [see INDIAN *n.* sense 1].

B. *adj.* INDIAN *adj.* sense 1.

1837 'N. POLSON' *Subaltern's Sick Leave* 78 Every Cape *spinster* (to use the elegant Indian term) is looking out for a Hindoo husband!

hippo /ˈhɪpəʊ/ *n.* Also with initial capital. [Special sense of colloq. Eng. *hippo* hippopotamus; one of a series of animal names used for such vehicles, perh. alluding to its shape or size.] An armoured vehicle used by the police as a personnel-carrier. Also *attrib.* See also BUFFEL sense 2, MARY DECKER sense a, ZOLA BUDD sense a.

1976 *Drum* July 28 Rocks were thrown. Shots were fired. And the anti-terrorist squad came onto the scene in their hippos. **1976** *E. Prov. Herald* 2 Aug. 2 Some pupils associated the 'hippo' trucks and camouflage uniforms with shootings and these reminded them of their dead colleagues. *Ibid.* 5 Aug. 1 Police .. swarmed into Soweto in vehicles ranging from conventional vans to 'Hippo' personnel carriers. **1977** J. HOFFMAN in *Quarry '77* 55 Pictures from the air showed students (marchers) moving around obstacles (police, hippos or buildings), regrouping and persisting in their flow to distant Johannesburg. **1982** *Jane's Armour & Artillery 1982–3* 316 South Africa has a large number of locally built 6x4, 4x4 and 4x2 APCs used primarily for internal security operations. These have various names such as Hippo and Rhino. **1984** D. PINNOCK *Brotherhoods* 81 The first urban units were formed as Riot Squads early in 1976 and soon forced their way to public attention as the men in camouflage and Hippo gun-wagons at the heart of the Soweto upheavals in June that year. **1985** S. TRENTBRIDGE-SMITH in *Frontline* Dec. 11 Every time some poor little black boy stays home from school PW sends in five casspirs, six hippos and three helicopters to smoke the little beggar out. **1988** K. BARRIS *Small Change* 78 There was a Hippo pulled off the road – a high, armoured, mine-proof vehicle. **1991** *Weekly Mail* 24 May 8 Witnesses say they saw police hippos in the area, either just before the shooting began or just afterwards.

hissing tree *n. phr.* [See quot. 1966.] MOBOLA sense a.

1917 [see MOBOLA]. **1966** C.A. SMITH *Common Names* 248 *Hissing tree, Parinari curatellifolia* s.sp. *mobola* ... The vernacular name is probably derived from the rustling noise produced in the tree by the wind. **1972** [see MOBOLA].

‖**hlala kahle** /ˌɬala ˈɡaːɬe/ *int. phr.* Also **hlala gahle**. [Zulu, *hlala* live, stay, remain, stop + *kahle*, see GASHLE.] SALA KAHLE.

1898 B. MITFORD *Induna's Wife* 298, I am old now, and my time is at hand for a longer sleep than that which now awaits me underneath your waggon. *Nkose! Hlala gahle!* **1907** J.P. FITZPATRICK *Jock of Bushveld* (1909) 404 When it was all over Jim recovered rapidly, and at parting time there was the broadest of grins and a stentorian shout of 'Hlala Kahle! Inkos!' [**1949** J. MOCKFORD *Golden Land* 267 As the Mother City and the mountains and the clouds, and all South Africa, grow misty before my eyes, I first murmur 'Hlala kahle!' which is for Zulu [*sic*] 'Rest gently!' .. and then 'Tot siens!' which is Afrikaans for 'see you again!'] **1961** T.V. BULPIN *White Whirlwind* 330 As they rode away, the chiefs called after them the customary *Hamba Kahle!* or 'Travel contentedly.' They replied *Hlala Kahle* – 'Remain contentedly', and the first peace indaba was over. **1964** G. CAMPBELL *Old Dusty* 34 'Inkosi, I thank you, but you have made a mistake. This is red money. I only want to buy snuff. This will buy blankets. It is for me? Inkosi, I thank you. You are indeed generous. Hlala kahle, Inkosi.' 'Hamba kahle, Mgwaza, son of Magoila,' and he was gone.

hlonipha /ɬɔˈniːpa, ˈhlɒnɪpə/ *n.* and *adj.* Also **hlonipa**, and (as noun) **ukuhlonipa**. [fr. *hlonipha* (see HLONIPHA v.), or fr. Xhosa *intlonipho*, Zulu *inhlonipho* 'respect', 'reverence', a word substituted for another in terms of hlonipha custom.]

A. *n.* A system of ritual avoidance observed as a mark of respect esp. by Xhosa and Zulu wives towards their male relatives by marriage; a code of manners, observed esp. in the avoidance of names and similar-sounding words.

Youths undergoing circumcision rites also observe this custom.

1850 J.W. APPLEYARD *Kafir Lang.* 70 The Kaffir *women* have many words peculiar to themselves. This arises from a national custom, called *ukuhlonipa.* **1857** J. SHOOTER *Kafirs of Natal* 221 Individuals affected by the custom of *uku-hlonipa*, may not pronounce each other's *i-gama* [proper name]. **1860** W. SHAW *Story of my Mission* 425 The custom called hlonipa requires that certain relatives by marriage shall never look on each other's face, .. more especially a daughter-in-law and all her husband's male relations ... She is not allowed to pronounce their names, even mentally; and, whenever the emphatic syllable of either of their names occurs in any other word, she must avoid it, by either substituting an entirely new word, or at least another syllable, in its place. This custom has given rise to an almost distinct language among the women. **1875** D. LESLIE *Among Zulus* 102 A wife must never speak to her husband's male relations, but must hide, or *appear* to do so, whenever she sees them. The husband must not speak to, look at, or eat with his mother-in-law. And neither husband nor wife must utter their relations' names. This is called 'Hlonipa'. **1937** B.H. DICKE *Bush Speaks* 167 Hlonipa is the name for a tabu which forbids females to use certain words, in particular the names of their husbands and chiefs. **1948** E. HELLMANN *Rooiyard* 86 The avoidance of the name of the parent-in-law of the opposite sex seems to be the whole extent of the urban Native's observance of *hlonipa.* **1967** O. WALKER *Hippo Poacher* 6 The dignity is threadbare, the *hlonipa*, or code of manners, rudely upset by the contacts of the migrant young men selling their labour in the towns. **1967** J.A. BROSTER *Red Blanket Valley* 160 When he spoke again his voice had changed to a solemn semi-ritual tone, and the words were hlonipa, the court language reserved for God and all that is revered or feared. **1976** WEST & MORRIS *Abantu* 40 She is expected to behave respectfully to her husband's kin and has to practise hlonipa, the avoidance of senior relatives in front of whom she has to keep her eyes lowered and whose names she has to refrain from using. **1981** B. MFENYANA in M. Mutloatse *Reconstruction* 300 Dialect and slanguage probes are fun: as long as the scholar respects people's desire for a little privacy, secrecy, hlonipha.

B. *adj.*

1. *obs.* (Predicative use.) Taboo; forbidden as a mark of respect.

1895 H. RIDER HAGGARD *Nada* 181 'Mindest thou of the last words of the Great Elephant, who is dead?' This he said meaning Chaka his brother, only he did not name him, for now the name of Chaka was hlonipa in the land, as is the custom with the names of dead kings ... It was not lawful that it should pass the lips.

2. *attrib.* Of or pertaining to the hlonipha tradition.

1902 G.M. THEAL *Beginning of S. Afr. Hist.* 31 First there was the hlonipa custom, by which women were obliged constantly to invent new words, so that each dialect underwent gradual dissimilar changes. **1937** B.H. DICKE *Bush Speaks* 167 Hlonipa Names. **1948** E. HELLMANN *Rooiyard* 86 The *hlonipa* laws seem to be observed by the majority of urban Natives in so far as a woman will not use her father-in-law's name, and a man will avoid the name of his mother-in-law. **1955** E.A. RITTER *Shaka Zulu* 370 Both sexes and all ages must observe the *hlonipa* custom in the case of the chief of the clan. **1978** A. ELLIOTT *Sons of Zulu* 172 Apart from a display of basic humility, she pays respect in specific ways according to *hlonipha* requirements ... She refrains from using many everyday Zulu words in her conversation and instead uses a special vocabulary of substitute words in their place.

hlonipha /ɬɔˈniːpa, ˈɬɒnɪpə/ *v.* Also **hlonipa**. [A verb common to the Nguni languages, meaning 'pay respect to', 'observe a system of ritual avoidance in speech'.]

a. *trans.* To pay (someone or something) respect; to avoid (a sound, word, or name which is regarded as taboo) in order to show respect.

1870 H. CALLAWAY *Religious System of Amazulu* (1884) 316 The women must respect (*hlonipa*) her husband's name: she does not call him by name, but as here, when addressing him or speaking of him, says, 'Father of so-and-so,' mentioning one of his children by name. *Ibid.* 426 We abstain from calling the tree umdhleve: for we do not take its name in vain, for it is an awful tree. [*Note*] That is, its name is hlonipad. It is 'tabu', and must not be called by name. **1875** D. LESLIE *Among Zulus* 173 At the King's kraal it is sometimes difficult to understand his wives, as they *Hlonipa* even the very sound of the name of the King's fathers. **1925** D. KIDD *Essential Kafir* 237 A woman may not sit in the same hut with the people whom she has to hlonipa, and she must be specially careful not to uncover in their presence any part of her body which is usually covered up. **1959** L. LONGMORE *Dispossessed* 27 They do not *hlonipha* (pay respect to) their mothers-in-law, and in many cases they even assault them. **1967** J.A. BROSTER *Red Blanket Valley* 70 By this strange custom a daughter in law is required to Hlonipha (reverence) her father in law and all her husband's adult male relatives. She is not allowed to pronounce their names, and when the emphatic syllable of either of their names occurs in any other word she must avoid it by substituting an entirely new word or another syllable in its place. **1970** J.P. VAN S. BRUWER in *Std Encycl. of Sn Afr.* II. 96 A wife must hlonipha her in-laws, in other words she must act humbly and respectfully toward them and shun them.

b. *intrans.* To practise the system of ritual avoidance as observed esp. by Xhosa and Zulu wives as a mark of respect towards their male relatives by marriage.

1934 P.R. KIRBY *Musical Instruments of Native Races* (1965) 266 Immediately after the completion of the ceremony, the people *hlonipha*, or 'abstain from the use of certain words'. Accordingly for *unyaga* (year) they say *umKhosi weKosi* (feast of the chief).

Hlubi /ˈɬuːbi/ *n.* Pl. **-s**, **Amahlubi**, or unchanged. [Named for an early leader; see quot. 1912.] A member of a people of the Nguni group, living in northern KwaZulu-Natal. Also *attrib.*

Some of the Hlubi migrated southwards during the MFECANE, and became part of the MFENGU group.

1902 [see MBO sense 2 a]. **1912** AYLIFF & WHITESIDE *Hist. of Abambo* 2 The whole tribe numbered about 250,000 ... It was divided into clans, each with a distinctive name. The largest were the Amahlubi (people who tear off), whose chief was Bungane, and they lived in the upper portion of the Buffalo River Valley. **1930** S.T. PLAATJE *Mhudi* (1975) 95 You understand the language of the Basuto, and of the Qoranna and the Hlubis, and the Boers down in Graaff Reinet, don't you, Rantsau? **1936** *Cambridge Hist. of Brit. Empire* VIII. 454 The Hlubi clan had been driven by the Zulus into Natal. There, under their great chief, Langalibalele ('the sun is shining'), they had been allowed to settle on the north-west frontier, bordering Basutoland. **1940** P.R. Kirby *Diary of Dr Andrew Smith* II. 169 Mpangazita, chief of the Hlubi, another Nguni tribe. **1954** W.D. Hammond-Tooke in A.M. Duggan-Cronin *Bantu Tribes* III. v. 17 The name Hlubi appears to be of comparatively recent origin. Previously the tribe was known as the imiHuhu .. even this was not the original name. *Ibid.* 19 The two sections united under the name Hlubi, that of Dlomo's maternal grandfather. In the second decade of the nineteenth century the Hlubi were probably one of the most powerful tribes in Natal. **1965** M. Hansen in *Sunday Chronicle* 7 Feb. The Hlubis, a small tribe of Basutos in Northern Zululand .. were settled in the Nqutu area in 1870 after the Zulu War. **1979** *Sunday Tribune* 3 June 30 The short-lived reign of Langalibalele II, the self-styled king of the AmaHlubi tribe in the Estcourt district, is over. **1980** Lye & Murray *Transformations* 31 The first major refugee from Shaka's fury was the Hlubi chiefdom, possibly the largest among the Northern Nguni. **1986** P. Maylam *Hist. of Afr. People* 87 The first half of the nineteenth century had been a traumatic period for the Hlubi. They had suffered severe disruption during the *difaqane*. **1993** C. Stagg in *Sunday Times* 10 Apr. 4 Among the claims under consideration by Acla is that of the Amahlubi people, who occupied 90 000ha of land in Natal.

HMSAS see SAS.

HNP /eɪtʃ en 'piː, hɑː en 'pɪə/ *n.*[1] *hist.* [Afk., abbrev. formed on *Herenigde Nasionale Party*, 'Reunited National Party'.] *Herenigde (Nationalist) Party*, see HERENIGDE. Also *attrib.*

1943 *Star* 3 Aug. 4 The much publicised struggle of the H.N.P. is either a holy war or an unholy fraud. **1948** *George & Knysna Herald* 21 May 1 The two candidates are Prof. M.C. Botha, United Party, and Mr. P.W. Botha, H.N.P. **1949** *Blueprint for Blackout* (Educ. League) (*pamphlet*) 28 On the war issue in 1939 General Hertzog and his followers disagreed with General Smuts, and reunited with Dr. Malan; the party became the Reunited Nationalist Party (H.N.P.) ... *Dr. Malan*: H.N.P. leader, and Prime Minister of the Union of South Africa. **1958** G. Carter *Politics of Inequality* 33 The pressure for unity was sufficient to result in an agreement between the two parliamentary parties in January 1940, and even into efforts to recast their organisation into a single body called *Die Herenigde Nasionale of Volksparty* (the Reunited National Party) and commonly known as the H.N.P. *Ibid.* 35 The election was equally significant for the H.N.P. In the first place, it decisively annihilated its rivals: the H.N.P. won 43 seats in place of its former 40: neither the Afrikaner Party nor the members of the New Order won a single seat. **1977** [see HERTZOGITE *n.* sense 1]. **1989** *Reader's Digest Illust. Hist.* 361 The flame of Afrikaner nationalism .. finally triumphed on 28 May 1948 when the *Reunified National Pary* (HNP; NP in 1951) took power.

HNP /eɪtʃ en 'piː, hɑː en 'pɪə/ *n.*[2] Also **H.N.P.** [Afk., abbrev. formed on *Herstigte Nasionale Party* 'Reconstituted National Party'.] A far right-wing breakaway from the National Party, formed in 1969. See also HERSTIGTE. Also *attrib.*

1969 *Rand Daily Mail* 27 Oct. 1 The foundation congress of Dr Albert Hertzog's Herstigte Nasionale Party (H.N.P.) in Pretoria was of more than sufficient calibre to warn the Prime Minister .. that the new group constitutes a grave danger to the National Party. **1969** [see HERTZOGITE *n.* sense 2]. **1970** *Argus* 30 Jan. 1 The main topic of discussion was the H.N.P. **1976** [see DONNER *v.* sense 2]. **1982** *Annual Register: Rec. of World Events 1981* 262 His ruling National Party did not lose any seats to the extreme right-wing HNP .. but the NP did lose a surprising number of *votes* to HNP candidates. **1987** [see 'K. de Boer' quot. at OOM sense 3]. **1989** *E. Prov. Herald* 1 June 16 So the dodo lives. Just when you thought the country was finally safe from the HNP up it pops making election noises in the Eastern Cape ... Dead though the HNP may be, it refuses to stay buried. **1989** *Reader's Digest Illust. Hist.* 484 The ultra right-wing *Herstigte* (Reconstituted) *Nasionale Party* (HNP) of Jaap Marais .. failed to gain a single seat.

ho var. HOT.

hock see HOK.

HoD *n.* Also **HOD**. Written abbrev. of *House of Delegates*, see HOUSE sense 2. Also *attrib.*

1989 *Progress* Mar. 8 HoD campaign ... The campaign for a stronger liberal opposition presence in the House of Delegates is in full swing. **1989** F. Meer in *Daily Dispatch* 21 Apr. 4, I believe the HoD to be an irrelevant organisation. Its entire five-year period of existence has been characterised by mud-slinging, infused with the culture of corruption, co-option, coercion and despotism. **1990** *Stanger Mail* 19 Jan. 3 HOD spokesman, Mr Ramkishan M— has .. stated that all departmental hearings cannot be held in public. **1994** R.W. Johnson in *London Review of Books* (U.K.) 6 Jan. 9 The HoD (commonly known as the House of Dogs) is a chamber in which corruption has been so general and the tendency of MPs to switch parties so frequent .. that its sole merit .. lies in the way it has brought to the wider nation an entertainment hitherto enjoyed by Natalians alone.

Hodmadod *n. obs.* Also **Hodmandod**, **Hodmontot**. [Perh. ad. HOTTENTOT (or the source of that word); or rel. to obs. Eng. *hodmandod* a deformed person; or imitative of an unknown Khoikhoi word or phrase.] KHOIKHOI sense 1.

1697 W. Dampier *New Voy. round World* I. (1729) 536 The Natural Inhabitants of the Cape are the *Hodmadods*, as they are commonly called, which is a corruption of the word *Hottantot*; for this is the Name by which they all call to one another .. as if every one of them had this for his Name. **1697** *Ibid.* (1699) 464 The Inhabitants of this Country [New Holland] are the miserablest People in the World. The Hodmadods of Monomatapa, though a nasty People, yet for Wealth are Gentlemen to these. [**1699** W.A. Cowley in R. Raven-Hart *Cape G.H. 1652–1702* (1971) II. 309 We walked .. to the Village inhabited by the Hodmandods, so called by the Hollanders, to view their Nasty Bodies ... The Hodmandods are born White, but make themselves Black with Sut, and besmear their Bodies all over.] **1710** E. Ward *Vulgus Britannicus* III. 40 So Hodmontots, because their Feasts Chiefly consist of Gutts of Beasts. **1729** W. Dampier *New Voy. round World* (7th ed.) 34 The Hodmandods .. make themselves Black with Sut.

hoek *n.*[1] var. HOK.

hoek /hʊk, huk/ *n.*[2] Also **hook**, **huik**. [Afk., angle, corner, hook, glen.]

1. A bend in a river, an angular part of a mountain, a coastal inlet, or any topographical feature in which a bend or angle is prominent: used as an element in place names, as *Fish Hoek, Franschhoek, Gannahoek*.

1731 G. Medley tr. *P. Kolb's Present State of Cape of G.H.* II. 28 The greatest Plenty of all is found at a Place, call'd the Fish-*Huik*, just under the Rock, call'd *Hang-Lips*. **1795** C.R. Hopson tr. *C.P. Thunberg's Trav.* I. 13 *Hoek*, added to the end of certain words, such as Mostertshoek, denotes a projecting angle, or point of a mountain. **1839** J. Collett Diary II. 6 Feb., *Tracked* to day from Kline fontien to Lombards hook. **1852** M.B. Hudson *S. Afr. Frontier Life* 246 The Keiskamma Hoek is the basin of the Keiskamma River at its source. **1989** P.E. Raper *Dict. of Sn Afr. Place Names* 213 *Houhoek Pass*, Explained as *hout hoek* or 'wood corner', *hou hoek* or 'hold corner'.

2. *obsolescent.* A valley bounded on three sides by hills or mountains; a glen.

1827 G. Thompson *Trav.* I. 59, I got upon the ridge which divides this *hoek* from another winding glen called Gannahoek. **1834** T.H. Bowker Journal. 26 Dec., The church to be a place of rendezvous for the boors in the hook. **1838** J. Collett Diary. I. 30 Apr., Tracked to day with my Oxen out of the hook to Kline Fontien. **1852** M.B. Hudson *S. Afr. Frontier Life* 21 Somerset Town .. is built in a vale, Or hoek of the mountain so hidden from sight. **1855** G. Brown *Personal Adventure* 59 A hoek, in South Africa, is not exactly what you would know by a vale at home; it is rather a cleft in a mountain, or between a range of mountains. **1900** B. Mitford *Aletta* 99 We might take guns and go down to the *hoek*. It's swarming with duiker and blesbok. **1913** C. Pettman *Africanderisms* 213 *Hoek*, A narrow glen or corner formed by the junction of hills or mountains, the entrance to it being also the exit. **1937** C.R. Prance *Tante Rebella's Saga* 75 His sinfulness cost almost every man in the hoek the price of a new hat. **1949** L.G. Green *In Land of Afternoon* 21 There is the hoek which is easy to enter but hard to leave save by the way you came.

hoekai var. HOKAAI.

‖**hoekie** /'hʊki, 'huki/ *n.* [Afk., *hoek* corner + dim. suffix -IE.] A corner, a nook. Also *fig.*

1970 J.L. Cousins *Informant, Vryburg* Hoekie. Corner. You'll find it in the hoekie! **1974** *Sunday Times* 15 Dec. (Mag. Sect.) 8 The more personal corners of the house remain much as they were in Royal Navy days, when the C-in-C, while using the house as a whole, had what Flam describes as 'our private hoekies'. **1988** B. Kgantsi in *Frontline* Apr.-May 31 All that Blacks are asking for is a small hoekie in the sun. **1989** D. Bristow in *Weekly Mail* 21 Apr. 29 If you are lucky, a funeral march will wake you up on Sunday morning, all oompah and pentecostal wailing — a touch of New Orleans in this strange, forgotten *hoekie*.

‖**hoender** /'hunə(r)/ *n.* [Afk., fr. Du. *hoenders* (pl. of *hoen* fowl).]

1. 'A domestic fowl', in the Special Comb. **hoenderpoot** /-puət/ *slang*, also **hoenderpoort**, [Afk., *poot* foot; so called because the leaf supposedly resembles the foot of a chicken], DAGGA *n.*[2] sense 1; **hoenderspoor** /-spuə(r)/ [Du., *spoor* track, trail; so called because parts of the plant resemble a chicken's footprint], the tree *Scolopia zeyheri* of the Flacourtiaceae; **hoenderspoor-karee**, see KAREE *n.*[2] sense 2.

1952 *Drum* Sep. 12 Scientifically known as Indian hemp, dagga .. is known in the slang as .. 'zol' .. 'bangi' .. '**hoenderpoort**' .. 'boom'. **1963** L.F. Freed *Crime in S. Afr.* 207 Dagga .. was known to them by a variety of names, such as .. 'bambalacha', 'hoenderpoot', .. 'pot', or just plain 'reefer'. **1843** J.C. Chase *Cape of G.H.* 160 **Hoenderspoor**, .. General Height without branches .. 12 to 14 ft.

2.a. The flesh of a domestic fowl: chicken.

1890 [see sense b below]. **1972** L.G. Green *When Journey's Over* 134 Hoender .. roasted in a pot until it falls apart and comes out devoid of flavour. **1985** J. Cloete in *S.-Easter* Oct.-Nov. 17 When everybody else now eats Kentucky Fried, I stick to *hoender*, thank you. **1990** *Style* June 79 Darryl started making cracks about eating *hoender* which Caroline didn't find funny.

b. *comb.* **hoenderkerrie** /-ˌkeri/ [Afk., *kerrie* curry], chicken curry; **hoenderpastei** /-pas'teɪ/ [Afk., *pastei* pie], chicken pie.

1913 D. Fairbridge *Piet of Italy* 292 There is **hoenderkerrie** and rice for dinner, and pumpkin fritters with cinnamon to follow. **1890** A.G. Hewitt *Cape Cookery* 15 Chicken Pie. **Hoender Pastei**. Make a nice puff-paste, line the pastei pan and put in the stewed fowl. **1957** L.G. Green *Beyond City Lights* 9 The *hoenderpastei* .. is the dish which is the special pride of the old Cape districts, a chicken pie with a difference .. the crushed coriander seeds and wine .. the lean pork and herbs, the blade of mace .. the puff pastry. **1972** *E. Prov. Herald* 15 Nov. 12 Do you like roast beef and Yorkshire pudding? Or turkey and cranberry sauce? Or hoenderpastei and geelrys?

‖**hoer** /huːr/ *n. Derog.* and *offensive.* [Afk.] Not in polite use.

1. A whore, a 'tart'; also used as a term of abuse.

1963, 1976 [see sense 2]. **1990** G. Slovo *Ties of Blood* 308 Rosa backed away. In doing so she bumped into the table where the youth was seated. '*Hoer*' he said. He got up abruptly and took one step towards her. **1991** P. Slabolepszy Braait Laaities. 19 (*He chuckles and wiggles his hips and feels himself up, provocatively. She* *backs away, horrified.)* Moira: You calling me a slet? ... You calling me a bladdy hoer!?

2. *comb.* **hoerhouse**, a brothel; **hoermeid** /-meɪt/ [Afk., *meid* an insulting term for a black woman], a term of abuse, 'black whore'.

1963 A. FUGARD *Notebks* (1983) 85 Had a lot to say about Klipplaat, that tough, dusty hot-as-hell railway junction here in the Eastern Cape. 'Put a roof over it and a redlight outside and you got a **hoerhouse**' ... Standard greeting at Klipplaat: 'How's your wife and my children?' **1976** M. MELAMU in *New Classic* No.3, 3 Anyway, Georgina tells me she knows I'm running after some filthy **hoermeid**. This woman's language, *hayi!*

‖**hoërskool** /ˈhʊərskʊəl/ *n.* [Afk., *hoër* higher + *skool* school.] An Afrikaans-medium secondary school.

'Hoërskool' is almost invariably part of the names of these schools, e.g. *Hoërskool Malherbe, Hoërskool Transkei.*

1955 *Pietersburg Eng. Medium School Mag.* Nov. 27 The next match against the local Hoërskool was, unluckily, no anti-climax. **1970** *Daily Dispatch* 11 Dec. 6 Umtata's Hoërskool Transkei will be able to offer English higher to junior and senior certificate candidates next year ... This is the first time this Afrikaans medium school has been able to offer this to senior school students. **1979** M. MATSHOBA *Call Me Not a Man* 77 When the two older children had gone to the Hoërskool they had promised to write.

hoes druppels see DRUPPELS sense b i.

hoesit, -zet varr. HOWZIT.

Hoffmansdruppels /ˈhɒfmənzdrəpəlz, ˈhɔfmansdrœpəls/ *n.* Also **Hoffmannsdruppels**, **Hoffman's droppels**. [Afk., 'Hoffman's anodyne'; combining form of *Hoffman* name of a German physician *F. Hoffmann* (1660–1742) + *druppels* drops.] A mixture of ether, alcohol, and ethereal oil, used as a medicine for the treatment of heart complaints, nervous tension, and headaches. See also DRUPPELS.

1884 *B.G. Lennon & Co.'s Catal. 1884* 65 Hoffman's Droppels. **1919** *Dunell, Ebden & Co.'s Price List* Oct. 20 Hoffman's Droppels. **1943** I. FRACK *S. Afr. Doctor* 118 When a badly advised Government .. decided to put a tax on patent medicines, the imposition nearly resulted in its downfall. The millions of bottles of 'borsdruppels,' 'Hoffmans druppels,' pain elixirs, 'duivels drek,' 'levens-essens,' .. that are sold must really be staggering. **1958** E.H. BURROWS *Hist. of Medicine* 191 *Hoffmann's droppels,* (*Spiritus Aetheris Compositus* B.P.C.): used as an anti-spasmodic remedy, in convulsions and for headaches. **1972** N. SAPEIKA in *Std Encycl. of Sn Afr.* VII. 302 A list of .. traditional remedies .. includes .. Hoffmannsdruppels (spirit of ether). **1989** D. SMUTS *Folk Remedies* 51 Heart, Drink 1 teaspoon of Hoffmansdruppels in water 3 times a day. *Ibid.* 64 *Nerves,* Rooilaventel, yellow balsem vita, Hoffmansdruppels. **1991** [see *krampdruppels* (DRUPPELS sense b i)].

hofstaad var. HOOFSTAD *n.*[1]

hogayi var. HOKAAI.

Hoggenheimer /ˈhɒgən,haɪmə/ *n. Derog.* and *offensive.* [The name of a cartoon character created in 1915 by D.C. Boonzaaier, cartoonist for *Die Burger*, prob. fr. a 1902 stage character (see Std Encycl. of Sn Afr. quot. 1972).] An insulting name for a stereotypical Jewish figure personifying organized capitalism, esp. that of Johannesburg. Also *attrib.*

[**c1895** in G. Viney *Col. Houses* (1987) 142 I'll marry Hoggenheimer of Park Lane .. And ev'ry one that sees me will explain That I'm Mrs Hoggenheimer of Park Lane.] **1934** *Sunday Times* 25 Feb. (Swart), That the leopard cannot change its spots – which is equivalent to saying that Dr. Malan cannot abandon his racialism – is shown by his current references to Parasites, Hoggenheimers and fusion. **1941** *Forum* 20 Sept. 29 This time it was clear to everyone that the so-called capitalists and imperialists (the Hoggenheimers) had nothing to do with the troubles of Afrikanerdom. **1943** 'J. BURGER' *Black Man's Burden* 238 He is fanatical in his anti-semitism, and .. blames the Jews for both communism and capitalism. The name of 'Hoggenheimer', or 'Hoggie' for short, and the political cartoonists depict a fat Jew dictating to the Government. **1972** L. HERRMAN in *Std Encycl. of Sn Afr.* V. 559 Hoggenheimer symbolised foreign capitalist exploitation and the less admirable aspects of acquisitive imperialism. The character first appeared as 'Hoggenheimer of Park Lane' in the musical comedy *The girl from Kay's*, produced on 15 Nov. 1902 at the Apollo Theatre in London, running for 432 performances. **1972** *Sunday Times* 3 Sept. 2 This is the Transvaler's old standby. Whenever it is in need of a scapegoat, it takes Hoggenheimer out of the cupboard, dusts him off and dangles him like a bogyman in front of its readers. **1979** *Ibid.* 1 Apr. 15 It's a far cry from the bad old days of the 30s and 40s when, with the Afrikaner excluded from South Africa's entrepreneurial class, the Hoggenheimer image ruled supreme as the ultimate Nationalist bogyman. **1981** *Ibid.* 25 Oct. 29 In years past it was fashionable in National Party circles to condemn Mr Oppenheimer as the 'Mr Big' of opposition politics, the 'Hoggenheimer' detested by Afrikanerdom. **1985** *Financial Mail* 18 Jan. 35 Nor last week was it the Rand Lords or Big Business that spoke out. It was not those whom the Nats delight in calling the Hoggenheimers that told government it must get down to real political and economic reform.

hok /hɒk, hɔk/ *n.* Also **hoek**. Pl. **-s**, or **hok(k)e** /ˈhɔkə/. [Afk. (earlier S. Afr. Du.), enclosure for domesticated animals.] Freq. (esp. formerly) in Englished form **hock**.

1. An enclosure for domestic animals: a pen, sty, run, hutch, or kennel; HOKKIE sense 1. Often with distinguishing epithet, denoting the kind of bird or animal kept in the enclosure, as **calf -**, **fowl -**, **ostrich -**, **pigeon -**, **rabbit hok**, etc. Also *fig.*, a prison cell. See also *skuthok* (SKUT sense 2).

1835 T.H. BOWKER Journal. 18 Feb., Making Calf hoke. **1839** T. SHONE Diary. 23 Mar., This day I made a Hock for Beauty the Cow. **1861** T. SHONE Diary. 29 June, In the Morning he was building a calf Hock. **c1881** A. DOUGLASS *Ostrich Farming* 204 If kept too much in the hock – especially if it is small, and has been long in use – the calves get lousy. [**1894** E. GLANVILLE *Fair Colonist* 80 The cows were bellowing continuously for their calves, and, without staying to milk, he turned the latter from the hoek, or smaller kraal where they were penned, and let them suckle. *Ibid.* 188 In the rear was the usual cattle-kraal and calves'-hoek, open to the skies.] **1900** H. BLORE *Imp. Light Horseman* 304 The motherly cows, in spite of past experience that man's rules forbade such indulgence, bellowing to their calves within the narrow limits of the kalver-hok to come with them to pasture. **1911** J.F. PENTZ in *Farmer's Weekly* 11 Oct. 159 If there are tape worms in the calf, you will see them in the 'hok' the next morning. **1919** J.Y. GIBSON in *S. Afr. Jrnl of Science* July 4 The cattle-kraal was furnished with a separate compartment called the *kalver hok*, or calves' pen, from which they were called by name in turn. **1920** S. BLACK *Dorp* 219 He has seen with his own eyes photographs of Kitchener, Sir Edward Grey and Churchill tied fast in a fowl-hok in Germany, where they are prisoners. **1925** P. SMITH *Little Karoo* (1936) 212 Aantje was driving her hens into their hock for the night. **1935** —— *Platkop's Children* 29 We took him to .. the hens-hock an' the pig-stye. **1948** V.M. FITZROY *Cabbages & Cream* 23 We had buff birds in the duck-hock. *Ibid.* 37 We relinquished the idea of a Kitchen Garden as such, and R.F. fenced off the whole area to make two hocks each for the fowls and ducks. **1951** H.C. BOSMAN in L. Abrahams *Bekkersdal Marathon* (1971) 106 Just look about how careful you had to be where you put your feet down on Chris Welman's front stoep. Half the time you didn't know if it was a front stoep or a fowl hok. **1953** D. JACOBSON *Long Way from London* 9 My brother and I kept homing pigeons ... We had a hok at the bottom of the back yard. **1958** I. VAUGHAN *Diary* 47 It was a long church, when we came home Ellen said The vark has got out of its hok and is eating Masters potatos. **1964** M.G. McCOY *Informant, Port Elizabeth* Dad and Piet got the bunny hok finished. **1967** E.M. SLATTER *My Leaves Are Green* 120, I took a couple of fowls from the hok and pushed the money under the door. **1971** *Informant, Langkloof* There's a nice ostrich hok. **1971** V. KELLY *Informant, Grahamstown* He opened the pigeon hok door, and all the birds came out. **1972** S. ROBERTS in *Contrast 28* Vol.7 No.4, 8 The stench from the chicken hoks was awful. **1975** —— *Outside Life's Feast* 53 Chickens milled about gossiping and complaining in a tiny hok. **1980** A. FUGARD *Tsotsi* 119 After a whimpering, desperate moment of indecision, he dived into a deserted fowl hok where he closed his eyes and his ears. **1982** *Daily Dispatch* 11 Jan. 6 As for all those fancy rabbit hokke he is putting in – who ever heard of rabbit farming in this district, on that scale? **1988** W. ODENDAAL in Bunn & Taylor *From S. Afr.* 113 What about your fowls, Ouma, you keep them in a hok? **1989** J. HOBBS *Thoughts in Makeshift Mortuary* 304 Back yards filled up with old cars and lean-to shacks and fowl hoks in the make-do anarchy of places where too many people live. **1990** L. BEAKE *Tjojo* 65 First they did the hen-hok – and *that* hadn't been clean for a while. **1991** D. ZAKE in *South* 14 Nov. 5 The mere fact of being 'shut up in a hok like an animal' had a detrimental psychological effect on prisoners. **1993** J. THOMAS in *House & Leisure* Nov. 50 This is a world of chicken hokke and rotting Valiant Barracudas, duplicated wherever the outer skirt of a city begins to fray.

2. *fig.* A shanty or hovel; HOKKIE sense 3.

1930 N. STEVENSON *Farmers of Lekkerbat* 23 The roof was always broken and the tin walls had parted company. In winter when .. the Westhuizens indulged in free fights .. in order to keep warm, it appeared as if the *hok* .. might fall to bits and bury them from sight. **1980** *Cape Times* 12 Sept. 4 'When I started moving with the gang I left home. We lived in "hokke" (shanties),' he recalls. **1984** *Drum* Jan. 6 They had already left for another place, or they had gone to fetch reinforcements, but we trapped four of them in a 'hok' (shack) in the backyard.

hokaai /ˈhɔkaɪ/ *int.* Also **hoekai**, **hogayi**, **hokai**, **hook haai**, **wokhai**. [Afk. *hokaai* stop (perh. ad. S. Sotho *hok* stop, stand motionless).] 'Whoa', 'stop', originally a command to draught animals, but now freq. used as a command to a person to pause or desist. So **hokaai** *n.*, a cry of 'hokaai'.

1958 A. JACKSON *Trader on Veld* 57 It was not long before the loud 'hook haai! hook haai!' (the order for stopping the oxen), were heard. **1970** BEETON & DORNER in *Eng. Usage in Sn Afr.* Vol.1 No.2, 23 *Hokai*, .. 'whoa!, halt there!' chiefly used to bring draught-animals to a halt, but also used in the sense of 'wait a minute!' **1971** *Informant, Grahamstown* Hokai! Don't drive so fast. **1979** F. DIKE *First S. African* 36 Thembi: Get a job and get us out of this mess. Rooi: O.K. O.K., hogayi. **1983** *E. Prov. Herald* 26 Feb. 4 (*caption*) Hokaai! .. Wait for Fanie. **1985** *Cape Times* 30 Dec., If the government refused .. 'teachers, parents, workers, church leaders, university staff and students must all combine in a concerted effort to say wokhai (stop)'.

hokkie /ˈhɔki/ *n.* [Afk., *hok* (see HOK) + dim. suffix -IE.]

1. HOK sense 1. Also with distinguishing epithet, designating the kind of animal kept in the enclosure.

1960 J. COPE *Tame Ox* 145 Go out and clean the chicken-hokkie. **1973** *Ibid.* 22 Sept. 9 The two geese .. escaped from their *hokkie* early in January. **1983** J.A. BROWN *White Locusts* 189 Why don't you go down to the *hokkies* and learn the pigs to read? **1983** *Daily Dispatch* 2 May 8 (*caption*) She says a bird in your hokkie is worth ten in the bundu. **1990** P. CULLINAN in M. Leveson *Firetalk* 9 'If I find one of her pigs in the dry mill again .., I'll shoot it!' 'No, Boss Skokiaan. I'll make a nice hokkie and then they will stay in it.'

2. *fig.* and *transf.* A booth or nook; a small, restricted space, a compartment.

1963 K. MACKENZIE *Dragon to Kill* 119 Tony went in through the back, past Petrus, the pleasant, intelligent Coloured youth who was now doing Abel's work. Tony resented him sitting in Abel's little *hokkie.* **1971** C.W. EGLIN *Informant, Cape Town* The government aims to keep us all in our separate ethnic hokkies. **1973** *Cape Times* 5 Feb. 8 As a poet and a philosopher does Mr Adam Small really believe that we who have perforce to live in a separate '*hokkie*' cannot understand him or those who are placed in *his* '*hokkie*'? **1973** on Radio South Africa 22 Mar. (Take a Chance), Put him in one of those klein hokkies they've got there. **1980** J. SCOTT in *Cape Times* 22 May 9 He had allowed the SABC to persuade him to be televised in a *hokkie* in Cape Town while 'ghost voices' interrogated him from Johannesburg. **1987** S.A. BOTHA in *Frontline* Oct.-Nov. 10 The gomma-gomma travelled .. with its load of .. prisoners under the eye of a uniformed boy with an automatic weapon in his own steel hokkie in the corner.

3. *fig.* HOK sense 2.

1973 *Cape Times* 16 June 11 They'll come with bulldozers and knock down our hokkies, then we'll have to sleep in the street. **1985** *Argus* 29 Aug., Susan worked as a servant and lived in a 'hokkie' in the yard. It was so small that she couldn't lie down with her legs straight. **1990** *Weekly Mail* 30 Mar. 13 Can somebody explain .. to me .. what this advertiser in the *Cape Times* has in mind? *Windows* ... Ideal for African hokkie. R10 ea.

holbol /ˈhɔlbɔl/ *adj. Archit.* [Afk., *hol* hollow + *bol* rounded, convex.] Of a style of gable used in Cape Dutch architecture, 1750–1800: concavo-convex in outline. Also *absol.* See also CAPE DUTCH *adj.* sense 2 a.

The holbol gable is called the 'florid' gable by C. de Bosdari (*Cape Dutch Houses & Farms*, 1971).

1968 H. FRANSEN in D.J. Opperman *Spirit of Vine* 200 The roof .. was neatly rounded off at both ends by a gable which protruded slightly, following the line of the pitch of the roof, or else with the characteristic *holbol* (concave-convex) outline. *Ibid.* 207 The cellar gable, which according to its date of 1804 should have been classical, is *holbol*, but it is not only grammar rules that have their exceptions! **1972** L.G. GREEN *When Journey's Over* 26 The present missionary's home, a fine thatched building with a *holbol* gable of alternate convex and concave curves and mouldings. **1975** *Wine: Guide for Young People* (K.W.V.) 68 There are various types of gables, among others, the *holbol* (concavo-convex), the *bell*, and the *neck gables*. **1979** C. PAMA *Wine Estates of S. Afr.* 42 The front with the beautiful holbol gable, looks very fine indeed. **1981** P. DANE *Great Houses of Constantia* 19 A fine new gable was built in front of the house, a '*holbol*', which Nicolaas chose for its unusual lines. **1987** G. VINEY *Col. Houses* 67 The manor at Morgenster was given six of the most beautiful gables to be found at the Cape. The *holbol* or concavo-convex style may here be seen at its most elegant. **1988** D. HUGHES et al. *Complete Bk of S. Afr. Wine* 260 Jan Theron .. enlarged and modified the house, adding the fine *holbol* gable, dated 1790.

hold *v. trans.* In the colloq. phr. ***to hold thumbs*** [tr. Afk. *duim vashou*, lit. 'hold a thumb', to wish someone luck]: 'to keep one's fingers crossed', to hope for luck or success; to fold one's fingers over one's thumb to bring good luck.

'Holding thumbs' is the standard expression in *S. Afr. Eng.* for 'keeping one's fingers crossed'.

1953 D. ROOKE *S. Afr. Twins* 53 'Hold thumbs that the train is late,' shouted Tiensie, dashing into the house. **1971** N.G. SABBAGHA in *Std Encycl. of Sn Afr.* IV. 326 'To hold thumbs' frequently occurs, even in print, as a variant of 'to keep one's fingers crossed'. **1980** *Sunday Times* 7 Dec. 33 It seems they knew that disaster was about to strike — rescue workers said the three passengers were 'holding thumbs' when their bodies were found. **1982** *Ibid.* 31 May, *I'm holding thumbs for you!* .. (The rest of the world crosses fingers.) **1984** *Daily Dispatch* 2 Aug. 1 Zola Budd received a very special 'luck packet' from .. David Kramer before she left Britain for the Olympic Games ... Kramer told [her] .. that he was 'holding thumbs'. **1987** C. NAIDOO in *Sunday Times* 12 Apr. 21 They say they are holding thumbs for her and praying that the pregnancy will be trouble-free. **1987** M. POLAND *Train to Doringbult* 191, I must fly or I'll be late for the doc! Hold thumbs hey? **1990** *Personality* 23 July 15 As she kissed her daughter good-bye for the last time, Yolanda said 'Mama, you must please hold thumbs for me today.' **1992** *Weekend Post* 15 Aug. (Leisure) 6, I would like copies of the recipes they supply ... I will be holding thumbs as I have lost my ring-binder containing these excellent recipes.

holism /ˈhəʊlɪzm/ *n.* [fr. Gk *hol-* combining form of *hólos* whole + Eng. n.-forming suffix *-ism.*] A term coined by J.C. Smuts to designate the tendency in nature to produce 'wholes' from the ordered grouping of units. So **holistic** *adj.*, **holistically** *adv.*

Now in general Eng. use, occurring often in phrr. such as 'holistic medicine'.

1926 J.C. SMUTS *Holism & Evol.* 99 The whole-making, holistic tendency, or Holism .. is seen at all stages of existence. *Ibid.* 127 There is a synthesis which makes the elements or parts act as one or holistically. **1945** *Outspan* 6 June 41 The principles of Holism — that in this universe we are all members one of another, and that selfishness is the grand refusal and denial of life. **1970** *Cape Times* 16 May (Weekend Mag.) 2 Smuts the soldier-philosopher developed the concept of 'Holism', which derived from Humanism — the linking of all good things in one perfect whole. Holism was Smuts's intellectual attempt to give a meaning to the world, and man's place in it. **1989** B. HUNTLEY et al. *S. Afr. Environments into 21st C.* 119 The Chinese talk of the 'yin' and the 'yang', the Africans speak of 'ubuntu' and a former Prime Minister of South Africa, Jan Smuts, called it 'holism'. **1990** P. SPIES in *Sunday Times* 4 Mar. 25 Current developments in systems thinking are strongly influenced by Smuts's holism ... His Holism and Evolution is used as a standard reference book for systems thinking in American universities today.

Hollander /ˈhɒləndə/ *n.* [Eng. or Du., *Holland* + *-er* suffix expressing the sense 'a native of'.] A Dutch-speaking immigrant who was born in Holland, as contrasted to a Dutch- or Afrikaans-speaking South African. Also *attrib.* Cf. DUTCHMAN sense 1 a.

'Hollander' is freq. *derog.*, esp. from the late 19th century onwards (Hollanders being judged to show a loyalty less secure than that of the older South African Dutch or Afrikaans community).

1699 W.A. COWLEY in W. Hacke *Collect. Voy.* (1729) 34 The Village inhabited by the Hodmandods, so called by the Hollanders. **1731** G. MEDLEY tr. *P. Kolb's Present State of Cape of G.H.* I. 27 Several .. *Hollanders*, who had been long acquainted with Persons and Things in the several *Hottentot* Nations. ***a*1875** T. BAINES *Jrnl of Res.* (1964) II. 169 It is said that an embassy has been, or is to be, dispatched, for the purpose of getting the word Hollanders changed to 'the Dutch African Emigrants'. **1896** PURVIS & BIGGS *S. Afr.* 74 The existence of a powerful and numerous body of imported Dutchmen (usually termed Hollanders) in the South African Republic presents one of the many anachronisms with which that unfortunate Republic abounds. The Boer .. is related to the Hollander by descent, yet .. the Boer hates him almost as much as he does the other foreigners. **1899** J.P. FITZPATRICK *Tvl from Within* 287 The Cape Colony Dutchmen, Hollanders, Germans, and individuals of other European nationalities associated themselves with the Boer party. *Ibid.* 330 His place was filled by a Hollander official in the Mining Department. **1899** R. DEVEREAUX *Side Lights* 79 During the past few years, .. many of the more prosperous Boers have sent their sons either to Bloemfontein or to Europe to be educated, and thus there has grown up a young generation, indigenous to the soil, who bitterly resent the Hollander element and its influence in the councils of State. **1899** [see SMEERLAP]. **1924** L. COHEN *Reminisc. of Jhb.* 74 This Dr. Leyds, of the frosty smile, was a weed that could have flourished in no other country but the Transvaal. The wily Hollander was out for money, and nothing else. **1933** S.G. MILLIN *Rhodes* (1936) 253 Of course, Kruger hated the Uitlanders and did what he could to hinder them. His officials were either Boers or Hollanders. **1936** *Cambridge Hist. of Brit. Empire* VIII. 463 Civil dissension had been created by the presence of the Dutchmen of European birth, or 'Hollanders', whom President Burgers had introduced, and whose advanced political and religious views conflicted with the rigid Puritanism of the old 'Dopper' Boers. **1948** [see AFRIKAANS *n.*]. **1965** C. VAN HEYNINGEN *Orange Days* 36 For years we had to put up quite a number of Hollanders sent out to my father — black sheep mostly of good families — remittance men — having left Holland for the good of Holland. **1979** T. PAKENHAM *Boer War* (1982) 40 They [*sc.* Joubert's party] baited Kruger for giving his country away to foreigners: the plum jobs were given to the Hollanders (Dutch immigrants) who acted as the administrators and technicians of the young state.

Hence **Hollanderism** *n. nonce*, the introduction of Dutch colonists as a means of securing political power.

1924 L. COHEN *Reminisc. of Jhb.* 70 It is no wonder .. that Kruger .. interpreted British Liberty as meaning Boer Thraldom. It was a redoubtable phantom that kept this son of the soil awake at nights, and led him into Hollanderism.

Hollands /ˈhɔlants/ *n.* [Afk.] The Dutch language, esp. as spoken in the Dutch province of Holland. See also NEDERLANDS.

1903 D. BLACKBURN *Burgher Quixote* 2 My fame as a reader of difficult letters in the Taal, Hollands, and English .. was great. ***c*1936** *S. & E. Afr. Yr Bk & Guide* 36 Afrikaans has ousted 'Hollands' and 'Nederlands' Dutch. **1977** F.G. BUTLER *Karoo Morning* 220 In addition to their Afrikaans set books the Higher Grade pupils had one or two in Hollands.

Hollard Street *n. phr. Hist.* [A former address of the Johannesburg Stock Exchange.] Used allusively to refer to the Johannesburg Stock Exchange (see JSE). Also *attrib.*

This name was current until 1978, after which it was replaced by DIAGONAL STREET.

1948 *Story of Jhb. Stock Exchange* (Comm. of Jhb. Stock Exchange) 73 Financial conditions improved until 1913 when the first major labour troubles in the history of the Witwatersrand caused an upheaval in Hollard Street. **1971** *Argus* 24 Apr. 2 The week in Hollard Street. **1972** S. LYNNE *Glittering Gold* 29 The idea is to prevent a drastic fall or rise in our stocks and shares in Hollard Street. **1974** *Daily Dispatch* 18 May 7 The first price rise seen on the gold bullion market in a week gave Hollard Street gold shares a boost yesterday. **1979** *S. Afr. Panorama* Nov. 29 The new stock exchange had to be built precisely because the old Hollard Street floor was too small to accommodate all the brokers.

home *n. Obs.* exc. *hist.* [Special sense of general Eng.] Among South African-born English-speakers: England; Great Britain. Also *attrib.*

At one time common among the inhabitants of all former British colonies and territories.

1863 LADY DUFF-GORDON in F. Galton *Vacation Tourists* (1864) III. 180 How I have caught the colonial trick of always saying 'home' for England! Dutchmen who can barely speak English, and never did or will see England, equally talk of 'news from home'. **1865** *Star* 26 Dec. 3 (*advt*) A lady recently from Home seeks a situation as Housekeeper. Best references. **1913** C. PETTMAN *Africanderisms* 213 *Home*, This word is employed by English colonists throughout South Africa when speaking of England, often even when they are African born and their parents too. **1920** R.Y. STORMBERG *Mrs Pieter de Bruyn* 73 Believe me: when it comes to a matter of hospitality we Home people don't know anything about it. **1934** A.J. BARNOUW *Lang. & Race Problems* 17 'Home', in South African usage, is .. a mere synonym for England .. ; I have heard a South African of Norwegian extraction speak of England as 'home', though he had never visited the British isles. **1949** *Blueprint for Blackout* (Educ. League) (*pamphlet*) 18 Can we believe that if we let the children of the two language-groups mix .. the sixty-three percent of Afrikaans-speaking children will soon all be speaking English, and talking of England as 'Home'? **1969** M.W. SPILHAUS *Doorstep-Baby* 114 Well-to-do colonials sent 'home' for their clothes, and were apt to out-English the English in ceremonial observances. **1974** *E. Prov. Herald* 16 July 2 'We Afrikaners are proud that the English people are proud of being South Africans. Only their talk of "home" (Britain) upsets us,' said Mr Fouche. **1981** A. PATON in *Optima* Vol.30 No.2, 93 Afrikaner nationalists were angered by the way in which the English-speaking gave their first loyalty to the Empire and to the royal family .. by the use of the word 'home', by the words 'colony' and 'colonists' ... I cannot remember having heard a born South African talk of Britain as 'home' for many years.

home-boy *n.* [tr. Xhosa and Zulu *umkhaya*, see MKHAYA.] In urban (esp. township) Eng.: a youth or man from one's home region, or belonging to one's clan; MKHAYA. Also *attrib.*, and *transf.*, a South African. Cf. HOME-GIRL.

Used also in *U.S. Eng.* (particularly in the African-American community) and *Bahamian Eng.*

1953 LANHAM & MOPELI-PAULUS *Blanket Boy's Moon* 40 Ntoane .. also came from Lesotho. Ntoane looked up as the Induna brought Monare into his room, and seeing the blanket round Monare's shoulders said: 'Welcome home-boy'. **1963** WILSON & MAFEJE *Langa* 14 The migrants .. subdivide on the basis of where they live in the country, and groups of home-boys are formed, based on the village of origin. **1963** *Ibid.* [see MOEGIE]. **1972** *Drum* 22 Oct. 18 When I came to Johannesburg in 1949 .. I stayed with homeboys in Sophiatown who also got me a job with a garage. **1976** WEST & MORRIS *Abantu* 173 More often than not they find their way to a large 'single men' barracks, where they tend to form small groups of 'home-boys', amakhaya, from the same rural area. The amakhaya live and eat together, assist one another in adjusting to the demands of urban living, and help one another in various other ways. **1980** J. COCK *Maids & Madams* 61 Men .. often come to employment and accommodation found for them by the group of men from their local area who are already in town. This arrangement and the continual help of homeboys mitigates what might otherwise be a complex and bewildering experience. **1980** D.B. COPLAN Urbanization of African Performing Arts. 433 *Homeboys, Homegirls*, A group of young men or women from the same rural area, residing in a distant town. They frequently form not only a social category, but also a tightly-knit network maintaining ties to the rural area among urban migrant workers. **1983** *Frontline* Sept. 27, I back Gerrie because he is the home boy who is challenging America all the time. **1984** *City Press* 13 May 14 Homeboys piece of the action. Promoter Joe .. is staging a professional boxing tournament featuring local fighters. **1990** P. GARSON in *Weekly Mail* 8 Feb. 7 The conflict .. is complicated by vigilante groups .. who are drawn into the fray to wage war on criminals and protect their 'homeboys' caught in the conflict. **1990** *Weekend Post* 19 May (Leisure) 5 The interaction between the 'homeboys' and the returned exile is more than symbolic in its unity. **1994** [see HOME-GIRL].

home-girl *n.* [See prec.] In urban (esp. township) Eng.: a girl or woman from one's home region, or from the same clan. Also *attrib.* Cf. HOME-BOY.

*a***1956** H.I.E. DHLOMO in Visser & Couzens *Collected Works* (1985) 402 Bob had married his 'home' girl, Zodwa Valo, whom he had known since childhood. **1979** *Voice* 4 Mar., The old days at boarding school when there was a strong bond between guys and dolls from the same town: we often formed strong links with a 'homegirl' or a 'homeboy'. **1980** J. COCK *Maids & Madams* 62 In Johannesburg it was found that the networks of most domestic workers were both socially and spatially closed. They tended to interact with persons similarly employed in the same locality. 'Homegirls' played no particular part in these networks. **1980** [see Coplan quot. at HOME-BOY]. **1987** M. MATSHOBA in *New Nation* 10 Dec. 13 For many newcomers to the city, working 'in the kitchens' provided a way into city life ... To get jobs many of them used the 'homegirl' contacts. **1994** L.Y. COKO *Informant, Grahamstown* When I'm in PE, and a woman comes from Grahamstown, I say its my 'home-girl'. If you're a man at Johannesburg and you see a PE man there, you say its a 'home-boy', because you come from the same town.

homeland *n. hist.* [Special sense of general Eng. *homeland* the land which is one's home, one's native land, prob. influenced by the official Afk. equivalent *tuisland* (*tuis* at home, 'at ease', fr. Du. *thuis*, blend of *te* at + *huis* house, home).]

1. Any of ten quasi-autonomous regions – one for each of the officially recognized black peoples of South Africa – which, during the apartheid era, became or were intended to become self-governing (or 'independent') states, and which for a time were the only areas in which blacks born in South Africa were legally entitled to claim citizenship and permanent residence; BANTUSTAN sense 2; NATIONAL STATE sense 1; *stan* (see *n.* at -STAN *suffix*); cf. *Blackstan* (see -STAN). Also *attrib.*, and *transf.*, denoting any similar ethnically-based region. See also CITY STATE, SELF-GOVERNING, RESERVE, SEPARATE DEVELOPMENT, TERRITORIAL AUTHORITY, TRIBAL AUTHORITY.

The creation of ten ethnic 'homelands' was the main feature of GRAND APARTHEID; Transkei, Bophuthatswana, Venda, and Ciskei later became 'independent' states, funded by South Africa, before the policy was abandoned; Gazankulu, KaNgwane, KwaNdebele, KwaZulu, Lebowa, and Qwaqwa had, for a time, a certain local autonomy within South Africa. These 'states' were recognized by few foreign governments. See also TBVC.

Although all 'homelands' were re-incorporated into South Africa in 1994, the word is still sometimes used of any area which was formerly independent or semi-autonomous.

1959 *Memorandum: Promotion of Bantu Self Govt Bill* 8 The objects can be outlined as follows ... The creation of homogeneous administrative areas for the Bantu by uniting the members of each Bantu national group in one national unit, concentrated in one coherent homeland where possible. **1960** A.J. LUTHULI in H. Spottiswoode *S. Afr.: Rd Ahead* 114 White South Africa with only 3,000,000 Whites has 87 per cent of the land, the rest is supposed to be the homeland of 10,000,000 Africans. **1971** *Time* 13 Dec. 23 One of the 29 scattered patches of land that make up the Zulu Bantustan, a separate homeland set up by the *apartheid* government in Pretoria. **1974** R. SMALL in *Argus* 4 July (Woman's Argus) 5 Sometimes I have visions of a Coloured Homeland. **1974** L.M. MANGOPE *Place for All* (*c*1979) 134 The Black man sees in the Homeland concept a positive acknowledgement and vindication of his particular stamp of Black identity. **1977** *Cape Times* 29 Mar. 2 New homelands legislation introduced in Parliament yesterday will provide for 'internally autonomous' countries with legislative authority over all internal affairs. **1977** *Optima* Vol.3, 28 It is very doubtful if many of the homeland leaders have particularly strong bases of electoral support given the widespread rejection of the homelands concept by Africans. **1980** *Rand Daily Mail* 23 Aug., What were once the 'reserves' became 'Bantustans', then the 'homelands'; now they are 'national states'. **1983** J.S. MOJAPELO in *Ibid.* 13 Jan. 2 More than three-quarters of the total population of the homelands of Transkei, Bophuthatswana, Venda and Ciskei (TBVC) lived outside the four states on a continuous basis during 1980. **1989** P. CULL in *E. Prov. Herald* 7 Oct. 4 The National Party's first attempt at a constitutional solution to the 'race question' was the Verwoerdian ideal of grand apartheid with Africans all safely stowed away in bantustans. This 'imposition' phase resulted in the creation of four 'independent' homelands – one of which was a geographic farce, and all of which were riddled with corruption and economically dependent on South Africa. **1990** *Weekend Mail* 28 Sept. 2 The visionaries of the new white homelands have retreated to much diminished claims. **1992** *Weekly Mail* 24 Apr. 8 Are the citizens of the homelands, who were never asked if they wanted independence, now entitled to vote on whether they want to return to South Africa? **1994** *Natal Witness* 3 Jan. 2 Chairman Yasser Arafat .. likened Israel's self-rule plans for Palestinians to South Africa's black homelands or bantustans.

2. Special Comb. **homeland(s) policy**, the National Party's plan of creating self-governing black states; **homeland(s) system**, the homeland policy as implemented.

1974 *Post* 28 July 2 It was unanimously agreed to challenge Mr Sam Solomon the elected Labourite for Newclare to resign his CRC seat and re-contest it on his **'homeland' policy**. **1977** *S. Afr. Panorama* May 11 Politically, the Black homelands policy will have to be pursued with all possible vigour as a means of devolving and decentralizing power among the Black peoples. **1987** 'A. AMAPHIXIPHIXI' in *Frontline* Feb. 15 Hasten on the final collapse of the shambles of the homeland policy. **1993** *Africa S. & E.* July 35 South Africa's pernicious homeland policy. **1983** *Pace* Oct. 54 The **homeland system** has been used as a reason for excluding Africans from taking part in South Africa's law-making process. **1987** *New Nation* 19 Nov. 4 If my party wins the next elections, it will negotiate with Pretoria from a position of power to declare the homeland system null and void. We want one unitary South Africa and not bits and pieces of land called homelands. **1990** *Drum* May 23 The clamour for the dissolution of the homeland system is gathering such momentum that Transkei, Ciskei and Venda, three so-called independent states, are to hold referendums to elicit public opinion on the issue. **1992** *Natal Witness* 6 Nov. 2 The minister of constitutional development .. yesterday rejected the notion that the government wants to retain the present homeland system by way of regionalism in a new constitution.

Hence (*nonce*) **homelander** *n.*, one supporting the idea of a homeland.

1986 *Sunday Times* 20 July 18 The white homeland prophets are hard at work .. trying to secure the town [*sc.* Morgenzon] as the growth point for their whites-only Oranjeland ... Apart from the ultra-right-wing white homelanders, few people know where Morgenzon is.

homestead /ˈhəʊmsted/ *n.* Also with initial capital. [Special sense of general Eng. *homestead* dwelling, farm-stead.]

1. *obs. Law.* In the n. phr. ***homestead law***, see quot.

1876 F. BOYLE *Savage Life* 2 The curious law called 'Homestead' enacted that each farm occupied should be circular, and should enclose three thousand *morgen*, about six thousand acres, *around* the farm house, which must always be the central point. The object of this law was to prevent .. the assembly of men together in towns or villages.

2. KRAAL *n.* sense 2 a. Also *attrib.*

1970 H. KUPER *Witch in my Heart* p.xii, Describing the ideal homestead, informants say, 'There should always be a headman with his mother, his wives and his children.' **1981** J.B. PEIRES *House of Phalo* 33 The homestead-head decided what and when to plant, supervised the herding and milking of the cattle, and chose whether to hunt, trade or stay at home. **1985** *Frontline* Sept. 10 On the hill above the town the king's homestead and kraal, burnt by the British in 1879, have been recreated ... My guide enjoins me to make a careful distinction between 'homestead' and 'kraal', to reserve the latter for describing a cattle enclosure. **1986** P.A. MCALLISTER Xhosa Beer Drinks. 6 People came to know that I had a hut in Mzilikazi's homestead and frequently dropped in to say hello and to chat. **1990** *Sunday Times* 17 June 26 Willie Mtolo cools off at his homestead in the Drakensberg foothills after a long, thirsty day.

honey-badger *n.* [See quot. 1959.] The RATEL (sense 1), *Mellivora capensis*.

This animal is found throughout Africa, and in parts of Asia and India, but the name appears to have originated in *S. Afr. Eng.*

1884 J.S. KINGSLEY *Stand. Nat. Hist.* V. 392 The ratels or honey-badger .. surpass the skunk in burrowing activity. **1944** MARAIS & HOGE (tr.) in H.J. Mandelbrote *O.F. Mentzel's Descr. of Cape of G.H.* III. 57 A honey badger came along to hide itself under a heap of stones. **1953** R. CAMPBELL *Mamba's Precipice* 130 It [*sc.* the ratel] lives .. on honey which it shares with the honey-guide; for the latter reason it is sometimes known as the honey badger. **1959** C. LAGUS *Operation Noah* 174 Ratel is another name for the Honey Badger, which, as its name suggests, is a badger-like animal partial to wild honey. **1966** [see quot. at *wild cat* (WILD sense b)]. **1987** [see RATEL sense 1]. **1989** L. BADENHORST in *Motorist* May 5 A vicious honeybadger going round in defiant circles uttering menacing growls, no doubt after .. a tin of golden syrup.

honey-beer *n.* [Perh. tr. Du. *honingbier*.] A drink similar to mead, made of honey fermented by the addition of leaven and, occas., the larvae of bees; BOJALWA sense 1; *Hottentot beer*, see HOTTENTOT *n.* sense 6 b; cf. KARRIE *n.*³ sense 1 a.

1731 G. MEDLEY tr. *P. Kolb's Present State of Cape of G.H.* II. 57 Doubtless, they owe not their Healths a little to the Simplicity of their Drink, which is only Water, Milk, and Honey-Beer. **1824** G. BARKER *Journal.* 21 Apr., Jan Wildeman came to me like a man under a sense of his sin, but I was told afterwards that he had been drinking honey beer. **1824**, **1834** [see BOJALWA sense 1]. **1844** J. BACKHOUSE *Narr. of Visit* 596 The Bushmen intoxicate themselves with honey-beer. **1883** M.A. CAREY-HOBSON *Farm in Karoo* 149 'Do they make mead?' said Fred. 'Oh, yes. Honey-beer they call it. Some of the larvae are used in the fermentation, and also the root of a curious little plant which possesses the fermenting property in a wonderful degree.' **1898** *Act 28* in *Stat. of Cape of G.H.* (1906) 3959 'Kafir beer' shall, in addition to the liquor commonly so-called, include .. fermented liquor, made from honey, called 'Honey-beer.' **1910** *E. Prov. Herald* 18 Apr., Honey Beer seems to be the author of the majority of their woes. It tickles the palate and fuddles the brain. **1920** F.C. CORNELL *Glamour of Prospecting* 218 Our gang was never full — except of honey beer — which they made from big hauls of wild honey .., and on which they got gloriously drunk every day. **1949** L.G. GREEN *In Land of Afternoon* 161 Much wild honey is gathered because honey means honey beer. Coloured people in the Piketberg Sandveld still make it every year. **1972** *S. Afr. Panorama* Nov. 36 The chilled and distilled lagers and ales as we know them are a far cry from, for instance, the honey beer relished by the Bushmen. **1988** *Weekend Argus* 1 Oct. 22 Honeybeer? It's good stuff, but we're not allowed to make it anymore. You take the honeycomb with the young bees still in it and strain it through a cloth by pouring hot water over it .. mix in some bread and let it stand. **1992** *Weekend Post* 24 Oct. (Leisure) 1 Kareedouw's Karrie Festival may well be over but the taste of its honey-beer lingers on. The smooth yellow liquid, first brewed by the Strandloper Bushmen, is unique to the Kouga and Tsitsikamma regions, since the vital ingredient — the boesman flower — only grows in this area.

honey-bird *n.* *obsolescent.* HONEY-GUIDE.

1804 R. PERCIVAL *Acct of Cape of G.H.* 168 The honey bird, or indicator, is common here in the woods. **1829** C. ROSE *Four Yrs in Sn Afr.* 233 The noise of the honey-bird was heard, which a Hottentot quickly answered by a whistle, and followed .. and the bird conducted him to the nest. **1860** A.W. DRAYSON *Sporting Scenes* 166 Sometimes the position of a beehive is discovered by the aid of a honey-bird ... This useful little creature is, of course, rewarded with a share of the honey. **1880** E.F. SANDEMAN *Eight Months in Ox-Waggon* 236 A small grey bird with a reddish beak, the size of a sparrow, had flown alongside and round the waggon for the last mile of our trek, making a shrill hissing cry ... This little insignificant visitor was the far-famed Honey-bird. **1893** F.C. SELOUS *Trav. & Adventure* 445 Gone in pursuit of a honey-bird. **1911** L. COHEN *Reminisc. of Kimberley* 390 The honey .. was procured .. through the aid of the far-famed honey-bird. **1925** D. KIDD *Essential Kafir* 104 With the Hottentots it is almost a religion to leave any important work unfinished and immediately to follow the honey-bird. **1958** S. CLOETE *Mask* 111 Whenever he saw a honey bird fluttering from branch to branch and calling him he followed it to the nest in a hollow tree or rock cleft that it had found. **1969** F. GOLDIE *River of Gold* 82 That is the honey-bird, N'kosana. It wants to show us where the honey is.

honeybush *n.* Also with initial capital. [tr. Afk. *heuningbos*; so called because of the sweetness of the tea made from the leaves of the plant.] a. In full *honeybush tea*: HONEY TEA sense b. b. HONEY TEA sense a.

1919 *Dunell, Ebden & Co.'s Price List* Aug. 30 Tea .. Colonial ... Honey Bush [per lb.] 4 1/2d. **1982** *S. Afr. Jrnl of Science* Vol.78, 472 Herbal tea-drinking is rapidly increasing. This consumption includes over 14 imported herbal teas as well as indigenous Honey Bush Tea. **1989** *Weekend Post* 7 Oct. 4 Herbal tea fans will soon be able to enjoy a sweet 'cuppa' made from an indigenous Cape plant, commonly called the honey-bush ... Honeybush tea was first discovered and brewed up in the Kouga mountains from the honey-bush by Boer pioneers over 200 years ago. **1989** *Product packaging* Honeybush Tea contains no harmful alkaloids or caffeine.

honey cake see CAKE.

honey-guide *n.* [Interpretation of S. Afr. Du. *honingwijzer*, fr. Du. *honing* honey + *wijzer* one who shows or points out (something).] Any of several small tropical birds of the Indicatoridae, esp. *Indicator indicator* (the greater honey-guide), which feeds on insects, honey, and beeswax, and guides man (and possibly other mammals) to bees' nests; BEE-CUCKOO; HONEY-BIRD; HONEY-SUCKER sense 1; HONINGWIJZER; INDICATOR; SPARM. Also *attrib.*

'Honey-guide" is also used in *U.S. Eng.* of American species.

Not all species of honey-guide lead man to bees' nests.

1777 A. SPARRMAN in *Phil. Trans. of Royal Soc.* LXVII. 43 The Dutch settlers thereabouts have given this bird the name of *Honig-wyzer*, or Honey-guide, from its quality of discovering wild honey to travellers. **1786** *Chambers's Cycl., Cuculus indicator*, a species of cuckow found in the interior parts of Africa .. called by the Dutch settlers *honig-wyzer* or *honey-guide*. **1798** *Sporting Mag.* XII. 89 A remarkable bird called the Honeyguide. a**1827** D. CARMICHAEL in W.J. Hooker *Botanical Misc.* (1831) II. 37 The hive is usually revealed to them by a bird, called, on this account, the *Honey-guide*, (*Cuculus Indicator*). **1841** B. SHAW *Memorials* 325 Sparrman offered the natives .. an ample recompense if they would assist him in catching a honey-guide, but they rejected the proposal, saying, 'the bird is our friend'. **1857** D. LIVINGSTONE *Missionary Trav.* 547 We began to be frequently invited by the honey-guide (*Cuculus indicator*) ... I am quite convinced that the majority of people who commit themselves to its guidance are led to honey. **1897** H.A. BRYDEN *Nature & Sport* 92 We had with us the little honey-guides, those strange feathered friends (also numbered among the cuckoos) which insist — not entirely from disinterested motives — in conducting mankind to the nests of bees. **1905** W.L. SCLATER in Flint & Gilchrist *Science in S. Afr.* 141 The Honey Guides (*Indicatoridae*) .. are remarkable for the fact that they will lead the traveller to the situation of bees' nests in the hope of sharing with him some of the spoil in the shape of honey or wax. **1927** E.N. MARAIS *Rd to Waterberg* (1972) 84 The honey-guide, like the cuckoo, is a parasite. It never makes its own nest and never rears its own young. **1949** L.G. GREEN *In Land of Afternoon* 161 Bushmen and Hottentots always leave a share of the honey for the honey guide. They say it is a vindictive bird which will lead the way to a snake or a leopard next time if it is cheated. **1953** R. CAMPBELL *Mamba's Precipice* 39 The bird was a honey-guide; a bird which lives on honey and bees. It calls both human beings and honey badgers or ratels, and guides them .. to hives .. which require to be dug out from difficult places either in the ground or in hollow trees. **1971** K.B. NEWMAN *Birdlife in Sn Afr.* (1979) 18 The honeyguides ... are small, inconspicuous birds whose drab appearances conceal some interesting and unique behaviour ... They have a special predilection for beeswax, and are the only known birds able to digest and benefit from it. **1985** *Flying Springbok* July 64 The honey-guide waits above while the bee-hunters rob the hive ... The birds have thick skins to protect them from the bees' stings. It has been suggested that this man-bird relationship is an example of co-evolution.

honey-guiding *n.* [Formed on prec.] The behaviour of the HONEY-GUIDE. Also *attrib.*

1923 HAAGNER & IVY *Sketches* 271 The stories told of the honey-guiding instincts of these little birds are innumerable, dating from the days of Sparrman and Livingstone.

honeypot *n.* Also with initial capital. [Calqued on S. Afr. Du. *hanepoot*, see quots 1913 and 1975.] HANEPOOT sense 1. Also *attrib.*

1798 LADY A. BARNARD in Lord Lindsay *Lives of Lindsays* (1849) III. 403 The Honipot grape .., a fleshy white grape, which is of the Muscatel nature and excellent. **1847** 'A BENGALI' *Notes on Cape of G.H.* 86 The 'Honey pot' is a very fleshy grape, and is dried for raisins. **1855** W.R. KING *Campaigning in Kaffirland* 190 The most deliciously flavoured grapes, one sort, called the 'honey-pot', .. of immense size. **1878** T.J. LUCAS *Camp Life & Sport* 213, I tasted .. delicious muscatels and sweet-water grapes, with crystal honey-pot and other kinds. **1908** M.C. BRUCE *New Tvl* 78 Grapes whether of the Muscat of Alexandria or the sweet and popular 'honey-pot' .., are amongst the most successful fruits grown in the colony. **1913** C. PETTMAN *Africanderisms* 214 The Dutch name for this richly flavoured grape, the muscat of Alexandria, is Haanepoot ... This name has been corrupted by English colonists into 'Honey-pot,' approaching the Dutch name in sound, but having reference to the lusciousness of the fruit. **1975** *Daily Dispatch* 20 Sept. 5 Its distinctive flavour and rich sweetness have led many a newcomer to the country to mistake the name and refer to the grape as 'Honeypot'. **1990** *Stanger Mail* 16 Feb. 1 (*advt*) 'Honeypot' Grapes 99c per kg.

honey-ratel *n. obs.* [Eng. *honey* + RATEL.] The RATEL (sense 1), *Mellivora capensis*.

1816 KIRBY & SPENCE *Intro. to Entomology* (1843) I. 238 The honey-ratel .. has a particular instinct enabling it to discover bees. **1835** W. KIRBY *On Power of God as Manifested in Creation of Animals* II. 463 Bee cuckows .. indicating to the honey-ratel .. the subterranean nests of certain bees. **1900** W.L. SCLATER *Mammals of S. Afr.* I. 110 *Vernacular Names*: Ratel or Honey-Ratel of Colonists.

honey-sucker *n.* [Special senses of general Eng. *honey-sucker* a name used of any creature feeding on honey, including various birds; or formed in S. Afr. Eng.]

1. HONEY-GUIDE.

[**1731** G. MEDLEY tr. *P. Kolb's Present State of Cape of G.H.* II. 155 These Gnat-snappers, or Honey-eaters are a sort of guides to the Hottentots in the search of honey.] **1835** A. STEEDMAN *Wanderings* I. 189 The little honey-sucker, or *indicator*, kept fluttering before us with its cry of *cherr, cherr*.

2. Any of several species of small, long-beaked sunbirds of the Nectariniidae, the males of which have brightly-coloured plumage, often containing metallic green feathers; SUGARBIRD sense 2; SUIKERBEKJE. See also JANGROENTJIE sense 1.

See note at SUNBIRD.

1853 F.P. FLEMING *Kaffraria* 76 The many species of gaudy little humming-birds, honey-suckers .. would amply claim and repay the .. talents of a second

'Gosse.' **1891** R. Russell *Natal* 36 Honey-suckers or sun-birds, that flit like living gems from flower to flower. **1904** *Argus Christmas Annual* (Cape Colony Sect.) 20 A long-tailed honey-sucker. **1907** J.P. Fitzpatrick *Jock of Bushveld* (1909) 269 Golden cuckoos there were also and beautiful little green-backed ruby-throated honey-suckers, flitted like butterflies among the flowers on the sunlit fringe of the woods. **1937** M. Alston *Wanderings* 105 When he was drinking his morning cup of coffee, the honeysuckers would come to the trailing jasmine overhead. **1967** S.M.A. Lowe *Hungry Veld* 93 Tiny, long-beaked honeysuckers were the noisiest of all. Their brilliant green and red plumage flashed in the sunlight as they darted about screeching their concern in urgent grating sounds. **1978** McLachlan & Liversidge *Roberts' Birds of S. Afr.* 622 Honeysucker, see Sunbird. **1983** K.B. Newman *Newman's Birds* 444 Popular bird names in general use ... Honeysuckers, Sunbirds.

honey tea /ˌhʌni 'tiː/ *n. phr.* [tr. Afk. *heuningtee*.]
a. Any of several fragrant plants of the genus *Cyclopia* of the Fabaceae, esp. *C. genistoides*; *heuning(blom)bos*, see HEUNING; HONEYBUSH sense b.
b. The herbal tea infused from the leaves of these plants; HONEYBUSH sense a. In both senses also called BUSH TEA. See also *vlei tea* (VLEI sense 2).

1917 R. Marloth *Common Names* 80 Tea, The most frequently employed shrublet is *Cyclopia Vogelii* (Honey -, Boer -) from the mountains of Swellendam, etc. Ibid. 111 *Cyclo'pia genistoides* .. *C. latifolia* .. , *C. longifolia* .. , *C. Vogelii* ... Boer-tea, bush -, honey -. c**1951** Rice & Compton *Wild Flowers of Cape of G.H.* Pl.42, *Cyclopia genistoides*. Bush Tea, Honey Tea, Honingtee ... The leafy twigs, fermented and dried, serve as a 'bush tea'. **1965** S. Eliovson *S. Afr. Wild Flowers for Garden* 219 *Cyclopia*. Bush Tea, Honey Tea, Heuningtee. This is a small genus of 12 species .. coming from the south-western Cape and as far east as Uitenhage. **1966** C.A. Smith *Common Names* 249 Honey tea, *Cyclopia genistoides* .. and *C. burtonii* .. , see heuningtee. **1971** *Horticultural Terms* (Dept of Nat. Educ.) 97 Honey tea, (bush tea, *Cyclopia genistoides* ..). **1987** T.F.J. Van Rensburg *Intro. to Fynbos* 30 Most South Africans know rooibos tea .. or honey tea ... Rooibos tea .. was relatively unknown .. one generation ago. Honey tea from the Swartberg, Baviaanskloof and Kouga was even less well known ... Honey tea is still picked mainly in the veld ... Like many other fynbos species, honey tea is adapted to survive fires.

honing var. HEUNING.

honing-wijzer *n. obs.* Also **heuning-wyser, honing-wyzer.** [S. Afr. Du., fr. Du. *honing*, (dial.) *heuning* honey + *wijzer* guide.] HONEY-GUIDE. Also (Englished pronunciation-spelling) **hony vyzer.**

[**1777** see HONEY-GUIDE.] **1786** G. Forster tr. *A. Sparrman's Voy. to Cape of G.H.* II. 190, I had previously promised an ample reward, consisting of glass beads and tobacco to my *Zwellendam* Hottentots, on condition that they would assist me in catching and shooting a *honing-wijzer*, yet I found them too much the bird's friends to betray it ... This bird .. is called by the colonists *honing-wyzer*, or the honey-guide. c**1808** C. von Linné *System of Natural Hist.* VIII. 236 The small indicator is about six inches long ... The colonists at the Cape .. call it *heuning-vogel*, or *heuning-wyser*, 'indicator of honey,' which is a literal translation of the Hottentot name. **1883** M.A. Carey-Hobson *Farm in Karoo* 146 Will master go too, if we can only get the 'Hony Vyzer' to show us again? **1913** C. Pettman *Africanderisms* 215 *Honingwijzer*, .. See Honeybird.

Honorary White *adj. phr.* and *n. phr. Hist.* Also with small initials.
A. *adj. phr.* Of a person: not a member of the white group by descent, but given certain white rights normally reserved for members of the white group under apartheid laws (such as the right to reside or carry out business in 'white' areas). See also WHITE *adj.* sense 1 a.

Used esp. of people of Japanese origin or descent (who were allowed most of the rights which the white group had), and people of Chinese origin or descent (who had the right to use certain amenities usually reserved for whites). Such rights were granted during the apartheid era from the 1960s onwards, and the nature and extent of the rights changed over time.

1965 D. Marais *Ag, Sis Man!*, (caption) Greetings. I am Honorary White man. Old South African tradition. **1970** *Drum* Sept. 8 Get an Honorary White tag to your name and the world is yours. **1973** *Sunday Times* 9 Dec. 5 They are impertinently classified as honorary White. **1992** *E. Prov. Herald* 11 Mar. 4 Chinese South Africans were not allowed to vote, even though they had been given honorary white status under a number of recently-scrapped apartheid laws.
B. *n. phr.* One who is not registered as 'white' according to apartheid laws, but who is given rights normally reserved for a member of the white group; a Japanese person. Hence (*nonce*) **Honorary Whitemanship** *n. phr.*, the status of being an 'Honorary White'.

1970 *Drum* Sept. 8 We introduced the fantastic title of Honorary White to these oriental buyers ... Their Indonesian crew were liberally showered with Honorary Whitemanship to overcome the all-too-true fact that they looked like any of the locals. **1972** *Daily Dispatch* 3 June, A Chinese diplomat was called an honorary white and an Italian diplomat a 'Mafia ice-cream boy'. **1976** A.P. Brink *Mapmakers* (1983) 129 Because Japan has enormous trade agreements with South Africa .. Japanese are regarded — for the duration of the contracts — as 'honorary whites'.

hony vyzer see HONING-WIJZER.

hoofbestuur see BESTUUR sense 2.

hoofdpijn druppels see DRUPPELS sense b i.

‖**hoofleier** /ˈhʊəfleɪə(r)/ *n.* Also with initial capital. [Afk., *hoof* chief + *leier* leader.] The chief executive or leader of a predominantly Afrikaans commercial enterprise, organization, or political party.

1948 *Press Digest* No.5, 37 Dr Diedrichs was retiring as hoofleier of the RDB [*sc.* Reddingsdaadbond] but would remain on as a member of the Executive. Ibid. No.7, 50 Mr. L.T. Weichardt, Hoofleier of the Blanke Werkers Party (Greyshirts) will address a public meeting in the City Hall, Brakpan. **1952** B. Davidson *Report on Sn Afr.* 159 Of commercial organizations then founded, the Reddingsdaadbond is probably the most important; according to a statement by Dr. Diedrichs, the Hoofleier of the Reddingsdaadbond. **1977** *Sunday Times* 27 Nov. 3 Now the question I wish to put to the Hoofleier is this: With these two trains racing towards each other at 100 miles an hour on a single-track railway, how would the Hoofleier avoid a head-on collision? **1984** *Frontline* Mar. 44 The office marked 'Hoofleier' is extravagantly long. Quite enormous. The Hoofleier himself is seated at a desk so far away, haloed against the window behind him, that it is difficult for a moment to make him out.

hoofstad *n.*[1] *obs.* Also **hofstaad, hoofstadt,** and with initial capital. [ad. Afk. *hoofstat* the 'great place' of a chief, fr. *hoof* principal, main + *stat* a black settlement.

There exists some confusion in S. Afr. Eng. concerning Afk. usage, in which *stat* is used to refer to a black settlement or township, and *stad* to a city.]
Great place, see GREAT.

1898 C. Rae *Malaboch* p.xvii (Jeffreys), The Commissioner sent some of the missionary Kafirs up to to the Hoofstadt with a request for Malaboch to come down as he wanted to take the census of the tribe. **1911** Blackburn & Caddell *Secret Service* 162 From the day he left Pretoria until the day he reached the hofstaad of Magato .. his doings were known to the chief as completely as if he had been supplied with the traveller's diary. **1953** B. Fuller *Call Back Yesterday* 7 He kept a mountain hoofstad overlooking the little kopje.

‖**hoofstad** /ˈhʊəfstat/ *n.*[2] Also with initial capital. [Afk., *hoof* principal, main + *stad* town, city; cf. prec.] A capital city (here referring to Pretoria).

1953 B. Fuller *Call Back Yesterday* 9 Commandant Henning Pretorius, Mr Carl Potgieter and Mr de Souza were at the Hoofstad under the stronghold on Thursday. **1967** W.A. De Klerk *White Wines* 71 One often saw this colourful young couple in the streets of the old *hoofstad* in those days. They would especially enjoy their walks on a Sunday afternoon through the broad streets of Pretoria.

Hooge Veld *n. phr. Obs.* Also **Hooge Veldt.** [S. Afr. Du., fr. Du. *hoge* attrib. form of *hoog* high + *veld(t)* open, undeveloped countryside.] HIGHVELD sense a.

1856 *Cape of G.H. Almanac & Annual Register* 291 What the farmers term the 'hoogeveld' .. is covered with a sour wiry grass. **1877** F. Jeppe *Tvl Bk Almanac & Dir.* (1976) 29 This plateau, called Hooge Veldt, extends through the whole breadth of the republic, and forms the watershed between the rivers flowing South to the Vaal and North to the Limpopo. **1882** J. Nixon *Among Boers* 288 The 'Hooge Veld' is the only locality where a lung patient ought to settle. Fortunately it occupies a wide district, and leaves a large choice. **1888** *Encycl. Brit.* XXIII. 518 The Hooge Veld, or uplands, comprising the southern districts drained by the Vaal and the Drakensberg highlands as far north as Lipalule, about 35,000 square miles altogether. **1902** D. Van Warmelo *On Commando* 137 The treeless Hoogeveld had been almost exhausted by the many large commandos which had visited the 'uitspan' places. **1907** J.P. Fitzpatrick *Jock of Bushveld* (1909) Glossary, Highveld, properly Hoogeveld (D), high country; the plateau, about 5000 to 6000 ft. above sea-level.

‖**hoogte** /ˈhʊəxtə/ *n.* [Afk., *hoog* high + n.-forming suffix *-te*.] A rise or height; higher terrain. See also RANDJIE.

1935 H.C. Bosman *Mafeking Rd* (1969) 13 If you walk over my farm to the hoogte, and look towards the north-west, you can see Abjaterskop behind the ridge of the Dwarsberge. **1958** A. Jackson *Trader on Veld* 158, I could almost name the hour when he would emerge from a certain 'hoogte' (rise) with his goatskin bag on a stick slung over his shoulder. **1974** A. Small in S. Gray *On Edge of World* 185 Just up the slope, slanting on the hoogte (rise) on the other side of the farm labourers' hovels, was the graveyard.

hook var. HOEK *n.*[2]

hook haai var. HOKAAI.

hook-thorn *n.* Also with initial capital. [tr. S. Afr. Du. *haakdoorn*.] HAAKDORING sense 1. Also *attrib.*

1822 W.J. Burchell *Trav.* I. 336 The Hook-thorn (*Acacia detinens*) before described, was found growing here. **1846** R. Moffat *Missionary Labours* 98 They are sometimes hedged into a fold made of hook-thorn bushes. **1937** C.R. Prance *Tante Rebella's Saga* 86 Up a .. narrow track beset with 'hook-thorn', 'hook-and-stab', and 'cat-claw bush'. **1960** U. Krige (tr. J. van Melle) in D. Wright *S. Afr. Stories* 132 Stretches of blue hookthorn straddled the slopes. **1983** K.C. Palgrave *Trees of Sn Afr.* 233 *Acacia caffra*, .. common hook-thorn. **1990** [see SWEET THORN].

‖**hoor** /hʊər/ *int.* [Afk., 'hear', ellipt. for *hoor jy my?* do you hear me?] 'Do you hear'; cf. HEY (in several senses).

1984 [see KAK *adj.*]. **1987** *Informant*, Pretoria Sorry for all the hassles, hoor. **1989** *Frontline* Mar. 13 'Hoor?' is used by whites to talk to blacks. Next time a white person 'baby talks' you, retort 'hoor?', and relish his/her blushing as you turn the tables in the word game. **1990** Ibid. Mar.-Apr. 21 'This combi is from Johannesburg,' says Toby, conferring guest status upon it. 'Keep watch, hoor.'

||**hoor hoor** /hʊər ˈhʊər/ *int.* and *n.* [Afk., tr. Eng. *hear, hear.*] 'Hear, hear'.

A. *int.* An exclamation of approval or agreement; also used ironically.

1901 W.S. SUTHERLAND *S. Afr. Sketches* 23 May they have a Merry Christmas in their own capitals .. (cries of 'Hoor, hoor'). **1915** D. FAIRBRIDGE *Torch Bearer* 62 'This, ladies and gentlemen,' she said in solemn tones, 'this is a map of the world.' 'Hoor, hoor,' in encouraging tones from the mayor. **1920** R.Y. STORMBERG *Mrs Pieter de Bruyn* 42, I swallowed the cheer 'Hoor-hoor!' **1940** F.B. YOUNG *City of Gold* 74 Burgers had been dealing with .. matters of administrative routine, which the Raad approved perfunctorily with gruff rumblings of 'Hoor! Hoor!' **1955** W. ILLSLEY *Wagon on Fire* 105 'If we can take heed in time to warnings such as we have received today we need not lose our freedom on the good earth the Lord has given to use.' 'Hoor, Hoor!' ejaculated Pieter MacDermott. **1971** *Daily Dispatch* 18 Nov. 5 South Africans yelled 'hoor hoor' when Eartha Kitt sat on the knee of a White South African to sing C'est si Bon in the Royal Swazi Casino last week. **1978** *Drum* Apr. 2 There were shouts of 'hoor hoor' as rector Professor J. de Villiers welcomed blackstan and mlungu parents and students. **1980** *Sunday Times* 9 Mar. (Extra) 3 Quicker than you can say Federale Party and Hoor! Hoor! they built a multi-million rand masterpiece of a mansion. **1987** *Pace* June 4 They had slogans like 'This land is our land' and 'We've had enough (of the Nats and their policies)'. I'm sure you too will say 'Hoor! Hoor!' to that.

B. *n.* A shout of 'hoor hoor'.

1915 D. FAIRBRIDGE *Torch Bearer* 147 The minister sat down to the accompaniment of a few perfunctory hoor-hoors. **1917** S.T. PLAATJE *Native Life* 131 The open air rang with the loud cheers and 'Hoor, hoors' from hundreds of leather-lunged Boers. **1923** B. RONAN *Forty S. Afr. Yrs* 75, I do not know what I said, but the tumultuous 'Hoor! Hoor!' which ascended at intervals from all sides lured me on my desperate way. **1934** *Cape Argus* 29 Mar., The 'Hoor, hoor' came from Mr. Erasmus. **1973** *Cape Times* 8 May 9 Not even Nationalist members, except for the occasional Minister, receive as many 'hoor hoors' as Mr. Malan got yesterday. **1991** B. SEARY in *Sunday Tribune* 19 May 9 Hall G in the Pretoria showgrounds reverberated to a wave of emotional applause and 'hoor hoors!' as the farmers got to their feet in a standing ovation.

hooze(e)t var. HOWZIT.

horries /ˈhɒriːz, ˈhɔriːz/ *pl. n. Slang.* [Afk., fr. Eng. *horrors*; it may be that the word existed as a S. Afr. Eng. var. of 'horrors' before it was used in Afk.] ***The horries***:

1. 'The horrors', delirium tremens.

1959 A. DELIUS *Last Division* 75 My brother, from drinking, once had the horries ... It was like there'd been a donderse battle With Loch Ness Monsters and people and cattle, And spooks and goggas and in-betweens, And elephant cray-fish and skokiaan-queens. **1977** D. MULLER *Whitey* 11 A grassy, treey, flowery place that was not at all like the usual gloomy places where the horries get at you when the booze has destroyed all the vitamins in your system, .. and the things come. **1989** B. RONGE in *Sunday Times* 17 Sept. (Mag. Sect.) 6 The 'horries' for those of you who still stubbornly deny yourself the idiomatic juiciness of Afrikaans, is a colloquial term for that state which English describes as 'The DTs' or delirium tremens.

2. *transf.* A fear, phobia, horror, or strong aversion. Also *attrib.*

1971 *Cape Times* 3 July (Mag. Sect.) 4, I watch the activity for a while, and then I get the horries that the rodents might eat me. **1972** *Informant, Grahamstown* 'Don't they want any padkos for the train?' 'No they've got the horries about how much they've been eating here as it is.' **1989** *Sunday Times* 24 Sept. (Mag. Sect.) 8 Last week I started dispensing my own personal 'Horries' awards, an inversion of the advertising industry's Loeries which are meant to praise and reward excellence. The Horries do exactly the opposite.

horse-sickness *n. Pathology.* [tr. S. Afr. Du. *paardeziekte*, see PAARDEZIEKTE.] An acute, frequently fatal, viral disease affecting horses, mules, and donkeys, and characterized by a fever which may be followed by a swelling of the head, neck, and tongue, or by an accumulation of fluid in the lungs; PAARDEZIEKTE; *the sickness*, see SICKNESS. See also DIKKOP sense 2 a, DUNKOP.

Known internationally as 'African horse sickness', the disease is transmitted by a midge (*Culicoides*) which is endemic to some of the lower-lying regions of central and southern Africa.

1822 J. CAMPBELL *Trav. in S. Afr. Second Journey* I. 32 The horse sickness .. was prevailing much at that time. **1837** 'N. POLSON' *Subaltern's Sick Leave* 163 A disease sometimes prevails among the horses .. styled the 'horse sickness' and has proved incurable hitherto. **1841** J.W. APPLEYARD *War of Axe* (1971) 7 This evening I lost my faithful riding horse Caesar, by that mysterious disease termed Horse-sickness. **1857** D. LIVINGSTONE *Missionary Trav.* 101 The disease passing under the name of horse-sickness (peripneumonia) exists in such virulence over nearly seven degrees of latitude, that no precaution would be sufficient to save these animals. *Ibid.* 136 Great numbers .. of Zebra are found dead with masses of foam at the nostrils, exactly as occurs in the common 'horse-sickness'. **1877** LADY BARKER *Yr's Hsekeeping* 70 Instead of the horses being left out night and day .. they need to be carefully housed at night, and well fed with oaten straw and mealies, to secure them from the mysterious and fatal 'horse sickness' which kills them in a few hours. **1887** [see BLUE TONGUE]. **1892** W.L. DISTANT *Naturalist in Tvl* 95 The horse sickness was now prevalent; a few days previously when travelling to Johannesburg, we had to unharness a horse and leave it on the veld. **1918** C. GARSTIN *Sunshine Settlers* 29 Horses were considered a luxury in our country on account of the horse-sickness, a devastating disease which killed off about fifty per cent. per annum. *c*1936 *S. & E. Afr. Yr Bk & Guide* 326 *Horse-sickness* is at times a terrible plague. It first appeared in 1719 and has never been stamped out. **1953** D. ROOKE *S. Afr. Twins* 23 She was valuable, for she was salted, which means that she was immune to horse-sickness. **1957** [see DUNKOP]. **1974** *E. Prov. Herald* 27 Feb. 4 Vaccine against horse sickness should .. be applied early in summer, and in cases where this has been neglected stock losses could be expected. **1976** [see BLUE TONGUE]. **1993** *Weekend Post* 16 Oct. 2 Horse owners have been warned not to vaccinate their horses against horse sickness and to take precautions against their horses contracting the often fatal illness. The warning .. follows adverse reactions .. to the current batch of horse-sickness vaccine. **1994** M. ROBERTS tr. *J.A. Wahlberg's Trav. Jrnls 1838–56* 19 The horse-sickness had been rampant here too.

Hence **horse-sick** *adj. nonce.*

1896 R. WALLACE *Farming Indust. of Cape Col.* 320 This organism has been distinguished and separated from a host of nameless organisms present in horse-sick blood.

Horutsie var. and pl. form of HURUTSHE.

hostel *n.* [Special senses of general Eng.]

1.a. A single-sex barrack or dormitory for the accommodation of black migrant workers in urban areas; BACHELOR QUARTERS. **b.** Similar living quarters for mine-workers. Cf. COMPOUND sense 1. Also *attrib.*, and *comb.* **hostel-dweller**, one living in a hostel. See also MIGRANT LABOUR sense 1.

1943 'J. BURGER' *Black Man's Burden* 180 In Durban .. the accommodation for Natives consists largely of hostels for single men and women and about 140 cottages for married couples. **1950** D. REED *Somewhere S. of Suez* 270 There is a single hostel, much overcrowded, for the female Native population. Women with children are debarred. **1957** [see LOCATION sense 3 b]. **1959** L. LONGMORE *Dispossessed* 317 The Johannesburg Municipality has one hostel for African women — namely, Wolhuter Women's Hostel, established in 1930, which can accommodate 160 tenants. **1973** *Sunday Times* 18 Feb. (Mag. Sect.) 3 Because of our inhuman laws they are herded into bleak hostels and townships, and kept apart from their families — but near factories. **1977** J. SIKAKANE *Window on Soweto* 9 Separately built in some of the 26 locations are the most notorious and depressing barracks known as hostels. These long narrow-built compartments accommodate 'single' men i.e. migrant workers. In Soweto 60,000 men are hostel dwellers. **1983** *Fair Lady* 16 Nov. 170 Family accommodation was to be eliminated entirely and 18 hostels were to be built for 'single' men and women. **1984** E. MPHAHLELE *Afrika my Music* 176 There are no apartment houses for Africans in South Africa. Single male hostels for migrant labourers, yes — dormitory style. **1987** S. NYAKA in *Weekly Mail* 3 Apr. 1 Defiant miners .. have unilaterally moved their wives or girlfriends into the single-sex hostels. **1990** *New African* 18 June 8 Each night, more than 17 000 workers finish off a day's work and head back to the KwaMashu Men's Hostel just north of Durban. Overcrowding, prostitution, and deplorable maintenance is what they come home to. **1990** *Weekend Argus* 29 Sept. 19 South Africa's widely discredited hostels system has earned a large measure of blame for the violence on the Reef ... Hostel-dwellers pay R6 a bed to secure a roof over their heads. **1991** [see COMPOUND sense 1]. **1992** *Weekly Mail* 16 Apr. 35 As the [mining] industry entered the 1990s the compounds, now renamed hostels, were occupied primarily by workers from South Africa and the 'homelands'.

2. A boarding-house for pupils at a primary or secondary school; those living in the hostel. Also *attrib.*

1956 A. BASKIND in *Pietersburg Eng. Medium School Mag.* 31 On Saturday .. the School House hostel held a tickey-evening to raise funds for .. a new radiogram. **1959** C.F.P. HERSELMAN in *Ibid.* 15 In 1957 there were 240 children living in a hostel that was planned for 180. **1959** L.N. SALOMON in *Ibid.* 21 At the hostel the senior girls have responded to her understanding, while their genuine respect for her has led to the disciplined behaviour so essential in their 'home from home' ... The staff, pupils and hostel will miss her greatly. **1964** C. KRIKST in *Capricorn High School Mag.* 12 Despite numerous and frequent changes in hostel staff, we have combined very well. **1986** [see HERNHUTTER]. **1991** *Grocott's Mail* 10 Sept. 9 The schools could do well to organise table tennis into a local inter-school league competition, as many of their hostels already have tables. **1993** [see SARMIE].

hot *n.*, *int.*, and *adj. Obs.* Also **ho(tt)**. [Du.] 'Right'. Cf. HAAR.

A. *n.* A cry of 'hot'.

1786 G. FORSTER tr. *A. Sparrman's Voy. to Cape of G.H.* I. 127 Each ox .. will pay attention, and go to the right or to the left, merely upon hearing its own name pronounced with a *Ho* or a *Ha* added to it.

B. *int.* 'Turn right' (a call to a draught-ox).

1812 A. PLUMPTRE tr. *H. Lichtenstein's Trav. in Sn Afr.* I. 14 The drivers manage the animals with merely calling to them; every ox has his particular name, and by pronouncing the word *hot* or *haar*, they turn to the right or left according to the signification of the word used. **1821** C.I. LATROBE *Jrnl of Visit* 54 He continually calls to his cattle by their names, directing them to the right or left by the addition of the exclamations of *hott* and *haar*, occasionally enforcing obedience to his commands by a lash. **1913** [see sense C]. **1919** J.Y. GIBSON in *S. Afr. Jrnl of Science* July 5 The descriptive *hot* and *haar* was employed in calling the names; thus *Hot* Bandom! or *Haar* Donker!

C. *adj.* Of or pertaining to the right-hand position of an ox in a team of draught-oxen; the right-hand or 'off' side.

1868 W.R. THOMSON *Poems, Essays & Sketches* 172 The sly old fellow gave his '*hot*' and '*haar voor*' oxen a smart cut with his whip, and as the cattle broke into a trot, looked round triumphantly at me from the *voor-kist*. **1870** R. RIDGILL in A.M.L. Robinson *Sel. Articles from Cape Monthly Mag.* (1978) 22 Literally, I did not know my right hand from my left when *hot* stood for one and *haar* for the other — sounds intelligible enough to the most stupid bullock that ever bore the yoke. **1913** C. PETTMAN *Africanderisms* 216 *Hot en haar*, .. These words are equivalent to the 'off' and 'near' of English drivers, and are employed: (1) To describe the position of the oxen in a span or team. (2) To direct the oxen which way to turn: *hot*, to the left; *haar*, to the right. **1919** J.Y. GIBSON in *S. Afr. Jrnl of Science* July 5 The words *hot* and *haar* described whether they were on the near or off side; thus *hot* or *haar achter* signified left or right wheeler.

Hotantot, Hotentot, Hotnetot varr. HOTTENTOT.

Hotnot /ˈhɔtnɔt/ *n. offensive.* Also with small initial. [S. Afr. Du., contracted form of Du. *Hottentot*, see HOTTENTOT.]

1. *obs.* KHOIKHOI sense 1. Also *attrib.*

[**1812** A. PLUMPTRE tr. *H. Lichtenstein's Trav. in Sn Afr.* (1928) I. 118 A Hottentot .. expects to be called Hottentot (which he pronounces *Hotnot*) or boy.] **1846** A.G. BAIN *Jrnls* (1949) 201 Our *sweet* Hotnot *ladies*. **1946** P. ABRAHAMS *Mine Boy* (1954) 65 She was called Hotnot Annie and claimed to be pure Hottentot.

2. *derog.* An insulting term of address or reference to a COLOURED person. Also *attrib.*

1947 C.R. PRANCE *Antic Mem.* 76 Oom Jurie and Neef Japie must dig a 6-foot hole and bury it properly, if there were no Hotnots available as grave-diggers. **1956** A. SAMPSON *Drum* 201 They joked .. about apartheid, and about .. being called bushmen, hotnots, coolies, with compulsory wounding laughter. **1955** [see GAMMAT sense 1]. **1956** A. LA GUMA in *New Age* 27 Sept. 6 Who did you kill? A white man or a hotnot or a kaffir? **1960** J. COPE *Tame Ox* 27 Nico had made the 'law' to keep Crispus from contamination by the coloureds ... No mixing whatever with .. the two little Hotnots. **1969** A. FUGARD *Boesman & Lena* 19 Shake his hand! Fancy *Hotnot* like you. **1974** J.M. COETZEE *Dusklands* 108 I'm just a poor hotnot, master, only one more chance, my master, my father. **1973** A. SMALL in *Evening Post* 16 July 3 Racists who thought in terms of 'hotnots' .. had no place on the University of the Western Cape campus. **1975** *Sunday Times* 21 Sept. 21, I was .. ordered to go to the 'Hotnot' cafe down the road, and told bluntly: 'We don't allow Hotnots to walk around here.' **1978** *Daily Dispatch* 24 Nov. 9 Five knife-bearing white vigilantes .. jumped out of a car shouting: 'Leave that hotnot maid.' **1987** B. PEARSON in *Weekly Mail* 17 July 11 In South Africa they had been 'Cape Coloureds', voteless, politically powerless, neither oppressed black nor privileged white .. 'just Hotnots born on the wrong side of the track'. **1992** M. TYALA in *Evening Post* 27 Mar. 10 They were not going to let any kaffirs, hotnots or koelies even think of coming near the suburb.

3. In full ***Hotnot fish***: HOTTENTOT *n.* sense 2. Also occas. dim. form **Hotnotjie** /ˈhɔtnɔiki/ [see -IE].

1951 L.G. GREEN *Grow Lovely* 84 'Hotnot!' came the high-pitched call of the hawker. When the housewives came to their doors, they found not only hotnot fish but snoek .. and penguin eggs. **1970** C. KINSLEY *Informant, Koegasbrug (N. Cape)* Hotnotjies. Fish. **1973** J. COPE in S. Gray *Writers' Territory* 115 Mr Katz pulled up two more [fish] in quick succession. 'My, but you good. The hotnots is skelm but you more skelm, mister,' he said. **1977** *Darling* 8 June 118 Hotnotjies, a round, dark, most tasty fish resembling a small galjoen.

‖**4.** Special Comb. (usu. with Afk. combining form *-s-*). **hotnotskooigoed** /-ˈkʊɪxut/ [Afk., *kooigoed* bedding, *kooi* bed + *goed* stuff], any of several species of *Helichrysum*, a laxly-branched aromatic shrub found in dry regions, used by the Khoikhoi and some modern campers as bedding and occas. medicinally; **hotnotskool** /-ˈkʊəl/ [Afk., *kool* cabbage], *veldkool* (see VELD sense 5); **hotnotskoolbredie** /-ˌbrɪədi/ [Afk., see BREDIE], a stew of meat and any of several species of edible wild plant; **hotnotstaal** /-ˌtaːl/ [Afk., *taal* language], a derogatory name for AFRIKAANS *n.*; **hotnot(s)vis** /-ˌfəs/ [Afk., *vis* fish], *Hottentot fish*, see HOTTENTOT *n.* sense 2; **hotnotsvy(g)** /-ˌfeɪ(x)/ [Afk., *vy* (earlier *vyg*) fig], *Hottentot('s) fig*, see HOTTENTOT sense 6 a.

1947 L.G. GREEN *Tavern of Seas* 199 **Hotnotskooigoed**, a shrub campers use as bedding, is also a remedy for colds and asthma. **1966** C.A. SMITH *Common Names* 251 *Hotnotskooigoed*, .. Formerly used by vagrant Hottentots as bedding (Afr.: kooigoed) and still used by campers as bedding. **1979** *Sunday Times* 15 July 5 This is *hotnotskooigoed*, it's good for a weak heart. **1917** R. MARLOTH *Common Names* 41 **Hotnots'-kool**, *Anthericum hispidum* and *A. revolutum*. **1950** H. GERBER *Cape Cookery* 87 **Hotnotskool Bredie**. Use the young unopened flower shoots of 'hotnotskool' (Anthericos longifolium). They look like asparagus ... You could use any cauliflower recipe for 'hotnotskool' as it resembles cauliflower in flavour. **1975** *Argus* 17 Sept. 28 If you care for waterblommetjie bredie you would find Hotnotskoolbredie (made from Hottentot cabbage) just as delicious, she says. 'One picked off the snake-like stalks and used them with onions, small young potatoes and fresh lamb chops.' **1987** W.A. DE KLERK in *Sunday Times* 25 Jan. 32 The *Taalmanne* .. recognised that the vernacular Afrikaans despised as a **hotnotstaal** was in fact the true language of the Afrikaners. **1989** *Reader's Digest Illust. Hist.* 299 To the majority of Boers, Afrikaans was a mishmash of bastardised Dutch, English, Xhosa and Malayan words — 'Hotnotstaal' (Hottentot's language). **1975** *S. Afr. Panorama* July 17 The surf is the place for catching galjoen .. while **hotnotvis** .. can be landed from the rocks. **1985** J. BARON in *Frontline* Feb. 30 Clean the hotnotsvis, not worrying too much about the scales and fins. **1971** R. RAVEN-HART *Cape G.H. 1652–1702* 503 **Hotnotsvyg** .. is not 'Sword-lily', nor could leaves be so used.

Hottentot /ˈhɒt(ə)ntɒt/ *n.* and *adj.* Also **Hattentote, Hotentot, Hotnetot, Hot(t)antot, Hottendod, Hottentod, (H)ottentoo, Hottentote.** [Du., perh. fr. G. *hotteren-totteren* to stutter. 'The name *Hottentots* .. it is generally assumed .. is derived from the term *Hüttentüt* ("stammerer" or "stutterer"), applied to this people by the early Dutch settlers on account of the peculiar "clicks" which gave their speech its distinctive character.' (I. Schapera, *Khoisan Peoples of S. Afr.*, 1930, p.44). Some claim that the word is imitative of an incremental dance chant heard by early European visitors at the Cape, see quot. 1696. The relationship between this word and HODMADOD is not clear.]

The word 'Hottentot' is seen by some as offensive, and KHOIKHOI is sometimes substituted as a name for the people, particularly in scholarly contexts. However, use of 'Hottentot' does not seem to be avoided in the names of plants, fish, birds, etc. (see e.g. quot. 1994 at sense A 2).

In addition to the senses given below, there are senses of 'Hottentot' which have developed outside South Africa and which are used internationally; these will be found in general dictionaries of English.

A. *n.*

1.a. KHOIKHOI sense 1.

Since early visitors to the Cape seldom distinguished between the Khoikhoi and the San, some of the earlier citations for this sense might belong at sense 3 a.

1677 T. HERBERT in R. Raven-Hart *Before Van Riebeeck* (1967) 119 Upon their feet they have a sole or piece of leather tied with a little strap, which while these Hatten-totes were in our company their hands held, their feet having thereby the greater liberty to steal, which with their toes they can do exactly, all the while looking us in the face, the better to deceive. **1688** G. TACHARD *Voy. to Siam* II. 72 Other Nations were Slaves to the Earth .. the *Hotentots* were the Masters of it .. they ate when they were hungry, and followed no other Rules but what nature taught them. **1696** J. OVINGTON *Voy. to Suratt* 284 If there's any medium between a Rational Animal and a Beast, the *Hottentot* lays the fairest claim to the Species ... They retain the vulgar name of *Hotantots*, because of their constant repetition of that word in their hobling Dances. **1698** W. DAMPIER *New Voy. Round World* I. 537 *Hottantots* are People of a middle Stature, with small Limbs and thin Bodies, full of activity. Their Faces are of a flat oval Figure. **1731** G. MEDLEY tr. *P. Kolb's Present State of Cape of G.H.* I. 25 The name of Hottentot does by no means belong to them any other wise than as a nick-name given them by the Europeans. *Ibid.* 28 The Hottentots are of a dingy olive colour. **1795** C.R. HOPSON tr. *C.P. Thunberg's Trav.* I. 130 A widow at the Paarl had three Hottentots in her service; they spoke with much delicacy and softness, clacking lightly and rapidly with their tongues both before and while they pronounced their words. **1804** R. PERCIVAL *Acct of Cape of G.H.* 154 The Dutch do not allow blacks or Hottentots the use of this bath. There are other springs contiguous which are thought good enough for them. **1810** G. BARRINGTON *Acct of Voy.* 186 Various causes have contributed to the depopulation of the Hottentots: and their impolitic custom of hording together in families, and not marrying out of their own kraals, has no doubt tended to .. reduce them to their present degenerated condition. **1823** W.W. BIRD *State of Cape of G.H.* 67 The Hottentot is quick in capacity, and the progress of his intellect rapid, but there is an unconquerable fickleness of disposition throughout that horde. **1835** G. CHAMPION *Jrnl* (1968) 13 The Hottentot is known by his sallow complexion, resembling the color of a fallen leaf of autumn. The hair is in knots upon the head. The cheek bones are quite prominent. The forehead broad. The face tapers from the cheek bones downward. **1837** 'N. POLSON' *Subaltern's Sick Leave* 109 Wild Hottentots live in the woods and subsist on roots and the produce of the chace; a very diminutive and savage race. **1846** R. MOFFAT *Missionary Labours* 1 The Hottentots .. are .. of a sallow colour, and in some cases so light, that a tinge of red in the cheek is perceptible. **1857** 'P.B.B.' in *Cape Monthly Mag.* II. Oct. 226 The fleet had horses on board, to be left here. [*Note*] In charge of an Ottentoo, who spoke English. **a1862** J. AYLIFF *Jrnl of 'Harry Hastings'* (1963) 20 Who could live at the Cape of Good Hope .. when the people of that country are Boars, Hotnetots and Kaferees? **1866** [see TRONK sense a]. **1878** T.J. LUCAS *Camp Life & Sport* 91 The Hottentots no longer exist as a people, having become completely absorbed amongst the mixed population of the colony, where they are only to be found as dependents, .. and are .. the most reckless and degraded of mortals. **1898** G. NICHOLSON *50 Yrs* 24 Within Colonial limits, a purebred Hottentot is very rarely seen. **1904** H.A. BRYDEN *Hist. of S. Afr.* 8 When the Dutch first landed they came into contact only with a race of aborigines who called themselves Khoi-Khoin (Men of men), but were dubbed by the Europeans Hottentots. **1948** H.E. HOCKLY *Story of Brit. Settlers of 1820* 8 The Hottentots .. inhabited the coastal belt from Table Bay to the Fish River and for some considerable distance inland. **1961** O. LEVINSON *Ageless Land* 56 Originally the Hottentots were a nomadic people, consisting of many tribes that wandered through Southern Africa before the arrival of the Europeans. **1989** *Reader's Digest Illust. Hist.* 45 The plague of 1713 effectively decimated the Khoikhoi population of the south-western Cape. Those who survived lost their old clan names and became known collectively as 'Hottentots'. **1991** J. COULTER in *Weekend Post* 4 May (Leisure) 3 The name Hottentot is derived from the chant which accompanied a characteristic dance .. which Dutch settlers encouraged homeless Khoikhoi to perform in exchange for liquor.

b. *Obs.* exc. *hist.* A member of the Hottentot Corps, a military corps of Khoikhoi soldiers. See also PANDOUR.

1796 J.H. CRAIG in G.M. Theal *Rec. of Cape Col.* (1897) I. 455 The Hottentots .. must on no account whatever be permitted .. to be guilty of any sort of Insolence or outrage towards the Inhabitants. **1809** R. COLLINS in *Ibid.* (1900) IV. 20 A steady active Hottentot might be placed at the foot of the mountain, and another at the Palmiet River's drift. **1835** C.L. STRETCH *Jrnl* (1988) 56 Two companies of Hottentots were ordered to scour the bush in the vicinity of the Amatola. **1846** J. HARE in *Imp. Blue Bks* Command Paper 786–1847,

171 A force .. should proceed from the Tarka side to co-operate with Captain Hogg's force, and to be joined by the Klip Plat Hottentots from Shiloh. **1852** J.F. CHURCHILL *Diary.* (Killie Campbell Africana Library MS37) 20 Jan., All the Hottentots in the Camp at P.M. Berg were disarmed on news of this coming down. **1972** N. ORPEN in *Std Encycl. of Sn Afr.* III. 28 The Hottentots .. became the Cape Corps under the British, and in 1802 .. became known as the Hottentot Light Infantry.

c. Any of the languages of the Khoikhoi: KHOIKHOI sense 2.

1836 A.F. GARDINER *Journey to Zoolu Country* 102 The .. terms *caross, kraal* and *assegai* .. are generally believed to have been a corruption of Dutch and Hottentot. **1862** W.H.I. BLEEK *Comparative Grammar* p.viii, The importance of .. Kafir and Hottentot for .. the so-called 'Science of Language' cannot well be overvalued. **1881** *Encycl. Brit.* XII. 312 The easiest Hottentot clicks, the dental and the cerebral, have been adopted by the Kaffres. **1885** D. MULLER *Science of Lang.* II. 11 Dr Bleek .. tries to show that the Hottentot is a branch of the North African clan of languages. **1910** *Encycl. Brit.* IV. 871 Their language .. has in common with Hottentot .. the peculiar sounds known as 'clicks'. **1916** B. SHAW *Androcles & Lion; Overruled; Pygmalion* 157 I've tried her with every possible sort of sound that a human being can make — Continental dialects, African dialects, Hottentot clicks, things it took me years to get hold of. **1921** E. SAPIR *Language* 55 Certain languages, like the South African Hottentot and Bushman, have also a number of inspiratory sounds. **1953** J.B. CARROLL *Study of Lang.* 57 He .. doubts very much the validity of certain early theories that such languages .. as Bantu and Hottentot are in any way related to the Semitic-Hamitic group. **1961** H.A. GLEASON *Intro. to Descriptive Ling.* 468 In South Africa .. the *Bushman* language and *Hottentot* occupy a large area of sparsely populated desert and scrub. **1972** G.S. NIENABER in *Std Encycl. of Sn Afr.* V. 605 Afrikaans and South African English have taken over words from Hottentot, such as *buchu, dagga, kanna*. **1986** M. PICARDIE in *S. Gray Market Plays* 93 Go back .. to the time when .. talking Malay or Hottentot or Bushman or even Xhosa didn't matter.

2. In full *Hottentot fish*, also with small initial, [so called because of their predominantly brown, bronze, or copper colouring; but see quot. 1731]: any of three species of seabream of the Sparidae, *Pachymetopon* spp., esp. *P. blochii*. **a.** *P. aeneum*; BLUE FISH sense 3 b; BRONZE BREAM sense a; JOHN BROWN sense b. **b.** *P. blochii*; HANGBERGER sense 2 (formerly also called HAMBURGER); ROCK-FISH sense 2. **c.** The BRONZE BREAM (sense b), *P. grande*. In these senses also called HOTNOT (sense 3), and *hotnot(s)vis* (see HOTNOT sense 4).

In Smith and Heemstra's *Smiths' Sea Fishes* (1986), the name 'hottentot' is used for *Pachymetopon blochii*, and 'blue hottentot' for *P. aeneum*.

1731 G. MEDLEY tr. *P. Kolb's Present State of Cape of G.H.* II. 196 The Cape *Europeans* call 'em *Hottentot* Fish. That Name was given 'em by the first *Dutch* settlers there, on Account of the said Settlers buying some of them of the *Hottentots*. **1798** S.H. WILCOCKE tr. *J.S. Stavorinus's Voy. to E. Indies 1768–71* I. 560 The Hottentot-fish, which is like a sea-bream, is daily brought to market in great plenty. **1806** *Gleanings in Afr.* (anon.) 33 Nature has also acted her part, by storing the surrounding bays with variety of excellent fish, such as the steen brash, Hottentot and Roman fish. *a*1823 J. EWART *Jrnl* (1970) 13 Hottentot fish, a small fish of the shape of the perch, covered with scales of a dirty brown colour. **1838** [see STUMPNOSE sense 1]. **1872** C.A. PAYTON *Diamond Diggings* 74 Fishing with some bait and tackle .. I caught a good many of the so-called Hottentot fish, a fat little fellow, somewhat like a black bream, with very sharp prominent teeth. **1880** 'C.W.' in *Cape Monthly Mag.* II. Mar. 161, I beheld swarms of large plethoric aldermanic Hottentot fish swimming lazily below, not a fellow under five pounds weight. **1891** H.J. DUCKITT *Hilda's 'Where Is It?'* p.ix, Some kinds of fish broiled are very good, such as the Cape 'Harder,' 'Hottentot Fish' or 'Snoek'. **1902** — in M. Kuttel *Quadrilles & Konfyt* (1954) 16 A breakfast of a broiled 'Hottentot' fish, just caught — most delicious and juicy. **1905** *E. London Dispatch* 24 Oct. 2 A large number of people in this district .. would possibly mistake a largely marked *mud fish* (tottie or Hottentot) for a trout. **1919** M.M. STEYN *Diary* 32, I bought a line .. and some hooks and then got out to Sea Point again to fish for 'Hottentots' with the incoming tide. **1921** *Annals of S. Afr. Museum* XXI. 721 The Hottentot is one of the commonest Cape fishes. **1930** C.L. BIDEN *Sea-Angling Fishes* 274 Teeming millions of small hottentot .. concentrate round the bait, and .. everything is nibbled off the hook except the varnish. **1949** J.L.B. SMITH *Sea Fishes* 276 The Hottentot slipped away with the next wave. **1972** [see DAS sense 2]. **1987** *E. Prov. Herald* 28 Mar. 6 Many anglers might be biased in favour of the hottentot as our national fish as it is found only from the Western Cape to just North of Natal and is a much sought-after light-tackle angling fish and makes good eating. **1993** *Flying Springbok* Apr. 123 It may be regarded by aficionados as the poor relation of more superior fish flesh, but a humble hottentot .. is best fried and braaied. **1994** *SA Commercial Marine* Sept.-Nov. 32 One of the Cape's many tasty fish, the hottentot, has, because of its nomenclature, become the target of verbal cleansing. Some fisherman have taken to calling them hangbergers or in English, sentinels. Black fish and Cape galjoen to impress unwary northern neighbours has been attempted, but according to the Department of Sea Fisheries, Margaret M Smith's book South African Sea Fishes remains the definitive work on local names. Fisherman know and identify the fish by this name and there is little likelihood of it being changed ... Pachymetopon blochii.

3.a. *Obs. exc. hist.* KHOISAN sense 1.

See note at sense 1 a.

1795 C.R. HOPSON tr. *C.P. Thunberg's Trav.* I. 185 Hottentots is the common denomination of all those nations which inhabit the southern angle of Africa, and are extended on either side of the Cape of Good Hope ... Though they are divided into a multitude of tribes, which differ from one another in many respects, yet it is clearly to be seen that they all originate from one and the same stock. **1846** J. TINDALL *Jrnl* (1959) 96, I employed a Bushman-Hottentot. **1881** T. HAHN *Tsuni-‖Goam* 2 The appellation Hottentot is now *en vogue* ... All we can do is to define it more accurately. We should apply the term *Hottentot* to the whole race, and call the two families, each by the native name, that is the one, the *Khoikhoi*, the so-called *Hottentot proper*; the other the *Sān* (*Sā*) or *Bushmen*. **1901** *Natives of S. Afr.* (S. Afr. Native Races Committee) 9 Population of Cape Colony ... (From Census of 1891) ... 50,388 'Hottentot' includes Hottentots 42, 891 Namaquas 70, Bushmen 5,296 and Korannas 2, 131. **1933** I. SCHAPERA (tr. O. Dapper) *Early Cape Hottentots* 33 The Sonquas .. steal from other Hottentots all the cattle they can get. **1973** P.A. WHITNEY *Blue Fire* 118 'Hottentot' itself meant 'stammerer,' and was what the Dutch had called the Bushmen because of their odd language. **1977** R. ELPHICK *Kraal & Castle* 23 For decades after 1652 .. white observers applied the word *Hottentot* (or *Hottentoo*) indiscriminately to all brown-skinned, noncultivating natives of South Africa ... Cattleless people were conceived of as a subspecies of Hottentot. **1983** [see CAPOID *adj.*].

b. Any of the languages of the Khoisan peoples: KHOISAN sense 2. Also *attrib.*

1884 W.D. WHITNEY *Language* 341 They fall into three groups: the Ethiopian .. the Libyan .. and the Hottentot, embracing the dialects of the degraded tribes of Hottentots and Bushmen. **1983** *S. Afr. Panorama* Apr. 33 There are .. tours .. to .. the forests and lakes of Knysna, the numerous rivers with their valleys and strange Hottentot names, and the dense indigenous bush of the Eastern Cape Province.

4.a. *hist.* COLOURED *n.* sense a. See also BASTARD *n.* sense 1, BASTARD HOTTENTOT.

Offensive to some.

1824 W.J. BURCHELL *Trav.* II. 6 Beyond this kraal we found .. a large proportion of inhabitants .. of the race of Mixed-Hottentots. **1828** *Ordinance 50 in Cape of G.H. Stat. Ordinances & Proclam. 1806–1828* 463 Certain laws relating to and affecting the Hottentots and other free Persons of colour, lawfully residing in this Colony, require to be consolidated, amended, or repealed. **1850** J.D. LEWINS *Diary.* 25 Mar., Intend to hire the Hottentot or Bastard that was with Whitehead. **1850** J.E. METHLEY *New Col. of Port Natal* 38 If your waggon driver be a Hottentot, or Mulatto, he will be able to interpret your orders, as they can generally speak the Zoola as well as Dutch, and a little English. **1852** W. PORTER in *Grocott's Mail* (5 May 1987) 2 I would rather meet the Hottentot at the hustings voting for his representative than meet him in the wilds with his gun on his shoulder. **1862** LADY DUFF-GORDON *Lett. from Cape* (1925) 99 The Hottentots .. of mixed Dutch and Hottentot origin (correctly 'Bastaards') — have a sort of blackguard elegance in their gait and figure which is peculiar to them. **1871** J. McKAY *Reminisc.* 87 It .. still is the chief pride of the Hottentot, or swarthy bastard, to procure wives or husbands of a lighter complexion than themselves in marriage. **1907** J.P. FITZPATRICK *Jock of Bushveld* (1909) 342, I had an old cross-bred Hottentot-Bushman boy once — one could not tell which lot he favoured. **1907** W.C. SCULLY *By Veldt & Kopje* 39 Danster was a Hottentot — or rather what is called by that indefinite term at the Cape. In his much-mixed blood that of the Bushman evidently preponderated. **1909** *Rand Daily Mail* 1 Oct. 7 He [sc. Mr Merriman] had often been horrified in the north-west district to find children of white parents living like Hottentots and worse than Hottentots. **1936** *Cambridge Hist. of Brit. Empire* VIII. 274 The Hottentots were a much mixed people, perhaps predominantly Hottentot in origin, but including also strains of Bushman, Malay, negro and European .. the people — with whom the freed slaves ultimately merged — now distinguished by the epithet Cape Coloured. **1948** E. HELLMANN *Rooiyard* 11 Apart from eleven Indians, four Cape Coloureds and one 'Hottentot' (mixed Hottentot and Coloured), the remainder of the population is of Bantu stock. **1956** F.C. METROWICH *Valiant but Once* 118 His choice fell on Andries Stoffles, a Gonah Hottentot. [Note] The offspring of a Kafir-Hottentot union. **1966** J. FARRANT *Mashonaland Martyr* 6 The Hottentots .. had forgotten their own language. They spoke Cape Dutch. **1976** D.M.B. PRESTON *Story of Frontier Town* 7 'Hottentots' in the context of the Kat River Settlement means Cape Coloureds, who were no longer of pure Hottentot descent. **1988** A. SHER *Middlepost* 268 Pulling at the ropes were the Hottentot and half-caste children of Middlepost.

b. *Derog.* and *offensive.* An insulting form of address or reference to a COLOURED person. See also sense B 3.

1964 G. CAMPBELL *Old Dusty* 6 If I cannot get some of his yarns out of him, you can call me a Hottentot. **1970** M. WILSON *1000 Yrs before Van Riebeeck* 1 The pejorative term Hottentot has been used .. to imply a pastoral economy, a language .. and a physical type. *Ibid.* 4 'Hottentot' has become a term of abuse comparable to 'Kaffir.' **1977** A. ROSCOE *Uhuru's Fire* 227 We don't want any educated hottentots in our town. **1980** E. JOUBERT *Poppie Nongena* 153 God, my sister, that Hottentot hit me with a plank, he got me flat on the ground. **1986** [see GAMMAT sense 1]. **1990** *Daily News* 26 Apr. 26 The Supreme Court .. held .. that to call a white person .. a Hottentot .. is defamatory. **1990** R. MALAN in *Cosmopolitan* Apr. 167 He called the white girl a 'slut' and demanded to know why she was hanging out with a 'Hottentot'.

5. *rare.* [See quot.] A hot drink similar to Irish coffee, made of coffee and whisky.

1987 H. ST BLAIZE-MOLONY in *Style* Mar. 54 The Plett set's 'In' drink is ... Hottentot (hot-in-a-tot), which is Irish coffee without the cream.

6. Special Comb.

a. Plants and animals: **Hottentot('s) bean (tree)**, the tree *Schotia afra* of the Fabaceae; also called BOERBOON; **Hottentot bonnet** *obs.*, the orchid *Disperis capensis* of the Orchidaceae; also called MOEDERKAPPIE; **Hottentot('s) bread** [tr. S. Afr.

Du. *Hottentotsbrood*], any of several widely differing plant species, parts of which were formerly used to produce a food resembling bread, esp. (*a*) the BREAD TREE, and (*b*) the *elephant's foot* (see ELEPHANT), *Dioscorea elephantipes*; also, this food; **Hottentot's cabbage**, also **Hottentots' cabbage**, any of several plants (*Trachyandra* spp. of the Liliaceae) with edible asparagus-like inflorescences; also called *veldkool*, see VELD sense 5; **Hottentot's candle**, BUSHMAN'S CANDLE; **Hottentot's cherry**, the shrub *Maurocenia frangularia* of the Celastraceae; **Hottentot('s) fig** [tr. S. Afr. Du. *Hottentotsvijg*], the hardy, creeping plant *Carpobrotus edulis* of the Aizoaceae, with medicinal properties; the edible fruit of this plant; GOCUM; *hotnotsvy(g)*, see HOTNOT sense 4; also called SOUR FIG; also *attrib.*; **Hottentot(s) god**, also **-God**, [tr. S. Afr. Du. *Hottentotsgod*], any of several species of insect formerly venerated by the Khoisan peoples, esp. the praying mantis; **Hottentot head**, the cycad *Stangeria eriopus* of the Stangeriaceae, with a thick turnip-like trunk; **Hottentots rice**, (*a*) BUSHMAN RICE; (*b*) the succulent plant *Gasteria nigricans* of the Liliaceae; **Hottentot sore** *obs.*, *veld sore* (see VELD sense 5); **Hottentot's poison bush**, BUSHMAN'S POISON; **Hottentot('s) tea**, BUSHMAN'S TEA; **Hottentot teal**, the small duck *Anas hottentota* of the Anatidae, with blue bill, spotted breast and back, and head dark above, light below; **Hottentot watermelon** *obs.*, KAMBRO.

1801 J. BARROW *Trav.* I. 188 The **Hottentot's bean**: This plant is the African lignum vitæ, the *guajacum Afrum* of Linnæus and the *Schotia speciosa* of the *Hortus Kewensis*. **1833** S. KAY *Trav. & Researches* 106 The Hottentot's bean tree ... Clusters of scarlet flowers, intermingled with the small and elegant green foliage, give it a remarkable pre-eminence over the tall trees of the ravines. **1921** T.R. SIM *Native Timbers* 192 Hottentots Bean Tree. *Schotia*, sps. **1976** A.P. BRINK *Instant in Wind* 93 They trekked past the fringe of a dense forest, .. reaching .. thickets of .. Hottentot's bean .. and the ubiquitous euphorbia. **1987** F. VON BREITENBACH *Nat. List of Indigenous Trees* 327 *Schotia afra*, .. Hottentot's Bean ... The roasted beans are eaten by some tribes. **1848** C.J.F. BUNBURY *Jrnl of Res. at Cape of G.H.* 188 *Disperis Capensis* .. is known by the name of the **Hottentot Bonnet**, on account of the peculiar shape of its purple and green flowers. **1731** G. MEDLEY tr. *P. Kolb's Present State of Cape of G.H.* II. 223 The Root of the *Arum*, among the Cape *Europeans*, is ordinarily call'd **Hottentot-Bread**; the *Hottentots* frequently eating it in the Place of Bread. They boil out its Acrimony .. then dry it in the Sun. Afterwards they roast it in Embers. **1818** [see UINTJIE sense 1 a]. **1824** W.J. BURCHELL *Trav.* II. 147 These mountains are the native soil of an extraordinary plant called *Hottentots Brood* (Hottentot's Bread). Its bulb stands entirely above ground, and grows to an enormous size, frequently three feet in height and diameter. **1844** J. BACKHOUSE *Narr. of Visit* 326 Hottentots-bread, found on the Karroo about Uitenhage. **1858** R. HOGG *Vegetable Kingdom & its Products* 718 The root-stock of *Testudinaria elephantipes*, called Elephant's Foot or Hottentot's Bread, forms a large, fleshy mass covered with a rough and cracked bark. **1887** [see *elephant's foot* (ELEPHANT)]. **1929** D. REITZ *Commando* 240 A strange growth known as 'Hottentot's bread' (*Encephalartos Altensteinii*), a wild fruit not unlike a large pine-apple. **1987** F. VON BREITENBACH *Nat. List of Indigenous Trees* 1 Cycad family ... *Encephalartos altensteinii* Lehm ... *Eastern Cape Cycad*, Hottentot's Bread. **1991** D.M. MOORE *Garden Earth* 198 The massive corky tubers of Hottentot bread (*Dioscorea elephantipes*), a type of yam, are also eaten. **1856** *Cape of G.H. Almanac & Annual Register* 346 The flower heads of this plant which thrives abundantly in the deep sands near the sea-shore, furnish a kind of culinary vegetable, which somewhat resembles asparagus, and is known as **Hottentot's cabbage** ... When stewed and properly prepared, they make no contemptible dish. **1982** FOX & NORWOOD YOUNG *Food from Veld* 253 *Trachyandra revoluta ... Common names:* English — Hottentots' cabbage. **1991** *S. Afr. Panorama* Jan.-Feb. 39 The Namaqualanders gladly welcome visitors to their home — a fine opportunity to .. feast on .. Hottentot's cabbage and candied sweet potatoes. **1975** *Sunday Times* 12 Oct. (TV Mag.) 5 Did he know the **Hottentot's candle** .. the waxy-stemmed xerophyte once used by the Nama for lighting these huts? **1818** H.J. TODD *Dict. of Eng. Lang. by Samuel Johnson* **Hottentot Cherry**. **1860** L. PAPPE *Florae Capensis* I. 465 *M.[aurocenia] capensis* ... Engl. name Hottentot cherry. **1880** *S.W. Silver & Co.'s Handbk to S. Afr.* 138 Hottentot Cherry .. is the fruit of *Maurocenia Capensis* .., a shrub growing in the ravines of Table Mountain. **1982** FOX & NORWOOD YOUNG *Food from Veld* 152 This fruit, called *Hottentot's cherry*, is edible and was once eaten by Hottentots. **1731** G. MEDLEY tr. *P. Kolb's Present State of Cape of G.H.* I. 141 Women go into the Fields to gather the Stalks of what they call **Hottentot-Figs**. With the juice .. they wash the Child all over. **1795** C.R. HOPSON tr. *C.P. Thunberg's Trav.* I. 163 *Mesembryanthemum edule* grew here in abundance, and especially in the sandy plains, and was called Hottentots figs .. the fruit when ripe and peeled, tasting tolerably well. **1821** T. PHILIPPS *Lett.* (1960) 85 The Hottentot Fig .. is a runner, the leaf is very thick and juicy, and is used by the Hottentots as a sovereign remedy for any bruise or sore, and they take it for many complaints. **1822** W.J. BURCHELL *Trav.* I. 54 The Hottentot fig .. produces plentifully .. a fruit of the size of a small fig, of a very pleasant acid taste ... The fruit when unripe has a disagreeably saline and austere taste. *a*1827 D. CARMICHAEL in W.J. Hooker *Botanical Misc.* (1831) II. 264 The mucilaginous capsules of the .. *Hottentot Fig*, are the chief material of an agreeable preserve. **1858** 'P.B.B.' in *Cape Monthly Mag.* IV. July 11 By an immoderate use of the Hottentot fig, some .. people were attacked with a dangerous flux. **1862** LADY DUFF-GORDON *Lett. from Cape* (1925) 83 Hottentot figs are rather nice — a green fig-shaped thing, containing .. a salt-sweet insipid glue, which you suck out ... The plant has a thick, succulent, triangular leaf. **1862** 'A LADY' *Life at Cape* (1963) 78 It puzzled everybody how to fix them [*sc.* sand-dunes], until the late Colonial Secretary hit upon the device of planting them with Hottentot fig — a wild succulent plant, like a lot of fingers moulded in green jelly, and which will grow anywhere. **1891** H.J. DUCKITT *Hilda's 'Where Is It?'* 176 Preserve ('Hottentot Fig,' or 'Sour Fig') ... (The Hottentot Fig is the fruit of a kind of mesembryanthemum which grows wild at the Cape.) **1910** R. JUTA *Cape Peninsula* 112 We .. kept close up to the sand-dunes, the white sand protected from the tearing gales of the 'South-easters' by a network of creeping 'Hottentot fig'. **1927** C.G. BOTHA *Social Life in Cape Col.* 103 Where the Hottentots fig .. was found, few other plants were so common in domestic use ... The juice from the succulent leaves was taken internally to check dysentery and acted as a mild diuretic. It was used as .. a lotion in burns and scalds. **1947** L.G. GREEN *Tavern of Seas* 66 Home recipes included a Hottentot fig gargle for sore throats. **1965** S. ELIOVSON *S. Afr. Wild Flowers for Garden* 287 Several species [of 'vygie'] have sour, fig-like fruits that are edible ... The edible types were called *Hottentot figs*. **1972** L.G. GREEN *When Journey's Over* 44 My coloured wagon crews gathered herbs and other veld medicines: .. grilled Hottentot fig for ear-ache. **1988** M. BRANCH *Explore Cape Flora* 19 The huge purple flowers of the .. Hottentot's fig grow well in sand near the seaside. Their soft, edible fruits have hundreds of little black seeds in a sticky sour syrup. [**1731 Hottentot God**: G. MEDLEY tr. *P. Kolb's Present State of Cape of G.H.* I. 98 The *Hottentots* .. adore .. a certain Insect ... To this little winged Deity, when ever they set Sight upon it, they render the highest Tokens of Veneration.] **1786** G. FORSTER tr. *A. Sparrman's Voy. to Cape of G.H.* I. 211 There is a genus of insects (the *mantis*) called by the colonists the *Hottentot's god*; but so far are they from worshipping these insects, that they have more than once catched some of them, and given them to me to stick needles through them by way of preserving them. **1796** C.R. HOPSON tr. *C.P. Thunberg's Trav.* II. 65 A small grey species of grasshopper (*Mantis fausta*) was found .. which has obtained the name of the *Hottentots God*, and is supposed to be worshipped by them. **1853** F.P. FLEMING *Kaffraria* 79 If touched, it immediately stops, and, rising on the hinder part of the body, it puts the two fore-legs, slightly bent, in an attitude of prayer, which has gained for it the cognomen of the praying Mantis, or Hottentot god. **1865** 'A LADY' *Life at Natal* (1972) 51 The most extraordinary insects were the .. 'Hottentot Gods', which grow here to an immense size. Some were eight inches long, and exactly like bits of dry twig. **1887** A.A. ANDERSON *25 Yrs in Waggon* I. 116 The mantis family, commonly called in Africa, Hottentot gods, as they always appear to be praying, having their two arms held as if in that act. **1890** A. MARTIN *Home Life* 264 In spite of being the Hottentot God, and of possessing such a pious-sounding scientific name as *Mantis religiosa*, he is a most pugnacious little beast. **1907** J.P. FITZPATRICK *Jock of Bushveld* (1909) 340 Hottentot-gods .. reared up and 'prayed' before him; quaint things, with tiny heads and thin necks and enormous eyes. **1918** S.H. SKAIFE *Animal Life* 61 Some of our most remarkable insects .. receive their popular name of 'Hottentot gods,' or praying insects from the manner in which they carry their front legs. **1939** *Outspan* 26 May 13 The common Hottentot God, the praying mantis (*Mantis religiosa*), so well-known .. in South Africa, is also found in .. the south of Europe. **1955** A. DELIUS *Young Trav.* 33 There were .. praying mantises with two front legs lifted in front of sinister triangular heads (as if in prayer) and known .. as 'Hottentot Gods'. **1961** L. VAN DER POST *Heart of Hunter* 161 When they noticed the reverence in which the Mantis was held by some of the aborigines of the Cape, they inaccurately called him the Hottentot's God. **1976** A. DELIUS *Border* 52 He's like one of those sinister insects .. like a pink, sweaty Hottentot God with green glasses. **1980** A.J. BLIGNAUT *Dead End Rd* 57 The Hottentot's god .. was praying for you. But .. you're past praying for. **1884** W. MILLER *Dict. of Eng. Names of Plants*, **Hottentot's-head**, Stangeria paradoxa. **1973** BEETON & DORNER in *Eng. Usage in Sn Afr.* Vol.4 No.2, 21 *Hottentot head*, .. Cycads with thick trunks; .. single cones develop on the stems with a silvery pubescence at first, but turn brown with age. **1775** F. MASSON in *Phil. Trans. of Royal Soc.* LXVI. 315 The eggs of a large species of ant, which they dig out of the ground in great quantities, washing them in water, and afterwards boiling them .. are commonly called **Hottentots rice**. **1970** BEETON & DORNER in *Eng. Usage in Sn Afr.* Vol.1 No.2, 27 *Hottentot's rice*, .. (*Gasteria nigricans*) succulent plant .. with pendulous coral-pink flowers with green-tipped segments; the Hott[entots] .. boiled the young buds as rice. **1822** W.J. BURCHELL *Trav.* I. 371 The most dangerous malady is a kind of cancerous sore or ulcer, called in the colony the *Hottentots Zeer* (**Hottentot Sore**). **1885** A. SMITH *Contrib. to Materia Medica* 12 *Strychnos*, **Hottentot's poison bush** ... This plant is used by the natives for the cure of snake-bite, but it has many uses. **1913** [see BUSHMAN'S POISON]. **1973** F.J. VELDMAN in *Std Encycl. of Sn Afr.* VIII. 610 The so-called Bushman's or Hottentot's poison-bush or gifboom (*Acokanthera oblongifolia* and *A. oppositifolia*) grows especially in the warm Bushveld along rivers, and the sap of the fruit was used by Bushmen for rendering their arrows poisonous. **1850** L. PAPPE *Florae Capensis* 17 *Helichrysum serpyllifolium* .. goes by the name of **Hottentot's tea**, .. and is much liked by the coloured people, who infuse it as tea. **1972** M.R. LEVYNS in *Std Encycl. of Sn Afr.* V. 611 *Hottentot Tea*, (*Helichrysum orbiculare* = *H. serpyllifolium*.) ... The shrub occurs in bushy places in the coastal regions from Cape Town to Natal. Another species, which is also called Hottentot tea, is *H. nudifolium*. **1937** M. ALSTON *Wanderings* 165 My eyes alighted on a pair of rare birds ... They were **Hottentot teal**, the smallest of ducks, and beautiful little brown and black creatures. **1993** G.L. MACLEAN *Roberts' Birds* 88 Hottentot Teal ... *Anas hottentota*. **1796** C.R. HOPSON tr. *C.P. Thunberg's Trav.* II. 135, I heard .. of a **Hottentot Watermelon** .. a large and succulent root, called Kou by the Hottentots, who grind it down to meal, and bake it like bread.

b. Products of the Khoikhoi: **Hottentot beer** *obs.*, HONEY-BEER.

1821 G. BARKER Journal. 2 June, One of the people had been drinking .. **hottentot beer**, made from honey. [**1976** A.P. BRINK *Instant in Wind* 105 Men .. drinking tea or the Hottentot beer of honey and *gli-roots*.]

c. Physiological features associated with the Khoikhoi: **Hottentot('s) apron**, an excessive elongation of the *labia minora* in Khoikhoi women; APRON sense 2.

[**1797** see sense B 1.] **1909** *Cent. Dict.* Suppl., **Hottentot's apron**. **1933** I. SCHAPERA tr. *O. Dapper's Kaffraria* 45 The labia minora are sometimes considerably elongated, and may project .. 60mm beyond the rima pudendi. This hypertrophy, the so-called Hottentot apron, has been regarded .. as artificially produced by manipulation. **1956** C. WINICK *Dict. of Anthropology* 33 There is some controversy as to whether the Hottentot apron is a genetic trait or an intentional deformation. **1964** R. RAVEN-HART in *Quarterly Bulletin of S. Afr. Library* Vol.18, 99 The Hottentot 'Apron' has been one of the most disputed of subjects, some writers even denying its existence altogether ... Many say that it was natural .. others that it was entirely artificial. **1974** *Rand Daily Mail* 28 Jan. 5 An unfortunate aspect of the publication is the exclusion of four sketches illustrating the 'Hottentot's apron' – a sex peculiarity in women. **1975** J. & I. RUDNER (tr.) in V.S. Forbes *A. Sparrman's Voy. to Cape of G.H.* 183 The so-called Hottentot's Apron .. appears to be a physiological feature and not artificially produced by manipulation ... It is not peculiar to Hottentots, for it is common among Bushwomen as well as among various East African peoples. **1992** P. CULLINAN *Robert Jacob Gordon* 25 *(caption)* François le Vaillant's drawing of the much disputed 'Hottentot apron'.

B. *Attrib.* and as *adj.*

1. Of or pertaining to the KHOIKHOI or KHOISAN peoples.

1718 *Entertainer* No.28, 187 The Spiritual is reduc'd to a Hottentot Way of Government. **1731** G. MEDLEY tr. *P. Kolb's Present State of Cape of G.H.* (1738) I. 33 The Generality of words or sounds in the *Hottentot* Tongue, yielding to no form of Writing or Pronunciation known in *Europe*, 'tis next to impossible to deliver any Thing of it for the Press that can merit the Name of a Specimen. *Ibid.* 62 Of the several *Hottentot* Nations, at the *Cape*, the first is the *Gunjeman* Nation, who sold their territories to the *Dutch*. *Ibid.* 63 Adjoining to the *Sussaqua's*, are the *Odiqua's* or *Udiqua's*. *Ibid.* 76 The *Sonquas* .. take up, for the most part, the Military Profession, and are Mercenaries to the other *Hottentot* Nations in their wars. *Ibid.* 81 The Hottentot stammering or clashing of the tongue in speaking. **1797** *Encycl. Brit.* VIII. 684 The Hottentot language is .. said to be a composition of the most strange and disagreeable sounds. *Ibid.* 685 A general opinion has prevailed that the Hottentot women have a kind of natural vail which covers the female parts. *Ibid.* 687 In a craal, or Hottentot village, the huts are most commonly disposed in a circle. **1836** *Penny Cyclopaedia* VI. 257 The latter [*sc.* the Koranna] are one of the few Hottentot tribes that have retained their independence. **1862** [see sense A 4 a]. **1866** WATERMEYER in *Trans. of Philol. Soc.* 17 The Hottentot national name is 'Khoikhoip', plural 'Khoikhoin', and is still in use among the Namaquas. **1897** J. BRYCE *Impressions* 77 From unions between Hottentot women and the Dutch sprang the mixed race whom the Dutch call Bastards and the English Griquas. **1924** *Internat. Jrnl of Psycho-Analysis* V. 41 It might perhaps be not without significance that three of the five patients informed me of their own accord that they possessed 'Hottentot nymphae'. **1933** I. SCHAPERA *Early Cape Hottentots* p.xii, In Hottentot mythology ‖Gaunab figured as a malevolent chief. **1933** W. PLOMER in *Best of S. Afr. Short Stories* (1991) 179 Mrs Stevens used to say she had no doubt that Plaatje had Chinese blood, but Stevens smiled and said it was Hottentot. **1968** M. MULLER *Green Peaches Ripen* 40 Christiaan's Hottentot ancestry was apparent in his flat-nosed, yellow-brown face, toothless and wrinkled like an old apple. **1977** R. ELPHICK *Kraal & Castle* 14 Hottentot culture is still recognizably Bushman in all its basic patterns, and its deviations are about the minimum to be expected in a hunting people adapting to a more stable pastoral economy.

2. Often *pejorative*. Indigenous; inviting contempt, inferior.

1828 J. PHILIP *Researches* I. p.xviii, The missionaries .. were called .. 'Hottentot predicants' (ministers), by way of contempt. **1963** R. LEWCOCK *Early 19th C. Archit.* 283 In the Cape Town church rows of mediaeval battlements were linked to the tower by baroque scrolls; a Roman Tuscan portico framed a pointed Gothic fanlight over the side door, and a baroque arched entablature framed the Gothic fanlight of the main doors. It was a style well worthy of the term 'Hottentot Gothic' which the Settlers invented to express their feelings about it! **1971** B. BIERMANN *Red Wine* 146 In the hands of strangers the buildings fell on evil days ... They [*sc.* the Cape Dutch homesteads] were dubbed 'Hottentot style' buildings; one by one the great gables fell. **1988** C. MARAIS in *Personality* 19 Dec. 34 In the old days a Cape Dutch house was considered second grade, and dubbed 'The Hottentot Style'. Nowadays .. the sweep and flow of Hottentot Style is being used in many urban centres around the country.

3. *Derog.* and *offensive*. Of or pertaining to one of mixed ethnic origin (see sense A 4 b).

1986 M. PICARDIE in S. Gray *Market Plays* 87 You Hottentot rubbish .. You Bushman piece of dirt ... You are not fit to judge .. this Afrikaner.

Hottie /ˈhɒti, ˈhɔti/ *n. ?Offensive. colloq.* [Formed on HOTTENTOT + Eng. (informal) n.-forming suffix *-ie*; cf. TOTTIE.] An affectionate or derogatory term of reference to a KHOIKHOI (*n.* sense 1) or a COLOURED (*n.* sense a). Also *attrib.*

1970 *Informant, Misgund (W. Cape)* Hotties. Hottentots. **1977** J. HEYNS in *Drum* July 6 When the settlers called on at Khore's village, it was the Hottie moffies who led the entertainment, providing food, liquor and other pleasures. **1987** B. PEARSON in *Weekly Mail* 17 July 11 Neville .. describes himself as a Cape Hottie. **1988** R. MARSDEN *Informant, Swakopmund (Namibia)* Hottie is an irreverent name for a coloured person whose features tend towards the Bushman look, i.e. high cheekbones, yellowish skin, smallish. **1992** *Informant, Cape Town* Hottie. A Coloured.

Hottniqua var. OUTENIQUA.

hou *int.* var. HAU *int.*

‖**hou** /həʊ/ *v. trans.* In the interjectional phr. ***hou moed*** /həʊ ˈmʊt/ [Afk., *hou* hold + *moed* courage], an injunction not to lose heart. Cf. VASBYT.

Used most commonly in speech.

[**1900** P.J. DU TOIT *Diary* (1974) 13 After riding a small distance we off-saddled and the General addressed the men, encouraging them to 'hou goede moed'. [*Note*] Keep their courage up.] **1936** C. BIRKBY *Thirstland Treks* 252 As after the 1925 floods, so now the women urged their men to *hou moed*, to be courageous in facing the future. **1944** 'TWEDE IN BEVEL' *Piet Kolonel* 113 As .. the goal of going North seemed more unattainable than ever, it would have been no wonder had our oft-repeated cry of 'Hou moed' fallen on deaf ears. [**1973** *Star* 2 June 13 Happy birthday, however. (It was on Thursday, if you remember.) Hou moed – en die blink kant bo.] **1978** *Het Suid-Western* 6 Dec., Go to it P.W. – Hou moed. **1991** A. VAN WYK *Birth of New Afrikaner* 33 The smiling faces would transmit: '*Hou moed!* Do not lose heart!'

‖**houbok** /ˈhəʊbɔk/ *n.* Pl. **-ke** /kə/, or unchanged. [Afk., *hou* keep, retain, store + *bok* antelope.] A springbok which remains in a particular area throughout the year. See also SPRINGBOK sense 1 a. Cf. *trekbok*, see TREK *n.* sense 12 b.

1955 L.G. GREEN *Karoo* 44 Karoo farmers last century firmly believed in two varieties of springbok – the lean *trekbok* and the fatter *houbok* (about fifteen pounds heavier), which remained in one area. **1958** S. CLOETE *Mask* 94 This was a springbok trek. The houbok, the residents as it were of the district, had been augmented by the trekbok. **1966** E. PALMER *Plains of Camdeboo* 162 They pointed out also that however many buck migrated, there were also some that did not – the '*houbokke*' or 'stay-at-homes', the farmers used to call them, and they divided into a completely different category from the travelling buck.

hou jou bek see BEK sense 2.

hour *n. Obs.* exc. *hist.* [Special use of general Eng. *hour* (a measure of time), influenced by Du. *uur* a measure of distance.] A measurement of distance: the distance which can be covered in an hour.

1785 G. FORSTER tr. *A. Sparrman's Voy. to Cape of G.H.* II. 81 This place is situated at the distance of two hours (uurs) from that which we had just quitted. **1792** E. RIOU tr. *J. Van Reenen's Jrnl of Journey from Cape of G.H.* p.xii, Throughout the journal the word hour is to be considered as distance, and not time. Travellers at the Cape of Good Hope reckon distance by hours: one hour being supposed equal to about a league. **1798** S.H. WILCOCKE tr. *J.S. Stavorinus's Voy. to E. Indies 1768–71* I. 58 A Dutch mile, which they in general call an hour, is about three miles and a half English. **1801** W. SOMERVILLE *Narr. of E. Cape Frontier* (1979) 64 From Commando fonteyn we proceeded to a place near the banks of the Sack River distance 9 Hours. **1809** R. COLLINS in G.M. Theal *Rec. of Cape Col.* (1900) VII. 136 The distance should be laid down by miles, to put an end to the absurd practice of measuring by hours. **1838** J.E. ALEXANDER *Exped. into Int.* I. 29 They have perhaps to ride a distance of fifty or sixty hours, and the same distance back on bringing an offender to justice. *a***1875** T. BAINES *Jrnl of Res.* (1964) II. 85 Informed them that it was customary to obtain a passport from the Field-Cornet, who lived three hours on horseback – eighteen miles – distant. **1886** W.H. MIDDLETON *Map of OFS* (Bloemfontein Cathedral Archives), (*legend*) This map of the Orange Free State Republic .. is based on one I published in 1880, and [I] have kept the mode of reckoning by hours, (not miles) as it is the custom of the country to which it relates. **1893** *Brown's S. Afr.* 15 The reply to inquiries regarding distance will invariably be so many 'hours', the Dutchman having no knowledge of miles and measuring all distances by the time it will take him to ride them. The hour may be reckoned as a little more than 6 miles. **1916** J.M. ORPEN *Reminisc.* (1964) 302 This [land] included a piece which I was required to lay out in the form of a square, of which each side was to be an 'hour on horseback' in length, around Makawaanstad, with that kraal as centre. **1920** K.M. JEFFREYS tr. *Memorandum of Commissary J.A. de Mist* 231 Take the average breadth to be twenty hours, and we find that the district contains more or less 2,500 hours of land. *c***1936** *S. & E. Afr. Yr Bk & Guide* 26 In the 18th century the '*hour*' was sometimes used as an actual measure of distance, approximating two miles. **1955** L.G. GREEN *Karoo* 76 Those were the days when karoo distances were reckoned in terms of hours on horseback.

house *n. hist.* [Special senses of general Eng. *house* the building in which a legislative or deliberative assembly meets, (*transf.*) this assembly.]

1. ***House of Assembly***:

a. From 1852 to 1910, the lower house of the parliament of the Cape Colony; VOLKSRAAD sense 1 b.

1852 *Ordinance 29* in G.W. Eybers *Sel. Constit. Doc.* (1918) 45 There should be within the settlement of the Cape of Good Hope a Parliament, to consist of the Governor, a Legislative Council, and House of Assembly. **1872** J.L. BABE *S. Afr. Diamond Fields* 75 The Parliament consists of two representative bodies called the Legislative Council and the House of Assembly. **1897** P.A. MOLTENO *Sel. from Correspondence* (1981) 51, I have two brothers in the Cape House of Assembly. **1909** H.E.S. FREMANTLE *New Nation* 38 A representative Select Committee of the Cape

House of Assembly unanimously agreed to insert clauses in an Education Bill providing that .. every English or Dutch child should learn both languages.

b. From 1910 to 1961, the lower house of the parliament of the Union of South Africa; from 1961 to 1984, the lower house of the parliament of the Republic of South Africa.

1909 *S. Afr. Act* in G.W. Eybers *Sel. Constit. Doc.* (1918) 537 There shall be a provisional council in each province consisting of the same number of members as are elected in the province for the House of Assembly. 1926 M. NATHAN *S. Afr. from Within* 241 Legislation vests in the Parliament of the Union. This consists of two Houses: the Senate, and the House of Assembly ... The House of Assembly consists of a variable number of members. c1936 [see ADMINISTRATOR sense b]. 1939 *Star* 4 Sept. 11 (*caption*) House of Assembly. Monday. 1972 W.P.L. VAN ZYL in *Std Encycl. of Sn Afr.* V. 613 *House of Assembly,* The lower house of the South African Parliament, now composed of directly elected White representatives of the White people of the four provinces of the Republic and of South-West Africa. c1988 *S. Afr. 1987-8: Off. Yrbk* (Bureau for Info.) 121 The bicameral legislature comprised a House of Assembly whose members .. were elected by simple majority .. and a senate.

c. In the TRICAMERAL parliamentary system (1984–1994): the chamber consisting of, and representing, white people. Also *attrib.*

1983 *Act* 110 in *Govt Gaz.* Vol.219 No.8914, 26 The House of Assembly shall consist of- (a) 166 members, each of whom shall be directly elected by the persons entitled to vote. 1985 [see sense 2]. 1987 L. LIGHTFOOT in *E. Prov. Herald* 1 May 2 The SABC is putting on the largest outside broadcast it has ever undertaken to cover the results of the House of Assembly election on May 6. c1988 *S. Afr. 1987-8: Off. Yrbk* (Bureau for Info.) 107 The House of Assembly consists of 178 members of whom 166 are elected by simple majority .., while four are nominated by the State President .. and eight are elected on the basis of proportional representation of the various political parties by the 166 directly elected members once they meet in Parliament. 1989 [see sense 3].

2. *House of Delegates*: In the TRICAMERAL parliamentary system (1984–1994), the chamber consisting of, and representing, South Africans of Indian descent; HoD.

1983 *Act* 110 in *Govt Gaz.* Vol.219 No.8914, 28 The House of Delegates shall consist of- (a) 40 members. 1984 *Rhodeo* (Rhodes Univ.) Oct., The House of Delegates has even less credibility. Of more than 500 000 Indians eligible to vote, only 83000 did so. 1985 *Afr. Review* 296 Parliament will be made up of three chambers, a house of assembly (178 members) for whites, a house of representatives (85 members) for 'coloured' (mixed race) people, and a house of delegates (45 members) for Indians. 1989 [see sense 3]. 1991 A. MAIMANE in *Weekly Mail* 15 Feb. 17, I asked the only other person in the lift if he was a member of the House of Delegates. He might look like one of them, he replied, but he wasn't an Indian: he, too, was coloured.

3. *House of Representatives*: In the TRICAMERAL parliamentary system (1984–1994), the chamber consisting of, and representing, those officially classified as COLOURED persons.

1983 *Act* 110 in *Govt Gaz.* Vol.219 No.8914, 28 The House of Representatives shall consist of- (a) 80 members each of whom shall be directly elected. 1984 *Evening Post* 22 Aug. 1 Voting in the elections for the House of Representatives got off to a painfully slow start around South Africa today. 1985 [see sense 2]. 1988 B. STREEK in *Cape Times* 20 Jan. 1 President P.W. Botha has refused to dismiss Mr Carter Ebrahim as the Minister of Education and Culture in the House of Representatives. 1989 *Reader's Digest Illust. Hist.* 467 Under the 1983 Constitution Act the South African Parliament consists of three legislative houses: the House of Assembly for Whites; the House of Representatives for Coloured people; and the House of Delegates for Asians.

housekeeper *n.* [Special sense of general Eng. *housekeeper* a woman who manages or superintends the affairs of a household (which is also used in S. Afr. Eng.).] A domestic worker; HELPER.

1982 Z. MAYAT *Indian Delights* 5 The help of several persons who have been deeply involved with this project and foremost amongst these is my housekeeper Mildred Mdladla. 1985 L. SAMPSON in *Style* Feb. 103 She has spent much of her life, working as a domestic servant; she prefers to call it a housekeeper. 1987 G. SILBER in *Style* Nov. 52 Housekeeper, Upwardly-mobile maid. 1988 L. JEANNES in *Style* Feb. 54 Somehow .. 'my domestic worker' doesn't roll as easily off the tongue or the teacups as 'my maid' ... The vogue word seems to be housekeeper. It has a round, rich upmarket feel. And it leaves the listener in doubt as to the exact colour of the person keeping house. There is a lot of status in having a white or even a dark beige housekeeper.

Housuana, Houswaana varr. HOUZOUANA.

hout /haʊt/ *n. Derog.* and *offensive. slang.* Shortened form of HOUTKOP. Also occas. **houtie** [see -IE].

1970 *Informant,* Grahamstown Houtie. Native. 1977 *Rhodeo* (Rhodes Univ.) 1 Aug. 15 In confirming that black and white students tend to mix socially largely with members of the same race groups, he commented that 'some white goody-goodies try and mix and hang around only with "houts"'. 1979 *Ibid.* 25 May 2 (*caption*) The houts have too many babies. 1985 [see GOOI sense 2]. 1987 M. POLAND *Train to Doringbult* 84 A coon got squashed by a truck this afternoon ... Silly hout fell off the back.

Houteniqua var. OUTENIQUA.

houtkapper /'haʊtkapə(r)/ *n. obsolescent.* [Afk., *hout* wood + *kapper* chopper, cutter; see quot. 1905.] Any of several species of termite of the Hodotermitidae and Termitidae, esp. *Hodotermes mossambicus.* Also *attrib.*

1904 *Cape of G.H. Agric. Jrnl* 471 (Pettman), The trouble here is not the small white ant, but the large brown black head, locally known as *Houtkapper* or wood-chopper. 1905 L. PÉREINGUEY in Flint & Gilchrist *Science* in *S. Afr.* 158 A subterranean, eyed, grass or twig-cutting one [*sc.* termite] .. works in the open in the daytime. Owing to its habit of piling up at the entrance little heaps of twigs of grass or dry wood cut to a short length, it has received here the cognomen of 'Hout-kapper,' or wood-cutter. 1911 *Farmer's Weekly* 15 Mar. 9 The insects causing the damage are I presume the large termites often called the 'Houtkapper'. 1913 C. PETTMAN *Africanderisms* 221 *Houtkapper,* .. The name is .. given to a species of termite — *Hodotermes havilandi,* which is destructive to growing crops. 1918 S.H. SKAIFE *Animal Life* 71 All termites, except the marching termite, or *houtkapper,* are blind. 1979 T. GUTSCHE *There Was a Man* 344 A certain white or 'Houtkapper' ant harboured a worm in its bloated body.

houtkop /'haʊtkɔp/ *n. Offensive. slang.* Pl. **-koppe** /-kɔpə/. [Afk., 'blockhead', *hout* wood + *kop* head.] A derogatory and insulting term for a black person.

1950 E. PARTRIDGE *Dict. of Underworld Slang* 348 *Houtkop,* An aborigine or coloured native. 1970 *Informant,* Johannesburg Houtkop. Bantu. 1973 *Daily Dispatch* 6 Aug. 8 The days of 'bloody kaffir' and 'houtkop' are definitely past ... Bantu are people. Respect their human values. 1980 C. HOPE *A Separate Development* (1983) 130 Jacko would ... start calling Joerie a coloured, a klonkie, a houtkop, a moffie, an Abo, a kaffir. 1983 *Times* (U.K.) 6 June 6 The court heard how .. Mr van der Merwe expressed a desire 'to hit a "houtkop" (thickhead)' an abusive term for a black. 1987 *Frontline* Mar. 22 Jonas is 'unskilled'. He can drive a tractor although he doesn't have a licence. The baas thinks that if you help a houtkop get a licence he will run away. 1989 *Informant,* KwaZulu-Natal They poisoned that dog ... They killed him because he used to wait until the houtkop had walked past and then attack from the back. 1991 M. KANTEY *All Tickets* 73 Van Eiselen's systematic hewing of the houtkoppe.

Houzouana *n. obs.* Also **Housuana, Houswaana.** Pl. unchanged, or **-s.** [Unkn.] SAN sense 1. Also *attrib.*

1790 tr. F. Le Vaillant's *Trav.* II. 347, I propose to give some further account of these Houswaana when, passing under the tropic, I come to visit their hordes. 1802 LADY A. BARNARD in D. Fairbridge *Lady Anne Barnard* (1924) 48 The Housuanas, or Wilde Boshiesmen, .. I have already seen enough of to raise my curiosity to a prodigious degree. 1810 G. BARRINGTON *Acct of Voy.* 367 The head of the Houzouana, though it exhibits the principal characteristics of that of the Hottentot, is .. rounder towards the chin. Their complexion, not so black, exhibits the lead colour of the Malays. 1879 tr. J.A.L. De Quatrefages's *Human Species* 52 This steatopygia reappears however in certain tribes situated much further north than the Houzouana races.

howzit /'haʊzət/ *int. colloq.* Also **hoesit, hoezet, hooze(e)t, howsit.** [Contraction of Eng. salutation *How is it?* Forms representing the pronunciations /'huzət/ or /hu'zi:t/ reflect the influence of Afk. and the Sintu (Bantu) languages.]

1. A salutation, equivalent to 'hello', but also containing the inquiry 'how are you?'

1975 'BLOSSOM' in *Darling* 29 Jan. 103, Howzit, cherries and okes. 1979 A. HARRISON in *Frontline* Dec. 17, I never get lonely. In a city lift I can give the manne a 'hora hora hoozeet' and I'm assured of a good conversation. 1980 E. PATEL *They Came at Dawn* 9 Howsit Mister Black ... I am Miss White. 1980 M.W. SEROTE in M. Mutloatse *Forced Landing* 171 'Hoozeet?' He looked at me. 'Fine,' I said. 1986 M. MANAKA in S. Gray *Market Plays* 58 Danny: Heitha Jimi. Jimi: Hoesit? 1986 T. THOKA in *Eng. Usage in Sn Afr.* Vol.17 No.2, 20 'Heita' is a popular greeting used by the Mapantsula ... One can go further by saying 'Heita hoezet majita?' ' (Hello, how are you, friends?). 'Hoezet' is a corruption of the Afrikaans phrase 'Hoe is dit', or the English adoption of this ('Hello, how's it?'). 1988 I. STEADMAN in *Weekly Mail* 9 Dec. 32, I can use that, man. It's much better than opening your play with a line like 'Howzit have a drink'. 1988 LAMPERT & FOURIE in *You* 21 Jan. 102 Howzit my china! Lekker surprise, hey? 1989 B. LUDMAN *Day of Kugel* 9 'Repeat after me: Hello, howzit.' 'Hello what?' 'Howzit,' Diana said, through her nose. 'Hello, howzit?' ... 'What happens if somebody says "Hello, howzit" to me? What do I say?' 'Okaynyu,' Diana said. 'Okaynyu?' Michelle asked. 'Perfect,' Diana said. 'Okay. And You? That's what it means.' 1992 C.M. KNOX tr. E. Van Heerden's *Mad Dog* 137 'Howzit.' 'Hello.'

2. In the interrogative phrr. *howzit for -, howzit with (something),* 'how about (something)', 'how's about': used to ask for something, or to suggest something.

1983 *Frontline* Feb. 12 So please, my china. I had a hard ride from Joeys and I got no chick to dance with so howzit for like a small loan of your old lady? 1987 *Scope* 6 Nov. 33 Wollies was .. coming off a pipe trip. 'Howzit with a pipe, man?' Wollies called as Jimmy walked by.

HSRC *n.* Initial letters of *Human Sciences Research Council,* a statutory body established in 1969 to sponsor and promote research projects in the humanities. Also *attrib.*

1974 *Std Encycl. of Sn Afr.* X. 39 In terms of the Human Sciences Research Act .. the Human Sciences Research Council (H.S.R.C.) was established as an independent body on 1 April 1969. Its functions comprise research on behalf of the State or any person or authority, as the Minister may approve; and advice to the Government upon the promotion of research and utilisation of its results. 1981 G. REILLY in *Rand Daily Mail* 30 June 3 (*caption*) Politics 'could block' HSRC school schemes. 1982 *S. Afr. Panorama* Feb. 23 The HSRC's Institute of Manpower Research has been working for more than two years on the collection and processing of career guidance data. **1986** *E. Prov. Herald* 19 Aug. 8 The HSRC said the results of the investigation would .. contribute to improving the quality of life of all South Africans. **1993** *Weekly Mail* 8 Apr. 15 The HSRC's centre for constitutional analysis. **1994** *HSRC Register of Graduates (brochure)*, The HSRC Register of Graduates is one of the most comprehensive sources of information on high-level resources in South Africa. The data base has been in existence since 1965 ... Information such as graduates' age, population group, gender, occupation, qualifications and the institute where qualifications were obtained, is recorded.

huik var. HOEK *n.*[2]

huilba(l)ken pl. form of HUILEBALK.

huilboom /'hœılbʊəm, 'heıl-/ *n.* [Afk., *huil* weep + *boom* tree; see quot. 1966.] The deciduous shrub or tree *Peltophorum africanum* of the Fabaceae, with acacia-like foliage and dense, erect sprays of yellow flowers; *African wattle*, see AFRICAN *adj.*[1] sense 1 b i; HUILBOS.

1961 PALMER & PITMAN *Trees of S. Afr.* 175 This beautiful deciduous tree is found in the dry bush country of the northern and eastern Transvaal, Swaziland, Portuguese East Africa, Rhodesia, and Angola ... The huilboom often has a stout, crooked or forked trunk which .. gives the tree a gnarled .. appearance. **1966** C.A. SMITH *Common Names* 253 *Huilboom (-bos)*, .. An abundance of nectar drips from the flowers and hence conveys the impression of weeping. **1990** M. OETTLE in *Weekend Post* 29 Dec. (Leisure) 7 *Peltophorum africanum*, weeping wattle or huilboom.

huilbos /'hœılbɔs, heıl-/ *n.* [Afk., *huil* weep + *bos* bush.] The HUILBOOM, *Peltophorum africanum*.

1924 *Off. Yrbk of Union 1923* (Union Office of Census & Statistics) 44 The most conspicuous and characteristic trees in this bush country are ... The huilbos .. *Peltophorum africanum*. **1966** [see HUILBOOM]. **1974** *Personality* 27 Dec. 33 *Huilbos* or weeping bush.

huilebalk /'hœıləbalk/ *n. Obs.* exc. *hist.* Pl. **huilebalken, huilba(l)ken** [Du.] Usu. in *pl.*: Professional mourners, employed to walk, weeping, in funeral processions. See also TROPSLUITER.

1926 P.W. LAIDLER *Tavern of Ocean* 157 Funerals were pageants not soon forgotten. Professional mourners – 'huilbaken,' as they were called – accompanied the coffin and were paid to weep copiously. **1927** C.G. BOTHA *Social Life in Cape Col.* 65 At a funeral there were paid mourners or weepers called 'huilebalken,' who had to weep and exhibit great distress. **1952** G.M. MILLS *First Ladies of Cape* 76 Her funeral, conducted by the Rev. Mr Hough with great privacy, was one of the last attended at the Cape by huilebalken or professional mourners. These persons were hired to walk at the head of a funeral procession and perform certain ceremonies at the interment. **1965** A. GORDON-BROWN *S. Afr. Heritage* III. 10 Funerals were accompanied at one time by professional mourners known as 'huilebalken', whose duty it was to exhibit signs of grief.

huis-apotheek /'hœısapɔ,tıək/ *n. hist.* Also **huisapatheek, huisap(o)teek**, and with initial capital. Pl. **-apotheeks, -apteke** /-aptıəkə/. [Du. (later Afk. *huisapteek*), *huis* house, home + *apotheek* dispensary, pharmacy.] A medicine-chest of patent remedies, formerly used in many rural (Afrikaans) households. Also *attrib.* See also BOERERAAT, TROMMEL sense 1.

1868 W.R. THOMSON *Poems, Essays & Sketches* 167 At a bare little table .. sits the *huisvrouw*, with .. a coffee or tea kettle on the table beside her, and the *huisapotheek* .. on the window-ledge near her. **1871** J. MACKENZIE *Ten Yrs* (1971) 110 Before leaving home, they purchase .. a small tin box, gaudily painted, and labelled 'huis-apotheek', being an assortment of medicines for domestic use. **1884** *B.G. Lennon & Co.'s Catal. 1884* 65 Huis Apotheeks, small, each 10s.6d. **1908** J.M. ORPEN *Reminisc.* (1964) 27 The ordinary medicine chest of a Boer's house was a well-known japanned tin box with 'Huis Apatheek' printed upon it. **1914** L.H. BRINKMAN *Breath of Karroo* 260 Nettie was ordered off to bed, and given a dose from Tante Let's 'Huis Apotheek'. **1919** *Dunell, Ebden & Co.'s Price List* Oct. 20 Huis Apotheeks, small 10/6 .. large 15/- Per doz. **1933** W. MACDONALD *Romance of Golden Rand* 214 There were many farmers, like the old Boer just mentioned, who kept thousands of pounds sterling in their houses, very often in the Dutch medicine canister – (Die Huis-apteek). **1940** BAUMANN & BRIGHT *Lost Republic* 227 The treatment did not kill him, as it might have done when one thinks of all the patent medicines usually found in the 'Huis Apteke'. **1958** [see TROMMEL sense 1]. **1968** K. MCMAGH *Dinner of Herbs* 47 There must have been a stout little wooden chest kept handy, a little box that held medicines. This was known as 'Die Huis Apteek', the medicine chest that took the place of the family doctor, honoured by the name of 'The Home Pharmacy' and usually imported from Germany. **1972** N. SAPEIKA in *Std Encycl. of Sn Afr.* VII. 303 The 'huisapotheek' remedies were used empirically and mainly for symptomatic treatment. **1991** *Best of S. Afr. Short Stories* (Reader's Digest Assoc.) 112 Every wagon and country home had its *huis-apotheek* or 'home pharmacy' of patent remedies, many of them with a remarkably high alcohol content.

huisbesoek /'hœısbəsuk/ *n.* Formerly also **huisbezoek(ing)**. Pl. **-s, -besoeke** /-bəsukə/. [Afk., earlier S. Afr. Du. *huisbezoek* (fr. Du. *huisbezoeking*), *huis* house, home + *besoek* visit.]

1. Parish or district visiting by clergy; a house call by a doctor or teacher. Also *attrib.*

1824 W.J. BURCHELL *Trav.* II. 154 Four times a year, he undertook journeys through his district .. for the convenience and instruction of those whom distance prevented from coming to the church. These pastoral visits were called *huisbezoekings*, or domiciliary visitations. **1927** C.G. BOTHA *Social Life in Cape Col.* 77 Periodically the minister accompanied by one of his elders or deacons, went on 'huisbezoek' or visitation amongst the congregation. *a***1951** H.C. BOSMAN in L. Abrahams *Unto Dust* (1963) 122 Even if this huisbesoek was not part of my after-school duties, I would have gone and visited the parents in any case. **1955** I. ABRAHAMS in Saron & Hotz *Jews in S. Afr.* 18 He paid pastoral visits, often in connection with a local religious celebration ... The Jews living in the platteland were deeply appreciative of this *huisbesoek*. **1957** L.G. GREEN *Beyond City Lights* 218 Hofmeyr was also a skilful amateur doctor, and while on *huisbesoek* he extracted many a tooth. **1958** [see DIAKEN]. **1965** C. VAN HEYNINGEN *Orange Days* 9 He came home from a 'huisbesoek' journey (visiting his flock). **1967** L. MARQUARD in M. Marquard *Lett. from Boer Parsonage* 24 Since his parishioners did not often come to town it was natural that the minister should spend much time travelling to visit them. This was called *huisbezoek*. **1975** W.M. MACMILLAN *My S. Afr. Yrs* 132 Pastoral visitation (*huisbesoek*) .. was a highly organized duty: families in the outlying districts were duly notified of the intended visit, and woe betide anyone who failed to muster the whole family for this solemn occasion. **1989** F.G. BUTLER *Tales from Old Karoo* 12 He was hiding from the Dominee who'd come on a couple of hours' *huisbesoek*.

2. House-to-house canvassing by political party workers or election candidates. Also *attrib.*

1948 *George & Knysna Herald* 1 The two candidates – have both made themselves widely known by way of public meetings and 'huisbesoek.' **1970** *Evening Post* 3 Oct. 3 The United Party feels it is having far greater success with the 'huisbesoek' method in its Provincial Council election campaign ... Mr Rossouw said: 'You don't convince anyone at meetings ... My people are busy doing "huisbesoek" and I don't want to take them off it.' **1972** *Argus* 26 Feb. 1 Nationalist predictions were based on huisbesoek figures and records kept by party workers at the polls. **1977** *Sunday Times* 30 Oct. 12 Political *huisbesoek* can be a hazardous business – particularly if almost every house in the constituency has a 'Beware of the Dog' sign. **1980** *Cape Times* 9 July 9 The Progressive Federal Party's candidate .. re-emerged from the farmhouse, shaven and showered and in the 'huisbesoek' suit that had taken the place of his farming gear.

Hence (*nonce*) **huisbesoek** *v. intrans.*, to pay a pastoral visit.

1955 W. ILLSLEY *Wagon on Fire* 183, I 'huisbesoek' (pay pastoral calls) on the farms.

‖**huisgodsdiens** /'hœıs,xɔtsdins, 'heıs-/ *n.* [Afk., *huis* house + *godsdiens* religion, worship.] Family prayers; a religious service held at home. See also BOEKEVAT.

1958 A. JACKSON *Trader on Veld* 33 Living so far from any village, most farmers could not go to church on Sundays, but had to content themselves with Huisgodsdiens or family prayers, at which the head of the household would generally read from a volume of sermons. **1981** *Sunday Times* 7 June (Mag. Sect.) 1 He and his wife have their 'quiet time' which has taken the place of huisgodsdiens. **1988** SMUTS & ALBERTS *Forgotten Highway* 182 *Huisgodsdiens* was also held at home, at Kromfontein, in the Koue Bokkeveld.

‖**huismiddel** /'hœısməd(ə)l, 'heıs-/ *n.* [Afk. (earlier S. Afr. Du.), *huis* house + *middel* remedy.] BOERERAAT. Formerly also **huysmiddeltje** /-ki/ [see -IE].

1861 P.B. BORCHERDS *Auto-Biog. Mem.* 197 Great faith was placed in small boxes of medicine prepared at Halle, in Germany ... They are known as huysmiddeltjes (domestic medicines), and are sometimes applied with good success. **1941** N. DEVITT *Concentration Camps* 48 There were some terrible cases among those treated by means of 'huis-middels'. **1958** A. JACKSON *Trader on Veld* 31 These farmers were miles away from any doctor and had to fend for themselves ... Some of their 'Huismiddels', although drastic, were extremely effective.

‖**huistoe** /'hœıstu, 'heıs-/ *adv.* and *int.* [Afk., *huis* home + *toe* towards.]

A. *adv.* Homewards, home.

1887 J.W. MATTHEWS *Incwadi Yami* 263 Mr. Jeppe went 'huis toe', or home. **1902** D. VAN WARMELO *On Commando* 38 Many of the burghers were discouraged, and rode 'huis-toe', and nothing came of the great battle that was to have been fought. **1986** J. BROUARD in *Style* Sept. 54 South Africans cannot remain in Australia to work temporarily while the paperwork gets done ... So it's huistoe and vasbyt until the work permit plops into your postbox. **1987** L. BEAKE *Strollers* 104 'I'm going home', he said. 'Huistoe'.

B. *int.* 'Home(ward)'; 'let's go home'.

1887 J.W. MATTHEWS *Incwadi Yami* 445 President Burgers .. went to the front himself, but all in vain. Deserted by the burghers, who raised the now proverbial cry of 'huis toe,' .. he had to return to Pretoria. **1901** W.S. SUTHERLAND *S. Afr. Sketches* 24 Let us also have a war cry! .. (Cries of 'Huis toe' and 'More beer,' several of the staff evidently getting mixed up in their ideas). **1929** H.A. CHILVERS *Out of Crucible* 6 'Huis toe!' (home) was the cry, however, and the farmers went back beyond Sekukuni's boundaries and dispersed to their homes. **1937** B.H. DICKE *Bush Speaks* 44 Over the Boer laager in the lowveld fever had reigned ... 'Huis toe' (homeward) went up the cry from frightened people .. and the laager dispersed. **1949** A. KEPPEL-JONES *S. Afr.: Short Hist.* 99 The weary commandos dispersed with the cry of '*huis-toe*!' **1958** I. VAUGHAN *Diary* 14 Sanna said 'huis toe'. We ran home and sat in the dark. [**1963** S. CLOETE *Rags of Glory* 113 Things were slack and he was going to profit by it to go home. *Huis toe* was the Dutch for it, for going home.] **1979** T. PAKENHAM *Boer War* (1982) 443 '*Huis toe*' had been intermittently heard ever since the capture of Bloemfontein.

Hence **huistoe** *adj. nonce*, 'going-home'.

1987 *Cosmopolitan* Apr. 28 If I were overseas and I heard a moppie being sung, or a mbaqanga guitar riff, .. I'd be able to say, 'Hey, that's my music. That's where I come from. That's huistoe music!'

‖**huisvrou** /'hœısfrəʊ, 'heıs-/ *n.* Formerly also **haus-vro(u)w, huisvrouw**, and with initial capital. [Afk., earlier Du. *huisvrouw*, *huis* house +

vrouw wife, woman, mistress. The spelling *haus-* shows the influence of G. *hausfrau*.] The mistress of a house; a housewife; a wife; cf. VROU.

Usu. denoting a speaker of S. Afr. Dutch, or subsequently Afrikaans (but see quot. 1948).

*a*1801 LADY A. BARNARD *S. Afr. Century Ago* (1925) 65 We then set to .. to make our month as comfortable as might be. This, as a careful haus vrow, devolved on me. **1827** G. THOMPSON *Trav.* II. 140 The huis-vrouw smiled at this proposal, and told me that we should have a bed-room to ourselves. **1834** T. PRINGLE *Afr. Sketches* 175 During this refreshment, I carried on a tolerably fluent conversation in broken Dutch with my host and his *huisvrouw*. **1852** M.B. HUDSON *S. Afr. Frontier Life* 11 He led the way by His wagon containing his huis-vrouw and baby. [*Note*] Huis Vrouw (pronounced Huis Frow) – wife. **1868** [see HUIS-APOTHEEK]. **1882** J. NIXON *Among Boers* 202 You must shake hands .. with every person in the room, beginning with the good lady, or haus-vrouw, who sits in state by the coffee urn. **1883** M.A. CAREY-HOBSON *Farm in Karoo* 171 When they were at length seated .. they found they were near the 'Huis Vrouw,' or hostess. **1904** H.A. BRYDEN *Hist. of S. Afr.* 37 The Boer woman, or huis vrouw, of 1807, sat much at home. **1910** D. FAIRBRIDGE *That Which Hath Been* (1913) 264 The baas and huisvrouw .. came out on their stoeps and sank into the capacious chairs and rust-banks. **1924** — *Gardens of S. Afr.* 41 To begin with, the huisvrouw retrieved a small patch in front of the house, railed it in .. and packed it as full as it could hold with Roses and Violets. **1934** J.G. VAN ALPHEN in Stokes & Wilter *Veld Trails* 17 The heartsore *huisvrou* abstains from eating and keeps out of sight. **1948** O. WALKER *Kaffirs Are Lively* 208 The *huisvrou*, Dutch or English, in her own kitchen. **1977** S. ROBERTS in E. Pereira *Contemp. S. Afr. Plays* 232 Jong, whoever invented weekends never had the huisvrou in mind, that's for sure.

huit var. HEIT.

humba var. HAMBA.

humraad var. HEEMRAAD.

180-day *adj.*

Cf. 90-DAY (see under 'N'). See also EMERGENCY.

a. Of or pertaining to Section 215 *bis* of the Criminal Procedure Act of 1965, providing for the detention of political prisoners for up to 180 days without trial or recourse to law.

1966 *Survey of Race Rel. 1965* (S.A.I.R.R.) 46 At 1.27 p.m. on 10 September he had been released from arrest, but at 1.30 p.m. had again been detained under the 180-day clause. *Ibid.* 48 During the last week of October and early in November three more people were detained under the '180-day clause'. **1967** H. SUZMAN in *Hansard* 1 June 7042 The jurisdiction of the court is completely excluded, as it was in the 90-day and the 180-day measures. However, unlike the 180-day law there is no doubt that people will be detained for purposes of interrogation. **1971** *Post* 6 June 21 A refugee from the Transkei was handed over to the South African Police by Lesotho cops in April last year and held for 55 days in Bloemfontein under the 180-day law. **1971** *Cape Times* 6 Nov. 10 The 90-day law was virtually replaced in 1965 by the 180-day law. The 180-day law (or Section 215 bis of the Criminal Procedure Act) is not as far-reaching in that instead of a commissioned police officer acting independently and without warrant, the attorney-general is required to issue a warrant for the arrest and detention of a person.

b. Of detainees: held under this Act.

1969 *Drum* June 51 South Africa's penal island for 180-day detainees.

c. Of detention: imposed and administered according to the terms of this Act.

1971 *Rand Daily Mail* 31 May 12 In August, 1966, Mr. Vorster, then Minister of Justice, told the House that no fewer than 125 people were currently being held in 180-day detention. **1971** *Sunday Times* 14 Nov. 2 At least she wasn't put under house arrest or given 180-day detention.

Hence **180 days** *n. phr.* (alluding to this legislation).

1969 M. BENSON *At Still Point* (1988) 205 Nathaniel Qaba has been taken. A hundred and eighty days. **1986** *Style* Dec. 41 Any talk of multiracialism, in any form, got you 90 days or 180, or early retirement on Robben Island. **1987** J. MERVIS in *Sunday Times* 15 Nov. 21 Q: Can I speak to the Minister of Law and Order? A: Of course you can. Come back in 180 days. **1993** A. GOLDSTUCK in *Rhodent* (Rhodes Univ.) 29, 180 days, no option of a fine.

hunger-belt *n. girdle of famine*, see GIRDLE.

Recorded earlier in *Austral. Eng.*

1864 T. BAINES *Explor. in S.-W. Afr.* 467 (*caption*) Makalaka, with the first reef in his hunger-belt. **1865** *Daily Telegraph* (U.K.) 21 Dec. 7 'Tis a device of savages to cheat an empty stomach and is called 'the hunger belt'. *a*1878 J. MONTGOMERY *Reminisc.* (1981) 72, I did not dress like one who wore the hunger belt from dire necessity, or one who was accustomed to soil his fingers. I thought a decent appearance would recommend me, but I was mistaken. **1913** C. PETTMAN *Africanderisms* 221 *Hunger-belt*, A thong of hide (according to Krönlein the Namaqua words for hunger and for riem are from the same root, *a, to hunger), worn as a belt by the Namaqua Hottentots which in times of scarcity is gradually tightened to deaden the gnawings of hunger. **1968** G. CROUDACE *Silver Grass* 7 Asa Riarua drew his hunger-belt tighter, feeling the richly-plaited leather biting into his stomach. *Ibid.* 112 Asa Riarua was in Herero dress: an aristocrat of other days, his beautifully-plaited hunger-belt drawn tight about his belly.

Hurutshe /hʊˈrʊtʃi, -tʃe/ *n.* Pl. usu. unchanged, or **Bahurutshe**. Forms: *sing.* **Moharootzie, Morutze**; *sing.* and *pl.* **Harootzi(e), Harutse, Harutsi, Horutsie, Huruthse, Huruts(h)e, Hurutsi, Hurutze, Hurutzi, Morootzee**; *pl.* **Bafurutse, Baharootzi(e), Baharutse, Baharutsi(e), Baharutzi, Bahuruts(h)e, Bahurutsi, Bahurutze, Bakhurutse, Marootze(e)s**. [SeTswana name. See also BA- and MO-.] A member of a people descended from the BAROLONG, now part of the Tswana group and living mainly in the western Transvaal and in Botswana. Also *attrib.*

1821 B. SHAW in *Missionary Notices* (1882) Feb. 214 One of these visitors having frequently travelled amongst the *Manketsens, Boschuanas*, and *Marootzes*, .. gave us much more information respecting that country. **1827** G. THOMPSON *Trav.* I. 369 They .. formed an amicable junction with the Morootzee tribe, whom they had formerly plundered. **1835** A.G. BAIN in A. Steedman *Wanderings* (1835) II. 233 Various Bechuana tribes, such as the Baharutsie, Wanketzie, and Barolongs, all of whose countries Masilikatsie has conquered. [**1835** J.C. CHASE in *Ibid.* 180 The capital of the Bamorutze tribe of Bechuana. **1835** G. CHAMPION *Jrnl* (1968) 11 The station is called Moriah (incorrectly called Baharootze in my letter to Mr. A.).] **1835** A. SMITH *Diary* (1940) II. 37 One or two Baharutse visited us after halting; stated that no Matabeli had been seen this side of Molopo since Bain's wagons were seized. *Ibid.* 152 The Moharootzie who spoke on the subject of the commando says that at most of the posts there are not more than one or two Matabeli. **1840** [see MORENA sense 1]. **1857** D. LIVINGSTONE *Missionary Trav.* 45 The other tribes will not begin to eat the early pumpkins of a new crop until they hear that the Bahurutse have 'bitten it'. **1871** J. MACKENZIE *Ten Yrs* (1971) 142 The Bakhurutse at first refused to act as guides. **1905** *Native Tribes of Tvl* 31 The Baharutse in Moilo's location are a peacable people, fully occupied by the care of their cattle, and the cultivation of their very fertile lands. **1930** S.T. PLAATJE *Mhudi* (1975) 125 The allies were joined en route by large numbers of Bakwena, Bakhatla and Bahurutshe who lived in the neighbourhood through which they marched. **1940** P.R. KIRBY *Diary of Dr Andrew Smith* II. 223 Hurutshe. **1951** W.S. MATSIE in *Drum* Apr. 12 Other tribes began to spring up in the country .. thus the Bafurutse, Batuang, Bakoena [etc.] came about. **1960** C. HOOPER *Brief Authority* 128 Courtesy is bred into the Bafurutse from their birth. It is seldom violated. **1974** F.J. LANGUAGE in *Std Encycl. of Sn Afr.* X. 73 In the Western Transvaal there are the following Tswana tribes: the Hurutshe in Marico, the Kgatla and Tlokwa in Rustenburg, [etc.]. **1977** T.R.H. DAVENPORT *S. Afr.: Mod. Hist.* 7 One sub-group, the Hurutshe, who without question developed iron-smelting on a considerable scale, moved to the headwaters of the Marico river. **1979** P. MILLER *Myths & Legends* 173 The baRolong fell to fighting and quarrelling among themselves .. and .. the great tribe disintegrated ... One of these offshoots, the baHurutshe, moved to the slopes of the Enzlesberg mountain. **1986** P. MAYLAM *Hist. of Afr. People* 45 Around the end of the fifteenth century Masilo's lineage divided into two, and from this split arose the Hurutshe and Kwena chiefdoms. **1990** *Weekend Post* 10 Mar. 13 The belief that the Government is cheating them has made many Bafokeng very hostile to Mangope, who is a chief of the Bahurutshe people. **1993** S. GRAY in *Weekly Mail & Guardian* 5 Nov. 48 The Hurutshe who built cities.

hut tax *n. phr. Hist.* [So named because the tax was originally levied per hut (or group of huts) owned by the head of a family.] A tax instituted during the 19th century and imposed on black people by various southern African governments and authorities.

1851 R. GRAY *Jrnl of Bishop's Visitation* II. 76, I propose .. that the Government should help forward the work, out of the fund collected through the hut-tax. **1855** J.W. COLENSO *Ten Weeks in Natal* p.xxviii, This hut-tax was first sanctioned by Earl Grey in 1848. **1881** F.R. STATHAM *Blacks, Boers & Brit.* 152 All he pays, in recognition of his obligation to the State, is fourteen shillings a year as 'hut-tax'. **1892** J.E. RITCHIE *Brighter S. Afr.* 186 Now, says a local paper, the hut-tax, which is a direct tax, brings in about £72,000 per annum. **1897** 'F. MACNAB' *On Veldt & Farm* 260 The first move to check population was made by the levy known as the Hut Tax. **1907** W.C. SCULLY *By Veldt & Kopje* 269 An attack was projected upon Seccocoeni, chief of the Bapedi, who had refused to pay hut-tax. **1923** G.H. NICHOLLS *Bayete!* 185 Martha told me that the men were going to be doctored for war, but that they would not fight until the hut tax was being collected. **1936** C. BIRKBY *Thirstland Treks* 324 Every native in the Territory is liable for hut tax of £1 a year. **1949** O. WALKER *Proud Zulu* (1951) 226 Hlubi, the Basuto 'kinglet' to the north also instituted a hut tax which he used for his own purposes. **1953** [see VENDA *adj.*]. **1976** R. ROSS *Adam Kok's Griquas* 120 The Africans under Griqua rule were required to pay a hut tax, variously reported as 5s. or 7s.6d. per hut. **1985** J. MAKUNGA in *Staffrider* Vol.6 No.2, 35 Tribalized in a pass-book. Name and present address? Place and date of birth? Name of chief? Name and address of last /present employer? Wages? Fingerprints? Income tax? Native tax? Hut tax? **1986** P. MAYLAM *Hist. of Afr. People* 87 From 1849 those who lived in locations had to pay a hut-tax of 7s. a year. **1989** *Reader's Digest Illust. Hist.* 230 Only in 1870 did the volksraad (parliament) decide that all Africans must pay a hut tax .. 2s 6d for those living on a white-owned farm and providing labour for the Boer household; 5 shillings for those not living on the farm but providing labour; and 10 shillings for those not providing labour at all.

huysmiddeltje see HUISMIDDEL.

hykona var. AIKONA.

hyraceum /haɪˈreɪsɪəm/ *n.* Also **hyracium**. [fr. modern L. *hyrax*, once used as the genus name for the DASSIE.] The crystallized urine of the hyrax (see DASSIE sense 1), used medicinally and as a fixative for perfume; DASSES PISS; DASSIEPIS; KLIPSWEET.

1866 BRANDE & COX *Dict. Sci., Lit. & Art* II. 182 *Hyracium*, An article imported, as a substitute for castor, from the Cape of Good Hope, and derived from one of the species of *Hyrax*. **1868** [see DASSIEPIS]. **1892** P.L. SIMMONDS *Commercial Dict. of Trade Products*

(Suppl.) 462 Hyraceum, a secretion of the Cape badger, at one time considered to have medicinal properties. **1923** W.A. POUCHER *Perfumes & Cosmetics* 3 Hyraceum is a secretion having a most disagreeable odour of excreta and urine, and is obtained from a species of monkey [*sic*]. It is occasionally used as a substitute for Castor. **1955** [see DASSIEPIS]. **1966** C. SWEENY *Scurrying Bush* 34 The faeces of the rock rabbit .. contains a substance called hyraceum, which is .. incorporated in various perfumes. **1971** D.J. POTGIETER et al. *Animal Life in Sn Afr.* 394 These deposits [of the dried urine of the dassie] contain hyraceum, a valuable material used in perfumery. **1990** SKINNER & SMITHERS *Mammals of Sn Afr. Subregion* 557 It was claimed that crystallised dassie urine has medicinal properties and was marketed at one time under the name 'hyracium'.

I

i- /i/ *pref.* A Xhosa, Zulu, and Ndebele singular noun prefix found in some words originating in these languages. For examples, see IBANDLA, IBUTHO, IDLOZI, IKHOWE, IKRWALA, IQABANE, ITONGO. Cf. UM-.

In Xhosa, Zulu and Ndebele, the plural of words beginning *i-* is formed by replacing this prefix with *ama-*. In *S. Afr. Eng.* this pattern is not always observed, the plural sometimes being formed by adding the English plural suffix *-s* to the singular form; less often, the singular form is used, unchanged, as a plural. See also AMA- and ILI-.

ibandla /iˈbaːnɟa/ *n.* Also **bandhla**. Pl. unchanged, or **amabandla**. [Zulu and Xhosa *ibandla* assembly; leader's retinue; church congregation; army division (pl. *amabandla*). For an explanation of sing. and pl. forms, see I- and AMA-.] In the context of Nguni society: a meeting, committee, court, or congregation of a village, area, clan, or people; the following of a chief. Cf. KGOTLA senses 2, 3, 4, and 5. See also INKUNDLA sense 1.

1895 H. RIDER HAGGARD *Nada* 90 On the first day of the new moon I summon a great meeting, a *bandhla* of all the Zulu people. **1954** W.D. HAMMOND-TOOKE in A.M. Duggan-Cronin *Bantu Tribes* III. v. 34 In times of national emergency a council of all the adult men of the tribe is called (*ibandla*). **1955** E.A. RITTER *Shaka Zulu* 45 It was the feature of these ibandla, or councils of war, that everyone was entitled freely to voice his opinions. **1978** *Voice* 8 Nov. 10 Whoever came with the suggestion to form an ibandla — residents' committee — and why, nobody can tell with certainty. **1981** J.B. PEIRES *House of Phalo* 34 The state apparatus of a Xhosa chief was not a standing bureaucracy of named officers, but a variable and shifting aggregation of people, usually referred to as his *ibandla*, or following. **1982** M. MZAMANE *Children of Soweto* 194 The Methodists, the Lutherans and members of other denominations .. would all await their turn after the Anglicans whose territory, as it were, this was, as Muntu's parents belonged to their *ibandla*. **1985** L. DU BUISSON in *Avenue* May 89 King Goodwill called an *ibandla* of all his people at the royal capital at Nongoma. **1986** P.A. MCALLISTER *Xhosa Beer Drinks.* 6 Meetings of the sub-ward court (*ibandla*) and of the Tribal Authority. **1988** S. MEINTJES in Laband & Haswell *Pietermaritzburg 1838–1988* 66 Conflicts between village members were solved in the customary court, *ibandla*.

ibangalala var. BANGALALA.

ibari var. BARI.

ibe(t)shu var. BESHU.

Ibhayi /iˈbaːji/ *n.* Also **eBhayi** /e-/. [Xhosa *iBhayi* (locative form *eBhayi*) ad. Afk. *die Baai* 'the Bay' (see BAAI).] Esp. among Xhosa-speakers, a name for the city of Port Elizabeth; a collective name for the black townships in and around that city. Also *attrib.* See also PE.

1982 *Voice* 21 Mar. 5 Plague hits eBhayi … Bubonic plague has broken out in a Black settlement at Coega, about 32 km from Port Elizabeth. **1986** *E. Prov. Herald* 7 Oct. 6 The security forces may .. re-introduce the notorious 'dompas' in a different form (as they admit to doing in Ibhayi). **1990** T. DANIELS in *New African* 27 Aug. 2 Port Elizabeth .. township residents are holding their breath as thousands of wooden houses are mushrooming … The Ibhayi City Council, which administers the townships, seems to be unable to stem the tide. **1993** F. FRESCURA in *Weekly Mail & Guardian* 29 Oct. 12 Most Afrikaners refer to Port Elizabeth as Die Baai — and black people call it iBhayi, which means the same thing: the bay.

ibheshu var. BESHU.

iboma var. BOMA *n.*²

ibongi var. IMBONGI.

ibutho /iˈbʊːtɔ, iˈbuːtəʊ/ *n.* Also with initial or medial capital. Pl. **amabutho**; formerly also **amabooto(es)**, **amabuthi**, **amabuthos**, **amabuto**. [Zulu. For an explanation of pl. forms, see I- and AMA-.]

1. In the context of Zulu society: a regiment of young soldiers from one age-group; a member of such a regiment; a warrior. Also *attrib.*

1836 N. ISAACS *Trav.* (1937) II. 182 He was surrounded by a body of Amabootoes or young warriors. **1949** A.T. BRYANT *Zulu People* 494 The practice of regularly banding together into 'groups' (*amaButo*) all clan youths of a similar age, continued as before. **1955** E.A. RITTER *Shaka Zulu* 8 So soon as there seemed to the king a sufficiency of unenlisted youths in the military kraals, a brand-new guild or regiment, i-butho, was created for their enrolment, with a brand-new barrack-kraal for their reception and a brand-new uniform for their distinction. **1957** B. FRASER *Sunshine & Lamplight* 98 In the cattle kraal they find meat ready and the aMabuthi (warriors) dancing. **1961** T.V. BULPIN *White Whirlwind* 73 Membership of a particular iButho or regiment was always signified among the Zulus by some item of dress special to that group. **1976** *Drum* June 29 He was a member of the Royal household and therefore a member of the King's own ibutho. **1985** *Cape Times* 30 Sept. 1 Three-quarters of the way through Chief Buthelezi's speech, three buSloads of amabutho (warriors) .. in tribal dress and many of them armed, left the Umlazi stadium .. and crossed .. into .. Lamontville. **1987** *New Nation* 28 May 9 The Zulu became the dominant power in south-east Africa. Their strength was based on the amabutho or 'regiments' … Men from a large number of different chiefdoms were brought together in the amabutho under the direct authority of the Zulu king. **1989** *Reader's Digest Illust. Hist.* 81 The reorganisation of armies into an *amabutho* system (an age-grade basis) .. meant that young men .. could now be assembled by chiefs and formed into regiments with names of their own. **1991** G. MCINTOSH in *Sunday Times* 13 Jan. 16 Conscription is established in the English-speaking military tradition, in the Zulu *amabutho* and regimental call-up tradition, in the commando tradition of the Afrikaners and no doubt in other communities.

2. In *pl.* In the Durban area: **a.** Armed vigilantes who grouped together during the 1980s in opposition to the 'comrades'. **b.** Occas., the comrades (see COMRADE). Also *attrib.* See also VIGILANTE.

1986 T. MAKHOBA in *Learn & Teach* No.3, 5, I saw a large group of 'Amabutho' chasing my eldest son, Mandla. He ran into my house and locked the door. The 'Amabutho' chopped down the door. **1987** *New Nation* 5 Nov. 4 A 200-strong amabutho group patrolling the streets of the township. **1991** *Weekly Mail* 28 Mar., Police moved in against a crowd of 'amabutho', or 'comrades', who were arming themselves to protect residents against the Inkatha launch.

ID /aɪ ˈdiː/ *n. colloq.* Also **I.D.** [Initial letters of *Identity Document.* Cf. general Eng. *ID* 'identification', 'identity (card)' (*OED*).] An identity document initially issued (in terms of the Population Registration Act of 1950) to white, 'coloured', and Asian people only, but which, in 1986, became the identity document for all South Africans; cf. BOOK OF LIFE.

1976 M. THOLO in C. Hermer *Diary of Maria Tholo* (1980) 159 All African families have a few strange relatives. Gus's are no exception. Half of them are passing for coloured. Gus and his two brothers carry passes but his sisters and two other brothers have I.D.'s. **1986** *Grocott's Mail* 15 July 1 The first black man to receive an identity document in the Eastern Cape in terms of the Population Identification Act of 1986 which replaced the old passbook for blacks was handed to Mr Mvuselelo Lawrence Dyibishe … Mr Bristow said he hoped the relationship between Mr Dyibishe and his new ID would be better than his relationship with his old passbook. **1986** *Rhodeo* (Rhodes Univ.) Aug. 13 Students from Durban's Lamontville High were barred from entering the school premises after they had burnt their IDs. **1986** 'JOSEPH' in *New Nation* 17 July 11, I am one of those people who needs the common ID. As a citizen of Bophuthatswana I would therefore like to know whether I will be allowed to have it? **1987** *Pace* Nov. 14 The new ID may be the same as that carried by white, Indian and coloured South Africans but it does not entitle blacks to work and live where they want. **1994** P. BAUER *Informant, Springs* A question often asked when one visits a Bank or Post Office or some other institution where identification is required: 'Have you got your ID?'

Idasa /iˈdɑːsə/ *n.* [Acronym formed on *Institute for a Democratic Alternative for South Africa.*] An organisation founded in 1986 to explore strategies for achieving a non-racial democracy in South Africa. Also *attrib.*

1987 F. VAN ZYL SLABBERT in *Sunday Times* 12 Apr. 2 What we (Idasa) do is perfectly legal and above board. The Government itself gets overseas funds. **1988** C. RYAN in *Star* 30 May 9 He described Mr Malan's decision to meet the ANC as 'very courageous' — particularly in the light of the massive Government propaganda campaign after last year's meeting between the ANC and Dr van Zyl Slabbert's Idasa movement in Dakar, Senegal. **1989** *Race Rel. Survey*

1988–9 (S.A.I.R.R.) 675 According to its national co-ordinator .. the role of IDASA was educative. He said, 'Our work is to convince the white population that there is a democratic alternative and to indicate how they can work towards it.' **1990** *City Press* 8 July 4 On Idasa's future, Boraine said it had to remain independent and become a 'critical ally' of the transition process towards democracy in South Africa. **1994** A. Boraine in *Democracy in Action* Vol.8 No.4, 11 People underestimate the courage and initiative of the Idasa team in breaking new ground.

IDB *n.* Also **I.D.B.** [Initial letters of *illicit diamond buying* or *illicit diamond buyer.*]

Cf. IGB.

1. An illicit diamond buyer: one who trades illegally in uncut diamonds.

1881 *Diamond News* in *Diggers' Ditties* (1989) 16 For half-a-dozen years or more I've been an IDB. **1886** G.A. Farini *Through Kalahari Desert* 25 The I.D.B, as the 'illicit diamond-buyer' is called, flourishes still. **1893** C.A. Goade in *Cape Illust. Mag.* Vol.4 No.9, 314 Here [*sc.* in prison] may be seen the tall gentlemanly form of the latest I.D.B. (Illicit Diamond Buyer), a man brought up in and bred to good Society. **1899** 'S. Erasmus' *Prinsloo* 16 When the detectives came up they ordered the waggon to stop, and while two of them made the two 'I.D.B.'s' strip off every bit of their clothing, the others searched the waggon. **1916** S. Black in S. Gray *Three Plays* (1984) 228 Peace: Now then, Von Kalabas, turn out your pockets. Van K: Look here, I'm not a bally I.D.B. *c***1936** *S. & E. Afr. Yr Bk & Guide* 496 The trapping system .. can only be defended on the ground of the great difficulty in bringing a conviction against an I.D.B ... by the ordinary methods of justice. **1939** [see STONE]. **1946** S. Cloete *Afr. Portraits* 134 Only by organisation could the thefts of the natives and the operations of the IDB – illicit diamond buyers – be controlled. **1955** T.V. Bulpin *Storm over Tvl* 31 Both republics had been strongholds for illicit diamond buyers, and so many of these gentry had .. settled in the little town of Christiana that if any of its inhabitants so much as visited Kimberley they were regarded by the authorities as I.D.B.s without further investigation. **1968** S. Tolansky *Strategic Diamond* 91 Illicit diamond buyers (I.D.B.s) .. are pursued fiercely by penal laws in many African states. Often the I.D.B. must offer lower prices than world prices.

2. Illicit diamond buying: illegal trading in uncut diamonds by unlicensed persons. Also *attrib.*

1882 C. Du Val *With Show through Sn Afr.* I. 95 The principal white prisoners are those who have been convicted of I.D.B., which cabalistic letters translated mean 'illicit diamond buying', a fascinating species of occupation much in vogue on 'the Fields'. **1886** W.M. Kerr *Far Int.* I. 15 In spite of the vigilance of the detective department a great deal of illicit diamond buying is successfully carried on; hence the well-known 'IDB', which refers to the illegal trade. **1897** *E. Prov. Herald* 22 Jan., The white woman, Lane, charged with I.D.B. was remanded for Trial before the Special Court. **1924** L. Cohen *Reminisc. of Jhb.* 249 Oliphantsfontein, which drips of history, is about six miles from Kimberley, and, being in the Orange Free State, was immune from the I.D.B. laws. **1937** H. Klein *Stage Coach Dust* 42 Kimberley and the diamond fields coined this new phrase: I.D.B. – illicit diamond buying. The crime was considered to be one of the most serious that could be committed in South Africa. **1949** O. Walker *Wanton City* 68 Made a fortune in I.D.B. and selling liquor to the natives. **1957** C. Birkby *Airman Lost in Afr.* 28 A little yellow tobacco bag seemed to be the badge of the trade: uncut stones were always kept in one, and the I.D.B. fellows called the little bag a 'parcel'. **1973** A. Hocking *Diamonds* 22 The importance attached to diamonds in South Africa can be judged from the serious view taken of Illicit Diamond Buying, or IDB for short. **1989** D. Carte in *Sunday Times* 8 Oct. (Business Times) 13 With huge sums at stake, the IDB racket, like the illicit drug trade, is sophisticated and violent.

3. *comb.* **IDB Act**, the Diamond Trade Act (No.48 of 1882) passed by the Cape Parliament to regulate trade in diamonds.

1913 C. Pettman *Africanderisms* 223 *I.D.B. Act*, The common name of the Diamond Trade Act, .. framed to suppress, if possible, the nefarious traffic above described. **1919** M.M. Steyn *Diary* 184 At this period the I.D.B. Act (Illicit Diamond Buying) was not in force, and diamonds could be bought from anyone.

Hence **IDBism** *n. nonce*, illicit diamond buying.

1895 R.H.S. Churchill *Men, Mines & Animals* 45 A law of exceptional rigour punishes illicit diamond buying, known in the slang of South Africa as I.D.B.-ism.

IDC *n.* [Initial letters of *Industrial Development Corporation.*] A parastatal corporation established in terms of the Industrial Development Act of 1940 for the promotion and financing of the industrial sector. Also *attrib.*

1968 *Post* 17 Nov. 7 The I.D.C. chairman, Dr. H.J. van Eck, one of the most respected non-political Afrikaners. **1971** *Daily Dispatch* 21 May 19 The remaining R60-million will be loaned by the IDC so that it becomes the IDC's largest investment in mining. **1978** *S. Afr. Panorama* Mar. 1 On October 1, 1977 the Industrial Development Corporation of South Africa – widely known as the IDC – completed 37 years of promoting industrial development in South Africa. The IDC is the biggest promoter of private enterprise in South Africa. *c***1988** *S. Afr. 1987–8: Off. Yrbk* (Bureau for Info.) 453 A number of public corporations are .. financed directly by the central government or indirectly through the Industrial Development Corporation (IDC). **1994** D. McCormack *Perm Bk of 'Test the Team'* 167 The first loan made by the IDC was for today's equivalent of R3 000.

identity *n. hist.* [Special sense of general Eng. *identity* 'absolute or essential sameness, oneness' (*OED*).] A principle of government by which all people are regarded as the same despite any cultural or other differences which might exist.

1924 E.H. Brookes *Hist. of Native Policy* 62 Most modern thinkers on the Native question argue as if there were no *via media* between the principle which refuses to acknowledge any real difference between Europeans and Natives, the policy of identity as we may call it, .. and the principle which insists on the subordinate position of the Native in the body politic, the policy of subordination. **1961** *Listener* (U.K.) 30 Nov. 808 These influences .. led in South Africa to the policy sometimes known as 'identity', of regarding all men as much the same ... The earlier British policy of identity broke down.

idhlozi var. IDLOZI.

idle *adj.* In the obsolete n. phr. ***Idle Dick*** (or ***Idle Jack***): a nickname for the grassbird *Sphenoeacus afer* of the Sylviidae; *Lazy Dick*, see LAZY.

1884 Layard & Sharpe *Birds of S. Afr.* 281 It [*sc. Sphenoeacus afer*] .. will suffer itself to be taken with the hand rather than rise again; for this reason it has acquired the name of Idle Jack or Lazy Dick. **1893** A. Newton *Dict. of Birds* 458 Idle Jack, a local name in the Cape Colony for *Sphenoeacus africanus* (Grass-bird). **1901** Stark & Sclater *Birds of S. Afr.* II. 168 *Sphenoeacus natalensis*, Natal Grass-Bird .. 'Idle Dick' and 'Lazy Dick' of English Colonists. **1913** C. Pettman *Africanderisms* 223 *Idle Dick or Lazy Jack, Sphenœcicus natalensis.* The common names of this bird in Natal.

idlozi /iˈɮɔːzi/ *n.* Pl. usu. **amadlozi**, or **madlozi(s)**. Forms: *sing.* **ehlosé**, **id(h)lozi**, **ihloze**, **ndhlozi**; *pl.* **amad(h)lozi**, **amadlosi**, **amaHlose**, **amahlosi**, **a'Mahlozi**, **amahlozi**, **madlosis**, **madlozi(s)**, **mahlose**, **mathlosi**. [Zulu. For notes on sing. and pl. forms see I-, AMA-, and MA- *pref.*[3]] Among Zulus: an ancestral spirit; a guardian spirit. Also *attrib.* See also ITONGO.

1855 J.W. Colenso *Ten Weeks in Natal* 99 They said that 'amaTongo and amaHlose were certainly not the same as umKulunkulu: for *they* could not be till man was created; in short, they were departed spirits, but umKulunkulu made all things.' **1857** W.H.I. Bleek in *Cape Monthly Mag.* I. May 293 They seldom pray to any but to the *a'Mahlozi*, or spirits of their departed great people. **1857** J. Shooter *Kafirs of Natal* 161 The Kafirs believe that, when a person dies, his *i-hloze* or *isi-tute* survives. These words are translated 'Spirit'. **1895** H. Rider Haggard *Nada* 9, I prayed to my *Ehlosé*, to the spirit that watches me. **1899** A. Werner *Captain of Locusts* 127 'Surely the Amadhlozi were protecting thee, child!' cried the old woman. **1918** H. Moore *Land of Good Hope* 109 A child of Christian parents has no itongo, though he has his own idhlozi, or personal spirit. **1923** [see ITONGO]. **1948** E. Hellmann *Rooiyard* 102 The ancestors are a living reality to them and they give proof of the constancy of their faith in the religion of their fathers by invoking the *amadlozi* in joy and in distress. **1955** E.A. Ritter *Shaka Zulu* 88 The amadlozi (ancestral spirits) have given me a clear vision, and I can see you as a mighty tree. **1968** *Post* 28 Apr. 11 To qualify as a top witchdoctor, he had to leave town life to call his amadlozi (spirits) of his dead ancestors near a spruit at Protea. **1972** *Drum* 22 Oct. 18 Now your game's up big boy, I said to myself ... But the madlozis of Malinde were working overtime. I was offered R600 bail in court, and the case was postponed. **1976** *Ibid.* 15 May 2 The mbongis have retired to the caves in the hills to commune with their madlozi muses for inspiration. **1987** *Pace* Oct. 4 They say his [*sc.* Prince Charles's] idlozi is Sir Laurens van der Post. **1989** S. Motimele in *Staffrider* Vol.8 No.1, 43 The following day, early in the morning, I set out with grandfather to complete the *madlozi* rituals.

idoda var. INDODA.

idumbi var. MADUMBI.

-ie /i/ *suffix.* Also **-etjie**, **-jie**, **-kie**, **-pie**, **-tjie**. [Afk., fr. Du. *-je.*] An Afrikaans suffix found in words originating in that language, forming a diminutive, affectionate, or informal term; occas. also added to words of English origin with similar effect. The Afrikaans rules governing the use of the variant forms are as follows: If the word ends:

1. with *-f*, *-g*, *-k*, *-p*, or *-s*: add **-ie**. If the preceding vowel is short, double the final consonant and add **-ie**.

2. with *-d* or *-t*: add **-jie**.

3.a. with *-ng*: if monosyllabic, or if polysyllabic with the stress on the last syllable, add **-etjie**.

b. with *-ng*, in cases not covered by 3 a: replace the final *-g* with **-kie**.

4. with a vowel, add **-tjie** (in S. Afr. Eng. sometimes represented by the pronunciation spelling **-kie**).

5.a. with *-l*, *-n*, or *-r*, preceded by a diphthong, long vowel, or unaccented neutral vowel (schwa), add **-tjie**.

b. with *-n*, preceded by *-oe-* or *-ie-*, add **-tjie**.

c. with *-l*, *-m*, or *-r*, preceded by *-oe-* or *-ie-*, add either **-tjie** or **-etjie**; there is no fixed pattern to be found in these cases.

d. with *-l*, *-m*, *-n*, or *-r*, preceded by a short, accented vowel apart from *-oe-* or *-ie-*, double the final consonant and add **-etjie**.

6. with *-m*, preceded by *-l* or *-r*, or by a long vowel, diphthong or unaccented neutral vowel (schwa), add **-pie**.

For examples, see AGRETJIE, BOETEBOSSIE, BOETIE, BOKHORINKIE, DUIWELTJIE, LIEDJIE, PRUIMPIE, WATERBLOMMETJIE, and, added to an English word, BOYKIE.

ifafa lily /iˈfɑːfə ˈlɪli, ə-/ *n. phr.* Freq. with initial capital(s). [Named for the *Ifafa* river, in KwaZulu-Natal; see quot. 1975.] Any of several species of plant of the genus *Cyrtanthus* (family Amaryllidaceae) with umbels of white, yellow or reddish flowers, esp. *C. mackenii*. See also FIRE LILY.

1913 C. PETTMAN *Africanderisms* 223 *Ifafa Lily*, The name given in the Transkeian territories to *Cyrtanthus lutescens, Herb.* **1934** *Friend* 15 Mar. (Swart), Ifafa lilies (Kaffir lilies) with their scarlet, yellow and white spikes or blooms are particularly pleasing subjects in the early spring. **1946** K.C. STANFORD in *Farmer's Weekly* 30 Oct. 48 The cream Ifafa lilies .. begin to bloom about the same time. **1962** S. ELIOVSON *Discovering Wild Flowers in Sn Afr.* 160 *Cyrtanthus o'brienii* ... The graceful drooping flowers of the Red Ifafa Lily appear in August and September ... The well-known Ifafa Lily (*C. mackenii*) is similar in appearance, but has white, pink or apricot flowers, while there is also a yellow variety. *c*1968 S. CANDY *Natal Coast Gardening* 71 Ifafa lily must be guarded against attack from the black-and-yellow Amaryllis caterpillar at all times. **1975** J.M. GIBSON *Wild Flowers of Natal* 15 Found in damp places near the Ifafa lagoon, there used to be large colonies of Ifafa lilies. **1982** W.G. SHEAT *A-Z of Gardening* 91 The ifafa lily .. bears spring umbels ranging from white through cream to yellow, apricot and on to deep red.

IFP *n.* [Initial letters of *Inkatha Freedom Party*.] A political party formed in 1990 from the cultural movement *Inkatha Yenkululeko Yesizwe* (see INKATHA sense 2). Also *attrib.*

1990 *Clarion Call* Vol.3, 7 The IFP believes that various scenarios could produce awesome dangers in South Africa. **1990** *Weekend Post* 29 Sept. 10 In a show of force, the Inkatha Freedom Party (IFP) today proved it had strong support. **1991** *E. Prov. Herald* 30 Jan. 1 Mr Mandela went on to say that the parties 'solemnly call upon our people, members of the ANC and IFP as well as our allies, to cease all attacks against one another with immediate effect'. **1991** L. KAUNDA in *Natal Witness* 28 Mar. (Echo) 1 This week IFP president Mangosuthu Buthelezi said hopes for peace were becoming slimmer by the day. **1992** *Weekly Mail* 16 Apr. 5 The mostly IFP-dominated hostels in the Transvaal and many areas of Natal. **1994** W. HARTLEY in *Natal Witness* 8 Jan. 1 The possibility of open confrontation between the IFP and the transitional executive council was increased.

IGB *n.* Also **I.G.B.** [Initial letters of *illicit gold buying* (or, rarely, *illicit gold buyer*).]

Cf. IDB.

1. Illicit gold buying. Also *attrib.*

1893 *Poster, Witwatersrand Mine Employees & Mechanics Union*, Gold Thefts Bill! I.G.B., the shadow of the I.D.B. **1897** G. ALBU in *Mining Industry: Report of Industrial Commiss. of Enquiry* (Witwatersrand Chamber of Mines) 26 A large number must be thriving on the ill-gotten gains of I.G.B. The proof of that we have in the quantity of people who are doing absolutely nothing, and they live in a very good manner. **1899** F.R.M. CLEAVER in M.M. Cleaver *Young S. Afr.* (1913) 27 We shall have some most glorious work before us, exterminating the illicit sale of liquor to natives. We shall also tackle the I.G.B. (illicit gold buying). Both of these evils have assumed such gigantic proportions as to be a menace to the life of the State. **1899** W.F. MONEYPENNY in C. Headlam *Milner Papers* (1931) I. 344 Thieving from the mine and I.G.B. (illicit gold buying) was estimated by the Industrial Commission as costing the industry no less than three-quarters of a million sterling a year. **1900** T. FROES *Kruger & Co.* 6 No doubt can possibly exist as to the reality of the evil in question, and .. as the enormous sums stolen represent an absolutely dead loss to the industry and a consequent curtailment of dividend-paying power, this matter of 'I.G.B.' is one which directly concerns every shareholder in 'The Witwatersrand Gold Mining Companies'. **1979** J. GRATUS *Jo'burgers* 256 I.G.B. was the poor man's passport to .. the life of sweet idleness such as he believed the magnates lived. I.G.B. was the magic that could turn a black man into a white man and a white man into a king. I.G.B. was illicit gold buying. **1983** J. DE RIDDER *Sad Laughter Mem.* 131 He knows the I.G.B. squad's reputation as well as I do. The Illicit Gold Buying branch of the South African Police is one of the cleverest and hardest teams to beat. **1990** J.G. DAVIS *Land God Made in Anger* 178 Unlicensed dealing in gold is a serious offence in South Africa – IGB.

2. *rare.* An illicit gold buyer.

1945 N. DEVITT *People & Places* 146 A prosecution of the big I.G.B. – illicit gold buyer – is rarely heard of.

igogog var. GOGOG.

Igoli var. EGOLI.

igqira *n.*[1] var. IGQWIRA.

‖**igqira** /i'ǂi:xa/ *n.*[2] Pl. usu. **amagqira**. Forms: *sing.* **agika**, **gqir(h)a**, **igqir(h)a**, **igqiya**, **igquira**, **inqira**, **iqika**, **iquira**; *sing.* and *pl.* **amaqira**; *pl.* **amagqi(g)ha**, **amagqir(h)a**. Also with initial capital. [Xhosa *igqira* (pl. *amagqira*) healer, diviner, smeller-out of witches, fr. a Khoikhoi word (see quot. 1966).] A traditional Xhosa healer or priest-diviner who, through seances and the interpretation of dreams sent to him by the ancestral spirits, may 'smell out' enchantment, and both diagnose and treat disease. Also *attrib.* Occas. in the feminine form **igqirakazi** [Xhosa, feminine suffix *-kazi*]. See also WITCHDOCTOR.

Sometimes confused with IGQWIRA.

1833 *Graham's Town Jrnl* 8 Aug. 3 At the kraal where I belong, a man .. was very ill with a pain in his head, when the people of the place sent for an 'Iqika' (witchfinder) .. to come and see the man. **1835** A. STEEDMAN *Wanderings* I. 266 The Amaponda Caffers have three professions – that of the 'Amaqira,' or witch-doctor; of the 'Abanisi-bamvula,' or rain-maker; and of the 'Agika,' or doctor of medicine, which may be considered the most valuable of the three. **1860** W. SHAW *Story of my Mission* 512, I have no doubt that they had .. been directed .. by the great *Igqira*, Priest or doctor, who, according to custom, had prepared them by his charms and other ceremonies for their warlike proceedings. **1918** H. MOORE *Land of Good Hope* 119 The white man has stopped .. the awful practice of 'smelling out'. The Igqira goes on finding lost cattle, and using his remedies to heal sickness, if he can. **1937** C. BIRKBY *Zulu Journey* 282 The most powerful people in Pondoland, powerful even above the Chief, are the practitioners of black magic. The 'xwele' are the male magicians; but they even are not so powerful as the strange women who deal in mtagati – the gqira woman of Pondoland. **1937** B.J.F. LAUBSCHER *Sex, Custom & Psychopathology* p.xiv, Through the assistance of one of the native attendants, I made the acquaintance of Solomon Daba, a prominent *igqira* (or witch-doctor). **1949** L. HUNTER *Afr. Dawn* 9 Were these things any more wonderful than the magic of a *gqira* (diviner) who, by plastering a man's stomach with specially prepared medicine, could remove the lizard that had been the cause of the ache in his bowels? **1954** W.D. HAMMOND-TOOKE in A.M. Duggan-Cronin *Bantu Tribes* III. v. 39 Another type of 'doctor' derives his skill from communion with the spirits. This is the *isangoma* (*igqiya*), usually a woman, who 'smells out' wizards and diagnoses sickness at special seances (*iintlombi*) held in huts at night. **1966** A.T. BRYANT *Zulu Medicine* 11 The Kafirs call their medicine man, in Zulu, an *i-nyanga*, and in Xosa, an *i-nyangi* (although in the latter language a totally different term, viz. *i-gqira*, is in more common use nowadays, probably derived from the Hottentot: cf. Nama-Hot. *gqeira*, pertaining to witchery, from *gqei-di*, bewitch, from *gqei*, belch). **1978** *Daily Dispatch* 29 June 10 The term 'Witchdoctor' is a misnomer; the doctor is no more a witch than a detective is a burglar ... The Amagqira, or priest-diviners, searched for witches as detectives searched for burglars. **1982** *Ibid.* 25 May 16 The functions of the igqirha (more often than not an igqirhakazi – a woman) are threefold: religious, magical and medicinal. **1984** *S. Afr. Panorama* Dec. 41 The role of the igqira is closely associated with the ancestor cult of the Xhosa. The ancestral spirits, or 'living dead', .. communicate through dreams, the interpretation of which is the vocation of the iqgira. **1990** M. OETTLE in *Weekend Post* 16 June (Leisure) 7 All *amagqirha* believe in God the Creator, uThixo – the name also given in the Church to God the Father – but hold that He has little interest in the affairs of men, and that a family's ancestral spirits are more directly involved with that family's day-to-day life.

igqirakazi see IGQIRA *n.*[2]

‖**igqwira** /i'ǂwi:xa/ *n.* Also **egeerha**, **egqwira**, **igqira**, **igqwire**, and with initial capital. Pl. **amagqwira**, or (occas.) **amagqira**. [Xhosa *igqwira* malevolent sorcerer (pl. *amagqwira*).] Among the Xhosa: a malevolent wizard or sorcerer; also used as a title. Also *attrib.* See also WITCHDOCTOR.

Sometimes confused with IGQIRA.

1836 A.F. GARDINER *Journey to Zoolu Country* 247 Umyaki had dispatched two men to Faku, for the alleged purpose of procuring beads, but they were at the same time accompanied by an Egeerha or Bewitcher. **1860** W. SHAW *Story of my Mission* 452 The Priest is expected to expose the bewitching matter, *ubuti*, and to declare who is the *igqwire* or wizard that has been exercising malevolent influence over the person or property of others. **1866** W.C. HOLDEN *Past & Future* 308 When all their arts are exhausted without success, they impute their failure to the amagqira, or sorcerers, by whose malicious influence the rain is prevented from falling. **1891** T.R. BEATTIE *Pambaniso* 42 With him the word *Igqwira* not only meant wizard, sorcerer, or dealer in witchcraft, but it comprehended or applied to all those who boasted of efficiency in anything, or who were reputed to be adepts in any art, and who, when a trial of the skill was made, failed to maintain their reputation. **1908** [see QAMATA]. **1978** A.P. BRINK *Rumours of Rain* 37 'So you murdered him?' 'I went to see the witchdoctor, the *igqira*. And he spoke to the *izinyanya*, the spirits of the ancestors. And then my father died ...' **1980** E. JOUBERT *Poppie Nongena* 83 A witch, or what you call an igqwira, is the one who does the wicked things, but she became an igqira, a doctor who helps people.

igubu var. UGUBU.

‖**igxagxa** /i'ǁa:ǁa/ *n.* Pl. **amagxagxa**, occas. **gxagxa**. [Xhosa, 'one who has become poor, a poor white', fr. *ukugxagxa* to become poor and squalid.]

Usu. in *pl.*

1. A poor white; a derogatory term for a white person (esp. one who shows hostility to black people). See also POOR WHITE.

1956 A. SAMPSON *Drum* 158 To most Africans, white men are enormously rich. The rudest word for a white man is Igxagxa, 'poor white man': an Igxagxa is like a hen which doesn't lay eggs. **1983** *Frontline* June 29 In Xhosa there is a long-standing distinction between Izingamula, 'gentlefolk', and Amagxagxa, poor whites ... Amagxagxa has taken on a connotation of hostility towards blacks and has also, say various Xhosa-speakers, come to be generally applied to all whites. **1987** *Ibid.* Aug.-Sept. 36 We would have to stop calling poor and sloppy whites 'amagxagxa' ... Now it is only low-class whites who are amagxagxa.

2. One who falls between two cultures.

1980 [see MASKANDA]. **1987** *Frontline* Aug.-Sept. 36 To start with, the 'amagxagxa' were the people who came to the towns and began to behave half-way like whites. This was around the early years of the century, when those people would wear a white-type suit, but with Zulu-type sandals. **1988** K. SOLE in Bunn & Taylor *From S. Afr.* 263 They [*sc.* migrant workers] still find their creative identity to some degree in the rural areas .., although many of them spend their lives mainly in the urban centres ... Known as 'the people between' (*amagxagxa*), they play a significant role in a number of recent cultural developments .. as they assimilate and mould elements of their own Western and urban township life-styles into something which has meaning for them.

‖**ihlambo** /iˈɬaːmbɔ/ *n.* [Zulu *i(li)hlambo*.] In traditional Zulu society: a purification ceremony which ends a period of mourning.

> **1934** *Sunday Times* 25 Feb. (Swart), This ceremony is known as ihlambo to the Zulus, to whom it is of great importance and significance. **1937** C. BIRKBY *Zulu Journey* 70 The nation mourned him for eighteen months and its was not until the great ceremony of Ihlambo which 'cleansed' the nation and ended the mourning period that the successor to the throne was chosen. **1955** E.A. RITTER *Shaka Zulu* 329 This campaign .. would now also serve as the i-hlambo or mourning hunt for his mother's death.

ihloze var. IDLOZI.

ii-, iim-, iin- /iː, iːm, iːn/ *pref.* A Xhosa plural noun prefix found in some words originating in that language.

> In Xhosa, the singular of words beginning *ii-*, *iim-*, or *iin-* is formed by replacing the prefix with *in-* or *im-*; in S. Afr. Eng. this pattern is not always observed, and words in the plural forms are sometimes treated as singular nouns to which an English plural *-s* is added. See also IM- and IN-.

iibari pl. form of BARI.

iim- see II-.

iimbongi pl. form of IMBONGI.

i'impundulu var. IMPUNDULU.

iin- see II-.

iingcibi pl. form of INGCIBI.

ijna var. EINA.

ijuba /iˈdʒʊːba, iˈdʒuːbə/ *n.* Also **Ijuba, iJuba, juba, jubu**. [Zulu, 'dove'.] **a.** With initial capital. The proprietary name of a brand of sorghum beer. **b.** Loosely, any such beer: TSHWALA sense a. Cf. JABULANI.

> **1973** *Drum* 22 Apr. 12 'Do you drink jubu?' she asked the Drum reporter. The reply was a firm No. 'You talk like you do,' came the calm rejoinder. **1975** M. MUTLOATSE in *Bolt* No.12, 32 Alongside the rails, Ijuba upon Ijuba. The train itself? A mobile black market ... Ijuba, carton — of white-brewed concoction — 15 cents. **1984** *E. Prov. Herald* 24 Mar. 1 We've had a problem with black women selling iJuba (sorghum beer) to workers outside the factory at lunchtime, and we have asked police to remove them. **1986** M. RAMGOBIN *Waiting to Live* 155 The profits from the sale of juba in the beer halls are used to run this township, don't you know that? **1990** W. BOTHA in *Frontline* Sept. 19 You know, our Zulu men's kingdom is beer and braai meat ... Shabalala gives the men Ijuba and meat, then he says, 'Come and fight'.

ijzer vark var. YSTERVARK.

ikankat(h)a var. IKHANKATHA.

ikaya var. KAYA.

ikazi var. IKHAZI.

Ikey /ˈaɪki/ *n. colloq.* [Special sense of general Eng. *Ikey* (dim. form of *Isaac*), used derog. of a Jew (see quot. 1984); reportedly first used by Stellenbosch University students in songs at an intervarsity rugby match in 1919.]
a. A student of the University of Cape Town; a member of a sports team representing this university. Also *attrib.*

> **1921** *Cathartic* (Univ. of Cape Town) Sept. 4 We believe that the recent protest on the part of the S.R.C. to the Maatie University, re the name 'Ikey,' which has been applied to us at Inter-'Varsity, has caused considerable criticism in 'Varsity circles. **1971** *Cape Times* 15 May 24 The chances of John le Roux and his green-horned underdog Ikeys pulling off an upset win in the 58th intervarsity at Newlands to-day look slim indeed. **1984** P. BEALE *E. Partridge's Dict. of Slang & Unconventional Eng.* 592 Ikeys, Students of the old South African College, now the University of Cape Town, so called by their rivals of Victoria College, Stellenbosch, because of their large Jewish enrolment. **1987** S. ROBERTS *Jacks in Corners* 148 'After my training,' said Will, 'I worked among students, Witsies and Ikeys, from 1972 through 1974'. **1988** *E. Prov. Herald* 23 July 3 Excesses such as those at last year's Ikey-Matie intervarsity rugby match would 'put the annual event in direct danger of cancellation'. **1990** T. PARTRIDGE in *Sunday Times* 12 Aug. 20 On paper an Ikey victory yesterday appeared to be about as feasible as an igloo in the Sahara desert — the last time the UCT students had beaten their arch enemies was in 1976.

b. Always in pl. The University of Cape Town; a sports team from this university. Also *attrib.* See also UCT.

> **1971** C. HOOGENDIJK *Informant, Welkom* It's really wet down here now and I don't blame you for leaving Ikeys. **1973** *Star* 8 June 13 At Ikeys, too, there is a lot of indifference. But that is universal. In our parents' day they had something to fight for. **1981** *Campus Sport* Vol.5 No.5, 2 Huge crowd watches Ikeys thrash Maties. **1990** T. PARTRIDGE in *Sunday Times* 12 Aug. 20 If Western Province had played this season with as much fight and spirit as Ikeys did in yesterday's intervarsity at Newlands, they would already have been well on their way to the Currie Cup final.

‖**ikhankatha** /ˌikanˈkɑːta, -tə/ *n.* Also **inkankat(h)a, kankata, khankatha, nkantata**. [Xhosa.] In traditional Xhosa society: the guardian in charge of youths undergoing the initiation rite of circumcision. See also ABAKWETHA.

> Sometimes an INGCIBI may perform the work of the 'ikhankatha'.
> **1866** W.C. HOLDEN *Past & Future* 183 To this hut the boys are taken, having been placed in charge of a person appointed to that office, and who is called the inkankata, and under whose charge they continue during the whole time of their initiation. **1939** N.J. VAN WARMELO in A.M. Duggan-Cronin *Bantu Tribes* III. i. 32 The initiates (abakhwetha) stay in a grass hut (isuthu) built for the occasion at a distance from dwellings, under the charge of a master (ikhankatha) who instructs them and trains them in endurance and other qualities of manhood. **1952** H. KLEIN *Land of Silver Mist* 48 They are taken charge of by the nkantata, the warder, who together with the old men of the tribe instructs the abaKweta, as the initiates are now called, in the rites and lore of their people. **1976** *Daily Dispatch* 20 Aug. 4 He preferred to use his own 'warden' or 'ikhankatha' to avoid any carelessness that might affect the initiates' health while they were training. **1976** R.L. PETENI *Hill of Fools* 122 Girls often visited their lovers when their khankatha was satisfied that the circumcision cuts of all of them had healed. **1978** *Voice* 15 Nov. 8 A certain person with experience in circumcision rites is appointed to take charge of the boys during this period. He is called 'ikhankatha' (teacher). **1989** [see INGCIBI].

ikhaya var. KAYA.

‖**ikhazi** /iˈkɑːzi/ *n.* Also **ikazi, khazi**. [Xhosa, 'dowry', 'marriage cattle'.] In Xhosa society: LOBOLA *n.* sense 2.

> **1858** *Cape Monthly Mag.* IV. Oct. 218 The dowry, or price paid for a wife, is called the 'ikazi.' **1891** T.R. BEATTIE *Pambaniso* 102 Frequently a match is arranged through the negotiations of friends, as to the number and quality of the cattle to be given as a dowry. This custom is known as that of Ikazi or ukulobola. **1897** 'F. MACNAB' *On Veldt & Farm* 272 Among these semi-civilized Kaffirs the custom of giving 'ikazi' (cattle in payment for wives) is becoming rare. **1905** [see LOBOLA *n.* sense 1]. **1931** F.C. SLATER *Secret Veld* 311 The cattle so tendered are known as ikazi (dowry). Should a wife have reasonable cause for complaint she may always return to her father (or his heirs) who, having received *ikazi*, are bound to protect her. **1962** W.D. HAMMOND-TOOKE *Bhaca Soc.* 132 The marriage ceremonies of the Bhaca have shown the important part played by the handing over of cattle ... The verb ukulobola is used to express this action, and the cattle which are handed over are known collectively as ikhazi.

ikhowe /iˈkɔːwe, iˈkaʊwi/ *n.* Also **ikowe, i'kowe**, and with initial capital. Pl. **-s**, or **amakhowe** /ama-/. [Zulu. For an explanation of pl. forms, see AMA- and I-.] Any of several species of large edible mushrooms of the genus *Termitomyces* (family Tricholomataceae), esp. *T. umkowaanii*; BEEFSTEAK MUSHROOM sense a.

> *T. umkowaanii* is also known as *Schulzeria umkowaani*.
> **c1948** *S. & E. Afr. Yr Bk & Guide* 313 The Natal Beefsteak Mushroom or I-kowe (*Schulzeria umkowaan*). **1953** E. STEPHENS *Some S. Afr. Edible Fungi* p.vii, The well-known 'Kaffir mushroom' (Ikhowa, Ikowe). **1954** BOTTOMLEY & TALBOT *Common Edible & Poisonous Mushrooms* 43 Natal Beefsteak or I'kowe Mushroom, (*Termitomyces* species.) ... Although this mushroom occurs fairly frequently in the Transvaal, its natural home appears to be Natal. **1967** S.M.A. LOWE *Hungry Veld* 132 Four enormous amakhowe (*a type of giant mushroom*). **1972** G.C.A. VAN DER WESTHUIZEN in *Std Encycl. of Sn Afr.* V. 101 The beefsteak mushroom or ikowe, and various species of *Termitomyces* grow on termite nests in summer. **1979** W. EBERSOHN *Lonely Place* 133 He could see in what profusion the late mushrooms, the *ikhowe* as Freek had called them, were still growing. **1985** H. LEVIN et al. *Field Guide to Mushrooms* 153 *Termitomyces umkowaanii* (I'kowe) are large, fleshy mushrooms which require a longer cooking time than other species — about 20 minutes. They can be braised, braaied or used in frikkadels. I'kowes can also be left raw, sliced finely and added to salads. **1987** *Ibid.* 20 The fruit-body of the I'kowe (Beefsteak Mushroom) grows up through the termite nest on an extraordinarily long stem and produces a giant mushroom at the surface.

ikona var. AIKONA.

ikowe, i'kowe varr. IKHOWE.

‖**ikrwala** /iˈkxwaːla/ *n.* Pl. **amakrwala, amarwela**, or (occas.) unchanged. [Xhosa (pl. *amakrwala*). For note on sing. and pl. forms, see I-.] In traditional Xhosa society: a newly circumcised youth. Also *attrib.* See also ABAKWETHA.

> **1963** WILSON & MAFEJE *Langa* 50 Cooking and washing up is done by the young men, *amakrwala* (newly circumcised), or boys *amakhwenkwe*, and the young men are served with a dish separate from that of the senior men. *Ibid.* 155 The ikrwala refused to cooperate with his room-mates because he felt that he was being overworked. **1967** [see UMFAAN sense 1]. **1971** P. MAYER *Townsmen or Tribesmen* 86 The *amakrwala* (youths in transitional stage after initiation). *Ibid.* 91 Senior boys (approaching initiation) and *ikrwala* (youths in the transition stage just after initiation) go away to work for short periods to show their manliness. **1976** *Financial Mail* 22 Oct. 3 The boys are still regarded [*sc.* after circumcision] .. as no more than *amarwela* or unripe fruit. Tribal elders must instruct them in social behaviour, rituals, traditional responsibilities and tribal law. **1978** *Voice* 15 Nov. 8 Different ones from the elderly men take turns in lecturing to the 'amakrwala' young men, as they are now called. Gifts .. are given by relatives and friends to enable them to set out in their new way of life.

ilala /iˈlɑːlə/ *n.* Also **lala**. [Zulu, fr. *lala* (v.) sleep; see quots. 1978 and 1988.] In full *ilala palm*: the fan palm *Hyphaene coriacea* of the Arecaceae. Also *attrib.*

> **1868** J. CHAPMAN *Trav.* II. 464 Ilala, Hyphæne. **1884** E.P. MATHERS *Trip to Moodie's* 29 There is a natural drink .. which .. goes by the name of kaffir beer .. it is the exudation of a native palm tree (*ilala*). **1911** *Encycl. Brit.* XIX. 253 Of palms [in Natal] there are two varieties, the ilala (*Hyphaene crinita*), found only by the sea shore and a mile or two inland, and the isundu (*Phoenix reclinata*). **1929** J. STEVENSON-HAMILTON *Low-Veld* 44 Rope is made from the bark of several acacias and from that of the bush known as tshishumbana .. while the fibre of the ilala, or fan palm

(Hyphoene crinita) is used for the same purpose. **1954** T.V. BULPIN *Ivory Trail* 44 He .. passed the hot hours in plaiting a hat from lala palm leaves. *Ibid.* 114 The elephants .. also had a liking for this potent lala palm wine. **1966** C.A. SMITH *Common Names* 254 *Ilala palm*, Natives use the leaves for making basket-ware, rope, etc. The trunk is tapped and the sap caught in small calabashes and fermented into a very potent liquor. **1978** A. ELLIOTT *Sons of Zulu* 129 They .. make a brew from the sap of a fan-palm tree which they call lala palm. In their language *lala* means to sleep, so no doubt the tree got its name originally from the soporific delights which its juices gave to those who partook of them. **1980** *S. Afr. Digest* 17 Oct. 15 Ilala Palm, also known as the Fan Palm or Gingerbread Tree (*Hyphaene natalensis*). Occurs from the Natal South Coast, through KwaZulu, the Transvaal to as far north as tropical Africa. The nut is known as vegetable ivory, from which buttons are made. **1988** P. WILHELM *Healing Process* 25 One thing you have to know about this area .. is its ecology of drunkenness. Have you heard of the lala-palm? .. They collect its sap and within twenty-four hours the stuff ferments and you can drink it. Palm wine. **1993** G. SILBER in *Flying Springbok* June 79, I watched him [*sc.* an elephant] tear off a couple of fronds and a giant cluster of orange dates from the top of an ilala palm.

iland var. ELAND.

ili- /ili/ *pref.* A Xhosa, Zulu, and Ndebele singular noun prefix found in some words originating in these languages.

In Xhosa, Zulu, and Ndebele, the plural of words beginning *ili-* is formed by replacing this prefix with *ama-*; in *S. Afr. Eng.* this pattern is not always observed, and the plural is sometimes formed by the addition of the English plural suffix *-s* to the singular form. See also AMA- and I-.

Ilindebele *n. obs.* [In the Nguni languages, a variant of *iNdebele* (see NDEBELE).] MATABELE sense 1 b.

1872 T.M. THOMAS *11 Yrs in Central S. Afr.* 170 The Ilindebele is not wanting in good taste in respect to beauty, cleanliness, and dress. *Ibid.* 201 These facts account for the ease, fluency, and effect with which an Ilindebele can speak.

illegal *adj.* and *n. Hist. colloq.* [Special senses of general Eng.] During the apartheid era:

A. *adj.* Of a black person: present or resident in an urban area in contravention of Section 10 of the Natives (Urban Areas) Consolidation Act. See also SECTION 10 sense 1.

1977 J. SIKAKANE *Window on Soweto* 25 The law states that no-one may lawfully reside in Soweto or other locations without being in possession of several appropriate permits ... The search for 'illegal' natives is carried out by the 'blackjacks,' the notorious municipal police. **1977** *Survey of Race Rel.* (S.A.I.R.R.) 159 Employers .. engaged 'illegal' Blacks at a low wage. **1979** *Rand Daily Mail* 14 July 1 Govt. will relax law on 'illegal' workers. In a dramatic move yesterday, the Government announced that employers have until October 31 to register blacks who have been working illegally for them for at least a year. **1980** C. HERMER *Diary of Maria Tholo* 197 When their reports were first presented to parliament as bills, the recommendations were considerably watered down. The definition of 'illegal blacks' was changed. **1983** *Frontline* Feb. 39 He was present on a wintry day near Cape Town when officials razed the shanties of 'illegal blacks'. **1985** *Sunday Star* 27 Oct. 1 She went to jail this week for a principle – she refused to register her illegal maid.

B. *n.* [Absol. use of *adj.*] One who is considered 'illegal' in terms of Section 10 of the Natives (Urban Areas) Consolidation Act. Cf. LEGAL.

1980 *Rand Daily Mail* 5 Feb. 1, 72-hour limit on illegals to go – as test. **1981** *Ibid.* 13 Feb. 9 Dozens of former Johannesburg municipal workers – forcibly bused to their homelands after their strike last July – have come back to the city .. but are now stranded in Johannesburg as 'illegals'. **1982** *Voice* 1 Aug. 5 The fine for a person found guilty of this law is R500 or six months imprisonment. This also applies to anyone, whether Black or White, who allows that person (an illegal), to be in his house from 10pm to 5am. **1982** *Argus* 22 Oct. 14 If journalists are forbidden to report what happens in the townships in the early hours of the morning – when most of the raids on 'illegals' are carried out – how will anyone know what is going on under the cloak of night? **1983** *Pretoria News* 28 Sept. 1 Illegal squatter huts would not be tolerated anywhere in the Cape Peninsula, but it had to be realised that there was lots of shelter for 'illegals' in the bush. **1985** PLATZKY & WALKER *Surplus People* 61 Others said they were moved because .. they did not have papers to be in town – they were 'illegals'. **1987** M. CHALLENOR in *Star* 30 Oct. 15 Right-wing whites and the black illegals are defending the same thing: their homes. **1988** *Now Everyone Is Afraid* (Catholic Inst. for Internat. Rel.) 71 It was only when the government announced that illegals could move to serviced sites and get temporary legal status, that significant numbers of people moved to Khayelitsha willingly. **1989** [see ALREADY].

ilobola var. LOBOLA *n.*

im- /im/ *pref.* A singular noun prefix common to the Nguni languages and found in some words originating in these languages.

In the Nguni languages, the plural of a word beginning *im-* is formed by replacing the prefix with *ama-*, *ii-*, *iim-*, or *izim-*; in *S. Afr. Eng.* this pattern is not always observed, and the plural is sometimes formed by the addition of the English plural suffix *-s* to the singular form. See also AMA-, II-, and IZIM-.

imali var. MALI.

imamba var. MAMBA.

‖**imbeleko** /imbeˈleːkɔ/ *n.* [Zulu, formed on *beleka* carry (a child) on one's back.]

1. A piece of animal-skin or other strong material, used for strapping a baby onto its mother's back.

1948 E. HELLMANN *Rooiyard* 10 Even the time-honoured *imbeleko* (cradle-skin in which children are carried on back) is giving way to the blanket. *Ibid.* 60 A goat is slaughtered by the father ... Friends and relatives eat the goat and the skin forms the *tari* (Sotho) or *imbeleko* (Zulu) in which the mother will carry her baby. **1951** *Afr. Drum* Mar. 55 When a woman carries an infant on her back she binds it to herself with a thong or part of her dress. This support is called *imbeleko*. **1977** P.C. VENTER *Soweto* 55 A goat was killed, the blood symbolizing the mother's loss of virginity ... Her mother presented her with the imbeleko, a rectangle of strong material with straps so that she could one day carry a baby on her back. 'You must not use any old blanket,' her mother said. 'Too many township women have forgotten the imbeleko. It will protect your child.'

2. *rare.* A ceremony celebrating the birth of a child, in which a goat is killed and its skin made into a support for carrying the child.

1988 I. DARBY in Laband & Haswell *Pietermaritzburg 1838–1988* 166 The ceremony of *imbeleko* which followed the birth of a child gave it personhood and identity.

Imbhokoto var. MBOKODO.

imbira var. MBIRA.

‖**imbizo** /imˈbiːzɔ, ɪmbiːzəʊ/ *n.* Also **'mbizo**. [Zulu, fr. *biza* call, summon.] A meeting, esp. a gathering of the Zulu people called by a traditional leader. Cf. KGOTLA sense 3.

1975 M. MUTLOATSE in *Bolt* No.12, 24 There was this foreboding 'mbizo at the bugged hovel of Matlambani Kahle ... And she prayed that Nkulunkulu bless those who were brave enough to attend. **1982** *Pace* Oct. 70 When King Goodwill Zwelithini called the Zulu nation together for an *imbizo* to discuss the Ingwavuma issue, tribesmen turned out in large numbers dressed in traditional garb and carrying their shields and spears. **1991** D. NTOMBELA in *Sunday Tribune* 15 Dec. 5, I don't think anyone can say that shields, knobkerries and spears cannot be carried when the amakosi (chiefs) call an imbizo (meeting) or if the Chief Minister calls an imbizo. **1993** J. ZUMA in *Weekly Mail* 10 Dec. 3 If an *imbizo* (meeting of the Zulu nation) is called and some political parties are attacked, that will be most unfortunate. **1994** D. KANDLOVU in *Sidelines* Dec. 23 One day there is an imbizo of all the Natal Midlands people ... Here at the imbizo all he wants to do is lead his warriors in war chants.

Imbo var. MBO.

Imbokodo, Imbokotho varr. MBOKODO.

‖**imbola** /imˈbɔːla/ *n.* [Xhosa.] In Xhosa society: red ochre, burnt, pounded, mixed into a paste, and used as a body paint both by women and by newly circumcised youths.

1937 B.J.F. LAUBSCHER *Sex, Custom & Psychopathology* 69 The mother is hereafter smeared with fat and *Imbola* (red ochre) and the *Ukufukama* [*sc.* lying-in] is completed. **1978** B.J. MOTAUNG in *Staffrider* Vol.1 No.2, 22 Men, women and children .. cover their bodies And put a daub of imbola on their faces, Making them look like circus clowns and Coon Carnivals of the Cape. **1979** M. MATSHOBA *Call Me Not a Man* 166 Both to protect her skin and to enhance her beauty, her face was smeared with *ingxwala*, the white stone, the rest of her with *imbola*, the red ochre.

‖**imbongi** /imˈbɔːŋgi/ *n.* Also **ibongi, imbonga, imbongo, mbongi**, and with initial capital. Pl. usu. **-s**, or **izimbongi**; also **iimbongi, isibongi, izibongi, izimbonga, sbongi, 'sbongi, zebõngas**, or unchanged. [Xhosa and Zulu, praise-poet (pl. *iimbongi* in Xhosa, *izimbongi* in Zulu).] Esp. in the context of traditional African society:

1. A praise poet or public orator; MBONGO sense 1; PRAISER. Also *attrib.* See also BONGA *v.*

1836 A.F. GARDINER *Journey to Zoolu Country* 65 We were accompanied by the two Imbõngas, or professed praisers of the King. *Ibid.* 124 The leopard skin .. would be given to one of the Zebõngas, or praisers, to make a new dress for the dance. **1839** W. C. HARRIS *Wild Sports* 116 We .. were .. preparing to start when a herald, called, in the Matabili language, *Imbongo*, a proclaimer of the king's titles, suddenly made his appearance outside the kraal. **1871** in T. Baines *Northern Goldfields Diaries* (1946) III. 687 His Imbonga, or court flatterer .. recounted the battles of the Matabele. **1888** D.C.F. MOODIE *Hist. of Battles & Adventures* 474 An amusing scene was taking place outside between two Izibongi (jesters or praisers), each yelling out the string of praises of their respective Chiefs – Mr. Shepstone and Cetewayo – and trying to outdo each other. **1898** B. MITFORD *Induna's Wife* 132 The King .. came forth .. , preceded by the *izimbonga*, running and roaring, and trumpeting and hissing, as they shouted aloud the royal titles. **1913** W.C. SCULLY *Further Reminisc.* 270 The 'imbonga,' or 'praiser.' *c*1948 H. TRACEY *Lalela Zulu* p.ii, A good Zulu *Imbongi* would be expected to string off a round of praises lasting five minutes or more without repeating himself, though many individual lines were repeated for poetic reasons. **1968** *Post* 28 Apr. 3 (*caption*) A mbongi ululates before the smiling Heads of State (Kaunda and Khama). **1973** *Drum* 8 Mar. 53 The mbongis are out in their colourful dresses dancing and singing, shouting 'Bayete' to Mnumzana Vorster ... The mbongis .. climb up his ancestral tree singing the praise poems of Vorster's illustrious forebears. **1976** *Drum* 15 May 2 The mbongi laureate will .. be able in his praises to climb right up Chief Matanzima's ancestral tree to the first Matanzima since creation. **1980** M. MUTLOATSE *Forced Landing* 1 The part the black writer has to play is rather demanding ... He has to be tradesman, docker, psychologist, nurse, miner, *matshigilane*, *tshotsha*, teacher, athlete, toddler, mother, musician, father, visionary, *imbongi* and – above all – oral historian. **1986** A. SITAS in Bunn & Taylor *From S. Afr.* (1988) 277 His performances initiated a revival of *imbongi* poetry in union gatherings in Natal and beyond. [*Note*] Praise-singer. **1988** SPIEGEL & BOONZAIER in Boonzaier & Sharp *S. Afr. Keywords* 55 Inkatha now has its own izimbongi (praise poets) who are called upon to praise the organisation and its leaders at various public gatherings. **1991** N. MBATHA in *Pace* Feb. 28 Before the chief takes the floor, a praise-poet (imbongi) will introduce the chief by reciting. **1992** *S. Afr. Panorama* Nov.-Dec. 75 In Transkei, the *iimbongi*, the public orators or praise poets, have gradually shifted their allegiance from royalty to political figures.

2. *rare.* Pl. unchanged. ISIBONGO sense 2.

1965 M. HANSEN in *Sunday Chronicle* 7 Dec., The ancient Zulu .. intoned the Imbongi of Cetewayo (the praises of Cetewayo).

imfe /ˈɪmfi, ˈiːmfe/ *n.* Also **imfa(y)**, **imfé**, **imfer**, **imfi**, **impfie**, **imphe(e)**, **imphey**, **imphi**, **imphye**. [Xhosa and Zulu.] A cultivar of the cereal grass *Sorghum bicolor*, grown for the sweetness of its culms; SOETRIET; SWEET CANE. See also SORGHUM sense 1.

1828 W. SHAW Diary. 28 Feb., We found a number of the men assembled at one of the Kraals, chewing Imfay, or sweet cane. **1832** *Graham's Town Jrnl* 15 June 100 Two kinds of *Impfie* or Sugar-cane are mentioned by the travellers; one as thick as the little finger, and the other as thick as the wrist. **1833** S. KAY *Trav. & Researches* 123 A species of sugar cane, called *imfe*, is grown in great abundance. **1836** A.F. GARDINER *Journey to Zoolu Country* 27 A bundle or two of imphi (a spurious sugar cane). **1844** J.M. BOWKER *Speeches & Sel.* (1864) 135 The sweet cane (imphe), which the Kafirs grow with their other corn merely for the sake of the saccharine matter contained in the stem .. is quite as sweet as the sugar cane itself, and requires little cultivation. **1850** J.E. METHLEY *New Col. of Port Natal* 81 We were supplied with quantities of 'imphi,' a kind of spurious sugar-cane, which is cultivated for its sweet and juicy qualities. **1857** *Country Gentleman* (U.K.) 11 June 379 A plant bearing the name of *Imphee*, or *Imphey*, or *Imphye* .. which it is alleged is identical with the Chinese Sugar Cane, has been introduced by Mr. Leonard Wray, from Southern Africa. **1864** T. BAINES *Explor. in S.-W. Afr.* 438, I .. spent the intervening time with a circle of old fellows, who gave me imphi (holcus saccharatus) stalks to chew. [**1880** S.W. SILVER *Handbk for Australia & New Zealand* 273 The imphee, or Planter's Friend, is well adapted to the Queensland climate.] **1893** WATT *Dict. Econ. Prod. Ind.* VI. iii. 277 This .. is said to be extensively grown in Africa and America, the plant of the former country being the Imphee, and of the latter the Sorgho, which is mainly cultivated on account of sugar. **1897** F.W. SYKES *With Plumer in Matabeleland* 21 Amongst other articles that ran short .. was sugar. A capital substitute for this was found in many of the kraals in the shape of 'imfi,' or native sugar-cane. **1923** W.C. SCULLY *Daniel Vananda* 112 In a corner of the field nodded the plumes of a patch of 'imfé' or Native sugarcane. **1937** B.J.F. LAUBSCHER *Sex, Custom & Psychopathology* 109 The crops .. consist of mealies, caffir corn, pumpkins and *imfe*. The *imfe* is a miniature sugar-cane, thin of stem and very similar to the kaffir corn. *c*1963 B.C. TAIT *Durban Story* 155 All along the coast the natives cultivated an indigenous reed for the sweet juice contained in the stalks which they liked to chew. They called the reed 'imphi' and it made excellent cattle fodder. **1966** C.A. SMITH *Common Names* 254 *ImFi*, .. Cultivated over a long period by Natal natives for the sweet culms. The species was known on the old Kaffrarian frontier long before 1800. **1987** J. MUNDAY *Grasses, Grains & Conservation* 14 Two kinds of sugar cane, *umoba* and *imphe*, were grown in Natal by the indigenous people long before the arrival of the white man in 1823.

Imfecane /(ɪ)mfeˈkɑːni, ɪmfeˈlaːne/ *n. hist.* Also **Imficani**, and with small initial (and capital m). [See MFECANE.]

1. FETCANI sense 1.

1828 W. SHAW Diary. 21 June, The confused state of the country occasioned by the approach of the Amazooloo, commonly called the Imficani. **1946** U. LONG *Chron. of Jeremiah Goldswain* I. 63 Rumours of Zulu terrorism continued through 1827 and 1828 and were confused with stories of the advance of people called Fecani or Fitcani (iMfecane – the Matiwane and Amangwane tribe).

2. MFECANE.

1979 M. MATSHOBA *Call Me Not a Man* 175 *Abe*Suthu .. are ruled by a wise king *u*Moshoeshoe. The land to which they moved had been laid open by *imfecane*.

imfi var. IMFE.

Imficani var. IMFECANE.

imfino var. IMIFINO.

imfofo var. IMPOFU.

Imidange /imiˈdaŋge/ *pl. n.* Also **imiDange**. [Named for the founding leader *Umdange*.] Collectively, the members of a Xhosa chiefdom with traditional lands in the Suurberg region of the Eastern Cape. Also *attrib.*

As is the case with many names of peoples and groups in *S. Afr. Eng.*, this word has been found only in plural uses; however, it may be that it has also been used in unrecorded singular forms.

*c*1847 H.H. DUGMORE in J. Maclean *Compendium of Kafir Laws* (1858) 16 The formation of the Imidange tribe dates a generation still farther back. Umdange, its founder, was the 'right hand' of Gconde. **1924** G.E. CORY *Rise of S. Afr.* I. 35 The Imidange tribe under Mahota, the son of Umdange, and the Amambala tribe under Langa, crossed into the Zuurveld, dispossessing the Amangqunukwebi under Tshaka. **1978** *E. Prov. Herald* 24 Mar. (Indaba) 7 Brownlee explains clearly that the ImiDange were the very first inhabitants of Peelton. **1986** P. MAYLAM *Hist. of Afr. People* 37 He [*sc.* Ndlambe] drove the imiDange, another autonomous Xhosa chiefdom, into a conflict with the white colonists who were expanding from the west. In the First Frontier War of 1779–81, the imiDange were defeated by the boers.

imifino /imiˈfiːnɔ, ɪmiˈfiːnəʊ/ *n.* Also **(i)mfino**. Usu. *noncount*, but occas. with pl. **-s**. [Xhosa *imifino*, Zulu *im(i)fino* (sing. *umfino*), edible herbs cooked as a vegetable.] MOROGO.

1941 'JUANA' in *Bantu World* 25 Jan. (Suppl.) 3 The next dish .. was .. a kind of Native Spinach but ever so much nicer than Spinach. This was the 'Imifino' which the women take so much trouble to gather in the fields. Just a weed to those who do not know it. **1970** HEARD & FAULL *Cookery in Sn Afr.* 477 African Spinach (*Imifino*) ... Amadumbi shoots – this is the most delicious of all the imifinos. **1980** *S. Afr. Digest* 16 May 16 This porridge is the favourite of the Zulu, Swazi and Xhosa people who traditionally serve it with sour milk (*amasi*) or wild green vegetable stew (*imfino/marogo*). **1986** J. CONYNGHAM *Arrowing of Cane* 26 Moses .. serves my dinner of steak and kidney pie and imfino. I have loved the latter since childhood when, like the black women, I picked it between rows of cane. **1991** on M-Net TV 4 Aug. (Carte Blanche), It is believed that eating these wild plants, or imifino as they're called here, inhibits the body's absorption of calcium.

imikhuhlu pl. form of UMKHUHLU.

imishologu pl. form of UMSHOLOGU.

imit(h)ombo var. MTOMBO.

Immo /ˈɪməʊ/ *n.* Also with small initial. [Journalistic abbreviation of *Immorality* (*Act*), see IMMORALITY.]

1. In the phr. ***Immo Act***, *Immorality Act* (see IMMORALITY sense 1). Also *attrib.*

1971 *Post* 30 May 25 Sam, a 29-year-old lorry driver, was found guilty of having broken the Immo Act with Liverpool-born .. 42-year-old twice divorced mother of 4. **1971** *Ibid.* 10 Oct. 3 He was questioned by a senior police officer, in connection with the alleged breaking of the Immo Act. **1972** *Drum* 22 Mar. 31 K–s' advocate .. questioned Bernadette about the Cape Town Immo Act case. **1985** K. NGWENYA in *Ibid.* June 48 When Drum staffer the late Can Themba campaigned for the lifting of prohibition, he exhorted: 'Let the people drink .. they are drinking anyway.' The same could be said for the Immo Act.

2. IMMORALITY sense 2.

1977 *Cape Herald* 22 Oct. 2 Ex-cop on immo charge.

immorality *n. hist.* Also with initial capital. [Special senses of general Eng., fr. *Immorality Act* the short title of Act 5 of 1927 (see quot. 1927).]

1. In the phr. ***Immorality Act***, the law which prohibited sexual relations between a white person and a member of any of the other officially-defined racial groups; *Immo Act*, see IMMO sense 1. Also *attrib.*

The 1927 Immorality Act was exclusively concerned with inter-racial sexual relations. The 1957 Immorality Act repealed the earlier Act, but included most of its provisions, re-worded, in Section 16. This section was repealed in its entirety in 1985. Although the 1957 Act deals with sexual relations in general (e.g. prostitution), most references to it allude to the provisions of Section 16.

1927 *Act 5* in *Stat. of Union* 15 Act to prohibit illicit carnal intercourse between Europeans and natives and other acts in relation thereto ... This Act may be cited as the Immorality Act, 1927, and shall come into operation on the thirtieth day of September, 1927. **1949** W.H. STUART in *Hansard* 19 May 6201 In getting that Immorality Act placed on to the Statute Book, I had saved perhaps half-a-dozen decent European women by that legislation but I also had saved .. over 2,000 Native women per annum. **1950** *Act 21* in *Stat. of Union* 217 Sections *one, two* and *three* of the Immorality Act, 1927 .. is [*sic*] hereby amended by the substitution for the word 'native', wherever it occurs, of the word 'non-European'. **1954** *Drum* Dec. 29 Regina B–, a European woman, and Richard K–, an African, were charged under the Immorality Act with living together in a house at Orlando. **1956** A. SAMPSON *Drum* 214 The Immorality Act of 1927 (amended in 1950 to include Coloureds), and the Mixed Marriages Act of 1949, forbade relations between Europeans and non-Europeans, with a maximum penalty, nearly always applied, of six months' hard labour, without the option of a fine. **1963** B. MODISANE *Blame Me on Hist.* (1986) 215 'The Immorality Act' prohibits all sex between black and white, labelling such acts as sinful, immoral and unlawful. **1971** *Personality* 5 Mar. 54 The Immorality Act was introduced primarily to safeguard White South Africans from 'mongrelisation'. **1971** *Sunday Times* 28 Mar. 12 Mr. O– .. shot himself in the bedroom of his Bloemfontein home on the eve of his court appearance on an Immorality Act charge. **1978** *Sunday Post* 9 Feb. 4 A Motion calling for the repeal of the Mixed Marriages Act and the section of the Immorality Act prohibiting sex across the colour line will be introduced next month. **1985** *Act 72* in *Govt Gaz.* Vol.240 No.9804, 2 Section 16 of the Immorality Act, 1957, is hereby repealed. **1987** *S. Afr. Digest* 10 July 2 A major step in removing discriminatory legislation from the Statute Book was taken in 1985 with the repeal of Article 16 of the Immorality Act. **1990** P. FENSTER in *Sunday Times* 22 July 6 Forty years on, especially for anyone under 30, the Immorality Act seems so absurd that even mentioning it seems immoral. **1993** L. HOLMES in *Sunday Times* 16 May 19 What about those who suffered under the Immorality Act? Our scars run deep. We were treated worse than lepers.

2. Sexual intercourse between a white person and one of another race; IMMO sense 2. Also *attrib.*

1962 *New African* Apr. 8 The Ontug Act (.. this law should be known by its Afrikaans appellation, since it has nothing to do with the accepted meaning of the word 'immorality' in other languages). **1970** *Post* 25 Jan. 12 We were patrolling that well-known Immorality rendezvous, Doornfontein. **1973** *Cape Times* 13 Jan. (Weekend Mag.) 3 They made love, the woman turned out to be Coloured and they were each sentenced to nine months' jail suspended, for immorality. **1976** A.P. BRINK *Mapmakers* (1983) 129 A white South African marries a Vietnamese girl abroad ... Should he bring his wife home with him, both of them can be jailed for 'immorality' because they do not belong to the same race. **1977** *Drum* Oct. 20 Hand in hand, a white man and his black wife stroll into the Holiday Inn. There is no furtive looking over the shoulder to see if big brother from the Immorality Squad is following. **1978** *Survey of Race Rel.* (S.A.I.R.R.) 53 Immorality and Mixed Marriages ... 417 cases of suspected contravention of Section 16 of the Immorality Act (dealing with intercourse across the white-black colour line) were investigated during the year ended 30 June 1976. **1980** E. PATEL *They Came at Dawn* 48 Can't you see that blerry whitey, met a black bokkie? .. See them kissing. Quick, take a picture ... That's the evidence for an act of immorality.

imoogie var. MOEGIE.

impala /ɪmˈpɑːlə/ *n.* Also **impalla**, **mpala**, and with initial capital. Pl. unchanged, or **-s**. [Zulu.] **1.a.** The antelope *Aepyceros melampus* of the Bovidae, esp. the subspecies *A. m. melampus*, russet in colour, with a white belly and a curved black stripe on the haunch, the ram having ridged, lyre-shaped horns; PALLAH; RED-BUCK; ROOIBOK; ROOIBUCK. Also *attrib.*

1875 W.H. DRUMMOND *Large Game & Nat. Hist. of S. & S.-E. Afr.* 330 The roibok or impalla .. is about the size of a small reed-buck doe, though more slenderly made. *Ibid.*, These impalla .. could easily distance any dog I possessed. **1888** P. GILLMORE *Days & Nights by Desert* 136 The Mpala Antelope (*Æpyceros Melampus*). **1896** R. WARD *Rec. of Big Game* 142 *Impala Antelope*, .. Few antelopes in South Africa excel the elegant Pallah, or Impala, in grace and beauty. For its size .. its horns are considerable ... In the good days .. impala were to be found abundantly amid the bush. **1907** W.C. SCULLY *By Veldt & Kopje* 206 The little russet impala, the very embodiment of sylvan grace. **1915** *Chambers's Jrnl* (U.K.) Nov. 700 The curious Hunter's hartebeest or herola, having horns which somehow suggest a connecting link with the fleet and supremely graceful impala. **1937** C. BIRKBY *Zulu Journey* 111 The little lanterns .. were the shining eyes of a hundred impala, the red, leaping buck of the bush country. **1947** J. STEVENSON-HAMILTON *Wild Life in S. Afr.* 87 The impala (*Æpyceros melampus*) – Discovered by .. Lichtenstein more than a hundred years ago, and variously termed impala, pallah, and rooibok, this antelope may claim to be one of the most beautiful and graceful members of the existing African fauna. **1951** [see NIGHT-AAPPIE]. **1979** *Antelope of Sn Afr.* (Wildlife Soc. of Sn Afr.) 40 Impala are the finest jumpers of all our antelopes; leaps of 10 metres long and more than 3 metres high have been recorded. **1988** N. RICHARDS in *Fair Lady* Mar. 98 On the Hippo Haunt restaurant menu in Mlilwane is impala or warthog stew with phutu or rice, vegetables and salads. **1990** C. GITTENS in *Farmer's Weekly* 4 May 14 The Swazi herdsmen have developed a picturesque way of gathering the cattle by blowing impala horns.

b. With distinguishing epithet: **black-faced impala**, the antelope *Aepyceros melampus petersi*, distinguished by its relatively heavy body and a dark blaze, and restricted in its distribution to south-western Angola and northern Namibia.

1970 *News/Check* 24 July 31 The Kaokoveld is also the haven of at least three unique animals – the mountain zebra, the **black-faced impala** and the South West elephant. **1979** ZALOUMIS & CROSS *Field Guide to Antelope* 41 In northern South West Africa the very rare sub-species, the black-faced impala occurs – the only Southern African antelope on the I.U.C.N. Endangered species list. **1988** A. HALL-MARTIN et al. *Kaokoveld* 36 The black-faced impala is endemic to an area stretching from Otjovasandu on the south eastern corner of Kaokoland to the Moassamedes district of southwestern Angola ... In appearance they are much like the impala of South Africa, though they are somewhat heavier and have a more pronounced black blaze on the face. **1990** SKINNER & SMITHERS *Mammals of Sn Afr. Subregion* 670 The black-faced impala originally was considered to be worthy of full specific status .. but Ellerman .. and Ansell .. both considered it as a subspecies. This has been confirmed in a pilot cytogenetical study by Grimbeek.

c. *comb.* **impala lily**, either of two low, succulent shrubs of the Apocynaceae: (*a*) *Adenium multiflorum*; (*b*) *Pachypodium saundersii*; *kudu lily*, see KUDU sense 1 b.

1966 C.A. SMITH *Common Names* 254 **Impala lily**, .. *Adenium obesum* var. *multiflorum* .. ; *Pachypodium saundersii* ... Shrubby succulent, with a ball-shaped bole, and spiny branches. Flowers showy, white or tinged with pink, sweetly scented. *c*1968 S. CANDY *Natal Coast Gardening* 133 *Adenium multiflorum*, 'Impala Lily' ... An indigenous relation of the Frangipangi. **1981** *S. Afr. Garden & Home* June 116 The Impala Lily, *Adenium obesum* var. *multiflorum*, blooms in late winter. **1984** J. ONDERSTALL *Tvl Lowveld & Escarpment* 152 Impala Lily ... In full bloom this striking succulent shrub provides welcome colour in the drab winter landscape. **1988** C. INNES *Handbk of Cacti & Succulents* 80 *Adenium multiflorum* ... Flower funnel-shaped, white with crimson edges. The milky sap is poisonous ... Known as the Impala lily.

2. *Military.* Usu with initial capital. Either of two models of jet fighter aircraft manufactured in South Africa under licence from an Italian company. Also *attrib.*

1970 *Daily News* 8 May, Citizen Force squadrons throughout South Africa will be equipped with Impala jet aircraft to replace the Harvard trainers within the next two to three years. **1976** [see KUDU sense 2]. **1979** *Weekend Post* 12 May 1 A light aircraft, piloted by an American, was yesterday forced to land by two South African Air Force Impalas in northern SWA/Namibia. **1985** *E. Prov. Herald* 25 Mar. 6 A formation of Impala jet fighters streaked over Port Elizabeth on Saturday as 6 Squadron of the South African Air Forces bade farewell to the city before being officially disbanded. **1990** *Armed Forces* Nov. 6 The Impalas were able to operate despite the Soviet-supplied and maintained air defence system that covered the Angolan airspace.

impee, impey varr. IMPI.

impfie, imphe(e), imphey, imphi, imphye varr. IMFE.

impi /ˈɪmpiː/ *n.* Also **impee**, **impey**. [Zulu.] **1.a.** An army or regiment (usu. of Zulu warriors); a ceremonial Zulu regiment. Also *attrib.* See also COMMANDO sense 3.

1836 N. ISAACS *Trav.* (1937) II. 77 In the evening one of my boys ran away, and joined the 'impee' (army) which had lately passed. **1846** *Natal Witness* 24 Apr., Mr Hans de Lange, .. having learned that an *impey* (commando) had been sent out by Panda, very promptly and properly returned to town and informed the authorities of the fact. **1862** G.H. MASON *Zululand* 200 There is always an 'Impi', (or army,) preparing for an attack on some neighbouring district. **1881** *E. London Dispatch* 5 Jan. 3 Chief Dunn was written to by the Cape Government as to the expediency of raising a Zulu impi for service against the Basutos. **1900** H. BLORE *Imp. Light Horseman* 142 The black muzzles of the guns gaped vengefully, ready to shatter the dense crowds of scurrying Boers, when the whole impi was signalled to cease fire. **1907** J.P. FITZPATRICK *Jock of Bushveld* (1909) 193 Ketshwayo, after years of arrogant and unquestioned rule, had loosed his straining impis at the people of the Great White Queen. **1925** D. KIDD *Essential Kafir* 400 No one who has happened to get in the way of a Swazie or Zulu impi, when it was on the warpath, will be inclined to call the natives lazy. **1941** C.W. DE KIEWIET *Hist. of S. Afr.* 60 Not even the power of Matabele and Zulu impis, the scourge of all the High Veld and Natal, could prevail against the Boers. **1947** C.R. PRANCE *Antic Mem.* 44 Quarter and his amateur cavalry, spread out in Zulu-impi 'horns' already threatened to cut off all hope of retreat from McGlusky and his awesome Mule Artillery. **1964** G. CAMPBELL *Old Dusty* 32 Yes, Inkosi, .. I was a soldier in the impis of the amaZulu. Ah! that was an army. To be a soldier in those impis was to be a man. **1971** *Rand Daily Mail* 4 Dec. 3 Dressed in full tribal regalia of leopard skin and feathers he led the dancing and singing impis who paid homage to their king.

b. *fig.*

1953 LANHAM & MOPELI-PAULUS *Blanket Boy's Moon* Not only did he notice the already familiar fumes of petrol and oil, but a whole impi of unidentified odours attacked his nostrils. **1986** S. HARRIS in *Sunday Times* 26 Jan. 15 Rugger impis set for kick-off. **1990** P. GREGSON in *New African* 9 July 12 Amazulu plunged to a disastrous 3–1 defeat at the hands of lowly Pretoria City in an NSL Castle Soccer league game. The green impi went in search of those both points [*sic*] but unexpectedly came empty handed.

2. An armed band (esp. one made up of Zulu men) involved in urban or rural (political) conflict.

*c*1948 H. TRACEY *Lalela Zulu* 19 In recent time the Zulus have brought firearms to their faction fights instead of assegais only. The sound of fighting was heard far off and the 'impis' were *in* at each other over by the hill, Mthashana. **1970** *Daily News* 29 July, Faction Fight Arrests. Two well-armed impis assembled, but were dispersed by a police mobile unit before they clashed. **1973** *Sunday Times* 11 Mar. 3 A common sight in Durban during the strikes as a factory 'impi' of Zulus takes to the streets to demonstrate their dissatisfaction with their low rates of pay. **1980** *Weekend Post* 24 May 2 Thousands of uniformed Inkatha members lined the entrance to the campus to welcome their president, Chief Buthelezi. There were also several Zulu impis present in an apparent attempt to prevent the students from disrupting the ceremony. **1985** *Financial Mail* 18 Oct. 35 There have even been charges that Zulu (not necessarily Inkatha) 'impis' have been deployed by the police in regions such as the Cape Flats to bring recalcitrant, youth-led populations in upheaval to a standstill. **1988** J. SIKHAKHANE in *Pace* Nov. 61 In other townships around Durban notably KwaMashu and Lamontville, vigilante groups called 'amabutho' or impi, were allegedly responsible for deaths and attacks on the amaqabane, mostly youths belonging to the UDF, or politically neutral. **1990** M. TYALA in *Sunday Times* 12 Aug. 2 Inkatha-phobia is increasing in Transvaal townships as the Zulu cultural group's adversaries portray it as a terror force, impis who run amok attacking ANC sympathisers and township residents at random. **1990** *Sunday Times* 10 Mar. 1 Angry ANC supporters confronted police while Inkatha impis with sticks, pangas and dustbin-lid shields assembled near their hostels.

impimpi /imˈpiːmpi/ *n. slang.* Also **mpimpi**. Pl. unchanged, **izimpimpi**, or **impimpis**. [Xhosa and Zulu (pl. *izimpimpi*), fr. any of several possible origins: ad. Eng. *pimp* provider or procurer of immoral or unlawful services (cf. Austral. and N.Z. Eng. *pimp* informer); or fr. Zulu *umbimbi* conspiracy, ill-intentioned collaborative effort; or fr. Zulu *iphimpi* a species of cobra.] In urban (esp. township) Eng.: a police informer or collaborator; PIMP *n.* Also *fig.*, and *transf.* See also PIMP *v.*, SELL-OUT.

1969 M. BENSON *At Still Point* (1988) 157, I guess even the informers were won over ... Impimpis! Informers! What has been done to my people! **1970** A. FUGARD *Notebks* (1983) 184 Whole of Serpent Players session devoted to discussing informers (impimpi). Impossible to believe, but the Group suddenly find X. very suspect. **1979** *E. Prov. Herald* 13 Nov. 9 Miss Mkona said Miss Mambinja claimed she was a police informer – 'impimpi' – who deserved to be burnt in her home. **1982** *Pace* Feb. 26 Sergeant Albert G— T—, of the Transkei security police, was kicked, punched, booted and battered to death by a frenzied mob after a tape recorder was found in his possession. 'Kill, kill the impimpi,' the mob screamed as the blows rained down. **1982** *Grahamstown Voice* Vol.6 No.4, 1 They write about what they see .. brutality, discrimination, violence, unemployment, izimpimpi. **1986** *Learn & Teach* No.2, 4 Bishop Tutu said the children must stop burning so-called 'impimpis'. He said, 'One day we will be ashamed to read our history books.' **1990** *City Press* 11

Feb. 8 They would come to their schools and in full view of their schoolmates throw the 30 pieces of silver at them and openly identify them as informers. We all know to our eternal regret and agony the fate of mpimpis in the ghettoes. **1993** *Weekly Mail & Guardian* 5 Nov. 9 The Big Five Gang, known in prison as the *'impimpis'* (stooges) because they help the warders by informing on other groups. **1994** [see SELL-OUT].

impiti var. IPITI.

‖**impofu** /imˈpɔːfu/ *n.* Also **empofos, imfofo, impoof, impo(o)fo, impophoo, mpofu.** [Xhosa and Zulu *impofu*, formed on adj. stem *-mpofu* tawny.] ELAND sense1 a.

[**1785** G. FORSTER tr. *A. Sparrman's Voy. to Cape of G.H.* II. 205 In one of the places above referred to, I have mentioned, that it [*sc.* the eland] is called by the Caffres *empofos*; I have since found in my manuscript notes, that it is likewise called by the same nation *poffo*, and by the Hottentots *t'gann.* **1789** *Encycl. Brit.* (1797) IV. 147 The Caffres call this species *empofos* and *poffo.* **1834** *Penny Cyclopaedia* II. 89 The Canna, .. improperly called *eland* or elk by the Dutch colonists of South Africa and *impoof* by the Caffres.] **1839** W.C. HARRIS *Wild Sports* 83 During the day I killed another impoofo, which actually measured nineteen hands two inches at the shoulder. **1875** *Encycl. Brit.* II. 101 The eland or impophoo (*Boselaphus Oreas*) is one of the largest of the antelopes. **1884** *Cassell's Nat. Hist.* III. 21 Writing on the hunting of these creatures, known in South Africa as the *Impoofo*, the same author [*sc.* W.C. Harris] remarks that, 'notwithstanding the unwieldy shape of these animals, they had at first greatly exceeded the speed of our jaded horses'. [**1900** SCLATER & THOMAS *Bk of Antelopes* IV. 198 *Eland* of the Dutch at the Cape ... *Impofo* of the Amandabele, Zulu, and Kafirs ... *Mpofu* (Swaheli).] **1967** E.M. SLATTER *My Leaves Are Green* 138 'Not Mpofu, Nkosi,' he grumbled as an eland came in sight. 'The Nkosi knows a Zulu does not eat the flesh of Mpofu.'

impoon var. IMPUNZI.

‖**impundulu** /impʊnˈdʊːlʊ/ *n.* Also **i'impundulu, mpundulu, umpundulu,** and with initial capital. [Xhosa and Zulu.] In Xhosa and Zulu mythology: an evil spirit which most often appears in the form of a bird; LIGHTNING BIRD. Also *attrib.* See also *lightning (and hail) doctor* (DOCTOR sense 1 b).

Several species of bird are associated with the 'impundulu', the most common one being *Scopus umbretta* (see HAMMERKOP).

1894 E. GLANVILLE *Fair Colonist* 289 The Mpundulu flying high in the darkness has seen us ... The lightning bird swooped from his watch above us like an eagle with fiery wings. **1908** F.C. SLATER *Sunburnt South* 207 He spoke .. of Impundulu, the Lightning Bird, with white plumes and flapping wings. How it descends to the earth in a flash, accomplishes its fatal errand and is gone in a moment of time. **1937** B.J.F. LAUBSCHER *Sex, Custom & Psychopathology* 13 The *Impundulu* plays the most prominent part in persecutory witchcraft, and is reputed to be merciless in its attacks on the victim. People so attacked cough up blood and frequently die. In consequence, pulmonary tuberculosis is considered as the work of the *Impundulu.* **1950** [see LIGHTNING BIRD]. **1955** J.B. SHEPHARD *Land of Tikoloshe* 11 As everybody in Africa knows, the Umpundulu is a fabulous fowl that lives up in the sky: the flapping of its huge wings produces thunder, and lightning is caused by the hot fat which drips from its breast, falling to earth. **1961** H.F. SAMPSON *White-Faced Huts* 27 My brother's wife said the 'mpundulu' (the lightning bird) belonged to the deceased. The 'mpundulu' stole the sick woman and placed her in front of the deceased's hut. **1976** WEST & MORRIS *Abantu* 20 Perhaps one of the most fascinating of these beliefs among the Xhosa-speaking peoples was that in witch 'familiars' ... *Impundulu*, a lightning bird, who appeared in the form of an extremely handsome man. Both Uthikoloshe and Impundulu were supposed to have sexual intercourse with witches and they have a highly sexual aura about them. **1982** *Pace* Feb. 12 Her revelations that some of the corpses are *impundulus* have already caused loss of life. In Port Elizabeth three women were killed by an angry mob which accused them of witchcraft. **1990** J. KNAPPERT *Aquarian Guide to Afr. Mythology* 120 The Impundulu is a large bird, sometimes described as a vulture, but with a penis, shaped like an ox tongue ... If a woman who 'has' an Impundulu at night, takes a human lover as well, the Impundulu will attack him, suck his blood and so cause him to cough up blood and die.

impunzi *n. obs.* [Zulu.] The *common duiker* (see DUIKER sense 1 b), *Sylvicapra grimmia.* Also (Englished form) **impoon.**

1839 W.C. HARRIS *Wild Sports* 386 *Cephalopus Mergens.* The Duiker. Duikerbok *of the Cape Colonists.* Impoon *of the Matabili.* **1860** D.L.W. STAINBANK Diary. (Killie Campbell Africana Library KCM8680) 12 June, I went out early in the morning to see if I could get a buck but only saw one impunzi. **1868** *Chambers's Encycl.* X. 570 *Impoon* (*Antilope* or *Cepahlopus mergens*), .. a small species of antelope, very plentiful in South Africa, in wooded districts. **1908** F.C. SLATER *Sunburnt South* Glossary, *Impunzi*, A species of Antelope.

in- /in/ *pref.* A singular noun prefix common to the Nguni languages and found in some words originating in these languages. For examples, see INDODA, INDUNA, INKUNDLA, INKWENKWE.

In the Nguni languages, the plural of a word beginning *in-* is formed by replacing the prefix with *ama-*, *ii-*, *iin-*, or *izin-*; in *S. Afr. Eng.* this pattern is not always observed, and the plural is sometimes formed by the addition of the English plural suffix *-s* to the singular form. See also AMA-, II-, and IZIN-.

inboek /ˈənbuk, ˈɪnbʊk/ *v. trans. Hist.* [Afk., fr. Du. *inboeken* to register, enter in a book.] APPRENTICE *v.* Also (Englished form) **inbook.**

The forms 'ingeboeked' and 'ingeboekt' reflect the influence of both Dutch (later Afrikaans) and English grammatical conventions governing passive voice and past tense.

1846 *Natal Witness* 6 Mar., I remember being (ingeboekd) bound apprentice to Mr. Maritz. **1857** J.M. ORPEN *Hist. of Basutos* 73 He then went and gave Boshuli a riding-mare and a horse, for which he got two children, whom the magistrate 'inboeked' (apprenticed). **1882** C.L. NORRIS-NEWMAN *With Boers in Tvl* 57 The children so procured were indentured (or as it is called 'Inboeked' [*printed* Inbocked] up to the age of twenty-two or twenty-five years' — and as the Kaffirs rarely knew their age, this indentureship lasted as long as the master pleased. **1946** S. CLOETE *Afr. Portraits* 55 Some Kaffir children were captured and these were ingeboekt — that is to say, apprenticed to various Boer families, where they would be kept under supervision till they came of age. **1968** E.A. WALKER *Hist. of Sn Afr.* 155 It only needed Somerset's permission to landdrosts to inboek orphans to reduce the Hottentots to the level of serfs at the disposal of the local officials. *Ibid.* 291 The laws seem to have been observed in republican Natal. There apprentices had to be *ingeboekt* (registered) before an official.

Hence **inboeked** *ppl adj.*; **inboeking** *vbl n.*, APPRENTICESHIP.

1896 M.A. CAREY-HOBSON *At Home in Tvl* 255 Under the specious name of 'inbooking' (a form of apprenticeship) they were actually made slaves for an indefinite number of years. *Ibid.* 405 'That is what it is makes the English say we Boers will have slaves,' remarked Cobus; 'but it's not true. My father and I give decent wages to our people, and we always find them willing to work for us, inboeking or no inboeking.' *Ibid.* 522 He must have been one of those *inboeked* children that never grew out of their apprenticeship. **1913** C. PETTMAN *Africanderisms* 224 *Inbooking*, .. The anglicized form of the word used by the Dutch in the Transvaal for a system of apprenticing natives that was open to great abuse.

‖**inboekseling** /ˈənbʊksələŋ/ *n.* [Afk., *inboek* to apprentice + linking phoneme *-s-* + (often pejorative) n.-forming suffix *-eling* indicating a person or thing belonging to or concerned with (what is denoted by the primary n.).] APPRENTICE *n.* Also *attrib.*

1982 DELIUS & TRAPIDO in *Jrnl of S. Afr. Studies* Vol.8 No.2, 239 *Inboekselings* might — in attempting to free themselves from settler society — attach themselves to autonomous or semi-autonomous African communities ... The ending of the *inboekseling* system in the years before the first British occupation of the Transvaal in 1877. **1989** *Reader's Digest Illust. Hist.* 116 During commando onslaughts .. thousands of young children were captured to become *inboekselings* (indentured people). These children were indentured to their masters until adulthood.

inbook see INBOEK.

incha var. INJA.

inchie var. UINTJIE.

incibe, incibi varr. INGCIBI.

incosa-case var. INKOSIKAZI.

incose, incosi varr. INKOSI *n.*

incubhe, incubi varr. INGCUBHE.

indaba /inˈdɑːbə/ *n.* Also **en-daba, n'daba,** and with initial capital. [Xhosa and Zulu, subject, topic, matter, affair, business, doing; pl. *iindaba* (Xhosa) *izindaba* (Zulu), affairs, communication, news.]

1. A meeting or discussion. Cf. BOSBERAAD, PITSO.

a. A Zulu council meeting. **b.** *transf.* Any conference, meeting, or discussion. Also *attrib.*, and *fig.*

1827 G. THOMPSON *Trav.* II. 408 A domestic now informed us, that the king was holding an en-daba (a council) with his warriors. **1882** C.L. NORRIS-NEWMAN *With Boers in Tvl* 24 The Dutchmen were .. invited to make a farewell visit to the King .. and to leave their arms outside ... To this Retief incautiously acceded, and after they had partaken of some native beer, and had a short 'indaba,' they were set upon. **1885** H. RIDER HAGGARD *King Solomon's Mines* 249 It was a few days after this last occurrence that Ignosi held his great 'indaba' (council), and was formally recognised as king by the 'indunas' (head men) of Kukuanaland. **1894** *Pall Mall Gaz.* (U.K.) 26 Dec. 3 A message was .. conveyed .. to the King, inviting Umtassa to come in to an indaba at Umtali. **1896** *Westminster Gaz.* (U.K.) 30 Mar. 5 They will .. attack Gimgem's kraal, where the chief Ulimo is holding an indaba, or consultation. **1899** 'S. ERASMUS' *Prinsloo* 93 Although Piet had tried to keep Jan du Toit away from the indaba by holding it when he thought Jan was in Krugersdorp, his plans fell through. **1900** F.D. BAILLIE *Mafeking Diary* 177 They had a sort of 'indaba' this morning. I only trust it was bad news for them. **1903** D. BLACKBURN *Burgher Quixote* 221 A long and angry indaba began on the proper colour of good medicine, Charlotte holding out for blue and Mrs du Beer for black. **1910** J. BUCHAN *Prester John* (1961) 199 He had a message sent to the chiefs inviting them to an indaba, and presently word was brought back that an indaba was called for the next day at noon. **1913** C. PETTMAN *Africanderisms* 224 *Indaba*, .. Native council meeting for the discussion of business of importance to the tribe. It seems as if the word were likely to pass into South African slang. **1920** R.Y. STORMBERG *Mrs Pieter de Bruyn* 63 We're having a last little indaba all together, and then Gwenno Cape-carts it back home. **1939** M. RORKE *Melina Rorke* 138 The great indaba tree, beneath whose shade Lobengula used to sit when he administered justice. **1940** F.B. YOUNG *City of Gold* 355 He saw, as a culmination of the British surrender, the indaba of native chiefs, to whom the High Commissioner, Sir Hercules Robinson, presented the Boer triumvirate as their new leaders. **1971** P.S. WALTERS *Informant, Grahamstown* We're going to have an indaba to decide whether to go to the sea or not. **1973** *Star* 30 June 12 Traffic cases could be established fairly easily by a prompt indaba of all those involved ... The indaba procedure might have a less intimidatory effect on the potentially wicked driver. **1978** *Sunday*

Times 22 Oct. 16 Diplomatic indabas only rarely produce neatly wrapped, comprehensive solutions to problems. **1989** *Ibid.* 12 Nov. 28 Mme Danielle Mitterand, whose invitations to an indaba in Paris fluttered through selected South African mailboxes this week. **1990** *Daily News* 20 Apr. 12 A proposal for all parties to sit down, indaba-style, and devise something they can live with. **1991** *Weekly Mail* 20 Dec. (Suppl.) 13 Church unity starts to gel in a year of great indabas. **1991** F.G. BUTLER *Local Habitation* 244 Far from being without 'ghosts', the poem is an indaba of shades on the headland known as Kwaai Hoek, where Dias planted his *padrao* half a millennium ago.

c. With qualifying word: **great indaba** [tr. Xhosa and Zulu *indaba inkulu*], an important meeting; a meeting of important people; a gathering of the people of a village, area, or group for discussion on an important matter; *transf.*, a national convention.

[**1860** D.L.W. STAINBANK Diary. (Killie Campbell Africana Library KCM8680) 8 Apr., Easter Sunday ... Indaba Inkulu.] **1910** *Cape Times* 8 Oct. 12 They had come .. to invite the leaders to a great indaba concerning the joint interests of the country. **1930** S.T. PLAATJE *Mhudi* (1975) 44 Their business was to cook and to prepare the eatables for the festival which was to follow the great indaba in the assembly. **1960** J. COPE *Tame Ox* 12 The college boys .. began to marshal the people into a wide mass about the platform. It would be like a great indaba, a people's council. **1979** *Sunday Times* 18 Nov. 4 The Department of Foreign Affairs .. is co-ordinating the 'great indaba'. **1989** *E. Prov. Herald* 7 Mar. 4 De Klerk's conciliatory attitude and his personal eagerness for what he calls the great indaba are greatly encouraging to all in this country. **1989** *Weekend Argus* 11 Nov. 17 A promise of negotiation pervades the political scene. On all sides moves seem to be afoot to set the scene for a 'great indaba'. **1990** W. OLTMANS in *Sunday Times* 27 May 18 All South Africans .. should express a view as to who will speak on their behalf at the Great Indaba.

2. *obs.* News, affairs.

1836 A.F. GARDINER *Journey to Zoolu Country* 382 Having satisfied their questions respecting indaba (news), etc. we rode on. **1862** G.H. MASON *Zululand* 10 (Jeffreys), As soon as the place is full, then begins the cookery; with uproarious singing and merriment .. discussing the *indaba*, or news of the day.

3. Often in the phr. ***one's (own) indaba***. Concern, problem, affair, business.

1899 B. MITFORD *Weird of Deadly Hollow* 72 'We want more rain – another good thunderstorm or two.' 'Yet that will bring the Van Niekerk *indaba*,' said Custance, with a queer smile. **1958** F.H. SIBSON in A.D. Dodd *Anthology of Short Stories* 107 It should be safe enough to let 'Tipperary' across ... But that's Stewart's indaba. **1964** G. CAMPBELL *Old Dusty* 31 Hou, Inkosi! Do you remember that? I have forgotten it. It was the white man's indaba. **1969** I. VAUGHAN *Last of Surlit Yrs* 25 Mom refrained from adding that there was also an East wind, which .. blew, .. sweeping across the hillside to hit the small cottage bang on. Anyway she felt it was their indaba, put the cheque in her purse, and left them. **1970** BEETON & DORNER in *Eng. Usage in Sn Afr.* Vol.1 No.2, 30 *Indaba*, .. in S Afr coll[oquial] usage, a 'problem' or 'worry', eg 'I don't know how he is going to get out of this difficulty but that is his *indaba*, not mine'. **1972** *Drum* 8 Dec. 18 Their sex needs are their own indaba. **1974** *Ibid.* 22 Dec. 2 Asking the rest of the world to leave South West Africans to sort out their own indabas. **1976** K. MATANZIMA in *Evening Post* 24 Apr., Those who do not register – well, that is their own indaba, not ours. **1976** *Drum* Mar. 47 The railways say that they have delivered the goods and that it is not their indaba if there is nobody to receive them. **1978** I.J. PATEL in *Ibid.* July 9 We no longer share each other's troubles. If Indian shopkeepers are being moved from Fordsburg it is their own indaba, some will say. **1980** M. MELAMU in M. Mutloatse *Forced Landing* 51, I don't see that I matter so much for Georgina to take the trouble of going to a *nyanga* on my account. If she goes to bone-throwers, that's her own *indaba*. **1989** J. HOBBS *Thoughts in Makeshift Mortuary* 196 The battles of Africa must be fought in Africa, by Africans, face to face. This country is our indaba, not anybody else's.

4. *hist.* Usu. with defining word (and initial capitals), **KwaNatal Indaba, KwaZulu/Natal Indaba, Natal(-KwaZulu) Indaba** [see KWA-]: a convention organised by the government of KwaZulu and the Natal Provincial Council during 1986, at which proposals for a non-racial and united provincial government were drawn up; also *attrib.*; see also *KwaNatal* (KWA-).

1986 *Daily Dispatch* 3 Apr. 9 Thirty-one delegates from a wide range of political, business and union organisations will attend the first meeting of the KwaZulu/Natal indaba in the Durban City Hall today. **1986** M. BADELA in *City Press* 20 Apr. 2 The Congress of SA Trade Unions says it could never become involved in the 'KwaNatal indaba' being held in Durban – because the meeting in 'undemocratic'. *Ibid.* 13 July 2 The Natal/KwaZulu 'indaba' met yesterday to discuss a bill of rights to be included in the proposed new constitution for the area. **1986** T. WENTZEL in *Argus* 1 Dec. 1 The Government was today urged to think again about the Kwanatal Indaba plan for a multiracial provincial structure following its swift rejection by the leader of the National Party in Natal, Mr Stoffel Botha ... The report of the Indaba has not yet been handed to the Government officially. **1987** P.W. BOTHA in *Time of Challenge & Decision* (National Party) 12 The Natal/KwaZulu Indaba .. took place at the joint initiative of the KwaZulu Government and the Natal Provincial Council. **1987** *Cape Times* 3 Feb. 3 Stand for election as an Independent in Natal on a pro-Indaba ticket. **1987** A. PATON in *Sunday Times* 17 May 23, I hope that P.W. Botha .. will give earnest and favourable consideration to the proposals of the KwaZulu/Natal Indaba. At the present moment they offer the only hope to be seen on our dark horizon. **1987** E.K. MOORCROFT in *Grocott's Mail* 10 Feb. 1 By rejecting the Indaba proposals the government has slammed the door to genuine reform in the face of moderate South Africans. **1990** *Daily News* 20 Apr. 12 The Government's copy of the proposals of the Natal Indaba must be getting very well-thumbed by now. **1990** *Weekend Argus* 9 June 14 Joint convenor of the Natal/KwaZulu Indaba.

independent *adj. hist.* [Special sense of general Eng. *independent* autonomous.] Of or pertaining to any of four ethnically-based territories within South Africa which were granted self-government in terms of the policy of SEPARATE DEVELOPMENT. Often in the special collocation ***independent (Black) state***. See also HOMELAND sense 1, TBVC. Cf. SELF-GOVERNING.

The former 'independent' states of Transkei, Bophuthatswana, Venda, and Ciskei were not recognized by the international community, and were viable only because of substantial monetary support from South Africa. They were reincorporated in 1994.

1963 *Annual Register: Rec. of World Events 1962* 314 A series of 'independent' Bantu 'homelands', where each ethnic group would have a vote. **1973** *Daily Dispatch* 16 June 1 The government's plans for the so called consolidation of the homelands – the independent states envisaged by Dr. Verwoerd. **1978** *Survey of Race Rel.* (S.A.I.R.R.) 311 Transkei was granted independence on 26 October 1976 and Bophutha-Tswana became an independent state on 6 December 1977. All other homelands have self-governing status. **1979** *Survey of Race Rel. 1978* (S.A.I.R.R.) 265 By 1978 Transkei and Bophuthatswana had become independent states in terms of SA legislation although they had not received international recognition. **1980** *Survey of Race Rel. 1979* (S.A.I.R.R.) 305 The Inkatha movement called on Africans in 'independent' homelands not to take out citizenship of those areas. **1982** P.W. BOTHA *Keynote address* 13 Sept. 5 We have .. formulated a policy for regional development in consultation with the independent Black states which are co-operating with us in this regard. **1984** L.N. DYWILI in *Drum* Jan. 42, I have been forced to leave my 'independent country' to come and lead a better life here in South Africa. **1987** *Financial Mail* 22 May 40 Minister of State in the Foreign and Commonwealth Office Linda Chalker reiterated her government's policy of non-recognition of the 'independent' homelands. **1987** N. WEST in *Sunday Times* 1 Nov. 2 Favouring a form of federation is .. the inability of the homelands and independent black states to exist without South African support. **1988** *Pace* Dec. 12 South Africa's so-called independent black states .. the legislative centerpiece of the bantustan policy. **1989** J. HOBBS *Thoughts in Makeshift Mortuary* 302 Bophutatswana, one of the black areas promoted to 'independent' homelands that began to spread like patches of fungus on the map of South Africa after 1976.

indhlunkulu var. INDLUNKULU.

Indian *n.* and *adj.* [Special senses of general Eng.]

A. *n.*

1. *Obs.* exc. *hist.* In the Cape colony: a European (usu. British) resident of India; HINDOO *n.* Also *attrib.*

Not exclusively *S. Afr. Eng.*

1830 *Cape of G.H. Lit. Gaz.* I. June, Take her as your free servant, no longer a slave. Take her as your friend ... God bless you both, and when you supplicate on high, ask heaven's mercy for Wilkinson the Indian. **1833** *S. Afr. Almanac & Dir.* 137 The Indians are warm supporters of this, as they are of almost every Philanthropic Institution. **1834** *Cape of G.H. Lit. Gaz.* July 103 The number of matches that have taken place between the fair Africanders (the general term for natives of European descent ..) and *'Indians,'* proves that their attractions are appreciated. *Ibid.* Many Indians have complained of a want of hospitality and attention to strangers at the Cape; but, in reality, the English residents have not the means of exercising an indiscriminate hospitality among so numerous a class. **1837** [see HINDOO *n.*]. **1862** M. TRUTER in A. Gordon-Brown *Artist's Journey* (1972), Arrived at Mr du Toit's place where I had the pleasure to meet a large company of Indians. **1972** L.G. GREEN *When Journey's Over* 121 The visitors who widened the vocabulary were white military officers and officials of the Honourable East India Company, and they were nicknamed 'Hindoos' or 'Indians.'

2.a. A South African of Indian or Pakistani descent. See also ASIAN *n.*

Quot. 1980 reflects the use of 'Indian' as a racial designation in terms of the Population Registration Act.

1942 *Off. Yrbk of Union 1941* (Union Office of Census & Statistics) 984 The population is divided for census purposes into four racial groups ... Asiatics – natives of Asia and their descendants; mainly Indians [etc.]. **1946** *Act 28* in *Stat. of Union* 194 'Indian' means any member of a race or tribe whose national home is in India or Ceylon. **1953** *Drum* Jan. 14 Indian merchants have been warned not to exploit Indians and Africans. **1961** H.F. VERWOERD in *Hansard* 10 Apr. 4192 If it were possible to get the Indians out of the country completely, if one could have settled the Coloureds in a part of the country quite on their own, in their own areas like the Bantu, we would certainly have done that. **1971** *Rand Daily Mail* 31 May 6 Durban Indian Papwa Sewgolum, won the Natal Open Golf championship, becoming the first Non- White to win a major South African golf title. **1976** *Daily Dispatch* 6 Feb. 14 Imagine how baffled a foreigner must be to learn that there are South Africans called Indians. **1980** *E. Prov. Herald* 27 July 2 Other applications were by .. two whites who wanted to be Indian, ten coloureds who wanted to be Indian, ten Malays who wanted to be Indian, eleven Indians who wanted to be Malay, [etc.]. **1990** *New African* 11 June 12 Black is beautiful was coined to unite Amazulu, Basotho, Mashangana, Indians, so-called 'Coloureds', etc.

b. *comb.* **Indian time**, see quot. Cf. AFRICAN TIME.

*c*1983 R. MESTHRIE Lexicon of South African Indian English. 64 *To run on Indian time*, To be behind schedule. Usually said of weddings, prayers and public functions which often begin a good half-hour after the advertised commencing time.

B. *adj.*

1. *Obs.* exc. *hist.* (Of a foreign visitor of European descent.) Resident in India; from India (see sense A 1); HINDOO *adj.*

Not exclusively *S. Afr. Eng.*

1834 A.G. BAIN in A. Steedman *Wanderings* (1835) II. 227 As my Indian friends were bound to Lattakoo .., I was here reluctantly obliged to part with these amiable and worthy gentlemen. **1835** G. CHAMPION *Jrnl* (1968) 25 The Temperance Society here owes its existence & efficiency to the Indian residents of the Cape. These gentlemen are officers in the army, & others in government service in India who have left that sultry clime for a few months, to enjoy the healthy air of the Cape ... They retain their salaries, if they proceed no further than the Cape. **1840** [see SOPIE]. **1843** *Cape of G.H. Almanac & Annual Register* p.xii, Wynberg is truely [*sic*] the 'Sweet Auburn' of South Africa ... Here our Indian Visiters [*sic*] generally reside, and breathe the life-giving and health-restoring properties of its .. air. **1885** L.H. MEURANT *60 Yrs Ago*, Mr Advocate Cloete, two Indian residents, two medical gentlemen and two English merchants of Cape Town. **1965** A. GORDON-BROWN *S. Afr. Heritage* III. 5 Higher up the street was the Society House .. usually with a group — largely of 'Indian Visitors' — standing round the doorway. These visitors, who came to the Cape to recuperate from the effects of the Indian climate, represented a large and wealthy section of Cape society.

2. (Of a South African.) Of Indian or Pakistani descent (see sense A 2).

1892 W.L. DISTANT *Naturalist in Tvl* 117 We reached Heidelberg about 10 a.m., a small and very established town ... It has a considerable 'coolie' or Indian population. **1941** C.W. DE KIEWIET *Hist. of S. Afr.* 148 The difficulties caused by Natal's Indian population. **1953** *Drum* Jan. 14 In the past the Indian merchants succeeded in persuading the Indian masses to keep aloof from the political troubles of the blacks. **1961** *Govt Gaz.* Vol.1 No.71, 4 Creation of a Department of Indian Affairs and Provision for the Appointment of a Head of Department. **1970** *Daily News* 18 May 22 (*advt*) Young Indian or Coloured Lady Required for clerical work. **1982** *S. Afr. Panorama* Feb. 8 South African groups representing the Swazi, Xhosa, Zulu, Shangaan, Indian and Malay communities took part in .. the festival. **1990** J. MCCLURG in *Star* 11 Sept. 11 A graphic illustrating the operation of the racket also depicted 'an Indian businessman' ... Mr Kaka is .. unhappy about the use of 'Indian' to denote a South African of Indian descent.

3. *comb.* **Indian shop, - store**, a shop (usu. a GENERAL DEALER) owned by one of Indian origin.

1935 H.C. BOSMAN *Mafeking Rd* (1969) 23 It was a good blue flannel shirt that I had bought only a few weeks ago from the Indian store at Ramoutsa. **1950** [see METHI]. **1972** *Sunday Times* 24 Sept. 5 My first trouble with the law began when I was 15. I stole something from an Indian shop. **1974** *Daily Dispatch* 3 Aug. 9 There's a little Indian shop fairly near her home in front of which is a stretch of soft sand about the size of a tennis court.

indicator *n. Obs.* exc. *hist.* [Modern L., 'one who guides or points out', fr. former scientific name *Cuculus indicator*.] HONEY-GUIDE.

[**1786** G. FORSTER tr. *A. Sparrman's Voy. to Cape of G.H.* II. 181 A little bird, which flies on by degrees with the alluring note of *cherr, cherr, cherr*, and guides its followers to the bees' nest .. the little *cuculus indicator*, which I have described and given a drawing of in the Phil. Trans.] **1790** tr. *F. Le Vaillant's Trav.* I. 372 Naturalists, for what reason I know not, place the indicator among the cuckoos. *c*1808 C. VON LINNÉ *System of Natural Hist.* VIII. 235 The small indicator is about six inches long. The bill is conical, pointed. **1828** W. SHAW Diary. 22 May, The Chief gave me a quantity of honey in the comb, which one of the young men, had just taken from a rock, having been guided thereto, by that singular bird, called the 'Indicator' and described by many of our Naturalists. **1835** A. STEEDMAN *Wanderings* I. 190 The trunk of the tree over which the indicator was hovering. **1923** HAAGNER & IVY *Sketches* 271 The nestling Indicator has the swollen nostrils characteristic of the Cuckoo-nestling, but instead of being rounded as in the Cuculidae, they are elongated. **1994** M. ROBERTS tr. *J.A. Wahlberg's Trav. Jrnls 1838–56* 36 Saw a Kaffer following an Indicator.

‖**Indlovu** /ɪnˈɡ̊ɔːvu/ *n.* Also **Ndlovu**, and with small initial. [Xhosa and Zulu *indlovu* elephant.] 'Elephant', an honorific title used in Nguni society of kings and princes, as a clan name, praise name, or surname. See also NDLOVUKAZI, NGONYAMA sense 1.

[**1934** *Friend* 23 Feb. (Swart), The natives then gave the Prince the name of 'a ngangendlovu' (hail, mighty elephant), and by this name His Royal Highness will, in future, be known throughout the Ciskei by this and future generations.] **1975** *Daily Dispatch* 27 Mar. (Suppl.) 12 In a deep memory of my father .. who passed away on the 20th February, 1971. Ndlovu, Msutu, You are still in mind of your daughter. **1978** A. ELLIOTT *Sons of Zulu* 99 The king is still the father figure and hereditary sovereign of the nation. His people call him *Ngonyama* or Lion and sometimes he is called *Ndlovu* (elephant). This latter title, however, today appears to be less used except when referring to the past 'father' kings. [**1987** H. GOOSEN in *S. Afr. Panorama* May 18 The elephant features as the centre-piece of the Zulu coat-of-arms .. while its Zulu name *indlovu* is traditionally an honorary title for kings.]

Indlovukati, -zi varr. NDLOVUKAZI.

‖**indlunkulu** /ˌinɡ̊uŋˈkʊːlʊ/ *n.* Also **indhlunkulu, intunkulu, ndlunkulu**. [Zulu, lit. 'great (or big) house', 'great (or big) hut'.] *great hut*, see GREAT.

1891 *Law 19* in *Stat. of Natal* (1901) II. (Native Law) 13 The word 'Indhlunkulu' (the great house) denotes the chief house in a kraal. **1885** H. RIDER HAGGARD *King Solomon's Mines* (1972) 201 Behind this again were the *Emposeni*, the place of the king's women, the guard house, the labyrinth, and the *Intunkulu*, the house of the king. **1960** J.J.L. SISSON *S. Afr. Judicial Dict.*, *Indhlunkulu*, a native term signifying the great house. **1962** W.D. HAMMOND-TOOKE *Bhaca Soc.* 38 If the husband is away from home for any reason all the wives are supposed to sleep together in one hut, usually in the indlunkulu (great hut). **1976, 1978** [see *great hut* (GREAT)].

indoda /inˈdɔːda/ *n.* Pl. usu. **amadoda**. Forms: *sing.* **idoda, (i)ndoda, mdoda, umdodi(e)**; *pl.* **amadoda(s), amadodo, amatontos, indodas, madoda**. [Xhosa and Zulu (pl. *amadoda*); voc. *ndoda* (pl. *madoda*). For notes on pl. forms, see AMA- and IN-.]

Occas. in dim. form **ndodana, amadodana** [Xhosa and Zulu, dim. suffix *-ana*].

1. A man; one who has been initiated into manhood; in some traditional African societies, esp. one who has undergone ritual circumcision.

1835 A. SMITH *Diary* (1940) II. 67 The nation is divided into three classes — amadodo or amatontos, machaha and .. boys who take care of cattle. **1837** F. OWEN *Diary* (1926) 8 A Kafir youth, having gone thro' this ceremony is now reckoned an 'indoda' or man and is permitted to acquire cattle, or to possess a kraal for himself. **1855** G.H. MASON *Life with Zulus* 121 An old greyheaded Caffre (an Umdŏdie) pointed his finger towards me. **1855** R.J. MULLINS Diary. 11 June, One old man asked me to play [the harmonium] very low and then very high, and then said 'It is like Indodas (men) and Intombis (girls)'. **1857** J. SHOOTER *Kafirs of Natal* 47 No man can marry until he belongs to the class of *ama-doda* or men, the sign of which is the head-ring. **1866** W.C. HOLDEN *Past & Future* 322 The regiments consisted of three divisions. The first, amadoda men; these were veterans, — tried men — the men on whom chief reliance was placed to bear the shock of battle, and bravely win the victory. **1875** C.B. BISSET *Sport & War* 53 The rite of circumcision is performed on all the young men at the age of sixteen who are thus made men or amadodas. [**1920** S.M. MOLEMA *Bantu Past & Present* 265 On that lavatory you see written 'Gentlemen,' and there only white men may go. On that other lavatory you see written 'Amadoda' (men), and this is meant for black men.] **1939** N.J. VAN WARMELO in A.M. Duggan-Cronin *Bantu Tribes* III. i. 32 They are now young men, *abafana*, who will shortly look out for wives; having secured whom, they become *amadodana*, and finally family men, *amadoda*. **1949** C. BULLOCK *Rina* 25 If they looked for gold as well as elephants, as did Hartley, they were never free from the *amadoda* sent with them by the King. **1971** *Drum* July 5 Here and there behind some back-street bush there will be 'White Amadodas this way' and 'White Abafazis the other way.' **1983** *Ibid.* Jan. 40 When he graduated from piccannin to ndoda I was the best man at his wedding. *c*1985 M. STRACHAN in *Eng. Academy Rev.* 3 138 So baas, this mdoda, he too wants to sell shimyane. **1988** *Frontline* Aug.-Sept. 12 The respect youth are expected to pay the fathers or *amadoda*.

2. Usu. in the form **ndoda** (pl. **madoda**): a form of address, 'man'.

1976 *Drum* June 2 Mlungu approaches a man and says — 'Hey ndoda are you a Bantu or are you a Transkei citizen?' Funny? **1976** *Ibid.* July 26 Hey madoda, it is bad. **1976** M. THOLO in C. Hermer *Diary of Maria Tholo* (1980) 60 The black policeman said, 'Ai indoda, where are you going?' **1980** M. MATSHOBA in M. Mutloatse *Forced Landing* 119 Somdali, is right, *ndodana* (son). *Ibid.* 122 Yes, *ndoda*, I should be running away before my people decide to go looking for me at the police-stations. **1982** *Pace* Apr. 158 This, madoda, would be quite normal, if Mr Goldberg could also come around and enjoy beer with me at my township concrete slab. **1985** *Ibid.* Aug. 4 There are many examples like 'Aimbabane' for Mbabane and 'Ensumalo' for Nxumalo. Phew! Madoda! **1994** [see HAU].

indoona var. INDUNA.

‖**induku** /ɪnˈdɔːkʊ/ *n.* [A word common to several Nguni languages.] KIERIE. Also *attrib.*

1960 J.J.L. SISSON *S. Afr. Judicial Dict.* 387 *Induku*, a type of native stick. [**1973** J. MEINTJES *Voortrekkers* 76 Another weapon used for throwing and clubbing was a stout stick with a knob, called a *knopkierie* by the Boers and *induka* by the Matabele.] **1989** *Weekend Post* 9 Dec. 7 A group of *abakwetha* pose for a picture with their *induku* sticks.

induna /ɪnˈduːnə/ *n.* Also **entuna, indoona, intuna, nduna, tuna**. Pl. usu. **-s**, but also (infrequently) **isinduna, (i)zinduna, lintuna, zintuna**. [Xhosa and Zulu (pl. *izinduna*).]

1.a. Esp. in traditional Zulu society: a headman, councillor, or officer under a chief, often responsible for overseeing the affairs of a district made up of a number of villages. Cf. LETONA. See also UMNUMZANA sense 1 a.

1835 A. SMITH *Diary* (1940) II. 79 Masalacatzie has two grades amongst his chiefs, viz.: *numzan* and *tuna*, the former the highest. **1836** N. ISAACS *Trav.* (1937) II. 108 Our conversation was interrupted by the arrival of the induna, Amastanger, with seven head of cattle, which the king gave to me. **1836** in D.J. Kotze *Lett. of American Missionaries* (1950) 129 Under the king there are a number of officers of different grades, called Zintuna. Intuna is the singular. Every town is directly under the control of some Intuna. **1837** F. OWEN *Diary* (1926) 28 A regiment is stationed at each town under several Indoonas or Captains. **1846** R. MOFFAT *Missionary Labours* 141 He was a man of rank, and what was called an Entuna (an officer,) who wore on his head the usual badge of dignity. **1857** J. SHOOTER *Kafirs of Natal* 322 The English settlers proceeded with their natives against the kraals of Sotobe and another *induna*, situate between the Mooi River and Tugela. **1887** *S.W. Silver & Co.'s Handbk to S. Afr.* 418 We sent word to the 'indunas,' or heads of the principal kraals round us, to assemble their men the next day. **1895** H. RIDER HAGGARD *Nada* 3 Suddenly Chaka was seen stalking through the ranks, followed by his captains, his indunas, and by me. **1898** B. MITFORD *Induna's Wife* 14 The King himself came forward, and making a sign to myself and two or three other izinduna to attend him, sat himself down at the head of the open space. **1907** W.C. SCULLY *By Veldt & Kopje* 289 A large military kraal .. was situated about two days' journey from the 'Great Place,' and was under the command of a favourite induna, or general. **1934** B.I. BUCHANAN *Pioneer Days* 120 A band of Zulu isinduna (heads of kraals) came down to Maritzburg and begged the Governor to annex their country. **1939** R.F.A. HOERNLÉ *S. Afr. Native Policy* 61 He happened to be the son of an aristocratic English father and the daughter of a Xhosa Induna. **1958** S. CLOETE *Mask* 143 The induna who brought the message was of royal blood. **1971** *Time* 13 Dec. 23 The lead *induna*, or head man, resplendent in hyena tails and impala, monkey and civet skins. **1979** *Bona* Apr. 26 'I'm one of the new chief's indunas,' he told me, 'one of his selected warriors and councillors'. **1986** P. MAYLAM *Hist. of Afr. People* 28 He appointed a large number of *izinduna*, state officials who performed various administrative functions. **1990** R. MALAN *My Traitor's Heart* 170 He was a figure of great power and influence. He was the chief induna, or prime minister, if you will, of the Thembu tribe.

b. *transf.* A black foreman, head servant, mine overseer, or policeman. Also *attrib.*, and *comb.* **induna-clerk**. Cf. BOSS-BOY.

1857 J. SHOOTER *Kafirs of Natal* 93 A man's head-servant is called his *in-duna* — a name applied to the principal officers of a chief. **1887** J.W. MATTHEWS *Incwadi Yami* 494, I was especially fortunate in my *induna* (head man and guide), who was a tall, fine, strapping Swazi and knew every inch of the country. **1925** [see MABALANE]. **1946** *Tribal Natives & Trade Unionism* (Tvl Chamber of Mines) 6 The tribal pattern is the Chief, the Induna, the headman and the kraal head. **1946** P. ABRAHAMS *Mine Boy* (1954) 55 In front of the long column marched an induna, a mine policeman, whose duty it was to keep order among the boys ... The indunas all carried knob-kerries and assagais. **1953** LANHAM & MOPELI-PAULUS *Blanket Boy's Moon* 116 A big factory, where he had obtained the job of *Induna* or head-boy. **1962** A.P. CARTWRIGHT *Gold Miners* 221 There are, too, the *indunas* who act as liaison officers between the compound manager and the tribal groups. **1971** *Sunday Tribune* 14 Nov. 6 We loaded sacks of mielies on to a lorry. The induna .. kicked and hit us all the time. **1972** *Star* 24 Mar. 27 Mr Makwena is an 'induna' train marshaller — one of the first Africans to be trained at Elsburg shunting yards. **1978** *Voice* 13 Dec. 9 His father was an induna at the Modder East mine. **1980** *E. Prov. Herald* 29 Aug. 9 Mr Godlo .. worked at Jaggersfontein mines (today's Welkom), as induna-clerk from the age of 20. **1980** M. LIPTON in *Optima* Vol.29 No.2, 166 There have .. been reports of homosexuality within the compounds, said to be widespread among the long-serving and influential indunas who use their position to demand favours from younger men. **1984** L. MSHENGU in *Staffrider* Vol.6 No.1, 26 Indunas are workers but they do not go along with the workers' struggle. They .. tend to side very much with the employers. **1986** J. CONYNGHAM *Arrowing of Cane* 11 A black induna, dressed in a navy blue overall and not in the hessian shift of a cutter, walks towards me as I near the labourers. **1987** S. NYAKA in *Weekly Mail* 13 Mar. 2 The South African Railway and Harbour Workers' Union (Sarhwu) has vowed to destroy the compound housing system, migrant labour and the *induna* system. **1990** G. SLOVO *Ties of Blood* 30 The *indunas* — black overseers who did the white man's dirty work, their knobkerries and assegais always at hand. **1990** [see BOSS-BOY].

2. *fig.* One in authority, a leader.

1897 F.W. SYKES *With Plumer in Matabeleland* 6 'We no sooner get to know the big white induna than he goes away.' Thus said the native. **1899** [see MALKOP *adj.*]. **1941** *Bantu World* 25 Jan. 12 Mr J.S. Hardy .. Headman or Induna of Pelindaba to receive all the complaints of the inhabitants. **1970** *News/Check* 4 Sept. 9 The attack on the Press by rugby induna Dr Danie Craven for blowing up the incidents of rough play in the second Test. **1979** C. ENDFIELD *Zulu Dawn* 282 Disraeli, Chief in *Duna* of the white Queen of the whole world. **1982** *Voice* 18 July 4 Nafcoc's nduna Sam Mutsuenyane had some pertinent things to say about Black/White business partnership at Nafcoc's annual indaba last week.

Hence **indunaship** *n.*, the office or dignity of an induna.

1955 in M. Gluckman *Judicial Process among Barotse* 87 This is indunaship — this is ruling.

indwe /ˈiːndwe, ˈɪndwi/ *n.* Also **indwa**, and with initial capital. Pl. **iziindwe**, or unchanged. [Zulu *indwa*, Xhosa *indwe*.]

1. The BLUE CRANE, *Anthropoides paradisea*. Also *attrib.*

1854 R.B. STRUTHERS St. Lucia Hunting Diary. (Killie Campbell Africana Library KCM55079), Went out on the flat to look for game but saw nothing except a few cranes (Indwa). **1902** G.M. THEAL *Beginning of S. Afr. Hist.* 69 The two wings of a blue crane (the indwe) .. are regarded as an emblem of bravery only to be worn on this occasion and by veterans in times of war. **1939** N.J. VAN WARMELO in A.M. Duggan-Cronin *Bantu Tribes* III. 26 Outstanding fighters wore on each side of the head the black wing-feathers of the Stanley Crane (Tetrapteryx Paradisea; indwe). **1975** *S. Afr. Panorama* Oct. 16 The crane is known to the people of the Ciskei as the 'Indwe' and has great significance as a symbol of the will of the people to be courageous and constant. Traditionally anyone who has proved himself to have these qualities is often decorated by the chief with the feathers of the 'indwe'. **1979** *Ibid.* Dec. 12 The blue and white flag with the spindly-legged *indwe* (crane) bird, symbol of the self-governing Black state of Ciskei. **1981** M. OETTLE in *Weekend Post* 3 Oct. (Family Post) 4 Ciskei's national bird, the blue crane, or *indwe*, features prominently in the designs of the two stamp issues this new state will make on Independence Day, December 4. [**1986** *Motorist* 2nd Quarter 25 Indwe is the Xhosa word for blue crane .. a town .. named after the blue crane, South Africa's national bird and Ciskei's national emblem. Indwe was founded in 1896 when this stately bird occurred in large numbers along the Indwe River.]

‖**2.** Always in *pl.* A ceremonial headdress of blue crane feathers worn by someone who has shown prowess in battle.

1968 G. CROUDACE *Silver Grass* 39 The Plumed Ones came first; they were the counsellors. All wore the coveted iziindwe — the blue crane's feathers awarded to them for bravery in battle. The feathers, two foot long, curved back on either side of the head like the horns of a buck.

influx *n. Hist. rare.* Ellipt. for INFLUX CONTROL. Also *attrib.*

1971 *Drum* Mar. 68 What worries me is that I do not qualify to be in Johannesburg as I was born in Durban. Does influx also apply in marriage? *Ibid.* May 50 Helping men and women who fall foul of the pass and influx laws. **1971** *Argus* 4 June 12 These patient, long-suffering victims of our pernicious influx system. **1971** *Rand Daily Mail* 9 June 1 The government is planning to introduce a new system of dealing with influx and pass law offenders. **1973** *Drum* 22 Jan. 18 Yet another victim of the Influx laws.

Hence (*nonce*) **influx** *v. trans.*, to give permission (to a black person) to stay in an urban area.

1982 D. TUTU *Voice of One* 90 The growing frustration with unemployment, the long queues to get 'influx-ed'.

influx control *n. phr. Hist.* During the apartheid era, the rigid limitation and control imposed upon the movement of black people into urban areas; INFLUX. Also *attrib.*

Carried out mainly in terms of the Natives (Urban Areas) Consolidation Act (No.25 of 1945), by means of the pass system, and through the Group Areas Act, influx control was abolished in 1986. See also ENDORSE, *Group Areas Act* (GROUP AREA *n. phr.* sense 2 a), PASS sense 3 a, SECTION 10.

[**1949** J.S. FRANKLIN *This Union* 67 Limitation of the number of detribalised Natives in urban area; control of the influx of Natives into these areas.] **1955** *Report of Commission for Socio-Economic Dev. of Bantu Areas* (UG61–1955) 93 Influx Control is gradually being applied more strictly in accordance with the labour requirements of urban employers. **1963** WILSON & MAFEJE *Langa* 51 To many Africans directed labour, combined with influx control, appears as forced labour, and the system arouses intense bitterness. **1971** *Rand Daily Mail* 27 Mar. 2 The vast majority of short-term prison sentences are for minor statutory offences connected with Bantu influx control, taxation and reference book regulations. **1971** *Evening Post* 5 June 6 A man who had nothing against his wife applied .. this week for a decree of divorce because influx control regulations had made it impossible for him to live with her since they were married two years ago. **1973** [see DOMPASS]. **1980** M. LIPTON in *Optima* Vol.29 No.2, 75 Blacks were attracted to the towns, where wages were higher and conditions freer. To counter this, curbs over movement — influx controls or 'pass' laws — were introduced to divert Black labour towards, and to bind it to, the mines and particularly the White farms. **1986** *E. Prov. Herald* 20 June 4 The Abolition of Influx Control Bill was read yesterday for a second time to a chorus of 'hear, hears' from the PFP benches after an amendment by the Conservative Party Chief Whip .. that it be read 'this day six months' was defeated. **1989** A. BERNSTEIN in *Optima* Vol.37 No.1, 18 The abolition of influx control has *not* resulted in mass migration to the PWV. **1990** *Weekend Argus* 29 Sept. 19 From the time influx control was abolished about five years ago, families have been legally allowed to be together.

Info *n. hist.* [fr. *Department of Information.*] Often in the phr. ***Info scandal***. MULDERGATE.

1980 *Rhodeo* (Rhodes Univ.) Feb. 7 While the English papers have claimed this sweeping role, it is significant to note that black newspapers largely ignored Info ... Info helped spruce up the shining white image of the P W Botha administration. **1980** *Rand Daily Mail* 27 Nov. 16 For the fourth time since we first began exposing the Info scandal, the police called on this newspaper yesterday to investigate our reports relating to it. [**1984** see DONS.] **1987** *New Nation* 10 Sept. 5 The Info Scandal of 1978 confirmed that the government had pumped thousands of rands into the anti-Nusas campaign. **1988** G. SILBER in *Style* Mar. 39 He had been fired for 'tendentious and unacceptable' reporting when he stumbled across a story which he believed to be of interest to readers back home. He joined SAAN, taking the story with him. It was the Info Scandal. **1990** [see MULDERGATE].

Hence (*nonce*) **Info-ish** *adj.*, reminiscent of the Info scandal.

1990 *Sunday Times* 25 Feb. 22 The almost daily revelations have acquired a distinctly Info-ish flavour. Public disquiet is high.

informal *adj.* [Special senses of general Eng. *informal* not according to order, not observing forms.]

1. Of economic and business activity:

a. In the special collocation **informal sector**, a euphemism for those (such as street traders and hawkers) involved in tax-free trading not covered by normal business legislation; that part of the economy to which such traders belong. Cf. *formal sector* (see FORMAL sense 1 b). See also SPAZA.

1980 D.B. COPLAN Urbanization of African Performing Arts. 142 Gradually these rural-based peasant marginals were joined by urban proletarians drawn from the informal sectors of the economy. **1984** *Probe* Nov. 20 They are the street traders — those people forced onto the streets to earn a living. They include hawkers of all goods and are referred to in more fine intellectual language .. as the informal sector. **1990** [see FORMAL sense 1 b]. **1991** *S. Afr. Panorama* Jan.-Feb. 4 The informal sector flourishes in Hillbrow, bringing to the pavements everything from apples to oil paintings. **1991** *Bulletin* (Centre for Science Dev.) Mar. 6 Many early studies of the informal sector suggest that it might provide an adequate and secure alternative income to employment ... People enter the informal sector out of necessity rather than from choice.

b. Outside the conventional legal and economic structures of (Western) society. Cf. FORMAL sense 1 a.

  1990 *Weekly Mail* 21 Sept. 9 Some desperate people among the newly unemployed turn to crime as their 'informal' alternative for making a living. **1990** [see Maimane quot. at SPAZA]. **1991** [see Brokensha quot. at SPAZA]. **1991** *Bulletin* (Centre for Science Dev.) Vol.3, 6 The more successful informal operators had access to the formal wage of a family member.

2. Of settlements and shelters:

  Often a euphemism for 'squatter'. Cf. *squatter camp* (see SQUATTER sense 3).

a. Of settlements (freq. in the collocation **informal settlement**): erected in an unregulated and unplanned manner upon unproclaimed land, with no infrastructure provided by the local authority. See also SHACKLAND.

  1989 *Optima* Vol.37 No.1, 19 Informal settlement is a generic term used to describe a wide variety of different forms of shelter. Informal settlers differ in respect of the length of time they have been in their present location .. ; the size of their settlement; their location .. ; .. the nature of their shack (corrugated iron, breeze block, lean-to against a formal house) ... The Urban Foundation estimates that the number of urban people living in informal circumstances is some seven million. Throughout the country formal black residential areas are overcrowded and further population growth .. will have to be accommodated mainly in free standing informal settlements. **1991** T. VAN DER WALT in *Sunday Times* 10 Mar. 7 Mr P— is able to pinpoint every informal settlement in the Durban area.

b. Of housing: owner-built, made of a variety of unsubstantial materials. Cf. FORMAL sense 2.

  1991 A. BENJAMIN in *Daily News* 26 Mar. 26 Less formal townships are in fact squatter communities ('informal housing' and 'orderly urbanisation' are the other ways of putting it). **1991** *Weekly Mail* 24 Mar. 12 There could be up to seven million people leading squalid lives on 'informal housing' sites — shanty towns, without the official euphemism. **1994** B. MONK in *Weekend Post* 8 Oct. 4 Dwellings erected along the coast included a mix of formal and informal structures apparently built by both blacks and whites from within and outside Transkei.

inganga var. INGQANGA.

ingcibi /i'ŋli:bi/ *n.* Also **incibe, incibi**. Pl. **iingcibi**. [Xhosa *ingcibi* (pl. *izingcibi*) a skilled worker, artisan.] In traditional Xhosa society: a man responsible for circumcising initiates. See also CIRCUMCISION sense 1.

  See note at IKHANKATHA.

  1866 W.C. HOLDEN *Past & Future* 284 The name of these witch doctors or priests, amongst the Amaxosa Kaffirs, is *amaqqira* and *incibe*; among the Natal and Amazulu [*sic*], *isanusi* and *inyanga*. **1937** B.J.F. LAUBSCHER *Sex, Custom & Psychopathology* 114 The next office to be filled is that of *incibi*, the operator, more commonly known as the expert. A necessary qualification for an incibi is that he should have dreamt that he circumcised boys; after which he must have acquired experience by circumcising his own relatives before he is allowed to circumcise others. **1956** A. SAMPSON *Drum* 50 When he was twenty, in the holidays from Lovedale College, he underwent the Xhosa initiation ceremony. 'Say, "I am a man,"' said the *Ingcibi*, or tribal surgeon, after the painful circumcision. **1962** W.D. HAMMOND-TOOKE *Bhaca Soc.* 81 Elaborate initiation ceremonies are held annually at which large numbers of boys are circumcised at one time ... The operation is performed by experts (iingcibi) and the whole ceremony is still an important and vigorous element of social life. **1976** *Daily Dispatch* 20 Aug. 4 An 'ingcibi' .. said Port Elizabeth Africans were keen to take their sons for manhood training but the custom was not done properly. **1979** *Daily Dispatch* 9 Feb. (Indaba) 7 Mr Mdledle suggested the operation could be done by a medical doctor while Mr Tyamzashe still favoured a traditional ingcibi. **1980** E. JOUBERT *Poppie Nongena* 272 On the first day in the bush the boys are cut ... A special man, an incibi, is hired to do it and we paid him three rand and a bottle of brandy. **1989** J. MATYU in *Weekend Post* 9 Dec. 7 The *ingcibi*'s fee covers the surgical operation which is R25, R25 for his guardian (*ikankatha*) duties to nurse the *umkwetha* until he heals completely, and R5 for his medicine consisting of herbal salves and soft medicinal leaves (*isicwe*) used to bind the wound.

‖**ingcubhe** /iŋ'lu:be/ *n.* Also **incubhe, incubi, (i)ngcube, ncuba**, and with initial capital. [Xhosa.] Among the Bhaca people: a festival celebrating the first harvest of a new season; cf. UMKHOSI. Also *attrib.*

  1907 W.C. SCULLY *By Veldt & Kopje* 298 At the annual 'incubi', or 'feast of the first-fruits', which is held by the Bacas — .. the chief rushes out of his hut after being doctored, and flings an assegai towards the rising sun. **1913** — *Further Reminisc.* 269 The Baca tribe carried on the ritual of its ancient tribal customs long after such had fallen into disuse among other Natives. Most notable among these may be mentioned the 'incubi', or Feast of the First Fruits. **1954** W.D. HAMMOND-TOOKE in A.M. Duggan-Cronin *Bantu Tribes* III. v. 35 Even today among the Baca .. the annual first-fruit festivals (*ingcube*) are held to bless the new crops and strengthen the tribe against its enemies. **1962** — *Bhaca Soc.* 175 The possession of the *incubhe* medicines contributes greatly to the power and prestige of the Bhaca chief. **1967** S.M.A. LOWE *Hungry Veld* 143 The Ntombis of the village are giving a Ncuba (*harvest feast party*).

ingeboek(e)d, ingeboekt see INBOEK.

‖**ingelegde vis** /'ənxə,lexdə 'fəs/ *n. phr.* Formerly also **engelegte vis(ch)**. [Afk., *ingelegde* pickled, preserved + *vis* (earlier *visch*) fish.] PICKLED FISH. Formerly also part. tr. **ingelegde fish**.

  1890 A.G. HEWITT *Cape Cookery* 9 Pickled fish. Engelegte-Visch. For this geelbek is best. **1891** H.J. DUCKITT *Hilda's 'Where Is It?'* 70 Fish (Pickled, or 'Engelegte'). (Cape way of preserving fish.) **1902** — *Hilda's Diary of Cape Hsekeeper* 65 Geelbek, commonly called Cape salmon .. makes good fish-pie, 'smoorfish,' 'engelegte,' or pickled fish. **1909** *Rand Daily Mail* 16 Nov. 2 (*advt*) Perfectly Delicious Curried Fish, Ingelegte Visch (Pilot Brand). In 1-lb. and 7 lb. tins. **1945** N. DEVITT *People & Places* 16 Pickled fish, called at the Cape 'ingelegde vis' is essentially a South African dish. It is delicious and popular. **1958** L.G. GREEN *S. Afr. Beachcomber* 115 Dr Louis Leipoldt always said that geelbek was the only fish suitable for a really superb dish of ingelegde vis (pickled fish curry). **1977** *Fair Lady* 8 June (Suppl.) 11 Ingelegde Vis — Cape Malay Pickled Fish.

Ingelsman, Ingilsman VARR. ENGELSMAN.

‖**ingogo** /iŋ'gɔ:gɔ/ *n. slang.* Also **nongogo**. [Zulu, 'half-crown'.] In urban (esp. township) Eng.: a cheap prostitute.

  1974 A. FUGARD *Dimetos & Two Early Plays* (1977) 58 Nongogo: a woman for two-and-six, a term especially used for prostitutes soliciting amongst the lines of gold-mine workers queuing for their pay. **1982** *Sunday Times* 28 Nov. (Mag. Sect.) 17 Women who frequent hostels are mainly *ingogos* which is the word for those who can be lured for 25 cents. [**1987** *New Nation* 23 July 10 These parties were not healthy places, says Dikobe — people drank from Friday to Sunday night and women sold themselves for 'ngogo' (half a crown or fifty cents) a night.]

ingoma /iŋ'gɔ:mə, iŋ'gɔ:ma/ *n.* Also **(i)ngomo, ngoma**, and with initial capital. [Zulu, royal dance-song, hymn, song.

  In Döhne's *Zulu-Kafir Dict.* (1857), *ingoma* is defined as '2. A military exercise, a manoeuvre ... This exercise usually takes place at the ukwetjwama [*sc.* the festival of first fruits] .. , and, as a special part of it consists in the praises of the chief which are sung, hence 3 ... A song of war, a warlike song.' The military song subsequently became a royal dance-song, and then a hymn.]

1. Always with initial capital. The traditional Zulu national anthem, a royal dance-song performed esp. at 'first-fruits' festivals; the dance performed to this song.

  1875 D. LESLIE *Among Zulus* 92 They danced the 'Ingoma.' This is the national song of the Zulus ... It is a very old song, but became all of a sudden famous in Chaka's time, who made it his war song. **1885** H. RIDER HAGGARD *King Solomon's Mines* (1972) 34 Hark! the war song, the *Ingomo*, the music of which has the power to drive men mad. *Ibid.* 201 Now the regiment began to dance, singing the *Ingomo*, that is the war chant of us Zulus. **1949** O. WALKER *Proud Zulu* (1951) 143 At a given signal, the captains sitting near the king's sacred seat .. struck up the royal dance-song (iNgoma).

2. In full ***ingoma dance***: a traditional or neo-traditional Zulu dance in the 'ingoma' style, as performed esp. by troupes of migrant workers; also *attrib.*; so ***ingoma dancer*** *n. phr.*, one who performs such a dance; ***ingoma dancing***, the performance of this style of dance.

  1955 *Off. Visitors Guide* (Durban Publicity Assoc.) 18 Ngoma dancing is the popular amateur sport of the African and serves as a valuable outlet for his energies. Though purely recreational, membership of a recognised team is regarded as an honour. Many of the steps and movements employed in the Ngoma Dances are traditional, though .. they are subject to modification and new styles. **1966** *Std Bank Pocket Guide to S. Afr.* 22 The Ngoma dancing by Zulus may be seen any weekend at the Bantu Recreation Grounds. **1977** F. MTSHALI in *Speak* Dec. I. 51 The ngoma dances, although tribal, are laced with Western touches and this gives them a style of their own, making them a thrill to watch. **1980** D.B. COPLAN *Urbanization of African Performing Arts.* 434 *Ingoma*, (Zulu: 'dance, song') In urban areas, a form of dance and song in traditional idiom developed by Zulu male migrant workers in the mines, factories, and domestic service. **1985** *Afr. Review* 303 There are Zulu ngoma dances performed most weekends in the city. **1990** *Pace* May 36 They have some recreational facilities: sports fields and halls for ingoma dancing — a craze in the hostels. **1990** *Bulletin* (Centre for Science Dev.) Nov.-Dec. 11 Ingoma dancers and their response to town. A study of Ingoma dance troupes among Zulu migrant workers in Durban.

ingoma busuku /iŋ'gɔ:mə bu'su:ku, -bʊ'sʊ(:)-gʊ/ *n. phr. Music.* Also **ingoma ebusuku, ngoma busuku** [Zulu, contraction of *ingoma ebusuku*, *ingoma* see prec. + *ebusuku* at night.] MBUBE. Also *attrib.*

  In Zulu, the earliest widespread name for this style.

  1978 *Speak* Vol.1 No.5, 5 This style of music, first called Ingoma Ebusuku (night music) and later mbube or 'bombing', was performed live in Western dress in a stage context imitative of European or elite African choral music. **1980** [see ISICATHAMIYA]. **1980** D.B. COPLAN *Urbanization of African Performing Arts.* 153 The *ingoma ebusuku* male choral style came from Zulu and Swazi industrial and domestic workers with rural backgrounds and little or no Western education. They added only mission-school concert traditions from Natal ... The original model for *ingoma ebusuku* appears to have been performance of turn of the century rural or small town weddings. **1984** S. ZUNGU in *Pace* Oct. 64, I like choral music, ngoma busuku, Black Mambazo and all those things. **1990** [see *Tribute* quot. at ISICATHAMIYA].

Ingonyama var. NGONYAMA.

ingoobo, ingoobu, ingouboo VARR. INGUBO.

ingoose var. INKOSI *n.*

‖**ingqanga** /i'nt̪a:ŋga/ *n.* Also **inganga, ingquanga**. [Xhosa.] The BERGHAAN (sense 2), *Terathopius ecaudatus*.

1937 B.J.F. Laubscher *Sex, Custom & Psychopathology* 15 The *Inganga*, a species of vulture, portends, by its presence, a coming catastrophe such as war, pestilence or severe and prolonged drought. **1939** N.J. Van Warmelo in A.M. Duggan-Cronin *Bantu Tribes* III. i. 26 It was thought a good omen if an eagle (ingqanga) flew over the army in the direction of the enemy, but bad if it approached from the front. **1970** A. Fulton *I Swear to Apollo* 28 High above, hanging motionless on widespread wings was the dark, dread shape of Ingqanga, the mountain eagle.

‖**ingubo** /iŋˈgʊːbɔ/ *n.* Also **ingoobo, ingoobu, ingouboo, (i)nguba, ingubu, ungoobo.** [Zulu and Xhosa *ingubo* cloak, blanket; western clothing.]

1. KAROSS sense 1.

1833 S. Kay *Trav. & Researches* 37 He maintained that every thing around him, mountains, rivers, grass, cattle, and even his *ingubu*, 'beast-skin garment', proved the truth of what had been said respecting the being of a God. **1836** A.F. Gardiner *Journey to Zoolu Country* 90 He (Charka) immediately rose and attempted to throw off his ingoobo (skin mantle) but fell in the act. **1837** F. Owen *Diary* (1926) 25 They [*sc.* the tribesmen] asked in exchange for their fowls, Indian corn and pumpkins, either handkerchiefs, blankets or 'ingubo' i.e. a mantle or carosse. **1837** J.E. Alexander *Narr. of Voy.* I. 386 From the shoulder hangs the *ungoobo*, kaross, or mantle of softened hide, worn with the hair next to the body, and fastened with a thong at the neck. **1860** W. Shaw *Story of my Mission* 406 A Kaffir wears this ingubu, or 'kaross,' with the hairy side next to his skin, throwing it over his shoulders, from whence it hangs down to his ancles, being fastened in front of the throat by means of a thong. **1983** *S. Afr. Digest* 20 May 24 Natalie Knight, creator of *Ndebele Images*. Behind her is the huge *Nguba* — a fully beaded blanket consisting of white beads and geometric designs.

2. *transf.* Clothing; second-hand clothing.

1837 F. Owen *Diary* (1926) 77 He .. abruptly asked me what was the use of giving all that ingoobu to the children, alluding to the Kilts of Dingareen with which I have clothed the boys. **1855** G. Brown *Personal Adventure* 92 Not an article of the pillaged clothing was anywhere to be seen. The men had stolen away .., laid aside whatever they had on or about them and appeared again in their own ingubo. **1899** G. Russell *Hist. of Old Durban* 187 Cast-off articles of European attire, known to the Natives as 'Ingouboos'. **1913** C. Pettman *Africanderisms* 226 *Ingubu*, .. A dress or garment of any kind is offered for sale to the Natal natives under this name. **1967** E. Rosenthal *Encycl. of Sn Afr.* 260 *Ingubu*, Name used by Africans in Natal for second-hand garments. The word was derived from an expression meaning 'skin'.

Ingwenyama var. NGONYAMA.

inie var. IRONIE.

initiation school *n. phr. circumcision school*, see CIRCUMCISION sense 2. Also *attrib.*

1939 R.F.A. Hoernlé *S. Afr. Native Policy* 84 Initiation into manhood and womanhood through participation in an Initiation School [was] the only stage in this tribal education during which the boys and girls were very literally and completely segregated from the common round of daily life in the tribe. **1948** O. Walker *Kaffirs Are Lively* 42 Bavenda people keep very much alive their dark old customs of initiation schools and 'python dances' for young girls. **1965** P. Baragwanath *Brave Remain* 3 He had been out hunting with his initiation school friends. **1976** S. Fugard *Rite of Passage* 39 These were the rites of the *Mediti* in the Pedi initiation school. **1978** *Daily Dispatch* 14 July (Indaba) 4 He asks the chief to allow his youngest son, Jacob, to forego the initiation school as his studies are important because Jacob wants to go to university to study medicine. **1982** *Sunday Times* 2 May 3 The gang has already nabbed the private secretary of the homeland's Chief Minister and dragged him off to an initiation school. **1988** M. Saliso in *E. Prov. Herald* 13 Feb. 3 It was against African custom for an initiate to be removed from the initiation school and taken to a place where he would be exposed to some form of contact with women. **1992** M. Mabusela in *Ibid.* 25 Jan. 5 Parents should take their sons to a doctor who could recommend the use of blood cleaning pills and medicines before going to the initiation school.

‖**inja** /ˈiːndʒa/ *n.* Also **ainga, incha, inJa, injah.** Pl. **zinja.** [In the Nguni languages, *inja* (pl. *izinja*).]

1. *rare.* A dog.

1833 S. Kay *Trav. & Researches* 134 On these occasions, the *inja*, (dog,) although of the most wretched description, appears to render essential service. **1834** *Makanna* (anon.) III. 183 One relic was .. left behind, in the shape of 'a little yellow "inja" (hound) of a Bosjesman'. **1855** [see FOOTSACK]. [**1861** J.W. Colenso *Zulu-Eng. Dict.* p.v, The Zulu for dog is commonly spelt *inja*.]

2. Used of human beings.

a. *obs.* A term of praise used by a chief of a loyal subject.

1855 J.W. Colenso *Ten Weeks in Natal* 52 With the Kafir, every one is either *inKose* (chief) or *inJa* (dog); and many, who think they ought all to be placed on terms of perfect equality, cannot brook that others should receive this distinguishing honour, rather than themselves. **1861** E. Casalis *Basutos* 177 The word *incha* (dog) has two meanings, diametrically opposed to one another in the metaphorical language of these tribes. To call a man 'a dog' would be the most unpardonable insult; but a chief will say of one of his subordinates, 'That man is my dog!' and the appellation will be received with a smile of assent by the person on whom it is bestowed. **1913** C. Pettman *Africanderisms* 226 *Inja*, .. As employed .. by a chief of any of his indunas or people it is regarded as a compliment, indicating loyalty and fidelity.

b. *derog.* A term of contempt.

1861 [see sense 2 a]. **1911** P. Gibbon *Margaret Harding* 118 'Voetzaak,' she ordered shrilly. 'Hamba wena — ch'che! Skellum! Injah! Voetzaak.' **1972** *Drum* 8 Apr. 20 They ordered drinks and started calling us zinja. They said we were slumbanes and they wanted to nyusa us.

‖**Inkanyamba** /ˌinkanˈjaːmba/ *n.* Also **Inkhanyamba.** [Xhosa and Zulu.] In Xhosa and Zulu mythology: the deity of tornadoes, taking the form of a black snake.

1984 *Drum* Jan. 62 Other elders, those who survived the tornado .. looked up into space and one by one agreed the Inkanyamba — Black Snake — had come at last in search of blood and would come again ... While the belief still existed among both Zulus and Xhosas, educated people no longer feared the Inkanyamba 'because it did not exist and was pure fiction.' **1986** Qabula & Hlatshwayo in Bunn & Taylor *From S. Afr.* (1988) 290 Here it is: The tornado-snake — Inkhanyamba with its floods! Its slippery torso! **1990** J. Knappert *Aquarian Guide to Afr. Mythology* 243 The tornado, a terrible revolving storm, was regarded as a god in many parts of Africa where it occured. In southern Africa it is represented in the shape of a long snake because that is what it looks like, a snake reaching from heaven to earth. The Zulu name for this deity is Inkanyamba.

inkatha /ɪŋˈkaːtə/ *n.* Also **inkata.** [Zulu, in full *inkatha yesizwe* 'inkatha of the nation'.]

1.a. A Zulu national emblem in the form of a grass coil entrusted to the king, symbolising the nation's unity and strength.

1914 B. ka Silwana in *Jrnl of Sn Afr. Studies* (1978) Vol.4 No.2, 188 The *inkata's* purpose is to *keep our nation standing firm*. The binding round and round symbolizes the binding together of the people so *that they should not be scattered*. **1949** O. Walker *Proud Zulu* (1951) 52 'They tell me .. that you're about as close to the Royal councils as the king's inKata.' (the sacred grassring on which Mpande sat for certain ceremonials). **1970** J.P. van S. Bruwer in *Std Encycl. of Sn Afr.* II. 119 The paramount chief of the Zulu .. possessed the *inkatha* or sacred headring, which was made of special components and was supposed to imbue the paramount chief and the nation with strength. **1978** S. Marks in *Jrnl of Sn Afr. Studies* Vol.4 No.2, 188 The *inkatha ye[si]zwe*, or 'grass coil of the nation', .. was an actual ritual object, 15 or 18 inches in diameter, which was inherited by Shaka's successors, and kept at the royal headquarters. **1981** M. Kunene *Anthem of Decades* p.xx, The Zulu national symbol is the sacred band (inkatha yesizwe) shaped in a circular form and representing the national ethos. **1987** *Clarion Call* (Special ed.) 7 An 'Inkatha' is so powerfully woven together that it does not crumble and break, it does not slip and dislodge its burden. An 'Inkatha' carries the weight of the nation, the treasures of the nation, and the burdens of the people.

b. A grass or cloth coil placed on the head to cushion the burden of a water vessel or other load.

1978 S. Marks in *Jrnl of Sn Afr. Studies* Vol.4 No.2, 188 An *inkata* or *inkatha* is literally 'a grass coil placed on the head for carrying a load'. **1979** [see Frontline quot. at sense 2]. **1982** *Optima* Vol.30 No.3, 141 *(caption)* Zulu woman .. is cushioning weight of container with a cloth *inkatha*. **1985** *Fair Lady* 6 Feb. 82 An *inkatha* is the coronet of twisted cloth that eases the burden and helps to balance a heavy load carried on the head.

2. Always with initial capital. [Short for *Inkatha ya k(w)a Zulu* 'Coil of the Zulu Nation', and later *Inkatha Yenkululeko Yesizwe* 'Coil of the Freedom of the Nation'.] A Zulu national cultural movement, orig. founded in the early 1920s by King Solomon Dinizulu, recreated in 1975 by Chief Mangosuthu Buthelezi, and transformed into the Inkatha Freedom Party (see IFP) in 1990; a member of this movement or party. Also *attrib.*

[**1924** L.E. Oscroft in *Jrnl of Sn Afr. Studies* (1978) Vol.4 No.2, 188 The real object [of the newly-formed Zulu National Council, *Inkatha*] is to unite all black races ... They consider that the native is victimised in many ways and receives unfair and unjust treatment from the white man.] **1976** *Sunday Times* 9 May, Inkatha .. is termed a Zulu National Liberation Movement ... Inkatha is seen as a means for Blacks, significantly not just Zulus, unilaterally to determine political policies independently of the White Government. **1977** *Ibid.* 25 Sept. 19 The Zulu ladies, immaculate in their Inkatha uniforms of green, gold and black — the colours of the old ANC in the days when Chief Albert Luthuli held centre stage as Chief Buthelezi does today. **1979** M.G. Buthelezi *Power Is Ours* 61, I have been elected by the assembly twice without any division. I am the President of Inkatha, the largest liberation movement of its type within South Africa. **1979** *Frontline* Dec. 21 Zulu women, carrying waterpails or other burdens on their heads, use a soft pad or strip of blanket to soften the discomfort of the burden. That pad is an Inkatha. The pad symbolised the purpose of Inkatha kaZulu when King Zolomon ka Dinizulu founded it in 1928. Today, Inkatha claims bigger designs. It's purpose is no longer to soften the burden, but to throw it off altogether. **1984** R. Davies et al. *Struggle for S. Afr.* II. 388 The origins of *Inkatha* date back to the 1920s when the Zulu monarch, King Solomon, formed *Inkatha Ya Ka Zulu* (Zulu national movement) in an attempt to generate mass support for the monarchy faced with the disintegration of pre-capitalist social relations. It was revived by Buthelezi in 1975 and its name modified to *Inkatha ye Nkululeko Ye Sizwe*. **1986** *New African* May 11 Gatsha Buthelezi, the Chief Minister of KwaZulu and leader of the *Inkatha* movement, convened a conference — a 'grand *indaba*' — last month to discuss establishing a multi-racial government and assembly in Natal. **1987** *Clarion Call* (Special ed.) 32 The Constitution Of Inkatha: .. We .. declare ourselves a non-violent national cultural liberation movement .. desiring to abolish all forms of discrimination and segregation based on tribe, clan, sex, colour or creed. **1990** *Weekend Argus* 17 Feb. 13 The worst of these conflicts is between the United Democratic Front, an ally of Mandela's own African National Congress, and Chief Mangosuthu Buthelezi's tribally-based Inkatha movement. **1990** S. Ntshakala in *New African* 10 Oct.

6 Dr Frank Mdlalose, KwaZulu Minister of Health and national chairperson of the Inkatha Freedom Party. **1991** S. MACLEOD in *Time* 5 Aug. 10 Inkatha, a predominantly Zulu group battling the African National Congress for the support of South Africa's 28,5 million blacks. **1991** C. SMITH in *Sunday Times* 22 Sept. 29 ANC 'sojas' leap from an alley between two shacks and after a dusty, confused battle put the 'Inkathas' to flight. **1992** *Race Rel. Survey 1991–2* (S.A.I.R.R.) 32 In Ulundi .. at a special conference in December 1990 .. Inkatha transformed itself into a fully fledged political party, the IFP, and adopted a new constitution.

inkhosi, inkoos(e), inkoosi varr. INKOSI *n.*

inkoosikaas var. INKOSIKAZI.

inkors var. ENKOSI *int.*

‖**inkosana** /ˌɪŋkɔˈsɑːn(ə)/ *n.* Also **'nkosana**, and with initial capital. [Xhosa and Zulu, *inkos(i)* chief + dim. suffix *-ana.*]
1. 'Little master'; a title or respectful form of address to a boy or young man perceived to be of superior status; occas. used with a first name. See also INKOSI.

1913 J.J. DOKE *Secret City* 202 'Inkosana,' he said, looking me full in the face .. 'Lumkile is not a witch-doctor trained to live by deception'. **1948** A. PATON *Cry, Beloved Country* 224, I am just laughing, inkosana. — Inkosana? That's little inkosi, isn't it? — It is little inkosi. Little master, it means. **1958** R. COLLINS *Impassioned Wind* 18 He saw me and paused and raised his hand in greeting. 'Nkosana.' I smiled and nodded. **1961** D. BEE *Children of Yesterday* 60 It was not only to draw his pension that Temba Zondi came to the 'town'. He came to ask .. when the inkosana was expected home from Pietermaritzburg. **1967** O. WALKER *Hippo Poacher* 43 Speaking to Willie, the messenger said, 'Are you the *inkosana* of Jantoni, who is a great hunter?' **1967** E.M. SLATTER *My Leaves Are Green* 1 Nkosana David-Paul! Wake up! It is late and the horses are nearly ready. **1987** M. POLAND *Train to Doringbult* 24 'I wish to speak to *Nkosana*.' 'I will call him.'

2. The son and heir of a chief.

1974 C.T. BINNS *Warrior People* 83 The inKosana, (the eldest son of the chief wife), together with the iKohlo, (the eldest son of the wife second in dignity), had to proceed to the isiBaya where the animals had been kraaled.

‖**inkosazana** /ˌɪŋkɔsaˈzɑːn(ə)/ *n.* Also **inkosasana, inkosazan', inkosezan, 'nkosasaan, nkosaza(a)n, nkosazana**, and with initial capital. [Xhosa and Zulu, *inkos(i)* chief + fem. suffix *-az(i)* + dim. suffix *-ana.*] 'Young lady': a title for, or respectful mode of address to, a girl or young unmarried woman peceived to be of superior status; also used of or to the daughter of a chief. See also INKOSIKAZI sense 2.

1899 A. WERNER *Captain of Locusts* 193, I bade him begone; and he began to utter evil words of the abelungu, which it was not fitting that the Inkosazana should hear. **1909** N. PAUL *Child in Midst* 93 'Inkosazan'!' he called at length. 'You good gearl; you no let me die.' **1912** W. WESTRUP *Land of To-Morrow* 362 A step sounded in the passage and he stood at attention as Olga came into the room. 'Inkosezan!' he said, and raised his hand. **1951** O. WALKER *Shapeless Flame* 265 She had said 'Sala Kahle' and given him a shilling. She was a very nice missis, an inkosazana. **1953** R. CAMPBELL *Mamba's Precipice* 29 'Oh, what a darling little buck!' cried Mary. 'It is for you, Inkosasana,' said Vemvan. **1968** K. MCMAGH *Dinner of Herbs* 114 There was always a big plate of dinner, with plum-pudding to follow, set aside especially for them by the 'nkosasaan. **1977** P.C. VENTER *Soweto* 50 'Nkosazana', he told the girl of his dreams, 'I must have you for my wife.' 'I am not your princess,' teased the delicate Maria. **1987** BHENGU & BECKETT in *True Love* Mar. 29 Before we came to Johannesburg we had such a wonderful girl. She looked on me as her mother and called us 'Nkosana' and 'Nkosazana'. **1987** S. MOTJUWADI in *Drum* Dec. 22 Stella Sigcau was born into royalty, but her mother was very strict ... 'She did not want me called inkosazana, princess,' she explained. **1989** J. HOBBS *Thoughts in Makeshift Mortuary* 16 Gertrude chuckled 'Ai, Nkosazaan, don't worry!'

inkose kosi var. INKOSIKAZI.

inkosi *int.* var. ENKOSI *int.*

‖**inkosi** /ɪŋˈkɔsi/ *n.* Also **encossi, enkosi, (in)-cose, incosi, ingoose, inkhosi, inkoos(e), inkoosi, inkos(a), inkose(e), inkosu, inquose, ko(o)si, kos(e), kousi, nkhosa, (n)khosi, n'koos, nkos(e), nkosi**, and with initial capital. Pl. **-es, -s**, or **amak(h)osi**. [Xhosa and Zulu (pl. prefix *ama-*, see AMA-).] In traditional Nguni society:
1.a. A chief or ruler; *transf.*, God. Cf. KGOSI, MORENA sense 1 b. See also PARAMOUNT.

1836 N. ISAACS *Trav.* (1937) II. 245 When the monarch is firmly seated on his throne .. he becomes an absolute king, or 'Inquose'. [**1838** tr. S. van der Stel in D. Moodie *Record* I. 419 The English say that a certain chief named Ingoose wore a bracelet which was much heavier than the copper neck rings, from which circumstance they conjectured it to be gold.] **1846** J.C. BROWN tr. *T. Arbousset's Narr. of Explor. Tour to N.-E. of Col.* 301 As if a zula inkhosi could show clemency! **1855** [see INJA sense 2 a]. **1866** W.C. HOLDEN *Past & Future* 315 They (the Kaffirs) .. allow of no lamentation being made for a person killed by lightning; as they say it would be a sign of disloyalty to lament for one whom the inkosi had sent for. **1885** H. RIDER HAGGARD *King Solomon's Mines* 46 The Inkoosi (chief) saw my face at the place of the Little Hand (Isandhlwana). **1905** *Westminster Gaz.* (U.K.) 8 June 2 All the members of the kraals concerned will .. form, .. with the 'inkosi', his several wives and their brothers and sisters and children and dependent relatives, a formidable audience. [**1937** I. SCHAPERA *Bantu-Speaking Tribes* 174 At the head of the whole tribe is the Chief (Nguni *inkosi*; Shangana-Tonga, *hosi*; Venda, *khosi*; Sotho, *morêna, kxosi*.).] **1949** O. WALKER *Proud Zulu* (1951) 235 The Chiefs say: 'the English are amakosi (chiefs), indeed, since a man may live again after they have killed him'. **1959** G. & W. GORDON tr. *F.A. Venter's Dark Pilgrim* 112 He wishes he could understand .. about the Great Inkosi and the Good Book from which the white man reads, but he cannot. **1990** *Clarion Call* Vol.1, 5 The King told the chiefs that their ancestors would turn in their graves if they saw the extent to which the strapping Amakhosi and their warriors were fleeing before children. **1990** S. SANGWENI in *New African* 16 July 1 The KwaZulu government's proposed legislation to amend laws relating to Amakhosi and Iziphakanyiswa (chiefs and dignitaries). **1994** F. MDLALOSE in *Natal Witness* 23 Dec. 1 Nothing could be more insulting to the autonomy of the province, and to the integrity and dignity of the kingdom of KwaZulu, than the notion of putting *amakhosi* of our kingdom on the payroll of the central government.

b. A respectful form of address or reference to a chief, ruler, or one perceived as being of superior status. Cf. KGOSI, MORENA sense 1 a.

1827 G. THOMPSON *Trav.* I. 118 Calling the king, Kousie, which is not his name, but his title, *kousie* signifying king or principal chief in their language. **1871** J. MACKENZIE *Ten Yrs* (1971) 208 Khosi (chief)! you white people ought to come in here and fight with these Bechuanas, and overcome them. *Ibid.* 445 Addressing himself to Macheng, he said: 'Khosi! (king), it would appear that I along of all the Bamangwato am to speak unpleasant words to you this day.' **1882** LADY F.C. DIXIE *In Land of Misfortune* 209 With the salutation 'Inkos' they took their departure. *Ibid.* 341 The inhabitants greeted us with smiles and obeisances, and the stately sounding salutation 'Inkōse,' accompanied by the hand of the speaker raised towards the heavens, met us on all sides. **1891** R. SMITH *Great Gold Lands* 196 The Zulu .. hails you with just so much jocosity as he feels your bearing towards him will permit of. One arm is thrown up in the air straight, and the word pronounced is 'Cose,' an abbreviation of 'Ecossi,' or lord and master. **1900** B. MITFORD *John Ames* 96 Policeman he want to see Inkose. **1910** J. BUCHAN *Prester John* (1961) 215 Courage, Inkoos; in an hour's time you will be free. **1925** D. KIDD *Essential Kafir* 72 'Do you believe there is a God?' you ask. 'Yes, Nkos,' he answers. **1925** *E. Prov. Herald* 9 July 7 Deep shouts of 'Inkoos' greeted the Prince, and the chiefs bowing their heads to the ground clapped their hands in further Royal greeting. **1941** 'R. ROAMER' in *Bantu World* 1 Feb. 4 They befriend only those who 'Yes, Nkosi' them and try to ruin those who have moral courage to stand for themselves. **1964** G. CAMPBELL *Old Dusty* 27 Because, Inkosi, the white man's head is so full of clever things he will not believe the things the black man tells. [**1977** *Daily Dispatch* 23 Aug. 1 'Nkosi' was a Xhosa term of respect that had no racial connotations.]

c. Always in *pl.*: The spirits of the dead. Cf. IDLOZI.

1978 *Daily Dispatch* 25 Apr. 19 A herbalist .. said the guardian 'amakhosi' spirits had used Mr Nkohla T—, of Mdantsane, as an agent to assault the evil 'mafufunyane' spirits which had possessed Miss Kondokondo M—. Mr Woko said the gathering of mystics .. called on the amakhosi to drive out the mafufunyane.

2. In the phr. **inkosi inkulu** /- ɪŋkuːlu, -kʊːlʊ/ [Xhosa and Zulu *khulu* great, important], a 'great chief', a 'great king'; *transf.*, God.

1835 A. STEEDMAN *Wanderings* I. 255 The Umkumkani is usually a lineal descendant from the first great patriarchal chieftain of the tribe, and the title of Inkose enkulu is enjoyed exclusively by himself. **1837** F. OWEN *Diary* (1926) 44 He said it was the grave of an 'Inkosi inkulu,' a great king who lived many years ago. **1849** R. GRAY *Jrnl of Bishop's Visitation* I. 42 The Great Father of the Christians — the Lord Bishop .. to whom all the Christians looked up as their great chief (Inkosi Inkulu) in religion, had ridden ninety miles yesterday from Graham's Town. **1916** *E. Prov. Herald* 12 July 7 He was the Inkoos Inkulu (King). **1959** G. & W. GORDON tr. *F.A. Venter's Dark Pilgrim* 11 She .. has gone before through the Dark River, but beside the great Inkosenkulu she awaits him. *c***1963** B.C. TAIT *Durban Story* 16 Competition waxed among these one-time comrades — now self-appointed native chiefs — to see which could be the 'Inkosi Inkulu'. **1967** O. WALKER *Hippo Poacher* 110 The old man quavered finally that he had been sent to find Tom by the *amakosi amakula* (very high chiefs).

inkosikazi /(i)ŋˈkɔs(i)kɑːz(i)/ *n.* Also **incosacãse, inkoosikaas, inkose kosi, inkosigas, inkosigaze, inkos(i)kaas, (i)nkosikasi, inkosikaze, inkosikosi, inkosikozi, inkozikas, inkozikazi, inquosegose, khoskhaz, n(i)kosikazi, nkosikaas, nkozkazi**, and with initial capital. Pl. unchanged, or **-s**. [Xhosa and Zulu *inkosi* chief + feminine suffix *-kazi.*]
1. A married woman of status (in a polygamous family): **a.** The highest-ranking wife of an African chief or king, and mother of his heir; *great wife* sense *(a)*, see GREAT. **b.** Any of the wives of an African chief or king. **c.** The highest-ranking wife of a commoner; *great wife* sense *(b)*, see GREAT. Also used as a title, and occas. *attrib.* or *fig.* See also RIGHT HAND.

1835 A. STEEDMAN *Wanderings* I. 256 The Chief having many wives .. the sovereignty devolves on the offspring of the *Inkose kosi*, female chieftain, or queen. **1836** N. ISAACS *Trav.* (1937) II. 63 In the afternoon the Messrs. Fynn repaired to Umpenduin to celebrate the nuptials of a chief and Ningwas: all the inquosegoses were present. [*Note*] All the queens. **1855** G. BROWN *Personal Adventure* 115 At a small kraal a very eligible place presented itself, the hut of the Inkosikozi chiefess, the mother of Macomo. **1887** J.W. MATTHEWS *Incwadi Yami* 37 The *Inkosikazi* is the wife of the greatest rank, her hut is placed in the centre opposite the gateway of the kraal, and her eldest son is heir. **1895** H. RIDER HAGGARD *Nada* 130 Fastened to his arm by a thong of leather was the great axe Groan-Maker, and each man as he came up saluted the axe, calling it '*Inkosikaas*,' or Chieftainess. **1956** F.C. METROWICH *Valiant but Once* 197 A man came to tell Brown that Unoxima, one of the inkosikosi (wives of the chief), wanted to see him. **1978** A. Elliott *Sons of Zulu* 175 A chief's main wife, or *nkosikazi*, is chosen in consultation with his clan who provide the *lobolo* cattle for her and this marriage invariably takes place after the chief already has several wives. She is therefore likely to be younger than any of his first wives and she provides the heir for the chief ... The first wife of a commoner as opposed to that of the chief, is his main wife or *nkosikazi*.

2. *transf.* A respectful form of address or reference to any married woman (often an employer) who is perceived to be of superior status; also used as a title, with a name, and as a common noun. See also INKOSAZANA.

1836 A.F. Gardiner *Journey to Zoolu Country* 146 The appellation Incosa-căse (literally female chief) is applied to all women of high rank ... These are .. generally placed as pensioners, one or two together, in the different military towns where they preside, and are particularly charged with the distribution of provisions. **1866** H. Robertson *Mission Life among Zulu-Kafirs* 103 Look, Inkosikazi, here is Mary putting this in my best trousers. **1878** H.A. Roche *On Trek in Tvl* 246 He [*sc.* the 'washing Kaffir'] acquits himself at his task better than the *Inkosigas* (white mistress) who bungles hers so sadly. **1897** J.P. Fitzpatrick *Outspan* 86 One boy replied: 'Inkosikaas.' .. 'I asked who sent them with the food.' 'Well who did?' 'He says "The missis"!' **1908** D. Blackburn *Leaven* (1991) 26 It is not wise to let the white baas or the inkozikas (mistress) know that you can do clever things, for then they will make you work the harder. **1923** G.H. Nicholls *Bayete!* 238 She went to the door and beckoned Mukwasi 'Have you any coffee ready?' 'Yes, Nkosikasi,' he replied. **1948** A. Paton *Cry, Beloved Country* 175 My heart holds a deep sorrow for you, and for the inkosikazi, and for the young inkosikazi, and for the children. **1961** D. Bee *Children of Yesterday* 13 'Call the Inkosikasi, ..' he commanded. Then the girl disappeared and returned with the lady of the house. **1963** A.M. Louw *20 Days* 98 Mrs. Shuba .. Nkozkazi Shuba, the wife of the chief Bantu detective – a woman of importance. **1969** I. Vaughan *Last of Sunlit Yrs* 25 'Nkosikaas,' Moses had asked, 'what sort of a table is this?' **1978** A.P. Brink *Rumours of Rain* 277 On the stoep the voice went on calling softly but insistently: '*Nkosikazi! Nkosikazi! Nkosikazi!* – Madam!' At last Ma's voice, sleepy and surprised, answered. **1986** F. Karodia *Daughters of Twilight* 9 Noting Ma's heat-induced irritation, Gladys gave a sheepish grin, her dark cheeks glittering with perspiration ... 'Hienie, Khoskhaz, almost finished now.'

inkruip plaas /ˈənkreɪplɑːs, -krœip-/ *n. phr. Obs.* exc. *hist. Law.* [Afk., *inkruip* creep in + *plaas* (earlier Du. *plaats*) farm.] A farm obtained by squatting upon and claiming disputed land between two adjoining farms. See also UITVALGROND.

*a***1912** *Bloemfontein Post* (Pettman), Floores Tromp, .. under the impression that the owners of Boschhoek and Waterval claimed more land than they were entitled to, squatted on the south side of the Incandu River, near the Drift, and put in an application for any spare land which might be held by the original grantees. When the surveyor, Mr. Bell, came along a couple of years later, he cut off nearly 3 000 acres from the adjoining farms, and Tromp obtained the *inkruip plaats*. **1913** C. Pettman *Africanderisms* 227 In early days in the Orange Free State and the Transvaal when an applicant for a Request farm .. could find no suitable vacant site, he would sometimes squat between two such farms the owners of which had included (not an uncommon occurrence) within their boundaries much more than the stipulated 3 000 morgen, and at the survey would claim the excess land from each or both to make up his required area. Such a farm was known as an Inkruip plaats. **1967** E. Rosenthal *Encycl. of Sn Afr.* 260 *Inkruip Plaas*, (literally 'Creeping-in Farm'). A farm established in the early days on a piece of ground, the neighbouring owners of which were in dispute about their boundaries. **1990** C. Laffeaty *Far Forbidden Plains* 275, I question him about *uitvalgrond*, .. and he told me that under Roman-Dutch law the land may be claimed by an outsider as what is called an *Inkruip-plaas*.

‖**inkululeko** /ˌiŋkʊlʊˈleːkɔ/ *n.* [Xhosa and Zulu, emancipation, deliverance, freedom.] Freedom; independence.

1977 *S. Afr. Panorama* Jan. 26 'Inkululeko' (Independence) came to Transkei at midnight on October 25, 1976. **1982** *Pace* Feb. 29 An unwelcome inkululeko. The Ciskei celebrations were marred by ill omens. **1983** *Ibid.* Oct. 174 On the stroke of midnight the Republic of Ciskei was born ... At that fateful hour, the sacrificial beast refused to bellow ... According to custom, you .. should have called off the ceremony ... But .. you carried on with the unwelcome inkululeko. **1983** D. Martins in *Staffrider* Vol.5 No.3, 10 Azania .. let the seed of chimurenga .. take root .. to blossom bloom and bear inkululeko. **1989** B. Krige in *Sunday Times* 8 Oct. 25 The cardinal features of Transkei haven't changed since *inkululeko* (independence) in 1976.

inkundla /iŋˈkʊ(ː)ndla, -lə/ *n.* Also **inkudhla, nkundla, umkandhlu**, and with initial capital. [Xhosa and Zulu.]

1. In traditional Nguni society: a meeting of the people of a village or area, held in the public courtyard at the gate of the cattle enclosure. Cf. KGOTLA sense 3. See also IBANDLA.

1897 W.C. Scully in E.R. Seary *S. Afr. Short Stories* (1947) 33 He took his departure for the 'great place' of the paramount Pondo chief, for the purpose of attending an umkandhlu, or 'meeting for talk', of which general notice had been given. **1923** —— *Daniel Vananda* 20 The 'inkundla' of Dalisile – the great court held at the entrance to the cattle enclosure, – where all important appeals from the decisions of the minor chiefs were finally adjudicated. **1979** A. Kana in *E. Prov. Herald* 9 Feb. (Indaba) 7 The crucial issue is whether the initiant can accept and act according to the instructions he receives from his elders at the inkundla. **1981** *Voice* 22 Apr. 2 The conference table or inkundla is always the best place or method of solving issues. **1990** *City Press* 11 Feb. 6 Rolihlahla seemed to enjoy listening to elders arguing in the traditional Inkundla.

2. In a traditional Nguni homestead: the public courtyard before the gate of the cattle enclosure. Cf. KGOTLA sense 1.

1907 W.C. Scully *By Veldt & Kopje* 61 A few days afterwards the great council met at Kreli's 'Great Place,' the exact spot of assembly being the 'inkundhla,' or gate of the big cattle enclosure. **1930** S.T. Plaatje *Mhudi* (1975) 87 At the end of three days Mzilikazi was up at an early hour. His inkundla was full of warriors. **1939** N.J. Van Warmelo in A.M. Duggan-Cronin *Bantu Tribes* III. i. 25 The Chief and his mapakathi met in Council in the principal hut (isigqeba), but lawsuits and gatherings of the people took place in the nkundla, the space between the huts and the cattle-kraal. **1955** J.B. Shephard *Land of Tikoloshe* 22 The *inkundla* – the space between the dwelling huts and the cattle kraal – was devoid of old tins, bones, rags, and empty bottles. **1970** A. Fulton *I Swear to Apollo* 47 The doctor's jeep .. pulled up in a great cloud of dust in the in-kundla between the cattle-kraal and the huts of Debe's u-mizi. **1988** M. Mxotwa in *Daily Dispatch* 17 Dec., This was followed by a disciplined Xhosa dance (umtyityimbo) on the inkundla (the wedding arena).

‖**inkwenkwe** /iŋˈkweːŋkwe/ *n.* Pl. usu. **amakwenkwe**, but also **amacanquas, amakh(w)enkwe, makhwenkwe**, and unchanged. [Xhosa (pl. *amakwenkwe*).] KWEDINI. Also *fig.*

Occas. found in dim. form **inkwenkwana** [Xhosa dim. suffix *-ana*].

1875 C.B. Bisset *Sport & War* 53 Up to the age of sixteen the boys remain boys, or, as they are called, amacanquas. **1937** B.J.F. Laubscher *Sex, Custom & Psychopathology* 9 Many stories are told by boys (*amakwenkwe*) of the wonderful games they have had. *Ibid.* 179 The small boys or *amakwenkwana* receive the large bowel, and the small girls or *intwanazana* are given strips from the neck and trotters. **1954** in A.M. Duggan-Cronin *Bantu Tribes* III. Pl.174, *Inkwenkwe* (uncircumcised boy). **1959** L. Longmore *Dispossessed* 159 Among the Xhosa, when a man does not behave himself, he is called inkwenkwe, an uncircumcised boy – one who has not been given the training to prepare him to be a worthy member of the community. **1963** [see IKRWALA]. **1970** A. Fulton *I Swear to Apollo* 46 The in-Kwenkwe will need a mug of coffee and some bread. I suppose the little fellow walked all the way? **1987** S.D. Tirivanhu in *New Coin Poetry* June 25, I work singing the ancient songs of my long forgotten youth of Amakhenkwe passing the day warming from the morning's dew.

in laager see LAAGER *n.*

inqira var. IGQIRA *n.*²

inquose var. INKOSI *n.*

inquosegose var. INKOSIKAZI.

inqutu var. NGQUTHU.

insangoma var. SANGOMA.

insangu, intsangu /inˈ(t)sa(ː)ngu/ *n.* Also **in(t)sango, itsangu, msangu, 'nsangu, ntsangu.** [Xhosa *intsangu*, Zulu *insangu*.] DAGGA *n.*² sense 1.

1897 Schulz & Hammar *New Africa* 201 The smoking of 'insangu' or 'dacha,' as it is variously called, is a widely distributed habit throughout South Africa amongst the natives. **1909** N. Paul *Child in Midst* 198 Smoking insangu, a kind of wild hemp which makes them half crazy. **1955** B.B. Burnett *Anglicans in Natal* 97 He had run amok, and, temporarily deranged by smoking *insango* had killed his father and several others. **1966** C.A. Smith *Common Names* 329 The cultivation of dagga is prohibited by law in South Africa, yet it is commonly found as a weed round native kraals in Natal and is known as *insangu*. **1969** A. Paton *Kontakion* 94 A handful of boys charged with more serious matters, such as smoking the weed called dagga or *insangu* (called in America marijuana). **1971** *Argus* 5 May 2 Drugs completely banned, known as 'prohibited dependence-producing drugs' are .. cannabis (Indian hemp), including cannabis resin, 'dagga', 'itsangu' and the whole plant or any portion thereof. **1975** S.S. Mekgoe *Lindiwe* (1978) 17, 2nd Constable: .. Look at this parcel, Sarge ... It's dagga .. intsangu, Sarge. **1979** *E. Prov. Herald* 5 Oct. (Indaba) 1 Dagga – intsangu – is available all over the country despite strict measures taken by the authorities to stamp out drug smuggling. [**1982** *Voice* 16 May 1 Bushes, shop backyards, school toilets or any other hidden places are used as venues for smoking 'intsango' as the drug is known in Zulu.]

inspan /ˈɪnspæn/ *v.* Also **enspan, inspand, inspann.** [Du. *inspannen.*]

Cf. OUTSPAN *v.*

1.a. *intrans.* To prepare for a journey (by harnessing draught animals to a vehicle); *to span in*, see SPAN *v.* sense 2 b.

1827 G. Thompson *Trav.* I. 86 A storm of snow and hail raging .., we delayed *inspanning* till it had blown past. **1834** T.H. Bowker Journal. 27 Dec., Inspan for the Church, return with Merai to his place for his Cattle and horses, and sheep. **1838** J.E. Alexander *Exped. into Int.* I. 179 On inspanning we had a battle with a young ox, which would not submit its neck to the yoke. **1838** T. Shone Diary. 18 July, Inspan'd for town. Call'd at Jolly's Canteen. **1839** J. Collett Accounts. II. 14 Feb., Inspanned about midday and rode on to the Field Cornet Ans Delange. **1851** R. Gray *Jrnl of Bishop's Visitation* II. 88 We were just inspanning in the morning, and I had settled with Mr. Shepstone that he should not go on further with us. **1860** D.L.W. Stainbank Diary. (Killie Campbell Africana Library KCM8680) 12 June, We inspanned and started at sunrise crossing the Amanzimtoti about breakfast time. **1871** E.J. Dugmore Diary. 27 Nov., As we were preparing to inspan this afternoon my brother came. **1881** *E. London Dispatch* 15 Jan. 3 Inspanning at daybreak, we again started, but after driving about for some hours across country I told the escort we would stop where we were. **1893** F.C. SELOUS *Trav. & Adventure* 93, I determined to inspan and hold on my course to the south. **1896** R. WALLACE *Farming Indust. of Cape Col.* 269 The practice is to inspan an hour before sunset, and to go on till say eleven o'clock, then outspan for a few hours, tying up the cattle in the yoke where they lie. **1901** P.J. DU TOIT *Diary* (1974) 30 The English are moving down to Klerksdorp from Lichtenburg and have already had a skirmish with result one killed and two wounded. Inspan and off. Artillery, horsemen, waggons, cattle, carts every living thing is being got out of the way. **1915** D. FAIRBRIDGE *Torch Bearer* 202 Not another half-hour do we stop by this place. Tell Koos to inspan. I will pack at once. *c***1936** *S. & E. Afr. Yr Bk & Guide* 36 Inspan — to harness, to start. **1938** F.C. SLATER *Trek* 18 Now must we inspan and up-saddle, Saddle-up, inspan and travel afar, For aloft in the East is the morning-star! **1976** V. ROSENBERG *Sunflower* 13 After the last Sunday service the farmers would inspan and disappear in different direction, leaving no trace behind them but their wagon tracks and a littered market place.

b. *trans.* To yoke or harness (draught animals) to a vehicle; to ready (a vehicle) for travel by harnessing draught animals to it; *transf.*, to make (oneself) ready for a journey; to couple (a tractor or other towing vehicle) to a trailer; SPAN *v.* sense 1 b; *to span in*, see SPAN *v.* sense 2 a.

1834 T.H. BOWKER Journal. 25 Dec., Arrive at [M]erais after sunset find the waggons inspanned ready for going away. **1835** A. STEEDMAN *Wanderings* I. 126 The oxen which we had engaged made their appearance, and were immediately *inspanned*. **1838** T. SHONE Diary. 8 Oct., We enspan'd the Oxen and draged a bush to Town. **1849** N.J. MERRIMAN *Cape Jrnls* (1957) 68 Mr Heugh, one of the churchwardens, kindly inspanned his mules and proposed taking me the first 15 or 20 miles of my long journey to Colesburg. **1852** *Blackwood's Mag.* (U.K.) LXXI. 294 (Cape Colony) At noon, the cattle, which have been turned out to graze, are 'inspanned', and the march continues. **1871** 'JNO' in A.M.L. Robinson *Sel. Articles from Cape Monthly Mag.* (1978) 129 We directed our coachman to 'inspan' the horses. **1883** O.E.A. SCHREINER *Story of Afr. Farm* 276 Gregory carried her out in his arms to the waggon which stood 'inspanned' before the door. **1887** A.A. ANDERSON *25 Yrs in Waggon* II. 122 It was arranged to inspann the waggon, and bring it round the best way we could through the forest to as near the dead giraffe as possible. **1895** A.B. BALFOUR *1200 Miles in Waggon* 74 Our oxen were inspanned (harnessed) about 6 p.m., and we all walked behind. **1900** A.W. CARTER *Informant, Ladybrand* 8 Feb., I had the spider inspanned and went forth. **1911** L. COHEN *Reminisc. of Kimberley* 100 They inspanned horses to Rossmore's cape cart, and away the three jolly souls went. **1934** B.I. BUCHANAN *Pioneer Days* 90 The farmer forthwith inspanned his wagon and returned to Maritzburg. **1955** A. DELIUS *Young Trav.* 141 The two white boys helped Charlie and an older boy ... to *inspan* a team of oxen for the early ploughing. **1962** F.C. METROWICH *Scotty Smith* 27 A party of four Boers with their wives and families were trekking and had stopped for the night. When Scotty joined them they were already inspanned and ready to move. **1975** *Sunday Times* 10 Aug. 7 She need not be clever, but she must know how to inspan a team of donkeys. **1986** *S. Afr. Panorama* Feb. 14 The history of South Africa is the history of its people; people who did not hesitate to load their wagon, inspan their oxen and trek when circumstances at the Cape no longer suited them. **1991** F. LE ROUX in *Ibid.* Jan.-Feb. 83 A sturdy and powerful tractor was 'inspanned' to pull the trailer.

2. *trans. fig.* To enlist the help of (someone); to 'round (someone) up'; to make use of (resources); *to span in*, see SPAN *v.* sense 2 c.

1883 E.L. PRICE Letter. 25 June, I think I must inspan him tomorrow to bake me a loaf of bread for he knows how to do it. **1900** E. ROSS *Diary of Siege of Mafeking* (1980) 101 They did not lose much time in inspanning me at my new redoubt, for I had no sooner arrived there .. than I was ordered to do sentry-go. **1914** R. KIPLING in *Geog. Jrnl* Apr. 373 One man, apparently without effort, inspans the human equivalent of 'three blind 'uns and a bolter' and makes them do miracles. **1925** D. KIDD *Essential Kafir* 324 The gathering-in of the harvest is a great event, and all hands are 'in-spanned' for it. **1937** C.R. PRANCE *Tante Rebella's Saga* 176 As it was all in English the schoolmistress was inspanned to translate it *viva-voce* for the edification of the crowd. **1949** *Cape Times* 13 Sept. 8 To rescue the Coloured man, all forces will have to be inspanned to raise him economically. **1955** W. ILLSLEY *Wagon on Fire* 80 The Bantu Worker's Christian Union will inspan every worker, young or old, male or female. *c***1966** J. HOBBS in *New S. Afr. Writing* 161 The one successful farmer works like a slave for five months of the year, toiling from before dawn till well into the night with teams of relatives inspanned to pack. **1971** J. FRYE *War of Axe* p.x, He had been trained as a printer early in life, and in the completion of his task he had to inspan all of his talents. **1972** *E. Prov. Herald* 12 Aug. 8 The UP did not inspan the party machine but the NP's public representatives were not shy in working openly in some wards for the people they favoured. **1980** *S. Afr. Panorama* Dec. 46 It awaited only the courage and ingenuity of the pioneers to inspan these natural resources in the service of civilisation. **1981** *Daily Dispatch* 8 June 11 Nationalist newspapers have suggested that some senior SABC officials are blocking attempts to inspan the Corporation in support of Mr P.W. Botha's reform programme. **1990** M. KENTRIDGE *Unofficial War* 166 Vlok .. scoffed at the efforts of clergymen involved in peace initiatives, and said they had been 'inspanned by the ANC-SACP to do their devilish work'.

Hence **inspan** *n. obs.*, and **inspanning** *vbl n.*, the preparations for a journey, esp. the harnessing of draught animals to vehicles; also *attrib.*

1849 E.D.H.E. NAPIER *Excursions in Sn Afr.* II. 12 A 'spann' means, I believe, in Dutch, a team of oxen, or other draught animals; hence the terms 'inspanning' and 'outspanning,' or yoking and unyoking. **1871** J. MCKAY *Reminisc.* 161 We passed the night, drinking coffee and telling yarns until the *reveille* sounded, and the 'inspan' followed, reminding us of our day's duty. **1872** [see *outspanning* (OUTSPAN *v.*)]. **1876** T. STUBBS Reminiscences. 19 A large bush was fastened to the end of a stout rope which was to answer for a trek tow and yokes fastened on, the inspanning commenced. **1879** R.J. ATCHERLEY *Trip to Boerland* 62, I had been sound asleep at the time of inspanning. *Ibid.* 68 We managed to get along until next morning's sunrise and inspan. *Meteor* 27 Nov. 4 Inspanning and saddling up was now the order and thus ended the pleasantest day's outing your truly has had at a cricket match. **1887** H. RIDER HAGGARD *Jess* p.ix, John went .. to see the inspanning of the Cape cart. **1891** W. SELWYN *Cape Carols* 3 The 'inspanning' finished Jack shoulders his rifle. *c***1900**, **1924** [see *outspanning* (OUTSPAN *v.*)]. **1925** L.D. FLEMMING *Crop of Chaff* 3 The two oxen that the boy went to fetch last week come up at a briskish walk .. and then — inspanning begins. **1934** B.I. BUCHANAN *Pioneer Days* 31 This was the first time that we saw the inspanning, and we watched the novel performance with keen interest. **1949** L.G. GREEN *In Land of Afternoon* 132 Driving a team of mules is not so easily learnt as the control of a motor-car. Inspanning and outspanning are often difficult. **1968** K. MCMAGH *Dinner of Herbs* 79 We watched the inspanning with amazement and wondered how any human being could sort out the tangle of harness lying on the ground. **1977** F.G. BUTLER *Karoo Morning* 11 She expressed a keen longing to experience a trek by oxwagon — the whole slow ritual of inspanning and outspanning, of moving over vast spaces. **1986** *S. Afr. Panorama* Feb. 16 Seldom before have oxen been the cause of so much interest with everyone in the camp taking a close look at the inspanning process.

‖**intelezi** /ˌinteˈleːzi/ *n.* [Zulu and Xhosa.] Collectively, traditional African herbal medicines or charms which are believed to have protective properties, esp. in battle. Also *attrib.* See also MUTI sense 2 a.

1870 H. CALLAWAY *Religious System of Amazulu* 435 He washes himself .. with intelezi, that, though he should meet with danger whilst travelling, he may not be quickly injured. **1918** H. MOORE *Land of Good Hope* 109 Some of the same intelezi is put into waters, and stirred with a stick. **1925** D. KIDD *Essential Kafir* 14 The chiefs .. give their warriors special medicines, called Intelezi, with which to wash their bodies. **1966** A.T. BRYANT *Zulu Medicine* 18 He [*sc.* the 'medicine man'] would stand aghast .. if you were bold enough to ridicule his ability to confound the knavery of the *umThakathi* by plentifully sprinkling *inTelezi*-medicine about the kraal. **1989** *Greater Dict. of Xhosa* III. 255 *Gasteria* spp.: traditionally warriors were treated with an infusion of *intelezi* to render them invulnerable; chiefs are washed with it to give them charisma; employees use it to ensure acceptance by their employers; [etc.].

international *adj.* [Special senses of general Eng. *international* pertaining to relations between nations.]

See also NATION.

1. Also **inter-national**. Inter-racial, intergroup.

1824 W.J. BURCHELL *Trav.* II. 112 The boors occasionally suffer heavy losses: but the Bushmen, in exculpation, declare that they rob in retaliation of past injuries. Thus, the recollection of injustice on both sides, still operates to produce an international enmity. **1960** J.H. COETZEE in H. Spottiswoode *S. Afr.: Rd Ahead* 70 An inter-racial society .. means an inter-ethnic and *inter-national* society. **1990** S. GRAY in *Staffrider* Vol.9 No.1, 49 That week, to much publicity, some prestigious restaurants had succeeded in becoming 'open' to 'international' diners of colour.

2. Of bars and licensed hotels, restaurants, and trains, in terms of the Liquor Act: open to all races. Also *transf.*

1975 J.T. KRUGER in *Hansard* 22 May 6563 Provision is being made in this clause for the establishment of what I shall call 'international hotels' and other on-consumption distribution points to which non-Whites may be admitted ... Application for international status will have to be made annually. **1978** *Pace* Dec. 86 The Carlton is .. an *international* hotel, which means the staff has been trained not to notice people's colour, except amongst themselves. **1978** *Financial Mail* 10 Mar. 734 Desegregating licensed premises requires their being granted 'international' status under the Liquor Act. **1979** *Survey of Race Rel. 1978* (S.A.I.R.R.) 364 At this year's Liquor Board hearings, 'international status' was granted to 58 of SA's 1 448 hotels, 23 in the Cape, 19 in the Transvaal, 13 in Natal and 3 in the OFS. **1981** *Cape Times* 28 Dec. 9 The zoo and surrounding facilities are open to all races, but the hotel does not have an 'international' licence. **1982** *Pretoria News* 24 Nov. 14 Durban established the province's first multi-racial beach last month and an 'international' beach is expected to be opened at Richards Bay early next year. **1983** B. HARTDEGEN in *Outeniqualander/Herald* 21 Dec. 12 Tootsie is an international train with no race barriers. **1985** *Weekly Mail* 1 Nov. 17 One thing which certainly jars with the colonial past are the 'international status' bars. And while even with the upcoming change in the liquor laws some bars will stay segregated, it should lead to greater choice for all of us who don't like racial separation.

intje var. UINTJIE.

into laager see LAAGER *n.*

intombazana /intɔmbaˈza(ː)na/ *n.* Also **ntombazana, ntonbizani, tombazaan, tombesan, tombozane.** Pl. **-s, amantombazana.** [Xhosa and Zulu, *intombi* girl + feminine dim. suffix *-azana*.] A little girl; also used as a respectful form of address. See also INTOMBI.

1836 N. ISAACS *Trav.* (1937) II. 101 We were not a little amused by some 'tombesans', or girls, who assembled and danced round us. **1929** M. ALSTON *From Old Cape Homestead* 249 A number of plump, pleasant-faced 'tombozanes' came flocking round the verandah. **1957** B. FRASER *Sunshine & Lamplight* 8 The young amantombazana (girls) and izinsizwa (youths) were crowded around near the sweet counter. **1979** F. DIKE *First S. African* 26 Austin: .. Ntombazana come ... If we don't take you back your father will expect a bride's price. **1982** *E. Prov. Herald* 4 May 1 Princess Di will have a ntonbizani – a little queen. [**1987** M. POLAND *Train to Doringbult* 53 Elsa took the baby and brought it to Chrissie. 'Yintombazana, Chrissie. It's a girl,' she said.] **1988** 'A. AMAPHIXIPHIXI' in *Frontline* Apr.-May 28, I have heard a radio announcer speak of Zola and fondly refer to her as 'Intombazana' meaning the little girl. **1991** *Style* Dec. 92 Speculating mischievously about the absurdity of a system which would jail the sun worshippers of Sandy Bay for doing what the *tombazaans* do with impunity at Gatsha's rallies.

‖**intombi** /in'tɔːmbi/ *n.* Also **entombie, intombe, intomebi, ntombi, tumbee, tumbi**. Pl. **-es, -s**, or **izintombi**. [Xhosa and Zulu (pl. *izintombi*).]
1. A young woman of marriageable age; a young girl. See also INTOMBAZANA.

1809 R. COLLINS in D. Moodie *Record* (1841) V. 46 Cattle are never given for a Tumbee, but her father or brother is supplied with assagays by her keeper. **1833** S. KAY *Trav. & Researches* 470 'That,' said he, 'contains the body of an intombi (young woman) who was killed by lightning from heaven, about two years ago.' **1836** A.F. GARDINER *Journey to Zoolu Country* 97 An unmarried woman is called *Intomebi*. **1855** G.H. MASON *Life with Zulus* 228 A knot of marriageable young ladies (Entombies), clustering thick about the bride. **1855** J.W. COLENSO *Ten Weeks in Natal* 26 There is another special one [*sc.* reason] for the young men wishing to go home from time to time – namely, to make acquaintance with the *intombies*, or young women, whom they will one day acquire for wives. **1866** W.C. HOLDEN *Past & Future* 186 The next morning she is pronounced to be an intombi; that is, she is entered into the state of womanhood, and is considered marriageable. **1882** LADY F.C. DIXIE *In Land of Misfortune* 364 The remainder of our visit to the kraals was spent in endeavouring to induce some of the Zulu intombes, or girls, to mount into my saddle. **1887** A.A. ANDERSON *25 Yrs in Waggon* II. 177 The young Intombies (girls) are all excitement to see their sweethearts so brave. *a*1931 S. BLACK in S. Gray *Three Plays* 139 She is now a big woman .. umfazi. Last time she came home from school she was a little intombi. **1947** L. HASTINGS *Dragons Are Extra* 118 The little girls, the intombis, were busy with bunches of twigs tidying up the huts. **1949** J. MOCKFORD *Golden Land* 189 A few beads and the loin strings suffice for the intombis, the maidens. **1967** O. WALKER *Hippo Poacher* 100 The *intombis*, or young girls, round about made a point of bringing clay pots full of newly-brewed Kaffir beer and baskets of mealie-cobs and wild spinach to trade for meat. **1971** J. MCCLURE *Steam Pig* (1973) 112 'Hey, Johannes, you old skelm,' Pop brawled. 'Don't tell me you've been at the ntombis again?' **1986** PRESTON-WHYTE & LOUW in Burman & Reynolds *Growing Up* 364 Indigenously-based forms and processes of political control obtain there, as do some other structural features such as the organization of girls between puberty and marriage (*izintombi*) into recognized age groups under a designated leader (*ighikize*).

2. *obs.* See quot.

1809 R. COLLINS in G.M. Theal *Rec. of Cape Col.* (1900) VII. 62 It is perhaps only through custom that a couple of tumbies, the name here given to concubines, are attached to his household.

intonga /in'tɔːŋga/ *n. obs.* Also **itonga**. Pl. unchanged. [Xhosa (pl. *iintonga*) and Zulu (pl. *izintonga*).] FIGHTING STICK sense 1.

1833 S. KAY *Trav. & Researches* 269 The only weapon .. carried by any of them was the *itonga* or fencing-stick. **1835** A. STEEDMAN *Wanderings* I. 39 At least seven hundred men and women assembled, and forming themselves into a large circle, the former commenced their preparatory ceremonies by striking on the shafts of their lances with their *intonga*, or fencing sticks. **1860** W. SHAW *Story of my Mission* 462 Now and then the crowd of Pato's people commenced beating time, also, upon their bundles of Javelins, with the long *intonga*, or fencing-stick, which they always carry with them.

intonjane /ˌintɔn'dʒɑːne/ *n.* Also **intonjani, ntonjane**. [Xhosa.] An initiation rite marking the transition from girlhood to young womanhood; the initiated woman. Also *attrib.* See also BOYALE. Cf. ABAKWETHA.

1858 J.C. WARNER in J. Maclean *Compendium of Kafir Laws* (1906) 105 Intonjane ... When the time of her separation has expired, the girl .. proceeds .. to a .. spot .. where she .. hides under ground the fork with which she has been accustomed to eat her food during .. her separation. **1860** W. SHAW *Story of my Mission* 454 The *intonjane*, when a young girl of a certain age, with various absurd and licentious ceremonies, not to be described here, is declared to be marriageable. **1865** *Proceedings of Commission on Native Aff., Cape of G.H.* 57 What is the reason that the natives – or at least the 'school people,' or Christians, have abandoned the *intonjani*? **1891** T.R. BEATTIE *Ride through Transkei* 32 Nqwiliso killed seven head of cattle in honour of one of his daughters having gone through the intonjane ceremony. **1891** [see ABAKWETHA]. **1896** *Cape Argus* 2 Jan. 5 Seventeen men and twenty-two women were charged before the Magistrate last Friday for taking part in an 'intonjane dance' on the farm. **1937** B.J.F. LAUBSCHER *Sex, Custom & Psychopathology* 143 There are two forms of *Intonjane* ceremonies with a slight variation in the beginning of the rites. **1939** N.J. VAN WARMELO in A.M. Duggan-Cronin *Bantu Tribes* III. i. 33 The proper observance of the intonjane was believed to ensure fecundity, and to promote good health and normal delivery in childbirth. **1955** J.B. SHEPHARD *Land of Tikoloshe* 45 She will not hear of school until her time comes to be 'Intonjane' – a girl initiate. **1980** J. COCK *Maids & Madams* 284 Other Xhosa customs involving women that the missionaries found offensive were the marriage ceremony .. and the initiation ceremony for young girls, the intonjane.

intsango, intsangu varr. INSANGU.

intuna var. INDUNA.

intunkulu var. INDLUNKULU.

inyal(l)a var. NYALA.

inyanga /in'jæŋgə, in'jaːŋga/ *n.* Also **enyanga, inyanger, inyanya, (izi)nyanga**, and with initial capital. Pl. **-s**, or ‖**isinyanga**, ‖**izinyanga**. [Zulu *inyanga* (pl. *izinyanga*) doctor, herbalist, diviner, Xhosa *inyangi* (obs.) doctor, diviner, formed on *nyanga* treat, heal, cure; the word is found in various forms in other Sintu (Bantu) languages. For explanation of sing. and pl. forms, see IN- and IZIN-.]
1. A traditional healer or diviner, esp. one specializing in herbalism; also used as a title. Also *attrib.* See also WITCHDOCTOR.

The term is applied mainly to Zulu traditional healers.

1836 N. ISAACS *Trav.* (1936) I. 82 The 'inyangers,' or water doctors, arrived to take us across the river. **1836** *Ibid.* (1937) II. 82 During her accouchement, she being ill and despaired of, they had been obliged to call in the 'inyangers' or prophets, who suggested that a cow should be sacrificed to appease the Spirit for her recovery. **1852** R.J. GARDEN Diary. I. (Killie Campbell Africana Library MS29081) 21 Apr., An Inyanga or Witch Doctor is a man or woman who administers medicine to people and who pretends to perform cures by means of spells and other ridiculous tricks. He is also supposed to have the power of Divination and is consulted when any one who dies is supposed to have been bewitched. **1862** G.H. MASON *Zululand* 180 An 'Enyanga', as the said professor is called, is a formidable foe; merely as being master of the most deadly poisons in the world. **1875** A. LANG in *Encycl. Brit.* II. 204 The inyanga, or second-sighted man. **1877** LADY BARKER *Yr's Hsekeeping* 176 The witch-finders, .. 'Isinyanga' or 'Abangoma'. **1895** H. RIDER HAGGARD *Nada* 289 Well I knew the arts of healing, my father; I who was the first of the *izinyanga* of medicine. **1897** W.C. SCULLY in E.R. Seary *S. Afr. Short Stories* (1947) 36 He was rich in cattle, and was now celebrated for generosity and hospitality to the i-sanuse and inyanga fraternities, members of which were generally to be found at his kraal. **1928** R.R.R. DLOMO *Afr. Tragedy* 28 On the following day they went with Jane to the Inyanga ... The 'Nyanga, like the rest of his kind, subjected the poor girl to various, humiliating and disgusting examinations and questionings. **1946** *Archit. Rev.* (U.K.) C.22 Before the first stick or stone is cleared the headman has the new site approved and then treated by an inyanga – a specialist in various types of native medicine, a man usually labelled by the ethnocentric European as 'magician'. **1954** W.D. HAMMOND-TOOKE in A.M. Duggan-Cronin *Bantu Tribes* III. Pl.164 (*caption*) A distinction should be drawn between the herbalist (inyanga) and the witch doctor proper (isangoma), sometimes called a diviner, who communes with the ancestral spirits (amathongo). **1956** L. LONGMORE in *S. Afr. Jrnl of Science* Vol.52 No.12, 281 They patronise *izinyanga* (African medicine men) who provide them with drugs to bring luck. **1959** —— *Dispossessed* 233 The doctor or *inyanga* must diagnose and prescribe remedies for ordinary ailments and diseases, prevent or alleviate misfortune, bring prosperity and good luck, and provide protection against bad luck, accidents and witchcraft. **1970** *Post* 28 June, Millionaire inyanga Sethuntsa Khotso, who last year threw the bones and successfully tipped Naval Escort, says that Golden Jewel will win the Durban July next Saturday. **1971** *The 1820* Vol.43 No.12, 26 An inyanga, or medicine woman. **1978** A. ELLIOTT *Sons of Zulu* 24 A medicine-man (nyanga). **1989** *Personality* 29 May 29 Experts estimate that about two thirds of South Africa's population is making more or less regular use of the inyanga and the magico-medical herbs available. **1990** *Bulletin* (Centre for Science Dev.) Jan.-Feb. 7 The Professional Herbal Preparations Association of Inyangas (Pty) Ltd ... Membership: Only bona fide qualified Inyangas. **1990** *Weekly Mail* 23 Mar. 10 Shop stewards at a large metal factory near Johannesburg used routinely to consult an *inyanga* (traditional healer) for 'cleansing medicine' that would fortify them during wage negotiations with management. **1990** R. MALAN *My Traitor's Heart* 185 In 1985 .. some 10,000 sangomas and inyangas were practicing [*sic*] in greater Johannesburg, consulted by 85 percent of all black households.

2. *obs. rare.* An expert, one skilled in a particular craft.

1852 R.J. GARDEN Diary. I. (Killie Campbell Africana Library MS29081) 21 Apr., The word Inyanga is applied strictly speaking to any person skilful in a particular line. **1852** H. FYNN in J. Bird *Annals of Natal* (1888) I. 108 The term 'Inyanga' has a more extensive application, and is not only used to denote a native dispenser of medicines, but a smelter of iron or copper, a blacksmith .. or any one exercising an occupation in which much skill is required.

‖**inyoka** /in'jɔ(ː)ka/ *n.* Also **nhoca, nyoka**. [Xhosa and Zulu.] A snake. Also *attrib.*

1866 W.C. HOLDEN *Past & Future* 300 This was the highest kind of sacred inyoka, or 'serpent'. **1891** R. MONTEIRO *Delagoa Bay* 114, I described the noise to Jack in the morning, and he at once said it was made by a *'nhoca'* snake as thick as his arm. **1894** W.C. BALDWIN *Afr. Hunting* 112 One of the Amatongas .. gave a most unearthly howl, .. saying that an inyoka snake had bitten him. **1937** [see IZINYANYA]. **1958** R. COLLINS *Impassioned Wind* 60 Inyoka! Snake! Where's the snake?

‖**inyongo** /in'jɔ(ː)ŋgɔ/ *n.* [Xhosa and Zulu.] In Nguni society:
1. A gall-bladder, worn by a diviner as part of his traditional dress.

1962 W.D. HAMMOND-TOOKE *Bhaca Soc.* 110 The groom's sister and the sister of the bride have a special part to play in these ceremonies. Each wears an inflated inyongo (gall-bladder) and acts 'just like a witness in a church marriage'.

2. Bile; biliousness.

1966 A.T. BRYANT *Zulu Medicine* 23 Practically all those common attacks of passing indisposition .. are ascribed by them to the bile (*iNyongo*), and their first step is to clear the excess of this fluid out of the system. **1968** *Post* 7 Apr. 12 (*advt*) Sparkling Eno 'Fruit Salt' takes away inyongo in seconds ... You can tell how quickly Eno takes away bile by the fresh, clean taste in your mouth. **1971** *Drum* Jan. 22 (*advt*) Two-action Master Pills act fast to purify kidneys and blood. They get rid of the inyongo that makes you feel sick and weak. **1984** *City Press* 29 Aug. 9 (*advt*) Just one small bottle of Tonika Bile Tonic helps stop that feeling of wanting to be sick. It acts quickly to relieve Inyongo.

IP /aɪ 'piː/ *n.* Initial letters of *Independent Party*, a short-lived party formed in 1988 by breakaway members of the National Party.

One of three groups which merged in 1989 to form the Democratic Party (see note at DP *n.*[2]).

1988 *E. Prov. Herald* 15 Apr. 8 If the new Independent Party thinks it can persuade the Government to allow the SABC to adopt an 'apolitical' line .. it clearly has a lot to learn. But full marks to the IP for trying anyway. **1989** *Race Rel. Survey 1988–9* (S.A.I.R.R.) 595 Mr Luyt asked the leaders of the Progressive Federal Party (PFP), the Independent Party (IP) and the National Democratic Movement (NDM) to meet under his auspices in an attempt to unite them. **1989** D. WORRALL in *Progress* (P.F.P.) Mar. 2 The I.P.'s ability to cut into the National Party's base is clearly necessary if we are going for power — which we certainly are.

iphakathi var. UMPAKATI.

ipiti *n. obs.* Also **epiti, (im)piti, ipi(e)te, iputi, peetie, peté, pootie.** [Zulu *iphithi*, Xhosa *iphuthi*.] The *blue duiker* (see DUIKER sense 1 b), *Philantomba monticola*. Also *attrib.*

1836 R.M. MARTIN *Hist. of S. Afr.* 138 They display considerable taste in the arrangement of their dress, particularly for the head, which is covered by a turban made of the skin of the *'ipiete'*, a species of antelope. **1870** C. HAMILTON *Life & Sport in S.-E. Afr.* 67 We made a permanent stand for a few days to hunt ipiti buck, the smallest of all South African antelopes. **1878** T.J. LUCAS *Camp Life & Sport* 101 Immediately around Pietermaritzburg the game is comparatively scarce, consisting principally of the small Ipite Bok, a graceful little antelope. **1879** R.J. ATCHERLEY *Trip to Boerland* 26 There is little shooting to be obtained near Durban, except in the shape of birds and small buck ... I shot a few small buck known as *impiti*, .. not much larger than a hare, and of a mouse-grey colour, with short spiked horns. **1900** W.L. SCLATER *Mammals of S. Afr.* I. 163 *The Blue Duiker* ... Peté of the Natal Colonists. **1905** D. BLACKBURN *Richard Hartley* 244 The beautiful little ipiti, no bigger than a toy-terrier and quite as sprightly and alert. **1907** W.C. SCULLY *By Veldt & Kopje* 266, I doubt if you would find an 'iputi' in the Didima Forest. **1908** *E. London Dispatch* 18 Nov. 4 (Pettman), The presence in Swaziland of the delicately formed little Natal bluebuck, more generally known as the *piti*, was not suspected until recently. **1912** *Ibid.* 4 Oct. 9 (Pettman), I was after *pooties* at the time. [**1926** R. LYDEKKER *Game Animals Afr.* 143 (heading) Blue Buck or Blue Duiker ... Ipiti, Zulu.] **1934** B.I. BUCHANAN *Pioneer Days* 33 Twice we saw some of the fairy bucks — the darling little ipiti — which immediately won our hearts. **1953** R. CAMPBELL *Mamba's Precipice* 25 Vemvan had found the python fast asleep and scarcely able to wake up, because it had just swallowed a whole peetie-buck.

iqaba var. QABA.

iqabane /ˌiɬa'baːne, iˌka'baːne/ *n.* Pl. usu. **(a)maqabane.** Forms: *sing.* **iqabane**; *sing.* and *pl.* **qabane**; *pl.* **amaqabani, amaq(u)abane, maqabane(s).** Also with initial or medial capital. [Prob. orig. Xhosa, subsequently also Zulu, 'friend', 'companion': sing. prefix I- + *-qabane*, fr. *qabana* be close friends (lit. 'paint, smear each other'), *qaba* paint, smear + reciprocal suffix *-ana* (cf. QABA). For notes on pl. forms, see AMA-, I- and MA- *pref.*[3]] Usu. in *pl.*, as a collective term: *the comrades*, see COMRADE. Also *attrib.*

1985 *E. Prov. Herald* 8 Oct. 3 Youths were enforcing the consumer boycott through manning .. 'maqabane roadblocks', meaning comrades' roadblocks, where passing cars were being stoned if they failed to stop. **1986** [see Cape Times quot. at FATHERS]. **1986** *Cape Times* 3 Jan. 9 The 'fathers' had abducted at least three 'maqabanes' (comrades) .. and were holding them prisoner in a shipping container in Crossroads. **1986** *Learn & Teach* No.3, 2 In New Crossroads near Cape Town, the 'fathers' beat the 'maqabane' because 'maqabane' said people must boycott white shops. **1988** K. MKHIZE in *Frontline* Feb. 12 He explained: '... Where I stay .. you meet someone at night who greets you "Qabane, Qabane heyta!" Whatever you do, you may receive a bullet hole ... If you deny you are a qabane then you are in trouble if the strangers are in fact comrades.' **1988** J. SIKHAKHANE in *Pace* Nov. 61 In other townships around Durban .. vigilante groups called 'amabutho' or impi, were allegedly responsible for deaths and attacks on the amaqabane, mostly youths belonging to the UDF, or politically neutral. **1989** *Frontline* Apr. 11 'Nobody is neutral ... If you are not a member of Inkatha then you are an iQabane.' I said: 'You mean everybody must either be Inkatha or UDF?' **1990** *Weekly Mail* 9 Mar. 9 He saluted the crowd with the novel 'Viva Maqabane!' The crowd was too goodnatured to care much and responded enthusiastically. **1990** [see Kaunda quot. at HEIT sense a]. **1990** *Weekend Argus* 29 Sept. 1 The youths, mostly in African National Congress T-shirts and calling themselves 'amaqabani' (comrades), were addressed by four special constables.

iqika, iquira varr. IGQIRA *n.*[2]

iron *n. obs.* Ellipt. for IRONWOOD.

1892 W.L. DISTANT *Naturalist in Tvl* 43 Trees are more plentiful, but are principally long-spined acacias and 'iron' and other hard-wooded species.

iron hog *n. phr. Obs.* [tr. of S. Afr. Du. *ystervark*.] YSTERVARK.

1786 G. FORSTER tr. *A. Sparrman's Voy. to Cape of G.H.* I. 151 The *hystrix cristata* of *Linnaeus*, called by the colonists here *yzer-varken* (or the *iron-hog*,) is the same animal as the Germans carry about for show in our country by the name of the *porcupine*. **1810** G. BARRINGTON *Acct of Voy.* 282 They have .. an animal that burrows in the ground, called the *yzer varke*, or iron hog, the flesh of which, when salted and dried, is esteemed by the Dutch as a great delicacy. **1835** A. STEEDMAN *Wanderings* I. 81 On returning we fell in with a porcupine, *hystrix cristata* .. : the Dutch call it *yzer varke*, or the iron hog.

ironie /'aɪ(ə)ni/ *n.* Also **inie.** [Formed on Eng. *iron* + (informal) n.-forming suffix *-ie* (or Afk. -IE).] In the language of schoolchildren: a large ball-bearing used as a marble. Cf. GHOEN sense a. See also ARLIE.

1948 V.M. FITZROY *Cabbages & Cream* 135, I have a fellow-feeling for .. Terence when he comes to me in despair and says that his inie and his blood-alley have gone again. **1970** A.J. DU PREEZ *Informant, Misgund (W. Cape)* Ironie. Iron marble, usually the ball of a ball bearing. **1971** K. HOBSON *Informant, Grahamstown* On Wednesday we're going all round the garages to ask for ironies, .. ball bearings to use as marbles. **1972** *E. Prov. Herald* 3 Apr. 17 Watching the youngsters 'sticking up' their ghoens, precious king sizes and ironies, there was little doubt of the seriousness of it all. **1973** *Argus* 2 Apr. 20 Hoffie and the grubby children watched with awe and admiration as the General's 'ironie' scattered the marbles with deadly accuracy. **1985** *E. Prov. Herald* 27 Feb. 1 Ready to catch the marbles of hopefuls taking shots at his monster 'ironie' in Grey Junior School's 'arlie patch'. **1988** [see ARLIE]. **1990** *Fair Lady* 6 June 11 They stagger off to school with bank bags bulging with ironies and alies.

ironwood *n.* [tr. S. Afr. Du. *ysterhout*, fr. Du. *yster* iron + *hout* wood.]

a. Any of several trees characterized by their very hard wood, esp. species of *Olea*, *Millettia*, and *Vepris*; the timber itself; IRON; YZER; YZER HOUT. Also *attrib.* See also UMZIMBEET.

'Ironwood' is also in general English use, as a name for other species.

1693 *Phil. Trans. of Royal Soc.* (U.K.) XVII. 621 An Iron-wood from the Cape. **1731** G. MEDLEY tr. *P. Kolb's Present State of Cape of G.H.* II. 248 *Sideroxilum Africanum, Cerasi folio.* i.e. African Iron-wood, with a Cherry Leaf. This Wood is so call'd because, when dry, 'tis as hard as Iron, and not to be clove by the most furious Strokes with the Hatchet. **1804** R. PERCIVAL *Acct of Cape of G.H.* 148 The iron wood, or yezer hout, is very common, and grows very high. The wood is hard, heavy, and of a dark brown colour. **1821, 1822** [see YZER HOUT]. **1836** A.F. GARDINER *Journey to Zoolu Country* 238 A wood of very handsome trees, chiefly umzani, and what are known in the Colony by the name of sneeze and iron-wood. **1850** J.E. METHLEY *New Col. of Port Natal* 31 There is also the ironwood (olea undulata), which for its hard grain and durability is used for the axles of waggons. **1859** R.J. MANN *Col. of Natal* 157 The hardest and toughest of the woods of Natal is that known under the native name *'Umsimbiti' (iron-wood)*. **1870** C. HAMILTON *Life & Sport in S.-E. Afr.* 6 The wheels are made of the famous Natal wood called 'umsimbiti' or ironwood, from its strength and durability. **1916** *Farmer's Weekly* 20 Dec. 1456 Wagons. Hand-made Buckwagons, made from the best seasoned Colonial Hardwoods, Stinkwood, Assegai, Ironwood and Hickory. **1919** *Dunell, Ebden & Co.'s Price List* Aug. 35 *Disselbooms.* Ironwood. **1936** E. ROSENTHAL *Old-Time Survivals* 10 Ironwood, a type of rare African timber so heavy that it will not float in water, was (and is) selected for the 'onderstel' or under-frame. **1955** [see UMZIMBEET]. **1973** *E. Prov. Herald* 28 May 13 Wake up .. to the smell of a smouldering ironwood fire and old ash. **1990** *Weekend Post* 14 July (Leisure) 4 He makes to order from popular woods like stinkwood, oak and imbuia, and wild woods like ironwood and wild pear.

b. With distinguishing epithet: **bastard ironwood** [see BASTARD *adj.*], *Olea capensis L.* subsp. *capensis* of the Oleaceae; **black ironwood,** *(a) O. capensis L.* subsp. *macrocarpa*; *(b)* less commonly, the KERSHOUT (sense 2), *Rothmannia capensis*; **bushveld ironwood,** *O. capensis L.* subsp. *enervis*; **white ironwood,** *(a) Vepris lanceolata* of the Rutaceae; *(b)* the UMZIMBEET, *Millettia grandis*.

1913 C. PETTMAN *Africanderisms* 49 **Bastard ironwood,** *Olea foveolata*, a common South African forest tree. **1988** *Conserva* Oct. 28 The bark of the bastard ironwood is dark grey with white and black patches, longitudinally striated, and becomes corky and rough with age. The wood is dull grey-brown, close-grained and very hard and heavy. **1796** C.R. HOPSON tr. *C.P. Thunberg's Trav.* II. 109 **Black iron wood** *(Zwarte Ysterhout, Gardenia Rothmannia)* is hard and strong; it is used for axle-trees and the poles of waggons. **1920** [see OUTENIQUA sense 2]. **1955** A. DELIUS *Young Trav.* 114 The most abundant is the black ironwood. They call it that on account of the toughness of its timber. **1988** H. GOOSEN in *S. Afr. Panorama* Aug. 49 The black ironwood, *O. capensis* subsp. *macrocarpa*, reaches a height of 40 m and grows in indigenous forests from the Transvaal to the Cape Province. The false ironwood, *O. capensis* subsp. *capensis*, and the **bushveld ironwood,** *O. capensis* subsp. *enervis*, also prefer wooded areas. **1989** *Conserva* Vol.4 No.4, 22 *Olea capensis* subsp. *enervis*. Bushveld ironwood. It has not been possible to germinate this seed. **1843** J.C. CHASE *Cape of G.H.* 160 Iron Wood; black and **white.** **1891** R. SMITH *Great Gold Lands* 179 Perhaps it may be useful to say what the timber-yielding plants of Natal are. The best known are .. black iron-wood, an olive (*Olea latifolia*); white iron-wood, allied to the rues. **1902** G.S. BOULGER *Wood* 335 Umzimbit .. Known also as 'White Ironwood'. **1951** N.L. KING *Tree-Planting* 71 *Vepris (Toddalia) lanceolata (White ironwood)*, A medium- to large-sized, evergreen tree with pretty foliage. **1961** PALMER & PITMAN *Trees of S. Afr.* 274 The white ironwood is found in most of the forests of the Union as a tall evergreen tree; or in open forest or scrub as a spreading tree or bush. **1989** *E. Prov. Herald* 25 Feb. 5 The 'Cape chestnut' is .. one of the several South African

isakubula var. SAKABULA.

isangoma var. SANGOMA.

isanusi /ˌisaˈnuːsi/ *n.* Also **(i)sanuse, izanusi, sanusi,** and with initial capital. Pl. unchanged, or **-s**. [Zulu *isanusi* (pl. *izanusi*), Xhosa *isanuse* (pl. *izanuse*), diviner, formed on *nusa* contraction of *nukisa, nuka* divine, 'smell out' + causative suffix *-isa*. For notes on the use of Nguni pl. prefixes, see ISI- and IZI-.] A traditional healer or diviner, often an aged practitioner who has developed his or her psychic gifts, and whose clairvoyant powers enable him or her to 'smell out' evil; *smeller out*, see SMELL; *smelling doctor*, see DOCTOR sense 1 b; also used as a title, and *attrib*. See also WITCHDOCTOR.

> 1852 H. FYNN in J. Bird *Annals of Natal* (1888) I. 107 The Kafir term employed to designate the person called a 'witchdoctor' is 'Isanusi'... This designation is specific, and indicates one who is not only gifted with an extraordinary power of discernment, but who has also an intercourse with the spiritual world. 1885 H. RIDER HAGGARD *King Solomon's Mines* 163 Are your senses awake, Isanusis — can ye smell blood, can ye purge the land of the wicked ones who compass evil against the king and against their neighbours? 1891 T.R. BEATTIE *Pambaniso* 24 The witchdoctor to whom the task of smelling out the guilty one has been entrusted, was of the Izanusi class, and many brave men in the crowd trembled, lest this terrible personage should adjudge them guilty of the crime. 1897 [see INYANGA sense 1]. 1937 B.J.F. LAUBSCHER *Sex, Custom & Psychopathology* 35 The *i-sanuses* thus form the specialist group of this profession and their healing is mostly done by psychic means and the performance of certain rituals. They conform to what are known by us as mediums. 1949 O. WALKER *Proud Zulu* (1951) 54 As for the invisible — that was for the izinyanga and izanusi to resolve with their frenzied dancing, their communion with the spirits, their subtle powers of smelling-out evildoers, their mastery of the elements that could bring rain, thunder and hail, their medicines gathered in lonely places that could heal or kill, according to their purpose. 1955 E.A. RITTER *Shaka Zulu* 38 He forthwith gave orders for the killing of an ox, as a propitiatory offering to the spirits, and sent for a renowned isanuse (witchdoctor) living close by. 1974 C.T. BINNS *Warrior People* 259 The term isaNusi is derived from the now obsolete Zulu verb uku-*Nusa* meaning to smell... Thus the *isaNusi* is the person whose chief task is to 'Smell Out', or track down the wrong-doer, the wizard or witch... The word *isaNusi* is also used to indicate one who is not only gifted with extraordinary powers of discernment but who is also able to hold intercourse with the spiritual world through his own particular spirit or Familiar. 1977 *S. Afr. Panorama* Oct. 22 The highest order.. is the *Isanuse* who has gone through a process of psychic development and is able to foretell events and communicate with ancestral spirits. He also has second sight and can see into the unseen. 1983 *Pace* Dec. 23 In the language of the Hitites a high priest is known as a 'sanusi' or 'sanuzi.' In the language of the Hindus a holy man is known as a 'sanyasi'. In Zulu he is known as a 'sanusi' or an 'isazi,' which immediately connects the Hitites' 'sanasi' and the word 'sanusi'.

iscamto var. ISICAMTHO.

iscathamiya var. ISICATHAMIYA.

Iscor /ˈɪskɔː/ *n.* [Acronym formed on *Iron and Steel (Industrial) Corporation*.] A corporation producing iron and steel, established (as a parastatal) in 1928. Also *attrib.*, and *fig.*

> [1928 *Act 11* in *Stat. of Union* 160 Upon a date to be determined by the Governor-General and notified by proclamation in the *Gazette* there shall be constituted and incorporated a company, under the name of the South African Iron and Steel Industrial Corporation, Limited.] 1936 R.J.M. GOOLD-ADAMS *S. Afr. To-Day & To-Morrow* 143 'Iscor' (South African Iron & Steel Corporation) is.. a Government concern. 1943 'J. BURGER' *Black Man's Burden* 199 At the Iscor (Iron and Steel Corporation) works, in 1939, Afrikaner workers, organised by the Nationalists, held protest meetings against the alleged discharge of European workers who were to be replaced by Natives. 1951 *Yr Bk & Guide to Sn Afr.* 1951 97 (Advt), Iscor, the primary producer of iron and steel in South Africa. 1972 *Weekend Post* 14 Oct. 1 Senator Horwood said an agreement.. was being negotiated between Iscor and the Steelworkers Union. c1988 *S. Afr.* 1987–8: *Off. Yrbk* (Bureau for Info.) 431 Iscor was established in Pretoria in 1928 to promote the development of the iron and steel and allied industries. Iscor today has three plants.. which produced 6,2-million tons of liquid steel in 1984/85. 1990 *Staffrider* Vol.9 No.1, 32 High-ranking public officials in our land must be made of very firm material. Iscor steel. 1991 I. BERELOWITZ in *Weekend Argus* 26 Jan. (Weekender) 2 He gained a concession to collect all old scrap iron and formed the Union Steel Company, the forerunner of Iscor.

isi- /isi/ *pref.* A Xhosa and Zulu singular noun prefix found in some words originating in these languages.

In Xhosa and Zulu, the plural of words beginning *isi-* is formed by replacing this prefix with *izi-*. In S. Afr. Eng. this pattern is not always observed, the plural sometimes being formed by adding the English plural suffix *-s* to the singular form; less often, the singular form is used, unchanged, as a plural. See also IZI-.

‖**isibonda** /ˌisiˈbɔːndɑ/ *n.* Pl. **izibonda(s)**, or unchanged. [Zulu (pl. *izibonda*), head or principal member.] Among Nguni people:

1. A civic leader; a government official.

> 1907 W.C. SCULLY *By Veldt & Kopje* 61 He called a great council of the 'Izibonda' (lit. 'poles,' such as those which support the roof of a hut) or elders, as well as the numerous petty chiefs who owned his sway. 1983 *Frontline* Feb. 38 Often the Izibonda (civic leaders) or Bomabalane, act in concert with Abelungu officials. 1985 BLONDEL & LAMB *Parrot's Egg* 60 The magistrate ruled the people with the help of the headmen paid by the white government. The Xhosa called them 'izibonda' — supportive poles — existing only to support a system above their heads. 1988 SPIEGEL & WELDT in Boonzaier & Sharp *S. Afr. Keywords* 50 Headmen came to be 'commonly regarded as instruments of alien control, and earned themselves the title of *isibonda* or "poles" supporting the colonial administration'.

2. The elected representative of each unit of rooms in a mining hostel, acting as an arbitrator of complaints. Also *attrib*. See also HOSTEL sense 1.

> 1946 *Tribal Natives & Trade Unionism* (Tvl Chamber of Mines) 7 In the mine compound the pattern is the compound manager, the Induna, the tribal representative — called the Isibonda — and the room headboy, who takes the position of the kraal head. 1962 A.P. CARTWRIGHT *Gold Miners* 221 Each room has an *isibonda* who is elected by the occupants and who conveys complaints and suggestions to the headman. 1977 C. HEEVER in *Optima* Vol.27 No.2, 126 The *izibondas*.. that is communications committees comprising representatives elected by employees,.. which will be spokesmen elected by the occupants of each room, who will have an important two-way communications role. 1988 RAMPHELE & BOONZAIER in Boonzaier & Sharp *S. Afr. Keywords* 157 A system of discipline.. involves electing one bed-holder from each 'door' (a unit of rooms, usually six, which shares one external door) to act as convener, arbitrator and chairman of disciplinary hearings... Such conveners are called *izibonda*, since their role closely resembles that of men in rural areas who are often used by government authorities to control local villages. *Ibid.* 160 The *izibonda* system.. is monopolised by older men.

isibongi pl. form of IMBONGI.

‖**isibongo** /ˌisiˈbɔːŋɡɔ, ˌisiːˈbɔŋɡəʊ/ *n.* Also **esebongo, (i)sibonga, sibongo,** and with initial capital. Pl. usu. **izibongo**; occas. **isibongos, izi-(m)bongi, izimbongo.** [Xhosa and Zulu. In these languages, the sing. form *isibongo* is used only with reference to a clan name or praise name; the pl. form *izibongo* is used of clan names, but also of a praise poem, which is made up of numerous praises.]

1. A clan name, praise name, or surname used among Xhosa- and Zulu-speakers. Also *attrib*. See also *bonga-name* (BONGA *v.* sense 2).

In this sense, forms in *izi-* always represent the plural.

The 'isibongo' name usu. constitutes the first word or words of a praise poem (see sense 2 below).

> 1857 J. SHOOTER *Kafirs of Natal* 220 The other name is called *isi-bonga* — a noun formed from *uku-bonga* to praise. This is an honorary name, borne in addition to the i-gama, and independently of it. 1870 H. CALLAWAY *Religious System of Amazulu* 337 These words are *izibongo* or praise-giving names, by which the doctor addresses the bone which is taken from the porcupine. Each bone has its *isibongo*, one or more. 1875 D. LESLIE *Among Zulus* 146 Each tribe has its own 'Esebongo,' name of thanks; for instance, one tribe is called Emtetwa, or scolders. *Ibid.* 204 This 'Isibongo' is taken from some trait in a man's character, from his bravery, his strength, or his comeliness. 1895 H. RIDER HAGGARD *Nada* p.ix, I give you your 'Sibongo'.. and that royal salute, to which you are alone entitled. [Note] Titles of praise. 1936 *Cambridge Hist. of Brit. Empire* VIII. 45 In the south-eastern tribes all the people claiming descent from the same ancestor in the male line bore a common *isibongo*, or laudatory name, which was usually that of the common ancestor. 1967 O. WALKER *Hippo Poacher* 49 A man came to Laita's kraal at this time claiming to be of the same *sibongo*, or praise name, as Laita. 1978 A. ELLIOTT *Sons of Zulu* 15 One reason why a surname or family name (*sibongo*) is not.. used more.., is that clans generally live grouped together in specific areas under their own chieftains and.. have the same clan names or 'surnames'. *Ibid.* 46 Zulu took a wife from a clan in the neighbourhood and his son or sons took the name Zulu as their *sibongo* or family name. 1993 K. MAKAKA Informant My first name is Kasiya, my father's name is Henry, my grandfather's names are Chitamba and Makaka and his 'Isibongo' is Banda. I prefer to drop the 'Isibongo' because it belongs to millions [of] other people and because.. I should get my 'Isibongo' from my maternal grandmother.

2. Freq. *pl.* (sometimes with a singular construction). A collection of praises together constituting a praise poem; praise poetry; IMBONGI sense 2. Also *attrib.* See also BONGA *n.*

As oral poetry, izibongo are considered one of the principal art-forms of the Zulu- and Xhosa-speaking peoples. The term is now also applied to printed poems written in the style of traditional izibongo, including some in English.

> 1903 *Ilanga* 9 Oct. 4 The Izibongo, or 'praises', in which the deeds of ancestors and great men are recited, were.. valuable storehouses of historic fact. 1937 C. BIRKBY *Zulu Journey* 72 The assembled men chanted the famous Isibongos — the official paeans of praise which are accorded to each of the Zulu kings. Chaka, Dingaan, Mpande, Cetywayo, Dinizulu and Solomon each have their own personal Isibongo, fulsome and repetitive, but nevertheless sacred and immutable as the full name and title of England's sovereigns. c1948 H. TRACEY *Lalela Zulu* 17 This Zulu song.. is in the style of all Izibongo, the familiar Zulu praises to their heroes. 1949 O. WALKER *Proud Zulu* (1951) 186 'Thou glancest and grazest them with spears,' said Sibebu's own 'isibongo' in honour of Mbuyana. 'Quick stabbing is best, O Mbuyana!' 1959 L. LONGMORE *Dispossessed* The bride sat down and an old man.. stood up to bonga her with izibongo, that is, to laud her with praises. The izibongo at urban weddings are dying out because the old people who

live in town today cannot remember the family incidents of olden times. **1978** *Speak* Vol.1 No.5, 4 Selections included .. African hymns .. and traditional praise singing (izibongo) in the vernacular, and traditional rural African music. **1980** D.B. Coplan Urbanization of African Performing Arts. 276 Most missionary teachers ignored the elaborate improvisational mime and dramatic recitation of indigenous *izibongo* (Zulu: praise poetry) and *izintsomi* (Zulu: storytelling). **1983** *Rand Daily Mail* 26 May 9 His tale varied from time to time but never failed to be recounted to the shouting and pantomime of an African praiser proclaiming his chief's *isibongo*. **1987** *NELM News* (Nat. Eng. Lit. Museum) May 1 The traditional praise poem or *izibongo* has enjoyed a particularly vital renascence in the context of the labour movement. This is reflected in the recent publication of .. a collection of verse by 'worker poets' .., originally performed at trade union meetings in Natal. *Izibongo* of this sort are a unique tool in raising workers' consciousness of their union and its role in their lives. **1988** A. Sitas in Bunn & Taylor *From S. Afr.* 278 After hearing Qabula perform his *izimbongo* of Fosatu, he realized that one did not need to be somebody from the university to write poetry.

||**isicamtho** /ˌis(i)ˈlaːmtɔ/ *n.* Also **(i)scamto, isiqamtho, scamtho.** [Xhosa or Zulu, see quot. 1987.] FLAAITAAL; but see quot. 1993.

See note at FLAAITAAL.

1980 *Voice* 20 Aug. 14 Scamto goes hand in glove with Jit, khwela, marabi, mbaqanga, soul, jazz, disco-jive. **1981** [see SASAFRIKA]. **1981** [see OKAPI]. **1982** *Star* 11 Nov. (Tonight) 4 In Soweto .. 'die majitas' indulge in a colourful 'taal' called scamtho. This is a concoction of Zulu merged with other dialects and a bit of English. It also swallows other European words. **1987** C.T. Msimang in *S. Afr. Jrnl of Afr. Langs* Vol.7 No.3, 85 Tsotsi terms from inflected Zulu words ... *Isiqamtho* comes from the verb *-qamutha* or *-qamunda* (talk volubly or maintain a constant flow of language) ... Never refer to their medium as Tsotsitaal ... Among themselves, their medium is *isiqamtho* (or *isicamtho*), which implies that they really have a gift of the tongue. There is a possiblity that this word is derived from Xhosa, a sister language of Zulu, where to speak volubly is to *qamtha*. **1993** M. ka Harvey in *Weekly Mail* 23 Dec. 15 The Sophiatown influence can .. be seen in township lingo, which varies from group to group. There is '*tsotsi taal*' (mainly spoken in Meadowlands and Rockville), '*isicamtho*' (spoken by the youth), 'jive lingo' (influenced by African Jah) and pristine '*wietie*', directly from Sophiatown.

isicathamiya /(ɪ)s(i)kataˈmija, ˌis(i)-, -lata-/ *n. Music.* Also **(i)scathamiya, sic(h)athamiya,** and with initial capital. [Zulu, lit. 'stalking movement', formed on n. prefix ISI- + *cathama* stand or walk stealthily or on tip-toe (referring to the movements of the singers).] MBUBE. Also *attrib.*

1980 B. Mthethwa in *Papers, Symposium on Ethnomusicology* (Internat. Library of Afr. Music, 1981) 24 The secular version of the hymn resulted in today's black popular music. The more serious, emotional text of this secular hymn became known as *ingomabusuku* (night song) or, as we call it today, *sicathamiya*. **1982** *Pace* Feb. 69 They call themselves The Lovely Brothers, they are a group of seven, and they say their bag is *Scathamiya* (Zulu choral folk music). **1988** J. Khumalo in *Ibid.* May 7 Everybody knows that Isicathamiya has all these years been regarded as music of the rustics. Sophisticated blacks wouldn't be seen dead appreciating this kind of 'junk'. **1989** G. O'Hara in *Weekly Mail* 20 Jan. 25 Leader of the 10-man *isicathamiya* (or *mbube*) group, Joseph Shabalala, .. is 'very happy that people overseas have accepted our music, our singing without instruments ... In New York, many ladies and gentlemen .. are singing *isicathamiya*'. **1989** A. Tracey *Informant, Grahamstown* Isicathamiya grew out of mbube and the name refers to the movement associated with singing the songs ... The songs are often gospel songs, but isicathamiya does not necessarily have to be gospel music. **1990** *Tribute* Apr. 24 A'capella music became harmonised and then that was the birth of Ngomabusuku/Sicathamiya, which evolved into what Ladysmith Black Mambazo is doing today. **1990** *Weekly Mail* 21 Dec. (Suppl.) 31 We have seen Grammy-award-winners Ladysmith Black Mambazo put *'sichatamiya* (antiphonal/choral call and response/*mbube*) music back on the map. **1994** *Weekly Mail & Guardian* 13 May 9 A spirited African interpretation of Ravel's *Bolero*, complete with drums and gumboot dancing; *isicathamiya* and doo-wop choruses.

isichwe /iˈsiːɬwe, iˈsiːtʃwe/ *n.* Also **isicwe.** [Xhosa.] The bulbous plant *Ammocharis coranica* of the Amaryllidaceae; the bulb sheaths of this plant, used medicinally. Also *attrib.*

1967 J.A. Broster *Red Blanket Valley* 127 The initiates were taken by their *amakhankatha* to gather the bulbs of *isichwe*. These bulbs .. belong to the genus Boophane of the family Amaryllidacae. The medical properties of this bulb were known to the Bushmen and Hottentots long before the arrival of the ama-Xhosa. **1976** S. Fugard *Rite of Passage* 43 Find the bulbs of the *isichwe* plant. Search for these bulbs. Three or four times the size of an onion. **1989** *Weekend Post* 9 Dec. 7 Soft medicinal leaves (*isicwe*) used to bind the wound.

||**isicoco** /ˌisiˈlɔːlɔ/ *n.* Also **esikoko, isigcoco, isig(c)oko, issigoko.** [Zulu.] HEAD-RING.

1836 A.F. Gardiner *Journey to Zoolu Country* 100 Both men and women shave their heads close, the former leaving only sufficient to attach the issigoko, or *ring*. **1839** W.C. Harris *Wild Sports* 121 All their heads were shaven, sufficient hair only being left to attach the *issigoko*, which is composed of sinews sewn to the hair, and blackened with grease. **1855** J.W. Colenso *Ten Weeks in Natal* 10 He has cut off his *isigcoco*, (ring of hair upon his head, worn by married heathens), and dressed himself like a Christian. **1860** A.W. Drayson *Sporting Scenes* 58 A ring, composed of grease, wax and wood, is worn on the head of the kaffir men. I believe it to be a sign of a man having arrived at the dignity of marriage; it is called esikoko, the two k's signifying two clicks of the tongue. **1940** F.B. Young *City of Gold* 114 The magnificent figure of an *induna* stepped out and towered over him ... Encircling his head he wore the *isigoko*, a ring of fibre covered with twisted sinews attached to the roots of unshaven hair and blackened with beeswax. **1949** O. Walker *Proud Zulu* (1951) 106 The king had his black-shielded regiments of single men, and his white-shielded regiments of married men who had his permission to take wives and wear the isicoco, or head-ring. **1974** C.T. Binns *Warrior People* 183 *Note on the Isicoco* ... It was built up from .. a latex, collected from certain bushes indigenous to Zululand, which the craftsman worked in the palm of his hand until it took on the texture of putty ... It was .. kneaded and shaped into a long sausage which was carefully wound round an oval framework ... It was then sewn firmly to his hair with threads of sinew which, when completely cold, formed a solid, hard, black, latex ring. Finally this was rubbed with grease and polished with a small stone until it took on the appearance of polished jet. **1981** M. Kunene *Anthem of Decades* p.xx, The headring (isicoco) symbolic of the ultimate wisdom.

isidwaba /ˌisiˈdwaːba/ *n.* Also **sidwaba.** [Zulu.] A pleated hide skirt or kilt worn by a Zulu woman as a sign of betrothal or marriage; *transf.*, the woman who wears such a skirt.

1956 J. Chatterton *Return of Drums* 22 She has large holes in the lobes of her ears, a sign that she had at one time been a heathen, a sidwaba – one who wears a skin skirt. **1964** G. Campbell *Old Dusty* 2 We hailed them at this unexpected strip-tease exhibition to warn them of our presence, when, with a great deal of screaming and giggling, they grabbed up their *isidwabas*, while we strolled back to .. our camping site. **1967** O. Walker *Hippo Poacher* 128, I undid my *isidwaba* (hide skirt) gently and rolled it up. **1976** West & Morris *Abantu* 40 The bride wears her new black leather skirt, the isidwaba of a married woman. **1978** A. Elliott *Sons of Zulu* 169 Important developments take place in the courtship sequence ... She .. has to discard her girl's skirt and don the leatherpleated skirt or sidwaba of a woman. **1988** L. Kaunda in *Pace* Oct. 50 A black isidwaba (cowhide skirt), leopard skins and intricate beadware.

isiDwadwa var. DWADWA.

isigcoco, isig(c)oko varr. ISICOCO.

||**isigodlo** /isiˈgɔːɮɔ/ *n.* Also **isigo(d)hlo.** [Zulu.] The Zulu king's private enclosure within the royal kraal, containing the huts of his wives and children.

1835 A.F. Gardiner in J. Bird *Annals of Natal* (1888) I. The road branched off, one path leading to the principal gate of the town, and the other to the 'Isigodhlo', or King's quarter. **1855** J.W. Colenso *Ten Weeks in Natal* 108 The fence .. separated the *isiGodhlo*, or royal parts, from the central area. **1857** J. Shooter *Kafirs of Natal* 116 The *isi-gohlo*, or palace .. which is appropriated to the king and the women of his family, is furnished with several huts. **1898** B. Mitford *Induna's Wife* 32 With these words Umzilikazi rose and retired within the *isigodhlo*. **1949** O. Walker *Proud Zulu* (1951) 10 During his 40 years in Zululand Dunn acquired great wealth in cattle ... and girls from the Zulu king's own isigodhlo or harem who were presented to him as gifts. **1983** *Pace* Dec. 85 Even in a changed form .. the *isigodlo* or forecourt, which they have used, sadly seems to be missing from their architecture in the homeland.

isijita /isiˈdʒi(ː)ta/ *n. nonce.* Also **sjita,** and with initial capital. [Coined by Buntu Mfenyana; *isi-* in the Sintu (Bantu) languages a prefix denoting a language + *-jita* see MAJITA.] FLAAITAAL.

1979 B. Mfenyana *Neo-Sintu: Dynamic Challenge*, Bra Biza's Test Yourself Quiz ... Write a 200-word essay on *isijita*. **1980** *Voice* 20 Aug. 14 Buntu Mfenyana .. has carried out research into what he interestingly refers to as: 'Isijita-Scamto: the Black Language Arts in Sasafrika.' **1980** B. Mfenyana in *Ibid.* 14 We can speak of language wars, struggles, courts, conventions, festivals and revolutions. Our discussion of these would not be complete if we left out Sjita-scamto: a creole with mainly Afrikaans, Sintu and English elements – used by 15 million people in Sasafrika alone. Sjita raises its own unique questions, but it is also part of the rapid change that has swept across the sub-continent since 1900. **1981** — in M. Mutloatse *Reconstruction* 300 The international side of Sjita .. makes it even more fascinating.

isikorokoro var. SKOROKORO.

isiNdebele var. SINDEBELE.

isinduna pl. form of INDUNA.

isiNtu var. SINTU.

isinyanga pl. form of INYANGA.

isiqamtho var. ISICAMTHO.

isishimyana, isishishimeyane varr. SHIMIYANA.

isishweshwe var. SESHWESHWE.

is it *int. phr. Colloq.* [Calque formed on Afk. *is dit?* is that so?] A rhetorical expression equivalent to 'really?' 'is that so?', conveying polite interest, astonishment, or incredulity. Cf. ISN'T IT.

1970 Beeton & Dorner in *Eng. Usage in Sn Afr.* Vol.1 No.2, 33 *Is it?* Meaningless S. Afr. colloquialism for 'Is that so?', eg 'I am going to town this morning' – '*Is it?*' **1970** J. Stodel *Informant, Cape Town* 'I came by car you know.' 'Oh, is it?' ('Is that so?' 'really?' 'You don't mean to say?') **1972** R. Malan *Ah Big Yaws* 55 *Uzzit? Uzzitay?* Very useful in the sort of conversation where you're not quite sure what your reaction should be. As in: A: 'You see, this cable leads from the carburettor to the distributor and that activates the differential.' B: 'Uzzit?' **1972** *Star* 15 Nov. 18 In South Africa one can actually carry on a conversation quite easily by using only four words: 'Shame,' 'Hey' and 'Is it?' **1973** J. Cope *Alley Cat* 96 'Next time you see him he may have begun to talk.' 'Is it!' 'Yes, God willing.'

1978 M. TLALI in *Staffrider* Vol.1 No.3, 4 'They're *so* mad about it. Even Maria read it.' 'Is it. I am very happy to hear that.' 1987 *Informant*, Grahamstown 'The people bought it in 1920 and converted it into a house.' 'Is it?' 1990 [see KIF].

Isithwalandwe /ˌisitwaˈlaːndwe/ *n*. Also **Isitwalandwe**. [Xhosa.] A high honour awarded originally among Xhosas for bravery in battle, and in recent times by the African National Congress for service to the people.

1955 *Bantu World* 2 July 1 Three people were decorated with the Isithwalandwe at the Congress of the People last Sunday ... 'the highest honour that Africans can bestow for meritorious services to the community. In the olden times, .. this honour was given to African heroes who distinguished themselves on the field of battle. It is a feather which they wore on their heads. It was only given on rare occasions.' 1962 A.J. LUTHULI *Let my People Go* 158 The people bestowed a great honour on Dr. Dadoo, the Indian leader, on Father Huddleston, and on me. The Xhosa title *Isitwalandwe* was conferred on each of us. 1963 M. BENSON *Afr. Patriots* 214 The *Isitwalandwe* — the feather worn by the heroes of the people symbolizing the highest distinction in African society. 1989 *SR Scene* (Rhodes Univ., Nusas SRC) Oct. 1 She [sc. Helen Joseph] has also been awarded the Isithwalandwe — the highest honour accorded by the ANC.

isitongo pl. form of ITONGO.

‖**isituta** /ˌisiˈtʊːta/ *n*. Also **isi-tute, issetator, issitata, issitoota**. Pl. unchanged. [Zulu *isithutha*.] Among Zulus: an ancestral spirit; a snake embodying such a spirit. Also *attrib*. See also ITONGO.

1836 A.F. GARDINER *Journey to Zoolu Country* 152 The transmigration of souls .. was universally believed among them ... The breath or spirit then passed into the body of some animal, generally a snake, called issitata, which is harmless. *Ibid*. 314 They knew not how long the issitoota, or Spirit of the deceased person, existed after its departure from the body. 1836 N. ISAACS *Trav.* (1937) II. 248 These are also sworn to tell the truth, by an appeal to the 'Issetator' or Spirit of their forefathers, which is their most sacred oath. 1857 [see Shooter quot. at IDLOZI]. 1866 W.C. HOLDEN *Past & Future* 284 The name of ghosts or departed spirits is, Amaxosa, *imishologu*; Natal, *isituta*. *Ibid*. 285 Other crimes relate to the body and time; these, to the manes of the dead, and the mysterious dwelling-place in which the *isituta* reside. 1934 C.P. SWART *Supplement to Pettman*. 79 *Isituta*, A Zulu term meaning a family or ancestral spirit ... The spirit of the dead man calls out to his brother to perpetuate his memory, and the brother buys a wife with the dead man's property and establishes in his .. kraal an Isituta House (Spirit House) and the eldest son of the wife of the House succeeds to the dead brother's property.

Isitwalandwe var. ISITHWALANDWE.

isityimiyana var. SHIMIYANA.

isiXhosa see XHOSA.

isiyanya var. IZINYANYA.

isiZulu var. ZULU *n*. sense 2.

Island *n. colloq*. Also with small initial. *The Island*: ROBBEN ISLAND sense 1. Also *attrib*.

1969 M. BENSON *At Still Point* (1988) 159 There are days on the Island when the warders are 'greedy for violence'. 1982 A.P. BRINK *Chain of Voices* 210 'If I'm lucky, it's the gallows.' 'And if you're not?' 'Then it's the island.' 'The island?' 'Robben Island.' 1990 G. SLOVO *Ties of Blood* 611 'Are you a political?' one asked. 'Been to the Island?' said the other. 'Do you know Mandela?' 1990 *Independent* (U.K.) 12 Feb. 6 Nelson always insisted on the island that we had to forget all our factionalism ... We had a common enemy, the white prison authorities.

Hence **Islander** *n*., one imprisoned on Robben Island; *Robben Islander*, see ROBBEN ISLAND.

1990 X. SIGONYELA in *New African* 18 June 2 Police threats at Islander's welcome in PE.

isn't it *int. phr. colloq*. [Formed on IS IT.] A rhetorical question, 'Is that not so?' Cf. IS IT.

1956 A. SAMPSON *Drum* 85 The English just use long words and big talk, isn't it? 1990 R. GOOL *Cape Town Coolie* 135, I am giving my *whole* life for other people. You get the point isn't it?

‖**isona** /iˈsɔːna/ *n*. [Zulu, lit. 'that which spoils, damages, corrupts'.] The WITCHWEED, *Striga asiatica*.

1907 J.M. WOOD *Handbk to Flora of Natal* 92 The 'Witchweeds,' known to the natives as 'Isona,' which are found in mealie fields and are parasitical on the roots of the mealies and other species of the grass family. 1917 R. MARLOTH *Common Names* 90 *Witchweed*, .. A parasitical herb of mealie-fields, also called Rooiblom or Isona or Matabele flower. 1966 [see WITCHWEED].

isongoma var. SANGOMA.

Israelite *n. hist*. [Transf. use of general Eng. *Israelite* a member of the people of God, of the spiritual Israel; perh. influenced by the American Church of God and Saints of Christ, who named themselves 'Israelites' after the Sabbatarian-Baptist belief that black Africans are descended from the ten lost tribes of Israel.] Usu. in *pl*.: (The) members of a millenarian sect founded in 1918 by Enoch Mgijima, in the Bulhoek district near Queenstown (Eastern Cape). Also *attrib*.

1926 M. NATHAN *S. Afr. from Within* 177 Under the influence of supersitition and credulity, a number of misguided natives, led by a 'prophet' named Enoch, and calling themselves Israelites squatted on the commonage at Queenstown, where they attempted to put a communist system into practice, and waited for 'the coming of the Lord.' c1936 *S. & E. Afr. Yr Bk & Guide* 84 A religious movement among a small section of the natives, who styled themselves 'Israelites' culminated, in May, in a collision with the police at Bulhoek. 1943 'J. BURGER' *Black Man's Burden* 207 In 1918 a Native, Enoch Mgijima, saw visions of a battle between two white Governments, with a baboon crushing them both. The obvious interpretation of this vision disturbed the Native religious sect to which Enoch belonged. He then founded his own sect, called the Israelites. 1961 T. MATSHIKIZA *Choc. for my Wife* 26 There was a religious sect back home in the Cape Province. They were known as the Israelites ... He and his followers refused to yield the land they had occupied in the Bullhoek district near Queenstown. They regarded this district as their spiritual home. But the South African Government wanted that piece of land for re-allotment and White occupation. Mgijima said he would not budge. If they were to be forced out of the land the bullets would turn into water. God had told him so. General J.C. Smuts mowed the Israelites down and out of the territory. 1963 M. BENSON *Afr. Patriots* 51 The Israelites armed with rough tools charged; the police fired, killing 164 Israelites and wounding nearly as many. 1970 B.A. PAUW in *Std Encycl. of Sn Afr*. II. 54 A seceding group [from the Church of God and Saints of Christ] ... , using the same name [sc. Israelites], was involved in armed conflict with the police .. when 153 'Israelites' were killed. 1980 D.B. COPLAN *Urbanization of African Performing Arts*. 184 His [sc. Enoch Mgijima's] squatter community of 'Israelites' was fired upon by police in the notorious Bullhock [sic] Massacre in 1921. Mgijima's Israelite hymns were a blend of mission hymnody and the Afro-American religious music of the Baptists. 1986 P. MAYLAM *Hist. of Afr. People* 162 The Israelite Sect was founded in 1918 ... In 1920 they set up a more permanent encampment on the commonage in order to await the end of the world. 1989 *Reader's Digest Illust. Hist*. 326 On 24 May, while the Israelites were at their morning prayers, police armed with machine guns and artillery took up positions on the surrounding hills.

issetator, issitata, -toota varr. ISITUTA.

issigoko var. ISICOCO.

ithongo var. ITONGO.

‖**itola** /iˈtɔːla, iˈtəʊlə/ *n. hist*. Also with initial capital. Pl. **amatola** /amaˈtɔːla, æməˈtəʊlə/. [Xhosa (pl. *amatola*).] In traditional Xhosa society: a war-priest or diviner. See also WITCHDOCTOR.

1844 J. BACKHOUSE *Narr. of Visit* 230 These are distinct from the persons who profess to be makers of rain; and from others who are called Amatola, or in the singular Itola, who practise augury by burning certain roots. 1891 T.R. BEATTIE *Pambaniso* 19 There are at least seven classes of doctors or priests among the Kaffirs — namely, the Amagogo, the Amatola, the Abuvumisi, the Izanusi, the Awobulongo, the Awolugxa, and the Abaqubuli ... The Amatola are the army doctors. 1937 B.J.F. LAUBSCHER *Sex, Custom & Psychopathology* 34 Apart from the *ama-tola* or war priests, who do not exist any more, there are still to be found the *awe-mvula* or rain makers ... The various grades of native doctors existing today can be adequately classified as follows: 1. *Amatola* or *Isanuses*: Diviners, [etc.].

itolofiya var. TOLOFIYA.

itonga var. INTONGA.

itongo /iˈtɔ(ː)ŋgɔ/ *n*. Pl. usu. **amatongo**. Forms: *sing*. **ithongo**; *sing*. and *pl*. **itongo**; *pl*. **amat(h)onga, amat(h)ongo, isitongo**. [Xhosa and Zulu *ithongo* (pl. *amathongo*). For notes on pl. forms, see AMA- and I-.] Among Zulus and Xhosas: an ancestral spirit, venerated as an agent of guidance, protection, and prophecy. See also BADIMO, IDLOZI, ISITUTA, IZINYANYA, UMSHOLOGU.

1855 J.W. COLENSO *Ten Weeks in Natal* 58 All the Kafirs of the Natal district believe in iTongo (plural, ama-Tongo) and amaHlose; .. the former may be regarded as having .. universal *tribal* influence ... These words are certainly used by them only with reference to the *spirits of the dead* — not to the Great Being, whom they regard as their Creator. 1870 H. CALLAWAY *Religious System of Amazulu* (1884) I. 5 Itongo, p. Amatongo — An itongo is properly the spirit of the dead, — a disembodied spirit. The notion that it is in the form of snake, or becomes converted into a snake, is probably something superadded to the original tradition. *Ibid*. 146 The *Itongo* — a collective term meaning the inhabitants of the spirit world .. are also said to 'live underground' ... They are also, like the Abapansi, called ancestors. 1895 H. RIDER HAGGARD *Nada* 24 We heard the *Itongo*, the ghosts of the dead people. *Ibid*. 84 Ah! my father, there, as I rolled among the ashes, I prayed to the Amatongo, to the ghosts of my ancestors. 1918 H. MOORE *Land of Good Hope* 117 It is better, they say, to honour the amatongo, the spirits of people we know and remember. 1923 W.C. SCULLY *Daniel Vananda* 58 He had accepted, as a child, the current theories regarding the 'itongo' and the 'idhlozi' the spirit of the clan and the spirit of the individual. 1954 W.D. HAMMOND-TOOKE in A.M. Duggan-Cronin *Bantu Tribes* III. v. 39 Bantu religion consists of the worship of the ancestral spirits (*amathongo*) who are believed to take a deep interest in the affairs of their children and who, if annoyed, send sickness and death. 1963 A.M. LOUW *20 Days* 114 The one who sleeps must not be woken suddenly. For then his itongo will not have the time to return. 1979 M. MATSHOBA *Call Me Not a Man* 167 To learn the laws of life, to heal, to gain immunity against witchcraft, the power to know the future and to bring the messages of *amathongo* unto the people. 1986 P.A. McALLISTER *Xhosa Beer Drinks*. 43 In Pondoland such beer was left to mature for three days at the back of the hut (a place closely associated with the shades), where 'the *amathongo* are thought to come and drink it at night' (Hunter 1936, 256). 1987 L. NKOSI *Mating Birds* 48 He prayed to the ancestral spirits, *amathonga* .. for guidance, for prudence in the government of his household, for wisdom in the conduct of his personal affairs.

itopi var. TOPPIE.

itoyi-toyi var. TOYI-TOYI.

itsangu var. INSANGU.

itungulu var. AMATUNGULU.

itywala var. TSHWALA.

‖**ixhwele** /iˈǀǀweːle/ *n.* Also **ixwele, izhwele**. [Xhosa.] Among Xhosa-speakers: one who dispenses or deals in medicinal herbs and other traditional remedies for sickness or misfortune. See also WITCHDOCTOR.
    1955 J.B. SHEPHARD *Land of Tikoloshe* 3 'My father was an Ixhwele (herbalist) and his father too. It is a family profession,' he replied. **1978** *S. Afr. Digest* 8 Sept. 20 Port Elizabeth witchdoctor Mr Ashley Totana Mashego, a licensed 'izhwele', showed some of his wares during a recent lecture. **1983** *Fair Lady* 2 Nov. 137 My father had trained to become *ixwele*, a herbalist. He knew the land and the herbs.

ixia /ˈɪksɪə/ *n.* Pl. **-s**, occas. **ixiae**. [Modern L., fr. Gk *ixios* birdlime, mistletoe.] Any of several bulbous plants of the genera *Dierama* (harebell) and *Ixia* of the Iridaceae, with showy flowers of various colours; KALOSSIE; also called PYPIE. See also AANDBLOM, SPARAXIS, WEESKINDERTJIES.
    1775 [see GLADIOLUS]. **1794** T. MARTYN *Rousseau's Botany* 154 There are some very beautiful genera in .. this class, particularly the Ixia and Iris. **1796** [see GLADIOLUS]. **1804** C. SMITH *Conversations* II. 119 An almost endless variety of ixias. **1806** J. BARROW *Trav.* I. 296 Several species of the Ixia, of the Morea, and Gladiolus, now in full bloom, adorned the sides of the hills. **1810** G. BARRINGTON *Acct of Voy.* 341 The tribe of *ixias* are numerous and extremely elegant; but none more singular than the species which bears a long upright spike of pale green flowers. **1812** A. PLUMPTRE in Smuts & Alberts *Forgotten Highway* (1988) 29 The valley .. is called the Uye, or Bulb-valley, because many sorts of *Iris* and *Ixia* grow here, the bulbs of which the Hottentots eat, and are very fond of them. **1841** DUNCAN *Hist. Guernsey* 557 The innumerable species of ixia, sparaxis, and other cognate genera of Cape bulbs. **1847** [see AANDBLOM]. **1852** *Johnson Cottage Gard. Dict.* 517 The true Ixias are known from *Sparaxis* by not having, like it, a jagged sheath. **1856** R.E.E. WILMOT *Diary* (1984) 35 A pretty pink and yellow centred *ixia* and a pure white but fragile orchid of large size. **1890** A. MARTIN *Home Life* 21 Another of our favourites was the *aantblom*, a kind of ixia. **1913** C. PETTMAN *Africanderisms* 246 *Kalotjes, Ixias* — the popular name of these pretty wild flowers. **1928** *Jrnl of Botanical Soc.* XIV. 7 Many of our 'bulbous' plants may be considered safely established in cultivation. The number is steadily increasing — more especially in the case of the family, *Iridaceae*, whose *Sparaxis, Tritonia, Ixia*, are acknowledged favourites. **1957** L.G. GREEN *Beyond City Lights* 104 Green ixia, an iris grown in many pots in England last century, is becoming rare at Tulbagh; but this is the pride of local flower-lovers. **1966** C.A. SMITH *Common Names* 256 Ixia, Many species of *Dierama*, see harebell, and *Ixia*, see kalossie. **1972** A.A. MAUVE in *Std Encycl. of Sn Afr.* VI. 167 Ixia, The 44 species which comprise this endemic Cape genus, belonging to the *Iridaceae*, are often called kalossies or klossies.

izangoma pl. form of SANGOMA.

izanusi var. ISANUSI.

izhwele var. IXHWELE.

izi- /izi/ A Xhosa and Zulu plural noun prefix found in some words originating in these languages.
    In Xhosa and Zulu, the singular of words beginning *izi-* is formed by replacing this prefix with *isi-*. In *S. Afr. Eng.* this pattern is not always observed, and words in the plural forms are sometimes treated as singular nouns, an *-s* being added to form the English plural. See also ISI-.

izibonda(s) pl. form of ISIBONDA.

izibongi *n.*[1] pl. form of IMBONGI.

izibongi *n.*[2] pl. form of ISIBONGO.

izibongo pl. form of ISIBONGO.

iziindwe pl. form of INDWE.

izim- /izim/ *pref.* A Xhosa and Zulu plural noun prefix found in some words originating in these languages. See also II-.
    In Xhosa and Zulu, the singular of words beginning *izim-* is formed by replacing the plural prefix with *im-*; in *S. Afr. Eng.* this pattern is not always observed, and words in the plural forms are sometimes treated as singular nouns, an English pl. *-s* being added to form the plural. See also IM-.

izimbonga, izimbongi *n.*[1] pl. forms of IMBONGI.

izimbongi *n.*[2], **izimbongo** pl. forms of ISIBONGO.

izimpimpi pl. form of IMPIMPI.

izin- /izin/ *pref.* A Xhosa and Zulu plural noun prefix found in some words originating in these languages. See also II-.
    In Xhosa and Zulu, the singular of words beginning *izin-* is formed by replacing the plural prefix with *in-*; in *S. Afr. Eng.* this pattern is not always observed, and words in the plural forms are sometimes treated as singular nouns, an English pl. *-s* being added to form the plural. See also IN-.

izinduna pl. form of INDUNA.

izinja pl. form of INJA.

izinyanga var. and pl. form of INYANGA.

izinyanya /ˌizinˈjaːnja/ *pl. n.* Also **isiyanya**. [Zulu; also Xhosa, var. of *iminyanya* (sing. *umnyanya*).] Ancestral spirits. See also ITONGO.
    1937 B.J.F. LAUBSCHER *Sex, Custom & Pyschopathology* 32 In these so-called *ukutwasa* will be found early communications from *Izinyanya* (ancestors), as well as associations with the *Impundulu, Tikoloshe* and *Inyoka*, which are not supposed to occur in a genuine *ukutwasa*. **1975** [see UMSHOLOGU]. **1977** F.G. BUTLER *Karoo Morning* 206, I wish I had known then the little I know now about the African feeling for their dead — their izinyanya, their amadhlozi — they do not forget them, lose touch with them, neglect them, as we do. The Communion of the Saints is real to them. **1978** A.P. BRINK *Rumours of Rain* 357, I went to see the witchdoctor, the *igqira*. And he spoke to the *izinyanya*, the spirits of the ancestors. And then my father died. **1980** E. JOUBERT *Poppie Nongena* 75 If a woman walks bare-headed at her in-laws's place, she is naked before the izinyanya, which means the old people lying under the soil, the forefathers who must be respected.

‖**Izwe lethu** /ˈi(ː)zwe ˌleːtʊ/ *int. phr.* Also **izwe elethu**. [Xhosa and Zulu, *izwe* land, country + possessive concord l(a)- + *-ethu* ours.] An Africanist slogan, 'our land', 'the land is ours'. Hence **Izwe lethu** *n. phr.*, used allusively, referring to the Africanist movement. Cf. AFRIKA *int.*
    1960 BERRY & TYLER in *Contact* 2 Apr. 2 Many people shouted the Pan-Africanist slogan, 'Izwe Lethu', which means 'Our Land', or gave the thumbs up 'freedom' salute and shouted 'Afrika!' **1963** A.M. LOUW *20 Days* 8 One of the Native men on the bench called out: 'Afrika! Izwe lethu!' ... Everybody knew it was the slogan of the black African nationalist and that it meant 'Africa! Our Land!' **1987** *Learn & Teach* No.2, 4 You must remember that it was also the time of 'Izweletethu' and 'Mayibuye'. Many people in Sharpeville were members of the Pan African Congress — the PAC. **1988** N. MATHIANE in *Frontline* Oct. 30 It is no longer strange to hear people greeting with the Africanist slogan 'Izwe Lethu' (Our Land). **1990** *Weekly Mail* 24 Aug. 1 'Amandla!' they call ... then they wait for the answer .. 'Awetu' (power ... to the people). Then 'Izwe' ... 'Elethu' (the country .. is ours). *Ibid.* 21 Dec. (Suppl.) 8 Whether the Africanist cry of 'Izwe Lethu — The Land is Ours' will emerge as a major, if not the major, voice in the 1990s is a moot point.

J

ja /jɑː/ *adv.* and *n. Colloq.* Formerly also **ya(h)**, **yaw**. [Du.] 'Yes'.

A. *adv.*

1. Used to indicate assent or consent to a request, proposal, or order; repeated, may indicate irritation at being nagged.

1832 *Graham's Town Jrnl* 18 Oct. 165 Capt. Damant asked Mr. Uys to claim the winning horse for him, and Uys said '*Ja Ja*'. **1871** J. McKay *Reminisc.* 87 Their invariable answer is 'yah,' without a second thought; the promise to fulfil an agreement is given, but when the time arrives for its accomplishment, they either neglect or have forgotten all about it. **1899** G.H. Russell *Under Sjambok* 85 'There are six of us here, and he has no rifle; let us surround the bush and put the dogs in.' 'Ja, ja, good!' yelled another, 'let the dogs go in'. **1949** O. Walker *Wanton City* 61 Where's our blerry scoff, eh? Hamba. Go on, man. Jijima! Tchecha! .. 'Yah, yah, baas!' grinned Ephraim, .. and trotted off to the canteen. **1987** *Scope* 20 Nov. 39 Marie Korf .. begged her brother to throw away the dynamite ... '*Ja, Ja, Ja*. I will, don't worry, I'll drop it.' **1988** M. Orson in *Fair Lady* 16 Mar. 128 'Listen, let's swim in our pyjamas.' 'Ja!' I almost bellowed.

2. 'It is so': a simple affirmative.

a. An affirmative reply to a question.

1835 A. Steedman *Wanderings* II. 27, I experienced great difficulty in making my Bushman companion comprehend my questions rightly, his constant replies being nothing more that *Yah, yah!* to the most opposite inquiries. **1877** R.M. Ballantyne *Settler & Savage* 10 'This is pleasant!' said Charlie ... '*Ja*, it is pleasant,' replied Hans. **1897** J.P. Fitzpatrick *Outspan* 6 'What, in winter time, and with lions about?' '*Yah!* Well, you get used to that.' c**1929** S. Black in *S. Gray Three Plays* (1984) 58 Lynda: Il sont tres a la mode, n'est ce pas! Van K: Oh ja ... I mean, we we. **1935** P. Smith *Platkop's Children* 61 He asked them, would they trust this man a little? An' they said Ja. **1959** J. Packer *High Roof* 179 'You know what that means?' 'Ja, I know.' **1973** M. Philip *Caravan Caravel* 29 'Pete, are you awake?' she whispered. '*Ja*,' he answered softly. c**1985** P. Firth in *Eng. Alive* '86 32 'Oh. You're in standard nine, hey?' 'Ja. You as well?'

b. An affirmative response to a statement.

1900 W.S. Churchill *London to Ladysmith* 120 'Think of a great Afrikander Republic ...' Their eyes glittered. 'That's what we want,' said one. 'Yaw, yaw,' said the others. **1910** D. Fairbridge *That Which Hath Been* (1913) 51 He said .. 'He will need to work with sympathy ... Practical sympathy ..' 'Ja,' added the vrouw, emphatically. **1931** V. Sampson *Kom Binne* 258 'Your sheep are looking well, Oom Tias.' 'Ja,' replied Oom Tias with a broad smile. **1957** D. Jacobson *Price of Diamonds* 129 Groenewald began to fear that .. he had offended his superior. So, as a placatory contribution to the discussion, Groenewald threw in, 'Ja, that's something to think about'. **1973** *Sunday Times* 1 Apr. (Mag. Sect.) 11 'It seems that this is a unilingual country, or that you wish it to be,' retorted Mr. Campbell, and there were shouts of 'Ja'. **1990** G. Slovo *Ties of Blood* 41 Zelig smiled. 'Sometimes these *kaffirs* get me down,' he replied. The assistant looked relieved. 'Ja, I know just what you mean.'

3. An indication that the speaker has heard, noted, or understood (something).

a. 'I understand', 'I see': used to indicate that the speaker has taken note of a statement, action, or event; sometimes indicating impatience.

1838 J.E. Alexander *Exped. into Int.* I. 65 Would hint how much I had to do; — shewed my writing materials, which would merely produce a drowsy 'yaw;' — would look at my watch. **1892** *Cape Illust. Mag.* Dec. 112 'Don't think that I am ungrateful, sir, or that I don't appreciate your kindness for —' 'Yah, yah, ' interposed the Dutchman, rising to his feet. 'I understand; do the best for yourself, of course.' **1899** J.P. Fitzpatrick *Tvl from Within* 108 The old President jumped up in a huff and said, 'Ja, ja, ja! You always say it is somebody else!' **1971** *Daily Dispatch* 30 June 10 Hilary said, 'I believe I am the first man to have climbed this peak and I claim it in the name of Her Britannic Majesty.' 'O ja,' said Koos. **1973** *Drum* 8 May 24 'Mmmmm ... mm yaaa. I see,' the withered hand stretches out for another bone, he squints, and places it next to the bull. **1973** Y. Burgess *Life to Live* 65 He did not enjoy his daily bread, but he was expected to say '*Ja, Boet Ben*', that is, 'Yes, Brother Ben,' whenever Ben paused, to show that he was awake and listening.

b. Acknowledging that the speaker has heard a summons or call, and is paying attention.

1882 C. Du Val *With Show through Sn Afr.* II. 112 Yells for Sixpence would result in a guttural 'Yah, Baas — yah, Baas!' **1884** B. Adams *Narr.* (1941) 58 Master: 'Hendricus.' Servant: 'Yah, myneer.' **1892** *The Jrnl* 31 Mar. 4 'Klaas! ..' 'Ja, baas.' 'Take those cattle to the skit at once.'

c. Used (interrogatively or as an exclamation) to show that what has been said is of interest to the speaker.

1900 B. Mitford *Aletta* 25 'Who is it?' 'The Patriot,' burst forth the other. 'Ja, that is good! I have wanted so much to see him.' **1949** O. Walker *Wanton City* 128 'There he is, Danie. That's the funny man on *The Comet*.' 'Ja?' said Danie Vos ... 'Another blerry rooinek, eh?'

d. Used to show that the speaker has understood a statement or has anticipated and understood an objection to something that he or she has said; indicating disagreement or only partial agreement, and usu. introducing a counter-argument.

1920 R. Juta *Tavern* 139, I let you kiss me, but I closed my eyes and .. imagined it was someone else. Ja! Ja! I know, they wish the vineyards to join ... Should I marry you, it would be just like this kiss; I would always close my eyes. **1929** V.L. Cameron *Reverse Shield* 11 'No-one can visit a country without being .. influenced by it.' 'Ach, ja, but he would never ape the English,' declared Oom Jan stubbornly. **1982** *Fair Lady* 22 Sept. 117 Ja, but I'm more likely to go *boom* and kick someone else, then stagger. **1989** E. Frank in *Scope* 10 Mar. 98 The witness looked at her doubtfully. 'Ja, she's about the right height. But the oke who robbed us was Coloured, .. and he had dark hair.'

e. In the phr. *ja, well*, an apologetic, embarrassed, or world-weary response.

1980 *Sunday Times* 25 May (Mag. Sect.) 5 'We've been married for a year ... He's terrific ... He even does the washing up ...' Joe squirms. 'Ja, well,' he said. 'I tell you these kids today don't know what they missed by missing rock and roll.' **1987** *Scope* 20 Nov. 44 'Are you full of drugs again, Jimmy?' 'Ja, well, you know me.' **1990** G. Slovo *Ties of Blood* 326 Ja, well, I can't feel sorry for Nicholas. He's made his bed, and a very comfortable one it is, too. **1990** K. Pather in *Cue* 5 July 2 Ja well, you've seen it all you say; lots of amandlas, toyi-toyi and just another struggle story line.

f. In the expression *ja well no fine* /jɑː ˌwel nəʊ ˈfaɪn/ *int.* and *adv.*, also *jawellnofine*, *yar-*, [coined in 1978 by R.J.B. Wilson of the SABC ('My youngest brother was in the habit of saying "no fine" to everything that really required a "c'est la vie" or "that's the way the cookie crumbles". It had a nice South African feel to it. I added "Ja, well ... " to it to reinforce the South Africanism when I was looking for a title for my radio series "*Jarwellknowfine*" (my original spelling)')], an expression equivalent to 'all right', 'c'est la vie', 'that's life': used to indicate a non-committal, resigned, or ironical response, or parodying *S. Afr. Eng.* speech.

1982 *Sunday Times* 31 May, '*Ja well no fine*' (also *No, fine*): to explain this to non-South Africans is a challenge. **1982** D. Kramer *Short Back & Sides* 57 They took the tray from the window, And I said 'Was yours OK?', And you said 'Ja well, no fine'. **1983** *Star* 15 Sept. 1 How many voters find it all very bewildering, among them Smitty — Mr Average Ou — who, instead of voting either a straight 'ja' or 'Nee' would really prefer to vote a 'Jawellnofine'. **1983** *Sunday Times* 18 Dec. 16 Jawellnofine — that was 1983. **1986** V. Cooke et al. in *S. Gray Market Plays* 16 Tony: Who's Bob? Tony: Hey, you should be on TV. Anna: Yar well no fine. Tony: Oh stop it. You killing me. **1987** R. Cutler in *Style* May 107 The next morning she asked him if he had had a good night. 'Ja, well no fine,' said True Butch, 'I swear I never ever sleep so good before.' **1989** *Sunday Times* 24 Dec. 23 Gwen Gill's A-to-Z of the decade: Jamie Uys, Jimmy Cook, *Jawellnofine*. **1990** *Sunday Times* 8 Apr. 6 'My wife .. says she heard this song with *that* four-letter word in it on the radio the other day.' His jovial face slips into outraged surprise. It won't be *Ja well, no fine* to that kind of smut here tonight. **1990** M. Fassler in *Fair Lady* 21 Nov. 81 Charles tried to pluck up the courage to pop the question ... He asked me just before dinner and I said something like 'Ja well, no fine'. **1992** S. Gutknecht in *Sunday Times* 19 Apr. (Mag. Sect.) 28 Jawellnofine. I'll check you later, broer. Me and my chick are off to the flicks. **1993** *Weekend Post* 9 Oct. 9 Ja, well no fine. No Queen's English for us Sefricans, just a little bit of this and a little bit of that.

4. Used to emphasize or affirm one's own words or thoughts.

1911 Blackburn & Caddell *Secret Service* 87 'Ja, I have wonderful eyes' was his only answer to our question, 'How do you know all this?' **1913** D. FAIRBRIDGE *Piet of Italy* 62 'Always I drink coffee,' he said in the Taal, 'and always I sleep by night. Ja, and by day, too.' **1924** L. COHEN *Reminisc. of Jhb.* 18 The .. Dutchman .. scooped all the money in sight ... *'Ja, you have all paid.'* *c*1966 J. HOBBS in *New S. Afr. Writing* 161 Here were pearls of wisdom, the precious fruit of years of experience. 'A tomato is a bugger, ja,' he said. **1970** M. DIKOBE Marabi Dance. 67 December 16, Ja, it's Dingaan's Day. Ja, it will be his day off. **1987** L. BEAKE *Strollers* 98 Johnny allowed the purchase of cake and sweet sticky cooldrinks. He sipped his while they strolled along the quiet dusty streets. Ja, this was the life! **1988** *Frontline* Apr. 24, I do not want to go to heaven when I die, fancy meeting Ou Strydom, Smuts, Malan, Verwoerd and who's the ancestor of the boers? Ja, the great pirate Ou Jan van Riebeeck and his fancy hair-do. **1993** *Pace* July 54 Lancelot — *ja*, that was the weakling's name.

5. Used without particular meaning to open a conversation.

1936 C. BIRKBY *Thirstland Treks* 57 *'Naand, oom.' 'Naand, neef.'* We drank coffee. The old man talked. *'Ja,'* he said, *'Ja,* we left the old village'. **1972** *Drum* 8 Oct. 14, I expected him to ask me: 'Ja, you skelm so you are still alive, you bloody bastard?' **1984** *Sunday Times* 11 Nov. (Lifestyle), Ja, so I was saying *all* the collections show these amazing outfits from the Japanese designers. **1992** *Weekend Post* 26 Dec. 11 Ja, we were all different, but we were a united community.

6. A reprimand: 'I told you so', 'you should have known better'.

*c*1966 M. JABOUR in *New S. Afr. Writing* 91 'Now what's the matter with the thing, hey? Cohen said it was in perfect condition.' Ouma leaned forward ... 'Ja, ja, I warned you not to trust that Jewboy, Jannie.' **1993** *Sowetan* 22 Jan. 8 Ja! I told you she's bringing strange animals into Progress!

7. In the phr. ***oh, ja***, used to indicate that one has just remembered something which one had intended to mention earlier.

1974 'BLOSSOM' in *Darling* 9 Oct. 95 But where was I? Oh ja, about greasy hair. **1988** *Time* June-July 5 Give fate a gentle shove. You may become the next boy/girl wonder of local pop. Oh ja, and if you don't have the right equipment, they supply that as well.

B. *n.* An utterance of 'ja'.

1971 *Rand Daily Mail* 18 Feb., The 450 workers present shouted a loud 'Ja' when Mr .. asked if they were prepared to strike if all negotiations failed.

jaag var. JAG.

jaagsiekte /ˈjɑːxsiktə/ *n. Pathology.* Formerly also **jachtziekte, jagsiekte, jag(t)ziekte.** [Afk., *jaag, jag* pant, draw quick laboured breaths (fr. Du. *jagen* hunt, pursue) + *siekte* (Du. *ziekte*) disease.] Either of two livestock diseases which cause an increased rate of respiration:

1. Crotalariosis, a disease of horses caused by the ingestion of either of two plants of the genus *Crotalaria* of the Fabaceae, *C. dura* or *C. globifera.*

1899 *Natal Agric. Jrnl* 31 Mar. 4 'Jachtziekte' (hunting or galloping sickness) a rapidly fatal ailment of horses. **1930** *Outspan* 31 Oct. 69 'Gousiekte' and 'geel dikkop' in sheep, 'staggers' or 'rushing disease' of cattle, 'jagsiekte' in horses, and possibly also 'dunsiekte,' are all caused by plant poisoning. **1937** *Handbk for Farmers* (Dept of Agric. & Forestry) 357 'Jaagsiekte' in horses is caused by the plants Crotalaria dura and C. globifera ... the first noticeable symptom is the increase in the rate of respiration (breathing), which may vary from 100 to 120 per minute. A dry cough is present. **1966** C.A. SMITH *Common Names* 257 These species [*sc. Crotalaria dura* and *C. globifera*] have been incriminated in causing the disease, known as 'Jaagsiekte', in horses, whence the vernacular name.

2. A lung disease of sheep.

1905 *Cape of G.H. Agric. Jrnl* 526 In the later stages the poor beast stands with its ribs fixed and flanks heaving, panting for breath, hence the Dutch name *jagziekte* or droning sickness. **1913** C. PETTMAN *Africanderisms* 232 *Jagziekte*, (D. *jagen*, to hunt; *ziekte*, sickness.) Chronic catarrhal pneumonia in sheep is thus designated, the panting of the animal making it look as if it had been hunted. **1914** *Farmer's Annual* 223 There is strong evidence that in certain conditions jagziekte is infectious or contagious, but all attempts to communicate it artificially by innoculation of the blood with inflammatory products from the lungs have failed ... Jagtziekte is a pneumonia — that is, an inflammation of the lungs, but of a peculiar character. [**1934** C.P. SWART Supplement to Pettman. 80 A herb that causes 'jaagsiekte' in sheep i.e. chronic catarrhal pneumonia which causes the affected animal to pant and give it the appearance of having been hunted. The herb, whose botanical name is Crotalaria dura, is found in the Midlands of Natal.] **1976** MÖNNIG & VELDMAN *Handbk on Stock Diseases* 276 The cause of jaagsiekte in sheep is as yet unknown, but it is possible that susceptibility to the disease is hereditary. It is characterized by a continuous growth of the tissue of the smallest air passages, which later have the appearance of a tumor invading the lung.

3. *comb.* **jaagsiektebossie** /-ˌbɔsi/ [Afk., *bossie* (see BOSCHJE)], any of several shrubs of the genus *Crotalaria* of the Fabaceae, esp. *C. dura* and *C. globifera.*

1930 *Farming in S. Afr.* Dec. 454 (Swart), The 'Jaagsiekte-bossie' (Crotalaria dura) belongs to the same genus as the preceding. **1966** C.A. SMITH *Common Names* 257 *Jaagsiektebossie, Crotalaria dura, C. globifera* .. and *C. brachycarpa* ... Shrubs with erect stems from a woody perennial and thickened rootstock.

jaagspinnekop var. JAGSPINNEKOP.

jaap /jɑːp/ *n. slang.* [Transf. use of Afk. name *Jaap*, see JAPIE.] JAPIE sense 3.

1963 M.G. MCCOY *Informant, Port Elizabeth* As the Springboks pulled ahead some very drunken white jaaps started jeering & throwing bottles over at the N.-E. stand, where drunken coloureds had been barracking the Springbok team, so of course chaos ensued. **1971** *Informant, Coalbrook (OFS)* You sound like a right proper jaap and it's terrible. **1987** C. HOPE *Hottentot Room* 38 'Cretin!' he said to Gerrie. *'Jaap!'* 'Don't call me a *jaap*,' said Gerrie.

jaapie var. JAPIE.

ja baas /ˈjɑː bɑːs/ *adj. phr.* and *n. phr. Colloq.* Also **ja-baas.** [Afk., see JA and BAAS.] 'Yes master', 'yes sir'.

A. *n. phr.*

1. The utterance 'Ja baas', seen as the epitome of the language and attitudes of one who is servile; cf. YES BAAS *n. phr.* sense 2.

1882 C. DU VAL *With Show through Sn Afr.* I. 145 He was to acknowledge his hour of servitude by answering 'Yah, Baas!' when I addressed him. **1926** L.D. FLEMMING *Fun on Veld* (1928) 226 Hendrik's 'Yah, Baas,' is reassuring. **1956** A. SAMPSON *Drum* 31 'It makes me boil having to say "Ya, baas" to a white man who's inferior to me,' he said. 'God, I feel sick when I see an educated African grovelling in front of a white man.' **1960** *Europeans Only (caption)*, The mythical Bantu of legend — a people of touching and childlike simplicity whose vocabulary was limited to *Ja, baas.* **1962** A.J. LUTHULI *Let my People Go* 142, I wonder if they believe us — left to ourselves — capable of more than *'Ja, Baas!'* **1972** A. PATON in *E. Prov. Herald* 8 Apr. 9 Black voices are going to be heard more loudly and more compellingly and they won't be saying 'Ja baas'. **1974** *E. Prov. Herald* 4 Mar., Days of 'ja baas' are over. **1980** *Voice* 10 Dec. 13 Forever ja-baas ... All black people are supposed to do — always — is never to say no. **1980** N. FERREIRA *Story of Afrikaner* 48 If only the Prime Minister was willing to talk to the real black leaders, not the ones who say *'ja baas'* all the time. **1984** *Frontline* Mar. 14 Pass offices, crowded trains, ja-baas/nee-baas. When you have so little potency, that which you have is understandably precious.

2. A black person who is servile in his behaviour towards whites; YES BAAS *n. phr.* sense 1.

1972 *Drum* 8 Aug. 8 In Saso lingo a non-White is regarded as a Ja-Baas, a sell-out. Saso take strong exception to be [*sic*] called in the negative term 'non-White' and call themselves Blacks. **1980** E. JOUBERT *Poppie Nongena* 378 Ja, they say, you are the ja-baas, the yes-men, so they don't trust us no more. They say the whites tread on us. **1989** *Pace* Dec. 4 The leadership position is for the learned and not for bo 'Dom Jan' and bo 'Ja Baas'.

B. *adj. phr.* Of persons, attitudes, or actions: servile and fawning (referring to the obsequiousness demanded in the past by whites of black people); YES BAAS *adj. phr.*

1960 C. HOOPER *Brief Authority* 103 We do not want war with the europeans; but even less do we want ja-baas chiefs, who are merely the Native Commissioner's voice. **1970** *Sunday Times* 22 Mar., South Africa's school children are in danger of educational influences which are narrow, bigoted and conditioned to a 'ja baas' attitude to the government in power, Mr. Harry Brigish, chairman of the Witwatersrand Central School Board, said in Johannesburg yesterday. **1974** *Daily Dispatch* 2 Dec. 1 Except for a few 'ja-baas' type [*sic*] of Africans, no black face was ever admitted into the educational councils or committees that framed the educational policy of South Africa. **1977** M.P. GWALA *Jol'iinkomo* 45 The ja-baas jive scares cowards with Frankenstein monstereyes. **1981** *Pace* Sept. 32 There is too much 'baaskap' in the SAAAU hierarchy. I was not given the chance to put my case. Perhaps they realised I am no 'ja baas' man. **1987** *New Nation* 3 Dec. 11 The Genuines have chucked out Goema's ja-baas connotations, but have emphasised its humour, anger, sensuality and subversiveness.

Hence **ja-baas** *v. trans.*, or (*rare*) *reflexive*, to agree (to something) without resisting; to ingratiate oneself in this way.

1977 *Het Suid-Western* 24 Aug., Mr. Vorster will have placed his opponents at the psychological disadvantage of being a one-in-four minority with the Cape, Natal and Free State having meekly 'ja-baased' his proposals. **1981** *Frontline* May 28 Idi Amin was a loyal soldier in the colonial forces, ja-baasing himself into a sergeant-majorship.

jabroer /ˈjɑːbruːr, -bruə/ *n.* Also **ja-broer.** [Afk., see JA and BROER.] Esp. in politics: one who goes along with the views and decisions of those in authority, either not forming or not acting upon independent opinions; a 'yes-man'. Also *attrib.* See also MBONGO sense 2.

1934 *Cape Argus* 29 May (Swart), Surely the taxpayers do not pay their representatives just to be so many 'ja-broers', I trust that the men elected will give value for the pay they receive. **1939** *Outspan* 26 May 53 Here he was, bothered by authority and compelled to submit to law and convention just like any ordinary jabroer of the laager. **1940** F.B. YOUNG *City of Gold* 445 Paul Kruger was sitting in his accustomed place on the stoep, surrounded by a group of men whom Adrian had called Ja-broers. *Ibid.* 478 He sat down heavily, amid long-continued applause. The Ja-broers had got their cue, and two of them .. excitedly challenged the genuineness of the Memorial's signatures. **1950** VAN DER BYL in *Hansard* 31 May 7693 It must be a very poor party if the Ministers won't even explain to their caucus what the Bill contained. If that is the way that hon. members opposite are prepared to be treated and are merely *'ja-broers'* then I am extremely sorry for them. **1973** *Weekend Post* 24 Mar. 10 The conformist atmosphere of the Afrikaans universities and the *ja-broer* attitude of the Afrikaner Studentebond. **1984** *Daily Dispatch* 21 June 3 When the PFP trooped across the floor to vote with government members, the Conservative Party jeered at them for being 'ja-broers'. **1988** 'K. DE BOER' in *Frontline* May 38 Ja-broers of the Party and the Regering.

jabula /dʒəˈbuːlə, dʒaˈbʊːla/ *n.* [Shortened form of JABULANI.] TSHWALA sense a.

1977 *Weekend Post* 18 June (Suppl.) 2 The first-aid officer himself is also in charge of the adjoining tea room and kitchen, where miners wishing to can drink 'jabula', a fortified drink, or help themselves to stew or soup.

jabulani /ˌdʒabʊˈlɑːni/ *n.* Also **jabulaan**, and with initial capital. [Xhosa and Zulu, imperative pl. form of *jabula* be joyful, rejoice.] **a.** With initial capital: The proprietary name of a brand of sorghum beer. **b.** Loosely, any such beer: TSHWALA sense a. Also *attrib.* Cf. IJUBA.

1974 *Daily Dispatch* 22 Nov. (Indaba) 5 He had gone to a shebeen and become involved in an argument .. over a can of jabulani. 1975 *Ibid.* 11 Apr. 7 Jabulani is blamed for an increase in venereal disease ... 'I propose that the jabulani beer hall be replaced by a dairy where people can buy milk and Amasi ... We don't want Jabulani here. It must go immediately, bad things occur because of it.' 1979 *E. Prov. Herald* 6 Apr. (Suppl.) 5 Sorghum not Jabulani, MP told. Chief G.N. N— asked what the department was doing about the sale of jabulani, which was now sold under the name of 'Mqomboti' and 'Xhosa beer' in cartons although it had been banned by the Assembly. 1980 [see BANTU BEER]. 1982 C. VAN WYK *Message in Wind* 12 Aunt Lilian had made a pot of Vusi's favourite drink, *jabulani*, to celebrate the good news that had arrived that afternoon.

Jacaranda City *n. phr.* [See quot. 1970.] A nickname given to the city of PRETORIA.

1970 BEETON & DORNER in *Eng. Usage in Sn Afr.* Vol.1 No.2, 33 *Jacaranda*, tropical Amer[ican] trees of the fam[ily] *Bignoniaceae*, .. extensively cultivated in Pretoria wh[ich] is sometimes referred to as the 'Jacaranda City'. 1978 *Reader's Digest Illust. Guide to Sn Afr.* 228 The Jacaranda City. 1982 *S. Afr. Panorama* Mar. 32 The Bernardi brothers of Pretoria .. recently auctioned costly items from the estates of well-known South Africana collectors in the Jacaranda City. 1990 P. APPELBAUM in *Weekly Mail* 2 Nov. 29 It's hard to avoid purple prose while jacarandas are still blooming in Johannesburg ... They're already past their prime in Pretoria. Trees in the 'Jacaranda City' bloom two weeks earlier than they do here.

jachtziekte var. JAAGSIEKTE.

jackal buzzard *n. phr.* ['The cry of this species is singularly like that of the common Jackal (*Canis mesomelas*) whence its name, and when its wings are expanded shewing the light colour, together with the reddish-brown breast-feathers, they greatly resemble the colours and markings of a jackal's skin; moreover this bird occupies just about the same position in the tribe of rapacious birds as the jackal fills in that of rapacious animals.' (M.E. Barber in Layard & Sharp's *Birds of South Africa*, 1884, p.27.)] The buzzard *Buteo rufofuscus* of the Accipitridae, slate grey in colour, with white bands, and dark red-brown to chestnut breast; JACKHALSVOGEL.

1884 LAYARD & SHARPE *Birds of S. Afr.* 26 *Buteo jakal*. Jackal Buzzard. 1923 HAAGNER & IVY *Sketches* 97 The Jackal Buzzard (*Buteo jakal*) is fairly common throughout South Africa. It derives its name from its howl-like cry, which somewhat resembles that of the Black-backed Jackal. 1936 E.L. GILL *First Guide to S. Afr. Birds* 126 *Jackal Buzzard*, .. In the air it does a great deal of soaring with stiffly-spread wings .. ; in doing so it shows a white band in the wing ... The name refers to its cry, which is very like a jackal's. 1971 *Personality* 2 Apr. 26 Jackal buzzards, yellow-billed kites and drongoes by the dozen made up the balance of our feathered friends. 1985 *S. Afr. Panorama* Oct. 34 In the surrounding koppies there are zebra, gemsbok, springbok, ostriches, steenbok, duiker, klipspringer, jackals, wild-cats and jackal buzzards. 1988 M. NEL in *Personality* 25 Apr. 54 If the day is clear you might see jackal buzzards wheeling overhead.

jackal-proof *adj.* Also **jakhal-proof**. Of fencing or other barriers: erected to provide protection against predators; of an area: protected against predators by the use of such fencing. Usu. in the Special collocations *jackal-proof fence*, *jackal-proof fencing*, *jackal-proof wire*.

1905 E.A. NOBBS in Flint & Gilchrist *Science in S. Afr.* 385 The best remedy .. is the construction of jackal-proof wire fences round whole farms or groups of farms, within whose shelter stock can graze at will. c1911 J.W. KIDDALL in S. Playne *Cape Col.* 689 Kraaling the flocks .. is necessary unless the lands are secured by a jackal-proof fence. c1911 S. PLAYNE *Cape Col.* 323 The farm is entirely fenced and divided into camps, jackal-proof wire being used in camps where chicks are reared. *Ibid.* 702 There are about 1200 Merino sheep, which .. are herded by day and confined in jackal-proof camps at night. 1972 *Daily Dispatch* 4 Mar. 19 (advt) Six land camps and four veld camps jackal proof fencing in very good condition with abundant stock water. 1972 *Grocott's Mail* 16 May 1 The farm is divided into 12 grazing camps which are stock-proof. The boundary fencing is jackal-proof. 1977 F.G. BUTLER *Karoo Morning* 87 Mr Gilfillan .. sent him up to the Eastern Transvaal .. whence he returned to kill jackals for the four farmers whose boundaries converged on Doornberg. Jackal-proof fencing was still a thing of the future. 1979 M. PARKES *Wheatlands* 31 The end of the war .. enabled Arthur to get on with the enormous task of fencing his farm with jackal-proof netting, which he had seen during a visit to America and had begun to work on as early as 1896. 1985 J. DEACON in *S. Afr. Panorama* Sept. 30 Jackal-proof fences have put many Coloured herdsmen out of a job.

jackalsbesjie var. JAKKALSBESSIE.

jackal's kost see JAKKALSKOS.

jackhalsvogel *n. obs.* Also **jack(h)alsvogel**. [S. Afr. Du.] The JACKAL BUZZARD, *Buteo rufofuscus*.

1834 A. SMITH *Diary* (1939) I. 137 The Vultur frilous occurs here, many being seen to-day; also the Aquila vulturina, jackalsvogel. 1856 F.P. FLEMING *Sn Afr.* 380 Some time after .. a '*Jackall-vogels*' nest came to view, built on the top of a large tree, which grew out of the face of a perpendicular and lofty '*krantz*,' or precipice. 1908 *E. London Dispatch* 4 Dec. 4 Hear our jackhalsvogel and groote visch-vanger vociferously vaunting.

jack hanger *n. phr.* Also **jackie hanger**, and with initial capitals. [See quot. 1913.] The FISCAL (sense 2), *Lanius collaris*.

1890 A. MARTIN *Home Life* 252 The butcher bird, called by the colonists Jack Hanger, likes to eat his game high; and you often come across mimosa-bushes which, stuck all over with small birds, beetles, locusts, etc, impaled on long stiff thorns, from his well-stocked larder. 1913 C. PETTMAN *Africanderisms* 231 *Jack Hanger*, *Lanius collaris*. This designation has reference to the bird's habit of hanging his captures on thorns until they are to his taste. 1966 F.G. BUTLER *S. of Zambezi* 17 A single jackhanger cursing made the air go brittle. 1975 *Dict. of Eng. Usage in Sn Afr.* 92 *Jack hanger* see: butcher bird.

jackie *n.* Ellipt. for JACKIE HANGMAN.

1961 *Red Wing* (St Andrew's College, Grahamstown) 15 The habitation of doves, jackies and mossies. 1989 *Weekend Post* 4 Nov. (Leisure) 3 Don't condemn the .. jackie or the boubou when you see them nest-robbing — it's nature's way of maintaining a good balance.

jackie hangman *n. phr.* Also **jack(e)y-hangman**, and with initial capitals. [See quot. 1945.] The FISCAL (sense 2), *Lanius collaris*.

1913 C. PETTMAN *Africanderisms* 231 *Jacky Hangman*, Natal name for the above bird [*sc.* Jack hanger]. 1936 [see JANFISKAAL]. c1936 M. VALBECK *Headlong from Heaven* 206 Outside, the brilliantly plumaged sunbirds and 'Jackie Hangmans' sang. 1945 N. DEVITT *People & Places* 145 Jacky Hangman is .. the Natal name for the butcher bird, known in the Cape as the fiskaal. Its quaint name was bestowed upon it from its habit of catching the locusts, beetles, and small birds upon which it lives, and impaling them upon long, sharp thorns. 1951 [see FISCAL sense 1]. 1963 S. CLOETE *Rags of Glory* 423 On a low branch a jackie hangman .. predatory as an eagle, watched for tiny insect game to eat or impale, still living, on the sharp spikes of the thornbush that was his larder. 1964 J. COPE in C. Millar *16 Stories* 35 A handsome black-and-white bird .. a .. jackey-hangman, a terrible greedy pirate of a bird. 1973 *Weekend Post* 28 Apr. 4 The big brass scale showing how many grass-hoppers, mice and lizards are eaten by two shrikes (Jackie Hangman) which in turn feed one hawk. 1977 [see JANFISKAAL]. 1988 LABAND & HASWELL *Pietermaritzburg 1838–1988* 177 The symbolic waiting and watching of the 'Jackie Hangman'. 1989 *Informant, Grahamstown* We had a budgie .. but eventually a Jackie Hangman killed her.

jackroll /ˈdʒækrəʊl/ *v. trans. Slang.* [Special sense of general Eng. slang *jack-roll* to rob one's companions while they are drunk or asleep. According to D. Blow (in *City Press* 11 Feb. 1990 p.3), the term is thought to have been introduced into township slang from a song by American duo Womack and Womack: 'Love is just a ball game, sometimes you lose — jack-roll'.] In township parlance: to abduct and rape (a young woman). Hence **jackroller** *n.*, a member of any of several gangs which abduct and rape young women; **jackrolling** *vbl n.*, the action of abducting and raping young women.

1990 D. BLOW in *City Press* 11 Feb. 3 More and more schoolgirls are being 'jackrolled' — abducted by youths and raped — for up to a week at a time. Police estimate that during the past two years when jackrolling began, hundreds of schoolgirls have been held captive and gang-raped ... Jackrollers are not one gang, but youths — aged from 14 years old — getting thrills by hi-jacking or stealing cars and using them to abduct school-girls, often by threatening them with a firearm ... Two Soweto Murder and Robbery policemen .. have arrested some of the worst jackrolling gangs ... 'The jackrollers warn them that if they testify they will kill them when they come out of prison.' 1990 *Tribute* Apr. 1 Have we not seen boys 'jackrolling' girls in front [of] their fathers, and school children stabbing teachers? 1990 *Drum* May 110 She was the victim of a gang rape by the feared jackrollers. 1991 *Sowetan* 29 July 13 T— .. is alleged to be the kingpin of the notorious 'Jackroller' gang.

Jacob Evertson /ˌjɑːkɔb ˈiːəfə(r)tsən/ *n. phr.* Obsolescent. Also **Jacob Eversson**, **Jacob Evert(sen)**, **Jacop Evertsen**, **Jakob Evertsen**. [See quot. 1731.]

1. An early form of JACOPEVER: **a.** The JACOPEVER (sense 1 a), *Helicolenus dactylopterus*. **b.** The JACOPEVER (sense 1 b), *Sebastes capensis*. **c.** The JACOPEVER (sense 1 c), *Trachyscorpia capensis*. **2.** The FRANSMADAM, *Boopsoidea inornata*.

[1727 J.G. SCHEUCHZER tr. *E. Kaempfer's Hist. of Japan* I. 136 *Ara* is what the Dutch in the Indies call *Jacobs Ewertz*.] 1731 G. MEDLEY tr. P. Kolb's *Present State of Cape of G.H.* II. 197 *Francisci* .. related how the *Red Stone-Brassem* at the Cape came by the Name of *Jacob Eversson* ... 'There was, .. at the Cape, many years ago, a Master. of a ship, whose name was *Jacob Eversson*. This man had a very red Face .. so deep-pitted with the Small Pox, that his Beard, which was black, could never be shav'd so close, but that several hairs would remain in the Pock-Frets. So that his Face .. had the colour, and seemed to have the Specks of the Red Stone-*Brassem* ... The crew dining .. very jovially upon this Sort of Fish, one of them took it in his Head, in a Fit of Mirth, to call it the *Jacob Eversson* ... The Settlers .. very merrily agreed to call a Red Stone-*Brassem* a *Jacob Eversson* ever after'. [1798 S.H. WILCOCKE tr. *J.S. Stavorinus's Voy. to E. Indies 1768–71* II. 352 There is likewise, it is said, a large fish near the pier-head at Amboyna, to which the name of Jacob Evertsen has been given.] 1801 J. BARROW *Trav.* I. 31 The *Scorpoena Capensis*, here called Jacob Evertson, is a firm, dry fish, but not very commonly used. 1823 W.W. BIRD *State of Cape of G.H.* 159 The hottentot, jacob evert, elft, hake or stockfish, the king klipfish, the steen brazen and the stompneus are all of excellent quality. 1831 [see MAASBANKER]. 1853 L. PAPPE *Synopsis of Edible Fishes* 14 *Sebastes Capensis* ... Called Jacob Evertsen, after a Dutch Captain, remarkable for a red face and large projecting eyes. 1887 *S.W. Silver & Co.'s*

Handbk to S. Afr. 181 *Scorpaenidae. Sebastes Capensis* ... Jacob Evertsen ... A highly-prized fish for the table. Common in Table Bay. **1927** *Annals of S. Afr. Museum* XXI. 908 *Sebastichthys capensis* (Gmel.) Jacob Evertson. **1968** J.L.B. SMITH *High Tide* 36 Kolb .. gives quite reasonable accounts of .. Jacop Evertsen, Hottentot, Red steenbras, Red Stompnose, .. and rays. **1972** [see SANCORD].

3. With qualifying word: **bastard Jacob Evertson**, *(a)* The JACOPEVER (sense 1 b), *Sebastes capensis*; *(b) Kyphosus* spp.; see also BLUE FISH sense 2.

1887 *S.W. Silver & Co.'s Handbk to S. Afr.* 183 *Squammipennes. Pimelepterus fuscus* ... **Bastard Jacob Evertsen** ... Flesh well favoured. Caught in Simon's Bay, &c. **1913** C. PETTMAN *Africanderisms* 423 *Sancord, Sebastes maculatus.* Known as the bastard Jakob Evertsen.

Jacopever /ˌjɑːkɔˈpɪəvə(r), ˌdʒeɪkəˈpiːvə/ *n.* Also **Jacob(e)ever, Jakopewer, Jakopiver**, and with small initial. [ad. JACOB EVERTSON; see quot. 1973.] Any of several edible marine fishes of the scorpionfish and seabream families, characterized by their pink or red colour.

In the case of the seabream (sense 2 below), only juveniles have this colouring.

1. Scorpionfishes (family Scorpaenidae): **a.** *Helicolenus dactylopterus*; JACOB EVERTSON sense 1 a; SANCORD sense a. **b.** *Sebastes capensis*; occas. with defining word, **false Jacopever**; *Bastard Jacob Evertson* sense *(a)*, see JACOB EVERTSON sense 3; JACOB EVERTSON sense 1 b. **c.** *Trachyscorpia capensis*; occas. with defining word, **spiny Jacopever**; JACOB EVERTSON sense 1 c; SANCORD sense b. **2.** The FRANSMADAM, *Boopsoidea inornata*.

In Smith and Heemstra's *Smiths' Sea Fishes* (1986), the name 'jacopever' is used for *Helicolenus dactylopterus*, 'false jacopever' for *Sebastes capensis*, and 'Cape scorpionfish' for *Trachyscorpia capensis*.

[**1838** see STUMPNOSE sense 1.] **1927** *Annals of S. Afr. Museum* XXI. 908 *Sebastichthys capensis* (Gmel.) Jacob Evertson; Jacopever ... Red shading to orange below; several silvery-white or pinkish irregular spots on sides. **1927** *Annals of S. Afr. Museum* XXI. 910 *Sebastosemus capensis* ... Spiny Jacopever. **1945** H. GERBER *Fish Fare* 45 Jacopever, which is sometimes called Cape Red Fish or Red Jacob, is a small red fish with a large head, popping eyes and very large fins. **1949** [see FRANSMADAM]. **1973** *Farmer's Weekly* 18 Apr. 102 In the very early days of the Colony, the Dutch East India Company had as captain of one of its ships a certain Jacob Evert. When the local fishermen caught a fish with a red face, bulging eyes and thick lips they named it jacopever ... The Ugly Men's Club .. in piscatorial society would elect the jacopever unanimously as its president. **1979** SNYMAN & KLARIE *Free from Sea* 30 *Frans madame*, Jacobever/dikoog/peuloog /grootogie ... A member of the bream family and as the name implies, a most attractive small fish. **1979** [see SANCORD]. **1986** SMITH & HEEMSTRA *Smiths' Sea Fishes* 477 *Sebastes capensis* ... False jacopever.

‖**jag** /jax/ *n.* Also **jacht, jagt.** [Afk., earlier Du. *jacht* a hunt, the chase.] A hunt. Also *transf.* (see quot. 1949), and *attrib.*

1826 A.G. BAIN *Jrnls* (1949) 139 Our first day's hunt was very successful ... But I must not trouble you with all the particulars of our 'jagt'. **1910** D. FAIRBRIDGE *That Which Hath Been* (1913) 275 The Piets and Jeans and Pierres, who sat among the older men listening to tales of trek and jacht. **1950** E. PARTRIDGE *Dict. of Underworld Slang* 359 *Jag, the*, The Turf Club races (at Cape Town); South Africa: C. 20. *The Cape Times*, June 3, 1946, short article by Alan Nash. Lit., 'the Hunt'. [**1968** E.A. WALKER *Hist. of Sn Afr.* 95 So popular did elephant-hunting become that soon no borderland lass would look at a young fellow who had not been once at least *op jagt*.] **1977** F.G. BUTLER *Karoo Morning* 116 Uncle Norman told us stories of a genre difficult to define, but they were clearly related to old Boer 'jag stories'. They always involved man and the animal kingdom.

jag /jax/ *v. trans. Obs.* Also **jaag, yach, yag, yah.** [Afk. *ja, jag* to chase or hunt (fr. Du. *jagen* or *jachten*).] To chase, hunt, or pursue (game); to urge on (domestic animals).

1850 R.G.G. CUMMING *Hunter's Life* I. 119, I directed Cobus to ride round and 'jag' them up to me. *Ibid.* II. 362 These being very wild, I yached them on the Boer principle. **1853** W.R. KING *Campaigning in Kaffirland* 80 On the plain we had the good fortune to fall in with several herd of spring-bok ... A party of Dutch Boers *jagging* them and firing above, drove a herd in our direction, giving us some splendid shots. *a***1867** CAPTAIN HARRIS in C.J. Andersson *Lion & Elephant* (1873) 329 It is usual to 'yah' the elephant — that is, ride with him before firing. **1913** C. PETTMAN *Africanderisms* 567 *Yag, or Yah, To*, (D *jachten*, to hurry, to pursue eagerly.) To urge animals to a quicker pace; to drive animals in a certain direction. The two Dutch words *jagen* and *jachten* are etymologically the same, and as used in Cape Dutch their meanings overlap, if they are not confused.

jagd spinnekop var. JAGSPINNEKOP.

jagsick *adj. obs.* [Part. tr. S. Afr. Du. *jaagsiek*, see JAAGSIEKTE.] Suffering from JAAGSIEKTE.

1849 J.D. LEWINS Diary. 15 Nov., The jagsick wether still alive. **1850** *Ibid.* 2 Jan., The jagsick hammel dead.

jagsiekte var. JAAGSIEKTE.

jagspinnekop /ˈjaxˌspənəkɔp/ *n.* Also **jaagspinnekop, jagd spinnekop.** Pl. **-koppe** /-kɔpə/, and (formerly) **-koppen.** [Afk., *jag* hunting + *spinnekop* spider.] Any of several fearsome-looking nocturnal arachnids of the order Solifugae (or Solpuga), yellow-brown in colour and with large, pincer-like jaws; HAARSKEERDER; JERRYMUNGLUM; ROMAN sense 2; ROOIMAN sense 2.

Known as 'sun spider', 'wind-spider', or 'wind-scorpion' in general Eng.

1905 J. DU PLESSIS *1000 Miles in Heart of Afr.* 55 Horrible-looking *jaagspinnekoppen* (hunting spiders) to startle you. **1905** [see ROMAN sense 2]. **1918** S.H. SKAIFE *Animal Life* 161 Romans, *jagd-spinnekoppen*, or *haar-scheerders* .. are ugly creatures, generally some shade of yellowish-brown in colour, and vary in size from half an inch to about five inches in length. **1939** — *S. Afr. Nature Notes* 81 Everybody will agree that the creatures known as jerrymunglums, haarskeerders, jag-spinnekoppe, or romans are among the most repulsive and hideous of all living creatures. There are several different kinds of them. **1979** [see ROMAN sense 2]. **1991** J. RUMP in *Wildlife News* Aug. 8 Scream — 'It's a Solly'. This is what announces the arrival of a Solifugid in our house at Amsterdamhoek. The result will be nightmares from the children for the next week. What is this terrifying creature that is commonly called a 'sunspider', 'jagspinnekop', 'langhaarmannetjie' or 'wind scorpion'.

jag(t)ziekte var. JAAGSIEKTE.

jakhals kost var. JAKKALSKOS.

jakkalsbessie /ˈjakalsˌbesi/ *n.* Also **jakals bessie**, and (formerly) **jackalsbesjie.** [Afk. (earlier S. Afr. Du.), fr. Du. *jakhals* jackal + *besje* berry.] Either of two trees, or their fruit: **a.** The dense spreading tree *Diospyros mespiliformis* of the Ebenaceae, having small, greenish-white, fragrant flowers and oval, yellow fruit; *Transvaal ebony*, see TRANSVAAL; also called *wild apricot* (sense *(b)* see WILD sense a). **b.** The *milkwood* (sense *(a)* see MILK sense 2), *Sideroxylon inerme*. Also *attrib.*

1854 L. PAPPE *Silva Capensis* 22 *Sideroxylon inerme* Lin. (*Melkhoud*) ... The fruit (*Jackalsbesjes*) are edible. **1887** *S.W. Silver & Co.'s Handbk to S. Afr.* 139 Jackalsbesjies, which are edible, are the fruit of the Melkhout, *Sideroxylon inerme*, Lin., a tree common in the Cape, Swellendam, George, and Uitenhage districts. **1917** R. MARLOTH *Common Names* 42 *Jakkalsbessie, Diospyros mespiliformis*, but also *Sideroxylon inerme* (milkwood). **1929** J. STEVENSON-HAMILTON *Low-Veld* 37 Perhaps the most striking .. of the larger forest trees in the Low-Veld is the umtoma (Diospyros mespeliformis), called 'jakals bessie' by the Boers, and sometimes known as the Transvaal ebony tree. **1932** WATT & BREYER-BRANDWIJK *Medicinal & Poisonous Plants* 137 The Zulus take an infusion of the bark of *Sideroxylon inerme* L., White milkwood, Wit melkhout, Jakkals-bessie .. to dispel bad dreams. **1949** J. MOCKFORD *Golden Land* 232, I sat under the green canopy of a jakals-bessie, whose mighty trunk of Transvaal ebony had its roots in a far-spread anthill. **1953** [see GEELHOUT]. **1961** PALMER & PITMAN *Trees of S. Afr.* 134 The jakkalsbessie, a common and most striking tree of the lowveld, is found from Zululand and the Transvaal lowveld, northward to Abyssinia. **1963** S. CLOETE *Rags of Glory* 377 Here and there a giant tree, a baobab, jakkals-bessie, or fig, stood out. **1969** T.H. EVERETT *Living Trees of World* 285 A fine African member of the genus [*Diospyros*] is the jakkalsbessie, West African ebony or Transvaal ebony (*D. mespiliformis*), which becomes 70 feet tall with a trunk diameter of 3 feet. **1972** PALMER & PITMAN *Trees of Sn Afr.* III. 1795 The bar at Leydsdorp is made out of a solid piece of jakkalsbessie timber. **1988** A. HALL-MARTIN et al. *Kaokoveld* 12 The vegetation of the northeastern escarpment zone .. contains many species of plants that are either endemic to the kaokoveld or representative of the eastern mesic flora. Among the latter categories are the baobab .. jakkalsbessie [etc.]. **1991** *Style* Apr. 102 'Never camp under a fever tree,' a fellow guest tells us. 'Jakalsbessie is the best.'

jakkalskos /ˈjakalsˌkɔs/ *n.* Formerly also **jackals-kost, jakhal's kos, jakhals kost.** Pl. unchanged. [Afk., earlier S. Afr. Du. *jakhals kost*, *jakhals* jackal + *kost* food; see quots. 1894 and 1966.] The fleshy, offensive-smelling plant *Hydnora africana*, a parasite on the roots of various species of *Euphorbia*; KANNIP. Also partial translation **jackal's kost.**

1795 C.R. HOPSON tr. *C.P. Thunburg's Trav.* II. 133 This winter Alderman Berg shewed me a very curious Fungus (*Hydnora*) .. called *Jackal's Kost* (or Jackall's food) being, on examination, found to be, with respect to the parts of fructification, the most extraordinary plant of any hitherto known. [**1856** L. PAPPE in *Cape of G.H. Almanac & Annual Register* 343 Hydnora Africana. Thbg (*Cytineae*). This interesting and extraordinary plant which grows parasitically on the roots of *Euphorbia Tirucalli* and other succulent shrubs, is .. called *Kannip* or *Kanimp* by the Hottentots and *Jackals-Kost* by the Dutch Colonists.] **1869** J. MCGIBBON in R. Noble *Cape & its People* 259 Further along the coast .. is found the curious *Hydnora Africana*, or 'Jackal's Kost,' growing parasitically on the roots of *Euphorbia Caput-medusæ*. **1887** *S.W. Silver & Co.'s Handbk to S. Afr.* 159 The Jackal's kost .. are parasitical leafless, or scaly fleshy plants, with large flowers and scarcely any stems. The Jackal's kost, called by the Hottentots Kanimp [*printed* Kauimp], is known to botanists as Aphyteia Hydora. **1894** R. MARLOTH in *Trans. of S. Afr. Phil. Soc.* p.lxxxiv, The eatable part of Hydnora Africana, the curious parasite on the roots of Euphorbia bushes .. [is] eaten by jackals or Bushmen, .. in consequence of which the Colonial name of jackal's kost has been given to the plant. **1912** *E. London Dispatch* 29 Mar. 8 (Pettman), Not a few solved the problem as some higher beings have done since, by making others work for them — the mistletoe and loranthus, the dodder and *Jakhal's kos (Hydnora)* are examples of this class. **1966** C.A. SMITH *Common Names* 258 *Jakkalskos*, The vernacular name used in the sense of something worthless dates back before 1800 and was first used by the Hottentots who had come to speak Dutch. **1977** *Sunday Times* 2 Oct. 3 The flowers .. were more than one could possibly have hoped for — .. nemesias, jakkalskos, .. moederkappies. **1990** M. OETTLE in *Weekend Post* 19 Jan. (Leisure) 7 (*caption*) This weird object, *Hydnora africana* or jakkalskos, is the oddest of the parasitic plants featured by Transkei in its January 10 [stamp] issue.

Jakob Evertsen var. JACOB EVERTSON.

Jakopewer, Jakopiver varr. JACOPEVER.

jall var. JOL *v.*

jamboc, -bok varr. SJAMBOK *n.*

Jameson *n. hist.* [The name of *Leander Starr Jameson*, the leader of the expedition.] Almost invariably in the Special Comb. ***Jameson raid***, the abortive expedition (of about 600 men) which invaded the Transvaal Republic in 1895 with the aim of taking over the government, ostensibly at the request of the UITLANDER population of the Transvaal; RAID. Also *attrib.*

The Raid took place between 29 December 1895 and 2 January 1896.

1897 *E. Prov. Herald* 22 Feb., The Transvaal claim from either the British Government or the Chartered Company for the Jameson Raid was £677,938 for material damages, and £1,000,000 for moral damages. **1899** *De Volkstem* 9 Oct. 1 One of the Jameson Scoundrels Sir John Willoughby has sailed in the 'Mexican' for the Cape. **1902** B. VILJOEN *Reminisc. of Anglo-Boer War* 17 The Jameson Raid was primarily responsible for the hostilities which eventually took place between Great Britain and the Boer Republics. **1903** E.F. KNIGHT *S. Afr. after War* 293, I crossed the border into the Marico district and followed the Jameson Raid road as far as the place known as the Lead Mines. **1911** BLACKBURN & CADDELL *Secret Service* 32 Just after that landmark in the history of the Rand, the Jameson Raid, the authorities at Pretoria moved in response to the complaints of the Chamber of Mines. *a***1930** G. BAUMANN in Baumann & Bright *Lost Republic* (1940) 157 To this day we are still suffering from the effects of the Jameson Raid and the Anglo-Boer War. **1943** 'J. BURGER' *Black Man's Burden* 25 Rhodes and Jameson, probably with the full knowledge of Joseph Chamberlain, attempted to annex the Republic in 1896 by a sudden stroke. Ill-conceived and badly executed, the Jameson Raid was a complete failure, except in so far as it made war between Britain and the Republics almost certain. **1950** H. GIBBS *Twilight* 168 Cecil Rhodes, Premier of the Cape, resigns office following accusations of being involved in the Jameson Raid. **1973** *The 1820* Vol.46 No.11, Everyone knows about the Jameson Raid – but who was Jameson who gave his name to this infamous expedition? **1986** P. MAYLAM *Hist. of Afr. People* 196 The [British South Africa] Company was disgraced by its involvement in the Jameson Raid, and it was that single event more than anything else that kept Bechuanaland directly in the imperial fold. **1989** *Reader's Digest Illust. Hist.* 241 At the time of the Jameson Raid it was feared that there were not enough rifles to arm the commandos called up to resist the invasion.

Hence **Jameson raider** *n.*, a member of this expedition.

1903 E.F. KNIGHT *S. Afr. after War* 291 The road on which the Jameson raiders had ridden to their fate. *a***1930** G. BAUMANN in Baumann & Bright *Lost Republic* (1940) 156 We have had risings, rebellions, and revolutions – and in every instance the leniency of the Transvaal Government to the Jameson Raiders was expected in the case of these warlike actions. **1989** *Reader's Digest Illust. Hist.* 236 The Jameson raiders left Pitsani and Mafeking for the ride to Johannesburg – but surrendered at Vlakfontein farmhouse. **1993** S. GRAY in *Weekly Mail & Guardian* 5 Nov. 48 Migrations have ended here .. : the Hurutshe who built cities; .. the Jameson raiders from British soil across the border.

jammerlappie /ˈjamə(r),lapi/ *n. colloq.* Also **jammerlap**. [Afk. *jammer* sorry, sad + *lappie* see LAPPIE.] VADOEK sense 1. See also LAPPIE sense 1 a.

[**1873** F. BOYLE *To Cape for Diamonds* 294 There lay a rag in the middle of the table, to which everyone applied his hands and mouth when so inclined. With this, the mutton plates were wiped by the eldest daughter.] **1963** A.M. LOUW *20 Days* 80 Breakfast was served ... Oil-cloth table cover and clean, damp jammerlappie made from an old flour-bag. *Ibid.* 81 She handed him the jammerlap to wipe his fingers. **1970** M. VAN DEVENTER *Informant, Pietersburg*, I am covered in peach juice, would you pass me the jammer lappie? **1972** L.G. GREEN *When Journey's Over* 71 Table napkins were seldom provided in those days, but a special wet cloth known as the jammerlappie was passed round after a meal so that guests could wipe their hands. **1972** M. VOM DORP *Informant, Grahamstown* We should actually have a jammerlap here to use with these chops. **1989** *Informant, Grahamstown* This nougat is so sticky you need a jammerlappie with it.

jammy /ˈdʒæmi/ *n. slang.* Also **jammie**. [Perh. formed on Brit. Eng. rhyming slang *jam-jar* car + (informal) n.-forming suffix *-y* (or *-ie*).] See quot. 1971.

[**1963** see CHAFF sense 1]. **1970** [see HANG *n.* sense a]. **1971** M. COZIEN in *UCT Studies in Eng.* Feb. 29 In South African English slang, a Jammie was any sort of car, but particularly a rather well-worn one. **1977** C. HOPE in S. Gray *Theatre Two* (1981) 36 Some of the biggest *brekers* in town .. me an' the boet an' them .. until ou Paulie's *jammie* hopped the Swartkops Bridge that night. *Ibid.* 52 Jus' pass me the keys for your jammie. **1978** A. AKHALWAYA in *Rand Daily Mail* 10 July 7 The timer's left the tannie and vied with the suitcase in a jemmy ... His father's left his mother and gone off with the fat lady in a car. **1981** *Cape Times* 13 Nov. 4 The unhorsed speed cop's jammy .. had broken down and was being towed away for repairs. **1982** D. KRAMER *Short Back & Sides* 61 Got a twin-carb V-8 in this jammie that I drive. You can take me for a dice but you won't survive. I need new tyres, need new shocks. **1985** *E. Prov. Herald* 16 Apr., (advt) Rent a Jammy. Cars from R10 per day.

janbruin /janˈbreɪn, -ˈbrœin/ *n.* Also with initial capital. Pl. unchanged. [Afk., *Jan* John + *bruin* brown; but perh. orig. Du. *tambrijn*, ad. Malay *tambera* bronze (see quot. 1913).] Either of two species of seabream of the Sparidae, members of which are predominantly brown, bronze, or copper in colour: **a.** *Gymnocrotaphus curvidens*; JOHN BROWN sense a. **b.** Less commonly, the BRONZE BREAM (sense b), *Pachymetopon grande*. Also *attrib.*

In Smith and Heemstra's *Smiths' Sea Fishes* (1986), the name 'janbruin' is used for *G. curvidens*.

1902 J.D.F. GILCHRIST in *Trans. of S. Afr. Philological Soc.* XI. iv. 229 Jan Bruin, John Brown, Tambrijn? ... *Gymnocrotaphus curvidens*. **1913** C. PETTMAN *Africanderisms* 493 *Tambrijn, Jan Bruin, John Brown*, (? Have these names their origin in the Mal. *tambra, tambarah; tombra*, Java, names given to an edible fish in the Malay Archipelago.) *Gymnocrotaphus curvidens* is known by these various designations along the South African coast. **1930** C.L. BIDEN *Sea-Angling Fishes* 230 The Afrikaans name is Jan Bruin from which the English-speaking people took the literal translation 'John Brown' a few generations ago. **1972** [see DAS sense 2]. **1972** *Grocott's Mail* 13 Oct. 3 Recently the Kasouga coast has been the popular stretch for the janbruin fishermen. **1974** *Daily Dispatch* 29 May 27 Jan Bruin on the bite. Anglers believe .. that the jan bruin could well be starting to bite again. **1987** *E. Prov. Herald* 28 Mar. 6 It [*sc.* the Hottentot] must have the world's longest list of common names ... To add to the confusion it is also known as jan bruin, a name also given to another far more insignificant fish.

Jan Compagnie /jan kɔmpanˈ(j)i/ *n. phr. Hist.* Also **Jan Kompanie**. [Du., *Jan* John + *Compagnie* Company; see quot. 1786.] An informal name for the Dutch East India Company (see COMPANY). Also partial translation **Jan Company**.

1786 G. FORSTER tr. *A. Sparrman's Voy. to Cape of G.H.* II. 21 Many of the ignorant Hottentots and Indians not having been able to form any idea of the Dutch East-India Company and the board of direction, the Dutch from the very beginning in India, politically gave out the company for one individual powerful prince, by the christian name of *Jan* or *John* ... On this account I ordered my interpreter to say farther, that we were children of *Jan Company*, who had sent us out to view this country. **1832** [see WINKEL]. **1936** *Cambridge Hist. of Brit. Empire* VIII. 174 Not the least of the grievances of the colonists against 'Jan Compagnie' was this shoddy currency which was only exchangeable into hard money of foreign merchants at a discount of between 20 and 30 per cent. **1958** E.H. BURROWS *Hist. of Medicine* 17 Since the surgeons of the Company's vessels are the principal characters of our story .. it is necessary to examine their relationship to *Jan Compagnie* more closely. **1963** J. PACKER *Home from Sea* 58 They .. were already establishing outlying republics such as Swellendam, in the days of the Dutch East India Company, for they liked the rule of 'Jan Kompanie' no better than they did the British régime which followed it. **1973** M. PHILLIPS *19th Burgher* 29 The talk among us is of national independence and free trade ... It must come, and when it does it will mean the death of Jan Compagnie and the birth of a nation.

ja-nee /jɑ(ː)ˈnɪə/ *adv.* Also **ja-neh, ya(h)-nee**. [Afk. (lit. 'yes-no'), 'sure', 'that's a fact'; qualifying a response.]

In all senses equivalent to YES-NO.

1. A non-committal expression used when the appropriate reaction is not obvious, or when one wishes to avoid saying something hypocritical or unpleasant; a vague expression of agreement or assent.

1948 H.V. MORTON *In Search of S. Afr.* 51 The lady enriched my vocabulary by a glorious word, not in the phrase-book, which, by means of intonation, may express affirmation, negation, approval, disapproval, credulity, and incredulity at will. It is just 'ja-nee', which means yes-no. **1973** Y. BURGESS *Life to Live* 96 Ja nee, pull your arse in a bit more. **1980** M. MATSHOBA in *Staffrider* Vol.3 No.1, 6 'Ya, neh,' I said, for the sake of saying something. [**1985** C. CHARLES in *Staffrider* Vol.6 No.2, 19 'Good evening officer,' I said in my most endearing politeness. 'Ja no ..' was all he muttered as he pushed himself into the hallway, 'Are you the owner of this property?'] **1988** *Femina* Mar. 89 When I revisit the Karoo, I develop an instant accent. I say *Ja-Nee*. I eat dried sausage. And I love sheep. **1990** R. MALAN *My Traitor's Heart* 58, I couldn't afford to alienate them, so I always sighed and shook my head and said 'ja-nee', a Boer phrase that means 'yes-no' and comes in handy when nothing else comes to mind.

2. Used to express rueful resignation, disillusionment, or dejection resulting from an unpleasant realization (esp. from the discovery that something or someone is not as pleasant or innocuous as one at first believed).

1970 A. FULTON *I Swear to Apollo* 214 Ja, nee, he thought mournfully, it's the men outside that hit the headlines. **1980** *Fair Lady* 19 Nov. 384 Ah yes, or *ja-nee* as I have now learnt to say. I was not at High Rustenburg losing weight, but on the Heia Safari Ranch acquiring a new language. **1984** *Frontline* Feb. 34 JaaaaNeeee. If this is development, homeland style, something *is* wrong. **1988** J. HEYNS in *Sunday Times* 3 July (Extra) 2 The N., I discovered, stood for non-white! To give an N. jockey a full name was racetrack sacrilege in the Orange Free State. Ja nee.

3. An emphatic affirmation of what one has said or is about to say, or of what someone else has said.

*a***1971** C. EGLINGTON in *Contrast 43* Vol.2 No.3, 83 Among old men I've heard 'Ja-nee', 'Ja-nee' – Repeated like a chuckle or lament When, after rumination, they felt free To summarise and clinch all they had meant by Long discourse in praise or condemnation Of a current political situation. **1972** L. VAN DER POST *Story Like Wind* 143 Looking down at the elephant, he exclaimed, 'Ja-nee, he was *darem* a monument of his kind'. **1972** R. MALAN *Ah Big Yaws* 59 The inability to see paradox or contradiction in what they do or say which most Woozers [White Urban English-speaking South Africans] suffer from elicits the curious and, to 'outsiders,' doubtless confusing affirmation *Yahnee!* **1984** *Frontline* Feb. 27 Ja-nee, Koos, there's much to tell you about [this] weird and wonderful city. **1985** J. THOMAS in *Fair Lady* 1 May 20 Of course, boetie of course. Ja-nee. Yes, a great triomf. **1987** L. BEAKE *Strollers* 43 Abel wasn't going to be caught in the same trap with that Johnny! Ja, nee, wragtig! **1988** A. SICHEL in *Star* 27 May 13 De Wet isn't your mail-order boereseun, 'Not classic Boksburg,' he grins. Ja nee, he went to all the right schools.

4. Used to express the paradoxical or contradictory nature of a situation. Also *attrib.*

1972 L. VAN DER POST *Story Like Wind* 143 *Ja-nee* literally means 'yes-no' ... It was for him an expression in the here and now of the mysterious, inexpressible and abiding paradox that is at the heart of all inanimate and living matter. **1990** *Cue* 30 June (Suppl.) 2 Her brother is both a hunter and leading conservationist. This is the *Ja/Nee* contradictory situation in which so many South Africans find themselves.

5. Introducing a contradiction: 'I understand why you think that, but you are wrong.'

1987 *Frontline* Feb. 41 The current exchange rate is not a 'true' exchange rate, I hear you cry. Political factors have depressed it. In terms of buying power, the rand is really worth much more. Yes and no. Or Ja-nee. **1988** D. PAICE in *Femina* June 40 *Ja-Nee*, they tell me when I ask about upper-class Afrikaans, there is no such thing.

Hence **ja-nee** *n.*, vacillation; one who vacillates, or who contradicts himself or herself.

1983 *Sunday Times* 18 Sept. 34 The Ja-Nees must not have it. **1987** *Sowetan* 6 Oct. 9 Ja-nee on group areas. **1990** *Sunday Times* 19 Aug. 14 Doctor Ja-Nee ... A master of ambiguity, he relies on sleight of phrase and ideological double jointedness to wriggle out of potentially tight spots.

Janfiskaal /janfəs'kɑːl/ *n.* Also **Jan Fiscaal, Janniefiskaal.** [Afk., *Jan* John (+ -IE) + *fiskaal* bailiff; see quot. 1951.] The FISCAL (sense 2), *Lanius collaris.*

1936 E.L. GILL *First Guide to S. Afr. Birds* 50 Fiscal shrike *Lanius collaris. Synonyms*: Janfiskaal, Jacky Hangman, Laksman, Kanariebyter. **1951** L.G. GREEN *Grow Lovely* 45 For nearly two centuries Cape Town's chief of police was an official with the title of Fiscal — a name which survives in the shape of Janfiskaal, Jacky Hangman or butcher-bird. That shows you how popular the fiscal was. **1971** *Informant, Grahamstown* Isn't Jacky Hangman the same as Jan Fiscaal? **1977** F.G. BUTLER *Karoo Morning* 161 One day when I came .. with my specimen jar full of newly dead wonders, one of my cousins laughed and said, 'Here comes old Janfiskaal.' I was deeply .. hurt by this pleasantry. The habits of the butcherbird, Jacky Hangman, or Janfiskaal, were well known to me.

Jan Frederik /jan'frid(ə)rək, -'frɪəd(ə)rək/ *n. phr.* Also **Jan Fredric.** [Afk. (earlier S. Afr. Du.), onomatopoeic, for the sound of its call.] The *Cape robin* (see CAPE sense 2 a), *Cossypha caffra*; a representation of its call. Also *attrib.*

*c*1808 C. VON LINNÉ *System of Natural Hist.* VIII. 337 The John-Frederic is very common through all that fourth part of Africa reaching from the Cape-town to Caffraria along the east coast. *a*1867 C.J. ANDERSSON *Notes on Birds of Damara Land* (1872) 119 The male sings very pleasantly; and his notes have been likened to the following differently intoned syllables, jan-fredric-dric-dric fredric, whence its colonial name of Jan frédric. **1896** H.A. BRYDEN *Tales of S. Afr.* 109 You may see and hear the lively, inquisitive Jan Fredric thrush, with his pleasing song, and his curious note — 'Jan-fredric-dric-dric-fredric.' **1923** HAAGNER & IVY *Sketches* 170 The commonest member of the Robin-Chats is the 'Cape' species (*Cossypha caffra*) called the Cape Robin or Jan Fredric. **1936** E.L. GILL *First Guide to S. Afr. Birds* 64 *Cape Robin, Jan Frederik* .. Has a typical thrush-and-robin song, clear and ringing, delivered in phrases. **1983** K.B. NEWMAN *Newman's Birds* 324 *Cape Robin*, .. Has a pleasant and continuing song, each passage starting on the same note and with the phrase 'Jan-Frederik' often repeated.

Jangroentjie /jan'xruɪŋki/ *n.* Also **Jan groentje.** [Afk., lit. 'little green John', *Jan* John + *groen* green + dim. suffix -IE.]

1. Any of several species of sunbird, esp. *Nectarinia famosa* of the Nectariniidae; also called HONEY-SUCKER (sense 2).

In G.L. Maclean's *Roberts' Birds of Sn Afr.* (1993), *N. famosa* is called the 'malachite sunbird'.

1909 'ANDIAZI' in *E. London Dispatch* 2 Apr. 4 There is a reason .. and a very cogent one, for Jan Groentje to wear a fine coat. **1913** C. PETTMAN *Africanderisms* 233 *Jan groentje*, The name given to the exquisite little Sugar-birds .. which 'like emeralds feathered in flame' hover over the flowers of garden and bush. **1982** *S. Afr. Panorama* Sept. 50 *Jangroentjie* is a glossy green bird.

2. Peppermint liqueur: *Groen Mamba*, see MAMBA sense 2.

1949 L.G. GREEN *In Land of Afternoon* 58 Every farmer made three liqueurs for house-hold use — Jan Groentjie (peppermint), aniseed and Van der Hum.

japie /'jɑːpi/ *n. derog.* Also **jaapie, jarpie, yarpie, yarpy,** and (freq.) with initial capital. [Afk. personal name *Japie*, dim. of *Jaap* 'Jake', derived fr. *Jakobus* James.]

1. A contemptuous name for an Afrikaner.

1949 O. WALKER *Wanton City* 104 Peter had the slighting word 'rooinek' flung in his ear ... But the insult was either intended for, or intercepted by, another young man on his left, who halted and snarled something about 'bloody Japies'. **1968** *Eng. Alive* 63 Another question that might be asked here is why do people refer to the Afrikaans speaking population of South Africa as 'Dutchmen' or 'Japies'. **1980** D. BECKETT in *Bloody Horse* No.2, 14 They've taken up with some new kids along the road who come from Welkom or somewhere and hardly even speak any English. You wouldn't believe what Simon talks like now. He sounds like a real little Japie.

2. *transf.* A jocular, affectionate, or derogatory term for a South African.

Although presented by some South Africans as a term which is current in world English, no examples of the word in use by non-South Africans have been found.

1956 H. KOPS *Veld, City & Sea* 30 He'd had a fight with two South Africans. He'd cleaned them up, he said. Said he hated 'bloody jaapies'. **1970** R. NIXON *Informant, KwaZulu-Natal* Yarpy. English name for a South African. **1981** *Sunday Times* 6 Dec. 1 They left for Britain, where the couple managed to get a 'cold, damp flat' in the centre of Liverpool which they called 'Japies' Corner' to remind them of home. **1986** *Frontline* Mar. 34 G'day, mate. Yer new around here. Where yer from? *Morning. I'm from er, South Africa actually.* A Yarpie, huh.

3. A yokel, an unsophisticated person, esp. one from the rural areas; a low-class person; GAWIE; JAAP. See also PLAASJAPIE.

1964 J. MEINTJES *Manor House* 119 They referred to the backvelders as *duine-molle, japies, takhare, gawies* and so on. **1968** M. DOYLE *Impala* 101 He was a thirteen-year-old scholar and not a little *bywoner* 'Japie'. **1984** *Sunday Tribune* 22 July (Today) 4 We encountered many people who thought we were absolutely stark raving mad to go and muck about in the wilds ... Not only were you nuts but you were considered low-class: as in 'these Japies obviously can't afford to live in a hotel'. **1990** C. LAFFEATY *Far Forbidden Plains* 508 Abel was a *japie* from the farm with cow dung between his toes and didn't understand the ways of sophisticated city men. **1990** D. KRAMER in *Sunday Times* 5 Aug. 13 It's part of the South African identity to dress like a Japie and speak with a guttural accent.

jarwellnofine see JA *adv.* sense 3 f.

jaul, jawl *n.* and *adj.* var. JOL *n.* and *adj.*

jawl *v.* var. JOL *v.*

jawler var. JOLLER.

JC *n. Hist. colloq.* Also **J.C.** [Initial letters of *Junior Certificate.*] **a.** The Junior Certificate examination, an external (school-leaving) examination taken, in the past, at the end of the Standard Eight year (the tenth year of schooling); JUNIOR CERTIFICATE sense a. **b.** The certificate or qualification so gained; JUNIOR CERTIFICATE sense b. **c.** By metonymy: The Standard Eight year. Also *attrib.*

1939 J. LUDUS in *Outspan* 20 Oct. 53 Why 'shrink back appalled' because a J.C. question paper cannot be answered off-hand by 'an English university graduate of some 16 years standing'? **1947** [see MATRICULATION sense 1]. **1957** *Pietersburg Eng. Medium School Mag.* Dec. 85 Anthony left us at the end of 1956 having obtained his J.C. and followed in his two elder brothers' footsteps by going to the Air Force. **1962** M.G. McCOY *Informant, Port Elizabeth* She starts exams tomorrow, the J.C. trials I presume. **1974** [see TRIBAL COLLEGE]. **1976** M. THOLO in C. Hermer *Diary of Maria Tholo* (1980) 110 The oldest two were in Matric, another one in J.C. and the baby in Standard 2. **1981** *Rand Daily Mail* 3 Apr. 3 It could be the end of the JC exam. The phasing out of the Standard 8 examination in black schools from 1982 is to be investigated. **1982** M. MZAMANE *Children of Soweto* 8 Kgopo's two daughters had dropped out of school after several unsuccessful attempts at J.C. **1987** S. VAN DER MERWE in *New Nation* 23 Apr. 11 Did very well in JC — to become a good factory labourer. **1990** *Tribute* Sept. 139 'She probably doesn't even have JC,' I'd think, saying nothing, so angry I'd sometimes almost feel her neck in my slowly squeezing hands.

jeeslike var. JISLAAIK.

jems bok var. GEMSBOK.

jentoe var. GENTOO.

Jerepigo /ˌdʒerə'piːgəʊ/ *n.* Also **Cherupiga, Jerepico, Jeripigo,** and with small initial. [ad. Eng. *geropiga, jeropiga* a mixture of grape-juice, brandy, sugar, and red colouring, manufactured in Portugal and used to adulterate port-wine, ad. Pg. *jeropiga* (ultimately fr. Gk *hiera* feminine form of *hieros* 'sacred', a name given to many medicines in the Greek pharmacopoeia + *picra* feminine form of *pikros* bitter).] Any of several very sweet, heavy, fortified dessert-wines. Also *attrib.* See also CAPE WINE.

1862 LADY DUFF-GORDON *Lett. from Cape* (1925) 157, I have a notion of some Cherupiga wine for ourselves ... It is about one shilling and fourpence a bottle here, sweet red wine, unlike any other I ever drank. **1947** L.G. GREEN *Tavern of Seas* 52 White Jeripico, a wine with a high sugar content, is blended for the sweet sherry types. **1947** H.C. BOSMAN in L. Abrahams *Cask of Jerepigo* (1972) 37 They had a bottle of Jerepigo wine which they were passing backwards and forwards and .. taking surreptitious swigs. **1959** A. DELIUS *Last Division* 26 Cut from the sherried vines around Constantia The grapes are turning into Jerepigo, Vaaljapie, dop, Cape Smoke or something fancier That pierced Napoleon's gut but soothed his ego. **1972** A.G. BAGNALL *Wines of S. Afr.* 32 The sweet types [*sc.* sherries] have their flavour and colour imparted to them .. by the addition of a quota of jerepigo — a well-matured wine in which the sugar of the original juice has been conserved by fortification with grape spirit. **1982** J. PLATTER in *Fair Lady* 3 Nov. 181 *Jerepigo* .. is fortified and by law must be between 16,5 and 22 degrees alcohol by volume. It can be either red or white or pink and always very sweet and heavyish. The style is powerful. **1986** *Pretoria News* 24 Sept. 13 Life does not begin and end in Zeerust. And nor is jerepigo the only wine the connoisseur enjoys. **1990** *Excellence* Vol.6 No.2, 5 We're not talking port or sherry or noble late harvest here, we're talking jerepigo, the umbrella name for our sweet fortified wines, a type virtually unkown in the rest of the world. There's quite a variety available which is part of the charm ... Jerepigo are divided into muscat and non-muscat flavoured wines. **1992** *E. Prov. Herald* 18 May 2 The humble jerepigo and the lusty pinotage.

jerrymunglum /ˌdʒɛrɪˈmʌŋgləm/ n. [Unknown.] JAGSPINNEKOP.

c1939 S.H. SKAIFE S. Afr. Nature Notes 81 Everybody will agree that the creatures known variously as jerrymunglums, haarskeerders, jag-spinnekoppe, or romans are among the most repulsive of all living creatures ... Jerrymunglums is a delightful name ... Its origin is obscure; perhaps it was coined by someone with a sense of humour and has stuck because of its aptness. **1955** — Dwellers in Darkness 88 Larger ones [sc. sun spiders] are common in Egypt and the Near East and troops became familiar with these during the two world wars and it was they, apparently, who gave them their quaint but apt name of 'jerrymunglums'. **1993** D. VAN DER HORST Informant, Cape Town We used to call those huge spiders 'jerrymunglums' in the army.

Jerusalemganger /jeˈrysalem ˌxaŋə(r), dʒəˈruːsələm -/ n. hist. Also **Jeruzalemganger**. [Afk. Jerusalem (earlier Du. Jeruzalem) Jerusalem + ganger goer.] A member of a religious sect among the Voortrekkers (see VOORTREKKER n. sense 1) who believed that the GREAT TREK would lead to the discovery of an overland route to Jerusalem. Usu. in pl., used collectively.

[**1877** T. BAINES Gold Regions of S.-E. Afr. 83 In the earliest migrations of the Dutch Boers from the Cape Colony they entertained hopes of being able to reach the Beloofte land, i.e. the promised land or Canaan ... When the avowed Jerusalem trekkers or pilgrims came to the Maghaliquain and found it flowing north, they at once christened it the Nile.] **1928** E.A. WALKER Hist. of S. Afr. 271 So closely did some of them follow the historical parallel that Andrew Murray found the Jeruzalemgangers of Marico ready to trek down the river Nyl which should guide them to Zion. **1949** L.G. GREEN In Land of Afternoon 146 The Jerusalemgangers, a group of religious fanatics .. took part in the Great Trek .. because they wanted to reach Jerusalem overland. **1955** T.V. BULPIN Storm over Tvl 24 The famed Jerusalem-gangers of Adam Enslin .. were [so] impressed by the appearance and legends of this summit that they considered it to be the ruin of one of the pyramids, and confirmation positive of their notion that they had reached the upper reaches of the Nile.

jesslike, jess-laik varr. JISLAAIK.

‖**Jeugbond** /ˈjiœxbɔnt/ n. [Afk., ellipt. for Nasionale Jeugbond (National Youth League).] The youth wing of the National Party. Also attrib., and transf.

[**1955** Time in M. Rogers Black Sash (1956) 70 Just before Strijdom arrived, 100 husky members of the Nasionale Jeugbond, the Nationalists' youth group, shouldered the women aside, and formed a solid, muscular phalanx inside the Black Sashers' double lines.] **1970** Daily News 25 May, There is mounting concern in the Nationalist Party about the erstwhile energetic Jeugbond, the youth wing of the party, which is, on the present indications, dying a lingering death. [**1973** Sunday Times 27 May 6 Mr. P.W. Botha disbanded the Nasionale Jeugbond in the 1950s when it became known that most of them were Strijdom supporters.] **1978** Ibid. 19 Feb. 15 Gatsha's Zulu Jeugbond. Youth .. the crucial word in South African black politics since Soweto, June 16, 1976. **1989** W. EBERSOHN in Cosmopolitan Apr. 198 A 31-year-old attorney had been elected to the Transvaal leadership of the Nasionale Jeugbond, the NP's youth wing.

Hence **Jeugbonder** n., a member of the Jeugbond.

1955 Rand Daily Mail in M. Rogers Black Sash (1956) 82 Included among the Jeugbonders, said Mrs Curry, were children of six years of age, and youths up to 18 years of age.

jeuk skei var. JUKSKEI.

jevrouw var. JUFFROU.

Jewburg n. Obs. Derog. [A pun on JO'BURG; see quot. 1934.] An offensive name for Johannesburg. So **Jewburger** n., a (Jewish) Johannesburg magnate.

1902 I. HAMILTON in T. Pakenham Boer War (1982) 562 Do let us profit by our experience when we smashed the Zulus for the Boers, and not repeat the mistake by annihilating the Boers for the Jewburghers. **1934** C.P. SWART Supplement to Pettman. 80 Jewburg, A corruption of Jo'burg, humorously applied to Johannesburg where Jewry is well represented. **1951** O. WALKER Shapeless Flame 193 Johannesburg was writing its nickname 'Jewburg' large over the sands, and the air was thick with broken English.

Jewish /ˈdʒuːɪʃ, ʒʊʒ/ adj. and n. Slang. Also **j(o)uj, zchoosch, zhoozsh**, and with small initial. [fr. Isicamtho iJuwish 'excellent', 'stylish', also 'fashionable clothing', fr. Eng. Jewish, with spelling remodelled to the English root.

The term perh. reflects a perception that Jewish people dress with style, or records the early predominance of Jews in the Johannesburg clothing trade. The variant spellings are attempts by English-speakers to reflect the pronunciation of the Isicamtho word.]

Originally in township slang, but now more widely used:

A. adj. Excellent, 'cool'; well-dressed, elegantly dressed. Hence (nonce) superlative form **Jewishest**.

[**1962** W.S. MANQUPU in Star 22 Feb. 14 [In 'isicamtho'] 'beef' means to get drunk; 'guess' is bad luck, 'Jewish' is excellent; 'jumpers' is late afternoon.] a**1968** D.C. THEMBA in E. Patel World of Can Themba (1985) 36 The tsotsi turned round and looked out of the window on to the platform. He recognized some of his friends there and hailed them. 'O, Zigzagsa, it's how there?' 'It's jewish!' **1985** H. PRENDINI in Style Oct. 41 Blacks look at someone who's well-dressed and announce admiringly 'Mooi-Jewish!' **1989** M. BRAND in Fair Lady 25 Oct. 92 Zchoosch, elegantly cool. **1992** A. JAY on Radio Five 19 Nov., If you wear this tie you'll be the jujiest oke in Cape Town.

B. n. Expensive clothing; the latest fashions; style, chic.

1972 Drum 8 Apr. 19 Maybe they were jealous of our expensive jewish. We pay for the clothes because we can afford them. **1973** P. BECKER in The 1820 Vol.46 No.7, 33 Billy is always unimpeachably attired in the very best 'Jewish', meaning top class suits from Johannesburg's most thickly carpeted outfitting stores. **1981** New Dawn Dec. [Cover], The Latest 'Jewish'. [**1982** C. NXUMALO Informant, Johannesburg There's even a participle for Jewish – 'ujewishile' all dressed up.] **1982** D. BIKITSHA in Rand Daily Mail 14 Oct. (Eve) 5 Money terms were coined by the Jewish ... Dress or fashion: lap, ndwango, Jewish, dlik, mestern etc. [**1990** M.J.H. MFUSI Soweto Zulu Slang. Appendix A, iJuwish (Jewish), expensive clothing.] **1992** B. RONGE in Sunday Times 10 May (Mag. Sect.) 8 This was the jet-set and I definitely required a touch of what some hairdressers call 'zhoozsh'. So I set out for Sandton City, the world's largest supplier of 'zhoozsh' to the masses.

Hence **Jewish** v. trans., to dress (someone or something) up.

1963 B. MODISANE Blame Me on Hist. (1986) 50 The boys were expensively dressed in a stunning ensemble of colour; 'Jewished' in their phraseology. **1992** Style Feb. 82 A Queenspark bouclé jacket, R180, which was joujed up with beading by Dickie Longhurst and diamanté buttons from Liberty's.

jieke var. GEITJIE.

Jim n. Obsolescent. offensive. [Prob. U.S. Eng., perh. ellipt. for Jim Crow a black man, orig. fr. popular 19th C. African-American ballad.] An insulting term for a black African man; also used as a form of address; JIM FISH; JOHN.

1878 H.A. ROCHE On Trek in Tvl 21 Jim the Kafir, Sam the Coolie, or Tom the Little Oomfan, – all equally 'Boys'. **1936** WILLIAMS & MAY I Am Black 80 Do you think the white Baases care what your mother and father call you? ... If you have no real name they will make one for you. Otherwise they will call you 'Jim,' or 'boy!' **1948** [see JOHN]. **1949** [see SAMMY]. **1952** H. KLEIN Land of Silver Mist 58, I went with Radebe to the Inchcape Hall, the Bantu night club. We saw 'Jim' and 'Mary' of everyday life in evening dress on the ballroom floor. **1955** J.B. SHEPHARD Land of Tikoloshe 76, I don't call him 'Jim' or 'Boy' but 'Umteto', his real name. That is polite. **1961** D. BEE Children of Yesterday 274 'What's your name, Jim?' he asked. 'Johannes, Baas,' the man said. **1963** B. MODISANE Blame Me on Hist. (1986) 242 The African has been reduced to a symbol which has to answer to labels like, Jim, John and boy. **1987** Frontline Mar. 10 The Magistrate says: 'Certainly, Mr Tshabalala.' Mr Tshabalala. Those days there were no black Misters in the Magistrate's Court. There were Jims and Jacks.

Hence (nonce) **Jim** v. trans., to address (someone) as Jim.

1965 E. MPHAHLELE Down Second Ave 152, I was 'Jimmed' and 'boy-ed' and 'John-ed' by whites.

Jim Fish n. phr. Derog. and offensive. [Unknown; perh. ad. U.S. Jim Crow, see JIM.] JIM.

1930 L. BARNES Caliban in Afr. 121 Dr. E.G. Malherbe refers to 'the business man who sits at his office desk and rings the bell for Jim Fish, who is working in the yard, to bring him his spectacles, which lie just a little beyond his reach on the desk'. **1931** Nat. Geog. Mag. Apr. 412 Umtata's bunga, .. under whose dome 'Jim Fish' (which is Afrikander for Jim Crow) sits among his gaily blanketed yellow councillors, debating territorial questions. **1943** D. REITZ No Outspan 199, I was taken to a cinema show for the local natives that evening [in 1934] ... The fool of the piece was called Jim Fish. His role was to do everything in the wrong way in order to teach the others how to do it correctly. **1951** R. FARRAN Jungle Chase (1957) 114, I like Jim Fish, and he likes me. Duff him up when he is cheeky, give him a kind word when he does well and never treat him unjustly. **1951** E. DAVIS in B. Sachs Herman Charles Bosman (1971) 222 Safely ensconced in Bloomsbury, he [sc. Roy Campbell] could be as offensive as he pleased to any South African who displeased him. And we all displeased him, from Jan Smuts to Jim Fish. **1975** J. McCLURE Snake (1981) 83 Good God, at the rate we're going, I'm likely to find myself working with Jungle Jim alongside of me! .. Jungle Jim? .. O, my mistake! Jim Fish – that's it, isn't it? **1979** W. STEENKAMP in Cape Times 18 July, Those who believed that the average guerilla, in the immortal words of an overly sanguine soldier in the early days, was just 'Jim Fish with a knife'.

jintoe, -too varr. GENTOO.

jirr(a), jirre varr. YIRRA.

jis /jəs/ int. slang. Also **j(i)ss**. [Afk., shortened form of jislaaik (origin unknown), or euphemism for Jesus (Afk. pron. /ˈjiəsəs/).] JISLAAIK. Also **jissie** [see -IE].

1974 A.P. BRINK Looking on Darkness 51 To be alone en' me not quite seventeen, jiss. Ibid. 119 Jiss, but you're a deep lightie, hey? **1986** Style Dec. 41 But jis, they could kwela, hey? **1986** V. COOKE et al. in S. Gray Market Plays 36 Jiss, he stinks. **1987** Scope 20 Nov. 39 Jissie, I'm feeling blind, man! **1990** Style July 64, I never forget. Jis, it sounds like Joan Collins but its true.

jislaaik /ˈjəslaɪk, ˈjɪs-, ˈdʒəs-/ int. colloq. Also **je(e)slike, jess-laik, jigslaak, jislaik, jis-like, juslike, yesslik, yislaaik, yislike, yusslaik, yusslark**. [Afk.; ultimate origin unknown.] An exclamation conveying any of a range of feelings: wonder, delight, admiration, approval, distress, dismay, anger, reproval or regret; JIS; YISSUS. Cf. HANG int.

1960 D. MARAIS Hey! Van der Merwe (1961), (caption) Jislaaik! It's been New Year's Day for five days now. When will it be 1961? **1965** — Ag, Sis Man!, (caption) Jislike! The old Cape Tradition is taking a beating. **1970** Forum Vol.6 No.2, 27 'Yislike, its cold in here' he said, and slumped down heavily next to the other man. **1971** *The 1820* Vol.44 No.5, 25 First, let's explain the meaning of the word 'jislaaik' ... This, in the glossary of South Africanisms, hits the jackpot in the force of its meaning. Jislaaik (pronounced yislike) is a composite of the English equivalents, super, heavens, wacko, great Scott, by George, fabulous, unbelievable, gee whiz, etc. **1978** S. ROBERTS in *New Classic* No.5, 22 An ex-Police *Colonel*, and they set him in a back office and let him sort the post. 'Jis-like!' I whispered. **1980** *Sunday Times* 7 Dec. 40 They smote each other upon the shoulders, .. and uttered the ancient invocation 'Yislaaik!'. The significance of this cry is lost in the mists of time. **1981** *Fair Lady* 9 Sept., When particularly impressed by Gerrie Coetzee's left hook, they will exclaim 'Yusslaik!'. **1989** D. RORKE in *Ski-Boat* Jan.-Feb. 46 'Juslaaik!' said I .. 'He's in a hurry to get to the hotel'. **1990** [see Rosenthal quot. at LIGHTY sense 1]. **1993** S. DIKENI in *Cape Times* 21 Aug. (Top of the Times) 17 Jislaaik I miss the shebeen.

jisses, jissus varr. YISSUS.

jiss(ie) var. JIS.

jita var. and pl. form of MAJITA.

Jlambi var. NDLAMBE.

JMB *n. hist.* A short name for the *Joint Matriculation Board*, a statutory body created in 1916 to conduct a university entrance examination, to prescribe the conditions under which exemption from this examination might be granted, to issue school-leaving certificates, and (later) to control standards of marking and curriculum development at matriculation level. Also *attrib.* See also MATRICULATION.

From 1921, the four provinces began setting their own matriculation examinations. An Act to dismantle the Board was passed in 1984 but has yet to come into effect (1994).

1956 G.H. DURRANT in *Proceedings of Conference of Writers, Publishers, Editors* (Witwatersrand Univ. Press, 1957) 13 These measures .. apply only to the J.M.B.'s own examinations. **1985** *Diamond Fields Advertiser* 13 Apr. 6 Initially the Government decided to scrap the JMB matric exam, but protests from many private schools conducting the exam stalled this decision. **1991** P.R.T. NEL tr. *M.H. Trümpelmann's Joint Matric. Board* 2 The Joint Matriculation Board (JMB) presently [*sc.* in 1984] fulfils a most essential function by determining .. one joint set of standards for university admission. *Ibid.* 33 There is [*sc.* in 1966] such a difference in standards between the Departmental examination and the JMB examination, that comparison .. is highly dangerous. *Ibid.* 129 The JMB had fulfilled an important function in controlling and maintaining standards for university admission [but] .. the JMB had concerned itself too narrowly with universities only.

JMC *n.* Pl. **JMCs, JMC's**, or unchanged. Initial letters of *Joint Management Committee* (one of about 500 local organizations), or of *Joint Management Centre* (one of twelve regional bodies), components of a security structure established in 1985 under the control of the State Security Council, with the aim of defusing unrest, co-ordinating government action, and organizing welfare and social services at local and regional level. Also *attrib.*

1986 A. SPARKS in *Cape Times* 18 Dec. 12 A series of Joint Management Committees (JMCs) which are the local limbs of an elaborate intelligence network called the National Security Management System, have sought to re-establish the legitimacy of the state authorities by identifying and redressing local grievances. **1987** P. CULL in *E. Prov. Herald* 30 May 4 The JMCs in the Eastern Cape .. had links with both the Regional Development Advisory Committee for the Eastern Cape and the East Cape Strategic Task Force. **1987** *New Nation* 11 June 7 R90-million has been pumped into Alexandra, for example, through the Joint Management Centre (JMC) system, with the aim of appeasing the people and distracting them from their real political demands. *Ibid.* 22 Oct. 22 The military strategists around PW Botha have taken a hard line on the extra-parliamentary opposition and activated the National Security Management System (NSMS) with its several hundred Joint Management Committees (JMC). **1988** *S. Afr. Panorama* Jan. 14 The prompt action that .. provided immediate flood relief is largely due to the success .. of civil defence organisations, and the joint management committee (JMC) in Durban. **1988** *Race Rel. Survey 1986* (S.A.I.R.R.) II. 512 The minister of defence .. officially acknowledged the existence of 12 bodies designed to 'defuse unrest' ... These bodies, known as joint management centres (JMCs) were designed to provide the government with an 'early warning system' for internal threats to state security. **1988** *Now Everyone Is Afraid* (Catholic Inst. for Internat. Rel.) 11 The Joint Management Centres (JMC's) that fall under the SSC are made up of important bureaucrats and 'key people' at a local level. JMC's meet under the chairpersonship of the local head of the South African Defence Force (SADF) and try to address local security problems. From mid-1986 it appears that these structures took responsibility for all security decisions. **1989** *Race Rel. Survey 1988–9* (S.A.I.R.R.) 524 The chairmen or members of the JMCs .. are functionaries of state departments and provinces and officers of the security forces ... The aim of the JMCs was to provide departmental inputs at regional levels so that action could be coordinated. **1990** *Weekly Mail* 21 Dec. (Suppl.) 13 For five years a network of Joint Management Centres and mini-JMCs had become the SSC's eyes and ears, and had implemented its dictates.

jo var. YO.

joala /ˈdʒwaːlə, dʒɔˈaːla/ *n.* Also **jwala**. [S. Sotho *bjalwa*, N. Sotho *bjala*; however, in some quots the writers may be representing the pronunciation of Zulu *utshwala* (see TSHWALA).] Esp. among Sotho people: TSHWALA sense a.

1854 R.B. STRUTHERS *Hunting Jrnl* (1991) 56 The Kraals round to supply joalla in turns. **1909** *Illust. London News* (U.K.) 8 Jan. 4 In keeping all other liquors, except jwala, away from the Natives .., the very best interests of all sections of the population will be duly cared for. **1940** V. POHL *Bushveld Adventures* 22 No doubt he was dumbfounded when told of his escapades while under the influence of jwala. **1955** W. ILLSLEY *Wagon on Fire* 43 They were regaling themselves with joala in the 'den'. **1976** *Drum* Sept. 76, I don't sell joala. *a*1977 K.M.C. MOTSISI in M. Mutloatse *Casey & Co.* (1978) 69 The wells are dry. No more joala. No mahog or paraffin (gin). **1987** R. NTOULA in *City Press* 26 Apr. 7 Basotho men aimlessly roaming the streets hoping to be invited for a free jwala.

job reservation *n. phr. Hist.* The setting aside by law of certain (skilled) grades of employment for certain ethnic groups, particularly whites. Also *attrib.* See also *civilized labour policy* (CIVILIZED LABOUR sense 2). Cf. COLOUR BAR.

The first Acts to promulgate this policy were the Mines and Works Act of 1911, and the Mines and Works Amendment Act of 1926. Other Acts in the 1950s further extended the policy, which was finally removed from the statute books in 1986.

1960 A. HEPPLE in H. Spottiswoode *S. Afr.: Rd Ahead* 84 We are now complicating these [labour] laws further by writing into them devices such as job reservation to limit the avenues of employment for non-Whites. **1964** H.H.W. DE VILLIERS *Rivonia* 45 Work reservation (job reservation) laws are necessary to see that labour opportunities are equably and justly distributed amongst the various sections of the inhabitants of South Africa. **1964** O.D. SCHREINER *Nettle* 36 No Non-White person should be given or retained in a job that any white person would like to have. That is what job reservation amounts to. **1968** COLE & FLAHERTY *House of Bondage* 86 In part the color bar is a legal tactic enforced through 'job reservation' laws. **1970** [see GROUP AREA *n. phr.* sense 2 b]. **1970** *Survey of Race Rel.* (S.A.I.R.R.) 89 The only new official job reservation determination published in 1969 .. related to the work of driving motor vehicles of an unladed weight or more than, 8,000 lb. by persons in the employ of the Divisional Council of Port Elizabeth. This work was reserved for whites. **1973** *Time* 15 Oct. 26 In perhaps the most significant modification of *apartheid* since it became national policy in 1948, Prime Minister John Vorster last week virtually abandoned the Job Reservation Act, under which the best jobs in the country have long been reserved for whites. **1978** T.R.H. DAVENPORT *S. Afr.: Mod. Hist.* 362 The Mines and Works Amendment (or 'Colour Bar') Act of 1926 was Hertzog's way of securing the interests of the white skilled worker ... Job reservation appeared to favour the Coloured man, but in practice did not do so. *Ibid.* 363 To reassure the white electorate .. the appearance of job reservation was preserved ... The amendments to the Industrial Conciliation Act in 1956 and 1959 had those objects in view. **1980** M. LIPTON in *Optima* Vol.29 No.2, 184 The failure of a strike by the Mine Workers' Union in March 1979 over the relaxation of job reservation at a mine in the north-western Cape suggests that the job bar will not remain intact, even in mining. With job reservation — their major concern — crumbling, how will White workers react to Black stabilisation? **1985** C. RAMAPHOSA in *Learn & Teach* No.5, 4 We demanded an end to the laws that stop black workers from doing certain jobs. These are the Job Reservation laws and we are sick and tired of them. **1989** *Reader's Digest Illust. Hist.* 316 The Mines and Works Act [of 1911] .. became the cornerstone of job reservation .. by putting a wide range of skilled jobs beyond the 'competency' of blacks on the mines and the railways. **1991** D. CARTE in *Sunday Times* 3 Mar. 7 The skilled labour shortage obliged the scrapping of job reservation, enabling blacks to do more skilled work. **1991** E. VAN ZYL in *Race Rel. News* (S.A.I.R.R.) Vol.53 No.1, 22 Numerous aspects of the apartheid system .. adversely affected the socio-economic development of the country as a whole and the black population in particular. The most important of these were neglect of education and training .. , job reservation, [etc.].

Jo'burg /ˈdʒəʊbɜːg/ *n. colloq.* Also **Jo-Burg, Jo(h)-burg, Joh'burg**. [Shortened form of *Johannesburg*.] The city of Johannesburg; JOEYS; cf. JOZI. Also *attrib.* See also GOLDEN CITY.

1908 J.H. DRUMMOND Diary. 15 Nov., His letter proposed my coming to Jo'burg and staying with him on the chance of getting employment. **1925** F. SHAY in *Nat. Geog. Mag.* Feb. 259 The second day in Jo-Burg we detoured to .. Pretoria. Pretoria is 45 miles from Jo-Burg. **1934** [see JEWBURG]. **1939** K.O. SHELFORD in *Outspan* 6 Oct. 39, I could tell you come from Jo'burg even if I 'adn't seen your number plate. Always rushing about, you Jo'burg fellers. **1953** *Drum* Mar. 22 Good-bye Joh'burg, Here I come Durban! **1964** *Capricorn High School Mag.* 29 Ragged and quarrelled ever so To let him not to Jo'burg go. **1977** J. SIKAKANE *Window on Soweto* 56 We Jo'burg Africans were used to using the same doors in certain City restaurants which do not display segregated entrance signs. **1989** [see FIETAS]. **1990** M. MELAMU in *Lynx* 293 The magic word was 'Jo'burg', the 'City of Gold'. Those who had succeeded in going there .. related semi-credulous tales of the glamour of Jo'burg. If you were in quest of quick riches .. Jo'burg was the place. **1993** J. THOMAS in *House & Leisure* Nov. 51 Chartwell, north of Joburg.

Hence **Jo'burger, Jo'burgite** *ns*, JOHANNESBURGER.

1918 A.C. CRIPPS in *Best of S. Afr. Short Stories* (1991) 98 Two or three Rhodesians and Joburgers enriched the bar with faithful fondness. **1977** J. SIKAKANE *Window on Soweto* 21 My father is what I could describe as a typical schooled 'Johburger' at heart. **1987** *Fair Lady* 13 May 84 December — that's when other Jo'burgers are 'getting away from it all'. **1988** J. SCOTT in *Cape Times* 24 Dec. 6 Fortunately the mountain is one thing that Joburgites will never fit into the capacious boots of their cars. **1990** J. MICHELL in *Style* Nov. 62 Unlike Jo'burgers, Durbanites eat for enjoyment and energy rather than to impress their clients.

Joeys /ˈdʒəʊiːz/ *n. colloq.* Also **Joey's**, **Jo'ies**. [Shortened form of *Johannesburg*.] JO'BURG. Also *attrib.*

1972 P. O'BYRNE on Radio South Africa 27 Mar., You come from Brakkies? We always tend to expect our contestants to come from Joeys. **1973** J. COPE *Alley Cat* 162 'Well – so where've you fallen from, kid?' 'Joeys.' 'Johannesburg?' **1975** *Darling* 12 Mar. 4 (*letter*) The reason you dont' dig Bloss is 'cos yous never been to Joey's and heard the Sowthefrican Inglishe as it should not be spoke! **1978** *Sunday Times* 5 Nov. (Mag. Sect.) 17 He was 37 when his break came, but the Joeys boy had been singing since he was a teenager. **1983** *Frontline* Feb. 12 So please, my china. I had a hard ride from Joeys and I got no chick to dance with so howzit for like a small loan of your old lady? **1984** *Ibid.* Feb. 26 Apartheid in CA [Cape Town] is even more of a gemors and a generally lost cause than in Joeys. **1991** *Flying Springbok* May 168 The spread of decent Chinese restaurants in Johannesburg is being tentatively followed in our other large cities. In Joeys, you can find traditional Cantonese rooms, one or two kitchens serving Pekingese dishes. **1991** H.P. TOFFOLI in *Style* Nov. 90 Brian W– .. was rooting for Joeys ... 'Johannesburg has a lot of interesting women.'

Johannesburger /dʒəʊˈhænəzbɜːgə, dʒə-, -ˈhanəz-/ *n.* An inhabitant of Johannesburg; *Jo'burger*, see JO'BURG.

1896 'S. CUMBERLAND' *What I Think of S. Afr.* 8 Cape Town .. is .. not quite so lively as Johannesburg, and the people are not so go-ahead as the Johannesburgers. **1903** E.F. KNIGHT *S. Afr. after War* 204 Johannesburgers sometimes boast, and not without reason, that theirs is the 'brainiest' city in South Africa. **1957** D. JACOBSON *Price of Diamonds* (1986) 110 Susskind would go to Johannesburg, and he would sell options here and options there to other Johannesburgers. **1968** E.A. WALKER *Hist. of Sn Afr.* 450 Chamberlain .. promised that if the Johannesburgers would hoist the Queen's flag, they might choose their own Governor. **1987** *S. Afr. Holidays Guide (brochure)* 5 Johannesburgers make good use of their city's restaurants. **1990** *Sunday Times* 11 Nov. (Mag. Sect.) 8 For South Africans, especially Johannesburgers .. suffering from status anxiety has become a most elegantly ambivalent status-symbol.

Johburg, Joh'burg varr. JO'BURG.

John *n. Obsolescent. offensive.* [Perh. transf. use of Brit. Eng. *John* a servant or underling.] JIM.

1894 E. GLANVILLE *Fair Colonist* 76 'What is your name, John?' – all black men being Johns when they are not Boys. **1901** [see DANKIE sense 1 a]. **1948** O. WALKER *Kaffirs Are Lively* 27 Not all of them are strictly black, round-headed and answering to the generic names of 'John', 'Mary', 'Jim' or 'Annie'. **1951** *Natal Mercury* 11 Apr. 8 (*letter*) So far as the expression 'John' goes, what else could be nicer or more friendly than 'What can I do for you, John?' when serving a Native from behind a counter when you do not know his name. Would Mr Jill say to him, What can I do for you, Sir? as if he were a European? It is also incorrect to say that these two expressions ['John' and 'boy'] are used on Africans only: they are used on Indians also, in fact with any non-European. **1951** J.J. MKWANAZI in *Natal Mercury* 20 Apr. 10 (*letter*) I feel that when a person called me John, Jim, Jack, etc., while my name is not so, it hurts me a lot because such names are only used to Non-Europeans. *a***1958** K.M.C. MOTSISI in M. Mutloatse *Casey & Co.* (1978) 107 'Hello, John.' ... I answered: 'Just for the record, my name is Herbert ... You can call me John. Whites call every darkie "John" ... But .. for the record, my name is Herbert.' **1968** J. LELYVELD in Cole & Flaherty *House of Bondage* 15 A large proportion of whites don't trouble themselves to call their servants by their own names. Sometimes they use a common name like John whether it belongs to the man or not. **1973** *Star* 3 Nov., 'John' seemed a good enough name to call a Black guy if you wanted to draw his attention. **1977** *Weekend World* 31 July C1, None of these terms has ever found favour with blacks ... The days when we could be called 'John', 'Boy', 'Meid', and so on are over. **1980** A. FUGARD *Tsotsi* 64 The old woman with the white hair and the fat dog: 'John my poor boy!' 'Morris Medem.' 'Johnny poor boy, what happened to your legs?' 'Morris Medem. Morris Tshabalala.' **1982** *Staffrider* Vol.4 No.4, 14, I don't even know his real name. I just call him John because I know they all like being called John.

Hence (*nonce*) **John** *v. trans.*, to address (someone) as 'John'.

1965 E. MPHAHLELE *Down Second Ave* 152, I was 'Jimmed' and 'boy-ed' and 'John-ed' by whites.

John Brown *n. phr.* Pl. unchanged, or -s. [tr. Afk. *jan bruin* see JANBRUIN; see quot. 1902.] Any of several species of seabream of the Sparidae, dark brown in colour (esp. *Gymnocrotaphus curvidens*): **a.** The JANBRUIN (sense a), *G. curvidens*. **b.** The *Hottentot fish* (see HOTTENTOT *n.* sense 2 a), *Pachymetopon aeneum*. **c.** The BRONZE BREAM (sense b), *P. grande*. **d.** *Polyamblyodon germanum*; BRONZE BREAM sense c.

1902 J.D.F. GILCHRIST in *Trans. of S. Afr. Philological Soc.* XI. iv. 223 The John Brown and Jacob Swart stand in a category by themselves ... The names appear to refer simply to the colour of these fish. **1913** [see JANBRUIN]. **1930** C.L. BIDEN *Sea-Angling Fishes* 231 The John Brown's scale-pockets are brown ... John Brown are always in groups of families of from four or five to a dozen. *Ibid.* 235 The John Brown family reappeared .. and were lost to view. **1945** H. GERBER *Fish Fare* 47 *John Brown*, as its name denotes, has a brown colour. It is somewhat similar to a galjoen in shape. **1947** K.H. BARNARD *Pict. Guide to S. Afr. Fishes* 156 *John Brown*, (*Gymnocrotaphus curvidens*) ... A vegetarian or omnivorous feeder, well known to rock anglers at the Cape, but seldom seen in fish markets. **1955** C. HORNE *Fisherman's Eldorado* 105 John Brown, probably the commonest small bottom feeding fish at Port Alfred and adjacent areas, cause confusion, for Eastern Province anglers know no less than four distinct fish by the one common name, John Brown. The John Brown of the Cape .. is scarce ... The fish known at the Cape as hottentot is the second of the four Port Alfred John Browns. The third John Brown is a brilliant blue and bronze copper bream ... The fourth fish known locally as John Brown is called hottentot at Knysna, bluefish at East London, and bronze bream in Natal and along The Wild Coast. **1975** *S. Afr. Panorama* July 17 John Brown, wildeperd and kob can be landed from the rocks. **1979** SNYMAN & KLARIE *Free from Sea* 33 *John Brown*, .. This plump shapely fish is typically South African, and distinctive with its dark brown body, bright blue eyes and large, comical teeth. **1982** *Outeniqualander* 2 Sept. 2 Most meritorius catch .. went to Keith Stephenson for a John Brown weighing 1,05 kg.

John Company *n. phr.* [tr. JAN COMPAGNIE.] An informal name for the Dutch East India Company (see COMPANY).

In nineteenth-century *Brit. Eng.* the name 'John Company' was used of the British East India Company (taken over from the Dutch *Jan Compagnie*).

1941 C.W. DE KIEWIET *Hist. of S. Afr.* 27 The common picture of John Company – all purse and no conscience – is exaggerated. **1985** *S. Afr. Panorama* May 17 The Dutch East India Company began to decline during the war between England and the Netherlands (1780–1783), as a result of John Company's poor management.

Johnny Hangman *n. phr.* The FISCAL (sense 2), *Lanius collaris*.

1899 R.B. & J.D.S. WOODWARD *Natal Birds* 40 The boys call it 'Johnny Hangman' from the extraordinary habit it has .. of impaling its prey after killing it, on the thorns. **1967** *Some Protected Birds of Cape Prov.* (Dept of Nature Conservation) Pl.144, *Fiscal Shrike, Butcher Bird, Johnny Hangman*, The commonest true shrike found in South Africa.

Jo'ies var. JOEYS.

joil var. JOL *v.*

joila var. TSHWALA.

join-boy *n. offensive.* [Prob. fr. Fanakalo, *joyin* contract (ad. Eng. *join*), with spelling remodelled to the Eng. root + *boy* (see BOY sense 1 a).] A newly recruited mine-labourer. See also BOY sense 1.

1948 O. WALKER *Kaffirs Are Lively* 22 Half a dozen reasons can be given why tribal Natives become 'join-boys', as recruited miners are called. **1971** P. YOUNG *Informant, Grahamstown* He used to fill a plane with white labour from England and bring it out to South Africa – much like happens with the join-boys for the mines. **1989** B. GODBOLD Autobiography. 14 Groups of blanket-clad 'join boys' as they were called, walked for many days to railheads, to entrain for Johannesburg, for employment underground.

joiner *n.* Also with initial capital, and **yoiner**. [Special senses of Eng. *joiner* one who joins (an organization).]

1. *hist.* A derogatory term (equivalent to 'traitor') used by the Boers of one who defected and fought with the British forces during the closing months of the Anglo-Boer War; HANDS-UPPER sense 1 b; HENSOPPER sense 1 b; *khaki Boer*, see KHAKI *adj.* sense 1 b; cf. NATIONAL SCOUT.

1902 L. PAGE et al. in A.C. Martin *Concentration Camps* (1957) 106 We .. request you .. not to allow Yoiners of the National and Intelligence Scouts in the camp during the war ... They consider the ex-Yoiners as traitors. **1934** C.P. SWART Supplement to Pettman. 80 *Joiner*, A word coined by the Dutch during the Anglo-Boer war and signifying a renegade, or a Boer who has deserted and 'joined' the ranks of the enemy. **1944** C.R. PRANCE *Under Blue Roof* 65 Half his men were 'joiners' or 'handsuppers,' 'vyf-sjieling verraiers,' ever the harshest and least scrupulous in dealing with their own kin. **1957** A.C. MARTIN *Concentration Camps* 40 Men who .. had come to the conclusion that the continued prosecution of the war was against the interests of their own people and had thus thrown in their lot with the British ... known as 'Joiners'. **1970** S. DE WET in J.W. Loubser *Africana Short Stories* 92 It wasn't the khakies who treated us so badly ... It was the handsuppers and the joiners, our own people working for the English. **1974** [see NATIONAL SCOUT]. **1979** T. PAKENHAM *Boer War* (1982) 568 There were already 5,464 *handsuppers* (or 'ensoppers' or 'yoiners') – Boers recruited to fight in the British army as National Scouts, guides, transport drivers and so on. **1979** E. DRUMMOND *Burning Land* 411 There were many Boers .. who .. refused to fight on and expressed a willingness to accept British rule, wanting only to get back to their farms and families. These men were dubbed 'hands-uppers' or 'joiners' by the militants. **1982** [see HENSOPPER sense 1 a]. **1990** *E. Prov. Herald* 9 Feb. 5 It was not with the joiners and the hensoppers that peace was concluded then. It was with the bittereinders.

2. *transf.* A collaborator; an opportunist.

1973 M. VAN BILJON in *Star* 8 Sept. 6 There's Dr. Connie Mulder .. calling the members of Verligte Aksie and ASASA 'Joiners'. **1979** *Sunday Times* 15 June 10 A glum view of Afrikaans members of the PFP. 'Joiners and hensoppers,' is what Mr van der Merwe called his opposition namesake. **1979** *Sunday Times* 16 Sept. 21 Equally conspicuous was the hang-dog look of the *hensoppers* and *joiners*, the collaborators. Politically they were to be outcasts, skeletons well hidden away in the cupboard. **1987** [see GAT *n.* sense 1 b]. **1990** *Sunday Times* 1 July 31 There was some concern about B–'s intentions when he entered the recent Canadian Open as British ... The South African sports writers were disgusted ... At a Press conference, one openly called him a 'joiner' – an opportunist.

jointed cactus *n. phr.* The low-growing succulent *Opuntia aurantiaca* of the Cactaceae. Also *attrib.*

Identified in 1903 as a noxious weed, this plant belongs to the same genus as the prickly pear.

1911 *Farmer's Weekly* 4 Oct. 138 The jointed cactus has made its appearance in the Colesberg district. It is the lowest type of prickly pear. Farmers should make the acquaintance of this noxious weed, so that they can have it destroyed wherever it is found. **1913** C. PETTMAN *Africanderisms* 234 *Jointed Cactus, Opuntia pusilla*, a dangerous weed: it is a near relative of the prickly pear, and threatens to become a great pest. **1936** [see SLANGKOP]. **1957** I.D. HATTINGH in *Handbk for Farmers* II. 426 *Jointed Cactus* (*Opuntia aurantiaca*). This is a low-growing, widely-distributed succulent plant of the prickly pear family ... Being covered with countless spines $\frac{1}{2}$ an inch to $\frac{1}{4}$ inch in length, the plant cannot be eaten by livestock. **1971** *Grocott's Mail* 31 Aug. 3 The Jointed Cactus Committee reported on the situation with the persistent and hard-to-eradicate pest, and said present methods of getting rid of the cactus seemed hopeless. **1977** *E. Prov. Herald* 2 June 12 The jointed cactus problem was first perceived in the late 19th century ... All species of cactus in South Africa were introduced .. and .. some, like the jointed cactus and prickly pear, were serious weed problems in certain areas. **1983** *Grocott's Mail* 18 Jan. 2 Inside the boxes, in a sealed air-conditioned room, a variety of insects are happily breeding and feeding on jointed cactus plants.

jol /dʒɔ(:)l/ *n.* and *adj. Slang.* Also **jaul, jawl, joll, jorl.** [Afk. (/jɔl/), dance, party. The S. Afr. Eng. pronunciation is either derived from the Afk. accent of working-class Cape coloured people, or is an Englished pronunciation of the Afk. word.]

A. *n.*

1.a. A good time, a time of merry-making; a 'thrash'. **b.** Always *sing.* (The source of) an intensely exciting or pleasurable time, activity, or experience, 'a ball'. **c.** *noncount.* Revelry; merry-making; enjoyment; entertainment; fun and games. In the phr. ***on the jol***, in search of this.

1957 A. LA GUMA in *Best of S. Afr. Short Stories* (1991) 385 Classical stuff. Just a helluva noise. Give me a wakker jol any time. **1964** J.L. WALKER *Informant, Cape Town* We're on the Freshers' train – going down to look for digs and for a bit of a jawl. **1970** I. PALMER *Informant, Grahamstown* We decided to have a real joll at the dance. **1975** 'BLOSSOM' in *Darling* 12 Apr. 95 This oke sticks he's foot out .. so I trip over it and end up on my guava, then he checks me over and says all casual, 'Fancy a jol sometime, poppie?' **1978** 'BLOSSOM' in *Darling* 22 Nov. 106, I excelled in sports, dancing and yoga ... I played in the first teams. It was a joll. **1980** [see LIGHTY sense 1]. **1980** *Post* 9 Feb. (Family Post), When day is done and the jols are over, most people are content to stagger off to bed. **1982** *Sunday Times* 19 Dec., The party .. was unanimously voted the 'Jorl of the Year.' **1983** *Rhodeo* (Rhodes Univ.) 6 June *On the Jorl.* Junk food review. **1983** A. GOLDSTUCK in *Frontline* Oct. 61 A leading Boksburg skate, he denies that his life of 'jol' is meaningless. **1984** *Cape Times* 3 Feb. 9 There's no heavy statement .. ; just five boys having a light jol. **1984** J. SALTON in *Ibid.* 18 Oct. 12 He's from Johannesburg ... 'We came here to see her mother ... I never saw my tjêrrie after we got here. Now I'm on the joll.' **1984** I. SIAS in *Style* Nov. 106 It's an absolute jol. You really get the most interesting people here. **1985** R. GREIG in *Ibid.* Dec. 111 The Brass Bell restaurant beside the harbour is worth a jol by day and worth eating at by night. **1985** *Vula* Oct. 15 They're unable to slot in with the 'black' culture ... So the endless jorl and dop and skyf help provide middle ground. **1985** *Weekly Mail* 1 Nov. 17 In the first of a series on Jo'burg Jolls, *Reg Rumney* .. takes a stroll around the city's pubs. **1986** L. WESTBY-NUNN in *Style* Mar. 41 It's not all jol and fun. She works damn hard. **1986** J. WHYLE in S. Gray *Market Plays* 182 We've split the country ... Shaunie because of the army and me ... well just for the jol really. **1987** *Oppie Newsletter* (Rhodes Univ.) May 1 Remember Cinderella and what a jol she had at the ball? **1987** *Scope* 20 Nov. 46 'Boys, the *jol* is over,' Jimmy said, picking up all the dynamite. **1988** *Frontline* Jan. 12, I drive along Oxford Road and see the jet set lurching home from the night's jolls. **1988** A. SICHEL in *Star* 27 May 13 Top of the list is a ballet teacher to keep him .. in shape for 'Countryside' ... 'That's really something to look forward to ... It may be rough stuff but it's such a jol.' **1988** D. SONNENBERG in *Style* May 53 It's on the Sun City run for the Sandton ladies ... Part of the jol is finding something to spend their money on. **1988** *Sunday Times* 30 Oct. 6, I spoke to boys as young as 11 .. waiting to be picked up by men. 'It's an easy way of scoring a few bucks for a night of jol in Hillbrow,' one streetwise youngster said. **1989** J. ALLAN in *Ibid.* 22 Jan. 4 What kind of fodder is the Dalton doll for a columnist whose main *jorl* .. is ripping out the jugulars of her victims with claws so deadly they must be manicured by Black and Decker? **1989** *Personality* 29 May 17 With *Scope* Girl of the Year it's all a fat jol, no strings attached. **1990** A. BUMSTEAD in *Style* June 111, I joined as a guide just to meet people and have a bit of a jol. **1990** *Femina* June 126 For them life is one big jol. **1993** *Rhodeo* (Rhodes Univ.) (Intervarsity Special) Aug. 3 The atmosphere was friendly and relaxed, and the braai held afterwards was a great jorl. **1993** *Weekly Mail* 18 June 27 Are you tired of .. radio transmissions that go on the blink whenever you leave for a weekend jol?

2. A party, dance, concert, festival, or other lively social occasion. Also *attrib.*

1978 A. AKHALWAYA in *Rand Daily Mail* 10 July 7 Ek se, where y'all vying after the jol? ... I say, where are you all going after the party? **1982** *Star* 31 Mar., Joll .. now means any social occasion. At a jol you can have a 'fat rip' or good time. **1983** *Sunday Times* 18 Sept. (Mag. Sect.) 33 There are two jols a term in the school hall for the pupils. **1985** *Daily News* 11 Jan. 9 'The best part of the Dusi is the jol .. ,' philosophised one of the backmarkers. And jol it was. A camp of .. marquees .. dispensed food, cooldrinks and beer. **1986** H. PRENDINI in *Style* Apr. 92 The Grahamstown Festival culture jol starts on June 27. **1987** *Weekly Mail* 19 June 25 *Local Culture Mega-Joll* ... Benny b Funk, Khaki Monitor and Winston's Jive Mix-up will be playing at the Summit Club Ballroom. **1990** R. RANGONGO in *New African* 3 Sept. 9 Traditional musician and Juluka founder Sipho Mchunu is back in action ... Last weekend he launched his sound with a massive jol at Jameson's Drift. **1990** A. RICE in *Frontline* Dec. 15 It was a cheapo cokey pen-and-cardboard creation ... 'Jol of The Year' it announced ... This poster was advertising a jol in a hitherto jol-free zone – Camden Lock, London. That's .. a couple of continents north of normal jol country. **1993** *'Jimbo' programme insert, Napac* Joll. Discotheque, dance, party.

3. *rare*, perh. *nonce.* A place.

1981 *Rhodeo* (Rhodes Univ.) 19 Oct. 2 I was .. sitting down .. to check out some .. reading ... I had hardly had the time to wonder what .. the guy was going on about, in the article when something distracted me. Like the whole jorl was filled with rumblings and shakings.

4. A joke, a game; a stunt.

1982 *Cape Times* 4 Jan. 3 Jumping Jack's 'jorl' ... Jumping Jack launches himself into a series of trampoline stunts, each of which ends in a seemingly disastrous fall. **1985** P. SLABOLEPSZY *Sat. Night at Palace* 48, I was only joking. You think I need to bust this joint? Bit of a jol, man. I don't need to hit this place.

5. A (self-indulgent) trip or holiday.

1985 *Ibid.* 52 There's it! Take a jol over to Pretoria. Arcadia Pepsi. Those bastards need a striker. **1989** *Informant, Grahamstown*, I accept that Jane Soap went on a jol overseas after the Council meeting. **1992** S. BARBER in *Natal Mercury* 24 Nov. 8 A chance for yet another transatlantic joll.

B. *adj.* Of the music, language, etc. enjoyed by or associated with jollers (see JOLLER sense 1).

1985 D. KRAMER in *Cape Times* 16 May, The concert explores my songs. The full range, from rock 'n roll to sakkie-sakkie, jol music, kwela and more serious ballads. **1985** H. PRENDINI in *Style* Oct. 39 Student slang .. tends to be more entertaining and imaginative and less deliberately vulgar than southern suburbs jol talk.

jol /dʒɔ(:)l/ *v. colloq.* Also **jall, jawl, joil, jola, joll, jorl.** [Afk., to make merry.]

I. *intrans.*

1. To depart; to hurry; to run; to go (to a place, esp. in search of entertainment); to walk. In the phr. ***to jol around***, to stroll or drive about idly, or with the vague intention of finding something interesting to do. See also JOLLER senses 1 and 2 a.

1946 C.P. WITTSTOCK in E. Partridge *Dict. of Underworld* (1950) 371 Let's jol ... Shall we go? **1950** E. PARTRIDGE *Dict. of Underworld Slang* 371 *Jol*, v. To depart; make off: South Africa: C.20. **1970** OLIVIER & HINDS *Informants, Pietersburg* Let's jol – let's go. **1970** J. STODEL *Informant, Cape Town*, I had to jall to catch my bus. To run fast. When spelt *joll* it means to dance. **1972** R. MALAN *Ah Big Yaws* 25 *Jawl*, .. Various meanings attach to this word ... It could mean 'to hurry'. **1974** 'BLOSSOM' in *Darling* 9 Oct. 95 The German band *jols* off to pastures new. **1974** *Informant, Grahamstown* Ag, we sommer jorled around town. **1979** 'BLOSSOM' in *Darling* 16 May 131 He jols up to me where I'm lurking behind this potted parm-tree [*sic*] trying to make like a coconut. **1984** W. STEVENSON in *Sunday Times* 29 Jan. (Life Style) 9 Most of the time we just jorl to the 'Brow and suss the scene out. **1985** P. SLABOLEPSZY *Sat. Night at Palace* 41 I'm jolling out the back door I hear this one hell of a scream. **1986** *Crux* Aug. 43 He jols up to King Saul and tunes him: 'Never fear, I'm near.' **1990** R. MALAN *My Traitor's Heart* 52 If you were brave, you could jol to a shebeen in Soweto ... You could jol to Zoo Lake on a Sunday afternoon to laze on the greensward .. , and you could jol to Swaziland.

2. To flirt; to have a love affair; to be in love; to make love. See also JOLLING sense 1.

1969 J. MBONGWE in *Post* 5 Oct. 5 (*letter*) Is love and 'jolling' the same thing? .. Let me advise our girls who go around 'jolling' with every Tom, Dick and Harry ... You'll hear most girls say: 'I love nobody. I only "jol"' ... You will not be good housewives because you have wasted your time 'jolling'. **1969** S. MOTLOUNG in *Post* 7 Dec. 9 (*letter*) Mr. Mpongwe .. does not know the meaning of the word 'jol'. The word simply means 'to be in love.' It is a slang word. **1979** F. NTULI in *Staffrider* Vol.2 No.3, 9 'If we do not hate each other why don't we jola? People who love each other ...' and then she was in his arms. **1988** ADAMS & SUTTNER *William Str.* 17 The other sister started jolling with the manager of the bioscope and they ran away together.

3. To make merry; to revel; to 'party'; to dance; to go out on the town. See also JOLLER sense 2 a, JOLLING sense 2, MAL sense 2.

1970 E.J. LE ROUX *Informant, Bellville* Jol. The coloured people use this word meaning to have fun or a party. **1970** M. BURGER *Informant, Pietersburg* We were jolling around at the café (having a good time). **1978** *Darling* 26 April 16 Jagger jolls while Bianca broods. **1980** *Cape Times* 12 Sept. 4 At weekends the gang members would 'jol' (amuse themselves), sometimes by looking for enemy gangs to fight. **1985** *Fair Lady* 18 Sept. 38 When I tackled him he .. asked me where I thought the relationship was going – he wanted to 'jol' and be free. **1987** *Cosmopolitan* Apr. 28 (*caption*) David Kramer, whose musical *District Six* (co-written with Taliep Petersen) is going to make South Africans jol as never before. **1990** J. MICHELL in *Style* Nov. 62 Everyone goes on to clubs and pubs where they jol till it is seriously late. **1990** *Weekly Mail* 20 Dec. 49 Time to jol – and there's plenty happening .. to get you through the festive season. **1993** A. DODD in *Ibid.* 4 June 10 He spent some of the cash *jolling* and reinvested the rest in stock. **1993** *Weekly Mail & Guardian* 10 Dec. 42 It was time to jol, to lighten up.

4. To tease; to joke; to play.

1970 *Informant, Grahamstown* I'm only jolling man. **1970** OLIVIER & HINDS *Informants, Pietersburg* Let's jol with the ball. **1973** *Informant, Grahamstown* Let's jol on the lawn, rather.

II. *trans.* and *reflexive* (*rare*).

5. *trans.* To play (a game). See also JOLLER sense 3.

1970 *Informant, Edenvale* Let's joll soccer. **1981** *Cape Times* 28 Dec. 9 These holiday jollers .. jorl Asteroids and Puckman .. or gooi a line without any bait in our muddy waters.

6. *trans.* To court (someone); to make love to (someone). See also JOLLING sense 1.

1978 A. ESSOP *Hajji* 27 If any of you rich Indian bastards try to joll my wife I will put a knife into your guts. *Ibid.* 38 Asif began visiting Maimuna rather too often .. and Myrtle declared that Asif was 'jolling his second mother'.

7. *reflexive.* To entertain (oneself).

1993 S. GARRATT in *Cape Argus* 12 Aug. (Tonight) 6 Make your mark for peace this weekend. Jol yourself in sublime harmony with the world.

joller /ˈdʒɔlə(r)/ *n. slang.* Also **jawler**. [fr. JOL *v.* + Eng. (or Afk.) agential suffix *-er*.]

1. One who frequents low places of entertainment; an unsavoury, thuggish youth. Also *attrib.*

1963 L.F. FREED *Crime in S. Afr.* 105 A distinction is drawn in the half-world between the terms 'ducktail' and 'joller' ... The term 'joller' is believed to have originated from the Afrikaans word 'jol', meaning a festive party. People who attended such parties were accordingly referred to as 'jollers', but the word has degenerated in meaning and now signifies any person who 'celebrates' any and every occasion by fighting, swearing, drinking, and smoking dagga. *Ibid.* Down came a joller, singing the blues ... And out came the dagga as he asked for a light. 1970 M.E. TAMLIN *Informant, Cape Town* Jawler. A layabout. 1972 *Star* 26 Oct., A young thug, rather more 'joller' in his talk than this one, ruminates in the condemned cell on the impulses welling within him when he committed murder. 1977 C. HOPE in S. Gray *Theatre Two* (1981) 36 You heard of my boetie, Paulie — ? And ou Abba and those jollers — ? 1982 *Frontline* Nov. 18 The photographer was a character of exceptional colour. Bouncer, brawler, diver, drinker, jawler ... Billy M— might have been to photography what Hemingway was to literature. 1985 H. PRENDINI in *Style* Oct. 39 Southern Suburbs joller: No ways, my china! No ways I work under a black! GCM! 1989 *Weekly Mail* 20 Oct. 31 The audience was nothing if not average: *pantsulas* rubbing shoulders with Boksburg jollers, blue collar workers with their bosses. 1991 M. KANTEY *All Tickets* 53 The supercool joller who leans against the dividing wall, dreaming of sixguns in the sunset.

2.a. A hedonist; a fun-lover; one who often goes out to places of entertainment. Also *attrib.* See also JOL *v.* sense 3.

1963 [see sense 1]. 1971 E. HIGGINS *Informant, Grahamstown* The others in the residence .. think he is not enough of a joller ou because he takes his intellectual commitments too seriously. 1978 *Sunday Times* 8 Oct. (Mag. Sect.) 16 His pal, Stevie, is .. a 'joller' with a tremendous sense of fun whose attitude to life is one of careless abandon. 1983 *Sunday Times* 18 Sept. (Lifestyle) 1 Blossom — a dedicated joller from Bez Valley who for years graced (or disgraced) the pages of fashion mags. 1985 *Cape Times* 23 Oct., Francis of Assissi .. wasn't always saintly. In fact, he was something of a joller in his youth. 1986 *Style* May 41 I'm always gated. That's why I'm not a joller. 1986 *Cape Times* 28 Jan. 16 (*advt*) Ideologically sound joller required to share .. house. 1989 *Weekly Mail* 13 Oct. 36 A chic supper club attracting the older, more moneyed jollers. 1990 A. RICE in *Frontline* Dec. 15 Nine million potential revellers, nine million partygoers perhaps, maybe even nine million merrymakers, but jollers? You don't get many of them to the hectare in good old London town. 1993 S. GARRATT in *Cape Argus* 12 Aug. (Tonight) 6 Any experienced joller will tell you that there is one time when peace really does reign, and that's the morning after.

b. One attending a party, concert, or other social gathering; one of a group of people who are out on the town. See also JOL *v.* sense 3.

1986 A. DONALDSON in *Style* May 108 As we leave, fellow-joller Cheryl .. claimed that some jock had put some *thing* in her palm as she passed a table. 1988 *Weekly Mail* 18 Oct. 19 The band blueses along behind him. The jollers sway. 1990 *Top Forty* July 12 A lot of expectant *jollers* were upset that Johannes Kerkorrel had taken his '*gereformeerde* blues' off to Europe just before the concert.

3. A player (of a game). See also JOL *v.* sense 5.

1988 I. LOUW in *Talk* Sept. 1988 5 Enter number 2. First team jorler, renegade and real hot property. She was only in standard seven — he was in Matric.

jolling /ˈdʒɔːlɪŋ/ *vbl n. Slang.* [fr. JOL *v.*]

1. Flirting; having a series of inconsequential love affairs; being in love. See also JOL *v.* senses 2 and 6.

1969 J. MBONGWE in *Post* 5 Oct. 5 (*letter*) Is love and 'jolling' the same thing? The answer is *no* ... Loving is permanent and 'jolling' temporary. 1969 S. MOTLOUNG in *Post* 7 Dec. 9 (*letter*) Loving and jolling are permanent. 1993 *'Jimbo' programme insert, Napac* Jolling. Having an affair.

2. Merry-making, revelry; 'partying'. Also *attrib.* See also JOL *v.* sense 3.

1980 R. GOVENDER *Lahnee's Pleasure* 7 Saturday night! Jolling night! 1985 C. RASCH in *Fair Lady* 3 Apr. 150 You might come upon a raving ex-junkie .. informing the tight circle of faces around him of his jolling days. 1988 P. GAINES in *Cosmopolitan* May 177 The girls .. had lots to talk about. Parents, boyfriends, fashion, jolling — they all spoke the same language.

Jonas /ˈdʒəʊnəs/ *n. Geology.* [Etym. obscure; perh. Afk. *Jona* (the biblical *Jonah*) + possessive *-s* (see quot. 1950), alluding to the problems caused by dolomite in mining.] Always *attrib.* Dolomite.

1912 *S. Afr. Agric. Jrnl* July 39 (Pettman), It is stated where Jonas klip (dolomite) is present the disease (lamsiekte) will occur. 1950 E. ROSENTHAL *Here Are Diamonds* 198 Much of the digger's ingenuity has been bestowed on geological and mineralogical subjects ... 'Jona's Rock' is dolomite. 1971 *Golden Fleece* (S. Afr. Wool Board) June (Suppl.) 7 The Ghaap plateau north of Kimberley .. displays a mixed shrub-grassveld with local differences on lime (Kalkveld) and dolomite (Jonasveld).

jong /jɔŋ/ *n.* and *int. Colloq.* Also **jonge**, **yong**, **yung**. Pl. **-s**, (rarely) **jongen**. [Afk., fr. earlier S. Afr. Du. *jongen* boy, lad.]

A. *n.*

1.a. *hist.* A young (black) male slave or servant.

1615 W. PEYTON in R. Raven-Hart *Before Van Riebeeck* (1967) 71 Twoe yeongers of my Shipps companye .. conserted to carrye awaye my boat ... for which pretended plott the twoe yeongers .. weare .. aiudged to the each of them 50 lashes with a Whipp vpon their bare back. 1846 J.C. BROWN tr. *T. Arbousset's Narr. of Explor. Tour to N.-E. of Col.* 253 Tied his *jong*, or young bushman slave, to the wheel of his waggon, where he was severely flogged. 1849 J. TINDALL *Jrnl* (1959) 127 The master and mistress take a few draws and hand the pipe to a neighbour ... It is handed round until it is exhausted, and soon refilled by another 'jong' or servant. 1886 G.A. FARINI *Through Kalahari Desert* 279 These slaves were called 'yungs' or 'boys'. 1953 J. COLLIN-SMITH *Locusts & Wild Honey* II. 155, I .. shouted into the house for the 'jong', the coloured houseboy, to bring me coffee.

b. *obs.* A form of address to a slave or servant of any age.

1812 A. PLUMPTRE tr. *H. Lichtenstein's Trav. in Sn Afr.* I. 119 A Hottentot .. takes it extremely amiss if he is addressed by the words *Pay* or *Jonge*, as the slaves are; he expects to be called by his name if addressed by any one who knows it.

2. *offensive.*

a. A black man; cf. BOY sense 1 a.

1908 [see OUTA sense 1]. 1912 *E. London Dispatch* 13 Feb. 3 (Pettman), Presently a couple of jongs came along with dainty cigarettes in their mouths. 1926 E. LEWIS *Mantis* 88 He'd make you feel a piccanin yourself, a proper little *jong* that'd never been beyond the dorp. 1955 A. DELIUS *Young Trav.* 100 Outa and Aia were general names for more elderly coloured men and women respectively, Jong and Meid for younger people. *Ibid.* 101 Dick and Frank helped the dusty Jong to replenish the seed and fertilizer cannisters. 1963 A.M. LOUW *20 Days* 77 'Katrina,' the voice outside was soft, wary, cracked with age. 'Who is that jong — that boy — with you?' 1980 [see SEUN]. 1987 O. PROZESKY *Wrath of Lamb* 11, I am old now, but for most of my life white people have called me a 'jong' or a 'boy'.

b. *comb.* **ou jong** *obs.* [Afk., lit. 'old young'], a form of address to an elderly black man.

1913 C. PETTMAN *Africanderisms* 354 *Ou'Jong*, A curious combination applied to an old coloured servant. 1929 J.G. VAN ALPHEN *Jan Venter* 263 Don't worry about it, *ou jong* ... You won't die yet, and when you do, you will go to the Happy Hunting Ground of all Hottentots. [1970 E. MUNDELL *Informant, Pearston (E. Cape)* Ask the old jong to carry that heavy parcel for you.]

c. A form of address to any black man.

1917 S.T. PLAATJE *Native Life* 65 By his looks and his familiar 'Dag jong' we noticed that the policeman was Dutch, and the embodiment of affability. 1961 T. MATSHIKIZA *Choc. for My Wife* 37 'Can you drink, jong, hey?' 'Yes, Baas Smitty.' 1963 K. MACKENZIE *Dragon to Kill* 223 So you did it, Ndlala. Well, we will get you, *jong*. 1980 R. GOVENDER *Lahnee's Pleasure* 18 What you mean, you don't know? You must check these things before you drive, jong — I say, I'm sorry sir, I made a mistake sir. 1986 S. SEPAMLA *Third Generation* 132 'The baas has asked you a question, jong' said the aggressive Brink. 1990 J. NAIDOO *Coolie Location* 153 She speaks English to him, only English ... You know, .. no blerrys, no voetsaks, no bliksems, no hey jongs, no pas ops.

3. 'My (young) friend', a usu. friendly form of address to both men and women, but esp. to young men; sometimes conveying exasperation (cf. sense B).

1911 *E. Prov. Herald* 25 Nov. 5 We returned to the station and held sweet converse with diverse Kerels, to whom we were 'man' and 'jong' after the nature of the tribe. *c*1929 S. BLACK in S. Gray *Three Plays* (1984) 93 Hay-Whotte .. : Well, I fancy her ... Van K: Hey, play the bally game, jong. 1939 S. CLOETE *Watch for Dawn* 65 'Where is your whip, jong?' Coenraad asked. 'I do not ride with a whip, Coenraad,' Kaspar said. 1947 H.C. BOSMAN *Mafeking Rd* (1969) 14 'Yes, jong,' he said, 'I am feeling pretty shaky about talking to her, I can tell you.' 1959 J. MEIRING *Candle in Wind* 133 'Pas op, jong,' the prison guard had said to her as she left the goal one day. 'We watch all the dagga people.' *c*1966 M. JABOUR in *New S. Afr. Writing* 91 'Ja, ja, I warned you not to trust that Jewboy, Jannie,' she wheezed down his neck, 'jong, he'll skin you alive'. 1972 D. BROWN on Radio South Africa 24 Mar., Jong, that hairpiece doesn't suit you. 1975 S. ROBERTS *Outside Life's Feast* 28 What do you want with that stick says Jan. Nothing. Well throw it away. No jong I am going to keep it. 1987 'A. AMAPHIXIPHIXI' in *Frontline* Mar. 38 Then why the voters love him so I never could descry And thinking once I'd like to know I asked the reason why. They cried, 'We like his bluster jong It makes us feel so big and strong'. 1991 P. SLABOLEPSZY Braait Laaities. 16 There are sharks out there, jong. White men can also be skelms.

4. A young (Afrikaans) man; a boyfriend or lover; KÊREL.

1912 F. BANCROFT *Veldt Dwellers* 316 Whenever we see a *jonge* and a *meisje* together —' .. we can safely reckon that there Mother-Nature will be at .. her work of drawing male to female, female to male.' 1920 S. BLACK *Dorp* 222 Some of the Nationalist 'jongs' annoyed him .. by bleating 'ma-a-a!' to remind him of his 'goatee'. 1959 J. PACKER *High Roof* 62 Bok looked offended. 'A jong needs a res' after a whaling expedition.' 1970 M. DIKOBE Marabi Dance. 169 Yes, I know him. He was my jong. I have a child by him. 1984 in D. Pinnock *Brotherhoods* 62 Many of the gangs are BJs (*boere jongs*, farm youths) but .. the leader is always a local person.

B. *int.* An expression of surprise, delight, approval, exasperation, or anger.

1956 A.G. MCRAE *Hill Called Grazing* 55 Now if I can't get a permit to sell them, man, *jong*. I'll have to drive them up on to the main road. 1963 M.G. MCCOY *Informant, Port Elizabeth* Andy .. said it was a lekker picture, all those ou's fighting, jong! **1973** *Sunday Tribune* 1 Apr. 20 (*caption*) Jong, I've had enough of this! **1973** *E. Prov. Herald* 12 June 9 Boetie tilted his hat back with a greasy hand and shook his head. 'Jong, there's something I don't understand about this engine,' he said. **1978** M. MATSHOBA *Call Me Not a Man* 5 'Jong! You can't even speak Afrikaans?' the white man went on in the same language. He sounded as if he regarded it as a grave sin for the poor granny not to be able to speak his tongue. **1980** *E. Prov. Herald* 20 Nov. 1 Neels, who does not read music said: 'Jong, I never expected it, I'm happy for Port Elizabeth that we won.' **1981** *Fair Lady* 14 Jan. 98 'He looks nice.' 'Oh he *is*. But, *jong*, is he strict!' **1984** *Sunday Times* 29 Jan. (Lifestyle) 9 Lots of chicks come to me for lessons but, jong, they can't even begin to hold a bike up. **1986** *Informant, East London* Jong he's a big guy.

jonge vrouw *n. phr. Obs.* [See JUFFROU.] JUFFROU sense 2 a.

1802 LADY A. BARNARD in D. Fairbridge *Lady Anne Barnard* (1924) 306 Sitting with his wife and jonge vrouw in their bed-gowns. **1925** I. COLVIN in F.C. Slater *Centenary Bk of S. Afr. Verse* 47 The Fiscal pressed his hat .. And swept the pavement with a bow Before the lovely Jonge vrouw.

jongmanskas var. JONKMANSKAS.

jonis var. AMAJONI.

Jonkershuis /ˈjɔŋkə(r)shœis, -heɪs/ *n.* Also **Jonkerhuis**, **Jonkheershuis**, and with small initial. [Afk. *jonker* young man, youth (fr. Du. *jonkheer*) + linking phoneme or possessive particle *-s-* + *huis* house.] A small dwelling built for a farmer's eldest son and situated near the main homestead of a Cape Dutch farm house.

1954 M. KUTTEL *Quadrilles & Konfyt* 40 She was standing at the door of the Jonkerhuis, waving a letter. **1968** H. FRANSEN in D.J. Opperman *Spirit of Vine* 199 No *werf* (or farmyard) in the wine-producing districts of the Western Cape is complete without its gabled cellar-structure next to the homestead itself, together with its companions: the *jonkershuis* (a minor dwelling for younger sons), stables, slave quarters and other outbuildings. **1977** G. WESTWOOD *Bride of Bonamour* 140 Perhaps it had worried her more than she had liked to admit to be alone so much in the Jonkershuis and staying in the large ancient house. **1981** A. ALBRECHT in P. Dane *Great Houses of Constantia* 156 He lives with his wife and children in what might be called a modern version of the traditional *jonkheershuis*, next to his father. **1987** *Style* Nov. 173 (*caption*) The H-shaped plan of the house is easily detectable from this side view ... The old jonkershuis may be seen to the left. **1992** E. VOSLOO in *Sunday Times* 20 Sept. 15 A 265-year-old homestead, an adjacent jonkheershuis, stables and waenhuis.

jonkmanskas /ˈjɔŋ(k)manzˌkas, -mənz-, -mans-/ *n.* Also **jongmans kas**. Pl. **-kaste** /-kastə/. [fr. Du. *jonkman* bachelor + linking phoneme or possessive particle *-s-* + *kast* cupboard.] See first quot.

1971 BARAITSER & OBHOLZER *Cape Country Furn.* p.xiii, Jonkmanskas .. seems to be a fairly modern name for a smallish clothes cupboard, with about three shelves but not provision for hanging, and a couple of drawers side by side but in variable positions. *Ibid.* 193 In their fairly late form, Jonkmanskaste are quite plain; they have two upper drawers with round stinkwood knobs, two yellowwood doors and turned Cape-style feet. **1971** L.G. GREEN *Taste of S.-Easter* 54 The collector may still find the typical stinkwood and yellowwood furniture of the area ... the jongmanskas, a clothes-chest of unusual design. **1978** A.P. BRINK *Rumours of Rain* 160 The old Cape yellowwood jonkmanskas which I'd changed into a cocktail cabinet. **1981** J. KENCH *Cape Dutch Homesteads* 45 Facing each other across the room are .. a large beefwood and stinkwood Cape armoire from the Eighteenth Century and .. a 'jongmanskas' made of yellowwood and stinkwood, a favourite combination in Cape furniture making. **1987** P. SULLIVAN in *Living* June 24 Some rare discoveries including an eye-catching stinkwood *jongmanskas* inlaid with yellowwood. **1987** J. KENCH *Cottage Furn.* 40 An important local variant on the wardrobe is the 'jonkmanskas', which features a drawer or drawers at the top. *Ibid.* 41 Much play was made in the jonkmanskas with contrasting woods, the dark stinkwood knobs on drawers and doors setting off the sheen of the yellowwood.

jorl *n.* and *adj.* var. JOL *n.* and *adj.*

jorl *v.* var. JOL *v.*

joseph *n.* Also **josef**, **josep**, **josup**. [Etym. obscure; perh. ad. Du. *Jood's visch* (modern orthography *vis*) Jew fish; or fr. Malay; or an allusion to the biblical Joseph's many-coloured coat (see quot. 1913).] The *elephant fish* (see ELEPHANT), *Callorhinchus capensis*.

1795 C.R. HOPSON tr. *C.P. Thunberg's Trav.* I. 295 Among the various sorts of fish that appeared on the tables at the Cape, were the *Chimæra callorynchus* (*Dodskop* or *Joseph*) the flesh of which is white and well-tasted; and the *Raja miraletus* (or *Rock*). **1902** J.D.F. GILCHRIST in *Trans. of S. Afr. Philological Soc.* Vol.11 No.4, 224 (Pettman), There are a few [names] .. for which no plausible derivation can be discovered. These are bafaro, assous, zeverrim, katonkel, joseph, and its variations. **1913** C. PETTMAN *Africanderisms* 235 *Joseph* or *Josvisch*, .. How the fish came by its trivial name is not clear. Dr Gilchrist ('History of the Local Names of Fish') suggests that 'it may be a corruption of "Jood's visch" or "Jews" fish". The fishermen of the Cape suggest that the name is derived from the brilliant and varied colours of the living fish. **1918** S.H. SKAIFE *Animal Life* 203 The Joseph, or *Josep*, is a peculiar fish closely related to the sharks. **1947** K.H. BARNARD *Pict. Guide to S. Afr. Fishes* 31 The *Joseph, Josup* or *Doodskop* (Callorhynchus capensis) .. is a well-known shallow-water species often brought in by trek-netters. It is also called Elephant-Shark in allusion to the fleshy protuberance on the end of the snout. **1958** L.G. GREEN *S. Afr. Beachcomber* 111 The name Joseph is a riddle, though I have heard that it is a corruption of Joodvis. Now the Joodsvis is the Jew Fish of Australia, and this in turn is a corruption of Jewel Fish. **1973** J.L.B. SMITH in *Std Encycl. of Sn Afr.* IX. 253 Of the subclass *Holocephli*, the josup is a curious creature living in 5–100 fathoms over the whole Southern African region. **1977** K.F.R. BUDACK in A. Traill *Khoisan Ling. Studies 3* 37 Against skin diseases and ulcers, also of a syphilitic nature, the yolks of the eggs of the joseph or Callorhynchus capensis were used.

Josey, **Josie(s)** varr. JOZI.

josup var. JOSEPH.

jouj var. JEWISH.

jowalla var. TSHWALA.

Jozi /ˈdʒɔzi/ *n. colloq.* Also **Josey**, **Josie(s)**, **Jozie**. Esp. among Zulu-speakers: a nickname for the city of Johannesburg; cf. JO'BURG.

*c*1948 H. TRACEY *Lalela Zulu* 81 'Goli,' the place of gold, and 'Jozi,' short for Johannesburg, are the modern Zulu abbreviations. **1978** *Drum* Feb. 65 We three from *Josie* decided to take the waitress jobs just for fun planning to quit after our first pay day. **1979** C. VAN DER MERWE in *Frontline* Dec. 17 Johannesburg — Josies, that is. **1987** *Drum* July 46 The opening gambit is usually like this: Him: 'Hau, mfowethu you look a stranger in these parts.' You: 'Sure, I've just come down from Jozi.' **1987** J. KHUMALO in *Pace* July 26 With her mind finally made up to seek fame and fortune in Jozi, naive Mercy made it known .. that she was ready to .. make for the fabled city of gold-paved streets. **1990** O. MUSI in *City Press* 20 May 9 Jozi will soon look like Pretoria — where every second mlungu is in uniform and every darkie knows his place, if you see what I mean. **1993** J. KHUMALO in *Pace* July 57 Capetonian Vicky Sampson blew into Jozi two years ago.

Hence **Jozi** *n. ?nonce*, an inhabitant of Johannesburg.

1984 *Frontline* Feb. 25 Us Joseys sometimes forget that there are such places in South Africa.

JSE *n.* Shortened form of *Johannesburg Stock Exchange*. Also *attrib.*

The Stock Exchange is also often referred to by the name of the street or location in Johannesburg from which it operates: see *between the chains* (CHAINS sense 1 b), HOLLARD STREET, and DIAGONAL STREET.

1971 M.M. BORKUM in *Daily Dispatch* 21 May 16 On the JSE, .. we traded 300,6 million shares to the value of R605,2 million as against 544 million and R1 700 million the previous year. **1979** *Citizen* 16 July 17 Index of shares traded on the JSE over the past week was 176,97 compared with 189,63 a week ago. A year ago the index stood at 224,03. **1981** *Rand Daily Mail* 30 June 1 Heavy JSE gold sales. With gold slipping to a new 18-month low gold shares continued their steep slide on the Johannesburg Stock Exchange yesterday. **1987** R.A. NORTON in *Jhb. Stock Exchange Centenary* 9 The first JSE lasted for no more than two years. **1991** D. CANNING in *Weekend Argus* 26 Jan. (Business) 3 JSE warning on insider trading. **1992** *Natal Mercury* 3 Nov. 11 JSE shares ended mixed after drifting sideways in dull trade yesterday as the market waited for the outcome of today's US presidential elections.

jss var. JIS.

juba, **jubu** varr. IJUBA.

juckschee var. JUKSKEI.

‖**juffrou** /jəˈfrəʊ, ˈjəfrəʊ/ *n.* Also **jevrouw**, **juffer(o)**, **juff(e)row**, **juffrauw**, **jufvrouw**, and with initial capital. [Afk., fr. Du. *jongvrouw*, *juffrouw* (*jong* young + *vrouw* woman, madam, miss, mistress, lady).]

'Juffrou' was also borrowed into *Brit. Eng.* directly from Dutch, but is now obsolete.

1. 'Mistress', a form of address or reference formerly meaning 'Mrs', and now 'Miss'; a form of address or reference to a school teacher; also used as a title, with a surname; JUFFROUTJIE.

1824 W.J. BURCHELL *Trav.* II. 118 At taking leave, *Juffrouw* (Mrs.) *Vermeulen* .. repeated her invitation for us to stop there on our return. *a*1827 D. CARMICHAEL in W.J. Hooker *Botanical Misc.* (1831) II. 32, I knew that Juffrouw understood as little the meaning of these flowers of rhetoric, as did the poor culprit on whom they were so lavishly bestowed. **1827** G. THOMPSON *Trav.* I. 27 In the course of conversation our hostess, the Juffrouw Maré, gave an account of the recent death of one of her relations. **1834** T. PRINGLE *Afr. Sketches* 178 The Juffrouw Coetzer, sometimes manufactured leather dresses for sale .. bespoke a travelling Jacket and trowsers of dressed springbok skin. **1867** E.L. PRICE *Jrnls* (1956) 249, I suggested they shd. make it [*sc.* the food] them selves ... but they murmured at it, saying that no one cd. make it like Yeffrow Price! **1871** J. MACKENZIE *Ten Yrs* (1971) 15, I fancy however, Jufvrouw would prefer the charcoal 'komfoor' to a spinning-wheel. **1898** W.C. SCULLY *Vendetta* 62 Juffrouw du Plessis and her two daughters were sitting in their garden behind the oleander hedge. **1913** C. PETTMAN *Africanderisms* 235 *Juffer* or *Juffrouw* ... Juffer is equivalent to the English 'mistress'. **1919** M. GREENLEES tr. *O.F. Mentzel's Life at Cape in Mid-18th C.* 126 He drew Mistress van Kerwel, as she stood turning her back upon him, in so natural and realistic a manner that everyone who saw the picture at once exclaimed 'That's the jonge Juffrouw!' **1926** P. SMITH *Beadle* (1929) 87 If Juffrouw will but tell me where I can find her I will now take her my letter. **1948** V.M. FITZROY *Cabbages & Cream*, 'You must be reasonable, juffrou,' the agent said persuasively, 'what you are asking is more than double the market value of the place.' **1960** J. COPE *Tame Ox* 92 Juffrou du Preez, we black people know this book — do you understand? We have had it for more than a hundred years, two hundred. **1973** J. COPE *Alley Cat* 96 'You deserve our heartfelt thanks,' .. 'I shall mention you to our Church Council. Yours, juffrou, is a work of ..' the voice going jerkily on. **1981** *Sunday Times* 14 June 9 'He had two passions,' said a former school teacher, Mrs van Dyk, still called 'juffrou' by everyone, 'education and the mission field'.

2. As a common noun.

a. A young woman; JONGE VROUW.

1837 'N. POLSON' *Subaltern's Sick Leave* 1104 At about two o'clock the Dutch take their siesta and on rising from their beds the coffee or teapot is introduced and kept by the juffrouw's side till night. **1859** E.L. LAYARD in *Cape Monthly Mag.* V. Jan. 27 The jufvrouw was busy about the wagon, mynheer had pastured the cattle, and one of the boys was off to the rocks with his fishing-rod. *a***1862** J. AYLIFF *Jrnl of 'Harry Hastings'* (1963) 25 If a poor man goes to the farm house, the *juffero* (for you know, Hetty, that's the name for lady or mistress) invites him into the large hall and with her own hands pours him out a cup of tea. **1896** M.A. CAREY-HOBSON *At Home in Tvl* 311 They had come to live in Pretoria, where the sister of the Jevrouw and some other members of the family lived. **1955** V.M. FITZROY *Dark Bright Land* 82 A new chemise trimmed with Moravian work that the juffrow had but just completed making. *Ibid.* 240 Ample-skirted vrouws would prepare meals, slim juffrows would slip by on errands watched with interest by the young kêrels. **1976** A. DELIUS *Border* 322 We used to tease him .. saying he must have some beautiful juffrauw hidden in the woods.

b. A female teacher.

1980 *Het Suid-Western* 6 Aug., [A] Six-year-old .. this week handcuffed his nursery school principal .. 'I let him handcuff me. He was most proud because he had now caught his "juffrou".' **1984** B. JOHNSON-BARKER in *Wynboer* June 72 To learn to sign his name. If he had the time the next day, he might consider speaking to the juffrou about it.

juffroutjie /ˈjəfrəʊki/ *n.* Also **juffrouwkie.** [Afk., see JUFFROU + -IE.] The dim. form of JUFFROU sense 1.

1966 I. VAUGHAN *These Were my Yesterdays* 90 Thank you, juffrouwkie – you have given my much happiness. **1980** *Sunday Times* 4 May 3 Mr Botha had referred to student questioners as 'juffroutjie' (little girl) and 'mannetjie' (little man).

juj var. JEWISH.

jukskei /ˈjəkskeɪ, ˈjœk-/ *n.* Also **jeuk skei, ju(c)kschee, jukschei.** Pl. **-s, -skeie** /-skeɪə/. [S. Afr. Du., fr. Du. *juk* yoke + *schei* (see SKEY).]

1. SKEY sense 1.

1822 W.J. BURCHELL *Trav.* I. 151 The yokes are straight, and pierced with two pair of mortices to receive the *jukschei* which fits in loosely, and answer to what in English husbandry are called the *bows*: but are merely two straight pegs, one on each side of the ox's neck, and having notches on their outer sides to receive the *nek-strop* (neck strap). **1871** LORD & BAINES *Shifts & Expedients* 452 Near each end are two mortices .. through which to pass the 'jeuk skeis', or yoke keys, which keep it in place on the neck of the ox. **1947** F.C. SLATER *Sel. Poems* 99, I heard the rattle of chains and the creak of the jukskei. [*Note*] Small wooden shafts fitting into yokes. **1968** F.G. BUTLER *Cape Charade* 25, I never tried to turn a jukskei into a saddle; and I'm not trying to pave military roads with cannon balls. **1971** *Evening Post* 27 Feb. (Mag. Sect.) 2 A stinkwood yoke, with 'jukskeis', serves as a hat-stand.

2.a. A game in which a bottle-shaped peg or 'skey' (see SKEY sense 2) is thrown at a stake planted in a sand pit. Also *attrib.* See also BOERESPORT, SKOF $n.^2$ sense 2.

1879 *Cape Argus* 11 Feb., Have game of *juckschee* and other recreations until supper time. **1939** J.C. LAAS in H. Gibbs *Twilight* (1950) 181 Organizing gatherings such as target-practice .., playing jukskei, etc. **1942** *Cape Times* 10 Nov. 4 Saturday's jukskei results were as expected. **1950** S. DE WET *Hour of Breath* 69 In the late afternoon we used to play Jukskei on the river bank below our houses. **1955** V. DE KOCK *Fun They Had* 70 *Jukskei*, the popular game played with yoke-pins, is said by some to have its origin in the days of the Voortrekkers. *c***1965** *State of S. Afr. 1965* 106 A form of sport peculiar to South Africa is *jukskei*, a reminiscence of the pioneering days. It resembles deckquoits and is played with wooden pegs, representing the pegs in the yoke of an ox, which the old pioneers did in fact use in their games. **1970** *S. Afr. Panorama* June 31 The South African Jukskei Board defines the game of *Jukskei* as follows: 'A game in which an object, known as a skey, is cast from a point, over a fixed distance, in the direction of and at another object, called the stake, which is planted in a sandpit'. **1982** *Weekend Argus* 10 Apr. 11 Jukskei is played in America as South Africans play it, and it is called 'jukskei' there too ... [American] Jukskei originated .. after someone read about it in an encyclopaedia. **1984** R. DE BEER in *Sunday Times* 7 Oct. (Life Style) 2 That's about it – apart from a very strong jukskei interest. **1990** *S. Afr. Panorama* July-Aug. 63 Jukskei, which originated in South Africa, reflects a way of life that is closely intertwined with the Afrikaner's history and his pioneering spirit.

b. SKEY sense 2.

[**1934** C.P. SWART Supplement to Pettman. 81 *Jukskeigooi*, A game .. played by the Boers.] **1956** *Cape Times* 26 Jan. 1 A few minutes after throwing about six practice *jukskeie* at the Newlands circus grounds .. Mr. P.A. M– .. dropped dead. **1972** *Grocott's Mail* 20 Oct. 3 His would be the choice of weapons. My own preference would be jukskeis at thirty paces.

Hence **jukskeier** *n.*, one who plays the game of jukskei.

1991 *Sunday Times* 7 Apr. 26 The sport is looking forward to the day when South African jukskeiers can, again, become part of the international fraternity.

July *n.* [Special senses of general Eng. *July* the seventh month of the year.]

1. ***The July***: A short form of *Durban July Handicap*, an annual horse-race held on the first Saturday in July at the Greyville Racecourse in Durban; *Durban July*, see DURBAN. Also *attrib.*

First run in 1897, and now the country's premier horse-race.

1942 *E. Prov. Herald* 4 July, Special message by Gen. Smuts broadcast after 'July' today. A special message from Gen. Smuts will be broadcast at Greyville racecourse tomorrow afternoon immediately following the running of the July handicap. **1948** H.C. BOSMAN in L. Abrahams *Cask of Jerepigo* (1972) 232 The boss had gone to Durban for the July. **1955** *Official Visitors Guide* (Durban Publicity Assoc.) 50 *Greyville*, mecca of South African racegoers during the famous 'July' Season, is unique in two respects. **1959** R.E. VAN DER ROSS in Hattingh & Bredekamp *Coloured Viewpoint* (1984) 66 Driving through the Karoo, as many have done recently to and from the 'July', we often come across little parties of Coloured farm labourers. **1972** *Sunday Times* 25 June (Mag. Sect.) 6 Held in the middle of Durban's superb winter, the July draws people from all corners of South Africa and Rhodesia. **1978** M. HARTMANN *Shadow of Leopard* 34 'What is the July, a local classic?' 'The premier race in South Africa, Mr Dryden, the equivalent of your Derby.' **1990** *Sunday Times* 1 July 22, I am glad to say that, as has happened every year for the past 45 years, I have the 'July' result absolutely and irretrievably tied up. **1992** E. VAN WIJK in *S. Afr. Panorama* Nov.-Dec. 57, I have one vice – gambling. I don't drink, I don't smoke, but come July time ... You can't beat it. **1994** G. WILLOUGHBY in *Weekly Mail & Guardian* 8 July 38 Our hopes, like those of hundreds of thousands round the country, are pinned firmly on the big one – race 7, the July.

2. *comb.* **July day**, the day upon which the Durban July Handicap is run (being the first Saturday in July); **July fever**, the intense interest and excitement surrounding the race.

1971 *Daily Dispatch* 30 June 1, July runners and jockeys, jackpot selections for **July Day.** **1981** R. MITCHELL in *Argus* 3 July 1 Last year we handled R496000 on July day. **1971** *Daily Dispatch* 30 June 1 **July fever** rises for big race. **1972** *Sunday Times* 25 June (Mag. Sect.) 6 Parking attendants, vegetable sellers, hotel porters and waiters are all subject to July Fever, and often show a remarkably sound knowledge of the finer details of the racing game. **1982** *Drum* July 45 Like everyone else, I have 'July Fever'. For those who don't know what that is, you catch it round the time the Durban July Handicap is about to take place. **1989** *Motorist* 2nd Quarter 14 Thousands of visitors .. find themselves in the grip of what Durbanites term 'July Fever'. One of the first events on the July calendar is the Rothman's July Handicap. **1991** *Sunday Times* 2 June (Mag. Sect.) 39 Get dressed for Winter in Durban ... Catch July Fever in a packed programme of exciting events in the funshine city.

jumping bean *n. phr. Colloq.* [Special senses of general Eng.; see quots. 1974 (sense 1) and 1974 (sense 2 a).]

1. A gall upon the shrub *Rhus lucida* (see TAAIBOS), formed by a grub.

*c***1939** S.H. SKAIFE *S. Afr. Nature Notes* 184 A smaller, oval gall will be found on taaibos plants, mostly on the leaves. These are hollow and will be found to contain a fat white grub that kicks vigorously when its home is destroyed. These galls are the 'jumping beans' familiar to every schoolboy. They are due to the activities of a curious little moth. **1974** B. DE WINTER in *Std Encycl. of Sn Afr.* X. 396 *Taaibos*, .. There are often galls upon the leaves of *Rhus lucida*, owing to a moth which punctures them and lays a single egg in each puncture ... If the gall is placed on the hand, the grub inside causes it to jump, and for this reason children often call the gall a 'jumping bean'.

2.a. In full ***jumping bean tree***: the TAMBOTIE (sense 1), *Spirostachys africana*.

1961 PALMER & PITMAN *Trees of S. Afr.* 239 *Spirostachys Africanus, Tamboti*, sandalwood, jumping-bean tree. **1972** —— *Trees of Sn Afr.* II. 1157 Tamboti, Cape sandalwood, jumping-bean tree. **1974** G.L.F. HARTWIG in *Std Encycl. of Sn Afr.* X. 405 *Tamboti. Jumping-bean tree, (Spirostachys africanus.)* ... The fruit is trilobate, is often attacked by an insect before it ripens, and falls off by Christmas. The larva of the insect develops in the seed and by convulsive action causes the seed to jump a few centimetres into the air. **1975** [see sense b]. **1987** [see SANDALWOOD].

b. The poisonous fruit of the tambotie tree, so called when the breeding place for larvae (see quot. 1974 at sense a).

1972 PALMER & PITMAN *Trees of Sn Afr.* II. 1157 The tamboti is widely known for three reasons – its fine wood, its toxic properties, and its 'jumping beans'. **1974** *S. Afr. Panorama* Apr. 24 Among the many other species are the tamboti .. whose 'jumping beans' feature in many Bushveld tales. **1975** *Ibid.* Sept. 5 The 'jumping beans' of the tamboti, which is also called the jumping-bean tree, are a source of great amusement to young and old.

3. The marine angel-fish *Centropyge acanthops* of the Pomacanthidae, being yellow, orange, and blue-black in colour.

1975 M.M. SMITH in Smith & Jackson *Common & Scientific Names of Fishes* I. 45 *Xiphipops acanthops* .. jumpingbean. **1986** SMITH & HEEMSTRA *Smiths' Sea Fishes* 624 *Centropyge acanthops* .. Jumping bean.

jumping jack *n. phr.* [Transf. sense of general Eng. *jumping jack* a toy which jumps.] The *blue porpoise shark* (see PORPOISE SHARK), *Isurus mako*.

1957 S. SCHOEMAN *Strike!* 144 The so-called 'Tornynhaai' (Porpoise Shark) of South Africa, also known as 'Jumping Jack' at Mossel Bay, is identical to the Mako shark of New Zealand. These Jumping Jacks or tornynhaaie are fairly plentiful in the littoral between Cape Infanta and Plettenberg Bay.

June 16 *n. phr.* **a.** Used allusively to refer to the start of the Soweto uprising of 1976. **b.** *Soweto Day*, see SOWETO sense 3. Also *attrib.* See also YOUTH DAY.

1977 *Rand Daily Mail* 16 June 1 Brigadier Jan V–, the head of the Soweto Police, last night appealed to blacks to commemorate the first anniversary of June 16 today peacefully. **1986** *Times* (U.K.) 16 June 16 All other meetings, both indoors and out, to commemorate June 16 are banned. **1987** M. BADELA in *Weekly Mail* 19 June 7, June 16, the anniversary of the 1976 Soweto uprising, has become a *de facto* public holiday for most South Africans. The massive stayaway across the country .. showed that support for June 16 is growing annually. **1989** *Sunday Times* 18 June 20 Another June 16 has passed in relative peace .. acknowledged, even by many white South Africans, as a day to reflect upon events that made a profound impact on the political history of our country. **1990** *New African* 18 June 1 In the first June 16 commemoration service since the unbanning of the African National Congress .. , tens of thousands of people attended peaceful rallies in Southern Natal. **1992** *Pace* Aug. 29 The City Hall was the destination of the June 16 march which began at Curries Fountain Stadium.

Junior Certificate *n. phr. Hist.* **a.** JC sense a. **b.** JC sense b. Also *attrib.*

1939 J. LUDUS in *Outspan* 20 Oct. 53 If they [*sc.* young South Africans] do not obtain their matriculation, or at the very least junior certificate, adult South Africa assumes that they are incapable of doing so. **1961** H.F. SAMPSON *White-Faced Huts* 20 Selbourne was 30, and had passed his Junior Certificate examination when at school. **1963** S.H. SKAIFE *Naturalist Remembers* 59 Children began to take biology in the Junior Certificate, Senior Certificate and Matriculation examinations. **1970** *Daily News* 12 May The commission has suggested that a Junior Certificate or its equivalent should be laid down as a minimum educational qualification. **1970** [see HOËRSKOOL]. **1979** M. MATSHOBA *Call Me Not a Man* 191 Learn something new .. rather than repeat in English for matric purposes what I did in *si*Sotho for primary school purposes and in Afrikaans for Junior Certificate purposes. **1980** C. HERMER *Diary of Maria Tholo* 141 Only 1,6 percent of African schoolteachers had university level qualifications, eight per cent had a Junior Certificate.

jurre, jur-ruh varr. YIRRA.

juslaaik, -like varr. JISLAAIK.

jussis, jussus varr. YISSUS.

just now *adv. phr.* [Special sense of general Eng. *just now* exactly at this point of time, precisely at present, only a very short time ago, directly, immediately; influenced by Afk. *netnou*.] In a while, presently; by and by, after some time, later. See also NOW-NOW sense 2.

Used also as in general Eng., meaning 'a short while ago'. See also NOW-NOW sense 1.

1900 H. BLORE *Imp. Light Horseman* 198 Go but inside, I shall follow just now. *a***1931** S. BLACK in S. Gray *Three Plays* (1984) 139 Katoo: Where is Miss Helena? Grietje: Gone in the veld, Miesies. She come yis now back. **1934** C.P. SWART *Supplement to Pettman.* 81 *Just now,* This expression, in the sense of presently or by and by, is in constant use all over South Africa and has been doubtless influenced by Scotch usage. **1939** 'D. RAME' *Wine of Good Hope* 40 'Well, eat then,' said Lowell. 'I'll come just now.' **1953** N. GORDIMER *Lying Days* 92 'Well,' I said, 'I'll open it just now —.' **1957** D. JACOBSON *Price of Diamonds* 7 'You must go,' Gottlieb said abruptly ... He stared above Gottlieb's head. 'Just now,' he said .. 'When we've done our business.' **1966** A. SACHS *Jail Diary* 143 'Would you mind switching off the light after you lock up.' 'The men on cell duty will do that just now.' **1969** A. FUGARD *Boesman & Lena* 12 Just now you get a bloody good *klap.* **1970** S. DEANE *Informant, Bloemfontein* I'll ring you back just now. **1979** A.P. BRINK *Dry White Season* 57 'Why don't you come to bed with me?' ... It wasn't often she conveyed it so openly. 'I'll be coming just now.' **1982** *Sunday Times* 31 May, 'Just now' — this, of course, changes meaning depending on how much the 'juuust' is drawn out: 'I'll come just now' could mean 'I'll come in a moment'; or 'I'll come in two hours ...' You could also use 'now now' in the same way as 'just now' to indicate that you'll be doing something 'soon soon'. **1987** M. POLAND *Train to Doringbult* 135 'Daddy! Daddy! Come and see where I buried the kingfisher!' ... 'Just now. I'm going to eat my breakfast, first.' **1990** *Estcourt High School Mag.* No.49, 17 After many months of careful observation I think I am safe in defining 'now' as meaning 'soon', 'now now' as meaning 'in a few minutes', 'now, now, now' as meaning 'now', and finally 'just now' as meaning 'later'. **1991** T. BOWLES *Informant, Grahamstown* Phone them just now. They should be back by just now.

juvenal /ˈdʒuːvənəl/ *n. Ostrich-farming.* [Prob. ad. Eng. *juvenile.*] A feather from the third plumage of a young ostrich, after the birth and chick plumages. See also CHICK. Also *attrib.*

1909 J.E. DUERDEN in *Agric. Jrnl of Cape of G.H.* XXXIV. 519 Juvenal feathers ... are of a uniformly dark grey or slate colour, and the tip is rounded, not pointed ... All the feathers of the juvenal plumage are not fully ripe until the birds are about sixteen months old, the last to ripen being the wing quills, which are known as 'first-after-chicks,' or, better, as *juvenals.* **1930** M.F. WORMSER *Ostrich Industry.* 9 The ostrich has 4 plumages, viz. natal, chick, juvenal, adult.

jwala var. JOALA.

jwarlar var. TSHWALA.

jysis var. YISSUS.

K

K /keɪ/ *n. colloq.* The eleventh letter of the alphabet, used as an abbreviation:
1. *offensive.* The initial letter of the offensive word KAFFIR, used *attrib.* (and euphemistically) in the following phrr.: *K-beer*, TSHWALA sense a; *K-factor derog.*, stupidity or inefficiency, as offensively attributed by some to black people; *K-form*, a word or combination formed with the word 'kaffir'; *K-rations derog.*, cheap foodstuffs supplied to farm labourers or domestic workers (see RATION); *K-sheeting*, KAFFIR-SHEETING; *K-word*, the word 'kaffir'.

1981 *Argus* 27 Aug., 'K' sheeting R3,25 m. 120 cm wide. Plain dyed in beautiful shades of Apple Green, Biscuit, Rust, Olive, Red, Sky, Natural & Unbleached (White). 1984 *Fair Lady* 25 Jan. 51 All self-respecting radicals of the time had a couple of huge art nouveau posters, a batik lampshade and tie-dyed k-sheeting curtains. 1984 *Sunday Times* 8 July (Lifestyle) 9 The kos, hardly five-star, consists of a reasonable potato hash, cabbage, a vegetarian concoction, plain salad and a fish dish which ran out. Perhaps K-rations would be more suitable. 1985 H. PRENDINI in *Style* Oct. 40 There is another taboo in Jilly's vocabulary. She gets around it by abbreviating it to the first letter and then managing to talk quite happily about K-sheeting, K-beer and the K-factor. 1988 E. *Prov. Herald* 30 July. 7 Natural K-sheeting (1st quality) m R6,40. 1990 L. BRANSBY *Homeward Bound*, I was a fool to think .. Solomon wouldn't know K-factor stood for 'Kaffir'. 1991 B. RONGE in *Sunday Times* 26 May (Magazine) 8 While the ANC was banned and Mandela was imprisoned there was a genuine attempt on the part of most South Africans to curtail racist language and jokes. Now .. the K-word has become a commonplace one. 1991 J. BRANFORD *Dict. of S. Afr. Eng.* 143 It [*sc.* the word 'Kaffir'] is avoided by most educated speakers and writers, though many K-forms continue in colloquial use. 1992 *Grocott's Mail* 16 Oct. 1 It's the 'k' word that's causing conflict. 1992 M. GRIFFIN in *Weekend Post* 31 Oct. 9 Debate about the K-word flared up again this month.

2. Also **k., k.** Pl. **-s, -'s.** The initial letter of *kilometre* and (in *pl.*) *kilometres-per-hour*; KAY.

1983 G. PIENAAR in J. Johnson *S. Afr. Speaks* 41, I do a lot of road running in the early mornings. I run five k's a day, for stamina. 1984 *Frontline* Feb. 33 It's about ten minutes to the school. That is, at 120 Ks it takes ten minutes. 1987 L. BENNETT in *Personality* 18 Nov. 76 The apprentice .. gets into his dad's car and *drives* a few hundred k's risking life and limb. 1988 T.J. LINDSAY *Shadow* (1990) 39 'On clearing the line, how far ahead were you?' 'About 3.5 Ks, sir.' 1990 *Frontline* Mar.-Apr. 34 Watch out for kudu. They jump for the headlights. We just had a case, about 30 Ks on. 1990 K. GILBERT *Informant, Westminster* (OFS), I went to the 'Allotment' — taking Nina in her push chair, it is about a k. away.

kaai(i)ngs, kaains varr. KAIINGS.

kaak var. KAK.

‖**kaal** /kɑːl/ *adj. colloq.* Also **carl, kall.** [Afk.]
1. Bare; naked; cf. KAALGAT sense 1.

c1881 A. DOUGLASS *Ostrich Farming* 66 Select a farm that has on it especially plenty of spec boom and carl prickly pear. 1911 A.H. FROST in *Farmer's Weekly* 4 Oct. 134 You don't want a long legged flat sided sheep with a weak back and a kaal pens. 1966 S. CLOUTS *One Life* 46 The bitter stars, I've tasted them, My backside is mos kaal. 1969 A. FUGARD *Boesman & Lena* 54 You should have thrown it on the bonfire. And me with it. You should have walked away kaal! 1970 C.S. HENDRY *Informant, Somerset West* We swam kaal (bare). 1975 [see KLOMP]. 1986 B. SIMON in *S. Gray Market Plays* 116 I'm just out of the bath all wet my hair dangling and this little hand-towel around me ... I see there's this girl on the other side with a face like a box of bladdy tomatoes ... I always walk kaal here. You know, a man likes to feel free.

2. Special Comb. **Kaal Kaffir** *n. phr. Obs. offensive* [see KAFFIR], NDEBELE sense 1 a; **kaalkop** /-kɔp/ [Afk., *kop* head], a bald person; also *fig.* and *transf.*; **kaalsiekte** /-siktə/ [Afk., *siekte* disease], alopecia in lambs.

1899 J.G. MILLAIS *Breath from Veldt* 152 (Swart), Oom said they were 'Kall Kaffirs', the Dutch appellation for Matabele. 1930 S.T. PLAATJE *Mhudi* (1975) 75 But in the summer months no Matebele ever puts on anything. They only carry spears and shields; for the rest they walk about just like children! 'Oh,' said an elderly Boer, 'they are the kaal-Kaffers.' 1894 W.C. BALDWIN *Afr. Hunting* 301 The bush was very good, a moderate breeze of wind, which I kept always below, but I had great difficulty in getting the bull out from the company of the 'carl kop' (naked head). 1896 R. WALLACE *Farming Indust. of Cape Col.* Kaalkop wheat, a beardless variety well liked by millers. c1936 *S. & E. Afr. Yr Bk & Guide* 1022 On the silver coins of the Union, the King's head is crowned. The lack of this in British Silver has earned them the name of 'Kaalkop,' bare head. 1932 M.W. HENNING *Animal Diseases* 662 (Swart), The veld in Colesberg is far superior, so that animals are seldom tempted to eat the plant and **kaalsiekte** is but rarely observed.

kaalblad /ˈkɑːlblat/ *n.* Also **kaalblaar, kahlblad.** [Afk., *kaal* bare + *blad, blaar* leaf.] Any of several spineless or semi-spineless plants of the genus *Opuntia* (prickly-pears).

1877 *Queenstown Free Press* 4 Sept., The *Kaalblad* is not only safe, but the birds evince a decided liking for its leaves and fruit. [c1881 see KAAL sense 1.] 1885 *Handbk S. Afr. Exhibition* 290 (Pettman), The *Kaal-blad* is a 'sport' of the 'prickly pear,' but the seeds yield for the most part the original prickly pear. 1890 A. MARTIN *Home Life* 57 One kind [of prickly pear], the *kahlblad*, or 'blad leaf,' has no thorns. 1906 F. BLERSCH *Handbk of Agric.* 256 In some localities the thornless *Opuntia*, or *kaal blad*, is considered a valuable plant during seasons of drought. 1913 C. PETTMAN *Africanderisms* 237 Kaalblad, .. The variety of the prickly pear (*Opuntia*), the leaves of which are almost bare of thorns. Whether this is really a variety or only a 'sport' is not quite clear; it appears to revert very quickly to the prickly type. 1917 R. MARLOTH *Common Names* 43 Kaalblad, The thornless variety (by artificial selection) of the common Prickly pear. 1942 S. CLOETE *Hill of Doves* 7 The orchard wall was backed by a thick hedge of kaalblad, whose big leaves were like flat, dull-green hands. *Ibid.* 328 'Brandy made from the fruit of the kaalblad.' 'I have never had brandy made from prickly pears.'

‖**kaalgat** /ˈkɑːlxat/ *adj. slang.* [Afk., *kaal* bare + *gat* hole, 'arse'.]
1. Not in polite use. Naked; cf. KAAL sense 1.

1969 A. FUGARD *Boesman & Lena* 4 Sitting there in the dust with the pieces ... Kaalgat! That's what it felt like! 1975 S. ROBERTS *Outside Life's Feast* 95 'I'll wait till you've put on your dress,' said Joey. 'No ... Come in! Do you think I want to stand kaalgat like this all day, getting gooseflesh down my arms and legs?' 1976 *Daily Dispatch* 6 Feb. 14 Everyone was required to admire the non-existent suit and nobody was expected to proclaim the unpalatably true fact that the emperor was actually kaalgat. 1982 D. KRAMER *Short Back & Sides* 8 It was there that we went kaalgat-swimming in the Breede River. 1985 P. SLABOLEPZSY *Sat. Night at Palace* 41 Vince: Finally I got her kaalgat — Forsie: Kaalgat!? No, man — Vince: Look, shut up, man! Anyway. I got her where I want her. 1989 on Radio 5, 14 Nov., As a prize we're giving away a pair of sleeping shorts. You could call us 'No Kaalgat' radio. 1991 G. DE BEER *Informant, Port Nolloth* (N. Cape) He ran kaalgat down the street.

2. Special Comb. **kaalgat peach, kaalgatperske** /-pɛrskə/ [Afk., *perske* peach], a nectarine. Also *attrib.*

[1913 C. PETTMAN *Africanderisms* 237 Kaal perske, The Cape Dutch name for the nectarine.] 1975 S. ROBERTS *Outside Life's Feast* The leaves on our kaalgatperske tree are just old pieces of rag. 1977 E.M. MACPHAIL in *Contrast* 44 Vol.11 No.4, 15, I knew I wouldn't be able to resist crossing the road later to buy a big kaalgat peach and black grapes. 1980 A.J. BLIGNAUT *Dead End Rd* 94 Complaining about what the ruspes had done to his yellow kaalgat peaches. 1984 *Cape Times* 15 Mar., Well meerem, see I is not allowed to call them 'kaalgat' perskes any longer like in the old days, cause why it is too rude! 1989 *Style* Dec. 80 Kaalgatperske or peach: a nectarine.

kaalvoet /ˈkɑːlfut, -fʊt/ *adj. colloq.* [Afk., *kaal* bare + *voet* foot.] Barefoot.

1899 F.R.M. CLEAVER in M.M. Cleaver *Young S. Afr.* (1913) 26 You were a comparatively young man then, and I a little 'kaalvoet Hotnot'. [1968 L.G. GREEN *Full Many Glorious Morning* 219 It was a mixed train, known along the river as 'Ou Kaalvoet' because it carried so many bare-footed school children.] 1970 J.L. COUSINS *Informant, Vryburg* Children like going kaalvoet (barefoot). 1970 *Daily News* 28 May, It is not illegal to drive barefoot. Would you have thought it was an offence to drive a car kaalvoet? 1977 *Argus* 31 Dec. 5 Pint-sized 'kaalvoet' athlete Elsa Kok, the 13-year old daughter of a Paarl farm labourer, is a girl with a big stride and a bright future. 1980 *Sunday Times* 14 Dec. 45 The 'Kaalvoet kids' were at it again last week when they flew through the air at a terrific rate .. behind the 355Hp V8 Barefoot Supreme boat at the Southern Transvaal Waterskiing Championships. 1982 D. KRAMER *Short Back & Sides* 52, I grew up in the Boland, I was kaalvoet and carefree. 1983 *Frontline* Feb. 12 He was running up and down on the trestle tables *kaalvoet*, stubbing his toes on the empty beer-cans and tripping over the full ones. 1983 *Sunday*

Times 18 Sept. (Lifestyle) 9, I climbed up first, kaalvoet, leaving my shoes half way down the cliff. **1984** *Rand Daily Mail* 29 Mar. 1 A proud dad wins kaalvoet wager .. 'I won a bet today. The rest of our group all said Zola would wear running shoes. I said she would not.' **1990** *Sunday Times* 5 Aug. 10 TV fame has turned 'kaalvoet kids' into overnight celebrities and given their families a cash windfall. **1991** G. De Beer *Informant, Port Nolloth (N. Cape)* You can't mountain climb kaalvoet. **1993** *Weekend Post* 1 May 3 Mr Nqakula .. said he had learnt to love the Afrikaans language and rugby as he grew up in his 'kaalvoet days' at Cradock.

kaama var. KAMA.

kaa-nap var. KANNIP.

||**Kaap** /kɑːp/ *n.* [Afk.] ***The Kaap, d(i)e Kaap***: *the Cape*, see CAPE sense 1.

1912 F. Bancroft *Veldt Dwellers* 82 These devils from Australia and the Kaap are just as tough as we Boers. **1975** D.H. Strutt *Clothing Fashions* 30 There were several separate and distinct classes of people, namely: the Company officials, the servants of the Company in de Kaap itself, and the Free Burghers. **1990** *Star* 11 Sept. (Tonight) 10 What .. have a girl from *die Kaap* and a boy from Cardiff in common?

KaaPee /kɑːˈpɪə/ *n. colloq.* Also **Kapee, KP.** [Pronunciation-spelling of Afk. *KP* initial letters of *Konservatiewe Party*.] An informal name for the Conservative Party, or for a member of that party; CP. Also *attrib.*

1988 J. Scott in *E. Prov. Herald* 5 Mar. 6 You think that nobody in his right mind .. really wants the KaaPee ... If things go on like this, the KaaPees will soon take over the Government. **1989** *Frontline* Apr. 25 Lefty is saying 'Ag, you KPs, you're poep-scared of the kaffirs, that's why you want to chase them away.' [**1990** *Sunday Times* 11 Feb. 12 Sir, I am a Kay-Pee and I hereby give notice to De Klerk .. that we will fight the new dispensation tooth and nail.] **1990** *Style* July 64 These KP people are the most incredible material for a study of the ways of human behaviour. **1992** C. Leonard in *Sunday Times* 16 Feb. 6 On the campus, where one of the special polling booths is situated, .. are two caravans packed with enthusiastic party workers, one with young Nats and the other with young Kapees.

Kaapenaar /ˈkɑːpənɑː(r)/ *n.* Also **Capenaar, Kapenaar**, and with small initial. [Afk. (earlier S. Afr. Du.), *Kaap* Cape + n.-forming suffix *-enaar*.] **1.** An inhabitant of Cape Town, or of the Cape Peninsula and its environs; an inhabitant of the Cape Province; *Capeite*, see CAPE; CAPER sense 1. Cf. CAPEY sense 2. Also *attrib.*, passing into *adj.*

1834 *Cape of G.H. Lit. Gaz.* IV. Nov. 180 (Pettman), The *Capenaars* have always attempted to justify the holding of human flesh in bondage by appeals to Scripture. **1837** 'N. Polson' *Subaltern's Sick Leave* 80 'Kaapenaars,' as the Dutch and other natives of Cape Town delight to call themselves, in contradistinction to the other native white inhabitants of the colony whom they style 'Afrikaanders'. **1915** J.K. O'Connor *Afrikander Rebellion* 82 The desire for a republic among the Boers had grown stronger during recent months, and whether they be Transvaalers, Free Staters, or Kaapenaars. **1926** P.W. Laidler *Tavern of Ocean* 192 At the Koopmans de Wet House .. are collections of all that pertained to the old-time Kapenaar's home life, furniture, china, ornaments, silver plate, glass and jewellery. **1934** N. Devitt *Mem. of Magistrate* 29 The true Boer .. looked upon a man from the Cape, the 'Kaapenaar' as he called him, with some dislike born of mistrust. **1949** L.G. Green *In Land of Afternoon* 212 Kaapenaars, the people of the Cape Peninsula called themselves in the seventeenth century and long afterwards. **1955** A. Delius *Young Trav.* 68 A 'Kaapenaar' was an inhabitant of the Cape, but the word generally meant an inhabitant of the south-western areas of that province. **1973** M. Van Biljon in *Star* 16 June 6 Breeding is added to the long list of attributes lacking in the Transvaaler, and abundantly granted to the Kaapenaar. **1978** *Sunday Times* 5 Mar. (Mag. Sect.) 1 A Kapenaar naval wife .. finds Pretoria's stormy seas rough going. Transvalers and folk from other provinces might just find that Capeys, too, are a breed apart. **1982** D. Bikitsha in *Rand Daily Mail* 14 Oct. (Eve) 5 It was about this time that I made my acquaintance with the Tsotsi Taal. There was no skollie or Kaapenaar element about it. **1982** *Cape Times* 21 Dec. 17 If there is antagonism between the Transvalers and the Kaapenaars, it has deep, historical roots. **1984** *Reader's Digest* Jan. 40 Kapenaars like their meat finely minced with subtle flavouring, while Freestaters do not consider it real boerewors unless the spek (fat of the pork) comes in chunky bites. **1988** D. Hughes et al. *Complete Bk of S. Afr. Wine* (ed.2) 315 The South African Society of Wine-Tasters, now one of the most energetic in the country and one particularly dear to expatriate *Kaapenaars* far from home. **1991** A. Maimane in *Weekly Mail* 15 Feb. 17, I only realise they consider themselves coloured when I hear the *Kaapenaar* accents. **1993** J. Khumalo in *Pace* July 57 Word soon got around that there was this Kapenaar session singer who was world-class.

2. On the east coast: the CARPENTER, *Argyrozona argyrozona*.

1913 C. Pettman *Africanderisms* 238 *Kaapenaar*, The Port Elizabeth name for the fish *Denex argyrozona*, known at Cape Town as the silver fish. *c*1936 *S. & E. Afr. Yr Bk & Guide* 347 The names given vary locally, the Capetown 'silver fish' for instance being known as 'kaapenaar' in Port Elizabeth and 'sand silver' in East London. **1942** *Off. Yrbk of Union 1941* (Union Office of Census & Statistics) 770 The brilliantly coloured seventy-four (*Dentex undulosus*), more abundant in the warmer waters of the east coast, where it is known as the Silverfish, the Silverfish of the west coast being known as the Carpenter (a corruption of Kaapenaar). **1949** J.L.B. Smith *Sea Fishes* 278 *Argyrozona argyrozona* ... *Karpenter* or *Kaapenaar* (East London to Natal). **1979** Snyman & Klarie *Free from Sea* 50 *Silver Fish*, Doppie /Rooitjie/Karp/Karpenter or Kaapenaar. Silver fish are pretty fish with fairly firm, strongly-flavoured moist flesh. **1981** *E. Prov. Herald* 23 Apr. 11 The original name of the carpenter, a common reef fish, was kaapenaar, indicating that it was caught in Cape waters and this became anglicised to carpenter.

Kaapmans /ˈkɑːpmans/ *pl. n. Hist.* Also **Caapmen, Caepmans, Kaapmen**, and with small initial. [Du., *Kaap* Cape + *mans* men.] (The) members of any of several Khoikhoi peoples formerly living in the south-western Cape. See also SALDANHA sense 1 a, STRANDLOPER sense 2 a.

As is the case with many names of peoples and groups in *S. Afr. Eng.*, this word has been found only in plural uses; however, it may be that it has also been used in unrecorded singular forms.

1838 D. Moodie *Record* I. 247 *Goringhaiquas*, whose Chief is named Gogosoa, and who are the Caepmans; they are, exclusive of women and children, about 300 men capable of bearing arms. **1912** (tr. *J. van Riebeeck's Jrnl*) in I.D. Colvin *Cape of Adventure* 220 Herry and the Caapmen had spoken only evil of our people wherever they went. **1926** P.W. Laidler *Tavern of Ocean* 14 The Hottentots were the chief offenders against this law ... The Kaapmen stole anything they saw. **1930** H.A. Chilvers *Seven Lost Trails of Afr.* 173 A clan of Hottentots, known to the Dutch as Kaapmans, visited the bay with horned cattle. **1952** [see GORINGHAIQUA]. **1968** [see GORINGHAIKONA]. **1972** [see SALDANHA sense 1]. **1982** (tr. *J. Van Riebeeck's Jrnl*) in *Voice* 11 July 9 At the Fort today, peace was renewed with the chiefs and overlord of the kaapmans (Gogosoa).

||**Kaapse** /kɑːpsə/ *adj.* Also **Kaaps, Kaapsche.** [Afk., earlier S. Afr. Du. *Kaapsch(e)* 'of the Cape'.]

Cf. CAPE sense 1.

1. Of, pertaining to, or with the atmosphere or flavour of Cape Town, the Cape peninsula, the western Cape, the Cape Province, or South Africa.

1913 C. Pettman *Africanderisms* 238 *Kaaps*, .. Used by the Cape Dutch of anything South African. *a*1963 *Drostdy at Swellendam (pamphlet)* 11 When the older generation wished to indicate great age, they said: 'as old as the Kaapse Wapad' — the wagon road to Cape Town. **1988** J. Crwys-Williams in *Style* Mar. 18 Also available .. are first courses of the like of ou Kaapse snoek pâté. **1988** *Weekly Mail* 3 June 23 Die Drein, a play performed by workers for workers, explores the lives of Kaapse 'kleurlinge'.

2. Of or pertaining to the 'coloured' people of the Western Cape.

1946 *Cape Times* 3 June, Up in .. the cobbled roads off Hanover-street, .. the speakers of Kaapse English have been revising and classifying their vocabularies. **1974** *To the Point* 12 July 41 A play whose language vividly conjures up .. poor Coloureds. And when the actors perform using the Kaapsetaal, this is more true. **1988** *Weekly Mail* 3 June 23 Draining pathos in Kaapse patois. **1991** *Weekend Post* 1 June 5 The text-book does not promote any particular dialect, for example 'Kaapse Afrikaans'.

3. Special collocations. **Kaapse draai** /- ˈdraɪ/ [Afk., *draai* turn], a flamboyant turn executed in a horse-drawn cart; *fig.*, any touch of the flamboyant; **Kaapse Jongens** /- ˈjɔŋəns/ [S. Afr. Du., *jongens* young men], BOEREJONGENS; **Kaapse nooitjie** /- ˈnɔɪki/ *obs.* [Afk., *nooitjie* young girl], the PAMPELMOESIE, *Stromateus fiatola*; **Kaapse sesry** /- ˈsesreɪ/ [Afk., *ses* six + *ry* row], Cape Six-row barley; **Kaapse smaak** /- ˈsmɑːk/ [Afk., *smaak* taste], CAPE SMOKE.

[**1934** C.P. Swart Supplement to Pettman. 82 **Kaapse Draai**, .. To make a short sharp turn is so designated by the Afrikaner.] **1949** L.G. Green *In Land of Afternoon* 174 On arrival at the homestead the driver of the bruidswa reached the height of his skill by making the fancy curve known as a Kaapse draai. It took a fine driver to carry out that 'figure eight' flawlessly at full gallop. **1982** *Pretoria News* 22 Sept. 5 It'll be oh, là, là and magnifique and a touch of the Kaapse draai in Pretoria on Friday. **1983** *Sunday Times* 6 Mar. 16 Hanepoot [grapes] in brandy, known as **Kaapsche Jongens** — the young men of the Cape ... Fill the jars with brandy ... Leave for at least six months then serve, taking care to tell the guests that, eaten like olives, your Kaapsche Jongens are lethal. **1913** C. Pettman *Africanderisms* 238 **Kaapsche nooitje**, .. The Riversdale and Knysna name for the Pompelmoosje. **1932** *Farming in S. Afr.* June 105 (Swart), Of all varieties of barley, Cape Six-row (known also as **Kaapse Sesry**, Ougars [or] Laatgars, is without doubt the best for malting purposes. [**1834** — *Afr. Sketches* 515 Some of the lighter Cape wines are occasionally found of good quality and agreeable flavour, though seldom *altogether* free of the earthy taste, or *Kaap smaak*, which seem peculiar to the soil or climate.] **1988** D. Hughes et al. *Complete Bk of S. Afr. Wine* 332 '*Witblits*' otherwise known as Dop, White Lightning, Boerblits, Cape Smoke, or **Kaapse Smaak**. **1991** *Best of S. Afr. Short Stories* (Reader's Digest Assoc.) 92 Brandy has been part of South African life since it was first distilled about 20 years after Jan van Riebeeck arrived and its evocative local names have included *boerblits* and 'Cape Smoke', which is thought to be a corruption of *Kaapse smaak* or 'Cape taste'.

Hence **Kaaps** *n.*, the dialect (of Afrikaans or English) spoken by the 'coloured' people of the Western Cape.

1976 S. Roberts in *Quarry '76* 113 There were subdued sniggers from the students and under-breath remarks in Kaaps.

Kaapse klopse see KLOPSE.

kaarshout var. KERSHOUT.

kaartjie *n.* [Afk., *kaart* card + dim. suffix -IE.] **1.** /ˈkɑː(r)tʃi, ˈka-, ˈkar-/ *slang.* Also **kachie, kaitchee, katjie.** [Afk., prob. tr. Eng. *card* small portion of opium; or perh. ad. Mexican Spanish *cachucha* 'a capsule of drugs; probably from the Chilean use of the word, which means a small comet' (H. Braddy in *American Speech* Vol.30

No.2, 1955, p.86).] (A small quantity of) marijuana, usu. sufficient to make one cigarette, and wrapped in a twist of paper.

1952 'Mr Drum' in *Drum* Sept. 12 Scientifically known as Indian hemp, dagga .. is known in the slang as .. ; tree of knowledge, 'parcel', '"n katjie', 'stops', 'boom', [etc.]. 1963 L.F. Freed *Crime in S. Afr.* 140 The street-corner loafers, with their pockets crammed with dagga kartjies. 1978 C. Van Wyk in *Staffrider* Vol.1 No.2, 37 Can we have so two kachies, please ... Make it three .. ; I wanna get lekker blou tonight ... Tell ou Blare to give three kachies dagga .. Sorry, gents. Die boom is leeg ... Not even a kachie? 1978 L. Barnes in *The 1820* Vol.51 No.12, 19 He is referring to the practice of preparing a *kaitchee* (zani or dagga cigarette). 1979 J. Rogers in *Staffrider* Vol.2 No.3, 24 A police sergeant at a roadblock .. found four *kaartjies* of zol in my bag, and arrested me. 1984 D. Pinnock *Brotherhoods* 28 The dagga is .. distributed by countless runners, mostly in the form of *kaartjies*, which cost only sixpence. 1986 L.A. Barnes in *Eng. Usage in Sn Afr.* Vol.17 No.2, 6 The sub-culture of the dagga smoker is .. rich in colourful expressions ... Let's have some *kaitchee*.

2. /kɑː(r)ki, -ci/ *colloq.* A card, ticket, or label. Also in the expression *kaartjies asseblief* [Afk., *asseblief* please], the Afk. phr. used by train conductors when inspecting tickets; used allusively of train conductors and train travel.

1971 *Argus* 13 May 18 Gone are the days of 'kaartjies asseblief — tickets please' when the train conductor weaved his way through the carriage. 1974 *Informant, Grahamstown* Now here you must buy kaartjies to put on your things. 1981 C. Barnard in *Daily Dispatch* 19 Oct. 8, I unwrapped the asparagus — and out fell a little kaartjie which told me that the succulent morsels were produkte van Suid Afrika.

Kaaskop /'kɑːskɔp/ *n.* Pl. **-koppe** /-kɔpə/. [Afk., *kaas* cheese + *kop* head.] A (derogatory) nickname for one from Holland.

1970 V.E. Pautz *Informant, Empangeni* Kaaskop, a Hollander. 1977 D. Muller *Whitey* 84 My late husband Hans Stilhuis was a Dutch marine engineer ... Trust my luck to marry the only Kaaskop in the world who was not a tightwad. 1985 *E. Prov. Herald* 22 Apr. 10 Klonkie, he told me, was no worse a term than Mick, Paddy, Jock, soutie, pom, spic, wop, kaaskop, kraut, kugel, rockspider, hairy-back and other words used to describe the various subcultures of sunny SA. 1988 C. Robertson in *Star* 31 May 4 We call one another Kaaskoppe, Boere, Hotnots, Porras or Seekaffers, Yanks, Pommies or *Rooinekke, Aitaais, Keffiegrieke*, Kafirs or Bantu ... Dias laid the cornerstone of the 'Porras'; Van Riebeeck that of the 'Kaaskoppe'.

kaatle var. KATEL.

kabeljou /kab(ə)l'jəʊ/ *n.* Also **cabaljao, cabeliau, cabeljauw, cabeljou, cableow, cobblejaw, gabeljouw, kabbelj(ia)auw, kabeljaau(w), kabeljau(w), kabeljou(w), kaboljou, keppeljou, kobeljauw**. [Afk., earlier Du. *kabeljauw* cod.] The marine fish *Argyrosomus hololepidotus* of the Scianidae, an important source of food; CAPE SALMON sense 1 b; also called COB (*n.*[1]), KOB (sense a).

1731 G. Medley tr. *P. Kolb's Present State of Cape of G.H.* II. 188 At the Cape there are several sorts of the Fish call'd Cabeliau ... The Cabelian, boil'd fresh, is very tender and delicate Food. But when 'tis boil'd salted, 'tis somewhat tough. 1790 W. Paterson *Narr. of Four Journeys* 80 A pleasant river called Cableows River, from a fish which goes by that name, and which is a species of cod, being found near its mouth. 1806 J. Barrow *Trav.* II. 37 One of these [fish] called the Cabeljou .. grows in weight of forty pounds. 1837 *Moderator* 17 Jan. 2 The varieties of fish were striking; viz. the harder, smelt, silver-fish, kabeljou, stock-fish, snoek, the sardyn (sprat), in countless myriads, and even the sole. 1838 J.E. Alexander *Exped. into Int.* II. At last we got a great prize in a stranded cabaljou, fifty pounds in weight, like a huge salmon. 1859 E.L. Layard in *Cape Monthly Mag.* Vol.5 No.1, 27 One of the boys was off to the rocks with his fishing-rod, where we were told he would catch abundance of cobblejaw, Hottentot, stumpnose, and other fish, with euphonious names and palatable flavours. 1890 [see GALJOEN sense 1]. 1906 H.E.B. Brooking in *E. London Dispatch* 26 June 3 Our well-known and very common kabeljaauw, called for briefness 'cob' or 'kob,' (sciaena acquila). 1915 D. Fairbridge *Torch Bearer* 138 'Some dreadful, unpronounceable name it had — "cobblestones," I think,' 'Kabbeljaauw,' amended Katherine, who had heard the Dutch for cod-fish. [1917 A.C.M. Orrey *Bottom Fishing in Cape Waters* 52 The geelbek is a far gamer fish than the kab., and fights well to the last.] 1930 C.L. Biden *Sea-Angling Fishes* 109 The kabeljou is often mistaken for the geelbek. 1954 L.G. Green *Under Sky Like Flame* 41 Some of the fish, like the kabeljou (Cape cod), geelbek (the so-called Cape salmon), and pilchards are of the South African species. 1968 J.L.B. Smith *High Tide* 34 Little remains about fishes but a few names, such as haarder, kabeljaauw and snoek, which are, however, names of fishes of their own homeland [sc. Holland], which they applied to Cape fishes because they thought they looked like their own. 1974 [see FISH-CART]. 1988 E. Withers in *Fair Lady* 22 June (Suppl.) 15 Main courses like poached kabeljou with a piquant sauce, stir-fried prawns and sweet-and-sour hake. 1990 *E. Prov. Herald* 12 Jan. 18 Kob, cob, or kabeljouw, choose your own name, are caught everywhere on the South African coast. They are also found in the Atlantic Ocean and the Mediterranean sea. On the West Coast of Australia they are called jewfish. 1993 P. Goosen in *Getaway* Nov. 127 The whole area .. is good for surf fishing, and you can expect to catch kabeljou (commonly called kob), elf, steenbras and galjoen.

kaboe mealie /'kabu 'miːli/ *n. phr.* Also **kabu mealie, koeboe mealie**. [Afk. *kaboe* ad. Xhosa *iqubu* heap of grain sorghum, Zulu *uqubhu* water in which mealie-meal has been steeped or boiled + MEALIE.] Usu. in *pl.*: Boiled (formerly also roasted) whole maize kernels. Also *attrib.*

1902 D. Van Warmelo *On Commando* 9 My uncle .. treated us to kaboe-mealies (roasted maize), the first we had on commando, and we ate with great relish. 1903 J.D. Kestell *Through Shot & Flame* 14 They gave me something to eat, just what they had ready — kaboe mealies (boiled maize). 1913 C. Pettman *Africanderisms* 239 Kaboe mealies, .. Mealies stripped from the cob and boiled without removing the skin. 1940 [see STERTRIEM]. 1945 N. Devitt *People & Places* 143, I have rarely met anyone who can give me the meaning of the words 'kaboe mealies'. The term comes from the Xosa. 'Iquba' is a heap of corn before it is winnowed ... The mealies are stripped from the cob and boiled in their husks. *a*1952 H.C. Bosman in L. Abrahams *Bekkersdal Marathon* (1971) An iron pot that a fire had been burning underneath ... All afternoon it had smelt to me like sheep's inside and kaboe mealies. 1980 *E. Prov. Herald* 1 Apr. 13 A customary Zulu openair kitchen where .. a South African dietician demonstrated recipes like kabu mealie fries, pumpkin pips, putu porridge and mopani worms. 1989 V. Owen in *Grocott's Mail* 20 Jan. 11 In winter .. we would gather around their wood fire in the open shed and beg 'koeboe' mealies from their pot, which was continually on the fire.

kaboljou var. KABELJOU.

kachie var. KAARTJIE.

kackela var. KAKELAAR.

kadel var. KATEL.

kadoesie var. KARDOESIE.

kaersbosch var. KERSBOS *n.*[1]

kæzschebyring var. KATJIEPIERING.

kafee /ka'fiə/ *n.* Also **kaffee**. [Afk., café, coffeehouse.] CAFÉ.

1973 *Weekend Argus* 21 Apr. 5 Filling station, hotel, church .. intermingle with stereotyped shops and 'kafees'. 1977 [see LARNEY *n.* sense 1]. 1978 S. Roberts in *New Classic* No.5, 26 Arrest of Bantoes without passes, arrest of Hobos in parks, arrest of noisy Bantoes outside kafees. 1979 *Sunday Times* 26 Aug. 3 The white couple behind the counter looked like retired pensioners who had invested their last penny in this ramshackle *kaffee*. 1990 *Sunday Times* 1 Apr. 19 The small-town *kafee* society of remote rural life which has no English equivalent. 1990 R. Stengel *January Sun* 43 The shop proved not much to look at (it was actually a *kafee*, the Afrikaans term for a simple café or coffee shop; tearoom was too genteel a description). *Ibid.* 59 Driving down Murray Avenue he passes Travolta's Take-Aways, a popular *kafee* among the young people because it has a video game. 'A Greek *kafee*,' de la Rey calls it ... All the *kafees* in Brits are run by Greeks or Portuguese immigrants.

kaffer, kafferboetie varr. KAFFIR, KAFFIRBOETIE.

‖**kaffermeid** /'kafə(r)meɪt/ *n. Derog. and offensive.* Also **kaffir meid**. [Afk., *kaffer* (see KAFFIR) + *meid* female servant.] An insulting form of address or reference to a black woman; *kaffirmaid*, see KAFFIR *n.* sense 2 e.

1963 B. Modisane *Blame Me on Hist.* (1986) 36 Because my mother was black she was despised and humiliated, called 'kafir meid'. *Ibid.* 58 This kaffir meid, my baas, was trying to trick me into sleeping in her room, but I know it is against the law. 1965 J. Bennett *Hawk Alone* 188 A young white man walked past his with his arm around a half-caste girl. 'What do you think of that ... A bloody kaffermeid. Man, a bloody meid.' 1977 B.L. Leshoai in E. Pereira *Contemp. S. Afr. Plays* 266 The other day in town a white thing — a woman as pale and dirty as dishwater — called me 'Kaffir Meid'. I said, 'No, I'm not a Kaffir Meid'. 1986 S. Sepamla *Third Generation* 53 Gots, *kaffermeid*, don't give me that bull!

‖**kafferpak** /'kafə(r)pak/ *n. offensive.* [Afk., *kaffer* kaffir + *pak* hiding.] An overwhelming defeat, usu. in sporting events or politics; a thorough thrashing. Occas., a physical beating.

1934 *Star* 9 Feb. (Swart), General Hertzog will .. help Mr. Fullard to give his opponent the biggest kafferpak that he had ever received. 1970 H.M. Musmeci *Informant, Port Elizabeth* The visiting rugby team were given a real kafferpak .. beaten without being able to score a single goal. 1973 *Het Suid-Western* 9 Apr. 14 The team .. seemed totally dejected after the 'kafferpak' they picked up at the hands of S.W.D. Police side. 1990 R. Malan *My Traitor's Heart* 111 He died of a kafferpak .. a brutal beating of the sort whites have been administering to blacks since the day we set foot on this continent.

‖**kaffertjie** /'kafə(r)kɪ, -ci/ *n. offensive.* Also **kaffirkie, kaffirtjie**. [Afk., *kaffer* (see KAFFIR) + dim. suffix -IE.]

1. *obs.* [See quot. 1972.] The small lily-like plant *Wurmbea spicata*, with very dark flowers.

1913 C. Pettman *Africanderisms* 243 Kaffirtjies, the Riversdale name for *Wurmbea capensis*, Thun. The flowers are nearly black. 1966 C.A. Smith *Common Names* 266 Kaffertjie, *Wurmbea spicata* ... A cormous plant with a long underground neck. 1972 M.R. Levyns in *Std Encycl. of Sn Afr.* VI. 262 The name kaffertjie .. derives from the purple-black colour of the flowers.

2. *obs.* Any of three species of finch-larks of the genus *Eremopterix*.

1972 G.J. Broekhuysen in *Std Encycl. of Sn Afr.* VI. 262 The males have a lot of black, hence the name 'kaffertjie'.

3. An insulting term for a young black boy.

1975 *Drum* 8 Aug. 1 He dished out posters .. he had bought from those 'kaffertjies' who sell newspapers. 1980 A.J. Blignaut *Dead End Rd* 76 You had better look after this kaffirkie. For if there's any more nonsense, I'll chain the pair of you to a wheel at night to watch over one another. 1982 *Voice* 6 June 4 How do we Africans feel .. being referred to as 'kaffirtjies'? 1988 *Cape Times* 27 Jan. 1 Mr Cruywagen denied that he referred to 'kaffertjies' in his lecture. 1991 *Sunday*

Times 10 Nov. 7, I saw the two kaffertjies walk right past us to the front. They sat on the floor.

kaffia var. KOFIA.

kaffir /ˈkæfə/ *n.* and *adj.* *Offensive* in all senses and combinations. Also with initial capital, and (formerly) **cafar, caffer, caf(f)ir, caffre(e), cafre, kaffer, kaffre(e), kafir, kafre.** [ad. Arabic *kafir* infidel. The form *kaffer* is influenced by Du. (and subsequently Afk).]

A. *n.*

1. *Obs.* exc. *hist.* Usu. with initial capital.

a. A black African inhabitant of the region now covered by KwaZulu-Natal and the north-eastern parts of the Eastern Cape, i.e. a member of any of the Nguni groups which in the eighteenth and nineteenth centuries became consolidated into the Xhosa and Zulu peoples.

1589 R. HAKLUYT *Voy.* II. 242 The Captaine of this castle [*sc.* Mozambique] hath certaine voyages to this Cafraria .. to .. trade with the Cafars. **1731** G. MEDLEY tr. *P. Kolb's Present State of Cape of G.H.* I. 28 The *Caffres*, who inhabit the *Monomotapa*, tho' encompas'd in a Manner by the *Hottentot* Nations, are a very different kind of People. **1841** [see sense b]. **1860** W. SHAW *Story of my Mission* 298, I must .. in this sketch employ the term 'Kaffir' as applying in a generic sense to the whole of the nations living along the line of coast. *a*1864 [see sense b]. **1949** H.E. HOCKLY *Story of Brit. Settlers of 1820* 9 The most formidable native tribes to oppose the onward march of the Europeans were .. the Kaffirs, a branch of the mighty Bantu race which was slowly advancing southwards down the eastern side of Africa.

b. XHOSA *n.* sense 1 a.

1776 F. MASSON in *Phil. Trans. of Royal Soc.* LXVI. 197 We were now on the borders of a powerful nation of Hottentots called Caffers. **1790** W. PATERSON *Narr. of Four Journeys* 70 The great nation of Caffres, which is about nine hundred miles to the south-east. **1799** H.W. BALLOT in G.M. Theal *Rec. of Cape Col.* (1898) II. 370 It was properly the man who has to deal with you, namely Van Jaarsveld, whose true purpose was to convey the Landdrost to the Caffer Country. **1801** H.C.D. MAYNIER in *Ibid.* IV. (1899) 61 On what terms are we with Gyka and the Caffres on the other side the Great Vis River? **1804** R. PERCIVAL *Acct of Cape of G.H.* 46 To the east a view is opened of the more distant Caffree country whose mountains .. of a bright copper colour close the sublime prospect. **1804** R. RENSHAW *Voy. to Cape of G.H.* 18 The eastern district of the colony .. is inhabited by a singular race of people called Kaffres. **1812** A. PLUMPTRE tr. *H. Lichtenstein's Trav. in Sn Afr.* I. 309 The tribe .. call themselves Koosas, or Kaussas ... These people are exceedingly offended at being called Caffres. **1822** W.J. BURCHELL *Trav.* I. 64 The word Caffre, or Kaffer, is generally, at the Cape, applied exclusively to the tribe inhabiting the country beyond the eastern boundary of the colony. **1824** *Ibid.* II. 530 In distinguishing those African tribes which inhabit the country immediately adjoining the eastern boundary of the Cape Colony, as the *Caffres proper*, I merely comply with the common custom of the Colonists. **1827** T. PHILIPPS *Scenes & Occurrences* 208 The Caffers and Tambookies were very much pleased at my calling them by their true titles ... The name of the former is *Kosa*, plural *Amakosa*, .. the latter is *Tymba*, plural Amatymba. **1834** J.C. CHASE in A. Steedman *Wanderings* (1835) II. 196 The first great political division of the interior, next to the Colonial limits, is that under the Amakosae tribes, or Caffers Proper, bounded from the Colony by the Keiskamma River on the west. **1840** *Echo* 8 June 2 The progress of civilization among the Caffers and other tribes beyond the boundaries. **1841** B. SHAW *Memorials* 36 The Kaffirs are a numerous race of men inhabiting that tract of country situated on the South-Eastern coast of South Africa. This appellation .. is applied by the Dutch and English colonists to the Amakosae tribe exclusively; but by Barrow, Thompson, and other travellers, it is extended to the Tambookies and neighbouring hordes. *a*1864 L. GROUT *Zulu-Land* 60 The numerous tribes which occupy this broad section of southern and central Africa .. all spring from a common stock ... For this group no name has yet been definitely adopted by the learned. Some would call it the *Kafir* .. but custom at the present day limits that term to a small district on the east coast between Natal and the Cape Colony. **1871** J. MCKAY *Reminisc.* 204 It was native against native — Fingoe against Kafir. **1892** J.E. RITCHIE *Brighter S. Afr.* 63 The men looked happy; they are of all races, Kaffirs being held to be the best if only they would work ... There was also a large number of Basutos. **1948** H.V. MORTON *In Search of S. Afr.* 171 The Ciskei and the Transkei .. stretches for hundred of miles north to the borders of Natal. This native territory .. includes the tribal territories of the Xosas — the original Kaffirs — the Tembus and the Pondos. **1949** J. MOCKFORD *Golden Land* 77 The migration of many became a flight from the marauding impis of the Zulus until the Xosas, the Kafirs, clashed with the Whiteman in the eastern regions of the Cape.

c. XHOSA *n.* sense 1 b.

1836 R. GODLONTON *Introductory Remarks to Narr. of Irruption* 4 We distinctly saw the dark cloud gathering over the Kafir country, but with that exception there was abundant cause for congratulation and thankfulness. **1837** J.E. ALEXANDER *Narr. of Voy.* I. 366 The so-called Kaffirs are divided into three great nations: the Amakosas, or the people of a chief Kosa, extending from the Keiskamma to the Bashee; the Amatembies, or Tambookies, between the upper Kye and Umtata; and the Amapondas .., from the Umtata to the south of Port Natal. **1857** D. LIVINGSTONE *Missionary Trav.* 95 The annual supply of rain is considerable, and the inhabitants (Caffres or Zulus), are tall, muscular and well made. **1896** M.A. CAREY-HOBSON *At Home in Tvl* 178, I had heard so much about the yells and war cries of the natives that I really thought we were surrounded by Kaffirs or Zulus. **1972** *Std Encycl. of Sn Afr.* VI. 263 In more recent history the 'Zulus' were distinguished from the 'Kaffirs'. The word 'cafres' .. was applied to the people now known as the Xhosas, who are composed of several tribes or tribelets including the Mpondo (Pondos), the Mfengu (Fingos) and many others.

d. *comb.* **Kaffirland** *obs.* exc. *hist.*, any or all of the territories on the eastern seaboard of Southern Africa (to the east of the Great Fish River) inhabited by people of the Nguni group, particularly those parts inhabited by Xhosas.

1786 G. FORSTER tr. *A. Sparrman's Voy. to Cape of G.H.* II. 146 These rivers .. probably run all together through the country called *Caffer-land*. **1800** G. YONGE in G.M. Theal *Rec. of Cape Col.* (1898) III. 339 One of the Missionaries lately come here has gone into Caffer-land, his name Vanderkemp. *a*1823 J. EWART *Jrnl* (1970) 48 To the eastward of the Great Fish river .. extends a fertile tract of country, broken into hill and dale and diversified with extensive woods of the finest forest trees .. inhabited by a nation called Kaffers or Caffres, the country being called Caffraria or Kafferland. **1832** A. SMITH in Donald & Kirby *Peddie* 13 Buttons and wire .. are the staple articles for barter throughout all Cafferland. **1837** F. OWEN *Diary* (1926) 89 The word [for God] used in Caffre land .. has been introduced *here* [*sc.* in Natal] by Europeans .. as Uteeko. **1841** B. SHAW *Memorials* 223 She was remarkably strong and healthy, but the hardships of the Kaffir-land Mission made .. inroads upon her constitution. **1857** *Cape Monthly Mag.* II. Sept. 190 Raising funds for the relief of the sufferers by famine in Kafirland. **1871** J. MACKENZIE *Ten Yrs* (1971) 518 Kaffir-land, convulsed with internal feuds, poured its people into the Zuurveldt .. from which they dislodged the Dutch. **1881** *Daily Dispatch* 29 Jan. (Suppl.) 1 Great numbers of Boers are in Kafirland, leaving everything to the mercy of the rebels, and going to the Kafirs for protection. **1891** T.R. BEATTIE *Pambaniso* 58 In a few days the whole of Kaffirland was ablaze with the torch of war. **1909** O.E.A. SCHREINER *Closer Union* (1960) 35 The hearts of a complex people will put on mourning .. from the kraal in Kafirland to... the cities where men congregate. **1913** W.C. SCULLY *Further Reminisc.* 306 The Natives .. obtain liquor at this canteen, and return with it into Kaffirland. **1926** M. NATHAN *S. Afr. from Within* 15 A barrier against the irruption of Kaffir marauders, who inhabited what was comprehensively known as Kaffirland. **1931** F.H. DUTTON tr. *T. Mofolo's Chaka: Hist. Romance* 2 In Kafirland the snake is a well-recognized messenger bringing tidings from the dead to their descendants. **1948** H.E. HOCKLY *Story of Brit. Settlers of 1820* 9 The main body of the Bantu migrants had not yet crossed the Fish River but had firmly established itself in the territory to the east of that river, covering a vast and undefined area generally referred to as Kaffirland. **1956** F.C. METROWICH *Valiant but Once* 96 The patrol .. saw a large body of Natives driving stolen cattle across the Kap River along the well-trodden route to Kaffirland.

2. A black person. **a.** *Obs.* exc. *hist.* Any black inhabitant of South Africa. **b.** *Derog.* and *offensive.* An insulting and contemptuous term for a black African, or occas. for any black person. Also *attrib.*

Originally simply descriptive of an ethnic group, 'kaffir' is now insulting and abusive, and its use is actionable (see CRIMEN INJURIA).

1607 W. KEELING in R. Raven-Hart *Before Van Riebeeck* (1967) 36 Wee found many of the Saldanians alias Cafares at our landinge place to speake wth us although wee could not onderstand one an other. **1731** G. MEDLEY tr. *P. Kolb's Present State of Cape of G.H.* I. 81 The Caffres .. are so far from bearing any affinity or resemblance with the Hottentots, that they are a quite different sort of people. **1798** B. STOUT *Narr. of Loss of Ship 'Hercules'* 59 We spoke at first to some *Caffree* women, who behaved kindly, and gave us one or two baskets of milk. **1822** W.J. BURCHELL *Trav.* I. 582 To the Caffre Race belong the Bichuanas, and the Dammaras, together with the Kosas or Caffres Proper, the Tambookies, and probably all the tribes on the eastern side of the Continent, as far as Delagoa Bay. **1835** J.W.D. MOODIE *Ten Yrs* II. 65 My companion had .. got thoroughly perplexed among a multitude of old Kaffre tracks crossing each other at all angles, and leading anywhere — or nowhere. **1843** J.C. CHASE *Cape of G.H.* 9 All their orders relative to the aborigines, whether Hottentot, Bushman, or Kafir, breathe the spirit of kindess and conciliation. **1851** H. WARD *Cape & Kaffirs* 10 Most of the associations connected in the mind of an European with the name of Kaffir, have been formed upon the represented bad character and conduct of the nation so called, .. and are consequently highly unfavourable to any people bearing a name which, by common consent, attributes all the cunning faithlessness of the savage, with an admixture of many of the depravities of civilized life, to its bearer. **1855** J.W. COLENSO *Ten Weeks in Natal* 8 The conversation turned naturally upon the question of Kafir education, and I found that my two friends had very little confidence in the success of Missionary operations among the Zulus. **1860** A.W. DRAYSON *Sporting Scenes* 18 'Kaffir' is .. a term unknown to the men so called; they speak of themselves by the designation of the tribe. **1864** 'A LADY' *Life at Natal* (1972) 22 These Zulus .. do appear to deserve their title as the gentlemen of the Kafir races. **1875** D. LESLIE *Among Zulus* 63 Cetchwayo is a stoutly built black Kaffir; and of him I shall have more to say anon. **1876** F. BOYLE *Savage Life* 212 The Kaffirs — they were Basutos - .. suffered an overwhelming defeat. *a*1878 J. MONTGOMERY *Reminisc.* (1981) 105 Mietjie was a civilised Kafir woman, and could speak Dutch and English fluently. **1882** C.L. NORRIS-NEWMAN *With Boers in Tvl* 57 It will not be surprising that they should make common cause against all Kaffirs, and .. should regard the natives as an entirely inferior race, only fit for slavery. **1899** D.S.F.A. PHILLIPS *S. Afr. Recollections* 125, I do not mean to say .. that I consider the English treatment of the Kaffir the right one either. They go too far in the other direction, and treat a kaffir as if he were a white man. **1902** G.M. THEAL *Beginning of S. Afr. Hist.* 203 The Mohammedan mixed breeds, living like Kaffirs and caring little whether they were one month or twelve on an expedition. **1913** C. PETTMAN *Africanderisms* 340 *Nigger*, A term of contempt applied to people of coloured blood, and as a rule as vigorously resented by them as the designation Kaffir is sometimes resented by the natives. **1925** D. KIDD *Essential Kafir* p.v, The word Kafir is used in its broadest sense, so as to include all the dark-skinned tribes of South Africa, though the word has been used by others in the most varied connotations. **1936** WILLIAMS & MAY *I Am Black* 200 Who are you to call me a kaffir? You are only a toad. If you call me that name again I will thrash you. **1941** A. MAQELEPO in *Bantu World* 15 Feb. 5 To be called a Kaffir or a Coloured is an insult to which we can never submit. **1941** J.A.B. NTI SANA in *Bantu World* 15 Mar. (Suppl.) 2 This floor is known as the Kafir-mud-floor because only Native people can make it properly. **1950** D. REED *Somewhere S. of Suez* 114 The disdainful word 'Kaffir' is seldom used today; .. to the Native [it] is a stigma and a reproach. **1952** P. ABRAHAMS in *Drum* July 10, I have heard illiterate Coloureds describing educated Africans as damn kaffirs. How do we cope with that? **1955** [see MLUNGU *n.* sense 3]. **1962** L.E. NEAME *Hist. of Apartheid* 84 Their concept of a Non-White person is that he is a 'Kafir', a 'Native', a 'boy', a 'girl', or a 'maid', a sub-human. **1966** J. FARRANT *Mashonaland Martyr* p.xxxi, Peter Paliso is described as a 'Kaffir', indicating that he came from Kaffraria. In those days the word did not cause offence, and was used in all innocence by the clergy and missionaries. Today, however, it .. is seldom used except as a malicious, contemptuous epithet. **1968** *Eng. Alive* 63 To call an African a 'Kaffir' is an insult in the worst taste and we can certainly not gauge the illfeeling and resentment this causes among those at whom these insults are directed. **1970** *Daily Dispatch* 6 Oct. 8 The African was referred to in the usual manner employed by insecure, ethnocentric people of low mentality. In short, he was called a 'Kaffir'. **1972** *Evening Post* 19 Aug. 8 In those days of long ago, the word 'Kaffir' was permissible ... It was spelt Caffre and denoted someone of the dark-skinned races. **1972** *E. Prov. Herald* 7 Nov. 1 A Johannesburg Regional Court adjourned in uproar after a White man shouted 'Kaffir' at an African attorney who was questioning him and then refused to apologise. **1975** J. MCCLURE *Snake* (1981) 56 The Colonel had very nearly said 'kaffir', which was now an officially banned word. **1976** *E. Prov. Herald* 25 May 19 The use of the word 'kaffir' when referring to an African in South Africa was sufficiently serious to constitute injuria. **1979** M. MATSHOBA *Call Me Not a Man* 197 The word 'kaffer' had been declared an offence in law some time ago. **1987** *Frontline* May 27, I myself was shouted at by a white man – 'Move, kaffir!' – a thing I have not come across for some time. **1989** *Sunday Times* 8 Oct. (Mag. Sect.) 8 That persistently obnoxious word 'kaffir' .. is a loathsome word, which exemplifies the very worst attitudes, assumptions and practices of recent history. **1991** P. HAWTHORNE in *Time* 20 May 8 'President F.W. de Klerk,' says Dirk, 'has given our country to the blacks ... Now kaffirs will tell us how to live our lives'. **1992** S. NTSHAKALA in *Weekend Mercury* 4 Jan. 6 He rose up and repeatedly said .. 'They think they now rule the world. Stupid kaffirs!' **1993** *Weekly Mail & Guardian* 29 Oct. 2 He said black personnel were still called 'kaffirs' behind closed doors.

c. *Fig.*, and in idiomatic expressions, including: ***kaffir appointment***, an appointment for which one does not trouble to be punctual; cf. AFRICAN TIME; ***to go to the kaffirs***, to deteriorate, 'to go to the dogs'; ‖**kaffer op sy plek** /ˌkafər ɔp seɪ 'plɛk/ [Afk., 'kaffir in his place'], an expression used to ridicule the racist attitude which demands white dominance over blacks, and which expects subservient behaviour from black people; also *attrib.*; ***to work like a kaffir***, to work extremely hard, esp. at manual labour.

1835 T.H. BOWKER Journal. 25 Mar., I'm affraid they'll have the Kafirs in England ere long – heavy taxes and light Meals will make a Kaffir of almost any man. **1951** R.B. PITSO in *Afr. Drum* Apr. 14 Zwane will think that I am used to keeping kafir appointments. **1977** FUGARD & DEVENISH *Guest* 51 Those first few years, Doors and the two boys worked like kaffirs on the land. **1980** *Sunday Times* 9 Mar. 13 We have men stomping the platteland spouting dangerous 'kaffer-op-sy-plek' politics! **1983** J. DE RIDDER *Sad Laughter Mem.* 23 Hell, we worked like Kaffirs getting the place ready. **1984** *Frontline* Mar. 39 The Afrikaner Nats, for whom a generation ago the policy of Kaffer op sy plek en Koelie uit die land summed up pretty well the entire philosophy. **1987** M. POLAND *Train to Doringbult* 225 'Funny how I never really knew what that curfew implied when I was at school,' said Elsa. 'It only meant half an hour to lights-out.' 'Kaffirs-into-bed,' said Jan wryly, remembering the schoolboy chant. **1990** *Sunday Star* 11 Mar. 14 To most whites at that time it [*sc.* apartheid] was just a more of less respectable way of saying 'kaffer op sy plek'. **1990** C. LEONARD in *Weekly Mail* 2 Nov. 29 The place was going to the kaffirs. It was in a bad condition, I tell you.

d. With distinguishing epithet: **mission(ary) kaffir** *obs.*, a black person taught by missionaries, or having been under their influence; a westernized black person; see also SCHOOL *adj.* sense 1; **white kaffir**, see as a main entry.

1875 D. LESLIE *Among Zulus* 145 **'Missionary Kaffirs'** have become a byword and a reproach, and are considered the greatest rascals in the colony. **1878** A. AYLWARD *Tvl of Today* 48 The mission Kafirs, fearing the King, spread the most alarming reports concerning his intentions. **1882** C. DU VAL *With Show through Sn Afr.* I. 158 In nine opinions out of ten you will find colonists denouncing what they call missionary Kaffirs in no measured terms, and there must be some grounds for so sweeping an opinion. **1908** D. BLACKBURN *Leaven* 87 Mr Hyslop suggested that a mission kafir having been taught to work more intelligently was surely worth more than a raw kafir.

e. *comb.* All *obs.* or *obsolescent* because of their offensive nature. With the following meanings (which often overlap): **i.** Used among the black peoples of southern Africa. **ii.** Esp. in the names of flora and fauna: indigenous, wild. **iii.** *derog.* Inferior, worthy of contempt. **kaffir almanac** [see quot. 1913], either of two species of lily, *Haemanthus katherinae* or *H. magnificus*; **kaffir brandy**, a potent liquor prepared for sale to black people; cf. *kaffir whisky* below; **kaffir buck**, see quot.; **kaffir cabbage** [see quot. 1966], the plant *Cleome gynandra*; **kaffir cat**, the African wild cat *Felis lybica* of the Felidae, with a tawny, striped coat; also called *wild cat* (see WILD sense b); **kaffir cattle**, (*a*) *hist.*, a breed of indigenous African cattle with distinctive horns and colouring; cf. NGUNI *n.* sense 3; (*b*) *derog.*, inferior cattle of mixed breed; **kaffir cherry**, the plant *Gardenia neuberia*; **kaffir chestnut**, *wild chestnut* (sense (*a*) see WILD sense a); **kaffir coffee**, the plant *Phoenix reclinata* of the Arecaceae; **kaffir-college** *derog.*, a segregated college for blacks under apartheid legislation; see also *bush college* (BUSH *adj.*[1] sense 2); **kaffir cow**, a cow of the type called *kaffir cattle* (see above); **kaffir crane**, a former name for the MAHEM, *Balearica regulorum*; **kaffir date**, *kaffir plum* (see below); **kaffir doctor**, WITCHDOCTOR; **kaffir fair** *obs.* exc. *hist.*, during the nineteenth century, a gathering to enable trade and barter between the colonists and the Xhosa; also *attrib.*; **kaffir farming**, a form of sub-tenancy outlawed in 1913, whereby white land-owners leased land to African squatters in return for labour (see also second quot. 1989); **kaffir fever** *Pathology*, an unidentified febrile illness; **kaffir fig-tree**, see quot.; **kaffir finch, -fink** [Englished forms of S. Afr. Du. *kaffervink*], (*a*) BISHOP-BIRD; (*b*) SAKABULA; **kaffir fowl** *derog.*, a scraggy domestic fowl of indeterminate breed; **kaffir god**, (*a*) *Hottentot(s) god* (*offensive*), see HOTTENTOT *n.* sense 6 a; (*b*) a flower (the precise species is unclear); its fruit; **kaffir hen**, *kaffir fowl* (see above); **kaffir hoe**, a simple iron hoe; ‖**kaffirhond** /-ˌhɔnt/ [Afk. *hond* dog], KAFFIR DOG; **kaffir honeysuckle**, the TECOMA, *Tecomaria capensis*; **kaffir horse**, *Cape horse* (see CAPE sense 2 a); **kaffir hut**, (*a*) a circular wattle-and-daub hut with a conical thatched roof (cf. RONDAVEL), or any traditionally-constructed African dwelling; (*b*) the dome-shaped Eastern Cape succulent *Euphorbia meloformis*; **Kaffir Jack**, an Eastern Cape name for the common hornbill; **kaffir lily**, (*a*) the water-loving perennial herb *Schizostylis coccinea* of the Iridaceae, with narrow leaves and slender stalks bearing deep pink flowers; (*b*) the perennial forest plant *Clivia miniata* of the Amaryllidaceae, cultivated for its large, showy, orange flowers; (*c*) IFAFA LILY; **kaffir-lover** *derog.*, KAFFIRBOETIE; **kaffir-maid** [Englished form of Afk. *kaffermeid*; cf. MAID] *derog.*, KAFFERMEID; **kaffirmanna**, BABALA; **kaffir mealie**, KABOE MEALIE; **kaffir melon**, TSAMMA; **kaffir mushroom**, IKHOWE; **kaffir orange**, KLAPPER *n.*[1] sense 1; **kaffir ox**, an ox of the type called *kaffir cattle* (see above); **kaffir path**, a rural footpath or track; **kaffir pear**, *wild pear* sense (*b*), see WILD sense a; **kaffir pick**, a simple home-made pick; **kaffir pillow**, a small wooden neck-rest, used while sleeping; **kaffir plum**, the evergreen forest tree *Harpephyllum caffrum*, its edible fruit, or its reddish timber; also called *wild plum* (sense (*a*) see WILD sense a); also *attrib.*; **kaffir pock** *Pathology*, see quots; **kaffir poison**, (*a*) BUSHMAN'S POISON; (*b*) *Pathology*, see quot. 1968; **kaffir police** *hist.*, any of several black police corps established during the nineteenth century (the first of which was founded in 1835); **kaffir pot**, POTJIE; **kaffir potato**, the Natal plant *Coleus esculentus*, and its edible tuber; **kaffir print**, *German print* (see GERMAN); **kaffir rail**, the bird *Rallus caerulescens*; **kaffir rope**, MONKEY-ROPE; **kaffir scimitar**, *kaffir plum* (see above); **kaffir sheep**, any hardy cross-bred sheep; **kaffir slangwortel** /-'slaŋvɔrtəl/, formerly also - **schlangenwortel** [Afk. *slangwortel* (fr. Du. *schlangenwortel*), *slang* snake + *wortel* root; see quot. 1860], the shrub *Polygala serpentaria*; its thick, woody root; **kaffir sorrel**, the plant *Pelargonium peltatum*; also called PELARGONIUM; **kaffir store**, a rural trading store carrying a wide variety of inexpensive merchandise for a black clientele; **kaffir tax**, HUT TAX; **kaffir taxi** *derog.*, (*a*) a motor vehicle used as a taxi by black people; (*b*) *transf.*, an old or run-down motor car or bus; **kaffir tea**, (the dried leaves of) any of several plants used for brewing medicinal teas, esp. (*a*) *Helichrysum nudifolium* and *Athrixia phylicoides*, but also (*b*) shrubs of the genus *Aspalathus* (see ROOIBOS sense 1 a); the tea made from these plants; see also BUSHMAN'S TEA; **kaffir-thorn**, the tree *Lycium tetrandrum*; **kaffir thread**, animal sinew used as thread; **kaffir tobacco**, DAGGA *n.*[2] sense 1; **kaffir tou**, MONKEY-ROPE; **kaffir trade**, the sale of manufactured goods to black people, or barter with black people; latterly called *African trade, black trade*; also *attrib.*; hence **kaffir trader** *n. phr.*, a merchant, often in remote districts, selling primarily to black people; **kaffir tree**, KAFFIRBOOM; **kaffir truck** *derog. hist.*, cheap (often inferior) merchandise intended for sale or barter to black people; also *attrib.*; **Kaffir war**, (*a*) *Frontier war*, see FRONTIER sense b; (*b*) *rare*, any war between blacks and whites (see quot. 1939); **kaffir watermelon**, TSAMMA; **kaffir whisky**, a type of liquor prepared for sale to black people; cf. *kaffir brandy* above; **kaffir('s) work** *derog.*, an offensive term for manual labour, or for any task considered by some to be too menial for whites to perform.

1913 C. Pettman *Africanderisms* 240 **Kaffir almanac**, So called in Natal, because the Zulus sow their mealies when this plant is in flower. **1967** E. Rosenthal *Encycl. of Sn Afr.* 278 *Kaffir Almanac*, Bulbous Cape and Natal plant with a single red tulip-like flower and fleshy spotted stem rising from two prostrate leaves. **1978** *Randlords & Rotgut* (Junction Ave Theatre Co.) in S. Gray *Theatre Two* (1981) 116 You and your **Kaffir brandy** are killing these people! **1983** *Sunday Times* 4 Sept. (Mag. Sect.) 2 '*Kaffir Brandy*' .. was prepared according to the following formula: '15 gal Delagoa proof spirit, 15 gal water, 1 gal cayenne pepper tincture, $\frac{1}{2}$oz sulphuric acid and 1oz nitric acid.' **1937** W. De Kok tr. *E.N. Marais's Soul of White Ant* (1973) 104 For the experiment I used a herd of sixty half-wild buck, known in South Africa as **Kaffir Buck**. **1966** C.A. Smith *Common Names* 267 **Kaffir cabbage**, *Cleome gynandra* ... The leaves and young shoots are cooked as a spinach by natives. **1988** A. Sher *Middlepost* 373 Plants .. casting a million different scents into the air ... Traveller's Joy, .. Mouse Bush, Harebell, Grapple Thorn, *Kaffir-cabbage*. **1900** W.L. Sclater *Mammals of S. Afr.* I. 43 The **caffer cat** is nocturnal, though sometimes seen in cloudy, cool weather, during day time. **1971** C.M. van der Westhuizen in *Std Encycl. of Sn Afr.* III. 127 The African wild cat or Kaffir cat .. was probably the same species which was domesticated by the ancient Egyptians. **1833** *Graham's Town Jrnl* 7 Mar. 3 Whichever way you travel in Cafferland you meet with thousands of colonial cattle, and the offspring of colonial cattle; the breed of **Caffer cattle** in many places appears almost extinct. **1834** A. Smith *Diary* (1939) I. 83 Three were taken out of a herd of Caffer cattle. **1896** R. Wallace *Farming Indust. of Cape Col.* 255 The thick-horned Kaffir cattle .. are broken in colour, and lack style and uniformity. **1914** E.N. Marais *Rd to Waterberg* (1972) 21 The finest Kaffir cattle .. were to be seen three years ago. **1913** C. Pettman *Africanderisms* 241 **Kaffir** or Hottentot **cherry**, *Maurocenia capensis*. The name given to the fruit of this shrub. **1966** C.A. Smith *Common Names* 267 *Kaffir cherry, Gardenia neuberia*. **1906** [**kaffir chestnut**: see *wild almond* (WILD sense a)]. **1966** C.A. Smith *Common Names* 267 *Kaffir chestnut, Brabeium stellatifolium*. **1827** T. Philipps *Scenes & Occurrences* 87 A very beautiful shrub called the **caffer coffee** which bears a small berry resembling coffee. **1829** C. Rose *Four Yrs in Sn Afr.* 125 The glossy palm-leaves of the Kaffer coffee. **1966** C.A. Smith *Common Names* 267 *Kaffir coffee, Tricalysia capensis*. **1988** P. Wilhelm *Healing Process* 24 'Were you at Wits?' ... 'I tried to get in,' the black went on, 'but the government wouldn't allow it — so I went to a **kaffir-college**.' **1942** S. Cloete *Hill of Doves* 143 As lean as a **Kaffir cow**. **1826** A.G. Bain *Jrnls* (1949) 93, I shot one of those beautiful birds called by the Caffres Mahem and by the Colonists **Caffre Crane**. **1856** R.E.E. Wilmot *Diary* (1984) 133 The 'Kaffir' or 'Balearic crane' .. gaudily dressed in his coat of blue and purple and his strange crest of grey bristles. **1899** R.B. & J.D.S. Woodward *Natal Birds* 174 The Crowned, or Kaffir Crane, as it is sometimes called, appears to be the commonest species in Natal. **1923** Haagner & Ivy *Sketches* 121 The .. 'Kaffir Crane' .. is easy of recognition in its slate, white and black plumage, velvety black crown, ornamented by a large crest of pale-yellowish bristles, and the patches of naked red and white skin on the cheeks. **1963** O. Doughty *Early Diamond Days* 42 Immense long feathers of the Kaffir Crane. **1961** Palmer & Pitman *Trees of S. Afr.* 288 **Kaffir date**, *Harpephyllum caffrum*. **1972** *Std Encycl. of Sn Afr.* I. 267 *Kaffir plum*, .. The small, white flowers give rise to a deep red plum-like fruit, sometimes called Kaffir date. **1994** [see *wild plum* (WILD sense a)]. **1836** R. Godlonton *Narr. of Irruption* 219 When an individual has had the misfortune to make him or herself obnoxious to a **Kafir doctor** .. he is marked down as a future victim to this horrid custom. **1860** W. Shaw *Story of my Mission* 447 Europeans .. call them [*sc.* the amaqqira] 'the wise men,' or 'the Kaffir doctors,' but neither of these designations is a translation of the names which the Kaffirs give to these persons. **1891** T.R. Beattie *Pambaniso* 17 Sometimes a Kaffir doctor will make many guesses before he names the subject his visitors have come about. **1931** [see MUISHOND sense 1]. **1989** *Informant, Grahamstown* She always sick sick, go to Kaffir doctor. **1827** T. Philipps *Scenes & Occurrences* (1960) 239, I saw a return of the **Caffre Fair** today, the whole amount is valued at about two thousand pounds sterling! Most astonishing and wonderful! In less than 8 or 9 months, Elephants' tusks, Hides, Gum and Curiosities. **1835** J.W.D. Moodie *Ten Yrs* II. 246 Our time not permitting us to remain to witness the Kaffre fair, after breakfast we continued our journey. **1957** H.E. Hockly *Story of Brit. Settlers of 1820* 109 The 'Kaffir fairs' which for the past two and a half years had been conducted regularly three days a week at Fort Willshire. **1968** E.A. Walker *Hist. of Sn Afr.* 154 Somerset still further relaxed the system of non-intercourse by permitting a Kaffir fair twice yearly at Grahamstown. **1923** G.H. Nicholls *Bayete!* 214 A law has been passed to limit '**Kaffir farming**'. **1941** C.W. De Kiewiet *Hist. of S. Afr.* 82 Many a landowner .. obtained an important income from 'Kafir farming'. **1989** *Reader's Digest Illust. Hist.* 332 '*Kaffir-farming*' was outlawed in the 1913 Natives' Land Act, which forbade more than five African families from living on each 'white' farm as peasant squatters. *Ibid.* 489 *Kaffir-farming*, The letting of land to Africans; creation of pools of African labour on Transvaal farms in the late 19th century, which were made available to mine recruiting agencies for a large commission. **1828** W. Shaw Diary. 15 Mar., I have had a severe attack of the **Caffre Fever**, in consequence of taking cold when at the Cattle place. **1836** A.F. Gardiner *Journey to Zoolu Country* 194 A large **Kafir fig-tree** (species of banian), growing near the ford of the Tugela. *a*1827 D. Carmichael in W.J. Hooker *Botanical Misc.* (1831) II. 275 A boor to whom I once gave some .. small shot to kill a **Caffre Finch** (*Emberiza longicauda*) for me, returned .. with a fine bird. **1827** T. Philipps *Scenes & Occurrences* 70 Two very singular birds, the Caffer finch and mousebird .. have two very beautiful marks on their wings ... At the commencement of spring their tails begin to grow, and get to such a length as to appear to be an absolute incumbrance; but in the winter the feathers fall and they look like other birds. **1844** J. Backhouse *Narr. of Visit* 202 The Caffer Finch of this part of the country is *Ploceus spilonotus*. **1836** A.F. Gardiner *Journey to Zoolu Country* 358 The Kafir finch, a singular bird, about the size of a sparrow, having two long tail feathers, which it sheds during the winter; the plumage is very glossy black. **1850** J.E. Methley *New Col. of Port Natal* 29 The cattle are teased with an insect called the 'tick' .. from which they are often relieved by a bird called the Kaffir finch. **1862** 'A Lady' *Life at Cape* (1963) 107 The two red and black Kafir-finches .. will serve to brighten up her best bonnet. **1878** T.J. Lucas *Camp Life & Sport* 83 The Kaffir finch, whose black and white plumage and red throat were set off by his long streaming tail, the feathers of which are so prolonged that they droop into a perfect arch, and when flying nearly overbalance him. **1888** *Cape Punch* 18 Apr. 30 Hark! How de Kaffir-finches sing? **1900** H.A. Bryden *Animals of Afr.* 160 One of the most beautiful of the many kinds of weaver birds in Africa is the splendid Red Kaffir Finch. **1940** Baumann & Bright *Lost Republic* 234 The black kaffir-finch, with his long tail and his red breast ... always has a lot of his drab little wives flying about with him for company. **1946** S. Cloete *Afr. Portraits* 80 The Deriders .. wore two plumes of Kaffir finch on the head pointing backwards. **1973** Brink & Hewitt ad. Aristophanes's The Birds. 4 You're so cocky. What are you — a kaffir finch? **1983** J.A. Brown *White Locusts* 97 A widow bird lifted from among the grasses its long black tail fluttering like a widow's crepe ... Father called it the 'Kaffir finch' and told her that before their defeat the warriors used to wear its plumes. **1822** W.J. Burchell *Trav.* I. 20 In the aviary I saw .. the **Kaffers Fink**. **1834** A. Smith *Diary* (1939) I. 168 Caffer fink common along the streams. **1861** Lady Duff-Gordon *Lett. from Cape* (1925) 66 Kaffir 'finks', which weave the pendant nests, are hardy and easily fed. **1867** E.L. Layard *Birds of S. Afr.* 185 The Red Kaffir fink though not an uncommon bird is certainly a very local one. **1884** Layard & Sharpe *Birds of S. Afr.*, I saw what I took to be a black silk neckerchief drifting down to us ... I called the attention of my companion to it, when, with a laugh, he told me it was a male Kafir fink. **1897** H.A. Bryden *Nature & Sport* 93 Pendant over the water-courses, or curiously fastened to the reeds, were the daintily-fashioned nests of weaver-birds. The handsome yellow Kaffir fink was one of the most striking of these weavers. **1902** H.J. Duckitt in M. Kuttel *Quadrilles & Konfyt* (1954) 12 The boughs of the poplars were festooned with numberless artistically woven nests of the little orange and black finches called here 'Kaffirfinks'. **1923** Haagner & Ivy *Sketches* 118 The Red Bishop-Bird or Kaffir-fink .. is so destructive to the Kaffir corn and wheat crops that it has earned the undying enmity of the Barolong natives. **1956** F.C. Metrowich *Valiant but Once* 118 A flock of scrawny **Kafir fowls** scratched optimistically in the dust. **1896** H.L. Tangye *In New S. Afr.* 269 Looking at my feet, one day, I see a large specimen of the 'Praying Mantis,' vulgarly called the '**Kaffir God**.' **1903** *Cape Times* (Weekly) 11 Mar. (Pettman), It graphically pictured the tawny Kaffir gods rising on slender stems, with soft, rich petals flaming in the long grass. **1937** C.R. Prance *Tante Rebella's Saga* 179 Gysbertus, lanky and scraggy as a **Kafir hen**. **1871** J. McKay *Reminisc.* 272 An article .. as useful to the colony, if not more so, than the plough .. instead of the **Kafir hoe** or pick. **1886** M.E. Barber *Erythrina Tree* (1898) 2 'Pick,' Kaffir hoe. **1912** Ayliff & Whiteside *Hist. of Abambo* 80 The old Kaffir hoe is never used except for cleaning crops from weeds, and breaking up ground that is either too steep or too stony to admit of a plough being used. **1914** S.P. Hyatt *Old Transport Rd* 59 In the store itself .. the Kaffir hoes were in a heap by the door. **1969** A. Fugard *Boesman & Lena* 24 Must have been a **Kaffer hond**. He didn't bark. **1974** B. Simon *Joburg, Sis!* 107 Helena didn't have no choice of how to come home but past the dogs. You should see them, Boerbuls, Mastiffs, Kaffirhonde. **1955** J.B. Shephard *Land of Tikoloshe* 37 He flung his stick, neatly decapitating a red **kaffir honeysuckle** a few yards away. **1966** C.A. Smith *Common Names* 268 *Kaffir honeysuckle, Tecomaria capensis* ... Flowers long, trumpet-shaped, orange to orange-red, in showy masses ... The vernacular name is in reference to that of the cultivated honey- suckle. **1835** T.H. Bowker Journal. 2 Oct., My baggage **Cafir horse** died at fort Warden. **1835** W.B. Boyce in A. Steedman *Wanderings* II. 271, I hope to be able, as soon as I get a **Caffer hut** to live in, to teach the people one hour every morning or evening. **1877** C. Andrews Reminiscences of Kafir War 1834–5. 31 Passed the wooded hill .. and bivouacked among some Kafir huts to the eastward of it. **1841** B. Shaw *Memorials* 38 The Kaffir huts are constructed in the form of a bee-hive ... In building these huts, strong poles are first firmly fastened in the ground; upon these a kind of mortar, composed of clay and the dung of animals, is plastered; and the whole is then overlaid with matting. **1851** T. Shone Diary. 4 May, We were all wet thro, the rain running thro all our kaffre huts flooding of us, making of us miserable. **1857** R. Gray *Jrnl of Visitation to Diocese of Grahamstown* 356 A circular dining hall, which is an improved Kafir hut on a large scale. **1875** C.B. Bisset *Sport & War* 105 They were buried on the heights .. inside a Kafir hut. **1903** E.F. Knight *S. Afr. after War* 148 Not even a Kaffir hut into which to crawl for shelter. **1923** B. Ronan *Forty S. Afr. Yrs* 88 The most delightful of South African residences, the kafir hut transformed to meet European requirements ... delightfully cool and comfortable. **1933** W.H.S. Bell *Bygone Days* 37 On an opposite ridge were the Kafir huts where the native servants lived. **1949** C. Bullock *Rina* 74 She disappeared among the huts of the kraal. Among the kaffir huts! The thing was .. absurd! **1966** C.A. Smith *Common Names* 268 *Kaffir hut, Euphorbia meloformis*. **1975** *Dict. of Eng. Usage in Sn Afr.* 95 *Kaffir hut*, .. Dome-shaped succulent resembling a special type of Af-r[ican] hut. **1906** 'Rooivlerk' in *E. London Dispatch* 4 Aug. 4 The nasal whistle of the Common Hornbill or **Kaffir Jack**, is almost certain to come from various quarters. **1900** W.D. Drury *Bk Gardening* 348 *Schizostylis coccinae* (Crimsom Flag; **Kaffir Lily**) is a lovely iridaceous subject with bright crimson gladiolus-like spikes of flower. **1934** [see IFAFA LILY]. **1946** M. Free *All about House Plants* 94 *Clivia miniata*, Kafir Lily. Give only enough water to keep leaves from wilting. **1970**

M. Allen *Tom's Weeds* 27 A feature of Number 1 greenhouse was the inantophyllum or Kaffir lily, renamed clivea by John Lindley in honour of the Duchess of Northumberland .. a member of the Clive family. **1972** J.U. Crockett *Flowering House Plants* 110 Kaffir lilies bloom in winter, bearing clusters of 12 to 20 brilliantly coloured lily-like flowers .. on top of .. stalks that rise from waxy, dark green, strap-like leaves. **1975** *Egerton's Postal Gift & Shopping Service Catal.* 3 Kaffir lilies .. flower in Autumn and the variety bears numerous small, pink, starlike flowers. **1974** J. McClure *Gooseberry Fool* (1976) 22 Does he think I'll say he's a **kaffir lover**? **1983** A. Paton *Ah, but your Land Is Beautiful* 221 You're a kaffir-lover and a worm. **1988** E. Mphahlele *Renewal Time* 37 Some of these kaffir-lovers .. hate the thought of having cheap labour within easy reach when we remove black servants to their own locations. **1990** G. Slovo *Ties of Blood* 308 Somebody grabbed her from behind. 'Kaffir lover,' hissed a voice. **1990** *Weekend Post* 24 Feb. (Leisure) 4 The town's white inhabitants .. labelled the Hoopers 'kaffir-lovers'. **1979** W. Ebersohn *Lonely Place* 104 Five minutes after you left that **kaffir maid** my men were there. **1983** F.G. Butler *Bursting World* 169, I remember question time best ... The contributions ranged from the archetypal racist ('why does General Smuts allow all these R.A.F.'s to come to South Africa and sleep with Kaffir-maids?') to the enlightened prophetic. **1986** S. Sepamla *Third Generation* 16 Sis Vi burst out .. 'Look at me properly: I'm none of your kaffir maids!' The lady with important looks turned white with rage. **1934** C.P. Swart Supplement to Pettman, 8 Babala, .. The Native name for a variety of manna known as **Kaffir manna**. [**1956** *Off. Yrbk of Union 1954–5* (Bureau of Census & Statistics) 520 N'Yati or Babala, also known as Cattail millet (*Pennisetum hyphoides*), known as *Kaffermanna* in Afrikaans.] **1966** C.A. Smith *Common Names* 265 *Kaffermanna(koring)*, *Pennisetum hyphoides* .. and *P. americanum* ... Large perennial grasses extensively cultivated by the natives for the grain which is used like the real Kafferkoring. *c*1963 B.C. Tait *Durban Story* 56 His children could not digest the tough, half-boiled, yellow **Kaffir mealie**. **1835** T.H. Bowker *Journal*. 31 Mar., Large fields of Caffer corn, Imfer, pumpkins, **Caffer melons** .. growing luxuriantly. **1844** J. Backhouse *Narr. of Visit* 249 The Caffer Melon, *Citrullus Caffer*, is a native of the country. **1948** V.M. Fitzroy *Cabbages & Cream* 208 Beyond the house was a barn filled with kaffirmelons. **1971** L.G. Green *Taste of S.-Easter* 89 Her atjar, bobotie and kaffir melon jam recipes are more appetising. **1950** H. Gerber *Cape Cookery* 102 In the Eastern Province the very large **kaffir mushroom** enjoys popularity. **1953** [see IKHOWE]. **1852** R.J. Garden *Diary*. I. (Killie Campbell Africana Library MS29081) 22 Apr., Mrs Wylder took up a **Caffir orange** & tried to explain to her that the earth was round. **1891** R. Smith *Great Gold Lands* 238 A kind of strychnia, called the Kaffir orange, bearing a hard-shelled fruit, filled with seeds embedded in a pleasant orange-like pulp. **1929** J. Stevenson-Hamilton *Low-Veld* 40 The umsala (*Strychnos spinosa*) and the umkwakwa (*Strychnos pungens*) both termed kaffir orange .. are small evergreen trees, bearing large globose fruits, three or four inches in diameter. **1932** [see KLAPPER *n*.[1] sense 1]. **1934** P.R. Kirby *Musical Instruments of Native Races* (1965) 128 *Shiwaya* .. is made from the shell of a .. 'kaffir orange'. **1972** M.R. Levyns in *Std Encycl. of Sn Afr*. VI. 267 Kaffir orange. Monkey orange. Klapper. Msala. (*Strychnos spinosa*) .. The fruit is large, much resembling an orange in form ... The fleshy part of the fruit is edible. **1948** H.C. Bosman in L. Abrahams *Unto Dust* (1963) 172 The spoor of a couple of **kafir oxen** that I smuggle across the Bechuanaland border. **1822** T. Philipps *Lett*. (1960) 117 We accepted the offer of the Hottentot guide on his Ox, as the **Caffre paths** were numerous, and we did not know which to take. **1850** N.J. Merriman *Cape Jrnls* (1957) 143 We had a long march over mountains by Kafir paths before us the following day. **1859** 'An Old Campaigner' in *Cape Monthly Mag*. V. Apr. 230 We threaded our way .. through the pleasant forest bridle ways or Kafir paths which at that time intersected the country between Graham's Town and the Fish River. **1864** 'A Lady' *Life at Natal* (1972) 40 We rode down to the place, crossed a wide sandy river, and then meandered up by crooked Kafir paths. **1877** R.M. Ballantyne *Settler & Savage* 299 A jungle so dense that it would have been impassable but for a Kafir-path which had been kept open by wild animals. **1885** Lady Bellairs *Tvl at War* 210 A mounted party was sent in advance to scale a Kafir path leading to the crest. **1887** [see AMATUNGULU]. **1903** D. Blackburn *Burgher Quixote* 107, I struck a kafir path, which I followed. **1936** P.M. Clark *Autobiog. of Old Drifter* 117 Though there was a road of sorts, we were able — having a guide — to make use of kaffir paths as short cuts. **1949** C. Bullock *Rina* 48 The winding kaffir path, so true in its main direction, so absurdly sinuous in detail. *a*1951 H.C. Bosman *Willemsdorp* (1977) 17 There was that Kafir path that he and his younger brother had walked along every afternoon back from the farm-school. **1853** F.P. Fleming *Kaffraria* 36 Amongst these various Kaffrarian trees may be enumerated the **Kaffir-Pear**, or *Oichna*, of a reddish wood, which bears a good polish, and works well into furniture, though not so durable as others. **1851** R.J. Garden Diary. I. (Killie Campbell African Library MS29081) 2 July, They made assegais & **Caffir picks** the customers bringing their own iron, but before the Colony of Natal was formed they used to smelt the ore from iron stone. **1887** A.A. Anderson *25 Yrs in Waggon* I. 106 They are very expert in metal, melting the ore for the manufacture of ornaments, assagais, Kaffir picks, and such things as they require. *c*1963 B.C. Tait *Durban Story* 66 Barter was the trade language of the country folk who exchanged calico, beads, salt, kaffir-picks and all sorts of odds and ends for pumpkin and mealies. **1852** R.J. Garden Diary. I. (Killie Campbell Africana Library MS29081) 21 Apr., Entering the hut I found a young girl about 16 or 17 lying on the floor on a mat her head resting on a **caffir pillow**. **1968** K. McMagh *Dinner of Herbs* 22 A 'kaffir pillow', a small saddle of wood [used] as a head rest at night. **1844** J. Backhouse *Narr. of Visit* 205, I visited a steep wood .. to see the tree known in the colony by the name of pruim or **Caffer-plum**, *pappea capensis*. **1875** C.B. Bisset *Sport & War* 76 One great fellow had got .. into the branches of a Kaffir plum tree. **1880** S.W. Silver & Co.'s *Handbk to S. Afr*. 132 The timber-yielding trees .. are these — . Kaffir Plum. **1881** [see KAFFIRBOOM]. **1892** A. Sutherland in *Cape Illust. Mag*. Vol.3 No.4, 134, I noticed the crimson gleam of some Kaffir plums amongst the foliage on the opposite bank. **1923** W.C. Scully *Daniel Vananda* 145 A large 'umgwenya' (Kafir plum) tree .. wide-branched and with dense, dark-green foliage. **1933** W.H.S. Bell *Bygone Days* 36 A kafir plum is .. chiefly composed of a large stone of nearly an inch in length, round this oblong stone is a thin covering of juicy, fleshy substance, and covering that is the skin; both the fleshy part and the skin have an attractive flavour. **1954** U. Van Der Spuy *Ornamental Shrubs & Trees* 134 The Kaffir Plum .. is grown for its handsome form and attractive foliage. Mature trees branch rather high above the ground level. **1972** Palmer & Pitman *Trees of Sn Afr*. II. 1195 The Kaffir plum, which so much resembled the dog plum or essenhout, *Ekebergia capensis*, in foliage, is an evergreen tree found in the forests of the Cape Province. **1977** *E. Prov. Herald* 16 Nov. 17 A Kaffir Plum .. is one of the familiar street trees of Port Elizabeth. **1990** *Weekend Argus* 14 July 7 The King is seen planting a kaffir-plum at the foot of Government Avenue in 1947. **1882** S. Heckford *Lady Trader in Tvl* 291 A disease much resembling scabies — called, I believe, **Kaffir-pock** — was very prevalent at Makapan's-poort. **1887** J.W. Matthews *Incwadi Yami* 109 Kafir pox, a varicelloid disease, believed to attack only natives, also known as 'Wacht en beitje' pock (Dutch, 'wait a bit,'), as it delayed them on their road. **1932** M.W. Henning *Animal Diseases* 644 (Swart), It [*sc. Acokanthera venenata*] is known popularly as 'Hottentot's poison', 'Bushman poison', '**Kaffir poison**' or merely 'poison bush', also as 'gifboom'. **1943** I. Frack *S. Afr. Doctor* 121 In the beginning I used to argue with the people that there was no such thing as kaffir poison, designed exclusively to annoy Europeans. **1968** Cole & Flaherty *House of Bondage* 153 Minor illness — including what white hospitals call 'Kaffir poison,' a physical and psychological malaise that resists Western-style treatment. **1836** C.L. Stretch *Journal*., Applied for a military escort to support the **Caffre Police**. **1845** J. Montagu Letter. (Cape Archives LG84, p.25) 12 Dec., The Governor's Dispatch to the Lieutenant Governor [in] relation to the Kafir Police, dated 30th May last. **1853** G. Cathcart (17 Apr.) in *Cape of G.H. Annexures* (1854), During the whole of the late war, a portion of the Kafir Police remained faithful, and did good service as levies and guides. **1878** T.J. Lucas *Camp Life & Sport* 49 There was a Kaffir police organized for .. purposes connected with the native administration. **1884** B. Adams *Narr*. (1941) 199 On reaching Fort Hare we found .. a Division .. there consisting of 50 Dragoons, 120 Cape Mounted Rifles, 250 of the 45th Regiment, 50 Kaffir Police and a few Burghers. **1941** A. Gordon-Brown *Narr. of Private Buck Adams* 202 Kaffir Police, A small body .. enrolled in 1835 .. was disbanded in 1846. Another body of 100 men .. formed in January 1847 .. was found so useful that the number was increased to 446 men. The Kaffir Police deserted early in the war of 1850–3. **1976** A. Delius *Border* 272 Duma seems to be endlessly useful as a member of the Kafir Police. **1878** P. Gillmore *Great Thirst Land* 425 He got a **Kaffir pot**, and built it in over an oven, had a condenser made, and for a worm substituted an old gun-barrel. **1882** C.L. Norris-Newman *With Boers in Tvl* 190 On Sundays .. a general stew was made in a large Kaffir pot, with the addition of a little rice and pumpkin .. to the meat. **1896** H.A. Bryden *Tales of S. Afr*. 260 The *kaptein* .. persuaded the *vrouw* to .. roast .. a joint of springbok in a Kaffir pot, with hot embers below and on the lid. **1900** E.E.K. Lowndes *Every-Day Life* 89 The Kaffir pot, a large iron pot with three legs .. can be stood right on the fire. **1922** S.G. Millin *Adam's Rest* 254 Over the fire stood a big black tripod Kaffir-pot. **1929** J.G. Van Alphen *Jan Venter* 148 Underneath the waggon swung .. a soot-blackened kettle and gridiron, and a three-legged Kafir pot. **1942** S. Cloete *Hill of Doves* 24 Outside, on the stoep, were .. three-legged Kaffir pots of various sizes, chained together by their handles. **1959** A. Fullerton *Yellow Ford* 177, I use a kaffirpot, a three-legged thing made of cast iron. **1964** J. Van Zyl in *New S. Afr. Writing* 47 Three great bulbous kaffir-pots brimming with hot soup for the African school children during the winter. **1973** M.A. Cook *Cape Kitchen* 43 The so-called 'Kaffir' pot .. introduced about the middle of the 19th century .. was intended for the cooking of mealie-meal. **1976** D.M.B. Preston *Story of Frontier Town* 59 Round-bellied iron pots .. commonly called 'Kaffir-pots' to this day .. were imported from England. **1986** W. Steenkamp in *Cape Times* 11 Jan. 5 A colleague of mine who is a *potjiekos* fan .. went into a shop up-country (catering mainly for the tribal trade) and asked for a cast-iron pot. 'Oh,' said the woman behind the counter with more honesty than tact, 'you mean a kaffir-pot'. My colleague .. made it clear that .. he did not like that ancient and time-dishonoured ethnic designation. **1988** H. Prendini in *Style* June 102 Homesick exiles .. including one .. who arrived complete with his kaffirpot, his mealie meal and a ball jar of homemade sousboontjies. **1993** [see THREE-LEGGED]. **1866** C. Barter *Alone among Zulus* 117 A long kidney potato, not originally indigenous, but which now goes by the name of '**Kaffir potato**'. **1966** C.A. Smith *Common Names* 268 *Kaffir potato*, *Coleus esculentus* ... The vernacular name is derived from the nature of the rootstock which is eaten like a potato by natives in Tropical Africa and in Natal. **1978** J. Branford *Dict. of S. Afr. Eng*. 109 Kaffir print, .. Inexpensive cotton material usu. of blue or brown, closely printed with geometrical or floral designs. **1906** Stark & Sclater *Birds of S. Afr*. IV. 244 **Kaffir rail**, *Rallus caerulescens*. **1923** Haagner & Ivy *Sketches* 254 The Kaffir Rail (*Rallus caerulescens*) is dark brown above, merging into slatey-blackish on the crown: throat white. **1832** *Graham's Town Jrnl* 1 June 92 They made a coffin for Mr. Green .. by getting a few spars laid down, into which Jacob placed the body, making it fast with **Caffer ropes**. **1970** Beeton & Dorner in *Eng. Usage in Sn Afr*. Vol.1 No.2, 39 **Kaffir scimitar**, .. see: kaffir plum. **1870** C. Hamilton *Life & Sport in S.-E. Afr*. 219 **Kaffir sheep**, a breed of animals with large ears, having the appearance of a cross with a goat. **1930** *Farming in S. Afr*. Jan. 505 (Swart), Throughout the bushveld the so called 'Kaffir' sheep are found in fair numbers. **1937** *Handbk for Farmers* (Dept of Agric. & Forestry) 136 The Kaffirsheep, as found in the northern Transvaal, is inferior for slaughter purposes. **1860** HARVEY & SONDER *Flora Capensis* I. 93 According to *Ecklon* and *Zeyher*, confirmed by *Dr. Pappe*, the root is a Caffir remedy for the bite of serpents, whence the specific name, and the colonial '**Kaffir Schlangen Wortel**.' [**1885** A. SMITH *Contrib. to Materia Medica* 9 *Polygala Serpentaria — Kaffir Snake-root*. Dutch, *Kaffer Schlangenwortel*.] **1966** C.A. SMITH *Common Names* 266 *Kafferslangwortel, Poly serpentaria* ... A lax procumbent shrub with a thick woody root. Flowers in masses, mauve to pinkish, the outer sepals yellowish. **1856** *Cape of G.H. Almanac & Annual Register* 344 *Pelargonium Scutatum*. Sweet (Geraniaceae). The juice of the petals produces a blue colour of the tint of Indigo and may advantageously be used for painting ... The vernacular name of this plant is **Kafir-Sorrel** (Kaffir Zuring). **1913** C. PETTMAN *Africanderisms* 243 *Kaffir sorrel*, .. The astringent sap of the leaves is used to relieve sore throats. **1895** *Star* 17 Dec. 2 Main Reef, near Town. Stand 50 x 50: just the right spot for **Kaffir Store**: near Compound; £125. **1900** 'ONE WHO WAS IN IT' *Kruger's Secret Service* 138 Bottles and jars full of things usually sold in a Kaffir store. **1903** [see COMPOUND sense 1]. **1923** G.H. NICHOLLS *Bayete!* 130 The two messengers .. were dressed in the long overcoats to be found in every Kaffir store. **1950** C. BULLOCK *Mashona & Matabele* 220 The local 'kaffir store' .. is now a commercial exchange in all but the remotest areas. It is also a rather poor sort of social centre. **1961** *Red Wing* (St Andrew's College, Grahamstown) 31 We had been to the Kaffir store and bought a baby's bottle. **1887** *S.W. Silver & Co.'s Handbk to S. Afr.* 467 The revenue of the Territory, derived chiefly from land sale, quitrents, licences, stamps, transfer dues, capitation tax, and **Kaffir tax**, was, in 1878, 105,130l., and the expenditure 152,000l. 10s. **1980** C. HOPE *A Separate Development* (1983) 12 The Yannovitchs drove an old green, hump-back Dodge to Sunday mass. Parked in among the Vauxhalls and Morrises it looked like a **kaffir taxi**. **1985** P. SLABOLEPSZY *Sat. Night at Palace* 17 We had this old '48 Dodge. Real kaffir-taxi. Took the old toppie a whole bladdy day to crack Durbs in that thing. **1989** D. MULLANY in *Scope* 21 Apr. 4 The sardine-stuffed, wrong-side-of-the road, won't-budge 'kaffir' taxi. **1851** J.J. FREEMAN *Tour* 362 One kind hearted woman .. prepared a Kaffir meal for us — a pot of sour-milk, some Kaffir corn bread and some **Kaffir tea**. *a*1862 J. AYLIFF *Jrnl of 'Harry Hastings'* (1963) 93 After a good supper of rice, some salt ration beef, and a bason of Kaffir tea, the family sang an hymn, Mr Trollip had prayers, and the family retired to rest. **1870** C. HAMILTON *Life & Sport in S.-E. Afr.* 253 We made some Kaffir tea from a plant which is a kind of mint, possessing a bitter flavour. **1899** G. RUSSELL *Hist. of Old Durban* 96 An indigenous herb both nutritive and refreshing, which is known to us as 'Kafir Tea' (*Athrixia Phylicifolia*). **1949** L.G. GREEN *In Land of Afternoon* 55 Bush tea is popular in the fashionable cafes of the United States. They call it 'Kaffir tea' over there. *c*1963 B.C. TAIT *Durban Story* 56 She dried and infused a local herb, Athrixia Phylicifolia, which belied its designation of 'Kaffir tea' by being nutritive as well as stimulating. **1978** *Sunday Times* 30 July 6 (*advt*) Kaffir 'tea' is the dried leaves of the rooibosch shrub which grows on the highlands above Cape Town. **1906** B. STONEMAN *Plants & their Ways* 258 *L[ycium] afrum* (**Kaffir thorn**) is used for hedges. **1958** R.E. LIGHTON *Out of Strong* 49 Even the leaves of the kaffir-thorn that crowned the school rockery did not stir. **1833** *Graham's Town Jrnl* 15 Aug. 3 This late Zoola attack on these tribes, was for the purpose of taking cattle to obtain the sinews, or **Caffer thread**, to sew rings on the heads of several of the junior Regiments. **1972** *Sunday Times* 13 Feb. (Mag. Sect.), When I was a lad dagga was known as '**kaffir' tobacco** and had a vast sale at 1s. a lb. **1841** J. COLLETT Diary. II. 10 May, Sail twine & **Kaffir Tow**. **1832** *Graham's Town Jrnl* 12 Oct. 159 Ball Buttons, Beads, and Handkerchiefs for the **Caffer trade**. **1837** J.E. ALEXANDER *Narr. of Voy.* I. 364 In eighteen months, the Kaffir trade in ivory, principally exchanged for beads, buttons, brass-wire, *c*, yielded thirty-two thousand pounds. **1877** R.M. BALLANTYNE *Settler & Savage* 399 Just look at the Kafir trade, which last year .. amounted to above £40,000 — that's *crushed* out altogether. **1882** C. DU VAL *With Show through Sn Afr.* I. 171 A large Kaffir trade is carried on here. *Ibid.* 220 The shelves of the stores devoted to what is called the 'kaffir trade'. **1903** *Ilanga* 10 Apr. 3, I might point out to manufacturers at Home the volume of business they were neglecting in the kafir trade. **1941** C.W. DE KIEWIET *Hist. of S. Afr.* 251 Bad brandy, good only for the Kafir trade. **1949** C. BULLOCK *Rina* 33 Bags of coarse salt, kaffir trade blankets, limbo, knives, beads, changes of boots and clothing. **1975** D.H. STRUTT *Clothing Fashions* 351 Mackintoshes cost 6/6 (65c) and a cheaper line was advertised in Johannesburg for the 'Kafir' trade. **1829** W. SHAW Diary. 17 June, The **Caffre Traders** have conceived a prejudice against the Store, and have used their utmost influence to put it down. **1832** *Graham's Town Jrnl* 6 Apr. 58 The Caffer Trader whose occupation may be dated from the first Caffre Fair held on the 24th of May 1822. **1836** *Albany Settlers 1824–36* (Soc. for Relief of Distressed Settlers) 16 Two persons of colour .. were waggon-drivers in the employment of Messrs. Simpson & Ford, Caffer traders. **1822** G. BARKER Journal. 17 Aug., Planted a large **Caffre Tree** behind the house. **1955** A. DELIUS *Young Trav.* 149 There were peach trees absolutely covered in blossom and red-flowering kaffir-trees and many other flowering plants. **1958** — in R.M. Macnab *Poets in S. Afr.* 32 It sees the logic of decaying rock, maturing soil and fumbling root concluding in the flagrance of a Kafir-tree. **1848** *E. Prov. Directory*, (*advt*) Ayliff and Co .. a large and varied assortment of Merchandize .. Fineries, Clothing, Hardware, Saddlery .. **Kaffir Truck**, Breadstuffs, Groceries. **1851** J. & M. CHURCHILL *Merchant Family in Natal* (1979) 19 Getting out of stocks very fast, especially in Caffir Truck as blankets, sheets, beads, etc. **1855** G.H. MASON *Life with Zulus* 133 Enterprising native races, dependent entirely on the P.M. Berg traders, for blankets, hatchets, rough agricultural implements, and 'Caffre truck.' **1877** C. ANDREWS Reminiscences of Kafir War 1834–5. 8 Kaffir truck was down in the market, brown Kafir cloth was cheap. **1882** C. DU VAL *With Show through Sn Afr.* II. 202 With their wonderful rolls of baggage containing all the various articles purchasable at a 'Kaffir truck' store carried on their heads. **1900** J. ROBINSON *Life Time in S. Afr.* 279 Glass beads, knives, scissors, needles, thread, small looking-glasses .. are the chief staples of 'Kafir truck' to-day. **1908** D. BLACKBURN *Leaven* 218 Bulalie was receiving fifty-three shillings a month ... and spent half of it at the kafir truck store in childish unnecessaries. **1936** *Cambridge Hist. of Brit. Empire* VIII. 818 Every trader who taught natives to buy cotton blankets and shirts, beads and all the range of kaffir truck .. added a new demand upon the scanty wealth and low productivity of the natives. **1941** *Bantu World* 15 Mar. 4 The days of 'Kafir' trucks [*sic*] are fast passing away. The ambition of the new African .. is to possess the good and higher things of civilisation. **1943** 'J. BURGER' *Black Man's Burden* 51 The trade with Natives is often referred to as the 'Kaffir truck' trade. *Ibid.* 219 The principal imports [into Swaziland] are maize and other foodstuffs, blankets, clothes, and what the official report calls 'kaffir truck'. **1949** C. BULLOCK *Rina* 70 Most of the stuff I had to present was cheap kaffir truck — Manchester blankets, lembo and suchlike. **1958** S. CLOETE *Mask* 86 Kaffir truck — axe heads, knives, blankets, beads, black three-legged iron cook-pots and small mirrors. **1968** F.C. METROWICH *Frontier Flames* 90 Before long the more sophisticated Xhosas refused to barter their possessions for red clay. They demanded beads, buttons, trinkets and other Kaffir truck in return for their goods. **1982** *Pace* May 43 He was in charge of what was then called the *kaffir-truck* — merchandise aimed mainly for the black market. **1990** *Sunday Times* 4 Mar. 17, I became a buyer in a department called the 'kaffir truck'. **1798** in G.M. Theal *Rec. of Cape Col.* (1898) II. 245 They have been ruined by the **Kaffir war** and Bushman depredations. **1805** R. SEMPLE *Walks & Sketches* 191 During the Caffre War three English deserters, ready to die of hunger, approached the house of a boor. **1812** A. PLUMPTRE tr. *H. Lichtenstein's Trav. in Sn Afr.* (1928) I. 210 A year after the flight of Buys the Caffre war began, but what part he had .. in .. it is not easy to decide. **1835** G. CHAMPION *Jrnl* (1968) 13 The Caffre war, it is tho', will soon end, & the country be settled. **1838** J.E. ALEXANDER *Exped. into Int.* II. 186 Before the Caffer war of 1835 the British settlers in Albany were in a very prosperous condition .. when suddenly the prospects .. were blighted by the destructive invasion of the Caffers. **1841** B. SHAW *Memorials* 234 Since the late Kaffir war, an extensive revival of religion has taken place at Graham's Town. **1857** D. LIVINGSTONE *Missionary Trav.* 93 Our route .. led us .. through the centre of the colony during the twentieth month of the Caffre War. **1878** T.J. LUCAS *Camp Life & Sport* 140 Some discriminating individual has truly observed .. that a Kaffir war is 'the snob of all wars'. **1889** *Vanity Fair* in S. Clarke *'Vanity Fair' in S. Afr.* (1991) 62 He served in the Kaffir War .. in the Zulu War .. , and in the [first] Boer War. **1891** T.R. BEATTIE *Pambaniso* 8 Their determination to keep possession of the rich lands of Kaffraria amid all the dangers and troubles coincident with the life of the early Settlers in the days of Kaffir wars. **1898** G.M. THEAL *Rec. of Cape Col.* II. 245 They have been ruined by the Kaffir war and Bushman depredations. **1923** B. RONAN *Forty S. Afr. Yrs* 81 What an important part that dull old town had played in the numerous kafir wars, particularly the Gaika-Galeka campaigns. **1939** R.F.A. HOERNLÉ *S. Afr. Native Policy* 5 Eleven successive 'kafir-wars', the last of which was the 'Zulu Rebellion' of 1906. **1943** I. FRACK *S. Afr. Doctor* 63 Those days of the Kaffir Wars when the natives objected strenuously to the occupation of their country by the white men. **1962** L.E. NEAME *Hist. of Apartheid* 14 This early attempt at segregation failed, for the Xosas crossed the river again and their incursion led to the first of the many so-called Kafir Wars. **1972** *Cape Times* 9 Nov. 7 An endless succession of 'Kafir Wars' and an ever-shifting boundary-line on the dim Kaffrarian border. **1980** D.B. COPLAN Urbanization of African Performing Arts. 77 In the Cape, evangelism fed on a series of 'Kaffir Wars' between the Xhosa and the British. **1980** C. HOPE *A Separate Development* (1983) 70 Everything is a question of black and white ... You'd think we were still fighting the Kaffir Wars. **1986** M. PICARDIE in S. Gray *Market Plays* 94 Tannie used to .. tell me stories of .. the Kaffir Wars. **1992** *Weekend Post* 31 Oct. 9 Kaffir Beer had been largely replaced by sorghum beer, .. and Kaffir War by Frontier War. **1993** *Sunday Times* 17 Oct. 25 The sixth, seventh and eighth Frontier Wars (still known hereabouts as the Kaffir Wars). **1826** A.G. BAIN *Jrnls* (1949) 5 Sibigho sent us two earthen vessels full of boiled **Caffre water melon**. **1832** *Graham's Town Jrnl* 1 June 92 When Cowie was sick all the Caffers .. were dispatched forward, that they might get Caffer water melons to make soup. **1868** W.H. HARVEY *Genera of S. Afr. Plants* 124 *C. vulgaris* .. is the 'Kaffir Water-melon' and 'Bitter Apple' of the colonists, and a wild variety of the common European and Asiatic Water-melon. **1887** *S.W. Silver & Co.'s Handbk to S. Afr.* 140 When edible or sweet, this is called .. Kaffir water-melon; when bitter, it is called .. bitter apple, and the pulp of this may be used like that of the Colocynth. **1890** A.G. HEWITT *Cape Cookery* 59 Kafir Water-melon Komfyt. **1891** H.J. DUCKITT *Hilda's 'Where Is It?'* 118 Jam (Kaffir Water Melon). **1951** S. VAN H. TULLEKEN *Prac. Cookery Bk* 327 Take the inside of a kaffir water-melon; mince it, and to every 8 lbs minced kaffir watermelon add 2 lbs minced pineapples. **1983** *Sunday Times* 4 Sept. (Mag. Sect.) 22 The recipe for '**Kaffir Whisky**' was just as horrific: '100gal Delagoa Bay proof spirit, 1gal tincture of prunes, 3lb glycerine, 1 pint green tea, ½oz acetic acid, 20 drops of creosote and 12 drops oil of cognac'. **1905** P. GIBBON *Vrouw Grobelaar* 253 Call it **Kafir work**, or what you please. **1908** M.C. BRUCE *New Tvl* 28 The British working man has a healthy repugnance towards doing 'Kafir's work' .. keeping himself in every way above the level of the native. *Ibid.* 59 To her mind certain duties were 'Kafir's work', and she would starve rather than touch them. **1909** R.H. BRAND *Union of S. Afr.* 28 The growth of a poor white class which is too ignorant for any skilled trade and yet refuses to do 'Kaffir work' is an ominous sign. **1920** S.M. MOLEMA *Bantu*

Past & Present 253 To do manual labour .. they call it 'kaffir work' .. would be degrading to their caste. **1939** R.F.A. HOERNLÉ *S. Afr. Native Policy* 23 The poor white is psychologically handicapped by his tradition of membership of the master-class, expressed in contempt for 'kafir-work' and unwillingness to undertake it, especially in public labour-gangs. **1943** 'J. BURGER' *Black Man's Burden* 195 Colour prejudice has helped to establish an economic ideology that uses such terms as 'civilised labour' and 'kaffir work'. **1958** R.E. LIGHTON *Out of Strong* 167 Their children went to school to learn, not to do kaffir work. **1963** M. BENSON *Afr. Patriots* 68 The Wall Street crash struck South Africa at a time of sever drought. The poorest people — white and black — were badly hit. Poor whites took kafir work and hundreds of blacks were thrown out of work. **1964** W.H. HUTT *Economics of Colour Bar* 35 They had been taught to regard any form of labouring as 'Kaffir work' and hence as beneath the white man's dignity. **1977** F.G. BUTLER *Karoo Morning* 132 White men in their thousands were forced to do what they regarded as menial work — kaffir's work — with picks and shovels. **1979** T. GUTSCHE *There Was a Man* 131 Ds Bosman's advice was that they should go back to the land and work with their hands; but that was 'kaffir work' and no one accepted it. **1980** C. HOPE *A Separate Development* (1983) 52 That's the trouble with this country, everyone wants to be a boss. Anything else is kaffir work. **1988** D. OWEN in Laband & Haswell *Pietermaritzburg 1838–1988* 129 Relief work, because it entailed manual labour — 'kaffir work' — remained extremely unpopular.

3. *Obs. exc. hist.* Usu. with initial capital. **a.** The Xhosa language. **b.** *rare.* Any (or all) of the Nguni languages (see NGUNI *n.* sense 2 a). **c.** Any (or all) of the Sintu (Bantu) languages (see SINTU, BANTU *adj.* sense 1). Also *attrib.*

1779 W. PATERSON in J.B. Bullock *Peddie* (c1960) 5 A pleasant river, called in the Caffre language, Mugu Ranie. **1828** W. SHAW Diary. 8 June, For the first time, I read a Sermon in Caffre at our forenoon service; the countenances of most of the people afforded pleasing evidence that they understood me. **1835** G. CHAMPION *Jrnl* (1968) 2 The Dutch it is said is .. absolutely necessary upon the frontiers, & at the stations, it being there, except the Caffre, the only spoken language. **1836** [see CLICK]. **1842** J.W. APPLEYARD *War of Axe* (1971) 29 A few days before our District meeting I finished my Kaffer grammar, which has occupied most of my time and study during the past year. **1849** J.D. LEWINS Diary. 22 Sept., Entered some more words in my Caffre vocabulary. **1850** E. WRIGHT Letter., Billy and Polly can ask for anything they want in kaffir, and will soon speak it as correctly as English. **1860** W. SHAW *Story of my Mission* 471, I translated what he said into Dutch, from which language one of our people, a very apt interpreter, rendered it into Kaffir. **1870** T.M. THOMAS *11 Yrs in Central S. Afr.* 194 The languages of South Africa are divided into two great families, of which the Hottentot and Kafir may be regarded as bases ... Dr. Bleek, in his comparative grammar, however, divides them into three classes — Kafir, Hottentot, and Bushman. **1877** C. ANDREWS *Reminiscences of Kafir War 1834–5.* 34 After a second warning in Kafir Southey fired a second shot which wounded him in the left side. **1880** S. LAKEMAN *What I Saw in Kaffir-Land* 73 Johnny Fingo, their chief, was a tall, powerful fellow, who spoke Kaffir perfectly well. **1898** J.F. INGRAM *Story of Afr. City* 52 It consists of five stars surmounted by an elephant, with the word 'Umgungunhlovo,' the Kafir name for the city, underneath. **1900** W.S. CHURCHILL *London to Ladysmith* 190 Worst of all, I could not speak a word of Dutch or Kaffir, and how was I to get food or direction? **1906** J. STEWART *Outlines of Kaffir Grammar* p.vi, Sometimes statements are made about the beauty of the Kaffir language. On this the writer can offer no opinion. **1909** G.Y. LAGDEN *Basutos* II. 653, 1. *The Kaffir* or Zulu sub-class; 2. *the se-Chuana* or *se-Suto* sub-class; and 3. *the Herero* and *otj-Ambo* sub-class. The *Kaffir* dialects are spoken by tribes residing on the East Coast, east and south of the Lebombo Mountains and the Drakensberg as far south as Port Elizabeth. **1912** *E. London Dispatch* 4 Sept. 7 (Pettman), You hear an Englishman speak of dobo grass, dongas, tollies, tsholo, etc., which are pure Kaffir. **1933** tr. in W.H.S. Bell *Bygone Days* 352 Opposite to me was a nice-looking old gentleman who spoke Kafir. **1949** *Principles of Internat. Phonetic Assoc.* (1967), Xhosa (Kaffir). **1955** J.B. SHEPHARD *Land of Tikoloshe* 127 John Bennie, a Scot, has been called the Father of Xhosa literature because the credit for reducing the 'Caffre' tongue to writing is largely due to him. **1979** A. GORDON-BROWN *Settlers' Press* 56 The long-expected Kafir grammar by the Revd W.B. Boyce was at once set up and was printed in time for Shaw to comment in the preface, dated 5 February 1834, that a few obvious errors had escaped correction.

d. With distinguishing epithet: **mine-kaffir**: a former name for FANAKALO. Also *attrib.*

1947 O. WALKER in *Vandag* Vol.1 No.9, 25 They live amid a welter of tongues — Bantu, mine-kaffir, Afrikaans and pidgin English. **1972** L.G. GREEN *When Journey's Over* 123 Fanagalo has many names. Known in its early days as Kitchen Kaffir or Mine Kaffir [etc.].

4. *obs.* The BLACK EAGLE, *Aquila verreauxii.*

*c*1808 C. VON LINNÉ *System of Natural Hist.* VIII. 25 The *Caffrarian Eagle* ... The caffre is as large as the golden eagle; the claws short, but not so much hooked ... The plumage is entirely black, except a few brownish reflections on the smaller wing-coverts towards the pinions. Its colour, and being found only in Caffraria, made Vaillant call it *Caffre*. **1867** E.L. LAYARD *Birds of S. Afr.* 12 *Aquila Verreauxii* ... Le Vaillant evidently founded his 'Caffre' upon this species.

5. As in general English: an infidel or unbeliever.

A relatively rare sense in S. Afr. Eng.

1827 T. PHILIPPS *Scenes & Occurrences* 116 They call themselves *Amakosæ* or the tribe of Kousa. Caffer is an Arabian word for infidel or bad man; and they themselves frequently so apply it. **1860** W. SHAW *Story of my Mission* 396 It is somewhat remarkable that the term 'Kaffir' is not a name used by the natives to designate either themselves or any other tribes in the country. The word is derived from the Arabic, and signifies an infidel or unbeliever. **1870** C. HAMILTON *Life & Sport in S.-E. Afr.* 58 The meaning of the word Kaffir, or Kafir, is 'unbeliever.' These men have no written laws, nor prescribed forms of religion. **1902** G.M. THEAL *Beginning of S. Afr. Hist.* I. 109 They [sc. communities of Asiatic origin on the East African coast] termed the Bantu inhabitants of the mainland Kaffirs, that is infidels, an epithet adopted by modern Europeans and still in use. **1937** B.H. DICKE *Bush Speaks* 52 The Bantu being 'kafirs' (unbelievers) and heathens — poor, doomed souls, according to the idea of people who harbour the presumption that they alone are the true believers. **1968** K. MCMAGH *Dinner of Herbs* 63 The whites were to learn to their cost that the 'Kaffirs' or unbelievers were not the noble savages pictured in the story-books of the day. **1972** *Grocott's Mail* 9 May 3 A kaffir is a person who does not believe in the existence of God ... There are no kaffirs today. We have all gone to school. We know God and we pray to him every day. **1982** *Sunday Times* 5 Sept. (Extra) 3 It is tantamount to heresy itself for one Muslim to call another Muslim a Kaffir (unbeliever). **1989** *Frontline* Mar. 13 *Kafir*, Arabic for a non-believer in Islam, applies to every non-Muslim, including Messrs Terre'Blanche and Treurnicht.

6.a. [Prob. used in this sense because the word was strongly associated with South Africa; in the context of the stock exchange, perh. first used in the name *Kaffir Circus*, see quot. 1948 at sense b.] Either *attrib.*, or *pl.*: South African mining shares traded on the London Stock Exchange.

1889 *Rialto* 23 Mar. (Farmer), Tintos climbed to 12¼, and even Kaffirs raised their sickly heads. **1895** *Nation* 19 Dec. 481 The mines floated on the London Stock Exchange which are classed under the general head of 'Kaffers'. **1896** PURVIS & BIGGS *S. Afr.* 133 The Kaffir boom of 1895 .. like its predecessors was the result of artificial movements on the part of the Stock Exchange riggers. *Ibid.* 151 Some of the big men of the Kaffir Market laid the foundation of their fortunes by illicit diamond buying. **1909** *Rand Daily Mail* 16 Nov. 7 Kaffirs closed dull. **1932** *Grocott's Mail* 2 Apr. 3 The rise in sterling will probably have the effect of causing prices of Kaffirs on the London Stock Exchange, to fall. **1936** *Rand Daily Mail* 6 Jan. 4 The Kaffir distributions are less interesting as a guide to gold share prospects than as yet another indication of South African prosperity. **1942** *Star* 30 Dec. 6 On the London Stock Exchange yesterday Kaffirs were quietly steady and a shade harder. **1946** S. CLOETE *Afr. Portraits* 326 Whenever there was a chance of trouble .. the Kaffir stocks rose in value, on the assumption that the trouble would be for others .. and the benefits for the British stock-holders. **1952** *Drum* Dec. 11 Kaffirs opened .. in rather a nervous condition under the influence of the news of the Port Elizabeth riots. **1968** E.A. WALKER *Hist. of Sn Afr.* 446 The 'Kaffir boom' in mining shares, following on the proving of the deep levels was at its height. **1976** *Sunday Times* 1 Aug. 18 The London gold share market — known as the 'Kaffir Market' since its inception — was dealt a critical blow when British Chancellor of the Exchequer, Mr Dennis Healey, refused to change the rules regarding foreign portfolio investment. **1983** J.A. BROWN *White Locusts* 315 The total effect has been a loss of confidence in the Kaffir market. The familiar cry has gone up: 'Johannesburg is a dangerous investment.'

b. Special Comb. **Kaffir Circus** *obs. exc. hist.*, (*a*) the market on the London Stock Exchange where South African mining shares were traded; (*b*) *rare*, a name given to South African mining magnates residing in London.

1896 M. DONOVAN *Kaffir Circus* 96 A big boom is on in the Kaffir Circus, and Laure's shares are worth £15000. **1899** *Sketch* 19 July 572 The Miscellaneous Market has acquired a reputation of closely sympathising with the Kaffir circus. **1901** C. DUGUID *How To Read Money Article* 121 The market in which they are dealt in the Stock Exchange is often called the 'Kaffir Circus.' **1902** *Encycl. Brit.* XXXII. 865 At first .. the 'Kaffre Circus' .. was regarded with contempt by the older *habitués* of the Stock Exchange. **1913** C. PETTMAN *Africanderisms* 241 *Kaffir circus*, A slang name for the market on the Stock Exchange, where transactions in South African land, mining and other stock are carried out. **1928** *Daily Chron.* (U.K.) 9 Aug. 6 The Kaffir Circus presented a very idle appearance. **1939** F.B. YOUNG *City of Gold* 482 A wild, indiscriminate boom in the Kaffir Circus; for war would mean the overthrow of the Republican Government. **1945** N. DEVITT *People & Places* 145 'Kaffir circus' .. was the name given in London to the market in gold shares when the Rand goldfields were first opened. **1948** *Story of Jhb. Stock Exchange* (Comm. of Jhb. Stock Exchange) 44 South African gold mining shares were dubbed 'Kaffirs' on the London Stock Exchange, and the section of the market devoted to business in them was first called the 'Kaffir Circus', which name stood for many years until the last part of the sobriquet was dropped and South African gold shares settled down under the name of 'Kaffirs'. **1967** E. ROSENTHAL *Encycl. of Sn Afr.* 278 *Kaffir Circus*, Expression for the section of the London Stock Exchange specialising in South African Gold shares. **1987** G. VINEY *Col. Houses* 142 The arrival of all these colonials was greeted with a certain amount of scorn .. and their frantic social efforts caused them to be collectively and slightingly referred to as 'the Kaffir Circus'.

7. *Obs. exc. hist.* In Cape Town: an armed, uniformed slave with various official duties, such as that of exciseman, peace-keeper, policeman, and executioner.

1925 H.J. MANDELBROTE tr. *O.F. Mentzel's Descr. of Cape of G.H.* II. 124 Slaves .. called 'Kaffirs' are armed with a sword with iron hilt, carrying a 'palang' or heavy club, wear a grey uniform consisting of a short coat with blue lapels, a waistcoat and trousers, and receive some petty perquisites as well. **1926** P.W. LAIDLER *Tavern of Ocean* 80 The Company's storehouse, a wing of which was occupied by the Provost and his 'kaffirs', faced the sea. *Ibid.* 105 He had .. ten constables, and nineteen under-constables, the latter

Kaffirs or men picked from among the prisoners on Robben Island. **1975** D.H. Strutt *Clothing Fashions* 143 Some of the more trusted male slaves .. employed as assistants to the police .. given a certain amount of authority and armed with a short sword, were called Kaffirs.

B. *adj.*

1. *rare.* Of or pertaining to the black peoples of South Africa.

1925 D. Kidd *Essential Kafir* p.v, The people have forgotten Umkulunkulu's praise-giving names, and so can hardly worship him in any sense which is adequately Kafir.

2. *derog.* With negative connotations:

a. In the n. phr. ***kaffir bargain***, a spurious bargain.

1934 'N. Giles' *Ridge of White Waters* 266 'Another kaffir bargain!' said Sir Alfred wearily. **1937** C.R. Prance *Tante Rebella's Saga* 67 He and the doctor drove a grim 'Kafir bargain', like a Jew speculator trying to sell a barren heifer as 'due to calve shortly'. **1979** T. Pakenham *Boer War* (1982) 67 Milner brushed aside Kruger's Reform Bill. It was a 'Kaffir-bargain'. *Ibid.* 487 This was the short-cut he [*sc.* Milner] dreaded: some kind of botched up settlement, a 'Kaffir bargain', he called it.

b. Bad, inferior, unreliable; clumsy, inept.

1948 O. Walker *Kaffirs Are Lively* 27 *Kaffir* .. is, in fact, an adjective of contempt in the ordinary speech of the South African when he speaks of a 'Kaffir' trick, or 'Kaffir' work. **1961** *Spectator* (U.K.) 14 July 53 'That was a real Kaffir shot.' .. This .. was the first time I had come across Kaffir, *adj.*: bad, clumsy, inferior .. etc.

c. In the phr. ***to go kaffir***, to go native (see Native *adj.* sense 3).

1956 J. Chatterton *Return of Drums* 36 He could not forgive those who hinted that he chose to lead this solitary life because he had gone 'kaffir', because he had taken to Native women.

Hence **kaffirdom** *n.*; **kaffirhood** *n.*; **kaffirish** *adj.*, see quot. 1941; **kaffirize** *v. trans. rare*, also **kaffirized** *ppl adj.*, of words, to render into a Xhosa or Zulu form; of people, to make inferior or subservient.

1858 B. Nicholson in J. Maclean *Compendium of Kafir Laws* (1906) 171 A Kafirized form of some tribal name given by the Hottentots. **1860** W. Shaw *Story of my Mission* 452 Dr. Colenso attempted to cut the knot of this difficulty by Kaffirizing the Latin name of God, and writing the word thus, 'Udio'. **1877** J.A. Chalmers *Tiyo Soga* 435 He was disposed to glory in his Kafirhood. **1891** T.R. Beattie *Ride through Transkei* 11 The surroundings of Cala seem to make one forget that one is in the heart of Kafirdom, with barbarian life and customs all around. **1908** B. Blackburn *Leaven* (1991) 75 The nature of the charge against him was known to every kafir in the jail before he had been there an hour, for news travels fast in kafirdom. **1941** W.M.B. Nhlapo in *Bantu World* 1 Mar. 9 There is something kaffirish about our shows. No matter how stale and washed-out the programme, the audience will .. still applaud with the same feverish enthusiasm. **1949** O. Walker *Proud Zulu* (1951) 250 Natal's determined policy of Kafirising the Zulu Nation and making of them a nation of servants and plantation workers.

kaffir bean *n. phr. Obsolescent. offensive.* [Kaffir + Eng. *bean.*]

1. The cow pea *Vigna sinensis*, cultivated as a vegetable, as a food for livestock, and for soil enrichment.

1839 T. Shone Diary. 13 Aug., Sarah planted some water melons and kaffre beans. **1913** H.A. Junod *Life of S. Afr. Tribe* II. 510 That year the Kafir beans were plentiful at Mpfumu. **1925** *Off. Yrbk of Union 1910–24* 441 The *Kaffir Bean* .. makes excellent hay or ensilage, and when ploughed in, builds up the fertility of the soil. **1936** P.M. Clark *Autobiog. of Old Drifter* 166, I roused some of the natives and asked for food ... Some Kaffir beans and some thick milk were brought. **1968** S. Cloete *Chetoko* (1976) 115 He grew his tobacco here, and marakas, mealies, Kaffir beans, and pumpkins. **1972** *Farmer's Weekly* 21 Apr. 55 The latest offical estimate of the dry bean crop excluding kaffir beans reveals that only about 5000 tons more than last year are expected.

2. Lucky bean sense 2 a. Also *attrib.*

1839 T. Shone Dairy. 29 Aug., This day Henry found the chain we lost at the top of a Kaffre bean tree where the Monkey had got fast when he ran away, and died there. **1972** *Std Encycl. of Sn Afr.* VI. 264 The large, poisonous seeds, scarlet with a black spot, are known as lucky beans, Kaffir beans, Kaffrarian peas or cocky-doodles.

kaffir beer *n. phr. Obsolescent. offensive.* [Kaffir + Eng. *beer.*] **a.** Tshwala senses a and b. **b.** See quot. 1898.

1837 R.B. Hulley in F. Owen *Diary* (1926) 174 About a hundred pots filled with Kaffir beer were brought and placed before the .. men. **1841** B. Shaw *Memorials* 39 Kaffir beer is made by malting, drying, grinding, boiling, and fermenting millet. **1851** R.J. Garden Diary. I. (Killie Campbell Africana Library MS29081) 29 June, The Queen .. drinks a great deal of Caffir beer & indeed takes little other sustenance. **1866** J. Leyland *Adventures* 53 The chief Mahura .. sent us some Kaffir beer, (made from Kaffir corn). **1875** D. Leslie *Among Zulus* 78 Kaffir beer is, in substance and taste, something like butter-milk, and about as intoxicating as thin gruel would be if made with sauterne and water. **1880** E.F. Sandeman *Eight Months in Ox-Waggon* 95 Kaffir beer .. has anything but an inviting appearance, in colour a pale pink, and very thick. It is made of Kaffir corn fermented with various herbs, and has a sour taste. **1883** J.A. Chalmers in *Blue Bk for Col.* No.G4, 136 The drink of Kafir beer has changed within the last few years, and it is no longer what it used to be among the Kafirs. **1894** E. Glanville *Fair Colonist* 139 The men .. returned with a great calabash of Kaffir beer. This beverage, brewed from the red corn, is not intoxicating in itself, but, unhappily, it is seldom now taken in its pure state. **1898** *Act 28* in *Stat. of Cape of G.H.* (1906) 3959 'Kaffir beer' shall, in addition to the liquor commonly so-called, include fermented liquor made from prickly pears .. and fermented liquor made from honey. **1900** S.T. Plaatje *Boer War Diary* (1973) 68 Kaffir beer to a common Morolong is 'meat vegetables and tea' rolled into one, and they can subsist entirely on it for a long time. **1907** [see Mtombo sense 1]. **1925** *E. Prov. Herald* 29 July 12 Native women were charged with being in possession of Kafir beer at Korsten. **1932** *Grocott's Daily Mail* 5 Apr. 2 We .. humbly request the local authorities of Pretoria humanely to consider the advisability of allowing a limited quantity of Kaffir beer for domestic consumption. **1943** 'J. Burger' *Black Man's Burden* 100 Concoctions that contain ingredients such as boot polish, carbide, raw spirit, or anything else that will supply the necessary 'kick' to kaffir beer. *c*1948 H. Tracey *Lalela Zulu* p.x, The municipal monopoly in the brewing of kaffir beer, made usually from millet or maize, from which much of the revenue of municipal administration is derived, must necessarily result in boot-legging. **1950** *Report of Commission to Enquire into Acts of Violence Committed by Natives at Krugersdorp* (UG47–1950) in L.F. Freed *Crime in S. Afr.* (1963) 130 The trade in these concoctions has grown and flourishes because the urban Native has now acquired a taste for something stronger than kaffir beer. **1959** L. Longmore *Dispossessed* 224 For births, ancestor-worship ceremonies, and so on, kaffir beer is bought from the municipal breweries and partaken of with due ceremony and circumspection by many urban Africans. **1966** L.G. Berger *Where's Madam* 80 Kaffir beer .. plays a very important part in the religious and social life of the Bantu, and it is imperative that .. he can obtain this most important beverage in a legal way. **1972** *Std Encycl. of Sn Afr.* VI. 263 There has .. been legislation to supersede the traditional term 'Kaffir beer' by 'Bantu beer'. **1976** A. Delius *Border* 179 There was no welcoming committee to see us in, not so much as a dish of sour milk or Kafir beer. **1992** [see Kaffirboom].

kaffirboetie /ˈkæfəbuti, -buti, ‖ˈkafə(r)-/ *n. Derog.* and *offensive.* Also **kafferboetie, kafir-boetie**, and with initial capital. [Afk. *kafferboetie* lit. 'little brother of a kaffir'.] An abusive form of reference or address to a white person who is perceived to be friendly with black people or working for their welfare. Also *attrib.* See also Boetie sense 5.

1939 [see Liberal *n.*]. **1943** 'J. Burger' *Black Man's Burden* 81 Farmers are eloquent about .. 'kaffirboeties' .. who advocate justice for the Bantu. **1948** A. Paton *Cry, Beloved Country* 166 All the welfare workers and this Father Beresford and the other Kafferboeties say it must not be so. **1952** G. Gordon *Let Day Perish* Glossary, 'Kafferboetie' means literally 'the Kaffir's little brother' and is used contemptuously for any European who sponsors the uplift of the Non-European. **1958** *Church Times* (U.K.) 21 Nov. 6 You can call a man a *Kaffir-Boetie* in Johannesburg and a nigger-lover in the Southern States; but both mean precisely the same thing and have the same accent. **1963** A. Fugard *Notebks* (1983) 80 Making a stand .. will result in all likelihood in your being dragged out and shot by the whites as a 'kafferboetie' traitor. **1964** G. Gordon *Four People* 103 If you have too many Non-Europeans coming to the house .. they'll say you are a Commie, or at any rate a *Kafferboetie.* **1971** C.W. Eglin in *Daily Dispatch* 6 Sept. 6 Ten years ago people who campaigned for equal pay for equal work were called 'kaffirboeties'. **1980** M. Lipton in *Optima* Vol.29 No.2, 186 They were openly critical of .. the *kaffirboetie* (liberal) attitudes of .. the mining companies. **1985** *Frontline* Sept. 27 A native will always come to your aid before a white man. I haven't got a soft spot for them. I mean I'm not a kaffirboetie or anything like that. **1990** *Weekend Argus* 14 July 15 At school he was called a 'kafferboetie' .. because he made friends with black children.

kaffirboom /ˈkæfəbʊəm/ *n. Obsolescent. offensive.* Also **caffer-boom, caffir boom, kaffir boem**, and with initial capital. Pl. **-s, -bome** /-bʊəmə/, and (formerly) **-boomen**. [S. Afr. Du. *kafferboom*, *kaffer* see Kaffir + *boom* tree; the explanation in quot. 1972 is prob. folk etymology.] The coral tree *Erythrina caffra* of the Fabaceae, a tall, spreading, deciduous tree with bright scarlet flowers and seeds; its soft wood; Boer-bean sense 1; Corallodendron; also called *lucky bean tree* (see Lucky bean sense 2 b). Also *attrib.*

As 'kaffirboom' is offensive to many, the general Eng. name 'coral tree' is often preferred.

1824 T. Pringle *Some Account of Eng. Settlers in Albany* 8 They pitched their tents under the shade of fragrant acacias, and groves of the gorgeous-blossomed caffer-boom. **1827** G. Thompson *Trav.* II. 31 The stakes of this fence, consisting chiefly of Caffer-boom (*Erythrina Caffra*) .. had in numerous instances struck root, and thrown out flourishing branches, which gave the palisade an uncommon and agreeable effect. **1835** *Graham's Town Jrnl* 20 Aug., Thatch ought never to be used on the frontier, if tiles, or Kafirboom shingles, can be obtained. **1836** A.F. Gardiner *Journey to Zoolu Country* 158 The Kafir Boom .. throws out short bossy thorns on every part of the trunk and branches .. the blossom .. appearing at the ends of the twigs like a shuttle-cock with crimson feathers. **1851** R.J. Garden Diary. I. (Killie Campbell Africana Library MS29081) 3 July, We passed trees of great height, amongst them Caffir Boomen. **1878** T.J. Lucas *Camp Life & Sport* 133 The Kaffir 'boem', with which the streets are adorned, is a very beautiful tree. The flower, which is bright scarlet, almost dazzles one's eyes to look at. **1881** *Meteor* 31 Oct. 1 High rock-crowned hills .. their bases thickly wooded with Kafir boom, yellow-wood, Kafir plum trees. **1887** *S.W. Silver & Co.'s Handbk to S. Afr.* 135 Kaffir-boom .. wood soft and light. *Ibid.* 150 It is impossible to avoid making mention of the Kaffirboom, *Erythrina Caffra*, with its splendid clusters of scarlet flowers. **1895** A.B. Balfour *1200 Miles in Waggon* 170 The Kaffir-booms, with their magnificent scarlet flowers, look gorgeous when growing .. among the boulders. **1911** D.B. Hook *'Tis but Yesterday* 145 They halted under the shade of a Kaffir-boom tree. **1937** M. ALSTON *Wanderings* 154 The Kaffir-boom bursts forth in all its brilliance. **1949** *Cape Argus* 15 Oct. 4 The Alexandria forests, red with giant kaffir-booms. **1954** U. VAN DER SPUY *Ornamental Shrubs & Trees* 117 The Kaffirboom .. is admirably suited .. to line the streets of towns, or as an avenue tree. **1964** A. ROTHMANN *Elephant Shrew* 19 Two large, spreading kaffirbooms. **1972** *S. Afr. Garden & Home* Oct. 145 The Kaffirboom .. so called because its bright red fowers .. resemble the red blankets worn by the Xhosas in the area. **1980** *Daily Dispatch* 20 Aug. 11 The wood of the kafirboom is soft and fibrous ... In the old days it was the standard timber for the huge brake blocks of the buck wagons. **1989** *E. Prov. Herald* 11 Jan. 8 The beans of the vivid orange-flowering *Erythrina caffra* .. (formerly Kaffirboom) are needed in medical research ... An enzyme extracted from them is used to isolate a remarkably quick anticlotting device. **1992** *Weekend Post* 31 Oct. 9 Kaffir beer had been largely replaced by sorghum beer, *kafferboom* by coral tree, [etc.].

Kaffir-bread /ˈkæfəbred/ *n. Obsolescent. offensive.* Also **Kaffir's-bread**, and with small initial. [KAFFIR + Eng. *bread*; see quot. 1971.] In full ***Kaffir-bread tree***: BREAD TREE.

1801 J. BARROW *Trav.* I. 189 Two plants of the palm tribe were frequently met with; one, the *zamia cycadis*, or Kaffer's bread-tree, growing on the plains. **1868** W.H. HARVEY *Genera of S. Afr. Plants* 354 Encephalartos .. species, natives of the Eastern district and the countries beyond. Colonial name 'Kafir Bread'. **1882** *Garden* (U.K.) 10 June 410 *Encephalartos*, or Kaffir Bread, is a genus confined to South Africa. **1908** [see BREADFRUIT]. **1958** L.G. GREEN *S. Afr. Beachcomber* 14 Beyond the Buffalo River lies the Wild Coast, with the frangipane and kaffir-bread trees growing down to the beaches. **1971** R.A. DYER in *Std Encycl. of Sn Afr.* III. 534 Kaffir-bread tree ... Several early travellers in the Cape refer to the making of crude bread from Encephalartos by Hottentots and Bantu, hence the common names indicating bread.

kaffircorn /ˈkæfəkɔːn/ *n. Obsolescent. offensive.* Formerly also **caffer-corn**, **caffre(e)-corn**, **kafir corn**. [Prob. tr. S. Afr. Du. *kafferkoring*, *kaffer* (see KAFFIR) + *koring* wheat.] SORGHUM sense 1. Also *attrib.*

1785 G. FORSTER tr. *A. Sparrman's Voy. to Cape of G.H.* II. 10 The kind of corn which they sow, is .. known to yield abundantly. The colonists call it caffer-corn. **1795** C.R. HOPSON tr. *C.P. Thunberg's Trav.* I. 294 Caffre-corn (*Holcus caffrorum*) .. grew to the height of a man, bearing large clusters of flowers. **1802** TRUTER & SOMERVILLE in G.M. Theal *Rec. of Cape Col.* (1899) IV. 382 Dinner was served, consisting in roast beef and in holcus, or Caffer corn, boiled in milk. **1803** J.T. VAN DER KEMP in *Trans. of Missionary Soc.* I. 438 The Caffree corn is, as I think, a kind of millet, but grows from seven to ten feet high ... The corn .. is eaten boiled ..; they also bruise it between two stones, and make unleavened bread of it; they likewise malt it, after which it is boiled, and the decoction fermented. This drink they call *tjaloa*. **1835** W.B. BOYCE in A. Steedman *Wanderings* II. 266 A large earthen pot of beer made from Caffer corn, which is not very bad, considering all circumstances. **1852** A.W. COLE *Cape & Kafirs* 157 The Kafir can do without us; he drinks pure water; he eats bruised Kaffir corn and milk. *a*1867 C.J. ANDERSSON *Notes of Trav.* (1875) 221 Indigenous to the country .. the so-styled Caffir corn (*Holcus Suluceni*), a flattened, roundish seed of a reddish yellow colour. **1882** W.R. LUDLOW *Zululand & Cetewayo* 73 Corn maas is made from the Kaffir corn, or millet. **1894** E. GLANVILLE *Fair Colonist* 80 Breakfasting off a dish of kaffir corn boiled in milk, and home-made brown bread. **1903** E.F. KNIGHT *S. Afr. after War* 140 Here the farmer, without any irrigation, raises not merely his summer crops of mealies, Kaffir corn, side oats and potatoes, but also his winter crop of wheat, barley, [etc.]. **1911** L. COHEN *Reminisc. of Kimberley* 288 Gallons of native beer, made from Kaffir corn .. were drunk .. I imbibed some with unfortunate results. **1925** D. KIDD *Essential Kafir* 57 This beer is made .. from Kafir corn, which is soaked and allowed to sprout; it is then dried and powdered up and soaked in water; sometimes special roots which contain a ferment are added to help the process. **1936** *Cambridge Hist. of Brit. Empire* VIII. 769 Kaffir corn is .. apparently indigenous to South Africa, and still forms in native agriculture an important grain and forage crop. **1941** C.W. DE KIEWIET *Hist. of S. Afr.* 81 From the time of the .. Frontier War of 1850–1 may be said to date the monotonous and insufficient diet of maize and Kafir corn porridge. **1955** A. DELIUS *Young Trav.* 50 The kaffir-corn porridge was a dark-brown colour. **1966** L.G. BERGER *Where's Madam* 80 In Lily's skokiaan-making days .. the recipe consisted of twenty cents worth of brown sugar, two loaves of brown bread mixed with warm water, two packets of yeast and twenty cents worth of crushed, sprouted kaffir corn. **1972** *Std Encycl. of Sn Afr.* VI. 265 Kaffir-corn and sweet-stemmed sorghums .. from Natal and other regions roused considerable interest in the U.S.A. **1973** D. JACOBSON *Through Wilderness* (1977) 158 Some kaffircorn malt which he used to brew his own beer. **1985** *Cape Times* 10 Oct., Sorghum — 'kaffircorn' they still call it - .. sold at the time for nearly £4 a bag. **1991** B. MACKENZIE (tr. F.P. Van den Heever) in *Best of S. Afr. Short Stories* 56 Three times a day it was Kaffir corn and ground acorn coffee; the Kaffir corn however boasted some trifling variations: first Kaffir corn porridge, then stamped Kaffir corn, and finally extra stiff Kaffir corn porridge. **1994** M. ROBERTS tr. *J.A. Wahlberg's Trav. Jrnls 1838–56* 34 The following plants are cultivated by the Kaffers: .. Kaffir-beans, Kaffir-corn, and Kaffir-manna.

kaffir dog *n. phr. Offensive.* [KAFFIR + Eng. *dog*; or perh. tr. Afk. *kafferhond*.]

1. *obsolescent.* A tan-coloured, short-haired hunting dog kept by indigenous peoples throughout southern Africa and characterized by its leanness, long tail, sharp muzzle, and drooping ears; *kraal dog*, see KRAAL *n.* sense 5.

1835 T.H. BOWKER Journal. 11 July, Cafir dogs attacked the sheep, the guard kills two of them. **1864** S. TURNER in D. Child *Portrait of Pioneer* (1980) 6 These Kaffir dogs eat anything; you must not leave your saddle or anything made of leather within their reach or it is gone directly. **1870** C. HAMILTON *Life & Sport in S.-E. Afr.* 61 The Kaffir dog is an active, wire-haired, long-nosed hound, which much resembles the lurcher. **1882** LADY F.C. DIXIE *In Land of Misfortune* 69 The dust rose in clouds and enveloped us in its choking veil, Kaffir dogs flew out from wayside kraals and barked defiance. **1911** P. GIBBON *Margaret Harding* 5 The Kafir dog is not a demonstrative animal, and his snuffle meant much. **1929** G.P. LESTRADE in A.M. Duggan-Cronin *Bantu Tribes* II. i., 'Kaffir' dogs abound in Bechuanaland. **1939** S. CLOETE *Watch for Dawn* 14 What had he done that he could be teased like this, like a lion surrounded by kaffir dogs? **1943** F.H. ROSE *Kruger's Wagon* 70 The barking of Kaffir dogs, as we call the gaunt, black, smooth-haired, ravenous-looking beasts which the natives use in buck hunting. **1949** H.C. BOSMAN in S. Gray *Makapan's Caves* (1987) 39 A yellow kafir dog was yelping excitedly round his black master. **1954** J. WILES *Moon to Play With* 5 The kaffir dogs were usually out hunting in the long grass and that meant they might be away for days. **1970** *Daily Dispatch* 30 Jan. 14 In the old days they called them 'kaffir-dogs' — those yellowish pooches lolling about the kraals yapping at the cattle. **1971** D. MARAIS in *Std Encycl. of Sn Afr.* IV. 53 Kaffir dogs .. vary considerably in coloration, coat and ear carriage, but some characteristics are constant: in their general conformation and slinking gait they strongly resemble jackals ... Most of them weigh from 50 to 60 lbs ... Usually they live as scavengers in Bantu villages. **1971** [see BOERBULL].

2. *derog.* A mongrel dog: BRAK *n.*[2]

1882 S. HECKFORD *Lady Trader in Tvl* 61 Did she see a half-starved Kaffir dog look in her kitchen door or crawl trembling towards the dresser, it was not 'Furtseck,' .. that she would cry, but .. a piece of bread or meat was sure to be offered. **1949** O. WALKER *Proud Zulu* (1951) 97 They treat us as Kafir dogs. They whip us — yes, even the sons of Zulu men, they whip. **1973** BEETON & DORNER in *Eng. Usage in Sn Afr.* Vol.4 No.1, 71 *Kaffir dog*, .. mongrel .. , usu. underfed, maltreated & very thin. **1977** F.G. BUTLER *Karoo Morning* 203 No trees in these streets. No pavements. And at intervals, communal latrines. And starved 'kaffir' dogs. **1979** T. GUTSCHE *There Was a Man* 331 He had immediately banished all 'Kaffir dogs' from the Armoedsvlakte area as they found and distributed bones and carrion. **1989** J. HOBBS *Thoughts in Makeshift Mortuary* 303 Scrawny dogs tied with ropes round their necks to running wires. Kaffir dogs.

kaffirkie var. KAFFERTJIE.

kaffir meid var. KAFFERMEID.

kaffir piano *n. phr. Obsolescent. offensive.* [KAFFIR + Eng. *piano*.]

1. Any of a wide variety of indigenous multiple-keyed wooden percussion instruments, sometimes with tuned gourd resonators attached to the keys. See also MBILA.

1891 R. MONTEIRO *Delagoa Bay* 253 This song had a rapidly played accompaniment on the 'Kafir piano'. **1895** A.B. BALFOUR *1200 Miles in Waggon* 64 Kaffir pianos .. consist of two logs of wood wrapped in rags, laid parallel to each other on the ground in front of the player. Side by side across these are placed a number of slats of wood about fifteen inches long, which are actively hammered upon with a couple of drumsticks. **1899** R. DEVEREUX *Side Lights on S. Afr.* 58 Others played wild airs on the row of graduated sticks, usually described as a 'Kaffir piano'. **1913** C. PETTMAN *Africanderisms* 242 *Kaffir piano*, .. Made of flat bars of hard wood fastened across a frame, beneath which a number of calabash shells are fixed. The bars of wood when struck emit sounds that are not at all unmusical. **1931** J. MOCKFORD *Khama* 157 To the throb and wail of these kafir pianos the big-bodied, lusty mine-boys dance freely in two long lines. **1948** H.V. MORTON *In Search of S. Afr.* 311 A native band was thrumming on 'Kaffir pianos', instruments like large xylophones. **1967** E. ROSENTHAL *Encycl. of Sn Afr.* 278 Made of strips of wood varying in length, but strung along a series of calabashes which serve as a sounding board ... Kaffir pianos are used for native dances.

2. MBIRA.

1897 J. BRYCE *Impressions of S. Afr.* 251 The so-called 'Kaffir piano', made of pieces of iron of unequal length fastened side by side in a frame. [**1925** D. KIDD *Essential Kafir* 332 The natives have two forms of 'piano'. One .. is made by supporting different lengths of a special wood over two strings; when the pieces of wood are struck with a hammer they emit musical notes which vary with the length of the piece of wood. The other .. is made by fastening a good many pieces of iron of different lengths into a hollow calabash; this is decorated with many pieces of shell which jingle when the apparatus vibrates.] **1949** E. HELLMANN *Handbk on Race Rel.* 626 Mbira (so-called kaffir pianos), upon which Africans may play their traditional music and interchange tribal compositions without having recourse to expensive foreign instruments. **1963** S. CLOETE *Rags of Glory* 347 Reeling a little as if drunk, singing to himself, and playing the Kaffir piano in his hand. **1968** L.G. GREEN *Full Many Glorious Morning* 153 He listened to a native playing the *mbira* or kaffir piano with such exquisite melancholy that he became homesick and decided to return at once.

kaffir-sheeting *n. Obsolescent. offensive.* [KAFFIR + Eng. *sheeting*.] A thick, soft, coarsely woven cotton fabric used for clothing and inexpensive curtaining; *K-sheeting*, see K sense 1.

Not usu. used for sheets.

[**1836** C.L. STRETCH Journal. 8 June, The articles furnished were of the most common material, a Jacket of 'Caffre baize', imitation moleskin trousers, a common black hat, 2 cotton shirts, and a tin jug. **1868** T. STUBBS *Reminisc.* (1978) 211 Levies .. generally received a few yards of Caffer duffel or coarse gursey, and for boots a pair of soles and a piece of sheep skin.] **1959** J. MEIRING *Candle in Wind* 161 She had had to wrap them both in an old piece of kaffir-sheeting. **1967** J.A. BROSTER *Red Blanket Valley* 7 A coarse white cotton cloth called 'Kaffir sheeting' from which all

Qaba dress is made. **1971** *Daily News* 4 Mar. (Trend) 6 The couch is in apple green and white floral linen and the curtains are of kaffir sheeting. **1972** on Radio South Africa 11 Sept. (Woman's World), Young Xhosa girls wear short skirts made of Kaffir sheeting, dyed with ochre and often decorated with beadwork. **1974** *E. Prov. Herald* 27 Mar. 10 First quality Kaffir Sheeting with a .. textured effect that goes with every decor. Available in 10 decorator shades. **1979** *Grocott's Mail* 21 Aug. 2 When shopping, the girls would wrap a piece of 'Kaffir' sheeting around the top parts of their bodies. **1980** C. HOPE *A Separate Development* (1983) 104 The art students one knew by their ponchos, rough woven kaffir-sheeting dyed red and black, draped over sky-blue jeans. **1992** *Weekend Post* 31 Oct. 9 Kaffir beer had been largely replaced by sorghum beer, .. kaffir sheeting by heavy sheeting, [etc.].

kaffirtjie var. KAFFERTJIE.

Kaffrarian /kæfˈreərɪən, kəf-/ *adj.* Also **Caffrarian**. [*Kaffraria* (formed on KAFFIR) + Eng. adj.-forming suffix -(a)n.] Of or pertaining to the south-eastern (predominantly Xhosa-speaking) areas of South Africa, particularly the Ciskei and Border areas of the Eastern Cape (see BORDER sense 1); CAFFRIAN. Often in special collocations, as **Kaffrarian eagle**, the BLACK EAGLE, *Aquila verreauxii*; **Kaffrarian pea**, LUCKY BEAN sense 2 a; **Kaffrarian yew**, the YELLOWWOOD (sense 2 c) *Podocarpus elongatus*.

'Kaffraria' was a name given first to southern Africa, then to *Xhosaland* (see XHOSA *n.* sense 1 c), and subsequently to 'British Kaffraria' (an area of the eastern Cape Province situated between the Kei and Keiskamma rivers; annexed by Britain and administered separately between December 1847 and 1865, it was subsequently incorporated into the Cape Colony). Although the name 'Kaffraria' was occas. extended to all of the territories inhabited by Nguni peoples (being the entire east coast of southern Africa, including what is now KwaZulu-Natal, and parts of Mozambique), 'Kaffrarian' was not used of these other areas.

*c*1808 C. VON LINNÉ *System of Natural Hist.* VIII. 25 The Caffrarian Eagle, .. Its colour, and being found only in Caffraria, made Vaillant call it *Caffre. Ibid.* 333 The Caffrarian Thrush .. *Turdus Cafer, Linn.* and Curonge, *Vaillant.* **1821** W. SHAW in *Missionary Notices* 36 Locally known as the Yellow-wood. This is the kaffrarian-yew (*Taxus Elongatus*) and grows to a great height, the timber being fine and hard, and, when well seasoned, a most substantial and durable wood. *Ibid.* 123 Your Missionaries shall be called to lay the axe to the root of Caffrarian ignorance and cruelty. **1853** F.P. FLEMING *Kaffraria* 35 A large population thus located .. would prove most beneficial in the future administration of Kaffrarian policy. *Ibid.* 36 Amongst these various Kaffrarian trees may be enumerated the Kaffir-Pear, or *Oichna*, of a reddish wood. *Ibid.* 51 The Kaffrarian gooseberry is also a very pleasant fruit. **1874** G. ELIOT *Legend of Jubal* 193 No lions then shall lap Caffrarian pools. **1882** C.F.G. CUMMING *Fire Fountains* I. 258 From Crimean winters to Kaffrarian summers. **1884** FRIEND *Flowers & Folk Lore* 524 The seeds of one kind are called Caffrarian Peas by Barrow. **1891** T.R. BEATTIE *Pambaniso* 163 There was something particularly sad in the fate of those early Kaffrarian settlers. **1913** C. PETTMAN *Africanderisms* 244 *Kaffrarian pea*, The seed of the Kaffir boom ... I have never known the Kaffirs to use the seed of this tree as an article of food. **1931** G. BEET *Grand Old Days* 70, I recollect a Kaffrarian Englishman, named Wilson, being offered a certain claim for £12 10s. **1966** C.A. SMITH *Common Names* 268 *Kaffrarian pea*, The seeds of *Erythrina caffra* ... Erroneously alleged by some writers (under the vernacular name) to have been used by natives in Kaffraria like peas. **1967** E. ROSENTHAL *Encycl. of Sn Afr.* 279 *Kaffrarian Pea*, The seed of the Kaffirboom. **1972** [see LUCKY BEAN sense 2 a]. **1972** *Cape Times* 9 Nov. 7 An endless succession of 'Kafir Wars' and an ever-shifting boundary-line on the dim Kaffrarian border. **1980** F. O'KENNEDY in *Weekend Post* 29 Nov. (Family Post) 2 The Border's attractive and popular Kaffrarian Coast with its beautiful unpolluted beaches.

kaffre(e) var. KAFFIR.

kafia var. KOFIA.

kafir, kafir-boetie, kafir corn varr. KAFFIR, KAFFIRBOETIE, KAFFIRCORN.

kafre var. KAFFIR.

kafula var. AMAKHAFULA.

kahale var. GASHLE.

kahlblad var. KAALBLAD.

kahle var. GASHLE.

kaia(h) var. KAYA.

kaiings /ˈkaɪəŋz, -s/ *pl. n.* Also **kaai(i)ngs, ka(a)ins, kaiangs, kyens**. [Afk., prob. fr. Du. *kaaien*, pl. of *kaan* residue of melted tallow.] Greaves or brownsels from which fat has been rendered down. Also *attrib.*

*a*1905 H.J. DUCKITT in M. Kuttel *Bk of Recipes* (1966) 25 Two cups kaiings (that is the dry scraps of any minced sheep-tail fat or suet after it has been fried, and the boiling fat drained from it). **1913** C. PETTMAN *Africanderisms* 245 *Kains*, .. The browned pieces of skin remaining after the internal fat of an animal has been melted out; these are eaten cold with a little salt. **1928** J.W.N. MOLLER *What Every Housewife Should Know* 76 Keep a paraffin tin handy, into which put all scraps of fat, bacon, 'kyens' (refuse from dripping), ends of soap. **1930** M. RAUBENHEIMER *Tested S. Afr. Recipes* 37 '*Kaiings*' is the residue of rendered fat. It is best and most economical to pass the fat through a mincing machine before frying it out. Then the 'kaiings' will be fine enough and must be used just as they are. **1951** S. VAN H. TULLEKEN *Prac. Cookery Bk* 271 Kaaings soap ... Put the kaaings in a soap pot .. Dissolve 1 lb. caustic soda in ¼ bucket of water ... Now stir into the kaaings .. boil for an hour and .. find out if all the kaaings have disappeared. **1958** A. JACKSON *Trader on Veld* 43 During the summer .. the main fare was mutton and mutton again, but the byproducts were by no means uninteresting .. 'kaains' (a tasty bit of Afrikaner fat-tailed sheep). **1972** *Fair Lady* 8 Sept. 174 '*Kaiing*' bread. **1973** H. BECK in *Farmer's Weekly* 25 Apr. 104 Kaiings are little bits of crisp fat which remain when sheep's fat is rendered down into dripping ... They must be eaten piping hot and, as they are very rich should be approached by anyone over the age of sixteen with great restraint. **1982** *S. Afr. Panorama* Aug. 37 A pan on the kitchen table full of kaiings (crackling) — how many city slickers have tasted this particular delicacy? **1985** *Cape Times* 7 Aug., With the pre-dinner drinks there were tasty 'kaiings' — made from thin strips of fatty meat cut from the ribs of Karoo mutton and rendered crisp in the oven.

kaitchee var. KAARTJIE.

kajat var. KIAAT.

kajatenhout *n. obs.* Also **coyatte hout, Kajate'hout, kehatenhout**. [S. Afr. Du., *kajaten* (see KIAAT) + *hout* wood.] KIAAT.

1801 J. BARROW *Trav.* I. 339 Catalogue of Useful Woods ... Coyatte hout ... Tough. [Uses:] Staves for butter firkins. **1862** L. PAPPE *Silva Capensis* 29 *Atherstonea Decussata* (Cape Teak, or Kajatenhout) ... This tree grows 20–25 feet high. **1907** T.R. SIM *Forests & Forest Flora* 6 Of trees which are endemic to the Eastern Conservancy, Umtiza .. and Kajatenhout .. are the only ones of economic importance. **1913** C. PETTMAN *Africanderisms* 245 *Kajatenhout, Strychnos Atherstonei.* See Cape teak. **1917** R. MARLOTH *Common Names* 44 *Kajate'hout* (Cape teak) ... Wood used for assegais, etc. [**1921** H.F. MANDELBROTE tr. O.F. Mentzel's *Descr. of Cape of G.H.* I. 123 The pulpit is formed of East Indian Chiaten wood.] **1921** D.E. HUTCHINS in T.R. Sim *Native Timbers S. Afr.* 108 The stem of Kajatenhout is not wanting in thickness. **1956** *Handbk Hardwoods* (Forest Prod. Research Lab.) 159 Muninga — *Pterocarpus angolensis*. Other names .. kajat, kajatenhout, kiatt (Union of South Africa). **1971** [see KIAAT].

kak /kak/ *adj., int.,* and *n.* Also **cac, kaak**. [Afk., fr. Du., excrement (fr. L. *cacare* to defecate); quot. 1816 prob. represents the Italian *cacca* excrement.]

Not in polite use.

A. *adj.* Worthless, bad, horrible, untrue.

1971 *Sunday Times* 12 Sept. 4 A former mayor of Naboomspruit once described Naboomspruit as a kak ou dorpie. **1981** *Student Informant*, Grahamstown Midsummer Night's Dream, Measure for Measure: they're kak notes. **1982** *Rhodeo* (Rhodes Univ.) 6 Apr. 2 This is a kak newspaper, what with your political raves and squatter problems and pop-music crits. **1983** J. CRONIN *Inside* 15 The pay's kak, The prisoners give bek. **1984** A. DANGOR in *Staffrider* Vol.6 No.1, 17 Jurre, don't start that kak story again, hoor. **1991** P. SLABOLEPSZY *Braait Laaities.* 10 How was that? *Kak*? If you think it was kak, you can say so. I have a very big heart. **1992** P.-D. UYS in *South* 27 Feb. 24 'All Eurocentric culture is kak!' came from a group of huddled forms. **1993** J. THOMAS in *Weekly Mail* 8 Apr. 26 Seventies LPs, where every second track was *kak*.

B. *int.* 'Rubbish', 'nonsense'.

1973 J. COPE *Alley Cat* 83 Doof! A stone lands and sends over him a fine spray of dust. The hornbill cackle of Jonkman's laugh — '*Kak*!' he jeers. **1977** L. ABRAHAMS *Celibacy of Felix Greenspan* 44 'He's the worst man in the world,' said Felix. 'Ag, kak, man!' Willem growled. **1985** P. SLABOLEPSZY *Sat. Night at Palace* 32 Forsie: They'd let me through. Vince: Kak. No ways. Forget it.

C. *n.* Excrement, dung; usu. *fig.*, equivalent to general English 'shit'. Also *attrib.*

[**1816** J. MACKRILL *Diary.* 124, I was given to understand .. that cow dung alone was the Fuel of the Inhabitants ... I .. attacked my first Mutton Chop a la Caca with some hesitation, but was most agreeably disappointed.] **1975** J. MCCLURE *Snake* (1981) 24 Reporters? Those bastards can't see what's under their noses — and their values, so called, are all up to *kak*! *Ibid.* 118 That's why I am worried to find you in this cold, dirty place, with dog *kak* and frikkies on the floor. **1975** M. MUTLOATSE in *Bolt* No.12, 20, I do not care a kak about being moved every ten years. They may send me anywhere but employment I'll find. **1976** J. MCCLURE *Rogue Eagle* 104 'You write kak,' Willem said, lifting his glass. 'I read what you put in the papers .. and that's what it was, pure kak.' **1977** M.P. GWALA *Jol'iinkomo* 64 This chief who has let himself and his people into some confused Bantustan kaak. **1977** P.-D. UYS *Paradise Is Closing Down* 141 Take your carrots or whatever .. sis, what is all this kak? **1980** A. DANGOR in M. Mutloatse *Forced Landing* 163 Stop talking kak! Who are you? **1982** FUGARD & DEVENISH *Marigolds in Aug.* 25 The police come, and what happens then? We all land in the kak. **1985** *Frontline* Aug. 54 You hear about guys who can never sleep again and that, but that's kak. **1990** G. SLOVO *Ties of Blood* 255 Jesus, Jacob, you're full of *kak* today.

kak /kak/ *v. intrans.* [Afk.] Not in polite use. To defecate. Also *fig.*

1988 A. SHER *Middlepost* 380 For years, years, the Bokkie is kakking onto the big masters ... For years, years, .. the Bokkie is living on this my land, so he knows where to kak ... He needs no food or water but still he kaks. **1991** *South News* 14 Nov. 5 They tell you they will let you out when you've kakked and pissed.

Kakabi var. RHARHABE.

kakebeen /ˈkɑːkəbɪən/ *n. hist.* [Afk., lit. 'jawbone'.] Used *attrib.* in Special Comb., as **kakebeen wagon, kakebeenwa** /-vɑː/, pl. **-waens** /-vɑː(ə)ns/, [Afk., *wa* wagon], a pioneer wagon with high, curving sides resembling in profile the jawbone of a horse or ox.

1946 *Forum* 2 Nov. 34 These oxen were to be used to haul the kakebeen wagon across the river. *a*1951 H.C. BOSMAN *Willemsdorp* (1977) 7 They must go still further northward, dragging with long teams of oxen their cumbrous *kakebeen*-wagons through endless grass plains and over rugged mountains. **1955** L.G.

GREEN *Karoo* 116 Ladismith .. provided the Voortrekker wagon 'Johanna van der Merwe,' the authentic *kakebeenwa* which is now preserved in the Pretoria [sc. Voortrekker] monument. **1974** A.A. TELFORD in *Std Encycl. of Sn Afr.* X. 568 Many generations of Trek Boers modified and adapted the wagon ... The typical *kakebeenwa* of the Great Trek was .. no more than 4,5 metres long and one metre wide, and tented throughout its length. *Ibid.* 569 The body consisted of the sides, resembling somewhat in shape the lower jawbone of a horse or ox .. and the white canvas tent. **1983** *S. Afr. Panorama* Apr. 17 The *kakebeen* wagon .. was developed for the Great Trek of 1836–1838 to the interior. It was a lighter wagon suited to the uncharted territory which the pioneers had to traverse. **1989** *Reader's Digest Illust. Hist.* 114 The trekkers .. set out in wagons which they called *kakebeenwaens* (literally, jawbone wagons, because the shape and size of a typical trek wagon resembled the jawbone of an animal). **1989** *Weekend Post* 30 Dec. (Leisure) 4 In its time, the Cape ox-wagon — the *kakebeenwa*, as it became — was a revolution in itself. Its early development, though slow, was essential to the conquest of the interior.

kakelaar /ˈkɑːkəlɑː(r)/ *n.* Also **kackela**. [Afk., lit. 'chatterer', 'cackler', fr. Du. *kakel(en)* to chatter, cackle + agential suffix *-aar*; see quot. 1884.] The wood hoopoe *Phoeniculus purpureus* of the Phoeniculidae, black with a red bill; MONKEY-BIRD.

In G.L. Maclean's *Roberts' Birds of Sn Afr.* (1993), the name 'Redbilled Woodhoopoe' is used for this species.

1884 LAYARD & SHARPE *Birds of S. Afr.* 137 Its voice is harsh and resounding, and has acquired for it the name of *'Kackela'* among the Dutch, which signifies the 'chatterer'. **1913** C. PETTMAN *Africanderisms* 245 *Kakelaar*, .. This bird has a loud and harsh voice — hence the name. **1923** HAAGNER & IVY *Sketches* 39 The Wood Hoopoes .. are represented in South Africa by two well-marked species, the first of which is the Redbilled Wood Hoopoe or Kakelaar (Chatterer). **1929** J. STEVENSON-HAMILTON *Low-Veld* 98 Almost as noisy as the babblers are the birds known as kakelaars or wood hoopoes. Small parties of three or four hop about .. accompanying their work with a continuous harsh chatter — the name 'kakelaar' is not an inapt one. **1937** [see MONKEY-BIRD]. **1982** *S. Afr. Panorama* Sept. 50 Particularly noisy is the *kakelaar*, or red-billed hoopoo, a sociable black bird with a long, white spotted tail and raucous, cackling call.

‖**kakie** /ˈkɑːki/ *n.* Also **kaki**, and with initial capital. [Afk., British soldier, fr. Eng. *khaki* dull brownish-yellow, the colour of their uniforms; cf. KHAKI.]

1. *hist.* KHAKI *n.* sense 1 a.

1949 A. KEPPEL-JONES *When Smuts Goes* 209 There haa been rumours .. that the invading *Kakies* and Yankees were displaying a strange flag that was neither the Union Jack nor Old Glory. **1958** I. VAUGHAN *Diary* 15 Willem said here is a kaki. The Tommy rode fast up to us and said what place is this. **1969** J. MEINTJES *Sword in Sand* 56 Once he was in British hands and felt himself unfairly treated, it gave him satisfaction to think how many Kakies he had despatched on that dramatic day. **1988** G.R. GOOSEN in Smuts & Alberts *Forgotten Highway* 137 He .. had to devise a plan to prevent the 'Kakies' from taking his draught horses off the land.

2. *comb.* **kakiebos** /-bɔs/ [Afk., *bos* bush], *khaki bush* (see KHAKI *adj.* sense 1 b); also *attrib.*, and occas. **kakiebossie** /-bɔsi/ [see -IE]; **kakieridder** /-rədə(r)/ *hist.* [Afk., *ridder* knight], an ironical term used by pro-German Afrikaners to describe government informers during the First World War.

1953 A. PATON *Phalarope* 146 He came to the place where the blue-gums are, and the **Kakiebos** weed in the vacant ground. **1962** D. MARAIS *I Got a Licence*, (*caption*) There's always hakea, kakiebos, Australian wattle, [etc.]. **1970** H.M. MUSMECI *Informant, Port Elizabeth* The veld is full of kakiebossie. **1974** *S. Afr. Panorama* May 35 Many a South African farmer who fights a losing battle trying to clear his fields of persistent 'kakiebos' would shed tears at the sight of the devotedly cultivated fields of 'tagetes' (kakiebos) on the farm. **1980** N. FERREIRA *Story of Afrikaner* 37 There were signs of the remains of a homestead and kraal now covered with kakiebos. **1993** I. VLADISLAVIĆ *Folly* 61 He .. breathed in a blend of BBQ Sauce and char-broiled lamb; .. the spicy marinade combined exquisitely with the delicate herby aroma of the heap .. tarragon .. cinnamon .. kakibos. **1978** J. LAWRENCE *Harry Lawrence* 138 Hertzog said he had made contact with Leibbrandt, who was doing good work — he had already given a few **kakieridders** a good hiding.

Kalahari var. KGALAGADI.

kalander /kaˈlandə(r), kəˈlændə/ *n.*[1] ?*obsolescent.* Also **klander**. [Du., grain weevil.] Any of several species of weevil, esp. the grain weevils (*Sitophilus* spp., of the Curculionidae); the larva of any of these weevils. See also CALANDRA.

1731 G. MEDLEY tr. *P. Kolb's Present State of Cape of G.H.* II. 185 There are Abundance of Weevils in the Corn-Lofts in the *Cape*-Colonies. The Cape-*Europeans* call 'em *Klanders* ... One would think, that Name was deriv'd from the Latin Word *Clandestinus*, signifying, *secret, hidden, private*; because this Insect, having entered a Grain of corn, hides it self in it, as it were. **1929** *Handbk for Farmers* (Dept of Agric.) 540 *Grapes*, .. Kalander .. *Phlyctinus callosus* ... Brown wingless weevil, about 1/4-in. long. Specially destructive to buds and young fruit. **1937** *S. Afr. Garden Manual* 8 If you are troubled by cutworms, Mole Crickets, Kalander, Cockchafer and other beetles .. get rid of them by using *Seekat Oil Fumigant.* **1937** *Handbk for Farmers* (Dept of Agric. & Forestry) 728 Wheat, maize and other cereals which are stored, are susceptible to attack, particularly by two small insects — the grain weevil or kalander, and the grain moth.

kalander /kaˈlandə(r)/ *n.*[2] [Afk., abbrev. and ad. *Outeniekwalander* 'one from Outeniqualand'.] The YELLOWWOOD (sense 2 a), *Podocarpus falcatus*; the wood of this tree (see also YELLOWWOOD sense 1). Also *attrib.*

1966 C.A. SMITH *Common Names* 270 *Kalander* (*geelhout*), .. The vernacular name is corrupted from Outeniqualander. **1974** *E. Prov. Herald* 21 Sept. 4 The highest prices a cubic metre of timber realised at the sales were: stinkwood R1360, yellowwwood R260, kalander yellowwood R230, blackwood R250. **1977** *Het Suid-Western* 19 Oct., Parkes and Sons paid R350 a cubic metre for Kalander (Outeniqua yellowwood). **1988** M. STANSFIELD in *Weekend Argus* 1 Oct. 22 People .. spent their whole lives chopping down giant Kalanders (Outeniqua yellowwood) and stinkwood trees in the forest.

kalhaas var. KOLHAAS.

kalifa, kalifer varr. KHALIFA.

kalkivain var. KELKIEWYN.

kalkoentjie /kalˈkʊɪŋki, -ˈkuɪŋci/ *n.* Also **calcoon, kalkoentje, kalkoontjie**, and with initial capital. [Afk., *kalkoen* turkey + dim. suffix -IE; see quot. 1936 at sense 1.]

1. An orange-throated bird, *Macronyx capensis* of the Motacillidae; *Cape lark*, see CAPE sense 2 a; CUT-THROAT LARK.

In G.L. Maclean's *Roberts' Birds of Sn Afr.* (1993), the name 'Orangethroated Longclaw' is used for this species.

1835 T.H. BOWKER Journal. 11 June, Shot three Calcoons this morning. **1862** 'A LADY' *Life at Cape* (1963) 79 To scamper across these Flats is like riding on the top of a Scotch or Yorkshire moor, and only for the scream of some excited kalkoontjie .. the scene is quiet and subdued. **1867** E.L. LAYARD *Birds of S. Afr.* 120 *Macronyx Capensis*, Swain ... *Kalkoentje* of Colonists, lit. Little Turkey ... This handsome lark is common throughout all the open country. **1884** [see CUT-THROAT LARK]. **1908** HAAGNER & IVY *Sketches* 120 The Orange-throated longclaw .. is known as the cut-throat lark or kalkoentjie (little Turkey). **1931** R. BOLSTER *Land & Sea-Birds* 93 *Orange throated long-claw* .. *Kalkoentjie*, Cut-throat lark. The prevailing colour is sufficiently described as brown, mottled and striped above, the orange-red throat with black band below being enough to distinguish it. **1936** E.L. GILL *First Guide to S. Afr. Birds* 78 *Cape Longclaw*, kalkoentjie, cutthroat lark ... The name Kalkoentjie (little turkey) presumably referring to its red throat. **1937** M. ALSTON *Wanderings* 21 Several 'Kalkoentjes' or orange-throated long-claws (handsome bird with a bright orange patch on the throat). **1967** E. ROSENTHAL *Encycl. of Sn Afr.* 280 *Kalkoentjie*, .. Cape Longclaw .. a brown bird of the Pipit and Wagtail family.

2.a. Any of several flowering plants of the genera *Gladiolus* and *Tritonia* (family Iridaceae), with flowers resembling a turkey's wattle, esp. *Gladiolus alatus, Tritonia hyalina, T. deusta* and *T. crocata*. **b.** The plant *Sutherlandia microphylla* of the Fabaceae.

1906 B. STONEMAN *Plants & their Ways* 198 *Gladiolus*, .. 'Painted ladies' and 'Kalkoentjes' belong here. Eighty-one species of this large genus are found in South Africa. **1910** D. FAIRBRIDGE *That Which Hath Been* (1913) 105 Flowers bloomed everywhere in the warm sunshine — gladioli, ixias, iris, heaths, every shade of colour, from the crimson kalkoentje to the pure white chincherinchees. **1917** R. MARLOTH *Common Names* 45 *Kalkoentje, Gladiolus alatus.* **1924** D. FAIRBRIDGE *Gardens of S. Afr.* 138 The Gladiolus which is known locally as *kalkoentje.* **1928** *Jrnl of Botanical Soc.* XIV. 9 The Kalkoentje-allies contain some species well worthy of mention here. Perhaps the most striking, both in colour and form, is *G. orchidiflorus*, commonly called Green Kalkoentje. **1929** M. ALSTON *From Old Cape Homestead* 24 As for the irrepressible little kalkoentjes, .. they even have the audacity to bob up again after the plough has devastated the land. **1937** —— *Wanderings* 77 We found yellow nemesias and a new kalkoentje — Gladiolus namaquensis. **1949** *Cape Times* 13 Sept. 14 Fields of gousblom, baby blue flax, lemon and mauve cineraria, lachenalias, blue bobbejantjies, kalkoentjies, .. and other veld flowers. **1964** J. MEINTJES *Manor House* 35 The children always accompanied us on our walks to collect wild flowers: kalkoentjies, viooltjies, bobbejaantjies, freesias and the exotic aandblom. **1966** C.A. SMITH *Common Names* 270 *Kalkoentjie*, Several species of Iridaceae are known by this name: *Tritonia hyalina; T. deusta* and *T. crocata* .. : Cormous plants ... *Gladiolus alatus* .. a cormous and dwarf species ... It was the first of the *kalkoentjies* of the south western Cape to be named and one of the earliest Cape plants to be figured (1680) ... The flowers and sometimes the plants of *Sutherlandia microphylla* .. are also *kalkoentjies* because the red flowers recall the red wattles of a turkey. **1967** E. ROSENTHAL *Encycl. of Sn Afr.* 280 *Kalkoentjie*, .. Name given to a wild flower in the Western Cape and in Namaqualand. **1977** *Cape Times* 28 Aug. 1 The display of cinerarias, .. vygies, gousblomme and kalkoentjies would not be a mass of colour till mid-September.

kall var. KAAL.

kalossie /kaˈlɔsi, kə-/ *n.* Formerly also **kalotje**. [Afk., ad. *kalotjie* (earlier *kalotje*) skull-cap, see quot. 1966.] IXIA.

1913 C. PETTMAN *Africanderisms* 246 *Kalotjes, Ixias* — the popular name of these pretty wild flowers. **1966** C.A. SMITH *Common Names* 271 *Kalossie* (*kalotje*), A general name for several species of *Ixia* and *Lachenalia* ... The vernacular name, which is derived from 'Kalotje', was originally applied to only a section of the Ixiae, the flowers of which with their narrow tube and bowl-shaped perianth suggest an olden day type of skull-cap .. , as also the head dress worn by the Cape Malays. **1972** [see IXIA].

kama *n. obs.* Also **ca(a)ma, kaama, kamma, kha(a)ma**. [Khoikhoi *khama*, N. Sotho and seTswana *kgama*.] *red hartebeest*, see HARTEBEEST *n.* sense b.

[1810 G. BARRINGTON *Acct of Voy.* 274, I must also mention an animal, the name of which is not known in the Colony, as they call it the unknown animal. The Hottentots call it kamma. **1824** W.J. BURCHELL *Trav.* II. 81 The *Hartebeest* of the Cape Colony, called *caama* (or *kaama*) by the Hottentots, was considered .. to be the same as .. a animal of Northern Africa. **1846** R. MOFFAT *Missionary Labours* 89 A fine large hartebeest (khama of the Bechuanas), the swiftest of the antelope species), darted close past the wagon.] **1857** [see TSESSEBE]. **1871** J. MACKENZIE *Ten Yrs* (1971) 199 In the distance we sometimes descried the shy khama (hartebeest), or the kukama (gemsbuck or oryx), fleetest of the antelopes. **1878** P. GILLMORE *Great Thirst Land* 294 Here the Macalaca shot a hartebeest, or kama.

kamaroo var. KAMBRO.

kamassi /kəˈmasi, ka-/ *n.* Also **camassie, gomassie, kamasi, kamass(i)e, kammassie.** [S. Afr. Du. *kamassie(hout)*, perh. fr. Khoi-khoi *!găn* tree or *!găn-nāsi* bush.] The evergreen tree *Gonioma kamassi* of the Apocynaceae; its hard yellow wood. Also *attrib.* Formerly occas. in full ***kamassi wood.***

1793 C.R. HOPSON tr. *C.P. Thunberg's Trav.* II. 110 Camassie wood (Camassie-hout), is merely a shrub, and consequently produces small pieces only, which serve for veneering. **1798** S.H. WILCOCKE tr. *J.S. Stavorinus's Voy. to E. Indies 1768–71* II. 80 *Camassiehout*, which is used for veneering. **1816** R.B. FISHER *Importance of Cape of G.H.* 84 The kamasse, a sort of bark, being the rhind or shavings of the tree of that name. **1843** J.C. CHASE *Cape of G.H.* 160 Statement of the various woods growing in the Western and Eastern Province of the Cape of Good Hope ... Gomassie ... [uses] Veneering. [**1860** HARVEY & SONDER *Flora Capensis* I. 459 An erect, greyish shrub, called, '*Kammassie-hout*' by the colonists.] **1905** D.E. HUTCHINS in Flint & Gilchrist *Science in S. Afr.* 392 *Goniami kamassi*, .. Kamasi is a Boxwood substitute exported from Knysna. **1917** R. MARLOTH *Common Names* 45 *Kamassie'hout, Gonioma Kamassi.* Contains a very bitter principle. (Knysna). The wood a substitute for Cape box (*Buxus*), but the exhalations of the fresh wood injurious to the workers. **1935** L. CHALK et al. *Forest Trees & Timbers Brit. Empire* III. 15 Kamassi attains about 40 ft. in height and generally a maximum girth of 2 to 3 ft. *Ibid.* 17 Kamassi is one of the two timbers exported from South Africa regularly in small quantities. **1951** *Dict. of Gardening* (Royal Horticult. Soc.) II. 908 *Kamassi*, Evergreen shrub ... Yields the hard Kamassi wood of S. Africa. **1984** A. WANNENBURGH *Natural Wonder of Sn Afr.* 94 Beneath the canopy is a lower storey, in which ironwood and kamassi prevail.

kamba /ˈkamba/ *n.* Also **(ma)khamba, ukhamba.** [Xhosa and Zulu *ukhamba.*] An earthenware pot for holding sour milk or beer.

1952 F.J. EDMONSTONE *Where Mists Still Linger* 5, I have often stood in the confines of our home and watched the womenfolk struggling up the steep path from the Gwala Gwala carrying water in their kambas, which they balance on their heads. *Ibid.* 143 *Kambas*, Earthenware vessels. **1955** V.M. FITZROY *Dark Bright Land* 267 Calabashes filled with thick milk beautifully prepared. A *kamba* of *amasi*, each decorated with its *imbanga* — this was the Zulu expression of gratitude, of goodwill, of hospitality. **1967** S.M.A. LOWE *Hungry Veld* 96 She was going to make ukhambas (*dishes made from river clay*) too. These were to be baked in the hot sand under the fire and then polished shiny black with dugo seeds ... Ukhambas of utywala (*native beer*) were handed round. **1978** A. ELLIOTT *Sons of Zulu* 79 The man called out to his youngest wife to bring 'such and such' a *khamba* (beer-pot) from his hut for the white lady. *Ibid.* 130 As the family head, he is given his own pot of beer or *khamba* in his hut in the early morning and he starts his drinking then. **1980** *E. Prov. Herald* 16 May (Suppl.) 4 One beerhall has a television set where eyes that can hardly see and a mind that can hardly discern after gulping some makhambas, are exposed to beauty and education for which they do not care. **1986** M. RAMGOBIN *Waiting to Live* 19 The contents of the *khamba* could also be obtained, but not, here in Durban, a whole big khambaful — there was no sharing and passing around of the wide-mouthed earthenware pot. The thick beer they were used to was sold in small tin mugs. **1987** *Scope* 6 Nov. 42 'Imagine my husband's face,' she said, 'if, when he sipped his beer, he found a tadpole floating in his kamba!'

kambro /ˈkæmbrəʊ, ˈkam-/ *n.* Forms: α. **kamaroo, kamero, kamerup, komaroo;** β. **camberoo, kambaroo, kambro(o).** [ad. Nama *camare(bi)*, perh. fr. *//gami* (or Khoikhoi *kama-*) water + *//hoe-* or *//ho-* container + dim.-forming element *-ro-*. Nienaber (in *Hottentots*, 1963) suggests that the β forms *kambro, kambaroo*, etc., result from the inclusion of a bridging *-b-* to facilitate pronunciation by Afk. and Eng. speakers.] Any of several plants of the Asclepiadaceae, particularly *Fokea edulis*, but also other plants of the genera *Brachystelma, Fokea*, and *Pachypodium*, characterized by large, edible tubers. See also KU.

α. **1790** tr. *F. Le Vaillant's Trav.* II. 82 That [root] .. known under the Hottentot name of kamero, is shaped like a radish, and is as large as a melon. It has a most sweet and agreeable taste, and is excellent for allaying thirst. **1795** C.R. HOPSON tr. *C.P. Thunberg's Trav.* II. 150 Kamerup was the name given here to the Hottentot's Watermelon, a large succulent root. **1897** EDMONDS & MARLOTH *Elementary Botany* 125 The natives of the central and northern districts know very well how to find such underground reservoirs of the precious liquid, *e.g.* the 'Komaroo' (*Fockea*) and 'Barroe' (*Cyphia*). **1912** *E. London Dispatch* 27 July 20 (Pettman), 'Have you seen a Cape Kamaroo?' asked the doctor, 'that enormous plant of milky tubers, of which locally, by the way, we make an alluring komfyt?' **1913** C. PETTMAN *Africanderisms* 274 *Komaroo* or *Kambroo*, A plant of the genus Fockea (glabra), the root of which contains a large quantity of water, of which the natives avail themselves during the long droughts ... The word is sometimes shortened to 'Koo'.

β. **1872** E.J. DUNN in A.M.L. Robinson *Sel. Articles from Cape Monthly Mag.* (1978) 54 The principal varieties consumed by them are two kinds of 'camberoo' and 'uintjes'. The 'camberoo' has but a tiny leaf on the surface. Following this down among the stones, .. for a few inches or a foot, a large root is found from half a pound to two or three pounds in weight. **1913** C. PETTMAN *Africanderisms* 247 *Kambaroo*, Several species of Fockea, which are eaten raw by the natives and made into preserve by the farmers' wives. **1924** L.H. BRINKMAN *Glory of Backveld* 53 The kambro is a large, thick root, like a sweet potato, very watery, but sweet and refreshing on a hot day. **1966** C.A. SMITH *Common Names* 272 *Kamb(a)roo*, A name applied to several of the larger tuberous-rooted species of Asclepiadaceae .., usually with some special habitat prefix. **1975** W. STEENKAMP *Land of Thirst King* 129 The baroe is a round milky fruit with a light-brown peel and the kambro looks like a sweet-potato but contains a very edible milky fruit. You can eat the kambro raw or make it into a fine jam which has a strange but pleasant flavour. **1976** A.P. BRINK *Instant in Wind* 196 It has lately become possible once again, for Adam to locate and dig out the rare barroe or ngaap or kambro on their way. **1988** SMUTS & ALBERTS *Forgotten Highway* 184 There are many little things: kambro (Fockea), now, it's like a sweet potato, it pushes up its shoot right in the middle of a bush. Now, if you find a kambro here, then ten paces this way or ten paces that way you'll find another one.

Kamdeboom var. CAMDEBOO.

kameel *n. obs.* [S. Afr. Du., shortened form of *kameelperd, kameelpaard* giraffe (lit. 'camel horse').] CAMELEOPARD.

1839 W.C. HARRIS *Wild Sports* 158 The Hottentots .. were leisurely returning, having come to the conclusion that 'Sir could not catch the kameel'. *Ibid.* 373 *Camelopardalis Giraffa.* The Giraffe. Kameel of the Cape Colonists. **1896** H.A. BRYDEN *Tales of S. Afr.* 70 Rather suddenly we came upon a klompje of giraffe, and as .. we wanted meat, I rammed the spurs in and galloped headlong for the kameels. **1897** [see CAMEL]. **1900** W.L. SCLATER *Mammals of S. Afr.* I. 264 The name giraffe, derived according to Skeet from the arabic Zaref or Zarefat, is practically unkown in South Africa where the term 'kameel' is always used. **1925** in F.C. Slater *Centenary Bk of S. Afr. Verse* 11 Through the forest ways where the wild things graze ... Where the tall 'Kameel' at sunset steal like ghosts to silent 'vley'. **1925** F.C. SLATER *Shining River* 234 *Kameel*, The Southern giraffe, formerly found throughout the country north of the Orange River. (There are no true camels in this region). **1936** E. ROSENTHAL *Old-Time Survivals* 36 Many a South African .. still calls a leopard a 'tiger'; while to some farmers a giraffe is still a 'kameel' or camel, as it was when zoology books were inaccurate, back in the sixteen-hundreds.

kameeldoring /kaˈmɪəlˌdʊərəŋ, kə-, -ˌdʊərəŋ/ *n.* Also **cameel-doorn, camile-dorn, kameeldoorn, kameeldorn.** [S. Afr. Du., *kameel(perd)* giraffe + *doring* (Du. *doorn*) thorn.] CAMEL-THORN. Also *attrib.*

1822 W.J. BURCHELL *Trav.* I. 453 A large solitary tree of *Kameel-doorn* (camel thorn, or tree upon which the Camelopardalis generally browses), the first I had seen of the species, was standing here. **1839** W.C. HARRIS *Wild Sports* 241 The range of its *habitat* is exclusively confined to those regions in which the species of mimosa termed mokaala, or *kameel-doorn*, is abundant. **1844** J. BACKHOUSE *Narr. of Visit* 441 The Kameeldoorn, *Acacia Giraffe*, is a handsome tree; in the places formerly inhabited by the Giraffe, the trunks of these trees are naked as high as the Giraffe could browse off the branches. **1864** T. BAINES *Explor. in S.-W. Afr.* 24 The mimosa, the kameel-doorn, (camel-thorn), and a tree like the shedak of Australia .. grew among the reeds that fringed the sandy bed of the Swa-Kop. **1872** C.A. PAYTON *Diamond Diggings* 18 Tents of the diggers are scattered in all directions over the 'veldt', and are generally pitched near one of the numerous *kameeldorn* (camel-thorn) trees. [**1880** E.F. SANDEMAN *Eight Months in Ox-Waggon* 292 The shade of some thick kameel-thorns, so called because they are taller than any of the other varieties of mimosa, and also have a shoot which the long-necked animals are specially partial to.] **1917** R. MARLOTH *Common Names* 45 *Kameeldoorn*, (Camel thorn). *Acacia Giraffae.* A stately tree of the Kalahari region, with very hard, dark-brown wood and nutritious pods. **1920** F.C. CORNELL *Glamour of Prospecting* 25 Larger trees .. called locally cameel doorn, a species of thorny acacia, which is usually found in or near watercourses. **1948** O. WALKER *Kaffirs Are Lively* 90 The whole of this huge magisterial district .. is naught but a wilderness of *cameeldoorn* — camel thorn — and hook-and-stick bushes. **1957** L.G. GREEN *Beyond City Lights* 182 An inquiry was ordered, and the Bastards gathered under the kameeldoring trees outside the magistrate's office at Clanwilliam, awaiting the proceedings nervously. **1981** *S. Afr. Panorama* Dec. 5 The flat landscape is relieved only by kameeldoring (camelthorn) trees and the communal nests of social weaver birds suspended from telegraph poles. **1989** F.G. BUTLER *Tales from Old Karoo* 37 He travelled hopefully, for several weeks, south, always south — out of the *mopani*, into the *cameeldorings* and sand, and then the Karoo-like landscape near Keetmanshoop. **1990** *Weekend Post* 6 Oct. (Leisure) 4 The sweet scent of the kameeldoorn or acacia blossom is typical of the lowveld. **1992** C. NORMAN in *Sunday Times* 20 Sept. (Mag. Sect.) 31 In the centre of our dry riverbed, *kameeldorings* put down deep roots to tap underground water sources.

kamero, kamerup var. KAMBRO.

Kami-nun see BONDELSWART.

kamma var. KAMA.

kammassie var. KAMASSI.

kamparang var. KAPARRANG.

Kamtours var. GAMTOUERS.

kana var. KANNA *n.*[3]

kanalah /ka'nala/ *v. intrans.* Also **kanala, kanallah.** [ad. Malay *karna Allah* with the help of God.] Esp. in the Cape Malay community: to help or care for (someone); to please. Also an element in *comb.*, as: **Kanalahdorp** /-dɔ:p/ [Afk. *dorp* a village], a name given to (a part of) District Six; **kanalahwerk** /-vɛrk/ [Afk. *werk* work], see quot. 1951.

1951 L.G. GREEN *Grow Lovely* 177 There is a strong camaraderie among the Malays, and when one builds a house he calls on the craftsmen among his friends to help him. This is called 'Kanalawerk', or done to please a friend. ('Kanala' is the Malay word for 'please'.) **1981** *Sunday Times* 12 July (Mag. Sect.) 1 'Kanalah' is such a word, and it is most descriptive of the attitudes in the community. 'To kanalah' means to help, and it places an obligation on the person asked, no matter how difficult it might be ... At one stage the practice was so widespread that District Six was known as 'Kanalahdorp'!

Hence **kanalah** *vbl n.*, caring.

1992 L. VAN HOVEN in *S. Afr. Panorama* May-June 4 The casual visitor is unaware that the spirit of *kanallah* — a Malay word referring to 'caring' or 'looking after each other' — is still active here.

kanga /'kæŋgə/ *n.* [Swahili *khanga.*] A colourful fabric originating in East Africa; a length of this fabric worn as a garment.

1971 N. GORDIMER *Guest of Honour* 449 He saw the Gala women swaying off, sweeping their kangas round their backsides, laughing rudely and shouting abuse the soldiers couldn't understand. **1972** *Drum* 8 Oct. 62 Made up in bright East African kanga, and great fun to wear, it can also keep you cool. **1982** *S. Afr. Panorama* Apr. 38 Colourful Swazi kaftans, swirling skirts and shawl-like *kangas* to wrap around the waist or sling over the shoulder. **1983** *Informant, Cape Town* Java print? Don't you mean kanga?

Kango var. CANGO.

kankata var. IKHANKATHA.

‖**kankerbos** /'kaŋkə(r)bɔs/ *n.* Formerly also **kankerbosch.** [Afk. (earlier S. Afr. Du. *kankerbosch*), *kanker* cancer + *bos* bush.] CANCER BUSH. Also *attrib.*, and in dim. form **kankerbossie.**

1924 D. FAIRBRIDGE *Gardens of S. Afr.* 155 Perhaps of all the leading herbs of South Africa, the greatest hopes have centred round *Sutherlandia Frutescens*, known to the Dutch as the *Kankerbosch*. **1931** *Farming in S. Afr.* Sept. 216 (Swart), They preferred by far the 'Klein Kankerbos' (Sutherlandia frutescens), in spite of the fact that most farmers believe that this bush is not touched by any animal. **1949** L.G. GREEN *In Land of Afternoon* 51 There is the kankerbos, which has failed to provide a cure for cancer ... Mrs Dijkman .. advised the silvery kankerbos leaves for ordinary stomach troubles. **1953** *Cape Times* 14 July 2 These [*sc.* existing plantings] will be followed by the introduction of more woody species, such as bitou, blombos, kankerbossie and waxberrie. **1966** C.A. SMITH *Common Names* 275 *Kankerbos(sie), Sutherlandia frutescens* ... The leaves .. are aromatic and very bitter, used medicinally by the Hottentots in decoctions for washing wounds and internally for fevers.

kanna *n.*[1] var. GANNA.

kanna /'kænə, 'kana/ *n.*[2] Also **c(h)anna, gonna, konna.** [Khoikhoi *koŋ.*]

1. Either of two species of succulents, *Sceletium anatomicum* or *S. tortuosum* of the Mesembryanthemaceae, the roots and stems of which were formerly chewed by various peoples, esp. the Khoikhoi, for their narcotic effect. Also *attrib.*

1611 P. FLORIS in R. Raven-Hart *Before Van Riebeeck* (1967) 55 Wee vsed great diligence in seeking of the roote Ningimm .. being called of these inhabitants Canna. **1688** G. TACHARD *Voy. to Siam* 73 *The captain .. sent us .. a certain herb which they call* Konna [*sic*]; it is probable that that famous Plant which the Chinese name *Ginsseng*; for *Monsieur Claudius* who hath seen it at *China*, affirms that he found two Plants of it upon the Cape ... *They use* Kanna *as frequently as the Indians do* Betle *and* Areka. **1731** G. MEDLEY tr. *P. Kolb's Present State of Cape of G.H.* I. 212, I have often seen the Effects of *Kanna* upon *Hottentots*. They chew and retain it a considerable Time in their Mouths. *Ibid.* 262 The *Kanna* Root .. is in such Esteem among 'em, that they hardly think any Thing too good to be given in Exchange for it. **1790** [see sense 2]. **1796** C.R. HOPSON tr. *C.P. Thunberg's Trav.* II. 175 These people first chew Canna (*Mesembryanthemum*,) and afterwards smoke it. **1838** J.E. ALEXANDER *Exped. into Int.* I. 100 We ate the thick and reddish root called *canna.* **1913** C. PETTMAN *Africanderisms* 248 *Kanna*, .. a Karoo plant = *Mesembryanthemum anatomicum.* **1966** C.A. SMITH *Common Names* 276 The properties ascribed to Kanna are decidedly those of some species of *Sceletium* of which Thunberg .. first recorded the vernacular name ... Thunberg .. and Sparrmann .. had .. described *Salsola aphylla* under the vernacular name of Kanna ... This .. confusion .. seems to have arisen from the rendering of the original Nederlands spelling Channa (for *Salsola aphylla*) as Kanna. **1972** M.R. LEVYNS in *Std Encycl. of Sn Afr.* V. 287 'Gonna' has .. been taken as the equivalent of 'kanna', which should rightfully be confined to species of *Sceletium*, a genus allied to *Mesembyanthemum* and much prized by the Hottentots for its stimulant action.

2. *comb.* **Kannaland**, see quot. 1989.

Some believe this name to be derived from KANNA *n.*[3], or from GANNA: see quots 1844, 1913, and 1967.

1790 W. PATERSON *Narr. of Four Journeys* 23 This is called, the Channa Land; and derives its name from a species of Mezembryanthimum, which is called Channa by the natives, and is exceedingly esteemed among them. **1844** J. BACKHOUSE *Narr. of Visit* 112 This country is called the Little Karroo or Kanneland; from its producing a bush abounding with soda called Kannabosch, *Caroxylon Salsola.* **1880** S.W. *Silver & Co.'s Handbk to S. Afr.* 526 *Kannaland or Little Karroo* is an elevated plain between the Langeberg and Zwartberg range of mountains. **1913** C. PETTMAN *Africanderisms* 249 *Kannaland*, The part of the colony lying between the little Zwaart Berg Range and Touws River, probably so called as being the habitat formerly of the kanna or eland. **1966** C.A. SMITH *Common Names* 276 Paterson about 1779 also records that Channaland was so named from the abundance of a plant, one of the Mesembryeae [*sic*] (Sceletium) growing there. **1967** E. ROSENTHAL *Encycl. of Sn Afr.* 280 *Kannaland*, Portion of the Cape Province between Touws River and the Swartberg. The name is derived from the fact that it used to be inhabited by many Eland (Kanna in Hottentot language). **1989** P.E. RAPER *Dict. of Sn Afr. Place Names* 86 *Cannaland*, Region extending from Ezeljachtpoort to Platte Kloof, situated north of the Outeniqua Mountains. The name is derived from Khoekhoen and refers to the canna root, an edible type of Mesembryanthemum. Also encountered as *Kannaland* and *Canaan's Land.*

kanna /'kænə, 'kana/ *n.*[3] *obs.* Also **canna, kana.** [fr. Khoikhoi *ǃkhan.*] The ELAND (sense 1 a), *Taurotragus oryx.*

[1790 tr. *F. Le Vaillant's Trav.* II. 332 I .. unexpectedly fell in with a small flock of eight elks ... Doctor Sparrmann has given a very accurate description of this animal, which the savages name *kana.*] **1822** [see GANNA sense 1]. **1824** [see ELAND sense 1 a]. **1846** J.C. BROWN tr. *T. Arbousset's Narr. of Explor. Tour to N.-E. of Col.* 65 The long grass and herbage .. shelter and support a multitude of animals, such as the springbok .. and the canna. **1913** C. PETTMAN *Africanderisms* 248 *Kanna*, (Hot. *kan *ga (with cerebral click before each word), adj. half-yellow, half-grey, the eland.) *Taurotragus oryx*. The Dutch form of the Hottentot name of this animal. See Eland.

kanniedood /'kanidʊət, -duət/ *n.* Also **canne doet, kannidood, kan-niet dood.** [Afk., *kan* can + *nie* not + *dood* dead (abbrev. *doodgaan* to die).]

1. Any of several succulents of the Liliaceae, esp. *Aloe grandidentata* and *A. variegata*, and various species of *Haworthia* and *Gasteria*, which are exceptionally drought resistant and appear to live without sustenance. Also *attrib.*

1878 *Trans. of S. Afr. Phil. Soc.* I. i. 24 (Pettman), Here we find .. several kinds of 'air plants,' *Canne doets* or aloes. **1897** EDMONDS & MARLOTH *Elementary Botany* 125 The so-called 'Kanniet dood' plants ... Suspended in the air, .. economize the water and food-materials originally contained in their leaves and stem so well, that they are able, not only to live a year or more, but also to produce flowers. **1913** C. PETTMAN *Africanderisms* 249 *Kannidood*, .. The popular designation of several varieties of aloe, especially *A. variegata*; it refers to the striking way in which these plants will exist and flourish for a long time apparently without sustenance. **1970** G.W. REYNOLDS in *Std Encycl. of Sn Afr.* I. 314 *A. variegata* (kanniedood, partridge-breast aloe) occurs in the arid Karoo and has trifarious leaves. It is said that plants suspended by their roots will flower for two to three years before dying. **1974** H. HALL in *Ibid.* X. 340 The aloes, gasterias and haworthias belong here [*sc.* in the lily family], some of them popularly known as 'kanniedood; (cannot die)'. **1974** *S. Afr. Panorama* June 39 A rich variety of fauna and flora, ranging from colourful lizards, klipspringers .. and a wealth of birds to drought-stricken 'kanniedood' (Haworthia). **1982** *Flying Springbok* Nov. 27 *Comiphora glaucens* (Kanniedood) .. a fat, stunted, twisted little plant, sprouting a dense tangle of twigs like roots growing upside-down, is hanging on for dear life.

2. *fig.* Also *attrib.*

1970 E. MUNDELL *Informant, Pearston (E. Cape)* That lady has been sick for very long, but she is a real kanniedood. **1986** *Sunday Times* 7 Sept. 26 Never say die. So the NRP is to soldier on. This *kanniedood* group — 'party' seems almost too grand a description — is undeterred by calamity at the polls.

kannip /'kænɪp/ *n.* Also **kaa-nap.** [Khoikhoi.] The JAKKALSKOS, *Hydnora africana.*

1790 tr. *F. Le Vaillant's Trav.* II. 85 In the rocky cantons there grows a kind of potato, which the savages call *knaa-nap*; it is of an irregular figure, and contains a milky juice exceedingly sweet. **1856** *Cape of G.H. Almanac & Annual Register* 343 Its fruit which is like that of the Earth-nut, is subterraneous, has the form, size and taste of a potatoe. It is of a reddish brown tint, thoroughly Farinaceous ... Some wild beasts and particularly the porcupine (Hystrix cristata) are very fond of this fruit which is called *Kannip* or *Kauimp* by the Hottentots and *Jackals-kost* by the Dutch Colonists. **1917** R. MARLOTH *Common Names* 46 *Kannip*, Other name for *Hydnora africana* (Jakhalskost). **1966** C.A. SMITH *Common Names* 277 *Kanni(p), Hydnora africana* ... The underground fruiting part was formerly eaten by Hottentots and was known to them by the vernacular name. **1975** *Dict. of Eng. Usage in Sn Afr.* 97 *Kanni*, .. alt: kannip.

kanoti /kə'nəʊti/ *n.* Also **kanot, konotie.** [ad. Xhosa and Zulu *ugonothi* a pliable stick or rod; the plant *Flagellaria guineensis.*] In full ***kanoti grass***: the forest climber *Flagellaria guineensis* of the Flagellariaceae, with bamboo-like stems.

1868 J. CHAPMAN *Trav.* II. 446 The bush on the coast is rendered impenetrable by a dense undergrowth of shrubs and climbers, .. or pliant monkey-ropes and kanot-grass. **1899** G. RUSSELL *Hist. of Old Durban* 90 The materials consisted of wattles, and the 'Konotie' tree-runner from the bush (for tying.) *c*1963 B.C. TAIT *Durban Story* 49 The thatch, which was tied with Konotie — a tree-runner from the bush — overhung the edges of the roof. **1966** C.A. SMITH *Common Names* 278 *Kanotgras (kanoti grass)*, .. The stems are used by the Pondos for making baskets and by other natives for tying down the thatch of their huts. **1975** *Dict. of Eng. Usage in Sn Afr.* 97 *Kanoti grass*, .. Plant with stems that become hard like bamboo & are approx. 1cm in diameter.

kaparrang /ka'parəŋ, -aŋ/ *n.* Also **caparran, ka(m)parang, kaparran, kapar(r)ing, kapparan.** [S. Afr. Du., ad. Javanese *gambarran* sandal.] A wooden sandal held on the foot by a knob or knot passing between the big and second toes, traditionally worn by Cape Malay people.

1861 'A LADY' *Life at Cape* (1963) 12 A Malay beauty .. clatters upon *'caparrans'* (a species of wooden buskin), and it is marvellous how firmly they can keep their footing upon these comical pattens. **1867** M. KOLLISCH *Musselman Population Cape of G.H.* 23 Both sexes in some instances carefully ignoring the use of shoes, rather preferring clogs, called Kaparrans. **1883** 'A CAPE COLONIST' *Cape Malays* 7 Clogs called *Kaparangs* (a small piece of wood with two slips joined underneath, and a wooden knob on the upper side, it is easily put on, and has a very slight fastening, as the knob is simply placed between the first two toes. **1913** D. FAIRBRIDGE *Piet of Italy* 24 He kicked off his wooden *kaparangs* and waded across. **1936** L.G. GREEN *Secret Afr.* 130 Soon the cobbled streets resound to the clatter of the wooden sandals called *kamparangs*. **1944** D. FAIRBRIDGE in I.D. Du Plessis *Cape Malays* 52 When Lady Duff-Gordon saw them the men wore the toudang — a wide, pointed straw hat — .. and on their feet kaparangs or clogs, as the old-fashioned Malays still wear them. **1944** I.D. DU PLESSIS *Cape Malays* 51 Kaparrings, wooden sandals with a knot to push between the big and second toes, are still in use. **1953** DU PLESSIS & LÜCKHOFF *Malay Quarter* 61 By the end of the nineteenth century Oriental dress had been discarded; but certain characteristic features have been preserved. *Kaparrings*, (probably from the Javanese *gamparan*: wooden sandals with a knot to push between the big and second toes) are still in use. **1960** G. LISTER *Reminisc.* 10 There seemed to be many more Malays in Cape Town then, and they wore their own distinctive dress — .. wooden pattens called kapparans, a most uncomfortable footwear, with a flat sole for the foot and a sort of door knob to fit between the big toe and its neighbour. **1968** K. MCMAGH *Dinner of Herbs* 45 The Kamparang had come from the East and was no more than a wooden platform sole with a heel-and-toe lift which was held to the foot by a thick screw, also of wood, that was gripped between the big and second toes and that made the wearer the noisiest of all pedestrians. **1971** L.G. GREEN *Taste of S.-Easter* 140 Both sexes wore the wooden sandals called kaparrings; but the women put on white shoes at weddings. **1972** A.A. TELFORD *Yesterday's Dress* 139 Both men and women were to be seen wearing 'kaparrings', or wooden sandals held to the foot by means of a knob between the toes.

kapater /kəˈpɑːtə(r)/ *n.* Also **ca(r)parter, capater, kaparter, kirpater.** [Afk., fr. Du. *kapater* (fr. *capade* eunuch, ad. Pg. *capado* castrated).] A castrated goat. Also *attrib.*

1833 *Graham's Town Jrnl* 20 June 1 On Saturday morning next, on the Market, will be sold .. 24 he Goats, (Capaters,) 44 she Goats. **1838** J. COLLETT Diary. I. 17 July, Rode this Evg to Vandevyfers to purchase Caparter Bucks. **1841** B. SHAW *Memorials* 126 She kindly invited us to supper, for which she had the head of a large Kirpater Bok. [Note] Goat. *a***1862** J. AYLIFF *Jrnl of 'Harry Hastings'* (1963) 77 He said he was anxious to get some breeding stock of goats ... Five were a large kind of goat; he said that the Dutchman told him that they were of the 'Carparter' breed of goats. **1870** H.H. DUGMORE *Reminisc. of Albany Settler* 22 So were the hamels and kapaters gradually gathered together for the return journey, sometimes (it has been waggishly asserted) under the idea that they would make excellent breeding stock! **1897** E. GLANVILLE *Tales from Veld* 228 One of the biggest goats — a great blue 'Kapater,' with long beard, massive horns. **1899** *Natal Agric. Jrnl* 31 Mar. 3 'Kapaters' (wether goats) is a useful word. **1911** J.H. SMITH in *Farmer's Weekly* 4 Oct. 130 Can you give me a good remedy for goats (kapaters) that cannot pass their urine, as I have every year about 5 or 6 kapaters that cannot do so. **1917** [see PISGOED sense 1]. **1932** *Grocott's Daily Mail* 13 Jan. 1 20 Angora Kapaters 60 Angora Goats. **1955** L.G. GREEN *Karoo* 142 A dignified *kapater* at the head of a long procession of the sheep bound for the kraal. The *kapater*, of course, is a castrated goat; and a well-trained *kapater* is the key to easy management of sheep. **1968** F.C. METROWICH *Frontier Flames* 45 One poor farmer decided to go in for breeding goats ... Proudly he returned to his location with them, only to be informed by a more knowledgeable friend that they were all kapater! **1970** D.M. MCMASTER *Informant, Cathcart (E. Cape)* Hamels (sheep), kapaters (goats), and tollies (young cattle). The first and second are Afrikaans, the third Xhosa. Curious that all the terms used for castrated males; for all the others the ordinary English words are used. The only place I have ever seen the word 'wethers' is on the Income Tax form! **1986** *Grocott's Mail* 13 June 3 He said he would like to import a good ram, 'then if they do the breeding, I'll buy the kapaters for hair'. **1988** *Farmer's Weekly* Jan. 70 *Golden Valley* ... Merino ewes R125,50, Angora kapaters R72,50, Boergoat kapaters R159.

Kapee var. KAAPEE.

Kapenaar var. KAAPENAAR.

kapitein var. KAPTEIN.

kapje var. KAPPIE.

kapok /kəˈpɒk, kaˈpɔk/ *n.* Also **capoc, kapock, kappoc(k).** [S. Afr. Du., ad. and transf. use of Malay *kapuq* the tree *Ceiba pentandra.*]

1. The downy, cotton-like hairs encasing the seeds of all shrubs of the genus *Eriocephalus* of the Asteraceae. Also *attrib.* Cf. *wild kapok* (see WILD sense a).

1913 C. PETTMAN *Africanderisms* 250 Cotton-wool is spoken of among the Dutch as kapok, as is also the woolly material which encloses the seed of a Karoo bush — *Eriocephalus umbellatus.* **1966** C.A. SMITH *Common Names* 278 *Kapok*, Originally derived from the Malay word 'Kapuk' for the Kapokboom. To-day applied to the material derived from various indigenous species of *Eriocephalus.* **1972** M.R. LEVYNS in *Std Encycl. of Sn Afr.* VI. 296 The woolly appearance of the fruiting heads gave rise to the name 'kapok'. **1988** M. BRANCH *Explore Cape Flora* 17 The wild rosemary or 'kapok' bush has fluffy seeds that are spread by the wind and collected by birds and mice to line their nests.

2. *comb.* **kapok bird** [tr. S. Afr. Du. *kapokvoël*], a tiny bird, *Anthroscopus minutus*, which builds nests of down-like materials; *kapokvoël*; **kapokblom** /-blɔm/ [Afk., *blom* flower], the plant *Lanaria lanata*, which has fine woolly hairs covering its stem and inflorescence; **kapokboom** /-buəm/ [Afk., *boom* tree] the large tree *Ceiba pentandra*, or any tree bearing the white, woolly hairs known as 'kapok'; **kapokbos** /-bɔs/ [Afk., *bos* bush], the shrub *Eriocephalus*; also **kapokbossie** /-bɔsi/ [see -IE]; **kapokvoël** /-fʊəl, -fuəl/, formerly also **-vogel**, [Afk., *voël* bird], *kapok bird*; also **kapokvoëltjie** /-fʊəlki, -fuəlci/, formerly **-vogeltje** [see -IE)].

1795 C.R. HOPSON tr. *C.P. Thunberg's Trav.* I. 136 The name of **Kapock-bird** was given to a very small bird, that forms its nest (which is as curious as it is beautiful, and is of the thickness of a coarse worsted stocking) from the down (*pappus eriocephali*) of the wild rosemary-tree (*wilde rosmaryn*). **1890** A. MARTIN *Home Life* 252 Even prettier and more wonderfully made is the nest of the Kapok bird, a little creature resembling a tom-tit. The material used in the construction of this small domicile is a kind of wild cotton, well named by the Boers *Kapok* (snow). **1972** M.R. LEVYNS in *Std Encycl. of Sn Afr.* VI. 296 **Kapokblom** .. is one of the many plants encouraged to flower by veld-burning ... Kapokblom is a name also applied to *Eriospermum burchellii*, better known as beesklou(tjie). *c***1808** C. VON LINNÉ *System of Natural Hist.* VIII. 429 They [*sc.* the colonists] denominate all plants that bear a down *capoc-boschje*, **capoc-boom**, down-tree or down-shrub. **1966** [see quot. at *kapokbos* below]. *c***1808** [**kapokbos**: see quot. at *kapokboom* above]. **1948** H.V. MORTON *In Search of S. Afr.* 257 There is the Kapokbos, which in seed-time sheds soft, fluffy wool. **1966** C.A. SMITH *Common Names* 278 *Kapokbossie*, A name applied to all species of *Eriocephalus* on account of the white woolly-hairy involucres which first suggested to the early colonists the 'kapok' obtained from the fruit of the Kapokboom. **1983** M. DU PLESSIS *State of Fear* 74 Could smell the *fynbos* too — .. kapokbos. **1984** *S. Afr. Panorama* July 48 Bits of woolly material from dry protea flowers and *kapokbossies* (*Eriocephalus* species). **1987** M. POLAND *Train to Doringbult* 55 At the edge of the culvert *kapokbos* flowered, the frosting of white down lying in drifts. **1988** LE ROUX & SCHELPE *Namaqualand: S. Afr. Wild Flower Guide* I. 166 *Eriocephalus ericoides, Kapokbos* ... The fruits are covered with long white hairs. There are about 26 species of Eriocephalus in Southern Africa. *c***1808** C. VON LINNÉ *System of Natural Hist.* VIII. 429 The *African Warbler.* The colonists at the Cape give the name of **capoc-vogel**, down-bird, to all birds who build their nests with the down of plants. **1822** W.J. BURCHELL *Trav.* I. 214 The Capoc vogel (cotton bird) so called on account of its curious bottle shaped nest, built of the cotton like down of certain plants; its manners and singing very much resemble those of the common wren: and a kind of finch, of a ferrugioneous brown colour, having a white collar and black head. **1883** M.A. CAREY-HOBSON *Farm in Karoo* 235 Do you see that tiny plain-looking bird? That is the 'Kappock Vogel;' it makes the cosiest nest that you can possibly imagine, and as white as the hoar frost, after which it is named. **1896** J. WOOD in *Scientific African* Mar. 76 Kapokvogel, the ingenious constructor of a wonderful nest. **1913** D. FAIRBRIDGE *Piet of Italy* 150 A silence broken only by ... the pee-eep of a *kapok-vogel* as he whirred through the bushes in his search for fragments of wool left by passing sheep on the wacht-een-beetje thorns. **1914** W.C. SCULLY *Lodges in Wilderness* 22 The 'kapok vogeltje,' no bigger than a wren, twittered at us from his seat of cunning on the outside of the simulated snowball which is his nest. **1923** HAAGNER & IVY *Sketches* 131 Those dainty little birds, called Kappoc-vogel (meaning cotton-wool bird) by the farmers, build a neatly woven nest of the downy seed of plants (in sheep districts wool is utilised). [**1933** J. JUTA *Look Out for Ostriches* 34 One day on the flats I found the beautifully made nest of one of the tit family called *Kapokvoël* in Afrikaans.] **1936** E.L. GILL *First Guide to S. Afr. Birds* 39 *Penduline Tit*, Minute Tit, kapokvoël ... This tiny bird is found .. over practically the whole country, but not as a rule in the moister districts. **1973** BEETON & DORNER in *Eng. Usage in Sn Afr.* Vol.4 No.1, 73 *Kapokvöel*, .. (*Anthoscopus minuta*) alt: Cape penduline tit.

kapparan var. KAPARRANG.

kappie /ˈkapi/ *n.* Also **capp(e)y, cappie, cappje, kapje, kappi, kappj(i)e.** [Afk., fr. Du. *kapje* little hood.]

1. A large cloth sunbonnet with a deep brim and a frill or flap protecting the neck, formerly often worn by Afrikaner women, but now used mainly on certain ceremonial occasions, as in re-enactments of events from Afrikaner history.

Similar in shape to a coal-scuttle bonnet.

1766 A. FOTHERGILL in D.H. Strutt *Clothing Fashions* (1975) 118 Two sets of lace caps and engageantes besides the handkerchiefs and palenteijns ... 6 Kapjes. **1834** A. SMITH *Diary* (1939) I. 66 Some few of the women were fashionably dressed, but most of them had on their head either small black bonnets or what are called 'cappies'. **1872** 'Z.' in *Cape Monthly Mag.* V. Oct. 230 'Cappy' we shall ever regard with respect, for its multifarious uses, for it is more than a sun-bonnet, being a sun-wind-dust-and-fly-screen all in one. **1873** F. BOYLE *To Cape for Diamonds* 327 Upon their heads is tossed the kapje (cappy), a hideous calico funnel, of which the coal-scuttle bonnet of our grandmothers was the refined and graceful model. **1883** M.A. CAREY-HOBSON *Farm in Karoo* 71 A fine comely Dutch Vrouw, with a pair of large brown eyes looking out from under a huge sun-bonnet or kapje. **1897** 'F. MACNAB' *On Veldt & Farm* 18 For the Boers he had a distinct class of goods — large cuckoo bonnets, which were worn by the Dutch 'vrows,' and are called 'kappies', though anything less like a cap could hardly be imagined. **1900** B.M. HICKS *Cape as I Found It* 140 A Hottentot girl in a clean kapje. **1901** E. HOBHOUSE *Report of Visit to Camps* 205 The 'Kapje' or sunbonnet generally used on Dutch farms. **1905** O.E.A. SCHREINER in C. Clayton *Woman's Rose* (1986) 116 His mother covered her face with the sides of her kappie and wept aloud. **1913** C. Pettman *Africanderisms* 250 *Kapje*, .. A useful article of female attire largely worn in the country; it is made to shade the face and to protect the back of the neck at the same time. It cannot be said to enhance in any way the appearance of the wearer. **1915** D. Fairbridge *Torch Bearer* 98 Little Mrs. Neethling was watering her sun-dried plants, a huge, frilled kapje of snowy whiteness on her neat head. **1936** E. Rosenthal *Old-Time Survivals* 25 The kappie is worn by some wives of farmers. Save that it is of more generous dimensions, it is the cowl preferred by the Dutch peasant women of Rembrandt or Adriaan van Ostade. Overshadowing the face in front, as was needed in a sunny climate, with wide flaps at the side and a system of tucks at the back, this glorified poke-bonnet is like those donned by the goodwives in the 'Covered Wagon' and similar American films. **1944** J. Mockford *Here Are S. Africans* 63 Usually the women wore big sunbonnets of .. fine white linen. These kappies with their hems and tucks and embroideries were their joy ... Quite apart from looks the kappie had its uses. It shaded the whole face and neck. **1958** S. Cloete *Mask* 98 They bought also some soft goods from which their wives made their clothes and kappies, or sunbonnets. **1958** [see SIS *n.*[1] sense 1]. **1965** A. Gordon-Brown *S. Afr. Heritage* II. 31 The fichu and the kappie were typical features of a Voortrekker woman's dress. The kappies, particularly, were beautifully embroidered in quaint original designs. **1968** K. McMagh *Dinner of Herbs* 81 The Griqua .. women wore the 'kappie', starched and beautifully ironed, of print or calico, based on the design of the sunbonnets of the Voortrekker women. **1972** A.A. Telford *Yesterday's Dress* 124 Probably the most distinctive item of clothing worn by Voortrekker women was the bonnet or 'kappie'. **1973** J. Meintjes *Voortrekkers* 61 A distinctive and decorative peaked bonnet called a *kappie*. **1975** D.H. Strutt *Clothing Fashions* 24 A black hood turned back at the front and descending to her shoulders in kappie-like fashion. *Ibid.* 141 A frill was added early in the 19th century that shaded the neck and was so useful that it persisted as part of the hood. Such was the birth of the kappie. **1981** *Sunday Times* 13 Sept. 7 Tannie Ralie peers out at the modern world from under an old starched Voortrekker kappie. **1982** C. Hope *Private Parts* 17 Grannie would send him to fetch the old black crêpe voortrekker 'kappie' from the stinkwood chest in her bedroom. **1986** W. Steenkamp *Blake's Woman* 91 A '*kappie*', a large cloth bonnet with wings, such as the colonial farmers' wives wore. **1989** J. Hobbs *Thoughts in Makeshift Mortuary* 203 The two older girls had to make sure that the child kept her deep-brimmed cotton kappie and her shoes and socks on at all times. **1991** O. Oberholzer in *Time* 29 July 28 'Wait' she said 'just let me put on my scarf .. and new pink kappie'. **1993** [see OSSEWA sense 2 a].

2. *rare.* Any hat or cap.

1970 C.B. Wood *Informant, Johannesburg* Put on your 'kappie' (hat or bonnet). **1983** *Frontline* Sept. 27, I can't go with a bare head – always with a doek or a kappie. I ask him why, but he says, no, it is his religion.

3. *fig. Grammar.* The circumflex used in Afrikaans to indicate a lenthening and lowering of the vowel (as in *kêrel* and *môre*). Also *fig.*

1972 *Informant, Grahamstown* Czech is full of diacritics – like kappies upside down. **1993** I. Vladislavić *Folly* 129 He formulated a question .. and was about to come out with it when Nieuwenhuizen raised his right hand to hush him, kinked his eyebrows into kappies (circumflexes) and formed a perfect O with his lips.

4. *colloq.* A member of the Kappie Kommando; also used allusively of this group or its members.

1983 *Evening Post* 2 May 6 No scrap of evidence linking the Conservative Party to the Nazified Afrikaner Weerstandsbeweging and the ultra-verkrampte Kappie-commando is overlooked by the NP-supporting newspapers .. An advertisement in .. Die Patriot: Kappies and AWB members will receive especially good service. **1988** *Cape Times* 28 Oct. (Suppl.) 2 Somebody laughed at my clothes and said I must be a *kappie vrou*.

Kappie Kommando /ˈkapi kəˌmɑːndəʊ, ‖- kɔˈmanduə/ *n. phr.* [Afk., *kappie* see prec. + *kommando* see COMMANDO.]

1. *hist.* See quot.

1939 *Star* 1 Oct. 6 Voortrekker costumes are to be worn by members of the 'Kappie Kommando,' which has been formed at Brakpan by a number of Afrikaner women with the object of honouring the Voortrekkers.

2. An ultra-conservative Afrikaner women's political organization: a member of this organization; KK. Also *attrib.* See also KAPPIE sense 4.

1981 *Cape Times* 18 Jan. 1 Kappiekommandos had received the 'call of God to save South Africa against a government that was ready to give in to the blacks'. **1981** M. Van Biljon in *Sunday Times* 19 Apr. (Mag. Sect.) 5 (*caption*) The Kappie Kommando .. declared 'war' on the Prime Minister (and others) at the opening of Parliament. **1981** *Het Suid-Western* 23 Mar., A few fortunate souls were .. treated to a rare glimpse of a kappiekommando outside the Magistrate's Court in George on Friday. **1982** *Sunday Times* 28 Feb. 1 Members of the Transvaal Head Committee .. were greeted by a demonstration of 'Kappie Kommando' women in traditional Voortrekker dress and children waving the Vierkleur flag of the Transvaal republic. **1983** *Evening Post* 2 May 3 The Prime Minister .. has sharply criticised the leader of the 'Kappie Kommando' .. for reportedly saying that blacks and whites had separate gods and would go to separate heavens. **1990** *Sunday Times* 11 Feb. 3 South African heroine Emily Hobhouse's Bloemfontein grave became the stage for a right-wing protest against reform this week. An angry group of Kappie Kommmando members tried to disrupt a memorial service for the South African War heroine as a British actress prepared to lay a wreath. **1990** D. Van Heerden in *Sunday Times* 10 June 8 Marie van Z– and her Kappie-kommando .. used to grace right-wing rallies with their appearances in full Voortrekker regalia. **1990** P. Cull in *E. Prov. Herald* 14 Sept. 6 One ally of the AWB is the Kappie Commando, led by Mrs Marie van Z–. It surfaced about 10 years ago as an all-women commando, making a dramatic entry on the the 'political stage' when five women in black Voortrekker dresses attempted to hand white carnations to then Prime Minister P W Botha at the opening of Parliament. **1990** R. Daniel in *Weekly Mail* 2 Nov. 25 And then there are irresistible instances of whimsy, such as the unlikely cameo by Vanessa Cooke as Kappiekommando mili-tante Wanda Stander. **1992** R.H. Du Pre *Making of Racial Conflict* 166 *Kappiekommando* Formed out of the AWB for the 'boervrou' to take up the fight beside her husband like the Voortrekker women of old.

kappj(i)e var. KAPPIE.

kappoc(k) var. KAPOK.

kapstylhuis /ˈkapsteɪlˌhœis, -ˌheɪs/ *n. Archit.* Also **kapsteilhuis**. Pl. **-e** /-ə/. [Afk., *kapstyl* roof-truss + *huis* house.] A temporary dwelling evolved by Cape frontiersmen, and built on an A-frame design with thatched roof extending to the ground in lieu of walls. Also part. tr. **kapstyl house**. See also *hartebeest house* (HARTEBEEST *adj.*).

1969 D. Child *Yesterday's Children* 113 The *kapsteilhuis* .. looked like a thatched roof standing directly on the ground. **1970** J. Walton in *Std Encycl. of Sn Afr.* I. 541 In the Western Province .. one type of roof house, the 'kapstylhuis', is still quite common ... In its simplest form the Puntjie kapstylhuis has no walls and is .. nothing more than the roof of a Cape house built at ground-level ... Inside, the kapstylhuis is divided by a simple partition into a bedroom and a living-room. **1971** D.F. Kokot in *Std Encycl. of Sn Afr.* IV. 101 At the Duiwenhoks mouth is situated the picturesque settlement of Puntjie, containing the largest collection of 'kapstylhuise' in the country. **1983** *S. Afr. Panorama* Apr. 21 A much earlier dwelling is the *kapstyl* house which can still be seen in the Riversdale area. Indigenous saplings of wild olive or thorn trees form the A-frame which is thatched with reed or bulrushes to ground level. **1989** *Weekend Post* 7 Oct. (Leisure) 3 On the drawing board are plans for a shepherd's *kapstylhuis*.

kaptein /kapˈteɪn/ *n. hist.* Also **capitein, kapitein, kapteen, kapteijn, kaptijn, kaptyn.** [S. Afr. Du., fr. Du. *kapitein* leader, chieftain.]

1. A title bestowed by the early Dutch colonists on the indigenous leader of a village or a people; also used as a form of address, often with a name; CAPTAIN.

1790 tr. *F. Le Vaillant's Trav.* I. 273 A crescent or gorget, formed of the same metal [*sc.* copper] upon which is engraven in large letters the word *capitein*, is put round his neck as a badge of his dignity. **1806** *Gleanings in Afr.* (anon.) 238 When they had conciliated the friendship of the chief, they acknowledged his authority, and dubbed him a *capitein*. **1824** W.J. Burchell *Trav.* II. 436, I was sometimes styled *Kaptéen* (Captain), a word well known to all the native tribes who have any connection with the Cape Colony, and understood by them in the sense of 'a chief', or 'a chieftain'. **1857** E.L. Layard in *Cape Monthly Mag.* II. July 58 A Griqua named Hans Waterboer, a nephew of the late Andries Waterboer, the well-known Griqua Kaptyn. **1896** H.A. Bryden *Tales of S. Afr.* 260 The *kaptein* .. persuaded the *vrouw* to follow his own example, and roast wild duck or a joint of springbok in a Kaffir pot. **1924** S.G. Millin *God's Step-Children* 82 This Kapteijn Adam Kok, as he chose to style himself, once ruled a great land in Africa, and, when that was taken from him, led his people, Moses-like (but across mountains, not deserts) to a new home. **1928** E.A. Walker *Hist. of S. Afr.* 135 Their tribal system was now far gone in decay; only two petty kaptijns and their clans still held land; the rest, .. were either vagrants or miserably paid .. farm-labourers. **1974** J.M. Coetzee *Dusklands* 66 Long ago I had given Klawer a medal, which he had bored a hole through and hung around his neck. It gave him authority, he said, like that of the Hottentot *kapteins* who carried staffs of authority from the Castle. **1976** R. Ross *Adam Kok's Griquas* 25 It is best to see the !Kora as those who followed a style of life which entailed nomadic cattle herding and raiding in smallish hordes, led by a, theoretically hereditary, *Kaptyn*. **1982** *Voice* 24 Jan. 4 Kaptein Mphephu's banana-and-mango authority has already .. claimed its first detention victim. **1987** B. Lau *Namibia in Jonker Afrikaner's Time* 47 The 'kaptein' as leader of the commando was able to extract tolls for the use of roads, royalties from European mining ventures, and fees for giving access to hunting velds. **1987** *Financial Mail* 22 May 6 KwaZulu is to abolish such titles as Chief, Paramount Chief, Kaptein and Hoofkaptein and replace them with Zulu terms.

2. The formerly hereditary, now elected, leader of the Rehoboth Baster people of Namibia (see REHOBOTH).

1946 L.G. Green *So Few Are Free* 198, I had to apply to the 'Kaptein' of the Rehoboths before I could gather the threads of their strange story on the spot. They guard their borders jealously against strangers. **1952** —— *Lords of Last Frontier* 204 Only one old Berg Damara was living at the hot springs when Kaptein Hermanus van Wyk led the Baster cavalcade up to the hill of pink granite where the present Rehoboth village stands. **1976** O. Levinson *Story of Namibia* 66 In June 1970 the seven-man Baster Council, an advisory body with parochial powers, informed the Rehoboth Magistrate that it no longer recognised him as its Kaptein or Chief, a position he held *ex officio*. **1984** *Daily Dispatch* 30 Oct. 13 The Rehoboth Liberation Front of Mr Hans Diergaardt, who was elected Kaptein of the Gebiet last month, took seven of the nine seats in the Volksraad.

Hence **kapteinship** *n.*

1987 B. Lau *Namibia in Jonker Afrikaner's Time* 28 Jager Afrikaner died in 1823 ... One of his younger sons, Jonker, was not prepared to cede the kapteinship to his older brother.

karamat var. KRAMAT.

karaminatze var. KARMENAADJIE.

karanteen /kærən'tiːn/ *n.* Also **karantine.** [Unkn.; perh. fr. an Indian language (see quot. 1949).]

1. Any of several species of seabream of the Sparidae. **a.** *obs.* The ZEBRA, *Diplodus cervinus hottentotus.* **b.** *Crenidens crenidens.* **c.** The STREPIE, *Sarpa salpa.*

In Smith and Heemstra's *Smiths' Sea Fishes* (1986), the name 'karanteen' is used for *Crenidens crenidens.*

1905 *Natal Mercury Pictorial* 334 (Pettman), The fish pictured to-day is a Karantine. It is a local species, and so far as I know had not been classified. **1930** C.L. BIDEN *Sea-Angling Fishes* 62 Mackerel, mullet, sardine, and bamboo-fish (Natal karanteen) are the best lures. **1949** J.L.B. SMITH *Sea Fishes* 275 *Crenidens crenidens* ... *Karanteen* ... Comes from Indian waters, extends to Durban, rarely as far as East London. **1955** C. HORNE *Fisherman's Eldorado* 210 False Bay anglers .. would not link the names karanteen or sasa with the fish they know as bamboo fish, but Natal anglers, who know this fish as karanteen and bamboo fish would probably not experience a similar difficulty. **1968** J.L.B. SMITH *High Tide* 42 One of the many queries I receive relates to live bait, commonly used for predatory fishes, notably leervis and kob. For this purpose, certain smaller fishes such as harders (mullets) and strepies (karanteen) are caught and, while still alive, usually impaled on a large hook through the muscles of the back. **1970** *Albany Mercury* 29 Jan. 15 Smaller fish — such as mullet and karanteen — making up his staple diet. **1971** *Grocott's Mail* 27 Apr. 31 Karanteen Haul. He cast his net for karanteen and really got a netful. He battled to bring his 59 karanteen onto the surf. The karanteen were much bigger than average. **1976** *E. Prov. Herald* 1 July 21 Pilchard is good bait but it is soft. So rather use a strip of freshly caught streepie (karanteen), or French Madam with a bit of sardine lashed to it with cotton or shirring elastic. **1979** SNYMAN & KLARIE *Free from Sea* 54 *Streepie*, Bamboo/Mooi Nooitjie/Karanteen. Most streepies are too small to rate as important table fishes; they must be cooked very fresh, as the flesh rapidly softens.

2. Formerly also with distinguishing epithet, designating a particular species of karanteen: **Natal -**, **silver -**, or **striped karanteen**, the STREPIE, *Sarpa salpa*; **white karanteen**, *Crenidens crenidens* (see sense 1 b above).

1930 C.L. BIDEN *Sea-Angling Fishes* 62 Mackerel, mullet, sardine and bamboo-fish (**Natal karanteen**) are the best lures. **1913** [**silver karanteen**: see STREPIE]. **1947** K.H. BARNARD *Pict. Guide to S. Afr. Fishes* 156 **Striped Karanteen** (Natal) (sarpa salpa) ... Silvery, greenish or bluish above, yellow-orange longitudinal stripes. *Ibid.* 152 **White Karanteen** (Crenidens crenidens) .. Silvery, greenish or bluish above narrow dark longitudinal stripes.

karbonatjie /ˌkarbə'nɑiki, ˌkɑː-, -ci/ *n. obsolescent.* Also **carabenatje, carbonaadtje, carbonaatje, carbonaatjie, carbonadj(i)e, carbona(i)tje, carbonardjie, carbonatjie, karbonaadjie, karbonaartjie, karbonaatje, karbonadj(i)e, karbonatj(i)e.** [S. Afr. Du., a choice piece of meat, a gift of meat after slaughtering, fr. Du. *karbonadje*, dim. form of *karbonade* grilled meat. (Although *karbonatje* is used in modern Afk., *karmenaadjie* (see KARMENAADJIE) is more common.)] Meat grilled over an open fire: **a.** A chop or other choice piece of meat; KARMENAADJIE sense 1. **b.** Small pieces of meat skewered on a stick.

1822 W.J. BURCHELL *Trav.* I. 514 My only food was 'karbonadjes' of hippopotamus, without bread or salt. **1826** A.G. BAIN *Jrnls* (1949) 149 After eating a small 'carbonatje', we again prepared to resume our journey. *a***1827** D. CARMICHAEL in W.J. Hooker *Botanical Misc.* (1831) II. 278 They .. cut it [*sc.* their meat] into steaks and broil it over the coals. The latter they call 'Carbonatjie', a term of extensive import. You have it in the various forms of beef-steak, mutton-chop, veal-cutlet, and pork-relish. **1838** J.E. ALEXANDER *Exped. into Int.* I. 197 We .. took our coffee and karbonatje (or pieces of meat roasted on twigs) in the evening. **1847** 'A BENGALI' *Notes on Cape of G.H.* 27 'Karbonatje' meat dressed in the open air on wooden spits. **1848** H. WARD *Five Yrs in Kaffirland* I. 80 A welcome meal of carbonatje. [*Note*] Meat toasted on a wooden prong before the fire, or broiled on the ashes. **1853** J. MCCABE in *Graham's Town Jrnl* 12 Mar. 3 Our kettle on the fire, and our *karbonatjes* well peppered and salted, and producing a rather savoury perfume. **1864** T. BAINES *Explor. in S.-W. Afr.* 397 A 'sticker up', or, in African parlance, a carbonadjie, had been roasted on a fork for me. **1870** in A.M.L. Robinson *Sel. Articles from Cape Monthly Mag.* (1978) 14 City epicure, .. what are your daintiest dishes compared to an exquisitely cooked carbonaatje? **1875** C.B. BISSET *Sport & War* 203 The Prince enjoyed nothing more than the cup of coffee, or bit of carabenatje which was always ready for him on these occasions. **1891** W. SELWYN *Cape Carols* 3 *Carbonaitje*, The Colonial designation of a piece of mutton roasted on a forked stick or live coals, in the absence of the more civilized gridiron. **1891** H.J. DUCKITT *Hilda's 'Where Is It?'* p.ix, Anyone who has travelled in South Africa will remember how good was the 'Sasatie' (Kabob) or 'Carbonatje' (Mutton Chop), steaming hot from the gridiron on wood coals, or two-pronged fork held against the coals. **1910** D. FAIRBRIDGE *That Which Hath Been* (1913) 53 *Karbonatjes*, grilled by the skilful hand of the Widow Tas over the embers of a wood fire. **1945** M. HONE *Sarah-Elizabeth* 37 They always stopped half-way for an alfresco meal of karbonaadjies, Boer beskuit, and coffee. **1949** L.G. GREEN *In Land of Afternoon* 127 Coffee and sausages, biscuits and ash cakes, meat for karbonaatjes (grilled chops) — such was the wagon's larder. **1958** A. JACKSON *Trader on Veld* 44 'Sosaties', a meat dish roasted on sticks, 'karbonatjes' (a sort of cutlet — quite a palatable dish). **1968** F.G. BUTLER *Cape Charade* 6 Karbonatjie? Let me see. It's mos meat you fries over a fire — not on a stove. It's very lekker.

kardoesie /ˌkar'dusi, ˌkɑː-/ *n.* Also **kadoesie, kardoesi.** [Afk., dim. form of Du. *kardoes* cartridge (fr. Fr. *cartouche* paper container), perh. reinforced in Cape speech by Malay *kardus* cardboard (box).] A small container (for food), made of paper.

1913 C. PETTMAN *Africanderisms* 252 *Kardoesi*, .. A paper bag, the paper cornet used by grocers. **1970** *Informant, Johannesburg* Kardoesie. Paper Container. **1970** F. PHILIP *Informant, Johannesburg* How excited we were when the smous paid the farm a visit ... He usually spent hours on the farm! He'd swirl his little paper cones and we'd buy tameletjies in the kardoesie for 1d. **1971** L.G. GREEN *Taste of S.-Easter* 159 The tammeletjies are set in the folded paper called kadoesies by the Malays. **1978** *Sunday Times* 21 May (Mag. Sect.) 3 Some guy .. peddling kardoesies full of food for our feathered friends. **1988** F. WILLIAMS *Cape Malay Cookbk* 68 To make rectangular paper cases, called *kadoesies*, cut out paper rectangles 7x12 cm and fold up along each side to form a casing.

karee *n.*[1] var. KARRIE *n.*[2]

karee /kə'riː, kə'rɪə, ǁka'rɪə/ *n.*[2] Also **caree, kari, karré(e), karree, karrie, kharee.** [ad. Khoikhoi *karré-, care-, kare-, caree-, karree-*, or *carru-* (in Koranna, *!gare-b*).]

1.a. i. In full ***karee tree***, occas. ***karee wood***: any of several evergreen trees of the genus *Rhus* of the Anacardiaceae, but particularly *R. lancea*, an evergreen tree with lance-shaped leaves, small berries, and gnarled trunk (resembling a willow), and less frequently *R. viminalis*; KAREEBOOM; KAREEHOUT sense b. Also *attrib.* See also *rosyntjiebos* sense (*b*) (ROSYNTJIE sense 2).

1802 W. SOMERVILLE *Narr. of E. Cape Frontier* (1979) 77 The banks are cloathed with wood, but only along the margin of the river, chiefly willow and Karee wood. **1822** W.J. BURCHELL *Trav.* I. 210 The number of Karrée trees growing along the course of the rivulet, give a more pleasing appearance to the Pass. **1834** A.G. BAIN in A. Steedman *Wanderings* (1835) II. 248 Two large Karee trees, with large pools of rain-water around them. **1846** R. MOFFAT *Missionary Labours* 2 Richly fringed with overhanging willows, towering acacias, and kharee trees and shrubs, umbrageous at all seasons of the year. **1859** W.J. BURCHELL in *Cape Monthly Mag.* V. June 359 The karree trees .. belong to the *rhus* genus, all the species of which have trifoliote leaves, and small, clustered berries of an acid, slightly turpentine flavour. **1876** E.E. FREWER tr. *Verne's Adv. in S. Afr.* 39 The karrees with dark green foliage. **1905** D.E. HUTCHINS in Flint & Gilchrist *Science in S. Afr.* 401 From a six-year-old plot of Kari on Cedar Ridge there has been a mean yearly production of timber amounting to 533 cubic feet. **1917** R. MARLOTH *Common Names* 47 *Karee*, (Karee'boom). *Rhus lancea*, but also *R. viminalis* (Nam.). Frequent along rivers and watercourses of the central and northern districts. **1936** W.B. HUMPHREYS in *Hansard* 10 Mar. 1008 The vaalbos, the wild olive, the karree are all indigenous fodder plants. **1955** L.G. GREEN *Karoo* 133 Karee trees grow in the sandy kloofs; their trunks are often used as fencing posts, while the wood makes good charcoal. **1961** PALMER & PITMAN *Trees of S. Afr.* 290 The full rounded shape of the karree and its evergreen, drooping, willow-like foliage, give a soft note to what is often otherwise a bleak landscape. **1966** E. PALMER *Plains of Camdeboo* 287 Along the river-beds across the plains are thorn trees and karees. **1971** [see DORINGBOOM]. **1987** M. POLAND *Train to Doringbult* 9 The ridge was dark, shadowed with euphorbias, with *gwarri* and *karee*. **1988** SMUTS & ALBERTS *Forgotten Highway* 26 The river banks are lined by the graceful karee tree (*Rhus viminale*) and by the true willow (*Salix*). **1991** H. HUTCHINGS in *Weekend Post* 23 Feb. (Leisure) 7 *Rhus lancea* (karee) makes an attractive shade tree.

ii. In full ***karee wood***: the timber of any of these trees; KAREEHOUT sense a.

1802 TRUTER & SOMERVILLE in G.M. Theal *Rec. of Cape Col.* (1899) IV. 403 We immediately cut a new one [*sc.* beam] of caree wood. **1861** P.B. BORCHERDS *Auto-Biog. Mem.* 110 The weapons of the Bushman tribes are the bow and arrow, assegai, and the kirrie. The bow is commonly made of Karee wood and very tough. **1872** E.J. DUNN in A.M.L. Robinson *Sel. Articles from Cape Monthly Mag.* (1978) 56 The deadly arrows tipped with puffadder poison, and the bow made of Karee wood. **1892** *The Jrnl* 9 July 1, 300 Karee Poles. **1958** L. VAN DER POST *Lost World of Kalahari* 15 In the rivers and streams he constructed traps beautifully woven out of reeds and buttressed with young karee wood or harde-kool. **1984** *S. Afr. Panorama* Feb. 36 During the ostrich feather boom thousands of karee fencing poles were cut on the banks of the Buffels River .. and sold to wealthy ostrich farmers in the Little Karoo.

b. In full ***karee bush***: **i.** The fodder shrub *Rhus ciliata; suurkaree* (see sense 2). **ii.** The shrub *Rhus viminalis.* In both senses also called *kareebos* (see sense 3).

1815 A. PLUMPTRE tr. *H. Lichtenstein's Trav. in S. Afr.* II. 223 Mimosas, .. willows, and *karree bushes.* Among the latter the colonists include several sorts of *rhus.* **1898** W.C. SCULLY *Vendetta* 177 A long, low ridge dotted with *karee* bushes and large arboreal aloes. *Ibid.* (Glossary), *Karee Bush*, A shrub: Rhus viminalis. **1974** *Evening Post* 17 Oct. 8 Massive replanting scemes with wild olives, rooiels, yellowwood, stinkwood, kareebush, [etc.]. **1992** A.B. MULLER *Informant, Graaff-Reinet* Karree bush is that low, grey bush. It smells horrible, but the sheep love to eat it. It is what gives Karoo mutton its special flavour.

2. With distinguishing epithet: **broom karee**, *Rhus erosa*; **hoenderspoorkaree** [see quot. 1966], *R. lancea*; **mountain karee**, *R. leptodictya*; **suurkaree** /'syːr-/ [Afk., *suur* sour], *R. ciliata*; **white karee**, *R. viminalis.*

1989 *Conserva* July 22 *Rhus erosa.* **Broom karee.** **1993** F. VAN RENSBURG in *Getaway* Nov. 93 Several Rhus species: the nana berry *Rhus dentata*, common taaibos *R pyroides* and broom karee *R erosa*, the last-mentioned being a very valuable tree in consolidating the soil. **1966** C.A. SMITH *Common Names* 2 In the name **hoenderspoorkaree** (*Rhus lancea L.*), .. 'hoenderspoor' refers to the .. mark on the equipment of the British forces during the Anglo-Boer War. The mark has a resemblance to the spoor of a fowl (Afrikaans *hoender*) .. , but its application to this particular species of *karee* was prompted by the resemblance to the three unequal leaflets of the plant. **1985** *S. Afr. Panorama* Feb. 33 The **mountain karees** are evergreen. **1993** *Grocott's Mail* 6 Aug. 10 Rhus leptodictya/Mountain Karee. **1913** C. PETTMAN *Africanderisms* 576 **Zuur-karee**, *Rhus tridactyla* is so called in Bechuanaland. **1968** *Farmer's Weekly* 3 Jan. 7 Grazing in good condition with olienhout, vaalbos, rosyntjiebos, suurkaree and mixed grazing. **1971** *Golden Fleece* (S. Afr. Wool Board) June (Suppl.) 8 Rhus ciliata – Suurkaree. **1991** *Sat. Star* 2 Nov. (Weekend Suppl.) 6 **White Karee** (rhus viminalis), mountain Karee (rhus leptodictya), pink flowering pom-pom tree.

3. *comb.* **karee-berry**, **kareebessie** /-ˌbesi/ [Afk., *bessie* berry], the berry of the karee tree, used to make alcoholic drinks; **kareebos** /-bɔs/ [Afk., *bos* bush], *karee bush* (see sense 1 b); **karee brandy**, a spirit distilled from karee berries; **kareedoring** /-ˌduərəŋ/ [Afk., *doring* thorn], any of a number of species of *Lycium*; **karee-mampoer** /-mamˈpuːr/ [Afk., see MAMPOER], *karee brandy*, see above.

1947 H.C. BOSMAN *Mafeking Rd* (1969) 122 It was good mampoer, made from **karee-berries** that were plucked when they were still green and full of thick sap. **1979** *Star* 17 Jan., There are some people who will try to tell you that **kareebessies** (berries) make the best *mampoer* but I, personally, would agree with Oom Daan that the best kind is the sort that is made from peaches. **1939** S. CLOETE *Watch for Dawn* 23 Thrown flesh-side upwards on acacia and **kareebos**, the crinkled skins of sheep lay drying. **1977** *Weekend Post* 23 Apr. (Suppl.) 5 Natural forks were made from the karriebos. **1947** H.C. BOSMAN *Mafeking Rd* (1969) 121 **Karee-brandy** is not as potent as the brandy you distil from moepels or maroelas. **1968** L.G. GREEN *Full Many Glorious Morning* 216 Thick bush along the banks, thorn bush and mimosa, **kareedoring** and willows. **1983** J.A. BROWN *White Locusts* 201 A jug of **karee-mampoer** was going the rounds.

kareeboom /kəˈriːˌbʊəm/ *n.* [S. Afr. Du., *karee* (see KAREE *n.*²) + *boom* tree.] KAREE *n.*² sense 1 a i.

1835 A. SMITH *Diary* (1940) II. 110 *Rus lancea*, or karreeboom. **a1858** J. GOLDSWAIN *Chron.* (1949) II. 97 One of my sons said that he beleved that (there were) under th(e) creayboumb. **1907** T.R. SIM *Forests & Forest Flora* 5 The higher ground there is devoid of tree vegetation except occasional Karee-boom (Rhus lancea). **1910** J. ANGOVE *In Early Days* 157 The kareeboom is a kind of willow, but the wood, which is red, is harder and tougher. **1942** S. CLOETE *Hill of Doves* 21 A place embowered by trees: the wild bush trees .. thorns, karree booms, willows and wild olives. **1947** H.C. BOSMAN *Mafeking Rd* (1969) 121 The berries of the karee-boom (Oom Schalk Lourens said) .. may not make the best kind of mampoer that there is. **1951** N.L. KING *Tree-Planting* 70 *Rhus lancea (Kareeboom)*: A small tree with graceful drooping foliage. **1961** PALMER & PITMAN *Trees of S. Afr.* 290 The kareeboom is a drought and frost resistant tree, and grown on chalky, or sandy soil, as well as in deep rich earth. **1971** L.G. GREEN *Taste of S.-Easter* 54 Local craftsmen seem to have found tables difficult though the reddish kareeboom was selected for a few rare specimens.

kareehout /kəˈrɪəˌhəʊt/ [S. Afr. Du., *karee* (see KAREE *n.*²) + *hout* wood.] **a.** KAREE *n.*² sense 1 a ii. **b.** KAREE *n.*² sense 1 a i.

1795 C.R. HOPSON tr. *C.P. Thunberg's Trav.* II. 171 Karré hout (*Rhus*) is a kind of wood which the Hottentots in this part of the country used for making bows. **1810** J. MACKRILL Diary. 89 The Hottentot Bow, karree hout, is a Sumach – Rhus. **1822** W.J. BURCHELL *Trav.* I. 179 Very large bushes of Karree-hout, which in growth and foliage, have a great resemblance to our common willows, grow along the banks. **1835** A. SMITH *Diary* (1940) II. 110 They eat no roots but only berries from the kareehout when they are ripe. **1961** PALMER & PITMAN *Trees of S. Afr.* 291 In 1811 Burchell when passing through Karro Port north-east of Ceres, camped under two large bushy trees of 'karreehout' near a small stream of water. **1971** BARAITSER & OBHOLZER *Cape Country Furn.* 75 They are made of kareehout, the wood of the bastard willow, and were inlaid with klapperbos, the wood of a small indigenous shrub. **1974** J.M. COETZEE *Dusklands* 128 He saw that the banks, clothed in trees (*zwartebast, karreehout*), might furnish timber for all the wants of colonization.

karem var. KEREM.

kari var. KAREE *n.*²

karie *n.*¹ var. KARRIE *n.*²

karie *n.*² var. KIERIE.

karinkeltjie /kəˈrəŋkəlki, ˌka-, -ci/ *n. Music.* Also **karinkelkie**. [Afk.; see quot. 1985.] The extension of the last note of a musical phrase by a precentor, used to assist the singers he leads in achieving the correct intonation; a song in which this technique is used.

1981 *S. Afr. Digest* 30 Oct. 12 The only Eastern element is found in the contribution of the cantors, or precentors, who lead the song in *'karinkeltjies'* (glosses), to be followed by the choir on the European scale. [**1985** A. DAVIDS in *Papers Presented at 5th Symposium on Ethnomusicology* (I.L.A.M.) 37 The Arabic influence of *Cape Malay Music* is evident from the *Karinka*, i.e. the dragging out of the end notes of a line or verse of a song in fluctuating intonation .. a very distinctive characteristic in the rendering of the *Athaan*, the Islamic call for prayer, to create musical effect.] **1989** C. CHAPMAN in *Edgars Club* Apr. 45 The roots of Cape music, according to Kramer can be traced to various influences. Firstly, European folk songs, or *Nederlands liedjies*, preserved by the Malay choirs, sung in Dutch and still sung today. Secondly, the Eastern influenced *karinkelkies*, brought in by the slaves from Malaysia. **1989** *Personality* 26 June 77 Cape Town .. is where teeming sprawling District Six gave rise to a new kind of South African culture and music. It had its roots in the beating of the *goema* drum on the slave ships sailing to Table Bay, the *Nederlandse liedjies*, the unique body movements of Hottentots and Bushmen, Coon Carnivals, *karinkelkies* and travelling minstrels.

‖**karkoer** /karˈkur/ *n.* [Afk., prob. fr. Khoikhoi, fr. San *|kɔrogən*, *|kɔroka* cucumber, *kakuŋ* pumpkin; or see quot. 1934.] TSAMMA.

1934 C.P. SWART Supplement to Pettman. 86 *Karkoer*, (According to Dr. S.P.E. Boshoff in 'Volk en Taal van Suid-Afrika' p. 382, the word is derived from Bantu cakulo, pronounced karkoer by the Hottentots from whom the Dutch colonists first heard it). A species of bitter melon or wild watermelon. **1937** C.R. PRANCE *Tante Rebella's Saga* 158 Only one watermelon was on sale ... Rube seized the prize, cut it greedily at once – and found that it was only a 'karkoer', the 'Kafir pumpkin' which grows as a weed amongst the mealie-crops. **1971** *Informant, Grahamstown* The karkoer grows wild and is very bitter – looks like watermelon ... Nothing eats them.

karmenaadjie /ˌkarməˈnɑɪki, ˌkɑː-, -ci/ *n.* Also **karaminatze**, **karmenaatjie**, **karminaatjie**. [Afk., earlier S. Afr. Du., ad. Du. *karbonaadje* collop of cooked meat.]

1. KARBONATJIE sense a.

1835 A. STEEDMAN *Wanderings* I. 92 The Hottentots .. made a cheerful fire, around which we partook of our Karaminatze. **1933** W. MACDONALD *Romance of Golden Rand* 201 Travellers would congregate around the camp fire where the tasty 'karmenaadjie' were fizzling merrily. [*Note*] Chops fried on a gridiron, on an open fire. **1970** C. KINSLEY *Informant, Koegasbrug (N. Cape)* Karmenaatjie. Rib marinated in vinegar & spices, with sliced onion added. **1971** L.G. GREEN *Taste of S.-Easter* 94 Sosaties and karmenaadjies must be placed on a gridiron on the open veld.

2. *transf.* A present of meat, given by one who has slaughtered an animal.

1970 I. PALMER *Informant, Grahamstown* It is customary in the North Eastern Cape and the Free State for the farmers to slaughter an ox or a pig in winter. The custom is then to give neighbours and friends a gift of meat which is called karminaatjie. **1977** FUGARD & DEVENISH *Guest* 17 Tant Corrie: Doctor! Doctor! (*Oom Doors halts the Doctor's progress to the car.*) A Karmenaadjie. We slaughtered yesterday. **1981** *Meat Board Focus* May, South Africans are well-known for their generosity in handing out .. 'karmenaadjies' ... A 'karmenaadjie' simply means any small choice piece of meat from any part of the carcase offered as a gift. In the olden days it was customary to present a 'karmenaadjie' to the dominee .. or receiver of revenue. **1984** *Informant, George* Some karmenaadjie! He's given me the whole leg.

karnemelk var. KARRINGMELK.

Karoo /kəˈruː/ *n.* Also **Karroo**; formerly **Caro(o)**, **Carouw**, **Carro(o)**, **Carrow**, **Kar(r)o**, and with small initial. [ad. Khoikhoi *karo-*, *karro*, *garo* hard, dry, or *!gar-b* desert.

The spelling *Karoo* may be seen as a compromise between the Afk. form *Karo* and a common Eng. form, *Karroo*.]

1.a. The vast, arid inland plateau extending from Langeberg in the south to Cradock, Pearston, Somerset East and Venterstad in the east and northwards into the Orange Free State; any tract of Karoo-like desert land. Also *attrib.*

The original Karoo probably lay entirely within the former Cape Province. Its boundaries are determined by the dominance of xerophytic vegetation and are in a constant movement outwards as desert encroaches on farming land.

1776 F. MASSON in *Phil. Trans. of Royal Soc.* LXVI. 287 On each side of this river lies an extraordinary track of land, which in the Hottentot language is called Carro. **1786** G. FORSTER tr. *A. Sparrman's Voy. to Cape of G.H.* II. 125 These large birds were .. chiefly to be found in such tracts of country as partook of the properties of the *carrow*, and produced succulent plants. **1790** W. PATERSON *Narr. of Four Journeys* 44 We proceeded through what the Dutch call Karo, the soil of which is a soft friable loam, chiefly producing succulent plants, and a few dwarf shrubs. **1790** tr. *F. Le Vaillant's Trav.* II. 357 The dry plains of Carouw begin in this place. **1822** W.J. BURCHELL *Trav.* I. 81 The hottest parts of the colony are to be found in those barren plains which are distinguished by the general appellation of Karro. **a1823** J. EWART *Jrnl* (1970) 34 Betwixt the Zwarteberg and Nieuveldt or last great chain, extend the immense arid deserts called by the Hottentot name of Karroo. **1833** *S. Afr. Almanac & Dir.* 167 *Namaqualand* .. includes a great extent of Caroo-plain. [**1841** B. SHAW *Memorials* 68 On leaving the banks of the Elephant River, we commenced our journey in the Karree or arid desert.] **1900** J.B. ATKINS *Relief of Ladysmith* 43 The kopjes and the great flat sandy karroo have a strain of deformity in their nature. **1920** K.M. JEFFREYS tr. *Memorandum of Commissary J.A. de Mist* 195 A series of barren deserts and karoos, on which not a morsel of food can be found for man or beast. **1948** H.V. MORTON *In Search of S. Afr.* 246 The Karoo – a Hottentot word which means 'dry place' – is an arid plateau lower than the plains of the Free State, lying within the Cape Province. **1971** *S. Afr. Panorama* Sept. 27 The Karoo, the semi-arid but healthy plateau that covers nearly one-third of South Africa's interior, and which supports the world's second-largest sheep population. **1990** *Philatelic Services Bulletin* 1 Nov., The Khoi word *karoo* means thirsty land, but many million years ago the Karoo was a lush jungle in which awesome mammal-like reptiles roamed. Their fossiled remains .. earned the Karoo a special place in palaeontology. **1993** *Getaway* Nov. 13 (*letter*) Those trucks pound through the Karoo town night and day.

b. With distinguishing epithet designating a region or sub-division of the Karoo: **Bokkeveld Karoo**, see BOKKEVELD; **Great Karoo** [tr. Afk. *groot* great], the main plateau north of the Swartberg; **Klein Karoo** /ˈkleɪn/ [Afk. *klein* little] and tr. **Little Karoo**, the southern portion of the Karoo, lying mainly between the Langeberg and the Swartberg; also *attrib.*

1790 W. PATERSON *Narr. of Four Journeys* 45 The people informed us of the danger of crossing the **Great Karo**, not only from its being a desert country, but also from parties of the Boshmen Hottentots, who were at war with the Dutch. **1809** R. COLLINS in G.M. Theal *Rec. of Cape Col.* (1900) VII. 119 Whoever reads the accounts that have been published of travels through the colony of the Cape, must be impressed with ideas of the Great Karoo. **1812** A. PLUMPTRE tr. *H. Lichtenstein's Trav. in Sn Afr.* (1928) I. 112 The great Karroo, as it is called, a parched and arid plain, stretching out to such an extent that the vast hills by which it is terminated are almost lost in the distance. **1828** T. PRINGLE *Ephemerides* 89 The Great Karroo is an uninhabitable wilderness, about 300 miles long by 80 broad, forming an elevated plain, or tract of table land, between the great ridges of the *Zwartbergen* .. and *Sneeubergen*. **1836** *Penny Cyclopaedia* VI. 257 The Great Karroo is one of the most barren and desolate spots imaginable. **1847** J. BARROW *Reflect.* 147 At the head of the Hex River valley, we were to take leave of every human habitation for at least sixteen days, the usual time required to cross the dreary and barren desert known by the name of the Great karroo, on which nothing .. is to be had except ostrich eggs and antelopes. **1900** H.C. HILLEGAS *Oom Paul's People* 4 Farther inland is the Great Karroo, a desert of sombre renown. **1955** L.G. GREEN *Karoo* 11 It must have been a drought year when the fist Hottentot tribes migrating southwards gazed on the Great Karoo for the first time. They named these plains Garob, meaning dry, unfruitful, uninhabited. **1985** J. DEACON in *S. Afr. Panorama* Sept. 30 Thus did the Reverend .. christen this oasis [*sc.* Bethesda] in the wilderness of South Africa's Great Karoo. **1971** *S. Western Herald* 14 Aug. 5 An American bird lover is one up on ostrich farmers, nowadays confined to the **Klein Karoo** only. **1987** *E. Prov. Herald* 6 May 9 The neglect of the Klein Karoo .. could play a major part in the result. **1844** J. BACKHOUSE *Narr. of Visit* 112 This country is called the **Little Karroo** or Kanneland. **1880** [see KANNA *n.*[2] sense 2]. **1948** H.V. MORTON *In Search of S. Afr.* 117 The best mutton in South Africa is raised on the small moisture-holding vygies of the Little Karoo and the Great Karoo. **1951** *Off. Yr Bk of Union 1949* (Union Office of Census & Statistics) 331 The little Karroo, stretching from the first mountain range to the Zwartberg, has a greater altitude, more severe climate and an average rainfall of 8 to 12 inches. **1975** J.P.H. ACOCKS *Veld Types* 61 Justice cannot .. be done to the Little Karoo flora. **1992** T. VAN RENSBURG in *S. Afr. Panorama* Mar.-Apr. 8 The agricultural potential of the area is low, with the exception of the Little Karoo which has become famous for its ostrich farms.

2. In full ***Karoo bush*** *noncount*, or with pl. **-es**: (any of) numerous species of scrub-like bushes occurring in the Karoo, esp. those of the genera *Chrysocoma* and *Pentzia*; also called SWEET KAROO. See also *bergganzie* (BERG sense 1 b ii), BITTER KAROO, SKAAPBOS.

Some species are toxic, semi-toxic, or noxious weeds; others are invaluable as grazing.

1835 A. STEEDMAN *Wanderings* I. 98 A dry, sunburnt plain; not a single vestige of vegetation was anywhere to be seen, except the *karroo* bush, almost as brown and barren as the ground on which it grew. **1843** *Cape of G.H. Almanac & Annual Register* 387 This grazing is principally heath known by the name of Karroo. **1852** M.B. HUDSON *S. Afr. Frontier Life* 236 The Karroo is a heathery shrub, and affords very good grazing for cattle, and stock that are used to it, but it must not be compared to grass. **1863** J.S. DOBIE *S. Afr. Jrnl* (1945) 120 The Karoo bush is about the size of heather, growing more or less thickly together, and is of a dark dusky green. **1872** *The Jrnl* 9 July 1 The Veld consists of the much-sought-after Karoo, Vygebosch, Granaat, Brakbosch. **1896** R. WALLACE *Farming Indust. of Cape Col.* 80 Most of the valuable Karoo bushes give off a sweet aromatic perfume when bruised between the fingers, and the flavour appears to be agreeable to the palates of herbivorous animals. **1908** F.C. SLATER *Sunburnt South* 72 Wandering airs of night, laden with pungent odours of Karroo-bush, began to whisper with tremulous solemnity over the desolate wilderness. **1910** [see DRAAIBOSSIE]. **1916** *Farmer's Weekly* 20 Dec. 1468 Thousands of morgen of veld, which consists of the best grass and karroo, with water for stock in all parts. **1920** E.H.L. SCHWARZ *Thirstland Redemption* 17 Most botanists maintain that the Karroo bushes are of such a peculiar type, that they must have taken untold ages to acquire their adaptive modifications. **1926** M. NATHAN *S. Afr. from Within* 208 The characteristic vegetation of the Karoo is the Karoo bush, a drought-resisting shrub, which, though uninviting in appearance, is wonderfully nutritious to sheep. **1938** F.C. SLATER *Trek* 51 On both sides of the Orange 'mixed-karroo,' Grass and karroo-bush, close together grew. But farther North 'karroo' was counted out. **1949** J. MOCKFORD *Golden Land* 216 The veld maintained its strength because the game trekked with the growth and decline of grass and the Karoo bush. **1958** A. JACKSON *Trader on Veld* 37 These animals .. thrived on the brown, lifeless karroo when every other animal starved. **1972** *Grocott's Mail* 3 Mar. 4 The veld consists of mixed Karroo and Sweet Grass. **1973** [see BITTERBOSSIE]. **1985** *S. Afr. Panorama* Oct. 41 Hardy Karoo bushes, so numerous that Afrikaners changed the Dutch saying 'money like water,' to 'money like bushes', are *made* for grazing. **1990** *Weekend Post* 13 Oct. 7 Autumn rains which promote Karoo bush growth for small stock did not materialise and they are approaching summer with depleted veld and reserves.

3. *comb.* and Special Comb. **Karoo ash** *colloq.*, burnt kraal manure used as a fertilizer; **Karoo beds** *Geology*, geological strata comprised of sandstone and volcanic matter, and believed to date from the Triassic period; **Karoo caterpillar**, the larva of the Karoo moth, *Loxostege frustalis* of the Pyralidae, which destroys Karoo grazing veld; also *attrib.*; see also RUSPER; **Karoo chat**, the small bird *Cercomela schlegelii*, predominantly grey in colour; **Karoo coal** *colloq.*, *Free State coal* (see FREE STATE *adj. phr.* sense 2); **Karoo field** [calque formed on S. Afr. Du. *Karo veld*], *Karoo veld*, see below; **Karoo ground** *Geology*, a yellow soil containing sand, clay, and particles of iron; **Karoo korhaan**, see KORHAAN sense 1 b; **Karoo oyster** *colloq.*, Karoo lamb's liver wrapped in fat; **Karoo quick grass** [see QUICK], the grass *Cynodon incompletus* of the Poaceae; **Karoo syndrome** *Pathology*, see quot.; **Karoo series, - System** *Geology*, the (structure and formation of the) geological strata characteristic of the Karoo but extending beyond it; also in *ellipt.* form **Karoo**, sometimes used *attrib.* to allude to the era in which this system was formed; see also DWYKA, ECCA; **Karoo thorn**, the SWEET THORN, *Acacia karroo*; **Karoo veld** /-felt/ [Afk. *veld* field, land], parched land typical of the Karoo, or the drought-resistant vegetation such land supports.

1925 *Off. Yrbk of Union 1910–24* (Union Office of Census & Statistics) 458 *Potassic* fertilizers are imported in the shape of slats of potash, and there is also a considerable production in the Union, burnt kraal manure ('**Karoo ash**') being largely utilized in this connection. **1937** *Handbk for Farmers* (Dept of Agric. & Forestry) 623 *Karroo Ash* is the name commonly given to the ash obtained by burning kraal manure on the sheep farms of the drier areas, notably the Karroo. **1876** *Encycl. Brit.* V. 42 The '**Karoo beds**' .. are believed from the abundance of fossil wood and fresh-water shells to be of lacustrine origin. **1886** H.C. LEWIS in *Papers on Diamond* (1897) 7 The diamond-bearing pipes [at Kimberley] penetrate strata of Triassic age which are known as the Karoo beds. **1896** [see ECCA]. **1961** *Webster's Third Internat. Dict.* I. 1233 **Karroo caterpillar**, .. the larva of a pyralidid moth (*Loxostege frustralis*) that seriously damages fodder in sheep-farming regions of southern Africa. **1973** *Cape Times* 30 June 11 There have been good rains this year, and the veld was fairly good although much devasted by the Karoo caterpillar. **1974** *E. Prov. Herald* 21 Dec., There was a bad drought and a karroo caterpillar plague. **1975** *Ibid.* 21 Mar. 4 Mr Pretorius said the Karoo caterpillar did extensive damage by defoliating Karoo bush. **1986** SCHOLTZ & HOLM *Insects* (1985) 417 Several ichneumonids .. are parasitic on the karoo caterpillar, *Loxostege frustralis* (Pyralidae). **1990** A. CRAIG in *Birding in S. Afr.* Vol.41 No.4, 123 Although he was little concerned with African birds, the **Karoo Chat** *Cercomela schlegelii* bears his name. **1929** J.G. VAN ALPHEN *Jan Venter* 16 'It's no joke starting a fire with only dry dung for fuel.' '**Karoo coal** we call it down at the Cape.' **1786** G. FORSTER tr. *A. Sparrman's Voy. to Cape of G.H.* I. 246 The **carrow-fields** .. are horridly parched up and arid. **1801** TRUTER & SOMERVILLE in G.M. Theal *Rec. of Cape Col.* (1899) IV. 417 The cattle were extrememly fatigued from the journey over hills and vales and sandy **Karoo grounds**. **1812** A. PLUMPTRE tr. *H. Lichtenstein's Trav. in Sn Afr.* (1928) 122 The soil throughout [the Karroo] is a sand mixed with clay or argilacious earth, and contains every where more or less of particles of iron, from which all yellow tinted soil throughout the colony has obtained the name Karroo ground. **1824** W.J. BURCHELL *Trav.* II. 44 Such land is called Karro ground by the Cape farmers. **1836** *Penny Cyclopaedia* VI. 257 The soil is a sand mixed with clay containing particles of iron, which gives it a yellowish colour: all soil of a similar colour in other parts of the Colony is called by the name Karroo ground. **1987** *Handbill, Connock's Butchery (Grahamstown)* Smoked chickens, '**Karoo oysters**' — liver rolled in caul. **1989** *Motorist* Aug. 5 For lunch, order what the locals jokingly call 'Karoo oysters', and you will be served the most succulent lamb you have ever tasted. **1991** G.E. GIBBS RUSSELL et al. *Grasses of Sn Afr.* 97 *Cynodon incompletus* **Karroo quick grass**. **1974** *Dorland's Illust. Medical Dict.* 1522 **Karroo s[yndrome]**, a condition observed in youth among Afrikaners in the Karroo region, consisting of high fever, alimentary tract disturbance, and tenderness in the lymph glands of the neck. *c*1936 *S. & E. Afr. Yr Bk & Guide* 134 The **Karroo series** covers the southern Karroo and a patch south of Worcester. **1945** [see MOGGEL]. **1905** H. KYNASTON in Flint & Gilchrist *Science in S. Afr.* 294 In the western, and particularly in its northern extension, the **Karroo System** diminishes very considerably in thickness. **1965** HAMILTON & COOKE *Geology for S. Afr. Students* 248 The rocks are undoubtedly pre-Karroo and largely terrestrial in character. **1972** D.F. KOKOT in *Std Encycl. of Sn Afr.* VI. 306 A large part of the Karoo .. is coterminous with what is known geologically as the Karoo System, which .. extends much farther northwards and covers a large part of Southern Africa. **1991** F.G. BUTLER *Local Habitation* 270 Andrew Geddes Bain, .. a pioneer geologist whose description of the Karoo system of rocks remains virtually intact. **1992** *Afr. Wildlife* Vol.46 No.6, 278 A sill of Karoo dolerite intersecting the Mzintlava River. **1822** W.J. BURCHELL *Trav.* I. 83 Cords made of the bark of the **Karro Thorn-tree**. *Ibid.* 386 A small spring very pleasantly situated amidst large trees of Karro-thorn. **1824** *Ibid.* II. 241 The principal shrubs about Ongeluks Fountain, are the Tarchorianthus, the Hookthorn, the Karrothorn. **1906** F. BLERSCH *Handbk of Agric.* 258 The *doornboom*, karroo thorn, or mimosa (*Acacia horrida*), become injurious by their getting into and spoiling wool and hair. **1960** U. KRIGE (tr. J. van Melle) in D. Wright *S. Afr. Stories* 133 The sweet scent of the Karoo-thorn flowers filled the air as you passed by. **1966** C.A. SMITH *Common Names* 282 *Karoo thorn, Acacia karroo*. **1973** [see BITTER BUSH]. **1795** C.R. HOPSON tr. *C.P. Thunberg's Trav.* II. 103 The plants as well herbs as bushes, stand very thin in the **carrow-veld**. **1837** 'N. POLSON' *Subaltern's Sick Leave* 152 Those reared in the 'karoo veld,' or parched lands destitute of all vegetation but a species of bush, eat and thrive on the bush. **1906** F. BLERSCH *Handbk of Agric.* 256 In the dry regions the bush veld, or *karroo veld* prevails, grasses rarely finding sufficient moisture to grow in such localities. **1910** A.B. LAMONT *Rural Reader* 252 Karoo veld is the name applied to the veld in the dry parts of Cape Colony, where grass cannot get enough moisture, but where certain bushes flourish. **1937** *Handbk for Farmers* (Dept of Agric. & Forestry) 386 The perennial bushes form the staple, and at times indeed the only, means of subsistence in the Karroo veld. **1958** A. JACKSON *Trader on Veld* 38 The Karroo veld had no trees to provide us with firewood. **1961** H.F. SAMPSON *White-Faced Huts* 19 On the scrub of the Karrooveld two Europeans .. lay asleep under a little mimosa tree, fanned by a strong berg-wind. **1975** J.P.H. ACOCKS *Veld Types* 60 The vegetation today is sparse Karoo veld .. with stunted shrubs, especially in rocky (as distinct from stony) places. **1988** P.E. RAPER tr. *R.J. Gordon's Cape Trav. 1777–86* I. 60 Travelling for a full hour through a fairly level 'caroveld' as it is called by the farmers.

Hence **Karoo, Karroid** *adjs*, of or pertaining to the Karoo; of Karoo-like structure, climate, vegetation, etc.

1786 G. FORSTER tr. *A. Sparrman's Voy. to Cape of G.H.* I. 197 In certain northern districts, such as *Roggeveld*, or *Bokkeveld* .. the land is, as it is called, carrow, or dry and parched. *c***1936** *S. & E. Afr. Yr Bk & Guide* 134 The Karroid Plateau covers the northern Karroo and reaches Kimberley. **1937** *Handbk for Farmers* (Dept of Agric. & Forestry) 384 A knowledge of the vegetation of the locality is essential, particularly so in parts like the Karroo and semi-karroo areas. **1951** N.L. KING *Tree-Planting* 66 *Carissa haematocarpa* (*ferox*) (*Num-num*), Very similar to *C. bispinosa*. Occurs in karroid scrub in eastern Cape. **1975** J.P.H. ACOCKS *Veld Types* 59 Karroid broken veld. **1978** *Sunday Times* 5 Mar. (Mag. Sect.) 3 The architecture is superb, pure early Karoo. **1978** *Ibid.* 12 Nov. 5 A taphouse at Robertson, where the food and style will be more Karoo than Boland. **1982** *S. Afr. Panorama* July 15 Interesting natural Karroid veld.

kaross /kəˈrɒs/ *n.* Forms: α. **cross, kross**; β. **carass, caross(e), carross, corrass, corrose, karo(o)s, kaross(e), karraos, karro(s)s, kerose.** [S. Afr. Du., fr. Khoikhoi *caro-s, karo-s, cro-s, kro-s* skin blanket, perh. dim. form of *kho-b* skin.]

1. A blanket of softened skins, used both as a cloak and (now more usually) as a covering for a bed or floor; INGUBO sense 1; KOBO; KOMBERS sense 1; VELKOMBERS. Also *fig.*

α. [**1731** G. MEDLEY tr. *P. Kolb's Present State of Cape of G.H.* I. 187 Their *Krosses* (as the *Hottentots* term 'em) or Mantles cover the Trunks of their Bodies ... They wear 'em the Year round; in Winter turning the hairy side inward; in Summer turning it outward. They lie upon 'em at Nights. And, when they die, they are tied up and interr'd in 'em.] **1776** F. MASSON in *Phil. Trans. of Royal Soc.* LXVI. 295 These Hottentots were all cloathed in *crosses*, or mantles, made of the hides of oxen, which they dress in a particular manner, making them as pliant as a piece of cloth: they wore the hairy side outwards. **1786** G. FORSTER tr. *A. Sparrman's Voy. to Cape of G.H.* II. 187 The Hottentots do not burden themselves with a great many changes of these cloaks or *krosses*, (as they call them in broken Dutch). **1790** tr. *F. Le Vaillant's Trav.* I. 386, I awoke, and went to visit my Gonaquas, who were all sunk in profound sleep, huddled together under their krosses. **1790** W. PATERSON *Narr. of Four Journeys* 115 We found .. a few skins of Seals, which are used for garments, and called Kerose. **1810** G. BARRINGTON *Acct of Voy.* 231 Their [*sc.* the Greater Nimiquas'] garment called a kross, except being longer, differs not at all in shape from the Hottentot cloak. **1839** F. MARRYAT *Phantom Ship* x, They wore not their sheepskin krosses. *a***1858** J. GOLDSWAIN *Chron.* (1949) I. 112 The Kaffer saw that he was nearley over taken run into a rownd bush and thrue his cross onto a bush.

β. **1786** G. FORSTER tr. *A. Sparrman's Voy. to Cape of G.H.* I. 188 The women have a long peak to their karosses. **1822** S. HECKFORD *Lady Trader in Tvl* 295 The dark and dirty room was furnished with two or three chairs, a little table, and a common bedstead, on which were thrown a mattress, some gaudy blankets, and a 'caross', or large mat made of skins curiously stitched together, with the hair left on. *a***1827** D. CARMICHAEL in W.J. Hooker *Botanical Misc.* (1831) II. 287 The mantle, or kaross, is usually made of calves' skins stitched together, and pared round the skirts into the shape of a blanket. **1836** C.L. STRETCH Journal. 26 Mar., After the war he sent his thanks to Mr. Bonabe for hiding them under '*his* Karraos'. **1841** B. SHAW *Memorials* 298 He was sleeping a few yards from his master, in the usual mode of his nation, wrapped in his sheep-skin carosse, with his face to the ground. **1852** A.W. COLE *Cape & Kafirs* 176 The proper dress of a Kafir chief is a Kaross of leopard skin. **1874** A.O. WOOD Letter. 26 July, You can buy nice Corroses for 15/- up here, for 6 sheep skins they will give you one. **1884** B. ADAMS *Narr.* (1941) 68 On leaving, Mr Webster made me a present of a very handsome kaross — a number of skins sewn together. **1892** W.L. DISTANT *Naturalist in Tvl* 12 A buckskin kaross kept them warm or provided the substitute for a carpet, whilst the same animals provided them with covering for furniture. **1905** O.E.A. SCHREINER in C. Clayton *Woman's Rose* (1986) 114 His mother was making him shirts and his grandmother was having a *kaross* of jackals' skin made that he might take it with him to Europe where it was so cold. **1927** C.G. BOTHA *Social Life in Cape Col.* 93 Instead of woollen blankets fur karosses, made from the skins of wild animals, were used and feather beds in place of hair mattresses. **1941** A. GORDON-BROWN *Narr. of Private Buck Adams* 68 *Kaross*, a skin blanket. Practically the only article of clothing worn by the raw native. **1955** V.M. FITZROY *Dark Bright Land* 16 A coverlid of deerskin called a carosse. **1978** *Sunday Times* 2 Apr. 14 The donors of cured skins and karosses to the former Minister of Bantu Administration .. must have been .. relieved to read his .. denial of claims .. that he had been asked to sell them on behalf of the former Minister. **1988** P. EDGAR in *Personality* 25 July 69 If it were not for these two men and myself, those cows would have ended up as karosses for some dusky maidens in Xhosaland by now.

2. *obs.* With distinguishing epithets designating smaller skins used to cover the pubic area, as **fore -, hind -, kull -, kut kaross**. Cf. APRON sense 1.

α. [**1731** G. MEDLEY tr. *P. Kolb's Present State of Cape of G.H.* I. 188 The *Verenda* .. they cover with what they call a Kull krosse, a square Piece of the Skin of a Wild Beast, generally of a Wild Cat; tied at Top, the hairy Side outward, by Two Strings, one at each Corner, going round the Waste. *Ibid.* 191 They cover the *Pudenda* with what they call a Kut-Krosse. This is always of Sheep-Skin, stript of the Wool or Hair; and is at least Three Times bigger than the *Kull Krosse* of the Men.]

β. **1822** W.J. BURCHELL *Trav.* I. 395 These aprons, which they distinguish into fore-kaross and hind-kaross, and which are tied just over the hips, are their only permanent clothing.

Hence **karossed** *adj.*, dressed in a kaross.

1992 L. VAN HOVEN in *S. Afr. Panorama* Nov.-Dec. 66 (*caption*) Karossed figures.

karpenter var. CARPENTER.

karper /ˈkɑːpə, ˈkarpə(r)/ *n. Obs.* exc. *hist.* Also **carper**. [S. Afr. Du., transf. use of Du. *karper* carp.] Either of two species of freshwater fish: **1.** *Cape kurper*, see KURPER sense 1. **2.** *Barbus burchellii* of the Cyprinidae; also called YELLOWFISH (sense a).

1823 W.W. BIRD *State of Cape of G.H.* 160 Few fish are found in the rivers, on the Cape side of the mountains, except small fish, called Karpers and springers, which are excellent, and eels. **1893** H.A. BRYDEN *Gun & Camera* 461 The karper or carp (Rooivlerk karper, red-finned carp, of the Dutch colonists; *Barbus* [*Pseudobarbatus*] *Burchellii* of Dr. Andrew Smith, first identified, as its name implies, by the traveller Burchell, *circa* 1812) is a handsome little fish, not unlike a perch in shape. **1896** H.A. BRYDEN *Tales of S. Afr.* 18 The pouch contained seven fresh fish — six smallish and carp-like, well known to the Boers as karpers. **1913** C. PETTMAN *Africanderisms* 253 *Karper, Spirobranchus capensis* is known by this name among the Dutch. **1971** L.G. GREEN *Taste of S.-Easter* 185 Joris van Spilbergen caught 'carpers of excellent flavour' at a river mouth in Table Bay early in the seventeenth century.

karraos var. KAROSS.

karré, karrée, karree *n.*[1] varr. KAREE *n.*[2]

karree *n.*[2] var. KARRIE *n.*[2]

karre-milk var. KARRINGMELK.

karreweijer var. KARWEIER.

karri var. KARRIE *n.*[2]

karrie *n.*[1] var. KIERIE.

karrie *n.*[2] var. KAREE *n.*[2]

karrie /ˈkari, ˈkæri/ *n.*[3] Also **karee, karie, karree, karri, kiri(e), kirrey, korree.** [Afk., ad. Khoikhoi ‖*kare*, ‖*kari*, the name of a root or plant (found in Nama *!kari-b* honey-beer).]

1.a. A fermented drink made of honey or prickly-pear syrup to which powder from the root of the *karriemoer* (see sense 2) is added as a leaven; cf. HONEY-BEER. **b.** Any of several plants whose roots are so used; the powder made from these roots. Also *attrib.*

1835 J.W.D. MOODIE *Ten Yrs* I. 229 A particular plant .. grows in some of the most arid situations of the interior of the colony ... This plant, as well as the drink which is made by its means, is called 'Karee'. **1866** —— *Soldier & Settler* 144 This plant as well as the intoxicating drink made from it, is called '*Karee*'. **1911** *E. London Dispatch* 20 Dec. 5 (Pettman), Out of the honey, young bees and bee bread which we acquired our men brewed a really good wine, which they termed *kirrey*. It was quite as strong as porter, and only took a few hours to make; the only addition besides water, being a whitish powder. **1913** C. PETTMAN *Africanderisms* 253 *Karee* or *Kiri*, A drink prepared by the coloured people from honey or prickly pear syrup, to which a small quantity of the dried and powdered root of a certain plant (concerning which they are very secretive, but which appears to be *Mesembryanthemum stellatum, Mill*) is added, and the whole fermented. *Ibid.* [see sense 2]. **1971** L.G. GREEN *Taste of S.-Easter* 164 This so-called bee wine is made to this day in certain parts of the Cape ... The modern recipe includes sugar and yeast and the potent drink is known as 'Korree' or 'Karie', pronounced curry. **1992** *Weekend Post* 17 Oct. 7 Honeybeer which is produced from karrie — the root powder of a flower only found in the Kouga and Tsitsikamma areas. *Ibid.* 24 Oct. (Leisure) 1 The more karrie (or root powder), the bigger the kick.

2. *comb.* **karrie-making** (objective); **karriemoer** /ˈkariˌmuːr/ [Afk., *moer* leaven], any of several plants of the genera *Trichodiadema, Euphorbia*, and *Anacampseros*, whose roots are powdered and used as yeast in the making of karrie; the powdered roots of these plants; MOER *n.*[1] sense 1 b. See also GLI.

1973 S. STANDER (tr. M. Versveld) in *A.P. Brink's Brandy in S. Afr.* 172 Strange that we make so little use of honey-beer, or karrie ... Most farmers don't talk too much about **karrie-making**, but .. if you want to bake a good 'mosbolletjie' you have to keep a bottle of karrie-lees on your shelf. **1913** C. PETTMAN *Africanderisms* 321 *Moer wortel*, .. The root of *Anacampseros ustulata, E. Mey.* employed in making 'karree' and '**karree moer**'. **1917** R. MARLOTH *Common Names* 49 *Kirie'moer, Mesembrianthemum stellatum* .. , used as an addition to kaffir beer. But in Griqualand West .. the natives apply a similar name to *Euphorbia decussata* and use it for the same purpose. **1925** *E. Prov. Herald* 27 Aug., The sample produced was 'karriemoer' with water. It was not exactly kaffir beer. **1930** M. RAUBENHEIMER *Tested S. Afr. Recipes* 55 Take a quantity of prickly pear and peel them, taking only the inside fruit .. Procure a teaspoon of 'Karee Mc..:,' and while the sediment is still warm but not hot, add the 'Moer' to it. **1949** L.G. GREEN *In Land of Afternoon* 161 Much wild honey is gathered because honey means honey beer. Coloured people in the Piketberg Sandveld .. use kareemoer, a powdered root, as yeast. **1966** C.A. SMITH *Common Names* 280 *Kareemoer, Trichodiadema stellatum* ... The tuber was used by the Hottentots in beer-making, the product obtained being a deliriant and intoxicant, with an earlier stimulating action.

||**karringmelk** /ˈkarəŋmelk, -mɛlk/ *n.* Also **karnemelk**. [Afk., fr. Du. *karnemelk*.] Buttermilk. Also part. tr. **karre-milk**.

1921 H.J. MANDELBROTE tr. *O.F. Mentzel's Descr. of Cape of G.H.* I. 112 Such things as omelettes, pancakes, a kerri-kerri prepared with fish, jams and preserves, some fruits like guavas, and 'Karre-milk' (buttermilk) were allowed to be given to the patients. [**1958** L.G. GREEN *S. Afr. Beachcomber* 116 You must have karnemelkwater, a disturbed sea coloured like buttermilk, to catch this fish. Even then half of them break away from the hook.] **1982** L. SAMPSON in *Sunday Times* 5 Sept. (Mag. Sect.) 29 Time sprawls, suspended in a between-train vacuum. A cut grapefruit and a carton of *karringmelk* are on the table in front of me. Some of the *karringmelk* has spilt.

Karro(o) var. KAROO.

karro(s)s var. KAROSS.

kartel var. KATEL.

kartonkel var. KATONKEL.

karveyer, karveying varr. KURVEYOR, KURVEYING.

||**karwats** /karˈvats/ *n.* [Afk., horsewhip, riding whip.] A short-handled riding whip; a quirt.

1913 C. PETTMAN *Africanderisms* 254 *Karwats*, (D. *karbats*, a scourge of leather; Pol. *karbacz*; Turkish *kyrbatsj*, a whip of rhinoceros hide.) A whip made of one piece of hide throughout. **1955** L.G. GREEN *Karoo* 141 When the shepherd cracks his old *karwats*, his short whip, the flock falls into line and wheels and bunches and obeys the order. **1980** *Cape Times* 16 July 1 The quirt is still being used experimentally in riot control ... A police statement referred to the instrument as a 'karwats' and in a subsequent note said this should be translated into a 'quirt'.

||**karweier** /ka(r)ˈveɪə(r)/ *n. hist.* Also **karreweijer**. [Afk., *karwei* to transport (transf. use of the Du. sense, to do odd jobs) + agential suffix *-er*; the meaning has perh. been influenced by *kar* cart.] TRANSPORT-RIDER.

1887 A. WILMOT *Geog. of S. Afr.* 230 A gentleman Karreweijer. **1959** L.G. GREEN *These Wonders* 149 A karweier of the early days, an English transport rider nicknamed John Bull.

karweyer, karweying varr. KURVEYOR, KURVEYING.

kas /kas/ *n.* Pl. **kaste** /ˈkastə/. [Afk., fr. Du. *kast* cupboard, or perh. *kas* box or chest.]

1. A cupboard. See also KOSKAS, MUURKAS.

1971 L.G. GREEN *Taste of S.-Easter* 46 The original Dutch kas was a sea-chest; and scores of them, if not hundreds, must have been carried on shore when Van Riebeeck landed. **1971** BARAITSER & OBHOLZER *Cape Country Furn.* 267 Most of the Riversdale kaste are so constructed that they can be dismantled — a necessity for easy transport. **1977** F.G. BUTLER *Karoo Morning* 81 The oubaas had told him No, he'd better maar choose a suit from the kas. **1984** S. GRAY *Three Plays* 132 Hendrik .. I found your kappie for you .. It was in the kas, the one with the flowers on. **1987** J. KENCH *Cottage Furn.* 41 As with other kinds of furniture, yellowwood and stinkwood versions of cupboards were made, including the imposing Cape 'kaste' and 'muurkaste'. **1993** A. VISSER in *House & Leisure* Nov. 72 Two porcelain vases from Martha's Vineyard perched on a Sandveld kas.

2. *fig. Army slang.* Detention barracks.

1971 C. BRITZ *Informant, Grahamstown* Don't get caught by the M.P.s wearing my army tackies in town. You'll get thrown in the kas, boy.

kat /kat/ *n.* Also with initial capital. [Du., raised battlement, siege defence works.]

1. The fortification wall which divides the CASTLE into an inner and outer court. Also *attrib.*

1946 H.C. BOSMAN in L. Abrahams *Cask of Jerepigo* (1972) 89 An interesting feature of the Castle is the kat, or curtain, a cross-wall about 2 yards in length and 40 feet in height and 10 feet thick, which was erected by the original builders as an afterthought, in order to divide the courtyard into two halves for additional safety. **1955** A. DELIUS *Young Trav.* 79 The great square in the interior of the Castle was .. cut in two by a *kat* — a big dividing block. **1965** A. GORDON-BROWN *S. Afr. Heritage* I. 9 Modern photograph of the 'Kat' balcony — a masterpiece of the architect Thibault and the early Cape sculptor, Anton Anreith. **1971** C. DE BOSDARI *Cape Dutch Houses & Farms* 48 The space within the walls [of the Castle] was divided in 1691 into two courtyards by a 'Kat' or wall on which cannon could be mounted — whence the name of the Balcony later built onto it. **1974** *S. Afr. Panorama* July 18 Guests awaited the president in 'The Kat', where a buffet supper was served. **1979** *Ibid.* July 8 In 1691 the courtyard within the Castle was divided in two by the 'Kat', a crosswall ... The most commanding feature of the first courtyard is the beautiful Kat balcony at the entrance to the Council Chamber.

2. *transf.* The ornate wooden balcony at the centre of the kat fortification wall in the CASTLE.

1969 I. VAUGHAN *Last of Sunlit Yrs* 50 De Kat, the place where the Burghers, two centuries ago, had pasted their placaats and read their announcements. **1971** [see sense 1]. **1973** BEETON & DORNER in *Eng. Usage in Sn Afr.* Vol.4 No.2, 73 *Kat, the*, .. Porch forming part of the Castle in Cape Town, the oldest fortification in S. Afr. **1990** *Light Years* Vol.1 No.3, 9 (*caption*) One of the most well-known features of the Castle, De Kat.

katdoring /ˈkatdʊərəŋ, -duərəŋ/ *n.* Also **katdo(o)rn**. [Afk. (earlier S. Afr. Du. *katdoorn*), *kat* cat + *doring* thorn, alluding to the shape of the thorns.] Any of several species of plants with hooked thorns.

1. The CAT-THORN (sense 2 a), *Scutia myrtina*.

1868 L. PAPPE *Florae Capensis* 12 *Scutia Commersoni*, .. (*Katdoorn*) ... Habit of growth usually shrubby, branches armed with hooked thorns. **1972** [see CAT-THORN sense 2 a].

2. The CAT-THORN (sense 3), *Acacia caffra*; the wood of this tree.

1868 J. CHAPMAN *Trav.* I. 24 The forest generally consists of various kinds of mimosas, acacia, and other thorny trees, such as the 'wagt-een-beetje' (wait-a-bit), .. 'kat-doorn,' *c* **1968** F.C. METROWICH *Frontier Flames* 240 She was buried in the bush on the farm and a stake of Katdoring was planted to mark her resting place. This took root and for many years it was the only sign to distinguish the place where she lay. **1973** *Evening Post* 27 Jan. 2 A peg of katdoring had been driven into the ground at the time of the burial to mark the spot as was the custom of the Xhosas. The peg had grown into a large tree at the head of the grave of the famous prophetess. **1983** T. BARON in *Frontline* June 29 The Umfolosi has more than its fair share of the various species that abound — they have the .. wag-'n-bietjie, .. katdoring, .. just to name a few.

3. CAT-THORN sense 1.

1913 C. PETTMAN *Africanderisms* 254 *Kat doorn*, .. *Asparagus retrofractus*. The Wild asparagus is so called because its thorns are hooked like the claws of a cat.

katel /ˈkɑːt(ə)l/ *n. Obs.* exc. *hist.* Also **cadel, cardell, carte(l)l, cartle, catel, kaatle, kadel, kartel**. [Afk., prob. ad. Malay *katil* bed. (Acc. to the *OED* this word was orig. S. Indian, Tamil *kattil* bedstead, and was adopted and diffused by the Portuguese as *catel, catle, catre* trundle bed.)] A light bedstead consisting of a wooden frame supporting interwoven leather thongs, particularly as formerly used on an ox-wagon. Also *attrib.* Cf. KATIL.

1849 N.J. MERRIMAN *Cape Jrnls* (1957) 75 He .. gave me a mattress and quilt stretched upon a 'catel' or wagon bed frame. **1852** F.P. FLEMING *Kaffraria* 47 The 'cardell' .. a frame of wood with 'riems;' or thin thongs, of ox-hide interlaced across it, and in size, is a few inches smaller than the inside of the waggon. **1864** T. BAINES *Explor. in S.-W. Afr.* 22, I accepted .. an invitation .. to avail myself of the cadel, or beds slung in the wagon. *a***1878** J. MONTGOMERY *Reminisc.* (1981) 85 My father-in-law, .. as was the custom, gave his daughter her katel (bedstead), feather bed, pillows, .. etc. **1882** J. NIXON *Among Boers* 171 Two seats ran down the side, and a cartel, or framework of wood and hide, on which our mattress was placed, fitted between them. **1890** A. MARTIN *Home Life* 70 For night journeys no Pullman car ever offered more luxurious sleeping accommodation than does the *kartel*, a large strong framework of wood, as wide as a double-bed, suspended inside the tent of the waggon. **1896** H.A. BRYDEN *In Praise of Boers* 257 Jacoba went to her *kartel* bed and dreamt of the alert, brisk Engelschmann. **1906** H. RIDER HAGGARD *Benita* 63 One morning Benita, who slept upon the cartel or hide-strung bed in the waggon, .. thrust aside the curtain and seated herself upon the voorkisse, or driving box. **1919** M. GREENLEES tr. *O.F. Mentzel's Life at Cape in Mid-18th C.* 26 He has also to buy himself a bed. This consists of a wooden frame covered by a seal-skin; it is called a 'catel'. **1926** P.W. LAIDLER *Tavern of Ocean* 74 The internal arrangements of the hospital were peculiar. Acute cases lay on two rows of cartel beds stretching down the centre of the upper wing. **1928** H. VEDDER in *Native Tribes of S.W. Afr.* 125 The furniture consists of the so-called 'Katel', a wooden frame with a network of leather straps connecting the four sides, used as a bed. **1934** B.I. BUCHANAN *Pioneer Days* 30 The kartel, a frame fitted snugly across the wagon, and laced with strips of ox-hide, spread with a mattress, furnished a comfortable bed at night. **1948** H.V. MORTON *In Search of S. Afr.* 83 The African trek wagon was really a caravan in which people lived as they travelled ... The katel, or bed, .. was a wooden frame on which rawhide thongs were interwoven. It was carried under the wagon-tilt by day and brought out at night. **1958** A. JACKSON *Trader on Veld* 44 The 'katels' (bedsteads) were wooden frames spanned by 'riempies' carrying mattresses filled with kapok. **1967** E.M. SLATTER *My Leaves Are Green* 115 The wagon was fitted with a 'kartel' — a frame laced with oxhide strips which took the place of a bed. **1975** *Sunday Times* 12 Oct. (Mag. Sect.) 10 The old Nama *katel* or bedstead .. carved from tree trunks and strung with skin straps no longer exists, for today people want only the White man's kind of bed. **1987** G. VINEY *Col. Houses* 62 The whole place was crammed with beds — two in the front right-hand room, three and a *kadel* in the one opposite, .. two and two *kadels* and a crib in the *klijnekamer*. **1989** B. GODBOLD Autobiography. 1 A full tented wagon, rather like the wagons of the Voortrekkers, but without the riempie-strung kartel, was my first real home.

katil /ˈkɑːtɪl/ *n.* [See prec.] In the Cape Malay community: a bier used for the dead.

1937 *Argus* in I.D. Du Plessis *Cape Malays* 30 A bench, which is known as a *katil*, is then brought into the room. Underneath this cane bench is placed a big bath, and there the corpse is laid with its face towards the ancient Mecca, known to the *Muslims* as Quiblah. **1949** E. HELLMANN *Handbk on Race Rel.* 595 The body is placed upon a bier, an imam chanting, and the bier (katil) is turned towards Mecca. **1953** DU PLESSIS & LÜCKHOFF *Malay Quarter* 39 The body is .. transferred to the stretcher or *katil*. **1985** *S. Afr. Panorama* Jan. 24 The body is bound up and placed on a katil so that it faces towards Mecca.

katjie var. KAARTJIE.

katjiepiering /ˌkaɪkiˈpirəŋ, ˌkaɪci-/ *n.* Also **catch-peeren, catjepiring, katjepeerang, katjepeering, kæzschebyring, katjepi(e)ring**. [Afk., *katjie* kitten + *piering* saucer (ad. Malay *katja-piring, kachapiring* lit. 'glass saucer': the gardenia).] Any of several species of *Gardenia* with sweetly-scented flowers, including *G. jasminoides, G. thunbergia*, and *G. florida*; the wood of these shrubs. See also *Cape jasmine* (CAPE sense 2 a).

1731 G. MEDLEY tr. *P. Kolb's Present State of Cape of G.H.* II. There is a Shrub at the *Cape*, transplanted from

Madagascar, which is call'd, by the Natives of that Island, *Kæzschebyring*; and such is the Name 'tis known by among the *Cape-Europeans*. **1795** C.R. HOPSON tr. *C.P. Thunberg's Trav.* II. 111 Wilde Catjepiring (*Gardenia Thunbergia*) is a hard and strong kind of wood, and on this account used for clubs. **1798** S.H. WILCOCKE tr. *J.S. Stavorinus's Voy. to E. Indies 1768–71* II. 79 Among the various sorts of timber, earlier unknown, or extremely rare in Europe, the following abound here, .. wilde catjepiering (*gardenia thunbergia*), a strong kind of wood used for clubs. **1809** J. MACKRILL Diary. 74 Gardenia florida, produces that elegant & sweet flower called by the Dutch (Catchpeeren) they have a yellow & a white, the latter the sweetest. [**1837** ECKLON & ZEYHER *Enumeratio Plantarum Africae* 360 2290 *Gardenia florida* ... Ubique in totius Coloniae hortis, et ex India aut China versimiliter advecta Nov. Dec. — Incolis europaeis: katjepiering.] **1869** W.G. ATHERSTONE in R. Noble *Cape & its People* 373 The wagons .. stand on a bed of wild flowers .. fragrant clematis — the 'traveller's joy', — vying in sweetness with the wild 'katjepeering'. **1910** D. FAIRBRIDGE *That Which Hath Been* (1913) 269 Friends bring .. the richest purple violets, the sweetest katjepierings, until the house is heavy with the perfume of flowers. **1916** S. BLACK in S. Gray *Three Plays* (1984) 241 Here, come with your flowers into the chief's office ... He wants to order a big bunch of special katjepeerangs. **1949** *Cape Argus* 3 Dec. 18 Gardenias (Katjiepering), flowering, 4s. 6d. each. **1951** N.L. KING *Tree-Planting* 68 *Gardenia thunbergia* (*Katjiepiering*), A small bushy tree. Occurs in moist forests in eastern Cape and Natal. Bears strongly scented, snow-white flowers. Needs shade and is best suited to moist localities where frosts are not severe. **1966** C.A. SMITH *Common Names* 284 *Katjiepiering*, .. A shrub up to 5 ft high, cultivated for its sweet-scented flowers which turn brownish if touched and bruised. **1972** *Std Encycl. of Sn Afr.* V. 120 Gardenia. Katjiepiering. Genus of evergreen shrubs .. which bear sweetly scented white flowers.

katonkel /kəˈtɔŋk(ə)l, kəˈtɒŋk(ə)l/ *n.* Also **kartonkel, katonker, katunka, katunker.** [Afk., ad. Malay *kentangkai* or *ikan tĕnggiri* Spanish mackerel, fr. *ikan* fish + *tĕnggiri* mackerel; see also quot. 1930.] Any of several species of marine fish (but esp. *Scomberomorus commerson*). **1.** The PAMPELMOESIE, *Stromateus fiatola*. **2.** Any of several fish of the Scombridae: **a.** The SKIPJACK (sense 2), *Katsuwonis pelamis*. **b.** *Sarda sarda*. **c.** *Scomberomorus commerson*. **d.** *S. plurilineatus*; SNOEK sense 3. **e.** *Acanthocybium solandri*.

In Smith and Heemstra's *Smiths' Sea Fishes* (1986), the name 'Atlantic bonito' is used for *Sarda sarda*; 'king mackerel' for *S. commerson*; 'queen mackerel' for *S. plurilineatus*; and 'wahoo' for *Acanthocybium solandri*.

1853 L. PAPPE *Synopsis of Edible Fishes* 26 Stromateus Capensis Mihi. N. Sp. (*Katunker*) ... A good table-fish, but not common. It is caught with the hook and the net, chiefly east of Table Bay. **1893** [see PAMPELMOESIE]. **1930** C.L. BIDEN *Sea-Angling Fishes* 144 The word 'Katonkel' has been corrupted from what was known by the Port Elizabeth Malays as 'katunker' or 'katonker' which originated from the original Malay word 'kentangkai', a kind of sea-fish. **1945** H. GERBER *Fish Fare* 49 *Katonkel* which looks somewhat like mackerel or albacore has rather firm meat like the latter. It is a nice pickling fish. **1955** C. HORNE *Fisherman's Eldorado* 8 The first few casts were sufficient to prove casual observation wrong, for yellowtail .. had been replaced by the Western Province katonkel, always to be distinguished from the Eastern Province katonkel which is the barracuda of Natal and a much bigger fish than the katonkel found in False Bay. **1951** [see SANCORD]. **1959** *Cape Times* 18 Feb. 2 This is the first time in eight years that so many barracuda (katonkels) have been caught at one time. **1964** J. BENNETT *Mr Fisherman* (1967) 18 'These katonkel. They're what they call barracuda up in Natal?' 'Yes. But he's not really a barracuda. Proper barracuda's a different fish. Don't get them so far south.' **1971** *Argus* 14 May 14 Huge concentrations of yellowtail and katonkel stretching from Olifantsbos to Anvil Rock over the week-end provided spearfishermen with the best diving of the year. **1977** *E. Prov. Herald* 10 Feb. 17 At one time our only recognised game fish in Eastern Cape waters was the katonkel. **1979** SNYMAN & KLARIE *Free from Sea* 52 Spanish Mackerel, Barracuda/Katonkel /Natal Snoek/Wahoo. Members of the large tuna family, these exciting game-fish have rich, tasty flesh. **1987** *E. Prov. Herald* 28 Mar. 6 The Natal barracouda is not a member of the barracouda family. The name katonkel is a local name given by the old Cape Malay to this fish as it resembled a fish they knew .. in their home country. Confusion increases when it is realised that the name katonkel is also used in the Western Cape for the bonito. **1990** M. HOLMES in *Ibid.* 14 Sept. 18 Colin .. relaxes next to a 51lb katonkel while the diminutive Joy is dwarfed by poenskop of 58lb and 52lb.

Kat River /ˈkæt rɪvə, ˈkat -/ *n. phr.* Also **Katriva.** [The name of a river in the Balfour district of the Eastern Cape.]
1. In full ***Kat River tobacco***: a cheap pipe tobacco.

1910 J. RUNCIE *Idylls by Two Oceans* 48 He .. pulled out his pipe, whose bowl was bitten all round its brim by the burning particles of the cheap Kat River tobacco he smoked. *Ibid.* 177 He groped within his frayed pocket for a pinch of Kat River to fill a briar pipe charred down to half its depth. *Ibid.* 179 He went over to a tobacconist's and bought threepence worth of Kat River. **1989** V. OWEN in *Grocott's Mail* 20 Jan. 11 We would .. repair to the shop and buy .. what we knew as 'kartrief', which is what the natives called Kat River tobacco, which we would then smoke in a homemade pipe of a cut off bamboo branch with a hole bored in. **1991** M. PRETORIUS in *Weekend Post* 9 Feb. (Leisure) 5 Xhosa women .. bought rolled tobacco which they chewed or 'Katriva' (Kat River) which they smoked in long-stemmed pipes.

2. *comb.* **Kat River disease** *Pathology*, *Kat River wilt* (see below); **Kat River Levy** *hist.*, during the 19th century, a small auxiliary force composed of the Khoikhoi inhabitants of the Kat River area; **Kat River Settlement**, a settlement of formerly landless Khoikhoi people, established in the vicinity of the Kat River, Balfour district, from 1829 until 1853 (when the land was redistributed to white settlers); **Kat River wilt** *Pathology*, KROMNEK. Also *attrib.*

1957 K.M. SMITH *Textbk Plant Virus Diseases* 572 Tomato Spotted Wilt Virus ... Synonyms: T.S.W. Virus; Kromnek or **Kat River Disease** Virus. [**1846 Kat River Levy**: J. HARE in *Imp. Blue Bks* Command Paper 786–1847, 114 Captain Sutton to leave Eland's post with the Kat river people, proceeding via the Chumie post to Blockdrift, to take post in the seminary.] **1871** J. MCKAY *Reminisc.* 81 It would appear that the Hottentot Levies — for we had such auxiliaries .. — who were termed the 'Kat-river Levy', were composed of a few hundred men. *Ibid.* 82 The Kat-river Levy was a broken body of Bastards and Hottentots. **1835** J. WEIR in J. Green *Kat River Settlement in 1851* (1853) 64 He had told Hintza and the Tambookies that, if they came into the Colony, they must come below the Chumie Station, meaning that they were not to come through the **Kat River Settlement**. **1846** H. POTTINGER in *Ibid.* (1853) 34 On my arrival in Graham's Town .. it was reported to me .. that the Burghers of the Kat River Settlement were in a state of great insubordination. **1853** J. GREEN *Ibid.* p.vii, I became a resident of the Kat River Settlement in Nov., 1849, and remained at Balfour till the 22nd January, 1850. **1932** *Grocott's Mail* 2 Apr. 4 'Kromnek' or **Kat River Wilt** of tobacco is a disease which is not known to occur anywhere in the world outside the Cape Province. **1933** E.S. MOORE in *Sci. Bulletin Dept Agric.* No.123, 1 The disease known locally as 'Kromnek' or 'Kat River Wilt' is by far the most serious of the diseases of tobacco in the Stockenström division.

kattekruid /ˈkatəkreɪt, -krœit/ *n.* Pl. **-kruie** /-ə/, **-kruiden.** [Afk., transf. use of Du. *kattekruid* (*katte* cat's + *kruid* herb), the plant *Nepeta cataria*; see quot. 1913.] The aromatic medicinal herb *Ballota africana* of the Lamiaceae.

1913 C. PETTMAN *Africanderisms* 256 *Katte kruiden*, .. In South Africa this designation has been transferred to *Ballota Africana, Benth* .. , not because cats are supposed to be partial to it, but because it is covered with soft hairs. Decoctions of its leaves are used for coughs, colds, and asthma. **1917** R. MARLOTH *Common Names* 47 *Katte'kruid, Ballota africana*. Used as a tea and an emollient. Also *Stachys hispida*. The 'Kattekruid' of Holland is *Nepta Cataria*. **1966** C.A. SMITH *Common Names* 285 *Kattekruie*, An aromatic hairy herb ... Decoctions of the plant have a bitter taste and were formerly employed in pulmonary troubles and particularly in asthmatic affections. **1975** W. STEENKAMP *Land of Thirst King* 140 A herb called 'kattekruid' (cat's weed) was popular among those who suffered from rheumatic joints. The kattekruid's furry leaves would be warmed in a cloth bag and laid on the affected joint, the value obviously being in the heat-retaining qualities. **1975** *Argus* 17 Sept. 18 Kattekruie (cat's herbs or carming) has a sharp fragrance, pale mauve flowers and round leaves which we used to use in our doll's house as herbs.

kattie, katty varr. CATTY.

katunka, katunker varr. KATONKEL.

Kaussas pl. form of XHOSA.

kay *n. colloq.* [Representing the pronunciation of the letter *k*, abbrev. of *kilometre*.] K sense 2. Also *attrib.*

1983 M.A. BIRKIN in *Sunday Times* 13 Mar. (Mag. Sect.) 3 We can't even shorten the kilometre properly. The abbreviation is supposed to be km, in which case where do the young, in particular, get the expression: 'I was only doing 90 kays, man'? **1989** *Grocott's Mail* 31 Jan. 8 Increase in training kays for the Settlers [marathon]. **1990** M. SMIT in *Sunday Times* 2 Dec. 27 In a moment of madness during the night's endeavours, someone suggested a five-kay run to Frith on the golf course at 7am the next morning. **1991** *Pretoria News* 11 Apr. 9 Wouldn't it be nice to have so much money that it's a major hassle to drive a couple of kays to pick up a measly 15 grand? **1991** *Style* May 95 They stop at the first miserable, mosquito-infested bosveld ditch they can find when, instead, just a few kays further on they could porzie off at one of the biggest rivers in the country.

kaya /ˈkaɪə/ *n.* Also **ik(h)aya, kaia(h), k(ha)ya, k(h)ia, ki(y)a, kja, ky-ah.** Pl. **-s**, occas. ‖**amakhaya.** [ad. Xhosa and Zulu *ikhaya* (pl. *amakhaya*) home, dwelling, place to which one belongs.]
1.a. *obsolescent.* A traditional African hut. Also *attrib.*

1855 G.H. MASON *Life with Zulus* 224 After a short pause, he exclaimed, 'Kia, bos; kia!' (A hut, master; a hut!) and led us over the hill to a large Caffre craal. **1909** K. FAIRBRIDGE *Veld Verse* 85 Where the high-veld breaks to valley .. Stands a kaia looking Northward through the mountains to the plain. **1910** J. BUCHAN *Prester John* (1961) 257 Inanda's Kraal was a cluster of kyas and rondavels. **1911** *E. London Dispatch* 24 Nov. (Pettman), A native living in a kraal at Lydenberg quarrelled with another native, whom he accused of having fired his *kya* ... The first native .. set about two dozen newly made *kyas* alight and fled to the adjacent hills. **1919** R.Y. STORMBERG *With Love from Gwenno* 91 Together we trek for my future home, which is a glorified mud hut or stone kia, or something of that sort, I'm told. **1956** N. GORDIMER *Six Feet of Country* 38 Two white-washed servant's rooms (some white people called them kyas, .. wanting to keep in their minds the now vanished mud huts which the word indicated).

b. The separate (usu. single-roomed) living quarters for domestic workers on an employer's property. **c.** *transf.* Any small dwelling.

Often *derog.*, alluding to the basic nature of the rooms in which domestic workers are frequently accommodated.

1935 L.G. GREEN *Great Afr. Mysteries* (1937) 192 Each house has a separate *kya* in the back garden for the servant. 1936 P.M. CLARK *Autobiog. of Old Drifter* 72 Often of a Saturday night I would join these three fellows in their *kia* for a game of cards. 1941 *George & Knysna Herald* 20 Aug. 2 Required to Rent Furnished Bungalow with Crockery and Linen, with Boy's Kias. 1948 O. WALKER *Kaffirs Are Lively* 29 *Kja* means literally 'home', and [is] always used of the single rooms or sheds at the bottom of a garden where domestic servants live. 1949 A. KEPPEL-JONES *When Smuts Goes* 185 This apparently spontaneous movement .. had been anticipated and much discussed in kitchen and *kaya*. 1950 D. REED *Somewhere S. of Suez* 269 He lives in a little *kia*, or house, apart from his employer's, who might rest tranquil if he slept in servant's quarters within, but now worries often about undesirable guests in the kia. 1956 T. HUDDLESTONE *Naught for your Comfort* 92 They [*sc.* African servants] must live in 'Kayas' – single rooms of varying quality built away from the house. 1968 COLE & FLAHERTY *House of Bondage* 78 (*caption*) Living in her 'kaya' out back, servant must be on call six days out of seven and seven nights out of seven. 1971 *Guardian* (U.K.) 29 Sept. 19 The houseboys' Kias (usually one small room) at the bottom of the garden. 1984 *Fair Lady* 14 Nov. 166 There was lights on, steady in the big house, flickering in the *kayas*. 1989 E. BREGIN *Kayaboeties* 2 It was a pretty ugly place, even for a kaya; dark and small and stuffy – like a jail, I thought – with a concrete floor and a tiny window and walls so patched with damp and mildew that there was hardly any paint left on them. 1990 *Style* June 120 She .. has followed an almost entirely African theme for the interior of the house, which she describes, with a gust of laughter, as 'the modern *kaia* style, perhaps, and no doubt an interior decorator's nightmare!' 1990 H.P. TOFFOLI in *Ibid.* Nov. 51 Hall is now a practising sculptor ... He works from home in what he refers to as a kaya at the back of the house. 1992 *S. Afr. Panorama* Nov.-Dec. 52 Between 60 000 and 100 000 fortune hunters' kayas and tin shacks stood wall to wall for several square kilometres.

‖**2.**

a. Home. See also *hamba kaya* (HAMBA sense 3).

1947 F.C. SLATER *Sel. Poems* 79 I'm thinking of my kaya, On the slopes of Amatola. [*Note*] My home. 1951 L.G. GREEN *Grow Lovely* 156 The plague frightened Cape Town and thousands of native labourers shouted 'Hamba Kya' and clamoured for passes so that they could return to their homes. 1976 R. HAYDEN in *Sunday Times* 2 May (Mag. Sect.) 3 (*letter*) No matter how many years Bantu spend in urban areas, on returning to their ikayas they revert to the old ways. 1976 *Drum* June 2 'Verdomde Mandela and his gang can have the whole eiland as their khaya until this side of eternity,' is the message that rings from Pretoria. 1982 *Staffrider* Vol.4 No.4, 2 Kofifi was onse town. Never mind alles; hy was onse 'kaya'. Life was really adventurous. 1985 K. MKHIZE in *Pace* Aug. 46 She might get married and leave home and that would have meant a total collapse of what I knew as ikhaya.

b. In *pl.* form **amakhaya**: 'People from home'. Also *attrib.* See also HOME-BOY.

1980 J. COCK *Maids & Madams* 61 At work she lives, usually, in a detached room at the end of her employer's garden or adjoining the garage. This situation .. prevents the formation of 'amakhaya' clusters.

kaydaar var. KY'DAAR.

KB *n.* [Initial letters of *Kaffir beer*, used as a euphemism to avoid the offensive word KAFFIR.] TSHWALA. Also *attrib.*

1962 K.M.C. MOTSISI in M. Mutloatse *Casey & Co.* (1978) 47 He .. made a compromise – to drink only K.B., including the other homemade concoctions which are calculated to make you Nagasaky only after putting as little as a jam tin's amount under your belt. 1965 *Drum* Apr. 26 Boys have solved the day-to-day financial problems of the parents by buying gallons of KB from the council's beer hall depots, and selling it to guzzlers. *a*1968 D.C. THEMBA in E. Patel *World of Can Themba* (1985) 123 Simon is a man of sober habits. He has his occasional draught of KB at friendly parties on weekends. 1969 [see SCALE]. 1970 *Post* 10 May 13 We were given samp, porridge, and a pale suggestion of meat. They forgot the KB which would have nicely rounded off these Bantustan games. 1970 H. KUPER *Witch in my Heart* 70 'KB' is the so-called 'Kaffir beer', the name given to the African beer made from sprouted millet and corn. 1975 S.S. SEPAMLA in *New Classic* No.1, 9 For the K.B. drinkers in the lounge, there were wooden benches leaning on the walls.

k'daar var. KY'DAAR.

keerboom var. KEURBOOM.

keeri(e) var. KIERIE.

kee-vekie var. KIEWIETJIE.

keevit, -wit varr. KIEWIET.

kehatenhout var. KAJATENHOUT.

kehla /ˈkeːɬa, ˈkeːʃlə/ *n.* Also **kehle**, **keshla**, **kethla**, **khehla**, **ukhehla**. Pl. **-s**, occas. ‖**ama-**. [Zulu *ikhehla* a man with a head-ring, a man turning grey.]

1. A Zulu headman; one entitled, because of age, to the dignity of wearing the traditional HEAD-RING; also used as a respectful form of address. See also RINGKOP sense a.

1850 J. & M. CHURCHILL *Merchant Family in Natal* (1979) 11 A short active fellow with his head close-shaven with the exception of a narrow circle closely pressed down to the Crown like a cow-whip cord (He was a Kehle or 'ringed' man). 1875 D. LESLIE *Among Zulus* 24 I .. reached Machian's. He is a famous fellow – a tall, black 'Kehla' (top-knotted). 1885 H. RIDER HAGGARD *King Solomon's Mines* (1972) 46, I observed .. that he was a 'Keshla' (ringed man), that is, that he wore on his head the black ring, made of a species of gum polished with fat and worked in with the hair, usually assumed by Zulus on attaining a certain age or dignity. 1894 B. MITFORD *Gun-Runner* 182 The excited savages fell back, yielding place to a couple of tall *amakehla*, or head-ringed men, who, grim and ferocious of aspect in their war dresses .. advanced to the fore. 1907 J.P. FITZPATRICK *Jock of Bushveld* (1909) 248 One day .. there came to us a grizzled worn-looking old kaffir, whose head ring of polished black wax attested his dignity as a kehla. 1953 R. CAMPBELL *Mamba's Precipice* 22 He .. wore .. a big black ring of beeswax, like a black pudding, round the top of his head to signify his rank of kethla, or head-man. 1964 *Drum* Nov. 25 The old Zulu 'khehlas' and councillors felt that it was improper for a king of the Zulu nation to marry a divorcee.

2. *transf.* An elderly man; also used as a (respectful) mode of address.

1970 P. GWALA in *Ophir* Apr. 11 'Khehla, we don't own the day.' 'Son if I didn't know, I wouldn't have come so early'. 1974 J. MCCLURE *Gooseberry Fool* (1976) 148 An old *keshla* who handed spanners to the mechanic. 1975 J. MCCLURE *Snake* (1981) 132 'Ach, I'm not here to do your work for you – ask the *keshla* over there,' said the foreman. 1977 P.C. VENTER *Soweto* 172 An old man pushes a broom on the stoep. 'Ukhehla.' He stops the broom. And seems surprised to hear a white man address him as 'the old grey one'. 1986 *Drum* Aug. 55 Any old khehla in the ghetto who pulled rank on you and reminded you that you were still too wet behind the ears could not get away with it. 1987 O. MUSI in *Drum* May 47 A former British rail porter, Robert Kimberley ... at the ripe old age of 53, is one khehla who really went off the rails. 1987 *Ibid.* Dec. 32 Christmas is when an old khehla named Santa Claus comes over the roof-tops riding a sled. 1990 R. MALAN *My Traitor's Heart* 41 Some friends and I had a passing encounter with such a wise one – an old, yellow-eyed kehla who sold us some zol and invited us to sit down for a smoke outside his hut.

Kei /kaɪ/ *n.* [Khoikhoi *kei* sand (used as the name of the river forming the border between the old Cape Province and Transkei).]

1. *comb.* **Kei apple**, also with small initial, the densely spiny shrub or small tree *Dovyalis caffra* of the Flacourtiaceae; its edible bright yellow fruit; DINGAAN'S APRICOT; also called *wild apricot* (sense (*a*) see WILD sense a); also *attrib.*; **Kei lily**, the red lily *Cyrtanthus sanguineus* of the Amaryllidaceae; also called FIRE LILY.

1853 E. ARMITAGE in J. Chapman *Trav. in Int.* (1868) II. 449 The **Kei apple**, or Dingan's Apricot, invaluable for forming thorny fences and yielding a pleasant fruit. 1859 HARVEY & SONDER *Flora Capensis* II. 585 *Aberia Caffra*, hab. Eastern districts and Kaffirland. A shrub or small tree, .. fruit edible like a small yellowish apple. Colonial name, the Kei apple. 1868 W.H. HARVEY *Genera of S. Afr. Plants* 16 The 'Kei apple' (*Aberia Caffra* ..) has 6 (or probably more) styles and placentae. 1876 H. BROOKS *Natal* 185 This fruit is familiarly known as the kei apple, or in some places as Dingaan's apricot. 1887 *S.W. Silver & Co.'s Handbk to S. Afr.* 138 The Kei Apple is the fruit of the *Aberia Caffra*, Hk., a shrub or small tree found in the eastern districts of the colony and in Kaffirland. 1890 A.G. HEWITT *Cape Cookery* 68 Kei Apple Jelly. 1894 R. MARLOTH in *Trans. of S. Afr. Phil. Soc.* p.lxxxiv, Yellow, like the berries of the Kei apple. 1894 J.F. SEWELL *Private Diary* (1983) 152 By 4 p.m. we had got the Kei-apple all round [erven] No 18 & 20, and also as far as No 1 as far as the holes were dug. 1910 R. JUTA *Cape Peninsula* 93 Edging the road and hiding the beach from travellers are thick hedges of Kei-apple, a prickly red berry, and of a low shrub. 1913 A. GLOSSOP *Barnes's S. Afr. Hsehold Guide* 87 Serve with Tartar sauce ... or Kei apple jelly. 1924 D. FAIRBRIDGE *Gardens of S. Afr.* 55 Kei-apple forms an impenetrable fence, but it is more fitted for sheep-kraals than gardens. 1930 N. STEVENSON *Farmers of Lekkerbat* 7 In summer .. the mud was as thick .. as the dust in winter; especially near the hotel, where the kei-apple bush was always brown. 1958 I. VAUGHAN *Diary* 22 Round the Church is a green hedge with large lovely cherries on it, Gladys Long said that they are Kei apples and not poison .. but no one likes to eat Kei apples. 1989 *Weekend Post* 2 Dec. (Leisure) 3 Beside the main street of Hankey stands a beautiful old specimen of *Dovyalis caffra*, the kei-apple tree. 1991 [see *wild apricot* (WILD sense a)]. 1993 *Weekend Post* 20 Nov. (Leisure) 5 Acacia, Bougainvillea, Kei Apple, Veld Fig. 1913 C. PETTMAN *Africanderisms* 257 **Kei lily**, *Cyrtanthus sanguineus* is known by this name in some parts of the Transkei. *c*1969 E. GLEDHILL *E. Cape Veld Flowers* 82 *Cyrtanthus sanguineus* .. Kei Lily. Large Red Cyrtanthus ... From Port Elizabeth to Bathurst, now rare. Occurs also in Natal. 1971 *Reader's Digest Complete Guide to Gardening* II. 386 Kei lily ... Bears 3–4 in. trumpet-shaped scarlet flowers. 1985 K. PIENAAR *Grow S. Afr. Plants* 41 Kei lily, with salmon-red flowers. 1989 *E. Prov. Herald* 18 Mar. 8 For many years I have grown Kei Lilies, *Cyrtanthus sanguineus*. Many people in Port Elizabeth grow them, mostly in pots, and they flower very punctually in the middle of February. 1989 [see KNYSNA LILY sense b].

2. Also **'Kei**, and with small initial. In newspaper captions and headlines: ellipt. for **a.** Transkei (see note at TRANSKEI). **b.** Ciskei (see CISKEIAN *adj.*). Also *attrib.*

1979 *Voice* 23 Sept., Pamphlets flood 'Kei. 1982 *Rand Daily Mail* 23 Nov. 1 SAR men hit me – Kei Minister's wife. The wife of the Transkei Minister of Justice was allegedly assaulted by employees of the South African Railways. 1987 *City Press* 15 Feb. 5 (*headline*) Kei's 'roadside people' wait for a miracle. *Ibid.* (*caption*) Some of the 1 000s of Ciskeian refugees now living along the roadside in South Africa.

keil sick(ness) *n. phr. Obs. Pathology.* Also **kiel sick**. [Englished form of S. Afr. Du. *geilsiekte*.] GEILSIEKTE sense 1.

1838 J. COLLETT Diary. I. 23 July, Lost during my absence 3 Ewes in Lamb + 1 Wether from Keil Sick thro feeding in Delange Valey. *Ibid.* 27 July 2 Ewes died again with Kiel Sick. 1840 *Ibid.* II. 30 June, Keil Sick or some other disease killing numbers of sheep in different parts possibly the cold dew & Frost in the Valleys. 1842 *Ibid.* 8 Jan., A few young sheep has died about 3 or 4 with a sort of Kiel Sick swelling &

kejaat var. KIAAT.

kek var. KYK.

‖**kelder** /ˈkeldə(r)/ *n.* Pl. -s, occas. **kelderen**. [Afk., fr. Du.]
1. A wine-cellar. Also *transf.*

[1796 C.R. HOPSON tr. *C.P. Thunberg's Trav.* II. 136 Having arrived at the top from the eastern side we observed a place called the Company's Cellar (*Kelder*).] a1878 J. MONTGOMERY *Reminisc.* (1981) 81 The place of worship .. was an old, dilapidated 'kelder' or wine store. 1883 M.A. CAREY-HOBSON *Farm in Karoo* 57 They visited the vineyards ... They were next shown the 'Kelder', as it is called, where the pressing is done. *Ibid.* 268 They did not go through the 'kelderen', or cellars. 1967 W.A. DE KLERK *White Wines* 20 Foremen, workers and Kobus Jordaan, heir-apparent to the Theuniskraal domain, were all about the *werf* in front of the *kelder*, completing the last of the weekly chores, before *daar gepay word* (meaning 'they are paid'). 1982 J. KRIGE in *Staffrider* Vol.5 No.2, 20 What they really used to enjoy doing was chasing each other in the wine kelders.

2. *comb.* **keldermeester** /-ˌmɪəstə(r)/ *n.* [Afk., *meester* master], a cellarer.

1919 M. GREENLEES tr. *O.F. Mentzel's Life at Cape in Mid-18th C.* 8 The Under-Merchants ... The Keldermeester, who looks after the Company's wines and European beer.

kelkiewyn /ˈkelkiveɪn, ˈkɛlki-/ *n. colloq.* Also **kalkivain, kelkiewijn**. [Onomatopoeic, named for its cry, which is perceived to approximate Afk. *kelkie* (wine)glass + *wyn* (earlier S. Afr. Du. *wijn*) wine.] **a.** The bird *Pterocles namaqua*; also called *Namaqua sandgrouse*, see NAMAQUA *n.* sense 2. **b.** The call of this bird. Also *attrib.*

1898 W.C. SCULLY *Between Sun & Sand* The desert grouse .. throng over in countless myriads ... From their cry the colloquial name of 'kalkivain' is derived. 1913 C. PETTMAN *Africanderisms* 257 Kelkie wijn, .. The onomatopoetic name of the Namaqua partridge, by which it is known in the Karoo. 1918 S.H. SKAIFE *Animal Life* 231 Namaqua sandgrouse is the commonest species and is abundant in all parts of the Karoo ... The Dutch name *kelkiewijn*, is given to them in imitation of their call. 1955 L.G. GREEN *Karoo* 96 One of the finest meals of my life came out of a three-legged pot in which a *kelkiewyn* stew had been simmering all day. 1970 O.P.M. PROZESKY *Field Guide to Birds* 140 A trisyllabic call, usually heard when flocks are on the wing. Rendered in Afrikaans as 'kelkiewyn' (pronounced *cal-kee-vane*). 1983 K.B. NEWMAN *Newman's Birds* 194 *Namaqua Sandgrouse*, .. Flight call 'Kelkiewyn'.

kennetjie /ˈkenəki, -ci/ *n.* Also **kenneki, kennetje, kennikie**. [Afk., perh. fr. *ken* chin, or *kenner* master; or fr. E. Frisian *kunje*, Du. *kien(e)* wedge; or fr. Malay *kena* to hit, + -IE.] The outdoor game 'tipcat'; the peg, tapered at each end, with which the game is played. Also *attrib.* See also BOERESPORT.

1861 P.B. BORCHERDS *Auto-Biog. Mem.* 21 Relieved from school labour, I retired generally with my young school-fellows to the playground .. where kite and ball, and the 'kennetje' game, amongst others, amused us. 1934 C.P. SWART *Supplement to Pettman* 87 *Kennetjie*, .. Tip-cat, the popular boy's game, is so called in South Africa. 1947 *Cape Times* 21 June (Weekend Mag.) 22 Whether they were climbing in hedges .. or playing kennetjie or marbles, the youthful Miss H— and her companions were like all healthy children. 1953 *Cape Argus* 28 Feb. 3 On these grassy squares we played 'rounders' and on the paths marbles, tops, hop-scotch, and kennetjie. 1958 R.E. LIGHTON *Out of Strong* 78 He had to stop kennetjie because one morning Andries hit the bit of wood so hard that, whirring far, it struck Willempie .. on his forehead so that the blood flowed. 1959 *Cape Times* 2 May 9 A South African in England tells me that what they call *kennetjie* in the Boland is sweeping Lancashire, where it is known as tip-cat. 1969 D. CHILD *Yesterday's Children* 36 The *kennetjie* game .. was a great favourite ... Kennetjie or tip-cat was played with a piece of wood .. tapered at both ends. It was laid on the ground and struck smartly on one end with a stick, to make it rebound in the air. 1971 *Std Encycl. of Sn Afr.* III. 190 In his delightful memoirs P. B. Borcherds mentions the games of 'kennetjie' (tip-cat) in which he took part .. at the close of the 18th century ... The kennetjie itself was a piece of wood about 5 inches .. long and 112 inch .. in diameter, tapered off at both ends. 1975 [see FARM *n.*]. 1978 *Staffrider* Vol.1 No.4, 25, I would rather have been outside playing the last round of kenneki hitting the stick high into the air, watching it arch and land in the mud of the street. 1985 T.R. ADLAM in M. Fraser *Jhb. Pioneer Jrnls 1888–1909* 121 'Kennetjie' .. was played with a small, cylindrical piece of wood, the ends being of conical form ... Striking a pointed end sharply with a stick, caused the 'kennetjie' to jump up, spinning, from the ground and, while in mid-air, it was given a swipe with the stick. The winner of the game was he who got his 'kennetjie' across the playground with the least number of hits on the pointed end. 1990 *Sunday Times* 4 Feb. 17 Points are gained by calculating the number of lengths the kennetjie is flicked from the groove ... If a fielder catches the kennetjie, the batsman is out. 1990 R. GOOL *Cape Town Coolie* 114 Children were playing *kennikie*, tag, and a grim, intricate, District Six version of hopscotch.

keppeljou var. KABELJOU.

keree var. KIERIE.

‖**kêrel** /ˈkɛːrəl/ *n. colloq.* Also **carle, ker(e)l**. [Afk.]
1.a. A young man, a fellow; a boyfriend.

1837 J.E. ALEXANDER *Narr. of Voy.* II. 63 The general's excellent defensive arrangements .. soon put a stop to their proceedings; but not before the 'slim carles' had played .. an ugly trick. 1873 *Cape Monthly Mag.* Oct. 215, I have always known you to be a *slimme kerel*. 1896 M.A. CAREY-HOBSON *At Home in Tvl* 400 'Ach! God bedank! The carle lives. A dead body does not bleed like that!' exclaimed the old Boer. 1899 'S. ERASMUS' *Prinsloo* 3 He was a bold young kerel, and did many things that caused his father loss and sorrow. 1903 D. BLACKBURN *Burgher Quixote* 205 Is it in the orders for a great lump of a kerel like that to stand and look on while a lady has to carry her own beer? 1911 *E. Prov. Herald* 25 Nov. 5 We returned to the station and held sweet converse with diverse kerels, to whom we were 'Man' and 'Jong,' after the nature of the tribe. 1917 A.W. CARTER *Informant, Ladybrand* 20 Aug., Major Herbst is the Secretary and seems quite a lekker Boer Kerel. 1937 F.B. YOUNG *They Seek a Country* 238 What is the poor *kerel* raving about? Tell him this house is the house of a Boer, not a storekeeper. 1955 V.M. FITZROY *Dark Bright Land* 240 Slim juffrouws would slip by on errands watched with interest by the young kêrels. 1965 W. PLOMER *Turbott Wolfe* 159 I've seen some queer kerels in these parts, but Soper! 1970 H.M. MUSMECI *Informant, Port Elizabeth Jan* is my new kêrel (boyfriend). 1984 *Frontline* Mar. 14 We think of our kêrels up there on the Border, Pursuing Angolans to utter disorder, What a burden it is to be White! we cry out. 1986 *Drum* Aug. 82, I can hear some influences of Abdullah Ibrahim and Basil 'Mannenburg' Coetzee. I bet my shirt that we will be hearing a lot from these kerels. 1988 'K. LEMMER' in *Weekly Mail* 2 Dec. 15 Still there's always next year. Meanwhile, we're back in business kêrels, so let's skinner!

b. As a form of address, equivalent to 'chap', 'fellow'; often in the phr. *ou kêrel*, 'old chap'; see also OU *adj.* sense 1 c.

1896 H.A. BRYDEN *Tales of S. Afr.* 214 Kerel (my boy) you have never by chance heard the story of the vrouw there and her Frenchman? 1899 F.R.M. CLEAVER in M.M. Cleaver *Young S. Afr.* (1913) 25, I am not preaching at you, ou kerel, only the wind is in the wrong quarter to-day. 1900 B. MITFORD *Aletta* 163 'Who are you, *kerel*, and have you a permit to remain here?' interrupted, in Dutch, the peremptory voice of a Zarp. Now 'kerel' — meaning in this context 'fellow' — is a pretty familiar, not to say impudent form of address as proceeding from a common policeman. 1902 J.H.M. ABBOTT *Tommy Cornstalk* 81 It is that 'kerel' French who is coming. 1920 S. BLACK *Dorp* 42 'Well now, kerel,' said Van Ryn, after Alrin had disappeared, 'how about my little plan, hey?' 1931 H.C. BOSMAN *Mafeking Rd* (1969) 145 'No, kêrels,' he said, 'always when the Englishman comes, it means that a little later the Boer has got to shift'. 1939 S. CLOETE *Watch for Dawn* 41, I want no more than justice, kerels. 1965 K. MACKENZIE *Deserter* 55 'Come, kêrels, or we will miss the war,' said Hans, throwing his reins over his horse's head. c1966 M. JABOUR in *New S. Afr. Writing* 95 Every day I get up and say Jaap, ou kêrel, today's the day. But no .. that blerry sky stays as blue as ever. 1974 *Cape Times* 11 Nov. 9 Willem Prinsloo .. served his lekker peach brandy on the stoep as the kêrels gathered to bid good afternoon to the setting sun. 1979 J. GRATUS *Jo'burgers* 130 It's all right, ou kêrel. They're going to let us out. 1981 *Flying Springbok* Sept. 54 You will not have been in South Africa very long before some earnest local .. will offer you an object that looks like a chunk of the mahogany tree and say 'have a bite, ou kêrel'. You, the 'old man' of the injunction, will no doubt turn your sensitive teeth away.

2. *slang.* In *pl.*: The police.

1978 L. BARNES in *The 1820* Vol.51 No.12, 19 *Kêrel* is also used to refer to the police: *the kêrels are coming*. 1993 'Jimbo' programme insert, Napac *Kerels. Police*.

kerem, karem /ˈkerəm, ˈkɛr-/ *n.* Also **carom, ker(i)m, kirram**. [ad. Indian Eng. *carom* a popular Indian game, fr. Malayalam *karambal* (Pg. and Sp. *carambola*) fruit of a certain tropical tree. In U.S. Eng. this game is called *caroms* (fr. *Caroms*, the proprietory name, a shortened form of *carambole*).] A game played, in groups of two or four players, on a small board with four pockets, the object being to flick small discs into the pockets using a large disc. Also *attrib.*

1953 DU PLESSIS & LÜCKHOFF *Malay Quarter* 16 An old game known as *kirram* has recently become popular. It is played by two or four men on a smooth board three-and-a-half feet square with pockets at the corners. Nine red and nine white 'men' are used, each having the form of a disc. The player moves these discs with the aid of a cue and a larger disc. 1973 *S. Afr. Panorama* Oct. 37 Facilities include indoor sports and film shows. Kerm, dominoes and table-tennis are popular games. 1974 *Ibid.* Aug. Mr. Ishmail Floris (84), grandson of a Malay, invented the game Karem many years ago and he still makes boards for this game, as he has done for 25 years. The game has been played by Cape Malays for the last quarter of a century. 1978 *Cape Times* 11 Dec. 13 Kerim board complete with cues and chips, as new R8. 1980 *Het Suid-Western* 8 Aug., Indoor games and competitive indoor sports like dominoes, .. kerem and chess must be provided for. 1982 D. KRAMER *Short Back & Sides* 64 Awie plays the kerem board Stoned on cheap white wine. 1984 D. PINNOCK *Brotherhoods* 4 Small groups of young men in their late teens and twenties talking earnestly or playing karem. 1987 P. JOOSTE in *Fair Lady* 25 Nov. 139 Across the road .. men were playing kerim and the sound of their laughter and the loud, clicking sounds of the game came across to us. 1992 R. MESTHRIE *Lexicon of S. Afr. Indian Eng.* 9 *Carom/Carom board*, Game played in groups of two or four, with a small wooden board on which small discs ('beads') are flicked with a large disc by hand into one of four pockets.

keri(e) var. KIERIE.

Kerk /kɛrk/ *n.* Also **Kirk**, and with small initial. Pl. **-e** /-ə/, or **-s**. [Du.]
1.a. Church; a Dutch Reformed church. **b.** A church building. Also *attrib.*

1818 *Blackwood's Mag.* (U.K.) III. **406** It would .. have done the readers good, To see the pair to kerk or kermis going. **1820** W. SHAW in C. Sadler *Never a Young Man* (1967) 31 The Dutch farmers .. always honour me with the appellation which they give their own minister, viz. 'Predicant' .. and many .. have expressed to me their thankfullness that they shall now have an opportunity of attending Kerk. **1837** 'N. POLSON' *Subaltern's Sick Leave* 105 On Sundays they sometimes attend the Kerk, and on others pay visits to their neighbours. **1862** LADY DUFF-GORDON *Lett. from Cape* (1925) 135 The Dutch farmers were tearing home from Kerk in their carts — well-dressed, prosperous-looking folks, with capital horses. **1888** *Cape Punch* 25 Jan. 35 Then let us to our Kerks adjourn And thank the God of Right (For damning men with swarthy skins And saving those with white). **1899** 'S. ERASMUS' *Prinsloo* 36 She would have Piet bring the money back every Saturday, lest robbers should break in on Sunday, when the bank people were at Kerk. **1905** P. GIBBON *Vrouw Grobelaar* 123 He had .. a kerk on his land, where his nephew, the Predikant, used to preach. **1913** J.J. DOKE *Secret City* 10 A spacious stone sanctuary has replaced the dear old kerk, and other ministers preach there to other congregations. **1935** P. SMITH *Platkop's Children* 173 It was Sunday, an' the people goin' past the house to the Dutch Kerk. **1948** *Press Digest* No.5, 36 A number of Afrikaans bodies and institutions, foremost among them the Universities of Pretoria and Stellenbosch and the three Afrikaans Kerke, had taken the lead. **1948** *Ibid.* No. 13, 79 Apartheid has Blessing of Kerk. **1948** *Ibid.* No.14, 84 The Kerk never expressed its views on political matters, 'but when times of great emergency for the volk arrive, .. the Kerk has never scrupled to make its voice heard when it is forced to do so.' **1967** J.G. DAVIS *Hold my Hand* 43 Suzanna de Villiers did not go to kerk any more. She did not go to church because the Dominee had told her she was a wicked woman and she was doomed. **1979** *Fair Lady* 10 Oct. 57 Xavier came out for the full *kerk* wedding in Potchefstroom. **1988** P. LAWRENCE in *Weekly Mail* 17 July 7 The racially-stratified society of the Boer Republics and the dubious virtues of *volk, kerk* and family. **1992** *Sunday Times* 20 Sept. 18 The government's decision to outlaw gambling casinos .. may satisfy the *kerk* lobbies, but surely there is no legal or moral ground for putting hundreds of small operators out of business, while leaving the homelands' gaming centres intact.

‖**2.** *comb.* **kerkdorp** /-dɔː(r)p/ [Afk., *dorp* village], see quots; **kerkhof** /-hɔf/ [Afk., *hof* court], churchyard, cemetery; **kerkhuis** /-heɪs, -hœɪs/ (pl. **-e**, **-es**), also part. tr. **kerk-house** [Afk., *huis* house], SUNDAY HOUSE; **kerkstoel** /-stʊl/ [Afk., *stoel* chair], see quot. 1927; **Kerk(e)raad** /-rɑːt/, the parish council of a Dutch Reformed church; **Kerkwet** /-vet/ [Afk., *wet* law], church law.

1913 C. PETTMAN *Africanderisms* 257 **Kerkdorp**, .. A small village, consisting of a church and a few small cottages, which are only used by those who have built them, at service time. **1953** B. FULLER *Call Back Yesterday* 133 Bethlehem began as a 'kerkdorp,' or a township which arose gradually about a church. **1906** DE V. HUGO *In the Kerkhof (pamphlet)* 5 'Ghost or not ghost' he muttered impressively, 'I shoot anything that comes,' and set forth determinedly for the **Kerkhof**. **1935** P. SMITH *Platkop's Children* 95 There was Ockert an' Alida nearly cryin' .. an' Ou-ma waitin' for him in the **kerk-house**, an' what would the Predikant say when he heard about it. **1965** C. VAN HEYNINGEN *Orange Days* 29 During 'Nachtmaal', when all the farmers who could came into town, the shops did a roaring trade. The wealthy farmers all had 'kerkhuises' (small houses in the dorp to live in while they were in the dorp — 'Nachtmaal' was every three months). **1974** *Evening Post* 2 Nov. A group of old 'nagmaal huise' .. the oldest buildings in Alexandria were built by the early Boers .. to live in when they came together for 'nagmaal' .. Her last purchase is the 'kerk' or 'nagmaal huis' of the Scheepers family. **1927** C.G BOTHA *Social Life in Cape Col.* 53 The '**kerkstoel**,' or special chair for use in church on Sunday, made of ebony or stinkwood. [**1827** G. THOMPSON *Trav.* I. 60 My host, a jolly consequential looking person, was, I found, a Mynheer Van Heerden, a *heemraad* and **kerkraad** of the district (i.e. a member of the district-court and a churchwarden).] **1856** E.R. MURRAY in J. Murray *Young Mrs Murray* (1954) 53 The Kerkraad are going to board four of my floors. **1865** *The Jrnl* 24 Feb., One of the honourable members for the district of Bethulie was discovered by the Raad to have acted as the agent of the Kerkeraad of that place and to .. 'do' the government out of a farm. **1878** H.A. ROCHE *On Trek in Tvl* 143 They submit with much humility to the recognized authority of their 'Kirk Raad' or Council, composed of men like themselves. **1899** M. MARQUARD *Lett. from Boer Parsonage* (1967) 49 As the Kerkraad filed in there was the deacon Philip Meyer with his head all bandaged up yet — wounded at Modderspruit. **1906** *E. Prov. Herald* 4 May, At yesterday's meeting of the Dutch Reformed Church synod .. a delegate asked what action should be taken in cases of members of the Kerkraad who participated in dances and races. **1914** L.H. BRINKMAN *Breath of Karroo* 54 They constituted the much-dreaded Kerkraad of the Dutch Church. **1920** R.Y. STORMBERG *Mrs Pieter de Bruyn* 62 The Kerkeraad took the affair up and presumed to lecture her on the subject of her dangerous attractions. **1934** M.E. MCKERRON *Hist. of Educ.* 16 (Swart), These Kerkraden had the right of visiting and examing the schools in order to guard against the dissemination of false doctrines. **1950** H.C. BOSMAN in S. Gray *Makapan's Caves* (1987) 159 What I can't understand is how the *kerkraad* allowed Jacques le Français to hire the church hall for a show like that. **1955** W. ILLSLEY *Wagon on Fire* 60 They were compelled to face a painful interview with the Dominie and Kerkraad, who reprimanded, reproved, and disciplined very severely. **1975** *Sunday Times* 7 Sept. 3, I have nothing to say at this stage as the matter is sub judice until the Kerkraad had discussed it. **1993** *Weekend Post* 26 June (Leisure) 4 The affairs of the church are run by a Kerkraad of 18. **1849** N.J. MERRIMAN *Cape Jrnls* (1957) 66 In the **Kerkwet** of the Dutch Reformed Church, 1846, the minister of a church is referred to both as a *Leerar* and *predikant*.

kerl var. KÊREL.

kerm var. KEREM.

kerose var. KAROSS.

kerper var. KURPER.

kerre var. KIERIE.

kerrematata var. KREMETART.

kerri, kerrie *n.*[1] varr. KIERIE.

‖**kerrie** /ˈkeri, ˈkɛri/ *n.*[2] [Afk., fr. Malay *karie* or Tamil *kari*.]

1. Curry; curried food of various kinds. Also *attrib.*

1885 L.H. MEURANT *60 Yrs Ago* 28 A Soup plate of 'kerrie' (mullagatawny), two 'sasaatjes' (diamond-shaped inch-sized pieces of mutton, curried, and about half-a-dozen stuck upon a bamboo skewer). **1927** C.G. BOTHA *Social Life in Cape Col.* 56 Who has not enjoyed what may be considered typical South African foods, although they originated in the East, such as various stews known as 'bredie,' 'sosaties,' 'kerrie' (curried meats) and 'bobotie.' **1965** A. GORDON-BROWN *S. Afr. Heritage* IV. 19 The meal, which consisted of a plate of 'kerrie' (mulligatawny), two sosaties and boiled rice, and half a pint of Cape wine, cost a quarter of a rix-dollar (4 cents). **1971** L.G. GREEN *Taste of S.-Easter* 178 Kerrie patats, small pieces steeped in brine, cooked and served with a hot curry sauce. **1979** *Sunday Times* 8 Apr. (Mag. Sect.) 5 Her strongly religious household .. is nourished on foods like sosaties, pinang kerrie, snoek and cabbage bredie, and pootjies-en-tamatie.

2. *comb.* **kerrierys** /-reɪs/ *n.* [Afk., *rys* rice], curry-flavoured rice; **kerriesop** /-sɔp/ *n.* [Afk., *sop* soup], soup made with curry.

1979 *Capetonian* May 9 Any foreigner found without his pass will be sentenced to say **kerrierys** *en roosterbrood* in a thick Malmesbury accent 500 times. **1968** L.G. GREEN *Full Many Glorious Morning* 13 Potage Dubarry boils down to *blomkoolsop* while Crème Africaine is simply **kerriesop**.

kerry var. KIERIE.

‖**kersbos** /ˈkɛrsbɔs/ *n.*[1] Also **kaersbosch, kerzbosch.** [Afk., *kers* (fr. Du. *kaars*) candle + *bos* (fr. Du. *bosch*) bush.] BUSHMAN'S CANDLE.

1890 A. MARTIN *Home Life* 60 The *Kerzbosch*, or candle-bush, a stunted, thorny plant, if lighted at one end when in the green state, will burn steadily just like a wax candle. **1913** J.J. DOKE *Secret City* 160 Stoffel suggested torches made of such inflammable herbs as the kaersbosch and other materials of a like nature. **1955** L.G. GREEN *Karoo* 133 *Kersbos* burns steadily like a wax candle if lighted when green. It is often used as a torch for burning off the prickly pear thorns.

kersbos /ˈkɛrsbɔs/ *n.*[2] [Afk., formed on *kersie* cherry + *bos* bush.] Any of various species of shrub of the genus *Euclea*, esp. *E. polyandra*, and *E. tormentosa*, an evergreen arborescent shrub. Also *attrib.*, and dim. form **kersiebos** [see -IE].

1966 C.A. SMITH *Common Names* 287 *Kersiebos, Euclea polyandra* ... Fruits round, .. red when ripe and then resembling cherries .., whence the vernacular name. **1972** M.R. LEVYNS in *Std Encycl. of Sn Afr.* VI. 369 *Kersbos, Bush guarri* (*Euclea racemesa*) ... The name kersbos or kersiebos is sometimes also applied to *Euclea polyandra* and *E. tormentosa.* **1975** W. STEENKAMP *Land of Thirst King* 130 The tkoenoebee and its equally popular companion, the kersbos berry, grow on shrubs, but two one-time favourites, the bokbessie (goat-berry) and skilpadbessie (tortoise-berry) grow on bushes.

kershout /ˈkɛrshəʊt/ *n.* Also **kaarshout, ker-s(i)ehout.** [Afk. formed on *kersie* (fr. Du. *kers*) cherry or *kers* (fr. Du. *kaars*) candle + *hout* wood.

Pterocelastrus tricuspidatus is called both *candlewood* and (occas.) *cherrywood* in S. Afr. Eng., illustrating the confusion surrounding the origin of the name.]

Either of two species of forest tree or shrub:

1. *Pterocelastrus tricuspidatus* of the Celastraceae, with hard, dark red wood; CANDLEWOOD sense 2.

1887 J.C. BROWN *Crown Forests* 237 Timber Valued Standing. Per cubic foot ... Kershout, .. 0 0 3. **1913** [see sense 2]. **1917** R. MARLOTH *Common Names* 48 *Kerse-'hout*, .. *Pterocelastrus variabilis.* **1937** F.S. LAUGHTON *Sylviculture of Indigenous Forests* 56 *Celastraceae. Pterocelastrus tricuspidatus*, .. (*Kershout*) is an extremely variable species, found as a shrub on the coastal dunes and in other dry localities. **1966** C.A. SMITH *Common Names* 287 *Kers(ie)hout, Pterocelastrus tricuspidatus* ... The vernacular name .. is derived from the resemblance of the wood of the species of *Pterocelastrus* to that of the European cherry .. and was seemingly first applied (c. 1750) to *Pterocelastrus tricuspidatus.* **1972** M.R. LEVYNS in *Std Encycl. of Sn Afr.* VI. 369 *Kershout*, (*Pterocelastrus tricuspidatus*) ... The wood is dark red, hard and heavy, and is used for spokes and for pick- and axe- handles. **1977** E. PALMER *Field Guide to Trees* 194 *Kershout, Pterocelastrus tricuspidatus.* Capsules: bright orange-yellow with 3 wing-like horns which sometimes divide futher. **1977** *Het Suid-Western* 19 Oct., Although on average prices realised were good, there was little interest in .. kershout .. which went for bargain prices. **1989** *Afr. Wildlife* Vol.43 No.2, 79 Xhosa warriors are said to have fixed the iron blades to the assegai handle with sticky resin obtained by heating the roots of the cherrywood or *kershout.* **1990** *Weekend Post* 19 May (Leisure) 7 Back along the terrace .. was a well-grown kershout (*Pterolastrus tricuspidatus*) not yet bearing its attractive orange seed capsules. **1992** H. HUTCHINGS in *Weekend Post* 1 Mar. (Leisure) 7 *Pterocelastrus tricuspidatus* (kershout), a many-branched evergreen bush tree with leathery leaves and orange seed pods in autumn and winter.

2. Less commonly, *Rothmannia capensis* of the Rubiaceae, which has creamy white flowers and large, woody, inedible fruit; AAPSEKOS; *bobbejaanappel*, see BOBBEJAAN sense 2; CANDLEWOOD sense 1; *wild gardenia*, see WILD sense a.

1913 C. PETTMAN *Africanderisms* 238 Kaarshout, .. According to Sim ('Forest Flora') this is another name for *Gardenia Rothmannia* ... But the name is universally applied to *Pterocelastris variabilis*, .. which is very resinous. *Ibid.* 258 *Kersehout*, .. *Pterocelastrus variabilis*. **1917** R. MARLOTH *Common Names* 48 *Kershout*, .. candle wood (*Gardenia*). **1966** C.A. SMITH *Common Names* 287 *Kershout, Rothmannia capensis* ... The vernacular name is derived from some real or fancied resemblance of the wood to that of the European cherry. The wood burns with a smoky flame, suggestive of that of a candle. **1972** M.R. LEVYNS in *Std Encycl. of Sn Afr.* VI. 369 The name kershout is also applied to *Rothmannia capensis*, which is better known as aapsekos ... Other common names of *R. capensis* are candlewood and wild gardenia.

kersiebos var. KERSBOS *n.*[2]

kerzbosch var. KERSBOS *n.*[1]

keshla, kethla varr. KEHLA.

kettie var. CATTY.

kettle *n.* [Calqued on Afk. *ketel*.] A still. See also *brandewyn ketel* (BRANDEWYN sense 2).

1973 S. STANDER tr. *A.P. Brink's Brandy in S. Afr.* 158 They hid their small farm 'kettles', barely large enough for two half-aum, in poplar plantations, in the vineyards or the vleis. *Ibid.* 159 One day he and an excise man arrived at a farm where, they knew, the 'kettle' was often on the boil. **1976** G. & G. FAGAN in *Optima* Vol.26 No.2, 79 In 1823 Paul .. distilled five-and-a-half leaguers of brandy in the kettle under the oak trees. **1980** C. MARAIS in *Rand Daily Mail* 7 Oct. 5 'The kettle will be dry until late in February, when the fruit is out.' What Tant Mart would clearly love to do is keep the kettle and her stilling rights.

keur /ˈkiœ(r), ˈkɪə/ *n.* Shortened form of KEURBOOM (sense a).

1907 T.R. SIM *Forests & Forest Flora* 204 Keur is often cultivated for its ornamental evergreen foliage and sweetly scented flowers. **1909** *George & Knysna Herald* 22 Dec. 3 Two Keurs and two stinkwood tree-trunks ready for sawing. **1951** N.L. KING *Tree-Planting* 71 *Virgilia oroboides (capensis) (Keur)*, A quick-growing tree found in south-western Cape.

keurboom /ˈkiœ(r)bʊəm, ˈkɪəbʊəm/ *n.* Also **keerboom, keureboom, queur-boom**, and with initial capital. Pl. **-s, -e** /-ə/. [Afk. (earlier Du.), *keur* choice, pick + *boom* tree.] **a.** Either of two small trees of the genus *Virgilia* of the Fabaceae, *V. oroboides* or *V. divaricata*, with pendulous scented pink to rosy-lavender flowers; KEUR. **b.** The wood of these trees. Also *attrib.*

1731 G. MEDLEY tr. *P. Kolb's Present State of Cape of G.H.* II. 258 This Tree the Cape-Europeans call *Keur-boom* ... The Blossoms are of a Whitish Red, like those of the Apple-Tree, and of a fragrant Smell. **1786** G. FORSTER tr. *A. Sparrman's Voy. to Cape of G.H.* I. 261 *Keurebooms-rivier* is perhaps so called, after a tree of the same name (the *sophora capensis*, Linn.). On this kind of tree there is found a great quantity of gum, resembling that of the cherry-tree, but not so adhesive. **1798** [see DORINGHOUT]. **1829** C. ROSE *Four Yrs in Sn Afr.* 265 The beautiful winding stream .. flowed beneath the purple-scented blossoms of the Queur-boom, from which tree it takes its name. **1833** *S. Afr. Almanac & Dir.* p.xlvii, Seeds of keureboom sown at this season, thrive well, other native leguminous trees should also be sown now. **1854** L. PAPPE *Silva Capensis* 13 *Virgilia Capensis.* Lamk. (*Keurboom*) ... Wood rather light and soft. Looks well when polished. **1871** W.G. ATHERSTONE in A.M.L. Robinson *Sel. Articles from Cape Monthly Mag.* (1978) 90 Nowhere in the Colony have I seen so wonderful a pass .. fringed with green trees — keurboom and wagenboon, aloes, succulents nestling in the rock-fissures. **1887** *S.W. Silver & Co.'s Handbk to S. Afr.* 130 Most of the Knysna woods are of a good durable character .. The woods reckoned the best are those of the Ironwood, .. Keurboom (*Virgilia Capensis*), [etc]. **1910** D. FAIRBRIDGE *That Which Hath Been* (1913) 148 Table mountain lifted its face towards heaven, .. clothed almost to the summit with forests of shining silver-trees or sweeps of peach-pink keurboom. **1926** C.G. BOTHA *Place Names in Cape Prov.* 66 The Keurboom is a tree that grows along river courses or in damp places, and bears a bright purple flower. **1955** V.M. FITZROY *Dark Bright Land* 79 Rafters of keurboom taken from the river banks. **1966** *Cape Times* 24 Sept. (Weekend Mag.) 9 A strong encouragement to other gardeners to plant slower-growing indigenous trees than the keurboom beyond which some gardeners' thinking cannot progress. **1971** *Personality* 5 Mar. 83 The new source of income was to be found in the keurboom logs which were brought into the house daily and used as fuel. **1972** PALMER & PITMAN *Trees of Sn Afr.* II. 903 Botanists, foresters, and gardeners have not yet decided to their mutual satisfaction whether the genus *Virgilia* is composed of one, two or three different species of keurboom. **1989** *Afr. Wildlife* Vol.43 No.2, 77 The indigenous keurboom (*Virgilia divaricata*) is now found only in isolated spots, even though the river is named after this particular tree. **1991** H. HUTCHINGS in *Weekend Post* 23 Feb. (Leisure) 7 The faster growing kinds like *Virgilia oroboides* (keurboom), .. and *Dodonea viscosa* (sand olive).

keuvitt, -witt varr. KIEWIET.

keveky, -vitje, -wiche varr. KIEWIETJIE.

kewit var. KIEWIET.

Kgalagadi /ˌxalaˈxɑːdi/ *pl. n.* Also **Bakalahadi, Bakalahari, Bakgalagadi, Bakgalagalis, Kalahari, Kgalagadi, Kgalakgari**. [SeTswana *baKgalagadi* people of the Kgalagadi (the Kalahari desert); see also pl. n. prefix BA-.] (The) members of a people of the Tswana group. See also VAALPENS sense 1.

The Kgalagadi are thought to be of Sotho origin, although they have at times been believed to be San or Khoikhoi. They were probably the earliest Sotho people to migrate into southern Africa, arriving by the 15th century, and were later absorbed under the Tswana group.

As is the case with many names of peoples and groups in *S. Afr. Eng.*, this word has been found only in plural uses; however, it may be that it has also been used in unrecorded singular forms.

1835 A. SMITH *Diary* (1940) II. 188 They did not inhabit the Kalahari. There were Bechuanas who lived in it called Bakalahari. **1857** D. LIVINGSTONE *Missionary Trav.* 49 The Bakalahari are traditionally reported to be the oldest of the Bechuana tribes, and they are said to have possessed enormous herds of the large horned cattle .. until they were despoiled of them and driven into the Desert by a fresh migration of their own nation. **1871** J. MACKENZIE *Ten Yrs* (1971) 53 Their fellow-countrymen to the south affect great contempt for their restless connections on the frontier, and sometimes call them Vaalpensen, which is the Dutch for Bakalahari, the ill-favoured and lean vassals of the Bechuanas. **1899** S.T. PLAATJE *Boer War Diary* (1973) 38 These Bakgalagalis reported having heard at the laager that there was a heavy fight between Kimberley and [some] river or other — probably the Vaal. **1912** A.W. HODSON *Trekking Great Thirst* 33 The Bakalahadi make their villages in the neighbourhood of these pits. **1928** E.H.L. SCHWARZ *Kalahari & its Native Races* 179 The Bakalahadi are so primitive, that there is strong reason for believing they are pre-bushman, while the fact that they speak a Bantu tongue illustrates the fallacy of applying the language test, rather than proves their Bantu origin. *c*1936 *S. & E. Afr. Yr Bk & Guide* 528 The Bakgalagadi (generally subject to the Bechuana) pasture cattle, collect skins, feathers, etc., and cultivate a little land near the wells. **1970** *Std Encycl. of Sn Afr.* II. 222 The Kgalagadi, descendents of the first Sotho invaders in Southern Africa, .. were formerly often serfs of Tswana masters. This servile condition has now largely disappeared, but the Kgalagadi are still regarded as socially inferior to the Tswana. **1976** WEST & MORRIS *Abantu* 119 The Kgalakgari are usually portrayed as degenerate Tswana but were in fact descendants of the first wave of Sotho immigrants to the area who had fallen on hard times and lost their stock. **1986** P. MAYLAM *Hist. of Afr. People* 42 The Kgalagadi were eventually forced westwards into the desert where they adopted a hunter-gatherer lifestyle.

Kgatla /ˈga(ː)tɬa/ *n.* Also **Kxatla**. Pl. now usu. unchanged, but also **Bagatla, Bakatla(s), BaKatlha, Bakgatla, Bakhatla, Batklaka**. [Tswana (pl. pref *ba-* +) *kgatla* monkey, 'they of the monkey'.] A member of a clan of the Tswana people, living mainly in Botswana and around Pilanesberg, in the North West Province. Also *attrib.*

1835 A. SMITH *Diary* (1940) II. 152 Palanie, the chief of the Batklaka, has left his country. *Ibid.* 184 They were Bakatlas. **1857** D. LIVINGSTONE *Missionary Trav.* 13 The different Bechuana tribes are named after certain animals ... The term Bakatla means 'they of the monkey'. **1881** E.L. PRICE *Jrnls* (1956) 457 If the Bakhatla were to hear of this, they would be tempted to try their side of the battle — but as yet they keep very still. **1905** *Native Tribes of Tvl* 30 Politically the most important tribe is the portion of the Bakhatla located in the Pilanesberg. **1928** E.H.L. SCHWARZ *Kalahari & its Native Races* 223 As the nations grew, other sections hived off, under separate seretos; the Ba-Kwena, the crocodile people; the Ba-Katlha, the monkey people, and so on. **1930** S.T. PLAATJE *Mhudi* (1975) 125 The allies were joined en route by large numbers of Bakwena, Bakhatla and Bahurutshe who lived in the neighbourhood through which they marched. **1943** 'J. BURGER' *Black Man's Burden* 217 Bechuanaland contains a number of tribes, such as the Bamangwato, the Bakhatla, the Barolong, and the Bakwena. **1948** E. HELLMANN *Rooiyard* 123 Christine, an attractive and bright young Kxatla woman, .. married early — before she was twenty — a Kxatla from a neighbouring kraal. **1986** P. MAYLAM *Hist. of Afr. People* 42 The Kwena and the Kgatla .. became dominant in the sixteenth century. Most of the later Sotho-Tswana chiefdoms can trace their origins back to the Kwena or Kgatla. **1989** *Reader's Digest Illust. Hist.* 66 The principal group among the northern Sotho were the Pedi, a branch of the iron-working Kgatla people.

‖**kgosi** /ˈkɔːsi/ *n.* Also **kosi**, and with initial capital. [Sotho and seTswana.] In traditional Sotho or Tswana society: a chief or ruler; also used as a form of address, and as a title. Also *transf.* Cf. INKOSI senses 1 a and b.

1824 W.J. BURCHELL *Trav.* II. 272 The word *kosi* in the Sichuàna language signifies *rich*, and is by metonymy therefore used to imply a *chief. Ibid.* 364 The different members of his family, and the kosies or subordinate chieftains, formed round us a circle two or three deep. **1908** *Rand Daily Mail* 11 Sept. 7 Grades of rank [in the Amalaita] were established. Every leader became a 'kgosi' or 'morena' with sergeants and corporals beneath him. **1984** D. BECKETT in *Frontline* May 14 There were more unintroduced outsiders coming to plead with Kelly. 'The Boer has given me until tomorrow night to get off his farm. Please, kgosi (chief), what can I do?' **1990** *City Press* 11 Mar. 7 The urbane Mr Botha said the Bop dust-up was the work of 'the criminal element' and that the doors of the Rre Kgosi Lukas Mangope .. were 'always wide open'.

kgotla /ˈkɔtɬə, ‖ˈxɔtɬa/ *n.* Pl. usu. **ma-** or **-s**. Forms: *sing.* **cotla, khot(h)la, kotla, (le)kgotla, lekhothla**; *sing.* and *pl.* **makgotla**; *pl.* **k(g)otlas, makgotlas, makhotla(s)**. [Sotho and Tswana (*le*)*kgotla* courtyard, place of assembly, council chamber or enclosure (pl. *makgotla*). For an explanation of singular and plural forms, see LE- and MA- *pref.*[2]]

I. In the context of traditional (rural) Sotho and Tswana society:

1. A meeting place, esp. an enclosure in a village used for villagers' assemblies, court cases, and meetings of the village's leaders. Cf. INKUNDLA sense 2.

1840 B. SHAW *Memorials* 303 Morokos Kotla had no attractions yesterday; we went and sat down in it, but we could not bear to remain. **1846** H.H. METHUEN *Life in Wilderness* 253 We .. reached the cotla, or place of assembly, set apart in all native tribes for the purpose of holding public meetings. **1857** D. LIVINGSTONE *Missionary Trav.* 15 Near the centre of each circle of huts there is a spot called a 'kotla', with a fireplace; here they work, eat, or sit and gossip over the news of the day. **1871** J. MACKENZIE *Ten Yrs* (1971) p.xxii, The proceedings at which Mackenzie made his speech were not in church but in the *khotla*, or public courtyard. **1878** P. GILLMORE *Great Thirst Land* 305 At eight we breakfasted, and at nine went down to the kotla to visit the young King. **1895** J. WIDDICOMBE *In Lesuto* 55 All trials are held in public in the open Khothla, to which every full-grown man has access. **1923** G.H. NICHOLLS *Bayete!* 98 The Queen .. began to enter the Lekhothla. The chiefs stared aghast at this breach of their customs ... Were women to take part in their pitsos? **1930** S.T. PLAATJE *Mhudi* (1975) 95 Unlike the rest of the crowd massed in the khotla, these three apparently had not not come from their homes. **1951** H. DAVIES *Great S. Afr. Christians* 107 Khama called the tribe together, told them that he disliked but would not prohibit heathen ceremonies, but they must not be performed in the *kgotla* or public courtyard. **1968** A. FULTON *Dark Side of Mercy* 27 The Chief had summoned the men of the clan to the Khotla and opened the pitso by telling those assembled that the season had been poor, the crops bad, the cattle infertile. **1984** *Sunday Times* 1 Apr. 21 The white Lady Khama, other members of the famous Khama family and chiefs met in an immensely moving, impressive ceremony in the enclosure of the dusty Kgotla — chief's meeting place — beneath the towering rocks of the holy hill and royal graveyard in the traditional, picturesque village of Serowe. **1990** *City Press* 17 June 17 The next day, villagers assembled at the Kgotla to ask Lotlangtirang about the money.

2. A court of law composed usu. of important people from a village or area. Cf. IBANDLA.

1924 E.B. FORD *Waterfalls* 10 To-morrow shall the 'Khotla' try thy case .. ? **1934** *Cape Argus* 29 Jan. (Swart), A native who feels himself wrongly punished by a kgotla — a native court such as that recently was the origin of the Tshekedi trouble — may appeal. **1961** M.A. WALL *Dominee & Dom-Pas* 22 When the Dinokana men came from the Rand in two chartered buses the following Saturday (13th April), they held an illegal *kgotla* in the absence of the deposed Chief, where they 'tried' the 'rebels' who had denounced the Chief's domestic misgovernment, and condemned them to death. **1974** *Sunday Express* 30 June 20 The accused is not allowed a defence when he appears before the makgotla, a tribal bush court. **1974** *Sunday Times* 27 Oct. (Mag. Sect.) 2 An indication of local concern with crime has been the re-emergence of the traditional legkotla, or tribal court. *c*1976 H. FLATHER *Thaba Rau* 215 Meriama's father Mashale had just finished presiding over the *kgotla* or tribal court. **1982** *Pace* Apr. 35 Speaking to villagers at Bapong, Pace discovered the strongroom has come to be accepted as the village jail, especially reserved for people who needed 'softening' up before they appear before the kgotla.

3. An assembly of the people of a village or area, usu. for the discussion of some important matter. Cf. IBANDLA, IMBIZO, INKUNDLA sense 1.

1950 H. GIBBS *Twilight* 56 He showed acumen by calling a *kgotla* (assembly) of the tribe, numbering roughly 500,000, and asking them to accept Ruth, his white wife, as their chieftainess. **1958** A. SAMPSON *Treason Cage* 46 There was a slow and heavy ritual of formality, in keeping with the traditions of *kgotlas*, or tribal debates. **1970** P. BECKER in *SABC Bulletin* 23 Feb. 25 But the kgotla serves another significant purpose: It gives all Bantu, even the very humblest among them, the right to bring their grievances to the notice of their superiors. **1978** *Daily Dispatch* 24 Oct. 6 Following the spate of lightning incidents, the villagers asked for a kgotla (meeting) to be held and summoned 30 traditional witchdoctors to cast their bones and find out who was responsible for the lightning. **1991** *Weekend Argus* 26 Jan. 8 Some of the crowd that attended the 'Battle of the Okavango' kgotla (village gathering).

4. A council, usu. one comprising a chief and the elders of his people and ruling over the people. Cf. IBANDLA. Also *attrib.*

1951 H. DAVIES *Great S. Afr. Christians* 124 He had mastered the proverbial lore and vivid expressions of Sotho and he took his place as adviser in the *khotla*. **1957** A.A. MURRAY *Blanket* 26 Phiri turned to Lepotane. 'Come into the khotla hut,' he said. **1961** M.A. WALL *Dominee & Dom-Pas* 21 A complaint made against him years before, in 1952, by members of his own *kgotla*, was revived by the Native Affairs Department in 1956. **1974** *Drum* 8 Apr. 10 'After this incident, we were not allowed to keep cattle on our land,' says Mr. Simon Makodi, who is a khotla delegate. **1977** *Weekend World* 13 Mar. B1 The lekgotla is responsible to the Lebowa Government for the control of unauthorised influx of people into its area and for the prevention and detection of crime. **1981** *Sunday Times* 14 June 3 In an interview with the chief and Kgotla councillors at Saulspoort, one disillusioned councillor maintained that Sun City brought no advantages. **1987** M. HOLMES in *Leadership* Vol.6 No.4, 49 The inter-racial marriage was an event beyond the ken of the conservative tribal council, the *kgotla*. Yet by June 1949, most members of the *kgotla* had accepted it. Many in 'enlightened' Britain frowned on it. **1988** E. MPHAHLELE *Renewal Time* 168 Madam and those who think like her also wanted my people who have been to school to choose those who must speak for them in the — I think she said it looks like a *kgotla* at home who rule the villages.

II. *Transf.* senses, used mainly among Sotho and Tswana peoples.

5. Any gathering. Cf. IBANDLA.

1970 M. DIKOBE Marabi Dance. 19 The woman had had Marabi party dances and brandy gatherings of well dressed men, as well as a beer kgotla — meeting.

6.a. PEOPLE'S COURT sense 3. Also *attrib.*

1974 *World* 13 May 16 Yesterday .. the Zone 7, Meadowlands lekgotla flogged a 15-year-old youth after he had been found 'guilty' of molesting a school-girl. **1974** *Drum* 22 Aug. 7 We formed the first lekgotla here in Naledi during December last year. There are now 20 makgotla in Soweto, each with its executive committee. More are being formed weekly. **1977** P.C. VENTER *Soweto* 156 The measure dates back to the early forties, when strong-armed men ruled in the squatter camps and shanty towns; bloody floggings were inflicted, and the makgotla courts saw to it that the punishment fitted the crime. **1984** *Frontline* Feb. 13 The Ward Four lekgotla, started in 1977 after a local woman was assaulted by a man who although turned in to the police was released and not prosecuted.

b. A group or gang of vigilantes, often composed of members of a people's court, which patrols a township, ostensibly to maintain law and order; a member of such a group or gang. Also *attrib.*

1976 *Scotsman* in J. Sikakane *Window on Soweto* (1977) 30 The Justice Minister .. is considering giving legal status to tribal vigilante groups in the townships ... These groups, known as makgotla, have operated unofficially in Soweto for several years. They work by tribal law and occasionally administer public floggings. **1982** *Reader* Dec. 6 A makgotla beats a young man in Soweto. *Ibid.* 7 The makgotla group is also trying to fight crime. But the way they fight crime makes some people worried. People say makgotla go in groups and carry dangerous weapons. **1983** *Argus* 29 Dec. 13 A newly elected Soweto councillor .. has called for a halt to the makgotla (vigilante) activities in the townships. **1990** R. MALAN *My Traitor's Heart* 65 Mrs Ramathlape claimed that the men behind the kidnapping were makgotla — members of a tribal vigilante movement that had recently been dispensing rough justice in the townships.

7. A burial society.

1982 C. MVUBELO in *Frontline* Nov. 21 The importance of death is shown by the Makhotlas, or Burial Societies. These, the real, traditional, makhotla, have nothing to do with the vigilante groups you see of in the newspapers. The real makhotla are supported by everyone ... When death occurs among one of the members, they bury the deceased with all expenses arranged and paid.

Kgung var. KUNG.

khaama var. KAMA.

Khakhabe var. RHARHABE.

khaki /ˈkɑːki/ *n.* and *adj.* Also with initial capital. Pl. **khakis**, occas. **kakhies**, or unchanged. [fr. Afk. *kakie*, ad. of general Eng. *khaki* dust-coloured (fr. Urdu), with spelling remodelled to the Eng. root; alluding to the colour of British army field-uniforms.]

A. *n.*

1.a. *hist.* The Boer name for a British soldier during the Anglo-Boer War; KAKIE sense 1. Freq. in *pl.*, the British army. See also ROOIBAADJIE sense 1.

1900 F.R.M. CLEAVER in M.M. Cleaver *Young S. Afr.* (1913) 148 The khakis had probably anticipated that we should take this road. **1901** P.J. DU TOIT *Diary* (1974) 43 A brisk skirmish had taken place at Geduld, where approximately 50 Khakis fell and about an equal number were taken prisoner and disarmed. **1902** MRS DICKENSON in E. Hobhouse *Brunt of War* 211 He was in his farm with his sister, who was also blind, when the Khakis (i.e. the British) arrived. **1902** D. VAN WARMELO *On Commando* 44 It was a happy time — away from khaki, far beyond the reach of the roar of the cannon. *Ibid.* 166 Our wives and children and our exiled men we cannot get out of khaki's hands, and that is the greatest difficulty in our way. **1903** E.F. KNIGHT *S. Afr. after War* 43 The Dutch bitterly resented the establishment of the military camp at Middelburg, and practically the entire population .. petitioned that the 'khakis' should be removed from the country. **1944** J. MOCKFORD *Here Are S. Africans* 100 Her husband and his commandos were riding to orders from Pretoria and engaging the khakis wherever they might be found. **1955** W. ILLSLEY *Wagon on Fire* 35 Engaged in skirmishes against the Khakies, .. sniping the enemy from mountain fastnesses which the British Tommy could not penetrate. **1961** D. BEE *Children of Yesterday* 230, I can see them coming at me in my dreams sometimes — the Khakis. I can see them falling from their horses, with their swords shining and flashing in the sun. **1980** N. FERREIRA *Story of Afrikaner* 27 One day the British soldiers, the hated Khakis, arrived. **1988** J. BOEKKOOI in *Frontline* Oct. 23 Those Cape Afrikaners who stayed behind in comfort, .. talking English with the imperialists, while their trekking cousins braved lions and crocodiles and blacks and khakis.

b. *transf. derog.* An English-speaking South African; also called ROOINEK.

1940 *Forum* 7 Sept. 3, I wonder if Dr. van Nierop's statement that one Boer is enough for ten Khakies is not perhaps true? **1972** *Sunday Times* 11 June 15 We are fighting the English. The fight has been declared against the khakis — the battlefield is wide open. **1980** *Cape Times* 29 Apr., This list included lying; bad temper and naughtiness in general; Judas; dirty hands; Milner, Kitchener, Jameson and Rhodes; all Khakies; all Englishmen.

B. *adj.*

1.a. Of or pertaining to the British army, esp. during the Anglo-Boer War of 1899–1902; British; English(-speaking).

1902 D. VAN WARMELO *On Commando* 156 Some did not wait to find their horses. Some even escaped on khaki horses that had strayed from the camp. **1903** R. KIPLING *Five Nations* 207 Ubique means the tearin' drift where, breech-blocks jammed with mud, The khaki muzzles duck an' lift across the khaki flood. **1913** J. BRANDT *Petticoat Commando* 41 Mother, I vow I shall never be seen with a khaki officer as long as our men are in the field. **1920** S. BLACK *Dorp* 5 When an Afrikander's turned khaki like that — King George and the Union Jack stuck all over him — .. he's a smeerlap (blackguard). *Ibid.* 225 It's a khaki trick, Johannes — boycotting is thing the English invented. **1937** C.R. PRANCE *Tante Rebella's Saga* 35 Tante Katrina van Ammenies .. chased him with insult and contumely, threatening to loose the dogs on him, because, by his breeches and leggings he must be a khaki-Englander. **1972** *Cape Argus* 16 Sept. 9 My Pyper predicted the three 'emotional' fronts the national Party would employ were 'khakigevaar, swartgevaar, and rooigevaar.' **1976** [see MBONGO].

b. As a qualifier in Special Comb.: **khaki Boer** *hist.*, pl. **-Boers, -Boere** /-ə/ [Afk. *kakieboer* (see BOER)], JOINER sense 1; **khakibos**, [Afk., *bos* bush], *khaki bush* (see below); also *attrib.*; **khaki brandziekte** *?obs.* [S. Afr. Du., see BRANDSIEKTE], see quot. 1914; **khaki bush, khaki weed** [see Pettman quot. 1913], any of several species of alien weed, esp. *Tagetes minuta* and *Inula graveolens* of the Asteraceae, and *Alternanthera pungens* of the Amaranthaceae; *kakiebos*, see KAKIE sense 2; see also AFRIKANER *n.* sense 9.

1906 G.B. BEAK *Aftermath of War* 227 There are the so-called '**khaki Boers**' — those who surrendered before the end of the war. **1946** V. POHL *Adventures of Boer Family* 121 The advance guard of a British cavalry force .. mistook him for one of the Khaki Boere (traitors who had joined the enemy). **1934** H.C. BOSMAN *Mafeking Rd* (1969) 136 He seemed to have picked out all the useless bits for his pictures — a krantz and a few stones and some clumps of **khaki-bos. 1945** *Outspan* 3 Aug. 49 Against these intruders, especially the persistent and ubiquitous 'khaki bos', a cohort of picannins is marshalled. **1966** C.A. SMITH *Common Names* 288 *Khakibos*, .. The vernacular name is derived from the current belief that the species was introduced by British troops who wore khaki coloured uniforms. **1978** C.M. RIP *Contemp. Social Pathology* 94 The so-called 'Khaki-bos' weed. **1982** *Sunday Times* 3 Jan. (Mag. Sect.) 2 My father .. once told me .. that .. in his opinion even a khakibos would wither under my ministrations. **1986** *Farmer's Weekly* 25 July 6 Khakibos silage? It's enough, you would think, to make a cow wish it had only one stomach. **1991** 'BP' in *Weekly Mail* 28 Mar. 39 'Rub "green-flea-flee" thoroughly into the dog's fur .. then dance around waving a sprig of khaki-bos, chanting "fleas be gone".' **1993** *Rhodos* (Rhodes Univ.) 1 July 4 Pupils .. used onion skins, lichen, khakibos and cochineal to dye commercial hand-knitting wool. **1914** *Farmer's Annual* 181 What is the best remedy for scab in equines — '**Khaki brandziekte**,' as it is known by farmers owing to its having been very severe among horses shortly after the war? **1947** C.R. PRANCE *Antic Mem.* 75 'Flag' the next train, whether passenger or goods, to return to Bloemfontein in quest of further orders to investigate anthrax, glanders, 'khaki-brandziekte,' etc., etc., in the map's blank spaces to north, south, east or west. **1907** R.W. THORNTON in *Agric. Jrnl Cape of G.H.* 7 Jan. 76 The **Khaki Bush** is a species of *Aplopappas* ... The plant is an annual shrub. **1913** *Times Lit. Suppl.* (U.K.) 24 July 309 A certain weed which came from the Argentine with imported fodder is called the 'Khakibush.' The name cannot be more that a dozen years old, but it will no doubt endure, since the weed apparently shows no signs of departing. **1913** C. PETTMAN *Africanderisms* 258 *Khakibush*, A species of *Aplopappus*. The name has reference to the dull fawn colour the withered leaves assume ... The name is also applied to *Alternanthera Achyrontha*, .. now spread widely throughout South Africa, the seeds having been introduced from the Argentine Republic with imported fodder. The name was given to this plant because it made its appearance in military camps during the late war in places where it was previously unknown. **1917** R. MARLOTH *Common Names* 48 *Khaki bush, Tagetes minuta.* One of the Mexican marigolds which has become a troublesome weed. **1925** L.D. FLEMMING *Crop of Chaff* 18 With consummate tact he says nothing about the price of cattle, gielziekte, the khaki bush. **1956** P. BECKER *Sandy Tracks* 118 Tall, damp, tamboekie grass and pungent-scented khaki-bush. **1981** *Daily Dispatch* 13 Feb. 10 Khaki bush (Mexican marigold) and Afrikaners suppressed eelworm incidence. **1907** H.G. MUNDY in *Tvl Agric. Jrnl* V. 939 **Khaki-weed** or Amaranthus weed (*Alternanthera echinata*). **1928** N. STEVENSON *Afr. Harvest* 27 The side of the hill was overgrown with khaki weed and thornbushes. **1949** L. HUNTER *Afr. Dawn* 5 Even the khaki weed, growing everywhere in profusion and usually so robust, looked forlorn. **1966** L.G. BERGER *Where's Madam* 3 We peered across the dense screen of khaki weed which smelt like marigolds. **1971** *Daily Dispatch* 4 Sept. 6 The plants [*sc.* dagga] are somewhat similar in appearance to the Mexican marigold or khaki-weed. **1972** M.R. LEVYNS in *Std Encycl. of Sn Afr.* VI. 373 *Khaki-weed*, .. Tall khaki-weed or khaki-bush .. (*Tagetes minuta*). This plant is by some termed the 'true khaki-bush' ... (Cape) khaki-weed or khaki-bush .. (*Inula graveolens*). Introduced from the Mediterranean region ... Khaki-weed, .. Kakiebos (*Altenanthera pungens* = *A. repens*). Prostrate perennial belonging to the family *Amaranthaceae*. **1983** D.A.C. MACLENNAN *Reckonings* 25 We .. approached through crackly grass and khaki weed, beer cartons, broken glass. **1991** *Dict. of Horticult.* (Dept of Nat. Educ.) 330 *Khaki weed*, (*Inula graveolens*) ... *Khaki weed*, (*Tagetes minuta*, Mexican marigold, stinking Roger). **1994** *Weekend Post* 1 Jan. (Leisure) 6 To prevent fleas from invading a vacant house, scatter khaki weed branches in every room before going on a trip.

2. Patriotic; militaristic; jingoistic. Found esp. in the phr. ***khaki election*** (used orig. of the war spirit in England at the time of the Anglo-Boer War of 1899–1902).

[**1913** *Everyday Phrases Explained* 164 **The Khaki Election**, This was the General Election of 1900, when the Government appealed successfully to the country for its approval of the South African War.] **1948** *Press Digest* No.10, 64 A khaki election ... General Smuts wants to make the following election a 'sort of war election again' since he hopes that such an election will once more ensure him the success which he attained in the previous election. **1948** *Ibid.* No.13, 81 The Afrikaner front is afraid of a khaki-election. **1979** T. PAKENHAM *Boer War* (1982) 464 Polling for the election — the 'Khaki election', as people called it, alias the 'patriotic election' — would start in a fortnight. **1989** *Reader's Digest Illust. Hist.* 384 It was a typical 'khaki election', held in the shadow of war, in which the UP won 89 seats. **1990** *Sunday Times* 3 June 4 Down at the Waterval Festival Showgrounds .. on Republic Day, Eugene talked khaki patriotism. Talked soldiers for God and Fatherland ... Talked armed struggle.

Hence **khakidom** *n. hist.*, a derogatory term for the English governing bureaucracy in South Africa.

1921 W.C. SCULLY *Harrow* 464 He felt that he and his puppet the Commandant, the staff and, in fact, the whole of the amateur khakidom were outclassed.

khalifa /kəˈliːfə, kaˈlifa/ *n.* Also **califa, chalifah, kalifa, kalifer, khalifah**, and with initial capital. [Arabic *khalīfah* a caliph, the chief civil and religious leader in an Islamic society.]

1.a. A Cape Muslim ceremony at which a sword-ritual is performed by worshippers while they are in a trance-like state. **b.** This sword-ritual; also called RATIEP. Also *attrib.*

1856 *Cape Monitor* 16 Jan. 3 Several Malay priests have been examined .. and it would seem from their evidence that the Califa is by no means part of the Mahomedan religion, and .. ought only to be played on a certain night in each year. **1861** *Cape Monthly Mag.* Dec. 356 The most characteristic of their customs is the 'Khalifa', a religious ceremonial of the highest solemnity. **1862** LADY DUFF-GORDON *Lett. from Cape* (1925) 82 English Christians were getting more like Malays, and had begun to hold 'Kalifas' at Simon's Bay. These are festivals in which Mussulman fanatics run knives into their flesh, go into convulsions, etc., to the sound of music. **1867** M. KOLLISCH *Mussulman Population Cape of G.H.* 59 Performance of the ceremony called the Khalifa ... The feats which the 'Khalifa' involved were highly amusing. **1884** J.S. LITTLE *S. Afr.: Sketch Bk* II. 407 The Kalifas of the Malays are curious religious ceremonies ... Half-a-dozen men play tambourines, and a dozen or more fanatics, stripped to the waist, dance about the room .. incising themselves between their ribs with small short-pointed spears. **1900** *Diamond Fields Advertiser* 31 May 2 Khalifa Representation in aid of the fund for the relief of the sick and wounded in the Transvaal war. **1913** H. TUCKER *Our Beautiful Peninsula* 81 More grim and startling to the spectator is the now almost abandoned practice known as the Khalifa, wherein the performers, after dancing into a frenzy to the music of tom-toms and chanting voices, gash themselves with knives and inflict other self-injuries. **1944** I.D. DU PLESSIS *Cape Malays* 37 The Malay sword dance known as the *Chalifah* should really take place on the 11th day of Rabi-l-achier in honour of Abdul Kadir Beker, a follower of the prophet; but its original religious implications have been modified ... The *Chalifah* now amounts to a skilful exhibition of sword play. **1950** M. MASSON *Birds of Passage* 142 The pièce de résistance of the whole affair was a kalifa dance by two hundred Malays. **1953** DU PLESSIS & LÜCKHOFF *Malay Quarter* 62 During the previous century .. there were many bands of Chalifah-players. **1965** K. THOMPSON *Richard's Way* 32 The Malay Khalifa was famous at the Cape. As a religious hypnotic dance it was famous with tourists and truly interesting among historians. **1970** *Cape Times* 6 June (Weekend Mag.) 2 The khalifa originated at the Cape, and is not an import from the mysterious East as many think. **1972** *Std Encycl. of Sn Afr.* VII. 147 The most spectacular custom of the Cape Malays is the performance of the Chalifah. **1989** C. CHAPMAN in *Edgars Club* Apr. 45 These hypnotic rhythms are still heard in the *Khalifa*, a display of faith ritual. **1991** *Best of S. Afr. Short Stories* (Reader's Digest Assoc.) 217 The strange rituals of the *Khalifa* (originally a religious ceremony), when swords and skewers pierce flesh, yet draw no blood and cause no pain.

2. The priest or leader conducting the Khalifa ceremony; a participant in the ceremony.

1861 *Cape Monthly Mag.* in I.D. Du Plessis *Cape Malays* (1947) 36 During this time, the Khalifa, or schoolmaster, was divesting himself of his upper garments ... He .. took in each hand a peculiar sort of dagger .. flung both his armed hands to their full height above his head, and then dashed them down, as if driving both daggers .. through his stomach! **1944** [see RATIEP]. **1953** DU PLESSIS & LÜCKHOFF *Malay Quarter* 62 The chief priest .. is designated by the term *Chalifah*, which has now, through common usage, come to be applied to the performance itself. **1965** K. THOMPSON *Richard's Way* 81 The Khalifa himself, chief priest tonight, was moving now behind the 'bank'. **1970** *Cape Times* 6 June (Weekend Mag.) 2 The ritual obtains its name from the khalifas or leaders of performing troupes who are chosen for their clean living, strong spiritual beliefs and dedication to the art of physical stoicism. **1985** *S. Afr. Panorama* Jan. 22 Kalifa is really the name of the leader who blesses the sword, leads the performance, and prays continuously while it is under way.

khama var. KAMA.

khamba var. KAMBA.

khankatha var. IKHANKATHA.

kharie var. KAREE *n.*[2]

khaya var. KAYA.

khazi var. IKHAZI.

khehla var. KEHLA.

khia var. KAYA.

Khoe var. KHOI.

Khoe-Khoe, Khoekhoen varr. KHOIKHOI.

khofija var. KOFIA.

Khoi /kɔɪ, xɔɪ/ *n.* Also **Khoe, Khoin.** Pl. unchanged. [Shortened form of KHOIKHOI.]

1. KHOIKHOI sense 1. Also *attrib.*

1976 R. ROSS *Adam Kok's Griquas* 7 The belief was current that the Moravian mission at Genadendal locked up Khoi labour that would be better employed on white farms. **1977** K.F.R. BUDACK in A. Traill *Khoisan Ling. Studies* 3 20 Like the Cape Khoe, the Aonin are said to have eaten fish raw. **1980** V.C. MALHERBE in *Afr. Studies* XXXIX. 60 Another Khoi, Jan Swart, ..

later died. **1980** Lye & Murray *Transformations* 40 The second Khoi group to settle the frontier were the Griqua, the creation of irregular unions of Khoi women and white and slave males. **1981** Newton-King & Malherbe *Khoikhoi Rebellion* 14 Many Khoi .. absconded from their masters during the war of 1793, when there were no British troops from whom they might seek protection. **1982** A.P. Brink *Chain of Voices*, 'Yes, I'm of the Khoin', I said. 'The Dutch call me Hottentot.' **1986** *S. Afr. Panorama* June 22 Paths used by the indigenous Hottentot (Khoi) and Bushmen (San) peoples. **1989** R. Finlayson Changing Face of isiXhosa. (Unpubl. thesis, Unisa) 5 The missionaries, especially the Dutch made use of Khoi interpreters to communicate with the Xhosa. **1993** S. Hall in *Natal Mercury* 29 Dec. 7 The more robust dogs found among the Khoi and San were described as being very 'plucky' and protective.

2. Khoikhoi sense 2. Also *attrib.*

*c*1978 *S. Afr. 1977: Off. Yrbk* (Dept of Info.) 99 The Khoe languages constitute a language family. They include Nama (or Namaqua), Xiri (or Griqua) and !ora (or Korana). **1989** R. Finlayson Changing Face of isi-Xhosa. (Unpubl. thesis, Unisa) 2 There is no way of us ascertaining just when the Khoi and San-speaking people first had an impact on the Xhosa, but earliest records note the click (or clack) sounds as an intrinsic part of the language. *Ibid.* 4 Certain Khoi morphemes have been adopted into Xhosa and hence we have suffixes such as *-rha*, *-sha* and *-sholo* in the language.

Khoikhoi /ˈkɔɪkɔɪ/ *n.* Also **Khoe-Khoe, Khoe-khoen, Khoé-Khoep, Khoikhoin, Khoi-Khooi, Khoikoi, Koi-Koi, Xhoi-Xhoi**, and (formerly) **Quaiquae**. Pl. unchanged. [Khoikhoi *khoe-khoen*, the Khoikhoi people, *khoe* person + *khoen* people.]

In modern Nama this word is written 'khoe-khoen', which is also the form preferred by some scholars writing in English.

1. A member of a southern African people distinguished by short stature, yellow-brown skin, and tightly-curled hair, and speaking a language characterized by click sounds; Hodmadod; Hottentot *n.* sense 1 a; Khoi sense 1. Also *attrib.* Also called *free person of colour* (see colour sense 1). See also Khoisan sense 1, Nama *n.* sense 1, Saldanha sense 1 a.

Groups of Khoikhoi migrated to various parts of southern Africa from what is now northern Botswana approximately 2 000 years ago; at that time they were predominantly nomadic pastoralists. The only branch surviving as a group and still speaking a Khoikhoi language are the Nama of Namibia.

Recently, the division between the Khoikhoi and the San (Bushmen) has come to be seen by some as a false one, and is understood as describing differences of lifestyle rather than of ethnicity.

1791 tr. *F. Le Vaillant's Trav.* II. 154 A Hottentot man .. Khoé-Khoep ... A Hottentot woman .. Toraré-Khoes. **1801** J. Barrow *Trav.* I. 151 Each horde had its particular name, but that by which the whole nation was distinguished, and which .. they bear among themselves in every part of the country, is *Quaiquae*. **1847** — *Reflect.* 163 In their own language, it [sc. the name 'Hottentot'] has neither place nor meaning: they call themselves, in every part of the country over which they are scattered, *Quaiquae*. **1877** J. Noble *S. Afr.* 16 The weak and scattered Hottentot tribes – the Khoi-Khoin, as they termed themselves. **1880** *Encycl. Brit.* XII. 310 Women were held in high repute: the most sacred oath a Khoi-Khoi could take was to swear by his sister or mother. **1908** J.M. Orpen *Reminisc.* (1964) 24 The Hottentots called themselves Khoin Khoin, (men of men). **1925** D. Kidd *Essential Kafir* 409 The word Koi-koi means Men of Men, or Men par excellence, the Bantu or Kafirs being in their estimation creatures of a very low order, whom they call things or dogs. **1930** I. Schapera *KhoiSan Peoples* 44 The Hottentots .. all .. apparently owned to the common name *Khoi-khoin* (men of men, i.e. men *par excellence*, people of pure race), by which they distinguished themselves from other peoples. **1963** Wilson & Mafeje *Langa* 1 The Coloured people count among their ancestors the aborigines of the Cape, the Khoikhoin people, or so-called Hottentots. **1966** W.P. Carstens *Social Structure Cape Coloured Reserve* 2, I prefer to use the term Khoi Khoin because the word Hottentot has become a derogatory stereotype in South Africa, symbolising the undesirable characteristics attributed to people of Khoi Khoin descent. **1976** Cubitt & Richter *South West*, Today's .. Nama .. are descendants of the Xhoi-Xhoi, the 'men of men', who share the Bushman's linguistic clicks and mongoloid eyes, peppercorn hair, bridgeless nose and yellow skin. **1976** *HSRC Newsletter* June, The Khoe-khoen spoke languages characterised by click sounds and the omission or alteration of these sounds may change the meaning of a word .. completely. **1977** K.F.R. Budack in A. Traill *Khoisan Ling. Studies* 3 1 It is their annual harvesting of the *!nara* melon and sea-fishing that makes them [sc. the Topnaar] different from any other Khoe-khoe tribe. **1977** R. Elphick *Kraal & Castle* 25 This Bushman-Hottentot (or Khoikhoi-San) dichotomy has become one of those time-honoured pairing mechanisms by which scholars automatically organize, but also distort, the complexities of historical reality. **1980** J. Cock *Maids & Madams* 173 The Khoikhoi were caught in the middle between the Xhosa and the colonists. **1983** P. Warwick *Black People & S. Afr. War* 11 As well as participating in the commandos, Khoikhoi and Coloureds entered into professional military service at the Cape. **1983** P.S. Rabie tr. *Nienaber & Raper's Hottentot Place Names* 12 There were the Khoekhoen who had become *Oorlam, Baster, Griqua* or *Coloured* and adopted the culture of the Europeans, and .. the traditional Khoekhoen. **1985** *Weekly Mail* 16 Aug. 16 The fatal confrontation of Dutch and Khoikhoi began the long and often bitter story which has since formed the main theme of South African history. **1988** C.A. Hromnik in *Weekend Argus* 18 June 5 *Khoikhoi* is a name *ex academia*. It was created by European writers out of their misunderstanding of the historical sources and reality ... To include women in history, another hyphenated name, *Tararekhoes*, would have to be invented. **1991** *Bulletin* (Centre for Science Dev.) Mar. 3 The missionaries failed to transform the nomadic Khoikhoi into sedentary agricultural and trading communities.

2. Any of the group of languages or dialects spoken by this people; Hottentot *n.* sense 1 c; Khoi sense 2. Also *attrib.* See also Khoisan sense 2, Nama *n.* sense 2, and the note at San sense 2.

1881 T. Hahn *Tsuni-‖Goam* 5 The Khoikhoi language is entirely void of prefixes. **1897** A.J. Butler tr. *Ratzel's Hist. Mankind* II. 247 The Khoi-Khoi (Bushmen and Hottentot) group of languages. **1969** *Oxford Hist. of S. Afr.* I. 10 Blood group studies suggest .. that certain Khoikhoi speakers are closely allied in their blood-group patterns to African negroids. *Ibid.* 43 There were .. groups of herders, most of whom spoke Khoikhoi. **1976** *E. Prov. Herald* 6 July 11 We were talking about Khoekhoen, the languages spoken by the Hottentot people. **1977** R. Elphick *Kraal & Castle* 29 As Jan Danckaert noted in 1660, 'there [was] also one language which all their great ones understand but which the common people do not.' This lingua franca was doubtless Khoikhoi. **1981** A. Paton in *Optima* Vol.30 No.2, 86 They called a great part of it [sc. the land] by its Khoikhoi name, the 'Karoo'. **1983** P.S. Rabie tr. *Nienaber & Raper's Hottentot Place Names* 21 Even experts on Khoekhoen often give explanations based on assumption .. in areas where Khoekhoen has become obsolete and no local assistance can be obtained. **1989** P.E. Raper *Dict. of Sn Afr. Place Names* 9 An obviously English name such as *The coombs* is not English at all, but Khoekhoen; it means 'river of wild olive trees'. **1990** *Weekend Post* 21 July (Leisure) 7 The stream rising from the springs gave it [sc. Windhoek] both its Khoikhoi name of Ai-gams and the Herero one, Otjomuise.

Khoin var. Khoi.

Khoisan /ˈkɔɪˌsɑːn, -ˌsæn, ˈxɔɪˌsɑːn/ *pl. n.* Also **Xhoisan**. [Coined in German in 1928 by L. Schultze, fr. *Khoikhoin* (see Khoikhoi) + *San* (see San).]

1. The Khoikhoi and San peoples collectively; Hottentot *n.* sense 3 a; cf. Boschman Hottentot. Also *attrib.* See also Capoid *n.*

See note at San sense 1.

1930 I. Schapera *KhoiSan Peoples* 5 The term Khoisan, recently coined by Schultze to denote the racial stock to which the Bushmen and the Hottentots belong, has .. been accepted .. as a convenient generic name for these people. The term is compounded of the names Khoi-Khoin, by which the Hottentots call themselves, and San, applied by the Hottentots to the Bushmen. **1966** J.P. van S. Bruwer *S.W. Afr.: Disputed Land* 21 The Khoisan peoples of the click languages, namely Bushmen, Dama and Nama, were experiencing the clash of cultures between nomadic hunters and pastoralists. **1976** A.R. Willcox *Sn Land* 119 In recognition of the similarity in some physical characteristics of the *khoikhoi* and the *san*, the term *khoisan* has been invented to describe the common features and a possible ancestral race or sub-race from which they originated. **1980** D.B. Coplan Urbanization of African Performing Arts. 434 *Khoisan*, The aboriginal, non-Bantu-speaking, non-Negro inhabitants of South Africa. Colloquially known as Hottentot (Khoi, pastoralist) and Bushman (San, hunter-gatherer). **1982** M. Mzamane *Children of Soweto* 25 He asked what difference it made to me whether Jan van Riebeeck had met the Khoisan or the Incas when he landed at the Cape. **1983** *S. Afr. 1983: Off. Yrbk* (Dept of Foreign Affairs & Info.) 77 The Bushman (San) and Hottentots (Khoikhoin), collectively known as Khoisan. **1985** A. Tredgold *Bay between Mountains* 149 There were .. crude stone choppers and other indications that this had been the home of Khoisan strandlopers. **1985** *Weekly Mail* 12 July 11 The original inhabitants of much of South Africa were of Khoisan origin and they were slaughtered by invaders both black and white. **1987** B. Lau *Namibia in Jonker Afrikaner's Time* 19 Boer farmers .. won their new freedom and property largely at the expense of the local Khoisan population who were dispossessed of their land, lost their stock, became servants or slaves, and generally suffered a great measure of violence. **1991** J. Coulter in *Weekend Post* 4 May (Leisure) 3 All witnessed .. the agility of the Khoisan. They would identify themselves with a buck bounding across the .. veld with flying leaps .., or mime the inimitable gait of the baboon lumbering along. [**1994** 'Hogarth' in *Sunday Times* 18 Sept. 22 PAC general secretary Benny Alexander's new name !Khoisan X, might not be as politically correct as he thinks it is ... His new name translates roughly into poor rascal. It is derived from the Nama word Khoi, meaning simply person, and their derogatory term, San, for someone who owns no cattle, or is a rascal. The name is mired in racist and colonial overtones, being a portmanteau word coined by a German anthropologist to lump together people once known as Hottentots or Bushmen.]

2. The group of languages or dialects spoken by these peoples; Hottentot *n.* sense 3 b. Also *attrib.* See also Khoikhoi sense 2, San sense 2.

1930 I. Schapera *KhoiSan Peoples* 438 The vocabularies of the Khoisan languages are necessarily very restricted along certain lines. **1977** C.F. & F.M. Voegelin *Classification & Index World's Lang.* 201 South African Khoisan. Central ... 36. San = Saan. **1977** E.A. Gregersen *Language in Africa* 125 The traditional notion of Khoisan actually encompasses five independent and unrelated language groups. **1978** *Annual Bulletin of Logopedics* (Univ. of Tokyo) XII. 113 Click sounds characterized by the ingressive velaric airstream .. are found in the Khoisan (the Hottentot and Bushman) languages. **1990** *Weekly Mail* 21 Sept. 7 The American Committee on Africa took .. exception ... Why, they ask, is there 'no mention of the .. extermination of San and Khoisan-speaking peoples and cultures'.

Hence **Khoisaniform** *adj.*; **Khoisanoid** *adj.* and *n.*; see also Capoid *adj.*, Gariepine.

1971 P.V. Tobias in *Std Encycl. of Sn Afr.* III. 95 The Capoids comprise the Bushman and, in a mixed state, the Hottentots, Korana and Sandawe of Tanganyika. Thus the term covers the congeries of people commonly grouped as the Khoisanoid or Khoisaniform race or complex of races. The Capoids or Khoisanoids were formerly regarded as one of the five major subdivisions of living mankind. 1986 P. MAYLAM *Hist. of Afr. People* 34 The archeological evidence .. does suggest, according to Derricourt, an 'admixture of Khoisanoid, Negroid and Caucasoid'. 1991 J. COULTER in *Weekend Post* 4 May (Leisure) 3 These unique African people are the descendants of the ancient Capoid or Khoisanoid division of man.

khoko var. GOGGA.

kholwa /ˈkɔːlwa/ *n.* Also **kolwa, m(a)kolwa.** Pl. **amakolwa** /ama-/, **amakholwa(s), kholwas.** [Xhosa and Zulu *ikholwa* believer. For an explanation of plural forms, see AMA-.] A name given (esp. in the past) to a Christian African. Also *transf.*, a westernized or middle-class black person. Also *attrib.* See also SCHOOL *adj.* sense 1.

1899 A. WERNER *Captain of Locusts* 179 These Amakolwa girls — with a spiteful emphasis (Nono was a former pupil of the Mission school, and a regular church goer) — every one knew what they were, for all the airs they gave themselves with their frocks and their starched cappies. 1903 *Ilanga* 8 May 3 Christian Natives ... The following clippings .. may prove interesting to our readers especially in reference to the behaviour of *kolwa* Natives. 1903 Ibid. 22 May 4 Kolwa Natives would be willing to pay a reasonable fee for a clean place to sleep in ... Civilized Natives cannot go into any of the Restaurants because of their colour. 1903 Ibid. 20 Nov. 4 Nearly all the Amakolwas some time ago possessed wagons and spans of oxen. 1906 *E. London Dispatch* 14 Feb. 4 Accused is a 'Mkolwa' or Christianised native. 1908 D. BLACKBURN *Leaven* 33 My God, a makolwa! (Christianised native). 1911 M.S. EVANS *Black & White in S.E. Afr.* 84 At one time either a native was tribal .. or he was a mission Christian, a kolwa or believer. 1944 C.R. PRANCE *Under Blue Roof* 56 The 'Kolwas' have lit a fire which flames like a sudden lighthouse beacon. 1949 O. WALKER *Proud Zulu* (1951) 202 Through another messenger, a 'kolwa' or Christian Zulu, Cetewayo sent his bound copy of the rules read out to him by .. Shepstone. 1962 W.D. HAMMOND-TOOKE *Bhaca Soc.* 64 Christians are called by pagans 'amakholwa' (believers) or, occasionally, amagqoboka (the pierced ones), while pagans are referred to as amaqaba (those smeared with red ochre). 1980 D.B. COPLAN *Urbanization of African Performing Arts.* 159 The *amakholwa* ('believers') as African Christians were called, became increasingly bitter about White resistance to their advancement in every field. 1986 P. MAYLAM *Hist. of Afr. People* 85 The ranks of the *kholwa* also produced resourceful, enterprising people. In the last three decades of the nineteenth century *kholwa* aspired to positions of leadership in the church. 1988 B. GUEST in Laband & Haswell *Pietermaritzburg 1838–1988* 125 The enterprising *kholwa* (convert) members of the black community .. were quick to extend their transport-riding activitoes inland to the diamond fields. 1989 *Frontline* Apr. 12 Edendale is one of the few places where blacks have always owned land. There are wealthy people known as the amaKholwa, (that is, bourgeois), whose ancestors were given land as a reward for siding with the English in the war of 1879. These people are resented.

khonia var. GHONYA.

khonza var. KONZA.

khora(a)n var. KORHAAN.

khori var. KORI.

khosi var. INKOSI *n.*

khoskhaz var. INKOSIKAZI.

khot(h)la var. KGOTLA.

‖**khotso** /ˈxɔːtsɔ/ *int.* [S. Sotho.] A traditional Sotho greeting, 'peace'. See also PULA *int.*

1934 *Friend* 2 Mar. (Swart), The High Commissioner then greeted the Natives with the salute, 'pula' and 'khotso', and back it was chorused by the Basutos. 1953 LANHAM & MOPELI-PAULUS *Blanket Boy's Moon* 17 After the Chief's speech, the tribesmen shout out 'Pula! Khotsa! Morena!' — Rain! Peace! Chief! 1968 A. FULTON *Dark Side of Mercy* 14 'Khotso.' Together they voiced the customary greeting as Michael dismounted. 1985 *S. Afr. Panorama* June 6 Zion in the Transvaal is a City of Peace. *Khotso* (Peace) is the traditional greeting. 1988 *Pace* Mar. 58 Here you will be greeted with welcome cries of 'Khotso — peace be with you', as you are offered a friendly beaker of joala, the local beer. 1990 T. WA MOLAKENG in *Frontline* Dec. 18 Sothos are friendly, respectful and peaceful. They greet each other with 'Khotso' (Peace), and respond 'A e ate' (May it — peace — reign). 1992 R. NXUMALO in *Weekly Mail* 24 Apr. 21 Mandela's speech was cleverly sprinkled with the ZCC's axiomatic salutation 'Khotso', which means 'peace unto you'.

Khoza var. XHOSA.

Khu var. KUNG.

khune var. KUHNE.

Khung var. KUNG.

khwedini var. KWEDINI.

khwela var. KWELA.

khwela-khwela var. KWELA-KWELA.

khwetha var. ABAKWETHA.

khwidini var. KWEDINI.

kia var. KAYA.

kiaat /kiˈɑːt/ *n.* Also **chiaten, coyatta, kajat, kejaat, kiatt, kijaat.** [Du. *kiaat, kiaten* (earlier *kajaten*) fr. Sundanese *ki jati*, Javanese and Malay *kayu jati, kayu* wood + *jati* teak. Cf. KAJATENHOUT.] The hardwood tree *Pterocarpus angolensis* of the Fabaceae; the wood of this tree; BLOODWOOD; DOLF; KAJATENHOUT; *Transvaal teak*, see TRANSVAAL. Also *attrib.*

1843 J.C. CHASE *Cape of G.H.* 160 Coyatta. A species of the teak. 1934 C.P. SWART Supplement to Pettman. 87 *Kejaat,*.. The South African teak; the wood is dark-brown, with a conspicuous grain, presenting a beautiful appearance. The wood is extremely durable and is extensively used for furniture and high-class joinery. 1951 N.L. KING *Tree-Planting* 70 *Pterocarpus angolensis* (Kiaat), A small to medium-sized tree with sweetly scented, yellowish flowers which appear before the leaves. 1969 I. VAUGHAN *Last of Sunlit Yrs* 53 The huge old stable door of polished Kiaat, with giant steel locks. 1971 BARAITSER & OBHOLZER *Cape Country Furn.* 279 Kiaat is also known as blood wood, Transvaal teak and Kehatenhout. Kiaat is a medium sized tree, usually not exceeding 13m in height. 1984 *S. Afr. Panorama* Feb. 39 Of all the indigenous woods used for furniture, kiaat has one of the most beautiful grains. 1987 Ibid. Sept. 15 Stately kiaat trees covered with yellow sweetpea blooms. 1989 *Daily Dispatch* 11 Mar. 16 Kiaat Morris chair, Teak Double Bed.

kief var. KIF.

kiel-back var. GEELBEK.

kiel sick var. KEIL SICK(NESS).

kiep, kiepie /kɪp, ˈkɪpi/ *n.* Also **kepi, kip(i), kippie.** [Afk., fr. Du. *kip(per)* chicken, hen.]

1.a. In the language of children: a chicken.

1866 E.L. PRICE *Jrnls* (1956) 224 He alone feeds our fowls ... He seeks his wee beker everywhere and runs to Monagen or whoever is at hand and says 'Miri — beker! kepi' & they never are hungry I am sure — our fowls ... One day he took the beads to a man who brought [a fowl] & seeing the man give up the 'kipi' to him on the receipt of the beads, he is always busy at the bead box trying to get some. 1956 U. LONG *Jrnls of Elizabeth Lees Price* 224 'Kepi' is perhaps derived from the sound made when calling the chickens. 1970 M.E. TAMLIN Informant, Cape Town Kiepie. Fowl, child's name for it. 1975 S. ROBERTS *Outside Life's Feast* 53 'Let's go and see the kiepies,' said Ann. They .. stood hand-in-hand looking at the shabby, self-important chickens that milled about gossiping and complaining in a tiny hok.

b. In the reduplicated form **kiep-kiep**: a call to gather farm-yard chickens together; a child's term for a chicken. So **kiep-kiep** *v. intrans. nonce*, to make a clucking noise, esp. in order to call chickens together.

See note at NOW-NOW.

1907 J.P. FITZPATRICK *Jock of Bushveld* (1909) 94 He would crow and cluck-cluck or kip-kip. 1934 C.P. SWART Supplement to Pettman. 89 *Kiep, kiep,* An onomatopoetic expression, extensively used in Southern Africa, to call fowls together. c1966 M. JABOUR in *New S. Afr. Writing* 91 It's not sweets. It's fowl food for Kosie's Kiep Kiep. 1968 M. MULLER *Green Peaches Ripen* 29 When they heard her strange high-pitched cry 'Kip! Kip! Kip! Kip!', they'd appear from every direction — wings flapping, scraggy necks stretched out, running, flying and cackling.

2. *comb.* In the names of plants: **kiepiebos** /-ˌbɔs/ [Afk. *bos* bush], *Sutherlandia frutescens* or *S. tomentosa;* **kiep(ie)mielie** /-ˌmiːli/ [Afk. *mielie*, see MEALIE], a variety of maize, *Zea mays*, the grain of which is used as poultry food; *colloq.*, popcorn; **kipkippers**, also **kiepkiepies, kip-kippies**, a name given to several plants because of the appearance of their flowers or fruit, e.g. *Nymania capensis, Gladiolus alatus*, and *Sutherlandia frutescens*.

1917 R. MARLOTH *Common Names* 49 *Sutherlandia frutescens* (**Kippie'bos**). 1966 C.A. SMITH *Common Names* 290 Kiepiebos, *Sutherlandia frutescens; S. tomentosa.* 1966 C.A. SMITH *Common Names* 290 Kiepmielie, Zea Mays, ... A particular variety of which the grain is used as food for fowls (Afr.: kiepies), whence the vernacular name. The term 'kiepie' is derived from the Nederlands 'kip' (a fowl). 1973 BEETON & DORNER in *Eng. Usage in Sn Afr.* Vol.4 No.2, 24 *Kiepiemielies*,.. means 'chicken maize', a variety of grain used as chicken food; .. means 'popcorn'. 1913 C. PETTMAN *Africanderisms* 261 *Kip-kippies*, A wild fuchsia-like flower is so called in Namaqualand. 1917 R. MARLOTH *Common Names* 49 *Kipkippers* (Kipkippies) meaning 'chickens'. *Gladiolus alatus* (flowers); in other districts *Nymania capensis* (capsules). Also *Sutherlandia frutescens* (Kippie'bos). 1966 C.A. SMITH *Common Names* 290 Kiepkiepies, *Nymania capensis* .. see *kipkippers*. The vernacular name is strictly applied to the fruits only. Ibid. 291 Kipkippers (-kippies), A name applied by children to several plants, chiefly on account of their fruits ... In the two species of *Sutherlandia*, the vernacular name has reference to the resemblance of the bright red flowers to the wattles of fowls (Neth.: kipper).

kiepersol /ˈkipəsɒl, ˌkipəˈsɒl/ *n.* Also **kiperso(l)l, kippe-sol.** [Afk., ad. obsolete Indian Eng. *kittisol* parasol, esp. a Chinese parasol of paper and bamboo, fr. Pg. *quitasol, quitar* to take away, ward off + *sol* sun, see quot. 1966; but see also quot. 1954.] Any of several evergreen trees of the genus *Cussonia* of the Araliaceae, with umbrella-shaped crowns; CABBAGE TREE; NOOISBOOM; SAMAREELBOOM; UMBRELLA-TREE. Also *attrib.*

1879 O.E.A. SCHREINER in C. Clayton *Woman's Rose* (1986) 19 Upon the summit of the precipice a kiepersol tree grew, whose palm-like leaves were clearly cut out against the night sky. 1883 M.A. CAREY-HOBSON *Farm in Karoo* 120 The place was full of wild pigs ... Generally they had plenty of bulbs and the roots of the Kippersoll trees to eat. 1893 R. IRON *Dream Life* 26 A kippersol tree. Ibid. 29 She .. cut at the root of a kippersol, and got out a large piece .. and sat down to chew it. Kippersol is like raw quince. Ibid. 34 No food but kippersol juice for two days. 1913 C. PETTMAN *Africanderisms* 261 *Kippersol,*.. The name has been given in South Africa to a tree — *Cussonia Thyrsiflora* — which grows something like an umbrella in shape. 1954 K. COWIN *Bushveld, Bananas & Bounty* 78 We discovered that the name of our district, Kiepersol, meant more than that of an indigenous tree. The tree itself is of two varieties .. *cussonia spicata* and *cussonia umbellifera*, and according to legend the umbellifera .. was first called Kiepersol by the Cape Malays, whose word for monkey is *kie* and for umbrella is the Afrikaans word *persols* and the combination results in the picturesque name of Monkey's Umbrella. **1966** C.A. SMITH *Common Names* 290 *Kiepersol (boom)*, .. The vernacular name is an interesting corruption of the Portuguese 'quita-sol' (excluding the sun), though more directly from the Indian 'Kitty-sol' or 'Kippe-solis', names used for a type of light bamboo and paper parasol, the 'Chinese umbrella'. These terms are in themselves corruptions of 'quita-sol' introduced by the Portuguese in the 16th century, the Indian term being eventually employed at the Cape for *C. thyrisiflora* on account of the umbrella-like crown of leaves and so gave origin to the alternative name of Sambreelboom. **1970** D.E. ABOUD *Informant, Bloemfontein* The Kippersol tree is a common sight in the veld. (Kippersol is the Afrikaans word for the parasol tree.) **1972** PALMER & PITMAN *Trees of Sn Afr.* III. 1691 Most of the species [of *Cussonia*] are known as 'kiepersol' ... The name travelled to the Cape where it was first used for the *Cussonia* species common around Cape Town, *Cussonia thyrsiflora* Thunb., and is now a general name for all the cussonias with their parasol-like mops of leaves at the ends of the branches. **1976** A.P. BRINK *Instant in Wind* 93 They've been forced to rely on what Adam could provide to quench their thirst, mainly wild figs and the watery bulbs of *kiepersol* roots. **1987** *S. Afr. Panorama* June 49 The *kiepersol*, also known in English as the cabbage tree, has been named .. as the tree of the year of 1987. **1991** [see CABBAGE TREE].

kiepie see KIEP.

kierie /ˈkiri/ *n.* Also **car(ri)e, cary, kar(r)ie, keeri(e), keree, keri(e), kerre, kerri(e), kerry, kieri, kierrie, kiri(e), kirri(e), kur(r)ie.** [ad. Khoikhoi *karrie, keeri(e), kirri, kurie* (cf. Nama */káru-p, /káru-s*) (walking) stick.

The Afk.-influenced *kierie* has displaced *kerrie* as the most common orthography; however *kerrie* is still seen in KNOBKERRIE.]

A traditional weapon of the indigenous peoples of South Africa: a short, thick stick with a knobbed head, used as a club or missile (but also as a walking stick); FIGHTING STICK sense 2; INDUKU; KNOBKERRIE; KNOB-STICK; KNOPKIERIE; KNOPSTICK. Also *attrib.*, and *comb.* **kierie-play** *n.*, **kierie-toting** *ppl adj.* (objective), **kierie-stick** (*obs.*).

1731 G. MEDLEY tr. *P. Kolb's Present State of Cape of G.H.* I. 188 In their Right Hands, when they go abroad, they generally carry Two Sticks of Iron- or Olive-Wood. One they call *Kirri* ... The *Kirri* is about Three Foot long; and about an Inch thick. *Ibid.* 292 The Hottentots use their *Kirri-* and *Rackum*-Sticks .. as martial Weapons ... The *Kirri*-Sticks are for Warding off the Arrows .. and Whatever is thrown by the Enemy. *Ibid.* 330 The women rarely trouble themselves to interpose when the men fight only with Kirri sticks. **1786** G. FORSTER tr. *A. Sparrman's Voy. to Cape of G.H.* II. 9 They were all of them armed with one or more of the javelins, which they call *hassagais*, as well as with short sticks, to which they gave the name of *kirris*. **1812** A. PLUMPTRE tr. *H. Lichtenstein's Trav. in Sn Afr.* (1928) I. 218 A short stick of Hassagai wood, so cut, that a knob is made at the end by a part of the thick root of this stem. With the latter weapon, which the Hottentots call a *Kirri*, they turn aside the Hassagai by a strong side blow. They use the Kirri equally as a weapon of defence, in the way of a bludgeon, when they come to close fighting. *a*1823 J. EWART *Jrnl* (1970) 50 Their arms consist of a long spear called a hassagai which they throw in the manner of a javelin .. and a small club called a keerie which they use when closely engaged. **1833** *Graham's Town Jrnl* 4 Apr. 3 A Caffer .. struck him several blows with a kierie. **1835** J.W.D. MOODIE *Ten Yrs* II. 269 They also show great dexerity in throwing the 'kurie,' which is a stick with a large knob on the end of it. **1836** R. GODLONTON *Narr. of Irruption* 48 The others said 'Stop, we will beat him to death with our kierries.' **1841** B. SHAW *Memorials* 300 They had but one musket, which Keudo took himself, his companions being armed with their assagais and keeries. **1857** N.J. MERRIMAN *Cape Jrnls* (1957) 90 After a little talk, on his admiring my kerie, a walking stick, I proposed an exchange with him. *a*1858 J. GOLDSWAIN in L.F. Casson *Dialect of Jeremiah Goldswain* (1955) Thear *Cares* or knobed sticks. **1891** T.R. BEATTIE *Pambaniso* 134 The youths .. had prevailed upon the chiefs to allow them to display their skill with the kerries, or long sticks. **1918** C. GARSTIN *Sunshine Settlers* 240 What is this woman talk? This is no Kaffir kerrie-play; it is a white man's war I tell you of. **1931** V. SAMPSON *Kom Binne* 139 The kerrie .. was a heavy stick two and a half feet long, with a round knob at one end, as large as an orange; .. a most dangerous bludgeon in the hands of a Kaffir. **1942** S. CLOETE *Hill of Doves* 622 In his hand he carried a black-and-white ox-hide shield, .. two long assegais, a short stabbing spear, and a kerrie. **1953** D. JACOBSON *Long Way from London* 61 Twelve black policemen, armed with heavy *kieries*. *Ibid.* 168 He stooped low to pick up his cane, a slender *kierie* of dark African wood. **1959** *Cape Times* 10 Nov. 1 Two other Europeans had been discharged after being treated for kierie wounds. **1963** L.F. FREED *Crime in S. Afr.* 76 Police squads have often to carry our day-and-night raids to stop the illicit liquor traffic, and also to suppress the stabbing and kerrie fights which invariably ensue. **1976** M. THOLO in C. Hermer *Diary of Maria Tholo* (1980) 59 They said, 'It was your children who made us stay away from work and lose our pay and now you go to work ...' And their kieries got busy. **1977** F.G. BUTLER *Karoo Morning* 55 Brandishing his kerrie. **1982** *Sunday Times* 28 Nov. (Mag. Sect.) 17 Dangerous tribesmen, for example, kierie-toting Zulus or South Sothos. **1985** *Argus* 31 Aug., He's the kierie king, is 75-year-old Abraham de Vries ... Oom Abraham knows all the secrets of kierie craft. **1986** *Pace* May 4 She chased them out of the house naked while letting fly with a kirrie. **1990** *Tribute* Sept. 56 The search for political support and group survival through the barrel of the gun .. the point of the spear, or the knob of a kierie. **1993** A.P. BRINK *First Life of Adamastor* 21, I jumped at him and grabbed the *karba*; but when I turned round there was a half-moon of people waiting with their *kieries*. *Ibid.* 88 In one *kierie* fight two men were badly wounded, and afterwards no one could explain what had caused it in the first place.

Hence (*nonce*) **kierie** *v. trans.*, to beat (someone) with a kierie.

1897 J.P. FITZPATRICK *Outspan* 97 You had a lucky escape. Umketch would have had you kerried.

kiesieblaar /ˈkɪsi͵blɑː(r). ˈki-/ *n.* Also **kissieblaar, kissi blad, kissie-blad.** Pl. **-blare** /-blɑːrə/, and (formerly) **-blaren, -bladeren.** [Afk., ad. S. Afr. Du. *keesjesblad* fr. Du. *kaasje blad* 'cheese leaf'.] The wild mallow *Malva parviflora* of the Malvaceae, a weed used for medicinal purposes.

1911 *E. London Dispatch* 9 June (Pettman), The plant known as *kissie-blad*. **1912** *Queenstown Rep.* 30 Aug. 8 (Pettman), Graaff Reinet. A farmer of this district reports losing seventeen ostriches and a horse through feeding them with mallows (*Kiesie bladeren*). **1914** *Farmer's Annual* 235 In connection with the poisonous nature of the mallow, or 'kissie blaar' ... He cut up mallows (kissie bladeren) .. and fed his ostriches and one horse systematically with the same, with the result that seventeen ostriches and a horse died. **1932** *Farming in S. Afr.* Nov. 378 (Swart), Experiments with 'kiesieblaar' (Parviflora) and milkweed were carried out with hamels and in both cases the animals remained healthy. **1966** C.A. SMITH *Common Names* 290 *Kiesieblaar*, A weed introduced from Europe about 1700 and now naturalized all over the Republic. The leaves were formerly used in decoctions for throat troubles or as fomentations and poultices in cases of neuralgia. **1973** [see KRIMPSIEKTE]. **1993** MILTON & DEAN in *Afr. Wildlife* Vol.47 No.1, 28 Their taste for such alien plants as Mexican poppy .. , stinkblaar .. , kissieblaar (*Malva parviflora*) and saltbush .. ensures the future of leopard tortoises on Karoo rangeland.

kievietje var. KIEWIETJIE.

kiewiet /ˈkivit, ˈkɪvɪt/ *n.* Also **keevit, keewit, keuvitt, keuwitt, k(i)ewit, kivi(t).** [Afk., onomatopoeic fr. its shrill, piercing cry.] The plover *Vanellus coronatus* of the Chariadriidae; KIEWIETJIE. Also *attrib.*

1785 G. FORSTER tr. *A. Sparrman's Voy. to Cape of G.H.* I. 153 Flocks of *keuvitts* .. towards the dusk of the evening screamed out a disagreeable sound resembling that of the name they bear. **1818** C.I. LATROBE 131 Some kivits, or plovers, were the only birds .. we saw, during several hours' ride. [**1824** W.J. BURCHELL *Trav.* II. 346 The armed plover .. is a very noisy bird; by night, as well as by day, uttering a sharp cry which was fancied to articulate the words *Brother Keevit! Brother Keevit!*] *a*1827 D. CARMICHAEL in W.J. Hooker *Botanical Misc.* (1831) II. 56 Numbers of .. *Koorhaans, (Otis Afra,)* and *Kewits, (Charadrius coronatus)*. **1827** T. PHILIPPS *Scenes & Occurrences* 17 We killed a few brace of partridges and a peewit, or as it is called here, a *keewit*; in moonlight nights they are constantly crying on the wing. **1835** E.A. KENDALL *Eng. Boy at Cape* III. 187 Birds of the peewit species, or, by the Dutch variation, *keewit*. **1867** E.L. LAYARD *Birds of S. Afr.* 294 *Hoplopterus Coronatus* .. *Kiewit* of the Dutch Colonists ... As soon as the cool shades of evening fall on the earth, the 'Kiewit' makes known its presence by its loud plaintive call. **1873** 'F.R.' in A.M.L. Robinson *Sel. Articles from Cape Monthly Mag.* (1978) 105 That birds and animals assume the colour of the soil in which they are found is well exemplified in the Karoo, where the *bont* or particoloured korhaan become the *vaal* or coloured one, and the kieviet the dik-kop, and the pauw (or buzzard) all differ in the same manner from those found near the sea-board. **1936** E.L. GILL *First Guide to S. Afr. Birds* 139 Crowned Lapwing, Kiewiet; *Stephanybix coronatus*. **1964** P.A. CLANCEY *Birds of Natal & Zululand* 156 *Vanellus coronatus* ... Not normally shy, but extremely vociferous, uttering a harsh cry which has given rise to its local name of 'kiewiet'. **1976** W. HÉFER in *Optima* Vol.26 No.2, 46 The kiewiet, or crowned plover, which lays its eggs in the orchards. **1986** F. FALLER *Weather Words* 9 Among tangled willow stands, kiewiets clamour. **1990** *Staffrider* Vol.9 No.1, 85 Like a kiewiet's wing his fingers brush my throat. **1993** R. GUY *Informant, Underberg* Well-found bird names like 'kiewiet' .. have come in quite naturally from Afrikaans ... Though the bird books don't recognize them as English words, they are widely used as such and are often more evocative of the real thing. Crowned plover forsooth.

kiewietjie /ˈkɪvɪki, ˈkiviki, -ci/ *n.* Also **kee-vekie, keveky, kevitje, kewiche, ki(e)vietje, kiewitje, kivike, kiviky, kivitje, kiwikie.** [Afk., *kiewiet* see prec. + dim. suffix -IE.] KIEWIET. Also *attrib.*

1835 T.H. BOWKER Journal. 16 Oct., Shot kevekys. **1891** E. GLANVILLE *Fossicker* 142 Clouds of long-legged, white-winged Kee-vekies, the pest of the hunter. *a*1885 T.H. BOWKER in M.E. Barber *Erythrina Tree* [Ms. insertion], The stars too are twinkling above in the sky And the night owl is screaming and kivikys cry. **1896** H.A. BRYDEN *Tales of S. Afr.* 121 The cry of one or two night birds may be heard — the dikkop and the kiewitje plovers. **1911** D.B. HOOK *'Tis but Yesterday* 57 Little birds called 'kevitjes'. [Note] The lively little plover-like singer familiar to many travellers. **1931** G. BEET *Grand Old Days* 15 Goodly gatherings of the gentle red-legged plover, or 'kiewietje' which even yet pays friendly visits to our farmers. [**1937** M. ALSTON *Wanderings* 61 Crowned lapwings ... The Dutch name for this bird is 'kiewetje' from the cry.] **1939** *Outspan* 22 Sept. 55 The kiewietjie is .. one of the easiest birds to photograph at the nest. **1940** BAUMANN & BRIGHT *Lost Republic* 234 The kivike .. flew about just after the sun had set, and screamed as if he were being hurt. **1959** J. MEIRING *Candle in Wind* 46 The high, shrill, piercing cry of the kiewietjie in the veld as it ran on its long thin legs through the grass. **1974** *E. Prov. Herald* 7 Nov. 5 The wide-eyed appearance of this 'kiewietjie' yesterday, nesting on a lawn .. , is understandable after it had to sit through the surrounding Guy Fawkes celebrations this week. **1982** *Ibid.* 9 Oct. 1 Golfers .. keep a sharp lookout for the flags that dot the fairways, marking the nests of the club's friendly kiewietjies. **1993** A.C. BROWN in

Afr. Wildlife Vol.47 No.2, 83 One of the kiewietjies had built a nest just inside the school fence, where we could clearly see it from the pavement.

2. *fig. colloq.* In the phr. ***kiewietjie beentjies*** [Afk., *been* leg + dim. suffix -IE + pl. -*s*], very thin legs.

1970 S. SPARKS *Informant, Fort Beaufort* That child has real 'kiewietjie beentjies' as she has such a poor appetite. (Very thin legs.)

kif /kɪf, kəf/ *adj. slang.* Also **kief, kiff.** [Transf. use of Eng. underworld slang *kef, kif* cannabis, fr. (in Morocco and Algeria) *kief, keef* cannabis or any other substance smoked to produce a state of well-being, fr. Arabic *kaif* (colloq. *kef*) good humour, pleasure, well-being.

The similarity in sound between *kief* and Afk. *gif* (poison) perh. led to the use of 'poison' as an adj. expressing approval; see quot. 1978 (where Afk. *gif* is suggested as the source of *kif*), and cf. *Durban poison* (see DURBAN).]

Esp. among schoolchildren: good, nice, fine; 'cool'; great, fantastic. Also as *int.*, 'great'.

1978 L. BARNES in *The 1820* Vol.51 No.12, 19 One should not forget that Durban is the home of *Durban poison*, the best dagga (cannabis) in the southern hemisphere ... And while on the subject of *poison*, it .. appears in expressions like *she's a poison bokkie*, or in its translated and further transliterated forms *gif* and *kif* – *she's a kif chick*. That means .. she's an attractive girl. **1983** A. GOLDSTUCK in *Frontline* Oct. 61, I tune you, mate, if I can get one mamba chow a day, I scheme life is kif. **1987** *Scope* 6 Nov. 36 Jimmy schemed that 'suicide by dynamite' would be a *kiff* idea. **1987** S. SMITH in *Fair Lady* 8 July 160 'Let's play some kiff vibes' is an invitation to enjoy some music. **1988** *Weekend Argus* Mar. (Suppl.) 3 The two teenagers with me pronounced the food very 'kif'. **1988** N. DEAN in *Style* June 101 It's really *kif* to go around in bare feet, but most have to relax their standards a little and wear leather sandals. **1988** A. DONALDSON in *Ibid.* Aug. 118 Hell, we could drink up a storm and catch fish. I know a *kif* spot to get galjoen. **1990** *Estcourt High School Mag.* No.49, 17 Kylie is from Australia. South African: Is it? Kiff hey! Which part of Australia are you from? **1991** E. WILLIAMS *Informant, Cape Town* Gee Ma, look at that Ninja Turtle T-shirt, Ma, can I have it, it's so smart, it's kif, ag please Ma. **1991** G. HERBERT *Informant, Durban* So you're able to attend? Kif! **1992** 'CHANTAL' on Radio 5, 'How are you?' 'I'm kif ... I haven't spoken to you for lank days.' **1993** C. TILNEY in *Rustenburg Girls' High School Mag.*, She called him over and they had this kiff rap and they both put in some major spadework.

kijaat var. KIAAT.

kijk var. KYK.

kill-me-quick *n. slang.* Esp. in township Eng.: a potent alcoholic drink made of sour porridge, bread, syrup, brown sugar, yeast, and bran. Also *attrib.* Cf. MBAMBA.

1948 E. HELLMANN *Rooiyard* 48 At the present time *babaton* comes first in popularity, with *shimeya* or *shimeyani* as close second. *c*1948 H. TRACEY *Lalela Zulu* 69 These potent drinks are special concoctions known to the Zulus by the speed of their action. 'Kill-me-quick' they say will make you drunk in a few minutes. **1952** *Drum* June 10 Africans .. are not allowed to buy wine in the bottle-stores; so they either get Coloured workers to buy it for them, or brew skokiaan or 'Kill-me-quick' for their weekend drinking. **1963** L.F. FREED *Crime in S. Afr.* 204 The concoctions which are sold to Natives in our large urban centres include 'isigomfana' ('kill me quick'), 'chechisa' (hurry), .. and others. **1968** COLE & FLAHERTY *House of Bondage* 140 For .. the oppressed and rootless of the cities who trudge from day to day without hope, drinking is a fast escape ... The name of one popular concoction is 'Kill Me Quick'. **1989** *Reader's Digest Illust. Hist.* 355 Drinking *skokiaan* and *isiqatavika* ('kill me quick') in order to forget the drabness of life in urban ghettos. **1992** *Daily News* 14 Sept. 1 It is called Indiza, .. one of the 'kill me quick' group of alcoholic drinks .. produced by inventive shebeen queens, and .. rumoured sometimes to include additives such as methylated spirits and battery acid.

kimbaars var. KOMBERS.

Kimberley Club *n. phr.* [See quot. 1936.] A dry sherry-type aperitif produced locally before the importation of European flor culture. Also *attrib.*

1934 *Cape Argus* 29 Jan. (Swart), The 'Kimberley Club' sherry we drink in South Africa is a pleasant substitute for the famous Spanish appetiser. **1936** L.G. GREEN *Secret Afr.* 166 In South Africa all the best dry wines of the type are called Kimberley Club. Even the club secretary could not tell me how the name became associated with the wine. Probably it is a relic of the great days of Cecil Rhodes, when Kimberley was one of the most prosperous towns in the world, and the wine cellar of the Kimberley Club was regarded as the standard of excellence. **1955** H. BECK *Meet Cape Wines*, The Cape developed a wine of its own, different from the Spanish, with a sherry character which was and still is widely used as an aperitif. Much of this type is sold as Kimberley Club sherry ... Some brands of Kimberley Club .. although they are dry have as much colour as some of the sweet sherries. **1966** *Ibid.* (ed.2) 35 Before the arrival of the flor sherries, those at the Cape fell into two classes, dry and sweet. The dry, for some reason unknown to me, was, and still is, often sold under the name of 'Kimberley Club' ... Some of these Kimberley Club sherries and similar ones under brand names can be really enjoyed. **1976** S. CLOETE *Chetoko* 177 There was an unopened bottle of Kimberley Club sherry on the sideboard beside the glasses.

kimberlite *n. Geology. Diamond-mining.* Also with initial capital. [Coined in 1886 by H.C. Lewis, being named for the place of its discovery, *Kimberley* (+ Eng. suffix *-ite* forming names of minerals).] BLUE GROUND. Also *attrib.*

In worldwide use.

1887 H.C. LEWIS in *Papers on the Diamond* (1897) 50 There appears to be no named rock-type having at once the composition and structure of the Kimberley rock ... It is now proposed to name the rock *Kimberlite* ... Kimberlite is a rock *sui generis*, dissimilar to any other known species. **1899** *Edinburgh Review* (U.K.) Apr. 319 This 'blue' rock – named 'Kimberlite' by Professor Carvill Lewis – is really of a dull green tint, due to its impregnation with iron oxides. **1905** [see BLUE GROUND]. **1920** F.C. CORNELL *Glamour of Prospecting* 37 He had just returned from a trip south to the Gibeon district, and he showed me some samples of excellent 'blue ground' – Kimberlite – he had found there. **1931** G. BEET *Grand Old Days* 97 For the exploitation of the kimberlite pipes, or craters, elaborate methods of open-cast and underground mining have been evolved in the past fifty years. **1968** S. TOLANSKY *Strategic Diamond* 27 The diamond .. has usually been brought to the surface region encased in a rock called 'blue ground' (from its colour) or alternatively called 'kimberlite'. **1973** A. HOCKING *Diamonds* 5 Volcanic diamond-bearing kimberlite shoots to the surface, cools to form the pipe. The elements erode exposed blue ground, thus scattering the diamonds it contains. **1976** A.R. WILLCOX *Sn Land* 219 The soft substance in which the first in situ diamonds were found (later called Kimberlite) was known as the 'yellow gravel'. Below it was the hard 'blue ground'. This was actually the same material in unweathered form. **1984** A. WANNENBURGH *Natural Wonder of Sn Afr.* 157 *Kimberlite pipe*, a cylindrical mass of rock formed when magma drilled from the interior of the earth to the surface by gas explosions cooled together with rock fragments plucked from the formations through which it passed. **1985** A.J.A. JANSE in Glover & Harris *Kimberlite Occurrence & Origin* 29 Kimberlites are rare rocks because their surface expressions are very small in extent, but they are widely spread theoughout all continents. **1993** *Business Day* 23 Nov. 7 UK company Reunion Mining has found two clusters of kimberlite near the shores of Lake Kariba.

Hence **kimberlitic** *adj.*

1972 *Daily Dispatch* 14 July 10 This time the geologists found abundant evidence of ilmenites and garnets of kimberlitic quality – the two chief indicators of diamond.

‖**kind** /kənt/ *n.* Pl. **kinders** /ˈkən(d)ə(r)s/, formerly also **kinder(en).** [Du. (pl. *kinderen*), later Afk. (pl. *kinders*).] Usu. in *pl.*: Children. Hence **kinderkins** *obs.* [Eng. dim. suffix *-kin*], little children.

1798 LADY A. BARNARD in Lord Lindsay *Lives of Lindsays* (1849) III. 454 We had a good many kinder baptized, the boys in their little man's nightcaps. **1827** T. PHILIPPS *Scenes & Occurrences* 12 The boor puts his vrouw and kinders into the wagon, lights his pipe and sets off to travel five hundred miles with as much ease as we should ten in England. **1852** A.W. COLE *Cape & Kafirs* 53 A stout, happy-looking old boer and his *frouw* and *kinderen*. **1872** C.A. PAYTON *Diamond Diggings* 106 He has with him not only his 'vrouw' and 'kinders,' i.e. wife and children, but a lot of Kafirs. **1879** R.J. ATCHERLEY *Trip to Boerland* 78 You are not supposed to shake hands with him [*sc.* the Boer] alone, but to extend the same form of salute to his vrouw and to every one of the kinderkins present. **1881** P. GILLMORE *Land of Boer* 106 Pater and Henrick want to see their frows and kinderkins. **1882** C. DU VAL *With Show through Sn Afr.* I. 87, I had large numbers of non-English-speaking Dutchmen, their 'vrouws' and their 'kinderen', amongst my audiences. **1882** [see KLEIN sense a]. **1911** L. COHEN *Reminisc. of Kimberley* 70 'Here's your money, Piet; give these to your frau and kinder as a present'. **1931** G. BEET *Grand Old Days* p. xv, Even the phlegmatic old Boer .. trekked forth from his 'plaas' at the back of beyond, along with his vrouw and kinders, intent on acquiring riches.

kinderbewys /ˈkən(d)ə(r)bəˌveɪs/ *n. Law.* Also **kinderbew(e)ijs.** Pl. **-bewyzen.** [Afk., earlier S. Afr. Du., fr. Du. *kinder* children + *bewijs* warranty, deed, proof.] A deed or bond made by the surviving spouse of a couple married in community of property, in order to secure the amounts due to minor children.

1821 C.I. LATROBE in P. Dale *Great Houses of Constantia* (1981) 148 He took out a special Deed of *Kinderbewys*, which allowed him to borrow money left to his children by their mother. **1824** in *Stat. Law of Cape of G.H.* (1862) 71 Deeds for securing the portion of children from former marriages .. stamps on deeds of kinderbewys. **1833** in *Stat. Law of Cape of G.H.* (1862) 293 Privileges of bonds passed by surviving spouses previously to their remarriage for securing the inheritance due to the minor children of their predeceased spouse (kinderbewyzen). **1862** in *Stat. Law of Cape of G.H.* 29 That the registration of kinder-bewyzen, and ante-nuptial contracts, although expressly ordered by a proclamation of the 23rd April, 1793, does, notwithstanding not take place universally. **1866** *Cape Town Dir.* 89 On Deeds of 'Kinderbewys' and General Mortgage, commonly called 'Notarial Bonds': Amount secured not exceeding £15 .. £0. 1. 0. **1873** *Cape Monthly Mag.* VII. 208 No widower having a minor child .. is allowed to marry unless he can show, by a document from the proper authority, either that the maternal portion coming to his minor child has been duly paid into the Guardian's Fund, or, what is oftener done, that the amount has been secured by a bond, called a *kinderbewijs*. **1894** *Stat. of Cape of G.H.* 260 Every general or notarial bond and every deed of kinderbewys which shall hereafter be tendered for registration at the Deeds Registry shall be accompanied by a duplicate or notarial copy to be filed of record. **1913** C. PETTMAN *Africanderisms* 260 *Kinderbewijs*, A bond passed by the surviving spouse of two persons married in community of property, to secure the property of the children accruing from the deceased parent. **1961** G. WILLE *Law of Mortgage & Pledge* 44 A *kinderbewijs* is the security given by a surviving parent for the portion of inheritance retained by him or her and belonging to the minor children. The word 'bewijs' means proof, and hence the term 'kinderbewijs' may be translated as 'proof of the inheritance due to a child.' **1975** H. SILBERBERG *Law of Property* 329

The so-called *Kinderbewys* which signifies the security which a surviving spouse, as guardian of a minor child, may be called upon to provide if and when she receives the inheritance due to such child from the estate of the predeceased spouse.

kinderen pl. form of KIND.

Kindergarten *n. hist.* [Transf. sense of general Eng. *kindergarten* school for the instruction of young children: in this sense first used by John X. Merriman (see quots 1902).] A nickname given to a group of young Oxford graduates recruited by Alfred, Lord Milner, British High Commissioner in South Africa, to work under him in the administration and reconstruction of the former Boer republics after the South African War of 1899–1902. Freq. *Milner's Kindergarten.*

[1902 J.X. MERRIMAN *Case Against Suspension of Constitution* 9 Lord Milner was good enough to describe the nature of the Government that was to be set up. It was a Council. I wonder what sort of a Council it would be ... Was the idea to set up a sort of kindergarten of young Balliol men? 1902 *Cape Times* 12 Sept. 6 He (Mr. Merriman) wondered what sort of rag-tag and bob-tail they would have got to sit on that Council ... What did he expect to set up? A sort of kindergarten of young Balliol men — laughter — to govern this great country.] 1913 W.B. WORSFOLD *Reconstruction New Colonies* I. 259 Mr Curtis was one of the most flagrant examples of Lord Milner's 'kindergarten'. 1958 *Spectator* (U.K.) 22 Aug. 244 The ideas of Milner and his dedicated 'kindergarten' about the treatment of the African. 1958 *Listener* (U.K.) 6 Nov. 739 The group of Englishmen who helped to bring order out of chaos and to prepare the way for the future came to be nicknamed Lord Milner's 'kindergarten'. 1963 M. BENSON *Afr. Patriots* 20 The British Government was influenced considerably by Milner's Kindergarten .. who lobbied passionately for Union. 1971 *Oxford Hist. of S. Afr.* II. 331 Locally he appointed young Oxford graduates – 'Milner's kindergarten' – to the administrative positions. *Ibid.* 346 To Selborne and the members of the Kindergarten .. unification was desirable. 1979 T. PAKENHAM *Boer War* (1982) 484 He [*sc.* Lord Milner] had an exciting task: to recruit imperially minded young men .. , his own 'Kindergarten' they would be called, for the .. task of nation-building in modern South Africa. 1987 G. VINEY *Col. Houses* 198 Lionel Curtis, one of the Kindergarten, came to the rescue.

kinders pl. form of KIND.

King *n. colloq.* An informal name for *King William's Town*, a town in the Eastern Cape, once the capital of the 19th century provinces of Queen Adelaide and British Kaffraria. Also *attrib.*

1880 F.G. BROWNING *Fighting & Farming* 118 He was immediately sent on to the hospital at 'King'. *Ibid.* 119 A waggon with liquor on board .. had come from 'King'. 1886 *See* BORDER sense 1]. 1897 G.A. PARKER *S. Afr. Sports* 14 Cape Town, King, and Kimberley took part [in the tourney] with the Bayonians. 1913 C. PETTMAN *Africanderisms* 260 King, Abbreviated form of King William's Town in general use. This town, named after William IV, is situated at the foot of the Amatolas, on the Buffalo River. 1923 B. RONAN *Forty S. Afr. Yrs* 80 At length we lumbered into 'King', and I made the acquaintance of my new comrades. 1956 M. ROGERS *Black Sash* 169 From 'King' the convoy .. will make its way to the Cape via Grahamstown, Port Elizabeth. 1958 I. VAUGHAN *Diary* 18 We must go on .. to a place called King where the Kafirs live always in red blankets. 1971 *Daily Dispatch* 11 May 10 There is naturally a chance that the King councillors might decide they agree with the Schornville removal scheme. 1973 *Weekend Post* 27 Oct. (Parade) 2 A train service was also available from East London .. on race days at 'King'.

Hence **Kingite** *n.*, an inhabitant of King William's Town.

1993 *Daily Dispatch* 26 Aug. 4 Kingites accuse traffic dept. of selective fining. 1994 *Weekend Post* 22 Oct. 5 Kingites are doing more than painting the town red.

kingfish *n.* [Perh. transf. use of Austral. and N.Z. Eng. *kingfish* a name applied to the carangoid fish *Seriola lalandii*.] Any of several marine fishes of the Carangidae, but particularly *Pseodocaranx dentex*. See also MAASBANKER.

In Smith and Heemstra's *Smiths' Sea Fishes* (1986), the name 'kingfish' is used for fishes of the Carangidae.

1862 *Argus* in V. DE KOCK *Fun They Had* (1955) 164 Here they cast a big net over the side, gazing down as it sank .. where inquisitive fish 'swarmed over and around it .. but presently one little bold "kingfish", gleaming in bronze armour, came nibbling at the bait'. 1906 *E. London Dispatch* 26 July (Pettman), A '*kingfish*' is illustrated, the particular specimen weighing 28 lb. 1930 C.L. BIDEN *Sea-Angling Fishes* 55 In South Africa Carangidae has 36 known species including Maas banker - .. King-fish of Natal and East Africa waters *Caranx carangus* (Bl.) *c*1936 *S. & E. Afr. Yr Bk & Guide* 347 The most valuable fish .. on the South African Coast are the sole, silver-fish, .. stockfish, harder or mullet, kingfish, mackerel, etc. 1951 R.D. CAMPBELL in A.C. Partridge *Lives, Lett., Diaries* (1971) 170 The kite was still climbing. It was a mere speck in the sky ... The natives saw it glinting and flashing yellow in the sun as we played it like some gigantic kingfish in the wind. 1955 C. HORNE *Fisherman's Eldorado* 156 Among those light tackle men are anglers who seek the kingfish. 1968 J.L.B. SMITH *High Tide* 82 One advantage of these coastal waters is the abundant free swimming surface fish easily caught by trolling, chiefly kingfish (Caranx), serra (the Natal barracuda, Scomberomorus), wahoo, small tunny and bonito and barracuda (the Natal snoek, Sphyraena). 1970 *Daily Dispatch* 16 June 17 Unusual catch – a kingfish – taken in the Nahoon River. Kingfish are thought to be found only in Natal and Pondoland waters and are rated among the finest fighters in the sea. 1988 *S. Afr. Panorama* Dec. 40 Shore fishermen seek the shad (*Pomatomus saltator*), kabeljou (*Argyrosomus hololepidotus*), grunter and inshore gamefish such as garrick (*Lichia amia*) and kingfish (*Caranx* species). 1989 J. PARNELL in *Ski-Boat* Jan.-Feb. 44 At low tide this is an idyllic spot for snorkeling, with beautiful coral, clams and all manner of sea creatures, including large kingfish, clearly visible in the crystal water.

kingklip /ˈkɪŋkləp, -klɪp/ *n.* [Short form of *kingklipfish*, part. tr. Afk. *koningklipvis* 'king rock fish'; see *king klipfish* (KLIPFISH sense 2).] Any of several species of marine fish (but esp. *Genypterus capensis*). **1.** Any of three species of rock cod of the Serranidae: **a.** *Acanthistius sebastoides*; **b.** *Epinephelus andersoni*; **c.** *E. guaza*. **2.** The eel-like cuskeel *Genypterus capensis* of the Ophidiidae, an esteemed table fish; formerly called *king-* or *koning klipfish* (see KLIPFISH sense 2), *king rock-fish* (see ROCK-FISH sense 3), KLIP (*n.* sense 3), KLIPFISH (sense 2), and KLIPVIS (sense 1). Also *attrib.* In both senses also called KONINGKLIP.

In Smith and Heemstra's *Smiths' Sea Fishes* (1986), the name 'kingklip' is used for *G. capensis*; the name 'koester' is used for *A. sebastoides*, and 'catface rock-cod' for *E. andersoni*.

[1801 J. BARROW *Trav.* I. 30 Another Blennius, called the King Rock-fish.] 1834 *Cape of G.H. Lit. Gaz.* July 103 Of fish abundance and great variety .. ; the best, the kingklip and stokfish. 1949 J.L.B. SMITH *Sea Fishes* 193 *Acanthistius sebastoides* (Castlenau). Soup-bully (East London). *Kingklip* or *Koningklip* (Knysna) ... Found only in South Africa from the Cape to Natal in shallow water among rocks ... Flesh excellent. *Ibid.* 195 *Epinephelus Andersoni* ... Rock-cod. *Kingklip* or *koningklip* (Knysna) ... Found only in our area from Knysna to Delagoa Bay, often in quite shallow water about rocks. Sluggish, but good eating. *Ibid.* 364 *Genypterus Capensis* ... Kingklip. Koningklip ... Found from Walfish Bay around to Algoa Bay in 30–250 fathoms. A rather slimy, quite unmistakable species, sometimes abundant. Flesh excellent, an important food-fish of Cape waters. 1956 M. ROGERS *Black Sash* 161 Parliament's two chefs prepared 15 turkeys, 30 ox-tongues, sole and king-klip, plus mixed salads and dessert. 1960 J. COPE *Tame Ox* 40 The trawlers came in from the deep sea loaded down to the gunwales with stock-fish, not to mention soles, silver, gurnet, kingklip, cob, white and red stumpnose, skate, yellowtail and tunny. 1966 J.L.B. & M.M. SMITH *Fishes of Tsitsikamma Coast National Park* 81 This almost eel-like fish is one of the best known first class eating fishes of our seas, from Walvis Bay round to Algoa Bay, and as it is nowhere abundant, far more fish named 'Kingklip' [*printed* Kingglip] on menus is eaten than is ever caught. 1975 *E. Prov. Herald* 27 May 34 Grapefruit adds a piquant flavour to kingklip steaks, baked crisp with buttered crumbs. 1975 M.M. SMITH in Smith & Jackson *Common & Scientific Names of Fishes* 24 *Xiphurus capensis* Koning-klip, Kingklip. 1975 [see KREEF]. 1977 *World* 27 Sept. (Suppl.) 2 We tried the kingklip fish which, although it came in smaller pieces, was served rich in a selection of vegetables and sauces to suit individual taste. 1982 *Fair Lady* 6 Oct. 6 Grilled kingklip, perlemoen fritters on the beach at Onrus River and shoulder of impala in cream and sherry in the bush are about the only dishes we would dare to put before those looming gastronomes. 1985 [see KLIPFISH sense 2]. 1988 *Style* Feb. 18 One of the most popular dishes for health conscious executives is the filleted grilled kingklip. 1989 E. PLATTER in *Style* Dec. 18, I have much enjoyed, here, good old kingklip and chips, the fish exceptionally succulent yet firm. 1990 *City Press* 11 Feb. 5 The ANC leader enjoyed a breakfast of kingklip fishcakes and cereal. 1994 *Weekend Post* 1 Jan. (Leisure) 6 Kingklip in Cider ... Cut kingklip into serving portions.

king klip fish see KLIPFISH sense 2.

kippersol(l), **kippe-sol** varr. KIEPERSOL.

kiri *n.*[1] var. KIERIE.

kiri *n.*[2], **kirie** varr. KARRIE *n.*[2]

Kirk var. KERK.

kirpater var. KAPATER.

kirram var. KEREM.

kirrey, kirri *n.*[1] varr. KARRIE *n.*[2]

kirri *n.*[2], **kirrie** *n.*[1] varr. KIERIE.

kirrie *n.*[2] var. KARRIE *n.*[2]

‖**kisklere** /ˈkəsˌklɪərə/ *pl. n. Hist.* [Afk., *kis* chest, box + *klere* clothes; see quot. 1975.] Best clothes, worn only on special occasions.

1944 J. MOCKFORD *Here Are S. Africans* 63 Every man .. would try to have at least one suit of *kisklere*, a carefully tended Sunday best. 1964 J. MEINTJES *Manor House* 29 On the afternoon of the funeral I was dressed in my black *kisklere*. 1972 A.A. TELFORD *Yesterday's Dress* 120 For special occasions like Church services and weddings, men kept at least one suit of 'kisklere', perhaps a tailcoat of broadcloth, a fancy waistcoat and cashmere trousers. 1975 D.H. STRUTT *Clothing Fashions* 211 Even the humblest families carried with them .. kisklere for church and very formal occasions. The latter, as the name indicates, were stored in a wagon chest away from dust and damp.

kissi blad, **kissie-blad**, **kissieblaar** varr. KIESIEBLAAR.

kist /kɪst/ *n.* [S. Afr. Du., fr. Du.] A chest or coffer, used usu. for storing clothes and linen. Also *attrib.*, *transf.*, and *fig.* See also WAKIS.

Found also in Scottish and northern Eng. dialects as a result of Scandinavian influence.

1838 J.E. ALEXANDER *Exped. into Int.* II. 293 It is hoped .. that the few public establishments which have been lately formed in the colony will .. draw the idle and unproductive capital from its slumbers in their *kists*, into active use in public improvements. 1927 C.G. BOTHA *Social Life in Cape Col.* 52 A large brass-bound kist or chest upon heavy carved feet, from the

Indies, was the general receptacle for the best clothes of the family. **1930** *Outspan* 25 July 63 Anna climbed once more to the loft and she took out all the neatly folded things from the kist. **1946** S. CLOETE *Afr. Portraits* 34 In each there would be a kist – a chest of fine hardwood with beautifully ornamented brass locks and hinges in which the Boers kept their best clothes. **1952** G.M. MILLS *First Ladies of Cape* 25 The elegance and workmanship of the locks and the silver work decorating the massive kists and camphor boxes. **1965** M.G. ATMORE *Cape Furn.* 215 The Cape kists were directly descended from these 17th Century Dutch chests and the earliest are indistinguishable from them. **1980** M. MATSHOBA in M. Mutloatse *Forced Landing* 117 You sleep .. on the door-like lid of a brick kist in which you are supposed to keep your belongings. **1985** *S. Afr. Panorama* Feb. 14 The Nourse, Geldenhuys, Jumpers and Meyer-and-Charlton mines were once dubbed 'the jewel *kist* (chest) of the Witwatersrand.' **1991** D. GALLOWAY in *Weekend Argus* 26 Jan. 18 Most of the old Cape furniture, from beds and dressers to kists and riempie chairs, was collected from second-hand shops and homes. **1993** *House & Leisure* Nov. 75 The Oregon and yellowwood kist at the foot of the brass bed.

kitchen *n.* and *adj. Derog.* Also with initial capital. [Special senses of general Eng.; prob. fr. literal tr. of S. Afr. Du. (and Afk.) *kombuis-*, see KOMBUIS.]

A. *n.*

1. In the offensive phr. ***kitchen kaffir*** /-'kæfə/ [see KAFFIR], also (occas.) ***kitchen Zulu, -Xhosa***, etc.: **a.** An inferior or pidgin variety of an African language. **b.** A former name for FANAKALO. See also KOMBUIS sense 1 a.

1862 G.H. MASON *Zululand* 38 The Bishop has been guided by one of the chief's clerks in the native department; who was born and reared amongst the Cape Colony's Caffres, and, consequently, prefers it to learning Zulu proper; which, or course, is held in contempt by all officials, and sneeringly called '*Kitchen Kaffir*'. **1885** H. RIDER HAGGARD *King Solomon's Mines* (1972) 109 Sir Henry and Umbopa sat conversing in a mixture of broken English and Kitchen Zulu in a low voice. *Ibid.* 261 'Art thou coming, Foulata?' asked Good in his villainous kitchen Kukuana. **1899** J.P. FITZPATRICK *Tvl from Within* 53 The man who interpreted knew a smattering of 'kitchen' Kaffir. **1907** [see GASHLE]. **1911** P. GIBBON *Margaret Harding* 2 'Kitchen Kafir,' the *lingua franca* of the Cape .. a sterile and colourless tongue – the embalmed corpse of the sonorous native speech. **1913** C. PETTMAN *Africanderisms* 262 *Kitchen Dutch or Kaffir*, The mixture of English and Dutch or English and Kaffir words frequently employed when speaking to servants by those who understand neither Dutch nor Kaffir perfectly. **1923** G.H. NICHOLLS *Bayete!* 344 Kitchen Kaffir, a vile hotch-potch of English, Dutch and Zulu, with a vocabulary of from twenty to fifty words. **1924** E.T. JOLLIE *Real Rhodesia* (1971) 261 Kitchen Kafir, the *lingua franca* of the natives in South Africa, is used on all mines and acquired by the majority of adult male natives. It consists of Zulu, Dutch and English, the proportion of words of each language used being according to the speaker's knowledge. **1936** P.M. CLARK *Autobiog. of Old Drifter* 127 At this time I knew nothing of the Barotse language, but got along with some of the natives who could talk what was called Kitchen Kaffir. **1943** F.H. ROSE *Kruger's Wagon* 47 He spoke .. what is known as 'Kitchen Kaffir,' which is a compendium of three languages, English, Dutch and Zulu, and is known and understood all over the country. **1949** C. BULLOCK *Rina* 102 He called out some light remark to the girl in his vile kitchen-kaffir gibberish. *Ibid.* 120 'For a kitchen-kaffir linguist you've learnt a good deal,' I said, 'unless, perhaps, your fertile imagination helps you as you go along with your tale.' *c*1955 M. HUME *Sawdust Heaven* 22 Kitchen Kaffir, that useful *lingua franca* of the border country that was a mixture of Zulu, Dutch, English, German, and a word here and there from no known tongue. **1957** [see FANAKALO]. **1961** D. BEE *Children of Yesterday* 25 They spoke in many different languages, these men ... And many understood the common lingua franca of the mines – 'fanagalo' or 'kitchen kaffir' – derived from the Zulu-Swazi-Xhosa languages mixed with corrupted English and Afrikaans words. **1972** L.G. GREEN *When Journey's Over* 123 Fanagalo has many names. Known in its early days as Kitchen Kaffir or Mine Kaffir, it has also been called .. Isilololo and Silunguboi. **1989** J. HOBBS *Thoughts in Makeshift Mortuary* 17 She greeted her staff .. and spoke to them in well-enunciated English rather than the kitchen Zulu most Durban madams used. *Ibid.* 92 She did not use the pidgin Zulu once known as kitchen kaffir, but now that the word 'kaffir' was acknowledged as insulting, called Fanagalo.

2. *Obs.* exc. *hist.* In the phr. ***kitchen Dutch***, or (occas.) ***kitchen Afrikaans***:

a. A derogatory name for the Afrikaans language (see AFRIKAANS *n.*).

1882 J. NIXON *Among Boers* 209 The language in vogue among the Boers and the semi-civilised native tribes of South Africa is a patois of Dutch, known as Kitchen Dutch. It contains a considerable proportion of Hottentot and English words, but the groundwork is Dutch, from which the inflections have been largely removed. Kitchen Dutch is a barbarous and uncouth dialect and I observed with pleasure that it was giving place to English. **1894** F.A. BARKLY *Among Boers & Basutos* 109 By this time they [*sc.* our two children] could both speak Sesuto and 'Low' or 'Kitchen Dutch' (as it is called in those parts) well. **1924** S.G. MILLIN *God's Step-Children* 286 He spoke English with a strong kitchen-Dutch accent, and with, now and then, a word of Dutch .. for Dutch was his home language. **1943** 'J. BURGER' *Black Man's Burden* 241 It is .. to be deprecated that Afrikaans is still spoken of slightingly as an inferior language, as 'kitchen-Dutch', as the 'taal', by people who ought to know better. **1964** V. POHL *Dawn & After* 102 What delighted us most was the originality of Gashep's speech. To us he spoke a kind of kitchen Dutch into which he introduced English and Sesuto words. **1972** N. HENSHILWOOD *Cape Childhood* 79 The coloured people, who spoke their version of it [*sc.* Afrikaans] which we referred to as 'Kitchen Dutch', spoke English to us in our homes. **1981** A. PATON in *Optima* Vol.30 No.2, 91 Dutch was spoken by hundreds of servants and slaves, and .. hundreds of Dutch children spent hundreds of hours with servants and slaves. The linguistic changes that came about through the use of this 'kitchen Dutch' were resisted by the church, the older generations, the purists. **1987** G. VINEY *Col. Houses* 104 The time when only English or *Hoer Duits* [*sic*] was spoken in the household and 'kitchen Dutch' punished by the offender's being sent down from table. **1987** *Ibid.* [see GEK]. **1992** Y. MAAKENSCHYN *Informant, Johannesburg* The use of 'kitchen' when referring to poor or little knowledge of a language, such as 'kitchen Dutch', 'kitchen German' etc.: ... When I have been overseas and told locals that I only have 'kitchen German' or 'kitchen French' they have stared at me blankly.

b. A derogatory name for the form of Afrikaans spoken by Cape 'coloured' and black people, and in the past by Khoikhoi people; cf. *kombuistaal* (see KOMBUIS sense 1 b).

1896 R. WALLACE *Farming Indust. of Cape Col.* 162 The people who were not Boers were Hottentots, and this servile race spoke kitchen Dutch. **1899** [see KOMBUIS sense 1 a]. **1915** D. FAIRBRIDGE *Torch Bearer* 66, I am proud to think that the language of my ancestors was French. What claim on us has this mixture of kitchen-Dutch and slave-talk which we call the Taal? **1979** W. EBERSOHN *Lonely Place* 79 He thought over what Lesoro's sister had told him in her awkward kitchen-Afrikaans.

B. *adj. obsolescent.* Of languages: inferior, emanating from the kitchen, or used in the kitchen, i.e. by or to servants:

1910 J. BUCHAN *Prester John* (1961) 39 The Dutch .. is a sort of kitchen dialect you can learn in a fortnight. **1958** A. JACKSON *Trader on Veld* 28, I learnt not only to speak but to write the 'Taal' fluently, but I must admit that it was the purest kombuis or Kitchen variety that I knew.

kitke /'kɪtkə/ *n.* Also **kitka**. [Etym. unkn.; perh. fr. Hebrew *kikkar* loaf.] In the Jewish community: the soft white Sabbath loaf or 'challah', braided and glazed with egg-white. Also *attrib.*

1977 *Fair Lady* 11 May 63 Especially on Fridays, their .. home would be filled with the aroma of kitke and cheese-cake for the Sabbath meal. **1980** C. HOPE *A Separate Development* (1983) 118 The baker hanged himself. His customers found him the next morning swinging 'directly above the doughnuts and a little to the left of the *kitke* loaves,' to quote the newspaper report. **1983** J.E. KAHN *Informant* A S. African in London bought a uniquely (Yiddish?) term to my attention in *kitke/kitka* .. the braided, poppy seeded loaf .. blessed and eaten on the Sabbath. In England it's called *challah* ... They don't know what you're talking about if you talk of *kitke*. **1985** *S. Afr. Cookbk* (Reader's Digest Assoc.) 380 *Kitke*, A plaited loaf of bread that is traditionally eaten on the Jewish sabbath. Also known as challah. **1987** *E. Prov. Herald* 17 Sept. 3 Kitke Long Each 99c **1988** *Fair Lady* 23 Nov. (Suppl.) 12 Bread! Bread! Bread! Milly's Mister Crusty Makes It – baguettes, kitka, rye, seed loaves, pitta and many-flavoured bagels. **1990** J. EDELMUTH *Hooked on Cooking* 179 Divide dough into three for 3 kitkes. Divide each piece into three. Roll each piece into a sausage shape and plait, pinching ends together ... Brush unglazed section on top of kitke with more egg mixture and replace in oven for last 10–15 minutes.

kits /'kəts, 'kɪts/ *combining form. Colloq.* [Afk., 'instant'; formed by analogy with *kitskonstabel* (see KITSKONSTABEL).] An element in various names for a KITSKONSTABEL, as **kitsconstable, kitscop** (being nouns which are also used attributively).

1987 *Progressive Trust for New S. Afr.* (Progressive Federal Party) (*pamphlet*), Lack of discipline evident amongst the poorly trained Special Constables (Kitsconstables) deployed in the townships. **1987** *Rhodeo* (Rhodes Univ.) Mar. 13 A Phillipi woman, .. was shot dead by her 'Kitskop' husband. **1987** *South* 2 July 1 (*caption*) Man blinded in kitscop shooting. **1988** *Argus* 20 Jan. 13 (*caption*) 'Kitscops' curbed in Oudtshoorn township. **1988** *Cape Times* 8 Aug. 1 Kits cops killed in city townships. Two special constables were killed in Cape Town townships at the weekend. **1993** [see KITSKONSTABEL]. **1993** *Weekly Mail & Guardian* 29 Oct. 1 What's a kitskop's life worth? R26 a day and pay for your own funeral.

kitskonstabel /'kətskɔnˌstɑːb(ə)l/ *n.* [Afk., *kits* trice, moment, instant + *konstabel* constable.] A derogatory name for a black police assistant or Special Constable assigned to the policing of the townships after only a short period of training; BLOUPAK.

1986 *E. Prov. Herald* 24 Sept. 1 The row over the 1 000 'kitskonstabels' undergoing a three-week crash course at Koeberg raged on yesterday. **1987** *Rhodeo* (Rhodes Univ.) Mar. 15 Since the imposition of the State of Emergency the state has begun arming and training black people to contain opposition in the townships. These 'kitskonstabels' as they have been called, because of their brief and inadequate training, are a cause for grave concern throughout the country. **1988** B. ORPEN in *E. Prov. Herald* 15 Jan. 5 In his affidavit, Mr N— said the township had been peaceful until the advent of the 'kitskonstabels' toward the end of June 1987. **1988** *Now Everyone Is Afraid* (Catholic Inst. for Internat. Rel.) 21 The kitskonstabels are second class members of the SAP. They are paid weekly wages that amount to under R400 per month and have no benefits. They are not treated as full members of the police team and are easily dismissed. Kitskonstabels need no educational qualifications. **1989** *Weekly Mail* 17 Mar. 5 Opposition spokesmen in Parliament .. have strongly criticised the kitskonstabels, not only because they receive only six weeks' training, but also because of their reputation for brutality in the townships and their record of abuses and irregularities. **1990** *New African* 25 June 10 We know of the dirty work done by the kitskonstabels and the KwaZulu Police and these other South African forces who are supposed to be keeping peace in the country. **1993** *Sunday Times* 11 July 22 There is a distinct risk we shall end up with another force of unready 'kitskonstabels', or 'kitsgeneraals', adding another dimension of disillusion, distrust, and freelance 'peacekeeping' by the semi-criminal gangs of the townships.

kivietje, kiviky varr. KIEWIETJIE.

kivi(t) var. KIEWIET.

kivitje, kiwikie varr. KIEWIETJIE.

kiya, kja varr. KAYA.

KK *n.* Initial letters of KAPPIE KOMMANDO.

1982 *Sunday Times* 28 Mar. 40 Angry ex-servicewomen this week blasted Kappiekommando leader Marie van Zyl for her 'outrageous' accusation .. A Cape Town lawyer .. has been briefed by the Ex Servicewomen's League to investigate what action to take against the KK leaders for their remarks.

klaar /klɑː(r)/ *adj. colloq.* [Afk., ready, finished, done, exhausted.] Finished, in the following senses:

1. Ready, prepared, completed; GEDAAN sense 2.

1852 M.B. HUDSON *S. Afr. Frontier Life* 208 I, as a guest, no enjoyment to mar, Lie slumbering on, till the coffee is 'klaar'. **1872** 'Z.' in *Cape Monthly Mag.* V. Oct. 229 Would any of us wish to get rid of the expressive 'disselboom' and revert to the unsuggestive 'pole?' Can we do anything else than 'trek,' when we have packed our wagons, and made all 'klaar' to start for the Diamond-fields? *a***1875** T. BAINES *Jrnl of Res.* (1964) II. 33 In a few minutes more, coffee was pronounced klaar, or ready, and the edibles .. were soon discussed. **1912** *E. London Dispatch* 2 July 8 (Pettman), It is anticipated that in six months' time the long-talked-of bridge will be *un fait accompli*, or to suit the times should one say it will be *klaar*? **1913** C. PETTMAN *Africanderisms* 262 Klaar, .. This word is in every-day use in the Midland Districts of the Colony, both among English and Dutch, in both its meanings — clear and ready.

2. Over; all gone.

1960 J. COPE *Tame Ox* 180 Well, that's how it is. Finished, *klaar*. Take my kit out of Swart's boat and put it back in the shed. **1970** *Informant, Grahamstown*, I am klaar with this work now. **1978** C. VAN WYK in *Staffrider* Vol.1 No.2, 36 When you want the stuff, it's klaar. Don't lieg, man, it's all still there by the possie.

3. 'Finished', exhausted, depleted; ruined, 'done for'. Cf. GEDAAN sense 1.

1964 J. BENNETT *Mr Fisherman* (1967) 100 'We're klaar,' said Pillay. 'That's what it is.' He felt all his strength, all the reserve of endurance which he had been nursing so jealously, ebb slowly away. *Ibid.* 119 'You're finished, old man, he said. Finished, *klaar*. You're no use for nothing any more.' **1971** *Sunday Times* 14 Nov. 15 When Sir De Villiers dealt with B— and his legal costs several members of the audience voiced the opinion that 'B— is klaar'. [**1987** L. BEAKE *Strollers* 37 Koosie spoke then, eventually, and Johnny thought that his words did him great credit. 'En André? .. En Pieter?' he gasped. 'Klaar,' Abraham said, with great relish. (Finished? Johnny thought in great alarm, not *dead*, surely?) 'Klaar,' his brother continued, '*in* Jo-hann-es-burg.']

4. In the phrr. ***finished(ed) and klaar***, or ***finish(ed) en klaar*** [Afk. *en* and]:

a. An emphatic interjection of finality, 'that's that', 'all done', 'nothing more to be said'.

1969 A. FUGARD *Boesman & Lena* 16 'Take her' .. finish en klaar. They know the way it is with our sort. **1971** F.G. BUTLER *Informant, Grahamstown* It's interesting to think how the Elizabethans used synonyms from Anglo-Saxon and Latin — they've got their 'will and testament' and we've got our 'finished and klaar'! **1974** A.P. BRINK *Looking on Darkness* 20 Now we're done for, it's all up with us, we've had it. Finish and klaar. **1974** *Evening Post* 25 Oct. 1 'I shot the bastard, finish and klaar,' he wrote in a statement to the police. **1979** *Voice* 7 Oct. 5 He was served with the first of two restriction orders in February 1973. Those moves meant that he had to stop writing there and then, finished and klaar. **1984** S. GRAY *Three Plays* 134, I tell you, I won' sell, finish and klaar! **1985** K. NGWENYA in *Drum* June 49 We want equal rights. Finish and klaar. **1986** S. SEPAMALA *Third Generation* 90 Sometimes I think he wishes he could simply get rid of me you know, *finish and klaar*. **1987** *Scope* 9 Oct. 36 Sakkie Enslin put him down in one. Finished and *klaar*, as they say in Budapest. **1989** J. HOBBS *Thoughts in Makeshift Mortuary* 74 Jo'burg is closed this year to applications from Natal female Bantu, finish and klaar. **1991** P. SLABOLEPSZY Braait Laaities. 12 That's very nice and all that, but it's all over now, OK? Finish and Klaar.

b. Used predicatively: 'had it'; 'done for'; 'over', 'final'; cf. TICKETS.

1970 R.S. GIBSON *Informant, N. Tvl* It's finished and klaar (*finis*). **1970** A. FULTON *I Swear to Apollo* 208 All patients sign a form consenting to post-mortem in the event of death ... One of the rules. All finished and klaar, as the locals say. **1972** *Sunday Times* 12 Mar. 4, I am finished and klaar with this Government and from now on ek stem Sap. **1974** A.P. BRINK *Looking on Darkness* 54 He tole me I was finish' en' klaar, it's no use, I'm rotten with the cencer [*sic*]. **1976** S. ROBERTS *Outside Life's Feast* 88 I'm finish an' klaar here. Van Staden will let it get around. I mus' move on. **1980** M. MELAMU in M. Mutloatse *Forced Landing* 47 Damn it all, I decide, I'm caught red-handed and it's *finish en klaar*. I can't do anything about it. **1982** *Sunday Times* 31 May, '*Finished and klaar*', literally 'finished and finished' this tautology is used to express the absolute finality of something. 'I'm finished and klaar with that man — he hasn't called me since Tuesday.' **1989** *Informant, Grahamstown* The prodigal son had spent all his money, his friends had left him, he had nothing left, he was finished and klaar.

klaar /klɑː(r)/ *v.* [ad. Afk. *uitklaar* to clear; or *klaar* finished.]

1. *intrans. Army slang.* In the phr. ***to klaar out*** [part. tr. Afk. *klaar uit, uitklaar* to get clearance to leave (as used *spec.* of the army), which was in turn perh. influenced by Eng. *clear out* to get out (of an unpleasant situation)], to be discharged from the army, having completed the compulsory term of national service; *to clear out*, see CLEAR. Hence **klaaring out** *vbl n. phr.*, discharge from the army; *clearing out*, see CLEAR; also *attrib.*; so **klaar uit** /- 'eɪt, -'œit/ *n. phr.* [Afk. *uit* out], discharge from the army.

1977 *Informant, Grahamstown* Klaar out. Be discharged (from the Army). **1980** *Armed Forces* May 9 Gary will be in army terms 'Klaaring out' in December. **1983** *Sunday Times* 4 Sept. (Lifestyle) 1 The Vietnam Syndrome. It occurs often — obviously, since there is a new batch of ex-soldiers 'klaring out' every six months. **1984** *Cape Times* 19 Jan. (Car Finder) 8 No GST! If you have just klaared out from the army .. come to Subway Renault ... Your 'klaaring out' papers could save you a bundle. **1986** *Uniform* 16 June 9 Klaaring out soon doesn't mean that you can start wearing some of your 'civvies'! **1989** *Personality* 6 Mar. 72 Well, *min dae* came along at last and after *klaar uit* and beers and braais with the family I was ready to put my plan into action. **1989** *Sunday Times* 24 Dec. 23 Gwen Gill's A-to-Z of the decade: Koo Starke, Kupido, Kubus, Koeberg, .. *klaaring out* (now much sooner than expected). **1992** E.M. MACPHAIL *Mrs Chud's Place* 71 He hoped by going into the army straight after school, and later call-ups, that he could get out of doing the course his father wanted him to do ... But he needn't have worried because by the time he *klaared* out, his father wasn't interested anymore. **1994** *E. Prov. Herald* 25 June 2 (*caption*) 'We came, we saw and we *klaared* out', said some of the relieved national servicemen who have been demobilising from Eastern Province Command.

‖**2.** *trans. slang.* To finish (something).

1991 *Scope* 31 May 54 Women are happy to stand barefoot and pregnant at the kitchen sink, boetie, never mind waiting in the car with the kids while an ou *klaars* his dop.

Klaas's cuckoo /ˌklɑːsəz 'kʊkuː/ *n. phr.* Also **Klaas' cuckoo.** [tr. Fr. *Coucou de Klaas, Coucou* cuckoo + *de* of + Du. *Klaas*, abbrev. of *Nikolaas*; so named by the French explorer Francois le Vaillant (see quots 1800 and 1899).] The green and bronze cuckoo *Chrysococcyx klaas* of the Cuculidae; MIETJIE. Also *attrib.*

[**1800** F. LE VAILLANT *Histoire Naturelle des Oiseaux d'Afrique* V. 54 Ce fut Klaas qui .. tua prés de la rivière *Platte* l'espèce de coucou auquel je donne son nom ... Je ne balance pas á regarder le Coucou de Klaas comme une espèce particulière et bien distincte du coucou didric.] *c***1808** C. VON LINNÉ *System of Natural Hist.* VIII. 240 *Klaas's Cuckoo*, So named by Vaillant from his favourite Hottentot servant, who brought him the species here described. **1867** E.L. LAYARD *Birds of S. Afr.* 250 Klaas's cuckoo is not uncommon in most wooded parts of the colony. **1899** R.B. & J.D.S. WOODWARD *Natal Birds* 118 Klaas's Cuckoo ... Monsieur Le Vaillant named this Cuckoo after his Hottentot servant Klaas, who was almost as fond of birds as himself ... He saw Klaas's Cuckoo perched on a twig. **1903** STARK & SCLATER *Birds of S. Afr.* III. 188 Klaas's Cuckoo frequents both bush and thorn lands. **1923** HAAGNER & IVY *Sketches of S. Afr. Bird-Life* 284 (*caption*) Klaas' or Bronze Cuckoo. **1936** E.L. GILL *First Guide to S. Afr. Birds* 108 Among the birds parasitized by Klaas's Cuckoo are various sunbirds, warblers and kingfishers. **1953** J.M. WINTERBOTTOM *Common Birds of S.-E.* 10 Klaas's Cuckoo (*C. klaas*) .. has white outer tail-feathers. **1964** P.A. CLANCEY *Birds of Natal & Zululand* 222 The young Klaas' cuckoo ejects the nestlings of the foster parent a few days after hatching. **1978** MCLACHLAN & LIVERSIDGE *Roberts' Birds of S. Afr.* 250 *Klaas's Cuckoo* ... A common species of the savannas and rocky hills. **1989** *Weekend Post* 4 Nov. (Leisure) 3 We recently had to raise a Klaas cuckoo chick.

klaauw zickte, klaauwziekte varr. KLAUWZIEKTE.

klaberjas /'klabə(r)jas/ *n.* Also **klabbe(r)jas, klab(e)jas, klaberjaas, klaberjass, klaverjas, klawerjas.** [Either Afk., fr. Du. *klaverjas, klaver* club + *jas* knave of trumps; or fr. Brit. Eng. *klobbiyos* ad. G. *klaberjass* (*OED*), fr. Du.] A type of piquet in which the knave of clubs is the highest card, and all knaves are trumps. Also *attrib.*

1925 H.J. MANDELBROTE tr. *O.F. Mentzel's Descr. of Cape of G.H.* 105 Sometimes an invitation follows to take a hand at L'Ombre or Gravejas. [*Note*] Probably from 'Klavernaas', known in Afrikaans as 'Klawerjas'. **1954** A. SEGAL *Jhb. Friday* 232 He cupped both hands over his mouth and shouted .. 'Klabberjas! Klabberjas!' ... 'As you say, as you say,' he shouted in his turn, falling into a chair with the enthusiasm of the card lover. **1955** V. DE KOCK *Fun They Had* 59 Card-Playing, it seems, has always been an important feature in our social life ... L'ombre, whist, quadrille, piquet, lanterloo, klawerjas .. these were all popular in their turn. **1972** *E. Prov. Herald* 10 Feb. 11 Players of Klabberjas will tell you (as will bridge players of their game) that it is the *only* card game ... In the bistros of Paris they call it 'Belotte', the Dutch call it 'Klaviarsz' and in South Africa it's often called just 'Klabjas'. **1974** *Ibid.* 18 July 3 The Eastern Province Klaberjaas championships .. Klaberjaas is .. similar to bridge or German whist, and is believed to have originated in Holland. It is usually played by four people, playing in two pairs. **1980** *Daily Dispatch* 5 July 3 Klaberjass, a card game many centuries old, is played in one form or another all over the world ... Its origins are believed to be Flemish or Dutch and the word klaberjass refers to the Jack of clubs — the most valuable card in the pack. **1980** *Sunday Times* 26 Oct. 7 Our favourite game was four-hand klabberjas at tournaments. **1989** F.G. BUTLER *Tales from Old Karoo* 39 Long after the rest were snoring, they'd play klabejas by storm lantern. **1990** *Weekend Argus* 24 Nov. (Business) 10 Klabbejas competition. Sunday 9.12.90. Great prizes.

klander var. KALANDER *n.*[1]

klap /klap/ *n.*[1] *colloq.* Formerly also **klopje**. Pl. **-s**, occas. **klappe** /'klapə/. [Afk. (pl. *klappe*), fr. Du.

klop a blow, a stroke.] A blow, cuff, or slap. Also Englished form **clap**.

1838 J.E. ALEXANDER *Exped. into Int.* II. 299 One discontented farmer said .. 'If I give a kloppé (klopje, or a little blow) to a slave, he immediately runs off to a magistrate and complains'. **1897** H.A. BRYDEN *Victorian Era in S. Afr.* 7 (Pettman), When I get home I cannot help giving the Hottentot another *klopje*, when I am fined £10. **1913** C. PETTMAN *Africanderisms* 269 *Klopje*, (D. *klop*, a knock.) A hit or blow. **1960** C. HOOPER *Brief Authority* 236 'Hell!' said the policeman under his breath, greatly to the delight of the twenty-five accused, 'I'll give that man such a klap!' **1965** E. MPHAHLELE *Down Second Ave* 47 'But Blacks are Blacks and whites are whites all over.' 'But I am telling you the whites do the thinking here.' 'Like the one that gave me a hot clap at the market this morning?' **1969** A. FUGARD *Boesman & Lena* 12 Just now you get a bloody good *klap*! **1976** M. THOLO in C. Hermer *Diary of Maria Tholo* (1980) 73 One of the teachers was found writing on the board, so they gave her a few claps and said, 'Next time you take heed of warnings'. **1982** *Daily Dispatch* 31 Mar. 6 A T-shirt with the AWB emblem. 'It looks like a swastika that's had a klap,' he declared, holding up the shirt for the House to see. **1988** S. SOLE in *Style* Apr. 49 Me and the foreman had words. I gave him a couple of klappe and we went to our caravan. **1989** D. CAPEL in *Personality* 16 Oct. 10 Some computers never grow up. They deserve a fat *klap* right where it hurts most. **1991** *Weekly Mail* 30 Aug. 11 The white workers were much disgruntled .. about Moolman giving one of the workers the occasional 'klap'. **1993** *Weekly Mail & Guardian* 23 Dec. 8 Keeping his wig on after the televised *klap* from one of Eugene Terreblanche's Ystergaarde.

klap *n.*[2] *obs.* Also **clap**. [S. Afr. Du., tent-flap.] A canvas curtain hanging at the front or rear of a covered wagon. See AFTER-CLAP, FORE-CLAP.

*a*1858 J. GOLDSWAIN *Chron.* (1949) II. 38, I had ordered .. the claps of the wagon sale to be put down. *a*1875 T. BAINES *Jrnl of Res.* (1964) II. 30 Hardly had we halted when the pitiless storm fell upon us; the oxen were hastily cast loose, the claps — loose sails with which the ends of the wagon-tents are closed — made fast. **1882** J. NIXON *Among Boers* 47 While the cart was in motion, we were able to keep them [*sc.* flies] at bay by opening the 'klap' or curtain, at the back, and allowing a breeze to circulate through. *Ibid.* 72 At the back was a door a curtain or 'klap' fitting on the upper half.

klap /klap, klæp/ *v.* Also Englished forms **clap**, **clup**. [Afk.]

1. *obs.* To make a cracking sound.

a. *trans.* To crack (a whip).

1880 *S.W. Silver & Co.'s Handbk to S. Afr.* 227 The drivers 'clap' their long whips, and the teams, eight pairs of oxen labouring at each wain, move briskly over the way.

b. *intrans.* To crack, bang.

1890 F.C. SELOUS *Hunter's Wanderings* 232 The bullet clapped loudly, and I saw her stagger, but recovering immediately, she went on.

2. *trans. colloq.* To slap, hit, or strike (someone or something).

1961 T. MATSHIKIZA *Choc. for my Wife* 83 The two white men closed in on me ... The one on the left .. had frying-pans for hands. He said, 'If you move I'll clap you dead with these.' **1979** F. DIKE *First S. African* 39 Shut up! ... No I won't ... (*Claps Rooi very hard*) I said, shut up! **1986** F. MCLACHLAN in Burman & Reynolds *Growing Up* 345 There was a lot of fighting in the cells ... They make you blow out your cheeks and then *klap* [slap] them so hard that your mouth bleeds. **1988** B. HOUGH in *Frontline* Oct. 24 *Klapping the volk.* Afrikaans theatre consists of a long line of assault on old Afrikaner values. **1990** *Frontline* Mar.-Apr. 17, I say: 'How about black people who want to vote for De Klerk?' They are shocked, and ponder. One says: 'They won't be allowed to.' The other, the guy who klapped the drunk, ponders longer and finally pronounces: 'They won't want to.' **1991** P. SLABOLEPSZY *Braait Laaities.* 22 Blacks are not allowed in our house. Not even for work. One day a maid came to borrow something from next door and he klapped my mother. **1991** *Weekly Mail* 30 Aug. 11 Accused of 'klapping' a worker. **1992** M.J. SILVA *Informant, Grahamstown* This umpire was killed — the guy klapped a cover drive and hit him on the temple. **1992** J. PHILIPS in *Style* May 10 Don't even think of *klapping* your kid in Checkers here, you'll probably be arrested. **1993** M. RAMPHELE on TV1 12 Sept. (Agenda), One of the security policemen we didn't respect took the opportunity of klapping him as soon as he got into detention. He turned round and walloped him right back. **1993** *'Jimbo' programme insert, Napac* Clup. To slap someone.

‖**klapbroek** /ˈkla(p)bruk, -brʊk/ *n. hist.* Pl. **-broeke** /brukə/. [Afk., *klap* flap + *broek* trousers.] Men's trousers with a front flap fastened by buttons on both sides; FLAP-TROUSERS. Also *attrib.*

1936 E. ROSENTHAL *Old-Time Survivals* 25 The idea of the klapbroek or flapped trousers, which carry a strap at the waist, is a survival on African soil of a garment worn by Continental 'villeins' in the 16th century. **1937** F.B. YOUNG *They Seek a Country* 404 Nobody would have taken him for an Englishman in his check shirt, his flapped leathern *klapbroek* trousers and thong-sewn veld-schoens and wide brimmed straw hat. **1937** S. CLOETE *Turning Wheels* 417 Scorning belts or braces, [these men] held up their trousers, which were of the klapbroek kind with a flap in the front, by means of draw-strings. **1944** J. MOCKFORD *Here Are S. Africans* 62 Trousers were of the *klapbroek* type with a flap that buttoned up in front like navvies' corduroys. **1958** A. JACKSON *Trader on Veld* 35 The old adherents of the Dopper sect preferred a Klapbroek. **1972** A.A. TELFORD *Yesterday's Dress* 119 Trousers were of the 'klapbroek' type, and had in place of the centre fly opening, a flap (hence the name) fastened at the sides with buttons. **1975** D.H. STRUTT *Clothing Fashions* 213 Leather *klapbroeke* were made short because if allowed to get wet, when dried they were harsh and stiff — hence the English name for them, *crackers* ... Klapbroeke were sometimes called *nierknypers* (kidney-pinchers).

klapper /ˈklapə(r)/ *n.*[1] Also **clapper**, **klopper**. [Afk., earlier S. Afr. Du., ad. Malay *kelapa* coconut.]

1. [Named for the similarity between the fruit casing and the shell of a coconut; or (see quot. 1917) influenced by Afk. *klapper* rattler, see KLAPPER *n.*[2]] Either of two small trees, *Strychnos pungens* or *S. spinosa* of the Loganiaceae, bearing hard-shelled edible fruit; this fruit; MONKEY ORANGE sense 1; also (esp. formerly) called *wild orange* (see WILD sense a). Also *attrib.*

1863 W.C. BALDWIN *Afr. Hunting* 199 We had a capital lunch from some wild fruit about three times the size of an orange, called a clapper. It has a hard shell outside, which one must batter against a tree to crack or break. **1868** W.R. THOMSON *Poems, Essays & Sketches* 113 'O! What was that?' 'A klapper fell.' 'Does that Give the poor klapper pain?' 'I think not, love; They say that fruits and stones want feeling.' **1917** R. MARLOTH *Common Names* 49 *Klappers*, .. Name .. applied to some species of *Strychnos*, e.g., *S. pungens* (wild orange), as the seeds rattle in the old fruits. **1921** T.R. SIM *Native Timbers* 120 *Strychnos pungens*, .. Klopper, Wild orange. **1932** WATT & BREYER-BRANDWIJK *Medicinal & Poisonous Plants* 140 The pulp of the fruit of *Strychnos pungens* solered., Wild orange, Kaffir orange, Klapper .. *Strychnos spinosa* ham. (*Brehmia spinosa* Harv.), Kaffir orange, Klapper .. and *Strychnos gerrardi* N.E. Br .. is very refreshing. **1958** R.E. LIGHTON *Out of Strong* 59 The thorn-tipped leaves of the tart-tasting klapper and the wild plum, the powdery leaves of the wild pear. **1966** E. PALMER *Plains of Camdeboo* 177 The spekboom, the wild plum and the klapper, now bright with colour. **1971** E.C.G. MARAIS tr. *E.N. Marais's My Friends the Baboons* 29 Wild peaches, sour klappers .. medlers, moepels, and various other kinds of fruit made our wilderness a veritable orchard. **1972** PALMER & PITMAN *Trees of Sn Afr.* 1857 The monkey orange, or klapper as it is often known .. is an evergreen tree. **1993** S. BRINK in *House & Leisure* Dec. 59 My ever-inventive mother decorated a wonderful tree with gold-painted klappers (a hardy subtropical fruit the size of a tennis ball) and blood-red pomegranates.

‖**2.**

a. The coconut. Also *attrib.*

1891 H.J. DUCKITT *Hilda's 'Where Is It?'* 238 Tart (Cocoa-nut). ('Klapper-Taart.' From a very old Dutch Book.) **1925** H.J. MANDELBROTE tr. *O.F. Mentzel's Descr. of Cape of G.H.* II. 132 The klapper 'nut is much larger in size than the average ostrich-egg ... The rind is hard as wood ... While the fruit is still immature it is filled with a milky fluid which oozes out immediately the shell is pierced.

b. *comb.* **klapper oil**, **klapperolie** /ˈklapərˌuəli/ [Afk., *olie* oil], coconut oil; **klappertert** /-tɛrt/, formerly also **klappertaart**, and dim. form **klappertertjie** /-tɛrki/ [Afk., *tert* fr. Du. *taart* (+ -IE)], a traditional sweet tart filled with coconut.

1920 R. JUTA *Tavern* 104 Sis! man! I hate the smell of a Malay girl's hair; **klapper oil** — foulest smell on earth. **1979** *Weekend Post* 10 Mar. (Family Post) 6 Malay women in their bright coloured clothes, men with their red fezzes and girls with their long black hair made soft and shiny with the popular '**klapperolie**' (coconut oil), made a striking contrast with the sombre surroundings. *a*1905 H.J. DUCKITT in M. Kuttel *Bk of Recipes* (1966) 133 Tart, Cocoanut, **Klapper-tert**. From a very old Dutch book. **1913** C. PETTMAN *Africanderisms* 263 *Klapper taart*, .. A tart, the contents of which are chiefly coco-nut. **1939** S. CLOETE *Watch for Dawn* 284 She thought of geel rys, of klapper tert. **1973** *Cape Times* 13 Jan. (Weekend Mag.) 4 The baskets of food contained two traditional New Year items to relish — curried pickle fish and *Klappertert* (coconut tart). **1979** *Sunday Times* 8 Apr. (Mag. Sect.) 5 The list of goodies to be made includes klappertertjies, jamtertjies, krapkoekies. **1988** F. WILLIAMS *Cape Malay Cookbk* 95 The ladies sample a colourful assortment of cakes, biscuits, melktert and klappertert.

klapper /ˈklapər/ *n.*[2] Also **clapper**. [Afk., 'rattle', 'chatter (of teeth)'.]

1. Either of two shrubs with rattling seed-pods, *Crotalaria burkeana* or *C. lotoides* of the Fabaceae.

1911 *S. Afr. Jrnl of Science* VII. 269 (Pettman), It [*sc. Crotalaria burkeana*] is .. called *klappers* from the character of the somewhat horny pods, in which the seeds rattle about. **1913** C. PETTMAN *Africanderisms* 122 *Clapper*, The name given to *Crotaliaria Burkeana* in the neighbourhood of Graaff Reinet, the seed-pods of which make a rattling sound when shaken by the wind. **1917** R. MARLOTH *Common Names* 49 *Klappers, Crotalaria Burkeana* ... (The pods are inflated like little rattles).

2. In full ***klapperbos*** /-bɔs/ [Afk., *bos* bush; see quot. 1971]: the tree *Nymania capensis* of the Meliaceae, with papery, lantern-like seed-capsules; CHINESE LANTERN sense 2 a i; *Christmas Tree* sense (*a*), see CHRISTMAS.

1917 R. MARLOTH *Common Names* 49 *Klapper'bos, Nymania (Aitonia) capensis*. The capsules papery and inflated, often bright red. **1931** [see CHINESE LANTERN sense 2 a i]. **1951** N.L. KING *Tree-Planting* 69 *Nymania capensis* (*Klapperbos*), An attractive shrub the seed vessels of which become inflated. They turn red as they ripen and hang like Chinese lanterns. Occurs in scrub in the karroid belt known as the Little Karoo. **1955** L.G. GREEN *Karoo* 14, I could walk away among the driedoring bushes, the brosdoring and klapperbos. **1961** PALMER & PITMAN *Trees of S. Afr.* 279 Passing through the Karroo in spring, travellers often pause in astonishment at splashes of pure and vivid colour ... This is the famous klapper or Chinese lanterns, *Nymania Capensis* ... The flowers .. develop into inflated fruits with a papery covering like that of a large gooseberry ... These fruits give the tree its common names of klapper and Chinese lanterns. **1966** E. PALMER *Plains of Camdeboo* 177 The spekboom, the wild plum and the klapper, now bright with colour. **1971** BARAITSER & OBHOLZER *Cape Country Furn.* 75 This small tree is found in the Karroo. In spring it produces pods which, when compressed, make a bang; hence the name Klapperbos. **1979** *Daily Dispatch* 25

Oct. 19 The wild flowers everywhere are too beautiful. Bright red klapperbos, Nymania capensis, is the most striking. **1989** F.G. BUTLER *Tales from Old Karoo* 81 The dry sand bank, half in shade, half sun, had a *klapperbos* with its red pods transparent as jelly jubejubes on it. **1992** H. HUTCHINGS in *Weekend Post* 22 Aug. (Leisure) 7 *Nymania capensis*, the Chinese lantern bush or klapperbos, .. bears pink blooms which are followed by inflated membraneous seed pods. These are green, fading to pale cream and are tinged with pink.

klauwziekte *n. Obs. Pathology.* Also **klaauw zickte, klaauwziekte, klaw-sikte, klaw-ziekte**, and with initial capital. [S. Afr. Du., fr. Du. *klauw* claw, paw + *ziekte* sickness.] Foot-rot, a disease primarily of cattle and sheep, arising from infection by a micro-organism and varying in degrees of severity; CLAWSICKNESS; KLOW SICK(-NESS).

1790 tr. *F. Le Vaillant's Trav.* II. 79 The *Klaw-sikte* attacks the feet of oxen, causes them to swell prodigiously, and often produces a suppuration. **1795** C.R. HOPSON tr. *C.P. Thunberg's Trav.* I. 209 The *Klaw-ziekte* is a disease, in which the hoofs of the cattle grow loose, so that they cannot walk. **1798** S.H. WILCOCKE tr. *J.S. Stavorinus's Voy. to E. Indies 1768–71* II. 63 He had lost one hundred and twenty head of cattle, a few days before, by the diseases called the *klaauw* and *tong-ziekte*. **1844** J. BACKHOUSE *Narr. of Visit* 305 Many sheep perished this season from the Klaauw Zickte or Foot-rot. **1859** 'B.' in *Cape Monthly Mag.* V. May 297 The 'Tong' and 'Klauw Ziekte' .. created such havoc throughout the western districts in 1858. **1896** R. WALLACE *Farming Indust. of Cape Col.* 496 Driving sheep over young swarms [of locusts] tramples them to death, but there is a danger of the sheep becoming lame or taking 'klawziekte,' owing to irritation set up between the digits.

klaver-, klawerjas varr. KLABERJAS.

klaw-sikte, -ziekte varr. KLAUWZIEKTE.

kleen var. KLEIN.

||**kleilat** /ˈkleɪlat/ *n.* [Afk., *klei* clay + *lat* stick.] A children's game in which balls or pellets of clay are flicked at an opponent with a flexible stick; the flexible stick used in this game.

1955 V. DE KOCK *Fun They Had* 80 When no other sport presented itself, young South Africans often amused themselves by fighting with sticks, and, more especially, with the so-called *kleilat* or clay-stick. **1970** BEETON & DORNER in *Eng. Usage in Sn Afr.* Vol.1 No.2, 47 *Kleilat*, .. flexible stick used to flick a pellet of clay at an opponent in a game played by S. Afr. schoolboys particularly in rural areas. **1970** *Informant, Pietersburg* His body was a patchwork quilt of bruises after a game of 'kleilat'. **1982** T. BARON in *Frontline* Nov. 45 *Kleilat* was popular and extremely multi-national. There were kids named Llewllyn, Marais, Van Niekerk, McLeod, Lazlo Magyar. [*Ibid.* He put rocks in his *klei* and aimed them like an artilleryman.]

||**klein** /kleɪn/ *adj.* Also **clyne, kleen, kleina.** [Du. (and later Afk.).]

a. Small, young; 'lesser'. See also KLEINTJIE.

Common in place-names, and in the names of plants.

1798 LADY A. BARNARD *S. Afr. Century Ago* (1925) 209, I spied a poor *clyne* Hottentot in a chair which had lost the matting. [**1862** LADY DUFF-GORDON in F. Galton *Vacation Tourists* (1864) III. 151 The boots here is a mantatee, very black, and called Kleen-boy, because he is so little. **1871** W.G. ATHERSTONE in A.M.L. Robinson *Sel. Articles from Cape Monthly Mag.* (1978) 95 *Only* 24000 acres, adjoining the gold farm on the west, quite '*een kleine plaats*', said he; and so in sooth it was, comparing it with others.] **1882** C. DU VAL *With Show through Sn Afr.* I. 271 The 'Vrouw', with a 'kleina Kind' (little child) in her arms, debouched on the front 'stoep'. **1914** L.H. BRINKMAN *Breath of Karroo* 227 'Where is the Klein Nooi going?' enquired the woman .. as her husband led the horse away. **1920** R. JUTA *Tavern* 12 Dear Georgie, perhaps the klein doctorje is a little 'fey'. *Ibid.* 47, I like Klein Adonis best; Adonis is the newest, littlest slave; as small as me, so we play together. **1924** S.G. MILLIN *God's Step-Children* 205 If only she were not eaten up with this jealousy. If only the servants did not call her, May, as the head of the household, 'Missis,' and herself, the elder sister, 'Klein Missis' — 'Little Missis.' If only Darrell were not so grotesquely satisfied with May. **1968** M. MULLER *Green Peaches Ripen* 40 Why don't *Klein Nooi* plant fuschias in pots? (he always called me 'little mistress'). **1972** *Sunday Times* 22 Oct. 16 Dawie de V. drops a klein clanger. **1987** *Learn & Teach* No.5, 17 They say Hillbrow is mos a klein America. Darkies and Lanies live together.

b. *comb. colloq.* **kleinboet** /-bʊt/ [Afk., *boet* brother (see BOET)], young(er) brother, 'young fellow'; **kleingoed** /-xʊt/ [Afk., *goed* things], youngsters, 'small fry'. See also KLEINBAAS, KLEINHUISIE, *klein missus* (MISSUS sense 3), *klein-nooi* (NOOI sense 1 c).

1953 U. KRIGE *Dream & Desert* 9 It was wonderful news. He was going to have a brother, a new brother! **Kleinboet** ... Yes, that was what he was going to call him, Kleinboet, little brother. **1987** M. POLAND *Train to Doringbult* 9, I wish my wife would make me coffee in the morning. She'll be burrowed in that bed till ten if you don't throw her out. Farm girls are worth their weight in gold — not so, *kleinboet*? **1973** N. DESMOND on Radio South Africa 16 Oct. (Woman's World), Pieter, the man, did not want to have anything to do with the **kleingoed**.

klein apartheid see APARTHEID sense 1 b.

kleinbaas /ˈkleɪnbɑːs/ *n.* [Afk., *klein* little + *baas*, see BAAS.]

See note at BAAS.

I. A common noun.

1. *obs.* One not fully in authority.

1896 E. CLAIRMONTE *Africander* 15 The next morning I went for a walk with Smith, who was the *klein-baas* of the farm. *Klein-baas* is the term used for the sub-manager, and 'baas' is the manager or proprietor. **1913** C. PETTMAN *Africanderisms* 264 *Klein baas*, .. The designation given by farm labourers to the eldest son of the farmer, and also to a sub-manager.

2. BAASIE sense 2.

1910 D. FAIRBRIDGE *That Which Hath Been* (1913) 47 Even with such childish songs did I sing the *klein baas* to sleep when he was a baby in my arms. **1913** —— *Piet of Italy* 8 The *klein baas* will be drowned. Call Oom Magmoet. I can't pull him out. **1963** D. JACOBSON *Through Wilderness* (1977) 63 How incredulous their friends must be to hear their stories about the kind white kleinbaas who gave them food and toys and clothing. **1973** S. CLOETE *Co. with Heart of Gold* 122 The old Kaffirs who remembered him would come up to greet the Klein Baas who had come back. **1988** J. BENTLEY in *Style* Apr. 30 The Kadett GSE, a budget priced little brother to the top-of-the-range GSI. The latter having been dubbed The Boss in .. advertising campaigns, it comes as no surprise that the small performance model has unofficially been called Kleinbaas. **1993** S. DIKENI in *House & Leisure* Nov. 42 As a kid I walked into the Grobbelaars' Spar, and the *kleinbaas* called me and asked if I was Magdalena's child. I said, 'Ja, baas'.

II. A form of address.

3. BAASIE sense 1 a.

1899 G.H. RUSSELL *Under Sjambok* 259 'Ja, my Klein Baas,' said the old man, rising from the ground, 'Babijan will be quick for the young master, and he shall have of the best'. **1914** L.H. BRINKMAN *Breath of Karroo* 24 The master of the house is addressed as 'Ou baas' and a young man, 'Klein baas'. **1935** H.C. BOSMAN *Mafeking Rd* (1969) 73 'I can see you go far away, my kleinbaas,' he said, 'very far away over the great waters'. **1958** A. SAMPSON *Treason Cage* 148 The Afrikaners forced the Africans, who were smaller, .. to call them '*klein baas*' — little boss. **1965** E. MPHAHLELE *Down Second Ave* 84, I stopped him and I said, Greetings, Kleinbaas, remember Petros from the farm? I saw in those eyes that he remembered me, but he said, 'Get out of my way, Kaffir!' and he passed on. **1980** N. FERREIRA *Story of Afrikaner* 41 Do you still remember me as *kleinbaas* or do you despise that word? **1982** A.P. BRINK *Chain of Voices* 85 To all the others I was .. superior — Baas or Kleinbaas, 'Master' or 'Little Master' to the slaves. **1992** C.M. KNOX tr. *E. Van Heerden's Mad Dog* 67 Old Pyp came up to me and grinned, 'Face jus' like an old Bushman, hey, kleinbaas?'

III. A title.

4. Used with a name.

1937 C.R. PRANCE *Tante Rebella's Saga* 200 In time he became a sort of 'adjutant' to Klein Baas Willem, Oom Willem's son ... Klein Baas Willem had succeeded to the title of 'Oom Willem' in his turn.

kleinbasie /ˈkleɪnbɑːsi/ *n.* [Afk., *kleinbaas* see prec. + dim. suffix -IE.]

1. BAASIE sense 2.

1970 M. MULLER *Cloud across Moon* 156 He gave a wide toothless smile. 'Ai, Klein nooi, but the new klein basie is pretty!' **1982** *Weekend Post* 27 Mar. 3 The kleinbasie had told her that the guttering and downpipes were also part of the roof, so I had to do that as well.

2. BAASIE sense 1 a.

1982 M. MZAMANE *Children of Soweto* 182 A *kaffir* maid of the old generation .. had called him *klein baasie* from about the time he was five.

kleinhuisie /ˈkleɪnheɪsi, -hœisi/ *n. colloq.* [Afk., *klein* small + *huis* house + dim. suffix -IE.] A privy, usu. an outdoor pit or bucket lavatory; any outdoor lavatory. See also *piccanin(ny) kaya* (PICCANIN *adj.* sense 2).

1966 VAN HEYNINGEN & BERTHOUD *Uys Krige* 94 They chatter to Luis about the house they have built for themselves high up in an old oak tree, a house that even has a 'kleinhuisie' (a little house, or lavatory). **1972** *Cape Times* 28 Feb. 7 The N9 may be the smiling Gateway to Cape Town; the main line is surely the way out of the back door, past the dustbin and the Kleinhuisie. **1978** *Sunday Times* 14 May 6 The second cobra to call on an occupied 'Kleinhuisie' (outside lavatory) in Anysberg .. this week was routed by shouts of a housewife. **1981** C. BARNARD in *Daily Dispatch* 6 July 6 Sometimes the rain fills up the hole you dug for the 'kleinhuisie' and the pools lie around the shack. **1989** F.G. BUTLER *Tales from Old Karoo* 23 He did not have to inspect the kleinhuisie, because the door was open. **1994** [see *piccanin(ny) kaya* (PICCANIN sense 2)].

Klein Karoo see KAROO sense 1 b.

||**kleintjie** /ˈkleɪŋki, -ci/ *n. colloq.* Also **kleinkie, kleintje**, and (formerly) Englished form **clynie**. [Afk., earlier S. Afr. Du., fr. Du. *kleintje*.]

1. A small child; any small creature or object.

1797 LADY A. BARNARD *Lett. to Henry Dundas* (1973) 94 While the partners ate and drank heartily, the Clynies, viz. the Moye Kinders — (pretty little children ..) were busy in their way. **1910** D. FAIRBRIDGE *That Which Hath Been* (1913) 48 Oh, he was but a kleintje when he was last here, and a very tiresome one at that. **1913** —— *Piet of Italy* 63 Once, when I was a *kleintje*, there came a Frenchman to the Paarl. **1917** S.T. PLAATJE *Native Life* 83 Good morning, Auta Gert, how is Mietje and the Kleintjes (little ones)? **1942** S. CLOETE *Hill of Doves* 279 Do not take the kleinkies. The little ones must be allowed to grow.

2. As a term of endearment: 'little one'.

1905 P. GIBBON *Vrouw Grobelaar* 170 'No,' he cried, bending to her lips. 'No! It is a true charm that, my kleintje.' **1911** —— *Margaret Harding* 143 Marry me, my kleintje, and you shall be nobody's fool. **1913** D. FAIRBRIDGE *Piet of Italy* 8 'What is it then, my *kleintje*?' she cried, clutching the brown baby to her breast. **1963** R. GEDYE in C.M. Booysen *Tales of S. Afr.* 159 'What was she saying? Pa, what's happened to Jan?' 'He's in trouble, kleintjie.' **1987** M. POLAND *Train to Doringbult* 140 Talk to me kleintjie. Tell me what else you've been doing. Why haven't you been playing tennis and why haven't you been eating?

klepkous var. KLIPKOUS.

kleurling /ˈklœ(r)ləŋ, ˈklɪə(r)-/ n. Also with initial capital. Pl. -s, occas. -e /-ə/, and (formerly) -en. [Afk., *kleur* colour + *-ling*, the (often pejorative) n.-forming suffix indicating 'a person or thing belonging to or concerned with (what is denoted by the primary n.)'.]

1. Often *derog.* COLOURED *n.*

1908 I.W. WAUCHOPE *Natives & their Missionaries* 3 The Dutch are a very logical people. In their logic a *Kleurling*, or coloured person, is not 'man' but a 'creature'. 1955 [see GAMMAT sense 1]. 1969 J.M. WHITE *Land God Made in Anger* 197 There are perhaps two thousand of these coloured or *Kleurling* people in South West Africa... An off-shoot of the million-and-a-half strong Coloured community in the West Cape, they are intelligent and clever with their hands. 1975 *Sunday Times* 21 Sept. 21 To them I was just a man who happened to be a Kleurling from Kaapstad. 1979 *Ibid.* 26 Aug. (Extra) 3 This kleurling who was sitting like a proper white man at one of his rickety tables. 1981 *Ibid.* 22 Feb. (Extra) 3 As mixed, you can [be] a bank manager, a street sweeper or city council member. Such is the exclusive scope of us kleurlinge. 1987 M. MELAMU *Children of Twilight* 50 When the baby was born, it was a kleurling... A bastard in the family. The father must be a verdomste Kaffer! 1990 *Frontline* Mar.-Apr. 22 When we get to Harmony Park the coloured guy is telling me about nomenclature. This thing about 'bruinmense' is bad news, he says, 'We're Coloureds, Kleurlinge, that's what we should be called, not "bruinmense".' 1991 [see BANTU n. sense 1].

2. *comb.* **Kleurling-Afrikaans**, a derogatory name for Afrikaans as spoken by (Cape) 'coloured' people. See also *kitchen Dutch* (KITCHEN *n.* sense 2 b).

1981 V.A. FEBRUARY *Mind your Colour* 95 The 'coloured' objection to Small's exploitation of a particular brand of Afrikaans is worthy of a closer look. It has been variously called Kaaps (i.e. the language from the Cape), even facetiously Capey language, and Kleurling-Afrikaans (Coloured-Afrikaans). It is looked upon as a mark of low social status and cultural inferiority.

klew sick var. KLOW SICK.

klick var. CLICK.

klimop /ˈkləmɔp/ *n.* [S. Afr. Du., transf. use of Du. *klimop* ivy, *klim* climb + *op* up.]

1. Any of several species of *Clematis* of Ranunculaceae, esp. *C. brachiata*.

1860 HARVEY & SONDER *Flora Capensis* I. 2 *Clematis* ... One species is wild in England, and many are cultivated in gardens. The colonial name for the Cape species is 'Klimop'. 1906 B. STONEMAN *Plants & their Ways* 214 *Clematis*, Flowers white or delicate green in definite clusters. No petals or honey secretion. Climbing by means of the sensitive perioles. 'Klimop' or 'Traveller's Joy.' 1913 C. PETTMAN *Africanderisms* 264 *Klimop*, .. The name is also given to the wild clematis. 1966 C.A. SMITH *Common Names* 296 *Klimop*, .. All the species of *Clematis* have vine-like climbing stems ... The vernacular name was first recorded for *C. brachiata* .. but was in use about 1770, and is the original Nederlands name for the 'ivy'. 1974 M.R. LEVYNS in *Std Encycl. of Sn Afr.* X. 617 Traveller's Joy, Klimop. (*Clematis brachiata.*) Klimop belonging to the family Ranunculaceae. 1983 M.M. KIDD *Cape Peninsula* 62 *Clematis brachiata*. Ranunculaceae. Klimop. Woody climber; rare in Constantia Valley.

2. Any of several species of creeping or climbing plants, esp. species of *Cynanchum* (family Asclepiadaceae), all of which are poisonous to livestock, causing KRIMPSIEKTE; also called MONKEY-ROPE. Also *attrib.* See also DAWIDJIES sense 2.

1893 HENNING in D.G. Steyn *Toxicology of Plants* (1934) 347 This stage .. of krimpsiekte .. endures a longer or shorter time depending upon the quantity of the Klimop eaten, and the individual susceptibility to the poison. 1904 *Cape of G.H. Agric. Jrnl* Oct. 399 (Pettman), Cattle and sheep when tied up at the *Klimop* .. showed fifteen or thirty hours afterwards, the first symptoms of 'krimp-ziekte'. 1905 D. HUTCHEON in Flint & Gilchrist *Science in S. Afr.* 356 *Cynoctomum Capense* or 'Klimop', This creeper grows plentifully in the Caledon and other of the South-Western districts of Cape Colony. 1917 R. MARLOTH *Common Names* 49 *Klimop*, This name (meaning 'climber') is in Holland used for the ivy. Here several other climbing plants bear this name, most frequently species of *Cynanchum*, e.g., *C. africanum* and *C. capense*, both twining herbs with milky juice, injurious to animals eating them. 1932 WATT & BREYER-BRANDWIJK *Medicinal & Poisonous Plants* 150 *Cynanchum africanum* R. Br., Excelsior, Klimop, Bobbejaanstou, Dawidjies, is also toxic, and causes loss of stock ... *Cynanchum obtusifolium* L.f., Klimop, is toxic to stock, producing .. symptoms of gastro-enteritis. 1934 STEYN *Toxicology of Plants* 343 Farmers refer to 'cynanchosis' as 'klimop' poisoning, 'krampsiekte' or 'krimpsiekte'. 1966 C.A. SMITH *Common Names* 296 *Klimop*, A name rather loosely applied to many scandent or rambling species, so-called 'creepers' .. for example *Cynanchum africanum*; *C. obtusifolium*; *C. ellipticum* and *C. natalitium* ... All the species have been reported as poisonous to stock. 1972 M.R. LEVYNS in *Std Encycl. of Sn Afr.* VI. 413 *Klimop*, Bobbejaantou. Monkey-rope. (*Cynanchum obtusifolium; C. africanum.*) Common twiners of the family Asclepiadaceae, found in the bushes near the coast.

3. *comb.* **klimopgras** /-xras/ [Afk. *gras* grass], see quot. 1966.

1966 C.A. SMITH *Common Names* 296 *Klim(op)gras*, *Olyra latifolia* .. : A perennial grass, with culms up to 15 ft high and scrambling over other plants ... *Potamophila prehensilis* ... A perennial grass, up to several feet high ... The vernacular name is in allusion to the climbing habit. Said to be a good fodder plant. Both species are found only in damp places in bush or woods.

klinker /ˈklɪŋkə, ˈkləŋkə(r)/ *n.* [Du., a very hard, pale-coloured brick, fr. *klinken* to sound, ring.]

Found in general Eng. as *clinker*.

1. [Transf. use of Du. sense.] Any very hard biscuit.

1874 A. EDGAR in *Friend* 23 Apr., After performing such a good morning's work, we solaced ourselves with 'klinkers' and cold beef. 1900 G. MOLL in E. Hobhouse *Brunt of War* (1902) 49 They brought us food because we were almost starved, which consisted of six tins of bully beef, and some biscuits (Klinkers) in a dirty grain bag ..; the poor children could not eat the biscuits as they were too hard. 1902 C.R. DE WET *Three Yrs War* 48 On some of the wagons we found *klinkers*, jam, milk, sardines, salmon, cases of corned beef, and other such provisions in great variety. 1970 M. VAN RENSBURG *Informant*, Port Elizabeth, Klinker. Army biscuit.

2. A clinker, a small, exceptionally hard, pale-coloured brick used esp. for exposed work, steps, or paving; KLOMPIE *n.*[2] Also *comb.* **klinkerbrick**.

1913 C. PETTMAN *Africanderisms* 265 *Klinkers*, .. A brick that has been partially vitrified in the kiln used for paving courtyards. 1963 [see KLOMPIE *n.*[2]]. 1971 *S. Afr. Panorama* Sept. 8 Brick klinkers and wood make an attractive combination. Like face bricks their biggest advantage is that they do not require plastering or painting. 1981 P. DANE *Great Houses of Constantia* 39 Caused some experts .. to believe that Van der Stel had built the homestead of imported Dutch klinker bricks. 1984 *Sunday Times* 1 Apr. (Mag. Sect.) 34 (*advt*) Luxury Living: Superb klinker-brick home commanding .. sea views. 1990 *E. Prov. Herald* 5 Mar. 9 (*advt*) Klinkers and Red building bricks available at all times. 1991 G. SILBER in *Style* Nov. 173 These walls do a magnificent job of hiding poorly designed klinker-brick townhouse complexes from public view. 1992 *Grocott's Mail* 22 May 8 (*advt*) Somerset Heights. Klinker brick home with many unusual features.

klip /kləp/ *n.* Pl. -s, and (formerly) **klippen**. [Afk., earlier S. Afr. Du.]

1. A rock, stone, or pebble; KLIPPIE sense 1.

1835 T.H. BOWKER *Journal.* 13 Jan., Fall in with CB at the Barracks .. sell klips for goods. 1835 A. SMITH *Diary* (1940) II. 26 As a woman's husband dies the Dr. must make red klip and medicine into a mixture if she will marry another man. 1852 C. BARTER *Dorp & Veld* 50 Stooping to set large klips (stones) behind the wheel, to prevent the wagon from slipping back. 1925 H.J. MANDELBROTE tr. *O.F. Mentzel's Descr. of Cape of G.H.* II. 30 *Klippen*, Submerged rocks or those exposed at low tide. 1931 G. BEET *Grand Old Days* 113 Schalk van Niekerk .. happened to call on my mother, and, noticing the pretty stone, said, 'Give me this klip. I think it may be a diamond.' 1992 G. ETHERINGTON in *Weekend Post* 9 May (Leisure) 4 We sat, backs to the *klip* looking at the greenery around us until it was dark.

2. A diamond; BLINK KLIP sense 2; BLINK KLIPPIE; KLIPPIE sense 2; STEENTJIE sense 2; cf. STONE.

1873 F. BOYLE *To Cape for Diamonds* 108 Ye who have despised the lowly pebble, go ye to the Dutoitspan road ... What might of pain and terror lies in the smooth, round product of the brook! .. I do allege these klips to be a thing of downright dread. 1887 J.W. MATTHEWS *Incwadi Yami* 186 The natives had not yet acquired a knowledge of the value of diamonds or *klips* as they were then termed. 1892 J.R. COUPER *Mixed Humanity* 48 Flogged to death for stealing a 'klip' (as the Dutch and many of the Kaffirs call a diamond). 1897 *Pearson's Mag.* July 67 Fifteen years on that blathted breakwater, just for being found with a few little klips on you. 1911 L. COHEN *Reminisc. of Kimberley* 35 'Alamachtig,' he ejaculated, 'I'll show you the "klip". Here it is.' With that he pulled out his snuff-box ..; inside was a fairly sized beautiful octahedron diamond, called in the trade a glassy stone. 1962 F.C. METROWICH *Scotty Smith* 53 His Hottentot 'achter-ryer' said, 'Baas, take off the cups of the cartwheels and see if the klips are not to be found there.' They did so, and sure enough the parcel was there. 1983 R.L. FISH *Rough Diamond* 11 A Hottentot shepherd, tending his flocks not far from where Erasmus Jacobs had found his pretty glasslike *klip*, found another shining stone .. to become the famous Star of Africa.

3. The KINGKLIP (sense 2), *Genypterus capensis*.

1873 *Cape Monthly Mag.* VII. July-Dec. 147 Fish there were in plenty, The Klip, the Hottentot. Busily they plied their lines And very many caught.

4. KLIP-KLIP.

1976 *E. Prov. Herald* 9 Feb. 6 Call it 'klip' or 'five stones' or 'potjie-kook' it's all the same as the game called 'knuckles'.

5. *slang.* CLIPPER.

1992 M.D. PRENTICE *Informant*, Durban Klip – R100.

klip *v. trans. obs.* [fr. KLIP *n.* (sense 1), or fr. Afk.] To place a stone before or behind a (wagon) wheel in order to prevent a vehicle from moving down a slope.

1878 H.A. ROCHE *On Trek in Tvl* 91 Crawling into the wagon, the wheels of which were 'klipped', to keep us from running down the hill, trying to nap at intervals. 1913 C. PETTMAN *Africanderisms* 267 *Klip, To*, To place a stone behind a wheel to prevent the vehicle running backwards.

Hence **klipping** *vbl n.*

1878 P. GILLMORE *Great Thirst Land* 114 As it was the start, the oxen were comparatively fresh, and no stones were required; but in fifty yards more 'Klip!' was called out, and my friend and I did the klipping ... Now, this klipping may be a playful amusement for some people, but Morris and myself very soon came to the conclusion that it bore a very strong resemblance to hard work, with every probability of getting your fingers crushed or yourself run over.

klip-bok /ˈkləpbɔk/ *n.* [Afk., *klip* rock + *bok* antelope.] The KLIPSPRINGER, *Oreotragus oreotragus*. Also *occas.* **klip-bokkie** [see -IE].

1886 G.A. FARINI *Through Kalahari Desert* 4 Not even the beasts of the desert, the klip-bok (rock buck), or steinbok (stone buck) .. are to be seen. **1920** F.C. CORNELL *Glamour of Prospecting* 125 On the higher peaks the chamois-like klip bok was plentiful. **1936** C. BIRKBY *Thirstland Treks* 126 *Klipbok* climb chamois-like and alone among the *krantzes*. **1947** *Cape Argus* 23 Oct. (Mag. Sect.) 1 The dog .. brought down a klipbok. **1953** J.R. ELLERMAN et al. *S. Afr. Mammals* 188 *Oreotragus oreotragus* Zimmerman, 1783. Klipspringer. Klipbokkie. **1968** G. CROUDACE *Silver Grass* 29 Jeremy saw the cloven imprints of a small buck – a *klipbok* perhaps – that had passed that way only a few moments before.

klip-buck *n. obs.* [Part. tr. Afk. *klipbok*, see KLIPBOK.] The KLIPSPRINGER, *Oreotragus oreotragus*.

1895 J.G. MILLAIS *Breath from Veldt* 92 The most curious thing about the klipbuck is the shape of its feet and the manner in which it uses them in springing up and down its native rocks. **1936** L.G. GREEN *Secret Afr.* 75 Klip-buck sprang up in the track. **1939** tr. *E.N. Marais's My Friends the Baboons* 59 The troop must often have had the chance of catching little klipbuck, dassies, and red hares.

klipdagga see DAGGA *n.*[2]

‖**klipdas** /ˈkləpdas/ *n.* Pl. unchanged. [S. Afr. Du., *klip* rock + *das* hyrax.] Either of two species of hyrax: **a.** The DASSIE (sense 1 a), *Procavia capensis*. **b.** The DASSIE (sense 1 b), *Heterohyrax brucei*.

It is possible that the plural forms *dasses* or *dassen* (see DAS) also occur but have not been recorded.

*c*1808 C. VON LINNÉ *System of Natural Hist.* VIII. 52 A small quadruped very common among these barren mountains .. called *klip-das* by the colonists at the Cape. **1853** *Edin. New Philos. Jrnl* (U.K.) IV. 214 Basking themselves on the sunny side of the krantzes .. may generally be seen several of the Klipdas, Cony, Rock Rabbit, or Cape Hyrax (*H. capensis*). [**1886** P. GILLMORE *Hunter's Arcadia* 248 From this descendant of Holland .. I bought the skins of some rock rabbits, the *klip das* of the Dutch.] **1900** H.A. BRYDEN *Animals of Afr.* 57 The rock-rabbit or hyrax, known all over South Africa by its Boer name, Dassie, which is a diminutive of *Klip das* (literally, rock-badger), .. is a most amusing and interesting little beast. **1953** J.R. ELLERMAN et al. *Afr. Mammals* 157 *Procavia capensis* Pallas, 1766. Dassie; Hyrax, Klipdas. Distribution: one of the commonest mammals in the Union.

klip dassie see DASSIE sense 1 a.

klipfish /ˈkləp-, ˈklɪpfɪʃ/ *n.* Also Englished form **clipfish**. [Part. tr. S. Afr. Du. *klipvisch*, see KLIPVIS.]

1. Any of a number of small, brightly-coloured fishes of the Clinidae, found usu. in shallow water or rock pools; KLIPPIE sense 3; KLIPVIS sense 2; ROCK-FISH sense 1.

1801 J. BARROW *Trav.* I. 30 *Klip* or rock-fish, the *Blennius viviparus*, makes no bad fry. **1831** [see CRAYFISH]. **1838** [see STUMPNOSE sense 1]. **1861** 'A LADY' *Life at Cape* (1963) 22 Presently one little bold klipfish, gleaming in bronze armour came nibbling at the bait. **1880** 'C.W.' in *Cape Monthly Mag.* II. Mar. 157 A .. box of tackle containing everything for catching fish of any size from a klipfish to a red steinbrass. **1913** D. FAIRBRIDGE *Piet of Italy* 6 The cuttlefish spread out their long arms and lift their cruel faces to peer .. into quiet corners in which small and foolish klipfish may be dozing. **1919** M.M. STEYN *Diary* 1 In Dixby's Bay I have hauled, with a small net, seventy klipfish in one haul. **1930** C.L. BIDEN *Sea-Angling Fishes* 158 The migration of the steenbras fits in well with the natural cycle of propagation of the most common species of klipfish (*Clinus superciliosus* one of the few sea fishes giving birth to its young) and of octopus. *c*1933 J. JUTA in A.C. Partridge *Lives, Lett. & Diaries* (1971) 159 A small, delicate-flavoured fish called *klipfish* – literally, 'stone fish' by reason of its haunts in the rocky weed-covered pools along that stretch of coast. **1949** [see ROCK-FISH]. **1968** J.L.B. SMITH *High Tide* 37 The wonderful variety of easily caught klipfishes that are such a feature of the tide pools of the Cape. **1971** A.C. PARTRIDGE *Lives, Lett. & Diaries* 163 *Klipfish* (*Clinus superciliousus*). The *blenny*, a small rock-fish of bright colours that gives birth to its young. It is the staple food of cormorants. **1979** *Signature* Dec. 17 The reduction of the seaweed, may serve to drive the little lobsters, the crabs, the klipfish, the mussels and other sea creatures from the area. **1985** A. TREDGOLD *Bay between Mountains* 109 The water stirs the bright green leaves of the sea lettuce ... Through them dart the speckled klipfish.

2. *obsolescent.* Usu. with qualifying words, **king -** or **koning klipfish** /ˈkʊənəŋ -/ [part. tr. S. Afr. Du. *koning klipvisch*, *koning* king + *klipvisch* see KLIPVIS]: the KINGKLIP (sense 2), *Genypterus capensis*.

1823 W.W. BIRD *State of Cape of G.H.* 159 The king klipfish, the steen brazen, and the stompneus, are all of excellent quality. **1843** [see ROCK-FISH sense 3]. J.C. CHASE *Cape of G.H.* 169 Koning Klip Fish, King Rock Fish. Scarcer than the preceding [*sc.* klipfish], very considerably larger, and less delicate, but in much repute. **1876** H. BROOKS *Natal* 141 Klipvisch, kingklip fish .. are held in very high estimation. **1887** *S.W. Silver & Co.'s Handbk to S. Afr.* 185 Xiphiurus Capensis, King Klip fish. One of the best of all Cape fishes. Caught with hook amongst rocks in our bays. Mentioned by Barrow. **1910** R. JUTA *Cape Peninsula* 95 During the Van Riebeeck reign a corporal went fishing for 'Klip' fish amongst the brown seaweed which lies like a barren reef round the South-West Coast. **1930** C.L. BIDEN *Sea-Angling Fishes* 2 Snoek, stockfish and king klipfish are hooked in great numbers from boats whenever the state of the bar permits of fishermen going half a mile or more to sea. **1945** H. GERBER *Fish Fare* 50 *Klipfish* is a tasty, scaleless fish, which goes up to about 2 lbs. **1950** [see STEENBRAS sense a]. **1985** J. HELLBERG in *S.-Easter* Oct.-Nov. 4 Those were .. the days when there were 'plenty of fish but no market .. When we caught kingklip we just threw them back because we couldn't sell them. In the 32 years of fishing I never sold a single klipfish' he recalls wryly.

klipje var. KLIPPIE.

Klipkaffir /ˈkləpkafə(r)/ *n. obsolescent.* [Afk. *klip* rock + KAFFIR; see quot. 1966.] An offensive name for a BERG DAMARA.

*c*1936 *S. & E. Afr. Yr Bk & Guide* 175 The Bergdamaras, or Klip kaffirs, of Negroid origin, are found in all the central districts, where they dwell in families of ten to forty. **1947** M. OLDEVIG *Sunny Land* 53 There were also the Dama people, living in the mountains further to the north who were capable of forging iron weapons – the Hilldamaras or Klipkaffirs of the present day. **1966** J.P. VAN S. BRUWER *S.W. Afr.: Disputed Land* 19 The Dama's only refuge was in the inaccessible regions of the arid mountains where they were ultimately discovered, living in a state of dire poverty. For this very reason they have been named Bergdama, (Mountain People), Klipkaffirs (Rock People) and Heuningkaffers (Honey People). [**1976** O. LEVINSON *Story of Namibia* 25 The Hottentots call the Bergdamas Xou-Daman ... When the fortunes of their Nama masters waned, they led a hazardous existence in mountain caves. For this reason they came to be termed disparagingly 'Berg (Mountain) Damaras', or else 'Klip-kaffers' (Stone Kaffirs).]

klipkaus var. KLIPKOUS.

klip-klip /ˈkləpkləp/ *n. colloq.* [Afk., reduplication of *klip* stone.] A children's game, 'five-stones', in which the aim of the players is to throw one pebble in the air and pick up the remaining four before catching the first, using one hand only; KLIP *n.* sense 4.

See note at NOW-NOW.

1931 G. BEET *Grand Old Days* 113 It was a very pretty klipje (pebble), and as I thought it might be useful to my sisters in their games of klip-klip, I handed it over to them. **1933** W. MACDONALD *Romance of Golden Rand* 15 The children were playing the game of 'klip-klip' with their pebbles on the kitchen floor. **1966** I. VAUGHAN *These Were my Yesterdays* 6 The girls .. played .. 'Klip Klip', skipping contests and hop scotch. **1978** M. VAN BILJON in *Sunday Times* 24 Dec. (Mag. Sect.) 1 One moment I would be playing 'klip-klip' with the younger children.

‖**klipkoppie** /ˈkləpˌkɔpi/ *n.* [Afk., *klip* stone + *koppie* see KOPPIE.] KOPPIE sense b.

1986 *Personality* 3 Nov. 32 An arid region of *harde veld, sandveld,* and *klipkoppies.* **1991** R. LANDMAN in *Sunday Times* 27 Jan. (K-TV Times) 14, I grew up in a small town in the Northern Cape at the foot of a stone koppie ... a klipkoppie.

klipkous /ˈkləpkəʊs/ *n.* Also **klepkous, klipkaus, klipkoes, klipkos.** Pl. unchanged, or (formerly) -**kousen.** [S. Afr. Du., fr. Du. *klip* stone, rock + *kous* stocking.] The PERLEMOEN, *Haliotus midae.*

1731 G. MEDLEY tr. *P. Kolb's Present State of Cape of G.H.* II. 209 The *Klip-Kousen* are sometimes call'd, by the *Virtuosi*, *Nabel*-Snails. These are frequently found at the *Cape*. **1785** G. FORSTER tr. *A. Sparrman's Voy. to Cape of G.H.* I. 26 A sort of snail or cockle, *klipkous* (*Haliotis*, Linn.) from half a foot to a foot and a half in diameter, is usually stewed, but makes in my opinion a very unsavoury dish. **1790** tr. *F. Le Vaillant's Trav.* I. 33 Crayfish I never saw; but the people eat sea ears, which are called *klepkousen*. **1843** J.C. CHASE *Cape of G.H.* 168 Klip Kous, .. A shell fish, most delicious, but requiring much trouble in the preparation. **1863** LADY DUFF-GORDON in F. Galton *Vacation Tourists* (1864) III. 169, I found a handsome Malay, with a basket of 'Klipkaus', a shell-fish much esteemed here. **1890** A.G. HEWITT *Cape Cookery* 8 Stewed Klipkaus. The only parts used are the tough parts which adhere to the rocks ... To every klipkaus, allow 1/2 pint of water, and to 4 klipkaus put 2 shanks of mutton. **1891** H.J. DUCKITT *Hilda's 'Where Is It?'* 164 The Paarl Lemoen, or Klip Kous ('Stone-stocking'), a species of shellfish found on many parts of the South African coast, adhering to the rocks. The shells are lovely, with a mother-of-pearl lining. The fish is most delicious if properly cooked. **1913** D. FAIRBRIDGE *Piet of Italy* 163 What she doesn't know about cooking isn't worth knowing ... Do you remember the heavenly klipkous she gave us one day? **1926** P.W. LAIDLER *Tavern of Ocean* 77 Strange dishes appeared on the tables: stewed 'klip kos,' a large Venus-ear shellfish; sea-cat soup; and mussels from the rocks below Lion's Head. **1930** C.L. BIDEN *Sea-Angling Fishes* 260 The crushed remains of klipkoes or venus ear – a shellfish, *Haliotis*. **1945, 1946** [see PERLEMOEN]. **1950** M. MASSON *Birds of Passage* 41 Souvenirs, among which was a Venus ear or klipkos whose brown crust had been scraped away to reveal the iridescent shell. **1979** [see PERLEMOEN]. **1985** A. TREDGOLD *Bay between Mountains* 101 If the fishing was poor there were perlemoen and klipkous on the rocks.

klipkrans *n. obs.* [S. Afr. Du., fr. Du. *klip* rock, stone + *krans* see KRANTZ.] See quots. See also KRANSKOPPIE, KRANTZ sense 2.

1786 G. FORSTER tr. *A. Sparrman's Voy. to Cape of G.H.* I. 258 At a very small distance from the water, appears .. a klip-krans .. or a rocky hill flat on the top, and perpendicular on the side towards the sea. *Ibid.* II. 48 He looked out for a *klipkrans*, (so they commonly call in this country a rocky place level and plain at the top, and having a perpendicular precipice on one side of it).

klippen var. KLIP.

klippenspringer var. KLIPSPRINGER.

klippie /ˈkləpi/ *n.* Formerly also **klipje**. [Afk., KLIP + dim. suffix -IE.]

1. KLIP *n.* sense 1.

1899 A. WERNER *Captain of Locusts* 63 The boys and I could only cut a cross on the thorn-tree .. and put a heap of klippies to mark the spot. **1931** [see KLIP-KLIP]. **1970** V. YOUNG *Informant, Queenstown*, I tripped on some klippies (small stones).

2. KLIP *n.* sense 2.

1908 D. BLACKBURN *Leaven* 43 This is a klippie, from Vaal River, .. what the white man call diamond, and it is worth more cattle than there is in the location. **1970** M. WOLFAARDT *Informant, Stilfontein* He smuggles klippies. (He smuggles diamonds.) **1983** *Frontline* Sept. 51 Greek tycoons with tankers, .. Kimberley Jims with a sharp eye for the klippies .. bring 'em all and I'll give you two to one on Sol.

3. KLIPFISH sense 1.

1973 M. PHILIP *Caravan Caravel* 66 We'll make a dam and try and catch *klippies* for it from the pools ... Peter pretended that he had at last actually caught a *klippie* in his hands.

klippspringer var. KLIPSPRINGER.

klip-salamander /ˈkləpsælə,mændə/ *n. obsolescent.* [Afk., earlier S. Afr. Du., fr. Du. *klip* rock + *salamander*, fr. L. *salamandra* reptile resembling a lizard.] The spiny girdle-tailed lizard *Cordylus cordylus* of the Cordylidae.

1838 J.E. ALEXANDER *Exped. into Int.* I. 143 The country now got worse every mile ... 'A dassé could not live here,' said a Boor, 'only a klip salamander'. **1911** *State* Sept. 251 (Pettman), A species of lizard with a long name, *klip-salamander*, whose sole occupation is to lie all day on a rock in the blazing sun – though not asleep, for its eyes are always open. **1911** D.B. HOOK *'Tis but Yesterday* 124 None of the parasites they harboured made any impression on Piet, whose skin was like that of a klip salamander. **1950** W. ROSE *Reptiles & Amphibians* 149 The type most commonly met with in Cape Province is *Cordylus cordylus*, sometimes misleadingly referred to as the Klip Salamander ... Stretched out on a rock these Zonures have the appearance of diminutive crocodiles, but the tail is proportionately far more spiky and is not flattened. **1970** BEETON & DORNER in *Eng. Usage in Sn Afr.* Vol.1 No.2, 47 *Klip-salamander*, .. (*Cordylus cordylus*) spiny girdle-tailed lizard widely distributed in rocky uplands.

klipspringer /ˈkləpsprəŋə(r), -sprɪŋə(r)/ *n.* Also **klipp(en)springer**. Pl. **-s**, or unchanged. [Afk., earlier S. Afr. Du., *klip* rock + *springer* leaper, jumper.] The small mountain antelope *Oreotragus oreotragus* of the Bovidae; CHAMOIS; KLIPBOK; KLIP-BUCK; ROCK-GOAT. Also *attrib.*, and occas. *fig.*

1785 G. FORSTER tr. *A. Sparrman's Voy. to Cape of G.H.* II. 224 The *klipspringer* has obtained the name it bears, from .. its running with the greatest velocity, and making large bounds even on the steepest precipices and in the most rocky places. **1812** A. PLUMPTRE tr. *H. Lichtenstein's Trav. in Sn Afr.* (1928) I. 72 At the very edge of the overhanging crags skipped the nimble antelope, called here the *klippenspringer*. **1835** A. STEEDMAN *Wanderings* II. 10 This peculiarity of structure in the hoof, and the rigid form of the pastern joints, account for the amazing agility which the klip-springer displays in bounding among the most dangerous rocks and precipices. **1847** [see DUIKER sense 1 a]. **1862** LADY DUFF-GORDON in F. Galton *Vacation Tourists* (1864) III. 156 The 'klip springer' ... Such a lovely little beast, as big as a small kid, with eyes and ears like a hare, and a nose so small and dainty. **1878** T.J. LUCAS *Camp Life & Sport* 227 The klip springer, a little antelope only found in rocky districts; which we find provided with a most perfect atmospheric apparatus in the hoof, which being pressed upon the smooth rocky surface, and being provided with a series of minute spongy cells, creates a temporary vacuum, and enables the antelope to maintain its footing. **1885** *Macmillan's Mag.* (U.K.) 24 Feb. 280 The klip-springer, the little chamois that is so clever at eluding dogs and men. **1896** R. WARD *Rec. of Big Game* 116 Klipspringer venison is excellent. **1900** W.L. SCLATER *Mammals of S. Afr.* I. 167 The klipspringer ... General colour speckled yellow and brown; hair very coarse .. close lying and thick, forming a species of cushion all over the body of the animal. *c*1936 [see CHAMOIS]. **1949** J. MOCKFORD *Golden Land* 226 The tiny klipspringer .. leaps nimbly from rock to rock on the slopes of the koppies. **1964** G. CAMPBELL *Old Dusty* 156 We .. had been watching two klipspringers jumping daintily from rock to rock along the kopje face, their pointed toes giving them a wonderful security on the sloping boulders. **1971** J.A. BROWN *Return* 153 Above them on a ledge were a pair of klipspringer, regarding them curiously; then whistling they leapt away. **1973** *Daily Dispatch* 1 May 2 Mr. Basson had changed his political affiliation so many times he was nothing but a political klipspringer. **1990** J. HEALE *Scowler's Luck* 67 A klipspringer darted onto a pinnacle of rock, gazed at them and then disappeared on tiny hooves that seemed to float down the crags. **1992** A. DE KLERK in *S. Afr. Panorama* Mar.-Apr. 74 Among the mammal inhabitants are klipspringer (*Oreotragus oreotragus*), steenbok [etc.]. **1994** M. ROBERTS tr. *J.A. Wahlberg's Trav. Jrnls 1838–56* 34 The Klippspringer is said, when leaping down steep slopes, to assume an upright position, and to land on his hind legs.

‖**klipsweet** /ˈkləpswɪət/ *n.* [Afk., *klip* rock, stone + *sweet* sweat.] HYRACEUM.

[**1857** D. LIVINGSTONE *Missionary Trav.* 22 A variety of preparations, such as .. inspissated renal deposit of the mountain Coney (Hyrax capensis) (which by the way is used in the form of pills as a good anti-spasmodic, under the name 'stone-sweat').] **1955** [see DASSIEPIS]. **1973** Y. BURGESS *Life to Live* 29 Even 'klipsweet', the dehydrated, tar-like residue of the urine of dassies, or rock-rabbits (who relieved themselves always, for some unknown reason, at the same place) was dissolved in boiling water and taken for the 'flu. **1975** W. STEENKAMP *Land of Thirst King* 139 Even worse to contemplate was 'klipsweet', the dark, puttylike layers of ancient dassie excreta the farmers gathered from fissures in the rocks. Melted in hot water, klipsweet was known as a specific for menstrual pains and other female complaints. **1989** D. SMUTS *Folk Remedies* 58 *Kidney problems:* (1) 2 oz klipsweet (rock rabbit or dassie secretion – ask the chemist) in 2 bottles gin. Drink a mouthful every morning and 3 mouthfuls in the evenings.

klipvis /ˈkləpfəs/ *n.* Formerly also **klipvisch**. Pl. **-visse** /-fəsə/. [Afk., earlier S. Afr. Du. *klipvis(ch)*, fr. Du. *klip* rock, stone + *visch* fish.]

1. *obs.* The KINGKLIP (sense 2), *Genypterus capensis*.

1790 E. HELME tr. *F. Le Vaillant's Trav. into Int.* I. 22 The *klepvis* .. is without scales, .. and taken among the rocks on the sea shore. **1876** H. BROOKS *Natal* 141 Klipvisch, kingklip fish .. are held in very high estimation.

2. KLIPFISH sense 1. Occas. also **klipvissie** [see -IE].

1887 *S.W. Silver & Co.'s Handbk to S. Afr.* 185 *Blennius versicolor* (several varieties) ... Klipvisch ... All very delicious. Flesh fat and firm when cooked freshly caught. **1902** J.D.F. GILCHRIST in *Trans. of S. Afr. Philological Soc.* XI. 224 Several names, or parts of names, are derived from the localities in which the fish are found. Thus we have .. Klip Visch, Steen Klip Visch (a peculiar redundancy). *Ibid.* 229 Klip-visch ... *Clinus*, 12 *sp.* **1949** [see ROCK-FISH]. **1953** U. KRIGE *Dream & Desert* 14 They had .. gazed into rockpools full of starfish, slowly waving sea plants and green-and-gold *klipvissies* drifting lazily from crevice to crevice. **1977** K.F.R. BUDACK in A. Traill *Khoisan Ling. Studies* 3 15 The so-called 'klipvisse' (various genera and species of the family *Clinidae*). **1994** *Afr. Wildlife* Vol.48 No.5, 31 (*advt*) Crowned Cormorants feed in shallow waters on bottom-dwelling prey such as *klipvis*, crustaceans and polychaete worms.

klis grass *n. phr. Obs.* [Englished form of S. Afr. Du. *klisgras*, Du. *klis* any of several weeds with hooked fruits + *gras* grass.] KLITS.

1906 B. STONEMAN *Plants & their Ways* 150 Fruits of Burr Weed (*Xanthium*) and Klis Grass (*Panicum verticillastre*) become very troublesome when the fruits become fastened into the wool of sheep or goats. **1909** 'ZWARTBAST' in *E. London Dispatch* 23 July 5 The fruits of such plants as the Burr-weed and Klis grass are a source of trouble and loss. **1913** C. PETTMAN *Africanderisms* 267 *Klis or Klits grass*, .. *Setaria verticillata, Beauv.*, a grass very common in some parts of the country, the seeding part of which, furnished with numerous minute hooks, knots and tangles in the most curious fashion. It is a source of much trouble and annoyance to farmers and gardeners.

klits /ˈkləts/ *n.* [Afk., ad. Du. *klis* (see prec.).] In full ***klitsgras*** /-xras/ [Afk. *gras* grass] or ***klits grass***: any of several species of grass having hooked fruits which adhere to all that they touch, esp. *Tragus racemosus* and *Setaria verticillata* of the Poaceae; KLIS GRASS.

1894 R. MARLOTH in *Trans. of S. Afr. Phil. Soc.* p.lxxxi, The klitsgrass (*Paniceum verticillastre*) bears .. hooks on its spikelets. **1905** J. DU PLESSIS *1000 Miles in Heart of Afr.* 139 Grasses and seeds of evil repute are conspicuous by their abundance, vitality, and pertinacity. *Klitsgras* may be disregarded and *weduwenaars* don't excite much remark. **1917** R. MARLOTH *Common Names* 50 *Klisgras* (klits), *Setaria verticillata* ... Other kinds of klits belong to Amarantaceae, e.g., *Achyranthes aspera, Cyathula globulifera*. **1966** C.A. SMITH *Common Names* 299 *Klitsgras*, .. The dense cylindric spike is particularly troublesome in wool and mohair in which it forms compact masses impossible to disentangle. **1977** F.G. BUTLER *Karoo Morning* 117 He just dragged them along like two feathers of klitsgras towards a shallow hole which he had started digging the day before.

kloaf, kloff varr. KLOOF.

‖**klomp** /klɔmp, klɒmp/ *n.* [See next.] KLOMPIE *n.*[1]

1920 F.C. CORNELL *Glamour of Prospecting* 170 Poulley spotted the *klomp* of springbok on the sandy, kopje-studded plains over which we were now travelling. **1975** *Darling* 12 Feb. 119 The very thought of a whole klomp of nudists jolling around kaal – I mean sis!

klompie /ˈklɔmpi, ˈklɒmpi/ *n.*[1] Also **clompie, clompje, clumpjie, clumpy, klompj(i)e, klumpjie.** [Afk. (earlier Du. *klompje*), a (small) lump, crowd, lot, bunch, heap, *klomp* + dim. suffix -IE.] A group or cluster of people, animals, plants, or other objects; CLUMP; KLOMP.

1853 W.R. KING *Campaigning in Kaffirland* 215 Even at three quarters of a mile, we were able to disperse small 'clumpjies' of Kaffirs and cattle. **1864** T. BAINES *Explor. in S.-W. Afr.* 241 Snyman also saw nothing except one 'klumpjie' of kameels. *Ibid.* 453 The chief was killed and his tribe utterly dispersed, .. and now they are here and there in clumpjies. **1884** *Queenstown Free Press* 19 Feb., His neighbours .. were continually losing small and large 'clompjes' of sheep. **1896** H.A. BRYDEN *Tales of S. Afr.* 70 Suddenly we came upon a *klompje* of giraffe. **1900** [see VELD sense 2 a i]. **1900** B. MITFORD *Aletta* 108 The mimosa and prickly pear *klompjes* were a favourite haunt of those splendid game birds. **1900** *Ibid.* [see DRAAI sense 1 b]. **1910** R. JUTA *Cape Peninsula* 112 Tall flowering reeds grow in klompjes. **1911** D.B. HOOK *'Tis but Yesterday* 205 A 'clumpy' of bush was allotted to the captives, underneath which there was shelter from dew. **1913** J.J. DOKE *Secret City* 257 Since the destruction wrought by the great flood, the klompje of native huts .. had been rebuilt on higher ground. **1917** C.G. CARTER *Informant, Westminster (OFS)* 8 July, There are a good many South Africans here [*sc.* in London], and whenever you see little klompies together you can bet they are refreshing their dutch vocabulary. **1920** F.C. CORNELL *Glamour of Prospecting* 79 Paauw, that most magnificent of bustards, was abundant .. ; klompjes of four or five together rising repeatedly a few dunes ahead of us, but always well out of gunshot. **1937** S. CLOETE *Turning Wheels* 180 Each clompie of beasts had its own herders, black or coloured, who looked after them. **1945** M. HONE *Sarah-Elizabeth* 42 They sat in the shade of a klompie of weeping willows. **1963** S. CLOETE *Rags of Glory* 44 Great *klompies* of them [*sc.* stallions] could live together with hardly a serious quarrel till a female came along. **1973** *The 1820* Vol.46 No.9, 10 A dry, arid, barren waste of illimitable distances .. , with every now and then a klompie of trees, very green against the sombre background of brown veld. **1990** G. HARESNAPE in M. Leveson *Firetalk* 30 They disturbed a good-sized klompie of baboon.

klompie /ˈklɔmpi, ˈklɒmpi/ *n.*[2] Also **klompje**. [Afk., fr. Du. *klomp* a small blue brick (typical esp. of the Antwerp area) + dim. suffix -IE.] KLINKER sense 2. Also *attrib.*

1926 P.W. Laidler *Tavern of Ocean* 91 In November, 1768, a new hospital was begun ... Most of the material for its construction, small Dutch bricks called *klompjes*, was sent out from Holland. **1926** S.G. Millin *S. Africans* 111 Over-mantled and over-mirrored green or red tiled fireplaces to open hearths outlined in stone or in small bricks called klompjes. **1932** *Grocott's Daily Mail* 12 Jan. 2 The coastal towns .. we have always regarded as being a natural market for our bricks, klompjes, paving tiles and roofing tiles. **1945** *Outspan* 3 Aug. 47 The lounge fire-place is built of facebrick in modern klompjie style. **1949** J. Mockford *Golden Land* 47 The formative process is clearly to be seen in the use of .. local 'stock' bricks for walling and imported 'klompjes' for special work. **1950** *Cape Times* 4 Mar. 11, (*advt*) Golden Brown Klompies 9 in. x 4 in. x 134 in. and 2,500 face bricks. **1951** L.G. Green *Grow Lovely* 35 Large shipments of bricks arrived until late in the eighteenth century. You find them mainly in stoeps and face works, with the yellow klompjes that have weathered so well. **1963** R. Lewcock *Early 19th C. Archit.* 379 In the days of the Company small hard yellow bricks, 'geele klinkers' — locally called 'klompjes' — were imported from Holland in large quantities and used for all exposed work, and for reinforcing arches over openings. **1969** I. Vaughan *Last of Sunlit Yrs* 51 The high wide stoeps of square Batavian tiles and the steps of smooth small klompie bricks had echoed to the sound of busy footsteps. **1971** C. De Bosdari *Cape Dutch Houses & Farms* 48 An example of the decorative effect obtainable from the use of the small imported Dutch bricks (klompjes). **1976** V. Driver-Jowitt in *Living & Loving* May 8, I ordered 100 'klompie' bricks ... These I stacked outside the rim of the sandpit. **1987** G. Viney *Col. Houses* 84 Entrance showing the semi-circular steps of *klompie* bricks (imported as ballast in the ships of the Dutch East India Company).

klong /klɔŋ/ *n. offensive.* [See next.] KLONKIE.

1913 C. Pettman *Africanderisms* 268 *Klong*, .. The word is in common use in various parts of South Africa, and is applied to coloured males without reference to age, much as the word 'boy' is among the English colonists; indeed so far has the original sense disappeared that the expression 'ou' klong' (lit. 'old small youngster') is by no means uncommon. **1963** A.M. Louw *20 Days* 71 'He is a big klong now. I can't work for him any more. He must work for me. What does a mother bring children up for?' she said.

klonkie /ˈklɔŋki/ *n. Derog.* and *offensive.* [Afk., *klong* (contraction of *klein-jong*, *klein* small + *jong*, see JONG *n.* senses 1 and 2) + dim. suffix -IE.] Of black or 'coloured' people: a patronizing name for a youth; an insulting name for a man; KLONG.

1953 A. Paton *Phalarope* (1963) 25 The *klonkies* there, the small black boys, having learned it from the soldiers who camped in Venterspan during the war of 1939, saluted him. *Ibid.* 58 The small *klonkies* from the black people's location .. liked to hang around the store. **1955** A. Delius *Young Trav.* 104 After tea most of the Klonkies and the Klimmeide went off to help their parents with the feeding of cattle, horses and pigs, while the white children wandered off to help their mothers with such things as separating cream, [etc.]. **1955** D. Jacobson *Trap* 32 Strained and shy, the boy's voice came: 'Good night, baas. Thank you, baas.' 'Good night, *klonkie*,' Van Schoor replied. **1960** D. Lytton *Goddam White Man* 102 Don't tell me the coloured klonkie living in those huts on the farm feels shame at his failure to provide better for his kids. **1963** J. Packer *Home from Sea* 24 'How do you clean them?' I asked. 'A man goes in' said Dudley. 'For the little tasks a boy does the job — a *klonkie*.' **1974** F. Forsyth *Dogs of War* 155 He had learned to stalk birds and shoot in the valley with Pieter, his klonkie, the coloured playmate white boys are allowed to play with until they grow too big and learn what skin colour is all about. **1980** [see HOUTKOP]. **1984** *Cape Times* 14 Dec., He would not be prepared to share the Sea Point swimming pool with 10 000 klonkies from Guguletu. **1985** *E. Prov. Herald* 22 Apr. 10 When I told him that words like 'coon' and 'klonkie' were a form of racial abuse, he told me I was a 'kayjayell'. A KJL .. stands for 'knee jerk liberal' .. another term for an inverted racist. **1986** P. Jooste in *Fair Lady* 22 Jan. 108 Newspaper billboards headlined the latest news of the Suez crisis and barefoot *Argus* 'klonkies' would sell the full story for a tickey. **1989** J. Hobbs *Thoughts in Makeshift Mortuary* 277 'The klonkie up the ladder?' He jerked his head at Jake. 'He's just a painter who was recommended to us.'

kloof /klu:f, kluəf, klʊəf/ *n.* Also formerly **cleugh, clo(e)f, cloff(e), cloof, clough, clufe, cluff, clugh, kloaf, kloff, klooft, kluff, klugh.** [Afk., earlier S. Afr. Du., fr. Middle Du. *clove* cleft (in which form it is found in U.S. Eng.).]

1. *Obs.* exc. in place-names such as *Bain's Kloof, Brickmaker's Kloof, Tamboerskloof*: a narrow natural or man-made pass between mountains.

1731 G. Medley tr. *P. Kolb's Present State of Cape of G.H.* II. 18 As the *Lion-* is separated from the *Table-Hill* by a small *Kloof*, as the *Dutch* call it (i.e. Cleft or Descent) so is the *Wind-* or *Devil's-Hill* from the *Lion-Hill*. **1776** F. Masson in *Phil. Trans. of Royal Soc.* LXVI. 273 Kloof, is a narrow passage over a lower part of a chain of mountains, or sometimes a narrow passage between mountains. **1790** W. Paterson *Narr. of Four Journeys* 7 Here may be said to be one of the most difficult passes into the country, called Hottentot Holland's Kloaf. [*Note*] Kloaf signifies a narrow pass through the mountains. **1796** C.R. Hopson tr. *C.P. Thunberg's Trav.* II. 183 From Roode Zand we took the usual way through its kloof, which has a considerable eminence that must be crossed. **1801** J. Barrow *Trav.* I. 63 Of these passes, or *kloofs* as they are called by the colonists, there are but three that are ever used by wheel-carriages. **1812** A. Plumptre tr. *H. Lichtenstein's Trav. in Sn Afr.* (1928) I. 64 The reader is probably aware from other travels that the term *kloof* is not appropriated solely to the passage of which we are here speaking; it is a general name given to all mountain-roads of a similar kind. *a*1823 J. Ewart *Jrnl* (1970) 62 We crossed a range of mountains called the How Hoek, by a pass or klooft more dreaded by the Boors, than that of Hottentot Holland though neither so steep or long. **1829** [see sense 2]. **1835** G. Champion *Jrnl* (1968) 32 The village of B.[ethelsdorp] is situated at the entrance of one of the kloofs or clefts through the range of hills before described. A stream of water issues from the same forming a kind of valley. **1838** J.E. Alexander *Exped. into Int.* I. 75 The shepherd of the field-corporal, a Bush boy, in returning home with the flock one evening through a kloof or pass, stayed behind to bring up some of the lame. **1862** 'A Lady' *Life at Cape* (1963) 90 What is meant by a 'kloof' is the gap between two mountain chains that threaten to touch. At best, they are very narrow and tortuous, now contracting till the crags almost exclude the light, now opening into glorious vistas of rock and river. **1878** T.J. Lucas *Camp Life & Sport* 45 Anon, our road led through some rocky pass, or kloof, from whose summit came the harsh grunts of the enormous baboons which regarded us with evident curiosity.

2. A (wooded) gorge or valley; a ravine running down a mountainside.

1796 C.R. Hopson tr. *C.P. Thunberg's Trav.* II. p.xiii, *Kloof* signifies a valley, or such a cleft in the mountains as is either inhabited by the Colonists, or admit of a passage through it on horseback or with a carriage of any kind. **1815** G. Barker Journal. 2 Sept., Br. P. left us in the afternoon to go to a farm hous[e] in the kloof and prepare for us bread *c* **1822** W.J. Burchell *Trav.* I. 15 This pass is defended by a block-house, and is called the Kloof, a word of frequent occurrence in this colony, and signifying a pass, either over or between mountains, and often a deep ravine down the side of a mountain. *Ibid.* 36 The woody kloofs, or ravines in this range, contain many of the forest trees and other plants which, according to common opinion, are only to be found in more distant parts of the colony. **1829** C. Rose *Four Yrs in Sn Afr.* 17 Kloof, in the country round the Cape, generally means a pass among the hills and mountains; in Albany, a deep wooded hollow, frequently the retreat of savage animals. *Ibid.* 300 Soft, cool moss and fern, in the shade of a steep, wooded kloof. **1834** T. Pringle *Afr. Sketches* 164 Gave Scottish names to several of the subsidiary glens and cleughs, or kloofs, as the colonists call them. **1841** J. Collett Diary. II. 13 May, Some Flocks Folded in the Kloofs on acct. of the wet Kralls. **1845** S. Dennison in D.R. Edgecombe, Letters of Hannah Dennison. (1968) 209 They found him in a cloef at the foot of an imence crance of[f] wich he had thrown himself. **1850** N.J. Merriman *Cape Jrnls* (1957) 144 After a hard day of precipitous climbing [we] found ourselves at nightfall quite entangled amongst the kloofs on the west side of the Great Winterberg. **1852** M.B. Hudson *S. Afr. Frontier Life* 237 The name 'kloof' is applied to any valley; but it seems more particularly to refer to the hollows cut out (as it were) in the sides of mountain ranges. **1856** G. Grey in *Imp. Blue Bks* Command Paper 2352–1857, 36 The seaward side of the range is intersected by deep rocky kloofs, clothed with forests of large trees, in which many rivers rise; these kloofs open, even in the mountain range, into wide and fertile valleys. **1861** Lady Duff-Gordon *Lett. from Cape* (1925) 46 What a divine spot! Such kloofs, with silver rills running down them! **1871** J. McKay *Reminisc.* 66 Woody-sided kloofs striking off now and again to your right in the direction of the Kroome range. **1877** R.M. Ballantyne *Settler & Savage* 159 A grand background of wooded gorges, — or corries, as you Scotch have it, or kloofs, according to the boers. **1882** J. Nixon *Among Boers* 10 The air was so clear that we could plainly discern the indentations, or kloofs as they are called, in the sides of the distant mountains. *Ibid.* 269 The sides of the mountain consisted of long bare ridges with deep kloofs between, devoid of vegetation. **1899** (tr. J.A.U. de Mist) in G.M. Theal *Rec. of Cape Col.* (1899) V. 179 The burgher senate is particularly enjoined to give every encouragement to the planting of trees for timber and fuel .. in the flat, the sidelings and 'cloofs' (ravines) — alongside and on the top of Table Mountain, Lion's Head and Lion's Rump. **1899** H. Rider Haggard *Swallow* p.iv, Her face was rich in hue as a kloof lily. **1908** J.M. Orpen *Reminisc.* (1964) 60 The stream .. rises on the top of the mountain and comes down a kloof near its eastern end and the path to reach the top goes up the kloof. **1925** D. Kidd *Essential Kafir* 157 He wanders off into the veldt alone and hides in kloofs, dives into deep pools of which others are afraid. **1948** H.E. Hockly *Story of Brit. Settlers of 1820* 18 Between the rolling grass-covered hills, dotted with mimosa trees and thickets, were deep, thickly wooded 'kloofs' affording protection to wild animals of endless variety. **1962** *Bokmakierie* June 20 From the berg heavily wooded kloofs lead down to the flatter plains at the edge of the dam. **1968** K. McMagh *Dinner of Herbs* 82 The kloofs were filled by a thick bush of mighty trees which made a fairyland of fern and flowers where man seldom if ever ventured. **1976** A.P. Brink *Instant in Wind* 46 To one side lie the Company's gardens; to the other, the fountains fed by water running from Table Mountain down a ravine or kloof visible from town. [**1985** A. Tredgold *Bay between Mountains* 195 Another threat to the old village .. has been a plan to cram 28 'luxury' flats onto three plots in the kloofie between the end of Loch Road and Godfrey Road.] **1988** J. Scott in *Cape Times* 8 Aug. 6 The foolhardy .. often commit themselves with irresponsible abandon to kloofs and gullies which even a trained climber would not attempt. **1993** F. Van Rensburg in *Getaway* Nov. 93 The vegetation in the protected kloof differs a lot from that of the exposed mountain slopes.

Hence **kloofing** *vbl n.*, exploring and hiking in kloofs.

1986 *Argus* 11 Jan., A definition of kloofing — if there is one — is hard to find, but .. it is an adventure which offers excitement, exercise and outdoor fun. **1990** A. Bumstead in *Style* June 111 Last year, we tried mountain bikes (.. ideal for the nearby hills and mountains around Swellendam) ... Next year, who knows? Hiking? Kloofing? Pogo stick safaris.

klop *n. obs.* Also **klopje.** [Afk. (now *klap*), fr. Du. *klop(je)* blow, stroke (echoic).

Cf. general Eng. *klop* or *clop*, 'the sound of the impact of something solid on a hard surface' (*OED*).]

The thudding sound made by a bullet striking flesh.

1884 'E.V.C.' *Promised Land* 17 'Klop,' I heard the bullet strike, but not then knowing the merits of that lovely sound, thought it merely the ground I had fired into. **1893** *Blackwood's Mag.* (U.K.) Sept. 444 The crack was heard, again followed by the fatal 'klop'. **1900** B. MITFORD *Aletta* 107 Bang! .. The 'klop' made by the bullet as it rushed through the poor little beast – through ribs and heart – was audible to them there at upwards of four hundred yards. **1913** C. PETTMAN *Africanderisms* 269 *Klopje*, .. The noise which a bullet makes when it finds its billet in the body of an animal is .. spoken of as the *klop* of the bullet. **1914** W.C. SCULLY *Lodges in Wilderness* 92, I knew well enough that the bullet had fetched him; I heard its 'klop' distinctly.

Hence **klop** *v. intrans.*

1900 B. MITFORD *Aletta* 47 'That's good!' observed Colvin; I knew he'd got it, heard the bullet 'klop'.

‖**klopjag** /ˈklɔpjax/ *n.* Pl. **-s**, **jagte** /-jaxtə/. [Afk., *klop* knock, tap, beating + *jag* hunt, pursuit, chase.] A police raid.

[**1971** *E. Prov. Herald* 27 Feb. 13 Newspapers which had .. described .. activities of the South African Police as 'raids', 'swoops', or 'klapjagte' were .. doing tremendous damage to the image of the Republic.] **1971** *Rand Daily Mail* 21 May 12 Lottery klopjag. **1971** *Ibid.* 28 Aug. 10 Non-Nationalists shrink away in revulsion and anger .. when there is another Security police klopjag with a whole lot a decent, ordinary citizens being raided at dawn. **1987** *New Nation* 28 May 4 They claim police have staged an almost daily 'klopjag' (raid) at the houses of Bisco activists and SRC members. **1990** *City Press* 4 Feb. 6 The echoes of De Klerk's words had hardly vanished from the airwaves nor the ink hardly dried on newspaper reports of his words than the boys in blue were out on klopjag.

klopje *n.*[1] var. KLAP *n.*[1]

klopje *n.*[2] var. KLOP.

klopper var. KLAPPER *n.*[1]

klopse /ˈklɔpsə/ *n.* Also **kloppse**, **klops**. [Afk., prob. ad. Eng. *clubs*: 'The scintillating "Klopsdans" (Club Dance – klops, pronounced "klawps" – being a corruption of the English word "club". The clubs in question .. are essentially music clubs.' (Van Heyningen & Berthoud, *Uys Krige*, 1966, p.116); or perh. ad. Du. *klop* audible bang on a hard surface, referring to the sound of the ghomma drum.] Often in the phr. ***Kaapse klopse*** [Afk., Klops of the Cape].

1. *pl. n.* Esp. in Cape Town: troupes of Cape Malay street singers who sing traditional songs, bitter-sweet but laced with humour, accompanied usu. by a ghomma drum, and by particular body movements. See also COON, GHOMMA sense 1, GHOMMALIEDJIE. Also *attrib.*

1981 *Cape Times* 10 Jan. 12 Some called it 'coons', and others 'klopse' and they surged through the streets in the wake of the traditional adult coon bands. **1981** *S. Afr. Panorama* July 34 A lower level of music for the masses .. consists of three divisions – the Klopse, commonly known as Coons, the 'Dutch' (Malay) night troops, and the Christmas choirs. **1987** [see E. Prov. Herald quot. at sense 2]. **1987** *New Nation* 3 Dec. 11 As a tribute to the Kaapse-Klopse tradition, the group has just released an album with Mac's father, Sam McKenzie, one of the original Goema leaders ... 'Mac and The Genuines' .. is a combination of moppies and sopvleis (klopse-lingo for humorous and serious music respectively). **1990** *Staffrider* Vol.9. No.1, 14 A voice from an open doorway shouted, 'What does *Meneer* want?' 'I'd like to know where Mr Levy lives, the one who makes clothes for the coons.' 'It's too early for the klops-gear, *Meneer*.' **1991** *Cosmopolitan* Jan. 40 Ibrahim grew up with the *goema* beat of the *klopse* troops, the Malay choirs and the gospel influences of the family church in which his grandmother and dressmaker mother were pianists.

2. *transf. Music.* The style of music performed by these troupes; also called GHOMMA (sense 2). See also MOPPIE, SOPVLEIS. Also *attrib.*

1987 *E. Prov. Herald* 31 Oct. 7 Now the Genuines .. have gone to the roots of traditional Cape Music. Known as *moppie* and *sopvleis* and played by klopse (clubs or troops), although *klopse* has become the general term, it is to the coloured community what Highlife is to Lagos or what *mbaqanga* is to Soweto. **1987** *Personality* 15 June 66 With the exception of Dollar Brand, klopse-inspired music has never been played commercially in clubs. **1989** *Fair Lady* 18 Jan. 15 A jazzy blues sound with an understated dash of township jive, a spot of Kaapse klop and a hint of something Eastern. **1989** M. BEHR in *Fair Lady* 12 Apr., Bubbling banjo from one of the few surviving exponents of Kaapse Klopse makes for a memorable indigenous experience. **1989** C. CHAPMAN in *Edgars Club* Apr. 45 There were the unique body movements of the indigenous Cape people, the Hottentots and Bushmen. They used a kind of shoulder-shake, a trembling body and shuffling foot movement. This body movement translates into the characteristic rhythms employed by the troupes, and known as *klopse*, which also involves a highly developed singing tradition. This klopse music developed out of the freedom of the slaves, who were then allowed to sing and dance through the streets. **1989** *Personality* 26 June 77 That dinkum old Coon Carnival player, Mr Mac, and his son and friends The Genuines do a more honest rendition of *Kaapse Kloppse*.

klow sick, **klow sickness** *n. phr. Obs. Pathology.* Also **klew sick**. [Calque formed on S. Afr. Du. *klauwziekte*.] KLAUWZIEKTE.

1789 W. PATERSON *Narr. of Four Journeys* 96 Many of our oxen .. had caught a disease called Klow sickness, which rages among the horned cattle in the summer, and affects their hoofs so much that they drop off, and numbers of the cattle die. **1839** J. COLLETT Diary. II. 22 Feb., Cattle nearly well of klew sick many sheep yet cripled.

kluff, **klugh** varr. KLOOF.

‖**kluitjie** /ˈklœiki, ˈkleɪki, -ci/ *n.* Formerly also **kluitje**. [Afk., earlier S. Afr. Du., dim. form of *kluit* clod, lump (see -IE).]

1.a. A dumpling. See also SOUSKLUITJIES.

1890 A.G. HEWITT *Cape Cookery* 58 Have ready a saucepan of *boiling* water and drop a spoonful at a time of the batter into the water; as each kluitje rises to the surface, take it out, put it into a dish kept hot. **1891** H.J. DUCKITT *Hilda's 'Where Is It?'* 55 In this gravy was stirred some of the above *Milk Kluitjes* a few minutes before serving. **1913** C. PETTMAN *Africanderisms* 269 *Kluitjes*, (D. *kluit*, a lump, clod.) The South African name for small dumplings. **1972** L.G. GREEN *When Journey's Over* 143 Most of the old Cape soups appeared on Klaas Muller's menus. He had a splendid green mealie soup, a sheep's head soup with forcemeat balls and kluitjies (dumplings) and a venison soup in season.

b. *obs.* With distinguishing epithet: **broodkluitjie** [Afk., *brood* bread], a dumpling made with breadcrumbs; **rice -** or **rijstkluitjie** [Du., *rijst* rice], a dumpling made with rice.

1891 H.J. DUCKITT *Hilda's 'Where Is It?'* 15 **'Brood Kluitjes'** (Bread Dumplings). **1934** *Cape Argus* 4 Jan. (Swart), Brood Kluitjies are delicious served with stewed chicken. **1954** M. KUTTEL *Quadrilles & Konfyt* 94 She would find those typically South African dishes of yellow rice, Angel's food, Zoet Koekies, Smoor fish, .. broodkluitjies, koeksisters, poffertjies, frikkadels, pickled fish and many other dishes. **1890** A.G. HEWITT *Cape Cookery* 58 **Rice Kluitjes**. Make a stiff batter, with cold rice, milk, a little flour and eggs. **1891** H.J. DUCKITT *Hilda's 'Where Is It?'* 55 Dumplings (Rice). (Very old Cape Recipe. Cape name, 'Rys Kluitjes.') **1913** C. PETTMAN *Africanderisms* 402 **Rijstkluitjes**, .. Dumplings or rolls made of rice.

2. *comb. obs.* **kluitjiesop** /-sɔp/ [Afk., *sop* soup], dumpling soup.

1949 L.G. GREEN *In Land of Afternoon* 63 Kluitjiesop is a heavy dumpling soup.

klumpjie var. KLOMPIE.

knecht /knɛxt/ *n. Obs.* exc. *hist.* Also **kneg**. Pl. **-s**, ‖**knechte** /ˈknɛxtə/. [S. Afr. Du., fr. Du., perh. fr. G. *knecht* knight, in the orig. sense of 'servant', esp. a military servant. (The modern Afk. form is *kneg*).] A bondman or man-servant, usu. seconded from the army to work as a farm overseer or foreman. Cf. *slagter's knecht* (see SLAGTER sense b). See also MANDOOR.

1798 LADY A. BARNARD *Lett. to Henry Dundas* (1973) 106 We only regretted that we could not make our knecht sit down at table with us, and pass him off as a cousin, – but a trick of this sort would never have been forgiven in this place, had we lived for two thousand years. **1850** R.G.G. CUMMING *Hunter's Life* I. 5 The trader then instructs his knecht, or head servant, to make a parade of the goods. **1861** P.B. BORCHERDS *Auto-Biog. Mem.* 46 Obliged to take up quarters at a shoemaker's, one Mulder, who had a large family, besides some visitors, butcher's knechts or travelling servants. **1913** C. PETTMAN *Africanderisms* 269 *Knecht*, (D. *knecht*, a man-servant. Etymologically this is the same word as the English 'knight'.) An overseer, a head servant. **1921** H.J. MANDELBROTE tr. *O.F. Mentzel's Descr. of Cape of G.H.* I. 164 We come next to the class of soldier who does not perform any military duties and who is not in receipt of pay, but who is, nevertheless, required to serve the specified period, and who is bound to step into the ranks at a moment's notice. These are either 'Knechte' or schoolmasters. Whenever a farmer finds that he cannot supervise his whole farm by himself, or if he owns several farms, he usually applies to the Company for an overseer of the slaves and general estate manager. A suitable man is selected from the soldiers in the garrison .. ; he is styled a 'Knecht'. **1928** E.A. WALKER *Hist. of S. Afr.* 72 Others .. were men set free to work as *knechts* or overseers of farms or as *meesters* or both, subject to recall to the colours at a moment's notice. **1955** A. DELIUS *Young Trav.* 72 The young man .. informed them in cautious, shy English that he was a 'kneg' – a farm foreman. **1977** T.R.H. DAVENPORT *S. Afr.: Mod. Hist.* 18 To cheapen its costs it [*sc.* the Company] released potential settlers from its service, or encouraged its servants to hire themselves to free farmers as Knechts. **1983** *Daily Dispatch* 22 Apr. 25 My father lost his farm and became a knecht, looking after someone else's for £3 a month and rations. **1989** *Reader's Digest Illust. Hist.* 53 Other supervisors were the *knechte*, unskilled European labourers or soldiers of the lowest rank, who were not far above the slaves in the social hierarchy.

kneealtre, **kneeaulter** varr. KNEE-HALTER.

knee-band *v. trans.* [Calque formed on S. Afr. Du. *knieband*, knee-halter.] KNEE-HALTER *v.*

1825 W. THRELFALL in B. Shaw *Memorials* (1841) 15 The people set up a loud shout, got from their horses, off-saddled, knee-banded them, and then we set off after him.

knee-halter *v. trans.* and *intrans.* Also **kneealtre**, **kneeaulter**, **kneehalt**. [Calque formed on S. Afr. Du. *kniehalter*.] To hobble (a horse) by tying the bridle to the knee or to the foreleg above the knee, thus allowing the animal to graze freely but preventing it from straying; KNEE-BAND.

1827 G. THOMPSON *Trav.* I. 124 Our horses were hastily *knee-haltered* (i.e. tied neck and knee to prevent their running off) and turned to graze till the night closed in. **1833** *Graham's Town Jrnl* 14 Feb. 4 If his [*sc.* the Pound Master's] right to knee-halter be established, it is high time that some laws are enacted to compel him to apply *proper reins*, and not such as cut the legs of horses *to the very bone*. **a1858** J. GOLDSWAIN *Chron.* I. (1946) 32 Found they Horse kneealtred his head made fast to one of his frunt legs with a strap. *Ibid.* 38 As soone as I had taken sum refreshmen I on [*sc.* un-] kneeaulter my Ox and returned to the Bush ware I rived jest at dark. **1860** A.W. DRAYSON *Sporting*

Scenes 68 When a traveller halts in Africa, .. he takes off the saddle and bridle, and knee-halters his horse; .. fastening the animal's head to its leg, just above the knee. **1882** LADY F.C. DIXIE *In Land of Misfortune* 317 The horses were at once watered, knee-haltered, and turned out to graze. **1884** B. ADAMS *Narr.* (1941) 193 We .. 'kneehalted' them, which is done by fastening the head to within about 18 inches of the knee by means of a rhiem — strip of hide — just allowing them sufficient length to reach the grass to eat. **1900** B. MITFORD *Aletta* 119 'Don't have him put in the camp' as a Hottentot came up to take the horse. 'Just knee-halter him, and let him run.' **1907** J.P. FITZPATRICK *Jock of Bushveld* (1909) 308 Horses are differently treated when 'offsaddled'; some may be trusted without even a halter, and can be caught and saddled when and where required; others are knee-haltered. **1919** R.Y. STORMBERG *With Love from Gwenno* 64 Pieter knee-haltered the horses, and then we proceeded on foot to where the grass gives way to a kind of platform. **1931** G. BEET *Grand Old Days* 93 He knee-haltered his horses as usual and left them feeding on the veld. **1937** [see OFF-SADDLE *v.* sense 2]. **1963** S. CLOETE *Rags of Glory* 519 Some burghers out of habit had knee-haltered their mounts. **1977** F.G. BUTLER *Karoo Morning* 84 His hunting was almost ruined by the carelessness of his Hottentot grooms, who let some of the horses graze without knee-haltering them.

Hence **knee-halter** *n.*, a hobble; **knee-haltered** *ppl adj.* (and *quasi-adv.*); **knee-haltering** *vbl n.*, the method of hobbling a horse by tying a thong from neck to foreleg.

1839 W.C. HARRIS *Wild Sports* 69 Knee-haltering is the colonial method of securing a horse when turned out to graze; a leathern thong attached to the neck, is passed round the knee, and tied. **1849** E.D.H.E. NAPIER *Excursions in Sn Afr.* II. 16 The 'knee-haltered' horses, and out-spanned oxen, were busily engaged. **1862** E.L. PRICE *Jrnls* (1956) 87 The horse was grazing quietly and knee-haltered. **1908** *Animal Management* 126 The practice of grazing may be taken advantage of to accustom horses to knee haltering. **1936** P.M. CLARK *Autobiog. of Old Drifter* 80 Oxen, tied to the trek chains, stood or lay all about, with knee-haltered horses in great number. **1963** S. CLOETE *Rags of Glory* 464 There was no need for a knee halter. They were very tame and too tired to wander far. **1991** *Best of S. Afr. Short Stories* (Reader's Digest Assoc.) 150 Tying the bridle to the foreleg of a horse — knee-haltering — prevents it from raising its head fully.

kneg var. KNECHT.

knobby thorn *n. phr. Obs.* [Calqued on Afk. *knoppiesdoring*, see KNOPPIESDORING.] KNOBTHORN sense 2.

*c*1936 *S. & E. Afr. Yr Bk & Guide* 324 *Knobby thorn (Acacia nigrescens)*, a very handsome tree usually found near the Mopani. **1949** C. BULLOCK *Rina* 39 The knobby thorn .. was already in bloom and putting out new leaves, delicately beautiful as those of the silver birch.

knobkerrie, **knobkierie** /ˈnɒbkeri, ˈnɔb-, -kiri/ *n.* Also **knobcarrie**, **knobcary**, **knobkeerie**, **knobkerry**, **knob-kiêri**, **knobkier(r)ie**, **knobkirrie**, **knob-kurrie**, **nob kerie**, **nob kerry**. [Eng. *knob* + *kerrie*, (anglicized form of) *kierie* (see KIERIE), after S. Afr. Du. (later Afk.) *knopkierie*.] KIERIE. Also *attrib.*, and *fig.*

1844 *United Service Mag.* July 337 With the precious book .. in one hand, and his knob-kurrie in the other, away he trudged. **1849** E.D.H.E. NAPIER *Excursions in Sn Afr.* II. 82 The 'knob keerie' .. hurled with unerring aim, brings the smaller animals to the ground. **1855** J.W. COLENSO *Ten Weeks in Natal* p.xvii, The Boers, their sons, and servants, were all massacred, being knocked upon the head with knob-kirries. **1855** N.J. MERRIMAN *Cape Jrnls* (1957) 224 This man had .. destroyed many of his subjects by the cruel death usual in the case of those who are accused of withcraft — viz., roasting by a slow fire, and beating to death with Nob Keries. *a*1867 C.J. ANDERSSON *Notes of Trav.* (1875) 181 If a gun be not at hand, a blow with a *knob-kiêri* on the nose or chest will prove sufficient. **1878** T.J. LUCAS *Camp Life & Sport* 94 The game .. is eventually despatched with 'knob kerries,' and 'assegais', the former, a long knobbed stick of heavy wood, which they throw with great dexterity. **1882** S. HECKFORD *Lady Trader in Tvl* 133 A stick with a heavy knob at the end of it, here called a 'knob-kirrie'. **1905** *Native Tribes of Tvl* 129 'Knob-kerries' (clubs or throwing sticks) are .. in general use by the natives. They throw the lighter varieties with some skill. **1920** R.Y. STORMBERG *Mrs Pieter de Bruyn* 19 Her hair .. would be quite pretty if she didn't drag it so painfully to the back of her head, screwing it up into a knobkerrie lump and stabbing it through with hideous black hairpins. **1948** O. WALKER *Kaffirs Are Lively* 164 They .. beat him with a knobkerrie — heavy knobbed stick — and left him lying dead. **1963** S. CLOETE *Rags of Glory* 518 A group of men armed with rifles and battle-axes, knobkerries and assagais rode threateningly toward them and watched them ride by. **1971** *Argus* 5 June (Weekend Mag.) 2 A sandy-haired, blue-eyed Afrikaner .. unbeatable in knob-kierie fighting. **1987** *Sunday Times* 6 Sept. 7 A knobless stick carried to indicate peace, in contrast to the knobkierie which was an instrument of war. **1990** M. KENTRIDGE *Unofficial War* 52 Inkatha vigilantes use a variety of weapons. The most common are the knobkerrie — a wooden stave with a heavy bulb at one end — and the assegai — a short stabbing spear used in hand-to hand combat. **1993** [see NP sense 2].

knobkerrie /ˈnɒbkeri/ *v. trans.* Also **knobkerry**. [See prec.] Usu. *passive*: to be beaten with a knobbed stick.

1914 S.P. HYATT *Old Transport Rd* 81 We should smash up our wagon; we should die of fever or be knobkerried. **1937** H. SAUER *Ex Afr.* 217 He earnestly advised us to turn back with the coach and recross the Limpopo, assuring us that we would be assegaied or knobkerried before we could reach Fort Victoria. **1970** A. MCGREGOR in *Outpost* 66 One man .. had been knobkerried and left for dead on the veld.

Hence **knobkerrying** *vbl n.*, a beating with a knobkerrie.

1918 C. GARSTIN *Sunshine Settlers* 164 Those who came along quietly were invited to a revival singsong in my goat kraal, those who demurred got a description of hell from the Reverend and a Knobkerrying from Sixpence.

Knobneus /ˈnɒbniœs, -nɪəs/ *n.* Pl. **-neusen**. [Part. tr. Afk. (earlier S. Afr. Du.) *Knopneus*, see KNOPNEUS.] SHANGAAN sense 1 a. Also *attrib.*

1951 H. DAVIES *Great S. Afr. Christians* 154 These people were known as the *Knobneusen* (knobbly-nosed, because of their curious nasal tattooing) by the Boers. **1953** B. FULLER *Call Back Yesterday* 15 Eventually, the forces at the General's disposal included no fewer than 5,000 burghers and 3,000 Native allies, largely of the Knobneusen tribe.

Knobnose /ˈnɒbnəʊz/ *n. Obs.* exc. *hist.* Also with small initial. [tr. S. Afr. Du. (later Afk.) *knopneus*; see quot. 1905.] Often *attrib.* in the offensive phr. ***Knobnose(d) kaffir***. SHANGAAN sense 1 a.

1839 W.C. HARRIS *Wild Sports* 350 A friendly tribe of natives, whom, from a peculiarity in the nasal prominence, they dignified with the appellation of 'knob-nosed Kafirs'. **1877** F. JEPPE *Tvl Bk Almanac & Dir.* (1976) 33 Tons of iron, a friend informs us, were carried out of a Kafir kraal near Matzibandela's which was ransacked by the Knobnoses. **1888** W.J. PRETORIUS in J. Bird *Annals of Natal* I. 231 After a while Rensenburg and Triegaart separated. The first and all his followers were murdered by the 'Knob-nosed' Kafirs. **1892** [see MAGWAMBA]. **1900** A.H. KEANE *Boer States* 99 Hence the extraordinary differences that are observed between .. the degraded Magwamba ('demons' or 'devils'), called 'Knobnoses' by the Transvaal Boers, and the Basutos. **1905** *Native Tribes of Tvl* 64 They [*sc.* the Shangaans] used to be called 'Knob-noses' from the custom of lacerating their faces, especially the nose, in such a manner as to produce a number of raised scars or knobs, but this practice is now dying out. **1943** D. REITZ *No Outspan* 59 We went up the Sami river to Sibasa's country and then to the chief of the knob-nose kaffirs. **1958** S. CLOETE *Mask* 131 Albini was a Portuguese of good family who .. had collected a number of knob-nose Kaffirs or Shangaans who regarded him as their chief. **1974** A.P. CARTWRIGHT *By Waters of Letaba* 20 Joao Albasini, native commissioner of the eastern district, chieftain of the 'Knobnose Kaffirs', as the Mashangana were nicknamed by the Boers, offered refuge to all in his fortress-like trading post.

knob-stick *n.* KIERIE.

1822 W.J. BURCHELL *Trav.* I. 354 A *kéeri* (a short knobstick) in his hand. **1839** W.C. HARRIS *Wild Sports* 167 The dexterity of the Matabili in the use of the knobstick is also wonderful: they rarely miss a partridge or a guinea-fowl on the wing. **1846** R. MOFFAT *Missionary Labours* 95 Their weapons were war-axes of various shapes, spears, and clubs; into many of their knobsticks were inserted pieces of iron resembling a sickle, but more curved, sometimes to a circle, and sharp on the outside. **1867** S. TURNER in D. Child *Portrait of Pioneer* (1980), When his mother complained to him .. he knocked her down with a knobstick. **1885** H. RIDER HAGGARD *King Solomon's Mines* (1972) 46 Presently a very tall, handsome-looking man .. very light-coloured for a Zulu, entered, and, lifting his knob-stick by way of salute, squatted himself down in the corner on his haunches. **1894** B. MITFORD *Curse of Clement Waynflete* (1896) 241 The warrior's heavy knobstick, hurled with deadly precision. **1898** — *Induna's Wife* 114 For arms he had a broad assegai and three or four casting ones, and a great short-handled knob-stick, which he had brought especially for me. **1934** *Sunday Times* 11 Feb. (Swart), He then got up and struck the deceased a blow on the head with a knob stick. **1958** A. DELIUS (tr. D.J. Opperman) in R.M. Macnab *Poets in S. Afr.* 76 Three outas from the High Karroo .. Took knob-sticks, and three bundles with and set forth along a jackal path. **1961** H.F. SAMPSON *White-Faced Huts* 22, I drove the accused to the Police at Bizana and made them carry the knobsticks and the assegais. **1989** *Advertisement, Sun International* Swazi warriors carry shields, knobsticks, spears and battle axes as part of their traditional dress.

knobthorn *n.* [tr. Afk. *knoppiesdoorn* (see KNOPPIESDORING); see quot. 1977.]

1. KNOBWOOD.

1913 C. PETTMAN *Africanderisms* 270 *Knob-thorn* or *-wood, Xanthoxylon capense, Hars.* One of the well-known indigenous trees of South Africa, the trunk of which is covered with a profusion of bluntly pointed protuberances, which give it a very curious appearance. *c*1968 S. CANDY *Natal Coast Gardening* 53 *Fagara capensis*, 'Knobthorn', Native tree of charm with large thick thorns along the trunk.

2. In full ***knob-thorn tree***: the tree *Acacia nigrescens* of the Fabaceae, with thorns borne on distinct knobs on bole and branches, and bearing creamy, sweetly-scented flowers; the wood of this tree; KNOBBY THORN; KNOPPIESDORING sense 1. Also *attrib.*

1917 R. MARLOTH *Common Names* 50 *Knobthorn* = Knoppies'doorn. **1975** *S. Afr. Panorama* Dec., Furniture was mainly of wood indigenous to the Transvaal such as tambotie, .. knoppiesdoring (knobthorn) and red and white syringa. **1977** E. PALMER *Field Guide to Trees* 130 *Knobthorn*, .. *Bole*: usually unbranched for some distance, .. often (but not invariably) studded with conspicuous knobs, each tipped with a hooked thorn. **1987** *S. Afr. Panorama* Sept. 15 The first acacia to bloom is the knob-thorn .. it has pink buds and spikes of delicate creamy flowers which have a sweet fragrance. **1988** E. SMITH in *Conserva* Feb. 17 We make camp under a giant strangler fig. I find a knobthorn-tree to hang clothes out to air. **1990** [see LEADWOOD]. **1990** CLINNING & FOURIE in *Fauna & Flora* No.47, 8 Another common tree in this area is the knob thorn *Acacia nigrescens* with thorns which develop to form egg-sized knobs on its rough bark. **1991** J. HUNTLY in *Sunday Star* 16 Feb. (Weekend) 4 The protective thorns of the acacias reach their most fearsome development in the knob-thorn (acacia nigrescens). **1991** [see

KNOPPIESDORING sense 1]. **1993** *Getaway* Nov. 77 (*caption*) Knobthorns, marulas, tambotis, bush willows and other species create a filigree in the evening sky.

knobwood *n.* [tr. Afk. *knophout, knop* knob + *hout* wood.] Any of several trees of the genus *Zanthoxylum* of the Rutaceae (wild cardomum) having horn-like protuberances on the trunk, esp. *Z. capense* and *Z. davyi*; the close-grained wood of this tree; KNOBTHORN sense 1; KNOPPIESDORING sense 2.

[**1837** ECKLON & ZEYHER *Enumeratio Plantarum Africae* 118 *Fagara capensis* ... Lignum fruticus solidum incolae ad utensilia varia facienda adhebent vocantque Knobhout.] **1887** in *Kew Bulletin* (UK) Sept. 11 *Knobwood* (*Xanthoxylon Capense*), Tree averaging 15 to 20 feet, but sometimes attaining 50 to 60 feet high. **1894** T.R. SIM *Flora of Kaffraria* 14 The curious warted stems of the knobwood (Xanthoxylon) attract attention. **1913** [see KNOBTHORN sense 1]. **1917** R. MARLOTH *Common Names* 50 *Knoppies'doorn* ... In the coastal forests it is another name for Knobwood. **1961** PALMER & PITMAN *Trees of S. Afr.* 272 Among the most unusual of our trees are the several species of knobwoods, easily identified by the knobs which stud the stems. **1986** *Motorist* 2nd Quarter 38 Dense indigenous forest, unusually rich in yellowwoods, .. knobwoods, .. and Cape chestnuts flood the moist slopes below. **1990** *Weekend Post* 31 Mar. (Leisure) 7 A reader at Kenton-on-Sea .. who had discovered what seemed to be a borer attacking a knobwood (*Fagara capensis*) in her indigenous garden ... Knobwood belongs to the citrus family and is notable for the thorns on its branches, which develop into large knobbly lumps on the trunk as the tree matures. **1990** *Ibid.* 11 Aug. (Leisure) 4 Indigenous woods, among them yellowwood, Camdeboo stinkwood, assegai and knobwood.

knolkool /ˈknɔlkʊəl, -kuəl/ *n. obsolescent.* Also **knohlkole, knol kool, nole-kole.** Pl. unchanged. [Afk., fr. Du., *knol* tuber, turnip + *kool* cabbage.

'Nol-kole .. is the usual Anglo-Indian name of a vegetable a good deal grown in India.' (Yule & Burnell, *Hobson-Jobson*, 1886, p.830); and see *OED* entry at *noll-kholl*.]

The turnip-cabbage or kohl-rabi, *Brassica oleracea* var. *caulopa*. Also Englished form **knol-cole**.

1833 *S. Afr. Almanac & Dir.* p.lix, About the full moon plant out onions, cabbage, lettuce, knolcole, leeks, celery, and potatoes. **1893** J.F. SEWELL *Private Diary* (1983) 140 Old Catherine brought me .. mulberries and knohlkole (Brussels sprouts). **1910** *S. Afr. 'Inquire Within'* (Cape Times) 92 Cabbage, knol kool, beet, onion, parsnip and lettuce to be sown this month [*sc.* in July], care to be taken that the seeds are colonial. **1913** A. GLOSSOP *Barnes's S. Afr. Hsehold Guide* 274 Broad beans, beet .., knol-kohl, lettuce .. may still be sown. **1913** C. PETTMAN *Africanderisms* 341 *Nole-kole*, .. Toward the root the stalk of this vegetable expands into a turnip-like mass, which is the edible part. **1950** H. GERBER *Cape Cookery* 101 *Knolkool* (*Kohlrabi*), These look like purple or green turnips with leaves sprouting from the sides and top. Both the green leaves and the thick parts are used.

knoo var. GNU *n.*[1]

knoorhaan var. KNORHAAN.

knopjes-doorn, knopjie-sdoorn, knopji(e)s doorn varr. KNOPPIESDORING.

‖**knopkierie** /ˈnɔpkiri/ *n.* Also **kanop kerie, knop kieri.** [S. Afr. Du., *knop* rounded end or protrusion + *kierie* (see KIERIE).] KIERIE.

1832 *Graham's Town Jrnl* 15 Nov. 179 Tembo had no assegaais with him that morning, but a knop kieri, and a Knife. **1835** C.L. STRETCH Journal. 18 Sept., The Boers have all .. affirmed that .. the Caffres would Kill every Englishman with 'Kanop Keries'. **1940** BAUMANN & BRIGHT *Lost Republic* 220 When a Basuto beats his wife, he does it with a knopkierie. **1951** *Cape Times* 26 Nov. 8 If it is his fundamental nature to grab for knopkierie or hatchet when angered, no teaching and no evangelization would be worth the trouble. **1961** *Reader's Digest* Feb. 142 On the river-bed lay the weapon — an African knopkierie. **1975** *S. Afr. Panorama* Jan. 14 On the wall of the entrance hall was a gun rack which supported a 'Voorlaaier' (Muzzle loader) 'Knop Kierie' (Walking stick) [etc.]. **1986** F. KARODIA *Daughters of Twilight* 36 At Mohamed's General Store the African customers milled around the doorway or sat on the sidewalk, knopkierie in one hand.

‖**Knopneus** /ˈknɔpniœs, -nɪəs/ *n.* Pl. **-neuse** /-niœsə/, and (formerly) **-näse, -neusen, -neuses.** [Afk. (earlier S. Afr. Du.), *knop* knob + *neus* nose.] SHANGAAN sense 1 a.

1882 S. HECKFORD *Lady Trader in Tvl* 258 Kaffirs [came] in from the neighbourhood to buy. Some of these were 'Knopnäse', perfect savages, with tassels of fur tied on to their woolly heads, and a girdle, with a fringe of wild cats' tails, as their only garment. **1952** H. KLEIN *Land of Silver Mist* 166 Deep-seated friction .. developed between him and the Boers .. over his Shangaan followers, who, because of their squat noses, the Boers called Knopneusen. **1970** E.B. VAN WYK in *Std Encycl. of Sn Afr.* II. 106 Transvaal Tsonga is spoken by various tribes such as the Gwamba or Knopneuse of the Northern Transvaal. **1971** H. ZEEDERBERG *Veld Express* 90 Fifty armed Shangaans (Knopneuses) were hired to guard the convoy from attacks by wild animals. [**1973** H.P. JUNOD in *Std Encycl. of Sn Afr.* IX. 600 The characteristic tribal mark of the Shangana-Tsonga is the pierced ear-lobe .. while other forms of tattooing have been developed and adopted, notably the big black keloids of the Chopi, farther north — a custom which caused the Voortrekkers to call them 'Knopneuse' (Knob-noses).]

knoppiesdoring /ˈknɔpisˌduərəŋ, -ˌduərəŋ/ *n.* Also **knopjes-doorn, knopjies-doorn, knopji(e)s doorn, knoppies-doorn.** [Afk., fr. S. Afr. Du. *knopjesdoorn, knopje* small knob + *doorn* thorn.]

1. KNOBTHORN sense 2.

1887 A.A. ANDERSON *25 Yrs in Waggon* II. 132 Out all day in the bush, looking for a suitable tree to cut down to make desselboom; the knopjies-doorn or lignum-vitae is the best. *Ibid.* 210 Knopjis doorn or lignum vitae. *Ibid.* 225 Knopjes doorn, wild olive, saffraan. **1897** [see SWARTHAAK]. **1913** C. PETTMAN *Africanderisms* 271 *Knopjies doorn*, .. *Acacia nigrescens pallens*, Benth. **1928** E.H.L. SCHWARZ *Kalahari & its Native Races* 122 Often found growing in association with the makoba tree, or knoppies doorn. **1929** J. STEVENSON-HAMILTON *Low-Veld* 50 The umkaiya, also called knopjes-doorn, is one of the most useful of Low-Veld trees. **1972** L.G. GREEN *When Journey's Over* 45 Some men chose the tough knoppiesdoring for a disselboom, a yellow-coloured acacia. **1991** M. OETTLE in *Weekend Post* 29 Dec. (Leisure) 7 *Acacia nigrescens*, knobthorn or knoppiesdoring.

2. KNOBWOOD.

1966 C.A. SMITH *Common Names* 302 *Knoppiesdoring*, .. The vernacular name was first applied to the species [*Acacia nigrescens*] about 1750, while in the south coastal districts the name is given to *Fagara capensis* and *F. davyi*, both of which are now generally referred to as *knophout*.

knopstick *n. obs.* [Eng., *knop* (archaic form of *knob*) + *stick*, influenced by S. Afr. Du. *knopkierie*, see KNOPKIERIE.] KIERIE.

*a*1858 J. GOLDSWAIN *Chron.* I. (1946) 102 The father will go into the hut ware his Daughter is and if she refuses to go with the man that as bought her that the father will comence beeting her with knopstick. *Ibid.* II. (1949) 20 To strike Mr. Bradshaw on the head with a Knopstick.

knorhaan /ˈknɔrhɑːn/ *n.* Also **knoorhaan, knorha(e)n, knor(rh)aan, knorr-haen.** Pl. unchanged, **-s**, or (rarely) **-hane** /-hɑːnə/. [Transf. use of Du. *knorhaan*, see KORHAAN.]

1.a. *obsolescent.* KORHAAN sense 1 a. Also *attrib.*

1731 G. MEDLEY tr. *P. Kolb's Present State of Cape of G.H.* II. 139 The *Knorhan*. Among the Wild Fowls at the *Cape*, there is a Sort of Birds, a Male of which the *Europeans* there call *Knor-Cock*: A Female they call *Knor-Hen*. These Birds are a Sort of Centries to the other Birds at the *Cape*. **1777** G. FORSTER *Voy. round World* I. 85 The knorhaan .. is not a gelinote or grous, as he calls it, but the African bustard. **1786** —— tr. *A. Sparrman's Voy. to Cape of G.H.* I. 153 *Knorr-haen* is the name of a kind of *Otis*, which conceals itself perfectly, with great art, till one comes pretty near to it, when on a sudden it soars aloft. **1810** J. MACKRILL Diary. 87 Knorhaan Otis .. derives his name from an incessant Cry of 'Grac'. Knorhaan in the Dutch language signifies, a scolder, he warns all other Birds in his Neighbourhood of an enemy. **1819** [see KORHAAN sense 1 a]. *a*1867 C.J. ANDERSSON *Notes of Trav.* (1875) 35 The Cape Knorhaan Bustard (*Eupodotis Afra*, Gmel.), is in length nineteen inches, the wing twelve inches, and the tail five inches. **1872** C.A. PAYTON *Diamond Diggings* 38 The 'knorhaan' (*Otis afra*) a small species of bustard. [**1890** A. MARTIN *Home Life* 226 A smaller bustard, with beautifully-variegated plumage, is about the size of a large fowl. His Dutch name of *knorhaan* — .. 'scolding cock', or 'growling fowl' — is very justly bestowed on him.] **1905** W.L. SCLATER in Flint & Gilchrist *Science in S. Afr.* 143 The Bustards (*Otidae*) are represented by no less than twelve species, ranging from the large Gom Paauw (*Otis kori*) .. to the smaller Knorhaan (*Otis afra*), about the same size as a partridge. **1907** J.P. FITZPATRICK *Jock of Bush-veld* (1909) Glossary, *Knoorhaan*, commonly, but incorrectly, *Koorhaan* or *Koraan*, (D), the smaller bustard (*lit.* scolding cock). **1913** [see KORHAAN sense 1 a]. **1918** H. MOORE *Land of Good Hope* 12 The knorhaan, or 'scolding fowl', springing up in your path with deafening clamour. **1931** G. BEET *Grand Old Days* 15 The knorhaan, which with its rusty 'kruk-kruk-kruk,' has come to be looked upon by sportsmen as 'the sentry of the veld.' **1937** H. SAUER *Ex Afr.* 53 The bustard family, divided into two sections: the great bustard, or paauw, of which there are six varieties in Africa, and the lesser bustard, or knoorhaan (grumbling cock), of which there are no less than eleven varieties. **1948** H.V. MORTON *In Search of S. Afr.* 262 Upon this road there was .. a bird known as the korhaan, or knorhaan, the 'scolding cock,' and a good name it is, for I think the meercats employ him as a watchman!

b. With qualifying word denoting a particular species: **dikkop knorhaan** [Afk. *dikkop, dik* thick + *kop* head], the *vaal knorhaan*, (see KORHAAN sense 1 b), *E. vigorsii*; **red-crested knorhaan**, the *red-crested korhaan* (see KORHAAN sense 1 b), *E. ruficrista*; **vaal knorhaan**, the *vaal korhaan* (see KORHAAN sense 1 b), *E. vigorsii*.

1913 C. PETTMAN *Africanderisms* 144 **Dikkop knorhaan**, .. *Otis vigarsi* [*sic*]. **1906** STARK & SCLATER *Birds of S. Afr.* IV. 291 The **Red-crested Knorhaan** is found singly or in pairs. **1867** E.L. LAYARD *Birds of S. Afr.* 284 The **Vaal Knorhaan** is common on the Karroo ... If it fancies itself unobserved, it will suddenly squat ... So great is its similarity to the soil and stones among which it is found that it is next to impossible to detect it.

2. [See quot. 1986.] Any of several marine fishes. **a.** Any of several species of gurnard of the genus *Chelidonichthys* (family Triglidae); KORHAAN sense 2. **b.** Any of several species of grunter of the genus *Pomadasys* (family Haemulidae); see also TIGERFISH sense 2 b.

1806 J. BARROW *Trav.* II. 38 The Knorhaen, a species of *Trigla*, or Gurnard .. is not a bad fish. **1900** J.D.F. GILCHRIST in *Trans. of S. Afr. Philological Soc.* Vol.11 No.4, 215 The Gurnard or *Knorhaan* (*Trigla peronii*) not unlike its European representative (*T. gurnardus*). **1949** J.L.B. SMITH *Sea Fishes* 259 *Trigla Capensis* ... *Gurnard. Knoorhaan.* **1979** SNYMAN & KLARIE *Free from Sea* 31 *Grunter*, Silver Grunter/Bull or Cock Grunter/Knoorhaan/Tiger/Spotted Grunter. So named, because when it comes from the water, spasms of the throat muscles cause the teeth to rasp together, which sounds like a man — not a gentleman — clearing his throat! .. *Gurnard*. Knoorhaan. Quaint-looking with its large head encased in a bony shield. It grunts or croaks when taken from the water. [**1986** SMITH &

HEEMSTRA *Smiths' Sea Fishes* 486 The American name 'sea robins' and Afrikaans 'knorhane' come from the bird-like chirping noise some species make when they are taken from the water.]

knorha(e)n, knorrhaan, knorr-haen varr. KORHAAN.

knum-knum var. NUM-NUM.

Knysna lily /ˌnaɪznə ˈlɪli/ *n. phr.* Also **Nysna lily**. [Named for *Knysna* (Khoikhoi name), a town on the Western Cape coast.] Either of two plants of the Amaryllidaceae.
a. The justifina *Cyrtanthus obliquus*, a bulbous flowering plant with strap-shaped leaves and umbels bearing pendulous flowers, yellowish at the base, merging into bright red, and tipped with green; SORE-EYE FLOWER sense d.

1824 W.J. BURCHELL *Trav.* II. 637 Nysna lily (Cyrtanthus obliquus). 1982 W.G. SHEAT *A-Z of Gardening* 91 The sore-eye flower, or Knysna lily, is indigenous to the Cape ... Its 70 mm-long flowers, borne in summer, are yellow and green with red tips. 1985 K. PIENAAR *Grow S. Afr. Plants* 41 *C. obliquus* (Knysna lily), a beautiful plant with drooping red flowers tipped with green.

b. The widely cultivated bulbous flowering plant *Cyrtanthus purpureus*, with strap-shaped leaves, and umbels bearing funnel-shaped flowers with a yellow throat; berglelie, see BERG sense 1 b ii; GEORGE LILY. See also FIRE LILY.

Formerly *Vallota purpurea* or *V. speciosa*; known as 'Scarborough lily' in Britain.

1917 [see berglelie (BERG sense 1 b ii)]. 1932 M.W. HENNING *Animal Diseases* 639 (Swart), This plant .. known popularly as berglelie, George lily or Knysna lily .. has an ovoid bulb with brown membranous tunics. 1967 COURTENAY-LATIMER & SMITH *Flowering Plants, Knysna Lily, George Lily*, This beautiful flower is in serious need of preservation. The .. plants .. formerly grew in profusion in the forest. 1972 M.R. LEVYNS in *Std Encycl. of Sn Afr.* VI. 640 The evergreen Knysna or George lily .. has strap-shaped leaves and brilliant red flowers, and grows in the divisions of Mossel Bay, George, Knysna and Uniondale. 1982 [see GEORGE LILY]. 1989 'BABIANA' in *E. Prov. Herald* 18 Mar. 8 The .. Knysna Lily .. bears several flowers on a stalk whereas the Kei Lily rarely has more than one. 1991 *Best of S. Afr. Short Stories* (Reader's Digest Assoc.) 174 The indigenous Knysna or George lily (*Vallota speciosa*) likes to grow on mountain slopes. In England, the plant is known as 'Scarborough lily' — it is thought because it was grown in Scarborough after bulbs were washed ashore after a shipwreck.

Knysna loerie see LOERIE sense 1 b.

kob /kɒb/ *n.* Pl. usu. unchanged, occas. -s. [Abbrev. of Afk. *kabeljou* (see KABELJOU), with anglicization of the vowel (see quot. 1917).]
a. Any fish of the family Sciaenidae, esp. the KABELJOU, *Argyrosomus hololepidotus*; COB *n.*[1] See also GEELBEK sense 1 a.

In Smith and Heemstra's *Smiths' Sea Fishes* (1986), the name 'kob' is used both in this sense and, with distinguishing epithets, to designate individual species of the family Sciaenidae.

1906 *E. London Dispatch* 26 June 3 Our well-known and very common kabeljaauw, called for briefness 'cob' or 'kob'. 1913 W.W. THOMPSON *Sea Fisheries of Cape Col.* 155 Kabeljaauw .. cob or Kob (East London). [1917 A.C.M. ORREY *Bottom Fishing in Cape Waters* 52 The geelbek is a far gamer fish than the kab., and fights well to the last.] 1930 C.L. BIDEN *Sea-Angling Fishes* 113 One hears them mentioning the word 'kob' — not that they can see the fish, but the surface indications a mile away portend the coming of the kob. 1949 J.L.B. SMITH *Sea Fishes* 226 *Johnius hololepidotus* ... Salmon. Salmon Bass. Kob. Kabeljou. Rietbul. Boerkabeljou. Jewfish. Attains 6 ft. and a weight of over 150 lbs .. Found virtually over our whole region .. enters and lives freely in estuaries .. One of our most important food fishes taken in great numbers on lines and by trawl. 1955 C. HORNE *Fisherman's Eldorado* 71 In 1951, an angler trolling at Cape Agulhas for elf .. hooked a 72 lb kabeljou, the first kob recorded caught by trolling at Cape Agulhas. On the east coast his catch would not have caused surprise, for kob, or salmon as these fish are known there, are regularly taken by spinnermen north-east of East London. 1971 *Daily Dispatch* 28 Aug. 21 Hamburg is renowned for kob fishing in the river and many a fish of well over 100 pounds in weight has been taken. 1972 *Grocott's Mail* 15 Sept. 3 Kobs too should soon be heard chopping, and anglers will expecting runs from the big 'uns. 1975 *E. Prov. Herald* 28 Aug. 3 With the arrival of chokka in the bay, the kob cannot be far behind. Any day now we should see our seasonal run of big kob in Algoa Bay. 1979 SNYMAN & KLARIE *Free from Sea* 34 Kabeljou, Kob/Salmon/Salmon Bass/Rietbul/Boerkabeljou. One of our most important and versatile food-fishes, with all but the largest having delicate, tasty flesh. Kabeljou have been known to reach 1,8 m in length. 1988 P. GOOSEN in *Argus* 1 Sept. 19 A good sign for the spring and summer fishing season is the early arrival of kob over a wide area of the Western Cape coast. 1991 *Weekend Post* 5 Jan. 4 Longing for a nice fresh piece of hake or a whole small kob to put on the braai. 1993 *Getaway* Nov. 127 Kabeljou (commonly called kob).

b. Special Comb. **kob-water**, disturbed or discoloured water, in which the kob is often caught.

1930 C.L. BIDEN *Sea-Angling Fishes* 113 On the south-east coast particularly they keep a watchful eye on what is known as '**kob-water**' — a discoloration of the sea, either milky, dirty yellow, or what one would liken to pea soup. 1957 S. SCHOEMAN *Strike!* 71 Kob-water usually results from a disturbance of the seabed. 1974 *Argus* 31 Dec. 4 The familiar, ginger-beer coloured water known to anglers as 'kob water' is moving in along parts of the Strandfontein coastline.

kobeljauw var. KABELJOU.

kobo *n. obs.* Also **kobe**. Pl. **-s, -es**. [Sotho and Tswana.] Among the Sotho and Tswana: KAROSS sense 1.

1824 W.J. BURCHELL *Trav.* II., I may here remark that *kaross* and *kobo* are but two words for the same thing; the former belonging to the Hottentot, and the latter to the Sichuana, language. *Ibid.* 382, I found the chief .. employed in scraping the hair off from a skin intended for a kobo. 1839 W.C. HARRIS *Wild Sports*, The skins of both these animals .. are in great demand amongst the savages, for kobos, or fur cloaks. 1866 E.L. PRICE *Jrnls* (1956) 185 The only thing in the shape of a shawl or kobo, was an old sheet — tho' a bitter cold day.

kobomvu var. KUMBOMVU.

Kochaqua var. COCHOQUA.

kockervick var. KOKKEWIET.

kodoe var. KUDU.

koeboe mealie var. KABOE MEALIE.

koedo(e), koedoo varr. KUDU.

koek(e)makranka var. KUKUMAKRANKA.

koekerboom var. KOKERBOOM.

koekie /ˈkʊki/ *n.* Also **cokie, koekey, koekje**. [Afk., fr. Du. *koekje* little cake.]
1. Any small (flat) cake or biscuit. See also COOK-IE.

a1867 C.J. ANDERSSON *Notes of Trav.* (1875) 212 It is now more than a month since I touched meat; bread, or rather 'cokies', and now and then a little arrowroot. 1905 O.E.A. SCHREINER in C. Clayton *Woman's Rose* (1986) 111 His mother made him koekies and sosaties, and nice things every day. 1913 C. PETTMAN *Africanderisms* 306 *Makrolletje*, ... A variety of 'koekey' made with almonds, macaroon. 1930 M. RAUBENHEIMER *Tested S. Afr. Recipes* 37 Let the dough stand for half-an-hour, roll out on a floured board, and cut with a round cutter into 'koekies'. 1938 [see LEKKER adj. sense 1 c]. 1955 L.G. GREEN *Karoo* 98 It [*sc.* breakfast] started with hot springbok fry, followed by cold springbok haunch, cold korhaan, steaming coffee with goat's milk, *koekies* of boer meal, springbok biltong planed thin, wild honey, stewed peaches, tomato and lettuce. 1959 J. MEIRING *Candle in Wind* 34 She was bustling about the house, filling the borrowed plates with buns and bright, pink-iced koekies. 1967 E.M. SLATTER *My Leaves Are Green* 60 Good coffee came, and little red koekies — the kind I had not seen for years. 1973 *Fair Lady* 26 Dec. 120 The wakis of koekies and the barrel of beer were placed at strategic points. 1983 *Daily Dispatch* 11 May 6 Curry favour they did with the best of home-made koekies and snacks.

2. An endearment, usu. for a woman.

1977 FUGARD & DEVENISH *Guest* 51 Marais: I've seen them, Koekie. Little Corrie: My name is not 'Koekie'. Marais: I'm going to call you 'Koekie'. Little Corrie: My name is 'Corrie'.

koekoek /ˈkʊkʊk/ *n.* Also with initial capital. [Afk., prob. ad. Xhosa and Zulu *inkuku* chicken (Du. *koekoek* having the meaning 'cuckoo').] In full **Potchefstroom koekoek**: (one of) a poultry type developed mainly from White Leghorn and Black Australorp crosses. Also *attrib.*

1971 *Farmer's Weekly* 12 May 107 (advt) Pure-Bred Koekoek. Not the old fashioned Barred Plymouth Rock with its small eggs. A purebreed bred by Potchefstroom Agricultural College as a tablebird with stamina and high egg production. 1973 *Ibid.* 30 May (Suppl.) 22 Amazing Growers: Heavy Leg Koekoek Cockerels ... Austra-White Pullets giving the same results as the Koekoek but with white eggs. 1973 *Grocott's Mail* 14 Aug. 1 Pure Breeds: Black/Swart Australorps ... Plymouth Rock/Koekoek. 1976 *E. Prov. Herald* 6 July 11 South Africa has produced its very own, indigenous kind of fowl ... called .. the Potchefstroom koekoek ... It produces chickens which can be readily identified as boys or girls immediately they hatch out ... The cockerels have a spot on the head, which the hens do not. 1988 *Farmer's Weekly* Jan. 78 (advt) Koekoek ... The ideal farm bird. A good producer and table bird. 1991 *Philatelic Services Bulletin* No.8075, Potchefstroom Koekoek, This breed of fowl was developed at the Agricultural Research Institute at Potchefstroom .. from White Leghorn and Black Australorp crosses and the colouring was improved by a few crossings with breeds with barred plumage. In 1976 the Koekoek was registered as an acknowledged breed.

koekoemakranka var. KUKUMAKRANKA.

koeksister /ˈkʊksɪstə, -səstə(r)/ *n.* Also **koek sister, koeksuster, koesijster, koesister, koesyster**. [Afk. *koeksister, koesister*, etym. obscure: perh. fr. Du. *koek* cake, or fr. Malay *kuih* cake, sweetmeat, seen in the form *koesister*) + *sister*, perh. fr. *sissen* sizzle + agential suffix *-er*.]
1. A twisted or plaited doughnut, deep-fried and immediately dipped into cold syrup. Also *attrib.* See also KOSSITER.

1891 H.J. DUCKITT *Hilda's 'Where Is It?'* 128 Koesisters. (Batavian or old Dutch Sweetmeat Recipe.) 1913 C. PETTMAN *Africanderisms* 272 Koesijsters. A confection or sweetmeat which has been boiled in fat and dipped in powdered sugar. 1930 M. RAUBENHEIMER *Tested S. Afr. Recipes* 48 Just dip the 'Koek Sisters' into the syrup and remove at once, else they will be too sweet. 1944 I.D. DU PLESSIS *Cape Malays* 42 Contact with the Dutch colonists has left its mark. Many old Cape dishes, such as *melktert* and *koeksisters* are still to be found in the Malay home. 1949 L.G. GREEN *In Land of Afternoon* 63 Koesisters are doughnuts of Malay origin, but the derivation of the name is not so easy. Some say that a mother was busy in the kitchen one day when her little daughter asked her what she was making. 'Koek, susterjie,' was the reply — hence the name. 1955 A. DELIUS *Young Trav.* 111 The children had a hamper of ... sandwiches, ... biltong, ... and finally some syrup-soaked cakes called koeksisters. 1974 *E. Prov. Herald* 18 June 14 The lives of a dozen schoolchildren who use a school bus in the Salem district could be in danger, claims .. the bus driver, 'In parts the road looks like a koeksuster'. **1981** *Ibid.* 30 Apr. 2 The legendary koeksisters and melkterts that have graced innumerable South African elections are no more ... At not one of the six polling stations in the area was there any sign of these traditional delicacies. **1987** C. HOPE *Hottentot Room* 92 When she baked she became a farmer's daughter again: milk tart, plum pudding, fly cemetery and *koeksusters.* **1988** F. WILLIAMS *Cape Malay Cookbk* 6 Saturdays were spent frying koesisters because my grandmother was also a koesister vendor. **1994** *Sunday Times* 23 Jan. 28 (*advt*) For the sweetest treat you're ever likely to eat, there's nothing like a koeksister. A traditional Cape confection thought to be of Malay origin, this deep-fried twisted doughnut dipped and basted with lashings of syrup .. is mos seriously addictive.

2. *fig.* Often used allusively, suggesting the traditions and values of the Afrikaner people. Also *attrib.*

Quot. 1990 is a pun on Eng. 'sister'.

1986 *Personality* 15 Sept. 16 The man who really takes the *koeksister* for all-round twisted meanness. **1987** *Ibid.* 21 Oct. 78 She continued to perform regularly on the 'crimplene and koeksuster' circuit. **1989** G. SILBER in *Sunday Times* 30 Apr. 17 The polished pectorals of a gallery of koeksuster-muscled female body-builders. **1989** *Sunday Times* 17 Dec. 11 Sometimes it seems that this survivor would be dishing out political koeksisters, negotiating and meeting misplaced Popes no matter who was in power. **1990** *Top Forty* July 12 Kim Irwin-Pack was there with his camera to catch the *koeksisters* and *bier-manne* having a *fris* time. **1991** *Weekly Mail* 19 Apr. 15 The koeksuster tannies of the ANC?

Hence (*nonce*) **koeksisterish** *adj.*, **koeksisterism** *n.*

1990 H.P. TOFFOLI in *Style* Nov. 50 They call themselves the Cook Sisters but there's nothing remotely koeksisterish about them. Stylish Sloane Rangers rather. **1993** J. PEARCE in *Weekly Mail & Guardian* 22 Oct. 45, I found myself trying to get profound concerning the implications of the former high dominee of hippie-punk-twisted-koeksusterism ending up doing an after-dinner slot in a venue which .. might even attract the odd Stellenbosch academic.

‖**koelie** /ˈkʊli, ˈkuli/ *n.* *Derog.* and *offensive.* [Afk., ad. COOLIE.]

1. COOLIE sense 1. Also *attrib.*

1956 D. JACOBSON *Dance in Sun* 26 The kaffirs and the *koelies* will know their places. **1959** L. LERNER *Englishman* 220 It was his girl the other one took, the one who slept with koelies. *Ibid.* 226 You won't, you koelie girl. **1959** J.A.L. BASSON in *Hansard* 16 Apr. 4076, I hope he will .. reproach the Minister of Labour who .. referred to Mrs Nehru as a 'koelie-meid'. **1963** D. JACOBSON *Through Wilderness* (1977) 85 All Lipi's neighbours in the street were Afrikaner railwaymen or mineworkers; and their children sometimes shouted '*Koelie-Jood*' after him — *Koelie* being an insulting term for an Indian, and thus being a disdainful way of referring to Lipi's trade [as a fruit hawker]. **1974** S. ROBERTS in S. Gray *On Edge of World* 144 She's helluva narrow minded ... She'll put up with a 'rooi-nek' .. an Englishman, but Jews and Portuguese, never mind Kaffirs and koelies, are out. **1980** C. HOPE *A Separate Development* (1983) 53 Don't get cheeky with me you bloody *koelie*, he says. **1983** *Daily Dispatch* 10 May 6 There is hope for places like Ellisras and Vaalwater, where 'kaffir' and 'koelie' are still in daily use. **1992** [see HOTNOT sense 2].

2. *comb.* **koelie creeper**, see *coolie creeper* (COOLIE sense 2).

1970 A. PALMER *Informant, King William's Town* Peter Pollock bowled a koelie-creeper (ball runs along the ground).

koerhaan var. KORHAAN.

koesi(j)ster, koesyster varr. KOEKSISTER.

koevoet /ˈkʊfʊt, ˈkufut/ *n.* [Afk., crowbar.]

‖**1.** *rare.* A crowbar.

1980 J.C. SKAIFE *Informant, Grahamstown,* I have just demolished a built in cupboard to retrieve some photographs that had slipped down behind .. Amazing what one can do with a hammer and koevoet. **1986** *Rhodeo* (Rhodes Univ.) May 8 A 'koevoet' used to mean a crowbar but is now a word which is 'hated and feared by the people of Namibia'.

2. With initial capital. A paramilitary counter-insurgency unit of the police force deployed in South West Africa (Namibia), officially from 1979 to 1989; occas. (with pl. -s), a member of this force. Also *comb.* **koevoet-style** *adj.*, and *attrib.*

1982 *E. Prov. Herald* 4 Dec. 3 The SWA Ministers' Council has appealed to South African Minister of Law and Order, Mr Le Grange, to give his personal attention to the recent deaths in detention of two men held by the special task force of the police, called 'Koevoet'. **1983** *Frontline* June 42 Plans and Koevoets might give each other the evil eye, but apparently they'll usually wait until they're back on duty before shooting each other up. **1984** D. PINNOCK *Brotherhoods* 82 Nobody is recruited into the Riot Squads without first having seen service against guerillas ... The cream of the local squads are then picked to serve in the Special Task Force, which is in turn the recruiting-ground for an even more élite unit known simply as Koevoet. **1985** *Sunday Times* 10 Mar. 7 Koevoet, the crack police counter insurgency unit operating in the war zone ... Koevoet (it means crowbar) was probably never an ideal name, in public relations terms, for a counter-insurgency unit. **1985** *Vula* Oct. 12 Special Unit K of the SA Security forces — the men who call themselves Koevoet! **1989** P. KENNY in *Sunday Times* 26 Feb. 2 The Koevoet unit was started 10 years ago with five people to counter the burgeoning bush war by Swapo. Some Swapo members .. say police who were in Koevoet are politicising the people to vote anti-Swapo. **1989** M. VERBAAN in *Weekly Mail* 20 Jan. 11 *Koevoet* has consistently been accused of perpetrating atrocities in its self-proclaimed battle against guerrillas of the Swapo nationalist movement. **1989** *Weekly Mail* 17 Mar. 1 Among the claims made in the court papers is that the the notorious *Koevoet* counterinsurgency unit is still in effective operation, despite widely-publicised claims that it had been disbanded. **1989** *Reader's Digest Illust. Hist.* 462 SADF counter-insurgency operations inside Namibia continued to attract wide controversy .. particularly the secret operations of a unit name *Koevoet* (Crowbar) officered by many former members of the Rhodesian military. **1989** *Sunday Times* 19 Nov. 6 Nestling on the banks of the Hennops River, Vlakplaas serves as a base camp for South Africa's own Koevoet-style unit. **1990** P. VAN NIEKERK in *Weekly Mail* 12 Oct. 5 At the weekend African National Congress leader Nelson Mandela .. angrily blamed the violence in the townships on the 'Third Force' whom he identified as the askaris, military intelligence, the National Intelligence Service and Koevoet. **1991** J. PAUW *In Heart of Whore* 113 In Namibia, Koevoet was established in 1976 and concentrated on 'offensive action on the tracking and eradication of terrorists'. **1992** *Sowetan* 17 Dec. 19 The man in charge .. appeared popular among the Koevoets.

‖**koffie kar** /ˈkɔfikar/ *n. phr.* Pl. **-kara** /-kara/ [Afk., *koffie* coffee + *kar* car, cart.] Esp. in township Eng.: a small stall, usually on wheels, from which snacks and drinks may be served hot. See also CAFÉ DE MOVE-ON.

1980 M. DIKOBE in *Staffrider* Vol.3 No.1, 7 He ran an unlicensed Koffie-Kar. 'I did not sleep,' he would say, 'I baked fat cakes on returning from work'. **1981** *Voice* 12 Aug. 13 Of course I was still a five-year-old laaitie then, but I can still picture those '*koffie kara*' next to the then dark-soiled Wemmer Sports Ground. **1991** on TV1, 24 Apr. (The Big Time), 'Koffie kar — oven with wheels — we use them in the location to sell pap and vleis, magheu, smiley.' 'What is smiley?' 'Half sheep's head, with tongue sticking right out, and big smile.'

‖**koffie-moffie** /ˈkɔfiˌmɔfi/ *n.* *Offensive. slang.* [Afk., *koffie* coffee + *moffie* (see MOFFIE).] A derogatory or joking name for an airline steward or cabin attendant. See also MOFFIE *n.* sense 1.

1985 *Sunday Times* 16 June (Mag. Sect.) 14 Pieter confesses that he feels most at home in the role of the *koffie-moffie* De Kock. 'But I don't actually like that overtly queeny type of moffie.' **1986** P. CRAMS in *Style* Dec. 10 Your story on Local Lingo .. was tops ... Here are a few others — steam queen (captain), Sarie switchboard (flight engineer) and the age old koffie moffie.

kofia /kɒˈfiːə/ *n.* Also **kaf(f)ia, k(h)ofija, kufiya**, and with initial capital. [Prob. ad. Indonesian *kopiah* beret, untasselled fez.] **a.** A skull-cap worn by Muslim men. **b.** Among Cape Muslims, a fez.

1951 L.G. GREEN *Grow Lovely* 189 Cape Malays call the fez a kofija. **1970** T. JAMES *Informant, Cape Town* Kaffia. **1971** L.G. GREEN *Taste of S.-Easter* 141 The flaming scarlet fez is in great demand, but some Moslems prefer maroon, others black. They talk of a kofija rather than a fez and order the style they favour; tall or flat. **1974** J. MATTHEWS *Park* (1983) 49 The eldest one cautioned the other two to take care lest their khofijas be blown away by the wind. **1974** *S. Afr. Panorama* Nov. 31 The Malay men were wearing their 'kofias'. **1976** 'KAFIA' in *E. Prov. Herald* 2 Nov. 2 Referring to 'Gassan's Kafia' .. I wish to emphasize that the Kafia is worn by all Moslems throughout the world. **1976** G.K. MAJOMBOZI in *Ibid.* 29 Oct. (Indaba) 2 It is a kafia, neither a cap not a hat, and that is that. **1980** A. DANGOR in M. Mutloatse *Forced Landing* 164 There were many young men at your house, suitors who wore spotless kufiyas over their Brylcream gladdies.

Kofifi /kɔˈfi(ː)fi/ *n.* *Hist. colloq.* [Isicamtho, perh. fr. Sotho (*le*)*fifi* darkness, obscurity, or (*se*)*fifi* carcass, corpse, or (*bo*)*fifi* mourning.] Esp. in township English: a nickname for Sophiatown, a black residential area in Johannesburg which was razed during the 1950s after residents had been forcibly removed.

1975 *Drum* 22 Sept. 44 Kid, ek is a ou clever van Sophiatown. Kofifi. Blackjacks are not my worry. **1982** D. BIKITSHA in *Rand Daily Mail* 14 Oct. (Eve) 5 As we danced and sang our way to Apartheid the Tsotsi language flourished ... Former famous black residential areas like Sophiatown, Western Native Township and Alexandra went under quaint names like 'Kofifi', 'Casbah' and 'Dark City'. **1988** *New Nation* 11 Feb. 17 The author paints a vivid picture of Kofifi before the forced removal of Dr Hendrik Verwoerd's government. Interestingly, the destruction of the community did not matter much to him then. **1990** M. ISAACSON in *Staffrider* Vol.9 No.22, 16 Now all that remains of 'Casbah' or 'Kofifi', other slang names for Sophiatown, is our home — this cheap white suburb with the name that means 'triumph'. **1992** O. MUSI in *Drum* Dec. (Then & Now) 54 The hurly-burly razzmatazz that was the life in townships like Sophiatown, better known as 'Kofifi'.

kofija var. KOFIA.

kogel-tas *n.* *Obs.* exc. *hist.* Also **kogeltache, kugel-tas.** [Du., *kogel* cartridge, bullet + *tas* bag or pouch.] A bullet-pouch.

1824 W.J. BURCHELL *Trav.* II. 246 Having first learnt from the boors, to carry their powder in a horn, and their bullets in a *kogel-tas* (bullet-pouch) they were now either too awkward, or too lazy, to practice any new method. **1835** C.L. STRETCH *Journal.* 15 Aug., A mounted force of 300 armed with guns from the appearance of their 'Kugel tases' there was no scarcity of ammunition. *a*1875 T. BAINES *Jrnl of Res.* (1964) II. 148 My ball told audibly, and I saw that he was crippled; but for want of my belt and kogeltache, I could not reload. **1972** A.A. TELFORD *Yesterday's Dress* 92 A 'kogel-tas' (bullet pouch) of leopard skin was fastened about his waist and a blue handkerchief about his neck.

koggelmander /ˌkɔxəlˈmandə(r)/ *n.* Formerly also **cogolomander, koggelmanner.** [Afk., blend formed on *koggel* to mimic + *salamander* lizard.]

1. Any of several species of non-venomous lizards of the genus *Agama* of the Agamidae; KOGGELMANNETJIE sense 1.

1895 R.H.S. CHURCHILL *Men, Mines & Animals* 87 Jumping up he threw the lizard to Mr De Beer, who loudly exclaimed 'Mr Chairman, there is a cogolomander here,' and ran away. **1896** *Scientific African* Feb. 61 The leguan, a large animal of the lizard tribe; the kogelmanner, of two sorts, one dull greyish black, the other with dark blue head, usually seen on large stones. **1940** V. POHL *Bushveld Adventures* 151 We found that they much preferred koggelmanners and lizards in any shape or form as a staple article of diet. **1953** D. JACOBSON *Long Way from London* 10 He told us about the *koggelmander* that snatched at people walking through the veld. **1956** H. KOPS *Veld, City & Sea* 144 The naked hill was .. infested with mambas ... To keep them company were scorpions and lizards – particularly the hideous jumping koggelmander. **1967** E. ROSENTHAL *Encycl. of Sn Afr.* 293 *Koggelmander,* South African name for a lizard and sometimes also for a chameleon. **1984** *Informant, Grahamstown* There used to be hundreds of lizards in my garden, not just the common lizard, also the koggelmanders – you know those ones that poke their neck out in a jerky way. **1987** PATTERSON & BANNISTER *Reptiles of S. Afr.* 37 The agamas, or 'koggelmanders' as they are known colloquially, are fairly robust lizards that have distinct heads like those of toads, movable eyelids and ear openings that are usually clearly seen.

2. With qualifying word: **bloukopkoggelmander** /ˌbləukɔp-/, formerly also **bla(a)uwkop koggelmander** [Afk. *bloukop* (earlier S. Afr. Du. *blauwkop*), *blou* blue + *kop* head], a male koggelmander, with bright blue back and head; *black koggelmannetjie,* see KOGGELMANNETJIE sense 2.

[**1889** H.A. BRYDEN *Kloof & Karroo* 278 The Boers call it the **'Blaauw kop salamander'** (blueheaded salamander), and look upon it with feelings of awe and horror. They will tell you solemnly .. that this reptile is deadly poisonous, and that from it all the snakes obtain and renew their poison.] **1939** [see KOGGELMANNETJIE sense 2]. **1950** W. ROSE *Reptiles & Amphibians* 145 Found from North Cape Province to the Tropics is *A. aculeata* ... commonly called the 'Blaauwkop Koggelmander,' which, though fond of perching on the tops of thorn trees, also lives on the ground. **1955** L.G. GREEN *Karoo* 16 Each day brings the oppresive thunder weather, with everyone staring at the sky, or at the blue-headed lizard, the *bloukopkoggelmander,* that is supposed to gaze steadfastly into the north when rain is on the way. **1970** H.M. MUSMECI *Informant, Port Elizabeth* There is a bloukopkoggelmander on that rock (blue-headed lizard). **1985** *Grocott's Mail* Apr. (*advt*) We've adopted the Bloukopkoggelmander as our symbol. Legend has it that this colourful creature can predict the changing conditions.

koggelmannetjie /ˌkɔxəlˈmanəki, -ci/ *n.* Also **koggelmanne(r)jie, kokelmannetjie, kokkelmanetj(i)e.** [Afk., *koggel* to mimic + *mannetjie* little man, perh. ad. *koggelmander* (see prec.).]

1. KOGGELMANDER sense 1.

1903 A.F. TROTTER *Old Cape Col.* 234 The lizards, grey 'Kokelmannetje,' the little cooking man, and the blue blinking Agora, have hardly yet crept out to bask in the sun. **1905** W.L. SCLATER in Flint & Gilchrist *Science in S. Afr.* 145 They are spiny lizards and bask in full sunlight on smooth rocks often nodding their head, and have thus gained the name of 'Kokkelmanetjie' or Little Bowing Man among the Dutch. **1905** W.L. SCLATER in Flint & Gilchrist *Science in S. Afr.* 145 The *agamidae* have eight representatives, all assigned to the typical genus; they are spiny lizards and bask in full sunlight on smooth rocks often nodding their head, and have thus gained the name of 'Kokkelmanetjie' or Little Bowing Man among the Dutch. **1918** S.H. SKAIFE *Animal Life* 216 The little *kokkelmannetje* is very common, and receives its name from the habit it has of moving its head up and down as it rests on the rock. Thus it has been named the 'little mimicking man,' because it is supposed to return the bow of the observer. *c*1939 — *S. Afr. Nature Notes* 22 The lizards known as 'koggelmannetjies' do not appear to have any popular English name ... There are nine different species of koggelmannetjies found in this country. **1947** J. STEVENSON-HAMILTON *Wild Life in S. Afr.* 318 There are nine species of so-called Rock Lizards (*Agama*) known as koggelmannetjies in South Africa. **1950** W. ROSE *Reptiles & Amphibians* 142 The agamas, familiarly called in South Africa 'koggelmannerjies', are a large genus numbering about fifty species. **1970** V.F.M. FITZSIMONS in *Std Encycl. of Sn Afr.* I. 218 The Afrikaans name 'koggelmannetjies' refers to their characteristic habit of bobbing their heads up and down, especially when nervous or curious.

2. With qualifying word: **black** - (*rare*) or **bloukop koggelmannetjie**, formerly also **blauwkop koggelmannetjie** [Afk., *bloukop* (earlier S. Afr. Du. *blaukop*), *blou* blue + *kop* head], *bloukopkoggelmander* (see KOGGELMANDER sense 2).

*c*1939 S.H. SKAIFE *S. Afr. Nature Notes* 22 The commoner [species] is the **Black koggelmannetjie** (*Agama atra*) ... The scales on his head and chest are a bright turquoise blue .. hence the name 'bloukop koggelmander'. **1913** C. PETTMAN *Africanderisms* 66 **Blaukop** *salmander* or **Koggelmannetje**, A lizard .. of somewhat striking colours, the head and back being a bright blue and the throat of an exquisitely delicate rose colour. **1963** S.H. SKAIFE *Naturalist Remembers* 172 For some time past two *koggelmannetjies* have lived in the garden. They do not seem to have a popular name in English ... The Afrikaans name means 'little mimicking man' and refers to the habit these lizards have of bobbing the head up and down when peering over the edge of a rock ... The male's head is a bright blue during the breeding season. Many people are convinced that the *bloukop koggelmannetjie* is poisonous but they are wrong.

Koi-Koi var. KHOIKHOI.

kokama var. KUKAMA.

Kokani /kɔˈkɑːni/ *n.* [ad. Eng. *Konkani* an inhabitant of Konkan (southern Maharashtra), a coastal region of western India; the language spoken by the Konkani.] COCKNEY.

*c*1983 R. MESTHRIE Lexicon of South African Indian English. 20 *Kokani/Konkani,* .. 1. An Indic Language of South Maharashtra, spoken by some South African Muslims. Erroneously called *Cockney,* occasionally. 2. A speaker of Kokani. Sometimes known as a *Cockney.* **1987** *Argus* 4 July 1 (Classified Sect.) Moslem, Kokani introductions, 22–60.

kok-a-viek var. KOKKEWIET.

kokelmannetjie var. KOGGELMANNETJIE.

kokerboom /ˈkʊəkə(r)bʊəm/ *n.* Also **koekerboom, koker boem, kookerboom.** Pl. **-s, -bome(n)** /-bʊəmə(n)/. [S. Afr. Du., *koker* case, sheath, quiver + *boom* tree; see quot. 1776.]

1. The tree aloe *Aloe dichotoma* of the Liliaceae, growing in arid regions to a height of nine metres, and having a tapered trunk with porous, cork-like timber, upward-growing branches, and a roundish crown; QUIVER TREE. Also *attrib.*

1774 F. MASSON *Jrnl.* 2 Nov. in *Phil. Trans R. Soc.* (1776) LXVI. 309 We found a new species of aloe here, called by the Dutch Koker Boom, of which the Hottentots make quivers to hold their arrows; it being of a soft fibrous consistence, which they can easily cut out. **1790, 1806** [see QUIVER TREE sense 1]. **1841** B. SHAW *Memorials* 102 Along the stony sides of most of the mountains grow many trees, which are a species of the *aloe*; each branch is divided and subdivided into pairs; each of these subdivisions is terminated by a tuft of leaves, and the whole forms a large hemispherical crown, supported upon a tapering trunk, which is generally of large diameter, but short in proportion to the vast circumference of the crown. It is here called *kookerboom,* or quivertree. **1870** R. RIDGILL in A.M.L. Robinson *Sel. Articles from Cape Monthly Mag.* (1978) 31 A parched and sandy plain, surrounded by barren hills, on which no vegetation was visible, save the weird kokerboom. **1914** W.C. SCULLY *Lodges in Wilderness* 26 Huddled in irregular patches .. were the 'koekerboome'. These were gigantic aloes of archaic form and immense age. **1920** F.C. CORNELL *Glamour of Prospecting* 116 We outspanned about sunset on an open plateau covered with vegetation and studded with many of the queer looking aloes known as koker boomen, or 'quiver trees'. **1931** O. LETCHER *Afr. Unveiled* 120 We had broken down an old and rotting Koekerboom tree (a species of wild aloe of enormous size). **1950** *Cape Argus* 5 Aug. 7 As you drive northwards through the mountains to Springbok you may see that weird tree-aloe, the kokerboom, flowering beside the road. **1959** J.D. CLARK *Prehist. of S. Afr.* 226 The arrows were usually kept in a quiver made from leather .. or bark, in particular the bark of the 'Kokerboom' tree which is a species of aloe. **1976** CUBITT & RICHTER *South West,* Biggest and most impressive of all the aloes is the kokerboom, the so-called quivertree, its fibrous core providing pincushion-type quivers for the Bushman hunters. **1985** [see VLAKTE sense 1 a]. **1989** [see QUIVER TREE]. **1993** *Weekend Post* 17 July (Leisure) 7 A solitary kokerboom stands in the foreground.

2. With defining word: **baster kokerboom** [see BASTER *adj.*], *Aloe pillansii; giant quivertree,* see QUIVER TREE sense 2.

1990 [see BASTER *adj.*].

kokevic var. KOKKEWIET.

koki /ˈkəuki/ *n. colloq.* Also **cokey.** In full ***koki pen***: the proprietory name (with capital initial) of a particular make of fibre-tipped pen; also (with small initial) applied loosely to any fibre-tipped colouring pen. Also *attrib.*

1990 A. RICE in *Frontline* Oct. 15 It wasn't much of a poster, really ... It was a cheapo cokey pen-and-cardboard creation. **1992** C.M. KNOX tr. *E. Van Heerden's Mad Dog* 42 Above the urinal, someone had written in koki pen: *Enjoy the last great white erection.* **1993** V. COHEN in *Natal Witness* 7 Jan. 14 A quotation on a basic school kit .. reveals that a suitcase or satchel containing glue, .. kokis and so on, costs R80.94 and R86.94 respectively. **1994** G. VISSER in *Natal on Saturday* 8 Jan. 21 (*letter*) This letter's to all those among us who are .. 'Shocked by the naked flesh!' ... Haul out the black koki! The reverend hordes are on the march.

kokkelmanetjie, -mannetje varr. KOGGELMANNETJIE.

kokkewiet /kɔkəˈvit/ *n.* Also **cock-o-veet, cock-o-viek, kockervick, kok-a-viek, kokevic, kook-a-vic.** [S. Afr. Du., onomatopoeic.] Either of two bush-shrikes of the Malaconotidae, or their calls: **a.** *Laniarius ferrugineus,* with black head, back, and wings, creamy-white chest, and cinnamon-buff lower belly and flanks. **b.** The BOKMAKIERIE, *Telophorus zeylonus.*

1882 O.E.A. SCHREINER Diamond Fields. 88 She could not hear the cock-o-veets sing, even when she had the ear-trumpet in, for she was very deaf. **1896** E. CLAIRMONTE *Africander* 126 The *Kook-a-vic* was piping his shrill note in a bush hard by – 'Kook-a-vic, kook-a-vic, kook-a-vic'. **1900** B. MITFORD *Aletta* 147 A 'kok-a-viek', the yellow African thrush, was calling to his mate in his melodious triple hoot. **1908** HAAGNER & IVY *Sketches* 98 The well-known Bakbakiri (*Laniarius gutturalis*), called by most Colonials the 'Kokevic', from its call. *a*1920 O.E.A. SCHREINER *From Man to Man* (1926) 49 A cock-o-veet came flying up to her. *Ibid.,* Kokkewiet: The Bush-shrike, a very handsome bird with resonant call notes of great beauty. **1931** *Guide to Vertebrate Fauna of E. Cape Prov.* (Albany Museum) I. 100 Telephorus zeylonus .. Kokevic (kockivit) .. Olive green above, but crown and nape grey. **1936** E.L. GILL *First Guide to S. Afr. Birds* 49 Bokmakierie, Bacbakiri, Kokkewiet ... The calls are duets by the inseparable pair. **1940** A. ROBERTS *Birds of S. Afr.* 299 *Laniarius ferrugineus ferrugineus.* Boubou shrike .. Kokkewiet .. Remains concealed in the tangles and its presence is made known only by its loud duets, 'ko ko,' '*kweet*,' and other less noisy clucking notes. **1947** E.R. SEARY *S. Afr. Short Stories* (Glossary), *Kokkewiet*, .. one of the many bush shrikes. It is yellow and green with black patches and has a distinctive call .. variously described: 'bok, bok kiririe', pirrevit, quit, quit, quit. **1967** E. ROSENTHAL *Encycl. of Sn Afr.* 67 Bokmakierie or Kokkewiet (Telophorus zeylonus). [**1970** O.P.M. PROZESKY *Field Guide to Birds* 266 *Common Bou-bou Shrike*, .. The most common [duet] is antiphonic: a loud, clear bisyllabic '*koko*' from the male, immediately followed by a '*weet*' from the female.] **1970** *Std Encycl. of Sn Afr.* II. 401 Bokmakierie .. is sometimes locally referred to as bakbakiri, kokkewiet, janpierewiet or bush-shrike. **1982** *S. Afr. Panorama* Sept. 50 There is, too, the typically South African *witboskraai* (pied crow), the *kokkewiet* — better known as *bokmakierie*. **1982** *E. Prov. Herald* 1 Oct. 15 A male kokkewiet (bokmakierie) is boisterously proclaiming that the entire area around my homestead is his domain. **1989** F.G. BUTLER *Tales from Old Karoo* 201 In spite of the cold, there were butterflies about the aloe roads, and Kokkewiet cries echoing in the kloof. **1991** —— *Local Habitation* 303 His pondering pause was filled with doves and kokkewiets.

Kokney var. COCKNEY.

kokok var. GOGOG.

kokoon *n. obs.* Also **kokong**, **kokūn(g)**. [ad. S. Sotho *kgokong*, seTswana *kgokon* wildebeest.] The *blue wildebeest* (see WILDEBEEST sense b), *Connochaetes taurinus*.

[**1806** J. BARROW *Voy. to Cochinchina* 409 It was called by the *Booshuanas* the *Kokoon*. **1824** W.J. BURCHELL *Trav.* II. 278 The Bichuanas call it *Kokūn* (Kokoon), or rather, with a nasal sound of the *n*, *Kokūng* (Kokoong).] **1824** *Ibid.* 315 We saw a solitary *kokūn* (kokoon) in the open plain, prancing about, exactly in the manner of the gnu. **1834** *Penny Cyclopaedia* II. 91 The habits and manners of the kokoon closely resemble those of the gnu. **1835** A. SMITH *Diary* (1940) II. 39 From the chin of kokoon some long black and white hairs or bristles; upper lip turned inwards. [**1839** W.C. HARRIS *Wild Sports* 375 Kokoon of the Bechuana and Matabili.] **1857** D. LIVINGSTONE *Missionary Trav.* 135 The kokong or gnu.

kokopan var. COCOPAN.

Kokoqua var. COCHOQUA.

kokun(g) var. KOKOON.

‖**kolhaas** /'kɔlhɑːs/ *n.* Also **kalhaas**. [Afk., *kol* spot, patch + *haas* hare.] The hare *Lepus saxatilis*, the largest of three indigenous hare species, characterized by a white patch on the forehead.

1911 *Farmer's Weekly* 4 Oct. 120, I have done a great deal of springhaas shooting with gun and bull's-eye lantern ... On several occasions I .. , after pulling the trigger, have found the animals to be a 'muishond', 'kol-haas', or 'duiker'. **1912** *E. London Dispatch* 18 Oct. 6 Backed into the shelter of an untidy bunch of what looked like coarse 'grass' ... there lay in his well couched 'form' a fine big *kalhaas*. **1918** S.H. SKAIFE *Animal Life* 254 The rock hare, or *kol haas*, is similar in appearance to the Cape hare, but it is larger and found only on hill tops. **1948** A.C. WHITE *Call of Bushveld* 202 The dog never moved until I was close up to him, when a big kolhaas sprang out. **1970** M. VAN RENSBURG *Informant, Port Elizabeth* Kolhaas. Mountain hare.

Kolonie /kə'luəni/ *n.* Also with small initial. [Afk., colony, as found in the phr. *die Kolonie*, a name given to the Cape Colony.] COLONY. Also *attrib.*

[**1861** P.B. BORCHERDS *Auto-Biog. Mem.* 168 The landdrost of Swellendam .. had been obliged to order all the inhabitants of his district (kolonie) to proceed to the distant parts of the settlement, in order to oppose the attacks of the Kafirs and Hottentots, and to disperse them.] **1912** F. BANCROFT *Veldt Dwellers* 202 So foolish are the *rooinecks*, but yet so stiff-necked ... Why, where would they be in this war if they had not the *Kolonies* men to help them? **1971** *Cape Times* 3 July (Mag. Sect.) 3 Many people still call the Cape 'die Kolonie' ... Even in the towns they still refer sometimes to the Cape as '*Kolonie*'. **1975** *Sunday Times* 2 Nov. (Mag. Sect.) 2 It was too high a price to pay to listen while pa took us on a trip through the eating habits of the old kolonie.

kolwa var. KHOLWA.

‖**kolwyntjie** /kɔl'veɪŋki, -ci/ *n.* [Afk., ad. Du. *kolumbijntje*.]

1. See quot. 1973.

1973 M.A. COOK *Cape Kitchen* 58 The word 'kolwyntjie' is derived from *kolumbijntje* meaning a small cake or tartlet baked on the day of St. Columbine. **1975** *E. Prov. Herald* 20 Feb. 18 Mr van Tonder and companions entered the shop and that he asked for something which sounded to Mrs Howard like 'kolwyntjie'.

2. *comb.* **kolwyntjie-pan**, a pan with shaped depressions, used to bake kolwyntjies.

1973 M.A. COOK *Cape Kitchen* 58 Tart-pans and kolwyntjie-pans: these are possibly the most typical of all old Cape kitchen utensils, and the most eagerly sought after by collectors. **1974** *S. Afr. Panorama* Sept. 37 There are .. wafer and waffle irons, pancake slicers .. copper pots and 'kolwyntjie' (a small cake) pans, skimmers, mortars and coffee pots with their 'konfore' (warming stands). **1987** J. KENCH *Cottage Furn.* 81 The Victorians were obsessive inventors of kitchen gadgets ... On the local front, these innovations ran parallel to a long-standing tradition of sturdy simplicity, with Cape-style cooking pots in iron or copper, .. tart pans and 'kolwyntjie pans'.

‖**kom** /kɔm/ *v. intrans.* [Afk., *kom* come.]

1. In the interjectional phr. ***kom binne*** /-'bənə/, formerly also ***kom binnen*** [Afk., *binne* (Du. *binnen*) inside], 'come in(side)', an invitation to enter; a response to a knock.

Used by writers to represent Afrikaans dialogue.

1871 J. MACKENZIE *Ten Yrs* (1971) 38 Half awake, .. Philip shouted out 'Kom binnen!' — 'Come in!' — awaking both himself and me with the earnestness of his hospitality. **1882** J. NIXON *Among Boers* 202 Having thus satisfied his curiosity, the invitation follows, 'Kom binnen', ('Come in,') and you are requested to place yourself on the seat of honour or 'rustbank'. **1910** D. FAIRBRIDGE *That Which Hath Been* (1913) 75 As though in response to his thoughts, the stout lady opened her eyes, smiled benignly, and said 'Kom binnen.' **1931** V. SAMPSON *Kom Binne* 13 'Kom Binne' (pronounced Kom Binner) was sufficiently near 'come ben the hoose' of Scotch for the stranger to comprehend the invitation to enter. **1963** A.M. LOUW *20 Days* 52 Adriaan knocked on the door of his father's study and opened when he heard the voice calling 'Kom binne — Come in!' **1974** *E. Prov. Herald* 27 Nov. 37 An enormously stout woman was seated in the voorkamer and made no attempt to rise, but called out hospitably, 'Kom binne, you are welcome.'

2. In the phr. ***to kom klaar*** /-'klɑː(r)/ [Afk. *kom klaar*, *klaar* finished (see KLAAR)], to succeed; to get on together.

1883 'M.R.C.' in *Meteor* 30 Jan. 3 Have completed the 4th chapter, but have had to pull up there, owing to having placed the heroine in a very difficult situation, in fact, if she and all the other characters 'kom klaar,' (come clear) it will be a caution. **1940** E. BRIGHT in Baumann & Bright *Lost Republic* 221 Simon had told her how he and the ou baas had managed to 'kom klaar' (get on together).

komaroo var. KAMBRO.

‖**kombers** /kɔm'bɛrs/ *n.* Also **cambeass**, **comberse**, **cumbess**, **kimbaars**, **kombāars**, **kombaase**, **kombars(e)**, **kombasse**, **komberse**. Pl. **-e** /-ə/, **-en**, or unchanged. [Afk., fr. Du. *kombaars* coverlet, rug.]

1. KAROSS sense 1.

1824 W.J. BURCHELL *Trav.* II. 175 This *kombáars*, or coverlet, is a genuine South-African manufacture, being nothing more than a Hottentot *karóss* of large dimensions; but which has been adopted by the boors in every district. [*Note*] This word, agreeably to Colonial pronunciation, would be written by an Englishman, *Combáirce*. **1830** T. PRINGLE in *Cape Lit. Gaz.* 16 June 2 From Keiskahama's farthest springs, Where savage tribes pursue their game, His *kombaars* tied with leathern strings, This hunter of the *woestyn* came. **1850** R.G.G. CUMMING *Hunter's Life* I. 186 In the evening I took my pillow and 'komberse', or skin-blanket, to the margin of a neighbouring vley, where I had observed doe blesboks drink. **1851** N.J. MERRIMAN *Cape Jrnls* (1957) 231 The wolf's nightly howl, and quick jackal's cries Are music as under the kombarse he lies. **1855** G.H. MASON *Life with Zulus* 148 A few of these [people] bore traces of civilisation, being partially clothed and able to speak broken English, the rest being wrapped in their 'cumbess's' (Caffre blanket). *a***1858** J. GOLDSWAIN *Chron.* I. 20 We saw thear several Hottentot women from the age of 18 to 25 years old with nothing on but the sheep skin cambeass .. on. **1872** 'Y.' in *Cape Monthly Mag.* V. Sept. 183 Most certainly, when night came, far from any 'place,' he would be thankful for the comfort of a 'kaross' or 'kombaars,' without troubling his sleepy senses about the meaning of the word. **1913** [see sense 2].

2. A blanket.

[**1870** H.H. DUGMORE *Reminisc. of Albany Settler* 22 The qualities of the linebayi and the wolkombersen were elaborately discussed.] **1878** T.J. LUCAS *Camp Life & Sport* 137 The bed's .. clothing consisted of .. a felt *comberse* or quilt sewn up in a sheet of cotton print and apparently never washed. **1896** M.A. CAREY-HOBSON *At Home in Tvl* 346 The central curtain was taken down, the bedding on the kartel made level, and a large coloured kombasse, or coverlid, spread over it. **1913** C. PETTMAN *Africanderisms* 126 *Comberse*, A blanket, rug. *Ibid.* 274 *Komberse*, .. A rug, blanket; sometimes a kaross is so styled. **1979** *Daily Dispatch* 22 Oct. 6 The blanket tip came from an elderly member of the family who spent her days almost motionless wrapped in an old kombers.

kombi, combi /'kɒmbi, 'kɔmbi, 'kʊmbi/ *n.* Also **combie**, **kombie**, and with initial capital. [Transf. use of proprietory name *Kombi* a Volkswagen minibus (abbrev. of G. *Kombiwagen*, fr. *Kombination* combination + *Wagen* car).]

1. Any minibus, esp. one used to transport passengers commercially. Also *attrib.*, and *comb.* **kombi-load** *n.*, **kombi-type** *adj.*

1964 H.H.W. DE VILLIERS *Rivonia* 41 He arranged with one Suliman to bring two Kombis (small motor buses) to a garage at Orlando. **1975** *Drum* 22 Sept. 44 Ask them to help push the kombie which does not seem to want to start. **1979** W. EBERSOHN *Lonely Place* 166 He saw the *Kombi* first — a small bus — standing at 45 degrees with the road. **1983** *Commission of Inquiry into Bus Passenger Transport* (RP50–1983) 24 The 'taxi industry' .. consists of the ordinary legal taxi .. , the legal kombi-type taxi that is normally used as a minibus and the pirate taxi that is in most cases a kombi-type of vehicle and used illegally. **1984** H. ZILLE in *Frontline* Mar. 10 He no longer drives his gold Valiant. Along with thousands of township taximen throughout South Africa, Jabu now runs a kombi (and like the rest, he pronounces it koombi). **1989** D. BRISCOE in *Motorist* Oct.-Dec. 5 The road is in fair to good condition and negotiable by car and combi. **1990** D. BECKETT in *Frontline* Mar.-Apr. 10 We lash our broken Starwagon behind his Landrover and cover the 60 kilometres to Beaufort West ... We have a chaotic combi-load of bags and blankets and buckets and spades. **1990** R. STENGEL *January Sun* 22 Buda owns the township's largest taxi service — six cars. The taxis, known as kombis, are actually small vans that can seat about eight comfortably, but usually carry twelve or thirteen. **1992** E. JAYIYA in *Pace* Sept. 168 Dumisani Buthelezi believes his new sleek combi will be a hit. 'It's a modified version of the Hi-Ace.'

2. *comb.* **kombi taxi**, TAXI sense 1. Also *attrib.*

[**1983** M. Du Plessis *State of Fear* 4 The police are intimidating the people from the townships who run combi-bus taxis, demanding to see their licenses.] **1984** H. Zille in *Frontline* Mar. 12 What justification could there be to crush the burgeoning kombi-taxi business, that creates thousands of jobs unaided? **1988** *Star* 26 Apr. 4 The incidence of combi taxi accidents was no higher than other passenger vehicles, the Minister of Transport said yesterday. **1988** *Technical Info. for Industry* (C.S.I.R.) Sept. 2 The 'combi-taxi' has become an increasingly popular form of public transport. The .. CSIR has researched this form of minibus-transport, and the reasons for its rapid growth and success. **1990** C. McCaul *No Easy Ride* (S.A.I.R.R.) 35 From about 1977 .. taxi-operators – new entrants as well as those formerly operating sedan vehicles – began introducing 10-seater minibuses (kombitaxis) on to feeder and commuter routes ... Ten-seater minibuses were legalised as taxis (but to carry only eight passengers) in 1978 and 16-seaters (to carry 15 passengers) in 1986. **1990** *New African* 11 June 8 Are kombi taxis as safe as their owners maintain? **1991** S. De Villiers on M-Net TV 12 Mar., A new initiative to establish a working liason with the combi-taxi association. **1993** *Africa S. & E.* July 10 The legal traders come by bus, many by kombi taxi and a few by plane.

‖**kombuis** /kɔm'beɪs, -'bœɪs/ *n.* Also **combuys**. Pl. **-e** /-ə/, **-en**. [Afk., transf. use of Du. *kombuis* galley of a ship (however, in P.G.J. van Sterkenburg's *Een Glossarium van Zeventiende-Eeuws Nederlands* (1977), *kombuis* is glossed as 'een bijgebouwtje', an outbuilding).]

1.a. Used before the names of languages, as ***kombuis-Engels, kombuis-Hollands*** implying a pidgin variety of that language. See also KITCHEN *n.* senses 1 and 2.

1899 W.S. Logeman *How to Speak Dutch* Preface, My friend J.F. van Oordt .. has tried to strike the happy medium between 'High Dutch', not often understood by the people, and the 'Kombuis-Hollands' (Kitchen-Dutch) of the uneducated coloured servants. **1937** C.R. Prance *Tante Rebella's Saga* 40 Oom Sampson could only speak kombuis-Engels and some High Dutch and the old Cape Dutch. **1971** L.G. Green *Taste of S.-Easter* 76 It has been suggested that the first book printed in Afrikaans (then known as Cape Dutch or Kombuis Hollands) was a pamphlet intended for Malays. **1972** J. Packer *Boomerang* 24, I learn Afrikaans from Lizzie – that's kombuis Afrikaans – kitchen Afrikaans.

b. *comb.* **kombuistaal** /-tɑːl/ [Afk., *taal* language], a form of Afrikaans considered non-standard; cf. *kitchen Dutch* (see KITCHEN sense 2 b).

[**1958** A. Jackson *Trader on Veld* 28 During my 12 years' sojourn in the Backveld, I learnt not only to speak but to write the 'Taal' fluently, but I must admit that it was the purest Kombuis or Kitchen variety that I knew.] **1986** K. McCormick in Burman & Reynolds *Growing Up* 293 The local dialect of Afrikaans is referred to pejoratively as 'broken Afrikaans', 'not proper Afrikaans', '*kombuistaal*' (kitchen language) ... *Kombuistaal* has many loan-words from English and other languages, thus facilitating code-switching. **1989** *Weekend Post* 9 Dec. (Leisure) 5 Koos Kombuis sings about everything from Aids, oppression and hypocrisy to family murders in a 'kombuistaal' which is unlikely to find favour in polite company. **1990** S. De Waal in *Weekly Mail* 23 Feb. 22 He is bravely contributing to the unfettered growth of the one-time *kombuistaal* – he's helping to take it out of the mouths of ministers of constitutional development .. and return it to the kitchen, to the people. **1990** *Sunday Times* 3 June 4 Strangers embraced, danced together and declared undying loyalty in the name of harmony, brotherhood, kombuis taal, the end-conscription campaign – or wherever the next six pack was coming from.

2. A kitchen. Also *attrib.*

[**1913** C. Pettman *Africanderisms* 274 *Kombuis,* (D. *kombuis, kabuis,* a nautical term for the cooking place aboard ship; cf. Eng. *caboose.*] Cape Dutch for the kitchen. The word used in Holland is *keuken.*] **1921** H.J. Mandelbrote tr. *O.F. Mentzel's Descr. of Cape of G.H.* I. 64 We must note besides the 'Combuysen,' or kitchens, where the cooking was done for the garrison ... All these buildings had flat roofs in the Italian manner. **1948** H.V. Morton *In Search of S. Afr.* 285 We have no Coffee! Let us go to the kombuis! Now that's an interesting word! Seafaring Dutchmen turned their backs on the sea and became farmers, but they still called their kitchens by that word 'Kombuis' which is the ship's galley of a Seventeenth Century East Indiaman. **1969** D. Child *Yesterday's Children* 27 At the back the two wings of the dwelling partially enclosed a paved courtyard. One wing contained the nurseries, and the other the *dispens* (pantry) and the *kombuis* (kitchen). **1980** A.J. Blignaut *Dead End Rd* 26, I had told the four white men a few stories while I was seeing to their coffee in the kombuis. **1985** L. Sampson in *Style* Feb. 100, I remember sitting beside the range in her kitchen. She still had one of those old kombuise. **1986** *Argus* 15 Feb., Pine refectory table, 10-seater witels kombuis-tafel with stinkwood legs, large Yellowwood Kombuis pestle and mortar. **1987** P. Sullivan in *Living* Jun. 24 The Ruperts' dining room resembles a traditional *kombuis* .. with quarry-tiled floor, yellow-wood table, stink-wood chairs, country dressers and an open hearth. **1990** *Style* May 40 Leaning against the wall of his purple and orange kombuis in Rockey Street, Yeoville, he was an assimilated Afrikaner, a 'South African' rather than a Boer.

komeky, kometjie varr. KOMMETJIE.

komfoor /'kɔmfʊə(r)/ *n.* Also **comfore, confoor, komfore, komvoor, konfoor**. Pl. **-s, komfore** /'kɔmfʊərə/. [Du. (Afk. *konfoor*).] A charcoal brazier, in one of two forms:

a. A warmer for a kettle or pot, usu. of brass, with decorative perforations; TESSIE sense a. **b.** A foot-warmer in the form of a small (wooden) box with perforated lid; STOOF; STOOFIE; STOVE; VOETSTOFIE.

1841 *Cape of G.H. Almanac & Annual Register,* (advt) Tools of all descriptions ... Coffee and Pepper Mills, Strykyzers, Brushes, Kettles, and Komfores. **1844** J. Backhouse *Narr. of Visit* 84 To preserve warmth, the Dutch women use an apparatus to set their feet upon, called a Komfoor. **1871** J. Mackenzie *Ten Yrs* (1971) 15 Jufvrouw would prefer the charcoal 'komfoor' to a spinning-wheel. **1910** D. Fairbridge *That Which Hath Been* (1913) 95 The inevitable coffee, in a graceful brass vessel, simmered over the komvoor. **1926** P.W. Laidler *Tavern of Ocean* 77 After drinking he re-lit his pipe with charcoal from a komfoor. **1927** C.G. Botha *Social Life in Cape Col.* 54 Silver spoons, forks, teapots, .. candlesticks, tea kettles with 'confoors,' [etc.]. **1940** 'B. Knight' *Walking the Whirlwind* 144 She signalled to the slave near the door to hand round charcoal from the komfoor to relight some of the pipes. **1951** *Cape Times* 6 Sept. 16 Samovars are almost as common in Cape Town as komvoors and spittoons used to be in the salesrooms. **1957** L.G. Green *Beyond City Lights* 229 Many a copper kettle (and *konfoor* to keep the coffee hot) was hammered out in the early days. *Ibid.* 230 To-day you can pay as much as twenty-five guineas for a small, artistic *koffieketel* with its *konfoor,* simply because such things seldom come on the market. *c*1963 B.C. Tait *Durban Story* 137 There was my best after ox, old Blueberg, with his hind foot jammed in the old missus' 'comfore' (a brass charcoal brazier used as a foot-warmer or to boil a coffee kettle). **1963** A.M. Louw *20 Days* 10 Adriaan noticed that the spirit lamp was still burning in the konfoor under the antique silver coffee urn. **1965** M.G. Atmore *Cape Furn.* 84 The footwarmers or komvoors fall into a different category ... Since these komvoors were accepted in society in winter, they were probably used without heating as footstools in the summer months. The shapes are rather similar to the brass komfoors or stoofjes used in Holland in the first half of the 18th century. **1965** A. Gordon-Brown *S. Afr. Heritage* II. 23 Three old Brass Konfoors intended to contain burning coals to keep a kettle hot. **1972** A.A. Telford *Yesterday's Dress* 81 She sits drinking coffee with her bare feet upon a 'komfoor' which as its name implies was wooden 'chauffette' containing a pan of charcoal, a comfortable footwarmer. **1973** M.A. Cook *Cape Kitchen* 100 The coffee pot was an important piece of Kitchen or pantry or breakfast-room furniture, and was kept continually hot on a konfoor. **1974** *S. Afr. Panorama* Sept. 37 Pans, skimmers, mortars and coffee pots with their 'konfore' (warming stands). **1982** *Ibid.* Sept. 15 The coffee pots, dish warmers, jugs, candlesticks, *konfoors* (coffee pot stands), milking pails, .. were just as good in all respects as those made abroad. **1986** *Ibid.* Aug. 48 'Konfore' (small braziers on short legs on which the tea or coffee pots were kept warm).

komfyt var. KONFYT.

komikie var. KOMMETJIE.

‖**kommandant** /ˌkɔman'dant/ *n.* Also with capital initial. [Afk., see COMMANDANT.]

1. COMMANDANT sense 1.

1881 G.F. Austen *Diary* (1981) 38 Received by Kommandant M Wolmarhans. **1946** H.C. Bosman in L. Abrahams *Cask of Jerepigo* (1972) 165 When the commandant addressed a veld-kornet directly .. , the veld-kornet would say, 'Ja, Kommandant,' .. shuffling .. awkwardly. **1971** *Daily Dispatch* 16 Dec. 10 Kommandants Koos Potgieter and Greyling came from Pietermaritzburg, as did kommandant Jacobus Uys.

2. COMMANDANT sense 2.

1971 H. Zeederberg *Veld Express* 155 Commandant Tjaardt Kruger, the chief of the Republic's Intelligence Service .. told Pieter Zeederberg, then Hoofd Kommandant of Pretoria, that Jameson's original plan was to use the coaches for the 'invasion' of the Transvaal.

3. COMMANDANT sense 6.

1975 *E. Prov. Herald* 9 Aug. 4 The bazaar was opened by the leader of the Voortrekker Movement in Fort Beaufort, Kommandant Izak Malan.

kommandeer var. COMMANDEER.

‖**kommando** /kɔ'mandəʊ, kə'mɑːndəʊ/ *n.* Also with initial capital. [Afk., fr. S. Afr. Du. *commando, kommando* (see COMMANDO).] A small fighting force; a member of such a force.

1.a. COMMANDO senses 4 and 5. Also *attrib.*

1971 J.A. Brown *Return* 113 The police force was small but sound ... The district *kommandos* could be called up if trouble spread .. the farmers and traders, they were men who had fought two or three wars already. **1972** *Star* 17 Mar. 17 Here [*sc.* at Cottesloe hill] the 1700-strong Knopkierie Kommando, rough Afrikaner men, were shelled and rifled into submission. **1988** D. Haarhof in *Staffrider* Vol.7 No.1, 42 Snorting horses unlaagered at dawn carry the Kommando across bordering bloodrivered waters. **1988** S.A. Botha in *Frontline* Apr.-May 25 No-one came up with a plan of action to satisfy the blooming kommando spirit. **1992** 'K. Lemmer' in *Weekly Mail* 3 July 12 Every last man knows one thing: when the Groot Mariko Kommando says 'Kom!' you come, on the double.

b. With defining words denoting particular types of kommando, particularly in right-wing paramilitary organizations: **blitskommando** /'bləts-/ [Afk., *blits* lightning], a strike force; **boerekommando** /buːrə-/ [Afk., *boere* see BOERE], a name for the military wing of the Afrikaner Weerstandsbeweging (see AWB); cf. *wenkommando* (below); see also COMMANDO sense 7; KAPPIE KOMMANDO, see as a main entry; **skietkommando** /'skit-/ [Afk., *skiet* shoot], a commando of soldiers bearing rifles; **wenkommando** /'ven-/, also **winkommando** /'vən-/, [Afk., *wen* to win], historically, the Boer commando which fought and won the battle of Blood River; later, a name for the military wing of the AWB; cf. *boerekommando* (above).

1981 *Sunday Times* 23 Aug. 21 We do have a special motorcycle unit, the Stormvalke, and a marching unit, called the **Blitskommando**. **1981** *Pretoria News*

26 Nov. 26 Today it operates openly and even boasts its own vigilante groups like the 'Blitskommando' and the 'Stormvalke,' a leather-jacket squad of motorbike troops. **1990** D. VAN HEERDEN in *Sunday Times* 10 June 8 The **Boerekommandos** .. are the latest in a long list of failed attempts by the AWB to get a military wing off the ground. Their predecessors were the Stormvalke and Aquila. **1993** *Sunday Times* 12 Dec. 5 Tuesday went by with the men of the Pretoria Boere Kommando dug in at the fort. **1972** *Sunday Times* 3 Dec. (Mag. Sect.) 1 Now, although many do not realise it, there are no such things as '**skietkommandos**'. They are all commandos. **1953** B. FULLER *Call Back Yesterday* 135 He sold his farm at short notice, trekked northwards with his herds, and joined the **Wenkommando**. **1971** *Daily Dispatch* 16 Dec. 10 At the head of this commando, afterwards termed the 'winkommando' because they won the Blood River battle, stood kommandant-general Andries Pretorius. **1972** *S. Afr. Panorama* Mar. 30 On December 3, 1838, at the head of 463 fighting men, Andries Pretorius crossed the Tugela River at Skietsdrif. The Wen-Kommando (Victory Commando), as it was prophetically called, was committed to one of the most decisive battles ever fought in Southern Africa. **1991** L. VENTER in *Sunday Times* 6 Jan. 7 The AWB's official militant wing is now called Wenkommandos — named after a trekker commando which fought the Zulus ... AWB sources told him the Wenkommandos' predecessor, Aquila, had about 300 fully-trained men. **1993** *Sunday Times* 25 Apr. 21 Police sources believe the AWB may be able to muster 15 000 members of its fanatical and highly-drilled Wenkommandos. **1993** *Star* 22 July 3 The honour confers on the Wenkommando the right to parade in the town once a year with fixed bayonets, and have free drinks afterwards.

2. In the Voortrekker youth movement: COMMANDO sense 9.

1975 *E. Prov. Herald* 9 Aug. 4 A bazaar in the Nico Malan Hall of the Fort Beaufort High School organised by the Fort Beaufort Voortrekker Kommando brought in R403. **1984** *Daily Dispatch* 18 May 8 Prof B— said Mr Chris H— had done the Voortrekker movement a disfavour by using his privilege to officiate at a kommando to create anxiety within the movement.

kommetjie /ˈkɔməki, -ci/ *n.* Also **comage, comet(i)e, comiche, commatje, commigee, commitj(i)e, komeky, kometjie, komikie, kommeky, kommiekie.** [Afk., fr. Du. *kommetje* a small cup or basin (*kom* + dim. suffix -IE); in Afk., also with the transf. sense of a shallow, basin-like depression in the ground.]

1. A cup or small basin. Also *comb.* **kommetjieful** *n.*

1859 *Cape Monthly Mag.* VI. Nov. 277 A dish of boiled fossil remains — alias bucksteaks; a tin of sweet potatoes, .. a cometje of rocky salt, formed a repast, of which we breakfastless wayfarers made almost a clean sweep. **1872** C.A. PAYTON *Diamond Diggings* 108 A Homeric repast had been eaten, and numberless glasses of Boer brandy been consumed by the men, and 'kommetjes' of coffee by their fair and fat spouses. *a***1875** T. BAINES *Jrnl of Res.* (1964) II. 16, I then sent one of the Kafirs to wash the commigee. **1878** T.J. LUCAS *Camp Life & Sport* 136 The meal usually consisted of kid-flesh, .. little 'commitjies', or bowls of milk, being placed by the side of each person in the absence of liquor. **1882** S. HECKFORD *Lady Trader in Tvl* 247 My customers now expressed their desire to see some 'kommekies' (be it understood that a 'kommeky' is a small bowl used by the Boers instead of a cup — handles being inconveniently given to breaking on trek). **1882** J. NIXON *Among Boers* 178 I .. found him sitting up in his nightshirt, catching the water, which was trickling through the waggon tilt, in a small 'cometjie' or basin. **1896** H.A. BRYDEN *Tales of S. Afr.* 137 She .. drank a bare half *kommetjie* of coffee, parched though she was. *Ibid.* 139 Hendrika .. gave him .. the last kommetjeful of weak coffee. **1910** C. MEREDITH *Peggy* 20 The old lady always inspected the kommetjes in which it was the custom for the servants to take food to their homes. **1920** S. BLACK *Dorp* 165 She declared that her stomach was faint and that she needed something to 'keep herself up'. A large kommetje full of butter-milk and a bunch of grapes contributed towards this. **1936** P.M. CLARK *Autobiog. of Old Drifter* 119 The gargantuan Hebrew angel brought out a *comiche* of proportions worthy of his own remarkable bulk, and started pouring gin into his huge enamel mug. **1938** *Star* 9 Dec. 19 The babies were baptised with water from a Voortrekker 'kommetjie'. After each christening the water .. was decanted into another bowl and the 'kommetjie' used was given to the mother in remembrance. **1939** M. RORKE *Melina Rorke* 90 Another Hottentot servant appeared with coffee in komikies — crockery basins, decorated in appallingly gaudy designs, with a bowl-like bottom and a wide rim ... A wayfarer was certain of receiving a hearty welcome and a komikie of coffee. **1949** C. BULLOCK *Rina* 33 Knives and forks, cooking pots, tin plates and kommetjies. *Ibid.* 92 The boy brought us tea. Cooked in a kettle and poured into enamelled tin kommetjies, it was so rankly strong that a teaspoon would almost stand up in it. *Ibid.* 159 The boy .. asked me if I would not take a little of the beer. He poured some into my tin kommetjie and I drank. **1960** G. LISTER *Reminisc.* 20 His old coloured servant, Harry, signalled that he had only his own *kommetjie* (basin) left .. (the Prince declared) he would not have the coffee unless it was in the *kommetjie*. **1963** A.M. LOUW *20 Days* 10 He held one of the kommetjies, arranged on a silver tray around the coffee-urn .., and watched greedily whilst the amber liquid welled up against the translucent sides of the kommetjie. **1980** A.J. BLIGNAUT *Dead End Rd* 100 With the second kommiekie, he began to relate the story of Tjaart and the snake.

2. *Geology.* A shallow, saucer-like depression in the ground.

[**1840** J.E. ALEXANDER *Western Afr.* II. 74 Passing the Debe Nek we came upon a plain full of strange holes like large basins, hence this plain is called Commatje Flats.] *a***1858** J. GOLDSWAIN *Chron.* I. 113 We soon came to the comages flat .. these comages or holes in the ground are from 6 to 10 feet Long and from 3 to 4 feet [across]. **1875** C.B. BISSET *Sport & War* 149 For the sake of shelter from the bullets I was deposited in one of these kometjes, or basins in the ground. **1907** T.R. SIM *Forests & Forest Flora* 2 Towards the coast shale and mudstone are more frequent, the soil is often very shallow, and a feature of this part is the peculiar surface conformation known as 'kommetjes' in which flat or gently sloping ground overlying an impervious ironstone-gravel pan has the surface closely but irregularly pitted to a depth of about two feet while the adjoining ground is similarly elevated, it is said by the action of earthworms. [*c***1933** J. JUTA in A.C. Partridge *Lives, Lett. & Diaries* (1971) 159 The bay is called *Kommetjie* or 'little saucer,' for it lies shallow and transparent against the cream-coloured sand.] **1962** C. BOARD *Border Region* 19 A peculiar feature which is perhaps confined to this area is the occurrence of what are called kommetjies ... They rather resemble a network of ancient gravel pits a foot or two in depth and are associated with the existence of giant worms. **1968** F.C. METROWICH *Frontier Flames* 117 His stretcher-bearers thankfully deposited him in a kommetjie (a round saucer-like depression in the ground from which the plain takes it name), while they rested their weary limbs.

kommissie trek see COMMISSIE TREK.

konfyt /kɔnˈfeɪt, kɒnˈfeɪt/ *n.* Also **cómfáát, comfyt, confeit, conf(e)yt, confijt, convyt, komfyt, konfeit, konfijt.** [Afk., fr. Du. *konfijt.*] A preserve or conserve of fruit in its own syrup, either whole or in large pieces. Also *attrib.*, and *comb.* **konfyt-jar.** See also MOSKONFYT.

1861 'A LADY' *Life at Cape* (1963) 59 They have a long 'siesta' in their darkened rooms: after which Coffee and cakes, tea and cómfáát. **1862** LADY DUFF-GORDON *Lett. from Cape* (1925) 157, I have bought some Cape 'confyt'; apricots, salted and then sugared, called 'mebos' — delicious! **1888** *Cape Punch* 18 July 12 The ladies were .. much skilled in the arts of making a delicious dish, called by them comfyt, meaning come fête or feast. **1891** H.J. DUCKITT *Hilda's 'Where Is It?'* 149 'Naartje Comfyt.' (Mandarin Orange Preserve ..). **1896** R. WALLACE *Farming Indust. of Cape Col.* 9 A delightful Afrikander custom .. a cup of tea, with a liberal supply .. of some beautifully preserved home-made *confyt.* **1908** M.C. BRUCE *New Tvl* 79 Beyond the making of the family 'comfyt', at which the Dutch women are exceedingly skilful, there was no use for an abundant supply [of fruit]. **1910** C. MEREDITH *Peggy* 32 She made sasaarties, moss-bolletjes, komfyt, and the Lord knows what, and invited nearly everyone in the place to her house. **1913** D. FAIRBRIDGE *Piet of Italy* 156 It was barely four o'clock when .. Piet .. set out, well fortified with coffee, zoet-cookies and *konfyt.* **1913** A. GLOSSOP *Barnes's S. Afr. Hsehold Guide* 171 Take weight for weight of sugar (to each pound of sugar 1/2 pint of water; this is the rule for all konfyt). **1920** S. BLACK *Dorp* 42 Anita now entered with komfyt, an exquisitely flavoured preserve made from melon skins. **1925** P. SMITH *Little Karoo* (1936) 71 On the long trestle-table in front of the church door the women spread their offerings of baked meats and pastries, their konfijts and waffels. **1931** V. SAMPSON *Kom Binne* 218 The Dutch tradition, especially at Cape Town, is to have preserves of all kinds, called komfyts, with afternoon tea, if visitors are present. *c***1933** J. JUTA in A.C. Partridge *Lives, Lett. & Diaries* (1971) 154 She will give you some of the watermelon 'konfijt' you all like,' she said .., remembering my weakness for this highly-spiced preserve. *Ibid.* 161 *Watermelon konfyt.* Slices of melon preserved in their own syrup, first by the Malays, then the local farmers. **1944** I.D. DU PLESSIS *Cape Malays* 45 The Malay has a fondness for sweets. All kinds of *konfyts* and sweets are prepared. **1947** L.G. GREEN *Tavern of Seas* 87 Malay families sometimes sell these fine eighteenth century saucepans, kettles and konfyt pots. **1951** S. VAN H. TULLEKEN *Prac. Cookery Bk* 301 Konfyt is fruit preserved in a heavy syrup, either whole or cut into large pieces. **1955** A. DELIUS *Young Trav.* 102 With tea there was always served either preserved oranges or melon, known as *konfyt*, or hard, white rusks called beskuit. **1968** W. FEHR in D.J. Opperman *Spirit of Vine* 221 Exquisite examples of English, Irish, Dutch or Flemish konfyt-jars. **1968** K. MCMAGH *Dinner of Herbs* 15 No konfyt of green fig or watermelon had been as transparant; crisply green without and tender and juicy within. **1974** [see MEBOS]. **1980** A. DANGOR in M. Mutloatse *Forced Landing* 162 In your home you were taught that watermelon, like life, had to be turned into *konfyt*, calcified, preserved in sugar, and eaten demurely. **1986** M. KLINZMAN in *Style* Apr. 140 Preserves are a traditional South African delicacy, colloquially referred to as 'konfyt'. They differ from jam in that the whole small fruits or portions of fruit are cooked in a syrup until this becomes thick and clear. **1988** F. WILLIAMS *Cape Malay Cookbk* 63 Konfyts are usually served on their own as a sweet at weddings and feasts. **1992** P. DOBSON *Informant, Cape Town* Watermelon konfyt. A preserve made with the rind of a watermelon.

koning aasvoel see AASVOEL sense b.

koningklip /ˈkʊənəŋkləp/ *n. ?obsolescent.* [Ellipt. for *koning klipfish* (see KLIPFISH sense 2).] KINGKLIP.

1949 [see KINGKLIP]. **1975** [see Smith quot. at KINGKLIP].

konka /ˈkɔŋka/ *n.* [Afk. *konka(drom)*, prob. ad. Xhosa *(in)konkxa* jam tin.] A drum or large tin, often one with perforated sides, used as a brazier; MBAULA.

1950 E. ROSENTHAL *Here Are Diamonds* 199 The explanations for some of the words found on the diggings have yet to be found. Why should a fire-bucket be a 'Youka' and a drum be a 'Konka'? **1970** H.M. MUSMECI *Informant, Port Elizabeth* This konka is ideal for cooking purposes (drum or tin). **1980** E. JOUBERT *Poppie Nongena* 108 In the evenings Poppie lit a fire in the konka ... When the coals were glowing in the brazier she carried it into the house. **1988** S.A. BOTHA in *Frontline* Apr.-May 24 Security guards sit with mangy dogs in front of the factories. During winter every corner is occupied by a konka glowing with a bellyful of coal and wood scraps.

‖**konkel** /'kɔŋkəl/ *v. intrans.* [Afk.] To plot or intrigue.
> **1916** J.M. ORPEN *Reminisc.* (1964) 314 They said these men would 'konkel' (intrigue) with the natives. **1974** *Informant, Grahamstown* It's much easier to konkel when there isn't a bright light on you.

Hence **konkeling** *vbl n.*
> **1985** J. MALCOMESS in *E. Prov. Herald* 20 Mar. 4 Quite obviously, there has been a lot of 'konkeling'. The alternative is that they have gone behind the scenes and used the big stick... I would love to be a fly on the wall when that 'konkeling' takes place or when that big stick is wielded. One wonders what is offered. **1994** C.W. EGLIN on TV1, 15 Aug., The process [of constitution-making] has also got to be transparent. It mustn't be seen that there was a bit of konkeling behind closed doors.

konna var. KANNA *n.*[2]

konotie var. KANOTI.

konsa var. KONZA.

konstabel /kɔn'sta:b(ə)l/ *n.* [Afk., constable.] An Afrikaans-speaking policeman; also as a title, with a name.
> **1971** on Radio South Africa 4 May, This show was set in the mythical dorp of Witblits, where the Konstabel was always asking 'Did you got a license?' **1971** A. MENDELOW in *Daily Dispatch* 30 June 10 Looking up he saw none other than Konstabel Koos van der Merwe. **1978** P.-D. UYS in *Theatre One* 147 Molly: .. I know a nice konstabel in Simonstown ... Anna: .. Molly, a konstabel in Simonstown is about as useful as a millionaire on the moon. **1987** L. BEAKE *Strollers* 76 The konstabel clicked the handcuffs onto Katjie's wrists. **1988** M. DE PARAVICINI in *Style* Dec. 52 Hendrik Ignatius Botha, the ex-SAP konstabel from Pretoria, is learning Italian and teaching local kids to speak English. **1989** *Star* 9 Dec. 6 It seems the legendary South African konstabel who told a motorist she had just been past a sign that spelt S.T.O.P. and not P.A.W.S. has spiritual brothers among British bobbies.

‖**kontant** /kɔn'tant/ *n.* [Afk., fr. Du.] Cash, ready money.
> **1830** *Cape Lit. Gaz.* I. 16 June 3 The slave was knocked down to the Stranger, and the auctioneer demanded — kontant — cash. [**1870** H.H. DUGMORE *Reminisc. of Albany Settler* (1958) 34 Occasionally a few of the hoarded *rixdaalders* were added as *kontante geldt*, when the goods were specially attractive.] **1949** L.G. GREEN *In Land of Afternoon* 104 It was not always sheer ignorance that led people to keep large amounts of money on their farms. 'Kontant', hard cash, was the rule of the veld .. and men buying farms and stock in distant places simply had to have the money close at hand. **1973** *E. Prov. Herald* 5 May 15 (*advt*) Cash (kontant) for your clean used car. **1981** *Ibid.* 26 May 28 (*advt*) Ah! cash (kontant) for your clean used car, present hire purchase account settled. **1988** *Sunday Times* 5 Jun. (Mag. Sect.) 26 It was when Mr Fred K— paid R225000 *kontant* for ten roan antelope that my animal instincts told me I was in the presence of a type of homo sapiens that is (possibly) an endangered species.

‖**kontrei** /kɔn'trei/ *n.* [Afk.] Region.
> **1967** W.A. DE KLERK *White Wines* 25 Considering the merits and demerits of a neighbouring 'kontrei'. **1977** *Cape Times* 23 Dec. 8 He acted as honorary veterinary surgeon .. for much of the livestock of the *kontrei*. **1980** *Sunday Times* 27 July (Extra) 3 Abraham de Vries .. comes from the same 'kontrei' as Ou Paai and .. farms near Ladismith.

konza /'kɔ(:)nza/ *v.* Also **khonza, konsa.** [Nguni *khonza* pay homage, serve, wait upon.]

1. *intrans.* To pay homage, show respect; often in the phr. *to konza to* (*someone*).
> **1836** N. ISAACS *Trav.* (1937) 123 The people of the outer kraals .. generally come to 'conser,' (pay their respects,) with the view of getting cattle. **1875** D. LESLIE *Among Zulus* 93 It is the custom for all the young men in the country to spend a few months every year 'Konsaing,' i.e. paying their respects at court; but .. this means in fact that they have to hoe the King's corn. **1895** H. RIDER HAGGARD *Nada* 140 Now the councillors and the captains of the People of the Axe konzaed to him whom they named the Slaughterer, doing homage to him as chief and holder of the axe. **1897** J.P. FITZPATRICK *Outspan* 14 Mahaash was a big induna, and had about five to seven thousand fighting men. He used to konza to Umbandine, but paid merely nominal tribute, and was jolly independent. **1898** B. MITFORD *Induna's Wife* 130 Is the Black Bull of the North growing old and weak that he sends to konza to the elephant who trumpets at Nkunkundhlovu? **1913** C. PETTMAN *Africanderisms* 276 *Konza, to,* .. To pay one's respects to the chief; to act as a minister of the chief; to attend to the request or command of another. **1939** R.F.A. HOERNLÉ *S. Afr. Native Policy* 51 The Native commoner is trained to khonza to his chief ... Some of the forms in which this respect and submission have to be shown are, according to White notions, humiliating to a man's self-respect. **1949** C. BULLOCK *Rina* 27 You might meet Ratshatsha the BaXanwana Chief who won't *konza* to us Boers, foolish fellow. **1949** O. WALKER *Proud Zulu* (1951) 61 Already there were .. families who, when they came asking for land, 'konza-ed,' or paid homage in cattle for the right to build a hut and graze stock. **1982** *Financial Mail* 9 July 161 The chief of the Tembe-Tonga is .. now an old man ... Tongas in Mozambique even today 'Khonza' (pay deference) to him.

2. *trans. rare. to konza* (*someone*): To pay (a chief or king) homage; to show (a superior) respect.
> **1852** R.B. STRUTHERS *Hunting Jrnl* (1991) 15 An old man who used sometimes to go hunting with me at the lake came today saying he wanted to Konza (serve) us. **1952** H. KLEIN *Land of Silver Mist* 104 She sat quietly in her mountain kraal ... Her indunas konza-d her. They sang praises of their queen.

3. *comb.* **konza-attitude; konza name,** a courtesy title.
> **1937** B.H. DICKE *Bush Speaks* 35 If, in time, Schiel has proved himself as great chief, the natives might have accorded him, as one of his 'konza'-names, the name of Cetywayo, (Konza-names are respect-titles). [*Note*] Konza-Names: The Bantu consider it disrespectful to address a man by the name they have given him. Therefore, 'konza-names' are invented, i.e. courtesy-titles. **1939** R.F.A. HOERNLÉ *S. Afr. Native Policy* 51 The transfer of the *khonza*-attitude from the chief, as its object, to a White superior has a natural basis in Native tribal tradition. **1952** H. KLEIN *Land of Silver Mist* 172 The tribesmen, .. in the ordinary course of events, first gauge a man's capabilities and character before bestowing a konza name (courtesy title).

koo var. KU.

koodo(o) var. KUDU.

kookaam var. KUKAMA.

kookamakranka var. KUKUMAKRANKA.

kook-a-vic var. KOKKEWIET.

kookerboom var. KOKERBOOM.

koolganna see GANNA sense 2.

kooper /'kuəpə(r), ?'ku:pə/ *n. Obs. exc. hist.* [ad. Afk. *koper* buyer, fr. *kopen* to buy.] KOPJE-WALLOPER.
> **1873** F. BOYLE *To Cape for Diamonds* 229 The koopers sit silent in their canvas dens, and miserably estimate their losses probable ... What do I stand to lose with diamonds down one-third? **1911** L. COHEN *Reminisc. of Kimberley* 215 Undoubtedly, Mr. J.B.R. was a bold and rather careless diamond kooper, and would often make an offer for a large parcel of diamonds, close the envelope, *without weighing the diamonds*, and return same to the broker to permit him to submit the bid to his principal. **1913** C. PETTMAN *Africanderisms* 277 *Kooper*, .. In the early days of the diamond fields the diamond buyers were known as 'koopers'. **1963** [see KOPJE-WALLOPER].

koopman /'kuəpman/ *n. Obs. exc. hist.* Pl. -s, -men. [Du., *koop* (fr. *kopen* to buy) + *man* man.] A merchant or trader; see quot. 1823.
> **1772** G. FORSTER *Voy. round World* I. 71 The second Governor has the direction of the Company's whole commerce here ... He and the Fiscal have the rank of *upper koopman. Ibid.* 72 The major .. has the rank of *koopman* or merchant. **1790** tr. F. *Le Vaillant's Trav.* II. 101 The name of Koopmans was also given to those who first carried on trade by barter. These two words signify, in very good Dutch, a merchant or dealer. **1806** J. BARROW *Trav.* II. 96 Koopman or merchant was a title that conferred rank at the Cape, to which the military even aspired. **1823** W.W. BIRD *State of Cape of G.H.* 120 An unproductive harvest .. is not more to be regretted by the boer than by the dealers, or koopmen, as they are called. *Ibid.* 148 On the address of a letter to an Englishman, after the word esquire, they sometimes add, by way of compliment, the appellation koopman (or merchant) as the superlative distinction. **1911** L. COHEN *Reminisc. of Kimberley* 398 These people recognized no superior in rank to themselves, except .. the nearest Koopman .. whose office was in their eyes a sacred calling, as in the old Dutch East India Company trade was a complete monopoly. **1949** L.G. GREEN *In Land of Afternoon* 197 Strand Street was once known as 'the street of the koopmans' (the merchants) who lived there because they were close to the shipping.

koor haan, koor-haen, koor(h)an varr. KORHAAN.

koorn kriek var. KORINGKRIEK.

koors druppels see DRUPPELS sense b i.

koosi var. INKOSI *n.*

Koos(s)as pl. form of XHOSA.

kop /kɔp/ *n.* Also **kope, koup.** [Afk., fr. Du., head; peak, hill.]

1. A prominent hill or peak; a hill crest. See also KOPPIE.

a. Used as an element in place names.
> **1835** A. STEEDMAN *Wanderings* I. 115 We *uitspanned* at a place called Rhenoster Kope, from the supposed resemblance which the mountain bears to the head of a rhinoceros. **1835** C.L. STRETCH *Journal.* 1 Apr., On the following morning the troops .. advanced in the direction of T'Slambies Kop, a high point visible from the heights near Graham's Town. **1900** A.W. CARTER *Informant, Ladybrand* 24 Jan. 3 Watched shell after shell fall on and round Cronje's Kop, sometimes three at a time. **1902** 'LINESMAN' *Words Eye-Witness* 81 The rocky bush-covered foot of Schwartz Kop. **1903** R. KIPLING *Five Nations* 209 From Colesberg Kop to Quagga's Poort — from Ninety-Nine till now. **1955** D.L. HOBMAN *Olive Schreiner* 175 Buffels Kop stands over her, buttressing his powerful summit into the sky. **1971** *Rand Daily Mail* 26 June (Home Owner) 5 Two of Johannesburg's most famous 'kops' — Langermann's Kop .. in Kensington, which had been cited as an example of a 'forgotten' area, and Pullinger Kop .. on the Berea. **1989** P.E. RAPER *Dict. of Sn Afr. Place Names* 339 *Meintjeskop*, .. Hill in Pretoria, on which the Union Buildings are situated.

b. Used as a common noun.
> *a*1858 J. GOLDSWAIN *Chron.* (1946) I. 91 We saw several Horses greasen on the Kop and thought that we could get them without danger. **1860** A.W. DRAYSON *Sporting Scenes* 144 Karl and I trudged on for some miles to a little 'kop', where we hoped to get a better view round. **1878** H.A. ROCHE *On Trek in Tvl* 303 One fine Kop or Kopjie we passed upon which grazed an immense herd of fine oxen and heifers. **1882** J. NIXON *Among Boers* 124 The town is placed between a kop and a kopjie. On one side is a hill with a flat, long top, covered with patches of bush; and on the other a small irregular elongated ridge. **1882** C. DU VAL *With Show through Sn Afr.* I. 136 This little Dutch town, sleeping quietly at the feet of the mountain Kops, that stand sentinel over its slumbers. **1901** L. JAMES in J. Ralph *War's Brighter Side* 347 The three field batteries then came into action against a high tableland *kop*

which formed the right of the held position. **1903** R. KIPLING *Five Nations* 159 Me that 'ave watched 'arf a world, 'Eave up all shiny with dew, Kopje on kop to the sun. **1929** D. REITZ *Commando* 64 For a time there had been talk of an attack by the Free State forces against a loose-standing kop called Wagon Hill. **1939** tr. *E.N. Marais's My Friends the Baboons* 14 On one side the kloof was bordered by a krans, two to three hundred feet high, and on the other by a kop so steep that it could almost be called a krans too. **1949** H. GIBBS *Twilight* 126 Wide, flat lands which stretch from horizon to horizon, with only the sudden rise of a table-mountain or a kop, sharply pointed, breaking the view and shaping the hot sky's blueness. **1955** D.L. HOBMAN *Olive Schreiner* 124 Give back my dead! They who by kop and fountain, First saw the light upon my rocky breast! **1965** A. GORDON-BROWN *S. Afr. Heritage* II. 24 Behind the town of Swellendam are found conspicuous peaks which form a natural sundial, and for more that two hundred years these have been known to local farmers as 10 uur, 11 uur, 12 uur and 1 uur Kop. **1970** R. MAYTHAM *Informant, Empangeni* We traversed the kop and surveyed the scenery. **1971** [see sense a]. **1990** A. GOLDMAN in *Motorist* 4th Quarter 7 The tribe [of baboons] .. had time to scramble to the top of the kop from where they could roll rocks down the hill to frighten off attackers.

‖**2.** *colloq.* Head; intelligence.

1881 *E. London Dispatch & Frontier Advertiser* 19 Jan. 3 Why! what is this, a night cap, a scotch cap, or what? .. Here is some writing: 'for anyone suffering from rheumatics in the kop'. **1906** H. RIDER HAGGARD *Benita* 83 'Too much in his kop,' and she tapped her forehead. **1909** N. PAUL *Child in Midst* 123 An' presently 'is missus come in an' chucked some water on my kop, an' tied a rag round it. **1937** S. CLOETE *Turning Wheels* 348 That young man has something in his kop. He was right and we were wrong. **1958** I. VAUGHAN *Diary* 57 Mr H. said Mr Vaughan she jes took a mok and kepped me on my koup. Look how she scryched me. **1970** A. VAN DEN BERG *Informant, Pretoria* My father says that when doing arithmetic I must use my kop. **1970** C. BANACH *Informant, Port Elizabeth* Use your kop before you answer back. **1973** *Cape Times* 8 Mar. 7 A tight little *bollatjie* of hair at the top of the *kop*. **1973** J. COPE *Alley Cat* 167 'Did Bruce Young bring you?' 'Yeh ... crazy ou with a bald kop.' **1976** J. MCCLURE in *Sunday Times* 19 Feb. (Mag. Sect.) 8 'Er, well sort of like a hobo, sir. There's cuts on his *kop* from falling down in the gutter. **1989** B. RONGE in *Sunday Times* 19 Feb. (Mag. Sect.) 8 This is a competition I could win. This one takes a bit of *kop*, you have to respond to words and images to piece together clues. **1991** G. DE BEER *Informant, Port Nolloth (N. Cape)* One day you'll leave your kop behind too ... That guy really has kop (intelligence).

3. *slang.* A head-butt.

1972 *Sunday Tribune* 16 July 3 Squawk just swore at him. 'So the CID man gave him three quick kops ('butted him in the face) ..'

kopdoek /ˈkɔpduk, -duk/ *n.* [Afk., *kop* head + *doek* cloth, scarf.] DOEK sense 2. Also **kopdoekie** [see -IE].

1908 *Rand Daily Mail* 11 Sept. 7 They adopted a most attractive dress; a kop doek (each gang with a distinctive colour), low-necked blouse, [etc.]. **1911** *State* Dec. 642 He deposited his shapeless hat on the floor, tapped his red kopdoek with a clawlike forefinger, and waited for an inspiration. **1914** L.H. BRINKMAN *Breath of Karroo* 32 He .. undid his 'kopdoek,' and took from it a number of very small bundles each tied in a little rag, and handed the doek to Tante Let. **1946** L.G. GREEN *So Few Are Free* 60 Their daily life is bound up with the church which has fathered them. They are as old fashioned as the kopdoeks worn by the women. **1952** L.G. GREEN *Lords of Last Frontier* 149 Frau Bullik and her daughters all wore skin trousers such as the Bechuanas make ... But even more remarkable were their kopdoeks, padded handkerchiefs worn round the head. **1953** U. KRIGE *Dream & Desert* 55 In the vineyards coloured folk were working, the *kopdoekies* of the women bright flecks of colour against the dark earth. **1957** *Cape Times* 6 Apr. (Weekend Mag.) 3 The Swazis barter the bones for food and clothing .. ; half a monkey means a new kopdoek. **1974** *S. Afr. Panorama* Feb. 10 In their bright blue-and-pink 'kopdoeks' (head scarves), they lend a colourful note to an already colourful scene. **1975** W. STEENKAMP *Land of Thirst King* 76 The older women wear their dresses conservatively long and still cling to the brightly-coloured 'kopdoek' (headcloth). **1987** S. KNOTT in *Style* Feb. 68 Barend has on a brown Voortrekker *vrou* number with padded bosom and *kopdoek*.

kope var. KOP.

kop-en-pootjies /ˌkɔp(ə)nˈpʊɪkiz, -ˈpuɪkis, -cis/ *n.* Also **kop en poitjes**, **kop-en-pooitjies**, **kop en pootje(s)**. [Afk., *kop* head + *en* and + *poot* foot of animal, hoof + dim. suffix -IE + pl. suffix -*s*.] A traditional dish of sheep's head and trotters; OFFAL sense a. Cf. PENS EN POOTJIES.

1890 A.G. HEWITT *Cape Cookery* 24 Engelegte Kop en Pootjes. Take a well-cleaned sheep's head and feet, put them in a deep saucepan. **1913** A. GLOSSOP *Barnes's S. Afr. Hsehold Guide* 321 Kop en Pootjes. Take a well-cleaned sheep's head and feet. **1913** C. PETTMAN *Africanderisms* 278 *Kop-en-pootje*, .. The designation of a favourite Dutch dish, the principal ingredients of which are sheep's head and feet. **1925** L.D. FLEMMING *Crop of Chaff* 58 Find farmer friend with whom I discuss 'kop and poitjes' and rust in oats. *c*1937 E. CRAIG *Cookery Illust. & Hsehold Management* 649 Kop-en-Pootjies. (Sheep's head and Trotters) 1 Sheep's head. 4 Trotters. 2 tablespoons Vinegar. 4 Onions. Salt. Pepper. Cloves. **1945** *Outspan* 20 July 37 The Transvaal Bushveld can boast the best cooking in South Africa .. but the best kop-en-pooitjies comes from the Karroo. **1958** A. JACKSON *Trader on Veld* 43 During the summer the main fare was mutton and mutton again, but the by-products were by no means uninteresting – the 'kop en pootjes' (head and trotters), the tripe, liver, kidney and 'kaains'. **1973** *Farmer's Weekly* 25 Apr. 101 Kop en pootjies (sheep's head and trotters) and pens en pootjies (tripe and trotters) are two more traditional dishes of the Cape which may be classified as stews – but what stews! **1979** M. PARKES *Wheatlands* 49 The dogs and cats enjoying a feast of 'kop en pooitjies' which had found its way to the floor in the pot in which it had been cooking on the stove. **1985** T. BARON in *Frontline* Feb. 30 Hardened farmers stood back in awe at the sight of our attack on Mrs Paxton's kop en pootjies, or rather the kop en pootjies she had been cooking for the past couple of days.

koperdraad /ˈkʊəpə(r)drɑːt/ *n.* [Afk., *koper* copper + *draad* wire.] Any of several species of grass which become hard and wiry when mature. See also *sour grass* (SOUR sense 2).

1896 R. WALLACE *Farming Indust. of Cape Col.* 103 *Koper draad*, or copper-wire grass. *Andropogon excavatus* becomes so hard and bristly as it matures that it has been favourably mentioned as a suitable material from which to manufacture paper. **1907** T.R. SIM *Forests & Forest Flora* 41 The wiry class of grasses, known as 'Koper-draad'. **1913** C. PETTMAN *Africanderisms* 278 *Koper draad*, .. *Aristida sp.* This name describes this grass when ripe ... When ripe it is hard and wiry and of little worth as food for stock. **1937** *Handbk for Farmers* (Dept of Agric.) 400 Once the grain crops have been reaped, stock find a fair amount of grazing on the stubble, consisting of .. a little grass .. , weeds such as koperdraad (*Polygonum aviculare*) and small bushes. **1966** C.A. SMITH *Common Names* 307 *Koperdraad*, Several species of grasses, generally of the 'sour' type, are known by this vernacular name on account of their wiry culms or leaves. Stock not partial to any of the grasses .. which are useless from the stockman's point of view. **1986** *Farmer's Weekly* 13 June 13 During my farming apprenticeship with him I knew only two types of grass – koperdraad and steekgras.

kopij, kopje varr. KOPPIE.

kopje-wallop /ˈkɔpiˌwɒləp/ *v. intrans. Hist.* [Back formation fr. KOPJE-WALLOPING or KOPJE-WALLOPER.] To buy diamonds directly from diggers on their claims, and sell the stones to traders.

1911 L. COHEN *Reminisc. of Kimberley* 33 One windy day, .. I was kopje-walloping in Kimberley, feeling more depressed and dispirited than usual, when .. I came across a Dutchman sorting at his table. **1944** J. MOCKFORD *Here Are S. Africans* 92 In that era, such a man as Barney Barnato, a penniless Jew from Whitechapel, could establish himself in Kimberley .. by koppie-walloping, as they called tramping the fields in order to buy the rough diamonds for their finders.

kopje-walloper /ˈkɔpiˌwɒləpə/ *n. hist.* Also **koppie walloper**. [Deriv. of KOPJE-WALLOPING; see quot. 1897.] A diamond-buyer who bought stones directly from diggers on their claims, before this trade was outlawed by the Diamond Trade Act of 1882; KOOPER.

1886 G.A. FARINI *Through Kalahari Desert* 21 It was found that the wily Jew was a 'partner' in a 'company' of ten 'Koppje wallopers,' to whom a single licence was issued on payment of 10*l.* or 1*l.* per head. **1887** J.W. MATTHEWS *Incwadi Yami* 227 The 'kopje walloper,' who was generally a gentleman of the Hebrew persuasion .. was one of those who, when diamond buying was as legal in the open air as in a properly registered office, used to haunt the edge of the mine. **1897** H. RAYMOND *B.I. Barnato* 14 The slang camp term indeed for this [*sc.* dealing in diamonds] was 'kopje walloper' ... The diamonds were obtained from a number of kopjes or small hills in the neighbourhood of the camp, and the dealers travelled on foot from one to the other purchasing the finds as they were turned out at the sorting tables. **1910** J. ANGOVE *In Early Days* 64 In the early seventies there was a class of diamond buyers known as 'Kopje-Wallopers' – that is to say, having taken out a licence for the purpose, they were allowed to go where they pleased and buy diamonds whenever opportunity offered. **1923** B. RONAN *Forty S. Afr. Yrs* 166 He went up to the diamond fields to join his brother, and there became a 'Kopje Walloper,' or dealer in diamonds. **1931** *Nat. Geog. Mag.* Apr. 421 'Kopje-wallopers' – those who bought other men's finds on speculation – hurrying to and fro among the sorting tables. **1947** *Cape Argus* 20 Dec. 2 A 'koppie walloper' was a diamond buyer who went from claim to claim buying stones. The name was used in Kimberley in the early days. **1955** E. ROSENTHAL in Saron & Hotz *Jews in S. Afr.* 114 A 'koppie-walloper', that is one who went from claim to claim buying diamonds as the diggers produced them. **1963** O. DOUGHTY *Early Diamond Days* 119 The lowest class of diamond buyers were known by the rather contemptuous name of 'diamond koopers', or more commonly, by the yet more contemptuous name of 'kopje-wallopers' ... Too poor to buy an office they perambulated the mines in search of sellers on the spot ... Many were so successful that before long they graduated into the highest ranks of the diamond-buying hierarchy. **1976** B. ROBERTS *Kimberley* 123 Most 'kopje-wallopers' were simply small-time opportunists who, without claims or much capital, toured the diamond-sorting tables in the hopes of picking up (or fiddling) a bargain. **1983** R.L. FISH *Rough Diamond* 75 A 'kopje walloper' .. goes from claim to claim .. buying the day's find from the miners, offering as little as he can for their stones, and then selling them for as much as he can to the diamond traders. **1989** *Personality* 13 Mar. 38 A koppie-walloper, a go-between running from claim to claims office and selling diamonds to the buyers for a commission.

kopje-walloping /ˈkɔpi ˌwɒləpɪŋ/ *vbl n. Hist.* [Du. *kopje* see KOPPIE + Eng. *walloping* thrashing; see quot. 1897 at KOPJE-WALLOPER.] The practice of buying diamonds directly from prospectors (see KOPJE-WALLOP). Also *attrib.*

1876 in J. Angove *Early Days* (1910) 645 From and after this date the practice known as 'Kopje-walloping' or otherwise the purchasing of diamonds in places other that the offices of Licensed Bankers or Diamond Dealers, will be strictly prosecuted by the police. **1911** L. COHEN *Reminisc. of Kimberley* 63 The great envy of some Aaronic gents in the kopje-walloping profession who daily watched us through a telescope from a neighbouring mound. **1963** O. DOUGHTY *Early Diamond Days* 122 Another, after being an unlucky digger, had taken to kopje-walloping almost by accident. **1974** *The 1820* Vol.47 No.8, 31 They lived in the most primitive conditions, powdered daily with red dust from head to foot, with Barney making his daily rounds of *kopje walloping* – the purchasing of the rough stones from the sorting tables of the diamond miners.

koppie /ˈkɔpi, ˈkɒpi/ *n.* Also **copjie, coppie, coppy, kopij, kopj(i)e, koppj(i)e, kopy.** [Afk., fr. Du. *kopje*.] A small hill, a hillock. See also KOP, KRANSKOPPIE, RANDJIE.

The Du. spelling 'kopje' is still used, and is the standard form of this word in Zimbabwe.

a. An element in place names.

1822 W.J. BURCHELL *Trav.* I. 285 [We] halted for the night in the plain at *Kopjes Fontein*, so called on account of several low hills in the surrounding distance. **1882** J. NIXON *Among Boers* 255 The only hill of importance I passed was 'Kopjie Aleen', or the 'Lone Hill', a solitary sugar-loaf hill which rises out of the vast plain. **1897** H. RAYMOND *B.I. Barnato* 13 The alluvial workings were much neglected in favour of mining the yellow surface earths in the neighbourhood of the Colesberg Kopje. **1939** J.F. BENSE *Dict. of Low-Dutch Element in Eng. Vocab.* 170 When the hills are low or small the dim. *kopje* is always used. Cf. the name *Kopjes Fontein*.

b. A common noun; KLIPKOPPIE. Also *attrib.*

1849 R. GRAY *Jrnl of Bishop's Visitation* I. 76 Large dreary plains interrupted by rocky koppies abounding with the springbok and the gnu. **1850** N.J. MERRIMAN *Cape Jrnls* (1957) 135 Retiring behind a koppie to pitch our tent. **1857** *Cape Monthly Mag.* II. July 47 The greenstone caps, locally known as *kopjes*, which form so marked a feature in the Karroo. *a*1867 C.J. ANDERSSON *Notes of Trav.* (1875) 200 Ascended a small granite '*Kopy*', or rocky eminence, in the neighbourhood. **1878** T.J. LUCAS *Camp Life & Sport* 153 The Kaffirs are now seen collecting on the hills ... On one tall 'copjie' a group of mounted Kaffirs watch the course of the column. **1881** P. GILLMORE *Land of Boer* 244 The stronghold of the Kaminyani is on a coppy, or hill, about eight hundred feet high, and probably a mile and a half in circumference at the base. **1883** O.E.A. SCHREINER *Story of Afr. Farm* (1960) 18 The little cicada-like insects cried aloud among the stones of the kopje. **1895** A.B. BALFOUR *1200 Miles in Waggon* 85 One day we had a pretty view of low hills, and twice we have been near low kopjes (little hills). **1900** F.D. BAILLIE *Mafeking Diary* 142 Incendiary Boer shells provided the kopje contingent with fireworks gratis. **1900** R. KIPLING in J. Crwys-Williams *S. Afr. Dispatches* (1989) 164 Spiked koppies, heartbreaking to climb under a hot sun at four thousand feet above sea level. **1903** E.F. KNIGHT *S. Afr. after War* 54 Rolling open spaces of veldt studded with high rugged kopjes. **1908** M.C. BRUCE *New Tvl* 3 The karoo .. under a new moon has its ugliness and barrenness changed as if by magic into soft browns and fawns, merging into the pink and purple of distant kopjes, which again are topped by sunset streaks of yellow. **1916** *Farmer's Weekly* 20 Dec. 1469 Partly kopjes Veld, partly flat. *a*1920 O. SCHREINER *From Man to Man* (1926) 290 You will creep on hands and knees over rough koppies. **1920** R. JUTA *Tavern* 127 When a giant was killed, he was buried just where he fell, a big mound was erected over him, and you see, that is why all over the veld there are little and big kopjes. **1935** P. SMITH *Platkop's Children* 74 Always kopjes an' stones an' little brown bushes, an' always when you got the top of one kopje there was another one in front of you jes' ensackly like it. **1937** W. DE KOK tr. *E.N. Marais's Soul of White Ant* (1973) 68 If the termitary is an old one and placed on tip of a dry kopje or hill, this passage descends to an incredible depth. **1947** E.R. SEARY *S. Afr. Short Stories* Glossary, Kopjes, in the Karroo, are hillocks of stones, that rise up singly or in clusters, here and there; presenting sometimes the fantastic appearance of old ruined castles or giant graves. **1966** F.G. BUTLER *S. of Zambezi* 20 Ironstone kopjies like dead volcanic islands rising purple and black from oceans of grass. **1987** G. VINEY *Col. Houses* 199 Hard, rough, koppie quartzite, which he instructed eight local masons to quarry and dress to display its varied tints. **1988** M. URSON in *Personality* 6 June 60 Their sturdy little dorp, nestling amid granite koppies and ridges. **1990** W. SMITH *Golden Fox* 226 A flamboyant Karoo sunset lit the gaunt kopjes with a ruddy glow and set the clouds on fire. **1991** [see KLIPKOPPIE]. **1993** J. THOMAS in *House & Leisure* Nov. 50 Paul bought a house in the Greymont koppies and lives in close communion with his two cats.

korà var. GORAH.

Kora /ˈkɔrə/ *n.* Also **Cora, !Kora, !Ora.** Pl. unchanged, or **-s.** [Khoikhoi, prob. fr. the name of the first chief of the clan, named *!Kora, !Khora*, or *!Ora*: see KORANNA (Std. Encycl. quot., 1975).]

1. A member of a KHOIKHOI people who migrated from the southern and central regions of the Cape Province to their final home near the Orange, Vaal, and Harts rivers; KORAQUA sense 1; cf. KORANNA sense 1. Also *attrib.* See also GORACHOUQUA.

1802 TRUTER & SOMERVILLE in G.M. Theal *Rec. of Cape Col.* (1899) IV. 403 We were visited by several Coras. **1806** J. BARROW *Voy. Cochinchina* 373 The native inhabitants which are settled on the banks of the Orange River .. are a variety of the Hottentot race .. called the *Koras* ... What the Gonaquas were on the eastern coast the *Koras* seem to be to the northward, a mixed breed between the Hottentot and the Kaffer. **1822** [see KORAQUA sense 1]. **1824** W.J. BURCHELL *Trav.* II. 212 This difference of stature in those [Bushmen] who inhabit the vicinity of the river [*sc.* the Gariep], is probably to be attributed to a mixture of Kora blood. **1834** T. PRINGLE *Afr. Sketches* 16 The Corannas, Koras, or Koraquas, are a tribe of independent Hottentots, inhabiting the banks of the Gareep, or Great Orange River. They are naturally a mild, indolent, pastoral people. **1928** [see Vedder quot. at KORANNA sense 1]. **1930** [see GORACHOUQUA]. **1936** J.A. ENGELBRECHT *Korana* 83 Kora tribes .. left the Cape to seek new pastures. **1955** J.H. WELLINGTON *Sn Afr.: Geog. Study* II. 234 The tribes occupying the Cape Peninsula and adjacent areas at the time of Van Riebeeck's arrival were the Goringhaiqua and the Kora (later known as the Koranna). **1976** R. ROSS *Adam Kok's Griquas* 25 Although various criteria in terms of physical type, historical grouping and language have been suggested for the !Kora, these do not inspire confidence, and rather it is best to see the !Kora as those who followed a style of life which entailed nomadic cattle herding and raiding in smallish hordes, led by a, theoretically hereditary, *Kaptyn*. **1978** T.R.H. DAVENPORT *S. Afr.: Mod. Hist.* 25 The Kora, or Khoikhoi people who had largely preserved their identity and got on well with the Griqua, .. later became involved in conflict with the Cape government on the Orange River in the 1860s. **1986** P. MAYLAM *Hist. of Afr. People* 111 In the years 1833–4 about 12 000 people migrated from this direction into Moshoeshoe's sphere of influence. These were mostly Tswana, but also included Kora, Griqua and 'Bastards'.

2. The Khoikhoi language spoken by the Kora people; KORANNA sense 2; KORAQUA sense 2.

1824 [see KORAQUA sense 2]. **1881** *Encycl. Brit.* XII. 312 The Kora dialect, spoken by the Korannas, or Koraquas, dwelling about the middle and upper part of the Orange, Vaal, and Modder Rivers. **1928** E.H.L. SCHWARZ *Kalahari & its Native Races* 185 In Kora, as in Namaqua, there is the singular, dual and plural, with some interesting modifications from normal Hottentot. **1936** J.A. ENGELBRECHT *Korana* 197 A complete linguistic survey of all the areas in which Kora .. is still spoken at the present day could not be undertaken. **1968** *Encycl. Brit.* XI. 751 Hottentot is the European name for the Nama, Kora and other languages comprising 14 or 15 subdivisions of the main Hottentot speech. *c*1980 *S. Afr. 1979: Off. Yrbk* (Dept of Info.) 101 *Khoe-(kowab) or Hottentot Languages.* This language family includes Nama with Dama, Xiri (Griqua), !Ora (Korana), Hai-n//um (Heikom), [etc.].

kora(a)n var. KORHAAN.

Korachoqua var. GORACHOUQUA.

Koranna /kɔˈrænə, kɔˈranə/ *n. hist.* Also **Coran, Coran(n)a, Corran(n)a, Corunna, Gorona, Korana, Qoranna.** Pl. unchanged, or **-s.** [See Vedder quot. 1928.]

1. A colonial name for a member of the Kora peoples: see KORA (sense 1). Also *attrib.*

1801 J. BARROW *Trav.* I. 403 The country to the eastward of the Roggeveld, is inhabited by different hordes of Bosjesmans. One of these, called the *Koranas*, dwelling on the right bank of the Orange river, .. is represented as a very formidable tribe of people. **1822** W.J. BURCHELL *Trav.* I. 345 The people usually called Koranas, are a numerous, and distinct, tribe of the Hottentot race. **1827** G. THOMPSON *Trav.* II. 29 The Korannas are a race of pure Hottentots, who have attached themselves to the vicinage of the great River. **1831** *Graham's Town Jrnl* 30 Dec. 3 At a Koranna kraal .., the first cases of Small Pox presented themselves. **1834** [see KORA sense 1]. **1841** B. SHAW *Memorials* 304 Thus lived and thus died Jan Kapitein, a converted Coranna, the fruit of missionary labour, and a crown of rejoicing to the friends of missions in the day of the Lord. **1867** *Blue Bk for Col. 1866* JJ4, In the northern part, adjacent to the Orange river, several robberies and assaults have been committed by bands of Korannas upon traders and others. **1871** [see *clicking* (CLICK)]. **1881** [see KORA sense 2]. **1899** *Grocott's Daily Mail* 12 July 2 The Bushmen and Korannas are a nomadic people, and live for the greater part of the year in the Kalahari, existing upon the Tsame and wild potatoes of the desert. **1905** G.W. STOW *Native Races of S. Afr.* The great tribe of the Koranas took its name from !Kora, an ancient chief under whom they had formerly lived. **1924** S.G. MILLIN *God's Step-Children* 14 Although he had been told that these were a tribe called Korannas, he had not before realised that there were different kinds of Hottentots. **1928** E.H.L. SCHWARZ *Kalahari & its Native Races* 182 Kora's successor .. realizing the hopelessness of exposing .. his men to the bullets from the guns of the Dutch, trekked away northwards, settling eventually on the Orange River, where his tribe became the Koranas. **1928** H. VEDDER in *Native Tribes of S.W. Afr.* 113 Gorona, also written Goraqua, Gorachouqua, whose real name is !Khora, out of which Koranna has been made through the omission of the click and the addition of the suffix for the 3rd pers., plur. **1930** S.T. PLAATJE *Mhudi* (1975) 63 Two of the Qoranna men could speak a few Sechuana words. **1930** [see GORACHOUQUA]. **1930** *Friend* 25 Aug. 14 A Free State Koranna farm labourer, was charged before the magistrate with malicious injury to property. **1955** [see KORA]. **1961** *Encycl. S. Afr.* 278 Today pure Korannas are almost extinct. **1961** L.E. VAN ONSELEN *Trekboer* 112 These Koranna Hottentots were a fierce clan led by a succession of halfbreed captains. **1975** *Sunday Times* 12 Oct. (TV Mag.) 10 The supremacy of Griqua, Koranna and Bergenaars dwindled during the 1830s. **1975** *Std Encycl. of Sn Afr.* VI. 444 *Korana*, Nomadic Hottentot tribe. The name is most probably derived from that of a famous chief, Kora or Gora, or possibly Ora, originally a leader of the Gorachouqua, who .. became the first big chief of the Korana ... Actually the name Korana may not even be derived from that of a chief, but may signify that this tribe was 'the real thing', representing the thoroughbred Hottentots.

2. KORA sense 2.

1835 A. SMITH *Diary* (1940) II. 282 The Griqua and Coranna languages are nearly allied, but in some words there is considerable difference. **1990** *Frontline* Mar.-Apr. 34 Prieska means 'place of the lost she-goat' in Coranna. 'Coranna?' I ask the lady. She studies the word in the booklet. 'I suppose that's Boesmantaal,' she says.

Koraqua /kɔˈrakwa/ *n. Obs. exc. hist.* Also **Goraqua.** [Khoikhoin, *!Khora* (see KORA) + *-qua* man, see quot. 1822.]

1. KORA sense 1.

1822 W.J. BURCHELL *Trav.* I. 345 The name by which they themselves call their nation, is Kora, or Koraqua. The adjunct qua, signifying man or men in most of the Hottentot dialects, is, in some cases, as in this, used or omitted indifferently. The word Koraqua means a man wearing shoes, as distinguished from sandals. **1834** [see KORA sense 1]. **1881** [see KORA sense 2]. **1928** [see Vedder quot. at KORANNA sense 1].

2. KORA sense 2.

1824 W.J. BURCHELL *Trav.* II. 251 The following specimen of the *Kora*, or *Koraqua, dialect*, was obtained.

Korea /kəˈrɪə, kɔˈrɪə/ *n. slang.* [See quot. 1959.] In township Eng.: a home-distilled spirituous liquor.

[**1951** *Drum* Nov. 10 Nearly every hut there is a shebeen — specialising in 'Barberton' and 'Korean' booze.] **1952** 'SKAPPIE' in *Ibid.* Nov. 7 Of late, some Eastern folk have been brewing a very potent and harmful ersatz brandy which goes by the name of Korea. **1959** L. LONGMORE *Dispossessed* 220 False labels and correctly trade marked bottles give all the appearance of authenticity. Larger quantities are contained in thirty-six gallon barrels. Such types of spirits are called 'Korea' because they are manufactured by Chinese traders. **1972** *Drum* 8 Apr. 23 Qash reeled back as though he had drunk a mixture of baberton, korea and chillis. **1985** D. BIKITSHA in *Sunday Times* 1 Sept. 4 Will they succumb to offers of doctored liquor or 'Korea' (Mickey Finn), as we call it in the townships.

korenkrekel var. KORINGKRIEK.

korhaan /kɔˈrɑːn, kɔrˈhɑːn/ *n.* Also **coran(ne)**, **corha(a)n**, **khora(a)n**, **koerhaan**, **koor haan**, **koor-haen**, **koor(h)an**, **kora(a)n**, **korha(e)n**, **korhane**, **korr(h)an**, **kor-rhaan**, **korr-haen**. Pl. unchanged, **-s**, or (formerly) **-hanen**. [Imitative of the bird's call; transf. use of Du. *korhaan* or *knorhaan* a name for the male of the black grouse *Lyrurus tetrix*, fr. *korren* to coo + *haan* cock; cf. KNORHAAN.]

1.a. Any of several species of bird of the Otididae, esp. *Eupodotis cafra* (the *black korhaan*, see sense b below); CORE-HEN; KNORHAAN sense 1 a; *vlak(te)pou*, see POU sense 2.

1776 F. MASSON in *Phil. Trans. of Royal Soc.* LXVI. 317 The fields abounded also with korhaans (a kind of bustard), partridges, hares &c and great flocks of ostriches. **1786** G. FORSTER tr. *A. Sparrman's Voy. to Cape of G.H.* I. 153 *Korr-haen* is the name of a kind of *Otis*, which conceals itself perfectly, with great art, till one comes pretty near to it, when on a sudden it soars aloft, and almost perpendicularly into the air, with a sharp, hasty, and quavering scream, of the repetition of *Korrh, Korrh*, which is an alarm to the animals throughout the whole neighbourhood. **1795** C.R. HOPSON tr. *C.P. Thunberg's Trav.* I. 148 Difficult as it is to come within reach of it, we at last shot a *korhaan*, a bird which in its flights cries *kok-karri, kok-carri*. **1800** G. YONGE in S.D. Naudé *Kaapse Plakkaatboek Deel V* (1950) 208 In order to define what animals in this Colony, come under the description of game the following are to be considered as such, hares, partridges, pheasants, korans, wild peacocks, [etc.]. **1819** J.F. STEPHENS *Continuation of Shaw's Gen. Zoology* XI. 451 [*Otis afra*] Native of the country north of the Cape of Good Hope, where it is called *Korhane*, or *Knorhaan*, from its cry. **1822** W.J. BURCHELL *Trav.* I. 186 A small species of Otis, or bustard, called Korhaan .. (or Knorhaan), a name which is given also to two or three other kinds of Otis. **1827** G. THOMPSON *Trav.* II. 99 No living thing to relieve the monotony of the scenery, except the korhaan, .. screaming forth its hoarse, discordant cry. **1841** B. SHAW *Memorials* 65 Mrs. S. had for some time been indisposed, and could eat but little; I therefore, occasionally pursued hares, partridges, doves, khorans, *c* **1850** R.G.G. CUMMING *Hunter's Life* I. 49, I saw and shot the black koran, an excellent game-bird, allied to the bustards, so abundant throughout South Africa. **1856** R.E.E. WILMOT *Diary* (1984) 132 Here .. we find the various kinds of *coran* or *koraan*, a fine specimen of game bird much like a large grouse in general appearance. **1860** A.W. DRAYSON *Sporting Scenes* 59 Two species of bustards were common; viz: the coran and the pouw, both excellent eating. *c***1881** A. DOUGLASS *Ostrich Farming* 146 It was discovered that the guinea-fowls, pows, corhans, fowls, and many of the small birds throughout the country had contracted the disease, and were spreading it in all directions. **1912** *Report for 1911* (Dept of Justice) 107 Korhaan were the most plentiful of the game birds, and did a considerable amount of damage to the crops. **1913** C. PETTMAN *Africanderisms* 271 *Knorhaan* or *Korhaan*, .. *Otis afra* .. is exceedingly noisy when disturbed, and well deserves the name of 'Scolding-cock'; its raucous cry has been fairly described as resembling a 'shrill-voiced woman's nagging heard afar, so that the words are not intelligible'. **1920** F.C. CORNELL *Glamour of Prospecting* 79 Most frequent and .. annoying .. was the koorhaan, whose irritating croaking cackle could be heard on all sides, and which seemed to take a mischievous delight in disturbing other game of a less suspicious nature. **1936** L.G. GREEN *Secret Afr.* 229 Hunters in the North-West Cape usually open the gizzards of the large game birds, the paauw and korhaan, in the hope of finding diamonds. *c***1936** *S. & E. Afr. Yr Bk & Guide* 1105 The korhaan is a bustard and varies in size from a pheasant to a good-sized fowl. It is a great runner and fairly abundant everywhere in South Africa. **1942** S. CLOETE *Hill of Doves* 108 A korhaan, its white breast red in the sunset, flung chattering into the sky. **1985** *Style* Oct. 90 There's a rich bird life .. ; from the korhaans, blue cranes and secretary-birds to the small multi-hued rollers.

b. With distinguishing epithet denoting a particular species of korhaan: **Barrow's korhaan** *obs.*, *white-bellied korhaan*, see below; **black korhaan**, *Eupodotis afra*, the most common species of korhaan; **black-bellied korhaan**, *E. melenogaster*; **blue korhaan**, *E. caerulescens*; **bont korhaan** *obs.* [Du. *bont* variegated, see BONT], an unidentified species of korhaan, prob. the *black korhaan* (see above); **bush korhaan** [tr. Afk. *boskorhaan*, *bos* bush], *red-crested korhaan*, see below; **Karoo korhaan** [see KAROO], *vaal korhaan* (see below); **red-crested korhaan**, *E. ruficrista; red-crested knorhaan*, see KNORHAAN sense 1 b; **vaal korhaan**, *E. vigorsii; dikkop -, vaal knorhaan*, see KNORHAAN sense 1 b; **white-bellied korhaan**, *E. cafra*; POU sense 1 c; **white-quilled (black) korhaan** or **white-winged (black) korhaan**, *black korhaan*, see above.

1923 HAAGNER & IVY *Sketches* 215 **Barrow's Korhaan** (*Otis borrovii*) can be distinguished .. by the patches of tawny on either side of the chest and the white abdomen. **1936** E.L. GILL *First Guide to S. Afr. Birds* 154 A related species is: *Barrow's Korhaan, Eupodotis cafra*, in which all the colours are much paler, and only the male has any blue, a pale grey-blue band down the front of the neck. Underparts white. **1823** T. PHILIPPS *Lett.* (1960) 191 We gave up shooting ... A **black Korrhan** was our only success. **1866** J. LEYLAND *Adventures* 40, I also shot .. a smaller species, called the Black Koran by the Colonists. **1923** [see quot. at *white-bellied korhaan* below]. **1962** *Bokmakierie* June 20 Black korhaan is everywhere and every other bush has its ant-eating chat. **1980** J.O. OLIVER *Beginner's Guide to our Birds* 53 In spring, male Black Korhaans fly noisily over the veld and then land with their wings held high and their yellow legs dangling. **1992** T. VAN RENSBURG in *S. Afr. Panorama* Mar.-Apr. 11 Birds are plentiful and species such as the black korhaan, the blue crane, guinea-fowl and other grasslands birds are typical of the area. **1992** [see quot. at *white-quilled korhaan* below]. **1923** HAAGNER & IVY *Sketches* 214 The **Black-bellied Korhaan** (*Otis melanogaster*) is easily distinguished by the characteristic indicated by its trivial name, viz. the black under parts. **1978** MCLACHLAN & LIVERSIDGE *Roberts Birds of S. Afr.* 227 Black-bellied Korhaan ... frequents the savannas and even rather marshy ground bordering them. **1835** A. STEEDMAN *Wanderings* I. 135 We found for the first time several of the **blue korran**, a species of *Otis*, which has only been recently described. **1866** J. LEYLAND *Adventures* 34 On route I shot a Blue Koran, (Otis Caerulescens,) at 150 yards, with ball. *Ibid.* 40, I also shot several of the Blue Koran, or Leaden-tinted Bustard. **1964** P.A. CLANCEY *Birds of Natal & Zululand* 143 The blue korhaan occurs sparingly in the interior of Natal. **1873** 'F.R.' in A.M.L. Robinson *Sel. Articles from Cape Monthly Mag.* (1978) 105 In the Karoo, .. the **bont** or particoloured **korhaan** becomes the *vaal* or coloured one. **1896** H.A. BRYDEN *Tales of S. Afr.* 250 The **bush koorhaan** .. are playing their strange aerial pranks. **1940** V. POHL *Bushveld Adventures* 57 We had gone about fifty yards when a bush korhaan suddenly flew out from almost beneath my feet. **1963** P.J. SCHOEMAN in C.M. Booysen *Tales of S. Afr.* 198 He heard a whistle. It was Xan-bib, the bush Korhaan. **1838** J.E. ALEXANDER *Exped. into Int.* II. 149 The **Karoo Koran**, or small red bustard, flew up here and there to tempt us, but the cold took sporting out of us. **1980** J.O. OLIVER *Beginner's Guide to our Birds* 53 *Karoo Korhaan*, Plain coloured .. these korhaans are generally seen in pairs or threes, walking over dry, stony ground where there are scattered bushes. **1990** A. CRAIG in *Birding in S. Afr.* Vol.42 No.1, 4 The Karoo Korhaan *Eupodotis vigorsii*. **1937** M. ALSTON *Wanderings* 224 We saw the gom pauw and the white-quilled and the **red-crested korhaan**. **1975** *Dict. of Eng. Usage in Sn Afr.* 143 *Red-crested korhaan*, .. bird commonly seen in the bushveld; the male has a characteristic red crest and is known for its vertical tumblings in the air. **1857** E.L. LAYARD in *Cape Monthly Mag.* I. June 386 The **Vaal Korhaan**, recently presented by J. Rose Innes, Esq., of Riversdale, is a valuable addition to the collection of birds. **1899** R.B. & J.D.S. WOODWARD *Natal Birds* 175 Pink Bustard — (*Heterotorax vigorsi*). This bird is called the 'Vaal Koran'. **1900** B. MITFORD *Aletta* 149 How many birds have you got? 'Brace of partridge and two koorhaans. One is *vaal* koorhaan, and a fine one too.' **1955** V. DE KOCK *Fun They Had* 160 The Vaal Korhaan .. can be, as Bryden found, 'very uncertain birds' to shoot. **1978** MCLACHLAN & LIVERSIDGE *Roberts Birds of S. Afr.* 156 **White-bellied Korhaan** ... The only small Korhaans with a white belly in both sexes ... A bird of open grassveld. **1923** HAAGNER & IVY *Sketches* 213 The Black Korhaan .. is confined to the Cape Province, being replaced north of the Orange River by the **White-quilled Korhaan** (*O[tis] afroides*), which .. has the primary wing feathers *white* on the *inner* web, only the tips being black. **1937** [see quot. at *red-crested korhaan* above]. **1992** B. RYAN in *Sunday Times* 26 Apr. 14 The recreated Whitewinged Black Korhaan is .. already being referred to in some birding circles .. as the White-quilled Korhaan. **1993** [see quot. at *white-winged korhaan* below]. **1992** B. RYAN in *Sunday Times* 26 Apr. 14 The biggest change for Transvaal birders is that what they have known as the Black Korhaan — common in grasslands throughout the Transvaal, Free State, Northern Cape and Botswana — has become the **Whitewinged Black Korhaan** because the Black Korhaan is now held to be restricted to the Western Cape. **1993** G.L. MACLEAN *Roberts' Birds of Sn Afr.* 211 *Black Korhaan* ... *Status*: Very common resident. Populations outside of sw Cape winter-rainfall area have white in remiges [*sc.* flight feathers of wing]; may be separate species, Whitequilled (or Whitewinged) Korhaan *Eupodotis afraoides*.

2. *rare.* KNORHAAN sense 2 a.

1913 W.W. THOMPSON *Sea Fisheries of Cape Col.* 12 It was so easy to catch them that one could not quickly enough throw the hooks into the water in order to draw them up again with 'Korhanen', red, spotted, and other fish.

kori /ˈkɔːri/ *n.* Also **khori**. [SeTswana *kgori*.] In full ***kori bustard***: the very large bustard *Ardeotis kori* of the Otididae, greyish-brown in colour, with neck and breast finely barred in black and white; *bush -, wild pou*, see POU sense 2; GOMPOU; GUMPAAUW; POU sense 1 a.

1822 W.J. BURCHELL *Trav.* I. 393 We shot a large bird of the bustard kind ... The present species, which is called *Kori* in the Sichuana language, measured, in extent of wing, not less than seven feet ... A representation of the head of the Kori Bustard .. is given at the end of this chapter. **1846** R. MOFFAT *Missionary Labours* 93 Here we remained the whole day, and, to supply our wants, shot two *khoris*, called by the colonists, wild peacocks, a species of bustard. **1847** 'A BENGALI' *Notes on Cape of G.H.* 81 On the Gariep is a very large bird called the 'Kori-bustard', which is said to be better eating than the turkey. *a*1867 C.J. ANDERSSON *Notes of Trav.* (1875) 31 The Kori Bustard (*Eupodotis Kori*, Burch), usually called the '*wilde pauw*,' or wild peacock, a name, however, very wrongly applied; .. as it also attaches to the *Balearica Regulorum*, or southern-crowned crane. **1872** L. LLOYD tr. *Andersson's Notes Birds of Damara Land* 258 Kori Bustard ... This splendid bird is found throughout the year in Damara. **1889** H.A. BRYDEN *Kloof & Karroo* 306 Among the bustards stands pre-eminent the great Kori bustard — the gom paauw of the Dutch colonists. **1891** R. WARD *Sportsman's Handbk* 123 Kori Bustard (Otis Kori), the largest of the genus, upwards of five feet high, very fine game, found especially in the countries on the banks of the Orange river. **1923** HAAGNER & IVY *Sketches* 215 The .. largest of all the Bustards is the stately Gom Paauw or Kori Bustard (*Otis kori*), which has a total length of nearly 5 feet, and weighs about 30 lbs. **1936** E.L. GILL *First Guide to S. Afr. Birds* 150 *Kori Bustard*, .. Said to have been shot weighing 50 or even 60 lbs., but anything over 30lbs is a large male. **1966** E. PALMER *Plains of Camdeboo* 209 The Kori bustard, a dweller of the desert or semi-desert, a gigantic creature weighing up to fifty pounds or more, heavier than the great bustard of Eurasia which is usually held to be the heaviest bird of the air. It has a wing span of up to eight feet, and it stands nearly five feet high. **1972** *Etosha Nat. Park (brochure)*, Birds seen by tourists every day are ostriches, kori bustards, black korhaan, guinea fowls, pheasants, partridges, blue cranes. **1973** P. GINN *Birds Afield* 28 A .. Kori Bustard has to run across the veld to get enough speed to become airborne. **1980** J.O. OLIVER *Beginner's Guide to our Birds* 53 Kori Bustards prefer to walk over the veld with long strides rather than to fly. **1991** *Best of S. Afr. Short Stories* (Reader's Digest Assoc.) 11 Another game bird favoured by hunters in the Karoo .. was the kori bustard (*Ardeotis kori*), often called the *gompou* or *paauw*.

koringkriek /ˈkʊərəŋkrik/ *n.* Also **korenkrekel**, **koorn kriek**. Pl. **-s**, **-krieke** /-krikə/. [Afk., fr. Du. *koren* corn + *krekel* cricket, or *kriek(en)* to chirp.] Any of several species of armoured ground cricket of the Tettigoniidae, esp. *Eugaster longipes*.

[**1864** T. BAINES *Explor. in S.-W. Afr.* 376 A kind of wingless insect somewhat between a locust and a cricket .. which I have heard in the Cape called koren beestje (a little corn beast).] **1911** J.D.F. GILCHRIST *S. Afr. Zoology* 120 The 'Korenkrekels,' e.g., *Eugaster* .. are, however, common enough; these are rather stoutly-built insects with the first pair of wings much reduced and the second absent. **1913** C. PETTMAN *Africanderisms* 277 *Koorn kriek*, .. *Eugaster longipes*, an insect belonging to the *Locustidae*; it is very destructive to pumpkins, mealie cobs, etc., and does at times great damage to crops. **1950** W. ROSE *Reptiles & Amphibians* 157 If handled carelessly when first caught it [*sc.* the Crag Lizard] can inflict a severe nip, its jaws being powerful enough to crush up even those spiney-armoured wingless locusts known as Korenkrekels. **1954** S.H. SKAIFE *Afr. Insect Life* 30 Many people in South Africa fear the koringkrieks because they have the reputation of being poisonous. **1956** D. JACOBSON *Dance in Sun* 135 When a sleepy koringkriek trilled one long note the sound came through the air as sharp as a drill. **1966** E. PALMER *Plains of Camdeboo* 13 The koringkrieks lurching on immense and crooked legs. **1977** F.G. BUTLER *Karoo Morning* 41 Of the many new insects that I met .. there was one I .. could not warm to: the koringkriek. He is corn coloured, his bloated abdomen is bigger than an acorn, he is rough and spiky all over like a lobster, he twiddles sinister feelers at you .. and worse than all these, he is a cannibal. **1986** SCHOLTZ & HOLM *Insects* 83 The Hetrodinae (armoured ground crickets, koringkrieke ..) are endemic to Africa being most abundant in arid areas in southern Africa. **1987** M. POLAND *Train to Doringbult* 138 He reminded Elsa of a *koringkriek*, for he sat with his hands on his knees, his elbows stuck out, his shoulders hunched, his head thrust forward. **1994** M. ANDERSON et al. in *Afr. Wildlife* Vol.48 No.2, 18 In the northern Cape, koringkrieke are always present during summer, albeit usually in low numbers ... With the approaching winter, the koringkrieke disappear as quickly as they emerged from their dormancy beneath the ground.

Korporaal var. CORPORAAL.

korran var. KORHAAN.

korree var. KARRIE *n.*²

‖**korrel** /ˈkɔr(ə)l/ *n.* [Afk., grape; grain; bead.] **1.** A grape.

1970 S. SPARKS *Informant, Fort Beaufort* Please give me a korrel from your bunch of grapes (one grape). **1982** J. KRIGE in *Staffrider* Vol.5 No.2, 20 Doekvoet's father was standing on a ladder in the vat, stirring the korrels, as he so often did.

2. *comb.* **korrelkonfyt** /-kɔnˌfeɪt/ [Afk., *konfyt* jam, preserve], grape jam; also dim. form **korreltjiekonfyt** /ˈkɔr(ə)lkikɔnˌfeɪt/ [see -IE]; **korrelkop** /-kɔp/ *offensive*, pl. **-koppe** /-kɔpə/, [Afk., (*kop* head), a quarrelsome person; a head with woolly tufts of hair], one with PEPPERCORN hair; also *attrib.*

1983 *Sunday Times* 6 Mar. (Mag. Sect.) 16 **Korrelkonfyt** again made from hanepoot grapes, is traditionally eaten with baked snoek and sweet potatoes. **1984** *Fair Lady* 30 May 176 So we do not have *korreltjiekonfyt* or *bredies* and we do not make a Barbara Cartland romance out of a liking for the rather dull galjoen. **1988** *Ibid.* 16 Mar. 14 Grapes are delicious — fresh, pickled or in the form of *korrelkonfyt* or homemade wine. **1990** *Handbill, Die Muisbosskerm Restaurant, Lambert's Bay*, Some of the West Coast's most sought after seafood dishes fresh from the sea. 'Bakbrood' straight from the oven, fresh farm butter and the region's famous Hanepoort 'korrelkonfyt'. **1958** I. VAUGHAN *Diary* 12 Hans is a **korrelkop** bushman. **1961** D. BEE *Children of Yesterday* 11 The fair boy looked up .. at the dark one, .. his eyes narrowed ... 'Gamat!' he cried, his voice shrill, teeth clenched, 'Coloured! I'll kill you for that! Yellow korrelkop!'

korrel /ˈkɔrəl/ *v. trans.* Also **korral**. [Afk., to pick (from a bunch of grapes).] To select and pick (a grape) from a bunch.

1896 M.A. CAREY-HOBSON *At Home in Tvl* 378, I korralled half-a-dozen grapes this morning for poor old Hans. **1970** S.E. NATHAM *Informant, Cape Town* Korrel. Pick, e.g. 'To korrel grapes from a bunch'. **1970** S. SPARKS *Informant, Fort Beaufort* Let us go to the vines and 'korrel' some grapes.

kor-rhaan, **korr-haen**, **korrhan** varr. KORHAAN.

kos *n.*¹ var. INKOSI *n.*

‖**kos** /kɔs/ *n.*² Also **cos(t)**, **koss**, **kost**. [Afk., fr. Du. *kost* food.]

1. Food, victuals. Also *attrib.* See also PADKOS, VELDKOS.

1828 J. PHILIP *Researches* I. 156 'Lebricht Aris' .. engaged with the Boor .. to work six months on his farm, at two dollars (three shillings) per month, and his *cost*, (victuals,) on condition that the Boor should immediately discharge his debt. **1840** *Inn sign, Farmer Peck's (nr Muizenberg, Cape)* in A. Gordon-Brown *S. Afr. Heritage* (1965) Lekker kost as much as you please, excellent beds without any fleas. **1845** W.N. IRWIN *Echoes of Past* (1927) 235 I .. take the opportunity of the first off saddle to stretch myself in the Shade, and, while my orderly sits Smoking or Cooking some Cos (flesh), read your welcome epistle. **1850** J.D. LEWINS Diary. 20 Sept., People cutting rushes & Ponas grumbling for kost. All he gets from me won't choke him, damn his eyes. **1899** G.H. RUSSELL *Under Sjambok* 259 But drink, Baasie, drink, and the koss will soon be ready. **1900** A.W. CARTER *Informant, Ladybrand* 8 Mar. 14 Most of the men had had nothing to eat or drink from Tuesday night and their first cry was 'Kos' — Pohl gave away everything he had but of course it was not nearly enough and those that came late got nothing. **1910** D. FAIRBRIDGE *That Which Hath Been* (1913) 80 Mevrouw seated him on her right hand at the long table, creaking under the weight of *lekker kost*, served in deep dishes of blue and white Nankin. **1966** I. VAUGHAN *These Were my Yesterdays* 4 At each outspan a new team of horses and a new driver took over, while we ate a picnic meal packed in what we called the 'kos box'. **1982** [see GOOSIE sense 2]. **1984** *Sunday Times* 8 July (Lifestyle) 9 The kos, hardly five star, consists of a reasonable potato hash, cabbage, a vegetarian concoction, plain salad and a fish dish which ran out. **1985** *Rand Daily Mail* 15 Mar. (Funfinder) 10 Closer to home-styled *kos* — Leipoldts, named after the South African poet C. Louis Leipoldt, is now open on Sundays.

2. *comb.* **kos geld** [Du. *geld* money], an allowance for food; but see also quot. 1857; **koshuis** /-hœɪs/ pl. **-huise**, [Afk., *huis* house], a boarding house or school; also *attrib.*; **kos-mandjie** /-maɪŋki/ [Afk., *mandjie* basket], a food-basket.

1795 'J.H.C.' in G.M. Theal *Rec. of Cape Col.* (1897) I. 217 What he received was an allowance .. for his maintenance, .. 30,000 Dutch florins per annum, together with his **Costgeld**, the whole amounting .. to 1,116 dollars 5 schellings and 2 stivers per month. **1857** J.M. ORPEN *Hist. of Basutos* 73 'Kost geld' (food money) is the slang term among the Boers for the purchase-money of a slave, and is supposed to mean payment for the food the seller has been at the expense of providing for the slave before the sale. **1926** P.W. LAIDLER *Tavern of Ocean* 51 The soldiers in Nassau bastion .. received weekly about six pounds of bread, and an allowance of one penny three farthings *kost geld* with which to buy other food. **1977** F.G. BUTLER *Karoo Morning* 132 Some of them came in wagons .. wearing old-fashioned but spotless clothes — to hand over their children to the free **Koshuis**. **1986** *Personality* 1 Sept. 34 By the time they get back to their *koshuis* dinner is long since over — but they've still got to eat. **1988** V.R. JACOBS in *Style* Apr. 6, I once lived in one of the 'Residences' so prevalent in Pretoria — a cross between an hotel and a boarding house with a dash of the old '*koshuis*' thrown in. **1989** *Sunday Times* 22 Oct. 23 More Conservative Party mutterings, this time about Free State *koshuise* being opened up. **1913** D. FAIRBRIDGE *Piet of Italy* 23 Everyone was packed into the Cape cart waiting at the door, the **kost-mandje** was roped on behind. *Ibid.* 24 Shouldering the *kost-mandje* as lightly as though the solid food inside were feathers. *Ibid.* 30 Come, Gamdin, it is time for lieffin and our *kost-mandje* holds enough for twelve. **1972** L.G. GREEN *When Journey's Over* 7, I can remember the days of the *kosmandjie* and the station coffee stalls.

Kosa, **Kósa** varr. XHOSA.

kose var. INKOSI *n.*

kosi *int.* var. ENKOSI *int.*

kosi *n.*¹ var. INKOSI *n.*

kosi *n.*² var. KGOSI.

koskas /ˈkɔskas/ *n.* Pl. **-te**, **-se**. [Afk., *kos* food + *kas* cupboard.] A low cupboard used in the past for storing food. See also KAS sense 1.

1971 BARAITSER & OBHOLZER *Cape Country Furn.* 261 Country koskas with one gauze door ... In modern usage, the word koskas refers to small cupboards irrespective of whether they incorporate a method of ventilation or not. There seems to be no doubt that some small cupboards without ventilation were used as koskaste. **1972** *Grocott's Mail* 19 Sept. (*advt*) 4 Yellowwood Kitchen Dresser, Yellowwood Koskasse; a large number of Stinkwood chairs. **1973** M.A. COOK *Cape Kitchen* Glossary, *Food Cupboard*, Low wooden cupboard usually with two doors in which food was kept. Also known as Koskas. **1974** *Weekend Post* 27 Oct. 23 (*advt*) Yellowwood Table; Yellowwood Washstand; Yellowwood Koskas. **1974** *S. Afr. Panorama* Sept. 38 The trestle table and 'bakkis' (baking trough), wall shelves and 'koskaste' (store cupboards). **1975** *Ibid.* Jan. 15 A pine 'koskas' (food cupboard). **1980** *Rand Daily Mail* 4 Dec. (Eve) 12 You should be able to pick up a riempie chair, a wakis or a koskas for anything from R75 to about R400. **1987** P. SULLIVAN in *Living* June 24 Amongst the Africana furniture .. is a *koskas* dated around 1720. Not only is it the most valuable article in the house, but it is the only known example of its kind.

‖**kosmos** /ˈkɒzmɒs, ˈkɔzmɔs/ *n*. [Afk., ad. Eng. *cosmos*.] The pink or white flowering annual, *Cosmos bipinnatus* of the Asteraceae, commonly called 'cosmos'.

[1971 C. CLAASSEN in *Std Encycl. of Sn Afr.* III. 447 *Cosmos*, Kosmos. Mieliepes (. . *Cosmos bipinnatus* . .) . . . Although it is a weed in South Africa, the fields covered by these colourful flowers are a beautiful sight in autumn.] 1988 W. ODENDAAL in Bunn & Taylor *From S. Afr.* 113, I wandered and dashed and hid among the kosmos, and tall winter grass. 1990 *Weekly Mail* 4 May 23 A small table with a large vase of 'kosmos' on top. 1991 H. AULT *Informant, Port Alfred* The khaki-bush and dubbeltjies next to the rondavel will have to be skoffeled and the ground levelled . . . We'll leave the kosmos as it's quite pretty.

koss var. KOS.

Kossa var. XHOSA.

kossiter /ˈkusətə(r), ˈkɒ-/ *n*. [See KOEKSISTER.] A sweetmeat similar to a KOEKSISTER, but made in a ball; BOLLA sense 2.

1890 A.G. HEWITT *Cape Cookery* 48 Kossuters . . . Roll it [*sc.* the mixture] out and make it into balls the size of a walnut; pop the balls into a deep saucepan of boiling lard. 1990 R. GOOL *Cape Town Coolie* 44 She . . circulated bowls of kossiters, mebos, sourfigs and other sweetmeats.

kost var. KOS.

koster /ˈkɔstə(r)/ *n*. [Du., verger, beadle.]

1. The verger or caretaker of a DUTCH REFORMED church.

1786 G. FORSTER tr. *A. Sparrman's Voy. to Cape of G.H.* I. 67 (Pettman), A little further on lived a *koster* or sexton, a set of people that are more respected by the colonists than with us. 1909 *George & Knysna Herald* 11 Aug. 3, I have to pay the Predikant and the Koster their fees, then there would have to be swell clothes and carts and eetmaal . . no, I prefer the court to the Koster. 1934 *Week-End Advertiser* 10 Mar. (Swart), After the funeral address the koster requests the bearers to bring the corpse forward, and the coffin is placed with its two extremities on the seats of two chairs until the sterflys is read by the koster. 1951 L.G. GREEN *Grow Lovely* 30 Cape Town has only one trilogy of eighteenth-century buildings — the Dutch Lutheran Church with the koster's (sexton's) house on one side and the Martin Melck, formerly the parsonage, on the other. 1957 — *Beyond City Lights* 23 Paarl said farewell shortly after World War II to an oak planted in the main street in 1824 by Mr J.J. Luttig, *koster* of the Dutch Reformed Church. 1991 H. AULT *Informant, Port Alfred* We're thinking of asking the dominee, the landdros, the diakens and ouderlinge, and the koster. 1993 C. LOUW in *Weekly Mail* 4 June 8 Walking up and down like a Dopper *koster* . . , making sure that everything was in order.

‖**2**. *comb. hist*. **kosterhuis** /-hœɪs/ [Afk., *huis* house], a house provided for a beadle; **koster school** [Du. (pl. *scholen*)], see quot. 1934.

1873 W.L. SAMMONS in A.M.L. Robinson *Sel. Articles from Cape Monthly Mag.* (1978) 267 The Kosterhuis stood on the site of the present Groot Kerkgebou and slightly in front of the Church. 1934 C.P. SWART *Supplement to Pettman*. 96 *Koster Scholen*, . . In the nineteenth century schools in sparsely populated areas were run by Church clerks who received an annual government grant of £60 and a plot of land. 1934 M.E. McKERRON *Hist. of Educ.* 18 Schools run by Church clerks, and known as Koster Scholen (i.e. beadle schools) were instituted.

kostgelt see GELD sense b.

kotch var. COTCH.

kotla var. KGOTLA.

koudou var. KUDU.

koup var. KOP.

kouseband *n. obs.* Also **kousband**, and with initial capital. [S. Afr. Du., fr. Du. *kouseband* garter, fr. *kouse* socks + *band* band.] GARTER SNAKE. Also **kousebandje** [see -IE].

Although *kouseband(slang)* is current in Afrikaans, the term is obsolete in S. Afr. Eng., having been replaced by 'garter snake'.

1789 [see GARTER SNAKE]. 1819 G.M. KEITH *Voy.* 71 There are six species about the Cape, namely: the horned snake, . . the Kouseband or garter snake. 1849 A. SMITH *Illust. of Zoo. of S. Afr.: Reptilia* Appendix 21, *Elaps Hygeae* . . . Kouseband of the Cape Colonists. Individuals of this species are found in all parts of Southern Africa. 1860 J. SANDERSON in *Jrnl of Royal Geog. Soc.* XXX. 237 Within a fortnight I saw some seven or eight more of the ringhals, and three or four of a small brown kind called the 'kousband' [*printed* kousbaud] or garter-snake. 1913 C. PETTMAN *Africanderisms* 280 Kousbandje, . . *Elaps Hygae* . . . A small, vicious snake, marked in transverse bands of scarlet and black, is thus named in the Midland districts.

kousi var. INKOSI *n*.

Koussie, Koza(s) pl. forms of XHOSA.

KP var. KAAPEE.

kraaibos /ˈkraɪbɔs/ *n*. Formerly also **kra(i)je bosch**. [Afk. (earlier S. Afr. Du.), fr. Du. *kraai* crow + *bosch* bush.] Any of several species of small shrub, esp. of the genera *Diospyros* of the Ebenaceae, and *Heteromorpha* of the Apiaceae. Occas. also **kraaibossie** [see -IE].

1795 C.R. HOPSON tr. *C.P. Thunberg's Trav.* I. 149 The black berries of a bush called *kraije-bosch*, or crow-bush, were greedily devoured by the crows at the Cape. 1809 J. MACKRILL *Diary*. 60 Kraje bosch, Royena glabra grows near the Cape town. 1966 C.A. SMITH *Common Names* 310 Kraaibos, *Diospyros austro-africana var. austro-africana*; *D. glabra* . . : Small, rigid bushily branched shrubs . . . The dried and pulverized roots were used by the Hottentot as a purgative. *Heteromorpha trifoliata* . . . A tallish shrub . . . In Natal and the Eastern Cape the inner bark and roots are used in native medicines. 1976 *E. Prov. Herald* 21 Oct. 4 Invader plants that caused the greatest problem in the mountainous parts of the Eastern Karoo Region were the broom-bush, taaibos or kraaibossie, leucosidea [etc.].

kraakelen var. KRAKELING.

kraal /krɑːl/ *n*. Also **chraal, c(o)raal, crael, krael, krail, krale, krall**. [Du. k(o)raal fr. Pg. *curral* corral, enclosure, fold.]

1.a. A traditional African village or extended settlement; CRAWL sense a; STAT sense 1; cf. UMZI. Also *attrib*. passing into *adj*., now often pejorative, meaning 'unsophisticated', 'rural' (see quots 1946, 1957, and 1974).

1731 G. MEDLEY tr. *P. Kolb's Present State of Cape of G.H.* I. 75 The Kraals, as they call them, or villages, of the Hassaquas are larger. 1786 G. FORSTER tr. *A. Sparrman's Voy. to Cape of G.H.* I. In a Hottentot's camp, or village, the huts are all built exactly alike. 1797 [see HOTTENTOT *adj.* sense 1]. 1798 S.H. WILCOCKE tr. *J.S. Stavorinus's Voy. to E. Indies 1768–71* I. 547 [Hottentots] . . dwell together in villages, called *kraals*, and are under a chief. a1823 J. EWART *Jrnl* (1970) 46 Thirty or forty of these [habitations] usualy form'd a kraal or village over which presided a chief. 1828 W. SHAW *Diary*. 28 June, Several Kraals or Native Villages, where all the huts were burned down to the ground. 1835 W.B. BOYCE in A. Steedman *Wanderings* II. 268 Mr. Shepstone counted a hundred kraals, each of which contained from twenty to forty houses. 1849 R. GRAY *Jrnl of Bishop's Visitation* I. 39 The Kraal of the Kaffir, several of which we passed, is very similar to the village of the Fingoe. 1860 A.W. DRAYSON *Sporting Scenes* 18 Kraal is a Dutch term, and means an inclosure for animals. I fancy that they call the Kaffirs' residences by this name to indicate their contempt for the

people; the Kaffirs call their villages 'umsi'. 1860 W. SHAW *Story of my Mission* 410 The dwellings of the Kaffirs consist of huts, a collection of from five to thirty of which constitute what the Colonists call a kraal. 1877 F. JEPPE *Tvl Bk Almanac & Dir.* (1976) 33 Tons of iron . . were carried out of a Kafir kraal near Matzibandela's which was ransacked by Knobnoses. 1885 H. RIDER HAGGARD *King Solomon's Mines* (1972) 35 Red sandhills and wide sweeps of vivid green, dotted here and there with Kafir kraals. 1891 R.W. MURRAY *S. Africa* 194 A kraal is . . a collection of huts surrounded by mud walls or palisading. 1899 G.M. THEAL *Rec. of Cape Col.* V. 134 The kraal was found to consist of five or six hundred huts, and to contain about five thousand people. 1907 W.C. SCULLY *By Veldt & Kopje* 1 The District Surgeon had . . been busy riding from kraal to kraal in these locations where the disease existed. 1925 D. KIDD *Essential Kafir* 12 The word kraal does not connote a single hut; it is a collection of huts. It is sometimes called a village. 1934 B.I. BUCHANAN *Pioneer Days* 156 The kraal was a very large one, about a mile in circumference, built in the usual Zulu style — a double stockade of rough poles with huts between. 1938 E. ROSENTHAL in D.B. Coplan, *Urbanization of African Performing Arts*. (1980) 54 The simple-minded black from the kraal was immensely impressed by the sophisticated dress of his brother from the far side of the Atlantic. 1941 C.W. DE KIEWIET *Hist. of S. Afr.* 219 For many natives there links between the old life of the kraal and the new life of the city corroded and snapped. 1946 T. MACDONALD *Ouma Smuts* 51 The black man was coming out of his kraal. 1957 D. JACOBSON *Price of Diamonds* 26 Asking her why she had called the offending boy a lazy kraal kaffir. 1958 — *Through Wilderness* (1977) 22 He was a good boy, come straight from the kraal. 1974 *Sunday Times* 23 Feb. 9 An eloquent dramatisation of the obstacles in the way of success for the kraal African who migrates to the city in search of work. 1980 D.B. COPLAN *Urbanization of African Performing Arts*. 348 In 1952, a commercial company installed a rediffusion service in Soweto's Orlando township and met with opposition . . . The African National Congress feared that radio would become an instrument of government propaganda. Others attacked it as a 'back-to-the-kraal, apartheid and never-never-land service' that used African languages (rather than English). 1983 P.S. RABIE tr. *Nienaber & Raper's Hottentot Place Names* 7 At first the Hottentots were like free burghers, were never enslaved and retained their own kraal civilization fully intact. 1990 *E. Prov. Herald* 19 Jan. 2 The bodies of 11 people between the ages of 11 and 48 were found at four different kraals in the Natal Sweetwaters area. 1990 G. SLOVO *Ties of Blood* 43 This customer was going to be a difficult one. He was a real *kraal* type with his thick blanket around his shoulders.

b. *transf*. ?*obs*. The community inhabiting a traditional village.

1731 G. MEDLEY tr. *P. Kolb's Present State of Cape of G.H.* I. 279 On these and the like Occasions the whole *Kraal* testifies its Joy in Dancings. 1786 G. FORSTER tr. *A. Sparrman's Voy. to Cape of G.H.* I. 173 We met with a refusal likewise from them, on our sending to a couple of *craals*, or communities. 1804 R. PERCIVAL *Acct of Cape of G.H.* 81 Still indeed there are some Kraals or tribes of these people living quietly. 1808 R. COLLINS in G.M. Theal *Rec. of Cape Col.* (1900) VI. 340 The other kraals of that part of the country were said to be mostly hostile. 1821 J. AYLIFF *Journal*. 22 That every Chraal May Unite to praise the Lord. 1852 M.B. HUDSON *S. Afr. Frontier Life* 36 Rescued a fine of four cattle imposed on a Kraal for a theft. 1876 F. BOYLE *Savage Life* 209 The Zulu kraals under his father's sovereignty had *treked* thither. 1899 *Natal Agric. Jrnl* 31 Mar. 4 'Kraal,' . . a community of kafirs (whose huts are generally arranged in circles or sections of circles).

2.a. A hut or cluster of huts occupied by one family or clan, either standing alone or as part of a traditional African village; the labourers' huts on a farm; HOMESTEAD sense 2; WERF sense

2 a; cf. UMZI. **b.** *transf.* The family or clan inhabiting these dwellings. Also *attrib.* (sometimes pejorative, implying a lack of sophistication). Hence **kraalful** *n.*

'Homestead' is the preferred term among anthropologists.

1786 G. FORSTER tr. *A. Sparrman's Voy. to Cape of G.H.* I. 197 The order or distribution of these huts in a craal or clan, is most frequently in the form of a circle with the doors inwards. **1790** tr. *F. Le Vaillant's Trav.* I. 159 At the distance of a league, I found a Kraal, consisting of four huts, in which was a Hottentot family. **1790** PENNANT in W. Paterson *Narr. of Four Journeys* 20 The order or distribution of these huts in a craal or clan, is most frequently in the form of a circle with the doors inwards. **1795** C.R. HOPSON tr. *C.P. Thunberg's Trav.* I. 164 They encamp there with their cattle, and make huts (*Kraals*) of Mesembryanthemum bushes or of mats. **1798** LADY A. BARNARD in Lord Lindsay *Lives of Lindsays* (1849) III. 434 We have prevailed on each family to have a spot of ground round its craal to rear things on. **1801** — *Jrnl* (1973) 191 Saw no house for five miles, and then another of the Landdrost's, with kraals around it of Hottentots belonging to the farm. **1801** W.S. VAN RYNEVELD in G.M. Theal *Rec. of Cape Col.* (1898) IV. 90 There are some who have Cattle and dwell with their families in Huts (kraalen). **1821** C.I. LATROBE *Jrnl of Visit* 240 The kraal consisted of a circular building of reeds and rushes, covered with grass, a garden near the brook, and a small enclosure for cattle. **1827** G. THOMPSON *Trav.* II. 30 They are divided into a great number of independant clans, or *kraals.* **1836** C.L. STRETCH Journal., The population .. amount to about 500 souls, who reside in the village; but the inmates of several kraals in its vicinity have also the benefit of instruction. **1841** B. SHAW *Memorials* 24 Each tribe is again subdivided into clans or kraals, governed by petty chiefs. *Ibid.* 242 The chief Pato .. has this year put that beyond all doubt, by fining several kraals for working on the Sabbath, which has had a very general effect throughout the tribe. **1856** G. GREY in *Imp. Blue Bks* Command Paper 2352–1857, 37 Throughout Kaffraria the natives live along the ridges and slopes of the hills .. in collections of huts termed kraals. **1860** W. SHAW *Story of my Mission* 317 He was allowed by Gaika to fix his residence at a place at no great distance from the principal kraal or residence of that Chieftain. **1890** in *Cape Law Jrnl* VII. 226 When I related what I knew to friends I met at the different kraals I visited, I would imagine I was before the judge. **1912** AYLIFF & WHITESIDE *Hist. of Abambo* 81 Their children were useful to the parents in many ways in kraal life. **1926** M. NATHAN *S. Afr. from Within* 54 The principal kraal was at Zombode, though the kraals at Lobamba (the residence of the Present Paramount Chief) and at Embekelweni have also been occupied. **1937** C. BIRKBY *Zulu Journey* 23 These homes, merely thatched huts, are all grouped within the family enclosure — the kraal. **1948** V.M. FITZROY *Cabbages & Cream* 126 People living on real farms with a kraalful of piccanins. **1948** A. PATON *Cry, Beloved Country* 266 *Kraal*, .. a number of huts together, under the rule of the head of the family, who is of course subject to the chief. **1955** J.B. SHEPHARD *Land of Tikoloshe* 14 Because that pen or kraal is the social and often the religious centre of life in a Xhosa community, the whole homestead is usually referred to as 'So-and-So's kraal'. **1955** E.A. RITTER *Shaka Zulu* 2 The single homestead, popularly called kraal, was the basic unit of the old Zulu State, a microcosm of the whole clan system. **1967** J.A. BROSTER *Red Blanket Valley*, The average kraal consists of three huts, these being a store room and two living rooms. **1972** *Std Encycl. of Sn Afr.* VI. 453 Among the Bantu peoples the kraal was the basic social and economic unit and had a personal significance. **1977** J. SIKAKANE *Window on Soweto* 15 My grandfather .. was the eldest son in the whole family 'kraal' unit. **1978** A. ELLIOTT *Sons of Zulu* 97 The word 'kraal' is the long established name for the homes of the country tribespeople of Southern Africa ... It is a word which is used broadly and may mean the single hut of a newly married couple, the larger establishment of a many-wived man, or it may even be used to indicate a tribal village and also a byre. **1984** *Frontline* Mar. 22 His kraal, his huts, were set alight, so showing his broken wife and their bewildered children they were no longer wanted in the village. **1992** E. JAYIYA in *Pace* Sept. 15 Another pretty woman has become the fifth wife in the kraal of King Goodwill Zwelethini. **1993** *Weekend Mercury* 2 Jan. 17 Since becoming self-employed, he has built and furnished his own kraal.

c. With distinguishing epithet denoting a particular type of kraal: **royal kraal**, a homestead where the chief of an African people lives and holds court, or where his wife and children live; cf. *great place* (see GREAT).

1926 M. NATHAN *S. Afr. from Within* 36 Invaded the country with three columns, Ulundi, the **royal kraal**, being their objective. **1958** J.J.R. JOLOBE in R. Macnab *Poets in S. Afr.* 49 A spear betrothal's sign was left in court. Report was made it came from royal Kraal. **1971** *Sunday Tribune* 5 Dec. 23 Thousands of Zulus accompanied the new Paramount Chief to the Royal Kraal for the traditional feast of oxen. **1975** *Drum* 22 Sept. 8 Nobody in Swaziland, it seems, can give the exact number of queens and princes at the eight royal kraals. **1987** *Ibid.* Mar. 13 The king then called his first meeting of the nation at the Royal kraal, Ludzidzini. Thousands of Swazis gathered at the royal place from the early hours of the morning.

3.a. An enclosure, fold, or pen for domestic or other animals; CRAWL sense b. Also *attrib.* See also *cattle-boma* (BOMA *n.*[1] sense 3 b), SKUTKRAAL.

1795 C.R. HOPSON tr. *C.P. Thunberg's Trav.* I. 164 A place or fold where sheep or cattle were enclosed in the open air was called a *kraal.* **1812** A. PLUMPTRE tr. *H. Lichtenstein's Trav. in Sn Afr.* I. 107 The Kraals for the horse and oxen are enclosed by a wall five or six feet high, those for the sheep are only enclosed by thorn hedges. **1827** T. PHILIPPS *Scenes & Occurrences* 106 Each flock had its separate *kraal*, fenced round with the thorny mimosa, piled high and impenetrable to wild beasts. **1834** W.H.B. WEBSTER *Narr. of Voy. to Sn Atlantic Ocean* 267 The kraal forms an important part of the establishment of every farmer; and each ox in it hath his name. **1843** T. PRINGLE *Afr. Sketches* 180 He led us out towards the kraals or cattle-folds. **1876** T. STUBBS Reminiscences. II. 17 Found a Kraal in the thick bush a lot of Cows and Calves in the Kraal. **1884** B. ADAMS *Narr.* (1941) 80 At sunset all the cattle was brought in and enclosed in Kraals — large circles formed of the mimosa tree. **1898** J.F. INGRAM *Story of Afr. City* 19 As the morning advanced the kraal gates were opened, and the cattle driven forth. **1900** R. KIPLING in J. Crwys-Williams *S. Afr. Despatches* (1989) 160 We made a kraal for the two little ones — a kraal of thornbushes, so that they should not be bitten by anything. **1926** P. SMITH *Beadle* (1929) 152 Riding about the farm with mijnheer or visiting distant lands, camps and kraals with Frikkie. **1949** T. MOFOLO *Chaka Zulu* 7 The cattle will come here in great numbers and the kraals will soon be full. **1957** S. SCHOEMAN *Strike!* 227 The Ordinance and the Regulations *inter alia prohibit:* .. The use of Nets or Kraals for the capture of fish except under licence. **1968** R. GRIFFITHS *Man of River* 93 Have I a kraal of fish, like a kraal of cattle or sheep or goats, that I can select some each day for slaughter? **1974** *S. Afr. Panorama* Dec. 5 A supplementary 'kraal' system where some 20000 sheep can be accommodated. **1990** R. STENGEL *January Sun* 13 About two dozen cows and bulls .. stand in the muddy kraal next to the barn. Kraal is the Afrikaans word for what an American cowboy would call a corral, a term with the same Latin root, *currale*, meaning 'enclosure'.

b. With distinguishing epithet.

i. Designating enclosures for various kinds of domestic or other animals, as ***cattle-kraal, fish-kraal, goat-kraal, lamb-kraal, sheep-kraal, turtle-kraal***, etc. See also *beast-kraal* (BEAST sense 2).

1817 G. BARKER Journal. 19 Nov., Went to the cattle kraal to settle some differences among the people. **1827** T. PHILIPPS *Scenes & Occurrences* 188 A fire blazing on a little hill which we rode up to and discovered it to be a cattle Kraal. **1832** J. COLLETT Accounts I. 64 Whether krale, Lamb krale, Kid krale. **1841** B. SHAW *Memorials* 35 The chief, at his death, is buried in the cattle kraal: his grave being filled up, the cattle are driven over it, in order that the place may not be discovered. **1843** J.C. CHASE *Cape of G.H.* 150 The field is generally at a convenient distance from the cattle kraal, from whence he procures a dressing for his land whenever it may be required. **1849** E.D.H.E. NAPIER *Excursions in Sn Afr.* I. 313 At the door of the Calf kraal. **1903** R. KIPLING *Five Nations* 153 Giving and taking counsel each Over the cattle-kraal. **1924** S.G. MILLIN *God's Step-Children* 292 That was the cattle kraal, said Gert. And the smaller one next to it was the sheep kraal. **1953** U. KRIGE *Dream & Desert* 175 Then walked slowly towards the sheepkraal where he slaughtered six sheep. **1958** L.G. GREEN *S. Afr. Beachcomber* 109 Long, long ago the first beachcombers were .. baiting their fish-kraals wherever the rocks allowed them to trap the shoals as the tides went out. *Ibid.* 191 Turtle kraals, built early last century in a creek where the tide ebbs and flows ... The seamen .. of old would often capture a hundred, two hundred turtles in a night and keep them in those kraals. **1961** T.V. BULPIN *White Whirlwind* 295 There'll be streets and theatres and fine shops standing on the site of his old goat kraal. **1981** *Sunday Times* 15 Mar. 11 From cattle kraals to concrete parking lots ... that is the changing world of the black mineworker. **1985** *Fair Lady* 6 Feb. 79 A cattle kraal near the first set of highly efficient security gates lends a practical homely air to the place. **1993** *Weekly Mail & Guardian* 23 Dec. 15 Although we do not have our cattle kraals in the township, traditional weddings still take place.

ii. Designating particular uses, as ***keep-kraal***, a kraal for segregating or holding game; ***out-kraal***, a kraal far from a farm homestead; ***skut-kraal***, see as a main entry; ***sorting kraal***, a kraal for sorting and separating animals into groups; ***wash-kraal*** *nonce*, an open-air bathing enclosure.

1850 J.D. LEWINS Diary. 5 Oct., Had a visit from Kew. To give him my wash-place. He will send poles for wash-kraal & make me also a spout. **1891** O.E.A. SCHREINER *Thoughts on S. Afr.* (1923) 171 Cattle to see to, or out-kraals to visit. **1894** — in S.C. Cronwright-Schreiner *Life of Olive Schreiner* (1924) 263 Went to an out-kraal right away in the Hoek, a beautiful valley on the farm. **1971** *Daily Dispatch* 28 May 7 The animals are trapped .. and moved to 'keep-kraals' in the reserve. **1972** *Grocott's Mail* 16 May 1 There is a cattle dip as well as a sheep dip tank with sorting kraals.

c. *Fig.* and *transf.* In sense 3 a, but referring to a place used or inhabited by people, or to a grouping of people.

i. A contained area, an enclosure.

1853 *Report* (12 Dec.) in *Cape of G.H. Annexures* (1854) 74, I was put into the kraal with the lunatics. **1896** PURVIS & BIGGS *S. Afr.* 169 Each division was subdivided into military kraals. **1905** P. GIBBON *Vrouw Grobelaar* 172 How some have striven for the home kraal. **1961** T.V. BULPIN *White Whirlwind* 214 They called the ship 'the great kraal that pushes through the water'. **1961** H.F. SAMPSON *White-Faced Huts* 36, I saw Vamsinya in a little kraal in the centre of the Court ... The old gentleman who spoke kaffir put up two fingers of his right hand, and told me to speak the truth, so help me God!

ii. A social grouping based on economic, political, linguistic, ethnic, or other differences, and serving to separate people from one another.

1938 A.H. MURRAY in *Star* 16 July 10 The Afrikaner kraal is being drawn so narrow that it is almost impossible to move within it. You must not dance and you must not play cards, [etc.]. **1949** J.S. FRANKLIN *This Union* 87 Carefully shepherded in separate kraals, the one shut off and excluded from the language and culture of the other. **1953** LANHAM & MOPELI-PAULUS *Blanket Boy's Moon* 274 The white man places all who do not possess white skins in one kraal, and calls them 'non-Europeans'. **1969** J. MERVIS in *Sunday Times* 24 Aug. 13 The English Press are trying to chase the Afrikaners, like cattle, into separate 'verligte' and 'verkrampte' kraals. **1970** *News/Check* 4 Sept. 8 Too long have English-speakers taken a superbly bland view of politics, and this has merely kept them (and consoled them) in their own kraal. **1979** F. Dike *First S. African* 18 Are you a coloured? Hayi maan, your son has broken into my kraal. **1982** *Pace* June 66 These women .. are a permanent feature of this kraal designed exclusively for men. **1985** *Argus* 4 June 10 So many whites are running into Mr P W Botha's kraal. **1990** Siramo in *Staffrider* Vol.9 No.2, 79 Let my right hand not forget you, Saf' Afrika, the kraal of no mercy. **1991** F.G. Butler *Local Habitation* 100 These Christian Nationalists were going to legislate all education into a monolithic master-plan of separate linguistic kraals.

d. *comb.* **kraal bird** *rare*, the small bird *Pytelia melba*; **kraalbos** /-bɔs/, also **kraal-bosch**, [Afk., *bos* (earlier S. Afr. Du. *bosch*) bush], any of several shrubs used for making enclosures for livestock, esp. *Galenia africana* and *Eretia rigida*; also **kraal bosje** [see BOSCHJE]; **kraal fuel**, *Free State coal* (see FREE STATE *adj. phr.* sense 2); **kraal manure, -mis** /məs/, [Afk., *mis* manure], dung taken from animal enclosures, dried, and used for fertilizing lands or gardens, or as building material; see also MIS sense 1; **kraalward** *adv.*, towards a kraal; **kraal-wood**, wood used for building rough animal enclosures.

1900 Stark & Sclater *Birds of S. Afr.* I. 90 This Finch [*sc. Pytelia melba*] is found sparingly in Damara and Great Namaqua Land ... Its favourite resort is low bush and old abandoned village fences, whence the Damaras call it the '**Kraal bird**'. **1795** C.R. Hopson tr. *C.P. Thunberg's Trav.* I. 310 The *Galenia Africana* was known under the appellation of **Kraal-bosch**, and in some places was used for fences about the inclosures for their cattle. **1913** C. Pettman *Africanderisms* 280 *Kraal bosje, Galenia africana*, and other plants. **1917** R. Marloth *Common Names* 52 *Kraalbos*, .. A frequent bushy herb of the Karoo, eaten by stock in times of drought. **1932** *Farming in S. Afr.* Apr. (Swart), 5 Kraalbos was one of the plants sampled. **1966** C.A. Smith *Common Names* 310 *Kraalbos*, .. *Eretia rigida* ... Frequently found round native kraals. The vernacular name has reference to the use made of the plants, or perhaps it has been prompted by the globose fruits, each of which suggests a bead (Afr.: kraal). **1972** *Std Encycl. of Sn Afr.* VI. 453 *Kraalbos*, Two shrubs are known by this name. **1988** Le Roux & Schelpe *Namaqualand* 76 *Galenia african[a]*, Kraalbos ... This plant .. can be the only remaining species after the veld has been heavily overgrazed. [**1815** J. Mackrill Diary. 101 Having preserved a Quantity of dry dung from my Kraal, I sow the dung .. liberally over my land.] **1904** *Argus Christmas Annual* (Competitions Sect.) p.viii, Where wood is scarce, people use coal .. and are more fortunate than those who are compelled to use **kraal fuel** and pay well for it. **1905** E.A. Nobbs in Flint & Gilchrist *Science in S. Afr.* 383 Facilities for the sale of .. '**Kraal manure**' exists [*sic*] in the form of specially low charges for carriage by rail from the Karroo to the grain and fruit areas. **1905** *Blackwood's Mag.* (U.K.) Mar. 389 The room was floored with dagga — anthill earth brought to a high stage of hardness and mahogany-like polish by frequent dressings of bullock's blood and kraal manure. *c***1911** E. Glanville in S. Playne *Cape Col.* 661 He was also manuring his ground with kraal manure and it was possible for him to put down 1000 acres of lucerne. *a***1951** H.C. Bosman *Willemsdorp* (1977) 61 With kraal manure in his trouser turn-ups. **1970** *Grocott's Mail* 5 June 4 (*advt*) Sweetveld Kraal Manure (goat). **1987** *E. Prov. Herald* 13 Nov. 21 (*advt*) Manure: Fresh farm manure. Kraal manure R3 per grain bag. **1989** J. Hobbs *Thoughts in Makeshift Mortuary* 222 Despite the day's heat, the well dug-over soil is still damp under a thin layer of kraal manure. **1991** H. Hutchings in *Weekend Post* 9 Feb. (Leisure) 7 The rose beds are covered with a thick mulch of kraal manure — as are all other beds of shrubs and flowers. **1977** M.P. Gwala *Jol'iinkomo* 42 Let me drink from the khamba of the elders. Let me blow my nose into **kraalmis**. **1991** J. Farquharson in *Sunday Times* 10 Mar. 22 Fine houses are razed; many shops with enchanting facades are being 'done over' and plastered with an apparent mixture of mud and kraalmis. **1947** F.C. Slater *Sel. Poems* 85 The lowing cows plod **kraalward** with full udders. **1888** *Cape Punch* 7 Sept. 119 Timber, firewood, wattles, **kraal-wood**, branch-wood. **1907** T.R. Sim *Forests & Forest Flora* 68 No Kraalwood or Firewood shall be cut within twenty (20) yards of the edge of the Crown Forest.

4. In senses 1, 2 and 3: an element in place names.

1838 J.E. Alexander *Exped. into Int.* I. 41 The site of the institution of Ebenezer was formerly called Doorn Kraal (thorn village or pen). **1875** C.B. Bisset *Sport & War* 10 In the valleys near and about Buck Kraal. **1882** J. Nixon *Among Boers* 53 We reached S's camp at Vlak Kraal (pr Krawl) after a 30 miles drive. **1986** *E. Prov. Herald* 9 Apr. 1 Lawaaikamp residents said Sandkraal is 'further away from the white town'. **1988** O. Oberholzer *Ariesfontein to Zuurfontein*, This idea came to me — a pictorial journey from Ariesfontein to Zuurfontein. Sure, I admit, it could have been place names ending in 'spruit' or 'kraal' or 'berg'. **1989** P.E. Raper *Dict. of Sn Afr. Place Names* 217 *Hooge Kraal*, Former name of *Pacaltsdorp*. Of Dutch origin, the name means 'high-lying byre', 'village at a high elevation'.

5. *comb.* **kraal dog**, KAFFIR DOG sense 1; **kraal-head** [Eng. *head* leader], the head of a traditional African village; the head of a family or clan.

1970 *Daily Dispatch* 30 Jan. 14 Kaiser the tribal terrier — once a mangy **kraal dog** with his ribs showing. **1982** *E. Prov. Herald* 29 Apr. 13 Each selected a kraal dog, often the most vociferous. **1911** M.S. Evans *Black & White in S.E. Afr.* 67 The wives take their status according to ancient custom, and both they and their children are under the direct rule of the **kraal head**. **1946** *Tribal Natives & Trade Unionism* (Tvl Chamber of Mines) 6 The tribal pattern is the Chief, the Induna, the headman and the kraal head. **1959** L. Longmore *Dispossessed* 113 The will of the kraal-head was tempered and, to a great extent, influenced by the individual and collective views of his wife or wives, and the male adult members of his household. **1962** W.D. Hammond-Tooke *Bhaca Soc.* 36 Informants insisted that if a kraalhead so wished he could select a son from any of his minor houses if there was no heir in the great house. **1967** O. Walker *Hippo Poacher* 71 He must pay his respects to the kraal-head. **1978** A. Elliott *Sons of Zulu* 45 It is tribal custom that when a kraal head or senior man dies, then his family keeps a rigid ritual of mourning in which they may not, for a time, till their lands, eat certain foods or do certain types of work. **1985** Platzky & Walker *Surplus People* 146 A press statement .. listed convictions for '291 kraal heads (2246 souls)' who were squatting illegally on their former land.

kraal /krɑːl/ *v. trans.* Also **krall**. [fr. prec.] Sometimes in the phr. ***to kraal off***. Often *passive*.

1. To drive (animals) into an enclosure; to keep (animals) in an enclosure.

1822 T. Philipps *Lett.* (1960) 136 Our Cattle are kraaled every night before sun down, and we have determined not to defend them if the Caffres make an attack in the night, but allow them to carry them off. **1827** G. Thompson *Trav.* I. 401, I found the lady of the mansion *kraaling* her flocks and herds. **1836** R. Godlonton *Introductory Remarks to Narr. of Irruption* 11 For some time were permitted even to graze and kraal their cattle as far westward as the banks of the Fish River. **1850** J.D. Lewins Diary. 24 Oct., Ordered Fengou to kraal the horses at night, as they are every night in the corn. *a***1858** J. Goldswain *Chron.* II. 170 Your sheep can be Kraaled within the square. **1863** E.L. Price *Jrnls* (1956) 120 After kraaling the oxen, the men gathered round the fires & cooked their suppers. **1865** *Pall Mall Gaz.* (U.K.) 16 Oct. 6, 25,000 cattle and 8,000 horses were thus kraaled on the top of a mountain. **1877** T. Baines *Gold Regions of S.-E. Afr.* 8 The necessity of kraaling the cattle at night within the village. **1882** J. Nixon *Among Boers* 87 In South Africa the practice of kraaling the sheep at nights appears to be universal. **1896** M.A. Carey-Hobson *At Home in Tvl* 95 It was absolutely necessary that they should be kraaled, for fear of the wolves and jackles. **1904** *Argus Christmas Annual* (Orange River Colony Sect.) 12 The sheep were kraaled. **1924** S.G. Millin *God's Step-children* 14 He saw that the huts acted as a barrier for the cattle kraaled within the circle. **1910** H. Rider Haggard *Queen Sheba's Ring* 35 Their only resource was to kraal their animals within stone walls at night. **1926** J. Kirkman in S.N.G. Cory *Diary of Francis Owen* 163 No cattle had been Kralled for many days. **1937** *Handbk for Farmers* (Dept of Agric. & Forestry) 517 To prevent the disease, do not kraal the animals but leave them in the open veld. **1944** J. Mockford *Here Are S. Africans* 21 Even as he .. kraaled the Hottentots' cattle, Jan van Riebeeck looked over his shoulder and frowned his annoyance at the bay. **1954** K. Cowin *Bushveld, Bananas & Bounty* 28 He kraals his cattle at night partly because they may stray, but chiefly from the habit of protecting them from wild animals. **1961** H.F. Sampson *White-Faced Huts* 16 Manjusa arrived at dusk after the donkeys and cows were kraaled. **1974** *E. Prov. Herald* 9 Aug. 6 Because of past attacks by killer dogs, the Bouwers kraal their sheep every night.

2. *Transf.* and *fig.* To separate (people) into groups of similar type; to restrict (people); to enclose (an area).

1898 G. Nicholson *50 Yrs* 25 Converted kaffirs .. kept 'kraalled' within institutional limits. **1911** Blackburn & Caddell *Secret Service* 284 Arresting a few ringleaders and kraaling the crowd in the old jail at Doornfontein. **1949** *Rand Daily Mail* 27 July 6 Kraaling off the children. *c***1963** B.C. Tait *Durban Story* 21 Captain Smith and his 'rooibaadjies' were kraaled in the Fort and there the Boers meant to starve them into surrender. **1970** *Argus* 26 Sept. 5 Children of the two language groups are deliberately kraaled off and are, therefore, unable to learn one another's language properly and to become true South Africans. **1974** *Sunday Times* 24 Nov. (Mag. Sect.) 18 There would be no such thing as kraaling off the beaches in my brave new world. **1986** *Drum* Mar. 18 More than three decades ago mlungu came up with the Bantu Authorities Act to kraal us into our little bantustans.

Hence **kraaled** *ppl adj.*, **kraaling** *vbl n.*

1899 H. Rider Haggard *Swallow* p.vi, Now I go out to see to the kraaling of the cattle. **1910** A.B. Lamont *Rural Reader* 118 Kraaling is not a good method; for it injures the wool. **1915** J.K. O'Connor *Afrikander Rebellion* 78 His child .. must help with the milking and kraaling of the cattle. **1919** R.Y. Stormberg *With Love from Gwenno* 73 To-day the two native boys had permission to leave early ... On such occasions the young 'baases' finish up the kraaling between them. **1942** S. Cloete *Hill of Doves* 7 The kraaled beasts were restless. **1963** R. Lewcock *Early 19th C. Archit.* 167 Few proper precautions had been taken for the safe kraaling of the livestock. **1979** M. Parkes *Wheatlands* 85 Kraaling of stock was all wrong and .. was not only bad for the stock but for the veld as well. **1990** B. Nixon in *Weekend Post* 3 Nov. (Leisure) 3 This was the pioneering life — complete with a kraaled flock of black-faced sheep and goats.

kraants var. KRANTZ.

krael var. KRAAL *n.*

‖**kragdadig** /krax'dɑːdəx/ *adj.* Also (*attrib.*) **kragdadige** /-ə/. [Afk., resolute, firm, vigorous.] Usu. of politicians or government policies: uncompromising, autocratic, heavy-handed.

1952 *Cape Times* 21 May 5 The Government wanted to make scapegoats of himself and Mr. C— so that it could claim *kragdadige* (strong) steps against communism. **1958** *Ibid.* 18 Feb. 8 Mr. Sauer's answer was that the inquiry was merely United Party propaganda and he was not going to answer it ... That is at least a nice *kragdadige* answer. **1962** A.J. Luthuli *Let my People Go* 163 The Nationalists encourage their followers to look forward to show-downs .. with their opponents. No doubt these will become progressively more *kragdadig*. **1973** *Sunday Times* 15 Apr. 17 Even the Minister of Sport .. could not restrain himself from issuing one of those kragdadige statements that get no one anywhere. **1974** *Cape Times* 28 Sept. (Suppl.) 1 By its very nature a kragdadige Government acts and enacts but seldom enlightens or consults its electorate on what is being done and why. **1979** *Sunday Times* 18 Nov. 21 While he bluntly advocates a heavy-handed, '*kragdadige*' approach to terrorism, he also tells the politicians that the real solution is not a military one. **1981** *Ibid.* 25 Jan. 4 The party cannot help showing its true colours in the typical kragdadige action we have seen in the closure of Post and Sunday Post this week. **1986** R.A.F. SWART in *Hansard* 9 June 7951 'Kragdadige Minister Le Grange' virtually telling the security forces to carry on doing whatever they have been doing and that he will answer the 'questions at the top'. **1993** P. VAN NIEKERK in *Weekly Mail* 18 June 15 De Klerk .. is, after all, a man who broke with the *kragdadige* tradition of his predecessors to engage in a debate about what the future South Africa should look like.

||**kragdadigheid** /krax'dɑːdəx,heɪt/ *n.* [Afk., *kragdadig* (see prec.) + n.-forming suffix *-heid* -ness.] Heavy-handed, uncompromising autocracy; brute force. Also *attrib.*

1949 *Cape Times* 21 Sept. 8 Where any evidence can be found in this rigmarole of tentativeness for the *kragdadigheid* which is supposed to distinguish Nationalist Ministers we fail to see. **1957** *Cape Argus* 11 Feb. 8 Signs of that kragdadigheid of which Cabinet spokesmen claim a monopoly. **1963** H. SUZMAN in *Hansard* 29 Apr. 4924 As extreme white nationalism is fed by crisis situations and tough measures which are then taken to deal with those situations, so too does Black nationalism feed on this type of so-called 'kragdadigheid'. **1974** *Daily Dispatch* 4 Feb. 8 Already there are distressingly clear pointers that it will be the season for kragdadigheid. On at least four fronts the government has indicated that tolerance of dissent from Nationalist policy will be in short supply. **1976** *Time* 28 June 19 The dour, stocky political patriarch of South Africa .. has the iron-fistedness his fellow Afrikaners call *kragdadigheid.* **1985** *Cape Times* 21 Sept., Let us forget 'kragdadigheid', whether it be governmental in origin or township-inspired. **1988** in *Star* 28 May 10 (*letter*) The white teachers at the school are used for ulterior motives. Their 'kragdadigheid' mentality is being exploited in clearing up the mess in the department. **1990** R. MALAN *My Traitor's Heart* 341 This was an old Afrikaner philosophy called kragdagidheid, the act of power: you took what you wanted, and held it with your gun and fists. **1991** *Personality* 18 Mar. 14 *Kragdadigheid*, i.e. 'ruling by kicking backsides seriously hard'. **1991** A. VAN WYK *Birth of New Afrikaner* 100 P.W. Botha's so-called Rubicon speech .. was as unseemly and untimely an exhibition of *kragdadigheid* (power play) as a brawl at a prayer meeting. **1993** A. SPARKS in *Weekly Mail* 4 June 6 De Klerk's stand is in line with the government's new *kragdadigheid.* The NP is terrified of a massive haemorrhage to the right, and so it is showing that it is the boss. **1993** H. TYSON *Editors under Fire* 9 Balthazar Johannes Vorster's reputation of cool *kragdadigheid* (untrammelled power) had become his key to fame.

kra(i)je bosch var. KRAAIBOS.

krail var. KRAAL *n.*

krakeling /'krɑːkələŋ/ *n.* Pl. **kraakelen, krakelinge.** [Afk. (fr. Du., 'pretzel'; cf. Brit. Eng. *cracknel*).] A traditional biscuit made from a sweet dough and shaped into a figure eight.

1891 H.J. DUCKITT *Hilda's 'Where Is It?'* 265 'Zoete Krakeling' (Sweet Cracknels). (Old Dutch.) ... Roll out and make in shapes like the figure 8, and bake on flat pans for twenty minutes. **1950** H. GERBER *Cape Cookery* 37 Krakelinge. Roll out puff pastry to about $\frac{1}{4}$inch thickness. Cut it into strips and form these into the figure 8. **1951** L.G. GREEN *Grow Lovely* 72 The Malay quarter, source of the cookery secrets that have survived the centuries. There .. the origin of many of the old Cape sweets and pastries .. may be traced, the tammeletjies and bossuiker, kraakelen and sugared mebos. **1977** *Fair Lady* 8 June (Suppl.) 6 Krakelinge ... To shape each krakeling, gently pinch and fold long edges of one strip of dough together ... When all of the krakelinge have been shaped, spread beaten egg-white mixture lightly over tops with a pastry brush. **1991** L. POPPER *Sunday Times* 20 Oct. (Mag. Sect.) 30 Elegant *krakelinge* — traditional South African biscuits — have graced our tea tables since the Cape's early days ... Cut strips and form each strip into a figure 8.

krale, krall *n.* varr. KRAAL *n.*

krall *v.* var. KRAAL *v.*

kramat /kra'mat/ *n.* Also **karamat.** [ad. Malay *keramat* holy place or person, or (adj.) of a miraculous nature, sacred, fr. Arabic *karamat*, pl. form of *karama* a miracle worked by a holy man other than a prophet.] In the Cape Malay community: an Islamic shrine, usu. the tomb of a holy man. Also *attrib.*

Also occas. called *mazaar* (see quot. 1984), a word found also in *Indian Eng.*

[**1833** *S. Afr. Almanac & Dir.* 156 A tomb of a celebrated Malay Priest, near the farm Zandvliet, is frequently visited by the Mahomedans, and where they perform Divine Service, or what is called Grammat.] **1883** 'A CAPE COLONIST' *Cape Malays* 10 About twenty-five miles from Cape Town, near the mouth of the Eerste River, is a spot designated the Kramat, the grave of an influential priest who was buried there, and to whose shrine a visit is often paid by the Malays. **1900** W.W. SKEAT *Malay Magic* 61 There is usually in every small district a holy place known as the kramat. **1910** D. FAIRBRIDGE *That Which Hath Been* (1913) 270 Near the sand hills and the sea lies the kopje on the summit of which is the little white mosque, the kramat, which marks to this day the resting-place of Sheik Yussuf. **1910** R. JUTA *Cape Peninsula* 111 There is a sepulchre which is called the 'Kramat,' or resting place of a holy man. **1926** C.G. BOTHA *Place Names in Cape Prov.* 87 The Sheik, his family and a large number of followers were located near the place where he lies buried and [which] is now known as the *Kramat.* **c1936** *S. & E. Afr. Yr Bk & Guide* 466 In 1930, the Malay community announced the discovery by revelation of a *Kramat* (burial place of a saint) at a spot about the high level road. **1944** I.D. DU PLESSIS *Cape Malays* 7 This *karamat* is one of a series which stretches round the Cape peninsula to form a rough circle. Every Muslim believes that all followers of the prophet who live within this circle are safe from fire, famine, plague, earthquake and tidal wave. **1947** L.G. GREEN *Tavern of Seas* 136 Followers of the Prophet listening to the reading of the Koran within the 'kramat'. **1949** E. HELLMANN *Handbk on Race Rel.* 591 The vast majority live within a half-moon area bounded by these holy Karamats (shrines) to which pilgrimages by the Faithful are made. These tombs are on Robben Island in the north, Signal Hill, Faure in the East, Constantia and Oude Kraal in the South. **1969** *Drum* June 51 With .. 1,000 South African political prisoners just a stone's throw away, this 'kramat' for a political refugee from Java was sanctified with ceremony and prayers. **1971** *Ibid.* July 55 The Karamat singers will chant the sacred Islamic music. **1984** *Cape Times* 17 Oct., (*advt*) The Cape Mazaar (Kramat) Society (Est. 1982) Wish to inform the public the abovenamed society is the only official body maintaining most of the kramats/mazaars including the kramat on Robben Island. **1985** *S. Afr. Panorama* Jan. 20 The sheik's *kramat* (sacred tomb) at Faure .. is more greatly esteemed by the Cape Malays than any other in the Cape Peninsula. **1987** *Flying Springbok* Oct. 49 A green-domed kramat. **1990** *Weekend Argus* 10 Feb. (Weekender) 4 We would pass a Malay kramat where there were always vases of everlastings, stone jars containing strange concotions and cloth coverings. **1992** *S. Afr. Panorama* Nov.-Dec. 8 Another regular visitors' group is the Moslems who go there to worship at the Kramat, or sacred grave, of Abdurahman Motura, a Moslem leader who died on the island.

kram-a-tat var. KREMETART.

krampdruppels see DRUPPELS sense b i.

krans see KRANTZ.

||**kranskoppie** /'kranskɔpi/ *n.* [Afk., *krans* (see KRANTZ) + *koppie* (see KOPPIE).] A small hill with a steep cliff face. See also KLIPKRANS, KOPPIE.

1994 M. ROBERTS tr. *J.A. Wahlberg's Trav. Jrnls 1838–56* 61 Our road diverged due north, while he continued on his way to Sandrivier; a short while .. before we diverged we passed two kranskoppies.

krantz, krans /krans, krɑːns, krʌns/ *n.* Also **crance, kra(a)nts, kranse, krantze, kranz.** Pl. **-es,** occas. **-e** /-ə/, or (formerly) **-en.** [S. Afr. Du. *krantz, krans* fr. Du. *krans* (earlier *krants*) fr. Middle Du. *crans* coronet, chaplet.]

1. *?obsolescent.* A vertical wall of rock crowning the summit of a mountain.

1795 C.R. HOPSON tr. *C.P. Thunberg's Trav.* I. 166 This bitumen was to be found in great abundance in the cracks and crevices of the mountain, especially at one large projecting *krants*, or summit. **1798** S.H. WILCOCKE tr. *J.S. Stavorinus's Voy. to E. Indies 1768–71* I. 31 A narrow ridge of the mountain .. ended about halfway up abruptly, against the side of a precipice. This place, the inhabitants of the Cape call the *krants* or wreath. **1852** C. BARTER *Dorp & Veld* 88 (Pettman) We passed this morning under a mountain whose summit is garlanded with a ring of perpendicular rocks appropriately termed *kranz. Ibid.* 93 We had been directed to look out for a white krans in the mountain. **1893** 'AFRICANUS' in *Cape Illust. Mag.* July 418 It resembles Table Mountain in form, but has no large 'kransen,' and is verdant up to the top. **1908** J.M. ORPEN *Reminisc.* (1964) 63 There is a small flat topped hill there, with a little irregular krantz all round the top. **1910** J. BUCHAN *Prester John* (1961) 46 The top was sheer cliff; then came loose kranzes in tiers, like the seats in a gallery. **1913** *Times Lit. Suppl.* (U.K.) 24 July 309 How are we to describe the curious crowns of rock so common on the Cape mountains except by the word 'kranz'? **1916** J. BUCHAN *Greenmantle* 283 A little hill split the valley, and on its top was a *kranz* of rocks. **1925** H.F. MANDELBROTE tr. *O.F. Mentzel's Descr. of Cape of G.H.* II. 93 A phenomenon appeared below the krantz of the mountain that looked like a veritable carbuncle to some and a crowned serpent to others. **1949** L.G. GREEN *In Land of Afternoon* 21 A krantz is not merely a cliff, but a steep, rocky place near the summit of a berg. **1956** A.G. MCRAE *Hill Called Grazing* 64 You see the pale azure of the sky just touching the top of the Hill Called Grazing, you see the shape of the little *krantzes* which crown it. **1972** *Daily Dispatch* 4 Sept., The billowing Themeda triandra in autumn looks like a great field of wheat rising right up to the basalt krantzes of the Drakensberg.

2. A sheer rock face, a precipice; an overhanging cliff. See also KLIPKRANS.

1834 T. PRINGLE *Afr. Sketches* 515 Kranz, in colonial usage, signifies a steep cliff or overhanging rock, such as the Bushmen often select for depicting their rude sketches on. **1835** T.H. BOWKER Journal. 22 Apr., Corporal Kelly of the engineers fell drunk over a krantz last night. He is to be buried to night. **1845** [see KLOOF sense 2]. **1853** F.P. FLEMING *Kaffraria* 39 Rising up, here and there, from some of these deep and gloomy kloofs, appear immense perpendicular *krantzes* (or precipices) of iron-stone and granite rock. **a1858** J. GOLDSWAIN *Chron.* (1946) I. 100 He fell over a Crance or a rockey precipice and the next morning was found quit dead. **1861** *Queenstown Free Press* 16 Jan. (Pettman), Five horses were precipitated down a *krans* (or precipice) by the same wind and killed. **1877** R.M. BALLANTYNE *Settler & Savage* 144 Started the echoes of the precipices — which he styled Krantzes — and horrified the nearest baboons with shouts of bass laughter. **1892** *Midland News & Karroo Farmer* 4 Mar. 6 The krantz that overhangs the Maraisburg road .. is in a very dangerous state, and yesterday a large stone .. fell into the road. **1911** D.B. HOOK *'Tis but Yesterday* 56 He could scale any 'krans' and find nests .. in the rocky precipices. **1937** C. BIRKBY *Zulu Journey* 175 Twenty-five miles of precipitous kranzes cut off the Oribi Flats from the outside world of Natal. **1956** J. CHATTERTON *Return of Drums* 1 The burning noon silence was broken by the sudden, shrill chatter of monkeys disturbed from their midday rest in the shade of the krantz. **1964** V. POHL *Dawn & After* 30 Presently two big black horses inspanned to an empty Cape cart came careering past, heading straight for the edge of the plateau, where the kranz dropped about thirty feet.

3. Used as an element in place names: see quots.

1847 G.H. BERKELEY in *Imp. Blue Bks* Command Paper 969–1848, 8 I had intended making a combined movement on Murray's Krantz at daybreak to morrow morning. **1853** T. SHONE Diary. 12 Dec., Our Jack and horse was carried down the river at Blue Kraants, he lost Henry Greatcoat. **1956** F.C. METROWICH *Valiant but Once* 206 His headquarters were a peak of almost perpendicular rock in the Eastern Amatola mountains. This peak, afterwards known as Murray's Krantz, was a natural fortress and appeared to be well-nigh impregnable. **1974** *S. Afr. Panorama* Nov. 11 This krans was also known as the 'Skietkrans' (shot precipice) because when the north wind blew, it made sounds like shots.

Krechie var. GRIETJIE.

kreef /ˈkrɪəf/ *n.* Also **kreeft**, **krief**. [Afk., crayfish, ad. Du. *kreeft* lobster (langouste).] The spiny rock lobster *Jasus lalandii*; also called CRAYFISH. Also *attrib.*

1863 *Queenstown Free Press* 30 June, A new theological schism has sprung up amongst the Malays, touching the important question whether 'kreef' or crawfish is to be considered ceremonially unclean or not. **1871** *Cape Monthly Mag.* II. Feb. 81 Hawkers screaming their wares mid ear-splitting cries of *'Kreef! kreef!' 'Snoek! snoek!'*. **1884** J.S. LITTLE *S. Afr.: Sketch Bk* I. 151 The Krief, which resembles our cray fish, and which abounds in the waters of Table Bay .. is in itself but a poor libel upon the lobster. **1890** A.G. HEWITT *Cape Cookery* 5 To Boil Kreeft. Wash the kreeft quickly. **1891** H.J. DUCKITT *Hilda's 'Where Is It?'* 42 Creef (Potted). (Cape Crawfish.) Boil the creef, mince in the sausage machine, adding all the red meat. **1902** [see *Cape lobster* (CAPE sense 2 a)]. **1915** D. FAIRBRIDGE *Torch Bearer* 139 'It is a crustacean,' said Miss Lumsden kindly, 'Red when boiled, and with protruding eyes.' 'Ach!' a flash of inspiration came to Cornelia. 'A crayfish, klein kreef,' she added. **1936** *Nature* II. 74 *(heading)* The Natural History and Utilisation of the Cape Crawfish, Kreef or Spiny Lobster, *Jasus (Palinurus) lalandii.* **1942** *Off. Yrbk of Union 1941* (Union Office of Census & Statistics) 771 Research work dealing with the canning processes of the Cape crawfish or Kreef was completed during 1935. **1959** *Cape Argus* 7 Nov. 11 The three months open season for kreef fishing .. opened last Sunday. [**1961** see CRAWFISH.] **1968** G. CROUDACE *Black Rose* 60 The dinner was magnificent, the course Jeremy liked best being baked *kreef*, served whole, the delicately-flavoured flesh of the tails drenched with a cheese sauce. **1970** G. CROUDACE *Scarlet Bikini* 73 'And no *kreef*,' Tony said, referring to the rock lobster. **1975** *Financial Mail* 11 Apr. 112 The company called on a local white fish trawling company to buy kreef bait (which consists largely of stockfish and kingklip heads). **1978** *S. Afr. Panorama* Feb. 45 To comply with the European and US marketing requirements, legislation had to be passed in South Africa to change this delectable crustacea's [*sic*] name from the local 'kreef' or 'crayfish' to that of 'rock lobster'. One reason was that in Europe and the US there are several species of freshwater crustacea, some of which are not edible, known there as 'crayfish'. **1981** C. BARNARD in *Daily Dispatch* 16 Nov. 8 Fishermen will tell you that kreef are more efficient than undertakers at removing corpses. In fact, if you loll around on the bottom long enough, you'll soon realise there's no scarcity of crayfish. **1989** E. PLATTER in *Style* Aug. 108 If you don't eat a kreef within, at the most 24 hours of catching it, .. you'll never get the luscious leg meat to slip out as easily as it ought. **1990** J. CULLUM in *Weekend Post* 7 Apr. 3 Eating crayfish these days means forking out megabucks ... This is the sombre news for lovers of the delicate taste of *kreef.* **1993** J. NEL in *Getaway* Nov. 52 Collectors of kreef and perlemoen .. should come armed with permits.

kremetart /ˈkremətart, -tɑːt/ *n.* Also **kerrematata**, **kram-a-tat**, **kremata(r)t**, **krimmetart**. [Afk., fr. Du. *kremetart* or *krimmetart*, apparently ad. *cremortart*, fr. L. *cremor tartari*; or ad. Eng. *cream-of-tartar*.]

1. In full ***kremetartboom*** /-buəm/ [Afk., *boom* tree]: the CREAM OF TARTAR, *Adansonia digitata.* Also *attrib.*

1860 J. SANDERSON in *Jrnl of Royal Geog. Soc.* XXX. 243 The baobab, called by them the krematatboom, or cream-of-tartar tree, is abundant. **1931** H.C. BOSMAN *Mafeking Rd* (1969) 101 In company she hardly ever talked, unless it was to say that the Indian shopkeeper .. put roasted kremetart roots with the coffee he sold us. *c***1936** *S. & E. Afr. Yr Bk & Guide* 707 The country to the north of the mountains is dotted with baobab, locally known as the 'Kerrematata' or 'cream of tartar' trees, so called from the acid powder with which the fruit is filled. **1944** [see SWARTHAAK]. **1950** [see MOEPEL]. **1966** C.A. SMITH *Common Names* 311 *Kremetartboom*, .. The large pendulous fruits contain a pleasantly acidulous pulp which contains citric acid and which is often mixed with hot water to prepare a pleasant wholesome beverage. **1980** A.J. BLIGNAUT *Dead End Rd* 21, I had cut the forked stick from the kremetart for his first catapult. **1991** I. & F. DE MOOR *Informants, Grahamstown* Cremetart tree — Baobab tree.

2. *obs.* The fruit of this tree; its acidic white pulp. Also *attrib.*

1868 J. CHAPMAN *Trav.* II. 441 In this capsule numerous kidney-shaped seeds are imbedded, between fibrous divisions, in a white, pulpy, acid substance, somewhat resembling cream of tartar in taste, and hence called by the Boers 'kram-a-tat'. **1888** D.C.F. MOODIE *Hist. of Battles & Adventures* II. 342 With this meat we had to eat 'krimmetart,' a fruit resembling a cocoanut, but sour, and full of small pips. **1913** C. PETTMAN *Africanderisms* 282 *Krimmetart*, This word is a corruption of the English 'cream of tartar,' and is the name given by the Dutch to the fruit of the Baobab.

kreupelboom /ˈkrɪəp(ə)lbuəm, ˈkriœp(ə)l-/ *n.* Also **kreuple boom**, **kreuppelboom**. [S. Afr. Du., fr. Du. *kreupel* cripple + *boom* tree; so named for the twisted appearance of the lower branches.] Either of two small trees of the Proteaceae: **a.** *Leucospermun conocarpodendron*; CRIPPLE-WOOD; KREUPELHOUT; also called KREUPELBOS, PINCUSHION. **b.** *rare.* The red-and-yellow bottlebrush *Mimetes hirtus.* Also *attrib.*

1796 C.R. HOPSON tr. *C.P. Thunberg's Trav.* II. 112 The Kreupelboom (*Protea speciosa*). The bark is used by tanners for dressing and tanning leather. **1806** *Gleanings in Afr.* (anon.) 31 What the colonists call the Kreupel Boom, and seemingly adapted for no other use, is what they mostly cut down for this purpose [*sc.* firewood]. **1822** W.J. BURCHELL *Trav.* I. 25 An uncultivated plain extending to the foot of Table Mountain, and, in some parts, abounding in low scrubby trees of Kreupelboom, much used for fire-wood. **1848** C.J.F. BUNBURY *Jrnl of Res. at Cape of G.H.* 57 *Kreupel boom*, a large shrub or small tree, with greyish hairy leaves and compact heads of tawny yellow flowers. **1869** T. MCGIBBON in R. Noble *Cape & its People* 258 *Leucospermum conocarpum*, (the *kreupel boom*) is plentiful in groups on the lower slopes. **1880** *S.W. Silver & Co.'s Handbk to S. Afr.* (ed.3) 127 It covers extensive grounds .. associating with the Kreupel-boom, the Sugar-bush and other shrubs. **1888** *Castle Line Handbk & Emigrant's Guide* 62 There are numbers of Cape plants which yield tannin, and some of them such as kreuppelboom, wagenboom, kliphout .. are unequalled for tanning purposes. **1906** B. STONEMAN *Plants & their Ways* 31 Unfortunately for the tree, tannin is excellent for preserving leather also, and so the beautiful *Protea cynaroides* .., *Leucospermum conocarpon* (Kreuple boom) and *Rhus lucida* .. are destroyed for this substance which was intended for their protection. **1957** L.G. GREEN *Beyond City Lights* 236 The *kreupelboom* bark was used for dressing and tanning leather. **1966** C.A. SMITH *Common Names* 311 *Kreupelboom, Leucospermum conocarpodendron.* A small tree up to 10ft high, with showy golden-yellow heads of flowers ... *Mimetes hirta* (Cape), see Red-and-Yellow Bottlebrush. **1991** *Dict. of Horticulture* (Dept of Nat. Educ.) 450 *Kreupelboom*, (*Mimetes hirtus*, ..): red-and-yellow bottlebrush.

kreupelbos /ˈkrɪəp(ə)lbɔs, ˈkriœp(ə)l-/ *n.* Also **kreupel-bosch**. [Afk., earlier S. Afr. Du., fr. Du. *kreupel* cripple + Afk. *bos* (Du. *bosch*).] Any of several species of shrub or small tree of the Proteaceae, particularly the KREUPELBOOM (sense a), *Leucospermum conocarpodendron.* Also *attrib.*, and **kreupelbossie** [see -IE].

1821 C.I. LATROBE *Jrnl of Visit* Glossary, *Kreupel-bosch*, Leucospermum conocarpum, (the fire-wood grown under the Table-Mountain.) **1946** *Cape Times* 5 Feb. 6 He is collecting waboom and kreupelbos seeds above the Camps Bay slopes so that the bare areas .. can be covered with these handsome proteas. **1966** C.A. SMITH *Common Names* 312 *Kreupelbos(sie), Protea speciosa* ... The vernacular name was first recorded by Thunberg .. as an alternative to the kreupelboom. **1972** L.G. GREEN *When Journey's Over* 17 The explorers discovered a land of eternal sand with kreupelbos and thorn trees. **1981** M. MALAN in P. Dane *Great Houses of Constantia* 69 *Leucospermum conocarpodendron* or Kreupelbosch. **1987** F. VON BREITENBACH *Nat. List of Indigenous Trees* 25 *Leucospermum rodolentum*, .. Kreupelbos.

kreupelhout /ˈkrɪəp(ə)lhəʊt, ˈkriœp(ə)l-/ *n.* [Afk., *kreupel* cripple + *hout* wood; perh. transf. use of Du. *kreupelhout*, see quot. 1913.] KREUPELBOOM sense a. Also *attrib.*

[**1812** A. PLUMPTRE tr. *H. Lichtenstein's Trav. in Sn Afr.* (1928) I. 216 We rested near the river under the shade of Kruppelholz (*Protea Conocarpa*).] **1913** C. PETTMAN *Africanderisms* 281 *Kreupelhout*, .. *Leucospermum conocarpum.* In Holland the word appears to be applied to brushwood or undergrowth generally; in Cape Dutch is is limited to the above wood and has reference to its contorted appearance. **1917** R. MARLOTH *Common Names* 52 *Kreupel'hout, Leucospermum conocarpum.* A dwarf tree of the South West with yellow flower heads. Bark used for tanning. **1963** A.M. LOUW *20 Days* 184 Covering the .. hillock and reaching almost down to the sea, was a thick, sub-tropical growth of taaibos, .. kreupelhout, [etc.]. **1974** *S. Afr. Panorama* Nov. 9 Rough rocks. Thorn trees. Dense bushes of kreupelhout ... It is densley wooded with thick kreupelhout bushes. **1977** E. PALMER *Field Guide to Trees* 98 *Keupelhout, Leucospermum conocarpodendron* ... A shrub or tree up to 6m, often branching from the base ... Flower Heads: at tips of young branches partially hidden by leaves, cone-shaped, about 9 cm long, bright yellow. **1988** [see SWEET THORN]. **1988** M. BRANCH *Explore Cape Flora* 6 The yellow kreupelhout is a common gnarled bush found growing on mountain slopes near the sea. [**1991** *Dict. of Horticulture* (Dept of Nat. Educ.) 450 *Kreupelhoutbome*, (*Leucospermum* spp., ..): pincushion bushes, pincushion trees.]

kreuple boom, **kreuppelboom** varr. KREUPELBOOM.

krief var. KREEF.

kriging /ˈkriːgɪŋ, ˈkrɪxɪŋ/ *vbl n. Geology.* [Coined in 1960 by the French geologist Georges Matheron and named for *D.G. Krige* of Johannesburg, developer of the procedure.] A geostatistical technique of evaluating the economic potential of an area within an ore deposit. Also *attrib.*

'Kriging' is the international name for this procedure.

1979 *World Mining* June 105 This volume is by Dr. D. G. Krige developer of the lognormal kriging technique. **1979** I. CLARK *Practical Geostatistics* 1 The simplest application of the Theory of Regionalised Variables, that of producing the 'best' estimation of the unknown value at some location within an ore deposit. This technique is known as kriging. **1981** D.G. KRIGE *Lognormal-De Wijsian Geostatics* 25 Kriging was the name given in 1960 by Matheron to the *multiple regression* procedure for arriving at the *best linear unbiased estimator* or best linear *weighted moving average* estimate of the ore grade for an ore block (of any size) by assigning an optimum set of weights to all the available and relevant data inside and outside the ore block. **1987** *S. Afr. Panorama* Oct. 14 Internationally, the term 'kriging' is associated with Professor Krige's pioneering work in the field of geostatistics – the application of mathematical statistics in the earth sciences. 'Kriging', derived from his surname, refers to statistical methods for ore valuation developed by Professor Krige in the sixties. Today 'kriging' is part of the international mining vocabulary.

Hence **krig** *v. trans.*, to obtain (data) by the application of this technique.

1979 I. CLARK *Practical Geostatistics* 114 Block averages kriged from the set of regular samples *Ibid.* 115 Contour map kriged from random samples.

krij(g)sraad var. KRYGSRAAD.

krimmetart var. KREMETART.

krimpsiekte /'krəmpsɪktə, -siktə/ *n.* Also **krimpsiek, krimpziekte.** [Afk., *krimp* shrink + *siekte* (earlier *ziekte*) disease; see quot. 1966.]

1. *Pathology.* A disease affecting the muscular and nervous system of livestock and caused by the ingestion of any of a variety of poisonous plants; LÊSIEKTE; NENTA sense 2. Also *attrib.*

1893 HENNING in D.G. Steyn *Toxicology of Plants* (1934) 347 This stage .. of Krimpziekte .. endures a longer or shorted time depending upon the quantity of the klimop eaten, and the individual susceptibility to the poison. **1904** [see KLIMOP sense 2]. **1920** B. VAN DER RIET Letters. 29 Mar., The plant Cynanchum Africanum .. is responsible for the condition known to some farmers as krimpziekte. There is another disease known as krimpziekte, or neto, affecting goats throughout the Karoo, but the cause of this is a Cotyleden (plakkies). The scientific name for the former is Cynanchosis, and for the latter Cotyledenesis. **1929** *Handbk for Farmers* (Dept of Agric. & Forestry) 208 All our domestic animals are susceptible to krimpsiekte, but goats suffer chiefly as the krimpsiekte areas are mostly suitable for goat farming ... Two forms of krimpsiekte, namely the acute or 'opblaas' krimpsiekte, and the chronic or 'dun' krimpsiekte, are encountered. **1932** *Farming in S. Afr.* Apr. 11 (Swart), The only reliable preventative remedy against 'krimpsiekte' is to eradicate the krimpsiekte-bossie. **1934** D.G. STEYN *Toxicology of Plants* 345 'Cotyledonosis', which is also referred to by farmers as 'nenta', 'krimpsiekte', or 'krampsiekte'. **1966** C.A. SMITH *Common Names* 312 Dogs eating meat from the carcasses of herbivores poisoned by the plant [*Cotyledon wallichii*] will also develop krimpsiekte symptoms. The vernacular name is derived from the peculiar arching of the back and bending of the neck to one side .., as if these conditions had been brought about by a shrinkage of the muscles. **1973** F.J. VELDMAN in *Std Encycl. of Sn Afr.* VIII. 607 Several other plants produce symptoms resembling those of 'krimpsiekte', e.g. horse-tail grass .. and kieseblaar ... Even prussic acid poisoning is sometimes wrongly called 'krimpsiekte'. **1978** [see NENTA sense 1]. **1988** SMUTS & ALBERTS *Forgotten Highway* 184 *Pruimkougoed* ('chewing tobacco') .. is .. a good thing for sheep with *krimpsiek*. **1988** LE ROUX & SCHELPE *Namaqualand* 100 *Tylecodon paniculatus*, This plant, though not often eaten by stock .., causes severe stomach cramps ('krimpsiek') and even death.

2. Used *attrib.* in combinations designating some of the poisonous plants associated with this condition, as ***krimpsiektebos*** /-bɔs/ [Afk. *bos* bush], ***-bossie*** [see -IE], ***-bush, -plant***: (*a*) any of several poisonous plants of the Crassulaceae, including species of *Tylecodon* (or *Cotyledon*), esp. *Tylecodon cacaliodes*, or of *Kalanchoe*, esp. *Kalanchoe brachyloba;* (*b*) the poisonous plant *Lessertia annularis* of the Fabaceae. In both senses also called NENTA (sense 1).

Various species of *Cynanchum*, esp. *Cynanchum africanum* (see KLIMOP sense 2), are also thought to be responsible for krimpsiekte but are not named 'krimpsiektebos'.

1917 [see NENTA sense 1]. **1932** *Farming in S. Afr.* Apr. 11 (Swart), *Krimpsiektebossie*, .. A poisonous herb the Lessertia annularis that causes the disease in cattle known as krimpsiekte characterised by symptoms indicating an affection of the muscular and nervous system. **1966** C.A. SMITH *Common Names* 312 *Krimpsiektebos*, .. The vernacular name was assigned in more recent times to several species of *Cotyledon* and *Kalanchoe*, which are regarded as being the cause of krimpsiekte in stock. **1973** F.J. VELDMAN in *Std Encycl. of Sn Afr.* VIII. 607 *Cotyledon poisoning*, (Afr. krimpsiekte). This disease (also known as nenta poisoning) is caused by several species of 'krimpsiekte'-bush. **1991** *Dict. of Horticulture* (Dept of Nat. Educ.) 450 *Krimpsiektebos*, (*Tylecodon cacalioides*) nenta.

krissy var. CRISSY.

Kriste-mensch pl. form of CHRISTENMENSCH.

kroes /krʊs/ *adj. derog.* [Afk.]

1. Frizzy; an offensive mode of reference to tightly curled African hair; CRISSY. Occas. also **kroesie** [Eng. adj.-forming suffix *-y*, with spelling influenced by Afk.].

1949 H.C. BOSMAN in L. Abrahams *Unto Dust* (1963) 16 The British Government wanted to give the vote to any Cape Coloured person walking about with a *kroes* head and big cracks in his feet. **1971** J. BRANFORD *Informant, Grahamstown* Her hair is long and curly, not *kroesie*, but twisty. **1975** S. ROBERTS *Outside Life's Feast* 17 Her hair was black and tightly curled. Kroes, they call it. There's a touch of the tar-brush there, Mom once said. **1977** —— in E. Peirera *Contemp. S. Afr. Plays* 250 You favour him because he's got black kroes hair. **1989** V. OWEN in *Grocott's Mail* 20 Jan. 11 One of our number in an argument with him (who unfortunately had very curly hair) said it was obvious from his kroes hair why he could speak the lingo – from then on he never spoke one word.

2. *comb.* **kroeskop** /-kɔp/ [Afk., *kop* head], an offensive term for (one with) frizzy or tightly-curled hair (used esp. of the hair of black or 'coloured' people).

1913 C. PETTMAN *Africanderisms* 283 *Kroeskop*, Another nickname applied to the Hottentots. **1964** R. RIVE *Mod. Afr. Prose* 59 Do you want Soufie with her black skin to sit in the dining-room? Or Ou Kaar with his *kroeskop*? **1970** C.B. WOOD *Informant, Johannesburg* Look at that 'kroes-kop' (curly head).

krombek, kromebec varr. CROMBEC.

kromnek /'krɔmnek/ *n.* [Afk., *krom* crooked + *nek* neck (stalk).] **a.** A disease of tobacco plants caused by the tomato spotted-wilt virus; *Kat River wilt*, see KAT RIVER sense 2. **b.** Occas., this disease in tomato plants. Also *attrib.*

1931 *Farming in S. Afr.* Aug. 187 (Swart), *Kromnek*, This is a local name given to a serious wilt disease of tobacco which occurs in the Cape. **1932** [see *Kat River wilt* (KAT RIVER sense 2)]. **1933** E.S. MOORE in *Sci. Bulletin Dept of Agric.* No.123, 1 The disease known locally as 'Kromnek' or 'Kat River Wilt' is by far the most serious of the diseases of tobacco in the Stockenstrom division. *Ibid.* 15 The evidence indicated not only that the tomato disease is of virus nature but that probably it is caused by the same virus which is responsible for the tobacco kromnek. **1937** *Handbk for Farmers* (Dept of Agric. and Forestry) 1034 *Tobacco*, Kromnek. A very destructive disease which attacks plants at any age. Growth suddenly stops. **1941** *Nature* 19 Apr. 480 Control of the Kromnek (Spotted Wilt) Disease of Tomatoes. **1957** [see *Kat River disease* (KAT RIVER sense 2)].

kross var. KAROSS.

Kruger /'kruːgə/ *n.* [The name of *Stephanus Johannes Paulus Kruger* (1825–1904), president of the Transvaal (or South African) Republic from 1883 to 1901.]

1. Special Comb. **Kruger Day** *hist.*, the 10th of October, a public holiday commemorating the birthday of President Paul Kruger. Also *attrib.*

Scrapped as a public holiday in December 1994.

[**1889** F. JEPPE *Tvl Almanac & Dir.* 24 October, 31 days. The 10 *President Krüger born, 1825, Holiday.*] **1952** *Act 5* in *Stat. of Rep. of S. Afr.*, The days mentioned in the First Schedule to this Act shall be public holidays ... *First Schedule* .. Kruger Day (tenth day of October). **1980** *Rand Daily Mail* 9 Oct. 3 Kruger day celebrations will be held at different venues around the country. **1985** *Weekly Mail* 18 Oct. 9 Kruger Day is traditionally a day of rededication to the ideals of the Afrikaner nation .. commemorating the Afrikaner hero who led the Boers in their losing battle against British imperialism. **1987** P. RONAN in *E. Prov. Herald* 13 Nov. 2 A large number of black persons believe that Kruger Day is a celebration of apartheid. **1988** N. MATHIANE in *Frontline* Oct.-Nov. 32 The morning of Kruger Day – Saturday, October 10. *c*1988 *S. Afr. 1987–8: Off. Yrbk* (Bureau for Info.) 613 The Economic Affairs Committee of the President's Council in September 1987 recommended that Kruger Day and Founders' Day be abolished as public holidays and that a heroes' day be introduced in September. **1990** E. CLOETE in *Weekly Mail* 12 Oct. 1 Our idea was to de-mystify Kruger's or Heroes Day. **1993** M. BURGER in *Sunday Times* 10 Oct. 22 The entire 45-minute slot on what is likely to be the last Kruger Day will be devoted to what promises to be a heated exchange of views on such sensitive matters as the Springbok emblem, the flag and the national anthem. **1994** *E. Prov. Herald* 8 Sept. 1 A number of public holidays, including Sharpeville Day, Kruger Day and Republic Day, will be scrapped next year.

2.a. In full ***Krugerrand***, also ***Kruger rand*** /-rænd, rant/ [see RAND sense 3 a]: a coin of legal tender consisting of one ounce of gold, first minted in 1967 and bearing the portrait of Paul Kruger on the obverse side; any one of the fractional Krugerrands (see sense b). Also *attrib.*

1967 *Govt Gaz.* Vol.25 No.1793, 1 Design On Kruggerrand Gold Coin. Under and by virtue of the powers vested in me .. I hereby declare .. that the design on the obverse and on the reverse of the Kruggerrand gold coin (1 ounce fine gold) .. will appear on the said coin. **1967** *S. Afr. Digest* 14 July 3 The first gold Krugerrand coin was struck at the South African Mint in Pretoria last week by the Minister of Finance, Dr. N. Diederichs ... The Krugerrand is to be minted in limited numbers and is intended for overseas issue. **1971** *Std Encycl. of Sn Afr.* III. 313 The Krugerrand, a gold coin of 32.7 mm diameter containing 1 troy oz. of fine gold. **1972** *Evening Post* 26 Aug. 8 The recent sharp rise in the price of gold has made more people aware of the investment value of South Africa's prestige gold coin, the Kruger rand. [**1974** *E. Prov. Herald* 2 Sept. 8 A Kruger gold rand.] **1978** *Financial Mail* 9 June 805 This year Intergold expects a surge of demand for Krugers in West Germany ... A big upturn in Kruger sales is expected next year in Switzerland. **1978** *Sunday Times* 3 Feb. (Mag. Sect.) 3 If an ex-stripper like Kathy K— had the *nous* to stock-pile Krugers, why didn't a supposedly in-the-know journalist? **1982** *Pretoria News* 21 Sept. 21 The Krugerrand lost R12 at R550, and the tenth R6 at R58, but the quarter held steady at R140. The half Kruger was untraded. **1985** *E. Prov. Herald* 11 Jan. 16 Kruger sales down. **1985** *Sunday Times* 17 Nov. 28 It was announced this week that the minting of Krugerrands had been suspended. **1987** *Motorist* 1st Quarter 11 (*advt*) A lifetime Investment in Solid Gold ... Each piece of this unique collection is designed around a genuine 22 carat solid gold 1/10th Kruger rand. **1989** A. HOGG in *Style* Dec. 30 Some years back, the authorities realised that the price of a full one-ounce Krugerrand was putting the investment out of people's reach. So it gave the green light for the mintage of fractionals which carry, respectively, one tenth, a quarter and a half of an ounce of gold. **1992** *You & Your Bank* (Standard Bank) No.20, 6 Five years ago, ordinary Krugerrands traded at R1 140 and proof coins at a considerable premium. Today they trade at around R1 000, proof coins at much the same price.

b. With defining word: **mini-Krugerrand**, any one of the fractional Krugerrands made available in 1980.

1982 *E. Prov. Herald* 1 May 5 A new row over mini-Kruger rands broke in Parliament yesterday. 1982 O. HORWOOD in *E. Prov. Herald* 15 May 1 The wholly unfounded and scandalous allegations .. made .. against me .., certain senior officers of the Chamber of Mines and the director of the South African Mint (who had far more to do with the launching of the mini Krugerrands in September 1980 than I had).

3. Ellipt. for *Kruger National Park*, the largest South African game reserve, situated in the Eastern Transvaal.

1994 *House & Leisure* June 110 The Kruger charges R160 for two sharing, accommodation only. 1994 *Conserva* Vol.9 No.3, 20 (*heading*) Make the most of Kruger.

Krugerism /ˈkruːgərɪzm/ *n. Hist. derog.* [*Kruger* (see prec.) + Eng. abstract n.-forming suffix *-ism*.] The conservative, nationalistic, isolationist policy followed by President Kruger in the former Transvaal (or South African) Republic.

1897 *Times* (U.K.) 4 Feb. 3 Pure and unadulterated Krugerism. 1900 *The Jrnl* 13 July 2 'The Rise and fall of Krugerism' .. a goodly volume of more than 300 pages lies before us. 1903 E.F. KNIGHT *S. Afr. after War* 233 In the Transvaal the narrow fiscal system of Krugerism has been swept away. *Ibid.* 258 This centre of fanatical hatred – the headquarters of Krugerism and 'Dopperism'. 1923 B. RONAN *Forty S. Afr. Yrs* 183 It was Rhodes who was recognised as the only leader capable of checking the spread of Krugerism in South Africa. 1946 S. CLOETE *Afr. Portraits* 380 Rhodes addressed an anti-Boer meeting in Cape Town and told his audience that the Boers were not beaten. Only Krugerism was beaten. 1979 T. PAKENHAM *Boer War* (1982) 40 Joubert's party .. hammered home the message: 'Krugerism' was corrupt, inefficient and a ridiculous anachronism; high time Kruger was put in a museum.

Krugerite /ˈkruːgəraɪt/ *adj.* and *n. Obs.* exc. *hist.* [*Kruger* (see KRUGER) + Eng. n.- and adj.-forming suffix *-ite*.]

A. *adj.* Adhering to the ideology or policies of President Paul Kruger (of the former Transvaal Republic).

1896 *Westminster Gaz.* (U.K.) 3 Dec. 5 Those who have effusively championed Mr. Chamberlain for what they imagined was his agreement with their Krugerite sympathies. 1897 *Daily News* (U.K.) 24 Mar. 7 The conflict between the two ideals – the Rhodesian or British, and the Krugerite or non-British. 1899 J.P. FITZPATRICK *Tvl from Within* 146 The visitors were men who although officially associated with the Government were not at all in sympathy with the policy of the Krugerite party, and they were .. desirous of liberal reform. 1900 *Pall Mall Gaz.* (U.K.) 11 June 2 In the spring of last year he denounced the corruption of the Krugerite gang.

B. *n.* A follower of President Paul Kruger or his policies.

1897 *Daily News* (U.K.) 25 Jan. 5 Krugerites we know, and Rhodesites, but the Schreinerites (politically) all seem to live in London. 1903 E.F. KNIGHT *S. Afr. after War* 258 The fact is that the Krugerites are not accepted as prophets in their own country. 1900 *Pall Mall Gaz.* (U.K.) 29 Mar. 8 There are those who suggest that, perhaps, if the scrutineers had not been Krugerites, Joubert would have been found at the head. 1902 R. KIPLING *Traffics & Discov.* (1904) 33 Van Zyl wasn't any Krugerite. 1972 *Sunday Times* 11 June (Mag. Sect.) 9 My father was not a Krugerite, he was a follower of Joubert, who would be called a Progressive today, I suppose.

kruidjie-roer-my-nie /ˌkreɪkiˈruːrmeɪni, ˌkrœɪki-, -ci-/ *n.* [Afk., transf. use of Du. *kruidje-roer-mij-niet*, *kruid* herb, plant + dim. suffix -IE + *roeren* touch, stir + *mij* me + *niet* not, the plant *Mimosa pudica*, or (fig.) a touchy or irascible person.

The name is said to refer to the smell the plant emits when touched: the plant so called in Dutch has leaves which close up when touched.]

Any of several species of shrub of the genus *Melianthus* of the Melianthaceae, esp. *M. major*, *M. minor*, and *M. comosus*, with foul-smelling leaves which are held to have certain medicinal properties; TRUIDJIE-ROER-MY-NIE.

[1896 J. WOOD in *Scientific African* Mar. 76 A few nests of the *N. Famosa* were discovered among the 'roer-mij-niet' bushes.] 1917 R. MARLOTH *Common Names* 52 *Kruidje-roer-mij-niet*, Several species of *Melianthus*, used med[icinally]. In the S.W. *M. major* (very ornamental foliage), in the central districts *M. comosus* (poisonous to stock). The latter yields a black, but otherwise quite tasty and harmless honey. [1936 L.G. GREEN *Secret Afr.* 231 Traditional country remedies for the bite [*sc.* of the button spider] ... Many people boil up the weed called, in Dutch, *kruidjie-roer-my-niet* and make the patient drink a concoction.] 1949 —— *Land of Afternoon* 51 Leaves of Kruidjie (or Truidjie) roer my nie, in spite of the unpleasant odour, yield a decoction which is taken as a gargle or applied to skin diseases. 1970 D.E. ABOUD *Informant, Bloemfontein* Kruidjie-roer-my-nie is a shrub up to four feet, unpleasantly scented, which secretes much nectar. 1975 W. STEENKAMP *Land of Thirst King* 130 The kruidjie-roer-my-niet .. which translates as 'little herb, touch me not' .. is a sizeable growth and not unhandsome in appearance, but bruise its leaves in any way and it exudes a ghastly rank smell that would make a polecat blanch. Nevertheless, the children of old Namaqualand were always willing to brave the kruidjie-roer-me-niet's stench .. in order to get at the delicious brown nectar in its leaves. 1979 *Sunday Times* 9 Dec. (Mag. Sect.) 7 A television series with Willem doing the commentary in the accent that is as strongly flavoured as the kruidjie-roer-my-niet.

kruisbessie /ˈkreɪsbesi, ˈkrœɪs-/ *n.* Formerly also **kruisbesje, kruysbesjie.** [Afk., earlier S. Afr. Du. *kruysbesje*, Du. *kruys* cross + *besje* (fr. Du. *bes*) berry; see quot. 1913.] **a.** The fruit of *Grewia occidentalis* of the Tiliaceae; FOUR CORNERS sense b. **b.** The small tree or shrub *Grewia occidentalis*, with mauve-pink flowers and characteristic four-lobed berries; BUTTONWOOD; CROSS-BERRY; DEW-BERRY; FOUR CORNERS sense a. **c.** *rare.* Any plant of the genus *Grewia*. Also *attrib.* See also ASSEGAI WOOD, ROSYNTJIE.

1887 *S.W. Silver & Co.'s Handbk to S. Afr.* 139 Kruysbesjies are the fruit of the *Grewia occidentalis*. 1894 R. MARLOTH in *Trans. of S. Afr. Phil. Soc.* p.lxxxiv, *Greewia flava* (Kruisbesje). 1913 C. PETTMAN *Africanderisms* 284 *Kruisbesjes*, .. The fruit of *Grewia occidentalis* is known in the Cape Colony by this name, the reference being apparently to the cross-like arrangement of the four-lobed drupe. 1934 *Sunday Times* 25 Feb. (Swart), The three children were on their way from school and passed through a patch of 'Kruisbessie' bushes, which had just been sprayed. 1934 C.P. SWART Supplement to Pettman. 99 *Kruisbessie*, .. Grewia occidentalis or four-corners is so designated on account of its shape. 1966 C.A. SMITH *Common Names* 314 *Kruisbessie(boom)*, *Grewia occidentalis*. A shrub or small tree ... The branches were much favoured by Bushmen for making their bows .. and by natives for their assegai shafts. 1972 I.C. VERDOORN in *Std Encycl. of Sn Afr.* V. 83 *Kruisbessie. Rosyntjebos*, (Grewia sp.) ... The one common name refers to the arrangement of the fruits, which usually occur in fours and form a cross. 1983 H. THESEN in *Outeniqualander/Herald* 21 Dec. 26 The bush-buck ram .. can eat the most juicy tips of 'kruisbessie' .. to his heart's content. 1990 *Weekend Post* 17 Feb. 7 A small tree which deserves to be grown more frequently in our gardens is *Grewia occidentalis*. It .. bears pretty many-petalled pinky/mauve flowers .. and these are followed by red berries borne in fours in the form of a cross. Hence the common name crossberry or kruisbessie. 1992 H. HUTCHINGS in *Weekend Post* 22 Aug. (Leisure) 7 The shape of the berries gives rise to the common name of cross berry or kruisbessie.

‖**kruithoring** /ˈkreɪthʊərəŋ, ˈkrœɪt-, -huərəŋ/ *n.* Formerly also **kruithoorn.** [Afk., *kruit* gunpowder + *horing* (earlier *hoorn*) horn.] **a.** *hist.* A powder-horn made of the horn of a cow or antelope, fitted with a lid or cap, and worn on a belt. **b.** *Transf.*, and *fig.* A symbol of the National Party. Also *attrib.*

1948 *George & Knysna Herald* 28 May 3 The Nationalist candidate headed the procession with the Kruithoring banner. 1971 *Daily Dispatch* 16 Dec. 10 Each man had three rifles, ready primed with small bags of slugs at hand and the horns (kruithorings) filled with dry powder. 1973 J. MEINTJES *Voortrekkers* 106 To a belt was attached a powder-horn or *kruithoring*. 1975 *S. Afr. Panorama* Jan. 14 on the wall of the entrance hall was a gun-rack which supported .. the 'kruithoring' which was traditionally used to store gunpowder. 1975 *Drum* 8 Aug. 1 How else can you explain their throwing a braai and sounding the kruithoorn after losing the recent by-elections at Middelburg and Gezina. 1978 *Sunday Times* 14 May 14 In the Transvaal he held sway over the strongest principality in the party, and those who wore the kruithoring were his followers almost to a man. 1982 *Rand Daily Mail* 25 Feb. 11 The Kruithoring Rebellion. 1988 J. SCOTT in *E. Prov. Herald* 5 Mar. 6, I even had to take off my kruithoring badge. It's bad for business, and a man mos has got to live. 1988 [see OSSEWA sense 2 a]. 1989 *Reader's Digest Illust. Hist.* 116 Armed with rifles on their backs and a *kruithoring* (powder horn) .. formidable groups of trekkers would ride into battle.

krummelpap /ˈkrəm(ə)lpap/ *n.* [Afk., fr. Du. *krummel* crumbly + *pap* porridge.] PUTU sense b. See also MEALIEPAP sense 1.

1968 *Fair Lady* 30 Oct. (Suppl.) 6 A real old time South African favourite – perfect at braais. Make the firm stywe pap or the dry and crumbly Krummelpap. 1970 HEARD & FAULL *Cookery in Sn Afr.* 476 There are many ways of making mealie pap, from the dry crumbly 'krummelpap' beloved of the Zulus to the thick, smooth porridge. 1972 *Sunday Times* 2 Sept. (Mag. Sect.) 4 For four servings of krummelpap, add 1 teaspoon salt to 1 cup water and boil. Add 2 cups maize meal. 1979 HEARD & FAULL *Our Best Trad. Recipes* 62 Krummelpap. Crumbly porridge .. for Two ... Boil slowly for 15 minutes. Stir with fork until mixture becomes crumbly. 1986 C. KIRSTEIN *Best S. Afr. Braai Recipes* 84 If you are eating firm 'stywepap' you are probably in the Transvaal, whereas if you are served the more crumbly 'krummelpap' or 'putupap', chances are you are braaiing in the Orange Free State or Natal. 1991 P. BOSMAN *Informant, George* We're the maize generation! We enjoy stywe pap and krummelpap, also known as putu, with a braai.

krygsraad /ˈkreɪxsrɑːt/ *n.* Formerly also **kriegsraad, krij(g)sraad.** [Afk., fr. Du. *krijgsraad* Council of War, *krijg* war, strife + *raad* council.]

1. *obs.* Under Dutch rule at the Cape: the Council of Burgher Officers (see BURGHER sense 1 a).

*c*1795 W.S. VAN RYNEVELD in G.M. Theal *Rec. of Cape Col.* (1897) I. 248 The Council of Burgher Officers under the name of Burgher council of War (Krijgs Raad), was composed of the officers of cavalry and infantry, together with the commandant of the Garrison as their President. *Ibid.* 251 The College of Officers of the Burgher Militia, or Krijgsraad.

2. *hist.* Esp. in the former Boer republics: a war council; a meeting of such a council; a court-martial of such a council. Also *fig.*

1880 *Grocott's Penny Mail* 28 Dec. 3 Paul Kruger had a meeting of the Krysoraad [*sic*] and it was unanimously resolved to starve the garrison with women and children out. 1881 *E. London Dispatch & Frontier Advertiser* 22 Jan. 2 The *Friend* gathers from a reliable man .. that Major Clarke and High Sheriff Raaff are to be tried by Krijgsraad, and that their fate will be decided by twenty-two jurymen. 1881 G.F. AUSTEN *Diary* (1981) 23 Today the Krygsraad made demand on the merchants of the town for the supply of various articles of consumption .. for the rise of the Boer army. 1882 C.L. NORRIS-NEWMAN *With Boers in Tvl* 192 There were great rejoicings that night throughout all the camps, and an important Kriegsraad was held to consider the final terms of peace offered by General Wood. 1885 J. NIXON *Complete Story Tvl* 220 A number of them were brought up before the 'krijgsraad,' or council of war, on a charge of high treason. **1899** J.P. FITZPATRICK *Tvl from Within* 186 It lay with the Commandant-General and Krijgsraad (or War Council) to decide what should be done with the prisoners. **1901** P.J. DU TOIT *Diary* (1974) 40 We arrived at Syferpan, where a Krygsraad (Council of war) was held. It transpired that a general attack on Lichtenburg was decided upon. At sunset we trekked, not knowing whither. **1909** LADY S. WILSON *S. Afr. Mem.* 102 The magistrate wrote me a miserable letter, saying his office had been seized by the Boers, who held a daily Kriegsraad there, and that he had received a safe-conduct to depart. **1916** E.H. SPENDER *General Botha* 64 He was now readily, in spite of his youth, granted a right to speak in the 'Krijgs-raad.' **1927** E.N. MARAIS *Rd to Waterberg* (1972) 164 Within a short while — a very short while — I shall appear before the Great Court martial (*Krygsraad*), where false evidence will avail no man. *Ibid.* 165 He stipulated that he would only surrender if he received a written undertaking from the Triumvirate that he would be tried by a *Krygsraad* of his own people; he refused to be tried by a British court martial. *a*1930 G. BAUMANN in Baumann & Bright *Lost Republic* (1940) 166 Besides receiving all telegrams, seeing people who wished to interview the 'Krygsraad' (War Council), receiving coded messages .. I had to inaugurate the Red Cross Department and the Scout Corps. **1933** W.H.S. BELL *Bygone Days* 279 When war was imminent in 1899, he joined the Vryheid Commando and was appointed to the staff of his old friend General Lucas Meyer and became a member of his Krijsraad (war council). **1957** B. O'KEEFE *Gold without Glitter* 25 Get hold of Kornet de Villiers, and three of the senior burghers to sit with me on the *kriegsraad*. **1969** J. MEINTJES *Sword in Sand* 41 At a krygsraad De la Rey had painstakingly outlined to the men under his command what he had in mind. **1973** J. MEINTJES *Voortrekkers* 86 As Commandant, Potgieter was also chairman of any Krygsraad or council of war, while Maritz was chairman or president of the Volksraad or parliament. **1977** R.J. HAINES in R.J. Bouch *Infantry in S. Afr. 1652–1976* 1 Each administrative district had a council of war, a *Krygsraad*, of superior officers who generally supervised the militia and junior officers. **1979** T. PAKENHAM *Boer War* (1982) 542 The *Krijgsraad* took place at Blijdschap, near Reitz. The leaders decided to seize the first chance to launch a concentrated attack. **1987** W. STEENKAMP *Blockhouse* 7 The average commando was democratic to the point of virtual anarchy ... Battle-plans were usually discussed and voted on at a 'krygsraad' or council of war at which every man had his say. **1990** C. LAFFEATY *Far Forbidden Plains* 97 The *Krygsraad* cannot even afford to feed the burghers for long, let alone equip them.

ku /kuː/ *n. Obs.* exc. *hist.* Also **koo**. [Khoikhoi *!ku(u)*, *!ko(o)*, the name of a plant. Despite Pettman's contention (see quot. 1913), 'ku' is etymologically unrelated to the word KAMBRO.] The tuberous plant *Fockea edulis* of the Asclepiadaceae; also called KAMBRO.

1795 C.R. HOPSON tr. *C.P. Thunberg's Trav.* II. 102 Besides the above-mentioned plant called Kon or Gunna, they use two others, viz. one called Kamekà, or Barup, which is said to be a large and watery root; and another called Ku, which is likewise .. a large and succulent root. **1913** C. PETTMAN *Africanderisms* 274 *Komaroo* or *Kambroo*, A plant of the genus Fockea (glabra), the root of which contains a large quantity of water ... The word is sometimes shortened to 'Koo'. **1966** C.A. SMITH *Common Names* 316 *!Ku(u), Fockea edulis* ... Tuber up to 2 ft in diameter ... In former days were eaten by the Hottentots who knew the species by the above vernacular name.

kubombu, ku bomvu varr. KUMBOMVU.

kubus /ˈkʊbʊs/ *n.* [Khoikhoi plant name.] **a.** *hist.* A fungus cultured in milk, claimed by its promoters to possess anti-ageing properties, and sold to investors during the mid-1980s as part of a fraudulent money-making scheme. **b.** Used allusively of any such scheme. Also *attrib.*, and *comb.* **kubus-type** *adj.*

1984 *Cape Times* 13 July 2 The secret use of the kubus plant has been unveiled — it is to be exported to the United States where it will be made into a range of cosmetics to be known as Cleopatra's Secret. **1984** *Grocott's Mail* 21 Sept. 1 Kubus .. Kubus .. Kubus. Agency opening in Grahamstown ... Activators, envelopes, cheese/milk powder mix available. **1987** S. BARBER in *E. Prov. Herald* 7 May 5 A Kansas City Court sentenced the South African kubus king .. for his role in a nationwide 'ponzi' scheme that milked American investors of up to R200-million. **1989** *E. Prov. Herald* 17 Feb. 9 Too many people in South Africa had a 'Kubus mentality' in that they believed that they could use their hard-earned savings to make the proverbial 'quick buck,' rather than investing them sensibly and soundly. **1991** M. STANDFIELD in *Sunday Times* 17 Feb. 7 Evidence given to the commission showed that Mr V— operated a 'Kubus-type scam'.

Hence **kubusy** *adj. nonce*, suspect, doubtful.

1987 E. MOOLMAN in *You* 22 Oct. 8 The so-called 'grocery clubs' are starting to smell just a little .. well .. 'kubusy', shall we say. And anyone who lost his boots in the kubus ripoff will certainly recognise the smell.

kudu /ˈkʊduː, ˈkuduː/ *n.* Also **coedoe, coodoo, coudou, cuddu, ko(e)doe, koedo(o), kood(o)o, koudou.** [ad. Khoikhoi *kudu-b* or *kudu-s*, Xhosa *iqudu*. *Koedoe* is the S. Afr. Du. (and subsequently Afk.) form.]

1.a. The large antelope *Tragelaphus strepsiceros* of the Bovidae, characterized by long spirally-curved horns in the male animal. Also *attrib.*

1773 J. HAWKESWORTH *Acct of Voy.* III. 384 A beast called by the Hottentots 'Coe-doe', which is as large as a horse, and has .. fine spiral horns. **1777** G. FORSTER *Voy. round World* I. 84 The Coodoo, or Kolben's *bock ohne namen* (goat without a name). **1785** —— tr. *Sparrman's Voy. Cape G.H.* II. 213 Koedoe is the name given by the colonists to a beautiful tall gazel with long and slender shanks. **1789** W. PATERSON *Narr. of Four Journeys* 27 We found here many .. Koedoes ... These animals are about the size, or rather larger than our deer, and of a mouse colour, with three white stripes over the back; the male has very large twisted horns. **1801** W. SOMERVILLE *Narr. of E. Cape Frontier* (1979) 133 The horns differ from all the antelope species .. but has something of the spiral turn of the Coodoos Horn. **1802** *Sporting Mag.* XX. 141 The n'gou and koudou are also inhabitants of Caffraria. **1822** W.J. BURCHELL *Trav.* I. 337 Antilope strepsiceros, of modern writers. The Hottentot name is written Koedoe, according to Dutch orthography: Kudu, in German: and Koodoo or Coodoo in English. **1835** T.H. BOWKER Journal. 14 Oct., Go a shooting but find nothing but spoors of cuddu Sea Cow & &. **1854** R.B. STRUTHERS *Hunting Jrnl* (1991) 45 Presently we fell in with some Koodus .. a buck & doe of which I shot — they are splendid Buck & have magnificent horns (the male). **1874** D. LIVINGSTONE *Last Jrnls* I. 161, I got a fine male Kudu. **1879** R.J. ATCHERLEY *Trip to Boerland* 155 Advancing .. with their beautiful spiral horns towering high above them, were two magnificent koodoos. **1896** R. WARD *Rec. of Big Game* 204 Although one of the largest of the antelopes, .. it is astonishing how, in bushy country, this animal is able to conceal itself. **1900** W.L. SCLATER *Mammals of S. Afr.* II. 245 The Kudus .. seem to be particularly fond of rocky and stony hills covered with thick thorny shrubs, but are also found along the densely wooded river banks. **1929** D. REITZ *Commando* 127 Koodoo comes from the Xhosa word Qhude. Non-Xhosas finding it difficult to pronounce the aspirated click qh went on and pronounced it as koo-. **1936** C. BIRKBY *Thirstland Treks* 296 The old hunter spoke of .. the kudu's graceful horns and stripes. **1947** L. HASTINGS *Dragons Are Extra* 176 A Kudu bull with his great spiral horns a good sixty inches long. **1951** A. ROBERTS *Mammals* 308 The Kudu occurs usually in the rather dry acacia veld, seldom far from water. **1951** D. LESSING in D. Wright *S. Afr. Stories* (1960) 99 It was more than the ordinary farm living-room. There were koodoo horns branching out over the fireplace, and a bundle of knobkerries hung on a nail. **1971** *Daily Dispatch* 2 Sept. 2 At night, the car lights attract the kudu, which then tend to jump on to the vehicle. With these animals weighing up to 800 lbs, severe damage can be inflicted and lives endangered. **1985** T. BARON in *Frontline* Feb. 31 That's how it is with potjiekos. Steenbok is best but anything else will do .. kudu, springbok, warthog. **1990** *Farmer's Weekly* 8 June 41 Species available to hunters today include impala, kudu.

b. *comb.* **kudu foot**, a style of foot in furniture and silverware; **kudu-berry**, the tree *Pseudolachnostylis maprouneifolia* of the Euphorbiaceae; **kudu-bush**, either of two shrubs, (*a*) *Combretum apiculatum* of the Combretaceae, (*b*) *Haworthia viscosa* of the Liliaceae; **kudu lily**, the *impala lily* (sense (*b*) see IMPALA sense 1 c), *Pachypodium saundersii*; **kudu-milk** *slang*, in the Grahamstown district, a name for brandy; **kudu-wors** /-vɔːs, -vɔrs/ [Afk. *wors* sausage], sausage made of kudu meat.

1972 *Farmer's Weekly* 21 Apr. 84 Lounge suites made in ball and claw, Queen Anne or **Kudu feet**. **1961** PALMER & PITMAN *Trees of S. Afr.* 235 The **kudu-berry**, *Pseudolachnostylis maprouneifolia* is a tree of the bushveld and lowveld. **1987** F. VON BREITENBACH *Nat. List of Indigenous Trees* 90 *Pseudolachnostylis maprouneifolia*, .. Kudu-berry. **1971** B.J.G. DE LA BAT in *Std Encycl. of Sn Afr.* IV. 395 A great variety of trees, including .. **kudu-bush** (*Haworthia viscosa*) .. grow in the deeper soil of the eastern sector. **1974** W. GIESS in *Ibid.* X. 150 The berg-thorn .. grows here together with the kudu-bush (*Combretum apiculatum*). **1966** C.A. SMITH *Common Names* 316 **Kudu lily**, *Pachypodium saundersii* .. , see *Impala lily*. **1984** J. ONDERSTALL *Tvl Lowveld & Escarpment* 152 *Pachypodium saundersii* Kudu Lily ... This impressive succulent shrub resembles the Impala Lily but differs in having slender sharp spines along the branches. **1971** F.G. BUTLER *Informant, Grahamstown* **Kudumilk**. Albany [name] for brandy. **1993** S. GRAY in *Weekly Mail & Guardian* 5 Nov. 48 That was actually **kudu-wors** we were gorging on. Gamey, as the Bushvelders like it, fat spattering.

2. *Military.* A light transport aircraft developed for the defence force.

1976 *Std Encycl. of Sn Afr.* XII. 14 Atlas was taken over by Armscor, and .. has built many impala jet aircraft and the Kudu, a light transport aircraft. **1980** A. ROBINSON *Air Power* 276 A few Bosbok developments, the C4M Kudu with similar wing and tailplane, are attached to No 41 from the 40 aircraft so far produced.

kufiya var. KOFIA.

kugel /ˈkʊg(ə)l, ˈku-/ *n. slang.* [Special sense of general Eng. *kugel* a starchy pudding of potatoes or noodles, fr. Yiddish, lit. 'ball', fr. Middle High G. *kugel(e)* ball, globe.] A (usu. *derog.*) term for a young, spoilt, wealthy (Jewish) woman who is preoccupied with materialism or frivolities, and is characterized by nasal, drawling speech. Also shortened form **kug** (see quot. 1992), *attrib.*, and *comb.* (objective) **kugel-spotting**. Cf. BAGEL.

1970 *New Nation* Oct. 17 He married, quite thoughtlessly, a middle-class Kugel, but soon sees that her eccentric zany charm is merely slovenly vacuousness. **1971** *Personality* 29 Jan. 49 *Kugel* is a Yiddish word meaning pudding, but in this country it now also means daughters of wealthy parents whose only interest in life is their appearance and how to spend more money. Kugels have developed a jargon and accent of their own. **1975** *Rhodeo* (Rhodes Univ.) Vol.29 No.6, 2, I regretfully observe that a fair number of *kugels* are managing to infiltrate the Rhodes Campus .. all dolled up to the nines. **1981** B. RONGE in *Fair Lady* 2 Dec. 352 'A kugel is not a radical or ethnic phenomenon' he said. 'It is really a state of mind. And an accent of course.' **1982** *Sunday Times* 28 Mar. (Mag. Sect.) 1 He took to the business the way a kugel takes to Krugerrands. **1982** I.H. KLEVANSKY *Kugel Book* 6 How to spot a kugel. She's well-dressed. She wears diamond studs in her ears. She smells expensive. She speaks through her nose ... Thursday nights make for good kugel-spotting. **1986** FRANKENTAL & SHAIN in

Burman & Reynolds *Growing Up* 220 Some Jewish girls will virtually act out a fascinating stereotype which has been named and articulated in recent years. This is the 'kugel' phenomenon, a caricature of a young woman with 'the latest' in everything and a single-minded determination to find the 'right' husband, the 'perfect' home in the best area and to raise 'perfect' children. Clearly, the 'kugel' is a product of urban affluence associated with the *nouveau riche*, to be found in many countries and not restricted to Jews. The word, however, has become a code reference for young Jews (and increasingly for non-Jews) in South Africa, with the user aspiring sometimes to the status, but more often rejecting association with the category. **1986** *Style* Aug. 146 Ran into a kugel friend last week. Expressed surprise that she hadn't *already left for Australia*. 'Never!' she shrieked. 'As I said to Merv, I'd be rather killed in my bed than have to get up and make it.' **1989** *Flying Springbok* Sept. 14 She has a wardrobe that would make a kugel blanch (1 200 000 pairs of shoes). **1989** B. LUDMAN *Day of Kugel* 8 'Kugels are mostly from the wealthy northern suburbs of Johannesburg ..' Clive said. 'If you're a kugel, you're doing a BA degree while you look for a medical student to marry. Your heart is as big as all outdoors and your head is an empty as the Karoo.' **1991** C. SAMPSON on TV1, 11 June, In America we call the kugel the JAP – the Jewish American princess. **1991** I. & F. DE MOOR *Informants, Grahamstown* Kugel (probably originated at the University of the Witwatersrand) – a rich, spoilt, shallow female. Usually a first year University student, often Jewish. Has a particular accent and manner of speaking, epitomised in Pieter Dirk Uys's send up in his many satirical reviews. Definitely associated more and more with Johannesburg than anywhere else in the country. **1991** H. PHILLIPS *Informant, Johannesburg* 'It's outstanding', the ultimate mark of kugel approval. **1992** B. RONGE in *Sunday Times* 10 May (Mag. Sect.) 8, I hung around .. observing the shopping patterns of the kugels because I was looking for a jet-set, you see, and if the Sandton kugs can't set your jet for you, then 10-to-one it can't fly at all. **1993** H.P. TOFFOLI in *Ibid.* 16 May 15 Studies show the black-tipped hanging fly chooses her man .. on the size of the prey he provides. A regular kugel.

Hence **kugel** *adj.*; also as *v. intrans.* and *reflexive*, to be concerned with frivolities, to dress (oneself) smartly or ostentatiously; **kugeldom** *n.*, kugels collectively; **Kugelese** *n. nonce*, the language of kugels; **kugelism** *n.*, the state of being a kugel; **kugelly** *adj.*; **kugel up** *v. phr. intrans.* (*nonce*), to dress up, to over-dress.

1978 G. ARON in S. Gray *Theatre Two* (1981) 15 Phone and cancel – and if that *kugelly* cousin of mine whines, tell her it's all my fault. **1979** *Sunday Times* 9 Sept. (Mag. Sect.) 4 Being at .. University, I spend half my life in faded jeans, but that doesn't give me the right to condemn the few who do turn up dressed to kill. I indulge in 'kugeling-up' myself occasionally. **1985** *Cape Times* 15 July, The girls are .. on their way to the Girls' Army unit at George. One is a 'kugelly townie,' joining the army to fill in time between leaving school and finding a husband. **1987** *Fair Lady* 18 Feb. 143 My daughter .. went one step further by opting, as a gentile, to study Hebrew at the University of the Witwaterstrand, and in that temple of intellectual kugeldom marched off with first prize. **1987** R. CUTLER in *Style* Mar. 28 Afrikaans will be made up of not only English and Afrikaans, but also of our indispensable Kugelese which has so handsomely enriched the language of this country. **1989** M. BRAND in *Fair Lady* 25 Oct. 90 *Kugel*, materialistic, Jewish person; there are varying degrees of kugelism, from baby kugels (five year olds comparing outfits and parents' wealth), to minor kugels (nice girls inclined to overdress), to major kugels (prime snobs). **1990** S. JORDAN in *Style* Aug. 40, I hate kugel places where you sit for hours drinking coffee with your girlfriends. **1991** C. SAMPSON on TV1, 11 June, Now we're going to stop kugeling and get down to some serious business.

kugel-tas var. KOGEL-TAS.

kuhne /ˈkuːni/ *n.* Also **khune**, **kuny**, and with initial capital. [See quot. 1977.] In full ***kuhne meal***: a name given to coarsely crushed wholewheat flour, particularly in KwaZulu-Natal. Also *attrib.*

1951 S. VAN H. TULLEKEN *Prac. Cookery Bk* 350 Khune Meal Porridge. This is the best of all a wonderful help against constipation. Khune meal is crushed wheat. **1974** *Sunday Times* 22 Dec. (Mag. Sect.) 3 It's supposed to be made from something called kuny meal but I just used flour. **1976** *Darling* 18 Aug., If you're just feeling peckish, how about honey and sunflower seeds between slices of kuny bread? **1977** L.H.M. HOOD *Informant* Although we are a firm of Millers who produce and pack Kuhne crushed wheaten meal, .. we too have experienced great difficulty in establishing the derivation of the name 'Kuhne'. Popular belief .. is that the name Kuhne was that of a German Doctor who developed a loaf of bread to 'clear up the illnesses prevalent at the time – during the turn of the century – it was called the health loaf and was made of the following ingredients: whole wheat flour, salt, yeast and water'. **1978** *Sunday Times* 23 July (Mag. Sect.) 3 Uncrushed wheat (called kuhne meal in Natal) is an excellent source of fibre.

kuickendieff var. KUIKENDIEF.

kuier /ˈkeɪə, ˈkœiə/ *v.* Also **kuyer**. [Afk., fr. Du. *kuieren*, to walk, stroll.]

a. *intrans.* To call, stop by, pay a visit.

1822 W.J. BURCHELL *Trav.* I. 329 They soon began to feel themselves at home, as they were allowed to visit, or as they call it, kuyer, at the kraal. **1971** *Informant* Frikkie even sent his kids over there one day to kuier and ask when he would be selling his farm. **1978** J. HOBBS *Darling Blossom* 115 We use up some of Sherman's extra petrol on kuiering with other parties .. where the beer never stops flowing and the braai's never go out and .. such funny Van der Merwe jokes. **1982** J. KRIGE in *Staffrider* Vol.5 No.2, 20 We would sleep till four o'clock, have a quick cup of tea to wake up and then go kuier on the farms. **1985** D. KRAMER in *Cosmopolitan* May 102 When the Kriels settled down for a 'little nap' on Sundays after lunch, that's when the rugby Romeo came to kuier. **1994** C.J. DRIVER *In Water-Margins* 17 And so he came to visit, *Kom kuier*, in the language of childhood we still use. **1995** C. LAWRANCE in *Natal Witness* 3 Jan. 7, I knew they hadn't come to *kuier* (visit socially).

b. *trans. Rare*, perh. *nonce*. To visit (someone).

1994 C.J. DRIVER *In Water-Margins* 31 Flood-lights Leap at tentative footfalls; to *kom kuier* Even the most patiently waiting friend What glass-topped walls would one climb.

So **kuier** *n.* [Afk.], a visit.

[**1913** C. PETTMAN *Africanderisms* 284 *Kuier*, .. In Cape Dutch this word means a visit, an outing.] **1971** M. BRITZ *Informant, Grahamstown* Margie came for just a short kuier on Saturday.

kuikendief /ˈkeɪkəndif, ˈkœiken-/ *n.* Also **kuickendieff**, **kuikenduif**, **kuyken-dief**. [S. Afr. Du., fr. Du. *kuiken* chicken + *dief* thief.] Any of a number of birds of the kite, harrier, or hawk families, particularly the yellow-billed kite *Milvus migrans parasitus* of the Accipitridae.

*c*1808 C. VON LINNÉ *System of Natural Hist.* VIII. 44 The settlers at the Cape called it [*sc.* the Parasite Kite] *kuyken-dief*, which signifies fowl-stealer. **1810** [see KWIKSTAART]. **1822** W.J. BURCHELL *Trav.* I. 502 A kite, which in size, manners, and appearance, much resembles the common kite of Europe, .. is known by the name of *Kúikendief* (chicken thief). **1834** A. SMITH *Diary* (1939) I. 165 Many of the birds common in the Colony are also found here, the Elanus melanopterus .. and kuikenduif common. **1913** C. PETTMAN *Africanderisms* 285 *Kuikendief*, .. *Milvus aegypticus*, a species of kite. **1923** HAAGNER & IVY *Sketches* 102 The Yellow-billed Kite (*Milvus aegyptius*) is a migrant from North Africa and Arabia ... According to Major Stevenson Hamilton, the Game Warden of the Transvaal Game Preserves, its Dutch name of *Kuikendief* (Chicken thief) is not merited. **1994** A. CRAIG in M. Roberts tr. *J.A. Wahlberg's Trav. Jrnls 1838–56* 36 A common name for the yellow-billed kite is still 'kuikendief'.

kuil /keɪl, kœil/ *n. obsolescent.* Also **kuyl**. Pl. **-s**, occas. **kuile** /ˈkœɪlə/. [Afk., earlier S. Afr. Du., fr. Du., pit, hole.]

1. A pool or water-hole. Also *attrib.*

1827 G. THOMPSON *Trav.* I. 425 At length .. we reached a spot .. called the *kuil* or pit, where we found a small natural reservoir of tolerable water. [*a*1873 J. BURROW *Trav. in Wilds* (1971) 76 This place is called the *'Kuyl'* (hole) from an extraordinary pit several feet deep.] **1911** *Farmer's Weekly* 18 Oct. 194 Some large cattle farmers .. held that cattle drinking the running river water never took lamziekte, whilst those animals drinking shallow kuil water frequently did. **1916** *Ibid.* 20 Dec. 1455 For Immediate Sale – Four miles from Devon, Transvaal – about 800 morgen grand grazing and arable land – nine paddocks, kuils, dam, spring borehole and windmill. **1925** P. SMITH *Little Karoo* (1936) 174 Every kuil or water-hole they passed was dry, and near every kuil were the skeletons of donkeys and sheep which had come there but to perish of their thirst. **1966** C.A. SMITH *Common Names* 261 *Kaainanblom*, .. Very common in most pools, kuile, dams, vleis and slow-flowing streams and rivers of the south west to the Transvaal.

2. *comb.* **kuilgras** /-xras/ [Afk., *gras* grass], either of two grasses, *Eragrostis plana* or *Diplachne fusca.*

1931 E.P. PHILLIPS *S. Afr. Grasses* 78 (Swart), *Kuilgras*, .. A species of grass, Eragrostis plana, growing in the Fauresmith district is so called. **1966** C.A. SMITH *Common Names* 316 *Kuilgras, Diplachne fusca* ... *Eragrostis plana* ... Occurs in vleis where it is generally found fringing the deeper pools ... The vernacular name for both species is derived from their occurrence in vleis.

kukama *n. obs.* Also **kokama**, **kookaam**. [Se-Tswana.] The GEMSBOK (sense 1), *Oryx gazella.*

1839 W.C. HARRIS *Wild Sports* 264 The species [*sc.* the sable antelope] was evidently not recognised by the natives, although .. they pronounced it to be *kookaam*, which signifies the oryx, an animal of such extremely rare occurrence in Moselekatse's country, that they had in all probability never seen it. **1852** J.E. GRAY *Catal. of Specimens of Mammalia in Brit. Museum* III. 105 *Oryx gazella*. The Kookaam or Gemsboc. Horns straight, shelving backwards. **1857** D. LIVINGSTONE *Missionary Trav.* 136 The zebra, giraffe, eland, and kukama, have been seen mere skeletons from decay of their teeth as well as from disease. **1871** J. MACKENZIE *Ten Yrs* (1971) 260, I gave chase under the impression that the half-dozen creatures before me were elands, but as I approached I could see that they were gemsbucks or kukamas. **1883** —— *Day-Dawn in Dark Places* 48 The kukama (gemsbuck or oryx) fleetest of the antelopes. [**1888** J.S. KINGSLEY *Riverside Nat. Hist.* V. 326 The *Oryx capensis* of South Africa, or Gemsbok of the Dutch colonists, Kokama of the Bechuanas, is even more striking in its colouring.]

kuka shop var. CUCA-SHOP.

kukumakranka /ˌkʊkəməˈkræŋkə/ *n.* Also **cokimakranki**, **koek(e)-**, **koekoe-**, **kooka-**, **kukamakranka**, **kukumakrănki**. Pl. **-s**, occas. unchanged. [Prob. a Khoikhoi name; *koekoemakranka* is the Afk. form.

An unlikely etym. is provided by L.G. Green in *Beyond the City Lights*, 1957, p.14: 'This quaint name, which sounds like Hottentot, appears to have been corrupted from the Afrikaans words *"goed vir my krank maag"* (good for my sick stomach).']

Any of several species of the small perennial bulbous plant genus *Gethyllis* of the Amaryllidaceae, bearing fragrant white flowers and an edible underground fruit; this fruit. Also *attrib.*

1793 tr. *C.P. Thunberg's Trav. Europe, Afr. & Asia* I. 116 Kukumakranka (*gethyllis*) is the name given to the legumen or pod of a plant, that grew at this time among the sand-hills near the town, without either leaves or flowers. This pod was of the length of one's finger, somewhat wider at top than at bottom, had a pleasant smell, and was held in great esteem by the ladies. The smell of it resembled in some measure that of strawberries, and filled the whole room. **1798** LADY A. BARNARD in Lord Lindsay *Lives of Lindsays* (1849) III. 424 May On these banks there grows .. the Cokimakranki; or what I call Hottentot pine-apple; it has the same colour, the same flavour, and is filled with an aromatic juice and seeds. **1809** J. MACKRILL Diary. 59 Kukumakranka, Gethyllis ... is Gethylis not wrong. I believe it a Renealmia/Wild Pine. **1822** W.J. BURCHELL *Trav.* I. 55 In the neighbourhood of Cape Town, grows a celebrated little plant which still preserves its original Hottentot name being known by no other than that of *Kukumakrānki.* **1850** L. PAPPE *Florae Capensis* 39 The elongated, club-shaped, orange-coloured fruit of this plant has a peculiar fragrance, and still preserves its old Hottentot name of *Kukumakranka.* **1868** W.H. HARVEY *Genera of S. Afr. Plants* 384 *Gethyllis*, .. is known to colonial children by the name 'Kukumakranka'. **1887** *S.W. Silver & Co.'s Handbk to S. Afr.* 140 There are some fruits which have not as yet got names from any of the languages of Europe. One of these is the Kukamakranka; it is the Gethillis spirilis. **1894** R. MARLOTH in *Trans. of S. Afr. Phil. Soc.* p.lxxxiv, *Gethyllis spiralis* (kukumakranka). **1906** B. STONEMAN *Plants & their Ways* 152 My hostess brought in a flower — a beautiful, cream-white, six-pointed star, borne at the top of a long tube. 'That is surely a Kukumakranka,' .. 'You have left part of it in the ground — the Kukumakranka — the part we hunt to wear in our hats and enjoy the scent, and press in books.' **1913** C. PETTMAN *Africanderisms* 285 *Kukumakranka, Gethyllis spiralis* and other species. The peculiar, strongly scented berry of this field plant is thus designated in the neighbourhood of Cape Town. **1917** R. MARLOTH *Common Names* 53 *Kukumakranka, Gethyllis spiralis*, etc. Several species. The life-cycle of the plant is completed in three distinct phases. **1924** L.H. BRINKMAN *Glory of Backveld* 53 In course of time she received koekemakranka bulbs and uintjies from the coast. **1932** WATT & BREYER-BRANDWIJK *Medicinal & Poisonous Plants* 28 An alcoholic infusion of the fruit of the *Gethyllis spiralis*, .. Koekoemakranka (Bramakranka), Koekmakranka, was taken by the early Cape colonists for the relief of colic and flatulence. **1947** L.G. GREEN *Tavern of Seas* 199 The medicine chest of the Cape Flats is not without virtue. The kukumakranka, a strongly scented seed-pod, is still steeped in brandy and given to sufferers from colic. **1950** *Cape Times* 15 May 14 Before I found a palate for mushrooms, it was the kukumakranka we used to go seeking in the veld. **1957** L.G. GREEN *Beyond City Lights* 14 The *koekmakranka* is not gathered as a decoration. It is a medicine. **1960** G. LISTER *Reminisc.* 13 We went for walks on Green Point Common, where we used to find a strange scented plant called *Kookamakranka.* **1970** E. STUART *Informant, Pinetown* As children we would scour Green Point common for kukumakrankas ... Long strong-smelling seed pod. **1971** *Cape Argus* 29 May (Weekend Mag.) 1 Another pastime of ours was to dig for *Koekemakrankas*, a long tube-like plant that only showed a small pink section above the ground ... A jar .. half filled with brandy, each koekemakrankra placed in the liquid, and the jar tightly screwed. **1973** Y. BURGESS *Life to Live* 179 When the drug did not help she asked the old women to gather 'kukumakranka' leaves for her, and she asked Magriet for brandy to steep them in. **1982** FOX & NORWOOD YOUNG *Food from Veld* 71 Gethyllis afra L. and Gethyllis ciliaris L.f. along with other members of the genus are the well-known *kukumakrankas* of the Cape and Namaqualand. The fruits ... are .. pleasantly aromatic and good to eat. **1986** *Style* Mar. 79 Southern Suburbanites stroll on the Common looking for tadpoles and scented kukumakranka. **1990** *E. Prov. Herald* 3 Mar. 8 The joke plant whose name makes people laugh, the kukumakranka. **1991** *Ibid.* 5 Jan. 7 Following up last week's reports of the sightings of kukumakrankas, I pondered the behaviour of these strange little plants, which seem to spend most of their lives underground and appear as flowers only after a good shower of rain in December.

‖**kultuur** /kəl'ty:r, kœl-/ *n.* [Afk., culture.] Afrikaner culture; often used allusively, with (ironic) reference to its perceived exclusivity and notions of superiority. Also *attrib.*

1943 I. FRACK *S. Afr. Doctor* 103 He is hastily persuaded by the orator to pay more attention to this 'Verhoogte Stateus,' his new flag or his new 'Kultuur'. *Ibid.* 152 The ubiquitous 'kultuur' association took charge and turned the whole affair, including the laying of the foundation stone of the koppie outside Pretoria, into a gigantic political demonstration. **1964** J. MEINTJES *Manor House* 57 We Afrikaners with our obsession about *kultuur* have neglected and destroyed some of the best *kultuur* we possess. **1972** *Star* 26 Oct. 27 Just once, while guarding me and mine from the infidels waiting to destroy my 'kultuur', he .. may take a new look at what exactly is being destroyed. **1989** K. SUTTON in *E. Prov. Herald* 25 Feb. 4 'This fair land of ours' .. meant the Afrikaner Nationalist and his kultuur, not the actual rocks and veld. **1993** A. VINASSA in *House & Leisure* Dec. 54 Just yesterday, we had Afrikaner National fanatics trying to keep 'die kultuur' alive.

kulu var. MAKHULU *n.*

‖**ku:mbomvu** /ˌkʊm'bɔ:mvʊ/ *int.* Also **kobomvu, kubombu, ku bomvu.** [Xhosa and Zulu, subjectival concord *ku* it (is) + adj. stem *-bomvu* red.] Among Xhosa- and Zulu-speakers: beware; look out; 'danger', a warning cry to signal danger (particularly the approach of police).

1972 *Drum* 8 Oct. 19 In the township the aunties shouted Kobomvu to warn one another. **1977** P.C. VENTER *Soweto* 8 Liquor was prohibited in black areas and the police kept a close watch. 'Kumbomvu!' was the warning shout. Literally translated, the word means 'red'. It was enough to scatter the brewers. **1980** *Staffrider* Vol.3 No.1, 46 When somebody saw the police coming they would say 'kubomvu', that's a sign telling there is danger coming. **1985** D. BIKITSHA in *Sunday Times* 15 Sept. 6 A three pronged sharp whistle call meant the police were about. The cry 'Ku Mbomvu' [*printed* Ku Mbonvu] (it is red) meant an alarm whenever there was police presence in the area.

Kung /kʊŋ/ *n.* Also **Kgung, !Khu(ng), !Kun(g), Qung.** Pl. unchanged. [Khoikhoi *!Kung* persons, people.]

1. *pl.* Collectively, the members of a San people living in the Kalahari desert and in Namibia. Also *attrib.*, now usu. in the n. phr. ***Kung Bushmen.*** See also SAN sense 1.

As is the case with many names of peoples and groups in *S. Afr. Eng.*, 'Kung' has been found only in plural uses; however, it may be that it has also been used in unrecorded singular forms.

1928 E.H.L. SCHWARZ *Kalahari & its Native Races* 165 The Qung are a small — not pigmy — race, with slender limbs. The body colour is a Venetian red. Their ears are without lobes, but elongated, the lower margin running into the cheek. Their hair, though short and kinky, is longer than that of the San, so that the head is covered with a continuous mat. **1930** I. SCHAPERA *KhoiSan Peoples* 33 Immediately north of them, and speaking a closely-related language, live the !Khu or !Kun, commonly called Kung, one of the largest and most independent of the Bushman tribes. Their tribal name means simply 'persons, people', but when used without an adjective signifies 'Bushmen' to them. **1960** *Africa* 4 Oct. 343 It always amuses me to speak of residence when I visualize the nomadic !Kung .. building their nest-like grass shelters (scherms) for a stay of a few weeks. **1966** J.P. VAN S. BRUWER *S.W. Afr.: Disputed Land* 8 A considerable stretch of government land gives ample scope for the nomadic habits of a few thousand !Khung Bushmen. **1969** J.M. WHITE *Land God Made in Anger* 225 In the north, between Namutoni and Lake Ngami, taking in the many salt-pans of the north-east corner of South West Africa, live the Kung Bushmen. **1983** *Flying Springbok* Apr. 107 He and his wife spent 18 months with the !Kung people in the north-west Kalahari. **1985** [see BUSH *n.*[2]].

2. The language spoken by the Kung people. Also *attrib.*

1928 E.H.L. SCHWARZ *Kalahari & its Native Races* 144 In Qung, there is no 'p,' nor labial click; .. in Hottentot, the 'p' has become fully developed, but the labial click has vanished. **1971** *S. Afr. Panorama* Dec. 3 Work is progressing on two new translations, namely in Kwangali and the Kung Bushman tongue.

kuny var. KUHNE.

Kureechane var. KURRICHANE.

kurie var. KIERIE.

kurper /'kɜ:pə, 'kərpə(r)/ *n.* Also **kerper, kurpur.** Pl. unchanged. [Afk., fr. Du *karper* (see KARPER).] Any of several freshwater fishes, esp.: **1.** Usu. with defining word, **Cape kurper**: the labyrinth fish *Sandelia capensis* of the Anabantidae; KARPER sense 1.

1831 *S. Afr. Quart. Jrnl* Oct. 19 Kurper ... Inhabits most of the rivers towards the Southern extremity of Africa. **1913** C. PETTMAN *Africanderisms* 285 *Kurper* or *Kerper*, .. *Spirobranchus capensis*, a well-known freshwater fish. **1947** K.H. BARNARD *Pict. Guide to S. Afr. Fishes* 80 The Cape Kurper (*Sandelia capensis*). **1952** *Cape Times* 31 Jan. 9 The casualties include .. mudfish, carp and kurpur. **1967** R.A. JUBB *Freshwater Fishes* 175 *Sandelia capensis* ... Cape kurper ... Confined to the South Coastal drainage basin from the Langvlei River .. to the Coega River. **1987** *E. Prov. Herald* 22 Aug. 5 A survey of the river life conducted by the Cape Department of Nature Conservation in September, 1984, showed that the indigenous fish, the Cape kurper, could no longer be found. **1993** P. SKELTON *Freshwater Fishes* 338 Cape kurper .. *Sandelia capensis.*

2. Any of several species of cichlid of the genus *Tilapia.*

1967 R.A. JUBB *Freshwater Fishes* 161 *Tilapia mossambica* .. Bream or kurper ... This species .. is widely distributed .. in the rivers of the east coast. **1973** *Farmer's Weekly* 13 June 11 These simple plants could .. provide food for the weed-eating fish such as the moggel (sand fish) or tilapia (kurper). **1973** [see GEELVIS]. **1982** *S. Afr. Fishing* Apr.–May 22 In October Roodeplaat dam starts coming to life ... Bass, barbel and sometimes .. a kurper will snatch a lure or a porridge bait. Carp are active as well. **1988** C. NORMAN in *S. Afr. Panorama* Dec. 367 The indigenous angling fishes include several species of tilapia, or kurper, a family of broad, flat, silvery fish which in their many forms are found throughout the continent ... The sweet white flesh .. is such good eating flesh that several species now form the basis of fish-farming projects in far corners of the world. **1993** H. BOUWMAN in *Afr. Wildlife* Vol.47 No.1, 11 Butter fish and blue kurpur from Mzinyeni Pan .. had higher levels of DDT when compared with the same species from other pans.

Kurrichane /'kʌrɪˌtʃeɪn, ˌkʌrɪ'tʃeɪn, ˌkʌrɪ'keɪn, 'kʌrɪˌkeɪn/ *n.* Also **Kureechane, Kurrichaine,** and with small initial. [Named for *Kurrichane*, ad. obs. Sotho place name *Kaditshwene* (fr. Sotho locative prefix *ka-* + sing. n. prefix *di-* + *tshwene* baboon), in former times a capital city of the Hurutshe people, near Zeerust.

The naturalist Sir Andrew Smith collected and named several species of mammals and birds in the surrounding area.]

Used *attrib.* in the names of two bird species:

1. ***Kurrichane buttonquail***, also (*obs.*) ***Kurrichane hemipode***: the buttonquail *Turnix sylvatica* of the Turnicidae.

[**1849** A. SMITH *Illust. of Zoo. of S. Afr.: Aves* Pl.17, *Hemipodius lepurana* ... Only a very few specimens of this Quail were obtained ... The grassy valleys south-east of Kurichane were the only localities in which they were discovered.] **1906** STARK & SCLATER *Birds of S. Afr.* VI. 240 The Kurrichane Hemipode seems to be everywhere somewhat scarce. **1967** C.J. SKEAD in *Bokmakierie* Vol.19 No.3, 61 How many times have you pondered over the names Kurrichane Thrush, .. and Kurrichane Button-quail, *Turnix sylvaticus*, and wondered why they should have the unusual name of Kurrichane? **1978** MCLACHLAN & LIVERSIDGE *Roberts*

Birds of S. Afr. 137 *Kurrichane Button-quail* ... The commoner Button-Quail in South Africa, found in dry parts of the country, including the Kalahari. **1989** A.N.B. Masterson in P.J. Ginn et al. *Complete Bk of Sn Afr. Birds* 192 *Kurrichane Buttonquail* ... The name 'Kurrichane' which this species shares with our common dry-country thrush is normally pronounced as 'curry-cane'.

2. ***Kurrichane thrush***: the thrush *Turdus libonyana* of the Turdidae.

[**1836** A. Smith *Report of Exped. for Exploring Central Afr.* 45 *Merula Libonyana* ... Inhabits the country about and beyond Kurichane.] **1923** Haagner & Ivy *Sketches* 22 The Kurrichaine Thrush (*T. libonianus*) is somewhat similar to the two preceeding species, differing mainly in having the centre of the belly white and the bill bright orange-red ... It is common in the precincts of the Pretoria Zoo. **1924** *Ibis* 770 *Turdus libonianus*. Kurrichane thrush. This thrush is common in Nyasaland. **1936** D.A. Bannerman *Birds Trop. W. Afr.* IV. 314 The Kurrichane Thrush is not unlike a female European blackbird. **1960** G. Durrell *Zoo in my Luggage* 32 A kurrichane thrush treated us to a waterfall of a sweet song. **1984** G.L. Maclean *Roberts' Birds of Sn Afr.* 505 *Kurrichane Thrush* ... S Africa to Angola, Zaire and Tanzania; in s Africa from Natal to Mozambique, Transvaal, Zimbabwe, e and n Botswana and Caprivi. **1989** P.J. Ginn et al. *Complete Bk of Sn Afr. Birds* 476 Although shy in the wild, Kurrichane Thrushes become very tame and confiding in gardens and public parks. **1993** L. McGill in *Birding in SA* Vol.45 No.1, 31 The type specimen of the race of Kurrichane Thrush *Turdus libonyanus libonyana* came from 'the country about and beyond Kurrichane – near Zeerust'.

kurrie var. kierie.

kurvey *v. intrans. Obs.* [Englished form of S. Afr. Du. *karwei* to transport, carry, fr. Du. *karweien* to do odd jobs (perh. influenced by Du. and Afk. *kar* cart) or fr. Du. *karwei* hard work, big job (ad. F. *corvée*).] *to ride transport*, see ride sense 1 b.

1873 *Queenstown Free Press* 8 Aug., For various reasons not a single farmer 'kurveys' between either Concordia or Springbok and Port Nolloth. **1913** C. Pettman *Africanderisms* 286 *Kurvey, To*, To convey goods by wagon.

kurveying *vbl n. Obs.* Also **karveying, karweying**. [fr. prec.] transport-riding. Also *attrib.*

1876 T. Stubbs Reminiscences. I. 49, I tryed a trip at Kerveying, I took a load to Fort Wiltshire. *Ibid.* 50 We got the waggon and I reach Town in two days, and gave up Kerveying. **1886** *Grocott's Penny Mail* Nov. 29 Karweying in South Africa. **1896** M.A. Carey-Hobson *At Home in Tvl* 29 'I know there will be an end to those visits one of those days,' said the merchant, 'and then good-bye to your karweying, Walters.' *Ibid.* 515 I've been obliged to take to the karveying (transport riding) again. **1902** *Encycl. Brit.* XXXI. 81 'Kurveying' (the conducting of transport by bullock-waggon) in itself constituted a great industry. **1907** T.R. Sim *Forests & Forest Flora* 58 The Wagonwood of the Cape is not excelled by that from any other country, the extraordinary endurance of local wagons during the old Kurveying days before railways existed .. having given complete satisfaction to the most fastidious. **1913** C. Pettman *Africanderisms* 285 During the last thirty or forty years the railways have wrought a change, but kurveying is still a remunerative employment in some parts. *c*1960 J.M. Donald in J.B. Bullock *Peddie* 40 It is .. to be surmised that his occupation at Peddie was trading, and 'karveying' or transporting.

kurveyor *n. obs.* Also **karveyer, karweyer, kurweyer**. [Englished form of Afk. *karweier* transport rider, fr. *karwei* (see kurvey).] transport-rider.

1871 'R.M.R.' in *Cape Monthly Mag.* III. Dec. 372 The foundations of some of the largest fortunes in the East were laid by *kurweyers*. **1871** W.G. Atherstone in A.M.L. Robinson *Sel. Articles from Cape Monthly Mag.* (1978) 78 Strangers and visitors can't repress an audible hope .. that some 'kurweyer' of taste will run his wool-wagon against it by accident. **1877** [see tulp sense 1]. **1885** W. Greswell in *Macmillan's Mag.* (U.K.) Feb. 285 The *kurveyor* or carrier who drags the trade of the country about in his ponderous ox waggon with spans of 16 to 20 oxen. **1886** *Grocott's Penny Mail* 29 Nov., All the karweyers came out as we passed the crowd of wagons, and assured us that it was impossible to go up. **1894** E. Glanville *Fair Colonist* 318 Jimmie wants to be a karveyer; but she says, rather than see him a driver of oxen, she would apprentice him to a tailor. **1896** *Blackwood's Mag.* (U.K.) May 645 It was a very paying thing for the individual 'transport-rider' or 'Kurveyor' to convey goods to and from Kimberley. **1896** M.A. Carey-Hobson *At Home in Tvl* 27 A fine, independent young fellow was Robert Walters, the transport rider, or karweyer as they are called in South Africa. **1912** *E. London Dispatch* 2 July 8 (Pettman), It is anticipated that in six months' time the long-talked-of bridge will be *un fait accompli* ... Shades of old Kurveyors, what wouldn't you have given for that bridge.

kusting *n. Obs. Law.* [S. Afr. Du., mortgage.] kustingbrief.

1827 *Reports of Commissioners upon Finances at Cape of G.H.* II. 103 The bank was authorized from these sources to discount at six per cent per annum the vendue rolls, .. and private bonds called 'kustings'. **1910** *E. Prov. Herald* 2 May, *Bond List*. Kustings. General. Donation. Contracts. **1913** [see kustingbrief].

kustingbrief /ˈkəstəŋbrif, ˈkœs-/ *n. Hist. Law.* Pl. **-brieven** /-brivən/. [S. Afr. Du., *kusting* mortgage + *brief* letter.] A mortgage bond registered simultaneously with the transfer of property, and offering the mortgagee certain privileges should the mortgagor become insolvent; kusting. See also bond *n.*[1]

1862 *Stat. Law of Cape of G.H.* 3 There hath hitherto remained unused and not adopted in practice in this government, the registration of Kusting Brieven, Obligations before Schepenen .. 'inasmuch as it can never be seen what may be due by any persons by Kusting Brieven or Obligations before Schepenen, Orphan Masters, and writings of Mortgage on their immovable property'. **1884** *Cape Law Jrnl* I. 323 It can never be seen what may be due by any persons by Kustingbrieven. **1913** C. Pettman *Africanderisms* 286 *Kusting* or *Kustingbrief*, .. A mortgage bond upon a property covering the balance due on the purchase price of the property. **1918** *Act 13* in *Stat. of Union* 242 The provisions of this section shall not apply to bonds intended to secure the purchase money of land and passed simultaneously with the transfer thereof (kustingbrieven). **1944** G. Denoon in *S. Afr. Law Jrnl* 190 The kustingbrief still figures in Section 88 of the Insolvency Act, 1936, where the special privilege appertaining to the true kustingbrief has been retained, in ignorance of the fact that the instrument has been dead for over a century. *Ibid.* 287 In 1823 transfer and bond forms were translated into English ... As no exact equivalent for kustingbrief was found in English, the translated kustingbrief forms were also headed 'Mortgage Bond'. *Ibid.* 289 The name persisted ... It is therefore not surprising that before a generation had passed the term should have been applied to the mortgage bond which supplied the place of kustingbrief with greater efficiency. **1961** G. Wille *Law of Mortgage & Pledge* 44 A kustingbrief is a particular variety of special mortgage bond. It is a bond intended to secure the purchase money of land and passed simultaneously with the transfer thereof. **1975** H. Silberberg *Law of Property* 330 A *kustingbrief* is a mortgage bond passed to secure the purchase price (or any portion thereof) of land. It need not be in favour of the seller, but may be passed in favour of any person that has lent and advanced money to the mortgagor towards the purchase price of the land to be mortgaged. It is of the essence of a *kustingbrief* that it is passed .. simultaneously, with the transfer of the property. It is distinguished from ordinary mortgage bonds by the fact that it confers certain privileges on the mortgagee in the event of the mortgagor's insolvency.

kuyer var. kuier.

kuyl var. kuil.

Kwa- /kwa, kwɑː/ *pref.* Also with small initial. [In the Nguni languages, 'at the place of'.

In the Nguni languages, usu. prefixed to the name of a person or a people, the word to which *Kwa-* is prefixed usu. retaining its initial capital, as *KwaZulu*, formed on the Zulu n. stem *-Zulu* (see Zulu), and *KwaMashu*, formed on the name of *Marshall Campbell*, on whose farm the township of KwaMashu was built.]

A prefix used to form place-names; now also prefixed to company names, as *KwaTeba* [see Teba], and to existing place names, as ***KwaNatal*** *hist.*, the composite name of a proposed re-unified region of the province of Natal and the self-governing state of KwaZulu (see also *KwaNatal Indaba* at indaba sense 4).

1899 A. Werner *Captain of Locusts* 169 Nono's husband was working far away – kwa Mabunu, in the Boer country. **1977** *E. Prov. Herald* 10 June (Indaba) 1 All 51 houses in the new KwaFord scheme are to be fully electrified. **1982** *Voice* 30 May 2 The first steps towards possible independence for KwaNdebele will be taken shortly. **1986** *E. Prov. Herald* 19 Apr. 1 Govt accepts joint KwaNatal in principle. **1986** [see City Press quot. at indaba sense 4]. **1987** L. Capstickdale in *S. Afr. Panorama* Aug. 43 The large Black township outside Durban is called Kwa-Mashu, meaning 'the place of Marshall'. **1990** *Sunday Times* 13 May 17 The KwaNatal experience contained useful material for South Africa's current constitution builders.

kwaai /kwaɪ/ *adj.* Formerly also **kwaad, kwaaje, kwaat, kw(a)i, quaai, quei**. [Afk., earlier S. Afr. Du. *kwaad* bad, evil.]

‖**1.**

a. Bad-tempered, aggressive, fierce. Also *attrib.*, and *transf.*

1827 G. Thompson *Trav.* I. 129 Next, that the lions on the opposite side were more *kwaad* (angry or fierce) than those where we now were. **1851** N.J. Merriman *Cape Jrnls* (1957) 175 The Boer informed me .. I should come to the 'Kwai' or *Fierce* river, and I should be very lucky if it did not take me off my legs. **1852** Barter *Dorp & Veld* 57 (Pettman), The Boers meanwhile smiled and said that Mr ... was a *kwaad* (angry) man. [**1890** A. Martin *Home Life* 111 When the birds are savage – *quei*, as the Dutch call it – they become very aggressive.] **1900** B. Mitford *Aletta* 29 'Now we have made him *kwaat*,' said Andrina. 'See now, I'll get him to laugh again.' ... 'That has made him more *kwaat* than ever,' whispered Condaas. *Ibid.* 52 Krantz Kop is at the far end of the *berg*, sir. Boer *menschen* up there very *kwaai*. **1908** F.C. Slater *Sunburnt South* 152 She was a *kwaai* old *vrouw*, but, if she took a fancy to you, she would prove a very good friend. **1911** P. Gibbon *Margaret Harding* 184 *Quaai* – that means bad-tempered. **1929** J.G. Van Alphen *Jan Venter* 282 The Baas is very good but the Missus is a bit *kwaai*. [**1934** C.P. Swart Supplement to Pettman. 101 President Kruger .. spoke of Queen Victoria as a 'Kwaaje Frau', an expression which caused a good deal of offence in England at the time but which obviously was not meant by Kruger as insulting.] **1955** L.G. Green *Karoo* 127 It takes courage of a high order to break the neck of a *kwaai* ostrich as a coloured mother did. **1987** *E. Prov. Herald* 26 Aug. 2 The 'kwaai' months – August, September and October, when the weather at sea is rough and catches are poor.

b. *comb.* **kwaai-vriende** [Afk., *vriende* friends], bad friends.

1969 A. Fugard *Boesman & Lena* 28 Don't say anything. Just sit still. Pretend we're still *kwaai-vriende*.

2. *slang.* A term of approval, equivalent to 'great' or 'fantastic'.

1974 *Eng. Usage in Sn Afr.* Vol.5 No.1, 6 *Kwaai*, .. a general term of approval, retaining only the force of 'kwaai' not the meaning – denotes anything from 'good' to 'beautiful' .. *a kwaai movie. She's a kwaii goose. Kwaai, man, thanks.* **1980** E. Patel *They Came at Dawn* 9 The music is kwaai.but nobody wants to *d-a-n-c-e*. **1981** *St. Martin's Chron.* 3 June, *Kwi*, adj ... extremely good, marvellous — 'a kwi hamburger.' **1989** M. BRAND in *Fair Lady* 25 Oct. 92 *Kwaai*, groovy.

kwag(g)a, kwakka varr. QUAGGA sense 1.

kwarrie var. GUARRI.

kwedini /kwe'di(:)n(i)/ *n.* Also **khwedini, khwidini, kwedien, kwedin(g), kween dine, quedien, quedine**. Pl. usu. **-s**; occas. ||**ama-**, ||**ma-**, or unchanged. [Xhosa, voc. equivalent of *inkwenkwe* uncircumcised boy, but found also in the nominative and objective form *ikwedini*.] Esp. in areas where Xhosa is spoken: a young boy; a boy not yet of an age to be initiated into manhood; INKWENKWE. Also *attrib.* See also PICCANIN *n.* sense 1. Cf. UMFAAN sense 3.

1912 *Queenstown Rep.* 27 Jan. 5 A young native boy was badly hurt with a blow from the pole .. ; and this '*kween dine*' was walking behind the pole driving the bullocks on. **1913** C. PETTMAN *Africanderisms* 287 *Kwedini*, .. A term applied on the Border to a native boy, but never by the Kaffirs to a circumcised lad, however young he may be. **1946** *Spotlight* (S.A.I.R.R.) 23 Aug. 6 A twelve-year-old *kwedini* asleep across some sacks. **1955** J.B. SHEPHARD *Land of Tikoloshe* 37 Many a white school-boy might envy Africans in the Khwidini stage. A Khwidini is 'not yet old enough for a man, nor young enough for a boy' ... He has few responsibilities, precious little work and even less supervision. *Ibid.* 59 Abakhweta .. do not mix with the younger Khwedinis. **1966** I. VAUGHAN *These Were my Yesterdays* 78 Orchard fences broken by 'quediens' from locations stealing all your fruits. **1970** G. WESTWOOD *Bright Wilderness* 8 The labour force consisted of a few quedines, young boys not yet initiated into manhood. **1970** *Daily News* 18 Dec. 13 One White trader complained that kwedings (boys) had destroyed more than 1000 white telephone cups. **1976** *Weekend World* 9 Sept. A 16-year-old kwedini was this week sentenced to six cuts for culpable homicide. **1980** E. JOUBERT *Poppie Nongena* 139 I'll always be the small boy, although I'm your age. Boys that haven't been to the bush show you respect, but they call me the old man who is still kwedini. **1981** M. MZAMANE in *Best of S. Afr. Short Stories* (1991) 397 'Where can I refill this bottle, *makwedini*?' The boys laughed derisively at being called pickaninnies. **1987** M. POLAND *Train to Doringbult* 205, I always said that those *kwedinis* who're allowed in the house when they're small get too big for their boots when they grow up. **1989** M. BALL in *Weekend Post* 14 Jan. (Funfare) 3 The little farm boys, the *amakwedini*, were soon there to meet them, grinning from ear to ear. **1992** C.M. KNOX tr. *E. Van Heerden's Mad Dog* 69 With his strange bundle he set off to the farmyard trailed by the excited mob of kwedini. **1993** *Weekend Post* 26 June 13 (*letter*) A church elder said to me: 'Kwedini, you will never satisfy all the people.'

kweek /kwɪək/ *n.* Also with initial capital. [Afk., couch- or quick-grass.] In full ***kweek grass*** or ***kweekgras*** /-xras/ [Afk., *gras* grass]:

a. Any of several species of creeping grass of the Poaceae, esp. *Cynadon dactylon* (see QUICK sense 1 a).

*a***1928** C. FULLER *Trigardt's Trek* (1932) 36 This mound, covered with kweek grass, is said to have remained unchanged .. until today. **1929** J.W. BEWS *World's Grasses* 184 It [*sc. Cynodon dactylon*] is commonly known .. in S. Africa as 'Kweek grass', though that name is applied to other species of creeping grasses as well. **1937** *Handbk for Farmers* (Dept of Agric. & Forestry) 450 A large number of pasture grasses .. develop dangerous amounts of prussic acid when they are wilted. The most dangerous of these are the 'quick grasses' or 'kweekgras' — different species of *Cynodon*. **1942** S. CLOETE *Hill of Doves* 7 Looking back from the orchard gate she saw her spoor, green on the kweekgras that surrounded the house. **1946** H.C. BOSMAN in L. Abrahams *Cask of Jerepigo* (1972) 173 A donga dense with all sorts of vegetation, blue lobelia and river reeds and rushes and kweekgras and yellow gazanias. **1947** *Cape Times* 2 May 9 Only 342 acres were planted to marram grass and kweek. **1950** H.C. BOSMAN in L. Abrahams *Jurie Steyn's Post Office* (1971) 96 The mealie planter doesn't seem to work so well on the lands, behind a plough, going over kweekgras sods and pieces of turned-up anthill. **1954** K. COWIN *Bushveld, Bananas & Bounty* 178 Covered with kweek grass and ploughed up to expose the roots. **1954** C.E. HUBBARD *Grasses* 335 Like other well-known grasses it [*sc. Cynodon dactylon*] has numerous common names, being known as 'Kweek' in S. Africa, 'Doob' in India, 'Couch' in Australia, 'Bermuda Grass' in the United States, and in the British Isles sometimes as 'Creeping Dog's-tooth-grass' or 'Creeping Finger-grass'. **1969** E. ROUX *Grass: Story of Frankenwald* 56 (*caption*) *Cynodon dactylon* (kweek, a runner grass) forms a thick mat on the surface of the ground, with surface and subterranean runners. **1972** *S. Afr. Garden & Home* Oct. 19 Your best lawn grass will be the local kweek which is adapted to your conditions. **1979** M. PARKES *Wheatlands* 64 The whole area at the time being covered with thorn trees with 'Kweek gras' growing luxuriously beneath the trees. **1983** H. THESEN in *Outeniqualander/Herald* 21 Dec. 26 Kweek grass comes in like a colonising vanguard to win the land back to its primeval state. **1988** R. BILLET in *Farmer's Weekly* 1 Jan. 7 The grazing is kweek and wild buffalo grass. **1989** M. ROBERTS *Herbs for Healing* 34 Make a tea .. using either *Celery, Borage, Kweekgras* rhizomes or *Parsley*. **1992** [see BUFFALO GRASS sense 1].

b. With defining words designating various species of grass (all of the subfamily Chloridoideae): **kwagga kweek**, *Eragrostis bergiana*; cf. *quagga quick* (see QUAGGA sense 2); **pan kweek**, *Sporobolus tenellus*; **regte kweek**, *Cynodon incompletus*; **Transvaal kweek(gras)**, see TRANSVAAL.

1933 *Farming in S. Afr.* May 190 (Swart), **Kwagga-kweek** is utilised in winter to a large extent after the other grasses have ceased to be eaten. **1981** G.B. SILBERBAUER *Hunter & Habitat* 41 Game animals .. favour the pans because the palatable **pan kweek grass** (*Sporobolus tenellus*) grows there. **1935** J.W. MATHEWS in *Jrnl of Botanical Soc.* XXI. 13 In a publication on Lawns and Lawnmaking, by the Division of Botany, it says of the **Regte Kweek** (Cape Province) *Cynodon incompletus*: 'A surface creeping grass of the coastal districts of the Cape that resembles very much the Transvaal Kweek (*Cynodon hirsutus*), but is less hairy and a deeper green in colour'.

kween see QUEEN *n.*[1]

kween dine var. KWEDINI.

kwela /'kwelə, 'kwe:la/ *n.* Also **khwela, quela, qwela**, and with initial capital. [Xhosa and Zulu *khwela* climb on.

Several factors led to the use of this word as a name for the music. Firstly, it was used in the fig. senses 'join in', 'get going', as a call to dancers or band members. Secondly, it was used in the slang word *kwela-kwela* (police van), which is to be heard in the spoken introduction to the 1956 recording 'Tom Hark', by Elias Lerole and his Zig-Zag Flutes; it may have been due to the popularity of this record that the term became widely associated with the music. 'Some African informants argue that it was Whites, who by 1956 were buying pennywhistle recordings also .. , who first picked out the word *kwela* from "Tom Hark" and used it as a general term for the music.' (D.B. Coplan, Urbanization of African Performing Arts, 1980). Thirdly, among speakers of Nguni languages, the use of the word *kwela* was prob. reinforced by association with the Zulu and Xhosa word *ikhwelo* (whistling, a shrill whistle).]

1. *Music.* A rhythmical, repetitive popular music style in which the lead part is almost invariably played on the penny-whistle, and which developed out of MARABI (sense 3), TSABA-TSABA (sense a), and traditional southern African music; also called PATA-PATA (sense 2). Also *attrib.* See also MBAQANGA, PENNY-WHISTLE.

'Kwela' music developed in Soweto during the 1940s and 1950s.

1958 *Time* 16 June 37 The haunting sound of penny-whistle jazz has become the favorite music of South Africa's slum-caged blacks — and of a great many white hipsters. In the dusty streets, urchins rock to the penny-whistle's fast *kwela* beat. **1963** K. MACKENZIE *Dragon to Kill* 132 It was *kwela* music, much of it from penny whistle combinations: an insistent, unvarying, endlessly repetitive beat that sounded at first drearily monotonous, but which became hypnotically fascinating after a while. **1965** *Drum* Dec. 19 The Xhosa verb -kwela is in this context used to mean to begin, to get moving. The word, which originally meant to climb, assumed this different meaning during the time of the pennywhistle music. Before the famous pennywhistle group, the Black Mambazo .. began playing, their leader .. to notify his band that .. they should begin playing .. would say 'Kwela' meaning begin. From this .. the name 'Kwela music' was given to pennywhistle music. **1977** [see MBAQANGA]. **1980** D.B. COPLAN Urbanization of African Performing Arts. 343 *Kwela* music consisted of a rhythmic ostinato chord sequence, usually C-F-C-G[7] .. on a string bass and guitar, backed by a standard drum set in place of shakers. Above this was a strong melodic line played by several pennywhistles ... Above the two parts played by the rhythm section and pennywhistles, a solo pennywhistle plays an improvised third part. **1985** A. GOLDSTUCK in *Frontline* Feb. 21 Kwela music, the township rhythm that had its heyday in the fifties, has more in common with boeremusiek than any imported 'white' musical form. It has the same vibrance, the same uninhibited rawness, and a very similar musical structure. **1988** *New Nation* 25 Feb. 11 It was the development of kwela music during the mid-1940s which influenced him the most. It was just after this period that people started classifying any music with township rhythms as kwela, without realising that it referred specifically to penny whistle music. **1989** *Research News* (H.S.R.C.) Vol.1 No.7, 3 It was .. in Sophiatown that the styles of music called 'kwela' and 'mbaqanga' had their origin. **1990, 1991** [see PENNY-WHISTLE]. **1993** B. SUTER in *Natal Mercury* 26 Mar. (Funfinder) 4 The sounds of 1950s Sophiatown, when urban big-band jazz first learned to absorb and accommodate traditional kwela-mbaqanga, pata-pata and marabi music. **1994** *Sunday Times* 30 Jan. (*advt*) 34 Kwela. Who can forget the Sofiatown buzz of the fifties. And the inimitable sounds of Spokes Mashiyane — the King of Kwela himself. Playing probably the simplest wind instrument ever conceived, he and his African penny-whistle are today a legend.

2. *rare.* PENNY-WHISTLE. Also *attrib.*

1958 *Gramophone* Dec. 328 Those addicted to the shrill squawking of the Kwela flute will have to hear .. Something New From Africa. [**1965** P.R. KIRBY *Musical Instruments of Native Races* 276 It is interesting to note that performances upon this instrument, [*sc.* the penny whistle] and indeed the instrument itself, called *Kwela* by the Natives, should be associated with the Xhosa verb *uku-Kwela*, which means 'To hiss or whistle by drawing in the air.' From this verb is derived the noun *i-Kwelo*, which signifies 'a shrill whistling sound, made to incite cattle to run, or to induce cows to give their milk, or — to encourage people to attack!']

3. A dance-style accompanied by kwela music. Cf. PATA-PATA sense 1.

1960 *Guardian* (U.K.) 1 Apr. 10 When night falls, she can dance the kwela, mambo, or high-life with any or all of them. **1961** T. MATSHIKIZA *Choc. for my Wife* 55 She did half a shimmy, half a wobble, half a jive. She put her sherry in my hands and said, 'That's what they call the Kwela'. **1970** M. WEITZMAN *Informant, Johannesburg* It is fascinating to watch the Bantu children do the Qwela. **1970** V. JAQUES *Informant, Pietersburg* Kwela. A type of dance. **1971** on Springbok Radio 24 July, The Kwela, you know, being the African dance.

kwela-kwela /ˌkwela'kwe:la, ˌkwelə'kwelə/ *n. slang.* Also **khwela-khwela**. [In the NGUNI languages, *khwela* climb on or in, mount (see sense 1, quot. 1960); but see also quot. 1990.] In urban (esp. township) English:

1. A police van; *transf.*, any similar vehicle used for law-enforcement; NYLON; PICK-UP; PICK-VAN. Also *attrib.* See also MELLOW YELLOW.

1957 in Karis & Carter *From Protest to Challenge* (1977) III. 404 If a woman is found without the book or if all the papers inside are not in order, she will be pushed into the Kwela-Kwela and taken to gaol. 1960 C. HOOPER *Brief Authority* 209 Because of the appearance of their perspex panels they were soon known as 'Nylons'; or they were referred to by the city name of 'kwela-kwela' — an imitation of the police herding prisoners aboard with shouts of 'Kwela! get on!' 1962 W.S. MANQUPU in *Star* 22 Feb. 14 The lorry used as a pick-up van is called the 'Khwela-Khwela,' as the police call out 'Khwela, bo, khwela!' ('Ride, man, ride!') after making an arrest. 1963 B. MODISANE *Blame Me on Hist.* (1986) 35, I saw my mother insulted, sworn at and bundled into the kwela-kwela, the police wagon. 1967 *Post* 23 July 15 Over 20 women were rounded up by Municipal 'Kwela-kwela' trucks at dawn on Thursday. 1976 *Drum* 15 May 6 The accused sang freedom songs when the kwela-kwela drove off and Black Power salute fists shot from the ventilation holes of the kwela-kwela sieve. 1977 J. SIKAKANE *Window on Soweto* 27 Should some people get caught in an area we would hear voices of wailing children as women and men were escorted into the kwela-kwela vans with all the confiscated booze. 1979 M. MATSHOBA *Call Me Not a Man* 21 The large *kwela-kwela* swayed down Mohale Street at breakneck speed ... The driver of the *kwela-kwela*, the only uniformed constable among the group, clanged the door shut. 1981 *Voice* 29 July 2 The policemen dragged me into the waiting kwelakwela and locked me in there together with other Blacks. 1984 *City Press* 29 Apr. 1 It's the taxi kwela-kwela! Soweto taxi 'tsotsis' are in for a shock — the Witwatersrand Taxi association has introduced a squadcar to check on them! 1986 S. SEPAMLA *Third Generation* 153 Those prisoners and awaiting-trialists downstairs in the cells waiting for the kwela-kwelas to remove them to the cells all around Johannesburg and Benoni. 1990 G. SLOVO *Ties of Blood* 160 He had been pushed into an overcrowded *kwela-kwela* and the first thing he noticed was the stench of fear. 1990 *New African* 11 June 13 Kwela-kwela is a name that was given to the notorious pick-up police vans. Juveniles gambling at street corners would, at the first approach of kwela-kwela, take out their penny-whistles and begin to play music until the danger of being arrested was over.

2. Esp. in the Eastern Cape: TAXI sense 1. Also *attrib.*

[1960 C. HOOPER *Brief Authority* 265 The new parish vehicle — a miniature bus seating eleven passengers which, from the day of its arrival .. was known as kwela-kwela ya Modimo, God's Pick-up van.] 1985 I. MACDONALD *Informant*, Grahamstown There's no doubt at all that the Kwela drivers are exploiting their fares. 1987 *E. Prov. Herald* 16 June 1, I had just begun walking when I saw the kwela kwela (pirate taxi) come straight at us. I didn't even hear brakes. 1988 A. JACOT-GUILLARMOD *Informant*, Grahamstown The Kombi taxis which run all over the town have a new name, besides their old one of '*kwela-kwela*'. 1991 *Informant*, Grahamstown Kwela-kwela. Black taxis. We went to .. Port Elizabeth by kwela-kwela ... White employers take their employees to the Kwela-Kwela taxi rank when they work late. 1991 N. GODDARD *Informant*, Port Elizabeth Kwela-Kwela. Name given to taxis that ply to and from the townships/homelands in the Eastern Cape.

Kwena var. BAKWENA.

kwetha var. ABAKWETHA.

kwetha dance /ˈkwe(ː)tədɑːns, -ta-/ *n. phr.* Also **abakweta dance**. [fr. Xhosa *umkhwetha* (see ABAKWETHA) + Eng. *dance*.] TSHILA. Hence **kwetha-dancing** *vbl n.*

1891 *Stat. of Cape of G.H.* 1889-93 (1894) 254 Act To prohibit the Native Dances known as the 'Abakweta' and 'Intonjane' Dances. 1974 P. BECKER *Tribe to Township* 81 The boys .. are taught the delicate movements and steps of an ancient initiation dance. This, the *Kwetha* dance, will climax the festivities to be held on the closing day of the lodge. 1989 *Greater Dict. of Xhosa* III. 391 *ín.tshílí*, .. an outstanding performer of the traditional *khwetha* dance ... *uku.tshílísà*, .. make (circumcision initiates, *abakhwetha*) dance the *khwetha* dance .. ; hold a khwetha-dancing competition.

‖**kwêvoël** /ˈkweːfʊəl, -fuəl/ *n.* Also **kwévoël**, **quay vogel**. [Afk., echoic *kwê* + *voël* bird.] The grey *loerie* (see LOERIE sense 1 b), *Corythaixoides concolor*.

1895 J.G. MILLAIS *Breath from Veldt* 120 (Swart), The Dutch hunters declare that the quay vogel is a most inveterate disturber of game, and these birds give wild animals due warning of the approach of the hunter. 1940 A. ROBERTS *Birds of S. Afr.* 138 The names of 'Goway Bird' and 'Kwévoël' are derived from its alarm call, which it is fond of uttering when intruded upon, often following the hunter and thus alarming the animals. 1968 M. DOYLE *Impala* 31 A frightened *kwê-voel* dived out of the way, shrieking its raucous call, 'Go-a-way, go-a-waaaay!'

kwi var. KWAAI.

kwikstaart *n. obs.* [Du., *kwik* lively, brisk, spirited + *staart* tail.] QUICKSTERTJE.

1810 G. BARRINGTON *Acct of Voy.* 302 The kuikendief [printed kwickendreff] and kwikstaart are also known in Europe, but I know not their English names. 1822 W.J. BURCHELL *Trav.* I. 30 In most countries there are some few birds to which man has allowed the privilege of approaching him without molestation ... At the Cape, the familiarity .. of the Cape wagtail is greatly owing to the same cause. [*Note*] *Motacilla capensis* ... It is called Kwikstaart in the colony.

KWV *n.* Also **K.W.V.** [Initial letters of S. Afr. Du. *Ko-operatieve Wijnbouwers Vereniging (van Zuid-Afrika Beperkt)*.]

1. The Co-operative Winegrowers Association of South Africa Ltd., established in 1918 to control, encourage, and develop wine production. Also *attrib.*

1932 *Grocott's Daily Mail* 13 Jan. 2 Grape juice, the new by-product of the vine, which has been so successfully manufactured by the K.W.V. 1967 W.A. DE KLERK *White Wines* 104 Today the K.W.V. exports its whites, like its dry reds, sherries, ports, muscadels and brandies, to the United Kingdom, and some thirty other countries. 1968 C.J. ORFFER in D.J. Opperman *Spirit of Vine* 128 Farms which do not have a K.W.V. quota, may not produce wine. 1972 *House & Garden* Feb. 100 KWV Late Vintage .. is slightly spritzig, and has a very fresh taste. 1978 *Signature* June 16 Paarl is the headquarters of KWV, the cooperative Wine-growers association whose cellars are the largest in the world. KWV controls the export of spirits and wines in South Africa. 1979 *S. Afr. Digest* 14 Sept. 14 KWV was established in 1918 as a result of farmers' agitation against constant overproduction and the subsequent financial slump in the wine industry. 1988 D. HUGHES et al. *Complete Bk of S. Afr. Wine* 32 The 'Ko-operatieve Wijnbouwers Vereniging van Zuid-Afrika, Beperkt' — the sonorous full title of what is commonly referred to as the KWV. *Ibid.* 34 All transactions between merchants and producers had to carry the approval of the KWV; and all payments for wine had to be made through the organization ... No person might produce wine except under a permit issued by the KWV. 1992 C.M. KNOX tr. *E. Van Heerden's Mad Dog* 37 A brace of chic little female media assistants draped around the table and a bottle of the KWV's finest brandy.

2. *transf.* Brandy distilled by the KWV.

1963 A. DELIUS *Day Natal Took Off* 130 He walked abruptly to the door and called his driver: 'Van Jaarsveld, bring that bottle of K.W.V.' He came back bearing the bottle of K.W.V. 1980 M. MZAMANE *Best of S. Afr. Short Stories* (1991) 389 Mazibuko has brought the bottle of our special K.W.V. What I like about this brandy is that it really has no hangover to speak of. 1982 — *Children of Soweto* 72 Meikie produced a sealed bottle of KWV from her handbag ... 'A stiff tot of this brandy will do him some good.' 1993 *Sunday Times* 12 Dec. 11 The KWV flowed generously as the hopes and dreams of a peaceful future came spilling out.

Kxatla var. KGATLA.

kya, ky-ah varr. KAYA.

ky'daar /ˈkeɪdɑː(r)/ *n. colloq.* Also **kaydaar**, **k'daar**, **kydar**, **kyk-daar**. [Ellided form of Afk. *kyk* look + *daar* there, supposedly a common exclamation among (Afk.) tourists.] A derogatory term (esp. in coastal resorts) for tourists from the inland provinces. Also *attrib.*, and *fig.* See also VAALIE.

1982 R. GREIG in *Cape Times* 21 Dec. 17 In Natal and the Eastern Cape they have a different name for the polite 'tourists'. It's 'K'daars' as in 'Kyk, daar!', said by urchins in grubby khaki pants to fathers in grubby khaki pants ... To the locals k'daars are people with stomachs over shorts, strange accents and combs and cheque books in their socks. 1983 T. MCALLEN *Kyk Daar*, The term 'Kyk-daar' is a nickname given by the people of Durban to Free State and Transvaal visitors. Although originally it applied only to the Afrikaaner it has over the years grown to embrace all up-country visitors, regardless of culture or language. 1985 *Style* Oct. 88 It's the *ky'daar* syndrome in reverse, as I learnt to my cost in the early hours of the morning when two elephants .. had their freehold rights threatened by an aggressive rhino. 1989 S. SOLE in *Sunday Tribune* 1 Jan. 2 'Bleddy Kydars,' muttered CA drivers stuck behind T registrations meandering through the scenery. 1989 D. MULLANY in *Scope* 21 Apr. 4 We sit simmering in our motor cars and curse the national stereotypes we see swarming round us: .. the lunkheaded Transvaal 'kaydaar' in his Datsun Laurel, Toyota Cressida, or gold-wheeled Sierra; [etc.]. 1991 C. BARRETT in *Weekend Post* 5 Jan. 7 Transvalers earned the nickname ky'daar (look there) because they cruised slowly down Beach Road in their cars with passengers hanging out of the windows, oblivious to the minor traffic jams they caused. 1991 E. *Prov. Herald* 8 Mar. 18 Having never visited Struisbaai before I was turned into a proper 'kyk daar!' What strikes the newcomer most are the dazzling colours of the sea and landscapes.

kyens var. KAIINGS.

‖**kyk** /keɪk/ *v. intrans.* Formerly also **kek**, **kijk**. [Afk., earlier S. Afr. Du. *kijk*, to look, peep, view.]

1. 'Look'; used to command attention.

Often used in reporting Afrikaans speech.

1900 B. MITFORD *Aletta* 48 'Kyk! Do you know Mynheer Botma, then?' asked the old Boer, in round-eyed astonishment. 1906 H. RIDER HAGGARD *Benita* 65 Hans ceased from his occupation of packing up the things and said in a low voice: 'Kek! Baas'— that is 'Look!' 1927 *Outspan* 22 Apr. 63 Jesophat called me to the dashboard 'Kyk, Baas,' I kyked, and swallowed a lump. The switch key was turned off. 1979 J. GRATUS *Jo'burgers* 306 Kyk, meneer, look. I have five lumps of sugar. 1991 P. SLABOLEPSZY *Braait Laaities*. 24 Kyk, when we are sitting by my home in Pietersburg — the men are coming with all the stories from Jo'burg. *Ibid.* 28 Kyk, jong — I'm looking for the Bright Lights.

2. In the idiomatic expression *kyk hoe lyk hy (hulle, ons) nou* /ˌkeɪk hu ˌleɪk heɪ (hələ, ɔns) ˈnəʊ/, [Afk., lit. 'look how he (they, we) appear(s) now'], an expression with a range of meanings, as 'just look (at him)'; 'what else do you expect', or 'I told you so'; 'that's life'.

1982 *Drum* Jan. 2 Kyk hoe lyk hulle nou! That is what we shout when some pigheaded oafs with wax-laden ears come a cropper. 1988 A. SICHEL in *Star* 27 May 13 Ja nee, he went to all the night schools .. maar kyk hoe lyk hy nou. 1990 *City Press* 25 Feb. 8 The King left for a brief period and 'Popompo' was a dictator — en kyk hoe lyk hy nou. 1990 *Weekly Mail* 22 June (Suppl.) 7 Oberholzer is unrestrained in subject choice: anything and everything, from spectacular landscapes to AWB stalwarts, are sucked into the emulsion and spat out in a powerful documentary of the times. *Kyk hoe lyk ons nou!*

kyk-daar var. KY'DAAR.

‖**kyk weer** /ˈkeɪk vɪə(r)/ *n. phr.* [Afk., *kyk* look + *weer* again.]
a. A replay of a television sequence, usu. in slow motion. **b.** A reappraisal.

   1983 K. SHIPPEY in *Style* May-June 19 Those 'kyk weers' on television lost their enchantment; we'd seen Transvaal and Western Province so often on the screen that it was a bit like watching an old movie. **1985** *Vula* Oct. 36 Having looked at Via Afrika's music, maybe we should take a kyk-weer at their lyrics. **1987** D. CARTE in *Sunday Times* 15 Nov. (Business Sect.) 1 The stadium will also soon have another huge TV screen for 'kyk-weers'. **1988** *E. Prov. Herald* 12 Dec. 1 It was far from funny at the time, but the whole thing would look hilarious in a 'Kyk Weer,' he said laughing. **1989** *Informant, Grahamstown* Oh Ailsa, you'll have to have a kykweer.

Hence **kyk weer** *v. phr. intrans.*, to look again.

   1984 J. ALLAN in *Sunday Times* 23 Sept. 26 Andy will cause you to 'Kyk Weer' and coo with delight at his Renaissance revisited.

kysed var. CASED.

KZP *n.* [Abbrev. formed on *KwaZulu Police*.] The police force of the former 'homeland' of KwaZulu. Also *attrib*. See also ZP.

   1990 C. RICKARD in *Weekly Mail* 27 July 2 The supreme court has granted a final order against the kwaZulu Police (KZP) barring them from assaulting an Umlazi family. **1990** G. EVANS in *Ibid.* 12 Oct. 1 Madi claims he has received death threats and is in hiding in the Transvaal to avoid 'being hunted down by the SADF, KZP or Inkatha'. **1992** *New Nation* 7 Aug. 8 They complained that the KZP did nothing when Inkatha supporters attacked them. **1993** *Daily News* 9 Dec. 26 The Goldstone Commission revelation of a suspected five-man hit-squad of KZP members.

L

laager /ˈlɑːgə/ n. Also **lager**, and (formerly) **la(a)rger, largaar, lawger, leger**. [S. Afr. Du. *la(a)ger* (cf. Afk. *laer*), fr. Du. *lager, leger* camp.]

I. *hist.* Nineteenth century senses.

1.a. A defensive encampment surrounded and fortified by wagons lashed or chained together, particularly an encampment of emigrant Boers (see VOORTREKKER *n.* sense 1); the fortifying ring of wagons; occas. with qualifying word, **wagon laager**. Also *attrib.*, and *comb.* **laager-camp** (*rare*).

1834 T.H. BOWKER *Journal.* 29 Dec., About dusk the Kafirs commence taking the Cattle down from the *lawger-Camp* — which they endeavour to storm by violently driving herds of Cattle down the hill upon the waggons. 1845 W.N. IRWIN *Echoes of Past* (1927) 385 Fancy at one Lager (Boers' Camp) taking away 21,000 sheep. 1877 J. NOBLE *S. Afr.* 81 The Matabele retired, sweeping away .. the whole of the cattle and sheep which the farmers had been unable to get into their 'laager'. 1879 G.C. CATO *Letter.* (Killie Campbell Africana Library MS1602b), The Volunteers soon brought the waggons into a Laarger position. 1881 G.F. AUSTEN *Diary* (1981) 36 Today the Boers have increased their force by the addition of about 200 men drawn from the outside Lagers. 1898 B. MITFORD *Induna's Wife* 1 The conical ridge, once crested with fort and waggon laagers .. and the stir and hum of troops on hard active service, now desolate and abandoned. 1900 F.D. BAILLIE *Mafeking Diary* 280 In half an hour all there was left of the laager, which had vexed our eyes and souls so much for long months, was a cloud of dust on the horizon. 1929 D. REITZ *Commando* 23 The veld .. was dotted with tents and wagon-lagers. 1949 L.G. GREEN *In Land of Afternoon* 127 In laager formation, with thorn-bushes packed between the wagons, small bodies of voortrekkers defeated the mass attacks of Zulu impis. 1967 E.M. SLATTER *My Leaves Are Green* 95, I have always considered a laager essential when camping in enemy country. The wagons were placed in a circle and chained together with the pole of one thrust in between the wheels of the wagon in front. 1971 *Sunday Times* 19 Dec. 5 A crowd of about 25000 came to the bronze laager at Blood River .. the controversial monument of 64 bronze wagons. 1973 J. MEINTJES *Voortrekkers* 77 The laager system was still being perfected. 1990 *Personality* 4 June 42 White children may listen enthralled to recordings of how the Trekkers formed a laager for the massacre of the Zulus at Blood River. 1991 G. ZWIRN in *Settler* Vol.65 No.2, 11 A laager was an encampment formed by ox-wagons lashed together and drawn end to end, thus making a circle or square for the protection of the people and animals inside.

b. Collectively, the occupants of a fortified encampment.

1851 T. SHONE *Diary.* 17 Jan., I went to Bathurst .. about the rations, Mr Currie declares he will give none, untill the whole Larger as enrolled their names. 1877 F. JEPPE *Tvl Bk Almanac & Dir.* (1976) 36 A commandant-General is chosen by the whole laager. 1942 S. CLOETE *Hill of Doves* 19 He .. had survived the massacre of Uys's laager by the Zulus.

c. In the adv. phrr. *in laager, into laager*: in, or into, a defensive and fortified state.

1879 MRS HUTCHINSON *In Tents in Tvl* 48 In the event of an attack, the inhabitants would have to 'go into laager' as they call it. 1882 J. NIXON *Among Boers* 92 They drew their waggons into 'laager'. 1900 F.D. BAILLIE *Mafeking Diary* 35 Six hundred Boers were in laager. 1953 B. FULLER *Call Back Yesterday* 15 It was believed that .. some 40,000 Natives would join M'Pefu. So most of the whites gathered at agreed spots and there went into laager. 1974 *Sunday Times* 24 Nov. 2 The consular corps .. representing 13 foreign countries in Luanda, is preparing to go into laager if civil war comes. 1977 *S. Afr. Panorama* Nov. 19 Bowker designed the town with a hexagonal space in the centre .. where the inhabitants could go into laager to defend themselves.

d. A convoy of wagons, of a number large enough to form a defensive encampment if necessary.

1900 W.S. CHURCHILL *London to Ladysmith* 452 The great white tilted waggons of the various laagers filed along the road. 1900 P.J. DU TOIT *Diary* (1974) 18 Sure enough there is a big laager moving slowly towards the beleaguered camp with a mounted troop leading the advance. 1902 D. VAN WARMELO *On Commando* 93 It took our little lager nearly all day to reach the plateau. 1933 W.H.S. BELL *Bygone Days* 118 Women and children had preferred .. to accompany the commandos and .. lived in nomadic laagers.

e. Special Comb. and phrr. **cattle laager**, an encampment used for the safeguarding of cattle in time of war; ‖**vroue laager** /ˈfrəʊə-/ [Afk. *vroue* women] or **women's laager**, an encampment in which women and other non-combatants live during times of war.

1901 P.J. DU TOIT *Diary* (1974) 37 An unexpected attack was made on the women's laager, about 37 waggons with families captured, besides large flocks of cattle and some prisoners. 1902 D. VAN WARMELO *On Commando* 174 The others might have been saved if the women's lager had not impeded their flight. 1929 D. REITZ *Commando* 184 The women's laager consisted of some fifty wagons and carts, with over two hundred women and children, the collective non-combatant population of the district. 1949 O. WALKER *Proud Zulu* (1951) 199 Several new charges made against the cattle laager defences won another portion of it for the Zulus. 1982 *Sunday Times* 16 May 22 The commando had two laagers — the 'vroue laager' consisting of women, children and those too old or infirm to fight, and the 'perde commando', the fighting laager.

2. *transf.* Any fortified place, either of a permanent nature (in which residents of a district customarily gather for safety in time of war) or of a temporary nature (in which groups of people shelter on a short-term basis).

[1846 *Natal Witness* 11 Dec. 1 These people were compelled, for several years, to remain concentrated in encampments, or 'legers'.] 1850 R.G.G. CUMMING *Hunter's Life* (ed.2) I. 202 Their tents and waggons were drawn up on every side of the farm-house ... The Boers informed me that all their countrymen, and also the Griquas, were thus packed together in 'lagers', or encampments. 1851 N.J. MERRIMAN *Cape Jrnls* (1957) 151 At the last play 300 souls were gathered on the premises of Mr Dell — men, women, and children, of all ages, races and colours. It is one of the largest laagers in Albany. 1851 J.F. CHURCHILL *Diary.* (Killie Campbell Africana Library MS37) 29 June, The larger which was erected at the time of the Caffre alarm is still ready for any emergency mounted with two pieces of Cannon. 1852 M.B. HUDSON *S. Afr. Frontier Life* 233 Many families congregate together on one farm, and drawing their wagons up into the most defensible position form what is termed 'a Laager'. This colonial expression comprehends any description of camp, formed either for defensive or military purposes. 1856 F.P. FLEMING *Sn Afr.* 98 This farm, during the war, was formed into a 'largaar,' or place of rendezvous, for the burghers of the surrounding district. 1882 S. HECKFORD *Lady Trader in Tvl* 85 A great outbreak of the Kaffirs was close to hand, and .. all who did not wish to be murdered had best go into lagers. 1882 C. DU VAL *With Show through Sn Afr.* I. 206 The laager in the town still stands, its loopholed walls and sentry-boxes giving evidence of the scare that must have been felt. 1902 G.M. THEAL *Beginning of S. Afr. Hist.* 269 The invaders constructed a rough lager or enclosure of bushes and earth, within which they attempted to defend themselves. 1903 E.F. KNIGHT *S. Afr. after War* 35 The men of the Essex Regiment succeeded in hauling up two 15-pounder guns, which harassed the Boer laagers and could have driven the enemy out of Colesberg itself had it not been out of the question to shell our own town. 1923 G.H. NICHOLLS *Bayete!* 191 In all the smaller centres the people were rushing into lager. 1942 *Cape Times* in J. Crwys-Williams *S. Afr. Despatches* (1989) 282 We formed a laager at about 5 o'clock in the afternoon. We had more than a dozen tanks, a number of 25-pounders and two dozen armoured cars in the laager. 1971 H. ZEEDERBERG *Veld Express* 82 One of the main camps (they soon developed into 'laagers') with a six-feet high thorn enclosure, was established about twenty miles from the Umzingwani River. 1973 *E. Prov. Herald* 9 Feb., The farmhouse had formed a valuable laager and refuge for other neighbouring members of the Bowker family during these Kaffir Wars, as it was best suited for protection purposes.

II. Modern figurative senses.

3. Any more or less circular arrangement of objects or persons, esp. one intended to form a barrier; the area enclosed by this. Also *attrib.*

1910 J. BUCHAN *Prester John* (1961) 94 My laager of barrels was intact. 1971 J.A. BROWN *Return* 179 About a hundred oxen were breaking out from the circling *laager* of thornbush. 1974 J. MCCLURE *Gooseberry Fool* (1976) 190 Parties of intrepid, elderly shoppers .. built laagers of parcels around them as if anticipating an attack by the Zulu waiters. 1976 M. THOLO in C. Hermer *Diary of Maria Tholo* (1980) 112 The police .. collect everybody they meet .. and take them towards Nyanga East where there are bushes and then they form what the Voortrekkers called a laager with the boys in the middle. They either set dogs on them or beat them up. 1978 *S. Afr. Digest* 19 Oct. 19 South Africa has a word for it — laager housing ... The managing director .. told *The Citizen* that simplex or laager housing had got off to a bad start ... Laager living was a single-level ground floor development. 1987 *Uniform* 7 Apr. 2 In the centre of the laager lies a small pool. The pool is situated near an open air pub. **1987** *Style* Mar. 44 Outside, beyond the bookies' lazy lager, a tombola barrel waits for offerings from the unlucky. **1991** *Weekly Mail* 24 May 11 They had been thrown out of their classes .. to make way for .. riot police apparently lurking in the blockhouses that make up the campus. Inside the concrete laager a .. character called Viljoen .. was waiting for us. **1993** *Motorist* 1st Quarter 15 Bush was cleared, vehicles parked to form a laager, a generator was kicked into action.

4. Usu. in a political context, and often *attrib.* **a.** Allusively, isolationist thinking or intransigence in groupings, attitudes, or policies, particularly as found among right-wing Afrikaners, and in the South African polity during the era of apartheid. Cf. BOMA *n.*[1] sense 4.

1939 [see JABROER]. **1940** *Forum* 8 June 3 General Smuts appeals to us to drop our political differences and form laager against the common foe. **1960** [see BLACK PERIL sense 2]. **1962** L. GANDAR in J. Crwys-Williams *S. Afr. Despatches* (1989) 342 The next state of emergency will be the time, and there will surely be another state of emergency ... When it comes .. the White population of South Africa will go streaming into the Nationalist laager, stripped of the power of resistance. **1971** S. LENKOE in *Post* 15 Aug. 5 (*letter*) To say that Black consciousness is a 'laager' and an 'anti-whitism' movement is utter rubbish. **1971** *Rand Daily Mail* 18 Feb., The reaction .. one would expect of .. authoritarian bigots, in whom years of laager worship have .. bred a pathological fear of foreigners. **1972** *Sunday Times* 5 Mar. 3 A gulf is developing between the party's verligtes and verkramptes over whether the party should close or open their ranks to ensure survival. The more purposeful .. favour a 'closing the laager' move. **1973** *Cape Times* 16 June 10 We should use an Order of Service which is not in danger of driving people into one *laager* or another. **1975** *Sunday Times* 27 July 20 Even the laager has a worm eating at its heart. Afrikaans books and plays are being banned. **1977** *World* 13 Oct. 5 If white South Africa withdraws into the laager during the coming elections, the country is likely to drift into a Rhodesian-type situation, with confrontation and isolation. **1981** *Guardian Weekly* (U.K.) 23 Aug. 1 People in laagers can't make U turns. **1982** *Drum* Oct. 105 Now that he has come out of the laager, Ds Smit says he can talk boldly about injustices like the Mixed Marriages Act. **1986** *Economist* (U.K.) 14 June 15 The laager men on South Africa's far right .. will feel nothing from sanctions beyond a mild thickening of the skin. **1987** *Frontline* Aug.-Sept. 25 Fissures within even the Afrikaans-speaking population .. make it very hard for the regime to follow a defiant '*laager*' strategy. **1988** *Sunday Times* 10 Apr. 18 Government is still seen as something that is run for Afrikaners by Afrikaners ... English speakers were invited into the laager ... But, once inside, many resent having been treated like *bywoners*. **1991** J. KANE-BERMAN in *Ibid.* 10 Feb. 13 Ernie Wentzel and Laurie Schlemmer and I decided to liberate ourselves from the liberal laager. **1991** G.J. CHURCH in *Time* 22 July 13 Some analysts suspect that .. sanctions .. might have produced a laager backlash. **1992** R.H. DU PRE *Making of Racial Conflict* 162 Because the Afrikaner could not withdraw into the 19th century, he now forms a 20th century laager (a political attitude of isolationism against a hostile environment). **1992** H. YOUNG in *Guardian Weekly* 2 Oct. 12 After four decades in the laager, the whites now spectacularly failing to run this country do crave the assistance of the outside world. **1993** M. SHAIK in *Weekly Mail & Guardian* 29 Oct. 2 Bashing the police force pushes the hardliners into the laager, while the good people leave the force.

b. In the phr. ***laager mentality***, an attitude of isolationism and intransigence born of fear or anger.

1958 *Times Lit. Suppl.* (U.K.) 14 Feb. 87 That the leaders of the Nationalist Party have created a 'laager' mentality and hate all opponents of apartheid is a fact. **1963** J. SINCLAIR in *Black Sash* Oct.-Nov. 28 We have had to contend with fear and the 'White laager mentality' of the public. **1970** *Evening Post* 8 June, In the victory of the verligte .. strain in Afrikaner thinking, .. some observers have claimed to detect that South Africa is shedding the laager mentality. **1977** D. OWEN in *Cape Times* 14 Apr. 14 If we drive the South Africans into a total laager mentality we could force one of the most right wing and loathsome regimes to develop. **1983** A.P. BRINK *Mapmakers* 139 The Afrikaner continued to feel threatened. Once again the '*laager* mentality' came to the fore, asserting itself in the sad saga of repressive legislation which has come to characterize the regime. **1984** W. GREENBERG in *Frontline* May 44 They were told that racial identity could be preserved without the laager mentality. **1991** G.J. CHURCH in *Time* 22 July 13 It had been widely forecast that the embargo would provoke a laager (circling the wagons) mentality among whites, a nose-thumbing determination to defy world opinion. **1993** B. MAHABIR in *Sunday Times* 10 Oct. 18 One can safely conclude that most Afrikaners will not go along with the laager mentality of the right wing.

||**5.** A group of VOLKSPELE dancers.

1974 *S. Afr. Panorama* Nov. 19 The National Council for Folk Singing and Dancing chose 36 'volkspelers' (folk dancers) from different 'laers' (laagers) to accompany the overseas dancers and perform with them.

Hence (all modern *nonce* uses) **laagerism** *n.*, the manifestation of an insular or intransigent attitude; **laageritis** *n.*, a 'disease' characterized by insularity or intransigence; **laagerize** *v. trans.*, to cause (a person, persons, or organization) to become insular and intransigent; so **laagerizing** *vbl n.*

1975 *Sunday Times* 20 Apr. 16 Unlike RAU and Stellenbosch – which, by opening the academic doors .. to Black post-graduate students, have traded in the symbolic wa [*sc.* wagon] .. – Tuks continues to suffer from an advanced case of laageritis. **1977** *Ibid.* 29 May 16 It will 'laagerise' the whites (indeed, Mr Mondale has already strengthened the NP by enabling Mr Vorster to corral his dissident verligtes). **1987** *Frontline* Feb. 29 The obvious effect would be another boost to the laagerising of South Africa and the general sense of polecattery. **1989** *Style* Dec. 151 Botha .. underwent all the regular conditioning and was exposed to all the laagerisms of any Vrystaat Afrikaner boy.

laager /ˈlɑːgə/ *v.* Also **lager**. [fr. prec.]

1. *trans. hist.* To form (wagons) into a laager, as a defensive fortification.

1879 *Daily News* (U.K.) 1 Mar., The waggons were not 'laagered' or drawn up so close as to make it difficult to force the camp. **1882** C. DU VAL *With Show through Sn Afr.* II. 46 There was no time to 'laager' the waggons. **1885** LADY BELLAIRS *Tvl at War* 93 The waggons were laagered, double sentries and look-outs placed. The march was continued with the greatest caution, the waggons being kept closed up, so that they could be quickly laagered on the first appearance of intended attack. **1934** B.I. BUCHANAN *Pioneer Days* 112 He ordered the wagons to be inspanned, but left where they were, and refused requests to allow them to be laagered. **1949** O. WALKER *Proud Zulu* (1951) 176 He listened in Maritzburg and D'Urban to the tales of colonials who had fought against the Zulus in the long ago, and their eternal prating about 'laagering' the wagons. **1958** S. CLOETE *Mask* 147 Before long the wagons came up and were laagered – wagon tongue to wagon bed in a great defensive circle. **1968** R. KEECH in *New Coin Poetry* Vol.4 No.4, Dec. 12 Too late we laager their forty-five waggons As tourniquet around that disembowelling plain. **1988** [see OSSEWA sense 2 b].

2. *trans.* and *reflexive.* To encamp (persons, or oneself and one's companions) in a strong defensive position in a laager. Usu. *passive.*

1883 *Standard* (U.K.) 17 May 5 Four hundred Boers, laagered in Stilleland, have threatened to attack Mankoroane. [**1895** *Westminster Gaz.* (U.K.) 28 Aug. 1 What, then, can be more absurd, to adopt Mr. Healy's picturesque phrase, than 'to laager the Postmaster-General in the Lords?'] **1897** F.R. STATHAM *S. Afr. as It Is* 41 The Europeans, believing themselves to be attacked by the Griquas, laagered themselves in the town.

3. *intrans.* To camp; to set up camp (within a ring of wagons). Also *fig.*, and in the phr. ***laager up***.

1885 LADY BELLAIRS *Tvl War* 93 With difficulty the waggons were passed over Sand Spruit, then halting, and laagering for breakfast. **1896** *Tablet* (U.K.) 22 Feb. 290 We stopped firing at about seven o'clock, and laagered up for the night. **1897** F.W. SYKES *With Plumer in Matabeleland* 132 About half an hour before laagering, a party of officers will be sent forward to reconnoitre the ground to be selected. **1937** C.R. PRANCE *Tante Rebella's Saga* 118 Armed farmers .. clamorous for advice whether to defend their farms, to bring their families to laager at the Post. **1953** B. FULLER *Call Back Yesterday* 129 Near this division of the roads is the site of the encampment where Piet Retief laagered after crossing the Berg. **1956** M. ROGERS *Black Sash* 175 A total of 321 Black Sash women in 86 cars laagered in the historic town tonight. **1970** P.B. CLEMENTS in *Outpost* 40 After about half-an-hour's fighting, in which time we suffered several casualties, we were ordered to laager up. **1980** *E. Prov. Herald* 17 June 8 Eventually the battle petered out, and we had laagered for the night. As we lay, the crew of the vehicle despondently discussed the day's events. **1989** J. CRWYS-WILLIAMS *S. Afr. Despatches* 6 By midday, all was over: the royal kraal was fired and the troops recrossed the Umfolozi to laager for the night.

4. *trans. rare.* To enclose (an encampment) in a laager.

1891 R. RUSSELL *Natal* 229 Had the camp been at once laagered in Dutch fashion on the first indication of the enemy's presence. **1934** B.I. BUCHANAN *Pioneer Days* 112 He would inevitably incur disaster if the camp were not laagered (that is, barricaded with parked wagons) wherever and whenever it was pitched.

Hence **laagered** *ppl adj.*, (of wagons) disposed so as to serve as a laager; (of camps or persons) enclosed in a laager or behind a defensive barrier (also *fig.*); **laagering** *vbl n.*, the action of forming a laager.

1881 *Contemp. Rev.* (U.K.) Feb. 222 The laagered waggon their sole protection. **1894** *Daily News* (U.K.) 14 Sept. 5 The Army Service Corps were drilled in laagering. **1901** *Grocott's Penny Mail* 3 Jan. 3 Piet Swart, the Origstad Veld-cornet is laagered in the vicinity of Kruger's Post. **1926** M. NATHAN *S. Afr. from Within* 22 On the 16th, while laagered on the Umhlatusi (since known as Blood River), they were attacked by the main Zulu army. **1937** S. CLOETE *Turning Wheels* 40 Yes, I am laagered. I was waiting for you, Paul. **1942** — *Hill of Doves* 21 There was no tragic history of massacre, or laagered camps. **1948** H.V. MORTON *In Search of S. Afr.* 30 The assegais whistling towards Boer and Briton; the bullets thumping from the wheels of laagered wagons. **1949** *Cape Times* 27 Apr. 10 Are we really going to keep ourselves laagered when other countries in Africa get together on economic expansion projects?

laagte, leegte /ˈlɑːxtə, ˈliəxtə/ *n. obsolescent.* Also **lichter**. Pl. unchanged, or **-s**. [Afk., 'valley, low ground'.] A low-lying plain or valley; a shallow dip or depression.

1868 J. CHAPMAN *Trav.* I. 25 We emerged on a sandy elevation or 'buet' [bult] overlooking an extensive undulation or *leegte*. **1887** A.A. ANDERSON *25 Yrs in Waggon* II. 99 There are many streams and laagte which intersect this extensive and swampy region. **1897** 'F. MACNAB' *On Veldt & Farm* 87 There was a wide laagte which stretched right across the veldt through the centre of the native village of Genesa. **1897** SCHULZ & HAMMAR *New Africa* 188 As far as I could see up the open laagte the ground was teeming with heavy game. *a***1928** C. FULLER *Trigardt's Trek* (1932) 136 Tall grass on the *bults* – not so thick as near the mountain – with the *laagtes* in between, for the most part, wet and boggy. **1937** S. CLOETE *Turning Wheels* 14 A herd of wildebeeste and zebra were grazing in a leegte. **1946** V. POHL *Adventures of Boer Family* 68 Dudley decided that .. they should turn left .. and take shelter in a *laagte* where they might easily shake off their pursuers in the dark. **1949** M. LEIGH *Cross of Fire* 89 On the laagte between ourselves and the main encampment other dim figures moved evenly. **1950** H.C. BOSMAN in L. Abrahams *Bekkersdal Marathon* (1971) 155 He emerged from his cottage in the *leegte* that was all grown about with the thorniest kind of cactus. **1968** S. STANDER *Horse* 63 Two leopards, a male and a female, trotted down the easy slope of a three-mile-wide laagte. **1970** M. VAN RENSBURG *Informant, Port Elizabeth* Laagte. Low-lying part of even stretch of land.

laaitie, laaity varr. LIGHTY.

laamziekte var. LAMSIEKTE.

laani(e) var. LARNEY.

laarger var. LAAGER *n.*

laas var. LAS.

laatlammetjie /ˈlɑːtlaməki, -ci/ *n.* Also **laat lammertjie**. [Afk., *laat* late + *lam* lamb + -IE.]
1. A child born long after the other children in a family, an 'afterthought'; a first child born late in a marriage; LATE LAMB. Also *attrib.*
    1970 A. PALMER *Informant, King William's Town* That girl is a laat lammertjie because her youngest brother is twenty years older. **1973** *Fair Lady* 30 May 113 Dr Lee Salk .. provides valuable guidelines for parents on explaining new arrivals, sibling rivalry, adoption, and 'laat lammetjies'. **1975** *Fair Lady* 17 Sept., She told me that she was born when her mother was 40. 'I was a *laatlammetjie* — twelve and sixteen years behind my two brothers and I cried and nagged for a little brother or sister to play with'. **1979** *E. Prov. Herald* 27 Apr. 20 To Manny and Willie a 'laatlam' daughter .. and sister to Jeanine and Haideé. **1980** *Fair Lady* 23 Apr. 61 Michelle was the start of a new life to Daphne and her husband ... They felt quite up to the challenge of their 'laatlammetjie'. **1981** *Sunday Times* 25 Oct. 53 Mrs Parkin said Rudie was a 'laatlammetjie' child who was full of life and 'the apple of his father's eye'. **1987** H. PRENDINI in *Style* Feb. 33 Rossouw is the Bothas' 18-year-old laatlammetjie. There are almost 25 years between him and the oldest. **1987** L. BEAKE *Strollers* 2 Ma was determined that Johnny, the laatlammetjie, last and final of her many sons, would not go the same way. **1988** *Personality* 22 Feb. 4, I was a 'laat-lammetjie,' there is a 40-year age gap between my parents and myself. **1989** A. DOMAN in *South* 7 Sept. 16 The laat-lammetjie seventh and last of the Herberts' offspring came kicking and screaming into the world. **1990** *Sunday Times* 21 Oct. 3 They had waited 13 years for their laatlammetjie. **1991** D. ASHMAN *Informant, Cape Town* Jane and Betty were almost finished with High School, when, to their intense embarrassment, they were presented with the news that mommy, who was almost 40, was going to have a baby! However, when the 'laatlammetjie' arrived they doted on him as if he was their own child and not just their brother.
2. *fig.* A latecomer.
    1980 *Cape Times* 30 Aug. 8 It is a pity that the National Party's *laat lammetjie* Mr John W— is too busy to reply to the voters of Simon's Town.

Labarang /laˈbaraŋ, -ran/ *n.* Also **Labaran, Lebaran**. [ad. Malay *lebaran* religious feast.] Esp. in the Western Cape: EID.
    There are in fact are two 'Labarangs' during the Islamic year: 'Labarang Ramadan' (Eid-ul-Fitr), and 'Labarang Hadjie' (Eid-ul-Adha).
    1944 I.D. DU PLESSIS *Cape Malays* 16 Locally and in Java the Feast of *Eid-ul-Fitr* is known as *Lebaran*. **1949** E. HELLMANN *Handbk on Race Rel.* 593 The feast day Labaran or Eid-ul-Fitr. This is celebrated with pomp and ceremony throughout the world of Islam. **1976** *Cape Herald* 14 Sept. 16 (*advt*) Special offer for labarang!! A discount of 10% on cash purchases over R30. **1976** *Sunday Times* 3 Oct. (Extra) 3 The eve of Labarang became a night of terror when a man .. threatened to knife him. **1988** ADAMS & SUTTNER *William Str.* 13 The Malay holidays and festivals. I loved them and at their holidays like Labarang I too would get special treats. **1992** P. DOBSON *Informant, Cape Town* Labarang. Eid.

labola, -bolo varr. LOBOLA *n.*

labour tenant *n. phr. Hist.* See first quot. Also *attrib.* Cf. BYWONER sense 1.
    The labour tenant system was made illegal in 1969.
    1931 [see TREK *n.* sense 2]. *c*1970 C. DESMOND *Discarded People* 15 Labour-tenants are Africans over the age of 15 years who occupy certain parts of white farms, for which, instead of paying a money rent, they and other members of their families work for the farmer for a very low cash payment, or none at all, for a part of the year, varying from 3 to 9 months. **1970** *Survey of Race Rel.* (S.A.I.R.R.) 101 The Government is pursuing its objective of abolishing the labour tenant system in favour of full-time labour. **1985** PLATZKY & WALKER *Surplus People* 30 Labour tenants .. supplied their labour to the land owner for part of the year .. as a form of rent, in return for the use of some of the land for themselves. **1988** *Afra Newsletter* (Assoc. for Rural Advancement) No.1, 2 A 'labour tenant' family lived on the land of a white landlord and worked for him for six months of the year for no wages ... This was the dominant form of farm labour in the Natal Midlands and northern districts as well as the Eastern Transvaal until the abolition of the system in the 1960's.
Hence **labour tenancy** *n. phr.*
    1985 PLATZKY & WALKER *Surplus People* 123 By January 1969 labour tenancy had been abolished throughout the Orange Free State.

ladies' bar *n. phr.* Also **ladies bar**. [See quot. 1955.] Historically, a lounge or other public area in a hotel in which the sale of liquor to women was permitted (public bars being in the past closed by law to women); loosely, a hotel lounge or public area. Also *attrib.*
    [**1955** LANSDOWN & BROEKSMA *S. Afr. Liquor Law* 162 Since, by section 104 of the Liquor Act 1928, a licence holder is prohibited .. from permitting any female .. from being at any time in his bar or any other part of the premises which the licensing board has declared to be restricted, it follows that sales of liquor, in so far as permitted to be made to females, must take place in some other portion of the premises, *e.g.* the dining room, or a lounge outside the bar or restricted portion, or a part which the board .. has set aside as a place in which females shall be served.] **1972** *S. Afr. Law Reports* 1972(3) July-Sept. 386 The said accused sold, supplied or dealt in liquor in the ladies' bar, known as the Café de Paris, .. a restricted portion of the licensed premises, contrary to the conditions imposed by the Liquor Licensing Board .. in that the said sale .. was made .. by .. a barmaid in respect of whom no certificate had been issued as required. **1981** W.A. JOUBERT *Law of S. Afr.* Vol.15, 148 The restricted portions [of licensed premises] covered by this provision [sc. the minister's granting of permission to the licensee to admit women or children] are commonly known as 'ladies' bars'. The holder of an on-consumption licence who wishes to have a 'ladies' bar' on his premises has to make an application to the liquor board describing the restricted portion. **1983** M. FAIRALL *When in Durban* 74 Good linefish, casseroles and stews from á la carte/ladies bar menu. [*Ibid.* 79 This is not men-only terrain .. Many hotels will let you order a pub lunch in ladies' lounges, cocktail bars and public terraces.] **1994** *Informant, Grahamstown* 'Is there somewhere we can sit and have a drink before eating?' 'There is a ladies' bar in the restaurant.'

lady *n.* [Special senses of general Eng.]
1. [Influenced by Afk. *dame* a lady; 'madam, ma'am', the most courteous Afk. form of address to a woman.] Esp. in the Eng. of Afrikaans-speakers: 'madam, ma'am', a respectful mode of address to a woman.
    Although sometimes intended respectfully, the word is sometimes misinterpreted as being impolite (cf. *U.S. Eng.* 'lady').
    1956 N. GORDIMER in *Best of S. Afr. Short Stories* (1991) 221 'My God,' said Mrs Hansen, 'My God. So she died, eh?' 'Yes, lady,' he held out his hand for her ticket. **1963** J. PACKER *Home from Sea* 171 One of our drunks. Drunk and disorderly, lady, truculent with the constable who arrested him. **1971** D.A.C. MACLENNAN *Wake.* 31 That's quite all right lady. I jus' come to visit. Don't worry about me. **1975** J. MCCLURE *Snake* (1981) 162 'Do I make myself clear?' 'Yes, lady, I'm sorry, hey?' **1982** *Informant, Bible Society* Dear Sir/Lady, Two scholars are cycling from Johannesburg to Port Elizabeth to raise funds for Bible distribution. **1987** M. POLAND *Train to Doringbult* 100 'What the hell's going on?' she demanded. 'Lady, this is not your business.' **1989** J. HOBBS *Thoughts in Makeshift Mortuary* 232 'What do you want her for, lady?' The official voice on the phone sounded deeply suspicious.
2. *Special Comb.* **Lady Billie** [formed by analogy with OLD BILL], a title given to the leader of the Women's Auxiliary of the Memorable Order of the Tin Hats (see MOTHWA). See also OLD BILL.
    1979 *E. Prov. Herald* 26 June 12 Mrs Ann Lawent, Deputy National Lady Billie.

laemer-vanger var. LAMMERVANGER.

lagavaan var. LEGUAAN.

lager *n.*[1] var. LAAGER *n.*

lager *n.*[2] var. LEAGUER.

lager *v.* var. LAAGER *v.*

lagewaan var. LEGUAAN.

lahnee var. LARNEY.

laitie var. LIGHTY.

lakavan var. LEGUAAN.

lala *n.* var. ILALA.

‖**lala** /ˈlaːla, ˈlɑːlə/ *v. intrans.* [Xhosa and Zulu, lie down, rest, sleep, spend the night.] To sleep; to lie down; to rest; cf. DOEDOE. Occas. in the phr. *lala kahle* /-gaːɬe/ [see GASHLE], sleep well.
    Used esp. when speaking (or singing) to children.
    1902 F.C. SLATER *Sel. Poems* (1947) 78 Then lala, lala, my little son, You'll soon be a man of might. [*Note*] Sleep. **1970** S.E. NATHAM *Informant, Cape Town* Lala. Sleep. **1975** *Daily Dispatch* 27 Mar. (Suppl.) 12 Rest in holy peace. Lala Kahle. [**1977** P.C. VENTER *Soweto* 70 'My wife will not support me,' he once growled ... So now I say, 'Lala lulaza.' Let sleeping dogs lie!] **1991** M.L. MCCAFFERY *Informant, Durban* Lala. Sleep.

lamajita see MAJITA sense a.

‖**lambile** /lamˈbiːle/ *adj.* Also **lambele**. [In the Nguni languages, -*lambile* hungry, perfective of *lamba* become hungry.] Hungry. Occas. in the collocation **lambile strap** /-stræp/, *girdle of famine* (see GIRDLE).
    1839 W.C. HARRIS *Wild Sports* 293 The leathern strap worn round the waist is called by the savages a lambele strap, or hunger-girdle. **1860** A.W. DRAYSON *Sporting Scenes* 218 They showed a great disinclination to move after their repast, although they complained that they were still lambile (hungry). **1966** I. VAUGHAN *These Were my Yesterdays* 101 Progress hampered by a crowd of ragged native urchins who rush beside me proclaiming loudly 'Lambile,' Am hungry.

lamesick *adj. Obs. Pathology.* Also **lamsick**. [Calqued on S. Afr. Du. *lamziek.*] Of, pertaining to, or afflicted with LAMSIEKTE.
    1823 W.W. BIRD *State of Cape of G.H.* 98 Every boer, having a farm of usual extent, possesses many yokes; but in most farms they require change of pasture for a few months every year, without which they become *lamziek* (lame-sick), or paralytic in all their limbs. **1911** J.F. PENTZ in *Farmer's Weekly* 11 Oct. 158, I have heard of a 'gallsick' microbe, but not of a 'lam-sick' microbe.

lamesickness, lamsickness /ˈlamsɪknəs/ *n. Pathology.* [(Part.) tr. Afk. *lamsiekte.*] LAMSIEKTE.
    1905 D. HUTCHEON in Flint & Gilchrist *Science in S. Afr.* 361 Cases similar to the above frequently occur

in veld-fed cattle, more especially where 'stiffsickness' and 'Lamsickness' prevails. **1974** R. Clark in *Std Encycl. of Sn Afr.* X. 299 Lamsiekte ('lame-sickness') was known in South Africa as early as 1796 and became the greatest obstacle to cattle-farming in the North-Western Cape and Western Free State. **1979** T. Gutsche *There Was a Man* 5 A worse scourge since it affected both food and transport was the equally noted 'lame-sickness' among cattle.

lammervanger /ˈlamə(r),faŋə(r)/ *n.* Also **laemervanger**. Pl. **-s**, or unchanged. [S. Afr. Du., fr. Du. *lam(mer)* lamb + *vanger* catcher; so named because reputed to feed on young lambs.] Any of several large raptors of the Accipitridae, esp. the MARTIAL EAGLE, *Polemaetus bellicosus*, the tawny eagle or GOLDEN EAGLE, *Aquila rapax*, and the bearded vulture or lammergeyer, *Gypaetys barbatus*. Formerly also (*rare*) **lammetjievanger** /ˈlamәki-/ [see -IE], or **lamvanger** /ˈlam-/. Also *attrib.*

1830 *S. Afr. Quarterly Jrnl* Jan.-Apr. 105 *Gypaetys Barbatus*, Cuv. — Arend and Lammervanger of the Colonists. **1835** A. Steedman *Wanderings* II. 7 On the previous night some jackals had attacked and bitten off the tails of several lambs .. others had been destroyed by the *Laemer-vanger*, or bearded vulture. [**1846** see GOLDEN EAGLE.] **1864** T. Baines *Explor. in S.-W. Afr.* 194 The bird, .. called by some the Lammijie-vanger, (Lamb catcher,) and by others the Golden Eagle, differs, so far as I can find, only in the lighter colour of its plumage from the European kind. **1906** W.S. Johnson *Orangia* 17 We have a good many birds, including eagles, some of which attack lambs and are called Lammervangers. [**1923** Haagner & Ivy *Sketches* 8 The peculiar Lämmergeyer (*Gypaëtus ossifragus*) is called by the Boers the Lammervanger (Lamb-catcher), but the stories told of its attacking sheep, and even human beings, are exaggerated!] **1946** V. Pohl *Adventures of Boer Family* 117 The *lammervanger* is one of the wariest, shyest and most keen-eyed of all birds. **1959** *Cape Times* 20 June 2 Mr. Sonny Waks .. saw an eagle — commonly known as a *lammervanger* — catching one of his young lambs. **1961** A. Fugard *Notebks* (1983) 24 The wildest, most beautiful of all animals, the Martial Eagle, Lammervanger. **1965** J. Bennett *Hawk Alone* 124 Right about then two black specks flew in wide circles; lammervanger eagles from the cliffs across the valley. Their high harsh cries drifted down from the sky. **1970** [see GOLDEN EAGLE]. **1975** *Daily Dispatch* 10 Apr. 8 Suddenly a lammervanger, or martial eagle, swooped down and picked up a baby baboon in its talons.

‖**lammetjie** /ˈlamәki, -ci/ *n.* Also **lamme(r)tje**. [Afk.] A term of endearment, 'little lamb'.

1908 F.C. Slater *Sunburnt South* 21 Klaas, who was about half a head shorter than she, used often to make us laugh by calling her, 'Lena, my *lammetje*'. **1920** R.Y. Stormberg *Mrs Pieter de Bruyn* 111 The wicket people wot calls her precious lammertje ugly! **1968** G. Croudace *Black Rose* 113 We are of one blood, *lammetjie*, of one language, of one church.

lammijie-vanger see LAMMERVANGER.

lamsick, lamsickness varr. LAMESICK, LAME-SICKNESS.

lamsiekte /ˈlamsiktә/ *n. Pathology.* Also **la(a)mziekte, lam-sikte, lumsiehte**. [Afk. (earlier S. Afr. Du. *lamziekte*), *lam* paralyzed + *siekte* disease.] Botulism, a paralytic disease primarily of cattle, caused by the bacterium *Clostridium botulinum*, and usu. resulting from the eating of decomposed organic material, esp. bones, in phosphorus-deficient areas; GALLAMSIEKTE; LAME-SICKNESS. Also *attrib.* See also LAMESICK.

1790 tr. *F. Le Vaillant's Trav.* II. 78 The first [malady], called at the Cape *lam-sikte*, is a real palsy. **1798** S.H. Wilcocke tr. *J.S. Stavorinus's Voy. to E. Indies 1768–71* II. 64 The *lamziekte*, is when the cattle are not able to stand. **1809** J. Mackrill Diary. 61 Laam ziekte, The lame distemper comes on slowly & deprives the Bones of all medulla & strength. **1812** A. Plumptre tr. *H. Lichtenstein's Trav. in Sn Afr.* (1928) I. 49 A disease among cattle called the *lamziekte* (a sort of murrain of the most pernicious kind, since the animal infected with it becomes entirely lame). **1896** *Cape Argus* 2 Jan. 6 Cattle are dying from lamziekte on many farms. **1911** L. Knoblauch in *Farmer's Weekly* 18 Oct. 194 About 1880 .. we again totalled 180 head of cattle. Then all of a sudden lamziekte broke out, and in 18 months' time my father had not a cow to milk. **1937** S. Cloete *Turning Wheels* 272 Quarter evil, lamsiekte in which cows went about eating bones and animal refuse, struck at them. **1948** *Cape Argus* 6 Nov. 1 The Division of Veterinary Services .. will shortly make available a new, improved and concentrated lamsiekte vaccine. **1962** F.C. Metrowich *Scotty Smith* 225 One of the farm boys arrived and informed his master that two of the donkeys had died of lamsiekte. **1973** [see PAARDEZIEKTE]. **1975** G.P. West *Black's Veterinary Dict.* 418 The best means of preventing lamziekte is to feed sterilised bone meal to cattle during the winter months. **1978** *S. Afr. Panorama* May 37 Years ago Theiler noticed that cattle suffering from 'lamsiekte' (paralysis disease) .. were prone to chew old bones and carrion. **1989** J. du P. Bothma *Game Ranch Management* 233 Botulism, also known as 'Lamsiekte', is caused by the toxins of a bacterium *Clostridium botulinum*. The bacteria multiply in putrid and decaying bones that lie around in the veld. If these bones are eaten, usually by cattle with a phosphate deficiency, the toxins produced by the bacteria are absorbed and cause paralysis of the nervous system.

lamvanger see LAMMERVANGER.

land /lænd/ *n.* [Calque formed on Du. (and subsequently Afk.) *land* a piece of ground, a field; a country.]

1. A field; a portion of farm land under crops, or suitable for cultivation. Freq. in *pl.*

1731 G. Medley tr. *P. Kolb's Present State of Cape of G.H.* I. 358 The Colonies are encreasing daily, and daily taking in new Lands for Tillage. **1806** J. Barrow *Trav.* I. 5 At the feet of the hills .. are several pleasant farms, having gardens well stored with vegetables for the table, vineyards, and extensive corn lands. **1810** [see Gie quot. at LEENINGS EIGENDOM]. **1821** G. Barker Journal. 11 Sept., Began to cut down thorns to fence my wheat land, the cattle being every day in it. **1841** B. Shaw *Memorials* 243, I came to a number of *women working in a garden*, or, as it might with more propriety be called, a small corn land. **1842** J. Collett Diary. II. 6 Apr., Ploughed one Land and sowed Barley. **1851** N.J. Merriman *Cape Jrnls* (1957) 172 Not so the Dutchman, who either welcomes you, or at the most comes and tells you, he hopes you will take care that your horse does not get upon 'the land', that is, among the standing corn, which is never *enclosed* as it is in England. **1871** E.J. Dugmore Diary. 19 Oct., The huts of the natives further on with their lands and gardens about them looked quite picturesque. **1896** H.A. Bryden *Tales of S. Afr.* 248 She had .. some good tobacco 'lands', which yielded no mean profit each year. **1905** E.A. Nobbs in Flint & Gilchrist *Science in S. Afr.* 378 Even in our more highly-cultivated grain-growing districts, the 'lands' — that is, the cultivated fields — only occupy a fraction of the whole farm. **1905** P. Gibbon *Vrouw Grobelaar* 46 One day the Kafirs came in from the lands and would not work any more. *c***1911** S. Playne *Cape Col.* 39 The bulk of the heavy work at the home and in the mealie 'lands' is done by the women. **1926** P. Smith *Beadle* (1929) 20 Her youngest son .. remained at the homestead working the lands with his father. **1930** *Friend* 25 Aug. 12 Lands — Excellent for all kinds of grain; at present there are lands for 16 bags of mealies, but more lands can be made. **1956** F.C. Metrowich *Valiant but Once* 12 About forty years ago the grave was dug up by some farmers while they were making a land. **1966** E. Palmer *Plains of Camdeboo* 297 Dust enveloped the world. Maurice and Sita could not even see where the lands had been. **1971** *Farmer's Weekly* 12 May 102 The farm Delarey .. measuring 603 hectares (702 morgen), comprising approximately 256 hectares lands, and the rest grazing. **1971** *Rand Daily Mail* 25 May 3 Mr Colombera .. returned to the potato lands on the farm after lunch. **1977** [see LEAD]. **1988** H. Vickery in *Quagga* Vol.20, 24 There have been reports of up to 70 dead cranes found in a single land. **1988** H. Dugmore in *Personality* 18 July 32 He was out in the lands one morning when his wife brought him his morning coffee. **1991** F.G. Butler *Local Habitation* 52 There was the silhoutte of Rhebokberg and the tree-lined course of the Great Fish River, the dam, the poplar bush and the lands. **1993** *Informant, Grahamstown* 'Do you cut this wood on your farm?' 'Yes, I cut it on my farm. I'm clearing some old lands, you know.'

2. A commonly used synonym for 'country' or 'nation'.

Used in other varieties of English, but usu. in poetic or dramatic contexts.

1900 [see NAAR sense 1]. *c***1937** *Title of publication, United Tobacco Co.* Our Land. **1948** [see ASIATIC *n.*]. **1969** [see LEKKER *adj.* sense 3]. **1990** [see ISCOR]. **1992** H. Ashton on Radio South Africa 11 Nov., The crying need in this land is for primary education. **1993** *Weekend Post* 25 Sept. 11, I have had to learn to respect him as my grandfather without justifying what he and like-minded people did to people in this land. **1994** [see *Durban July* (DURBAN)].

Land Act *n. phr. Hist.* [Shortened form of the name of each Act.] Either of two Acts of Parliament: **a.** The *Natives Land Act* (No.27 of 1913) which prohibited black people from owning or leasing land except in areas reserved for them, or in areas to be added to these on the recommendation of a commission set up in terms of the Act. **b.** The *Native Trust and Land Act* (No.18 of 1936), which added land to the areas already set aside for black occupation, and appointed a Trust to control the ownership, leasing, and acquisition of such land; see also HERTZOG BILLS.

The 1913 Act set aside 10,5 million morgen (approx. 7,4 percent of South Africa's total area) for occupation by blacks; the 1936 Act added a further 7,25 million morgen, bringing the percentage to approx. 12,5 per cent. Both Acts were repealed by the Abolition of Racially Based Land Measures Act (No.108 of 1991). See also *pillar(s) of apartheid* (PILLAR).

[**1913** *Act 27* in *Stat. of Union* 436 To make further provision as to the purchase and leasing of land by Natives and other Persons in the several parts of the Union and for other purposes in connection with the ownership and occupation of Land by Natives and other Persons. *Ibid.* 448 This Act may be cited for all purposes as the Natives Land Act, 1913.] **1916** S.T. Plaatje *Native Life* (1982) 60 We have dealt with the history of the Land Act from its commencement, and all the speeches and official documents we have mentioned hitherto say nothing about restricting Europeans in their ownership of land. **1931** W.A. Cotton *Racial Segregation* 58 It might as well be admitted that the efficient motive behind the 1913 Land Act, as behind the later Colour Bar Act and all the policy of parallel institutions and domiciliary segregation, was and is, that we want the Natives' labour, but we don't want them. [**1936** *Act 18* in *Stat. of Union* 90 This Act and the Natives Land Act 1913 (Act No.27 of 1913), hereinafter referred to as the 'principal Act', as modified by this Act, shall be construed as if they formed one Act. *Ibid.* 142 This Act shall be called the Native Trust and Land Act 1936.] **1963** M. Benson *Afr. Patriots* 290 There was the Land Act — restricting millions of African peasants to small tight reserves. These .. have grown ever more crowded, denuded, struck by famine. **1977** J. Sikakane *Window on Soweto* 11 They were forced off the land by .. economic and political measures such as the Land Act of 1913 which displaced thousands of Africans from 'white-owned' land. **1980** D.B. Coplan Urbanization of African Performing Arts. 168 The widespread popularity of Caluza's compositions among African choirs throughout the Union was largely due to the topicality of his lyrics ... *Umteto we Land Act* .. protests the injustice of the Land Act of 1913. **1990** *New African* 11 June 4 The 1913 and 1936 Land Acts scheduled areas for black settlement — a mere 13 percent of South

Africa — and ended black purchase of land outside the homelands. **1991** B. SEERY in *Sunday Tribune* 19 May 9 The battlecry at this week's conference was opposition to the government's plans to repeal the Land Acts of 1913 and 1936 which would effectively allow blacks to buy white farming land.

Land Bank *n. phr.* [Shortened form of *Land and Agricultural Bank of South Africa*.] A financial institution making loans to farmers, agricultural co-operatives, and statutory agricultural institutions, established in 1912 by the Land Bank Act. Also *attrib.*

1911 J.F. PENTZ in *Farmer's Weekly* 11 Oct. 156 Let the next Parliament .. vote for Land Banks and .. for scientific veterinary research, to solve our cattle diseases. [**1912** Act 18 in *Stat. of Union* 370 There shall be established in the Union a bank under the name of 'The Land and Agricultural Bank of South Africa'.] *Ibid.* 412 This Act may be cited for all purposes as the Land Bank Act, 1912. **1915** J.K. O'CONNOR *Afrikander Rebellion* 88 A Land Bank on a larger scale than the existing Bank was to be established. **1927** *Outspan* 18 Mar. 63 Farmers who are not in a position to afford double fences along the trunk-road over their farms may be assisted with loans bearing a lower rate of interest than that charged by the Land Bank. **1936** *Cambridge Hist. of Brit. Empire* VIII. 799 Provision was made in each of the colonies before Union for advances of capital by a Government Land Bank to farmers on first mortgages of their land, and to agricultural co-operative societies. The Land Banks were absorbed by a Union Government Act of 1912 in a new Land and Agricultural Bank of South Africa. **1937** [see *bond v.* (BOND *n.*[1])]. **1951** *Afr. Drum* Mar. 24 Loans from the Farmers' Home Administration (F.H.A.), a federal agency of the United States Government (equivalent to South Africa's Land Bank). *c*1967 J. HOBBS in *New S. Afr. Writing* 67 He paid a formal visit to the Land Bank, .. and rode back from the Dorp in a snorting red Massey-Ferguson, brand new. **1973** *Farmer's Weekly* 13 June 13 The Land Bank grants four types of loans to farmers: Mortgage loans, charge loans, hypothec loans and loans in the form of cash credit accounts. The Land Bank and Agricultural Bank of South Africa is an autonomous institution and is responsible to Parliament through the Minister of Finance. **1976** V. ROSENBERG *Sunflower* 39 Jim Flattery had bought the farm in 1906 at four shillings and sixpence a morgen in terms of a Land Bank scheme designed to assist Bushveld farmers. **1986** J. CONYNGHAM *Arrowing of Cane* 88 Back came the Afrikaners, accustomed to hardships and bolstered by a benign Land Bank and faith in their government. **1992** *Financial Mail* 13 Mar. 71 The Land Bank .. often holds first bonds.

landdrost /ˈlændrɒst/ *n. hist.* Pl. -**s**, occas. -**en**. Formerly also **land(d)rest**, **landdroost**, **landros(t)**, **landruest**, **llandrost**, and with initial capital. [S. Afr. Du., fr. Du. *land* country + *drost* bailiff. (In Afk., *landdros* magistrate).]

The first landdrost was appointed in 1685; in 1827, landdrosts were replaced by civil commissioners and magistrates, but the title was revived in the Boer republics (see sense 2).

1. Under Dutch East India Company rule: the magistrate and chief administrator of a district or 'drostdy' (see DROSTDY sense 1), and chairman of the board of heemraden; DROST. Also *attrib.* See also HEEMRAAD.

1731 G. MEDLEY tr. *P. Kolb's Present State of Cape of G.H.* II. 10 He gave this *Land-Drost* the Powers of a Fiscal Independent (an Officer in the *Capian* Colony) to seize and prosecute all Criminals, Vagabonds and disorderly Persons in the Colonies for which he was appointed. **1776** F. MASSON in *Phil. Trans. of Royal Soc.* LXVI. 286 Dined with the Land Drost, who is a justice of peace, and collects different taxes from the peasants. **1786** G. FORSTER tr. *A. Sparrman's Voy. to Cape of G.H.* II. 144 The *land-drost* has appointed one of the farmers, with the title of *veld-corporal*, to command in these wars. **1790** W. PATERSON *Narr. of Four Journeys* 20 Zwellendam .. is the residence of a Land Drost, or chief justice. **1795** C.R. HOPSON tr. *C.P. Thunberg's Trav.* I. 167 Arrived at *Zwellendam*, the residence of one of the company's land-drosts, whose jurisdiction extends over all the interior part of the country that lies beyond this spot, and whose office is in some respect, though not absolutely, similar to that of the governor of a province. **1801** [see HEEMRAAD sense 2]. **1811** [see FIELD CORNET sense 1]. **1822** W.J. BURCHELL *Trav.* I. 75 Each [district] is placed under the superintendance of either a Landdrost or a deputy landdrost, who administers the government, in most respects, as the representative of the governor; and it is through him that all laws, proclamations, and inferior regulations, are carried into effect. **1823** W.W. BIRD *State of Cape of G.H.* 22 The landdrost, who is the chief officer of the district, or drostdy, holds, together with six heemraden, as assessors, a court for petty cases, both criminal and civil; and also a matrimonial court. **1830** in *Stat. Law of Cape of G.H.* (1862) 31 Oct., The office of landdrost was abolished on the 31st day of December, 1827. **1832** *Graham's Town Jrnl* 22 June 102, I hope the Civil Commissioners of both the districts will order immediate repairs. In the old times of Landdrosts such complaints would not be long unattended to. **1837** J.E. ALEXANDER *Narr. of Voy.* I. 355 Before civil commissioners were appointed for the Cape districts, the *landrost* was the chief officer in each; and his residence was styled 'the drostdy'. **1943** 'J. BURGER' *Black Man's Burden* 18 In 1834 .. the old Dutch local courts of Landdrost and Heemraden were abolished and paid magistrates appointed, and a few years later popularly elected municipal councils were instituted. **1955** L. MARQUARD *Story of S. Afr.* 64 Local government for this whole area centred in the village of Stellenbosch. The chief government official was the *landdrost* who was assisted by a district secretary and an unpaid board of *heemraden* to administer the district, try petty cases, collect taxes, register wills and notarial deeds, pay out 'lion and tiger money' as a reward for the destruction of wild animals, and organize and control the burgher militia. **1985** *S. Afr. Panorama* Oct. 15 Building started in 1804 when the first *landdros* (magistrate), Hendrik van de Graaff was appointed to the Land of Waveren and the newly proclaimed town of Tulbagh.

2. In the former Boer republics: a magistrate. Also *attrib.*

1846 *Natal Witness* 8 May, A further sum .. which he also owes .. by virtue of a certain Deed .. signed by him .. before Johan Philip Zietsman, then Landdrost of this District of Pietermaritzburg. **1856** *Cape of G.H. Almanac & Annual Register* 291 British authority again having been withdrawn from the whole of this country [*sc.* the Orange River Sovereignty] on the 23rd February 1854 .. its government is now in the hands of a President, freely elected by the inhabitants, assisted by an Executive Council and Landdrosts and Heemraden in the several districts while the Volksraad exercises legislative functions. **1877** F. JEPPE *Tvl Bk Almanac & Dir.* (1976) 35 The chief officer in each district is the 'Landdrost' who acts as Magistrate and Civil Commissioner with the assistance of a Landdrost Clerk, who is at the same time Public Prosecutor, Postmaster and Distributor of Stamps. Each district is further provided with a baljuw or sheriff, gaoler, and staff of constable. *Ibid.* 37 Landdrost Court — This Court has police, criminal, and civil jurisdiction, regulated by law, the latter in all cases up to £37 10s. From this court of Landdrost or Resident Magistrate, there is an appeal to the Landdrost and Heemraden Court. **1880** G.F. AUSTEN *Diary* (1981) 7 Through the whole of this day, hostilities were actively carried on between the Llandrost's office and the Boers. **1895** *Star* 30 Dec. 2 Government this morning received telegrams from the Landdrost of Potchefstroom .. that a large force of mounted men had crossed the Bechuanaland border into the Transvaal and were evidently *en route* for Johannesburg. **1900** H.C. HILLEGAS *Oom Paul's People* 204 In Johannesburg and Pretoria the land-drosts are men of eminent station in the legal profession of South Africa, and are drawn from all parts of the country, regardless of their political or racial qualifications. **1923** B. RONAN *Forty S. Afr. Yrs* 173 One of the most conspicuous figures of the early days of the Rand was its first Landdrost, Major von Brandis. **1925** [see LAW AGENT]. **1934** N. DEVITT *Mem. of Magistrate* 30 In the Transvaal and Free State the Landdrost and Predikant were the two men always most looked up to. **1947** L. HASTINGS *Dragons Are Extra* 35 Any old leader or landrost of the Free State or Transvaal had just Botha's sort of serenity. **1965** C. VAN HEYNINGEN *Orange Days* 24 Anton was afterwards magistrate (landdrost) of Hoopstad. **1971** [see FIELD COMMANDANT]. **1973** *The 1820* Vol.46 No.11, The landdrost was a well-known figure in Johannesburg, in his flat-topped hat, morning coat, light trousers and with his characteristic limp.

Hence **landdrostdy** *n.*, DROSTDY sense 1; **landdrostship** *n. nonce*, the office of landdrost.

1821 T. PHILIPPS *Lett.* (1960) 104 Capt. Trappes having Bird's interest expected to have succeeded to the Landdrostship, and in this state matters were when the Govnr determined to come up here. **1972** *Evening Post* 19 Feb. (Weekend Mag.) 2 The veldkornetcy of Achter Bruintjes Hoochte .. was by then the eastern section of the Graaff-Reinet landdrostdy.

langarm /ˈlaŋar(ə)m/ *adj., adv.,* and *n.* [Afk., *lang* long + *arm* arm.]

A. *adj.* Occas. also **lang arme** (*attrib.*). Of, in, or pertaining to a style of dancing, often accompanied by BOEREMUSIEK (sense 1), in which the dancing partners, with hands clasped, extend their leading arms horizontally and move rapidly round the dance-floor; LONG-ARM.

1977 *Dance with Meteors* (record cover) The diamond city's Meteors are falling stars with a difference for Kimberley's 'langarm' dancing public have seen to it that they are here to stay. **1982** *E. Prov. Herald* 29 Dec. 11 Old Year's Eve to New Year. Lang Arme Ball at Reflections, Hotel Jubilee. **1985** D. SMUTS in *Fair Lady* 18 Sept., A whole row of Stellenbosch ballgowns .. redolent of exhilarating evenings of real langarm dancing. **1987** *Sunday Times* 12 Apr. (Extra) 4 Bobby .. just smiled as Jerry Sloane of Gallo handed him his gold disc .. for his contribution to *langarm* music. **1987** *Ibid.* 12 Apr., On the look-out for a marimba band, a langarm band, .. and any other band or singer who plays music that is distinctively South African. **1987** *Grocott's Mail* 14 Aug. 12 Ruby's Dance Club — Saturday Night. Langarm dancing. Live Band. **1989** C. CHAPMAN in *Edgars Club* Apr. 45 Traditional sounds .. are expressed today in many different forms, from the singing of the troupes to jazz to *langarm* dance music. **1990** M. VAN KUIK in *Fair Lady* 15 Aug. 65 The Turkish Riviera ... *Langarm* dancing ... Chilled grapes. [**1990** see SKOFFEL *n.*[2] sense 2.] **1992** *Weekend Post* 9 May (Leisure) 1 The hotel has the largest dance floor I have seen in many years — the old-fashioned *langarm* kind.

B. *adv.* In the dance style described above.

1982 D. KRAMER *Short Back & Sides* 8, I watched the grown-ups on a Saturday night dancing langarm across the sawdust floor and listened in awe to the squeal of the saxaphone, the slap of the double bass and the thud of the drums of the local jazz band. **1987** *Informant, Jeffrey's Bay* Let's go langarm around the dance floor.

C. *n.* This dance-style. See also SAKKIE-SAKKIE *n.* sense b.

1994 *Sunday Times* 30 Jan. 34 (*advt*) Tiekiedraais and sakkie sakkie. When it's time to skop 'n bietjie, wragtig there's nothing like a boereorkes and a concertina to bring out the 'vastrap', 'langarm' or 'tiekiedraai' in you.

lang tande /ˌlaŋ ˈtan(d)ə/ *n. phr. Colloq.* [fr. Afk. idiom *eet met lang tande*, lit. 'eat with long teeth', to eat with distaste or reluctance.] In the phr. **with lang tande**, with long teeth (see LONG TEETH).

1973 *Farmer's Weekly* 9 May 13 A bloodied mess .. which even a dog would eat with *lang tande*. **1983** *Frontline* May 32 Chemically, the water is quite as pure as any other, but many a Windhoeker still .. drinks the city's water with very lang tande.

langwa /ˈlaŋvɑː/ *n. Wagon-making.* Formerly also **langwagen.** [Afk., earlier Du. *langwagen.*] LONG-WAGON. Occas. also part. tr. **lang-wagon.**

1822 W.J. BURCHELL *Trav.* I. 150 The *langwagen* is that beam which connects the two axletrees together. [**1835** A. SMITH *Diary* (1940) II. 158 The wagon wheel was yesterday put together and .. the band put on, and also a new long way was fixed.] **1893** [see ONDERSTEL]. **1914** S.P. HYATT *Old Transport Rd* 262 The 'lang-wagon,' the wooden bar which connects the fore carriage with the after carriage, is far more easily replaced. *Ibid.* 263 The only tools used by the transport-rider .. in getting düsselbooms or 'lang-wagons' were an auger and a side-axe. **1974** A.A. TELFORD in *Std Encycl. of Sn Afr.* X. 570 This [trolley] was usually a lighter vehicle ... There was no *langwa* and the body was on springs. *Ibid.* 571 The invention of the elliptic spring eliminated the need for the perch (*langwa*), thus lightening the weight.

lani(e) var. LARNEY.

lank /læŋk/ *adj.* and *adv. Slang.* [Etym unkn.; perh. fr. Afk. *lank* long (used of both time and proportion).] Used esp. by schoolchildren and young adults.

A. *adj.*

1. [Perh. rel. to Afk. *geld lank* money galore, pots of money.] Plenty of, lots of, many. Also *demonstrative.*

1970 K. NICOL *Informant, Durban,* I haven't seen him for lank ages ... You need lank practice to become expert in the game. **1981** *Informant, Grahamstown* Lank people do 'Legals' in English III. **1982** *Star* 31 Mar., Do you know what your children are talking about when they come home from school with 'lank homework'? **1982** J. ALLAN in *Sunday Times* 6 June (Mag. Sect.), This guy's been getting *lank* praise for this *lekker* play everyone is checking at the Market Theatre. **1983** *Frontline* May 14 The Fast Eddies, of which every bike club has at least half a dozen, came to Kyalami to check it out — *lank speed, my china.* **1985** *Vula* Oct. 32 Traditional songs .. are sung, strange garb is donned and lank vodka is drunk. **1991** M.A. KARASSELLOS *Informant, Cape Town* Come and share our braai — we've got lank meat. **1992** C. BOJARSKI *Informant, Grahamstown* We saw kudu, hartebees, lank ostriches. **1992** H. DUGMORE in *Scope* 13 Nov. 46 'She took lank time,' he says ... For five weeks he spent every available moment cutting up hundreds of *Scope* pin-ups to stick together his unique, all-paper nude.

2. [Perh. rel. to Afk. *lank nie sleg nie* not at all bad.] Good, nice, fantastic, etc.

1970 K. NICOL *Informant, Durban* The hotel food was lank (delicious, very enjoyable). **1983** *Cape Times* 9 Dec. 16 David .. starts tuning you lank Boland stories about his youth and his observations of life in suburbia. **1985** H. PRENDINI in *Style* Oct. 40 'He's got lank ninja stars' which could mean he's got plenty or they're nice. **1987** S. SMITH in *Fair Lady* 8 July 160 In the field of language, or rather, idiom the gap feels as wide as the Fish River Canyon. 'Hey, that was a really lank joll' translates into 'That was a terrific party'. **1991** K. SULLIVAN *Informant, Cape Town* Hell, those cars are lank! (nice). **1991** G. PAUL *Informant, Weltevreden Park* Lank. Much used by pre-teens and teenagers = superb/lovely/fantastic/wonderful. My Dad's got a lank new car.

B. *adv.* Very.

1987 *Informant, Grahamstown,* I am lank interested in the Hindus. **1989** M. BRAND in *Fair Lady* 25 Oct. 92 *Lank* ... Very, extremely. **1991** *Fair Lady* 8 May 63 *Lank* = very, as in 'lank cool'. **1991** C. CLARKSON *Informant, Johannesburg* It was a lank kif jol at Susan's last night, hey! After the exams we're only going to have a lank lekker peace-out on the beach, man. **1991** M.A. KARASSELLOS *Informant, Cape Town* There are lank suspicious characters outside the bank on pay-days. **1992** A. UTTLEY *Informant, Somerset West* Lank. A superlative meaning 'very': The exam was lank hard (heard on UCT campus and in Rondebosch high schools). **1993** *Informant, Grahamstown* That's lank rude, hey!

lannie var. LARNEY.

‖**lap** /lap/ *n.* [Afk.]

1. *noncount.* LAPPIE sense 2.

1920 R. JUTA *Tavern* 53 A small piece of dirty 'lap' long treasured by a woman slave .. , said to be a portion of the robe of Sheik Joseph, the holy man. **1972** M. BRITZ *Informant, Grahamstown* It's a warning — printed on lap — telling the farmers about brand-siekte.

2. LAPPIE sense 1 a.

1970 G. MARTIN *Informant, Bloemfontein* Fetch a lap to clean this mess up. **1970** C. DE VILLIERS *Informant, Bloemfontein* Where is the floor-lap?

lapa /ˈlɑːpə, ˈlaːpa/ *n.* Also **lappa,** ‖**lelapa.** [Sotho *lelapa.*]

1. In a traditional Sotho homestead: the forecourt, the first of two courtyards in the walled enclosure which contains the cluster of huts belonging to one family, providing an area for cooking, eating, and recreation. Also *transf.,* used of any enclosure, and *attrib.*

1924 E.B. FORD *Waterfalls* 10 My boy! My son! He brought me everything His mealie-cart, his whip, his earthen cow And I played with him in the 'lapa' ring. **1948** E. HELLMANN *Rooiyard* 9 Six Sotho women have each constructed a *lapa* (courtyard) of clay and cow-dung in front of their rooms. **1960** C. HOOPER *Brief Authority* 34 The low lelapa wall which surrounds each family's group of buildings. **1974** *S. Afr. Panorama* May 20 Each complex is integrated in an individual fashion. In some, the units are grouped about a centralised forecourt — or 'lapa' — with entrance through a gateway in the decorated 'lapa' wall. **1976** WEST & MORRIS *Abantu* 138 A typical homestead had another wall dividing the area into two courtyards: the front, *lapa,* being the cooking and entertaining area; and the rear one, *mafuri,* a private area for the family. **1982** *Voice* 21 Mar. 10 We dug a hole in the middle of the lapa (courtyard) and plastered the walls with dung. **1985** *Style* Oct. 150 His sunlit south-facing living room: 'I call this westernised African lapa.' ... From this lapa spaces fan out to a marvellously appointed kitchen; a cool diningroom [etc.]. **1990** E. KOCH in *Weekly Mail* 30 Mar. 11 With that [*sc.* R200 a month] he tries to feed his wife, nine children and a horde of grandchildren who scamper around the *lapa* of his homestead.

2. BOMA *n.*[1] sense 2.

1982 *S. Afr. Panorama* Dec. 13 Dinner is served in a reed walled *boma,* or *lapa,* within which tables are arranged in a big semi-circle. In the centre burns a log fire. **1987** *You* 3 Sept. 104 Paradise Game Ranch is an exclusive, private game reserve on the Lowveld ... Dinner around the braai in the *lapa* is an unforgettable experience. **1990** 'T. EQUINUS' in *Weekly Mail* 2 Nov. 54 We realised that we had driven into the wrong camp ... Five Dobermans shepherded us into a lapa where we were given a Bible quiz, intermediate level. **1990** *Weekend Post* 8 Dec. 12 Game spotting and bird-watching can be arranged .. and traditional delicacies like *potjiekos* and braais are held on farms in thatched structures called *lappas.* **1991** C. URQUHART in *Weekend Post* 16 Mar. (Leisure) 4 These 'safari farmers' offer a variety of activities, including game viewing, .. lapa braais, conducted tours and night game spotting drives.

‖**lapa** /ˈla(ː)pa/ *adv.* and *adj. Colloq.* Also **lapha.** [Fanakalo, 'here', 'there', 'at', 'to', fr. Zulu, Siswati, and Ndebele *lapha* here.]

A. *adv.* There, over there; also in the n. phr. **lapa language** [so called because of the frequent use of the word 'lapa' in the language], FANAKALO; **lapa-lapa** *n.,* fancy talk, 'beating about the bush'.

1957 J.D. BOLD *Dict., Grammar & Phrase Bk of Fanagalo* 7 It [*sc.* fanakalo] is known as 'the Lapa Language' or even .. as the 'Lo Lo Language'. **1976** M. MELAMU in *New Classic* No.3, 4 But that's how she is, this Georgina. Straight-talk and no *lapha-lapha,* as she says. **1990** P. CULLINAN in M. Leveson *Firetalk* 7, I was trying to get .. boards stacked in an orderly manner. The team I was working with were raw and had never been in a factory before ... I was shouting at them: 'Ai lapa, you bloody mompara, sit hom daarso.'

B. *adj.* (demonstrative). In the phr. ***lapa side*** [fr. Fanakalo *lapasayid* there (*sayid* ad. Eng. *side*), with spelling remodelled to the Eng. root], 'that side', over there, in that place.

1970 N. CONWAY *Informant, Salisbury* (*Harare, Zimbabwe*) Lapa side. Over there. **1982** 'HOGARTH' in *Sunday Times* 2 May 28 Munnik? 'Lapa side!' .. Dr Munnik .. is not one of them. He is a product of UCT. **1985** P. SLABOLEPSZY *Sat. Night at Palace* 45 Vince: Why isn't he here? September: He is by the home ... Is down the road here. Vince: Where? September: Lapa side. **1985** *Vula* Oct. 16 Whites whinge that side, please. Blacks, lapa side. **1991** L. PAROLIS *Informant, Grahamstown* You want Mike's address lapa-side? In America? **1994** on CCV TV 20 Aug., (*advt*) Hey chief, park it as close to the fountain as possible, lapa side.

lapje var. LAPPIE.

lappa var. LAPA *n.*

lappie /ˈlæpi, ˈlapi/ *n. colloq.* Also **lappy,** and (formerly) **lapje.** [Afk. (earlier Du. *lapje*), (small) rag or cloth, *lap* + -IE.]

1.a. A rag or cloth; a small piece of fabric or patchwork (cf. sense 2); LAP sense 2. See also JAMMERLAPPIE.

*c*1892 J. WIDDICOMBE *Fourteen Yrs in Basutoland* 106, I kept them rolled up in a *lappie* (old piece of rag). **1899** S.T. PLAATJE *Boer War Diary* (1973) 50, I sent back to them St. Leger's cream coloured lappie. **1908** J.H. DRUMMOND *Diary.* 7 Nov., This evening we got a lappy at the end of a pi[e]ce of cotton and frightened people .. but they thought it a huge joke when they found out. **1913** J.J. DOKE *Secret City* 255 'Pas op, Johannes!' she cried, mopping her face with a lapje, 'how you do frighten me'. **1925** *E. Prov. Herald* 10 July 5 Did she say anything about putting this money in a lappie and wearing it round your neck? **1926** E. LEWIS *Mantis* 208 Pouring out a saucerful of water and using his handkerchief for a 'lappie' as he called it, he cleaned the cup. **1935** P. SMITH *Platkop's Children* 22 Rubbin' the schoolroom floor with a terpintiny lapje an' a bottle that had water in it, to make it shine. **1937** S. CLOETE *Turning Wheels* 253 'Ach', she sighed, 'to think that Gert Kleinhouse, whose nose I used to wipe with a lappie, has verneuked me out of a lovely little pig'. **1939** —— *Watch for Dawn* 325 It was a beautiful little dress .. and Kaspar never gave back the lappie in which it was wrapped. **1941** M.G. GILBERT *Informant, Cape Town* Everybody sitting hunched at their tables dressed in peculiar clothes & with old lappies or bits of string tying up their hair. **1970** *Cape Times* 16 Sept. 7 There had been 'dramatic evidence about the finding of the *lappie* and the hair stuck in the middle'. **1970** L. DU TOIT *Informant, Bloemfontein,* I had to get a lappie to wipe up the milk which I had messed in the kitchen. **1978** *Sunday Times* 5 Nov. (Mag. Sect.) 5, I was cured of a headache with a lappie on my forehead soaked in buchu and vinegar. **1982** *Ibid.* 28 Feb. (Mag. Sect.) 5 Mrs Hough used 3420 'lappies' to make the rosetted quilt. **1989** *Informant, Johannesburg* Look at this cloth, I washed it this morning and now it looks like a lappie; I'll have to wash it again.

b. *fig.* Anything resembling a piece of rag or patchwork.

1955 B.B. BURNETT *Anglicans in Natal* 21 On the small *lappies* around the lonely homesteads of the Dutch pastoralists, the cultivation of the soil began for the first time. **1977** T. SHEARING in *Fair Lady* 16 Feb. 23 In the farming world wet lappies abound, Every Friday they come to town. **1990** S. MAXWELL *Informant, Grahamstown* Those milk skins in coffee, I call them 'lappies'.

c. *comb.* **lappie-legs,** used to designate (one with) an un-coordinated gait, or very thin or gangly legs; ‖**lappie-pop** [Afk., *pop* doll], a rag doll; ‖**lappieskombers** [Afk., *kombers* blanket, cover], a patchwork quilt; also *fig.*; ‖**lappies smous** [Afk., *smous* see SMOUS *n.*], a rag man.

1973 *Informant, Grahamstown* That girl walks as though she's got real **lappie-legs!** **1977** F.G. BUTLER

Karoo Morning 182 He was growing tall and rangy .. and his socks were usually round his ankles. He was nicknamed 'Sigaret-beentjies' or 'Lappy-legs'. **1935** P. SMITH *Platkop's Children* 111 Dinka's brought her piccanin, Dill the coffee-kettle, Light has brought her **lapje-pop**. **1957** L.G. GREEN *Beyond City Lights* 41 There is also a decorative **lappieskombers** (patchwork quilt) in the museum which shows how the women spent their evenings. **1990** *Sunday Times* 4 Mar. 25 The policy of protection through division is still strong in the NP philosphy and practice ... It envisages a future of a *lappieskombers* of black, white and khaki (a colour coding for the so-called open group) with the white sector small and threatened. **1989** *Grocott's Mail* 10 Mar. 7 (*letter*) I have seen the local shopkeeper stand hand-in-pockets .. all because an out of town **'lappies smous'** has been allowed to open a 'store' on the Church Square.

‖**d.** With defining words denoting a specific use for the cloth or rag: **koerant-lappie** [Afk., *koerant* newspaper], a cloth used as a cover to prevent soiling from newsprint; **vet lappie** [Afk., *vet* grease], a greased or oiled rag loaded into the barrel of a gun and rammed home with the bullet.

1978 *Sunday Times* 3 Sept. (Mag. Sect.) 5 A rectangular piece of material which in black ink bore the legend: **Koerant-lappie** ... It keeps the ink off the sheets and the frown off matron's face. **1949** J. ROSE-INNES in F.G. Butler *When Boys Were Men* (1969) 272 The favourite firearm was a heavy double-barrelled piece, right barrel shot, left barrel bullet, and each charge had to be rammed home, accompanied by its wad, or its oil rag (**vet lappie**). **1987** G. TYLDEN in *Africana Notes & News* Vol.12 No.6, 206 Rifles like the Baker nearly always have some form of flap backsight .. or hinged lid closing a small box cut in the right side of the butt for holding greased patches and 'vet lappies' loaded with the bullet.

2. *noncount.* Fabric, cloth; LAP sense 1. Also *attrib.*

1900 B.M. HICKS *Cape as I Found It* 179 The dishcloth is a great institution in the Boer household. A dirty bit of 'lapje' (rag) it is. **1973** *Grocott's Mail* 9 Nov. 3 Think of that 'lappy' nightcap with a tassel and those nightshirts below the knees. **1982** *Drum* Mar. 100 'Back in your homeland and village the girls are topless every day.' 'Yes,' I said, 'but they wear a little piece of lappie in front'. **1986** L.B. HALL in *Style* July 97 As she stoops, her lappie hat falls to the ground.

largaar, larger varr. LAAGER *n.*

large-tailed Cape sheep see *Cape sheep* (CAPE sense 2 a).

larney /lɑːni/ *n.* and *adj. Colloq.* Also **laani(e)**, **lahnee**, **lani(e)**, **lannie**, **larnie**, **lorny**. Pl. **-s**; occas. ‖**ama-**. [ad. Isicamtho *lani(e)* white man; ultimate origin unknown, perh. rel. to Malay *rani* rich, a queen, or Hindi *rani* queen (see Green quot. 1982 at sense B).

The replacement of /r/ by /l/ is common in the adaptation of foreign words by speakers of the Sintu (Bantu) languages. The spelling forms *laani, lahnee* and *lanie* are more frequently found in the n. form, while the Englished *larnie* and *larney* are more common as adj. forms.]

A. *n. derog.*

1.a. A white man. **b.** A boss or employer. (These two senses sometimes overlap.) Also as a term of address, and *attrib.*

1956 A. SAMPSON *Drum* 101 As I sat down, between Bill and Can, I heard a murmur behind me of 'Laanis,' the *tsotsi* word for white men. **1963** L.F. FREED *Crime in S. Afr.* 127 The tsotsis have a variety of words for money ... Their word for an old man is 'toppie', for a young girl 'tjerrie', for a European 'lani'. **1965** PATON & SHAH *Sponono* (1983) 22 Walter: I thought you wanted to work for the *lanie*. Sponono: Well, if I wanted to work for the *lanie*, I don't want to work for him now. **1977** D. MULLER *Whitey* 34 The larnie at the kafee is a good man – a Portjie [Portuguese]. **1979** A.P. BRINK *Dry White Season* 53 How's it? Is this your Boer, Emily? This the lanie? ... 'You may be a lanie' – his red tongue caressed the syllables of the taunting tsotsi word – 'but you've got it right here'. **1980** R. GOVENDER *Lahnee's Pleasure* 4 In another twelve and a half years you might get yourself a gold watch. Sunny: My lahnee will give it to me, man. Stranger: Your? Sunny: My boss, man. **1982** V. KHUMALO in *Pace* May 158 'Come here Lanie, let me tune you sum'-thin'. So the 'Lanie' .. comes around a crowded local fish and chips shop. 'Hey lanie, gimme a smoke, gee man, lanie man.' **1983** *Natal Mercury* 8 June, The 'situations' can go to their 'larnies' (white superiors) and complain about corruption ... If a bra is working in a shop, he can slip a little extra into another bra's parcel without letting the larnie know. *c***1985** M. GARDINER in *Eng. Academy Rev.* 3 114 How does a literary critic, especially a 'lanie', explore poetry which dramatises the complex and developing perceptions of a street-wise .. skollie? **1987** *Learn & Teach* No.5, 18, I tell you, he was a real lanie – white, just like Terre-blanche. **1989** E. MALULEKE in *Pace* Mar. 56, I am my own boss here – no 'larney' (white) to shout at me, and I don't have to say 'boss' to anyone. **1989** J. HOBBS *Thoughts in Makeshift Mortuary* 171 'Where did you go to school to get this education that has you writing poetry and speaking –' ... 'Like a lanie? I'm flattered.' **1989** *Weekly Mail* 15 Dec. 6 He learnt his trade by standing around in the boat yard and watching what the *larnies* (white men) were doing. **1990** J. NAIDOO *Coolie Location* 104 Shushila .. was a junior school teacher, real sophisticated, light-skinned, spoke like a *laanie*, was, actually more European than the Europeans. **1993** I. POWELL in *Leadership* Vol.12 No.2, 122 'She doesn't play the larnie like the way some of the other trustees do,' is the way one long time employee put it.

2. A member of the upper classes.

1978 L. BARNES in *The 1820* Vol.51 No.12, 19 Terms derived from the Indian languages can be found to cover the whole social spectrum: The *lahnees* and the *motas* are the wealthy. **1982** [see Green quot. at sense B]. **1990** *Frontline* Mar.-Apr. 16 We might think we're plain folks, but in this context, that's a ludicrous affectation. Here we're larneys – gentry – like it or not.

B. *adj.* Uppercrust, 'posh'; elegant, smart.

1975 L. HOGG *Informant, Pietermaritzburg* Larney. Used as an adj. meaning elegant, sophisticated, eg. That's a larney outfit ... It is commonly used by students. **1977** 'BLOSSOM' in *Darling* 31 Aug. 131 Blue eye shadow, orange blusher, .. her best diamante drop ear-rings. Talk about larny! Auntie Vilma would put a rainbow to shame any day. **1978** J. HOBBS *Darling Blossom* 64 Hang of a Romantic, get it, with larney graze and candles. **1982** *Sunday Times* 6 June (Mag. Sect.), The Bee-ems and other larney cars filled with businessmen and their birds out for a bit of this and that. **1982** M. GREEN *Informant, Durban* 1 The word lahnee. I have a feeling that this word (used by white youngsters to mean 'posh', smart, in a vaguely derogatory sense) is more generally used now than it was in the past. I gather it is of Indian origin and was originally used by the Indian community in Natal to refer to white people, especially upper class people. **1985** *Weekly Mail* 1 Nov. 17 Very *laanie*, and so it should be at the prices of the drinks, is Churchill's in the Landdrost. **1986** L.A. BARNES in *Eng. Usage in Sn Afr.* Vol.17 No.2, 3 The word *lahnee* .. has been adopted into general SAE slang (*larney*) with the usual meaning of 'smart' or 'grand'. **1991** H. MENDES *Informant, Johannesburg* Larney means 'upper-class', 'moneyed' or 'intellectually sophisticated': It was a really larney dinner party: we ate caviar, everybody but me wore R900 dresses, and most of the conversation went right over my head. **1993** D. BIGGS in *Rhodent* 24 *Plonk de plonk*: .. Known in larney circles as Blanc de blanc, but that's very pretentious and means more or less the same.

las /las/ *n. slang.* Also **laas**. [Afk., *las* to weld, join, pool resources; (colloq.) to augment, increase.] A contribution; a loan. Usu. in the v. phr. ***to make a las***, to contribute money, to make a loan. Hence **las** *v. trans.*, to lend. Cf. GAZAAT.

1970 G.E.Q. ABSOLOM *Informant, Germiston* Make a las you blokes (contribution). **1970** J.R. BENNETT *Informant, Krugersdorp* Las me a Rand (lend). **1970** K.M. BRAND *Informant, East London* Make me a las of five rand! (loan). **1970** B.C. MARITZ *Informant, Port Elizabeth* Gooi me a las so I will have enough money for ice skating. **1977** *Family Radio & TV* 23 Jan. 19 They were thirsty. Old Chris looked around meaningfully and said: 'Well, gentlemen, between us we should be able to make a *las* for a *dop*,' meaning we should have enough money to buy a drink. **1979** F. DIKE *First S. African* 30 Rooi: Yeerrrr Solly, you've cleaned us out. Max: Well Solly my laitie, make 'n laas daar. Solly: O.K. gents, let's go and have a drink. **1987** *Scope* 6 Nov. 33 Let's *waai* to Joubert Park and sit for a while. I'm sure we'll make a *las* from one of the chinas. **1991** G. DE BEER *Informant, Port Nolloth (N. Cape)* He made me a las (gave me a loan).

lash *v. trans. Mining.* [Special sense of general Eng. *lash* to dash, throw, or move violently.] To load (ore, broken rock, etc.) on to a car for transporting to the surface; to fill (a car) in this way.

1932 WATERMEYER & HOFFENBERG *Witwatersrand Mining Practice* 348 The snatch-block is moved nearer the face .., the object being to lash the rock directly from the pile into the truck. **1949** *Aptitude Tests Native Labour Witwatersrand & Gold Mines* (Nat. Inst. for Personnel Res., Pretoria) 35 Figures 1 and 2 show the lashing efficiency of these groups, average number of cars lashed being plotted against total time on lashing duty. **1964** A. NELSON *Dict. Mining* 249 *Lashing*, .. Loading broken rock or ore with shovels (South Africa). **1981** *Miners' Dict.* 30 *Lash! (Load!)* Layisha! **1983** *Mining Dict.* 148 *Lash*, 1 laai (*met graaf*) [load (with spade)] 2 wegruim [remove, clear away]. **1989** B. COURTENAY *Power of One* 474 The back-breaking labour of drilling and lashing a freshly blasted haulage could bring grown men to total exhaustion and, many a time, to the point of mutiny. *Ibid.* 479 The grizzly man works in the dark; his miner's lamp attached to his hard hat with the battery clipped to his webbing belt is the only source of light. He has five Africans to help him lash the rock through the grizzly bars and to prepare mud for the explosives.

Hence **lasher** *n.*, one who performs this task; **lashing** *vbl n.*, the action of shovelling and loading (a truck etc.) with broken ore from a mine; also *attrib.*

1932 WATERMEYER & HOFFENBERG *Witwatersrand Mining Practice* 347 Lashing or shovelling. Except where advantage can be taken of the angle at which an end dips, all the ore is usually loaded into trucks by shovel. **1946** C.B. JEPPE *Gold Mining on Witwatersrand* I. 688 Such cleaning out was largely done on night shift, some 4 to 6 natives being allocated to each end for lashing and tramming, depending on the distance to be trammed and the supply of cars. **1949** [see above]. **1974** *S. Afr. Jrnl Econ.* XLII. 293 The National Institute for Personnel Research has also demonstrated that even on a simple manual task like lashing (shovelling or loading broken rock) output can be appreciably increased by continuous practice. **1989** B. COURTENAY *Power of One* 474 The Northern Rhodesian Department of Mines required that all miners obtain their blasting licence, a process which required that we learn not only how to use dynamite but that we were trained as lashers, timber men, drillers and pipe fitters ... Lashing was the process of removing blasted rock by hand and shovel and loading it into underground trucks.

Last Outpost *n. phr.* [In this sense, coined by Tommy Bedford in the early 1970s, responding to a perceived bias against Natal players by the national rugby selectors, who were said to look on Natal as though it were not a part of South Africa but still belonged to the British Empire.] In full ***the Last Outpost of the British Empire***: a jocular name for the province of KwaZulu-Natal (formerly called Natal), or sometimes for the city of Durban, alluding to a perceived isolationism, and a supposed adherence to all things British, among its English-speaking inhabitants. Also *attrib.*

1988 E. PLATTER in *Style* Aug. 58 Is Natal the Last Outpost? Are Natalians a breed apart? .. Our Last Outpost image died years ago. We were very anti-Republic here. **1990** *Sunday Times* 1 Apr. 29 They might call his province the Last Outpost of the British Empire, but Mac is no whingeing Pom. **1990** D. VAN HEERDEN in *Sunday Times* 10 June 8 Umlazi with its 75 percent of English-speakers showed that the CP can come within the thickness of a banana peel of victory in the heartland of the Last Outpost of emergency rule. **1990** A. JAY on Radio 5, 6 July, In the Last Outpost this morning, fine and mild, Durbs 15 to 23. **1990** M. EDWARDS in *Flying Springbok* July 23 Bedford, whose most famous pronouncement came when he said that Natal was 'The last outpost of the British Empire', and whose rugby career seemed always clouded in controversy, was one of Natal's greatest captains. **1990** *Sunday Times* 14 Oct. 25 Not every 100 years that Natal wins the Currie Cup. In the Last Outpost they are more used to defeat and the stiff upper lip that should go with it. **1991** on TV1, 31 May, Natal has always been a sporting province, but the Last Outpost has really excelled itself over the last two years. **1991** A. VAN WYK *Birth of New Afrikaner* 11 An ardent Afrikaner, initially ill at ease in the 'last outpost of the British Empire', as Durban has humorously been called. **1993** *Sunday Nation* 8 Aug. 30 So why come to Durban, the 'Last Outpost' .. ?

Hence **Last Outposter** *n. phr.*, an inhabitant of KwaZulu-Natal.

1992 W. KNOWLER in *Weekend Mercury* 4 Jan. 6 New year saw the New South Africa cocking one helluva snook at the Last Outposters.

late *adj.* [Special use of Eng. *late* recently deceased (always used attrib. of a particular person, e.g. 'the late Mr Smith', 'my late father').] Among speakers of Sintu (Bantu) languages, used freq. in non-standard ways, esp. predicatively, as a euphemism for 'deceased', 'dead'. Also *absol.*, 'the departed (person)'.

1959 K.M.C. MOTSISI in M. Mutloatse *Casey & Co.* (1978) 27 Kid Playboy is making a hurried exit .. , and the bride tearing at her .. dress and hurling all sorts of names at Kid Playboy and his family including the late ones. **1979** *Pace* Sept. 28 His father is late, .. his mother .. is his only guardian. **1982** *Staffrider* Vol.4 No.4, 37 My father was John Piliso and my mother's name was Emily. Both are late. *Ibid.* 38 The band comprised two altos, tenor sax, trumpet, trombone, second trumpet, drums, and string bass. Trombonist was Dingane — he's late. **1983** A. NYATHIKAZI *Informant, KwaZulu-Natal*, I don't remember whether I told you that Mrs Garnett is late. She passed away in January. **1984** *Frontline* Mar. 10 'You see, .. Two-minutes-to-Town is late.' That doesn't mean he took three minutes or even twenty minutes to get to town. It is the idiomatic way of explaining that Two-minutes-to-Town is no more. **1988** M. MATSHOBA in *Staffrider* Vol.7 No.3, There's no father. Only the old lady. The old man is late. **1991** R.M. ELLIOT *Informant, Addo* In referring to a deceased person, people don't say 'The late Phindile Nxopho,' but simply 'The late'. So you can ask the question 'How's your mother,' and receive the answer 'Oh, she's late,' meaning dead. **1991** H. PHILLIPS *Informant, Johannesburg* Telephone conversation between relative of a woman student and the student's somewhat bemused house warden, c.1987. Caller (from the Transkei): 'Please tell Thandi her uncle is late.' Warden, trying to be helpful: 'Oh, was he coming to fetch her, has he been delayed?' Caller: 'No. She must come by taxi, the funeral is on Saturday.' **1992** W. MANDELA on M-Net TV 26 Apr. (Carte Blanche), I had a sister at the time — she is since late. **1992** A. BRIDGE *Informant, Soweto* When the bereavement committee heard that Sipho Sithole's mother was late, it immediately organised a collection to help with the funeral expenses. **1993** *Weekly Mail* 18 June 12 The late usually played bass guitar in his time.

late harvest *n. phr.* [See Platter quot. at sense 1.]

1. Any of several full-bodied sweet and semi-sweet white wines, made from late-harvested grapes; see quot. 1988. Also *attrib.*

This designation is officially regulated, the requisite residual sugar content being stipulated by legislation.

1966 H. BECK *Meet Cape Wines* 46 Even among the semi-sweet wines there are grades of sweetness ranging up to what the Germans know as spätlese, which has been appropriately named late harvest by the Germans who first produced this type at the Cape. **1980** J. PLATTER *Bk of S. Afr. Wines* 10 *Late Harvest*, Full-bodied, fruity white with long sweet aftertaste made from a number of late-harvested cultivars. **1981** *Oude Libertas* (Stellenbosch Farmers' Winery) Vol.9 No.4, 12 The new legislation of December 1980 provided for three categories of 'Late Harvest' wines. **1982** *S. Afr. Digest* 8 Jan. 9 Two late harvest wines from Nederburg of Paarl have been awarded superior certification by the Wine and Spirit Board, thus achieving a new distinction in wine industry history. **1982** J. PLATTER in *Fair Lady* 3 Nov. 181 *Late Harvest*, A loose designation (no official stipulations) for unfortified white wine, varying from semi-sweet to very sweet. Made from grapes harvested in late summer, or even autumn, which are riper and therefore sweeter. **1988** D. HUGHES et al. *Complete Bk of S. Afr. Wine* 328 'Late Harvest' is a specifically South African usage and refers to a sweetish, medium-to full-bodied white wine with sugar levels of more than 20 but less than 30 grams per litre.

2. With defining word: **noble late harvest**, see quot. 1982; **special late harvest**, see quot. 1982.

1981 *Oude Libertas* (Stellenbosch Farmers' Winery) Vol.9 No.4, 12 The requirements for producing a **noble late harvest** wine state that the residual sugar content has to be derived solely from the grapes from which the wine was produced. **1982** J. PLATTER in *Fair Lady* 3 Nov. 181 *Noble Late Harvest*, Unfortified and natural, but much sweeter and more intense that 'Special'. Needs to be awarded 'Superior' by the Board's tasting panel before it can be called Noble Late Harvest. Must show typical 'Noble Rot' or fungus-infected grape style, usually called 'Botrytis', the name of the fungus that denudes the grape of moisture and intensifies the sweetness. Must contain at least 50 g sugar per litre, but if balanced by acidity need not taste cloying. Invariably very expensive. **1988** D. HUGHES et al. *Complete Bk of S. Afr. Wine* 331 *Noble Late Harvest*, Residual sugar more than 50 grams per litre. **1982** J. PLATTER in *Fair Lady* 3 Nov. 181 **Special Late Harvest**, The official Wine and Spirit Board classification for natural, unfortified sweet wines, containing no less than 20 g of sugar per litre. Should be delicate and light and about a very manageable 10 degrees alcohol by volume. Usually made from Chenin Blanc (Steen) grapes. **1988** D. HUGHES et al. *Complete Bk of S. Afr. Wine* 331 *Special Late Harvest*, Residual sugar more than 20 but less than 50 grams per litre.

late lamb *n. phr.* [tr. Afk. *laatlammetjie.*] LAATLAMMETJIE sense 1.

1971 *Informant, Grahamstown* I've got a little sister — she's a late-lamb, only four years old. She's a real little afterthought. **1979** T. GUTSCHE *There Was a Man* 30 Nine years later, a 'Laatlammetjie' (or 'late lamb' as such an event was called in Arnold's future home) was born and christened Alfred. **1991** V. WARREN *Informant, Alberton* Late lamb. Child born years after completion of family.

laurie var. LOERIE.

laventel /la'fent(ə)l/ *n.* Ellipt. for ROOILAVENTEL.

1974 Y. BURGESS in S. Gray *On Edge of World* 31 'Mustn't we get a doctor now?' 'The *laventel* ..' Alida begged weakly. **1984** B. JOHNSON-BARKER in *Wynboer* Feb. 64 If a man was even to suggest that lavente was really a good remedy for the palpitations, he was likely to snap his bag at you and order you out.

‖**lawaai** /la'vaɪ, lə-/ *n.* Also **lawai.** [Afk.] Disturbance, racket, fuss. See also *to skop lawaai* (SKOP *v.* sense 2).

1908 J.M. ORPEN *Reminisc.* 16 Now, please, father, leave it all to me and don't touch the whip or make any 'lawai.' **1969** A. FUGARD *Boesman & Lena* 24 This morning in all the *lawaai* and mix-up — gone! **1972** *Drum* 22 June 26 Of all the examples of civilisation that have been dangled before our envious eyes in recent weeks, surely the most illuminating is the affair of the lavatorial lawaai. **1975** S. ROBERTS *Outside Life's Feast* 85 We arrive at this house really at the right moment it was blarry good luck for him there was a bliksemse lawaai coming from the bathroom an' we somaar walk in they were struggling with a razor. **1979** *Sunday Times* 2 Dec. (Extra) 2 They went into one of the classrooms and we heard a commotion (lawaai) coming from the room.

law agent *n. phr. Hist. Law.* [Special sense of general Eng. *law-agent* a legal practitioner.] One who, having no legal qualification but being an adult of good character, could, on payment of a fee, be enrolled in a magistrate's court to defend those who could not afford the more expensive services of an ATTORNEY. Also *attrib.*

[**1856** *Act 20* in *Stat. of Cape of G.H.* (1906) 613 It shall and may be lawful for every Court of Resident Magistrate to admit and enrol, as agents in the said Court, so many persons of full age, and of good fame and character, as shall be desirous to be so enrolled, and shall pay for such enrolment .. the sum of twenty pounds.] **1903** D. BLACKBURN *Burgher Quixote* 12 Although I am what is called a lawyer, I never was a proper one, being only a law-agent, which is not so high as an attorney, and requires only that one pay fees but pass no examination. **1925** W.H.S. BELL *S. Afr. Legal Dict.* 316 *Law agent*, .. In Cape Colony a *law agent* might not be admitted in a district where not less than two attorneys were in practice. None could be admitted in Natal since the passing of Act 22 of 1896. In the Transvaal only *law agents* who were entitled to practice in the courts of the landdrost of the late South African Republic, or who had passed the examinations which under the laws of the Republic would have entitled them to admission, could be admitted ... In the Orange River Colony Ordinance 7 of 1902 authorised the enrolment of persons of full age and of good fame and character to practise in the courts of the resident magistrate in districts where less than three attorneys were carrying on practice as such independently of one another ... *Law agents* are not authorised to practise in the superior courts. **1934** C.P. SWART Supplement to Pettman. *Law Agent*, Law agents .. were enrolled in a court of a magistrate to practise therein on payment of a small fee, their status being lower than that of a solicitor. **1960** HAHLO & KAHN *Union of S. Afr.* 226 To Natal's credit she ended future admissions of law agents fairly early — in 1896. From 1876 as elsewhere in South Africa these quite unqualified individuals had been admitted by the magistrates' courts. *Ibid.* 230 Law agents, the lowest species, unable to appear before the High Court, were admitted by the President on the passing of an elementary legal examination, so easy that 'anyone able to speak and write Dutch was sure to have a profession.' **1982** H.F. MELLET et al. *Our Legal Heritage*, The lowest category of practitioner was the so-called 'law agent' who could appear in the lower courts without any legal training whatsoever. **1990** *Weekly Mail* 21 Sept. 7 Motivating the 'law agent' concept the ALS said it would enable a large number of practitioners to qualify who would charge less than attorneys and could represent those accused presently undefended.

lawger var. LAAGER *n.*

lay-by *n.* Also **lay-bye.** [Perh. fr. Austral. or N.Z. Eng.] A system of payment whereby a deposit is made on an article which is then reserved for the buyer until the full price has been paid. Also *attrib.*

1947 *Monitor* 21 Mar. 8 *(advt)* Use Our Lay-Bye Plan of purchase ... Pay an initial deposit, and we will reserve and store your purchases for you in our special warehouse until required. **1973** *E. Prov. Herald* 11 June 5 Shopping on the lay-by system has pitfalls for the unwary buyer. **1981** *Voice* Aug. (Reader) 5 The Stokvel way is better than the Lay-by way. This is because you can buy cash. **1987** *Splargie* (Pretoria Technikon) 53 What is lay-by. When you want to buy a certain article but do not have the cash to pay for it, you could secure it by lay-by. This means that the article is set aside by the seller while the purchaser pays it off. **1989** *Weekend Post* 28 Oct. 3 He described North End as a 'land of laybyes and Christmas bonuses'. **1994** on Radio Algoa 29 Dec. (*advt*) They take credit cards, Buy-Aids, and Lay-bys.

Hence **lay-by** *v.*, to reserve an article by paying a deposit.

1983 M. Du Plessis *State of Fear* 144 A sheet of cardboard .. had pictures of holly on it, with the command, 'Lay-bye now for Christmas'. **1992** on Radio Algoa 4 Sept., (*advt*) Everything carries a money-back guarantee — and you can lay-by too.

lazy *adj.* In the obsolete n. phr. ***Lazy Dick*** (or ***Lazy Jack***): Idle Dick, see IDLE.

1884, 1901, 1913 [see IDLE].

le- /le-/ *pref.* A Sotho and seTswana singular noun prefix found in some words originating in these languages.

For examples, see KGOTLA, LEKGOA, MAKATANE. In Sotho and seTswana, the plural of words beginning *le-* is formed by replacing this prefix with *ma-* . This pattern is not always observed in *S. Afr. Eng.*, and the plural is sometimes formed by the addition of the English plural suffix *-s* to the singular form. See also MA- *pref.*[2]

lead /li:d/ *v. trans.* [Calqued on S. Afr. Du. *water lij* (subsequently Afk. - *lei*) to irrigate.] In the phr. ***to lead water*** (occas. ***to lead out water***): to irrigate; to obtain household water by bringing it from its source through furrows constructed for this purpose. See also SLOOT sense 1.

Not exclusively *S. Afr. Eng.*, but differing from general usage in that it is commonly used without a prepositional phrase.

1827 G. Thompson *Trav.* II. 27, I observed with regret the impracticability of leading out the water for irrigating the adjoining lands by dams and ditches, — the usual and only method of cultivating the soil in the interior of Southern Africa. **1832** *Graham's Town Jrnl* 12 Oct. 160, I sent her home to lead water into the garden; she was alone. **1846** J. Collett Diary. II. 8 Oct., Interesting day all hands busy leading Water. **1894** E. Glanville *Fair Colonist* 125 The man looked up a minute, then resumed his work of leading water to the roots of each tree. **1913** J.J. Doke *Secret City* 244 A native boy was leading water, and the smell of dampness and fresh, sweet life was wonderfully refreshing. **1939** S. Cloete *Watch for Dawn* 150 On the day of the fight Gerrit Bezuidenhout had been leading water. **1940** [see FURROW]. **1958** A. Jackson *Trader on Veld* 24 Presently we started a so called garden, fencing in about two acres of ground and leading water from our fountain. **1960** G. Lister *Reminisc.* 29 We loved having tea there and watching Van Eeden 'leading' water along the numerous furrows in the garden. **1976** [see FONTEIN sense 1 a]. **1977** *Fair Lady* 25 May 107 Outside she found Eli leading water in a walled lucerne land near some old pear trees. **1990** R. Malan *My Traitor's Heart* 32 Once a week, water came running down the roadside furrows, and my granny would lead it into her backyard to irrigate her corn, tomatoes, and peaches.

leader *n.* [tr. S. Afr. Du. *leier*, prob. ellipt. for *touwleier* (lit. 'rope-leader') wagon-leader.] VOORLOPER sense 1. Also *attrib.*

1786 G. Forster tr. *A. Sparrman's Voy. to Cape of G.H.* I. 175 As the road was good and even all the way, and my Hottentot assured me that he could do very well without any leader, we let him go forward. **1804** R. Percival *Acct of Cape of G.H.* 60 Little Hottentot boys .. usually run before and guide them ... The attachment of the animals to their little leaders is very great. **1816** G. Barker Journal. 26 Aug., Set out for Bethelsdorp, had Jan Boezak for a driver, Plaatje Laberlotte for a leader. **1822** W.J. Burchell *Trav.* I. 552 Old Hans had engaged a Half-Hottentot, named Daniel Kaffer, and his son, to be the driver and leader of my waggon. **1835** G. Champion *Jrnl* (1968) 32 The oxen knew the way home, & the leader was not much wanted. The driver sat with his long whip in front of us. **1839** T. Shone Diary. 19 June, I thought of plowing, but could not, on account of all the children being ill, I went to Bathurst to try to get a leader but could not. **1852** A.W. Cole *Cape & Kafirs* 141 My 'leader,' (as the boy is called who leads the two front oxen of the span), on my first wagon journey, was a Bushman. **1879** [see FIELD sense 2 a]. **1883** O.E.A. Schreiner *Story of Afr. Farm* 72 When they drew near the house he threw the whip to the Kaffir leader, and sprang from the side of the waggon. **1895** A.B. Balfour *1200 Miles in Waggon* 72 There are no reins, except for a little bit of reim fastened to the front pair of oxen, by which the 'leader' or boy, who walks in front in difficult places, pulls them in the required direction. **1907** J.P. Fitzpatrick *Jock of Bushveld* (1909) 417, I was left with three leaders and two drivers to manage four waggons. **1936** E. Rosenthal *Old-Time Survivals* 15 The mode of harnessing has not changed since 1652 ... Nor has the institution of the leader-boy varied — usually a native piccanin known as the voorloper. **1955** V. De Kock *Fun They Had* 32 Several wagons, bringing Dutch visitors, were outspanned hard by; their Hottentot drivers and leaders .. had gathered round the bonfire. **1971** *Daily Dispatch* 16 Dec. 10 During the firing, wagon drivers and leaders would help load the guns.

leadwood /'ledwʊd/ *n.* [Alluding to the weight of the wood.] HARDEKOOL. Also *attrib.*

1961 Palmer & Pitman *Trees of S. Afr.* 246 The leadwood is a tall deciduous tree of the Transvaal bushveld and lowveld, Natal, Swaziland .., often growing up to 70 feet with a stem diameter of 3 feet. It is commonly supposed to be one of the slowest-growing trees in the lowveld. **1972** — *Trees of Sn Afr.* I. 195 Probably the most revered tree of Southern Africa belongs to South West Africa. It is the Omumborombonga, the leadwood or hardekool (*Combretum imberbe*), the ancestral tree of the Herero people who believe that from it came human beings, their flocks and herds, and all wild animals. **1977** *S. Afr. Panorama* Sept. 42 A number of tables were arranged in horseshoe fashion that evening round the large leadwood camp fire for staff and guests. **1978** A.P. Brink *Rumours of Rain* 353 And then the nights in the camp, the meat strung up in the trees and the heavy leadwood logs burning as high as a house. **1988** A. Hall-Martin et al. *Kaokoveld* 11 Along watercourses which cut through the rugged terrain the dominant trees are mopane, .. and leadwood (*Combretum imberbe*). **1990** *Farmer's Weekly* 8 June 108 Unspoiled indigenous bush with magnificent big trees such as leadwood, tambotie and knobthorn.

leaguer /'li:gə/ *n.* Also **leagar**, **l(e)ager**, **leagre**, **legger**, **liggar**, **ligger**. [ad. Du. *legger* unit of liquid capacity (equivalent to 582 litres).] **a.** *hist.* A unit of liquid measurement formerly in use at the Cape, sometimes reckoned as four aums (see AUM sense a), being approx. 120 to 136 imperial gallons (545 to 620 litres), but said by some to represent 150 imperial gallons (682 litres). **b.** In the modern wine industry, a measure of 127 imperial gallons (approx. 577 litres) **c.** A vessel containing a leaguer.

Not exclusively *S. Afr. Eng.*: see note at AUM.

1777 G. Forster *Voy. round World* I. 71 The company allows the sum of forty dollars for each leagre, of which the farmer receives but twenty-four. **1786** — tr. *A. Sparrman's Voy. to Cape of G.H.* I. 40 According to M. de la Caille's account, not more than sixty *liggars* of red, and ninety of the white Constantia wine are made, each *liggar* being reckoned at six hundred French pints, or about one hundred and fifty Swedish cans. **1797** Lady A. Barnard *Lett. to Henry Dundas* (1973) 77 They have to draw .. one or two Leagars of wine .. which I should reckon four oxen quite equal to. **1804** R. Percival *Acct of Cape of G.H.* 186 A leager is a measure of one hundred and fifty gallons. **1878** A. Trollope in D.J. Opperman *Spirit of Vine* (1968) 295 Wine was then no more than £3 the 'ligger' or leaguer, being a pipe containing 126 gallons. **1881** F.R. Statham *Blacks, Boers & Brit.* 61 You want to see what can be done with South African wine? .. Visit a great airy shed not far from the Cape Town docks, .. the rough and ready wine has become — what? Look at it and see it as it is drawn from the huge casks — leaguers they call them here. **1896** R. Wallace *Farming Indust. of Cape Col.* 155 Only one leaguer of sweet wine can be got from grapes which would produce three leaguers of dry wine. **1919** M. Greenlees tr. *O.F. Mentzel's Life at Cape in Mid-18th C.* 111 To each company of soldiers in the garrison was given a slaughtered sheep, enough vegetables to go with it, and a legger or pipe of wine. **1920** R. Juta *Tavern* 121 Such wine, being as good as original Constantia, was now sold by the farmers by the lager. **1926** P.W. Laidler *Tavern of Ocean* 64 Each company was given a leaguer of wine, and the remainder of the day was given up to festivities and rejoicing. **1959** *Cape Times* 14 Mar. 2 Two lorries, one carrying a 5-leaguer tank of wine (some 800 gallons) collided here yesterday. **1967** E. Rosenthal *Encycl. of Sn Afr.* 311 *Leaguer*, South African measure for liquor, 126 gallons. **1970** *Cape Times* 28 Oct. 20 (*advt*) A wine quota of 320 leaguers. **1972** A. Scholefield *Wild Dog Running* 101 On massive shelves behind the counter stood half-aum and anker barrels, while set against the wall and resting on the dung-and-mud floor were the great wine leggers. **1976** G. & G. Fagan in *Optima* Vol.26 No.2, 79 In 1823 Paul made 102 leaguers of wine at the Boschendal cellars and distilled five-and-a-half leaguers of brandy in the kettle under the oak trees beside the river. **1981** P. Dane *Great Houses of Constantia* 100 She leaves her son a wine-press .., ten empty leggers and the slave Damon. **1988** G. Levin *Informant, Bramley* A leaguer = 127 Imp. Galls. = 5.7734 hl. **1988** D. Hughes et al. *Complete Bk of S. Afr. Wine* 328 One leaguer equalled slightly more than 577 litres, or 127 gallons. However, the traditional measure of Cape wine is now superceded by metrication.

Lebaran var. LABARANG.

lecker, leckers varr. LEKKER, LEKKERS.

leegte see LAAGTE.

leenings eigendom /'lɪənəŋs ˌeɪxəndɔm/ *n. phr. Law.* [Du., *leenings* combining form of *leening* loan + *eigendom* ownership.]

a. *Obs.* exc. *hist.* Loan freehold tenure, a form of tenure under which 60 morgen (about 50 hectares) of a farm was converted into freehold after survey to give the farmer greater security, the balance of the land being hired to him for an annual amount of 24 rixdollars. Also *attrib.* See also EIGENDOM, LOAN.

1809 Lord Caledon in G.M. Theal *Rec. of Cape Col.* (1900) VII. 184 Leenings Eigendom or Loan Property. The nature of this tenure is not materially different from the Eigendoms Land or freehold, except .. that the possessor pays an annual rent to Government of 24 Rixdollars. Land granted in this manner is usually attached to an Eigendom and partakes of the advantages of the extent of the Loan place and the permanent tenure of the eigendom. **1974** Davenport & Hunt *Right to Land* p.v, Loan freehold (leeningseigendom) tenure. A form of loan farm tenure under which 60 morgen of the farm was converted into freehold after survey .. introduced by Governor-General van Imhoff in 1743 to give loan farmers greater security.

b. *obs.* Pl. **-dommen**, or unchanged. A farm so held.

1810 M.C. Gie in G.M. Theal *Rec. of Cape Col.* (1900) VII. 431, I observe with regard to the Leening Eigendommen .. that many Corn lands differ in extent. **1810** C. Bird in *Ibid.* 467 The origin of perpetual loan places (Leenings Eigendom). **1811** J.A. Truter in *Ibid.* (1901) VIII. 94 The origin of perpetual loan places (Leenings Eigendom) and their rights.

leenings-plaats /ˈlɪənəŋsplɑːts/ *n. Law.* Also **leningplaats**. Pl. **-plaatsen**. [Du., *leenings* see prec. + *plaats* place, farm.]

a. (*Obs.* exc. *hist.*) *loan farm*, see LOAN.

1795 J.H. CRAIG in G.M. Theal *Rec. of Cape Col.* (1897) I. 255 The lands (leeningsplaatsen) or Loan Land, are in general granted to the farmers from year to year, so much so that they are every year under the necessity of taking out a sort of new grant. [1809 see LOAN. 1812 A. PLUMPTRE tr. *H. Lichtenstein's Trav. in Sn Afr.* I. 187 This mode of living on the territory of the government, cultivating the land, and enjoying its produce without any property in it, or even being regularly tenanted to it, is called here an *Erbe*, in contradistinction to the tenure by lease, when the domain is called a *Lehnplatze*.] 1902 J.W. WESSELS in Martin & Friedlaender *Hist. of Surveying & Land Tenure* I. 77 The nearest approach to *emphytensis* in South Africa were the *leenings plaatsen* (loan farms). 1936 *Cambridge Hist. of Brit. Empire* VIII. 766 In 1795, almost the whole of the quarter of the total revenue that the Government derived from land was in respect of the annual rent of loan farms, or *leeningsplaatsen*, of over 6000 acres each. 1968 E.A. WALKER *Hist. of Sn Afr.* 91 Farmers had learnt to prefer the leenings plaatsen – great cattle runs of 3000 morgen and upwards held on loan from the Company first for six months and then for a year at a time. 1989 *Reader's Digest Illust. Hist.* 55 The Company decided to grant the colonists land on loan, known as *leningplaatsen* (loan farms), each with an area of 2420 hectares. 1989 *Ibid.* [see PLACAAT sense a].

b. *obs.* The form of tenure under which a loan farm was held.

1929 W.M. MACMILLAN *Bantu, Boer & Briton* 21 (Swart), The normal tenure was leenings-plaats, or one year lease for which the uniform charge was 24 Rix Dollars per annum, regardless of the value of the land.

Leeraar *n. obs.* Also **Lehrer**. [Du., teacher, fr. *leren* to instruct, teach.] PREDIKANT sense a.

1821 C.I. LATROBE *Jrnl of Visit* 63 During the whole day, parties of Hottentots came to wish their Teachers a happy new-year. Lehrer or Teachers, is the name they generally give to the missionaries. 1841 B. SHAW *Memorials* 290 Andries myn Leerar (my teacher) is dead; he died on a journey through the Karree Mountains. 1849 N.J. MERRIMAN *Cape Jrnls* (1957) 66 That evening they perplexed me much by an enquiry to which I afterwards became very familiar – namely whether Mynheer (i.e. myself) was a Leerar as well as a Predikant ... In the Kerkwet of the Dutch Reformed Church, 1846, the minister of a church is referred to both as a *Leerar* and *predikant*.

leerboom *n. Obs. Wagon-making.* Also **le'erboom**. Pl. **-s**, **-en**. [Afk. (earlier S. Afr. Du.), *leer* ladder, rack + *boom* beam.] The upper rails of a *leerwa* or rack-waggon, a waggon with high sides.

Cf. *Brit. Eng.* 'cart-ladder'.

1824 W.J. BURCHELL *Trav.* II. 318 The fur coverlet .. seemed the only covering which could enable a person to sleep with tolerable warmth in one of these waggons; for along both sides, there was between the upper *le'er-boom* and the mats, a wide opening through which the wind found free entrance. 1870 *George Advertiser* 14 Apr., Wagon and Cart Wood, Yellow-wood and Stinkwood Planks, Leerbooms, Disselbooms, *c* 1919 J.Y. GIBSON in *S. Afr. Jrnl of Science* July 6 The length of the wagon was about 15 feet; the height of the tilt from the floor 5 feet 6 inches. The upper rails of the sides, *leerboomen*, were curved upwards from about the second third ... The *boogen*, or tent bows, arched between *standers*, or standards, which were fastened on the outer sides of the leerboomen.

leerfisch var. LEERVIS.

leerfish /ˈlɪəfɪʃ/ *n.* Pl. unchanged. [Part. tr. S. Afr. Du. *leer-visch* (see next).] The GARRICK, *Lichia amia*.

1843 J.C. CHASE *Cape of G.H.* 169 Leer Fish ... A species of Pike, affording considerable sport to the angler. 1902 J.D.F. GILCHRIST in *Trans. of S. Afr. Philological Soc.* XI. iv. 217 Probably the Cape Leer-fish was so named by the early Dutch sailors, who brought the name from the East Indies. 1930 C.L. BIDEN *Sea-Angling Fishes* 62 Leerfish take up the coloration of the bottom – a power shared by the galjoen and dassie – hence in sandy places the silvery sheen is brilliant and .. it has been mistaken for some strange visitor from its dark and almost black colour as seen against a rocky bottom. 1945 [see GARRICK]. 1955 C. HORNE *Fisherman's Eldorado* 107 Young leerfish which, on light outfits, will display traces of the courage and speed that have made the mature fish outstanding among the game fish of South Africa. 1971 *S. Afr. Panorama* Jan. 27 The big fighting leerfish (garrick). 1971 *Daily Dispatch* 14 Sept. 20 The flesh of the leerfish has an excellent taste. 1973 *E. Prov. Herald* 28 Nov. 37 Out in the darkness came the unmistakable sound of a leerfish hurling itself in frenzy after its prey. 1982 *S. Afr. Fishing* Apr.-May 20 The Eastern Province team decided to move into the warm green water off St Croix Island and look for big leerfish. 1983 *Sunday Times* 31 July 17 She's .. livelier than a leerfish on a line. 1994 R. SIMPSON on Radio Algoa 23 July, Robberg is teeming with marine life, with seals, sharks, and leerfish.

leervis /ˈlɪə(r)fəs/ *n.* Formerly also **leerfisch**, **leervisch**. [Afk., earlier S. Afr. Du. *leervisch*, fr. Du. *leer* leather + *visch* (modern orthography *vis*) fish.] The GARRICK, *Lichia amia*.

1853 L. PAPPE *Synopsis of Edible Fishes* 24 Lichia Amia, Cuv. & Val. (Leervisch.) .. Taken occasionally in Table Bay, but not in great repute, its flesh being deemed dry and rather insipid. 1913 W.W. THOMPSON *Sea Fisheries of Cape Col.* 156 *Lichia amia* L ... Leer-visch; Leather-fish; Garrick (Natal). *c*1936 *S. & E. Afr. Yr Bk & Guide* 559 Lake and river fishing include the Leerfisch (Garrick) up to 20 lbs., also Steenbras, Grunter and other varieties. 1949 J.L.B. SMITH *Sea Fishes* 222 Leervis .. is one of the finest game fishes, fighting fiercely to the end. 1959 J. PACKER *High Roof* 191 Kaspar is sure we'll get leervis or elf – both good eating. 1968 J.L.B. SMITH *High Tide* 52 Live bait, commonly used for predatory fishes, notably leervis and kob. 1974 *S. Afr. Yachting* Dec. 29 A recently-developed sport is trolling for leervis (garrick), or lying out with live bait for them just outside the mouth of the river. 1979 SNYMAN & KLARIE *Free from Sea* 35 No doubt about it, leervis is the best game fish in our seas, eagerly hunted by anglers. The smaller fish are good eating, but the flesh becomes coarser and dryer as they get bigger. 1989 *Weekend Post* 23 Dec. 5 A 5kg leervis has been landed from the canal bank. 1991 *E. Prov. Herald* 8 July 1 Virtually the entire marine population of the .. main tank was wiped out .. when the water was overdosed with chlorine ... A ragged tooth shark, a large leervis and an aggressively territorial galjoen .. had been favourites with visitors to the oceanarium.

legal *n. hist.* [Absol. use of Eng. *legal* founded upon or permitted by law.] One legally entitled to live in an area, according to the provisions of the Group Areas Act. Freq. in *pl.* Cf. ILLEGAL *n.*

1984 *Cape Times* 18 July 14 Dr Koornhof and his officials have gone a long way to meeting the objections by allowing 'legals' and 'illegals' alike to put up shelters. 1984 *E. Prov. Herald* 3 Oct. 1 Core housing will continue to be restricted to 'legals' only. 1985 PLATZKY & WALKER *Surplus People* p.xxvii, While the government conceded that (part of) Crossroads could stay, this concession, which divided the people into 'legals' and 'illegals', would force the majority to move.

leger var. LAAGER *n.*

legger var. LEAGUER.

leg(g)evaan, **-waan**, **legouane**, **legovaan** varr. LEGUAAN.

legplaats /ˈlɛxplɑːts/ *n. Obs.* exc. *hist.* Pl. **-e** /-ə/. [Du., *leg* lying, laying + *plaats* place.] An outstation used for winter grazing; LEGPLEK.

1812 A. PLUMPTRE tr. *H. Lichtenstein's Trav. in Sn Afr.* (1928) I. 99 Every colonist of the Roggeveld has .. besides his proper habitation, a place in the Karroo, which is called a *legplaats*, and for which no duty, as for a regular farm, is paid to the government. 1822 W.J. BURCHELL *Trav.* I. 207 In the winter season, .. the boors of that country .. remove, with their families and cattle, to certain temporary huts, called Legplaats (which may be translated Cattle-place). 1988 SMUTS & ALBERTS *Forgotten Highway* 11 Farmers from the Warme Bokkeveld (Ceres Basin) .., between 1750 and 1800, were establishing 'legplaatse' and even permanent farms over the Koedoesberg along the foot of the Roggeveld Range.

legplek /ˈlɛxplek, ˈlɛxplɛk/ *n. Obs.* exc. *hist.* Pl. **-ke** /-kə/, **-ken**. [Du., *leg* lying, laying + *plek* place.] LEGPLAATS.

1861 P.B. BORCHERDS *Auto-Biog. Mem.* 55 A suitable resting-place (legplek) in the karoo, with plenty of grass in the season. 1867 *Blue Bk for Col. 1866* JJ38, About 120 pieces of ground, called legplekken, have been given out for one year for which the parties pay a stamp of £1 for each lot. 1884 *Cape Law Jrnl* I. 317 These loan places were in some cases .. granted together with the right to an outstation or 'leg-plek,' to which the stock might be moved with the change of seasons ... The land situate immediately around the head station, homestead or centre of the loan place, was called the 'Ordonnantie,' to distinguish it from the outstation or leg-plek. 1972 L.G. GREEN *When Journey's Over* 59 A *legplek* with plenty of grass in season.

leguaan /ˈleg(ə)wɑːn, ˈlegəvɑːn, ˈlegjuɑːn, ‖ˈləkəvɑːn/ *n.* Forms: α. /ˈleg(ə)wɑːn, ˈlegəvɑːn, ˈlegjuɑːn/ **legouane**, **legua(a)n**; β. /ˈlegəvɑːn/ **lagavaan**, **lagewaan**, **lakavan**, **leg(g)evaan**, **leg(g)ewaan**, **legovaan**; γ. /ˈlegəvɑːn, ‖ˈləkəvɑːn/ **lekkewaan**, **likawaan**, **likkewan**. [Du. *leguaan* fr. Fr. *l'iguane*, *le* the + *iguane* iguana.

Despite long and well-established use in S. Afr. Eng., neither the spelling nor the pronunciation of this word has become standardized. (The modern Afk. form is *likkewaan*.)]

Either of two species of large monitor lizard, *Varanus niloticus* (also called **water leguaan**), or *V. exanthematicus* subsp. *albigularis* (also called **berg leguaan** /bɜːg -/, [Afk., *berg* mountain] and **rock leguaan**), with robust bodies and strongly-clawed, stocky limbs. Also *attrib.*

V. exanthematicus subsp. *albigularis* is associated by some with the mythical *das-adder* (see DAS sense 1 b).

α. 1790 tr. *F. Le Vaillant's Trav.* I. 391 My Hottentot wits .. tried to persuade him he had fired at a *Legouane* (a kind of large lizard, common in the rivers of Africa). 1812 A. PLUMPTRE tr. *H. Lichtenstein's Trav. in Sn Afr.* (1928) I. 189 The *Leguan* is not a crocodile at all. It is .. an animal of the *Lacerta* class, and amphibious, but perfectly harmless. 1827 G. THOMPSON *Trav.* I. 10 A tremendous ravine .. frequented by the leguaan, a species of amphibious lizard, growing to the length sometimes of six feet, but quite innoxious. 1834 T. PRINGLE *Afr. Sketches* 286 A large amphibious lizard, called the *leguan*, a species of guana, is found in the rivers. 1849 A. SMITH *Illust. of Zoo. in S. Afr.: Reptilia* Appendix 6 *Varanus niloticus*, .. Leguan of the Cape Colonists. *a*1875 T. BAINES *Jrnl of Res.* (1964) II. 285 A Hottentot with a fishing rod on his shoulder .. had pointed out a 'leguan', or guana, sleeping beneath a tree. 1926 *E. Prov. Herald* 24 Feb. 10 Boss, the leguans ate up all the little pythons just like worms. *c*1936 *S. & E. Afr. Yr Bk & Guide* 1108 The *Leguan*, probably a corruption of the French ('L'Iguane') or Monitor Lizard, is common in South Africa. 1945 *Outspan* 3 Aug. 49 Leguaans and meercats. 1950 W. ROSE *Reptiles & Amphibians* 196 Although the name leguaan is a corruption of the words 'L'iguana', iguanas belong to a totally different, vegetarian and mainly arboreal family that is not represented on the African continent. 1958 R. COLLINS *Impassioned Wind* 113 I .. pointed out a leguan – a giant, five foot lizard – swimming slowly up against the current with the water forming a tight, green ruff around his sinuous throat. 1972

N. SAPEIKA in *Std Encycl. of Sn Afr.* VII. 303 Vulture fat or leguan fat was used as an embrocation for lumbago. **1978** *E. Prov. Herald* 7 Nov. 6 When threatened, the water leguan inflated its body and hissed loudly through its mouth, lashing its tail from side to side. **1985** H. GOOSEN in *S. Afr. Panorama* Aug. 22 The berg leguaan is best-suited to a mountainous, Karoo-like environment and feeds on large insects and Karoo animals. **1986** J. CONYNGHAM *Arrowing of Cane* 12 Past the bank where the kingfishers nest, the lower holes deserted after leguaan raids. **1987** R. PATTERSON *Reptiles of Sn Afr.* 37 On adult size alone, the Water Leguaan and the Rock Leguaan could not be mistaken for any other lizard in southern Africa. Being the largest lizards on the African continent (adults easily exceed 1 m), they are readily distinguished by their sheer size. **1989** *Personality* 29 May 11 George tackled an enraged leguan which tried to attack children in the Friedemann family backyard. **1990** *Weekend Post* 5 May 8 One could easily lose oneself in the timelessness of nature, watching .. a leguaan slip its lazy body silently into the dark, cool depths of a river pool. **1994** M. ROBERTS tr. *J.A. Wahlberg's Trav. Jrnls 1838–56* 31 One Leguan .., lying on the bank, which tried to get away by running swiftly into the water.

β. **1834** T.H. BOWKER Journal. 23 Dec., Shoot rabbits — swim horses in the river below the garden. Shoot two Lakavans. **1894** E. GLANVILLE *Fair Colonist* 87 A deep wide pool, still haunt of the lagavaan, beneath a tall precipice. **1907** J.P. FITZPATRICK *Jock of Bushveld* (1909) 315 Found deeper water .. no break in the bank; there was not even a lagavaan slide, a game path, or a drinking place. **1958** [see PLATANNA]. **1967** E.M. SLATTER *My Leaves Are Green* 265 Nyoni's quick eye had caught a movement in the reeds. 'Look, Nkosana, ' he whispered, 'a legavaan'. **1976** A. DELIUS *Border* 35 Made acquaintance with a variety of creeping, crawling, or darting creatures, some of which have been identified for us .. as scorpions, puffadders, .. leggewaans (like monstrous lizards), [etc.].

γ. **1913** J.J. DOKE *Secret City*, Why, man, I'm as stiff as a lekkewaan, every bone seems broken. **1914** *Farmer's Annual* 334 Likawaan skin. How to cure it. **1936** WILLIAMS & MAY *I Am Black* 183 The boy watched the likkewan with its shiny brown-green skin and its little lizard eyes. [In 1949 ed. changed to 'likkewaan'.] **1943** *Outspan* 9 July 23 They went away as lounge lizards and came back as big, brown likkewans. **1949** *Cape Argus* 14 May (Mag. Sect.) 10 The dour old likkewaan with his whip-lash of a tail, can still be seen creeping through the shadows in search of birds' eggs to suck. **1951** H.C. BOSMAN in L. Abrahams *Bekkersdal Marathon* (1971) 123 Push a small likkewaan down the back of the visitor's neck, and .. pretend to him that it's a mamba. **1960** D. ROOKE in D. Wright *S. Afr. Stories* 198 The intense stillness had brought a likkewaan to the wire screen where it hung like a monstrous ornament. **1977** F.G. BUTLER *Karoo Morning* 175 The likkewaans of the Karoo .. had toned their colours down to match the grey of the veld. **1987** D. KENMUIR *Tusks & Talisman* 102 A black-and-yellow water likkewaan was retreating cautiously, a piece of rotten fish skin dangling from its jaws. [**1989** *Personality* 29 May 14 This is the terrain of Crocodile Dundee's cousin, Likkewaan Labuschagne.]

Lehrer var. LEERAAR.

leke var. LEKKER.

‖**Lekgoa** /lə'kɔ(w)ə, le'xɔ:(w)a/ *n.* Pl. usu. **Makgoa**. Forms: *sing.* **Lekgoa, Lekhoa, Machoa, Macooa, Magoa**; *pl.* **Macooas, Makgo(w)a, Makho(w)a, Makoa, Makoöas**. Also with small initial. [Triple derivation: seTswana *lekgóa* (pl. *makgóa*), N. Sotho *lekgówa* (pl. *makgówa*), and Ndebele (see quot. 1871). It is not always clear from which of these languages particular instances of the word in S. Afr. Eng. are derived. For an explanation of plural forms, see LE- and MA- *pref.*[2]] Esp. among speakers of Sotho and seTswana: a white person. Cf. MLUNGU.

1824 *S. Afr. Jrnl* I. Jan.–Feb. 78 The matchless wisdom and superiority of the 'Macooas,' or civilized men. **1827** [see EAT]. **1827** G. THOMPSON *Trav.* I. 225 Mr. Moffat told them that they might depend implicitly upon the correctness of my information; .. and that my report was not the report of a *Bechuana*, but the true statement of a *Macooa*. **1834** *Makanna* (anon.) II. 161 For some time previously Makanna, forseeing the struggle about to ensue with the false-hearted ally of the 'Macooas' (white men), had trained a select number of his followers to the use of fire-arms. **1846** R. MOFFAT *Missionary Labours* 92 We must not act like Bechuanas, we must act like Makoöas (white people). **1850** R.G.G. CUMMING *Hunter's Life* (1911) 291 All the natives shouted out 'Machoa' (signifying white man). **1866** E.L. PRICE *Jrnls* (1956) 225 This little speech of Roger's caused thunders of applause and several people meeting him since have greeted him heartily as the Lekhoa who made the stir in the pico. **1871** J. MACKENZIE *Ten Yrs* (1971) 281 The Matebele called out, 'These are "Makhoa"' (white men), and that some might still labour under this impression. [**1912** W. WESTRUP *Land of To-Morrow* 177 You must speak to Penite, your herd boy. He came here yesterday and said to Raphofoolo: 'Lumela, Lekhoa' instead of 'Morena'.] **1946** S. CLOETE *Afr. Portraits* 50 Suddenly a Kaffir shouted 'magoa!' — white man — and all fled deeper into the cave. **1988** 'A. AMAPHIXIPHIXI' in *Frontline* Apr.–May 33 Meanwhile the Basotho word for whites is also under assault. Basotho people used the word 'makhowa', which means bossy people who always find fault with everything you do.

lekgotla, lekhothla varr. KGOTLA.

lekker /'lekə, 'lɛkər, 'lækə, 'lʌkə/ *adj.* and *adv.* *Colloq.* Also **lecker, leke, lekka**. [Afk. (earlier Du.), in the sense 'delicious' (of food).]

The pronunciation /'lʌkə/ is commonly heard in Kwazulu-Natal.

A. *adj.*

1.a. A term of general approbation: 'nice', 'pleasant', 'good', 'lovely'. So comparative forms **lekkerder** [Afk.] or **lekkerer**, and superlative form **lekkerest**.

Initially used only of food and drink, but subsequently broadened in usage.

1847 J. BARROW *Reflect.* 188 Mr. Bresler, having heard that the gelatinous hoof of the hippopotamus was delicious, had one of them cooked in his iron pot ... The landrost .. got through the whole foot, exclaiming repeatedly how *lekker* (delicious) it was. **1861** P.B. BORCHERDS *Auto-Biog. Mem.* 27 Music was introduced, and many a pipe of *lekker kanaster* [tobacco] smoked during this animating scene. **1898** M.E. BARBER *Erythrina Tree* 10 He knows his exchequer, Has grown fat and 'lecker,' Since all of you came to Pretoria. **1901** *Grocott's Penny Mail* 29 Apr. 3 While the rebels were paying visits to the unprotected and loyal farmers and looting their stock and wantonly destroying their household goods, one of the lawless rascals declared the enterprise to be 'lekker'. **1911** D.B. HOOK *'Tis but Yesterday* 91 Piet asked why the 'baas' did not hunt the gemsbok for the sake of the biltong, which was so 'lekker' (nice). **1926** E. LEWIS *Mantis* 123 To Mr Dan Hugo nothing tasted so lekker as a good cup of coffee at that hour. **1952** *Drum* July 21 Galima get some tea and lekker koeksisters for the madams and masters. **1953** F. ROBB *Sea Hunters* 137 'Fish soup and baked fish to follow. Lekker!' Olley drooled. **1960** J. TAYLOR 'Ballad of the Southern Suburbs'. (*lyrics*) Ag, pleeze, Deddy, won't you take us off to Durban, it's only eight hours in the Chevrolet. There's spans of sea and sand and sun, and fish in the Aquarium, That's a lekker place for a holiday. **1961** *Personality* 16 May 27 It's a lekker language. **1971** *E. Prov. Herald* 15 Sept. 13 I'd prefer to let him continue with his own mod vocabulary of 'lekka,' 'deck,' .. and 'sight.' **1973** *Star* 11 Apr. 18 (*advt*) My chickens are really lekker ... My chickens are lekkerder because although they're available in your shop they're fresh from my farm. **1975** *E. Prov. Herald* 19 Sept. 7 Graze — the lekkerest thing between meals. **1978** M.J. MTSAKA *Not his Pride* 13 Find me a place that is *lekker* — if not *lekkerer* than this one. I mean, there must be good things. **1985** *S. Afr. Panorama* May 39 With apologies to a famous advertising slogan, we'll call it liplicking *lekker*. **1987** *Cosmopolitan* Dec. 89 White South African audiences tend to regard anything South African as unlekker. **1987** E. MAKHANYA in *Sowetan* 28 Dec. It has been *leke* being with you. Have a *leke* New Year and avoid all kinds of troubles. **1990** R. STENGEL *January Sun* 52 When people say 'How's it?' to him, he often replies, 'Lekker, lekker'. **1992** *Style* Oct. 108 It wasn't a *lekker* experience seeing ourselves as others saw us. **1992** H. DUGMORE in *Scope* 13 Nov. 46 'It [*sc.* the magazine] has interesting articles, and the chicks are lekker,' says this British boy from Dorset in mock Saffrican. **1994** *Sunday Times* 23 Jan. 28 (*advt*) We can't always keep the lekker local flavour of South Africa to ourselves ... If you don't believe biltong is the lekkerest, best loved snack in the land, try this; put down a bowl of peanuts, a bowl of crisps and a bowl of biltong.

b. In the expression ***local is lekker***: a slogan expressing or calling for pride in South African achievements; used also as *adj. phr.* and *n. phr.*

Used orig. of local popular music.

1983 *Sunday Times* 4 Sept. (Mag. Sect.) 30 At 702, they call Neil Johnson 'The Local Hero'. Just a dash of irony there, of course. Because the fact is, the station doesn't really go for the Local is Lekker Affirmative Action programme. **1987** J. KHUMALO in *Pace* May 140 Local is lekker says Kamazu. Out with the phony American influence and in with the home grown stuff. **1988** H. PRENDINI in *Style* Feb. 8 Chris Barnard .. has such a local-is-lekker charm that after a while no-one notices the Karoo accent. **1988** *Personality* 25 July 80 We see a very high percentage of America's best shows. But what's good for Americans is not necessarily good for us. Local is lekker. **1988** *Cape Times* 29 Dec. 4 She's a firm supporter of 'local is lekker'. She prefers to work with the resident company rather than with famous names. **1989** P. LEE in *Sunday Times* 26 Feb. (Mag. Sect.) 36 What more can I say about a runner who's pure poetry in motion once he gets going, and who can show those foreigners a thing or two. Local is really lekker. **1989** S. MOSTERT in *Flying Springbok* Sept. 30 Three seasons of the musical, *District Six*, were sold out, making it the longest-running show in South African history. So, the time was ripe for 'local is lekker' and the troupes marched again. **1990** *Style* June 120 Perhaps it is simply the old South African chip on the shoulder which has led us to swallow the line that local may be *lekker* when you're speaking of the white rhino but is somehow vastly inferior when it comes to the inside of our homes. How else to explain the extraordinary absence of indigenous arts and crafts from the interior decor of most South African homes? **1990** *Top Forty* July (Suppl.) 1 The time for the 'local is lekker' syndrome is long gone. We have to compete with the best from overseas on their own terms. No more excuses that it is a local product and that the public should accept it out of sympathy or patriotism. **1993** [see Daily News quot. at LOERIE sense 2]. **1993** *SABC Radio & TV* July–Sept. 15 Local is very 'lekker' and the station regularly uses local artistes. **1995** *Natal Witness* 3 Jan. 7 Local is lekker! The Woza '95 festival held .. in Durban yesterday proved that South African music is highly appreciated.

c. Special collocations. ‖**lekkergoed** /'lekə(r)xʊt, -xut/ *n.* [Afk., *goed* stuff, things], sweet things, esp. sweets; cf. LEKKERS; ‖**lekkerjuk** /'lekə(r)jək/ *n.* [ad. Afk. *lekkerjeuk*, *jeuk* itch], also **lekkerkrap** /-krap/ [Afk., *krap* scratch], scabies, infectious itch; **lekker lewe** /'lekə(r)ˌlɪəvə/, formerly also **- leven**, [Afk. *lewe*, earlier Du. *leven* life], 'the good life'; **lekker ou** /'lekə(r) ˌəʊ/ [Afk. *ou*, see OU *n.*], 'fine fellow', 'nice chap'; also *attrib.*

1938 F.C. SLATER *Trek* 45 He would stir About the camp to find them koekies sweet, Raisins and other **lekkergoed** to eat. **1958** A. JACKSON *Trader on Veld* 35 The average farmer had a sweet tooth and we carried varied stocks of lekkergoed (sweets). **1970** H.M. MUSMECI *Informant, Port Elizabeth* The children enjoy eating lekkergoed (sweets). **1970** *Post* 21 June (Home Post) 11 Your wife would appear to have something called **lekker-yuk**, and this can be cured with anti-scabies lotion. **1971** *Informant, OFS* One of the kids was itching so, and she said 'That's lekkerjuk'. **1969** *Rand Daily Mail* in C. Desmond *Discarded People* (c1970) 253 The most prevalent disorder is known locally as '**lekker-krap**' (scratch nicely, a good scratch) ... 'People are always scratching their bodies ... Everybody gets lekkerkrap.' **1928** E.A. WALKER *Hist. of S. Afr.* 204 What could cattle-farmers do but look around for a way of escape from changing conditions which promised to make the old style of life, the **lekker leven**, impossible? **1937** S. CLOETE *Turning Wheels* 260 They had come to lead a 'lekker lewe' and considered themselves happy because they were free to live a comfortless life, to hunt and to fight without let or hindrance. **1944** J. MOCKFORD *Here Are S. Africans* 61 They called it .. the *lekker lewe*, the nice life, the pleasant life. **1949** C. BULLOCK *Rina* 26 Enjoying the *lekker lewe* of the trek-boer who stays only for so long as the pasture is good. **1952** B. DAVIDSON *Report on Sn Afr.* 115 Such is the setting of the drama. The curtain goes down at last on the sweetly lingering *lekker lewe* of rural solitude. **1981** *E. Prov. Herald* 13 May 8 They stayed on the land, enjoying the old traditional *lekker lewe* as long as they could, which was well into the 20th century. **1990** R. STENGEL *January Sun* 34 Farming in the Transvaal was not the *lekker lewe* — the sweet life — that it had been in the Cape. **1970** C.B. WOOD *Informant, Johannesburg* He is a '**lekker ou**' (nice chap). **1972** *Cape Times* 1 Aug., To rank as a lekker ou at Bishops, Michaelhouse or St. Andrews is surely not to have lived in vain. **1990** 'HOGARTH' in *Sunday Times* 22 July 16 Mr S— has a persuasive lekker-ou manner which enables him to make even the most outrageous ideological codswallop sound mildly plausible to uncritical ears. **1990** J.G. DAVIS *Land God Made in Anger* 266 He knew the type: the lower-class whites which this country protected with its Apartheid, the *lekker ous* with their leather lumberjackets and their zoot suits.

2. *transf.* Usu. predicative. Of people: lightly intoxicated, 'happy', tipsy.

1913 W.C. SCULLY *Further Reminisc.* 66 For upwards of a quarter of a century Jacomina had spent more than half her time in gaol — for drunkenness or violent incontinence of speech when only 'lekker' or half-tipsy. **1934** *Sunday Times* 17 June (Swart), They were not drunk, he said, but only 'lekker'. **1934** C.P. SWART Supplement to Pettman. 105 *Lekker*, .. Figuratively it means half-tipsy or convivial. **1952** H. KLEIN *Land of Silver Mist* 96 When we got to the Letaba we were all lekker — lovely ... I can't help it, baas, if the gentlemens are lekker and jump out of the coach and falls down the mountain. **1968** F.G. BUTLER *Cape Charade* 10 At midnight .. the whole country was lekker-happy. **1974** *Evening Post* 11 Sept. 1 They had drunk a bottle of wine together and Mr Geswindt was 'lekker' when he last saw him. **1978** *Post* 12 Oct. (Woman's Post) 8 The cheese helped keep everybody just 'lekker' and not too stoned to make them rowdy.

‖**3.** Of water: 'sweet', wholesome.

1936 C. BIRKBY *Thirstland Treks* 117 '*Lekker water*,' she cried, her arms outstretched. 'Sweet water.' Can you imagine a child begging not for a crust or a penny, but for a drink of water that is not *brak*, bitter to the mouth? **1969** J.M. WHITE *Land God Made in Anger* 53 The land pants eternally for moisture. It is not for nothing that the talk here is all of *lekker* water — sweet water — a monologue concerning dams and barrages, canals, pipelines and storage tanks.

B. *adv.*

1. Well; delightfully.

1900 A.W. CARTER *Informant, Ladybrand* 8 Feb., On Monday these left and in moving round the mountain was 'verneuked' as Hannes said 'lekker'. **1968** G. CROUDACE *Silver Grass* 90 'I couldn't sleep.' 'But your ma and pa ..' 'Oh, they're sleeping *lekker*, very nice.' **1982** D. KRAMER *Short Back & Sides* 9 Ja, we grew up with the Shadows and Beatles and .. fell in love and got drunk and bunked school .. and did all the things that made our parents worry, but growing up so lekker. **1986** *Vula* July 19 In 1974 I met Dudu Pukwana overseas. We got on lekker. **1989** D. KRAMER in *ADA* No.7, 8 Why is he called Jan Mockingbird? Because he sings so lekker. **1991** *Sunday Times* 23 June (Mag. Sect.) 14 My new go-faster-stripes really work lekker, hey?

2. Very, incredibly, wonderfully; 'nice and ...'.

1916 S. BLACK in S. Gray *Three Plays* (1984) 210 Mrs H: Oh, I suppose you'd sooner she showed you the rooms than me? Van K (*embarrassed*): She's a ripper — lekker fet. **1975** G. HARESNAPE in *Bolt* No.12, 12 Weekends I'se gonna be lekker lazy. **1986** J. SCOTT in *Cape Times* 5 Feb. 11 The Cape skollie .. got on the train 'lekker dronk' and was told by the conductor to 'go to hell'. **1987** *E. Prov. Herald* 29 Apr. 14 (*advt*) Weekend Fish Specials! 'Lekker Fresh!'.

Hence **lekkerness** *n.*, pleasantness.

1974 *Weekend Post* 31 Aug. 6 Expressed his satisfaction with the increasing lekkerness of Parliament.

lekkers /ˈlekəz, ˈlɛkə(r)s/ *pl. n.* Also **leckers**. [Afk.] Sweets; sweetmeats; also called *lekkergoed* (see LEKKER *adj.* sense 1 c).

1846 *Natal Witness* 15 May, The Boers .. appeared perfectly satisfied that — *a plan had been laid by the Hottentots for despoiling them of their new years lakkers!* **1879** R.J. ATCHERLEY *Trip to Boerland* 78 As pocket handkerchiefs are the exception, and leckers (a kind of sticky sweet-meat) the rule, your hand, at the finish of a family 'How do you do?' has something of the adhesiveness and consistency of a glutinous fish. **1891** J.P. LEGG in *Cape Illust. Mag.* I. 96 The universal term among children 'lekkers,' and again 'mebos' dried apricot. **1901** W.S. SUTHERLAND *S. Afr. Sketches* 46 It is their duty to see that the fighting burghers at the front are .. supplied with creature comforts, .. lekkers. **1913** C. PETTMAN *Africanderisms* 293 *Lekkers*, .. Confections made of sugar; sweets. **1957** L.G. GREEN *Beyond City Lights* 195 The population .. were inordinately fond of *lekkers*, and enormous quantities were consumed. **1970** [see BONSELLA sense 3]. **1985** A. TREDGOLD *Bay between Mountains* 162 One penny would buy quite a number of lekkers out of the big glass jar.

lekkewaan var. LEGUAAN.

lekuka *n. obs.* Pl. **makuka(s)**. [SeTswana (pl. *makuka*). For an explanation of plural uses, see LE- and MA- *pref.*[2]] Among the Tswana people: *milk-sack*, see MILK sense 1. Also *attrib.*

1846 R. MOFFAT *Missionary Labours* 86 They boasted of .. filling their *makukas* (milk sacks) with milk, making every heart to sing for joy. *Ibid.* 122 The *lekuka*, or Bechuana milk-sack, .. is made of the hide of an ox, or that of a quagga, which is said to give the milk a better flavour. **1871** J. MACKENZIE *Ten Yrs* (1971) 263 The woman .. had stolen some sour milk from a 'lekuka,' or leathern bottle, which was hanging in the sun. **1879** E.L. PRICE *Jrnls* (1956) 346 We have bought some Lekuka milk tonight, too, at this cattle outpost. **1880** *Ibid.* 399 The skimmed milk goes into the makuka or milk sacks.

lelapa var. LAPA *n.*

Lemba /ˈlembə/ *n.* Pl. unchanged, **-s**, **Balemba** /ba-/. [Unkn.] A member of a people, apparently of mixed Semitic and black African origin, living mainly among the Venda of the Northern Transvaal and in parts of southern Zimbabwe, Zambia, and Mozambique. Also *attrib.*

The Lemba have no language of their own, but speak the language of the people among whom they live. Both physiological characteristics and cultural elements suggest East African and Arab origins.

1928 G.P. LESTRADE in A.M. Duggan-Cronin *Bantu Tribes* I. 20 They [*sc.* the Venda] are excellent smiths (the Balemba who dwell amongst them are noted copper-workers). **1952** H. KLEIN *Land of Silver Mist* 191 It is evident from Lemba legend and tribal custom that somewhere in the distant past these people were closely allied to the Semitic clans of North-Eastern Africa. **1972** J.F. ELOFF in *Std Encycl. of Sn Afr.* VI. 581 *Lemba*, .. Bantu ethnic group living in the Northern Transvaal and Rhodesia and displaying certain Semitic traits in their physical appearance and way of life ... In South Africa there are probably fewer than a thousand who may still be considered to be of pure Lemba stock. *Ibid.* 582 A marriage between a Lemba and a non-Lemba meets with the strongest disapproval. **1982** *S. Afr. Panorama* Sept. 17 (*caption*) The traditional apron, adorned with copper beads, is worn prior to initiation by young Lemba maidens in the North-Eastern Transvaal. **1985** G.T. NURSE et al. *Peoples of Sn Afr.* 164 The Lemba, a dispersed people living mainly among the Venda and the Karanga, show morphological and cultural features very suggestive of an East African and Arab-related origin ... The derivation of their name is uncertain. **1986** K. NGWENYA in *Drum* Sept. 50 An estimated 40 000 black Jews — the Lembas — are preparing themselves for a ceremonial gathering at Sweet Waters near Louis Trichardt later in the year.

lemoenhout /ləˈmʊnhəʊt/ *n.* [Afk., *lemoen* orange + *hout* wood; named for the colour of its wood.] LEMON WOOD. Also *attrib.*

1966 C.A. SMITH *Common Names* 322 *Lemoenhout*, *Xymalos monospora* ... A large or small dioecious, evergreen tree or shrub. **1971** BARAITSER & OBHOLZER *Cape Country Furn.* 55 These chairs are commonly called lemoenhout chairs because they were most often made from the wood of the Cape Orange tree. **1971** L.G. GREEN *Taste of S.-Easter* 54 Chairs are made of lemoen-hout from the orange groves of the Olifants River valley.

lemon wood *n. phr.* [Calque formed on Afk. *lemoenhout*, see prec.] The tree *Xymalos monospora* of the Monimiaceae; its yellow-hued wood; *borrie yellow*, see BORRIE sense 2; LEMOENHOUT.

1906 B. DAVY in C.A. Smith *Common Names* (1966) 159 The Lemonwood or Borie. **1913** C. PETTMAN *Africanderisms* 294 *Lemon wood*, *Xymalos monospora*, *Harv.*, common in Transvaal forests. **1966** C.A. SMITH *Common Names* 322 *Lemon wood*, *Xymalos monospora*. **1972** G.L.F. HARTWIG in *Std Encycl. of Sn Afr.* VI. 583 *Lemonwood*, .. (*Xymalos monospora*.) Large tree belonging to the family *Monimiaceae* and found in the mountain forests of the Eastern Cape Province. **1974** [see SANDVELD sense 2]. **1990** CLINNING & FOURIE in *Fauna & Flora* No.47, 10 Evergreen high forests clothe the southern slopes. The wild quince *Cryptocarya liebertiana*, red stinkwood *Prunus africanus*, .. Lemonwood *Xymalos monospora*, [etc.].

leningplaats var. LEENINGS-PLAATS.

leopard-crawl *v. intrans. Military.* To move stealthily along the ground, keeping very low and using elbows and knees for leverage.

1980 *Daily Dispatch* 3 July 2 He slung the AK 47 he had taken off a tree and leopard-crawled undetected right through a village where the terrorists were. **1985** *Sunday Times* 11 Aug. (Lifestyle) 5 Leopard-crawling and bent-double, they set off in search of the elusive herd. **1987** A. SOULE et al. *Wynand du Toit Story* 21 Wynand could feel the skin come away from his knees and elbows as they leopard-crawled to a point where he and his men hoped for a brief moment of safety. **1988** T.J. LINDSAY *Shadow* (1990) 263 He leopard-crawled painfully slowly along one of the lower slopes, in and out of rock cover. **1990** C. SHERLOCK *Hyena Dawn* 52 Desperately he had tried to leopard-crawl to the open back door, but he hadn't stood a chance. **1992** *Sunday Times* 13 Sept. 20 They were .. driven to a place .. flooded with effluent from a leaking pipe and ordered to leopard crawl through it.

Hence **leopard-crawl** *n.*, this stealthy movement along the ground.

1985 J. THOMAS in *Fair Lady* 1 May 20 Boetie, lies and skande are punishable by 20 km pole PT and leopard crawl.

‖**lêsiekte** /ˈleːsiktə/ *n. Pathology.* [Afk., *lê* lying + *siekte* sickness.] KRIMPSIEKTE sense 1. Also *attrib.*

1978 *E. Prov. Herald* 6 Mar. 8 There was an outside chance that campanulata could be responsible for local cases of lêsiekte due to its containing, during dry seasons, cotyledontoxin ... Goats are most susceptible because conditions in lêsiekte veld are suitable practically only for goat-farming.

leting /leˈti(ː)ŋ/ *n.* [S. Sotho.] A mild beer derived from a second brewing of sprouted grain which has been used to make strong beer. See also TSHWALA sense a. Cf. TING.

1957 A.A. MURRAY *Blanket* 130 One of the police wives .. brought him fuel for a fire and a can of thin, sour beer – leting. 1964 V. POHL *Dawn & After* 35 Before the day had ended a bag of green mealies and a large pot of leting, which is a milder drink than kaffir beer, found its way to our doorstep. *c*1976 H. FLATHER *Thaba Rau* 216 Before you go .. I'll get you a drink! What would you like? I've got both *leting* and *yoala*! 1991 E.A.S. LESORO *Informant, Grahamstown* When you've poured off the first beer, you can make leting with the same grain. It's not as strong, of course – leting is a mild beer.

‖**letona** /le'tɔ(:)na/ *n.* [Sotho.] A headman, councillor, or officer under a Sotho chief. Cf. INDUNA sense 1 a.

1953 LANHAM & MOPELI-PAULUS *Blanket Boy's Moon* 18 Monare's behaviour won him the confidence of his Chief, who at length appointed him to be his second Headman or letona. 1968 A. FULTON *Dark Side of Mercy* 27 The Letona, the Chief's headman .. instructed them. *c*1976 H. FLATHER *Thaba Rau* 224 They run around the village at night screaming and banging tins, making the most dreadful noises. They would do harm even to my father, the *Letona*.

‖**letsemma** /le'tse(:)ma/ *n.* [SeTswana *letseme* seed-time.] A ritual inauguration of seed-time, planting, or sowing. Also *attrib.* See also UMKHOSI.

1872 J. MACKENZIE in A.J. Dachs *Papers of John Mackenzie* (1975) 39 Why .. should not a Christian Chief issue his 'letsemma' – inaugurate the seed-time in his town – by public prayer to Almighty God, the Maker of Heaven and Earth. 1953 LANHAM & MOPELI-PAULUS *Blanket Boy's Moon* 17 At such *letsema* [*printed* letsoma] times, kaffir beer is brewed and small livestock killed to provide drink and food for the working-parties; tribal songs – such as the Mokorotho, or Chant of Praise – are sung, and every man and woman in the village has to attend. 1971 C. NORTHCOTT *Ten Yrs* p.xxii, Khama .. made a speech .. asking the people to regard the act of public worship which Mackenzie was leading as their *letsemma*, after which they might dig as they pleased. 1980 D.B. COPLAN Urbanization of African Performing Arts. 176 A fusion of economic and social activities parallel to that involved in traditional work-for-beer parties such as the Tswana *letsema*.

lewensessens /'lɪəvəns,esəns/ *n.* Also **levens-essens**. [Afk., *lewens* combining form of *lewe* life + *essens* essence.] 'Essence of Life', a patent household remedy for stomach and digestive complaints. Also part. tr. **lewens essence**. See also (*old*) *Dutch medicine* (DUTCH *adj.* sense 2).

1919 *Dunell, Ebden & Co.'s Price List* Oct. 20 Levens Essence, Kiesow's, small 11/6. 1934 *Sunday Times* 24 June (Swart), Paregoric, krampdruppels, lewensessens and the host of other old Dutch remedies and patent medicines can now only be brought from chemists. 1934 C.P. SWART Supplement to Pettman. 106 *Lewensessens*, .. The name of a well-known Dutch medicine – an essence with curative properties. 1943 I. FRACK *S. Afr. Doctor* 118 The millions of bottles of 'bors-druppels,' .. 'levens-essens,' .. that are sold must really be staggering. 1949 L.G. GREEN *In Land of Afternoon* 44 When 'Lewens Essence' ceases to give instant relief to the troubled stomach. 1958 E.H. BURROWS *Hist. of Medicine* 191 *Levens essens* (lit., Essence of Life): used for indigestion, biliousness, headache and for 'swellings'. 1972 S. LYNNE *Glittering Gold* 16 '*Levensessens*,' an old Dutch remedy – very good; puts you right in two ticks; one of the few medicines my old Voortrekker forefathers took with them when they trekked north to get away from the English. 1992 *Guide to Lennon's Dutch Medicines*, Lewensessens – A famous stomach tonic. For constipation, stomach disorders resulting from incorrect diet or excessive eating or drinking.

liberal *n.* and *adj.* [Special use of general Eng.] As a term of abuse:
A. *n.* LIBERALIST *n.*

1939 R.F.A. HOERNLÉ *S. Afr. Native Policy & Liberal Spirit* p.vii, To plead for fuller knowledge, or for more humane consideration, of non-European needs and interests, is to earn .. the title of 'negrophile,' *kafirboetie*, or – most scathing of all – 'liberal'. 1962 L.E. NEAME *Hist. of Apartheid* 8 A White population most of whom are too engrossed in business or sport to pay serious attention to those they regard as 'alarmists', or even worse, 'liberals'. 1962 L.J. CLARKE in *Black Sash* Dec.-Jan. 21 *Liberal*, A Communist belonging to the Liberal Party. *Communist*, A Liberal belonging to the Communist Party. 1971 *Sunday Times* 14 Nov. (Mag. Sect.) 12 It seems that Christianity as we see it in the Bible has joined the ranks of that other dirty world 'liberal,' and is something to be despised rather than admired. 1981 A. PATON *Ah, but your Land Is Beautiful* 71 It is hard to describe the detestation in which the words *liberal*, *liberalism*, and *liberalist* are held in white Pretoria. Liberalism denotes moral looseness and degeneracy. White liberals are people who will hop into bed with blacks at the drop of a hat.

B. *adj.* LIBERALIST *adj.*

1943 'J. BURGER' *Black Man's Burden* 238 Anyone who advocates non-European rights is dubbed 'liberal' or 'negrophilist' by the Nationalists. 1956 *Times* (U.K.) in M. Rogers *Black Sash* 268 The Christian and idealistic wing of Nationalism (one cannot say 'Liberal wing,' since 'Liberal' is a term of abuse among Nationalists). 1958 A. PATON *Hope for S. Afr.* 7 Further, the word 'liberal' has for the white enemies of South African Liberalism another meaning; it shares this further meaning with the words 'liberalist' and 'liberalistic'. This meaning is derogatory and carries the stigma of 'loose', 'careless', 'promiscuous'.

liberalist *n.* and *adj.* [Calqued on Afk. *liberalis* a liberal, or *liberalisties* liberal.] Esp. in the Eng. of Afrikaans-speakers:
A. *n.* An abusive term for: **a.** One holding liberal political views. **b.** A member of the former Liberal Party. **c.** An opponent of apartheid or of the National Party. **d.** A leftist. In all senses also called LIBERAL *n.*

1939 R.F.A. HOERNLÉ *S. Afr. Native Policy* 103 The spokesmen of the Nationalist section of the Afrikaner people are especially fond of hurling the word 'liberal', or 'Liberalist' (*liberalis*) as they like to say, at everyone and everything they regard as most *on-afrikaans*. It is a word surpassed in abusive vigour only by 'Communist' and 'Bolshevik'. 1963 K. MACKENZIE *Dragon to Kill* 57 Is this what you liberalists want? We will have a demonstration, you say, nonviolent *en so voort*, just like it is in Hyde Park and then they are throwing stones at the police. 1970 *Evening Post* 20 Oct. 7 This arch-liberalist was pleading for co-operation between the National Party and the United Party on the eve of the Provincial Council elections. 1971 [see BEK sense 2]. 1972 *Evening Post* 21 Oct. 2 You criticise the National Party – you point out the injustices in our society and they turn round and shout 'liberalists, communists, terrorists'. 1981 [see LIBERAL *n.*]. 1990 I. CREWS in *Sunday Times* 15 Apr. 17 The ousted NP members are claiming 'liberalists' in their own party supported the DP and they were 'stabbed in the back'.

B. *adj.* Of or pertaining to liberals and their beliefs; LIBERAL *adj.*

1972 *Times Lit. Suppl.* (U.K.) 27 Oct. 1272 Liberal or (in the pejorative corruption of her Afrikaner opponents) liberalist. 1972 *Sunday Times* 3 Dec. 17 Protection of the *status quo* backed by churchmen, Cabinet Ministers and editors standing firm against 'terrorist impis, communist threats, liberalist lies and Anglican bishops'.

licence *n.* In the interrogative phr. ***did you got a licence?***: 'do you have a licence?', a jocular imitation of the obstructively bureaucratic behaviour (and poor command of English) of some civil servants and police force members. Made popular by Kenneth Taylor, scriptwriter for the 1960s radio programme *The Caltex Show.*

1962 J. TAYLOR 'Hennie van Saracen'. (*lyrics*) A traffic cop came up to me and said as he scratched his ear, 'Well, did you got a licence to park that blerrie thing here?' 1981 *E. Prov. Herald* 4 May 12 A particularly virulent form of a new disease is sweeping South Africa. It is called scientifically Habes potestatem or, when translated into the South African vernacular, it is known as 'Did you got a licence?' 1991 *Sunday Times* 12 May 20 Did you got a licence? With murder and mayhem rife, 250 detectives .. have swooped on – gamblers ... How absurd .. do the raids appear when it is possible to have a flutter perfectly legally only 30 minutes from Pretoria in what is *de facto* the same country.

lichter var. LAAGTE.

lidjes ganna see GANNA sense 2.

lieck var. LIEG.

‖**liedjie** /'liki, 'lici/ *n. Music.* Also (occas.) **liedtjie**. [Afk., *lied* song + -IE.] A song, particularly an Afrikaans folk-song. Also occas. *fig.* See also BOERELIEDJIE, GHOMMALIEDJIE, LUISTERLIEDJIE.

1934 *Star* 26 May (Swart), He .. has arranged numerous Afrikaans liedjies and deuntjies [tunes], already popular here. 1937 C.R. PRANCE *Tante Rebella's Saga* 94 The girls .. provided tasteful items in the programme in the intervals between burgher 'liedjies' and soldier-songs. 1948 *E. Prov. Herald* 6 Mar. 6 Afrikaans liedjies and some of the Bantu singing that made an impression during the Royal Tour will be a feature of a £25,000 'Meet South Africa' exhibition due to open in London. 1949 *Cape Times* 10 Jan. 2 He hoped that the Cape 'moppies' or comic songs and the *liedjies* would become a regular feature of future carnivals. 1951 L.G. GREEN *Grow Lovely* 193 This is the place to watch the coons, in the sunlit streets ... Here they .. give you moppies in Afrikaans, their own Cape liedtjies. 1963 A.M. LOUW *20 Days* 198 The boys and girls .. were circling round each other bobbing to the rhythm of the 'liedjie'. 1976 *Drum* June 2 Pretoria replied in so many words: 'You can sing your October song you know when. But now I am paying the piper so I'll call the liedjie.' 1980 A. PATON *Towards Mountain* 207 Prayers were said over the wagons, meat and *boerewors* were cooked over the fires, nostalgic Afrikaner *liedjies* were sung. 1989 C. CHAPMAN in *Edgars Club* Apr. 45 The roots of Cape music .. can be traced to various influences. Firstly, European folk songs, or *Nederlandse liedjies*, preserved by the Malay choirs, sung in Dutch and still sung today. 1990 [see ENGELS *n.* sense 3 a]. 1991 *Weekly Mail* 30 Aug. 11 They play hymns and Afrikaans liedjies on a Yamaha electric keyboard someone set up in the café's dining room.

‖**liefie** /'lifi/ *n. colloq.* [Afk., *lief* dear, beloved + -IE.] Among Afrikaners: an endearment, 'little love'.

1971 *Sunday Times* 21 Mar. (Suppl.) 14 Haremse did his best to comfort his distraught wife. 'They'll catch him, liefie.' 1972 J. PACKER *Boomerang* 54 'You're the girl in my life, liefie – no one else.' *Liefie* – I was glad to be his 'little love,' the girl in his life. 1985 P. DIAMOND in *Style* Dec. 26 Liefie, you *must* believe me. I've just come from the city and there it all was. 1987 L. BEAKE *Strollers* 75 For the thousandth time Van Jaarsveld explained to her about being a policeman. 'There's a big panic on, liefie! I must go!'

‖**lieg** /lix/ *v. intrans.* Also **lieck**. [Afk.] To tell a lie or lies.

1911 L. COHEN *Reminisc. of Kimberley* 14 She exclaimed: 'Yer lieck (you lie), we all do it, and so must you'! and .. the sensuous syren dragged me into the giddy maze. 1969 A. FUGARD *Boesman & Lena* 5 Lena: No Boesman. This time you *lieg*. Boesman: Don't say to me I *lieg*! *Ibid.* 7 'Three bob my *baas*. Just dug them out!' *Lieg* your soul into hell for enough to live. 1978 C. VAN WYK in *Staffrider* Vol.1 No.2, 36 Don't lieg, man, it's all still there by the possie.

lieta var. AMALAITA.

lifaqane var. DIFAQANE.

liggar, ligger varr. LEAGUER.

lightee, lightie varr. LIGHTY.

lightitjie see LIGHTY.

lightning bird *n. phr.* Also with initial capitals. [So named because, according to Zulu lore, the bird is left behind on the ground when lightning strikes.] IMPUNDULU.

1870 H. CALLAWAY *Religious System of Amazulu* (1884) 383 When it thunders and the lightning strikes the ground .. the bird remains where the ground was struck ... 'Is it not really that bird which it is said exists, the lightning-bird which goes with the lightning?' **1894** E. GLANVILLE *Fair Colonist* 289 A streak of summer lightning darted across the horizon ... Then darkness ensued blacker than before. 'It is Mpundulu, the lightning bird,' muttered Makanna. **1908** [see IMPUNDULU]. **1930** I. SCHAPERA *KhoiSan Peoples* 167 When .. a 'hammerkop' (*Scopus umbretta*, the 'lightning bird' of other South African tribes) flies, calling out, over the camp, the people know that someone belonging to them has died. **1934** P.R. KIRBY *Musical Instruments of Native Races* (1965) 100 He calls it the 'Flute of Heaven' because the doctors used it to ward off lightning. It was made from a bone (supposed to be from the *ndlati* or 'lightning bird' itself). **1939** J.K. GODFREY in *Outspan* 24 Nov. 71 They hold in dread the fatal lightning bird; they believe that any wandering hammerhead bird or bromvoël that settles on their huts must be a messenger of evil sent by a wizard. **1950** A.W. BURTON *Sparks from Border Anvil* 174 Witchdoctors and people associate with lightning an evil and hideous monster known as the 'Lightning Bird' or 'i'Impundulu'. **1970** B. DAVIDSON *Old Afr.* 243 The effigies vary .. because the 'lightning birds' vary: the Southern Sotho imagine the lightning bird as a *hamerkop*, the Venda imagine it as an eagle, and the peoples of the north-western Transvaal imagine it as a flamingo; but the cult is in any case widespread. **1975** *Evening Post* 2 Apr. 7 Three brothers charged with the desecration of their father's body .. were acquitted .. because the court accepted that they believed it was an evil spirit (a lightning bird) in their father's coffin and not his body. **1982** *Sunday Times* 21 Feb. (Mag. Sect.) 1 The queen agreed the mixture did include the lightning bird's feathers and that horns filled with the mixture were put on the ground to bring rain and lifted to stop it.

lighty /'laɪti/ *n. colloq.* Also **laaitie, laaity, laitie, lightee, lightie, litie.** ['App. ex Eng. adj. *light* (of heart, mind, head)' (E. Partridge, *Dict. of Underworld*, 1950) + Eng. (informal) n.-forming suffix *-y*. The *-a(a)i-* forms show the influence of Afk.]

1. A (male) child, adolescent, or young adult.

1946 *Cape Times* in E. Partridge *Dict. of Underworld* (1950) 409 No 'lighty' .. should presume to call her a 'jintoe' .. the lighty would be guilty of using 'opposite' (obscene) language. **1970** M. BENNETT *Informant, Krugersdorp* Litie. Small boy. **1974** A.P. BRINK *Looking on Darkness* 119 She was struck dumb when I told her about University. 'You? Jiss, but you're a deep lightie, hey?' **1980** R. GOVENDER *Lahnee's Pleasure* 14 When we was lighties we couldn't catch a joll like today's lighties. We used to get it — one day my father hit me with a sjambok. **1986** *Vula* July 33 They are always looking for the easy way out. You get a laaitie coming to you and saying, 'Bra Vic, what is the formula for producing a hit?' **1990** J. NAIDOO *Coolie Location* 25 It was the Location way for us *lightees* to associate ourselves with someone three to five years older than ourselves. These older boys were our mentors and protectors. **1990** J. ROSENTHAL *Wake Up Singing* 61 A Standard Six lightie .. came in for an innocent leak, and said in staring amazement, '*Jislaaik!* What's happening?' **1991** K. MACDONALD in *Style* Nov. 67 A platteland lightie, Leon L— was born into a strict Afrikaner Calvinist clan, a fact not evident from his impeccable English accent.

2. *Prison* and *underworld slang.* A young convict, esp. the catamite of an older convict; a junior gang member. Cf. GOOSIE sense 1.

1974 *Eng. Usage in Sn Afr.* Vol.5 No.1, 10 The general term *laitie* now gets specific application. **1975** *E. Prov. Herald* 8 Aug. 1 Witnesses further alleged that prisoners at St Albans had rank systems within gangs, and the lowest ranks, called 'lighties', were used by senior convicts for acts of sodomy. **1987** [see HASIE sense 2]. **1987** L. BEAKE *Strollers* 38 It was them what started it — the Spider men. Wanted us to be lighties, you know, join the gang.

3. A term of address, not necessarily to someone younger than the speaker; sometimes expressing a sense of superiority. Often in the phrr. ***my lighty***, or (less commonly) ***my lightitjie*** [see -IE].

1978 A.P. BRINK *Rumours of Rain* 325 Don't underestimate our boys, lightie. We had a very good look before we made up out minds. **1981** *Voice* 8 Apr. 2 Ya, 'Terror', my laaitie, there you are. What do you have to say to all these accusations and criticisms? **1982** M. MZAMANE *Children of Soweto* 17 'See me after school, my laititjie,' Phakoe said.

Hence **lighty** *adj. nonce*, young.

1980 R. GOVENDER *Lahnee's Pleasure* 38 Char ous were working there for years — longer than some of the wit ous, but they weren't earning more than even the lightie wit ous.

likawaan, likkewan varr. LEGUAAN.

limbo /'lɪmbəʊ/ *n. Obs.* exc. *hist.* [ad. Zulu *ulembu* web, gossamer material, gauze, muslin.] A coarse, brightly-coloured calico.

1886 W.M. KERR *Far Interior* 50 For some small strips of cotton cloth — limbo it is called by the traders — we bought some potatoes. **1891** *Pall Mall Gaz.* (U.K.) 9 Nov. 6 This present is accompanied by a quantity of limbo (a coarse quality of calico). *c***1894** WILLS & COLLINGRIDGE *Downfall of Lobengula* 187 *(caption)* The native in the foreground is wearing the distinguishing mark — yellow 'limbo' round his head, as worn by our 'friendlies'. **1895** R.H.S. CHURCHILL *Men, Mines & Animals* 153 A small group of Makalaka .. brought pumpkins, milk, mealies, and beans, for which they took in exchange pieces of coarse blue calico ('limbo'). **1899** B. MITFORD *John Ames* 14 A dark blue fabric, commonly called by the whites 'limbo', being a corruption of the native name 'ulembu', which signifieth 'web'. **1914** S.P. HYATT *Old Transport Rd* 60 The table-cloth, a piece of white limbo, trade calico, remained on from meal to meal, forming a favourite promenade for the flies. **1968** L.G. GREEN *Full Many Glorious Morning* 132 Fairbridge said that even Dr. Jameson had to be content with coarse cotton material known in pioneer slang as 'limbo'. **1974** P. GIBBS *Hist. of BSAP* II. 174 He had already tried ritual offerings to the Rain God of limbo and beer but these had proved unavailing.

linaby var. LINNEBAAI.

line /laɪn/ *v. intrans. Slang.* [Isicamtho, origin dubious: perh. rel. to Afk. *'n lyn sny* to run away, to move off quickly.] Esp. in township English: to walk; to leave, to move off; to run away; *to cut a line*, see CUT.

1979 A.P. BRINK *Dry White Season* 178 'You know I don't keep drink in the house,' she said. 'Well, let's line,' he said to Ben. 'We can fill up at a shebeen.' **1982** *Sunday Times* 4 July 21 When he saw her, he said she was already dead. 'I told Gerry we had better "line" (walk).' [**1982** D. BIKITSHA in *Rand Daily Mail* 14 Oct. (Eve) 5 [In Isicamtho] to walk assumes names like: mova, nyauka, line, tleri, slice, dak or digosh.]

linebayi var. LINNEBAAI.

linefish *n.* [Back-formation fr. general Eng. *line-fishing*.] See quot. 1977. Also *attrib.*

1977 *Fair Lady* 8 June (S. Afr. Cookery Suppl.) 29 Line fish, rock fish or angling fish normally means the smaller (and tastier) species of fish either caught by anglers from the rocks or with hand-lines from boats — not the ubiquitous larger fish .. which are usually caught with nets by trawlers. **1983** *S. Afr. Panorama* Jan. 12 Apart from the three main branches of the industry already mentioned, there are others of lesser importance such as bait, shrimps and prawns, perlemoen and line fish. **1983** M. FAIRALL *When in Durban* 69 Baked linefish (fresh off the ski-boats and into the oven). **1984** *E. Prov. Herald* 10 May 21 Detailed research under the auspices of the South African National Committee for Oceanographic Research is at present under way into about 50 linefish species in our waters. **1988** *Fair Lady* 16 Mar. 116, 2 cm-thick slices linefish (kabeljou, snoek, steenbras, yellowtail). **1990** J. MCARTHUR in *Sunday Tribune* 21 Oct. (Today) 4 My companion decided to have the fresh linefish of the day and I was given a good report on the more than generous portion. **1992** *Weekly Mail* 3 July 12 Most inland consumers will at some time or another have ordered 'fresh fish' or 'line fish of the day' in a restaurant. **1992** *SA Commercial Marine* Vol.1 No.2, 33 Drastic changes in linefish regulations .. which severely restrict the bag limit of certain species, are the result of recommendations from the SA Linefish Management Association which consists of representatives of sport and commercial anglers, researchers, law enforcement authorities, the Cape Provincial Administration and the Natal Parks Board. **1993** *Natal Mercury* 1 Jan. (Funfinder) 4 Linefish is 'scaled' with sliced potatoes and served on spinach with a creamy herb sauce.

linenbaai var. LINNEBAAI.

lingaka pl. form of NGAKA.

linnebaai *n. obs.* Also **linaby, linebayi, linenbaai, linnebaay.** [Afk., earlier S. Afr. Du., *linne* linen + *baai* baize, coarse woollen cloth.] A fabric of wool and linen, used during the 19th century for clothing.

1832 *Graham's Town Jrnl* 18 May 80 (b), On Friday, the 25th May, a Public Sale will be held .. of .. Duffles, Baize, Linnebaai, Flannels, worsted and cotton Hose. **1832** J. COLLETT Accounts. I. 4 Aug., To 6 pieces Linaby @ 9/ — 54 0 0. **1833** *Graham's Town Jrnl* 18 July 4 Chintz, plain and printed Muslins, Voerchits, Linnebaay, sail Canvass. **1833** *Ibid.* 5 Sept. 1 Voerchits, brown Punjums and Baftas, Linenbaai, sail Cloth. **1870** H.H. DUGMORE *Reminisc. of Albany Settler* (1958) 33 The qualities of the *linebayi* and the *wolkombersen* were elaborately discussed.

lintuna pl. form of INDUNA.

Lion and Tyger *n. phr. Hist.* Also **Lion and Tiger**, and with small initials. [Prob. tr. Du. *Leeuw en Tijger*; see quot. 1798.] In the phrr. ***Lion and Tyger money, Lion and Tyger tax***: a per capita tax levied at the Cape, the proceeds being used as prize money to encourage the hunting of predatory game. Also *attrib.* See also TIGER sense 1.

The tax was instituted by Jan van Riebeeck, who noted it in his *Daghregister* (16 July 1656) as follows: 'Is op dato ten aansien het wild gediert aan Compagnies vee dus veel schade doet, bij resolutie goedgevonden tot premie te stellen: voor een leeuw die gevangen off schoten wordt 6 [realen van 8], een tijger off wolff 4, ende een lupert 3 ra van 8.'

[**1708** (tr. F. Leguat) in R. Raven-Hart *Cape G.H. 1652–1702* (1971) II. 431 The Company gives twenty Crowns to anyone that kills a Lion, and ten to him that kills a Tigre.] **1795** C.R. HOPSON tr. *C.P. Thunberg's Trav.* II. 19 The farmer continues paying to the Company the old tax, called Lion and Tyger Money .. out of which fund, at the time when the colony began to extend itself, .. a certain premium was paid to everyone who killed or caught any of these animals. **1797** EARL MACARTNEY in G.M. Theal *Rec. of Cape Col.* (1898) II. 103 The Burgher Senate have represented to me that in order to enable them to levy and collect the annual assessment of Lion and Tyger money, for the supply of the Colony's fund, they have affixed advertisements requiring all inhabitants of the Cape District that shall have attained their sixteenth year to cause themselves to be entered into the Registers of this Colony. **1798** S.H. WILCOCKE tr. *J.S. Stavorinus's Voy. to E. Indies 1768–71* III. 460 A tax was .. levied by the Dutch Company, under the denomination of lion and tyger-money; this tax was paid by each burger, at the rate of four rixdollars for lion, and two guilders for tiger-money; out of this fund, at the time when the colony began to extend itself, and when the colonists were much infested by wild beasts, a certain premium was paid to everyone who killed or caught any of these animals. **1806** J. BARROW *Trav.* II. 104 A kind of capitation tax was levied under the name of Lion and Tyger money. The fund so raised was applied to the encouragement of destroying beasts of prey, of which these two were considered as the most formidable. **1951** L.G. GREEN *Grow Lovely* 142 Rewards were paid on the evidence of skins. The Burgher Council financed all its activities by levying a single tax known as 'Lion and Tyger money'. Rewards were paid out of this fund. **1955** [see LANDDROST sense 1]. **1990** R. MALAN *My Traitor's Heart* 14 Dutch governors .. sent bailiffs to collect the 'lion and tiger' tax, the 'pontoon' tax, and the quitrent on farmland.

lion dog *n. phr.* [See quot. 1991.] RIDGEBACK.

In *Brit. Eng.* usu. called the *Rhodesian lion dog.*

[**1930** *Observer* (U.K.) 9 Feb. 13 Such rarities as .. Rhodesian lion dogs, distinguished by the ridge of hair running along the back the reverse way of the rest of the coat.] **1938** E.C. ASH *New Bk Dog* 466 *(caption)* A Rhodesian Ridgeback (Lion Dog). **1971** [see RIDGEBACK]. **1979** A. PRICE *Tomorrow's Ghost* 182, I think we ought to have dogs ... A pair of Rhodesian Ridgebacks — 'Lion Dogs'. **1991** *Philatelic Services Bulletin* No.8075, *Ridgeback Dog* ... First known as the Van Rooyen or lion dog (because of its hunting ability).

liretla, -lo varr. DIRETLO.

list *v. trans. Hist.* [Special sense of general Eng. *list* to place on a list, see quot. 1969.] Almost invariably *passive.* To have one's name placed on a consolidated list of those who are considered by the government to be a danger to the state, and whose words and opinions may thus not be publicly quoted. Cf. BAN *v.*

1966 *Survey of Race Rel. 1965* (S.A.I.R.R.) 46 On 1 September Security Branch policemen detained Mr. I. H— of Johannesburg, a married man with two young sons, whose name had previously been 'listed' as a Communist. **1971** *Rand Daily Mail* 16 Mar. 11 Another brother .. was detained under the 90-Day Clause in 1964 and listed as a communist the following year. **1987** *E. Prov. Herald* 7 Nov. 1 Mr Coetsee has muzzled the 77-year-old Mr Mbeki, released after 23 years from Robben Island on Thursday, by stressing that he is listed and may not be quoted without permission. **1990** *E. Prov. Herald* 3 Feb. 11 Of those people de-listed today, 65 fall under Section 27 (3) of the Internal Security Act. The other 110 were listed in terms of section 28 of the Act, or Section 8 of the old Internal Security Act of 1950 — namely, office bearers of the ANC, PAC and Communist Party.

Hence **listed** *ppl adj.*, named on the consolidated list, silenced; also *transf.*

1978 P.-D. UYS in S. Gray *Theatre Two* (1981) 145 International boycott is a listed phrase. **1982** *Sunday Times* 19 Dec. (Extra) 3 Books which have been judged by the Directorate of Publications to be 'not undesirable' cannot be published because their authors are listed persons and may not be quoted. **1987** C. BAUER in *Weekly Mail* 19 June 14 Mark Uhlig's compilation of essays, *Apartheid in Crisis*, was passed on appeal last week, despite contravening the Internal Security Act by quoting 'listed persons' including Oliver Tambo. **1989** *Ibid.* 26 Jan. 2 The aim of the law was not only to stop the voices of subversive individuals but to keep their opinions from being heard ... The Internal Security Act covered the reproduction of any opinion, meaning or argument of a listed person. **1989** P. GARSON in *Weekly Mail* 1 Sept. 3 Newspapers can be found guilty of quoting listed persons whether they intended to do so or not. **1990** *E. Prov. Herald* 3 Feb. 11 Oliver Tambo can speak again — and be heard in South Africa. So can dozens of other banned or listed people given voice once more by a Government Gazette published in Pretoria today.

litie var. LIGHTY.

Liverpool *n. obs.* [Alluding to the industrial growth of Port Elizabeth, considered comparable to that of the port of *Liverpool* in England.] Usu. in the phrr. ***Liverpool of the Cape, -of South Africa,*** the city of Port Elizabeth (Eastern Cape); PE.

1844 J. EVATT in R. Godlonton *Mem. of British Settlers* 73 A rising City — the Liverpool of the colony; and I trust that I do not presume when I say, I hope to live to see Port Elizabeth *the Capital of the Colony.* **1870** H.H. DUGMORE *Reminisc. of Albany Settler* (1958) 15 Algoa Bay spread its broad bosom, and ship after ship bore its living freight to the last anchorage ... The 'Liverpool of the Cape' was not yet in existence, and a dreary barren looking waste met many a disappointed eye. **1881** F.R. STATHAM *Blacks, Boers & Brit.* 78 Port Elizabeth, the 'Liverpool of South Africa,' is the next point we have to aim at. **1884** *Cape Law Jrnl* I. 6 Mercantile men .. have .. vigorously pushed colonial commerce from the Liverpool of the Cape Colony to the distant and inaccessible parts of South Africa. **1888** *Cape Punch* 18 July 7 Possibly I, Tony Pearson, the relict of the South African Liverpool, might not have been born, dontcherknow, a poet. **1891** W. SELWYN *Cape Carols* 154 The Liverpool of Africa Has reached a sorry pass When country cousins laugh, 'Ha! ha! 'Yer can't pay fur yer gas.' **1893** *Cape Illust. Mag.* Jan. 182 [Port Elizabeth] is undoubtedly the principal maritime centre of South Africa, and has very aptly been termed 'The Liverpool of the Cape'. **1913** C. PETTMAN *Africanderisms* 297 *Liverpool of South Africa*, Port Elizabeth is sometimes so designated, but whether the designation is intended to be taken humorously, or as being anticipative, is somewhat uncertain. **1913** [see BAYONIAN]. **1934** C.P. SWART Supplement to Pettman. 107 *Liverpool of South Africa*, The popular name for Port Elizabeth, the chief trading centre of the Cape Province.

llandrost var. LANDDROST.

loan *n. hist.* [tr. Du. *leening* (found usu. in the comb. *leeningsplaats* loan farm, place).] A system of land tenure whereby farmers paid the Dutch East India Company 24 rix-dollars per annum for the use of a farm of about 3 000 morgen (approx. 2 400 hectares). Usu. *attrib.*, esp. in the n. phrr. ***loan farm, loan place*** [see PLACE], designating a farm held under such tenure; LEENINGS-PLAATS sense a. See also LEENINGS EIGENDOM, ORDONNANTIE, QUITRENT sense 2 a.

Introduced in 1717, the system was phased out under British rule, from 1813.

1798 EARL MACARTNEY in S.D. Naudé *Kaapse Plakkaatboek 1795–1803* (1950) 140, I am informed that many irregularities are practiced by the farmers, in the present mode of noting new places, intended for loan-places in the office of the collector of land-revenue. **1804** J. BARROW *Trav.* II. 380 The number of these loan farms registered in the office of the receiver of the land revenue, on closing the books in 1798, were .. 1832. **1806** *Ibid.* II. 56 Loan-farms .. are the usual kind of tenure in the colony. *Ibid.* 84 The most ancient tenure is that of Loan lands. These were grants made to the original settlers, of certain portions of land to be held on yearly leases on condition of paying to Government on arrival rent of twenty four rix-dollars. **1809** LORD CALEDON in G.M. Theal *Rec. of Cape Col.* (1900) VII. 185 *The Leening or Loan Place*, A loan place is generally speaking a grazing farm which embraces a space of one hour's walking (about three English miles) in diameter or half an hour's walking in each direction from the house or beacon whence it is to be measured. **1811** J.A. TRUTER in *Ibid.* VIII. (1901) 93 Under these three principal titles of possessions namely *loan, property, quit rent*, I conceive all lands in this Colony which are possessed with any right may and ought to be arranged. **1813** *Proclamation* in *Stat. Law of Cape of G.H.* (1862) 47 Every holder of a loan place, on his making application by memorial to the government for the purpose, shall have a grant on his place, on *perpetual quitrent.* **a1823** J. EWART *Jrnl* (1970) 42 Land Tax or Rent of Estates, which (with the exception of a few freeholds) are all held of government under the denomination of Loan Lands or Places, and at a rent for each place of twenty four rixdollars per annum, and the regular payment of this rent insures a perpetuity of the lease. **1843** J.C. CHASE *Cape of G.H.* 132 The tenures at present in use are — 1st, Freehold; 2nd, Loan; and 3rd, Perpetual Quitrent. **1844** *Ordinance* in *Stat. Law of Cape of G.H.* (1862) 689 The term 'land-rents due and in arrear' shall extend to and comprise quitrents, loanrents, and all other sorts of periodical payments to the colonial government arising out of lands and due and in arrear. **c1881** A. DOUGLASS *Ostrich Farming* 190 They continued to allow the Company's discharged servants and others to occupy patches of land, upon the payment of a small annual rental of £416s., called 'Quitrent,' and these patches were known as 'loan places'. As the community spread farther inland, and stock-raising became the main industry of the people, the size of these places came to be about 3, 000 morgen, or a little over 6,000 acres, which is recognised at the present day as the size of a full farm. **1902** [see LEENINGS-PLAATS sense a]. **1927** C.G. BOTHA *Social Life in Cape Col.* 11 The stock farmers .. occupied 'loan' places. A 'loan' place was one granted on lease for a year; the lease had to be renewed annually. The farmer chose a suitable grazing place for his stock and registered this with government. **1936** [see LEENINGS-PLAATS sense a]. **1941** C.W. DE KIEWIET *Hist. of S. Afr.* 16 In 1717 the Company decided to halt the issue of freehold land. Instead the farmer could obtain a 'loan farm' in return for an annual rent. **1963** R. LEWCOCK *Early 19th C. Archit.* 222 By October, 1814, Dr. Mackrill .. had chosen two loan farms which together might form the nucleus of the experimental agricultural station. **1966** E. PALMER *Plains of Camdeboo* 21 Probably in the 1770's the land was issued as a loan place and became the temporary property of one farmer. Loan farms were apportioned in the simplest possible way and were held at a nominal rent. **1980** *E. Prov. Herald* 30 May 3 Lombard's Post was a government loan farm granted to Peter Lombard in 1790. **1985** A. TREDGOLD *Bay between Mountains* 142 Bruyns applied in 1818 for the loan place of Vischhoek, measuring 1 308 morgen, to be granted to him under quit-rent. **1991** *Settler* Vol.65 No.1, Col. John Graham .. established military headquarters nearer the Fish River. The site he chose was De Rietfontein, a loan farm formerly occupied by Lucas Meyer.

Lobedu, Lovedu /lɔˈveːduː/ *n.* Also **loBedu.** Pl. **ba-**, unchanged, or **vha-**; occas. also **Balobelu.** [fr. N. Sotho *BaLobedu*, pl. form of *MoLobedu* a member of this people, prob. an early var. of *molobedi* one who pays tribute or homage (pl. *balobedi*), fr. *lobela* pay tribute or homage for, fr. *loba* pay tribute or homage; forms with *vha-* and *-vedu* are fr. the Venda spelling *VhaLovedu* (sing. *MuLovedu*). See also quot. 1979.] A member of a people of the Northern Sotho group, living mainly in the Northern Transvaal, among whom the RAIN QUEEN lives and over whom she rules. See also *North(ern) Sotho* (SOTHO sense 1 c). Also *attrib.*

1931 E. KRIGE in *Bantu Studies* V. 207 Among the Balobedu whose queen Modjadge is renowned for her great rain-making powers, rain ceremonies predominate. **1933** J. JUTA *Look Out for Ostriches* 97 Her Tribe, known as the *Lovedu*, is said to be an offshoot of the great migration of the Bantu race. **1943** E.J. & J.D. KRIGE *Realm of Rain-Queen* 52 The Lovedu is an individualist, but life is hardly regarded as a competitive struggle, even in respect of the things that are limited in supply. **1949** J. MOCKFORD *Golden Land* 156 The people Mujaji rules over are the Lovedu, peaceful tillers of the soil. Against warlike tribes such as the Zulu and Swazi, Mujaji balances her higher wisdom and supernatural mysteries. **1955** [see RAIN QUEEN]. **1974** A.P. CARTWRIGHT *By Waters of Letaba* 24 The tribe who call themselves the Lovedu, or 'the Modjadji's people', came into being early in the seventeenth century when one of the sons of Monomotapa quarrelled with his father and established a kingdom of his own. **1976** WEST & MORRIS *Abantu* 133 The Lobedu are not entirely typical of the North Sotho – in some ways they stand mid-way between the Sotho and the Venda. They are also unique in Southern Africa in that they are ruled by a queen. **1979** P. Miller *Myths & Legends* 203 Out of the hazy annals of tradition comes the strange, mystic story of Modjadji, the rain queen, and her people, the Lobedu. *Ibid.* 204 Modjadji's people waxed prosperous and contented from the wealth and gifts showered on their queen by the tribes who sought her magical talents. The land of Modjadji became known as *LoBedu* (the land of offerings), and her people as the baLobedu. **1980** *Sunday Times* 16 Nov. 11 The Vhalovedu were kept safe by their queens because chiefs from all over Southern Africa sent emissaries for help when their lands were hit by drought. **1982** *Ibid.* 21 Feb. (Mag. Sect.) 1 When she is installed as Modjadji V, Mokope will be expected to live out her years in seclusion in her village – also called Modjadji, the headquarters of the 100 000 strong Balobelu tribe. **1986** P. Maylam *Hist. of Afr. People* 50 The Lobedu chiefdom also falls within the northern Sotho area ... After 1800 the Lobedu were ruled by 'rain-queens', who attracted Pedi into their domains through their rain-making abilities. Gradually the Pedi language came to predominate among the Lobedu. **1988** H. Goosen in *S. Afr. Panorama* March 38 (*caption*) Modjadji the legendary rain queen. A dense cycad forest near her kraal has been protected for many generations by the Lovedu tribe. **1990** J. Knappert *Aquarian Guide to Afr. Mythology* 205 The Lovedu pride themselves on their female ancestry and give a high status to women, which is quite exceptional in Africa.

Hence (*nonce*) **Lobeduize** *v. trans.*, to assimilate (someone) into this people.

1943 E.J. & J.D. Krige *Realm of Rain-Queen* 174 The queen has accepted wives even from the Shangana-Tonga, .. and after a time they become sufficiently Loveduized to be given in marriage to commoners.

lobola /lɔˈbɔ(ː)la, lə-, ləˈbəʊlə/ *n.* Also **ilobola, labola, labolo, lobolo, lubolo.** [Zulu and Xhosa, see LOBOLA *v.* Forms ending *-lo* are fr. Zulu *ilobolo* the goods (etc.) given.]

1. The custom among many southern African peoples of giving cattle, goods, or (now usu.) money to the parents of a woman or girl in order to secure her hand in marriage; BOGADI sense 1; UKULOBOLA. Also *attrib.*

1892 J.E. Ritchie *Brighter S. Afr.* 160 These courts recognise, and are often called upon to adjudicate upon, cases arising out of .. the custom of paying cattle for the wives the Kaffir male desires so ardently, not as a matter of affection, but that they may save him from the need of working for his own living, which custom, by-the-bye, is denominated lobola. **1897** F.W. Sykes *With Plumer in Matabeleland* 7 In exchange for cattle he can purchase a wife or wives – the recognised ratio being ten to one; this matrimonial custom, known as 'lobola,' can be directly traced to their Zulu ancestry. **1905** *Westminster Gaz.* (U.K.) 19 Apr. 9 The native custom of passing cattle, known variously as 'lobolo', 'ikazi', and 'bohadi', in connexion with marriage. **1918** H. Moore *Land of Good Hope* 58 We must not think of this 'lobolo' as simply a matter of buying and selling flesh and blood. *c*1936 *S. & E. Afr. Yr Bk & Guide* 241 *Lobolo*, the regulations affecting marriage, has been described as supporting the whole social structure of the race. The cattle, which pass to the bride's family, are in effect a kind of dowry with added religious significance, and the Economic Commission (1932) deprecates in strong terms any interference with the custom. **1947** E.R. Seary *S. Afr. Short Stories* 230 Lobola .. may be defined as a contract between a father and the intending husband of his daughter, whereby the father promises his consent to the marriage of his daughter, and by which he receives from the bridegroom-elect valuable consideration (usually several head of cattle) partly to compensate him for the loss of his daughter's services, and partly as a guarantee by the intending husband of his good conduct towards such daughter as wife. **1948** A. Paton *Cry, Beloved Country* 240 The custom of lobola, by which a man pays for his wife in cattle. **1968** E.A. Walker *Hist. of Sn Afr.* 250 Why was lobola, the basis of their family life, the giving of the sacred cattle which legitimised the children of the wife for whom they were given, condemned as 'the sin of buying wives'? **1982** *Voice* 18 July 4 Lobola leads to exploitation. **1982** *Drum* Oct. 60 Let's face it, lobola has gone commercial. And while most of our youth acknowledge that it is a custom to be revered, they are increasingly beginning to question the fact that parents are using it to make huge profits. **1988** *Style* June 96 Among African tribes, the system of Lobola exists whereby gifts are given, not so much to the couple, but to the bride's family as compensation for their loss. **1991** N. Mbatha in *Pace* Sept. 49 Perhaps because of its inescapable link to money, lobola is seen as the most controversial of all old customs.

2. Goods, cattle, or money given as dowry according to traditional African custom; BOGADI sense 2; IKHAZI. Also *attrib.* Cf. NGQUTHU.

1898 B. Mitford *Induna's Wife* 91 She was young and good-tempered, and was a daughter of Xulawayo, an induna of rank, and a commander of high standing in the army, by reason of which he demanded much cattle in lobola for her, all of which I paid him without objection. **1899** A. Werner *Captain of Locusts* 50 I'd not long been married. I'd paid the last of the lobola cattle, but I hadn't brought her home, and that was just as well, as it turned out. **1936** *Cambridge Hist. of Brit. Empire* VIII. 818 Cattle played an essentially important part in marriage customs. Lobola or the bride price was paid in cattle to the family of the young man's bride ... While the lobola for chiefs on the eastern frontier could be as high as twenty head of cattle, for an ordinary tribesman the amount lay between four and ten head. This figure would appear to hold for most native tribes and does not seem to have varied greatly during the century. *c*1948 H. Tracey *Lalela Zulu* 40 The young man who wishes to get married must first find the lobolo, or 'bride sum'. It represents a kind of social security between the two families involved. In the old days it was usually found in cattle and gifts but nowadays the young townsman who has no cattle has to find money instead. **1955** J.B. Shephard *Land of Tikoloshe* 32 *Lobola* is as much an insurance premium as a payment, for, if a wife is so badly treated by her husband that she runs back to her father's kraal for protection, her husband will find it difficult to get his money back. In so far as it safeguards the woman, the custom of *lobola* is wholly good. **1957** G. Muldoon *Trumpeting Herd* 95 According to the Angoni custom, the aunts and not the parents are responsible for fixing the Lobola, or payment for the bride. **1967** J.A. Broster *Red Blanket Valley* 144 Lobola is often paid on the instalment system. When the girl is taken in marriage it is common practice to pay four or five cattle, and then a year or two later or maybe twenty years later, the final instalment is paid. **1971** *Nat. Geog. Mag.* Dec. 754 This bridegroom has presented lobolo – bridewealth – to the girl's father. The payment, usually 11 head of cattle, legalizes the marriage and legitimizes children born to the couple. **1974** *Drum* 8 July 48, I not only paid R300 lobola but used to send her money to support her as my wife. **1976** West & Morris *Abantu* 38 Like that of the Xhosa, Zulu marriage is a contract between families and clans as well as between individuals. Its traditional form involves elaborate protocol, exchange of gifts, lobola, ritual killings, dancing and feasts. **1977** S.M. Maphobole in *Weekend World* 19 June 131, I read that your readers suggested that lobolo should be abolished. But I am very much against this ... In my opinion the girls' parents should take the lobolo, but hand it back on the wedding day to the newly weds. **1978** A. Elliott *Sons of Zulu* 168 In the present times 'ten plus one' head of cattle is the lobolo figure for a virgin. The 'one' is to compensate her mother for the sadness of losing a daughter and the 'ten' cattle are for her father. **1982** *Pace* June 2f, I .. support the anti-lobola campaign. I say to African fathers and mothers that no daughter of Africa is worth R2000 or more because no daughter owes her father her life. **1982** *Drum* Oct. 60 My parents put me through university and now they want R4 000 from the man who wants to marry me. How can they expect us to raise a family and build a home when the lobola debt will keep us in poverty for the rest of our lives? **1984** *Ibid.* Jan. 42 Lobola is a cultural thing to us Africans not only in South Africa alone but on the whole continent, Mother Africa. We are not paying lobola, we are giving lobola. Paying lobola has negative connotations. Lobola is the means of bonding two different families and making them one. **1990** R. Stengel *January Sun* 154 *Lobola*, Life says, is actually a Zulu word, but it has been accepted by the Tswanas. *Lobola* is the dividend paid to parents for their investment in their daughter. Nowadays *lobola* is paid in money. Formerly, it consisted of cattle and goods. **1992** N. Mbatha in *Pace* Sept. 49 While an overwhelming majority of Africans still agree on the payment of lobola, the area of dispute is the ever-rising 'fee' that grooms must pay.

3. *Fig.*, and *transf.*

1972 *Evening Post* 22 July 2 Mr J.J. Barkhuizen of Despatch successfully offered 'lobola' for his 'lonely year-old dog, looking for a wife'. **1973** *E. Prov. Herald* 26 Mar. 7 'Lobola' system illegal on frontier. Three of Pakistan's four provinces are taking steps to end or curb the wedding dowry custom. **1982** *Voice* 10 Jan. 4 Lobola will always be a contentious issue whichever way one looks at it. However, in Nigeria it is handled with a difference ... No lobola will exceed the stipulated $90 price, following a recommendation by the National Council of Women's Societies. **1987** *New Nation* 24 Sept. 3 Evidence has been heard that Prime Minister George Matanzima was paid R1-million 'lobola' by a construction firm which later got a R30-million contract. **1992** J. Drew in *Weekly Mail* 24 Apr. 11 It is a heavy price to pay for two relatively mediocre meetings ... But this is the *lobola* that has had to be paid to gain Nebiola's approval for the South African entry into the IAAF ahead of the Barcelona Olympics.

lobola /lɔˈbɔ(ː)la, lə-, ləˈbəʊlə/ *v.* Also **lubola, lubolo.** [Zulu and Xhosa, give (goods, cattle, etc.) to a woman's parents in order to secure her hand in marriage.]

1. *intrans. rare.* To pay a dowry according to the custom of lobola.

1836 N. Isaacs *Trav.* (1936) I. 40 Jacob had become enamoured of Enslopee's sister, and had sent three head of cattle to 'Loboler,' [*printed* lololer] when it was understood, that the girl was to have been sent by the persons who drove the cattle. **1908** F.C. Slater *Sunburnt South* Glossary, *Lobola*, To pay dowry.

2. *trans.*

a. To secure the hand of (a girl or woman) in marriage by giving lobola to her parents; to marry (her) in this way.

[**1857** J. Shooter *Kafirs of Natal* 48 The verb for buy is *tenga*; but when a Kafir speaks of 'buying' a wife, he uses the verb *lobola*, which means to take away a cutting, and figuratively to remove a pain. It would seem therefore that the word, when applied to the giving of cattle for a girl, refers to the pains which the mother endured in bearing and nurturing her; and that they were originally given to remove those pains – that is, to reward her for them.] **1875** D. Leslie *Among Zulus* 170 The one just lobola'd or married – goes into the house of her from whom he took the first cattle. **1923** G.H. Nicholls *Bayete!* 121 It was generally known tha Mbojoni had lubolo'd Martha, and she was therefore considered as his wife. Nobody would come forward with more cattle unless he were a stranger. **1937** B.H. Dicke *Bush Speaks* 269 The doctor claims the girl as a wife whom he has lobolaed (paid the woman's value to her family for). But, no lobola has passed. **1948** E. Hellmann *Rooiyard* 81 As one informant explained it, 'if a man *lobola* a woman, he can *lobola* many more. If he married her in court he can't take more wives. Because then I can put him in trouble.' **1965** P. Baragwanath *Brave Remain* 4 As you did not work for those cattle with which the young girl is to be lobolaed, or herd them in your youth, you must be guided by your mother. **1970** M. Dikobe Marabi Dance. 107 She wanted to find out whether the Ndalas had cattle to lobola her.

b. *transf. rare.* To secure custody of (an illegitimate child) by giving cattle, money, or goods to the family of the child's mother.

1952 *Drum* Feb. 23 In some tribes there is a practice whereby the natural father can 'lobola' or 'buy' such child and in this way obtain the custody of it.

local is lekker see LEKKER *adj.* sense 1 b.

locate *v. trans. Obs.* [Special sense of general Eng. *locate* to establish oneself in a place, to settle.] Usu. *passive.* Of persons: to be placed in or on a LOCATION (senses 1 a and 2); to be allocated land in a location.

1846 *Natal Witness* 10 Apr. 1 At present the natives are located – according to their own choice of land – they grow more than sufficient for their own consumption. **1851** J.J. FREEMAN *Tour* 361 They are located by the Government, and on these locations they cultivate lands and build their native huts. **1858** J. GOLDSWAIN *Chron.* (1946) I. 21 The place ware we was Located [was] just in a line with jargers Drift. **1875** D. LESLIE *Among Zulus* 306 These natives are *located* i.e., portions of the land of Natal are laid off for occupation by them.

location *n.* [Special senses of general Eng. *location* place.]

I. Rural.

1. *Obs.* exc. *hist.* A smallholding or farm.

a. An area of land granted in 1820 to a group (or 'party') of British settlers on the eastern frontier of the Cape Colony, and divided up for individual possession; PARTY sense 2. **b.** The farm granted to an individual settler (or settler family) from the party's land.

1820 G. BARKER Journal. 17 Apr., Mr Bailey's party left the Bay for their location. **1820** E.S. PIGOT Journal. 25 Dec., The D[algairn]s went to Mr Bailey's location to a dance. **1827** G. THOMPSON *Trav.* II. 171 Many families were .. reduced to great distress ... They naturally clung to their own locations; for .. they were all that remained to them of property. **1835** C.L. STRETCH Journal., The Govt had to issue a Proclamation forbidding Settlers to leave their Locations without a written pass signed by the Landdrost. **1870** H.H. DUGMORE *Reminisc. of Albany Settler* 9 But now to return to the first arrival 'on the location'. It was a forlorn-looking plight in which we found ourselves, when the Dutch waggoners had emptied us and our luggage on to the green-sward, and left us sitting on our boxes and bundles. **1870** *Ibid.* [see PASS sense 1]. **1876** T. STUBBS Reminiscences. 11 After the Settlers arrived on their Locations, they were not allowed to go to Town without a pass except the heads of Parties. **1936** *Cambridge Hist. of Brit. Empire* VIII. 237 Ox-waggons were hired from farmers .. to convey the settlers to the locations which had been allotted to them. **1948** H.E. HOCKLY *Story of Brit. Settlers of 1820* 59 The Settlers .. were literally dumped down on the locations. **1963** R. LEWCOCK *Early 19th C. Archit.* 145 After December 1821, when those settlers who wished to were at last permitted to leave their locations and to settle in the near-by towns, crafts were established. **1970** *Cape Times* 7 Sept., When the Settlers arrived .. they found themselves shepherded into various 'locations' to provide a buffer strip against the Caffres ... The word 'location' persists to this day, and its application is not all that different to its application to the Settlers, for they were indeed placed in position and told to stay put. **1988** P. EDGAR in *Personality* 25 July 68 The removing of all military protection from the Coombs Valley locations had allowed cattle theft to grow alarmingly.

c. *transf. obs.* A small area of land owned or occupied by any group or individual.

1828 J. PHILIP *Researches* II. 253 An industrious Hottentot .. possessed a small location in this vicinity. **1833** *S. Afr. Almanac & Dir.* 191 The population consists of a mixture of Bastards and Hottentots, who are divided into about 60 parties, each of which has a distinct location allotted to it. **1837** J. AYLIFF Journal. 19 Aug., I found it [*sc.* Fort Beaufort] in a state of the greatest excitement and confusion, arising from the forcible removal of the Fingoes from their Locations. **1841** B. SHAW *Memorials* 243 If government give them any thing like protection, the location of the Clusie River will soon become a fruitful village. **1843** *Cape of G.H. Almanac & Annual Register* 344 A tract of land situated on the S side of the town has been divided into 24 locations occupied chiefly by labourers of Hottentot descent.

d. *hist.* An area of land on a farm, set aside by the farmer for his labourers to occupy and cultivate. Also *attrib.*

1843 J.C. CHASE *Cape of G.H.* 253 One extensive wine-merchant possesses a good farm, several small locations, 2500 wool sheep, 150 cattle and two waggons. **1894** E. GLANVILLE *Fair Colonist* 209 That is what our politicians ask us to do when they amended the Location Act ... They will not have native locations on private farms. *c*1953 P. ABRAHAMS *Return to Goli* 18 Each house stood in a small piece of fenced-off land. And the land belonged to the farmer for whom the people of the location worked. **1985** PLATZKY & WALKER *Surplus People* 75 Most of the Africans living on white farms were fulltime servants. Some were cash tenants or sharecroppers on what came to be known as 'private locations' – white-owned land given over entirely by its owner to African tenants.

2. *Obs.* exc. *hist.* Esp. in Natal: RESERVE. Occas. with qualifying word, **rural location**. Also *attrib.*

1846 'MYSON' in *Natal Witness* 13 Mar., Presuming that it is the intention of the Government to appoint them spots for permanent locations .. , a land tax will be .. reasonable. **1846** *Natal Witness* 10 Apr. 1 Among other supposed disadvantages that may be anticipated from the Location System, will be the abstraction of the labouring population from the midst of those colonists who can now obtain their services at a moderate rate of remuneration. **1852** M.B. HUDSON *S. Afr. Frontier Life* p.xi, The port of the Buffalo (East London) is situated in his [*sc.* Pato's] location. **1855** W.C. HOLDEN *Hist. of Col. of Natal* 176 The plan of government devised was, to preserve the Natives distinct from the whites; and, for this purpose, large tracts of country were set aside, under the designation of 'Locations for the Natives.' On these Locations the Natives were to be collected, and governed by their own laws, through the medium of their own chiefs. **1856** G. GREY in *Imp. Blue Bks* Command Paper 2352–1857, 37 Each tribe inhabits a separate district of country, called here a location. **1860** D.C.F. MOODIE Letter. 31 Dec., The Lieut. Governor could not properly have allowed you to take that land in a locality which has long been said to be part of a Native Location. **1864** 'A LADY' *Life at Natal* (1972) 36 Close behind is a 'kafir location', a tract of country set apart for natives. **1875** D. LESLIE *Among Zulus* 306 Each tribe holds a title from the Government. The people, however, are at liberty to, and thousands of them do, reside on private property, if they prefer the locality, and can arrange with the proprietor. Much has been said against this system of locations. **1884** *Cape Law Jrnl* I. 333 These cattle were registered by the Inspector of Locations, under the Native Locations Act. **1901** *Natives of S. Afr.* (S. Afr. Native Races Committee) 75 A .. similar system was prepared for the Glen Grey location. The land had been surveyed into thirty farms, each farm had its headman, and each four or five farms had a superior headman over them. **1909** *Illust. London News* (U.K.) 8 Jan. The 32 Native areas which equal 2421 square miles – are probably enough for the present; but eventually .. will become what the Native Locations are in Natal. **1913** W.B. BERRY in *Hansard* 5 June 3134 Apart altogether from the locations, there were in his district natives who owned large farms. **1913** C. PETTMAN *Africanderisms* 298 *Location,* In Natal the term refers to certain large tracts of land which are firmly secured by Government to the natives. Each such 'location' is suitable for a population of from 10,000 to 12,000, and is the property of the tribe collectively. **1941** C.W. DE KIEWIET *Hist. of S. Afr.* 74 The Commission worked in the popular belief that Natal's natives should be expelled northwards .. , leaving behind only enough to satisfy the need for labour ... It was an important achievement for the Commission to establish eight locations with a total area of 1,168,000 acres. **1948** O. WALKER *Kaffirs Are Lively* 45 Bokwe did not seek a practice in the cities. He returned to the location he had known as a child. **1969** *Survey of Race Rel.* (S.A.I.R.R.) 132 The planning of rural locations (tribal areas) .. involves the demarcation of arable, grazing, and residential areas; the fencing of grazing camps and provision of watering points. **1971** *The 1820* Vol.43 No.10, 13 My father, as Chief Inspector of Locations in Natal, had gone up to northern Zululand to settle a grazing dispute. **1973** M. HORRELL *Afr. Homelands* 137 After a rural location has been planned, the residents are persuaded gradually to move their dwellings to demarcated residential areas. **1979** DUMINY & ADCOCK *Reminisc. of Richard Paver* 3 All the countryside this side of the Great Kei River will .. in all probability be divided into farms and locations, some of which will be peopled with its original possessors. **1989** *Reader's Digest Illust. Hist.* 155 In 1846 a so-called Locations Commission was set up [in Natal] to explore a proposal .. to establish 'six or more locations, keeping them, if possible, a little way removed from the contaminating influence of the chief town and port'.

II. *obsolescent.* Urban.

3.a. TOWNSHIP sense 2 a. Also *attrib.*

Occas. used of a residential area for any group which was not white (see quots 1903, 1956, 1977). 'Location' is now avoided by many, being replaced by 'township'.

1880 E.F. SANDEMAN *Eight Months in Ox-Waggon* 31 At seven o'clock at night the 'curfew' bell tolls. After that every kaffir found in the town, or away from his location, is put in 'trunk,' as the goal is denominated throughout South Africa. **1882** J. NIXON *Among Boers* 131 The natives are not allowed to live in the town, but reside in a 'location' assigned to them outside it. **1899** B. MITFORD *Weird of Deadly Hollow* 215 For the rest, this important centre boasted a population of about four hundred persons – white, that is; for a squalid 'location' just outside the town proper, harboured as many more of every shade and colour. **1903** LORD MILNER in *Indian Opinion* 4 June (Suppl.), Suppose for a moment that some great Indian aristocrat, some man of wealth and education, .. were to come to live here, .. would you insist upon his being sent to a location? **1908** M.C. BRUCE *New Tvl* 12 The coloured races have their own locations, customs and schools, and the laws regarding colour are very stringent. **1914** S.P. HYATT *Old Transport Rd* 72 The native population lived outside the township, in a filthy collection of hovels called the Location. **1922** S.G. MILLIN *Adam's Rest* 67 Sometimes Miriam took it on herself to visit the location. It lay, like an eruption, on the face of the hill. Not anywhere near the location was there a tree or any green thing planted by a living agency. **1942** *Star* 30 Dec. 5 The death roll in the native riot in Marabastad location, near Pretoria, .. has risen to 17. **1953** LANHAM & MOPELI-PAULUS *Blanket Boy's Moon* 33 'Is the Moruti staying in Johannesburg?' 'Yes, I stay at Orlando township – that big location we are now approaching.' **1956** N. GORDIMER in D. Wright *S. Afr. Stories* (1960) 71 He had accompanied Jake to a shebeen in a coloured location. **1968** COLE & FLAHERTY *House of Bondage* 54 The term, 'location' is deliberate: Since the African is regarded as an abstraction, without status or meaning in society, his physical displacement is also defined vaguely, rather than in terms of an entity whose inhabitants have legal rights and real responsibilities. **1977** A. ROSCOE *Uhuru's Fire* 233 Coloured locations are generally more salubrious than the infamous ghettoes of Orlando, Soweto and Marabastad. **1978** A.P. BRINK *Rumours of Rain* 110 You will be allowed to work in our industrial areas, provided you leave your families behind, you live in locations or in compounds, and you be excluded from performing skilled work. **1979** W. EBERSOHN *Lonely Place* 64 It was the standard South African pattern. There was no town that did not have its location close by. Without it where would the shops find delivery boys, or the coal-yard its labourers, or Mrs van Schalkwyk her kitchen maid? **1980** D.B. COPLAN Urbanization of African Performing Arts. 434 *Location,* Obsolete official and colloquial designation for an authorized African residential area.

1982 D. Bikitsha in *Rand Daily Mail* 14 Oct. (Eve) 5 New styles and modes of living mushroomed all over locations before we called them townships. 1986 *Learn & Teach* No.3, 9 If we give up, they will put us in a location. But we are farmers. You cannot keep cows in a location. 1988 E. Mphahlele *Renewal Time* 110 It was a letter from the location's white superintendent telling Karel that he would have to leave house No. 35 Mathole Street where he was known to live, and was forbidden from occupying any other house in Corner B as he was registered 'coloured' and should not be in a 'Bantu location'. 1990 *Weekend Mail* 14 Sept. 7 The first townships, known then as 'locations', were given names that were memorials to people — Sophiatown outside Johannesburg after the wife of a land developer; Lady Selborne beyond Pretoria for the wife of a colonial master, and kwa-Mashu in Durban is the Zulu corruption of Marshal, the name of the farmer who previously owned the land.

b. In the phr. ***location in the sky***, see quot. 1967.

1957 D. Rycroft in *Afr. Music* Vol.1 No.4, 33 Any evening of the week in Johannesburg, small groups of Bombing enthusiasts are to be heard rehearsing in hostel rooms, on balconies, in back yards or in the servant's quarters at the top of luxury blocks of flats (nicknamed 'locations in the sky'). 1968 Cole & Flaherty *House of Bondage* 92 In luxury apartment buildings the servant's quarters are usually built atop the flat roof — a double row of connecting cell-like rooms humorously referred to as 'locations in the sky'.

c. *comb.* **location boy** *rare*, see quot. See also TSOTSI sense 1. Cf. BOY sense 1 b.

1963 Wilson & Mafeje *Langa* 22 The *townees* or *tsotsis* are also called *'location boys'*.

Hence **locationized** *adj. nonce*, placed in locations.

1971 *Daily Dispatch* 16 Oct. 8 The Coloureds in the Kliptown-Eldorado are locationised with rows upon rows of bee-hive type homes, no sidewalks, dusty streets with dark streets.

lock-shoe *n. Hist. Wagon-making.* [tr. Du. *remschoen*, see REMSKOEN.

The English word 'brake' in the sense 'motion-retarding device' first appeared in 1782 (according to the *OED*), so a translator of the time would have been influenced by the idiom of the language being translated (Swedish for both Sparrman and Thunberg) in his choice of a word for this device. Dutch is, however, the ultimate origin.]

REMSKOEN sense 1.

1786 G. Forster tr. *A. Sparrman's Voy. to Cape of G.H.* I. 124 In order that .. the wheel that is to be *locked* may not be worn, .. a kind of sledge carriage, hollowed out on the inside, and called a lock-shoe is fitted to it. 1795 C.R. Hopson tr. *C.P. Thunberg's Trav.* II. 111 Dorn-hout (*Mimosa nilotica*) is used for *Lock-shoes*, to put under waggon wheels. 1804 R. Percival *Acct of Cape of G.H.* 60 Sometimes they are obliged to drag all four wheels, and have for this purpose a machine they call a lock-shoe being a kind of sledge or trough shod with iron into which the wheels are set. 1822 [see REMSKOEN sense 1]. 1913 C. Pettman *Africanderisms* 299 Sometimes a 'lock-shoe' or 'riemschoen' was employed into which the wheel was slipped and secured, saving enormously in wear and tear. All this has .. been superceded by the patent-screw brake. 1927 C.G. Botha *Social Life in Cape Col.* 91 This lockshoe, or as the Dutch called it 'remschoen,' was a great destroyer of the roads. 1967 E. Rosenthal *Encycl. of Sn Afr.* 320 *Lock-Shoe*, A device locked into the side of a wheel to prevent wagons skidding downhill.

locust-bird *n.* Also with initial capitals. Any of several birds that feed on locusts. **1.** Formerly also with distinguishing epithet, **great locust-bird**: either of two storks of the Ciconiidae, the white stork *Ciconia ciconia*, or the whitebellied stork *Ciconia abdimii*. **2.** Formerly also with defining word, **small locust-bird**: **a.** Any of several species of Pratincole, esp. *Glareola nordmanni* of the Glareolidae; **b.** the wattled starling *Creatophora cinerea* of the Sturnidae. In these senses also called LOCUST DESTROYER, LOCUST-EATER, *sprinkaanvoel* (see SPRINKAAN sense 2).

The name 'locust-bird' is also used elsewhere, but refers to a bird not found in South Africa.

1832 *Graham's Town Jrnl* 24 Feb. 34 The Locust Bird has at last visited this district in such numbers, that there is every prospect of a deliverance from the Locusts now in their larval state. 1856 R.E.E. Wilmot *Diary* (1984) 39 It is curious to see the enormous numbers of so-called *'locust birds'* which hang about the veld now. They are really storks, with black tipped wings, red beaks and legs, and very similar to the Asia Minor variety. *Ibid.* 133 The great *locust bird* or red legged stork ... More abundant this year than has ever been known. 1867 E.L. Layard *Birds of S. Afr.* 291 Glareola Nordmanni ... Small Locust-bird of Colonists. *Ibid.* 314 Ciconia Alba, .. The White Stork, Gould .. Great Locust-Bird of Colonists. 1874 Froude *S. Afr. Notes* 13 Dec., An army of locust-birds. *a*1875 T. Baines *Jrnl of Res.* (1964) II. 30 McCabe shot a locust bird about the size of a small pigeon but in almost every other respect resembling a swallow. 1881 E.E. Frewer tr. *E. Holub's Seven Yrs in S. Afr.* I. 42 The bird was really the South African grey crane, to which the residents have given the name of 'the great locust bird'. 1899 R.B. & J.D.S. Woodward *Natal Birds* 200 It [*sc.* the white stork *Ciconia alba*] consumes large quantities of locusts, and so earns for itself the title of 'Great locust-bird.' 1900 Stark & Sclater *Birds of S. Afr.* I. 23 *Dilophus carunculatus*, Wattled Starling ... 'Locust Bird' of English Colonists. 1903 A.R.E. Burton *Cape Col. for Settler* 11 The white stork of Europe is known here as the 'great locust bird.' 1910 A.B. Lamont *Rural Reader* 31 The smaller locust birds follow swarms, cleverly snip off the wings of the locusts as they fly. 1923 Haagner & Ivy *Sketches* 10 The next two species which are also known by the vernacular name of Small Locust Bird, are the two Pratincoles (*Glareola pratincola* and *G. melanoptera*). *Ibid.* 13 The last of the 'Locust' Birds is the White-bellied Stork (*Abdimia abdimii*), a slightly glossy black bird with a white back and white underparts. 1936 E.L. Gill *First Guide to S. Afr. Birds* 141 *Wattled Starling*, .. Locust-Bird ... Roving birds, appearing almost anywhere for a time in flocks and disappearing again. Called Locust-bird because they used (before man tried his hand at controlling the pest) to follow the swarms of locusts, living on them and nesting *en masse* wherever the locusts happened to settle and breed. 1949 U. Long *Chron. of Jeremiah Goldswain* II. 104 Several species are colloquially called 'Locust birds'. Goldswain refers to Wattled Starlings — *creatophora carunculata*. 1953 R. Campbell *Mamba's Precipice* 47 Flocks of .. locust birds, descended and perched among the reeds. 1967 E. Rosenthal *Encycl. of Sn Afr.* 533 The wattled starling .. is a fawn-grey bird .. ; known too as the Locust-bird from its habit of following swarms of locusts and nesting in crowds where they settle. 1972 G.J. Broekhuysen in *Std Encycl. of Sn Afr.* VII. 19 *Locust-Bird*, A number of birds belonging to different families are called locust-birds in Southern Africa ... They include the pratincoles .. , the wattled starling .. , and storks, particularly the white stork .. and the white-bellied stork. 1978 McLachlan & Liversidge *Roberts Birds of S. Afr.* 524 *Creatophora cinerea* ... *Habits:* A locally abundant species which moves restlessly about the country in small parties or very large flocks ... Follows locust swarms ... *Food:* Locusts — hence the popular name 'locust-bird'.

locust destroyer *n. phr. Obs.* LOCUST-BIRD (prob. sense 2).

1801 G. Yonge in G.M. Theal *Rec. of Cape Col.* (1898) III. 428 An Immense Flight of Birds .. fell upon them and in a short time, there was not a Locust left alive ... The Boors call them emphatically, the Locust Destroyers, and have no other name for them.

locust-eater *n. obs.* LOCUST-BIRD sense 2.

1806 J. Barrow *Trav.* I. 211 Our boors .. immediately recognised the bird to be the locust-eater ... This species of thrush .. is only met with in places where the migrating locust frequents ... Its whole food seems to consist of the larvae of this insect. 1810 G. Barrington *Acct of Voy.* 300 The African thrush, or locust-eater, .. is about the size of a common sky-lark.

loeper var. LOOPER.

loerie /ˈluːri, ˈlʊəri/ *n.* Also **louri(e)**, and (formerly) **laurie**, **loeri**, **loorie**, **lori(e)**, **lorrie**, **lo(w)ry**, **luri(e)**. [Afk., fr. S. Afr. Du., fr. Du. *lori*, ad. Malay *luri* (dial. form of *nuri* parrot).]

1.a. Any of several species of touraco, birds of the Musophagidae which are characterized by their prominent crests and often brilliant plumage. Also *attrib.*

Ornithologists now prefer the anglicized spelling 'lourie', but general usage tends to follow the Afrikaans form 'loerie'. (In *Brit. Eng.* the form 'lory' is commonly used.)

1776 F. Masson in *Phil. Trans. of Royal Soc.* LXVI. 294 At night we came to Lory's River, so called from a species of parrot, which is found here. 1790 W. Paterson *Narr. of Four Journeys* 81 The Lorie River derives its name from a species of that bird, which is found in the woods on its banks. 1798 [see SUGARBIRD]. 1804 R. Percival *Acct of Cape of G.H.* 168 Besides the common lowries there is a species peculiar to the Cape. 1812 A. Plumptre tr. *H. Lichtenstein's Trav. in Sn Afr.* (1928) I. 195 The *cuculus persa*, a beautiful bird, called by the colonists *loeri* or *luri*. It has brilliant green feathers, with scarlet wings, a green crown tipped with red, and a red bill. 1850 J.S. Christopher *Natal* 33 The beautiful and soft-voiced loerie, the golden cuckoo, the green pigeon .. and many others too numerous to particularise. 1853 F.P. Fleming *Kaffraria* 73 Another local misnomer is that of the Lory of the Amatola, whose short, high, compressed beak, raised crest, and rounded, short wing, but long fan-like tail, all of a dark purple green, and crimson and violet quills, at once claim for it the genus of *Corythaix*, or Touraco. 1860 A.W. Drayson *Sporting Scenes* 59 Many birds, brilliantly adorned, frequented the forests, amongst which the golden cuckoo and the lowry were conspicuous. 1862 'A Lady' *Life at Cape* (1963) 107 He was kind enough .. to give me the lovely 'lourie' wing, which he tells me is obtained from a rare bird in the Knysna forests ... When flying in the sun, they glitter all over like burnished metal with the lustrous green and deep claret hues of their feathers. 1893 *Brown's S. Afr.* 162 The slopes are densely wooded and afford shelter to many beautiful birds, foremost among which is the lori, a large bird of the parrot tribe with green and red plumage. 1907 W.C. Scully *By Veldt & Kopje* 46 The red-winged, green-crested lories flitted with noiseless undulations from tree to tree or waked strident echoes with their hoarse- throated calls. 1923 Haagner & Ivy *Sketches* 182 The family Musophagidae (*Plaintain* [*sic*] *Eaters*) contains some of the handsomest birds in South Africa, the best known of which is the Knysna Plaintain Eater or Common Lourie. 1940 A. Roberts *Birds of S. Afr.* 135 The Louries or Touracoes are peculiar to Africa and their relationship to other birds is not quite clear, though they are placed between the Parrots and Cuckoos by most authorities. 1968 G. Croudace *Black Rose* 88 'Go'way, go'way.' The sudden alarm call of the lourie startled her. 1981 P. Ginn *Birds Afield* 75 We have three species of loerie in southern Africa ... They all have harsh calls which are distinctive. 1988 M. Stansfield in *Weekend Argus* 1 Oct. 22 Loeries? Best-tasting bird in the bush — 'course we aren't allowed to catch them for food anymore. 1991 *Settler* Vol.65 No.1, Except for festival wear, leopard skin is reserved for chiefs as are the red feathers of the loerie bird.

b. With distinguishing epithet, denoting a particular species of the Musophagidae: **grey loerie**, the bushveld bird *Corythaixoides concolor*, unusual in its plain grey colouring and strident warning cry; GO-AWAY sense 1; KWÊVOËL; **Knysna loerie**, the forest bird *Tauraco corythaix*, distinguished by its predominantly green plumage and white-tipped crest; **purple-crested loerie**, the tropical bird *Tauraco porphyreolophus*, distinguished by its purple crest, black bill, and the lengthy sequence of its call. See also BUSH LORY, *vlei loerie* (VLEI sense 2).

1881 [grey loerie: see GO-AWAY sense 1]. **1928** E.H.L. SCHWARZ *Kalahari & its Native Races* 66 There is the grey lorrie, who looks at you and utters a querulous 'Why?' **1933** J. JUTA *Look Out for Ostriches* 154 From the denser thickets .. the Grey Lourie kept uttering its cry of 'Go away, go away.' **1948** A.C. WHITE *Call of Bushveld* 257 The grey lourie is probably spoken of more often by visitors to the bushveld than any other bird. This is due to their persistent ordering of human beings from their own domain. **1951** T.V. BULPIN *Lost Trails of Low Veld* 268 Among the less co-operative birds, or perhaps just one that understands the human being, is Nkwenyane, the Grey Lourie, with his harshly unmistakeable cry of 'go away.' **1967** E. ROSENTHAL *Encycl. of Sn Afr.* 323 The Grey Lourie (Go-Away Bird) of bush country gives a warning cry when disturbed by hunters, and is seen in small groups. **1971** [see GO-AWAY sense 2]. **1987** D. KENMUIR *Tusks & Talisman* 60 A grey lourie landed in a nearby tree and called out harshly, 'Go way, go way!' **1993** S. GRAY in *Weekly Mail & Guardian* 5 Nov. 48 Penetrate past the jacarandas a few yards and the Grey Loeries hurl abuse. [**1923** **Knysna loerie**: see sense 1 a.] **1940** A. ROBERTS *Birds of S. Afr.* 137 *Knysna Lourie* ... This species is restricted to South Africa, occuring only in the evergreen forests of Knysna eastwards to Natal. **1976** WEST & MORRIS *Abantu* 66 (*caption*) The dancers are joined by the royal princesses who are distinguished by the vivid red feathers of the Knysna Loerie worn in their hair. **1986** *Fair Lady* 30 Apr. 24 For bird watchers, there's abundant bird-life including the famed Knysna loerie which flashes green and crimson through the trees. **1990** *Evening Post* 2 Feb. 5 You may see the unforgettable scarlet brilliance of a Knysna loerie. **1908** HAAGNER & IVY *Sketches* 109 (Pettman), The **Purple-crested Lourie** (*Gallirex porphyreolophus*) is the commoner species in the Northern Transvaal, ranging from Natal to the Zambesi along the Eastern Line. It has the top of the head and crest glossy purple. **1980** A. PATON *Towards Mountain* 5 The purple-crested loerie. When it is in flight, in its colours of red, green and purple, it is one of the most beautiful sights in nature. **1986** J. CONYNGHAM *Arrowing of Cane* 120 Colour-flashes in an umdoni announce a purple-crested loerie which hops through the branches, eyeing me quizzically. **1992** T. VAN RENSBURG in *S. Afr. Panorama* Mar.-Apr. 8 The subtropical and coastal areas show off Knysna and purple-crested louries and green pigeons.

2. *transf.* Always with initial capital. The name of the major award presented by the local advertising industry. Usu. in *pl.*

1991 *Sunday Times* 9 June 7 South Africa's premier advertising awards, the Loeries, will be presented at a glittering ceremony in Sun City's Superbowl tomorrow. **1993** *Daily News* 14 Jan. 6 (*advt*) For all those advertising creatives who still think local is not 'lekker', a reminder that winners of Silver Quills invariably go on to land Loeries and other international awards. **1993** *Weekly Mail* 4 June 14, June is major award time in the advertising industry. Our own Loeries take place on June 11.

‖**lokaas** /ˈlɔkɑːs/ *n.* [Afk., *lok* attract, entice + *aas* bait.] Chopped or crushed bait.

1955 C. HORNE *Fisherman's Eldorado* 20 Two methods, which will effectively attract and hold shoals .. are widely employed in the Cape Peninsula. The first .. is to scatter what Cape anglers call 'lokaas' .. usually obtained by crushing a crawfish body to pulp. *Ibid.* 185 Anglers regard one preliminary operation as absolutely essential. They will never cast their bait unless they have used 'lok-aas', the term used at the Cape to denote chum. **1980** *E. Prov. Herald* 31 Jan. 15 Some people caught many mullet by an ingenious method. They rolled congealed blood in the sand and threw this into the surf as lokaas.

long-arm /ˈlɒŋɑːm/ *adj.* [tr. Afk. *langarm.*] LANGARM *adj.*

1988 L. STAFFORD in *Style* Apr. 42 He warned her .. that dinner was formal, and formal meant stuffy ... Yes, there'll be dancing, but strictly of the long-arm variety.

Long Cecil *n. phr.* [Named for *Cecil John Rhodes*, by analogy with Brit. Eng. *Long Tom* a large gun with a long range.] A 28-pounder long-range gun improvised during the siege of Kimberley in response to the 'Long Tom' guns of the Boers.

1900 H.C. NOTCUTT *How Kimberley Was Held* 27 The workshops of De Beers were .. put on their mettle, and on January 19th the new gun, which had been christened 'Long Cecil', was tried for the first time. **1930** H.A. CHILVERS *Seven Lost Trails of Afr.* 232 (Swart), On the stylobate stands Labram's gun, 'Long Cecil'. **1972** L. HERRMAN in *Std Encycl. of Sn Afr.* VI. 514 During the siege of Kimberley he [*sc.* George Labram] was one of the defenders and made a famous gun, popularly known as 'Long Cecil', in De Beers' workshops. He constructed it from steel shafting and within 24 days it was shelling the Boer lines. Named after Cecil Rhodes, it is still preserved in Kimberley. **1979** T. PAKENHAM *Boer War* (1982) 323 George Labram, De Beers' enthusiastic American engineer, had succeded in improvising a 4-inch gun ... On 19 January, 'Long Cecil', as the gun was christened, first opened his mouth, and out came a 28-pound shell that flew, accurately enough, five miles through the air, smack into a Boer laager.

longdavel see RONDAVEL.

long drop *n. phr. Colloq.* A pit lavatory. Also *attrib.*

1979 *Het Suid-Western* 7 Feb., In October, 1972, they dug up the old pit lavatory or 'long drop' near the cottage. **1979** J. MULLINS in *Fair Lady* 5 Dec. 256 Tables under the trees and the inevitable boma for big camp-fire gatherings. In the nearby thicket are reed walled long drops (with no doors). **1982** *Rhodeo* (Rhodes Univ.) 6 Apr. 8 Matchbox houses placed one on top of another, with an outside, 'long drop' toilet, barely three feet away from the house. **1988** D. KENMUIR *Song of Surf* 8 Even the long-drop loo, perched over the gobbling tide, had a quaint and amusing charm. **1989** *Personality* 29 May 15 Hot showers! with a couple of twigs acting as vanity boards .. and, of course, a 'Kalahari wishing well' – the long drop. **1990** A. EMBLETON in *Style* May 94 Roni wanted to turn her elegant lavatory into a typical bottom-of-the-garden *long-drop.* **1990** R. MALAN *My Traitor's Heart* 287 A hole in the ground behind my hut led down to an underground chamber, in the center of which stood a 'long drop' – a plastic toilet on a wooden platform suspended above a deep pit of shit. **1993** G. SILBER in *Flying Springbok* June 74 It's a small, remote camp, .. and you stay in five-star army tents with adjoining bucket-showers and long-drop toilets.

long teeth *n. phr. Colloq.* [tr. Afk. *lang tande*, see LANG TANDE.] In the phr. ***with long teeth***, reluctantly, without enthusiasm; *with lang tande*, see LANG TANDE.

1974 *Weekend Post* 30 Nov. 2 He gave a warning which will ensure that Pretoria's hog snobs will eat with long teeth when they have a braai in future. **1984** J. RYAN in *E. Prov. Herald* 21 July 6 We lunched – with long teeth – on a tin of bully beef and a packet of diet crackers. **1984** *Informant, Grahamstown* At the official banquet the ice cream was in three stripes – orange, white and blue. I noticed most people left the blue till last and were eating it with very long teeth. **1985** *E. Prov. Herald* 26 Oct., The Afrikaans language contains a splendid idiom about 'supping with long teeth' ... Rats I could never attempt to stomach. **1991** R. HILTON-GREEN *Informant, Grahamstown* One often attends school plays with 'long teeth', but this superb production .. will hold your interest.

long-wagon *n. Wagon-making.* [tr. Du. *langwagen.*] The beam (or perch-pole) joining the front and rear axles of a wagon; LANGWA.

1858 T. SHONE Diary. 14 Sept., Henry put a new Long waggon to J. Allen waggon. *a***1875** T. BAINES *Jrnl of Res.* (1964) II. 23 The iron 'long wagon', or connection between the fore- and after-axles, of the same unfortunate vehicle .. had given way. **1895** A.B. BALFOUR *1200 Miles in Waggon* 138 Extra delay was caused by the 'long-waggon' (perch-pole) of the buck-waggon getting badly cracked in crossing a spruit on the wrong road. **1919** *Dunell, Ebden & Co.'s Price List* Aug. 35 Long wagons, Ironwood, Square 20/0 rough, 23/6 dressed. **1973** [see FORE-TONGUE].

long-ziekte *n. Obs. Pathology.* [S. Afr. Du., fr. Du. *long* lung + *ziekte* sickness.] LUNGSICKNESS.

1852 in *Stat. Law of Cape of G.H.* (1862) 987 Ordinance to prevent the spread of the Cattle Disease, commonly called 'Long Ziekte' ... The owner of every animal which shall have or be commonly deemed and taken to have the said disease called the 'long ziekte,' .. shall cause the same to be shut up in some kraal. **1883** M.A. CAREY-HOBSON *Farm in Karoo* 227 Every now and then a case of *Long-ziekte* is reported, and then .. immediate measures are taken to prevent its further spread. **1896** [see LUNGSICKNESS].

‖**loop** /lʊəp, ləʊp/ *v. intrans.* Also **lo(o)pe, loup.** [Afk., earlier S. Afr. Du. fr. Du., imperative of *lopen* to walk.]

1. In the imperative.

a. *Obs. exc. hist.* TREK *v.* sense 1 a.

1822 W.J. BURCHELL *Trav.* I. 169 Phillip mounted his seat, and taking in his hand the great whip .. made the street echo with one of his loudest claps at the same moment, with an animated voice, calling out to the oxen, Loop! **1841** B. SHAW *Memorials* 121 Having, with difficulty, got Mrs. Shaw and the children into the wagon, I immediately cried, – 'Trek, trek, – Loop, loop,' and the oxen set off at full speed. **1876** T. STUBBS Reminiscences. 20 He had noticed on the road from the Bay the Boers called out Trek, Trek lope. **1927** W. PLOMER *I Speak of Afr.* 40 'Loop!' he ordered in a loud voice. Shilling cracked his whip and shouted to the oxen. **1937** F.B. YOUNG *They Seek a Country* 162 'Trek, you lazy troop of mares!' (The long lash curled in the air like a salmon cast and stung the off-leader's muzzle.) *'Loop, you devils, loop!'* **1939** S. CLOETE *Watch for Dawn* 33 First .. came the clap of whips .. then the cries of his drivers ... Now he could distinguish the names of the oxen as his boys called to them ... Loop .. Loo-oop, you duiwels!

b. Go away, 'push off', 'get lost'. Cf. VOETSAK sense 1 a.

1829 C. ROSE *Four Yrs in Sn Afr.* 173 He .. repeated again and again, amber – get on, and then went to the extent of his Dutch in loup, bearing the same meaning. **1888** *Cape Punch* 25 Apr. 43 Go, Voila, Loop, and English learn, Man with the horrid name! And when that is accomplished quite You then my hand may claim. [**1913** J.J. DOKE *Secret City* 238 'Mynheer looks ten years younger today!' Goed zo! ... 'Johannes', said his sister severely, 'hush! you make a noise like a mule. Loop maar!'] **1969** A. FUGARD *Boesman & Lena* 9 Then they found our place there in the bush. *Loop Hotnot! So Hotnot loops* ... to Swartkops. **1979** *Daily Dispatch* 23 May 11 So he had to leave the chamber ... 'Loop, loop' cried Nationalist members.

2. To leave; to go; to walk or run.

1838 J.E. ALEXANDER *Exped. into Int.* I. 11, I was furiously assailed by dogs and the shrill voice of an old woman, intimating that the master was not at home, and desiring me also to 'loop', or take myself off. **1876** T. STUBBS Reminiscences. 103 One of the caffers had taken a shawl out of the wagon, put it round Mrs Mahoney's shoulders and told her to lope. **1882** C. DU VAL *With Show through Sn Afr.* I. 77 His gun in one hand, and his bay'net in the other, chargin' the kopje, and the Boers 'loopin' before him. **1897** 'F. MACNAB' *On Veldt & Farm* 123 The Baralong never hesitated to cut his slave with the waggon-whip indicating thereby to which side he wished him to 'loope'. **1910** 'R. DEHAN' *Dop Doctor* 303 If any of mine have hung back when I told them to loop and do a thing .. did I fail to whack them as a mother should? *Ibid.* 305 Boys can't loop about without breeches. **1920** [see HAMBA sense 1]. **1963** L.F. FREED *Crime in S. Afr.* 105 When he says he is 'looping' away from a 'bottle and stopper' or from a 'copper' he means he is running away from a policeman. **1969** [see sense 1 b]. **1976** S. CLOETE *Chetoko* 54 *'Ja,* my friend,' he said 'you are a Boer horse again. A free horse, with less food but all Africa in which to *loop.'*

looper /ˈluːpə(r), ˈlʊəpə(r)/ *n. Obs.* exc. *hist.* Also **loeper, lo(u)per, luper, lyper.** [S. Afr. Du., fr. Du. *looper* runner (see quot 1936).] Usu. in *pl.*: Large buckshot. Also *attrib.*

1822 *Game Law Proclamation* in *Stat. Law of Cape of G.H.* (1862) 60 A gun loaded with shot of a smaller size that those which are commonly known and called by the name of *loopers.* **a1827** D. CARMICHAEL in W.J. Hooker *Botanical Misc.* (1831) II. 275 Balls and buckshot are the only kinds of shot they ever use. The latter the call 'Loupers'. **1835** A. SMITH *Diary* (1939) I. 255 He fell from his pack ox in consequence of receiving a lot of lupers in the shoulder. **1852** C. BARTER *Dorp & Veld* 47 (Pettman), With plenty of powder, buck-shot, *loepers*, or slugs. **1869** J. MONTGOMERY in *Friend* 22 July, It could be seen where the balls had penetrated the head or the ribs; some had *looper* holes in the side. **1871** J. MCKAY *Reminisc.* 32, I will put some loopers (ounce ball cut into four parts) into my musket, and if any Kafir comes within range, he will not run far afterwards. **1886** P. GILLMORE *Hunter's Arcadia* 18, I quickly substituted cartridges of lopers (buckshot) for the No. 3 that my chambers had previously contained. **1889** H. RIDER HAGGARD *Allan's Wife* 47 Now, boy, the gun, no, not the rifle, the shot-gun loaded with loopers. **1893** G. BERKELEY in *Cape Illust. Mag.* Mar. 260 A strong leather belt with pockets for ammunition (cartridges for his carbine, and 'loopers' for his shot gun). **1907** J.P. FITZPATRICK *Jock of Bushveld* (1909) 49 He had taken the big 'looper' cartridges from his gun and reloaded with No. 6. **a1928** C. FULLER *Trigardt's Trek* (1932) 120 They espied a fully armed Native and scared him away with a charge of *lopers.* **1936** E.C. LLEWELLYN *Influence of Low Dutch* 169 *Looper* (1889), a kind of large buckshot, called in Du. *looper*, runner, because of its greater range than the smaller shot. **1949** L.G. GREEN *In Land of Afternoon* 206 Buckshot of a large size were called lopers. **1968** W. SMITH *Shout at Devil* (1970) 141 Lying beside Flynn was his shotgun, double-loaded with big loopers, lion shot, and he had every intention of using it. **1979** A. GORDON-BROWN *Settlers' Press* 28 He recommended the use of bell-mouthed blunderbusses 'loaded with loopers or slugs above the ball'. **1986** W. STEENKAMP *Blake's Woman* 99 Bags filled with 'lopers', or slugs, instead of single bullets.

loorie var. LOERIE.

lootjie /ˈlɔɪki, ˈluɪki, -ci/ *n. Sheep-farming.* [Afk., lottery token.] A token used by a shearer to keep tally of the number of sheep shorn.

1955 L.G. GREEN *Karoo* 143 A tin is nailed to the wall of the shearing shed. Into the tin the farmer drops a number of *lootjies*, fragments of punched cardboard. **1970** *Informant, Jansenville* Lootjies. One given to each shearer as a sheep is shorn and later counted for payment. Can be bottle tops, large seeds or flat discs, to be used year after year. **1971** M. BRITZ *Informant, Orange Free State* On the farm the shearers used mealie pips as lootjies when they sheared. **1984** C.J. SKEAD *Informant, Grahamstown* Lootjie. (Sounds like loykie). Applicable in sheep-farming circles to the token used to register each shorn sheep as it leaves a shearer. **1992** A. MURRAY *Informant, Graaff-Reinet* Lootjie. A token, used when shearing, usually a bean or a seed or stone. 'The shearers all handed in their lootjies and fortunately the number balanced with the number of sheep shorn.'

lope, loper varr. LOOP, LOOPER.

Lords Seventeen *n. phr. Hist.* [tr. Du. *Here Seventien*, see HERE SEVENTIEN.] SEVENTEEN.

1976 A.P. BRINK *Instant in Wind* 37 One gets entangled in many trifles here in the Cape ... The Lords Seventeen must give permission for every single thing. **1985** A. TREDGOLD *Bay between Mountains* 31 The favourable accounts that travellers .. had brought back of the well-waters and fertile country .. persuaded the Lords Seventeen in Holland to consent to the occupation of the area.

lori(e), lorrie, lory varr. LOERIE.

lorny var. LARNEY.

los /lɔs/ *v. trans. Slang.* [Afk.] To leave (a person or persons) alone; to drop (a matter). Also in the phr. ***to los uit*** /- ˈeɪt, -ˈœit/ [Afk., *uit* out, alone], in the same senses.

1983 *Fair Lady* 19 Oct. 48 There's nothing like a whitey trying to be a blackie. You know, *los uit.* [**1987** *Personality* 4 Nov. 31 They kept on urging me to have a drink with them ... They .. insisted, calling me a spoil-sport and worse names. They got very abusive but I told them to *los die saak.*] **1991** P. SLABOLEPSZY Braait Laaities. 15 Boikie: I phone downstairs. There was no answer. Moira: Well, then you must los them. It's not happening. **1993** *'Jimbo' programme insert, Napac,* Los me! Let me go!

‖**losieshuis** /lʊəˈsisheɪs, -hœis/ *n.* [Afk., *losies* accomodation, lodgement + *huis* house.] A boarding-house providing accommodation and meals, but having no liquor licence.

1942 [see SKINDER *v.*]. **a1951** H.C. BOSMAN *Willemsdorp* (1977) 55 Usually .. she went for supper to Ben's Losieshuis, a boarding house run by Mavis Clarke's mother. **1984** L. SAMPSON in *Style* July 118 A double room with bath in the main hotel costs between R35 to R44 per room, sleeps two. In the Losies Huis it is as little as R23 for a double room.

lospit /ˈlɔspət/ *n.* [Afk., *los* loose, free + *pit* stone, pip, seed.] A freestone peach, a variety in which the stone or kernel is free from the flesh. Also *attrib.*

1913 C. PETTMAN *Africanderisms* 302 *Lospit*, .. The name given to a variety of peach the flesh of which does not adhere to the stone. [**1975** S. ROBERTS *Outside Life's Feast* 11 He joked about Mom's maiden name being Freestone and said her mother would have to call herself Mevrou Lospit now.] **1980** A.J. BLIGNAUT *Dead End Rd* 55 The glow of lospit peaches, ripe in the sun, turned the bottle into a lantern.

lost generation *n. phr.* [Special sense of the general Eng. expression, which refers particularly to the generation of the 1914–18 period, and more generally to any generation thought to have 'lost' its values, etc.] ***The lost generation***: A name given to the generation of black people who left school at the time of the Soweto uprising of 1976, and either went into exile or became involved in the country-wide turbulence of the 1980s.

1990 *Sunday Times* 30 Sept. 23 The 'lost generations' – those blacks who dropped out of school and society after 1976, many of whom are unemployed (and often unemployable) and who are largely beyond the reach of the main political organisations. **1990** *Weekend Post* 27 Oct. 7 Intensive literacy and training courses could form a bridge to help South Africa's 'lost generation', trapped in a hopeless life of poverty and unemployment, to find jobs. **1991** K. OWEN in *Sunday Times* 22 Sept. 29 The townships are too turbulent, and the 'lost generation' is too wild. **1991** A. VAN WYK *Birth of New Afrikaner* 102 Thousands of black children – the so-called lost generation of youths who have been boycotting or burning their apartheid schools in protest against a government they despise – had nothing to live for but their hatred of all whites. **1992** A. SPARKS in *Guardian Weekly* 26 June 17 Her explanation begins with the 'lost generation' of young blacks who abandoned school and got caught up in a lawless revolutionary culture during the unrest of the 1980s. **1992** *Pace* Aug. (Queen) 3 They call them the 'lost generation'. Township youth whose apartheid heritage has left them without education, without jobs and, worst of all, without hope. **1993** M. MZONQWANA in *Democracy in Action* 31 Aug. 32 Skollies or tsotsis take advantage of any situation ... Such people eagerly embrace the terms 'lost generation' and 'marginalized youth'. They think they are justifications for criminal acts.

loup, louper varr. LOOP, LOOPER.

louri(e) var. LOERIE.

Lovedu see LOBEDU.

low country *n. phr. Obs.* Also with initial capitals. [tr. Afk. *Laeveld.*] LOWVELD. Also *attrib.*

1879 *Chambers's Jrnl* (U.K.) 1 Mar. 134 For big game, the low country and Bushveld is that part of the Transvaal which the hunter must seek. **1911** *Farmer's Weekly* 4 Oct. 127 That cotton will grow up north [from East London], especially in the Low Country, is undeniable ... I see no reason why famers should not be equally successful in the Low Country of the Transvaal. **1929** D. REITZ *Commando* 126 Our road ran through the Sabi low country teeming with big game of all descriptions. **1930** *Off. Yr Bk of Union 1929* (Union Office of Census and Statistics) 18 The Low Country stretches from the Limpopo valley behind the escarpment past the eastern end of Zoutpansberg southwards to meet the South-Eastern region below the escarpment east of Carolina. **c1936** *S. & E. Afr. Yr Bk & Guide* 715 Leydsdorp, 2,200 feet, at one time the principle township in the Low Country, was proclaimed as a gold digging in 1887. **1937** J. STEVENSON-HAMILTON *S. Afr. Eden* 160 There was a land boom, and for the first time there began to arise a demand for the opening up of the low-country fever belt. **1940** F.B. YOUNG *City of Gold* 100 That trackless expanse of bush and savannah which men called the Low Country. **1947** J. STEVENSON-HAMILTON *Wild Life in S. Afr.* 189, I have weighed a good number of low-country leopards immediately after death.

lowry var. LOERIE.

lowveld /ˈləʊfelt, -fɛlt/ *n.* Also with initial capital, and (formerly) **low veldt.** [Part. tr. Afk. *laeveld, lae* low + *veld* (see VELD).] The sub-tropical region of north-eastern South Africa, lying mostly at an altitude of under 600 metres, esp. the Eastern Transvaal part of this region; LOW COUNTRY. Also *attrib.* See also BUSHVELD sense 1, HIGHVELD sense a.

One of the major Southern African physiographic regions, the lowveld is situated mainly in the Eastern Transvaal, but extends also into northern KwaZulu-Natal and into Swaziland and Zimbabwe. The boundaries of the region, based on vegetation, altitude, and prominent physical features, are not clearly defined.

1878 A. AYLWARD *Tvl of Today* 44 It is unnecessary for me here to go at great length into the distinction of Highveld and Bushveld. It is sufficient for the purpose of this narrative to state that northward and eastward from Lydenberg, Bushveld and Lowveld are convertible terms. **1897** J.P. FITZPATRICK *Outspan* 34 We were .. trekking with loads from Delagoa Bay to Lydenburg, trekking slowly through the hot, bushy, low veld. **1903** E.F. KNIGHT *S. Afr. after War* 286 We were still in the low veldt, but throughout this trek we ever saw ahead of us the dark, well-defined ridge that forms the edge of the healthier, cooler, but less fertile and drier high veldt, 1,000 feet above us. **1905** *Tvl Agric. Jrnl* Oct. 141 (*heading*) Notes on the native flora and crops of the Lowveld of the Eastern Transvaal. **1923** *S. Afr.: Land of Outdoor Life* (S.A.R. & H.) 125 The term Low Veld has been given to that portion of the country which lies below the 1,500 feet contour line, and which produces a more tropical vegetation. **1932** *Farming in S. Afr.* Sept. 233 (Swart), The Low Veld extends as far northwards and westwards as the Limpopo Valley. **1944** J. MOCKFORD *Here Are S. Africans* 69 The swamp-miasma and the tsetse-fly killed off his sheep, cattle and horses; while the lowveld mosquito gave malaria to the members of his clan. **1951** N.L. KING *Tree-Planting* 58 The low veld is sub-tropical ... Altitude about 500 to 2,000 feet. Frostless. Temperatures up to 120°F in the shade during summer. Rainfall 15 to 20 inches in north increasing to 20–25 in southern portion. Area occupied by dry savannah-like type of bush consisting mainly of Acaciae. **1964** V. POHL *Dawn & After* 131 The winter holidays, when the low veld proper was free from malaria, were set aside for expeditions into what was then wild country. **1972** J.D. KEET in *Daily Dispatch* 6 May 10 (*letter*) Farmers trekked their sheep from the Free State to the better winter grazing of the Natal lowveld. **1974** A.P. CARTWRIGHT *By Waters of Letaba* 1 The true Lowveld (officially defined as all the land that lies at the foot of the eastern escarpment of the Drakensberg at

an altitude of less than 700 metres above sea-level). **1989** *Cape Times* 4 Sept. 6 Within my lifetime, the deep Lowveld .. was the refuge of adventurers, dirt farmers and dipsomaniacs. **1992** *Pace* Sept. 72 Siteki looks down to the west on Swaziland's harsh, dry lowveld. **1993** *Getaway* Nov. 77 (*caption*) The mixed woodlands of the southwestern corner of the Kruger National Park has perhaps the greatest diversity of trees found anywhere in the Lowveld.
Hence **Lowvelder** *n.*, an inhabitant of the lowveld. Cf. *bushvelder* (see BUSHVELD).
　1937 J. STEVENSON-HAMILTON *S. Afr. Eden* 67 The General Manager .. leaving his drink unfinished — almost a criminal act in the eyes of any old time lowvelder — rushed off to stay the impending calamity. **1990** *Weekend Post* 6 Oct. (Leisure) 4 The Lowvelders were often referred to as 'those people from the mosquito country'. **1990** 'MRS POLLY' in *Sunday Times* 14 Oct. 20 (*letter*) Us Lowvelders see only half of what people on the Rand do, so why can't we pay half the price?

LP *n.* Abbrev. name for the *Labour Party of South Africa*, a political party formed in 1965 for COLOURED people. Also *attrib*.
　1984 *Cape Times* 16 July 2, LP launches campaign in South Cape. **1987** *E. Prov. Herald* 20 Aug. 1 The Labour Party and the Government stood poised for another blunt showdown .., with the LP leader .. threatening to thwart attempts to postpone the 1989 white general election. **1990** W. KRIGE in *Sunday Times* 12 Aug. 2 The political shifts are reflected in local issues with supporters of both the ANC and LP locked in struggles. **1994** *Weekly Mail & Guardian* 16 Sept. 5 The Labour Party of South Africa will hold a special congress .. where it is likely the party will dissolve … The dissolution of the LP comes at a time when coloured people are once again feeling marginalised.

lubola *n.* , **lubolo** *n.* varr. LOBOLA *n.*

lubola *v.* , **lubolo** *v.* varr. LOBOLA *v.*

lucky bean *n. phr.* [See quot. 1966.]
1.a. The scarlet, black-eyed seed of the creeper *Abrus precatorius* of the Fabaceae. Also *attrib*.
　1966 C.A. SMITH *Common Names* 326 Lucky bean, *Abrus precatorius* … The plants are reported as being toxic to stock … The beans are a brilliant red, with a black 'eye' and were used as ornaments and worn in necklaces or armlets as charms for luck, whence the vernacular name. **1972** I.C. VERDOORN in *Std Encycl. of Sn Afr.* VII. 57 Lucky Bean, .. (*Abrus precatorius*) … The most striking feature is the bright, shiny, red seed with a black patch at one end. **1984** [see sense b]. **1991** *Dict. of Horticult.* (Dept of Nat. Educ.) 337 *Lucky bean*, (*Abrus precatorius* subsp. *africanus*).
b. In full *lucky bean creeper*: the creeping plant which bears these seeds.
　1984 J. ONDERSTALL *Tvl Lowveld & Escarpment* 110 *Abrus precatorius* subsp. *africanus*. Lucky Bean Creeper. The clustered pods are very striking … , splitting open to display the shiny red-and-black 'lucky bean' seeds … The seeds are extremely poisonous.
2.a. The scarlet, black-eyed seed of any of several species of coral tree (*Erythrina* spp.), esp. *E. caffra* of the Fabaceae; *Kaffrarian pea*, see KAFFRARIAN. Also *attrib*.
　1970 J. MCINTOSH *Stonefish* 231 He .. brushed away fallen red, black-eyed lucky beans. **1972** G.L.F. HARTWIG in *Std Encycl. of Sn Afr.* VI. 264 The large, poisonous seeds, scarlet with a black spot, are known as lucky beans, Kaffir beans, Kaffrarian peas or cocky-doodles. **1975** *E. Prov. Herald* 21 May 22 The *Erythrina humeana* seeds are red 'lucky beans' which should germinate easily and are best planted in spring. This is a shrubby form of Kaffirboom flowering spectacularly in summer not winter. **1984** *Scientiae* Vol.25 No.2, 25 South African researchers have discovered that the use of an extract from the 'lucky bean', the seed of the coral tree (*Erythrina latissima*), simplifies the method of preparing an experimental drug used successfully to dissolve blood clots blocking the flow of blood to the heart. **1989** *E. Prov. Herald* 11 Jan. 8 Only the highest quality 'lucky bean' seeds, and only 50kg of them.
b. In full *lucky bean tree*: a tree bearing such seeds. See also KAFFIRBOOM (*offensive*).
　[**1960** W. PLOMER in D. Wright *S. Afr. Stories* 188 Frant stood under the bean tree with his feet among the open pods and little black-and-scarlet beans that had fallen from it.] **1970** J. MCINTOSH *Stonefish* 16 There were splashes of scarlet on the hillsides, the sprays of lucky-bean trees. *Ibid.* 230 A lucky-bean tree whose split pods showed bright-red drops. **1972** G.L.F. HARTWIG in *Std Encycl. of Sn Afr.* 264 Coral-tree, Lucky-bean tree, (*Erythrina caffra* and *E. lysistemon*.) These two closely related species of *Erythrina* are among the best-known South African trees. **1984** *S. Afr. Panorama* Nov. 26 A decoction of the leaves of the common lucky bean tree, *E. lysistemon*, is highly regarded as a cure for earache. **1984** A. WANNENBURGH *Natural Wonder of Sn Afr.* 16 In late winter, even before its new leaves have sprouted, a lucky bean tree growing beneath the remnants of a castle kopje raises dense heads of scarlet flowers on the ends of naked stalks. **1985** *E. Prov. Herald* 27 Feb. 10 The count of Coral or Lucky Bean trees in Port Elizabeth has risen to 450. **1993** *Grocott's Mail* 6 Aug. 9 *Erythrina lysistemon* .. Lucky Bean Tree.

Lucy *n.* [Unkn.] In the Eastern Cape: the *red stumpnose* (see STUMPNOSE sense 2), *Chrysoblephus gibbiceps*.
　1930 C.L. BIDEN *Sea-Angling Fishes* 169 The red stumpnose is known as 'Lucy' by many anglers at East London and Port Elizabeth. **1957** S. SCHOEMAN *Strike!* 36 There seems to have been a tendency in certain quarters to give it [*sc.* the red stumpnose] the name of a person whose features it resembled to a marked degree. At Port Elizabeth and East London, for instance, anglers refer to the red stump as 'Lucy'.

luisterliedjie /ˈlœɪstə(r)ˌliki, ˈlœɪstə(r)-, -ˌlici/ *n.* [Afk., *luister* listen + *liedjie* little song.] An Afrikaans song with lyrics which contain a serious message, or which are considered more meaningful than those of most popular songs. Also *attrib*. See also LIEDJIE.
　1982 *E. Prov. Herald* 1 Mar. 9 He [*sc.* David Kramer] has taken over from Anton Goosen the leadership in the new 'luisterliedjie' movement. **1983** *Sunday Times* 18 Sept. (Mag. Sect.) 35 Karin Hougaardt is the little swallow of the new Afrikaans luisterliedjie. **1984** B. RONGE in *Fair Lady* 18 Apr. 9 The *Musiek and Liriek* movement produced 'luisterliedjies'. The composers and lyricists were trying to write songs of relevance, not meaningless pop lyrics. **1989** H.P. TOFFOLI in *Style* Feb. 41 A quantum leap from the oozy lyrics of Bles Bridges and all those other luisterliedjie crooners we're subjected to on the airwaves between ads.

lumela var. DUMELA.

lumsiehte var. LAMSIEKTE.

lungsick *adj.* and *n. Obs. Pathology*. [See next.]
A. *adj.* Infected by LUNGSICKNESS.
　1856 T. SHONE *Diary*. 19 May, T. Pike fine'd £2.00 for a lung sick ox. *a*1867 C.J. ANDERSSON *Notes of Trav.* (1875) 247 'Lung-sick' meat .. is easily detected by a yellowish fluid and little pimples of the same colour disseminated throughout it.
B. *n.* LUNGSICKNESS.
　1880 E.F. SANDEMAN *Eight Months in Ox-Waggon* 209 The oxen die by the thousand every year from either lung-sick or red-water. **1887** A.A. ANDERSON *25 Yrs in Waggon* II. 69 Salt .. is a great preventative also against that common sickness the lungsick, which is very fatal to oxen all through South Africa. **1899** *Strand Mag.* (U.K.) Mar. 270 For 'lung-sick' had reduced the .. team of sixteen [bullocks] to .. five.

lungsickness *n. Pathology*. Also with initial capital. [tr. S. Afr. Du. *longziekte*, see LONG-ZIEKTE.] Contagious bovine pleuro-pneumonia, a usu. fatal disease of cattle; LONG-ZIEKTE; LUNGSIEK *n.*; LUNGSIEKTE.
　1852 T. SHONE *Diary*. 10 May, Henry had one of Mr. Woods Cattle die of the Lung sickness. **1856** *Cape of G.H. Almanac & Annual Register* 230 During 1855, the Fingoes of this division have sustained a ruinous loss of cattle by the lung-sickness. **1864** T. BAINES *Explor. in S.-W. Afr.* 8, I asked how so many of the oxen had lost their tails, and was told it was the lung sickness .. it was usual to inoculate healthy cattle by passing a needle and thread previously steeped in the virus of the deceased lung, through the skin of their tails. [**1870** see FATHERLAND.] **1878** A. AYLWARD *Tvl of Today* 35 The Englishman .. obtains cattle he cares little how or where, and may at any moment be the cause of great loss to his neighbours by contaminating their herds with lung sickness and worse diseases. *c*1881 A. DOUGLASS *Ostrich Farming* 205 Lung-sickness is the great bugbear with cattle, as from its terribly communicative nature the farmer never feels safe. **1882** [see HEARTWATER sense 1]. **1885** A. SMITH *Contrib. to Materia Medica* 18 Lungsickness is undoubtedly caused by poison germs present in the blood. **1896** R. WALLACE *Farming Indust. of Cape Col.* 282 Lung-sickness, 'longziekte', or *pleuro-pneumonia*, a highly infectious disease in cattle, is one of the most severe stock scourges in the Colony. **1914** *Farmer's Annual* 118 Lung-sickness, or Bovine Contagious Pleuro-Pneumonia, is a disease, fortunately, confined exclusively to cattle, which has at various times caused enormous losses to the pastoralists of South Africa. **1940** F.B. YOUNG *City of Gold* 39 Look at the froth on their mouths and the way they fight to breathe. This is no poison. This is the lung-sickness. **1968** F.C. METROWICH *Frontier Flames* 236 In 1855 the deadly lung sickness spread from the Cape Colony across the border with calamitous results, and the simple Africans were only too ready to believe that the hated European was using witchcraft to ruin them utterly. **1972** L.G. GREEN *When Journey's Over* 51 You had to guard your oxen against redwater, meltsiekte and lung sickness, and the rinderpest put an army of transport riders out of business. **1987** B. LAU *Namibia in Jonker Afrikaner's Time* 122 Lungsickness brought the cattle trade to a near standstill.

lungsiekte *n. Obs. Pathology*. Also **lung ziekt**. [Part. tr. of Du. *longziekte*, see LONG-ZIEKTE.] LUNGSICKNESS.
　1859 'D.' in *Cape Monthly Mag.* V. Feb. 107 Here, you Cobus, take this horse. How are the oxen? none gone? no lungsiekte? **1886** G.A. FARINI *Through Kalahari Desert* 64 We have sickness among the flocks and herds to contend with. First, the *lung ziekt*, or lung-sickness. **1920** [see PAARDEZIEKTE]. **1937** H. KLEIN *Stage Coach Dust* 172 A closer inspection disclosed that 'Lungsiekte' (lung disease) had broken out among the herd.

luper var. LOOPER.

luphoko var. PHOKO.

luri(e) var. LOERIE.

lus /ləs/ *adj.* and *n. Slang*. [Afk., desirous; lust, enthusiasm.]
A. *adj.* In the phr. *to be lus for*, to long for (something).
　1970 C.S. HENDRY *Informant, Somerset-West* I'm so lus for some sweets. **1971** *Informant, Grahamstown*, I bought some bacon yesterday because I was so lus for bacon.
B. *n.* Enthusiasm.
　1994 *Sunday Times* 18 Dec. 10 People close to Mr de Klerk have said that he has lost his *lus* for politics.

lyper var. LOOPER.

M

m- /m̩, əm/ *pref.* A Xhosa and Zulu singular noun prefix, the vocative form of UM-, found in some words originating in these languages.

For examples, see ABAKWETHA, MLUNGU. In Xhosa and Zulu, the plural vocative prefix corresponding to *m-* is *ba-*; in *S. Afr. Eng.* this change in prefix is not always observed, and the plural is sometimes formed by the addition of the English pl. *-s* to the singular form.

Ma- /ma, mɑː/ *pref.*[1] [Prefix common to the Nguni languages; in the sense 'mother of', also Sotho.] Among speakers of the Nguni languages, used as a woman's title: **a.** 'Mrs'; 'Mother'; 'Ma' (prefixed to the woman's surname or clan name). **b.** (Also in the Sotho languages.) 'Mother of', prefixed to the first name of one of the woman's children (esp. of her firstborn son). **c.** 'Daughter of': after the woman's marriage, prefixed to the first name or clan name of her father, making a name with which to address the woman; used esp. in traditional contexts among Zulus. Cf. MAMA sense 1 a, MMA-, MME.

Usu. indicating respect or affection.

1852 R. SPEIRS *Diary.* 2 Aug., Left my Kaffers and Pack .. at Umdingans and started for Mrs Halley (Mahalley her Kaffer name) a missionary about 30 miles South East of Umdingans. **1857** D. LIVINGSTONE *Missionary Trav.* 126 The parents take the name of the child, and often address their children as Ma (mother), or Ra (father). Our eldest boy being named Robert, Mrs Livingstone was, after his birth, always addressed as Ma-Robert, instead of Mary. **1871** J. MACKENZIE *Ten Yrs* (1971) 111 So Khosimore was not a little proud that he had succeeded in bringing it close to the waggon road, where, as he said, Ma-Willie (Mrs. Mackenzie) could see it. **1953** LANHAM & MOPELI-PAULUS *Blanket Boy's Moon* 15 Why are you worrying? I am worrying about my wife Ma-Libe and my son Libe. **1963** B. MODISANE *Blame Me on Hist.* (1986) 167 Because African mothers are known by the names of their first-born children my mother has since — and shall henceforth — come to be known as Ma-Bloke. **1970** [see AUNTIE sense 2]. **1981** *Voice* 24 June 1 Soweto's prominent Black leader and social worker, Mrs Ellen 'ma-K' Kuzwayo — the former actress. Ma-K, as she is fondly called. **1982** M. MZAMANE *Children of Soweto* 80 MaVy herself, who ran a spot (which is our eupemism for a drinking joint) .. was already there ... she was called MaVy after her eldest daughter, Violet. **1983** *Drum* Oct. 90 The unveiling ceremony of the tombstone of the late Lillian Ngoyi ... The tombstone will serve as a tribute to MaNgoyi, as she was affectionately known. **1985** W.O. KAMTETWA in *Staffrider* Vol.6 No.2, 45 Vuyo had been given a hiding .. MaVuyo could see why the boy was crying so bitterly as the belt was still dangling in Mangethe's hand. **1990** M. MELAMU in *Lynx* 278 Baba Mkhize .. took umbrage at these activities of the devil, as he described them, when he was about God's work ... Ma-Mkhize was also a lovable woman who had never got herself involved in the kind of tongue-wagging that was so much a characteristic of the women of Wanderers.

ma- /ma/ *pref.*[2] A Sotho and seTswana plural noun prefix found in some words originating in these languages.

For examples, see KGOTLA, LEKGOA, MAKATANE, MATABELE. In Sotho and seTswana, the singular of words beginning *ma-* is formed by replacing this prefix with *le-* or by dropping the prefix. In *S. Afr. Eng.*, this pattern is not always observed, and words in the plural forms are sometimes treated as singular nouns, an *-s* being added to form the English plural. See also LE-.

ma- /ma/ *pref.*[3] A prefix found in some words originating in Ndebele, Xhosa, and Zulu: **a.** An anglicized form of the plural noun prefix AMA- found in these languages. **b.** The vocative form, in these languages, of the prefix AMA-.

For examples, see MABELA, MABURU, MADUMBI, MAFUFUNYANA, MAFUTA. Although this prefix is derived from an Ndebele, Xhosa, and Zulu plural prefix, words including it are sometimes treated as singular nouns in *S. Afr. Eng.*, an *-s* being added to form the plural.

‖**maagbom** /ˈmɑːxbɔm/ *n.* Pl. **-bomme** /-bɔmə/, **-bommen.** [Afk., *maag* stomach + *bom* bomb.] A flour dumpling fried in fat; also called STORMJAER (sense 1). Cf. VETKOEK.

1902 C.R. DE WET *Three Yrs War* 11 The burghers utilized the flour supplied to them in making cakes; these they cooked in boiling fat, and called them *stormjagers*, or *maagbommen.* [Note] Storm-hunters; so-called from being rapidly cooked ... Stomach-bombs — a reflection on their wholesomeness. **1963** S. CLOETE *Rags of Glory* 41 Moolman taught the boys how to cook the flour they drew in boiling fat. These delicacies were known as storm jagers or maagbommen, that is to say, storm hunters because they were rapidly cooked, or stomach bombs, owing to their effect on the digestion. **1975** W. STEENKAMP *Land of Thirst King* 127 The high fat content has been known to play merry old hell with various sensitive stomachs, and in fact stormjaers were often known by the graphically descriptive name of 'maagbomme' (stomach bombs) in other parts of the country.

maagtig var. MAGTIG.

maahoom var. MAHEM.

maak *adj.* var. MAK.

‖**maak** /mɑːk/ *v.* [Afk., 'make'.]
1. *intrans.* In the interjectional phr. ***maak gou*** /mɑːk ˈxəʊ/, formerly also ***mak gauw, mak hoe*** [Afk. *gou* (earlier *S. Afr. Du. gauw*) quick(ly)], 'hurry up', 'buck up', 'make haste'.

[**1901** A.R.R. TURNBULL *Tales from Natal* 177 One horseman drew rein .. while the other cantered on shouting, 'Kom, vriend, laat ons rei! Mak hoe!' [Note] 'Come, friend, let's ride on! Make haste!'] **1913** C. PETTMAN *Africanderisms* 306 Mak gauw! .. Be quick! Make haste! In common use in Dutch-speaking districts. **1937** C.R. PRANCE *Tante Rebella's Saga* 97 Here's your Medical Certificate. Mak gou — getamoveon. Next man! **1969** M. BENSON *At Still Point* (1988) 101 He unlocked the gate of the wire cage. 'Maak gou!' he commanded the invisible occupant. A woman emerged. **1978** C. VAN WYK in *Staffrider* Vol.1 No.2, 38 Say it's for me, Kiet. He knows me, ou Blare. Maak gou, bra. **1980** E. PATEL *They Came at Dawn* 48 Maak gou hurry up, bring that camera here. **1990** R. MALAN *My Traitor's Heart* 213 Koekemoer fired until his gun was empty, and then ducked back inside the Chevy's cab. He grabbed the radio and screamed, 'Maak gou, boys!' — 'Hurry boys, they're killing us.'
2. *trans.* In the phr. ***maak 'n plan*** /mɑːk ə ˈplan/ [Afk., *'n* a + *plan* plan, strategy], *make a plan* (see MAKE). Cf. *'n boer maak 'n plan* (see BOER sense 1 d).

1986 *Learn & Teach* No.7, 26 You tell me about danger! What about my bonus? Maak 'n plan man! **1986** *Thousand Ways to Die* (Nat. Union of Mineworkers) Sept. 18 When I complain to the white miner, he does not come. He says that we must 'maak 'n plan'. **1990** C. BARRETT in *Weekend Post* 19 Jan. 1 It is your bounden duty to tell me where my local suppliers are or *maak 'n plan* to get the stuff to Lanseria. **1994** A. SACHS in *Proceedings of the 'Languages for All' Conference* (Dept of Arts, Culture, Science & Technology) 56 There is a very good Afrikaans, South African, term for what is involved here, and it is called 'maak 'n plan'. That is really what is involved. If the good will is there, you will find an answer.

maanhaar /ˈmɑːnhɑː(r)/ *n.* [Afk., *maan* mane + *haar* hair.] In full ***maanhaar jackal***, or (less frequently) ***maanhaar jakkals*** /jakəls/ [Afk. *jakkals* jackal]: the AARDWOLF, *Proteles cristatus*.

[**1892** NICOLLS & EGLINGTON *Sportsman in S. Afr.* 93 The 'Mona (maned) jackal,' by which name it is most commonly known, may be found all over South Africa.] **1896** R. WALLACE *Farming Indust. of Cape Col.* 338 The Maanhaar (maned) jackal .. an animal intermediate in appearance between the hyena and the common jackal, has recently been the subject of discussion, as to whether it attacked sheep or not. **1900** W.L. SCLATER *Mammals of S. Afr.* I. 80 Aard Wolf *Proteles cristatus* ... *Vernacular Names* — ... Aard Wolf or Maanhaar (*i.e.,* Mane-hair) Jackal of the Colonists. **1913** C. PETTMAN *Africanderisms* 20 Aardwolf, .. called more frequently the Maanhaar. **1918** S.H. SKAIFE *Animal Life* 267 The aard-wolf, or maanhaar jackal, is found in many parts of South Africa, both in the open plains and in the bushy veld. It is nocturnal, lying up during the day in some hole in the ground or amid thick bush. **1970** R. MAYTHAM *Informant, Empangeni* A maanhaar entered the yard and stole a fowl. **1970** *Daily Dispatch* 6 June 9 He said many of the poachers killed for the sake of killing, especially animals like the maanhaar jackal. **1974** *Rand Daily Mail* 31 July 4 The animal, commonly known as a maanhaar jakkals sought safety in the backyard of a home in Linton Road, Morningside Manor, after being chased by dogs.

maar /mɑː(r), ma:(r)/ *conjunction* and *adv.* [Afk., 'but', 'yet', 'only', 'just'.]
‖**A.** *conjunction.* But, yet.

Often used to indicate that Afrikaans speech is being reported.

1892 *The Jrnl* 12 Jan. 3 One day as he sat upon his stoep, he saw a number of bovines in the field. 'Klaas' ... 'Ja, baas', 'Take these cattle to the skit at once.'

'Maar baas —' 'Don't baas me, take them off.' 'Maar, baas —'. **1896** M.A. CAREY-HOBSON *At Home in Tvl* 280 'Maar, Sieur,' remonstrated the man; 'Sieur forgets that I told him there were two young ladies in the waggon.' **1912** F. BANCROFT *Veldt Dwellers* 83 *Maar* this man — a devil at fighting — is still at large on our borders, and able to do us mischief. **1920** R. JUTA *Tavern* 175 Allemachtig! Maar Georgie, I myself begin to think these are mysteries you and I will never discover. **1931** F.C. SLATER *Secret Veld* 300 Jan Woest laughed ... 'Maar, Oom Piet' he said, 'you are losing all the interest upon your money.' **1974** A.P. BRINK *Looking on Darkness* 50 If it must break my poor old far'er's heart, it's ok maar just too bed for I love you. **1982** M. MZAMANE *Children of Soweto* 132, I went there before coming here. *Maar* before that I'd been to Inhlazane.

B. *adv. colloq.* Often used redundantly.

1. *rare.* Used as an intensifier; cf. DAREM, ONLY.

1913 A.B. MARCHAND *Dirk, S. African* 77 (Swart), The bearer of bad tidings is maar unwelcome. *a***1931** [see STONE]. **1970** E. MUNDELL *Informant, Pearston (E. Cape)* The sheep are maar pretty thin.

2. Simply, merely, just; cf. SOMMER.

*a***1931** S. BLACK in S. Gray *Three Plays* (1984) 167 Ja, I used to have pains in my belly ... The doctor said I've got maar a stone inside. **1938** *George & Knysna Herald* 19 Oct. 1, I been living quietly lately, so last week I said to Agapantha we could maar go to the Rugby Ball just to see a little bit of life. **1949** [see BLERRY *adv.*] **1963** M. KAVANAGH *We Merry Peasants* 14 *Ag, ja wat, lady.* It's all right. I'm just *maar* thinking what it is that you must send to the Transvaal for. **1970** S. ROBERTS in *Ophir* 12 Sept. 12 He is arrested it's maar for the best i'm not going to be sucker to bail him out. **1977** FUGARD & DEVENISH *Guest* 46 'Louis, I'm beginning to lose my temper with you.' 'Then you must maar lose it, Pa, because .. I've had enough.' **1979** D. SMUTS (tr. *E. Joubert's Swerfjare van Poppie Nongena*) in *Fair Lady* 9 May 112 Then the Lord must maar look after me. **1991** on TV1, 27 July (News), I suppose we'll never be ready. We're going to maar find out the hard way what to do.

maart, maartjie varr. MAAT, MAATJIE.

maas, amasi /mɑːs, əˈmɑːsi, aˈmaːsi/ *n.* Also **ama(a)s, amaaz, amarsa, masi, mazee.** [Zulu and Xhosa *amasi.* The form *maas* may have come into Eng. via Afk., and is considered more colloquial than 'amasi'.]

1. Thickened curdled milk; SACK-MILK; SOUR MILK; THICK MILK.

A traditional staple food among the black peoples of southern Africa. While similar in taste and appearance to yoghurt, maas is allowed to ferment and curdle naturally, rather than by the addition of bacteria. See also *calabash milk* (CALABASH sense 2), *milk-sack* (MILK sense 1).

1809 R. COLLINS in G.M. Theal *Rec. of Cape Col.* (1900) VII. 58 We passed through several villages, at one of which we stopped to procure *mazee*, or curdled milk. **1833** S. KAY *Trav. & Researches* 121 Their general diet extremely simple. This ordinarily consists of milk, which .. they invariably use in a sour curdled state. It is called *amaaz*, and rendered thus thick and acidulous by being kept in leathern sacks or bottles. **1838** [see SOUR MILK]. **1855** G.H. MASON *Life with Zulus* 224 He bade his wife fetch .. Amarsa (a delicious Caffre beverage made of fermented milk). **1857** W.H.I. BLEEK in *Cape Monthly Mag.* I. May 289 Another peculiar custom among the Zulus and kindred tribes is, that the men are not allowed to drink any amasi or thick sour milk from a kraal of which they may think of courting a girl; or, more strictly speaking, they are not allowed to pay their addresses to a girl belonging to a kraal from which they may have drunk amasi. **1882** W.R. LUDLOW *Zululand & Cetewayo* 73 Maas, which is the chief food of the Zulus, where there are large herds of cattle, is most delicious and nourishing food. *Ibid.* Corn maas is made from the Kaffir corn, or millet. **1887** J.W. MATTHEWS *Incwadi Yami* 506 Here we rested .. during the intense heat, refreshing ourselves with cool delicious 'amasi' (sour milk), which we were fortunate enough to procure from the natives. **1905** R. PLANT *Zulu in Three Tenses* 14 His father would offer him a spoonful of what he was eating, probably *Amasi*, curded milk. **1913** [see *milk-sack* (MILK sense 1)]. **1949** E. HELLMANN *Handbk on Race Rel.* 182 Amasi, or curdled milk, was a plentiful source of proteins and fat soluble vitamins to supplement an otherwise starchy diet. **1953** R. CAMPBELL *Mamba's Precipice* 24 They solidified the milk in calabashes and called it *Maas*. **1967** E.M. SLATTER *My Leaves Are Green* 77 The men brought in a couple of reed-mats for sleeping, and two clay pots filled with 'amasi' (sour milk) and mealie-meal. **1970** [see MNGQUSH(O)]. **1978** A. ELLIOTT *Sons of Zulu* 111 Most of the taboos of the kraals are tied to rules which necessitate an abstention from taking of sour milk or *amasi*. **1981** *Daily Dispatch* 19 June 3 Mr Mama said he had been perturbed to see Xhosa words like 'amasi' being changed to 'maas', 'amarhewa' spelt 'amahewu' by advertisers. **1989** *Pace* Dec. 21 (advt) Delicious, thick, pure, creamy, home-made Maas. Introducing new Nestlé Make-it-Yourself Maas. Made from real milk to give you all the taste of traditional, creamy homemade maas.

2. *comb.* **amasi bird**, see quot.

1987 M. MAHLABA in *Weekly Mail* 12 June 23 The motif used to illustrate this is a bird-creature called the *Amasi* Bird which, in African mythology, was supposed to supply rivers of curdled milk.

maasbanker /ˈmɑːsbaŋkə/ *n.* Also **maasbancker, maasbank, ma(r)sbanker, massbanker, mossbanker.** [Du. *marsbanker.*] The fish *Trachurus trachurus* of the Carangidae. See also KINGFISH. Also *attrib.*

The name 'maasbanker' is used for this species in Smith and Heemstra's *Smiths' Sea Fishes* (1986).

[**1727** J.G. SCHEUCHZER tr. *E. Kaempfer's Hist. of Japan* I. 136 *Adsi* is the *Maasbancker* of the Dutch.] **1831** *S. Afr. Almanac & Dir.*, June, Fish in Season — Ray, Maasbanker, Jacob Evert etc. **1843** J.C. CHASE *Cape of G.H.* 169 Maasbank like Mackarel [*sic*] but stronger, not always wholesome. **1887** *S.W. Silver & Co.'s Handbk to S. Afr.* 184 *Caranx trachurus*, Bastard Mackerel, Maasbanker. Flesh well formed and wholesome. Caught in winter at both ends of Colony. **1905** J.D.F. GILCHRIST in Flint & Gilchrist *Science in S. Afr.* 193 The familiar Stock-fish (*Merlucius vulgaris*) and the Maasbanker (*Caranx trachurus*) are examples from the group of the fishes illustrating identity of Cape and European forms. **1910** D. FAIRBRIDGE *That Which Hath Been* (1913) 36 The white sea-gulls and the gannets wheeled overhead, dropping every now and then from the blue sky into the bluer sea in search of harders and mossbankers. *c***1929** S. BLACK in S. Gray *Three Plays* (1984) 95 I'm no good at fishing. I once caught a mossbanker, but he got off the hook. **1949** J.L.B. SMITH *Sea Fishes* 213 *Trachurus trachurus* ... *Maasbankers. Horse Mackerel* ... On the west coast large numbers are captured. **1958** L.G. GREEN *S. Afr. Beachcomber* 114 The harder is a mullet, of course, and this is one of the fish selected in the Cape for kippering. Marsbanker is another, and a marsbanker soaked in brine and cunningly smoked will stand comparison with Scotland's famous product. **1960** G. LISTER *Reminisc.* 14 There was a big shoal of Maasbankers coming in, and numbers of Malay boys and men were catching them with hook and line. **1969** J.R. GRINDLEY *Riches of Sea* 76 The most important pelagic fish in our waters are the south African pilchard (Sardinops ocellata) the maasbanker (Trachurus trachurus) the mackerel (Scomber japonicus) and the anchovy (Engraulis japonicus). **1970** [see BOKKEM]. **1976** *E. Prov. Herald* 19 Feb. 18 Fleets of boats accompanied by factory ships from many parts of the world, converge on the pilchard, anchovy, maasbanker and mackerel shoals and clean them up with vacuum cleaner thoroughness. **1979** SNYMAN & KLARIE *Free from Sea* 36 *Maasbanker*, Horse Mackerel Small, bony fish with a strip of sharp, prickly scales down each side which must be cut out. The flesh is dark, rich and tasty, and is invaluable to our canning industry. **1986** *Conserva* Aug. 11 The deep-sea industry targets mainly on Cape hake, and to a lesser extent horse mackerel (maas-banker), although profitable by-catches of species such as king-klip, monk and snoek are also made. **1986** SMITH & HEEMSTRA *Smith's Sea Fishes* 660 *Trachurus Trachurus*, Bluish green, grey or nearly black above, shading to silvery white below; black opercular spot ... The maasbanker is an important commercial species with 100–250 thousand tons trawled annually by west coast fishermen; it is also considered to be an excellent bait for large game fish. **1989** *E. Prov. Herald* 14 Sept. 3 A limit on the number of catches of redeye round-herring and South Coast maasbanker will be imposed from January 1.

maaster var. MASTER.

maat /mɑːt/ *n.* Also **maart.** [Afk., fr. Du. *maat* friend, comrade, companion, partner, mate.]

1. *obs. rare.* A formally selected or appointed partner in business or other matters.

1824 W.J. BURCHELL *Trav.* II. 466 Barends's waggon was stationed in Serrakutu's mootsi, and Hendrick's in that of Another chieftain who was his *maat* (partner, or agent). *Ibid.* 555 He .. goes directly to the house of his correspondent, whom he calls his *maat* (a Dutch word identical with, 'mate'). **1827** G. THOMPSON *Trav.* I. 238 Many of the Bechuanas selected *maats* or comrades, after their manner, from among their allies, presenting, in a formal manner, an ox to the individual pitched upon.

2. *colloq.* Usu. used as a term of address: mate, friend, comrade, companion; MAATIE *n.*[2]; MAATJIE sense 2. Often in the phr. ***ou maat*** /əʊ-/ [Afk. *ou* old], old friend, old chap; see also OU *adj.* sense 1 c.

1900 B. MITFORD *Aletta* 66 By the time they are found the English will not be here to hang anybody, and we, *ou' maat* — we shall have deserved the thanks of all true patriots. **1913** A.B. MARCHAND *Dirk, S. African* (Swart), Hullo, ou maat, cried Edouard coming in with a rush. *a***1928** C. FULLER *Trigardt's Trek* (1932) 124 (Swart), We drank it as my maats had just come to the waggon. *c***1929** S. BLACK in S. Gray *Three Plays* (1984) 49 Frikkie: ... Come out, soldat. Smith (*coming out*): Hello mate. Frikkie: Don' you call me maat. **1961** D. BEE *Children of Yesterday* 93 'Dolf, ou maat — here's to you.' Perhaps it was the first sign of the drink in him, that 'ou maat' — old friend. **1964** L. HITZEL in *Capricorn High School Mag.* 59 Suddenly the bell goes, and a stream of yelling 'maats' pour out of the science and biology classes. **1977** C. HOPE in S. Gray *Theatre Two* (1981) 52 Sorry, ou *maat*, jus' pass me the keys for your jammie. **1983** *Frontline* Feb. 12 'Jeez, I'm sorry,' said the captain, owning up immediately, 'I just kicked your friend in the head.' 'S'okay, *ou maat.* He's feeling no pain.' **1986** S. SEPAMLA *Third Generation* 114 It was a brief, dramatic encounter which Lambert ended with the words: 'He's finished me, *ou maat.*' And he fell into the arms of Bruil. **1990** R. GOOL *Cape Town Coolie* 59 The man poked aggressively at Henry's chest ... 'Come on, you remember me. I was an old *maart* of yours. We ooze to go fishing.' *Ibid.* 60 Okay, *maart.* I 'ave to cut a line now. I'll give you a look-up when I hit the Cape, you 'ear?

3. *obs.* An assistant officer on a ship, the mate.

1919 M. GREENLEES tr. *O.F. Mentzel's Life at Cape in Mid-18th C.* 125 The Bottelier's maat and the little boy were .. saved. **1925** H.J. MANDELBROTE tr. *O.F. Mentzel's Descr. of Cape of G.H.* II. 18 The second bottelier, the second cook, the assistant cooper. Each of these is styled 'maat' of his corresponding superior officer, e.g. the bootmann's maat, the schiemann's maat, etc.

Maatie *n.*[1] var. MATIE *n.*[2]

maatie /ˈmɑːti/ *n.*[2] *slang.* Also **matie.** [MAAT + -IE, influenced by Afk. *maatjie.*] MAAT sense 2.

1970 D.J. OLIVIER *Informant, Johannesburg* We are 'maaties', aren't we (we are chums). **1974** *Drum* 22 Sept. 10, I tell you, matie, if she could get hold of a panga herself, she sure would have enjoyed using it!

maatjie /ˈmaɪki, -ci/ *n. slang.* Also **maartjie.** [Afk. *maat* (see MAAT) + -IE.]

1. On Citizens Band radio: a 'good buddy', i.e. another Citizens Band radio user.

1979 *Sunday Times* 8 July (Mag. Sect.) 3 'Gooi me a zero,' chirped the robin and my own good buddy went bug-eyed. 'What the hell ... ,' he muttered as the robin went on fluting about his mike maatjies. [1979 B. MOLLOY S. Afr. CB Dict. 107 Maatjie, good buddy, as in 'enige maatjie vir 'n praatjie?' (any good buddy for a chat).]

2. MAAT sense 2.

1990 C. BARRETT in *Weekend Post* 19 Jan. 1 Tell me, O Half Beer makers, why we Vaalies have to wait for the parsimonious goodwill of our Cape *maatjies* before we can get a sip of your highly esteemed .. brew? 1990 R. GOOL *Cape Town Coolie* 10 How's your heart, *maartjie*? You remember me! Moodley. John Moodley. *Ibid.* 59 Ow's it, *ou maartjie*? Ow's it, man?

Maatschappij /ˌmɑːtskɑˈpeɪ/ *n. Obs. exc. hist.* Also **Maatschappy**. Pl. **-ijen**. [Du., partnership, company.] A name given to an early form of local government among the Boers in the regions that were to become Orangia, the Transvaal Republic, and the Republic of Natalia.

1857 J.M. ORPEN *Hist. of Basutos* 22 The Boers were, at this time, divided into parties, the greater portion under a rude form of government, called the 'Maatschappy'. 1878 A. AYLWARD *Tvl of Today* 10 Potgieter and his followers, in declaring their new government — the 'Maatschappij' — claimed absolute independence. 1908 J.M. ORPEN *Reminisc.* (1964) 224 Much the same sort of Government had existed a few years before in Winburg and Harrismith, when they, as well as the Transvaal, were loosely united under that sort of government which was called the Maatschappij (association or partnership) and there was a wish among a good many, as it appeared, in the Free State, to revert to it. 1973 *Std Encycl. of Sn Afr.* IX. 299 In March all the 'maatschappijen' or communities in the Transvaal ratified an agreement which brought into existence a united Transvaal republic.

‖**mabalane** /ˌmabaˈlɑːn(e)/ *n.* Also **mabhalana, mbhalane, mbalan, mo-bhalane, umabalane**. Pl. **o-, bo-**. [Zulu *umabhalane* (and siSwati *mabhalane*) clerk, secretary (pl. *omabalane* (Zulu), *bomabalane* (siSwati)), fr. *bhala* write. Cf. Fanakalo *mabalan* mine clerk.] A clerk or secretary; one who has a task which includes the keeping of written records.

1925 *E. Prov. Herald* 18 Sept. 10 Corruption was practised on the mines. Police boys' or boss boys' jobs were 'bought' by paying £1 to £2 to the induna or head native clerk (mabhalana). 1959 K.M.C. MOTSISI in M. Mutloatse *Casey & Co.* (1978) 28 'Those who have presents for the bridal couple may now see the "mabalane" (the M.C. of the wedding).' ... A few folk .. stand in line before the 'mabalane', who jots down the name and address of .. everyone who dumps a parcel on the table. 1971 P.J. SILVA *Informant, Coalbrook* (OFS) Mabalane. Chief clerk on the mine. 1978 *Speak* Vol.1 No.5, 3 Relatively small groups of 'mission-school' Africans from the Transkei-Eastern Cape, Rustenburg, and Natal areas .. worked in Johannesburg as clerks (umabalane), teachers, preachers, and tradesmen. 1979 M. MATSHOBA *Call Me Not a Man* 61 My parents wanted me to go to school and qualify for a white collar job, to be a *mabhalane* (clerk) they said. 1983 *Frontline* Feb. 38 Their relatives stealthily wrench quick service from bomabalane (clerks) with bribes. 1984 D. PINNOCK *Brotherhoods* 73 This prison-gang thing started on the mines. Each gang has a judge, a magistrate, a doctor and an office man they call a *mbalan* who takes the names of new recruits. 1986 O. MUSI in *Drum* Oct. 51 For the millionth time like so many darkies I found myself in a queue while a mabhalane, looking very important and extremely busy, although he seemed to be standing in one place all the time, peered at a big book containing the names of job-seekers/pensioners and other victims of the recession. 1987 *New Nation* 30 July 10 Teachers and 'omo-bhalane' (clerks) preferred the quieter atmosphere of the Bantu Men's Social Centre, Springbok Hall in Vrededorp, and the New Inchape Palace de Dance, where, according to one observer, 'the European type of dance was followed exclusively'.

mabela, mabele /məˈbe(ː)lə, ‖maˈbeːle/ *n.* non-count. Also **amabele, mabbele**. [A word found in varying forms in many Sintu (Bantu) languages, as Xhosa and Zulu *amabele*, seTswana *mabele* (pl. nouns).] **a.** Any of several species of *Sorghum*: SORGHUM sense 1. Also *attrib.* **b.** The porridge made from this grain; MEALIEPAP sense 2. See also TSHWALA sense a.

[1824 W.J. BURCHELL *Trav.* II. 586 The Bichuanas call it [*sc.* sorghum] *mábbele* (mábbaly) and are fond of chewing the stalk, or rather, cane. [*Note*] Sometimes pronounced *mabbeli*.] 1852 [see TSHWALA]. 1866 W.C. HOLDEN *Past & Future* 278 This utyalla is made from the amabele or Kaffir corn; and being long boiled in large beer-making pots, inbeza, and subjected to fermentation, it becomes intoxicating, acquires a sour taste, and is much liked by the people. 1912 W. WESTRUP *Land of To-Morrow* 91, I haven't got much 'mabele', .. Kaffir-corn you know. They use it for making the best beer. 1939 A.W. WELLS *S. Afr.: Planned Tour* 228 (*caption*) Natives in a valley of mealies and mabela corn near the Caledon River. 1946 *Cape Argus* 14 Dec. 4 He set before him on a stool a bowl of mabela, a flat scone toasted on the coals and a calabash bowl of milk. 1952 F.J. EDMONSTONE *Where Mists still Linger* 62 The ripened mabele plants had waged their annual fight against burr and khaki bush for the meagre nourishment from the soil. 1957 B. FRASER *Sunshine & Lamplight* 132 She loves her brother .. very much and grinds the mabela very fine for him to eat. 1960 C. HOOPER *Brief Authority* 33 Cattle thrive, and the staple crop, mabela (kaffir-corn), does fairly well, except in occasional years of drought. 1976 B. HEAD in *Quarry '76* 17 Corn or mabela always lasted longer than half a bag of mealie meal. 1984 M. NKOTSOE in *Staffrider* Vol.6 No.1, 33 They are groups of men moving through fields of mielies and mabela, reaping where they did not sow, a constant source of danger to the women working in the fields. *Ibid.* 35 From her childhood comes the story of the making of 'matebelekwane', a home-made bread. Mabele meal was ground with warm water, to which a pinch of salt was added, then a small quantity of bread flour. 1985 M. TLALI in *Fair Lady* 26 June 84, I opened the door and a smiling neighbour walked in holding in her hand a dishful of steaming hot soured brown mabela porridge which she knew I liked very much. 1994 A. CRAIG in M. Roberts tr. *J.A. Wahlberg's Trav. Jrnls 1838–56* 34 Several species of sorghum; mabela; *Sorghum caffrorum*.

mabhalana, -lane var. MABALANE.

Maboela var. AMABHULU.

ma Bunu var. AMABHUNU.

‖**Maburu** /maˈburu/ pl. *n. Rare.* [Sotho, ad. Afk. *Boer* Afrikaner.] Among Sotho-speakers, a derogatory name for Afrikaners. Cf. AMABHULU sense 1.

1960 J. COPE *Tame Ox* 57 South Africa, to her, was the land of the *maburu* (Boers).

mace ont var. MUISHOND.

machaha var. AMAJAHA.

Machoa var. LEKGOA.

machonisa var. MASHONISA.

machtig var. MAGTIG.

mackatan var. MAKATANE.

Macooa var. LEKGOA.

ma coola var. AMAKULA.

madala /maˈdɑːla, məˈdɑːlə/ *n. and adj.* Also **mdala, m'dala, medalla**. [Zulu, vocative of *u-madala* old one.]

A. *n.* Old man; 'old one'; often as a term of address, esp. to an old black man.

1960 N.H. BRETTELL in *P.E.N. 1960: New S. Afr. Writing* 62 A slow-moving one, a grey mdala raggedly shambling by, with sleeping mat and little calabash. 1968 M. DOYLE *Impala* 6 Not that his calloused soles needed protection, but the shoes gave him a dignity befitting a *madala* of his years. *Ibid.* 134 *Umfaans* and *madalas*. 1970 *Forum* Vol.6 No.2, 48 Now I myself have become old, you do not give me, an old madala, time to stop working, because without work, and you, I myself would die. 1970 Y. WINTERS *Informant, Kimberley* You are too much of an old m'dala to dig up the garden. 1975 M. MUTLOATSE in *New Classic* No.1, 57 The madala was unashamed to say he had a wife and child in nearly every town in South Africa he had toiled. 1986 *Thousand Ways to Die* (Nat. Union of Mineworkers) Sept. 32 But madala we can't work here! It's dangerous! 1991 *Personality* 11 Mar. 4, I went to the front door to see an old beggar walking away. 'Ho, madala,' I called out, and he turned and came back. 1992 K. SUTTON in *E. Prov. Herald* 2 May 4 Who was that old Madala there Beside you on the bench?

B. *adj.* Old; used esp. of old men.

1980 A. PATON *Towards Mountain* 88 A little old man approached me in the main street of Durban with the question, 'Do you remember me?' ... Then he said to me, 'My you are *madala*, madala being a corrupted Zulu word for 'old'. He was puzzled that I thought his remark so amusing, but I did not describe to him just how he looked to me. 1985 P. SLABOLEPSZY *Sat. Night at Palace* 21 Forsie (*laughing*): Voetsak, you mad, man. September: Ai-ai-ai-mdala. Forsie: This!– September: Too old. Forsie (*tapping his head*): You madala up here, yes.

madam *n.* Also with initial capital. [Special senses of general Eng.] The (usu. white) mistress of a household; a white woman employer or superior at work; a white woman. Cf. MASTER sense 2.

1. A term of address.

a. Used when addressing someone directly; MEDEM sense 1; MERREM sense 2 a.

1943 *Outspan* 23 July 22 (*advt*) A: You must be using a lot of polish on the floors, John. They shine so brightly. B: No, Madam see how much there is left in the tin. 1952 MANUEL & VAN DE HAER in *Drum* Aug. 6 The most hurtful remark I ever heard was made by a girl in a factory to her 'Pass-for-White' forelady. 'Madam,' she said, 'Whatever is happening to your skin? You seem to be getting blacker every day.' 1963 B. MODISANE *Blame Me on Hist.* (1986) 226 This house servant .. was talking to her 'madam' with whom I was friendly: 'You know, madam,' she said, 'it's true what they say. Natives is Natives.' 1969 M. BENSON *At Still Point* (1988) 136, I was appalled at how appreciative Mr. Qaba was of my visit, and relieved to notice he no longer addressed me as 'madam'. 1986 *Style* Feb. 62 They tell all their servants to call them Sarah and Jim instead of Master and Madam.

b. Used in the third person, as a deferential term of address; MERREM sense 2 b. Cf. MISSUS sense 2.

1968 F.G. BUTLER *Cape Charade* 28 Ai! Madam gave me a fright! 1973 M. PHILIP *Caravan Caravel* 24 Madam's palace is ready for madam. Madam can now sit on her throne and watch the sea.

2. A common noun; MADDIE; MEDEM sense 2; MERREM sense 1. Cf. MEVROU sense 3, MISSUS sense 1.

1952 *Drum* July 21 When Mrs. 'So-and-so' says: 'Galima get some tea and lekker koeksisters for the madams and masters, and leave ours in the kitchen,' she is not practising *apartheid*. 1963 M. BENSON *Afr. Patriots* 251 As soon as they were arrested they climbed happily into the police vans, some calling out: 'Tell our madams we won't be at work tomorrow!' *a*1965 N. NAKASA in Cole & Flaherty *House of Bondage* (1968) 14, I could .. find a comfortable job in the northern suburbs. I'm sure some 'madam' would find me intelligent and give me one of those incredible 'kitchen boy' suits. 1976 M. THOLO in C. Hermer *Diary of Maria Tholo* (1980) 55 Even for domestics it is worse to work for a black than a white madam in terms of kindness and time off. 1980 C. HOPE *A Separate Development* (1983) 111 We sold Jacaranda Blossom Perfume, White Winda Washing Powder, Smart *Madam* Wigs ('Each Hair guaranteed 100 percent Human & Fully European'). 1980 E. JOUBERT *Poppie Nongena* 100, I got sick at the work, but the madam said to me: You can't be sick here, you must go to Nyanga,

I'm too busy to look after a sick person. **1985** *Frontline* Sept. 15 For the madams of Musgrave the bread strike has meant an irrevocable shift in the tense dynamic of the master-serf relationship. **1986** *Style* July 63 She raises a pale finger in the candlelight: 'Hercules, bring me a clean spoon for that madam.' **1991** K. SWART in *Sunday Times* 13 Jan. 13 He and the 13 other 'new kids' made friends – some, like Collen, the sons and daughters of Emmarentia 'maids', others the children of the suburb's 'madams'.

3. Used as though the word were a name, with no article, and with a verb in the third person; MERREM sense 3.

1968 COLE & FLAHERTY *House of Bondage* 70 'When madam returns from her tea date,' they say, 'you can be sure of two things: She will be in a terrible temper and she will have a brand new recipe for handling her servants'. **1986** *Style* Dec. 41 Monologue with the servants, the boys and the girls, was limited to that magic word from Zululand, 'fanagalo'. And while Jim did pusha lo plam, Madam did hamba chiya golef, at the club. **1988** J. WELLINGTON in *Cape Times* 29 Dec. 6 The poor maid, when willing to work on Christmas Day, receives a carton of chicken livers for lunch, while 'madam' and her family go to an expensive restaurant.

Hence **madamhood** *n. nonce*, the state of being a madam.

1985 D. BOUTALL in *Fair Lady* 27 Nov. 89 'Viva Molly! Viva Molly!' .. Into the midst of the black multitude .. came Molly Blackburn, at first sight the very epitome of affluent, white, middle class madamhood.

maddie /ˈmædi/ *n.* Colloquial form of MADAM (sense 2).

1985 J. MAKUNGA in *Staffrider* Vol.6 No.2, 36 He crept towards Tsidi's 'dog's-meat' home, so-called because when the maddie went shopping, part of the meat she bought was allotted the servant. **1988** *Pace* May 4 One day he brought his son to work and the maddies assumed he's a darkie like his daddie ... The maddies as usual instructed the poor boy as they always do to darkies to clean the machines.

Madiba /məˈdiːbə, maˈdi(ː)ba/ *n.* [Xhosa, the clan name of the Thembu chiefdom.] A name used informally or affectionately to refer to Nelson Mandela, President of South Africa from 1994 and leader of the African National Congress. Also *attrib.* See also MANDELA.

1990 E. KOCH in *Weekly Mail* 27 Apr., A bright red top-of-the-range Mercedes Benz 500 SE .. dubbed the *Madibamobile* ... 'It has just been sent off for a carphone to be fitted. When it comes back, we will ask Madiba to come and collect it.' **1990** *Sunday Times* 1 July 26 The Mandela party has apparently banned Coca-Cola from the Madiba-jet in protest against the company still doing business in South Africa. **1990** M. TYLALA in *Ibid.* 12 Aug. 7, I am agonizing over how to address the man. Madiba, Comrade Nelson, Baba (Father), Chief, Com (short for comrade) – there is such a plethora of salutations in use here that plain Mr Mandela sounds out of place. **1990** T.V. NXELE in *New African* 13 Aug. 10 (*letter*) You said Mandela has done nothing since his release ... You want Comrade Madiba to live in a shack. **1994** N. MEHLOMAKULU in *Tribute* May 12 Nelson Mandela vowed to go on his knees to prevent a threatening bloodbath ... In short, good luck Madiba and God Bless. **1994** D. STREAK in *Sunday Times* 29 May 15 'Madiba's speech was inspirational,' she said. **1994** *E. Prov. Herald* 11 Nov. 1 With glistening eyes, [Whitney] Houston responded, 'I love you, Madiba,' using Mr Mandela's clan name.

Madjadja var. MODJADJI.

madlosis, madlozi(s) pl. forms of IDLOZI.

madoda pl. form of INDODA.

madombe var. MADUMBI.

madressa /məˈdresə/ *n.* Also with initial capital. [ad. Arabic *madrasa* college, school. Cf. general Eng. *madrasah*.] A Muslim school, operating after normal school hours and teaching children subjects such as Islamic history, Islamic belief, and the reading and reciting of the Arabic Qu'ran.

1949 E. HELLMANN *Handbk on Race Rel.* 582 The Muslims have their mosques and *madressas* where religion is formally taught to the young and old. **1979** *S. Afr. Panorama* Dec. 25 Muslim educational institutions such as the madressas attached to the mosques. **1981** *Sunday Times* 12 July 1 Children attend secular schools in the morning, the madressa in the afternoon, where they are instructed in the Koran.

madumbi /maˈdʊːmbi, mə-/ *n.* Pl. usu. **madumbies.** Forms: *sing.* **idumbi, madombe, madumbi**; *sing.* and *pl.* **amadumbe, amadumbi**; *pl.* **amadoombies, amadumbies, amadumbis, madombes, madumbe(s), madumbies.** [Zulu *amadumbe* (sing. *i(li)dumbe*). For explanations of sing. and pl. usages, see AMA- and MA- *pref.*[3]] The edible root of the plants *Colocasia esculenta* and *C. antiquorum* of the Araceae, similar to the sweet-potato. Also *attrib.*

Introduced from the East Indies, the plant is cultivated mainly in KwaZulu-Natal.

1851 R.J. GARDEN Diary. I. (Killie Campbell Africana Library MS29081) 30 June, For dinner yesterday we had some amadumbe, a kind of succelent [*sic*], they require a great deal of boiling. **1852** *Ibid.* 24 Apr., Sweet Potatoes, Amadumbis, Sugar Cane, Matingolas, & Pineapples. **1856** *Cape of G.H. Almanac & Annual Register* 282 An edible root resembling the wild turnip (arum) called 'idumbi'. **1899** G. RUSSELL *Hist. of Old Durban* 146 Cash .. was scarce, consequently people in the country bartered .. Pumpkins, Amadoombies (an edible potato-like root). **1925** D. KIDD *Essential Kafir* 323 There is also a waxy sort of potato called amadumbe, which seems to be made of a specially tough kind of guttapercha, so fearfully solid and indigestible is it. **1951** *Off. Yrbk of Union 1949* (Union Office of Census & Statistics) 473 Of the root crops, madumbies are generally grown on the North coast of Natal. **1953** R. CAMPBELL *Mamba's Precipice* 148 He fished a hot *madumbi*, or native potato, out of the pot. *c*1963 B.C. TAIT *Durban Story* 66 A root of the potato family known as Amadoombies. **1970** HEARD & FAULL *Cookery in Sn Afr.* 477 Amadumbi shoots – This is the most delicious of all the imifinos. **1990** H. HUTCHINGS in *Weekend Post* 26 May (Leisure) 7, I had some difficulty in finding out what exactly *madombes* were, except .. that they were a highly nutritious form of food.

maffick /ˈmæfɪk/ *v. intrans. Rare* exc. *hist.* [Back-formation fr. *Mafeking* (now *Mafikeng*), a town besieged by Boer soldiers during the Anglo-Boer War.] To celebrate in a boisterous and jubilant manner.

First used in *Brit. Eng.* of the celebration of the relief of Mafikeng in London in 1900.

1900 *Pall Mall Gaz.* (U.K.) 21 May 2 We trust Cape Town .. will 'maffick' today, if we may coin a word, as we at home did on Friday and Saturday. **1901** W.S. SUTHERLAND *S. Afr. Sketches* 34 Of course we 'Mafficked' with the best of them when the news came. In a small way, we considered ourselves comrades with our good friends in Mafeking – brother-besieged, so to speak. **1904** 'SAKI' in *76 Short Stories* (1956), Mother, may I go and maffick, Tear around and hinder traffic? **1963** S. CLOETE *Rags of Glory* 307 The [Mafeking] siege of seven months was over, and all England was in an uproar. London had gone mad and the verb 'to maffick' was born. **1977** J. PODBREY in *Quarry '77* 115 This was my night for stopping traffic, .. This was my time to roar and maffick. **1980** *S. Afr. Panorama* Dec. 23 The Tswanas were mafficking (celebrating uproariously), as had the British 80 years previously in London when they first heard of the Relief of Mafeking. **1991** S. CLARKE *'Vanity Fair'* 190 Mafeking was finally relieved on 17 May 1900 by a combined force ... Rejoicing continued for two days, and a new word describing frenzied jubilation – to 'maffick' – was added to the English language.

Hence **maffick** *n.*, a boisterous celebration; **mafficker** *n.*, one who celebrates in a boisterous manner; **mafficking** *vbl n.*, riotous celebration.

1902 *Westminster Gaz.* (U.K.) 4 June 7 The Peace 'maffick' has not yet been completely worked off. **1902** *Daily Chron.* (U.K.) 9 July 6 We have no wish to advocate the hysteria of which the name is 'mafficking.' **1910** *Blackwood's Mag.* (U.K.) July 9 The 'Mafficker' may hereafter come within sight of the enemy. **1957** D. GRINNELL-MILNE *Baden-Powell at Mafeking* 218 The verb 'to maffick', the noun 'mafficking' were presently coined and thrust hastily into the dictionary to reprehend hooliganism and to denounce the 'noisy rejoicing of the mob'. **1986** *Cape Times* 22 Jan. 8 There is .. no mention here of 'mafficking' – a word widely used up to and during World War II to describe riotous rejoicings like those that followed the relief of Mafeking in 1900. **1991** G. ZWIRN in *Settler* Vol.65 No.2, 10 A linguistic curiosity from the time of the Boer War is *mafficking* ... London newspapers seized upon the gerund suggested by 'Mafeking' and, by changing the spelling, produced *mafficking*. Then, as now, the meaning is extravagant or excessive jubilation.

mafufunyana, mafufunyane /ˌmafʊfʊˈnjɑːnə, -ˈnjana, -ne/ *n.* Also **(ama)fufunyane, fufunyana, mafofonyane, mafunyana.** Pl. unchanged. [Zulu *amafufunyane, amafufunyana* (sing. *ufufunyane, -na*). For notes on sing. and pl. forms, see AMA- and MA- *pref.*[3]]

1.a. An emotional disorder, characterized by hysteria and hallucinations and often believed to be caused by witchcraft.

1952 B. DAVIDSON *Report on Sn Afr.* 123 Mafufunyana is widely feared and results often in death, being an especially powerful form of self-hypnosis induced by an acute sense of guilt. **1968** *Post* 4 Feb. 14 Son died after Priest's mafufunyane water cure. *Ibid.* 16 Masemola told him Charles was suffering from mafufunyane (lunacy). **1970** M. DIKOBE Marabi Dance. 12 I am going to send her Mafufunyane – the madness that causes one to see chimpanzees. **1978** *Daily Dispatch* 26 July 18 Miss J– told the court she was being treated for 'mafufunyana' (hallucinations) and that evil spirits drove her to do things against her will. **1988** RAMPHELE & BOONZAIER in Boonzaier & Sharp *S. Afr. Keywords* 162 She had developed *mafufunyane* (a temporary mental illness said to be brought about by evil forces). **1993** *Weekend Post* 1 May 7 Professor Dan Mkize, head of psychiatry at the University of Transkei, spoke on two culturally-bound syndromes, Twasa and Fufunyana.

b. *pl.* The evil spirits which are believed to possess one suffering from this disorder. Also *attrib.*

1963 A.M. LOUW *20 Days* 131 He said: 'It is the igqira – the diviner. There are mafufunyana – evil spirits – in this house .. !' **1978** *Daily Dispatch* 25 Apr. 19 A herbalist .. said the guardian 'amakhosi' spirits had used Mr Nkohla T–, of Mdantsane, as an agent to assault the evil 'mafufunyane' spirits which had possessed Miss Kondokondo M–. Mr Woko said the gathering of mystics .. called on the amakhosi to drive out the mafufunyane.

2. *rare.* A stomach-ache.

1980 *E. Prov. Herald* 22 Feb. (Suppl.) 7 One of the girls was taken to him as a faith healer as she was suffering from stomachaches (amafufunyana).

mafuta /maˈfʊːta, məfuːtə/ *n.* and *adj.* [ad. *amafutha* fat, oil, a word common to several Nguni languages; see also MA- *pref.*[3]]

A. *n.* Often with initial capital.

1. A fat person; now often a term of address.

1899 G.H. RUSSELL *Under Sjambok* 31, I have been there, I know the mafuta (fat man) of the canteen, I have eaten in his yard. **1908** D. BLACKBURN *Leaven* 41 So it came that the boss, whom the boys called 'Mafuta' because he was fat, said Bulalie was the best horse boy he ever had, and very rarely threw things at him. **1957** B. O'KEEFE *Gold without Glitter* 79 They .. heard the women clap their hands and cry 'What is this? Mafuta, the Fat One, has come home.' **1970** M.J. MATULOVICH *Informant, KwaZulu-Natal* Hello Mafuta!

2. In *pl.*: Fats of various creatures. Part of the stock-in-trade of a herbalist.
 1971 *Post* 24 Oct. 33 (*advt*) African Herbal College for 20 years has taught the people how to use African Mutis and Mafutas. 1987 *City Press* 26 Apr. 6 (*advt*) We supply a range of herbs and Mafutas.
B. *adj.* Fat, obese.
 1943 F.H. ROSE *Kruger's Wagon* 48 'There is a woman at that place where we are going,' Falooti had said. 'She is "mafoota" (fat), of the same race as my master'.

magageba /ˌmaɡaˈɡeːba/ *n. slang.* Also **magegeba, magegebe(s)**. [Isicamtho; perh. rel. to Zulu *amakhekheba* flat rigid objects, as honeycombs, sheets of ice (sing. *ikhekheba*).] In urban (esp. township) parlance: MAPHEPHA sense 1 b.
 1974 K.M.C. MOTSISI in *Drum* Jan. 17 Kid Fall .. orders more spirits in the form of litre and boasts that we will never finish his boodle. He explains this by saying that he is in the magegebes. 1977 P.C. VENTER *Soweto* 153 A stranger to the tsotsi's dangerous world could still save his throat if he has some knowledge of basic words and phrases: .. Magageba — money. 1979 A.P. BRINK *Dry White Season* 84 You pick them up, listen to their sob stories, you're their bank when they need some magageba. [1982 D. BIKITSHA in *Rand Daily Mail* 14 Oct. (Eve) 5 Tsotsi taal: a fly patois passes away. Money terms were coined by the dozen .. zak, miering, kuzat, tsang, chin, malazanas, mazuzu, magagebas, [etc.].]

Magaliesberg /məˈxaliːzbɜːɡ, maː-, -ˈxaːliːz, -ˈxalis-/ *n.* [Afk., name of mountain range and village, fr. *Magali(e)* ad. *Mohale* a Sotho leader of the mid-19th century + possessive *-s-* + *berg* mountain.] A tobacco grown in the Magaliesberg area of the North-West Province, used orig. as pipe tobacco but now also in the manufacture of cigarettes. Also *attrib.*, esp. in the phr. *Magaliesberg tobacco.*
 1899 J.G. MILLAIS *Breath from Veldt* 44 (Swart), There sits the old Boer on the top of his waggon, solemnly blinking in the sun as he puffs away at his Magaliesburg. 1910 J. RUNCIE *Idylls by Two Oceans* 79, I gathered a handful of Magaliesberg from my pocket, and held it to him. With plenty of the Transvaal's delightful sedative at only 2s. a lb. and less, a handful of tobacco is not missed. 1919 *Dunell, Ebden & Co.'s Price List* Aug. 32 *Tobacco, Transvaal* ... Guaranteed best Magaliesberg. 1924 H.W. TAYLOR *Tobacco Culture* 28 (Swart), The pipe tobacco manufactured from Magaliesberg leaf might be described as a mild smoke. 1937 H. SAUER *Ex Afr.* 28 During question time tobacco pouches were freely handed round by the men, everybody filling his pipe from the pouch of someone else .. but as the tobacco was usually the same brand of Magaliesberg there was not much in it. a1951 H.C. BOSMAN in L. Abrahams *Unto Dust* (1963) 135 Each time I got back to my own farm, and I could sit on my stoep and fill my pipe with honest Magaliesberg tobacco, I was pleased to think I was away from all that sin that you read about in the Bible. 1958 A. JACKSON *Trader on Veld* 52 Before returning I visited the market square in Johannesburg, where I was intrigued into buying a wagonload of cut Magaliesburg tobacco, packed in grain bags for 3d a lb. 1970 'R.C.G.' in *Outpost* 159 My citizens smoked Magaliesberg tobacco, manufactured in the form of chopped twigs, which when ignited smelt like the exhaust of a diesel truck ... Magaliesberg was sold in cotton bags which were tied to the belt. 1980 [see SPAN *n.²*]. 1990 R. STENGEL *January Sun* 110 Beginning in the 1970s, the quality of Magaliesberg tobacco deteriorated ... In 1979, the tobacco companies informed the farmers that Magaliesberg tobacco was no longer up to snuff.

magayo var. MAHEWU.

magegeba, -gebe varr. MAGAGEBA.

mageo, magewu, mag(h)eu varr. MAHEWU.

maghtag var. MAGTIG.

Magoa var. LEKGOA.

magoduka pl. form of GODUKA.

‖**magogo** /maˈɡɔːɡɔ/ *n.* Also **m'gog**, and with initial capital. Pl. **-s**, or unchanged. [Vocative of *umagogo* 'ancient one' (pl. *omagogo*), a word common to several Nguni languages.] An old woman, esp. a grandmother; also used as a term of address. Cf. GOGO *n.²*, MAKHULU.
 1978 M. MATSHOBA in *Staffrider* Vol.1 No.2, 12 The frail .. old woman tottered painfully from where she had been sitting. It took her some time to reach the door and in the meantime the clerk coaxed her dryly, 'C'mon, c'mon *magogo, phangisa*' (hurry up). 1987 *Learn & Teach* No.2, 39 Who looks after the children of working mothers? Lucky mothers leave their children with their grandmothers. But other women must pay. They send their children to the 'magogo' who look after many children. 1988 O. MUSI in *Drum* Sept. 70 Many cattle were slaughtered and the magogos brewed highly potent traditional beer, that would have rattled the decayed bones of old Hintsa himself. 1989 *Frontline* Nov. 21 He gives a great indulgent laugh. 'Oh. that's all right, M'gog!' His kindness eases the hurt of the journey home. 1993 M. KA HARVEY in *Weekly Mail* 23 Dec. 15 Although we do not have our cattle kraals in the township, traditional weddings still take place, with the '*magogos*' and '*mkhulus*' (grandmothers and grandfathers) taking the centre stage as the custodians of tradition.

Magossees pl. form of XHOSA.

magou(w) var. MAHEWU.

‖**magtie** /ˈmaxti/ *int. colloq.* [Afk., fr. *magtig* (see MAGTIG).] MAGTIG.
 1870 in A.M.L. Robinson *Sel. Articles from Cape Monthly Mag.* (1978) 11 Good-night. Magtie! it's dark for the passenger. 1965 S. DEDERICK *Tickey* 17 '*Magtie*, Tickey, that same old story.' 'But I like to hear it.' *Ibid.* 77 She looked down at Tickey's flushed face and felt her forehead. '*Magtie*,' she murmured. 1968 F.G. BUTLER *Cape Charade* 13 Magtie, if only Klaas were free, he could be your guide, and your agterryder! 1987 *Informant*, Grahamstown Magtie, this is an enormous job!

‖**magtig** /ˈmaxtəx/ *int.* Also **maagtig, machtig, mag(h)tag**. [Afk. (earlier Du. *machtig*), ellipt. for *alamachtig, allemachtig*, see ALLEMAGTIG.] 'Lord', 'Heavens above': an exclamation expressing surprise, delight, dismay, admiration, or reproach; MAGTIE. Sometimes in the phr. *my magtig* /meɪ -/, formerly also *mij magtig* [Afk. *my my*, fr. Du. *mij*], having a similar but intensified meaning. Cf. ALLEMAGTIG.
 1871 W.G. ATHERSTONE in A.M.L. Robinson *Sel. Articles from Cape Monthly Mag.* (1978) 81 '*Magtig*!' exclaimed the old Frontier Boer, when he first heard of the *iron* rail, 'our roads are so heavy already, what will our poor oxen do with *iron roads*!' 1899 B. MITFORD *Weird of Deadly Hollow* 103 *Magtag*! .. Whoever heard of bringing *vrouw-menschen* out springbok-hunting! 1925 L.D. FLEMMING *Crop of Chaff* 68 'For heaven's sake don't say he's swallowed it.' 'Mij magtag!' I said, 'I hope not — it's one of my most treasured possessions that tickey.' 1931 V. SAMPSON *Kom Binne* 157 'Mij machtig!' ejaculated Nicholas with exasperation, 'how long is it all going to be?' 1958 S. CLOETE *Mask* 22 Rape, magtig, plenty of girls were raped — a matter usually of not saying yes in time. 1967 E.M. SLATTER *My Leaves Are Green* 127 'Magtig, how fat I am,' she said good-humouredly. She put on her grey kappie and waddled away across the veld. 1979 J. GRATUS *Jo'burgers* 11 With a shout of triumph, the two men approached the fallen beast. 'Magtig! What a shot,' .. 'Thanks ... Bit of luck, I reckon.' 1985 *Style* Dec. 41 Liberated quote of the year 'Magtig, are you serious?' from an elderly passenger when told his Magnum flight from Pietersburg to Jan Smuts would have a woman pilot at the controls. 1989 J. HOBBS *Thoughts in Makeshift Mortuary* 283, I was homesick. Magtig, I was so homesick!

Magwamba /maˈɡwamba/ *n. obsolescent.* Also **Gwamba, Ma-gwamba.** Pl. unchanged, **ama-Gwamba**, or **-s**. [Unkn.; but see quot. 1900, and second quot. 1905. For notes on singular and plural forms, see AMA-, MA- *pref.²*, and MA- *pref.³*] SHANGAAN sense 1 a. Also *attrib.*
 1892 W.L. DISTANT *Naturalist in Tvl* 100 The Magwambas, or 'knob-noses' so-called from having their noses originally ornamented with notches or scars, were the tribe or clan of the Bantu race with which I was principally thrown in contact. 1900 A.H. KEANE *Boer States: Land & People* 99 The degraded Magwamba ('demons' or 'devils'), called by the Transvaal Boers. 1905 W.H. TOOKE in Flint & Gilchrist *Science in S. Afr.* 88 As fugitives the ama-Gwamba fled over the Lebombo Mountains into the Lydenberg district, where they are known as 'Knobnoses'. 1905 *Native Tribes of Tvl* 64 Ma-gwamba, a name by which they are often known, was given to the Shangaans by the Bavenda and Basuto peoples on account of their habit of swearing by 'Gwamba' who according to them was the first man created. 1937 [see HEAD-RING]. 1970 J.B. DE WAAL in *Std Encycl. of Sn Afr.* I. 288 He [sc. Albasini] established a model farm .. where he lived from 1857 in feudal fashion in a fort, surrounded by his Magwamba followers.

magwetha var. ABAKWETHA.

mahaan, maha(e)m varr. MAHEM.

mahala /maˈhaː)la, məˈhɑːlə/ *adv.* and *adj.* [Zulu and S. Sotho *adv.*]
 More common in speech than in written contexts.
A. *adv.* For nothing, gratis. Cf. *basela adv.* (see BASELA *n.*).
 1941 'R. ROAMER ESQ.' in *Bantu World* 1 Mar. 4 Jos: And who gave her away in marriage? Jer: She gave herself away — mahala. *Ibid.* 8 Mar. 4 She says a man with a car can do anything with her. He can just have her mahala, without even seeing her parents about the matter. 1948 E. HELLMANN *Rooiyard* 40 Many domestic conflicts are occasioned by the desire of a man to give his friends beer *mahala* (free of charge), while his wife demands that his friends, who form the nucleus of her beer-custom, should pay for their drinks. *Ibid.* 60 The host and hostess dispense beer and food *mahala*. 1991 I.E.G. COLLETT *Informant, Pilgrim's Rest* Nothing for mahala: Nothing for gratis.
B. *adj.* Free; obtained without payment or difficulty.
 1977 *Weekend World* 31 July C1, There lies my bid for an easy R25. That's mahala money you might say.

mahayo var. MAHEWU.

mahem /məˈhem, maˈhem, ?ˈmeɪhem/ *n.* Also **amahen, maahoom, mahaan, maha(e)m, mayhem.** Pl. unchanged, or **-s**. [Xhosa *amahemu* crowned cranes (sing. *ihemu*); said to be imitative of their call. For an explanation of singular and plural forms, see AMA- and MA- *pref.³*] The crane *Balearica regulorum* of the Gruidae. Also *attrib.*
 [1810 G. BARRINGTON *Acct of Voy.* 302 The honey bird, unknown in Europe; .. the pekwe, the segizi, the heem ... The last, I think, is mentioned by Van Rhener, and called hemoe. 1826 see kaffir crane (KAFFIR *n.* sense 2 e).] 1827 G. THOMPSON *Trav.* II. 353 If a person kill by accident a mayhem, (or Balearic crane), .. he is obliged to sacrifice a calf or young ox in atonement. 1845 W.N. IRWIN *Echoes of Past* (1927) 232 I .. have a pair of the most beautiful birds in Africa (Amahens) which are even here very rare ... They are about three feet six inches in height. 1878 A. AYLWARD *Tvl of Today* 246 The crested crane, called 'mayhem,' should .. never be shot; it is a snake-killer. 1882 LADY F.C. DIXIE *In Land of Misfortune* 178 Two stately Mahaan birds .. were standing by a deep sedgy pool, with their long necks half buried in the water. 1905 W.L. SCLATER in Flint & Gilchrist *Science in S. Afr.* 143 The Mahem or Crowned Crane (*Balearica chrysopelargus*). 1936 E.L. GILL *First Guide to S. Afr. Birds* 176 *Mahem*, The name 'mahem' is supposed to be an imitation of its call. 1960 G. LISTER *Reminisc.* 83 My lovely golden-crested crane, the Mahem from Natal. 1980 J.O. OLIVER *Beginner's Guide to our Birds* 45 When in flight they stretch their necks and legs, and often

give their loud call as they fly away. The sound of this call has earned them the name of 'Mahem'. **1994** A. CRAIG in M. Roberts tr. *J.A. Wahlberg's Trav. Jrnls 1838-56* 35 Crowned crane *Balearica regulorum*, known as 'Mahem' from its call.

mahewu, mageu /maˈheːwʊ, maˈxe(w)ʊ/ *n.* Also **amageu, amahewu, (a)marewu, magayo, mageo, magewu, magou(w), mahayo, mah(-l)eu, mahou, mama(r)ghew, marewa, marhewu**, and with initial capital. [Xhosa *amarewu* (the 'r' being pronounced /x/), Zulu *amahewu*.] A non-alcoholic home-brewed drink made of thin, slightly fermented maize-meal porridge, often with wheat flour added; a similar, commercially manufactured drink sold in cartons, or in the form of an 'instant mix'. Cf. TSHWALA sense b.

[**1826** A.G. BAIN *Jrnls* (1949) 56 In the afternoon Siligho sent us .. large wooden dishes containing a mess something like Scotch porridge, but made of Caffre Corn boiled in thick milk. This they called Maghaby.] **c1913** J.M. ORPEN *Natives, Drink, Labour: Our Duty* (pamphlet) 88 [Hand-written note] Final best *Ama-Rewu* as used in East London Native Location. **1936** R.J.M. GOOLD-ADAMS *S. Afr. To-Day & To-Morrow* 176 Sip at a glass from the fermenting vats of mahewu. **1941** 'R. ROAMER' in *Bantu World* 1 Mar. 4 He says he'll ask for ginger-beer. I told him it would be better to ask for 'mahewu'. **1952** *Drum* Mar. 7 In the morning we had had 'maheu' (liquid fermented porridge), and in the evenings we had .. dry porridge. **1955** J.B. SHEPHARD *Land of Tikoloshe* 110 Of the two kinds of beer in common use, Marewa is the less potent; when it is freshly brewed it has little alcoholic content, being made from finely ground mealie meal which is boiled up into a thin porridge and then allowed to cool. Afterwards a little wheaten meal is stirred into the brew which is left to stand and form a head. **1962** W.D. HAMMOND-TOOKE *Bhaca Soc.* 20 Kaffir corn .. is reaped .. with a sickle, and a certain amount is gathered, before the reaping proper, for beer and marewu (fermented gruel). **1967** S.M.A. LOWE *Hungry Veld* 1 The Xhosa tribes .. provided him with cool refreshment in the form of their mahewu (*corn malt drink*) and maas (*their own most delicious kind of yoghourt*). **1973** *Evening Post* 2 Nov. 7 The children had interrupted their lessons at about 10am on Wednesday for the traditional drink of 'maheu', the vernacular name for their nutritional drink. **1979** *E. Prov. Herald* 26 Jan. (Indaba) 7 (*advt*) Instant Powdered Mahewu. It's the fantastic new thirst-quenching Mahewu that is ready to mix and drink immediately. **1980** E. JOUBERT *Poppie Nongena* 216 They'd baked bread and cooked samp mealies and made the sour magou drink with yeast and cornmeal and water. **1982** *Pace* May 36 Mageu was a non-intoxicating African brew ... Her friends loved it because it was a food-drink, it quenched your thirst while filling your tummy. **1986** P.A. MCALLISTER *Xhosa Beer Drinks.* 41 Apart from the common *utywala* (Xhosa), *utshwala* (Zulu) or *bjalwa* (Sotho), made in earlier times almost exclusively from sorghum but nowadays mainly from maize, a variety of similar but non-alcoholic beverages were made. These include *marhewu* (Xhosa), *igwele* and *isibebe* (Zulu), and *kepye* (Lovedu), which are fermented drinks made from maize meal. **1990** C. LAFFEATY *Far Forbidden Plains* 19 It gave him great pleasure to press upon her a bowl of *magouw*, made from fermented mealie-meal. **1991** G. HOFMEYR on TV1, 24 Apr. (The Big Time), Koffie car — oven with wheels — we use them in the location to sell pap and vleis, magheu, smiley. **1994** *Sunday Times* 18 Sept. 8 Packets of mealie-meal, boxes of mageu and a half-empty tray of *vet-koek* sit on the shelf.

mahli var. MALI.

mahlose pl. form of IDLOZI.

mahog /məˈhɒg, maˈhɔːg/ *n. slang.* Also **mahoga**. [Prob. abbrev. of Eng. slang *mahogany* brandy and water.] In urban (esp. township) parlance: brandy; HA-JA sense b.

1962 T. HOPKINSON *In Fiery Continent* 371 The favourite spirit was 'mahog', usually a sticky sweetish brandy which you could feel easing its claws into your liver and stomach as soon as it got inside. **1972** *Drum* 8 Feb. 26 We made arrangements to meet at a well-known shebeen to celebrate with mahog and beers. **1973** [see HA-JA sense a]. **1974** K.M.C. MOTSISI in M. Mutloatse *Casey & Co.* (1978) 52 He collects a whole straight of mahog and a case of be-ahs. *a***1977** [see MAIL v. sense 1]. **1980** [see HA-JA sense a]. **1990** O. MUSI in *City Press* 20 May 9 He .. was now wondering how he would pay Zandi for the straight of mahog he had just slugged.

mahoohoo var. MOHOHU.

mahou var. MAHEWU.

mah wo var. MAWO.

mai var. MAYE.

maid *n. offensive.* [Calqued on Afk. *meid* female servant, black woman.]
1. A demeaning term for a black woman (of any age, and not necessarily in domestic service).

1961 T. MATSHIKIZA *Choc. for my Wife* 126 They laughed into their big police van ... 'The maid is now called wife, caw, caw'. **1962** L.E. NEAME *Hist. of Apartheid* 84 A Non-White person .. a 'maid', a subhuman, a member of a child race created by a benevolent Deity to serve the material interests of the superior race. **1978** [see HOTNOT sense 2]. **1987** O. PROZESKY *Wrath of Lamb* 11 My mother was a teacher once, but all her life she was a 'girl' or a 'maid'. **1988** A. VAN NIEKERK in *Staffrider* Vol.7 No.2, 39 The resoluteness, the sacrifice and suffering of women, ranged against tyranny of those who call us maids. **1991** *Informant, Grahamstown* Please get me some tomatoes from the maids outside Checkers.
2. *comb.* **maid's meat**, **boy's meat** (see BOY sense 1 c).

1975 *Sunday Times* 12 Oct. 16 This syndrome is as South African as boerewors and pap — or rather, maid's meat.

mail *n.* see MAILER.

mail *v. slang.* [Back-formation fr. MAILER.]
1. *trans.* To send (someone) to buy or deal in liquor illicitly.

*a***1977** K.M.C. MOTSISI in M. Mutloatse *Casey & Co.* (1978) 64 Once in a while you found a gweva who was as dirty as his face and his rags. You mail him for a bottle of mahog. What does he do? He creeps back with a bottle of cheap vino. Gives it you on the sly at a street corner and scuttles.
2. *intrans.* To act as a go-between in the purchase of illicit liquor.

1980 E. JOUBERT *Poppie Nongena* 209, I know this man, I see him walking up and down, he's a mailer. For whom does he mail? He carries drink to the shebeen queens.

mailer *n. Hist. slang.* [Prob. transf. use of Eng. *mailer* one who conveys mail.] A liquor-runner who bought from a regular outlet, for resale to an illicit liquor dealer or drinking establishment. Also *occas.* shortened to **mail**. See also GWEVA.

Under the Liquor Act (Act No. 30 of 1928) the supply of spirituous liquor to anyone but a white person was outlawed; this led to the employment of lighter-skinned or white people as liquor-runners.

1950 E. PARTRIDGE *Dict. of Underworld Slang* 428 Mail, A liquor-carrier for an illicit saloon, etc. **1950** *Cape Times* 17 June (Weekend Mag.) 5 As soon as the bottle-store opens, the *mailer* is there. He gets his regulation two bottles and takes this to the shebeen. Then he goes to another bottle-store for a further two bottles. And so he goes on the whole day. **1950** *Ibid.* [see DOP *n.* sense 2 a]. **1952** 'SKAPPIE' in *Drum* Nov. 6 Shebeens always depended on the 'mail'. Before all liquor purchases were recorded, your 'mail' was a white, or near-white, who supplied on a commission basis ... These 'mails' .. often spent a considerable part of their lives in jail. **1959** *Drum* Jan. 27, I have to rely on the services of 'mailers'. These are ordinary white men who are allowed to enter bottle stores, and for a small fee will buy liquor for us. **1959** *Cape Argus* 14 Nov. 2 When we stopped the delivery the shebeens arranged for mailers to get the liquor for them. **1962** T. HOPKINSON *In Fiery Continent* 101 A couple of hardcase whites. These last were 'mailers', purveyors of illicit liquor. They buy drink, chiefly brandy and beer, at liquor stores as if for themselves, and turn it over to the shebeen 'queens'. **1974** in *Eng. Usage in Sn Afr.* Vol.5 No.1, 10 Various social practices are reflected in the terminology ... The outside term 'mailer' was common before the liquor-for-all days. **1977** D. MULLER *Whitey* 32 By this time the legal bottle-stores would be open, and the 'mailers' — the runners from shebeens big and small — would be at the counters, buying supplies for the long-week-end-thirst. **1986** D. CASE *Love, David* 110 'Yes, Oupa,' David explained. 'I was working with a mailer. The day that they caught us, I had a few parcels on me.'

main man /ˈmeɪn man/ *n. phr. Colloq.* Also **mynman**. Pl. **-manne** /-nə/. [Eng. *main* chief + Afk. *man*, *manne*, guy; perh. ad. U.S. Eng. *main man* best friend, hero.] An important or dominant person (usu. male); a man who has an exaggerated sense of his own importance; BRA sense 3; BROER sense 6; MAIN OU; OU *n.* sense 4 b. See also BREKER, MAN *n.*[2] sense 1.

1970 *Forum* Vol.6 No.2, 27 'That ou's just thinking he's a mynman,' replied the drunk and added, 'Kriste, he mustn't start with me.' **1972** M. DEVELIN on Radio South Africa 25 Jan., That ou schemes he's like a mainman. (That gentleman considers himself to be a big cog in a small machine.) **1982** J. ALLAN in *Sunday Times* 6 June (Mag. Sect.), Face-to-face with one of the 'main manne' over a road house menu ... So you see, what better place to interview the main man than at a roadhouse? **1983** *Frontline* Sept. 50 Frank Sinatra, Lisa Minelli, Linda Ronstadt, George Benson, Mike Weaver, Jimmy Connors, Ivan Lendl .. these are all main manne, and how. **1983** *Daily Dispatch* 7 Nov. 1 While ministers and main manne speeched and speeched and speeched in the corrugated iron-roofed barn, you could see the mampoer drinkers a mile away. **1986** H. PRENDINI in *Style* May 43 Piepiejoller is a word that crops up often among the over-15s and seems to refer to anyone under 15. The opposite end of the scale are the *main manne*, South African version of big deal. **1989** *Cape Times* 4 Sept. 6 Don't hold your demo just after 4 pm when all the main *manne* in the police are on their way home and cannot be phoned. It really delays things. **1994** on Radio South Africa 10 Oct., You always get the guys who argue, 'Let's do this, let's do that', you know, the main manne.

main ou /ˈmeɪn əʊ/ *n. phr. Colloq.* Pl. **main ous**, **— ou's**, **— ouens** /əʊəns/ [Eng. *main* chief + OU *n.* sense 1 a.] MAIN MAN.

1978 A. AKHALWAYA in *Rand Daily Mail* 10 July 7 Ask any of his 'maats', and they'll tell you he is the 'main ou' or the 'dada' ... And our main ou, who is also a 'chaar ou' (Indian), has friends of all races. **1984** *Frontline* Feb. 27 Apparently the main ou is a Cape ou, and the Cape ous are winning so far. **1987** S. BAGLEY in *Cosmopolitan* Dec. 168, I can't even take a lady out to dinner or walk down Church Street without almost being lynched because I'm a 'main ou' in leathers. **1990** *Personality* 16 July 14 The kids catch on .. fast, learning how to operate from the main ou's long before they're ten years old. **1993** *Weekly Mail* 8 Apr. 3 She said: 'We won't get raided tonight because they're showing the main *ouens* how the whores operate.' Then .. she added that she found one policeman's bandy legs 'so cute'.

mais-hand, -hond varr. MUISHOND.

maiza /ˈmaɪza/ *n.* Also **miza**. [Isicamtho, ad. Eng. *maize*.] In urban (esp. township) slang: (commercially manufactured) beer made from sprouted maize; cf. TSHWALA sense b. Also *attrib.*

1968 *Drum* Sept. 30 The local maiza in Germiston, which sells for 10c a scale. *a***1977** K.M.C. MOTSISI in M. Mutloatse *Casey & Co.* (1978) 133 Next time the quack and nurses call around this 'Bara' bed of mine they will find me singing — *Show me the way to go home* with a smile as wide as a two-up of maiza. **1979** *Pace* Sept. 28 The calabash goes round and round, and everybody shakes it and gulps down the only beverage of immortality 'mbamba,' some call it 'maiza,' the Afrikaner call it 'Bantoe bier'.

maizena /mə'ziːnə, meɪ-/ *n.* Also **mazina**, and with initial capital. [Formed on *maize*; not originally S. Afr. Eng., but apparently now obs. elsewhere.] The proprietary name (with initial capital) of a brand of fine maize flour or corn flour; applied loosely to any similar flour, which is used in cooking as a thickener.

[**1863** *Rep. Juries Exhib. 1862* III. A. 13 Maizena or corn starch used for food.] **1867** T. SHONE Diary. 2 Aug., Mrs Roberts sent Me. Viz 3 papers Mazina 2lb Sperm Candles. **1890** A.G. HEWITT *Cape Cookery* 54 Rub the baking powder into the flour and maizena, add to the eggs and butter. *Ibid.* 56 Thicken the sauce with a little maizena. **1891** H.J. DUCKITT *Hilda's 'Where Is It?'* 193 Set the milk to boil .. keeping half a cup to mix with the maizena and butter and the yolks of the eggs. When the milk boils pour in the maizena, etc.; stir till quite done, which can be told by the maizena coming off from the bottom of the saucepan. **1913** A. GLOSSOP *Barnes's S. Afr. Household Guide* 76 If, when ready, the curry needs thickening, mix into a smooth paste a little maizena or flour, and stir into it. **1918** *D.S.G. Bk of Recipes* (ed.3) 78 Maizena Cake. **1928** M. MOLLER *What Every Housewife Should Know* 5 Make a paste by using 2 tablespoonfuls (level measure) maizena and ½ pint water. **1950** H. GERBER *Cape Cookery* 62 Thicken the soup with a little maizena dissolved in water, and a lump of fresh butter. **1970** A. THERON *More S. Afr. Deep Freezing* 173 *Maizena*, This is a brand name for only one of several makes of corn flour. But I have never heard any South African speak of corn flour — its always Maizena. **1973** *Weekend Post* 27 Oct. (Parade) 7 Mix the maizena, salt and lemon juice. Then add the orange juice and stir over boiling water until mixture thickens. **1977** *The 1820* Vol.50 No.12, 15 You have probably searched in the supermarket for items which are marketed in this country under a different name, and certainly you have heard unfamiliar sounding names for foods — e.g. maizena which is cornflour and frikkadel which is rissole, etc. **1991** F.G. BUTLER *Local Habitation* 74 He was like an extra juvenile member of the party. He had to be fed on baby foods and maizena.

majaha var. AMAJAHA.

majat /ma'dʒat/ *n. slang.* [Unkn., perh. ad. Malay *madat* opium.] Marijuana (see DAGGA *n.*[2] sense 1), esp. that of an inferior grade.

1956 A. LA GUMA in *New Age* 4 Oct. 6 Ingenious methods have been discovered to secrete tiny things which make life a little more tolerable. Even dagga, known as 'majat' in prison slang, finds its way into the cells. **1969** *Drum* Aug. 43 Between R75 and R100 is paid per bag, depending on the quality and particular strain of the plant. The first grade is called 'Rooipoortjie', second grade is 'Jong Dagga' or 'Pieper' and the third grade is called 'Majat' in the Cape. **1974** J. MATTHEWS *Park* 20 The air was heavy with the pungent smell of dagga ... 'Gran' stuff dis,' Orkas said, exhaling twin streams of smoke. 'Not like de majat Bones sell us las' night.' .. 'Majat Bones sells only good forra sheep.' **1978** C. VAN WYK in *Staffrider* Vol.1 No.2, 36 Tell him, good dagga. Good dagga for Kiet. Not majat. **1987** *Scope* 6 Nov. 33 At Jeppe, they scored two pokes of dagga ... It was Majat, not the best quality, but who cared on that Sunday morning. **1990** *South* 27 Feb. 6 Brands and quality vary from the despised 'majat' to the internationally valued Swazi Gold and Durban Poison.

majita /mə'dʒitə, ma'dʒiːta/ *n. slang.* Forms: *sing.* **majika, mjieta, mjita**; *sing.* and *pl.* **(ama)jita, majieta, matji(e)ta, mayita**. Pl. also **-s**. [Isicamtho, prob. coined *c*1951 in the form *majika*, ad. *magic*, fr. *The Magic Garden*, the title of a film released in that year which depicts, among other things, the life of a black South African petty thief. For notes on the variety of (esp. pl.) forms, see AMA-, MA- *pref.*[2], and MA- *pref.*[3]] In urban (esp. township) parlance: 'chap', 'guy', used in the following ways:

a. As a common noun: a black youth or a black adult male. Also **lamajita** /ˌlama'dʒita/ *pl. n.* [Isicamtho and Zulu enclitic *la-* this, these], 'these chaps', 'these guys'.

[**1956** 'MR DRUM' in *Drum* Apr. 6 Take this spice-and-pepper language known as the Lingo or 'Die witty van die reely-reely majietas' (The language of the real McCoy bright-boys).] **1963** L.F. FREED *Crime in S. Afr.* 126 If he becomes a criminal tsotsi, he is known as a 'majita' or a 'majika'. **1978** M.P. GWALA in *Staffrider* Vol.1 No.2, 6 Playboy Joe was already at Umgababa, pulling dagga zol with other matjietas. **1984** [see BRA sense 5]. **1984** C. MATHIANE in *Staffrider* Vol.6 No.1, 30 The following day was Friday which meant, like most majitas, he had to end the week well by downing a bottle or two with the guys at the joint. **1987** *Learn & Teach* No.5, 17 They say Hillbrow is mos a klein America. Darkies and Lanies live together. It is a 24 hour place — good for a young mjita like me. **1989** *Weekly Mail* 20 Oct. 28, I felt the power of the ex-prisoners in my bones in the ensuing theatre. The glory of that day was summed up by one of three youths at the back of my car when he remarked: 'Lamajita (these guys) are great. By the way, we did not even exist when they were jailed.' **1994** on TV1, 30 July (The Line), The situation was a mess until we, the majitas, moved in.

b. As a term of address to a black man or youth.

1979 M. MATSHOBA *Call Me Not a Man* 50, I looked at my comrades and said, 'There we go, majita. Let the hammers pound while the sickles swish.' **1981** B. MFENYANA in M. Mutloatse *Reconstruction* 298 Are you one of those characters that flip, freak or fret everytime they hear another new word like botsotso, devushka, shishkebab or halaal? Well mjita, you've got a friend right here. **1986** [see HEIT sense a]. **1990** M. MELAMU in *Lynx* 291 'Ja, majita,' Oupa concluded, 'the mpimpi is hinty, They say the Duke got him at last.' *Ibid.* 305 My father and his friend came to a dead stop. The tsotsis looked them over, and the one who appeared to be the leader of the group turned to his companions and said, in the racy jargon of the breed of animal: 'Majita, it seems we are in for an easy pay-day, of hoe sê ek?'

majoni var. AMAJONI.

Majuba Day /mə'dʒuːbə ˌdeɪ/ *n. phr.* [Named for the scene of the battle at *Majuba* mountain (ad. of its Zulu name *Amajuba* 'the doves', 'the pigeons') near Volksrust in KwaZulu-Natal.] The 27th of February, the date of a significant Boer victory against British forces in 1881, during the first Anglo-Boer War.

[**1891** J. KELLY *Coming Revolt of Eng. in Tvl* 6, I will not .. dwell longer on the great and crowning day of Majuba, but go straight to the events which transpired afterwards.] **1902** C.R. DE WET *Three Yrs War* 361 On the 27th of February, 1902 — 'Majuba Day' — Commandant van Merwe [*sic*] and four hundred men fell into the hands of the enemy. On that very day, in the year 1881, the famous battle of Majuba had been fought. **1969** J. MEINTJES *Sword in Sand* 72 The following day would be the 27th, Majuba Day ... And it was on that day that General Piet Cronje .. surrendered to Lord Roberts ... 'Why not a day sooner or a day later.' General de la Rey lamented in Bloemfontein. 'Why on Majuba Day!' **1988** *E. Prov. Herald* 31 Mar. 2 Mr Botha was replying to the militant organisation's [*sc.* the AWB's] petition to the Government on Majuba Day demanding the return of Boer land. **1993** B. KRIGE in *Sunday Times* 4 Apr. 17 The Bush Pub will .. close for Republic Day, the Day of the Vow and Majuba Day.

‖**mak** /mak/ *adj. colloq.* Also **maak**. [Afk., fr. Du.] **1.** Docile, tame, tractable.

[**1822** W.J. BURCHELL *Trav.* I. 227 They were Bushmen belonging to a kraal near the Zak river. The people of this horde being in amity with the boors, were therefore denominated Makke Boschjemans (Tame Bushmen). **1846** R. MOFFAT *Missionary Labours* 30 'Why!' I asked, 'did you not bring her sooner?' 'She was afraid to see you, and would not come, till I assured her that you were a *maak mensche*.'] **1937** C.R. PRANCE *Tante Rebella's Saga* 153 The Police Commandant might be so 'mak' and friendly as almost to entitle him to rank as 'een van onse mense' — one of us. **1963** S. CLOETE *Rags of Glory* 427 An ox, a gelding, a hamel, a cut thing, mak, tame, able to make war on women. **1970** *News/Check* 4 Sept. 31 Rowan is no radical. He is the South African equivalent of a *Mak Sap.* **1977** *Sunday Times* 13 Nov. 16 For years the Progs have been accused of attracting only 'mak Afrikaners' to their ranks.

2. In the special collocation **mak Engels(e)** /- 'ɛŋəls(ə)/ [Afk., *Engels* English (pl. *-e*)], white South African English-speakers who either support the National Party or are ineffectual in their efforts to oppose it. See also ENGELS *n.* sense 2 a.

1948 P.V.G. VAN DER BYL in *Hansard* 20 Jan. 111 Should it bring them into power they will then pick up the hidden Republican policy and deal with the English-speaking section and particularly the 'mak-Engels' who were foolish enough to vote for them. **1978** *Sunday Times* 19 Mar. 10 Mr Kruger is deliberately having a crack at Natal. One of these days the so-called 'mak-Engelse' (tame English) will tell the likes of Jimmy Kruger where to get off.

makatane *n. obs.* Also **mackatan, makata(a)n, makatani, mangatan**. Pl. usu. unchanged; occas. **-s**. [SeTswana, pl. form of *lekatane* tsamma melon. For notes on singular and plural forms, see LE- and MA- *pref.*[2]] TSAMMA; freq. *pl.*

1833 J. ARCHBELL in A. Steedman *Wanderings* (1835) II. 35 The houses had in them the furniture and utensils usual to the country, and a few melons (*makatani*). **1835** A. SMITH *Diary* (1940) II. 38 They bought skins and mackatan for barter, also a few ostrich feathers. **1900** S.T. PLAATJE *Boer War Diary* (1973) 110 Some women went out in the direction of Signal Hill to gather green makatane, etc. from their fields. **1912** A.W. HODSON *Trekking Great Thirst* 39 There were a few *makatane* amongst them, which we put carefully on one side for ourselves, and the *kgeñwe* we cut up to give to our horses. **1913** C. PETTMAN *Africanderisms* 305 *Makatan*, A variety of water-melon from Bechuanaland which makes splendid feeding for stock, and is now being grown in the Karoo. *c*1929 L.P. BOWLER *Afr. Nights* 110 Hitherto, Piet had been forced to subsist on *makatane* or kgenwe, the marvellous water-melon that grows in the arid, sandy wastes of the Kalahari Desert ... Without these makatanes certain areas of the Kalahari would be impenetrable to animals or people. *c*1936 *S. & E. Afr. Yr Bk & Guide* 528 Explorers during part of the year have to rely for drink upon the fruit of the Tsama, a species of melon .. also known by the name of Makatan.

Makatees *pl. n. Obs.* Also **Makatese**. [Afk., prob. ad. Sotho *MmaNtatisi* (see MANTATEE).] (The) members of the MANTATEE section of the Tlokwa people.

As is the case with many names of peoples and groups in *S. Afr. Eng.*, this word has been found only in plural uses; however, it may be that it has also been used in unrecorded singular forms.

1892 W.L. DISTANT *Naturalist in Tvl* 107 The Makatese, originally fugitives from the Basuto and Bechuana countries and taking their name from the supposition that they were all subjects of Ma Ntatisi, are now the most numerous in Zoutpansberg. **1905** W.H. TOOKE in Flint & Gilchrist *Science in S. Afr.* 93 Individual members of this extinct clan, driven as fugitives hither and thither, are still called by the Boers 'Makatees'. Hence probably the Kafir word for Bechuana, 'amahadi'.

make *v. trans.* In the phr. ***to make a plan*** [calqued on Afk. *maak 'n plan*], to devise a way of doing something, esp. of overcoming some difficulty; *maak 'n plan*, see MAAK sense 2.

1905 P. GIBBON *Vrouw Grobelaar* 115 Instead of going out to be shot like a fool, he made a plan. **1937** C.R. PRANCE *Tante Rebella's Saga* 34 His wagon was unfortunately away, but if the Commandant would drink coffee and rest awhile, he would try to make a plan. **1946** S. CLOETE *Afr. Portraits* 71 A Boer when in difficulties always makes a plan — plan maak — and he allowed his enemies to think that he was so enchanted with their country that he intended to settle in it. **1957** D. JACOBSON *Price of Diamonds* 113 What have I ever had in my life except what I grabbed and held on to with both hands and made a plan for, at once? *c*1967 J. HOBBS in *New S. Afr. Writing* 74 We will make a plan to show that Uitlander a thing or two, nè? **1976** A.P. BRINK *Instant in Wind* 220 'It's all right.' he said. 'You can stay here until we make a plan.' *c*1977 [see Okes quot. at NOU JA]. **1979** *Star* 17 Jan., It's not that the farmers aren't making a plan either. At is already in the export business — exporting bricks to that place the Government likes to call Bophuthatswana. **1990** *Frontline* Mar.-Apr. 21 'Leave it to me,' he says. 'I'll make a plan.' **1991** *Sunday Times* 7 Apr. 26 Sadly, these days the *skeis* are not made from wood. When the bottom dropped out of the ox-wagon market, the *boere* were forced to make another plan. Now the *skeis* are composed of some kind of rubber compound.

make a draai see DRAAI sense 1 c.

mak gauw, - hoe varr. *maak gou* (see MAAK v. sense 1).

makgotla var. and pl. form of KGOTLA.

Makgo(w)a pl. form of LEKGOA.

makhamba var. KAMBA.

makhotla(s) pl. form of KGOTLA.

Makho(w)a pl. form of LEKGOA.

makhuloo var. MAKULU.

‖**makhulu** /maˈkʊːlʊ/ *n*. Also **kulu**, and with initial capital. [Xhosa and Zulu *umakhulu* (pl. *omakhulu*), n. prefix *u-* + MA- pref.¹ + *-khulu* great, big.] Grandmother; old woman; also used without an article, in place of a name. Cf. MA-GOGO.

1978 *E. Prov. Herald* 4 Mar. 8 Ward Able, Olga ... passed away on 2nd March ... Loving kulu of Richden and Denrich. **1980** E. JOUBERT *Poppie Nongena* 244, I must cook for tatomkhulu and makhulu. **1981** *Voice* 8 July 5 Sindi .. wondered why Makhulu should remember her in a time of need.

makhulu adj. var. MAKULU.

makhwenkwe pl. form of INKWENKWE.

Makoa, Makoöas pl. forms of LEKGOA.

makolwa var. KHOLWA.

makora, makor(r)o varr. MOKORO.

makoti /maˈkɔːti/ *n*. Also **makothi**, and with initial capital. Pl. *-s*, occas. **omakoti** /ˌɔmaˈkɔːti/. [Zulu *umakoti* (pl. *omakoti*).] Esp. among speakers of a Sintu (Bantu) language:
1. A bride; a newly-wed woman.

1949 L. HUNTER *Afr. Dawn* 187 Although she missed her husband, she was never lonely .. and there was no lack of friends to call on the *makoti* — the newly married woman. **1959** L. LONGMORE *Dispossessed* 95 They sang the whole night, and had by custom to be fed by the people of *makoti* (the bride). **1970** M. DIKOBE *Marabi Dance*. 40 'George, you call me a woman.' 'Yes I do, because you are dressed like an old auntie. Long German print dress, headgear fastened like a makoti — bride.' **1982** M. MZAMANE *Children of Soweto* 178 I'm only sad because I'm being deprived of my new *makoti*, barely twelve hours after I've inherited her. **1989** J. KHUMALO in *Pace* Mar. 19 'Durban people have always welcomed me with love,' says Brenda, 'and I'm thrilled to bits to be their "Makoti" (bride).'

2. A daughter-in-law; a term used by the family of a woman's husband to refer to her.

1963 B. MODISANE *Blame Me on Hist.* (1986) 45 When a relative died in Alexandra Township Princess accompanied her to the tebello, working in the catering; she was the ideal makoti, the African daughter-in-law. **1979** *Voice* 23 Sept. 5 That old debate about the Mother-in-law-Makoti Syndrome ... It would .. be welcomed, if mothers-in-law would stop regarding their makotis as total strangers in the home. **1982** [see GOGO n.²]. **1987** M. POLAND *Train to Doringbult* 124 Once he too stayed with Ngubane, but he had run away with the money the makoti had given him to buy her bread and sugar. **1988** J. KHUMALO in *Pace* Nov. 83 Old Ngcobo, Bheki's father, would be horrified if his makoti sought permission to take time off from her society-decreed household chores to go and prance around the country's stages in the company of men other than her husband.

makuka pl. form of LEKUKA.

makulu /məˈkuːlu, maˈkʊːlʊ/ *adj. colloq.* Also **makhuloo, makhulu, mukulu**. [Fanakalo, fr. Xhosa and Zulu sentence *makhulu* they are big, pl. subjectival concord *ma-* + adj. stem *-khulu* big.]

1. Also with initial capital. In the special collocation **makulubaas** /-ˌbɑːs/ [see BAAS; prob. first used in Fanakalo], 'big boss':

a. A male employer; a powerful official in an organization; (occas.) any white male. Now usu. ironical.

[1899 G.H. RUSSELL *Under Sjambok* 195 You will give this letter to the Baas mukulu (manager).] **1953** LANHAM & MOPELI-PAULUS *Blanket Boy's Moon* 121 Libe .. asked his Makulu Baas for a day's unpaid leave. **1970** S.E. NATHAM Informant, Cape Town You'd better be good all day as the Makulubaas will be coming sometime. **1978** *Voice* 25 Nov. 16 The 'makhulubaas' of Black soccer. **1979** *Ibid.* 7 Oct. 2 For a moment, one of our Makulu baases, Dr Andries Treurnicht, must have wondered what he was all about. **1987** *Pace* May 4 This mlungu .. curses the day he decided to settle in this .. continent. The bad luck makhulu baas .. now walks with a limp because of a mysterious accident. **1987** [see PARAMOUNT sense a]. **1991** O. MUSI in *Drum* Dec. 18 The driver will .. explain to her in terse terms the 'makhulubaas' wants his stove back unless she forks out the balance of R500. **1991** S.I. ABRAHAMS Informant, Port Elizabeth Makulu baas. The big boss or head of the firm or institution. eg. Did you know that 'so-and-so' is the new makulu baas of the factory?

b. As an ironical title for a government minister, esp. a head of state; also used as a form of address. Also part. tr. **makulu boss**.

1982 *Voice* 21 Mar. 4 Makhulubaas Influx Throttle is virtually telling Cape Town's Black refugees .. : don't starve here, starve in the Sebes' and Matanzimas' paradises. **1985** *Pace* Aug. 4 The heads of the .. neighbouring states of Venda, Bophuthatswana, Transkei and Ciskei have come together to have talks with 'makhulu baas' in Pretoria. **1986** *Drum* Apr. 36 It would be .. presumptuousness on the part of this scribe to try to interpret makhulubaas PW Botha's Rubicon II speech. **1987** *Ibid.* July 11 Makhuloo Baas you must realise that some of our white brothers .. have come to realise that their destiny is tied up with our destiny. **1991** P. SLABOLEPSZY *Bright Laaities*. 8 A French Dutchman who became Makulu Boss Prime Minister of South Africa.

2. Big; important; impressive; foremost.

1959 E. MPHAHLELE *Down Second Ave* 108 Why-for you maker so much *makulu* troble-troble. **1977** *Argus* 13 Jan. 10 (*advt*) Mr McCrae is a makulu manager, and he drives a makulu car. **1981** *Voice* 18 Feb. 2 After the raid which left many mutilated bodies, the Bishop is reported to have smiled: 'That's nothing! That's peanuts! More is coming.' What words from a cleric! Nogal from a makhulu-mfundisi. **1987** *Weekly Mail* 11 Sept. 21 September is *makulu*-boy, another way of saying he's a reliable worker. **1991** G. HOFMEYR on TV1, 24 Apr. (Big Time), You must get Papademos — he's the makhulu man.

makwedini pl. form of KWEDINI.

makweta var. ABAKWETHA.

mal /mal/ *adj. colloq.* [Afk.]
Common in spoken contexts.
1. Mad, crazy; angry.

1970 V. YOUNG Informant, Queenstown He makes me mal (mad — angry). **1987** L. BEAKE *Strollers* 21 He whistled. 'You must be mal, man. Going with Katjie se mob!' **1991** A. JAY on Radio 5, 8 May, Listen to that noise out there — the boys are going completely mal.

2. In the phrr. *to maak mal* [Afk. *maak* make], *to make mal*, to make merry, to revel. See also JOL v. sense 3.

1991 G. DE BEER Informant, Port Nolloth (N. Cape), I chowed and schemed about maaking mal later ... I ate and thought about enjoying myself later. *Ibid.* We went to Joburg and made mal.

malagas, -gash, -gos varr. MALGAS.

malaita var. AMALAITA.

Malalapipe /maˈlaːlaˈpaɪp, məˈlɑːlə-/ *n. slang.* Also with small initial. Pl. unchanged, or -s. [ad. Zulu *umalalepayipini* tramp, homeless child (pl. *omalalepayipini*), *uma-* one who + *lala* sleeps + *epayipini* in a drain (loc. prefix *e-* + *ipayipi* drain, pipe, ad. Eng. *pipe*).] In urban (esp. township) English: STROLLER. Also *attrib*.

[1962 K.M.C. MOTSISI in M. Mutloatse *Casey & Co.* (1978) 44 Sis Curls simply doesn't like my guts. Just on account of this pal of mine called Kid Malalapipe — which means a guy of no fixed abode.] **1973** M. DIKOBE in *New African* (4 June 1990) 13 The skokiaan enabled the hen to fight more bravely ... They knew marabi as a dance party for persons of a 'low type' and for 'malalapipe' homeless ruffian children. **1986** E. NKOSI in *Pace* May 32 They call themselves the 'Malalapipes', these kids. Look in any South African city and you'll find them, living rough, sniffing glue and smoking dope. At night they sleep in derelict buildings, or in abandoned cars, or even in dustbins.

‖**mala mogodu** /ˌmaːla mɔˈxɔːdʊ/ *n. phr.* Also **mala le mogodu**. [Sotho, *mala* intestines + *mogodu* (see MOGODU).] MOGODU.

*a*1978 K.M.C. MOTSISI in M. Mutloatse *Casey & Co.* (1978) 69, I must have a manly slug of the waters of immortality to feel for favourite diet of pap and mala le mogodu [chitterlings] liberally spiced with mixed masala or chillies. Yum. **1977** *World* 23 Sept. 19, I missed little things which I took for granted when I was still in South Africa. I longed for 'mala le mogodu' and walking down the dusty streets of the townships. **1986** M. MASIPA in *Pace* May (Queen) 25 Here under the open sky her business is booming. Mandawo has been selling 'mala mogodu' since 1975. **1987** *Learn & Teach* No.3, 45 Hey! My malamogodu's gone! Look, who's the thief? **1988** *Ibid.* No.1, 9 The pavement is buzzing. It's alive. A woman is frying mala mogodu on a dustbin lid.

Malanite /məˈlanaɪt/ *n. hist.* [The surname of D.F. Malan (1874–1959), prime minister of South Africa (1948–54) and National Party leader, + Eng. suffix *-ite* denoting a follower or adherent.] A supporter of D.F. Malan and his policies. Also *attrib*.

1933 *Rand Daily Mail* 15 Feb. 9 The feeling between the Prime Minister and the Malanites is strained. **1934** *Times* 20 Jan. 9 A manifesto expressing unshakable confidence in General Hertzog and deprecating Malanite agitation. **1938** [see UP]. **1968** W.K. HANCOCK *Smuts* II. 253 In October 1933 at Bloemfontein the Malanites repudiated Hertzog. **1971** D. WORRALL *S. Afr.* 201 After the election the opposition of the Malanites stiffened as the trend towards fusion quickened. **1977** T.R.H. DAVENPORT *S. Afr.: Mod. Hist.* 253 The Malanites had not agreed with all aspects of Hertzog's policy in 1936–7, standing out in particular against the continued presence of Coloured people on the Cape electoral roll.

Malay *n*. and *adj.* [Eng., tr. Du. *Maleier* fr. Malay *Melayu* person of Malayan origin, speaker of the Malayan language. See quot. 1979.]

A. *n.*

1. CAPE MALAY *n. phr.* **2.** *rare.* CAPE COLOURED *n. phr.*

1765 MRS KINDERSLEY *Lett.* (1777) 65 Some of them are called Malays or Malaynese, brought from the country of Malacca, and the islands to the eastward of India, subject to the Dutch company. **1786** G. FORSTER tr. *A. Sparrman's Voy. to Cape of G.H.* I. 12 To the south .. are seen the burial grounds of the Chinese and free Malays that live at the Cape. **1804** R. PERCIVAL *Acct of Cape of G.H.* 86 The Hottentots .. are both more ordinary in their faces, and not so well made in their persons as the Malays. **1822** W.J. BURCHELL *Trav.* I. 73 The Malays have .. a house dedicated to the Mahometan form of worship, with a regular priest established and supported by themselves. *a*1823 J. EWART *Jrnl* (1970) 27 The Malays form no inconsiderable part of the population of Cape Town. These have been brought at different periods from the Dutch settlements in Java and neighbouring islands. They are a very ingenious people and are the only artificers in the place. **1827** A.J. JARDINE *Fragment of Church Hist.* 34 The Malays in Cape Town are said to amount to 3000, and converts are almost daily added. **1835** G. CHAMPION *Jrnl* (1968) 2 Have commenced studying the Dutch. Its harsh guttural sounds are constantly annoying us as the numerous tribes of servants, Hottentots, Malays, .. children &c are passing & repassing our narrow streets. *Ibid.* 28 The Malays or Mahometans are a large & distinct body, consider themselves a grade above the others, & in some respects are accessible by the Christian Teacher. **1861** LADY DUFF-GORDON *Lett. from Cape* (1925) 33 Malay here seems equivalent to Mohammedan. They were originally Malays, but now they include every shade, from the blackest negro to the most blooming English woman ... Emigrant girls have been known to turn 'Malays' and get thereby husbands who know not billiards and brandy — the two diseases of Cape Town. **1877** R.M. BALLANTYNE *Settler & Savage* 35 He stormed in Dutch at three of his unfortunate people, or rather slaves. One was a sturdy Hottentot, named Ruyter, one a Malay named Abdul Jemalee. **1883** [see MEBOS]. **1904** H.A. BRYDEN *Hist. of S. Afr.* 11 As small traders, shopkeepers, artisans, horsekeepers, and fishermen, the careful Malays have thriven ..; during a period of more than two centuries they have preserved their own customs and the Mohammedan religion. **1936** *Cambridge Hist. of Brit. Empire* VIII. 263 Malays .. were found in useful employment as skilled tailors, carpenters and cobblers. **1949** E. HELLMANN *Handbk on Race Rel.* 588 It [*sc.* Islam] welded its adherents into a compact group and if to this group the term 'Malay' has come to be applied, it denotes a religious and not a racial group. **1951** L.G. GREEN *Grow Lovely* 187 About 150 Malay words .. remained in the Afrikaans spoken by the Malays, and some are more widely used — such words as atjar, blatjang and katel. **1953** *Drum* May 44 There are about 30,000 Malays and one million Coloureds. **1973** *Cape Times* 7 Feb. 10 In Cape Town the terms 'Malay' and 'Mohammedan' are often used as synonyms. Strictly speaking, however, 'Malay' refers to that section of the Coloured community in which the descendants of the Eastern Malays are to be found. **1979** 'J.C.' in *Natal Witness* 2 Feb. 11 The number of slaves' names examined was 4890, only 0,31 percent of which (16 persons) came from Malaysia. Yet the majority of the slaves were described as Malays. In his summing up Dr Bradlow suggests that they were called Malays for linguistic reasons, the Malay language being the trading medium (like Swahili in East Africa) for a vast geographical area stretching from Madagascar to China. **1981** *Sunday Times* 12 July (Mag. Sect.) 1 'We speak the most beautiful Afrikaans in the country,' said Mr Ebrahim Schroeder, a prominent Malay. 'We use words drawn from Malay, Arabic and English.'

3. *comb.* **Malay cart**, a small, two-wheeled cart formerly much used in the Cape Malay community; **Malay magic**, occult arts, esp. involving poltergeists and psychokinesis, supposedly practised by Cape Malays; cf. GOËLERY; see also SLAMAAIER sense 2; **Malay Quarter**, a residential area of Cape Town, situated below Signal Hill, in which Cape Malays have traditionally lived, see quot. 1989; **Malay-tricked** *ppl adj.*, affected by *Malay magic*; **Malay trickery**, **Malay tricks**, see *Malay magic*.

1861 LADY DUFF-GORDON *Lett. from Cape* (1925) 49 A light **Malay cart** (a capital vehicle with two wheels) and four horses. [*Ibid.* 50 The cart is small, with a permanent tilt at top, and moveable curtains of water-proof all round; harness of raw leather, very prettily put together by Malay workmen.] **1900** W.W. SKEAT (*title*) **Malay Magic**. **1934** *Cape Argus* 27 Jan. (Swart), Malay 'magic' assumes a hundred different forms. **1966** I.D. DU PLESSIS *Poltergeists* 53 Malay magic goes further than the use of charms and love potions. *Ibid.* 83 Whether we believe in these supernormal phenomena or not, .. what is locally known as 'Malay Magic' or 'Malay Tricks' is to be found not only in Cape Town or in South Africa but all over the world. **1970** [see GOËLERY]. **1971** L.G. GREEN *Taste of S.-Easter* 146 The kris (or creese), a dagger either straight or curved and elaborately decorated, plays a large part in Malay magic. **1920** R. JUTA *Tavern* 29 Above the square, almost honeycombed into the hill behind, the tiny mosques and white and pink and yellow houses of the **Malay Quarter** showed. **1989** T. BOTHA in *Style* Dec. 158 The real Malay Quarter isn't really a quarter. It's not even an eighth. Of the Bo-Kaap, that is. Lots of people, even residents, talk about it generally as the neighbourhood on the Signal Hill side of the city. But .. it's located between Chiappini and Buitengracht to the top and bottom. Between Strand and Wale to the side. Next door are the lesser known, but bigger quarters: Stadzicht, Schoon Kloof and Schotse Kloof. Together they're the Bo-Kaap, home to some 6000 Cape Muslims. **1990** *Weekend Argus* 10 Feb. (Weekender) 4 The girl's face had been changed into that of a jackal. My mother said it was a lot of nonsense, but Mattie insisted that the girl had been **Malay-tricked** ... Anyway, said Mattie, she couldn't stay there because she too would be Malay-tricked. **1970** [**Malay trickery**: see GOËLERY]. **1944** I.D. DU PLESSIS *Cape Malays* 69 Poltergeist phenomena ('**Malay tricks**'). **1966** [see quot. at *Malay magic* above].

B. *adj.* CAPE MALAY *adj. phr.*

1815 *Afr. Court Calendar & Dir.*, Abdol Garis, Malay priest, 23 Langa Street, Abdol Malik van Batavia, Malay Doctor, 22 Dorp Str. **1823** W.W. BIRD *State of Cape of G.H.* 73 Slaves at the Cape may be divided into three classes: the Negro, the Malay and the Africander ... The Malay slaves are coachmen, tailors, painters, shoemakers, carpenters, and fishermen. **1832** *Graham's Town Jrnl* 13 July 112 A Malay Priest waltzed with a tight little Quaker, and the Imaum of Muscat flung the handkerchief alternatively to little loves from Alp and Appenine. **1847** J. BARROW *Reflect.* 155 He stuck to his waggon nearly the whole journey, but spurred on his Malay cook in the preparation of our evening's repast. **1875** 'M.E.' *Life on Diamond Fields* 6 A number of gaily-dressed Malay girls got out here .. most of them sporting the Prophet's colour — bright green. **1892** J.E. RITCHIE *Brighter S. Afr.* 7 As fast as the coloured people become Mohammedans .. they call themselves Malays, and adopt Malay ideas and habits. **1919** M.M. STEYN *Diary* 7 The Malay boy .. was our constant companion and taught us how to make kites in the Malay fashion. **1936** [see MEDORA]. **1952** G.M. MILLS *First Ladies of Cape* 75 The pattern of the furniture made and carved at the Cape by the Malay craftsmen. **1960** J.P. VAN S. BRUWER in H. Spottiswoode *S. Afr.: Rd Ahead* 53 Of the two groups the Brown people are numerically the stronger, numbering over one million — and for practical argument also including the Malay people. **1971** *Daily News* 24 Apr. 9 His remaining sisters were classified 'Malay' as was his mother. **1985** J. CLOETE in *S.-Easter* Aug.–Sept. 21 Malay music, as we know it in the Cape, is fundamentally a sung music, .. a simple expression of a love of life. **1987** *Star* 30 Oct. 18 Its decor, in the finest tradition of the Old Cape is equalled by the excellence of its menu — a splendid combination of authentic Cape Dutch and Malay. **1990** R. GOOL *Cape Town Coolie* 97 'Why aren't you working?' he asked, in the racy, sing-song Afrikaans peculiar to Malay fishermen.

malgas /ˈmalxas/ *n.* Also **malagas(h)**, **malagos**. Pl. unchanged, or **-es**. [Afk., earlier S. Afr. Du., ad. and transf. use of Pg. *mangas de veludo* 'sleeves of velvet' (alluding to the bird's black wing tips), the wandering albatross, *Diomedea exulans*.] The large marine bird *Morus capensis* of the Sulidae, white, with a strikingly coloured head and black wing tips; *Cape gannet*, see CAPE sense 2a. Also *attrib.*

[**1611** P. FLORIS in R. Raven-Hart *Before Van Riebeeck* (1967) 55 Wee sawe dyvers foules that keepe aboute the cape; which we had not seene att sea before, as mangas de veludo.] **1731** G. MEDLEY tr. *P. Kolb's Present State of Cape of G.H.* II. 143 There is a Water-Bird, which is frequently seen on the Sea and on the Rivers about the *Cape*, and which the Cape-*Europeans* call *Malagos*. **1867** E.L. LAYARD *Birds of S. Afr.* 379 *Sula Capensis* ... *Malagash* of Colonists ... It visits Table Bay in vast numbers in the months of April and May, in pursuit of the shoals of fish that then appear on the surface. **1872** C.A. PAYTON *Diamond Diggings* 76 Birds were wonderfully numerous, thousands of cormorants, .. and two large birds, termed by our natives 'mollimauks' and 'malagasses.' **1906** STARK & SCLATER *Birds of S. Afr.* IV. 17 *Sula capensis*, Malagash. *Ibid.* 19 The Malagash is found along the coasts of South Africa. **1913** C. PETTMAN *Africanderisms* 306 *Malagas, Sula capensis*. The common gannet of South Africa found round the coast in countless thousands. **1936** E.L. GILL *First Guide to S. Afr. Birds* 186 *Malagas*, Malgas, Cape gannet; *Morus capensis*. This is the gannet of the South African guano islands. **1955** [see STERRETJIE sense 2]. **1964** J. BENNETT *Mr Fisherman* (1967) 69 They were big black and white birds and they wheeled flashing in the sunlight, dropping into the water like bombs. 'Malgas,' said the serang. **1974** *E. Prov. Herald* 7 Nov. 22 There are vast colonies of malgas (gannets) and other birds which live off the shoals of fodder fish in our waters. **1985** A. TREDGOLD *Bay between Mountains* 16 The big malgas, so handsome in its white plumage, with black-tipped wings and yellow-streaked blue head, dives like a plummet from great heights to take its pick of the fish. **1987** [see STERRETJIE sense 2].

‖**mali** /ˈmɑːli/ *n.* Also **imali**, **mahli**, **marlie**. [Xhosa and Zulu *imali*, ad. Eng. *money*.] Money.

1851 J.F. CHURCHILL Diary. (Killie Campbell Africana Library MS37) 14 One Caffir .. came to ask for work and when asked how much marlie replied one pound a month. **1852** C. BARTER *Dorp & Veld* 214 (Pettman), The Kaffir has .. made the discovery that .. a certain number of threepenny pieces is the most desirable of possessions; and nothing which is not readily convertible into *mali*, or hard cash, has now much attraction for him. **1899** G.H. RUSSELL *Under Sjambok* 50 A native will go through fire and water for mali (money). **1911** P. GIBBON *Margaret Harding* 66 Picanin all right; plenty *scoff*, plenty *mahli*, plenty everything. **1913** C. PETTMAN *Africanderisms* 307 *Mali*, .. A word in constant use among the natives, and frequently heard among the colonists also, for money. *a*1931 S. BLACK in S. Gray *Three Plays* (1984) 141 Maningi mali, Baas. Plenty money! *Ibid.* 142 Baas, if I take now this — ten pound — and afterwards you make plenty mali out of the gold, you must give me and Grietje a job by Johannesburg and one hundred pound! [**1948** A. PATON *Cry, Beloved Country* 225 And money is imali. — Right also.] **1970** R. MAYTHAM *Informant, Empangeni* Lots [of] mali (money).

malkop /ˈmalkɔp/ *n.* and *adj.* Formerly also **mall-koppen**. [Afk. (fr. Du.) 'crazy (person)', *mal* mad + *kop* head.]

A. *n.*

1. *obs. Pathology.* The staggers, a disease of livestock induced by the ingestion of poisonous vegetable material. Also *attrib.* Cf. DOMSIEKTE sense b.

1731 G. MEDLEY tr. *P. Kolb's Present State of Cape of G.H.* I. 128 When the Sheep of a *Kraal* are seiz'd with the *Megrims* (the *Hottentots* call the Distemper by the *Dutch* Terms, *Mall-Koppen* i.e. *disorder'd in the Head*) the Inhabitants make propitiatory Sacrifices. **1830** A. SMITH in

S. Afr. Quarterly Jrnl I. 189 The third [poison] is of vegetable origin and called the malkop poison on account of the peculiar effects it produces upon the senses. **1914** *Farmer's Annual* 137 Gid, Sturdy, or 'Mal-Kop' ... Owing to the brain disturbance, the animal seems to lose the power of governing its movements.

2. An insane, crazed, or foolish person.

1913 C. PETTMAN *Africanderisms* 308 Malkop, .. A wrong-headed, foolish person; also one who is insane. **1931** V. SAMPSON *Kom Binne* 72 You are a mal-kop (mad head) not to know that the springbuck would never allow you to get near them that way. **1976** J. MCCLURE *Rogue Eagle* 209 'Do you know where this path leads?' 'Didn't the boy say?' 'He's a *malkop* — just that it went to the west.'

B. *adj.* Crazy.

1899 A. WERNER *Captain of Locusts* 22, I can't very well make it out. Something about his being the Great Induna of all the locusts; they are his impis, and he tells them when to come and go. The man is malkop, I think. [*Note*] Crazy.

malmok /ˈmælmɒk, ˈmalmɔk/ *n.* Also **malmock, malmuck.** [Afk. (earlier S. Afr. Du.), ad. and transf. use of Du. *mallemok* mollymawk, *malle* (attrib. and combining form of *mal* foolish) + *mok* gull.] Any of several species of albatross, esp. the blackbrowed albatross *Diomedea melanophris* of the Diomedeidae.

1795 C.R. HOPSON tr. *C.P. Thunberg's Trav.* I. 91 On the 26th, the large birds called *malmucks*, which are brown and white underneath, passed us in great numbers. **1960** J. COPE *Tame Ox* 44 A lovely broad-winged malmock flew up with a big fish, dropped it and caught it again in mid-air as if to prove himself no mere scavenger. *Ibid.* 159 The women who go to collect feather-down of the malmocks blown up from the sea on to the beaches sometimes find the bone of a drowned man there. **1987** *E. Prov. Herald* 26 May 11 Malmok is the common name in South Africa of the mollymawk, which is found along the west coast and the east coast. It is larger than a blackbacked gull but not as big as the biggest albatross.

malombo /maˈlɔːmbɔ, məˈlɒmbəʊ/ *n.* Also **molombo,** and with initial capital. [Venda, 'spirit'.]
1. A Venda rite of exorcism and healing conducted by a diviner, accompanied by drumming, singing, dancing, and creating a high state of nervous excitement. Usu. *attrib.*

The drums used in this rite are now also used in the popular music style of the same name: see sense 2.

1931 H.A. STAYT *BaVenda* 303 He .. summons a drummer who knows the *molombo* beat ... When the *maine vha tshele* begins to sing the words of the *molombo* song and to dance wildly to the sound of the drums .. each old *molombo* dancer takes her part. *Ibid.* 306 A person once possessed of the *tshilombo* spirit .. belongs to the fraternity of *molombo* dancers and is always liable to be repossessed by the spirit. *Ibid.* 307 The *molombo* performance is .. stage-managed by the *maine vha tshele. Ibid.* 308 The *molombo* dance is regarded with an ambivalent attitude. The people fear it .. but it possesses a magnetic attraction. **1934** P.R. KIRBY *Musical Instruments of Native Races* (1965) 9 This diviner is responsible for singing the special *malombo* song of exorcism, accompanied by a drum-player who is familiar with the particular rhythms used for casting out spirits. **1964** *Drum* Nov. 35 The malombo drums send out their jungle-like sound. **1985** *S. Afr. Panorama* May, South African participants discussed subjects such as .. the Malombo Possession Cult.

2. *Music.* [Named for the group *Malombo* who pioneered this style in the mid-1960s.] A style of music combining elements of the music performed in traditional malombo ceremonies, esp. the drums and drumming style, with elements taken from jazz and African popular music. Also *attrib.*

1964 *Drum* Nov. 35 On the blistering hot afternoon of September 26, a new jazz sound was born in the Orlando Stadium, Johannesburg ... It is simply called 'Malombo!' There has been .. what is loosely termed 'Mbaqanga', or pop jazz. But the Malombo sound is unique. It is hard to pinpoint. **1971** *Post* 6 June 21 The Malombo duo of Philip Tabane and drummer Gabriel Thobejane will be hitting the United States of America soon. Real groovy malombo music the fans will get from these two. **1974** *Drum* 8 Apr. 32 The other mlungus just don't dig this kind of malombo jazz and that is why the Nkosikazi Progressive will be a voice in the wilderness for a long time. **1988** V. KHUMALO in *Pace* Apr. 16 Godfather icon of malombo music .. (which is an in-depth investigation into indigenous jazz).

malongoes pl. form of MLUNGU.

malo(o)nga var. MLUNGU.

malpitte /ˈmalpətə/ *n.* Also **malpita.** Pl. unchanged. [Afk., *mal* mad + *pit* pip + pl. suffix *-(t)e.* Although a pl. form in Afrikaans, *malpitte* is often interpreted as a sing. noun in S. Afr. Eng.] The highly poisonous seed of the thorn-apple *Datura stramonium* of the Solanaceae, containing the narcotic alkaloid known as hyoscyamine; occas., the thorn-apple plant itself (also called STINKBLAAR). Also *attrib.*

1948 [see STINKBLAAR]. **1949** L.G. GREEN *In Land of Afternoon* 51 Stinkblaar .. a weed which must be treated with respect ... Generations of South African school boys have known these seeds as *malpitte* because of the queer behaviour and delirium they produce. **1973** *E. Prov. Herald* 27 Apr. 1 A nightmare four-day hallucinatory drug trip induced by a common garden weed, known as 'malpitte' (mad pips), which grows wild in gardens and open ground. **1973** on Radio South Africa 29 May (Woman's World), There is the Jimson weed ... Very often it's called malpitte by children because the pips when eaten cause hallucination. **1973** *E. Prov. Herald* 7 Nov. 7 The tin contained a mixture of dagga, fine tobacco and 'malpitte', an intoxicating seed. **1975** *Ibid.* 3 Jan. 6 The authors .. investigated 10 cases of malpitte (madseed) madness treated at the Johannesburg General Hospital and Crisis Clinic, Johannesburg. The patients were schoolchildren aged between 14 and 18. **1978** *Darling* 22 Nov. 84 They're chewing morning-glory seeds, and malpita, which was originally imported from South America and planted on our plains to prevent soil erosion. *Ibid.* 109 Malpita can derange you for ever ... You see people that aren't really there, you do things without knowing what you're doing. **1987** *Party invitation,* Grahamstown Bring your own Obbies, Tas, or SAB, Pure Ethanol, Malpitte or Bags of Weed.

maltziekte var. MILTSIEKTE.

malunga var. MLUNGU.

malva pudding /ˈmalvə -, ˈmalfa -/ *n. phr.* [Part. tr. Afk. *malvapoeding, malva* marshmallow + *poeding* pudding.] A traditional dessert, consisting of a baked pudding over which a syrup or sauce is poured as it is removed from the oven.

*a***1981** *Our Favourite Recipes.* (Pinelands Methodist Mothers' Morning Fellowship) 30 Malva Pudding. **1985** *S. Afr. Cookbk* (Reader's Digest Assoc.) 265 Malva Pudding. **1986** *Style* Oct. 12 A chocolate mousse so light it almost floats from the spoon; malva pudding — a sweet, spongy delight. **1988** *Fair Lady* 22 June (Suppl.) 39 A delicious dessert — moist malva pudding, a rich chocolate cake or cheesecake. **1990** *Style* July 18 And the malva pudding — well, it's famous, and I've never tasted better. **1994** *Your Family* Oct. 34 Malva Pudding ... This dessert can be made in advance and frozen without the sauce.

Mama /ˈmɑː(ː)mɑ/ *n.* Also with small initial. [Zulu and Xhosa *umama* (pl. *omama*), seTswana *mama.*] Among speakers of Sintu (Bantu) languages: 'Mother'.

1. Always with initial capital, used as a respectful title. **a.** Prefixed to a woman's first name; cf. MA- pref.¹, MMA-, MME. **b.** *spec.* **Mama Africa, -Afrika:** the singer Miriam Makeba, so called because of her importance as a political and cultural figure.

1977 *Drum* Oct. 57 (*caption*) Peter Davidson and Gabriel Thobejane meet the first lady of jazz, Mama Ella. **1977** *Daily Dispatch* 8 Dec. 13 Mothers who have borne eight or more children are automatically referred to Mama Effie. **1987** *New Nation* 19 Nov. 9 You are hated by the pillars of apartheid; Loved you are by freedom-lovers ... You exposed our African music abroad. You, Mama Africa, took them by surprise. **1989** *Weekly Mail* 15 Dec. 27 The next rhyme was on Helen Joseph: 'Mama Helen, Mama Helen. What do you see? .. I see a new land for Soraya, Cecily, Bongani and me.' **1990** P. TSHUKUDU in *New African* 18 June 12 Mama Afrika back after 30 years ... Lady Africa Miriam Makeba jetted in from Paris last week after three decades in exile ... Makeba (57) — affectionately called the 'Empress of African Song' or 'Mama Africa' — arrived for a two week private visit. **1994** *Sunday Times* 24 July (Mag. Sect.) 30 Mama Afrika — a documentary on Miriam Makeba airs on NNTV at 20.30.

2. A respectful or familiar term of address.

a. Used to address any adult woman.

1979 W. EBERSOHN *Lonely Place* 71 'Did Small-boss Marthinus never, never hit Musikei, Mama?' he repeated. His using of the respectful 'mama' had done something to the old woman. **1984** *Sunday Times* 29 Jan. (Mag. Sect.) 10 She is pregnant. She says Paulus hit her on the head with a bottle. Eric says: 'Nice and easy, mama. How are you now — okay?' **1987** E. MAKHANYA in *Sowetan* 21 Dec. 12 He moves so fast he looks like he is going through an Oriental ritual, ya see, mama.

b. Used to address one's mother.

1982 M. MZAMANE *Children of Soweto* 41 His mother said they'd been woken up about three a.m. by the police who took him away ... 'Did they say when he'll be back, Mama?' **1984** E. MPHAHLELE *Afrika my Music* 141 Our children have grown up to say, 'Yes Mama,' or 'Yes, Ntate.'

3. Usu. with small initial, as a term of reference: a black woman.

1984 *Frontline* Feb. 37 Outside there are several aged mamas selling the same wares from the old-style stalls ... Both shop and mamas seem to be doing good business, the mamas selling their apples for one cent less than the shop. **1987** A.K. HORWITZ in *New Coin Poetry* June 24 Phineas would whisper, rising from a whore's imboia bed, (we'd take the pick of the mamas), that his doctor was right. **1989** J. HOBBS *Thoughts in Makeshift Mortuary* 122, I like to work hard, sir, but maybe Mrs Kimber will not like me. Or the mama who brings me to you. *Ibid.* 173 The old mealie mamas .. used to go past in the street with big bulging sacks on their heads, calling 'Meeeeealies!' **1990** D. STANLEY in *Frontline* Sept. 12 Mammoth-breasted mamas shriek at each other, jovially scolding, while selling apples, tomatoes, and oranges from makeshift tables.

mama(r)ghew var. MAHEWU.

mamba /ˈmambə, ˈmæmbə/ *n.* Also **imamba, momba.** [Xhosa and Zulu *imamba.*]
1. Either of two deadly snakes of the genus *Dendroaspis* of the Elapidae, with a bite that is almost invariably fatal: **a.** *D. polylepis,* noted for its aggressiveness; *black mamba,* see sense 2 below; or **b.** *D. angusticeps; green mamba* sense (a), see sense 2 below. Also *attrib.,* and *fig.*

1860 D.L.W. STAINBANK *Diary.* (Killie Campbell Africana Library KCM8680) 23 Apr., A large snake rushed by me into the hut ... It proved to be a large mamba (black) between 8 and 9 feet long and two or three inches in diameter. **1878** T.J. LUCAS *Camp Life & Sport* 104 The imamba, a small species of boa, is the most dangerous. **1890** P. GILLMORE *Through Gasa Land* 23 The mamba frequently grows to the length of ten or eleven feet ... There are two varieties, the green and the brown. **1905** W.L. SCLATER in Flint & Gilchrist *Science in S. Afr.* 148 The justly-dreaded mamba (*Dendraspis angusticeps*) is only found in Natal and the low country in the east. It is more of a tree-snake than the others, and sometimes reaches a length of 10 feet. **1926** *E. Prov. Herald* 11 Mar. 3 On ploughing through an ant heap he cut a large mamba in two. Unfortunately the mamba, before dying, bit Botha on the leg. Botha expired within two hours. **1937** C. BIRKBY *Zulu Journey* 113 A mamba-bite remedy made by the natives from pounded root of the inkwa-kamuti bush mixed with the dried powdered spleen of the mamba. **1940** V. POHL *Bushveld Adventures* 147 There is little doubt that the mamba is the most dangerous snake in existence. **1953** R. CAMPBELL *Mamba's Precipice* 19 Mambas can move with the speed of a galloping horse. Their bite is absolutely fatal and there is no remedy for it. **1965** P. BARAGWANATH *Brave Remain* 133 She was a woman who was going to do battle with the mamba, the lion, the raiding Swazi! **1982** C. HOPE *Private Parts* 17 Grannie would .. talk to him of her great-grandfather who died with Retief at the hands of the mamba, Dingaan, King of the Zulus. **1982** *Sunday Times* 19 Sept. (Mag. Sect.) 25 Just sit and watch the fun with a vetkoek in one hand and a fizzy mamba-green cooldrink in the other. **1988** J. MICHELL in *Style* Mar. 46 Anyone who lives in Africa is sooner or later going to meet a mamba in the bathroom. **1991** *Best of S. Afr. Short Stories* (Reader's Digest Assoc.) 168 About 1 – 1,5 m long, the boomslang resembles a mamba, except for its very large eyes, which are grey or brown in adults and iridescent green in hatchlings. **1993** A.P. BRINK *First Life of Adamastor* 28 This rearing mamba in my loins.

2. With defining word: **black mamba**, see sense 1 a above; also *fig.*; **green mamba**, *(a)* see sense 1 b above; *(b) fig. colloq.* [see quot. 1980], a nickname for a Putco commuter bus; also *attrib.*; see also PUTCO; **Groen Mamba** *fig. colloq.* [Afk. *groen* green; referring to the colour and potency of the drink], the liqueur crème de menthe; JANGROENTJIE sense 2.

1878 P. GILLMORE *Great Thirst Land* 346 A **black mamba** – a description of snake common in Natal, and reported to be very deadly – I killed to-day. **1897** J. BRYCE *Impressions of S. Afr.* 23 The black *momba*, which is nearly as large as a rattlesnake, is a dangerous creature. **1910** J. BUCHAN *Prester John* (1961) 80 A black mamba might appear out of the tangle. **1928** L.P. GREENE *Adventure Omnibus* 691 A black momba passed very close to him. He struck at it, missing, and the snake .. turned, incensed. **1938** F.C. SLATER *Trek* 113 Warnings from those who knew Black-mamba-Dingaan, that the king was bent On treachery and murder. **1955** A. DELIUS *Young Trav.* 118 There were vivid red and black coral snakes, the green lash-like boomslang which was as poisonous as the dreaded black mamba. **1978** C.L. REITZ *Poisonous S. Afr. Snakes* 22 Two drops ($\pm \frac{1}{4}$ml) of venom is regarded as fatal for man and an adult black mamba has a capacity of 20 drops or more per venom fang. **1987** R. PATTERSON *Reptiles* 91 Rarely black despite its name, it is dull olive, gun metal or leaden coloured ... The Black Mamba inhabits bushveld and tropical areas. **1988** M. GWALA in *Staffrider* Vol.7 No.1, 91 In 'The Black Mamba Rises' the lethal black mamba becomes a metaphor for the strategic astuteness of the organized workers' movement. [**green mamba**: sense *(a)*] **1862** J.S. DOBIE *S. Afr. Jrnl* (1945) 44 He called it a green mamba and [it] was about 9 feet long. **1864** 'A LADY' *Life at Natal* (1972) 37 Having just killed a large green 'mamba' that was taking its siesta in an oleander bush opposite my window. These snakes are the deadliest known. **1913** L. LYSTER *Ballads of Veld-Land* 69 Back and forth that deadly bay'net swung Like the green mamba's swiftly darting tongue When o'er her hole she battles for her young. **1925** D. KIDD *Essential Kafir* 189 If the person had been bitten by a green mamba, then he would have to be treated with green mamba-head dried and powdered. **1946** H.C. BOSMAN in *S. Afr. Opinion* Dec., Jurie Steyn's mind seemed to have grown all curved like a green mamba asleep in the sun. **1979** C. ENDFIELD *Zulu Dawn* 19 Mamba, deadly green mamba! But if it really had been there, it failed to show itself during the beating-out he had ordered. **1990** *Weekly Mail* 2 Feb. 21 Asbestos is like a green mamba. It is very dangerous. [**green mamba**: sense *(b)*] **1975** S. ROBERTS *Outside Life's Feast* 12 Having lived .. in Johannesburg in a tiny house .. on a busy street down which incessant traffic and 'green mambas' screamed. **1980** C. HOPE *A Separate Development* (1983) 44 Racketing kikuyu green buses jammed to the eyeballs with blacks from the Location. The buses were called Green Mambas. I think because they appeared from nowhere and hit you without warning. [**1981** *Frontline* Sept. 15, I have seen changes. For example Putco buses are no longer mamba green but light blue.] **1985** *Frontline* Sept. 15 Domestic servants .. have been crowding the pre-dawn Green Mamba buses with their shopping baskets laden with fresh Umlazi bread for The Madam. **1987** S. ROBERTS *Jacks in Corners* 61 Wobbly buses known as Green Mambas would woosh by spewing diesel fumes. **1968** W. KEMPEN in D.J. Opperman *Spirit of Vine* 281 Words denoting liquor: Chwala, .. **Groenmamba** (Peppermint liqueur). **1978** *Pace* Dec., The lunch menu: Crayfish cocktail, filet mignon .. Van der Hum, Drammie, Groen Mamba.

3. *fig.* An unusually talented, skilful, or intelligent person.

1978 L. BARNES in *The 1820* Vol.51 No.12, 19 A *mamoo* – known also as a 'mamba' or 'a good thing' .. is one who excels in academics, sport or some special skill. **1992** E.R.A. ESSERY *Informant, Durban* She sews like a mamba; she's really good ... You have to be a mamba of a bricklayer to make a circular wall.

4. *fig. slang.* A home-brewed alcoholic drink. Cf. MBAMBA.

1981 B. FAIRBROTHER in *Sunday Times* 15 Nov. 41 In the jungle the mighty mamba rules. Only this 'jungle' is on the outskirts of Arlington race-course ... And mamba is the name of a potent homebrew made by squatters.

Hence **mamba** *adj.* (*slang*), big.

1983 A. GOLDSTUCK in *Frontline* Oct. 61, I tune you, mate, if I can get one mamba chow a day, I scheme life is kif.

mambakkie var. MOMBAKKIE.

Mambo var. MBO.

Mambookie *n. obs.* Also **Mambu(c)ki**. [Unkn.; perh. ad. MBO + -IE. (Cf. TAMBOOKIE).] PONDO sense 1 a. Also *attrib.*

1786 G. FORSTER tr. *A. Sparrman's Voy. to Cape of G.H.* II. 147 Adjoining to this nation, towards the north, there is, according to them, a still more warlike and intrepid people, whom they call *Mambukis*. **1812** A. PLUMPTRE tr. *H. Lichtenstein's Trav. in Sn Afr.* (1928) I. 367 Proceeding along the coast, the next tribe to the Koossas is one which is called by many different names; that by which it is most generally known is the Gonaaquas, but by the colonists they are usually called Mambuckis. **1828** [see MBO sense 1]. **1829** W. SHAW Diary. 16 May, It is impossible to estimate with accuracy the number of people forming the Mambo or Mambookie Nation, but if all the clans and tribes are included I think they are quite as numerous as the Caffres or the Tambookies. **1835**, **1836** [see PONDO sense 1 a]. **1841** B. SHAW *Memorials* 308 When the Mambookies build their houses .. the floor is raised at the higher or back part of the house, until within three or four feet of the front, where it suddenly terminates, leaving an area from thence to the wall, in which every night the calves are tied to protect them from the storm or wild beasts. **1860** W. SHAW *Story of my Mission* 315 The time might soon follow, when you would see on your lists Stations among the Tambookies, the Mambookies, and the various tribes of people between us and Delagoa Bay.

mamele var. MOMELA.

||**Mamlambo** /maɱˈlaːmbɔ/ *n.* Also **Momlambo**, and with small initial. [Zulu *umamlambo*, lit. 'one of the river' (pl. *omamlambo*).] In Zulu mythology: a female water spirit, usu. in the form of a snake or a woman requiring sacrifice, sometimes of human life, in return for her favour.

1937 B.J.F. LAUBSCHER *Sex, Custom & Psychopathology* 32 The *Mamlambo* demands a sacrifice before she bestows her favours on a man, and this penalty or sacrifice takes the form of someone dying in his family. **1955** J.B. SHEPHARD *Land of Tikoloshe* 84 'Your son is indeed sick .. to death .. he has a Mamlambo.' .. A Mamlambo is not the sort of creature you like to keep in a respectable family. I cannot describe it .. for nobody has seen one, though it is well known to assume different shapes; at times it appears as a baboon, or a skunk, or a wild pig, but it is just as likely to be a lovely woman. It is always female. **1962** W.D. HAMMOND-TOOKE *Bhaca Soc.* 285 The snake is perhaps the most sinister of all .. familiars, for when it is obtained 'something must be slaughtered for it – but not a beast or a goat'. This is said to mean that the owner of a *mamlambo* must kill his father or mother to propitiate it. **1967** J.A. BROSTER *Red Blanket Valley* 48 Mamlambo the mother of the river is a mythical snake that lives under the water in river pools. She escapes from the river as a beautiful woman. **1978** A.P. BRINK *Rumours of Rain* 356 If a man desires the Momlambo, if you want to sleep with her under one kaross and untie her *inciyo*, then you must kill your own father in your heart. **1982** B. MASEKO in *Staffrider* Vol.5 No.1, 22 Mamlambo is a kind of snake that brings fortune to anyone who accommodates it. One's money or livestock multiplies incredibly. This snake is available from traditional doctors ... Certain necessities are to be sacrificed in order to maintain it. **1990** J. KNAPPERT *Aquarian Guide to Afr. Mythology* 150 Mamlambo means 'the River Mother'; she is the goddess of the rivers of Natal and will appear to those who sacrifice to her.

mampar(r)a var. MOMPARA.

mampoer /mamˈpuːr, mamˈpʊə/ *n.* Also **mapoer**. [Afk., perh. ad. *Mampuru* the name of a former Pedi chief in a region where an abundance of marulas led to much distilling of spirits.]

1. A raw brandy originating in the Transvaal and distilled, often illicitly, from fruits such as peaches, karee-berries, and marula fruit; WITBLITS sense a. Also *attrib.*

1934 *Sunday Times* 13 May (Swart), Mampoer, as this home-distilled brandy is commonly called, has been very popular. **1943** I. FRACK *S. Afr. Doctor* 29 *Mampoer* is a home-made alchoholic beverage with a pleasant smell, yellowish, and a soapy consistence like strong nitric acid ... I have known it to have a beneficial effect on sufferers from Tape-worm. **1946** H.C. BOSMAN *Mafeking Rd* (1969) 122 It was good mampoer, made from karee-berries that were plucked when they were still green and full of thick sap. **1968** W. KEMPEN in D.J. Opperman *Spirit of Vine* 284 *Mapoer*, fiery brandy illicitly distilled on farms. **1976** *S. Afr. Panorama* May 24 What is moonshine white, has the kick of a pack of crazed mules and is in essence liquid folk-lore? Mampoer, my friend, mampoer. **1987** *Investing Today (pamphlet)*, The Tzaneen distillery .. now produces six popular mampoer spirits – peach, orange, pineapple, litchi, naartjie and marula .. Mampoer has come of age and is a smooth, velvety spirit that is clean on the palate .. with the same alcohol volume (43%) of its brothers cane, vodka and whiskey. **1987** D.W. POTGIETER in *Sunday Times* 12 Apr., Moonshiners get mampoer lovers in impotent rage ... Mampoer is traditionally distilled in the Transvaal from peaches, apricots, .. in fact, any fruit except grapes. Grapes are used for making witblits. **1987** *Weekly Mail* 19 June 26 In the past excise men made access to mampoer difficult. **1990** M. SHAFTO in *Weekend Argus* 9 June 11 Mampoer stoking was very much part of his life – indeed, part of his earliest recollections.

||**2.** *comb.* **mampoerfees** [Afk., *fees* festival], a fair at which mampoer is tasted and prizes awarded for the best distillation; **mampoer-stoker** /-ˈstʊəkə(r)/ [Afk., *stoker* distiller], a distiller of mampoer; see also STOKER.

1983 *Frontline* May 18 Down the road, there is another gate with a small sign saying '**mampoerfees**'. **1988** *Weekly Mail* 27 May 3 (*caption*) About the only stall at the annual Mampoerfees in Pretoria last week to offer wares to rival the sharpness of the infamous throat-blistering brew was this selection of cutlery, perfect for the serious biltong-gnawer. **1988** *Sunday Star* 5 June 2 In the above right picture **mampoer-stokers** distill their precious brew of distilled juice and alcohol. **1990** *Motorist* 1st Quarter 16 There are [*sic*] a plentiful supply of mampoer-stokers in our north-western Transvaal, most operate with a licence, some brew the clear liquid under cover of the bushes in the backyard, all their booze has the kick of a mule.

man /mæn/ *n.*¹ and *int.* Also **mann.** [tr. Du. (later Afk.) *man* man, husband.]

A. *n.* A husband.

1798 LADY A. BARNARD in Lord Lindsay *Lives of Lindsays* (1849) III. 465 In this house I saw the first trait of female industry, the vrows being employed in making clothes for their 'men'. **1829** C. ROSE *Four Yrs in Sn Afr.* 263 The wife broke out, 'You lament a brother, and you a child, but I have lost my man.' *a***1858** J. GOLDSWAIN *Chron.* (1949) II. 4 One of them told her to look out for her man — meaning her husband — should kill her that night. **1899** J.G. MILLAIS *Breath from Veldt* 133 (Swart), My man is too good-natured, and people humbug him; but once roused he is the devil. **1902** 'THE INTELLIGENCE OFFICER' *On Heels of De Wet* 52 'Where is your man?' asked the Tiger. **1920** R.Y. STORMBERG *Mrs Pieter de Bruyn* 72 The country lady strolls in to buy a hat, grabs at anything she likes, .. tells them to put it down to her 'man's' account. **1926** P. SMITH *Beadle* (1929) 167 She had in readiness also both her shroud and her coffin and the shroud and the coffin of her 'man'. **1937** S. CLOETE *Turning Wheels* 35 Danke kerls. Ja, baie danke for bringing back my man. **1946** P. ABRAHAMS *Mine Boy* (1954) 15 He is the brother of my man, Leah replied. **1947** C.R. PRANCE *Antic Mem.* 91 The eldest, a widow whose man had fallen on the British side in the war, apologized for Pa. **1967** E.M. SLATTER *My Leaves Are Green* 127 She nodded ponderously. 'My man has a place on the high bank there ..' and she pointed down the creek. **1970** *Farmer's Weekly* 16 Dec. 61 'How is your man, Mevrou?' he asked anxiously. **1975** *E. Prov. Herald* 6 June 12 Her man is .. balancing 10 metres up on a rickety platform surrounded by lethal galvanised sails.

B. *int.* Freq. in the phr. ***ag man*** /ax -/ [Afk.], an interjection used (regardless of the gender of the one being addressed) for emphasis, to express irritation or frustration, or pleadingly. Hence *n.*, an utterance of this phrase. See also AG.

1897 E. GLANVILLE in E.R. Seary *S. Afr. Short Stories* (1947) 20 'Man,' said Lanky John, the ostrich farmer, 'I killed a snake, a ringhals, yesterday morning back of the kraal, and in the evening when I went by there was a live ringhals coiled round the dead one.' **1900** F.R.M. CLEAVER in M.M. Cleaver *Young S. Afr.* (1913) 73 Man! I wish you were here! **1912** *E. London Dispatch* 13 Feb. 3 With many *mans*! and other fashionable interjections they carry on their brainy conversation. **1913** C. PETTMAN *Africanderisms* 309 *Man*, An exclamatory form of address in common use all over South Africa, employed often enough quite irrespective of either the age or the sex of the person addressed. **1948** O. WALKER *Kaffirs Are Lively* 48 The people iss too poor, man. **1960** C. HOOPER *Brief Authority* 76 Man, Padre, they will like it over there, where they can grow things and live as in the reserve. **1965** K. MACKENZIE *Deserter* 22 Come on, help him get up, man Sannie! What are you just standing there for? **1966** J. TAYLOR 'Mommy I'd Like to Be'. (*lyrics*) Ag man, won't you come down to the shops, we'll have some fun. **1972** *Sunday Times* 3 Dec. (Mag. Sect.) 15 Agh man lady, there's nothing nobody can do. **1975** *Darling* 9 Apr. 95 'Ag, dry up, Trix, man,' I hiss. **1985** *Frontline* Aug. 54, I realise I could have been killed and that. I think jissus man, what was I doing? **1988** M. ORSON in *Fair Lady* 16 Mar. 128 Oh man Lisa, your nails are digging into my arm again man. **1989** H. HAMMAN in *Scope* 24 Mar. 57 Man, I look at those guys who have just come off selection and they think they're through the worst. **1989** J. HOBBS *Thoughts in Makeshift Mortuary* 311 Don't take a huff now, Rose, man. We haven't got time for a fight. **1994** C. HARPER in *Flying Springbok* June 108 'Ag Man' is a South Africanism meaning 'oh dear' or, alternatively 'get lost, you idiot'.

man /man/ *n.*² *slang.* Pl. **manne** /'manə/, occas. **mannes** /'manəs/. [Afk.]

The word occurs in both the sing. and pl. forms in spoken *S. Afr. Eng.*; the sing. has not been found in written contexts, as the distinction between /mæn/ and /man/ is not apparent in writing.

1. As a term of reference.

a. Usu. in *pl.*: 'Real men', 'man's men', 'macho men': men who are ostentatiously virile or manly; men who are engaged in, or excel in, activities considered to be typically masculine. See also MAIN MAN, RUGGER-BUGGER.

1963 B. MODISANE *Blame Me on Hist.* (1986) 51 'O Broad-derick is de manne,' one of them said, imitating the bubbling speech of the actor. 'Did you hear him when he said: "I'm the fastest gun there is." .. ?' **1972** *Drum* 8 Aug. 20 He was one of the real manne when young. And what the real manne usually do is spin around town. Be seen around the city often. **1975** J. DAVIDS in *New Classic* No.1, 41 Rollicking full of life, you met all the manne, everywhere. **1981** *Frontline* May 15 The various sides of our culture .. of which the down-and-out meths drinker is as much a part as the manne in the Royal Hotel kroeg. **1985** D. LAUTENBACH in *Argus* 28 Sept., On the veld under a Boland Saturday afternoon sky, the manne from Meerlust meet the manne from Mooiplaas. **1987** *Weekly Mail* 12 June 31 While rugby's *manne* get in some practice .. there are two potentially close contests to sort out the boys from the bigger boys. **1990** C. LEONARD in *Weekly Mail* 2 Nov. 28 The manne compete to produce the highest number of decibels from their music systems in their Cortinas. **1992** J.S. SILVA *Informant, Grahamstown* Look at him, how he walks — he thinks he's a real *man*.

b. ***The manne***: 'The boys', 'the guys', men with whom one shares a sense of camaraderie; the (important) men of a community (esp. an Afrikaans-speaking community). See also MAIN MAN.

1979 A. HARRISON in *Frontline* Dec. 17, I never get lonely. In a city lift I can give the manne a 'hora hora hoozeet' and I'm assured of a good conversation. **1985** T. BARON in *Frontline* Feb. 30 Pofadder .. where the manne were recklessly ordering dam to go with their dop because it had rained the day before, the first rain in seven years. **1989** *Weekly Mail* 15 Dec. 7 'I don't wake my wife when I get up at four in the morning .. just give her a kiss ..' he says. 'Then I go out and join the other *manne* on the way to the harbour.' **1990** B. COHEN in *Weekly Mail* 22 June (Suppl.) 7 The photograph is innocent, stoned amateurish, a happy snap of the manne taken with a self-timer. **1990** T. VAN DER WALT in *Sunday Times* 21 Oct. 11 War veterans and colonial types with bushy moustaches rubbed shoulders and shared jokes with the bearded *manne* from the platteland. **1990** *Sunday Times* 21 Oct. (Mag. Sect.) 38 Des Park, president of the SACF, collected the top canoeing *manne* for a brainstorm .. and programme of safety exercises. **1991** 'K. LEMMER' in *Weekly Mail* 15 Feb. 17 These guys from the Organisation for African Unity come to Cape Town this week, meet with the *manne* that matter, and then say they aren't here because of anything to do with politics. **1993** *Sunday Times* 31 Oct. 31 There's nothing shy about the *manne* up here ... Government of the Volk, by the Volk, for the Volk .. is the only democracy you can safely mention in these parts.

2. As a form of address, always in *pl.*: 'Men', 'guys'; used (by a man) to address a group of men, usu. indicating or inviting a sense of male camaraderie.

1974 C. HOPE on Radio South Africa 7 Sept., OK manne, let's push now. **1982** V. KHUMALO in *Pace* May 158 Ek sê, mannes, how's yu'wol? Hoezit chana, hoe's ou Pedro daar? **1983** G. SILBER in *Sunday Times* 28 Aug. (Mag. Sect.) 18 Al says: 'Listen, you *manne*, I don't want to be a spoilsport. But please, no dancing on the grass. It's the Sunday law, okay?' **1985** D. BAUER in *Frontline* Dec. 6 Okay manne, today I'm going to learn you about riot control.

management committee *n. phr. Hist.* A committee consisting of appointed or elected members, or both, being responsible for the administration of a 'coloured' or Indian township or area (see GROUP AREA *n. phr.* sense 1). Also *attrib.*

1963 *Local Authorities Ordinance* in *Ord. of Prov. of Cape of G.H.* II. 2124 The Administrator may .. establish for any group area (other than a group area for the white group) .. within the area of jurisdiction of a local authority, .. either a consultative committee or management committee ... Any such .. committee shall consist wholly of members of the group for which such group area or group areas have been established ... Any management committee shall within the area for which it has been established have such powers, functions and duties of the local authority .. as may be conferred .. upon it by or under regulation. **1977** *Survey of Race Rel.* (S.A.I.R.R.) 175 There were .. 109 Coloured management committees .. in the Cape and one in the Transvaal ... All .. had both elected and nominated members ... In the OFS .. all Coloured consultative committees .. would be converted into management committees, with provision for them to become fully elected bodies. **1983** *Financial Mail* 16 Sept. 49 Extremely low polls were recorded in western Cape coloured management committee elections last week. **1988** K. BENTLEY in *E. Prov. Herald* 23 June 3 These are the criteria for receiving a pension in terms of the municipal pension scheme introduced .. this year ... Members of management committees (Mancoms) who have served eight years or more will receive a proportion of the full pension, worked out on a pro-rata basis. **1991** D. FOX in *Weekly Mail* 15 Dec. 12 We need to raise some money to replace the floor in the village hall, otherwise the management committee will be holding their meetings below ground.

manatoka var. MANITOKA.

Manchatee var. MANTATEE.

Mandebele pl. form of NDEBELE.

Mandela /mæn'delə, man'de:la/ *n.* [Surname of *Nelson Rolihlala Mandela*, President of South Africa from 1994 and leader of the African National Congress.] Used *attrib.* in Special Comb. (mostly *nonce*). **Mandelamania, Mandela-Mobile, Mandela Plan** (see M PLAN), **Mandelarand, Mandela release fever, Mandela University**: see quots. See also MADIBA.

1990 *E. Prov. Herald* 12 Feb. 6 As '**Mandelamania**' sweeps the world, two anti-apartheid leaders who recently spent a day at his prison home say the man is greater than the myth that has built around him. **1990** *Weekly Mail* 22 June 1 New York's newest hero from abroad moves through the streets ... Ticker tape rains down on the curiously shaped '**Mandela-Mobile**' as it drives through the streets of lower Manhattan. **1987** M. DESMIDT in *E. Prov. Herald* 14 May 2 The organisation of street committees based on the so-called **Mandela Plan**, whose objective was the violent overthrow of the existing order and the introduction of their own committees. **1985** *City Press* 23 June 1 Meet the **Mandelarand** — anti-apartheid campaigners' answer to the Krugerrand. Minted in their thousands in Holland, the brass Mandelarands are part of a massive campaign to make banks aware of the implications of trading in Krugerrands ... Needless to say, the Mandelarands worked. Dutch banks no longer trade in South Africa's prime gold coin. **1990** *E. Prov. Herald* 12 Feb. 8 The possible release of .. Nelson Mandela .. has for a number of years sent the international and local Press .. into frantic and often wild frenzy ... David Beresford .. called this phenomenon **Mandela release fever**, 'an affliction which bears a resemblance to malaria for the way in which it afflicts sufferers periodically'. **1991** S. MACLEOD in *Time* 22 July 8 Despite the hardships, Robben Island became known as '**Mandela University**' to younger inmates because of the lessons in politics that Mandela taught them.

Hence (*nonce*) **Mandela** *adj.*, of the release of Nelson Mandela in February 1990, and the changes which followed.

1990 *Sunday Times* 27 May (Mag. Sect.) 6, I needed respite from the New South Africa .. so I sought frivolity in the company of acquaintances who struck me as being fairly safe custodians of the Old South Africa ... They had both been at Sol's entire birthday bash, and you don't get more pre-Mandela than that, babe.

Mandela United *n. phr.* [Surname of *Nomzamo Winnie Mandela* + Eng. *United*, as used in the names of football teams.] Often in the phrr. *Mandela United Football Club, - Football Team, -Soccer Team*: a nickname for a group of young ANC activists who in the late 1980s acted as bodyguards for Nomzamo Winnie Mandela, a prominent ANC leader married to Nelson Mandela. Occas. also shortened to *Mandela Football Club.*

1989 *Race Rel. Survey 1988-9* (S.A.I.R.R.) 639 Mr Oliver Tambo and Mr Mandela strongly urged that Mandela United football team, a group of young 'comrades' who acted as bodyguards for .. Mrs Winnie Mandela, be disbanded in the light of widespread controversy surrounding it. **1990** C. MUNNION in *London Evening Standard* (U.K.) 12 Feb. 7 It was necessary to have .. protection ... Hence the formation of her own 'presidential guard', .. who, with the dark humour of South Africa's townships, called themselves the Mandela United Football Club ... The Mandela Football Club disappeared overnight. **1992** *Race Rel. Survey 1991-2* (S.A.I.R.R.) p.xxxix, Mr Jerry R—, former coach of the Mandela United Football Club.

mandoor /ˈmandʊə(r)/ *n. hist.* Also **mandor(e), mandur, mantoor.** [Du., fr. Malay *mandor, mandur* overseer, foreman fr. Pg. *mandador* one who gives orders.] A foreman or overseer of slaves or labourers during the early years of the Dutch settlement at the Cape. See also KNECHT.

Used also in Malaysia and Indonesia with the same meaning.

1802 *African Kalendar,* Department of the Slave Lodge ... Mandoors August Nederland Johan Mich. Berthold Anthon Jonker Phil. Tiftel. **1913** C. PETTMAN *Africanderisms* 309 Mandoor, (Port. *mandador*, an overseer, superintendent.) A foreman. This is the Malay form of the word current in the Archipelago, whence it was brought in the early days to South Africa by Malay slaves. **1974** A.P. BRINK *Looking on Darkness* 44 He must have been twenty or so when he became *mantoor* or overseer on a farm in Klapmuts district. **1982** — *Chain of Voices* 126 At Lagenvlei it's Ontong and Achilles who keep an eye on me, but there on Houd-den-Bek I'm made mantoor over them. **1989** *Reader's Digest Illust. Hist.* 52 Farm slaves often worked under the immediate supervision of a *mandoor* (overseer) who was himself a slave, usually Cape-born and chosen for this senior position by his owner.

manekie var. MANNETJIE.

manel /maˈnel/ *n.* [Afk., prob. ad. Du. *manteljas* caped great coat; but see also quot. 1913.] A black frock-coat worn by elders and deacons of the DUTCH REFORMED churches.

1913 C. PETTMAN *Africanderisms* 309 Manel, (F. *mandille*, footman's cloak, great-coat; Lat. *mantrellum*, a cloak.) A dress-coat, a frock-coat. **1916** S. BLACK in S. Gray *Three Plays* (1984) 239 Dear old Vanny, you ought to have seen him in his long manel and tophat. **1927** *Outspan* 29 Apr. 17 The figure which was that of an old man walked swiftly past him and in passing tugged at the coat-tails of the minister's manel. **1950** H.C. BOSMAN in L. Abrahams *Bekkersdal Marathon* (1971) 11 When Elder Landsman came back into the church he had a long black bottle half hidden under his *manel*. **1955** A. DELIUS *Young Trav.* 107 Oom Thys, who was one of the elders of the church, appeared very carefully groomed and dressed in his black manel, a tail-coat suit something like an undertaker's. **1958** [see OUDERLING sense 1]. **1965** C. VAN HEYNINGEN *Orange Days* 92, I was wearing a smart tweed coat and skirt that I had just bought in England — long tails at the back, like a 'manel'. **1975** D.H. STRUTT *Clothing Fashions* 213 In the Pretoria Cultural History Museum there is an example of a frock coat (*manel*) of the 'thirties made of fine black melton cloth lined with linen.

mangatan var. MAKATANE.

mangpara var. MOMPARA.

'Mangwato see BAMANGWATO.

‖**maningi** /maˈniːŋgi, məˈnɪŋgi/ *adj.* and *adv. Colloq.* [Zulu pl. adj. concord *ma-* + *-ningi* many; prob. entering S. Afr. Eng. through Fanakalo.]
A. *adj.* Much; great. Also *absol.*

a**1931** S. BLACK in S. Gray *Three Plays* (1984) 141 Abraham: If you come to Johannesburg you'll get three pounds in the month. Jeremiah: Wow! (*Whistles*) Maningi mali, Baas. Plenty money! **1978** *E. Prov. Herald* 23 Nov. 19 Tembo once informed Greenfield's brother, Niels, that he was 'maningi gentleman', pointing out that the seat of his trousers had become worn out. The implication was that gentlemen sit about more than the working man. **1991** G. HOFMEYR on TV1, 24 Apr. (Big Time), They come in for bread, they go out with maningi.

B. *adv.* Very, exceedingly.

1939 C. DELBRIDGE in *Outspan* 20 Oct. 71 The Baas hit you 'maningi sterrek' N'kos, and when you fell across the pump 'asleep' the Baas told me to put you in the skip and take you quickly to the top. **1949** C. BULLOCK *Rina* 159 'Maningi sick, Inkosi?' he enquired anxiously. 'No, you old fool,' I laughed. **1971** *Sunday Times* 21 Mar. (Mag. Sect.) 5 The gardener arrived at my study window and said it was 'maningi hot' and could he have shorts like the cook?

manitoka /ˌmænəˈtəʊkə, -tɔkə/ *n.* Also **manatoka, manitaka, manitokka, man(o)toka.** [A name perh. created by the botanist P. Macowan; not used in Austral. Eng.] In full **manitoka tree,** also **-boom** /bʊəm/ [Afk. *boom* tree]: the large shrub *Myoporum insulare* of the Myoporaceae, bearing small white flowers followed by edible blue berries, indigenous to Australia but naturalized in parts of the Western Cape. Also *attrib.*

1906 F. BLERSCH *Handbk of Agric.* 267 Hedge shrubs and trees ... Manatoka (*Myoporum insulare*). **1913** C. PETTMAN *Africanderisms* 310 Manotoka boom, .. The Western Province name for *Myoporum acuminatum.* **1948** H.V. MORTON *In Search of S. Afr.* 48 The old buildings and houses of former occupants .. were standing roofless and deserted in a jungle of manitaka trees. **1949** L.G. GREEN *In Land of Afternoon* 175 Manitoka trees curled over by years and years of south-easter. **1956** *Cape Times* 1 Mar. 8 The English myrtle hedge .. is far more interesting, is greener and less likely to dry out. This can also be said of the manitoka and tecoma hedges. **1957** L.G. GREEN *Beyond City Lights,* I remember the blue gum trees with their colonies of finches and the twisted old manitoka trees where the weaver-birds nest. **1973** M. PHILIP *Caravan Caravel* 19 Hedges of fleshy, narrow-leaved manitokkas bushing out between the caravan sites. **1984** R.J. POYNTON *Characteristics & Uses of Sel. Trees* 155 Manatoka *Myoporum insulare.* Manatoka, Dotted-leaf *Myoporum laetum.*

Manketsens see quot. 1822 at NGWAKETSE.

mann var. MAN *n.*[1] and *int.*

manne pl. form of MAN *n.*[2]

‖**mannetjie** /ˈmanəki, -ci/ *n.* Also **manekie, mannikee.** [Afk., fr. Du. *mannetje.*]
1. A male animal.

1837 'N. POLSON' *Subaltern's Sick Leave* 136 She was savage as her '*mannikkee*' had just been shot. Lions are met in pairs and in troeps. **1886** G.A. FARINI *Through Kalahari Desert* 325 We picked up the spoor of a clump of six [ostriches], of which Kert said he could tell from their footprints that four were *manekies* (males). **1919** F.W. FITZSIMONS *Natural Hist. of S. Afr.* I. 35 (Swart), It is presumed some old 'mannetjie', more clumsy that the rest, must have slammed to the upper half, or perhaps it was the wind. **1963** M. KAVANAGH *We Merry Peasants* 172 The seller was as ignorant as we were about their sex and to make sure I called on a coloured farmer ... He kindly drove with me to inspect and pronounced: 'hens'. He .. regretted that he could not supply a '*mannetjie*' for them. **1964** J. BENNETT *Mr Fisherman* (1967) 99 While the whales were around his fear had made him forget his tiredness ... 'The prop,' said Pillay. 'That old killer, that old mannetjie, he snapped a blade right off.' **1977** F.G. BUTLER *Karoo Morning* 46 The lands were suddenly full of ostriches — the black ones were men, the grey ones ladies. They were different colours? 'They say it's for protection ... The mannetjie sits on the eggs at night; and because he is black, his enemies can't see him at all.'

2. A little man; a disparaging term of address.

1974 in *Eng. Usage in Sn Afr.* Vol.5 No.1, 5 Frequent use in Central [Prison] English or Afrikaans diminutive (eg. *My Cherrytjie ... well my mannetjies.*) **1977** *Family Radio & TV* 4 Apr. 46 My four brothers and four sisters were fine, nothing wrong with them; then I came along ... But I'm telling you *mannetjie* what you can do I can do better. **1977** S. ROBERTS in E. Pereira *Contemp. S. Afr. Plays* 240 And who do you think you're talking to, mannetjie. **1988** *Informant, Cradock* They took this Mars mannetjie to their leader in the space ship. **1990** *Sunday Times* 6 May 1 He said he would one day meet this 'Emiel-mannetjie' (Emiel character).

man of the blanket see BLANKET sense b.

man(o)toka var. MANITOKA.

Mantatee /manˈtɑːtiː, mæn-/ *n. Obs. exc. hist.* Also **Manchatee, Mantati(e), Manteti.** [ad. *MmaNtatisi,* the name of a leader of this people (see quot. 1928).] A member of a section of the TLOKWA people who, under their chieftainess MmaNtatisi, migrated through parts of what is now the Orange Free State during the Mfecane, conquering other peoples as they moved. Also *attrib.* See also FETCANI, MAKATEES.

1823 [see MATABELE]. **1824** *Cape Chron.* in *S. Afr. Jrnl* I. 76 Mr. Moffat .. Missionary of the Kuruman .. has lately arrived in Cape Town .. accompanied by .. five women and a boy of the marauding nation called 'Mantatees', who recently made so formidable an inroad upon the less warlike tribes of the Barolongs and Bechuanas. **1826** [see OPGAAF sense 1]. **1828** T. PRINGLE *Ephemerides* 188 In the years 1824 and 1825, owing to the devastation occasioned in the countries north-east of the Colony, by the hordes called Mantatees and Ficani, .. many of the Bechuana tribes were broken up. **1833** *Graham's Town Jrnl* 6 June 3 The greater part .. of these aliens, are destitute people of the Bechuana tribes, usually designated by the Frontier farmers 'Mantatees'. **1838** J.E. ALEXANDER *Exped. into Int.* II. 221 The invasion of the Bechuana country, in 1823, by an immense horde which came from the eastward, driven from their own country by the warlike Zoolas, and called *Mantatees.* **1841** B. SHAW *Memorials* 47 Dr. Smith .. states that the Mantatees were known by the name of Backlokwa, or Bakora, previous to their coming into contact with the Bechuanas, and that their present designation was first given them by the Bechuanas, from the name of their Chief, Mantatee ... It is ascertained that Mantatees in the Bechuana language, and Ficani in the Kaffir, are synonymous terms, both signifying invaders. **1843** J.C. CHASE *Cape of G.H.* 238 The Mantatees, the remnants of tribes broken up and dispersed by the Zoolah conquests in 1822 to 1824. **1862** LADY DUFF-GORDON in F. Galton *Vacation Tourists* (1864) III. 151 The boots here is a mantatee, very black, and called Kleen-boy, because he is so little. **1867** *Blue Bk for Col. 1866* JJ30, By the great influx of Mantatee and other Kafirs, agricultural labour is abundant and cheap. **1905** *Native Tribes of Tvl* 9 The 'Mantatis' took their name from Ma Ntatisi the chieftainess of the

Basuto tribe, said to be the original Batlokwa, which till about 1821 dwelt in or near the present district of Harrismith. [1928 E.H.L. SCHWARZ *Kalahari & its Native Races* 225 Mokotjo, a Bechuana chief of the tribe of the Batlokoa, married his cousin Monyalue ... She gave birth to a daughter, Ntatisi, and .. became known herself as her daughter's mother — Mantatisi; later, she bore a son who was called Sekonyela. This boy became the leader of the Batlokoa in a series of raids throughout the country .. but his mother was the directing force; to such an extent indeed that the marauders came to be called after her.] 1941 C.W. DE KIEWIET *Hist. of S. Afr.* 50 A common explanation of the confusion of Bantu life at this time was the sudden emergence of highly disciplined warrior tribes — Zulu, Matabele and Mantatees — who carried death and destruction far and wide. 1953 B. FULLER *Call Back Yesterday* 144 Towards the close of the year 1833 Edwards, Archbell, and Moroka set out to interview Chief Moshesh of the Basutos, and Chief Sikonyela of the Mantatees. 1979 M. MATSHOBA *Call Me Not a Man* 147 The land that had been left barren of populace ... Left barren by the Mantatee Hordes. 1980 J. COCK *Maids & Madams* 200 Somerset arranged for the original 13 Mantatee women and children to be apprenticed for seven-year periods in Graaff Reinet. 1985 *Weekend Post* 27 July 5 The building .. was built for and by a group of Southern Sothos called the Mantatees. The Mantatees had fled across the Orange River and settled in the area. 1989 J. CRWYS-WILLIAMS *S. Afr. Despatches* 14 A general assembly of the tribes making up the Bechuana nation .. was called together at Kuruman to meet the threat of advancing Mantatees.

mantoor var. MANDOOR.

‖**mantshingilane** /ˌmantʃiŋiˈlɑːne/ *n*. Also **mantshingelane**, **(u)mantshingelani**, **matshingilane**, and with initial capital. [Zulu *umantshingelana* (pl. *omantshingelana*).] Esp. among speakers of Sintu (Bantu) languages: a night watchman or security guard.

a1968 D.C. THEMBA in E. Patel *World of Can Themba* (1985) 72 An old Zulu, clad in a greenish-khaki military overcoat, huddling over a glowing brazier. He was the *matshingilane* — the nightwatchman. 1980 M. MUTLOATSE *Forced Landing* 1 The part the black writer has to play is rather demanding .. jack of all trades — and a master of all! He has to be a tradesman .. psychologist .. *mantshingelane*, *tshotsa*, teacher .. visionary, *imbongi* and — above all — oral historian. 1982 M. MZAMANE *Children of Soweto* 108 Rathebe had once applied for guns for all his petrol attendants plus his nightwatchman, but a licence had been granted for only one. Even the Zulu *mantshingilane* had to rely on his *knobkierie* and *assegai*. 1983 *Frontline* May 39 Labour order: 'Three garden boys, six bricklayers, two painters, three mantshingilanes, one teaboy, two floor-cleaners, eight street-sweepers and a dozen night-soil and ash collectors,' is made. 1983 *Pace* Dec. 114 A new breed of watchmen. The time-honoured image of the stubborn old matshingilane is on the way out. The new breed of security guard are tough, ruthlessly efficient men. *Ibid.* 117 The new breed of matshingilanes — security guards to be correct — are trained at the highest level to guard what are called National Key Points against saboteurs, and to kill if need be in the discharge of their duties. 1989 O. MUSI in *City Press* 7 May 14 Did I hear you ask how a mantshingilane like Mkhize came to be advancing the cause of science when he should have been standing at the factory gates with his knobkerrie and an unfriendly look; ready to repel unwanted guests. 1993 L. MADIKANE in *Weekly Mail & Guardian* 22 Oct. 17 Multitudes of Mantshingilanes, 'daga-boys', 'baas-boys', 'garden boys', and 'kitchen maids' .. traditionally make the only visible 'black' input into the economy.

Manyano /manˈjaːnɔ, manˈjaːnəʊ/ *n*. Also **Manyane**, **Umanyano**, and with small initial. Pl. **-s**, or (occas.) unchanged. [Xhosa *umanyano* union, association, fr. *manya* join, unite.] In any of several black churches, the name given to the women's association. Also *attrib*.

Each Manyano has a distinctive uniform, and usu. accepts only married women as members.

1941 *Bantu World* 8 Mar. 12 Manyano presidents of various churches .. attended with Manyano members in uniforms of their respective churches. 1955 W. ILLSLEY *Wagon on Fire* 239 'It is the church choir,' she cried excitedly, peering through the window. 'They are followed by the Women's Manyano and .. Moruti Tsotetsi and .. Moruti Etherton.' 1962 M. BRANDEL-SYRIER *Black Woman* 15 Manyano is originally a Xhosa word. It is the noun of the reciprocal form of the verb *Ukumanya*, which means, 'to join', to 'unite'. Possibly the word was first coined amongst the Xhosa peoples of the Ciskei, which is the region of the earliest missionary concentration in South Africa ... It remained for a long time the general term used by the Methodists for their Church-women's organizations, even amongst peoples speaking other Bantu languages. *Ibid.* 29 The Manyanos are the strongholds of the older African women — the mothers and grandmothers. *Ibid.* 80 With the Stockfel, the Manyano affords by far the most popular and most frequent occasions for social outings available to urban women. 1963 WILSON & MAFEJE *Langa* 93 Far the most vigorous of the church associations are those for married women: all the larger churches have such associations (*manyano*) whose members hold weekly meetings for prayer and discussion. 1978 M. MABOGOANE in *Staffrider* Vol.1 No.2, 18 There might be a talk about the church. They were in the same women's association, the Manyane, of the Methodist Church. 1978 *Voice* 13 Dec. 1A, Churches must organise seminars on marriage and family life. Mothers unions (manyanos) should be involved. 1981 *Grocott's Mail* 16 Apr. 4 The Manyano (black Methodist women's organisation) exhibit at the Commemoration Church Easter Flower Festival. 1982 M. MZAMANE *Children of Soweto* 194 The older men would come before the younger ones, the lay preachers before members of the women's *Umanyano* and so on, all in strict vigil protocol. 1986 S. SEPAMLA *Third Generation* 24 If she began to be nasty .. I raised the spectre of the Methodist church Women's *Manyano*. I'd remind her that she wore the red blouse of that honourable group. 1987 L. DELLATOLA in *S. Afr. Panorama* May 27 The aims of the Women's Manyano are 'to control and direct the life of the home in accordance with Christian principles and example, with special reference to cleanliness, respect for elders, and for training of children for the service of home, in purity of thought, word and deed'. 1987 *New Nation* 10 Dec. 13 Almost every domestic worker belongs to a 'manyano'. Every Sunday and Thursday, suburban churches, parks, rivers and fields come alive with church meetings, singing and prayers ... These manyanos have not only been spiritual and social homes to their members. They have sometimes provided a focus for political organisation. 1990 *S. Afr. Panorama* Nov.-Dec. 6 During the week, meetings by the women's movements (*manyano*) are held in classrooms and in private homes.

mapakathi pl. form of UMPAKATI.

mapani var. MOPANI.

mapansula pl. form of PANTSULA.

mapantsula var. and pl. form of PANTSULA.

maphepha /maˈpe(ː)pa/ *n*. Also **mephepha**. Pl. unchanged, or **-s**. [Xhosa *amaphepha*, pl. form of *iphepha* paper.] In urban (esp. township) English:
1. *slang*.
a. RAND sense 3 a.

1970 O. MUSI in *Post* 11 Oct. 2 These people must fork out a thousand maphephas for costs and the cops want their pound of flesh. 1981 *Voice* 24 June 2 Those guys are not playing games ... The fine is 600 maphepha or six months and, wait for it, both. *Ibid.* 8 July 2 They won't listen to any application for a site unless .. you have at least 6 000 maphepha in the bank. 1987 *Drum* Oct. 86 Our pal says he can divulge this heavenly secret to you if you send him something like 20 mephepha.

b. *noncount*. Money; MAGAGEBA.

1978 *Voice* 8 Nov. 2 Bearing in mind that Queen Elizabeth II has a lot of maphepha I frankly don't see why she shouldn't .. fork out income tax. 1979 *Ibid.* 31 Jan. 2 A White guy .. ordered the tellers to fork over the maphepha after telling them to kneel on the floor. 1983 O. MUSI in *City Press* 28 Aug. 8 Putco, of course has made a lot of maphepha from us, being virtually the only means of transport for many workers. 1987 *Drum* Jan. 51 Divorce our speciality. Your maphepha refunded if wifey decides to hang on to you in spite of the fact that she's lost the divorce action. 1987 O. MUSI in *Drum* Nov. 93 The smooth-talking shysters would spot a wealthy-looking and obviously greedy-for-more maphepha mlungu in the city and quickly make his acquaintance. 1990 — in *City Press* 17 June 9 That whopping increase in the cops' maphepha announced last week.

2. *rare*. An official document; in *pl.*, 'papers'.

1985 D. BIKITSHA in *Sunday Times* 15 Sept. 6 Anybody ordinarily or shabbily dressed was a work-seeker who had to have all his papers or 'maphephas' (official documents) in order.

mapoer var. MAMPOER.

mapone var. MOPANI.

mapusa /maˈpʊ(ː)sa, -za/ *n*. *slang*. Also **maposa**, **mapuza**, and with initial capital. Pl. unchanged. [Contraction of the words for 'policemen' in various Sintu (Bantu) languages, e.g. Xhosa *amapholisa*, Zulu *amaphoyisa*, Tswana *mapodisa*, these in turn being derived fr. Eng. *police*. The contraction prob. originated in township slang.] The police; a policeman; a night watchman.

1970 M. WEITZMAN *Informant, Johannesburg* He is a maposa at night at the factory. 1973 *Eng. Alive* 53 A shadow lurks — mapuza, and the people crouch in clenched fists of black terror. 1984 *E. Prov. Herald* 18 June 13 We never carried our weapons around because we knew we would get grabbed by the Mapusa (police), so we kept them at scattered arsenals. Fortunately, one was close.

maqabane(s) pl. form of IQABANE.

maqueta, **maqweta** varr. ABAKWETHA.

marabaraba var. MORABARABA.

marabi /məˈraːbi, maˈraːbi/ *n*. Also **maraba**. [Perh. fr. *Marabastad*, the name of a township (now no longer in existence) on the outskirts of Pretoria; or S. Sotho *marabi* pl. of *lerabi* gangster (indicating the disapproval with which the sub-culture was regarded); or rel. to S. Sotho *raba* fly around, perh. referring to the energetic dance style.]
1. *hist*. A working-class township culture of the 1930s and 1940s: see quot. 1989. Also *attrib*.

1933 *Umteteli* 11 Nov. in D.B. Coplan, *Urbanization of African Performing Arts.* (1980) 247 The 'marabi' dances and concerts, and the terrible 'jazz' music banged and wailed out of the doors of foul-smelling so called halls are far from representing real African taste. 1948 [see Walker quot. at BEER-DRINK]. 1980 D.B. COPLAN *Urbanization of African Performing Arts.* 205 Marabi was .. a category of people with a low social status and a reputation for immoral behaviour. 1982 *Pace* May 103 The Doornfontein slums were amongst the worst in the world in the Twenties and were the first to be cleared for removal to Orlando Township in the Thirties. Before this it was the favourite shebeen area in Johannesburg, and the home of Marabi. 1985 *Learn & Teach* No.3, 10 Wilson Silgee was of my old days. He was my schoolmate. He was also of the Marabi Period. 1986 KALLAWAY & PEARSON *Johannesburg* 36 The pictures of Ferreira's Town in the 1930s capture the context of the 'Marabi Culture' — without the romantic gloss it is sometimes given. 1986 P. MAYLAM *Hist. of Afr. People* 150 Liquor formed a central part of a wider African working-class urban culture, often known as *marabi*. 1989

Reader's Digest Illust. Hist. 355 Out of the mire of these teeming, reeking, violent and tumble-down acres of apparently hopeless misery rose a spirit of proud survival. Africans called it *marabi*. *Ibid.* 358 The heart of *marabi* was its music – a throbbing blend of Christian spirituals, Negro rags, Boer *vastrap* .. and traditional rural rhythms and harmonies. But *marabi* was not only about music. Other vital components were home beer-brewing, weekend shebeen parties and drinking *skokiaan* and *isiqatavika* ('kill me quick') in order to forget the drabness of life in urban ghettos.

2. *hist.* A township drinking and dancing party of the 1920s, 1930s, or 1940s, esp. one at which marabi music (see sense 3) was played. Usu. *attrib.*

1946 P. ABRAHAMS *Mine Boy* (1954) 108 They would relax and dance till daybreak at some maraba, egged on by the thumping noise of a broken-down piano. **1970** M. DIKOBE Marabi Dance. 2 She loved George and he attracted her to the Marabi parties, which were run by the well-known Ma-Ndlovu and were very popular, but not favoured by respectable people. **1978** *Speak* Vol.1 No.5, 3 No 'stokvel' (working class savings and self-help club 'rent party') or 'marabi' party could attract paying customers without someone pounding out African melodies and rhythms on a battered organ, piano or guitar, to the rattle of milk-cans filled with pebbles. **1984** *Staffrider* Vol.6 No.1, 34 Mrs S— didn't go to Marabi parties, didn't join a dance club, and rather regrets that she didn't queue for 'bioscope' with her sister. **1987** *New Nation* 23 July 10 It was one of the areas in the city centre where blacks were allowed to live close to the wild shebeen and marabi centre of Doornfontein.

3. *Music.* A style of popular dance music common in townships in the 1920s, 1930s, and 1940s, consisting of a blend of African, Afrikaans, and 'coloured' folk music styles adapted to performance on the organ or piano, with the addition, in later years, of elements of American jazz. Also *attrib.*

At that time, often played in shebeens and at parties and dances, at first usu. by a keyboardist, later also by guitarists, penny-whistlers, and bands. A forerunner of KWELA and its derivatives.

1941 W.M.B. NHLAPO in *Bantu World* 15 Mar. 9 The Jazz Maniacs .. were regarded as a 'marabi' or 'Tsaba-Tsaba' band. **1953** *Drum* Jan. 40 'Marabi' Guitar .. the three-chord 'marabi' style which draws crowds to every gramophone and cycle shop in town. **1953** T. MATSHIKIZA in *Drum* Feb. 37 The choir sings first a short little introductory piece, Marabi-like. **1958** *Time* 16 June 37 In the dusty streets urchins rock to the penny-whistle's fast *kwela* beat; in the shabby speakeasies, women shuffle to its slower *marabi* rhythm. **1959** E. MPHAHLELE *Down Second Ave* 96 The name 'Marabi' came from Marabastad. From there it went to the Reef ... Bring your gal, spin your gal for the palpitating marabi rhythm of u-no-mes at a Daybreak Dance at Columbia Every Night. **1976** W. SILGEE in D.B. Coplan, Urbanization of African Performing Arts. (1980) 212 *Tickey draai* plus *tula n'divile* equals *marabi*. **1977** P.C. VENTER *Soweto* 8 Here they danced to marabi tunes, a form of earthy music which preceded the jive and rock 'n roll. **1977** T. COUZENS in *Quarry '77* 35 Doornfontein and Prospect Townships produced a particular music in the early Thirties: marabi. It was shebeen music played to be drunk to. **1981** B. MFENYANA in M. Mutloatse *Reconstruction* 295 The broad topic of language arts cannot be discussed in isolation from drama, story-telling (folk-lore), music, dance, sculpture and other performing and expressive arts. So Scamto goes hand in hand with Jit, Khwela, Marabi, Mbaqanga, Soul, Jazz and Disco-jive. **1982** A. OLIPHANT in *Staffrider* Vol.5 No.2, 22 Discordantly we sing long forgotten maraba songs. *c*1985 J. CRONIN in *Eng. Academy Rev.* 3 35 This poem closely resembles the rhythmic qualities of contemporary 'township' music in South Africa ... This music (in all its varieties – *Marabi*, *Mbganga* [*sic*], *Kwela*, etc.) is characterised by a basic riff repeated many times over, with small subtle variations. **1986** T. THOKA in *Eng. Usage in Sn Afr.* Vol.17 No.2, 19 Tsotsie-taal goes hand in hand with Marabi (township jazz) and disco music, and with general life in the township. **1987** *New Nation* 9 July 10 Marabi music was born in the ghettos of early Johannesburg. It is the basis of South African jazz. Jacob Moeketsi, the .. pianist, said: 'Marabi music is a type of music that does not compare with European music. It has much more movement physically and rhythmically. It forms the core of African music.' ... 'King Force' Silgee confirms the .. influence ... 'If you listen to that "Mannenberg" of Dollar Brand, that's marabi, marabi straight.' *Ibid.* 16 July 10 Composer and critic Todd Matshikiza wrote in Drum magazine: 'Ntebejana .. exploited the three-chord form of marabi, consisting entirely of the major chords in C and F and their sevenths. This was marabi – a simple form of improvisation on the piano, organ or sometimes guitar.' **1990** *Sunday Tribune* 14 Jan. (Today) 7 Mango Groove is not just another ethno-trendy band. It has taken the marabi-kwela sound and popularised it. **1990** [see PENNY-WHISTLE].

maranka /mə'ræŋkə/ *n.* Also **marak(k)a, marake, maranki**. [ad. Pedi *moraka* the name of this plant (the fruit being called *leraka*).] The bottle gourd *Lagenaria siceraria* of the Cucurbitaceae; its fruit. Also *attrib.* See also CALABASH sense 2.

1934 C.P. SWART Supplement to Pettman. 112 *Maranki*, .. A vegetable, indigenous to South Africa, resembling a squash and when prepared tasting very much like sweet potatoes. **1937** L. LEIPOLD *Bushveld Doctor* 319, I met him tilling his mealie lands, his little patches of sweet potatoes and marankas. **1951** S. VAN H. TULLEKEN *Prac. Cookery Bk* 183 Stuffed Marakes. Peel marakes; cut a hole in the top and scrape the pips, etc., out. **1966** C.A. SMITH *Common Names* 332 *Marakka*, .. see maranka, of which it is another version ... *Maranka, Lagenaria siceraria* .. used by natives as a vegetable and regarded by some Europeans as superior to vegetable marrow. **1982** *S. Afr. Panorama* May 39 These traditional foods include *maranka* squash, sorghum beer and sour milk.

Mardyker /'mɑːdaɪkə, 'mɑːdeɪkə/ *n. hist.* Also **Mardycka, Mardycker**. [Afk., earlier Du. *Mardijker*, fr. Malay *Campon-Maredhika*, an area in the East Indies; see quot. 1883.] Usu. in *pl.*: The name given by Dutch colonists to freed Malay slaves who fought with them against the indigenous peoples of the Cape, and later against the British, in the days of Dutch East India Company rule.

1883 'A CAPE COLONIST' *Cape Malays* 3 The word Mardycker needs some explanation. Valentyn says: 'Mardycka, or Maredhika, in the East Indies belongs to Amboyna ... Between the town Amboyna and Soya in the neighbourhood of the river Waytomo, there is a hamlet commonly called Campon-Maredhika, inhabited by strangers who first arrived with the Portuguese from the Moluccas proper, and were employed to help in strengthening the position of the latter against the Amboineese.' On the same principle the Amsterdam Chamber was most anxious that free Malays should settle at the Cape to strengthen the position of the Dutch against the Hottentots and other natives, *i.e.*, to be employed in a similar manner as the Mardyckers had been by the Portuguese at the Moluccas. **1936** L.G. GREEN *Secret Afr.* 132 They were called 'Mardyckers,' and it was hoped that their proved fighting ability would help to strengthen the Dutch against Hottentot raiders. **1944** I.D. DU PLESSIS *Cape Malays* 46 The Malays who took part in this engagement at Blaauwberg were known as Mardyckers: servants of high officials of the Dutch East India Company. **1971** L.G. GREEN *Taste of S.-Easter* 139 Some free Malays attended Dutchmen of rank on visits to Europe and learnt to speak Dutch. Such men often remained at the Cape on their return and were known as Mardykers.

marena var. MORENA.

marewa, mar(h)ewu varr. MAHEWU.

Maritzburg /'mærɪtsbɜːg/ *n. colloq.* Shortened form of *Pietermaritzburg*, the capital city of the former province of Natal. See also SLEEPY HOLLOW.

At time of writing (1994) the issue of the capital of the new province of KwaZulu-Natal had not yet been decided.

1846 'A CORRESPONDENT' in *Natal Witness* 26 June, They .. bear the same relation to Maritzburg with regard to distance, as the districts of Tulbagh, Worcester, Swellendam, *c*, do to the Cape. **1852** C. BARTER *Dorp & Veld* 26 Maritzburg .. an English town rising out of the ruins of a Dutch *dorp* or village. **1855** J.W. COLENSO *Ten Weeks in Natal* 188, I saw in a humble shed at Maritzburg handsome chairs of yellow-wood. **1887** A.A. ANDERSON *25 Yrs in Waggon* I. 56 We had a very narrow escape on our return journey from Maritzburg. **1893** 'CHARLOTTE' in *Cape Illust. Mag.* May 310, I am going to live in Maritzburg, Miss Donnington. **1911** *Farmer's Weekly* 11 Oct. 171 Farmers are now able to inoculate their sheep with 'blue-tongue' virus prepared at the Government laboratories at Pretoria and Maritzburg. **1926** M. NATHAN *S. Afr. from Within* 235 They opened stores in Durban and Maritzburg, and acquired property. **1939** M. VERITY in *Outspan* 6 Oct. 55 She wondered if they would see anything of David in Natal. They themselves were going on to Maritzburg. **1980** A. PATON *Towards Mountain* 4 We British shortened the name to 'Maritzburg', and pronounced it in English fashion. **1990** A. GOLDSTUCK *Rabbit in Thorn Tree* 59 Everyone in Maritzburg is scared and they're watching their kids, especially ones under about the age of seven. **1992** J. DUNN in *Drum* Dec. (Then & Now) 75 The Maritzburg-born weightlifter .. left the country after refusing to accept apartheid.

market master *n. phr.* A municipal official who administers the market of a town.

1831 *S. Afr. Almanac & Dir.* 166 The proceedings of the Market to be under the control of a Market Master ... The following Tariff of fees shall be exacted for the purpose of paying the Market Master a salary. **1845** S. DENNISON in R. Edgecombe, Letters of Hannah Dennison. (1968) 210 H had just obtained the Market masters Place. **1859** *Queenstown Free Press* 3 Aug. (Pettman), I should advise them to send the market-master .. to visit our market. **1877** F. JEPPE *Tvl Bk Almanac & Dir.* (1976) 49 Market and Poundmaster: J.G.C. Wagner; Gold Commissioner at Suikerbosch-fontein (Blaauwbank): W.S. Sanders. **1882** J. NIXON *Among Boers* 130 A market was held every morning, at which the market master, a municipal official peculiar to South African towns, sold produce for all comers at a fixed rate. **1955** V.M. FITZROY *Dark Bright Land* 121 Mevrouw appealed to her husband .. to back up her statement that the Market Master had assessed her berry wax. **1971** *Farmer's Weekly* 12 May 47 The recent conference of the Institute of Market Masters of South Africa. **1974** *Grocott's Mail* 11 Apr., Market Report. The Market Master .. reports as follows on the sales held at Grahamstown for the week ending April 5.

marlie var. MALI.

maroela, -roola varr. MARULA.

marog(o) var. MOROGO.

Marootze(e)s pl. form of HURUTSHE.

marretje see quot. 1812 at NAARTJIE *n.* sense 1 a.

marsbanker var. MAASBANKER.

marsh rose *n. phr.* [Prob. tr. Afk. *vleiroos*, *vlei* (see VLEI) + *roos* rose.] A very rare species of plant of the Proteaceae, *Orothamnus zeyheri*, bearing coral to bright red flowers shaped like a rose.

1957 L.G. GREEN *Beyond City Lights* 214 Caledon has the rarest and choicest wildflowers; nearly all the most exquisite heaths; the coral-red pincushion protea, the Marsh Rose and other proteas on the verge of extinction. **1975** [see VELDKOS]. **1977** *Weekend Argus* 9 Apr. (Mag. Sect.) 1 The marsh rose – a plant so rare that since its discovery it was twice thought to be extinct ... The Orothamnus zeyheri was discovered by the intrepid collector, Carl Zeyher, in marshy places, on the summit of the Hottentots-Holland Mountains in the month of July. **1985** A. TREDGOLD *Bay between Mountains* 16 High up, in a restricted damp and misty region of the Kogelberg, in the Hottentots Holland Mountains, is another of the rarest flowers in the land, the rich red marsh rose, clinging to its tall, woody stem. **1992** RICHARDSON & VAN WILGEN in *Afr. Wildlife* Vol.46 No.4, 160 Fire was necessary to prevent the extinction of certain species, e.g. the endangered blushing bride (*Serruria florida*) and the marsh rose (*Orothamnus zeyheri*).

martevaan /ˈmɑːtəvɑːn/ *n.* Also **martavaan**, and with initial capital. Pl. **-s**, **-vanen** /-vɑːnən/. [Du., ad. of *Martaban*, see quot. 1965.] A large glazed earthenware jar, used in the past on Dutch East India Company ships to store oil and wine. Also *attrib.*

Elsewhere called 'martaban', 'mortaban', or 'mortivan'.

[**1698** J. FRYER *New Acct of E. India & Persia* 180 An huge Heap of long Jars like Mortivans. **1711** C. LOCKYER *Acct of Trade in India* 35, 35 Mortivan and small Jars.] **1963** W. FEHR *Treasures at Castle of G.H.*, A selection of large and small 'Martevanen' or 'Voorraad-spotten' dating to the Ming Period .. came to the Cape from Batavia. **1965** A. GORDON-BROWN *S. Afr. Heritage* II. 13 Martavanen were large earthenware jars of Chinese origin used on board Dutch East Indiamen for carrying oil and wine. They were mostly shipped from Pegu in the Gulf of Martaban, Burma, of which the name is a corruption. **1968** M. MULLER *Green Peaches Ripen* 24 She lifted a heavy brown jar and lovingly polished its bright glaze. 'Look at this martavanen jar, Anna. It dates back to the Ming period.' **1973** *Cape Times* 26 Jan. 2 A magnificent pair of Martevaans in brown glaze decorated with panels of flowers R625 the pair.

martial eagle *n. phr.* The largest African eagle, *Polemaetus bellicosus* of the Accipitridae; also called LAMMERVANGER.

1923 HAAGNER & IVY *Sketches* 94 The Martial Eagle (*Spizaetus bellicosus*) is dark sepia above and below, except the abdominal regions, which are white spotted with brown. **1936** E.L. GILL *First Guide to S. Afr. Birds* 126 *Martial Eagle*, Lammervanger ... Such a powerful bird (it has massive muscular feet and terrible talons) has a great choice of prey; it commonly takes small buck, hares, meercats, and sometimes, unfortunately, lambs and kids. **1962** W.R. SIEGFRIED *Some Protected Birds* Pl.29, *Martial Eagle, Polemaetas bellicosus* ... This large and powerful bird is found in the wilder open or mountainous country. Deserves protection for its value in combating the dassie plague. **1973** J. COWDEN *For Love* 43 'There is everything in the sky,' he said, 'but they refuse to come in. They fly round .. lammergeyer, Cape vultures, martial eagles. Even black eagles.' **1982** *E. Prov. Herald* 23 Aug. 11 Two of Africa's largest birds of prey, the martial eagle and the crowned eagle. **1983** K.B. NEWMAN *Newman's Birds* 168 Martial eagle ... Distinctive large long-legged eagle ... Singly in bushveld, woodland, grassland and hill country. **1987** *Eagles & Farmers* (Endangered Wildlife Trust) 12 The Martial Eagle is found in open country and bushveld throughout Africa. It is currently classified as 'vulnerable' in the *S.A. Red Data Book – Birds*. **1990** *Farmer's Weekly* 8 June, Black eagles, martial eagles, bateleurs, African hawk-eagles, [etc.].

martingola var. MATINGOLA.

marula /məˈru(ː)lə/ *n.* Also **maroela**, **maroola**, **marul(l)o**, **marulla**, **merula**, **meruley**, **meruli**, **morala**, **morula**. [ad. Afk. *maroela*, N. Sotho *morula* (pl. *merula*).]

a. In full *marula tree*: the tree *Sclerocarya birrea* (subsp. *caffra*) of the Anacardiaceae found in the tropical and sub-tropical areas of central and southern Africa, having glossy, dark green foliage and edible, yellow, plum-like fruit (see sense 2). Also *attrib.*

1857 D. LIVINGSTONE *Missionary Trav.* 165 Another tree, the 'Morala' .. has never been known to be touched by lightning. [**1868** D. OLIVER *Flora Trop. Afr.* I. 449 S[*clerocarya*] *Caffra*. Native name 'Morula'.] **1878** P. GILLMORE *Great Thirst Land* 346 A tree that I have noticed before, but paid little attention to, now becomes abundant – it is the meruley. **1907** J.P. FITZPATRICK *Jock of Bushveld* (1909) 443 It was there, lying between two rocks in the shade of a marula tree, that I got one of those chances to see game at close quarters of which most men only hear or dream. **1928** E.H.L. SCHWARZ *Kalahari & its Native Races* 150 They carve their jugs and bowls out of the soft wood of the marula tree. **1937** B.H. DICKE *Bush Speaks* 136 Kaffir beer was brought made of the marula fruit fermented with rapoko grain, a very potent beverage. **1940** V. POHL *Bushveld Adventures* 64 There .. was Mosillikaas, and his last words were, 'We will wait for you, masters when the berries are falling from the marulo trees.' **1949** J. MOCKFORD *Golden Land* 143 Here grow .. sturdy, shady, *marulas* dropping yellow plums so sun-fermented that elephants, having feasted on them, stagger tipsily. *a***1951** H.C. BOSMAN in L. Abrahams *Unto Dust* (1963) 171 If the bark of the maroelas turned black before the polgras was in seed, we would know that it would be a long winter. **1951** R. GRIFFITHS *Grey about Flame* 164 The three squatted round the pot of stodgy mealie-meal in the shade of a marula tree. **1976** V. ROSENBERG *Sunflower* 35 There were marulas with their potent fruit. **1982** *S. Afr. Panorama* Dec. 13 Elephants are reputed to get intoxicated on ripe marula fruit – the ponderous beasts have been observed staggering drunkenly around marula trees. **1985** H. GOOSEN in *S. Afr. Panorama* Feb., A utility tree in every sense is the marula, *Scletocarya birrea* subsp. *caffra*. Its golden fruit provides food and drink, its foliage is favoured cattle fodder. From the wood are fashioned bowls, spoons, other utensils and ornaments. **1991** *Style* Apr. 102 Did you know that the maroela can give you everything you need, from the bark to the fruit, and even the pips when roasted make delicious nuts?

b. The fruit of the marula tree, from which beer and other liquors are brewed. Also *attrib.*, and *comb.* **marula beer**.

1877 T. BAINES *Gold Regions of S.-E. Afr.* 9 The Marula, as large as a peach and with a kernel almost like one, has a pleasant flavour. **1897** F.W. SYKES *With Plumer in Matabeleland* 48 By this time we were half famished, as, since the first night we had eaten no food except berries, wild apples, and 'maroolas', a kind of wild plum. **1917** R. MARLOTH *Common Names* 59 *Morula* (*meroola*), *Sclerocarya caffra*. The fruit with an acidulous pleasant pulp. **1940** F.B. YOUNG *City of Gold* 358 It was the season of the ripening of the marula, that yellow plum-shaped fruit which the natives call *umgana* or 'friend'. **1951** T.V. BULPIN *Lost Trails of Low Veld* 45 It was potent, tasty Maroela beer and the trekkers drank it with relish .. first making the bearer of the gift sample it. **1961** T. MACDONALD *Tvl Story* 96 The fruiting time of the marulla is of special significance in the life of the Pedi. When the marulla juice flows potent beer is brewed from it. **1965** P. BARAGWANATH *Brave Remain* 67 At home the owner of the land would provide marula beer which, although not very intoxicating, made everybody happy. **1976** [see MOEPEL]. **1980** *Sunday Times* 19 Oct. (Mag. Sect.) 5 Marula beer, says pa, is not only potent, it's lethal .. 'but the fruit is delicious. I love it. It's a smooth fruit, rather like a litchi, but the meat adheres more firmly to the pip.' **1985** H. GOOSEN in *S. Afr. Panorama* Feb., The marula liqueur marketed by a South African distilling company is becoming increasingly popular. **1991** *Leisure Books Catal.* Apr.-June, Do you know that you can use elderberries, violets, oranges, marulas and other fruits, as well as roses, spices, nuts and even leaves to make your own liqueurs?

maruti var. MORUTI.

mar-whow, marwow varr. MAWO.

Mary *n. offensive.*

1. [See quot. 1973.] A demeaning generic name given to a woman of Indian descent.

1927 R. JOHNSTON in *Outspan* 15 Apr. 37 To me there is always something fascinating in this part of Durban. On a Saturday morning I go for a walk along its garbage-littered streets where 'Marys' and 'Sammies' are feverishly chaffering for vegetables. **1968** K. MCMAGH *Dinner of Herbs* 18 Their women folk, each called Mary, just as the Indian males were known as Sammy, hawked fruit and vegetables in flat baskets. **1970** P.C. CHAMBERS *Informant, Durban* Every African male is a 'boy'; every African female is a 'girl'; every Indian male is a 'Sammy' and every Indian female is a 'Mary'. **1971** J. MCCLURE *Steam Pig* (1973) 88 'Shut up, Mary!' Every Indian woman was Coolie Mary. **1973** *Cape Herald* 22 Sept. B2, Because 'Mariamma' was a common name among Indian women and 'Munsamy' among the men, we were referred to as 'Marys and Sammies'. This was considered to be insulting.

2. ?*transf.* A demeaning generic name given to a black woman (esp. a domestic worker).

In *Austral. Eng.*, 'Mary' is an offensive name for an aboriginal woman.

1952 H. KLEIN *Land of Silver Mist* 58, I went with Radebe to the Inchcape Hall, the Bantu night club. We saw 'Jim' and 'Mary' of everyday life in evening dress on the ballroom floor. **1970** G. WESTWOOD *Bright Wilderness* 24 When they came home Mary would have set the table and prepared the meals and Jim would polish the floors and mow the lawns. **1986** S. SEPAMLA in S. Ndaba *One Day in June* 23 Thixo! we want to rejoice Celebrating the birth of a new age ... No more Sixpence, John is neither here nor there, Mary lives no more for tea only!

Mary Decker *n. phr. slang.* [The name of a U.S. middle-distance athlete of the 1980s, considered a rival of S. Afr. athlete Zola Budd.] In urban (esp. township) Eng.: **a.** A police vehicle, the HIPPO, esp. a fast one; cf. ZOLA BUDD sense a. **b.** A small bus, seating between ten and fifteen passengers, and used for taxi shuttle services; also called TAXI (sense 1); cf. ZOLA BUDD sense b.

In sense b, this name was at first applied mainly to Mitsubishi minibuses.

1985 H. PRENDINI in *Style* Oct. 41 'Johnnies' (soldiers), 'Zola Budds' (slow SADF hippos) and 'Mary Deckers' (fast hippos). Township people try and avoid the 'gatta' (police) and the 'kwela-kwela' (black maria) by always carrying their 'stinkers' (reference books). **1987** G. O'HARA in *Weekly Mail* 19 June 21 A Zolabud, by the way, is a Toyota taxi. A Mary Decker is a Mitsubishi. So you make your allegiances clear every time you take a ride. **1990** M. MALUNGA in *Ibid.* 8 June 9 It is just after four in the morning and the streets of Soweto are already filled with roaring Zola Budds and zooming Mary Deckers flying up and down to swallow as many workers .. as possible. **1991** C. VAN ULMENSTEIN in *Weekend Argus* 12 Jan. (Suppl.) 5 Taxis are called Zola Budds and Mary Deckers, but these are not linked to any specific brand name of minibuses.

masadi var. MOSADI.

Masarwa /maˈsarwa/ *n.* Also **Masara**, **Masaroa**, **Masowar**, **Mosarwa**. Pl. unchanged, or **-s**. [SeTswana; see quot. 1928.] Esp. among seTswana-speakers: a derogatory name for a member of the SAN people living in the northern Kalahari desert. Often *attrib.*, esp. in the phr. ***Masarwa Bushman***.

1871 J. MACKENZIE *Ten Yrs* (1971) 128 The other subject race is that of the Bushmen, called Barwa by the Bechuanas in the south, and Masarwa by those in the north of the country. **1894** [see STEL sense 1]. **1896** H.A. BRYDEN *Tales of S. Afr.* 42 You may never .. see a Masarwa Bushman .. who does not show marks of fireburn upon the nether limbs. **1897** 'F. MACNAB' *On Veldt & Farm* 130 For many years the Masowars, Bakalahari and Vaalpens, who were the original owners of the country, have been habituated to live on locusts, roots, bark, berries and any creatures, even reptiles, which they may snare. **1905** G.W. STOW *Native Races of S. Afr.* 205 Bushman speaking peoples as the Masarwa. **1912** A.W. Hodson *Trekking Great Thirst* 272 We had with us an important headman of these Masarwa Bushmen in the person of Inkabiki, quite one of the best native hunters I ever met. **1928** E.H.L. Schwarz *Kalahari & its Native Races* 172 The term Masarwa or Masaroa, Baroa, Abatwe, is used for all Bushmen in the Northern Kalahari. *Ibid.* 173 The word means 'abandoned' and was applied originally to the Bechuana by the Bantu, but as they became powerful they transferred the appellation to their slaves as a title of opprobrium. *Ibid.* 174 There were several Masarwa women about the palace precincts. **1930** S.T. Plaatje *Mhudi* (1975) 64, I have never met anyone who could master the clicks and gibberish of the Masarwa. **1931** J. Mockford *Khama* 60 The rich tribute in hides, ivory, and ostrich-feathers which the Masarwa bushmen and other vassals occupying the game-land .. brought annually to Shoshong. **1936** C. Birkby *Thirstland Treks* 315 The Bamangwato, the people whom Khama ruled so wisely, have reduced another tribe, the Masarwas, to a state of serfdom. **1943** 'J. Burger' *Black Man's Burden* 217 Bechuanaland contains a number of tribes ... There are also vassal tribes, such as the Masarwa, who are, for practical purposes, slaves. **1971** *Sunday Times* 28 Mar. (Mag. Sect.) 3 The people of Dilepe .. are not prepared to receive a Masarwa in their midst. **1974** P. Gibbs *Hist. of BSAP* II. 74 The Masarwa — Bushmen from Bechuanaland. **1981** *Voice* 11 Oct. 13 Margaret was teased and tormented by the Batswana children, because she was a 'Mosarwa'. Many Batswana people despised the Bushmen. **1982** *Drum* Sept. 34 Although Botswana boasts of a democracy, it still has a hangover of a caste system that discriminates against Masarwa-bushmen. In the past they were treated like India's Untouchables.

masbanker var. MAASBANKER.

Masbieker /mas'bikə(r)/ *n. Obs.* exc. *hist.* Also **Mosbieker**. [Afk. (earlier S. Afr. Du.), contraction of *Mosambieker* one from Mozambique, 'slave'.] MOZAMBIQUER.

1868 J. Chapman *Trav.* II. 182 Their [*sc.* the people of Mazhanga's] language is .. very like that spoken by most of the prize negroes brought from the east coast to the Cape. They have consequently been called, very appropriately, I think, Mosbiekers — a corruption of Mosambique — from this resemblance. **1913** C. Pettman *Africanderisms* 326 *Mosbieker* or *Masbieker*, A corruption of Mozambiquer, a native from the neighbourhood of Mozambique, many of whom are employed in South Africa as labourers at the mines and elsewhere. **1972** *Std Encycl. of Sn Afr.* VI. 26 The slaves from Mozambique ('Masbiekers') were .. very untrustworthy; the free burghers felt disinclined to bid for them, and after ten years their import ceased.

Mashangane pl. form of SHANGAAN.

mashonisa /ˌmaʃɔ'niːsa/ *n. slang.* Also **machonisa**. [Prob. Zulu, *ma-* (see MA- *pref.*[3]) + *shonisa*, causative form of *shona* lose heavily, become bankrupt (see quot. 1982).] In urban (esp. township) parlance: a money-lender.

1979 M. Matshoba *Call Me Not a Man* 12 What I'll do tomorrow is to go and borrow the ten rand from the *mashonisa* where I work. **1982** *Voice* 23 May 6 Do you know that money-lenders are sometimes called 'mashonisa' because they want interest on the money they lend. **1987** *Pace* Sept. 13 This incredible machonisa (money lender) affectionately known as Mr Money .. near Tzaneen .. never writes down who owes what and when it must be paid.

masi var. MAAS.

maskanda /mas'kandə, -kaːnda/ *n. Music.* Also **mazkande**. [ad. Zulu *umasikanda*, fr. *umasikandi* (pl. *omasikandi*) choir conductor, skilled guitarist, ad. Afk. *musikant* musician.] Zulu traditional music played on Western instruments, such as the combination of a guitar with concertina or violin. Freq. *attrib.*

1980 J. Clegg in *Papers Presented at Symposium on Ethnomusicology* (Internat. Library of Afr. Music, 1981) 2 The *gxagxa* are people who .. are somehow problematically situated between what we call a really fervent traditionalist, *Ibhinca*, somebody who wears the skins, and *Ikholwa*, a Christian. He's somebody who has mixed both music forms and has developed a '*mazkande*' tradition. **1980** B. Mthethwa in *Ibid.* 24 The marriage of Western instruments with African music has become known as *maskanda* music ... Maskanda music is not Western music nor does it have any Western influences. The *maskanda* resulted as an interaction of the Zulu musicians with the Western instruments. **1989** C. Scott in *Weekly Mail* 13 Oct. 31 Sipho Mchunu .. Juluka co-founder will give a lecture/demonstration on *maskanda* style, exemplified in the traditional strolling musician using guitar and concertina ... The programme will begin with an audiovisual presentation on a predecessor of *maskanda*, traditional *amahubo* clan songs. **1992** A. Dodd in *Ibid.* 28 Aug. (Jo'burg Alive) 12 This is a rare opportunity to catch the unique sound and energy of mbaqanga and maskanda music.

‖**masonja** /mə'sɔndʒə, ma'sɔːndʒa/ *pl. n.* [Shona *masondya* (sing. *sondya*), *mashondy(w)a* (sing. *shondy(w)a*).] Mopani worms. See also *mopani worm* (MOPANI sense 3).

1964 D. Varaday *Gara-Yaka* 182 Crawling, fat, three-inch-long worms! Mopani worms — Masonja — as the Bantu call these brightly coloured insects, are regarded by them as a great delicacy ... The 'masonja' feeds mainly on the turpentine flavoured leaves of the mopani trees. **1984** *Pace* Oct. 55 A humble dish of stiff porridge and masonja (mopani worms).

Masowar var. MASARWA.

massbanker var. MAASBANKER.

master *n.* [Special senses of general Eng.]
1. *Law.* Always with initial capital. Ellipt. for *Master of the Supreme Court*, an officer of the court primarily responsible for the administration of deceased and insolvent estates, the supervision of guardians of minors, and the control over curators of persons unable to look after themselves.

1832 *Graham's Town Jrnl* 2 Mar. 37 All persons claiming to be Creditors under this Estate, are required to take Notice, .. that the Master has appointed the third Meeting to be held before the Resident Magistrate at his office. **1877** F. Jeppe *Tvl Bk Almanac & Dir.* (1976) 52 *Orphan Chamber*, Representatives of the Master, The Landdrosts of the different Districts, the Gold Commissioner, and the commissioner of Lichtenburg. **1968** E.A. Walker *Hist. of Sn Afr.* 163 The Chief Justice .. took over the duties of the Vice-Admiralty Court, the Attorney-General those of the Fiscal, and, in 1834, the Master those of the Orphan Chamber. **1970** H.H. Hermans *Law my Master* 107, I took him up for a personal chat to the Master of the Supreme Court ... The unhappy answer was easier for the Master to put across as he did not know all the family circumstances as I did. **1987** [see ORPHAN CHAMBER].

2. Also **maaster**. Often with initial capital. Now offensive to many: a deferential term of address or reference used by black people of or to their white employers or white people in general; used as a title with a first name. See also MADAM. Cf. BAAS senses 2 and 3.

1833 *Graham's Town Jrnl* 6 June 2, I know that they beat the old master, and that he fell. **1841** B. Shaw *Memorials* 95 Boor: 'What kind of singing and praying is this you have had? I never heard any thing like it, and cannot understand.' Jacob Links: 'I think master, you only come to mock at us, as many of the farmers say we ought not have the gospel.' **1857** 'A.' in *Cape Monthly Mag.* II. Sept. 140 Master was not yet up, but if I came back in half an hour I might see him. **1877** R.M. Ballantyne *Settler & Savage* 3 The Bushman looked vacant and made no reply. 'Where is your master's house?' asked the youth. **1902** H.J. Duckitt in M. Kuttel *Quadrilles & Konfyt* (1954) 22 Our faithful old Hottentot ox-herd came in, gravely saluting 'the master', and .. said, 'Master, I have found a nest with seventeen ostrich eggs a little way inside your boundary.' **1904** C.G. Dennison *Fight to Finish* 12 One of my despatch bearers, David, came to me and said, 'Master, the chiefs Cobus and Frederick Nagalie have sent me to tell you that on Monday morning at day-light you must have your wagons loaded.' **1948** A.C. White *Call of Bushveld* 166 My boy excitedly exclaimed, 'There he is master.' **1952** [see MADAM sense 2]. **1954** A. Segal *Jhb. Friday* 18 'Sixpence,' she said, thumping the three packages in turn. 'This one is for the Master. This one is for Miss Jessie. This one is for Baas Phillip.' **1966** S. Clouts *One Life* 54 I'm sorrie sir: are you married, maaster? **1969** A. Paton *Kontakion* 104 Elizabeth came to see me, a big strong coloured woman who called me *master* but quite clearly had a mind and personality of her own. **1973** *Sunday Times* 29 Apr. 13, I talked to quite a few Black people — domestic servants, drivers, and people I met in Soweto ... Most of them called me baas or master. I know they called me those things because I am White. **1985** *Staffrider* Vol.6 No.2, 24, I got a job as a domestic. I was there five years. The madam was nice, the master was nice. I liked the work. **1986** M. Picardie in S. Gray *Market Plays* 79 I'm moving to a nice house, master. I'm getting a job with master. Oh he's a good master, master. **1988** L. Jeanes in *Style* Feb. 53 After searching him for drugs, bemused officials brought him back to Michael Spilkin with the words: 'This man says you're his master.' 'That,' says Edward with a large laugh, 'was my last time to say Master. Now I say Boss or Sir'. **1989** J. Hobbs *Thoughts in Make-shift Mortuary* 277 'Get down man! Show me your ID.' 'I'm coming, Master, Don't make me fall, Master. Please, Master, I'm coming.' **1989** B. Ludman *Day of Kugel* 4 The master is at university and the madam is playing squash. Master Clive is out.

Masutu var. MOSOTHO.

Matabele /ˌmætə'biːli, ˌmat-/ *n.* Also **Matabeli**, **Matabili**, **(ma)Tebele**, **Matebele(y)**, **Matibili**. Pl. unchanged, **-s**, or **Amatebele**. [Sotho *matebele* (sing. *letebele*), 'term applied by the Sotho-Tswana people to invading Zulu sections, so-called because they sank down (*teba*) behind their large shields when fighting' (Doke & Vilakazi *Zulu-English Dictionary*, 1948, p.537); or fr. Sotho and seTswana *thebe* shield. For an explanation of forms used, see MA- *pref.*[2]]
1.a. NDEBELE sense 1 a. **b.** A member of an Nguni people who, led at the time by Mzilikazi, were displaced during the MFECANE and eventually settled in the Bulawayo region of present-day Zimbabwe after fleeing north of the Limpopo in 1837; ILINDEBELE; NDEBELE sense 1 b. Also *attrib.*

Despite Moffat's claim of a link between 'Matabele' and MANTATEE (quot. 1823), no other evidence of this link has been found.

1823 R. Moffat in I. Schapera *Apprenticeship at Kuruman* (1951) 84 The Mantatees had driven the Barolongs from their town, .. the Mantatees .. name is properly Matabele ... Several men from the Barolongs had just passed them on their way to Mahumapeloo to request their assistance .. to endeavour to make the Matabeles retreat. **1835** A.G. Bain in A. Steedman *Wanderings* II. 238 When the Matebeley (for that is the name of Masilikatsie's tribe) were within two hundred yards of us, I perceived the villain Piet Barends. **1835** A. Smith *Diary* (1940) II. 106 The Bechuanas who have from necessity been forced to adopt that portion of dress use much more tails than the regular Matabeli. **1839** W.C. Harris *Wild Sports* 22 Moselekatse, king of the Abaka Zooloos, or Matabili, a powerful and despotic monarch. *Ibid.* 111 Numerous Matabili villages, having all the same form and appearance, though varying considerably in size and extent. **1847** 'A Bengali' *Notes on Cape of G.H.* 22 Their [*sc.* the Boers'] dealings with the Caffre, Matabili, and other powerful native tribes have always been marked by the greatest want of tact, temper, and judgement. **1857** D. Livingstone *Missionary Trav.* 10 In going north again, a comet blazed on our sight, exciting the wonder of every tribe we visited. That of 1816 had been followed by an irruption of the Matabele, the most cruel enemies the Bechuanas ever knew. **1871** J. MACKENZIE *Ten Yrs* (1971) 2 They had indeed some misgivings about returning to a country which they had evacuated through fear of their sworn enemies the Matebele Zulus. **1882** J. NIXON *Among Boers* 93 The Amatebele were part of the Zulu tribe, who had expatriated themselves some ten years before, and had taken refuge in the country across the Vaal. **1900** H.C. HILLEGAS *Oom Paul's People* 49 Moselekatse and his Matabele warriors having been driven out of the country by the other 'trekking' parties, the extensive region north of the Vaal River was then in undisputed possession of the Boers. **1930** S.T. PLAATJE *Mhudi* (1975) 155 It was a hopeful nation that moved forward, and for months afterwards the Bechuanaland forests were alive with swarms of Matabele travelling persistently towards the land of promise. **1951** R. GRIFFITHS *Grey about Flame* 57 The people of Kwenaland .. cried ... 'See, they hide behind long shields and carry only one spear ... We are not afraid of the Ama Te Bele.' It was thus that Mzilikatze's people became known as the Amatebele, the people who crouch behind long shields. **1961** T.V. BULPIN *White Whirlwind* 198 They had cut the Sotho tribes of the Transvaal to pieces, and gathered rich booty in cattle, women, slaves, and youths to press into their growing army. They had also received their name of *Matabele*, given to them by the Sothos, and meaning The Refugees, because they were foreigners in the new land going before the wrath of Shaka. **1974** *Drum* 8 Apr. 35, I am a Matabele guy, aged 23 and I would like to hear from girls who are interested in settling down. **1975** [see Lye quot. at NDEBELE sense 1]. **1982** N. PARSONS *New Hist. of Sn Afr.* 74 After Mzilikazi's Khumalo attacked the Phuting in 1822, they passed northwards .. to the Steelpoort (Thubatse) river. Here Mzilikazi temporarily .. settled among Ndzundza 'Tebele' (Transvaal-Nguni) ... The size of the Khumalo nation was swollen by the Ndzundza and by other 'maTebele', so that the Khumalo nation itself eventually became known as the Tebele or Ndebele. **1990** R. STENGEL *January Sun* 34 Mzilikazi, the former lieutenant to Shaka, .. led a fierce tribe in the Magaliesberg region of the western Transvaal. They were known as the Matabele: *Ma*, meaning people, and *tebele*, referring to the tall, ox-hide shields they carried into battle.

2. *comb.* **Matabele flower** [see quot. 1966], the WITCHWEED, *Striga asiatica*.

1913 C. PETTMAN *Africanderisms* 312 *Matabele flower*, Species of *Striga* is so called. **1917** R. MARLOTH *Common Names* 57 *Matabele flower, Striga lutea*. Known under this name in Bechuanaland, because it devastates the mealie fields (= Witch-weed, rooiblom). **1966** C.A. SMITH *Common Names* 333 *Matabele flower, Striga asiatica* ... The vernacular name is said to be an allusion to the havoc created by this parasite in mealie (maize) lands, suggestive of the destruction wrought by the Matabele impis of the [18]70's but also said to refer to the appearance of the species in northern Bechuanaland after a Matabele raid during the same period.

Matchappee pl. form of BATLHAPING.

matchbox *n.* [Transf. use of general Eng. slang *matchbox* a small house.] In full ***matchbox house***: a small house, one of many built to the same plan as part of a mass housing scheme in a township. Also *attrib.*

1963 M. BENSON *Afr. Patriots* 288 During the night helicopters flew low over townships flashing searchlights down on the matchbox houses and rough roads. **1968** COLE & FLAHERTY *House of Bondage* 54 The Government .. simply erected two noisome tent cities, reminiscent of Boer War concentration camps, and put the people in them until their matchboxes should be ready. **1977** J. SIKAKANE *Window on Soweto* 5 Inside the matchbox houses the inmates have woken up. **1982** [see LONG DROP]. **1982** M. MZAMANE *Children of Soweto* 67 The matchbox houses seemed to have been simply planted amid rocks and debris. **1985** *Frontline* Sept. 21 Those successful ones who manage to liberate themselves from 'Matchbox house' existence to modern suburbia are accused of displaying 'bourgeois' tendencies to the accompaniment of ominous threats. **1982** I. HUDSON in *Leadership* Vol.5 No.4, 74 It is a match box house — one of a row of identical homes — with four rooms, concrete floors and an asbestos roof. **1992** S. MEMELA in *Pace* Sept. 176 The common ordinary folk .. are imprisoned in the squatter camps and matchbox houses.

matchetoe, -too, -tow varr. MATJIESTOU.

Matclhapee pl. form of BATLHAPING.

maTebele, Matebele(y) varr. MATABELE.

‖**matekwane** /ˌmateˈkwaːne/ *n.* Formerly also **matekoane, motekwane, mutakuane, mutokuane**, and with initial capital. [Sotho.] Esp. among Sotho-speakers: DAGGA *n.*² sense 1.

Livingstone is writing of an area to the north of South Africa.

[**1857** D. LIVINGSTONE *Missionary Trav.* 330 Reaching the village of Kabinje, in the evening he sent us a present of tobacco, Mutakuane or 'bang' (Cannabis sative) and maize.] **1953** LANHAM & MOPELI-PAULUS *Blanket Boy's Moon* 30 Who can say how a man becomes a *tsotsi*? Perhaps because the man .. takes to the smoking of *matekoane* — dagga. **1968** A. FULTON *Dark Side of Mercy* 105 Libe himself grew matekoane, or dagga as they called it here in the Union ... Matekoane is a weed but law forbids its growth. **1978** M. WA NTHODI *From Calabash* 11 Moditi gives them *motekwane* to smoke and beer to drink. **1981** *Voice* 20 May 17 I .. wouldn't mind to have a legalised puff of matekwane under medical control.

mathlosi pl. form of IDLOZI.

mat-house *n. hist.* [tr. S. Afr. Du. *matjieshuis*, see MATJIESHUISIE.] A beehive-shaped temporary shelter consisting of poles planted in the ground in a circle and drawn together at the top, and with rush mats stretched over them; MATJIESHUISIE.

1824 W.J. BURCHELL *Trav.* II. 7 The situation of this little village .. was exceedingly sheltered and rural: .. enclosed by a rocky precipice, under which stood their mat-houses and the cattle-kraals. **1872** E.J. DUNN in A.M.L. Robinson *Sel. Articles from Cape Monthly Mag.* (1978) 48 A shed built of poles and reeds doing duty as a school-house, a 'wattle and daub' mansion for the Chief .. and a score or so of the national 'mat houses' for the people, constitute the settlement. **1898** W.C. SCULLY *Between Sun & Sand* 2 These people are dwellers in tents and bee-hive-shaped structures known as 'mat-houses', a form of architecture adopted from the Hottentots. The latter are constructed of large mats made of rushes strung upon strands of bark or other vegetable fibre, and are stretched over wattles stuck by the larger end into the ground in a circle, the diameter of which may vary from fifteen to twenty-five feet. **1907** — *By Veldt & Kopje* 230 The only people I met were the few wandering Boers who lived in wagons and mat-houses and moved about on the track of the rains. **1913** C. PETTMAN *Africanderisms* 312 *Mat house*, .. The temporary shelters used by natives and Boers when on trek. **1941** C.W. DE KIEWIET *Hist. of S. Afr.* 184 Less enterprising families lived in 'mat houses', made of woven rushes on a light framework of poles. [**1957** see SKERM sense b]. **1975** [see Steenkamp quot. at MATJIESHUISIE].

Matibili var. MATABELE.

matie *n.*¹ var. MAATIE *n.*²

Matie /ˈmɑːti/ *n.*² Formerly also **Maatie**. [Prob. abbrev. of Afk. *tamatie* tomato, alluding to the colour of Stellenbosch University's rugby jersey.]

1.a. A student or alumnus of Stellenbosch University, Western Cape; esp., a member of this university's rugby team. **b.** Often in *pl.*, used collectively: Stellenbosch University. Also *attrib.*

1921 *Cathartic* (University of Cape Town) Sept. 4 We believe that the recent protest on the part of the S.R.C. to the Maatie University, re the name 'Ikey,' which has been applied to us at Inter-'Varsity, has caused considerable criticism in 'Varsity circles. **1934** *Cape Argus* 20 Apr. (Swart), The Maties should be able to field an excellent pack, especially now that their difficulty of a hooker has been solved. **1971** *Argus* 26 June, It is the sixth such visit by Matie students to give free medical assistance to neighbouring countries. **1978** *E. Prov. Herald* 9 Feb. 3 The first black Maties joined their white first-year counterparts in loud cheering .. at the University of Stellenbosch here yesterday. **1978** *Sunday Times* 12 Feb. 8 Maties opens to all. *Ibid.* 12 Having produced the last four South African Prime Ministers, Maties are trying to make sure they produce the next one as well. **1983** [see OORBELIGTE]. **1985** *Sunday Star* 27 Oct. 16 As one of the eight Maties who wanted to meet the ANC youth, I do not understand the grounds on which our visit is opposed. **1986** *City Press* 13 Apr. 3 Matie Rag magazine editor Dawid van der Merwe was arrested in Stellenbosch this week for wearing a pair of camouflage pants, according to his flatmate. **1991** G. SPENCE in *Sunday Tribune* 19 May 5 The Maties students' call has enraged the Conservative Party, which said the authorities had no right 'even to consider' the request. **1992** J. MOMBERG in *Cape Times* 20 May 9 As a member of the ANC, I am proud to be an old Matie.

2. *comb.* **Matieland**, Stellenbosch University; the town of Stellenbosch.

1966 *Cape Argus* 8 Mar. 7 Matieland banishes Jumbo. A farewell ceremony was held at Wilgenhof hostel, Stellenbosch, yesterday in honour of a resident who has been suspended by the university authorities. **1979** C. NQAKULA in *Daily Dispatch* 12 Oct. (Indaba) 7 Down Matieland [way] they call it wine tasting, but upstairs in my head I knew I was drinking wine — a distinct difference between tasting the stuff and pushing the glass away.

matingola /ˌmɑːtɪŋˈgəʊlə, mæ-, -ˈguːluː/ *n.* Also **martingola, matingula**. [Englished form of Zulu *amathungulu*.] AMATUNGULU.

1851 R.J. GARDEN Diary. I. (Killie Campbell Africana Library MS29081) 2 June, Of fruits besides the Matingola, there is a tree called Ummaki. **1852** *Ibid.* 24 Apr., His garden contained .. Sweet Potatoes, Amadumbis, Sugar Cane, Matingolas, and Pineapples. **1855** G.H. MASON *Life with Zulus* 70 Growing, in wild profusion, the huge cactus, the deep crimson martingola, starch and castor-oil plants. **1960** J. COPE *Tame Ox* 11 At some distance from the back of the building was a straggling row of thorny matingula shrubs, once a hedge, and behind them the tin roof of a privy. **1994** M. ROBERTS tr. *J.A. Wahlberg's Trav. Jrnls 1838–56* 36 Matingola or Numnum, the flesh red, when bitten a white milk runs out.

matjiesgoed /ˈmaɪkisxʊt, -cis-, -xut/ *n.* Formerly also **matjes goed**, occas. **matjes goederen**. [Afk., earlier S. Afr. Du. *matjesgoed, matjes* comb. form of *matje* little mat + *goed* stuff, material (pl. *goederen*).] Any of several species of reed or rush used for making mats and baskets, and for thatching. **a.** The river reed *Cyperus textilis* of the Cyperaceae; occas., any of several other species of *Cyperus*; MAT-RUSH. See also MATJIESTOU. **b.** *rare.* Either of two rushes, *Typha domingensis* or *T. capensis* of the Typhaceae. **c.** *rare.* Either of two reeds, *Scirpus corymbosus* or *S. inanis* of the Cyperaceae. Also *attrib.*

[**1795** C.R. HOPSON tr. *C.P. Thunberg's Trav.* II. 37 Matware (*Matjegoed*) is the name given here to a kind of rush that grew in the river, and of which mats were made, that were used by the husbandmen for the tilts of waggons, and also to lie on.] **1812** A. PLUMPTRE tr. *H. Lichtenstein's Trav. in Sn Afr.* (1928) I. 87 *Matjesgoed* is the name given to a sort of rush, of which very pretty mats are made in this country. **1822** W.J. BURCHELL *Trav.* I. 263 Of this rush, which is called the Hard Matjes-goederen, the Hottentots, in these districts, make all their mats, which are much more durable than those made of Cyperus textilis, distinguished by the name of Sagt (soft) Matjes goederen, the material of all the mats made near Cape Town. 1856 [see MAT-RUSH]. 1913 C. PETTMAN *Africanderisms* 312 *Matjesgoed, .. Cyperus textilis.* This reed is so called because it is largely used for making mats and baskets. 1917 R. MARLOTH *Common Names* 57 *Matjesgoed, Cyperus textilis.* In some districts *Typha australis.* [1934 P.R. KIRBY *Musical Instruments of Native Races* (1965) 236 This 'string' is made from a swamp grass called *nala* (called by the Dutch *matjesgoed*, a name given by them to several species of grasses, but in this instance to *Typha capensis*).] 1955 L.G. GREEN *Karoo* 63 Matjesfontein takes its name from the rush called Matjesgoed from which mats are made. 1963 R. LEWCOCK *Early 19th C. Archit.* 155 The roofing material was still generally thatch, made from 'matjes goed' reed. 1966 C.A. SMITH *Common Names* 333 *Matjesgoed, Cyperus textilis* ... The long culms were extensively used by the Hottentots for making mats .. for their houses, whence the vernacular name .. *C. sexangularis; C. marginatus* and *C. sphaerospermus* .. are similarly used. *Scirpus corymbosus* .. : The tallish culms are used by natives for mat-making, whence the vernacular name ... The name sometimes applied to *Typha australis* and *T. capensis* ... The vernacular name here applied from the use of the long leaves for making mats used for shelters, etc ... *Scirpus spathaceus.* 1971 L.G. GREEN *Taste of S.-Easter* 182 Missions sent produce to the Early Morning Market, not only fruits and vegetables but articles made of taaibos and matjiesgoed. 1973 M.A. COOK *Cape Kitchen* 19 These cross-reeds, known as loopriete, were then tied to the reeds of the ceiling proper with lashing made of a small rush *Cyperus textilis*, i.e. matjiesgoed.

‖**matjieshuisie** /ˈmaɪkisˌhœisi/ *n. hist.* [Afk., *matjie* little mat + linking phoneme (or pl.) -s- + *huis* house + -IE.] MAT-HOUSE. Also **matjieshuis**.

1955 L.G. GREEN *Karoo* 238 It is nothing unusual in Namaqualand for a rich man to live in a *matjieshuisie*; many a wealthy white sheep farmer prefers this type of dwelling to the most solid farmhouse. 1975 W. STEENKAMP *Land of Thirst King* 64 (*caption*) A typical Namaqualand 'matjieshuis' or mat house, in traditional beehive form. The people .. were on trek .. , and like all Namaqualanders took their matjieshuis along with them. 1975 *Argus* 17 Sept. 18 Gharra beer, .. on a hot day a wonderfully refreshing drink faintly aromatic from the smoke of the matjieshuisie (hut of reed mats) in which the aia lived.

matjiestou /ˈmaɪkizˌtəʊ, -cis-/ *n. hist.* Formerly also **matchetoe, matchetoo, matchetow.** [Afk., fr. S. Afr. Du. *matje* little mat + linking phoneme (or pl.) -s- + *touw* rope.] Rope made from the culms of the reed *Cyperus textilis* (see MATJIESGOED sense a), formerly used for tying or binding thatch.

1839 T. SHONE *Diary.* 11 Jan., I was not long thatching before my Matchetow was done. And I was obliged to leave off and go in search of more matchetow. 1857 *Ibid.* 17 Feb., Bought from R. Bradfield a bar of soap paid 1/-, a stick of tobacco /3, 2 Bundles of matchetoe 1/-. *Ibid.* 28 Feb., For Mat Dixon a bundle of matchetoo /6. 1966 C.A. SMITH *Common Names* 333 *Matjiestou(e), Cyperus textilis* .. : The name applied to the rope .. made from the culms. 1973 M.A. COOK *Cape Kitchen* 19 Lashing made of a small rush *Cyperus textilis*, i.e. matjiesgoed; when beaten, softened and slightly twisted to a string-like consistency, it was known as matjiestou.

matji(e)ta var. and pl. form of MAJITA.

Matok see quot. 1835 at TLOKWA.

matric /məˈtrɪk/ *n. colloq.* [Shortened form of MATRICULATION.]

1.a. MATRICULATION sense 1. Freq. *attrib.*

[1934 see BOER MATRICULATION.] 1941 *Bantu World* 15 Feb. 15 Preference will be given to an applicant .. who has passed Matric Afrikaans or the Hoer Taalbond. 1953 R. CAMPBELL *Mamba's Precipice* 121 Mary had passed her Matric. 1957 *Pietersburg Eng. Medium School Mag.* Dec. 84 She is now at the Tom Naude High School and is writing her matric this year. 1973 [see AFRIKAANS *n.*]. 1973 *Daily Dispatch* 16 July 12 A plea that the study of science be made compulsory in the education of blacks up to Matric level, was made. 1982 *Voice* 10 Jan. 1 The initial poor matric results had hit the Black community hard. 1984 *Fair Lady* 25 July 7 (*letter*) I have a child writing Matric and once again tension, trauma, drama and neuroses are rearing their ugly heads. 1988 C. BATEMAN in *Cape Times* 22 Oct. 1 On the eve of matric exams, police yesterday raided one Peninsula school and fired teargas to disperse demonstrating pupils at another. 1994 *Sunday Times* 9 Oct. (Mag. Sect.) 8 When I advised a female student to study engineering after passing matric, she nearly collapsed with shock.

b. *comb.* **matric exemption,** MATRICULATION EXEMPTION.

1994 *Weekend Post* 22 Oct. 10 Entry qualifications for a Unisa degree .. matric exemption and at least three D symbols.

2. MATRICULATION sense 2.

1955 A. DELIUS *Young Trav.* 37 If you want to get a decent job of any sort, or go to a university, you've got to get your standard ten, that's matric, or senior certificate. 1970 *Personality* 12 Feb. 6 Best thing to do is act promptly and realise that your Matric is a very important asset. 1977 *Scope* 1 July 29 A man with Matric has the pick of jobs. 1979 [see JUNIOR CERTIFICATE.] 1986 *Grocott's Mail* 9 Sept. 3 (*advt*) A minimum of matric is required and previous admin/retail experience would be a distinct advantage. 1987 K. OWEN in *Daily Dispatch* 22 Oct. 14 By now, it turns out, a TED matric is about as good as one from Bantu Education. 1990 R. STENGEL *January Sun* 36 Of our grandparents, the only one with a matric (a high-school degree) is my wife's mother. 1991 KOCH & BLECHER in *Weekly Mail* 15 Feb. 5 Toughman describes himself as a 'middle' student, but is sure he will get his matric one day.

3.a. By metonymy: The final year of high school, Standard Ten. Often *comb.*, as **matric dance** (occas. **matriculation dance**, see MATRICULATION sense 3), or **matric farewell**.

1976 [see JC]. 1980 C. HOPE *A Separate Development* (1983) 60 Looking back to the big night of the Matric dance I tremble at my ignorance, my gullibility. 1985 [see BOLLEMAKIESIE *adv.*]. 1986 *New Dawn* Oct. 7 In matric I became aware of the importance of the law degree. 1987 *New Nation* 21 May 13 Spider, .. and Myrtle .. were returning home from their matric farewell party when the accident happened. 1989 *Conserva* Vol.4 No.6, 21 For teachers of any subject, from kindergarten to matric, this book should prove invaluable. 1990 P. SIDLEY in *Weekly Mail* 8 Feb. 36 Failed matriculants have once again found that they may not re-enrol for matric at their schools. 1990 *Weekend Argus* 29 Sept. 3 He .. had no interest in sport, but had captained the hockey team in matric. 1994 *Sunday Times* 23 Oct. (Mag. Sect.) 71 Dress Suit .. to hire for Matric Dances and Weddings.

b. MATRICULANT.

1984 *Sunday Times* 11 Nov. (Business Times) 1 A large proportion of more than 54 000 black matrics .. are on the verge of looking for work. 1985 *Evening Post* 25 Feb. 10 Matrics and graduates are tramping the streets looking for work. 1987 *You* 22 Oct. 20 Please let this be a warning to all future matrics. Don't end up like me. 1992 *Natal Mercury* 18 Dec. 1 (*caption*) Matrics flock to schools. 1993 [see DET].

matriculant *n.* [Transf. use of Eng. *matriculant* one who has qualified to register at a university or college.] A pupil studying for the matriculation examination; one who has passed this examination; MATRIC sense 3 b.

1957 D. JACOBSON *Price of Diamonds* 89 As a matriculant with a good scholastic record, .. Groenewald had entered the Police College at an early age. 1977 *Sunday Times* 9 Oct. 8 A month before matriculants write their final examination, prospects for thousands writing the new practical school-leaving certificate look gloomy. 1985 *Sunday Star* 27 Oct. 2 Parents and matriculants (also in Soweto) would prefer the matriculation examination to be offered in November instead of at a later date. 1987 *Star* 24 Oct. 4 Hundreds of black matriculants will .. not be writing their examinations, which began yesterday. 1988 S. CHETTY in *Sunday Times* 10 July (Extra) 6 (*caption*) Matriculant Dayanthri helps Tess with her homework after school. 1990 [see MATRIC sense 3 a].

matriculate *v. intrans.* [Transf. use of Brit. Eng. *matriculate* to be entered as a member of a university or college.] To pass the final school-leaving (or MATRICULATION) examination; to leave school.

1972 *Evening Post* 27 May 10 Mr Du Preez matriculated with distinctions at the old Humansdorp High School, and obtained a bursary to further his studies. 1974 *Post* 28 July 9 Each year we have many students matriculating and I am sure that they will work hard to show how good the Indians are. 1980 *Sunday Times* 30 Mar. 27 (*advt*) Matriculated. Where now? 1985 *Evening Post* 25 Feb. 10 The Divisional Inspector of Manpower said a total of 123 boys and girls who matriculated last year were registered with his department. Hence **matriculated** *ppl adj.*, possessing a matriculation certificate.

1977 *Friend* 30 June 14 (*advt*) The General Tyre and Rubber Co .. require the services of a matriculated male clerk. 1985 [see NON-EUROPEAN *adj.* sense 1]. 1987 *Personality* 7 Oct. 16 Piet was a 19-year-old, freshly matriculated 'greenhorn'.

matriculation *n.* [Transf. use of Eng. *matriculation* formal admission into a university or college.]

1. A school-leaving examination taken at the end of Standard Ten (the twelfth year of schooling) and used also as the criterion for university entrance; the studies undertaken in order to pass this examination; MATRIC sense 1 a. Also *attrib.* See also JMB, POST-MATRIC *n.*

[1916 *Act* 12 in *Stat. of Union* 198 Such board [*sc.* the joint matriculation board] shall issue matriculation certificates to successful candidates .. and may also grant certificates (called school-leaving certificates) and other certificates, to such candidates at the matriculation examination as have satisfied the examiners in such subjects as may be prescribed by the joint statutes. 1924 see BOER MATRICULATION.] 1937 *Report of Educ. Commission: Prov. of Tvl* (1939) 189 The problem of the examination at Standard X stage is much more complicated. This examination, commonly called the matriculation, was originally conducted by the university authorities for the purpose of selecting students capable of profiting by a university career. 1947 'MONIK' in *Vandag* Jan. 13 Forty blank-faced children who wish above all else to pass their J.C. or matriculation examination. 1971 *S. Afr. Panorama* July 7 Since 1964 .. the matriculation candidates [have increased] by 180 per cent, from 167 to 465. 1972 *Ibid.* Mar. 34 An agricultural high school .. which offers all the usual matriculation subjects plus many other things.

2. A pass in the matriculation examination; the school-leaving certificate so obtained; MATRIC sense 2; SENIOR CERTIFICATE.

1939 [see JUNIOR CERTIFICATE]. 1980 J. COCK *Maids & Madams* 272 Whereas 12 percent of the males attained Matriculation, only three percent of the females did.

3. *comb.* **matriculation dance,** *matric dance* (see MATRIC sense 3 a).

1980 C. HOPE *A Separate Development* (1983) 55 The idea of the matriculation dance following on the Saturday night clearly displeased him.

matriculation exemption *n. phr.* [MATRICULATION + Eng. *exemption* the act of exempting, the state of being exempted.] A certificate providing proof of the holder's qualification for appointment in the public service, service with an attorney under articles, or entry to a professional examination; loosely, a good pass in the matriculation examination, allowing a candidate entrance to a university. Also *attrib*.

1920 *Act 30 in Stat. of Union* 128 Whenever under any law or regulation the passing of .. the matriculation examination of the University of the Cape of Good Hope; or .. any examination declared to be equivalent to such first-mentioned examination, .. the holding of a certificate of exemption issued by the joint matriculation board .. shall be regarded as a qualification alternative to the qualification aforesaid ... This Act may be cited .. as the Matriculation Exemption Act, 1920. **1960** *Act 9 in Ibid.* 83 The holding of a full certificate of exemption issued by the said matriculation board .. shall be regarded as a qualification alternative to the said qualification: Provided that .. the dispensation granted shall not prejudice any special requirements for admission prescribed for candidates by the regulations governing such professional examination ... This Act shall be called the Matriculation Exemption Act, 1960. **1979** W.A. JOUBERT *Law of S. Afr.* Vol.8, 184 In terms of the Matriculation Exemption Act certain privileges are conferred upon holders of exemption certificates ... Where the passing of the matriculation examination of the former University of the Cape of Good Hope or recognized equivalent examination, or of the examination controlled and conducted by the joint matriculation board is necessary for appointments in the public service, .. then the certificate of exemption is regarded as such necessary qualification. **1988** *Personality* Sept. 27 (*advt*) Matriculation exemption in two months!

matrimonial court *n. phr. Hist.* Also with initial capitals. A court established at the Cape (in 1676) by the Dutch East India Company, before which every engaged couple had to appear in order to establish the legality of their forthcoming marriage. Also *attrib*.

[**1731** G. MEDLEY tr. P. Kolb's *Present State of Cape of G.H.* I. 340 The Court of Marriages, as it is call'd, looks to the Lawfulness of all Marriage-Contracts, before the Celebration of Marriage. **1806** *Cape Town Gaz. & Afr. Advertiser* 26 Apr. The Court for Matrimorial Affairs in Cape Town.] **1808** EARL OF CALEDON in G.M. Theal *Rec. of Cape Col.* (1900) VI. 386 To constitute a legal marriage by the colonial law it is necessary for the parties to appear in the matrimonial court. **1819** G. BARKER *Journal.* 1 Oct., Mr Arnot passed on his way to Uitenhage to appear before the matrimonial court. **1831** S. *Afr. Almanac & Dir.* 236 Two couples had been Married, with regular Matrimonial Court Certificates. **1861** P.B. BORCHERDS *Auto-Biog. Mem.* 23 There was but one matrimonial court in the colony, holding session every Saturday in an upper room of a building occupying the site of the late Cape Town prison. **1873** *Cape Monthly Mag.* VII. 208 They might appear before the Matrimonial Court next morning. **1898** W.C. SCULLY *Vendetta* 128 In the days we tell of no marriage could be solemnized in the Cape Colony unless the parties had previously appeared before the matrimonial court in Cape Town. **1921** H.J. MANDELBROTE tr. *O.F. Mentzel's Descr. of Cape of G.H.* I. 147 The Matrimonial Court (Raad van Huuwelijke Saaken) had for its duty to inquire into the legality of proposed marriages. **1949** L.G. GREEN *In Land of Afternoon* 88 The records of the Matrimonial Court. **1955** V. DE KOCK *Fun They Had* 29 Before banns of marriage could be published, it was necessary for the parties to appear before the Commissioners of the Matrimonial Court. **1966** F.G. BUTLER *Take Root or Die* (1970) 45 We have walked .. thirty miles, because we are told the Dutch law of the country states we have to pass a thing called a matrimonial court, which meets in Grahamstown, once a month. **1979** L. GORDON-BROWN *Settlers' Press* 4 The 1822 edition contains a heading, 'District of Albany' in large capitals, with Harry Rivers, Landdrost, six Heemraaden, a Matrimonial Court.

mat-rush *n. obs.* [Perh. transf. use of Eng. *mat-rush* a name for the bulrush *Scirpus lacustris*; or coined in this country, influenced by S. Afr. Du. *matjesgoederen* (see quot. 1856).] MATJIESGOED.

1822 W.J. BURCHELL *Trav.* I. 401 Our guides .. brought me .. to a part of the river where the mat-rush grew in great abundance. **1824** *Ibid.* II. 123 The mat-rush grows here in abundance; .. with this rush, all the houses in these parts of the Colony, are thatched. **1856** L. PAPPE in *Cape of G.H. Almanac & Annual Register* 324 *Cyperus textilis* ... A rush 2 or 3 feet high, which grows in marshy localities and in the beds of rivulets. From it baskets and mats are manufactured by the natives who call it mat-rush (*matjesgoed*).

MaTshangane pl. form of SHANGAAN.

matshingilane var. MANTSHINGILANE.

Mavenda pl. form of VENDA.

mawo *int. obs.* Also **mah wo, mar-w(h)ow, mawoh, maw-wah, mow-wah.** [Xhosa.] Esp. among Xhosa-speakers: an exclamation of astonishment or wonder. Cf. HAU.

1835 T.H. BOWKER *Journal.* 6 Sept., It was Botma who stood on the road on Wellington Hill, the Galeka from beyond the Kei were here too, Gasela from beyond the Kabousie & Umhala from the sea side, Eno was here too!!! Mawo! **1875** C.B. BISSET *Sport & War* 89 These Kafirs were equally astonished, for I heard the exclamations of Oh, Marwow meaning a wonder, an apparition. **1883** O.E.A. SCHREINER *Story of Afr. Farm* 51 The Hottentot maid sighed, the Kaffir girl who looked in at the door put her hand over her mouth and said 'Mow-wah!' **1894** E. GLANVILLE *Fair Colonist* 112 'Mawoh,' exclaimed the Kaffir as he saw the long wound. **1907** W.C. SCULLY *By Veldt & Kopje* 256 We had no guns, but .. we used to drive the game into stalked pits. *Mawo*, but these were great days.

Hence **mawo** *n.*, an utterance of this exclamation.

1931 G. BEET *Grand Old Days* 61 A tremendous shout of surprise at once arose from the Kaffirs, and their many 'Maw-wahs' sounded and resounded throughout the mine.

‖**maye** /ˈmaːˈjeː/ *int.* Also **mai, my.** [Zulu, int. expressing grief, dismay, terror.] Often in the phr. **maye babo** /-ˈbaːbɔ/ [Zulu *babo* int. expressing grief, surprise, pleasure], a cry of distress or pain.

Usu. included by writers to suggest Zulu speech.

1907 J.P. FITZPATRICK *Jock of Bushveld* (1909) 332 The victim flapped his hands on the ground and hallooed out 'My babo! My babo!' but he did not struggle. **1909** N. PAUL *Child in Midst* 53 The Kafir .. kept on ejaculating: 'Ubi! Ubi! Ubi! Maye-ba-bo!' as he followed the horse cautiously into the stable yard. **1923** G.H. NICHOLLS *Bayete!* 125 A terrific burst shook the hut and loosened their tongues. 'Maye! maye! maye! the chief is angry to-night. Why does he afflict us?' they cried in terror. *Ibid.* Glossary, Maye Babo! 'Alas, my fathers.' The usual wail at a funeral. *c*1948 H. TRACEY *Lalela Zulu* 64 The correct way of writing 'Mai Mai' is 'Mayemaye!' a cry of grief and pain.

Mayebuye var. MAYIBUYE.

mayhem var. MAHEM.

Mayibuye /ˌmajiˈbuːje/ *v. intrans.* Also **Mayebuye, Mayibuya.** [A sentence common to Nguni languages: hortative prefix *ma-* 'may' + linking phoneme *y* + subjectival concord *i-* + *buye*, subjunctive form of *buya* come back, return.] A rallying-cry of the African National Congress (see ANC *n.*[1]), esp. in the phrr. **Mayibuye (i)Afrika** or **Afrika Mayibuye,** 'Come back Africa', 'Africa, may it return'. See also OPERATION MAYIBUYE. Cf. AFRIKA *int.*

1949 E. HELLMANN *Handbk on Race Rel.* 491 It was this paper .. that was largely responsible for popularizing the stirring slogan, *Mayibuy'iAfrika* (Let Africa Come Back). **1956** A. SAMPSON *Drum* 131 As the last harmonies of the song died down, Moroka lifted up his thumb and shouted: *Mayibuye!* the crowd shouted: *Afrika!* — pronouncing the word in the African way, with long a's. 'Mayibuye Afrika — that means "Come back, Africa" ... It's one of the slogans of Congress; it means back to the old days of freedom before the white man came.' *Ibid.* 134 'Mayibuye — Afrika,' with thumbs up, became a greeting in the street. **1960** *Rand Daily Mail* 31 Mar. 5 There were shouts of 'Afrika mayibuya' (Africa return) after the treason trial hearing yesterday when all the accused were arrested. **1961** T. MATSHIKIZA *Choc. for my Wife* 60 She said, 'Heil,' each time she raised her glass then she sipped slowly ... She said, 'Heil, Gesondheid, Mayibuye.' **1963** M. BENSON *Afr. Patriots* 173 As the singing died away, Moroka, immaculate as always, rose quietly, lifted his hand in the Congress salute, and shouted 'Mayibuye' with a long rumble on the last sound 'Boo-Yáa' and the crowd roared back — 'Afriká'. **1974** A.P. BRINK *Looking on Darkness* 226 A single word — *Mayebuye!* — could lead to imprisonment on Robben Island. And they were prepared to take the risk. **1976** M. THOLO in C. Hermer *Diary of Maria Tholo* (1980) 114 In 1948, .. people had spirit — umoya. It was the 'Let's get Africa back' movement — Mayibuye iAfrica. You could be arrested just for saying that. **1982** M. MZAMANE *Children of Soweto* 218 An old Congress warrior from our street, old man Kumalo (everybody called him ANC), who had marched in the Defiance Campaign, called 'Afrika!' and the people responded, 'Mayibuye!' (May it come back). **1986** *Rhodeo* (Rhodes Univ.) May 20 Mayibuye! is more than a word which is shouted with jubilation at mass rallies and funerals. It's a vibe, a spirit of liberation. **1987** [see FREEDOM SONG]. **1990** *Pace* May 4 As the whole world cheers, black, white and yellow say in unison, 'Mayibuye I Africa'.

mayita var. and pl. form of MAJITA.

mazaar see KRAMAT.

mazee var. MAAS.

mazina var. MAIZENA.

mazkande var. MASKANDA.

mbalan var. MABALANE.

mbamba /m̩ˈba(ː)mba, əm-/ *n.* Also **mbhambha.** [Perh. fr. Zulu *bamba* belabour, strike with a heavy stick.] Mainly in urban (esp. township) slang: an illicitly brewed raw liquor, made usu. of yeast, brown bread, brown sugar, and water. Cf. BARBERTON sense 2, KILL-ME-QUICK, MAMBA sense 4, SHIMIYANA, SKOKIAAN sense 1 a.

*a*1968 D.C. THEMBA in E. Patel *World of Can Themba* (1985) 138 African men come from the neighbouring mines, the town, and industrial concerns for their mugful of *mbamba* (barberton). But barberton is a poison made in such a way as to give a quick kick. It is made of bread, yeast and sugar. **1970** H. KUPER *Witch in my Heart* 40 Have you tasted mbamba? *Ibid.* 70 All sorts of intoxicating potions, such as *skokiaan, mbamba* and *kill-me-quick.* **1979** [see MAIZA]. **1980** M. MATSHOBA in M. Mutloatse *Forced Landing* 115 The poisonous brew of yeast, brown bread, brown sugar and water, mbamba or *skokiaan* and other variations of the same thing, which were readily available and out of sight of the people of the location. **1981** M. MZAMANE in *Best of S. Afr. Short Stories* (1991) 398 Took him to their favourite shebeens in the township where they drank *mbhambha.* **1982** *Pace* May 34 All the illegal concoctions being brewed by domestic servants in their quarters — skomfaan, mbamba, skokiaan, barberton, what have you. **1982** [see Sunday Times quot. at FACTION sense a]. **1985** [see Ngwenya quot. at AI-AI]. **1990** G. SLOVO *Ties of Blood* 143 The deadly *mbamba* — a drink brewed from yeast, so vicious that it could waste a man within the space of one short year. **1990** M. MELAMU in *Lynx* 284 She had actually fallen into the pit in which Ntsoaki had stored her mbamba.

mbaqanga /mbaˈɬa(ː)ŋga, əm-/ *n.* Music. Also (occas.) **mbaquanga.** [Zulu *umbaqanga* steamed maize bread; app. first applied to the musical style by trumpeter Michael Xaba, see quot. 1980.] **a.** A rhythmical popular music style developed in the 1950s, in essence KWELA, but with brass instruments in place of penny-whistles and with the addition of a strong jazz element. **b.** A style derived from this music, but more strongly influenced by traditional southern African styles, and often featuring vocal arrangements patterned after western close harmony singing. **c.** Loosely, township dance-music in general. Also *attrib.*

A forerunner of MGQASHIYO and SIMANJE-MANJE.

In quot. 1954 the word represents the title of a song, a sign that 'mbaqanga' was probably being used in Zulu as the name of the musical style by this time.

[**1954** *Bantu World* 8 May (Suppl.) 11 Mayibuye Record Review ... *Special* ... *Umbaqanga* ... *Golden City Six* ... They have the same way of using the 'Majuba' idiom and yet making it sound disarmingly unpretentious and tuneful.] **1964** *Drum* Nov. 37 There has been the Zulu-idiom, which forms the basis of what is loosely termed 'Mbaqanga', or pop jazz. **1969** *Post* 15 June, 'Cats' .. are raving mad with mbaqanga, the Soweto originated song-dance mood, which came soon after phatha phatha (touch-touch), a dance tempo popularised by the famous Miriam Makeba. **1977** M. MZAMANE in *New Classic* No.4, 30 Mbaqanga dubbed Kwela by white critics who hear the music as nothing more than an expression of the noisy happiness of simple-minded township natives and a gold mine for recording companies. **1980** D.B. COPLAN Urbanization of African Performing Arts. 348 By the early 50's the S.A.B.C. was presenting different African languages and musical styles on separate days. Once each week jazz pianist-composer Gideon Nxumalo entertained urban Africans with his regular feature, 'This is Bantu Jazz.' He was principally responsible for the wide distribution of the term for the *kwela*-derived *majuba* African jazz, *mbaqanga*. This term, coined by Jazz maniacs' trumpeter Michael Xaba, originally referred in Zulu to a kind of traditional steamed maize bread. Among musicians, it meant that the music was both the Africans' own, the homely cultural sustenance of the townships, and the popular working-class source of the musicians' 'daily bread'. **1982** *Voice* 31 Jan. 16 Jazz with a strong African accent — the mixture of jazz and township music known as mbaqanga — avante garde, and unique. **1986** *Style* Mar. 97 American Disco-Soul has now crept into Mbaqanga (basic 'township' music) in a big way. **1987** *Cosmopolitan* Apr. 28 If I were overseas and I heard a moppie being sung, or a mbaqanga guitar riff, or a klopse banjo, or a township sax, or a mbube choir, or a concertina vastrap, I'd be able to say, 'Hey, that's my music, That's where I come from.' **1987** R. HYDE in *Flying Springbok* Aug. 29 Mbaqanga boasts a variety of rhythmic styles, rich with subtle tribal differences and teasing urban inflections. **1987** *E. Prov. Herald* 31 Oct. 7 Traditional Cape music ... Known as *moppie* and *sopvleis* and played by *klopse* (clubs or troops), .. is to the coloured community of the Cape what Highlife is to Lagos or what *mbaqanga* is to Soweto. **1989** *Reader's Digest Illust. Hist.* 418 The new music soon earned a new name, '*mbaqanga*' (Zulu for African maize bread), which by the mid-50s was shouldering aside the older, large jazz bands — and attracting the commercial attention of local record companies. **1990** *Weekly Mail* 21 Dec. (Suppl.) 31 In the local (upper) middle-class environment, an increasing number of young urban whites are perking up to *mbaqanga* — or what they think is 'happening' in the townships. **1993** *Sunday Times* 11 July 21 She gave a concert that ranged from Bach to mbaqanga.

‖**mbaula** /m̩baˈʊːla/ *n.* Also **mbauula**, **mbawula**. [Zulu *imbawula*.] Among speakers of Sintu (Bantu) languages: KONKA.

1963 B. MODISANE *Blame Me on Hist.* (1986) 21 I .. neglected my duties and was away until an hour before sunset; then, I hurriedly started the fire in the mbaula, brazier. **1977** P.C. VENTER *Soweto* 8 When winter came, the families would carry the mbawula inside; stoves were an impossible dream and the brazier had to keep the bitter winds at bay. But a smoking mbawula was also a health hazard. **1980** *Voice* 23 July 2 The man died after he had slept next to a brazier (mbaula) in order to keep warm. The mbaula was placed among a heap of bags of coal in a tiny room. **1987** P. QOBOZA in *City Press* 25 Oct. 8 Usually people living in shacks had their mbawulas (braziers) burning at full speed outside where they cooked their night meals. **1988** M. TLALI in *Staffrider* Vol.7 No.3, 354 You'll see all those women sitting there roasting mielies on the 'mbaulas' (braziers).

mbhambha var. MBAMBA.

Mbhokodo var. MBOKODO.

mbila /m̩ˈbi(ː)lə, -la/ *n. Music.* [Venda (pl. *dzimbila*).] Esp. among the Venda people: a marimba, an African xylophone with wooden keys and hollow gourd resonators.

[**1901** G.M. THEAL in P.R. Kirby *Musical Instruments of Native Races* (1965) 47 The best and most musical of their instruments is called the *ambira*, which greatly resembles our organs; it is composed of long gourds, some very wide and some very narrow, held close together and arranged in order.] **1928** in A.M. Duggan-Cronin *Bantu Tribes* I. i. Pl.15, (*caption*) The *mbila*, the finest and most perfect of the Venda musical instruments, consists of a number of carved wooden slabs of from three to four inches wide and of various thicknesses, which are beaten with india-rubber hammers by one or two players. The sounding-board consists of a number of calabashes, the apertures of which are closed by thin membranes of thick cobweb. **1931** H.A. STAYT *BaVenda* 316 Drums and wind instruments, chiefly pipes and horns, form a band for most dances, and are, with the *mbila*, the instruments of social value. *Ibid.* 320 Players of the *mbila* are becoming increasingly rare; formerly every chief had a player in his village, who, in the evenings, would often amuse the chief and his guests with his instrument. **1934** P.R. KIRBY *Musical Instruments of Native Races* (1965) 47 Two varieties [of xylophone] are met with, the first among the Venda and the second among the Tshopi. Both are called by the same name, *mbila*, and both are constructed on the same principle. **1985** *S. Afr. Panorama* May, The Venda xylophone, *mbila mutondo*, can be played by as many as four musicians at once.

mbira /m̩ˈbi(ː)rə, əm-, -ra/ *n. Music.* Also **imbira**. [Shona (Zimbabwe), prob. by metathesis of *rimba, limba*, a note.] Any of several small hand-held African musical instruments, having metal tongues of varying lengths which are plucked with the thumbs and forefingers, sometimes over or inside a hollow gourd.

Originating in the countries to the north of South Africa.

1951 H. TRACEY in *Drum* Apr. 18 The Mbira is the only instrument of quality which is unique and peculiar to Africa alone. It is of small size, being held comfortably between the palms of the hands and consists of a number of metal tongues set out upon a resonating body. The tips of the tongues are plucked by the thumbs and forefingers and emit a clear dulcet tone. **1963** B. MODISANE *Blame Me on Hist.* (1986) 44 Like most women I loved she could play on me like an mbira, manoeuvre me into any situation. **1968** L.G. GREEN *Full Many Glorious Morning* 153 Posselt might have remained longer at Zimbabwe but he listened to a native playing the mbira or kaffir piano with such exquisite melancholy that he became homesick and decided to return home at once. **1973** *S. Afr. Panorama* May 33 (*caption*) Dr Tracey holding one of the Mbiras which he has designed. This instrument is often wrongly called a thumb piano. **1976** *Daily Dispatch* 6 Feb. (Suppl.) 2 The marimba originated in East Africa and imbira (a Shona instrument) is played in worship of ancestors. **1978** *Grocott's Mail* 25 Apr., (*caption*) Andrew Tracey with Kalimba Mbira made by the Nsenga tribe in Zambia, which belongs to the Albany Museum collection of African musical instruments. **1987** *Cosmopolitan* Apr. 28 South Africa has no instrument other than the mouth bow that it can truly call its own. Instruments easily associated with Africa such as the drums, the marimbas, the akadindas and the mbiras are all indigenous to countries north of us. [**1990** *Weekly Mail* 8 Feb. 17 The traditional instrument known all over Africa — less so down here — the 'hand-piano', called *mbira* by the Zimbabweans. It sounds like a crystal rivulet rushing over pebbles.]

'mbizo var. IMBIZO.

Mbo /m̩ˈbɔ(ː)/ *n.* Also **Embo**, **Hambona**, **Imbo**, **Mambo**, **Mbu**, **Umbo**. Pl. unchanged, **-s**, **aba-Mbo**, **Abambu**, or (occas.) **aba-s-eMbo**, **Abasembu**, **Amabambo**. [Zulu and Xhosa *umuMbo* (pl. *abaMbo*). For an explanation of sing. and pl. forms, see ABA- and MA- *pref.*[3]]

The Pondo and the Mfengu (see sense 3 below) were originally part of the large Mbo people (sense 2), and retained the name 'Mbo' for themselves for a period after they had migrated down the eastern coast of South Africa during the MFECANE.

1. PONDO sense 1 a.

1803 J.T. VAN DER KEMP in *Trans. of Missionary Soc.* I. 441 They [*sc.* the Xhosa] use shields of an oblong square form .. ; whereas the Imbo use circular ones. **1812** [see GONAQUA sense 2]. **1828** W. SHAW in A. Steedman *Wanderings* (1835) II. 262 There are four entirely distinct nations, who all speak the Caffer language, and occupy .. the coast from the Colony to Port Natal. The Amakosa, commonly called Caffers; the Amatembo, called Tambookies; the Amabambo, called Mambookies; and the Amaponda. **1829** [see MAMBOOKIE]. **1832** *Graham's Town Jrnl* 8 June 96 They entered a nearly depopulated territory, formerly belonging to the Hambona or Amapondo nation, which had been swept by the spear and firebrand of the Zoolah conqueror. **1971** BEETON & DORNER in *Eng. Usage in Sn Afr.* Vol.2 No.2, 15 *Pondos*, .. tribe of the Xhosa fam[ily] .. , also known as the Aba-Mbo.

2.a. *hist.* A member of a large NGUNI people, dominant in northern Natal from the mid-16th to the early 19th centuries. **b.** A member of a small Zulu clan, a remnant of the formerly powerful Mbo group. Also *attrib.*

1857 J. SHOOTER *Kafirs of Natal* 377 Abasembu or Abambu. Branched from the Quabies. Lived near the junction of Tugela and Umzinyati. Routed by Tshaka. **1902** G.M. THEAL *Beginning of S. Afr. Hist.* 301 The Makalapapa .. lived about the St. Lucia lagoon. South of them was a tribe termed the Vambe by the Portuguese, which was to a certainty the Abambo of Hlubi, Zizi and other traditions, from whom Natal is still called Embo by the Bantu. **1912** AYLIFF & WHITESIDE *Hist. of Abambo* 1 The Abambo, at one time a numerous and powerful Bantu tribe, living in Natal, .. included many clans, each under a well known chief. *Ibid.* 3 The life of an Umbo .. was overshadowed by a dread of witchcraft and death. **1937** N.J. VAN WARMELO in I. Schapera *Bantu-Speaking Tribes* 49 Before 1815 one would have classified them into .. : (*a*) the true Nguni or Ntungwa, with perhaps a subdivision for (*b*) the Mbo; and (*c*) the Lala tribes. But today .. one can say neither which tribes are of Lala stock, nor which were originally Mbo. **1949** A.T. BRYANT *Zulu People* 17 The Embos .. occupied .. the flat country between the southern Lubombo hill-range and the sea. There the abaMbo remained (their country being spoken of as *eMbo*, and they, as 'the people of eMbo' or *aba-s-eMbo*) ... At the end .. only one comparatively insignificant clan still retained (and does .. today) the ancient tribal-name of *aba-s-eMbo* (or *abaMbo*). **1972** A.M. MCGREGOR in *Std Encycl. of Sn Afr.* VII. 381 *Mfengu*, .. Variously described as being of the AbaMbo or the AmaLala section of the South-Eastern Bantu, this tribe was defeated and broken during the wars of Shaka. **1986** P. MAYLAM *Hist. of Afr. People* 27 Both the Mbo and Ngcolosi chiefdoms soon submitted to Shaka. The ruling lineage of the Ngcobo chiefdom .. was forcibly incorporated into the loyal Mbo chiefdom.

3. MFENGU.

1912 AYLIFF & WHITESIDE (*title*) History of the Abambo Generally Known as Fingoes. **1913** C. PETTMAN *Africanderisms* 170 *Fingos*, .. As a people they call themselves Aba-Mbo.

Mbokodo /m̩bɔˈkɔ(ː)dɔ, əm-/ *n. hist.* Also **Imbhokoto, Imbokodo, Imbokotho, Mbhokodo, Mbokhodo, Mb(h)okhoto, Mbokotho.** [Ndebele *imbokodo* grindstone.] A uniformed vigilante force which operated in the former 'homeland' of KwaNdebele during the period 1985–6. Also *attrib*. See also VIGILANTE.

1985 *New Nation* 21 May 1 'I moved carefully through the bush, scared of being caught by the Mbokodo,' said the victim of kwaNdebele's repression. **1986** *Learn & Teach* No.3, 1 In other townships vigilantes have different names – the A-Team in Tumahole, the Pakathis in Thabong, the Amabutho in Durban, the Mbhokhoto in Kwa Ndebele and the 'fathers' in Cape Town. **1986** *Sowetan* 13 Aug. 1 The Imbhokoto is allegedly responsible for a reign of terror in the homeland to force people to accept the independence plan of chief Simon Skhosana. **1988** N. MATHIANE in *Frontline* May 20 The real life of Ndebele people has become dominated by something which will never be seen in postcards – a police force called Imbokodo. 'Imbokodo' is an ancient word for a stone used for crushing and grinding. It has taken a new meaning in KwaNdebele. **1988** *Now Everyone Is Afraid* (Catholic Inst. for Internat. Rel.) 110 The government of this tiny and impoverished area stubbornly pressed ahead with their independence plans in spite of massive opposition from most of the residents. The government-created Mbokodo vigilante group and kitskonstabels have been the main tools used in attempts to crush this opposition. S.S. Skosana, Kwandebele's Chief Minister, announced on May 7 1986 that the independence date was to be December 11 of that year. Just over three months later this decision was reversed after a bloody civil war and the defeat of the Mbokodo vigilantes. *Ibid.* 122 Some Mbokodo members were killed in public necklacings. *Ibid.* 125 In August 1986, the Kwandebele legislative assembly unanimously voted to both cancel independence and outlaw Mbokodo. The defeat of Mbokodo meant that a great popular victory had been won. **1990** *Drum* May 22 The notorious Mbokotho – a vigilante group – wreaked havoc during its reign of terror. Mbokotho was used to intimidate people who were opposing the independence of KwaNdebele.

mbombela var. BOMBELA.

mbongi var. IMBONGI.

mbongo /m̩ˈbɒŋɡəʊ, əm-/ *n. colloq.* Also **bongo, m'bonga, 'mbongo,** and with initial capital. [ad. Zulu and Xhosa *imbongi*, see IMBONGI.]

1. *rare.* IMBONGI sense 1.

1875 'P.' in A.M.L. Robinson *Sel. Articles from Cape Monthly Mag.* (1978) 198 The humdrum tones of the chief's 'bongo', who chanted his praise in the Kafir tongue. **1982** *Argus* 22 Oct. 14 The high-and-the-mighty and minor pooh-bahs alike move around with Mbongos (Zulu praise-singers) preceding them with out-bursts of toadying sycophancy.

2. *transf.* Often derisive. A representative, or an enthusiastic supporter, of a political group; a political 'yes-man'. See also JABROER.

1911 *E. Prov. Herald* 12 Oct., Ministerial 'mbongo talks at Grahamstown. Professor Fremantle addressed a fairly large gathering of citizens this evening in the Town Hall. **1945** *Cape Times* 29 May, Municipal mbongo ... The Mayor made quite a good case for the appointment of an official who would be a sort of professional praiser. **1948** *Cape Argus* 16 Sept. 7 Government supporters have danced around their Ministers like dutiful, adoring and disciplined mbongos. **1957** *Ibid.* 15 June 1 They were .. a lot of mbongos to hymn the praises of the incompetent Nationalist hierarchy. **1959** *Hansard* 14 Apr. 3883 Mr Raw: It is typical of the contempt with which they regard the problems of those who do not travel round in luxury as the stooges, the M'Bongos ... Mr Speaker: Order! The hon. member must withdraw the word M'Bongos. **1976** M. VAN BILJON in *Sunday Times* 3 Oct. (Mag. Sect.) 4 A fair sample of expressions which have been disallowed in the House of Assembly including 'he has a yellow streak', 'agitator', 'gangster', 'stooge', 'mbongo', 'khaki pest', 'fat-head'. **1989** *Sunday Times* 3 Sept. 29 Windhoek advocate and long-time Swapo *mbongo* Mr Anton Lubowski has visited South Africa to reassure businessmen that a future Namibia will be a good place to invest.

Mbu var. MBO.

mbube /m̩ˈbuːbi, m̩ˈbʊ(ː)be, əm-/ *n. Music.* Also with initial capital. [Zulu, vocative of *imbube* lion (pl. *izimbube*); so named after the title of a song in this style, composed by Solomon Linda and recorded in 1939 by his group 'The Evening Birds', which became very popular both in South Africa and abroad (where it was adapted and given the name 'Wimoweh').] A style of male choral music, usu. unaccompanied, combining traditional Zulu song with hymns and American gospel music, often featuring the vocal style known as BOMBING, and performed to slow, synchronized dance movements patterned after Zulu regimental dancing; INGOMA BUSUKU; ISICATHAMIYA. Also *attrib*.

The style first emerged during World War I; the 'bombing' element was apparently introduced during World War II.

*c*1948 H. TRACEY *Lalela Zulu* p.x, 'Mbube' songs .. are composed upon the slightest of lyrics. But this does not matter. They are designed to show off the immaculate suitings and the fine team-work of the half-dozen or so young men who .. strut archly to and fro across the stage. **1952** *Drum* Dec. 29 Someone said to me 'Mbube' tunes were so primitive, too tribal for piano accompaniment .. an 'Mbube' is about twenty years old. To settle the argument the 'Durban Evening Birds' have done it. **1954** *Bantu World* 8 May (Suppl.) 14 This factory makes thousands of records a day – everything from mbube and jazz to American crooners and world famous symphony orchestras. **1978** [see INGOMA BUSUKU]. **1986** *Learn & Teach* No.5, 14 'Mbube' music started long ago. 'Mbube' groups only use their voices. We never use guitars or pianos. So our voices must sound very beautiful. **1987** *Drum* Apr. 6 An amalgam of African mbube music, mbaqanga rhythms and American pop sound was at home in Harare and a huge crowd .. turned out. **1989** G. O'HARA in *Weekly Mail* 20 Jan. 25 Golden-voice mbube artists Black Mambazo look set to scoop their second Grammy Award. **1989**, **1990** [see ISICATHAMIYA]. **1991** N. MBATHA in *Pace* Feb. 28, I used to go with my father to single male hostels over the weekends. He was an ardent mbube follower. I would accompany him to mbube sessions, which exposed me to praise-poetry.

mchana var. MTSHANA.

mdala, m'dala varr. MADALA.

MDM *n. hist.* Initial letters of *Mass Democratic Movement*, an alliance of organizations working against apartheid (see quot. 1990). Also *attrib*.

The alliance was formed in the late 1980s, and was dissolved once banned organizations were again able to operate legally (after February, 1990).

1989 McINDOE & PERKINS in *Sunday Times* 20 Aug. 1 One MDM activist carrying the ANC tricolour yelled to a solitary white girl ..: 'Can't we swim together?' **1989** *Sunday Times* 5 Nov. 22 One day it's MDM leaders calling by for an indaba with Mr Nelson Mandela, the next he's sorting out the troubles between the ANC and the PAC. **1989** *Stanger Mail* 17 Nov. 3 Reaction to MDM presence at meeting ... MDM men, strongly opposed to the tricameral system of government, attended a meeting chaired by nominated House of Delegates MP, Mr M F Cassim. **1990** [see Kentridge quot. at UDF n.²]. **1990** *Race Rel. Survey 1989–90* (S.A.I.R.R.) 725 The Mass Democratic Movement (MDM) is an alliance of anti-apartheid organisations, with the United Democratic Front (UDF) and the Congress of South African Trade Unions (COSATU) as the core ... The MDM emerged when the UDF and its allies were restricted in February 1988 ... The .. publicity secretary of the UDF .. said that the MDM, which did not have a constitution or a list of members, enabled anti-apartheid organisations to operate without fear of restriction or banning. The idea of the MDM originated at COSATU's annual congress in 1987. **1991** K. OWEN in *Sunday Times* 26 May 27 The young men and women who led the UDF and the MDM .. bore the brunt of the battle against apartheid.

mdoda var. INDODA.

meal-ball *n. obs.* [Calque formed on *meelbol*.] MEELBOL.

1915 D. FAIRBRIDGE *Torch Bearer* 74 Members .. teach women of the poorer classes to look after their babies .. and the women bring up their children on meal-ball. It's very wholesome.

mealie /ˈmiː(ː)li/ *n.* Also **mielie,** and (formerly) **mealea, meali, mealy, meele, meeli, m(e)ilie, meli(e), miele, milli, mily.** [ad. S. Afr. Du. *milie, mily*; according to J.F. Bense, *A Dict. of the Low-Dutch Element in the Eng. Vocab.* (1939), the word *milie* is found in Du. from 1554, ad. Old Fr. *mil*, ad. L. *milium*. However, it prob. became obs. in standard Du. by the late 17th C. (esp. since the word *maïs* was well established in standard Du. and other European languages by that time). In addition, the forms *milie, milies* and *milies* are all listed in early Afrikaans dictionaries as being S. African rather than Du. Other dictionaries claim that it is ad. Pg. *milho*, but that etymology could not be verified.

The Afk. form *mielie* is often used.]

1.a. Usu. in *pl.*, treated as a *noncount n.*: Maize or Indian corn, the gramineaceous plant *Zea mays*. **b.** A maize ear or cob. Also *attrib*. **c.** Usu. in *pl.*: Maize kernels, either green (see *green mealie* at sense e), or hardened and used crushed (see SAMP) or as seed.

The plant was introduced into South Africa in the mid-17th century.

1801 'C.F. DAMBERGER' *Trav.* 71 (Pettman), *Melis* (Indian corn) were .. distributed for food. **1812** J.T. VAN DER KEMP *Acct of Caffraria* 15 There is another kind of corn which they call *bona*, and known in the Colony by the name of *meelis*. **1835** C.L. STRETCH Diary. 6 Apr., The country was covered with good corn and melies. **1837** 'N. POLSON' *Subaltern's Sick Leave* 104 This meal is similar to the dinner with the addition of stewed fruit and *mealies* or Indian corn stewed in milk. **1844** J. BACKHOUSE *Narr. of Visit* 98 Indian Corn, called in this country *Meeles*, and Dwarf Kidney-beans are the chief produce of the gardens. **1846** *Natal Witness* 3 Apr., The Caffers grow mealies and potatoes in abundance. **1860** A.W. DRAYSON *Sporting Scenes* 203 Bucks so plentiful that they often destroyed the mealeas (as the Indian corn is here called), if it were not regularly watched. **1865** T. SHONE Diary. 6 Oct., Henry is in Town, the men are hoeing of Mieles. **1877** R.M. BALLANTYNE *Settler & Savage* 99 The active brothers had already planted a large quantity of Indian corn, or 'mealies,' entire, without knocking it off the cobs. **1877** LADY BARKER *Yr's Hsekeeping* 70, I hear that 'mealies' – the crushed maize – are also much more expensive than they used to be. [**1889** F. GALTON *Trav. in S. Afr.* 111 The Ovampo .. eat corn (milice) steeped in hot water.] **1896** R. WALLACE *Farming Indust. of Cape Col.* 462 The *mealie*, maize, or Indian corn crop supplies the staple food of the black population of South Africa. *Ibid.* 464 Mealies are largely *consumed* during the growing season in a *green* state. When fully ripe, they are often ground into meal, made into thick porridge or 'pap,' and eaten either alone or with milk. **1898** J.F. INGRAM *Story of Afr. City* 17 Forage or Hay Presses, Mealie Shellers, Single, Double, and Three-Furrow Ploughs, Harrows. **1900** W.S. CHURCHILL *London to Ladysmith* 184 We cherished the hope that with .. a great deal of luck, we might march the distance in a fortnight, buying mealies at the native kraals and lying hidden by day. **1916** L.D. FLEMMING *Fool on Veld* (1933) 95 You planted a bag of mealies and got anything from 100 to 200 in return. **1925** D. KIDD *Essential Kafir* 47 Some of the children are busy roasting mealies in the ashes of the fire. **1933** W.H.S. BELL *Bygone Days* 40 Our Breakfast consisted of crushed mealies and milk with some moist black sugar. **1941** C.W. DE KIEWIET *Hist. of S. Afr.* 257 The Mealie Control Act of 1931, the Meat Trade Control Act of 1932. **1955** A. DELIUS *Young Trav.* 50 Alice was eating a white-coloured porridge. 'This is made from maize, or *mealies* as we call it.' **1968** *Farmer's Weekly* 3 Jan. 92 Lovely 1,000-acre .. farm, 350 acres deep red soil lands planted to mealies, groundnuts and Eragrostis. **1973** *Weekend Post* 27 Oct. (Parade) 14 Though it is not indigenous to South Africa, the mealie could almost qualify as our national vegetable. **1979** *Grocott's Mail* 21 Aug. 2 A type of mielie samp was produced in a home made mortar, .. a hollowed out stump of a tree. **1980** C. HOPE *A Separate Development* (1983) 104 Huge cheerleaders, their blonde heads cropped close as mealie cobs. **1990** N. MANDELA in *Weekly Mail* 27 Apr. 3 Some of the mielie fields that could be seen now had been villages then. **1994** M. ROBERTS tr. *J.A. Wahlberg's Trav. Jrnls 1838–56* 21 Fires visible in various directions; they are lighted by the Caffres to get rid of the grass so that they may begin their cultivation of pumpkins and millis.

d. *comb.* **mealie-bag**, a bag, formerly usu. of hessian, of a size to carry the regulation weight of maize grains, 70 kg or 180 lbs; **mealie beetle** *obs.*, see quot.; **mealie-boer** [Du. *boer* farmer], a farmer who grows maize as his main crop; **mealie bread**, coarse bread made with maize kernels; **mealie-cob**, the head or ear of the maize plant, bearing the kernels; **mealie-cob worm** *obs.*, the caterpillar of the moth *Heliothis armigera* of the Noctuidae; **mealie land** [see LAND], a farm field planted with maize; **mealie pip** *colloq.*, one of the white or yellow seeds on the cob of the maize plant; **mealie-pit**, an underground storage pit for maize in a traditional African village; **mealie planter**, an implement for planting maize seed at the correct depth and spacing; **mealie-sack**, see *mealie bag*; **mealie-stalk borer**, the caterpillar of the moth *Busseola fusca* of the Noctuidae; **mealie-stamper** [Afk. *stamper* pounder, crusher], a large wooden pestle and mortar used in traditional rural African households for pounding maize into a coarse meal. Also *attrib.*

1883 O.E.A. SCHREINER *Story of Afr. Farm* 47 The room, once a storeroom, had been divided by a row of '**mealie' bags** into two parts. **1949** O. WALKER *Proud Zulu* (1951) 183 Those still standing swung around the back of the storehouse hospital and made a rush at the mealie-bag wall. **1967** E.M. SLATTER *My Leaves Are Green* 104 At the outpost men were hurriedly building a connecting wall of mealie-bags between the hospital and the storehouse. **1971** *Seek* June 11 The M.U. members in the Taung area of the Kimberley diocese make clothing — even cottas — from mealie bags and scraps of material. **1889** E.A. ORMEROD *Notes & Descr. of Injurious Farm & Fruit Insects* 111 *Psammodes obliquatus*, Sol. **Mealie Beetle.** **1937** C. BIRKBY *Zulu Journey* 227 The Northern Free-State, the home of the **mielie boer**, is cultivated but sparsely compared with the mealie belts of Basutoland. **1975** *Daily Dispatch* 19 Apr. 2 You won't believe it, but the mielieboere met us with a bodyguard of 2 000 tractors. **1986** *Personality* 15 Sept. 14 Like any other fit young schoolboy of Western Transvaal mealie-boer-stock, Jan Wilkens played rugby. **1941** 'JUANA' in *Bantu World* 25 Jan. (Suppl.) 3 The gravy was brought in cups, and slices of steamed green **mealie bread**. **1971** *S. Afr. Panorama* May 36 Some people like eating slices of mealie bread with butter, others prefer it with gravy, and the children love honey or syrup with it. **1971** L.G. GREEN *Taste of S.-Easter* 90 Mealie bread is a Natal contribution to the South African cuisine. **1977** *Fair Lady* 8 June (Suppl.) 25 Mealie Bread ... 6 green or yellow mealies ... Choose young fresh mealies. **1989** *Woman's Focus* (Spar) 17 July 1 Mealie Bread. To make this quick bread even quicker, bake in a microwave oven. **1994** E. BADENHORST in *Flying Springbok* June 9 The couscous, *pap*, rice and mealie-bread staples are there, as are those spicy stews. **1859** R.J. MANN *Col. of Natal* 137 The young **mealie cob** .. is generally preferred to bread. **1861** T. SHONE Diary. 27 May, Food as usual, plenty of Milicopes, Green heads of indian Corn. **1912** AYLIFF & WHITESIDE *Hist. of Abambo* 5 A white man, who had long hair, like the tress of a mealie cob. **1913** D. FAIRBRIDGE *Piet of Italy* 130 Shook her till her gleaming white teeth — polished every morning on a mealie-cob — chattered in her head. **1977** *Sunday Times* 27 Feb. 15 Fuel was mealie cobs — appropriate for that maize and wheat growing area. **1989** M. BALL in *Weekend Post* 14 Jan. (Funfare) 3 As he smoked his mealie cob pipe, Jim told him stories about the clever hare who outwitted all the forest animals. **1911** J.D.F. GILCHRIST *S. Afr. Zoology* 150 The **Mealie-Cob-Worm**, attacks buds and pods and does extensive damage to mealies, peas, tomatoes and lucerne. **1900** F.R.M. CLEAVER in M.M. Cleaver *Young S. Afr.* (1913) 123 Menton remarks the **mealie lands** are looking well all along the road, but I prefer the kafir koorn. **1916** L.D. FLEMMING *Fool on Veld* (1933) 97 Although I have from year to year fenced off lands .. from cattle, .. most of the mealie lands are as yet open. **1970** M. HOBSON *Informant, Tzaneen*, I sent Andries to skoffel the mealie land. **1973** *E. Prov. Herald* 18 Apr. 34 Natal smothered under sugarcane, the highveld .. endless mielielands, the Boland one huge wheatfield. **1985** *S. Afr. Panorama* May 9 Nearby was a large mealieland (maize field) with two women farm workers whose sole job it was to chase away hill-dwelling baboons. **1971** *Farmer's Weekly* 12 May 85 The yellowfish .. tricked themselves with a single **mealie pip** .. which was like a snare at the barb of the hook. **1976** S. CLOETE *Canary Pie* 114 When they are sick they are as alike as mielie pips from the same cob. **1987** L. BEAKE *Strollers* 12 Maybe a tokolosh would appear and turn them all into mealie pips or something. **1925** D. KIDD *Essential Kafir* 128 He .. begged to be placed in the **mealie-pit**, which is excavated in the ground of the cattle kraal. **1933** W.H.S. BELL *Bygone Days* 78 For the first few days lived on mielies that we found in the native mealie pits ... The natives used to dig pits in the cattle kraals, fill them with mealies to protect them from weevils, place a large stone over the mouth of the pit, and this in turn was covered with the usual kraal litter. **1986** *Daily Dispatch* 1 Nov. 17 (*advt*) 1 John Deere 26 **Mielie Planter** with Cotton Seed Plates. **1989** *Grocott's Mail* 4 Aug. 4 (*advt*) Cream cans, mealie planters, disc plough, and other articles. **1918** C. GARSTIN *Sunshine Settlers* 48 High on the load, his legs straddled firmly round the topmost **mealie-sack**, rocked the brown puppy. **1951** H.C. BOSMAN in L. Abrahams *Unto Dust* (1963) 86 And instead of a jacket, he was now wearing a mealie sack with holes cut in it for his head and arms. **1965** J. BENNETT *Hawk Alone* 91 They brought him back up to Unda Maria in a mealie sack and the next day he was buried in the public cemetery at Nelspruit. **1913** C. PETTMAN *Africanderisms* 314 **Mealie-stalk borer**, The larva of a moth, *Sesamia fusca*, which eats out the core of the growing mealie, and sometimes destroys large quantities. **1890** A. MARTIN *Home Life* 228 The centre of an old waggon-wheel did duty very effectually as our **mealie-stamper**. **1925** P. SMITH *Little Karoo* (1930) 237 Aantje was stamping mealies for the evening meal ... By the side of the mealie-stamper he paused. *a*1959 — in Lennox-Short & Lighton *Stories S. Afr.* (1969) 110 The worn mealie-stamper, cut out of a tree-trunk and shaped like an hour-glass, in which the mealies were pounded into meal. **1985** *Cape Times* 20 Sept., Grabbing a 'mielie stamper' club, the former Iron Man contestant rushed outside to surprise three burglars.

e. With defining word: **green mealie**, the young head or cob of the maize plant, picked for eating before the kernels have dried and hardened (cf. *U.S. Eng.* 'corn on the cob'); also *attrib.*; **yellow mealie**, any of several varieties of maize which produce yellow seeds (as distinguished from the white varieties), used esp. for animal feeds.

1881 G.F. AUSTEN *Diary* (1981) 43 The Boers in the trenches nearest the Fort have observed the loose leaves or shucks of **green mealies** thrown away out of the Fort. **1889** 'A HOUSEWIFE OF THE COLONY' *Col. Hsehold Guide* 50 Green Mealies, to boil ... Boil till tender in salted water. Serve hot with butter. Green Mealies, to roast. Strip the cob of its husks, and put it in the hot ashes of the fire until it is nicely done without being burnt. **1891** H.J. DUCKITT *Hilda's 'Where Is It?'* 165 Take cabbage cut in small pieces; green 'mealies' (heads of Indian corn) in rings; tiny carrots, [etc.]. **1900** G.W. LINES *Ladysmith Siege* 46 Green mealies, each 3s. 8d.; small plate grapes, £1 5s. **1906** H. RIDER HAGGARD *Benita* 157 Fresh meat was also brought to them daily, and hauled up in baskets .. and green mealies to serve as vegetables. **1913** C. PETTMAN *Africanderisms* 314 The young cob is boiled or roasted whole, and is much esteemed being known as 'Green mealies'. **1925** D. KIDD *Essential Kafir* 326 The famous dish known as 'green mealies'. *c*1936 *S. & E. Afr. Yr Bk & Guide* 297 *Green Mealies*, (Sweet corn) ... There is every prospect that a large demand will arise for this delicious vegetable. **1941** [see quot. at *mealie bread* above]. **1949** L.G. GREEN *In Land of Afternoon* 139 The meal he enjoyed most was the green mealie bread made for him by a trader's wife in Pondoland. **1973** *Farmer's Weekly* 13 June 69 White maize, at the semi sweet stage, known as the good old 'green mealie' has been sold as a substitute for sweet corn in this country for many years. **1977** [see quot. at *mealie bread* above]. **1994** *Weekend Post* 19 Feb. (Leisure) 6 There are .. many way of using green mealies, apart from the popular boiled mealies with butter, pepper and salt. **1926** P. SMITH *Beadle* (1929) 11 Klaartje's fair, glossy hair, the colour of ripe **yellow mealies**. **1968** *Farmer's Weekly* 3 Jan. 75 With what other ingredients could I mix a good feed for poultry using yellow mealies? **1970** *E. Prov. Herald* 4 Sept., 9.2. million bags of white mealies and 5.1 million bags of yellow mealies. **1977** *Ibid.* 13 July 11 Good things like yellow mielies, wheat bran, sunflower seeds, groundnuts.

2. In various *fig.* or *transf.* uses.

a. *derog. rare.* An offensive term for an Afrikaner. Also (*comb.*) **mealie-muncher**.

1970 V.R. VINK *Informant, Florida* The litter at the picnic spot was caused by a bunch of mealies (a derogatory term describing an ignorant, common type of Afrikaner). **1970** *Informant, Pietersburg* Mealie-muncher. Afrikaner.

b. In idiomatic expressions: ***to eat (something or someone) like a mealie***, to dispose of (something or someone) with ease; ***to work (one's) mealie off*** (prob. euphemistic), to work extremely hard.

1988 J. GILBERT *Informant, Westminster (OFS)* He ate him like a mealie, man, he didn't stand a chance. **1993** *Informant, Grahamstown* Don't laugh, I'm exhausted! I've worked my bladdy mealie off here.

mealie-meal /ˈmi(ː)liˌmiːl/ *n.* [MEALIE + Eng. *meal*; or tr. Afk. *mieliemeel* (*meel* flour, meal).]

1. Maize meal, white or yellow in colour and either coarsely- or finely ground. Also *attrib.* Cf. MAIZENA.

1846 *Natal Witness* 10 July, Market Intelligence ... Mealie Meal, 7s. 6d. per muid. **1852** *Natal Times* in W.C. Holden *Hist. of Col. of Natal* (1855) 282 The consumption of mealie (maize) meal in D'Urban has increased. **1882** C. DU VAL *With Show through Sn Afr.* II. 198 A forward jerk of the bullocks toppled it over .. the Boer tobacco-rolls .. and a large bag of mealie meal being liberally distributed over the adjacent 'Veld'. **1907** *Zululand Times* 5 Jan., (*advt*) Always in stock or to arrive: Boer meal, Bran, .. Crushed Mealies, Mealie Meal. **1910** J. BUCHAN *Prester John* (1961) 73 The native gave me good-day in Kaffir, then begged for tobacco or a handful of mealie-meal. **1911** M.J. PULLEN in *Farmer's Weekly* 4 Oct. 119, I beg to state that the best food for young ducks .. is mealie meal (raw) or mealie porridge. **1928** M. MOLLER *What Every Housewife Should Know* 67 In making cakes or biscuits for which rice flour is asked — and is not to hand, try mealie meal. **1937** C.R. PRANCE *Tante Rebella's Saga* 124 His mill .. is another boon .. enabling him to take mealie-meal contracts for road-gangs. **1949** H.C. BOSMAN *Cold Stone Jug* (1969) 59 You get your supper — a kind of mealie-meal soup and a hunk of bread, and you are locked up again for the night, and the day is over. **1955** A. DELIUS *Young Trav.* 137 These trading stations ... were the chief sources of supply for the Bantu of everything from canned foods, mealie-meal and blankets to beads, banjos and mouth organs. **1971** *Evening Post* 27 Feb. (Mag. Sect.) 2 The only food in the house that day was a loaf of mealie-meal bread. **1972** *Fair Lady* 19 Apr. 11 Why is it so difficult to buy yellow unrefined mealie meal? **1982** *E. Prov. Herald* 18 June 13 That first night we had to go and beg for food ... A week later we got rations — half a bucket of mielie meal. **1983** *Daily Dispatch* 21 Mar. 8 Per capita income is below the 'mealie meal line'. To them the breadline would be 'pure luxury'. *Ibid.* 16 June 3 Doctors have unanimously agreed that mealie-meal .. should be vitamin-enriched to combat two widespread diseases among blacks whose staple diet is primarily based on the product. **1989** J. HOBBS *Thoughts in Makeshift Mortuary* 263 Mealie meal is the staple food of Southern Africa, cooked with water in a three-legged pot over an open fire to make the stiff crumbly porridge called phuthu. It is eaten with the fingers, unaccompanied if the family is poor, but preferably with a spicy meat and vegetable sauce.

2. In full ***mealie-meal pap*** [part. tr. Afk. *mielie-meelpap, mielie* maize + *meel* meal + *pap* porridge], ***mealie-meal porridge***: MEALIEPAP sense 1.

1880 E.F. SANDEMAN *Eight Months in Ox-Waggon* 20, I was able to walk from sunrise to sunset, .. often with no more strengthening food to work on than mealie-meal pap. **1882** S. HECKFORD *Lady Trader in Tvl* 178 Mr Higgins told me .. that I could feed my Kaffirs on nothing but mealea meal. **1899** D.S.F.A. PHILLIPS *S. Afr. Recollections* 148 The food .. consisted of a tin pannikin of mealie meal pap (porridge), at six in the morning .. [etc.]. **1925** L.P. GREENE *Adventure Omnibus* 471 The beer brewed by the women grows stale, and mealie meal — three times a day, look you — is no proper food for a man. **1951** [see Griffiths quot. at MARULA sense a]. **1951** S. VAN H. TULLEKEN *Prac. Cookery Bk* 4 Mealie Meal. 4 cups boiling water, ½ teaspoon salt, 3 heaping spoons of mealie meal. **1961** T. MATSHIKIZA *Choc. for my Wife* 101 A four gallon paraffin tin loaded with mealie meal, a porridge of crushed corn. **1966** L.G. BERGER *Where's Madam* 79 Add a gigantic pot of mealie meal porridge .. as a side dish. **1968** J.T. MCNISH *Rd to Eldorado* 236 After a hasty breakfast of mealiemeal and coffee he went off to his claim with his boys. **1976** J. BECKER *Virgins* (1986) 13 Left-overs of hard-cooked mealie-meal scraped from the bottom of the servants' lunch-pot. **1976** J. MCCLURE *Rogue Eagle* 150 The old devil came to be treated for damages his wives had inflicted with hot mealie meal! **1985** *Financial Mail* 18 Oct. (Fedics Suppl.) 40 You still have to consider differences in ethnic tastebuds. I would not serve salt in a Sotho's mealie-meal because that's like putting a curse on him. **1987** R. HYDE in *Flying Springbok* Aug. 29 Even in Paris, capital of gourmet refinement, steamed yellow mealie-meal from South Africa is the latest taste sensation.

mealiepap /ˈmi(ː)liˌpap/ *n.* Also **mi(e)liepap.** [Part. tr. Afk. *mieliepap, mielie* maize + *pap* porridge; perh. ellipt. for *mieliemeelpap* (see MEALIE-MEAL sense 2); or MEALIE + Afk. *pap* porridge.]

1. Maize-meal porridge, prepared in any of several ways, including crumbly (KRUMMELPAP), stiff (STYWE PAP), or soft; MEALIE-MEAL sense 2; PAP *n.* sense 1 a; cf. PUTU. Also *attrib.*

1880 E.F. SANDEMAN *Eight Months in Ox-Waggon* 273 Guinea fowls .. form a very relishing change from the never-varying menu of bôk or mealie pap. **1892** W.L. DISTANT *Naturalist in Tvl* 25 The Kafirs began ill-treating the poor woman, but on the suggestion of one of their number, ordered her at once to cook a large pot of mealie pap. **1897** 'F. MACNAB' *On Veldt & Farm* 243 It is a pity that .. oatmeal porridge is not commoner than the disgusting mealie pap which is everywhere provided so liberally. **1900** H. BLORE *Imp. Light Horseman* 135 He no drink millik 'way from hims own Kraal. Drink Kaffir beer, yes. Eat mealie-pap, yes. **1918** C. GARSTIN *Sunshine Settlers* 240 Clustered round the compound fires, stirring away at the black pots in which steamed their ration of mealie pap, the staple food of the country. **1925** D. KIDD *Essential Kafir* 326 Mealie pap is made by stirring the meal into a large pot of boiling water, any dirty old piece of stick that is at hand being used as a spoon. **1932** in C.W. DE KIEWIET *Hist. of S. Afr.* (1941) 204 If you have a diet of mealie-pap (porridge made of ground mealies or maize; the American corn mush) without any fat, the balance is all wrong. **1949** H.C. BOSMAN *Cold Stone Jug* (1969) 89 How the hell can I keep working all morning in the tailors' shop at that blessed machine, just on one ladle of mealie-pap? **1955** J.B. SHEPHARD *Land of Tikoloshe* 43 A nurse, perhaps seven years old, feeding a young baby with mealie pap by .. scooping up a fistful and clapping her hand over the baby's mouth. **1968** *Fair Lady* 30 Oct. (Suppl.) 6 (advt) Mieliepap for every taste: Have you tried it with meat and gravy? .. Mieliepap — a good South African name for a great South African custom! **1971** *S. Afr. Panorama* May 36 Lavish helpings of 'miliepap' (maize porridge) made as stiff as bread. **1971** *Personality* 22 Oct. 157 Traditional recipes plus new ones like mieliepap fritters. **1973** *Sunday Times* 16 Dec. (Mag. Sect.) 25 The difference between a barbecue and a braai is mieliepap. **1978** *Drum* July 67 They were as unsexy as cold mielie-pap on a winter morning. **1985** *Sunday Times* 5 May 24 The sooner the immutable rules of a market economy are introduced into the maize idustry, the better. There is no such thing as a free lunch — mieliepap or otherwise. **1987** S. WOODGATE in *Star* 27 Feb. 3 Lights go out for 'mielie-pap people' ... For most of the tenants in the area they call 'the mealie-pap place', repaying the arrears is a dream as remote as having white bread every day of the week. **1988** *Personality* 27 June 80 Dolly playing the part of Dixie, as homely as 'grits' (which is American for mieliepap). **1988** B. FORDYCE in *Era* Sept. 44 The body .. will steer the famished marathoner towards the complex carbohydrates, such as the pastas, potatoes, breads, mielie-paps.

2. *nonce.* Sorghum porridge: MABELA sense b.

1905 J. DU PLESSIS *1000 Miles in Heart of Afr.* 148 A village for them .. means the chance .. perhaps of a mouthful of 'mealie-pap' or millet-porridge.

mealie rice /ˈmi(ː)liˌraɪs/ *n. phr.* [MEALIE sense 1 c + Eng. *rice.*] Crushed maize kernels, used as a cheap substitute for rice.

1936 M. HIGHAM *Hsehold Cookery* (1941) 165 Hominy or mealie rice, a finer form of samp. **1950** H. GERBER *Cape Cookery* 57 Use rice, mealie rice, semolina, barley, oats, .. [etc.]. **1966** L.G. BERGER *Where's Madam* 79 Lily thrives on this diet and only varies it to add a gigantic pot of mealie meal porridge, .. or mealie rice, as a side dish. **1968** *Fair Lady* 30 Oct. 12 Wash the mealie rice well and put into boiling water. Add salt .. and cook gently till tender and thick. **1972** *S. Afr. Garden & Home* Feb.-Mar. 12 We have been feeding them regularly for five years on mixtures of all sorts, .. bread crumbs, bird seed, cooked mealie meal, sunflower seeds. They love mealie rice. **1979** *Voice* 2 June 11 The first signs of hardship were experienced when mealie-meal .. went up. This was succeeded by increases in the price of maize by-products such as samp and mealie-rice. **1985** *Weekly Mail* 16 Aug. 7 We ate all our meals in our cells ... Supper (mielie rice, a vegetable, bread and a piece of meat and coffee) was at 3pm. **1989** *Woman's Focus* (Spar) 3 July 7 Maize Meal (includes super maize meal, sifted and unsifted maize meal, samp and mielie rice; *excludes* maize flour).

mealy var. MEALIE.

mebos /ˈmiːbɒs, ˈmeɪbɒs, -bɔs/ *n.* Also **mee(r)bos, meibos(s).** [S. Afr. Du., prob. ad. Japanese *umeboshi* plums pickled in salt and dried; but see quot. 1948.] **a.** A confection made from apricots soaked in brine, stoned, pulped, sugared, and sun-dried. **b.** Minced and sugared dried fruit, usu. presented in the shape of a slab or roll; TAMELETJIE sense 2. Also *attrib.* See also PERSKESMEER.

[**1796** C.R. HOPSON tr. *C.P. Thunberg's Trav.* III. 120, I saw several kinds of fruit, the produce of this country [*sc.* Japan], either dried or preserved in yeast, in a mode which is, I fancy, only practiced at Japan and China. The fruit that was only dried, such as plums and the like, was called *Mebos.*] **1862** LADY DUFF-GORDON *Lett. from Cape* (1925) 157, I have bought some Cape 'confyt'; apricots, salted and then sugared, called 'mebos' — delicious! **1883** O.E.A. SCHREINER *Story of Afr. Farm* 47 'Here Sampson,' said his mother, 'go and buy sixpence of "meiboss" from the Malay round the corner'. **1891** H.J. DUCKITT *Hilda's 'Where Is It?'* 4 Apricots, Dried and Salted. (*Commonly called 'Mebos.'*) ... At the Cape it generally dries and becomes 'Mebos' in three or four days in the sun ... To crystallise the Mebos, lay them in lime water .. for five minutes, .. wipe dry on a soft cloth, and rub coarse crystallised white sugar well into each. **1905** [see BOEREBESKUIT]. **1910** D. FAIRBRIDGE *That Which Hath Been* (1913) 115 No one could make such meibos .. and when the apricots were ripe every available pair of hands on the farm are pressed into the work of stoning, drying, salting and sugaring the fruit. **1927** C.G. BOTHA *Social Life in Cape Col.* 57 Apricots were dried and made into 'mebos,' no doubt an art learnt from the East. **1936** [see BAADJIE sense 1]. **1948** H.V. MORTON *In Search of S. Afr.* 293 Mebos is not common ... Some believe that the word is derived from the Arabic mushmush, an apricot, but others, and this is more likely, from umeboshi, a Japanese word given to preserved plums. **1951** S. VAN H. TULLEKEN *Prac. Cookery Bk* 266 Mebos Chutney. 1lb. mebos ... Soak mebos in 1 bottle vinegar, boil soft next day. **1955** J. HENDRIE *Ouma's Cookery Bk* 136 Quince Mebos. Grate quinces, put in pot with sugar ... Pour into wetted tin and leave to set, cut into pieces, roll in sugar. **1966** C.A. SMITH *Common Names* 334 *Mebos,* Not a plant but a confectionery prepared from stoned apricots, which are dried with sugar and salt, generally in the form of a roll made from the pulp. **1972** *Std Encycl. of Sn Afr.* V. 77 *Mebos* is prepared by putting whole, well-ripened apricots into a concentrated salt solution until the skin loosens. **1974** D. ROOKE *Margaretha de la Porte* 229 'Konfyt and meerbos, what a typical Dutch spread', Fanny commented .. ; but she was quick enough to help herself to the glazed watermelon and sugary apricots. **1987** I. DAVIS in *S. Afr. Panorama* Aug. 11 The French Huguenots .. produced mebos, a delicacy made from dried apricots, and encouraged by governor Simon van der Stel, exported mebos and raisins to his fatherland. **1990** R. GOOL *Cape Town Coolie* 44 She .. circulated bowls of kossiters, mebos, sourfigs and other sweetmeats.

MEC /em iː ˈsiː/ *n. hist.* Abbrev. of *Member of the Executive Committee* (of a province).

See also MPC.

1942 *Off. Yrbk of Union 1941* (Union Office of Census & Statistics) 1149 Members of the Provincial Councils ... S.F. Malan, M.E.C. **1970** *Daily News* 28 May, Maj. G. Leonard Arthur, MEC in charge of hospital services. **1988** *Stanger Mail* 23 Dec. 3 Members of the Town Board invited MEC Mr Peter Miller .. to do an in loco inspection. **1989** *E. Prov. Herald* 26 Jan. 2 Tolcon's agreement .. was described as 'fair and reasonable' by MEC for Roads Mr Val Volker. **1994** *Weekly Mail & Guardian* 16 Sept. 25 Though the provincial director general has formal directing powers, MECs do work closely with their respective officials, much as at national level.

medalla var. MADALA.

medem /ˈmedem/ *n.* Also **meddem,** and with initial capital. [ad. MADAM, representing a common pronunciation of the word among speakers of the Sintu (Bantu) group of languages.]

1. A term of address: MADAM sense 1 a.

1969 I. VAUGHAN *Last of Sunlit Yrs* 11 'Medem', he would say, 'it is of no use to have that small tenk for water'. **1970** J. PACKER *Veronica* 73 'Good morning, Minnie. This damp weather gets into your bones, doesn't it?' 'Ja, Meddem, it's terrible.' **1990** *Tribute* Sept. 139 On the last day of the month, she gives you your money and you say, 'Thank you, Medem,' walk out of her kitchen and close the door.

2. A common noun: MADAM sense 2.

1990 *Tribute* Sept. 138 Not only a harsh *medem*, she was, by far, the most unreasonable and, I thought, least blessed with any intelligence.

medicine *n.* [Special senses of general Eng.]

1. MUTI sense 2 a.

'Medicine' is used also by the indigenous peoples of North America in this sense.

1890 *Cape Law Jrnl* VII. 231 All of us who can afford it are provided with a medicine which is supposed to bring good luck, and preserve the family from misfortune; and in cases such as the one in which we were engaged the medicine (piece of root) is kept in the mouth and carefully chewed while the case is going on. **1904** D. KIDD *Essential Kafir* 174 The diviner is supposed to be bound to find not only the culprit but also the magic medicine used. He will then grub some hairs from a cow's tail, and declare that these were the bewitching medicines which were used. **1957** A.A. MURRAY *Blanket* 70 'The medicine,' Phiri repeated, and his voice shook with horror. **1964** R. OWEN in *Capricorn High School Mag.* 69 We could not stop in the towns, for the Bantu pulled out the hairs of his [*sc.* the giraffe's] legs for 'medicine'. **1991** J. PAUW *In Heart of Whore* 44 To obtain the goodwill of the witch doctors, he visited the Kruger National Park and obtained animal material that they needed for their medicine ... Criminals would visit the witch doctors for medicine for protection.

2. *comb.* **medicine boy**, the bearer of a container of this medicine; **medicine horn**, a container, usu. a horn, containing medicine supposed to guarantee the prosperity of a people; **medicine man**, a HERBALIST or sorcerer; **medicine murder**, *ritual killing* (see RITUAL).

1907 W.C. SCULLY *By Veldt & Kopje* 71 The Chief, accompanied by his 'isicake se 'nkosi,' or '**medicine boy**,' now stalked majestically forward. The 'medicine boy' lifted the pot and carried it slowly into the large kraal. **1953** [**medicine horn**: see MOFOKENG]. **1957** A.A. MURRAY *Blanket* 147 Then the medicine horn. Had he ever seen this medicine horn? What knowledge had he that it had been filled with medicine brewed from his brother's flesh? **1968** A. FULTON *Dark Side of Mercy* 27 The ancient medicine horns had grown feeble with the passage of time. No longer could they protect the clan against the scheming of malevolent spirits nor thwart the spells of the enemies ... A new medicine horn must be prepared without delay and it would require as one of its ingredients the blood and flesh of a young and fertile woman, preferably heavy with child. **1824** [**medicine man**: see MORIMO]. *c*1929 [see MOLIMO]. **1951** R. GRIFFITHS *Grey about Flame* 108 Medicine men wove spells to bring the rain. **1972** *Daily Dispatch* 4 Aug. 2 The farmer sacked him for insolence. Khotso .. told his fellows he was a strong medicine man and they should see what happened to the farm. 'It so happened a cyclone hit the farm .. and that established Khotso as a medicine man,' Mrs Lamb said. **1988** J. KHUMALO in *Pace* June 7 The missionaries .. lumped the unfortunate traditional medicine man with some derogatory names. **1952** *Drum* Apr. 25 The murders are not part of a ritual, and they should really be called *diretlo*, or **medicine murders**. **1957** A.A. MURRAY *Blanket* 36 Maburu is to be the victim of a medicine murder? **1983** D. AMBROSE *Informant* Liretlo. A better definition is 'medicine murder'.

medora /mə'dɔːrə/ *n.* [Etym. dubious: perh. fr. Arabic *mudawwar* round, circular; or named for *Madura*, an island off Java.] An ornamental headdress worn by Cape Muslim brides, and by Muslim women who have completed their pilgrimage to Mecca. Also *attrib.*

1936 L.G. GREEN *Secret Afr.* 136 A Malay wedding .. is one of the most gorgeous sights of Cape Town ... The Malay girl .. is not present at the simple ceremony in the mosque; but you may see her driving through the streets in an open carriage afterwards wearing the golden *medora* headdress of the bride. **1944** I.D. DU PLESSIS *Cape Malays* 28 On the wedding day the bride wears a headdress reminiscent of the golden ballets of Bali — the *medora* — and a veil, and receives her guests in her first wedding dress. **1981** *Sunday Times* 12 July (Mag. Sect.) 1 The young women are beautiful .. their dress modern, their faces often framed in a new version of the traditional medora.

meebos var. MEBOS.

meelbol /'mɪəlbɔl/ *n.* [Afk., *meel* flour + *bol* ball.] Infant food, made by either boiling a bag of tightly-packed flour, or baking it in an oven, after which it is finely crushed and mixed with milk; MEAL-BALL.

1913 C. PETTMAN *Africanderisms* 315 *Meelbol*, Flour or meal pressed hard into a cloth and boiled, after which it is crushed fine, mixed with milk and used as food for infants and invalids. **1930** M. RAUBENHEIMER *Tested S. Afr. Recipes* 119 'Meel-bol' or Baked Meal for Baby. From the fourth month this is a very safe and nourishing food for a normal baby ... For a young baby a teaspoon to a breakfast cup of water is sufficient. **1941** FOUCHE & CURREY *Hsecraft for Primary Schools* 46 Meelbol (Dextrinized Flour). Pack .. tin or cup tightly with white flour. Put into a cool oven. Bake till biscuit coloured ... Roll to a fine powder ... Use for infants and invalids. For infants' food milk must be used .. and .. only given after the teeth begin to appear. **1948** V.M. FITZROY *Cabbages & Cream* 59 'What are you feeding it on?' 'Meelbol, missis.' I remembered Meelbol. I had once tried the boiling and baking of that ball of meal for Digory at weaning time. **1968** K. MCMAGH *Dinner of Herbs* 60 There were no baby foods as such in Granny's young days so, after infants had been weaned, they were given 'meel bol'. **1974** *Bona* Mar. (*advt*) The richest part of the wheat and nourishing natural bone meal in Ouma Meelbol.

meele, meeli varr. MEALIE.

meelkis /'mɪəlkəs/ *n.* Pl. **-kiste** /-kəstə/. [Afk., *meel* flour + *kis* chest.] A large wooden bin with compartments, formerly used for storing different types of flour and meal; a dough trough.

1965 M.G. ATMORE *Cape Furn.* 217 Dough or Kneading troughs (meelkiste). **1971** BARAITSER & OBHOLZER *Cape Country Furn.* 227 Storage chest or meelkis in Swellendam Museum with compartments for fynmeel, growwemeel and semels. **1974** *S. Afr. Garden & Home* June 29 On the right is the *meelkis* (meal chest for flour and maize) with two sieves on top of it. **1987** J. KENCH *Cottage Furn.* 118 Flour bin ('meelkis') in Oregon pine, 625mm high.

meerbos var. MEBOS.

meercat /'mɪəkæt/ *n.* Formerly also **mere-cat**. [Englished form of S. Afr. Du. *meerkat*, see MEERKAT.]

1. MEERKAT. Also *attrib.*

1801 J. BARROW *Trav.* I. 231 Upon these parched plains are .. found a great variety of small quadrupeds that burrow in the ground, and which are known to the colonists under the general name of *meer-cats*. **1850, 1853** [see MOUSE-HUNT]. **1873** F. BOYLE *To Cape for Diamonds* 330 We found a sick meercat by the road, the prettiest, but most ferocious little brute I ever saw. Of these animals there are several kinds, only to be classed together by their habit of living in holes upon the veldt, and standing on hind legs to survey the prospect, in a very droll manner. **1878** T.J. LUCAS *Camp Life & Sport* 219 His horse .. suddenly encountered in his course a nest of mere cat holes — a nimble little animal .. which lives gregariously like the prairie dog in burrows. **1880** E.F. SANDEMAN *Eight Months in Ox-Waggon* 85 The holes of the ant-bear are .. generally conspicuous, they do not prove so dangerous as the smaller holes of the mere-cat, a pretty little animal between a rat and a stoat, found all over South Africa. **1887** A.A. ANDERSON *25 Yrs in Waggon* I. 65 Meercats abound all over the Veldt, they are grey, some have very bushy tails, others long and smooth, but along the river-banks they are red with black tails. **1900** S.T. PLAATJE *Boer War Diary* (1973), We dodged like a couple of meercats. **1911** L. COHEN *Reminisc. of Kimberley* 113 The veldt was very unsafe, and one morning my pony put his foot in a merecat hole, broke his leg, and nearly broke my back. **1930** S.T. PLAATJE *Mhudi* (1975) 136 As she picked her way along the hillside, she frightened several coveys of meercats which, scampering away from her, never stopped until well out of her sight. **1936** [see MARTIAL EAGLE]. **1945** *Outspan* 3 Aug. 49 Leguaans and meercats. **1947** J. STEVENSON-HAMILTON *Wild Life in S. Afr.* 207 The bushy-tailed meercat. **1964** A. ROTHMANN *Elephant Shrew* 76 The common meercat has a grizzled grey-brown coat with dark cross stripes ... The bushy-tailed meercat is .. yellowish-brown, but its coat is more furry. **1978** C.L. REITZ *Poisonous S. Afr. Snakes* 5 No animal is naturally completely immune to snakebite, although certain predators of snakes, such as the meercat (*Suricata spp*) .. have an increased resistance. **1986** *Sunday Times* 20 July 17 As a rule, nothing much happens in the vast open spaces of the Karoo. Sheep wander about aimlessly .. and meercats play hide-and-seek among the dried-out bushes.

2. *Mining*. A vehicle developed for underground use in mines.

1979 *S. Afr. Digest* 19 Jan. 11 The Meercat is powered by a twin-cylinder diesel engine, is fully automatic and all-hydraulic, and can be fitted with a light or heavy duty bucket, a roof bolter drill, a scissors lift, a mobile crane, and a personnel carrier.

meerkat /'mɪəkæt, 'mɪərkat/ *n.* [S. Afr. Du., transf. use of Du. *meerkat* a long-tailed monkey of the Cercopithecidae, *meer* sea, ocean + *kat* cat; *meer* is sometimes erron. tr. 'ant' or 'termite' (cf. modern Afk. *mier*), see MIERKAT.] Any of several small mammals, esp. the suricate: **1.** (Viverridae family) **a.** The suricate, *Suricata suricatta*. **b.** Any of several species of mongoose, esp. the yellow mongoose *Cynictis penicillata* and the banded mongoose *Mungos mungo*; cf. MUISHOND sense 1 b. **2.** The ground squirrel *Xerus inauris* of the Sciuridae. **3.** The MUISHOND (sense 1 a i), *Ictonyx striatus*. In all senses also called ANT-CAT, MEERCAT (sense 1), MIER-CAT, MIERKAT. Also *attrib.*, and (formerly) **meerkatj(i)e** [see -IE].

1822 W.J. BURCHELL *Trav.* I. 343 The holes of the Aardvark, those of the Springhaas (Springhare), and Meerkatje (Weasel), were very frequent. **1824** *Ibid.* II. 241 In the vicinity, a number of *Meerkats* have their burrows: these are a species of *squirrel* of about the size of our common squirrel. **1833** OGILBY in *Trans. of Zool. Soc.* (1835) I. 34 The name *Meer-kat* .. is of very general acceptation in South Africa, being applied indifferently to the present species [*sc. Cynictis sp.*], the Cape Herpestes, Ground Squirrels, and various other burrowing animals. **1872** C.A. PAYTON *Diamond Diggings* 38 These [holes] are generally found twenty to forty together, and are the entrances to the abodes of the 'meerkat,' a small feline animal, something like a weasel, with a nice furry coat .. and fine bushy tails. **1897** A. PAGE *Afternoon Ride* 62 Meerkat skins sewn together, as pouches for tobacco. **1901** W.S. SUTHERLAND *S. Afr. Sketches* 73 There are three kinds of Meer-Kat. One is yellow in colour, .. with pointed ears, a sharp nose, mouth and eyes like a fox ... The second variety is .. much brighter in colour, and striped like a hyena ... The most interesting variety is the third .. which in many ways resembles our home ground squirrel. **1914** [see PICCANIN sense 1]. **1936** WILLIAMS & MAY *I Am Black* 72 He saw the wide eyes of the children peeping out of the hut entrances where they had run to cover ... Like frightened meerkats. **1948** H.V. MORTON *In Search of S. Afr.* 261 Wherever there are ant-hills there is a delightful-looking animal called the meerkat, a cross between a weasel and a squirrel. He sits bolt upright, his small front paws hanging loosely against his stomach, watching the road with two large eyes ringed with black fur and set in an inquisitive snouted face. **1956** D. JACOBSON *Dance in Sun* 156 It had been Joseph who had told him stories, played with him, hunted hares and meerkats with him. **1976** *E. Prov. Herald* 26 Jan. 11 The bushy tailed meerkat is perhaps the most common and most widely spread of the little animals known as meerkats in South Africa ... The slender-tailed meerkat is the little animal one sees sitting on its hindquarters as one drives through the Karoo, the Free State, the highveld of the Transvaal. **1980** *Rand Daily Mail* 9 Aug. 3 In most areas of the Transvaal rabies is carried by meerkats. **1987** *Personality* 30 Sept. 69 We moved in absolute silence, leaving our horses because of the many antheaps and meerkat warrens. **1990** SKINNER & SMITHERS *Mammals of Sn Afr. Subregion* 481 *Suricata suricatta*, .. In English, meerkat is often used, but as the name is applied to other mongoose species as well, suricate is more appropriate. **1994** M. ROBERTS tr. *J.A. Wahlberg's Trav. Jrnls 1838–56* 64 Took a shot at a meerkat.

meerkus var. MUURKAS.

meester /ˈmɪəstə(r)/ *n.* Also **meister**, and with initial capital. [Du. *meester* master, or obs. dialect *meister* schoolmaster, teacher, leader.]

1.a. *hist.* A resident tutor hired by rural families; an itinerant schoolmaster. Also with qualifying word, **school-meester**.

1798 LADY A. BARNARD in Lord Lindsay *Lives of Lindsays* (1849) III. 439 Here was another civil schoolmaster, the tutor of the *yonge vrow* ... The good *meister* gave us some of his private bottle of punch. **1822** W.J. BURCHELL *Trav.* I. 199 The daughters .. were under the tuition of an itinerant tutor, or Meester, as he was called, who had been for several months an inmate of the family. **1824** *Ibid.* II. 114 This *meester* .. (that is; *schoolmeester*, or schoolmaster) considered it part of his profession .. to let every person know the extent of his acquirements. **1829** C. ROSE *Four Yrs in Sn Afr.* 254 The Meester deserves a separate notice. The tutor, who teaches the ingenuous youth of Southern Africa, is generally a discharged English soldier, and leads a kind of middle life, a connecting link between the family and the slaves. **1835** J.W.D. MOODIE *Ten Yrs* II. 301 When a farmer wishes to have his children taught to read and write, he gets some of his neighbours to join him in hiring a schoolmaster at the lowest rate of wages ... The 'meester,' as he is called, is generally referred to when his learning is required to solve any difficult point in the course of conversation. **1835** A. STEEDMAN *Wanderings* II. 63 The 'Meister' was generally found in the family of the Boor whose circumstances would allow of such an addition to the household; but .. his qualifications were seldom of much consideration. **1847** 'A BENGALI' *Notes on Cape of G.H.* 27 The Dutch .. are generally .. instructed by 'Meesters' as they call them, — itinerant pedagogues of little knowledge and of dissolute habits. **1871** J. MACKENZIE *Ten Yrs* (1971) 25 Those parents who can afford the paltry salary secure the services of a 'meester,' or family tutor. **1883** M.A. CAREY-HOBSON *Farm in Karoo* 185 The 'Meester' or tutor, an institution on all Dutch farms of any size .. is, or was until lately, very often a man totally unfitted for the post of tutor to youth of any sort. *Ibid.* 186 The Meester's salary is paid in sheep. **1896** —— *At Home in Tvl* 302 He knew the old school 'Meester' too — the one we have called the English-speaking Boer. **1911** D.B. HOOK *'Tis but Yesterday* 126 George was twenty years of age, with a clever brain, and with the knowledge he had acquired from the meester was fairly, if roughly, equipped for life's battle. **1912** F. BANCROFT *Veldt Dwellers* 60 The men were .. both educated by the same worthy pedagogue — the broken-down-gentleman *school-meester* — speaking both the *taal* and English with equal fluency. **1937** F.B. YOUNG *They Seek a Country* 326 There were many men of his kind, old soldiers, English and German, attached to the households of frontier Boers in those days ... They acted as 'meesters,' being allotted the task of instructing the children of the family in reading and writing and ciphering. **1949** L.G. GREEN *In Land of Afternoon* 145 Itinerant teachers. Known as 'meesters', they were nevertheless expected to help in the farm work after school hours. **1958** R.E. LIGHTON *Out of Strong* 46 'It must be a good thing to be on the school committee.' 'Not always ... It's that way if the other members and the meester are reasonable people.' **1969** D. CHILD *Yesterday's Children* 50 The eighteenth century saw the emergence at the Cape of a type of schoolmaster mercifully long vanished .., the itinerant *meester* who moved from farm to farm in the wild interior .. where schools were non-existent. **1976** A.R. WILLCOX *Sn Land* 165 The *meester* had low standing, had to help the farmer with his figuring and writing and do any other odd jobs about the place. **1990** *Sunday Times* 25 Mar. 5 The .. English girl arrives in the village like a blackboard bombshell ... But she wins their respect and sparks a romance with their Meester.

b. As a term of address or reference to a teacher; a title, used with a surname.

1943 I. FRACK *S. Afr. Doctor* 107 The farmer is so taken up with his own troubles that he leaves everything to 'Meester'. The teacher's training is provided free. **1944** 'TWEDE IN BEVEL' *Piet Kolonel* 120 'Meester' Cilliers, ex-schoolmaster, was a great find as lecturer. **1966** W.P. CARSTENS *Social Structure Cape Coloured Reserve* 100 Various titles are given to people holding special positions in the community. All teachers and former teachers are addressed as *Meester*. **1980** E. JOUBERT *Poppie Nongena* 20 The teacher, Meester Riet, came to school on his bicycle. **1982** C. BARNARD in *E. Prov. Herald* 20 Sept. 8 At school I can remember addressing men teachers as '*meester*'. Nobody thought it demeaning. **1990** C. LAFFEATY *Far Forbidden Plains* 47 It was *Meester* who taught at the farm school which had been established four years ago.

2. [Du.] *Obs.* exc. *hist.* A doctor.

1812 A. PLUMPTRE tr. *H. Lichtenstein's Trav. in Sn Afr.* (1928) I. 88 The Dutch ship surgeons are called in the sailor's language *meester*, (master) and this term, with many others used by the sailors, has been adopted as the language in common use among the colonists. **1958** E.H. BURROWS *Hist. of Medicine* 19 Apart from the guild surgeons and the *doctoren* .. there were also lesser types of practitioners abroad in the countryside ... The *operateurs*, the itinerant *meesters* who made a living by removing gravel and operating for cataract or hare-lip. **1972** N. SAPEIKA in *Std Encycl. of Sn Afr.* VII. 303 The popularity of patent medicines inland, and the earlier activities of the 'wonder-doeners', 'meesters', and itinerant 'doctors' who travelled among the Trek Boers.

meibos(s) var. MEBOS.

‖**meid** /meɪt/ *n. offensive.* Pl. **meide** /ˈmeɪdə/. [Afk., fr. Du. *meid* servant girl, maid.] Among Afrikaans-speakers: an insulting term of address or reference to a 'coloured' or black girl or woman; MEIDJIE.

[**a1858** J. GOLDSWAIN *Chron.* (1949) II. 4 When I was a bout two yards off her I ordered he to stop but she told me to 'fung the underMaid' (catch the other woman).] **1908** I.W. WAUCHOPE *Natives & their Missionaries* 4 A female Native was called 'Meid,' i.e. girl, or as a term of endearment 'Ou-ma,' i.e. grandmother or 'Ayah.' **1955** [see JONG *n.* sense 2 a]. **1959** [see BOESMAN]. **1963** B. MODISANE *Blame Me on Hist.* (1986) 58 'You must watch these meide,' the constable said. **1969** A. FUGARD *Boesman & Lena* 21 Some sports. You and him. They like *Hotnot meide*. **1974** A.P. BRINK *Looking on Darkness* 54 So they take me en' one of them show me a stick en' he say: *Meid* where's de money?' **1980** *Sunday Times* 4 May 6 Senior white medical and nursing staff treated them with contempt, often referring to them as 'meide'. **1980** [see SEUN]. **1982** *E. Prov. Herald* 3 May 10 It didn't matter that she was of royal descent and the well-educated daughter of an ambassador. She was a *meid* even if her family had been wearing shoes long before our forebears stopped wearing skins. **1987** *Learn & Teach* No.1, 22, I have had enough of your Baasmiesieskleinbasskleinnooi minds This meid means business.

‖**meidjie** /ˈmeɪki, -ci/ *n.* [Afk., *meid* (see MEID) + -IE.] MEID.

[**1960** M. MULLER *Art Past & Present* 121 His sensitivity .. is seen in his carving of a Coloured girl, Meidjie.] **1975** S. ROBERTS *Outside Life's Feast* 85 Sometimes you feel sorry like the time we kruisvra a meidjie I was convince she was innocent she was maybe eighteen an' very light skin. **1987** L. NKOSI *Mating Birds* 80 The *meidjie* says she was as naked as the day she was born.

meilie var. MEALIE.

meineer var. MENEER.

meinheer var. MIJNHEER.

meisie /ˈmeɪsi/ *n.* Formerly also **meisj(i)e**, **mysie**. [Afk., fr. Du. *meisje* girl.] Esp. among, or with reference to Afrikaans-speakers:

1.a. A girl or young woman. Also dim. form **meisietjie** /ˈmeɪsiki/ [see -IE]. See also MEISIEKIND.

1838 J.E. ALEXANDER *Exped. into Int.* I. 130 The vrouws and meisjes were accordingly at work day and night .. preparing biltong and dried meat, and baking bread for their men. **1870** in A.M.L. Robinson *Sel. Articles from Cape Monthly Mag.* (1978) 18 A most rotund Boer *meisje*, of athletic structure, about as broad, indeed, as she was tall. **1896** H.A. BRYDEN *Tales of S. Afr.* 183 Now Kate .. was in no mind to suffer herself to rust dully through existence like some Boer meisje. **1904** *Argus Christmas Annual* (Cape Colony Sect.) 19 The gay proteas .., flaunting their apparel like a meisje in her best pink blouse. **1908** F.C. SLATER *Sunburnt South* 21 When she was young .. she was the prettiest *meisje* you could wish to meet in a long day's ride. **1919** J. BUCHAN *Mr. Standfast* 287 One night I told him about Mary. 'She will be a happy *mysie*,' he said, 'but you will need to be very clever with her'. **1919** R.Y. STORMBERG *With Love from Gwenno* 62 Ben has started blazing a fresh wooing trail — the neighbouring meisjes have been heartlessly neglected of late. **1924** S.G. MILLIN *God's Step-Children* 72 He will not have you. He does not want you ... He said he would not think of marrying a brown *meisje* — a brown girl. **1930** *Outspan* 25 July 63 Said others, shaking their heads 'A good wife *he* lost when he ran off with that Kaapse meisje and sold the land of his fathers to strangers'. **1946** E. ROSENTHAL *General De Wet* 14 She was a typical Boer meisie — healthy, kindly and with no other ideas of a home than those of a farm-house. **1959** J. PACKER *High Roof* 196 Her parents had been upset when she married a Malay, for .. when a Coloured meisie married into a Moslem family she was lost to her own. **1967** E.M. SLATTER *My Leaves Are Green* 147 'Good-bye, my meisie,' she said as Anna-Marie clung to her hand. **1983** *Cape Times* 9 Dec. 16 The meisie who shaves her legs so smooth, her knees look like ostrich eggs. **1984** *Drum* July 35 His woman, .. a naive, innocent and blissfully ignorant Afrikaner meisietjie. **1988** J. KHUMALO in *Pace* May 32 As the Kaapse klonkies and meisies do their thing on stage one is hit by a twinge of nostalgia for the colourful places like Hanover Street, Allie's High class Tailors, Jet Set Hairdressing Saloon and the Seven Steps of Stone. **1991** *Sunday Times* 7 Apr. 26 At top level, the *okes* (and the *meisies*) all throw so straight they keep cancelling each other out.

b. As a term of address to a girl or young woman.

1905 P. GIBBON *Vrouw Grobelaar* 139, I will ask the girl once more if she will come out ... Meisje, will you not come out? I ask you to. *c***1964** M. JABOUR in *New S. Afr. Writing* 21 'Cheeky', Ouma glared, 'you're getting too big for your boots, meisie'.

2. Ellipt. for BOEREMEISIE (sense 1).

[**1896** see sense 1 a.] **1920** R.Y. STORMBERG *Mrs Pieter de Bruyn* 25 Neither was there any incongruity in his making persistent love to a be-kappied unilingual meisje who was anything but polite to him. **1937** C.R. PRANCE *Tante Rebella's Saga* 94 The girls who provided tasteful items in the programme in the intervals .. were a refreshing novelty in Afrikander life, not shy like the backveld 'meisje'. *Ibid.* 168 What of the girls, including meisjes of unimpeachable Voortrekker ancestry, cavorting on public tennis-courts in curt divided-skirts, or even in (very) shorts. [**1946** see sense 1 above.] **1970** *Sunday Times* 15 Nov. 7 Hannatjie (a meisie of the eighteen-thirties). **1984** *Ibid.* 8 July 6 Zola Budd .. has .. been telling all who ask .. that she is a runner, not a politician .. a meisie from die plaas who misses her pets. **1989** *Style* Feb. 41 On the Cover of *Voelvry* a Trekker meisie jumps for liberated joy above the Joeys skyline.

3. A girlfriend or wife.

1972 P. O'BYRNE on Radio South Africa, 25 Sept., A little bird tells me that you haven't managed to find yourself a meisie yet – you're still a bachelor, right? **1975** *Sunday Times* 10 Aug. 7, I need a meisie to warm the cockles of my heart. Also, I need a son to carry on the business when I hang up my hatchet. **1990** *Ibid.* 11 Feb. 9 Mrs A–, whom Mr B– called his 'meisie', said the two intended getting married and planned to buy a farm in the Karoo. **1992** C. LEONARD in *Ibid.* 16 Feb. 6 Fanie L– and his 'meisie', Anet M–.

‖**meisiekind** /ˈmeɪsikənt/ *n.* Pl. **-kinders** /-kənərs/. [Afk., *meisie* girl + *kind* child.] Esp. among Afrikaans-speakers: a young girl. See also MEISIE sense 1 a.

1986 D. CASE *Love, David* 92 'What time did the meisiekind come home?' Dadda asked. *Ibid.* 93 The meisiekind said that he was going to look for a job. **1987** L. BEAKE *Strollers* 80 Abel was not pleased, when he returned .. to find that Mesana had disappeared. But he had more to think about than naughty meisiekinders at a time like this.

meister var. MEESTER.

meitjie, me-it-je varr. MIETJIE.

mekaar /məˈkɑː(r)/ *adj. rare.* Short for DEURMEKAAR (sense 1).

1990 J. NAIDOO *Coolie Location* 5 Gambling is no good. Dice and fight gaan altyd saam. You know that man they stabbed, ag, he was so mekaar that he wanted to walk home.

mekoro var. MOKORO.

melee /ˈmeleɪ/ *n. Diamond-trade.* Also **melée, mêlée, mélèe.** [Unkn., perh. fr. Fr. *mêlé(e)* mixed; the word *mêlée* is also found in Dutch in the sense of 'mixed small diamonds'.] Small diamonds (usu. of less than one carat each in weight). Also *attrib.* See also CLEAVAGE, SPLINT.

1911 L. COHEN *Reminisc. of Kimberley* 267 On a certain day I entrusted him with two or three hundred carats of melée – small stones – to sell. **1931** KRAUS & HOLDEN *Gems & Gem Materials* 82 The term *melee* is applied to stones cut from small fragments of the diamond, the result either of cleavage or sawing. Many of these small stones, of which from eight to sixteen are required to make a carat, are cut with the usual fifty-eight facets. Smaller stones are called *small melee.* *Ibid.* 86 The smaller portions of the stone resulting from cleavage or sawing may be cut and polished as *melee.* **1946** J.R. MCCARTHY *Fire in Earth* 110 One great diamond importing house moaned that if melee weren't supplied soon it would have to go out of business. **1962** SMITH & PHILLIPS *Gemstones* 264 Mélée are small stones of mixed sizes, weighing less than 1/4 carat, and mélange is the term used for larger stones of mixed sizes. **1969, 1971** [see CLEAVAGE]. **1972** [see STONE]. **1973** A. HOCKING *Diamonds* 9 When it comes to gemstones .. the first step is to divide them into two broad categories according to bulk. The division comes at about the one carat mark. Anything above this limit is 'size', anything below is 'melee'.

meli(e) var. MEALIE.

melkbalie see BALIE sense b.

melkboer see BOER sense 1 b.

melkboom /ˈmelkbʊəm, ˈmɛlk-/ *n.* [Afk. (earlier S. Afr. Du.), *melk* milk + *boom* tree.] Either of two species of tree exuding a milky latex when injured. **a.** The *milk-bush* (sense (*a*) see MILK sense 2), *Ficus cordata.* **b.** The *milkwood* (sense (*a*) see MILK sense 2), *Sideroxylon inerme.*

1917 R. MARLOTH *Common Names* 57 *Melkboom, Ficus cordata* ... At the coast the same name applies to *Sideroxylon inerme.* **1957** L.G. GREEN *Beyond City Lights* 225 An old *melkboom* gives shade, and under the tree you are more likely to find a wagon than a motor-lorry. **1966** C.A. SMITH *Common Names* 335 *Melkboom,* A name applied to several trees with milky latex in the bark and to nearly all the arborescent species of *Euphorbia* .. ; *Sideroxylon inerme* .. ; *Ficus cordata.* **1972** M.R. LEVYNS in *Std Encycl. of Sn Afr.* VII. 324 *Melkboom,* (*Ficus cordata.*) Native fig-tree of the family *Moraceae,* with simple, cordate leaves. **1977** E. PALMER *Field Guide to Trees* 90 *Melkboom, Ficus cordata* Thunb ... The commonest species of fig from the Cedarberg northwards.

melkbos /ˈmelkbɔs/ *n.* Formerly also **melkbosch.** [Afk. (earlier S. Afr. Du. *melkbosch*), *melk* milk + *bos* forest, bush.]
1. Any of several species of low, shrubby plants which produce a white (often poisonous) latex when injured. **a.** Any of several species belonging to the milkweed family (Asclepiadaceae): **i.** Either of two species of *Asclepias, A. fruticosa* or *A. physocarpa.* See also *wild kapok* (WILD sense a). **ii.** Any of several species of *Sarcostemma.* **b.** Any of several species of the genus *Euphorbia* of the Euphorbiaceae, esp. *E. mauritanica,* and including *E. hamata* (see sense c below); see also *milkbush* sense (*b*) at MILK sense 2. Also *attrib.*, and (occas.) **melkbossie** [see -IE].

1862 'A LADY' *Life at Cape* (1963) 100 Here .. you find tufts of reed called the 'melkbosch', which are full of a milky fluid, only grateful to goats, for sheep will not touch it. **1887** *S.W. Silver & Co.'s Handbk to S. Afr.* 161 While the designation *Melkbosch* is given to the Euphorbiaceae, or Spurge-plants, it is applied to any plant having a milk-like sap. **1917** R. MARLOTH *Common Names* 57 *Melkbos,* Various plants with a white latex in the bark or young wood, belonging either to the genus *Euphorbia* or to some genera of Asclepiads, mostly bearing also some other name. **1920** F.C. CORNELL *Glamour of Prospecting* 46 Tattered, torn, dusty, covered in melkbosch-juice from the thickets we had traversed. **1936** C. BIRKBY *Thirstland Treks* 126 The melkbos (like gigantic asparagus) and the aloes are undisturbed by passers-by. **1940** V. POHL *Bushveld Adventures* 24 In the first place, no other weapon than the full-leafed branch of a melk-bossie might be employed in the attack; and more often than not your bossie was smashed on your own head long before the enemy had been subdued. *Ibid.* Glossary, *Melkbossie,* Shrub, with a white resinous sap. **1958** L.G. GREEN *S. Afr. Beachcomber* 24 Often they camped in the melkbos on the south side of the vlei at Betty's Bay. **1971** D.H. WOODS in *Std Encycl. of Sn Afr.* IV. 560 The flora is highly xerophytic, including the quiver-tree or kokerboom .., the halfmens .., while communities of melkbos (*Sarcostemma* spp.) occur on valley slopes and plateaus. **1973** [see GIFBOOM]. **1974** H. HALL in *Ibid.* X. 339 *Euphorbiaceae,* The succulent members of this large family usually belong to the cosmopolitan genus *Euphorbia,* popularly known as melkbos ('milk-bush' – referring to the latex). [**1988** J. MUNDAY *Poisonous Plants in S. Afr. Gardens & Parks* 32 *Asclepias fruticosa,* Gansies, Melkbos, Milkweed, Tonteldoosbos, Wild swans ... *A. physocarpa,* Balbossie, Melkbos, Milkweed, Wild cotton, Wildekapok.] **1989** M. ROBERTS *Herbs for Healing* 79 Warts. Apply any of the following directly onto the wart, at regular intervals: the milky juice of *Melkbos* or a Fig leaf.

2. With defining word: **olifant(s)melkbos** [Afk., *olifant* elephant (+ linking phoneme (or pl.) *-s-*)], the plant *Euphorbia hamata* of the Euphorbiaceae; see also sense 1 b above.

Used as a food for livestock (see quot. 1966).

1898 in T.R. Sim *Forests & Forest Flora* (1907) 316 The local name of the plant [*Euphorbia cervicornis*] is Olifant Melkbosch. **1913** C. PETTMAN *Africanderisms* 347 *Olifant melkbosch,* .. *Euphorbia cervicornis.* **1961** PALMER & PITMAN *Trees of S. Afr.* 235 The olifants melkbos of Namaqualand, a shrub with a large succulent root and small crown, played an important part in the early economy of the country. **1966** C.A. SMITH *Common Names* 355 *Olifantsmelkbos, Euphorbia hamata* .. : A unisexual plant, forming large, spreading growths from a tuberous rootstock. Stem succulent with copious latex ... An excellent fodder plant which is much valued and carried as food for stock when trekking through the arid parts .. where the plant is not found.

3. In full ***melkbos tree***: **a.** The small tree *Diplorhynchus condylocarpon* of the Apocynaceae. **b.** the *milkwood* (sense (*a*) see MILK sense 2), *Sideroxylon inerme* of the Sapotaceae.

1939 'D. RAME' *Wine of Good Hope* I. 92 They camped below melk-bosch trees. **1951** L.G. GREEN *Grow Lovely* 199 An even more historic landmark .. is the gnarled melkbos tree known as the 'old slave tree'. **1957** — *Beyond City Lights* 160 Before the seventeenth century ended a wagon track was built over Constantia Nek so that timber from the great melkbos and wild olive and yellowwood trees could be transported to the Table Bay settlement. **1957** *Cape Times* 18 Feb. 2 Seedlings from the old Melkbos tree at Mossel Bay should be cultivated. *Ibid.* 12 Sept. 2 The Board decided to give a melkbosch tree for an afforestation scheme. **1964** L.G. GREEN *Old Men Say* 261 Behind the house grew two melkbos trees, and one ancient specimen is still there. **1972** PALMER & PITMAN *Trees of Sn Afr.* III. 1911 One of the features of the tree [*Diplorhynchus condylocarpon*] is its milky latex which when 'dry' is soft, sticky and rubber-like, and which gives it the common names of 'rubber tree' or 'melkbos'. **1982** J. KRIGE in *Staffrider* Vol.5 No.2, 21 Tired and exhausted we flopped down under the shade of a melkbos. **1988** G. CROUDACE *Secret of Rock* 36 The wind was still raging .. tossing the branches of the melkbos, though their camp in the lee of the slow-growing tree was fairly sheltered.

melkhout /ˈmelkhəʊt, ˈmɛlk-/ *n.* [Afk. (earlier S. Afr. Du.), *melk* milk + *hout* wood.] In full ***melkhout tree***, or ***melkhoutboom*** /-bʊəm/ [Afk. *boom* tree]: (the timber of) any of several species of tree of the Sapotaceae which exude a milky sap upon injury, esp. **a.** the *milkwood* (sense (*a*) see MILK sense 2), *Sideroxylon inerme*; also with distinguishing epithet, **white** or **wit(te) melkhout** /vət(ə)/ [Afk., *wit(te)* white]; and **b.** *Mimusops obvata*; also with distinguishing epithet, **red melkhout,** formerly also **roode melkhout** /rʊədə/ [Du., *roode* attrib. form of *rood* red]; also called *milkwood* (see *milkwood* sense (*b*) at MILK sense 2).

*a*1823 J. EWART *Jrnl* (1970) 81 Three very large trees of a species I had never before seen grew seemingly from one root, they were called the melk hout or milk wood; their foliage had a resemblance to that of the box-wood with the dusky colour of the yew. **1887** *S.W. Silver & Co.'s Handbk to S. Afr.* 125 Thorn trees .. and a few trees of the Melkhout, Sideroxylon inerme. *Ibid.* 130 In those of Klein and Van Stadans rivers are found .. Melkhout (*Sideroxylon inerme*) .. Red Melkhout (*Mimusops obovata*). **1913** C. PETTMAN *Africanderisms* 317 *Melkhout boom,* .. *Sideroxylon inerme* is so called in the Riversdale District. *Ibid.* 409 *Roode melkhout, Mimusops obovata.* See Red Milkwood. *Ibid.* 564 *Witte melkhout,* Sideroxylon inerme, the timber of which is much esteemed for boat building, mill, and bridge purposes. **1932** [see *milkwood* (MILK sense 2)]. **1933** W.H.S. BELL *Bygone Days* 38 The barrel and lock were treasure trove ... We lost no time in making a stock from a piece of melkhoutboom which we cut in the bush. This wood is very hard and .. very suitable for the purpose. **1949** L.G. GREEN *In Land of Afternoon* 99 This captain .. found a melkhout tree near the highwater mark; so he posted his letter in an old shoe, which he hung on a branch of the tree. **1963** A.M. LOUW *20 Days* 184 Covering the .. hillock .. was a thick, sub-tropical growth of taaibos, melkhout. **1966** *Cape Times* 24 Sept. (Weekend Mag.) 4 Whenever .. I have mentioned the planting of melkhout or yellowwoods .., someone is always certain to say: 'Oh but aren't they too slow-growing?' **1971** BARAITSER & OBHOLZER *Cape Country Furn.* 259 Other woods used are melkhout and yellowwood. They do not last as long and are inclined to crack, rot or become infested by beetles. **1985** A. TREDGOLD *Bay between Mountains* 174 A big melkhout tree, called the trekboom, grows on the headland. **1990** *Weekend Post* 19 May (Leisure) 7 Back along the terrace past a very large melkhout tree (*Sideroxylon inerme*) was a well-grown kershout.

‖**melkkos** /'mɛlkɔs/ *n.* Also **melkos.** [Afk., *melk* milk + *kos* food.] *melk snysels*, see SNYSELS sense b.

1969 S.J.A. DE VILLIERS *Cook & Enjoy It* 414 Serve the 'melkkos' in soup plates and sprinkle with a cinnamon-and-sugar mixture. **1986** M. KLINZMAN in *Style* Apr. 138 Melk Kos ... This lovely noodle dish served as a pudding or as a particularly comforting breakfast dish on a cold day. **1990** *You* 14 June 15 Melkos is a traditional South African dish that was enjoyed by farm folk at about 8pm on winter evenings. It is easily digestible and has as its main ingredient 'snysels', a home-made pasta.

melkpens /'melkpens, 'mɛlk-/ *n. slang.* [Afk., 'milk stomach', perh. alluding to the role of the abomasum in the digestive process of a young calf or lamb.] A young, naive, or inexperienced person.

1974 *Drum* 22 Mar. 28, I always get very worried when I see some 'melkpens' in Western Township thinking that there is some glamour in the underworld. **1978** *Pace* Dec. 74 Among them is a youngster in oversized trunks. To some .. he is a visible picture of a 'melk pens,' but his lanky, imposing and athletic physique is that of a human volcano.

melktert /'mɛlktert/ *n.* Pl. **-e** /-ə/, **-s.** [Afk., *melk* milk + *tert* tart.] A traditional baked custard tart, flavoured with spice; MILK TART. Also *attrib.*

1938 'MRS GOSSIP' in *Star* 1 Dec. 12 Pannekoeke, braaiwors, melktert, mosbolletjies, beskuit and coffee could be had in plenty. **1949** L.G. GREEN *In Land of Afternoon* 61 She was able to bake a cake and prepare melktert and poffertjies for Queen Mary and her ladies-in-waiting. **1958** A. JACKSON *Trader on Veld* 44 I .. recall .. 'melk tert' (milk tart) .. and many other specialities of the old South African kitchen. **1964** L.G. GREEN *Old Men Say* 120 Grilled snoek with butter sauce, pickled fish, tomato bredie, melktert and other old favourites appear regularly on the railway menus. **1971** *Argus* 5 June 1 The Cape Malays excelled in the art of baking, especially the melktert with crushed cardomons [*sic*] and cinnamon lightly strewn on the egg and milk filling. **1981** *E. Prov. Herald* 1 June 3 South Africa, with its cuisine firmly based on the bredie, the bobotie, the melktert and the tjop. **1988** M. LE CHAT in *Flying Springbok* Apr. 27 'It was so *lekker* working with somebody else for a change,' says David Kramer, giving his trademark, melktert-sized grin. **1989** T. BOTHA in *Style* Dec. 158 Davids talks about how Afrikaans has taken part of its structure from the old Malayo-Portuguese language spoken by the slaves and political exiles from the East ... Foods like *bobotie, blatjang, bredie, melktert, koeksisters* and *konfyts*. **1990** *Weekly Mail* 21 Dec. (Suppl.) 21 The guests ate bobotie, yellow rice, melktert and koeksusters. **1994** on M-Net TV 24 Aug. (Egoli), Do I really have to have tea with koeksusters and melktert to make me feel welcome?

mellow yellow *n. phr. Slang.* Also with initial capitals. [Transf. use of the proprietary name of a yellow-coloured soft drink, which in turn was prob. named for the song 'Mellow Yellow' by Donovan.] In urban (orig. township) parlance: a police vehicle (so called because the vans are painted yellow); YELLOW MELLOW. Also *attrib.* See also KWELA-KWELA sense 1.

1986 *Anon. Pamphlet* 25 June, Hullo hullo hullo. This is your friendly casspir Mellow Yellow with this morning's unrest report. **1988** *Now Everyone Is Afraid* (Catholic Inst. for Internat. Rel.) 94 JM said a police hippo and 'mellow yellows' had pulled up outside her house after a group of vigilantes came looking for her brother. **1990** *Weekly Mail* 21 Dec. (Suppl.) 32 The mellow-yellow was part of a fleet of seven police vehicles which monitored the occasion throughout.

melongas, -longgoes pl. forms of MLUNGU.

melt sickness *n. phr. Obs. Pathology.* [Prob. (part.) tr. S. Afr. Du. *meltziekte* (see MILTSIEKTE); but cf. Eng. *melt* (var. of *milt*) the spleen.] MILTSIEKTE.

1867 *Blue Bk for Col. 1866* JJ23, There has been a good deal of sickness amongst the cattle during the year – lung-sickness .. ; melt sickness, which has carried off a considerable number [etc.]. **1882** *Times of Natal* 8 June, An ox suffering from melt-sickness.

Hence **melt-sick** *adj.*, suffering from miltsiekte.

1882 *Times of Natal* 8 June, He never knew of a case of illness from eating a melt-sick ox.

melt sicte, meltsiekte, melt zicte, meltziekte varr. MILTSIEKTE.

meneer /mə'nɪə(r)/ *n.* Formerly also **meineer.** Pl. **menere** /-ɪərə, -ɪərə/. [Afk., fr. S. Afr. Du., reduced forms of Du. *mijnheer*, see MIJNHEER.]

1. MIJNHEER sense 1.

1899 'S. ERASMUS' *Prinsloo* 32 'Meneer Prinsloo,' said he, 'show me where this water is got.' *a*1951 H.C. BOSMAN *Willemsdorp* (1977) 121 It's the Gawd's truth, the Gawd's own truth, meneer Stein. **1956** D. JACOBSON *Dance in Sun* 114 Nobody had ever seen young Meneer Bester until the Noordhuizen girl met him on holiday. **1974** J. MATTHEWS *Park* 73 'Meneer Du Toit,' the farmer stiffened at the omission of the customary 'baas' and looked hard at Herman. **1980** S. SEPAMLA in M. Mutloatse *Forced Landing* 80 This is the Stirtonville of Meneer Taylor. To get to Mnr Taylor's place, one had to turn right at the very first street. **1993** K. MALGAS in *Weekly Mail & Guardian* 10 Dec. 43 'I'm planning to do something by myself ... I know something will come but I haven't caught it yet – but working with Meneer Beezy has pushed me towards it.'

2. MIJNHEER sense 4.

1910 J. RUNCIE *Idylls by Two Oceans* 115 'Come to de house, come to de house, de Missis is awake. Come inside, meineer.' **1946** S. CLOETE *Afr. Portraits* 110 'Meneer,' he said, 'there are no minerals in the moon, for if there were you British would have annexed it long ago.' **1956** A. SAMPSON *Drum* 184 A white policeman demanded his permit. 'I haven't got one, meneer.' (It always annoys an Afrikaans policeman to be called meneer – mister – and not baas). **1965** PATON & SHAH *Sponono* (1983) 27 Sponono: Meneer. Principal: .. What's your trouble, Sponono? Sponono: I've no trouble, meneer. **1971** *Sunday Times* 28 Mar. 1 She addressed a policeman as 'Meneer' (sir or mister) and he told her: 'If you call me "meneer" I won't speak to you. You know what you should call me.' **1982** M. MZAMANE *Children of Soweto* 182 'Yes sir.' 'Yes, what?' the younger man asked. 'Yes, *Meneer*.' ... 'Yes, what?' 'Yes, *Baas*.' **1990** F. BATES in *Style* Oct. 76 That's when I decided I wanted out. '*Meneer*,' I said in what I hoped was *suiwer* Afrikaans, 'I would prefer to drive back and sleep at the side of the road.' **1992** *Living* Feb. 82 'Pack out everything including your pockets please Meneer,' said the youngster.

3. MIJNHEER sense 2.

1936 C. BIRKBY *Thirstland Treks* 146 *Meneer* the magistrate says that there are hundreds of other men like me. [**1958** A. JACKSON *Trader on Veld* 33 When Meneer die Predikant turned up in person in his rounds .. there was a period of intensive worship.]

4. MIJNHEER sense 5.

1949 H.C. BOSMAN *Cold Stone Jug* (1969) 22 Didn't meneer perhaps think, with that funny smell about, that the body of some prison officer might be lying there under those sacks? Didn't meneer smell something dead. **1987** L. BEAKE *Strollers* 87 'Meneer,' he said slowly. 'Can Meneer help that small madboy.' **1990** *Frontline* Mar.-Apr. 22 'If Meneer would like to stop for a minute,' he says, 'I'd like to buy Meneer a cooldrink.' **1990** M.C. D'ARCY in *Staffrider* Vol.9 No.1, 13 'What does *Meneer* want?' 'I'd like to know where I can find someone who knows all about the coons and their organizations.' '*Meneer* wants to join?'

5. MIJNHEER sense 6.

1980 *Sunday Times* 31 Aug. (Extra) 3 Our domineetype tells Fred that he will be away for 20 minutes ... Fred says .. he will hold the fort while the Meneer is away. **1981** *Voice* 29 Apr. 2 You'll remember that some outstanding meneers .. made an unsuccessful attempt to get their voices heard at New York's Security Council of the United Nations.

‖**mens** /mens, mẽs/ *n.* and *int.* Formerly also **mensch.** Pl. **-e** /-ə/; formerly **menschen** and occas. **menser.** [Afk., earlier Du. (obs.) *mensch* person.]

A. *n.*

1. *obs.*

a. Usu. in *pl.*: Afrikaners. Cf. CHRISTENMENSCH sense c. See also VOLK sense 3 b.

1871 J. MACKENZIE *Ten Yrs* (1971) 65 'Menschen' is used by Dutch colonists of themselves, to the exclusion not only of black people, but of Europeans also. [**1937** B.H. DICKE *Bush Speaks* 43 Why should he, being merely an 'uitlander,' be permitted to loot? If one of 'Onse Mense' (our people – meaning Transvaal Boers) had been looting, it could be overlooked and forgiven.]

b. A white person. Cf. CHRISTENMENSCH sense b.

1960 J. COPE *Tame Ox* 69 Mogamat said .. : 'The white people are a lot of —y swine!' ... There were two white people in the room but he was not thinking of them, he was thinking of the 'mense' in general ... He had a voice for the 'mense', a whine; he had a flicker in the eyes for them and a quick touch of his cap as a gesture.

2. Usu. in *pl.*

a. People, human beings; ordinary people.

1871 [see VOLK sense 2]. **1899** G.H. RUSSELL *Under Sjambok* 57 'The groote Baas is an Englishman' came the voice, 'and I believe him; the Boer menser lie, they all lie, and if the Baas was one I would not do it.' **1913** A.B. MARCHAND *Dirk, S. African* 270 (Swart), It was a bitter world and hard to be a mensch. **1955** L.G. GREEN *Karoo* 13 '*Mense*!' someone would shout in excitement as the car rumbled up. 'People!' **1981** C. BARNARD in *Daily Dispatch* 6 July 6 Just spend a goodly part of student years stitching up endless scalps, arms or hands .. and keep talking to the 'mense' at every opportunity. **1990** 'K. LEMMER' in *Weekly Mail* 30 Mar. 13 Local MP's renamed the roads – after themselves, naturally. The *mense*, in response, were not just content to paint them out. New names were also painted in.

b. Family members.

1963 A.M. LOUW *20 Days* 90 She had said that her 'mense' – her people – had dinner early and that she was usually finished with the washing up by half past seven.

3. Usu. in *pl.*: A term of address.

1982 *Pace* June 46 For all Manana's tiny prettiness one gets the impression that the matter is unlikely to remain in this unsatisfactory state. Grr, watch it, mense. **1982** *Voice* 6 June 4 It's only time that will say 'now I am ready mense to respond positively'. **1985** *Vula* Oct. 46 Please mense respect the message. People risk detention and arrest to get it to you. **1988** SMUTS & ALBERTS *Forgotten Highway* 132 An old custom from that time of territorial separation survives today: such people, especially in the desolate Karoo, address others as '*mens*'. 'Sir', 'Baas' or 'you' would either be too intimate or too subservient and therefore this extra-ordinary form of address evolved.

B. *int.* An exclamation used for emphasis, and equivalent to 'goodness'.

1986 S. SEPAMLA *Third Generation* 8, I dared not cross her path because she could lash violently with her ageing tongue. *Mense*! Mmabatho had a tongue.

mensetaal /'me(:)nsətɑ:l, -ta:l/ *n. slang.* [Afk., *mense* people('s) + *taal* language.] Esp. in township parlance: FLAAITAAL. Also *attrib.*

1963 WILSON & MAFEJE *Langa* 23 He uses a mixture of Afrikaans and Xhosa slang – indeed the language of the *tsotsis* in Johannesburg, *mensetaal*, is said to be identical with that of white 'ducktails', and in Cape Town tsotsi and 'ducktail' speech approximates. *Ibid.* 41 He likes to speak the *mensetaal*, the jargon of the young townees. **1979** B. MFENYANA *Neo-Sintu: Dynamic Challenge* 1, I found it difficult to choose from a myriad of terms like Township Sintu Talk, Black

Slang, 'Mensetaal', 'Flytaal', 'Tsotsitaal', 'Lingo'.. and 'Black European Vernacular'. **1981** — in M. Mutloatse *Reconstruction* 301 A last word: on dictionary-making. Has township lingo accumulated enough vocab to warrant the compilation of 'A Mensetaal Dictionary'? **1988** K. SOLE in *Staffrider* Vol.7 No.1, 82 His use of different regional forms of *mensetaal* also points to his understanding that the use of English must be extended in South Africa to embrace a wider reading and listening public.

mephepha var. MAPHEPHA.

Meraai /mə'raɪ/ *n. Derog.* and *offensive.* [Afk., ad. of the female given name *Maria*.] **a.** A woman of Cape Malay descent; a 'coloured' woman. **b.** A given name for a stereotypical Cape Malay folk-figure, often as the subject of jokes. Cf. GAMMAT sense 1.

1970 S.E. NATHAN *Informant, Cape Town* Meraai. Malay or Coloured girl. **1974** [see Drum quot. at GAMMAT sense 1]. **1987** *Scope* 20 Nov. 42 You go down and show them this. Tell them the switch is booby-trapped — if anyone tries to rip it off me, boom! Goodbye Meraai.

mere-cat var. MEERCAT.

merogo var. MOROGO.

merrem /'merəm/ *n.* Also **mêrrem**, and with initial capital. [Pronunciation-spelling of MADAM, reflecting esp. the accent of working-class 'coloured' people.]
1. A common noun: MADAM sense 2.

1966 VAN HEYNINGEN & BERTHOUD Uys Krige 122 The exact tone and accent of the vendor's 'Capey' Afrikaans, the tone of his relationship with the white 'Merrem,' with the Colored servants. **1978** P.-D. UYS in S. Gray *Theatre One* 134 Yes! No, sorry dear, she's just died! (puts down phone) 'Can I speak to the Mêrrem?' Not even 'please'! *Ibid.* My maid calls me 'darling'! That 'Mêrrem' means more than just the old bag whose broeks they wash. **1980** [see RONDLOPER]. **1986** D. CASE *Love, David* 11 'You've been listening to too much of your *merrem's* talk again,' Dadda says irritably.
2. A term of address.
a. MADAM sense 1 a.

1979 *Sunday Times* 15 July (Mag. Sect.) 5 Here Mêrrem, up to my tits in the ice-cold water to collect these flowers and the Mêrrem complains about the quality. **1990** S. BOJÈ in M. Leveson *Firetalk* 162 'You've been lying with the sun on your head, my girl.' 'Haai merrem, never! Merrem come see for self!' **1993** C. EDEN in *Food & Home* Aug. 138 'Come merrem, take the box.' If merrem still holds out, Pantie rolls his eyes and sighs. 'OK, merrem, I give you a bargain. Half a box.'
b. MADAM sense 1 b.

1979, 1990 [see above].
3. MADAM sense 3.

1993 C. EDEN in *Food & Home* Aug. 138 He loads 10 into a packet, names a sum a little more than half the original price, and hands them to merrem with such urgency that she can't possibly refuse the transaction. **1993** *Ibid.* [see sense 2 a].

merula, meruley, meruli varr. MARULA.

mesem /mə'zem/ *n. colloq.* Also **mesemb**, and with initial capital. [Shortened form of genus name *Mesembryanthemum*, 'first coined by Jacob Breyne in 1689 to convey the meaning "noon-flowering" from the Greek "mesembria" meaning midday; it was adopted by Linnaeus when he founded the genus.' (D. Court, *Succulent Flora of Sn Afr.*, 1981, p.31).] VYGIE. Also *attrib.*

1928 H.M.L. BOLUS *Notes on Mesembrianthemum* I. 7 By far the larger number .. are at the height of their glory when the sun is hottest. They are what might be called the 'normal Mesembs'. *Ibid.* 67 In these days everyone who observes flowers at all is familiar with the meaning of 'vijgie', 'Mesemb.' or even the formidable *Mesembrianthemum* or 'noon-flower'. **1934** C.P. SWART *Supplement to Pettman.* 184 *Vingerkanna*, .. The common name of Hymenocylus Smithii, a species of mesem. **1965** S. ELIOVSON *S. Afr. Wild Flowers for Garden* 287 There is scarcely a garden in South Africa that has not known the beauty and brilliance of the flowers of the *mesemb* or *vygie* in the spring. **1979** *Daily Dispatch* 25 Oct. 19 A blaze of many-coloured lampranthus and related plants of the 'mesem' or vygie family. **1985** [see SUURVY]. **1988** M. BRANCH *Explore Cape Flora* 18 They [sc. vygies] are succulents with fleshy leaves, and belong to the family Mesembryanthemaceae – 'mesems' for short – which means 'midday flower'. **1991** D.M. MOORE *Garden Earth* 195 'Mesems' (succulents of the family Aizoaceae), .. include *Mesembryanthemum*, with its daisylike flowers in brilliant pinks, oranges and yellows.

messenger *n.* Also with initial capital. [Prob. tr. S. Afr. Du. *bode (van de hof)* messenger (of the court); but cf. Brit. Eng. *messenger* 'a government official employed to deliver dispatches' (*OED*).] In full *messenger of the court*: an officer of a magistrate's court responsible for the execution of orders of that court.

1810 G. BARRINGTON *Acct of Voy.* 180 The next step is to apply for a commission, consisting of the Landrost, two members of the Council, the Secretary of the district, and a messenger. **1872** E. ROBERTSON *Hist. Essays* 114 The Bode or messenger of the Court. **1972** V.G. HIEMSTRA in *Std Encycl. of Sn Afr.* VII. 345 *Messenger of the Court*, Official who is responsible for the serving of process of the magistrate's court and for the execution of orders of that court, including attachment of goods in civil cases and sales in execution ... The process of the Water Court is also served by the Messenger of the Court. **1986** *Reader's Digest Family Guide to Law* 227 All magistrates' courts have members of staff called messengers of the court ... A messenger of the court is obliged to execute 'without avoidable delay' all processes handed to him by the clerk of the court.

mest var. MIS.

Met /met/ *n.* [Short for *Metropolitan Handicap*.] *The Met*: A horse race carrying a large stake and run annually at the Kenilworth race-course in Cape Town. Also *attrib.*

1960 D. MARAIS *Europeans Only*, (caption), I just want somebody to place me a small bet on the Met. **1983** E. *Prov. Herald* 22 Jan. 1 Debbie .. married Basil on St Valentine's day .. after his magnificent Met victory on Foveros. **1987** *Sunday Times* 12 Apr. 1 It's Met time.

‖**methi** /'meθi, 'meti/ *n.* Also **methee, meti, mettie.** [Hindi and Urdu.] Esp. among South Africans of Indian descent: fenugreek. Also *attrib.*

1950 H. GERBER *Cape Cookery* 126 Fenugreek is obtainable in Indian shops under the name of meti. **1961** Z. MAYAT *Indian Delights* 134 Pumpkin Curry ... ¼tsp methi seed (fenugreek) salt to taste 1 cup water. **1977** *Fair Lady* 20 July, (advt) Methee, Turmeric, Fennel [etc.]. **1980** *Argus* 28 Aug. 3 Three large onions if a kilo of fish is to be curried and sunflower oil is used – to which half a teaspoon of mettie (fenugreek) is added when the oil is hot. **1985** T. SHABALALA in *Drum* Sept. 70, 4 bay leaves 1 teaspoon mustard seeds 1 teaspoon methi (fenugreek) seeds 1 teaspoon jheera (cumin seeds).

Methode Cap Classique /me‚θɒd ‚kap kla'si:k/ *n. phr.* [Fr., *méthode* method + *Cap* Cape (see CAPE) + *classique* classic.] Bottle-fermented sparkling wine (*méthode champenoise*) produced in South Africa; CAP CLASSIQUE. See also CAPE WINE.

1992 I. VON HOLDT in *Sunday Times* 6 Sept. 13 The tasters thought that Methode Cap Classique (the new name for methode champenoise bubbly from the Cape) was impressive. **1992** P. DEVEREUX in *Style* Nov. 26 Cape bottle-fermented bubblies (now called Methode Cap Classique seeing France is huffed with folk using the term 'Méthode Champenoise') are indeed generally an astonishment to knowledgeable winelovers. *c*1992 J. PLATTER **1993** *S. Afr. Wine Guide* 14 *Methode Cap Classique* (MCC), New – from 1992 – South African term to describe sparkling wines made by the classic French 'méthode Champenoise' (MC).

meti var. METHI.

metsha var. UKUMETSHA.

mettie var. METHI.

‖**mevrou** /mə'frʌʊ, 'mʌfrəʊ/ *n.* Also (esp. formerly) **mevrouw, mi(j) vrouw, mynfrau, mynvrou, myvrou(w).** Pl. **mevroue,** (formerly) **mynvrouwen.** [Afk., fr. Du. *mevrouw*.] Among speakers of Afrikaans (or, formerly, of Dutch): 'Mrs'; 'mistress'; 'madam'. See also VROU. Cf. MENEER.
I. A form of address.
1.a. A respectful term of address in the third person (avoiding the pronoun 'you'), a convention used by Dutch- and Afrikaans-speakers when addressing superiors, older people, and strangers.

1797 LADY A. BARNARD in Lord Lindsay *Lives of Lindsays* (1849) III. 409, I cannot convince the cooks that so great a lady as 'my vrouw' understands anything of the kitchen. **1910** D. FAIRBRIDGE *That Which Hath Been* (1913) 79 Does Mevrouw like it too and – and your daughter? **1974** D. ROOKE *Margaretha de la Porte* 219 When he scored a bull's eye, he called out to me: 'For Mevrouw!' and bowed elegantly. **1990** R. GOOL *Cape Town Coolie* 97 'Couldn't we have the little old, little one?' 'If *mevrou* wishes.'
b. A polite or formal term of address: 'Madam'.

1862 LADY DUFF-GORDON *Lett. from Cape* (1925) 89 Wished 'Vrolyke tydings, Mevrouw', most heartily. **1910** 'R. DEHAN' *Dop Doctor* 297 Little Dierck will have something worse than the belly-ache, and you also, if you eat of broth or vegetables cooked in a vessel as unclean as that, mevrouw. **1910** D. FAIRBRIDGE *That Which Hath Been* (1913) 195 You cannot believe, mevrouw, the lengths to which some of these ungentle ladies go. **1915** — *Torch Bearer* 169 Excuse me, mynvrouwen, but I must send a letter to the post. **1926** V.L. CAMERON *Reverse Shield* 18 'It's all right, mij vrouw,' she said kindly, in Afrikaans, 'You are among friends.' **1936** C. BIRKBY *Thirstland Treks* 57, I listened for a while, and then called: 'Mevrou, is this Bowesdorp?' **1966** I. VAUGHAN *These Were my Yesterdays* 89 Says to me, 'Good morning Mevrouw.' Say, 'Good morning Mynheer — may I ask how old you are.' **1986** F. KARODIA *Daughters of Twilight* 27 'Mevrou,' Hermanus said, speaking directly to her. 'I will have your window replaced.'
II. A title.
2.a. As a respectful term of reference, used without the definite article, as if a name: 'Madam,' 'mistress'.

1862 LADY DUFF-GORDON *Lett. from Cape* (1925) 111 There is a fine handsome Van Steen, who is very persevering; but Sally does not want to fancy becoming Mevrouw at all. **1882** J. NIXON *Among Boers* 203 He refers you to 'mevrouw,' who, after turning the matter over carefully, comes to the conclusion that she can spare a leg of meat, i.e. mutton. **1926** P. SMITH *Beadle* (1929) 40 Preparations for these guests .. kept Mevrouw busy in her kitchen with Andrina in constant attendance upon her there. **1955** V.M. FITZROY *Dark Bright Land* 121 Mevrou appealed to her husband when she found him at her side, to back up her statement. **1965** D. ROOKE *Diamond Jo* 32 Van der Spuyt got his shot-gun while Mevrouw wrung her hands and wept. **1976** A. DELIUS *Border* 286 Camping here for the night, with a large cold-mutton joint given us by Myvrouw to feast upon. **1990** R. GOOL *Cape Town Coolie* 97 When she explained that she was a schoolteacher, he was impressed and began to call her *mevrou* ... 'Give for mevrou one from that *hottentot*,' the fisherman said.
b. With a surname: 'Mrs', 'mistress'.

1910 D. FAIRBRIDGE *That Which Hath Been* (1913) 183 Large sash windows each containing innumerable little panes of glass — Mevrouw Huysing's alternate pride and despair. **1920** R. JUTA *Tavern* 17 Mynfrau de

Wahl .. was one of the few Dutch ladies to brave the morning sun. **1955** V.M. FITZROY *Dark Bright Land* 31 Good myvrou Luckhoff keeps me comfortable and full fed. **1968** G. CROUDACE *Silver Grass* 28 The Dixons, father and son, shared the mutton stew that *Mevrouw* van der Bos had prepared. **1974** M. BALL in *E. Prov. Herald* 27 Nov. 37 Did not return to the Cape for 11 years. Then it was to visit Mevrou van Niekerk, who had once been their nearest neighbour. **1988** D. HIRSON in Bunn & Taylor *From S. Afr.* 100 Mevrou Duplessis in an orange polka-dot apron waves Totsiens to them all from the front door.

III. A common noun.

3. An Afrikaans woman, esp. an employer. Cf. MADAM sense 2.

1960 J. COPE *Tame Ox* 170 They would be a little tired rushing to and fro, waiting on the white people. He had seen his mevrou leave earlier in the evening. **1990** *Sunday Times* 25 Mar. 6 'What would I like after independence,' she asks. 'That when I go work for my mevrou, she looks at me like I'm a person' ... Someone will still sell swastikas. And plenty of people will still work for the mevrou.

mfana var. UMFAAN.

mfazi var. UMFAZI.

Mfecane /əmfeˈkɑːni, m̩feˈlaːne/ *n. hist.* Also with small initial. [ad. Xhosa *iimfecane* marauders (sing. *imfecane*), perh. ad. Sotho *difaqane*, see DIFAQANE.] ***The Mfecane***: The large-scale dispersal of groups of northern NGUNI people during the early 19th century to the south, north, and west of present-day KwaZulu-Natal, which led to the displacement or impoverishment of neighbouring people; the resultant wars and battles; the period during which this upheaval took place; DIFAQANE; FETCANI sense 2; IMFECANE sense 2. Also *attrib.*

The Mfecane has usu. been attributed to there having been insufficient land to accommodate the Zulu nation (which its leader, Shaka, was forcibly consolidating at the time), so that certain groups, unable to defend themselves against his large regiments and innovative strategies, but unwilling to accept him as their ruler, were forced to move away. Latterly, however, this interpretation has been challenged by scholars who note that the political consolidation of groups in Natal was influenced by environmental factors such as drought, and by the increased ivory and cattle trade with Portuguese traders (see quot. 1990).

1928 E.A. WALKER *Hist. of S. Afr.* 226 Moshesh's claims were wide. Northward they embraced a large belt of territory right across to the Vaal on the ground that the remains of the tribes which occupied it before the *Mfecane* were now under his rule in Basutoland awaiting an opportunity to reoccupy it. **1966** J.D. OMER-COOPER *Zulu Aftermath* 172 Probably the most striking political change brought about by the *Mfecane* is the change from the small clan-based tribe to the large kingdom uniting peoples of diverse tribal origin. **1972** [see FETCANI sense 2]. **1977** T.R.H. DAVENPORT *S. Afr.: Mod. Hist.* 10 Known in Sotho as the *Difaqane* ('hammering'), and in Nguni languages as the *Mfecane* ('crushing' ..) it was a cataclysmic event ... The Mfecane scattered African chiefdoms in fragments across half the continent of Africa. **1980** J. COCK *Maids & Madams* 201 The Mfecane or dispersal of the African tribes westwards by the rising Zulu tribe .. provided the Cape with significant numbers of black agricultural and domestic servants. **1981** J.B. PEIRES *House of Phalo* 85 War [between Thembu and Xhosa] was avoided only by the need to join forces against the Mfecane invaders. *Ibid.* 138 The wars of the Mfecane, in which people like the Bhaca fought for the sustenance of life itself were appreciably bloodier. **1983** [see MFENGU]. **1988** *NELM News* (Nat. Eng. Lit. Museum) May, Many historians hold that the Boer migration was a marginal affair in comparison with the vast upheavals in the demography of the indigenous population produced by the Mfecane. **1989** *Reader's Digest Illust. Hist.* 88 Shaka was one of the principal players in the drama of the *Mfecane*, an upheaval among the Nguni people of South-eastern Africa that rippled its way north, west and eastwards as displaced groups fought for the land on which they could graze their cattle and grow their crops. **1990** *Weekly Mail* 8 June 5 The argument presented is that the *mfecane* was a social revolution in Southern Africa, leading to the creation of new states, which was set off by the Zulu king Shaka, in a bid to seize control over a limited amount of resources in the context of an increasing population. Articles over the past five years .. have challenged this interpretation and referred to the *mfecane* as a colonial myth ... The slave trade at Delgoa Bay and the labour demands from the Cape Colony .. led to the subsequent upheavals. **1992** N. MOSTERT in *Natal Mercury* 25 Nov. 8 Conventional history attributed the entire military and social revolution to the rise of Shaka and gave a name to it, *mfecane*, 'the crushing'. It was seen as virtually one seamless event, which modern research disputes.

Mfengu /m̩ˈfe(ː)ŋgu, əm-/ *n.* Also **Fengu**. Pl. unchanged, **Ama(m)fengu**, or **-s**. [In the Nguni languages, (pl. prefix AMA- +) *mfengu* 'destitute wanderers seeking work and refuge', fr. *fenguza* to seek service; see quots 1850 and 1912.] A member of a Xhosa-speaking people descended from the remnants of several refugee groups displaced during the MFECANE, and who settled in the eastern Cape and southern Transkei during the 1830s; FINGO sense a; MBO sense 3. Also *attrib.* See also HLUBI.

Many Mfengu escaped serfdom among other black peoples by seeking protection from and alliances with whites (often serving during wars as British levies), for which they were rewarded with grants of land. Also *attrib.*

1850 J.W. APPLEYARD *Kafir Lang.* 41 The term *Amafengu* is a conventional national epithet, first applied to the Fingoes by the Kafirs, but now in general use amongst themselves. The root from which it is derived is *fenguza*, and signifies to 'seek service,' implying, at the same time, the total destitution of the person who uses it. The word *amafengu* will accordingly mean, 'destitute people in search of service,' and correctly characterizes their condition when they arrived amongst the Kafirs. **1855** J.W. COLENSO *Ten Weeks in Natal* 146 The Fingoes .. took refuge with Hintza and his people, who called them *ama-Fengu*, 'miserables or paupers,' and, though Kafirs themselves, made slaves of their black brethren. **1860** W. SHAW *Story of my Mission* 525 The refugees .. were called *Fingoes*, or 'Amamfengu,' — a designation referring to their abject and forlorn condition, as driven from their country and seeking refuge among strangers. **1882** J. NIXON *Among Boers* 94 Natal was originally inhabited by the Amafengu and kindred tribes, who were driven southwards by the Zulus under T'Chaka. **1902** *Encycl. Brit.* XXX. 3 The formerly degraded but now respected and civilized Fingos or Fengus, who gave their name to the district of Fingoland. **1912** AYLIFF & WHITESIDE *Hist. of Abambo* 15 When the fugitives entered lower Kaffirland they were asked, 'Who are you? What do you want?' They replied, 'Siyam Fenguza,' which means 'We seek service'. 'We are destitute.' The word *Amafengu* therefore means 'hungry people in search of work'. **1975** W.F. LYE *Andrew Smith's Jrnl 1834–6* Index, *AmaMfengu*, Refugee Nguni peoples who fled from the Northern Nguni country during the rise of the Zulu and sought a home amongst the Southern Nguni. **1977** F.G. BUTLER *Karoo Morning* 84 What would have happened if the Fingos, or Mfengu, had not stayed loyal to the whites, God alone knows. **1980** *Report of Ciskei Commission* 141 It was through the political manoeuvres of D'Urban and Smith that the Mfengu tribal cluster (Zulu fugitives) was incited against the Xhosa both in the Transkei and Ciskei. **1983** C. SAUNDERS *Hist. Dict.* 108 *Mfengu*, .. It is said that the scattered remnants of various Nguni groups (Hlubi, Zizi, Bhele and others), broken up and disrupted by the Mfecane, introduced themselves to the Xhosa of the Transkei in the 1820s by saying 'siyamfenguze' ('we are hungry and seek shelter'). **1985** W.F. TABATA in *Probe* July 26 The presence of amaMfengu in that area was vital for the defence of Fort Peddie and they were essential intelligence-gatherers for the Cape Colony rulers. **1986** P. MAYLAM *Hist. of Afr. People* 61 The inferior, dependent status associated with clientage soon rankled with many Mfengu, and they increasingly looked towards Cape colonial society as an avenue for their advancement. **1990** J. COLLINGE in *Weekly Mail* 8 Feb. 12 The Tsitsikamma land from which the Mfengu were removed at gunpoint in 1977 may soon be on the market again.

mfesi /m̩ˈfeːzi, əm-/ *n.* Also **m'fesi**, **m'fezi**, and with initial capital. [Zulu *imfezi*.] The spitting cobra *Naja nigricollis* of the Elapidae. Also *attrib.*

In B. Branch's *Field Guide to Snakes & other Reptiles* (1988), the name 'black-necked spitting cobra' is used for this species.

1955 P.A. CHRISTENSEN *S. Afr. Snake Venoms* 81 M'fesi venom is too difficult to obtain in South Africa to make large-scale production of specific antiserum a practical proposition. **1962** V.F.M. FITZSIMONS *Snakes of Sn Afr.* 37 Cobras that 'spit' or squirt their venom ... The Rinkals .. and the Black-necked Spitting Cobra or Mfesi. **1978** C.L. REITZ *Poisonous S. Afr. Snakes* 16 The m'fezi is mainly nocturnal and prefers areas near water. Its bite is very dangerous ... It is able to spit from virtually any position, not only from the reared-up position.

mfino var. IMIFINO.

mfo /ˈm̩fɔ/ *n. colloq.* Pl. **bafo**. [Zulu, see MFOWETHU.] Among speakers of Sintu (Bantu) languages: MFOWETHU sense 1. So **mfondini** [Zulu, *mfo* + *-ndini* (suffix indicating affection)], 'dear brother'.

1976 M. THOLO in C. Hermer *Diary of Maria Tholo* (1980) 82 The watchman wanted his money back ... He said to Mr. Gaga, 'Mfo, you told me three months. Well, .. I want my money back.' **1979** M. MATSHOBA *Call Me Not a Man* 9 South Africa! A cruel, cruel world with nothing but a slow death for us. I hate it, *mfo*, I hate it! **1987** S.D. TIRIVANHU in *New Coin Poetry* June 26 Mfondini how i miss home. **1987** M. MATSHOBA in *New Nation* 10 Dec. 14 Monde grinned and greeted: 'How's it mfo?' The other one grunted, 'Sweet,' and sheepishly returned the grin. **1990** M.B. KUMALO in *Sunday Times* 22 July 16 (*letter*) Mr Ray de V— claims: 'I am now happy to call him *Bafo*, which means brother'. Without giving linguistic reasons, what Mr de V— means is *Mfo* when addressing one brother, as against Bafo when addressing two or more brothers. **1990** M. MELAMU in *Lynx* 274 Mfo, what happened?

‖**mfowethu** /ˌm̩fɔˈweːtʊ/ *n. colloq.* Pl. **bafowethu**. [Zulu, vocative of *umfowethu* (pl. vocative *bafowethu*), *umfo* brother, kinsman + *wethu* our, 'my'.] Among speakers of Sintu (Bantu) languages:

1. 'My brother,' a term of address; MFO. Cf. BRA sense 1.

1979 F. DIKE *First S. African*, Hayi Kona Max mfowethu, I'm not a coward, do what you like .. do it now. **1979** M. MATSHOBA *Call Me Not a Man* 145 One needs something cool to drink. Here's a beer and a brandy, *bafowethu*. *Ibid.* 195 Give him the five cents, *mfowethu*. **1980** — in M. Mutloatse *Forced Landing* 106 Say it again, *mfowethu*. We are all used to it at one time or another of our lives. **1982** *Pace* Nov. 47 But mfowethu, do you think these days it's easy to get away with controversial rulings like that one? **1987** *Ibid.* June 4 Tell me, mfowethu, say you had been allowed to vote in the mlungu general elections, which party would you have made your X for? **1994** D. KANDLOVU in *Sidelines* Dec. 23 Mfowethu, it was on July 14, 1990, when we woke up to find the hostel surrounded by hundreds of children bent on destruction.

2. As a common noun: a close friend.

1987 O. MUSI in *Drum* June 58 Hau, I sympathised with him, treating him like mfowethu; after all he even knew my clan-name, knew our chief way back home and sounded genuine.

m'fundis, mfundisi, -dizi varr. UMFUNDISI.

m'gog var. MAGOGO.

mgqashiyo /m̩ɬa'ʃi:yɔ/ *n. Music.* Also **mqhashiyo**. [Zulu *umgqashiyo*, Xhosa *umqhashiyo*, fr. *gqashiya* (Zulu), *qhashiya* (Xhosa), to dance attractively, to dance in a modern style.] A style of popular music featuring close-harmony singing (usu. by a three- or four-woman group) of traditional or neo-traditional African (esp. Zulu) songs set to MBAQANGA rhythms and instrumentation. Also *attrib.* Cf. SIMANJE-MANJE.

The style became popular in the 1960s.

1976 *World* 14 Sept. 8 Mahotella Queens are pioneers of a music which later came to be called mgqashiyo. This music was taken from traditional pieces, given a new lease of life for urban consumption. **1976** N. KA MNYAYIZA in *New Classic* No.3, 27 Mgqashiyo is the in-music. **1978** *Pace* Dec. 44 The Dark City Sisters of 'Tamati yoyo' fame pioneered the 'mqhashiyo' close-harmony groups. **1988** J. KHUMALO in *Ibid.* May 7 At the centre of this new-found enthusiasm about South Africa's music is Paul Simon, whom Joe regards as the man who modernised Mgqashiyo. **1990** *Weekly Mail* 21 Dec. (Suppl.) 31 We have seen the delightful combination of Zulu street-guitar, *mbube*, *mgqashiyo* (the return of the female-contingent) and 1950s-style 'groaning' as espoused by the Lion of Soweto and his Queens make its way into the .. British pop-world via the new Art of Noise disc.

‖**mhlekazi** /m̩ɬe'ga:zi/ *n.* [In Nguni languages, the vocative of *umhlekazi.*] Among speakers of the Nguni languages: an honorific, 'Your Excellency'.

1979 F. DIKE *First S. African* 3 Nkosi, the birth certificate ... Do you think it will be alright ... I mean at Native Affairs? .. Nkosi, please mhlekazi, I beg of you, don't make my child suffer, he does not deserve it. **1983** *Pace* Oct. 174 Mhlekazi, Sir, I greet you in the honourable name of trade unionism and crime. **1986** G. DLUKULA in *Pace* Mar. 78 Mhlekazi! Comrade! I greet you in the Holy name of our Lord, in the name of your stunning rise to prominence.

michi var. MIETJIE.

middelman /'mɪdlman, -mæn/ *n.* [fr. Afk. *middelmannetjie.*] MIDDELMANNETJIE. Also part. tr. **middleman**.

1937 L. LEIPOLDT *Bushveld Doctor* 148 One has .. at times to take precautions against the central ridge, 'the middleman,' which is such an annoying feature of country roads everywhere in the Union. **1958** H. WICHT *Rd below Me* 77 The grass .. rose high on either side of the narrow road, while in the centre, the *middelman* — a foot-wide strip .. - was almost as high.

middelmannetjie /'məd(ə)l͵manəki, -ci/ *n.* Also part. tr. **middlemannetjie**. [Afk., *middel* middle + *man* man + dim. suffix -IE.] The ridge or hump between the wheel-ruts of an unsurfaced road or farm track; MIDDELMAN. Also *transf.*

1934 *Sunday Times* 18 Feb. (Swart), There is a strong agitation on foot here to keep donkey transport off the Johannesburg-Lichtenburg road because the wagons cut it up to such an extent that, when cars try to follow in their tracks the axles catch on the 'middel mannetjie'. **1936** C. BIRKBY *Thirstland Treks* 30 While the off-side wheels ploughed deep, the near wheels churned over the *middel-mannetjie*, the hump between the scores. **1937** — *Zulu Journey* 93 Rain had eaten away huge ruts ... There was a tall middelmannetjie that threatened sump and differential with disaster. **1965** J. BENNETT *Hawk Alone* 207 They were driving too fast along the narrow rutted road with its high sump-scraping middel-mannetjie. **1970** S. SPARKS *Informant, Fort Beaufort* Citroens are built specifically to negotiate the 'middelmannetjie' on farm roads (the ridge between the 2 wheel tracks). **1971** A. SCHOLEFIELD *Young Masters* 42 The car .. was moving gently along the pitted surface of a farm road, the long grass from the *middelmannetjie* swishing under the chassis. **1977** *Farmer's Weekly* 24 Aug. 59 Ground covers are ideal between stepping stones and as 'middel mannetjie' for the drive. **1985** *Cape Times* 20 June, It has a high clearance so is easy to drive on roads with high middlemannetjies. **1989** J. HOBBS *Thoughts in Makeshift Mortuary* 317 She drove too fast along the grassy road that ran through the trees, not caring that the car was scraping on the middelmannetjie. **1989** M. PALMER in *Grocott's Mail* 21 Mar. 1 The Bedford tarred road is breaking up to such a degree that it needs a grader to get rid of the 'middelmannetjie'. **1989** J. METCALF in *Edgars Club* July 11 Our chassis bottomed out on the middlemannetjie. **1991** *Sunday Times* 10 Mar. (Mag. Sect.) 2 The new Nissan Hi Rider. Designed around the middel-mannetjie. **1991** O. OBERHOLZER in *Time* 29 July 29 Lesotho was better than I expected. Lots of tracks with 'middelmannetjies'. (The bit in the middle where grass sometimes grows.)

middelskot /'məd(ə)lskɔt/ *n.* Pl. **-te** /-tə/. [Afk., *middel* middle + *skot* intermediate payment.] An intermediate payment for a crop or wool clip, made to a farmer between the initial payment (or VOORSKOT) and the final payment (or AGTERSKOT). Also *attrib.*, and (occas.) part. tr. **middleskot**.

1972 *E. Prov. Herald* 30 Sept. 8 The Wool Board could consider a 'middleskot' to set the position right, but then only if the market trend was unchanged or improved. **1972** *E. Prov. Herald* 31 Oct. 6 The Maize Board here announced that a middelskot (intermediate payment) of R15 per ton would be paid by the Maize Board to producers for buckwheat delivered during the 1972 season. **1972** *Cape Times* 9 Nov. 2 Buckwheat delivered during November and December will be purchased at the 'voorskot' price plus the 'middelskot' of R15,00 per ton. **1982** *Farmer's Weekly* 5 Nov. 103 Producers of three oil-seeds .. are receiving cheques totalling R18 million as a *middelskot* (intermediate payment) on their 1981-season deliveries to the Oilseeds Board ... The *middelskotte* per ton average R45 for groundnuts, R15 for sunflower seed and R30 for soybeans. **1985** *Cape Times* 7 Aug., The co-operative announced yesterday that interim 'middelskot' payments would total more than R1, 7m.

middleveld /'məd(ə)lfelt, -fɛlt/ *n.* Formerly also **middleveldt**; now freq. with initial capital. [Part. tr. Afk. *middelveld* (*middel* middle + *veld* open, undeveloped countryside).] That region between the HIGHVELD and the LOWVELD, mostly lying 600 to 1 200 metres above sea level and comprising a wide variety of vegetation and soil types. Also *attrib.*

One of the major southern African physiographic regions, the middleveld lies across the northern, north-western and north-eastern parts of the interior, and extends into neighbouring countries. The boundaries of the region, based mainly on altitude and prominent physical features, are not clearly defined.

1878 A. AYLWARD *Tvl of Today* 25 The same class of progress is everywhere visible .. in the nearer and more recently settled district called the 'Middleveld' of the Orange Free State. **1902** C. WARREN *On Veld in Seventies* 225 We arrived at a settlement station in the Middle Veldt, forty miles from Worcester, 2800 feet above it. **1926** M. NATHAN *S. Afr. from Within* 210 In the area, as in the Middle Veld (Barberton) and the western Bush Veld (Rustenburg and Waterberg), are the most suitable tracts for cultivation of citrus. **1931** *Discovery* Aug. 259 There are two cotton breeding stations in the Transvaal; one at Rustenberg, where problems connected with the improvement of cottons for middle-veld areas are dealt with. **1937** J. STEVENSON-HAMILTON *S. Afr. Eden* 111 It is fine open healthy country, about 3,000 feet above sea level, in what is known as 'middle veld'. **1955** J.H. WELLINGTON *Sn Afr.: Geog. Study* I. 72 These two regions .. have important points of dissimilarity, the chief of which are the greater altitude and humidity of the highveld and the greater areas of pre-Karoo surfaces in the middleveld. **1958** S. CLOETE *Mask* 92 They began to drop from the high country into the middle veld as the Boers called it, the land intermediate between the bitter highlands and the pestilential bush of the low country. **1959** [see FLORISBAD]. **1961** D. BEE *Children of Yesterday* 281 There had been no men here, no huts, no crops, no cattle. The middleveld had been a hard land then. **1972** *Farmer's Weekly* 21 Apr. 11 Normal dryland conditions in the Rhodesian middleveld. **1972** *Sunday Times* 21 May 15 (*advt*) In the tranquil, radiant warmth of the Transvaal Middleveld .. you become one with nature. **1988** N. RICHARDS in *Fair Lady* Mar. 96 Divided neatly into four strips — the highveld, middleveld, lowveld and Lubombo range — the scenery in Swaziland appears to do something different around every corner.

miel(i)e var. MEALIE.

mier-cat *n. obs.* [Part. tr. Afk. *mierkat*, see MIERKAT.] MEERKAT.

1897 'F. MACNAB' *On Veldt & Farm* 221 Different orders of hawks and owls also assist the work of destruction, and so it is said do hyenas, mier-cat, and, in fact, most of the cat tribe, who find locusts a delicious article of food. **1906** W.S. JOHNSON *Orangia* 16 The bright little mier-cat, not unlike a weasel, but much prettier and easily tamed.

mierkat /'mɪə(r)kæt, 'mi:rkat/ *n.* [Afk., calque formed on Du. *meerkat* (see MEERKAT), *mier* ant, termite + *kat* cat.] MEERKAT. Also *attrib.*

1901 O.E.A. SCHREINER *Thoughts on S. Afr.* (1923) 19 There was a possibility that the red African mier-kat might ultimately creep back into its hole in the red African earth. **1918** C. GARSTIN *Sunshine Settlers* 179 As we finished dinner, the dogs came home, bearing the corpse of a mierkat amongst them. **1937** C.R. PRANCE *Tante Rebella's Saga* 128 No other sign of life, save here and there a 'mierkat' like a ground-squirrel, bobbing out from his warren to stand upright. **1947** — *Antic Mem.* 132 The Commandant's pony had bolted across a 'mierkat' warren and turned a somersault. **1949** *Cape Argus* 3 Sept. (Mag. Sect.) 1 To most people it is just a 'mierkat', but in reality it is a rodent, a squirrel, and quite different from the insect-eating, slender-tailed mierkat that is to be found in the same vicinity. **1990** SKINNER & SMITHERS *Mammals of Sn Afr. Subregion* 490 Both *Suricata* and *Cynictis* are referred to as 'mierkat'; 'mier' = the Afrikaans for termite and 'kat' = mongoose; both species are associated with termite .. mounds in the Orange Free State.

mies /mis/ *n.* [Afk., shortened form of *miesies* (see MIESIES).]

a. As a title used with a name, esp. of an employer: 'Miss', 'Mistress'. Cf. MIESIES sense 2 b.

1963 A.M. LOUW *20 Days* 18 Hein had been an adoptive Hottentot boy ... Aia Meidjie had brought Hein at the age of two to be taught and reared by 'Mies Susanna'. **1964** J. MEINTJES *Manor House* 10 'Mies Julia,' she said to Mrs. Vorster, 'you must please go to the kitchen right now.' *Ibid.* 37 It's all Mies Julia's doing. Poor heart, she's taken the baas's death very badly. Maraai told me last night that Mies Julia seems to have become a bit funny in the head.

b. As a common noun: a white woman, esp. an employer; cf. MISSUS sense 1 a.

1978 *Speak* Vol.1 No.3, 26 '*Mies is die mies.*' Magda's tautology is not merely her own: it belongs to her position in the heart of her country. To the majority of those around her a 'mies' is a 'mies' is a 'mies', a definition needing no outside sphere of reference.

c. With qualifying word: **kleinmies** [Afk., *klein* small, young], NONNIE sense a; **oumies** [Afk., *ou* old], OUMISSUS sense b.

1970 D. PINCUS *Informant, Bloemfontein* The African called her madam **Kleinmies** as she was still very young. **1990** C. LAFFEATY *Far Forbidden Plains* 363 No, Nonnie. No. Your Mamma — the **Oumies** — she fall down dead.

miesies /'misi(:)s/ *n.* Also **missees, missies**, and with initial capital. [Afk., ad. Eng. *missus* (see MISSUS).]

1. As a common noun: MISSUS sense 1 a.

*c*1929 S. BLACK in S. Gray *Three Plays* (1984) 79 Der other day he got er accident — he fall on his mossels en I got such a pulpertation of der heart. If I didn' have der missees' smelling salts by me I would have been quite onderstebo. **1959** J. MEIRING *Candle in Wind* 167 Already a collection had been taken in the White Town, and there was a white Miesies up at the Church, with a big bath of hot soup. **1968** F.G. BUTLER *Cape Charade* 44 A person doesn't pick up such a miesies every day. And the pay is also good. **1973** Y. BURGESS *Life to Live* 34 The Baas had pinched her when the Miesies was not looking. **1974** *E. Prov. Herald* 30 Aug. 15 Van Zyl asked for a telephone directory, and phoned for an ambulance, explaining: 'The miesies is sick.' **1974** Y. BURGESS in S. Gray *On Edge of World* 21 Alida had stacked the breakfast dishes in a basin because the 'old Miesies' had always used a basin and Mieta had, like Alida, a respect for tradition. **1982** M. WA MMUTLE in Chapman & Dangor *Voices from Within* 167 My mother died a servant ... Wrapped in a shoal of bags Covered with rags from her Missies. **1989** [see sense 2]. **1990** *Weekend Argus* 14 July 13 Most of those fed on that racist diet now find it impossible to believe they are not .. superior to anyone ... They won't accept that the myth of baas and miesies was a figment of racist imagination. **1990** R. MALAN *My Traitor's Heart* 100 As the Homan's girl, Paulina was expected to cook, dust, wash dishes, make beds, polish shoes, clean windows, scrub floors, and mind the children while the baas and missies were at work.

2.a. A term of address to a (white) woman; also used in the third person, to show respect. **b.** A title for a (white) woman. Cf. MIES sense a, MISSUS sense 2.

1959 J. MEIRING *Candle in Wind* 25 'And what does the old Miesies want today?' the shopkeeper asked kindly. **1973** Y. BURGESS *Life to Live* 113 She was the one who came to me and said, Miesies, we have our children but we don't know how they will turn out because the wind bends the saplings. **1979** *Daily Dispatch* 9 Feb. 11 Miesies, I brought you the pumpkin to say thank you for giving my child money so that he would not lose his job. Thank you, miesies. **1986** F. KARODIA *Daughters of Twilight* 52 They did seem like nice people .. but I suppose eventually they'll also change and they'll become Baas Edward and Miesies Jill. After all, South Africa is the only country in the world where the term 'baas' is equated with colour. **1987** G. SILBER in *Style* Nov. 53 *Moderate black*, Fulltime domestic servant. 'Selina, isn't it terrible what these Comrades do to your people?' 'Yes Miesies.' **1987** *Learn & Teach* No.1, 22 I'm tired of hand-me-downs Shut-me-ups Keep-me-outs Messing-me-arounds. I have had enough from you, Miesies. **1989** J. HOBBS *Thoughts in Makeshift Mortuary* 279 He went up the back steps and knocked on the door. 'Can I have my pay now, Miesies?' ... 'I'd recommend you as a Miesies any day.'

mietjie *n. obs.* Also **michi**. [Afk., earlier S. Afr. Du. *mietje* onomatopoeic.] The KLAAS'S CUCKOO, *Chrysococcyx klaas*.

1853 *Edin. New Philos. Jrnl* (U.K.) IV. 82 The pretty notes of the *michi* and *diedrick*. **1867** E.L. LAYARD *Birds of S. Afr.* 250 *Chalcites Klaasii, Mietje* of Colonists. [**1936** E.L. GILL *First Guide to S. Afr. Birds* 108 The usual call of Klaas's Cuckoo is quite well represented by its Afrikaans name 'mietjie'.] **1939** [see DIEDERIK]. [**1984** G.L. MACLEAN *Roberts' Birds of Sn Afr.* 336 Afrikaans *meitjie* is onomatopoeic.]

miggie var. MUGGIE.

migrant *n.* Ellipt. for *migrant labourer* (see MIGRANT LABOUR).

1963 WILSON & MAFEJE *Langa* 47 For a migrant in town by far the most important group is that of his *abakhaya* or home-boys. **1978** *Randlords & Rotgut* (Junction Ave Theatre Co.) in S. Gray *Theatre Two* (1981) 121 The miners are still digging. The compounds are policed. The migrants still fulfill our needs. **1980** C. HERMER *Diary of Maria Tholo* 34 The Administration Board operated beerhalls selling 'jabulani' or 'bantu beer' mainly to migrants. **1987** *Rhodeo* (Rhodes Univ.) Mar. 10 'Stimela' a rich song about the train which carries migrants to work in the South African mines.

migrant labour *n. phr.* [Special use of general Eng.]

1. Often in the phr. ***migrant labour system***. The laws (many of which are no longer in force) and structures under which black contract labourers from rural areas, the 'homelands,' or neighbouring African states, were recruited to work in the cities and in the mines, usu. living without their families, often in single-sex hostels; MIGRATORY LABOUR sense 1.

1948 [see Report of Native Laws Commission quot. at TOGT sense 2]. **1952** B. DAVIDSON *Report on Sn Afr.* 95 The migrant labour system and starvation wages were fathered by Rhodes and his friends. **1984** E. MPHAHLELE *Afrika my Music* 10 Field husbandry has diminished considerably owing to the disruptive impact of the migrant-labour system and the lack of good land. **1985** PLATZKY & WALKER *Surplus People* 107 A further and necessary consequence of the policy of restricted African urbanisation was the entrenchment of the migrant labour system after 1948. **1986** *Nusas Talks to the ANC (pamphlet)* 25 A democratic state would have to control the mines if it were to end the migrant labour system, which they saw as one of the worst features of apartheid. **1987** *Learn & Teach* No.4, 3 The bosses must end migrant labour and allow workers and their families to live near their factories. **1990** *Sunday Times* 8 July 18 Migrant labour was not a creation of apartheid. It was started by the mine bosses in Johannesburg in the 1890s to secure cheap labour for the gold mines.

2. The black labour force working within this system, or in a situation resulting from this system; MIGRATORY LABOUR sense 2. Also *attrib.*

1986 P. MAYLAM *Hist. of Afr. People* 145 Until recently the Rand mines have been heavily dependent on the supply of migrant labour from South Africa's political boundaries. **1987** *New Nation* 5 Mar. 5 The campaign against appalling living conditions in the SA Transport services migrant labour hostels continues to gain momentum.

Hence **migrant labourer** *n. phr.*, a black worker employed within the migrant labour system; MIGRANT; cf. GODUKA.

1952 P. ABRAHAMS in *Drum* July 11 How much more can the hearts of those who rule 'us' be hardened? And what difference can it make to the lot of your migrant labourer, to your farm worker on the 'Bethals' of this land? **1963** M. BENSON *Afr. Patriots* 77 Migrant labourers usually remained barely educated and within a tribal fold. **1980** C. HERMER *Diary of Maria Tholo* 4 Migrant labourers could work in Cape Town on a yearly contract but had to return to the homeland between each contract. **1984** E. MPHAHLELE *Afrika my Music* 176 There are no apartment houses for Africans in South Africa. Single male hostels for migrant labourers, yes — dormitory style. **1986** P. MAYLAM *Hist. of Afr. People* 145 In the twentieth century the flow of migrant labourers to the Rand mines continued to increase dramatically.

migratory labour *n. phr.*

1. Usu. in the phr. ***migratory labour system***: MIGRANT LABOUR sense 1.

1952 B. DAVIDSON *Report on Sn Afr.* 94 Migratory labour .. has been .. condemned by official investigators. **1982** D. TUTU *Voice of One* 80 The anguished cries of black mothers and children, left behind in an unviable, barren 'homeland', trying to eke out a miserable existence in some rural backwater, because South Africa's economy is based on the Migratory Labour system. **1989** *Weekly Mail* 3 Feb. 12 The migratory labour system has not only given rise to violence, it has resulted in the suppression of the fundamental human rights that are the hallmarks of successful business enterprises and societies worldwide.

2. MIGRANT LABOUR sense 2.

1985 *S. Afr. Panorama* June 35 It was on the Kimberley diamond mines that the system of employing migratory labour from the Black homelands was introduced for the first time, later to spread to all of the country's gold and other mines.

‖**mijnheer** /meɪnˈhɪə(r)/ *n. Obs.* exc. *hist.* Also **meinheer, mi(j)nheer, m'nheer, myn(h)eer**, and with initial capital. Pl. **mijnheeren** /-ɪərən, -ɪərən/. [Du., *mijn* my + *heer* lord, master.] Esp. among speakers of South African Dutch: 'Mister'; 'sir'; 'gentleman'. See also HEER *n.* sense 1. Cf. MEVROU.

I. As a title.

1. Prefixed to a first name or a surname: Mister (Mr); MENEER sense 1; MNR.

1696 J. OVINGTON *Voy. to Suratt* 292 The Governour of the *Cape, Min Heer Simon Vanderstel*, labours much in Improvements and Accommodations for the Inhabitants and Sea-men. **1837** 'N. POLSON' *Subaltern's Sick Leave* 101 Mynheer Buffel and his ladies alike think he has kept silence too long. **1852** M.B. HUDSON *S. Afr. Frontier Life* 11 To proceed with my tale, I must introduce here, Mynheer V—. **1871** J. MACKENZIE *Ten Yrs* (1971) 49 It is resolved that Mynheer Suikerlippen .. should now be installed as Landdrost. **1888** *Cape Punch* 21 Mar. 165 Assisted by the heavy weight Mynheer Squarefacio. **1899** B. MITFORD *Weird of Deadly Hollow* 93 'That is certain, Mynheer Rendelsams,' agreed the young Dutchman. **1913** J.J. DOKE *Secret City* 60 'Tis Mihnheer Van Blerk, Missie, and his sisters. **1926** V.L. CAMERON *Reverse Shield* 4 Mynheer Abel Kok, the local predikant, his wife and his daughter Elsie. **1944** J. MOCKFORD *Here Are S. Africans* 90 The very treasure trove of the treasure-house itself was on Mynheer de Beer's farm. **1955** V.M. FITZROY *Dark Bright Land* 33 Mijnheer Cloete, the country gentleman whose daughter Col. Graham is to wed. **1990** R. GOOL *Cape Town Coolie* 1 His lips began .. to shape the word, 'Mister', but he decided instead on '*Mijnheer* van der Merwe'.

2. With a designation of office or rank: equivalent to 'My Lord' or 'His Honour'; MENEER sense 3.

1797 LADY A. BARNARD in Lord Lindsay *Lives of Lindsays* (1849) III. 163 By her was Mynheer the 'Secretarius'. **1919** M. GREENLEES tr. *O.F. Mentzel's Life at Cape in Mid-18th C.* 6 The first is the Vice-Governor, commonly called 'Mijnheer de Tweede.' **1923** B. RONAN *Forty S. Afr. Yrs* 171 The influence of Mynheer Sekretaris became more firmly rooted with every additional year of office.

3. Used in the third person and without a definite article, as a respectful term of reference: 'Sir', 'master'; sometimes used (in *sing.*) to represent Dutch or Afrikaans men collectively.

1798 LADY A. BARNARD in Lord Lindsay *Lives of Lindsays* (1849) III. 463 Mr Barnard is so fond of these dried peaches that he became the purchaser of Mynheer's whole stock. **1804** R. PERCIVAL *Acct of Cape of G.H.* 51 Those Dutch gentlemen .. offer their habitations as taverns ... Besides being very handsomely paid for board and lodging, Mynheer expects over and above a present .. for the Vrouw his wife. **1839** W.C. HARRIS *Wild Sports* 35 We found that Mynheer, although ignorant of all languages except Dutch, claimed a Scottish extraction. **1841** B. SHAW *Memorials* 297 A *slave* ran after the wagon, calling aloud to the driver, and enquiring if it were not the wagon of old Mynheer. **1849** N.J. MERRIMAN *Cape Jrnls* (1957) 66 Mynheer and his vrou retired to rest. **1870** R. RIDGILL in A.M.L. Robinson *Sel. Articles from Cape Monthly Mag.* (1978) 29 All enjoyed the joke amazingly; the Hottentots especially chuckled at the thought of having caught mynheer napping. **1878** T.J. LUCAS *Camp Life & Sport* 136, I found quarters for myself inside with Mynheer. **1900** B. MITFORD *Aletta* 2 On one side of him sat 'Mynheer', as the local *predikant*, or minister, is commonly known among his flock. **1924** S.G. MILLIN *God's Step-Children* 12 He habitually called the missionary 'Mijnheer'. **1924** D. FAIRBRIDGE *Lady Anne Barnard* 20 The serious Dutch ladies had developed a passion for dancing, which it is not recorded that Mynheer shared. **1937** F.B. YOUNG *They Seek a Country* 430 'Ask m'nheer what he will make use of, Lisbet' Jacoba said. **1955** V. DE KOCK *Fun They Had* 48 The *vrouws*, in a minuet, solemnly dance ... As a whale, in shoal water, flaps hard to get out, Mynheer, in cotillion, thus flounders about.

II. As a term of address.

4. A polite or formal term of address: 'Sir'; MENEER sense 2. Cf. BAAS sense 6.

1798 LADY A. BARNARD in Lord Lindsay *Lives of Lindsays* (1849) III. 463 'You will bring these to me,' he said 'when you come to the Cape, Mynheer.' **1829** C. ROSE *Four Yrs in Sn Afr.* 252 The good Vrouw rose from her easy cushioned chair, and welcomed us with 'Sit, Mynheer'. **1835** A. STEEDMAN *Wanderings* I. 115 The usual salutation of 'Dag Mynheer,' accompanied by a hearty shake of the hand. **1841** B. SHAW *Memorials* 111 Mynheer, before we received the gospel, we were like an egg, before the chicken is hatched; we were surrounded with darkness, and could see nothing. **1888** *Cape Punch* 29 Feb. 117 'Not now, mynheer,' he replied, 'my children are waiting for me over yonder.' **1899** G.H. RUSSELL *Under Sjambok* 227 'No, Mijn Heer, no,' was the reply, 'I am at fault; I shall not do it.' **1914** L.H. BRINKMAN *Breath of Karroo* 89 When Boer calls Boer 'Mr.' or 'Mijnheer' it is a clear sign that the two are strangers to each other. **1915** D. FAIRBRIDGE *Torch Bearer* 126 My wife, mynheeren, is a very refined and sensitive female. **1920** R. JUTA *Tavern* 122 Dear Mihnheer, it is no good telling me that.

5. A respectful term of address in the third person (avoiding the pronoun 'you'), a convention used when addressing superiors, older people, and strangers; MENEER sense 4.

1816 J. MACKRILL Diary. 125 Almost the first Question put to a stranger is how old is Myn heer. **1822** W.J. BURCHELL *Trav.* I. 216 Old Hans . . . exclaimed very fervently when we gained the banks; 'Thank God! Mynheer is safe.' **1822** *Missionary Notices* 326 What Mynheer preached about on Friday evening exactly agreed with his state before he knew God. **1835** J.W.D. MOODIE *Ten Yrs* II. 212 If it had not been for mynheer's shot and that good dog, I should have been trampled to pieces by this time. **1910** D. FAIRBRIDGE *That Which Hath Been* (1913) 77 No hour would be inconvenient at which to receive the honour of a visit from mynheer. **1955** V.M. FITZROY *Dark Bright Land* 120 What dress stuffs has mijnheer got that are new?

III. As a common noun.

6. A gentleman; an Afrikaans-speaking (or, formerly, Dutch-speaking) man; MENEER sense 5.

1841 B. SHAW *Memorials* 279 For many years after this occurrence, he would frequently allude to the circumstances, and gratefully exclaim, *'Eisey, eisey, de old Mynheer and the lilies'*. **1853** J. TINDALL *Jrnl* (1959) 177 They with many others had travelled more than 100 miles to meet the Groot Mynheer and to enjoy the meetings during the visit. *a***1862** J. AYLIFF *Jrnl of 'Harry Hastings'* (1963) 21 All that the Mynheer has to do is to walk out into the corn fields and vineyards. **1882** [see SMOUS *n.*]. **1868** W.R. THOMSON *Poems, Essays & Sketches* 154 Ou Baas asked if the jonge mynheer had forgotten that his birthday was the day after Christmas. **1944** J. MOCKFORD *Here Are S. Africans* 45 When they went walking, the mynheers and their good ladies were protected from the rays of the sun by large silk umbrellas.

mijnpacht /ˈmeɪnpaxt/ *n. Hist. Law.* Also **mihnpacht, mynpacht**. Pl. **-s, -en**. [S. Afr. Du., fr. Du. *mijn* mine + *pacht* lease, agreement.]

1. A mining lease granted, in terms of mining laws, to the owner or lessee of the mining rights on land proclaimed a public gold field, entitling this person to claim a certain percentage of the land prior to any other claims being registered; the area held under such a lease. See also VERGUNNING.

[**1889** see sense 2]. **1893** T. REUNERT *Diamonds & Gold* 151 A *mijnpacht*, or mining lease . . is granted to the owner, or in case the owner has leased the mineral rights on his property to another, then to the lessee of such mineral rights. Its extent does not exceed one-tenth of the farm or piece of ground. **1901** D.M. WILSON *Behind Scenes in Tvl* 165 These constituted what is technically known as the *Mijnpacht*, and as they were supposed to represent the pick of the bunch, a *Mijnpacht* was the most valuable portion of a proclaimed farm. **1913** C. PETTMAN *Africanderisms* 331 *Mynpacht*, . . The proprietor of a farm which was proclaimed as a gold-field, was allowed by the Transvaal Gold Law to reserve for himself a certain number of 'claims' – these were technically known as the Mynpacht. **1923** B. RONAN *Forty S. Afr. Yrs* 155 After much negotiation, surveyors were employed, mynpachts marked out and proper deeds registered. **1932** *S. Afr. Mining & Engineering Jrnl* 11 June 386 The proposed amendments to the Gold Law gave the owner of the mineral rights a substantially larger area as a mynpacht, and there would be future claims available for exploitation under a Government lease. *c***1936** *S. & E. Afr. Yr Bk & Guide* 382 The owner of the mineral rights of a proclaimed private farm in the past has been entitled to select one or two areas (called a *Mijnpacht*) aggregating not more than one-fifth of the land over which he had the mineral rights. **1940** F.B. YOUNG *City of Gold* 417 Meninsky took care that the *Mijnpacht*, the tenth share reserved for the owner, and the sixty *Vergunnings*, or Preference Claims, which the law allowed him to assign to his friends, should be grouped compactly around the rich area which he had assayed. **1957** *Act 68* in *Stat. of Union* 1046 No contract of sale or cession in respect of land or any interest in land (other than a lease, mijnpacht or mining claim or stand) shall be of any force. **1962** A.P. CARTWRIGHT *Gold Miners* 61 They chose the site of Johannesburg because it was roughly in the centre of the line of claims and *mijnpachten* that ran from Roodepoort almost to where Germiston is today. *Ibid.* 179 The Precious and Base Metals Act, No. 35 of 1908 (universally known as the Gold Law) . . provided that, where the owner of a *mynpacht* (normally not more than one-quarter of the land on which gold had been discovered) considered that this was not sufficient ground to provide a workable mining area, he might acquire a lease over a larger area. **1973** *The 1820* Vol.46 No.11, With his former assistant, Jan Eloff, now the Mining Commissioner, they sorted out the tangle of mihnpachten and diggers' claims.

2. *comb.* **mijnpacht brief** [S. Afr. Du., *brief* (pl. *brieven*) letter, document], the document recording a mining lease agreement.

1889 E.P. MATHERS *Golden S. Afr.* 321 When farms are proclaimed as public fields the Government allow the owners . . to take out **Mijn Pacht Brieven**, which entitles them to reserve from interference from diggers about a tenth portion of the ground. **1962** A.P. CARTWRIGHT *Gold Miners* 61 The Government . . allowed the owners of the farms, and those to whom they had granted leases, a month in which to make sure that their *mynpacht-brieven* were in order. The regulation under which a *mijnpacht-brief* was registered gave the owner of the land, or the purchaser of his mining rights, the right to beacon an area equal to about one-tenth of the total area of the farm on which he could conduct mining operations himself. **1974** J.P. BRITS *Diary of Nat. Scout* 77 A list of registered owners of the mining leases (mynpacht-brieven) in connection with farms which were situated on the Main Reef.

Hence **mynpachter** *n.*, the holder of such a mining lease.

1893 T. REUNERT *Diamonds & Gold* 151 To the credit of the Government, . . it has never yet imposed the charge of this commission, for although it would add a very large amount to the annual revenue of the State, it would, on the other hand, be a very serious imposition on the mijnpachter.

mij vrouw var. MEVROU.

milice see quot. 1889 at MEALIE.

milie var. MEALIE.

mili(e)pap var. MEALIEPAP.

milk *n.* As in general Eng., but in the following Special Comb. peculiar to *S. Afr. Eng.*:

1. Denoting containers for milk: **milk-basket**, BASKET; **milk-sack** *hist.*, also **milk sac**, a tightly-stitched bag of animal-hide used for the preparation of curdled milk (see MAAS sense 1); LEKUKA; also *attrib.*

1798 LADY A. BARNARD *S. Afr. Century Ago* (1925) 212 A **milk-basket** which I looked at with a covetous eye, in which the Kafirs carry their milk – which they weave so close with certain rushes that, after once using, the milk cannot get through. **1824** W.J. BURCHELL *Trav.* II. 507 Made, apparently of some species of rush . . . The manner in which it is wove together is the same as that which is practiced by the Caffres Proper, in the making of their milk-baskets. **1913** C. PETTMAN *Africanderisms* 318 *Milk basket*, Baskets made by the natives from a strong, reedy grass are used to hold milk; so well and closely are they plaited that no liquid can pass through them. [**milk-sack**: **1795** C.R. HOPSON tr. *C.P. Thunberg's Trav.* I. 197 The vessel . . is the hide of an antelope . . which is sewed up close together, and hung up against the wall . . . In one of these sacks . . , new milk is put, which turns sour and coagulates.] **1828** W. SHAW Diary. 22 May, At supper tonight, . . we had not less than five different Messes: —Boiled pumpkin, Pumpkin mixed with Indian Corn; Boiled Caffre corn, Meal porridge, and Curded Milk, from the Milk sack. **1835** A. STEEDMAN *Wanderings* I. 263 In that [*sc.* the hut] of a wealthy Caffer, there is usually a milk-sack made of bullock's hide, so closely sewn together as to prevent leakage, and capable of containing several gallons. **1844** J. BACKHOUSE *Narr. of Visit* 249 A milk-sack of oblong form, made of cow-skin, with the fresh side out, and having the hair carefully removed, was lying at the door of one of the huts. **1860** W. SHAW *Story of my Mission* 416 The 'master of the milk-sack,' umnini wentsuba, is an important functionary, . . especially at the kraal of a Chief. He alone fills the sack with the milk, declares when it is ready for use, and pours it out. **1898** B. MITFORD *Induna's Wife* 126 Presently the women brought me *tywala* . . , for they might not open the milk-sacks, the heads of the houses being absent. **1902** G.M. THEAL *Beginning of S. Afr. Hist.* 72 This is the last of the ceremonies, and the guests immediately begin to disperse, each man taking home the milk-sack which he had brought with him. **1913** C. PETTMAN *Africanderisms* 318 *Milk sack*, . . A bag made of ox or quagga hide in which Amasi . . is prepared. **1925** D. KIDD *Essential Kafir* 59 The hens and eggs should always be bought from the women or children, who, by the way, are not allowed on any account to touch the milk sac. **1985** *S. Afr. Panorama* May 5 Nokokwane, a musical bow with milk sac resonators which is extremely rare today.

2. Denoting plants which exude a milky sap when injured: **milk-bush**, [tr. Afk. *melkbos*, see MELKBOS], *(a) obs.*, the tree *Ficus cordata* of the Moraceae; MELKBOOM sense a; *(b)* any of several species of shrub of the genus *Euphorbia* (family Euphorbiaceae); see also MELKBOS sense 1 b, and NABOOM; **milkwood** [tr. S. Afr. Du. *melkhout*, see MELKHOUT], in full ***milkwood tree***, occas. **milk tree** (also simply *milk*): any of several species of tree of the Sapotaceae, *(a)* freq. with distinguishing epithet, **white milkwood**: the usu. low-growing shrub-like coastal and forest tree *Sideroxylon inerme*, bearing leathery, dark-green leaves, small creamy flowers, and round, purple-black fruit; JAKKALSBESSIE sense b; MELKBOOM sense b; MELKBOS sense 3 b; MELKHOUT sense a; *(b)* freq. with distinguishing epithet, **red milkwood**: a tree of the species *Mimusops caffra, M. obovata* or *M. zeyheri*; see also MELKHOUT sense b, WATERBOOM sense 2; cf. MOEPEL sense a.

1821 C.I. LATROBE *Jrnl of Visit* 133 The **milk-bush** (*ficus*), a tree not unlike a Portugal laurel. **1838** J.E. ALEXANDER *Exped. into Int.* I. 284 He said that the poison of euphorbia, or milk bush (boiled till it was black), which he used, took from sun-rise to mid-day to kill the game. **1870** R. RIDGILL in A.M.L. Robinson *Sel. Articles from Cape Monthly Mag.* (1978) 32 We had a long walk among the poisonous milk-bushes, and a fatiguing scramble among the mountains in the deepening darkness. **1879** O.E.A. SCHREINER in C. Clayton *Woman's Rose* (1986) 15 Before her and behind her stretched the plain, covered with red sand and thorny Karroo bushes; and here and there a milk-bush, looking like a bundle of pale green rods tied together. **1883** —— *Story of Afr. Farm* 3 The milk-bushes with their long, finger-like leaves .. were touched by a weird .. beauty as they lay in the white light. **1895** *Cape Times Christmas No.* 45 *(caption)* Milk bush, from which the Bushmen obtain Poison for their Spears. **1896** E. CLAIRMONTE *Africander* 52 The only green things visible were the milk bushes — an *euphorbia* of a poisonous nature — that grew like long thin fingers pointing to the cloudless sky. **1911** P. GIBBON *Margaret Harding* 61 Sometimes there is grass — a little — not much, and milk bushes and prickly pear .. but it is hard ground. **1922** J. GALSWORTHY *Forsyte Saga* 697 The trickle of river running by in the sands, .. the straggling milk-bush of the Karoo beyond. **1958** I. VAUGHAN *Diary* 12 We looked at the milk bushes near the brick fields and saw the men on horses bobbing and riding from one side to the great sloot on the other. *c*1968 S. CANDY *Natal Coast Gardening* 134 *Euphorbia*, 'Rubberbush', 'Milkbush'. All have milky sap, and many are spinous and Cactus-like in growth. **1974** [see MELKBOS sense 1]. **1987** T.F.J. VAN RENSBURG *Intro. to Fynbos* 22 A large variety of succulents such as milk bush (*Euphorbia mauretanica*) and vygies (Mesembryantheaceae) are also present. **1988** SMUTS & ALBERTS *Forgotten Highway* 26 The traveller descends by a gentle incline to the lower-lying Bokkeveld Karoo, and the vijge, the brakbos, the milk bush and the ganna are in summer the only stunted shrubs that welcome him. **1815** J. MACKRILL Diary. 119 **Milk Wood** is the Sideroxylon inerme. *a*1823 [see MELKHOUT]. **1833** *S. Afr. Almanac & Dir.* 195 For Wagon-work, the following are selected: — Fellies, White Pear; Spokes, Assegai or Red Milk-wood. *Ibid.* The other woods most in request, and found in Albany, are — Red and White Milk, Red and White Else, Red and White Pear, Saffran, Iron-wood, Assagai-wood and Sneeze-wood. **1841** B. SHAW *Memorials* 43 The stick which is perforated, is generally obtained from a bush called mahacha, and the other from the milk tree. **1846** R. MOFFAT *Missionary Labours* 86 Reference has been made to certain trees, especially the milkwood (*sideroxylum inerme*). *a*1858 J. GOLDSWAIN *Chron.* (1949) II. 60 Close to us he found in a read milkwood tree a bees neast. **1862** L. PAPPE *Silva Capensis* 24 *Sideroxylon Inerme Lin.* (Milk-wood; Melkhout) ... Wood whitish, very hard, close, and durable. **1876** T. STUBBS Reminiscences. I. 14 He cut one Pole to stand at the end to support the roof, it was Milk wood. **1912** AYLIFF & WHITESIDE *Hist. of Abambo* 34 At a later date, Mr Ayliff held a mass meeting .. near a large milkwood tree. **1913** C. PETTMAN *Africanderisms* 395 *Red milkwood, Mimusops obovata* and *M. caffra* are so named. **1932** WATT & BREYER-BRANDWIJK *Medicinal & Poisonous Plants* 137 The Zulus take an infusion of the bark of *Sideroxylon inerme* L., White milkwood, Wit melkhout, Jakkal's-bessie .. to dispel bad dreams. **1934** [see MOEPEL]. **1944** [see AFTER-RIDER]. **1951** N.L. KING *Tree-Planting* 69 *Mimusops caffra (Red milkwood)*, A small tree. Occurs on sand dunes along the coast in eastern Cape down to high water mark. **1953** R. CAMPBELL *Mamba's Precipice* 21 There was the red roof of their Beach Cottage, half overshadowed by a giant milk-wood tree. **1961** PALMER & PITMAN *Trees of S. Afr.* 141 The white milk-wood is an evergreen, low-growing tree, sometimes with shady, spreading branches, sometimes many-branched from the base, and forming a rounded mass of compact foliage. *c*1963 [see WATERBOOM sense 2]. **1972** *Std Encycl. of Sn Afr.* VII. 413 *Red milkwood*, .. *(Mimusops zeyheri.)* Large tree, belonging to the family *Sapotaceae*. **1974** *Weekend Post* 30 Nov. 10 Throughout South Africa the white milkwood was proclaimed a protected tree on any land by Proclamation No. 1467 dated August 8. **1977** E. PALMER *Field Guide to Trees* 251 *White Milkwood Family*, Sapotaceae ... Mostly good shade trees, the timber often hard and much used. **1987** T.F.J. VAN RENSBURG *Intro. to Fynbos* 20 Trees are scarce but white milkwood (*Sideroxylen inerme*) occurs as patches of low scrub in protected places. **1991** [see BOEKENHOUT].

milk tart *n. phr.* [tr. Afk. *melktert*.] MELKTERT.

1891 H.J. DUCKITT *Hilda's 'Where Is It?'* 238 Tart (Milk). (Old Dutch *Spécialité*.) **1930** M. RAUBENHEIMER *Tested S. Afr. Recipes* 79 The original Recipe is for a milk tart filling, but it is better as a pudding. **1958** [see MELKTERT]. *c*1968 J. HOBBS in *New S. Afr. Writing* 115 Learning to bottle peaches and .. konfyts and to make the lightest pastry in the district for her milk tarts. **1971** *Cape Argus* 10 July 8 It is wrong to talk of milk tart — an insipid, anaemic-sounding name for a really delicious old Cape delicacy. What is wrong with melktert? **1977** *The 1820* Vol.50 No.12, 15 Of Milk Tart I've never heard But I'll read on, yes every word .. In fact I'll buy the book to-day And cook the real South African way. **1985** J. CLOETE in *S.-Easter* Oct.-Nov. 30 The Crayfish tour includes .. a gastronomic introduction to Swartland *boerekos* — offal, milktart and sosaties.

milli var. MEALIE.

Milner's Kindergarten see KINDERGARTEN.

miltsiek /ˈmәltsik/ *adj.* and *n. Pathology.* Also **miltziek**. [Shortening (as n.) and back-formation (as adj.) of MILTSIEKTE.]

A. *adj. obs.* Infected with MILTSIEKTE.

1885 A. SMITH *Contrib. to Materia Medica* 9 Antibacterial plants used with *milt ziek* meat. *Ibid.* 16 To disinfect *milt ziek* meat they either boil the leaves with the meat, or .. they .. make an infusion .. which they drink along with the meat.

B. *n. ?obsolescent.* MILTSIEKTE.

1937 H.C. BOSMAN *Mafeking Rd* (1969) 165 A young man had no chance, really, in the Marico. What with the droughts, and the cattle getting the miltsiek, and the mosquitoes buzzing around so that you couldn't sleep. **1959** *Cape Times* 12 Mar. 2 Miltsiek has broken out in certain areas in the Bushmanland.

miltsiekte /ˈmәltsiktә/ *n. Pathology.* Also **maltziekte, melt sicte, meltsiekte, melt zicte, meltziekte, miltsiekte, miltziekte**. [Afk. (earlier S. Afr. Du. *meltziekte*) *milt* spleen + *siekte* disease.

Some of the spelling forms may have been influenced by Eng. *melt* (var. of *milt*) spleen.]

Anthrax, a disease of livestock caused by the bacterium *Bacillus anthracis* and communicable to people; MELT SICKNESS; MILTSIEK *n.*

1835 T.H. BOWKER Journal. 11 May, One Fingo died from eating beef which had died of the Melt Zicte. *Ibid.* 13 May, There is another fingo ill of the melt Sicte. **1877** *Queenstown Free Press* 1 Dec., The oldest and most experienced of kurveyors confess themselves 'flabbergasted' by meltziekte. **1885** A. SMITH *Contrib. to Materia Medica* 15 *Teucrium Africanum* ... When an ox or cow has died of *milt ziekte* the Kaffirs boil the flesh along with this plant, and believe they can eat it with impunity. **1892** *The Jrnl* 14 Jan. 2 It may be hoped that redwater, horse-sickness, maltziekte, heartwater and other scourges will be stamped out by means of inoculation. **1896** R. WALLACE *Farming Indust. of Cape Col.* 284 Anthrax, locally termed 'meltziekte' or 'gift-ziekte', .. in its well-known erratic and spasmodic way, appears .. in all districts of the Colony, and among all classes of stock. **1914** *Farmer's Annual* 117 Anthrax or Meltziekte is a virulent disease of the blood, caused by the entrance into the system of a micro-organism known as the Bacillus Anthracis ... It is communicable to man. **1945** H.C. BOSMAN *Mafeking Rd* (1969) 107 Six of my best trek-oxen died of the miltsiekte. **1972** L.G. GREEN *When Journey's Over* 51 You had to guard your oxen against redwater, *meltsiekte* and lung sickness. **1989** M. NEL in *Personality* 6 Feb. 60 The inhabitants of Douglas .. treated the disaster as if it was no worse than *miltsiekte* or the drought.

mily var. MEALIE.

min dae /ˈmәn ˈdɑː(ә)/ *n. phr. Army slang.* [Afk., *min* few + *dae* days.]

1. A name given by national servicemen to the last few weeks of (compulsory) military service. Also *attrib.*, and as an interjection.

1971 on Radio South Africa 31 Dec., The only reason we could bear to cross them [*sc.* weekends] off at all was that any crossing off of days brought us nearer and nearer to the end of yet another term — like the army and their 'min dae'. **1972** [see OUMAN]. **1975** J.H. PICARD in *Eng. Usage in Sn Afr.* Vol.6 No.1, 36 New recruits are called *roofies*, a *roof* becomes a *blougat* when he is halfway through his course, and when he has almost completed his training period he has *min dae* and is raised to the exalted ranks of the *oumanne*. **1977** G. HUGO in *Quarry '77* 95 'Don't tell anyone, hey, but you're going to be permanently discharged.' His thick face breaks into a grin. 'Min dae, hey.' **1979** P. WILHELM in *Staffrider* Vol.2 No.3, 15 Sometimes they listened to the radio, to the messages on 'Forces Favourites' all about 'missing you my darling'; and 'longing to see you' and '*vasbyt*' and '*min dae*'. **1985** W. STEENKAMP in *Cape Times* 23 Jan. 6 National servicemen who are suffering from galloping 'min dae' fever and don't give a hoot about anything. **1985** P. SLABOLEPSZY *Sat. Night at Palace* 19 You really are as thick as pigshit, hey? How long you been sitting on this? You know what this means? Army — border — vasbyt — min dae. This could be it, my china. The ultimate summons from that Great Cop in the Sky!! **1986** *Informant, Durban* He's got mindae in the army now. **1987** *Personality* 30 Sept. 10 Liebenberg had less than a month's national service to complete before his demobilisation — the *min dae* of affectionate letters and radio broadcasts to our troopies. **1989** [see Personality quot. at KLAAR *v.* sense 1].

2. *comb.* **min dae flossie** [*flossie* (orig. unkn.) a troop- and cargo-carrying aeroplane], see quot.

1982 A. JACOT-GUILLARMOD *Informant, Grahamstown* Min dae flossie. The plane that will be flying you back to the Republic after a Border stint.

mine captain *n. phr.* [Eng., overseer of a mine. First used in Eng. *c*1860, but rare.] The overseer of an area of a mine. Also *attrib.*

1899 J.H. CURLE *Gold Mines of World* 7 The mine captain .. is usually a most capable man. **1922** *Rand Daily Mail* in J. Crwys-Williams *S. Afr. Despatches* (1989) 237 She was the mother of a mine captain. **1955** A. DELIUS *Young Trav.* 43 In came a broad healthy-looking young man. He was a mine-captain, they learnt, and he would be their guide ... The 'captain' .. said 'Actually, I'm just plain Mister ... Most of the mine-workers have very unflowery names like shift-bosses, skipmen, onsetters.' **1971** *Sunday Times* 9 May 8 The famous Cullinan Diamond .. was found at the Premier Mine, Cullinan, by Mr. Frederick Wells, a mine captain, on June 12, 1905. **1971** *Daily Dispatch* 11 May 10 Workers at the Impala Platinum Mine here decided unanimously at a meeting to demand the sacking of a mine captain and a shift boss. **1972** *S. Afr. Panorama* May 37 Mining is an exacting profession demanding a great deal of fitness, as mine captain Ginger Kimmings .. can testify. **1989** *Sunday Times* 19 Nov. 9 Mine captain Harry Player took two overdrafts in his life.

mine dance *n. phr.* A dance performed by a troupe of mine workers, usu. incorporating elements of traditional African dances. Also *attrib.* See also GUMBOOT DANCE.

1968 COLE & FLAHERTY *House of Bondage* 23 A number of men participate in programs of tribal dances — the so-called 'mine dances' — which are a big tourist attraction for whites visiting Johannesburg. **1984** *Frontline* Feb. 40 Weinberg took refuge in the mine-dances ... All the sweat, plenty of excitement among the participants. **1991** P. SLABOLEPSZY Braait Laaities. 29 I'm singing like Eddie Murphy, but I'm dancing like Ken Gampu. *(Doing a few 'mine dance' steps in the mirror).*

mine dump *n. phr.* [Eng. *mine* + *dump* pile of earth which accumulates during mining operations. Cf. DUMP.] A hill of solidified crushed quartz, built up from the residue of gold-mining operations; DUMP. Also *attrib.*

A term also used elsewhere, but particularly common in *S. Afr. Eng.*, as mine dumps are a dominant feature of the landscape in certain areas, esp. near Johannesburg.

1909 *Westminster Gaz.* (U.K.) 11 Feb. 3 Such statements as that .. a mine dump can contain 40,000 tons, and that such a dump consists of 10 per cent.

of pitchblende. **1922** *Rand Daily Mail* in J. Crwys-Williams *S. Afr. Despatches* (1989) 238 A runner came in from the mine dump shouting: 'The police are round at the back.' **1936** R.J.M. GOOLD-ADAMS *S. Afr. To-Day & To-Morrow* 159 Almost on top of the heart of Johannesburg itself the mine-dumps began again . . , like yellow downs piled up not by God, but by the hand of man over half a century. **1946** P. ABRAHAMS *Mine Boy* (1954) 44 Those are the mine dumps. They are made of the sand that's dug out of the earth when the miners seek for gold. **1953** U. KRIGE *Dream & Desert* 143 The mine dumps, dominating the scene and continually changing colour, reminded me of brown pyramids, grey flat-topped hills in the Karoo, the ochre foundations of gigantic old temples never completed. **1965** C. VAN HEYNINGEN *Orange Days* 68 The town was surrounded by mine dumps – yellow mountains of sand spewed up from underground, where thousands of men, white and black, worked like moles digging out the gold-bearing rocks. **1972** *S. Afr. Panorama* May 29 It has been estimated that the mine dumps of the Witwatersrand are among the largest man-made landmarks, comparable perhaps to the pyramids or to Manhattan Island. **1978** 'BLOSSOM' in *Darling* 30 Aug. 123 The Golden City, Egoli, the mine-dump masterpiece of the west – in a word, Joeys. **1987** E. KEYTER in *S. Afr. Panorama* Oct. 26 On South Africa's goldfields, which stretch from Virginia in the Orange Free State to Evander in the Transvaal, there are 740 gold mine-dumps at present. Producing mining companies are responsible for the rehabilitation of sand and silt piled on mine-dumps so that it does not create a dust problem or cause water pollution. The gold mine-dumps in the RSA extend over 44 000 hectares. **1989** J. HOBBS *Thoughts in Makeshift Mortuary* 227 A mine dump off which the fine yellow sand blew in sheets when it was windy. **1989** *Weekend Post* 2 Dec. (Leisure) 5 On the Reef the youngsters learn how the city of Johannesburg grew from the mine dumps and learn how to bake Mine Dump Bread. **1990** P. ESTERHUYSEN in *Staffrider* Vol.9 No.1, 9 Clogged highways glistened like necklaces strung out over the city, suspended between the railway line and distant pink mine dumps.

mines *pl. n.* In the adv. phr. ***on the mines***, in the employment of a mining company; in or down a mine.

1943 'J. BURGER' *Black Man's Burden* 49 If the Bantu could make a decent living in the Reserves, they would not work for European farmers or on the mines. **1948** [see FANAKALO]. **1952** H. KLEIN *Land of Silver Mist* 90 Except for the boys who have gone out to work on the mines or on lowveld farms most of the Natives . . have never seen a white man. **1984** D. PINNOCK *Brotherhoods* 73 Their prison-gang thing started on the mines. **1991** *Sunday Times* 9 June 5 Fanie's grandfather was a shiftboss on the mines.

min heer var. MIJNHEER.

Minister *n.* [Eng., prob. influenced by Afk. usage.] The title given to a government minister, used with a surname.

1938 *George & Knysna Herald* 19 Oct. 1 Persons who put various schemes to Minister Fourie received a very sympathetic hearing. **1981** *E. Prov. Herald* 3 Oct. 2 Minister Botha immediately acceded to this request. **1989** M. MANLEY tr. *L.M. Oosthuizen's Media Policy & Ethics* 32 Minister Barend du Plessis . . cites free expression of opinion as a basic principle . . . In the light of the new constitutional dispensation, ex-Minister Chris Heunis . . used the term 'consensus democracy'.

Ministers' Council *n. phr. Hist.* Also with small initials. [Prob. tr. Afk. *Ministersraad*.] A council consisting of the ministers and deputy ministers of state of each of the three houses of the TRICAMERAL parliament, responsible for 'own affairs' matters only. See also OWN AFFAIR sense 1.

1983 *Act 110* in *Juta's Stat. of S. Afr.* Vol.5, 1–346 A Ministers' Council shall consist of – (*a*) the Ministers appointed to administer departments of State for own affairs of one and the same population group. **1985** *Cape Times* 29 Jan. 5 House of delegates. Today's business: Resumption of debate of no-confidence in Minister's Council. **1986** *Race Rel. Survey 1985* (S.A.I.R.R.) 54 The Ministers' Council in each house is responsible for 'own affairs'. **1987** *Evening Post* 20 Jan. 3 The chairman of the Ministers' Council in the House of Delegates . . said joint caucus meetings . . would increase coloured and Indian parliamentary strength. **1989** *Reader's Digest Illust. Hist.* 467 A Ministers' Council has been appointed for each of the three houses and consists of ministers and deputy ministers of state and specially nominated ministers.

mink and manure *adj. phr. Colloq.* [Eng. *mink*, alluding to wealth and *manure*, alluding to horsey pursuits.]

1. Of or pertaining to the wealthy, semi-rural, northern suburbs of Johannesburg, or the inhabitants of these suburbs.

1981 *Signature* May 9 Often I am asked how Cape Town – so far from the mink and manure belt – draws the cream of South African riding talent to the . . International Show. **1984** B. MOLLOY in *Style* Nov. 140 The first [Transvalers] to arrive jet in from the mink and manure belt of the Johannesburg northern suburbs. **1985** *Evening Post* 24 May 4 A prominent and wealthy businessman of 'mink-and-manure' Sandton was found dead yesterday in his bed, apparently gassed. **1986** *Fair Lady* 25 June 158 She grew up on a large plot in the then isolated and countrified Northern Johannesburg among the 'mink and manure' set. **1988** J. KHUMALO in *Pace* Nov. 27 Suddenly white surburbia was swaying to the rhythm of the townships and 'Hotstix' became the buzzword at those high-powered parties . . of the mink and manure set. **1989** S. SELLO in *Drum* Apr. 78 The election . . of Sifiso Ngwenya as junior mayor of Sandton, the ultimate mink and manure belt of Johannesburg's northern suburbs, raised many eyebrows. **1989** *Sunday Times* 15 Oct. 7 (*caption*) History in Rivonia's mink-and-manure belt.

2. Used loosely: Wealthy.

1985 *Frontline* Sept. 23 Our car eventually hits the clean smelling mink and manure black area called Diepkloof Extension. It is like another world. **1987** *Sunday Times* 23 Aug. 15 There are legions of hitherto ignored upwardly mobile professionals eager to grab a piece of the action and at long last join the older mink and manure generation. **1987** *Drum* Oct. 22 As sudden and dramatic as her entry was into the mink and manure circles, was her exit and ignominy. **1992** S. SHERRY in *South* 27 Feb., The Club is definitely not a mink-and-manure gathering place.

Hence (*rare*) **mink and manure** *n. phr.*, the wealthy.

1985 *Sunday Times* 23 Aug. 15 What a pother for mink and manure.

mirumba pl. form of MURUMBA.

mis /məs/ *n.* Formerly also **mest**, **mist**(**e**). [Afk., fr. Du. *mist* manure.] Animal manure (esp. cattle manure).

1. Dried manure, used as fuel or as building material. Also *attrib.* See also *Free State coal* (FREE STATE *adj. phr.* sense 2), *kraal manure* (KRAAL *n.* sense 3 d).

1852 C. BARTER *Dorp & Veld* 51 (Pettman), This evening our fire was of *mest* or dried cow-dung, which turns to a white ash, gives a great heat, and is no bad substitute for wood. **1864** T. BAINES *Explor. in S.-W. Afr.* 212 The sun . . heated the dry sandy surface till the barefoot sitters felt it inconveniently . . . Each of them chose a cake of 'kraiel mist,' and turning it up, stood upon its yet moist under-surface. [**1872** C.A. PAYTON *Diamond Diggings* 154 They are generally particularly averse to collecting dry bullock dung, or 'mest' as it is called in Dutch, which makes most excellent fuel.] **1896** R. WALLACE *Farming Indust. of Cape Col.* 482 Owing to . . the custom . . of shutting farm animals in kraal during night, large accumulations of dung . . occur . . . The heaps get dry, and it is the practice to cut the material, which resembles a light fibrous peat and is known as 'mist', into slabs 3 to 5 inches thick, and about 16 inches long and 12 broad. In this form it is used for the building of kraal fences or as fuel. **1900** O. OSBORNE *In Land of Boers* 187 We experienced much difficulty in obtaining water and fuel, being compelled for the latter to rely upon dry cattle manure, 'mest'. **1910** J. ANGOVE *In Early Days* 110 Besides wood, the boy brought a lot of *mest* or dry cow-dung. **1925** L.D. FLEMMING *Crop of Chaff* 111 Digging miste out of the kraal. **1937** S. CLOETE *Turning Wheels* 137 As the fire took he added bigger pieces of dung and the sweet, almost invisible smoke of the mis rose in a thick column. **1944** C.R. PRANCE *Under Blue Roof* 140 Our cuisine was based on 'mis' which is cow-dung in brutal English, collected and hand-pressed into cakes by the Native farm-labourers' womankind. **1958** I. VAUGHAN *Diary* 9 Here . . we burn a strange kind of coal. It is dung . . . In big squares. It is sheeps and goats dung tramped fast and dug out . . . It is called mis. **1968** J.T. MCNISH *Rd to Eldorado* 76 There is the aromatic scent of burning mis in the air, clean and fragrant, and appealing to the senses. **1989** *Weekend Post* 4 Nov. (Leisure) 4 The Free State . . was 'so devoid of wood that "mist fires" [dung fires] are the rule'. This dung was the 'Free State coal'.

2. Fresh manure used (in various combinations with ash, ox blood, mud, lime, and water) to make composition floors in rural homes, and used subsequently to smear or dress these floors. See also SMEAR.

1896 R. WALLACE *Farming Indust. of Cape Col.* 350 The floor must be level and paved with cobble-stones, or formed of some hard, dry material . . . If built of 'mist,' ventilation spaces should be left at the bases of the walls. **1925** P. SMITH *Little Karoo* (1936) 17 The floors . . she smeared regularly with a mixture of cowdung and ashes called *mist*. The little house smelt always of *mist*, of strong black coffee, . . and of griddle cakes. **1930** N. STEVENSON *Farmers of Lekkerbat* 17 The house . . was thatched as the native *rondawels* were with veld grass, and the floors were made of *mist*. **1958** I. VAUGHAN *Diary* 5 Every week the floors are smered [*sic*] with mis which is cowdung made soft like mud with water. It has a nasty smell. **1963** R. LEWCOCK *Early 19th C. Archit.* 160 Following traditional Cape practice, such composition floors were sometimes smeared at regular intervals with a mixture of cow dung and water known to the settlers as 'mist'. **1973** M.A. COOK *Cape Kitchen* 20 When thoroughly dry, the surface was 'smeared' with mis, i.e. a mixture of fresh cow-dung and water. **1991** *Best of S. Afr. Short Stories* (Reader's Digest Assoc.) 110 When quite dry, the floor was smeared – often in traditional, swirling patterns – with *mis* or '*mist*' . . , a cattle dung mix which might contain ash, mud, water and blood . . . *Mis* was applied as often as necessary to maintain the shiny, impervious surface.

3. *comb.* **misbredie** /-briədi/ [Afk., *bredie* (see BREDIE)], see quot. 1966; **miskoek** /'-kʊk, -kuk/, also **mest-kock**, pl. **-e** /-ə/ [Afk., *koek* cake], cow-pat; square of dried dung; **miskruier** /-kreɪə(r), -krœɪ-/ [Afk., *kruier* porter], any of several species of dung-rolling beetles of the family Scarabaeidae; **misrybol** /-'reɪbɔl/ [Afk., *ry* (earlier Du. *rij*) to ride + *bol* bulbous root], see quot. 1913; **misvloer** /-flu:r/ [Afk., *vloer* floor], a composition floor made of various mixtures of clay, oxblood, lime, and cattle-dung, and dressed with cattle-dung or oxblood at intervals to restore and coat the surface; cf. DAGHA *n.* sense a; also *attrib.*

1913 C. PETTMAN *Africanderisms* 317 **Mest bredie**, . . *Amarantus Thunbergii, Moq.*, which grows on manure heaps; a Riversdale name. **1966** C.A. SMITH *Common Names* 339 *Misbredie*, A name applied to several species of *Amaranthus* and *Chenopodium* from the fact that the plants are generally found in sheltered places in kraals where they germinate from seeds contained in the droppings . . of animals that fed on the plants. The leaves of nearly all are used for making of a 'bredie'. [**miskoek**: **1810** G. BARRINGTON *Acct of Voy.* 332 The fuel used by the inhabitants, is the dung of animals collected in the places where their cattle are nightly pent-up . . . This is dug out in long squares, as turf is cut up from the bogs in the Northern parts of England.] **1824** W.J. BURCHELL *Trav.* II. 82 The walls of these cattle-pounds, are at many farms here, built entirely of such pieces of manure piled up to dry; and which go by the name of *mest-koek* (manure-cake). **1937** F.B. YOUNG *They Seek a Country* 224 For the glow of sods from the *mest-kock* was fading; the night air seeped in to the hearth beneath the wicker door, and it grew mortally cold. **1958** A. JACKSON *Trader on Veld* 38 The manure .. was periodically cut out with spades in square cakes of about 18 inches. Packed on top of the kraal walls, where it soon dried ready for burning, these cakes were sold .. at fourpence each, and were called miskoeke. **1985** L. SAMPSON in *Style* Feb. 103, I had a stove, but in Fraserberg there was no wood so we had to burn dung pats, you know the miskoek. **1913** C. PETTMAN *Africanderisms* 320 **Mist-kruier**, .. The not inappropriate appellation of the various dung-rolling beetles. **1913** *Ibid.* 319 **Misrijbol**, .. A variety of *Haemanthus*, which appears to have received this inelegant appellation because it happens to be in flower just about the time that the mest (manure) is being carted, or in South African English, 'ridden' on to the vineyards. The name is also applied to a fragrant Amaryllis. **1966** C.A. SMITH *Common Names* 339 Misrybol, .. *Amaryllis belladonna* .. ; *Haemanthus coccineus* ... Plants of both species flower (March to April) when the wine farmers commence carting .. manure .. into the vineyards, whence the vernacular name. **1934** *Cape Argus* 21 June (Swart), The primitive floor, in most cases a '**misvloer**'. **1949** L.G. GREEN *In Land of Afternoon* 144 The living room had a misvloer, but the floor of the wagon formed the roof of the room. **1973** M.A. COOK *Cape Kitchen* 24 Note the steep staircase; .. the opening above the oven, the high ceiling and the misvloer. **1977** F.G. BUTLER *Karoo Morning* 38 He was sure that all his guests would sleep comfortably enough on the misvloer, which had been smeared with cow-dung the day before 'to fix the fleas'. **1981** C. BARNARD in *Daily Dispatch* 6 July 6 Lino lasts a long time if the floor is flat and hard ... In the old days you could have a 'misvloer' made of dung, but that's not so easy to come by these days. **1984** *S. Afr. Panorama* Feb. 33 Parts of the service areas have a traditional *misvloer* (hardened cow-dung which gives off a sweet odour), and this has been recreated with a natural looking cement. **1988** *NELM News* (Nat. Eng. Lit. Museum) 12 May, In the kitchen .. the *misvloer* has been worked with clay and fresh green manure to achieve an authentic colour and texture. **1989** *Ibid.* 14 June, She is .. an expert 'misvloer' maker and the kitchen floor is an old-fashioned delight. **1990** *Weekend Post* 8 Dec. 12 Visitors view a short video on Xhosa traditions in a *mis-vloer*-and-mud hut.

missees, missies varr. MIESIES.

misselyat-kat var. MUSKELJAATKAT.

Miss Lucy *n. phr.* Also with small initials. [Etym. unknown (cf. LUCY).] In the Eastern Cape: the *red stumpnose* (see STUMPNOSE sense 2), *Chrysoblephus gibbiceps*.

1949 J.L.B. SMITH *Sea Fishes* 272 *Chrysoblephus gibbiceps* ... Red Stumpnose .. Miss Lucy. **1976** *E. Prov. Herald* 23 Sept. 33 No second look is necessary to identify this fish as a miss lucy (red stump nose). **1991** M. HOLMES in *Ibid.* 8 Mar. 18 Red Steenbras and Miss Lucys which any bottom-fish angler would be proud to catch.

missus /ˈmɪsɪs, ˈmisɪs/ *n.* Also **misses, missis**, with initial capital, and (rarely) **missuse**. Pl. **-es**. [Special sense of Eng. *missus*.]

Also found in *U.S.* and *Indian Eng.*

1. A common noun. Cf. MADAM sense 2.

a. A female employer; MIESIES sense 1; NONNA sense 2 a; NOOI sense 1 a. Cf. MIES sense b.

1853 E. RUTHERFOORD in J. Murray *In Mid-Victorian Cape Town* (1953) 40 We found a very nice felt hat which we gave to one of our Coolies, telling him to keep it, in remembrance of his long walk, he gallantly replied, 'he should keep it in remembrance of the pretty young Missus'. **1861** LADY DUFF-GORDON *Lett. from Cape* (1925) 38 Abdul first bought himself, and then his wife Betsy, whose 'missus' generously threw in her bed-ridden mother. *Ibid.* 73 He told them he was sure I was a 'very great Missis'. **1894** E. GLANVILLE *Fair Colonist* 89 He wanted to see the missis. 'The missis!' remarked the cook, scornfully. 'Did he expect the missis would see a black fellow like him?' **1911** BLACKBURN & CADDELL *Secret Service* 69 His instructions were to find out if and where the missis wrote and posted letters during the day. **1929** [see KWAAI sense 1 a]. **1930** *Star* 24 Jan., What are we coloured girls .. to do? The behaviour of some tram conductors is unbearable. Some of them want to know where your 'missus' is. If told 'there's no missus,' they say, 'You can't get on my car.' **1943** *Weekend News & Sunday Mag.* 20 Mar. 4 'Well, my Missus is going to de Show Ball,' goes on Katjie, 'an if she is going dere, wat will I wear?' **1956** D. JACOBSON *Dance in Sun* 146 Mrs Fletcher now added .. several remarks about the ingratitude of kaffirs .. and of their disregard of the length of service they had had under one particular missus, or even the father of the missus. **1971** 'LM' in *Rand Daily Mail* 27 July 12 Whites would 'all get along very much better without Non-Whites' is a deliberate untruth — ask the Missus whose children are brought up by Black nannies? **1979** W. EBERSOHN *Lonely Place* 65 In their world it was normal .. to possess only the worn-out bits of clothing brought home by their mothers from the home of the missis after the missis' children had outgrown them. **1986** M. RAMGOBIN *Waiting to Live* 151 You can ask the missus to buy them and I will be able to pay her at the end of the week when I get my wages.

b. Any white woman.

1861 LADY DUFF-GORDON *Lett. from Cape* (1925) 65 An 'indulgence of talk', from an English 'Missus' seemed the height of gratification, and the pride and pleasure of giving hospitality a sufficient reward. **1887** A.A. ANDERSON *25 Yrs in Waggon* I. 18 Her father wanted to sell her .. to the old man, and she did not like it, .. therefore she fled from the Kraal .. , and she begged the 'misses' would let her stop and work for her. **1900** H. BLORE *Imp. Light Horseman* 312 Jafta pondered for a while .. and then replied, 'There are no baases there, only misseses'. **1942** P. ABRAHAMS *Dark Testament* 113 As soon as she saw it was a white person she ran, back into the house. 'Ma! Ma! There's a missus at the door!' **1961** T. MATSHIKIZA *Choc. for my Wife* 91 'He looks cheeky, too, my baas.' 'Aren't you the one there's a complaint about from a white missus?' **1970** M. DIKOBE Marabi Dance. 57 You can already dress like a white missus, and Jo'burg girls dress like that. **1980** E. JOUBERT *Poppie Nongena* 54 We bought milk from the old missus and fresh bread which she baked. **1987** *Pace* Aug. 4 When some verkramptes can't accept a darkie looking at a mere photograph of a white woman, what about the real affair between a missis and a darkie ou?

2. A term of address. Cf. MIESIES sense 2.

a. Used by servants to a female employer, often in the third person, as a sign of respect; NONNA sense 2 b; NOOI sense 1 b. Cf. MADAM sense 1 b.

1855 H. RABONE in A. Rabone *Rec. of Pioneer Family* (1966) 105 One girl said, 'You are drunk.' 'Yes Missis, ' was the reply, 'it's Christmas time, and I mean to be till New Year.' **1862** LADY DUFF-GORDON *Lett. from Cape* (1925) 127 The Malays have such agreeable manners ... They have an affectionate way of saying '*my* missis' when they know one, which is very nice to hear. **1878** H.A. ROCHE *On Trek in Tvl* 298 It would be, 'Would missus like the fire lighted?' or 'Did missus call?' 'Missus had better hold on, bad place coming'. **1888** *Cape Punch* 25 Jan. 60 W.L.: Well, Jim, any news? Jim: Yah, misses, much news. **1911** P. GIBBON *Margaret Harding* 44 She had caught from Mrs. Jakes the first rule of polite conversation ... 'Sun burning plenty; how's Missis?' was her usual opening gambit. **1926** S.G. MILLIN in *Voorslag* Vol.1 No.3, 11, I cheated missis to take from her money for things she did not want. Don't speak to me of more payment, my missis. **1930** N. STEVENSON *Farmers of Lekkerbat* 215 The first to come out was the native, Temba; .. he knew what had taken place. 'Oh! Missus!' he said gravely, 'you were not able to protect Elofshuis.' **1954** A. SEGAL *Jhb. Friday* 17 'Have the shoes been polished?' she demanded of Sixpence. 'Yes, Missus,' he said. **1963** A.M. LOUW *20 Days* 77 'It is my cousin from Swellendam, old missus,' Katrina lied glibly. **1976** S. CLOETE *Canary Pie* 121 With Francis ill she had to run the farm. She hated the farm, she hated the natives. They said, 'Ja, Missis ... No, Missis,' and then did exactly as they wanted.

b. Used in addressing any white woman.

1968 F.C. METROWICH *Frontier Flames* 229 She was awakened by a rough voice shouting 'Missus! Missus!' She .. found two men at the bedroom door. They had been sent by the chief to tell her that not a second was to be lost. **1976** J. BECKER *Virgins* (1986) 11 'What is your name?' 'Yes misses.' ... 'Your *name*. What are you called?' Susan interpreted, and Hannah said her name was Hannah. 'Can't you speak English?' 'Yes misses.' **1980** E. PATEL *They Came at Dawn* 9 But haanetjie wants to jingle - .. a dance is a dance .. howsit Mister Black ... I am Miss White .. lets jingle jangle ... 'norr missuse' 'y-not?' 'cos of aparthate.' **1986** J. WHYLE in S. Gray *Market Plays* 178 This guy walks behind her for about two blocks trying to force her into alleys and things. So eventually Linda loses her temper and .. says, 'Listen fuck off!' So he says 'Sorry missus' and he splits. **1990** R. STENGEL *January Sun* 45, I used to see my father referring to whites in — how should I say it? — he referred to them with awe and undue respect. To an old white man, he would say, *Oubaas*, and to a woman, he would say *Missus*.

3. With a qualifying word indicating age: **klein missus** /klem -/ or **small-missus** [(part.) translations of Afk. *klein miesies*], NONNIE sense a; also used as a title with a name. See also OUMISSUS.

1899 B. MITFORD *Weird of Deadly Hollow* 241 Maghtag, **Klein Missis**! I think we shall have a storm to-night. **1900** —— *Aletta* 290 And the *klein missis* told me that it didn't matter if I killed the horse if only we did that. **1924** [see KLEIN sense a]. **1979** W. EBERSOHN *Lonely Place* 193 You worked for the Old-boss from the time **Small-missis** Marie and Small-boss Marthinus were babies?

mist var. MIS.

Mist Belt *n. phr.* Also with small initials. Collectively, several areas in the eastern foothills of the Drakensberg, lying mainly between 1 100 and 1 500 metres above sea level, in which mist and high humidity are so common that they have a notable effect on vegetation and agriculture. Also *attrib.*

1928 *Farming in S. Afr.* Oct. 1031 (Swart), Citrus scab is widely distributed in citrus nurseries, especially in the regions known collectively as the 'mist belt'. *c*1936 *S. & E. Afr. Yr Bk & Guide* 715 The 'Mist-belt' region and the land lying along the foot of the Drakensberg Mountains are exceptionally fertile. **1951** *Archeol. & Nat. Resources of Natal* (Univ. of Natal) 56 The agricultural significance of these local scarps has given rise to a specific term, namely the 'mist belt', in which are to be found most of the wattle plantations, mixed-dairy farms and horticultural nurseries of Natal. **1957** *Handbk for Farmers* (Dept of Agric.) I. 19 The Mist Belt. Along a belt of high country (1,500 to 4,500 feet in altitude) traversing the Natal midlands the annual rainfall .. is both supplemented and rendered more effective by .. mists ... In summer .. they generally occur on about 10 days in the month. The moisture which is filtered out by condensation against the vegetation is an appreciable addition to the rainfall ... Largely on account of its humidity this is an area of intensive agriculture. **1967** D. EDWARDS *Plant-Ecological Survey of Tugela River Basin* 167 The Midland Mist Belt Region, from 3,500 ft to 4,500 ft. *Ibid.* 174 Evergreen *Podocarpus* Forests form the climatic climax vegetation of the Midland Mist Belt. *c*1988 *S. Afr. 1987–8: Off. Yrbk* (Bureau for Info.) 9 In the summer rainfall region, light orographic rains are common along the windward slopes of the eastern escarpment. Lower down, at heights of 1 100 to 1 500 m, orographic lifting of the moist air causes what is known as the 'mist belt'. **1990** W.R. TARBOTON in *Fauna & Flora* No.47, 1 The highest rainfall areas support 'mistbelt' type evergreen forests. *Ibid.* 2 These mistbelt forests fall within the Acocks veld-type known as 'north-eastern mountain sourveld' which is essentially a forest-grassland mosaic.

miste var. MIS.

mi vrouw var. MEVROU.

mixed veld /ˈmɪkst felt/ *n. phr.* Formerly also **mixed veldt**. [Eng. *mixed* formed by the mingling of different types + Afk. *veld* natural uncultivated vegetation (used as pasture).] Land used as pasture and consisting of a mixture of natural vegetation types, usu. either grass and scrub, or sweet and sour grass; GEBROKEN VELD. Also *attrib*. See also *sourveld* (SOUR sense 2), *sweetveld* (SWEET sense 2).

1880 S.W. SILVER & Co.'s *Handbk to S. Afr.* 155 No one can be long at the Cape, if he takes an interest in farms, without hearing of Sweet Veldt and Sour Veldt and Mixed Veldt. 1906 F. BLERSCH *Handbk of Agric.* 256 Where the annual rainfall is fairly evenly distributed and not too scanty, the pasturage is generally best, and may be classed as *grass veld* and *mixed veld* pasturage. 1910 A.B. LAMONT *Rural Reader* 252 Mixed veld is a mixture of grass and bushes. 1911 *Farmer's Weekly* 15 Mar. 4 The farm is flat and hilly and contains mixed veld suitable for all kinds of stock. 1955 J.D. SCOTT et al. in D. Meredith *Grasses & Pastures* 603 Mixed Veld types are intermediate types. They occur in areas with rainfall intermediate between that of the sour and sweet veld. There is an admixture of grass types found in the other two veld types. 1989 J. DU P. BOTHMA *Game Ranch Management* 600 For the effective management of the veld and the rest of the game ranch, the rancher should have a sound knowledge of .. the location and area of sweet veld, mixed veld and sour veld on the ranch. 1992 F.P. VAN OUDTSHOORN *Guide to Grasses* 39 Mixed veld represents an intermediate form between sweetveld and sourveld. Mixed veld of which the characteristics correspond to those of sweetveld, is known as sweet mixed veld, and vice versa as sour mixed veld.

miza var. MAIZA.

Mjanji, Mjantshi varr. MODJADJI.

mji(e)ta var. MAJITA.

MK *n.* Also **M.K.** Short for UMKHONTO WE SIZWE; also, a member of this organization. Also *attrib*.

1964 H.H.W. DE VILLIERS *Rivonia* 99 This witness stated that the M.K. (Umkonto we Sizwe) was looked upon as the military wing of the African National Congress. 1984 R. DAVIES et al. *Struggle for S. Afr.* II. 294 The formation of MK marked the beginnings of the armed struggle now based on a new formal organisational alliance between the Communist Party and the ANC. 1988 M. PETANE in *Frontline* Apr. 8 MK was formed when the ANC was banned. 1989 V. GUNENE in *Weekly Mail* 3 Feb. 4 As MK soldiers, we do not recognise this civilian court. 1990 *Sunday Times* 18 Feb. 22 In ANC parlance, MK is short for Umkhonto we Sizwe — the movement's military wing. 1991 G. MCINTOSH in *Ibid.* 13 Jan. 16 Comparing MK to the SADF is like comparing a mouse to an elephant. 1992 J. CONTRERAS in *Newsweek* 22 June 25 Mandela and other leaders were prepared to ignore the mayhem of some returned ANC guerrillas from .. MK as long as they confined themselves to gangsterism, like ex-MK's in a Durban township who call themselves the Russians and specialize in bank robbery. 1993 *Daily News* 15 Jan. 3 On his involvement in suppressing the mutiny [in ANC camps in Angola], Mr Hani said he stepped in to stop the disintegration of MK and saw his task as restoring authority through 'persuasive discussions and not the use of force' ... Mr Hani said several members were sentenced to death after the mutiny by a tribunal.

‖**mkhaya** /m̩ˈka(ː)ɪa/ *n.* Also **mkaya**. Pl. **abakhaya, amakhaya**. [Xhosa *umkhaya* (pl. *abakhaya*) a neighbour, Zulu *umkhaya* (sing. only) the family.] Mainly in urban (esp. township) parlance: HOME-BOY.

1963 [see MIGRANT]. 1963 WILSON & MAFEJE *Langa* 51 In Cape Town then, a group of men from a small country village tend to live, eat, and work together. They address one another as *mkhaya* or home-boy if they are men of some education. 1976 [see HOME-BOY]. 1981 *Voice* 8 Apr. 2 That promising young man .. is your 'mkhaya'. He also lives in Dobsonville, that is. 1981 B. MFENYANA in M. Mutloatse *Reconstruction* 301 Mr Man breezes into Boston, and starts asking for 'fags'. He is greeted by blank expressions (at the very least). Soon the pained expression on his homza's face makes him ask, 'But whatsepnin, mkhaya?'

Mkhonto we Sizwe var. UMKHONTO WE SIZWE.

‖**Mkhulu** /m̩ˈkuːlʊ/ *n.* Also with small initial. Pl. **abakhulu**. [In the Nguni languages, a term of respect, being the vocative case of *umkhulu*, 'one of rank', 'old one', 'great one'.] Esp. among speakers of the Nguni languages: a respectful form of address or reference to a man more powerful than oneself.

1961 T. MATSHIKIZA *Choc. for my Wife* 103 'Where is your rag?' the warder asked me. 'I got there late, Mkhulu, big chief.' ... 'How are you, Fana Wami (my son)?' ... 'Yes, Mkhulu, yes my father.' 1978 M. MATSHOBA in *Staffrider* Vol.1 No.2, 11 The dignity of old age overcame some of the visitors' bragadocio. 'It is abakhulu (the big ones) who have sent us, magogo.' 1980 C. NKOSI in M. Mutloatse *Forced Landing* 10 'Ho, ho, you boys do not know anything. Ask this one,' he said pointing at his chest. 'You say so Mkhulu?' 1993 *Sowetan* 22 Jan. 8 (cartoon) 'Do you think we are only saving for Christmas?' 'You are right, mkhulu. Most of us here want to save for the future.'

mkhwetha, mkweta var. ABAKWETHA.

mkolwa var. KHOLWA.

m'kula's var. AMAKULA.

Mkulunkulu var. UNKULUNKULU.

mlaba-laba var. UMLABALABA.

mlungu, umlungu /m̩ˈlʊ(ː)ŋgʊ, ʊm-/ *n.* and *adj.* Pl. usu. **abelungu** /abe-, æbə-/, or **-s**. Forms: *sing.* **malo(o)nga, malunga, moloonga, moolongo, m(u)lungu, simlunga, umlunga, umlungo, umlungu**; *pl.* **abalongo, abalo(o)ngu, abalungu, abe(h)lungu, malongoes, melonges, melonggoes, melongoes, umlungi, umlungos, (u)mlungus**. [Xhosa and Zulu *umlungu* (pl. *abelungu*, sing. vocative *mlungu*, perh. fr. *lunga* get or be in order, become or be correct or good; or rel. to the n. stem *-lungu* canoe, ship, found in some other Sintu (Bantu) languages; for notes on sing. and pl. forms, see ABA-, ABE-, and UM-.]

A. *n.*

1. A white person. Cf. LEKGOA.

Used esp. in the context of interactions between black and white South Africans. Now often *derog.* or ironic, esp. as used by black writers.

1826 A.G. BAIN *Jrnls* (1949) 108 The next also chose the Malunga, or white man, and of course I took the hint to kiss the hand of my fair one. 1836 A.F. GARDINER *Journey to Zoolu Country* 245 Being informed of my intentions and asked if he had any message to the Great Chief of the Abalungu (white people — literally people who do right). 1836 N. ISAACS *Trav.* (1937) II., He conversed with me .. on .. the bravery of the Malongoes or white people. 1856 R.J. MULLINS *Diary.* 22 Oct., I said his people would then eat aloe leaves. He said 'They will not, they will steal and then there will be war, but he would go to the Abalongu.' 1859 'B.' in *Cape Monthly Mag.* V. Jan. 43 These princesses came to beg a present from the Umlungu (white man). 1875 D. LESLIE *Among Zulus* 9, I heard that a Moloonga, with a boy, had just passed the day before. 1889 'MYNHEER STALS' in H.A. Bryden *Kloof & Karroo* 63 It could only have been English *ūmlūngos* or drunken men who would have taken the drift on such a night. [*Note*] *Ūmlūngos* is a very expressive Kaffir word, signifying a sort of gentlemanly know-nothing or green-horn. 1899 A. WERNER *Captain of Locusts* 193, I bade him begone; and he began to utter evil words of the abelungu. 1910 J. ANGOVE *In Early Days* 68 They would get as many diamonds as they could, in order to ingratiate themselves with the 'umlungu', who took such a great interest in them. 1919 *Illust. London News* (U.K.) 17 Oct. 5 We must therefore avoid waiting for the Abelungu to do everything for us: we must help ourselves and he will think the better of us. 1961 D. BEE *Children of Yesterday* 284 Who knows how these doctors of the Abelungu keep blood in bottles for so long that they can take it from one man this month and put it in another man the next month? 1973 *Sunday Times* 22 July 16 Near Ixopo we spoke to Norman Mkwayane who has worked for R6 a month for the past 18 years without leave. He said the mlungu 'became angry' when workers asked for leave — so he never asked. 1980 M. MATSHOBA in M. Mutloatse *Forced Landing* 115 'We live like hogs, wild dogs or any other neglected animals. The pets of *abeLungu* live better then we,' Somdali would say to me. 1983 C.Z. ROLO in *Daily Dispatch* 23 June 24 We blacks don't hate whites. We love them and call them *umlungu* (good person). 1987 I. FYNN in *Sowetan* 5 May 6 Black South Africans must be relieved that the all-white election is almost over. Whites themselves probably feel the same way ... It's a wonder the *mlungus* haven't called for a general stayaway yesterday to get over it all. 1988 *Pace* Nov. 11 There is what we call petty thieving. Abelungu call it habitual stealing. 1990 [see JOZI]. 1992 W. KNOWLER in *Weekend Mercury* 4 Jan. 6 Everyone seemed to be having far too good a time to worry about two stray *umlungus*.

2. *sing.*, often without an article. White people collectively.

1836 A.F. GARDINER *Journey to Zoolu Country* 349 How oft on Abaloongu's race were threats and bitter curses heaped. 1949 T. MOFOLO *Chaka Zulu* (1965) 124 Chaka said: 'It is your hope that by killing me you will become chiefs when I am dead. But your hopes are false, for Umlungu will come, and it is he who will rule, and you will be his slaves.' 1952 H. KLEIN *Land of Silver Mist* 71 He told him how the white man, the umlungu, had conquered the Zulu armies, but had never broken the Zulu spirit. 1959 L. LONGMORE *Dispossessed* 245 *Umlungu* (the white man)! Don't tell me about him. He is the biggest *umthakathi* (wizard) I have ever known of. He stabs you in order to stitch you up. 1973 *Drum* 18 Jan. 33 Then somebody decreed that I go to my bantustan and leave the mlungu in the towns. 1985 *Ibid.* July 25 While he is still pondering the double standards applied by mlungu, he is told that Cape Town has decided that he is a citizen of a nebulous republic called Bophuthatswana and is not entitled to a South African passport. 1987 C.L. KGAPHOLA in *Staffrider* Vol.6 No.4, 48 Jabulani, Jubilate, Mlungu loves you. 1988 O. MUSI in *Frontline* Oct. 32 It did strike me that the white guy singing lustily alongside would probably change his tune if he found me at the bar of the nearby Royal Hotel. That place had been a mlungu-only haven for ever.

3. As a term of address: 'white person'.

1855 G.H. MASON *Life with Zulus* 121 A simultaneous exclamation of Molonga! Molonga! (white man! white man!) was succeeded by an universal beckon for me to come in. 1878 A. AYLWARD *Tvl of Today* 202 The black villain saluted me as 'Umlunga' (white man) although he could plainly see by my dress I was an Inkosi and a teacher. 1940 F.B. YOUNG *City of Gold* 114 'Where are you going and what do you want here, Umlungu?' 'We go north, but more towards the rising sun. We do you no harm. We are travellers.' 1955 J.B. SHEPHARD *Land of Tikoloshe* 76 My friend went on. 'I don't call him "Jim" or "Boy" but "Umteto", his real name. That is polite, but if I called him "Kaffir" he would, quite rightly, think I was being rude, and then he would probably call me "Umlungu" — White man — and that would be rude too.'

4. *rare.* A member of a people of the Transkei coast (see quot.).

1945 N. DEVITT *People & Places* 124 In various parts of the coastal areas, and in particular about 60 miles west of St. John is to be found a small tribe of natives known as the Abelungu (the white men). Ironically enough these people are of an extremely dark pigmentation. They pride themselves on their racial forbears. They contend they are descendants of white men, ship-wrecked people.

B. *adj.* **a.** Of a person: white. **b.** Of or pertaining to white people.

1973 *Drum* 22 Dec. 40 Those faces of the hurt Mlungu reporters also keep playing tricks with my imagination. Something's gotta be done. 1975 *Ibid.* 22 Dec. 2 Not that we Blackstanians ever get much. The reason could be that Santa is mlungu and takes care of his kind first before visiting our pondokkies. 1976 [see UMFUNDISI]. 1983 [see HAU]. 1983 *Frontline* Feb. 38 Often the Izibonda (civic leaders) or Bomabalane, act in concert with Abelungu officials, men who have open access to records, as the medium through which the impossible is made possible. 1985 *Drum* Jan. 32 Peter is mlungu. His football buddies are pluralstanians. 1987 [see PARAMOUNT sense a]. 1990 O. MUSI in *City Press* 17 June 9 What do I see the other day — and on a mlungu newspaper's front page, no less — but three uniformed white cops giving that old ANC sign.

Mlungustan see -STAN.

‖**Mma-** /ˈm̩ma/ *pref.* [Sotho and seTswana.] Among Sotho and Tswana peoples, used as a woman's title, usu. indicating respect or affection: **a.** 'Mother of', prefixed to the first name of one of the woman's children, esp. of her first-born son. **b.** 'Mrs', 'Mother', or 'Ma', prefixed to the woman's surname, clan name, or (occas.) nick-name or husband's title. Cf. MA-*pref.*[1], MAMA sense 1 a, MME.

1961 M.A. WALL *Dominee & Dom-Pas* 48 'No, *Mmamoruti*,' replied one of the old women. 'We have been lucky, we are glad.' 1980 B. LESHOAI in M. Mutloatse *Forced Landing* 129 Ou Breench was brought up by his grandmother, MmaSelala. He loved her fondly. 1984 *Staffrider* Vol.6 No.1, 37 One day when I was busy selling, one man I was acquainted with shouted at me and said, 'Mma-Josefa, why do you stand here selling apples in the street when on the other hand Joseph is busy working to support you and the children?' 1987 *Learn & Teach* No.2, 1 Both Mma Diniso and Oom Jantjie had lived in Sharpeville for many years. Mma Diniso started talking first. 1988 N. SEBOLAO in *Drum* Apr. 80 For a woman who obtained her JC Certificate through correspondence, 47 year-old Mrs Nora Mmankudu Glickman, better known as Mma-Mopipi, has not done too badly for herself as an enterprising businesswoman. 1990 [see MORUTI].

‖**Mme** /ˈm̩me/ *n.* Also with small initial. [Sotho and Venda.] Among the Sotho and Venda: 'Mother' or 'mother of', prefixed to the first name of a woman's child, or used as a title, and usu. indicating respect or affection. Cf. MA-*pref.*[1], MAMA sense 1 a, MMA-.

1979 M. MATSHOBA *Call Me Not a Man* 73 'What is it now Mme Thandi?' she inquired when she came to the two women. Mme Thandi was equally confounded. 1980 M. MUTLOATSE in *Forced Landing* Dedication, To mme masediba lilian ngoyi, auntie fatima meer, for their resilience and resourcefulness, black mothers who forever inspire us lost souls. 1993 [see NTATE sense 2].

mngqush(o) /m̩ˈnǂʊ(ː)ʃ(o), əm-, nʊʃ/ *n.* Also **(g)nush, ngqush, noosh, umngqushu.** [Xhosa *umngqusho.*] Maize kernels, coarsely broken, and usu. cooked with dried beans. See also SAMP.

1962 W.D. HAMMOND-TOOKE *Bhaca Soc.* 44 Occasionally a light meal of stamped maize (umngqusho) and marewu (unfermented beer) is taken on returning from the fields. 1970 S. SPARKS *Informant, Fort Beaufort* Pour your maas over the 'nush' and sprinkle with sugar. Eat from a soup plate with a spoon. 'Nush' is samp. This is a favourite dish amongst Eastern Cape farmers. 1976 *Drum* 15 May 2 The old women are washing the calabashes for the biggest drink-in the country has ever known, and also preparing tons and tons of mngqusho and ncancwa. 1979 *E. Prov. Herald* 30 Oct. 1 Though they were fed mostly on vegetables, they missed their usual diet of stamped mealies (umgqusho) and mealie porridge (umphoqoqo). 1980 *Voice* 20 Aug. 14 Today the migrant workers bring 'high culture' and Town Talk to the bundu. But, the villagers hit back — by taking Umabatha (the drama) and mngqusho back to London. 1982 M. MZAMANE *Children of Soweto* 198 Women boiled water and cooked meat and *umngqusho* in huge black three-legged pots over open fires. Now and again they called on the men to shift the pots. 1986 *Anon. handbill* Why not sommer just come in, sit right down, and see what the potjiekos is like. You could meet some of your best friends there, over a lovely dish of congealed ngqush. 1986 *Learn & Teach* No.2, 29 The school is like *umgqushu*, all mixed up, the beans and the samp together. We are like that, Africans, and coloureds and whites, all together. 1987 *Rhodeo* (Rhodes Univ.) Apr. 4 A hundred and twenty litres of umqomboti, a Xhosa home brew, was served along with gnush samp. 1987 M. POLAND *Train to Doringbult* When they were small she and Chrissie had built shelters, cooked ngqush, played endlessly at hospitals.

m'nheer var. MIJNHEER.

‖**Mnr** *n.* [Afk., written abbrev. of *meneer.*] MIJNHEER sense 1.

1973 [see *nee n.* (NEE)]. 1980 [see MENEER sense 1].

mntwana var. UMTWANA.

mnumzana, -zane varr. UMNUMZANA.

mo- /mɔ-/ *pref.* A Sotho and seTswana singular noun prefix found in some words originating in these languages.

In Sotho and seTswana, the plural of words beginning *mo-* is formed by replacing this prefix with *ba-*. In *S. Afr. Eng.*, this pattern is not always observed, the plural sometimes being formed by adding the English plural suffix *-s* to the singular form or, less often, the singular form being used unchanged as a plural. See also BA-.

mobela var. MOBOLA.

mo-bhalane var. MABALANE.

mobola /mɔˈbɔla, məˈbəʊlə/ *n.* Also **mobela.** [Present in various forms in the Sintu (Bantu) languages, as seTswana *mola*, Ndebele *mbola*, Venda *muvhula*, etc.] In full **mobola plum: a.** Either of two species of tree of the Chrysobalanaceae, *Parinari curatellifolia* or *P. capensis*; HISSING TREE. **b.** The edible fruit of this tree. In both senses also called GRYSAPPEL. Also *attrib.*

1857 D. LIVINGSTONE *Missionary Trav.* 237 A much better fruit, called mobela, was also presented to us. This bears, around a pretty large stone, as much of the fleshy part as the common date. 1917 R. MARLOTH *Common Names* 58 *Mobola plum, Parinarium mobola.* (The Hissing tree or grijsappelboom). The fruit apple-like, very aromatic. 1929 J. STEVENSON-HAMILTON *Low-Veld* 46 Another plum-like fruit grows on the mobola (Parinarium mobola) or grys appel, a large evergreen tree with dark green foliage: the fruit looks rather like a mango, and has an even larger stone than the latter. 1961 PALMER & PITMAN *Trees of S. Afr.* 143 One of the most typical trees .. is the mobola plum or grysappel, a handsome evergreen tree, bearing one of the best of our wild fruits. 1966 C.A. SMITH *Common Names* 340 *Mobola plum*, .. The fruit of *Parinari curatellifolia* s.sp. *mobola* or the plant itself (Lowveld to Rdsa [sc. 'Rhodesia' (Zimbabwe)]). 1972 G.L.F. HARTWIG in *Std Encycl. of Sn Afr.* VII. 479 Mobola Plum, Grysappel. Cork-tree. Hissing tree ... The brownish grey fruit is plum-shaped, somewhat resembling an apple, and is very tasty. 1977 E. PALMER *Field Guide to Trees* 116 Mobola Plum, .. Typically a graceful tree up to 12m high ... Fruit very popular with people and animals. 1983 K.C. PALGRAVE *Trees of Sn Afr.* 211 The mobola plum is much sought after by local peoples and consequently the trees are seldom chopped down. 1989 J. DU P. BOTHMA *Game Ranch Management* 26 The high-lying western parts of the Transvaal Lowveld have a higher rainfall and trees such as *Pterocarpus angolensis* (wild teak) and *Parinari curatellifolia* (mobola plum) .. are fairly common.

Mochache var. MODJADJI.

Mochuana var. BECHUANA.

Model C *n. phr.* [Used first by the Minister of National Education in a letter explaining the new system to education departments and parents.] Used *attrib.*, esp. of a formerly 'white' state school which has chosen an administrative structure allowing discretion concerning the admission of pupils (including the option to accept pupils from all ethnic groups), and giving more freedom (under a Board of Governors), but less financial support from the provincial education department; loosely, a non-racial state school.

In the early 1990s various options were offered to (exclusively 'white') state schools in an attempt to resolve the issues of dwindling state resources and pressure for non-racial schooling: Model A (private and self-funding), Model B (provincially-funded but exercising its own admission criteria), Model C, and Model Q (retaining the status quo). 'Model D' was the name given to DET schools which operated as Model B schools. 'Model C' is the only designation which has assumed some importance in *S. Afr. Eng.*

1991 M. METCALFE *Desegregating Education in South Africa* (Education Policy Unit, Wits University) 17 On 10th September 1990, Minister Piet Case announced the new government admission policy options for white State schooling ... For each of the three models (designated A, B and C) it was stipulated that the total number of white children had to be at least 51% of the whole ... Model C offers the possibility of semi-privatisation. 1992 *Weekend Argus* 22 Feb. 19 The revised [parliamentary] programme for next week allows for the Education Affairs Amendment Bill, which provides for the conversion of white schools to Model C. 1992 A.B. OLMESDAHL in *Natal Witness* 9 Nov. 5 The salaries paid by the [Natal Education] department to teaching and non-teaching staff at Model C schools represents more than 80% of the costs. 1992 in *Weekend Mercury* 19 Dec. 4 Feeling the brunt of Model C fees. Parents face staggering school fee increases next month when the full brunt of the conversion to Model C will be felt for the first time. 1993 [see Sunday Times quot. at OWN AFFAIR sense 2]. 1993 A. RALPHS in *Weekly Mail* 8 Apr. (Suppl.) 4 A .. caretaker of a local church in one of the 'grey areas' of Johannesburg had his grandchildren refused entry into the local Model C school ... He now has to .. transport them to schools in Soweto ... The failure of the Model C option lies .. in its naive and dangerous attempt to isolate a small section of the population from the systemic nature of the education crisis in South Africa. 1993 P. MAURICE in *Ibid.* By last August, 98 percent of all previously white schools in the country had voted to become Model C. 1993 *DEC News* Vol.4 No.1, 6 In future Model C schools will be referred to by the Department as state-aided schools. 1994 G. KNOWLER in *Weekend Argus* 12 Feb. 7 Angry parents have threatened court action to overturn a decision barring black children from the Model C Hluhluwe Primary School in Zululand. 1995 K. STRACHAN in *E. Prov. Herald* 11 Jan. 3 The ANC was opposed to Model C schools insofar as they were used to maintain white privilege.

modelling *vbl. n. Slang.* [Transf. use of general Eng. *modelling* the action of working as a model in order to display clothes.] In urban (esp. township) English: the parading of an offender, naked through a public place, as a form of punishment. Also *attrib.*

1990 K. MKHIZE in M. Kentridge *Unofficial War* 69 Comrades have banned smoking in buses ... The new system of punishment is 'modelling'. This is where a person is stripped naked and forced to parade, confessing his or her offence. There are heated arguments about 'modelling'. Some elders are strongly for it. They say it has helped clean up crime ... Defenders of modelling admit it is humiliating but say it is better than the necklace ... Inkatha officials have told me that modelling is bringing them new supporters. They say Inkatha is being asked to stop the amaqabane's immoral punishment. **1990** M. NDWANDWE in *Tribute* Sept. 65 The police were .. not interested in intervening. They would, at times, be interested onlookers during a 'modelling' session. 'Modelling' was the practice whereby offenders would be forced to parade through the public streets naked while being stoned and beaten with sticks. **1994** R.W. JOHNSON in *London Review of Books* (U.K.) 6 Jan. 10 In addition, this being ANC territory, both sides operated 'people's courts', dispensing summary justice — sometimes death, but more usually whippings or 'modelling', in which the guilty party has to strip naked and walk through the camp amid a crowd of jeering onlookers.

Hence **model** *v. trans.* and *intrans.*, to (force one to) undergo the punishment of 'modelling'.

1990 K. MKHIZE in M. Kentridge *Unofficial War* 69 A comrade argues: 'Modelling the offender acts as a rehabilitating exercise to deter crime.' **1990** M. NDWANDWE in *Tribute* Sept. 65 A journalist from a Durban-based alternative weekly, *The New African*, dared to write about these apparent injustices and had to face the music. Attempts to get him to 'model' were subsequently abandoned.

Moderamen /ˌmɒdəˈrɑːmən/ *n.* Also with small initial. [Afk. (fr. Du.), the governing body of a protestant church, fr. L. *moderamen* a means of controlling; government.] The executive body of a synod in the DUTCH REFORMED churches.

1973 A.A. LOUW in *Std Encycl. of Sn Afr.* VIII. 145 Each synod [of the Nederduitse Gereformeerde Kerk] at its opening session elects an executive body, the Moderamen, which acts for it until the next synod. The chairman of the Moderamen, and of the synod, is termed the Moderator. **1983** B. STUART in *Argus* 31 Oct. 3 The Moderamen of the Western Cape Synod of the NGK also asked congregations to observe it as a day of prayer and humility on the eve of Wednesday's white referendum. **1985** *Cape Times* 21 Sept., The moderamen prays for genuine guidance from God for the State President. **1986** E. *Prov. Herald* 24 Sept. 4 The Archbishop of Cape Town .. has decided to confer with his fellow Anglican bishops before responding to an invitation to have talks with the Western Cape Moderamen of the Ned Geref Kerk.

‖**Modimo** /mʊˈdiːmʊ/ *n.* [Sotho and seTswana, 'God'; with small initial, also in the senses 'god', 'ancestral spirit' (pl. *badimo* (see BADIMO) and *medimo*).

In the orthography of Lesotho this word is represented as *Molimo* /mʊˈdiːmʊ/. It appears that the earliest form was *Morimo*.]

Esp. among speakers of Sotho or seTswana: the supreme being; the Christian God; also used as an interjection; MOLIMO; MORIMO. Cf. TIXO, MORENA sense 3. See also BADIMO.

[**1933** A. WERNER *Myths & Legends* 41 The Bapedi (a branch of the Basuto living in the Transvaal) say that their High God (*Modimo o mogolo*) is called Huveane, and they pray to him for rain.] **1963** A.M. LOUW *20 Days* 142 He seemed to be praying in the Sotho language ... She bowed her head reverently, but beyond the occasional Modimo — God — she heard little. **1970** A. SILLERY in *Std Encycl. of Sn Afr.* II. 223 In pre-Christian times the Tswana believed in a remote deity called Modimo and practised a cult primarily concerned with .. ancestor worship. **1974** M. MUTLOATSE in S. Gray *On Edge of World* 111 Ntate Moruti was praying unnoticed: 'Modimo, forgive them, for they know not ...'. **1976** WEST & MORRIS *Abantu* 122 Like the Pedi, the Tswana believed in a supreme being, *Modimo*, a creator too remote to be approached by ordinary men. **1981** *Voice* 1 Apr. 17 Modimo does at times reveal Himself in many subtle ways, and we as earthlings dismiss some of these revelations as insignificant.

1987 M. MELAMU *Children of Twilight* 25 'Modimo.' These children of today. Their hearts are hard as stones, I tell you. **1988** M. MANYANYE in *Pace* May 22 We know that our ancestors, whom we call 'badimo' are mediators between us and our God, whom we call 'Modimo'.

Modjadji /mɔˈdʒɑːdʒi/ *n.* Also **Madjadja, Mjanji, Mjantshi, Mochache, Modjadge, Modjadje, Mujaji.** [In N. Sotho, the name of the woman who became the first rain queen; perh. fr. personal prefix *mo-* + *tšatši* day, sun.]

I. A personal name.

1.a. The hereditary name adopted by the RAIN QUEEN of the LOBEDU people.

1897 C.W. MACKINTOSH tr. F. Coillard's *On Threshold of Central Afr.* 77, I had set off with two of the evangelists to Mochache's ... Mochache, you must know, is the high priestess of the neighbouring tribes. She has her sanctuary in a wooded gorge. **1929** A.T. BRYANT *Olden Times in Zululand & Natal* 210 To fall into disfavour with queen Mjanji was ever a matter of gravest concern; for she was the magician *par excellence* of those parts, and the fear she inspired and the extent of her fame surpassed those of Mantatisi herself ... She was the most extraordinary, most powerful and most mysterious female of her time — if indeed, as was asserted, she was not eternal — in all South Africa. *Ibid.* 211 It would appear that Mjanji is not a personal, but a class name, applied to each successive ruler of these people, all of which rulers, at least for some generations, seem to have been females. This perpetuation of the name will explain the supposed attribute of immortality. **1949** [see LOBEDU]. **1955** [see RAIN QUEEN]. **1956** T.V. BULPIN *Lost Trails of Tvl* 22 Among the many myths gathered round the person of Mujaji was the idea that she lived for ever. **1959**, **1979** [see RAIN QUEEN]. **1979** P. MILLER *Myths & Legends* 204 The female dynasty was founded. To his daughter-bride Mugado gave the hereditary name of *Modjadji*, meaning 'the ruler of the day', and into her keeping .. he entrusted the sacred rainmaking medicines and magic rituals. **1988** [see LOBEDU].

b. Followed by a numeral: a particular RAIN QUEEN, identified by her position in the succession.

1943 E.J. & J.D. KRIGE *Realm of Rain-Queen* 11 A cheerless panorama unfolds before us as Mujaji III ascends the throne ... When the white man, coming to arrange for the recognition of the new queen, sees old Mathogani, who had impersonated Mujaji II, the proceedings are stopped. **1979** P. MILLER *Myths & Legends* 204 Father Time .. cut Modjadji down some time in the 1860s, leaving her daughter to don the mystic mantle of her mother. Modjadji II maintained her power and her mystery .. as skilfully as her mother had done. **1980** *Sunday Times* 16 Nov. 11 Modjadji IV, Rain Queen of the Vhalovedu, had always wanted an umbrella ... 'I bring the rain for other people,' she complained bitterly. 'Why can't somebody think about keeping it off me?' **1982** *Sunday Times* 21 Feb. (Mag. Sect.) 1 When she is installed as Modjadji V, Mokope will be expected to live out her years in seclusion in her village — also called Modjadji, the headquarters of the 100 000 strong Balobelu tribe.

II. A common noun.

2. Pl. **-s**, or unchanged. RAIN QUEEN sense a.

1943 E.J. & J.D. KRIGE *Realm of Rain-Queen* 1 Amid the convulsions .. the kingdom of the Mujajis arose to prominence. **1974** [see LOBEDU]. **1977** [see sense 3 below]. **1982** *Sunday Times* 5 Sept. (Extra) 2 This Queen is said to have died childless and to have nominated her successor ... They accepted the black girl as the true Modjadji.

3. Usu. in the phrr. *Modjadji('s) palm*, or (less commonly) *Modjadji cycad*. The cycad *Encephalartos transvenosus*, protected by and sacred to the Rain Queen; also called BREAD TREE. Also *attrib.*

1965 S. ELIOVSON *S. Afr. Wild Flowers for Garden* 223 *Modjadji Palm*, A tall-stemmed species. **1974** C. GIDDY in *E. Prov. Herald* 13 Nov. 23 It has been my privilege

to stand in the swirl of cloud and mist among the age-old stems of the Madjadja Palms on the hill below the Kraal of the Rain Queen. **1977** E. PALMER *Field Guide to Trees* 67 *Modjadji's Palm, Encephalartos transvenosus* ... Tall, up to 13m, usually un-branched .. A handsome and famous species, protected by generations of Rain Queens (Modjadji), making the territory near Duiwelskloof the only cycad forest in Southern Africa. **1980** *S. Afr. Panorama* Sept. 43 The romance of Rain Queen country clings to this largest Modjadji forest, in the Duiwelskloof garden of Dr Louis Botha. **1988** H. GOOSEN in *Ibid.* March 36 (*caption*) Rain queen territory. Modjadji cycads (*E. transvenosus*) can grow 13m tall, with a stem diameter of 45 cm.

moeder *n. obs.* [Du., subsequently Afk.] A mother; also used as a respectful form of address to an older woman. Also (as an endearment) **moedertjie** [see -IE].

Usu. included by writers to suggest Afrikaans dialogue.

1798 LADY A. BARNARD in Lord Lindsay *Lives of Lindsays* (1849) III. 430 'Good morrow, moeder!' said Gaspar to an old Hottentot woman with a dog running by her side. *Ibid.* 468 Myhneer was at the Cape, but we were received by the old moeder, by his daughter-in-law, two daughters, and a granddaughter of her own. **1913** A.B. MARCHAND *Dirk, S. African* 226 (Swart), 'Come, moeder', he said, 'What do you think?' **1920** R.Y. STORMBERG *Mrs Pieter de Bruyn* 22 Dear Moeder, it's a crazy kind of letter you'll have this time. *Ibid.* 50 So don't distress yourself, dear Moedertje.

moederkappie /ˈmʊdə(r)ˌkapi, ˈmu-/ *n.* Also **moederkapje.** [Afk. (earlier S. Afr. Du. *moederkapje*), lit. 'mother-bonnet', fr. Du. *moeder* mother + *kap* hood + dim. suffix -IE; see quot. 1966.] A name given to any of several species of Orchidaceae which have bonnet-shaped flowers, esp. *Disperis capensis*, *Bonatea speciosa*, and *Pterygodium catholicum*. Also Englished form **muttercap**. See also *Hottentot bonnet* (HOTTENTOT *n.* sense 6 a).

1887 J. MACKINNON *S. Afr. Traits* 124 Here is the Pride of Table Mountain and the Muttercap, two of the twenty-five species of orchids that exist in South Africa. **1910** D. FAIRBRIDGE *That Which Hath Been* (1913) 270 Orchids in inexhaustible variety, from scarlet disas to yellow moeder-kapjes, from pink trevors to countless jewels of mauve or blue .. are still left to us. **1917** R. MARLOTH *Common Names* 58 *Moederkappie*, Various orchids e.g. *Pterygodium catholicum, Disperis capensis*, etc. **1924** D. FAIRBRIDGE *Gardens of S. Afr.* 138 A dull-green jar holds pale-yellow moeder-kapjes, .. and the perfume from the little hooded flowers fills the room. **1952** *Cape Times* 8 May 14 Pine trees, together with humans, have been too much for the nerines, the *moederkappies* and other veld things which used to flower there. **1966** C.A. SMITH *Common Names* 340 *Moederkappie*, A name given to various terrestrial orchids in which the upper sepal is conspicuously hooded ... The whole flower bears a striking resemblance to the old type of Dutch 'kappie' (bonnet) and the lateral sepals enhance the effect by their suggestion of ribbons for tying the 'kappie'. **1973** M.R. LEVYNS in *Std Encycl. of Sn Afr.* VIII. 382 *Moederkappie, Oumakappie*, .. These names are borne by two quite distinct species: *Pterygodium catholicum* .. is usually about 20cm high, with two or three leaves sheathing the somewhat fleshy stem. The few sulphur-yellow flowers are borne in a lax spike. As the flowers fade they turn dull red ... *Disperis capensis*. Common orchid, sometimes called 'granny bonnet', with magenta, greenish or cream-coloured flowers. **1977** *Sunday Times* 2 Oct. (Mag. Sect.) 3 The overpowering smell of moederkappies. [**1983** M.M. KIDD *Cape Peninsula* 78 *Disperis capensis ... Moederkappie. Ibid.* 116 *Disperis villosa ... Moederkappie.*]

‖**Moederkerk** /ˈmʊdə(r)kɛrk/ *n.* Also with small initial. [Afk., *moeder* mother + *kerk* church.] Often in the n. phrr. **Dutch Reformed Moederkerk, Nederduits Gereformeerde Moederkerk.** A name given to the oldest Dutch Reformed church (building) in a particular area.

*c*1970 *Stellenbosch (brochure)* 35 In Drostdy Street is the D.R. Moederkerk ('Mother Church'), consecrated in 1722 and therefore the second oldest surviving church building in the country. [**1974** *S. Afr. Panorama* May 26 The Dutch Reformed 'Mother' Church (Moederkerk), the oldest church in Bethlehem was built in 1910.] **1975** C. RAMUSI in T. Sundermeier *Church & Nationalism* 119 The church is white dominated: Authority rests with the white leader. Africans are always puppets or are intimidated: e.g. rule by the 'moederkerk'. **1979** *E. Prov. Herald* 14 June (Suppl.) 6 Further along Drostdy Street is the neo-gothic Dutch Reformed 'Moederkerk', which dates in its present form from 1863, although some walls were part of an earlier church built in 1722. **1988** A. CAMPBELL in *Fair Lady* 27 Apr. 93 The funeral .. is held in the Nederduitse Gereformeerde Moederkerk in George.

moeg /mʊx, mux/ *adj. colloq.* [Afk.] Tired, weary. Common in speech.

1920 R.Y. STORMBERG *Mrs Pieter de Bruyn* 49 Ek's jolly moeg, but my powers of endurance are steadily growing, glad to say. **1969** A. FUGARD *Boesman & Lena* 3 I'll keep on walking. I'll walk and walk .. until you're so bloody *moeg* that when I stop you can't open your mouth! **1975** *Informant, Grahamstown*, I feel so moeg today: it must be the heat. **1985** *Informant, Grahamstown* I'd like to walk in the evening after we close the shop, but I'm too moeg.

moegie /ˈmʊxi, ˈmuxi/ *n. colloq.* Also **(i)moogie**. [Afk. and Isicamtho, *moegoe* (see MOEGOE) + -IE.] MOEGOE.

1963 WILSON & MAFEJE *Langa* 71 He was sent home in 1955 .. by his senior home-boys whom he referred to as *imoogie* — country bumpkins. **1975** M. MUTLOATSE in *Bolt* No.12, 31 It meant catching another train, but since I was a 'moegie' in a strange land, I got what was coming. **1982** [see CLEVER]. **1983** *Frontline* Feb. 25 If the other party decides to be clever and regard them as 'moogies' (fools), then chaos is bound to follow. **1983** G. MVUBELO in *Natal Mercury* 8 June, There are the 'baris' or the 'moegies'. They are the dumb ones, who just speak the vernacular. You can't regard them as 'bras'.

moegoe /ˈmʊxʊ/ *n. Derog. colloq.* Also **mo(e)go, moggoe, mugu**. Pl. usu. **-s**, occas. ‖**ii-**. [Afk. and Isicamtho, perh. ad. of a Sintu (Bantu) word.] In urban (esp. township) English: a country bumpkin or rustic; a dull, foolish, or gullible person; MOEGIE. Also *attrib.* Cf. BARI.

1953 *Drum* May 40 They make sure, with their guns and knives, that they win everything or don't lose too much to any 'moggoe'. **1970** *Ibid.* Aug. 23 You can see I'm not a moegoe (country bumpkin). **1973** *Ibid.* 22 Mar. 60 But you're a moego. Why take yourself back to the stokkies when you're already free? **1979** A.P. BRINK *Dry White Season* 180 'I brought him here on Gordon's business' ... 'Gordon is dead ... What's this mugu got to do with him?' **1981** [see Voice quot. at GEMORS sense b]. **1987** B. KHUMALO in *Drum* Aug. 26 In the townships they call us *Plaas Japie, moegoes, zaos* and other derogatory terms. They seem to think that everything that is good is from the cities. **1990** *Sunday Times* 1 Apr. 5 Tempers flared at the City Hall when a disgruntled councillor called his mayor a 'moegoe'. 'When he said that (it means "lazy lout") my fuse blew,' said East London's first citizen. **1992** M. MTHETHWA in *Pace* Sept. 75 Joe thinks Harry is a *moegoe* — an 'idiot' and scoffs at him. **1993** *Pace* July 54 She was engaged to be married to a real *moegoe* — a weakling. This guy was as thin as a broomstick, short-sighted, and spoke with a squeaky voice.

Hence **moegoe** *adj.*, simple, stupid; distracted.

1974 in *Eng. Usage in Sn Afr.* Vol.5 No.1, 12 The terms for this state of intoxication are transferred to describe anybody who normally appears to be slightly *mugu* (African origin 'moegoe?' = mad). **1986** *Pace* Aug. 4 What of the Algerians who pulled the wool over some moegoe referee by feigning injuries.

moekul var. MOGGEL.

moenie /ˈmʊni, ˈmuni/ *v.* Also **moeni, mooni**. [Afk., contraction of Du. *moet niet* must not, do not.]

‖**1.** Don't; (you) mustn't.

1913 C. PETTMAN *Africanderisms* 321 *Moeni*, .. A contraction of *moet niet* = must not, do not. *c*1929 S. BLACK in S. Gray *Three Plays* (1984) 48 Smith: ..'Ow about a kiss? Sophie: Ach no, Corporal, moenie! Smith: No, I said, you moenie — dat's Dutch. **1966** *Cape Argus* 19 Sept. 9 A teacher once told his class that it 'moenie die languages so opmix nie!' **1971** P. FREEDMAN 'The Traffic Cop'. (*lyrics*) Move your car, meneer, Jy moenie park in here. **1985** [see SUKKEL sense 2].

2. *colloq.* In the v. phrr. ***moenie panic (nie)***, ***moenie worry (nie)*** /-ni/ [Afk. *moenie .. (nie)* don't + Eng. *panic* or *worry*], 'don't panic', 'don't worry.' See also ALLES SAL REGKOM.

*a*1931 S. BLACK in S. Gray *Three Plays* (1984) 140, I don' know where is my fadder so moenie worry nie. My mother ran away from him. **1968** A. FULTON *Dark Side of Mercy* 7 So you are not used to the saddle ... Moenie worry. After a few weeks in this country your arse will be as tough as raw hide. **1971** *Daily Dispatch* 23 Feb. 10 Moenie panic, dearest — it's probably only a frog in your throat. **1975** *Friend* 15 Oct. 21 'Look what you have done to my car — my husband is going to kill me tonight,' cried the woman. 'Moenie panic nie, the State will pay,' came the reassuring reply. **1978** M. VAN BILJON in *Sunday Times* 1 Jan. (Mag. Sect.) 1 If some of the events seem familiar enough to give you a feeling of deja vu, moenie worry nie. **1982** 'PLURAL STAN' in *Drum* May 39 Ag, moenie worry. The lyrics may have been changed somewhat but the meaning of the song is tog still the same. **1985** *Vula* Oct. 12 The world has watched once again to see how SA keeps order. They have seen bullets, bannings, detentions and deaths. Everything's in order, moenie worrie. **1990** M. NAWA in *Staffrider* Vol.9 No.1, 68 Moenie worry Comrades you are not dead but living in our hearts and respect. **1991** K. OWEN in *Sunday Times* 26 May 27 The break in negotiations will not, despite all the sound and fury, abort the process. Meanwhile *moenie panic nie*.

moent var. MUNT.

moepel /ˈmʊpəl/ *n.* [Afk., ad. seTswana *mmupudu*, N. Sotho *mmupudu, mmopudu*, Mimusops spp.] **a.** Any of the evergreen trees of the genus *Mimusops* of the Sapotaceae, esp. *M. zeyheri*; cf. *milkwood* sense (*b*) (see MILK sense 2). **b.** The edible fruit of these trees.

[**1850** R.G.G. CUMMING *Hunter's Life* (1911) 443 A delicious African fruit called moopooroo .. was now ripe ... The tree has a very dark green leaf; the fruit is about the size and shape of a large olive, and when ripe is a bright orange colour.] **1934** C.P. SWART Supplement to Pettman. 118 *Moepel*, The red milkwood tree, Mimusops Zeyheri, is so designated in the Transvaal. **1939** tr. *E.N. Marais's My Friends the Baboons* 38 Wild peaches, sour klappers, medlers, moepels, and various other kinds of fruit made our wilderness a veritable orchard. **1944** H.C. BOSMAN in L. Abrahams *Cask of Jerepigo* (1972) 161 When I first went to the Marico it was in that season when the moepels were nearly ripening. **1950** —— in S. Gray *Makapan's Caves* (1987) 141 Not that I haven't got all the time in the world for a *moepel* or a *maroela* or a *kremetart* or any other kind of bushveld tree. **1976** *S. Afr. Panorama* May 24 Made from wild fruits — including marulas, moepels .. in fact mampoer is distilled from any fruit or vegetable which ferments. **1977** E. PALMER *Field Guide to Trees* 253 *Mimusops* ... A genus known for its edible fruits — rich in Vitamin C — all the species often indiscriminately called moepel. **1980** *E. Prov. Herald* 3 Sept. 13 The trees described include .. a few that are pretty common and could easily become known: Ilala Palm, .. Moepel. **1990** [see Van Rensburg quot. at CROSS-BERRY].

moer /mu:r/ *n.*[1] Also **mo(o)r**. [Du., sediment, dregs, yeast.]

1. In full ***moer wortel*** /-ˌvɔrt(ə)l, -ˌvɔ:t(ə)l/ [S. Afr. Du., fr. Du. *moer* + *wortel* root]: any of several plants whose roots are used as a yeast. **a.** The GLI, *Peucedanum gummiferum*. **b.** *karriemoer*, see KARRIE *n.*[3] sense 2.

1796 C.R. HOPSON tr. *C.P. Thunberg's Trav.* II. 150 Moor wortel is an umbelliferous plant, from the root of which and honey the Hottentots make, by fermentation, an intoxicating liquor. **1838** J.E. ALEXANDER *Exped. into Int.* I. 155 The people .. were .. drinking honey beer, made with honey and water, mixed in a bambus, and fermented by means of a root called 'mor,' but which I only saw when ground. **1913** C. PETTMAN *Africanderisms* 321 *Moer wortel*, .. The root of *Anacampseros ustulata, E. Mey.* employed in making 'karree' and 'karree moer'. **1966** C.A. SMITH *Common Names* 341 *Moerwortel(tjie), Glia gummifera* .. see Gli. The root .. was formerly used by the Hottentots for making an intoxicating liquor (mead) ... Occasionally *Anacampseros* .., .. *Euphorbia decussata* .. *Orthanthera jasminiflora*.

2. *?obs.* Yeast; any raising agent.

1868 J. CHAPMAN *Trav.* I. 273 A little barm, or 'moer,' obtained from the Kuruman people. **1930** M. RAUBENHEIMER *Tested S. Afr. Recipes* 55 When required, use about one teaspoon of the 'Moer.' Dissolve in a cup of warm water. Make a sponge in the ordinary way in the morning by adding meal.

moer /mu(:)r, mʊr/ *n.*[2] *slang.* [Afk., 'mother', 'dam (of animals)' or 'matrix', 'womb'.] Not in polite use.

‖**1.** Usu. in the n. phrr. ***jou moer*** /jəʊ-/ [Afk., *jou* your] or ***your moer***, and ***se moer*** [Afk., *se* possessive pronoun (his, her, their)]. An obscene and abusive mode of address, equivalent to 'stuff (you)'; an expletive expressing rage, disgust, or contradiction.

1946 C.A. SMITH in E. Partridge *Dict. of Underworld* (1950) 444 *Moer*, A word used only in the worst of company. **1950** E. PARTRIDGE *Ibid.* 444 *Moer!* or *your moer!* Go to hell!: South Africa: late C. 19–20. **1963** K. MACKENZIE *Dragon to Kill* 127 'Jou moer!' Jan hissed from the other side of the table. 'Now you see what you have done. She is sick, man!' **1973** A. FUGARD *Boesman & Lena* (1980) 240 (*Staring up at a bird* ...) *Jou Moer!* ... (*She .. shakes her fist at it.*) *Jou Moer!! Ibid.* 296 *Jou moer!* ultimate obscenity; contraction of *Jou ma se moer*, Your mother's womb. **1978** [see GAT *n.* sense 1 a]. **1980** A. DANGOR in M. Mutloatse *Forced Landing* 160 Cosseted like a virgin, offered as noble sacrifice ... Destiny! Destiny! Destiny *se moer!* **1987** *Frontline* Mar. 13 The ordinary guy on the street can just mutter under his breath: 'Boer, jou moer'. We are meant to resolve these things.

2. In phrr.: ***moer and gone*** *adv. phr.* [intensification of *doer and gone* (see DOER)], 'to hell and gone'; ***the moer in*** *adj. phr.*, *the hell in* (see HELL sense 2); ***moer of a*** *adj. phr.* and *adv. phr.* [tr. Afk. *moer se*], used before nouns and adjectives: 'hell of a (blow, etc.)', 'bloody (difficult, etc.)'; ***moer se*** *adj. phr.* [Afk.], see prec.; so also the contractions **moersa** *adv.* and *adj.*, and **moer(s)e** *adv.*

1974 B. SIMON *Joburg, Sis!* 132, I said I'll fucken kick you down moer and gone that's what I'll do. **1976** [see BONEY]. **1978** S. ROBERTS in *New Classic* No.5, 20 You get the moer in with them though too specially when they run up and put five cents in the metre just as you're getting your pen ready to write out the ticket. **1982** *Grocott's Mail* 3 Aug. 10 Well I've got two kids and I'd dig to give them a moerse good grounding like my mother gave me. **1985** P. SLABOLEPSZY *Sat. Night at Palace* 13 Jeez! I mean, take last Saturday, Katz had that moersa argument with the ref. *Ibid.* 30 Check the moon. Looks like one moersa mine dump. Moersa cheese mine dump. *Ibid.* 54 There's this poster 'Visit Margate'. On it there's this man standing in the sea catching this moere big fish. *Ibid.* 78 *Moere/moersa*, massive, very big (Afrikaans slang). **1987** S. ROBERTS *Jacks in Corners* 73 It makes me the *moer in* to have to discuss it in students' writing, at my age, with a straight face. **1987** *Informant, Grahamstown* You could see she was moer of a angry. **1988** L. BRYER (tr. W. Odendaal) in Bunn & Taylor *From S. Afr.* 112 The way Kita tells it, old Baby takes the turn on the hill at a moer of a speed ... [*Note*] A *moer* of a speed: a hell of a speed. **1988** G. LATTER in *Staffrider* Vol.7 No.3, 113

Kourie whispered, 'Let them try, I'm the moer-in anyway'. **1988** *Informant,* Grahamstown It must've been a moer se spring. **1992** M. ESAU *Informant,* Grahamstown This guy is moerse wealthy. **1992** J. GOETSCH *Informant,* Grahamstown, *Oracle* is moer of a expensive. **1993** B. KRIGE in *Sunday Times* 4 Apr. 17 The notice board behind the counter advertises a forth-coming event, a *moersa-party*.

moer /muː(ː)r, mʊr/ *v. slang.* Also **moera, moerr, moor.** [Afk., fr. either *moor* murder, or *moer* (see MOER n.²).]

Not in polite use.

1. *trans.* DONNER *v.* sense 1.

1960 J. TAYLOR 'Ballad of the Southern Suburbs'. (*lyrics*) If you won't take us to the zoo, Then what the heck else can we do, But go on out and moera all the outjies next door. **1961** A. FUGARD *Notebks* (1983) 25 The old coloured women .. had stolen an armful of the best dahlias ... Mr X, Park Superintendent, said, 'Take her down, moer her and learn her a lesson'. **1977** S. ROBERTS in E. Pereira *Contemp. S. Afr. Plays* 241 I'll moer him! I'll moer him! Why can't he take his bladdy car out? **1979** A.P. BRINK *Dry White Season* 182 Now they've released Johnny Fulani ... They moered him until he signed. **1980** C. HERMER *Diary of Maria Tholo* 180 *Moer*, .. A swearword, in the sense, 'Hurt until it degrades him'. **1990** *Style* July 81 These two guys walked into the Harbour Cafe in Yeoville and just started *moering* everyone. I got hit on the head by a flying bar stool.

2. *trans.* To kill (someone).

1985 *Frontline* Aug. 54 When I saw what was left of him I just wanted to moer them. Even before that it was drummed into us that what we were there for was to moer the terrs. You feel nothing.

3. *intrans.* To hit, bang (into).

1986 *Informant,* Grahamstown, I threw my budgie with my koki and it moered into my file.

4. *trans.* To throw, shove (something).

1991 *Informant,* Grahamstown, I moered the chair through the ceiling ... It didn't come back.

moering tool /ˈmuːrɪŋ tuːl, ˈmʊr-/ *n. phr. Slang.* [S. Afr. Eng. *moering* 'beating up' (ppl adj. formed on MOER *v.* sense 1) + Eng. *tool.*] Among the police: a baton or truncheon.

1988 S.A. BOTHA in *Frontline* Apr.-May 25 His friend was carrying a baton — a 'moering tool' he called it. **1988** P. AUF DER HEYDE in *Weekly Mail* 27 May 1 The judge said De Villiers had ordered his unit to take 'moering tools' into the township.

moer koffie /ˈmuːr kɔfi/ *n.* [Afk. *moerkoffie, moer* dregs, sediment + *koffie* coffee.] Coffee made by boiling the grounds. Occas. also part. tr. **moer coffee.** See also *plaas koffie* (PLAAS sense 1 c).

1987 'K. DE BOER' in *Frontline* Oct.-Nov. 42 You can still win a vote or two with a superb piece of melktert and strong moerkoffie. **1988** ADAMS & SUTTNER *William Str.* 23 Dadda .. would get up at four and go to the big coal stove .. and put on water and make a big pot of moer coffee. **1990** F. BATES in *Style* Oct. 76 The pungent aroma of strong black coffee — muslin-filtered moer koffie — simmered up my nose from a billycan on the anthracite stove. **1991** *Personality* 6 May 25 After the *konfyt* and the *boere moer koffie*, .. Oom Pine Pienaar thought that we had not tasted the *mampoer*.

moerogo var. MOROGO.

moerr var. MOER *v.*

moers doed var. MORSDOOD.

‖**moes** /mʊs, mus/ *n.* [Afk.]
a. A fruit or vegetable puree.

1934 C.P. SWART Supplement to Pettman. 119 *Moes*, A kind of purée peculiar to South Africa.

b. With defining word: **pumpkin moes** [part. tr. Afk. *pampoenmoes*], *pampoenmoes* (see PAMPOEN sense 1 b).

1951 S. VAN H. TULLEKEN *Prac. Cookery Bk* 196 **Pumpkin 'Moes'** (as a Vegetable). Dice pumpkin, and place a layer in a saucepan, then a layer of bread broken in small pieces, pinch salt, 1 spoon sugar, and dot some butter over, and a few pieces of whole cinnamon broken up.

moeshie var. MUSHY.

mof /mɔf/ *n.* and *adj.* [Afk., 'crossbreed' (esp. one resulting from breeding with imported stock), transf. use of Du. *mof*, a derog. name for a German or other foreigner.] Among livestock farmers:

A. *n.* *obs.* An imported animal.

1910 *E. London Dispatch* June 6 (Pettman), A crossbreed from a yellow [*printed* fellow] *mof* and the second generation was a light yellow. **1913** C. PETTMAN *Africanderisms* 321 *Mof*, An imported animal; *mofschaap*, a merino sheep; *mofbeest*, an imported bull or cow.

B. *adj.*

1. Of livestock: unsuited to South African conditions (often because cross-bred with imported animals); MOFFIE *adj.* sense 1.

1970 Y. WINTERS *Informant,* Kimberley Nothing but mof cows on the sale today (cross-bred — not up to any standard).

2. *derog.* Of men: weak; effeminate.

1992 P. DOBSON *Informant, Cape Town* Moffie/Mof. Effeminate person, softie. e.g ... 'He's a bit mof'.

moffhartebeest see HARTEBEEST *n.* sense b.

moffie /ˈmɔfi/ *adj.* and *n.* Also **moffee.** [Afk.: perh. abbrev. of *moffiedaai*, dial. var. of *hermafrodiet* hermaphrodite; or (esp. in adj. sense) *mof* (see MOF) + *-ie*; see also quot. 1982.]

A. *adj.*

1. *obsolescent.* Of an animal: MOF *adj.* sense 1.

1948 O. WALKER *Kaffirs Are Lively* 33 The official delivered a homily on the dangers of *moffie* cattle — the Afrikaans word for soft breeds, unsuited to the tough African heat and veld, which derive from crossing with English stock.

2. *slang.* Of or pertaining to someone lacking in toughness, or to something perceived to be unmanly or 'delicate'.

1990 J. ROSENTHAL *Wake Up Singing* 39 What kind of moffie headmaster doesn't jack the boys? **1991** *Style* May 95 'You!' the sergeant-major screamed at him ... 'You with the moffie clothes ...'

B. *n. slang.*

1. *offensive.* A derogatory name for: **a.** an effeminate man; **b.** a homosexual man; **c.** a transvestite; **d.** a man perceived to be weak-spirited or lacking in the physical toughness associated by some with manliness. Also *attrib.*

Occas. used also in general Eng. (pronounced /ˈmɒfi/) in the sense of 'effeminate man'.

1954 *Drum* Jan. 12 'Madame' (as Joey is known on the stage) leads a troupe of brilliant Coloured female impersonators who perform their popular 'Moffee Concerts' to packed houses. **1960** D. LYTTON *Goddam White Man* 27 Moffies. They don't like women but they like women's clothes ... But Achmed was not a proper moffie; he just liked fooling with boys. He didn't have the moffie voice. **1971** *Post* 23 May 18 The life of Edward Shadi — described as a beautiful, sexy moffie with a sweet soprano voice — was a strange affair. **1977** D. MULLER in *Quarry '77* 59 Uncle Achmet saw two moffies holding hands .. in Loop Street. The sight of the two effeminate young men, dressed in quasi-feminine clothing, caused the old man considerable disquiet. **1980** *Sunday Times* 3 Feb. (Mag. Sect.) 4 I'm a Gay, not a Pouf or a Moffie. **1982** N.C. LEE in *Cape Times* 9 Sept. 11 (letter) 'Moffie' I understand to be a corruption of the old French 'Maufé', meaning bad fairy. **1986** *Cape Times* 29 Jan. 3 The transfusion service has erected signs .. which state in bold letters: 'If you are a "gay" or a "moffie" or have had sex with a "gay" or a "moffie" do not give blood.' **1987** S. BAGLEY in *Cosmopolitan* Dec. 168 In self-defence, Cobus claims, the gays formed a 'moffie-mafia' a couple of years ago. **1988** ADAMS & SUTTNER *William Str.* 7 It is a world where the 'moffie' Rachmat (here the word denotes not so much a homosexual as an effeminate man, or a transvestite) is mocked but not excluded. **1992** M. GEVISSER in *Weekly Mail* 6 Mar. 30 Any troepie who shows reticence or queasiness is branded a 'moffie'. **1992** K. RUTTER in *Style* May 46 What's important now is the phenomenon of the New Man ... Paula probably thinks they're moffies. And the rest of us post-Neanderthal feminists don't believe the hype. **1992** P. DOBSON *Informant, Cape Town* Moffie, .. Effeminate person, softie. eg. 'Last one in's a moffie'.

e. *comb.* **moffiegevaar** /-xəˈfɑː(r)/ *nonce* [Afk., *gevaar* danger; by analogy with SWART GEVAAR], 'moffie peril', used of attitudes or statements which incite fear or hatred of homosexuals.

1990 M. VENABLES in *Weekend Mail* 5 Oct. 15 Rooigevaar, Swartgevaar and even Moffiegevaar.

2. Denoting an animal: a hermaphrodite.

1971 M. BRITZ *Informant,* Grahamstown We had a pig that was a moffie — a real hermaphrodite. **1983** C. BARNARD in *Daily Dispatch* 21 Mar., A kind of fish species in which you can't tell the difference between male and female. I think the South African word is moffie.

Hence (sense B 1) **moffette** *n. nonce,* a lesbian; **moffiedom** *n.* homosexuals collectively; the homosexual lifestyle.

1977 *Drum* July 47 (caption) Moffies .. have been engaged in meticulous research to trace their ancestors right back to the days of Van Riebeeck. Jackie Heyns gives .. an exclusive insight into the early days of moffiedom. **1982** *Sunday Times* 30 May 26 (letter) I would like to lodge my objection towards the use of the word 'moffiedom'. **1983** *Ibid.* 8 May 29 Chris moves out of maison moffette, which hurts Tory, by now the junior partner in the relationship. **1990** S. GRAY in *Staffrider* Vol.9 No.1, 54 Moffiedom is a flourishing and flamboyant part of the Cape lifestyle.

mofhartebeest see HARTEBEEST *n.* sense b.

Mofokeng /ˌmɔfɔˈkeŋ/ *n.* Pl. **Bafokeng, Fokeng**; formerly also **Bafuking.** [Sotho, MO- + *fok-* ad. *phoka* dew (their totem) + locative suffix *-(e)ng* (pl. *Bafokeng*). For an explanation of the form *Fokeng* in modern S. Afr. Eng., see note at BA- on the use of this plural prefix.] A member of a Tswana people, living mainly in what was formerly the 'homeland' of Bophuthatswana. Also *attrib.* See also TSWANA sense 2 a.

1909 G.Y. LAGDEN *Basutos* I. 22 The Bafuking are considered real Basutos, and chiefs always try to marry Bafuking wives ... Their clans were much scattered through the Bakwena country, and their *Siboko* (coat-of-arms) was the Dew. **1930** S.T. PLAATJE *Mhudi* (1975) 46 The Great One has sent invitations to all the Bechuana chiefs ... The Bahurutshe are strongly represented and the Bafokeng have also sent delegates. **1953** LANHAM & MOPELI-PAULUS *Blanket Boy's Moon* 98 This medicine horn will require as one of its magic ingredients the blood and flesh of a man of the Bafokeng clan. **1977** T.R.H. DAVENPORT *S. Afr.: Mod. Hist.* 7 The original Sotho-speakers are not easy to identify. Among the first were the Fokeng. **1979** P. MILLER *Myths & Legends* 173 In the beginning — about 1400 A.D. — it would appear that two groups of Sotho-Tswana wandered down from .. Botswana ... One group revered the cold dew, a major source of life in the dry wilderness of Africa; from this dew (*fokeng*) they called themselves ba Fokeng. **1983** K. KALANE in *City Press* 22 May 2 A two-part rebellion by the Bafokeng tribe in Bophuthatswana prompted President Lucas Mangope's hurried appearance there last week. **1986** P. MAYLAM *Hist. of Afr. People* 43 The evidence of oral tradition .. suggests that the Fokeng and Kwena were among the first Sotho groups to move across the Vaal. **1988** M. NKOTSOE in *Staffrider* Vol.7 No.3, 372 The village of Phokeng is the heartland of the Tswana-speaking Bafokeng people. **1988** *Frontline* Nov. 20 Her husband is chief Edward Lebone Molotlegi, chief of the 300 000-strong Bafokeng, on whose territory lies most of South Africa's platinum. **1990** *Weekend Post* 10 Mar. 13 The belief that the Government is cheating them has made many Bafokeng very hostile to Mangope ... The only Mofokeng now in a prominent position is Deputy Law and Order Minister A N Segoe.

moggel /ˈmɔx(ə)l/ *n.* Also **moekul, mogel**. [Afk., perh. fr. Du. *moggel, mokkel* a plump child or woman; or an ad. of the generic name *Mugil*.] **1.** Any of several freshwater fishes of the genus *Labeo* (family Cyprinidae), esp. *Labeo umbratus*. **2.** YELLOWFISH sense a.

1838 J.E. ALEXANDER *Exped. into Int.* I. 144 When my people came back in the evening with two of three large moekul or flat heads, they were knocked up with the distance, the heat, and the sand. The flat head, or Silurus Gariepinus, (so named by my friend Mr Burchell) .. is about three feet long, of a dark green colour above, and white below .. The taste of this, the commonest of the Great River fish, and of the streams which flow into it, resembles that of the eel. [**1902** *Trans. of S. Afr. Phil. Soc.* XI. 214 [Barbus capensis] is now .. called by the Dutch 'Moggel' — a word which .. may be a corruption of the Latin Mugil, a generic name which has been applied to this fish, or it may refer to the general appearance and shape of this fish, 'moggel' in Dutch signifying a clumsy child. **1913** C. PETTMAN *Africanderisms* 322 Moggel, Barbus capensis has been thus named by the Dutch.] **1945** H. GERBER *Fish Fare* 77 Mudfish, Mud-Mullet and Moggel. These indigenous fish occur in the Gouritz river system and other rivers of the Karoo series. They are also found in the Orange River and the rivers of the Transvaal. They are very bony. **1973** *Farmer's Weekly* 13 June 11 These simple plants could be nourished in quantity by the excreta of the high-value eels and thus provide food for the weed-eating fish such as the moggel (sand fish) or tilapia (kurper) and these could then provide cheap protein food for the masses. **1980** *Grocott's Mail* 19 Dec. 4 Other South African fishes which grazed on algae included the Labeo or moggel which built up large populations in dams which were enriched with wastewater, thus providing valuable protein food at no cost. **1982** M.N. BRUTON et al. *Pocket Guide to Freshwater Fishes* 49 Moggel, *Labeo umbratus* ... A large labeo .. with a markedly rounded head, fleshy snout and small eyes. **1992** P. CULLINAN *Robert Jacob Gordon* 82 *(caption)* The 'moggel' or mud mullet (*Labeo umbratus*) — a common Cape fish found in river mouths.

moggoe, mogo varr. MOEGOE.

‖**mogodu** /mɔˈxɔːdʊ, -du/ *n.* Also **mogudu**. [Sotho, 'stomach', 'paunch'.] Among Sotho-speakers: tripe; MALA MOGODU.

1966 K.M.C. MOTSISI in *Post* 16 Jan. (Drum) 19 His wife always gives him pap and mogudu, breakfast, lunch and supper. **1982** *Voice* 21 Feb. 10 If you look for it, you'll get it in Marabastad. From sheeps head to mogodu. **1982** *Pace* June 37 They long for pap and steak and mogodu .. just seeing a plane with SAA and knowing that that plane .. is going home. **1990** *Weekend Post* 7 July 14 For Miriam Makeba, the internationally-acclaimed vocalist who left South Africa 31 years ago, one of the main things she said she had missed was eating her favourite traditional dish *mogodu* (tripe).

mogonono /mɔxɔˈnɔːnɔ/ *n.* Also **mohonono**. [SeTswana.] The *vaalboom* (see VAAL sense 2), *Terminalia sericea*. Also *attrib.*

1864 T. BAINES *Explor. in S.-W. Afr.* 441 Passing through a thick mopane and mohonono forest, [we] outspanned about 7 p.m. in a more open flat. **1878** K. JOHNSTON *Africa* 427 The silvery mohonono .. is in form like the ceder of Lebanon. **1930** [see MOKAALA]. **1949** K.L. SIMMS *Sun-Drenched Veld* 33 There is .. the cedar-spread of the mohonono. **1970** A. SILLERY in *Std Encycl. of Sn Afr.* II. 222 Other species are mogonono or wild guinea (*Terminalia sericea*), .. and various kinds of acacia.

mogudu var. MOGODU.

Moharootzie var. HURUTSHE.

mohohu *n. obs.* Also **mahoohoo, moho(o)hoo, mohuhu, monooho, muchocho, muchucho**. [SeTswana *mogohu*.] The white rhinoceros, *Ceratotherium simum* of the Rhinocerotidae.

1835 A. SMITH *Diary* (1940) II. 107 The Baquana say that two kinds [of rhinoceros] are only in this country. The black, which they call *muchli* and the white *mohohoo*. **1846** R. MOFFAT *Missionary Labours* 120 The lion flies before them like a cat; the mohohu, the largest species, has been known even to kill the elephant, by thrusting the horn into its ribs. **1849** A. SMITH *Illust. of Zoo. of S. Afr.: Mammalia* Pl.19, Localities abounding in grass are therefore the haunts of the Mohoohoo. **1850** R.G.G. CUMMING *Hunter's Life* I. 77 With considerable difficulty we separated the horn of the muchocho from the skin by means of a long sharp knife. **1866** *Chambers's Encycl.* VIII. 236 The White R[hinoceros] .. or Muchuco, or Monooho, is the largest of the well-ascertained African species. **1871** J. MACKENZIE *Ten Yrs* (1971) 300 The meat from the ribs of the rhinoceros is considered best; and it is said the flesh of the mohohu or white rhinoceros is very good. [**1875** W.H. DRUMMOND *Large Game & Nat. Hist. of S. & S.-E. Afr.* 84 *Rhinoceros simus*, the mohohu of the Bechuanas.] **1883** J. MACKENZIE *Day-Dawn in Dark Places* 189 It is said the flesh of the mohohu, or white rhinoceros is very good. [**1894** R. LYDEKKER *Royal Nat. Hist.* II. 480 The individuals exhibiting this form being known to the Bechuanas by the name of mohohu.]

mohonono var. MOGONONO.

mohoohoo, mohuhu var. MOHOHU.

moi var. MOOI.

mokaala *n. obs.* Also **mokgalo**. [SeTswana, *mokala* red camel-thorn, *mokgalo* hookthorn.] CAMEL-THORN. Also *attrib.*

1824 W.J. BURCHELL *Trav.* II. 412 This stick .. is generally taken from the heart of the *Mokaala-tree* or camel-thorn, as that part of the wood is extremely hard and of a fine black color. *Ibid.* 445 The eaves were supported five feet from the ground by unhewn posts of mokaala wood. **1839** W.C. HARRIS *Wild Sports* 55 Shaded by spreading *mokaalas* — a large species of acacia which forms the favourite food of the giraffe. **1930** S.T. PLAATJE *Mhudi* (1975) 136 She missed the compact mokgalo and mogonono trees, the leaves of which had provided her with excellent awning when it rained.

‖**mokoro** /mɔˈkɔrɔ/ *n.* Also **makora, makor(r)o, mekoro**. [SeTswana.] A dug-out canoe traditionally used by the Tswana people. Also *attrib.*

Orig. and predominantly used of such canoes on the waterways of the Okavango Swamps, Botswana.

1928 E.H.L. SCHWARZ *Kalahari & its Native Races* 45 In order to get to his shop, customers from the main road had to be ferried across in makoras. **1945** L.G. GREEN *Where Men Still Dream* 188 When the sergeant patrols the rivers and swamps he uses 'makorros' — a fleet of three dug-out canoes. **1971** *Personality* 10 Sept. 105 We find our only hope of hiring two mokoros (dugout canoes) is to go to .. a village .. inside the swamp itself. **1980** *Rand Daily Mail* 25 Jan. (Suppl.) 1 Our mokoros are waiting on the river bank. Visualise half a tree trunk painstakingly hollowed by hand into a needle-sharp canoe. It takes a month for one man to make a mokoro, transport for generations in this waterworld in the middle of the desert. **1985** D. BIGGS in *Weekend Argus* 17 Aug. (Suppl.) 1 The owners of dugout canoes, or makoros, follow the waters northward to their villages to tend their herds during the summer months. **1986** *Motorist* 3rd Quarter 12 You can .. take an inexpensive 16-minute flight to one of several camps that offer mokoro trips.

molerat /ˈməʊlræt/ *n.* [Transf. use of general Eng. *molerat* a name applied to any rodent of the Spalacidae, or (Brit. dial.) to the common mole; named for its burrowing habits.] **1.** Any of several species of rodent of the Bathyergidae, esp. **a.** the SAND-MOLE *Bathyergus suillus*; **b.** the *Common molerat* (see sense 2 below); and **c.** the *Cape molerat* (see sense 2 below).

In early writings, molerats are usu. called 'moles' (see quot. 1980).

[**1795** C.R. HOPSON tr. *C.P. Thunberg's Trav.* I. 213 The gardens both within and without the town, suffer great devastation from three or four different species of rats, which are generally termed moles ... Moles also are found in the sand-downs near the town.] **1822** W.J. BURCHELL *Trav.* I. 57 There is another kind of mole-rat .. peculiar to this country and .. known by the name of Bles moll (White-faced mole). **1901** W.L. SCLATER *Mammals of S. Afr.* II. 77 *Georychus hottentotus*, The Mole rat. **1912** *State* Sept. 229 (Pettman), The fur of the blesmols, mole rats, and sand moles is usually rusty grey above, whitish below, and without any sheen. **1913** C. PETTMAN *Africanderisms* 322 *Mole rat, Georychus hottentotus*. The members of this family are found only in Africa — *Bathyergidae*. **1939** [see BLESMOL]. **1951** A. ROBERTS *Mammals* 379 Family Bathyergidae ... Mole-rats. **1963** S.H. SKAIFE *Naturalist Remembers* 72 In South Africa there is a family of rodents which have taken to a life underground and become mole-rats. **1972** C.M. VAN DER WESTHUIZEN in *Std Encycl. of Sn Afr.* VII. 490 *Mole-rats, (Bathyergidae)*, an entirely African family of rodents, are widely distributed in Africa. **1980** C.J. SKEAD *Hist. Mammal Incidence* I. 20 *Mole and Molerat*, These two groups, the first belonging to the Insectivora, the second to the Rodentia, have been confused in early writings. Where mole has been indicated for the tunnelers in the soft sandveld of the Western Province the blesmol, *Georychus capensis* or dune mole-rat, is intended. **1990** SKINNER & SMITHERS *Mammals of Sn Afr. Subregion* 186 The molerats are related more closely to the porcupines than to any other animals. **1992** BENNETT & JARVIS in *Afr. Wildlife* Vol.46 No.4, 167 The mole-rats, family Bathyergidae, are endemic to the African continent.

2. With defining word designating a particular species of molerat: **(Cape) dune molerat**, the SAND-MOLE, *Bathyergus suillus*; **Cape molerat**, the rodent *Georychus capensis*; BLESMOL sense a; **Common molerat**, the rodent *Cryptomys hottentotus*.

1986 R.H.N. SMITHERS *Land Mammals* 55 **Cape Dune Molerat**, .. Occurs only in the extreme southwestern parts of the Cape Province, in sandy soil. **1988** M. BRANCH *Explore Cape Flora* 24 It can take days to dig up and follow the burrows of a huge Cape dune mole rat, for they run 30 centimetres below the surface and are about a third of a kilometre long. **1990** SKINNER & SMITHERS *Mammals of Sn Afr. Subregion* 188 *Cape dune molerat*, .. They are called the Cape dune molerat as they are confined in their distribution to the Cape Province. **1972** C.M. VAN DER WESTHUIZEN in *Std Encycl. of Sn Afr.* VII. 491 Of the six genera of African mole-rats, three occur in South Africa. The Cape dune-mole ... The **Cape mole-rat** (*Georychus capensis*) ... The Common mole-rat (*Cryptomys*). **1988** R. LUBKE et al. *Field Guide to E. Cape* 303 *Cape molerat*, .. *Georychus capensis*. **1990** SKINNER & SMITHERS *Mammals of Sn Afr. Subregion* 196 *Cape molerat*, .. The species was described originally from the Cape, hence the association of their name with this area. The Afrikaans *blesmol* refers to the conspicuous white frontal patch on the head. **1992** BENNETT & JARVIS in *Afr. Wildlife* Vol.46 No.4, 167 The Cape mole-rat is herbivorous, feeding on bulbs, corms and rootstocks. **1972** [**Common molerat**: see above]. **1990** SKINNER & SMITHERS *Mammals of Sn Afr. Subregion* 190 Common molerats are capable of using a wide diversity of substrates ... Over part of their range, in the southwestern Cape province, they occur sympatrically with *Georychus capensis, Bathyergus suillus* or *B. janetta*.

‖**Molimo** /mɔˈdiːmɔ/ *n.* [Sotho (Lesotho orthography), 'God'; see quot. 1861.] MODIMO; also used as an interjection.

1861 E. CASALIS *Basutos* II. 248 Every being, to whom the natives render adoration, is called *Molimo* ... It is evidently composed of the prefix *mo*, which belongs to almost all those words representing intelligent beings, and of the root *holimo — above, in the sky*. *Moholimo*, or the abbreviation Molimo, therefore, signifies, *He who is in the sky*. **1918** [see QAMATA]. *c***1929** L.P. BOWLER *Afr. Nights* 114 'The medicine men in those days,' said this Pondomise seer, 'called it "Umtagati, " the Devil's great secret, who used it to secure more spirits of men than "Umolemo," the Greater God.' **1957** A.A. MURRAY *Blanket* 125 Somewhere, in the blue outer space beyond this world, there was a molimo, a God, who cared for him, Lepotane, closely and personally. **1979** M. MATSHOBA *Call Me Not a Man* 108 *Molimo*! I remember the days of the Congress. I was this small then. **1981** *Drum* Aug. 100 Molimo, you know I was so glad that my kids are Nightingales and will never sing like canaries. **1982** M. MZAMANE *Children of Soweto* 118 *Molimo*! It doesn't seem as if there's any public building they haven't set on fire.

‖**molo** /ˈmɔːlɔ/ *int.* [Xhosa, ad. Afk. *môre* 'good morning'. The form *molo* is used when addressing one person, *molweni* /mɔlˈweːni/ (pl. suffix *-eni*) when addressing two or more people.] Among Xhosa-speakers: a general greeting, 'hello', used when addressing one person. See also MOLWENI.

1955 J.B. SHEPHARD *Land of Tikoloshe* 17 He .. made a gesture of salute as he replied .. 'Molo, Nkosi,' His greeting was self-assured, dignified, and polite. **1964** J. BENNETT *Mr Fisherman* (1967) 94 The few Africans they passed on the quiet dirt roads stepped aside and raised their hats and smiled .. and said 'Molo, Baas, Molo, Basie'. **1979** *E. Prov. Herald* 27 July (Suppl.) 7 'Most of the contestants liked me and were always urging me to speak my language,' she said ... They learnt to say 'molo' and click a bit. **1982** K. SUTTON in *Ibid.* 11 Oct. 7 The older black man was the last to leave. As he passed me I said: '*Bota mnumzana*'. '*Bota*' is the traditional Xhosa greeting, '*Molo*' being the modern form taken from the Afrikaans 'môre'. **1987** M. POLAND *Train to Doringbult* 163 She wound down the window a little way. 'Molo', she said. Her voice was high and hoarse.

moloi /mɔˈlɔi/ *n.* Pl. **baloi**. [Sotho and seTswana, fr. *loya* bewitch.] In the context of Sotho and Tswana society: a wizard, a practitioner of evil magic. See also BOLOYI, WITCHDOCTOR.

1871 J. MACKENZIE *Ten Yrs* (1971) 388 There is a certain amount of suspicion connected with the word 'ngaka' (doctor, sorcerer); but when the superhuman power is supposed to be brought into requisition for an evil purpose, .. the man is called a 'moloi' (wizard). But the wizard is always a doctor, and his crime is that he turns his knowledge to evil purposes ... 'The baloi' (the wizards) is an expression often used to frighten naughty children by the Bamangwato mothers. **1960** C. HOOPER *Brief Authority* 251 Pamphlets appeared in the village. Written in Tswana, they implied that anybody who continued to patronise the white merchant might expect death by lightning, and they further alleged that .. the shopkeeper was a moloi, a wizard. **1976** B. HEAD in *Quarry '76* 14 The baloi are troubling us. The baloi are those people with a bad heart. No one openly walks around with the mark of the baloi, so we don't know who they are. *c***1976** H. FLATHER *Thaba Rau* 157 The Basuto believe .. in the moloi, whose purpose is to kill the enemies of his clan or his chief. Some of them believe that the first duty of the moloi is to kill one of his own relations.

molombo var. MALOMBO.

molo(o)nga var. MLUNGU.

Molteno /mɒlˈtiːnəʊ/ *n.* [The name of the district in the Eastern Cape in which the disease was first investigated (see E. London Dispatch quot. 1912).]

a. *Pathology.* In the n. phrr. ***Molteno (cattle) disease***, ***Molteno sickness***, ***Molteno straining disease***, seneciosis, a disease of livestock, esp. of cattle, caused by chronic poisoning due to the ingestion of any of several species of *Senecio* which affects the liver of the animal.

Seneciosis in horses is usu. known as DUNSIEKTE (sense 1 b).

1912 *Queenstown Rep.* 27 Feb. 7 (Pettman), The results leave no doubt that the *Molteno disease* of South Africa can be caused by the consumption of *S. latifolius*. **1912** *E. London Dispatch* 5 Mar. 7 (Pettman), The name *Molteno disease* arose from the fact that the Molteno Farmers' Association was responsible for the first investigation into the cause of what is still often referred to as merely black gallsick. **1929** *Farming in S. Afr.* Apr. 20 *Molteno disease* .. very closely resembles Dunsiekte or Enzootic Liver Cirrhosis in horses. **1966** [see Smith quot. at DUNSIEKTE sense 1]. **1972** N. SAPEIKA in *Std Encycl. of Sn Afr.* VII. 296 Ingestion of certain *Senecio* plants has long been known to cause liver damage, which may result in death in cattle and horses (Molteno sickness; dunsiekte). **1976** MÖNNIG & VELDMAN *Handbk on Stock Diseases* 214 Chronic Senecio poisoning in cattle is known as Molteno cattle disease or purging disease. **1988** T.S. KELLERMAN et al. *Plant Poisonings & Mycotoxicosis of Livestock* 5 Seneciosis .. is caused by hepatotoxic pyrrolizidine alkaloids contained by *Senecio* spp ... It is .. responsible for chronic disease, locally known as Molteno straining disease in cattle and dunsiekte in horses.

b. *comb.* **Molteno disease plant**, any of several plants of the genus *Senecio* (family Asteraceae) which are toxic to livestock, esp. *S. retrorsus* and *S. latifolius; dunsiektebossie*, see DUNSIEKTE sense 2. See also DAN'S CABBAGE.

1934 *Farming in S. Afr.* Mar. 97 The following is a list of the various species of *Senecio* known to be poisonous ... *Senecio isatideus* .. (ragwort, Dan's cabbage) ... *Senecio retrorsus* .. (ragwort, Dan's cabbage, **Molteno disease plant**). **1966** C.A. SMITH *Common Names* 341 *Molteno disease plant, Senecio burchellii* .. and *S. retrorsus* ... Both species are regarded as the cause of Molteno disease in stock. **1976, 1981** [see DAN'S CABBAGE].

‖**molweni** /mɔlˈweːni/ *int.* [Xhosa: see MOLO.] Among Xhosa-speakers: a general greeting, 'hello', used when addressing two or more people. See also MOLO.

1979 F. DIKE *First S. African* 16 Rooi: Mama's here. Molo mama. Freda: Molweni.

momba var. MAMBA.

‖**mombakkie** /ˈmɔmbaki/ *n.* Also **mambakkie**, and (formerly) **mombakje**. [fr. Afk. *mombakkies* (Du. *mombakkes*), *mom* mask + *bakkies* face.] A mask, esp. of a type worn by children at carnivals and on Guy Fawkes Day.

1913 C. PETTMAN *Africanderisms* 323 *Mombakjes*, .. The masks such as are employed at carnivals and by English children on 5 November — Guy Fawkes' Day. **1946** V. POHL *Adventures of Boer Family* 99 A *mombakkie* is made (exactly like a Hallowe'en pumpkin), by scooping out pips and pulp from a pumpkin or watermelon, cutting holes in one side for eyes, mouth and nose, and placing a lighted candle inside; and we had on more than one occasion struck terror into our farm natives with a *mombakkie*. **1958** I. VAUGHAN *Diary* 40 This month is to be Guy Fox ... The big men make a great G. Fox ... They put a mambakkie on its face. We all buy the cheap mambakkies in the shop to wear for walking the guy.

‖**momela** /mɔˈmeːla/ *n.* Also **mamele**. [SeTswana and Sotho, 'malted grain'.] Among Sothos and Tswanas: MTOMBO sense 1. See also *mtombo-mmela* (MTOMBO sense 2).

1929 in A.M. Duggan-Cronin *Bantu Tribes* II. i. Pl.17, The beer is made from sprouted Kaffir corn (*momela*), and the thick gruel thus obtained is strained through a grass strainer. **1971** M. BRITZ *Informant, Petrusburg (OFS)* When I went in to town momela was always on my shopping list — the stuff they use to make .. beer. **1979** Y. BURGESS *Say Little Mantra* 112 The natives .. were making mamele, from corn, very strong but it was clean in those days, not like the skokiaan they put battery acid in today.

Momlambo var. MAMLAMBO.

mompara /mɒmˈpɑːrə, mam-, mɔm-/ *n.* Also **mampar(r)a**, **mangpara**, **mompaara**, **momparra**. [Fanakalo, 'a fool'; 'waste material'.

The origin is uncertain; the first part of the word is prob. made up of the Sotho personal n. prefix MO- + linking phoneme *-m-*; *-para* is perh. N. Sotho *-para* the stick on which a blanket is carried (referring to inexperienced recruits' luggage or, metaphorically, to recruits as objects which are of no use on their own). Other possible sources of *-para* are adaptations of: Afk. *baar* raw, inexperienced (see BAAR); Afk. *padda* frog, explained by the fact that in about 1876, after a time of drought, recruits arriving at the diamond-diggings jumped into the water 'like frogs'; Xhosa *iphala* wanderer; or Zulu *phala*, ideophone of searching with the eyes (perh. used of one who is confused or looking for work).]

1. *derog.* Used of black workers (esp. in the mining industry): a greenhorn or inexperienced recruit; an unsophisticated country person; an incompetent. Also *attrib.* Cf. BARI.

1899 G.H. RUSSELL *Under Sjambok* 29 Except for the ordinary Kafir mouchi, he wore no clothing, and I could see that he was a mompara. **1914** *Farmer's Annual* 130 The shepherd must be, not the recently engaged 'mompara' whose only language is unintelligible .. but the most intelligent native available. **1927** U. LAMB in *Outspan* 29 Apr. 25 Once she had wept in his absence on his desk. He had merely said in a manly grumble: 'If that *mompara* Jim will wash my desk, I wish to goodness he would dry it!' **1934** G.G. MUNNIK *Mem. of Senator* 187 Faithful natives who went in and out of Pretoria and acted the part of momparas dressed in kraal attire and with letters stitched in between the soles of their rough sandals. **1934** C.P. SWART Supplement to Pettman. 111 *Mampara*, .. A term very commonly applied, especially on the mines, to a clumsy, stupid native servant. **1939** C. DELBRIDGE in *Outspan* 20 Oct. 41 The white man laboured frantically beside them, alternately cursing and imploring — 'Come on — harder, harder! Pull, you "momparas!"' **1941** *Bantu World* in *Forum* 6 Sept. 21 When the players and their mampara supporters shout 'Offside, Referee,' he (the referee) may sit down, consult the book on 'Offsides' and then blow his whistle. **1962** A.P. CARTWRIGHT *Gold Miners* 223 A native actor plays the part of the mine worker who does everything wrong and there is no comedian living or dead who raises such howls of laughter as this 'mompara' (the Fanakalo word for one who is dimwitted). **1964** G. GORDON *Four People* 130 You can get clothes and there are nice shops, you can be a gentleman, not just a *mampara* like in the country. **1970** L. MANGIWATYWA *Informant, Durban* Mampara is somebody ignorant of his or her work or surroundings. **1974** *Evening Post* 9 Aug. 6 When I explained I had come from the toilet, he said something like, 'You are a lazy, stupid kaffir, baboon, mampara.' **1990** [see LAPA *adv.*].

2. *transf.* Used loosely, sometimes affectionately: a fool, an idiot; also used as a term of address.

1942 U. KRIGE *Dream & Desert* (1953) 119 It makes me sick .. when I think of those smug *mamparas* sitting there in Parliament six thousand miles away from the nearest bullet, making a decision like that! **1949** O. WALKER *Wanton City* 198 He just stood like a momparra looking up in the sky. **1954** A. SEGAL *Jhb. Friday* He had no leisure to waste on a mompara, on a fool. **1968** K. MCMAGH *Dinner of Herbs* 96 She promptly .. began howling. I told her not to be such a 'mompaara'. **1970** E.J. LE ROUX *Informant, Bellville* If you call someone a 'mamparra' it means he is stupid (in a nice way). **1973** *E. Prov. Herald* 7 July 2 One of them said he was a freedom fighter, to which I said 'No you are not, you are a mompara.' **1986** F. KARODIA *Daughters of Twilight* 62 'That man is a mangpara,' Papa said as they stepped in the door. **1987** *Informant, Grahamstown* My dad always told us not to be such a mampara if we did something stupid. **1989** J. HOBBS *Thoughts in Makeshift Mortuary* 300 'You and I are quite alike, considering.' 'Considering our different degrees of tan?' 'No, mompara! Our different backgrounds.' *Ibid.* 351, I can't risk some half-trained mompara wrecking the mission and messing up the life she's built for herself. **1991** V. WARREN *Informant, Alberton* She can't knit, she is a real mampara. (Said with fondness.)

mona var. MAANHAAR.

||**mondfluitjie** /ˈmɔntfleɪki, -flœiki, -ci/ *n.* [Afk., *mond* mouth + *fluitjie* flute, whistle.] FLUITJIE.

1973 on Radio South Africa 14 June (Take a Chance), You know, it's funny, I used to play the mond-fluitjie and the concertina. **1979** *Sunday Times* 4 Mar. (Mag. Sect.) 3 The raft was officially handed over .. to the strains of the Hallelujah Chorus played on a mond-fluitjie.

monkey-bird *n. obs.* [See quot. 1923.] In the Eastern Cape: the KAKELAAR, *Phoeniculus purpureus.*

1923 HAAGNER & IVY *Sketches* 39 In Grahamstown it [*sc.* the wood hoopoe] is often called the Monkey-bird, probably .. on account of its chattering, noisy habits. **1931** *Guide to Vertebrate Fauna of E. Cape Prov.* (Albany Museum) I. 155 *Phoeniculus purpureus* .. Wood-Hoopoe, Monkey-Bird ... They go about in pairs, feeding on the insects infesting bark, chattering continuously as they feed, and sometimes breaking out into a loud demonical laugh. **1937** M. ALSTON *Wanderings* 223 The noisy red-billed hoopoes .. well deserve the name of either 'kakelaars' or 'monkey-birds'.

monkey orange *n. phr.*

1. KLAPPER *n.*[1] sense 1.

1953 B. FULLER *Call Back Yesterday* 110 Kathleen recollects as a child going to the South Parade .. to hunt for wild monkey-oranges and dates. **1972** I.C. VERDOORN in *Std Encycl. of Sn Afr.* VII. 514 *Monkey Orange, Klapper. Botterklapper. (Strychnos pungens).* This species of *Strychnos*, family *Loganiaceae* (or *Strychnaceae*), bears the characteristic fruits of several species in the genus, a globose berry, about the size of an orange, with a hard woody rind. **1990** CLINNING & FOURIE in *Fauna & Flora* No.47, 17 Sharpe's grysbok .. have also been seen feeding on the opened fruit of monkey orange, *Strychnos* spp, discarded by either kudus or baboons. **1991** D.M. MOORE *Garden Earth* 198 Monkey oranges, from the tree *Strychnos spinosa*, are also a favorite fruit [of the indigenous people of the Kalahari Desert]. They .. fall to the ground, where they turn orange as they ripen.

2. With distinguishing epithet denoting a particular species of *Strychnos*: **green monkey orange**, *S. spinosa*; **spine-leaved monkey orange**, *S. pungens*; **spineless monkey orange**, *S. madagascariensis.*

1982 FOX & NORWOOD YOUNG *Food from Veld* 259 Loganiaceae, *Strychnos spinosa* Lam. *Common names:* English – **green monkey orange**. **1990** M. OETTLE in *Weekend Post* 19 Jan. (Leisure) 7 35c: Strychnos pungens, **spine-leaved monkey orange**, lerutia ... The ripe fruit is pungent, sour and not very tasty, but most refreshing. Unripe, it is poisonous. **1991** *Philatelic Services Bulletin* No.8075, *Strychnos pungens* Lerutla. Spine-leaved monkey orange ... The unripe fruit and the seeds are poisonous. The Greek word *strychnos* means deadly and refers to the lethal chemical substance strychnine, present in many species. **1984** J. ONDERSTALL *Tvl Lowveld & Escarpment* 148 Loganiaceae, *Strychnos Madagascariensis* **Spineless Monkey Orange**, *Botterklapper.*

monkey-rope *n.* [Etym. dubious: either transf. use of Eng. nautical term *monkey-rope* a safety-rope used by sailors; or tr. and ad. S. Afr. Du. *baviaanstou(w)* 'baboon's rope', either referring to the supposed use of these lianas by baboons, or with the meaning 'worthless (or spurious) rope'.] Any of a number of liana-forming species of climbing plants of the Apocynaceae, Asclepiadaceae, Convolvulaceae, Hippocrateaceae, Leguminosae, Rhamnaceae, Rubiaceae, and Vitaceae; the tough, pliant stem of any of these plants; BAVIAAN'S TOUW; *bobbejaanstou*, see BOBBEJAAN sense 2; *bush tou*, see TOU sense 2. See also DAWIDJIES sense 2, KLIMOP sense 2. Also *attrib.*

Cynanchum africanum of the Asclepiadaceae was probably the first species to be given this name.

[**1812** A. PLUMPTRE tr. *H. Lichtenstein's Trav. in Sn Afr.* (1928) I. 188 This plant is here called *Pavia-nentau* (monkey's cord), and was running about in every direction all over the forest.] **1827** T. PHILIPPS *Scenes & Occurrences* 64 Various creepers were entwined round the trees ... The monkey rope, the wild vine with the grapes ascending the branches, wild fig, geraniums etc. **1829** C. ROSE *Four Yrs in Sn Afr.* 300 From them trailed light, stringy creepers, and that large one, known in Africa by the name of the monkey-rope, hung around in its twisted strength far thicker than the largest cable. **1849** E.D.H.E. NAPIER *Excursions in Sn Afr.* II. 369 Noble forest-trees, mostly connected together by various lianes and creepers – here called 'monkey ropes'. **1871** J. MCKAY *Reminisc.* 38 No path could we find; miles of monkey-rope hung pendant from the stately trees. **1878** T.J. LUCAS *Camp Life & Sport* 172 Trees and bush, tangled with monkey-ropes and creepers of all kinds. **1883** [see BAVIAAN'S TOUW]. **1887** J.W. MATTHEWS *Incwadi Yami* 40 Festoons of monkey rope parasites and other climbers. **1898** G. NICHOLSON *50 Yrs* 61 Creepers which in the local patois are called monkey ropes. **1907** T.R. SIM *Forests & Forest Flora* 13 Tangled undergrowth and a profusion of 'monkey-rope' creepers impart a tropical character. **1913** H. TUCKER *Our Beautiful Peninsula* 36 Swaying monkey ropes and leafy twilight: .. a haunting sense of intrusion into the hiding place of elves and wood-sprites. **1950** *Jrnl of Botanical Soc.* XXXVI., Wild Vine, Monkey Rope, Bosdruif, Baviaanstouw. *Rhoicissus capensis.* **1968** K. MCMAGH *Dinner of Herbs* 82 Immense trees, their lichen-grown boles festooned with great monkey ropes as thick as your arm. **1972** *Std Encycl. of Sn Afr.* VII. 515 *Monkey-rope, .. (Secamone alpinii.)* Plant of the family *Asclepiadaceae*, a scrambler on bushes and trees. When it grows in a forest its old stems form the well-known 'monkey-ropes' hanging down from trees. **1980** *Fair Lady* 22 Oct. 149 Palm fronds and monkey-ropes spill over onto the sundeck that overhangs the stream. **1989** B. COURTENAY *Power of One* 155 Monkey rope strung from tall trees draped with club moss.

monkey's wedding *n. phr.* [Prob. ultimately fr. Pg. *casamento de rapôsa* ('vixen's wedding') which has the same sense.

In the Portuguese colonies in Africa, the word for 'vixen' (*rapôsa*) was presumably replaced by a word meaning 'monkey' (e.g. *macaco*), in the same way as *gambá* (opossum) is used instead of *rapôsa* in other parts of the Pg.-speaking world. The adapted phr. may have come into S. Afr. Eng. directly fr. Pg., or through Du. (see quot. 1963) or Zulu (see quot. 1973).]

The simultaneous occurrence of sunshine and rain. Also *attrib.*

1949 *Cape Times* 29 Nov. 16 The Peninsula had a 'monkey's wedding' rainfall yesterday with the sun shining at intervals and rain falling intermittently. **1953** D. ROOKE *S. Afr. Twins* 101 The clouds shifted and the sun peeped out. A fine silver rain was still falling. 'It's a Monkey's Wedding', cried Tiensie. [**1963** S. CLOETE *Rags of Glory* 336 A monkey's wedding day of love – that was how the Dutch described a day of alternate bright sunshine and showers.] **1971** K. SHIPPEY on Radio South Africa 20 Nov., As I speak to you we have a burst of late sunshine making this into a monkey's wedding and a half ... Lets hope this sunshine does sweep the rain away. [**1973** *Informant, KwaZulu-Natal* Just for a joke in Zulu we call it '*umshado we Zinkawu*' wedding for monkeys, if the sun comes out in the rain.] **1988** K. BARRIS *Small Change* 106 It was a wistful morning with the sun attempting to shine through a drizzle. When he was a child, that was called a monkey's wedding. **1989** J. HOBBS *Thoughts in Makeshift Mortuary* 362 'Dumela,' Sarah says, trying to smile at her though it is like a monkey's wedding, sunshine through rain. **1990** A.E. SILVA *Informant, Grahamstown* It's a monkey's wedding, 'cause it's rainy and it's sunny.

monkey thorn *n. phr.* [tr. Afk. *apiesdoring.*] APIESDORING.

1985 *S. Afr. Panorama* Feb. 35 A magnificent flowering monkey thorn, *Acacia galpinii.* **1991** J. HUNTLY in *Sunday Star* 16 Feb. (Weekend) 4 The *apiesdoring* or monkey thorn .. is the giant of the thorn trees and the yellow flowering spikes, which appear from October to January, make the monkey thorn one of the most beautiful of all veld trees.

monooho var. MOHOHU.

Mons Mensae /mɒnz ˈmensaɪ/ *n. phr. Obs.* exc. *hist. Astronomy.* [L. *mons* mount + *mensae* of the table; see quot. 1987.] The name formerly given to the constellation Mensa, visible below the Large Magellanic Cloud. See also CAPE CLOUDS.

1987 P. MACK *Night Skies* 5 The rather faint and obscure constellation of Mensa is of local interest. It was originally named Mons Mensae ('Table Mountain') by La Caille who formed the figure from the stars under the Large Magellanic Cloud, the name being suggested by Table Mountain in Cape Town which was also frequently capped by cloud. It is the only constellation named after a geographical feature on Earth. **1994** K. WALL in D. McCormack *Perm Bk of 'Test the Team'* 61 One of the constellations is named after a South African topographical feature. Which? *Ibid.* 168 Mons Mensae (Table Mountain).

moocha var. MUTSHA.

mooche var. MOOTJIE.

moochi /ˈmuːtʃi/ *n.* Also **moochie**, **mouche**, **m(o)uchi**, **mutshi**. [Englished form of Zulu *umutsha*, see MUTSHA.] In traditional African dress: **a.** MUTSHA sense a. **b.** A square of beads worn by women as a loin-covering; MUTSHA sense b; also *transf.*, see quot. 1971.

1878 H.A. ROCHE *On Trek in Tvl* 324 A wee little Kafir boy, with nothing upon him but his 'moochie', or tails. **1882** W.R. LUDLOW *Zululand & Cetewayo* 37 Garga had on a mouche, or apron, made of catskins, round his waist. **1898** [see APRON sense 1]. **1899** G.H. RUSSELL *Under Sjambok* 29 Except for the ordinary Kafir mouchi, he wore no clothing. [*Note*] Some calico or skins hung round the loins. **1909** N. PAUL *Child in Midst* 139 Presently he appeared .. with no clothing except a cow-hide mutshi, with flaps around his waist, and pieces of bamboo stuck through his ears. [*Note*] Loin-girdle. **1936** WILLIAMS & MAY *I Am Black* 76 Fat belly protruding above the thong of the leather *moochi.* **1957** H.J. MAY in *S. Afr. P.E.N. Yrbk 1956–7* 46 Not even the usual native blanket to cover his little body; only a little grubby *moochi.* **1970** *Rand Daily Mail* 29 Oct. 12 Beaded 'muchi' R3.50. **1971** *Daily Dispatch* 14 July 5 Moochies, which were first worn as loincloths by tribal women, have graduated to bead the necks of sophisticated fashion-conscious women around the world. **1975** *Sunday Times* 6 Apr. 4 Does this mean that harbouring Michelangelo's Boy David without a moochi will be a sign of communist infiltration .. ? **1979** C. ENDFIELD *Zulu Dawn* 15 The swaying beads of the tiny G-string moochies she and her sister dancers wore.

moochy var. MUSHY.

moogie var. MOEGIE.

mooi /mɔɪ/ *int.* and *adj. Colloq.* Also **moi**, **mo(o)y**. [Afk., fr. Du., handsome, pretty.]

Used in the past by writers to suggest the speech of *S. Afr. Du.* or Afrikaans-speakers, 'mooi' is now commonly used in colloquial *S. Afr. Eng.*

A. *int.* Expressive of pleasure or approval: 'wonderful', 'great'.

1812 A. PLUMPTRE tr. *H. Lichtenstein's Trav. in Sn Afr.* (1928) I. 118 At every object which excited their astonishment or gave them pleasure, they exclaimed *mooi! mooi!* (fine! fine!) .. pronounced with a slow and lengthened tone that was not unpleasing. **1916** J.M. ORPEN *Reminisc.* (1964) 306, I caught the little boy by the arm and swung him behind me astride on the horse ... The mite .. turned and cried 'Mooi!' (Beautiful). **1946** V. Pohl *Adventures of Boer Family* 66 Being a Boer he felt himself amply rewarded with a handshake, a slap on the back, and a laughing 'Mooi, Jan!' ('Well done, Jan!') from his leader. **1960** *Capricorn High School Mag.* Dec. 90 With cries of 'Mooi, mooi, shot, Oh! Well played!' we finished off our competitive basketball against the various schools in our league. **1971** *Informant, Grahamstown* 'We'll come and see you tonight, then.' 'Mooi!' **1979** *Daily Dispatch* 11 May 10 There would always be a potential for conflict, he added. 'Mooi,' interjected an opposition member, applauding not the potential for conflict but Mr Nothnagel's recognition of its cause. **1983** *Sunday Times* 8 May (Mag. Sect.) 23 The kid from Booysens hits home with a lucky right cut and the word '*Mooi*' echoes around the hall like a mortar blast. **1994** on TV1, 30 July (The Line), Jiss, look at that, hey! Mooi!

B. *adj.* Also (*attrib.*) **mooie**. Pretty; good; nice.

[**1797** Lady A. Barnard *S. Afr. Century Ago* (1910) 138 The *moye kinder* (pretty little children – to translate for you).] **1850** N.J. Merriman *Cape Jrnls* (1957) 106 He wanted to know .. why the Wesleyans did not wear the same 'mooie' garments that we wore (viz. the surplice). *a***1875** T. Baines *Jrnl of Res.* (1964) II. 43 The one objectionable part of their attire .. a quantity of leather thongs coiled about their ankles till the really graceful limb had the appearance of a gouty leg. They told me however that it was very 'mooi'. **1887** A.A. Anderson *25 Yrs in Waggon* I. 41 When I showed them a small drawing of the town, .. they held it upside down, and said it was *mooi* (pretty). **1894** E. Glanville *Fair Colonist* 87 Two English ladies, he said ... He thought one was called Miss Tamplin. He knew this, that they were both *mooi* (beautiful). **1904** *Argus Christmas Annual* (Orange River Col. Sect.) 13 A soft mooi bed. He sank into the mattress. **1910** D. Fairbridge *That Which Hath Been* (1913) 109 'Ja, the homesteads are mooi.' 'Mooi, my dear Madam,' exclaimed van der Stel, .. 'surely you don't call a house like Meerlust pretty?' **1912** F. Bancroft *Veldt Dwellers* 15 Father's going to give him a *mooi* fat heifer. [**1921** *E. Prov. Herald* 3 Mar. 7 He said it was just a 'Mooi Kleppje' ... He certainly had no idea of its being any more valuable than any other Mooi Klip (pretty stone). **1937** C.R. Prance *Tante Rebella's Saga* 18 In the year 1900 she was a mere girl, a 'mooi meisje' whose skirts could never keep pace with the growth of long bare legs.] **1963** J. Packer *Home from Sea* 126 'She's tame, that mooi animal', said Ben, who loved and admired her. **1979** *Informant, Grahamstown* That was a mooi rain, hey? **1983** *Sunday Times* 18 Sept. 33 The people are *mooi* – really nice. *c***1985** S. Cromie in *Eng. Academy Rev.* 3 18 Look at their fancy clothes, Lekker houses, Mooi braaivleis once a week – real meat too nogal! **1994** *Sunday Times* 23 Jan., (advt) We've got a .. culinary culture all of our own. And boy is it mooi.

mooi nooitje /ˌmɔɪ ˈnɔɪki, -ci/ *n. phr. ?Obsolescent.* Also **mooinooientjie, mooi nooi(nt)je**. [S. Afr. Du. (later Afk.), *mooi* pretty + *nooitj(i)e* little mistress, young girl.] Esp. in the Western Cape: the strepie, *Sarpa salpa*.

1913 C. Pettman *Africanderisms* 324 *Mooi nooije*, .. The Struis Bay and Hermanuspetrusfontein name for *Box salpa*. See Bamboo-fish. **1913** [see strepie]. **1917** A.C.M. Orrey *Bottom Fishing in Cape Waters* 57 If mackerel .. cannot be obtained [as bait], a small fish such as a mooi noointje or blauw koppie or harder may be caught and used whole in the same way as mackerel. **1949** [see strepie]. **1951** L.G. Green *Grow Lovely* 92 An appealing name is that of the mooinooientjie, a modest bamboo fish with golden stripes. **1958** — *S. Afr. Beachcomber* 111 [Pappe] defended the bamboo fish, or mooi nooientjie (pretty girl) also known as the stinkfish, explaining that [its] diet of seaweed gave out a peculiar smell when the fish was cleaned.

moolongo var. mlungu.

moonfish *n.* [Named for its silvery colour and oval body-shape.] Any of several marine and freshwater fishes: **1.** Either of two marine and freshwater fishes of the Monodactylidae: **a.** *Monodactylus falciformis*; cape lady sense 3. **b.** *M. argenteus*. **2.** The marine fish *Trachinotus botla* of the Carangidae. In all senses also called moony.

1905 *Natal Mercury Pictorial* 339 (Pettman), The fish photo this week is that of a *moon-fish* ... It is a bluish silvery fish without scales and grows to a weight of about 3 lb. **1913** C. Pettman *Africanderisms* 325 *Moon fish, Psettus falciformis*. The name appears to be applied to a different fish in Natal. **1930** C.L. Biden *Sea-Angling Fishes* 54 Natal moonfish – *Trachynotus ovatus* (Linn.). **1949** J.L.B. Smith *Sea Fishes* 233 *Monodactylus falciformis* Lacepede .. *Cape Lady* (Knysna). *Moon-fish. Moony. Kite-fish. Sea-kite* (Eastern Cape and Natal) ... Brilliant silvery with iridescence, the scales easily shed. *Ibid.* 234 *Monodactylus argenteus* (Linnaeus). *Moony. Moon-fish* ... Brilliant silvery, characterised by only 2 cross-bars which fade with growth. *Ibid.* 222 *Trachinotus russellii* Cuv ... *Moonfish. Ladyfish* ... Throughout the tropical Indo-Pacific, not uncommon in Natal and Delagoa Bay, occasionally reaches East London. **1957** S. Schoeman *Strike!* 221 Galjoen, blacktail (dassie), copper bream (hottentot) and moonfish are caught during the period September to December. **1967** R.A. Jubb *Freshwater Fishes* 193 *Monodactylus argenteus*, .. Moonfish ... Attains a size of 9 inches, being rare south of Pondoland. **1974** [see zebra].

mooni var. moenie.

moony /ˈmuːni/ *n. colloq.* Also **moonie**. Pl. **moonies**, or unchanged. [Formed on moonfish + Eng. (informal) n.-forming suffix *-y* (or *-ie*).] moonfish.

In Smith and Heemstra's *Smiths' Sea Fishes* (1986), the name 'Natal moony' is used for *Monodactylus argenteus*, 'Cape moony' for *M. falciformis*, and 'largespotted pompano' for *Trachinotus botla*.

1949 [see moonfish]. **1967** R.A. Jubb *Freshwater Fishes* 192 *Monodactylus falciformis*, .. Cape lady or Moony. **1970** *Albany Mercury* 29 Jan. 15 Brenda .. landed three moonie weighing 7 lb 3 oz. The lucky fish which took the sealed award was a moonie of the exact weight of 2lb 7 oz. **1971** *Daily Dispatch* 30 July 8 An ugly, unimpressive round fish that I would call a 'moony'. **1986** Smith & Heemstra *Smith's Sea Fishes* 607 Family No. 193: Monodactylidae ... Moonies ... Natal moony ... Cape moony. **1993** P.H. Skelton *Complete Guide to Freshwater Fishes* 358 Family Monodactylidae. *Moonies* ... A small family of distinctive deep-bodied fishes common in estuaries, with juveniles frequently entering freshwater reaches or rivers. One genus and two species in southern Africa.

moor *n.* var. moer *n.*[1]

moor *v.* var. moer *v.*

Mooreemo, Moorimo varr. Morimo.

moorootze var. moruti.

moors dood var. morsdood.

moosh, moosh(l)y varr. mushy.

moote, mooti(e) varr. muti.

mootjie /ˈmɔiki, -ci/ *n.* Also **mooche, mootchee, mootje, motjie**. [Afk., fr. Du. *moot* piece, fillet of fish + dim. suffix -ie.] A small slice or piece of fish.

1890 A.G. Hewitt *Cape Cookery* 11 Cut the fish into Mootjes ... Put the pieces to drain. **1904** *Argus Christmas Annual* (Cape Colony Sect.) 19 A great trade is done in 'mooches' – if that be the correct spelling. A mackerel makes two mootches, and a mootchee, that is a dried slab of salted mackerel, serves as a ration for a farm labourer. **1934** *Cape Argus* 12 Apr. (Swart), Salted in 'Mootjies' or small sections it had a great sale inland and among the Indian population in Mauritius. **1972** L.G. Green *When Journey's Over* 145 He used to .. buy dozens of snoek at a penny each. They cut them into motjies, salted and spiced them and stored them in barrels for the winter.

Mōōtshooānās pl. form of Bechuana.

mooy var. mooi.

mopani, mopane /məˈpɑːni, mɔ-/ *n.* Also **mapani, mapone, mopaane, mopané, mopanie, m'pani, mupani**. Pl. unchanged, or **-s**. [Setswana *mopane* (Venda *mupani*).]

1.a. In full ***mopani tree***: a tree of the Eastern Transvaal and North-West Province, *Colophospermum mopane* of the Caesalpiniaceae, distinguished by rough, flaking bark, pale green flowers, and butterfly-shaped leaves formed of a pair of triangular leaflets joined at the base, which fold together in intense heat; turpentine tree. **b.** The hard, dark-red wood of this tree. Also *attrib.*

1857 D. Livingstone *Missionary Trav.* 91 In some parts there are forests of mimosa and mopane. **1864** T. Baines *Explor. in S.-W. Afr.* 427 We rattled on over hard limestone country, thickly clothed with mopánēs. **1871** J. Mackenzie *Ten Yrs* (1971) 140 We at length found in a large mopane forest a well-beaten path. **1887** A.A. Anderson *25 Yrs in Waggon* I. 229 Many of the mapani-trees grow to a great size; the leaf has a sweet gummy sort of varnish, of which the elephants are very fond. **1896** H.A. Bryden *Tales of S. Afr.* 136 A low growth of parched mopani trees .. whose odd butterfly-like leaves, now shrivelled and scorched .. bore eloquent testimony to the nature of this terrible 'thirst-land.' **1917** R. Marloth *Common Names* 59 *Mopane, Copaifera Mopane*. A social tree of northern Bechuanaland and Rhodesia. **1929** J. Stevenson-Hamilton *Low-Veld* 36 The widely distributed mopani (Copaifera mopani); thornless and with a large scented double leaf. **1949** C. Bullock *Rina* 41 A belt of mupani .. the trees very beautiful, their smooth, green leaves giving them the semblance of miniature English beeches. **1961** Palmer & Pitman *Trees of S. Afr.* 173 As a fodder tree the mopane plays a vitally important role in these areas of low rainfall ... Most of the mopane in the Union are no higher than 15 feet. **1968** L.G. Green *Full Many Glorious Morning* 188 A comfortable house of mopani logs and thatch. *Ibid.* 190 This is the mopane country, a tree named because each leaf resembles a butterfly with outstretched wings. (Mopane means butterfly). **1978** *S. Afr. Digest* 3 Nov. 1 The area, which stretches towards the Botswana border about 90 km to the west, is covered with thick bush and massive mopani trees. **1985** *Style* Oct. 92 So begins our odyssey ... days spent traversing a kaleidoscopic landscape of semi-arid vegetation dotted with acacia, mopane, boabab and thorn trees. **1988** [see umbrella thorn].

2. Used *attrib.*, in the phrr. ***mopani bush(veld)***, ***mopani country***, ***mopani veld***, etc., a bush- or veld-type characterized by large numbers of mopani trees.

1928 E.H.L. Schwarz *Kalahari & its Native Races* 62 This is good grass, not like that of the mopane veld which withers and blows away. **1937** M. Alston *Wanderings* 159 The eighteen mile drive .. through the green and gold and copper-coloured mopani bush was a delight. **1946** S. Cloete *Afr. Portraits* 87 The country became more and more inhospitable as the mopani scrub gave way to rocks. **1949** C. Bullock *Rina* 41 Mupani veld, the most sodden in summer, is dry as a baked brick until the rains come. **1951** T.V. Bulpin *Lost Trails of Low Veld* 266 The hundred-mile long by fifty-mile wide stretch of flat mopani bush land lying between the Letaba River .. in the south and the Great Limpopo River in the north. **1966** C.A. Smith *Common Names* 342 The species [*sc. Colophospermum mopane*] grows socially in large numbers in the areas in which it occurs and has given the name 'mopane veld' to such areas. *Ibid.* 459 East Coast fever is said to be unknown in Mopani veld. **1977** S. Stander *Flight from Hunter* 159 Gradually the landscape changed, from grass plain to the mopani scrub they had encountered in the north and then to belts of mopani forest. **1980** *E. Prov. Herald* 1 Aug. 13 Low rainfall produces short-lived flushes of sparse grass among mopane scrublands and jesse-bush thickets. **1988** *S. Afr. Panorama* May, The hunting-grounds vary from red Kalahari dunes in the north-west Cape to grassy plains in the Free State, mopani bushveld and savannah in the Transvaal lowveld and baobab country beyond the Soutpansberg in the far north.

3. *comb.* **mopani bee**, any of several small, stingless bees of the genus *Trigona* (family Apidae); **mopani beetle**, some unknown cicada; **mopani fly**, see *mopani bee*; **mopani worm**, the caterpillar of the emperor-moth *Gonimbrasia belina* of the Saturniidae, which feeds on the mopani tree and is used as food particularly by the Tswana peoples; *bosveld garnaal*, see BOSVELD sense 3; *bushveld prawn*, see BUSHVELD sense 3; see also MASONJA.

[**mopani bee: 1857** D. LIVINGSTONE *Missionary Trav.* 614 The bees were always found in the natural cavities of mopane-trees.] *c***1936** *S. & E. Afr. Yr Bk & Guide* 303 The M'Pani bee does not sting. **1954** S.H. SKAIFE *Afr. Insect Life* 357 The stingless bees, or Mopani bees, as they are often called, that are found in Africa, belong to the genus *Trigona*. **1988** T.J. LINDSAY *Shadow* (1990) 14 Mupani bees .. collected in worrisome clouds. **1972** L. VAN DER POST *Story like Wind* 161 At about ten in the morning .. all the billions of **mopani beetles**, hidden behind the butterfly leaves of the trees, began to sing their Messiah to the day. **1972** C. BRITZ *Informant, Namibia* Honey from the mopane trees — made by **mopane flies**, which are like miniature bees — they don't sting. They make small combs in the hollow mopane trees ... It tastes different — not quite the same as bee's honey, a wilder, sweeter taste. **1979** *Daily Dispatch* 14 Mar. 9 Reality here was clouds of dust, swarms of mopani flies and mosquitoes. **1964** [**mopani worm**: see MASONJA]. **1974** *E. Prov. Herald* 6 May, When we were in the bundu on a safari, everything was served with *stywepap* — even mopani worms. **1980** *S. Afr. Panorama* July 32 The dishes included grilled mopani worms in onions and tomato — as an accompanying dish — with stiff maize porridge. **1986** SCHOLTZ & HOLM *Insects* 381 The larvae of many of the large species of Saturniidae are favoured by African tribes as relishes, e.g. the mopane 'worm' *Gonimbrasia belina*. **1986** C. O'TOOLE *Encycl. of Insects* 101 The larva of the Mopane moth is .. an attractive caterpillar with bright red, yellow and black markings on a white background ... 'Mopane worms' are often sold dried, and they have a rather nutty flavour. **1987** J. QUEST *Burning River* 67 I'm so hungry I'd eat any number of mopani worms and lizards. **1990** G. MOKAE in *Frontline* Sept. 28 We may partake of delicacies that seem odd to white eyes, like mopani worms and horse meat.

Mopedi var. PEDI.

moppie /'mɔpi/ *n. Music.* [Afk., fr. Du. *mopje* ditty.] A street-song of the Cape 'coloured' and Cape Malay people. Also *attrib.* See also KLOPSE sense 2.

1949 *Cape Times* 10 Jan. 2 He hoped that the Cape 'moppies' or comic songs and the *liedjies* would become a regular feature of future carnivals. **1951** [see LIEDJIE]. **1953** DU PLESSIS & LÜCKHOFF *Malay Quarter* 48 Moppies are little songs (often of doubtful content) sung in order to challenge, deride or irritate the listener, or merely as foolery. When singing a moppie, the singer often includes a person's name, and if the person referred to cannot respond in similar vein, he is laughed at by all present. **1962** [see GHOMMALIEDJIE]. **1966** *Cape Argus* 8 Mar. 12 Musical programmes would also be able to relay more of the typical 'moppies' which are heard far too seldom these days — and then only at New Year. **1981** *S. Afr. Panorama* July 37 The true *moppie* is a comic song, and frequently a *skemliedjie* (skit) with a continuous theme, a lively refrain and a strong rhythm. New songs originate every year. **1984** D. PINNOCK *Brotherhoods* 102 An identifiable musical preference was until recently the traditional *moppies* and liedjies of the Coon Carnival. **1987** [see E. Prov. Herald quot. at KLOPSE sense 2]. **1988** *South* 21 July 6 Basil's at the Nico putting the Swan Lake Ballet to moppie music. **1989** [see GHOMMALIEDJIE].

mor var. MOER *n.*[1]

mora var. MÔRE.

morabaraba /mɔˌraba'raba/ *n.* Also **marabaraba**. [Sotho.] A game played with stones, placed and moved on rows of small holes in the ground, or on lines on a board or large stone, arranged to form concentric squares with diagonal lines passing through their corners; similar in many ways to nine-men's morris; UMLABALABA; TSORO. Also *attrib.*

1953 LANHAM & MOPELI-PAULUS *Blanket Boy's Moon* 161 Mkize looked up from his game of morabaraba and answered him. **1957** A.A. MURRAY *Blanket* 28 This was the marabaraba stone, and the males of the village, from small herds upwards, would frequently gather around it for a game. **1965** E. MPHAHLELE *Down Second Ave* 26, I wish Sello's father was my father too ... He plays morabaraba with his boys. Father'd never do that. **1979** *Sunday Times* 28 Oct. 21 On the corner further along, a game of marabaraba, played with stones and holes in the ground. **1979** *Pace* Sept. 28 Friday and Saturday nights are for drinking, singing, gambling and playing 'morabaraba.' **1981** *Sunday Times* 27 Dec. 8 You'll soon be seeing a 'new' game on the goggle-box. It's the game that comes out in Zulu as umlabalaba and in Sesotho as marabaraba. Umlabalaba or marabaraba, take your pick, was known to me as a small boy back were I come from as Nine Men's Morris.

morala var. MARULA.

‖**môre** /'mɔːrə/ *int.* Also **mora**, **morre**. [Afk., 'morning' or 'tomorrow'.]

1. [Afk., ellipt. form of *goeie môre*.] GOEIE MÔRE.

1916 S. BLACK in S. Gray *Three Plays* (1984) 200 Maria: Mora, Mr van Kalabas. Van K: What the dickens are you doing here during office hours? **1917** S.T. PLAATJE *Native Life* 81 The morning coffee had been made right enough but the maid's 'Morre Nooi' (Good morning ma'am) was rather sullen and almost bordering on insolence. **1973** *E. Prov. Herald* 27 Mar. 17 'Goeie môre,' he said, materialising from nowhere. 'Môre,' we said, walking on. **1988** *Personality* 17 Oct. 26 (*advt*) Then, speed trap. A bush .. came alive as a traffic policeman leapt out from behind it, and waved me down ... I drove back to him. 'Môre, officer ..' I said cheerfully.

2. In the idioms ***môre is nog 'n dag*** /- ˌəs ˌnɔx ə 'dax/, also ***môre is nog a dag***, ***more's nog 'n dag***, and (*obs.*) ***môre is ook 'n dag*** /- 'ʊək-/ [Afk., *môre* tomorrow + *is* is + *nog* another (or *ook* also) + *'n* a + *dag* day], expressions used as an (often ironic) excuse for procrastination. Also *attrib.* Cf. ALLES SAL REGKOM.

Similar in meaning to Spanish (and Eng.) 'mañana'.

[**1909** LADY S. WILSON *S. Afr. Mem.* 213 When one of the veldcornets went and begged his permission to collect volunteers as reinforcements, all the General did was to scratch his head and murmur in Dutch, 'Morro is nocher dag' (To-morrow is another day).] **1919** M.C. BRUCE *Golden Vessel* 94 That lively good nature which .. banishes the duty of the day because 'Morrer is ook een dag,' wants some toning up to bring the character of the people into line with other nations. **1944** C.R. PRANCE *Under Blue Roof* 118 'Môre is ook 'n dag' (to-morrow is also a day) is the backveld motto, akin to 'Manana' of old Spain. **1959** M.W. SPILHAUS *Under Bright Sky* 49 Japie is the one who is stern with his children, and counteracts whatever notion of *môre is ook 'n dag* Flora's soft heart might let them get away with. **1969** I. VAUGHAN *Last of Sunlit Yrs* 74 Only in South Africa, I thought, where 'môre is nog 'n dag', could this happy atmosphere attend a roaring railway engine and coaches rushing through a small village. **1976** *Cape Times* 21 July 10 *Môre is nog 'n dag* just won't do any more. Complacency is irresponsible. **1980** *Daily Dispatch* 25 Feb. 8 Westerners seem to suffer more from workaholism than those who live in traditional eastern cultures where people seem to have a natural wisdom, a kind of 'môre is nog 'n dag' outlook. **1986** *Style* Feb. 31, 101 Reasons for staying in South Africa: ... 95. Môre is nog 'n dag. **1990** *Weekend Post* 13 Jan. 3 People here have an attitude of 'Môre is nog 'n dag,' and so although they are friendly and helpful it is terrible to try and get something done.

More(e)mo var. MORIMO.

‖**morena** /mɔ'reːna, -nə/ *n.* Also **marena**, **moreana**, and with initial capital. [Sotho and seTswana, sing. n. prefix *mo-* + *rena* be rich, be a chief.] Esp. among Sotho-speakers:

1. Used of or to someone in authority (but see also quot. 1912).

a. A respectful form of address or reference: 'Sir', 'Master'. Cf. INKOSI sense 1 b, UMNUMZANA sense 2 a.

[**1835** A. SMITH *Diary* (1940) II. 186 They walked boldly in though they saw the Matabeli, saluted all the white people with 'Moron' and then went towards the Matabeli fire.] **1840** J. CAMPBELL *Journey to Lattakoo* 87 Thirty-nine Marootzees joined us from Mashow ... On meeting them .. they saluted me with the word *Murella*. **1912** J.C. MACGREGOR tr. *D.F. Ellenberger's Hist. of Basuto* 292 One is agreeably surprised to see .. so much politeness, and so many rules of etiquette .. faithfully observed ... The chiefs often address their subjects as *marena* ('chiefs'), *benghali* ('my masters'). **1923** G.H. NICHOLLS *Bayete!* 54 The messengers formed up in a line in front of the two officials and saluted in their turn, by throwing up the right hand, fist clenched, straight above the head and shouting 'Morena'. **1924** G. BAUMANN in Baumann & Bright *Lost Republic* (1940) 137 All the boys whom I had had occasion to flog saluted me with upraised arm: 'Domela Morena' (Sesuto — 'Hail, Master'). **1937** B.H. DICKE *Bush Speaks* 123 Morena! Ghosi! (Sir! Chief!), a voice called out of a large maize field where the plants stood some eight feet high. **1952** H. KLEIN *Land of Silver Mist* 85 A Native policeboy doing his patrol on a bicycle came down to have a look at me. 'Morena', he greeted. **1974** *Sunday Times* 1 Sept. 3 The Bantu is a person, an entity with a name and a surname. If it is known, call him by his name and surname and add 'mister' (Morena), particularly if you are in his homeland. **1975** S.S. MEKGOE *Lindiwe* (1978) 17 No-no Sergeant, no-no morena. Asseblief my baas. **1989** *Weekly Mail* 27 Oct. 11 The insistence by whites to be called *baas* or *Morena* (chiefs) by the black policemen. **1990** G. SLOVO *Ties of Blood* 474 Moses did not deign to reply. For this transgression one of the constables guarding him kicked him in the back. 'Answer the *moreana*,' he ordered.

b. A common noun: a master; also used as a polite form of address in the third person. Cf. INKOSI sense 1 a.

1908 [see KGOSI]. **1942** U. KRIGE *Dream & Desert* (1953) 133 'Greetings, Morena Dumela!' he exclaimed in Sesuto. 'But the Morena speaks Sesuto. It is wonderful. Why did the Morena not tell me the other day he speaks our language?' *Ibid.* 135 Morena, give my greetings to the other Morena. To-night I shall come to the Morena's truck and we shall speak again of Mokhotlong. **1948** E. ROSENTHAL *Afr. Switzerland* 71 The white morenas adjourn for a whisky-and-soda. **1960** J. COPE *Tame Ox* 61 The *morena* was a young man with a pleasant sunburnt face and blue eyes. He made out the ticket without a word and then he came from his small office and chatted to Isaiah.

2. A title of respect given to a Sotho chief.

1861 E. CASALIS *Basutos* II. 214 The Basutos give to the princes who govern them the title of *Morena* ... He who watches over the public safety and welfare. **1953** LANHAM & MOPELI-PAULUS *Blanket Boy's Moon* 17 The Chief is highly respected by his subjects, who call him, *Morena*. **1957** A.A. MURRAY *Blanket* 192 'Morena — Chief,' he said. At once the others followed his lead, and the night rang to the deep cadence of their voices: 'Morena — Morena'. **1988** SPIEGEL & BOONZAIER in Boonzaier & Sharp *S. Afr. Keywords* 48 A chief in Qwaqwa is still called *morena*, the word used to describe nineteenth-century political leaders whose authority derived from their ability to maintain their followers' allegiance, as well as from their descent from particular lines.

3. God, 'the Lord'. Cf. MODIMO.

1882 J. NIXON *Among Boers* 248 As a rule, the natives have some crude idea of an Omnipotent Being, .. who is known by some of the tribes as 'Morena', i.e. the power in the skies. **1981** *Rand Daily Mail* 16 July 6 The two began to work on the idea of what would happen if 'Morena' (Sotho for the Lord) came down to earth here in South Africa.

more's nog 'n dag see MÔRE sense 2.

moretlwa /mɔ'retlwa/ *n.* Also **moretloa**. [Se-Tswana *moretlhwa*.] The rigid, bushy shrub or small tree *Grewia flava* of the Tiliaceae, bearing edible red-brown, stoney drupes with a sweet pulp which is fermented to make beer, distilled for brandy, and ground to make porridge; *brandewynbos*, see BRANDEWYN sense 2; BRANDY BUSH; *rosyntjiebos* sense (*a*), see ROSYNTJIE sense 2; *wild plum* sense (*f*), see WILD sense a. Also *attrib.*

1857 D. LIVINGSTONE *Missionary Trav.* 112 The soil consists of yellow sand and tall coarse grasses growing among berry-yielding bushes, named moretloa (Grewia flava), and motatla. **1871** J. MACKENZIE *Ten Yrs* (1971) 70 The berries of the moretlwa bushes are also very welcome when their season comes round. *Ibid.* 103 The little bushes of the Karroo had given place .. to an extensive belt of country covered with the larger moretlwa and mohatla bushes. **1988** DEDEREN & SHORT in *Quagga* No.20, 7 The Kgatla Tswana mention the shady moretlwa (*Grewia flava*) as the favourite of their Skybird tladi.

morgen /'mɔːgən/ *n.* Pl. unchanged, or occas. **-s**. [S. Afr. Du., fr. Middle Du. *morghen* (lit. 'morning') an area of land ploughed in a morning.] A unit of land measurement comprising just over two acres, or one hectare.

Used also in certain dialects of *U.S. Eng.*, from as early as 1674.

1797 EARL MACARTNEY in G.M. Theal *Rec. of Cape Col.* (1898) II. 122 The number of Morgen of Ground that they possess in property or loan and what quantity of the same they believe to be cultivated. **1801** J. BARROW *Trav.* I. 64 Sixty *morgens* of land, or 120 English acres. **1832** *Graham's Town Jrnl* 20 Apr. 66 The mere proposal to confine a Dutch farmer to two hundred and fifty morgen of land, would be scouted as an extravagant absurdity. **1837** J.E. ALEXANDER *Narr. of Voy.* I. 342 A full-sized farm is reckoned from two to three thousand *morgen*, or double that number of acres. **1843** J.C. CHASE *Cape of G.H.* 193 A morgen is generally reckoned to be equal to two English statute acres, but the true proportion is considered to be 49 71–100ths morgen to 100 acres. **1873** F. BOYLE *To Cape for Diamonds* 24 A settler could obtain three thousand morgen, or something more than six thousand acres, round the spot where he chose to build the homestead. **1899** *Natal Agric. Jrnl* 31 Mar. 3 'Erf' (a town plot of land) and 'morgen' (about two acres) will linger wherever land has been set off by Dutch measurement. **1917** S.T. PLAATJE *Native Life* 31 They got alarmed to hear that Natives had during the past three years 'bought' land to the extent of 50 000 morgen per annum. *c*1936 *S. & E. Afr. Yr Bk & Guide* 26 The square was supposed to measure rather more than three miles each way, which allowed about 10 sq. miles or 3,000 morgens to the farm. **1939** [see NABOOM]. **1948** V.M. FITZROY *Cabbages & Cream* 213 The smallholder has to work every bit as hard as the farmer on five hundred morgen. **1963** L.F. FREED *Crime in S. Afr.* 109 The township lies outside the Johannesburg municipal area, and .. consists of 415 morgen, which is divided into 2,525 stands. **1974** [see QUIT-RENT sense 1]. **1989** *Sunday Times* 10 Dec. (Mag. Sect.) 26 The record price of R40 000 was recorded for a 25 morgen stand on the seafront between Keurboom strand and the Keurboom River a few kilometres north of Plettenberg Bay. **1991** D. GALLOWAY in *Weekend Argus* 26 Jan. 18 Oranjevlei is still the same 1150 morgen it was then.

Hence **morgenage** *n. obs.*, an area measured in morgen.

1934 *Cape Argus* 22 May (Swart), An unusually large morgenage has been cut for silage and generally provision has been made for winter feed on a considerable scale.

Morimo *n. obs.* Also **Mooreemo, Moorimo, More(e)mo, Morim**, and with small initial. [Sotho and seTswana: see MODIMO.] An early form of MODIMO.

1824 *Cape Chron.* in *S. Afr. Jrnl* I. 79 They had indeed heard of the 'Moreemo', (Deity); but only from their physicians, or 'medicine men'. **1826** A.G. BAIN *Jrnls* (1949) 31 The natives .. called me by no other name but Moorimo (god), for they said no mortal could make things live as I did on paper. **1833** S. KAY *Trav. & Researches* I. 236 A few indeed there were who seemed to have some confused notion of invisible powers, whom they designated *Mooreemo* and *Booreemo*. **1835** A. SMITH *Diary* (1940) II. 109, I caused the interpreter to put several questions to them touching the Divine Being. They said they did not know the meaning of the word moremo. **1846** R. MOFFAT *Missionary Labours* 69 Among the Bechuana tribes, the name adopted by the missionaries is *Morimo*. **1857** D. LIVINGSTONE *Missionary Trav.* 641 All the natives of this region have a clear idea of a Supreme Being ... He is named 'Morimo,' 'Molungo,' 'Reza,' 'Mpambe,' in the different dialects spoken. **1871** J. MACKENZIE *Ten Yrs* (1971) 138 The Bushmen will tell you in Sechuana, which is to him a foreign language, that this Agency or Agent is Morimo (God). **1925** D. KIDD *Essential Kafir* 102 Morimo may be regarded as the god of the Bechuana.

morogo /mə'rɔ(ː)gɔ, -xɔ, mɔ-/ *n.* Also **marog(o), merogo, moeroga, morog, morongo, muroch**. [Sotho and seTswana, 'amaranthus', 'wild spinach', 'vegetables'.]

In both senses also called IMIFINO and *wild spinach* (see WILD sense a).

a. Any of several species of edible leafy plants, traditionally cooked and eaten as a vegetable by African peoples.

1940 V. POHL *Bushveld Adventures* 73 The leaves and tender tops of a certain plant, which they use to make a delicious bread — they call it muroch — now mature and so become unfit for consumption. **1946** P. ABRAHAMS *Mine Boy* (1954) 27 It is called Moeroga ... They grow among nettles. I studied the leaves of wild spinach. *a*1968 D.C. THEMBA in E. Patel *World of Can Themba* (1985) 98 Macala's eyes glittered as he saw the Ma-Ndebele women squatting in their timeless patience behind their huge dishes of maize-cobs, dried morogo. **1979** *Voice* Vol.3 No.22, 11 There is not even naturally growing 'morogo' to fall back on. We just have to eat mealie-meal and water. **1988** N. MATHIANE in *Frontline* May 23 The women can no longer plant 'morogo' (spinach) which is their staple diet. **1989** [see *wild spinach* (WILD sense a)]. **1989** M. ROBERTS *Herbs for Healing* 12 *Anaemia, Amaranthus* ('morog') Include fresh or cooked, in the diet. **1992** C. KUPPELWIESER in *Living* Mar. 33 The Carolina mission had a large garden in which wild spinach, called Morogo, used to grow.

b. A traditional dish made from these plants.

1970 E. SCHEARKOGEL *Informant, Hennenman (OFS)* Marog. A stew of vegetables cooked like spinach. **1980** [see IMIFINO]. **1982** FOX & NORWOOD YOUNG *Food from Veld* 38 The leaves of several cultivated plants are used as 'imifino' or 'morogo'. The most common of these are: *Cajanus cajan* .. ; *Cucumis africanus* .. ; *Cucurbitae pepo* .. ; *Ipomea batatas* .. ; *Lablab purpureus* subsp. *uncinatus* .. ; *Manihot esculenta* .. ; *Vigna unguiculata* ... Quinn quoted a Pedi saying, 'meat is a visitor but *morogo* is a daily food'. **1986** P. PIETERSE *Day of Giants* 12 He sat on one foot stirring marog, a stew of pigweed shoots bubbling in the small iron pot. **1988** E. MPHAHLELE *Renewal Time* 170, I could not eat some of the things I loved very much: mealie-meal porridge with sour milk or *morogo*, stamped mealies mixed with butter beans, sour porridge for breakfast and other things. **1994** K. BOTHA in *Sunday Times* 25 Dec. 15, I can eat pap and marog with squatters and drink a toast to our new President. I am a citizen of the new South Africa.

Morolong var. BAROLONG.

morongo var. MOROGO.

Morootzee var. and pl. form of HURUTSHE.

morre var. MÔRE.

mors var. MOZ.

morsdood /'mɔrsdʊət, 'mɔːs-/ *adj. Colloq.* Also **moors doed, moors dood**. [Afk., fr. Du., perh. fr. L. *mors* death + Du. *dood* dead.] 'Stone dead'. Cf. (*as*) *dead as a mossie* (see MOSSIE sense 2).

1893 H.A. BRYDEN *Gun & Camera* 176, I pulled up my pony, fired from the saddle, .. and next instant, to the general astonishment, the koorhaan fell dead as mutton — 'moors dood,' as a Boer would say. **1899** B. MITFORD *Weird of Deadly Hollow* 245 That tiger should have been moors doed (stone dead) at every shot. **1904** H.A. BRYDEN *Hist. of S. Afr.* 44 An old Boer .. has been heard to protest that .. he would shoot the first man who attempted such a thing moors dood ('stone dead'). **1969** A. FUGARD *Boesman & Lena* 48 Lena: *Ja!* he's dead ... He's dead Boesman ... Boesman: *Morsdood?* Lena: *Ja.* **1989** *Advertising sticker, Maybaker (Pty) Ltd* Vrek kills flies morsdood.

morula var. MARULA.

moruti /mɔ'ruːti, mə-/ *n.* Also **maruti, moorootze, muruti**. Pl. **baruti**. [Sotho and se-Tswana, sing. n. prefix *mo-* (see MO-) + *-ruti*, fr. *ruta* teach.] Among speakers of Sotho and seTswana: UMFUNDISI.

1866 E.L. PRICE *Jrnls* (1956) 246, I think they wd. take anything fr. Roger, or any 'Muruti' — so glad are they to get a teacher once more. *a*1875 T. BAINES *Jrnl of Res.* (1964) II. 94 Instead of taking me to the Moorootze, Mr. Cameron, he left me in Morroko's kraal. **1918** C. GARSTIN *Sunshine Settlers* 163 They've got a new *maruti* over at Kala's *Stad* .. from the missionary school .. with a description of hell at his tongue's tip that makes old Dante's prospectus sound like a garden city. **1937** B.H. DICKE *Bush Speaks* 43 This old warrior was a 'moruti,' a teacher of religion. **1953** LANHAM & MOPELI-PAULUS *Blanket Boy's Moon* 22 Yes, Moruti, I was baptised during childhood at the French Mission, by a Moruti who bore your name. **1967** M. MARQUARD *Lett. from Boer Parsonage* 84 He sent his sugar ration to the Parsonage with the message that the moruti's children should rather have the sugar since his own children were older. **1968** A. FULTON *Dark Side of Mercy* 28 The moruti, the priest who had baptised him, had poured scorn on the power of the Ngaka, deriding the magic of the medicine horn. **1974** [see MODIMO]. **1977** *S. Afr. Panorama* Dec. 46 Shadrack Maloka is Moruti (minister) of a congregation in Garankuwa near Pretoria. **1980** *Voice* 29 Oct. 13 We already have too many buffoons de-citizenshipping us. But now some baruti wish to add Amen! to all that. **1990** *Weekend Post* 24 Feb. (Leisure) 4 Their attempts to be on good terms with all their parishioners were soon rebuffed by the town's white inhabitants ... The Bafurutse, however, .. took the *moruti* and his *mma-moruti* into their hearts.

Morutze var. HURUTSHE.

mos /mɔs, mɒs/ *n.* Also **moss, most(o)**. [Afk., fr. Du. *most* must, new wine.]

1.a. New wine: the juice of the grape in its first stages of fermentation. Also *attrib.*

1862 LADY DUFF-GORDON in F. Galton *Vacation Tourists* (1864) III. 123 The people were not at work, but we saw the tubs and vats, and drank 'most'. **1891** [see MOSBOLLETJIE]. **1913** C. PETTMAN *Africanderisms* 326 *Most*, .. The unfermented juice of the grape. **1913** W.C. SCULLY *Further Reminisc.* 65 During the wine-pressing season we used to quaff foaming tankards of must, or 'moss' as it was called. **1936** E. ROSENTHAL *Old-Time Survivals* 36 Mosbolletjies are spongy buns, into the making of which goes 'mos' or the half-fermented juice of the grape. **1957** L.G. GREEN *Beyond City Lights* 12 Juice and husks .. went into the fermenting vat ... When this liquid cooled it became *soet mos*, pleasant and apparently harmless. **1964** J. MEINTJES *Manor House* 36 The room was close with the smell of sweat, wine and *mos*, but Father was used to it. **1977** *Family Radio & TV* 19 Sept. 51 Sweet grapes, usually Muscadel or Hanepoot, are pressed and fully fermented, resulting in a *mos* with a high alcohol content.

b. A raising agent in baking, either fermented raisin juice or new wine. Also *attrib.* See also MOSBOLLETJIE.

1890 A.G. HEWITT *Cape Cookery* 51, 3 lbs. raisins for moss. Wash the raisins, chop them up and put them into a dry seasoned calabash; pour some hot water over them, and let them stand for a day or two till the raisins are fermented; .. strain off the moss and set the sponge as if for bread. **1891** H.J. DUCKITT *Hilda's 'Where Is It?'* 143 This jar is .. only used for making the 'moss' in, as one is so much surer of its fermenting in a given time if made in a seasoned jar or calabash. **1936** M. HIGHAM *Hsehold Cookery* (1941) 262 Yeast No.IV. Most. (a) With fresh grapes ... (b) With raisins. Souring of most occurs very easily, the juice turning to vinegar, if not used at the right moment. *Ibid.* 273 Either fresh grapes or raisins may be used to make the most. **1979** HEARD & FAULL *Our Best Trad. Recipes* 90 *Mos* may be made with fresh grapes or raisins, whichever is most convenient. *Ibid.* 91 If intending to use *mos* yeast regularly for your bread, do not wash out the jar after removing the liquid.

2. *comb.* **mos-biscuit** *obs.*, MOSBOLLETJIE.

1875 C.B. BISSET *Sport & War* 12 This skin is filled on one side with **moss-biscuit**, or very dry and light biscuit made from the finest flour, and mixed up with mosto, or the unfermented juice of the grape. It makes a biscuit that will keep for ever and is very nutritious. **1896** M.A. CAREY-HOBSON *At Home in Tvl* 340 That fragrant beverage, with its accompaniment of moss biscuits.

mos /mɔs/ *adv. colloq.* [Afk., fr. West Flemish *mos* (a form of Du. *immers*) but, yet, indeed.]

Used for emphasis.

1. As an interpolation: 'after all'; 'of course'; 'you know'.

1900 H. BLORE *Imp. Light Horseman* 288, I know, mos, what girls are. **1979** M. MATSHOBA *Call Me Not a Man* 195 Give him the five cents, *mfowethu*. That's what they want, *mos*. **1982** M. MZAMANE *Children of Soweto* 20 Whites are correct, *mos*, when they say 'Tomorrow never comes'! **1986** S. SEPAMLA *Third Generation* 90 It's all starvation out here, you know what I mean, *mos*? **1993** [see FANAKALO].

2. With adjectives and adverbs: 'really'; 'actually'; 'after all'; 'indeed'.

1963 M. KAVANAGH *We Merry Peasants* 14 He shook his head, rubbed his chin, looked miserable: 'Ag, there's *mos* plenty of guinea fowl here in the Cape, lady.' **1969** A. FUGARD *Boesman & Lena* 21 He's mos better than nothing. Or was nothing better? **1973** M. PHILIP *Caravan Caravel* 40 Firstly, a person can't live on ice cream and with these teeth in my mouth I can *mos* only eat soft stuff like ice cream. **1978** C. VAN WYK in *Staffrider* Vol.1 No.2, 36 He don't feel blind about it ... How can he? He's mos mad. **1982** D. MQHABA in Chapman & Dangor *Voices from Within* 174 He must eat like a pig stuck in the mud, .. He's mos never taught any table decency! **1984** *Frontline* May 39 'After all,' I say, 'it is mos in your language. You ought to be grateful.' **1990** [see TOULEIER].

3.a. Before verbs: 'really'; 'actually'; 'truly'; 'after all'.

1968 A. FULTON *Dark Side of Mercy* 13 'Drink that,' he said, thrusting the glass into Michael's hand. 'You mos need it, man.' **1974** B. SIMON *Joburg, Sis!* Hell, 3 o'clock! No! That wasn't a hint man, don't go yet. This is when a man mos comes alive. **1977** A. ROSCOE *Uhuru's Fire* 227 A man must mos fight for his brother, don't I say? **1985** J. CLOETE in *S.-Easter* Oct.-Nov. 17 And now I do that for my students. That paradox, I believe in it. And I believe in myself as a teacher. Man, that's *mos* being realistic! **1987** *Scope* 20 Nov. 44 'You really went and did it?' 'Ja. I *mos* told you. Do you still want to party?' **1988** A. DANGOR in Bunn & Taylor *From S. Afr.* 183 It was because you joined the trade union. You want to mos show you also know something about politics.

b. After verbs: 'only'; 'just'; after all'.

1968 F.G. BUTLER *Cape Charade* 12 My mother was mos a child in George Rex's trek from Cape Town, 1804. **1981** V.A. FEBRUARY *Mind your Colour* 158 Africa then proceeds to identify words and slang expressions which are frequently used in the novel. They are as follows: .. bedonerd (crazy); bliksem (miscreant); mos (just). **1986** D. CASE *Love, David* 112, I was saving to buy .. some clothes for my sisters. They are mos girls — they must look nice sometimes. **1987** *Learn & Teach* No.5, 17 They say Hillbrow is mos a klein America. Darkies and Lanies live together. **1987** [see BOLOYI]. **1988** *E. Prov. Herald* 27 Feb. 6 'I intend advising him to ban floods.' 'Floods?' 'Totally. Floods endanger *mos* the safety of the public.'

mosadi /mɔˈsɑːdi/ *n.* Also **masadi**. Pl. **-s**, or **basadi**. [Sotho.] Among Sotho-speakers: a term of address or reference to a woman.

1930 S.T. PLAATJE *Mhudi* (1975) 141 The conversation was interrupted by a sensational movement in the camp. 'Basadi, basadi! (women, women!)' shouted the crowd. *Ibid.* 160 She said if she lived to have little ones of her own, surely they would be proud to have for an ayah such a noble mosadi as Mhudi. **1959** KNOBEL in *Hansard* 16 Apr. 4066 On our farm we do not talk of 'kaffirs' but about Natives and the Native women are called 'masadis'. **1978** M. TLALI in *Staffrider* Vol.1 No.2, 32 He said, 'John .. we are very thankful that you and your kind "mosadi" allowed us to come and see your beautiful house.' **1986** S. SEPAMLA *Third Generation* 38 They led her out of the house and as she lingered she was able to overhear Brink say to Mmabatho: 'You will never see her again, mosadi.' **1987** M. MELAMU *Children of Twilight* 104 Come on, mosadi, pay up or out you go. Too many people wanting house.

Mosambiquer var. MOZAMBIQUER.

Mosarwa var. MASARWA.

Mosbieker var. MASBIEKER.

mosbolletjie /ˌmɔsˈbɔləki, -ci, ˌmɒsˈbɒləki/ *n.* Also **mosbolitje**, **mosbolletje**, **mossbollet(j)(i)e**, **mostbollet(j)(i)e**. [Afk., earlier S. Afr. Du. *mosbolletje*, fr. Du. *most* (see MOS *n.*) + *bolletje* little ball.] A sweetish bun, made with a yeast of partially fermented grape- or raisin-juice, often flavoured with aniseed, and eaten fresh or as a rusk; *mos-biscuit*, see MOS *n.* sense 2. Occas. also **mosbol** (pl. **-bolle** /-bɔlə/).

1890 A.G. HEWITT *Cape Cookery* 51 Moss Bolletjes ... When it has risen work in the rest of the flour, sugar, fat and anise seeds; knead it well and bake either in loaves or bolletjes. **1891** H.J. DUCKITT *Hilda's 'Where Is It?'* 143 'Moss Bolletjes.' (An old Dutch recipe ..) 'Moss Bolletje' — so called from 'Moss,' juice of the grape in its first stages of fermentation, and 'Bolletje,' a bun. **1902** —— in M. Kuttel *Quadrilles & Konfyt* (1954) 13 We made 'Moss Bolletjies', a delicious bun which every housekeeper prides herself on making a good supply of, as the rusks .. are so much appreciated. **1910** D. FAIRBRIDGE *That Which Hath Been* (1913) Glossary, *Mostbolletjes*, Small square buns in which the must from grapes is used as leaven. **1928** N. STEVENSON *Afr. Harvest* 130 The tempting smell of the onions, and some *mosbolitjes* which Aunt Aletta had freshly baked. **1936** [see MOS *n.* sense 1 a]. **1945** N. DEVITT *People & Places* 15 Favourite old Cape Dutch confections were tameletjes .. and most bolletjes, the latter a sort of flavoured bun. The word 'most' means the juice of the grape in its first fermentation — bolletje is a bun. **1968** M. MULLER *Green Peaches Ripen* 21 All day long she rang the bell, demanding cookies, *watermelon konfyt, mosbolletjies*. **1976** *Sunday Times* 10 Oct. (Mag. Sect.) 4 We're in the co-op shop in Bredasdorp buying mosbolle and raisin bread. **1979** HEARD & FAULL *Our Best Trad. Recipes* 90 *The Mosbolletjie*, Introduced by the French refugees who came to settle in the Franschhoek district of the Cape in 1688. **1981** *Flying Springbok* Sept. 57 Another great traditional South African stand-by is the 'Mosbolletjie', or must-rusk. This semi-cake-semi-bun comes in two speeds .. the bun itself, soft and beguiling and very, very filling .. and the bun when it has been dried into a rusk. **1985** *Style* Feb. 103 Caught in the pale ark of colonialism and the covered coathanger, perhaps the WASP's only redemption against the vast hinterland of home fires and mosbolletjies and chicken soup, is the hope that, failing all else, their ancestors could at least be naughty. **1991** *Weekend Post* 10 Nov. 7 (*advt*) Bakery: Mosbolletjies 6's 99c.

mos comfeit, **- confyt**, **- konfijt** varr. MOSKONFYT.

Moselekatze, **Moselikatze** varr. MOSILIKATZE.

Mosgas var. MOSSGAS.

Moshootoo var. MOSOTHO.

Mosilikatze /ˌməzəliˈkɑːtzi/ *n. obsolescent.* Also **Moselekatze**, **Moselikatze**, **Mosilikatse**, **Mosilikatzi**, **Mozilikatze**. [Named for *Mzilikazi* (Englished form *Mosilikatze*), founder of the Ndebele people; see quot. 1913.] In the phrr. ***Mosilikatze's bird*** or ***Mosilikatze's roller***, the lilac-breasted roller *Coracias caudata* of the Coraciidae.

1864 T. BAINES *Explor. in S.-W. Afr.* 333 Henry Chapman shot a couple of blue rollers .. without the long feathers in the tail common to Moselekatze's bird, on the Zambesi. **1903** STARK & SCLATER *Birds of S. Afr.* III. 48 *Moselikatze's roller*, .. 'Moselikatze's Bird' of English. **1913** C. PETTMAN *Africanderisms* 326 *Moselekatze's bird, Coracias caudatus*. This bird .. is known by this name because Moselekatze (Umzilikazi, King of the Matabele, and father of Lobengula) claimed its feathers for his own exclusive use and ornament. **1940** A. ROBERTS *Birds of S. Afr.* 169 *Lilac-breasted roller or Mosilikatzi's bird*. **1975** *Dict. of Eng. Usage in Sn Afr.* 110 *Lilac-breasted roller*, .. alt: Mosilikatse's (Mosilikatze's) roller; colourful bird .. has a light mauve breast, blue wings and long, straight tail feathers ... Mosilikatse, King of the Matabele, claimed sole use of its plumage; hence the vernacular name. **1978** MCLACHLAN & LIVERSIDGE *Roberts Birds of S. Afr.* 296 It is often known as Mosilikatze's roller.

‖**moskonfyt** /ˈmɔskɔnˌfeɪt, ˈmɒskɒnˌfeɪt/ *n.* Also **mos comfeit**, **mos confyt**, **moskomfijt**, **mos(t) konfijt**. [Afk. (earlier S. Afr. Du. *mostkonfijt*) *mos* must, new wine + *konfyt* conserve.] A thick syrup prepared from grapes, used as a sweetener in cookery and in wine production, and as a spread. Also *attrib.* See also KONFYT.

1872 in A.M.L. Robinson *Sel. Articles from Cape Monthly Mag.* (1978) 282 We will undertake never to .. pull face at 'mos comfeit'. **1905** *Cape of G.H. Agric. Jrnl* 483 (Pettman), The first idea in planting vines is to provide *mos confyt*, a kind of grape sugar syrup, which is given as part of their rations to the coloured labourers. **1905** [see BOEREBESKUIT]. **1931** T.J. HAARHOFF *Virgil in Experience of S. Afr.* 3 '*Moskonfyt*' is used, as it was by the Romans, partly as a syrup and partly to break down the acidity of wines. *c*1936 *S. & E. Afr. Yr Bk & Guide* 306 Moskonfijt, or Grape Syrup. Several thousand tons of grapes are yearly made into syrup. **1950** H. GERBER *Cape Cookery* 36 Cream butter and sugar and add coffee essence, egg and moskonfyt. **1953** *Cape Times* 10 Mar. 2 A consignment of 600 110-gallon drums of *moskonfyt*, which will be processed into wine in Britain. **1967** W.A. DE KLERK *White Wines* 55 Whatever was in the glasses when we sat down, it was suitably coloured: a bright orange. It was also as sweet as liqueur, with the consistency of moskonfyt. **1968** D.J. OPPERMAN *Spirit of Vine* 221 (*caption*) Cape made most-konfyt bottle .. late nineteenth century. **1973** M.A. COOK *Cape Kitchen* 90 In the days when young and old alike in the countryside ate and enjoyed bread-and-fat (often with moskonfyt spread on it), the fat-pot was in daily use. **1981** *Oude Libertas* (Stellenbosch Farmers' Winery) Vol.9 No.4, 12 For ordinary late harvest wines, a sweetener like concentrated must (moskonfyt) is usually added. **1983** *S. Afr.*

Panorama Apr. 22 *Moskonfyt*, a golden syrup made from must or grape juice ... The juice must be skimmed as it boils rapidly, and must then be continuously ladled until it attains the consistency of honey. **1988** D. HUGHES et al. *Complete Bk of S. Afr. Wine* 277 Originally started in 1922 with the intention of concentrating on *moskonfyt* and processed fruits, the Villiersdorp Co-operative was expanded to include wine production in 1976. **1991** *Flying Springbok* May 71 At the Dagbreek Museum, you can buy the local speciality, moskonfyt (a grape syrup).

Mosotho /ˌmɔˈsuːtu, mə-/ *n.* Pl. usu. **Basotho**. Forms: α. *sing.* **Masutu, Moshootoo, Mosuthu, Mosuto, Msutu**; *sing.* and *pl.* **Basuto, Basutu**; *pl.* **Basatos, Bashootoo, Bashuta(s), Bassutos, Basuta(s), Basuto(o)s**; β. *sing.* **Mosotho, Mosothu, Musotho**; *pl.* **Basotho(s)**. [Sotho, perh. a hlonipha substitute for *motho* human being; or sing. n. prefix *mo-* (pl. *ba-*) + *sootho* brown one (see SOTHO). For notes on sing. and pl. forms, see MO- and BA-.

See note on pronunciation and forms at SOTHO.] A member of the South Sotho people, most of whom are resident in the Kingdom of Lesotho; *South(ern) Sotho*, see SOTHO sense 1 c. Also *attrib.*, passing into *adj.*

'Basotho' now usu. refers to the Sotho people of Lesotho (formerly Basutoland), and 'Sotho' to the Sotho-speaking people of South Africa (see SOTHO); in many 19th century texts 'Basuto' is used to refer to South Sothos living in South Africa.

Although α forms with *-sutu* are still used, esp. 'Basutu', the β forms 'Mosotho' and 'Basotho' are now the most widely accepted. See also combinations formed on the word 'Basotho'.

α. **1828** J. PHILIP *Researches* II. 82 This unfortunate man (the chief of the Bashootoo tribe . .) relates, that his town was unexpectedly attacked by a large party of men on horseback. **1835** A. SMITH *Diary* (1940) II. 278 The Matabeli apply the term Bashutu to all black nations not of their description. **1835** G. CHAMPION *Jrnl* (1968) 11 The station . . is among the Bassouto, the people whose chief took with him a thousand head of cattle in order to purchase a miss[ionar]y, as related by Dr. Philip. **1837** F. OWEN *Diary* (1926) 71 The Izinseezu or young soldiers who were sent out against the Busutoos returned yesterday, not having found their foe. *a*1838 A. SMITH *Jrnl* (1975) II. 55 On hearing of his success the half-starved Moshootoo was all anxiety for a feast, and nothing would satisfy him but a visit to the spot where the quagga lay dead in order to secure some of the meat. **1841** B. SHAW *Memorials* 257 Arrangements having been made with the chief of the *Bashutas*, for the cession of the territory selected, the people and missionaries, migrated with their flocks and possessions, to Thaba Unchu. **1855** J.W. COLENSO *Ten Weeks in Natal* p.xxv, A desperate battle took place in the year 1852 between the forces under Sir George Cathcart and the great Basuto chief, Moshesh, who has 60 000 people under his rule. **1871** J. MCKAY *Reminisc.* 256 The Basutos, numbering thousands, poured from kloofs and krantzes upon the scene, with apparent determination to defend their stock. **1895** J. WIDDICOMBE *In Lesuto* 27 A Mosuto and a Mochuana will understand one another without much difficulty, but a Mosuto and a Zulu find it very hard, in fact almost impossible, to converse together, so greatly have the two dialects diverged as time has gone on. **1897** [see SWAZI *n.* sense 1 a]. **1900** H.C. HILLEGAS *Oom Paul's People* 246 The Basutos, east of the Orange Free State, now the most powerful and the only undefeated nation in this country, would hardly allow a war to be fought unless they participated in it. **1905** W.H. TOOKE in Flint & Gilchrist *Science in S. Afr.* 92 The ba-Suto were originally ba-Kwena according to their chief Moshesh, who . . collected the waifs and strays of fugitive clans escaping from Tshaka, and by the force of his rare intellectual qualities welded them into a homogenous nation, formidable once to Boer and British, but now wealthy and prosperous. **1911** *Farmer's Weekly* 18 Oct. 193 No wonder a 'boy' who has worked in a town will not go onto a farm, yet the Mosuto for one would choose the farm every time if he were guaranteed half the wages and as good treatment. **1923** G.H. NICHOLLS *Bayete!* 96 The Kings of the Amandabele, the Basuta, the Amazulu, the Amaswazi, and all the others — are they mad? **1930** S.T. PLAATJE *Mhudi* (1975) 119 The Basutos inflicted upon the raiding Matabele such a severe punishment that they ran down the mountains . . and when after a very long run they halted for a rest, they were overtaken by a number of Basuto driving a herd of bullocks. **1938** [see FAH-FEE]. **1941** C.W. DE KIEWIET *Hist. of S. Afr.* p.vii, I have . . not hesitated to use a correct plural like Basuto side by side with an anglicized plural form like Zulus. **1949** C. BULLOCK *Rina* 37 My Basuto were very anxious to make a long stay at the big kraal on the slopes of the mountain. **1949** L. HUNTER *Afr. Dawn* 162 Here Mayeza (now to be known as Simon) found that one of his neighbours, also a new student, was a Msutu. **1949** A. PATON *Cry, Beloved Country* 28 She is a Msutu, but she speaks Zulu well. **1950** G. TYLDEN *Rise of Basuto* p.x, The language is Sesuto, belonging to the prefix-pronominal group of languages, the country being called Lesuto and the people Basuto, of which the singular is Mosuto. **1955** W. ILLSLEY *Wagon on Fire* 21 A Mosuto youth, swathed in a vivid red blanket, was barely thirty feet distant. **1957** A.A. MURRAY *Blanket* 18 'You are a heathen, Lepotane.' 'I am a Mosuto.' 'And I am a Christian.' 'I say that you too are a Mosuto.' ... 'It is not impossible to be both. Many of the Basuto follow the Christian faith.' **1960** J. COPE *Tame Ox* 98 She was black, or more nearly a dark, dull, earth colour, a Mosuto girl. *c*1976 H. FLATHER *Thaba Rau* 38 He had always found the Basutos pleasing to the eye, in their colourful blankets, with wavy patterns in blue, green, pink and purple. **1980** J. COCK *Maids & Madams* 205 Four passes were issued to women in their independent capacities: Zumba aged 30 and Hugiva aged 23 from Eno's tribe; Aliena aged 13 a 'Masutu' and Sibaku aged 20 a Bechuana.

β. **1953** LANHAM & MOPELI-PAULUS *Blanket Boy's Moon* 13 Monare the Mosotho walked along the street briskly, humming to himself a song of the Basotho people. *Ibid.* Glossary, *Basotho*, Basuto — plural of Mosotho; is used as Noun or Adjective . . ; members of the Basuto race. **1961** R.A. PAROZ *Sn Sotho-Eng. Dict.* p.ii, Mabille was in due time to become a great friend of the Basotho, a Mosotho at heart. *Ibid.* p.ix, [This book] is dedicated to the Basotho of the South, Moshoeshoe's Basotho, both within the borders of Basutoland itself and outside of them. **1964** A. PATON in C. Millar *16 Stories* 121 For one thing, Ha'penny was a Mosotho, and she was a coloured woman. **1972** *Evening Post* 20 Jan., Mr Pieterse's aged wife, Berlina, is registered as a Mosotho. **1973** *Drum* 22 May 31, I am a Mosotho girl aged 20 and would like to correspond with male or female penpals from 19 to 26 years. **1973** J. COWDEN *For Love* 32 Once, . . snow-bound at the top of Sani Pass, I spent ten days there, my only company a handful of Basotho and the giant predators of the sky. *Ibid.* 43 Home-made Basotho beer is strong and coarse and can be heard thumping its potency, day and night, as it brews in their huts. **1976** WEST & MORRIS *Abantu* 149 The South Sotho, commonly called the Basotho, are the southernmost group of the great Sotho family. They can be divided into two groups — those living in the Republic of South Africa and those that inhabit the Kingdom of Lesotho. **1980** M. LIPTON in *Optima* Vol.29 No.2, 165 These tensions were a factor in the conflicts in 1975 between Basothos and Xhosas on the Free States mines. **1982** L.N. MZAMANE in *Staffrider* Vol.5 No.2, 27 Oh you Mosotho girl, You black shadow by the riverside. **1986** P. MAYLAM *Hist. of Afr. People* 21 The Sotho can conveniently be subdivided into three main groups: firstly, the western Sotho, or Tswana; secondly, the northern Sotho, who comprise the Pedi and Lobedu; and thirdly, the southern Sotho, or Basotho, who occupy present-day Lesotho and adjacent areas. **1987** R. NTOULA in *City Press* 26 Apr. 7 Statistics today reveal that the average Mosotho's gross income has fallen by 10 percent since the kingdom's independence in 1966. **1987** *New Nation* 6 Aug. 9 In 1871, Britain gave the Cape power to rule Basotholand. Until 1880, the Basotho managed to maintain a degree of independence. **1990** G. SLOVO *Ties of Blood* 30 The baas will tell you that we are Swazi, baSotho, Zulus, Xhosas, Tswana . . but all I see are men: men who live under a common oppressor. **1990** M. MICHAELIDES in *Frontline* Sept. 11, I asked how the Basotho were buried, before whites arrived. They were wrapped in animal skins, he explained, and buried close to the house. **1990** M. MELAMU in *Lynx* 276 The inevitable stick which was a deadly weapon in the hands of a Mosotho.

moss var. MOS *n.*

mossbanker var. MAASBANKER.

mossbolletjie var. MOSBOLLETJIE.

Mossgas /ˈmɒsgæs/ *n.* Also **Mosgas**, and with small initial. [Blend of town and district name *Mossel Bay* + Eng. or Afk. *gas*.] Usu. in the phr. ***Mossgas project***. A project undertaken off the coast near Mossel Bay, Cape Province, for the recovery of undersea petroleum gas reserves; subsequently, the proprietory name of the company created to recover this gas. Also *attrib.*

1987 D.E.T. LE ROUX in *Hansard* 8 June 1154 In view of the mosgas project, time is of the essence. **1987** *E. Prov. Herald* 12 Dec. 1 Companies likely to be involved in construction work for the Mossgas project have been silenced by the authorities. **1991** *S. Afr. Panorama* May-June 11 The five-year Mossgas project was approved mainly for strategic reasons. **1993** A. GOLDSTUCK in *Rhodent* (Rhodes Univ.) 29 Designed to reduce South Africa's dependence on expensive foreign energy by making locally produced energy even more expensive and thus allowing the government to spend even more money on finding even more expensive alternatives, thus . . well then, *you* make sense of Mossgas. *a*1994 *Overview* (Mossgas Public Affairs Dept) 1 The Mossgas project for the production of synthetic fuels from offshore gas was launched in February 1987 by the South African Government as a strategic project to reduce South Africa's dependence on imported oil.

mossie /ˈmɒsi, ˈmɔsi/ *n.* [Afk., fr. Du. *mosje* dim. form of *mos* sparrow.]

1.a. The sparrow *Passer melanurus* of the Ploceidae; *Cape sparrow*, see CAPE sense 2 a. **b.** Any of several species of sparrow occurring in southern Africa. Also *attrib.*

1884 LAYARD & SHARPE *Birds of S. Afr.* 479 The 'Mossie,' like its cousin, the English bird, is essentially a 'cit.' **1908** HAAGNER & IVY *Sketches* 87 The Cape sparrow (*Passer melanurus*), or mossie as it is called by the Colonial (Dutch and English alike), is the South African equivalent of the English House Sparrow. **1936** E.L. GILL *First Guide to S. Afr. Birds* 21 The cock mossie, with his black head, white eye-stripe and cinnamon back, is a handsome and unmistakeable bird. **1959** *Cape Argus* 22 Aug. 5 The mossies in her neighbourhood never seem to stray more than a few blocks away. **1963** J. PACKER in C.M. Booysen *Tales of S. Afr.* 183 Mr. and Mrs. Mossie are a pair of Cape sparrows (*mossies* to you and me) and very different they are from their scruffy little London relatives. **1970** D.M. MCMASTER *Informant, Cathcart (E. Cape)* Who ever calls a sparrow anything but a mossie, or a Red-chested cuckoo anything but a Piet-myn-vrou? **1971** D.A.C. MACLENNAN Wake. 30 The Bible says, not even a little mossie can fall to the ground without our heavenly father knows it. **1972** *Star* 27 Oct. 1 A mossie nest on the pavement. **1983** K.B. NEWMAN *Newman's Birds* 444 Popular bird names in general use ... Mossie, A sparrow. **1989** T. BOTHA in *Style* June 112 Mossies kamikaze my windscreen. **1990** D. HOFMEYR *Red Kite in Pale Sky* 42 It was hard to imagine her as a bird. Certainly not a mossie. **1991** G. ZWIRN in *Settler* Vol.65 No.2, 11 *Mossie* or *Passer melanurus*, is SAE for your common-or-garden (mainly garden) sparrow.

2. *rare.* In the idiom (*as*) ***dead as a mossie*** [tr. Afk. *so dood soos 'n mossie*], 'stone dead'. Cf. MORSDOOD.

mossie(s) /ˈmɒzi(ːz), ˈmɒzi(ːz)/ n. slang. Also **mozzie(s)**. [Unkn.; perh. ad. MOZ.] In the adv. phr. *for mossie(s)*, for no special reason, for fun, 'just because'; *for moz*, see MOZ. Cf. SOMMER.

1973 *Informant, Grahamstown* Put it on a sale and see what it fetches — just for mossies! 1975 M. VAN BILJON in *Sunday Times* 2 Nov., It obviously was not a sommer-for-mossie job and one can only be grateful .. for their splendid contribution. 1987 *Jewish Language Review* No.7A 265 For mossie, (also *for mozzie, for moz,* and *sommer for mozzie*) South African slang 'for no special reason, just for kicks' (etymologized as being 'perhaps from Yiddish *mozel* "luck"' ..).

most var. MOS n.

mostbolletjie var. MOSBOLLETJIE.

most konfijt var. MOSKONFYT.

mosto var. MOS n.

Mosuthu, -suto varr. MOSOTHO.

Motchuana var. BECHUANA.

motekwane var. MATEKWANE.

Moth n. Also MOTH, M.O.T.H. [Acronym formed on *Memorable Order of Tin Hats*.]
a. An ex-servicemen's organization; often in *pl.*, with the same meaning. Also *attrib.* See also MOTHWA, OLD BILL, SHELLHOLE, WEE BILL.

The organization was founded in Durban in 1927 by Charles Evenden.

1929 [see DUG-OUT]. 1939 *Star* 5 Sept. 5 The Benoni branch of the Moths .. is holding its monthly meeting at 8 p.m. tomorrow. 1949 J.S. FRANKLIN *This Union* 101 The Moth organisation came into being only as recently as 1927. 1952 *Natal Mercury* 25 Nov. (Centenary Souvenir), In 1927 'The Natal Mercury' cartoonist, Evo, published probably one of the most significant cartoons on Remembrance ever drawn. From this cartoon he conceived the idea of the Memorable Order of Tin Hats ... Thus inspired, he wrote the rules of the M.O.T.H., leaving out all officialism. 1962, 1966 [see SHELLHOLE]. 1971 *Std Encycl. of Sn Afr.* III. 118 (caption) This cartoon led to the foundation of the M.O.T.H. ('Moths'). 1972 J.D. ROBINSON in *Ibid.* VII. 327 *Memorable Order of Tin Hats*, (M.O.T.H.) This Order was founded in Durban in May 1927 by Charles Alfred Evenden. *Ibid.* 328 (caption) M.O.T.H. insignia can be seen above the Gate. 1979 *E. Prov. Herald* 7 Dec. 3 Ex-servicemen's organizations such as the Moths. 1980 [see SHELLHOLE]. 1983 L. CAPSTICKDALE in *S. Afr. Panorama* Dec. 16 The story of the MOTH organisation .. is the story of one extraordinary man ... That man was Charles Evenden — MOTH 'O', or Evo, as he was affectionately known to all.
b. A member of this order.

1979 *Daily Dispatch* 15 Mar. 3 Moths elected Mr Mac-Ewan .. as the new Old Bill. *Ibid.* 11 June 1 A number of new Moths .. recently completed Border service and joined the order 1980 *Ibid.* 3 Dec. 2 The custom .. was started by the late Moth Ebbo Bastard in Kokstad in 1946. 1983 [see sense a]. 1983 *S. Afr. Panorama* Dec. 18 The famous British admiral, Evans of the *Broke* .. was himself a Moth. 1987 19 Moth Alf Gooden, national chairman of the Memorable Order of Tin Hats. 1989 *Grocott's Mail* 20 June 2 Moths have not forgotten their wartime leader and fellow Moth, Jan Christiaan Smuts. 1993 G. O'NEILL in *Ibid.* 22 July 4 These sombre thought were lightened by the knowledge that my brother M.O.T.H.S from the Makanaskop Shellhole would .. be holding a service, in lieu of the parade.

mother n. [tr. of the equivalent words in the Sintu (Bantu) languages, which are used in a wider sense than the Eng. *mother*; see MA- *pref.*¹, MAMA, MMA-, and MME.]
1. Among speakers of Sintu (Bantu) languages: any of the group of female clan members, including one's physical mother; a female contemporary of one's mother.

1966 P. BECKER in *Lantern* Sept. 3 In Bantu society, my father together with all his brothers would be my fathers, and my mother together with all her sisters, would be my mothers. 1978 A. ELLIOTT *Sons of Zulu* 167 All the boys and girls of contemporary age belonging to the same clan regard each other as brothers and sisters and all the joint *parents* are their parents. They are called 'father' and 'mother' as readily as those who bore them. 1983 N.S. NDEBELE *Fools* 66 That is where your grandmother and grandfather are. Your uncles. Your younger mothers. They are all there.

2. In the phr. *Mother of the Nation* (also with small initials), an honorific given to Nomzamo Winnie Mandela because of her leadership in the anti-apartheid struggle, her prominence in the African National Congress, and her marriage to Nelson Mandela, leader of the ANC, at the time this name was coined. Also *attrib.*

[1985 M.G. BUTHELEZI in N.W. Mandela *Part of my Soul* 19 Nomzamo Mandela is more than just another black person ... In a very deep sense she qualifies for the title of being 'The Mother of Black People'.] 1990 C. MUNNION in *London Evening Standard* (U.K.) 12 Feb. 7 Winnie Mandela is .. a personable and attractive woman. Had the timing been right, she could have laid claim to the title 'mother of the nation'. 1990 J. CARLIN in *Independent* (U.K.) 12 Feb. 8 Looking rather more wistfully than most on .. events would have been Eveline Mandela, Nelson Mandela's first wife ... No 'Mother of the Nation' status for her, no pomp, no bodyguards. 1993 *Daily News* 9 Dec. 4 The endearing name 'Mama Wetu' (Mother of the Nation) is rarely heard in reference to the controversial Winnie Mandela these days.

Mother City n. phr. Also with small initials. [Specific use of general Eng. *mother-city* metropolis, home town, here referring to Cape Town's status as the oldest city in S. Afr. and the first point of settlement by people from Europe.] *The Mother City*: Cape Town. Cf. *Tavern of the Seas* (see TAVERN sense 1).

[1908 *Westminster Gaz.* (U.K.) 4 Aug. 5 Capetown .. is in the truest sense .. the 'mother-city' from which the rest have sprung.] 1913 H. TUCKER *Our Beautiful Peninsula* 17 Those who believe that the Mother City has still its best days to come, are equally assured that .. fair women and brave men will never be lacking to grace and guard the Cape Town yet to be. 1936 E. ROSENTHAL *Old-Time Survivals* 23 The district of Malmesbury, near the Mother City, is to this day known as 'Zwartland' to crowds of South Africans. 1943 *Outspan* 9 July 11, I have watched the civic growth of our Mother city for over 40 years. 1955 A. DELIUS *Young Trav.* 74 (chapter heading) Cape Town, the 'Mother City'. 1973 *Drum* 8 Mar. 14 Unique to the Mother City the singing and dancing of her Brown children echoes through the main streets by day and re-echoes down her back-alleys by night. 1979 *Capetonian* July 20 It's up to everyone who prides himself on being a Capetonian .. to help in whatever way possible to put life back in that old girl, the Mother City. 1989 T. BOTHA in *Style* June 108 Driving between the mother city and the highveld is an emotional experience ... It's totally South African. 1992 *Living* Mar. 69 Table Mountain, Sentinel Rock of the mother city.

Mother-in-law n. colloq. In the phrr. *Mother-in-Law Exterminator, Mother-in-Law('s) Hell Fire, Mother-in-Law Masala* [see quot. 1992], the proprietary name for a particularly strong mix of curry-powder and other spices; applied loosely to any such mixture.

1988 *Fair Lady* 22 June (Suppl.) 13 Try the .. hottest curry powders this side of the Ganges: Mother in Law's Hell Fire and Heaven's Delight. 1990 J. EVANS in *Personality* 18 June 27 The Valies were sniffing Mother-in-Law Exterminator curry powder with a sort of desperate hope. 1992 R. MESTHRIE *Lexicon of S. Afr. Indian Eng.* 30 *Mother-in-Law masāla*, .. A particularly pungent *masāla* sold in Natal. Now rare. (A brand name, presumably created in jest, implying a sharp, bitter variety).

Mothwa /ˈmɒθwə/ [Formed on MOTH + initial letters of *Women's Auxiliary*.] (A member of) the Women's Auxiliary of the Moth ex-serviceman's organization, founded in 1935. Also *attrib.* See also *Lady Billie* (LADY sense 2), MOTH.

1971 *Rand Daily Mail* 16 Mar. 6,400 Moths, Mothwas and Moth children set out on a big march in an attempt to complete 20 km to raise funds for Moth charities. 1979 *E. Prov. Herald* 20 June 12 Sore feet were the main topic of conversation among Mothwa delegates.

motivate v. To request (something) and present a case in support of this request; to submit facts and arguments (in support of a proposal, request, application, or theoretical position).

Used very rarely in this sense in other varieties of English.

a. *trans.*

1975 *Dict. of Eng. Usage in Sn Afr.* 120 Civil servants are requested to *motivate* their demands for higher wages. 1991 D.G. GOUGH *Informant, Grahamstown*, I can see why you give that answer. As long as you can motivate that, I'm not saying the answer's wrong. 1990 [see LAW AGENT]. 1991 P. ROGERS on TV1, 7 Mar. (Agenda), You believe that dagga should be legalized. Can you motivate that? Can you justify that? 1992 *Argus* 19 May 5 Mr Van der Velde said that he would motivate funds to upgrade the food and meat stalls. 1994 *Bulletin No.3, Rhodes University Annual Wage Negotiations* 12 Aug., Staff requiring additional paid leave will .. be granted the opportunity of motivating their case to the Administrative Sub-Committee of Council.

b. *intrans.*

1991 P. BOTHA on TV1, 25 July (Agenda), The Minister of Finance can allocate funds to those Ministers who can come and motivate — who can come and make out a case. 1993 [see MOTIVATION]. 1994 W. HOLLEMAN *Informant, Grahamstown* We needed funds ... They said we should motivate this year.

Hence **motivated** ppl adj., supported by fact and argument.

1991 B.M.H. SMITH *Informant, Grahamstown* Fully motivated applications .. must reach this office by 8 May.

motivation n. [fr. prec.] Facts and arguments used to support a proposal or application; the proposal or application, including these facts and arguments.

1991 R. VAN DER MERWE *Senate document, Rhodes University* The following proposal and motivation is submitted for consideration. 1992 *Agenda, Board of Faculty of Arts, Rhodes Univ.* 10 Dec. 3 To consider a request from the Department of Drama to introduce two new honours papers in 1993: *Motivation is attached in Document A.* 1993 S. POPE on Radio South Africa 19 Feb. (Radio Today), Submit a motivation. You don't have to have a professional to motivate for you.

motjie var. MOOTJIE.

‖**motreën** /ˈmɔtrɪən/ n. [Afk., fr. Du. *motregen, mot* mist, fine dust + *regen* rain.] Very fine rain.

1969 M. BENSON *At Still Point* (1988) 119 Listen — 'motreën' — that soft soft rain. 1979 *S. Afr. Panorama* Aug. 16 The Cape winters with their .. black oaks drenched with 'motreën' (rain as fine as mist). 1988 A. DANGOR in *Staffrider* Vol.7 No.3, 86 At dusk the rain came; the type of '*mot-reën*' that lasted for days.

Motswana /mɒˈtswɑː(ː)na, mɒˈtswɑːnə/ n. Also **MoTswana**, and (formerly) **Motsoana**. Pl. **Batswana, baTswana**, and (formerly) **Motswanas**. [SeTswana *moTswana*, sing. n. prefix MO- + -*tswana* adj. stem (the fem. of *ntso* black), or v. stem (meaning 'be alike'); for an explanation of sing. and pl. forms, see MO- and BA-.] **a.** TSWANA sense 2 a. **b.** A citizen of Botswana. Also *attrib.*, passing into *adj.* See also BECHUANA sense 1.

1952 *Drum* Aug. 21 Matthews is a Motsoana and his constituency .. is chiefly Xhosa. **1953** A. SANDILANDS *Intro. to Tswana* p.xi, I .. express my gratitude .. to the multitude of Batswana men, women and children who have .. taught me what I know of their language. **1965** J.D. JONES in *Setswana Dict.* (1982) p.iii, A dictionary of this nature .. needs to be .. informed by a genuine understanding of the life and customs of the Batswana. **1975** W.F. LYE *Andrew Smith's Jrnl 1834–6* Index, *baTswana*, (rendered Bechuana, Bachuana, Bituana, Bishuana etc.) A major division of the Sotho peoples including most of the communities north of the Orange River and east of the Caledon. **1979** *Voice* 31 Jan. 3 A very thin Motswana woman speaking English with a squeaking Setswana accent. **1982** *Ibid.* 20 June 2 Mr Joseph Mazibuko said he had changed his surname so that he could be reclassified as a MoTswana. **1984** *Rand Daily Mail* 21 Feb. 9 The nearly 1,5-million Batswana who live permanently in South Africa should not be compelled to become Bophuthatswana citizens. **1985** *Drum* Aug. 4 It is not only Batswana who are living in fear of another commando raid by South Africa but several refugees are also .. apprehensive. They fear that another raid .. will force .. the Botswana government to move them out. **1987** *City Press* 25 Oct. 26 There are moves to sell Bophuthatswana overseas as a free country ... There is a belief that the Batswana are essentially a peace and freedom-loving people. There is Botswana, Africa's only democracy, .. a shining example of this. **1987** C. CLAYTON in *Staffrider* Vol.6 No.4, 14 Bessie Head was buried in Serowe, Botswana ... She was .. an 'exile' who rebuilt her personal identity amongst the multiracial benevolence and co-operative effort of Batswana society. **1990** *Afr. Wildlife* Vol.44 No.4, 191 Batswana are the people inhabiting Botswana. **1990** *City Press* 25 Feb. 8 Any Motswana who wished to return to South Africa is free to do so. **1990** *Sunday Times* 1 July 3 Lady Ruth had already warned her son and Margaret about the trouble their marriage may cause among the tribal Batswana people. **1990** *Weekly Mail* 14 Sept. (Weekend) 7 How could they believe that the jigsaw pieces of land allocated to the baTswana were enough to be a homeland for all of them when they obviously couldn't cope even for a weekend with a gathering of a fraction of all the baTswana. **1991** *Weekend Argus* 26 Jan. 8 The aim of virtually every Motswana is to own cattle ... A number of Batswana are becoming increasingly concerned over the depredations of the cattle industry on the environment and on Botswana's unique heritage of wildlife. **1992** P. CULLINAN *Robert Jacob Gordon* 114 *(caption)* An artist's impression of a Batswana kraal, taken from Gordon's 'great map'.

moucha var. MUTSHA.

mouche, mouchi varr. MOOCHI.

mountain *n.* [tr. Afk. *berg.*] Used *attrib.* in the names of fauna and flora, in Special Comb. **mountain cypress**, the shrub or small tree *Widdringtonia nodiflora* of the Cupressaceae; *berg cypress*, see BERG sense 1 b ii; **mountain goose** [tr. Afk. *berggans*], the *berggans* (see BERG sense 1 b ii), *Alopochen aegyptiacus*; **mountain zebra** [influenced by Afk. *bergquagga*, see QUAGGA], any of several zebras of the Equidae (although in earlier times the distinctions between the different zebras was not always noted, the name 'mountain zebra' is now used exclusively for *Equus zebra zebra*): *(a) Equus zebra zebra*, now often with defining word as **Cape mountain zebra**; *bergquagga*, see QUAGGA sense 1 b; DAUW; QUAGGA sense 1 a iii; *wild horse*, see WILD sense b; also *attrib.*; also called *wildepaard* (sense *(a)*, see WILDE sense b); *(b)* The QUAGGA (sense 1 a ii), *E. burchelli*. *(c)* The QUAGGA (sense 1 a i), *E. quagga*.

1966 C.A. SMITH *Common Names* 343 **Mountain cypress**, *Widdringtonia cupressoides*. **1971** J.A. MARSH in *Std Encycl. of Sn Afr.* III. 538 The mountain cypress differs from both the Clanwilliam and the Willowmore cedar in the shape of the adult leaf and the scales of the female cones. **1972** PALMER & PITMAN *Trees of Sn Afr.* I. 334 The mountain cypress is usually a shrubby tree, seldom — in South Africa — more than 30 feet (9m) high, and widespread in the mountains of the south, south east, and north. In tropical Africa this is a large tree up to 140 feet (43m) high. **1987** T.F.J. VAN RENSBURG *Intro. to Fynbos* 16 Mountain cypresses (*Widdringtonia nodiflora*) often reach tree size when they are protected against fire for long enough or when they grow in sheltered spots. **1990** M. OETTLE in *Weekend Post* 29 Dec. (Leisure) 7 *Widdringtonia nodiflora*, the mountain cypress. **1731** G. MEDLEY tr. *P. Kolb's Present State of Cape of G.H.* II. 138 There are Three Sorts of Wild Geese in the *Cape*-Countries ... The *Hill* or **Mountain-Goose** is larger than an *European* Tame Goose. **1889** [see *berggans* (BERG sense 1 b ii)]. **1937** H. SAUER *Ex Afr.* 183 River duck, solan goose, and the berg or mountain goose. **1994** M. ROBERTS tr. *J.A. Wahlberg's Trav. Jrnls 1838–56* 11 At Sand Valley hunted herons and mountain geese but in vain. **1844** J. BACKHOUSE *Narr. of Visit* 572 The **Mountain Zebra**, Equus Zebra, called Wilde Ezel or Wild Ass, is abundant here. **1878** T.J. LUCAS *Camp Life & Sport* 218 Burchell's zebra .. differs also from the mountain or true zebra, in the marking of the stripes, which is not continued down the legs as in the zebra proper. **1897** H.A. BRYDEN *Nature & Sport* 96 Here, upon inaccessible cliffs, and rugged hills, still finds shelter that rare beast, the true or mountain zebra, an animal now becoming very scarce. This quadruped (Equus zebra) gallops the mountains, and climbs from steep to steep. **1957** L.G. GREEN *Beyond City Lights* 32 In the Van Riebeeck diary you will see that the men found the tracks and droppings of an animal they had heard about, but never seen. It was the mountain zebra. **1971** *Argus* 10 May 4 One of the most rare species of mammal in the world — the mountain zebra. *c*1978 *Report No.34* (Dept of Nature & Environ. Conservation) 37 One Cape mountain zebra foal died. **1988** K. SUTTON in *Motorist* May 23 Mountain zebra need to migrate to better grazing to survive. **1990** SKINNER & SMITHERS *Mammals of Sn Afr. Subregion* 576 Only two subspecies have been described, the Cape mountain zebra *E. z. zebra*, from the Cape Province, and Hartman's mountain zebra, *E. z. hartmannae*, of Namibia and Angola.

mouse-and var. MOUSE-HUNT.

mousebird *n.* [tr. S. Afr. Du. *muisvoël*, see MUISVOËL.] A long-tailed fruit-eating bird of the Coliidae, predominantly dull brown or grey in colour, of the species *Colius colius, C. striatus*, or *Urocolius indicus*; COLY; MUISVOËL. Occas. also with defining words, see quot. 1984.

*c*1808 C. VON LINNÉ *System of Natural Hist.* VIII. 383 The colies live upon fruits only ... At the Cape they are called *muys-voogel*, mouse-bird, their plumage being soft and silky. These birds are extremely injurious to the gardens. **1822** J. LATHAM *Gen. Hist. of Birds* V. 196 These birds [*sc.* colies] are called at the Cape Mouse Birds. **1827** T. PHILIPPS *Scenes & Occurrences* 70 Two very singular birds, the Caffer finch and mouse-bird (the latter so called from being the colour of a mouse) ... At the commencement of spring their tails begin to grow, and get to such a length as to appear to be an absolute incumbrance. **1856** R.E.E. WILMOT *Diary* (1984) 131 Also may be noticed .. the sombre crests and long tails of the small mousebirds which throng the protea and mimosa bushes. **1867** [see MUISVOËL]. **1896** E. CLAIRMONTE *Africander* 2 A flock of long-tailed mousebirds, called *finks*. **1905** W.L. SCLATER in Flint & Gilchrist *Science in S. Afr.* 140 A small though interesting family is the *Coliidae* or Mousebirds, .. remarkable for their pamprodactylous toes — that is, all four toes are normally turned forwards, although both hallux and fourth toe can be turned backwards at will. All three species of Mouse-bird (*Colius striatus, C. capensis* and *C. erythromelon*) are found about Cape Town. **1936** E.L. GILL *First Guide to S. Afr. Birds* 95 The Colies or Mousebirds are smallish and very curious birds found only in Africa. The name Mousebird refers to their soft, rather hairy plumage .. as well as to the way in which they creep about among twigs. **1963** M. KAVANAGH *We Merry Peasants* 135 Mouse birds are finishing off the last of the berries on the syringa tree branches. **1979** M. PARKES *Wheatlands* 39 The unwelcome mouse birds, who do real damage to the fruit and vegetables, are the only birds which may be shot around the house. **1980** J.O. OLIVER *Beginner's Guide to our Birds* 81 Speckled mousebird ... Very common where there are fruit trees. **1984** G.L. MACLEAN *Roberts' Birds of Sn Afr.* 369 *Speckled Mousebird, .. Colius striatus* ... Bill dark above, pale below (all dark in Redfaced Mousebird, pale with black tip in Whitebacked Mousebird). *Ibid.* 370 *Whitebacked Mousebird, .. Colius colius* ... Lower back white, bordered black (diagnostic in flight). *Ibid.* 371 *Redfaced Mousebird, .. Colius indicus* ... Bare face red (other mousebirds have dark feathered faces) ... More wary than other mousebirds. **1990** *Weekend Post* 21 July (Leisure) 3 Several spectacled [*sic*] mousebirds .. and a dusky flycatcher.

mouse-hunt *n. obs.* Also **mouse-and.** [Calqued on S. Afr. Du. *muishond*, see MUISHOND. Cf. dial. Eng. *mousehunt* (ad. Middle Du. *muushont*) weasel.] MUISHOND sense 1. Also *attrib.*

1850 R.G.G. CUMMING *Hunter's Life* (ed.2) I. 103 The whole ground was undermined with the holes of colonies of meercat or mouse-hunts. **1853** F.P. FLEMING *Kaffraria* 67 The *Mustela-Furo*, or Wild Ferret, more commonly called the Mouse-hunt, or Merecat, is also very plentiful. **1856** R.E.E. WILMOT *Diary* (1984) We rode away again reaching Sundays River with no greater incident than stopping for the purpose of .. a hunt after a large red pole-cat, known here by the name of 'mousehunt'. **1862** A.W. DRAYSON *Tales at Outspan* 347 'Piet,' an old Hottentot of my uncle's, .. had as many dodges for defeating the Kaffirs, stalking an ostrich, or trapping a mouse-hunt, as any jackal has for stealing chickens. **1871** J. MCKAY *Reminisc.* 16 Having found a large mouse-and hole, they threw him in head foremost, and there let him lie, with his posterior sticking up.

mouti(e) var. MUTI.

Movenda var. VENDA.

mow-wah var. MAWO.

moy var. MOOI.

moz /mɔz, mɒz/ *n.* Also **mors.** [Unkn.; perh. fr. Yiddish *mazel* /ˈmɒzəl, mazəl/ luck.] In the adv. phr. *for moz*: *for mossie(s)*, see MOSSIE(S).

1976 'BLOSSOM' in *Darling* 4 Aug. 123 This hang-gliding ... You wouldn't catch me jumping off a hill jis for moz like that. **1984** *Frontline* Feb. 26 Anyhow, Koos, sommer for mors I went looking for what's left of Hanover Street.

Mozambique *n. obs.* Also **Mosambique.** [See next.] MOZAMBIQUER.

1819 G.M. KEITH *Voy.* 37 There are not such thick lips among the hottentots as among their neighbours the negroes the caffres and the Mozambiques. **1835** J.W.D. MOODIE *Ten Yrs* I. 201 The slaves from the coast of Mozambique .. are so proverbial for their extreme stupidity that the greatest affront a Dutch colonist can cast on another's understanding is to observe that he is .. as stupid as a Mozambique. **1835** G. CHAMPION *Jrnl* (1968) 8 When we were far out in the flats, .. one of the company happened to observe a black, a Mosambique apparently lying among the bushes. **1905** W.H. TOOKE in Flint & Gilchrist *Science in S. Afr.* 88 Many individuals of this group are favourably known as labourers in the Cape Colony, where they are included in the general term 'Mozambiques, ' applied to all natives of Portuguese East Africa.

Mozambiquer *n. obs.* Also **Mosambiquer.** [Pg. *Mozambique* name of a country + Eng. suffix *-er*, expressing the sense 'a native of', 'a resident in'.] A person born in or inhabiting Mozambique; MASBIEKER; MOZAMBIQUE.

1805 R. SEMPLE *Walks & Sketches* 40 Without the inactivity or dulness of the Mozambiquer or the penetrative genius of the Malay, he [*sc.* the Malabar slave] forms an excellent medium between the two.

1876 F. BOYLE *Savage Life* 271 Besides this, we had two .. cooks, a Malay and a Mozambiquer. 1883 O.E.A. SCHREINER *Story of Afr. Farm* 260 A door in the corner opened and a woman came out — a Mosambiquer, with a red handkerchief twisted round her head.

Mozilikatze var. MOSILIKATZE.

mozzie var. MOSSIE(S).

mpala var. IMPALA.

m'pani var. MOPANI.

mpantsula pl. form of PANTSULA.

MPC *n. hist.* Abbrev. of *Member of the Provincial Council.* See also MEC.

1914 *Rand Daily Mail* 21 Dec., Conroy (a Free State M.P.C.) has been searched for eagerly during the last few weeks. 1970 *News/Check* 29 May 4 An unofficial group of Natal MPCs — all verligtes — went to see Vorster. 1977 *E. Prov. Herald* 15 July 2 The Mayor of Port Elizabeth, Mr Dan Rossouw, MPC. 1982 *Cape Times* 24 Dec. 1 Mrs Molly Blackburn, MPC for Walmer.

mpimpi var. IMPIMPI.

M Plan *n. phr. Hist.* [The initial letter of *Mandela* (Nelson Mandela having played an important role in the plan's formulation) + Eng. *plan.*] The name given to the African National Congress strategy of organizing its membership into cells; *Mandela Plan,* see MANDELA.

The M Plan was adopted in the late 1950s as a means of ensuring the continued existence of the organization, should it be banned.

1963 M. BENSON *Afr. Patriots* 196 In Port Elizabeth .. the M Plan which Mandela had conceived, which meant street to street and house to house canvassing and organizing, was being carefully implemented. 1990 *City Press* 11 Feb. 6 Although Mandela .. was banned from gatherings, he continued to work with small .. congress meetings. He was instrumental in the formulation of the 'M' Plan, named after him. ANC branches were to be broken down into cells to cope with the possibility that it would have to work underground. 1990 *E. Prov. Herald* 12 Feb. 8 When the ANC was banned in 1960, the M-Plan was adapted to form the organisational base of *Umkhonto we Sizwe,* the organisation's military wing.

mpofu var. IMPOFU.

Mpondo var. PONDO.

Mpondomise /(m̩)ˌpɔndɔˈmiːse, ˌpɔndəʊˈmiːsi/ *pl. n.* Also **Amampondumisi, Amapondomisi, (M)pondomisi, Pondomise(s).** [Xhosa, origin unkn.] (The) members of a southern Nguni people of the Transkei region of the Eastern Cape, originally part of the PONDO people. Also *attrib.*

As is the case with many names of peoples and groups in *S. Afr. Eng.,* this word has been found only in plural uses; however, it may be that it has also been used in unrecorded singular forms.

1866 W.C. HOLDEN *Past & Future* 143 The Amampondumisi .. dispute the right of priority with the Abatembu affirming that they were in the country when the Tembus and the Xosas passed along above them. 1875 'P.' in A.M.L. Robinson *Sel. Articles from Cape Monthly Mag.* (1978) 193 The country we were in belonged to the 'Amapondomisi', at one time a powerful off-shoot of the 'Pondos'; but now it is divided and broken up by party strifes. 1880 [see TAMBOOKIE *n.* sense 1 a]. 1901 *Natives of S. Afr.* (S. Afr. Native Races Committee) 3 Of the remaining tribes, the Pondomises are chiefly to be found in the divisions of Qumbu, Tsolo, Engcobo, and Umtata. 1913 W.C. SCULLY *Further Reminisc.* 288 In Pondomisi history the chief most honoured is 'Ngwanya, who flourished some hundred and fifty years ago. 1927 *Workers' Herald* 6 Apr. 1 From information to hand, it appears that the Pondomise tribe are very sore about having no Paramount Chief of their own. 1949 M. WILSON in A.M. Duggan-Cronin *Bantu Tribes* III. ii. 13 Traditionally the Mpondo and Mpondomise were cattle people, setting great store by their herds, and milk was a most important article of diet. 1981 [see quot. at *southern Nguni* (NGUNI *n.* sense 1 b)]. 1986 P. MAYLAM *Hist. of Afr. People* 21 The Nguni can be divided into a northern group — basically the Zulu and the Swazi — and a southern group, including the Xhosa, the Thembu, the Mfengu, the Mpondo and the Mpondomise. 1991 J. COULTER in *Weekend Post* 4 May (Leisure) 3 As recently as 1886, remnants of a San family were discovered in Transkei ... They had been in the care of Mpondomise chiefs for a long time and were considered the official rainmakers of the western Mpondomise.

mpundulu var. IMPUNDULU.

mqhashiyo var. MGQASHIYO.

mqombot(h)i var. UMQOMBOTHI.

Mrs Ples /ˌmɪsəz ˈplɛs/ *n.* [Eng. *Mrs* + abbrev. of generic name *Plesianthropus.*] A nickname given to the skull of an Australopithecine man-ape of the lower Pleistocene period, found in 1947 at Sterkfontein in the former Transvaal (now in the province called Gauteng). See also AUSTRALOPITHECUS.

1959 J.D. CLARK *Prehist. of S. Afr.* 62 The skull was that of a female and had come to be affectionately known as 'Mrs Ples' ... Broom said, 'I have seen many interesting sights in my life, but this was the most thrilling.' 1970 R.A. DART in *Std Encycl. of Sn Afr.* II. 536 At the entrance to the Sterkfontein caves stands a bust of Broom with a replica of the so-called 'Mrs Ples', the 'missing link' which was found by Broom. 1984 *S. Afr. Panorama* Aug. 35 Sterkfontein, where the first adult ape-man (*Plesianthropus transvaalensis*) known as 'Mrs Ples' was found. Mrs Ples is considered to belong to the same species as the material from Taung, *Australopithecus africanus.* 1989 *Reader's Digest Illust. Hist.* 16 He found the almost perfectly preserved cranium of a female specimen, nicknamed 'Mrs Ples, ' that had lived some 2,5-million years ago. Later, Mrs Ples and others of her genus were to be reclassified as *Australopithicus africanus.*

msangu var. INSANGU.

mshana var. MTSHANA.

mshoza /m̩ˈʃɔ(ː)za, əmˈʃəʊzə/ *n. slang.* Also with initial capital. Pl. **-s, bo-.** [Isicamtho, ultimate origin unkn.; perh. fr. Eng. *shows* (see quot. 1982) with the connotation of 'well-dressed', 'showy', 'good-looking'.] In township parlance: a woman or girl of the 'pantsula' social group (see PANTSULA sense 1 a); also occas. used predicatively as an *adj.* Also *attrib.*

[1982 D. BIKITSHA in *Rand Daily Mail* 14 Oct. (Eve) 5 A woman [in a South African township of the 1940s and 1950s] went by such titles: moll, cherrie .. , shows, .. and others.] 1984 M. MTHETHWA in *Frontline* July 29 Pantsulas and Mshozas take great pride in their expensive clothes. Lizard-skin shoes and purses, cashmere pullovers and cardigans, leather coats, jackets and berets are top with them. 1986 *Drum* Aug. 70 Bomshoza are the first to show up at parties where they are not invited. 1986 H. PRENDINI in *Style* Nov. 191 The pantsula's female counterpart is the mshoza ... A certain style of pleated skirt .. is such typical mshoza gear that Arthur Mzozoyana breaks into a huge laugh as he describes it: '... It's just so mshoza!'

msimbithi var. UMZIMBEET.

msobo(sobo) var. UMSOBOSOBO.

Msutu var. MOSOTHO.

m'tagat, mtagati *n.* , **mtakati** *n.*, **mtakiti** varr. TAGATI *n.*

mtagati *adj.*, **mtakati** *adj.* varr. TAGATI *adj.*

mthakathi pl. form of TAGATI *n.*

‖**mtombo** /m̩ˈtɔ(ː)mbɔ/ *n.* Also **imit(h)ombo, mthombo.** [Xhosa and Zulu *imithombo,* malted grain.]

1.a. Sprouted sorghum millet used for brewing beer; see also SORGHUM sense 1. **b.** TSHWALA sense a. In both senses also called MOMELA.

1907 W.C. SCULLY *By Veldt & Kopje* 69 They had to appear at the 'Great Place' .. each bringing a contribution of 'imitombo,' or millet ... It is from this, after it has been boiled and fermented, that the liquor known as 'Kaffir beer' is made. 1951 *Drum* Nov. 10 My friend and I were drinking pineapple brew in Alexandra. It is made with mtombo, pineapple, sugar, oats, carbide and so on. 1978 A. ELLIOTT *Sons of Zulu* 129 This dry sprouted corn is called *imithombo.* It is now ground into powdered malt in a concave milling stone. 1980 E. JOUBERT *Poppie Nongena* 262 However much she strained so the mtombo boiled up and she couldn't keep ahead, straining the beer. 1985 W.O. KA MTETWA in *Staffrider* Vol.6 No.2, 45 Libazisa, a mthombo brewed beer.

2. *comb.* **mtombo-mmela** /m̩ˈtɔmbɔ m̩ˈme(ː)la/ [S. Sotho *mmela* malted grain; cf. MOMELA], the bilingual Nguni-Sotho name given to a commercially-produced beer.

1971 *Drum* Jan. 25 (advt) Now you can legally brew .. Mtombo-Mmela Home Brew. Stronger, smoother, richer. Guaranteed pure and healthy ... King Korn mtombo-mmela the strongest home brew. 1971 *Post* 14 Mar. 12 (advt) Famous people drink King Korn mtombo-mmela. Follow the leaders and entertain *your* friends too in the comfort and safety of your home. 1981 *Pace* Sept. 174 The hypothetical TV2 programme, shows .. SA's first black jet flyer in a commercial advertising 'mthombo mmela' or 'A1 mageu'.

‖**mtshana** /m̩ˈtʃaːna/ *n.* Also **mchana, mshana.** [Xhosa *mtshana* vocative of *umtshana* or Zulu *mshana* vocative of *umshana* a sister's or daughter's child; a nephew or a niece.] Among (urban) Xhosa- or Zulu-speakers: an informal term of address to a friend or relative.

1982 *Pace* Sept., Awu Mtshana! The latest yak-yak blah blah from the tiny state of Transkei leaves us cold. 1983 *Ibid.* Oct. 70 Heyi Mchana, they say in boxing on these shores you have to be white to matter. 1983 N.S. NDEBELE *Fools* 66 This whole land, mshana, I have seen it all. 1985 *Learn & Teach* No.5, 57 (cartoon) Let's get rid of these bottles, mshana! 1985 *Pace* Sept. 4 Mtshana, people like to talk off beat.

mtwana var. UMTWANA.

mucha var. MUTSHA.

much better *adv. phr. Colloq.* As an intensifier: 'really well', 'enthusiastically', 'energetically', etc.

1975 'Blossom' in *Darling* 29 Jan. 103, I had a ball that night — go-going on the table for this ring of chuckling ole dads in paper hats, most of them poegaai, all of them egging me on much better. 1985 P. SLABOLEPSZY *Sat. Night at Palace* 40, I was gripping this chick ... Her folks were out and we were fraying much better.

muchi var. MOOCHI.

muchocho, muchucho varr. MOHOHU.

mud *n. obs.* Also **mudd.** Pl. **-s, muddes, mudden.** [Du., fr. Fr. *muid* see MUID.] MUID.

1795 C.R. HOPSON tr. *C.P. Thunberg's Trav.* I. 232 A freight contains ten *muddes,* or about 20 bushels. 1795 in G.M. Theal *Rec. of Cape Col.* (1897) I. 172 He is not allowed to sell his Wheat to any but the Company and Burgher Commissioners for 25 Rix Dollars the 10 Mud or Sacks. 1798 S.H. WILCOCKE tr. *J.S. Stavorinus's Voy. to E. Indies 1768–71* I. 567 A mud of wheat amounted to about four gilders; the common wines were sold, from two to three and a half stivers per bottle. [Note] A mud is equal to about three bushels. 1800 *Cape Town Gaz.* 16 Aug. 1 On this Estate are 60 acres of Land, sowed with 50 muds of Corn, 13 muds of Barley and 7 muds of Oats. **1819** G. BARKER Journal. 18 Sept., Finished sowing 2 mudden of wheat. **1832** J. COLLETT *Diary* II. 16 To 1 Mudd Oats, 2 pair hinges, 1 Mudd meal. **1863** W.C. BALDWIN *Afr. Hunting* 30 Bought a mud of mealies for the horse. **1899** *Natal Agric. Jrnl* 31 Mar. 3 'Mud' (muid in South African Dutch) is a very elastic measurement of quantity, and is gradually being superseded by weight measurement.

mue(a)d var. MUID.

muggie /ˈməxi/ *n.* Also **miggie**. [Afk.] A midge or gnat. Also *fig.*

[**1964** J. MEINTJES *Manor House* 129 The boy never had a real home of his own, and he never let you forget it. Everybody called him Muggie (a *muggie* is a mite).] **1970** C. TUCKETT *Informant, Bloemfontein* In the evenings around the street lamps one finds many muggies flying about. **1984** *Fair Lady* 30 May 176 What about the ubiquitous *muggies* which settle in clouds on every glass of wine drunk on every stoep in the Boland? **1986** L.B. HALL in *Style* July 97 They sit sipping their tea, enchanted by the ducks on the pond. And because it is getting hot, the *miggies* start to bite so they bring out their bottles of eau-de-cologne. **1988** A. LENNOX-SHORT *Informant, Cape Town* The one muggie in your rich *wyn* is the cover of DSAE. **1991** I. & F. DE MOOR *Informants, Grahamstown* Muggies — small flies or midges — the term refers to flies belonging to both the Chironomidae and Simuliidae families. **1991** [see Hurt quot. at GOEF *n.*]. **1995** *Advertising pamphlet, Heritage Collection* Simply switch on the tube light, which sends currents through the wires over it — miggies, mosquitoes, gnats and other flying insects are attracted to its bright blue glow where they're electrocuted.

mugu var. MOEGOE.

muid /mjuːd, mœid/ *n. hist.* Also **mue(a)d**. Pl. **-s**, or **muiden**. [S. Afr. Du., fr. Fr. *muid* (fr. L. *modius* a peck) a dry and liquid measure.] A measurement of capacity equal to about three bushels, used at the Cape esp. during the 18th and 19th centuries, usu. for grain; MUD. Also *attrib.* Cf. SCHEPEL.

1795 T.H. CRAIG in G.M. Theal *Rec. of Cape Col.* (1897) I. 271 Corn, of which the quantity in store belonging to the Company is immense, no less than 36,166 muids which I am informed is equal to near two years consumption. **1806** J. BARROW *Trav.* II. 48 The following is an abstract of the Opgaaff for the Cape district in the year 1797 ... Stock and produce ... Muids of wheat sown in 1796, 3464 heaped. **1816** G. BARKER Journal. 8 July, Today my corn was all put into the ground, (2 muiden). **1823** W.W. BIRD *State of Cape of G.H.* 104 The price of wheat in those days may be calculated at from 40 to 50 rix-dollars per load of ten muids, weighing 1800lbs. Dutch. **1833** *Graham's Town Jrnl* 17 Jan. 1 A good Garden and Arable land, from which 13 muids of good Wheat has been cleared this season. **1841** B. SHAW *Memorials* 146 The Namacquas of Lily Fountain had sown latterly about one hundred muids, or twenty thousand pounds of wheat annually. **1859** *Cape Town Weekly Mag.* 11 Feb. 39 Verily, Burghersdorp is an expensive place to live in ... We shall just quote the present prices of articles of consumption:— .. meal, fifty shillings the muid! with every prospect of an increase in price. **1871** J. MCKAY *Reminisc.* 299 A muid of wheat, which at its place of production or nearest market, is sold at from seven to ten shillings, will cost about twenty shillings before the Bay merchant receives it. **1915** J.K. O'CONNOR *Afrikander Rebellion* 99 There are too many poor whites in the country at present, and the problem .. is of greater importance than the production of three muids of mealies where only one muid is now obtained. **1937** *Handbk for Farmers* (Dept of Agric. & Forestry) 754 Muid sacks are commonly used in this country for harvesting [cotton]. **1941** C.W. DE KIEWIET *Hist. of S. Afr.* 26 After just one hundred years of existence all the Cape managed to export was 75,000 muids (A muid equals three bushels) of wheat per year. **1949** M.W. SPILHAUS in A.C. Partridge *Lives, Lett. & Diaries* (1971) 11 The word *muid* (no longer a legal quantity) was a Dutch measure of capacity derived, through French, from Latin *modius*, 'a peck'. In the Cape, the measure was slightly less than three English bushels, or six pecks .. ; its use was confined to the measurement of grain or fruit. *c*1963 B.C. TAIT *Durban Story* 59 In the absence of laundry baskets, a muid sack stuffed full of clothes was considered an average week's wash. **1987** G. VINEY *Col. Houses* 62 The *werf* boasted a barn containing one hundred and seventy *muids* of wheat.

muishond /ˈmeɪs(h)ɔnt, ˈmœis(h)ɔnt/ *n.* Also **mace ont, mais-hand, mais-hond, muis-hunt, muyshond.** [S. Afr. Du., transf. use of Du. *muishond* weasel.]

1. Any of several small mammals, esp. any of various species of mongoose. **a.** (Mustelidae family) **i.** The striped polecat, *Ictonyx striatus*; MEERKAT sense 3; STINK-CAT. **ii.** The African weasel, *Poecilogale albinucha*; occas. also with distinguishing epithet, **stink muishond**. **b.** Any of several species of mongoose of the Viverridae; cf. MEERKAT sense 1 b; occas. also with distinguishing epithet, **snake muishond**. In these senses also called MOUSE-HUNT. Also *attrib.*, and *fig.*

1796 tr. *F. Le Vaillant's Trav.* I. 236 Different species of these small quadrupeds .. which at the Cape are known under the general name of *muyshond*. *Ibid.* III. 278 My Hottentots of the colony all recognized it as a muyshond (mouse-dog), a general name among the inhabitants of the Cape for all the little carnivorous quadrupeds. **1827** T. PHILIPPS *Scenes & Occurrences* 16 Our first victim was a muis-hond, a destructive little animal of the weasel species and very numerous. **1835** A. STEEDMAN *Wanderings* II. 97 It is a lively little creature, extremely active and graceful in its movements, and is called by the Colonists the Rooie Muis-hunt. [**1844** J. BACKHOUSE *Narr. of Visit* 311 In the course of our journey, we saw .. a species of Polecat, *Mustella Zorilla*? the Dutch name of the last is Muishond, which signifies Mouse-dog.] **1859** 'B.' in *Cape Monthly Mag.* V. May 296 During lambing time, the enclosure is drawn regularly every second or third morning by a pack of foxhounds under efficient discipline, and thus the jackals, wild cats, ratel, muishond, etc. etc., are kept down. **1880** F.G. BROWNING *Fighting & Farming* 37, I rushed up, and saw the dog had hold of a *stink-mais-hand*, and had already, to all appearances, killed it. **1881** *Meteor* 12 Aug. 1 He ran .. into the veldt to take part in despatching an aromatic little animal known as a '*mace ont*', which his dogs had captured. **1905** W.L. SCLATER in Flint & Gilchrist *Science in S. Afr.* 127 The last of the families of terrestrial Carnivora, the *Mustelidae*, contains five South African species, .. two Otters .. ; the Ratel ... The Striped Muishond (*Zorilla striata*), with its handsome livery of black and white and its skunk-like and fetid odour emitted from the anal glands, and finally the curious little Striped Weasel .. make up the tale of this family. **1912** F.W. FITZSIMONS *Snakes of S. Afr.* 30 Within two yards of us, was a striped Muishond, with his paws firmly planted on an adult Black-necked cobra (*Naia nigricollis*). The Muishond stood facing us menacingly, daring us to approach. **1918** S.H. SKAIFE *Animal Life* 265 The *muishond* is easily tamed, but seemingly it would make an undesirable pet because it might at any time produce its overpowering odour if it should be disturbed or irritated. A smaller, but very similar species of *muishond* is found in Natal. These are the true *muishonds*, and must not be confused with the little grey mungoose. **1919** F.W. FITZSIMONS *Natural Hist. of S. Afr.* II. 178 (Swart), If a nestful of young Springhares is found in the burrow, the Snake Muishond kills them all, although it may only be able to eat one or two. **1931** V. SAMPSON *Kom Binne* 193 A Kaffir doctor appeared on the scene, a weird old fellow in a huge cap made of muishond skins and tails. **1948** A.C. WHITE *Call of Bushveld* 207 Striped Muishond (Cape Polecat). **1970** *News/Check* 12 June 11 An assumption had grown up over the past year or more that South Africa was well and truly isolated, that it remained the *muishond* of the world with whom nobody wanted anything to do. **1982** *S. Afr. Panorama* Aug. 33 Skeletons of bats and a *muishond* (a type of mongoose). [**1990** SKINNER & SMITHERS *Mammals of Sn Afr. Subregion* 461 *Ictonyx striatus* ... As the coat is distinctively striped black and white, 'striped' very aptly describes this polecat. The Afrikaans *stinkmuishond* is descriptive, but *muishond* applies also to the weasel and the mongoose.]

‖**2.** *comb.* **muishondbos** [Afk., *bos* bush], any of several odiferous plants, esp. the oak-leaf pelargonium *Pelargonium quercifolium* (family Geraniaceae), and the shrub or small tree *Premna mooiensis* (family Verbenaceae).

In F. von Breitenbach's *Nat. List of Indigenous Trees* (1987), the name 'skunk bush' is used for *Premna mooiensis*.

1966 C.A. SMITH *Common Names* 344 *Muishondbos(sie), Pelargonium quercifolium* ... The plants have strong but not objectionable odour, the vernacular name (lit. = skunk bush) refers to the pungent odour. **1975** *Argus* 17 Sept. 28 And then there's the muishondbos (skunk bush) which stinks like a skunk, especially after heavy dew or rain ... also a means of protection, I suppose.

muisvoël /ˈmeɪsfʊəl, ˈmœis-/ *n.* Also **muisvoel**, and (formerly) **muisvo(o)gel, muizvogel, muysvoogel.** [Afk. (earlier S. Afr. Du. *muisvogel*), *muis* mouse + *voël* bird (see quot. 1955); but see also quot. 1913.] MOUSEBIRD.

*c*1808 [see MOUSEBIRD]. **1822** W.J. BURCHELL *Trav.* I. 214 Muisvogel (Mouse-bird). *Colius erythropus* of Linnaeus. **1849** A. SMITH *Illust. of Zoo. of S. Afr.: Aves* Pl.2, *Chizærhis concolor* ... As soon as it was observed, the Hottentots declared it to be a *muis vogel*, or *Colius*, Lin ... which was not surprising, since it evinces considerable similarity to birds of that genus. **1867** E.L. LAYARD *Birds of S. Afr.* 221 Of the three species of this genus found in South Africa and known by the trivial name of Muisvogel or Mouse-bird, this [*sc. Colius Erythropus*] is the only one that is found in the neighbourhood of Cape Town ... They creep among the branches like parrots and hang suspended, head downwards, without inconvenience. **1905** J. DU PLESSIS *1000 Miles in Heart of Afr.* 137 Butcher birds and 'muisvogels' and finches. **1913** C. PETTMAN *Africanderisms* 329 *Muis vogel*, .. The former part of the word has reference to the hair-like character of the breast feathers of the bird; some, however, regard it as a corruption of the Dutch word for the crest which the bird has, *muts*, and others as a corruption of the Dutch word for sparrow, *musch*. **1920** R.Y. STORMBERG *Mrs Pieter de Bruyn* 7 It [*sc.* peachblossom] has been vandalised by swarms of 'finks' and wretched little stiff-tailed 'muisvogels' who snip off the blooms most viciously. **1952** *Cape Times* 27 Nov. 2 Muisvoëls are destroying whole orchards of early ripening fruit. [**1955** V.M. FITZROY *Dark Bright Land* 78 Whole colonies of little birds the Dutch call *muizvogels*. They .. have an appearance almost of grey fur with a tufted crest and long tail.] **1970** M. MULLER *Cloud across Moon* 36 Twittering witoogies and muisvoëls squabbling greedily over the glistening magenta pips. **1973** *Daily Dispatch* 16 June 9 The muisvoels .. flock in large numbers during the winter and can very quickly strip trees and shrubs of their fruit. **1982** M. BRITZ *Informant, Grahamstown* Muisvoëls and white eyes were the only birds we were allowed to shoot on the farm because they used to ruin the fruit crops.

Mujaji var. MODJADJI.

mukulu var. MAKULU.

Muldergate /ˈmʌldəgeɪt, ˈməldə-/ *n.* [Formed by analogy with U.S. Eng. *Watergate*, and named for the then Minister of Information, *C. Mulder*.

The use of *-gate* to indicate a scandal 'was principally a feature of US English until 1978, when the South African *Muldergate* scandal brought it wider publicity' (*Oxford Dict. of New Words*, 1991).]

The scandal, and subsequent investigation, resulting from the misappropriation of funds within the Department of Information in 1978; INFO. Also *attrib.*

1979 *Daily Dispatch* 16 Feb. 12, I was astonished to hear some public personalities urging the country to put Muldergate behind them and get back to the job of discussing race policies. *Ibid.* 27 Mar. 13 The Prime Minister, Mr P.W. Botha, .. begins by explaining his view of the 'Muldergate' affair, which now poses a threat to his six-month-old premiership. 1982 D. TUTU *Voice of One* 80 It can make or break men and women, as we very well know from recent history in the United States and our own country, in those episodes known as Watergate and Muldergate. *Ibid.* 95 The Information Scandal ('Muldergate') shook many of the more principled members of the Afrikaans community. 1984 D. PINNOCK *Brotherhoods* 90 All three men were to be toppled from power in a prolonged but bloodless coup conducted by the military after the 'Muldergate' information scandal in the mid-1970s. 1990 *Sunday Star* 11 Mar. 16 If the great Info Scandal of 12 years ago was called 'Muldergate' (after the Minister who finally took the rap) then the stuff the Harms Commission is now investigating might as well be called Murdergate.

multinational *adj.* [tr. Afk. *veelvolkig(e)* consisting of many peoples (or 'nations'). In Afk., *volk* means both 'people' and 'nation' (although *nasie* is increasingly used for the latter).]

1. Applied to South Africa and to South African society: composed of several peoples or 'nations'. See also NATION.

Often used (esp. in the past) to justify apartheid as an appropriate policy for the country, the term has encountered much resistance.

1964 H.H.W. DE VILLIERS *Rivonia* 31 The .. exhibits produced .. gradually high-lighted the significance and gravity of a plot which normally aimed at the destruction of the centuries-old and normally peaceful and democratic way of life in South Africa's multi-national society. 1971 *Daily Dispatch* 13 May 12 One of the more zany premises upon which many political theories are founded in this land is that South Africa is a 'multi-national' country. 1973 *Drum* 22 Jan. 41 Mr. Vorster had said he was not against 'foreign aid' to the Coloured section of our multi-national society. 1973 *Sunday Times* 27 May 17 This might prove too high a price for the creation of an all-White Parliament in a multi-national and multi-racial country. 1983 F.E.O'B. GELDENHUYS in *Optima* Vol.31 No.3, 156 One example comes from the official reply of the Swiss Federation of Protestant churches: ' ... Every page evidences [their] concern to examine critically the problems presented .. by the relations between the "population groups" in the "multinational South African state".'

2. *hist.* Applied to sport and to sporting events, teams, and policies.

a. Of sport and sporting events: involving the participation of people from all ethnic groups in South Africa, each group being represented by its own team.

1971 *Rand Daily Mail* 5 Apr. 1 The newspaper's top sportswriter .. suggested that it could concern the introduction of 'multinational' (veelvolkige) sport at an international level in South Africa. 1972 *E. Prov. Herald* 3 Aug. 1 They will show films on multi-national sport in South Africa. 1972 *Argus* 16 Sept. 4 It will be hard put to explain on what grounds it justifies .. multiracial (though officials called it 'multinational') athletics competitions while barring mixed rugby trials. 1973 *Sunday Times* 1 Apr. (Mag. Sect.) 3 He was referring to what is being called the 'multi-national' as opposed to the multi-racial South African Games. 1974 *Drum* 8 Aug. 19 Even the multinational games don't prove anything. 1980 *E. Prov. Herald* 27 Sept. 1 Saru stressed that they would not participate in what they called multinational rugby until the laws prohibiting non-racial rugby were repealed.

b. Of sports policies: based on the concept that South Africa is comprised of several nations, each having its own sports teams.

1972 *Evening Post* 29 Jan. 2 (*letter*) Nothing shows up the hypocrisy and opportunism of the Government's race policies more than its new so-called 'multinational' sports policy. 1973 *E. Prov. Herald* 1 June 8 The tortuous 'multinational' and 'open international' formula continues to be used as the excuse for discriminating between different sports. Those that are arbitrarily favoured are allowed more relaxation of the colour bar than those that are not. 1973 *Argus* 16 June 4 The sports policy is an extension of the policy of multinational development, and not an example of 'multiracialism', 'mixed sport' or 'multicoloured sport'.

c. Of sports teams: multi-racial; including representatives of more than one South African ethnic group.

1972 *Sunday Times* 29 Oct. 10 Keep the Springbok title for White teams and build a new tradition .. of a multi-national touring team. 1975 *S. Afr. Panorama* Sept. 19 As far as variety was concerned, the multinational South African team scored a huge success. Hence **multinationalism** *n.*, a euphemism for SEPARATE DEVELOPMENT.

1971 *Daily Dispatch* 16 Oct. 8 They call separate development multi-nationalism or separate freedoms. 1973 *Drum* 8 May 14 We want non-racial sport at all levels. We reject multinationalism because it maintains the racial status quo in South African sport. 1973 *Star* 29 Sept., I .. want to know when once we are past the convoluted sentences about multi-nationalism and multi-racialism and world opinion, just what Indians and Coloureds must do to get anywhere. 1973 on Radio South Africa 17 Oct. (Current Affairs), Separate development — multinationalism. 1973 *Weekend Post* 3 Nov. 12 The concept of 'multinationalism' can be given neither *de jure* nor *de facto* status. 1974 *E. Prov. Herald* 1 July 12 To prate about multinationalism in sport will not suffice.

mulungu var. MLUNGU.

mum-mum see quot. 1883 at NUM-NUM.

munt /mʌnt/ *n. Derog. offensive. slang.* Also **moent**. [Shortened form of MUNTU, see next.] Used contemptuously: a term for a black African; MUNTU sense 2. Also *comb.* (objective), see quot. 1974.

Used also (by whites) in Zambia and Zimbabwe.

1948 O. WALKER *Kaffirs Are Lively* 77 It's the towns that muck the *munt* up. 1949 C. BULLOCK *Rina* 35, I knew what it was to travel with the kind of 'munt' who has wool inside as well as outside his head. 1951 R. FARRAN *Jungle Chase* (1957) 42, I worked as a ganger on building schemes, chasing up the munts to mix concrete. 1953 N. GORDIMER *Lying Days* 35 Man, there a whole lota niggers round Ocherts', all over the garden and in the street and everywhere. Just a lot of munts from the Compound. 1962 *New Statesman* (U.K.) 24 Aug. 218 The old 'munt', as the African is still widely and insultingly termed. 1967 J.G. DAVIS *Hold my Hand* (1969) 23 What good am I doing anyway, playing white chieftain over a few thousand munts. 1970 *Daily News* 14 May, Words like 'munt' and 'kaffir' are never heard. Racial discrimination and intolerance have all but disappeared from the capital. 1974 *Weekend Post* 12 Jan. 12 The Whites played a game called munt-scaring .. to see how close they could get to Black pedestrians or cyclists without actually mowing them down ... They grabbed a Black person, took him for a ride, gave him a hiding and then dumped him. This was called munt-bashing. *c*1976 H. FLATHER *Thaba Rau* 36 'The munts eat out of his hand. One day he'll lead the revolution.' Poulson frowned. 'I don't like that expression — "munts"'. 1978 [see MUNTU sense 2]. 1980 *Grocott's Mail* 1 Aug. 2 The word 'cripple' has negative connotations .. which are as degrading to orthopaedically disabled people as 'kaffir', 'wog' and 'munt' are to Blacks. 1987 M. POLAND *Train to Doringbult* 91 You must get those munts of yours to be more careful with the gate. 1990 P. CULLINAN in M. Leveson *Firetalk* 13 The bloody munts won't work, Bob. They need a damn good lesson.

muntu /ˈmʊntu/ *n.* Also **munthu, umntu,** and with initial capital. [Personal noun prefix *mu-* + noun stem *ntu* human being (pl. *bantu*), common to many Sintu (Bantu) languages. Cf. BANTU.]

1. A human being; a black person.

Cf. BANTU (esp. *adj.* sense 2 a); the term 'Bantu' was debased by its use as an ethnic label during the apartheid era.

1920 S.M. MOLEMA *Bantu Past & Present* 305 The average 'Muntu' (pl. Bantu) cares little and knows less about politics. 1926 [see UBUNTU sense a]. 1937 E.G. MALHERBE *Educ. Adaptations in Changing Soc.* 500 Standard of development will be judged by the extent to which the Native has ceased to be an Umuntu and has become a European. 1941 A. MAQELEPO in *Bantu World* 15 Feb. 5 We are confused as to whether we are to be described as Kaffirs, Coloureds, Bantu, Negroes or even Africans ... To be called an *umuntu* is far too general, but to call us African or Negro is honourable and precise. 1949 C. BULLOCK *Rina* 8 A coloured member of the skolly type swayed arm-in-arm with a native — a Black African, a Munthu. 1962 M. BRANDEL-SYRIER *Black Woman* 112 The concept Muntu is central for the understanding of the Bantu idea of 'man', and the basis of Bantu psychology. Only in so far as .. the individual has 'life strength', is he truly Muntu which is humanus rather than homo. [1965 D. MARAIS *Ag, Sis Man!*, (*caption*) Baas Nel, I hear South Africa's first astronaut will be a Zulu, so they can call him Moon-to.] 1972 S. LYNNE *Glittering Gold* 45 I'm telling you! I spotted him entering the cage. I grabbed this hard hat from a muntu's head and took the next cage down. 1973 *Daily Dispatch* 6 Aug. 8 One never hears white government officials referring to a particular 'umntu' so why the predilection for 'Bantu'. 1975 *Drum* 22 Apr. 4 When offered a palace he said without malice I'm not a play-white, I'm a muntu. *a*1956 H.I.E. DHLOMO in Visser & Couzens *Collected Works* (1985) 429 Any person who stands between the 'Muntu' and his cattle would be crushed to death. 1986 *Drum* Aug. 55 My colleague and I here have been arguing about you. He says you can walk around Thekwini because you are a coloured and don't carry a pass. I say haikhona, you are a muntu. 1987 'HIGH VOLTAGE VUSI' in *Pace* June 16 Really gave this voteless, voiceless, rubber-black muntu a bellyful of guffaws.

2. *Derog.* and *offensive.* MUNT. Also *attrib.*

1977 *Drum* Mar. 2 Always having our interest at heart, 20 years ago the mlungu decided that there must be a special type of education for the primitive muntu mind. 1978 *Het Suid-Western* 22 Feb., Today's in word incidentally — for the singular of 'bantu' is 'muntu'. But 'muntu' if anything is even more offensive than 'bantu' in that it often gets shortened to 'munt'. 1989 E. BREGIN *Kayaboeties* 13 'It's a muntu song, man!' he said disgustedly. 'What did you have to go and write a song about a muntu for?'

mupani var. MOPANI.

muroch var. MOROGO.

murumba /mʊˈrʊmbə/ *n.* Pl. **mirumba**. [Venda *murumbu* (pl. *mirumbu*).] A small drum of the Venda people of the Northern Transvaal.

1931 H.A. STAYT *BaVenda* 316 The small drum, *marumba*, is held between the legs at an angle, with the tympanum away from the body; it is beaten by being vigorously struck with the lower part of the palm of the hand and the fingers, giving a fairly high sharp note. 1951 T.V. BULPIN *Lost Trails of Low Veld* 20 Around the fire the dark, gleaming bodies of the girls move, shufflingly, sinuously, while the drums, the baritone of the mirumba and the deep bass of the ngoma, thud out an intoxicating symphony.

muruti var. MORUTI.

mushy /ˈmʊʃi/ *adj.* Also **moeshie, moochy, moosh, moosh(l)y, mush**. [Englished form of *muhle*, common to several Nguni languages.

The word entered S. Afr. Eng. originally fr. Zulu *muhle*, personal *adj.* concord *mu-* + *-hle* good, and later fr. Rhodesian (now Zimbabwean) Eng., fr. Ndebele.]

Pleasant, nice: a general term of approbation.

a. *obs.* Used when reporting the speech of Nguni language speakers.

1870 C. HAMILTON *Life & Sport in S.-E. Afr.* 19 Black draughts, as being the most nauseous, are their especial favourites .. over which they smack their lips with the relish of a true connoisseur, between whiles exclaiming 'mooshly, mooshly', an expression of approbation which is weakly translated by 'very good, very good indeed'. **1877** LADY BARKER *Yr's Hsekeeping* 315 I .. showed them all her Majesty's picture, to which they cried 'moochy' (nice) and gave the royal salute.

b. *slang.* (Used esp. by Zimbabweans.)

1973 *Weekend Argus* 24 Feb. 2 Of course he was also giving her one of those stupid rings .. but he knew the real 'moosh' present was this lovely knife. **1979** *Chronicle* 14 Oct. 1 If the words are appropriate and sound jolly, they give one's language a bit of colour which is not out of place. But over-used — when everything, for instance, is 'moosh' — it is wrong. **1982** *Star* 31 Mar., Mush — originating in Zimbabwe, this means nice, pleasant. **1987** J. CARRUTHERS in *Style* May 38 Anyone at a when-we reunion who doesn't know what 'mushy' means must be Zambian.

muskaliat kat var. MUSKELJAATKAT.

muskat var. MUSK CAT.

musk cat *n. phr.* Also **muskat, musk kat.** [tr. Du. *muskuskat* or S. Afr. Du. *muskeljaatkat*, see MUSKELJAATKAT.] Either of two species of genet of the Viverridae, the small-spotted genet, *Genetta genetta*, or the large-spotted genet *Genetta tigrina*; MUSKELJAATKAT. Also *attrib.*

1731 G. MEDLEY tr. *P. Kolb's Present State of Cape of G.H.* II. 127 There is another Sort of Wild Cat in the *Cape*-Countries, that is call'd the Musk Cat. The Skins of these Cats have a very fine Scent. [**1835** A. SMITH *Diary* (1939) I. 278 Duiker, roodekat, muskelcat.] **1900** W.L. SCLATER *Mammals of S. Afr.* I. 53 *Genetta tigrina*, .. Muskat or Misselyat-kat of Colonists. **1913** C. PETTMAN *Africanderisms* 330 *Musk kat*, *Genetta tigrina* and *G. felina* are both known by this name. **1918** S.H. SKAIFE *Animal Life* 268 There are two different species of genets, or *muskkats*, fairly common in most parts of the country. **1968** *Farmer's Weekly* 3 Jan. 88 (*advt*) One Musk Cat (muskeljaatkat), full grown, R10 or nearest offer. **1978** A.P. BRINK *Rumours of Rain* 417 The incredible, dark, stinking little shop specialising in herbs and *muti*, anything from *dolosse* to musk-cat fur, dried ostrich heads and monkey tails, the skins of porcupines and snakes and iguanas.

muskeljaatkat /ˌməsk(ə)lˈjɑːtkat/ *n.* Also **misselyat-kat, muskaliat kat, muskejaatkat, muskiliat-cat.** [S. Afr. Du., fr. Du. *muskuskat, muskus* musk + *kat* cat.] MUSK CAT.

1821 C.I. LATROBE *Jrnl of Visit* 426 A trap having been set in a ravine, to catch mongooses, a muskiliat-cat was found in it ... The skin was beautifully variegated with stripes and spots. **1835** A. SMITH *Diary* (1940) II. 196 The clear spotted Muskaliat Kat inhabits this country and skins of them are often seen patching the karosses of the natives. **1900** [see MUSK CAT]. **1919** F.W. FITZSIMONS *Natural Hist. of S. Afr.* II. 10 *Muskejaatkat*, The Afrikaans and common name of the Spotted Genet. 'It differs from the large-spotted Genet in having five rows of irregular black spots on each side of its body, and by the tip of its tail being white. Both species are popularly known as Misselyat-kats.' **1968** [see MUSK CAT].

Musotho var. MOSOTHO.

musselcracker *n.* Pl. **-s**, or unchanged. [Named for its powerful jaws.]

1. Any of three species of seabream of the Sparidae, the diet of which includes shellfish and crustaceans: **a.** The *white steenbras* (sense (*a*) see STEENBRAS sense b), *Lithognathus lithognathus*. **b.** The *black musselcracker* (see sense 2 below), *Cymatoceps nasutus*. **c.** The *white musselcracker* (see sense 2 below), *Sparodon durbanensis*. In these senses also called MUSSEL CRUSHER.

1905 H.E.B. BROOKING in *E. London Dispatch* 6 Nov. 7 Judging by the enormous incisors, and the perfect pavement of rounded molars with which the jaws of these white steenbras are armed, these fish live largely upon shell-fish, hence the local name 'mussel-cracker' and Durban name 'mussel-crusher'. **1932** *Grocott's Daily Mail* 11 Jan. 2 The catching of a mussel cracker, 62lbs in weight .. yesterday cheered the hearts of local fishermen. **1937** C. BIRKBY *Zulu Journey* 180 Enthusiastic anglers here will lead one before the mounted head of a mussel-cracker which weighed 53lbs and pause enraptured to gaze at the rows of great rounded molars, like polished marbles, with which the monster had made sure that his diet of mussels and oysters would not give him indigestion. **1949** J. MOCKFORD *Golden Land* 45 Heavy netloads of fish .. with formidable names such as musselcracker, kabeljauw and seventy-four. **1949** J.L.B. SMITH *Sea Fishes* 268 *Sparodon durbanensis* ... *Sand Stompkop. Sand Blouer. Mussel Cracker. Mussel Crusher* (Cape). *Silver Steenbras. Steenbras. Brusher* (Eastern Cape — Natal). *Ibid.* 271 *Cymatoceps nasutus* ... *Musselcracker. Musselcrusher. Biskop. Black Biskop. Swart Biskop. Blue Biskop. Blou Biskop. Poenskop. Stompkop* (Cape). *Blouer* or *Bank Blouer* (Knysna). *Witbek. Stembras. Steenbras. Black Steenbras* (Eastern Cape — Natal). **1955** C. HORNE *Fisherman's Eldorado* 89 The musselcracker is the fish which is also known to Western Province anglers as sand stompkop, the white musselcracker or the white biskop, .. the silver steenbras of the Eastern Province and Wild Coast, the brusher of Natal. **1971** *Daily News* 16 Apr. 3 Zululanders can expect best results operating out of Mtunzini, where good catches of deep-sea reef-fish — including some big musselcracker have been reported. **1981** *E. Prov. Herald* 23 Apr. 11 The name 'steenbras' is probably the most abused name in the whole of our fish nomenclature. What we call a mussel-cracker, Natal and Border anglers call a white steenbras. **1993** BENNETT & ATTWOOD in *Earthyear* (ed.5) Winter, 35 Since the prohibition of angling in the De Hoop Marine Reserve in 1986, the populations of .. white steenbras, blacktail, bronze bream, musselcracker, Cape stumpnose, wildeperd .. have recovered to densities .. comparable to those which were likely to have been experienced by anglers earlier this century.

2. With distinguishing epithet designating a particular species of seabream: **black musselcracker**, *Cymatoceps nasutus*, a large fish known for its characteristic fleshy protuberance which gives it the appearance of having a nose; *bank blouer*, see BLOUER sense b; BISKOP sense 1 a; *black -, blou -,* or *blue biskop*, see BISKOP sense 2; *black steenbras*, see STEENBRAS sense b; BLOUER sense a; *blue poenskop*, see POENSKOP sense 2 b; POENSKOP sense 2 a ii; STOMPKOP sense a; **silver -** or (more commonly) **white musselcracker**, *Sparodon durbanensis*, a large species considered a good game fish; BISKOP sense 1 b; BRUSHER; CRACKER; *sand blouer*, see BLOUER sense b; *silver steenbras*, see STEENBRAS sense b; STOMPKOP sense b; *white biskop*, see BISKOP sense 2; *white steenbras* sense (*b*), see STEENBRAS sense b; also *attrib.*

In Smith and Heemstra's *Smiths' Sea Fishes* (1986), the name 'black musselcracker' is used for *Cymatoceps nasutus*, and 'white musselcracker' for *Sparodon durbanensis*.

1986 B. GROBBLER in *Cape Times* 27 Mar., There is an unusually good run this year of poenskop or **black musselcracker**. **1993** R. VAN DER ELST *Guide to Common Sea Fishes* 346 The black musselcracker is a large, solitary species. **1982** *S. Afr. Fishing* Apr.-May 10 A **silver musselcracker** of 16kg .. was the heaviest fish landed for the week. **1955** [**white musselcracker**: see sense 1]. **1979** SNYMAN & KLARIE *Free from Sea* 38 White musselcracker steaks are most successful. **1993** R. VAN DER ELST *Guide to Common Sea Fishes* 369 The white musselcracker is found in coastal waters, especially along rocky shores.

mussel crusher *n. phr.* Also with initial capitals. [As prec.] MUSSELCRACKER.

1905 [see MUSSELCRACKER sense 1]. **1913** C. PETTMAN *Africanderisms* 330 *Mussel crusher*, The Natal name of the above fish [*sc.* musselcracker]. **1930** C.L. BIDEN *Sea-Angling Fishes* 257 *Sparus durbanensis* ... Port Elizabeth — Mussel-Crusher ... *Pagrus nasutus* ... Natal — Mussel-Crusher or Mussel-Cracker. **1949** [see Smith quot. at MUSSELCRACKER sense 1]. **1979** SNYMAN & KLARIE *Free from Sea* 38 *Musselcracker*, .. There are two types .. which between them, have seventeen common names! .. Mussel crusher .. Silver Steenbras.

mutakuane var. MATEKWANE.

muti /ˈmuːti/ *n.* Also **moote, mooti(e), mouti(e), muthi, umuti.** Usu. *noncount*, occas. pl. **-s.** [Zulu *umuthi* (pl. *imithi*), Xhosa *umthi* tree, herbal or patent medicine.]

1. *obs.* A tree.

1858 A.W. DRAYSON *Sporting Scenes* 165 They could see but a 'muti' (tree or plant), .. neither fit for food or physic. **1889** F. OATES *Matabele Land* 414 Muti, *tree; medicine.*

2. Any of a number of types of medicine, or of medicinal or magical charm.

a. A substance or object which has or is believed to have curative, preventive, protective, or harmful powers of a medicinal or supernatural kind; esp. medicines or charms traditionally used among the black peoples of Africa, made usu. of plants or animal parts, and sometimes, reportedly, of parts of the human body; MEDICINE sense 1. Also *attrib.* See also INTELEZI. Cf. UBUTI.

Usu. prepared and supplied by an INYANGA or SANGOMA. Different kinds of muti are used in different ways: they may be ingested, applied, inhaled, sprinkled on a person or place, burnt, or simply placed somewhere or carried with one; vendors of muti usually have a standard range for the treatment of common complaints, but also make up preparations for specific purposes. Mutis are used to cure illnesses, to increase one's strength or courage, to improve a particular ability, to bring good luck, to provide protection, to influence a person's feelings or actions, to cause harm to someone, etc.

1860 A.W. DRAYSON *Sporting Scenes* 275 My Kaffir seemed awed by the lightning and thunder; he ate a little of his '*muti*' (charmed medicine) that was round his neck. **1875** D. LESLIE *Among Zulus* 60 Asked .. what he is looking for amongst the grass, he disdains to answer in his own language, or even to use the 'Pigeon English' word 'Moote,' but says 'Medditsin'. **1880** E.F. SANDEMAN *Eight Months in Ox-Waggon* 291 The boys had been gathering .. plants and bulbs, which they boiled together to make some sort of 'mootie'. **1898** B. MITFORD *Induna's Wife* 5, I took for principal wife Lalusini, the sorceress, .. whom I had first found making strange and powerful *muti* among the Bakoni. **1911** M.S. EVANS *Black & White in S.E. Afr.* 5 A little white child .. was .. lost among the natives and never heard of again, presumably killed by a witch doctor for muti. **1933** W. MACDONALD *Romance of Golden Rand* 18 My stone is like muti (medicine), and cures sickness by its lightning flashes ... I do not wish to sell my muti stone. **1939** S. CLOETE *Watch for Dawn* 307, I gave her strong moutie, a medicine that would make her invisible. **1943** D. REITZ *No Outspan* 154 The mamba would hiss and make as if to strike but the stench of the muti was overpowering and it would draw back. **1955** J.B. SHEPHARD *Land of Tikoloshe* 102 His knowledge of the plants, roots, and herbs employed for *muti* is extensive. **1964** G. CAMPBELL *Old Dusty* 81 We came across a meteorite from which .. the native witch-doctors had been chipping fragments for muti. **1967** O. WALKER *Hippo Poacher* 17 Because crocodiles like human flesh, it was believed that a medicine made from their eyes mixed with some portion of the heart would produce a muti that could make a man irresistible to girls. **1971** *Drum* Aug. 28 There was muti in them ... Tefo believed that the belts would protect him, even from the consequences of murder. **1981** *Voice* 22 Apr. 5 (*advt*) Zulu

Muti Herbal Centre. **1986** *Cape Times* 25 Jan. 2 Seventy-six miners — all bearing 'vaccination' marks which when smeared with 'magic muti' were meant to make them invulnerable to police gunfire. **1986** *City Press* 20 Apr. 8 (*advt*) This Holy stick which is an Indian Muti, is the answer to all your problems! When lit it gives off a sweet fragrance .. , keeping away evil spirits, bringing good luck, improving love, sex life & solving problems of unhappiness. **1989** *Personality* 29 May 28 The list of herbal plants and trees threatened by over-use as muti (traditional medicine) is growing. *Ibid.* 29 Durban is the main centre of the muti trade in South Africa — and presumably the biggest market of its kind on the continent. **1990** W. BOTHA in *Frontline* Sept. 18 Richard Lyster asked some of the witnesses — 'sharp, streetwise comrades' — why they thought Shabalala won the case. 'They said it was because his muti was so strong. If you shoot at him, they said, the bullets turn into water.' *Ibid.* 19 He [*sc.* a church minister] tells me Shabalala uses a very good witchdoctor. 'In the court last year his muti was so strong that the magistrate fainted several times.' **1990** *S. Afr. Panorama* Nov.-Dec. 2 (*caption*) Containerised, blessed seawater (*muti*) is taken home for potent medicinal use. **1991** J. BERGER in *Focus on Afr.* Jan.-Mar. 40 Deshi Baktawer .. remembers making his debut against the [Kaizer] Chiefs [football team] ... 'I had a spare pair of gloves and some gum, and I left them in the goalmouth — for them, that's magic, that's muti.' **1992** B. BAKER in *Weekly Mail* 16 Apr. 7 The use of *muti* in resolving labour disputes is firmly believed by many workers and union leaders.

b. Pharmaceutical medicine.

1908 D. BLACKBURN *Leaven* 316 White muti no good, baas ... You know all about muti, and the doctor told you I should die. **1928** L.P. GREENE *Adventure Omnibus* 365 They'll all come to me for muti in the morning, Jim. **1937** C. BIRKBY *Zulu Journey* 43 One of the most pleasant gifts Chaka ever received from Lieutenant Farewell was a cask of medicine. That was strong muti indeed. **1952** *Drum* Sept. 25 (*advt*) A baby who is cross needs this muti .. Ashton & Parsons' Infants' Powders. **1970** R.M. ANDERSON *Informant, Port Elizabeth* Have you put muti on your cut? **1976** *Sunday Times* 6 June 11 He went to the servant's room with .. an antibiotic capsule — 'powerful White man's muti'. **1990** *City Press* 11 Feb. 10 Animal muti cancer cure. A drug used to deworm farm animals could save the lives of .. patients suffering from .. cancer of the colon. **1990** *Style* June 128 Multi-vitamins, cold tabs and tummy muti.

3. *transf.* Any chemical preparation.

1937 J. STEVENSON-HAMILTON *S. Afr. Eden* 198, I may get some mealies, but your *muti* has killed all my sweet potatoes. [*Note*] Anti-locust spray. **1971** *Informant, Cape Town* 'What's this stuff?' 'It's some muti for sticking.' **1991** C. MITCHELL in *Personality* 11 Mar. 20 While the places where pigeons roost are easily accessible to those who have wings, how does Allen get his wonder muti up there?

4. *fig.*

1948 O. WALKER *Kaffirs Are Lively* 188 Education is the white man's *muti* — medicine — which makes him powerful. **1970** *Drum* Feb. 49, I think my best muti is hard work and praying to God. **1973** F. CHISHOLM in *Cape Times* 9 June 7 One man's *muti* is another man's poison. **1979** *Sunday Times* 15 July 16 That was bad muti from Sam Buti when he opted out of the committee for urban Black-White consultation. **1988** A. MNISI in *Pace* June 158 The muti he uses in a fight is a powerful, devastating punch. **1990** *Sunday Times* 8 Apr. (Business Times) 2 Kroks the right muti for Premier. **1992** K. DAVIE in *Ibid.* 14 June (Business Times) 3 Stals' strong muti for revival ... He is proposing a programme which could bring drastic and sudden changes to the economy. **1992** *Natal Mercury* 3 Aug. 6 He is an optometrist by profession and was taken aback when a patient asked for new glasses because 'the muti in the old ones is finished'.

5. Used *attrib.* in n. phrr.: ***muti killer*** or ***-murderer***, *ritual killer* (see RITUAL); ***muti killing*** or ***-murder***, *ritual killing* (see RITUAL); ***muti man***, a man who makes or supplies muti (see sense 2 a); ***muti shop***, a shop trading exclusively or mainly in muti (see sense 2 a).

1968 *Post* 7 Jan. He went to a muti-man who treated him with herbs until he was cured. **1970** *Ibid.* 18 Jan. 20 An inyanga .. had been robbed of his bag of herbs and mutiman's diploma. **1971** *Sunday Times* 14 Nov. (Suppl.), The three Xabas were indicted for trial at the Rand Supreme Court for the muti murder of the tramp. **1972** *Daily Dispatch* 9 Mar. 10 Muti men find a ready market in gullible sports administrators and sportsmen who think they cannot achieve anything without the use of herbs. **1972** *Sunday Times* 6 Feb. (Mag. Sect.) 12 The muti shop is in colourful Diagonal Street. **1978** *Pace* Dec. 10 A frail, devout church man .. was .. mistaken for the 'muti murderer' and came close to paying for it with his life. *Ibid.* 13 With muti murders soaring .. , suspicion and violence are the order of the day in Pretoria. **1982** *Sunday Times* 2 May 17 Those who practise as both a medium and muti-man must indicate this by including both abbreviations behind their names to comply with the Traditional Medical Practitioners Act of 1981. **1984** *Evening Post* 22 Aug. 3 Police have confirmed .. that .. Mr Glen L— .. was the victim of a 'muti' or ritual killing. **1985** *Sunday Times* 5 May 1 Kidnap child: Muti killing feared ... An East London murder and robbery squad officer said: ' .. We are now exploring the possibility that he may be in the hands of muti-killers.' **1985** *Probe* Sept. 20 In Mdantsane .. a family was made to pay for the muti murder of their eldest son, only because he had rendered his unwed sweetheart pregnant. **1986** *Sowetan* 22 Oct. 1 Muti killer gets death sentence. **1988** J. KHUMALO in *Pace* June 8B, These backyard muti-men use European chemicals in their spuit (syringe) ... And they use the most corrosive chemical .. , Potassium Dichromate. **1992** P. GARSON in *Weekly Mail* 16 Apr. 6 A member of the Black Cats in Wesselton has given a gruesome account of *muti* murders committed by the gang to increase their fighting prowess in battles against 'comrades' ... He blames the *muti* for his and other gang members' inability to stop fighting. **1985** *Cape Times* 16 July 1 Alleged muti murderer Mr William K— .. caused an uproar in the Magistrate's Court here yesterday. **1987** *City Press* 25 Oct. 10 (*advt*) You can boost your sagging vitality with the Amandla range of trusted products. From your Chemist or Muti-shop now! **1988** B. NTLEMO in *Frontline* Oct. 9 Many people fell victims of the alleged muti murderers. **1989** *Personality* 29 May 29 Jeff and his helpers have propagated close to 120 000 plants of about 200 different species ... These impressive quantities cannot supply one thriving muti shop for one month! And in the Durban area alone there are more than 70 muti shops. **1991** H. GRANGE in *Daily News* 26 Mar. 26 A muti murderer .. was sentenced .. to 12 years in jail for the killing of his two-year-old step-daughter by cutting her throat. He wished to use her body for the purpose of curing him of illness. **1991** NGCOBO & ESHAK in *Sunday Times* 7 Apr. 5 A three-year-old boy has been found dead with his right arm and leg cut off. The boy's father .. believes his son was the victim of a muti killer.

mutokuane var. MATEKWANE.

mutsha /ˈmʊtʃa/ *n.* Also **moocha**, **m(o)ucha**, **mutya**, **umtcha**, **umatsha**, **umutsha**, **umutya**. [Zulu *umutsha* man or girl's loin-covering.] **a.** A loin-cloth of animal's tails or leather strips, part of traditional (Zulu) male dress; MOOCHI sense a. **b.** MOOCHI sense b. Cf. APRON sense 1, BESHU, STERTRIEM.

1836 N. ISAACS *Trav.* (1937) II. 258 The men wear 'Umtchas' .. strips of skins of animals, neatly fastened to a small strip of hide, reaching from hip to hip, fastened in front by cords. **1872** C.A. PAYTON *Diamond Diggings* 137 A Kafir's notions of dress are primitive in the extreme; his only garment the ancient *mutya* or loin-cloth. **1885** H. RIDER HAGGARD *King Solomon's Mines* 153 He slipped off the 'moocha' or girdle round his middle, and stood naked before us. **1905** *Native Tribes of Tvl* 132 They wear round their waists skins, with the hair outwards, after the fashion of the Zulu 'moocha'. **1911** M.S. EVANS *Black & White in S.E. Afr.* 93 The hereditary chief of the Qadi clan, followed by his counsellors and attendants, clad for the most part in the mutya of their ancestors. **1923** *Chambers's Jrnl* (U.K.) Apr. 222 The native kilt or moocha composed of strips of raw hide. **1934** B.I. BUCHANAN *Pioneer Days* 26 A number of stalwart Native men .. clad in only a mutya (a belt of ox-hide from which depended fore and aft a fringe of monkey tails). **1936** *Blackwood's Mag.* (U.K.) Mar. 304 All the bravery of the Zulu war-dress was there: .. the leopard-skin karosses, the embroidered moochas, the white goat-hide garters. **1937** C. BIRKBY *Zulu Journey* 124 Zulus wearing nothing but the umutya, the girdle of buckskin dangling from their lean loins. **1948** O. WALKER *Kaffirs Are Lively* 30 The menfolk stride along bare-thighed, in swinging *umutshas* of monkey-tails and hide-strips instead of trousers. **1967** E.M. SLATTER *My Leaves Are Green* 1 He wore only his 'mutsha' of monkey-skin tails, and his head-ring had been freshly larded. **1974** C.T. BINNS *Warrior People* 208 The *uMutsha* and the *iBeshu* form the attire commonly worn in the kraals of Zululand and are the national dress of the Zulu males, although unfortunately this is being .. supplanted nowadays by the cast-off clothing of Europeans.

mutshi var. MOOCHI.

muttercap var. MOEDERKAPPIE.

mutya var. MUTSHA.

muurkas /ˈmyːrkas/ *n.* Also **meerkus**. Pl. **-kaste** /-kastə/, occas. **-es**. [Afk., *muur* wall + *kas* (pl. *kaste*) cupboard.] Esp. in traditional Cape Dutch houses: a cupboard built into an interior wall. Also **muurkassie** [see -IE]. See also KAS sense 1.

1949 L.G. GREEN *In Land of Afternoon* 198 The reception room, with its stinkwood muurkas and pieces of Delft. **1963** R. LEWCOCK *Early 19th C. Archit.* 344 Where eighteenth-century furniture was often built-in (the 'muurkassie') or at least kept small and neat (the Georgian book-case) the new furniture was heavy and dominant. **1964** J. MEINTJES *Manor House* 66 In the long dining room there were two muurkaste or built-in cabinets in black stinkwood with gabled tops. **1965** M.G. ATMORE *Cape Furn.* 201 Wall Cupboards or Cabinets (muurkaste). **1972** *S. Afr. Garden & Home* Feb.-Mar. 57 The living-room .. has wall cupboards of the Cape Dutch Muurkas type, filled with hand-painted crockery. **1975** *Cape Times* 7 Jan. 8 This year closed with the same auctioneers selling a fine example of an 18th-century Cape stinkwood-framed 'Muurkas', bought for R5 500 for 'Nova Constantia' a historic house in the Constantia valley. **1981** J. KENCH *Cape Dutch Homesteads* 44 The stinkwood 'muurkas' to the right of the screen door is thought to have belonged to Huysing himself. *Ibid.* 51 In the agterkamer the bricked outlines of two alcoves, now visible in the finished house, were discovered. These housed the traditional *muurkaste* — wall cupboards — which were a feature of Cape Dutch homes. **1985** *Style* Dec. 193 Young Cape Wine Farmers are .. forever throwing open wildly old houses full of meerkuses and wakuses and wildly old bottles of wine grown on the estate. **1987** [see KAS sense 1]. **1987** G. VINEY *Col. Houses* 40 Behind the *voorhuys* was the *galdery* with two wall cupboards (*muurkaste*).

Muvenda var. VENDA.

muyshond, **muysvoogel** varr. MUISHOND, MUISVOËL.

mvelangqangi, **mvelingqangi** varr. UMVELINQANGI.

my var. MAYE.

my lighty see LIGHTY.

mynfrau var. MEVROU.

myn(h)eer var. MIJNHEER.

mynman var. MAIN MAN.

mynpacht var. MIJNPACHT.

mynvrou, **myvrou(w)** varr. MEVROU.

mysie var. MEISIE.

‖**mzala** /m̩'zɑːla/ *n*. Also **mzal'**. [Zulu and Xhosa *umzala* cousin.] Among speakers of any of the Sintu (Bantu) group of languages: a cousin, brother, comrade, or friend; also used as a term of address, and occas. as a title.

[**1980** B.S. Motjuwadi in M. Mutloatse *Forced Landing* 189 Hy kom by my kesta. 'Mzala, mzala help my!'] **1981** M. Mzamane in *Best of S. Afr. Short Stories* (1991) 397 My cousin, Jola, comes from Tsolo in the Transkei ... One day Mzal'uJola went to buy some cold drink. **1986** [see Pace quot. at STINKER]. **1987** *Drum* Apr. 48, I want to say just keep on saying phinda mzala Ray Phiri. **1992** *Pace* Aug. 6 Mzala, we must go to school in the homelands next year.

N

N *n.* The fourteenth letter of the alphabet, used in the following senses:

1. *rare.* Abbrev. of NON-WHITE *n.*; see quot. Also *attrib.*

1988 J. HEYNS in *Sunday Times* 3 July (Extra) 2 'Sammy N rode such-and-such a horse to victory, while Jimmy N ran a close second with Josias N on his tail. Gerrit Botha failed to impress and Hannes van der Merwe maintained his standard to come home last.' The N .. stood for non-white. To give an N. jockey a full name was racetrack sacrilege in the Orange Free State.

2. [Prob. initial letter of *national*.] Prefixed to a number: designating a particular section of the NATIONAL ROAD network.

1991 [see NATIONAL ROAD]. **1994** P. SNYMAN in *Weekend Post* 24 Sept. 2 Repairs are being carried out on the N2 and N10 routes at the Gamtoos and Olifantskop Pass sections. **1994** E. CLARK in *Ibid.* 12 Nov. (Leisure) 4 Farmlands speckled with sheep .. fringe the N6 to Queenstown.

naaboom var. NABOOM.

Naachtmaal var. NAGMAAL.

naar /nɑː(r)/ *adj. colloq.* [Afk.]

1. Unpleasant, disagreeable, nauseating.

1900 M. MARQUARD *Lett. from Boer Parsonage* (1967) 65 It is too *naar* that a man who has shown this house so much kindness during our long time of sickness last year, should be turned into an enemy of the land now: one's heart is sore. **1990** J. NAIDOO *Coolie Location* 45, I knew my mother .. was going to go out and sprinkle the liquid dung over the swept portion of the pavement ... I asked her point blank: why was she doing something so *naar*.

2. Queasy, sick, nauseated.

1968 *Informant, Grahamstown* Let her try another cough mixture: this one makes a lot of my patients feel *naar*. **1969** A. FUGARD *Boesman & Lena* 47 The earth will get *naar* when they push us in. **1970** I. CALLARD *Informant, Pretoria* The smoke causing her to feel *naar*. **1977** FUGARD & DEVENISH *Guest* 34 You've got walls between you and him. We're in the same room. And that medicine of his is beginning to stink now. I get *naar* when I go in there. **1990** [see Top Forty quot. at AFRIKANER *n.* sense 2 b].

Hence **naar** *v. intrans.*, to smell unpleasant.

1986 L.A. BARNES in *Eng. Usage in Sn Afr.* Vol.17 No.2, 2 It's *naaring* 'It smells bad'. My socks are *naaring* 'My socks smell'. [*Ibid.* 3 Whereas the word is only used as an adjective in Afrikaans, it has been turned into a verb in S[outh] A[frican] I[ndian] E[nglish]. (The word has been forced to fit an English syntactic pattern.)]

naartjie /ˈnɑːtʃi/ *n.* and *adj.* Also **naartje(e), naartye, naatje(e), narchet, naret(e)ye, naretje, nartchie, nartjee, nartjie, nautjee**. [Afk., earlier S. Afr. Du., prob. ad. Tamil *nārattai* citrus.]

A. *n.*

1.a. A soft, loose-skinned variety of tangerine or mandarin orange; the tree which bears it, *Citrus reticulata* of the Rutaceae. Also *attrib.*

1790 tr. F. Le Vaillant's *Trav.* I. 34 The citrons .. and the oranges, especially that Kind called *nareteyes*, are excellent. **1812** A. PLUMPTRE tr. *H. Lichtenstein's Trav. in Sn Afr.* (1928) I. 57 The mandarine apple, called at the Cape *narretjes* [printed *marretjes*], is a sort of sweet-orange unknown in Europe. **1847** 'A BENGALI' *Notes on Cape of G.H.* 86 They have two kinds of oranges at the Cape, china oranges, and 'nautjees'. **1849** N.J. MERRIMAN *Cape Jrnls* (1957) 66 Had it not been .. for the narchets which Miss Currie had put up for me at Somerset, I should have suffered .. from .. thirst before reaching Graaff Reinet. **1861** 'A LADY' *Life at Cape* (1963) 75 As to the 'Van Rhum', some say it is made out of 'naartjee' peel – a species of mandarin orange. **1890** A.G. HEWITT *Cape Cookery* 59 Naartje Komfyt. Pare the naartjes very thinly, cut 4 slits in each. **1891** H.J. DUCKITT *Hilda's 'Where Is It?'* 22 Some 'Naartje' (Tangerine Orange) Peel. **1899** E.L. PRICE Letter. (Cory Library, MS 5973) July, Neither the oranges or the naartyes tempt me in the least. **1900** B.M. HICKS *Cape as I Found It* 129 There were all kinds of fruit .. pomegranates, oranges, naartjies. **1913** D. FAIRBRIDGE *Piet of Italy* 127 Beyond the orchard lay the *naartje* plantation, the trees laden now with little green balls. **1919** M.C. BRUCE *Golden Vessel* 87 It was the beginning of August .. and the orange and naartjie trees were laden with golden fruit. **1930** M. RAUBENHEIMER *Tested S. Afr. Recipes* 26 Dried 'naartjie' peel, powdered or cut up finely, gives a delicious flavour to milk tart. **1947** L.G. GREEN *Tavern of Seas* 61 Van der Hum. You detect the naartjie flavour at once .. flavouring extracted from the peel of the Cape naartjie. **1968** M. MULLER *Green Peaches Ripen* 77 We sat .. unable to resist nibbling Bella's *naartjie* preserve. [**1971** *Sunday Express* 28 Mar. 11 Couldn't the orange [of air-hostesses' uniforms] be toned down a little and the blue be slightly deeper? No wonder the poor girls are referred to as naartjies.] **1971** *Evening Post* 11 Sept. 5 Oranges, naartjies, lemons and cumcuats are all suitable for this type of planting. **1990** L. SAMPSON in *Frontline* Dec. 26 We passed a wedding where the bridesmaids wore naartjie coloured nylon. **1994** G. WILLOUGHBY in *Weekly Mail & Guardian* 17 June 42 He wins gold this year for his delicious naartjie liqueur.

b. With reference to the throwing of naartjies or their peel onto a rugby field to express disappointment (naartjies being easily obtainable during the rugby season).

1971 *Rand Daily Mail* 31 May 1 It was Naartjie Day at Ellis Park on Saturday, when thousands of fans subjected fellow spectators to a hail of naartjie peels. **1974** *Daily Dispatch* 20 July 8 It will become the in-thing to throw the referee with a nartchie. **1978** *Ibid.* 28 June 23, I am sure that as much as his leg injuries, the verbal naartjie-throwing is responsible for his hanging up the most dangerous kicking boots the game of rugby has ever seen. **1986** *Style* Feb. 31 Reasons for staying in South Africa ... 96. You can't throw naartjies at the ref in England. **1988** L. SHAW in *Ibid.* Feb. 42 Welcome to the racetrack ... Did you remember the earplugs/cushions/blockout/naartjies? **1989** [see BEER-BOEP]. **1989** *Sunday Times* 3 Sept. 28 Sparks were expected to fly in the final election debate on TV between Mr Pik Botha and Dr Denis Worrall. One wag even predicted that it would be a 'sixpack and naartjies' affair. **1991** I. COOK *Informant, Springs* Take some naartjies to the rugby.

2. *slang.* In the expression *to feel a (real) naartjie*, to feel like a fool, to feel an idiot.

1975 'BLOSSOM' in *Darling* 9 Apr. 95 Jislaaik, but you only feel a naartjie riding in the back of a truck with three drums of pig swill and a stack of moulting lucerne bales for company. **1977** *Ibid.* 18 July 123 Telling you, I felt a proper naartjie.

3. *comb.* **Naartjie Republic** *nonce*, 'Banana republic'.

1982 *Voice* 1 Aug. 4 We are too ready and willing to ridicule the rest of Africa with the contemptuous phraseology of 'Banana Republics', but our 'Naartjie Republic' is no great example of justice, dignity and freedom.

B. *adj.* Of the colour dark orange or tangerine.

1971 *Daily Dispatch* 16 Oct., Replacing the 'naartjie' hat is a chic bowler, decorated with an orange and blue airline emblem. **1987** G. SILBER in *Style* Dec. 100, I do not mind the dustbinmen, who wear naartjie overalls and whistle.

naat /nɑːt/ *n. Diamond-trade.* [Afk. (fr. Du. *naad*), seam, suture.] An irregularity in the structure of a diamond, caused by a change of direction in the grain; a 'knot' or blemish; a diamond having such a feature.

Used in the diamond industry world-wide.

1945 *Industrial Diamond Rev.* Sept. 205 Knot, naat (Min.), irregularity of crystal structure in a single crystal diamond. Because the cleavage planes cannot easily be found, it is generally believed that such stones have a greater resistance to abrasion. **1962** S. TOLANSKY *Hist. & Use of Diamond* 147 If changes in grain direction are encountered on a crystal (naat is the word for such a change), the impregnated wheel can readily cope. **1970** E. BRUTON *Diamonds* 190 The sawyer .. has .. to watch for any changes of hardness through an area of different crystallization. These naats sometimes have rope formation or spider's web formation in a stone and will turn the blade and spoil the cut. **1984** G. DAVIES *Diamond* 228 The blade .. will find it very difficult to make any progress if it comes up against a piece of the diamond which has a different crystallographic orientation. These mis-oriented pieces, the 'naats', are analogous to knots in a piece of wood.

naatje(e) var. NAARTJIE.

naboom /ˈnɑːbʊəm/ *n.* Also **gnaarboom, naaboom**. Pl. **-s**, occas. ‖**-bome** /ˈ-bʊəmə/. [Afk., prob. fr. a Khoikhoi word (perh. rel. to Nama *!na-* /ǃnɑ/ big, strong) + *boom* tree.] Any of several species of tree of the genus *Euphorbia*, esp. *E. tetragona* and *E. ingens*. Also *attrib.* See also CHANDELIER sense 3, and *milk-bush* sense (b) at MILK sense 2.

1875 S.W. DELL in *Cape Monthly Mag.* XI. July 12 To whom two nests I should have shown, In gnaarbooms green, to you unknown. **1913** C. PETTMAN *Africanderisms* 189 Gnaarboom, (The first part of this word appears to be of Hottentot origin, having an initial click; the Kaffir name for the tree is *um Hlonhlo*.) Euphorbia tetragona. **1917** R. MARLOTH *Common Names* 60 Naaboom, Euphorbia tetragona, E. grandidens, etc. S.E. coast districts. In Tr[ansvaal] applied to E. Cooperi and

E. ingens. **1939** S. Cloete *Watch for Dawn* 114 These endless morgen of forest brightened by the light green of the spekboom, darkened by isolated naboom*s*. **1955** T.V. Bulpin *Storm over Tvl* 24 Twenty-five miles from Nylstroom the road passed a small stream of clear water flowing through the wilderness. On its bank grew a number of Euphorbia Ingens, known colloquially as Nabome. **1958** R.E. Lighton *Out of Strong* 22 The broad, hill-dotted valley where the spiny nabooms clustered. **1961** Palmer & Pitman *Trees of S. Afr.* 239 All the tree Euphorbias described are commonly known as 'naboom'. According to the authors of 'The Succulent Euphorbieae', 'na' is a corruption of a Hottentot word 'gnap' meaning strong or energetic, and emphasizes the vigorous habit of growth of the trees. **1968** L.G. Green *Full Many Glorious Morning* 24 The natives .. toiled by the light of candles made of *naboom* leaves. **1976** A.P. Brink *Instant in Wind* 56 The gnarled, thorny shrubs were green from the moisture sucked up from very deep down .. hedgehog euphorbia and naboom, aloes, kiepersol and karee. **1977** *S. Afr. Panorama* Jan. 21 *(caption)* The majestic naboom and picturesque aloes highlight this view.

Nachmaal var. Nagmaal.

nacht-(a)apie, -(a)apje varr. nagapie.

Nachtmaal, -ma(h)l varr. Nagmaal.

nachtslang *n. obs.* Also **nachtschlange, nachtslaang**. [S. Afr. Du., *nacht* night + *slang* snake, serpent.] Any of several nocturnal snakes. **1.** night-adder sense 1. **2.** Either of two snakes of the Elapidae: **a.** garter snake; **b.** the coral snake, *Aspidelaps lubricus lubricus*. **3.** night-adder sense 2. In all senses also called night-serpent, night-snake.

1821 C.I. Latrobe *Jrnl of Visit* 124 The bite of the Nachtschlange, or night-serpent, is said by the Hottentot poison-doctors, to be uncurable. It is .. marked with dark blue or black, vermilion, and yellow rings. **1828** T. Pringle *Ephemerides* 111 It is time to haste My homeward walk across the waste, Lest my rash tread provoke the wrath Of nachtslang coil'd across the path. **1834** —— *Afr. Sketches* 280 There are several species of snakes which have come under my own observation, such as the *nacht-slang* (night-adder). *Ibid.* 284, I stood prepared, and instantly smote him dead; and afterwards found him to be one of the venomous sort called *nachtslang*. **1841** [see night-serpent]. **1849** A. Smith *Illust. of Zoo. of S. Afr.: Reptilia* Appendix 19 This snake occurs throughout Southern Africa, but nowhere in abundance. In the Colony it is, from its moving much during the night, known .. by the name of Nacht Slang. **1883** M.A. Carey-Hobson *Farm in Karoo* 189 Those little hornsmansches and nacht slaangs are as bad as any, although they are so small. **1937** *Guide to Vertebrate Fauna of E. Cape Prov.* (Albany Museum) II. 54 *Lamprophis aurora Linn. Nachtslang*, .. Olive brown or light olive-green above, with a long golden yellow line or row of orange spots from the top of the head along the centre of the back to the tip of the tail.

Nactu /ˈnæktuː, ˈnak-/ *n.* Acronym formed on *National Council of Trade Unions*, a labour federation formed in 1986 by the amalgamation of CUSA and the Azanian Confederation of Trade Unions. Also *attrib.*

Broadly aligned to the black consciousness movement, the organization was at first known as *CUSA-AZACTU*.

1988 Camay & Skhosana in *Frontline* Apr.-May 30 NACTU stresses black leadership. **1990** *Weekly Mail* 4 May 7 Nactu representative Cunningham Ngcukana said: 'The government is not serious about negotiations.' **1990** *City Press* 17 June 1 The gathering .. was convened by the PAC-aligned Nactu. **1991** *South News* 14 Nov. 3 Last week's stayaway has thrown a spanner in the works of unity between Cosatu and Nactu, South Africa's strongest trade union federations.

‖**nadors** /ˈnɑːdɔrs, -dɔːs/ *n.* [Afk., *na* after + *dors* thirst.] The extreme thirst experienced after drinking too much alcohol. See also babalaas *n.* sense a.

1970 S.E. Natham *Informant, Cape Town* Judging by my nadors this morning, I must have had a lot more to drink than I realized last night. **1972** *Cape Times* 14 Dec. 11 This is the time of the year, alas, when people are prone to wake up feeling tired and listless with a headache, maybe even a little sick, and of course, with a great *nadors*. **1989** D. Bristow in *Weekly Mail* 21 Apr. 29 The farmhouse was built in a dry river bed that hasn't see flowing water since great-grandpa got drunk one night, stepped outside, and in the morning was found — drowned. They say he drank the river dry to relieve his *nadors*.

Nafcoc /ˈnæfkɒk/ *n.* Also **NAFCOC**. Acronym formed on *National African Federated Chambers of Commerce*, an organization formed in 1969 to promote growth in the black business sector. Also *attrib.*

1978 *Survey of Race Rel.* (S.A.I.R.R.) 397 In August a delegation of African businessmen, representing the National African Federated Chambers of Commerce (Nafcoc), met with the Deputy Minister of Bantu Administration to request .. that urban Africans should be recognised as permanent communities with full rights and citizenship. **1982** *Voice* 11 July 4 Reporting on Soweto's Blackchain store's progress at this week's Nafcoc conference, chairman Mr S J J Lesolang said it had shown a 59 percent sales increase last year. **1984** R. Davies et al. *Struggle for S. Afr.* I. 119 NAFCOC grew out of the African Chamber of Commerce formed in the Johannesburg area in 1955. *Ibid.* 120 NAFCOC has promoted the emergence of a number of new African enterprises in South Africa. **1990** *Sunday Times* 4 Mar. 17 As founder of Nafcoc and a SA Foundation trustee, his potential as a political leader seems self-evident. **1994** *Style* May 77 Consider the following targets proposed by Nafcoc, the black business association, for companies listed on the Johannesburg Stock Exchange: by the year 2002, the boards of directors should be at least 30 percent black.

nagaapie var. nagapie.

nagana /nəˈgɑːnə/ *n. Pathology.* Also **ngana**. [Englished form of Zulu *u(lu)nakane*.] An often fatal disease of domestic livestock which is characterized by fevers, lethargy, and oedematous swellings, and caused by the parasite *Trypanosoma brucei*, which is transmitted by flies of the genus *Glossina*; fly sense 2 a; tsetse sense 2 a. Also *attrib.*

1895 D. Bruce *(title)* Preliminary report on the tsetse fly-disease, or nagana, in Zululand. **1896** *Nature* 16 Apr. 567 Nagana pursues a much slower course in cattle than in horses. **1904** *Quarterly Review* (U.K.) July 120 The 'fly districts' where nagana disease is rife. **1921** *E. Prov. Herald* 22 Jan., In the course of a lecture on new aspects of the disease nagana, Dr. Du Toit .. said .. it had been shown that ordinary flies could transmit the infection ... Sir David Bruce's theory that nagana and sleeping sickness were identical, had to be abandoned. **1923** *S. Afr.: Land of Outdoor Life* (S.A.R. & H.) 274 Since the outbreak of nagana disease, caused by the tsetse-fly, certain species of game have been declared 'nagana' game, these being waterbuck, Koodoo, wildebeest, buffalo, zebra and male bushbuck. *c*1936 *S. & E. Afr. Yr Bk & Guide* 760 Apart from the question of sleeping sickness, where *Glossina morsitans* is prevalent, it is rare for any domestic animal to escape death from 'nagana'. **1946** *Cape Times* 23 May 6 Urgent measures to be taken to combat nagana cattle disease in Natal. The tsetse fly is the culprit. **1963** S.H. Skaife *Naturalist Remembers* 43 As long ago as 1875 Colonel D. Bruce studied the life history of the tsetse fly in Zululand, and proved that this insect is the carrier of nagana. **1965** *New Scientist* (U.K.) 26 Aug. 504 Wild game don't suffer from nagana, the tsetse-borne trypanosome disease that disastrously affects domestic cattle. **1976** *E. Prov. Herald* 29 Sept. 15 The tsetse fly causes sleeping sickness in man and the dreaded disease, ngana, in cattle and is spread when an infected fly sucks the blood of a host. **1988** T.J. Lindsay *Shadow* (1990) 35 The vehicles passed through the old tsetse fly gates that once indicated the Health Department's boundary fence preventing flies and infected, but immune, game from entering the unsprayed areas and bringing the menace of sleeping sickness to humans or *nagana* to cattle.

nagapie /ˈnaxɑːpi/ *n.* Also **nagaapie**, and (formerly) **nacht a(a)pje, - (a)apie**. [Afk., earlier S. Afr. Du. *nachtaapje* fr. Du. *nacht* night + *aapje* little monkey (see -ie).] bush baby. Also *attrib.*, and *fig.* Occas. also **nagaap**.

1835 A. Smith *Diary* (1940) II. 160 *Galago maholi* is the Bush Baby or nag-aapie. [**1900**, *c*1911 see night-ape.] **1918** S.H. Skaife *Animal Life* 270 The lemurs, or *nacht aapjes*, are the lowest members of this order, and two species are found in South Africa. One occurs in the wooded districts of the Transvaal and Rhodesia and the other is found in Natal and Zululand. **1933** J. Juta *Look Out for Ostriches* 46, I knew immediately those eyes belonged to only one creature, the shy, mysterious little *nagaapie*. **1947** H.C. Bosman in L. Abrahams *Cask of Jerepigo* (1972) 188 The various other members of the simian race (including that wonderful little creature, the nagapie), have always fascinated me. **1953** D. Jacobson *Long Way from London* 125 One of those small animals that people are always warned against domesticating, for there is such great danger of their becoming rabid: a nagaap or bush-baby, a meerkat, one of those. **1976** *Sunday Times* 11 Apr. 8 Who could bear to see the nagapie charms of Goldie besmirched by association with serious sin? **1984** *S. Afr. Panorama* Nov. 15 *(caption)* Like a cuddly Walt Disney creation, is this wide-eyed nagapie (night ape), closely related to the large bushbaby. **1991** *Weekend Post* 5 Jan. 3 *(caption)* It's watermelon time again. Ronel Louw .. shares the delicious pink fruit with her pet *nagapie* (also known as a night-ape or owl monkey).

Nagmaal /ˈnaxmɑːl/ *n.* Also **Naachtmaal, Nach(t)maal, Nachtma(h)l, Nag(h)t Maal, Nag mal, Naughmal**, and with small initial. [Afk., fr. Du. *nachtmaal*, *nacht* night + *maal* meal.]
1. In the Dutch Reformed churches: the sacrament of Holy Communion; the communion service; the occasion, usu. four times a year, during which this service is held. Also *attrib.*

1833 *S. Afr. Almanac & Dir.* 200 At certain periods appointed for the administration of the Sacrament (Nachtmaal) this village displays a scene of great activity. **1836** R. Godlonton *Introductory Remarks to Narr. of Irruption* 17 The sacrament of the Lord's supper .. is administered once every three months in the district churches. At such seasons (called the 'nachtmaal') there is usually a very large congregation, many attending from the remotest part of the district. **1843** H. Dennison Letters. 183, I have comparatively nothing in the shop Naght Maal is Just here and here am I without good[s] without Money. **1843** *Cape of G.H. Almanac & Annual Register* 458 The great season for traffic is the period for the quarterly administration of the sacrament (or *nachtmaal*) on which occasion large numbers of farmers .. assemble, and the place assumes the appearance of a fair rather than an assemblage for the celebration of a solemn religious ordinance. **1844** J. Backhouse *Narr. of Visit* 94 Several of the family were setting out for Caledon, to attend the 'Nacht maal', *Night Meal*, or what is termed 'The Lord's Supper.' **1852** N.J. Merriman *Cape Jrnls* (1957) 195, I arrived just as the Boers were beginning to assemble for the quarterly *Nachtmahl* (communion) of their Church. **1879** R.J. Atcherley *Trip to Boerland* 210 In obedience to an old custom, the Boers of the district had trekked hither to partake of the nachtmaal, or sacrament. **1882** C. Du Val *With Show through Sn Afr.* I. 115 Many of these religionists — as indeed, I may say, many Boers of both species of faith — possess houses in the town which they only occupy once every three months, on the occasion of their 'Nachtmaal', or Communion celebration. **1899** D.S.F.A. Phillips *S. Afr. Recollections* 13 The Boers in out of the way places usually do their shopping at 'Nachtmaal' (The Sacrament of the Lord's Supper), which takes place every three months. **1908** M.C. Bruce *New Tvl* 48 Coming round by the church in the square I noticed a great number of trek-waggons .. the conveyances of farmers, who, coming from a great distance, brought their families to the nachtmaal which was to take place the following day, Sunday. **1911** M.S. EVANS *Black & White in S.E. Afr.* 50, I have often been struck at meetings of large numbers of Dutch families on occasions such as Nachtmaals .. with the apparently pleasant .. relations between .. family and .. servants. **1937** C.R. PRANCE *Tante Rebella's Saga* 64 Four times a year, for the inside of a week, the Nagmaal camp was a thronged and talkative clearing-house for all the news and gossip and scandal of an area the size of Wales. **1942** S. CLOETE *Hill of Doves* 20 The day had come at last, as all days did, nagmaals, festivals, Christmas, and birthdays that one thought would never come. **1944** J. MOCKFORD *Here Are S. Africans* 98 Both before and after actual *nagmaal*, the night-meal, the supper, the Lord's Supper, there was much visiting in the outspan, relatives and friends rejoicing in this rare occasion of reunion. **1948** *Cape Argus* 5 June (Mag. Sect.) 2 At nagtmaal the farmers drove in from miles around and opened up their little dorp dwellings. **1958** A. JACKSON *Trader on Veld* 34 Far or near, farmers visited the nearest church for Nagmaal (communion) at least once a quarter. Every village would be crowded with ox wagons and other vehicles; the wealthier farmers possessing small houses which they only occupied for that occasion. **1968** K. MCMAGH *Dinner of Herbs* 53 In those days of difficult communications and great distances the Boers strove to attend nachtmaal, the quarterly celebration of Holy Communion, at least once a year. **1981** *Daily Dispatch* 21 Feb. 2 A special collection was taken up at the quarterly Nagmaal service in the Dutch Reformed Church when R3 600 was received and donated to the Laingsburg Disaster Fund. **1994** F. CHISHOLM in *Cape Times* 9 Feb. 8 Imagine the impact of a semi-naked Madonna zooming up for *nagmaal* in Ventersdorp on the back of a noisy Harley Davidson.

2. A small wagon similar to a stage-coach, drawn by horses. Also *attrib.*

1910 J. BUCHAN *Prester John* (1961) 47 The owners and their families were travelling with them in wagons. Accordingly I had a light *naachtmaal* fitted up as a sort of travelling store, and with my two wagons full of building material joined the caravan. **1985** *S. Afr. Panorama* Oct. 42 This nagmaal (holy communion) horse carriage, adorns one of the world's few horse museums, in Richmond.

3. *comb.* **nagmaal chair**, a plain chair, sometimes with a half-moon back; **nagmaal huis** /-hœis/ [Afk. *nagmaalhuis, huis* house], SUNDAY HOUSE; **nagmaal tent**, see quot. 1968; **nagmaal wine**, communion wine.

1994 *E. Prov. Herald* 10 Mar. 2 Private Sale. Antique Furniture ... A superb collection of pieces of Antique Furniture .. Rosewood **Nagmaal Chair.** [**1882, 1948, 1958 nagmaal huis**: see sense 1.] **1974** *Weekend Post* 2 Nov. (Parade) 2 This house was originally the 'nagmaal huis' of the Muller family. **1968** *Farmer's Weekly* 3 Jan. 68 New **Nagmaal** Cottage Waterproof **tents**, 7 x 6 x 6, green, R25. **1975** *S. Afr. Panorama* Oct. 20 A common sight from mid-19th century to early 1930s was reconstructed at Rustenburg – Nagmaal tents pitched beside the church for a weekend of worship and socialising. **1979** *Ibid.* 11 Apr. 122 Nagmaal, Scout, Frame Tents of all sizes. **1952** C.L. LEIPOLDT *300 Yrs Cape Wine* 140 His wine was in great demand as a '*Nagmaal*' or Communion wine ... Oom Abram Mouton .. of the historic farm Brakfontein .. made a '**Nagmaal' wine** almost, but not quite, equal to the Worcester wine. **1967** W.A. DE KLERK *White Wines* 19 There was the famous *Nagmaal* wine of Abraham Mouton of Brakfontein, near Clanwilliam, or the even more famous *Nagmaal* wine of Koos Hugo of Worcester. **1978** *Sunday Times* 5 Nov. 11 It was hardly a noble vintage. Sweet and red, almost straight off the vine ... Nella .. said it tasted just like nagmaal wine. **1987** *Fair Lady* 18 Mar. 112 He had run out of *Nagmaal* wine during the service, and left his congregation .. singing hymns of thanksgiving for the past 20 minutes. **1991** G. ETHERINGTON in *E. Prov. Herald* 16 Nov. (Leisure) 4 Throughout, the organist is fortified with nagmaal wine.

Hence (*nonce*) **nagmaalize** *v. intrans.* [Eng. v.-forming suffix *-ize*], to participate in nagmaal; **nagmaalist** *n.* [Eng. suffix *-ist*, designating a follower or adherent of (a movement, philosophy, etc.)], one who goes to nagmaal.

1920 R.Y. STORMBERG *Mrs Pieter de Bruyn* 12, I suspect that your benedict brother is not an habitual nachtmaalist – but that's by the way ... You wouldn't think from the tone of this that I am nachtmaalising, would you?

nagotie var. NEGOTIE.

Nagt Maal var. NAGMAAL.

‖**naloop** /ˈnɑːlʊəp/ *n.* [Afk., *na* after + *loop* run (as of a liquid).] The last 'feints' or final weak runnings of a brandy still. Also *attrib.* Cf. VOORLOOP *n.*

1913 C. PETTMAN *Africanderisms* 333 *Naloop*, .. The weak brandy that flows after distilling. **1970** M. WEITZMAN *Informant, Johannesburg* Naloop. Weak distilled brandy. The naloop is not pleasant to drink. **1977** *Family Radio & TV* 19 Sept. 51 Every farmer has his own infallible method of telling when his brew's reached the right strength and the *naloop* begins. *Ibid.* 53 All the stokers swear to its medicinal value. Tannie Serfontein has developed her herbal naloop practice to the point where she can administer a blend for any complaint. **1990** M. SHAFTO in *Weekend Argus* 9 June 11 He would open a tap and let the *naloop* run off.

Nama /ˈnɑːmə/ *adj.* and *n.* [See next.]

A. *adj.*

1. Of or pertaining to the Nama (see sense B 1); NAMAQUA *adj.*

1862 W.H.I. BLEEK *Comparative Grammar*, The Nama language .. is represented by a large amount of missionary literature. **1864** —— tr. *Hottentot Fables & Tales* p.xxix, To make our available stock of Nama Hottentot literature quite complete. **1881** T. HAHN *Tsuni-‖Goam* 3 In the Nama language, one of the Khoikhoi idioms, the Bushmen are called Sā-n (com. plur.). **1928** H. VEDDER in *Native Tribes of S.W. Afr.* 140 If one cannot think in the Nama language, one will never be able to learn to speak it. **1966** J.H. GREENBERG *Lang. Afr.* 68 Nama Hottentot indicates the past by an element *go* (in the usual orthography). **1978** *Drum* Aug. 58, I am a Nama-guy of Namibia, 21 years old and would like to correspond with ladies and gentlemen between the ages of 18 to 28.

2. *Geology.* Designating or pertaining to a Precambrian-Cambrian sedimentary rock formation found in the south-western part of Southern Africa. In the special collocations ***Nama Group, -System***: this geological formation.

1965 HAMILTON & COOKE *Geology for S. Afr. Students* 199 In the South African region no clearly identifiable fossil-bearing deposits of Cambrian age are known but the Nama System of South-West Africa extends southwards into the Cape and is almost certainly Cambrian. For this reason, the term 'pre-Nama' can be used as a rough parallel to Precambrian. *Ibid.* 327 The western geosyncline became active again in Nama times and in a shallow sea there were deposited coarse and fine sediments of various types. **1972** J.H. WELLINGTON in *Std Encycl. of Sn Afr.* V. 163 The radiometric age-dating of the granites intrusive into the Malmesbury beds to the north-east of Cape Town has shown this formation to belong to an orogeny of 550–610m year range and to be of Nama origin. With the Nama system Southern African geology passes from the Precambrian to the Cambrian. **1980** L.E. KENT *Stratigraphy of S. Afr.* (Dept of Mineral & Energy Affairs) I. 495 Schenck (1885 ..) introduced the terms 'Namaqua-Schiefer, -Sandstein und -Kalkstein' for the horizontally disposed strata of the Huib and Han-ami Plateaux of the central and southern parts of the former Deutsch-Südwest-Afrika. In a subsequent paper (1893) he shortened 'Namaqua' to Nama ... Wagner (1916 ..) considered that the Nama System was .. the equivalent of the Transvaal System. *Ibid.* 498 The first macrofossils from the Nama Group were discovered .. in 1908 and 1914.

B. *n.* Pl. unchanged, **-s**, or **Naman**.

1. A member of one of the four main Khoikhoi peoples of western South Africa and Namibia; NAMAQUA *n.* sense 1. See also BONDELSWART, CHINESE HOTTENTOT, KHOIKHOI sense 1.

1881 T. HAHN *Tsuni-‖Goam* 89, I afterwards made him a present of ammunition, and, as anxious as a Nama is to possess that most precious material, he said: 'No'. **1928** H. VEDDER in *Native Tribes of S.W. Afr.* 119 In about the year 1830, strenuous fighting was going on between the Nama and the Herero. *Ibid.* 127 The Nama has always considered himself to be a master and he has always deemed labour beneath his dignity. **1930** C.G. SELIGMAN *Races of Afr.* (1939) 34 The customary division of the Hottentots into four main groups – Naman, Korana, Gonaqua, and Old Cape Hottentots. **1930** [see NAMAQUA *n.* sense 1]. **1961** O. LEVINSON *Ageless Land* 25 He sent a member of his group, Pieter Brand, with seven Namas, mounted on oxen, to travel further north. **1970** M. WILSON *1000 Yrs before Van Riebeeck* 7 In 1661 Nama (a section of the Khoikhoi) living near the mouth of the Orange River, told the Dutch settlers at the Cape of a people, the Brijckje, living north of the Orange. **1975** J.P. VAN S. BRUWER in *Std Encycl. of Sn Afr.* V. 607 The Nama (also called Naman or Namaqua) consisted of two groups: the Little Nama, living in the North-Western Cape south of the Orange River, and the Great Nama, living in South-West Africa. The latter formed a number of tribes, six of which formed an alliance. *Ibid.* VIII. 28 'Namaqua' is the plural form of Nama, the name of the large Hottentot tribe who lived here when the first whites came to South Africa ... The Namas have always lived in the southern half of South West Africa ... They have always been pastoralists and do not practise agriculture. **1982** *Voice* 18 July 9 The Hereros and the Namas were almost exclusively pastoral peoples: they farmed mainly with sheep, goats, cattle and horses. **1988** A. HALL-MARTIN et al. *Kaokoveld* 56 At Sesfontein and Warmguelle .. a community of Nama, or Hottentots of the Topnaar and Swartbooi tribes, are found. **1991** *Bulletin* (Centre for Science Dev.) Mar. 3 The impact of mission work on the Nama and Oorlams was fundamental because it stimulated new needs outside the traditional redistributive system.

2. The language of this people.

1883 R.N. CUST *Mod. Langs of Afr.* II. 439 The Directors of the Rhenish Society .. wrote in 1882 to the British amd Foreign Bible Society to arrest any further printing of Books of the Old Testament in Nama, as that language was being superseded by Dutch. **1908** T.G. TUCKER *Introd. Nat. Hist. Lang.* 148 Hottentot dialects: viz. *Nama* (of the Namaqua) to the north-west, [etc.]. **1930** I. SCHAPERA *KhoiSan Peoples* 429 In the Southern Group and in Nama there are two forms for the pronoun in the first person plural, one including the person addressed with the speaker, the other excluding him. **1966** J.H. GREENBERG *Lang. Afr.* 68 In Nama there is no phonemic distinction between k and g. *c*1980 *S. Afr. 1979: Off. Yrbk* (Dept of Info.) 111 It is the form of these languages, especially Nama, that is our prototype of what a Khoe or Hottentot language should be. **1983** *S. Afr. 1983: Off. Yrbk* (Dept of Foreign Affairs & Info.) 107 The Khoe languages constitute a language family ... The major literary language is Nama.

Namaqua /nəˈmækwə, -ˈmɑːk-/ *n.* and *adj.* Also **Namaaqua, Namacqua, Namacque, Namagwa, Namaquoi, Namiquoi, Nimiqua.** Pl. **-s**, or unchanged. [Nama (Khoikhoi) *Nama*, prob. fr. *nami, nams* tongue (referring to the characteristic clicks in the Nama language) + masculine pl. suffix *-qua* men, people. (The preferred modern form is *Nama*.)]

A. *n.*

1. NAMA *n.* sense 1.

The Namaqua were described by the early settlers as consisting of two peoples, the 'Greater Namaqua' and the 'Lesser (or Little) Namaqua': see quot. 1930 (which includes a list of the principal Namaqua clans).

1688 G. TACHARD *Voy. to Siam* 74 The *Namaquas* .. are all tall of Stature and strong, have good natural sense ... They seldom laugh, and speak very little. **1670** [see COCHOQUA]. **1731** G. MEDLEY tr. *P. Kolb's Present State of Cape of G.H.* I. 66 We come now to the two Nations, call'd the *Greater* and *Lesser Namaqua.* The *Lesser* lies on the Coast; the *Greater* is the next Nation East ward. **1790** tr. *F. Le Vaillant's Trav.* I. 133 The country of the great Namaquois. **1795** C.R. HOPSON tr. *C.P. Thunberg's Trav.* I. 307 Two great and famous nations, the *Little Namaquas,* who live on the sea-coast, and the *Great Namaquas,* who reside farther from it. **1812** A. PLUMPTRE tr. *H. Lichtenstein's Trav. in Sn Afr.* (1928) I. 170 He was of the tribe called Grosse Namaaquas. **1821** *Missionary Notices* 119 The *figure* of the Namacquas is by no means without attractions. They are generally taller than the Hottentots within the Colony, and are quite erect, and well proportioned. **1838** J.E. ALEXANDER *Exped. into Int.* I. 56 We got milk for tobacco from the yellow faced and Chinese-looking Namaquas. *Ibid.* 192 The Great Namaquas are taller than the Little Namaquas, but have the same general resemblances, their colour being yellowish brown, hair crisp and curled, noses and eyes small, faces triangular, lips protruding. *Ibid.* 260 Henrick came from his huts to visit me; he was a spare and athletic Namaqua, of forty years of age. **1841** B. SHAW *Memorials* 20 The Namacquas .. are divided into two distinct tribes, called the Little and the Great Namacquas, but so far resemble each other, that it would be useless to treat of them separately. *Ibid.* 270 This Namacqua .. was a man of deep piety, and of fervent zeal for the glory of God. **1877** *Sel. Comm. Report on Mission to Damaraland* 95 The northern Namaquas were alone engaged in the war with the Damaras, and it is only amongst them .. that the ill-treating and robbery of traders and others have settled into a custom. **1883** F. GALTON *Inquiries into Human Faculty* 204 The Bantus, after endless struggles among themselves, were being pushed aside at the time I visited them by the incoming Namaquas. **1904** A.K. KEANE *Africa* II. 182 The Namaqua proper, formerly said to number several hundred thousand, are now reduced to little over 20,000 including 3,000 settled in Little Namaqualand south of the Orange River. **1920** S.M. MOLEMA *Bantu Past & Present* 31 The best known of the tribes are the Nama-qua, or people of Nama ('qua' meaning 'people or men of') the Kora-qua, better known as Korannas, and the Geri-qua or Griquas. **1930** I. SCHAPERA *KhoiSan Peoples* 47 The fourth and best known division of the Hottentots are the *Naman,* spoken of more frequently as the Namaquas. They were classified by the early Dutch settlers into two main groups: the Little Namaqua, living south of the Orange River in what is now Little Namaqualand, and the Great Namaqua, living north of the Orange River in the southern parts of what is now South West Africa. *Ibid.* 48 The Great Namaqua were subdivided into seven tribal groups ... These groups were the *Gei‖Khauan* (otherwise known by their Dutch name *Rooi Natie*) ... the *!Gami ≠Nun (bondelswarts),* in the district of Warmbad .. the *‖Haboben (Veldskoendragers),* round Koes and Hasuur; the *!Khara Gei Khoin (Simon Coppers* or *Franzmanns*) .. the *‖Khau/Goan (Swartboois),* who lived at Rehoboth till about 1870, when they removed first to Ameib, and then to Fransfontein in the southern part of the Koakoveld .. the *‖O Gein (Groot Doode),* who formerly roamed about the upper courses of the Great Fish River, but ceased to exist some fifty years ago .. and the *≠Aunin* (or *!Naranis Topnaars*), of whom some live round Zesfontein in the Kaokoveld and the others at Walvis Bay. **1977** R. ELPHICK *Kraal & Castle* 135 To modern scholars the Namaqua are the most familiar of all Khoikhoi peoples; however, in the seventeenth century they were only on the fringes of the Dutch consciousness.

2. *comb.* In the names of animals: **Namaqua Afrikander**, a hardy variety of Afrikander sheep (see AFRIKANDER *n.* sense 7), found in the relatively dry parts of the Cape; **Namaqua dove** [prob. tr. S. Afr. Du. *Namaquasduyf*], the dove *Oena capensis* of the Columbidae; **Namaqua grouse** *obs.*, **- partridge** *obs.* [prob. tr. S. Afr. Du. *Namaqua patrijs,* see quots 1867 and 1897], *Namaqua sandgrouse* (see below); **Namaqua pheasant**, the *Natal francolin* (see NATAL sense c), *Francolinus natalensis*; **Namaqua sandgrouse**, any of four species of African sand-grouse of the Pteroclidae, esp. *Pterocles namaqua* (see also KELKIEWYN sense a).

1957 *Handbk for Farmers* (Dept of Agric.) III. 221 The **Namaqua Africander**. Both the Ronderib and Namaqua were developed from the same parent stock and the difference must, therefore, be ascribed to the difference in climatic and feeding conditions in the areas where these breeds originated. [**Namaqua dove**: **1795** C.R. HOPSON tr. *C.P. Thunberg's Trav.* II. 34 A small dove .. called Maquas Duyv (*Colomba capensis*) frequented the gardens, and there sought its food.] **1801** J. BARROW *Trav.* I. 283 Along the road were numbers of that beautiful little pigeon, called here the Namaaqua dove, not larger than a sparrow. **1864** T. BAINES *Explor. in S.-W. Afr.* 124 A pretty Namaqua dove fluttered about in abortive efforts to sip the water. **1884** LAYARD & SHARPE *Birds of S. Afr.* 573 (Pettman), This exquisite little dove .. is known by the name of *Namaqua dove* to the Dutch Cape Colonists. **1905** J. DU PLESSIS *1000 Miles in Heart of Afr.* 137 As for the birds they abound in every bush .. turtle-doves and little black-eyed Namaqua doves. **1936** E.L. GILL *First Guide to S. Afr. Birds* 112 *Namaqua dove,* Usually seen on the wing, when its very small size, and great speed, its long tail, and the cinnamon in its wings make it very recognizable. **1947** J. STEVENSON-HAMILTON *Wild Life in S. Afr.* 291 Doves ... The little namaqua (*Oena capensis*) appears to be a winter migrant to the eastern Transvaal low country. **1972** *Shooting Times & Country Mag.* (U.K.) 27 May 24 Mourning, laughing and even tiny, wagtail-sized Namaque [*sic*] doves arrive to raid the crops. **1983** K.B. NEWMAN *Newman's Birds* 196 *Namaqua dove,* .. The call is a seldom heard, explosive 'twoo-hoo'. Commonly seen in grassland, fallow fields, thornveld and eroded areas, particularly in drier regions. **1993** M. OETTLE in *Weekend Post* 9 Oct. (Leisure) 7 *Oena capensis,* Namaqua dove, *isavukazana.* A small-bodied dove with a long, pointed, almost black tail and black face and throat, with white underparts and chestnut flight feathers. **1994** A. CRAIG in M. Roberts tr. *J.A. Wahlberg's Trav. Jrnls 1838–56* 46 Namaqua dove *Oena capensis,* a bird of the dry interior which appears in coastal areas irregularly. **1801** J. BARROW *Trav.* I. 264 Cape partridges and the **Namaaqua** [*printed* Hamaaqua] **grous**, were equally plentiful. **1887** A.A. ANDERSON *25 Yrs in Waggon* II. 20 Many kinds of beautiful birds, mocking-birds, swarms of the butcher-bird, namaqua-grouse. **1790** tr. *F. Le Vaillant's Trav.* II. 376 Moor-fowl of a very beautiful species, which were accustomed to come by thousands, and light on the borders of this fountain. The Hottentots of the colonies call them **Nimiqua partridge**. **1802** [see FOUNTAIN]. **1812** A. PLUMPTRE tr. *H. Lichtenstein's Trav. in Sn Afr.* (1828) I. 87 We had here a Namaqua partridge ... These birds .. are about the size of a small pigeon, and very delicate. **1822** W.J. BURCHELL *Trav.* I. 265 At this place we met with, for the first time, the *Namaqua Partridge,* a very small species of Grous. **1838** J.E. ALEXANDER *Exped. into Int.* I. 46 At the pools, flights of Namaqua partridges rose noiselessly from the stony ground, and .. winged their whirring flight in gyrations through the air. **1866** J. LEYLAND *Adventures* 141 Large flocks of Namaqua Partridges, or Sand-grouse, of which there are two or three kinds, were seen in the locality. [**1867** E.L. LAYARD *Birds of S. Afr.* 277 The *Namaqua Patrys* of the colonists is very abundant on the arid Karroo plains throughout the colony and Namaqualand.] **1882** J. NIXON *Among Boers* 76 R shot some Namaqua partridges near the dam. Split down the middle and cooked on a gridiron, they offer one of the most dainty titbits wild cookery can supply. **1897** H.A. BRYDEN *Nature & Sport* 33 The only species of sand-grouse found in Cape colony, south of the Orange River, is pterocles tachypetes, known all over South Africa by the name 'Namaqua Partridge,' long since erroneously bestowed upon it by the Dutch Boers. **1920** F.C. CORNELL *Glamour of Prospecting* 74 At the pools of shallow water lying in the roads were Namaqua partridges by the thousand. These little plump, pretty game-birds are really a sand-grouse. **1937** H. SAUER *Ex Afr.* 56 The Namaqua partridge or common sand-grouse. **1955** V. DE KOCK *Fun They Had* 159 Bryden .. writes [in 1897] of the strangely pigeon-like Sand-grouse, and the so-called Namaqua partridge, which gather at veld pools at sunset. **1892** W.L. DISTANT *Naturalist in Tvl* 105 (Pettman), The Natal Francolin, called by the Dutch the **Namaqua pheasant**. **1913** C. PETTMAN *Africanderisms* 334 *Namaqua pheasant, Francolinus natalensis.* It is known as the 'Coast pheasant' in Natal. **1893** H.A. BRYDEN *Gun & Camera* 477 This species drink only in the evening; the **Namaqua sandgrouse** between eight and ten in the morning, and sometimes in the afternoon. **1918** S.H. SKAIFE *Animal Life* 231 Namaqua sandgrouse is the commonest species and is abundant in all parts of the Karoo. **1923** HAAGNER & IVY *Sketches* 205 The Namaqua Sandgrouse (*Pteroclurus Namaqua*) needs no further description than the attenuated centre tail feathers. **1964** L.G. GREEN *Old Men Say* 164 You may .. see the little Namaqua sandgrouse drinking round the vleis before sundown. **1971** K.B. NEWMAN *Birdlife in Sn Afr.* (1979) 150 Scientists have seen Namaqua Sandgrouse males fly in from their morning drink, land near their chicks and give them a drink from their wet plumage. **1984** G.L. MACLEAN *Roberts' Birds of Sn Afr.* 298 *Namaqua Sandgrouse,* Kelkiewyn. *Pterocles namaqua* ... *Habits:* .. flies up to 60km or more to water in flocks of hundreds or thousands daily, 1–3 hours after sunrise. **1991** *Best of S. Afr. Short Stories* (Reader's Digest Assoc.) 10 The birds for which the hunter 'stood waiting in the rushes' could well have been Namaqua sandgrouse (*Pterocles namaqua*), which were called 'partridges' in the early days.

B. *adj. obs.* NAMA *adj.* sense 1. Always *attrib.*

1838 J.E. ALEXANDER *Exped. into Int.* II. 72 Our captives belonged to a large tribe of red men, speaking the Namaqua language. **1841** B. SHAW *Memorials* 18 The Hottentot family is composed of the original Hottentot, Little Namacqua, Bushman, and Coranna tribes. **1841** *Ibid.* [see CLAPPING]. **1842** [see BERG DAMARA]. **1851** J. TINDALL *Jrnl* (1959) 145 Great enmity is manifested because while I had a few cattle remaining, I took them from thievish Namaqua shepherds, gave them to the care of Basterds and Damaras. They do not do well. **1889** F. GALTON *Trav. in S. Afr.* 41 The agents in this history are Namaqua 'Oerlams,' or Namaquas born in or near the colony, often having Dutch blood and a good deal of Dutch character in their veins. The Namaqua Hottentots look at these Oerlams with great jealousy.

Namaqualand daisy /nəˌmækwəlænd ˈdeɪzi/ *n. phr.* [*Namaqualand* (see NAMAQUALANDER) + Eng. *daisy.*] The annual plant *Dimorphotheca sinuata* of the Asteraceae, orig. a wild flower indigenous to Namaqualand but now widely cultivated; its daisy-like yellow, orange, or white flowers; *Cape marigold,* see CAPE sense 2 a; also called AFRICAN DAISY. Also occas. **Namaqua daisy.**

[*c***1911** C.L. BIDEN in S. Playne *Cape Col.* 618 The Namaqualand marigold (*Dimorphotheca auratiaca*) seems to spring up in a single night; and the veld that was parched and dry a few days before the rainfalls resembles one continuous Persian carpet.] **1963** M.G. MCCOY *Informant, Port Elizabeth* 5 Sept. It's looking lovely again, lots of bokbaai and Namaqualand daisies, and sparaxis and bobbejaantjies and freezias. **1969** M. BENSON *At Still Point* (1988) 185 My news is: I have a garden! Small but flourishing. Namaqualand daisies, iceland poppies just over, phlox, sweetpeas coming on. And lettuce! **1973** *S. Afr. Garden & Home* Sept. 60 The Namaqualand daisies I scattered in every vacant patch are a carpet of yellow. **1983** *S. Afr. Panorama* Jan. [Back cover], The list of South African floral immigrants settled over the surface of the earth is impressive: proteas, gladioli, chincherinchees, arum lilies, erica, agapanthus, geraniums, the lowly Namaqualand daisy, and many others. **1986** G. HEARN in *Conserva* Dec. 13 Here we are in the Namaqualand broken veld and as we swing south towards Kammieskroon, the fields and hillsides are covered with the

Namaqualand daisy (Dimorphotheca sinuata). **1989** P. LEE in *Sunday Times* 26 Feb. (Mag. Sect.) 37 Namaqualand Daisies ... These magnificent flowers, also known as African daisies or Cape Marigolds, are Namaqualand's pride and joy. **1991** J. COOPER in *Weekend Post* 5 Oct. 7 The flowers of the daisy family called Namaqualand daisies are the most prolific, ranging in colour from white and creams, through all shades of yellow to a brilliant orange. **1994** *E. Prov. Herald* 26 Mar. 9 One of the most desirable annuals is the Namaqualand daisy. **1994** M. WASSERFALL in *S. Afr. Garden & Home* Sept. 4 How wonderful are the Namaqua daisies, the freesias, sparaxis, *bobbejaantjies*, felicias and all the other colourful flowers that greet us at this time.

Namaqualander /nəˈmækwəˌlændə/ *n.* [*Namaqualand* (fr. NAMAQUA + Eng. or Afk. *land*) + Eng. or Afk. suffix *-er*, expressing the sense 'a resident in', 'a native or'.] An inhabitant of Namaqualand, a large, sparsely-populated district of the Northern Cape.

1961 L.E. VAN ONSELEN *Trekboer* 93 Maritz suggested that the very least the Government could have done, was to compensate Namaqualanders for their losses. **1987** W. STEENKAMP *Blockhouse* 13 The people .. had a strange sort of pity for us because we were not Namaqualanders. **1988** M. URSON in *Personality* 6 June 62 Jopie Kotze, a big greying Namaqualander .. was raised on the farm *Mesklip* outside Springbok.

Namiquoi var. NAMAQUA.

nam-nam var. NUM-NUM.

nanny *n. Offensive*. Often *derog*. Also **nannie**. [Transf. use of general Eng. *nanny* nursemaid.] A demeaning term for a black woman; used also as a term of address.

1956 *New Age* 30 Aug. 6 It [*sc.* a recording of the song *Fanakalo*] carries the same stigma as the words used directly to them, 'Boy,' 'Jim' or 'Nannie.' **1966** L.G. BERGER *Where's Madam* 142 'Do you want a lift nanny?' I ask them, but apparently 'nanny' is a term that native girls hate — the same as their being called 'my girl' or 'Mary'. **1985** A. KLAASTE in *Frontline* Dec. 32 It is possibly the dread that their children should become a replication of 'Boys' and nannies, always shuffling the foot and scratching the head in front of authority (whites). **1993** *Informant, Grahamstown* My husband hated my Afro — he said it was like going to bed with a nanny.

Napac /ˈneɪpæk/ *n.* Also **NAPAC**. Acronym formed on *Natal Performing Arts Council*, a parastatal body established in the early 1960s to promote the performing arts in the then province of Natal (KwaZulu-Natal). Also *attrib.* See also CAPAB, PACOFS, PACT.

1970 *Daily News* 25 May, Hand-over to Napac urged. The Committee .. will recommend .. that the orchestra should be handed over to the Natal Performing Arts Council (Napac). **1971** *Personality* 28 May 84 Ian did three plays for NAPAC. **1990** *Stanger Mail* 2 Mar. 5 Brochures and further information are available from NAPAC's music organiser. **1992** C. DU PLESSIS in *Pace* Sept. 156 While he was studying, Raphael remained in the Napac chorus. **1993** H. TYLER in *Weekly Mail & Guardian* 5 Nov. 43 Napac has cut its staff, lost its drama company, survived a fire and death threats — and its troubles still aren't over.

naras /ˈnaras/ *n.* Also **(!)nara**, **'nara(s)**, **!naras**, **narra**. [Khoikhoi *!naras*.] A leafless, spiny, prostrate shrub of the Namib desert, *Acanthosicyos horrida* of the Cucurbitaceae; the large melon-like fruit of this plant, which provides both food and drink; *Wonder of the Waste*, see WONDER sense 1. Also *attrib.*

1838 J.E. ALEXANDER *Exped. into Int.* II. 67 We found the new fruit 'naras of which I had first heard from the Boschmans of Ababies. The 'naras was growing on little knolls of sand; the bushes were about four or five feet high, without leaves, and with apposite thorns on the light and dark green striped branches. **1841** — in B. Shaw *Memorials* 162 After allaying our hunger and thirst with some ripe 'naras, the entire support of the Bay people, for two or three .. months, .. we continued our march among the sand hills. **1853** F. GALTON *Narr. of Explorer in Tropical S. Afr.* 21, I have mentioned above the 'Nara, a prickly gourd, which .. is the staple food of these Hottentots. **1856** C.J. ANDERSSON in F. Goldie *Ostrich Country* (1968) Ostriches are at all times more or less numerous on the Naarip Plain, but more particularly so at this season, on account of the Naras being now ripe (Naras being a kind of desert water-melon). **1881** T. HAHN *Tsuni-||Goam* 47 'Naras. This fruit is a *Cucurbitacea*, almost as large as a new-born child's head. The flesh of it is eaten raw, and the seeds are kept for the dry season, when there is no fruit. The seeds taste almost like almonds. **1889** F. GALTON *Trav. in S. Afr.* 11 The 'Nara, with long runners, covered numerous sand hillocks. [*Note*] The comma before N means that the letter is preceded by a Hottentot click. **1894** R. MARLOTH in *Trans. of S. Afr. Phil. Soc.* p.lxxxiv, The 'Naras' (*Acanthosicyos horrida*). **1906** B. STONEMAN *Plants & their Ways* 276 The western coast strip is a weird desert producing .. the naras, or *Acanthosicyos horrida*. **1916** W. VERSVELD & G.F. BRITTEN in *S. Afr. Jrnl of Science* XII. vi. 234 (*title*) Notes on the chemistry of the !Naras plant (*Acanthosicyos horrida* Hook). **1917** R. MARLOTH *Common Names* 60 *Naras, Acanthosicyos horrida*. A remarkable cucurbitaceous leafless plant on some dunes of the Namib .. where subterranean water exists, even if brackish and at great depth. **1926** M. NATHAN *S. Afr. from Within* 216 Even the desert flora is full of interest, containing species which are rare, curious or beneficial such as .. the narra which grows in the sand-dunes of the western coast, and, with its fattening properties is the only plant of economic value. **1930** I. SCHAPERA *KhoiSan Peoples* 22 There is the *!naras* melon, whose fruit is sufficiently succulent to provide a substitute for water. **1946** L.G. GREEN *So Few Are Free* 165 The Hottentots rely on a strange desert plant for nourishment. This is the narra ... The ripe narra is full of edible seeds, which are treated in many ways by the Hottentots. Boiled, they make a porridge. Tough pancakes are formed by the narra fluid and stored for months. Narra beer may be brewed from the syrupy juice. **1959** G. JENKINS *Twist of Sand* 267 The trails of naras creeper would provide some sort of fuel. **1961** O. LEVINSON *Ageless Land* 12 The straggling .. thorny bush, called Naras or 'Wonder of the Waste' .. is found nowhere else in the world. In its battle with Nature, this pumpkin plant has ceased to grow any leaves at all, their function being fulfilled by big green thorns; while its main root searches hungrily for moisture some twenty to forty feet underground. **1972** I.C. VERDOORN in *Std Encycl. of Sn Afr.* V. 82 *Naras*, .. This fruit is eaten fresh or is buried, and so preserved for future use. A sugar beer is made of the pulp, and the seeds when roasted are relished as nuts ... Another method of utilising the fruits is to boil the entire contents in a pot and .. pressing the pulp into flat cakes. These are dried in the sun and later used for making a kind of soap. **1977** K.F.R. BUDACK in A. Traill *Khoisan Ling. Studies 3* 4 The annual harvesting of the *!nara* fruit. **1988** A. HALL-MARTIN et al. *Kaokoveld* 4 Plants such as the dollar bush .. , the low-growing coastal ganna .. and narra (*Acanthosicyos horrida*) have an extensive root system under the sand which helps to stabilise the dune hummocks.

narchet, **naret(e)ye**, **naretje** varr. NAARTJIE.

Narina /nəˈriːnə/ *n.*[2] Also with small initial. [So named by Francois le Vaillant after a Khoikhoi woman with whom he formed a romantic attachment, and who, at his request, adopted the name *Narina* (Khoikhoi 'flower'). Cf. NERINE.] In full ***Narina trogon***: the tropical and subtropical forest bird *Apaloderma narina* of the Trogonidae, noted for its bright metallic green and red plumage; BUSH LORY.

[**1790** tr. *F. Le Vaillant's Trav.* I. 382, I found her name difficult to be pronounced, disagreeable to the ear, and very insignificant according to my ideas; I therefore gave her a new one, and called her *Narina*, which, in the Hottentot language, signifies a flower. **1800** F. LE VAILLANT *Histoire Naturelle des Oiseaux d'Afrique* V. 104 *Le Couroucou Narina*, ... Ce couroucou d'Afrique auquel je donne le nom de *narina* qui en langue hottentote signifie *fleur*, a sans doute beaucoup de rapport avec le couroucou à ventre rouge de Cayenne.] *c*1808 C. VON LINNÉ *System of Natural Hist.* VIII. 214 *The Narina Curucui*, The African species has considerable resemblance to the Red bellied Curucui of America. **1856** R.E.E. WILMOT *Diary* (1984) 132 Here .. lives the rosy breasted trogon, a bird so beautiful that le Vaillant named it after his Hottentot love 'Narina'. **1903** STARK & SCLATER *Birds of S. Afr.* III. 122 The Narina, so called by Levaillant after a Hottentot beauty for whom he professed great admiration, is found only in thick bush, where it creeps about or sits motionless and voiceless. **1923** HAAGNER & IVY *Sketches* 182 Of the family Trogonidae, South Africa possesses but a single species, the beautiful Narina Trogon (*Apaloderma narina*). It is metallic green above and below as far as the chest, the remainder of the underparts being bright crimson. **1937** M. ALSTON *Wanderings* 54 The Narina trogon must .. have a chapter to its own beautiful self. **1989** A. CRAIG in *Birding in S. Afr.* Vol.41 No.4, 124 His [*sc.* Le Vaillant's] faithful servant Klaas and the Hottentot beauty Narina have .. been commemorated in Klaas's Cuckoo .. and Narina Trogon. **1992** *S. Afr. Panorama* Mar.-Apr. 120 Birds twitter in a lush botanical garden. Some are like flitting jewels — the red flash of the lourie or the rare orange-green narina trogon.

Narina *n.*[1] var. NERINE.

narra var. NARAS.

nartchie, **nartjee**, **-jie** varr. NAARTJIE.

Nasionale Jeugbond see JEUGBOND.

Nat /næt, ||nat/ *n.* and *adj. Colloq.* Also **NAT**, and with small initial. Pl. **-s**, **||-te(s)** /-tə(s)/. [Abbrev. of *National(ist)*, tr. Afk. *Nasionaal* National, *Nasionalis* Nationalist, referring to the National Party.]

A. *n.*

a. Abbrev. of NATIONALIST *n.* sense a.

See note at SAP *n.*[1] sense 2.

1926 M. NATHAN *S. Afr. from Within* 274 Of late there has been much talk of toenadering or rapprochement between the 'Saps' and the 'Nats'. **1934** W. SAINT-MANDÉ *Halcyon Days Afr.* 24 Labour had done right to join forces with the Nats. **1943** *Weekend News & Sunday Mag.* 20 Mar. 4 We is realising dat jou is de fren orf orl de peoples excep de blerry Nats. **1956** A. SAMPSON *Drum* 159 The English just use long words and big talk ... Segregation — ah — democracy — ah, civilised men ... The Dutchmen just say 'you blerry Kaffir, you, voetsak!' They both mean the same; but with the Dutchmen, you know where you are, man! Give me the Nats! **1973** *Sunday Times* 8 July 14 The review will find great appeal with the South African who votes Prog and Sap but who every day thanks the Lord for the Nats. **1977** F.G. BUTLER *Karoo Morning* 99 If you were a Nat it was your sacred duty to fight for your language and the Vierkleur; if a Sap, you knew you were fighting for Britain, the Union Jack and Progress. **1990** G. SLOVO *Ties of Blood* 224 The Nats had easily comprehensible aims: they promised to the country that they would save the whites from the three-fold threat of coloured blood, the black peril and the red menace. **1990** *Sunday Times* 30 Sept. 22 The *Nattes* and *Sappe* behaved as badly at political meetings in decades past. **1994** P. LEE in *Style* May 59 We are starting to grasp a future without the wagging finger of a Nat in a hat.

b. With qualifying word: **bloednat** /ˈblʊt-/ [Afk., *bloed* blood], an ultra-conservative, dyed-in-the-wool Nationalist; cf. BLOEDSAP; **brown Nat**, see BROWN *adj.* sense 2 a; **new Nat**, see quots 1990 and 1993; cf. *neo-Nationalist* (see NATIONALIST *n.* sense b).

1986 D. VAN HEERDEN in *Frontline* Mar. 35 The conservatives are large in number .. but relatively small in influence ... They are '**Bloednatte**' who will still vote Nat when Mangosuthu Buthelezi receives the Paul Sauer medal for service to the Party. **1987** H.

BARKER in *Frontline* Apr. 6 New Nats ... Do they not count Mandela among those with whom negotiation must take place? **1987** K. CARLEAN in *Grocott's Mail* 31 Mar. 1 There will be a very important base for new realignments in politics which might encourage new nats still lurking in the National Party to cross the floor. **1990** *Frontline* Jan. 1 In March 1986, *Frontline* coined the term 'the New Nats' for left-wing National Party members who planned to implement drastic change working within the NP. **1993** P. LAURENCE in *Leadership* Vol.12 No.2, 48 The real threat lies in the future rather than in the past; and it emanates from black nationalists — the 'New Nats' — rather than the Afrikaner nationalists.

B. *adj.*

1. In the collocation **Nat Party**: NP sense 1.

1938 *Forum* 25 Apr. 48 (caption) Nat Party. **1982** M.W. SEROTE in Chapman & Dangor *Voices from Within* 111 My father .. complaining about the prime minister and the laws and the nat party.

2.a. Abbrev. of NATIONALIST *adj.*

1955 *Rand Daily Mail* 2 May 11 West believes in Nat. Policy of 'Baasskap'. **1974** *Daily Dispatch* 27 Feb. 14 (caption) Now, now, Agatha, let's continue as a lawful gathering — no anti-Nat sentiments please! **1984** [see HARDEGAT]. **1987** P. WILHELM in *Optima* Vol.35 No.2, 63 Abandon Apartheid! Abandon Nat Rule! **1988** *Broadsheet* (Progressive Federal Party), Over the past forty years, Nat policies have driven our once proud nation further and further into the wilderness, into quarantine. **1991** *Sunday Tribune* 19 May 20 One knows, of course, that Maggie has friends in high Nat places. **1994** *Style* May 97 All those who thought a post-Nat government would at least be more purposeful are in for a horrible shock.

b. With qualifying word: **neo-Nat**, of or pertaining to a reformed, relatively liberal Nationalism. Cf. *neo-Nationalist* (see NATIONALIST *n.* sense b).

1985 *Sunday Times* 29 Sept. 12 C- could be described as a **neo-Nat** technocrat, a member of the President's Council and a former journalist.

Natal /nəˈtæl/ *n.* [Pg. *Natal* Christmas Day; the region being so named by Vasco da Gama because its coast was first sighted on Christmas Day, 1497.] A name given to that area of South Africa situated on the east coast between the Umtamvuna river in the south, and the Swaziland and Mozambique borders in the north.

Historically one of the four provinces of the Union (later Republic) of South Africa, Natal was formally renamed 'KwaZulu-Natal' in 1994. Used *attrib., comb.,* and in special collocations.

a. Natal Code *Law (hist.)*, a collection of laws promulgated in 1891 controlling all aspects of the lives of black people in Natal; **Natal Fever** *colloq.*, apathy or chronic languor, induced by heat and humidity; **Natal rum** *obs.*, a spirit distilled from sugar refuse; **Natal sore** *Pathology*, a bacterial skin condition characterized by spreading ulcers; cf. *veld sore* (see VELD sense 5).

1932 *Union Govt document* (title) Natal Code of Native Law. **1970** E. KAHN in *Std Encycl. of Sn Afr.* I. 477 The Governor-General .. became the Supreme Chief of all Bantu save those in the Cape Province, armed with all the extensive powers of control given to him by the Natal Code of Native Law. **1991** J. MACLENNAN in *Sunday Tribune* 15 Dec. 1 In the Natal judgment Mr Justice Didcott ruled as invalid a proclamation by Mr De Klerk which amended the Natal Code ... Now the situation reverts to what it was before .. and blacks may only carry 'cultural weapons' such as assegais, sword sticks and battle axes under specific circumstances. **1991** B. KING in *Ibid*. 5 For almost a century nobody had been at liberty to carry a dangerous weapon in terms of the Natal Code. **1909** *E. London Dispatch* 7 June 4 Unwillingness to work ... It's an old malady in South Africa, remarks the 'Argus.' We call it '**Natal fever**.' **1913** C. PETTMAN *Africanderisms* 336 *Natal fever*, An indisposition to exert one's self, induced by the intense heat of summer, is thus euphemistically designated. **1914** S.P. HYATT *Old Transport Rd* 174 Native Commissioners — most of them were Natal men, suffering from 'Natal Fever,' chronic tiredness. **1951** O. WALKER *Shapeless Flame* 223 What with war fever, Natal fever and this heat, my dear, I'm beginning to believe the poet. **1980** *Sunday Times* 14 Sept. (Mag. Sect.) 4, I come from Durban, where Natal Fever is another name for apathy and indifference. **1986** *Fair Lady* 5 Mar. 113 Natal Fever is a national joke. Everyone knows what it means. Or rather, what it *used* to mean .. because Durban is no longer the colonial backwater it used to be: its citizens are shaking off the sundowner syndrome. **1990** J. FARQUHARSON in *Sunday Times* 30 Dec. 12 One Maritzburg lady, roused in the middle of the night and told to take shelter in the jail because the Zulus were coming, retorted: 'I will do nothing of the kind! I am in bed and intend to remain there!' Of course, Natal fever gets due mention. **1993** *Business Day* 27 May (Centenarians) 9 A banana leaning against a wall, partly covered by a Mexican hat, said, 'Okay, so we've got Natal fever?' **1882** C. DU VAL *With Show through Sn Afr.* II. 177 The Canteen-keepers .. were nimbly pocketing the shillings of their defenders in exchange for .. '**Natal Rum**'. **1882** LADY F.C. DIXIE *In Land of Misfortune* 147 A great deal of singing seemed to be going on inside, and the fumes of tobacco and strong smell of that disgusting concoction, Natal rum, pervaded the air. **1885** W. GRESWELL *Our S. Afr. Empire* II. 204 No public analyst has, as yet, exposed to light the horrible ingredients of 'Cape smoke' and 'Natal rum.' **1913** C. PETTMAN *Africanderisms* 337 *Natal rum*, A vile spirit distilled from sugar refuse and nothing behind 'Cape smoke' in its effects. **1851** J. & M. CHURCHILL *Merchant Family in Natal* (1979) 32 Begin to suffer from **Natal sores**. Painful and disagreeable. **1852** C. BARTER *Dorp & Veld* 13 The Natal sore, a very painful boil. **1862** J.S. DOBIE *S. Afr. Jrnl* (1945) 32 Another evil of the country is 'Natal sores.' That boy Norton is a mass of ugly itchy-looking red spots produced by little ticks about the size of a pin's point which stick themselves into the skin, preferring the more tender parts, and torment considerably. If scratched they become very nasty sores. **1870** C. HAMILTON *Life & Sport in S.-E. Afr.* 50 An open blain or blister, generally ending in a running tumour. It is known among the natives and colonists as the 'Natal sore,' and is of so violent a kind as to have seriously affected those who have neglected its first appearance. **1887** J.W. MATTHEWS *Incwadi Yami* 16 As peculiar to this colony, I ought to mention the Natal sore, a species of inflammatory boil .. with which new arrivals were almost always troubled. These sores were often produced by the irritating bite .. of the tick .. and also by the bite of the mosquito. **1903** D. BLACKBURN *Burgher Quixote* 210, I never wash my hands, having Natal sores on them. **1915** O.S. ORMSBY *Pract. Treat. Dis. Skin* 360 As distinguished from the Natal sore, which was chiefly found in the lower part of that country, the veldt sore was most abundant in the high, barren table-lands. **1951** G. PANJA in *R.B.H. Gradwohl Clin. Trop. Med.* 641 *Tropical Phagedenic Ulcer,* .. Synonyms .. Natal sore.

b. In the names of plants: **Natal bottlebrush**, see BOTTLEBRUSH; **Natal cotton plant**, the plant *Ipomoea mauritiana* of the Convolvulaceae; **Natal ebony** *obs.*, the UMZIMBEET, *Millettia grandis*; **Natal ivy**, the succulent plant *Senecio macroglossus* of the Asteraceae; **Natal lily**, any of several bulbous plants: (a) *Gladiolus dalenii* of the Iridaceae; (b) *Clivia miniata*, any of several species of *Crinum*, or *Amaryllis belladonna*, all of the Amaryllidaceae; **Natal mahogany**, either of two evergreen, timber-bearing trees: (a) *Trichilia emetica* of the Meliaceae; its wood; *Cape Mahogany* sense (a), see CAPE sense 2 a; ESSENHOUT sense b; UMKHUHLU; (b) ?obs. *Kiggelaria africana* of the Flacourtiaceae; **Natal beefsteak mushroom**, see BEEFSTEAK MUSHROOM sense a; **Natal plum**, the AMATUNGULU, *Carissa macrocarpa*.

1868 W.H. HARVEY *Genera of S. Afr. Plants* 254 B[atata] paniculata, or '**Natal Cotton-plant**,' a widely-dispersed tropical species, grows at Natal. **1913** C. PETTMAN *Africanderisms* 335 Natal cotton plant, Batata paniculata. **1966** C.A. SMITH *Common Names* 348 Natal cotton plant, *Ipomoea mauritiana* ... The vernacular name is derived from the fact that the species was first noted in Natal. **1851** R.J. GARDEN *Diary.* I. (Killie Campbell Africana Library MS29081) 24 June, The Umzimbete or **Natal Ebony** grows in the kloofs of the Ilovu but does not attain the size it does in the Amaponda country. **1917** R. MARLOTH *Common Names* 60 **Natal ivy**, *Senecio Macroglossus*. Not allied to the European ivy. **1975** J.M. GIBSON *Wild Flowers of Natal* 112 *Senecio macroglossus*, .. At forest margins one sometimes sees this Natal Ivy draping trees and flowering in July. **1856** *Cape of G.H. Almanac & Annual Register* 283 The **Natal lily** is the perfection of beauty and fragrance. **1859** R.J. MANN *Col. of Natal* 152 Most places are commonly covered with another very beautiful amaryllid .. which is termed *par excellence* the 'Natal lily'. The flowers of this striking plant are large white pink-ribbed bells, hanging in enormous bunches round the summit of the flower-stalk. **1876** H. BROOKS *Natal* 169 Another very magnificent amaryllid, which is distinguished *par excellence* as the 'Natal lily' (*Amaryllis belladonna*), presents itself in moist spots. **1913** C. PETTMAN *Africanderisms* 336 Natal lily, .. *Gladiolus psittacinus* ... The pink veined perianth of this exquisite flower makes it a general favourite. *Amaryllis belladonna* is incorrect, as it is only found in the Cape Districts and does not extend farther East than Riversdale. **1966** C.A. SMITH *Common Names* 348 Natallelie (-lily), *Crinum moorei*. The vernacular name was recorded about 1850, though the plants were mistaken for *Amaryllis belladonna*. *Gladiolus cooperi* .. ; *G. psittacinus*. c**1968** S. CANDY *Natal Coast Gardening* 24 Gladiolus, The indigenous, Autumn-flowering *Gladiolus psittacinus* ('Natal Lily') .. should be grown. **1903** H. STONE *Timbers of Commerce* 3 (heading) Natal mahogany. **1907** T.R. SIM *Forests & Forest Flora* 128 *Kiggelaria africana*, Wild Peach, Natal Mahogany .. does best in open forest. Ibid. 161 This tree [sc. *Trichilia emetica*] .. is known in the Transkei as Cape Mahogany, Manuti Mahogany, or Natal Mahogany. **1972** PALMER & PITMAN *Trees of Sn Afr.* II. 1071 *Trichilia emetica* Vahl. Woodland mahogany, Natal mahogany ... One of the widespread trees of Africa. **1991** *Grocott's Mail* 8 Mar. 10 A specimen of the Natal Mahogany (*Trichilia emetica*) was planted ... The Natal Mahogany .. usually attains a height of 10m, but under ideal conditions can grow up to 24m high. **1859** R.J. MANN *Col. of Natal* 158 The *Amatungulu* (**Natal plum**) is the berry of an evergreen periwinkle (*Vinca*) growing as a small shrub on the sea-coast lands. The fruit is about the size of a damson. **1876** H. BROOKS *Natal* 168 A plant .. bearing a really valuable fruit which is familiarly known as the Natal plum. **1917** [see AMATUNGULU]. **1954** [see NUM-NUM]. **1970** *Country Life* (U.K.) 17 Dec. 1230 Scarlet ixoras and the spiny carissa (Natal plum) are used as evergreen hedges. **1972** PALMER & PITMAN *Trees of Sn Afr.* 1901 *Carissa macrocarpa*, .. Amatungulu, Natal plum .. is a common and often conspicuous species in coastal bush, on sand dunes and on the edges of coastal forest ... Although it is often a low bush, it can grow into a small tree up to 4 m high, many-branched, spiny, with dense evergreen foliage. **1989** *Gardening Questions Answered* (Reader's Digest Assoc.) 328 *Carissa*, .. Also called amatungulu or Natal plum.

c. In the names of birds and insects: **Natal fly** *obs.*, the Tumbu or skin maggot-fly *Cordylobia anthropophaga* of the Calliphoridae, the larvae of which burrow into and feed upon human flesh; **Natal francolin** (formerly also **Natal pheasant**), the francolin *Francolinus natalensis*; *bush partridge* sense (b) and *coast partridge*, see PARTRIDGE sense b; *coast pheasant*, see PHEASANT sense b; *Namaqua pheasant*, see NAMAQUA *n.* sense 2; **Natal robin-chat**, now usu. **Natal robin**, the bird *Cossypha natalensis* of the Turdidae, with greyish-brown back and orange breast.

1905 *Addresses & Papers* (Brit. & S. Afr. Assoc. Agric. Science) III. 532 (Pettman), The **Natal fly** is said to occur; its larva causes annoyance by burrowing into the human skin, where it pupates and causes painful inflammation. **1913** C. PETTMAN *Africanderisms* 336

Natal fly, One of the *Muscidea*, probably *Lucilia* or *Ochromya sp.*, which has the objectionable habit when in the larval condition of burrowing into and feeding upon living human flesh. **1892** W.L. Distant *Naturalist in Tvl* 105 (Pettman), The **Natal Francolin**, called by the Dutch the Namaqua pheasant. **1906** Stark & Sclater *Birds of S. Afr.* IV. 213 Natal Francolin, .. 'Coast Partridge' of Natal; 'Namaqua Pheasant' of Transvaal Boers. **1947** J. Stevenson-Hamilton *Wild Life in S. Afr.* 274 The Natal francolin (*Francolinus natalensis*) .. may be recognized by its red bill and legs, and white breast with V-shaped black markings. **1970** O.P.M. Prozesky *Field Guide to Birds* 88 *Natal Francolin*, .. Found mostly in acacia scrub. **1984** G.L. Maclean *Roberts' Birds of Sn Afr.* 175 *Natal Francolin*, ... Size medium; looks uniform dull brown above; below black, barred and scaled with white .. ; bill and legs orange-red. **1835** A. Smith *Diary* (1940) II. 144 The **Natal pheasant** is very common here (and is) to be seen running about the banks of the Marique in the evenings and mornings, and when disturbed flies to the thickets edging the stream. **1901** Stark & Sclater *Birds of S. Afr.* II. 210 **Natal robin-chat**, .. *Cossypha natalensis*. **1923** Haagner & Ivy *Sketches* 172 The Natal Robin-Chat (*Cossypha natalensis*) is blue-grey above; head orange-brown streaked with bluish; nape and rump orange-brown; upper tail-coverts chestnut; entire under-surface orange-red. **1973** G.J. Broekhuysen in *Std Encycl. of Sn Afr.* IX. 384 Some species, the Cape robin and the Natal robin, for example, are good singers. **1983** K.B. Newman *Newman's Birds* 328 *Natal Robin, Cossypha natalensis* ... Entirely orange from *above the eyes* and sides of head to undertail, no white eyebrow. **1990** *Weekend Post* 21 July (Leisure) 3 In the course of an hour three different types of sunbird were seen, plus a Natal robin. **1991** *Philatelic Bulletin* No.46, The Natal Robin frequents the evergreen forests, feeding on insects and arachnids on the dimly-lit forest floor ... It is most often noted by its repetitive bisyllabic purring call.

Hence **Nataliana** *n.* [Eng. suffix *-(i)ana* (fr. L.), denoting collectables], artefacts and collectables of historical interest pertaining to Natal; **Nataline** *adj. nonce*, Natalian *adj.*; **Natalite** *n. hist.* [Eng. technical name-forming suffix *-ite*], see quot. 1982.

1950 H. Gibbs *Twilight* 89 Nataline Tapestry. *Ibid.* 90 Only occasionally in the hundred years which follow does a European ship put in along the Nataline coast. **1963** *Natal Mercury* 28 Nov. Mr Clinton Collins, who owned the Old House, offered it to the Durban Corporation as a museum for the purpose of displaying Nataliana. **1982** G. Knox *Estate Wines* 16 During the last two years of the war, Natal sugar farmers were distilling ethyl alcohol from unwanted molasses. Together, the wine and sugar industries produced a combustible spirit which was used as a substitute for almost unattainable petrol. This product, named 'Natalite', was the KWV's first venture. It was .. a commercial failure.

Natalian /nə'tæliən/ *n.* and *adj.* [Natal + Eng. n.- and adj.-forming suffix *-ian* denoting 'a resident of (a place)'.]

A. *n.* One born in Natal (now KwaZulu-Natal); a Natal resident. Cf. *banana boy*, see banana sense 2.

1864 'A Lady' *Life at Natal* (1972) 16 Natalians are very proud of the fact that their railway was the first opened in South Africa. **1879** Mrs Hutchinson *In Tents in Tvl* 95 'I tell you, I am a Natalian' he shouted, absolutely dancing with rage. 'I never was so insulted before.' **1894** E.N. Thomas *How Thankful We Should Be* 24 The Natalians appear to have got much more for their money than East London, The Kowie, or Port Elizabeth. **1900** W.S. Churchill *London to Ladysmith* 45 Now at last there is war ... More than to any it comes home to the Natalian. **1908** [see garden sense 1]. **1934** A.J. Barnouw *Lang. & Race Problems* 14, I heard Natalians deny that this document, in declaring Afrikaans to be the official equal of English, made it obligatory for every State official to be versed in either language. **1941** C. Birkby *Springbok Victory* 108 It was a grim baptism for the Natalians. **1969** I. Vaughan *Last of Sunlit Yrs* 95 He laughed ... 'I am a South African, a Natalian by birth.' **1973** *Sunday Times* 18 Feb. 2 An independent Natal has long been the dream of many White Natalians. **1984** *Reader's Digest* Jan. 40 Natalians, despite modern refrigeration, still persist in preserving it [*sc.* boerewors] with vinegar. **1988** *Natal Witness* in M. Kentridge *Unofficial War* (1990) 88 The atrocities shed a bleak light on ideologically-inspired political structures which are neither democratic nor acceptable to growing numbers of black Natalians. **1990** W. Botha in *Frontline* Sept. 21 These days, 'top the atrocity' is a party game in suburban homes where Natalians meet. **1990** [see NRP]. **1991** G. Eichorn in *Natal Mercury* 3 Apr. 22 *Why* aren't you — or any other Natalian — a Banana Boy any more? **1994** B. Spender in *Flying Springbok* Dec. 44 Twenty-five years ago, it was a young Natalian called Barry Richards who took the world by storm, cracking two centuries in the four-test series.

B. *adj. obsolescent.* Of or pertaining to the province of Natal (now KwaZulu-Natal); *Nataline*, see Natal.

'Natal' (used *attrib.*) has largely replaced 'Natalian' in this sense.

1867 R.J. Mann in *Intellectual Observer* X. 186 In the year 1842, .. the Dutchmen within the Natalian territory became subjects of the British Crown. **1928** R. Campbell *Wayzgoose* 10 Seldom do suns such striking talents show as when they set Natalian woods aglow. **1935** S. Desmond *Afr. Log* 191 Throughout the day I see the lovely Natalian landscape roll past. **1950** H. Gibbs *Twilight* 114 Back in the comparatively quiet years of the 1920's, in 1922 to be exact, the Government spent £25,000 on educating Natalian Indians.

nation *n.* [tr. Afk. *volk* a people or nation.] A group of people sharing a common ethnic background, but not necessarily occupying a single clearly-defined region or state: **a.** A clan. **b.** A chiefdom. **c.** An ethnic group. See also international sense 1, multinational sense 1, national unit.

A sense largely obsolescent elsewhere, but retained in South Africa (esp. in sense c) mainly by those who choose to see the country as one composed of several nations, each occupying its own independent state. Opponents of this perspective argue that while South Africa's population is made up of people from several ethnic groups, their common experience as South Africans is more significant than the differences which divide them. It is also argued that some of the 'nations' identified by proponents of apartheid are artificial conglomerations of smaller groups which would not naturally have grouped together to form political entities.

1731 G. Medley tr. *P. Kolb's Present State of Cape of G.H.* I. 27 Several .. *Hollanders*, who had been long acquainted with Persons and Things in the several *Hottentot* Nations. **1790** tr. *F. Le Vaillant's Trav.* II. 345 Another nation, entirely different from that of the Hottentots, is confounded also under the name of Boshmen. **1795** C.R. Hopson tr. *C.P. Thunberg's Trav.* I. 304, I met with but small remains of the once more or less numerous Hottentot nations, which, as late as the beginning of this century, still inhabited these vast plains. **1824** W.J. Burchell *Trav.* II. 217 His successor, Mattivi, had sent to the Klaarwater chief, Adam Kok, a present of two oxen, as expressive of his desire that the two nations, or tribes, should continue on peaceable and friendly terms. **1829** W. Shaw Diary. 7 May, The whole Tambookie Nation, which is quite as large as the Caffre Nation, are entirely without the means of Instruction. **1837** F. Owen *Diary* (1926) 29 Congella is the second capital of the Zoolu nation. **1844** [see paramount sense a]. **1873** F. Boyle *To Cape for Diamonds* 30 The nation of the Griquas. **1882** W.R. Ludlow *Zululand & Cetewayo* 31 Nearly one fourth of the Zulu nation perished. **1915** J.K. O'Connor *Afrikander Rebellion* 93 Had the whole Afrikander nation risen in rebellion against England .. the Boers would have been the losers. **1944** J.C. Van Rooy in M. Rogers *Black Sash* (1956) 148 The Afrikaner Broederbond was born out of the deep conviction that the Afrikaner nation was planted in this country by the hand of God, and is destined to continue to exist as a nation with its own character and calling. **1950** D. Reed *Somewhere S. of Suez* 156 The Cape Coloured People are a small nation, formed by processes similar to those which other nations, big or little, once passed through but have forgotten. **1953** A. Paton *Phalarope* (1963) 137 Japie .. said, you take the black nation too much to heart. **1964** *Drum* Nov. 25 Majali was brought before the tribal court, charged with infringement of taboos of the Zulu nation. **1970** B.J. Vorster in *Sunday Times* 15 Nov. 12 Most people look on them as tribes of the same nation. They are not that at all. The Zulus are as different from the Xhosas as the Dutch are from the Germans ... Each nation is a nation in its own right ... Separate development implies that we Whites are leading the various Black nations to full independence. **1971** *Daily Dispatch* 13 May 12 The flimsy theory that the 'ethnic group[s]' of Xhosa, Zulu, Sotho, Venda and so forth are each a nation. **1972** *E. Prov. Herald* 9 Sept. 9 Dr Koornhof .. made it plain .. that when the Broederbond Government speaks of the 'White nation of South Africa' it means only the 2 000 000 Afrikaners. **1973** *Weekend Post* 30 June 3 'The Coloured is not an Afrikaner,' Dr Mulder said. 'He is a nation in his own right, or a nation in the making.' **1979** M. Matshoba *Call Me Not a Man* 182 'Is that not another distortion, my bro?' 'Of what?' ... 'Of the concept of nationalism, its being equated with tribalism? .. By turning tribes into nations. Tribes combine to form one nation.' **1983** *City Press* 18 Sept. 11 (*advt*) Learn to drive the easy way ... Welcome all nations: Xhosa, Zulu, Tswana, N. Sotho, S. Sotho, Tsonga, Venda, Coloured and others. **1985** Platzky & Walker *Surplus People* 113 The bantustan policy outlined in 1959 was very simple. Old divisions dating from a pre-conquest past were to be redefined to make 'nations' where before there had often been only loose groupings of chiefdoms and clans. **1992** S. Macleod in *Time* 16 Mar. 30 Treurnicht would recognize the independence of the Zulu, Xhosa and other black 'nations' and negotiate borders with their leaders. He fails to explain how scrambled-egg metropolitan areas like Johannesburg could be fairly partitioned.

Hence **national** *adj.*, **nationality** *n.*, **nationhood** *n.*

1949 J.S. Franklin *This Union* 68 The policy of safeguarding the White Race .. must go hand in hand with security for the Native — his own national development. **1950** H. Gibbs *Twilight* 230 'National' does not mean 'the South African nation'. It means only the Afrikaner, the Boer people. **1960** J.H. Coetzee in H. Spottiswoode *S. Afr.: Rd Ahead* 71 The native majority as a *national group* will submerge the white minority as a *national unity*. **1972** *Drum* 8 Oct. 17 The diplomats are .. supposed to make us 'national' conscious. *Ibid.* 8 Dec. 9, I myself, other Whites and Chief Modjadji and his tribe donated towards the building of that hospital ... We all worked together and did not bother about nationality. **1980** Lye & Murray *Transformations* 18 *The South Africa Official Yearbook* .. is permeated by a laborious effort to identify particular cultures with particular 'national' populations. **1986** P. Maylam *Hist. of Afr. People* 170 Africans are treated as ethnically heterogeneous, while whites are assumed to be homogeneous. In addition, the idea of African nationhood is not matched by territoriality. **1987** [see potjie].

National Assembly *n. phr. Hist.* Also with small initials. The legislative body of any of several ethnically-based territories which were granted 'independence' in terms of the policy of separate development. See also Bunga sense 2 a, homeland sense 1.

1978 *S. Afr. 1977: Off. Yrbk* (Dept of Info.) 895 The legislative authority is vested in a unicameral assembly of 150 members, of whom half are traditional leaders, i.e. the hereditary tribal leaders of the country who by virtue of their hereditary status automatically become members of the national assembly. **1986** *Daily Dispatch* 21 May 3 The Minister .. told the National Assembly that despite the ever present spectre of unemployment which plagued Ciskei, his department was able to place 27 000 workseekers in employment last year. **1988** *Pace* Dec.-Jan. 12 You certainly shook the benches in the National Assembly.

Nationalist *n.* and *adj.* Also occas. with small initial. [tr. Afk. *Nasionalis* a member of the *Nasionale Party* the National Party.]

A. *n.*

a. A member of any of the successive (predominantly Afrikaner) National Parties; in *pl.*, a collective name for the National Party or its government; NAT *n.* sense a; NP sense 2.

1911 *Farmer's Weekly* 4 Oct. 115 The good party man, whether he be Nationalist or Unionist whose political attitude is one of humble worship and genuflection. **1919** *Illust. London News* (U.K.) 6 June, The Natives .. kept loyal under strong temptation to make trouble for the Government from the Nationalists and pro-German Europeans. **1921** *E. Prov. Herald* 16 Feb., General Smuts will out-face the Nationalists with a nationalism bigger, broader, prouder and more inspiring than their own. **1933** *Star* 2 May 5 Mr Vorster said .. he was still a Nationalist, but now supported General Smuts as strongly as any S.A.P. man. **1950** H. GIBBS *Twilight* 237 The Nationalists' anti-Semitism in the 1930s cannot be ignored, neither can Dr. Malan's attempt to ban Jewish refugees in 1937 as prohibited immigrants. **1953** A.J. LUTHULI in *Drum* May 11 As the Nationalists themselves have said, the laws which we oppose were not passed by them alone. **1963** M. BENSON *Afr. Patriots* 211 The A.N.C .. still hoped they [*sc.* the United Party] might learn they could never return to power by trying to beat the nationalists at their own game. **1973** *Sunday Times* 27 May 17 No Opposition group managed to break the increasing grip of the Nationalists on the 80 per cent or so of the Afrikaners who vote for them. **1979** T. PAKENHAM *Boer War* (1982) 576 The party founded by Botha and Smuts had been replaced in 1948 by Malan and the Nationalists. **1984** *Frontline* Mar. 39 Most English-speaking readers are easily [able] to remember the days when 'Nationalist' was virtually a synonym for 'Afrikaner' ... English-speaking Nationalists were as rare as kudu in Eloff street. **1991** *Sunday Times* 10 Feb. 20 Like Alan Paton's Liberal Party, the Nationalists now put forward the vision of a non-racial South Africa .. as the only viable alternative to the revolutionary socialist vision of the ANC and its communist pilot fish. **1993** K. OWEN in *Ibid.* 7 Nov. 22 The Nationalists who destroyed South Africa's provincial system when it showed some timid independence from central government are now demanding a full-fledged federation.

b. With defining word: **neo-Nationalist**, a member of the National Party who supports old-style Nationalist thinking. Cf. *neo-Nat* (see NAT *adj.* sense 2 b), *new Nat* (see NAT *n.* sense b).

1987 *Star* 3 Feb. 15 Though a law-and-order hawk (which to some people makes him a neo-Nationalist), Mr .. has consistently been against the Nats' racial ideology and policies.

c. *comb.* **Nationalist Party** [fr. Afk. *Nasionale Party* National Party], *(a) hist.*, an early name for the South African Party (see SAP *n.*[1] sense 1 a); *(b)* NP sense 1.

1913 V.R. MARKHAM *S. Afr. Scene* 156 The first elections under the Act of Union were held in September 1910, and resulted in a majority for the **Nationalist Party**, General Botha becoming Prime Minister. **1933** W.H.S. BELL *Bygone Days* 332 General Hertzog was not included in the new Cabinet and he at once established the Nationalist Party which subsequently became a very powerful organization. **1936** *Cambridge Hist. of Brit. Empire* VIII. 645 General Hertzog .. ultimately found himself at the head of a new party under the name of the Nationalist Party which arose from the clothing of cultural aims with political forms. **1939** *Star* 4 Sept. 11 Last night when it was know[n] that Britain was at war, Dr Malan and other leaders of the Nationalist Party were invited to Groote [S]chuur where further discussion took place. **1947** G.A.L. GREEN *Editor Looks Back* 215 Hertzog .. declared that .. the Re-united Nationalist Party .. would work for peace with Germany. **1966** VAN HEYNINGEN & BERTHOUD *Uys Krige* 32 The two traditional political groups, the South African Party under General Smuts and the Nationalist Party under General Hertzog had coalesced to form a new combination, the United Party. The extreme wing of the Nationalist Party, led by Dr. Malan, had refused to cooperate and continued to be the repository of ancient grudges and resentments. **1977** F.G. BUTLER *Karoo Morning* 224 Dr D.F. Malan was on a visit to Cradock to get support for his Purified Nationalist Party. **1983** D. TUTU *Voice of One* 43 You are brainwashed by the South African Broadcasting Corporation (SABC) which constantly misleads you, as it does its propaganda work for the Nationalist Party.

B. *adj.* Of, belonging to, or characteristic of Nationalists or the National Party; NAT *adj.* sense 2 a.

1916 *Farmer's Weekly* 20 Dec. 1450 Wanted — Experienced reliable energetic single man (Nationalist) for general farming. **1930** *Friend* 25 Aug. 14 The .. Nationalist M.P. for Potchefstroom has refused to take any further part in the activities of the Workers' Bond. **1938** *Star* 2 May 9 Referring to the Nationalist spirit, Dr. Malan said the reception accorded him was proof that large numbers of young people were staunch supporters of his cause. **1943** D. REITZ *No Outspan* 147 The Nationalist Government's five yearly term of office expired in March 1929 and another general election was due. **1950** H. GIBBS *Twilight* 31 If Union can be revoked, what else may not be changed? That it will be done in Parliament, with a majority of Nationalist votes supporting it, is not doubted. *Ibid.* 46 Apartheid is the Nationalist dream. It will be pursued with vigour as a main political faith of men whose forefathers resented the abolition of slavery. **1962** L. GANDAR in J. Crwys-Williams *S. Afr. Despatches* (1989) 342 The White population of South Africa will go streaming into the Nationalist laager, stripped of the power of resistance which some genuine moral principals might have given them. **1969** S. UYS in *Ibid.* 396 The rousing of the Nationalist rank and file out of its apathy, the whole emotional mobilisation of the Afrikaner nation, is generating political intemperance and intolerance. **1970** *Rand Daily Mail* 2 Apr. 4 South Africa was being condemned to economic disaster by the policies of the Nationalist Government. **1980** N. FERREIRA *Story of Afrikaner* 129 Nationalist politicians will insist on equating the NP with South Africa. **1990** R. GOOL *Cape Town Coolie* 63 The next government will be Nationalist. **1991** *Sunday Times* 10 Feb. 20 To hear a Nationalist leader denouncing the racism of the Conservative Party with a passion and conviction worthy of Helen Suzman is to know that a profound and irreversible change has occurred in Afrikaner politics. **1993** H. TYSON *Editors under Fire* 11 Every Nationalist speech from every political platform across the country devoted much of its content to the evils — and the dangers — of the *Engelse pers*, the English press.

Hence **Nationalism** *n.*, the policies pursued by the National Party.

1961 M.A. WALL *Dominee & Dom-Pas* 64 These things should unite all South Africans, of all races, creeds and colours, all who do not wish to disgrace their humanity, in one common opposition to Nationalism and all it entails. **1983** M. DU PLESSIS *State of Fear* 41 We've lived under Afrikaner Nationalism all our lives.

national road *n. phr.* Also with initial capital(s). Any major intercity road financed by the National Transport Commission. Also *attrib.* See also N sense 2.

1935 *Act 42* in *Stat. of Union* 284 There shall be established a board to be known as the National Road Board, consisting of six members, appointed by the Minister. *Ibid.* 286 The Governor-General may, on the recommendation of the board .. declare to be a national road, any road or part of a road the immediate or early construction or reconstruction of which is, in the opinion of the Governor-General, necessary in the national interest. **1939** *Report of National Rd Board for 1938* (UG19–1939) 324 Some of the smaller Municipalities might not be in a position to finance the construction of the national roads through their respective areas. **1941** C. BIRKBY *Springbok Victory* 160 An unending column of transport was moving along a wide 'autostrada' which, for most of its length, was as good as a stretch of asphalted national road in the Union. **1948** *George & Knysna Herald* 21 May 3 The attention of the Provincial Administration has been drawn to devastation of the natural beauty caused by the construction of the National Road between George .. and Stormsriver. **1950** [see GARDEN sense 2]. **1955** L.G. GREEN *Karoo* 14 It was an intimate journey, never so monotonous as the modern rush along the tarred national roads. **1963** A. DELIUS *Day Natal Took Off* 9 He didn't realize that Sobisa would make straight for the national road to Durban and thumb a lift with a returning dagga-runner. **1971** *Argus* 4 May 9 National road engineers are not concerned about the scenic beauty, but are interested only in the straightest route. **1973** *Daily Dispatch* 12 May 2 It is the department's intention for existing tarred roads to be rebuilt to certain standards before being deproclaimed as national roads and handed over to the provinces. **1985** P. SLABOLEPSZY *Sat. Night at Palace* 18 There, that's the old National Road over there with the white lines painted on it. It tells you you are going somewhere important. **1991** J. COOPER in *Weekend Post* 5 Oct. 7 Namaqualand daisies grow profusely in bright drifts along the national road N7 between Garies and Kamieskroon. **1993** *Weekend Post* 15 May (Leisure) 5 Take the Jeffreys Bay-Mondplaas turn-off onto the old national road.

National Scout *n. phr. Hist.* Also with small initials. During the Anglo-Boer War (1899–1902): a member of a corps consisting of Boers who, having deserted to the British forces, were used as scouts in various British units; cf. JOINER sense 1.

The corps was raised in 1901; its members were looked upon with opprobrium by Boers, both during and after the war.

1900 A.C. DOYLE *Great Boer War* (1902) 519 The National Scouts, or 'tame Boers,' as they were familiarly called. **1902** P.J. DU TOIT *Diary* (1974) 92 We have about 70 National Scouts, who, I noticed, are always put in advance and sent out in different directions, showing what confidence is placed in them. **1913** J. BRANDT *Petticoat Commando* 148 The thought has occurred to me that the words 'National Scout' may convey nothing to my English reader ... The first downward step to becoming a National Scout was the voluntary surrendering of arms to the enemy, to become a 'Handsupper', as the burghers were called, who laid down their arms while the Boer leaders were still in the field. **1915** J.K. O'CONNOR *Afrikander Rebellion* 57 Had certain Afrikanders not joined the National Scouts, and had there been fewer 'hands-uppers', the Republican forces would have victoriously emerged from the war. **1921** W.C. SCULLY *Harrow* 197 Were the fires of our tribulation to be kindled again tomorrow, these men would without hesitation go over to the side of our oppressors. Beware of such and — thrice and three times thrice — beware of the infamous 'National Scout'. **1928** E.A. WALKER *Hist. of S. Afr.* 507 Farmers .. refused to allow *bijwoners* to return to their farms, especially as many of these tenants-at-will had been National Scouts. **1936** *Cambridge Hist. of Brit. Empire* VIII. 610 Prisoners of war, inmates of the Concentration Camps, 'hands-uppers' or even National Scouts in the service of the enemy. **1941** [see HANDS-UPPER sense 1 b]. **1943** I. FRACK *S. Afr. Doctor* 99 The most detested appellation of all was 'National Scout,' implying that a man had deserted to the enemy during the Anglo-Boer War. **1960** [see BITTER-EINDER sense 1]. **1974** J.P. BRITS *Diary of Nat. Scout* 3 The *joiners* .. were burghers who, instead of laying down arms and ceasing to fight, defected openly and accepted remuneration for services rendered to the enemy. Grouped together as Town Guards, Farmers' Guards, Volunteers, Orange River Colony Volunteers and National Scouts, they put their knowledge of the topography and of the Boers' military tactics at the disposal of their British overlords. **1977** T.R.H. DAVENPORT *S. Afr.: Mod. Hist.* 142 National Scouts and their families were particularly vulnerable to Boer retribution, and it was in the first instance to protect them that the British military authorities decided in the second half of 1900 to set up concentration camps. **1978** R. WELCH Brothers. (Unpublished MS), Robbers, murderers, adulterers and fornicators the Lord and I can forgive – but National Scouts? Never! **1980** *Cape Times* 29 Mar. 8 At the end of the war, 'for the sake of future generations', Generals Botha, De la Rey and De Wet agreed to destroy a list of National Scouts.

national state *n. phr.* [Prob. tr. Afk. *nasionale staat.*]

1. *hist.* HOMELAND sense 1.

[**1971** *Nat. Geog. Mag.* Sept. 769 Its [*sc.* separate development's] goal is the eventual creation of national states for South Africa's tribes through a staged process bringing more autonomy at each step.] **1980** *Act 102* in *Govt Gaz.* Vol.182 No.7147, 5 Section 17 of the Second Black Laws Amendment Act, 40 1978, is hereby amended by the substitution .. of the following paragraph: .. the words 'Bantu Homelands' or the words 'Black states' the words .. 'national states'. **1980** P. CROSEUR in *Rand Daily Mail* 8 Dec. 2 The Government's total strategy is that South Africa will be surrounded by nine 'national states', economically unviable and dependent on South Africa, but drawn into a constellation of states with her so that they can sell their labour and provide a market for her manufactured goods. **1981** P.W. BOTHA in *S. Afr. Digest* 14 Aug., With the gaining of independence the citizens of national states lose their South African citizenship and acquire the citizenship of the new independent state. **1981** P.G.J. KOORNHOF in *Hansard* 29 Sept. 5156 To say that homelands are such terrible places and that the people there are unhappy, is not true. There are places in the national States where people are suffering hardships, .. but we are not responsible for those places. **1982** *E. Prov. Herald* 19 Oct. 6 The idea is to create constituencies in South Africa which will elect representatives to national assemblies in the 'independent national states'. **1983** *S. Afr. 1983: Off. Yrbk* (Dept of Foreign Affairs & Info.) 227 For the purpose of this publication 'South Africa' denotes the RSA, together with the country's Black national states, i.e. excluding the republics of Transkei, Bophuthatswana, Venda and Ciskei. **1984** *Rand Daily Mail* 18 Jan. 2 The Office of the Prime Minister affirmed that the Chief Ministers of the six 'national states' – as distinct from the 'independent states' – had been invited to lunch and discussions. **1984** R. DAVIES et al. *Struggle for S. Afr.* I. 197 Under apartheid, the Bantustans are the only areas of the country in which the majority of South Africans have any political 'rights'. First known officially as 'Bantu Homelands' and now as 'national states', the Bantustans are overcrowded, eroded and fragmented rural slums. **1985** *S. Afr. Panorama* May 23 At this stage six Black national states have the status of self-governing nations within South Africa: KwaZulu, KwaNdebele, Kangwane, Qwaqwa, Gazankulu and Lebowa. **1985** *Drum* Nov. 13 These rights will be extended even to those blacks in the so-called national states or non-independent homelands and the four independent Bantustans of Transkei, Bophuthatswana, Venda and Ciskei. **1987** *Weekly Mail* 31 July 4 'Foreign' Blacks. A total of 1,2-million 'foreign' black workers, the majority of them citizens of the four 'independent national states', were employed in South Africa as at June 30 last year ... The total number of registered South African black workers, including those from 'self-governing national states', was 1,3-million. **1988** J. SHARP in Boonzaier & Sharp *S. Afr. Keywords* 107 The designation of specific national states, then, is largely a matter of political convenience ... The embryo national states created by the homelands policy did not contain homogenous populations. **1988** A. FISCHER in *Ibid.* 131 Constitutionally, homelands were 'developed' from self-managing (*selfbesturende*) to self-governing (*selfregerende*) homelands, and from self-governing homelands to self-governing or independent 'national states'. **1988** *Star* 30 May 8 Bedevilled by bureaucracy, beset by political, social and economic problems, three of the four 'national states' have become distinguished by instability and corruption, violence and oppression, poverty and hopelessness. **1990** *Evening Post* 2 Feb. 3 Future of national states is open to 'agreements'. The re-incorporation of the independent national states into the Republic was one of many possibilities for the future of these territories.

2. *transf.* BOERESTAAT.

1988 W. DE KLERK in *Sunday Times* 10 July 17 The tip of the iceberg. That is the image appropriate for Professor Carel Boshoff's Afrikaner 'national state'.

National Suicide *n. phr. Hist.* Also with small initial(s). In full ***National Suicide of the Ama-Xhosa***: CATTLE-KILLING.

See Peires quot. 1989.

a1874 J.W. APPLEYARD *War of Axe* (1971) 119 This Armageddon resulted in the death of displacement through famine of about a third of all the tribes west of the Fish River. This is what we knew as the Cattle Killing or national Suicide of the Ama-Xosa. **1887** [see XHOSA *n.* sense 1 a]. **1971** J. MEINTJES *Sandile* 16 The great cattle-killing delusion .. caused the national sucide of the ama-Xhosa. *Ibid.* 249 (*chapter heading*) National Suicide. **1989** R. FINLAYSON Changing Face of isiXhosa. (Unpubl. thesis, Unisa) 3 A tragic event which is purported to have had an influence on written Xhosa was the so-called National Suicide which took place in 1857. **1989** J.B. PEIRES *Dead Will Arise* p.x, I nowhere use the well-known term, 'The National Suicide of the Xhosa'. The Nongqawuse catastrophe was as much a murder as it was a suicide. Probably, it was a little bit of both.

national unit *n. phr. Hist.* [Prob. tr. Afk. *nasionale eenheid.*] In official terminology during the apartheid era: a name given to each of the eight ethnic groups into which black South Africans were divided (see quots 1961 and 1986). See also NATION.

1959 *Memorandum: Promotion of Bantu Self Govt Bill* 8 The objects can be outlined as follows ... The creation of homogeneous administration areas for the Bantu by uniting the members of each Bantu national group in one national unit, concentrated in one coherent homeland where possible. **1961** *Off. Yrbk of Union 1960* (Bureau of Census & Statistics) 325 The Bantu population shall, for the purpose of the Act [*sc.* the Promotion of Bantu Self Government Bill, 1959] consist of the following national units: (*a*) The North-Sotho unit; (*b*) the South-Sotho unit; (*c*) the Swazi unit; (*d*) the Tsonga unit; (*e*) the Tswana unit; (*f*) the Venda unit; (g) the Xhosa unit; and (*h*) the Zulu unit. *Ibid.* 326 *Commissioners-General*, These persons shall represent the Government with the national unit in respect of which they have been appointed. **1970** *Rand Daily Mail* 8 Sept. 7 Immigrant receptionists had been unable to reply in Afrikaans to the Commissioner-General to the Xhosa National Unit. **1986** P. MAYLAM *Hist. of Afr. People* 167 This measure proclaimed the existence of eight African 'national units', based on assumed linguistic and cultural diversity, but not on territoriality.

National Women's Day *n. phr.* The 9th of August, celebrated as a public holiday. Occas. also shortened form **Women's Day**.

1994 *E. Prov. Herald* 8 Sept. 1, August 9 would celebrate Women's Day. **1994** *Ibid.* 8 Dec. 2 The full list of public holidays is as follows: .. August 9 National Women's Day.

National Youth Day *n. phr.* *Soweto Day*, see SOWETO sense 3.

1986 *Grocott's Mail* 20 May 1 The Rhodes University Vice-Chancellor .. said the university authorities had .. gathered that there would be a three-day stayaway by workers from June 16 – the National Youth Day commemorating those killed in unrest in Soweto in 1976. *Ibid.* 3 The Easter meeting of the National Education Crisis Committee called for a Stayaway on June 16, 17 and 18 and for June 16 to be commemorated annually as National Youth Day. **1986** *Edact* (Nusas) (*pamphlet*) 25 May, Motion on June 16 .. noting .. the call made by NECC and endorsed by COSATU to commemorate June 16 as National Youth Day. **1987** *Learn & Teach* No.4, 3 Metal workers want paid holidays on Workers' Day (May 1), National Youth Day (June 16).

Native *n.* and *adj. Obsolescent. offensive.* Also with small initial letter. [Specialized senses developed fr. Eng. *native* 'one originating in a particular place', 'indigenous', which senses have largely fallen out of use in S. Afr. Eng. when referring to fellow South Africans.]

Although all of the country's ethnic groups (including the majority of whites) are South African 'natives' in the general sense, the word came to be used exclusively of black Africans. The sense-change from 'indigenous' to 'black' is not easy to discern in the earlier quotations, but they are included as evidence of early local usage. See also the note at BLACK *n.* sense 1 b.

A. *n.*

1. As an ethnic label: **a.** A member of one of the Sintu-speaking (Bantu-speaking) peoples of southern Africa. **b.** Any black African.

Used in the past as an official term in various systems of race-classification.

1826 W. SHAW Diary. 31 Dec., Baptized five Adult Natives, on their profession of faith in our Lord Jesus Christ. **1833** *Graham's Town Jrnl* 29 Aug. 2 Destitute Natives .. are continually forced, by an irresistable pressure, over the Colonial limits. **1836** A.F. GARDINER *Journey to Zoolu Country* 79 Afternoon, – Kafir service – One hundred and fifty natives. **1836** R. GODLONTON *Introductory Remarks to Narr. of Irruption* 6 Their struggles to defend their homes and their families against the continued invasions of the natives have been stigmatised as wanton aggressions. **1846** *Natal Witness* 10 Apr. 1 The natives will be impelled by ambition, and avarice, as well as stimulated by artificial appetites that will soon be acquired, in the pursuit of wealth, and the natural results – industry, enterprise, progress in knowledge, and competition will follow. **1851** T. SHONE Diary. 5 Jan., Henry Jack Thurston and some Natives, went to cut oats at Thurston place. **1866** [see TRONK sense a]. **1879** C.L. NORRIS-NEWMAN in J. Crwys-Williams *S. Afr. Despatches* (1989) 47 The corpses of our poor soldiers, whites and natives, lay thick upon the ground in clusters. **1899** A. WERNER *Captain of Locusts* 208 He was a small, skinny, elderly native with an anxious expression of countenance. **1909** H.E.S. FREMANTLE *New Nation* 136 For over fifty years natives have been free to sit in the Cape Parliament if elected. **1918** *Cape Times* in J. Crwys-Williams *S. Afr. Despatches* (1989) 219 Spanish Influenza. Many Cases Among Rand Mine Natives. *c*1928 R.R.R. DHLOMO *Afr. Tragedy* 22 According to the story of the arrested Natives, there were other boys in the room that night whose identities they do not know. **1930** *Friend* 25 Aug. 13 Fichards will demonstrate with the Wolseley sheep shearing outfit at the sheep show today ... To prove its simplicity a Native will do the shearing. **1942** [see NON-EUROPEAN *adj.* sense 1]. **1952** L.E. NEAME *White Man's Afr.* 87 The Bantu tribes, known in South Africa as the natives, are not, of course, of the pure Negro type. **1952** F.B. YOUNG *In S. Afr.* 6 A new race, no less alien than they [*sc.* the Dutch], had appeared on their eastern frontier: the Southern Bantu, whom South Africans now call 'natives'. **1953** H.F. VERWOERD in L.V. Tutu *Twilight of Struggle* (*c*1986) 25 When I have control over native education I will reform it so that Natives will be taught from childhood that equality with Europeans is not for them. **1961** T. MATSHIKIZA *Choc. for my Wife* 107 The law couldn't describe her as a native since she was very fair, blue-eyed rosy-cheeked and straight haired. So she was entered in the Population Registration Offices as Coloured. **1966** *Cape Argus* 8 Apr. 13 There are literally no places to sit down anywhere – apart from the Gardens and a square of grass among draughts-mad Natives. **1982** M. MZAMANE *Children of Soweto* 87 Bra P. was what the legal *gurus* usually describe as 'a native of no fixed occupation'. **1990** R. MALAN *My Traitor's Heart* 30 Natives cooked my meals, polished my shoes, made my bed, mowed the lawn, trimmed the hedge, and dug holes at my father's direction.

c. *comb.* All *offensive* (and now *obs.* or *obsolescent*). **Native Affairs** *hist.*, a forerunner of the government department of CO-OPERATION AND DEVELOPMENT; **Native area** *hist.*, RESERVE; **Native beer** *obsolescent*, TSHWALA sense a; **Native boy**, BOY sense 1 a; **Native foreigner** *obs.*, a black African whose place of origin is beyond the borders of the Cape colony; **Native girl**, GIRL sense a; **Native Law** *hist.*, a body of laws applicable only to blacks, and based partly on the traditional law of the black peoples of southern Africa; see also CUSTOMARY; **Native problem, -question** *hist.*, (from a white perspective) the social and political difficulties connected with inter-racial relations and the political aspirations of black people; **Native reserve**, see RESERVE; **Native trade**, commerce in which most or all customers are black; **Native work**, an offensive term for manual labour, or for any task considered by some to be too menial for whites to perform.

1857 C.H. WILLIAMS Letter to H.F. Fynn. (Killie Campbell Africana Library MS22887) 7 Jan., I have the honour to request you will be pleased to forward .. a receipt for 14 head of cattle sent to feed Refugees .. by order of the Secretary to Government for **Native Affairs**. **1882** C.L. NORRIS-NEWMAN *With Boers in Tvl* 283 The future Boer Government would .. act wisely if .. it appointed a Minister for Native Affairs. **1911** *Farmer's Weekly* 15 Mar. 13 In the Transvaal she found the natives co-operated, if well looked after by the magistrates and officers of native affairs. **1923** G.H. NICHOLLS *Bayete!* 55 The Secretary for Native Affairs wrote the other day to say he wanted his officials to keep their fingers on the pulse of the natives. *c***1936** *S. & E. Afr. Yr Bk & Guide* 244 The Native Affairs Bill of 1920, created the Native Affairs Commission. **1987** C. HOPE *Hottentot Room* 10 'He sounds like an Indian, speaks like a white man and looks like a black,' cried the perplexed Minister of Native Affairs, back in the old days when such departments were named for their function and not to disguise their real purpose. **1963** D. JACOBSON *Through Wilderness* (1977) 48 Though she had been born in Johannesburg, she was convinced that she was liable to instant deportation if she were ever caught by a policeman or a clerk in the Native Affairs Department vengeful or conscientious enough to follow up her case. **1913** T.L. SCHREINER in *Hansard* 5 June 3134 It would be impossible for the Commission to say that they were either European or **native areas**, because the races were so mixed up together. **1913** *Act 27* in *Stat. of Union* 438 From and after the commencement of this Act, no person other than a native shall purchase, hire or in any other manner whatever acquire any land in a scheduled native area or enter into any agreement or transaction for the purchase, hire or other acquisition, direct or indirect, of any such land or of any right thereto .. except with the approval of the Governor-General. **1941** C.W. DE KIEWIET *Hist. of S. Afr.* 142 The Glen Grey district of the native area known as the Transkei. **1837** F. OWEN *Diary* (1926) 72 A number of his servants sitting by him on the ground, and the rest of the men of the town at some distance ready to commence their breakfast, consisting of bowls of **native beer**, which the women bring every morning from a long distance. **1912** AYLIFF & WHITESIDE *Hist. of Abambo* 19 These articles they did not use, but reserved them for barter with other tribes for cattle, contenting themselves with earthen pots for cooking and brewing native beer, and with wooden implements for breaking up the soil. **1928** L.P. GREENE *Adventure Omnibus* 49 They drank occasionally from a large calabash of thick native beer. **1952** 'SKAPPIE' in *Drum* Nov. 6 Native beer needs time to mature and tins of fermenting beer are often seized by raiding police. **1962** L.E. NEAME *Hist. of Apartheid* 56 In the towns .. Bantu women brewed Native beer for sale and though the practice was illegal it was widespread. **1896** H.A. BRYDEN *Tales of S. Afr.* 12 At one of these fires were gathered our **native boys**, feasting and chattering. **1907** W.C. SCULLY *By Veldt & Kopje* 19 The place has an evil reputation; no native boy cares to go near it. **1917** *Grocott's Penny Mail* 25 Apr. 3 Very few native boys working in the stores put in an appearance, and late in the day large numbers of native domestic servants deserted their employers. **1924** G. BAUMANN in Baumann & Bright *Lost Republic* (1940) 134 Some three thousand native boys were employed by different mining companies. **1978** *Daily Dispatch* 9 Nov. 3 He replied by calling her by her first name. Astonished and angry, she reported the incident to a senior manager, complaining she felt terribly insulted by this young 'native boy'. It led to Joseph's dismissal. **1843** R. GODLONTON in J.C. Chase *Cape of G.H.* (1967) 37, 186 Hottentots, and other persons of colour, natives of the colony, and 120 aborigines (styled by the Government '**native foreigners**') of the country beyond the colonial boundaries. **1845** J.M. BOWKER *Speeches & Sel.* (1864) 197 The Lt.-Governor having received information that certain of the kafirs are in an unsettled state, I am directed by his Honor to .. take measures to ascertain whether there are any native foreigners lurking about their wards. **1867** [see PASS sense 1]. **1912** AYLIFF & WHITESIDE *Hist. of Abambo* 52 No Gcaleka, Gaika, Tembu or other Native foreigner, was to enter the Colony without a pass, signed by some officer or functionary appointed by the Government. **1911** *Farmer's Weekly* 4 Oct. 115 The system of native men working in our homes must cease as soon as possible and their places be taken by **native girls**. **1919** R.Y. STORMBERG *With Love from Gwenno* 75 The old native girl in the kitchen cried out that it was heavily snowing. **1954** J. WILES *Moon to Play With* 182 'I cannot just go and ask for the native girl. I do not even know her name. The white people will certainly throw me out,' he said 'or put the dog on me.' **1934** C.P. SWART Supplement to Pettman. 123 **Native Law**, .. Law which is specially applicable to natives and based on native custom. **1948** O. WALKER *Kaffirs Are Lively* 170 The presence of two codes — Common law and Native law (which applies as between natives and mostly in rural areas) — enhances the complexities of the law for many urbanised Africans. **1936** R.J.M. GOOLD-ADAMS *S. Afr. To-Day & To-Morrow* 29 Now there are only three possible ways for men of two colours to live in one country, and we should do well to bear each of them in mind as we steer through the snags and currents of what we are pleased to call 'the **native problem**'. **1949** J.S. FRANKLIN *This Union* 209 We have no Native problem in this country at all. The only problem we are concerned with is, I think, the European problem. **1960** E.H. BROOKES in H. Spottiswoode *S. Afr.: Rd Ahead* 44 The 'Native problem', the 'race problem', the 'Jewish problem', the 'Indian problem', then (*sotto voce*) the 'English problem' and (in the shocked silence of blasphemous thought) the 'Afrikaner problem', seem to haunt us. **1974** L.M. MANGOPE *Place for All* (*c*1979) 136 The 1936 Land Act .. was introduced to increase the then 'Native Reserves', or, if one prefers to put it that way, to solve the then 'Native Problem'. **1977** F.G. BUTLER *Karoo Morning* 195 It will pass, as the poor-white and the native problem will pass no doubt in some way. **1882** C. DU VAL *With Show through Sn Afr.* I. 107 The Boers have a decided method of solving the **native question**, which might act like an electric shock upon the telescopic philanthropists of Exeter Hall. **1882** J. NIXON *Among Boers* 105 Their state is a happy augury of the success of intelligent efforts to grapple with the native question — the pressing difficulty for South Africa. **1941** C.W. DE KIEWIET *Hist. of S. Afr.* 179 The language of public discussion and political debate freely uses such terms as 'native question' and 'segregation', as if native questions concerned only natives, and as if segregation meant a real separation between two distinct communities. **1948** *Press Digest* No.1, 8 A strong plea was made for the teaching of the native question, described as the most important problem confronting South Africa, in schools. **1903** *Ilanga* 8 May 3 (advt) Best store in Durban for **Native Trade**. **1955** *Pietersburg Eng. Medium School Mag.* Nov. 4 (*advt*) Northern Transvaal Wholesalers Caterers for Native Trade. **1971** *Daily Dispatch* 16 Oct., 10 Heifers and Tollies for Native trade. **1976** S. CLOETE *Chetoko* 8 There were the usual shelves of soft goods — rolled bale after bale of red and yellow and blue materials — .. stuff for the native trade. **1941** W.M.B. NHLAPO in *Bantu World* 1 Mar. 9 Europeans had given up jobs merely because the thought that the work they were asked to do was '**native work**'.

2. *nonce.* The Xhosa language.

1937 B.J.F. LAUBSCHER *Sex, Custom & Psychopathology* If you cannot write English, then reply in native (Xosa).

B. *adj.*

1. a. Of, for, pertaining to, or characteristic of the Sintu-speaking (Bantu-speaking) inhabitants of southern Africa. **b.** Of, for, pertaining to, or characteristic of black Africans.

1827 G. THOMPSON *Trav.* II. 87 Mr. Shaw, the missionary, being on a journey to Cape Town, I was hospitably received by two native teachers, who had the superintendence of the institution in his absence. **1832** *Graham's Town Jrnl* 27 July 119 As Commandant of the Frontier the influence of his character among the Caffers was extensive and salutary. The celerity of his movements whenever he has been required to punish their acts of aggression on the Colonists .. has rendered his name equally familiar throughout Cafferland with that of its Native Chiefs. **1833** W. SHAW in B. Shaw *Memorials* (1841) 234 The native congregation continues large ... It is composed of people belonging to a great variety of tribes. **1846** A. ADAMS in *Imp. Blue Bks* Command Paper 980–1848, 63 The native population of this colony is made up principally of the remnants of several different tribes who inhabited the country previous to the time of the Zoolah chief Chaka. *a***1858** J. GOLDSWAIN *Chron.* (1947) II. 127 The Kaffer is like all other Natives tribes. **1875** C.B. BISSET *Sport & War* 16 Sir H. Smith had in the meantime detached some companies of native battalions. **1884** *Cape Law Jrnl* I. 107 A retail license .. enables a hotel keeper to sell wines, etc., to any person, whether European or native, in a shop or canteen forming part of the hotel premises. **1892** *The Jrnl* 14 Jan. 2 The criminals are for the most part Coloured or Native men. **1902** G.M. THEAL *Beginning of S. Afr. Hist.* 273 He had a force under his command of about fifteen hundred blacks armed in the native manner. **1907** J.P. FITZPATRICK *Jock of Bushveld* (1909) 313 We .. carried .. some beads with which to trade for native fowls and thick milk. **1914** *Rand Daily Mail* in J. Crwys-Williams *S. Afr. Despatches* (1989) 207 The work of removing the stones from the mouth of the cave was recommended by Detectives Martin, Rudd, O'Neill and some native police. **1923** G.H. NICHOLLS *Bayete!* 155 They were housed in the native quarters near the cattle kraal so as to be near their work; but they took frequent opportunity of visiting their families at the chief's kraal. **1934** J. VAN DER POEL Education & Native. (Paper read at conference of the South African Teachers' Association, Cape Town) 2 By no body of persons in South Africa should the issues of native education be more realistically confronted nor more dispassionately discussed than by an association of professional teachers having Bantu as well as European members. **1935** R.S. GODLEY *Khaki & Blue* 112 Laws .. must be just and reasonable, and administered absolutely impartially, irrespective of race, politics or colour ... Our so-called native policy appears to be one of oppression, engendered by fear. **1947** C.R. PRANCE *Antic Mem.* In 1903 Native labour was deadly scarce on farms. *c***1949** *Survey of Race Rel. 1948–9* (S.A.I.R.R.) 6 The Native Military Corps has been disbanded and Africans in future will be employed by the armed forces for purely non-combatant services. **1950** J. SACHS in B. Sachs *Herman Charles Bosman* (1971) 156 While the European product is stereotyped and standardised, the Native song is remarkable for its spontaneity and vitality. **1960** J.J.L. SISSON *S. Afr. Judicial Dict.* 493 *Native medicines*, The term should be understood as meaning medicines such as natives can make for themselves. **1960** *Star* in J. Crwys-Williams *S. Afr. Despatches* (1989) 332 The six European and 429 Native miners lie in a common grave 522 ft. below the surface. **1977** [see THIRD-CLASS]. **1982** [see BLERRY *adj.*].

2. Applied to cattle: of the Nguni type (see NGUNI *n.* sense 3).

1827 T. PHILIPPS *Scenes & Occurrences* 13 The native cattle have extremely long branching horns, and long legs and are not so valuable as the crossed. **1967** J.A. BROSTER *Red Blanket Valley* 3 The so-called 'Native cow' produces daily two to three pints of milk, and this only in summer. **1971** *Daily Dispatch* 28 Aug. 21, 20 Tollies native type. **1973** *Ibid.* 12 May 19, 6 Tollies, 2 years and under, 4 Native Stock.

3. *Offensive* and *derog.* In the phr. ***to go native***, (of whites) to associate with blacks; to adopt a black lifestyle. Cf. *to go bush* (see BUSH *adj.*[1] sense 3).

1948 O. WALKER *Kaffirs Are Lively* 79 There were here and there white men who had 'gone native', as the saying is, and were living in remote kraals with a plurality of wives. **1954** *Drum* Dec. 29 Regina B—, a European woman, and Richard K—, an African, were charged under the Immorality Act with living together ... Regina's attorney .. claimed that she had 'gone native,' and could no longer be considered a European ... The public prosecutor replied that under the Immorality Act it did not help to show that a woman had 'gone native'. **1968** L.G. GREEN *Full Many Glorious Morning* 144 By this time Mauch had been robbed and was almost destitute while Render had 'gone native' and was living with a daughter of Chief Bika and their half-caste child. **1968** F.C. METROWICH *Frontier Flames* 14 With the loss of their leader the Du Buys volk deteriorated rapidly and for a time they went native.

Native commissioner's court see COMMISSIONER'S COURT.

‖**natuurlik** /na'tyːrlək, nə-/ *adv.* [Afk.] 'Naturally', 'of course' (used as an affirmative).

1939 S. CLOETE *Watch for Dawn* 105 He paused. '.. I am coming back. I want you to know that I am coming back.' 'Natuurlik,' she said. 'Of course you will come back.' **1945** M. HONE *Sarah-Elizabeth* 44 Papa now asked if Mevrau proposed remaining at the farm while her husband and son would be away in the Western Province. 'But natuurlik!' said Mevrau 'where then would I go ... to the dorp?' **1978** *E. Prov. Herald* 8 Feb. 15 *(advt)* At last! South Africa's own keyboard. From IBM. Natuurlik.

Naughmal var. NAGMAAL.

nautjee var. NAARTJIE.

'n Boer maak 'n plan see BOER sense 1 d.

ncuba var. INGCUBHE.

n'daba var. INDABA.

‖**ndabazabantu** /ŋ̩ˌdabaza'baːntʊ/ *n.* Pl. unchanged, or **abondabazabantu** /abɔ-/. [Zulu *undabazabantu* lit. 'one concerned with the matters of the people', a journalist (pl. *ondabazabantu*).] Esp. in township parlance:

1. A journalist. Also *attrib.*

1984 V. KHUMALO in *Pace* Oct. 4 The other day soccer fans saw a strange game at Ellis Park — soccer writers vs referees ... Referees .. are supposed to be fundis of the game, and we would have expected them to have thoroughly trounced the ndabazabantu guys. **1987** E. MAKHANYA in *Sowetan* 21 Dec. 12 Journalists, *abondabazabantu*, Joe, like their fun ... *Abondabazabantu* are made to face the wall as the law searches for dangerous weapons. **1988** *Pace* Apr. 4 One ndabazabantu tells me, that we can expect a lot of kids born around the time of the Bophawhatsname to be named Manolo (overthrow). *Ibid.* Nov. 11 Two budding journalists attended a seminar in the Jozi one day ... A lady confronted these two 'ndabazabantu' because she thought they were gatecrashers.

2. *rare.* A magistrate; the presiding official in a commissioner's court.

1987 O. MUSI in *Drum* Aug. 79 You'll be explaining to a cold-eyed ndabazabantu why you did not marry her at all.

Ndabele var. NDEBELE.

‖**ndambula** /ŋ̩dam'bʊːla/ *n. slang.* Also **ndambola**. [Isicamtho; ultimate origin unknown.] In township English: TSHWALA sense a.

1971 E. MLENGI in *Drum* Jan. 4 Our most loved beer ... Cast-out dolls are the only ones I know to inbibe [*sic*] in the 'ndambula'. Maybe the brewers of the place she went to do not know how to brew the stuff. **1973** 'KID CASEY' in *Ibid.* 8 Oct. 41 He will organise a nip for me at a certain joint if I can keep him company while he wets his tonsils with this ndambola at this beer hall. **1982** M. MZAMANE *Children of Soweto* 9 If it was not for what I make on the sidelines you'd still be drinking *ndambula*. *Ibid.* 11 Khulu, Monty and I drank at Shirley Scott's Shebeen ... She only sold white man's liquor and no *ndambula*.

Ndebele /ŋ̩də'beːli, ŋ̩də'biːli, ŋ̩'debele, ən-/ *n.* Also **Ndabele**, **'Ndebele**, **Ndebeli**. Pl. unchanged, **ama-**, or **-s**; occas. **Mandebele**. [In the Nguni languages *i(li)Ndebele* (pl. *amaNdebele*), ad. Sotho and seTswana *matebele* (see MATABELE).]

1.a. A member of either of two divisions of a people of Nguni descent who, during the 17th century, settled in what was later known as the Transvaal, and who during the 19th century harboured and gave their name to those refugee Nguni people under Mzilikazi's leadership; MATABELE sense 1 a. Often in *pl.*, with a qualifying word distinguishing this South African people from the Zimbabwean people of the same name (see sense b), as **South(ern) -**, **Southern Transvaal -**, **Transvaal Ndebele**. **b.** MATABELE sense 1 b. Also *attrib.*

1872 T.M. THOMAS *11 Yrs in Central S. Afr.* 153 The Amandebele are divided into three divisions ... The first class are the Abezansi ... These came originally from Natal, with Umzilikazi, and now form the aristocracy of the land. The second class are Abenhla ... This class is made up of fragments of Basutu and Bechuana tribes, which were attacked by the chief, Umzilikazi .. and incorporated into one body with those who were already his people. These are at present the middle classes of the Amandebele. The other division are the Amaholi ... These were the aborigines of the present Amandebele country ... These are the lower classes. **1878** A. AYLWARD *Tvl of Today* 177 Far north of the Republic .. but separated from it by Bechuanas and peaceable tribes, dwells another Zulu nation called the Amandebele. **1898** B. MITFORD *Induna's Wife* 5 At that place we met in fierce battle and rolled back the might of Dingane and thus saved the Amandebeli as a nation. **1923** G.H. NICHOLLS *Bayete!* 10 Have I not all my life led my impi to victory; and now that I am getting old you tell me that I have lost my skill? Did the Amandebele die with Mzilikazi? Did not the Deliverer take his place? **1930** S.T. PLAATJE *Mhudi* (1975) 51 Let this success be known among the nations so that foreign armies may tremble each time they hear the mention of the name, Amandebele. **1937** N.J. VAN WARMELO in I. Schapera *Bantu-Speaking Tribes* 53 Transvaal Ndebele. These Ndebele tribes must not be confused with the Ndebele now living in Matabeleland, Southern Rhodesia. The latter left the confines of Zululand only a century ago under the leadership of Mzilikazi, whereas the former had by that time already been settled in their present territory for at least several centuries. **1937** A.W. HOERNLÉ in *Ibid.* 86 Among the Southern Transvaal Ndebele, each .. clan has a species of animal .. which may not be named or eaten or used by the members of that clan. **1939** N.J. VAN WARMELO in A.M. Duggan-Cronin *Bantu Tribes* III. i. 10 The Transvaal Ndebele tribes have traditions pointing to an emigration from Natal three or four centuries ago, but prior to that all is blank. *Ibid.* 12 The [Nguni] sub-group of the Transvaal Ndebele .. in turn fall into two sections, a Southern and a Northern one. **1951** [see BAROLONG]. **1966** J.D. OMER-COOPER *Zulu Aftermath* 170 The Transvaal Ndebele .. appear to have established themselves on the plateau before the Mfecane. **1970** *Drum* Oct. 24 Chieftainess Esther Kekana, head of the 10, 000 strong Mandebele tribe in the Northern Transvaal .. is not herself a Ndebele. She is a Pedi from Potgietersrust, but the Mandebele of Hammanskraal have taken her to their hearts. **1975** *Drum* 8 Mar. 61 Opposition to the establishment of the Southern Ndebele Homeland. **1975** W.F. LYE *Andrew Smith's Jrnl 1834–6* 318 *AmaNdebele (Nguni), maTebele (Sotho)*, (rendered *Matabili, Matabeli*, etc.), Name applied by Sotho people to the invading people of Mzilikazi and other Nguni raiders. The name had not yet been adopted by Mzilikazi's people at the time ... They called themselves abakwaZulu, kwaMoshobana, amaKumalo, etc. **1976** WEST & MORRIS *Abantu* 77 Originally, the Ndebele stem from Nguni stock and have close links with the Zulu and Xhosa. There are three distinct groups, two live in the Transvaal and the third in Rhodesia. **1979** *Daily Dispatch* 9 Apr. 10 The Matabele, or Amandebele as they prefer to be called, had very little to contend with when they met the demoralised Mashona. Having made peace with the spirits .. the Matabele had an easy passage and were soon raiding the Mashona for slaves (Maholi) and women for the Matabele to marry. **1980** LYE & MURRAY *Transformations* 32 He [*sc.* Mzilikazi] built the Ndebele kingdom after Shaka's model ... Being relatively few in numbers, and in an alien land, the Kumalo found every opportunity to add to their strength. They often absorbed other refugees from Zululand, and also many of the young men of the Tswana clans which they destroyed. **1983** *Pace* Dec. 82 Meet one of the most culturally rich tribes of Africa, the Ndebele of South Africa, or South Ndebele. They are also known as the Ndebele of (Chief) Mapoch, so as not to be confused with the MaNdebele of Matabeleland in Zimbabwe. **1985** PLATZKY & WALKER *Surplus People* 38 In 1975 these [homeland consolidation] proposals were updated and approved by parliament ... A bantustan for the Southern Ndebele was to be created near Groblersdal in the Transvaal. *Ibid.* 179 It was not part of the original Nationalist plan for ethnic 'homelands'. The first mention of an Ndebele bantustan was only made in the late 1960s. *c*1988 *S. Afr. 1987–8: Off. Yrbk* (Bureau for Info.) 63 The Nguni comprise three major subgroups .. : North Nguni: the Zulu .. and the Swazi ... South Nguni: the Xhosa-speaking peoples ... Transvaal Ndebele: a northern and southern section. **1990** *Sunday Times* 25 Feb. 22, I have been in KwaNdebele for some time, and could not understand why tribalism was promoted. The so-called 'Amandebele' are the class racists. Only Ndebeles hold the highest posts in the government services. **1994** D. MATTHEWS in *Sunday Times* 9 Jan. 11 Mrs Mahlangu's mother insisted she learn traditional Ndebele painting.

2.a. SINDEBELE.

1939 N.J. VAN WARMELO in A.M. Duggan-Cronin *Bantu Tribes* III. i. 12 The Rhodesian Ndebele are by far the most important, for though the empire founded by Mzilikazi in Matabeleland was overthrown by the British, a modified Nguni language and culture (Ndebele) still flourishes there now, and shows no sign of decay. **1972** *Drum* 8 Oct. 30 They must be .. able to write in English, Ndebele, Shona or Nyanga. **1973** *Ibid.* 8 Jan. 18 My mother language is Shona and I can speak English and Ndebele. **1980** LYE & MURRAY *Transformations* 100 Chieftainess Ester Kekana and 60 000 Ndebele followers .. proposed .. to join the North Sotho 'homeland' of Lebowa. They had been using the Pedi language, since no books were available in Ndebele. **1981** *Fair Lady* 1 July 108 What makes life even more difficult for the KwaNdebele children is that although they speak Ndebele, the language has no written grammar, so they are taught in Zulu. **1983** *Star* 1 Mar. 2 Black citizenship must be clarified before another homeland became independent, says the South African Institute of Race Relations. The institute was reacting to the coming independence of kwaNdebele, which could mean about 700 000 Ndebele-speaking blacks losing their South African citizenship. **1987** *Pace* Sept. 19 Here was the opening band for the greatest show on earth singing in some language akin to Zulu but known as Ndebele in Zimbabwe. **1993** *Weekend Post* 9 Oct. 9 If this letter is anything to go by, multilingualism including North and South Sotho, .. Xhosa, Zulu and Ndebele is out.

b. With a qualifying word, distinguishing each dialect of this language, as spoken in certain areas of South Africa: **Northern Transvaal Ndebele**, **South(ern Transvaal) Ndebele**.

1952 N.J. Van Warmelo *Lang. Map of S. Afr.* (Dept of Native Affairs) 11 **Northern Transvaal Ndebele** ... This language is mainly spoken in Potgietersrus and Pieterstrus districts ... A number have emigrated to the Hammanskraal sub-district of Pretoria. 1952 *Ibid.* 11 **Southern Transvaal Ndebele** ... This language is spoken by members of two tribes only, the Manala and the Ndzundza. c1988 *S. Afr. 1987–8: Off. Yrbk* (Bureau for Info.) 68 Another Nguni language is South Ndebele with 394 000 speakers living mainly in KwaNdebele in central Transvaal. Though influenced by Northern Sotho (Sepedi),.. South Ndebele remains a Nguni language with strong ties with Zulu and Swazi.

Ndhlovukazi var. Ndlovukazi.

ndhlozi var. idlozi.

Ndlambe /ŋ'ɬaːmbe, ŋ'dlambi, ən-/ *pl. n.* Also **Amadhlambi, amaNdlambe, Dhlambi, Jlambi.** [Xhosa *amaNdlambe*, named for *Ndlambe* (c1740–1828), son of Rharabe.] (The) members of one of the major branches (and its consolidated chiefdoms) of the Rharhabe division of the Xhosa people; slambie. Also *attrib.*

The Rharhabe split into the Ngqika ('Gaikas') and the Ndlambe ('Slambies') in c1795–96, when Ngqika tried to claim his throne from his uncle Ndlambe who had been acting as regent since about 1782. See also Rharhabe sense a.

As is the case with many names of peoples and groups in *S. Afr. Eng.*, this word has been found only in plural uses; however, it may be that it has also been used in unrecorded singular forms.

1842 J.W. Appleyard *War of Axe* (1971) 12, I fear that Pati is in league .. with the Gaika and Jlambi chiefs. 1846 *Ibid.* 68 Stock's great Counsellor and many of the great men of the Amadhlambi, have been killed. *Ibid.* 103 Capt. Maclean .. has received a similar appointment in relation to the Dhlambi tribes. 1939 N.J. Van Warmelo in A.M. Duggan-Cronin *Bantu Tribes* III. i. 21 Ndlambe ultimately fled across the Bushman's river, and here great numbers joined him, not only from Ngqika's people, but also from the tribes that had previously seceded. The Ndlambe tribe thus became almost as powerful as the Ngqika. 1968 E.A. Walker *Hist. of Sn Afr.* 288 The Ndhlambis and the Galekas, Sandile's Gaikas and most of the Tembus slew and slew and .. the madness mounted higher. 1971 J. Meintjes *Sandile* 12 The powerful tribe of ama-Rarabe was badly weakened when it split up into the rival factions of ama-Ngqika and ama-Ndlambe. *Ibid.* 13 The serious split between the ama-Ngqika and the ama-Ndlambe took place in 1796. 1981 J.B. Peires *House of Phalo* 61 Ndlambe did his best to make a separate peace with the Colony ... Somerset and Cuyler .. turned a deaf ear. Well might the amaNdlambe complain. *Ibid.* 80 The Ndlambe and the Gqunukhwebe had been expelled from their territory in 1812. 1986 P. Maylam *Hist. of Afr. People* 99 Some Ndlambe chiefs continued an intermittent, harassing style of resistance into 1847. 1989 [see Ngqika].

Ndlovu var. indlovu.

‖**Ndlovukazi** /ŋɮovu'kaːzi/ *n.* Also **Indlovukati, Indlovukazi, Ndhlovukazi, Ndlovukasi.** [Zulu *indlovukazi*, siSwati *indlovukati,* (-*kazi*), elephant cow, 'Great She Elephant'.] In Swazi and Zulu society: an honorific title given usu. to the Queen Mother, but also to the Queen Regent, or to the wife of a king or paramount chief; also used with a name. See also indlovu.

1941 H. Beemer in A.M. Duggan-Cronin *Bantu Tribes* III. iv. 9 Privileges and responsibilities of citizens are conferred on everyone owing allegiance to the king, head of the Nkosi Dlamini, titled *Ingwenyama,* the lion, and to his mother, the *Indlovukati,* lady elephant. 1964 *Drum* Nov. 25 She was the 'Ndlovukazi' Emily Thokozile Majali, Queen of the Zulus, the wife of Paramount Chief Cyprian Bhekuzulu. 1975 *E. Prov. Herald* 22 Aug. 13 The Swazi Queen Mother ranks second to the King, and enjoys exclusive right to the title of Ndlovukasi, which means 'great-she-elephant'. She has a special and separate royal kraal with her own private regiment of warriors. 1983 *Cape Times* 5 Jan. 1 The prince will become king when he is 21, the sources said. Meanwhile, the king's senior widow or Ndlovukazi — The Great She Elephant — would continue as regent. 1983 C. Van der Merwe in *Pace* Oct. 26 Swaziland, ruled .. by King Sobhuza for so long, was inevitably plunged into a vicious power struggle by his death. At the centre of the row is the Ndlovukazi, or She Elephant, the Kingdom's traditional fellow ruler. *Ibid.* 28 In the reign of her husband, Mbandzeni, the Ndhlovukazi Labotsibeni Mdluli had been the proverbial power behind the throne. After his death in 1889, she had held the centre stage, first as Queen Mother for her son, Bhunu, then, on his death in 1899, as Queen Regent until 1921.

ndlunkulu var. indlunkulu.

NDM *n. hist.* [Initial letters of *National Democratic Movement.*] A political movement to the left of centre, founded in October 1987 by former National Party and Progressive Federal Party members who believed that more co-operation should be sought with extra-parliamentary political structures. Also *attrib.*

The NDM was one of three groups which merged to form the Democratic Party in 1989: see note at DP *n.*[2]

1987 *Daily Dispatch* 9 Oct. 1 NDM in trouble as dispute surfaces. 1987 *Ibid.* 22 Oct. 15 PFP hecklers dominate at Durban NDM meeting. 1988 *Star* 10 May 3 Time to talk to ANC, says NDM. 1988 *Race Rel. Survey 1987-8* (S.A.I.R.R.) 745 The leader of the PFP, Mr Colin Eglin, said that the NDM had 'philosophically borrowed very heavily from the PFP' but only its 'style differs'. 1989 D. Worrall in *Progress* (P.F.P.) Mar. 2 The NDM's credibility with extra-parliamentary groups is an enormous political asset.

ndoda var. indoda.

ndodana see indoda.

nduna var. induna.

ne var. nee.

nê /ne/ *int. colloq.* Also **ne, nè, né, neh, nie.** [Afk. *nè.*] An interrogative particle, 'isn't that so?', 'not so?'; also used redundantly for emphasis.

1891 J.P. Legg in *Cape Illust. Mag.* I. 95 A peculiar use of an enclitic 'neh' is often to be heard, though not so generally; thus 'you are coming with us — neh?' Serving the purpose of a note of interrogation in conversation. 1900 H. Blore *Imp. Light Horseman* 194 Then you are not come as a recruit to our ranks, but have already ducked your head to a bullet, nê? 1920 S. Black *Dorp* 65 After a long pause, Achteruit replied, 'Couldn't you arrange a salary somehow, neh?' 1958 A. Sampson *Treason Cage* 140 The same washing that was brought in through the back of white man's house was washed by black hands — black hands — in an African hut, neh? 1967 [see make]. 1974 D. Rooke *Margaretha de la Porte* 116 When she finished the doily she shook it out and then smoothed it lovingly ... Small red beads decorated this one. 'Like rubies, nè?' said Mevrouw. 1979 M. Matshoba *Call Me Not a Man* 158 'Give me your pass' ... I gave it to him and he paged through it .. 'You're Xhosa, neh?' I nodded. 1981 H. Smith in *E. Prov. Herald* 16 June 12 South West Africa has a grand ring to it, né? Go on, say it. Listen to the sound of it. It's big. Big like my country, né? 1985 *Sunday Times* 10 Mar. (Lifestyle) 3 *Foeitog* a lesser person would find herself at the end of her dither, *né,* but not this rare woman who faces total onslaught .. without a crease to her crimplene. 1985 [see Engels *adj.* sense 2]. 1990 T. Robb in *Top Forty* July 36 You're one of those guys that believes every metal album has hidden 'evil' messages in its grooves if you play it backwards, right? Well, only someone like you would play a record backwards, nê?! 1990 J. Naidoo *Coolie Location* 5 He didn't go far né. He fell just in front of our place. *Ibid.* 131 Bhiraj has been arrested. He sent someone here, né. He said you must hide his things.

NEC /en iː 'siː/ *n.* Also **N.E.C.** A shortened name for the *National Executive Committee* of the African National Congress. Also *attrib.*

1943 *Constitution of A.N.C.* in Karis & Carter *From Protest to Challenge: Hope & Challenge 1935–52* (1973) II. 206 Once every three years the national conference shall elect a national executive committee ... The N.E.C. shall meet on the day of its election and thereafter at least once in 6 months ... The N.E.C. shall be responsible for the activities of Congress between National Conferences. 1990 N. Kulati in *New African* 10 Sept. 1 ANC National Executive Committee (NEC) member Gertrude Shope read out a statement. 1990 *Weekly Mail* 21 Sept. 7 The NEC wields extraordinary power: it is able to take major decisions without reference to any other ANC organ ... NEC member Pallo Jordan had to rush to Robben Island last week. 1991 R.W. Johnson in *Sunday Star* 21 July (Review) 6 Some nervousness was felt that Indians might be knocked off the NEC by the scrum of ambitious Africans. 1992 C. Whitfield in *Natal Mercury* 23 Nov. 1 Much of the ANC NEC discussions will focus on the bilateral meeting with the Government.

NECC /en iː siː 'siː/ *n.* [Initial letters of *National Education Co-ordinating Committee* (or, until late 1989, of *National Education Crisis Committee*).] An organization formed to co-ordinate left-wing opposition to the government's education policies, and to devise alternative policies. Also *attrib.*

The NECC was formed in March 1986 as a result of a conference called by the Soweto Parents' Crisis Committee in December 1985 to discuss national education.

1986 K. Andrew in *Evening Post* 31 Mar. 5 It is pleasing that the NECC is not adopting a knee-jerk reaction. 1987 *Weekly Mail* 12 June 1 Some of the prominent individuals who had no more than a few seconds of freedom before being redetained were .. NECC officials Vusi Khanyile .. and Bill Jardine. 1987 *New Nation* 15 Oct. 1 'By his active involvement in the NECC your client endangered and undermined the maintenance of public order,' Vlok added. 1990 *New African* 13 Aug. 2 (*advt*) The Education Development Trust (EDT), the development section of the NECC is committed to a non-racial, democratic education system.

necklace *n.* [Fig. and transf. use of general Eng. *necklace* jewellery worn around the neck.] Often *the necklace*: **a.** A tyre doused or filled with petrol, placed round a person's shoulders or neck, and set alight. **b.** This method of lynching or unofficial execution; see also necklacing. Also *attrib.*

1985 *Weekly Mail* 16 Aug. 5 The cry went up: 'The necklace! The necklace!' A tyre was draped around his neck, doused with petrol and set alight. 1985 Setuke & Badela in *City Press* 18 Aug. 4 The 'necklace' was there at Mxenge's funeral .. for those who didn't 'belong'. 1985 *Sunday Times* 27 Oct. 19 In township patois the 'necklace' is the death sentence whereby people are doused in petrol and a tyre is placed round the neck. 1986 *E. Prov. Herald* 28 Oct. 2 Three counts of murder by 'necklace'. 1987 M. Benson *At Still Point* (1988) 245 A horrifying element through the years has been the role of *impimpis* — informers. Their betrayals .. caused excruciating suffering and not surprisingly it was in the Eastern Cape that revenge by the gruesome 'necklace' first occurred. 1989 N. Mathiane in *Frontline* Mar. 8 Many people at that time still perceived the necklace as a symbol of the struggle. 1989 *E. Prov. Herald* 15 May 4 The 'necklace' — the term has become one of those uniquely South African words, like veld or kraal, which mark us as different from the rest of mankind — was in use for a long time before it surfaced in print. 1989 *Reader's Digest Illust. Hist.* 480 The 'necklace' was .. forced over the victim's head and shoulders, trapping his arms against his side. It was then set alight. 1990 *Frontline* Jan. 14 Strikes and stay-aways increase. So do bombs and necklaces. 1990 D. Capel in *Personality* 21 May 16 People who have taken part in things like necklace murders often later express incredulity at their actions. **1991** T. Molefe in *Race Rel. News* (S.A.I.R.R.) Vol.53 No.1, 18 We were tried, found guilty and sentenced to death by necklace – to be executed on the spot. **1994** R. Malan in *Style* May 37 The disgust I once felt about the suppression of the ANC had long since been subsumed by the spectacle of thugs in ANC T-shirts terrorising anyone who disagreed with them, my rage over Steve Biko's murder obliterated by the horror of the necklace.

necklace *v. trans.* [fr. prec.] To kill (someone) by the necklace method. Often *passive*.

1986 *Cape Times* 12 Feb., If I'm seen with this party, I'll be necklaced in the township tonight. **1987** *Drum* Jan. 51 It was not long after that he was Okapied on the steps of the Senate – a reminder incidentally that necklacing those in power is as old as the hills. **1987** *Sunday Telegraph* (U.K.) 28 June 9 According to the British-born scholar, Dr Tom Lodge, the first person to be necklaced was .. a town councillor in the Eastern Cape township of Kwanobuhle. **1988** *Grocott's Mail* 13 May 1 The charred body of a black boy who had been 'necklaced'. **1988** P. Younghusband in *Inside S. Afr.* Apr. 12 He once flung himself into a lynch mob at a township funeral and saved a man from being necklaced. **1990** *Frontline* Jan. 18 Some alarmist .. had warned over the SABC (where else) that the 'comrades' would necklace black children who attended 'white' schools. **1990** R. Malan in *Cosmopolitan* Apr. 162 A mob of Wararas waylaid him on his way home from Sipho's funeral and necklaced him – put a tyre around his neck, poured petrol on him and burnt him alive. **1992** Malan & Beckett in *Guardian Weekly* 3 July 7 The first person to die was a woman .. whose sin was a romantic involvement with a Zulu hostel dweller ... A crowd cornered her .. and necklaced her – burned her alive.

So **necklaced** *ppl adj.*, **necklacer** *n.*

1986 *Star* 22 Apr., The 'necklaced' bodies of three men have been found in squatter camps on the Cape Flats. **1987** Collins & Dyan in *Leadership* Vol.6 No.3, 98 Young militant blacks may understand how the lynch-mob mentality of the necklacers arises, .. but no-one we have encountered regards the practice as being morally justified. **1987** *New Nation* 12 Nov. 4 The wife of the necklaced Uitenhage councillor. **1993** D. Beresford in *Weekly Mail* 29 Oct. 14 The charred body of a necklaced woman was found in Katlehong's Radebe section.

necklacing *vbl n.* [fr. prec.] The action of killing (someone) by the 'necklace' method. Also *attrib.*

1986 H. Suzman in *E. Prov. Herald* 10 Apr. 1 Horrendous crimes of black on black violence, such as necklacing. **1986** *Sowetan* 19 June 2 Security forces prevented several necklacings on Tuesday ... Police arrested several blacks attempting to set a black alight in Tembisa. **1986** *E. Prov. Herald* 19 Aug. 2 Two men were killed, one by the infamous 'necklacing' method and the other by stabbing, after Pondos and Zulus clashed at a beerhall. **1986** *Sunday Times* 15 June 28 South Africa suddenly fell in [*sic*] the grip of a terrible cycle of violence – a phenomenon that gave rise to 'necklacings' and 'Trojan horses'. **1987** O. Prozesky *Wrath of Lamb* 17 The unrest in Good Hope's non-white townships, intimidation, the burning of houses and the brutal stoning and fire-necklacing of people stopped virtually overnight. **1988** *Now Everyone Is Afraid* (Catholic Inst. for Internat. Rel.) 122 Some Mbokodo members were killed in public necklacings. **1989** S. Barber in *Cape Times* 29 Jan. 1 Conservative demonstrators staged a mock 'necklacing' to protest against Secretary of State Mr George Shultz's meeting with the ANC president, Mr Oliver Tambo. **1990** *Weekly Mail* 14 Sept. 7 The first necklacing murder was committed in a township whose name belied the gruesome act as well as the lives of its residents. It's called kwa Nobuhle – the place of beauty, near Uitenhage. **1990** *Ibid.* 21 Sept. 9 From Sharpeville to the State of Emergency, from the torturer's arsenal of interrogation tools to the streetfighter's necklacings, we have lived through so much brutality that it's a wonder we South Africans can even contemplate a peaceful future. **1994** R.W. Johnson in *London Review of Books* (U.K.) 6 Jan. 10 Much of the fighting has been done with knives and pangas, but the local gunsmiths have been doing a roaring trade too and there has been some necklacing.

neckstrap *n. obs.* [tr. S. Afr. Du. *nekstrop*, see NEKSTROP.] STROP *n.*[1] sense 1 a.

1863 W.C. Baldwin *Afr. Hunting* 103 From the beams hung kaffir ropes, .. neckstraps, and all the apparatus for wagoning. **1907** J.P. Fitzpatrick *Jock of Bushveld* (1909) Glossary, *Nekstrop*, .. the neck-strap, or reim, which, attached to the yokeskeys, keeps the yoke in place. **1936** E.C. Llewellyn *Influence of Low Dutch* 168 *Skey*, .. one of a pair of wooden bars passing through each end of an ox-yoke, to which the neck-straps are fixed.

neck strop *n. phr. Obs.* [Part. tr. S. Afr. Du. *nekstrop*, see NEKSTROP.] STROP *n.*[1] sense 1 a.

1853 *Natal Mercury* 13 Jan., Mr Landsdell .. cut as many of the neck strops adrift as he possibly could. **1916** *Farmer's Weekly* 27 Dec. 1564 (*advt*) Mule and Donkey Harness ... We have a full stock of:– Game Reins, Game Neck Strops.

Nederduits Gereformeerde Moederkerk see MOEDERKERK.

Nederlands /ˈnɪədə(r)lants/ *n.* [Afk., fr. Du. *Nederlandsch.*] The Dutch language of the Netherlands; cf. HIGH DUTCH. See also HOLLANDS.

[**1926** *Spectator* (U.K) 21 Aug. 278 Africaans resembles, in vocabulary, the Dutch of the seventeenth and early eighteenth centuries almost more than modern Nederlands does.] *c*1928 Botha & Burger *Grammar of Afrikaans* Intro., Wherever the terms Dutch and Nederlands are used, the language of Holland is to be understood. *Ibid.* 4 Although Afrikaans is essentially Nederlands in respect of vocabulary and syntax, it differs widely from Nederlands in respect of sounds and accidence. **1946** [see HIGH DUTCH]. **1953** [see GHOMMA]. **1959** *Cape Times* 8 June 8 Nederlands is an old and highly developed language with a wide literature. **1991** *Rhodes University Calendar 1991* (Grahamstown) 21 Academic Staff and Departments ... Afrikaans & Nederlands.

‖**Ned Geref** /ned xəˈref/ *adj. phr.* Also **Ned. Geref.** [Afk., written abbrev. of *Nederduitse Gereformeerde* Dutch Reformed.] 'Dutch Reformed': NG. Usu. in the phrr. ***Ned Geref Church, -Kerk*** /- kɛrk/ [Afk., *kerk* church].

Used only in written contexts.

1877 F. Jeppe *Tvl Bk Almanac & Dir.* (1976) 38 There are congregations belonging to two other Dutch denominations represented in the Republic, such as the 'Ned. Geref. Kerk,' and the 'Gereformeerde Kerk', which are known under the common appellation of orthodox Churches; the latter is called the Dopper Church. **1970** *Argus* 3 Oct. 2 A plea by the Ned. Geref. Church. **1986** *E. Prov. Herald* 7 Oct. 2 The Ned Geref Sendingkerk general synod yesterday decided not to break ecumenical ties with the white Ned Geref Kerk. **1987** *Ibid.* 23 Oct. 1 In a historic decision yesterday the Western Cape Synod of the Ned Geref Kerk expressed itself in favour of one unified Church. **1988** K. Stander in *Argus* 24 Mar. 1 A new row has broken out in the Ned Geref Kerk family over criticism of Dr Allan Boesak and Archbishop Desmond Tutu by the white NGK and President Botha.

‖**Ned Herv** /ned ˈhɛrf/ *adj. phr.* [Afk., written abbrev. of *Nederduits Hervormde* Dutch Reformed.] HERVORMDE. Usu. in the collocation ***Ned Herv Kerk*** /- ˈkɛrk/ [Afk., *kerk* church], *Hervormde Church* (see HERVORMDE).

Used in written contexts.

1982 *Pretoria News* 21 Sept. 3 The Ned Herv Kerk has rejected a 'unique opportunity to change its ways' by its withdrawal from the World Alliance of Reformed Churches. [**1987** *E. Prov. Herald* 14 May 2 Mr Golden is a former Ned Hervormde Kerk minister.]

‖**nee** /nɪə/ *adv.* Also **ne**, **ney**. [Afk.] No.

1. Expressing a negative response to a statement or question, or introducing a correction to a prior statement or assumption.

1888 *Cape Punch* 14 Sept. 139 'Good evening, Samuel. Don't forget to call round early tomorrow morning ...' 'Ne, baas. Good ebenning.' **1961** S. Cloete in *Best of S. Afr. Short Stories* (1991) 289 'I believe that our Japie is mad ...' 'Nee, Hendrik,' his wife said, 'our Japie is not mad.' **1963** R. Gedye in C.M. Booysen *Tales of S. Afr.* 156 'Are you going out to-night?' 'Nee, I don't think so ...' **1973** *E. Prov. Herald* 12 June 9 'Seems to be coming from here.' I indicated the small box near the spark plug. 'Ag, nee man' they both laughed, 'that's the impulse'. 'Nee, this is a different noise.' **1979** *Daily Dispatch* 11 May 18 'It is more a tribute to their well-oiled political machine in the Cape Province than to a genuine belief in their policies,' ... 'Ag, nee,' objected several Nats. **1989** W. Swing in *Sunday Times* 3 Dec. 27 'Apartheid – nee' and 'amandla – yebo'. Which is it? Or is it both? **1990** *Frontline* Mar.-Apr. 16 Does it trouble him, her driving with coloureds? 'Agge Neee, man. Her colleagues are very respectable people.'

2. In the adv. phr. *nee wat* [Afk., *wat* /vat/, 'what', as interjection, 'please', 'won't you']: 'oh, no'; 'no indeed', 'certainly not'; NO WHAT.

a. Used for emphasis with the force of an expletive, without implying negation.

1900 B. Mitford *Aletta* 34 'Maagtig! but they are liars, those English newspaper men' ... '*Nee wat.* I would like to get the miserable ink-squirter who wrote that, and make him run at five hundred yards from my Martini.'

b. As an expression of dismay, disagreement, or refusal.

1917 S.T. Plaatje *Native Life* 83 Anna leaving the farm, O, nee wat! (Oh, no). We must find out who it is. **1973** A. Fugard *Boesman & Lena* (1980) 21 *Ag nee wat!* You must try something there. **1979** F. Dike *First S. African* 30 Ney wat, ou Solly drinks scotch only. Ney Solly? **1991** B. Krige in *Sunday Times* 14 July 5 (*caption*) Ag nee wat, now the dominee won't let us drink and dance in Dealesville.

3. Used to emphasize a statement, without implying negation.

1958 S. Cloete *Mask* 59 Nee, a man like that is better dead. [**1988** G. Silber in *Style* Apr. 41 The ladies .. try hard to look awestruck ... 'O, nee, dis mooi,' says Tannie Margaret. 'It's a very nice one, Hugh,' says Tannie Marie.]

Hence **nee** *n.*, an utterance of the word 'nee'.

1973 *Drum* 22 Jan. 22 Mnr. Greyling is very clear. He gives a loud and big, 'Nee'.

‖**neef** /nɪəf/ *n.* Also **nief**. [S. Afr. Du., cousin, nephew.] In the reported speech of Afrikaans- or South African Dutch-speaking people:

1. 'Cousin', 'nephew': an informal term of address or reference to a male cousin or nephew, or to any younger man; NEFIE sense a; NEPHEW sense a. See also NIGGIE.

1838 J.E. Alexander *Exped. into Int.* I. 103 The field-cornets and the farmers are all related or connected: every one is oom or neef (uncle or nephew) to his neighbour. **1868** W.R. Thomson *Poems, Essays & Sketches* 178 Will you .. make Merry Christmas with the *ooms, tantes, neefs*, and *nichtjes* at one or other of these places? **1871** [see OOM sense 2]. **1899** G.H. Russell *Under Sjambok* 48 'Believe me, Nief' (nephew, an expression used to young Boer men), 'you are the first I have met who does not take it [*sc.* sugar].' **1903** D. Blackburn *Burgher Quixote* 131 'Ah, neef, so the khakis have not got you?' said he, kindly. **1912** [see HEER *int.*]. **1914** L.H. Brinkman *Breath of Karroo* 14 The elders .. address the younger men as 'neef,' and young girls as 'nicht,' both terms meaning 'cousin,' a friendly method which tends to .. put every one at ease. **1937** C.R. Prance *Tante Rebella's Saga* 196 Oom Christiaan was still hardly more than 'Neef', new-married and with only a golden shadow of his today's snowy apostolic beard. **1944** —— *Under Blue Roof* 150

Nephew Piet might be uncle-by-marriage to his own Uncle Karel's second wife, so that nephew and uncle might reasonably address each other indifferently as 'Oom' or 'Neef'. **1945** *Outspan* 20 July 37 Come, let us now go and help the neef. **1946** E. ROSENTHAL *General De Wet* 21 Officers would frequently be addressed as 'Oom' (Uncle) and in their turn would call their men 'Neef' or 'Nephew'. **1952** VAN DE HAER & MANUEL in *Drum* Aug. 7 One day a broadfaced, florid Afrikaner joined our Coloured friend a few yards away. At every piece of smart play the newcomer would .. call for support from his unknown neighbour whom he addressed as 'Neef.' **1958** R.E. LIGHTON *Out of Strong* 144 Suddenly she cackled with toothless laughter and .. cried triumphantly, 'Can't you see, Neef?' **1965** K. MACKENZIE *Deserter* 71 Commander Venter came round to encourage his soldiers. He said to Japie: 'Veldcornet Kritzinger tells me you did very well in the charge ... That is good work, *neef*, and you must keep it up.' **1975** *Sunday Times* 19 Oct. (Mag. Sect.) 8 The folkdancers show the way. Note the hand-embroidered waistcoats of the 'neefs'. **1978** *Ibid.* 20 Aug. 14 'Ou neef, .. I am looking for my daughter, who is supposed to be somewhere in this building. Have you perhaps seen her?' **1980** [see NIGGIE]. **1993** 'K. LEMMER' in *Weekly Mail* 18 June 12 A neef of Oom Krisjan recently went to Shell House to claim some petrol money from the ANC accounts department.

2. A title, with a first name; NEPHEW sense b.

1912 F. BANCROFT *Veldt Dwellers* 175 Then Tante Jacoba said: 'Do not take it to heart, *neef* Petrus.' **1934** N. DEVITT *Mem. of Magistrate* 17 A leading Boer went to Paul Kruger: 'President', he said, 'I want a post for my son!' The President .. replied: 'Neef Hans, your boy is not slim enough to be a clerk, and all the higher posts are filled!' **1947** C.R. PRANCE *Antic Mem.* 76 Oom Jurie and Neef Japie had to help the Vet. personally to corner a suspected mule. **1953** U. KRIGE *Dream & Desert* 180 What a contrary fellow Neef Kobus is! **1963** L. ABRAHAMS (tr. H.C. Bosman) in *Unto Dust* 36 There was something dignified about his appearance that prevented me from calling him bluntly 'neef Herklaas'.

‖**nefie** /ˈnɪəfi/ *n.* Also **neefie**. [Afk., *neef* cousin, nephew + -IE.] **a.** As a term of address: NEEF sense 1. **b.** *nonce.* An Afrikaner.

1951 L.G. GREEN *Grow Lovely* 11 It is seldom now that I meet a man twice my age, but there it was and he called me nefie. **1984** E. MPHAHLELE *Afrika my Music* 124 Remember you used to say to me, nefie, I just take soda water and my tummy sits easy on my belt. **1984** *Daily Dispatch* 30 Aug. 22 The 300 000 (plus) civil servants .. watch unconcernedly the certain impoverishment of those non-neefies and non-niggies and the rest of the population who are not government-subsidised.

negotie /nəˈxʊəti, -si/ *n.* Also **nagotie, negocie, negosie, niccoti**. [S. Afr. Du. (later Afk. *negosie*), commerce, merchandise.]

1. *obs.* Retail trading, commerce. Also *attrib.*

1832 *Graham's Town Jrnl* 10 Feb. 25 Proposed .. and carried unanimously by all the Winkeliers present;— *That* .. no Members of the Port Elizabeth Temperance Society be allowed to purchase Brandy except for *Negotie. Ibid.* 23 Mar. 51 The lucky man who gets the *prize* may make a good thing of it by *Negotie.* **1913** C. PETTMAN *Africanderisms* 338 *Negotie ware*, .. Groceries, hard or soft goods offered for sale; the stock-in-trade of a store-keeper or pedlar. **1920** R. JUTA *Tavern* 248 About a month ago Uncle's old Malay driver fell ill and we were forced to put up a 'Negocie' affiche in the George Tavern for a new one.

2. *obs.* Goods, merchandise.

1832 *Graham's Town Jrnl* 4 May 74 A storekeeper .. will give him only a small proportion .. in cash, and the remainder negotie (goods,) at an advanced price.

3. *comb. Obs.* exc. *hist.* **negotie winkel** /- ˈwɪŋk(ə)l, -ˈvəŋ-/, also **- winkle**, [S. Afr. Du., *winkel* shop], GENERAL DEALER sense 1 b; hence **negotie winkeler** *n. phr.* [Eng. n.-forming suffix *-er*], GENERAL DEALER sense 1 a.

1839 W.C. HARRIS *Wild Sports* 334 Having obtained permission from a Dutchman named *Humans* to unyoke in an unoccupied spot, we again opened our **negotie winkel**. **1840** C.A. KINLOCH in *Echo* 26 Oct. 2 We .. lost no time in opening a 'Negotie Winkel' for some sheep and goats, in lieu of which we gave tobacco, at a most profitable rate of exchange. [*a*1862 J. AYLIFF *Jrnl of 'Harry Hastings'* (1963) 81 There was one board above the shop door printed 'Negotie Winkle'. *a*1875 T. BAINES *Jrnl of Res.* (1964) II. 35 We sought the abode of Mr. Bauman, formerly a watchmaker but now a merchant and 'negotie winkeler', or retail dealer. **1876** T. STUBBS Reminiscences. 9 Old Bertram had a Store and had over his door Nagotie winkel — the Settlers thought it was his name, and always called him Old Nigerty Winkle. **1881** P. GILLMORE *Land of Boer* 208, I looked out for the best store; at length I decided on what appeared the cleanest and most promising, which bore the inscription — 'Niccoti Winkle'. **1884** B. ADAMS *Narr.* (1941) 66, I observed a young man about 28 years of age standing at the door of a shed on which was written Negotie Winkle — Retail Store.] **1920** R. JUTA *Tavern* 64 He read, 'a charming young widow makes known the death of a tender husband and adds a piece of "negotie winkle" — in consequence of the death will be sold, etc ..' (here followed a list of the advertised shop goods). [**1965** A. GORDON-BROWN *S. Afr. Heritage* IV. 4 A visitor to Cape Town in 1823 wrote that all shops were in private dwelling houses, distinguishable only by the notice 'Negotie Winkel' over the doors.] **1987** B. MAREE in *S. Afr. Panorama* July 37 In this store with its packed shelves, its unique colours and flavours and its large variety of goods, visitors experience the typical atmosphere of an old-fashioned *negosiewinkel* (general dealer), where virtually anything under the sun could be bought.

neh var. NÊ.

nek /nek/ *n.* [S. Afr. Du., prob. calqued on Eng. *neck* isthmus, promontory, mountain pass, but perh. tr. Fr. *col*, as used in this sense by the French Huguenots. It seems that *nek* was never used in standard Dutch in this sense.]

1. A narrow ridge or saddle of land, lower than, but joining, two mountains or hills.

1834 T. PRINGLE *Afr. Sketches* 223 They had to travel along the narrow ridge (nek) in order to reach the opposite highland. **1853** R.B. STRUTHERS *Hunting Jrnl* (1991) 27 Got the Dr. ashore to a Kraal across the nek of land dividing the lake from the Umpata. **1881** *E. London Dispatch & Frontier Advertiser* 26 Jan. 3 On reaching the nek we found the enemy posted on the mountains, with a few stragglers moving across it to join them. **1899** B. MITFORD *Weird of Deadly Hollow* 85 The wheel-track mounted a grassy nek or 'saddle,' uniting this giant pillar to the main range. **1906** H. RIDER HAGGARD *Benita* 12 Leaving the waggon on the hither side of the steep nek, over which it would have been difficult to drag it. **1920** F.C. CORNELL *Glamour of Prospecting* 150 We were faced by a low connecting granite nek, barring our progress, and abruptly ending the ravine. **1925** F.C. SLATER *Shining River* 235 Nek, A depression between two hills. **1946** L.G. GREEN *So Few Are Free* 65 The sea once covered large areas of the Cape Peninsula, including .. the narrow nek of land at Kommetje. **1957** —— *Beyond City Lights* 82 Halt on the nek and gaze at another reminder of this bold family — the castellated Du Toit's Kloof Peak. **1987** L. BEAKE *Strollers* 96 The sun glittered on the sea far below as they came over the Nek.

2. POORT.

1882 LADY F.C. DIXIE *In Land of Misfortune* 144 On nearing a pass or nek .. extra care was taken to guard against surprise. **1900** R. KIPLING in J. Crwys-Williams *S. Afr. Despatches* (1989) 163, I shall put *you* and four or five more on the nek (the pass), where the road comes from their camp into these koppies. *c*1936 *S. & E. Afr. Yr Bk & Guide* 37 *Nek/Poort*, .. opening between mountains or hills. **1972** *S. Afr. Panorama* Mar. 31 The Wen-Kommando breasted a low *nek*, or pass, between an imposing mountain .. and a smaller hill that the Zulus called Zonkgonka.

3. *comb.* An element in place names, e.g. *Brooke's Nek, Constantia Nek, La(i)ng's Nek.*

1881 *E. London Dispatch & Frontier Advertiser* 12 Jan. 3 They retired to a ridge and donga below Tsitsa's nek. **1914** C. PETTMAN *Notes on S. Afr. Place Names* 18 Commando Nek recalls the means that were often employed in earlier days to punish the common enemy. *Ibid.* 30 Only a few, and those among the most conspicuous of our veld birds, have found recognition in our place names: e.g., Duivenhoek River, .. Mahemspruit; the ostrich — Vogelstruispoort, Vogelstruisnek, [etc.]. **1989** P.E. RAPER *Dict. of Sn Afr. Place Names* 292 *Lang's Nek*, .. Low mountain pass in the Drakensberg, some 8 km south of Volksrust.

nekstrop /ˈnekstrɒp, -strɔp/ *n. obsolescent.* [S. Afr. Du., *nek* neck + *strop* halter, noose, rope, strap.] STROP *n.*[1] sense 1 a. Also part. tr. **neck strop**.

1822 W.J. BURCHELL *Trav.* I. 151 The jukschei .. are merely two straight pegs, one on each side of the ox's neck, and having notches on their outer sides to receive the nek-strop (neck strap). **1907** [see YOKE-SKEY sense 1]. **1909** N. PAUL *Child in Midst* 8 He removed the yoke and nekstrops from it and its mate ... The ox moved off slowly. **1916** *Farmer's Weekly* 27 Dec. 1564 (*advt*) Mule and Donkey Harness ... We have a full stock of:— Game Reins, Game Neck Strops. **1970** W. JACOBS *Informant, Bloemfontein* The oxen who were pulling the wagon all had nekstrops.

nemesia /nəˈmiːʒ(ɪ)ə/ *n.* Also with initial capital. [Modern L., fr. Gk *nemesion*, used of a similar plant.] Any of several plants of the genus *Nemesia* of the Scrophulariaceae, bearing brightly-coloured flowers of various hues.

1815 F. PURSH *Donn's Hortus Cantabrigiensis* 196 Nemesia, [English name] Nemesia. Germander-leav. [*sic*]. **1838** *Edwards's Bot. Reg.* XXIV. 39 (*heading*) Many-flowered Nemesia. **1868** W.H. HARVEY *Genera of S. Afr. Plants* 255 *Nemesia*, Annual, or more rarely perennial of suffruticose plants ... Bentham describes 25 species. **1892** *Gardeners' Chron.* (U.K.) 3 Sept. 269 There are many plants that vary to the extent of two or three colours in a wild state, but it is exceedingly rare to find them indulging in such wholesale variation as this Nemesia does. I have seen sixteen varieties of colour. **1906** B. STONEMAN *Plants & their Ways* 259 *Nemesia*, .. Herbs annual or perennial, bearing racemes of pretty flowers of many hues. Twenty-eight species ... Beautiful Nemesias in great abundance are found in the Malmesbury district. **1913** D. FAIRBRIDGE *Piet of Italy* 31 He hurried down to the sandy track fringed with blue nemesias and orange gazanias. **1949** L.G. GREEN *In Land of Afternoon* 72 Hybrid gladioli, nemesias, even the Hottentot fig, were all startling novelties. **1968** *Farmer's Weekly* 3 Mar. 57 A plant I feel that gardeners generally do not appreciate as much as they should is the nemesia. **1977** [see JAKKALSKOS]. **1984** Z. GILBERT *S. Afr. Garden Month by Month* 26 Winter flowering annuals. *Summer rainfall areas*: In the warmer parts of these areas sow: .. *Godetia* (satin flower), *Linaria maroccana* (toad flax) .., *Nemesia*, [etc.].

nenta /ˈnentə/ *n.* Also **ninta, t'nenta**, and with initial capital. [Khoikhoi plant name (the *t'* in the S. Afr. Eng. variant *t'nenta* representing a click in the original language).]

1. *krimpsiektebos*, see KRIMPSIEKTE sense 2. Also *attrib.*, and occas. *comb.* **nentabossie** /-bɔsi/ [Afk., *bos* bush + -IE].

1796 C.R. HOPSON tr. *C.P. Thunberg's Trav.* II. 97 The Hottentots called by the name of *Nenta*, a plant (*Zygophyllum herbaceum repens*), which was said to be poisonous to sheep, as also another, a shrub of the same genus, (*Zygophyllum sessilifolium*.) **1896** R. WALLACE *Farming Indust. of Cape Col.* 95 The *t'nenta*, *Lessertia annularis*, Burch., is an insignificant, purplish-flowered species, at times seen in quantity in the gebroken veld, where, if consumed, it poisons goats and sheep. **1897** *Cape of G.H. Agric. Jrnl* 308 (Pettman), The Russian moufik contracts neurotis through continued eating of the leguminous *Lathyrus*; .. and the Cape goat gets it .. from an undetermined leguminous *Nenta*. **1913** C. PETTMAN *Africanderisms* 339 *Nenta*, (Hot. *Nenta, with initial click.) *Cotyledon ventricosa*.

This plant is supposed to be the cause of a disease fatal to sheep and goats. **1917** R. Marloth *Common Names* 61 *Nenta'bossie*, (Krimpziekte-plant). MacOwen ascribes this disease to *Lessertia annularis*, but almost all farmers are of the opinion that it is caused by *Cotyledon Wallichii* and some allied species, e.g., *C. ventricosa*. **1978** *E. Prov. Herald* 6 Mar. 8 The plant which causes the sickness variously known as lêsiekte, krimpsiekte, nenta poisoning or cotyledonsis, had been identified as Cotyledon teretifolia or Cotyledon campanulata. **1993** Milton & Dean in *Afr. Wildlife* Vol.47 No.1, 27 They [*sc.* Karoo leopard tortoises] swallowed large chunks of the succulent stems of ninta (*Tylecodon wallichii*), a plant protected against most other herbivores by its poisonous leaves and spiny stem.

2. *Pathology.* krimpsiekte sense 1.

1905 D. Hutcheon in Flint & Gilchrist *Science in S. Afr.* 358 Cerebro-Spinal Meningitis or 'Nenta' in Goats. **1910** *Cape of G.H. Agric. Jrnl* 302 (Pettman), The well-known disorder in sheep and goats known at the Cape as *Nenta. Ibid.* 12 Sept. (Pettman), Whether t'Nenta and Stiff-ziekte are names for one and the same thing differing in degree, I cannot say. **1934** [see krimpsiekte sense 1]. **1937** *Handbk for Farmers* (Dept of Agric. & Forestry) 462 Krimpsiekte or Nenta. **1976** Mönnig & Veldman *Handbk on Stock Diseases* 208 *Cotyledon Poisoning (Krimpsiekte).* This disease (also known as Nenta) is caused by several different species of *Cotyledon*. **1979** T. Gutsche *There Was a Man* 20 Some goats now suffering from a disease called Nenta.

nephew *n. obs.* [Special sense of general Eng., influenced by Afk. *neef* cousin, nephew, used loosely of any young man.]

Usu. used to suggest the idiom of Afrikaans-speakers.

a. neef sense 1. Also in the phr. ***the nephew***, substituted for the second person pronoun 'you', reflecting a respectful form of address in Afrikaans (see quot. 1900).

1900 H. Blore *Imp. Light Horseman* 213 He had met everybody there but me before, and as formal introductions are unknown among the Boers, after we had solemnly shaken hands all round and begun the repast, he addressed me with the query, 'How is the nephew called?' **1936** C. Birkby *Thirstland Treks* 243 'Those are Oom Gert's peaches,' said Wiets. 'We row now across his lands.' Oom Gert spat over the gunwale. 'Let us pull, nephew,' he said. **1940** F.B. Young *City of Gold* 198 'Who's that you're talking to, nephew?' the Veld-kornet said. 'He's not one of our men.'

b. neef sense 2.

1944 C.R. Prance *Under Blue Roof* 150 Nephew Piet might be uncle-by-marriage to his own Uncle Karel's second wife, so that nephew and uncle might reasonably address each other indifferently as 'Oom' or 'Neef'.

Nerine /nə'riːn/ *n.* Also **Narina**, **Nerina**, and with small initial. Pl. unchanged, or **-s**. [Etym. dubious; either fr. Khoikhoi *narina* 'flower' (see Narina *n.*[2]), or fr. L. *Nerine* the name of a Greek water-nymph (see quot. 1986).] Any of several bulbous flowering plants of the genus *Nerine* of the Amaryllidaceae, esp. *Nerine sarniensis*, with umbels of bell-shaped pink, red, or white flowers; sore-eye flower sense c. Also *attrib.*

Called 'Guernsey lily' in *Brit. Eng.* since 1664; see quots 1966 and 1972.

1820 *Curtis's Bot. Mag. 1787–1844* XLVII. 2124 Rose-coloured Nerine ... Nerine is probably confined to South Africa. **1837** W. Herbert *Amaryllidaceae* 285, I have no hesitation in stating that it is a Nerine. **1886** G. Nicholson *Illust. Dict. of Gardening 1885–8* II. 446 When in flower, Nerines are amongst the most beautiful of greenhouse bulbous plants. **1910** R. Juta *Cape Peninsula* 83 Narina is the Hottentot word for flower, and the flower is a gorgeous species of lily in every shade of red, pink, and maroon, covered with shining gold dust. **1913** H. Tucker *Our Beautiful Peninsula* 94 The exquisite nerine, whose lily-like cluster of long-stamened flowers ranges in hue from salmon-pink to deep magenta, while each wavy, outcurving petal glistens with a delicate sheen as of gold-dust. **1917** R. Marloth *Common Names* 61 *Nerina, Nerine sarniensis.* There are numerous other species. **1925** F.C. Slater *Centenary Bk of S. Afr. Verse* 235 *Nerine*, A genus of lilaceous plants. The finest species is found on Table Mountain, and is known as the 'Guernsey Lily' in England. **1929** *Amateur Gardening* 3 Aug. 293 Nerines, or Guernsey lilies, are attractive flowering bulbs. *c***1933** J. Juta in A.C. Partridge *Lives, Lett. & Diaries* (1971) 159 Flowers from the cool gorges of Table Mountain – blue disas, and golden-spangled nerines. **1946** K.C. Stanford in *Farmer's Weekly* 30 Oct. 48 First I would put Nerine sarniensis, the big red Nerine of the Cape mountain slopes ... There are many other Nerines, mostly good cut flowers. **1948** *Jrnl of Botanical Soc.* XXXIV. 7, I remember .. when Nerinas were plentiful about Hout Bay. **1952** [see moederkappie]. **1953** M.L. Wicht in *Jrnl of Botanical Soc.* XXXIX. 13 The mountaineer, passing a bowl of nerine blooms in the florists' window, .. in his mind's eye .. will see them making a brilliant display on the mountain slopes where *Nerine sarniensis* is at home. **1966** C.A. Smith *Common Names* 239 *Guernsey lily, Nerine sarniensis* ... One of the earliest South African plants to be figured, the tradition attached to the species being that a vessel bound for Holland from the East Indies via the Cape had a quantity of bulbs on board and was wrecked on the Guernsey (formerly Sarnia) coast in the early part of the 17th century ... By 1659, the species was in cultivation in England ... It was then regarded as a native of Japan, since the vessel which was wrecked returned from that part of the Orient and there was as yet no permanent settlement at the Cape at the time of the catastrophe. Nearly a century later specimens were found on the slopes of Table Mountain and its true home thus settled. **1967** J.A. Broster *Red Blanket Valley* 94 Glades of giant mountain nerina, their roots deep in leaf mould, flourish as in a hot-house. The exquisite blooms of these lilies are four inches in diameter. **1972** M.R. Levyns in *Std Encycl. of Sn Afr.* VI. 641 *Lily, Guernsey. Nerina*, .. Linnaeus, who gave it the name *sarniensis*, thought that it was a native of Guernsey ... Thunberg added further to the confusion by stating erroneously that it had come from Japan. Nowadays no one disputes its South African origin. **1986** A. Batten *Flowers of Sn Afr.* 286 The genus *Nerine* is endemic in southern Africa ... Its present name was applied only when the English botanist W. Herbert recognized that the plant differed sufficiently from other members of the genus *Amaryllis* to justify the founding of a new genus which he called *Nerine*, the name of a Greek water nymph. **1989** *Gardening Questions Answered* (Reader's Digest Assoc.) 345 *Nerine*, .. Indigenous, deciduous and semi-deciduous bulbs with narrow, strap-like leaves and heads of bell-shaped, pink, red or white flowers with narrow, recurved petals in summer and autumn. Also called Guernsey lily. **1990** M. Hayter in *Flying Springbok* 118 Pink nerinas and their tumbleweed-like seeds. **1992** S. Johnson in *Afr. Wildlife* Vol.46 No.4, 178 Few flowers can compete with the beauty of .. nerina (*Nerine sarniensis*).

nersderm see derm sense b.

nerve *n.* In the colloquial adv. phr. ***on one's nerves*** [calqued on Afk. *op (sy) senuwees* tense but self-controlled (perh. influenced by the general Eng. usage *to get on one's nerves*)]: in an extremely tense state; likely to become angry or aggressive at the slightest provocation.

1913 J. Brandt *Petticoat Commando* 92 There is a Dutch saying which forcibly expresses that condition of tense self-control under circumstances of a particularly trying nature. We say we are 'living on our nerves'. Our Heroines, like so many other sorely tried women in South Africa, were 'living on their nerves,' those wise, understanding nerves, so knowing and so delicate. **1976** *Cape Times* 29 Dec. 2 The residents of Nyanga, fearing trouble 'because we are on our nerves', gathered together .. , and by the time the riot police arrived .. , had formed a 'protecting line' against the migrant workers. **1988** Adams & Suttner *William Str.* 69 This is the first time I had witnessed division amongst us coloureds, especially over religion, and Sarah being so on her nerves. **1991** D. Ashman *Informant, Cape Town* Teacher, you seem on your nerves today. Why are you so cross with us? **1991** C. Clarkson *Informant, Johannesburg* On one's nerves: Nervous. No doubt from Afrikaans 'op sy senuwees'. Jees, I was on my nerves the whole time that his kid would break something.

neuk /niœk, nɪək/ *v. slang.* Also **nierk**. [Afk., 'to beat up', ad. Du. *neuken* to knock.] Not in polite use.

1. *trans.* donner *v.* sense 1. So **neuked** *ppl adj.* (used *absol.*), **neuking** *vbl n.*

1910 *E. Prov. Herald* 24 May, They wound up by asserting that they would straightway 'nierk' him ... 'Nierking' not being a very pleasant proceeding for the 'nierked,' Barnard asked 'What for.' 'Never mind. We will nierk you,' was the only reply. **1913** C. Pettman *Africanderisms* 399 Neuk, .. This word survives in South Africa with the meaning to hit, strike ... It is regarded as a coarse word. **1970** J. Goosen *Informant, Queenstown* Johnny neuked the other ou at school today – gave the other fellow a good beating. **1970** M.S. Wagener *Informant, Strydenburg*, I neuked him flat out. He was knocked out flat. [**1983** F.G. Butler *Bursting World* 154 The round ended with the crowd involved, shouting occasional polite words of encouragement such as 'Moer hom', 'Neuk hom.'] **1984** T. Baron in *Frontline* Mar. 18 He and Ou Mike were neuking the souties all over the shop when they stopped the fight to disqualify both sides. **1990** P. Cull in *Weekend Post* 18 Aug. 10 Dr Ferdi Hartzenberg ... CP 'will neuk ANC op'. **1991** B. Carlyon *Informant, Johannesburg*, I will neuk you if you start with me.

2. *intrans. rare.* In the phr. ***to neuk with (someone or something)***: to interfere with or 'mess with' something or someone.

1980 *Capetonian* Aug. 26 Die Merrem, she sez 'Katie, take die Master's teef to die dentist in the Main Road ... Yerrah, I don' min tellin' you, I don't like to *neuk* wid teef'. **1991** E. Bruwer *Informant, Cape Town* Don't neuk with the child.

NEUM /en iː ju(ː) 'em/ *n. hist.* Also **N.E.U.M.** [Initial letters of *Non-European Unity Movement*.] A Trotskyite liberation group formed in 1943 as an alternative to South African Communist Party-influenced mass movements such as the African National Congress.

From 1961 the NEUM was active mainly through a splinter group, Apdusa. Revived in 1985 under the name New Unity Movement, the organisation was also occas. called the Unity Movement. See also AAC, Anti-CAD.

1959 *Ikhewizi Lomso* May 8 Both the Anti-C.A.D. and the South African Convention, together with all those organisations affiliated to the N.E.U.M. are pledged to the struggle against oppression. **1963** M. Horrell *Action, Reaction* 4 A section of the Coloured people .. established an Anti-C.A.C. movement, which later changed its name to the Non-European Unity Movement, with the aim of securing united action ... As time went by the N.E.U.M. grew increasingly radical and stood for complete non-co-operation with Whites. [**1971** see Anti-Cad.] **1971** *Drum* Aug. 10 Hassim had been a main official of the NEUM. **1984** R. Davies et al. *Struggle for S. Afr.* II. 311 Concretely, the NEUM was created by a merger of the All African Convention .. and a militant coloured federation known as the Anti-CAD (Anti Coloured Affairs Department). The South African Indian Congress was also initially associated with the NEUM.

Neutral Territory *n. phr. Hist.* Also with small initials. Ceded Territory.

1829 W. Shaw Diary. 6 Oct., The Governor held a Meeting with the Chiefs, Kye and Fundis, of the Amakakabi Tribe .. this morning, in the Neutral Territory. [**1829** C. Rose *Four Yrs in Sn Afr.* 81 The rich tract which Gaika had so unwillingly ceded to his allies, and from which the Kaffers had been expelled, .. called the Neutral Ground.] **1833** *S. Afr. Almanac & Dir.* 204 Interview between Lord C. Somerset and the

Caffer Chief Gaika. Neutral Territory ceded. **1834** A. SMITH in *Graham's Town Jrnl* 24 Aug. 136 Caffers inhabit this part of the neutral territory, and many visited our wagons. **1846** J.M. BOWKER *Speeches & Sel.* (1864) 261 The Neutral Territory is to be settled with Fingoes and Hottentots. **1852** M.B. HUDSON *S. Afr. Frontier Life* p.vii, The Kafirs .. had, on the restoration of peace, to vacate a certain portion of land previously held by them, and henceforth to be named 'the Neutral Territory.' **1860** W. SHAW *Story of my Mission* 383 The spring-bok, bush-bok, hartebeest, and qwagga, were frequently met with in troops and flocks in the grassy country of the neutral territory. **1875** C.B. BISSET *Sport & War* 55 A new military position .. had recently been established east of the actual colonial border, on what was formerly called the Neutral Territory, between the Kat and Keiskamma Rivers. **1913** G.E. CORY *Rise of S. Afr.* II. 108 The Neutral Territory, that is, the country between the Great Fish and Keiskamma rivers, which, according to the verbal treaty between Lord Charles Somerset and Gaika in 1819, was to be occupied by neither Kaffir nor colonist. **1977** T.R.H. DAVENPORT *S. Afr.: Mod. Hist.* 99 D'Urban proposed to make the 'neutral' territory between the Keiskamma and the Kei available for exclusively white settlement. **1989** *Reader's Digest Illust. Hist.* 72 In 1819 Cape Governor Lord Charles Somerset knocked another nail in Ngqika's coffin when he forced him to give up the land between the Kei and Keiskamma rivers as 'neutral territory', to be occupied by neither the settlers nor the Xhosas.

new oath *n. phr. Hist.* Also with initial capitals. [Perh. tr. Afk. *nuwe eed.*] ***The new oath***: The General Service Oath taken by those members of the armed forces willing to serve anywhere in the world during the second World War. See also RED OATH.

The oath was first taken in 1943.

1944 'TWEDE IN BEVEL' *Piet Kolonel* 210 Never can they take away from us those days we had in the 1st S.W.A. Inf.; we have now taken the new oath, lots of us have. *Ibid.* 213 And the New Oath .. ? .. No one knows all the factors and circumstances which have influenced the boys .. to come to their decision to take or not to take the new oath. [**1983** F.G. BUTLER *Bursting World* 163 On 26 January Parliament passed legislation authorising a new oath for service anywhere in the world.]

Hence **new oather** *n. phr.*, one who took the General Service Oath.

1944 'TWEDE IN BEVEL' *Piet Kolonel* 207 There is nothing uplifting in the present disturbing rumours about the future of the ex-SWAIS's new oathers.

New South Africa *n. phr.* Also **New SA**, and with small first initial. South Africa in the post-apartheid era. Now often used ironically.

Although this phrase has been used at various times with reference to real or proposed political changes, its present wide currency resulted from its use by the National Party during the election campaign of 1989, and, more particularly, by the then State President F.W. de Klerk on 2 February 1990, during a speech to Parliament in which he announced the unbanning of left-wing political organizations, and committed the government to the abolition of apartheid legislation.

1989 *Daily Dispatch* 5 Sept. 5 (*advt*) Vote for the NP for a great and just, a New South Africa. **1990** F.W. DE KLERK in *Hansard* 2 Feb. 2, I wish to ask all who identify yourselves with the broad aim of a new South Africa, and that is the overwhelming majority: – Let us put petty politics aside ... Help us build a broad consensus about the fundamentals of a new, realistic and democratic dispensation. **1990** *Weekend Argus* 17 Feb. 12 The 'new' South Africa is barely two weeks old and already a distinctly new political style is taking shape. **1990** *Sunday Times* 3 June 18 In the new South Africa – an expression that is rapidly being devalued through the tedium of repetition – military service will obviously have to be as non-racial as the politics. **1990** J. SCOTT in *Weekend Post* 16 June 14 Jan H– of Kuruman seized on the Peninsula squatter problem, declaring: 'The people of Hout Bay can't open their windows, because they smell the new South Africa.' **1990** [see POST-APARTHEID]. **1990** R. VAN TONDER in *Frontline* Sept. 27 The much-trumpeted 'New South Africa' perpetuates the same old concoction, with nothing changed other than the substitution of white rule by black rule – or power-sharing, on the basis of one rabbit to one horse. **1991** J. BERGER in *Focus on Afr.* Apr.-June 32 The Kloppers are refugees from the New South Africa, and everything it stands for: uncertainty, change, and equality. **1991** C. GREGORY in *Frontline* May 20 I've declared war on 'the New South Africa'. And I'm out recruiting. I'm not resisting the change, but the words: *New South Africa*. This phrase may constitute the largest single impediment to a settled future ... By casting their eyes skyward in the direction of the imagined glow, people seem to be prevented from thinking sensibly. **1992** S. SHERRY in *South* 27 Feb. 3 So you thought that crazy animal called the 'new' South Africa had something to do with politics and human rights? Well it doesn't. It's about dialling soft porn at R6,60 a minute, legal scratch cards that can win you 50 Grand, topless women on M-Net and on the beach and 'adult' magazines in sealed plastic bags. **1992** *Sunday Times* 7 June 15 'Should inter-racial adoption of orphans be encouraged?' ... 'Yes. This is what the new South Africa is all about. It's about learning to live together.' **1992** 'HOGARTH' in *Ibid.* 17 May 24 Hail to the new SA. With Chris Hani's kids at private school, Joe Slovo in the suburbs and Nelson Mandela in Houghton, it gets more like the old SA every day. **1993** C. DESMOND in *Daily News* 6 Jan. 8 The 'New South Africa' has yet to be born; conceived in secrecy, intrigue and elitism, umbilically tied to Western values, it could well be aborted. **1994** L. RAMPOLOKENG in *Tribute* May 30 This romantic NSA (New South Africa) has turned me into a globe trotter.

Hence **New South African** *n. phr.*, one living in the New South Africa; one living a changed life in South Africa; *adj.*, of or pertaining to the New South Africa; **New South Africanism** *n. phr.*, a spirit of co-operation, tolerance, and unity in South African politics and society.

1990 *Sunday Times* 4 Mar. 25 While there is much talk of a new South Africa, a new South Africanism is still lacking. This can only be embodied in a truly non-racial togetherness. **1990** B. BREYTENBACH in *Weekly Mail* June 5 The onus is on the ANC: .. to promote the 'new South African'. **1994** R. MALAN in *Style* May 35, I saw him play one night in a Johannesburg pub and it was the standard New South African lovefest of the late Eighties: lots of mixed couples, pale left-wingers and black leather-jacketed creatures from the art and fashion fringe cracking pipes with Sowetan Rastafarians in the alleys off Commissioner Street. **1994** C. BAUER in *Sunday Times* 12 June 16 Substance abuse can take the edge off the trauma of being a new South African.

ney var. NEE.

NG /en 'dʒiː, en 'xɪə/ *adj.* [Afk., initial letters of *Nederduitse Gereformeerde* Dutch Reformed. Cf. NGK.] 'Dutch Reformed'; of or pertaining to the NGK; NED GEREF. Freq. in the n. phr. ***NG Kerk*** /- 'kɛrk/ [Afk., *kerk* church], NGK.

1971 *Weekend Post* 11 Sept. 3 After being closed for six months the historic Paarl NG Kerk, known as the 'Strooi-dakkerk', will be reopened to-morrow. **1974** [see SENDINGKERK]. **1978** *Daily Dispatch* 25 Jan. 13 The viewpoint on racism expressed at the meeting .. appears in a report on the World Council of Churches Programme to Combat Racism, compiled by a study commission of the NG Sending Kerk. **1989** D. VAN HEERDEN in *Sunday Times* 5 Mar. 4 Representatives of the NG churches will this week converge in an historic meeting. **1990** *Sunday Times* 10 June 11 He was the rising star in the NG hierarchy ... After more than a quarter of a century in clerical purgatory, he will again preach before a NG Kerk congregation. **1990** *Ibid.* 14 Oct. 4 NG synods have always been an important barometer to determine the political mood of the Afrikaner volk. **1993** *Weekend Post* 24 July (Leisure) 1 Alexandria .. was established in 1840 and named after the Rev Alexander Smith, a Scottish minister of the NG Kerk who was then based in Uitenhage.

ngaap var. GHAAP.

ngaka /ŋ'gɑːkə, ŋ'gaːka, ən-/ *n.* Pl. **-s**, ‖**di-**, ‖**li-** /di-/. [Sotho and seTswana *ngaka* (pl. *dingaka*, or, in Lesotho orthography, *lingaka*).] Among Sotho- and seTswana-speakers: a traditional healer. Also *attrib.* See also WITCHDOCTOR.

1871 J. MACKENZIE *Ten Yrs* (1971) 381 As Ngaka or priest, the chief is supported by a class of men (lingaka) who not only practise the art of healing but are professors of witchcraft and have taken degrees in rain-making. **1952** *Drum* Apr. 25 Many people .. thought that the people at the bottom of ritual murders were the ngakas, or medicine men (or witch doctors, as corrupted by Europeans) ... Many of the ngaka societies are companies formed on the usual business line, with a board of directors, president and secretary. **1957** A.A. MURRAY *Blanket* 19 The Ngaka (Witchdoctor) will say: 'Do such and such, and evil will be averted from your hut.' **1966** A.T. BRYANT *Zulu Medicine* 12 Returning across the continent, we find *n-gaka* (doctor) among the Sutos. **1976** WEST & MORRIS *Abantu* 130 To protect them from sorcery and witchcraft people turned to the Tswana doctors, *dingaka*. **1976** S. FUGARD *Rite of Passage* 100 *Ngaka*, A witchdoctor practising the medicine and homeopathy of the Pedi tribe; also a diviner, and the intermediary between the tribe and its ancestors. **1982** *Fair Lady* 19 May 36 You are called to study as a *ngaka* (spirit doctor).

ngana var. NAGANA.

ngawethu see AMANDLA.

ngcube var. INGCUBHE.

NGK /en dʒiː 'keɪ, en xɪə 'kɑː/ *n.* Also **N.G.K.** [Afk., initial letters of *Nederduitse Gereformeerde Kerk* 'Dutch Reformed Church'.]

In both senses also called *Ned Geref Church* (see NED GEREF), *NG Kerk* (see NG). See note at DUTCH REFORMED.

1. The *Nederduitse Gereformeerde Kerk* (Dutch Reformed Church), the oldest of the Calvinist churches; the white branch of this church. Also *attrib.*

1970 *Cape Times* 3 June, NGK journal on 'deviations' in Holland. **1971** *Drum* June 56 Drum pointed out that very recently, a non-White was asked to leave a NGK service in Johannesburg. **1973** A. PATON *Apartheid & Archbishop* 4 The largest church was the Nederduitse Gereformeerde Kerk, the N.G.K., called commonly and erroneously the Dutch Reformed Church, there being two other smaller Dutch Reformed churches. **1978** *Daily Dispatch* 25 Jan. 5 The viewpoint on racism expressed at a meeting between the moderature of the Coloured branch of the NGK and a top church delegation from Holland. **1980** *Voice* 29 Oct. 13 Priests usually make the lousiest politicians, and those ous in the NGK can attest to that. **1986** *Sunday Times* 16 Mar. 2 The Dutch Reformed family of 13 churches ... These churches include the white NGK, the NGK Church of Africa and the Dutch Reformed Mission Church. **1990** *Style* July 79 The NGK establishment had considered his poem, a send-up of the *Lord's Prayer*, to be offensive and had filed a criminal charge. **1994** C. BARRON in *Ibid.* 10 Apr. 11 Liquor licenses for the adjacent restaurant have been turned down because the NGK regarded the monument as 'a sacred shrine where God is thanked each year for the maintenance of white civilisation'.

2. In the phrr. ***NGK in Afrika***, ***NGK in Africa***: the *Nederduitse Gereformeerde Kerk in Afrika* (Dutch Reformed Church in Africa), the black branch of this church. See also SENDINGKERK.

1986 [see sense 1]. **1988** C. LE GRANGE in *Star* 25 May 5M The Nederduitse Gereformeerde Kerk (NGK) is bound to face opposition from its sister black and coloured churches, the NGK in Afrika (NGKA) and the NG Sendingkerk (NGSK). **1989** D. VAN HEERDEN in

ngoma *n.*[1] var. INGOMA.

ngoma /ŋgɔːmə, əŋ-, -ma/ *n.*[2] Also with initial capital. [Venda.] A large, single-headed drum of the Venda, used esp. in certain religious ceremonies.

The same word is used for drums and dances in eastern Africa, derived from Swahili.

1931 H.A. STAYT *BaVenda* 316 The two types of drum .. are usually played by women, although anybody is allowed to play them. The large drum, *ngoma*, is beaten with one stick, the tone being modified by pressure of the left elbow on the tympanum. **1934** P.R. KIRBY *Musical Instruments of Native Races* (1965) 34 A drum .. found only among the Venda of the Northern Transvaal and their immediate neighbours .. is the *ngoma*, a single-headed drum with a hemispherical resonator carved out of solid wood. **1951** T.V. BULPIN *Lost Trails of Low Veld* 20 The baritone of the mirumba and the deep bass of the ngoma, thud out an intoxicating symphony in praise of sex and its mystic role in projecting the tribe on and on down through the centuries. **1975** *S. Afr. Panorama* Oct. 17 The drum on the crest of the Venda is known as 'Ngoma' and is used by the chief to assemble his people when an important message has to be conveyed to them; it is thus the symbol of national unity. **1982** *Pace* Feb. 110 In the distance I heard the drum. It was a deep belly-like sound one expects from the powerful Ngoma, the big one, one of the three holy drums of the Vhavenda.

ngoma busuku var. INGOMA BUSUKU.

ngomo var. INGOMA.

Ngonyama /ŋgɔnˈjaːma, əŋ-/ *n.* Also **Ingonyama**, **Ingwenyama**, **Ngwenyama**, and with small initial. [Zulu *ingonyama*, siSwati *ingwenyama*.]

1. Always with initial capital. 'The Lion', a hereditary title of Zulu and Swazi kings. See also INDLOVU.

1941 [see NDLOVUKAZI]. **1964** *Drum* Nov. 25 During all my days at the Zulu Royal kraal, I knew that many people did not like me, especially those closely attached to the Ngonyama. **1975** *E. Prov. Herald* 22 Aug. 13 King Sobhuza, known to his subjects as Ngwenyama ('the great lion') makes no concessions to effete European manners. **1978** [see INDLOVU]. **1982** *Pace* Nov. 90 On August 21 an unsuspecting Swazi nation was stunned by the news that the Ingwenyama — the Lion — was dead. **1986** J. DEACON in *S. Afr. Panorama* Aug. 21 King Mswati — the Ngwenyama (lion) is one of his titles ... sat in a blue armchair with the principal secretary for the Swazi Ministry of Foreign Affairs .. doing most of the talking. *c*1988 J. NXUMALO in *Proc. of Internat. Symposium: Nat. Parks, Nature Reserves & Neighbours* (Endangered Wildlife Trust), The Zulu Nation consists of a number of Tribes which all pay allegiance to the Zulu King or Ingonyama. **1994** KING G. ZWELITHINI in *Tribute* May 40 I, Zwelithini Goodwill Zulu ka Bhekuzulu, presently the Ngonyama of the Zulus, pledge .. my solemn word that I will withhold myself from any participation in any form of politics.

‖**2.** A lion.

[**1961** T.V. BULPIN *White Whirlwind* 55 'What is it?' Johan whispered. The guide inclined his head. 'Ingonyama,' he replied, using the Zulu name for a lion, which means a wild beast of prey.] **1978** A. ELLIOTT *Sons of Zulu* 95 The King at his formal installation ... The lion and the elephant on his throne (*Ngonyama* and *Ndlovu*) are symbolic of power and strength — characteristics always associated by the Zulu with their king. **1981** *Bona* Jan. 38 One night, the ngwenyama comes to a lonely tracker's camp in a northern Transvaal game reserve to eat his wife ... and the nightmare begins.

n'gou var. GNU *n.*[1]

Ngqika /ˈnǃi(ː)ka, -ga, -kə, (ə)ŋˈɡiːkə, (ə)nˈgikə/ *n.* Also **Nqika**. Pl. unchanged, or **AmaNgqika**. [Named for the founding leader *Ngqika* (*c*1775–1829), son of Mlawu and grandson of Rharhabe.] **a.** A member of one of the major branches (and its consolidated chiefdoms) of the Rharhabe division of the Xhosa people; GAIKA; RHARHABE sense b. **b.** *obs.* RHARHABE sense a (so called through confusion as to the composition and leadership of the two peoples). Also *attrib.*

For details about the formation of this people, see the note at NDLAMBE.

*c*1847 H.H. DUGMORE in J. Maclean *Compendium of Kafir Laws* (1906) 8 The Amangqika possess the whole of the Amatoli range of mountains, from the colonial frontier to the banks of the Kei. **1866** W.C. HOLDEN *Past & Future* 146 Of the various tribes .. the first in rank are the Amagcaleka (The tribe of Khreli), numbering about 70,000. The second is that of Amangqika (Sandili's tribe) which, including the smaller tribes of the Imidange and Amambala that are dependent upon it, may also be estimated at 70,000. **1920** [see RHARHABE]. **1939**, **1971** [see NDLAMBE]. **1978** T.R.H. DAVENPORT *S. Afr.: Mod. Hist.* 100 The year 1850 was one of drought and unrest, and the Ngqika were stirred by the utterances of Mlanjeni, a prophet who managed to awaken a spirit of resistance among the blacks to Smith's new paternalism. **1982** *E. Prov. Herald* 10 Aug. 9 Once the whole of the so-called Border Corridor was black land but after the frontier war of 1877–78 the Nqika people under Chief Sandile were driven across the Kei River to Kentani and the area was opened up for white farmers. **1986** J. CONYNGHAM *Arrowing of Cane* 18 He served briefly in Gibraltar before proceeding to the Cape for the Ngqika and Gcaleka Campaign. **1989** J.B. PEIRES *Dead Will Arise* p.xii, The Xhosa themselves were divided into various chiefdoms, grouped as follows. The Gcaleka Xhosa .. lived mostly east of the Kei River beyond the bounds of British territory. The Ngqika Xhosa .. and the Ndlambe Xhosa .. lived in British Kaffraria.

ngqush var. MNGQUSH(O).

‖**ngquthu** /nǃu(ː)tu, ən-, nǃʊ(ː)tʊ/ *n.* Also **inqutu**, **ngqutu**, **nqutu**, and with initial capital. [Zulu *ingquthu* (pl. *izingquthu*).] In full *ngquthu beast*: in traditional African contexts, a cow or bull paid to a woman by her daughter's lover as compensation for her seduction. Also *attrib.* Cf. LOBOLA *n.* sense 2.

1931 C.H. BLAINE *Native Courts Practice* 15 (Swart), The Nqutu custom is one peculiar to natives, by which, when a man seduces a girl, the women of her kraal are entitled to exact restitution from the seducer. **1952** *Drum* Feb. 23 The Inqutu (or Ngqutu) beast which was represented by the the first £5 which you paid is paid to the mother of the girl and is regarded as a fine. It is separate from the damages which are payable to the father of the girl. **1986** PRESTON-WHYTE & LOUW in Burman & Reynolds *Growing Up* 367 One or possibly two or more beasts can be and often are sued for in the courts. The first is the so-called 'mother's beast' (*ngquthu*) which is said to represent the girl's virginity.

nguba var. INGUBO.

Nguni /əŋˈguːni, ŋˈguːni/ *n.* and *adj.* [Zulu, n. stem of *umnguni* (a person of) the Nguni group (pl. *abanguni*, *abenguni*), and of *isinguni* the Nguni language group.]

A. *n.*

1.a. *pl.* (The) members of a subdivision of the Sintu-speaking (Bantu-speaking) peoples, comprising the Ndebele, Ngoni, Swazi, Xhosa, Zulu, and some smaller peoples, all of whom have a common historical origin and speak closely-related languages.

Orig. and mainly resident in the eastern regions of southern Africa.

1929 A.T. BRYANT *Olden Times in Zululand & Natal* 3 The natives of South-Eastern Africa we distinguish as of three separate families, which we call respectively Ngúni, in Zululand, the Transvaal, Natal and the Cape; Sutú .. and Tónga. **1939** N.J. VAN WARMELO in A.M. Duggan-Cronin *Bantu Tribes* III. i. 14 The cattle of the Nguni are tended and milked only by males, and for a female even to enter the cattle kraal would be the breach of a strict tabu. **1961** T.V. BULPIN *White Whirlwind* 171 You must know that we were then of the same people as the Zulus, and were known as the Nguni. Our chief was a warrior of great renown, a hero named Dlamini, who led us down in search of a new home. **1976** WEST & MORRIS *Abantu* 7 Within South Africa, where the most accurate statistical information is available, the largest group is the Nguni who make up 66% of the black population. Best known within this group are the Zulu, Swazi, Xhosa and Ndebele. **1979** *E. Prov. Herald* 30 June 7 Nguni people to meet in Grahamstown ... Material gathered will probably be used in a book to become the first comprehensive cross-cultural analysis on the Nguni. The Nguni people are widely spread over the subcontinent and include the Xhosa, Zulu, Swazi, Shangaa[n], Ndebele and Ngoni. **1986** [see MPONDOMISE]. **1986** P.A. MCALLISTER *Xhosa Beer Drinks*. 42 The ritual significance of beer, common throughout Africa, seems to have been greater among Sotho-speakers and Venda than among Nguni.

b. *pl.* With qualifying word: **Cape Nguni**, Southern Nguni (see below); **East** - or **Natal Nguni**, the Zulu; **Northern Nguni**, the Nguni living in KwaZulu-Natal and in areas further north; **Southern Nguni**, the Nguni living in the former Transkei and in areas further south. Also *attrib.*

1957 C.G. SELIGMAN *Races of Afr.* (1939) 168 This group [sc. Eastern Southern Bantu] consists of two main subdivisions Nguni and Tsonga. Further include the **Cape Nguni** of the Ciskei and Transkei .. together with the 'Fingo', fugitive remnants of tribes broken up in Natal .. ; the Natal Nguni or 'Zulu' of Natal and Zululand, with their offshoot the Ndebele (Tebele) of Southern Rhodesia; the Swazi of Swaziland and the Eastern Transvaal; and the 'Transvaal Ndebele' of Central and Northern Transvaal. **1980** [see quot. at Natal Nguni below]. **1955** E.A. RITTER *Shaka Zulu* 1 When the time came for the passing of that chieftain in 1816 it marked the end and the beginning of two distinct periods in **East Nguni** political history. **1980** D.B. COPLAN *Urbanization of African Performing Arts*. 57 Among these performers were a number of African men, particularly Cape or **Natal Nguni** (Amafengu, Xhosa, Zulu, Baca) from Cape Town or the towns of the Eastern Cape and Natal. **1980** LYE & MURRAY *Transformations* 30 As the frontier passed beyond the **Northern Nguni** clans, they had ever reducing opportunities to segment and move to unoccupied land. **1981** J.B. PEIRES *House of Phalo* 18 The creation of the major political groupings of the **southern Nguni** area, the Xhosa, the Thembu, the Mpondo and the Mpondomise, resulted from the rise of particular descent groups, respectively the Tshawe, Hala, Nyawuza and Majola, to a position of dominance over their localities. **1990** *Weekend Post* 7 July 4 Xhosa tribal art is breaking artistic records in Port Elizabeth. The exhibition of Southern Nguni art .. is set to become one of the most popular and longest-running ever held in the city.

2.a. Used collectively: the group of languages spoken by the Nguni, the dominant languages being Ndebele, siSwati, Xhosa, and Zulu.

Formerly called the KAFFIR group of languages (*offensive*).

1939 N.J. VAN WARMELO in A.M. Duggan-Cronin *Bantu Tribes* III. i. 13 Nguni .. occupies a unique position in the non-Bantu family of languages, in so far as words containing the non-Bantu clicks occur in great abundance. **1950** [see TONGA sense 2]. **1957** [see FANAKALO]. **1970** M. WILSON *1000 Yrs before Van Riebeeck* 1 From 1593 they spoke a language identifiable from the words recorded as Nguni, that is Zulu or Xhosa or a dialect close to them. *c*1980 [see XHOSA *n.* sense 2]. **1981** *Star* 18 June 3 Programmes, he said, would reflect black viewers' tastes and he expected black viewership to be about eight people a set, compared with about 3,5 white people a set. 'I see it as a service for black people, run and produced by black people.' It will start on one channel broadcasting in both Nguni and Sotho, but within a year will expand to two channels.

b. *comb.* (objective) **Nguni-speaking** *ppl* adj., having as a home language one of these languages. Also *attrib.*, and *transf.* (used of an area inhabited by speakers of any of these languages.)

1980 D.B. COPLAN *Urbanization of African Performing Arts.* 78 By this time, mission communities were well established throughout the southern Cape and Transkei, swelled by members of homeless Nguni-speaking clans pushed into Xhosa country by Zulu expansionism during the 1820's and 1830's. 1988 I. DAVIS in *S. Afr. Panorama* Feb. 48 Aubrey, an expert on traditions, tribal customs and clothing of the Nguni-speaking peoples (Xhosa, Zulu, Ndebele and Swazi) recently held an exhibition of his photographs in Pretoria. 1993 M. OETTLE in *Weekend Post* 20 Nov. (Leisure) 4 Vigne has .. collected accounts from all quarters .. but all need careful editing before being put together to tell about .. the activities of shipwreck survivors on the Nguni-speaking coasts. 1994 N. NAUDÉ in *Conserva* May-July 14 The same colours are found among .. the Nguni-speaking groups along the South African east coast.

3. In full ***Nguni cattle***, a breed of cattle related to the Sanga, indigenous to Africa and traditionally the breed most commonly kept by Nguni people; ZULU *n.* sense 3. Also *attrib.* See also NATIVE adj. sense 2. Cf. NKONE.

1939 N.J. VAN WARMELO in A.M. Duggan-Cronin *Bantu Tribes* III. i. 14 The Nguni Cattle .. belong to one distinct strain (termed Zulu cattle by investigators), whereas two other distinct strains (Tswana and Kalanga Cattle) were bred by the non-Nguni tribes of the interior plateau. 1975 B. ARNOTT in *Farmer's Weekly* 2 July 40 The KwaZulu Government is breeding a vastly improved strain of indigenous Nguni cattle for resale to Africans in order to increase the production of their stock. The Nguni is the 'other' indigenous breed in South Africa. 1981 *S. Afr. Panorama* Nov. 27 The .. Drakensberger .. is particularly resistant to disease and drought and able to live largely off the veld, as can the animal's Africander and Nguni cousins of Zulu fame. 1989 J. BLADES in *Sunday Times* 3 Dec. 3 He discovered his Garden of Eden a few years ago when he was looking for land to re-introduce the kingdom's traditional Nguni cattle which now make Mkhaya pay. 1990 [see *Weekend Post* quot. at AFRIKANDER *n.* sense 4]. 1994 S. CHETTY in *Ibid.* 30 Jan. 15 Among the livestock kept are Nguni cattle, goats and sheep.

B. *adj.*

1. In, of, or pertaining to one or more of the languages of the Nguni. See also sense A 2 a.

1929 A.T. BRYANT *Olden Times in Zululand & Natal* 5 Captured Bushwomen became common in their homes ... And the children .. adopted .. in a Bantuized form, much of the slave-girl's speech. Hence the clicks in Nguni speech. 1939 N.J. VAN WARMELO in A.M. Duggan-Cronin *Bantu Tribes* III. i. 13 The Nguni language, which is spoken in several fairly divergent forms, is yet basically uniform; for while vocabularly differs appreciably between, say, Xhosa, Zulu and Ndebele, in point of grammatical form the difference is remarkably small. 1977 [see MFECANE]. 1982 *Voice* 24 Jan. 16 Why did they have to squeeze all the African languages into one channel? .. If they had decided on one common Nguni language and one Sesotho one, it would have been much easier for them and less irritating for the viewer. 1988 [see SINDEBELE].

2. Of or pertaining to the Nguni (see sense A 1). Occas. in the collocation **Nguniland** ?*nonce* [Eng. *land*], that area of the province of KwaZulu-Natal generally known as 'Zululand'.

1939 [see sense A 3]. 1949 [see TOKOLOSHE sense 1]. 1959 L. LONGMORE *Dispossessed* 27 There were, also, antagonisms between Nguni groups. For example, the Xhosa despise the Zulu for not circumcising and maintain that the Zulu for this reason are never fully mature. 1962 [see BHACA]. 1975 [see MFENGU]. 1978 A. ELLIOTT *Sons of Zulu* 13, I refer to the country before about 1819 as 'Nguniland' because, until then, it was not ruled by the Zulu nor was there even a Zulu nation as such, only a tiny clan by that name. 1979 [see sense A 1 a]. 1980 J. COCK *Maids & Madams* 197 Nguni disintegration was a slow, uneven and painful process. Leftwich points out that they were more numerous, their economy more resilient, and their capacity to withstand military defeat greater than that of the nomadic Khoikoi and San people. 1989 [see DIFAQANE]. 1992 G. TEMPLETON in *Weekend Post* 8 Feb. (Leisure) 4 The path up the river bank leads to a cave, probably used by early San (Bushmen) and Nguni people, and across a wooden bridge to another cave from where the lovely Strandloper Falls can be seen.

ngwai var. GWAAI.

Ngwaketse /ŋgwaˈke(:)tse, əŋ-/ *pl. n.* Also **Bangoaketse, Bangwaketse, Bangwaketze.** [SeTswana (pl. *baNgwaketse*).] The members of a people of the Tswana group. Also *attrib.* See also TSWANA sense 2 a.

As is the case with many names of peoples and groups in *S. Afr. Eng.*, this word has been found only in plural uses; however, it may be that it has also been used in unrecorded singular forms.

[1822 *Missionary Notices* 29 Sept. 214 One of these visitors having frequently travelled amongst the *Manketsens, Boschuanas*, and *Marootzes* to the north and north-east of Griqua Town, gave us much more information respecting that country.] 1857 D. LIVINGSTONE *Missionary Trav.* 51 The Bakwains, the Bangwaketze, and the Bamangwato all fled thither; and the Matabele marauders, who came from the well-watered parts, perished by hundreds in their attempts to follow them. 1871 J. MACKENZIE *Ten Yrs* (1971) 102 The Bangwaketse were once a large and powerful tribe, and they still number perhaps six or seven thousand people. 1930 S.T. PLAATJE *Mhudi* (1975) 86 The Matabele were evidently meditating a raid of a similar nature upon the Bangwaketse ... Mzilikazi's army swooped down upon the evacuated city like so many vultures thirsting for Ngwaketse blood. 1941 C.W. DE KIEWIET *Hist. of S. Afr.* 73 On the western border of the Transvaal .. dwelt the Bamangwato, the Bakwena, the Bangwaketse, the Baralong, and the Batlapin. 1951 *Afr. Drum* Apr. 12 Other tribes began to spring up in the country either by breaking away from the older and larger tribes or by coming into the sheltered safety of Basutoland from the troubled world outside. Thus the .. Bangoaketse, Bahlatoana and the Makhoakhoa came about. 1973 J. MEINTJES *Voortrekkers* 70 At the same time he [*sc.* Mzilikazi] nearly exterminated the tribes of the Bakwena, Bangwaketse, Bahurutsi and Barolong. 1986 P. MAYLAM *Hist. of Afr. People* 45 In the eighteenth century two new important Tswana chiefdoms were founded after breaking away from the Kwena. First the Ngwaketse broke away.

Ngwato var. BAMANGWATO.

Ngwenyama var. NGONYAMA.

nhoca var. INYOKA.

nhoo var. GNU *n.*[1]

NIC *n.* /en aɪ ˈsi/ Also **N.I.C.** Initial letters of *Natal Indian Congress*, an organization formed in 1894 to work for the political rights and social welfare of people of Indian descent in the former province of Natal. Also *attrib.* Cf. CONGRESS sense 1.

1952 'NIPPY' in *Drum* Aug. 40 They have .. forced their accusers in the N.I.C. and the A.N.C. in Natal .. to acknowledge that 'they are now talking sense'. 1974 J. NAIDOO in Bhana & Pachai *Doc. Hist. of Indian S. Afr.* (1984) 259 Well-meaning friends of the N.I.C. have in private and in public called upon us to participate in these elections. 1985 A. AKHALWAYA in *Frontline* Dec. 26 One finds Azapo supporters who accuse the TIC and NIC of being racist, while TIC and NIC supporters accuse Azapo of being racist. 1989 *Stanger Mail* 6 Oct. 3 NIC spokesman .. said relations between the Indian community and the majority of black people in South Africa had always been close. 1990 *New African* 18 June 10 Most if not all members of the non-racial NIC .. feel it should continue to exist, at least for a while longer.

niccoti var. NEGOTIE.

nicht, nichtje varr. NIG, NIGGIE.

nicker ball var. NIGGERBALL.

nickie, nicks varr. NIKKIES, NIKS *n.*

Nicro /ˈnɪkrəʊ/ *n.* Also NICRO. [Acronym formed on *National Institute for Crime Prevention and Rehabilitation of Offenders.*] An organization which works for the prevention of crime, cares for the needs of prisoners, and assists released prisoners to re-integrate into society.

Nicro was formed by the merger of the Prisoner's Aid Association (founded in 1910) and the Probation League (founded in 1933); from 1935 to 1970 it was known as the Social Services Organisation.

1972 *Daily Dispatch* 31 May 7 Crime in South Africa had taken on enormous proportions, the assistant director of the National Institute for Crime Prevention and Rehabilitation of Offenders (Nicro), Dr. Touissant van Hove, said here yesterday. 1983 *Sunday Times* 4 Sept. (Lifestyle) 1 Mr John Pegge, national director of the National Institute for Crime Prevention and Rehabilitation of Offenders (Nicro) says: 'We are dealing with a situation where men suddenly have to cope with civilian life again'. 1990 T. SEALE in *Weekend Argus* 29 Sept. 6 Nicro's 80th birthday celebrations this week. 1993 P. DU TOIT in *Weekend Post* 26 June 2 She said Nicro would prefer to have children awaiting trial released into the custody of their parents, or accommodated in a place of safety. 1994 *Grocott's Mail* 9 Sept. 2 NICRO .. helps arrested and convicted persons by promoting and securing their welfare and that of their dependents and promoting the rehabilitation and aftercare of adult offenders.

nie var. NÊ.

‖nie-blanke /niˈblaŋkə/ *n.* [Afk., *nie* not (equiv. of 'non') + *blanke* white person.] NON-WHITE *n.* Usu. in *pl.* Also *attrib.* Cf. BLANKE.

Usu. reflecting official terminology (esp. on signs in public places) during the apartheid era.

1955 L. MARQUARD *Story of S. Afr.* 243 Notices announcing *Blankes* and *Nie-Blankes* (white and non-white) sprouted in post offices, on railway stations and in other public places. 1966 L.G. BERGER *Where's Madam* 144 After the show we went outside to find our car, passing heaps of Africans piling into the voluminous insides of sagging native taxis — back to the realities of apartheid, where officialdom would next day reduce them to the role of ordinary nie-blankes once more. 1968 *Drum* Sept. 6 Dear Juby, I miss the sunshine and the signboards reading 'Nie-Blankes Alleen.' 1973 *Ibid.* 41 Because of 'Blankes — Nie Blankes' signs there are places he just cannot enter. He is Black. 1977 *World* 3 Mar. (Woman's World), I'm sure you've seen them all — the crazy signs I mean. 'Bantus only', 'Nie Blankes' or is it knee buckets? 1988 S.A. BOTHA in *Frontline* Apr.-May 24 There are two subways under the tracks, some 300m apart. The one nearest the hotel is marked 'non-whites/nie blankes', and the other 'whites/blankes'. Nowadays, anybody uses whatever is more convenient. 1989 S. BILAC in *Personality* 10 Apr. 30 The good people of Boksburg voted the CP in to control their town council and brought out the dusters to polish up the *Net Blankes* and *Geen Nie-blankes* signs and put them back from where they had been removed. 1990 S. CILLIERS in *Frontline* Jan. 9 Sometimes I think it was almost better to have the Geen Nie-Blankes signs. Then you knew. 1992 J. QWELANE in *Weekend Argus* 22 Feb. 18 Zealots in the rightwing camp may be dusting off the recently discarded 'Whites-only' and 'Nie-blankes' signs.

nief var. NEEF.

nierk var. NEUK.

nieshout *n. obs.* Also **niez-hout**. [S. Afr. Du., fr. Du. *niezen* to sneeze + *hout* wood.] SNEEZEWOOD. Also *attrib.*

[1786 G. FORSTER tr. *A. Sparrman's Voy. to Cape of G.H.* II. 75 This vale is called *Niez-hout-kloof*, from a Kind of tree which is said to excite sneezing, if it be rubbed and then smelled to. **1803** J.T. VAN DER KEMP in *Trans. of Missionary Soc.* I. 434 When they have killed a man, they dress their meat on a fire made of a kind of wood, which they call *umthati*, but the Dutch *nieshout*, because its powder (though it has very little smell) is a strong errhine.] **1812** — *Acct of Caffraria* 63 There is a variety of timber, of which I will mention the names by which they are known in the Colony, viz: the .. nieshout [etc.]. **1827** G. THOMPSON *Trav.* II. 359 The ground is chiefly cultivated by the females. The implement used is a sort of spade made of the *nieshout* tree. [**1837** ECKLON & ZEYHER *Enumeratio Plantarum Africae* 54 *Pateroxylon utile* ... 'Nieshout.']

niet waar var. NIE WAAR (NIE).

nieuwjaarsblom var. NUWEJAARSBLOM.

nieuwziekte /ˈnjuːsɪktə/ *n. Obs.* exc. *hist. Pathology.* Also **nieusiekte**, **nieuweziekte**, **niewe ziekt**, **niew-zickte**. [Du., *nieuw* (later Afk. *nieu*) new + *ziekte* (later Afk. *siekte*) disease.]
1. Strangles, an infectious and contagious disease of horses, mules, and donkeys, caused by *Streptococcus equi.*

1867 *Blue Bk for Col. 1866* JJ21, The nieuw ziekte has carried off many of our horses, and lung-sickness among the horned cattle has also been prevalent. **1886** G.A. FARINI *Through Kalahari Desert* 64 There are two horse diseases: one called the *paarde ziekt* (horse sickness), and the other the *niewe ziekt* (new sickness). In the first the symptoms are a slight running at the nose, and hard breathing, and frequently the horses die in a few minutes after being attacked. In the other the nose symptoms are the same, accompanied by a swelling under the throat, and sometimes by hard lumps all over the body, which suppurate. If the horse does not die it is rendered unfit for use for some time after. **1914** *Farmer's Annual* 177 Strangles, or Nieuwziekte, is a contagious disease caused by a micro-organism (the Streptococcus of Schütz). It attacks horses, mules and donkeys, which are most susceptible when still young. **1916** *Farmer's Weekly* 20 Dec. 1537 Some of the donkeys in the district contracted 'nieuweziekte' in October and November, when that disease was so prevalent among horses; but, thanks to the paraffin cure, the disease was soon mastered. **1920** [see PAARDEZIEKTE]. **1944** [see GALSIEKTE sense 1 a]. **1979** T. GUTSCHE *There Was a Man* 196 Theiler produced at the end of 1902 'Some Diseases of the Horse in South Africa', .. dealing with Horse Sickness, .. Glanders, Strangles or Nieuwziekte.

2. *rare.* Glanders, an acute infectious disease of horses which may be transmitted to other mammals, and which is caused by the bacillus *Pfeifferella mallei.*

1907 *Trans. Agric. Jrnl* Jan. 391 (Pettman), Glanders is also commonly called *nieuwziekte*; consequently, it is often very difficult to convince the proprietor of a horse suffering from glanders that it is really infected with that disease and not strangles.

‖**nie waar (nie)** /ni ˈvɑː(r) (ni)/ *adv. phr.* Formerly also **niet waar**. [Afk. *nie waar nie?*, lit. 'not true?', fr. Du. *niet* not + *waar* true + *nie* neg. particle, part of the double neg. structure.] 'Isn't that so?', a tag question inviting assent.

1915 A.B. MARCHAND *Dirk, S. African* 55 (Swart), If a man steals my property and I don't steal his, and he goes unpunished he's better off than I — niet waar? **1963** M. KAVANAGH *We Merry Peasants* 18 They'll cope with three or four wives each, man. You know what we chaps can be like down here ... Big stuff, that's us, *nie waar nie?* **1963** M.G. MCCOY *Informant, Port Elizabeth* How I envy you your N.Y. Phil. concert ... They made a big hit in Russia a couple of years ago, nie waar?

niew(e) ziekt(e) var. NIEUWZIEKTE.

niez-hout var. NIESHOUT.

‖**nig** /nəx/ *n.* Formerly also **nicht**. [Afk., niece.] NIGGIE; also used as a title, with a given name.

1913 A.B. MARCHAND *Dirk, S. African* 113 (Swart), Tant Martjie remarked that she thought Nicht Gesina was better able to bear the burden of a few additional sins than Miss Booysen. **1914** [see NEEF sense 1]. **1934** C.P. SWART Supplement to Pettman. 125 *Nig*, .. The word is often applied by elderly people to young women to whom they are not related at all, as a term of affection. **1958** R.E. LIGHTON *Out of Strong* 16 'Come, children,' called Hendrina, 'and you too, Nig Alida.'

niggerball *n. offensive.* Also **nicker ball**. A large, round, black, aniseed-flavoured sweet which changes colour in successive layers when sucked. Also *attrib.*

1960 J. TAYLOR 'Ballad of the Southern Suburbs'. (lyrics) Ag Daddy how we miss Niggerballs and liquorice, Pepsi-cola, ginger-beer and Canada Dry. **1971** *South Western Herald* 14 May 7 'Life is like a nigger ball, hard but nice,' is the favourite quotation of a friend of mine. **1975** S. ROBERTS *Outside Life's Feast* 7 Bevvy .. saw a blue-pink palely purple nigger-ball sky ... Nigger-balls are the best sweets ... When the black is sucked off you get pink and blue and blue-green, but you can't bite them until you've sucked them small or you'll chip your teeth. **1983** J. ALLAN in *Sunday Times* 2 Jan. (Lifestyle) 5 She cheers up a bit when we stop at the Greek caffie on the corner and buy some nigger balls for her from the machine. **1986** P. LE ROUX in Burman & Reynolds *Growing Up* 185, I remember occasionally buying a penny's 'nicker' balls or some black toffees at the store in the mining compound only half a mile from our house. **1993** *Grocott's Mail* 20 July 4 In 1979 when it [*sc.* 'The Ballad of the Southern Suburbs'] was included in an Oxford book on South African verse, the editors changed the word 'niggerballs' in one of the choruses to 'acid drops'.

‖**niggie** /ˈnəxi/ *n.* Formerly also **nichtje**. [Afk., *nig* niece, cousin + -IE.] A term of address or reference to a female cousin or niece, or, loosely, to any young woman, esp. an Afrikaans (or, formerly, South African Dutch) woman. In both senses also called NIG. See also NEEF.

Usu. used to suggest the idiom of Afrikaans-speakers.

1868 W.R. THOMSON *Poems, Essays & Sketches* 154 Ou Bass .. explained .. that the ooms, and tantes, and neefs, and niggies, had been induced .. to come. *Ibid.* 167 Was your wife not the daughter or the *nichtje* of So-and-so? **1870** in A.M.L. Robinson *Sel. Articles from Cape Monthly Mag.* (1978) 17 He shortly afterwards was enchanted by another 'niggie' at nachtmaal. **1914** L.H. BRINKMAN *Breath of Karroo* 54 The store-keepers were busy displaying their wares .. for the allurement of the Tantes and Nichtjes who were sure to come from distant farms to lay in a stock of clothes and fineries. **1920** R.Y. STORMBERG *Mrs Pieter de Bruyn* 76 Ouma du Preez on the riempie settee .. said to me: 'Is dit nie mooi nie? — excuse — I mean toch isn't it beautiful mij niggie?' **1955** L. MARQUARD *Story of S. Afr.* 66 The polite custom that still exists in South Africa of addressing .. younger [men and women] as *neef* and *niggie* (cousin) dates from a time when to do so was as likely as not to be strictly accurate. **1974** *S. Afr. Panorama* Nov. 19 The wide flared skirts of the 'niggies' (female cousins) swirling around the 'neefs' (male cousins) in embroidered waistcoats and scarves formed a colourful tableau. **1979** *Sunday Times* 7 Oct. (Mag. Sect.) 1, I do not thank those bearded forbears with their virtuous wives who seemed to think that all Afrikaners are, or should be, related in the spirit .. and should therefore be each other's 'niggies', 'neefs', 'ooms' and 'tannies'. **1980** *Sunday Times* 14 Sept. 11 In the quaint manner of the old-timers they address each other as 'neef', 'niggie' or 'suster'. **1984** [see Daily Dispatch quot. at NEFIE].

night-aappie *n. obs.* Also **night-appie**. [Part. tr. Afk. *nagapie*, see NAGAPIE.] BUSH BABY.

1937 S. CLOETE *Turning Wheels* 74 A night-appie sprang from one tree to another, spreadeagling through the air and clinging to a branch, looked down at them with wide round eyes. **1951** R. FARRAN *Jungle Chase* (1957) 22 Away in the bush there was the occasional chatter of a night-aappie or the feminine whistle of impala.

night-adder *n.* [Eng. interpretation of S. Afr. Du. *nachtslang*, *nacht* night + *slang* snake.] **1.** Any of several nocturnal snakes of the genus *Causus* of the Viperidae, esp. the common night-adder *Causus rhombeatus*; NACHTSLANG sense 1. **2.** Any of several nocturnal snakes of the Colubridae, esp. the aurora snake, *Lamprophis aurora*, and the HERALD, *Crotaphopeltis hotamboeia*; NACHTSLANG sense 3.

1816 G. BARKER Journal. 12 July, Worked at my peice [*sic*] of Land, Killed the first serpent I had seen alive in Africa, called a Night Adder. **1832** *Graham's Town Jrnl* 23 Mar. 50 A man in the service of Mr. Bailie was last week bitten in the leg by a night adder. **1834** T. PRINGLE *Afr. Sketches* 280 There are several species of snakes which have come under my own observation, such as the nacht-slang (night-adder). **1853** F.P. FLEMING *Kaffraria* 82 The Whip Snake, the Black Snake, the Night Adder, and the House Viper, are all of them venomous in their nature, and fatal in the effect of their bites, if not taken in time. **1854** T. SHONE Diary. 15 Jan., This morning Henry came home, with the Melancholy news of the Death of Joseph Dixie From the bite of a night Adder. **1888** *Cape Punch* 29 Feb. 119 'It's a snake,' I yells in my terror, 'a bloomin' night adder.' **1907** J.P. FITZPATRICK *Jock of Bushveld* (1909) 347 A night adder rose up before his face and slithered out its forked tongue. **1915** *Chambers's Jrnl* (U.K.) July 437 The night-adder, as its name implies, is most in evidence after sundown. **1932** *Grocott's Daily Mail* 5 Apr. 2 Little Joyce Dunstan .. had a terrifying experience with a night adder over Easter, says the Natal Mercury. **1937** *Guide to Vertebrate Fauna of E. Cape Prov.* (Albany Museum) II. 62 *Crotaphopeltis hotamboeia*, Laur. Herald-Snake. Red-lipped Snake .. (sometimes miscalled Night-adder). **1947** J. STEVENSON-HAMILTON *Wild Life in S. Afr.* 329 The Night Adder (Causus rhombeatus) ... I have often seen my cats eating night adders which they have caught and killed. **1956** A.G. MCRAE *Hill Called Grazing* 103 Adders, particularly the sluggish night adders that hunted in the strawberries, she would pin with an intrepid forepaw behind the head and hold until help came. **1971** *Rand Daily Mail* 12 Jan., John had now been bitten four times by snakes — by a puffadder, a cobra, twice by a night-adder and now by the Berg-adder. **1989** J. HOBBS *Thoughts in Makeshift Mortuary* 86 One of our sergeants killed a night-adder by the fence this morning.

night-ape *n.* [tr. Afk. *nagaap*; cf. NAGAPIE.] BUSH BABY.

1895 A.B. BALFOUR *1200 Miles in Waggon* 87 This morning I saw two fascinating little creatures in a tree, like lemurs or small monkeys. They don't usually come out much by day ... They are popularly called 'Night-Apes'. **1899** *Girls' Collegiate School Mag.* Sept., Miss Forrest has a nice little night-ape and a canary. **1900** H.A. BRYDEN *Animals of Afr.* 14 The maholi is invariably called by up-country white colonists in South Africa, the 'night-ape,' from the Boer name 'Nagt-apje.' **1905** W.L. SCLATER in Flint & Gilchrist *Science in S. Afr.* 125 The Lemurs .. are represented by two species of Galago, the larger (*G. garnetti*) found in Natal, and the smaller (*G. moholi*) from the more wooded districts of the Western Transvaal, Bechuanaland and Rhodesia. The latter .. is nocturnal in habits, sleeping during the day in a nest or on the branch of a tree ... The Dutch term it the Nacht-apje or Night-ape. *c*1911 S. PLAYNE *Cape Col.* 548 From its nocturnal activity the Dutch farmers have christened the lemur the *nacht-apje*, or night-ape. **1959** C. LAGUS *Operation Noah* 175 Also known as Bushbabies and Nightapes, Galagos are delightful little lemur-like animals. **1973** N.J. VAN DER MERWE in *Std Encycl. of Sn*

Afr. VIII. 211 *Night-Apes. Bush-babies,* There are two species in Southern Africa, the night-ape or large grey bush-baby (*Galago crassicaudatus*) .. and the common bush-baby (*Galago senegalensis*) ... There is a marked difference in size between the two species. The night-ape .. is much bigger than the bush-baby .., its tail is thicker and bushier and its fur much longer. **1984** [see NAGAPIE]. **1990** SKINNER & SMITHERS *Mammals of Sn Afr. Subregion* 147 *Galago moholi,* A. Smith, 1836 ... There has never been a complete consensus in the use of a colloquial name for this species, as night ape, lesser galago and bushbaby have all been used. **1991** [see NAGAPIE].

night-serpent *n. obs.* [tr. S. Afr. Du. *nachtslang.*] NACHTSLANG.

1821 C.I. LATROBE *Jrnl of Visit* 124 The bite of the Nachtschlange, or night-serpent, is said by the Hottentot poison-doctors, to be uncurable. **1841** B. SHAW *Memorials* 312 The *nachtslang,* or night-serpent, is a dangerous one, because of its going out by night, when it may be trod upon.

night-snake *n. obsolescent.* [tr. S. Afr. Du. *nachtslang.*] NACHTSLANG.

1819 G.M. KEITH *Voy.* 71 The night snake, more beautiful than any of the others, about 20 inches long, very thin, belted with black, red and yellow, and when near, at night has the appearance of fire. **1849** A. SMITH *Illust. of Zoo. of S. Afr.: Reptilia* 21 *Aspidelaps Lubricus,* .. Nacht Slang of the Cape Colonists ... It moves about principally in the evening, or during the night, hence the Colonists call it Night-Snake. **1954** J.A. PRINGLE *Common Snakes* 12 Olive Night-snake .. non-venomous .. is a quiet, docile snake .. mainly confined to the coastal belt from Cape Town to north of Durban. **1962** V.F.M. FITZSIMONS *Snakes of Sn Afr.* 112 *Lamprophis aurora* .. Aurora — or Night-snake.

nikkies /ˈnɪkiːz/ *v. trans.* Also **nickie, nicky, nikkis.** [Prob. a children's form of NIKS *v.*] Esp. in the language of children's games: a 'truce-word', forbidding certain actions or exempting the speaker from certain unpleasant tasks; NIKS *v.*

1970 M. BRONSLOW *Informant, Cape Town* May I borrow your book — nickie stumps. (By saying nickie stumps the borrower doesn't accept any responsibility). **1970** R. NIXON *Informant, Durban* Nicky stomps — I bags first. **1970** S. SPARKS *Informant, Fort Beaufort* 'Nikkies' I have to do the washing-up (meaning 'I'm not doing the washing-up'). **1990** *Informant, Grahamstown* Okay, you can all come and watch the video at our house, but nikkis making coffee when the crowd arrives. **1994** R.J. SILVA *Informant, Grahamstown* If you say 'Nikkies seven stations' then you don't have to do it [*sc.* recite the names of seven stations].

nikosikazi var. INKOSIKAZI.

niks /nəks, nɪks/ *n. colloq.* Also **nicks, nix.** [Afk., reinforced by the general Eng. *nix.*]

1. 'Nothing', in various senses.

1860 A.W. DRAYSON *Sporting Scenes* 146 There we were, with a few biscuits, beltong, powder, shot, and guns, a hundred miles from help. This distance would have been 'nix' (nothing) if we could only have procured water. [**1864** S. TURNER in D. Child *Portrait of Pioneer* (1980) 20 Little things like that must be expected out here. If that were the worst it would be, as the Dutch say, nix (nothing).] **1897** E. GLANVILLE *Tales from Veld* 278, I could tell there was some crittur there that they didn't like .. but I could see nix beyond a rock or tree stump. **1899** 'S. ERASMUS' *Prinsloo* 118 Would it not be patriotic if you offered to give for nix sufficient of your outside stands to rebuild the offices on? **1900** S.T. PLAATJE *Boer War Diary* (1973) 103, I have been on horseback from early till late during the last 2 days — and all that for 'niks'. **1907** J.P. FITZPATRICK *Jock of Bushveld* (1909) Glossary, Nix, (D), nothing (from D. *niets*). **1913** D. FAIRBRIDGE *Piet of Italy* 150 'That is better then *nix,*' she said. **1924** L. COHEN *Reminisc. of Jhb.* 130 The shares .. went up to £9 10s., and now stand at nix — which is a very good quotation for them. **1956** D. JACOBSON *Dance in Sun* 68 'What's the matter with your eyes?' Frank asked. 'Niks' the man replied, sniffing. **1966** J. TAYLOR 'Mommy I'd Like to Be'. (*lyrics*) Eleven times eleven is 'leventy-'leven, And nought times nought is niks. **1975** 'BLOSSOM' in *Darling* 29 Jan. 103 You see? Fired. For niks. The story of my life. **1975** *Ibid.* 26 Feb. 111 'You wanna bet?' Sampie reckons, sticking out his jaw. 'That Boy's for niks, man. Couldn't hurt a fly.' **1977** F.G. BUTLER *Karoo Morning* 100 By lunch time Stone was near to tears. I asked him, 'What's up?' 'He says my arm makeers [is wrong] nicks.' **1980** J. MULLINS in *Fair Lady* 19 Nov. 384 Take four extremely mature students, with language skills ranging from *niks* to not bad. **1985** W.O. KA MTETWA in *Staffrider* Vol.6 No.2, 44 They knew nix about trade unions. **1989** F.G. BUTLER *Tales from Old Karoo* 120 Nothing has been prepared, .. no reassuring bastions of coffee, rusks and *koeksisters* .. niks, man, niks. **1990** J. NAIDOO *Coolie Location* 192 Without a regular income, I was nothing, *niks* and bugger-all. **1992** M. TYALA in *Evening Post* 27 Mar. 10 'I'm well, thank you,' I say patiently awaiting identification. *Niks.* The caller just fires away with his business. You are supposed to have recognised the voice, you see.

‖**2.** *comb.* **niksdoen** /ˈnəksdun/ [Afk., *doen* do], inaction, doing nothing; **niks-nie** /ˈnəksni/ [Afk., *nie* neg. particle, part of the double neg. structure], the emphatic 'nothing at all'; **niksnuts** /ˈnəksnəts/ [Afk., 'useful for nothing' (*nut* use, usefulness)], a useless, good-for-nothing person.

1968 W.K. HANCOCK *Smuts* II. 218 White civilization was in danger .. because Smuts stood for **niksdoen**, for 'letting the situation develop', which meant letting white civilization drift on to the rocks. **1910** J. RUNCIE *Idylls by Two Oceans* 98 The Boy .. demanded what the devil the coloured gentleman was laughing at ... '**Nicks-nie**,' said Mahommet Ali, sheepishly. **1913** C. PETTMAN *Africanderisms* 340 Nix, .. Nothing. Nix-nie, nothing at all. **1913** *Ibid.* 340 **Nixnuts**, .. Applied to (1) a person who is neither clever not capable; (2) it is used also of a rogue. **1970** M.B. SMIT *Informant, Johannesburg* He's a real niksnuts — I can't bear him.

niks /nɪks/ *v. trans.* [fr. Afk. *niks* nothing.] NIKKIES.

1970 M.J. MATULOVICH *Informant, KwaZulu-Natal* The boy with the cool-drink, surrounded by his friends, said: 'Niks ops!' (Not sharing). **1985** *E. Prov. Herald* 27 Feb. 1 Before a hopeful aims at your 'spider', .. it is the norm to yell .. : 'niks tips', meaning you have to make a direct hit'; 'niks bends', meaning you may not bend over to throw.

Nimiqua var. NAMAQUA.

90-day *adj. hist.*

Cf. 180-DAY (see under 'H'). See also EMERGENCY.

a. Of or pertaining to the General Law Amendment Act of 1963, or more particularly clause 17 of this Act, which stipulates that a police officer may, for the purposes of interrogation, detain one suspected of committing, intending to commit, or having knowledge of certain political offences, for up to ninety days without access to a court of law.

1964 *Black Sash* Vol.8 No.1, 56 Since then [*sc.* 1962] hundreds of South Africans have been detained under the now notorious '90-day clause'. **1966** *Survey of Race Rel. 1965* (S.A.I.R.R.) 46 Detained during the State of Emergency in 1960 and again in 1964 in terms of the '90-day clause'. *Ibid.* 48 It was provided in the General Law Amendment Act of 1963 that Section 17 (the '90-day clause') would be in operation until 30 June 1964 and for such further periods .. as the State President may determine. **1967** H. SUZMAN in *Hansard* 1 June 7042 When the then Minister of Justice introduced the 90-day law, he did give us the original impression that the words '90 days' had been put there for a purpose, to have some limiting effects on the detention of a person. **1971** *Rand Daily Mail* 16 Mar. 11 Another brother .. was detained under the 90-Day Clause in 1964. **1971** *Ibid.* 24 May 10 Eight years ago the Nationalist Government, revealing its contempt for the rule of law, introduced 90-day detention without trial. **1987** *New Nation* 21 May 14 His first brush with the apartheid state was in 1964, when he was detained under the notorious 90-day clause. **1991** J. PAUW *In Heart of Whore* 41 [Ruth] First, who was professor in African Studies at the Eduardo Mondlane University in Maputo and wife of South African Communist Party leader Joe Slovo, had been the first woman to be detained in the 1960s under the infamous '90-Day Act'.

b. Of detention: imposed and administered under the terms of this Act.

1971 *Rand Daily Mail* 24 May 10 Eight years ago the Nationalist Government, revealing its contempt for the rule of law, introduced 90-day detention without trial.

Hence **90 days** *n. phr.* (alluding to this legislation).

1964 D. MARAIS *I Like it Here, (caption),* I suppose because it's leap year we'll do 91 days instead of 90 days. **1971** C.M. SILVA *Informant, OFS* If you kids don't get 90 days, I don't know. **1975** L. WILSON in *New Classic* No.2, 33 When he had been under ninety-days, he had been in solitary. **1986** *Style* Dec.-Jan. 41 Any talk of multiracialism, in any form, got you 90 days or 180 or early retirement on Robben Island.

ninta var. NENTA.

nip *v. trans.* and *reflexive.* [Unknown; perh. intended to suggest the tight clenching of teeth or tensing of muscles of one who is nervous.] In the slang phrr. ***to nip oneself, to nip straws*** (usu. in the participial form ***nipping straws***): to be anxious or afraid. Also *absol.* Cf. NIPS.

1970 B. KIRK-COHEN *Informant, Pietersburg* Nipping straws. Scared, nervous. **1972** R. MALAN *Ah Big Yaws* 36 *Nippon strauce,* A nervous condition brought about perhaps by the unexpected, unaccustomed or unwanted proximity of the forces of authority, officialdom or law and order. **1974** 'BLOSSOM' in *Darling* 8 May 91 Now we reely nipping straws, hey, oupa shouting, Bert blubbing and me running up and down looking in all the compartments. **1975** *Ibid.* 12 Feb. 119 I'm only nipping the biggest straws you ever saw. **1976** *Ibid.* 17 Mar. Talk about nipping straws .. never been so poep-scared in my whole entire life. **1981** *St. Martin's Chron.* 3 June, He nipped himself before the exams. **1989** F. WOLFAART on TV1, 14 Oct., Some of the guys out there will be nipping straws that he'll get away. **1991** I.E.G. COLLETT *Informant, Pilgrim's Rest* Nips or nipping: nervous.

nipinyana /ˌnipinˈjaːna/ *n.* [Eng. *nip* quarter bottle + dim. suffix *-inyane* found in some Sintu (Bantu) languages.] In urban (esp. township) slang: a 200–250 ml 'nip' bottle of liquor. See also HALF-JACK.

1968 *Drum* Sept. 29 When you enter a shebeen you are accosted by a cutie who asks, .. 'How about a nipinyana?' (small nip). This is their opening gambit and if you fall for it, you're hooked. You don't end buying a nipinyana .. but hooch enough to get your lassie nice and high. **1974** *Ibid.* 8 Aug. 50, I decide to go to Rockville to say hello to the Old Girl, and probably touch her for the fare for a nipinyana of mahog. **1976** *Ibid.* 15 May 49 I've got these shakes in my hands which shakes I wish to dispose of via a nipinyana at this aunty's place across the street.

nips /nɪps/ *adj. slang.* [Presumably related to NIP.] Afraid, anxious; cowardly. Cf. NIP.

In use (according to an informant's recollection) before 1963.

1977 L. ABRAHAMS *Celibacy of Felix Greenspan* 46 In the changing pavilion Willem said, 'Sies! but you're a real coward you know? You're nips like a kaffir.' **1983** J.E. KAHN *Informant* Nips. Schoolboy slang meaning scared, cowardly, chicken. **1991** I.E.G. COLLETT *Informant, Pilgrim's Rest,* I was too nips to try my horse over those jumps. **1991** V. HUSTLER *Informant, Umtentweni* When we had our first [baby] I was nips (afraid) that I would drop her.

NIS /en aɪ ˈes/ *n. hist.* A short name for the National Intelligence Service.

See note at BOSS.

1982 *Sunday Times* 9 May 6 The NIS is headed by 33-year-old .. academic, Dr N Barnard. **1983** *Rand Daily Mail* 1 Feb. 6 Dr Slabbert posed .. questions for the Government to answer ... Was Martin D— in the employ of the National Intelligence Service when the raid took place? .. If so, did nobody at the NIS know where he was? **1984** R. DAVIES et al. *Struggle for S. Afr.* I. 193 After 1978 under Botha's premiership, BOSS was restructured and renamed (first the Department of National Security – DONS – and now the National Intelligence Service (NIS). **1988** *Race Rel. Survey 1987–8* (S.A.I.R.R.) 545 In June [1987] the state president, Mr PW Botha, refused to give information in Parliament concerning the total number of persons employed in the National Intelligence Service (NIS) and their salary scales. **1993** C. ROBERTSON in *Sunday Times* 14 Nov. 3 He spied on the ANC, he spied on the AWB, he spied on the SADF, SAP, MI, NIS and SB.

nix var. NIKS *n.*

nkantata var. IKHANKATHA.

nkhosa, **nkhosi** varr. INKOSI *n.*

Nkone /ŋ'kɔːne, əŋ-, ən-/ *n.* Also **Nkona**, **Nkoné**. [fr. Zulu *inkone* a piebald ox or bull with a white patch on the ridge of its back; (a cow of such colouring is called *inkonekazi*).] (One of) a breed of cattle distinguished by piebald colouring and a white patch on the ridge of the back. Also *attrib.*

'Nkone' is sometimes confused with 'Nguni' (see NGUNI *n.* sense 3).

1949 O. WALKER *Proud Zulu* (1951) 128 The parade of his cattle inheritance from the surrounding kraals ... Black-muzzled Nkones, white Nkones, brown and oyster-blues. **1973** *Daily Dispatch* 12 May 18 The Ngoni cattle of Red Nkona pattern have been improved over the past 20 years for beef, milk and hornless: bred and reared on controlled heartwater and redwater veld. **1979** E. *Prov. Herald* 9 Aug. 8 Nearby was another well-known farmer, Mr John Sneyd, of Alicedale, with his rare span of Nkone oxen, an indigenous breed descended from the sacred cattle of the Matabele kings. **1986** *Daily Dispatch* 1 Nov. 17 Production sale of outstanding store tollies and trade nkone heifers and tollies ... The following cattle comprising .. 4 trained oxen – red nkone. **1988** *Grocott's Mail* 15 Nov. (Coastal News) 4 (*advt*) Dispersal Sale .. 80 Nkoné and Mixed Cattle. **1989** *Daily Dispatch* 11 Mar. 16 Mooiplaas Monthly Sale ... Cattle comprising 1 Nkone Bull, 2 Nguni Bulls.

n'koos, **nkos** varr. INKOSI *n.*

'nkosana var. INKOSANA.

'nkosasaan, **nkosaza(a)n**, **-zana** varr. INKOSAZANA.

nkose, **nkosi** *n.* varr. INKOSI *n.*

nkosi *int.* var. ENKOSI *int.*

nkosika(a)s, **nkosikazi**, **nkozkazi** var. INKOSIKAZI.

Nkosi Sikelel' (iAfrika) /ŋ'kɔ(ː)si sige'lel (i'aːfrika), (ən)'kɔsi sɪkələl (i'æfrɪkə)/ *n. phr.* Also **Nkosi i sikeleli Afrika**, **N'kosi Sikelela**, **Nkosi Sikelele (Afrika)**, **- Sikelel' i-Afrika**, **- i Afrika**, **Nkosi Sikelel'iAfrika**, and with small initials. [Xhosa sentence, *Inkosi* Lord, God + *sikelela* bless + *iAfrika* Africa; the first line of a hymn composed in 1897 by Enoch Sontonga.] The music or words of a hymn long perceived as the national anthem of the black peoples of southern Africa; under the Government of National Unity (1994), one of the two official national anthems of South Africa. See also *die* Stem (STEM).

The poet S.E. Mqayi added seven additional stanzas to the hymn. Nkosi Sikelel' iAfrika was adopted as the anthem of the African National Congress in 1925; translated into many African languages, it is also the national anthem of Zimbabwe and Zambia.

1934 *Cape Argus* 17 Feb. (Swart), The most novel experience of the day for the Prince was the singing of N'kosi Sikelela, the Xosa anthem, by a large choir of Bantu men, women and children. **1941** W.M.B. NHLAPO in *Bantu World* 22 Feb. 5 He was carried shoulder high down Main Street by some Bantu singing beautifully our sacred national anthem .. 'Nkosi Sikelel' iAfrika'. **1948** A. PATON *Cry, Beloved Country* 267 *Nkosi Sikel'él' iAfrika* ... This lovely hymn is rapidly becoming accepted as the national anthem of the black people. At any mixed meeting therefore, where goodwill prevails, three such anthems are sung in conclusion, 'God save the King', 'Die Stem Van Suid-Afrika', and 'Nkosi sikelel' iAfrika'. **1955** W. ILLSLEY *Wagon on Fire* 219 Let us terminate this meeting with the African National Anthem. In a flash he struck up and led the crowd in singing: Nkosi i sikeleli Afrika. **1959** [see CONGRESS sense 1]. **1962** A.J. LUTHULI *Let my People Go* 81 *Nkosi Sikelel' i-Afrika*. [*Note*] This means 'God Save Africa'. The hymn is a sort of unofficial national Anthem of black South Africa, and the theme song of the African National Congress. **1963** K. MACKENZIE *Dragon to Kill* 138 'Nkosi Sikelel' i Afrika', the virtual national anthem of the Africans. **1981** *Evening Post* 26 Oct. 1 Apartheid has resulted in most whites considering *Die Stem* as the country's anthem, while all Blacks regard *Nkosi Sikelele Afrika* as their anthem ... Dr Motlana predicted that *Nkosi Sikelele Afrika* .. would one day become the official South African national anthem. **1987** *Sunday Times* 25 Jan. 2 In Lusaka, the ANC meeting kicked off with choirs and the audience singing the 'alternative national anthem', 'Nkosi sikelel.' **1992** *Natal Witness* 30 Dec. 9 There were strong arguments for adopting *Nkosi Sikelel'iAfrika* as the new national anthem. It was widely accepted in southern Africa because it was a prayer without political references.

Nkulunkulu var. UNKULUNKULU.

nkundla var. INKUNDLA.

nob kerie, **- kerry** varr. KNOBKERRIE *n.*

noë, **nöe-boom** varr. NOOI, NOOISBOOM.

noem-noem var. NUM-NUM.

nog /nɔx/ *adv. colloq.* [Afk., (as) yet, still, besides, further, more.]
1. *rare.* Still.

1961 T. MATSHIKIZA *Choc. for my Wife* 89 This one is nog worse, he is Gxambagxamba, ask them to say it. **1993** A.L. HAYCOCK *Informant*, Grahamstown [visiting Rome] 8 June 1993. Nog Rome.

2. NOGAL.

1972 on Springbok Radio 7 Mar., At the next stroke of the gong the time on Springbok Radio will be 7.30 nog. **1975** *Sunday Times* 27 July 20 The first demo the capital has seen in many a long, conforming day. At the feet of Oom Paul, nog. **1977** *Ibid.* 13 Nov. (Mag. Sect.) 3 No matter what the basic outfit, whether slinky black silk or stiff brocade, the inevitable stole was there. Fringed, nog. **1978** *Fair Lady* 30 Aug. 5 Marabel Morgan's Total Woman is a diatribe on how to keep your marriage 'happy' by being a complete creep. In drag nog. **1981** *Sunday Times* 13 Dec. (Mag. Sect.) 5 You might use one credit card as a book mark (a literary thief, nog) but hardly the whole caboodle that was sent back. **1983** *Ibid.* 4 Sept. (Lifestyle) 3 Who's been sleeping in J-'s bed? Who's been bathing in her bath – and writing graffiti on her bathroom wall, nog?

3.a. Usu. in the phr. *nog a*, also *nog 'n* [Afk., 'n a]. Another.

1971 *Informant*, Grahamstown Here is nog – two, I think. **1972** R. MALAN *Ah Big Yaws* 21 Ah mist – gimmie nogga chorns! [I missed – give me nog a chance!] *c*1985 S. CROMIE in *Eng. Academy Rev.* 3 19 Me? – I go back to the Shebeen. Here Mister have nog a dop. **1989** *Weekly Mail* 20 Oct. 30 Nog 'n film festival. **1990** *Style* May 55, I grew up (pause) separately. I was a (nog a pause) fat kid, so I grew up being perceived as a fat person. **1993** J. NEL in *Getaway* Nov. 54 Saunders Rocks is a small beach but well sheltered, with nog 'n tidal pool and large, dramatic rocks.

b. In the phr. *nog 'n piep* /'nɔxə pip/, also *nog 'n peep* [Afk., *piep* peep, squeak], 'another cheer', customarily (and almost inevitably) said after three cheers have been given, calling for an additional one; *fig.*, some more.

1975 'BLOSSOM' in *Darling* 15 Oct. 135 He also fixes it that this party gets to be held every year on the anniversary ... It only breaks up well after midnight, with the traditional three cheers for oupa. 'And nog 'n piep,' Uncle Fanie reckons. **1985** J. VIGOR in *S.-Easter* Aug.-Sept. 52 (column heading) Nog 'n Piep. **1985** P. DIAMOND in *Style* Dec. 6 It was announced that the SAAA fund-raising auction raised R11 995. Clap-clap-hurrah-hurrah and nog 'n peep next year please. **1993** J. VLADISLAVIĆ *Folly* 141 A button sprang off the belly of an armchair and ricocheted, hip, hip, louder and louder, hurrah ... Malgas tossed and turned with the tide *en nog 'n piep.*

nog a dag, môre is see MÔRE sense 2.

nogal /'nɔxal/ *adv. colloq.* Also **nog al.** [Afk., 'fairly, rather, quite'.] 'What is more', 'into the bargain', 'on top of that', used as an interpolation; NOG sense 2.

1963 M. KAVANAGH *We Merry Peasants* 18 Two cocks and three hens, laying hens nogal, man. **1973** [see TWEETALIG]. **1978** *TV Times* 19 Mar. 8 Kojak can do it [*sc.* strike a match with one hand]. With a lollipop in the other hand, nog al. **1978** P.-D. UYS *Paradise Is Closing Down* 142 He phones up and .. asks if he can pop round for a bath. Pop round! And nogal a bath, can you believe it! **1981** *Fair Lady* 9 Sept. The Lower Class mixes freely with its Afrikaans equivalent and borrows equally from its vocabulary. In contrast the Middle Class thinks it amusing to use 'nogal' at the end of a sentence now and then. **1981** *Voice* 18 Oct. 4 That 'Kaffertjie' remark by Mr. Hennie V–! Nogal in Parliament by a man who is supposed to have the interests of Blacks at heart. **1983** *Sunday Times* 18 Sept. (Mag. Sect.) 3 The world karate whiz who's *nogal* a girl! **1983** O. MUSI in *City Press* 6 Nov. 7 It was a Wednesday nogal and he was really under the weather. **1986** [see *Weekly Mail* quot. at GREEN AND GOLD *n. phr.*]. **1987** 'A. AMAPHIXIPHIXI' in *Frontline* Mar. 38 All one needed to do was to join the queue, hats off and no smiles and wham! The snap ready in three minutes and for free nogal. **1988** D. CHRISTIE *Informant*, Grahamstown Surely so detailed a specification of forms (noun clause in apposition nogal) is inconsistent with the communications approach? **1991** D. KRAMER on M-Net TV 3 Apr., It was a great moment for me because I discovered that the man was nogal shorter than me. **1991** [see HAPPY BOX]. **1994** M. MBATHA in *Sunday Times* 9 Jan. 18, I have a Master's degree (from an American institution, *nogal*).

nôi, **noi(e)** varr. NOOI.

nojeboom, **nojes boom** varr. NOOISBOOM.

nole-kole var. KNOLKOOL.

No Man's Land *n. phr.* Also **Nomansland**. [Special applications of general Eng. *no-man's land* a piece of waste- or unowned land.]
1. *hist.* The area straddling the boundary between what is now the Eastern Cape (formerly the Transkei), and KwaZulu-Natal (formerly Natal); so called from the mid-1800s, when it had no officially recognized local government or ruler.

In 1861 the inland section was offered by the Cape governor to the Griquas, and became known as Griqualand East; it was annexed to the Cape Colony in 1866. See also *Griqualand* (GRIQUA sense 2). The section nearer the coast was annexed, as Alfred County, to Natal in 1865.

1861 *Queenstown Free Press* 15 May (Pettman), The country which is called *No Man's Land* is claimed by two powerful governments; and Sir George Grey has written to Adam Kok stating that in consequence of the land being claimed as above mentioned, the case has been referred to the British Government. **1875**

'P.' in A.M.L. Robinson *Sel. Articles from Cape Monthly Mag.* (1978) 189 At present the country is so broken up under different chiefs that it is a matter of some difficulty to recognize the territory as a whole without enumerating the separate dependencies. A portion of it is known as Nomansland; but this again is rather vague, and the present innovation is certainly a success. **1876** H. BROOKS *Natal* 234 In 1866 .. the Government of the colony took possession of 'No-man's-land'. **1882** J. NIXON *Among Boers* 104 The Cape Authorities offered Adam Kok, the Griqua chief, a piece of land on the borders of Natal, known as No Man's Land. **1913** C. PETTMAN *Africanderisms* 341 *No Man's Land*, .. In Sir George Grey's time as Governor, the territory now known as Griqualand East was so called; but in later times the designation was transferred to the coast country between Zululand and Delagoa Bay. **1965** BROOKES & WEBB *Hist. of Natal* (1979) 121 The annexation of Nomansland (named Alfred County) in 1866 might, if it had stood alone, have been treated as almost a matter of routine, except for the fact that the High Commissioner had to intervene to prevent the annexation encroaching on Adam Kok's territory. **1968** E.A. WALKER *Hist. of Sn Afr.* 305 The Kaffrarians .. hoped .. to remain a distinct colony enlarged by the annexation of Nomansland (the northern half of Faku's Pondo treaty state). **1970** *Std Encycl. of Sn Afr.* I. 301 *Alfred, Natal*, Area 543 sq. m. Magisterial district in the southern corner of Natal abutting on the Transkei. It was formerly called No Man's Land, annexed in Sept. 1865 by the Lieutenant-Governor of Natal. **1972** H. POTGIETER in *Ibid.* V. 351 *Griqualand East, C.P.*, The largest region in the Transkei ... The region was formerly known as No Man's Land after the paramount chief of the Pondo had ceded it to the British government in 1844 and gradually evacuated it. In 1861 the governor of the Cape Colony offered it to the Griquas as a settlement area. **1989** *Reader's Digest Illust. Hist.* 190 Under Adam Kok III, the Griqua had trekked from the vicinity of Philippolis ... They crossed Basutoland .. and descended, after two years, to the territory known as No Man's Land, between the Cape and Natal, in 1862 ... Despite its name, No Man's Land was not an empty territory when the Griqua arrived, but was peopled by, among others, Mpondo and Sotho. *Ibid.* 490 *No Man's Land*, Between the Cape Colony and Natal, settled by the Griqua from 1862 and subsequently annexed by Britain. Now Griqualand East.

2. *obs.* The area between Zululand and Delagoa Bay, so called in the late 19th century.

Now southern Mozambique.

1900 J. ROBINSON *Life Time in S. Afr.* 361 There still remained the undefined country (still called 'No Man's Land' by the Republic) lying between Zululand and Delagoa Bay, and it was therein that President Kruger hoped to secure a footing on the seaboard. **1913** [see sense 1].

nona var. NONNA.

non-black *n.* and *adj.* Also with initial capital(s). [Cf. BLACK *n.* senses 1 b and 1 c.] An inversion of the term NON-WHITE, used as an affirmation of black identity and dignity.

A. *n.* A white person; one who is not a black African.

1953 G. MAGWAZA in *Drum* Apr. 29 I've tried a couple of collective nouns for the lot: *non-Europeans, non-whites* and whatnot. I'm fed up with these negatives. *Natives* is meaningless ... I'm now toying with *blacks* and *non-blacks*. **1970** *Daily News* 9 June, Students at the University of Natal Medical School .. have decided to call themselves 'black' rather than 'non-European' students ... The students no longer wished to be referred to as 'the negative of another group' ... In future, 'other students will be referred to as non-blacks'. **1971** *Rand Daily Mail* 27 July 12 If the few Whites were sent to Australia instead (it would be cheaper too), then there would be no question of Blacks and Non-Blacks and we Blacks would live happily. **1972** *Drum* 8 Mar. 8 Well a great many *Drum* readers already refer to Whites as Non-Blacks and the idea seems to be catching on. **1973** *Ibid.* 8 May 22 Yesterday there was an incident concerning what is called a Non-White. For one I am a non-Black. **1980** *Cape Times* 18 Oct. 6 The Botha strategy as presently conceived is to co-opt a coloured and Asian elite to the side of the whites by means of the President's Council, drawing white and coloured more closely together. This in itself is not a bad thing but it creates a dreadful danger of non-blacks appearing to gang up together against the blacks. **1980** [see sense B]. **1982** *Voice* 6 June 4 It seems even so-called liberal newspapers have fallen for Pretoria's terminology and political-thinking by always referring loosely to 'South Africans', whereas in fact they mean only non-Blacks!

B. *adj.* Of or pertaining to one who is white, or to one who is not a black African.

1980 C. HERMER *Diary of Maria Tholo* 2 The administrative section contained the post office and rent office as well as an office to issue permits without which no non-black person could enter the township. **1980** *Rand Daily Mail* 29 Nov. 1 At present, blacks appear in these courts. It seems that the intention is to make non-black offenders also go before them. **1980** *Staffrider* Vol.3 No.4, 27 You never find a rubbish heap, right in the middle of the town, in a non-black area. You see, those non-blacks don't like rubbish even if it is their own. **1987** COLLINS & DYAN in *Leadership* Vol.6 No.3, 97 As for full-blown Leninist communism we estimate that only one in 12 of those designated 'radicals' – both black and non-black – are persuaded of the truth of the revolutionary faith. **1993** *Sunday Times* 31 Oct. 17 It does .. raise a number of questions for 'non-black' liberals. Do they have to accept black leadership simply because black South Africans are a numerical majority?

non-European *adj.* and *n. Obsolescent.* [See EUROPEAN.]

See note at EUROPEAN.

A. *adj.*

1. NON-WHITE *adj.* sense 1.

1918 *Report of General Manager* (Railways & Harbours) 31 Considerable progress has been made in the direction of providing separate accommodation on trains for Europeans and non-European passengers. **1942** *Off. Yrbk of Union 1941* (Union Office of Census & Statistics) 984 The population is divided for census purposes into four racial groups as follows:- (1) Europeans – persons of pure European descent. (2) Natives – pure blooded aboriginals of the Bantu race. (3) Asiatics – Natives of Asia and their descendants; mainly Indians. (4) Coloured – this group consists chiefly of Cape Coloured, but includes also Cape Malays, Bushmen, Hottentots, and all persons of mixed race. The last three groups, when combined, form the group referred to as the 'Non-European' group. *c*1949 *Survey of Race Rel. 1948–9* (S.A.I.R.R.) 11 Should we fail to do all in our power to help the Africans and the other Non-European groups attain the highest development possible. **1949** H. FORTES in *Hansard* 24 May 6451 There is frequent disagreement between individuals as to where to classify another individual, whether a particular person is European or non-European ... It does not seem to me there is a single reliable popular concept of either one or the other. **1957** N. MANDELA in *City Press* (11 Feb. 1990) 5 The decision of the government to introduce university segregation is prompted not merely to separate non-European from European students. **1970** *Daily News* 9 June, Students at the University of Natal Medical School .. have decided to call themselves 'black' rather than 'non-European' students. **1985** *Cape Times* 7 Jan. (Jobfinder) 12 Experienced Storeman ... Non-European male, matriculated, 27 upwards.

2. NON-WHITE *adj.* sense 2.

1939 R.F.A. HOERNLÉ *S. Afr. Native Policy* 52 The Indians .. were now excluded from the 'European' room and compelled to use the 'Non-European' room in the company of Natives. **1952** P. ABRAHAMS in *Drum* July 11, I was told the story of the young African intellectual who has a coloured girl friend. Whenever they go to the non-European cinema they are segregated from each other. **1968** J. LELYVELD in Cole & Flaherty *House of Bondage* 7 A white in South Africa who has some need or, less likely, wish to enter an area where black people live must first apply to his local Department of Non-European Affairs for a permit. **1970** *Drum* Aug. 10 With his record of leadership in the Non-European Unity Movement, it would seem hardly likely that he would want to assassinate so amiable a monarch. **1986** M. RAMGOBIN *Waiting to Live* 114 'Yes, take both my maids to the non-European hospital, please.' .. 'Sorry ma'am, you'll have to call for one of *their* taxis, or a non-European ambulance.'

B. *n.* NON-WHITE *n.*

1925 *E. Prov. Herald* 15 Aug. 4 The population of the town proper was 24,750 Europeans and 13,134 non-Europeans. **1932** *Grocott's Daily Mail* 11 Jan. 3 There are 250,000 whites and 350,000 non-Europeans in this country depending on salaries and wages for their living. **1950** *Act 21* in *Stat. of Union* 217 In this Act .. 'non-European' means a person who in appearance obviously is, or who by general acceptance and repute is a non-European. **1951** *Drum* Oct. 8 They foster racial hatred among non-Europeans, and aim to split the Africans, Coloureds and Indians from each other. **1960** *Star* in J. Crwys-Williams *S. Afr. Despatches* (1989) 330 It was 115 hours since 435 miners – the official figure is now six Europeans and 429 non-Europeans – were trapped by rock falls. **1964** N. NAKASA in *Ibid.* 245, I don't see that there is any justification in calling me a non-European either. That is as silly as this business of South African Whites who insist that they are Europeans. Some of them have never set foot in Europe. Nor did their grandfathers. **1968** in Cole & Flaherty *House of Bondage* (facing page) 83 [*sign on lift door*] Non-Europeans & Goods. **1971** N. ORPEN *War in Desert* (1983) 21 Field-Marshal Smuts had laid down as final that all drivers except for armoured fighting vehicles were to be Non-Europeans. **1989** *Personality* 10 Apr. 33 (*caption*) Nie-Blankes, Non-Europeans. Europeans, Blankes.

nongogo var. INGOGO.

nonna /'nɔnə, 'nɔna/ *n. obsolescent.* Also **nona, nonje, nonne.** [S. Afr. Du. *nonje, nonna* woman, oldest daughter, prob. fr. Malay *n(j)ona, njonjah* an unmarried European girl, used also as a form of address, 'miss', 'madam'; or perh. ad. Pg. *dona* lady (or see quot. 1913).

A.N.E. Changuion (*Proeve van Kaapsch Taaleigen*, 1844) records *nonna* as the dim. form of S. Afr. Du. *nooi* (see NOOI).]

1. Young mistress.

a. NONNIE sense a.

[**1785** G. FORSTER tr. *A. Sparrman's Voy. to Cape of G.H.* II. 191 The cry of the young gnu was sometimes *onje*, .. a good deal resembling the *nonje* of the colonists, (meaning miss).] **1913** C. PETTMAN *Africanderisms* 341 *Nonna* or *Nonni*, (Port. *nona*, a nun. Crawford ('Malay Dictionary') says that the word is used by the Malays of an unmarried European lady; hence most probably its use and application in South Africa.) A young European lady, a young mistress. **1960** J. COPE *Tame Ox* 145 The maid watched her aslant. 'Ai, my nonna, what is the basie doing?' the girl suddenly asked. *c*1964 'KWELA' in *New S. Afr. Writing* 157 As for the nonnas of Glenalmond, many of them ripe for marriage, he had taken none of them, in a white veil, to church.

b. NONNIE sense b.

1965 D. ROOKE *Diamond Jo* 93 'Nonna Leah did the writing,' Stokkies told me.

2.a. MISSUS sense 1 a.

[**1903** L. HOTZ tr. *J.E. De la Rey's Woman's Wanderings Anglo-Boer War* 6 *Nonne*, A Dutch-Indian term meaning Mrs or mistress.] **1968** K. MCMAGH *Dinner of Herbs* 51 Karolus .. was Granny's especial property and was devoted to his nonna and to keep him happy and occupied she gave him little tasks that required her presence.

b. MISSUS sense 2 a.

1972 L. VAN DER POST *Story like Wind* 269 Nonnie was a dimutive of *Nonna*, the polite word for mistress used by the servants in Francois's world. The daughters of the houses inevitably became *nonnie* (little mistress).

nonnie /ˈnɔni/ *n. obsolescent.* Also **nonni.** [Afk., *nonna* (see NONNA) + -IE.]

a. Often *my nonnie.* A respectful term of address or reference used often by servants to a young unmarried woman or to a girl, often the daughter of the employer; *kleinmies,* see MIES sense c; *kleinnooi,* see NOOI sense 1 c; NONNA sense 1 a; also called *klein missus* (see MISSUS sense 3). Cf. NOOI sense 2. See also BAASIE sense 1 a.

1913 J. BRANDT *Petticoat Commando* 200 'Are you thinking of your wife and children, Paulus?' 'Oh yes, Nonnie, I am always thinking of them, but I was thinking also how sad it was to forget all my learning.' **1913** [see NONNA sense 1 a]. **1930** S.T. PLAATJE *Mhudi* (1975) 140, I saw her .. shyly devouring you with her dreamy eyes but not daring to give vent to her raptures in public. Phil, that's the nonnie for you! **1953** D. ROOKE *S. Afr. Twins* 16 Above all this noise, Aia Kobie was exclaiming, 'My nonnie, and my basie'. **1960** C. HOOPER *Brief Authority* 89 Isaac waited patiently to be served. 'Yes?' asked the young white female assistant. 'Good morning, my nonnie.' 'Morning.' The nonnie was melting under this old-world treatment. **1968** COLE & FLAHERTY *House of Bondage* 73 Servants obsequiously call the children *klein baas* (small boss) and *nonnie* (small madam). The kids soon get to like this. **1969** M. BENSON *At Still Point* (1988) 53 At home, .. Amos and Cornelius would come to me: 'Can I have a night pass, please, nonnie?' Then I would spell out on a piece of paper: *Please pass native Cornelius* with the curfew time, our address, the date. **1972** L. VAN DER POST *Story like Wind* 269 Nonnie was a dimutive of *Nonna,* the polite word for mistress used by the servants in Francois's world. The daughters of the houses inevitably became *nonnie* (little mistress). **1974** [see OUMISSUS sense b].

b. Used as a title, with a name; NONNA sense 1 b.

1953 D. ROOKE *S. Afr. Twins* 16 Nonnie Tiensie how pretty you are.

non-voter *n. hist.* [Coined by K.M.C. Motsisi in *Drum* magazine, referring to the fact that blacks had no vote during the apartheid era.] In urban (esp. township) English: a jocular term for a black person.

1966 K.M.C. MOTSISI in *Drum* 30 Jan. 20, I turn around and recognise this non-voter as none other than Sis Well — the doll at whose wedding we sang. **1974** *Ibid.* 22 Apr. 28, I am a very peace-loving non-voter and I never wish to witness a punch-up between husband and wife. **1974** *Ibid.* [see STOKKIE *n.*[1]]. **1978** M. MUTLOATSE *Casey & Co.* Introduction, Putting together this baby that's *Casey & Company* was one hell of a task for this non-voter. **1982** *Voice* 31 Jan. 3 The lack of land for non-voters and such legislation as the Urban Areas Act, made it impossible for Blacks to be in a position to generate the necessary finance to build their own houses. **1987** 'DEKAFFIRNATED STAN' in *Drum* Apr. 33 For a moment I thought this non-voter was either forgetting himself or had become certifiable. **1990** M. KENTRIDGE *Unofficial War* 141 He .. tended to feature centrally in everything he wrote, referred to either in the first person as the lower-case 'i', or in the third person as 'voteless', a reference to Motsisi's collective term for South African blacks: 'non-voters'.

non-white *n.* and *adj. Obsolescent. offensive.* Also with initial capital(s). [Also used elsewhere. The term was used extensively in the past as a blanket term referring to those groups disadvantaged under apartheid.]

A. *n.* One whose racial ancestry is not predominantly European; one who is dark-skinned; NIE-BLANKE; NON-EUROPEAN *n.* Also *attrib.* Cf. BLACK *n.* sense 1 c, NON-BLACK *n.*, WHITE *n.* sense 2 a. See also N sense 1.

1934 A.J. BARNOUW *Lang. & Race Problems* 29 It is only in the Cape Province that distinction is made between natives and coloured people, and that the latter are given a privileged position ... In the other Provinces all non-whites are counted among the natives. **1949** *Blueprint for Blackout* (Educ. League) *(pamphlet)* 7 We stand for the principle of the trusteeship of the White, and particularly of the Afrikaner, over the non-White. **1952** MANUEL & VAN DE HAER in *Drum* Aug. 6 After 300 years of contact with the non-Whites, it would be difficult to say who really are free from the tarbrush touch and who really do come within the pigment class. **1953** *Drum* July 44 He realised he was no longer in England — he was no longer a man: he was a non-white again. **1968** J. LELYVELD in Cole & Flaherty *House of Bondage* 15 The whites have methodically used legislation to strip non-whites of their rights. **1972** *Drum* 22 Feb. 6 Non-White is a terrible word for a description of us. It makes us appendages of Whites. If there were no Whites then there wouldn't be Non-Whites. **1972** *Fair Lady* 14 June 23, I heard this said on the SABC news 'A lorry struck three children and a non-White ...' Don't you think it sounds just too terrible? What is a non-White? Some kind of non-person? *Ibid. [editorial comment]* The SABC PRO in Johannesburg says: 'Wherever possible we would identify the victim as a Zulu, Xhosa or whatever, but if the accident is fatal and the victim isn't carrying any identification we refer to him or her as a non-White.' **1980** C. HERMER *Diary of Maria Tholo* 194 At Kenilworth Centre it used to say, 'Whites' and 'Non-whites'. Now on both it just says 'Women'. **1986** P. MAYLAM *Hist. of Afr. People* 183 Karis and Carter have remarked, 'Xuma was both an Africanist .. and a multiracialist, .. but turning increasingly to co-operation with nonwhites'. **1990** *Weekend Post* 3 Mar. 8 He had queued at the 'non-whites' counter in the Upington post office on a hot afternoon ... 'Since when do baboons receive telegrams?' asked the postmaster. 'Since monkeys became postmasters,' replied Mr Rabie. **1991** J. BORGER in *Focus on Afr.* Apr.-June 31 Non-whites will have no place in the *Boerestaat,* not even as domestic workers. **1992** R.H. DU PRE *Making of Racial Conflict* 159 If the non-whites threatened to penetrate the carefully constructed cocoon, he could easily form a laager and repel the threat.

B. *adj.*

1. Of a person or persons: of ancestry which is not predominantly European, being esp. of African, Asian, or mixed ethnic descent; of a social group not considered part of the white group; NON-EUROPEAN *adj.* sense 1. Cf. BLACK *adj.* sense 3 a, NON-BLACK *adj.*

1952 *Drum* July 21 Those who are non-white have to travel a long distance indeed before they can enjoy a seaside picnic. **1956** *Off. Yrbk of Union 1954–5* (Bureau of Census & Statistics) 679 White Persons — persons who in appearance obviously are, or who are generally accepted as white persons, but excluding persons who, although in appearance obviously white, are generally accepted as Coloured persons; .. Natives .. Asiatics .. Cape Malays .. Coloured ... The last four groups, when combined, form the group referred to as the non-white group. **1961** M.A. WALL *Dominee & Dom-Pas* 55 If the police had discovered the non-White journalist of the party, who first hid and then masqueraded as the servant of the White reporter, the menace might not have been mere show. **1968** J. LELYVELD in Cole & Flaherty *House of Bondage* 9 Thirty-six million of the forty-two million people who will be living in South Africa in the year 2000 will be non-white. **1973** *Cape Times* 19 May 6 'Non-White' (although, at times, it is necessary to use it as a blanket descriptive) is in truth absurd. It implies that 'White' is the norm from which all other skin colours deviate. **1973** M. REINHART in J. Crwys-Williams *S. Afr. Despatches* (1989) 371 The impression that unseemly displays of the female body must make on non-White men, many of whom are only half civilised, need not be mentioned. **1980** C. HERMER *Diary of Maria Tholo* 55 Before the riots the coloureds used to keep us away from them ... The fact is we are all under one blanket. We are all non-white. **1983** *Cape Times* 28 Dec. 1 Police have refused to make known the number of 'non-white' bathers turned away from, ordered off or summonsed for being on the Peninsula's 'white beaches' over the Christmas weekend. **1990** *Weekend Post* 7 July 6 The term 'non-white' was an anachronism and a racist South African term which was especially ludicrous when used to describe an American. **1991** G. SPENCE in *Sunday Tribune* 19 May 8 'Any encouragement' of squatting in the area would be a 'grave disservice to the non-white community'. **1991** J. ANDERSON in *Focus on Afr.* July-Sept. 81 We see ourselves as non-white — maybe on paper we're black or we're coloured or we're Asian, but in the eyes of the whites we're all the same, oppressed. **1994** B. KHUMALO in *Weekly Mail & Guardian* 16 Sept. 26 They thought it was an insult to call somebody 'black' so they came up with all sorts of euphemisms like 'people of colour' and 'non-white', thinking it was less offensive.

2. Of, pertaining to, meant for, or predominantly used by people whose racial ancestry is not European, or who are considered to be outside the white social group; NON-EUROPEAN *adj.* sense 2.

1957 D. JACOBSON *Price of Diamonds* 93 Two young men .. whose sensibilities had been offended by this raucous non-white voice entering the only way it could into their sanctuary. **1963** A. FUGARD *Notebks* (1983) 84 Going to the toilet a minute ago, the train was passing a cluster of non-white houses when I looked out of the window. **1974** J. MATTHEWS *Park* (1983) 31 He turned away in disgust and joined the queue at the ticket-box, glaring resentfully at the 'non-white' metal plate fixed above the window. **1980** R. GOVENDER *Lahnee's Pleasure* 3 The scene throughout the play is the 'non-white' (meaning Indian and 'coloured') bar of a white-owned hotel in a small Natal North Coast town. **1981** *Citizen* 28 Nov. 9 Non-white graduate salaries going up. **1986** F. KARODIA *Daughters of Twilight* 55 Indian films at the non-white bioscope. **1992** I. MANOIM in *Weekly Mail* 24 Apr. 8 The Cape Corps, for many years the only 'non-white' corps in the Defence Force, has been disbanded.

Noodhulpliga /ˈnʊəthəlpˌligə, -ˌliga/ *n.* [Afk., ellipt. for *Suid Afrikaanse Noodhulpliga* 'South African First-aid League'.] A government-subsidized Afrikaner first-aid organization similar to the Red Cross.

Established in 1935.

1960 E.G. MALHERBE in H. Spottiswoode *S. Afr.: Rd Ahead* 148 The *Voortrekkers* hived off from the Boy Scouts, and the *Noodhulpliga* hived off from the Red Cross, and latterly the *Rapportryers* are going to break away from Rotary. **1961** *Off. Yrbk of Union 1960* (Bureau of Census & Statistics) 128 In addition to the official health organizations there are numerous other bodies contributing effort in health fields, and subsidized in many instances by the Government. There are the South African Red Cross Society, the St. John Ambulance, the *Noodhulpliga,* [etc.]. **1977** F.G. BUTLER *Karoo Morning* 224 The Red Cross was supplemented by Die Noodhulpliga.

‖**nooi** /nɔɪ, nuɪ/ *n.* Also **noë, nôi, noi(e), noy.** [S. Afr. Du., perh. fr. Malay *non(j)a, njonja(h)* (see NONNA); or, as claimed by Mansvelt (*Idioticon,* 1884), fr. Pg. *noiva* bride.]

1.a. MISSUS sense 1 a.

Sometimes substituted for the second person pronoun 'you', reflecting the respectful mode of address in Afrikaans.

1850 R.G.G. CUMMING *Hunter's Life* I. 54 The kind-hearted noë, or lady of the farm, commiserating my condition, .. informed me that she had an excellent recipe for sunburn. **1910** D. FAIRBRIDGE *That Which Hath Been* (1913) 43 Abdol .. was diligently cutting up berry-wax preparatory to .. producing such a floor-polish as would satisfy even this new and particular *nooi. Ibid.* 47 I am pardoned by the *nooi*?' she said half-timidly. **1945** N. DEVITT *People & Places* 141 The counterpart [of *baas*], nooi, or nonnie, is said to come from the Portuguese, and is derived either from the word 'nona,' a nun, or from the Portuguese term for a bride. **1960** J. COPE *Tame Ox* 199 'Hai! hai!' he said intensely, 'a white *nooi,* and a child' ... 'Where is the *nooi* going?' the smaller man asked. **1963** J. PACKER *Home from Sea* 149 Marriage, birth, death. These fundamental events had been shared in the families of the *nooi* and her domestics. **1968** K. McMagh *Dinner of Herbs* 56 The servant came hurrying back to say that the man had gone, but the nooi must just come and seen the bed!

b. MISSUS sense 2 a.

1917 S.T. Plaatje *Native Life* 86 'Well, Nooi,' assented the Natives with some relief, 'if you say it is all right, then it must be so.' **1970** M. Muller *Cloud across Moon* 48 His fingers touched the brim of his hat as he came further in. 'Good morning, nooi.' **1982** A.P. Brink *Chain of Voices* 124 To me he was subservient. Yes, Nooi, No, Nooi. Right, Nooi. If you say so, Nooi.

c. With qualifying word indicating age: **klein-nooi** /ˈkleɪn-/ [Afk., *klein* small, young], NONNIE sense a; **ounooi** /ˈəʊ-/ [Afk., *ou* old], OUMISSUS.

Sometimes substituted for the second person pronoun 'you', reflecting the respectful mode of address in Afrikaans.

1913 A.B. Marchand *Dirk, S. African* 361 (Swart), 'Bridge is a falling **klein nooi**, so I heard,' said old Piet. **1914** L.H. Brinkman *Breath of Karroo* 24 Servants speaking to a young lady say 'Klein nooi,' little maid. **1968** M. Muller *Green Peaches Ripen* 40 'Why don't *Klein Nooi* plant fuschias in pots? (he always called me "little mistress".) They grow well here in the shade.' **1977** N. Okes in *Quarry '77* 132 The kleinnooi, Miss Frances, said it was the penicillin in the water butt, but the Oumissus .. had only shaken her head and said that beef tea with a dash of port worked wonders. **1986** *City Press* 23 Feb. 4 'White women use these schools to supplement their income. They are normally addressed as kleinnooi,' said the teacher, adding that white teachers were 'arrogant and conservative'. **1914** L.H. Brinkman *Breath of Karroo* 24 **'Ou nooi'** is a term used by servants in addressing an old lady, and is equivalent to the English 'Missus'. **1970** M. Muller *Cloud across Moon* 33 Lizzie .. looked at her feet. 'Please, ou nooi, Merrem Retief phone. She say she want to speak to ou nooi.' **1972** J. Packer *Boomerang* 63 Of course Ma continued to be mistress of the house and Annie, the cook, had her own ways of making it clear that she took her orders from the *die ounooi* — the old mistress. **1982** A.P. Brink *Chain of Voices* 59 The drowsy Sunday afternoon, the Oubaas and Ounooi gone to visit the neighbours. **1984** *Fair Lady* 14 Nov. 164 The ounooi's memory had died even before she had, with her two bottles a day.

2. An unmarried (Afrikaans) woman or girl; NOOIENTJIE. Occas. also with qualifying word, **boerenooi** /ˈbuːrənɔɪ, -nuɪ/ [Afk., *boere* Afrikaans]. Also *attrib.* Cf. NONNIE sense a.

1851 N.J. Merriman *Cape Jrnls* (1957) 174, I could easily tell tales .. about divers slaps and opprobrious words which I have witnessed an angry Noie bestow occasionally on these little creatures. **1867** E.L. Price *Jrnls* (1956) 257 She is just a Boer *noi* to all appearance — square — huge — coarse & uneducated, poor thing, but very kind & willing to help others, I think. **1894** W.C. Baldwin *Afr. Hunting* 155 Many of the Dutch *nöes*, or young maidens, are very pretty; and they are a very moral set of people. **1896** M.A. Carey-Hobson *At Home in Tvl* 280 No! no! We dont want the young noies (ladies), or any of their things, with us on commando. **1975** *E. Prov. Herald* 23 May 8 Margaret R— as a boerenooi. **1979** D. Child *Merchant Family in Natal* 112 They can say very little for themselves and sit a tremendous time with their hands before them, staring at De Vrouw and the Noy. **1980** *Sunday Times* 14 Sept. 11 She tells the history of Onverwacht again. 'I was a "nooi" Monare, born at Elim.' **1990** M. Stansfield in *Ibid.* 1 July 3 Seretse's son wins a boerenooi bride. An Afrikaner convent girl from Rustenburg is to marry into one of black Africa's aristocratic families.

3. A girlfriend or sweetheart.

1963 R. Gedye in C.M. Booysen *Tales of S. Afr.* 160 He had asked her once, when he was just fourteen, to be his nooi, always. **1963** J. Packer *Home from Sea* 108 A father can get twenty to thirty head of cattle for a good and beautiful girl. Cyrus, you'd have had to pay thirty beasts for your blond nooi.

nooidoorn var. NOORSDORING.

nooiensboom var. NOOISBOOM.

‖**nooientjie** /ˈnɔɪ(ə)ŋki, ˈnuɪ-, -ci/ *n.* Also **noointjie.** [Afk., *nooi* (see NOOI) + linking phoneme *-en-* + -IE.] NOOI sense 2. Occas. also with qualifying word, **boere nooientjie** /ˈbuːrə-/ [Afk., *boere* Afrikaans].

1949 C. Bullock *Rina* 36, I can't get away just at present. There's a nooientjie, a mooi meisie, you understand. **1960** J. Cope *Tame Ox* 38 'What's so sad then?' Rina burst out. 'The poor boy, my noointjie. He had to play with someone.' **1985** *Frontline* Aug. 7, I could take my Sotho sweetheart to the former [*sc.* a cinema open to all races], and my boere nooientjie to the latter [*sc.* a cinema restricted to one race only].

‖**nooisboom** /ˈnɔɪsbʊəm/ *n.* Also **nöe-boom, noje(s)boom, nooiensboom.** [Afk. (earlier S. Afr. Du.), *nooi* (see NOOI) + *-s-* (linking phoneme, or contraction of the possessive *se*) + *boom* tree; see quot. 1966.] KIEPERSOL. Also *attrib.*

1848 C.J.F. Bunbury *Jrnl of Res. at Cape of G.H.* 101 The *Nojeboom* (*Cussonia spicata*), a small tree of very singular appearance. **1853** W.R. King *Campaigning in Kaffirland* 134 In the huts were all sorts of odd things — calabashes, beads, .. large pieces of the root of the Nöe-boom root, peeled for food. [**1868** see CABBAGE TREE.] **1966** C.A. Smith *Common Names* 351 *Nooi(en)sboom*, A name applied to several species of *Cussonia* on account of the umbrella-like nature of the leafy crown of each branch which suggests a parasol carried by a lady.

nooit /nɔɪt, nuɪt/ *adv. slang.* [Afk.] The emphatic 'no'; 'never'. Also as interjection.

1970 S. Maclennan *Informant, Pietersburg* Are you going home? Nooit! **1974** G. Jenkins *Bridge of Magpies* (1977) 40 'Aren't you staying tonight?' '*Nooit nie!* — never! I'm pulling out as you're on your way ashore.' **1979** M. Anderson in *Sunday Times* 21 Oct. (Mag. Sect.) 1 Nosh is food, graze, chow. For real emphasis you now say *nooit* instead of 'no'. **1987** [see Fair Lady quot. at BOSSIES]. **1987** [see Silber quot. at SCHEME]. **1989** *Informant, Umtata* The other day I was standing at the bar and this guy comes along and says 'Can I have three crates of beer?' And I thought 'Nooit, this can't be true!', but the barman just said 'Ja, sure' and puts three crates on the counter. **1989** J. Hobbs *Thoughts in Makeshift Mortuary* 157 'Why did you come here tonight .. ? To find someone to pick on?' 'Nooit! I wouldn't even try with this bunch of Uncle Toms.' **1990** *Frontline* Mar.-Apr. 13 He finds I am from Johannesburg and pronounces: 'Well you can do what you want up there, but here apartheid is never going to end, nooit.' **1991** C. Broster *Informant, Cape Town* Nooit. Interjection. Not a chance, I refuse, I disagree completely. He says we must learn for a test tomorrow! Nooit! **1991** M. Kantey *All Tickets* 76 His ambition was .. to play sax for real ... Nooit, my bra. This is the big time I'm talking about, man, nè?

Nooitgedacht /ˈnɔɪtxəˌdaxt/ *n.* [Named for *Nooitgedacht* a Department of Agriculture breeding-station near Ermelo (Eastern Transvaal).] Used *attrib.* in the names of breeds associated with this research station: ***Nooitgedacht pony***, a breed of pony resulting from cross breeding between the BASOTHO PONY and the BOERPERD, and known for its hardiness, sturdy build, and quiet temperament; ***Nooitgedacht sheep*** ?obs., a breed of sheep bred between *c*1909 and 1913.

1920 R.Y. Stormberg *Mrs Pieter de Bruyn* 40, I had secret misgivings that the Nooitgedacht sheep wouldn't pass the test, even though Oupa Cloete is nearly stone blind. **1974** *S. Afr. Panorama* Apr. 12 Nooitgedacht pony, the only indigenous South African breed of horse and a descendant of the Basuto pony. **1989** *Motorist* Aug. 43 Nooitgedacht ponies, Boerperde and Basutho ponies are the most popular on many of South Africa's major trails. **1990** J. Theron in *Farmer's Weekly* 22 June 13 The Nooitgedacht Pony, one of the few South African horse breeds, was developed to save the legendary Basuto Pony from extinction and to fulfil the need for a farm and riding horse in this country. **1994** K. Kirkman *Informant, Ermelo* A Nooitgedacht Pony was bred here [*sc.* at the Nooitgedacht Research Station] during the 1950s.

noomnoom var. NUM-NUM.

noonoo var. NUNU.

noordkaper /nʊə(r)tˈkɑːpə(r)/ *n.* Also **noordcaper, noordkaaper, noordkapper,** and with initial capital. [Transf. use of Du. name for *Eubalaena glacialis* a whale of the northern oceans, *noord* north + *kaap* cape + n.-forming suffix *-er*.] The Southern Right whale *Eubalaena australis* of the Balaenidae.

The general Eng. form is 'nordcaper'.

[**1790** tr. *F. Le Vaillant's Trav.* I. 45 The *cachalot*, a kind of whale which the Dutch call *noord kaaper*, is always found in great plenty sporting in the bason.] **1913** C. Pettman *Africanderisms* 342 *Noordkaaper*, .. The name given by the fishermen to a variety of whale; the designation has been taken over from the early Dutch sailors, and applied, without any appreciation of the incongruity, to an animal whose habitat is the southern ocean. **1913** W.W. Thompson *Sea Fisheries of Cape Col.* 102 It was pointed out that the whales were .. 'noord-kapers' (small South Sea black or 'right' whale), and that they were not met with permanently either in Table or Saldanha Bays, but came in mostly during the rainy season. **1925** H.J. Mandelbrote tr. *O.F. Mentzel's Descr. of Cape of G.H.* II. 138 A species of whale, styled 'Noord-Capers,' abound in Cape waters. They can be seen almost daily in the vicinity of Table Bay and along the Southern promontories of the Cape of Good Hope. **1977** K.F.R. Budack in A. Traill *Khoisan Ling. Studies 3* 24 The 'Noordkapers' are considered the typical whales. In earlier times they must have been more common. The name was originally not meant for the species occurring in the South Atlantic, but for a close relative found in northern oceans (*Eubalaena glacialis*). Introduced by white whalers, the term was soon applied to the southern species (*Eubalaena australis*) also and was later taken over by the ≠Aonin (norkaper). **1985** A. Tredgold *Bay between Mountains* 81 Right whales (called Noordkappers by the fishermen). **1986** J. & I. Rudner (tr.) in V.S. Forbes *Carl Peter Thunberg 1772–5* 22 On the 14th, we saw *noordkapers* spouting, the seals (*phoca*) sporting, and trumpet-grass .. floating in great abundance.

noors /nʊərs/ *n.* Ellipt. form of NOORSDORING.

1966 E. Palmer *Plains of Camdeboo*, (*caption*) The noors — *Euphorbia ferox* — with its savage spines lives up to its scientific name. *Ibid.* 258 The noors .. has need of its spine. Like all Euphorbias, it has a silky latex, but unlike the latex of many, this is edible, and were it not for the spine it would never survive a single season.

‖**noorsdoring** /ˈnʊərsdʊərəŋ/ *n.* Also **nooidoorn, noors(e)-doorn, norsdoorn, norsdoring.** [Afk., earlier S. Afr. Du. *noorsedoorn*, fr. combining form of Du. *norsch* gruff, disagreeable + *doorn* thorn.] Any of several species of succulent *Euphorbia* with recurved spines; NOORS. Also *attrib.*

1839 in J.C. Chase *Natal, Re-Print of all Authentic Notices* (1843) II. 98 Trees as high as fir trees, and much resembling them, called the Noorsdoorn, are seen raising their lofty tops over the more humble trees. [*Note*] *Euphorbium*. **1872** E.J. Dunn in A.M.L. Robinson *Sel. Articles from Cape Monthly Mag.* (1978) 43 You would be advised, when riding or walking in their neighbourhood to give 'nooidorn' a wide berth ... These short but terrible recurved hooks have a grasp like steel. [**1883** M.A. Carey-Hobson *Farm in Karoo* 216 The principal growth was a most uninteresting-looking euphorbia, called by the Dutch *noorse doorn*, or 'spiteful thorn;' .. for thorns were ubiquitous — there was no escape for thin trousers or the flesh itself where the 'noorse doorn' abounded.] **1889** H.A. Bryden *Kloof & Karroo* 16 The milk of the *noorse-doorn* is not poisonous, and forms an excellent food for cattle, sheep, and goats. **1898** *Midland News and Karroo Farmer*

10 Nov. (Pettman), The drought continues in the Ruggens with unabated severity, and the *noorse-doorn* and finger-pol plants are now in daily requisition to keep stock alive. **1913** C. PETTMAN *Africanderisms* 342 *Noorse-doorn*, (D. *norsch*, gruff, disagreeable; *doorn*, a thorn.) *Euphorbia enopla*, and one or two other species are known by this name, which refers to the *noli me tangere* character of their spines. **1931** F.C. SLATER *Secret Veld* 79 Prickly-pear .. grew thickly .. while, here and there, flourished unsightly clumps of flabby and leprous *norsdoorn*. **1979** *Sunday Times* 9 Sept. (Mag. Sect.) 5 He and his brother once went to look at flowers Calvinia way because in Graaff-Reinet all you see are noorsdorings. **1993** MILTON & DEAN in *Afr. Wildlife* Vol.47 No.1, 27 The tortoises braved some fearsome spines to feed on the juicy flesh of such plants as noorsdoring (*Euphorbia stellaspina*).

2. *comb.* **noorsdoring veld** /- felt, -fɛlt/, also in contracted form **noorsveld**, [Afk., *veld* countryside, natural vegetation], natural vegetation in which the primary plant growth is *Euphorbia*; also *attrib.*

1913 C. PETTMAN *Africanderisms* 343 *Noorse or* **Noorse-doorn Veld**, Veld composed almost entirely of Noorse-doorn; in some parts of the country, lying between Jansenville and Pearston, the Noorse-doorn is so thick as to be almost impenetrable. **1979** *Sunday Times* 9 Sept. (Mag. Sect.) 5, I prefer .. the flavour of the noorsveld honey which I also found in the butcher's shop.

noosh var. MNGQUSH(O).

normalize *v. trans.* [Special sense of general Eng.] To desegregate and remove racial bias (from any activity, but particularly sport).

First used with reference to government moves, in 1976, to desegregate sport at certain levels but not others. These moves were widely criticized as superficial, and simply an attempt to effect a return to international sport.

1976 D. DALLING in *Daily Dispatch* 25 Sept. 11 It's a giant step for the National Party, but a small step towards normalising sport. **1977** *Cape Herald* 22 Oct. 22 Trying to 'normalise' sport will fail if relations between people of different colours are not 'normalised' first. **1988** B. KGANTSI in *Frontline* Apr.-May 31 'We have normalised golf in our country', said one PGA official.

Hence **normal** *adj.*, desegregated and free of racial bias; **normality** *n.*; **normalization** *n.*; **normalized** *ppl adj.*; **normalizing** *vbl n.*

1977 *Het Suid-Western* 2 Feb. 1 Rugby will be normal. *Ibid.* The opening of the Civic Centre for the Concerned Citizens meeting is the second big hurdle in the past few months in the abolition of petty apartheid and the 'normalising' of race relations. **1977** *Cape Herald* 22 Oct. 22 The three Sacu men came to the meeting to try to 'sell' normal cricket to the Rylands union. **1982** *Evening Post* 16 June 3 Mr Creighton said the policy of the Chamber of Commerce had always been that business should be on a completely 'normalised' basis. **1982** *Cape Times* 8 Sept. 10 What must still be the effect of discrimination in all those spheres of life not as advanced as sport on the road to 'normalization'? **1983** J.F. COLEMAN in *Grocott's Mail* 15 Apr. 5 Race or colour is now immaterial as far as the Club is concerned. We are now a little oasis of normality within our wider society and I would like to hope that all members of the University will take advantage of this situation to demonstrate that our 'normality' can indeed be seen as normal. **1989** *Reader's Digest Illust. Hist.* 450 Despite the legal requirements of the Group Areas Act, mixed teams received government blessing. However, this so-called 'normalisation' did nothing to take the sting out of the international boycott — simply because apartheid remained in force ... 'No normal sport in an abnormal society' became the clarion call of the South African Council on Sport.

norsdoorn, -doring varr. NOORSDORING.

notsung /ˈnɒtsəŋ/ *n.* Also **nutseng, nutzung,** and with initial capital. [Afk., ultimate origin unkn.; perh. fr. G. *nutzung* usufruct (see quot. 1966); or fr. an unidentified Khoikhoi name.] The tree or shrub *Halleria lucida* of the Scrophulariaceae, an evergreen bearing orange-red flowers and brown or black edible berries; also called OUHOUT (sense a). Also *attrib.*

Parts of the notsung tree are used for medicinal purposes.

In F. von Breitenbach's *Nat. List of Indigenous Trees* (1987), the name 'tree fuchsia' is used for this species.

1913 C. PETTMAN *Africanderisms* 343 Nutseng or *Nutzung, Halleria elliptica.* **1961** PALMER & PITMAN *Trees of S. Afr.* 321 The notsung, as *Halleria lucida* is most commonly known, has a tremendously wide distribution in South Africa. It reaches from Tanganyika southwards through the northern Transvaal to the Cape Peninsula, as a shrub in dry shallow soil, as a scrambler, or as a tree up to some 40 feet in forest. **1966** C.A. SMITH *Common Names* 353 *Nutseng (nutzung), Halleria elliptica* ... According to Marloth, the vernacular name was assigned to the plant by early German foresters who were employed by the Cape Government, and means 'usufruct' ... Perhaps here applied both in the legal and literal senses in that the foresters had the free use of the wood and fruits, as opposed to others for which a permit was issued. **1973** M.R. LEVYNS in *Std Encycl. of Sn Afr.* VIII. 235 *Notsung*, Tree fuchsia. Wild fuchsia. Ouhout. Kinderbessie. Wit Olienhout. Wit Olyf. (*Halleria lucida*) Shrub or small tree belonging to the family *Scrophulariaceae* and therefore not in fact a fuchsia. It is common in most parts of South Africa in places with a moderately high rainfall. **1990** *Weekend Post* 19 May (Leisure) 7 *Halleria lucida* (notsung tree or tree fuchsia) and *Halleria elliptica* (wild fuchsia) were plentiful in the ground and in containers.

‖**nou ja** /ˈnəʊ ˈjɑː/ *int. phr.* Also **nouja,** and (formerly) **nouwja.** [Afk., *nou* now + *ja* yes.] 'Now then', 'well, all right', 'very well, then', 'well then': an interjection which either introduces the consequences of a prior statement or set of circumstances, or expresses resigned acceptance.

1900 B. MITFORD *Aletta* 227 'Is he mad?' 'No. Only violent. Wants to fight everybody with his fists.' 'Nouwja. I would cure that "madness" with a sjambok if I were the Commandant' growled another. **1971** *Sunday Times* 31 Oct., (caption) Ja? Ha! Ha! Nou ja, that's intriguing news. Well done. **1972** on Radio South Africa 19 May (Short Stories from Sn Afr.), Ag nou ja, it doesn't really matter. **1977** I. MARGO in *Quarry '77* 158 'Here my girl, Christmas: a cake, two Cokes, some crackers and a blue pinafore.' Nouja, and also a bit of fun, Oude Meester, whisky and some red wine. **1977** N. OKES in *Quarry '77* 139 'Nou ja, toe,' he said to the youth. 'Greetings to September. We'll make a plan.' **1986** S. SEPAMLA *Third Generation* 21 'Tell me,' said the officer, 'where are you from and going?' 'Port Elizabeth to Johannesburg.' 'Nou ja, show me the permit?'

no what *adv. phr. Colloq.* [Calque formed on Afk. *nee wat.*] *nee wat*, see NEE sense 2.

1900 H. BLORE *Imp. Light Horseman* 242 'Allemag, little uncle, that will never do', said a young lieutenant of artillery. 'Shoot a man taken prisoner in a fight? No-what, we shall come into trouble about it.' **1916** S. BLACK in S. Gray *Three Plays* (1984) 191 Boetie: Four for sixpence, baas. Van K: No what, you're too dear. **1926** P. SMITH *Beadle* (1929) 50 'Jantje is not afraid?' 'No, what,' said Jantje, sticking out his chest and his stomach, and looking sternly ahead of him. 'No, what!' **1987** *Informant, Grahamstown* Ag no what. I'll eat later. I'm not really hungry now.

now-now *adv. colloq.* [Calque formed on Afk. *nou-nou* in a moment, a moment ago.]

Reduplication is common in *S. Afr. Eng.*: see also BOK-BOK, FOOTSIE-FOOTSIE, *kiep-kiep* (KIEP sense 1 b), KLIP-KLIP, KWELA-KWELA, PATA-PATA, PLAY-PLAY, TSABA-TSABA, VOETJIE-VOETJIE.

1. In the immediate past, 'a moment ago'. See also note at JUST NOW.

1948 A. PATON *Cry, Beloved Country* 85 They have been here. It was now, now, that they left. **1960** C. HOOPER *Brief Authority* 330 'When did it happen?' 'Now, Father, now-now-now. Almost this minute.'

2. In the immediate future, 'in a moment'. See also JUST NOW.

1970 J.R. BENNETT *Informant, Krugersdorp* I'm going to town now now. **1971** N. GORDIMER *Guest of Honour* 78 The bar would open now now. **1979** W. EBERSOHN *Lonely Place* 164 The spare keys are in Lieutenant's key cabinet. We'll fetch them now-now. **1982** [see JUST NOW]. **1984** *Sunday Times* 15 July 17 He addressed the bar waiter, and ordered three lamb chops .. 'Pronto and now-now,' he said. **1986** D. CASE *Love, David* 31, I won't be long. You'll see, I'll be back now-now. **1989** J. HOBBS *Thoughts in Makeshift Mortuary* 302 The gravel road had been recently widened and graded ... 'The gov'ment is fixing it up now-now for all the peoples coming to be living here.' **1990** *Estcourt High School Mag.* No.49, 17 After many months of careful observation I think I am safe in defining 'now' as meaning 'soon', 'now now' as meaning 'in a few minutes', 'now, now, now' as meaning 'now', and finally 'just now' as meaning 'later'. **1991** *Informant, Port Elizabeth* She's waiting for her husband — he's coming now-now.

noy var. NOOI.

NP *n.* Also N.P. [Initial letters of Afk. *Nasionale Party* or Eng. *National Party.*]

1. The predominantly Afrikaner political party (founded by General J.B.M. Hertzog in 1914) which, after entering several coalitions, came to power in 1948 and adopted APARTHEID as its policy until 1990, when it moved into a period of transition towards a wider democracy, becoming part of the Government of National Unity in 1994; *Nationalist Party* sense (b), see NATIONALIST *n.* sense c; *Nat Party*, see NAT *adj.* sense 1. Also *attrib.* See also *Herenigde Nationalist Party* (HERENIGDE).

1956 *Star* in M. Rogers *Black Sash* 205 Two Government members — Mr Steyn (N.P., Graaff-Reinet), and Senator Malan .. attended in the wheel-chairs. **1977** B.J. VORSTER in *Hansard* 20 Apr. 3751 My predecessor, the late Dr Verwoerd, said on many occasions .. that as the policy of separate development of the NP is put into effect more and more, the discrimination which existed in South Africa would disappear. **1979** *E. Prov. Herald* 20 July 2 The reason the NP had not split was that it believed Afrikaner solidarity should be maintained at any cost. **1986** *Style* Dec.-Jan 41 Bear in mind that the NP and PFP are passé, the CP and HNP declassé and liberalism merely réchauffé. **1987** P. WAGENER in *Grocott's Mail* 28 Apr. 3 The NP was too 'pap' to govern. **1989** *Sunday Times* 3 Sept. 1 At centre-left we have the DP and the NP, both committed to a negotiated future but differing on whom to negotiate with, and about what. **1990** *Weekend Argus* 17 Feb. 12 The political thinking of South Africans, and NP members in particular, had been conditioned by decades of high-powered propaganda from .. the NP's propaganda machine. **1994** R. MALAN in *Style* May 40 From the outside, the process resembled nothing so much as sumo wrestling, the resolute giants of the ANC and the NP locked arm-in-arm and eyeball-to-eyeball, neither giving an inch.

2. NATIONALIST *n.* sense a.

1993 *Sunday Times* 31 Oct. 31 Mr Grobbelaar's favourite weapon is a knobkerrie — 'it's my favourite cultural weapon for chasing NPs off my farm,' he chuckles ... His father-in-law .. an NP member, recently enjoyed a very pleasant stay at the Grobbelaar farm. And he's an 'NP'.

NPA *n.*[1] *hist.* Initial letters of *Natal Provincial Administration*, the regional government of the former province of Natal. Also *attrib.*

1970 *Daily News* 28 May, Allegations in the Provincial Council this week .. that terrorists threatening South Africa's northern borders had been found with the NPA dressing on their wounds. **1970** *Daily Dispatch*

18 Sept. 11 It was .. implied that the 'marked bandages' were being supplied to terrorists by employees in NPA hospitals. **1988** *New Nation* 30 June 3 The Natal Provincial Administration (NPA) has gone back on promises to turn a squatter camp on Rietvlei farm into a proper township. **1990** *Natal Witness* 12 Apr. (Echo) 2 Mayor Mr Mark Cornell has criticised the NPA and the KwaZulu government for not assisting the city council earlier with the refugee issue ... Mr Peter Miller said the NPA was not the authority in charge of Edendale Valley.

NPA *n.*² *hist.* Initial letters of *National Peace Accord,* an agreement brokered by the churches and the business community and signed in 1991 by the leaders of the National Party, the African National Congress, and the Inkatha Freedom Party, pledging abstention from violence.

1991 K. NYATSUMBA in *Star* 1 Nov. 12 Many South Africans have concluded that the National Peace Accord has failed to bring about peace in the country ... The real test for the NPA will come on Monday and Tuesday, when the anti-VAT general stayaway will take place. **1992** P. SIDLEY in *Weekly Mail* 24 Apr. 5 From September 14 last year, the day the National Peace Accord (NPA) was signed until the end of March this year, 1 533 people were killed in political violence.

NPP *n. hist.* Also **N.P.P.** [Initial letters of *National People's Party.*] A political party which formerly existed to accommodate people of Indian descent. Also *attrib.*

1984 *Survey of Race Rel. 1983* (S.A.I.R.R.) 39 With 34 of the 45 seats, the National People's Party (NPP) is the majority party in the South African Indian Council. c**1988** *S. Afr. 1987-8: Off. Yrbk* (Bureau for Info.) 171 In January 1984 an entirely new grouping — Solidarity — appeared on the scene to present the strongest challenge yet to the NPP. **1989** *Race Rel. Survey 1988-9* (S.A.I.R.R.) 695 He would use both debates in parliament and the NPP's power on standing committees to force changes to be made to the Group Areas Act of 1966. **1989** *Stanger Mail* 21 July 2 (*advt*) Grow with the People's Party. The N.P.P. The party for the people!

Nqika var. NGQIKA.

nqutu var. NGQUTHU.

N.R.C. *n.*¹ *hist.* [Initial letters of *Native Recruiting Corporation.*] An organization established in 1912 by the CHAMBER OF MINES to recruit black mine labourers from South Africa, Swaziland, Lesotho, and Botswana. Also *attrib.*

On 1 January 1977, the N.R.C. merged with the WNLA to form TEBA.

1942 *Off. Yrbk of Union 1941* (Union Office of Census & Statistics) 783 The Native Recruiting Corporation (the N.R.C.). This Corporation obtains labour from the Union, Swaziland, Basutoland and the portion of Bechuanaland south of Latitude 22° South. The system of N.R.C. offices which has been established throughout these areas, is supplemented by nearly 400 independent recruiting agents, usually traders, whose recruiting activities are supervised by the Government and the N.R.C. The natives obtained reach the mines through the central depot of the W.N.L.A. During 1940, the mines obtained 252,000 natives from these areas. **1948** E. ROSENTHAL *Afr. Switzerland* 192 H.M. Taberer may be regarded as the creator of the N.R.C. system. He belongs to that group of instinctively-skilled administrators of the African, who understand their every thought, and whom they rewarded with the title of 'Father'. **1962** A.P. CARTWRIGHT *Gold Miners* 216 The W.N.L.A. and the N.R.C. now bring some four-hundred thousand natives to the mines every year. **1972** W.P. KIRSTEN in *Std Encycl. of Sn Afr.* VII. 442 The mining industry has two labour organisations, the main objects of which are to recruit indigenous labourers and to facilitate their journeys to and from the mines. These are the Witwatersrand Native Labour Association (W.N.L.A.), established in 1902, and the Native Recruiting Corporation (N.R.C.), which was founded ten years later. Both organisations are under the same management.

NRC *n.*² *hist.* Also **N.R.C.** [Initial letters of *Natives' Representative Council.*] A body established in terms of the Representation of Natives Act of 1936 to advise the government on matters affecting black people.

The establishment of this body put an end to direct representation in Parliament for all but the white group, until 1994. The NRC consisted of twelve elected black members, four nominated black members, and five *ex officio* white members. It was abolished in 1951.

1952 *Drum* Aug. 21 Brilliant in debate, he has often guided the N.R.C. wisely. **1963** M. BENSON *Afr. Patriots* 158 Moroka warmly supported its advocacy of the boycott of the N.R.C. The N.R.C., he said, was an illusion and people must not think they could depend on it. **1986** P. MAYLAM *Hist. of Afr. People* 167 The NRC was abolished by the 1951 Bantu Authorities Act, a key measure in the creation of the Nationalist government's Bantustan system.

NRP *n. hist.* Also **N.R.P.** [Initial letters of *New Republic Party.*] A political party founded in 1977 by members of the defunct United Party (see UP) and the recently formed Democratic Party. Also *attrib.*

The NRP was based largely in the former province of Natal, and disbanded in 1987.

1977 *Daily Dispatch* 22 Aug. 3 The NRP differed with the PRP over the question of group identity in respect of cultural, religious, language, ethnic and racial groups. **1977** *E. Prov. Herald* 28 Nov. 5 A constitution will be developed in terms of N.R.P. principles. **1978** *Survey of Race Rel.* (S.A.I.R.R.) 8 The disbanding of the former United and Democratic Parties, (UP and DP) and the formation of the NRP as a synthesis of the UP and DP. **1981** [see PFP]. **1989** *Reader's Digest Illust. Hist.* 484 Those who still cherished the ideals of the United Party formed the Natal-based New Republic Party. **1990** M. KENTRIDGE *Unofficial War* 140 The now defunct New Republic Party (NRP) was a white political party whose constituency consisted of conservative, English-speaking Natalians caught indecisively between the PFP and the NP.

'nsangu var. INSANGU.

NSM *n.* Pl. unchanged. Esp. among members of the army: an abbrev. of *National Serviceman.* Also *attrib.*

1979 *Paratus* Jan. 16 The Vice-Principal of the secondary school said that the NSM play a significant rôle in the running of the school. 'Their attitudes are extremely positive. It is not as if they regard their stay at the school as only a temporary period. Each NSM tackles his job as if it was a permanent occupation.' **1979** *Cape Times* 25 June 4 (*letter*) I wonder if you can satisfactorily explain a gross injustice perpetrated on myself and thousands of other NSM of the 1977 intakes ... As a NSM, I do not feel free to disclose my name. **1989** H. HAMANN in *Scope* 10 Mar. 57 The first batch of NSM volunteers began training in Dukuduku in northern Natal.

NSRI *n.* Also **N.S.R.I.** [Initial letters of *National Sea Rescue Institute.*] A voluntary organization established in 1966 to co-ordinate sea-rescues. Also *attrib.*

1971 *Evening Post* 20 Mar. (Weekend Mag.) 1 The N.S.R.I. was established in November, 1966, under the sponsorship of the Society of Master Mariners. Its goal was to provide an inshore rescue service along the entire coastline of South and South-West Africa. **1978** *Het Suid-Western* 1 Nov. (Suppl.), The new R14 500 NSRI boathouse on Central Beach will be officially opened on Saturday. **1983** *E. Prov. Herald* 12 Aug. 2 Plet NSRI save man in sea 'just in time'. **1993** J. BRENNAN in *Daily News* 13 Jan. 2 Both men as well as NSRI crewmen battled to work in the water which was saturated with aviation fuel, burning their skin as well as their eyes.

‖**Ntate** /n̩'ta:te/ *n.* [Sotho.] Esp. among Sotho-speakers: father. Cf. BABA *n.*²

1. A respectful mode of address to an older man.

1948 E. ROSENTHAL *Afr. Switzerland* 198 'Ntate,' observed the official. 'I remember you came last month for a stamp. **1974** *Drum* 22 Aug. 4 'Ntate, I've got the letter to the superintendent typed. Can you sign it, please?' They all call him father. c**1976** H. FLATHER *Thaba Rau* 215 Leach responded with a smile and the highest term of respect that could be accorded an older Basuto. 'Ntate', he said. 'It is good to be back'. **1982** [see CHEESE-KOP *adj.*].

2. Used as a respectful title, either standing alone or before a name.

1974 M. MUTLOATSE in S. Gray *On Edge of World* 111 And over there Ntate Moruti was praying unnoticed: 'Modimo, forgive them, for they know not ...' **1980** C. NKOSI in M. Mutloatse *Forced Landing* 13 Eviction from home resulting from ntate's chronic unemployment and inability to pay the hovel rent. **1980** M. MUTLOATSE *Forced Landing* 151 Each time she left .. Ma-Nthato would innocently but deliberately lie that she was visiting Ntate — the children's father — at his place of employment. **1985** S. SELLO in *Drum* June 56 Ntate Nef is gradually becoming either a hero or a villain, depending on one's standpoint. **1987** *Learn & Teach* No.5, 29 'Our parents and grandparents sold their cattle to buy the land at Mogopa in 1912,' said Ntate Ephraim Pooe. **1990** *Tribute* Apr. 28 She would inquire and be told. 'Danny said he would be late today.' '*Danny*?' she wondered, not 'Ntate?' **1993** *City Press* 12 Dec. 15 'It was always Frank's wish to be laid to rest in the land of his birth, and with the generous help of Ntate and Mme' — as she called the Fines — 'his wish became reality.'

3. As a common noun: an older man.

1975 M. MUTLOATSE in *Bolt* No.12, 17 A carelessly-bearded ntate of about 40 going on for 60 and pretending to be 30 shook the commuters with a hail of laughter.

ntombazana var. INTOMBAZANA.

ntombi var. INTOMBI.

ntomboti var. TAMBOTIE.

ntonbizani var. INTOMBAZANA.

ntonjane var. INTONJANE.

ntsangu var. INSANGU.

ntwana var. UMTWANA.

num-num /'nʊmnʊm/ *n.* Also **knum-knum, nam-nam, noem-noem, noomnoom.** Pl. **-s,** or unchanged. [Khoikhoi ǃnum-ǃnum (cf. San ǃnum berry).

C.A. Smith postulates that the name is 'seemingly onomatopoeic, suggestive of the sound made when expressing pleasure at the taste of the fruits' (*Common Names,* 1966, p.352).]

Any of several spiny evergreen shrubs of the genus *Carissa* of the Apocynaceae, bearing fragrant white flowers, and fruits of various colours; the edible fruit of these shrubs. See also AMATUNGULU.

1822 W.J. BURCHELL *Trav.* I. 192 It [*sc.* the shrub] produces little bunches of small white flowers, which have both the form and the scent of the jasmine, and are succeeded by berries resembling those of the berberry. The Hottentots call this shrub 'Num'num (or Noomnoom, agreeably to English orthography), each syllable preceded by a guttural clap of the tongue. **1843** [see DUINEBESSIE]. [**1883** M.A. CAREY-HOBSON *Farm in Karoo* 141 A small branch of singularly thorny bush from which the Hottentot gathered a delicious berry, calling it Mum-mum, a name which they subsequently found was given by the coloured people to more than one edible berry.] **1897** [see SWARTHAAK]. **1913** C. PETTMAN *Africanderisms* 343 *Num-num*, (Hot. ˈnum ˈnum, each syllable with an initial click). *Carissa arduina.* The common name of shrub and fruit alike, the latter being very small and without any distinctive flavour. **1917** R. MARLOTH *Common Names* 62 *Num'num, Carissa arduina* (berries black) and *C. ferox* (berries red). *a***1920** O.E.A. SCHREINER *From Man to Man* (1926) 113 The nam-nams and jasmine shrubs made a thick wall on either side. [*Note*] A shrub with a small edible berry (also 'num-num'). **1951** N.L. KING *Tree-Planting* 66 *Carissa bispinosa* (*Num-num*), A spiny shrub with light green leaves and bright red fruits ... *Carissa edulis (Num-num)*, A shrub indigenous to S.W. Africa, Bechuanaland and northern Transvaal ... *Carissa haematocarpa (ferox) (Num-num)*, Very similar to *C. bispinosa*. Occurs in karroid scrub in eastern Cape. Bears dark blue or black fruits. **1954** U. VAN DER SPUY *Ornamental Shrubs & Trees* 83 *Carissa grandiflora*, Natal Plum, Num-Num or Amatungulu. **1964** A. ROTHMANN *Elephant Shrew* 33 There are miles and miles of bush, a dense, impenetrable mass of num-num, thorn bushes, 'taaibos', gnarled ghwarrie trees. [**1973** O.H. SPOHR tr. *F. Krauss's Trav. Jrnl* 59 Carissa grandiflora A Dc Arduina E Mey, called knum-knum by the Boers, amatungulu by the Kaffirs, a bush with white sweet smelling flowers and red gooseberry-like berries with a pleasant flavour.] **1976** A.P. BRINK *Instant in Wind* 93 Thickets of .. horse-piss bush, wild apricot, ghaukum and numnum and dry-my-throat and the ubiquitous euphorbia. **1987** D. MATTHEE *Mulberry Forest* (1989) 181 In the underbush, forest bramble, cross-berry, turkey-berry and num-num flowered in violet, pink and white. **1988** H. GOOSEN in *S. Afr. Panorama* Sept. 45 The bushveld pantry is well stocked ... According to the season, you can satisfy your hunger with veld fruits such as the medlar, marula, num-num, wild fig, stem fruit and sour plum. **1994** [see MATINGOLA].

numzan var. UMNUMZANA.

nunu /ˈnunuː/ *n. colloq.* Also **noonoo**. [fr. Zulu *inunu* (pl. *izinunu*) horrible object or animal; monster; bogy.] Esp. in KwaZulu-Natal:

1. *rare.* A term of endearment (particularly to a child); a nickname.

*c***1948** H. TRACEY *Lalela Zulu* 39 Nunu, my darling. I am troubled and know not what to do ... My heart is so disturbed by you, Nunu.

2. An insect: GOGGA sense 1. Also *fig.*

1970 A.K. LEYS *Informant, Durban* The children gathered round to inspect the nu-nu (insect or grub). **1991** P. BARTON *S. Afr. Environment Friendly Hsehold Hints* 105 Not only does it [*sc.* the cardboard box] break down, but it also forms a protection against worms and other garden 'nunus'. **1985** A. GOOSEN *Informant, Grahamstown* In Natal one might find a nunu in the kaya. **1992** A. ALEXANDER in *Afr. Wildlife* Vol.46 No.6, 261 The word 'nu-nu' was created in South Africa to denote a particular class of animals that are usually quite small, strange in their ways and little known. Bladder grasshoppers, or pneumorids .. fit this description almost perfectly. **1992** [see DEURMEKAAR sense 1]. **1993** *Weekend Post* 25 Sept. 4 If you also wonder what that noonoo, long-legged beastie or simple birdcall is, the museum is the place to be. Wednesday sees the creepy-crawlies feature in a talk on 'Goggas and NooNoos, Long-leggedy Beasties and Things that Go Bump in the Night'.

Nusas /ˈnjuːsæs/ *n. hist.* Also **NUSAS, N.U.S.A.S.** [Acronym formed on *National Union of South African Students.*] An association (1924–1991) of mainly English-speaking, liberal students at universities and colleges. Also *attrib.*

Merged with SANSCO in 1991.

1934 C.P. SWART Supplement to Pettman. 126 *Nusas*, The popular name of the National Union of South African Students. **1955** T.B. DAVIE *Educ. & Race Rel.* (Hoernlé Mem. Lecture) 10 As far back as 1924 the students .. created .. a National Union of Students (N.U.S.A.S.) which for many years operated successfully in the interests of students generally. **1963** M.G. MCCOY *Informant, Port Elizabeth* The latest Govt. attack is on Nusas – Vorster calling on all students to resign and to break its hold over universities where it still reigns. **1973** A.G. BAGNALL in *Std Encycl. of Sn Afr.* VIII. 91 During the decades following the Second World War the leaders of NUSAS increasingly felt it their duty to give voice to the student bodies they represented, concerning controversial State actions and legislation. **1978** *Sunday Times* 28 May 12 More than 15 student newspapers, posters and pamphlets, mostly left-wing or Nusas-oriented have been banned so far this year. **1982** K. JAGA in *Voice* 11 July 2 The aim of NUSAS July Festival was to mobilize students in the 'education struggle', to tackle issues off campus like detentions and strikes. **1986** P. MAYLAM *Hist. of Afr. People* 193 Black university students .. in the late 1960's became disillusioned with the National Union of South African Students (NUSAS), a body dominated by liberal white students. **1987** *Rhodeo* (Rhodes Univ.) Mar. 7 Rhodeo: What exactly is NUSAS? SK: Our three main spheres of work are student representation, student benefits, and political action. **1991** [see SANSCO].

nush var. MNGQUSH(O).

nutria /ˈnjuːtrɪə/ *n. Military.* [Special use of general Eng. *nutria* the mid-brown colour of the fur of the coypu (*Myocaster coypus*).] The brown uniform of the defence forces; cf. *browns* (see BROWN *n.* sense 2).

1977 B. MARKS *Our S. Afr. Army* 11 The fear of loss of identity, of becoming a faceless number in a sea of nutria. **1983** *Evening Post* 28 Mar. 3 About two years ago a squall blew through navy ranks when Defence authorities decided that Navy personnel would be fitted out in nutria, the Army's brown uniform.

nutseng, -zung varr. NOTSUNG.

‖**nuwejaarsblom** /ˈnyvəjɑː(r)zˌblɔm, -jaː(r)s-/ *n.* Also **nieuwjaarsblom**, and with initial capital. [Afk., earlier *nieuwjaarsblom*, fr. Du. *nieuw* new + *jaar* year + euphonic *-s-* + *blom* flower; so called because it flowers in mid-summer.] The plant *Gladiolus cardinalis* of the Iridaceae, known for its bright scarlet flowers.

1917 R. MARLOTH *Common Names* 141 *G. cardinalis*, Nieuwjaarsblom. **1957** L.G. GREEN *Beyond City Lights* 11 Among the prized growths of these mountains is the rare and lovely *nuwejaarsblom* (Gladiolus cardinalis), which Dorothea Fairbridge called 'Maid of the Mist' and others have named 'New Year Lily' or Waterfall Gladiolus'. The bright scarlet flowers appear in midsummer, as the Afrikaans name suggests, and the petals quiver on long stems. **1974** *Reader's Digest Complete Guide to Gardening* II. 395 *G. cardinalis*, (Waterfall gladiolus, nuwejaarsblom). S. Africa. Height 24 in. This species is the parent of many hybrids and bears arching stems of 3 in, flat, crimson flowers in mid-summer. **1979** *Weekend Post* 17 Nov. (Family) 2 The rare and beautiful red disa orchid and Nuwejaarsblom can be seen here in summer. **1992** S. JOHNSON in *Afr. Wildlife* Vol.46 No.4, 178 Few flowers can compete with the beauty of .. the nuwejaarsblom (*Gladiolus cardinalus*).

‖**nxa** /ŋǁa/ *adj., int.* and *n.* [N. Sotho (int. and n.).] Esp. among Sotho-speakers:

A. *adj.* [fr. N. Sotho n.] Unpleasant.

1974 *Drum* 22 Sept. 10 Everything is nxa – then somebody says something.

B. *int.* An exclamation of disgust, displeasure, or discord.

1979 M. MATSHOBA *Call Me Not a Man* 75 On their way home that evening Martha had told Monde about the arrangements. 'Nxa!' 'What's it, love?' Monde had asked with a ring of concern in his voice.

C. *n.* Disagreement, friction.

1980 *Voice* 29 Oct. 2 South Africa .. was a world model of how different groups could live together without a 'nxa'. This much she was going to tell to her countrymen when she returned home.

nyala /ˈnjɑːlə, ən-/ *n.* Also **inyala**, with initial capital, and (formerly) **inyalla**. Pl. unchanged, or **-s**. [Tsonga and Venda *nyala*, Zulu *inyala*.]

1. The antelope *Tragelaphus angasii* of the Bovidae, which inhabits low-lying and thickly-wooded country. Also *attrib.*

1848 G.F. ANGAS in *Proc. of Zool. Soc.* 89 This new and brilliant Antelope, the Inyala of the Amazulu. **1853** R.B. STRUTHERS *Hunting Jrnl* (1991) 32 He shot a buck (Inyalla). **1863** W.C. BALDWIN *Afr. Hunting* 92 A moment after I beheld a noble buck inyala walking leisurely away. **1891** R. WARD *Sportsman's Handbk* 123 In Zululand were to be found, a few years ago, Elephants, .. Inyalas (Tragelaphus angassi), [etc.]. **1899** H.A. BRYDEN *Great & Small Game of Afr.* 453 The bushbucks, Genus Tragelaphus. The harnessed antelopes, or bushbucks, .. may be arranged as follows:– A ... 1. The Bongo (*T. euryceros*). 2. The Nyala (*T. angasi*) [etc.]. **1918** H. MOORE *Land of Good Hope* 38 Pictures of seven different kinds of wild animals killed in sport; wart-hog, rhinoceros, leopard, nyala [etc.]. *c***1936** *S. & E. Afr. Yr Bk & Guide* 1096 *The Nyala or Inyala Bushbuck or Angas' Antelope, (tragelaphus angasi).* Height about 40 inches; colour of male, dark grey and fawn with white markings, amongst which vertical stripes on sides and white V between the eyes. **1947** J. STEVENSON-HAMILTON *Wild Life in S. Afr.* 109 Along the Pafuri River in the nyala bush they have become accustomed to motor traffic. **1949** J. MOCKFORD *Golden Land* 219 Farther on, a rarely seen antelope looked at me from between the grass tufts, and then pranced away – a lovely nyala ram, its dark body a-flicker with stripes. **1953** R. CAMPBELL *Mamba's Precipice* 49 A full-grown Inyala bull was drinking .. ; behind him, half-way down the bank, were two beautiful ginger-red Inyala cows with brilliant white stripes which flashed electrically in the evening light. **1964** G. CAMPBELL *Old Dusty* 132 The Livingstone antelope, inyala, bongo and puku are as rare as virgins in night-clubs. **1975** *Country Life* (U.K.) 20 Feb. 444 A visit to .. these [South African] reserves is always rewarded with views of zebra, nyala, impala, duiker, waterbuck. **1982** *Flying Springbok* Sept. 88 With trophy charges and licence fees, Cape buffalo cost R1 500 a head, nyala R670. **1990** SKINNER & SMITHERS *Mammals of Sn Afr. Subregion* 693 The colloquial name originates from the Zulu name for the species, *inxala* [*sic*]. The species was first brought to the notice of European naturalists by Mr. Douglas Angas and was at one time known as Angas' bushbuck ... Nyalas are medium-sized antelopes. **1992** *S. Afr. Panorama* Mar.-Apr. 120 The lordly nyala come down to drink from dense surrounding woods.

2. A small armoured personnel-carrier used by the police.

1993 J. MAKER in *Sunday Times* 17 Oct. 16 His partner in crime had already gone down the stairs to the cells below, to be hustled into an SAP Nyala and taken to Death Row.

nyanga var. INYANGA.

‖**nyatsi** /ˈnjatsi/ *n.* Pl. unchanged, or ‖**di-**. [S. Sotho.] Esp. among Sotho-speakers: a paramour; the lover of a married person. Also *attrib.*

1948 E. HELLMANN *Rooiyard* 50 Some married women form more permanent liaisons with a *nyatsi* ('back-door husband'), who gives them cash presents every month. Such a woman, unbeknown to her husband, succeeds in earning part of her alleged beer money by having one or more *nyatsi*. **1959** L. LONGMORE *Dispossessed* 268 In tribal areas, a *nyatsi* (concubine, paramour – man or woman) relationship worked according to certain rules. *Ibid.* 269 It was generally agreed that every man in the urban area had a *nyatsi*, where, however, the practice was more risky than in the tribal areas where there was seldom more that one *nyatsi* involved. **1980** M. MZAMANE in *Best of S. Afr. Short Stories* (1991) 389, I wish I was like the other fellows who have *dinyatsi* (mistresses) to whom they can escape. **1986** *Drum* Apr. 32 (*letter*) I discovered that she had a 'nyatsi'. I tried to persuade her to stop seeing her 'nyatsi' and she pretended to understand.

Hence **nyatsarize** *v. intrans.* ?*nonce*, to enter an extra-marital sexual relationship; **nyatsism** *n.*, the practice of having extra-marital relationships.

1959 L. LONGMORE *Dispossessed* 278 It is not true to say that among Africans *nyatsism* is an urban practice.

It is most decidedly not. *Nyatsism* is an age-old practice... The original practice was for a man who was married to '*nyatsarise*' with a married woman.

nylon *n.* [Fig. and transf. use of general Eng.; see quots 1960 and 1962.] Esp. in township slang: KWELA-KWELA sense 1.

1960 C. HOOPER *Brief Authority* 209 Because of the appearance of their perspex panels they were soon known as 'Nylons'; or they were referred to by the city name of 'kwela-kwela' — an imitation of the police herding prisoners aboard with shouts of 'Kwela! get on!' **1962** W. MANQUPU in *Star* 22 Feb. 14 The riot cars with their windows covered with wire mesh are picturesquely known as 'nylons'. **1980** E. JOUBERT *Poppie Nongena* 169 Things look bad at the location, mama said, but we're all still alive... We counted ten burnt-out nylons in front of the pass office. **1980** *E. Prov. Herald* 16 Sept. 11 Multilingual South Africanisms like 'ag' and 'doek', 'muti' and 'kwedine', or the township slang of 'nylons' (police vans) and 'skellums'.

nyoka var. INYOKA.

Nysna lily var. KNYSNA LILY.

O

o var. OU *n.*

oakie var. OKIE.

oaklip var. OUKLIP.

OB /əʊ ˈbiː/ *n.*[1] *hist.* Also **O.B.** [Initial letters of Afk. *Ossewa Brandwag, ossewa* oxwagon + *brandwag* sentinel.] **a.** A short name for the Ossewa Brandwag, an organization which was founded in 1939 by Afrikaner nationalists as a cultural movement, but which became increasingly militant in its adherence to Nazism; OSSEWA sense 1. Also *attrib.* **b.** A member of this organization. See also BRANDWAG sense 2, STORMJAER sense 2.

1940 *Forum* 13 Oct. 19 Several new Afrikaans student organisations had sprung up as a result of a dislike of 'the totally un-Afrikaans fuehrer principle' introduced by the O.B. 1941 *Forum* 20 Sept. 29 You pluck really nice propaganda stuff out of an empty top-hat. First an O.B. jacket, and now school children are spattered with swastikas. 1947 M. ROBERTS *S. Afr. Opposition* 73 The O.B. movement had been founded in Bloemfontein in October 1938, upon the occasion of the centenary of the Great Trek. 1948 *Press Digest* No.2, 12 One point which still has to be clarified is whether the O.B. will agree to any of its more senior 'officers' .. accepting nomination for seats in Parliament. 1950 H. GIBBS *Twilight* 179 Having started by announcing itself in favour of a republic, the OB was stated by van Rensburg to be 'the core and concentration of Afrikanderdom'. 1952 B. DAVIDSON *Report on Sn Afr.* 156 As the years passed, and all hopes of Hitler's final victory vanished from the scene, the earlier enthusiasms of the 'OB' became more and more embarrassing to the Nationalists. 1963 S.H. SKAIFE *Naturalist Remembers* 139 'It's not bees that are bothering us, but O.B.'s'. He meant members of the Ossewa-Brandwag that was very active at the time. 1973 A.J.H. VAN DER WALT in *Std Encycl. of Sn Afr.* VIII. 395 The O.B ... was founded on 4 Feb. 1939 in Bloemfontein and modelled on the Commando system in the erstwhile .. Boer republics, with a commandant-general as leader, appointed by a 'Groot Raad' (High Council) comprising representatives of provincial boards. 1977 [see STORMJAER sense 2]. 1986 T. WENTZEL in *Weekend Argus* 8 Mar. In the 40s the National Party broke with the militantly National-Socialist OB and opposed it as the OB became increasingly involved in politics while it was supposed to operate only culturally. 1989 *Reader's Digest Illust. Hist.* 349 Although it was founded to promote 'cultural activities' and ideals, .. the OB quickly took on a distinctly military flavour. 1993 S. BRANCA in *Sunday Times* 11 July 17 That the OB succeeded in setting up a network of subversives across the length and breadth of South Africa is clear from Beecroft's reports.

o.b. /əʊ ˈbiː/ *n.*[2] *rare.* [Abbrev. of Afk. *oubaas,* see OUBAAS.] A form of address to a prison warder. Cf. OUBAAS sense 2.

. 1983 J. CRONIN *Inside* 16 Johannes Stephanus Februarie! Gives a small stylized skip. — Ja, o.b. (Ou baas worn short with long use).

OB /əʊ ˈbiː/ *n.*[3] Initial letters of Afk. *Orde Boerevolk* (Order of the Afrikaner people), a militant organization of white rightwingers.

1990 P. RUDOLPH in *Weekend Post* 29 Sept. 1, I want to take this opportunity to call on the members of the Orde Boerevolk (OB) to do the following: Upon my request, the SAP has allowed me to hold discussions with the Executive Council of the OB about the question of arms, ammunition and explosives. 1991 *Ibid.* 5 Jan. 8 This call should make it clear the OB would no longer commit acts of violence in the present political climate and expects the Government to accept it has chosen the negotiation path. 1992 R.H. DU PRE *Making of Racial Conflict* 165 Boer Republican Army (BRA), Rightwing terrorist army in Transvaal ... Suggests all members of the OB, AWB and HNP should consider themselves de facto members of BRA.

obies /ˈəʊbiːz/ *n. slang.* Also **obbies, OB's.** [Formed on initial letters of *Old Brown* + Eng. *-ies,* used to form a slang or colloq. noun.] Esp. among university students: old brown sherry.

1979 *Informant, E. Cape* We've got some obies. We can share it with you if you like. 1987 *Party invitation, Grahamstown* Pull in to a solid jol ... Bring your own obbies, tas or SAB. 1987 *Fair Lady* 18 Feb. 92 We set off down the N2, then Clarence Drive, with Juluka blasting and a bottle of OB's, responsible second years. 1990 D.G. GOUGH *Informant, Grahamstown* Does anybody know what obies is? — Old Brown Sherry.

Obiqua var. UBIQUA.

oblietjie /ɔˈbliki, -ci/ *n.* Formerly also **oblietje, obletje, oblitje, oubleetjie, oubletjie, oublie, oublietje.** [Afk., earlier S. Afr. Du., fr. Du. *oblie* (fr. Fr. *oublié,* ult. fr. Eccl. L. *oblata*) wafer + dim. suffix -IE; forms with *ou-* are prob. S. Afr. Du. variants, influenced by the Fr. spelling. See also quot. 1954.] A wafer-thin tea-cake similar to a brandy-snap, cooked in a wafer pan and rolled when still warm. Also *attrib.*

1890 A.G. HEWITT *Cape Cookery* 50 Obletjes, .. Mix the ingredients into a dough and make into balls the size of a walnut, bake them quickly one at a time in an oblietje pan; roll each one .. from the pan. 1891 H.J. DUCKITT *Hilda's 'Where Is It?'* 153 'Obletjes' (or 'Oubliés'). (An old-fashioned Recipe for Tea Cakes brought to the Cape by the French Refugees.). *Ibid.* 243 Use also 'Obletjes,' Scones and Cakes, Puffs and Sandwiches. 1912 *Northern News* 27 Aug. (Pettman), The one word I feel sure of is *oublietje,* that delicious, crisp, wafer-like pastry to be invariably found at bazaars in the districts settled by the Huguenots. 1915 D. FAIRBRIDGE *Torch Bearer* 201 Crisp zoet-cookies and oublietjes, the delicious spiced cakes of South Africa. 1927 C.G. BOTHA *Social Life in Cape Col.* 57 Even to-day those who know the Cape cooking will recall the eating of 'koekies,' 'oblietjies,' 'wafels,' 'poffertjes' and 'pannekoek.' 1945 N. DEVITT *People & Places* 15 The French refugees were responsible for a teacake turned out as thin as a wafer on a pan called an 'oublie' pan. The Dutch called these 'oubletjes'. The English name for the pan was 'wafer pan'. 1947 L.G. GREEN *Tavern of Seas* 65 She also served the rolled wafer tea cakes called oblietjies, made with cinnamon and white wine — a Huguenot contribution to Cape Cookery. 1951 S. VAN H. TULLEKEN *Prac. Cookery Bk* 68 Oblitjes, ... Add beaten egg and brandy, then gradually the flour and spices. Cook in an oblitje pan. 1954 M. KUTTEL *Quadrilles & Konfyt* 94 Some of the recipes are of hoary antiquity, such as the French Huguenot one called *obletjes* — a variety of ginger snaps — which are rolled while warm round a form into a pipe shape, and perhaps from their dark colour reminded the French Protestants of those round, paved holes sunk in the stone floors of gloomy French dungeons, known as oubliettes, in which many of their ancestors had languished. 1960 G. LISTER *Reminisc.* 9 Every Thursday a cleanly dressed coloured woman, Rachel, came with a covered basket of oubleetjies, a kind of light, crisp biscuit rolled and baked brown. 1972 *Argus* 27 Nov. 4 An old fashioned deal chair was sold for R38 and an 'oblietjie' pan for R50. 1979 HEARD & FAULL *Our Best Trad. Recipes* 93 Oblietjie was derived from the Latin *oblatus* and the French *oblation* (offering to God). Apparently the Huguenot wafers were similar to those taken at communion. 1985 *S. Afr. Cookbk* (Reader's Digest Assoc.) 316 Oblietjies are rolled wafers that were made by the Huguenots in special oblietjie irons.

oddida var. HADEDA.

Odiqua /ɒˈdikwə, əʊ-/ *pl. n. Hist.* Also **Odiquas, Odiqua's, Otiqua, Udiqua's.** [Khoikhoi.] Collectively, the members of a Khoikhoi group living on the west Cape coast in the 17th century. Also *attrib.*

As is the case with many names of peoples and groups in S. Afr. Eng., this word has been found only in plural uses; however, it may be that it has also been used in unrecorded singular forms.

1731 G. MEDLEY tr. *P. Kolb's Present State of Cape of G.H.* I. 63 Adjoining to the *Sussaqua's,* are the *Odiqua's* or *Udiqua's.* These two Nations have enter'd into a perpetual Confederacy against their Neighbours the *Chirigriqua's,* with whom they have had many long and bloody Wars. 1795 C.R. HOPSON tr. *C.P. Thunberg's Trav.* I. 307 All along the sea-coast, and round about St Helena's Bay, in a low, steril, and sandy tract, the Odiquas nation borders on the Sussaquas. 1972 J.P. VAN S. BRUWER in *Std Encycl. of Sn Afr.* V. 606 Beyond Saldanha Bay were the Susequa, Hessequa .. and Otiqua.

oefenaar *n. obs.* [Du.] *oefening-holder,* see OEFENING sense 2.

1843 *Laws & Regul. for Direction of Dutch Reformed Church in S. Afr.* in *Stat. Law of Cape of G.H.* (1862) 624 Is care taken that no lay-preachers ('oefenaars') perform divine service in the congregation without the consent of the minister?

oefening /ˈʊf(ə)nəŋ/ *n. Obs. exc. hist.* Also **oeff(e)ning.** Pl. **-en.** [Du.]

1. *obs.* A prayer meeting.

1824 W.J. BURCHELL *Trav.* II. 174 In the evening, was held, what is called an oeffning (or, meeting; as distinguished from the regular church-service); which consisted in alternately reading and expounding parts of the New Testament, in extemporaneous prayers, and in singing psalms. 1861 P.B. BORCHERDS *Auto-Biog. Mem.* 56 The missionaries to the Bushman tribes sometimes .. conveyed religious instruction by assembling meetings known as 'oeffningen'. *Ibid.* 170 The regular attendance at church in

2. *comb.* **oefening-holder** or **oefening-houder** /-ˌhəʊdə(r)/ *obs.* [Du. *houder* a holder (of office)], a lay preacher; OEFENAAR; cf. SIEKETROOSTER; **oefeninghuis** /-ˌhœɪs/ *obs. exc. hist.* [Afk. *huis* house], a meeting house, sometimes used for educational purposes.

1827 A.J. JARDINE *Fragment of Church Hist.* 74 **Oefening holders**, (Lay persons who hold divine worship in private houses.) Such must undergo an examination before the Church-wardens, and receive permission to hold service. 1843 *Laws & Regul. for Direction of Dutch Reformed Church in S. Afr.* in *Stat. Law of Cape of G.H.* (1862) 632 Instructors, catechists, or lay preachers (**oefeninghouders**). 1844 J. BACKHOUSE *Narr. of Visit* 106 The inhabitants of Zwellendam, not liking to have their place-of-worship used for a school-house have erected a commodious building near it, called an **Oefening-huis**, *Exercise-house.* 1979 E. *Prov. Herald* 23 Jan. 4 Apart from the Drostdy, the town boasts of several more historical monuments. They include .. the Meeting House (**Oefeningshuis**) which was built in 1838 for the holding of 'religious services and prayer meetings and the education of the heathens'.

oenkje var. UINTJIE.

oere var. ORE.

oerlam var. OORLAM.

off *n. slang.* [Ellipt. for *day off* or *time off.*] In urban (mainly township) English: a 'day off'; free time.

1966 L.G. BERGER *Where's Madam* 183 The watchboy supplied by Norman's firm hadn't come back from his 'off' which is the native abbreviation for 'day off'. 1971 *Informant, Cape Town,* I get my off once a week, on Sundays. 1980 J. COCK *Maids & Madams* 27 The only time she sees her children is during her 'off' on Sunday afternoons. 1983 F.G. BUTLER *Bursting World* 156 We did have one lovely day with my sister Christine on her 'off' from Groote Schuur, lazing on the beach at Camps Bay. 1987 *Learn & Teach* No.1, 3 Agnes Vilakazi of Johannesburg .. said, 'We do not get nice "offs". We don't get week-ends and holidays off. This is not right.'

offal /ˈɒfəl/ *n.* [Special sense of general Eng. *offal* 'the parts which are cut off in dressing the carcase of an animal killed for food' (*OED*); influenced by Afk. *afval* with these senses.] **a.** KOP-EN-POOTJIES. **b.** This dish with tripe and brains added. In both senses also called AFVAL. See also PENS EN POOTJIES.

1901 D.M. WILSON *Behind Scenes in Tvl* 22 The whole holiday party had retired to sleep after indulging in a literal gorge on a mess of sheep's head and feet called offal, the signs of which were all over their persons. 1913 C. PETTMAN *Africanderisms* 345 *Offal,* (D. *afval,* refuse, offal.) Sheep's head and feet, cleaned and prepared for cooking, are offered for sale in Midland towns by this name, which is a corruption of the Dutch word. [1970 M. HOBSON *Informant, Tzaneen* 'Ofval' is a popular South African dish, consisting of 'pens', 'kop' en 'pookies'.] 1982 *Signature* Jan. 17 Whether its fresh fish, fillet steak or offal that takes the fancy, Kleinplasie will ensure a memorable meal. 1985 J. CLOETE in *S.-Easter* Oct.-Nov. 30 The Crayfish Tour includes .. a gastronomic introduction to Swartland boerekos — offal, milktart and sosaties. 1988 E. MALULEKE in *Drum* Apr. 37, I taught her how to cook pap, and we had offal together. 1994 *Weekend Post* 8 Jan. (Leisure) 6 Starters, meat, chicken, offal, making your own sausages .. are all dealt with in this excellent book.

off-colour *adj.* and *n. Obsolescent. Diamond-mining.*

A. *adj.* Of a diamond: neither pure white nor of a definite colour, and so of inferior value.

1860 A. DE BARRERA *Gems & Jewels* 164 If the manufactured diamond is found to contain a flaw, or what is technically termed 'off-color', its value is proportionately diminished. 1872 C.A. PAYTON *Diamond Diggings* 57 The vast majority of our large diamonds, i.e. of stones over 10 carats, are 'off-colour', being instead of pure 'white' — or rather transparent — tinged, apparently throughout, with a yellowish tint, varying from the palest straw-colour to that of the topaz, or pale sherry colour. 1873 F. BOYLE *To Cape for Diamonds* 356 When .. one talks of 'yellow stones,' one means 'coloured' of that tint, not 'fancy;' on the fields we incorrectly call them 'off-colour.' The true 'off-colour' has no distinct tinge at all. 1876 — *Savage Life* 21 In every digging known, large stones are apt to be 'coloured' or 'off-colour'. 1894 *Daily News* 7 July 6 Purchasing 'off-colour diamonds' and substituting them for others of the first quality. 1911 L. COHEN *Reminisc. of Kimberley* 36 Same old kopje walloping gabble from him. 'Cracked, spots, smoky, off-colour, etc.' At last I sold it to him for two hundred and ten pounds. 1933 W. MACDONALD *Romance of Golden Rand* 24 A few days after I had found my diamond it was declared to be off-colour, and, consequently, dropped greatly in value. 1968 J.T. MCNISH *Rd to Eldorado* 144 Many South African diamonds .. are off-colour and instead of being pure coloured are tinged throughout in colours varying from pale straw and light sherry to those as dark as very old acorns.

B. *n. rare.* An off-colour diamond.

1873 F. BOYLE *To Cape for Diamonds* 356 The true 'off-colour' has no distinct tinge at all.

Hence **off-coloured** *ppl adj.*

1872 C.A. PAYTON *Diamond Diggings* 118 Often higher prices have been paid on the Fields, for large *off-coloured* (i.e. yellowish) stones. 1885 H. RIDER HAGGARD *King Solomon's Mines* 279 Some of these biggest ones, .. we could see by holding them up to the light, were a little yellow, 'off coloured,' as they call it at Kimberley.

offgaft var. OPGAAF.

off-load *v.* [Calque formed on Du. *afladen.*]

Now also in general English usage.

1.a. *intrans.* To unload.

1850 R.G.G. CUMMING *Hunter's Life* I. 5 No, no, mynheer, you must not off-load. 1871 E.J. DUGMORE *Diary.* 7 At the McKay's where I am staying while Henry offloads at the New Rush the heat is almost unbearable. 1892 R.H.S. CHURCHILL *Men, Mines & Animals* 221 There was nothing for it but to 'off-load,' a most tedious and tiring business. 1912 W. WESTRUP *Land of To-morrow* 235 In at the open gate .. came a string of ponies .. loaded with wool and grain. The natives ... proceeded to off-load. 1968 *Post* 4 Feb. 15 A family offloads soon after the lorry had arrived.

b. *trans.* To unload (something or someone) from a wagon; to unload (a vehicle).

1877 *Sel. Comm. Report on Mission to Damaraland* p.xiv, I gave orders to my men to off-load the waggon. 1902 D. VAN WARMELO *On Commando* 148 A wagon was being inspanned .. An old man ... threatened to off-load all the women on the first available place, as he had never in his life had so much trouble. 1931 G. BEET *Grand Old Days* 13 About 10,000 pounds of weight of goods and impedimenta had to be off-loaded by the wayside. 1940 F.B. YOUNG *City of Gold* 99 The wagon, even off loaded, tilted so dangerously that it seemed as if the least jerk would sent it crashing to splinters. 1967 J.A. BROSTER *Red Blanket Valley* 75 On her head she was carrying a heavy load of firewood which she off-loaded. 1979 M. MATSHOBA *Call Me Not a Man* 98 Stand in the passage and watch the guys offloading mailbags out of a mail coach onto a Railway truck. 1988 E. KEYTER in *S. Afr. Panorama* Mar. 16 At the mill the sugar-cane is off-loaded directly onto conveyor belts.

2. *trans. Transf.* and *fig.* To dispose of or discard (a person or thing).

1900 B. MITFORD *Aletta* 130 One would think .. Government would have plenty to do without off-loading all these insane circulars upon us. 1924 L. COHEN *Reminisc. of Jhb.* 82 Espying a man who had some belief in philanthropy, I — without the least compunction and to my intense relief — off-loaded the whole five hundred at fifteen and six. 1961 T.V. BULPIN *White Whirlwind* 186 What they are really looking at is their bank balance … If they look an inch beyond that it's only to find a dupe on whom they can offload dud shares. 1972 *Sunday Times* 12 Mar. 4 For two years I have been trying to offload my clay deposits on to the Government. 1973 *Farmer's Weekly* 11 July 76 The indifferent quality which they off-load on to local markets would not even fetch a return as pig swill on the competitive and discriminating markets of Europe.

Hence **off-loading** *vbl n.,* unloading.

1971 *Grocott's Mail* 12 Feb., Engineers were summonsed to assist in the manual off-loading of the oven from the truck. 1973 *Farmer's Weekly* 13 June 12 Off-loading can be controlled for dumping or spreading.

off-saddle *n. obs.* [fr. next.] A break in a journey during which horses are unsaddled.

1845 W.N. IRWIN *Echoes of Past* (1927) 235 I .. take the opportunity of the first off saddle to stretch myself in the Shade, and, while my orderly sits Smoking or Cooking some Cos (flesh), read your welcome epistle. 1860 A.W. DRAYSON *Sporting Scenes* 72 My horse appeared much distressed. The day was intensely hot, and I thought an 'off-saddle' for half an hour might refresh the animal. 1874 [see AGTERRYER]. 1875 C.B. BISSET *Sport & War* 188 After a short off saddle we crossed the beautiful river of clear crystal water. 1882 LADY F.C. DIXIE *In Land of Misfortune* 394 For seventeen hours, with the exception of the two short off-saddles, the horses had been on the move. 1893 HARLEY in *Cape Illust. Mag.* Vol.4 No.10, 377 His horse, rather young and skittish for a trooper, broke away from him at the first off-saddle. 1907 J.P. FITZPATRICK *Jock of Bushveld* (1909) 309 It was at the 'offsaddles' on long journeys .. or during the rest in the day's hunt that trouble was most to be feared. 1912 W. WESTRUP *Land of To-morrow* 227 Even if they came right through, without an off-saddle, it's a four-and-a-half hours' trek. 1925 D. KIDD *Essential Kafir* 9 We suggest an 'off-saddle,' and so dismount close to a stream, and knee-halter our horses, allowing them to roll or graze at pleasure. 1937 J. STEVENSON-HAMILTON *S. Afr. Eden* 191 With donkeys I usually found it best to complete the day's trek without making a long halt with its necessary *off saddle,* and just to stop every hour, see that the loads were all right, and that the pack saddles had not slipped.

off-saddle *v. hist.* [Calque formed on Du. *afzadelen* unsaddle.]

In both *intrans.* and *trans.* uses, also *saddle off* (see SADDLE sense 1).

1. *intrans.* To unsaddle; to break one's journey. Cf. OUTSPAN *v.,* UPSADDLE sense 2.

1823 T. PHILIPPS *Lett.* (1960) 203, I rode up to the door and began the never varied question 'Can I offsaddle?' 1825 [see KNEE-BAND]. 1835 C.L. STRETCH *Journal.* 23 Aug., I wish from my soul it was peace and that I could mount my horse with only a sambock and ride and offsaddle where I liked instead of being armed as you see me. 1838 T. SHONE *Diary.* 16 Aug., Started on horse back for Graham Town. Off Saddle at Mr Curl canteen for one hour. 1849 E.D.H.E. NAPIER *Excursions in Sn Afr.* II. 12 Another term of Colonial import is that of 'saddling-up,' and '*off-saddling.*' If you pull up at a farmer's house, after inquiring your name, vocation, and destination, he requests you to 'off-saddle;' which literally means to partake of his hospitality. 1852 M.B. HUDSON *S. Afr. Frontier Life* 169 Crossed the Fish River Drift, gained the Rand top, and were Offsaddled, when lo! sharp report rent the air. 1856 R.J. MULLINS *Diary.* 18 Dec., The horse I led kept breaking away. We offsaddled in the Kei Poort and made breakfast. 1860 D.L.W. STAINBANK *Diary.* (Killie Campbell Africana Library KCM8680) 4 Sept., I offsaddled for an hour and then went with Byron to see the Kafir Dance. 1871 J. MACKENZIE *Ten Yrs* (1971) 15 It is when you arrive at a Dutch farm on horseback, and are requested to 'off-saddle,' and stay over night, that you can see Dutch hospitality and manner to perfection. 1905 P. GIBBON *Vrouw Grobelaar* 108 Christiana was a wild fanciful girl, with an eye to every stranger that off-saddled at the farm. **1936** H.F. TREW *Botha Treks* 126 If the commandos were on the march at daylight, they always off-saddled for ten minutes just as the sun rose. The believed that if they were caught by the sun in their saddles their horses would give in during the day. **1956** F.C. METROWICH *Valiant but Once* 201 As it was stiflingly hot they offsaddled in a shady thicket. **1962** — *Scotty Smith* 112 The man had offsaddled and his horse was standing next to him. **1970** 'R.C.G.' in *Outpost* 143 On our return we wrote a history of the patrol in the area book, and a more monotonous document would be hard to find. Most of it was 'Offsaddled at Rosebank Farm 3p.m.: Mr Brown had no complaints.'

2. *trans.* To unsaddle (one's mount) in order to rest it. Cf. UPSADDLE sense 1.

1849 N.J. MERRIMAN *Cape Jrnls* (1957) 60 We 'off saddled' and 'knee haltered' our steeds, after the colonial fashion. **1853** F.P. FLEMING *Kaffraria* 106 No other grooming is required for horses on the road in Kaffraria, than merely to 'Off-saddle' and 'Knee-halter' them. **1860** D.L.W. STAINBANK *Diary.* 4 Sept., Captain Bennett .. ordered the horses to be off-saddled for a couple of hours and fed and then to proceed. **1879** G.C. CATO *Letter.* (Killie Campbell Africana Library MS1602b), The Camp had halted for Brk'fst and volunteers off-saddled their Horses & camp life going on. **1884** B. ADAMS *Narr.* (1941) 193 We off-saddled the horses and let them have a roll on the grass, which refreshed them very much. **1905** J. DU PLESSIS *1000 Miles in Heart of Afr.* 99 Donkeys are off-saddled and turned off to grass. **1937** F.B. YOUNG *They Seek a Country* 168 Jan Botha off-saddled his horse, knee-haltering it and allowing it to stumble away in search of grazing. **1968** K. MCMAGH *Dinner of Herbs* 173 After off-saddling and knee-haltering his horses McMagh went to the house behind the store. **1987** W. STEENKAMP *Blockhouse* 25, I had off-saddled my horse and rubbed it down.

off-sales *n.* [ad. Brit. Eng. *off-sale* the sale of alcoholic liquors for consumption elsewhere than at the place of sale.] A retail outlet attached to, or owned by, an hotel, where liquor is sold by the bottle, for consumption off the premises; also called BOTTLE STORE.

1970 S.E. NATHAM *Informant, Cape Town* Off-sales. Retail liquor store attached to a hotel. **1972** *E. Prov. Herald* 18 Feb. 17 Liquor sales both in the bars and the off-sales had dropped compared with last year. **1976** *Sunday Times* 10 Oct. 4 He's stoned out of his skull on cheap muscadel and his friends are vainly trying to drag him away from the off-sales before there's trouble. **1987** L. VENTER in *Frontline* Oct. 18 Stopping at an off-sales in Greylingstad, they walked in on the 'white' side of the partition that separated customers served from the same counter.

OFS /əʊ ef 'es/ *n.* Also **O.F.S.** [Initial letters of *Orange Free State.*] FREE STATE *n. phr.* Also *attrib.*

1881 G.F. AUSTEN *Diary* (1981) 58 Escort to be provided by Boers to see troops safely to Cronstad OFS. **1899** [see SAR *n.*¹]. **1914** *Farmer's Annual* 20 The Hackney. What Breeders should aim at: Faults to be avoided. By an O.F.S. Stud Groom. c**1936** *S. & E. Afr. Yr Bk & Guide* 75 On March 17th, 1897, the defensive alliance existing between the O.F.S. and the Transvaal was confirmed at Bloemfontein. **1958** R.E. VAN DER Ross in Hattingh & Bredekamp *Coloured Viewpoint* (1984) 18 In Bloemfontein, OFS, there appeared to be only one area set aside for Coloured occupation. **1963** L.F. FREED *Crime in S. Afr.* 23 The crime rate was invariably highest in the Transvaal followed by Natal, the O.F.S. and the Cape, in that order. **1977** [see MANAGEMENT COMMITTEE]. **1989** [see CONQUERED TERRITORY].

og *var.* AG.

oh, ja see JA *adv.* sense 7.

ointjie *var.* UINTJIE.

okapi /əʊˈkɑːpi/ *n. slang.* Also **ou kappie**, and with initial capital. [Trade name, named for a rare Central African mammal of the Giraffidae.] In urban (mainly township) English: a single-bladed knife usu. with a pattern of stars on its handle. Also *attrib.* See also THREE STAR.

1974 K.M.C. MOTSISI in *Drum* 22 Mar. 56 Kid Nyaks is in the habit of assaulting non-voters with this 'ou kappie' he always wears in his buttock pocket. *Ibid.* 8 July 58 He tells me that he must .. raise money to pay his creditors one of whom promises to ventilate his body with a 'ou kappie' if he does not pay him. **1981** B. MFENYANA in M. Mutloatse *Reconstruction* 302 When we glorify iscamto are we not also praising the thug, the cowardly lout with an okapi in his backpocket? **1982** V. KHUMALO in *Pace* May 158 A guy walks into a shebeen, party or gathering. His wet hand is gently fondling an okapi in the depths of his khaki pants. **1987** *Learn & Teach* No.5, 16 Bra Mofere-fere is bad news. Once he takes out his Okapi it always goes back to his pocket with blood. **1990** *New African* 25 June 10 What happened to the proud, energetic cop who would stop you in the street, search you and arrest you for just an okapi (knife) should it be found in your possession? **1993** S. DIKENI in *Cape Times* 21 Aug. (Top of the Times) 17 The big discovery was the intuitive reach for the back pocket whenever I saw something that looked vaguely like brah skin head. The Okapi draw.

Hence **okapi** *v. trans. slang,* to stab.

1987 *Drum* Jan. 51 It was not long after that he was Okapied on the steps of the Senate — a reminder incidentally that necklacing those in power is as old as the hills.

oke /əʊk/ *n. colloq.* Also **ouk.** [Shortened form of OKIE.]

1. OU *n.* sense 1 a. See also OKIE.

1970 R. VAN DER MERWE *Informant, Beaufort West* Who is that oke talking to your sister? **1972** *Rhodeo* (Rhodes Univ.) 23 Mar. 5 Me and the ouks like, every night go out to have some chicks and look for a fight. **1975** [see 'Blossom' quot. at CHERRY]. **1977** L. ABRAHAMS *Celibacy of Felix Greenspan* 46 You've got my promise in front of all these okes as witnesses. **1982** *Sunday Times* 6 June (Mag. Sect.), I quickly suss that the taxi-driver oke .. is taking his cherrie .. for a 'hoddog' and chips. **1988** *South* 21 July 16 As far as this ouk is concerned, he has the unique power of telling us what we all know are the dominant white perceptions of people like Tutu and Mandela. **1989** H.P. TOFFOLI in *Style* Dec. 94 Oke is A) What snoek is smoked in. B) Someone who fixes your Fiat. C) Usually somewhere near a Lion. **1991** *Sunday Times* 7 Apr. 26 At top level, the okes (and the *meisies*) all throw so straight they keep cancelling each other out. **1994** *Ibid.* 23 Jan. 28 (*advt*) The waiting as it bubbles away, emitting an aroma that can render a hungry oke speechless at a range of at least a kilometre. That's when you say 'what a potjie'.

2. In *pl.*, used collectively: people of a particular type or origin; cf. OU *n.* sense 2 a.

1975 in *Darling* 12 Mar. 4 (*letter*) Hang, man, who does this Mrs Botha think she is? She must be one of those rich okes wot went to Oxford and finishing school. **1977** *Sunday Times* 24 Apr. (Mag. Sect.), She digs wearing trousers with braces straight from the junk shops — which the okes in Bloemfontein wouldn't smile on. **1991** K. OWEN in *Sunday Times* 17 Mar. 23 There are no leaders to be found, only ordinary okes like thee and me. I suggested that we okes start thinking about how to cope with change.

okie /ˈəʊki/ *n. colloq.* Also **oakie, oukie.** [Englished form of Afk. *outjie,* see OUTJIE.] 'Little chap': **a.** A form of address or reference to a young boy. **b.** An affectionate or slightly patronizing form of address or reference to a man. In both senses also OUTJIE. See also OKE, OU *n.* sense 1 a.

1943 *Weekend News & Sunday Mag.* 20 Mar., 'Rong ergain!' larfed Sofie Dikpens. 'Dats de wors orf er standard tree [*sc.* three] oakie taking de chair!' **1970** *Forum* Vol.6 No.2, 38 O is for a oaktree, oaktree for a o-kie coming witties girlie. **1974** 'BLOSSOM' in *Darling* 8 May 91 Three okies in the States was streaking through a convent school in nothing but takkies. **1975** *Ibid.* 9 Apr. 95 This farmer okie drops us right outside the gate at Syringa Spa. **1977** F.G. BUTLER *Karoo Morning* 142 We were trapped ... A thick voice commanded 'Now come on, you oukies, open up now'. **1989** J. ALLAN in *Sunday Times* 11 June 4 'Where is Studio Four and are all these people auditioning for Focus?' I asked the reception okie. **1990** D. HOFMEYR *Red Kite in Pale Sky* 72 Testing. Just testing okie. There's no fun in fighting with someone like you.

old baas /ˈəʊld bɑːs/ *n. phr. Obs.* Also with small initials. [Part. tr. of Afk. *oubaas,* see OUBAAS.]

1. OUBAAS sense 3.

1882 C. DU VAL *With Show through Sn Afr.* I. 63 'Lots of fruit in the orchard, and the old Baas says you can help yourselves,' says Rogers the guard. **1942** S. CLOETE *Hill of Doves* 37 Drive fast, indeed! They should have seen old Tanta Anna de Jong drive. You ask the Old Baas how she drove. Like Jehu. **1953** D. JACOBSON *Long Way from London* 109 Johannes said that it did not matter so much if Paulus knew no English, because the old baas, the ou baas, knew no English either. **1958** A. JACKSON *Trader on Veld* 44 After supper the old Baas would always read a chapter of the Bible. **1963** S. CLOETE *Rags of Glory* 248 It is in my heart that the old Baas left mevrou some gold. **1976** — *Chetoko* 112 When the old Baas and I were young, the world was beautiful.

2. OUBAAS sense 1.

1899 B. MITFORD *Weird of Deadly Hollow* 242 Old Baas Rendlesams will get the shower if there is one.

Old Bill *n. phr.* [Special sense of general Eng. *Old Bill* a veteran, an old soldier, fr. the name of a cartoon character created by British cartoonist Bruce Bairnsfather during World War I.] The title given to a regional leader of the MOTH (sense a) ex-servicemen's organization. See also *Lady Billie* (LADY sense 2), WEE BILL.

1973 *Weekend Post* 14 Apr. 8 The ex-servicemen's organisation, the Memorable Order of the Tin Hats (Moths) would not die 'for many years', Mr R.J. Palframan, Provincial Old Bill of the Eastern Province, said this week. **1979** *Daily Dispatch* 15 Mar. 3 Moths elected Mr MacEwan, the former Wee Bill, as the new Old Bill. Mr Fraser Finlaison was elected the new Wee Bill.

old-boss *n.* [Calque formed on Afk. *oubaas,* see OUBAAS.]

1. OUBAAS sense 3.

1843 J. SHIPP *Mem. of Extraordinary Mil. Career* (1890) 68 On each side rode the Dutchman's two sons; after his four Hottentots armed with muskets; then the old boss (the master).

2. OUBAAS sense 1.

1979 W. EBERSOHN *Lonely Place* 24 Old-boss Marthinus Pretorius held a braaivleis last week, on Tuesday, to celebrate his promotion to deputy minister. *Ibid.* 71 Anna who works for Old-boss Marthinus says Small-boss Marthinus hit Muskiet.

old Cape (furniture) see CAPE senses 2 b and 3.

Old Colony see COLONY.

old Dutch medicine, - remedy see DUTCH *adj.* sense 2.

Old Fourlegs *n. phr. Colloq.* Also **Old Four Legs**, and with small initial(s). [fr. the belief formerly held that the fish actually walked on its four leg-like pectoral fins.] A nickname for the coelacanth *Latimeria chalumnae* of the Latimeriidae, a prehistoric fish thought to be extinct, but rediscovered off the coast of East London (Eastern Cape) in 1938.

1956 J.L.B. SMITH (*title*) Old Fourlegs: the Story of the Coelacanth. **1970** J. MCINTOSH *Stonefish* 246 Wispy fish and bushy fish; and deformed ones like Old Four Legs, the coelacanth. **1988** *E. Prov. Herald* 27 Feb. 7 Fifty years after Old Fourlegs was caught near East London .. the coelacanth is to be the subject of a new documentary. **1991** J. Taylor in *E. Prov. Herald* 16 May 6 There, [sc. at the Chalumna River mouth, between Port Elizabeth and East London] the hunt for 'Old Four Legs', the prehistoric coelacanth, once thought to be extinct, will begin. **1992** *Academic Standard* Mar. 5 Old fourlegs, the famous living fossil fish, *Latimeria chalumnae.*

old man saltbush see SALTBUSH.

Old Year *n. phr.* In the phrr. ***Old Year's Day, -Eve, -Night*** [tr. Afk. *Oujaarsdag, -aand, -nag*], New Year's Eve, the 31st of December.

1983 *Frontline* Feb. 52 There was Old Year's Night in the Parys Hotel. About a hundred local people mixing in and having fun in the traditional platteland style. **1983** F.G. Butler *Bursting World* 278 On Old Year's Night we had a hell of a party. **1987** A. Soule et al. *Wynand du Toit Story* 119 My next surprise came early in the morning on Old Year's Day. **1993** G. Pearce in *Natal Mercury* 30 Dec. 18 There are those who describe tomorrow as 'Old Year's Eve', something I've never quite understood because tomorrow, like December 24th, is the eve of the Big Day. Therefore it follows .. that Today is Old Year's Eve, because it is the Day Before New Year's Eve, the eve of the final day of the Old Year. And tomorrow would then be on the eve of the New Year.

olien /ʊə'lin/ *n.* [Afk., see OLIENHOUT.] OLIENHOUT.

1987 *E. Prov. Herald* 5 Sept. 2 The tree of the Free State — the wild olive or olien .. — will be the 1988 Tree of the Year.

‖**olienhout** /ʊə'linhəʊt/ *n.* Also **olinhout**, and (formerly) **oliven-hout**, **olyvenhout**. [Afk. *olie(ve)nhout*, ad. Du. *olijven* olive + *hout* wood.] The small evergreen tree *Olea europaea* subsp. *africana* of the Oleaceae; the timber of this tree; OLIEN; *wild olive*, see WILD sense a. Also *attrib.*

1798 S.H. Wilcocke tr. *J.S. Stavorinus's Voy. to E. Indies 1768–71* II. 79 Olyvenhout, wild olive (*olea Europa*), which is a heavy, strong wood, of a brown colour, used in the construction of mills. **1821** C.I. Latrobe *Jrnl of Visit* Glossary, Oliven-hout, Olea similis B. (a large tree with long narrow leaves.) [**1822** W.J. Burchell *Trav.* I. 177 The place .. was called Olyvenhout-bosch (Olive tree wood), so named from the Olyf boom, a tree so much resembling the European Olive, as to have been mistaken for it by botanists … The wood, which is extremely compact and heavy, is very handsome, and well suited for cabinet work.] **1937** B.J.F. Laubscher *Sex, Custom & Psychopathology* 188 The *isiqebe* hut is first decorated with branches of the *olienhout* tree or *umquma*. **1937** H. Klein *Stage Coach Dust* 132 Khama's boys had been cutting down trees in Linchwe's territory, and in so doing had felled an ancient olienhout tree. **1949** L.G. Green *In Land of Afternoon* 197 The old stinkwood and olyvenhout, rosewood and satinwood went at bargain prices in those days. **1968** *Farmer's Weekly* 3 Jan. 7 Grazing in good condition, with 'Olienhout, vaalbos, rosyntjiebos, suurkaree' and mixed grazing. **1982** *S. Afr. Panorama* Feb. 20 Chess pieces of Cape ebony, whale ivory and *olienhout* (wild olive wood). **1988** *S. Afr. Digest* 15 Apr. 16 This year's Tree of the Year is the *Olea* (Latin for olive), of which the wild olive, or 'olienhout' is probably the best-known species … The following six species and subspecies of *Olea* are indigenous to South Africa: the wild olive or 'olienhout' (*Olea europa* subsp *africana*).

Olifant /'ʊəlifant, 'ɒ-/ *n. Military*. [Afk., 'elephant', prob. fr. appearance, size, and strength of the tank.] An armoured main battle tank, redesigned and re-built in South Africa from the old Centurion tank of British manufacture. Also *attrib*. See also BUFFEL sense 2.

1983 W. Steenkamp in *Leadership* Vol.2 No.4, 60 The Olifant tanks are thoroughly revamped ex-British Centurions which have been up-gunned, re-engined and generally worked over. **1986** *Sunday Times* 16 Mar. 14 The Olifant main battle tank (MBT). Over 200 MBTs, originally British Centurions, have been redesigned and modernised, having been equipped with new engines, gearboxes and armaments, all locally produced. **1988** *Cape Times* 27 Jan. 5 Thanks to the arms boycott and local manufacture, about the only British-origin weaponry the SADF still has in service are a few hundred 1950s-vintage Centurion medium tanks, now rebuilt and renamed 'Olifant'. **1988** *New Nation* 30 June 17 The British-made Centurion tanks, modified by the South Africans and renamed 'Olifant', are the best .. in the South African tank weaponry. **1990** *Armed Forces* Nov. 30 A simulated battle exercise was conducted, using an Olifant MBT equipped with a flail to detonate what appeared to be at least a 6kg mine.

olifant(s)melkbos see MELKBOS sense 2.

olikreukel var. ALIKREUKEL.

olinhout, **oliven-hout** varr. OLIENHOUT.

ollap var. OULAP.

ollycrock /'ɒlikrɒk/ *n.* Also **olycrock**. [Englished form of Afk. *alikreukel*.] ALIKREUKEL. Also *attrib.*

1961 *Redwing* (St Andrew's College, Grahamstown) 13 Other shellfish in the forms of olycrocks .. and limpets are very numerous and plentiful … Olycrocks are exceptionally plentiful and their presence prevents a number of other shellfish from occupying visible crevices and pools. **1970** M. Van Rensburg *Informant, Port Elizabeth* Allekruk, Shell fish (English pronounce it 'ollycrock'). **1975** [see SIFFIE]. **1976** A.P Brink *Instant in Wind* 118 Where does one look for ollycrocks and oysters, how does one catch crayfish? **1982** *E. Prov. Herald* 21 Sept. 2 A .. man .. convicted of possessing an excessive number of ollycrocks .. admitted having 130 ollycrocks — large sea snails — in his possession. *Ibid.* 27 Oct. 12, I found a small ollycrock shell on which two limpets were playing double piggy-back. **1982** Kilburn & Rippey *Sea Shells* 47 *Turbo sarmaticus*, .. The vernacular name 'ollycrock' is a corruption of the Western Cape name 'alikreukel' or 'arikreukel' (originally Alikruik, the Dutch word for periwinkle) and has itself been further corrupted in the East London area to 'cockle'. Another Eastern Cape name is 'paraclough'. **1988** *Izaak* in *E. Prov. Herald* 5 Mar. 8, I was fishing at the Flatrocks near Cape Recife using ollycrocks, one of my favourite baits, particularly for musselcrackers. When my friend noticed this he remarked: 'I stopped using periwinkles when I was a kid fishing for bullies in rock pools'.

olyvenhout var. OLIENHOUT.

om var. OOM.

omakoti pl. form of MAKOTI.

omie var. OOMPIE.

omschryving *n. Obs. Law.* [S. Afr. Du., *om* round + *schryving* writing (fr. *schryf* write).] A written description of the boundaries of a property, provided for the owner by the official body authorizing the sale.

1905 G. Baumann in Baumann & Bright *Lost Republic* (1940) 241 The owner was .. provided with a dual Title. The first part consisted of an 'Omschryving' (description, literally means 'written round') of the lines and beacons of the farm, and its approximate area; the second part of this Title was a rough and very inaccurate sketch of the ground. *Ibid.* 242 Moffat .. said in his 'Omschryving' .. that the first beacon stood in a certain magnetic direction from this point, and then proceeded to describe the other beacons of the farm. **1924** *Ibid.* 107 The beacon should have been some four or five hundred yards nearer the original farm … This my calculation and plotting verified, and it was also in accord with the old 'Omschryving'.

onderbaatjie *n. Obs. Ostrich-farming.* Also **onderbaatje**. [Afk. (earlier S. Afr. Du. *onderbaadje*) *waistcoat*, *onder* under + *baatjie* jacket.] The two rows of feathers taken from beneath the wing (or those from the underside of the wing) of an ostrich. See also BLACK *n.* sense 2, DRAB, FEATHER sense a, FLOSS, WING.

1896 R. Wallace *Farming Indust. of Cape Col.* 230 Drabs, two rows of body feathers from the upper side of the wing, and two rows below it, termed 'onderbaatje,' are pulled. **1910** [see DRAB]. **1934** C.P. Swart Supplement to Pettman. 127 *Onderbaatjie*, The undercoat of feathers of an ostrich, so called because it resembles a waistcoat.

onderdorp see DORP sense b.

onderstel /'ɒn(d)ə(r)stel/ *n. Wagon-making.* [Afk., *onder* below, lower + *stel* frame.] The chassis or underframe of a *trek wagon* (see TREK *n.* sense 12), on which the body is supported. Also Englished form **understel**.

Originally made of heavy ironwood, the onderstel consists of front and rear parts, the VOORSTEL and AGTERSTEL respectively.

[**1822** W.J. Burchell *Trav.* I. 150 The whole of the wheels, axletrees, and parts connected with them, constituting what the boors call the *onderstel* or carriage, is well covered with tar.] **1893** F.C. Selous *Trav. & Adventure* 24 When I went to buy corn I had taken the wheels and 'understel' from the waggon, and by putting in a short 'langwaggon' and making a false bed plank, constructed a small light vehicle. [Note] Understel is the lower part of a South African waggon upon which the body is supported. The langwaggon is a portion of the understel. **1907** [see BUIKPLANK]. **1919** J.Y. Gibson in *S. Afr. Jrnl of Science* July 2 Burchell, describing one [wagon] which he had acquired in 1811, says that 'The framework of the tilt was made of bamboo cane', that the sides or *leeren* were painted on the outside, but that the lower parts called the *onder stel*, were 'well covered with tar'. **1936** [see IRONWOOD sense a]. **1948** H.V. Morton *In Search of S. Afr.* 83 For the onderstel, or under-frame, the Boer wheelwrights in the old days employed a rare and heavy timber, now no longer used, called ironwood. **1974** A.A. Telford in *Std Encycl. of Sn Afr.* X. 569 The chassis or *onderstel* comprised two pairs of wheels, the axles of which were linked together with a timber perch or *houtlangwa*.

one hundred and eighty-day see under 'H' (hundred and eighty-day).

one settler, one bullet see SETTLER sense 3 b.

only *adv. colloq.* Used as an intensifier: 'really'. Cf. MAAR *adv.* sense 1.

1970 G. Hassett *Informant, Bloemfontein* Gosh, I only had sukkel to open that bottle. **1975** [see NAARTJIE *n.* sense 2]. **1975** [see SMAAK]. **1976** [see WOES]. **1978** [see SKRAAL sense 1]. **1982** *Sunday Times* 6 June (Mag. Sect.), I'm sitting there minding my own beeswax and watching all the comings and goings-on, and it's only funny. **1983** J. Allan in *Sunday Times* 21 Jan., There was only a gevalt .. the night Tannie M— found E— in Miriam's kia. **1983** *Sunday Times* 8 May 21 Bliksem, these outjies from the South can only box. **1984** *Frontline* May 38 Man but it's only lekker to be back in Joeys. **1987** M. Poland *Train to Doringbult* 106 'He was only in a flap!' Kobie laughed. 'Real old woman sometimes!' **1991** [see LANK *adv.*].

‖**ons land** /ɒns 'lant/ *n. phr.* Also (formerly) **onze land**. [Afk., *ons* our + *land* country.] 'Our country'; South Africa.

1912 F. Bancroft *Veldt Dwellers* 32 Kruger's calling for you again; *onze land* is calling for you again; fight you must. **1924** L. Cohen *Reminisc. of Jhb.* 175 Boers hastily sold their land .. and trekked far away from the strangers — to resume in peace the ancient customs and solitary life of *Ons land* which their grim ancestors had practised before them. **1958** S. Cloete *Mask* 132 This was his country, ons land, the middle veld with its covering of scrub and tall thorn. **1963** *— Rags of Glory* 18 All these strange men united in a common purpose — to defend their land. *Ons land*, as they call it. **1979** *Darling* 27 June 131 Let budding Blossoms spring up all over ons land, ek sê. Be proud of your verbal heritage, kids. **1984** R. Hulley in *Deurbraak* Dec. 10, I believe that the form of the loyal toast should in future be 'to South Africa' or 'Ons land' and I would therefore like to call upon our protocol officials to make the necessary changes. [**1988** *Star* 26 Apr. 6 As far as I can ascertain, the USA forces do not formally toast their President, but they toast 'America'. Surely we, in South Africa, irrespective of our politics or race, should toast 'Our Land' or 'Ons Land'.]

onslaught *n.* Ellipt. for TOTAL ONSLAUGHT (sense a); often used ironically.

1982 *Argus* 22 Oct. 14 The Minister of Law and Order .. has revealed a .. warped concept of justice by asserting .. that the many .. who oppose the idea of magistrates presiding over political trials, among them eminent jurists and lawyers, and the official Opposition, are part of the 'onslaught against South Africa'. **1986** A. Klaaste in *Frontline* June 6 The 'onslaught' makes a brief appearance ... To counteract the onslaught, the aims of Biblical Studies are listed. **1987** B. Ronge in *Sunday Times* 17 May (Mag. Suppl.) 6 'Onslaught' .. has now been reserved for such things as letters sent to Canadians living in South Africa by a Canadian politician. **1987** *Informant, Grahamstown* 'Are you on pass [from the army]?' 'No, illegal, but I don't think the onslaught will start tonight.' **1992** C.M. Knox tr. *E. Van Heerden's Mad Dog* 172 In the town hall the Prime Minister addressed us on Preserving Our Heritage and the Onslaught against our Country.

onze land var. ONS LAND.

ooclever pl. form of CLEVER.

ook 'n dag, môre is see MÔRE sense 2.

oom /ʊəm/ *n.* Formerly also **om.** [Du. (later Afk.), 'uncle', used respectfully of or to an adult male.] 'Uncle', not necessarily referring to a blood relation; cf. OOMPIE. See also TANTE.

In *S. Afr. Eng.*, usu. employed to represent the idiom of Afrikaans, or when referring to an Afrikaans-speaker.

1. Used as a title, with a name. Usu. with initial capital.

a. A respectful and affectionate title for an older man; UNCLE sense 1 a. Cf. OOMPIE sense 2 b.

Usu., but not always, with a first name.

1822 W.J. Burchell *Trav.* I. 433 Old Lucas, or as he was more familiarly called, Oom Hans (Uncle Hans), now turned back with us. **1880** [see UNCLE sense 1]. **1889** H.A. Bryden *Kloof & Karroo* 42 Mr. Pieter Maynier, familiarly called by Graaff Reinetters, 'Oom Piet' (Oom, or uncle, being a term of affection in South Africa). **1937** C.R. Prance *Tante Rebella's Saga* 29 Oom Jakob in middle age was firmly established as 'Oom' to every burgher young enough to be his nephew or his son. **1965** S. Dederick *Tickey* 38 'Look here,' he said aloud, 'don't keep calling me Mr Van Heerden all the time. Call me Oom — Oom Casper'. *c***1965** *State of S. Afr. 1965* 106 Family ties, even among distant relatives, are strong and it is a common practice for young South Africans to refer to elderly persons as *Oom* (uncle) and *Tante* (aunt) as a token of respect. **1974** *Drum* 8 Apr. 7 Rather than part with his 400 hectare farm and dairy cattle, Oom Freddie said that he would become a subject of the Africans who run Lebowa. **1982** *Sunday Times* 18 July 11 These are just some of the many facets of the man who eventually, as State President, was known affectionately to thousands of South Africans as 'Oom Blackie'. **1982** *Drum* July 82 Businessman Mohale M— denies he financed 'Oom Piet' M— and his rebel group in their bid to oust the Orlando Pirates leadership. **1987** *Learn & Teach* No.2, 1 When we got to her house, we found Oom Jantjie Keele with her. Both Mma Diniso and Oom Jantjie have lived in Sharpeville for many years. **1988** O. Oberholzer *Ariesfontein to Zuurfontein*, I love to travel and look ... To look so far that it hurts, to listen and watch old Oom Hennie tell a story thru his face, to rub khakibos between my hands .. and smell Africa. **1993** *Weekend Post* 26 June 13 (*letter*) Early in 1970 a church elder said to me: 'Kwedini, you will never satisfy all the people.' These words of the late Oom Cronje Vellem came to mind when I read the headline 'Downpour the worst in Port Elizabeth for eight years'.

b. Special Comb. **Oom Jannie**, OUBAAS sense 4; **Oom Paul**, an affectionate name for Paul Kruger, President of the old Transvaal Republic; also *attrib.*; hence **Oom Paulite** *obs.*, a nickname for a Transvaler.

1923 *Radio Times* (U.K.) 28 Sept. 8 '**Oom Jannie**', as he [*sc.* Smuts] is known among his own people. **1882** C.L. Norris-Newman *With Boers in Tvl* 385 *Stephanus Johannes Paulus Kruger*, .. '**Oom** (Uncle) **Paul**,' as he is affectionately called. **1888** *Cape Punch* 29 Feb. 117, I am Oom Paul, the Cromwell of South Africa. *Ibid.* 7 Mar. 140 K stands for Kruger, best known as Oom Paul. **1897** G.A. Parker *S. Afr. Sports* 74 The event of the week's football was the final match between the holders, Western Province and the Transvaal — the former up to this fixture leading the 'Oom Paulites' by one point. **1898** *Cape Argus* (Weekly Ed.) 2 Feb. 36 I am quite certain .. that if Oom Paul gets in, .. this prominent Transvaal official can afford to put his thumb up to his nose. **1900** H.C. Hillegas *Oom Paul's People* 141 There was less formality and red tape in meeting 'Oom Paul' [*sc.* Kruger] than would be required to have a word with Queen Victoria's butcher or President McKinley's office-boy. **1913** C. Pettman *Africanderisms* 349 *Oom*, .. This Dutch word is often used in South Africa when addressing an elderly man, as denoting respect; e.g. *Oom* Paul, the ordinary designation of the President of the late Transvaal Republic. **1923** B. Ronan *Forty S. Afr. Yrs* 169 I .. had plenty of opportunities of seeing Oom Paul .. and will not readily forget the sound of his deep, raucous voice as he addressed his burghers from the top of an ox-wagon. **1946** T. Macdonald *Ouma Smuts* 30 The beloved Oom Paul, uncle to all the people. **1955** L.G. Green *Karoo* 13, I can visualise many a hospitable voorkamer adorned with Biblical texts and portraits either of Oom Paul or Queen Victoria. **1975** [see NOG sense 2]. **1984** *Frontline* Feb. 39 There was place for guitars as well as for violins, short skirts as well as Voortrekker kappies, long hair as well as Oom Paul beards.

2. Used as a respectful form of address or reference to any man older than the speaker. Cf. OOMPIE sense 2 a, UNCLE sense 1 b.

Sometimes substituted for the second person pronoun 'you', reflecting a respectful form of address in Afrikaans (see quots 1976 and 1983).

1838 [see NEEF sense 1]. **1871** J. Mackenzie *Ten Yrs* (1971) 64 It was not then unusual for a Dutchman to give his hand in greeting to a Griqua, and call him 'oom' (uncle), or 'neef' (nephew) — in short, to treat him as an equal. **1878** [see TANTE sense 3]. [**1880** E.L. Price *Jrnls* (1956) 409 The Boers have a way of calling any gentleman to whom they speak '*Uncle*' — token of respect — and any lady, '*Auntie*'. 'Om' is uncle, & 'Tanta' is Aunt.] **1883** O.E.A. Schreiner *Story of Afr. Farm* 22 We deal not in titles. Every one is Tanta and Oom — aunt and uncle. **1888** *Cape Punch* 1 Aug. 39 'All there, Oom?' 'All there, Tal,' replied Oom, 'I carefully counted them'. [**1914** see TANTE sense 3.] **1924** G. Baumann in Baumann & Bright *Lost Republic* (1940) 119 'Oom, were you not afraid of the Zulus?' I asked. 'No, they were all tame [*mak*] by then.' **1926** P. Smith *Beadle* (1929) 9 In the long Aangenaam valley there was no man who called him friend, no child who called him Oom. **1931** [see TANTE sense 3]. **1976** A. Delius *Border* 136 Never fear! I will not forsake my people. But Oom must understand these are times when much is changing. **1982** *E. Prov. Herald* 20 Sept. 8 On my farm the klonkies used the word 'master'. If they were of primary school age they called me 'oom' even though I wasn't their mother's brother. **1983** A. Sparks in J. Crwys-Williams *S. Afr. Despatches* (1989) 446 'Oom,' it must be noted, means uncle, and everybody in these parts is called either uncle or aunt as a term of respect. The proper mode of address is in the third person. 'Good morning, uncle,' says the youngster in short pants at the farm gate. 'Will uncle please drive straight up the road and park uncle's car under the black wattles.' **1989** B. Ronge in *Sunday Times* 3 Dec. 30 One word in particular grated on my ear when the narrator referred to the patriarch as 'Oom' which is utterly alien to the English idiom. But it is utterly characteristic of the Afrikaans idiom, and emblematic of those role perceptions and assumed positions of hypocritical power and deference that are, after all, the subject of this play. **1990** G. Slovo *Ties of Blood* 208 'Be silent, *oom*,' he commanded, 'and nothing will happen to you. Otherwise ...' He moved the revolver up the man's skull. **1990** *Sunday Times* 18 Mar. 3 'I think my father first started to hate me when I called him "oom" instead of dad,' Flip recalled wistfully.

3. Used as a common noun: a man, esp. an older man; UNCLE sense 2. Cf. OOMPIE sense 1.

1868 [see NEEF sense 1]. **1883** O.E.A. Schreiner *Story of Afr. Farm* 257 At the farmhouses where he stopped the 'ooms' and 'tantes' remembered clearly the spider with its four grey horses. **1898** W.C. Scully *Vendetta* 25 Many a bulky bottle of nasty but innocuous mixture did he prescribe to amplitudinous *tanta* or corpulent *oom*, whose only complaint was the natural result of too much exercise of the jaw-bones and too little of the arms and legs. **1914** L.H. Brinkman *Breath of Karroo* 83 'Ma, why is that Oom talking such a lot?' referring to the reader. *Ibid.* 85 Ma, the Oom is throwing water in my face! **1945** [see OUPA sense 3]. *a***1951** H.C. Bosman in L. Abrahams *Unto Dust* (1963) 123 The Oom would knock out the ash from his pipe on to his veldskoen and he would proceed to relate .. a tale of terror or of high romance. **1961** [see TANNIE sense 3 b]. **1976** V. Rosenberg *Sunflower* 150 A child came to tell her .. that there was an 'oom' outside making enquiries about the next-door neighbour. **1977** *Family Radio & TV* 19 Sept. 5 There was even one *oom* in the Marico district who used onions [to make 'mampoer']. The result was stronger than battery acid. **1981** *Sunday Times* 1 Nov. 43 Driving force behind the team of tannies — plus the occasional oom .. is the dominee's wife. **1983** A. Sparks in J. Crwys-Williams *S. Afr. Despatches* (1989) 446 They come, many of the 'ooms' and 'tannies', in Mercedes-Benzes, for the Afrikaner is no longer the underdog in South Africa that he once was. **1987** 'K. De Boer' in *Frontline* Apr. 36 The blue-blooded Afrikaners of the HNP, the old Ooms en Tannies of the deep platteland, faces lined by the sun and the worry, their history near to the surface of their pale eyes. **1987** *Sunday Times* 21 June 9 A tannie has beaten the ooms at their own game. She is the Witblitz King of South Africa. **1990** *Personality* 1 Jan. 44 Another oom was not so lucky and rode his bakkie into a ditch. **1990** C. Leonard in *Weekly Mail* 2 Nov. 17 The congregants filed past: elderly *ooms* and *tannies*, black families, white families and domestic workers.

oomfa(a)n var. UMFAAN.

‖**oompie** /ˈʊəmpi/ *n.* Also **o(o)mie.** [Afk., *oompie* a patronising or condescending dim. form of *oom* (see prec., and -IE), or *omie* the dim. form of *oom*, used esp. by children.

English-speakers have tended to blur the distinction between these two diminutive forms.]

An affectionate or patronising diminutive of OOM.

1. As a common noun: an affectionate or patronising term for a man, particularly an older man. Cf. OOM sense 3.

1900 O. Osborne *In Land of Boers* 315 Opulent, simple-minded, old Dutch 'oompies', inveigled at last from the seclusion of their distant 'boerenplaats' to visit the wonders of the Northern Old World. **1963** M. Kavanagh *We Merry Peasants* 14 We became such regulars that an old *Omie* (Uncle) at the goods shed where we had to offload, would chant a welcome as we arrived. [**1971** *Sunday Times* 19 Dec. 5 A broadly smiling man who witnessed the commotion .. said .. that 'die omie' seemed to have forgotten about Jan van Riebeeck's long hair.] **1975** *Ibid.* 21 Sept. 20 Neither will it help your case to tell the oomie from Tweeling that the more things change the more they remain the same. **1983** *Daily Dispatch* 7 Mar. 1 You could see the mampoer drinkers ... They were the ones who slipped off to the still at intervals to 'check the fire' — ha! Pretty soon there were a number of slack-eyed oomies leaning against the barn pillars. **1984** *Frontline* Feb. 27 Pipe-smoking Oomies in the slopes of the Water-berg who read High-Dutch copies of the Old Testament out loud before aandete. **1987** *Pace* Sept. 33 All those *tannies* and *oompies*, maids and servants invade the Banana City in hordes for the July, pinning their hopes on a horse and a jockey. **1987** 'K. De Boer' in *Frontline* May 37 'En waar stem jy, Boetie?' eventually comes the inevitable question. I tell him in which constituency, hoping to buy peace. My evasiveness annoys the omie. No man, for which party?

2.a. An affectionate or patronising form of address or reference to any man older than the speaker. Cf. OOM sense 2.

1954 M. Kuttel *Quadrilles & Konfyt* 53 He was much older than she was — a short man affectionately called 'Oompie' by the Duckitts. **1965** E. Mphahlele *Down Second Ave* 38, I borrowed a bicycle from a tenant of ours we called simply 'Oompie' — uncle — when he was not using it on his rounds .. collecting numbers from gamblers for the Chinaman's *fah fee*.

b. As a title, with a name: an affectionate title for an older man. Cf. OOM sense 1 a.

1966 M. Kuttel *Hildegonda Duckitt's Bk of Recipes* 5 Her sister Annie and her husband 'Oompie' van Renen. **1979** *Fair Lady* 9 May 202 Jakkie was hiding in the wardrobe in oompie Tata's house. **1980** E. Joubert *Poppie Nongena* 12 The children were oompie Kaffertjie and oompie Domani and grootma Martha and grootma Mieta and Lena who was our own ma, and then kleinma Hessie and oompie Sam and oompie Pengi, ouma Hannie's last born, her dry-teat child, her t'koutjie, as the Namas say ... Oompie is uncle.

‖**oorbeligte** /ˈʊə(r)bəˌləxtə/ *n.* [Afk., *oor* over + *beligte* illuminated.] See quot. 1982. Cf. VERLIGTE *n.*

1982 *Sunday Times* 18 July 26 Verligte and verkrampte Afrikaners have been with us for a long time. But now we'll have to get used to yet another category: the oorbeligtes (literal translation: those who have been excessively illuminated). It is used, somewhat pejoratively, to describe verligtes who have become so enlightened that they are adjudged by your average run-of-the-mill verligte to be beyond the Afrikaner pale. **1983** *Ibid.* 30 Jan. 28 With Herman Giliomee going to occupy a chair at UCT (a loss to Maties, this, but then it tends to be uncomfortable with oorbeligtes), Ikeys will have one of the strongest political departments around. **1985** S. Uys in *Cape Times* 12 July, The verligtes operate from the Afrikaner power base (unlike the oorbeligtes who are outside that power base). They are seen to be engaged in the *realpolitik* of South Africa whereas the liberal's public image is of being outside it. **1985** *Frontline* Nov., A battle royal has been raging in *Die Burger* between verligtes and 'oorbeligtes' in Afrikanerdom. **1987** *Sunday Times* 8 Mar. 22 The rebellious Matie academics — sarcastically described as 'oorbeligtes' by more stick-in-the-mud elements — have devised their own response to conservative crititcs. 'Onderbeligtes' is the word they use to describe those who still dwell in the dead-end streets of the NP.

oorlam /ˈʊə(r)lam/ *n.* and *adj.* Also **o(e)rlam**, **urlam**. Pl. **-s**, unchanged, or **orlammen**. [S. Afr. Du., ad. Malay *orang lama, orang* person + *lama* long (of time), 'one who has been in a place (orig. the East) a long time', hence 'one with long and wide experience'. There have been other explanations of the etym., see e.g. quots 1889 (sense A 1), 1881 (sense A 2), also 1928 (sense B 1).]

A. *n. Obs.* exc. *hist.*

1. Usu. with initial capital. A name formerly given to a member of an indigenous people who, as a result of long contact, was familiar with the customs, standards, and language of the Dutch colonists. See also sense B 2.

1815 J. Campbell *Trav. in S. Afr.* 284 In his kraal there are, of persons who speak the Dutch language, and who are called Orlams — 215. **1846** I. Reid in *Imp. Blue Bks* Command Paper 786–1847 88 We are happy to hear that Booy, who is at the head of the few Oorlams at the Bushman station, as also the Fingoes connected with it, .. have made up their minds .. not to fire a single shot, nor to throw a single assegai unless it be in self-defence. *a***1867** C.J. Andersson *Notes of Trav.* (1875) 79 The Oerlams (people born or bred in the colony, or in a wider sense, simply brought up by white men). **1868** W.R. Thomson *Poems, Essays & Sketches* 207 Throughout the whole of India, they call those who have either been there before, returned to Europe and come back again, or those who have lived in those countries for several years, *Orlammen*; while newcomers, or those who have not been there long, are called *Baaren*. These two names are corrupted words, taken originally from the Malay language, in which *Oranglami* means an old person or acquaintance, and *Orang-baru*, a new person. An *Orlam*, therefore, who conducts himself properly, and is known as a steady and honest person, has many and good opportunities of earning something among the burghers; the *Baaren*, on the contrary, are not trusted at once because there is no saying what sort of characters they may be. **1882** S. Heckford *Lady Trader in Tvl* 78 He had several families of what are called Urlams, or civilized Kaffirs, living in mud houses on his property. These families dressed like Europeans, and had food like Europeans, even to the drinking of early coffee. **1889** F. Galton *Trav. in S. Afr.* 41 Oerlam was a nickname given by Dutch colonists to the Hottentots that hung about their farms; it means a barren ewe — a creature good neither for breeding nor fattening, a worthless concern. *Ibid.* 70 Oerlams are like children. **1939** R.F.A. Hoernlé *S. Afr. Native Policy* 174 They were the first truly 'detribalized' Natives; and they and their descendants, the so-called 'Oorlams,' became so completely assimilated, in a hereditary master-servant relationship, into the structure of Afrikaner society that their very mother-tongue became Afrikaans, and they took over .. their masters' religion, dress, food, ways of life. **1980** D.B. Coplan Urbanization of African Performing Arts. 55 The majority of professional Coloured musicians .. belonged to a broader social category known as *oorlams*.

2. [See quot. 1980.] Usu. with initial capital, and in *pl.*, used collectively: the members of a predominantly Khoisan people of Namibia, displaced from the Cape Colony in the mid-nineteenth century; AFRIKANER *n.* sense 3; OVERLAM. See also BONDELSWART.

*a***1838** A. Smith *Jrnl* (1975) 289 All the *Orlam* went to Barend. **1846** R. Moffat *Missionary Labours* 22 A mixed multitude of Namaquas and Bastards from the colony (called on that account Oorlams) ... They stood high in their own estimation, and despised the aborigines. **1881** T. Hahn *Tsuni-‖Goam* 153 The *Orlams* .. are Bastard Hottentots, who say that a trader, by the name of Orlam, came about a hundred years ago to Little Namaqualand, and afterwards stayed amongst the Namaquas and married a Hottentot girl. The truth is, that about 1720 there was a man at the Cape of the name of Orlam, who had come from Batavia. He was a trader, and visited chiefly Little Namaqualand and the Khamiesbergen. **1889** F. Galton *Trav. in S. Afr.* 41 'Oerlams', or Namaquas born in or near the colony, often having Dutch blood and a good deal of Dutch character in their veins. **1922** *Report of Administration on the Bondelzwarts Rising* (UG30–1922) 1 The Bondelzwarts .. originally came from the Cape, and like all Orlams, are not pure Hottentots. **1930** I. Schapera *KhoiSan Peoples* 49 A great number of men also spoke Dutch, and the general culture had in many ways been influenced by contact with the Dutch and other colonists. These groups are collectively termed *Orlams* by the indigenous tribes. **1961** O. Levinson *Ageless Land* 27 The Orlams were Hottentots, who for various reasons, ranging from a desire for freedom to flight from the police, had left the Cape in small groups. Their leaders were mostly of mixed European and Hottentot blood. **1968** G. Croudace *Silver Grass* 14 He had picked up enough of the Dutch dialect that the Oorlams spoke to be able to read Witbooi's letter, for Witbooi himself was an Oorlam, the name meaning 'clever' or 'handy' and referring to the group's superiority over the ordinary Hottentots. **1969** J.M. White *Land God Made in Anger* 57 Jonker was head of the Afrikaners, who in turn were one of the three tribes of a branch of the Nama people known as the Oorlam. **1975** W.F. Lye *Andrew Smith's Jrnl 1834–6* Index, *Orlam, Oorlam*, Name for the mixed Hottentot and European peoples who were well acquainted with European customs. Possibly of Malay origin meaning 'old and trusted servant' (*Orang lami*), or from the Dutch, meaning 'foreigners' (*Oorlandse mense*) as applied by the Nama to late arrivals from the colony. **1976** Cubitt & Richter *South West* 8 In the early 1800s five clans of mixed Dutch-Hottentot descent crossed the Orange River and settled among the Nama in the south. Called the Orlams, or 'Smart Guys', they were considerably more sophisticated than their hosts ... Among the Orlams were the Afrikaner and Witbooi clans which were to play a prominent part in South West Africa's strife-torn history. **1980** D.B. Coplan Urbanization of African Performing Arts. 55 A fondness for drink and clever manipulation of those in authority became closely associated with Khoisan *oorlams*, and the Nama Hottentots used it as a name for themselves, reputedly because they delighted in their own shrewdness and joked that many drinks make a person clever. **1986** W. Steenkamp *Blake's Woman* 5 A number of these clans were pure-bred Khoikhoi, while others — commonly known as '*Oorlams*' — were people of mixed blood who had trekked northwards out of the Cape Colony from the late 18th Century onwards. **1991** [see NAMA *n.* sense 1].

B. *adj.*

1. *Obs.* exc. *hist.* Always with initial capital. Of or pertaining to the 'Oorlam' people of Namibia (see sense A 2); OORLAMS sense 1.

1838 J.E. Alexander *Exped. into Int.* I. 137 He and the hunter were captured some months after by the Orlam Namaquas. **1842** J. Tindall *Jrnl* (1959) 40 The Great Namaqua and Oorlam tribes commenced oppressing them (the Great Damaras). **1877** *Sel. Comm. Report on Mission to Damaraland* p.ix, There I met with some Namaquas, who said they were Orlam Hottentots belonging to the Gobabis people. **1928** H. Vedder in *Native Tribes of S.W. Afr.* 116 The Orlam tribe, containing many hybrids of Dutch descent, who had adopted something of European civilization, possessing horses and supplied even with firearms, made on the Nama who had never been in contact with civilization, the impression that they were a highly developed people. That the meaning 'Oorlandse mense' is also attached to the word Orlam by the Nama would lead one to believe that the word means foreigners, people coming from across the Orange River, ie. people who are 'further off'.

2. *obs.* Clever, shrewd, knowing; experienced, worldly-wise; crafty; OORLAMS sense 2. Cf. BAAR *adj.*

Used esp. of indigenous people long exposed to, and familiar with, the customs, standards, and language of the Dutch colonists.

1881 T. Hahn *Tsuni-‖Goam* 153 If .. they give a traveller a man as a servant, they say, 'He is very *orlam*; he is not *baar*' (he is very handy; he is not stupid). **1913** C. Pettman *Africanderisms* 349 *Oorlam*, .. Also used of a coloured servant whose laziness prompts him to a variety of scheming either to dodge or to scamp his work.

oorlams /ˈʊərlams, ˈuər-/ *adj.* Also **oorlamsch**, **oorlamse**. [Afk., OORLAM + adj.-forming suffix *-s(e)*.]

1. *obs.* OORLAM *adj.* sense 1.

1905 *Native Tribes of Tvl* 35 The term 'Oorlamsch' is applied to the descendants of the slaves of the Zulu and other invaders, who were in some cases taken over by the Boers ... They are able to speak Cape Dutch, and there are some clever artizans and mechanics among them. **1908** J.M. Orpen *Reminisc.* (1964) 261 A family of 'Oorlams' (or tame) Bushmen, who had been for their whole lives in servitude .. and had never received wages, had come to the Court to claim their freedom. **1922** *Report of Administration on Bondelzwarts Rising* (UG30–1922) 1 The Bondelzwarts are a tribe of Oorlams Hottentots.

2. OORLAM *adj.* sense 2.

[**1943** D. REITZ *No Outspan* 112 Having spent much of his time with the Angola Boers, he speaks Dutch fluently as do several of his sons whom for this reason he refers to with pride as 'oorlams volk', meaning 'enlightened people'.] **1980** D.B. COPLAN *Urbanization of African Performing Arts.* 55 During the early years of Dutch settlement at the Cape, the term *oorlams* first referred to hard-drinking, veteran sailors of the Dutch navy and merchant fleet who raised havoc in the local taverns. Later it came to be applied to the tough, experienced Dutch colonials brought from the East Indies, as distinct from their more sober, *baar* (raw, naive) counterparts fresh from Holland . . . Soon, the term came to refer to Khoisan who had learned Dutch and acquired a worldly knowledge of the ways of Europeans . . . Dutch farmers . . found that *oorlamse* Khoisan were more useful but also more disingenuous household servants than *baar kaffirs* (raw, tribal Africans). *Ibid.* 56 Among urban Africans, *oorlams* came to refer to those who had undergone Westernization through Afrikaans and work experience in Afrikaner communities, rather than through involvement with English-speaking mission schools. [**1981** V.A. FEBRUARY *Mind your Colour* 202 The word used in Afrikaans is 'oorlams'. It is generally applied to a 'coloured' who, in Afrikaner eyes, is too clever and who does not stick to his ascribed role.] **1986** W. STEENKAMP *Blake's Woman* 79 '"Oorlams?"' Anne asked, savouring the exotic word. The word . . means 'a wide-awake fellow' . . . in any case, the oorlams Namaquas have long since adopted the white man's clothes, his language, even some of his customs and methods of government – and his guns.

oor-re var. ORE.

‖**oorskiet** /ˈʊə(r)skit/ *n.* [Afk.] Leftovers. Occas. noncount.

1971 K. BRITZ *Informant, Grahamstown* 'Oh, I'm not going to finish this pack of cards. I'll give the oorskiet to you.' **1971** V. KELLY *Informant, Grahamstown* These roses are oorskiets really — only leftovers — because my dad's starting pruning. **1977** J. BRANFORD *Informant, Grahamstown* I'll take my pick of the first and you can have the oorskiets. **1982** M. WA MNUTLE in Chapman & Dangor *Voices from Within* 167 She ate out of a broken plate Drank from a cup without handle Those were oorskiets and krummels From her divine master's table.

ooscuse-me pl. form of EXCUSE-ME.

oosibali pl. form of SBALI.

o'pa var. OUPA.

opblaas geilsiekte see GEILSIEKTE sense 2.

op die kop /ˌɔp di ˈkɔp/ *adv. phr. Colloq.* [Afk., *op* on + *die* the + *kop* head.] Of time: 'on the dot', precisely.

1965 S. DEDERICK *Tickey* 56 We leave one hour from now — *op die kop*. Don't be late, Tickey. **1970** M. WOLFAARDT *Informant, Stilfontein* It is six o'clock op die kop. **1971** *Informant, Grahamstown* I'll serve tea in Mrs Kelly's room at 10.30 op die kop. **1972** C. PAYNE on Radio South Africa 30 May, The time is exactly, op die kop, twenty to nine. **1973** D. BERRY on Radio South Africa, 21 May, At the next stroke of the gong it will be exactly — op die kop — a quarter past seven. **1975** C. FORTUNE on Radio South Africa, Feb., Time: 7.30 op die kop. **1989** M. GLYN in *Fair Lady* 18 Feb. 149 Lunch begins at one, *op die kop*, as they say, mainly out of consideration for the servants, who must be given time off to eat their own Sunday lunch.

open *adj. hist.* [Special sense of general Eng. *open* not limited to a few; that may be used, shared or competed for without restriction.] Of an (educational) institution, public facility, or residential area, during the apartheid era: available to people of all ethnic groups, not only to whites. Occas., of a group: non-racial. See also FREE, GREY. Cf. CLOSED.

1954 *Report of Commission of Enquiry in Regard to Provision of Separate Training Facilities for Non-Europeans at Univ.* 4 At two universities, namely, those of Cape Town and the Witwatersrand, non-European students are admitted, and . . in so far as attendance of lectures is concerned, the principle of non-segregation is applied . . . For convenience sake . . they may be called 'open' universities. **1957** *Open Univ. in S. Afr.* (Council of Univ. of Cape Town & Witwatersrand) 2 While conforming to the South African practice of separation in social matters . . these two universities admit students on the basis of academic qualifications only, and in all academic matters treat non-white students on a footing of equality and without separation from white students. They are therefore described as 'open' universities. **1957** N. MANDELA in *City Press* (11 Feb. 1990) 5 The Bill is a move to destroy the 'open' university tradition which . . has . . been consistently practised by leading universities in the country for years. **1960** E.G. MALHERBE in H. Spottiswoode *S. Afr.: Rd Ahead* 142 It was from the non-White University College of Fort Hare and from the so-called 'open' universities . . that nearly 3,000 non-White university-trained men and women came to fill important posts in non-White communities. **1972** *Daily Dispatch* 16 Feb. 1 After the planning stage the specific areas would be declared 'open areas' in terms of a Parliamentary decision to make purchases easier. **1972** *Evening Post* 11 Mar. 7 Before the Universities Apartheid Act of 1949, Indians were admitted to the 'open' universities on the same basis as Whites. **1981** *Ibid.* 18 Feb. 1 'Open' beaches were receiving his constant attention. He was concerned about resorts becoming overcrowded, and resultant anti-social behaviour, regardless of the race of beachgoers. **1987** *Evening Post* 20 Jan. 3 Pleas to scrap or amend the Group Areas Act so that Woodstock could remain 'open'. **1987** *Frontline* Feb. 5 As to the removal of so-called petty apartheid, . . things are still the same. Few facilities are 'open', but there are umpteen 'own' parks, 'own' libraries, own footbridges, etc. **1987** *New Nation* 10 Sept. 5 Despite mass protest and huge international support, the 'open' universities were closed to most people of colour and the bush universities were established. **1988** *Evening Post* 24 Feb. 2 Clearly the Government has decided the next step is open areas. Good . . . The Group Areas Act is an emotional symbol — a cornerstone, in fact — of apartheid. **1989** *Weekly Mail* 1 Sept. 3 There is always the prospect of membership in the 'open' group — part of the National Party's reform package which allows for living in a 'free settlement' area. **1989** *Sunday Times* 8 Oct. 7 The Government has fought an extraordinary rearguard action to keep beaches white — appealing against landmark court rulings and proclaiming 'open' beaches racially reserved. **1990** R. STENGEL *January Sun* 58 At the direction of Wimpy International . . the local establishments . . became 'open' and permitted non-whites to eat there. **1990** [see LAPPIE sense 1 c]. **1990** *Sunday Times* 18 Mar. 20 'Open' cities — cities free of the racial stranglehold of the Group Areas Act. **1991** C. BARRETT in *Weekend Post* 26 Jan. 5 It was the second day of 'open school' at Erica Girls' Primary and 41 new black, coloured and Indian pupils showed they were 'already part of the Erica family'. **1992** E. DE WAAL in *Church Times* 13 Mar. 8 In order for any school to become an 'open' school, . . it was necessary for 90 per cent of the parents to vote, with an 80-per-cent majority in favour. **1993** C. VAN ONSELEN in *Sunday Times* 11 July 22 If their policies deliberately exclude the funding of former 'open universities' merely on the grounds of their status as HWUs [*sc.* Historically White Universities] their neglect will contribute to the running down of the country's existing and proven capacity for tertiary education.

open *v.* [Special senses of general Eng.]
1. *trans.* [Calqued on Afk. *oopmaak*.] To turn on (a tap).

1974 A.P. BRINK *Looking on Darkness* 287 Every now and then I opened the tap to add some more hot water. **1979** *Star* 17 Jan., In a town you don't think – you just open the tap and there's water. **1988** D. SAMUELSON in *Fair Lady* 16 Mar. 124 When the big taps were opened the water rushed out with great force.

2. *intrans.* [fr. OPEN *adj.*] To become accessible to people of all ethnic groups.

1990 *Weekend Post* 8 Dec. 3 Of 97 schools in the Cape School Board area, . . 68 had applied to hold polls and 62 had voted to open. **1991** *Style* Mar. 119 People are associating more freely, schools are opening, and the Group Areas Act is showing distinct signs of self-destruction.

operational area *n. phr. Military.* Also with initial capitals. The official designation of any area of the country in which control is vested not in the police force but in the defence forces. See also BORDER sense 3 a.

1977 *Rand Daily Mail* 17 June 1 A shooting accident in the operational area. **1978** A.P. BRINK *Rumours of Rain* 291 One day a group of Top Brass arrived to look around the 'operational area'. We slaved away to make everything shine and then they arrived in their helicopters. **1978** *Fair Lady* 8 Nov. (Suppl.) 8 The fighting soldier sees service in the operational area as the culmination of his training. **1979** *Sunday Post* 8 July 7 ' . . challenged the validity of young South Africans fighting against blacks in the operational area.' . . . I'd always thought both the soldiers and the guerillas were South Africans. **1980** *Fair Lady* 3 Dec. 63 The ignorance of people who don't know what life in the operational area, on the border, is like. **1981** *E. Prov. Herald* 9 July 3 At least 700 people have died this year in the bush war in the operational area in northern South West Africa. **1982** *Sunday Times* 18 July 2 The South African Defence Force will open an operational area in the buffer zone between South Africa and Mozambique and eliminate incursions. **1983** [see GOOI sense 1 a]. **1985** *Weekly Mail* 12 July 13 In March, the Government slapped a three-month ban on all meetings. Cradock was declared an operational area and journalists were barred. **1987** *Star* 30 Oct. 3 Defining an operational area as one where the SAP was no longer in control, Commandant Rose said only the State President could proclaim such an area.

Operation Mayibuye /- ˌmaji'buːje/ *n. phr. Hist.* [See MAYIBUYE.] **a.** A plan for the overthrow of the National Party government, prepared by the military wing of the African National Congress in 1962; RIVONIA sense a. **b.** The document setting out this plan. See also MAYIBUYE.

1964 H.H.W. DE VILLIERS *Rivonia* 61 Operation Mayibuye means 'Operation Return' or Operation Comeback'. The full title is 'Operation Afrika Mayibuye', that is 'Operation for the Return of Africa', which the Rivonia conspirators represented to the masses as having been stolen from the Bantu by the White man. **1989** *Reader's Digest Illust. Hist.* 412 At the moment the police came through the door, the six men were studying Operation Mayibuye, an *Umkhonto* proposal for guerilla war, insurrection and revolution. **1990** *City Press* 11 Feb. 6 The police found documents relating to the manufacture of explosives, Mandela's diary of his African tour and copies of a draft memorandum entitled 'Operation Mayibuye' which outlined the possible strategy of the proposed guerrilla struggle.

opgaaf /'ɔpxɑːf/ *n. hist.* Also **offgaft, opgaaff, opgaf(f), opgraaf, oppgaaf**. [Du., statement, account.]

1. An annual return or account of livestock, produce, and land under cultivation, introduced at the Cape in 1796 for the purposes of taxation; the documents submitted for this return. Also *attrib.*

1800 in *Stat. Law of Cape of G.H.* (1862) p.lvii, Order of Opgaaf or return of the inhabitants and the stock or property in their possession. **1800** G. YONGE in G.M. Theal *Rec. of Cape Col.* (1898) III. 67 A considerable time has elapsed since an Opgaaf or Return has been given in to Government by the Inhabitants of this

Colony of the Property and Stock they possess. **1806** *Cape Town Gaz.* in G.M. Theal *Rec. of Cape Col.* (1899) V. 443 These lists are to be shewn at the yearly opgaaf to the Landdrosts and Heemraden. **1806** J. BARROW *Trav.* II. 26 According to an account of the stock, produce and land under cultivation, which every man is obliged annually to give in to the police officers, and which is called Opgaff list, it appears that .. not one fifteenth part of the surface is under any kind of tillage. **1811** J.G. CUYLER in G.M. Theal *Rec. of Cape Col.* (1901) VIII. 29, I have the honour to transmit a copy of their opgaff taken last week, which will show all these people have left. **1823** W.W. BIRD *State of Cape of G.H.* 317 The wine-growers shall be allowed to sell their wine and brandy on their estates, by small measure, .. provided they report the same to the landdrost of the district to which they belong .. at the time of making their opgaaf. **1826** R. BOURKE in G.M. Theal *Rec. of Cape Col.* (1905) XXVII. 76, I propose .. that five shillings each be charged for Hottentots, Mantatees and others employed on farms under contract or apprenticeship from the age now usually returned in the opgaaf rolls, males above 16 and females above 20 years of age. **1843** R.M. MARTIN *Hist. of Colonies of Brit. Empire* (1967) 477 The first authentic account of the state of the colony is furnished by the *Oppgaff* or *tax* lists for 1798. **1884** *Cape Law Jrnl* I. 318 No survey was required for fixing the Ordonnanties, nor were the terms of the tenure reduced to written grants, the grants being merely registered in an 'Opgaaf Boek'. **1968** E.A. WALKER *Hist. of Sn Afr.* 77 The annual *opgaaf* of the burghers' produce became more unreliable than ever.

2. The property-tax calculated from the annual opgaaf return.

1816 G. BARKER Journal. 12 Apr., B^r U— set out this morning to go to Grahams-town to pay the peoples opgaaf a sum of 337 Rd^s. **1827** *Reports of Commissioners upon Finances at Cape of G.H.* II. 58 From the extension of the colony by the occupation of new lands, and the necessity that hence arose of forming district establishments, another class of taxes was imposed on the inhabitants ... These taxes, under the name of 'opgaaf,' have been assessed upon the property of the inhabitants. **1827** G. THOMPSON in Davenport & Hunt *Right to Land* (1974) 7 The occupation is considered sufficient for all the purposes of Government, if he pays his quit-rent, and is enabled .. to keep a greater stock, and pay a larger *opgraaf.* **1829** C. ROSE *Four Yrs in Sn Afr.* 258, I would tell the people of England that the opgaaf, a tax on produce, pressed very heavily on the boors. **1831** *S. Afr. Almanack & Dir.* 152 The first Opgaaf taken in the district .. amounted to 1,027 guilders. **1838** J.E. ALEXANDER *Exped. into Int.* I. 67 The manner in which the opgaaf in this district is collected is most objectionable and oppressive ... All the heads of families, white men, Bastaards, or free Hottentots, are obliged to go to Clanwilliam personally, in the month of April .. with the amount of their opgaaf [*printed* opgaap], whether it be thirty dollars or five. **1839** J. COLLETT Accounts. II. 26 Mar., Rode to Beaufort & paid Offgaft. **1844** J. BACKHOUSE *Narr. of Visit* 584 A Hottentot .. accompanied us as far as Clan William, whither he was going to pay the Opgaaf, Taxes, for himself and a few others. **1857** F.W. REITZ in *Cape Monthly Mag.* II. Oct. 197 Not many years ago the very same process was gone through with the acknowledged object of levying an *opgaaf* on every sheep and head of cattle. *a***1862** J. AYLIFF *Jrnl of 'Harry Hastings'* (1963) 27 Once a year the 'Myneer' goes to the town to pay what they call 'opgaaf', but he don't care a fig about that. **1876** T. STUBBS Reminiscences. 11 There was a tax called Op Gaaf, which had to be paid every year. **1885** L.H. MEURANT *60 Yrs Ago* The Chief Clerk of the Civil Commissioners travelled usually in an ox-wagon to collect the 'opgaaf' (taxes). **1936** *Cambridge Hist. of Brit. Empire* VIII. 280 Institutions .. were liable .. to taxation (the *opgaaf*). **1982** A.P. BRINK *Chain of Voices* 165 At first there was the opgaaf, the tax on slaves. *Ibid.* 310 When there are new proclamations on grazing licences or the Opgaaf or regulations on slaves I'm instructed by Landdrost Trappes to spread the news through the district.

3. *transf.* Any tax.

1871 J. MACKENZIE *Ten Yrs* (1971) 59 Both the Bechuanas and the Basutos who preferred to remain in Griqua-land were protected in the enjoyment of their property on the payment of the same 'opgaaf' or tax which was paid by the other inhabitants of the country. **1943** I. FRACK *S. Afr. Doctor* 67 An alarming number of natives fall foul of some infringement of the tax laws. This 'opgaf' is to my mind extremely unfair. **1970** M. DIKOBE Marabi Dance. 108 My grandfather was also very rich, but he went to Kimberley to work for white people because some white men came to our village and arrested men, young and old, for opgaf – poll-tax.

oppas /ˈɔpas/ *int.* and *v. Colloq.* [Afk., fr. S. Afr. Du. *pas op*, see PAS OP *int. phr.*]

A. *int.* PAS OP *int. phr.*

1969 A. FUGARD *Boesman & Lena* 16 *Oppas!* You'll get too far one day. Death penalty.

B. *v. trans.* and *intrans.* PASOP *v.*

1969 A. FUGARD *Boesman & Lena* 7 Oppas they don't get you. **1992** D. MCCORMACK on Radio South Africa 1 Mar., We now know exactly what [to do], and we will oppas.

oppblazer *n. obs.* [Du. *opblazen* to inflate + agential suffix *-er.*] BLAASOP sense 1.

1795 C.R. HOPSON tr. *C.P. Thunberg's Trav.* I. 150 The oppblazers (*pneumora*) a kind of grass-hopper, were caught in the evening. After sun-set they begin to make a singular noise, by rubbing their barbed hind-legs against their empty and transparent stomach. **1809** J. MACKRILL Diary. 61 Pneumora, a species of Grasshopper (oppblazers) .. their whole Body is as a bladder, so void of substance that it cannot be preserved.

oppgaaf var. GAAF.

oprecht /ˈɔprext/ *adj. obs.* Also (*attrib.*) **oprechte**. [S. Afr. Du. *oprecht* (predicative), *oprechte* (attrib.) upright, sincere, genuine.]

1. Decent; of upright character.

1899 'S. ERASMUS' *Prinsloo* p.vii, The fair-minded, oprecht man will be bound to confess that if Piet Prinsloo had faults .. they were not part of his nature. **1903** D. BLACKBURN *Burgher Quixote* 189 When you know how to use him, a schelm is as good as an oprecht deacon of the Reformed Kerk. **1908** F.C. SLATER *Sunburnt South* 21, I felt comfortable in my own mind that Klaas, who was a steady *oprecht* young *kerel*, would make Lena a good husband, and would manage the farm well after my death. **1910** D. FAIRBRIDGE *That Which Hath Been* (1913) 49 What will such a gay young spark do in our *oprechte* and virtuous society? **1912** F. BANCROFT *Veldt Dwellers* 87 My son, you are a burgher of our beloved Republic and in her need you will never refuse to handle a *roer* on her behalf .. as every oprecht man must certainly be willing to do. **1915** D. FAIRBRIDGE *Torch Bearer* 43, I heard it said that some who should be oprechte Afrikanders are but lukewarm. *Ibid.* 62 No disrespect to Mrs. Neethling, who is an oprechte and godly woman.

2. Special collocation. **oprecht(e) burgher**, a true or genuine citizen of the Transvaal Republic, in contrast to an UITLANDER.

1899 'S. ERASMUS' *Prinsloo* 23 He rejoiced very much when the independence of the Transvaal was established, and from that day was a good and loyal oprecht burgher of the State. **1903** D. BLACKBURN *Burgher Quixote* 1, I have decided .. to put my full name and district to this truthful story of the struggles after righteousness of a once oprecht Burgher of the late South African Republic. **1911** BLACKBURN & CADDELL *Secret Service* 239 That zealous patriot remained in the service of the Government to the end, and was always bold in his assurances that he was an oprecht burgher and true friend to the State. **1926** M. NATHAN *S. Afr. from Within* 65 He kept a sort of informal court at his residence in Pretoria .. to which all who had complaints or requests, whether oprechte (genuine) burghers or uitlanders (as the new foreign population was termed), resorted.

‖**opsaal** /ˈɔpsɑːl/ *v. intrans.* Also **opzaal**. [Afk. (earlier S. Afr. Du. *opzaal*), to saddle up.] Usu. in the imperative.

1. 'Saddle up', often as an exhortation to hasten. See also UPSADDLE sense 2.

1916 E.H. SPENDER *General Botha* 95 (Swart), 'Opsaal Burghers' was the cry before the first grey streaks of light on the eastern horizon. **1929** D. REITZ *Commando* 216 (Swart), We had scarcely slaughtered a few sheep and broken our fast, when the well-known cry of 'Opsaal! Opsaal!' sent us scurrying to fetch our unfortunate animals. [**1931** G. BEET *Grand Old Days* 44 From afar the sight of it to the watchful Boer commandant was indeed 'terrible as an army with banners.' He turned pale and at once passed the word to 'opsaal 'n huis toe!'] **1937** H. KLEIN *Stage Coach Dust* 205 That night Alexander passed the word round to 'inspan' and 'opsaal', and with all their kit and gear the little commando took the road. **1963** S. CLOETE *Rags of Glory* 365 'Opzaal!' Saddle up! The Khakis are here!

2. *Transf.* and *fig.* 'Let's get moving!'; freq. in the phr. ***opsaal boere***, 'prepare (boere)', used as a political rallying cry among Afrikaners.

1965 D. MARAIS *Ag, Sis Man!*, (caption) Opsaal Kêrels! I don't mind boycotts and cancelled contracts, but when Wilson starts interfering with the *Boer* and his *roer* — that's too much! *c***1967** J. HOBBS in *New S. Afr. Writing* 68 He got into his truck so tense with rage that the starter knob came away in his fist and we all had to push. Muttering 'Opsaal!' under his breath, he let in the clutch and roared off down the road. **1972** *Sunday Times* 12 Mar. 4 We Nats are in a bad way. Day and night I go out into the veld shouting 'Opsaal, Boere!' But no matter how hard I shout, there is not a Boer to answer op my roepstem. **1975** *Friend* 10 July 6 Like those grizzly Boer guerrillas of 75 years ago, some 40 Afrikaans writers — many as well-haired and bearded as their forebears — are gathering in the bush at Broederstroom to 'opsaal' and take to the warpath. **1975** *Sunday Times* 27 July 20 Opsaal! To the cry of 'opsaal boere, the bulldozer cometh,' verligte and verkrampte joined hands .. in defence of Church Square. **1990** D. VAN HEERDEN in *Ibid.* 10 June 8 When ET brings his silver-tongued oratory to town everybody on the right wing will cheer him wildly. And when Oom Manie Maritz shouts 'Opsaal', those who can will.

opsit /ˈɔpsət/ *n. Obs.* exc. *hist.* Also **opzit**. [Afk., fr. next.] Courtship; a courtship visit. See also UPSITTING.

1882 J. NIXON *Among Boers* 211 He takes stock of all the marriageable lasses in the neighbourhood, and when he has found one to his liking he pays a state visit to the house of the fair creature's parents, and undergoes what is called an 'opzit'. **1928** N. STEVENSON *Afr. Harvest* 177 If she isn't keen on Koos it doesn't really matter ... They can begin the *opsit* at once, and marry soon after. **1932** —— *Farmers of Lekkerbat* 127 Uncle Eloff told Gys that Caroline was willing and that they could arrange the *opsit* when they pleased. **1940** F.B. YOUNG *City of Gold* 141 The scene revealed by the light of guttering candles which Sarie had selected to cover the duration of her *opsit* was one of the most decorous propriety. **1955** V. DE KOCK *Fun They Had* 27 Among the farming community a direct method of courting was observed. It was called *Opsit.* **1965** K. MACKENZIE *Deserter* 33 The first *opsit* had been a slow, shy-making affair in which they had punctuated long silences with little bits of polite conversation.

opsit *v. intrans. Hist.* Also **opzit, opsitt.** [Afk., earlier S. Afr. Du. *opzit* to sit up, to court.] *to sit up*, see SIT.

1882 [see VRYER]. **1887** H. RIDER HAGGARD *Jess* 72 How often do you 'opsit' (sit up at night) with Uncle Croft's pretty girl, eh? **1899** —— *Swallow* 6 After we had 'oppsited' together several times according to our customs, and burnt many very long candles, we were married. **1912** F. BANCROFT *Veldt Dwellers* 110 She says when I am a grown up maiden about to *opzit*, she will let me into a secret — a very great secret. **1915** D. FAIRBRIDGE *Torch Bearer* 86 When a young man likes a girl, and she doesn't dislike him, they agree to opsitt — to see whether they would like to be engaged. They light a candle, stick a pin into it, .. and sit up talking .. until the flame burns down to the pin. If she likes him very much she sticks the pin in low down so that they may have a long evening together. If she thinks that she is likely to be bored, she puts it near the top. But it's a very old-fashioned custom. **1924** G. BAUMANN in Baumann & Bright *Lost Republic* (1940) 115 If a young man rode up to a house, mounted on a good horse, with a well-kept saddle and bridle, everyone knew the purpose of his visit. He had come to 'opzit' (literally — sit up). **1939** S. CLOETE *Watch for Dawn* 377 Why, if you wanted to court her, could you not opsit like a Burgher in the sit-kamer with a candle between you? **1944** J. MOCKFORD *Here Are S. Africans* 96 The horseman .. would dress up to kill, stick a feather in his hat, offer the girl of his choice some sugar plums, and then, if his suit prospered, *opsit* (sit up) with her after supper for as long as a measured candle burned. **1945** M. HONE *Sarah-Elizabeth* 90 She asked Mamma if it were true Rosina was Opsitting with a Rooinek Kerel. **1955** W. ROBERTSON *Blue Wagon* 181 'In my young days I had to *opsit* for weeks'. He referred to the Boer custom of two young people sitting up by the light of a candle after the elders had gone to bed.

‖**opsitkers** /ˈɔpsətkɛ(r)s/ *n. Obs.* exc. *hist.* Pl. **-kerse** /-kɛ(r)sə/. [Afk., *opsit* (see OPSIT *n.* and *v.*) + *kers* candle.] In the past, esp. among rural Afrikaners: a candle which was burned to determine the length of a suitor's or sweetheart's visit. See also SIT.

1939 *Outspan* 11 Aug. 34 (*advt*) Traditional as the opsitkers ... This century-old Aristocrat of Brandies. **1948** H.V. MORTON *In Search of S. Afr.* 289 Another Boer custom which has vanished, except .. maybe far off among the poorer inhabitants of the backveld, is the picturesque and pleasing custom of the opsit-kers. **1949** L.G. GREEN *In Land of Afternoon* 173 The opsitkers, the celebrated candle put out by the girl's mother to indicate how long the man might stay after the parents had gone to bed. She stuck a pin into the wax, knowing very well that an inch would burn for thirty minutes. Salt weakened the flame and was often used to delay the man's departure. **1958** A. JACKSON *Trader on Veld* 33 If acceptable to the parents, he was given, as nightfall approached, a piece of 'opsitkers' (sitting up candle). **1961** T. MACDONALD *Tvl Story* 20 When she had stocked her medicine chest she would buy a packet of candles for the 'opsit kerse', the courting of any of the daughters. **1977** *Weekend Post* 26 Mar. There was a thing called the opsitkers. It was simply a candle. A candle which told the time — the time which young courting couples were allowed to spend whispering sweet nothings to each other. [**1990** J. HOBBS in *New Contrast* Winter 70 These flesh and blood people banging their heads against their flawed heritage shine out like *opsit* candles.] **1990** C. LAFFEATY *Far Forbidden Plains* 16 'Don't you think,' Mamma was saying, 'that it's time the girl had an *opsitkers*?'

opsitting /ˈɔpsɪtɪŋ/ *vbl n. Obsolescent.* [Afk., fr. *opsit* (see OPSIT *v.*).] UPSITTING.

1900 H.A. BRYDEN *From Veldt Camp Fires* 195 Tobias meant to make a bit of a splash today, .. although he was not prepared for the solemnity of an 'opsitting' (that all-night form of courtship, dear to the heart of the Boer). **1946** S. CLOETE *Afr. Portraits* 68 The Boers had many customs of their own. The opsitting or courtship was one which persists in many parts of the Backveld to this day. **1949** C. BULLOCK *Rina* 36 There was no chance of Piet going far until the opsitting ended one way or the other. **1969** D. CHILD *Yesterday's Children* 111 At the age of seventeen he married a girl named Maria du Plessis. He had to ride nearly two hundred miles for the traditional *opsittings* (courting by candlelight) with her.

opskop /ˈɔpskɔp/ *n.* [Afk., lit. 'kick up'.] **a.** An informal, lively party, with dancing to the accompaniment of BOEREMUSIEK (sense 1); BOEREDANS. Cf. VASTRAP sense 2. **b.** Any lively party. Also *attrib.*

1985 J. THOMAS in *Fair Lady* 3 Apr. 152 He bellows against the beat, over it, with it, while the funniest, most unexpectedly fluid sounds of an accordian [*sic*] wheeze over the top. It sounds like a great witblitz-fuelled boeremusiek opskop gone crazy in the heart of Marabbastad. **1985** *Newsletter* (George Lakes Yacht Club) Nov. 1 We will be holding a New Year's Eve Party/Opskop at the Club House on the 31st, don't miss it — remember last year? **1988** I. WENTZEL *Informant* I'll be off to Durbs-by-the-sea in August again since my Dad will be turning 60 on the 23rd — so we'll be having something of a family opskop then. **1989** *Grocott's Mail* 6 June (Coastal News) 2 Dancers at the NSRI Barn Dance/Boere Opskop were kept constantly on their toes by the first rate dancing music of Neels Matthys's 'second' band recently. **1990** W. HOLLEMAN *Informant, Grahamstown* We need a parish party. We don't mean an opskop. **1990** M. SHAFTO in *Weekend Argus* 9 June 11 They told stories, they sampled Oom Apies award-winning yellow peach mampoer, they sang and danced as the *opskop* by Pieter Wolmerans and his orchestra warmed to its midnight crescendo.

Hence **opskopper** *n.* [Afk.], one who attends an opskop.

1980 *Sunday Times* 23 Nov. 29 Soft-shoe Neels, opskoppers! Can you imagine it? A band had to come all the way from 1820 Settler country to demolish the finest talent from the north and south in the 1980 Boeremusiek Olympics.

‖**opskud** /ˈɔpskət/ *n.* Also **opskut**. [See next.] **a.** *Music.* A vigorous style of dance music in the BOEREMUSIEK tradition. **b.** The style of dancing performed to this music. See also OPSKUD *v.* sense 2.

1941 W.M.B. NHLAPO in *Bantu World* 1 Mar. 9 Dancing clubs deplore engaging Bantu dance bands .. on the false ground that Bantu bands play nothing but 'tsaba-tsaba'. Having heard Coloureds play their 'opskuds and draais and polkas', we challenge this supremacy. **1963** [see TICKEY-DRAAI sense 2]. [**1969** A. FUGARD *Boesman & Lena* (1973) Glossary, *Vastrap, Tickey-Draai, Opskud en uitkap*, traditional South African folk dances. **1986** *Style* Oct. 132 Kicking up the dust of a mine dump to the stomp of *opskiet-musiek*.]

‖**opskud** /ˈɔpskəd/ *v. intrans.* Also **op-skut**. [Afk., lit. to shake up; to get a move on, hurry.] **1.** Used as a rallying call among Afrikaners: 'hurry up', 'shake a leg', 'get going'.

1951 H.C. BOSMAN in L. Abrahams *Unto Dust* (1963) 90 '*Opskud, kêrels!*' I heard. But it was not Serfina who gave that command. **1973** BRINK & HEWITT ad. Aristophanes's The Birds. 4 He can have his nap later. Off you go! Opskud! **1977** G. HUGO in *Quarry '77* 91 'Opskud! Word wakker!' At four in the morning the delightful Byl ushers in the pre-dawn darkness and a last frantic return to cleaning and neurotic scrubbing.

2. To dance.

1970 D.J. OLIVIER *Informant, Johannesburg* Come, we are going to 'op-skut' tonight.

opslag /ˈɔpslax/ *n.* Also **opslaag**. [Afk., a rise or increase; a self-sown plant.]

1.a. *noncount.* Short-lived vegetation which springs up in dry regions after rain. Also *attrib.*

1871 F.W. REITZ in *Cape Monthly Mag.* III. Sept. 145 The destruction of more lasting grasses, and the increase of what we call 'opslag' grass, is accounted for by over-stocking. **1872** E.J. DUNN in A.M.L. Robinson *Sel. Articles from Cape Monthly Mag.* (1978) 51 That rapid spring vegetation known as 'Opslag'. [**1890** A. MARTIN *Home Life* 95 All these plants, which are of many different kinds, and some of which possess very minute and pretty flowers, are indiscriminately called by the Dutch *opslaag* ('that which comes up').] **1918** J.W. BEWS *Grasses & Grasslands* 103 After rains, they [*sc.* the grasses] tend to spread very quickly forming part of the 'opslag' type of vegetation. [**1920** E.H.L. SCHWARZ *Thirstland Redemption* 138 In South Africa .., one sees after rain the original vegetation spring up, green and tender, among the hardy, permanent bushes; this 'opslag', as the Boers call it, is very short-lived, for in a few days the hot winds come and wither it up.] **1937** *Handbk for Farmers* (Dept of Agric. & Forestry) 399 Grazing available is the 'opslag' (chiefly annuals) which comes up on braaklands, stubble-lands and 'ouland'. **1970** *Cape Times* 6 May, They are especially glad that the first young shoots have started growing ... Stock are voracious .. feeders on this *opslag*.

b. *rare.* With pl. **-s**. A self-sown plant.

1979 *Weekend Post* 31 Mar. (Family Post) 6 It seems strange that these 'opslags' are frequently tougher and more resistant to adverse conditions than those which are specially sown, planted out, staked, sprayed, watered and fed.

2. *noncount. Obs.* exc. *hist.* The preliminary upward bidding at a Dutch-style auction; cf. AFSLAG. Also *attrib.* See also STRYKGELD.

1927 [see STRYKGELD]. **1965** A. GORDON-BROWN *S. Afr. Heritage* IV. 12 The method of selling a house or farm was unusual. First it was put up by opslag, that is by advancing the bids in the usual way. But the highest bidder to whom it was knocked down did not wish to be the purchaser; his function was to help the auctioneer to increase the final selling price and for this he received a bonus or strykgeld. Next the property was sold by afslag, or downward bidding ... The final figure was generally well in advance of the opslag bid, but should it fail to reach that amount the man who had received the strykgeld was compelled to become the buyer at that figure. **1981** P. DANE *Great Houses of Constantia* 119 First the house .. came up for sale, by the traditional method of '*opslag en afslag*' — the rise and fall of the hammer, where the bidding opens twice and the best price is accepted.

‖**opstal** /ˈɔpstal/ *n.* Pl. unchanged, occas. **-le** /-lə/, **-len**. [Du. (later Afk.), lit. 'structure', 'construction', 'something built up'.] Any farm building and the ground around it, but particularly the farm house and its garden ground; often in *pl.* and used collectively, a farm's main buildings; UPSTALL. Also *attrib.*

1809 EARL OF CALEDON in G.M. Theal *Rec. of Cape Col.* (1900) VII. 187 A duty of only 2 1/2 per cent is charged upon the Opstal or buildings erected upon a Loan Land. **1811** J.A. TRUTER in G.M. Theal *Rec. of Cape Col.* (1901) VIII. 96 When he sells the opstal (buildings) to any person who makes the purchase .. the proprietor stands in want of special grant to himself. **1811** *Ibid.* [see QUITRENT sense 2 a]. **1818** M.C. GIE in *Ibid.* 429 It appears from grants of the year 1705 that they have sold to one another the premises thereon, called Opstallen. **1827** *Reports of Commissioners upon Finances at Cape of G.H.* II. 80 The transfer of loan places has constituted an exception, the buildings on them called the 'opstal' having at all times been allowed to be sold by the occupier. **1844** *Ordinance for Regulating Payment of Transfer Duty* in *Stat. Law of Cape of G.H.* (1862) 706 In respect of every sale whether private or public of the opstal of any loan-place a duty of two and one half *per centum* shall be chargeable upon and payable by the purchaser. **1884** *Cape Law Jrnl* I. 317 The homestead, that is buildings and garden ground, of the 'loan place' was called the 'Opstal', and the sale or bequest of such 'Opstal' was impliedly allowed by the Government. **1887** *S.W. Silver & Co.'s Handbk to S. Afr.* 19 All farm-buildings erected, fruit trees or vineyards, etc., planted, were called 'opstal', and were saleable like any other kind of property. [**1913** C. PETTMAN *Africanderisms* 352 *Opstal*, In Cape Dutch this word is used collectively of the buildings on a farm, house, stables, etc.] **1927** C.G. BOTHA *Social Life in Cape Col.* 11 The farmer was only an occupier of the land which he had no right to sell. The only part he could sell or bequeath was the 'opstal' or buildings which he had put up. **1938** —— *Our S. Afr.* 26 The lessee had no *dominium* in the ground and he could sell or bequeath nothing more than the *opstal* — that is the house, kraals and other improvements. **1941** C.W. DE KIEWIET *Hist. of S. Afr.* 40 All he owned was the 'opstal' or buildings upon the land. **1967** W.A. DE KLERK *White Wines* 74 The present *opstal* (homestead) has a main gable dated 1814. **1978** *Sunday Times* 5 Nov. (Mag. Sect.) 5 He .. discovered the buchu growing freely on the mountain slopes and the apparatus for distilling buchu oil in an old opstal. **1981** J. KENCH *Cape Dutch Homesteads* 15 The second half of the Eighteenth Century is the great period of *opstal* design, the period when its central feature, the 'holbol' gable, reached its finest expression. *Ibid.* 25 The homestead at Bokbaai .. exemplifies the unpretentious architecture from which the grander 'opstalle' of the great wine-estates emerged. **1983** D. HUGHES et al. *Complete Bk of S. Afr. Wine* 15 It was then that they built their splendid homesteads, the stately *opstalle* which have become a central feature of the winelands. **1986** *S. Afr. Panorama* May. 23 'Overberg opstalle' (homesteads), complete with peach-pip floor. **1989** *Reader's Digest Illust. Hist.* 490 Opstal, Homestead, farm building.

‖**opstoker** /'ɔpstʊəkə(r)/ *n.* [Afk., *opstook* to incite + agential suffix *-er.*] An agitator or troublemaker.

Used ironically, poking fun at official terminology.

1972 *Sunday Times* 22 Oct. 16 That well-known Boerehaat opstoker .. is at it again. This week he warned .. the English Press to stop mocking and cursing the Afrikaner and the things that were holy to him. **1977** *Time* 2 May 22 The .. National Party .. remains committed to *kragdadigheid* (forcefulness) against all *opstokers* (troublemakers). **1981** *Voice* 10 June 2 When will the .. Government learn by admitting simple truths, like realising that there was much more to the students [*sic*] marches than mere 'ring leaders' and opstokers? **1985** *Drum* Sept. 64 The report has made it clear .. that the machinery that churns out discriminatory pieces of legislation is the real culprit and not our leaders who have been branded 'opstokers'. **1989** *Personality* 6 Feb. 20 While the establishment could console itself that it was one thing for an *opstoker* (agitator) like Breyten Breytenbach (who everyone knew had a prison record) to hob-nob with the enemy, it was quite another when none other than an Afrikaner like rugby's Dr Danie Craven followed suit.

Hence **opstokery** /'ɔpstʊəkəreɪ/ *vbl n.* [Afk.], the action of stirring up strife or ill feeling.

1972 *Sunday Times* 5 Nov. 4 The Olympic Games gold medal for Boerehaat Opstokery.

opzaal, opzit varr. OPSAAL, OPSIT.

!Ora var. KORA.

orabee, -bi(e) varr. ORIBI.

orange-blanje-blou var. ORANJE-BLANJE-BLOU.

Orange Express *n. phr. Hist.* [See quot. 1979.] The former name of the Trans-Oranje Express, a luxury express train which travels through the Orange Free State from Cape Town to Durban and back, twice a week.

1952 F.B. YOUNG *In S. Afr.* 127 The Orange Express, which connects Cape Town with Durban, is of the same character [as the Blue Train], although not air-conditioned. **1964** J. BENNETT *Mr Fisherman* (1967) 10 He worked on the railways, too, as a bedding boy, although he was old for the job, and did a spell on the Blue Train and on the Orange Express. **1968** A. FULTON *Dark Side of Mercy* 210 She would go with him to the station in Pine Street, and see him off on the Orange Express at seven-thirty. **1977** *S. Afr. Panorama* Dec. 18 South Africa's special trains are the Blue Train, which travels between Pretoria and Cape Town; .. the Orange Express [etc.]. **1979** *Handbk* (S.A.R. & H.) 95 Orange Express ... This train derives its name from the Orange Free State – the central point of the train's journey between Durban and Cape Town. **1990** *Weekend Post* 20 Oct. 6 Could Spoornet please give us back our old South African Railways, .. Not to mention the old Union and Orange Expresses.

Orange Leaves *n. phr.* [See quot. 1970.] In the phr. ***Feast of the Orange Leaves***, a festival celebrated among Cape Muslims, at which sweet-smelling sachets are prepared in celebration of the birthday of the prophet Muhammad; *rampi-sny*, see RAMPI sense b. Also ***Festival of the Orange Leaves.***

1944 I.D. DU PLESSIS *Cape Malays* 14 Moulidu 'n-Nabi (birthday of the Prophet), which falls on the 12th day of Rabi-'u'l-auwal, but which may be celebrated at any time provided the necessary preparation is made. In connection with this the Feast of the Orange Leaves is held. **1953** [see RAMPI sense b]. **1970** *Cape Times* 18 May. Moslem women and girls dressed in their best finery yesterday observed Mohammed's birthday with the traditional Feast of the Orange Leaves ... They spent the afternoon till sunset cutting up orange leaves on small boards, using special knives. The pieces were put on trays and sprinkled with rare oils. **1971** L.G. GREEN *Taste of S.-Easter* 138 Only during the Feast of the Orange Leaves (in honour of the Prophet's birthday) do the women take part in the service. **1979** HEARD & FAULL *Our Best Trad. Recipes* 106 At the Feast of the Orange Leaves Malays usually serve delicious little sponge cakes topped with green and lemon curd. **1989** T. BOTHA in *Style* Dec. 161 One of the best-known celebrations, the Festival of the Orange Leaves, is not Islam but an animistic form of worship brought from Indonesia which, according to Davids, is practised only in the Cape.

‖**oranje-blanje-blou** /ɔˌranjə blanjə 'bləʊ/ *n.* Also **orange-blanje-blou, oranje-blanje-blaauw, oranje, blanje blou,** and with initial capitals. [Afk., 'the orange, white and blue' (*blanje* being a poetic word for 'white').] The (colours of the) former national flag; the title of a patriotic Afrikaans song; *fig.*, a symbol of nationalism. Also *attrib.*

1985 [see VOLKSLIED sense 1]. **1987** *Sunday Times* 25 Jan. 2 It all made one wonder whatever happened to Die Stem and good old 'oranje, blanje blou'? **1989** *Frontline* Apr. 32 In the young Reiger Park, parties like the Coloured National Party and the Federale Kleurling Volksparty fought coloured elections on coloured tickets under Oranje Blanje Blou banners. **1989** *Personality* 10 Apr. 40 He did not leave in a blaze of patriotic glory, carrying the *oranje-blanje-blou* to the peaks of distant music charts. His mission was simply to fulfil his own goals and his own dreams. **1989** L. STUART in *ADA* No.7, 59 Trevor Woodside's T-Shirt .. contains most essential elements for Suid-Afrikanerism: the eternal tannie, proteas and windmills and a dung-beetle in 'oranje, blanje blou'. **1989** *Personality* 11 Sept. 71 Without waving the Oranje-Blanje-Blaauw, South African nicknames are possibly the most amusing. **1993** I. POWELL in *Weekly Mail & Guardian* 29 Oct. 9 One of the suggestions submitted to the commission for an interim symbol was to simply string up a square of clear plastic, so everyone could see what he or she wanted ... Or maybe, against all aesthetic judgment, stick with the old orange-blanje-blou. At least you can hate it.

orbea, -bee, -bie varr. ORIBI.

Order of Ethiopia *n. phr.* [See ETHIOPIAN.] ***The Order of Ethiopia***: An African order of clergy and laity established within the (Anglican) Church of the Province of South Africa (see CPSA *n.*[1]) and subject to its control. See also ETHIOPIAN.

The Order now has its own bishop.

1906 *Question of Colour* 253 On August 25, 1900, the Episcopal Synod adopted a scheme for forming the Ethiopians into an order – 'The Order of Ethiopia' – within the Church, to be in each diocese under the direct control of the bishop. **1948** B.G. SUNDKLER *Bantu Prophets* 42 The Order of Ethiopia can hardly be said to have succeeded in attracting the broad masses of Ethiopians. It has remained exclusively Xhosa. **1963** P. HINCHLIFF *Anglican Church* 202 The Order of Ethiopia originated in 1892 when an African minister, Margea Mokone, left the Methodist church and established a separate 'Ethiopian Church' intending it to become the great National Church for the African ... In 1900 a compact was drawn up which created an order of clergy and laity within the Church governed by a Provincial and a Chapter, and subject to .. control of the Bishops of the Province ... It was never made clear to the Ethiopians that giving them 'valid orders' did not mean giving them their own bishops. **1963** WILSON & MAFEJE *Langa* 93 The Order of Ethiopia has its own separate organization, but its members are members of the Church of the Province and its Provincial is appointed by the Archbishop. It is therefore not a separate church, though many people speak as if it were one. **1979** *E. Prov. Herald* 18 June 11 The walkout followed a heated debate over a motion calling for the consecration of a bishop for the black-dominated Order of Ethiopia, which falls under the authority of the Church of the Province. Fears were expressed that the order might break away once it had its own bishop. **1983** *Daily Dispatch* 9 May 1 Eleven people were injured when violence erupted .. yesterday at the installation of the Rt Rev Dr Sigquoba Dwane as Bishop of the Order of Ethiopia. **1989** *Daily Dispatch* 21 Mar. 1 The Order of Ethiopia and the Methodist Church .. do not officially recognise the gatherings at the shrine and have never encouraged their members to attend.

ordonnantie *n. Obs. Law.* Also **ordonnancie.** [S. Afr. Du.]

1. The lease on a *loan farm* (see LOAN).

1811 J.A. TRUTER in G.M. Theal *Rec. of Cape Col.* (1901) VIII. 94 All the Ordonnancies (Leases) upon which loan places have been granted. *Ibid.* 97 The very nature of loan right, added to the letter of the ordonnantie (lease) upon which he obtains the possession.

2. The central point of a loan farm, at which the homestead was generally situated, and from which the extent of the farm was calculated; the area immediately around this point.

1884 [see LEGPLEK]. **1884** [see OPGAAF sense 1]. **1927** C.G. BOTHA *Social Life in Cape Col.* 79 The extent of his farm was measured by choosing a central spot called the 'ordonnantie,' generally a spring of water close by to which he intended to build his house, and riding from here on horseback at a walk a half hour's distance in all directions. This gave an area of approximately three thousand morgen.

ore /'uərə/ *pl. n. Slang.* Also **oere, oor-re.** [Afk., 'ears'.] A derogatory name for the police.

1963 L.F. FREED *Crime in S. Afr.* 105 Jolling on the corner with my razor and chain; Down came the ore, one took my name. **1970** V.E. PAUTZ *Informant, KwaZulu-Natal* Oor-re: The police. **1970** M. BENNETT *Informant, Krugersdorp* 'The ore'. The police. **1972** [see TOKOLOSHE sense 2]. **1975** 'JIGGS' in *New Classic* No.1, 41 And now they are bulldozing the place down here's hardly anyone left; except the whores and oere. **1979** T. EMMET in *Eng. in Afr.* Vol.6 No.1, 80 In Houghton it might be more polite to talk of the 'police', but in Doornfontein words like '*ore*', 'the system' or '*varke*' convey a great deal more about the social position, political attitudes and sentiments of the speaker.

oribi /ɒrɪbi/ *n.* Also **orabee, orabi(e), orbea, orbee, orbie, orebi, oreby, orib(i)e, ourebi(e).** [Khoikhoi *orebi, orabi, oribi, ourebi*; cf. Nama *!gore-b(i).*] The small, rare antelope *Ourebia ourebi* of the Bovidae, an inhabitant of open plains. Also *attrib.*

1796 C.R. HOPSON tr. *C.P. Thunberg's Trav.* II. 58, I saw the kid caught of a very small and extremely scarce goat, called *Orebi* ... It was of a brown colour. **1801** J. BARROW *Trav.* I. 138 Another species of antelope was here very plentiful, known by the Hottentot name of *orabie*, which, except in color and size, .. bore a considerable resemblance to the steenbok. **1827** T. PHILIPPS *Scenes & Occurrences* 58 The dogs gave chase to and killed an *orabi*, a very pretty kind of buck. *Ibid.* 87 Before the day was over we had destroyed pheasants partridges orabees. **1835** T.H. BOWKER Journal. 10 Feb., Tavers fires right & left at an Orbie and Misses him. **1860** A.W. DRAYSON *Sporting Scenes* 60 The ourebi (Oreotragus scopariuus): two feet high at shoulder, and four in length; horns annulated, and about five inches long; colour pale tawny, with white belly; female similar, but hornless and smaller.

1880 E.F. SANDEMAN *Eight Months in Ox-Waggon* 149 Orebi – a small yellow bôk, the best eating of any antelope. **1900** W.L. SCLATER *Mammals of S. Afr.* I. 172 The oribi is found chiefly in open grass country and treeless plains. **1923** *S. Afr.: Land of Outdoor Life* (S.A.R. & H.) 275 The oribi, which is practically extinct in Zululand, is also royal game. **1958** R. COLLINS *Impassioned Wind* 20 An oribi, a little fawn-coloured antelope, darted to one side with the celerity of a frightened hare. **1985** *Evening Post* 25 Feb. 17 The rare East Cape oribi is in danger of extinction with numbers dwindling to 237 scattered in a 10 000-hectare area in 1984. **1990** *Weekend Post* 29 Sept. 6 The foothold of the endangered oribi in the Eastern Cape has been strengthened and the numbers on some farms have grown by as much as 51% in two years. **1992** C. URQUHART in *Afr. Wildlife* Vol.46 No.6, 264 The first oribi census carried out in 1981 had revealed that only 251 were left in the Eastern Cape.

orkes /ɔrˈkes, ɔːˈkes/ *n.* [Afk., orchestra, band.] Ellipt. for BOEREORKES.

1980 *E. Prov. Herald* 20 Nov. 1 With the R1200 prize money comes the invitation for the winning orkes to take part in an hour-long SABC-TV variety show to be screened on New Year's Night. **1986** D. CAPEL in *Sunday Star* 8 June 5 It wasn't the vlak-vark, nor the orkes, that had brought more than 2 000 to an open field on a smallholding in Potchefstroom last Friday. **1986** *E. Prov. Herald* 15 Oct. 1 The orkes outplayed five other bands during a taped audition at the SABC's local studios earlier this year.

orlam var. OORLAM.

Orphan Chamber *n. phr. Hist. Law.* [tr. Du. *weeskamer*, see WEESKAMER.] A court which regulated the affairs of orphaned minors at the Cape from 1674 to 1834; WEESKAMER.

Similar in function to the English Court of Chancery.

1801 F. DUNDAS in G.M. Theal *Rec. of Cape Col.* (1899) IV. 12 Give notice thereof to the Secretary of the Orphan Chamber. **1806** *Cape Town Gaz. & Afr. Advertiser* July 19 The members of the Orphan Chamber of this Colony, intend .. to dispose of by Public Auction, the property of the Deceased Apothecary Leopold Mayer. *a***1823** J. EWART *Jrnl* (1970) 41 The Weeskamer or Orphan Chamber, a court consisting of a president, vice and four members like our Court of Chancery, regulates the affairs of orphan children, and takes charge of property which may be disputable, in order to have justice done to the parties concerned. *a***1878** J. MONTGOMERY *Reminisc.* (1981) 126 A few days after the death of either the father or mother of a family the property used to be sold by the so-called Orphan Chamber, and I have seen poor widows and orphans stripped of everything they possessed, and left to starve, under the pretence of securing the property for the children. **1887** *S.W. Silver & Co.'s Handbk to S. Afr.* 21 Far more beneficent in its operation was the Orphan Chamber, instituted to look after the interests of orphan children. **1928** E.A. WALKER *Hist. of S. Afr.* 45 The Orphan Chamber, .. two officials and two burghers under a president appointed by the Commander. No widow or widower might re-marry without satisfying this committee that the rights of their children had been safeguarded; the committee itself invested the orphans' money and thus played a useful part as a loan bank. **1936** *Cambridge Hist. of Brit. Empire* VIII. 154 An Orphan Chamber had been established as far back as 1674. **1969** D. CHILD *Yesterday's Children* 25 In 1674 a special Orphan Chamber was established at the Cape to safeguard the rights of children who had lost one or both parents. **1987** G. VINEY *Col. Houses* 99 The Orphan Chamber (the equivalent of today's Masters Office) maintained that it [*sc.* the will] was irregular. **1989** *Reader's Digest Illust. Hist.* 73 Maynier estranged him .. by sending him a letter demanding that he produce two guarantors for a loan that Van Jaarsveld had requested from the Orphan Chamber.

ossewa /ˈɔsəvɑː/ *n.* Pl. **-wae** /-vɑːə/, **-waens** /-vɑːəns/. [Afk., ox-wagon.]

1. *obs.* Always with initial capital. Short for *Ossewa Brandwag* (see OB *n.*[1]). Also *attrib.*

1941 *Bantu World* 22 Feb. 4 Ossewa Storm Troopers of Afrikanerdom. 'The members of the Ossewa Brandwag are, and shall always be, the Storm troopers of Afrikanerdom,' said Mr O. Pirow. **1943** A. CAMPBELL *Smuts & Swastika* 113 It became plain that the Ossewa, organised on military lines, with commandants and generals and 'Storm troops', was nothing more than a South African Nazi Party. **1947** G.A.L. GREEN *Editor Looks Back* 227 Hot-heads shriek for the complete suppression of the subversive organisation known as the Ossewa Brandwag (The Ox-Wagon Sentinel), but the Government .. wishes to avoid driving Ossewa underground.

‖**2.**

a. An ox-wagon.

1975 *Sunday Times* 20 Apr. 16 At the University of Pretoria there is an ossewa – the 100 per cent genuine article, as my friend the wholesaler would say. **1988** SPIEGEL & BOONZAIER in Boonzaier & Sharp *S. Afr. Keywords* 54 Monuments were erected, public holidays created, and even individual items such as the *ossewa* (oxwagon) and *kruithoring* (gunpowder flask) became powerful symbols of Afrikanerdom. **1990** *Weekend Mail* 6 July 11 *On the Wire* is the story of a community under siege. Where previously the *ossewa* fortified the laager, now the electrified wire fences of the title surround the dorp. **1993** 'NOT ONE OF THEM' in *Weekend Post* 19 June 9 (*letter*) There they will be able to discuss the good old days with *tannies* in their Voortrekker dresses and *kappies* and again be able to make use of their beloved *ossewaens*.

b. *fig.* OX-WAGON. Also *attrib.*

1975 *Sunday Times* 13 Apr. 4 Hansie explained to me that at Herstigte banquets in the Waterberg they did not have their dinner a la carte but a la ossewa. **1977** *Ibid.* 31 July 14 South Africa can no longer be .. excited by the belief that the verligtes will one day hijack the party ossewa and drag it into the future. **1980** M.Q. CARSTENS in *Cape Herald* 27 Dec. 12 We can no longer allow this sinful groot-trekker ossewa-mentality to preach love from the pulpit and set barriers in the pews. **1988** R. RUMNEY in *Weekly Mail* 18 Oct. 15 Townhouse complexes were built in the middle of the veld, like laagering the *ossewae* against possible total onslaught.

ostrich /ˈɒstrɪdʒ, ˈɒstrɪtʃ/ *n.* Used *attrib.* in Special Comb. **ostrich baron** *hist.*, a wealthy ostrich farmer; **ostrich camp** [see CAMP *n.*[2]], a large enclosed field in which ostriches are kept; **ostrich derby**, a race in which ostriches are used as mounts; **ostrich farm**, a farm on which ostriches are reared; hence **ostrich farmer, ostrich farming; ostrich palace** *hist.*, *feather palace* (see FEATHER sense b); **ostrich show-farm**, a farm where ostriches and ostrich products are displayed as a tourist attraction; **ostrich wool** *obs.*, see quot. 1833.

Because of the economic significance of the ostrich industry, many of these terms have become current in South Africa. Some are not found in general English; others are, but were first used in *S. Afr. Eng.* See also FEATHER.

1982 *S. Afr. Panorama* May 9 After the Anglo-Boer War, .. the Cape's **'ostrich barons'** were flourishing, building palatial residences for themselves. **1989** F.G. BUTLER *Tales from Old Karoo* 82 There was the farm, a huge Victorian ostrich baron's palace, with an ornate wooden verandah all round it. **1881** *Meteor* 31 May 2 To the east lay the thatched farmhouse of Mr H.B. Guest surrounded by a number of **Ostrich camps**, where could be see[n] the feathery lord of the arid plains stalking about his domains. **1883** M.A. CAREY-HOBSON *Farm in Karoo* 244 The next day they all went down to the ostrich camp. **1899** B. MITFORD *Weird of Deadly Hollow* 244 One night, a week or so later, the Baas heard something in the ostrich camp. **1933** W.H.S. BELL *Bygone Days* 42 The shrubbery had disappeared and the land it occupied had been converted into an ostrich camp. **1968** F. GOLDIE *Ostrich Country* 56 (*caption*) The famous **'ostrich derby'** on *Safari* farm. *c***1881** A. DOUGLASS *Ostrich Farming* 203 Cattle are an essential item on every **Ostrich farm**. **1885** A. NEWTON in *Encycl. Brit.* XVIII. 62 The great mercantile value of ostrich-feathers .. led to the formation in the Cape Colony .. of numerous 'Ostrich-farms'. **1930** M.F. WORMSER Ostrich Industry. Sect. viii. 19 Lasting fences .. cost a great deal of money, being .. one of the most expensive items in starting an ostrich farm. **1973** G.J. BROEKHUYSEN in *Std Encycl. of Sn Afr.* VIII. 397 Ostrich farms were established .. when the .. feathers .. were in great demand for women's hats. **1875** *S. Afr.* 223 **Ostrich farmers**, in domesticating the bird, have apparently a regard to moral training. **1896** R. WALLACE *Farming Indust. of Cape Col.* 221 Since the decline in value of ostrich feathers .. and the consequent narrowing of profits accruing to the ostrich farmer, artificial incubation had gone out of fashion. **1955** D.L. HOBMAN *Olive Schreiner* 95 Mattison had heard some rumours .. of her engagement to a young South African ostrich-farmer. **1971** B. BIERMANN *Red Wine* 143 The wealthy ostrich farmers of Oudtshoorn were building cast-iron palaces. **1875** *S. Afr.* 220 It is difficult to say who was the first to begin **ostrich-farming** at the Cape. **1880** *S.W. Silver & Co.'s Handbk to S. Afr.* 230 It may be considered a settled law of ostrich-farming that free space and good fences are essential to success. **1908** M.C. BRUCE *New Tvl* Ostrich farming is not .. a Transvaal industry, and has been confined chiefly to the Cape Colony and the Orange River Colony. **1970** C. VAN H. DU PLESSIS in *Std Encycl. of Sn Afr.* I. 246 Ostrich-farming made an important contribution to the development of the farming industry ... For the first time in South Africa pasture-land was fenced off. **1973** *Std Encycl. of Sn Afr.* VIII. 406 Of several **'ostrich palaces'**, built .. when the ostrich industry was at its peak, one named Pinehurst was proclaimed a historical monument in 1966. **1988** M. TRUMP in *Staffrider* Vol.7 No.1, 29 So-called ostrich-palaces .. were built at the end of the last century by Afrikaner farmers of the Oudtshoorn district with the wealth they had recently acquired during the ostrich feather boom. **1988** D. HUGHES et al. *Complete Bk of S. Afr. Wine* 294 In the town of Oudtshoorn a few examples still survive of the 'ostrich palaces', the ornately splendid Edwardian houses which sprang up here at the height of the ostrich feather boom at the beginning of the century. **1968** F. GOLDIE *Ostrich Country* 75 One of the great success stories of our day concerns the **ostrich show farms** .. outside Oudtshoorn. **1991** *Sn Afr. from Highway* 134 Ostrich show-farms .. fascinate many thousands of visitors each year. **1833** *S. Afr. Almanac & Dir.* 164 **Ostrich wool** .. is the soft down lying close under the feathers of the Ostrich. It is used in lieu of Beaver in Europe.

other coloured *ppl adj. phr.* and *n. phr. Hist.* Freq. with initial capitals. [See COLOURED.]

A. *ppl adj. phr.* Of or pertaining to a person who, during the apartheid era, was defined as 'Other Coloured' (see quot. 1959) in the system of race classification. See also COLOURED *ppl adj.*

1959 *Govt Gaz.* Vol.195 No.6191, 11 Other Coloured Group: In the Other Coloured Group shall be included any person who is not included in the Cape Coloured Group, the Malay Group, the Griqua Group, the Chinese Group, the Indian Group or the Other Asiatic Group, and who is not a white person or a native as defined in section *one* of the Population Registration Act, 1950. **1971** [see CLASSIFICATION]. **1989** *Frontline* Apr. 32 In my family there were brothers classified 'Cape Coloured' and others classified 'Other Coloured', which caused a problem because the 'Cape Coloureds' were supposed to be the real thing. **1991** B. ROBERTSON in *Sunday Times* 14 July (Extra) 8 There were many children of Oriental sailors and white prostitutes who were brought to welfare agencies ... The seamen were classified honorary whites and their offsprings were classified 'Other Coloured'.

B. *n. phr.* One who, during the apartheid era, was classified as a member of the officially-defined 'Other Coloured' group, a sub-group of the 'coloured' group in terms of the POPULATION REGISTRATION ACT. See also COLOURED *n.*

1978 *Drum* June 79 The offspring of a coloured guy and a black girl would usually be classified as an 'other coloured'. I say usually because there are some cases when the child is able to choose whether he wants to be classified as coloured or black.

Otiqua var. ODIQUA.

Ottentoo var. HOTTENTOT.

ou /əʊ/ *n. slang.* Formerly also **o**, and with initial capital. Pl. **-s**, **-ens** /-əns, -ənz/. [Afk., (pl. *ouens*) prob. fr. Du. *ouwe* an elderly man.]

1.a. 'Chap', 'guy', 'fellow', a general term of address or reference; OKE sense 1. See also OKIE.

Also common in township English.

Its (rare) application to a woman (see Drum quot. 1972) perhaps implies that she is 'one of the boys'.

1949 B.A. TINDALL in F.G. Butler *When Boys Were Men* (1969) 270 He was a strict disciplinarian, but always just, and .. we all loved the '*Ou*'. **1960** J. TAYLOR 'Ballad of the Southern Suburbs'. (*lyrics*) Ag, Pleeze, Deddy, won't you take us to the wrestling, We wanna see an ou called Sky-High Lee. **1962** — 'Jeremy Taylor.' (*record*), I was on the radio the other day, being interviewed, and this announcer ou, he said to me, he said, 'Mr Taylor', he said, 'do you really speak like this? I mean — hell!' **1964** [see *boomy* (BOOM *n.*)]. **1970** *Forum* Vol.6 No.2, 28 'Have any of you ous got a radio? ' he demanded. **1972** *Cape Times* 1 Aug., (*editorial*) To rank as a lekker ou at Bishops, Michaelhouse or St. Andrews is surely not to have lived in vain. **1972** *Drum* 22 Nov. 24 The gang was taken over by a woman. She is big and fat, and a blerry clever ou. [**1972** R. MALAN *Ah Big Yaws* 37 *Oh*, Nothing to do with the English exclamation .. but a general word for 'another man', 'a person', 'the other fellow' ... Variants exist, such as *Oke, Okie*, .. with pride of place going to the famous plural *Use-ose*.] **1975** 'BLOSSOM' in *Darling* 9 Oct. 95 Hang, if there's one thing turns me off a ou it's greasy hair. **1976** *E. Prov. Herald* 28 Sept. 5 (*advt*) If there's one thing this 'O' can't stand it's seeing good petrol go to waste. **1987** L. BEAKE *Strollers* 16, I remembered once when she got in a fight with the police. Three of them laid out, big heavy ous too. **1989** *Frontline* Apr. 26 White survival has got nothing to do with stopping a black ou from resting on the grass. **1992** C. DU PLESSIS in *Style* 95 Ironically, the Market Theatre has turned down his work, one in which 'the black *ou* is the villain'.

b. With qualifying word designating a particular sort of 'chap' or 'fellow': see *lekker ou* (LEKKER *adj.* sense 1 c), MAIN OU.

2.a. In *pl.*: Collectively, people of a particular type or origin; cf. OKE sense 2.

1961 *Personality* 16 May 27 It's a lekker language, and those overseas ous often sound pretty snaaks themselves. **1984** *Frontline* Feb. 25 The mountain and the sea and all that goed .. is actually quite lekker and gives these ous a bit of an edge over us ous who have to go shlepping to hellangorn off to the Magaliesberg for a bit of natural-type recreation ... You get these ouens from Joeys who make a big deal of taking holidays in Venice and Paris and such places. **1984** *Ibid.* May 38 Who else has ever come up with a TV station which only ouens of one race are meant to see? **1986** 'KNOCKESPOTCH' in *Ibid.* June 34 Opposition ous can't tell their arses from sedition. **1990** D. BECKETT in *Ibid.* Mar.-Apr. 10 'Jeez,' says the garage man, 'don't these railways ous know about computers?'

b. With distinguishing epithet: see quot. See also CHAR OU, *roti ou* (see ROTI sense 2), WIT OU.

1978 L. BARNES in *The 1820* Vol.51 No.12, 19 The Afrikaans word *ou* seems to have caught on in Natal just as much as in other parts of the country. There are *chaar ous* (Indians); *roti ous* (Hindi speakers) .. ; *wit ous* .. ; *bruin ous* (Coloureds) and *pekkie ous* (Blacks).

3. With the indefinite article: 'one'.

1963 A. FUGARD *Blood Knot* (1968) 15 What sort of a thing was that to do to a ou's own flesh and blood brother? *Ibid.* 94 Friday nights it was, when a ou's got pay in his pocket and there's no work tomorrow. **1969** — *People are Living There* 73 Susy: .. Do something! Shorty: But what? What must a ou do? **1970** *Forum* Vol.6 No.2, 28 The fat one's got a bust hey? God man, an ou could sit down on it for a rest! **1990** S. CILLIERS in *Frontline* Jan. 9, I felt terrible. I didn't want to go to the bar ... But an ou gets stubborn. I wanted to be allowed to go to the bar.

4. In urban (esp. township) Eng.: **a.** A friend.

b. MAIN MAN.

1972 *Evening Post* 30 Sept. 4 Most .. said they carried weapons because they were afraid of the 'skollies, or ouens' in their neighbourhood. **1980** *Voice* 20 Aug. 14 Township slang prefers the flashy, modern, up-to-date and hip. However .. it also has a tradition, conservatism, and certain basic terms and styles that never seem to go out of use. These are: ausi, bra, cherrie, dovola, .. ou, [etc.]. **1981** *Pace* Sept. 174 The next thing, imagine, you see him dishing out for 'die ouens' at Number Four Fort Prison. [**1986** T. THOKA in *Eng. Usage in Sn Afr.* Vol.17 No.2, 19 Tsotsie-taal has .. certain basic terms .. that never seem to go out of use. For example, the following words: ausie (sister), bra (brother), cherry (girl), ou (friend).]

‖**ou** /əʊ/ *adj.* Also with initial capital, and (formerly) **oud**. [Afk. *ou*, earlier Du. *oud* old.] Old, elder.

1. In collocations and special collocations, as a term of address or reference:

a. With a name or title, a respectful term of address or reference to an older person. See also OUBAAS, OUBOET, OUMA, OUPA.

1838 J.E. ALEXANDER *Exped. into Int.* II. 231 We had not been long among Henrick Buy's people, before his elder brother, 'oud Jan,' rejoined us. **1905** P. GIBBON *Vrouw Grobelaar* 197 They bore the body to the shade of the tobacco shed. 'And now,' said Peter .. 'who is to tell the ou tante?' **1939** 'D. RAME' *Wine of Good Hope* 80 Has Mis' 'Tonia seen the Ou-Missis? **1968** G. CROUDACE *Silver Grass* 27 *Ou* Adriaan, as he was called, welcomed them with the grave dignity of the Afrikaner patriarch. **1970** M. MULLER *Cloud across Moon* 14 Ou Christiaan and Ou Attie, who had worked for Trina for over thirty years, were busy in the garden. **1971** A. FUGARD *Hello & Goodbye* 13, I hate them when they're like that — fat and dressed in black .. because somebody's dead, and calling me Ou Sister. **1975** *E. Prov. Herald* 12 June 2 Mr Murray said he could not wait for the time when Dr Koornhof became 'Oom Piet'. 'As long as I don't become "Ou Piet",' Dr Koornhof interjected. **1980** C. HOPE *A Separate Development* (1983) 169 Pielletjies, *ou* Neels, Lubavitch and Stokkies all came with me on the day I was taken to see the terrible Mr. Dekker. **1985** *Fair Lady* 1 May 20 Ag, poor ou Wallaby. I always knew your memory wasn't too lekker. **1987** M. MELAMU *Children of Twilight* 43 Ou Johannes had been Ferreira's 'boss-boy'.

b. With a name, an affectionate or jocular term of address or reference.

1975 'BLOSSOM' in *Darling* 9 Apr. 95 She may be a moaner but she's not dumb, ou Trix. **1985** P. SLABOLEPSZY *Sat. Night at Palace* 29 We got to phone ou Dougie now. **1990** 'K. LEMMER' in *Weekly Mail* 8 Feb. 11 *Ou* FW said he was going to scrap all this race classification in the interests of a future that will at least be grey if not altogether rosy. **1991** — in *Ibid.* 19 Apr. 10 You know, I was probably a little harsh on *ou* Chris B— last week when I pointed out that he claimed to have called for the release of Nelson Mandela 30 years ago, three years before Nelson Mandela was jailed.

c. Special collocations. **ou china**, 'old mate'; **ou kêrel**, see KÊREL sense 1 b; **ou maat**, see MAAT sense 2; **ou pellie**, see PELLIE; **ou seun** /- siœn/ [Afk., *seun* son, boy], 'old son'.

1975 C. HOPE in *Bolt* No.12, 5 How's it **ou china**, ou bebops, ou maat — Ek se, major, can you battle us some start? **1960** C. HOOPER *Brief Authority* 225 'The Western Front — where's that?' 'Zeerust, **ou seun**. There where the kaffirs are making riots.'

2. Belonging to a time in the past.

1946 H.C. BOSMAN in L. Abrahams *Cask of Jerepigo* (1972) 162, I was also astonished at the extent of my familiarity with historical events .. that had taken place in the ou Transvaal.

3. Traditional, old-style.

1974 *Sunday Times* 12 May 14 Every patriotic South African is now under a duty to fill the lads up with anything and everything from buchu brandy to a flagon of ou dop. **1988** J. CRWYS-WILLIAMS in *Style* Mar. 18 Also available .. are first courses of the like of ou Kaapse snoek pâté.

oubaas /ˈəʊbɑːs/ *n.* Also **oû baas**, **oud baas**, and with initial capital(s). Pl. (rare) **oubase**. [Afk. (earlier S. Afr. Du.), fr. Du. *oud* old + *baas* master (see BAAS). Cf. OU *adj.* sense 1 a.] The elderly male owner of a home, farm, or business, the employer of the servants and labourers who work there; an elderly manager or supervisor; an elderly white man. Cf. OUMISSUS.

1. Usu. with initial capital, not preceded by an article: a title, with a proper name, or used as a deferential alternative to a proper name; OLD BAAS sense 2; OLD-BOSS sense 2.

1824 W.J. BURCHELL *Trav.* II. 95 She told me that *Oud Baas* had tied her up to one of the wheels of the waggon and flogged her for a long time. **1868** W.R. THOMSON *Poems, Essays & Sketches* 153 Oû Baas .. rushed out and nearly dragged the young man from his horse in the vehemence of his welcome. **1869** T. BAINES *Diary* (1946) 59 They recognised at once and were rather pleased with the likeness of 'Oud Baas', Mr. Hartley. **1959** *Cape Times* 5 June 13, I recognized him as *oubaas* De Greef. **1971** *Post* 28 Mar. 22 One of my two battered cars .. should be sent to Oubaas Piet van der Merwe of Warden, Free State. **1974** *S. Afr. Panorama* Sept. 41 His [*sc.* Craven's] game caught the attention of 'Oubaas' Markotter, then coach of the university teams. **1980** A. PATON *Towards Mountain* 181 Mr. H.C. Fick, known to all, boys and staff, as Oubaas, a man of about forty, was now put in charge of all the gardens. **1982** *Sunday Times* 30 May (Mag. Sect.) 1, Is this the right number for Oubaas Wilkinson, the veteran who fought in the Boer War?

2. A form of address; OUBASIE sense 2. Cf. O.B. *n.*[2]

Sometimes substituted for the second person pronoun 'you', reflecting the respectful third-person form of address used in Afrikaans (see quots 1953 and 1991).

1914 L.H. BRINKMAN *Breath of Karroo* 24 The master of the house is addressed as 'Ou baas'. **1940** F.B. YOUNG *City of Gold* 419 Never you mind, ou baas ... Why the hell should it matter to you if the farm goes to blazes? **1946** V. POHL *Land of Distant Horizons* 50 The Hottentot exclaimed indignantly: 'Oubaas, if I have never told the truth, I am telling it now.' **1952** [see OUPA sense 1]. **1953** U. KRIGE *Dream & Desert* 91 'Why on earth is Oubaas looking at a dead painted old tree,' she broke into his reverie. **1973** in *Hansard* 16 Mar. 2807 Old Koos .. said: 'Oubaas, .. I don't know why you should start so late.' **1979** F. DIKE *First S. African* 20 Oubaas I'm looking for my master oubaas. **1990** R. STENGEL *January Sun* 45, I used to see my father referring to whites in — how should I say it? — he referred to them with awe and undue respect. To an old white man, he would say, *Oubaas*, and to a woman, he would say *Missus*. **1991** B. MACKENZIE tr. F.P. Van den Heever in *Best of S. Afr. Short Stories* 58 How come the Oubaas travels tonight on Shank's old pony just like a Jew trader? What's happened to the transport?

3. A common noun; OLD BAAS sense 1; OLD-BOSS sense 1; OUBASIE sense 1.

1931 F.C. SLATER *Secret Veld* 44 He .. indicated that I would find the 'Ou Baas' at the house ... The 'Ou Baas' .. — as the phrase signifies — was a gentleman of venerable appearance. **1942** 'B. KNIGHT' *Sun Climbs Slowly* 286 No, it was not the *Oubaas*, she said, but someone she had not seen before. **1952** E.H. BURROWS *Overberg Outspan* 161 These were the people who congregated on Sundays with the family to hear the *oubaas* read a chapter of the Bible. **1959** *Cape Times* 14 Feb. 3 Joe told him that he and Moyisi had hit the *oubaas* with kieries. **1963** A.M. LOUW *20 Days* 18 The nasty oubaas on the next farm .. sent other people's stray animals to the pound. **1974** [see OUBASIE sense 1]. **1977** *Family Radio & TV* 25 Sept. 53 Most *oubase* don't drink heavily. **1980** E. JOUBERT *Poppie Nongena*

340 Just let the Oubaas say: O.K. I give you your rights, and I'll say: O.K. tomorrow I go to the border with a gun. **1982** M. MZAMANE *Children of Soweto* 184 'Now, you *blerry skelm*, will you tell the *Oubaas* who your student leaders are?' he asked. **1987** *Frontline* Mar. 22 Far from the rioting crowds of Soweto and light years away from the street-wise man about the township, the life of Jonas on the farm goes on much as it did when his grandfather worked for the Oubaas at the time of the Rinderpest. **1991** [see SPIDER]. **1993** N. WEST in *Sunday Times* 16 May 6 If the old ideologue and apartheid patriarch, Dr Hendrik Frensch Verwoerd had heard his grandson .. proclaiming the virtues of the ANC and denouncing the NP, the oubaas would surely have turned in his grave.

4. *hist.* An affectionate nickname given to Jan Christian Smuts, second Prime Minister of the Union of South Africa; *Oom Jannie*, see OOM sense 1 b. See also *Ouma Smuts* (OUMA sense 3 b).

1943 *Weekend News & Sunday Mag.* 20 Mar. 4 It was ergreed dat we soud send de Ou Baas er letter orf welkom an hold er Jan Smuts Ball. **1947** *Forum* 19 Apr. 1 The problems which faced the Oubaas this week ranged from the spreading boycott of Indian traders in the Transvaal .. to the need for separate trade unions for Africans. **1950** H. GIBBS *Twilight* 249 Henry Cooper .. has devoted his life to 'the Oubaas', as Smuts is called. **1950** *Star* in J. Crwys-Williams *S. Afr. Despatches* (1989) 300 As the first light glanced across the eastern hills on lovely Doornkloof farm, it fell on a house of grief. Who there but felt the pangs of loss at the Oubaas's passing? *c*1963 B.C. TAIT *Durban Story* 69 From here 'Oubaas' (Field-Marshal Smuts) stepped down at sunrise to bathe in the sea-girt pool across the railtrack. **1970** *Daily News* 19 May 3 Once again, South Africa will be able to hear the voice of 'Oubaas' when recordings of his speeches .. will be used in the programme. **1987** G. VINEY *Col. Houses* 183 Field Marshall and Mrs Smuts ('Oubaas' and 'Ouma') amongst the cannas during the Second World War. **1990** *Fair Lady* 7 Nov. 8 Ouma Smuts .. was darning a pair of Oubaas's socks when some American tourists arrived.

5. *Obs. Prison slang.* With initial capital. The former Roeland Street prison, Cape Town.

1956 A. LE GUMA in *New Age* 27 Sept. 6 In Roeland Street, Cape Town .. stands the mass of brick and stone which is the city jail ... Hardened old-timers refer to it with macabre humour as 'Oubaas,' and behind its walls exists a world ruled by stony-eyed guards who have become as cold as the iron bars over the windows.

6. *fig.* Always with initial capital: God.

1972 *Star* 8 Dec. 9 One hundred years old .. Mrs Annie Hayman .. explains her century by saying: 'The Oubaas likes me, and that's why he looks after me.' **1974** *Het Suid-Western* 25 Apr., Jackson .. with the help of the 'Oubaas in the sky' succeeded in smashing the plug and breaking the current. [**1984** E. EUVRARD in *Sunday Times* 11 Nov. (Life Style) 115, I used to feel sorry for *die Oubaas daar bo* because my mother and I used to sit, one on either side of the bed, each praying fervently for the exact opposite!] **1991** D. GUY in *City Press* 27 Oct. 31 The promises of the UDF, DTA and Swapo do not help. Only the Oubaas up there will help.

oubasie /ˈəʊbɑːsi/ *n. colloq.* Also **oubassy**. [Afk., formed on *oubaas* (see prec.) + -IE.]

1. OUBAAS sense 3.

1974 *E. Prov. Herald* 19 Apr. 5 Representatives of the South African Railways non-White staff yesterday paid tribute to their retiring 'Oubaas', Minister Ben Schoeman ... The non-Whites stated that as the 'children of the "oubassy"', they had never been better treated.

2. OUBAAS sense 2.

1979 M. MATSHOBA *Call Me Not a Man* 105 'They have just paid their mother a visit from their other mother, *oubasie*,' replied Angie with a smile by way of explanation.

ouble(e)tjie, oublie(tje) varr. OBLIETJIE.

ouboet /ˈəʊbʊt/ *n. colloq.* [Afk., *ou* old + *boet* see BOET. Cf. OU *adj.* sense 1 a.]

1. An affectionate form of address or reference to an older brother, or to a male friend; also used as a title before a man's first name; OUBOETIE sense 1. See also BOET senses 1 and 2.

[**1949** H. KEPPEL-JONES *When Smuts Goes* The Ministers have been summoned urgently; they arrive one by one, a little out of breath, flushed. '*Middat*, Mr President.' '*Middat*, Mr President'. '*Middat, ou Boet*.'] **1953** U. KRIGE *Dream & Desert* 10 Kleinboet would call him Ouboet, eldest brother. Ouboet ... It was such a good name, it had such a full round sound. **1961** D. BEE *Children of Yesterday* 203 I've still got my own elephants to get. You understand, don't you, ou boet. **1963** L. VAN DER POST *Seed & Sower* 75 When I begged his pardon awkwardly .. he would look at me warmly and say quickly, 'But it was nothing, Ouboet, nothing at all.' **1963** K. MACKENZIE *Dragon to Kill* 72 A policeman was saying to the drunk Coloured ... 'We will put the Flying Squad on to look for your bicycle ... If necessary, we will call out the military. As soon as we find it we will let you know, *ou boet*.' **1982** *Sunday Times* 5 Sept. 4 No, no Cappy ou Boet, this is certainly not 'the winter of my discontent'. **1983** *Ibid.* 8 May (Mag. Sect.) 23 If you could, you'd get right there in the ring with him .. and you'd grab hold of his arms and force the fists this way and that way and you'd damn well win the fight for him, *ouboet*. **1990** [see Leonard quot. at TOPPIE *n.*[2]].

2. *rare.* Used as a common noun.

1971 on Radio South Africa 4 June, There are seven of you? So you've got lots of ouboets?

ouboetie /ˈəʊˌbʊti/ *n. colloq.* Also **auboetie**. [Afk., *ouboet* (see prec.) + -IE.]

1. OUBOET sense 1. Cf. AUBUTI.

1913 A.B. MARCHAND *Dirk, S. African* (Swart), The family debt is mine ou Boetie, and if I spend my life over it I'm going to pay it off. *a*1968 D.C. THEMBA in E. Patel *World of Can Themba* (1985) 35 She looked around in panic; at me, at the old lady opposite her, at the hulk of a man opposite me. Then she whimpered, 'Ah, *Au-boetie*, I don't even know you.' **1978** M.J. MTSAKA *Not his Pride* 33 Now, stupid woman comes to me ... 'Ouboetie, tell me why they're counting us, do you know?' **1988** J. KHUMALO in *Pace* Nov. 21 After conferring with Ouboetie (big brother) Thabiso, leader of the Eagles Peak pilgrims, we agreed to take them along as they said they were only hitching a ride to our next port of call.

2. Used in the third person as a deferential form of address to a man.

1963 B. MODISANE *Blame Me on Hist.* (1986) 285 'Hau,' Daisy said, 'I was saying there is nobody — I come to take the tea things. Why is auboetie sitting in the dark? Was auboetie asleep?'

oudbaas var. OUBAAS.

oude(n)hout var. OUHOUT.

‖**ouderling** /ˈəʊdə(r)ləŋ/ *n.* Pl. **-e** /-ə/, and (formerly) **-en**. [Afk. (pl. *-e, -s*), earlier S. Afr. Du. (pl. *-en*) fr. Du.]

1. An elder of the Dutch Reformed Church.

1821 C.I. LATROBE *Jrnl of Visit* 503 He is now required once a year to visit the families in their dwellings, in company of an ouderling or deacon. [**1877** F. JEPPE *Tvl Bk Almanac & Dir.* (1976) 38 The Church is ruled by a general Church Meeting consisting of the clergy, the half of the serving Churchwardens (Dienst doende Ouderlingen) and two Deacons .. from each congregation.] **1906** A.H. WATKINS *From Farm to Forum* 34 He holds the highly honoured and responsible position of an 'ouderling' or elder in the church at Hopetown. [**1921** H.J. MANDELBROTE tr. *O.F. Mentzel's Descr. of Cape of G.H.* I. 124 Before the sermon is delivered two elders (ouderlinge) step up to the pulpit with collection plates in their hands.] **1935** H.C. BOSMAN *Mafeking Rd* (1969) 74 We had no predikant there; but an ouderling, with two bandoliers slung across his body, and a Martini in his hand, said a few words. **1948** [see DOMINEE sense 2 a]. **1949** L.G. GREEN *In Land of Afternoon* 143 When he entered a new district he selected a man of standing, a leading farmer or ouderling of the church. **1957** — *Beyond City Lights* 230 He became an *ouderling* in the Dutch Reformed Church. **1958** A. JACKSON *Trader on Veld* 34 All the leading farmers were ouderlings (elders), who, on the Sabbath, clad in their 'swart manel' .. took their duties very seriously. [**1965** C. VAN HEYNINGEN *Orange Days* 30 There were 'ouderlinge en diakens' to help him run the church, but he had to do all the christening and marrying and funeral services and often went visiting the sick and the bereaved.] **1972** *Cape Times* 8 Nov. 1 He was unhappy about the whole thing. As chief ouderling, he was also in trouble with his church. **1978** [see BONUS BOND]. **1980** A. PATON *Towards Mountain* 195 Mr Laas was a devout member of this powerful church, and held the office of *Ouderling*, or 'elder.' **1991** D. BECKETT in *Sunday Star* 3 Feb. (Review) 5 Dr Danie brought his bull mastiff, Bliksem, to his second wedding .. and seated Bliksem in the best man's pew, causing major upset among the ouderlinge — not so much because of the canine as because of the name. **1994** [see DRC].

2. Special Comb. **ouderlingpille** /-pələ/ *colloq.* [Afk., *pille* pills], peppermints.

1955 W. ILLSLEY *Wagon on Fire* 64 One cleared his throat noisily, the others sucked at their pipes or chewed tobacco or '**ouderlingpille**' (the name given to peppermints, to which, it was alleged, the Church Elders were very partial, since they sweetened the breath after surreptitious drinks).

‖**ouderwetse** /ˌəʊdə(r)ˈvetsə/ *adj.* Also **oudewetse**. [Afk.] Old-fashioned.

1891 H.J. DUCKITT *Hilda's 'Where Is It?'* 167 Pie (Old-fashioned Dutch). ('Ouderwetse Pasty' ..). **1913** D. FAIRBRIDGE *Piet of Italy* 156 He has pulled down the old homestead and built a fine new one with an iron roof and a striped verandah. 'What's the good of an oudewetse thatched roof?' he says. **1915** — *Torch Bearer* 26 Poor Mrs. le Sueur ... To think .. that she should have to live in that oudewetse house, just as it came from her husband's mother, without any modern improvements! **1971** L.G. GREEN *Taste of S.-Easter* 89, I like to think of Victorian housewives in Manchester poring over the mebos recipe and a Cockney 'bus-driver coming home to find Mrs J. Cloete's ouderwetse chicken pie on the table.

Oud Grietje var. OU GRIETJIE.

oud-hout, oudklip varr. OUHOUT, OUKLIP.

oud mamma see OUMA sense 1.

oudstryder /ˈəʊtstreɪdə(r)/ *n. hist.* Also **outstryder**. [Afk., *oud* old, former + *stryder* fighter.] A veteran who fought for the Boer Republics, esp. during the Anglo-Boer War of 1899–1902. Also *attrib.*, and *fig.*

1942 J.H. GROBLER in *Hansard* 23 Mar. 4326 Oudstryders receive pensions because they rendered recognised services to the country in the past. **1947** *Cape Argus* 29 Mar. 1 More than 1,600 Oudstryders to-day waited to give the Royal Family their own special welcome. **1956** L.G. GREEN *Secret Hid Away* 37 A restless spirit prevailed in the Western Transvaal after the outbreak of World War I, for it seemed to a section of the *oudstryders* that this was their chance of regaining the independence of the old republics. **1970** *S. Afr. Panorama* Nov., The unveiling .. was attended by a gathering of more than 1000 amongst whom were many oudstryders (veterans) of the Anglo-Boer War. **1975** *Friend* 4 June 6 Put a Nationalist MP on the platform in Gezina when battle is joined with Dr Albert Hertzog's political *oudstryders* and up goes the volume again, blasting out old-fashioned *verkramptheid* in gory stereo. **1975** *E. Prov. Herald* 13 Oct. 11 The uncompromising Boer *outstryder* .. told the Queen that he could never forgive the British for fighting against the Boers. The Queen was all sympathy; as a Scot, she said, she understood his feelings perfectly. **1982** *Sunday Times* 30 May (Mag. Sect.) 1 A boy who never actually fought, but still became a PoW qualified for an oudstryder, or veteran, pension. **1993** J. MERVIS in *Sunday Times* 16 May 20 *A member of the AWB*, an Oudstryder's hat, khaki shirt and shorts, velskoens, shotgun and a .. moustache calculated to frighten the daylights out of the selectors.

Ou Grietjie /ˌəʊ 'xriki/ *n. phr. Hist.* Also **Oud Grietje**. [Afk., *ou* (fr. Du. *oud*) old + *Griet* short form of woman's name *Magriet* (Margaret) + -IE; see quot. 1974.] A nickname given to a cannon used by the Boers; GRIETJIE.

It is not clear whether the name was given to one particular cannon, or to a type of cannon.

1899 *Mafeking Mail* 5 Dec., During the week the [polo] ground had been well levelled, notwithstanding oud Grietje and her colleagues. **1951** T.V. BULPIN *Lost Trails of Low Veld* 55 All its protective armament he seized as well, two muzzle-loading cannon of the variety known affectionately to the trekkers as Ou Grietjies (Old Margarets). **1967** E. ROSENTHAL *Encycl. of Sn Afr.* 402 *Ou Grietjie*, (Little Old Greta). Nickname for historic ship's cannon used by Voortrekkers in campaigns against Zulus and Matebele. **1971** F.V. LATEGAN in *Std Encycl. of Sn Afr.* IV. 534 With regard to the Battle of Blood River .. the commando had three small field-pieces — a small bronze cannon .. and two three-pounders ... One of these, known as 'Ou Grietjie', was later .. used effectively against the British camp at Potchefstroom. **1974** E.A. VENTER in *Ibid.* X. 14 'Ou Grietjie', a cannon used by the Free Staters in the Basuto wars and named after Margaret (Grietjie), wife of the gunner Robert Finlay, has been mounted in front of the magistrate's office. **1978** *Reader's Digest Illust. Guide* 307 An old relic in the town [of Smithfield] is a former ship's gun named Ou Grietjie ('Old Margaret'). The gun has an unknown origin, but it was carried about the Central Plains for many years and used in various wars against the Sotho, and even as a threat against the Transvaal (when two unsuccessful attempts were made to fire the gun). In 1860 the weapon was brought to Smithfield ... The gun was last used in 1868 to bombard Thaba-Bosiu during the final Basuto War.

ouhout /'əʊhəʊt/ *n.* Also **oude(n)hout, oudhout.** [Afk. (earlier S. Afr. Du. *oudenhout*), *ou(d)* old + *hout* wood; see quot. 1983.] Any of several shrubs or small trees: **a.** Either of two species of *Halleria* of the Scrophulariaceae, *H. lucida* or *H. elliptica*. See also NOTSUNG. **b.** *Cordia caffra* of the Boraginaceae. **c.** The DWADWA, *Leucosidea sericea*.

In F. von Breitenbach's *Nat. List of Indigenous Trees* (1987), the name 'septee tree' is used for *C. Caffra*; see also notes at DWADWA, NOTSUNG.

1862 L. PAPPE *Silva Capensis* 30 *Halleria Elliptica* .. (*Oudehout*) ... Used chiefly for plough-beams, axe handles, *c* **1911** *Agric. Jrnl of Union* June 717 (Pettman), Two good bee plants here (Lady Frere) are the tree *oudenhout* and the wild coffee, both flowering in the spring. **1913** C. PETTMAN *Africanderisms* 354 *Oudehout*, .. This name is applied to several different trees, among them being *Cordia caffra* and *Leucosidea sericea*. The name has reference apparently to the fact that the wood of these trees is seldom straight. **1977** E. PALMER *Field Guide to Trees* 115 *Leucosidea*, One species only. *Oudehout. Leucosidea sericea.* **1980** *E. Prov. Herald* 3 Sept. 13 A few [trees] .. are pretty common and could easily become known: Ilala Palm, Ouhout, [etc]. **1980** *S. Afr. Digest* 17 Oct. 15 Ouhout .. , also known as Oubos, isiDwadwa (*Leucosidea sericea*) ... The resemblance of the trunk and branches to either a wrinkled old man or to weathered wood probably accounts for its common name. **1983** K.C. PALGRAVE *Trees of Sn Afr.* 208 *Leucosidea sericea*, .. Ouhout ... The common name *ouhout* may refer to the old gnarled twisted trunks, or to the fact that the wood burns slowly as if it were old and rotting.

ouk var. OKE.

ou kappie var. OKAPI.

oukie var. OKIE.

‖**ouklip** /'əʊkləp/ *n. Geology.* Also (occas.) **oaklip, oudklip, outklip.** [Afk., *ou* old + *klip* stone (fr. S. Afr. Du. *ouderklip*).] An iron-rich lateritic conglomerate, formed from the decomposition of underlying rocks by subsurface chemical weathering. Also *attrib.*

1892 *The Jrnl* 20 Sept. 2 A few months ago it was discovered .. that large beds of Ou Klip (honeycomb gravel rock) on the farm were literally saturated with mercury. [**1926** A.L. DU TOIT *Geology S. Afr.* XVII. 361 In many parts of South Africa a peculiar ferruginous material can be observed resting either directly upon the decomposed underlying rocks or more usually with the intervention of sandy clays .. Called by the Dutch farmers 'ouderklip' or 'ouclip', it is supposed by them to represent a lava flow of great antiquity, whereas on the contrary it is generally the youngest formation present.] **1940** *Min. Resources of Union of S. Afr.* (Dept of Mines) IV. 458 There are many types of laterite or 'ouklip' in this country. The harder types of conglomerate ouklip generally form a very good basecourse for bitumen ... Some types of soft conglomerate ouklip which contain an appreciable quantity of sandy soil binder generally yield satisfactory sand-clay bases ... The pebble type ouklip .. consists mostly of fairly hard lateritic pebbles and soil binder. **1955** J.H. WELLINGTON *Sn Afr.: Geog. Study* I. 289 In the western highlands of Natal, Pentz recognizes a third grassveld type .. in which the infertile sandy soils, underlain by 'ouklip' (i.e. pirolitic ironstone) produce a poor type of veld. **1958** S. CLOETE *Mask* 186 The soil changed to oaklip. The veld changed. **1961** M. COLE *S. Afr.* 87 The weathering processes .. result in the formation of soils comprising an A horizon of some 12 to 24 inches of friable sand .. overlying a B horizon of mottled clayey-sand containing many ferruginous concretions which in the lower part are cemented to form a hardpan called 'ouklip'. **1970** Memorandum of Agreement. (A.R. Whiteley & Co.) Sept., No allowance is included for excavation in abnormal circumstances such as waterlogged soil, hard or soft rock, shale, ouklip or ground containing boulders. **1973** *Farmer's Weekly* 9 May 65 The soil is poor being yellow turf about 0,75m deep on ou klip conglomerate. The presence of 'ouklip' layers just under the surface of a soil means poor drainage and gives rise to 'drowning' of plants in wet seasons. **1983** *S. Afr. Garden & Home* Mar. 126 The plants .. probably have not been able to send their roots out into the outklip ... They may also be waterlogged — as the water would not drain away in the outklip. **1988** D. HUGHES et al. *Complete Bk of S. Afr. Wine* 55 Kroonstad has a sandy top layer with an iron-bearing pan of peculiar hard, nuggety forms known as *ouklip*, just above the clay.

Oukoolukoolu var. UNKULUNKULU.

oulap /'əʊlap/ *adj.* and *n. Colloq.* Also (occas.) **ollap, ou'lap.** [Afk., fr. Du. *oude lap*, 'old rag', something of little value.]

A. *adj. obs.* Of little worth.

1908 *E. London Dispatch* 29 Sept. (Pettman), Writes a correspondent (says the 'Worcester Standard') from one of the ou'lap districts of the South-West. **1913** C. PETTMAN *Africanderisms* 354 *Ou'lap*, .. The word is also used as an adjective in a disparaging sense.

B. *n. Obs.* exc. *hist.* A penny; a pennyworth. Cf. DUBBELTJE *n.*² sense 2.

1912 *Northern Post* 20 June (Pettman), Sixpenny bits were a rarity, and the penny or oulap was a practically useless coin. **1913** C. PETTMAN *Africanderisms* 354 *Ou'lap*, .. A penny is often called an 'ou'lap', as being a coin of little worth. **1926** [see DUBBELTJE *n.*² sense 2]. *c***1929** [see CAFÉ DE MOVE-ON]. **1947** L.G. GREEN *Tavern of Seas* 14 Some .. coloured phrase-maker early last century fixed the penny forever as an 'ou lap' — valueless old rag. **1965** D. MARAIS in *Cape Times* 14 May, (*cartoon*) No more penny, no more ollap, no more stuiwer and jus' now no tickey. Jislike! The old Cape tradition is taking a beating. **1970** S. SMUTS *Informant, Cape Town* The young boy asked me for an oulap (penny). **1981** *Cape Times* 10 Jan. 12 Many of us will remember with affection the use of the colloquialism ou lap for a penny ... The derivation is Nederlands oude lap, meaning something of little material value.

ouma /'əʊma/ *n.* Also **ou-ma, ou'ma, ou ma.** [Afk., *ou* old (fr. Du. *oud*) + *ma* mother. Cf. OU *adj.* sense 1 a.] 'Grandmother', 'granny', denoting a parent's mother, or, informally, any other elderly woman. Cf. OUPA.

1. A respectful form of address or reference; OUMATJIE. In the speech of children, formerly also **oud mamma**.

1841 B. SHAW *Memorials* 112 She appeared to be at least seventy years of age; and in the afternoon of the day she was surrounded by a group of children, who had undertaken the arduous task, of teaching '*oud mamma*', the new song of thanks-giving. **1926** P. SMITH *Beadle* (1929) 21 His grandmother .. could have made it to-day for only one person ... 'Ou-ma! Ou-ma!' he cried, 'Is it then for Magdalena?' **1937** S. CLOETE *Turning Wheels* 423 'I am sorry, Ouma,' he said, 'to find you like this.' **1944** C.R. PRANCE *Under Blue Roof* 136 Early marriage was desirable, .. to confer on eager parents the dignity of Ou-pa and Ou-ma. **1961** T. MACDONALD *Tvl Story* 109 He was very humorous. I heard him refer to Queen Victoria as Ouma ... He was asked about the franchise for the Uitlanders. He said that the time factor had to be considered 'because there is the danger that we shall find our cart in Ouma's wagon-house.' **1973** *Cape Times* 6 June 9 Farmer's wives gather the makings for ouma's gargantuan recipe for 100 metres of boerewors. **1979** M. MATSHOBA *Call Me Not a Man* 5 You want to say I'm lying *ouma*? It says here you are in arrears to the amount of one hundred rand with your rent, maan! **1981** *Oude Libertas* Vol.9 No.4, 11 Sosaties in their different sauces. Not perhaps like ouma used to make them, but they were pronounced most delicious. **1984** *Sunday Times* 29 Jan. 10 Debbie is holding a syringe. Come now, ouma. She's going to be all right. The old woman calms down. **1993** M. GEVISSER in *Weekly Mail* 8 Apr. 9, I visited a reconstructed home one step behind the Brand family from Pretoria ... 'Look at that bath! It's just like Ouma's!'

2. A common noun.

1905 P. GIBBON *Vrouw Grobelaar* 177 'Yes, it is money,' he said. 'The ouma sent it, if you should need it.' **1955** L.G. GREEN *Karoo* 30 One beloved ouma after another, sitting in her chair by the fire, has passed on these stories of the trek long ago from some pleasant corner of the old Cape. **1969** I. VAUGHAN *Last of Sunlit Yrs* 118 A small boy at one of the houses says only his Ouma and Oupa (grandather and grandmother) are at home, and yells to them to come out. **1974** D. MOORE in *The 1820* Vol.47 No.8, 17 The ladies approached, one by one, to pay their respects. I supported many an ouma as she struggled to straighten out after making her curtsy and wondered how the Princess would bear up under the strain on the following day. **1977** *Sunday Times* 27 Feb. (Mag. Sect.) 7 Oumas and oupas stood on the sidelines with sissies and tannies watching with mouths watering. **1977** P.C. VENTER *Soweto* 153 A stranger to the tsotsi's dangerous world could still save his throat if he has some knowledge of basic words and phrases: ... Ouma — wise old woman. **1985** *Style* Feb. 103 Is the whole shihi-pihi of ethnic triumph, is the bubbe and chicken soup, the ouma and the boerebeskuite, purely apocryphal? Nowadays grandmothers have a distressing habit of putting on lip gloss and taking a lover. **1989** J. HOBBS *Thoughts in Makeshift Mortuary* 281 The warm oily smell reminded Jake of the Sophiatown kitchen where his ouma had cooked on a paraffin stove.

3.a. A title, with a name.

1910 D. FAIRBRIDGE *That Which Hath Been* (1913) 45 A coloured person, mevrouw; — 'Ou'ma Jannetje' she calls herself. **1958** R.E. LIGHTON *Out of Strong* 15 'Ouma Cronje,' Ansie piped up, 'why don't you make it go any more? You could make jellies and ice-cream in it.' **1976** M. THOLO in C. Hermer *Diary of Maria Tholo* (1980) 56 There is Ouma Swartbooi who has a cracked arm because she was beaten up by a policeman on her way from school. **1980** E. JOUBERT *Poppie Nongena* 11 Great-grandma Kappie only had one girl child, our grandma Hannie. We called her ouma Hannie. **1981** *Pace* Sept. 62 You have been bedevilled by evil forces? Then you need to see Ouma Masekalaka immediately.

b. Special Comb. **Ouma Smuts** *hist.*, an affectionate name for Mrs Isie Smuts, the wife of Jan Christian Smuts, second Prime Minister of South Africa. See also OUBAAS sense 4.

1943 L. SOWDEN *Union of S. Afr.* 147 'Ouma' Smuts is the wife of General Smuts. **1946** T. MACDONALD *(title)* Ouma Smuts. [**1951** I.K. SMUTS *Informant, Irene* 27 Nov., Please call me Ouma, all of you, as I much prefer it to Mrs. & after all you are all my Girls]. **1976** *Weekend Argus* 9 Oct. 12 General Smuts had in Ouma Smuts a remarkable and intellectually brilliant wife whom he once described as 'the steam in my kettle'.

‖**oumagrootjie** /əʊma'xruɪki/ *n.* [Afk., *ouma* see prec. + *groot* great + -IE.] Great grandmother.

1959 J. MEIRING *Candle in Wind* 133 Lena left the gaol, dragging her legs, feeling a hundred years old. 'Oumagrootjie could not feel as I feel,' she thought.

ouman /'əʊman/ *n. slang.* Pl. **-manne** /-manə/. [Afk., *ou* old + *man* man.] An 'old hand', one who is no longer a novice. Used esp. in military contexts, in the following senses: **a.** A national serviceman who has completed six months or more of his compulsory military training. **b.** An experienced soldier. **c.** One who has completed his period of national service. Also *attrib.*

1970 M.A. COOK *Informant, Bloemfontein* Jim is an 'ouman' at the University this year. **1970** M. BRONSLOW *Informant, Cape Town* Your son is an ouman as he has had 6 months' service. **1972** on Radio South Africa 1 Apr. (Forces' Favourites), To the oumanne of E-Squadron, Tempe, mindae and vasbyt from Dave. **1975** [see MIN DAE]. **1979** *Sunday Times* 1 Apr., When a national serviceman becomes an 'ou man', he's served on white plates which are washed for him afterwards. **1983** *E. Prov. Herald* 20 May 1 The Minister of Defence .. yesterday came to the help of thousands of 'oumanne' in the Citizen and Commando Forces who have spent years of uncertainty about their part-time military obligations. **1986** J. WHYLE in S. Gray *Market Plays* 173 We lived in a large bungalow where we were liable to unofficial initiation by the oumanne. *Ibid.* 175, I had nearly done a year in the army and was due for a seven-day pass. The roofie ouman tension seemed to have abated and we were almost on friendly terms.

‖**oumatjie** /'əʊmaki/ *n.* [Afk., *ouma* (see OUMA) + -IE.] OUMA sense 1.

1953 U. KRIGE *Dream & Desert* 184 Carefully Adoons filled up the large gap at Mieta's feet with two of her own blankets, 'just to balance poor old Oumatjie'.

oumissus /'əʊmɪsəs, -misis/ *n.* Also **oumiesies, ou miesus, oumissis**, and with initial capital(s). [(Englished form of) Afk. *oumiesies, ou* old + *miesies*, see MIESIES.] The elderly female owner of a home, farm, or business, the employer of the servants and labourers who work there; an elderly white woman. In all senses also called *ounooi* (see NOOI sense 1 c). Cf. OUBAAS.

a. A respectful form of address or reference.

1940 E. BRIGHT in Baumann & Bright *Lost Republic* 221 You, see, ou Missus, it was this way. When I was in the wrong, the ou baas said: 'Simon, you have done so-and-so wrong' and I saw his point. **1953** D. ROOKE *S. Afr. Twins* 61 'The child is very clever,' conceded Ouma. 'Yes Oumissis,' said Aia Kobie, looking fondly at Sophie. **1978** D.A.C. MACLENNAN in *Contrast* 45 Vol.12 No.1, 54 The shepherd came to the kitchen door ... 'Baas,' he said, 'Ou missies doesn't answer.'

b. A common noun; *oumies*, see MIES sense c.

1970 M. WEITZMAN *Informant, Johannesburg* The old madame. How is the oumissus? **1974** D. ROOKE *Margaretha de la Porte* 122 'Do as he says. I will look after your nonnie.' 'I would like to go but it had better be the oumissis who tells me, not you.' **1977** N. OKES in *Quarry '77* 131 Dr. Hopkins had come in then, followed by the Oumissus. **1979** M. PARKES *Wheatlands* 41 An African maid, 'Sophie', .. unfortunately suffered from a cleft palate and was almost unintelligible, but she and the 'ou Miesus' understood each other. **1982** *Sunday Times* 21 Mar. 3 Mr Felix said: 'Bekke recognised us immediately and came charging up. The "ou missus" started crying and hugged the dog. My heart also melted when I saw how happy the mistress was to get the dog back again.'

c. A title, sometimes with a proper name.

1974 D. ROOKE *Margaretha de la Porte* 225 Oumissis has a muzzleloader too from the days of long ago. **1993** S. DIKENI in *House & Leisure* Nov. 42 He asked someone to give me a sweet right under the disapproving scrutiny of Oumiesies Grobbelaar.

oupa /'əʊpa/ *n.* Also **o(u)'pa**. [Afk. (Du. *opa*), fr. *oud* old + *pa* father. Cf. OU *adj.* sense 1 a.] Grandfather, grandpa; informally, any elderly man (but particularly an elderly Afrikaans man). Cf. OUMA.

1. A respectful form of address or reference.

Sometimes substituted for the second person pronoun 'you', the respectful third-person form of address in Afrikaans (see quot. 1963).

1915 D. FAIRBRIDGE *Torch Bearer* 71 'Ou'pa has gone for a drive and Ou'ma is sick in bed,' he said in jerky English. **1916** S. BLACK in S. Gray *Three Plays* (1984) 190, I say, Tickey, listen to Oupa, he's got some work to do. **1926** P. SMITH *Beadle* (1929) 288 'Come in then, Ou-pa' she said. 'Come in then and see the little grandson that you have with his round bald head.' **1936** [see BLOMMETJIE sense 1]. **1952** *Drum* Jan. 27 He was a real Christian, and said that we should call him 'oupa' instead of 'Oubaas', because we were all his children. He never called anyone a 'kaffir'. **1963** A.M. LOUW *20 Days* 268 Adriaan and the girl Lucille appeared in the door of the breakfast room. 'Is Oupa ill?' asked Adriaan. 'Is there anything we can do?' **1981** *Sunday Times* 15 Nov. 21 The Brits folk long ago lost faith in radio weather forecasts. They'd far sooner rely on their own feelings .. or the pain in the bones of 'Oupa' on the farm next door. **1982** *Fair Lady* 27 Jan. 141, I wallowed in the security, the unchanging ways of my Oupa's house. **1990** *Ibid.* 6 June 110 Our children have only benefited from having 24-hour grandparents. There is no pressure to visit Ouma and Oupa — they are there for the children and the children enjoy them.

2. A title, with a name.

1920 [see NOOITGEDACHT sense 1]. **1935** H.C. BOSMAN *Mafeking Rd* (1969) 44 By this time it was dark. Oupa van Tonder, an old farmer who was very keen on debates, lit an oil lamp that he had brought with him and put it on the table. **1953** U. KRIGE *Dream & Desert* 13 That only other death he had known, the death of his grandfather three years ago. Oupa Kotze had died in his sleep. **1970** *Forum* Vol.6 No.2, 46 They had been the pride of Oupa Marais and would last forever. **1975** *Sunday Times* 23 Mar. 4, 84-year old Oupa Phillip Robyntjies, one of the oldest and most respected residents of the village. **1979** *Pace* Sept. 28 Oupa Hlongwane spend his day basking in the sun and wondering where the next meal will come from.

3. A common noun.

1945 *Outspan* 20 July 37, I have shown my old film .. in hundreds of towns and dorps right through South Africa .. to the ooms and oupas of the platteland. **1948** O. WALKER *Kaffirs Are Lively* 71 The *Oupa* — grandfather — it seems, had a vivid dream that he went to heaven. **1959** J. MEIRING *Candle in Wind* 16 She laughed a little to herself as she remembered the old oupa who had come down from Middleburg [*sic*] to visit the Stompies family. **1965** K. MACKENZIE *Deserter* 83 My *oupa* fought the kaffirs to get this farm and he fought them to keep it, as did also my Pa. **1977** M.P. GWALA *Jol'iinkomo* 31 Heard a foreman say 'boy' to a labouring oupa.

4. Special Comb. **oupa clause**, a provision in legislation allowing for the age of retirement to be extended in certain professions; **oupa juice**, liquor.

1986 *Financial Mail* 17 Jan. 58 Estate agents, quantity surveyors and architects were among those allowed to continue working in terms of the **oupa clauses** when legislation was introduced to control their professions. **1990** *Sunday Star* 11 Mar. (Mag. Sect.) 26 A row of low built in cupboards against a wall hides a TV set .. , three shelves of what Marais describes as his '**Oupa juice**' and, finally, a built in fridge.

‖**oupagrootjie** /ˌəʊpa'xruɪki/ *n.* [Afk., *oupa* see prec. + *groot* great + -IE.] Great grandfather.

1971 BARAITSER & OBHOLZER *Cape Country Furn.* 173 The desk .. has stood there, says the owner, since he first opened his eyes and it belonged to 'Oupa Grootjie'.

ourebi(e) var. ORIBI.

‖**ousie** /'əʊsi/ *n.* Also **ausei, ausi(e), ausisi, ous**, and with initial capital. [Sotho *ausi* ad. Afk. *ousus, ousie* elder sister.] Among Sotho-speakers: 'sister'. Cf. OU SIS, SISI sense 1.

1. A form of address to a girl or woman, irrespective of age.

1960 J. COPE *Tame Ox* 67 Be strong now, *ausei*, more than other women. **1963** A.M. LOUW *20 Days* 7 'What's all this, ousie?' he asked. *a***1968** D.C. THEMBA in E. Patel *World of Can Themba* (1985) 158, I knocked and called: 'Ousie! Ousie!' A bolt screeched back, and a broad face peered at me. **1969** *Post* 7 Dec. 2 One night a person knocked on her door ... A voice said, 'Ousie, ousie open the door I want to give you something.' **1974** *Drum* 8 Aug. 50 Ausie, what are you doing with all those globes? Are you trying to blind us, hey? **1976** BEZUIDENHOUT & SIMON in *Quarry '76* 46 She watched me pass. I stopped and reversed for her. 'Dag ousie,' I said. **1988** M. TLALI in *Staffrider* Vol.7 No.3, 353 Yes, Ausisi, after you have sold them you are happy. You have something in your pocket.

2. A title, usu. with a name.

1970 M. DIKOBE *Marabi Dance.* 12 When the children saw Martha they spoke in low but audible voices. 'It's ausie Msipone!' **1972** L. VAN DER POST *Story like Wind* 41 Their cook, a redoubtable old Xhosa lady whom he always had to address most punctiliously as Ousie (old Mother) — Johanna. **1976** M. MELAMU in *New Classic* No.3, 4 Ous Tricy is in the nursing profession. **1978** M.W. SEROTE *Behold Mama, Flowers* 79 Your memory keeps throbbing behind your eyes otherwise why would you sing with ausi Miriam about the empty days and the nights which shattered your sleep. **1981** M. SEROTE in *Staffrider* Vol.3 No.4, 34 Ausi-Pule would sit there on the chair, her boy on her lap suckling. **1988** D. SAMUELSON in *Fair Lady* 16 Mar. 135 The child studied Ousie. Together with Oema, Ousie created the order of the house. Ousie did not speak much, but she did sing a lot — mainly church songs. The child could tell what day of the week it was by what Ousie was doing.

3. A common noun: a (black) woman.

1971 *Informant, Coalbrook (OFS)* That old ousie really makes me laugh sometimes. **1975** K.M.C. MOTSISI in *Drum* 22 Sept. 44 Sis Tsidza .. is a very well-proportioned and prettiful ousie and has her house in the same street. **1979** *Sunday Times* 19 Aug. (Mag. Sect.) 6 One sardonic observer of the social scene [in the Free State] noted that what they did have were 'ousies' and 'garden boys' as opposed to people. **1985** [see SHEILA sense 1]. **1986** [see OU *n.* sense 4]. [**1986** *City Woman* Nov. 11 Ramagaga — who three years ago joined the legal profession as Temba township's first woman prosecutor — .. recalls some of her 'nasty experiences' as a woman court official. In typical ghetto language, an alleged rapist told a male prosecutor to tell 'die ousie' (Ramagaga) he was innocent.] **1987** Z. MDA in *New Nation* 11 June 17 Budda Joe .. Played the piano at the Chicken Shack Where the outies and ousies Drank Danced And made love.

‖**ou sis** /'əʊsəs/ *n. phr.* Also **ousis, ousus**. [Afk. *ousus, ou* old + *sus* sister.] A respectful form of address or reference to a woman, esp. an elder sister. Cf. OUSIE, SUSTER.

*c***1902** BAGLEY *Informant, Kimberley* How is Ou Sis and her Babies they seem to be alright by the photo fat and plump. **1956** D. JACOBSON *Dance in Sun* 130 'Drink without food will make you so drunk ... Your head

‖**outa** /ˈəʊtɑ, ˈəʊtə/ *n. offensive.* Also **auta**. [Afk., lit. 'old father' (Afk. *ou* old + shortened form of Xhosa *utata* father, or Du. dial. *tate* father).] Esp. among Afrikaans-speaking people:
1. A form of address to an elderly black man; OUTATJIE.

1908 I.W. WAUCHOPE *Natives & their Missionaries* 4 A Native male is either a diminutive or a super-annuated specimen of humanity whom they [*sc.* the Dutch] could not logically call man or woman; therefore he was called a 'Jong,' i.e. a boy, or as a term of respect, 'Ou-ta,' i.e. grand father. 1911 [see BAASIE sense 1 b]. 1914 L.H. BRINKMAN *Breath of Karroo* 229 'I must go on, Outa, for I am fetching a doctor for a sick woman, and there is no time to lose.' The word 'outa', meaning 'old father,' is only used by Europeans when addressing elderly native males. Thus, should any one address a half-caste as 'outa,' it would be taken as an insult. Should a half-caste address a native as 'outa,' the indignant reply would be, 'I'm not your outa — you are as black as I am.' 1955 [see JONG sense 2 a]. 1961 L.E. VAN ONSELEN *Trekboer* 103, I looked into his wrinkled old face and knew that there must be a story there. Jokingly, I said to him, 'Outa! have you got any diamonds to sell?' 1965 E. MPHAHLELE *Down Second Ave* 149 Afrikaans literature that teems with offensive words like aia — for non-white women, outa — for non-white men, and a literature that teems with non-white characters who are savages or blundering idiots to be despised and laughed at; characters who are inevitably frustrated creatures of city life and decide to return 'home' — to the Reserves. 1968 K. McMAGH *Dinner of Herbs* 52 The young woman flew to old Karolus and taking his hand led him to the steep path ... 'Slowly Outa, slowly,' she warned. 'Slowly or you might stumble and fall.' 1969 A. FUGARD *Boesman & Lena* 20 Come sit Outa. Sit and rest. 1981 [see AYAH sense 2].

2. A title, often with a name.

1917 S.T. PLAATJE *Native Life* 85 Go away, Auta Gert; you are dreaming, my husband would never talk such nonsense. 1927 C.G. BOTHA *Social Life in Cape Col.* 44 Even the servants had their designations, Ayah was the nurse, Outa was the senior male servant. 1953 [see AYAH sense 2]. 1960 [see BAASIE sense 1 a]. 1980 A.J. BLIGNAUT *Dead End Rd* 21 The Boer War broke out shortly after he'd started calling me Hottentot, instead of Outa Ruiter. 1991 B. MACKENZIE tr. F.P. Van den Heever in *Best of S. Afr. Short Stories* 56 'Ag, Outa Sem,' Jannie had lamented, 'I would like a nice bit of meat, or a spoon of syrup over my porridge or a little sugar in my coffee!' ... He had been left behind alone on the farm under the care of Aia Koema, an elderly Griqua maidservant and her husband Outa Sem.

3. A common noun: an elderly black man.

1934 C.P. SWART *Supplement to Pettman.* 131 *Outa,* An old coloured servant is so called by Afrikaans-speaking persons. 1955 A. DELIUS *Young Trav.* 110 Back on the farm Dick and Frank helped the Outas and Jongs to feed the pigs. 1959 — *Last Division* 77 Remembered childhood where an outa might twang strange wonders from a high-strung heart. 1977 M. DU PLESSIS in *Quarry '77* 68 You deplored false worship of racial purity, exploitation; you made a lament over the black ones denigrated and despised: 'jong, outa, kaffer, skepsel' the terms which filthy those who use them. 1978 *Sunday Times* 20 Aug. 14 Those who objected to 'meide and outas' in the post office queue should remember that the congress agenda also called for compulsory military service for coloureds and Indians. 1978 A.P. BRINK *Rumours of Rain* 153 As I stood to one side to let him go out, she asked: 'Daddy, is he an uncle or an outa?' 1989 F.G. BUTLER *Tales from Old Karoo* 56 The old coloured got up politely as I approached, and said 'Good morning ... Do you want to go in?' ... He pointed .. to the gate, and there .. was the name 'Heaven's Gate' ... I turned to the outa and said jokingly: 'I suppose your name is Peter?' He smiled, and nodded.

outatjie /ˈəʊtaki/ *n.* [Afk. *outa* see prec. + dim. suffix -IE.] OUTA sense 1.

1948 tr. 'Boerneef' in Smuts & Alberts *Forgotten Highway* (1988) 186 You must hurry up my outatjie, after all, we must stand on our backs for a few hours before we get up to guard the sheep in the small hours.

outchualla, outchuella varr. TSHWALA.

outdorp see DORP sense b.

outee var. OUTIE.

Outeniqua /əʊtəni(ː)kwə/ *n.* Formerly also **Auteniqua, Auteniquois, Autinegua, Autinicqua, Hottniqua, Houteniqua**. [Khoikhoi, usu. interpreted as 'the people who carry bags of honey', prob. *au* carry in bags (cf. Nama *awa*) + *tine* honey (cf. Nama *danib*) + masculine pl. suffix *qua* men, people (G.S. Nienaber, *Hottentots*, 1963); the area in which the Outeniqua lived was reported from early times to supply honey to the Cape, and is still an important apicultural region.]

1. *hist.* A Khoikhoi people formerly resident in the Western Cape, in the region of the present-day city of George. Also *attrib.*

1731 G. MEDLEY tr. *P. Kolb's Present State of Cape of G.H.* I. 79 North East of the *Gauros,* on the Coast, lie the *Houteniquas;* in whose Territory are several Woods. 1790 W. PATERSON *Narr. of Four Journeys* 34 I .. proceeded towards the Hottniqua Land. 1798 B. STOUT *Narr. of Loss of Ship 'Hercules'* p.xxxii, In the eastern parts, which include Caffraria, the country of the Autiniquois, Genequois, and various tribes of the Hottentot nation, I perceived a most luxuriant soil. 1810 G. BARRINGTON *Acct of Voy.* 171 No roots or other vegetables are regularly cultivated in any of the inferior parts of Africa, except in the country of the Autenicquas. 1847 J. BARROW *Reflect.* 198 It [*sc.* the Kayman River] separates the division of Plettenberg's Bay from Autenicquas Land, which the Dutch Government appropriated to itself, on account of the grand forests and fine pasturage. 1989 *Reader's Digest Illust. Hist.* 227 Descendants of the early white trekboers and the Outeniqua and Attaqua Khoikhoi.

2. In full *Outeniqua yellowwood*: **a.** the YELLOWWOOD (sense 2 a), *Podocarpus falcatus;* **b.** the timber of this tree; also *attrib.*; also called YELLOWWOOD (sense 1).

1843 J.C. CHASE *Cape of G.H.* 161 Yellow wood, Autineguas. 1887 J.C. BROWN *Crown Forests* 237 Timber Valued Standing per cubic foot. Upright Yellowwood, £0 0s 3d. Outeniqua, £0 0s 1d. 1904 D.E. HUTCHINGS in *Agric. Jrnl of Cape of G.H.* Feb. 3 *Podocarpus elongata* — Outeniqua Yellow-wood, .. is the largest and most generally useful tree in South Africa. 1920 K.M. JEFFREYS tr. *Memorandum of Commissary J.A. de Mist* 215 Local hardwoods, such as the Outeniqua, black ironwood, and other woods suitable for building houses. 1934 [see UPRIGHT YELLOWWOOD]. 1977 E. PALMER *Field Guide to Trees* 69 Common yellowwood *Podocarpus falcatus* ... Outeniqua yellowwood ... The tallest forest tree, up to 60m high ... A noble tree, formerly much exploited for its generally useful, fine, yellow timber. 1987 A. VISSER in *Fair Lady* 11 Nov. 141 Whisky-crate wood was used and now Johnny Walker and White Horse lie side by side with the finest Outeniqua wood.

outers /ˈaʊtəz/ *n. slang.* [Perh. fr. Austral. Eng. *on the outer(s)* disadvantaged, excluded (orig. with reference to the area outside a race-course enclosure); see first quot.] The haunts of vagrants and the homeless. Often in the adv. phr. *on the outers,* in the open, without shelter. See also OUTIE.

1977 *Family Radio & TV* 23 Jan. 18, I was quickly introduced to the language of their world beyond the fringes of society. They aren't hoboes, they are outies, and their domain is the outers. I never learned whether this was an abbreviation for outside, out of luck, out of respectability or a combination of all these ... Two newcomers to the outers .. had been sleeping in parking garages, bus-shelters and behind bushes for only five weeks. *Ibid.* 19 If they have one philosophy in common, it is this ... 'Anything, but anything, is better than the outers' ... Moral standards have no place on the outers ... A lady shouldn't sleep on the outers. 1977 D. MULLER *Whitey* 83 She stood almost on top of him for a moment and she didn't smell all violets — smelled, in fact, as if she had been living on the outers for a couple of weeks.

outie /ˈaʊti/ *n. slang.* Also **outee**. [Eng. *out* + (informal) n.-forming suffix *-ie;* see quot. 1982.] A down-and-out; an inhabitant of the OUTERS. Also *attrib.* Cf. BERGIE sense 2.

1974 J. MATTHEWS *Park* 24, I doan mind to go to jug if I robba outie or stick him witta lem but I doan go to jug for rape. 1976 K.M.C. MOTSISI in *Drum* Sept., It's a sad Kid Boikie who rejoins me and shouts like this: 'Laat ons loop. Maybe ons meet die outies daar.' We leave and head on. We arrive and, well, there are the outies. 1977 *Family Radio & TV* 23 Jan. 19 A hardened outie becomes resigned to sleeping on cardboard in shop doorways, but he doesn't enjoy it. *Ibid.* 20 The behaviour of my own outie companions dramatically illustrated what Reg B— was talking about ... There was always that one overwhelming thought in an outie's mind: where is the next *dop* coming from? ... Young working girls on their way to the office, they looked us over and then the prettier girl shouted: 'Voetsek, you bleddie outies!'. 1977 [see GOFFEL]. 1981 *Sunday Times* 16 Aug. 13, I immediately contacted the city police who agreed to deliver the 'outies' they picked up here ... The success rate for bringing tramps back to the straight and narrow was not great ... 'But if I can rehabilitate just one out of 50 "outies" I will be happy,' he said. 1982 *Ibid.* 16 May (Mag. Sect.) 1 Jo'burg's 'outies' are reluctantly having to change their travel plans. Their outlawing by the Durban City Council means that few of these self-styled 'gentlemen of the road' will be making their annual trek to Durban ... Give the watchmen their due: the 'outies' (so-called because they're without homes or jobs) are an unprepossessing bunch. 1987 [see OUSIE sense 3]. 1990 L. MABER in *Weekly Mail* 22 June (Weekend Mail) 1 They insist they are not hobos; rather they prefer to be called *outies.*

outjie /ˈəʊki/ *n. colloq.* [Afk., *ou* (see OU *n.*) + dim. suffix -IE.] OKIE.

1960 [see MOER *v.* sense 1]. 1963 A. FUGARD *Blood Knot* (1968) 104 The wind turned and brought the stink from the lake .. and a clear memory of two little outjies in khaki broeks. 1971 E. HIGGINS *Informant,* Grahamstown If he accepted the sales talk of the Borstal he would become an acceptable outjie. 1975 [see DRONKLAP]. 1984 E. MPHAHLELE *Afrika my Music* 124 Listen to him, outjies, you'd say, just listen to him. That's no damn shebeen language. 1987 *New Nation* 28 May 11 When I was a child, I can remember a white man pointing to me and saying 'These outjies, I hate them more than poison'. 1988 A. CAMPBELL in *Fair Lady* 27 Apr. 96, I prayed for all those other *outjies* on the border.

outklip var. OUKLIP.

outlander *n.* Also with initial capital. [Calqued on Afk. *uitlander.* Cf. Brit. Eng. *outlander,* fr. Du. and G., from the early 17th century.] UITLANDER *n.* Also *attrib.*

1892 *Pall Mall Gaz.* (U.K.) 10 Oct. 3 At Johannesburg this National Union has been formed, comprising not only 'uitlanders' (outlanders) but Boers. 1896 *Daily Telegraph* (U.K.) 1 Feb. 6 The racial antagonism between Boers and Outlanders. 1899 *Westminster Gaz.* (U.K.) 25 Apr. 1 If this is so, we may indeed dry our eyes about Outlander grievances. 1936 E.C. LLEWELLYN *Influence of Low Dutch* 171 Outlander .. is the Anglicized form of Du. *uitlander,* an alien, foreigner, applied by the Boers of the Transvaal to the alien population attracted to the country by the goldfields of the Rand. 1940 F.B. YOUNG *City of Gold* 439 A man who .. hated from the bottom of his soul the outlanders, who had already made his bankrupt state rich. 1944 J.

MOCKFORD *Here Are S. Africans* 93 In the eyes of Paul Kruger .. these gold grabbers were *uitlanders*, outlanders, foreigners. **1962** L.E. NEAME *Hist. of Apartheid* 26 Secure better treatment for the British and other Outlanders in the Transvaal. **1974** D. ROOKE *Margaretha de la Porte* 23 The Transvaal .. was swarming with Englishmen, indeed with foreigners of all nationalities, clamouring for the franchise: Uitlanders the Dutch called us — Outlanders. **1990** *Style* June 127 The influx of fancy outlanders can, and usually does, overtax the system to a point where even hot water is unobtainable.

outspan /ˈaʊtspæn/ *n.* Also **outspaan, outspann.** [fr. OUTSPAN V.]

1. In full ***outspan place***: **a.** *hist.* In the days of waggon transport: land near a public road, set aside for public use, on which travellers broke their journey or camped while allowing their draught-animals to rest and graze. **b.** *transf.* COMMONAGE. **c.** *fig.* Any place at which one may break a journey (see Prance quot. at 1937). **d.** In recent times: any piece of land formerly designated as an outspan place. Also *attrib.* In all senses formerly also called UITSPAN *n.*

[**1812** A. PLUMPTRE tr. *H. Lichtenstein's Trav. in Sn Afr.* (1928) I. 19 One of the many stations to which the name of *Auspannplatze* was given, because they 'were established by the Government for the benefit of travellers as resting-places.'] **1821** C.I. LATROBE *Jrnl of Visit* 167 A team or set of oxen or horses put to a waggon, is called by the Dutch a Spann, and those places in the wilderness, where halt is made and the oxen unyoked, an Outspann-place. **1822** W.J. BURCHELL *Trav.* I. 92 These *uitspan* or *outspan places*, are, in fact, the caravanserays of the Cape. **1827** G. THOMPSON *Trav.* II. 100 Found another Bushman family at our *outspann*. *Ibid.* 304 The cattle are grazed on the outspann places set aside for public use. **1835** A. SMITH *Diary* (1940) II. 61 Went up to the front wagons and led them to a spot fixed as an outspan. **1835** H.I. VENABLE in D.J. Kotze *Lett. of American Missionaries* (1950) 70 Outspan places are established by law for the accommodation of travellers. **1836** *Ordinance for Defining Limits of Injury to Cape Flats & Downs* in *Stat. Law of Cape of G.H.* (1862) 369 Licence to graze horned cattle .. upon the aforesaid crown lands not being outspan-places. **1840** C.A. KINLOCH in *Echo* 26 Oct. 4 We reached an outspan or halting place situated on the bank of a partially dry rivulet. **1841** B. SHAW *Memorials* 65 To-day de Heer P. Van Aarde sent one of his slaves to our out span-place, to inform us that we might obtain supplies at his house. **1871** [see CLUMP]. **1872** *E. London Dispatch & Shipping & Mercantile Gaz.* 19 Nov. 2 Government notice 405, of 1859, provided for the establishment of well-conducted houses of accommodation on outspans. **1884** G.C. CATO in *Natal Mercury*, (letter), I must leave out a lot of matter that took place between the Surveyor-General and myself about roads, outspans, seaboards, reserves. **1898** W.C. SCULLY *Vendetta* 129 Its owner's intention being to wait for his travelling companion at the next outspan place, where water and pasturage were known to be good. **1903** E.F. KNIGHT *S. Afr. after War* 162 According to the old Free State law, each farm has to provide a public outspan where sheep and cattle can graze and water when travelling. **1910** *Act 11* in *Stat. of Union* (1911) 202 It shall not be lawful for any tick-infested cattle to be upon .. any public outspan or commonage. **1913** C. PETTMAN *Africanderisms* 355 At intervals along the roads in South Africa spaces are beaconed off, some public, others private, where animals may be allowed to be outspanned and allowed to graze; these spaces are known as 'outspans'. **1920** [see *Cape cart v.* (CAPE CART)]. **1936** E. ROSENTHAL *Old-Time Survivals* 9 By an ancient law, virtually every settlement in the country has its 'outspan' .. where passing travellers are allowed to spend the night. *Ibid.* 10 Smaller towns possess outspans, which also serve as the market squares. **1937** M. ALSTON *Wanderings* 36 Near Mossel Bay we found a good outspan on open veld sheltered by thick bushes. **1937** C.R. PRANCE *Tante Rebella's Saga* 28 A shilling a day per team for outspan-fee. **1937** *Ibid.* [see HARTEBEEST *adj.*]. **1948** H.V. MORTON *In Search of S. Afr.* 278 A brand new estate office has been erected on the outspan. **1948** *George & Knysna Herald* 21 May 8 Several more outspans falling under the control of the Divisional Council are to be advertised for lease. **1951** L.G. GREEN *Grow Lovely* 206 The old outspans are appreciated by picnic and braaivleis parties. If you have travelled not less than five miles you are legally entitled to outspan facilities, including the right to pitch a tent for twenty-four hours. **1952** B. DAVIDSON *Report on Sn Afr.* 58 Along the roadside at frequent intervals, now, there were crescent-shaped notices set on posts with the word *outspan* written on the crescent — the traditional camping sites for trek wagons. **1958** F.G. BUTLER in R.M. Macnab *Poets in S. Afr.* 12, I stopped at the outspan place to watch .. A little fire leaping near a wagon. **1961** D. BEE *Children of Yesterday* 2 Back at their outspan the Swazi was asleep in a few minutes, wrapped in his single blanket beneath the jeep. **1970** *S. Afr. Panorama* June 31 The transport-riders gradually disappeared from the scene and with them the game at the outspan places also disappeared. **1971** *Grocott's Mail* 11 June 3 Letting of Outspans. Notice is hereby given that in terms of Section 168 of Ordinance No. 15 of 1952 that it is the intention of the Divisional Council of Albany to let by Public Auction .. the grazing rights of the Outspans hereunder described for a period of five years ... (1) Fletchers Outspan, in extent 176.2022 Hectares situated alongside the Fort Beaufort Trunk Road, approximately 18 miles from Grahamstown. *Ibid.* 27 July 3 The days of the voortrekkers are gone, and divisional councils no longer need outspans. **1975** *Friend* 25 June 8 There were many places along those roads — mostly outspans — where transport riders could rest awhile before proceeding on their long journeys. **1982** *E. Prov. Herald* 23 June 3 Three outspans in the eastern sector of the Dias Divisional Council are to be turned into nature reserves. **1985** *S. Afr. Panorama* Feb. 33 The two caravan parks were formerly outspans for grazing horses and cattle. **1994** M. ROBERTS tr. *J.A. Wahlberg's Trav. Jrnls 1838–56* 64 Willem had seen 4 lions at our previous outspan-place.

2. *hist.* In the days of waggon transport: the occasion or period of breaking a journey, unhitching the draught animals, and resting or camping.

1822 W.J. BURCHELL *Trav.* I. 87 Finding some waggons at *outspan*, we asked the favor of one of the boors to leave my bundle at Fortuintje, which lay in his road. **1824** *S. Afr. Jrnl* No.1, 28 The ennui of a dreary journey or an evening outspann in the interior. **1838** J.E. ALEXANDER *Exped. into Int.* I. 18 We journeyed onward, .. enjoying our gipsy outspan in the middle of the day. **1871** W.G. ATHERSTONE in A.M.L. Robinson *Sel. Articles from Cape Monthly Mag.* (1978) 94 An old track .. led us all right until dark, when we lost it again, and wandered away till prudence suggested an outspan. **1882** S. HECKFORD *Lady Trader in Tvl* 12 Our evening outspann was on a bleak hilltop. **1896** R. WALLACE *Farming Indust. of Cape Col.* 269 The sun is well up and the air warm before the next outspan is made. **1897** J.P. FITZPATRICK *Outspan* 45 In our routine there was as a rule no eating during the night outspan. **1900** F.D. BAILLIE *Mafeking Diary* 288 Towards dark, after an outspan that was like a picnic, we reached Mr Wright's farm. **1924** G. BAUMANN in Baumann & Bright *Lost Republic* (1940) 130 On our way home, at one of our outspans, we bought a fowl. **1960** G. LISTER *Reminisc.* 1 The long treks, the outspans and all the excitement of pitching tents and cooking meals. **1969** P. SMITH in Lennox-Short & Lighton *Stories S. African* 113 They travelled slowly .. with frequent outspans to rest their oxen. **1973** S. CLOETE *Co. with Heart of Gold* 154 Not once save at the midday outspan did he rest his oxen. **1994** M. ROBERTS tr. *J.A. Wahlberg's Trav. Jrnls 1838–56* 57 From Bushman's River to the first outspan by a small spruit, three and a half hours' travelling.

3. *Fig.* and *transf.* **a.** A stop-over, a break in a journey; a rest; a pause or digression. **b.** A place at which one breaks a journey; a resting-place.

1878 H.A. ROCHE *On Trek in Tvl* 110 Treat this long digression, an' it please you, as a kind of 'outspan' on paper. **1936** H.C. BOSMAN *Mafeking Rd* (1969) 10 A ship isn't so comfortable, of course. And it is further between outspans. **1977** *E. Prov. Herald* 18 Nov. 8 He was photographed resting yesterday near Van Stadens River bridge, during his daily afternoon outspan.

outspan /ˈaʊtspæn/ *v.* [Calque formed on Du. *uitspan*, *uit* out, from + *spannen* to yoke, hitch.]

In all senses also UITSPAN *v.* Cf. INSPAN, OFF-SADDLE *v.*

There is some overlap in the *intrans.* senses.

1.a. *intrans. obs.* To unyoke or unharness oxen or other draught animals and allow them to rest; *to span out*, see SPAN *v.* sense 3 a.

1801 in G.M. Theal *Rec. of Cape Col.* (1899) IV. 361 Arrived at noon at the pasture place of Esterhuizen, where we outspanned and being provided with fresh relays we went on. **1816** G. BARKER Journal. 15 Feb., About 10 out-spanned soon after which several men belong [*sic*] to Bethelsdorp .. came up and spanned out likewise. **1832** *Graham's Town Jrnl* 9 Mar. 41 The Undersigned .. Hereby warns all Persons from Shooting, Hunting, Fishing, Out Spanning, Cutting Wood. **1852** A.W. COLE *Cape & Kafirs* 134 At about ten we 'out-span' — that is, take out the oxen and turn them loose to graze. **1871** W.G. ATHERSTONE in A.M.L. Robinson *Sel. Articles from Cape Monthly Mag.* (1978) 94 We outspanned and halted. **1886** G.A. FARINI *Through Kalahari Desert* 11 We overtook Mr. Caldecott's turn-out and the coaches, both of which had outspanned for a change of 'horses.' **1900** H. BUTTERWORTH *Trav. Tales* 57 To outspan is to unyoke oxen — hence to encamp. **1912** W. WESTRUP *Land of To-Morrow* 66 They got here two whole hours ago, so as to be able to outspan, and give the horses a rest. **1931** *Nat. Geog. Mag.* Apr. 469 'At breakfast time you'd outspan and —' 'Unhitch, you mean?' 'Ay, that's it, outspan.' **1951** R. GRIFFITHS *Grey about Flame* 161 Outspan, hobble the mules and then get on with it.

b. *trans.* To unyoke or unharness (oxen or other draught animals) from a wagon or plough; *rare*, to unhitch (a waggon) from its draught animals.

Quot. 1962 may be *intrans.*

1815 G. BARKER Journal. 4 Aug., We .. were oblidged to outspan our oxen before we could ascend the sand hills. [*a*1823 J. EWART *Jrnl* (1970) 62 We .. unyoked our oxen (or as the Boors call it outspan'd) which is usualy done twice or thrice a day .. , to allow the animals to feed and refresh themselves.] **1833** *Graham's Town Jrnl* 3 Jan. 1 All cattle strayed or out-spanned over any part of the property of Frederick Korsten, Esq. will be forthwith impounded. **1864** F. GALTON *Vacation Tourists* III. 167 To see a farmer outspan and turn the team of active little beasts loose on the boundless veld to amuse themselves for an hour or two .. would astonish him a little. **1878** T.J. LUCAS *Camp Life & Sport* 45 At night the oxen were outspanned and allowed to scatter whither they would in search of grass. **1895** A.B. BALFOUR *1200 Miles in Waggon* 71 One gets out at the end by a high step, or when the oxen are outspanned (unharnessed), by a ladder. **1926** P.W. LAIDLER *Tavern of Ocean* 184 Riebeeck Square was originally Boeren Plein, or Farmer's Plain, where the countrymen outspanned their wagons. **1934** B.I. BUCHANAN *Pioneer Days* 29 The wagons were drawn up beside the road, and the oxen outspanned .. and allowed to graze for a while. **1962** F.C. METROWICH *Scotty Smith* 130 'The horses are tired,' Herman replied. 'I think we should outspan and rest them for a while.' **1976** V. ROSENBERG *Sunflower* 13 They outspanned their oxen, securing them with a yoke hewn especially for this purpose and a peg driven into the ground. **1980** A.J. BLIGNAUT *Dead End Rd* 90, I was still outspanning the predikant's team. **1990** M.M. HACKSLEY (tr. E. Van Heerden) in *Lynx* 182 At every turn-off .. they had outspanned the donkeys, hobbled them and let them graze on the little patch of government servitude on either side of the road.

2. *intrans.*

a. *hist.* To rest or camp at the side of the road while travelling by wagon; *to span out*, see SPAN *v.* sense 3 b. **b.** *transf.* and *fig.* To break a journey; to relax, take a break.

1811 J.G. CUYLER in G.M. Theal *Rec. of Cape Col.* (1901) VIII. 91 The rovers passed Scheepers at night who lay close to the road outspanned with his waggon. **1820** T. PHILIPPS *Lett.* (1960) 50 We struck our tents after Breakfast, and out spanned as they call it, at two o'clock. **1822** W.J. BURCHELL *Trav.* I. 196 A little before dark, the drivers wanted to outspan for the night. **1827** T. PHILIPPS *Scenes & Occurrences* 15 The twosome proposed that they should accompany us in our sporting expedition, and that we should all agree to outspan at Assagai Bush. **1836** A.F. GARDINER *Journey to Zoolu Country* 152 Rested two hours and a half in the heat of the day; and outspanned again at sunset. **1838** T. SHONE Diary. 17 July, We .. proceeded to Town and out span'd at my Son's place. **1849** N.J. MERRIMAN *Cape Jrnls* (1957) 19 We set off .. for Graham's Town, which we reached on the sixth day, having outspanned for the Sunday by Bushman's River. [*a*1862 J. AYLIFF *Jrnl of 'Harry Hastings'* (1963) 77 'You go in then you ask for permission to outspaan — that's Dutch' said he 'it means that you want to stop there to trade'.] **1866** E.L. PRICE *Jrnls* (1956) 348 We generally outspan of a morning about sunrise, when the little folks are waking after a long night's rest. **1870** R. RIDGILL in A.M.L. Robinson *Sel. Articles from Cape Monthly Mag.* (1978) 23 It was not until we outspanned for the night, near Stellenbosch, that the last farewell was spoken. **1878** *Argus* 13 Apr., This was the half-way place, and we 'outspanned' here all day. **1883** M.A. CAREY-HOBSON *Farm in Karoo* 140 It is customary in the country, .. when travellers wish to outspan upon a farm to ask the farmer's permission to do so. **1883** O.E.A. SCHREINER *Story of Afr. Farm* 246 We always travelled all night, and used to 'outspan' for five or six hours in the heat of the day to rest. **1885** H. RIDER HAGGARD *King Solomon's Mines* 16 He outspanned alongside of me for a fortnight to rest his oxen. **1896** [see INSPAN sense 1 a]. **1900** [see sense 1 a above]. **1910** J. BUCHAN *Prester John* (1961) 49 We got to Umvelos' after midday, and outspanned for our three weeks' work. **1911** L. COHEN *Reminisc. of Kimberley* 399 Another Boer wanted to know, when he heard that a steamship service was proposed to be established between the Cape and Natal, where the vessels outspanned during the night. **1934** B.I. BUCHANAN *Pioneer Days* 169 We travelled gaily for two hours, then outspanned for a rest. **1941** C. BIRKBY *Springbok Victory* 174 On the fifth day .. the head of the column outspanned just short of Jijiga. And all that night the lights of the brigade's trucks played in the sky as the Springboks came up. **1966** F.G. BUTLER *S. of Zambezi* 21 'When I was a boy', he said, 'we always outspanned for the night, here, among these trees'. **1970** C.B. WOOD *Informant, Johannesburg* 'Outspan' (relax) and rest. **1971** H. ZEEDERBERG *Veld Express* 24 Gone were the days when they could 'outspan' at the home of a farmer or relative, and spend a few days on a hunting expedition. **1977** FUGARD & DEVENISH *Guest* 51 We outspanned and put up our tents there where the kraal is now.

Hence **outspanned** *ppl adj.*, unyoked, unharnessed, unhitched; encamped; **outspanning** *vbl n.*, the unyoking of draught animals; the breaking of a journey; also *attrib.*

1841 B. SHAW *Memorials* 220 The other side of the river is the proper outspanning or halting-place, and there you ought to go. **1852** M.B. HUDSON *S. Afr. Frontier Life* 169 While resting the night at our outspanning station, A farmer came up to report depredation Of twelve hundred sheep. **1866** E.L. PRICE *Jrnls* (1956) 165 We .. have never had very long outspannings and have always been late at night .. before we outspanned. **1872** in A.M.L. Robinson *Sel. Articles from Cape Monthly Mag.* (1978) 280 'Outspanning' and 'inspanning' include by one expression what an English groom would need two or three orders to perform, since harnessing the cattle does not necessarily imply attaching them to the vehicle they are intended to draw. **1876** T. STUBBS Reminiscences. 25 On our first outspanning I would find him out, and ask him what time he thought we ought to proceed. **1884** 'E.V.C.' *Promised Land* 32, I will not give an account of each day's inspanning and outspanning, and our shooting between Newcastle and Lydenburg. **1893** *Month* Feb. 197 He was standing by the out-spanned wagon. **1894** H. NISBET *Bush Girl's Romance* p.iii, I do not think we forget these 'out-spannings' while we are driving our cattle in other directions. **1899** *Strand Mag.* (U.K.) Mar. 270 [He] pointed to the outspanned bullocks. *c*1900 S. LYALL Reminiscences. (Killie Campbell Africana Library MS138), Here first I saw the outspanning and inspanning oxen and cooking by the side of the wagons. **1918** H. MOORE *Land of Good Hope* 32 You come to one of the public 'out spanning stations' which are arranged at convenient distances. **1924** L. COHEN *Reminisc. of Jhb.* 16 There were the usual inspannings and outspannings, during which operations the passengers snatched a hasty, coarse breakfast. **1949** [see INSPAN]. **1971** H. ZEEDERBERG *Veld Express* 32 Outspanned wagons, tents and 'shanties' of all description. **1972** [see VOORLOPER sense 1]. **1977** F.G. BUTLER *Karoo Morning* 11 A trek by oxwagon — the whole slow ritual of inspanning and outspanning.

outstryder var. OUDSTRYDER.

out-verkramp /ˌaʊtfə(r)ˈkramp/ *v. trans.* Also **out-verkrampt**. [Eng. *out-* an element combining with verbs, meaning 'to surpass, outdo' + Afk. *verkramp* narrow, bigoted.] To outdo (someone) in ultra-conservative views or behaviour. See also VERKRAMP.

1971 *Sunday Times* 26 June 6 The Nationalist Party tried to out-verkramp the HNP on almost every issue. **1972** *Evening Post* 9 Sept. 11 Mr Viljoen has decided .. that the way to defeat Dr Mulder is to out-verkrampt him. **1982** *Sunday Times* 28 Feb. 28 If Mr P W Botha .. even tries to outverkramp his new opponents, the split will have been little more than a messy and meaningless tribal squabble.

overberg /ˈəʊvəbɜːg/ *n.* [S. Afr. Du., *over* over + *berg* mountain.] Any region beyond mountains; used particularly in the Western Cape, and in Kwa-Zulu-Natal (see quot. 1973). Also *attrib.*, and occas. as *adv.*

1822 W.J. BURCHELL *Trav.* I. 88 The districts situated, with respect to the metropolis, beyond these mountains [*sc.* the Hottentots Holland], and also their inhabitants and produce, are often distinguished in a general way by the word *overbergsch* (tramontane). **1823** W.W. BIRD *State of Cape of G.H.* 99 The pleasure and draft waggon of the country .. is .. the general and only convenient way of travelling through the peninsula and *Overberg* in the distant *drostdys*. *Ibid.* 160 Shooting parties to the most distant parts of the colony, on the other side of the mountains (overberg), frequently take place. **1851** J.F. CHURCHILL Diary. (Killie Campbell Africana Library MS37) 13 May, Business pretty brisk at Maritzburg with the Overberg Traders. **1859** R.J. MANN *Col. of Natal* 170 The trade with the Dutch States beyond the Drakensberg, which is technically known as the Overberg trade. **1874** in A.M.L. Robinson *Sel. Articles from Cape Monthly Mag.* (1978) 214 The settlers who removed to the inland districts, then designated the 'Over-berg' (beyond the mountains), were absolutely blocked up in an isolated world of their own. **1879** R.J. ATCHERLEY *Trip to Boerland* 61 The sale of rum to over-berg travellers. **1900** *Blackwood's Mag.* (U.K.) Mar. 324 A railway which derives the bulk of its revenue from the overberg trade. **1902** *E. Prov. Herald* 3 Mar. (Pettman), Sir Albert Hime, the Natal Premier, interviewed on the question of congestion of traffic and stoppage of permits for civil trade Overberg, said .. the Government had taken action. **1973** *Std Encycl. of Sn Afr.* VIII. 414 *Overberg*, .. Old name of the coastal belt in the south-western part of the Cape Province east of the Hottentots Holland Mountains. Formerly the name was applied more particularly to the district of Swellendam, but it came to include the districts of Caledon and Bredasdorp. The old Dutch name is still in daily use for this region ... The name 'Overberg' was also used by the Voortrekkers in Natal to indicate the area beyond the Drakensberg, north of the Orange River. **1985** L. DU BUISSON in *Avenue* May 36 The debate .. occasionally drew derisive comment from what Natalians were now calling the 'Overberg' — meaning the rest of South Africa. **1987** *Argus* 14 Mar., He is a hero not just in Caledon, but in the Cape Flats, the Boland, the Overberg and all along the Southern Cape coast as far as Port Elizabeth and East London. **1990** E. PARKER in *You* 16 Aug. 22 The little Overberg town [*sc.* Swellendam], shaken and split by the sordid poison tragedy, is all abuzz over the fairytale romance. **1993** G. ETHERINGTON in *Weekend Post* 12 June (Leisure Suppl.) 4 The Overberg is the country stretching between the Hottentots Holland and Mossel Bay.

Overlam *n. obs.* [Formed on S. Afr. Du. *oorlam*, through the misinterpretation of *oor-* as Du. 'over' Cf. OORLAM.] OORLAM *n.* sense 2.

1838 J.E. ALEXANDER *Exped. into Int.* I. 252 The people of Habusomop being ten times the number of the Overlams .. had the advantage at first, but they did not enjoy it long. The Overlams united and drove the old Namaquas before them off the station, and over the plain like sheep.

ow var. AU.

own *adj.* [tr. Afk. *eie* own, characteristic of, peculiar to (and thus divergent from all others).] Of or pertaining exclusively to a particular ethnic group or 'nation', esp., since the mid-1980s, as formalized in 'own affairs' legislation (see OWN AFFAIR).

1962 A.J. LUTHULI *Let my People Go* 152 It came down to the Bantustan idea — 'political rights' in our 'own' area, and so on. **1976** *Sunday Times* 1 Aug. 15 The old apartheid policy that was re-written in 1958 by Dr Verwoerd as eie-soortige (own identity) development failed shortly after it was proclaimed. *c*1979 L.M. MANGOPE *Place for All* 18 We do not regard it as unreasonable to establish an own Central or Reserve Bank, so that the repatriation of profits to countries outside the 'Rand bloc' is not controlled entirely by Pretoria. **1986** *E. Prov. Herald* 17 Feb. 2 Mr Botha .. indicated he was not prepared to move away from 'self-determination for whites' which he defined as 'own schools, own residential areas and own way of life'. **1986** *Daily Dispatch* 14 Aug. 4 The leader of the NP in the Transvaal defined these cornerstones as being 'own' community life, 'own' residential areas and 'own' schools. **1987** [see Frontline quot. at OPEN]. **1987** [see GROUP sense 1]. **1991** E. TERRE'BLANCHE on TV1, 13 Mar. (Good Morning South Africa), A nation recognized by the world as an own nation.

own affair *n. phr. Hist.* Also with initial capitals. [tr. Afk. *eie saak*, *eie* see prec. + *saak* affair, business, as defined in the Republic of South Africa Constitution Act, No. 110 of 1983 (see quot.).]

1. A matter defined as being specific to a particular ethnic group, and thus controlled by that group through a chamber of the TRICAMERAL parliament, in terms of the Republic of South Africa Constitution Act of 1983; freq. in *pl.* Also *fig.* See also *group rights* (GROUP sense 2), MINISTERS' COUNCIL. Cf. GENERAL AFFAIR.

Schedule 1 of the 1983 Constitution Act lists fourteen areas of 'own affairs', including social welfare, education, art, culture and recreation, health matters, local government, and agriculture.

1983 *Daily Dispatch* 6 May 8 The appointment of marriage officers for a specific population group is an own affair of that group. **1983** *E. Prov. Herald* 6 May 4 Matters particular to one group only are to be known as 'own affairs' and can be decided solely by the chamber for that group. Issues of common interest are to be called 'general affairs' and must be passed by all three chambers. **1983** *Govt Gaz.* Vol.219 No.8914, 12 Matters which specially or differentially affect a population group in relation to the maintenance of its identity and the upholding and furtherance of its way of life, culture, traditions and customs, are, subject to the provisions of section 16, own affairs in relation to the population group ... Matters which are not own affairs of a population group in terms of section 14 are general affairs. *Ibid.* 14 Any question arising in the application of this Act as to whether any particular matters are own affairs of a population group shall be decided by the State President. **1984** *Daily Dispatch* 13 July 5 The bill organised the financial transfer of the state revenue account to other accounts of the state revenue fund to finance the own affairs of the three houses. **1986** C. Heunis in *Cape Times* 8 Feb. 11 Please remember, gentlemen, that hospitals are 'own affairs' rather than 'general affairs'. **1987** N.S. Ndebele in *Eng. Academy Rev.* 4 12 English, unlike the other languages in South Africa, is not 'an own affair' of the ESSAs. It is everybody's affair, because it is indispensable in a way that our other languages are not. **1987** *S. Afr. Digest* 10 July 2 The new Constitution established a tricameral Parliament. Each of the three Houses of Parliament (for Whites, Coloureds and Indians) is responsible for handling the 'own affairs' of its particular population group (such as education and housing). The three Houses are jointly responsible for general affairs (such as defence and foreign affairs). **1987** P. Cull in *E. Prov. Herald* 18 Sept. 7 Education is an 'own affair' in terms of the constitution, with an own affairs minister who exercises control over all schools, training colleges, and technikons. **1988** C. Legum in *Afr. Contemp. Rec.* 1986–7 B719, The Vanderbijlpark public library evicted a Black woman because the library is an 'own affair'. **1988** *Daily Dispatch* 23 Feb. 17 The pre-occupation with race was still with the government, and found expression in the whole concept of 'own' and 'general' affairs. **1988** J. Clarke in *Sunday Star* 22 May 8 Your island .. could be manoeuvred .. into a parking position off, say, Australia. Anywhere! .. Where you eventually anchor would, of course, be an 'own affair'.

2. In *pl.*: The system under which each of the three ethnically-based chambers of the tricameral Parliament was given control of those matters considered to be particular to it. Also *attrib.*, passing into *adj.*, of or pertaining to this system.

1983 *Financial Mail* 16 Sept. 51 If there is to be maximum devolution of power to the ethnic chambers there is every prospect that their demands for 'own affairs' funds will grow increasingly more strident. **1984** *Cape Herald* 25 Jan. 4 The intrusion of politics — and especially 'own affairs' politics — into education. **1984** *Rand Daily Mail* 10 Feb. 6 The whole basis of 'own affairs' under the new constitution is a multitude of separate bureaucracies. **1987** G.D.M. Deas in *Daily Dispatch* 4 May 10 Their pernicious apartheid system .. is not dead. It is simply called by another name — 'own affairs'. **1988** J. Joubert in *Ibid.* 23 Feb 17 Until apartheid in every form and guise — whether it be the old fashioned apartheid of 'blankes alleen' or the new mode of 'own affairs' — was rooted out, there could be no long-term peace or stability. **1990** A. Sachs in *Weekly Mail* 2 Feb. 23 While each one of us has a particularly intimate relationship with one or other cultural matrix, this does not mean that we are locked into a series of cultural 'own affairs' ghettos. **1990** *Sunday Times* 20 May 14 It is a system with an unlovely genealogy. Apartheid begat separate development and separate development begat own affairs. **1992** *E. Prov. Herald* 15 Sept. 2 The first steps towards the dismantling of apartheid structures such as the three Own Affairs administrations and the six non-independent homelands will be set in motion next month when Parliament reconvenes. **1993** K. Davie in *Sunday Times* 21 Mar. (Business Times) 1 White Own Affairs will spend R1-billion less, but then many white parents are now paying much more for education under Model C. **1993** W. Hartley in *Weekend Post* 12 June 8 This year the whole 'own affairs' structure began to crumble in advance of changes to the tricameral Parliament itself.

oxpecker *n.* Either of two birds of the Buphagidae, *Buphagus africanus*, distinguished by a predominantly yellow bill, or *B. erythrorhynchus*, with a red bill, both having sharp claws enabling them to cling onto grazing animals while devouring ticks and other parasites; *buffalo bird*, see BUFFALO sense 2; RHENOSTERVOËL; RHINOCEROS BIRD; *rhinoster bird*, see RHINOSTER sense 1 b; TICK-BIRD sense 2.

1884 Layard & Sharpe *Birds of S. Afr.* 419 During our stay in the bush Ox-peckers appeared in numbers about our oxen, and actually ate large holes in the fleshy part of their backs. **1923** Haagner & Ivy *Sketches* 199 Those [*sc.* the eggs] of the red-billed Ox-pecker are spotted with purplish-red. **1977** D. Livingstone in E. Pereira *Contemp. S. Afr. Plays* 25 We don't want the ox-peckers to give the alarm. *Ibid.* 26 Red-billed oxpeckers flap away from very near, crying … The large animal starts to lumber away. **1988** *Our Living World* 29 Oct. 3 Several rare and endangered species including cheetah, Cape hunting dog, suni antelope, brown hyena, and yellow-billed oxpecker. **1990** *Grocott's Mail* 30 Oct. 3 The oxpecker, whose appetite for ticks is seemingly insatiable, is also the farmers' friend.

ox-wagon *n.* [Fig. use of general Eng.] A heavy pioneer wagon drawn by oxen; used allusively as a symbol of conservative Afrikaner values and aspirations, representing conservatism and retrogressive thinking; OSSEWA sense 2 b. Also *attrib.*

1960 C. Hooper *Brief Authority* 25 For most of my life I had dreaded the vacuous, depopulated, waste regions of South Africa, with their dreary little dorps, their occasional windmills, their dusty aridity, their ox-wagon mentality. **1960** *Times* (U.K.) 8 Oct. 7 The ox-wagon has creaked a little farther away into the blue of the backveld: another stage has been passed in the still unended attempt of the present leaders of Afrikanerdom to put their neighbours' chimney smoke out of sight. **1971** *Sunday Express* 28 Mar. 11 Students to whom I spoke described the move as 'archaic and back to the ox-wagon'. **1980** *Daily Dispatch* 18 Mar. 3 Any criticism of the Botha Government's policies by the conservatives .. will be interpreted as a return to the former ox-wagon tempo of change and can be guaranteed to cause restlessness among the black youth. **1981** P. Qoboza in *Rand Daily Mail* 21 July 13 There is one national characteristic we refuse to abandon. It is the mentality of the oxwagon. The oxwagon played a significant role in this nation. It helped the founding fathers of the nation, both black and white, to open up new frontiers and visions … But in an age where spaceships and computers are zooming through space, the oxwagon has left us a terrible legacy. It has conditioned the minds of so many people, and has kept captive their spirit of adventure. We need to relegate the oxwagons to the age they belonged to.

P

paala var. PALLAH.

paapies var. PAPIES.

paardevoetje var. PERDEVOETJIE.

paardewagen n. obs. [Du., *paard* horse + euphonic -*e*- + *wagen* wagon.] See quot. 1824.

1822 W.J. BURCHELL *Trav.* I. 27 Horse-waggon. This is so called in contradistinction to the more common waggon drawn by oxen, which travels usually about three English miles in an hour; but the Paardewagen goes at a trot, estimated at six miles in an hour. 1824 *Ibid.* II. 135 A *paarde-wagen* is a light waggon drawn by horses, and used more frequently for the conveyance of persons, than for carrying any other loads: it is in fact the colonists' carriage of pleasure. 1924 H.C. NOTCUTT *Pioneers: Men Who Opened Up S. Afr.* 99 (Swart), It is a common sight in Cape Town to see a Malay standing in a long paarde-wagen, driving six horses at full trot, and turning the corners of the streets with facility. [1949 L.G. GREEN *In Land of Afternoon* 204 A voortrekker perdewa (horse-drawn carriage) built in 1837 at Murraysburg.]

‖**paardeziekte** /ˈpɑː(r)dəˌsiktə/ n. *Pathology*. Also **paarde-siekte, paarde ziekt, paard-ziekte, perdesiekte, perdeziekte.** [S. Afr. Du. (later Afk. *perdesiekte*), fr. Du. *paard* horse + euphonic -*e*- + *ziekte* disease.] HORSE-SICKNESS.

1822 W.J. BURCHELL *Trav.* I. 254 The Hantam-berg .. is remarkable for being one of the few situations in this part of the country where horses are not liable to the *Paardeziekte* (Horse distemper), which rages during the summer season, and annually carries off great numbers. 1846 J.C. BROWN tr. *T. Arbousset's Narr. of Explor. Tour to N.-E. of Col.* 113 At all events your horses will be replaced by us, if they die of the *paardesiekte*. 1886 [see NIEUWZIEKTE sense 1]. 1896 R. WALLACE *Farming Indust. of Cape of Col.* 319 Horse-sickness or 'paard-ziekte', *Oedema mycosis*, is a deadly epizootic disease which has been known in Cape Colony since 1719. It is annually in evidence in some places. *Ibid.* 321 There are at least *two* varieties of the disease: .. The *paard-ziekte*, the common form in which the lungs are most seriously affected ... The dikkop. 1920 F.C. CORNELL *Glamour of Prospecting* 73 In the near vicinity were to be seen several swollen, rotten carcasses of goats, cattle, sheep, or horses, dead of lungsiekte or nieusiekte or paardeziekte. 1973 O.H. SPOHR tr. *F. Krauss's Trav. Jrnl* 28 Lamziekte amongst the cattle and perdeziekte amongst horses are dreaded diseases. 1983 J.A. BROWN *White Locusts* 264, I have a remedy for the *perdesiekte*, the horse sickness.

paarl lemoen, paarlmoer varr. PERLEMOEN.

paauw var. POU.

PAC /piː eɪ ˈsiː/ n. Also **P.A.C.** [Initial letters of *Pan African Congress* or *Pan-Africanist Congress*.]
1. The Pan-Africanist Congress, a political organization formed in 1959 by a group which broke away from the ANC under the leadership of Robert Sobukwe. Also *attrib.* See also AFRICANISM, APLA, POQO.

[1959 *Rand Daily Mail* 7 Apr. 1 Nearly 300 Africans meeting in Orlando decided yesterday to form a new political organisation pledged 'to overthrow White domination.' It will be called the Pan Africanist Congress.] 1961 *Survey of Race Rel.* 1959–60 (S.A.I.R.R.) 15 Mr Sobukwe said that the P.A.C. rejected apartheid, but it also rejected multi-racialism. 1963 M. BENSON *Afr. Patriots* 258 Three hundred delegates unanimously elected Robert Mangaliso — 'wonderful' — Sobukwe .. as their President. In his address to the conference he said the P.A.C. aimed 'politically at the government of the African, by the African for the African, with everybody who owes his only loyalty to Africa and who is prepared to accept the democratic rule of an African majority, being regarded as an African. We guarantee no minority rights because we think in terms of individuals not groups.' 1963 A.M. LOUW *20 Days* 78 P.A.C. and A.N.C. headquarters had been raided by the police. 1964 H.H.W. DE VILLIERS *Rivonia* 61 This claim [that Africa had been stolen by the whites] is also put forward in the slogan of the P.A.C.: 'Africa for the Africans'. 1977 *Drum* Aug. 10 The PAC felt the ANC was being controlled by white communists. 1978 *Daily Dispatch* 21 June 3 PAC alive on Robben Island says witness ... The Pan-Africanist Congress had adopted non-racialism, Marxism and the re-distribution of wealth. 1982 *Govt Gaz.* Vol.204 No.8232, 99 Unlawful organizations in respect of which the provisions of section 69 (7) are applicable 1. The African National Congress, also known as the ANC, including Umkhonto we Sizwe. 2. The Pan African Congress, also known as the PAC or Poqo. 1983 *Pretoria News* 28 Sept. 5 Both had pleaded guilty to a charge of contravening the Internal Security Act in that they possessed PAC literature. 1984 *Daily Dispatch* 27 Sept. 5 One quarter of the fund ($100 000) goes to Swapo and the Pan Africanist Congress of Azania (PAC) gets $30000. 1986 P. MAYLAM *Hist. of Afr. People* 188 At the PAC's inaugural conference at Orlando in 1959 Sobukwe was elected as the first PAC president. 1987 *Learn & Teach* No.2, 4 Many people in Sharpeville were members of the Pan African Congress — the PAC. They said on the 21st March we must leave our passes at home. 1988 P. LAWRENCE in *Saturday Star* 9 July 11 The open palm, as distinct from the clenched fist symbol of black power .. is the fraternal sign of the prohibited Pan-Africanist Congress (PAC). 1989 *Reader's Digest Illust. Hist.* 400 Acts of terror, orchestrated by Poqo, the armed wing of the Pan-Africanist Congress (PAC). 1990 P. CULL in *E. Prov. Herald* 3 Feb., State President FW de Klerk threw down the gauntlet yesterday, unbanning the ANC, PAC and South African Communist Party. 1990 R. MALAN *My Traitor's Heart* 248 In exile, the ANC was kept alive largely by Moscow and the PAC by Peking. Both organizations virtually ceased to exist inside South Africa. 1992 M. MBATHA in *Pace* Aug. 69 Mlambo says the PAC will only negotiate in [sic] the sole purpose of formally transferring power from the white minority to the indigenous majority.

2. *nonce.* A member of the PAC.

1990 *Sunday Times* 12 Aug. 17 An NP/ANC coalition will usurp all power and suppress the living daylights out of AWBs, PACs, CPs, Azapo, Democrats and anyone else who dares express a dissenting view.

pacati pl. form of UMPAKATI.

pacht n. obs. Also **pagt**. [S. Afr. Du., fr. Du. *pacht, pagt* pact, leasehold (fr. L. *pactus* agreement).] During the 18th and early 19th centuries, a monopoly licence for the retailing of wine and spirits, sold by the authorities to only one retailer in any given area. Also *attrib.*

The pacht was abolished in Cape Town in November 1823, and in the country districts in 1828.

1823 W.W. BIRD *State of Cape of G.H.* 41 The Pagt is the monopoly of selling wine by retail, and the Pagter is the farmer of that monopoly. 1824 *S. Afr. Commercial Advertiser* 28 Jan. 31 The Pachters of the District of Albany offer a Reward of One Hundred and Fifty Rixdollars for such information as will lead to the detection and condemnation of persons violating the Pacht Regulations. 1826 R. BOURKE in G.M. Theal *Rec. of Cape Col.* (1905) XXVII. 80 The general substitution of licences to Retailers of Wine and Spirituous Liquors in lieu of the Pacht will .. occasion another loss of Revenue. 1827 *Reports of Commissioners upon Finances at Cape of G.H.* II. 57 The licences for retail of wine were annually directed to be farmed to four persons, who were not to be wine-growers. This monopoly under the name of 'Pagt,' was continued in Cape Town, in the hands of one person, and is still supported in the country districts. 1832 *Cape of G.H. Lit. Gaz.* 1 Feb. 243 We would seriously take into consideration the propriety of re-establishing the old *Pacht* for Cape Town. 1926 P.W. LAIDLER *Tavern of Ocean* 171 You may talk of your pachts ... The nectar you sip at the glorious Apollo Is drink for the Gods and will beat them all hollow.

pachter /ˈpaxtə(r)/ n. *Obs. exc. hist.* [S. Afr. Du., *pacht, pagt* see prec. + agential suffix -*er*.] One holding the monopoly license for the retailing of wine and spirits in a particular town or district.

1823, 1824 [see PACHT]. 1824 W.J. BURCHELL *Trav.* II. 145 There were .. a town butcher and baker, and a *pagter*, (pakter) or retailer of wine and brandy; who are appointed by licence from the landrost. 1827 [see WINE FARMER]. 1832 *Graham's Town Jrnl* 16 Feb. 30 Had the 'Pachter' thought of any thing but his annual monopoly ten years ago, meeting houses and Sunday Schools would not now be undermining us in the name of Religion. 1857 *Cape Monthly Mag.* II. Sept. 158 Their forefathers, having first deposited a tithe of their vintage at the Government stores as a 'royalty,' in vain sought buyers for the remainder, unless the Company, or the 'farmer' of the right to vend wines (pagter) were inclined to purchase at the prices which the Government fixed. 1862 *Abstracts* in *Cape Stat.* p.xliv, All persons carrying wine or brandy in the streets to be required to prove that they have purchased from the 'pachter' or farmer of the sale of wines. 1955 L.G. GREEN *Karoo* 93 There was also a town butcher and baker, and a *pagter* or a retailer of wine and brandy. 1972 A. SCHOLEFIELD *Wild Dog Running* 101 He turned to the *pachter* behind the counter and said, 'Two more of the same,' putting down a golden sovereign to pay.

pack v. *trans.* In the phr. *to pack out* [calqued on Afk. *uitpak, pak uit*], to unpack (a suitcase, clothes, etc.); to empty (a pocket).

1969 *Sunday Times* 9 Mar., I turned around to pack out the night clothes from the suitcases. 1969 *Albany*

Mercury 23 Dec. 1, I have had great difficulty keeping the shop fully stocked. As fast as the staff can pack out goods they are bought up. **1973** *Eng. Usage in Sn Afr.* Vol.4 No.2, 33 *Pack out*, lit. transl. of Afk. 'pak uit' ... *Unpack* is .. correct. **1982** *Cape Times* 8 Sept. 11 While Capetonians sweated it out in yesterday's heat, this street musician packed out his home-made guitar and mouth organ and kept things cool by entertaining pedestrians. **1992** *Living* Feb. 82 'Pack out everything including your pockets please Meneer,' said the youngster.

Pacofs /'pækɒfs/ *n.* Also **PACOFS**. [Acronym formed on *Performing Arts Council of the Orange Free State*.] A government-subsidized organization established in the early 1960s to promote the performing arts in the Orange Free State. See also CAPAB, NAPAC, PACT.

1971 *Rand Daily Mail* 8 Feb., Mr. Peter Curtis, artistic director of English drama, said the agreement would be mutually beneficial to CAPAB and PACOFS. **1971** *Argus* 10 May 2 International ballet dancer and choreographer Frank Staff – ballet master with Pacofs since the beginning of 1969. **1974** *Friend* 11 June 8 PACOFS (Incorporated Association not for gain). **1980** [see CAPAB].

Pact /pækt/ *n.* Also **PACT**. [Acronym formed on the initial letters of *Performing Arts Council of the Transvaal*.] A government-subsidized organization established in the early 1960s to promote the performing arts in the former Transvaal. Also *attrib.* See also CAPAB, NAPAC, PACOFS.

1971 *Personality* 2 Apr. 35 Pier has been in Italy for six years but has been back to South Africa once to join a Pact opera tour of the Northern Transvaal. **1980** [see CAPAB]. **1987** *Star* 3 June 14 The 'super orchestra' recently put together through merging the Pact and SABC symphonies. **1992** C. DU PLESSIS in *Pace* Sept. 156 He appears regularly in the Sunday Morning Opera Concerts and private soirees organised by Pact. At present he is in rehearsal for Pact's version of *Marriage of Figaro*.

padda /'pada/ *n.* Also **pada**, **parra**, **podder**. [Afk., toad, frog.]

1.a. A frog. Also *attrib.*

1897 E. GLANVILLE *Tales from Veld* 241 'It sounds like treacle,' said Abe with a puzzled look; 'but I don't see what the podder's got to do with it, anyhow.' **1913** C. PETTMAN *Africanderisms* 359 *Padda*, .. The South African name for all varieties of frogs, generally pronounced 'podder'. *Ibid.* 365 *Parra* or *Parrak*, .. A common corruption of Padda. **1950** W. ROSE *Reptiles & Amphibians* 8 Whilst the West Cape paddas are most active those in other localities may be hibernating. **1968** F.G. BUTLER *Cape Charade* 9 Why are you being sent to work on the road? Frogs master; the Paddas. Its all the fault of the frogs. **1970** R. MAYTHAM *Informant, Empangeni* At night all the paddas made an uproarious noise. **1982** D. CAPEL in *E. Prov. Herald* 6 Oct. 5 Now a 'Very Important Padda' has died – and left the frog world without a king. **1988** *Cosmopolitan* Apr. 8 Frog Wines. If you think that froggy wines are French, you're fooled. A range of five 'padda' wines come from Tulbagh's Paddagang Wine House. The charming 'padda' labels will bring a smile to your lips. **1990** *Weekend Post* 10 Mar. 5 'She's the frog among the lilies,' ... This has a nicer ring to it than 'le padda'. **1992** A.A. FERRAR in *Afr. Wildlife* Vol.46 No.4, 151 An artificial wetland treating the college's effluent had fooled a goliath heron into dropping in for an early morning padda patrol.

b. *comb.* **paddabos** /-bɔs/ [Afk., *bos* bush], the shrub *Cliffortia polygonifolia* of the Rosaceae; **paddaklou** or **-klauw** [Afk., *klou* (earlier Du. *klauw*) claw, paw], the shrub *Teucrium africanum* of the Labiatae; **padda slym** /-sleım/ or **-slime** [Afk., *slym* (earlier Du. *slijm*)], any of several species of fresh water algae, spirogyra, or duckweed; **paddaslyk** /-sleık/ [Afk., *slyk* slush, slime], the skin formed on hot milk; **padda-water** /-vɑːtə(r)/ [Afk., *water* water], a pool of stagnant water.

1973 M.R. LEVYNS in *Std Encycl. of Sn Afr.* VIII. 425 **Paddabos**, (*Cliffortia polygonifolia*). Erect, hairy shrub belonging to the family *Rosaceae*. **1913** C. PETTMAN *Africanderisms* 359 **Padda klauw**, .. *Teucrium africanum*. The flowers of this plant resemble in shape a frog's or toad's foot. **1973** M.R. LEVYNS in *Std Encycl. of Sn Afr.* VIII. 425 Paddaklou. Aambeisbos(sie). Akkedispoot. (*Teucrium africanum*) Small, branched shrub belonging to the family *Labiatae*. **1913** C. PETTMAN *Africanderisms* 360 **Padda slijm**, .. The fine filaments of several species of freshwater algae. **1977** F.G. BUTLER *Karoo Morning* 144 A muddy pool about six foot across, thick with paddaslime and alive with mosquito larvae, tadpoles, [etc.]. **1980** *Cape Times* July (Dine & Wine) 15 My coffee came with a dollop of **paddaslyk** – the sloppy top of the boiled milk. **1912** *S. Afr. Jrnl* July 40 (Pettman), Some farmers accuse the so-called **padda water** collecting after the rainfall. **1912** *S. Afr. Agric. Jrnl* July 46 (Pettman), Water of whatever description, river or rain (so-called *paddawaterjes*), could not be responsible for the disease.

c. With qualifying word: **donder padda**, see as a main entry; **reen-padda** /'riən-/, also (formerly) **regen-padda**, [Afk., *reën* (earlier Du. *regen*) rain], DONDER PADDA sense b.

1905 W.L. SCLATER in Flint & Gilchrist *Science in S. Afr.* 149 The commonest representative of the curious digging family *Engystomatidae* is *Breviceps gibbosus*, commonly known as the 'regen padda.' It is the most comical little figure imaginable, with its globular body, very short stout legs and blunt little face hardly projecting beyond the general rotund outline. **1918** S.H. SKAIFE *Animal Life* 214 There are six species of the curious digging-frogs in South Africa, and of these, the quaint little *regen-padda* is the commonest. **1937** *Guide to Vertebrate Fauna of E. Cape Prov.* (Albany Museum) II. Index, Reen Padda = Breviceps.

2. *obs.* [See Thompson quot. 1913.] Any of several species of angler-fish, a marine fish of the Lophiidae.

[**1900** J.D.F. GILCHRIST *Hist. of Local Names of Cape Fish* 219 (Pettman), Known in several places in the Colony as the Paddy, and in others as the Devil fish.] **1913** C. PETTMAN *Africanderisms* 360 *Paddy* or *Padda*, .. *Lophius upsicephalus*, known at East London as the devil-fish or angler. **1913** W.W. THOMPSON *Sea Fisheries of Cape Col.* 59 (Swart), We can easily see how the froglike body and expansive mouth of the padda (fishing-frog) should be responsible for the designation bestowed.

paddavanger /'pada,faŋə(r)/ *n.* Also **padda-fanger**. [Afk., *padda* frog, toad + *vanger* catcher.] The HAMMERKOP, *Scopus umbretta*.

1902 'X.C.' *Everyday Life in Cape Col.* 42 The crane put in a claim for high flying, also the *padderfanger*, and the owl too. **1909** *The Cape* 23 Apr. 13 The eccentric nest of that eccentric bird the hammerkop – a paddavanger as it is sometimes called. **1923** HAAGNER & IVY *Sketches* 139 The Hammerhead (Scopus umbretta), usually called the Hammerkop or Paddavanger (Frog-catcher) by the South African. **1937** *Guide to Vertebrate Fauna of E. Cape Prov.* (Albany Museum) II. Index, Paddavanger – Hammerkop. [**1965** W. PLOMER *Turbott Wolfe* 155 They used to call him Paddafanger, from that odd clucking noise he made when he was trying to get a word out.] **1967** *Some Protected Birds of Cape Prov.* (Dept of Nature Conservation) 11 Hamerkop, paddavanger, *Scopus umbretta* ... A common bird on open shallow water ... Builds a large dome-shaped nest of sticks and twigs. **1979** *E. Prov. Herald* 5 Nov. 9 Those tadpoles .. turn into frogs but they .. have to look out for such predators as herons, fish, kingfishers, padda-vangers.

padkos /'patkɔs/ *n.* Also **padkost**, **pat-koss**. [Afk., *pad* road + *kos* (earlier Du. *kost*) food.] Food for a journey; provisions. Also *attrib.*, and *fig.*

[**1786** G. FORSTER tr. *A. Sparrman's Voy. to Cape of G.H.* I. 70 A luncheon of bread and butter doubled together, and stuffed into my coat-pocket by my host and hostess, by way of (*weegkost*) or provision for my journey.] **1849** R. GRAY *Jrnl of Bishop's Visitation* I. 95 Having got careless as to our 'pat-cop' [*sic*] as we approached home, we fared but badly, and finished our meal by a draught of not the clearest water in the world. **1851** *Ibid.* II. 173, I was not allowed to depart without a good supply of pad-koss, and other comforts provided by the kindness of the parishioners. **1895** in *Funk's Std Dict.*, Padkost. **1913** C. PETTMAN *Africanderisms* 279 'Veld kos' is such food as the veld will furnish; 'Pad kos', provisions for a journey. **1950** *Cape Times* 19 Sept. 14 With apples, biscuits and fish and chips as padkos, Mr. C.J. Kirstein .. arrived .. from Cape Town .. in 12 hours, 45 minutes. **1957** *Ibid.* 3 Apr. 9 One thing the South African Railways have always had to contend with is South Africa's habit of taking along 'padkos' on a journey. **1966** F.G. BUTLER *Take Root or Die* (1970) 59 As I am about to embark on the most important journey of my life, your gifts are most opportune. I shall be needing padkos. **1968** L.G. GREEN *Full Many Glorious Morning* 12 There have always been travellers who have preferred to carry their own *padkos*, and Piggot recalled a family man who boarded the train with eight roast chickens and a bucket of baked potatoes. **1972** J. CLARKE in *Argus* 18 Mar. (Mag. Sect.) 6 Before it [*sc.* the swallow] can make the flight it must put on a large amount of fat – virtually 'padkos' food for the road. **1973** A. FUGARD in S. Gray *Writers' Territory* 130 Basket of padkos – buttered slices of bread, one cold mutton chop, flask of black coffee. **1974** *Daily Dispatch* 20 July 8 The vast numbers of people on the train were evidently well stacked with 'pad-kos' and there were only 20-odd (some very odd) people in the dining car. **1980** *E. Prov. Herald* 30 July, The continuing and increasing demand for South Africa's traditional 'padkos' snack – biltong. **1982** *Ibid.* 23 Sept., Any parent knows that travelling with children means taking 'padkos'. And 'Padkos', providing welcome change, is more than simple nourishment on a long car journey. **1989** T. BOTHA in *Style* June 11 The red bag on the back seat .. contains the soulfood of the long-distance driver. The valium of the N1. Padkos. Sarmies, biltong, beers, Cokes, chips, Nux bars and indigestion. **1994** R. KINNEAR in *Flying Springbok* June 32 Even the kids seemed relaxed on the way home, happy to admire the drifts of cosmos and wild flowers banked on the side of the road while munching a *padkos* picnic supplied by the hotel.

padloper /'patluəpə(r)/ *n.* Also **padlooper**, **patlooper**. [Afk. (earlier S. Afr. Du.), 'tramp, vagabond', fr. Du. *pad* path + *loper* runner (fr. *loop* go, walk); see quot. 1821.] Any of several species of land-tortoise of the genus *Homopus* of the Testudinidae, esp. the small land-tortoise *Homopus areolatus*, peculiar to the Western Cape, and the pale olive-brown-coloured tortoise *H. femoralis*. Also *attrib.* See also PADLOPERTJIE sense 2.

1821 C.I. LATROBE *Jrnl of Visit* 79 Here I saw the first land-tortoise, of the species called by the Dutch, Patlooper, from their generally keeping on the pathway or carriage-road. *Ibid.* 439 Many tortoises crawl about the waste ... A small species called Patlooper, is from four to five inches. **1913** C. PETTMAN *Africanderisms* 360 *Padlooper*, .. A small tortoise is so named. **1937** *Guide to Vertebrate Fauna of E. Cape Prov.* (Albany Museum) II. 9 *Homopus areolatus* Thunb. Lesser Padloper or Areolated Tortoise (Parrot-beak Tortoise). *Ibid.* 10 *Homopus femoralis* Blgr. Greater Padloper. Karroo Tortoise ... A plain-coloured tortoise. *c*1939 S.H. SKAIFE *S. Afr. Nature Notes* 45 There are three different kinds of tortoises found in the Cape Peninsula: these are the areolated tortoise, or *padloper*, the angulated tortoise, or *bont-skilpad* and the water tortoise, or Cape Terrapin. The areolated tortoise is the smallest and commonest of the three. It receives its Afrikaans name of *padloper* from its habit of frequently choosing the public highway for its walks abroad. **1988** M. BRANCH *Explore Cape Flora* 21 Tiny *speckled padloper tortoise* eats a beetle daisy. **1989** E. BAARD in *Afr. Wildlife* Vol.43 No.4, 181 Researchers .. tracked down and removed 292 padlopers (*Homopus areolatus*) and 52 geometric tortoises after several comprehensive searches of the area.

padlopertjie /'patluəpə(r)ki, -luəpə(r)ci/ *n.* Also **patluperk**. [Afk., *padloper* see prec. + dim. suffix -IE.]

1. *?obs.* Any of several species of bird (see quots).

1881 E.E. Frewer tr. *E. Holub's Seven Yrs in S. Afr.* I. 80 A few red-legged plovers and some small bustards (of the kind that the Boers call 'patluperks'), which we had shot in the course of the day, afforded us a meal that we thoroughly enjoyed. **1913** C. Pettman *Africanderisms* 360 *Padloopertje,* .. *Megalophonus cinereus, Lay.* The reference is to the habit which this bird has of running along the road. **1937** *Guide to Vertebrate Fauna of E. Cape Prov.* (Albany Museum) II. 80 The following popular terms apply both to Larks and Pipits in allusion to the habit of 'ducking' on alarm: Koester, Koosvoël, Kooskoetjie, Kootsee, Platlêer and Padlopertjie. When approached they run ahead in crouching ratlike manner.

2. The land-tortoise *Homopus signatus* of the Testudinidae, the world's smallest tortoise. Also *attrib.* See also PADLOPER.

1982 *S. Afr. Panorama* Jan. 41 The *padlopertjie* tortoise, endemic to the south-western Cape Province. **1983** *Ibid.* Apr. [Back cover], The lovely little speckled *padlopertjie* (tramp), *Homopus signatus,* .. is the smallest of the Southern African species and one of the smallest in the world. The carapace is about 100 mm long.

padrao /pəˈdraɔ/ *n.* Also **padrão, padrâo,** Pl. **padraos, padrãos, padroes, padraões.** [Pg., inscribed post or pillar, monument; standard, gauge.] An inscribed stone pillar or cross, erected at several points along the South African coast by Portuguese explorers of the 15th and early 16th centuries to mark Portuguese sovereignty, proclaim Christianity, and serve as a landmark. See also BEACON *n.* sense 2.

1900 E.G. Ravenstein *Voy. of Diogo Cão & Bartholomeu Dias 1482–88* (1986) 3 Cão was the first to carry 'padr&otilde.es,' or pillars of stone on an exploring voyage. Up to his time the Portuguese had been content to erect perishable wooden crosses, or to carve inscriptions into trees, to mark the progress of their discoveries. King John conceived the happy idea of introducing stone pillars, surmounted by a cross, and bearing, in addition to the royal arms, an inscription recording .. the date, the name of the king by whose order the voyage was made, and the name of the commander. The four padrões set up by Cão on his two voyages have been discovered *in situ.* *c*1936 *S. & E. Afr. Yr Bk & Guide* 447 Part of a 'padrao,' or marble cross erected by Bartholomew Diaz, at Angra Pequena, in 1486. **1964** L.G. Green *Old Men Say* 42 Portuguese explorers left inscribed pillars called *padrãos* to mark their discoveries, and one or two of these have been pieced together in recent years. **1968** *Dict. of S. Afr. Biography* I. 242 The squadron passed Cape Cross (lat. 21°47'S.) where Diogo Cão had placed his last *padrão,* an inscribed stone pillar of Portuguese limestone, surmounted by a cross, which proclaimed Portuguese sovereignty over the area. **1973** *Std Encycl. of Sn Afr.* VIII. 425 *Padrões,* Inscribed stone pillars which were erected by Portuguese explorers from the time of Diogo Cão to early in the 16th century. **1988** Lubke & La Cock *Vegetation & Ecology of Kwaaihoek: Site of Dias Cross (pamphlet),* Dias carried on board his caravels on this exploratory voyage a number of padraõs or beacons sculptured from limestone from a quarry in Portugal. **1988** R.A. Lubke et al. *Field Guide to E. Cape* 380 Fragments of the padrão were recovered from pools at the leaward base of the headland by Axelson in 1938. **1988** R.G. Shuttleworth in *Cape Times* 13 Jan. 8 Dias and his crew would have had no particular difficulty carrying the 250–300 kg padrao, since several of them would have carried it in a rope or canvas sling. [**1989** P.E. Raper *Dict. of Sn Afr. Place Names* 88 The name [Cape Padrone] is derived from the Portuguese *padrâo,* a stone cross to mark Portuguese possession.] **1991** F.G. Butler *Local Habitation* 244 Far from being without 'ghosts', the poem is an indaba of shades on the headland known as Kwaai Hoek, where Dias planted his *padrao* half a millenium ago.

pagate, pagatees, pagati pl. forms of UMPAKATI.

pagger var. BAGGER.

pagt, pagter varr. PACHT, PACHTER.

painted lady *n. phr.* [Transf. use of general Eng. *painted lady* the name of a variety of carnation; see also quot. 1966.] Any of several species of GLADIOLUS.

1906 B. Stoneman *Plants & their Ways* 198 Gladiolus ... 'Painted Ladies' and 'Kalkoentjies' belong here. Eighty-one species of this large genus are found in South Africa. **1910** J. Runcie *Idylls by Two Oceans* 9 Like the little Moederkapjes, That brushed against my knee; Like the friendly Painted Ladies, That nodded a bright 'Good-day.' *c*1911 S. Playne *Cape Col.* 49 The well-known 'Painted Lady' is found chiefly on the coastal borders. **1913** D. Fairbridge *Piet of Italy* 77 Baskets heaped with heaths and arums, 'painted ladies,' and white watsonias, purple iris and mountain anemones. **1917** R. Marloth *Common Names* 64 *Painted lady,* Applied to several species of *Gladiolus* with pink marks on the flowers, e.g., *G. debilis, G. hastatus.* Sometimes also *G. blandus.* **1933** J. Juta *Look Out for Ostriches* 21 The large gladiolus family which boasts the pink patterned 'painted ladies'. **1966** C.A. Smith *Common Names* 362 *Painted lady,* Several species of *Gladiolus* of the so-called 'blandus type' with graceful slender stems and showy inflated flowers usually arranged in second spikes ... The vernacular name is in allusion to the marking on the lower segments of the flowers. **1969** M.W. Spilhaus *Doorstep-Baby* 141 In the Spring arum lilies and orchids and delicate gladioli, which South Africans called Painted Ladies, grow wild in the black soil. **1985** *Veld & Flora* Vol.71 No.4, It' [*sc.* the sandlelie] would 'go native' there just as your own bavianis [*sic*] .. painted ladies, kalkoentjies etc. have along Australian sand dunes.

paint-stone *n.* [Perh. tr. S. Afr. Du. *verfklip, verf* paint + *klip* stone (cf. Du. *verfaarde* 'paint earth').] A stone which, when broken, provides powder which in the past was used as pigment; this powder.

1797 J. Barrow in D. Fairbridge *Lady Anne Barnard* (1924) 41, I send you a specimen of a paint-stone, which you may break if you like – you will find within a fine impalpable powder which when mixed with oil serves all the country people here as a paint for their houses, waggons etc. They are found of every possible colour except green ... The blue is the most rare, and is the Native Prussian blue. **1797** Lady A. Barnard *S. Afr. Century Ago* (1910) 121 The 'paint stone' is found in this neighbourhood [*sc.* Paarl] in quantities – namely, an impalpable powder .. contained within stones of different sizes, and on breaking them the powder comes forth, ground as fine as if it had been done in Bond Street. **1926** P.W. Laidler *Tavern of Ocean* 97 For paint to preserve the woodwork of his carts and waggons, the farmer mixed 'paint stones' (natural ochres) with oil. **1934** C.P. Swart Supplement to Pettman. 132 *Paint Stone,* Certain stones in the Cape Province that on being broken are found to contain finely ground powders, of all colours but green. These powders were extensively used.

pakati var. and pl. form of UMPAKATI.

paling /ˈpɑːləŋ, -ɪŋ/ *n.* Also **palang.** [Afk.] Any of several species of marine or freshwater eel (order Anguilliformes), particularly *Muraena mossambica.* Also *attrib.*

1947 K.H. Barnard *Pict. Guide to S. Afr. Fishes* 64 In South Africa there is only one species [of eel]: the South African *Fresh-water Eel,* or *Paling (Anguilla mossambica).* **1949** J.L.B. Smith *Sea Fishes* 388 *Muraena Mossambica* ... *Eel. Paling* ... Found in most inland waters of the Cape, Natal, and Transvaal and further north. Attains at least 30lbs in the rivers of the Eastern Cape. **1965** J. Bennett *Hawk Alone* 145 He and Stuart would go down to the winding river .. to catch eels, palings they called them. **1970** A. Palmer *Informant, King William's Town* We went palang fishing (eel fishing) on Saturday. **1972** *Grocott's Mail* 4 Mar., Landed a moray eel, the bont paling. They are not common in our area and one this size (one metre) is exceptional. **1981** *Ibid.* 10 Nov. 8 Local freshwater angler John Knoetze holds the huge one metre 'paling' (eel) which he caught at the Fish River Bridge ... The Fish River Bridge area is well-stocked with this edible fish, the usual size caught being up to ,75 metres. **1984** J. Breytenbach *Informant, Grahamstown* There was I with my line, my hook, and my proppie, fishing for palings.

pallah *n. obs.* Also **paala, p(h)alla.** Pl. unchanged, or **-s.** [SeTswana, Sotho, and Venda *phala* red antelope.] IMPALA sense 1 a. Also *attrib.*

1802 Truter & Somerville in G.M. Theal *Rec. of Cape Col.* (1899) IV. 384 Pieter Jacobs shot a handsome ram of a palla antelope, with fine horns. [**1815** A. Plumptre tr. *H. Lichtenstein's Trav. in Sn Afr.* (1930) II. 324 That beautiful species of Antelope .. which is called by the Beetjuans *Phalla.* **1827** G. Thompson *Trav.* I. 201 On the banks of this stream I observed a species of antelope, that I had not previously seen. It is called by the Bechuanas *Paala,* and Mr. Burchell has described it under the name of the red buck. It is, I believe, the same animal termed *Riet-bok* by the colonists.] **1857** D. Livingstone *Missionary Trav.* 56 The presence of the rhinoceros, the buffalo and gnu .. the giraffe, the zebra and the pallah (Antilope melampus), is always a certain indication of water being a distance of seven or eight miles. **1866** J. Leyland *Adventures* 144 Hartebeests, Sassabes and Pallahs. **1875** D. Leslie *Among Zulus* 107 The graceful Pallah will be seen in troops, gazing with evident wonder and terror in your direction. **1900** W.L. Sclater *Mammals of S. Afr.* I. 206 The pallah is never found in the open country or very far from a river. **1928** E.H.L. Schwarz *Kalahari & its Native Races* 57 There was .. any amount of palla, the bush springbok.

pallie var. PELLIE.

palmiet /palˈmit, ˈpalmiːt/ *n.* Also **palmi(e)te.** [Du., fr. Sp. and Pg. *palmito* dim. of *palma* palm.] **1.** The reed *Prionium serratum* of the Juncaceae, common in swamps and along river banks, esp. in the Western and Eastern Cape, and which has a woody stem topped by a cluster of long, narrow, serrated leaves. Also *attrib.*

The young shoots were formerly used as a vegetable, the stems to make ceilings, and the stiff, sharp-edged leaves to weave straw hats, and in thatching.

1786 G. Forster tr. *A. Sparrman's Voy. to Cape of G.H.* I. 42 *Palmites,* a kind of *acorus* with a thick stem and broad leaves, which grow out from the top, as they do in the palm-tree, a circumstance from which the plant takes its name. These palmites are found in great abundance in most rivers and streams. [**1790** tr. *F. Le Vaillant's Trav.* II. 122 The river *Palmit,* thus named by the Dutch, on account of the great quantity of reeds which grow on its banks.] **1800** Lady A. Barnard *S. Afr. Century Ago* (1910) 285, I am living out of town, .. removed from all party work, except working parties in our fields, rooting up of palmite roots and planting of fir trees and potatoes. **1822** W.J. Burchell *Trav.* I. 91 Most of the rivers which we passed in this excursion, are choked up with the plant called Palmiet by the colonists .. Some notion of the appearance of these plants, may be gained by imagining a vast number of .. pine-apple plants, without fruit, so thickly crowded together as to cover the sides and even the middle of the stream, standing seldom higher than three or four feet above the surface. *a*1827 D. Carmichael in W.J. Hooker *Botanical Misc.* (1831) II. 44 The channel of this river .. is encumbered with the *Palmiet,* a gigantic species of bog-rush, (*Juncus serratus*) that spreads and interlaces its creeping stem over the surface, forming a strong elastic net-work, upon which a man may walk without the least fear of sinking. **1829** *Govt Gaz.* 23 Jan. 8 The Slave Boy Adam .. had on when he absented himself white shirt, leather jacket and trowsers, and Palmiet hat. **1860** W. Shaw *Story of my Mission* 56 A broad-brimmed hat, made from the leaves of the Palmiet, which grew in some of the streams. **1862** Lady Duff-Gordon *Lett. from Cape* (1925) 132 A troop [of baboons] followed at a distance, hiding and dodging among the palmiets. **1893** 'Africanus' in *Cape Illust. Mag.* July 416 We have seen some palmiet shrubs on the high parts, but they are very rare, stunted and generally far from water. **1894** E. GLANVILLE *Fair Colonist* 177 A straw hat that Sally was weaving out of dried palmiet leaves. **1906** B. STONEMAN *Plants & their Ways* 182 The Restiaceae .. differ from the true rushes to which Palmiet belongs (*Prionum palmita*). **1910** R. JUTA *Cape Peninsula* 98 The Hout Bay Valley has a distinctive charm of its own; its river-bed is overgrown with palmiet. **1913** H. TUCKER *Our Beautiful Peninsula* 41 A river, veiled in palmiet, issues from the kloof and flows down to the bay. **1946** V. POHL *Adventures of Boer Family* 162 During the final year of the war the only hats they possessed were those made by my mother and Sophia from straw, *palmiet* (a water plant) or mealie leaves. **1957** L.G. GREEN *Beyond City Lights* 38 It [*sc.* Huguenot, a suburb of Paarl] was a palmiet jungle in the seventies of last century. **1971** —— *Taste of S.-Easter* 82 They .. gathered an edible palmiet in the vleis. **1985** *S. Afr. Panorama* Oct. 14 In sharp contrast to the 'De Wet House' is the reconstructed pioneer dwelling with its *palmiet* (rush) ceiling and yellowwood floors.

2. *nonce.* A hat made of the leaves of the palmiet.

1870 H.H. DUGMORE *Reminisc. of Albany Settler* 17 The beaver gave way to the home-made palmiet, or coffee straw, and the tiger-skin cap, flat-crowned generally.

PAM /piː eɪ 'em/ *n. hist.* Initial letters of *Pan-Africanist Movement*, an organization formed in December 1989 to represent the then-banned Pan-Africanist Congress (see PAC) within South Africa.

The PAM was absorbed by the PAC after the unbanning of that organization in February 1990.

1990 *City Press* 25 Feb. 2 The Pan Africanist Congress is to hold a consultative conference in Harare to discuss its expansion and working relations with the Pan Africanist Movement (PAM). **1990** *Tribute* Apr. 18 PAM, the new Africanist grouping, was fighting the MDM in the Cape. **1990** GOODENOUGH & SIGONYELA in *Weekly Mail* 27 Apr. 8 Five-person committees from the MDM and the PAM, set up in terms of the agreement, meet frequently. **1990** *Race Rel. Survey 1989–90* (S.A.I.R.R.) 734 The impending launch in December 1989 of the Pan-Africanist Movement (PAM) as the PAC's internal wing was welcomed by the PAC as 'a positive step in advancing the cause of liberation.' *Ibid.* 744 In March 1990, following the lifting of the ban on the PAC, the PAM announced that it would dissolve to form part of the PAC ... A statement said the PAM would be renamed PAC-Internal.

pampelmoes /ˌpampəl'mʊs, -'mus/ *n.* Also **pampelmoose**, **pampelmous**, **pamplemoes**, **pamplemousse**, **pompelmoes**, **pompelmouse**, **pompelmus**, **pumplemus**. [An Afk. form of a name for the shaddock (the more common form in Afk. being *pompelmoes*) which arose in the Du. Indies in the 17th C., prob. a compressed form of *pompoenlimoes* 'pumpkin-like citron', Du. *pompoen* pumpkin + Pg. *limoes*, pl. of *limão* lemon. Cf. obs. general Eng. *pompelmoose*).]

1.a. The usual name given to the shaddock, *Citrus decumana*, a large, fleshy, loose-skinned, lemon-yellow fruit with bitter-sweet taste; the tree bearing this fruit; loosely, the grapefruit or any similar citrus fruit. Also *attrib.*

1731 G. MEDLEY tr. *P. Kolb's Present State of Cape of G.H.* II. 275 An *Indian Orange-Tree*, bearing the largest Sort of Oranges; and ordinarily call'd, by the *Dutch* at the *Cape, Pompelmus*; in the *West Indies, Shaddock.* **1796** E. HELME tr. *F. Le Vaillant's Trav.* I. 40 (Jeffreys), The canton of the Twenty-four Rivers is the Eden of Africa where we walk through groves of pampelmoes. **1798** S.H. WILCOCKE tr. *J.S. Stavorinus's Voy. to E. Indies 1768–71* I. 235 The *pompelmoes*, or shaddock, the fruit of which is one of the most wholesome, on account of its refreshing quality and taste. **1843** J.C. CHASE *Cape of G.H.* 152 We have the fruits of the warmer climates in great perfection; Chinese and Seville oranges, lemons, pamplemousses, shaddocks, limes and citrons, [etc.]. **1858** T. SHONE Diary. 27 Sept., Billy came to see me. I gave Him some pumplemuses to give to his Mother. **1892** 'KAMEAHS' in *Cape Illust. Mag.* Nov. 90 Plums, Pomegranate, Pompelmouses, Pine Apples. **1910** D. FAIRBRIDGE *That Which Hath Been* (1913) 134, I cannot understand why your oranges and pamplemousses should grow so much finer than do mine. **1918** *Bk of Recipes* (Diocesan School for Girls, Grahamstown) 108 Pampelmousse Marmalade. **1933** W.H.S. BELL *Bygone Days* 35 There were hundreds of beautiful orange trees, also lemons of several sorts, pamplemoes, citron, naartjes of most exquisite flavour, and a small and tasty fruit we used to call 'half orange and half naartje'. **1944** J. MOCKFORD *Here Are S. Africans* 45 There were always dishes piled with fruit on the table — peaches, *nartjies* or tangerines, pears, grapes, *pompelmoes* or grapefruit, *spanspek* or muskmelon, figs, pomegranates. **1951** S. VAN H. TULLEKEN *Prac. Cookery Bk* 306 So few know the difference between shaddock and pampelmoes. Shaddock is the very large fruit with the thick peel .. while pampelmoes has much thinner peel, and is a smaller fruit, the colour exactly like those rough-skinned lemons; .. the fruit has a beautiful smell. **1951** L.G. GREEN *Grow Lovely* 91 The pampelmoes, which is not unlike the citrus fruit called shaddock. **1971** A. SCHOLEFIELD *Young Masters* 128 The garden was a dusty waste, the only green thing in it a *pampelmoes* tree that shaded one wall of the house. **1979** M. PARKES *Wheatlands* 45 One grove consisted of very large seedling orange trees, pompelmoes and naartjie trees.

b. *comb.* **pampelmoes konfyt** /- kɔn'feɪt/ [Afk., *konfyt* see KONFYT], a conserve or marmalade made of the pampelmoes fruit.

1913 J.J. DOKE *Secret City* 396 She produced sour milk and pampelmoes konfyt, ad libitum. **1930** N. STEVENSON *Farmers of Lekkerbat* 304 She treated her relations continually to fig and *pampelmoes konfyt.* **1977** *Sunday Times* 6 Nov., Lovely local delicacies in Graaff Reinet by the way — prickly pear syrup, .. lucerne honey, pampelmoes konfyt.

2. The PAMPELMOESIE, *Stromateus fiatola.*

1913 W.W. THOMPSON *Sea Fisheries of Cape Col.* 59 (Swart), Surely it was a Malay who named the pampelmoes, the mottled hues of whose sides bear a strong likeness to the rind of the melon beloved by the fraternity. **1934** C.P. SWART Supplement to Pettman. 133 *Pampelmoes*, .. The Cape name given to a variety of fish Stromoteus [*sic*] fiatola whose hues resemble those of a water-melon. **1947** K.H. BARNARD *Pict. Guide to S. Afr. Fishes* 193 *Butter-fish, Blue-fish, Pampelmoes (Stromateus fiatola).* **1949** J.L.B. SMITH *Sea Fishes* 303 *Stromateus fiatola ... Butterfish. Cape Lady. Pampelmoes. Bluefish.* **1979** SNYMAN & KLARIE *Free from Sea* 26 Butter Fish, Cape Lady/Pampelmoes/Bluefish.

pampelmoesie /ˌpampəl'mʊsi, -'musi/ *n.* Formerly also **poempelmoesje**, **pompelmoosje**. [Afk. *pompelmoes, pampelmoes* see prec. + -IE; the reason for the use of this word for the fish is unknown; it may be a (joking) ad. of Pg. *pampo, pamplo* or Fr. *pompile* a fish of the Carangidae, or of Sp. *pámpano* a fish of the Stromateidae; or fr. archaic S. Afr. Du. *pompe(l)moer* (sometime *pompelmoes*), ad. Fr. *pomme d'amour* gooseberry (see quot. 1971).] The marine fish *Stromateus fiatola* of the Stromateidae (the ruffs); BLUE FISH sense 1; CAPE LADY sense 2; *Kaapse nooitjie*, see KAAPSE sense 3; KATONKEL sense 1; PAMPELMOES sense 2.

In Smith and Heemstra's *Smiths' Sea Fishes* (1986), the name 'blue butterfish' is used for this species.

1893 H.A. BRYDEN *Gun & Camera* 449 Many of the Cape fish are endowed with the quaintest Dutch names. Here are a few of them: Kabeljouw, Baardmannatje, Poempelmoesje, Katunka, Elftvisch, Stinkvisch, Poeskop, Dageraad, and others. **1913** C. PETTMAN *Africanderisms* 379 *Pompelmoosje, Stromatus microchirus.* One of the edible fishes of the Cape waters, so called from some fancied resemblance, probably, to the Pampelmoose. **1971** L.G. GREEN *Taste of S.-Easter* 187 His favourite fish, a comparative rarity known as the butterfish ... 'Some call it a pampelmoesie because it is shaped and coloured something like a goose-berry, with orange and rose-red fins'.

pampoen /pam'pʊn, -'pun/ *n.* Also **pampoon**, **pompoen**. Pl. **-s**, **-e** /-ə/. [S. Afr. Du., pumpkin (cf. obs. Eng. *pumpion, pompion*).]

‖**1.**

a. The common pumpkin *Cucurbita pepo* of the Cucurbitaceae.

1798 LADY A. BARNARD *Lett. to Henry Dundas* (1973) 143 At some of the farmhouses they are even worse off, getting the fourth part of a raw pampoon, a sort of pumpkin or bad melon .. - it must last them for the day. **1812** A. PLUMPTRE tr. *H. Lichtenstein's Trav. in Sn Afr.* I. 189 *Pampoen* is the name given by the colonist to a species of gourd, which is very commonly to be found here, and which appears to be only the common European pumpkin, *Cucurbita Pepo.* **1886** G.A. FARINI *Through Kalahari Desert* 61 A few mealies and squashes (which they call 'pampoons') completed the stock of a garden.

b. *comb.* **pampoenkoek(ie)** /-'kʊk(i)/ [Afk., *koek* cake (+ dim. suffix -IE)], a (small) pumpkin fritter served with cinnamon; **pampoenmoes** /-'mʊs/ [Afk., *moes* fruit or vegetable puree], a traditional dish of pumpkin baked with cinnamon and breadcrumbs or slices of bread; *pumpkin moes*, see MOES sense b.

1964 L.G. GREEN *Old Men Say* 133 They can bake *mosbolletjies* and *boerebeskuit, roosterkoek* and **pampoenkoekies**. **1973** *E. Prov. Herald* 2 Apr. 13 London rush on pampoenkoek ... They are ordering .. bobotie, pampoenkoek, melktert .. and coming back for more. **1979** *Sunday Times* (Mag. Sect.) 26 Aug. 2 She might serve pampoenkoekies with cinnamon sugar, cabbage in a cheese sauce, beans done in the old boere fashion. **1955** J. HENDRIE *Ouma's Cookery Bk* 133 **Pampoen Moes** .. Take a marrow, peel it and slice thinly. Put a layer in an oven dish, cover with a layer of thinly cut white bread spread with butter. Sprinkle over a little sugar, a few pieces of cinnamon and three or four cloves. Repeat ... Bake. **1977** *Fair Lady* 8 June (Suppl.) 25 Pampoenmoes. 4 medium slices of pumpkin; 2 slices white bread .. sugar .. salt .. stick cinnamon. **1985** *Drum* Nov. 75 This month's winning recipe .. Pampoenmoes. **1986** M. VAN WYK *Cooking the S. Afr. Way* 29 Breaded pumpkin (*Pampoenmoes*) Peel and slice pumpkin. Cut bread into squares and pack alternate layers of pumpkin and bread into a greased dish. **1989** I. JONES *Woman's World Cookbk* 95 *Pampoenmoes* ... A traditional Cape Dutch pumpkin pudding. **1990** *You* 24 May 52 My longing is for perlemoen rissoles, .. pampoenmoes, bottled peaches with custard.

2. *fig. colloq.* A fool, an ass (sometimes used affectionately). Also *attrib.*

1949 O. WALKER *Wanton City* 19 Fancy that pampoen Whyte-Whyte putting up for Parliament again. *Ibid.* 165 Buckled my front mudguard, the big pampoen. **1970** E. MUNDELL *Informant, Pearston (E. Cape)* You pampoen, imagine being afraid of a cow. **1975** W. STEENKAMP *Land of Thirst King* 129 The pumpkin is not a highly-esteemed vegetable, and indeed a common Afrikaans insult is to call a man a 'pampoen', meaning he is a lumpish fool. [**1980** *Daily Dispatch* 3 Dec. 12 If badges proclaiming JR to be a bighead are now no longer to be displayed, without proper authority, what about 'Jy Are a Pampoen?'] **1982** M. MZAMANE *Children of Soweto* 179 'Listen, who's talking!' Nina said. 'Whoever knows what goes on in that *pampoen* head of yours?' **1983** J. SCOTT in *Daily Dispatch* 22 Feb., When your opponents criticise you, reject your political philosophy and say you have the mind of a 'pampoen', you may rest assured. **1987** *You* 22 Oct. 7 *Pam the pampoen* ... If she's an expert I'm her grandma. **1989** *Cape Times* 4 Sept. 6 Once I was in a demo where the cops never turned up ... We stood for hours looking like real *pampoens.*

pan /pæn/ *n.* [Eng., 'a hollow in the ground', prob. reinforced by S. Afr. Du. *pan* a small lake.]

See also SALT PAN.

a. A natural depression, often one in which a deposit of salt remains after water has evaporated.

1809 H. Alexander in G.M. Theal *Rec. of Cape Col.* (1900) VII. 16 It is hereby permitted to all persons to bring Salt into Cape Town .. without paying any compensation to the farmer of the Pans. **1833** *Graham's Town Jrnl* 1 Aug. 1 Good pasturage, a sufficiency of Water for the washing of the Sheep, and a Pan of the best Salt. *a***1838** A. Smith *Jrnl* (1975) 147 Seven waggons belonging to natives who had come for a supply of salt to a pan (salt-lake) in this neighbourhood. **1843** J.C. Chase *Cape of G.H.* 63 The most important natural substance .. found in this country is salt, of which there are four natural pans. **1860** J. Sanderson in *Jrnl of Royal Geog. Soc.* XXX. 254 Next day we .. began our descent into the lower ground; passing numerous round or oval hollows called 'pans.' **1873** F. Boyle *To Cape for Diamonds* 74, I saw that peculiar phenomenon of the country, a 'pan' ... As the name imports, it is a circular depression in the level of the veldt, with earthy bottom and sides. **1883** M.A. Carey-Hobson *Farm in Karoo* 103 These 'pans' or lakes of salt are a curious feature in the physical geography of South Africa. **1913** C. Pettman *Africanderisms* 362 *Pan*, .. A nearly circular depression, in which a saline incrustation generally remains after the water, which accumulates in it in the wet season, has either evaporated or been absorbed. **1926** P.W. Laidler *Tavern of Ocean* 127 In the old days the Company had a magazine for storing the salt gathered from the pan near by. *c***1936** *S. & E. Afr. Yr Bk & Guide* 427 There are 39 producing pans within the Union, employing a capital of nearly £250,000; output about 80,000 tons. **1945** L.G. Green *Where Men Still Dream* 117 There are thousands of pans scattered over the dry parts of South Africa. Wind action may have caused these shallow depressions; or possibly they were flattened by glaciers. **1952** — *Lords of Last Frontier* 44 Ohopoho seems to have been selected as the seat of government because the huge pans there make natural aerodromes. **1961** L.E. Van Onselen *Trekboer* 82 The Bushmanlander distinguishes between the vlei and the pan. The vleis contain fresh water after rain. The pans, which are encrusted with layers of salt, soon contaminate the water and make it unfit to drink. **1970** *News/Check* 24 July 31 The Etosha region .. is only 8,000 sq miles .., of which a quarter is barren pan. **1972** *Etosha Nat. Park (brochure)* 1 In good rain years large parts of the pan are under water. Then tens of thousands of aquatic birds make their appearance. **1984** *Flying Springbok* Sept. 33 Several dazzling white pans have formed here at the point where the river runs into the highest set of sand dunes in the world ... The pan surfaces are usually 'cobbled' or cracked into flakes. **1988** M. Spence in *Motorist* Nov. 4 The animals are often concentrated around the waterholes, but large herds can also be seen on the plains and the shimmering white pans.

b. A shallow periodic lake, formed in a natural depression by rain-water. Cf. vlei sense 1.

1871 W.G. Atherstone in A.M.L. Robinson *Sel. Articles from Cape Monthly Mag.* (1978) 147 A natural drainage flowing off by rivers, or, where obstructed by rock dykes or mounds, forming 'pans' and periodical lakes and 'vleis'. **1889** F. Jeppe *Tvl Almanac & Dir.* 31 There are numerous pans all over the country, but only one that may be called a lake on account of its size and extent. **1902** 'The Intelligence Officer' *On Heels of De Wet* 78 There was a pan, which meant water for the horses. **1911** L. Cohen *Reminisc. of Kimberley* 112 Partridge, plover, pau, which last, in flocks of hundreds, each morning hovered over the pans (huge ponds) to drink the waters. **1913** C. Pettman *Africanderisms* 362 *Pan*, .. The word is sometimes used as being synonymous with 'Vlei'. **1920** E.H.L. Schwarz *Thirstland Redemption* 26 The ground is very flat, and the rivers naturally spread out into vast shallow pans or 'vloers'. **1930** S.T. Plaatje *Mhudi* (1975) 136 Passing a miniature lake — called a pan in South Africa — filled with the waters of the recent flood, Mhudi paused to admire a flock of wild ducks swimming gracefully on the still water. **1940** V. Pohl *Bushveld Adventures* 245 A large pan (a kind of small natural lake, usually dependent on rainfall). **1941** A.G. Bee *Kalahari Camp Fires* (1943) 18 'Pan' .. is the South African name for a lagoon, shallow and silver with reeds about the shore. **1970** *Daily News* 16 Oct. 1 Fresh water pans in the floodplain are drying up. **1972** E.N. Marais *Rd to Waterberg* 45 Our own lake 'Ngami .. has been transformed from a permanent lake into a 'temporary' pan. **1972** *Sunday Times* 5 Nov. (Mag. Sect.) 5 More than 40 sable walking with grace .. across the turquoise-tinted pan to the still water to drink. **1987** *S. Afr. Holidays Guide (brochure)* 3 Of particular interest .. are the shallow pans in which a wide variety of birds have made their homes.

pandok, pandokkie varr. pondok, pondokkie.

Pandour /ˈpændʊə(r)/ *n. hist.* Also **Pandoer**, and with small initial. Pl. **-s**, **-e** /-ə/. [Transf. use of general Eng. *Pandour* a brutal Croatian soldier (hist.), fr. Serbo-Croatian *pandur* a Croatian soldier; or fr. S. Afr. Du. *pandoer*.] A member of a Khoikhoi regiment established on orders from the Dutch East India Company in 1793 to defend the Colony; in *pl.*, this regiment. See also Hottentot *n.* sense 1 b.

1800 J. Backstrom in G.M. Theal *Rec. of Cape Col.* (1898) III. 288 If the least word is said about pandours (Hottentots in service) Buys will fall upon them with the whole Caffraria. **1904** H.A. Bryden *Hist. of S. Afr.* 28 For two years Janssens was expecting an English descent. He had been preparing as best might, strengthening his corps of Hottentots — Pandours they were sometimes called — to the number of 600. **1910** E.C. Godee-Molsbergen *Hist. of S. Afr.* 84 (Swart), Instead of sending European soldiers to enforce the summons, the Government despatched a troop of Pandours, who were hated throughout the Colony. **1926** P.W. Laidler *Tavern of Ocean* 104 A Hottentot corps of 'Pandours' or foot soldiers was formed, two hundred and ten strong. **1934** C.P. Swart Supplement to Pettman. 133 *Pandours*, .. Hottentot regiment, first trained by the Netherlands Commissioners' orders in 1783. **1977** R.J. Haines in R.J. Bouch *Infantry in S. Afr. 1652–1976* 2 To supplement its forces, .. the Company resorted to freed slaves, Hottentots and other blacks. Freed slaves were initially used for fire prevention and guard duties, and later formed into a regular corps called *Pandoere*. **1982** A.P. Brink *Chain of Voices* 347 He'd brought a young Hottentot with him to interpret for us — a Pandoer very proud of his uniform. **1983** *S. Afr. Panorama* Sept. 32 The *Korps van Pandoere* was established in 1793 ... The Corps of Pandours was the forerunner of the Cape Corps which was raised by the Dutch East India company in 1795 to defend the colony and incorporated into the British Army when it occupied the Cape that year. **1989** F.G. Butler *Tales from Old Karoo* 14 The old Dutch East India Company tried to police the East Cape Frontier with pandoers — Malays and halfcastes from the Cape mixed with Hottentots .. — surviving as mercenaries in the pay of the powers that had taken their land and way of life from them.

panga /ˈpæŋgə, ˈpaŋgə/ *n.*[1] Formerly also **pangar**. [Prob. fr. Malay *ikan pangerang*; see Gilchrist quot. 1902.] Either of two species of marine fish: **a.** The seabream *Pterogymnus laniarus* of the Sparidae; dageraad sense c; dikbekkie sense b. **b.** The kingfish *Megalaspis cordyla* of the Carangidae.

In Smith and Heemstra's *Smiths' Sea Fishes* (1986), this name is used only for *P. laniarus; M. cordyla* is called 'torpedo scad'.

1902 J.D.F. Gilchrist in *Trans. of S. Afr. Philological Soc.* XI. iv. 218 As the name is chiefly used by the Malay fishermen, .. it may have been originally a Malay name ... Valentyn in his 'Old and New East Indies' mentions a fish which the natives called Ikan Pangerang or Pangarang (literally, prince) which seems to bear some resemblance to the Cape Panga, more especially in its having the protruding teeth. **1902** H.J. Duckitt *Hilda's Diary of Cape Hsekeeper* 142 Snoek is still in season; also pangar, a very nice fish for frying. **1913** W.W. Thompson *Sea Fisheries of Cape Col.* 61 Only one Malay name seems to be in use — unless, as is probable, some of the unknown designations may be traced to them — panga, the name given to a fish resembling the Cape Silverfish, but with some of the front teeth protruding, is said to be derived from a fish called in the East Indies ikan pangirang (prince). **1947** K.H. Barnard *Pict. Guide to S. Afr. Fishes* 149 *Panga (Pterogymnus laniarus)* ... A well-known Cape table-fish. **1972** L.G. Green *When Journey's Over* 148 Hotel-keepers went to Agmat for Cape Salmon, butterfish and panga. **1980** *E. Prov. Herald* 26 Sept. 1 Although there was no quota for maasbanker and pangas, the threatened ban was likely because hake and sole would be caught up in the trawling nets. **1985** A. Tredgold *Bay between Mountains*, The trawlers were accused of 'exterminating such fish as the panga, silver fish, red and white stumpnose'. **1988** G. Winch in *Ski-Boat* Vol.4 No.6, 9 They [*sc.* foreign vessels] are .. limited to catch no more than 15% of other species (carpenter, panga, steenbras) as a by-catch when trawling for hake or maasbanker.

panga /ˈpæŋgə, ˈpaŋgə/ *n.*[2] [Swahili; the word entered S. Afr. Eng. either fr. Kenyan Eng., or through the influence of East-African contract mine-workers.]

1. A heavy cane knife with a long, broad blade, used as an implement or a weapon. Also *attrib.*

[**1936** E. Hemingway *Green Hills of Afr.* 170 Chopping our way through with the long brush knives that are called pangas.] **1953** *Drum* June 6 Men .. who had been home brought back gruesome stories of murder by the *panga* and forced oath-taking. **1961** T. Matshikiza *Choc. for my Wife* 111 The accused .. drove between fifty to sixty holes through her prostrate body with a panga. *Ibid.* 119 Panga practice on Saturdays instead of football! **1969** M. Benson *At Still Point* (1988) 142 He said we must have guns, pangas, axes, weapons which would come from Russia and Ghana? **1973** A. Fugard *Notebks* (1983) 205 Five African men spent the night sleeping on the sand in front of a neighbour's house, all with pangas, ready in case the fire swept down again. **1980** *Weekend Post* 13 Sept. 1 The Divisional Inspector of Police in Port Natal .. said his men had taken possession of hundreds of knobkerries, battle-axes, sticks, pangas, sharpened pieces of iron, [etc.]. **1983** *Pace* Oct. 45 At that time I used to carry some of the biggest pangas ever seen in Mdantsane. All the tsotsis feared me. **1986** J. Conyngham *Arrowing of Cane* 10 The roar of tractors and the rhythmical slash-fall of pangas and cane. **1987** S.D. Tirivanhu in *New Coin Poetry* June 25, I the sugarcane cutter don't feel the least offended, .. For in the morrow we go, to the fields ahead the only friend being my Panga. **1992** D. Forrest in *Weekly Mail* 16 Apr. 3 Phola Park squatters all say the soldiers kicked down shack doors .. assaulting them with pipes, rifle butts and pangas.

2. *comb.* **pangaman**, one armed with a panga; (objective) **panga-wielding** *ppl adj.*

1968 *Post* 17 Nov. 9 Natal's **panga man** has moved south and struck again. **1977** *Sunday Times* 1 May 1 They discovered 20 men, one of whom Mr L— identified as the pangaman. **1982** *Ibid.* 2 May 11 A pangaman viciously slashed two youngsters early yesterday. **1985** *Grocott's Mail* 8 Nov. 1 Panga man holds up ambulance. A drunk **panga-wielding** man stopped an ambulance in the black townships on Wednesday, threatened to burn the vehicle ... A group of people arrived on the scene and told the pangaman that the ambulance .. should be allowed to pass.

‖**pannekoek** /ˈpanəkʊk, -kuk/ *n.* Pl. unchanged, or **-e** /-ə/. [Afk.] A pancake. Also *attrib.*, and (occas.) *fig.*

1900 F.R.M. Cleaver in M.M. Cleaver *Young S. Afr.* (1913) 161 The Germans and Hollanders have their Zangvereine; the Irish have their boxing and athletic exercises; the Afrikanders impartially take part in everything and bake stormjagers en pannekoek in the intervals. **1927** [see oblietjie]. **1931** *Nat. Geog. Mag.* Apr. 395 Collections of Dutch masters, stinkwood furniture, .. and kitchen utensils wherein of old were prepared .. pannekoek. **1938** 'Mrs Gossip' in *Star* 1 Dec. 12 Pannekoeke, braaiwors, melktert, mosbolletjies, beskuit and coffee could be had in plenty and everyone throughly enjoyed themselves. **1976** *S. Afr. Panorama* Feb. 35 Steaming cinnamon-strewn pannekoek (pancakes) have gradually given way to the more easily prepared jaffles and vetkoek (yeasty cakes) with sweet or savoury fillings. **1978** *Sunday Times* 20 Aug. (Mag. Sect.) 3 If you want to make pannekoek then toss them, of course, and cook on the other side. **1979** 'Blossom' in *Darling* 16 May 131 This lekker suave piece of pannekoek from Parys ... Six foot two, eyes of blue. **1982** *S. Afr. Panorama* Jan. 12 There were little pavement cafes and stalls selling .. home-made bread and *pannekoek* with cinnamon. **1990** *Cue* 5 July 3 Talking point at PJ's isn't the venue or the food (although the pannekoek is reputed to be the best in town). **1992** *Style* May 60 Feeding 85 children a day at a primary school, a *pannekoek* evening, perhaps, or a jumble sale to raise funds.

Hence (*nonce*) **pannekoek** *v. intrans.*, to eat pancakes.

1990 *Sunday Times* 3 June 4 Seeing the queue at the pannekoek stall was thinning out, I went to watch an army of cooks indulge in a fry-up of epic proportions. To pannekoek or not to pannekoek?

pansella var. bonsella.

pansy *n.* [Transf. sense of general Eng. *pansy* the common name of the flower *Viola tricolor*; see quots 1976 and 1990.] In full **pansy shell**: the sea-urchin *Echinodiscus bisperforatus* of the phylum *Echinodermata*; most commonly, the calcium carbonate test (or shell-like skeleton) of this sea-urchin.

1954 K.H. Barnard *S. Afr. Shore-Life* 45 A particular kind of Cake-urchin is called the Two-slit Cake-urchin or Pansy Shell .., and is common in many sandy bays on the south coast. **1971** J.H. Day in *Std Encycl. of Sn Afr.* IV. 193 The pansy-shell gets its name from the five petal-like markings where the tube-feet perforate the shell. **1976** *Het Suid-Western* 8 Sept., The pansy shells are named for their decorative underside which, in varying shades of purple and white, strongly resembles a pansy ... A pansy is born male and then becomes female at a later stage in order to lay eggs already fertile by itself ... When the pansies die, it takes about a week for them to be bleached white by the effects of the salt and sun. **1978** *Ibid.* 1 Nov., The pansy is a living creature and not a shell at all ... When it is alive it is purple in colour and is covered with short furry bristles. **1979** *Ibid.* 1 Nov. (Suppl.), Two years ago Mr Edgar Cooke of Plettenberg Bay kept two pansy shells as pets ... He kept his pet pansies in a plastic bowl filled with sea sand and sea water. And every second day he took them for a walk on the beach. **1982** Kilburn & Rippey *Sea Shells* 3 Highly prized by beachcombers is the flattened test of the 'Pansy Shell' or 'Sand Dollar' (*Echinodiscus bisperforatus*), a sand-dwelling echinoid most frequently found on the Mossel Bay-Plettenberg Bay coast. **1987** S. Ozinsky in *Underwater* 31 Pansy shells are in fact urchins, belonging to the phylum *Echinodermata* (Greek for 'spiny skinned') and are therefore more closely related to sea urchins, starfish and brittlestars than they are to molluscs ... Pansy shells have flat bodies supported by a calcium carbonate test. **1990** J. Raphaely in *Motorist* 2nd Quarter 13 They aren't shells at all but the cast-off skeleton of a type of starfish ... We call them pansies because of the flower design etched on the upper surface by the original owner's arterial system. **1992** A.C. Bentley in *Afr. Wildlife* Vol.46 No.2, 237 A small dead pansy shell is very light and can drift considerable distances with the tides and currents.

pantokkie var. pondokkie.

pantsula /pænt'suːlə, pant-, pant'sʊla, -lə/ *n. slang.* Pl. usu. **-s, ma-**. Forms: *sing.* **pantsola, pantsula, panzolla**; *sing.* (occas.) and *pl.* **mapantsula, pantsulas**; *pl.* **mapansula, mapantsulas, mpantsula, pantsolas**. Also with initial capital. [Isicamtho, ultimate origin unkn.; perh. rel. S. Sotho *patsola* split open, or N. Sotho *phasola*, S. Sotho *pasola*, Zulu *p(h)ansula*, 'slap, strike sharply (with a whip)', perh. referring either to pantsulas' sometime association with violent crime, or to elements of the dance style associated with them.] In urban (esp. township) parlance:

1.a. A young urban black person (usu. a man) whose attitudes and behaviour, esp. regarding speech and dress, are of the most popular current fashion. See also mshoza. **b.** tsotsi sense 1 a. Also *attrib.*

Although the term seems not to have been used in Isicamtho before the late 1970s, it is now sometimes applied retrospectively to the 'tsotsis' and 'bras' of the 1950s.

Among themselves, pantsulas normally speak Isicamtho. Their style of dress was formerly reminiscent of 1950s 'tsotsi' fashion, characterized by expensive clothing, particularly trousers with turn-ups (usu. worn above the ankles), fine shoes (often two-tone brogues), and a felt hat; more recently a diversity of styles has emerged.

[**1976** K.M.C. Motsisi in M. Mutloatse *Casey & Co.* (1978) 62, I tell her I'm off to Kid Pancholla's place.] **1982** W.S. Kwamthetwa in *Staffrider* Vol.5 No.2, 9 There were .. Mapansula, Ma-Amerikane and what have you ... These people are discerned from one another by their way of dressing. **1982** *Star* 11 Nov. (Tonight) 4 A pantsola, a custodian of scamtho, explained his delayed arrival to his boss. 'I come from London 727' (I come from Orlando East number 727) leaving the employer .. trying to figure out how the poor bloke travels ... Capture the miasma of township life including the heady dances of pantsolas and their intoxicating patois called 'scamtho'. **1983** *Drum* Sept. 39 It is ironic that these sexy female 'pantsulas' are the first to fill church seats on Sundays. **1984** M. Mthethwa in *Frontline* July 29 Pantsulas and Mshozas take great pride in their expensive clothes. Lizard-skin shoes and purses, cashmere pullovers and cardigans, leather coats, jackets and berets are top with them. *Ibid.* 30 The cheapest pair of shoes you will come across worn by a Pantsulas will cost about R150. **1985** J. Khumalo in *Pace* Sept. 18 (*caption*) Is the Pantsula style, with one-pleat trousers and Florsheim shoes, going out of fashion after 30 years of glory? **1985** L. Sampson in *Style* Dec. 44 He wears .. Panzolla trousers. **1986** T. Thoka in *Eng. Usage in Sn Afr.* Vol.17 No.2, 18 The label 'Mapantsula' is actually the newest word for the old term 'tsotsie', which refers to an urban thug ... Tsotsie-taal has become a street dialect, and is not confined to thugs. The Mapantsula are the main users of this dialect. **1986** *Drum* Aug. 70 Women pantsulas live far from a healthy morality. **1987** *Cosmopolitan* Dec. 88 Pantsulas .. don't want to wear their father's clothes, speak English and do not buy mbaqanga music. They buy 'Hotstix', Brenda Fassie, Yvonne Chaka Chaka, Chicco and CJB. **1991** in Schmitz & Mogotlane *Mapantsula* 38 Nathan: To what extent were you influenced by the 1950s mapantsulas' style? Mogotlane: Those mapantsulas had style. They were influenced mainly by the American gangster movies ... Dressing in labels was very important, so, John Stevens of London, Dobson and Stetson, was vital ... Schmitz: .. Why is this guy wearing old fashioned clothes? Mapantsulas today don't wear those sorts of clothes. Mogotlane: Those who are criticising don't know the mapantsula ... That style of mapantsula still lives today. Even the elderly .. still believe in the turn-up trouser, .. Florsheims, and a straw hat maybe, or a Stetson. It does influence the youngsters. Godfrey Moloi .. has a handkerchief hanging out of his suit pocket all the time ... He is still a mapantsula of the 1950s ... Nathan: The music, dress and dance in the film all draw strongly on contemporary mapantsula style. **1992** on M-Net TV 19 Apr. (Carte Blanche), Didi calls himself a pantsula ... They speak a special language called tsotsi-taal.

2. A dance-style in which each person performs a solo turn within a circle of dancers doing a repetitive, shuffling step; the music accompanying this dancing. Usu. *attrib.*

1990 *City Press* 17 June 16 Forget disco and pantsula jive, move into the quiet world of waltzes, foxtrots and quickstep. **1990** J. Michel in *Style* Nov. 61, I asked him where he found his inspiration ... 'It could be the Zulu thing. You see them practising for mapantsula competitions all the time ..'. **1991** Schmitz & Mogotlane *Mapantsula* 38 We linked the freedom songs with mapantsula music because the two are inter-related.

Hence **pantsulahood** *n. nonce*, the state or condition of being a pantsula.

1985 J. Khumalo in *Pace* Sept. 19 She told him in no uncertain terms that he was not a suitable dance partner as he was a thug. That was it. It put paid to our Pantsulahood.

paou(w), paow varr. pou.

pap /pap/ *n.* [Afk. (fr. Du.), porridge. (Cf. general Eng. *pap* gruel.)]

1.a. mealiepap. **b.** Occas., any porridge. In both senses also called papa, poop *n.*[2] Also *attrib.*

1858 T. Shone *Diary* 29 May, Nothing to do, dry bread and pap for dinner, with Coffee and tea. **1862** E.L. Price *Jrnls* (1956) 104 Their empty unfurnished huts, with several pots, varying according to the number of the family, wh. are their only eating vessels for meat, milk or pap. **1866** *Ibid.* 203 Fancy them tearing meat, and snatching lumps of pap out of each-others hands yelling curses all the while. **1872** C.A. Payton *Diamond Diggings* 139 They will frequently provide themselves with an extra in the shape of offal, .. but still have an appetite unimpaired for the discussion of their mealie porridge, or 'pap' as they call it. **1879** E.L. Price *Jrnls* (1956) 343 The boy was grinding some Sechwana corn wh., do you remember, is a red & round grain, and the old woman in the kitchen made pap of it – but it looked quite black, and our little folks .. would not taste the black pap. **1880** E.F. Sandeman *Eight Months in Ox-Waggon* 57 The ordinary boys are content with mealie meal and salt, with which they make 'pap' or porridge, and an occasional treat of meat when passing through a town. **1893** *Brown's S. Afr.* 200 A museum with many objects of interest, including Cetewayo's cooking pots and pap dish. **1896** R. Wallace *Farming Indust. of Cape Col.* 464 Mealies .. are often ground into meal, made into thick porridges or 'pap', and eaten, either alone or with milk, by means of large wooden spoons. *c*1904 E.L. Price *Jrnls* (1956) 63 The servants food was mealiemeal porridge – cooked with whey – occasionally varied by .. the head, liver etc. of the animal, a piece in each bowl of pap. **1920** F.C. Cornell *Glamour of Prospecting* 51 Boer meal was the staple food; a big three-legged pot of it boiled into steaming 'pap' made an excellent breakfast. **1968** K. McMagh *Dinner of Herbs* 80 This little fellow, like every other umfaan earning a few shillings a month and his pap from the post-cart people, had as his sole garment the tattered remains of a navy-blue army greatcoat minus buttons. **1979** *Sunday Times* 13 May 4 He was born in England, went to school and university here, but was, and I quote ... 'as South African as boerewors and pap'. **1982** C. Van Wyk *Message in Wind* 12 That evening the small household sat around the supper table eating their meal of pap, boerewors and tomato gravy. **1985** *Financial Mail* 18 Oct. (Fedics Suppl.) 40, I would not serve salt in a Sotho's mealie-meal because that's like putting a curse on him. In contrast, I won't forget to put it in a Zulu's pap as he won't eat it without it. **1990** R. Stengel *January Sun* 62 Pap is a porridge made from maize that is the staple of the local black diet (no meal is considered complete without it). **1990** M. Melamu in *Lynx* 294 A generous helping of mealiemeal *pap* three times a day, washed down with a jam-can of black, liberally sugared coffee. **1991** *Best of S. Afr. Short Stories* (Reader's Digest Assoc.) 388 Pap, of course, is porridge – traditionally mealie meal, a basic African food. A form of this, called stywe pap (stiff porridge), has become part of the great South African braaivleis tradition, when it is eaten with meat or wors (sausage). **1993** [see atjar]. **1994** L. Rulashe in *Tribute* May 90 This all came with a serving of baked potato smothered in sour cream, plus stiff *pap* and tomato gravy which was brought to the table in small three-legged pots.

2. In the names of popular dishes [the conjunction *en* in these phrr. is Afk., 'and']: ***pap and*** (or ***en***) ***boerewors*** [Afk. *boerewors* (see BOEREWORS sense 1)], maize porridge and boerewors; also *attrib.*; ***pap and*** (or ***en***) ***braaivleis*** [Afk. *braaivleis* (*braai* grill + *vleis* meat)], maize porridge and grilled meat; *nonce*, the social occasion at which such food is enjoyed; ***pap en*** (or ***and***) ***vleis*** /-'fleɪs/ [Afk. *vleis* meat], maize porridge and meat; also *fig.*, a simple task, see quot. 1989; ***pap en*** (or ***and***) ***wors*** [Afk. *wors* sausage], maize porridge and sausage, usu. boerewors; also *attrib.*

1980 M. Lorentz in *Rand Daily Mail* 14 Nov. 10 Promise of nectar and honey while the kitchen ultimately produces food only slightly above the **pap-and-boerewors** standard. **1982** M. Mzamane *Children of Soweto* 106 They brought us *pap* and *boerewors*. We ate in silence. **1986** *Star* 17 Oct. 11 As the pap and boerewors simmer on the fire, Lood Minnie's bushy moustache bristles with indignation. **1970** J. Goosen *Informant, Queenstown* Going to a pap and braaivleis tonight. **1974** *E. Prov. Herald* 15 May 1 They enjoyed 'pap' and braaivleis around a camp fire. **1986** *S. Afr. Panorama* Feb. 16 In a trice a fire is on the go and breakfast prepared. Bacon and eggs, .. or pap and braaivleis — who could ask for anything more! **1974** *E. Prov. Herald* 16 May 1 Last night .. 800 Afrikaanse Handelsinstituut delegates and guests forsook the cuisine of the upper floors for good old **'pap en vleis'** braaied in the hotel's parking basement. **1976** *S. Afr. Panorama* Feb. 35 Pap en vleis (porridge and grilled meat) stay top of the bill. **1984** S. Zungu in *Pace* Oct. 64, I really believe in the simple things in life like pap and vleis. **1986** *Learn & Teach* No.2, 30, I told him that I wanted pap and vleis ... I paid, then I saw that the meat was not cooked. **1987** H. Prendini in *Style* May 49 Nomsa was going to the theatre, she hadn't had supper, so .. we cooked a meal. You know, pap en vleis. **1987** S. Hinton in *Weekly Mail* 19 June 26 The South African indigenous cuisine is a mysterious and not easily accessible lineament of the cultural landscape ... Outside *waterblommetjie bredie* and *koeksusters, pap-en-vleis* and perhaps *vetkoek* what national dishes spring to mind? **1987** *Pace* Aug. 10 Mr Buthelezi is still very much African — you might say he's as traditional as pap en vleis. **1989** *Ibid.* Mar. 24 My father is a policeman and I used to watch him load his gun — it's not pap and vleis; it takes time. **1990** *Evening Post* 19 Feb. 3 It's not in fact terribly difficult to establish that feeling of common nationhood. You know, to sit and eat pap and vleis together. **1970** M. Van Tonder *Informant, Bloemfontein* We are having **'pap en wors'** for supper. **1974** C. Hope on Radio South Africa 7 Sept., Pap en wors morning noon and night, if you're lucky. **1980** *Sunday Times* 7 Sept. 18 'Little blighter,' Gran would say fondly. 'Who does he think he is? If he doesn't swallow that pap and wors pronto I'll shoot him in the patellas.' **1983** *Argus* 9 May, CNA bring you 5067 alternatives to pap and wors. **1984** *Sunday Times* 8 July (Lifestyle) 9 Leading the convoy was a vintage Rolls-Royce, gleaming black and ivory, with headlamps the size of pap en wors plates. **1990** *Ibid.* 27 May 4 Known to aficionados as the Big D ... It's in Johannesburg's CBD between used car salesrooms and pap and wors cafés. **1991** H.P. Toffoli in *Style* Nov. 84 A bunch of lumpen platteland proles if ever you saw one, this lot was unashamedly pigging out on vast plates of patriotic *pap en wors*.

pap /pap/ *adj. colloq.* [Afk.]
a. Weak, lacking substance; (of food) soft, tasteless.

1912 H.H. Juta *Reminisc.* 77 Judge: 'I can read and write and "reken", but I don't want to be a schoolmaster, thank you.' Farmer: 'No, of course not ... But it doesn't matter: your Dutch is too "pap".' **1958** L.G. Green *S. Afr. Beachcomber* 114 Snoek is one of the fish which must never be hung up to dry in the moonlight, or it will become pap ... Pap snoek is something to be avoided. **1963** S.H. Skaife *Naturalist Remembers* 17 He was investigating a destructive disease of snoek at the time, a disease well known to fishermen because it gives rise to what are known as 'pap snoek' — fish that are worthless because of their soft, watery, inedible flesh. **1970** C. Banach *Informant, Port Elizabeth* Seeing that the apple is so pap I will not eat it. **1973** *Informant, George* I've brought you the black cistern — the white ones are made of such pap plastic these days. **1982** *Sunday Times* 5 Sept. (Mag. Sect.) 6, I find it a bit 'pap' as a chip. They're too soft and airy. **1987** P. Wagener in *Grocott's Mail* 28 Apr. 3 The NP was too 'pap' to govern. Integration was rife in Johannesburg and Port Elizabeth where blacks and coloureds were living in white areas. **1991** N.P. Saunders *Informant, Scottburgh* Pap — soft or withered or just tired out. 'Don't buy those bananas they are pap.'

b. Of persons: physically exhausted, feeble; unassertive, weak; soft, flabby. See also PAPBROEK.

1934 C.P. Swart Supplement to Pettman. 133 *Pap*, .. In its adjectival sense 'soft', it is steadily gaining ground among English-speaking South Africans and one frequently hears such expressions as: the tennis balls are 'pap'; the tyres are 'pap'; I'm feeling 'pap' (exhausted). **1970** C. De Villiers *Informant, Bloemfontein*, I am tired and I feel so pap. **1970** M. Dikobe Marabi Dance. 121 She looked at George: 'Men like George are pap.' She thought of her father, still respected by the Malaitas as their king. **1972** *Evening Post* 10 June 4 There's another side to the problem of African Widows trying to find work. They're too pap, washed out, burnt-out. They have lost all incentive. Life's kicked them so hard they no longer have the initiative. **1973** *Informant, Grahamstown* This variety of flu makes people feel pretty pap. **1975** S. Roberts *Outside Life's Feast* 27 His chest hangs like soft tits in his vest. He is pap. I could easily hit him. **1987** [see NP sense 1]. **1991** H.C. Watts *Informant, Cape Town* In this heat I feel so pap — no energy at all.

c. Of tyres, balls, and other inflated objects: flat, under-inflated.

1934 [see sense b]. **1970** M. Burger *Informant, Pietersburg* My beachball got pap after I kicked it a few times. **1970** E. Lawry *Informant, Bloemfontein* Before the tyre was pumped up it was pap (flat, soft). **1987** A.K. Horwitz in *New Coin Poetry* June 24 Life should be a silver Mercedes gliding at all hours in the basin of hills — hard tyres for tarmac, pap ones for mud. **1991** G. Murray *Informant, Alberton* My wheel was pap so I had to push the bike home.

‖**papa** /'pa:pa/ *n.* [Afk. *pap* porridge + *-a*, a noun-ending common to many Sintu (Bantu) languages.] Mainly among speakers of Sintu (Bantu) languages: PAP *n.* sense 1.

1957 A.A. Murray *Blanket* 100 Stiff papa made from mealie-meal, and coagulated lumps of dried beans and peas, cooked to a glutinous solidity. **1981** B. Mfenyana in M. Mutloatse *Reconstruction* 294 If I pour cold papa into Dilly's suphu and he starts, 'This your recent act of causing that aqueous substance to commingle with my ...' he is not communicating. **1983** N.S. Ndebele *Fools* 14 Your family gets knocked down with all kinds of disease ... Softies, all of you ... Instead of eating *papa* and beans, you have too many sandwiches!

papagaai var. PAPEGAAI.

‖**papbroek** /'pa(p)brʊk, -bruk/ *n. colloq.* [Afk., *pap* soft, flabby + *broek* trousers, pants.] A weakling; a spineless person or coward. Also *attrib.* See also BANGBROEK, PAP *adj.* sense b.

[**1934** *Week-End Advertiser* 12 May (Swart), The Afrikaans expression, 'Papbroek', is not without its significance in test match rugby, especially on one's initial appearance.] **1937** C.R. Prance *Tante Rebella's Saga* 179 Boys will be boys, and none liked to be called 'pap-broek' or nincompoop, so there was soon a lot of money and 'Good-For' in the pool. **1968** F.G. Butler *Cape Charade* 10 It takes a lot to make Klaas drunk. He's not a papbroek to get drunk on nothing. **1973** *Informant, Grahamstown* He's such a helluva papbroek no one wants him in the house team. **1975** S. Roberts *Outside Life's Feast* 85 He was a miner an' a real papbroek but I was sorry for him. **1982** *Sunday Times* 28 Mar. 44 Diplomatically, I say: 'Gerrie will win.' 'No' he answers, 'he's a "papbroek"'. **1994** *Ibid.* 27 Nov. 5 The AWB would do the job if the 'papbroek' government .. did not act within 30 days.

papegaai /papə'xaɪ/ *n.* Also **papagaai**. [S. Afr. Du. (later Afk.), parrot.] A target in the shape of a parrot, traditionally used in Stellenbosch at marksmanship contests during the annual celebrations commemorating the birthday of Simon van der Stel. Also *attrib.*, and *comb.* **papegaai shoot**, such a contest.

1817 G.M. Theal in J. Mockford *Here Are S. Africans* (1944) 36 A figure resembling a parrot, and hence called a papegaai, was fixed upon a pole in the centre of a circle with a radius of sixty feet. The marksmen chose their positions upon the arc of this circle. [**1918** D. Fairbridge *Hist. of S. Afr.* 47 This target-shooting gave the name Papagaaisberg to a little hill near Stellenbosch, on the summit of which was the target in the form of a gaily painted wooden parrot — in Dutch papagaai.] **1944** J. Mockford *Here Are S. Africans* 36 Shooting with hand steadied muskets at a brightly painted papegaai and firing pistols from the backs of galloping horses — these competitions gave high moments to the fair. **1952** G.M. Mills *First Ladies of Cape* 33 He emphasized the importance of good marksmanship during the gay fortnight of his birthday when military exercises took place at Stellenbosch. The principal target of the practice was a clay bird called a parrot or papegaai. **1972** *Argus* 14 Oct. 8 Members of the South African Historical Arms Association take part in the traditional 'papagaai' shoot at the festivities marking the birthday of Governor Simon van der Stel in Stellenbosch today. **1975** *Sunday Times* 20 Apr. 16 It was a Pieter Bekker, who first inflamed official wrath as the 'leader of the unruliness at the annual Stellenbosch papagaai shoot'.

papie var. PYPIE.

‖**papies** /'pɑ:pis, -i:z/ *n. Pathology.* Also **paapies**, **papys**. [Afk., fr. Du. *paapje* cocoon + pl. suffix *-s*.] Enteric myiasis or bots, a gastric disease of horses, donkeys, and mules, caused by the larvae of the fly *Gastrophilus intestinalis* of the Gasterophilidae; *pl.*, these larvae.

1867 *Blue Bk for Col. 1866* JJ14, Early in the year nearly all the horses at grass died of horse-sickness and paapies. Sulphur in bran mashes was found to be an excellent remedy for paapies. **1912** *Farmer's Weekly* 17 Jan. 767 (Pettman), The *papies* is the outcome of the gad-fly or horse-fly which deposits its eggs or larvae on the quarters of animals and underneath the belly of the animal. The animal by biting and licking itself conveys them to the mouth and thence into the stomach. **1913** A. Glossop *Barnes's S. Afr. Hsehold Guide* 300 *Bots or Papys* ... Nature dislodges them herself in due course. **1914** *Farmer's Annual* 178 Bots (or 'papies') ... The eggs of the gad fly are deposited on .. the horse, and are hatched by the heat of the body. This causes an itching sensation ... In consequence of this, the horse licks the part, and the eggs thus getting into the mouth, pass into the stomach. Here the eggs turn into grubs, and remain until developed and pass away with the faeces. **1966** C.A. Smith *Common Names* 363 It was believed that horses developed 'papies' (bots) when grazing in vleis or marshy places where the plants grow. **1971** B. Smit in *Std Encycl. of Sn Afr.* IV. 590 *Horse Bot-Flies*, ... These 'papies' or maggots take several months to develop, and when full-grown are about 6mm long.

parabat /'pærəbæt/ *n. Military.* Also with initial capital. [Blend formed on *Parachute Battalion*.] A member of the Parachute Battalion of the defence forces. Also *attrib.*

1972 [see VASBYT]. **1977** B. Marks *Our S. Afr. Army* 49 (*caption*) Note the emergency parachute on the parabat's stomach. **1977** *Daily Dispatch* 26 Nov. 9 Parabats' death ... A regional magistrate found .. that the deaths of two members of 2 Parachute Battalion .. were caused by the actions of some person. **1978** *Ibid.* 8 Sept. 2 A 29-year-old Parabat company commander jumped to his death near Bloemfontein yesterday. **1986** *Cape Times* 28 Mar., The troops are believed to be paratroops who have been in the Peninsula for some time ... Six Buffels carrying the parabats were parked outside the Manenberg police station. **1987** *Personality* 30 Sept. 12 Louis exhibited none of the tough, *vasbyt* characteristics which the public (possibly incorrectly) have come to associate with the parabats and Recces.

paradise crane see BLUE CRANE.

parallel *adj.* [Special senses of general Eng. *parallel* side by side.]
1. *hist.* Of political practices and concepts: based on a policy of racial segregation; usu. in (or referring to) official government terminology, in the phr. ***parallel development***. See also SEPARATE DEVELOPMENT.

[**1950** *Annual Register 1949* 140 The conflict between the Southern Rhodesian policy of 'parallel development' with its emphasis on permanent European control, and the United Kingdom policy of partnership leading to self-government.] **1971** *Weekend World* 9 May 3 Chief George agreed with an Opposition claim that parallel development in the Republic meant that the Europeans were in the sky and Africans were in the mud. **1973** *Cape Times* 21 June 11 They felt the political development of the Coloured people should be rapidly accelarated but within the 'parallel' concept of a fully-representative Coloured Representative Council (CRC) with greater executive powers ... He suggested a middle course embracing rapid parallel development of the Coloured townships as 'equal towns and cities'.

2. In the phr. ***parallel-medium***, of or pertaining to schooling or a school in which two languages of instruction (usu. English and Afrikaans) are used, in separate classes. Cf. DUAL-MEDIUM.

1958 *Cape Argus* 10 Dec. 20 The classroom instruction given in Afrikaans-medium classes in a parallel-medium school would be as Afrikaans as instruction given in the classes of an exclusively single medium Afrikaans school. **1960** [see DUAL-MEDIUM]. **1971** *Sunday Times* 28 Mar. (Business Times) 4 (*advt*) Separate English and Afrikaans medium primary schooling, and parallel-medium schooling to matriculation standard is available. **1977** *Sunday Times* 2 Oct. 16 This Parallel-Medium School — Unique in South Africa — Offers *Five* Fields of Study. **1991** [see DUAL-MEDIUM].

paramount *n.* [Special sense of general Eng. *paramount* (one who is) superior in authority.] In full ***paramount chief***:
a. A designation given (esp. in the past by colonial authorities) to a senior African leader who is accepted as 'the first among equals' in the ruling structures of a traditional people or group of peoples; UMKUMKANI. Also *transf.*, see quot. 1987. See also INKOSI sense 1 a.

1844 in F. Brownlee *Transkeian Native Territories: Hist. Rec.* (1923) 92 Treaty of Amity entered into .. on behalf of Her Britannic Majesty, of the one part, and Faku, Paramount Chief of the Amapondo Nation. **1848** H. WARD *Five Yrs in Kaffirland* II. 30 A paramount chief's person is held sacred. *a***1867** C.J. ANDERSSON *Notes of Trav.* (1875) 220 The residences of the great .. are on a much more extensive scale — that of Chykongo, the paramount chief .. being something like half a mile in circuit. **1877** R.M. BALLANTYNE *Settler & Savage* 19 Lord Charles Somerset .. chose to enter into treaties with Gaika as paramount chief of Kafirland, although Gaika himself told him plainly that he was not paramount chief. *c***1882** G.W. STOW *Native Races of S. Afr.* (1905) 183 A Bushman captain .. was succeeded by 'Khiba, or 'Kheba, who was the paramount chief over the men of the caves. **1906** [see PITSO]. **1919** G.M. THEAL *Ethnography & Conditions S. Afr. before 1505* 212 Sometimes the heads of the clans were members of the family of the paramount chief. *c***1948** H. TRACEY *Lalela Zulu* 17 This Zulu song is sung all over the country and particularly so when the Paramount Chief is in the immediate vicinity. **1968** E.A. WALKER *Hist. of Sn Afr.* In theory, the 'great place,' the kraal of the paramount chief, was the centre of the tribal state. **1970** *Daily News* 15 May, Paramount chiefs are already directing government officers at various levels. **1978** T.R.H. DAVENPORT *S. Afr.: Mod. Hist.* 101 Whether the slaughter was a spontaneous act of misguided faith or a calculated political move by Sarhili, the Gcaleka paramount .. may never be known for certain. **1979** M. MATSHOBA *Call Me Not a Man* 175 The paramount has followed his father's road and has done much to keep the clans together. **1986** P. MAYLAM *Hist. of Afr. People* 197 Vilakazi argues that the king's status was reduced to that of paramount chief, who was subordinate to the resident commissioner. **1987** *Drum* July 10 According to mlungu constitution the State President is the makhulu baas of all chiefs. He is the very Paramount Paramount Chief. **1991** S. MACLEOD in *Time* 5 Aug. 13 Proud of his descent from the great Zulu warrior and paramount chief Shaka, who never surrendered, Buthelezi is not likely to yield to anyone.

b. (Always in full, and with initial capitals.) A title, often used before a name; P.C. *n.*[1]

1926 M. NATHAN *S. Afr. from Within* 55 Sobhuza himself, together with his principal chiefs and Indunas, went to England to endeavour to obtain the restoration of his title as King (he had latterly been styled Paramount Chief by the Administration). **1949** O. WALKER *Proud Zulu* (1951) 324 All titles like Regent, Paramount Chief, and so on are mere sops to Zulu sentiment. **1974** *Afr. Encycl.* 505 The policy of 'separate development' .. which led to the establishment of the Transkei has been opposed by the leader of the 'True' Thembu, Paramount Chief Sabata Dalinyebo.

paramountcy *n.* Also with initial capital. [PARAMOUNT + Eng. n.-forming suffix *-cy*.] The rule or position of a paramount chief.

1971 *Sunday Tribune* 5 Dec. 23 Involvement in politics would bring about the end of the Paramountcy. **1979** [see GONAQUA sense 1]. **1986** *Weekly Mail* 18 Apr. 14 Matanzima .. was angered when the semi-educated Dalindyebo .. inherited the Thembu paramountcy. **1986** P. MAYLAM *Hist. of Afr. People* 137 Supporters of the Pedi paramountcy freed themselves from Transvaal control.

parcel *n.* [Special senses of general Eng.]
1. *Diamond-trade.* A packet of diamonds of mixed sizes and qualities, offered for sale together.

1902 G.F. WILLIAMS *Diamond Mines S. Afr.* 51 The daily productions of diamonds are put away in parcels until there is an accumulation of about 50,000 carats of De Beers and Kimberley diamonds. **1911** L. COHEN *Reminisc. of Kimberley* 69, I call to mind a Dutchman coming to his office with a mixed lot of stones to sell, that is to say in the parcel, as they called it, there were some diamonds worth ten shillings per carat, others perhaps three pounds or probably ten pounds. **1920** F.C. CORNELL *Glamour of Prospecting* 63, I found this little 'parcel' to consist of an almost complete assortment of various minerals usually found in or associated with diamondiferous 'blue ground' — or Kimberlite. **1931** G. BEET *Grand Old Days* 148 Should a digger have a 'parcel' to dispose of without delay, he knew that by going straight ot Robinson's office he would receive the immediate and courteous attention of the principal. **1936** [see SPERRGEBIET]. **1957** C. BIRKBY *Airman Lost in Afr.* 28 Somehow a little yellow tobacco bag seemed to be the badge of the trade: uncut stones were always kept in one and the I.D.B. fellows called the little bag a 'parcel'. **1967** E. ROSENTHAL *Encycl. of Sn Afr.* 150 'Parcels' are made up of clearly defined groups of diamonds. **1973** A. HOCKING *Oppenheimer & Son* 30 Once the stones were sorted, the staff .. gathered them in 'parcels' .., a fixed quota of stones of different sizes, qualities and colours in each. **1987** *S. Afr. Panorama* Mar. 46 They never found the precious parcel and it was only made known long after where the diamonds had been hidden — on top of a cupboard in the room which the two detectives had occupied during their stay. **1988** K. SUTTON in *E. Prov. Herald* 5 Mar. 7 A diamond rush was under way on the commonage at Bloemhof, and a digger named Steyn had found a flawless 25 carat stone ... Other nice parcels had been found.

2. *slang.* DAGGA *n.*[2] sense 1.

1952 [see BOOM sense 1].

Parkmore prawn *n. phr.* PARKTOWN PRAWN.

1986 SCHOLTZ & HOLM *Insects* 80 In recent years *Libanasidus vittatus*, the so-called 'Parkmore prawns', which originally occurred only in indigenous forests, have become a nuisance in urban areas in the Transvaal. They enter houses and cause alarm due to their large size. **1994** E. BARTLETT in *Weekly Mail & Guardian* 27 Jan. 6 Toms .. prefers the name Parkmore prawn and points out that some people call them Parkhurst prawns.

Parktown prawn *n. phr. Colloq.* [The name of an elite Johannesburg suburb *Parktown* + Eng. *prawn* (prob. so called because, with their feelers and overall body shape and size, they supposedly resemble prawns).] The king cricket *Libanasidus vittatus* of the Stenopelmatidae, which grows to a length of seven centimetres; PARKMORE PRAWN.

1984 *Fair Lady* 30 May 176 What about the dreaded Parktown prawn that stalks Jo'burg's trendy suburbs? **1988** G. HOOD in *Personality* 30 May 23 The bantams keep the insect population down, especially the Parktown Prawns. **1988** *Style* June 99 Bill might just .. present you with a large, fat, lime-green, carbuncular, ceramic toad ... One wonders if it hasn't been created with the sole function of frightening away Parktown prawns. **1988** *Argus* 18 Dec., Officially called *Libanasidus vittatus*, or king cricket, Johannesburgers have dubbed it the 'Parktown Prawn' — after the northern parkside neighbourhood which it loves to infest. **1991** *You* 18 Apr. 112 It seems highly unlikely that sweet-and-sour Parktown Prawns and Cockroach Kebab will take over from chops, wors and ribs at the braai. **1991** *Sunday Times* 23 June (Mag. Sect.) 14 There's nothing worse than .. Hysterical Parktown Prawns. **1994** E. BARTLETT in *Weekly Mail & Guardian* 27 Jan. 6 The Parktown prawn, or *Libanasidus vittatus*, is not a mutant cockroach but a cricket.

‖**parmantig** /par'mantəx/ *adj.* Also **permantig**. [Afk., fr. Du. *permantig*.] **a.** CHEEKY. **b.** Arrogant, proud, conceited.

1871 J. MACKENZIE *Ten Yrs* (1971) 61 As to being 'parmantig' or conceited, I believe we must bring the Griqua and Hottentot in as guilty, at any rate from a caste standpoint. **1902** W. DOWER *Early Annals of Kokstad* 14 The grass was too long, the winter too cold, the rains too heavy, the markets too far, the money too scarce, the merchandise too dear, the Kaffirs too 'parmantig'. **1904** A. WILMOT *Life & Times of Sir Richard Southey* 69 Biddulph is not popular ... I hear some of his Dorp people are about to leave — he is so independent, and 'permantig' in his doings. **1939** R.F.A. HOERNLÉ *S. Afr. Native Policy* 135 We have no need for active persecution, beyond making an example, now and then, of an 'impudent' (parmantig) non-European who does not remain 'in his place'. [**1976** A. DELIUS *Border* 287 The Boer holding the white flag roared at him, 'Parmantige Hotnot!']

Hence **parmantig** *adv.*, impudently.

1966 F.G. BUTLER *Take Root or Die* (1970) 38 'Magtig!' you spoke 'permantig' like that to Mr Mountjoy?

parra var. PADDA.

parrot fish *n. phr.* [See quots 1913.] Either of two species of marine fish, characterized by their bright colouring and beak-like mouths. **1.** *Oplegnathus conwayi* of the Oplegnathidae; *banded -* or *bastard galjoen*, sense (*b*) see GALJOEN sense 2. **2.** The surge wrasse *Thalassoma purpureum* of the Labridae.

1905 H.E.B. BROOKING in *E. London Dispatch* 4 July 2 The commonest fish found [at Delagoa Bay] are rock cod, .. parrot-fish, long-finned dory. **1906** *Ibid.* 12 Mar. 3, I secured the head of the parrot fish which is somewhat rare on our coast, in fact it is rare anywhere, only one genus of this family being known to science. **1913** C. PETTMAN *Africanderisms* 365 *Parrot fish*, In the Cape Colony this name is given to *Hoplegnathus conwayi*. See Papagaai visch. But in Natal the name is given to *Julius umbrostigma, Ripp.*, the reference being to its gay colouring of green, blue and pink. **1913**

W.W. THOMPSON *Sea Fisheries of Cape Col.* 60 (Swart), Papegaai (parrot fish), a name given to two or three different fish in the Cape and Natal seas, but all characterized by the beak-like form of the mouth, at the Knysna it is called kraai-bek (crooked-mouth). **1930** C.L. BIDEN *Sea-Angling Fishes* 260 Lumps of ascidian skin that have been ripped open ... The work has undoubtedly been that of the biskop, for no other fishes (unless the parrot fish ..) are capable of causing such destruction among red bait. **1949** J.L.B. SMITH *Sea Fishes* 201 *Oplegnathus conwayi* ... *Bastard Galjoen. Beaked Galjoen. Pappegaaivis. Parrotfish. Golden Roman* ... Found only in South Africa from False Bay to Natal, in mostly shallow water ... Flesh good, but some people fear to eat it because of the beak. **1973** *Argus* 12 Jan. 20 Big red steenbras ghosted by in the distance and .. the parrot fish were so tame that they came and bumped against your mask.

pars /pars/ *n.* Ellipt. for PARSTYD.

1982 J. KRIGE in *Staffrider* Vol.5 No.2, 20 It was during the Pars, and Doekvoet's father was standing on a ladder in the vat, stirring the korrels.

||**parstyd** /ˈparsteɪt/ *n.* [Afk., *pars* to press + *tyd* time.] In the Western Cape: the wine-making season; PARS.

1964 L.G. GREEN *Old Men Say* 135 Once in my life I saw the old-fashioned *parstyd*, the pressing of the grapes by foot ... Certainly the *parstyd* has lost something of its charm now that the music has died away under the noise of the égrappoir. **1971** — *Taste of S.-Easter* 204 The old parstyd, the time of the vintage, was a joyous festival in the wine districts. [**1986** *Cape Times* 7 Feb. (Funfinder) 3 Marketed as *Parstyd*, it is pure, fermenting grape juice, known as 'grape must'. It .. will be available for about 10 weeks only during the grape harvesting season.]

partridge *n.* [Transf. use of general Eng. *partridge* a name for various species of game bird, esp. birds of the genus *Perdix*.]

a. Any of several species of game bird of the genus *Francolinus* of the Phasianidae.

See note at PHEASANT.

1785, 1790 [see PHEASANT sense a]. **1835** T.H. BOWKER Journal. 13 Feb., Miles shoots two hares two partridges and a monkey on Cattl[e] guard. **1899** R.B. & J.D.S. WOODWARD *Natal Birds* 161 (Pettman), Perhaps the commonest of our partridges is the well-known *Redwing*. **1908** HAAGNER & IVY *Sketches* 124 The Francolins .. are locally known as Pheasants and Partridges ... There are two genera of Francolins ... *Francolinus* .. [and] .. *Pternistes*. To the former belong the 'Partridges' and to the latter the 'Pheasants'. **1943** D. REITZ *No Outspan* 151, I shot birds, for partridge, pheasant and guinea fowl are plentiful. **1970** G.J. BROEKHUYSEN in *Std Encycl. of Sn Afr.* II. 345 Most of the birds on the open veld are well camouflaged, for example the pheasants, partridges and quails. **1991** [see quot. at *grey partridge* (sense b below)]. **1994** M. ROBERTS tr. *J.A. Wahlberg's Trav. Jrnls 1838–56* 22 Shot various small birds and one partridge.

b. With distinguishing epithet: **bush-partridge**, (*a*) the SWEMPI, *Francolinus coqui*; (*b*) the *Natal francolin* (see NATAL sense c), *F. natalensis*; **Cape partridge**, the greywing francolin *Francolinus africanus*; **coast partridge**, the *Natal francolin* (see NATAL sense c), *F. natalensis*; **grey(-wing) partridge** (occas. simply *grey-wing*), *Cape partridge* (see above); **red-necked partridge**, the *Cape pheasant* (see PHEASANT sense b), *F. afer*; **redwing partridge**, the redwing francolin *F. levaillantii*.

1899 R.B. & J.D.S. WOODWARD *Natal Birds* 162 (Pettman), The **bush partridge** measures 13 inches in length. **1937** H. SAUER *Ex Afr.* 55 Three kinds of partridges were fairly frequently encountered: the redwing, .. the greywing, and .. the *schwempe* or bush-partridge, a smaller bird always found in thin forest country. **1801** [**Cape partridge**: see *Namaqua grouse* (NAMAQUA *n.* sense 2)]. **1908** HAAGNER & IVY *Sketches* 125 In the Cape Colony the two best known species are the Cape Redwing (*Francolinus levaillantii*) and the Greywing or Cape Partridge (*F. africanus*). **1913** C. PETTMAN *Africanderisms* 113 *Cape partridge, Francolinus Africanus* .. South Africa possesses neither a true partridge nor a true pheasant among its birds. **1931** *Guide to Vertebrate Fauna of E. Cape Prov.* (Albany Museum) I. 187 *Francolinus africanus*, .. Grey-wing Francolin, Cape Partridge. **1911** J.D.F. GILCHRIST *S. Afr. Zoology* 255 (Pettman), *Francolinus natalensis* is the **Coast partridge** of Natal or 'Namaqua pheasant' of the Transvaal. **1878** T.J. LUCAS *Camp Life & Sport* 85 We had a sprinkling of red wing, but the game **grey partridge** was more predominant. **1904** *Argus Christmas Annual* 13 He crawled about searching for 'fritongs,' or small roots dear to the 'grey wing' and the red. **1908** [see quot. at *Cape partridge* above]. **1918** S.H. SKAIFE *Animal Life* 230 There are several species of the large, stoutly-built birds known as francolins ... Among these must be included the greywing or Cape partridge. **1991** *Best of S. Afr. Short Stories* (Reader's Digest Assoc.) 260 More than one South African game bird goes by the popular name of 'partridge', but the one referred to here is most likely the grey-wing partridge (*Francolinus africanus*) ... Grey-wing partridges are often seen in coveys of up to 18 birds, which rise with a loud, squealing cry when flushed. **1899** R.B. & J.D.S. WOODWARD *Natal Birds* 163 (Pettman), **Red-necked partridge** .. in the up-country districts this large francolin .. alights in the trees, and is called a *pheasant*. **1878, 1937** [**redwing partridge**: see quots at *bush-partridge* above]. **1958** L.G. GREEN *S. Afr. Beachcomber* 23 Such expert shots did they become that they picked off redwing partridges on the wing with their rifles.

party *n. hist.* Also with initial capital. [Special senses of Eng. *party* group.]

1. An officially constituted group of British settlers (esp. those of 1820) under the leadership of one person and initially settled together on contiguous farms.

1819 *Circular* (Colonial Office) in G.M. Theal *Rec. of Cape Col.* (1902) XII. 229 It is absolutely requisite that the details respecting the Individuals of your Party which you are called upon to state in the Returns, should be correctly specified. **1835** C.L. STRETCH Journal., In 1820 about 4,000 took possession of the Zuurveldt under certain arrangements between the Heads of the different parties with the Government. **1868** *Act 13* in *Stat. of Cape of G.H.*, Following the line of the Deal Party's grant to the sea. **1877** R.M. BALLANTYNE *Settler & Savage* 78 There was 'Baillie's party,' which crossed Lower Albany to the mouth of the Great Fish River. **1948** H.E. HOCKLY *Story of Brit. Settlers of 1820* 32 What came to be known as 'independent parties' consisted of a number of persons who, while maintaining complete independence and paying their own deposit money, formally contracted with the head of the party to act as their representative and on their behalf in dealing with the authorities ... The 'sole proprietor party,' on the other hand, was one in which the director — usually a person of substance — assumed all financial responsibility and paid the deposit on behalf of the members, who on their side indentured themselves to the director as servants for a specified number of years at an agreed remuneration and generally waived their rights to the hundred acres of land in favour of the director. **1956** F.C. METROWICH *Valiant but Once* 54 A well-educated man of good family, Bishop Burnett decided to take part in the 1820 Emigration to the Cape. He therefore joined Mr. Bailie's party. **1966** F.G. BUTLER *Take Root or Die* (1970) 8 Like all other parties we have been carried to our locations between the Bushmans and Fish rivers. **1971** *Grocott's Mail* 28 May 3 Members of the Lower Albany Historical Society visited Reed Fountain, original settlement of part of the Sephton party of 1820 Settlers, and Theopolis on their May expedition. **1975** D.H. STRUTT *Clothing Fashions* 168 Parliament voted £50,000 (R100,000) to pay for the passages of 57 parties, each under a leader.

2. LOCATION sense 1 a. Also an element in place-names.

1820 G. BARKER Journal. 27 Dec., Left Bushmans Rivier at day light and rode to Mr Sephtons party of settlers. **1824** G. BARKER Journal. 16 June, Saw the new chapel that is building in James's party and also the man who preached in that party. **1832** *Graham's Town Jrnl* 89 There is also to be Let or Sold, a Location at Clarke's Party, with a good House on the same. **1843** *Cape of G.H. Almanac & Annual Register* 406 At the distance of four miles, is a village called Eben Ezer and sometimes James's party. **1971** *Grocott's Mail* 27 Apr. 1 The Location of the Salem Party (sub-division No. 6) and Portion 23 of Salem Commonage, all situate in the Division of Albany.

pasel(l)a var. BASELA *n.*

pasganger *n.*[1] *obs.* [Afk., *pas* pace, step + *gang* gait + agential suffix *-er*.] A horse with an ambling gait. See also TRIPPLE *n.*

1858 W. IRONS *Settler's Guide to Cape of G.H. & Natal* 159 The performances of 'pasgangers' and 'trippelaars,' in former days, are probably lost to history. **1870** H.H. DUGMORE *Reminisc. of Albany Settler* 33 It was an ugly old mare, a 'pas-ganger,' that used to waddle along in most ungainly fashion. **1913** C. PETTMAN *Africanderisms* 365 *Pasganger*, .. A horse with a peculiar gait. [**1934** *Farming in S. Afr.* June 223 (Swart), Some horses are born amblers (pas gang) and this is one of the most uncomfortable slow paces known.]

pasganger /ˈpasxaŋə(r)/ *n.*[2] *hist.* Also **pasgänger**. [S. Afr. Du., *pas* pass, ticket + *ganger* one who goes.] Under Dutch East India Company rule: one who was excused from military service and permitted to work at a trade for himself, in exchange for a monthly payment to be shared among those soldiers performing his duties.

1868 W.R. THOMSON *Poems, Essays & Sketches* 207 Such soldiers as could, by some trade which they had learnt, or by other occupations, earn more than they could [by] standing on guard, went out as free-ticket men (*pasgangers*), and received a monthly pay of 9 florins 12 stivers, which money, called service-money, was equally divided among all the soldiers actually serving in garrison. **1919** M. GREENLEES tr. *O.F. Mentzel's Life at Cape in Mid-18th C.* 79 Those soldiers who know a trade .. are excused from military service and pay in return for this privilege nine gulden twelve stuivers monthly. These men are called 'Pasgangers, ' and the money they pay is dienstgeld. **1925** H.J. MANDELBROTE tr. *O.F. Mentzel's Descr. of Cape of G.H.* II. 27 Most pasgängers and freiwerkers draw very little of their salaries; those men who earn a pittance in their spare time, or are very economical can get along without drawing subsidiengeld. **1968** E.A. WALKER *Hist. of Sn Afr.* 72 Others [of these men] were *pasgangers* who paid for the privilege of working on their own account.

pas op /ˌpas ˈɔp/ *int. phr. Colloq.* Also **passop**, **passup**. [S. Afr. Du., fr. Du. *oppassen* to be on guard.] 'Beware', 'look out'; BOSS UP *int. phr.*; OPPAS *int.*

1835 J.W.D. MOODIE *Ten Yrs* II. 80, I was suddenly warned of approaching danger by loud cries of 'Pas op,' (Look out,) coupled with my name in Dutch and English. **1860** [see POENSKOP sense 1]. **1900** B. MITFORD *Aletta* 139 '*Pas op, Baas!* The bird!' ... Now he turned to behold a huge cock ostrich bearing down upon him. **1901** E. WALLACE *Unofficial Despatches* 98 If he once gives fight, makes a stand, and brings the whole of his force into action, then *pas op*, De Wet! **1903** D. BLACKBURN *Burgher Quixote* 178 '*Pas op*, Burghers! Lancers! Lyddite!' he shouted, riding right among the drowsy and half-drunken bodies. **1905** P. GIBBON *Vrouw Grobelaar* 235 'Burghers, Burghers!' she screamed. 'Pas op! The Kafirs are coming up the hill!' **1916** S. BLACK in S. Gray *Three Plays* (1984) 190 Van K: What sickens me is to see how frightened everybody is of the chief .. a damn lot I care for the chief .. Van Slaap: .. Pas op, Vanny, the chief! **1924** G. BAUMANN in Baumann & Bright *Lost Republic* (1940) 131, I audibly knocked up my gun and shouted: 'Pas op, Swartz!' 'Don't shoot, I'm only going to fetch my horse,' he said. **1937** S. CLOETE *Turning Wheels* 28 He heard Sannie shout 'Pas Op,' as a Kaffir carrying a shield and assegais jumped up beside him. **1949** C. BULLOCK *Rina*

26 'Over the wet season? Pas op, kerel!' warned Piet. 'There's bad sickness after the rains.' **1956** A.G. McRae *Hill Called Grazing* 116 'Baas, there he is. *Pas-op* Baas, he very bad mule!' **1959** [see JONG *n.* sense 3]. **1968** G. Croudace *Black Rose* 40 'Jeremy, *pas op!*' The urgency of the warning shout threw him to one side. **1971** *Medical Chronicle* Apr. 1 Pas-op — for sex. Doctor, your morals are in danger. *c*1976 H. Flather *Thaba Rau* 71 She uses a curious expression. *Pas op.* It's Afrikaans I believe'. 'What does it mean?' 'It means "take care".'

Hence **pas op** *n. phr.*, a warning; a cautious person; an utterance of the phr. 'pas op'.

1900 S.T. Plaatje *Boer War Diary* (1973) 75 The alarm bells still rang .. a ring to warn us ... Then a lively gentle finale or 'pasop' when we all dodge into our holes. **1910** *Rand Daily Mail* 12 Feb. 7, I hope it is united, but to me it seems as if there are 'pas ops' and 'push ons' in the Bond Party, to use Mr Merriman's own words. **1990** J. Naidoo *Coolie Location* 153 She speaks English to him, only English ... You know, .. no voetseks, no bliksems, no hey jongs, no pas ops.

‖**pasop** /pasˈɔp/ *v. intrans.* [S. Afr. Du. *pas op*, fr. its use as an interjection: see prec.] To look out, to take care; OPPAS *v.*; PASS-UP sense a. Cf. *boss up* (see *v. phr.* at BOSS UP *int. phr.*).

1860 A.W. Drayson *Sporting Scenes* 151 When you come across a wounded leopard, you 'pas-op' (take care), was Hendrick's moral. **1974** *Sunday Times* 16 June 4 Craven must pas op. **1982** *Voice* 23 July 1, I ask *The Voice* to tell the people to 'pasop' for those who say they are policemen wearing camouflage. **1990** M.C. D'Arcy in *Staffrider* Vol.9 No.1, 13 My son, Amien, studied science at school; almost turned him into a heathen. *Meneer* must *pasop* for science. **1994** C.J. Driver *In Water-Margins* 31 The old gardener Who used to ask the *basie* to *pasop* For the seedlings and succulents is now Armed Response in an Instant.

pass *n. hist.* [Special senses of general Eng. *pass* (written) permission or authorization to pass.] See also PASS LAW.

1. (Similar to general Eng. usage.) Esp. during the 19th century: a temporary permit in the form of a letter, certificate, or token issued by one in authority, allowing movement from one district to another, and required by law to be carried **a.** by visitors travelling through the Colony; **b.** by the settlers of 1820 when not on their own land; **c.** by KHOIKHOI persons, in terms of vagrancy laws; or **d.** by black persons entering the Cape Colony, or moving livestock within the colony. In all senses also called CERTIFICATE (sense 1).

1786 G. Forster tr. *A. Sparrman's Voy. to Cape of G.H.* I. 113 As the colonists here are enjoined by the laws to seize .. all such as travel about the country without being able to show a permission in writing for that purpose, I therefore solicited and obtained the governor's pass, requiring that I should pass every where free and unmolested. **1806** *Cape Town Gaz. & Afr. Advertiser* Mar. I., The Land-Drosts of the Country-Districts .. required, to call upon all strangers whatsoever travelling beyond the Kloofs, to show their Passes. **1816** G. Barker Journal. 5 Oct., Tys Jager who was out without a pass was confined at Grahamstown. **1827** G. Thompson *Trav.* I. 105 He provided me .. with a pass, and an official order addressed to all the Veld-Cornets .. to provide me with horses, guides, and every other assistance. **1827** *Reports of Commissioners upon Finances at Cape of G.H.* I. 50 The free blacks .. are required to take out a pass from the director of the fire-engines, to enable them to proceed to a short distance in the country. **1828** W. Shaw Diary. 3 Nov., Busy writing passes for Caffres to go to the Colony. **1828** J. Philip *Researches* I. 167 Among the many hardships to which the Hottentot is subject by this proclamation one must advert to the Law of Passes, contained in the 16th article. **1833** *Graham's Town Jrnl* 2 May 2 Every one is to ask a pass from any Hottentot that happens to come to his place. *Ibid.* 23 May 3 The British Settlers had to apply at the office for a pass to work all day at the stone quarries. **1835** [see LOCATION sense 1]. **1841** J.M. Bowker *Speeches & Sel.* (1864) 102 The lax and incessant granting of passes to Kaffirs to come into the colony enables them to carry off our property with so much alacrity. **1851** J.J. Freeman *Tour* 20 Efforts to revive a 'vagrancy law;' the design of which is to commit men as vagrants .. who might be found travelling about without some 'pass,' or ticket of permission to remove. **1857** R.J. Mullins Diary. 7 July, I suppose he will be transported for he was in the colony without a pass! **1866** [see TRONK sense a]. **1867** *Blue Bk for Col. 1866* JJ25, Passes have been examined, granted and endorsed to 1,138 kafirs who have entered the Colony. **1867** *Act 22* in *Stat. of Cape of G.H.*, It shall not be legal for any native foreigner to enter this Colony without a pass signed by some officer or functionary .. empowered to grant such passes. **1870** H.H. Dugmore *Reminisc. of Albany Settler* 24 To be obliged to procure a 'pass', in order to go merely from the location to Graham's Town, without incurring the risk of getting a night's lodging in the 'tronk' .. chafed the minds of Englishmen. **1877** R.M. Ballantyne *Settler & Savage* 242 Our being obliged to procure a 'pass' to entitle us to go about the country, as if we were Kafirs or Hottentots. *a*1878 J. Montgomery *Reminisc.* (1981) 53 It is the law of the country, you must have a pass, and he ought to have asked you for it. **1899** [see CERTIFICATE sense 1]. **1912** Ayliff & Whiteside *Hist. of Abambo* 37 No Native was to leave his country without a pass from the Resident. **1926** P.W. Laidler *Tavern of Ocean* 84 A decree in 1812 that all slaves cutting .. wood for fuel must carry signed passes. **1933** W.H.S. Bell *Bygone Days* 123 The British Settlers of 1820 were, .. not permitted to leave their allotted holdings at Bathurst and thereabouts without having a pass in their possession. **1936** *Cambridge Hist. of Brit. Empire* VIII. 239 All were prisoners on the locations. They could not leave without permission from the head of the party and then they had to show a pass to the Landdrost in Grahamstown. **1957** A.A. Murray *Blanket* 102 To obtain a 'pass' or 'bewys' from the District Commissioner for stock sold to a farmer across the border in the Free State. **1989** *Reader's Digest Illust. Hist.* 52 Slaves sent by their owners beyond a certain distance were obliged to carry a pass, signed by the owner, stating the particulars of the mission.

2. From the late 19th century: an official certificate or letter (often from an employer), required by law to be carried by black men (esp. in urban areas) as a means of controlling movement and enforcing liquor- and curfew-laws; CERTIFICATE sense 2; SPECIAL. Also *attrib.*

1900 W.S. Churchill *London to Ladysmith* 133 'Is it right that a dirty Kaffir should walk on the pavement — without a pass too?' **1901** *Natives of S. Afr.* (S. Afr. Native Races Committee) 165 Every native on entering a district, being in possession of the pass required by the existing Pass Law, was directed to repair to the district office and get a pass and badge. **1903** D. Blackburn *Burgher Quixote* 9, I have, as public prosecutor, seen so many cases wherein educated Kafirs use their learning to forge passes for liquor or staying out late. **1911** Blackburn & Caddell *Secret Service* 71 To the town Kaffir the pass is a thing of ever present concern. *c*1928 R.R.R. Dhlomo *Afr. Tragedy* 21 There was no necessity for him to go to the Pass Office and spend half a day there waiting for his pass to be endorsed. **1937** C.R. Prance *Tante Rebella's Saga* 203 A job in the Police where he felt quite safe, because no one would ever again ask him for his 'pass' or take his fingerprints. **1944** *Annual Report 1943–4* (S.A.I.R.R.) 5 A memorandum .. showed that there are at least eight different forms of passes, and that these are parts of an intricate system to render Native labour immobile .. and to control the African population. **1954** P. Abrahams *Tell Freedom* 177 Once, Jim had wanted to go out at night without the boss knowing. He had brought .. an old pass to use as model. I had .. copied the white man's words: *Please pass native boy Jim who is in my employ.* **1961** T. Matshikiza *Choc. for my Wife* 121 This, to whom it concerns, is to certify that my houseboy so-an'-so, was working late tonight till this morning ... This pass is valid till four a.m. **1990** A.A. George in *Weekend Post* 3 Mar. 6, I think back on how Africans pleaded with people to write a pass for them and when the curfew rang and the *bombella* sounded its whistle, how they ran down Jetty Street.

3. In full *pass book*. From 1952 to 1986: an identity book which had to be carried at all times by black men (and women, after 1956) over the age of 16, and which was central to the administration of apartheid, being used particularly to limit the movement of black people to the urban areas; DOMBOEK; DOMBOOK; DOMPAS sense 1; DOMPASS; REFERENCE BOOK; STINKER. See also ENDORSE, INFLUX CONTROL.

This document contained personal and official information (see quot. 1968), and failure to carry a 'pass' was a criminal offence. The pass was one of the most hated aspects of apartheid.

1952 B. Davidson *Report on Sn Afr.* 118 The business of the police in these settlements is simple and straightforward. They are charged with seeing that all Africans have the necessary passes. **1953** Lanham & Mopeli-Paulus *Blanket Boy's Moon* 14 There are so many crimes against the Law of the white man of which he might be guilty (from failure to carry a Pass to indulgence in Liquor). **1959** G. & W. Gordon tr. *F.A. Venter's Dark Pilgrim* 157 'Why must we carry passes?' someone asks in a subdued voice. 'The white man does not carry a pass. The Coolie does not carry a pass.' **1960** *Natal Mercury* 22 Mar. 2 Anti-Pass campaign was a 'flop' in Durban. **1961** T. Matshikiza *Choc. for my Wife* 88 The sergeant .. thumbed querulously through each ninety-six paged pass book. **1964** G. Gordon *Four People* 83 The pass is today probably the feature of rule by the white man that is most resented by the African. **1968** Cole & Flaherty *House of Bondage* 40 The African .. calls this reference book his 'passport to existence'. Without it a black man is nothing. He cannot get a job, find housing, get married, or even pick up a parcel at the post office. He must have an employer's signature on his pass to prove he is working ... A man's pass contains his life history in brief detail. It tells his name, where he comes from, which tribe he belongs to, the name of his tribal chief, the place and date of his birth, and his father's birthplace. The pass also gives a history of a man's past employment (too many jobs, briefly held, can be a mark against him), tells whether he has paid taxes and indicates his grade of employment — domestic servant, laborer, student, clerk, etc. *Ibid.* 41 The African must carry his passbook with him religiously, twenty-four hours a day. If he is caught without it, or if his papers are out of order .. , the result is always a fast trip to jail. **1973** P.A. Whitney *Blue Fire* 107 Without a pass none of the native population could move anywhere in South Africa, and passes must be presented on demand at any time. **1977** *Daily Dispatch* 3 Aug. 9 The Government would have .. to scrap discrimination by: Replacing the pass book system by common identity documents for all South Africans. **1978** A.P. Brink *Rumours of Rain* 427 If that pass-book had been washed away, he would have been nothing ... Everything he is, is in there ... Without it he can't go anywhere. **1978** *Speak* Vol.1 No.5, 9 Most irritating of the tools of this constant surveillance of his every move is the 'pass', a document which determines where he is allowed to live and to work, where he may travel. **1974** [see DOMPAS sense 1]. **1980** J. Cock *Maids & Madams* 245 Africans living in a prescribed area are compelled by law to take out a reference document (pass book) at the age of 16. **1980** C. Hermer *Diary of Maria Tholo* 5 Failure to produce a pass when requested was a punishable offence. *Ibid.* 159 Only blacks were required to carry passbooks. White, coloured and Asian people had identity cards. **1983** *S. Afr. 1983: Off. Yrbk* (Dept of Foreign Affairs & Info.) 219 The Minister of Co-operation and Development has said that these 'passes' will eventually be replaced by documents similar to those used by other population groups. **1985** Platzky & Walker *Surplus People* 32 In 1952 two central pieces of legislation were passed ... The first made it compulsory for all African people over the age of 16, men and women, to carry passes at all times. **1985** [see

FORGET]. **1986** *City Press* 2 Feb. 1 Pass books have served not just as identity documents, but also as proof of legal employment and of the right to be in an urban area. **1986** P. MAYLAM *Hist. of Afr. People* 178 Two important measures were passed in 1952. One consolidated passes into a single reference book. **1988** 'A. AMAPHIXIPHIXI' in *Frontline* Apr.-May 28 When the government announced that they had scrapped the pass, that black people were no longer going to be subjected to carrying passes, some gullible people heaved a sigh of relief. **1988** A. KLAASTE in *Sunday Star* 22 May 11 Getting a passbook was the final humiliation of the black male. The de-personalisation that was created by most of the trappings of apartheid were perfected at the pass office. **1990** J. NAIDOO *Coolie Location* 212 I'd seen my uncles on the market sign passes and sometimes provide specials ... I saw the way the 'boys' queued up to have their passes signed and I realized that if I didn't sign their books (why was the Pass called a reference book?) they'd all be liable for arrest. **1991** R. RIORDAN in *Crux* Feb. 4 A .. Native Commissioner's Court .. was a special court that only heard cases relating to pass book offences.

4. *Attrib.* and *comb.* **pass arrest**, an arrest made for failure to carry a pass book, or for presence in an area without the necessary endorsement in one's pass; **pass-burner**, one who burns his or her pass in protest against the pass laws; **pass-burning** *vbl n.*; **pass-law**, see as a main entry; **pass offence**, failure to produce a valid pass when required to do so, punishable by a fine or a gaol sentence; **pass offender**, one found guilty of a pass offence; **pass office**, the administrative centre in each town or district which oversaw the issuing and control of passes (and, during the apartheid era, which acted as an employment bureau); see also ADMINISTRATION BOARD; **pass raid**, a surprise police action to check that people in an area were in possession of valid documents and were thus entitled to be there; **pass system**, the legislation under which passes were issued, and the way in which this legislation was enforced; cf. *dompas system* (DOMPAS sense 2). See also PASS LAW.

1971 *Post* 21 Mar. 7 The learned doctor said .. that when the number of **pass arrests** were compared with the number of people carrying passes (that's us), the proportion was not high at all. **1971** *Daily Dispatch* 18 Aug. 11 Africans interviewed said pass arrests in Port Elizabeth alone sometimes ranged from 60 to 80 a day. *c*1953 P. ABRAHAMS *Return to Goli* 190 Strikers and **pass-burners** were jailed and shot down in large numbers. **1983** J. CRONIN *Inside* 11 Passive Resistance, the Congress Alliance, Defiance Campaign, **Pass Burnings**. **1960** C. HOOPER *Brief Authority* 133 Who will care for the crops when we are arrested for **pass offences**? **1977** J. SIKAKANE *Window on Soweto* 26 In the streets the workers arrested on pass offences are handcuffed in two's and marched in silence in a column from street to street until the officers on duty finish their shift. **1986** *Star* 25 July 1 The prisons are emptied of the victims of this unhappy system. No South African will ever suffer the indignity of arrest for a pass offence again. **1989** J. CRWYS-WILLIAMS *S. Afr. Despatches* 311 'Mr Drum' got himself arrested on a pass offence and was sentenced to five days in the Johannesburg Fort (it had been known as a fort during the Second Anglo-Boer War), known to blacks as 'Number Four'. **1952** B. DAVIDSON *Report on Sn Afr.* 90 It seems that the police .. are mostly busy at night, raiding the location for people who brew 'Kaffir beer' without a licence, and for **'pass offenders'**. **1968** COLE & FLAHERTY *House of Bondage* 48 *(caption)* Every morning, police trucks from all over the city and surrounding townships .. dump their loads of pass offenders to await trial. **1977** P.C. VENTER *Soweto* 61 The Bantu Commissioner's court, where pass offenders are processed and prosecuted. **1982** *Survey of Race Rel. 1981* (S.A.I.R.R.) 238 A report of gross abuses in the trial of pass offenders. **1903** *Ilanga* 11 Sept. 4 After losing a whole hour, waiting in the Government **Pass Office**, I found that the official for issuing passes is also Clerk of the Court. **1936** WILLIAMS & MAY *I Am Black* 208 Shabala used to pay his tax at the Pass Office, where also he had to go every month to renew his pass. *c*1948 H. TRACEY *Lalela Zulu* 53 The scene is any pass office, where all male Africans must go to get their Registration Certificates. **1952** *Drum* Mar. 7, I had been to the Pass Office to have my passes fixed up and there I had heard a rumour about a job in a kitchen. **1970** M. DIKOBE Marabi Dance. 74 The 'registering of Natives with the Pass Office and the signing of his Pass every month.' **1972** *Drum* 8 Oct. 14 There were no records of me. I could not blame them at the pass office, because I had last had a pass in 1952. **1980** L. CALLINICOS *People's Hist. of S. Afr.* I. 41 All information on the pass was also registered in the files at the Pass Office. **1985** J. MAKUNGA in *Staffrider* Vol.6 No.2, 35 If you don't get your ass to the pass-office and register for a job, don't come back here tomorrow night. **1990** G. SLOVO *Ties of Blood* 423 He had gone to the pass office with reluctance but without showing any great fear. **1958** *New Statesman* (U.K.) 8 Nov. 619 **'Pass raids'** are so commonplace in Johannesburg that even few liberal whites experience any real shock when they see a group of 10 or 20 Africans under police guard on a street corner, waiting to become part of the more than a thousand of the kind who, every day of the year, spend at least a day in custody because their papers are not in order. **1963** B. MODISANE *Blame Me on Hist.* (1968) 24 There was a Pass ráid and two white police constables with their African 'police boys' were demanding to see the Passes of all adult African males. **1971** *Rand Daily Mail* 27 Mar. 1 Perpetual insecurity, the harassment of pass raids and the miseries of life below the poverty datum line. **1985** PLATSKY & WALKER *Surplus People* 58 Pass raids have escalated dramatically .. an average of R52 000 per month was collected in fines imposed on Africans charged with being in the Cape Town area illegally. **1988** *Now Everyone Is Afraid* (Catholic Inst. for Internat. Rel.) 69 The state used pass raids, eviction notices and a media campaign in its efforts to clear Crossroads. **1859** *Queenstown Free Press* 2 Mar. (Pettman), I have endeavoured to bring to the notice of the public the evils of the **Pass system**. **1896** PURVIS & BIGGS *S. Afr.* 106 The pass system under which Natives have to register changes of address. **1936** *Cambridge Hist. of Brit. Empire* VIII. 614 The native pass system was made less onerous. **1941** C.W. DE KIEWIET *Hist. of S. Afr.* 231 The monthly pass system, which required each native to carry a permit to seek work or a registered service contract. **1955** *Report of Commission for Socio-Economic Dev. of Bantu Areas* (UG61 1955) 93 This system of issuing reference books, has certain advantages over the former 'pass' system. **1963** M. BENSON *Afr. Patriots* 44 The Government's most effective instrument in controlling their movement and maintaining their subjection was the hated pass system which turned any African outside the Native reserves into a vagrant unless he were working for a European. **1963** A.M. LOUW *20 Days* 145 We offered ourselves for arrest in great numbers, thus forcing the police to recall the pass system. **1972** *Evening Post* 2 Sept. 11 A shock Bill .. is likely to force all Coloured youths between the ages of 18 and 24 years to carry a 'certificate of registration' in a system similar to the pass system for Africans. **1986** P. MAYLAM *Hist. of Afr. People* 146 African mineworkers were strictly controlled by a pass system that severely curtailed their freedom of movement from one area to another. **1988** P. EDGAR in *Personality* 25 July 68 It did not matter to her in that moment that the hated pass-system was finally abolished.

Hence **passless** *adj.*, without a pass.

1915 *Transvaal Leader* in D.B. Coplan, Urbanization of African Performing Arts. (1980) 137 The haunt of the criminal, the passless native, the loafer. **1958** A. SAMPSON *Treason Cage* 53 The police arrived on the scene, baton-charged the crowd and arrested the pass-less men. **1966** L.G. BERGER *Where's Madam* 190 Living the life of a hunted passless native, one step ahead of the police.

passela var. BASELA *n.*

passenger *n. hist.* [Special sense of general Eng.] Usu. *attrib.*, often in the phr. ***passenger Indian***. An Indian immigrant of the merchant class who came to South Africa independently, and not as an indentured labourer. See also ARAB.

1907 V. LAWRENCE in Bhana & Pachai *Documentary Hist. of Indian S. Africans* 23 Your petitioner is a passenger from India, resident in the borough of Durban, and is anxious to obtain a letter of exemption declaring him exempt from the operation of the laws affecting Indians. **1961** Z. MAYAT *Indian Delights*, The Gujeratis who alighted as 'free' or 'passenger' Indians, were on a higher economic rung. **1969** F. MEER *Portrait of Indian S. Africans*, Free or passenger Indians as they came to be called, followed in the wake of the indentured to Natal. But white colonists became alarmed by the competition offered by these merchants. **1981** N. AIYER in *Staffrider* Vol.3 No.4, 5 Some were indentured. Others were passenger immigrants. They came and they .. toiled and they slaved. **1989** [see ARAB]. **1994** F. MEER on Radio South Africa 21 Aug., As well as the indentured labourers there was a very small community of what they called passenger Indians, people who had come to South Africa to try their luck.

pass law *n. phr. Hist.* Also with initial capitals. Usu. in *pl.*: A body of laws controlling the movement and residence rights of black people, differing from one period to the next, but particularly during the apartheid era implemented by endorsements in identity documents (the carrying of which was compulsory), and enforced by the imposition of fines and prison-sentences. Also *attrib.*, and *comb.* **pass law system**, these laws collectively, and the way in which they were implemented; see also *pass system* (PASS sense 4).

[**1828** see Philip quot. at PASS sense 1.] **1897** *E. Prov. Herald* 8 Feb., In the defence of a native charged with being without a pass, the defence was made that the Pass Law was not legal. **1897** A. MILNER in C. Headlam *Milner Papers* (1931) I. 194 Exempt Cape Boys from the degrading provisions of the Pass Law. **1899** 'S. ERASMUS' *Prinsloo* 115 When the new Pass Law was made, the boys were afraid to leave without their passes, for if caught they would be flogged for having none. **1908** J.M. ORPEN *Reminisc.* (1964) 268 The President spoke of a pass law regarding movements of natives and cattle entering the Free State. **1909** *State* Vol.2 No.7, 14 The native .. is also subjected to the Pass Law in the Transvaal, which enables his employer to control him with greater ease and to enforce performance of his contract to work. **1921** *Outward Bound* May 46, I would not report them, that was not my way, let the pass-law say what it pleased. I don't hold with pass-law slavery. **1927** *Workers' Herald* 18 Mar. 1 Pass Laws Must Go. Every I.C.U. Member must pay his or her 5/- National Levy to fight these Dog Licenses. **1943** I. FRACK *S. Afr. Doctor* 68 The irritating pass laws are another form of petty persecution. **1948** O. WALKER *Kaffirs Are Lively* 171 A pass then was a scrap of paper stating that the owner of it had been freely released by his *baas*. From such a humble beginning has been raised the formidable Pass Law system. **1950** H. GIBBS *Twilight* 72 The majority of their crimes involve theft, robbery with violence, assault, offences against women, drunkenness. And towering above all, failure to comply with the pass laws. **1958** A. SAMPSON *Treason Cage* 52 The chief instrument by which Africans were controlled and disciplined — the *pass laws*, which require every black man to carry a document, without which he is arrested and removed from the city. **1968** COLE & FLAHERTY *House of Bondage* 40 A policeman may at any time call upon any African who is sixteen or older to produce his reference book. If the African fails to produce it, or if his papers are not in order, he is committing a criminal offence and is liable to a fine or imprisonment. The last is the nub of the infamous 'pass laws,' a complex mesh of rules and regulations that restrict the freedom of movement of Africans. Compared to some of the other oppressive statutes of *apartheid*, the pass laws on paper seem modest enough. But in practice they are the keynote on which enforcement of the entire *apartheid* system is based. *Ibid.* 51 For an African to protest against the degrading pass laws can be a deadly offense. On March 21, 1960, a crowd of blacks gathered in Sharpeville .. to conduct a peaceful, unarmed protest against these despised laws. **1971** *Rand Daily Mail* 10 June 5 The Government's move to introduce a new system of dealing with influx and pass law offenders is seen by the Black Sash as another means of removing Black people from urban areas to homeland settlements. **1977** *Time* 2 May 22 The 'pass laws' .. cost South Africa no less than $130 million a year to administer. **1980** L. CALLINICOS *People's Hist. of S. Afr.* I. 39 The first pass laws were introduced more than 200 years ago, in 1760, and applied to slaves in the Cape. **1985** [see DOMPAS sense 1]. **1990** *Femina* June 108 Apartheid has to have a reservoir of cheap black labour, and the pass laws helped to provide this by controlling the movement of African people. **1992** [see COLOUR BAR].

passop var. PAS OP *int. phr.*

pass-up *v. obs.* [Calque formed on S. Afr. Du. *pas op*, see PASOP *v.*]
a. With a clause: PASOP *v.*
  1835 T.H. BOWKER *Journal.* 24 Oct, They'll passup that I don't get hold of them next time I'll warrant them.
b. *trans.* To take care of (someone or something); cf. *boss up* (see *v. phr.* at BOSS UP *int. phr.*)
  1877 LADY BARKER *Yr's Hsekeeping* 38 'Pass up the baby,' is the first order which I hear given; and that astonishing baby is 'passed up' accordingly.

pastorie /ˌpastuˈri/ *n.* [Afk. (fr. Du.), ad. medieval L. *pastoria*.] The residence of a minister of one of the Dutch Reformed churches; a parsonage.
  [1856 E.R. MURRAY in J. Murray *Young Mrs Murray* (1954) 11 Bloemfontein Parsonage (or Pastorie as the Dutch call it).] 1910 D. FAIRBRIDGE *That Which Hath Been* (1913) 262 On the stoep of his pastorie sat the minister, .. watching Dorp Straat come to life again after its mid-day sleep. 1915 D. FAIRBRIDGE *Torch Bearer* 97 Enlarged photographs of the Reverend Septimus van Schoor's predecessors at the Pastorie hung on the chocolate-tinted walls. 1930 *Outspan* 25 July 17 At daybreak the predikant had sent for her to the Pastorie, where poor little Sari Malan lay breathing out the last of her pitiful young life. 1950 H.C. BOSMAN in S. Gray *Makapan's Caves* (1987) 141 And the commandant-general and the dominee had words about whether the *plein* in the middle of the dorp should be for the *Dopper Church*, or a *pastorie* next to it. 1951 H. DAVIES *Great S. Afr. Christians* 45 Lindley and his family came to minister to the Boers in 1841. He received a salary of £100 per annum, with the free use of the *pastorie*. 1951 *Ibid.* [see GEM sense 1]. 1963 R. LEWCOCK *Early 19th C. Archit.* 227 The house was granted to the Dutch Reformed Church as a 'pastorie', which function it served until well into the present century. 1972 *Evening Post* 19 Feb. (Mag. Sect.) 2 In 1834 it became the Pastorie of the Dutch Reformed Church and so remained till 1944. 1983 D. HUGHES et al. *Complete Bk of S. Afr. Wine* 226 In 1743 a small church, described as 'a very humble and simple edifice', was built. Between it and its pastorie a row of about a dozen small houses was strung out. 1991 F.G. BUTLER *Local Habitation* 281 Now, right opposite the Pastorie, next to the Manse and a stone's throw from the Rectory, the inhabitants of Bree Street had to see and smell the ragged poor for hours at a stretch.

pata-pata /ˌpaːtaˈpaːta, ˌpɑːtəˈpɑːtə/ *n.* Also **patha patha**, **phata-phata**. [Xhosa and Zulu *phatha* to touch, feel.]
1. 'Touch-touch': A sexually suggestive dance-style in which pairs of dancers touch each other's bodies with their hands. Also *attrib*. Cf. KWELA sense 3.
  1968 *Drum* Sept. 5 She entertained audiences all over Europe with her exotic dancing. Here her excellent performances of pata pata, voodoo and the syncopated clock mambo attracted bold headlines. 1976 *Sunday Times* 4 Apr. (TV Times) 5 London's new disco craze, brought straight from South Africa, by the cast of the West End musical 'Ipi Tombi'. They call it the phata phata, pronounced patter-patter. 1980 E. PATEL *They Came at Dawn* 9 Die is mos a party nie a shebeen 'n haanetjie wants to dance rock-'n-roll-pata-pata-take-five the music is kwaai. 1987 G. SILBER in *Style* June 26 The black movie sausage-machine annually churns out hundreds of skop, skiet, and phata-phata flicks. 1988 B. O'REILLY in *New Nation* 14 Jan. 9 (letter) The young mingled with the old doing the cassanova, pata-pata or even a bit of fly jazz. 1990 *New African* 11 June 13 Popularised world-wide by the exiled song bird Miriam Makeba, patha-patha — an individualised, sexually suggestive form of jive dancing for boys and girls in which partners alternately touched each other all over the body with their hands in time with rhythm — was a direct result of the popular kwela music.
2. *Music.* A name given to kwela music (see KWELA sense 1), particularly when it is intentionally arranged to suit the pata-pata dance style. Also *attrib*.
  1969 *Post* 15 June, 'Cats' in Windhoek .. are raving mad with mbaqanga, the Soweto originated song-dance mood which came soon after pathapatha (touch-touch) a dance tempo popularised by .. Miriam Makeba. 1976 *Drum* 8 Mar. 46, I am doing some research into .. African music in South Africa, with emphasis on kwela, jive, pata-pata. 1990 *Learn & Teach* No.7, 10 In the 50s and 60s, Sparks and other musicians thrilled fans all over South Africa with their kwela and pata-pata records.
3. *transf. slang.* Sexual intercourse. Also *attrib*.
  1977 P.C. VENTER *Soweto* 127 A stranger to the tsotsi's dangerous world could .. save his throat if he has some knowledge of basic words and phrases ... Phata-phata — sex. 1979 A.P. BRINK *Dry White Season* 84 'Others looking for phata-phata' — illustrated by pushing his thumb through two fingers in the immemorial sign.

patat /pəˈtat, pa-/ *n.* Also **pattatta**, **petata**. [Afk., fr. Du. *pataat* (ad. Sp. or Pg. *batata*).]
a. The sweet potato or yam, the tuberous root of *Ipomoea batatas* of the Convolvulaceae.
  1846 J. SUTHERLAND *Memoir* II. 557 A despatch of the end of this year, refers almost exclusively to the improvement of the colony, in the growth of wine, indigo, olives, pattattas, &c. 1903 L. HOTZ tr. *J.E. De la Rey's Woman's Wanderings Anglo-Boer War* 123 As we had so little [coffee] left, I used to cut up petatas into small dice and dry and burn them. [Note] A species of potato. 1949 L.G. GREEN *In Land of Afternoon* 62 Sweet potatoes are reverenced in the platteland to a degree unknown in the towns. For centuries the 'patat' has ripened in patches of dark green vegetation towards the end of June. 1971 — *Taste of S.-Easter* 178 The sweet potato or patat was the favourite and true potatoes were neglected. 1981 *Sunday Times* 14 June (Mag. Sect.) 9 'Patats' and indeed, sweet potatoes baked or stewed with sugar, seem to form a staple part of the local diet. 1983 M. VAN BILJON in *Ibid.* 6 Mar. (Mag. Sect.) 16 To serve, put snoek on a platter, patats in a bowl, *korrelkonfyt* in a jar ... Just a smidgen of butter for the rest of your patat.
‖**b.** *comb.* **patat salf** /-salf/ [Afk., *salf* salve], a traditional Dutch remedy used in the treatment of skin infections. See also (*old*) *Dutch medicine* (DUTCH *adj.* sense 2).
  a1910 *Lennon's Dutch Medicine Handbk* 22 Patatsalf, An excellent ointment for veldsores or septic ulcers.
‖**c.** With qualifying word: **gestoofde patats**, also **stowepatats** [Afk. *gestoof*, *stowe* stewed, fr. *stoof* to stew], sweet potatoes with sugar, cinnamon and butter, a traditional dish.
  1977 *Darling* 16 Mar. 86 Perhaps you'd like to try Mrs Malan of Paddagong's recipe for Stowepatats. 1977 *Fair Lady* 8 June (Suppl.) 11 Gestoofde Patats. 1 kg. sweet potatoes, peeled and sliced; 4 tablespoons light brown sugar. 1988 F. WILLIAMS *Cape Malay Cookbk* 68 Gestoofde Patats. Stewed sweet potatoes with coconut brings back many childhood memories.

pat-cop see quot. 1849 at PADKOS.

patha-patha var. PATA-PATA.

pat-koss var. PADKOS.

patlooper var. PADLOPER.

pattata var. PATAT.

pau, pau(u)w varr. POU.

pay-day *n.* [Special sense of general Eng. *pay-day* the day on which wages are paid.] Esp. in the townships: the day on which pensioners collect old-age-, disability-, maintenance-, and other grants.
  1977 *World* 28 Sept. 9 For the old and disabled, it was another 'pay-day', which meant getting up early to stand in the queue. 1978 *Daily Dispatch* 3 Mar. (Indaba) 6 Pay day's hot soup ... When the aged go to Durban Village Community Centre to get their pensions, there are good Samaritans who take time off from 9am till 3pm, to give them a good meal. 1983 *Informant, Grahamstown* Pay day tomorrow for Welfare.

P.C. *n.*[1] *rare.* [Initial letters of *paramount chief.*] PARAMOUNT sense b.
  1954 G. MAGWAZA in *Talk o' the Rand* Jan. 49 Radio announcer Dan Twala was hauled over the coals by one of P.C. Sobhuza II's counsellors for addressing the P.C. 'His Highness' instead of 'His Majesty.'

PC *n.*[2] *hist.* [Initial letters of *President's Council.*] A journalistic abbreviation for PRESIDENT'S COUNCIL. Also *attrib*.
  1981 N. FRANSMAN in *Cape Times* 27 June 1 Three top officials .. had appeared before the PC in their 'private capacities' and had engaged in a question-and-answer session with the PC's Economic Affairs Committee. 1983 N. WEST in *Sunday Times* 18 Sept. 1 The present totally-nominated PC consists of 43 whites, 12 coloureds, four Indians and one Chinese. 1987 J. LE MAY in *Weekly Mail* 19 June 3 President's Council recommendations .. are acknowledged as a clear guide to government thinking. Legislation frequently follows PC recommendations. 1992 *Weekend Post* 24 Oct. 20 PC to bulldoze law that Parliament failed to pass.

PE /piːˈiː/ *n. colloq.* A common name for *Port Elizabeth*, the largest city in the Eastern Cape; *die Baai*, see BAAI; *the Bay*, see BAY sense a; *Bayonia*, see BAYONIAN; FRIENDLY CITY; *Liverpool of the Cape*, see LIVERPOOL; WINDY CITY. Also *attrib*. See also IBHAYI.
  a1892 G. MCKIERNAN *Narr. & Jrnl* (1954) 30 Uitenhage .. is the farthest I penetrated into the interior from that side of the country. It is a pleasant little town and is the market garden for P.E. 1920 R.H. LINDSEY-RENTON *Diary* (1979) 12 From Uitenhage we drove straight back to P.E. *Ibid.* 20 Today is the centenary of the landing of the first settlers in P.E. 100 years ago. 1950 H. GIBBS *Twilight* 129 Go again by train, the overnight train which leaves 'P.E.' shortly after seven o'clock in the evening. 1964 A. FUGARD *Notebks* (1983) 113 It is my understanding, my total knowledge of the shape, sizes and feel of these moments that makes P.E. what it is in my life: necessary. 1966 I. VAUGHAN *These Were my Yesterdays* 46, I can't sit straight up all night in a coat waiting! Think what I should look like tomorrow at P.E. station! 1971 *S. Afr. Panorama* Nov. 28 People who have their homes there and earn their living there call it 'P.E.' And so do the inhabitants of its hinterland, the Eastern Cape Province. For South Africans further inland .. it is 'Port Elizabeth', both an industrial centre and a holiday resort. 1982 *S. Afr. Digest* 18 June 9 The palletised cartons are inspected in the interior before being railed to the coast, with the result that less rejected fruit is being handled in PE. 1986 S. SEPAMLA *Third*

Generation 12 My mind turned on Sis Vi. She was by that time somewhere in New Brighton, PE.

peach-pip floor see PIP sense 2.

peach-stone floor *n. phr.* [tr. Afk. *perskepitvloer*, *perske* peach + *pit* pip + *vloer* floor.] *peach-pip floor*, see PIP sense 2.

1965 K. THOMPSON *Richard's Way* 98 Walking with Helen through the empty rooms, he pointed out to her the peach-stone floor of the little storeroom. 1973 M.A. COOK *Cape Kitchen* 20 Occasionally a floor was laid with peach-stones ... A peach-stone floor had a life hardly longer than that of thatch, i.e. about thirty years. It was laid by setting rows of peach-stones, very closely, upon clay still slightly moist and soft; after which the stones were forced into the clay to a uniform level by means of a board laid over them and firmly pressed down.

peau var. POU.

pecho var. PITSO.

peckie var. PEKKIE.

Pedi, Bapedi /(ba)ˈpeːdi/ *adj.* and *n.* Forms: α. Bapedi, Mopedi. β. Pedi. Pl. Bapedi, baPedi, Pedi, Pedis. [Sotho *Mopedi* a member of this people (pl. *Bapedi*); see quot. 1979. For notes on sing. and pl. forms, see MO- and BA-.]

A. *adj.* Of or pertaining to the Pedi (see sense B).

α. 1882 J. NIXON *Among Boers* 109 Sekkukuni, a Bapedi chief, commenced a series of cattle-lifting expeditions. 1905 *Native Tribes of Tvl* 74 Foremost among the Basuto of these parts is the great Bapedi tribe, commonly known as Sekukuni's and perhaps the best known in the whole Transvaal. 1965 P. BARAGWANATH *Brave Remain* 3 He had heard many versions of battles against the Swazis from both Mopedi and Shangaan sources. 1970 *Post* 18 Oct. 18 The Mokoena family were not at all happy there. Sekhukhuniland is the Bapedi 'homeland.' The Mokoena family are Ndebele.

β. 1931 W. EISELEN in A.M. Duggan-Cronin *Bantu Tribes* II. ii. 35 The greater part of the Pedi tribe lived in reserved areas situated in the Middelburg, Lydenburg and Pietersburg districts. 1958 A. SAMPSON *Treason Cage* 148 His parents were of different tribes — father Pedi, mother Bechuana — so that Peter felt himself happily detribalised.

B. *n.*

1. A member of the largest northern Sotho people, originating in what was formerly the Lebowa 'homeland'. Also called *North(ern) Sotho* (see SOTHO sense 1 c): see quot. 1975.

α. 1926 M. NATHAN *S. Afr. from Within* 33 Burghers was involved in hostilities with Seccocoeni, chief of the Bapedi, in the north eastern Transvaal. 1946 H.C. BOSMAN in L. Abrahams *Cask of Jerepigo* (1972) 165 It was necessary for the prestige of the Boer forces in the field, that a commandant shouldn't go about looking like a Bapedi. 1965 P. BARAGWANATH *Brave Remain* 25 Every Mopedi among the spectators who had or could acquire a whistle, joined whatever group he fancied. 1977 *Drum* Oct. 45 'They say my husband does not qualify to live in these areas because he is a Mopedi,' she explained. 1979 P. MILLER *Myths & Legends* 173 The baRolong people found a small metal-working clan of Karanga people, the Wambedzi, already occupying their chosen spot. They promptly conquered this clan, but .. prudently decided to take the name of the original inhabitants and called themselves the baPedi, the old Sotho-Tswana form of Wambedzi. 1991 S. DU TOIT in *Weekend Post* 9 Mar. (Leisure) 5 This little town .. was founded in 1849 by Voortrekkers who had fled from the hostile baPedi .. at malaria-ridden Ohrigstad.

β. 1975 *Std Encycl. of Sn Afr.* X. 64 There was a tendency to substitute the name 'Pedi' for Northern Sotho, because the Pedi .. are the strongest tribal unit, and particularly because Sepedi has become the written and school language of all Northern Sotho tribes. 1976 WEST & MORRIS *Abantu* 137 The Pedi were among the more recent Sotho immigrants to South Africa. They arrived in the Northern Transvaal by at least the 17th century. 1980 M. MATSHOBA in M. Mutloatse *Forced Landing* 126 The first sound of the tom-tom and the flutes of the Pedis brought people to watch from all corners of the hostel. 1986 P. MAYLAM *Hist. of Afr. People* 50 The 'core group' among the northern Sotho has for long been the Pedi. 1990 *Weekly Mail* 24 Aug. 1 There are Pedis, Shangaans, Tswanas, even Xhosas from his hostel who have become Inkatha members overnight ... The others who have refused to join — especially Pedis — have fled.

2. SEPEDI. Also *comb.* (objective) **Pedi-speaking** *ppl adj.*

α. 1965 P. BARAGWANATH *Brave Remain* 20 They did not seem to be Bapedi-speaking Sothos of the north, but a nondescript crowd who could have come from anywhere between Rustenburg and Bechuanaland.

β. 1963 B. MODISANE *Blame Me on Hist.* (1986), 'The wayside corn does not grow,' Ma-Willie said, in Pedi, a northern Sotho dialect. 1983 *Pace* Dec. 140 'To this day I cannot speak perfect Zulu, Xhosa or Sotho,' she quips. The family is Pedi-speaking. 1985 *Cape Times* 3 Jan. 1 A New Year raid by Ndebele vigilantes into the largely Pedi-speaking Moutse district north-east of Pretoria.

pee(t)cho, peetsh(r)e, peetso varr. PITSO.

peetie var. IPITI.

peit myn vrouw var. PIET-MY-VROU.

‖**pekel** /ˈpɪək(ə)l/ *n.* [Afk.]

1. A brine made of water, salt, sugar, and a little saltpetre, in which meat is pickled.

1973 M.A. COOK *Cape Kitchen* 110 Ordinary meat .. intended to be kept for a longer time, was put into pekel (pickle) (i.e. a solution of about 500gm (1lb) ordinary salt, 150gm (5oz) brown sugar, and slightly less than 30 gm (1oz) of saltpetre, to every 4,5 litres (1 gallon) of water) in a pekelbalie. 1984 [see BALIE sense a].

2. *comb.* **pekelbalie** [Afk., *balie* tub], a vat or tub used in old Cape kitchens for salting meat. See also BALIE.

1971 BARAITSER & OBHOLZER *Cape Country Furn.* p.viii, The teak tub for pickling meat .. the vinegar-smelling 'pekelbalie'. 1973 M.A. COOK *Cape Kitchen* 79 Still larger were the pekelbalies, in which meat was salted. These were usually oval, with lugs at each end which held the lid in place. 1974 *S. Afr. Garden & Home* June 31 Vats or *balies* in common use in the Cape kitchen. Large one at the back was a pickling vat (*pekelbalie*) with its own lid. 1975 *S. Afr. Panorama* Jan. 14 Kitchen shelves against one wall held crockery and items such as a candle mould, pudding moulds, 'pekelbalie' (tub for pickling meat).

pekelbalie see PEKEL sense 2.

pekkie /ˈpeki/ *n.* and *adj. Derog.* and *offensive.* Also **peckie, perkie**. [Unkn.; perh. fr. Zulu *umpheki* cook (pl. *abapheki*); or ad. Afk. *pik* pitch (see Akhalwaya quot. 1978); or see quot. 1970.]

A. *n.* An insulting term for a black person.

1963 B. MODISANE *Blame Me on Hist.* (1986) 53 'Kill a black man and it's three years,' Moffat said. 'They like it when the perkies, the monkeys, kill each other.' 1970 BEETON & DORNER in *Eng. Usage in Sn Afr.* Vol.2 No.2, 6 *Pekkie*, .. abbr[eviation] of piccanin, male Ba[ntu] of any age, used in Natal. 1988 S.A. BOTHA in *Frontline* Apr.-May 24 'I tjaaf you, the peckies are getting white these days,' said Don. 'You can't trust them, any of them.' 1991 V. HUSTLER *Informant, Umtentweni* We battled at work today, the pekkies (blacks) had a stayaway. 1991 A. KUTTNER *Informant, Johannesburg* Peckie: Means African, male or female. Probably comes from piccanin. 'You know, he treats his clerk like a bloomin' peckie.' Derogatory.

B. *adj.* Of a person: black. Also shortened form **pek**.

1978 L. BARNES in *The 1820* Vol.51 No.12, 19 There are .. pekkie ous (Blacks) — known also as *zims, zambis* and *ravens*. 1978 A. AKHALWAYA in *Rand Daily Mail* 10 July 7 The Natal pronunciation of Afrikaans words such as 'wit' and 'pik' come out as 'vet' and 'pek'. And our main ou, who is also a 'chaar ou' (Indian), has friends of all races — 'vet ous' (whites), 'pek ous' (blacks) and 'bruin ous' (coloureds).

pelargonium *n.* /ˌpelɑːˈɡəʊnɪəm, ˌpelɑː-/ Also with initial capital. [Modern L. (L'Heritier 1787), fr. Gk *pelargos* stork (see quot. 1952).] Any of several species of the large indigenous genus *Pelargonium* of the Geraniaceae, having brightly coloured flowers with narrow elongated petals, and fragrant leaves which are either serrated at the edges or ivy-shaped, often with horseshoe-shaped darker markings; often called GERANIUM.

Now cultivated worldwide.

[1819 *Pantologia; Complete Series of Essays, Treatises and Systems; with Gen. Dict. of Arts, Sciences & Words, Pelargonium*, Crane-bill, in botany. 1835 *Encycl. Brit.* XI. 686 Pelargoniums are of easy culture, propagating readily by cuttings. 1861 *Times* (U.K.) 23 May, The azaleas, pelargoniums, and other spring flowers being in particularly good condition.] 1906 B. STONEMAN *Plants & their Ways* 27 Some plants of this family [sc. the carrot family] continue their growth under ground year after year, the part above ground dying down every year. This is also the habit of many *Pelargoniums* ('Geraniums'). 1952 F.M. LEIGHTON in *Jrnl of Botanical Soc.* XXXVIII. 8 Pelargonium — a South African Contribution to World Gardens. As defined by Linnaeus .. it [sc. 'Geranium'] comprised three distinct genera, .. Geranium or Crane's Bill, Pelargonium or Stork's Bill and Erodium or Heron's Bill. These names are descriptive of the shape of the fruit ... Pelargonium, though largely South African in origin, extends to Madagascar and up the east coast of Africa to Arabia and western India. There are species in Australia and on Tristan da Cunha. From the South African species have arisen all the manifold varieties of Pelargonium and so-called 'Ivy-leafed and Zonal Geraniums' of horticulture. 1965 S. ELIOVSON *S. Afr. Wild Flowers for Garden*, Most of the 230 species of *Pelargonium* are found in South Africa and many of them were used as the parents of the numerous named garden hybrids which are now cultivated all over the world. 1976 U. VAN DER SPUY *Wild Flowers of S. Afr. for Garden* 119 There are more than two hundred species of pelargonium growing wild in different parts of South Africa ... Most gardeners refer to them as geraniums, which are quite different although belonging to the same family. In the true geranium the five petals are of equal size and arranged in a regular fashion making a cup-shaped .. flower, whereas in the pelargonium the petals are of unequal sizes and they are arranged in an irregular way. [1989 H.P. TOFFOLI in *Style* Dec. 57 Many of our exotic species appear in foreign botanical gardens and hothouses. I even found myself falling over them in the Jardin Botanique at Menton, all with their universally despised country of origin dutifully noted: 'Pelargonium, Afrique du Sud.'] 1993 *Grocott's Mail* 6 Aug. 10 Pelargonium Peltatum, Ivy Leafed Pelargonium.

pellie /ˈpeli, ˈpæli/ *n. colloq.* Also **pallie**. [Afk. pronunciation-spelling of Eng. *pal* 'chum, mate' + -IE.] Esp. in the Western Cape, among 'coloured' people: a good friend, a 'pal'; also used as a term of address. Often in the *n. phrr.* *pellie blou* or *pellie blue* (see quot. 1966), and *ou pellie*, old friend, old pal (see OU *adj.* sense 1 b).

1959 A. DELIUS *Last Division* 75 Often me and some old pallies from the war Drank a few doppies to the old Cape Corps. 1961 D. MARAIS *Hey! Van der Merwe,* (caption) A state within a State is jus' the beginning, ou pellie. Next he'll want to give us a Nuwejaar within a Nuwejaar. 1963 A. FUGARD *Blood Knot* (1968) 94 Zach, he says, Ou Pellie, tonight is the night. 1964 L.G. GREEN *Old Men Say* 61 'Het ou Pellie!' I suppose that is the most typical of the popular greetings that belong essentially to Cape Town; but the origin would be hard to trace. One expert thinks it falls into the Malay-Portuguese group. 1966 VAN HEYNINGEN & BERTHOUD *Uys Krige* 114 Most Cape Town 'Coloureds' use such words as 'pêllie-blou' (pronounced 'pally-blow') which presumably is made up of the English 'pal' and the Afrikaans 'blou' meaning blue, here as in 'true blue'. **1974** [see GOOSIE sense 2]. **1974** 'BLOSSOM' in *Darling* 9 Oct. 95 They all pally blues, see, what's travelling around seeing the world together in a old clapped-out Kombi. **1975** *Ibid.* 12 Feb. 119 Anyway, Vernon's he's ou pellie blue from back home so long. **1977** D. MULLER *Whitey* 108 The skolly's face grew solemn with concern as he squatted down and peered closely. 'You don't look so good, ou pellie,' said Boon. **1988** M. LE CHAT in *Flying Springbok* Apr. 24 There is a saying in Cape Town: You can take the people out of District Six, ou pellie, but you'll never take District Six out of the heart of the people. **1992** K. WILLIAMS in *South* 27 Feb. 23 The former 'Dollar' says he and Coetzee have been pellies since District 6.

peninsula *n.* Usu. with initial capital. [Special sense of general Eng.] ***The Peninsula***: The Cape Peninsula. Also *attrib.*

1919 J.Y. GIBSON in *S. Afr. Jrnl of Science* July 3 The settlers had made their way accross the 600 miles of rough, trackless country which separated them from the Peninsula by means of their wagons. **1926** M. NATHAN *S. Afr. from Within* 201 The Peninsula is entirely cut off from the mainland by a sandy isthmus, the Cape Flats. *c***1929** S. BLACK in S. Gray *Three Plays* (1984) 66 Van K: He's quite an intellectual, hey? Lady M: I've never troubled to enquire. The most presumptuous person in the whole Peninsula. **1936** *Cape Times* 2 Nov. 17 For the first time in the peninsula, two-way telephonic communications .. were established with an aeroplane in flight. **1953** DU PLESSIS & LÜCKHOFF *Malay Quarter* 31 The festival takes place .. in many Peninsula mosques. **1971** *Grocott's Mail* 15 Oct. 3 Phase one will reach 72 per cent of the White population, with concentration in the Peninsula, the Reef, East London, Port Elizabeth and the South Coast areas. **1981** *Argus* 3 July 14 Peninsula Administration Board officials raided the restaurant this week and took Miss H— away because they said they were investigating allegations that she was a black person 'passing as coloured'. **1983** [see NON-WHITE *adj.* sense 1]. **1988** *Style* May 8 Recently, some 11000 cyclists entered the 100-km jaunt around the Peninsula. **1990** G. HARESNAPE in M. Leveson *Firetalk* 26 These Flats, between the Peninsula and the mountains, are now saturated with water after two days' rain.

penkop /ˈpenkɔp/ *n.* Pl. **-koppe** /-kɔpə/. [Afk., 'youngster', *pen* pen + *kop* head, perh. referring to the very short-cropped hair often worn by young Afrikaans boys.]

1. *obs.* In the Voortrekker youth movement: a young member, the equivalent of a Cub member of the Scout Association. Also *attrib.* See also VOORTREKKER *n.* sense 2 a.

1934 *Friend* 23 Feb. (Swart), Mr. J. was elected commandant, while Mr. P. and Mr. H. and Mr. L. and Miss B. were appointed field-cornets and assistant field-cornet of the 'Penkop' and 'Drawwertjie' sections. **1934** C.P. SWART Supplement to Pettman. 135 *Penkop*, .. In the Voortrekker movement it is equivalent to the Boy Scout 'cub'.

2. *hist.* A boy soldier fighting in the Anglo-Boer War of 1899–1902. Also *attrib.*

1946 V. POHL *Adventures of Boer Family* 30 All the Penkoppe (boys of from fifteen to twenty years of age) seemed to have gathered here ... Attack after attack was repulsed by the merciless accuracy of those Penkoppe sharp-shooters. *a***1951** H.C. BOSMAN *Willemsdorp* (1977) 95 Old men riding side by side with young boys: just as it was in the Boer War — greybeards and penkop youngsters taking up their rifles against the English. **1987** W. STEENKAMP *Blockhouse* 5 To the immortal memory of the 'penkoppe', the boy soldiers of the Boer forces, who fought like men long before they were old enough to shave.

3. A young, inexperienced boy; also *derog.*

1971 *Argus* 4 May 22, I was a penkop in the Transvaal in the early 1930's when I helped Africans collect enough insects to make a meal. **1975** W. STEENKAMP *Land of Thirst King* 85 In any case he was a seasoned hunter of men and beasts and not a 'penkop' quivering with nerves and twitchy about the trigger-finger. **1986** B. NASSON in Burman & Reynolds *Growing Up* 109 There is a genuine stigma attached to coming from a farm school, believe me ... Would you like to be called *penkop* (pencil-head) or *plaasjapie* (country-yokel) in the classroom?

penny-whistle *n. Music.* Used *attrib.* in Special Combinations, as ***penny-whistle music***, ***penny-whistle group***, etc., designating KWELA music (in which this small metal flageolet features prominently), or the musicians who play it; KWELA sense 2.

The penny-whistle was popular among working-class township residents from the early nineteen-hundreds, initially because of its low cost. Over the years, in using it to play music of various styles, township musicians developed innovative techniques which extended its capabilities from both a musical and an expressive point of view. Their virtuosity on the instrument was one of the central features of kwela music.

1951 *Drum* Mar. 14 My feet just wouldn't stop beating out that Boogie-tempo of Cele's Penny Whistle phrasing. **1958** *Star* 3 Feb., Lemmy the 12-year-old leader of a penny whistle group, performs on a Johannesburg pavement. **1958** *Time* 16 June 37 The haunting sound of penny-whistle jazz has become the favorite music of South Africa's slum-caged blacks — and of a great many white hipsters. **1960** C. HOOPER *Brief Authority* 66 Boys .. would climb the mulberry trees, turn the hose on the delighted dog, kick a tennis ball about, teach each other penny whistle tunes. **1963** B. MODISANE *Blame Me on Hist.* (1986) 117 My life is like the penny whistle music spinning on eternally with the same repetitive persistency. *Ibid.* 173 White opinion .. had .. become concerned over the spectacle of white teenagers following black penny-whistle troupes to the zoo lake. **1980** E. PATEL *They Came at Dawn*, The penny whistle melodies and the rhythm of cataclysmic change whisper into grass huts, rickety shanties, brick and mortar houses, granite prisons. **1983** J. DE RIDDER *Sad Laughter Mem.* 63 There were five boys moving in slow circles, jiving in the dust in front of a penny-whistle player. **1984** *Sunday Times* 1 Apr. (Mag. Sect.) 35 The number is a sharp up-tempo electro-pennywhistle-jive ballad. **1988** *New Nation* 25 Feb. 11 The development of kwela music during the mid-40s .. influenced him the most. It was just after this period that people started classifying any music with township rhythms as kwela, without realising that it referred specifically to penny whistle music. **1990** *New African* 11 June 13 Combine Marabi music and the penny-whistle music of the black slums of South Africa, and you'll find the origins of kwela music — regarded as an authentic expression of black urban culture in South Africa ... Kwela was .. transformed by many musically literate jazz players who had performed marabi on penny-whistle as youngsters. They readily adapted to the new style, replacing the penny-whistle — regarded as a child's instrument — with the saxophone and creating jazz-kwela. **1991** P. ALEXANDER in *Weekly Mail* 28 Mar. 27 Mango Groove .. is a curious hybrid .. , leaning heavily on the penny whistle and kwela themes of the Fifties.

Hence **penny-whistler** *n.*, one who plays (kwela music on) the penny-whistle. See also KWELA sense 1.

1982 *Grocott's Mail* 18 May 3 It is an enthralling story peopled with the legendary pennywhistlers of Sophiatown and the early music moguls. **1987** *Weekly Mail* 12 June 28 *Peto* will be supported by *Sangema*, featuring penny whistler Robert Sithole. **1988** M. LE CHAT in *Flying Springbok* Apr. 28 District Six was a vibrant place where .. crooners, penny-whistlers and saxophonists would play on street corners.

pens en pootjies /ˌpens ŋ ˈpʊikis, -kiːz/ *n. phr.* [Afk., fr. Du. *pens* belly, tripe + *en* and + *pootjes*, *poot* animal's hoof or foot + dim. suffix -IE + pl. suffix -s.] Tripe and trotters. Also *attrib.*, and part. tr. **pens and pootjes**. See also OFFAL sense b. Cf. KOP-EN-POOTJIES.

1815 A. PLUMPTRE tr. *H. Lichtenstein's Trav. in Sn Afr.* II. 355 Two or three sheep were killed every day: the entrails and feet were cooked with the fat of the tail, for breakfast, after a fashion which is very much in vogue throughout the colony, under the name of *pens en pootjets* [*sic*]. **1890** A.G. HEWITT *Cape Cookery* 26 'Pens and Pootjes' Curry. Take a well-cleaned sheep's tripe and trotters. **1913** C. PETTMAN *Africanderisms* 369 *Pens en pootjes*, .. A dish composed of sheep's entrails and feet. [**1970** see OFFAL.] **1973** [see KOP-EN-POOTJIES]. **1985** *Newsletter* (W. Prov. Sports Club) July-Aug., Tripe and trotters (pens en pootjies) R4,20. Pork Khebabs with pineapple R5,50.

people's court *n. phr.* Also with initial capitals. [Special senses of general Eng.]

1. *obs.* Any of several proposed minor courts in black urban areas, to consist of persons appointed by the Minister (under the Community Councils Act No.125 of 1977), with powers similar to those of traditional chiefs. Also *attrib.*

These courts were never established.

1980 M. TYALA in *E. Prov. Herald* 2 May, Community Councils in Port Elizabeth, Grahamstown and Uitenhage have accepted a proposal by the Department of Co-operation and Development to establish judicial 'peoples' courts' in the African townships. **1980** *Grocott's Mail* 9 May 1 The envisaged People's Court will only be able to try minor crimes including contraventions of tribal customs and conventions. **1980** R. NUTTALL in *E. Prov. Herald* 10 July 2 The introduction of people's courts in black urban areas came a step nearer yesterday ... The measure .. will confer on selected blacks the same judicial powers as headmen or tribal chiefs.

2. SMALL CLAIMS COURT.

1983 *Rand Daily Mail* 21 Oct. 8 People's courts .. could enable the ordinary man to afford recourse to the judicial process. **1983** *E. Prov. Herald* 22 Oct. 3 Mr E. F— bought a car radio and could not obtain any satisfaction from the seller when something went wrong with it. He .. was sure a 'people's court' could have resolved his problem. **1984** *Ibid.* 28 Mar. 5 The 'people's courts' will deal with claims of up to R700 and there will be no legal representation.

3. An unofficial court set up by a vigilante group in a black (urban) area, ostensibly to re-establish law and order; DC *n.*[2]; DISCIPLINARY COMMITTEE sense b; KGOTLA sense 6 a. Also *attrib.* See also STREET COMMITTEE.

1984 *Frontline* Feb. 13 Apart from the police and formal court structure, there are unofficial 'people's courts' operating under the authority of rural chiefs. **1985** *Sunday Times* 27 Oct. 19 This is the face of township vigilante justice — a man is brutally flogged after being 'tried' in an open-air 'people's court' near Port Elizabeth. **1986** *New Statesman* (U.K.) 13 June 21 The strategy of making the townships ungovernable by Black councillors and white security forces — and replacing it by people's government as seen in the street committees and 'people's courts' — is a sign of the ANC's growing influence in many of the townships. **1987** *Weekly Mail* 31 July 4 Two Duncan Village men were .. sentenced for assaulting a woman as a result of a 'People's Court' decision. **1990** *New African* 13 Aug. 1 ANC slams 'barbaric' people's courts. **1990** M. NDWANDWE in *Tribute* Sept. 64 People's courts, or 'disciplinary committees' (DCs) were a phenomenon of life in the townships in the eighties ... People's courts were .. set up to attend to community issues that the government either failed or was not prepared to handle. **1991** E. MOSANEKE on Radio South Africa 14 May (Audio Mix), Children run so-called 'people's courts' with jungle justice. **1994** [see MODELLING].

‖**peperkorrel** /ˈpɪəpə(r)ˌkɔrəl/ *n.* Also **pieper koral**. [Afk., 'peppercorn', fr. *peper* pepper + *korrel* corn, grain, tuft of hair.] Usu. in *pl.*: *peppercorn hair*, see PEPPERCORN.

1926 *Report of Rehoboth Commission* (UG41–1926) 5 The Bushmen are a people of small stature ... The hair on the head grows in tufts, at distances from each other, the tufts (known colloquially as *'peperkorrels'* — pepper-corns) consisting of twisted woolly hairs. *c***1929** S. BLACK in S. Gray *Three Plays* (1984) 107 Frikkie: Ach wat, you cut off your own hair. Sophie: Well it's der fashion, can' I cut off my own hair if I like! Frikkie: After you spend ten pounds to make your pieper korals straight. **1961** F.G. BUTLER in *Forum* Oct. 9 Pure White and pitch Black, straight hair and peperkorrels. **1970** V.R. VINK *Informant, Florida* The old Bantu woman covered the peperkorrels on her head with a scarf.

Hence **peperkorrel** *adj. nonce.*

*a***1951** H.C. BOSMAN in S. Gray *Makapan's Caves* (1987) 184 The missionary's child by Mletshwa's wife would be dark lemon in colour, with its hair less peperkorrel than the average negro's.

peppercorn *n.* [See quot. 1857.] In *pl.*, or *attrib.* (esp. in the phr. ***peppercorn hair***): hair growing in sparse, tight, curly tufts, as characteristic of the Khoikhoi and San peoples; cf. PEPERKORREL. Also *transf.*

[**1857** D. LIVINGSTONE *Missionary Trav.* 379 The Bushman and the Hottentots are exceptions, .. for both the shape of their heads and growth of wool are peculiar — the latter, for instance springs from the scalp in tufts with bare spaces between, and when the crop is short, resembles a number of black peppercorns stuck on the skin.] **1868** J. CHAPMAN *Trav.* I. 16 Bushmen with peppercorn heads. **1893** F.C. SELOUS *Trav. & Adventure* 107 High cheek-bones, oblique eyes, and peppercorn hair. **1905** W.H. TOOKE in Flint & Gilchrist *Science in S. Afr.* 95 The woolly hair of the Hottentot is a dense dead black; the peppercorn tufts of the Bushman are a rusty brown. **1910** D. FAIRBRIDGE *That Which Hath Been* (1913) 192 In the place of hair small pepper-corns were scattered over his head. **1948** H.V. MORTON *In Search of S. Afr.* 251, I could see the road .. emerging again upon the face of the greyish-brown plain, which was dotted with small peppercorn bushes like a Hottentot's hair. **1958** L. VAN DER POST *Lost World of Kalahari* 12 His [*sc.* the Bushman's] hair was black and grew in thick round clusters which my countrymen called, with that aptitude for scornful metaphor they unfailingly exercised on his behalf, 'pepper-corn hair'. **1961** O. LEVINSON *Ageless Land* 25 Hottentots were a nomadic people ... Light-skinned, of a pale yellow colour, with prominent cheek-bones, flat noses, 'peppercorn' tufts of hair, and eyes that seem to slant. **1968** D.J. OPPERMAN *Spirit of Vine* 251 Kok's face is described in minute detail as looking like 'old biltong' with 'peppercorns of ash-grey hair and with little watery eyes'. **1976** A.R. WILLCOX *Sn Land* 119 The Bushmen .. are typically short and yellow-skinned, with 'peppercorn', not woolly, hair on the head. **1978** A.P. BRINK *Rumours of Rain* 225 A big, flabby man with an infinitely sad face ... Behind him stood his Black helper, an old man with greying peppercorns. **1990** R. MALAN *My Traitor's Heart* 45 She wore spectacles for knitting and sewing, and .. her stubby peppercorn hair was flecked with gray.

Hence (*nonce*) **peppercorn** *v. trans. fig.*, to cover with tufts (of vegetation); so **peppercorned** *ppl adj.*, covered with tufts (of peppercorn hair).

1924 S.G. MILLIN *God's Step-Children* 8 His life was to be spent among Hottentots in future, .. these little yellow fellows, .. with their triangular faces (Mongolian in type), and peppercorned heads. **1948** H.V. MORTON *In Search of S. Afr.* 117 The bald land peppercorned with its dry, dusty-looking plants ended abruptly, and I saw before me the extraordinary contrast of a green, lush landscape stretching forward to another mountain range.

perdepootjie see PERDEVOETJIE.

perdesiekte, -ziekte varr. PAARDEZIEKTE.

‖**perdevoetjie** /ˈpɛrdəˌfʊiki, -ˌfuici/ *n. colloq.* Formerly also **paardevoetje.** [Afk. *perd* (earlier Du. *paard*), horse + *voet* foot + dim. suffix -IE.

'The most easily recognized species is the Pear Limpet (*Patella cochlea*) .. the shell of which is pear-shaped in outline, and has a dark horse-shoe-shaped mark inside.' (K.H. Barnard, *S. Afr. Shore Life*, 1954, p.33). The modern Afk. name is *perdepootjie* (*poot* paw, animal foot).]

The limpet *Patella cochlea.*

1919 M.M. STEYN *Diary* 2 Should you yearn for 'Paarde voetjes' (limpets) to use for crayfish bait or delicious stews, you must go off to the 'Kasteel' and the surrounding rocks. **1958** L.G. GREEN *S. Afr. Beachcomber* 130 Limpets, the perdevoetjies of the fishermen, make a good, safe dish provided you clean them properly. **1971** — *Taste of S.-Easter* 189 She has fish recipes .. ranging from perdevoetjies (periwinkles) to braised crawfish. **1985** A. TREDGOLD *Bay between Mountains* 18 The shell fish on which they [*sc.* strandlopers] feasted included perlemoen, alikreukels, mussels and perdevoetjies (limpets).

perdewa see PAARDEWAGEN.

pere-lemoen, perelomen varr. PERLEMOEN.

peri-peri, piri-piri /ˌperiˈperi, ˌpɪriˈpɪri/ *adj.* and *n.* [Etym. obscure; perh. ad. Swahili *pilipili* pepper; or perh. Mozambiquan Pg.; in either case, the ultimate orig. may be Arabic *phil-phil* chilli. The forms *pil-pil* and *pilli-pilli* occur in Spain and West Africa.]

Perh. used in the English of East Africa earlier than in that of southern Africa; a standard term in *S. Afr. Eng.*

A. *adj.* Of or pertaining to hot red chilli seasoning; descriptive of foods made with this seasoning or sauce.

1959 L. MORRIS *World's Best* (Red Cross) 116 Chicken Peri-Peri ... Have at hand a piece of garlic and some cooking oil into which you put some chilli powder made by crushing or mincing or rubbing through a sieve the dry little common red chillies. **1969** *International Goodwill Recipe Bk* (Jhb. Women's Zionist League) 110 Grilled Chicken Peri Peri ... Pour 4 teaspoonsful of Peri Peri Sauce on each half and squeeze the lemon juice over the chicken. *c***1970** *Your Guide to Spices* (Robertson & Co.) 20 *Prawns Peri Peri*: Fry Prawns in butter to which has been added juice of half a lemon and $\frac{1}{4}$ tsp. Peri Peri ... *Peri Peri Steak*: ... Season with garlic salt and a very light sprinkling of Peri Peri ... *Chicken Peri Peri* ... *Peri Peri Sauce.* *a***1973** *Blesbok Recipe Bk* 73 Dash peri-peri powder. **1988** F. WILLIAMS *Cape Malay Cookbk* 20 Grilled Peri-Peri Prawns. *a***1990** *S. Afr. Cookbk* (Reader's Digest Assoc.) 135 Chicken Peri-Peri. A spicy dish of Portuguese origin, this is probably the best known of the 'hot' chicken dishes. *Ibid.* 175 *Peri-Peri Sauce* .. is an ideal basting sauce for chicken or prawns 'peri-peri'. The strength of the peri-peri flavour is determined by the number of times you anoint the food while grilling or braaing it. **1992** SMIT & FULTON *Complete S. Afr. Bk of Food & Cookery* 306 *Prawns peri-peri* .. 500 g fresh or frozen prawns; .. 5 ml peri-peri powder.

B. *n.* A hot sauce based on red chillies, peppers, and lemon juice; a seasoning of powdered red chillies; any dish made with this seasoning. Also *attrib.*

1967 Can You Beat It? (Anglican Church, Sasolburg) 28 Approximately $1\frac{1}{2}$ tablespoons Liquid Peri-Peri. *c***1970** *Your Guide to Spices* (Robertson & Co.) 20 To make curry really hot, lightly sprinkle Peri Peri over curry after serving. *a***1973** *Blesbok Recipe Bk* 73 Sprinkle with salt, pepper, curry powder, mustard, peri-peri and mixed herbs. **1977** L. VAN DER POST *First Catch your Eland* 177 Piri-piri was perhaps Mozambique's national dish and its main contribution to the art of cooking in Portuguese Africa. Piri-piri was, of course, not unknown in Angola ... It has achieved a certain popularity in Lisbon but nowhere was piri-piri so consistently eaten as in Mozambique, particularly in Beira and the capital ... The man who has become hooked on piri-piri hungers for his favourite dish like a junkie for heroin ... Piri-piri feasts, if not piri-piri orgies, were organised for visitors from the interior ... The restaurants and hotels, like the great Polana, always seemed full of piri-piri voluptuaries. **1988** E. CROMPTON-LOMAX *S. Afr. Menu & Kitchen Dict.* 58 *Peri-peri; piri-piri*, a spice blended from hot chillies; excellent seasoning for meat, chicken and prawns. **1988** F. WILLIAMS *Cape Malay Cookbk* 20 Peri-peri, a fiery mixture of red chillis, is a flavour unique to Africa ... Mix flour and peri-peri and sprinkle over chicken on both sides. **1992** SMIT & FULTON *Complete S. Afr. Bk of Food & Cookery* 306 Peri-peri is an African term for a mixture of fiery red chillies — or *piripiri* — pounded to make a hot chilli paste.

perkie var. PEKKIE.

perlé /pɜːˈleɪ/ [Fr. *perlé* beaded, set with pearls, perh. fr. Fr. *perlant* or abbrev. G. *perlwein* slightly sparkling wine.] An off-dry, semi-sweet, slightly sparkling wine. Also *attrib.*

[**1845** *Cape of G.H. Almanac & Annual Register*, (advt) Light and strong Sherries, Lachryma Christae, (Frontignac white and red muscadel or Perle Constantia) and the genuine Constantia wines. **1973** BRINK & HEWITT ad. Aristophanes's The Birds. 4 Every now and then he gets a hankering for a bit of boerewors or mieliepap or a drop of perlies or something — all these worms and goggas every day don't agree with him.] **1977** E.H. BOLSMANN *S. Afr. Wine Dict., Perlant,* French term for slightly sparkling wine. *Perlé Wine,* The same as perlant, slightly effervescent as distinct from sparkling wines ... *Perlwein*, German term for white semi-sparkling wine made in a pressure tank which retains carbon dioxide generated by fermentation. **1979** *E. Prov. Herald* 20 Mar., Witzenberg Late Harvest and Perle R1,55. **1981** *Time* 7 Dec. (Liquor Suppl.), We have had appreciable success in introducing perlé wines in East London and in South West Africa. **1982** *Ibid.* 29 Nov. (Wine & Spirit Report), Some time ago we developed the low alcohol perlé type of wine, which we hope will fill a gap in the local market and overseas. **1982** *Signature* Jan. 25 Then came the launch of the Cellar Cask, followed by a whole host of bag-in-box wines ... These factors, together with the revival of perlé wine and .. Crackling in particular, have brought wine sales to a figure exceeding 201000000 litres during the twelve months ending August, 1981. **1985** *Drum* Oct. 7 Autumn Harvest Crackling. A delightfully fruity, perlé wine with all the quality which makes the Autumn Harvest range so popular. *c***1990** J. PLATTER *S. Afr. Wine Guide* 295 Sparkling and Perlé Wines.

perlemoen /ˈpɛː(r)ləmʊn, ˈpɜː-/ *n.* Formerly also **paarlemoen, paarl lemoen, paarlmoer, per(e)l-le-moen, perelomen.** [Afk. *pêrel* pearl + *lemoen* orange (by folk-etymology), also (obs.) *perlemoer*, 'womb-of-pearl' or 'mother-of-pearl' (referring to the pearlised layer inside the shell), fr. Du. *pa(a)relmoer, perlemoer* (dial. *parlemoen, peerlemoen, perelmoen*) fr. M. Du. *perlenmoeder* 'mother-of pearl', 'pearl-producing oyster'.] The abalone, *Haliotis midae* of the Haliotidae, a large, edible, univalve shellfish having a shell lined with mother-of-pearl; KLIPKOUS. Also *attrib.*

1853 L. PAPPE *Synopsis of Edible Fishes* 12 Amongst the mollusca, none are more eagerly caught, and none have such a deserved reputation as *Haliotis Midae Lin.* (Klipkous; sea-ear), and a species of *Stomatia* (Paarlmoer). **1891** [see KLIPKOUS]. **1911** J.D.F. GILCHRIST *S. Afr. Zoology* 192 The ordinary Limpet .., the Perlemoen or Klipkoes of South African Seas .., and the common periwinkle. **1919** M.M. STEYN *Diary* 3 If you wanted 'klipkous' or 'perl-lemoen', they were procurable seaward, at very low tides. **1945** H. GERBER *Fish Fare* 70 *Perel-lemoen* (Klipkous). The meat of this large, beautiful shell is greatly prized. To prepare, pry the meat from the shell. **1946** L.G. GREEN *So Few Are Free* 52 A rarer delicacy is the perel-le-moen or klipkous, largest of all the Cape shellfish. This monster grows far out on the rocks ... It has a beautiful shell, but the meat must be scrubbed and put through a mincer. **1958** — *S. Afr. Beachcomber* 127 South Africans are compensated for the scarcity of scallops by an abundance of *perlemoen.* This is the abalone of America and the *ormer* of the Channel Islands. **1970** G. CROUDACE *Scarlet Bikini* 14 Perlemoen was said to have the effect of oysters upon the human libido. **1979** SNYMAN & KLARIE *Free from Sea* 41 *Perlemoen*, .. Abalone/Klipkous. Elsewhere in the world, perlemoen is known as 'Ormer', a corruption of French 'oreille de mer' or 'sea ear'. **1983** [see S. Afr. Panorama quot. at LINEFISH]. **1989** R.J.Q. TARR in *Conserva* Nov. 13 The abalone, locally called 'perlemoen' (*Haliotis midae*), is a marine snail belonging to one of the most primitive of living gastropod families. **1989** *E. Prov. Herald* 3 Nov. 25 Only five legal size perlemoen each and you must first buy a permit from the Receiver of Revenue ... The law states you may not transport them out of their shells nor may you keep in your home more than 20 perlemoen. **1990** S. ROWLES in *Weekend Post* 16 June (Leisure) 4 Sparks's speciality – perlemoen wors cooked on an open fire. **1992** SMIT & FULTON *Complete S. Afr. Bk of Food & Cookery* 306 The beautiful single ear-shaped shell of the perlemoen is lined with mother of pearl, which is used to make buttons. The tough, fleshy mollusc in the shell .. has a delicious clam-like flavour.

Permanent Force *n. phr.* Also with small initials. The standing army of South Africa (see quot. 1912); PF sense a. Also *attrib.*

1912 *Stat. of Union* 194 The Permanent Force shall consist of (a) persons engaged for continuous service in the organization and training of the Defence Forces; and (b) persons charged in time of peace with the maintenance of order within the Union. **1939** G. MAKEPEACE in *Outspan* 10 Nov. 11 The term 'National Reservist' includes citizens who are *not* members of .. 1. The Reserve of Officers. 2. The S.A. Permanent Force. 2. The S.A. Permanent Force Reserve .. 6. The Active Citizen Force. 7. The Citizen Force Reserve, Class A. 8. The Citizen Force Reserve, Class B. **1963** *Rand Daily Mail* 3 May 2 Members of both the Permanent Force and the Citizen Force were trained as military police. **1977** B. MARKS *Our S. Afr. Army* 10 The formation headquarters of the conventional force are staffed mainly by Citizen Force manpower with a small Permanent force nucleus. **1981** *S. Afr. Panorama* July 42 The South African Army is a veritable people's army ... Only a small percentage of its members belong to the Permanent Force. The rest are servicemen or hail from the Active Citizen Force or Commandos. **1986** *Sunday Times* 13 July 22 The SADF has ordered it permanent-force members to learn at least one black language, an excellent idea. **1989** H. HAMANN in *Scope* 10 Mar. 58 Be prepared to sign up with the Permanent Force for a minimum of three years, after completing two years of National Service.

permantig var. PARMANTIG.

Persian *n.* [So named because the breed was developed from stock originating in the *Persian Gulf*.] One of a breed of sheep, the *Blackhead Persian* (BLACKHEAD sense 2). Also *attrib.*

1912 R. LYDEKKER *Sheep & its Cousins* 209 The Persian fat-rumped sheep .. is a well-known breed, which has been carried to Cape Colony and Rhodesia, where it is now bred to a considerable extent. **1913** W.M. MCKEE *S. Afr. Sheep & Wool* 91 Cape Wool and Cross-Persian Breeding ... I am greatly opposed to the crossing of Persians with merino ... It would pay better to sell a certain number of Persians as opportunity offers. **1932** S. ZUCKERMAN *Soc. Life Monkeys & Apes* 206, I have seen Chacma baboons playing about and foraging in the midst of a flock of Persian sheep. **1937** [see RONDERIB]. **1945** L.G. GREEN *Where Men Still Dream* 144 The [Karakul] ram is a treasure to be protected against leopards and jackals; the rest of the flock of Afrikander, Persian or Blinkhaar ewes may cost no more than ten shillings each. **1966** E. PALMER *Plains of Camdeboo* 256 'I guess it is a black-head Persian from the Karoo.' 'You're right,' replied Sir Abe [Bailey] with delight. 'It is Karoo Persian.' When he travelled he took with him live Persian sheep from the Karoo to be slaughtered when he needed them.

‖**perskesmeer** /ˈpɛrskəsmɪə(r)/ *n.* [Afk., *perske* peach + *smeer* spread.] A sweetmeat consisting of a thin layer of minced peaches which is sun-dried, coated with sugar, and rolled. See also MEBOS.

1934 C.P. SWART Supplement to Pettman. 136 *Perske Smeer*, .. The name of a delicious S.A. sweet, made of peaches, which after being cooked are finely pulped and spread thickly on a greased board where they are left to dry. After being well sprinkled with sugar they are rolled and tied. **1934** *Star* 5 Feb. (Swart), Perske Smeer (peach spread), a favourite South African delicacy, was among the subjects at the Star demonstration last week. **1968** L.G. GREEN *Full Many Glorious Morning* 220 A hard and flavourless peach which was pulped after cooking, dried, sprinkled with sugar and rolled to form the sweetmeat known as *perske-smeer*. [**1972** *Evening Post* 4 Mar. 2 Yellow clingstone peaches are plentiful now and they can be served in salads, tarts .. and our traditional South African 'smeerperske' (a fruit sweet).]

person *n. colloq.* [Calqued on Afk. *'n mens* 'one', or (lit.) 'a person'.] ***A person***: 'I' (the speaker); less commonly, used in place of the Eng. indefinite pronouns 'you' or 'one'.

1776 F. MASSON in *Phil. Trans. of Royal Soc.* LXVI. 315 A person cannot walk ten paces without raising a brace of quails. **1883** O.E.A. SCHREINER *Story of Afr. Farm* 94 Presently she added, 'Aunt, why does the Englishman always knock against a person when he passes them?' **1937** C.R. PRANCE *Tante Rebella's Saga* 196 If only 'a person' could rely on the inefficiency of the Police and their infernal dogs. **1979** *Darling* 10 Jan. 48 One day he came into the building society where I work and said over the counter, very quietly, that he was going to marry someone else. I mean what can a person do? **1985** P. SLABOLEPSZY *Sat. Night at Palace* 23 Yassas, how many times must a person tell you. I don't smoke. I'm a non-smoker. OK!? **1986** [see SKOLLY]. **1990** *Sunday Times* 3 June 4 Ja well, maybe so. But a person can only take so much music, peace, dancing and rum.

person of colour see COLOUR.

Peruvian *n. derog.* [Prob. a fanciful extension of the acronym *PARU* Polish and Russian Union.

'Peruvian or Peruvnik .. originated in Kimberley during the Diamond Rush Days ... The Jews from Eastern Europe were looked down upon by English and German Jews. The Polish and Russian Jews were of course excluded from the Kimberley club so they formed their own club which they called Polish And Russian Union. The acronym is Paru, which was and still is an expression of contempt and an assertion of superiority on the part of those using the word.' (D. Schrire, Letter, 2 May 1989). But see also quots 1923 and 1944.]

1. *hist.* A contemptuous name for a Jew, particularly one from eastern or central Europe. Also *attrib.*

1897 *Star* 7 July 5 That the Government will not listen to the oily tongues of the numerous deputations financed by a clique of Peruvians .. must be the earnest wish of every person who has been waiting patiently for them to do something towards improving the morals of this town. **1898** L. SEARELLE *Tales of Tvl* 4 A 'Peruvian' standing by, whose name was Schadrach Levi. **1899** [see PRETORIA sense 1 a]. **1900** *Rand Daily Mail* (Pettman), Behold one of the most striking types of Johannesburg life – the Peruvian. **1905** [see sense 2]. **1912** W. WESTRUP *Land of To-Morrow* 218 At the opposite side of the road was a fruit store of sorts ... It was run by a Jew of the kind locally known as Peruvian, and .. was a very third-rate kind of place. **1923** B. RONAN *Forty S. Afr. Yrs* 163 Those early days saw the influx of that strange race, locally known as 'Peruvians'. How they obtained their title is not very clear. I believe it was first given to some Polish and Russian Jews who came out to South Africa after failing to make a living after the failure of Baron Hirsch's Jewish colonisation scheme in South America. **1944** A.A. ROBACK *Dict. of International Slurs* 58 *Peruvian Jews*, Jews, who having been unable to cope with colonization conditions in South America come to settle in South Africa. **1956** H.M. BATE *S. Afr. without Prejudice* 59 Kruger .. saw in this a deliberate move by Rhodes to dominate the polls with mine employees and .. 'Peruvians' (a term of contempt which is applied to Jews of low class). **1972** E. ROSENTHAL *Informant, Cape Town* According to Max Sonnenburg, the expression originated in the early days of Kimberley, where a body was set up, called 'The Polish and Russian Union,' the initials of which 'P.R.U.' gave rise to the word 'Peruvian'.

2. *transf.*

1905 P. GIBBON *Vrouw Grobelaar* 145 A Peruvian, for the Vrouw Grobelaar, was any one for whose nationality she had no name. In Johannesburg it means a Polish Jew. **1987** J. KUTTNER in *Jewish Chronicle* 26 June 4 Among 30 Yiddish words in common use in South African English (not only that spoken by local Jews) [is] .. *Peruvian* (a boor).

petata var. PATAT.

peté var. IPITI.

petso var. PITSO.

petty apartheid /ˌpeti əˈpɑːtheɪt/ *n. phr. Hist.* [Eng. *petty* + APARTHEID (either tr. of, or the origin of, Afk. *klein apartheid* 'small apartheid').] The manifestations of apartheid experienced in everyday life, esp. the segregation of public facilities (see quot. 1991); *klein apartheid, small apartheid*, see APARTHEID sense 1 b. Also *attrib.* Cf. GRAND APARTHEID.

1966 *Cape Argus* 8 Apr. 14 While separate development proceeds so slowly, the Government, for home consumption, makes demonstrations of strength on the petty apartheid front. **1973** *E. Prov. Herald* 9 Nov. 1 Petty apartheid was probably the widest front on which a man's dignity was assaulted and .. almost the entire population was acutely aware of how it operated. **1986** *New Statesman* (U.K.) 24 Jan. 18 While racial signs have been removed from public buildings and whites can buy in the same shops as blacks, 'petty apartheid' remains enforced on a local level ... Pretoria's public parks are still out of bounds to blacks. **1989** *Weekend Post* 18 Nov. 3 The controversial Reservation of Separate Amenities Act, which the National Party introduced in 1953 and is now to abolish, was one of the original petty apartheid measures. **1991** A. VAN WYK *Birth of New Afrikaner* 81 Petty apartheid was the way the grand design found gratuitous expression daily in a variety of measures which prescribed for blacks separate taxis, buses, trains, lifts, toilets, park benches, shop counters and entrances to public places, denying them admission to 'white' restaurants, hotels, cinemas, beaches, swimming pools, sporting clubs and other facilities.

pezoulu, pezulu varr. PHEZULU.

PF *n.* Also P.F. [Initial letters of *Permanent Force*.] **a.** A colloquial short form of PERMANENT FORCE. Also *attrib.* **b.** A member of the Permanent Force.

1944 'TWEDE IN BEVEL' *Piet Kolonel* 18 They were no longer without considerable experience, and they found themselves subjected to what they felt to be the indignity of being treated as recruits by P.F. instructors of limited qualifications, whose sole claim to fame rested on their parrot-like knowledge of Pamphlet 2, Lesson 3. **1979** *Uniform* June 5 SADF's Pf-members [*sic*] are well off with pensions. **1983** W. STEENKAMP in *Leadership* Summer 55 In the late 1970s it was authoritively estimated that to raise and maintain one PF brigade would cost at least R90 million a year. **1983** *Frontline* Sept. 22 The 'PF' is an eccentric creature at best, and a crude power maniac at worst: it's incomprehensible that anyone should want to be in uniform for *life*! *Ibid.* Sept. 23 For the professional soldier the regiment is more important than the party ... The SADF will serve the country well only to the extent to which its leaders subscribe to that ethos. It would appear that many English-speaking PFs do just that. **1988** *Cape Times* 27 Jan. 5 The ex-PF member's need might be less urgent in some cases, since he could qualify for a pension.

PFP *n. hist.* [Initial letters of *Progressive Federal Party*.] A political party to the left of centre, espousing liberal-democratic policies. Also *attrib.* See also PROG.

Formed in 1977 when some members of the defunct United Party (see UP) were absorbed into the Progressive Reform Party (see PRP), the PFP was one of three groups which merged to form the Democratic Party in 1989 (see note at DP *n.²*).

1977 *Daily Dispatch* 6 Sept. 1 Mr Eglin's address to the congress was adopted as a formal declaration of PFP policy. 1979 *Daily Dispatch* 21 Mar. 10 An image of Afrikanderdom that is no longer nurtured in the hearts of the average urban Afrikaner .. like Van Zyl Slabbert and Japie Basson of the PFP, both 'ware' Afrikaners. 1981 *Annual Register: Rec. of World Events 1980* 262 The National Party won a massive majority of 110 seats in Parliament, though losing six seats to the PFP ... and two to the NRP (the New Republic Party). 1990 M. KENTRIDGE *Unofficial War* 134 The Pietermaritzburg branch of the Democratic Party ... despite suffering setbacks in its previous incarnation as the PFP in the 1987 general elections, has been active in monitoring and exposing the situation in the townships.

‖**phalaphala** /ˌpalaˈpaːla, ?-faːla/ *n.* Also **phalaf(h)ala**. [SeTswana *phala*. The origin and meaning of the second element has not been discovered.] A wind instrument made from the horns of the sable antelope and originally used by the northern Sotho and Tswana peoples.

1931 H.A. STAYT *BaVenda* 317 The sable-antelope horns, *phala-fhala*, are the most important [musical instrument] and are played in the Ibondo and around the chief's village. They are blown through a small rectangular hole in the side about 8 inches from the point, to which the lips are pressed as with an ordinary bugle. 1980 D.B. COPLAN *Urbanization of African Performing Arts.* 187 Pedi and Tswana people regarded brass instruments as superior modern replacements for their reeds and drums ... In addition to reed-flutes, Pedi-Tswana signal horns (*phalaphala*) gave way to the bugle and trumpet. 1984 *Pace* Oct. 14 (caption) A lady blowing a phalafala at a UDF rally.

phalla var. PALLAH.

phata-phata var. PATA-PATA.

pheasant *n.* [Transf. use of general Eng. *pheasant* a name for any of several species of game birds of the genus *Phasianus*; prob. influenced by Afk. *fisant*, used of the francolins.]
a. Any of several species of game bird of the genus *Francolinus* of the Phasanidae. Cf. PARTRIDGE.

There exists some confusion in the application of the names 'pheasant' and 'partridge' to francolins, the most common explanation being that those species with bare facial and neck parts are referred to as 'pheasants', whereas 'partridge' is used of birds with feathered heads and necks.

1785 G. FORSTER tr. *A. Sparrman's Voy. to Cape of G.H.* I. 153, I found here two new species of the genus *tetrao*, one of which is called *partridge* and the other *pheasant*: either sort being nearly of the size of our partridges. 1790 tr. *F. Le Vaillant's Trav.* I. 157 Great numbers of partridges; particularly of that large species which the inhabitants of the Cape call *pheasants*. 1834 T. PRINGLE *Afr. Sketches* 515 The bird called a Pheasant at the Cape is a sort of grouse, or rather a species intermediate between the grouse and the partridge. 1837 'N. POLSON' *Subaltern's Sick Leave* 119 There is .. a bird, general all over the Colony, styled 'pheasant,' though about as like a pheasant of England as a Dutch Boer is to a Bond-street exquisite. 1859 E.L. LAYARD in *Cape Monthly Mag.* V. Feb. 72 By the side of the road we put up three of the 'pheasants' of this part of the country. They differ from the species which we find down here, being the *Francolinus Nudicollis*. 1899 [see red-necked partridge (PARTRIDGE sense b)]. 1908 [see PARTRIDGE sense a]. 1937 H. SAUER *Ex Afr.* 181 These are what we call pheasants in South Africa, but they are really francolins, of which family there are no less than nineteen varieties, including our so-called partridges, the redwing, the greywing, and that excellent little fellow the *schwempe* or bush-partridge. 1961 D. BEE *Children of Yesterday* 282 A pheasant called in the distance, a free, wild calling which he loved to hear. 1981 P. DANE *Great Houses of Constantia* 136 I'd gone up into the mountain looking for pheasant.
b. With distinguishing epithet: **bush pheasant**, some unknown francolin; **Cape pheasant**, the rednecked francolin *F. afer*; *red-necked partridge*, see PARTRIDGE sense b; **coast pheasant**, the Natal francolin (see NATAL sense c), *Francolinus natalensis*; **Natal pheasant**, see *Natal francolin* (NATAL sense c); **red(-necked) pheasant**, see *Cape pheasant*.

1897 J.P. FITZPATRICK *Outspan* 34, I was keeping an eye on the scrub on my side for the chance of a **bush pheasant**. a1823 J. EWART *Jrnl* (1970) 13 On the summits of the mountains are still to be found a few antelopes, hares, partridges, and **Cape pheasants**. 1827 T. PHILIPPS *Scenes & Occurrences* 4 We flushed and killed a brace of what are called Cape Pheasants, but by no means resembling the English pheasant. They have something of the grouse flavour. 1878 T.J. LUCAS *Camp Life & Sport* 84 For game birds we had the grey partridge and the Cape pheasant; the latter .. being almost tailless ... The head .. being more fowl-like, with its red wattles, and the legs clumsy, crimson coloured. 1906 STARK & SCLATER *Birds of S. Afr.* IV. 214 *Francolinus capensis*. Noisy Francolin or Cape Pheasant. 1985 *Weekend Argus* 30 Nov. (Suppl.) 6 Every so often a flock of Cape pheasant would explode out of the low scrub almost at my feet, protesting loudly as they glided to safety. 1913 C. PETTMAN *Africanderisms* 124 **Coast pheasant** or *partridge*, *Francolinus natalensis* is so called in Natal. 1790 tr. *F. Le Vaillant's Trav.* I. 183 Besides the three species of partridges above-mentioned, we observed another called the **red pheasant**, because its feet and the naked skin of its throat are of that colour. 1913 C. PETTMAN *Africanderisms* 395 *Red-necked pheasant*, *Pternistes nudicollis*, not a common species; found in Pondoland and Natal.

Phengoe var. FINGO.

‖**phezulu** /peˈzuːlu/ *adv.* Also **pezoulo**, **pezulu**. [Xhosa and Zulu.] Up, above, on, on top of.

[1803 J.T. VAN DER KEMP in *Trans. of Missionary Soc.* I. 433 When this man, whom the Caffrees call the Lord from above (*Pezoulo*) is seen, in a kraal, the people immediately retire from it. 1907 J.P. FITZPATRICK *Jock of Bushveld* (1909) 93 Pezulu — It is a Zulu word meaning 'up' or 'on top'.] 1970 T. HATTINGH *Informant, Bloemfontein* They perched the dove pezulu of the steel rod. 1982 M. MANAKA in *Staffrider* Vol.5 No.1, 43 Down goes our souls underground up goes phezulu the price of gold.

phoko *n. obs.* Also **luphoko**, **poco**, **poko**. [Zulu *u(lu)phoko* a species of millet used in beer-making.] Either of two species of millet of the Poaceae, used in beer-making and as a porridge:
a. Pearl millet *Pennisetum glaucum* (sub-family Panicoideae). **b.** African finger millet *Eleusine corocana* (sub-family Chloridoideae). Also *attrib*.

1836 G. CHAMPION in *J. Bird Annals of Natal* (1888) I. 202 He sent us .. a quantity of flour made from a plant called 'poko'. 1836 A.F. GARDINER *Journey to Zoolu Country* 165, I immediately desired Umpondombeeni to boil some lupoko meal which I had by me; but he was unable to borrow a vessel for the purpose. 1837 N. ADAMS in D.J. Kotze *Lett. of American Missionaries* 176 The principal productions of this place are Indian corn, Kafir corn, and poko — species of millet, — pumpkins, calabashes, sweet potatoes, beans, etc. 1856 *Cape of G.H. Almanac & Annual Register* (Natal) 282 The productions of the Native Gardens are Indian corn, .. an edible root resembling the wild turnip (arum) called 'idumbi,' beans, and a sort of millet called 'upoko'. 1925 D. KIDD *Essential Kafir* 323 Gourds, beans, yams, sugar-cane, sweet reed, and poco are grown, and in Zulu kraals pineapples are frequently to be seen near Lake St. Lucia.

phow var. POU.

phut(h)u var. PUTU.

phuza /ˈpuːzə, ˈpʊːza/ *n. slang.* Also **poosa**, **pusa**, **puza**. [fr. Xhosa and Zulu, 'drink', 'sip'.] Esp. among speakers of Sintu (Bantu) languages:
1. Liquor.

1908 D. BLACKBURN *Leaven* 100 Abstain from expensive luxuries in the shape of puza (liquor), white men's clothes and magisterial fines. *Ibid.* 193 Weldon addressed him. 'Will you go to Johannesburg and work on a mine? Plenty puza, plenty skoff, and five sovereigns a month.' 1928 L.P. GREENE *Adventure Omnibus* 54 'You are thirsty, headman,' 'I have brought you white man's puza.' Umbalose nodded and closed his eyes as if to shut out the vision of happiness the bottles had conjured up. a1931 S. BLACK in S. Gray *Three Plays* (1984) 141 Yoy yoy, he doesn't know vat is visky. I can see you not a Scotch Native! Visky is brandewyn — poosa! *Ibid.* 160 Tell him to send a reporter to write about my next party. Say there'll be lots of poosa. 1977 K.M.C. MOTSISI in *Drum* Nov. 133 They will ask how come I can become so gladful in this bemiserable room of moaning, weeping and no phuza. 1985 [see sense 2].
2. *comb.* **phuza face**, a face showing signs of heavy drinking; **phuza-joint**, a bar; **phuza-(phuza-)cabin**; SHEBEEN sense 1; **phuzawise** *adv.*

1987 E. MAKHANYA in *Sowetan* 28 Dec. 8 We have been moving together from *phuza-cabin* to *phuza-joint* converting ourselves into practising alcoholics. 1985 H. PRENDINI in *Style* Oct. 41 Sweet relief from these heavy pressures comes in the form of the 'phuza-cabin' or 'spot' (shebeen) where you drink .. with your 'phuza-buddies' or any good guy you can call your 'bra'. 1987 [see quot. at *phuza-joint*]. 1990 P. SEGONE in *Tribute* 116 Their eyes could not withstand The beers of her puza-puza cabin. You better beware, brother .. For you are not dealing with a doll But the boss of the puza cabin. 1986 *Pace* May 110, I pitied those sweety pies with rotund **phuza faces** and with figures like over-fed bed-bugs. 1988 *Frontline* Nov. 27, I approach another man pushing a wheelbarrow. He has a phuza face and he generally looks sickly. a1977 K.M.C. MOTSISI in M. Mutloatse *Casey & Co.* (1978) 132, I hate it every bit being away from my guys and dolls and being put in orbit **phuzawise**.

phuza /ˈpuːzə, ˈpʊːza/ *v. intrans.* [As prec.] To drink liquor.

1977 P.C. VENTER *Soweto* 124 Say, 'Auntie, what about a popla?' That means you would like a beer. Or, 'A dop of moonshine, sister!' .. Or even, 'I just want to pusa'. Meaning you want to fly high on something and you are not particular. 1978 *Randlords & Rotgut* (Junction Ave Theatre Co.) in S. Gray *Theatre Two* (1981) 92 Give yourself a silly grin, come and drink Imperial Gin ... Don't be a loser, come and phuza! 1982 *Voice* 23 May 4 Neither am I an extremist as to suggest that we don't phuza at all — ach that would be the day ... We go about boozing 'to hell and gone'.

phuzamandla /ˌpʊːzaˈmaːnɡa/ *n.* Also **puzamandla**. [Xhosa and Zulu *phuza* (v.) drink + *amandla* strength.] Among speakers of the Sintu (Bantu) languages: a name for an instant, highly nutritious, fortified soup-powder. Also *attrib*.

1977 *Daily Dispatch* 19 Nov. 7 Mr Biko drank a beaker of puzamandla (a vitamin drink) .. three days before his death. 1978 *E. Prov. Herald* 3 Mar. (Indaba) 6 They served phuzamandla, not as hot soup as the kind that had to simmer, but a type where hot water was added. It was full of nutrition.

piccanin, piccaninny /ˈpɪkənɪn, pɪkəˈnɪni/ *n.* and *adj.* Forms: α. **picaninni**, **picaninny**, **piccaninny**, **pickaninny**, **pikienienie**, **pikinini**. β. **pican(n)in**, **piccan(n)in**, **pickanin**, **pikkanien**. [fr. West Indian creole *picaninny*, ad. Pg. *pequenino* very little, tiny.]
A. *n.*
1. *Offensive to many.* **a.** A small black African child. **b.** A young black African boy. See also KWEDINI, UMFAAN sense 3.

The α forms are used of black children also in *U.S.* and *Austral. Eng.*

α. [**1851** J.F. CHURCHILL Diary. (Killie Campbell Africana Library MS37) 29 June, We were soon surrounded inside by men women and picannies laughing and chattering all the time.] **1855** in J.W. COLENSO *Ten Weeks in Natal* (Addendum) 3, 'What will the poor little *piccaninnies* do, Boy?' **1866** W.C. HOLDEN *Past & Future* 169 The mother .. gives birth to the child and afterwards proceeds on her journey with but little inconvenience, having her 'picaninni' tied to her back. **1905** P. GIBBON *Vrouw Grobelaar* 37 There was a little Kafir picaninny, as black as a crow, that was sent to play about near him every day. **1912** F. BANCROFT *Veldt Dwellers* 135 The little chocolate coloured piccaninnies crept out from under their karosses in the huts. **1939** M. RORKE *Melina Rorke* 141 Complained bitterly about his white baby having to live like a piccaninny. **1970** F. GUNTHORP *Informant, Bloemfontein* The piccaninny was half-starved, because his parents had been unable to scrape together enough money to purchase food. **1986** F. KARODIA *Daughters of Twilight* 76 'Please, Baas,' the man pleaded. 'How many pickaninnies you got?' the Afrikaner fired at the man. 'Five, Baas.'

β. **1908** *Rand Daily Mail* 11 Sept. 7 Some three years ago the Amalaita made its appearance. The nucleus was a number of piccanins. **1908** M.C. BRUCE *New Tvl* 33 Several hundreds of Kafirs have taken their places. Many of them are 'piccanins', half-grown lads. **1914** *Farmer's Annual* 130 The shepherd must be .. not the 'picannin' who spends the day catching meerkats or sleeping, but the most intelligent native available. **1920** R.Y. STORMBERG *Mrs Pieter de Bruyn* 38 This note shall be sent by piccanin as soon as day breaks. **1939** *Outspan* 20 Oct. 70 (advt) Jim is a pickanin learning to be a houseboy. And he's learning fast. **1947** C.R. PRANCE *Antic Mem.* 134 Plaatje the piccanin caught using his Missis's best face-cloth to swab out the bath. **1952** H. KLEIN *Land of Silver Mist* 116 Next morning when I tried to photograph a naked piccanin in the kraal the frightened father of the child dashed out yelling 'Tagati' (witchcraft) and snatched him away. **1961** T. MATSHIKIZA *Choc. for my Wife* 7 This girl with you is she your wife and these two piccanins are your children? **1961** A. FUGARD *Notebks* (1983) 23 My friends were the picannins on the farm. Race relations did not exist for me. **1972** *Evening Post* 5 Feb. 6 The few non-whites who braved the elements to follow battling golfers round the sand-blasted Wedgwood course, were vastly outnumbered by Black caddies and ragged piccanins. **1982** C. HOPE *Private Parts* 9 An unkempt little 'piccanin' ran to unhook the big farm gate. The truck chugged and waited. **1983** *Drum* Jan. 40 When he graduated from piccannin to ndoda I was the best man at his wedding.

2. A small child.

α. **1882** J. NIXON *Among Boers* 201 Three or four native huts with little black picaninnies and Kaffir dogs crawling about. **1917** S.T. PLAATJE *Native Life* 89 A kind Dutchman and his noble wife, on whose property .. little black piccaninnies still played about in spite of the law. *Ibid.* 273 The naughty white piccaninnies who always insult inoffensive black passers-by. **1970** *Forum* Vol.6 No.2, 48 You hit and kick me, me myself, an old man who has much love for you ... You yourself were my little pikinini. **1981** M. MZAMANE in *Best of S. Afr. Short Stories* (1991) 397 'Where can I refill this bottle, *makwedini* (boys)?' The boys laughed derisively at being called pickaninnies.

β. **1908** M.C. BRUCE *New Tvl* 7 The Kafir piccanin shouts the morning papers .. and as long as the sound is approximate, it does not matter about the sense. **1936** WILLIAMS & MAY *I Am Black* 190 He might not strike them, for though they were piccanins, they were white piccanins, children of his white Baas. **1936** E. ROSENTHAL *Old-Time Survivals* 15 The mode of harnessing has not changed since 1652, when the first wagons were put in use at the Cape ... Nor has the institution of the leader-boy varied — usually a native piccanin known as the voorlooper. **1940** F.B. YOUNG *City of Gold* 350, I had a strange dream: I thought I saw a white child among the other piccanins. **1956** D. JACOBSON *Dance in Sun* 25 I'm not a little Kaffir piccanin. You can't do what you like with me. **1970** K.M. BRAND *Informant, East London* My little piekanien will be three next month (small boy). **1991** S. RORKE *Informant, Port Elizabeth* Piccanin. A small child.

3. *transf. Offensive. Mining.* A black assistant who carries the bags of a white miner. Also *attrib.*

β. **1970** *Informant, Kimberley* Pikanin, go and fetch the can (little native boy, or on the mines the boy with the miner). **1987** P. VAN NIEKERK in *Weekly Mail* 3 Apr. 3 A dispute involving the refusal of black miner's assistants to carry the bags of white miners. The 'picanin' system, in which a black worker is forced to look after the welfare of a white miner or supervisor, is a long-established practice on South African gold mines ... The job of 'picanin' was to carry the 'masters' satchel which has food, clothes, newspapers and comics.

B. *adj.*

1. Small; young.

α. **1851** R.J. GARDEN Diary. I. (Killie Campbell Africana Library MS20981) 25 June, Riding along we soon came to the Igana or Infant River which has a pretty little mouth in which a stork was fishing. The river itself is in reality a piccaninny one.

β. **1961** T.V. BULPIN *White Whirlwind* 233 'How old are you?' 'Nineteen.' 'Oh, you are a piccanin white man.'

2. *slang.* Special collocation. **piccanin(ny) kaya** [fr. Rhodesian (now Zimbabwean) Eng., 'little house' (*-khaya* is the n. stem for 'house' in the Nguni languages)], an outside lavatory or privy; PK. See also KLEINHUISIE.

α. **1966** I. VAUGHAN *These Were my Yesterdays* 151 The old man went out late at night to 'pic-a-ninny kaiah', natives polite word for outdoor lavatory — no sewerage here in wilds. **1970** S. SPARKS *Informant, Fort Beaufort* The farm P.K. was situated in the backyard quite a way from the homestead. (Abbreviation of Picannini Khaya or Kia.) **1970** M.S. WAGENER *Informant, Strydenburg* Pikkanienie Kaaia. Outside Toilet. **1991** *Informant, Grahamstown* Picinniny Kaia. P.K. The toilet. **1994** R. SOAL in *Weekend Post* 8 Jan. (Leisure) 3 The WC, latrine, lavatory, convenience, [etc.] .. and even our own 'kleinhuisie' and PK (picaninny khaya) — all are acceptable terms for the same facility.

β. **1968** L.G. GREEN *Full Many Glorious Morning* 50 Such romantic survivals as the 'piccanin kias' rolled back the years. (I am not suggesting that many 'piccanin kias' are still in use but they are like historic monuments in suburban gardens.) **1991** N.P. SAUNDERS *Informant, Scottburgh* P.K. or Piccanin-kaya. A lavatory usually an outhouse with earth hole; privy. **1991** H. PHILLIPS *Informant, Johannesburg* The once-ubiquitous 'long-drop' or outside loo, i.e. 'the small room' or 'piccanin kya'. Still used occasionally by the older generation, despite modern inside plumbing.

picho var. PITSO.

pick-axe *n. Obs.* On the diamond fields, a potent 'cocktail' of Cape brandy, PONTAC wine, and ginger-beer.

1873 F. BOYLE *To Cape for Diamonds* 125 He withdraws to the ambulating canteen .. and cools his brow and whets his hopes in pontac and gingerbeer, 'pickaxe,' or some such compound. **1876** —— *Savage Life* 28 Before him, on a board smoothed with dirt, stood the filthiest of all glasses, containing a turgid compound of pontak wine, 'cape smoke', and home-made ginger-beer, called in our camp parlance a 'pickaxe.' *Ibid.* 170 The landlord comes up to me: 'Seems kinder dull you do!' says he. 'Have a pickaxe, and tell a friend about it!' **1887** A.B. ELLIS *S. Afr. Sketches* (Jeffreys), He was forced to take shelter behind the bowl of his pipe, and to reinvigorate himself with a 'pick-axe', by which designation a fiery mixture of Cape Smoke, Pontac, and ginger-beer, was known at the Fields. **1913** C. PETTMAN *Africanderisms* 370 *Pick-axe,* The slang name of a fiery mixture of Cape smoke, pontac, and ginger-beer, in much request in the Diamond Fields in the early days.

pickled fish *n. phr.* Also **pickle fish**. A traditional dish of fish prepared with onions in a vinegar sauce and flavoured with curry powder, turmeric, and other spices; INGELEGDE VIS.

1887 [see SHAD]. **1890** [see INGELEGDE VIS]. **1891** H.J. DUCKITT *Hilda's 'Where Is It?'* 71 Fish (Pickled) ... Lay your fish in layers in a jar, pour over each layer some of the mixture. Take care to have it well corked, and it will keep for months. **1950** H. GERBER *Cape Cookery* 74 Pickled fish: For this old Cape favourite choose any firm fish such as snoek, Cape Salmon, Kabeljou, albacore. **1964** L.G. GREEN *Old Men Say* 128 Pickled fish is another traditional Cape curry with a local origin. Vinegar, curry powder, cornflour, sugar and salt, thinly-sliced onions and bay leaves are cooked for a short period with fried fish. **1973** [see *klappertert* (KLAPPER *n.*[1] sense 2 b)]. **1977** *Darling* 8 June 118 Pickled fish .. must be one of our oldest traditional fish recipes and if you know how to make it, it comes in very handy on holiday, as it's also a way of preserving fish. **1982** D. KRAMER *Short Back & Sides* 21 We were offered bredies and pickled fish (recipes from Leipoldt's Cape Cookery) by women wearing bonnets and aprons in matching country floral prints probably designed by Mary Quant. **1988** F. WILLIAMS *Cape Malay Cookbk* 7 Malay cooks .. used the exotic spices of the land of their birth to create such well-known dishes as bobotie, sosaties and pickled fish, which were almost always accompanied by chilli atjars, blatjangs and sambals.

pick-up *n.* [fr. U.S. Eng. *pick-up truck* or *- van* a small truck for carrying light loads, or U.S. Eng. slang *pick-up* an arrest.] In full ***pick-up van***: KWELA-KWELA sense 1.

1941 W.M.B. NHLAPO in *Bantu World* 22 Feb. 11 We have .. the drama of pick-ups, the life in the zoo-like locations, the hooliganism and the like, subjects which are full of passion, of sorrow, of strife. **1942** P. ABRAHAMS *Dark Testament* 63 They all turn, and see a group of policemen jumping out of the moving pick-up van and running towards them. **1946** —— *Mine Boy* (1954) 30 Suddenly a Pick-Up Van swerved round a corner. Policemen jumped out and ran down the street. The crowds scattered. *Ibid.* 67 If I saw a policeman or a pick-up van I shouted a warning and ran. *c***1948** H. TRACEY *Lalela Zulu* 55 There comes the big van. All over the country they call it the Pick-up Van. There is the Pick-up. *Ibid.* 56 They had the misfortune to be raided by the police. Everyone ran for safety. The 'Pickups' failed to find Msila, who had dived into a hole and lay low. **1953** LANHAM & MOPELI-PAULUS *Blanket Boy's Moon* 50 'Police! Police! The pick-up van's coming.' Even as he shouted the warning, the police arrived in their closed van with a squealing of brakes. **1962** L.E. NEAME *Hist. of Apartheid* 59 The introduction of the 'pick-up-van' by the police led to disorders in Johannesburg and along the Rand. **1962** W.S. MANQUPU in *Star* 22 Feb. 14 The lorry used as a pick-up van is called the 'Khwela-Khwela,' as the police call out 'Khwela, bo, khwela!' ('Ride, man, ride!') after making an arrest. **1966** A. FUGARD *Hello & Goodbye* (1971) 3 Down Baakens Street past the police station where the bars on the windows and the pick-up vans give me the creeps. **1970** M. DIKOBE Marabi Dance. 56 Sergeant Van Rooyen of the Marabastad Police Station lifted a hand and ordered him to accompany him to an awaiting pick-up van. **1990** *New African* 11 June 13 Kwela-kwela is a name that was given to the notorious pick-up police vans.

pick-van *n. nonce.* [Short form of *pick-up van*, see PICK-UP.] KWELA-KWELA sense 1.

1941 *Bantu World* 12 Apr. 4 They move freely .. without fear of having to be locked up in a pick-van for no other reason than that they were found without passes.

pico var. PITSO.

piemp var. PIMP *v.*

||**pieperig** /'pipərəx/ *adj. colloq.* Also **pipperag**. [Afk., weak, frail.] Feeble, weak; finnicky, complaining.

1970 R.S. GIBSON *Informant, N. Tvl* That girl is too pipperag for my liking (finnicky). **1970** M. WOLFAARDT *Informant, Stilfontein* He is just pieperig (weak and sickly). **1971** A. SCHOLEFIELD *Young Masters* 6 'You too ...' He searched for the word, and, not finding it in

English, chose the Afrikaans word for weak and sickly. 'You too .. *pieperig*'. **1989** B. KRIGE in *Femina* July 72 In the forefront of the fray is a mild-mannered woman who formed her own ratepayers association because she found the existing ones *pieperig* ... 'They really have some fuddy duddies,' pronounced Mrs Shaw, now in her mid-60's. 'They're so darned *pieperig*.'

pieper koral var. PEPERKORREL.

piepiejoller /ˈpipi,dʒɔlə(r)/ *n. slang.* Also **pipijoller, pippie-joller**. [Afk., *piepie* (not in polite use) penis + *joller* a merry-maker.] An adolescent.

1977 C. HOPE in S. Gray *Theatre Two* (1981) 50 It was only a bunch of piepiejollers .. dicing round the garden. **1986** H. PRENDINI in *Style* May 43 Heaven is .. the only young club that isn't gay (except on Fridays) and a *piepiejollers* hangout. *Piepiejoller* is a word that crops up often among the over-15s and seems to refer to anyone under 15. The opposite end of the scale are the *main manne*, South African version of big deal. **1988** C. HOPE in *SA in Poetry* 545 He disappears into the ladies' bars .. And sits with the moffies and piepiejollers and primps his nice long hair. **1989** G. GILL in *Sunday Times* 24 Dec. 23 Gwen Gill's A-to-Z of the decade: .. Packing for Perth .. Prince, *piepie jollers*, the Pope's unexpected visit, potjiekos. **1991** D. BOSWELL *Informant, Giyani (N. Tvl)* Piepiejoller (also PJ), an adolescent; a youngster; someone still 'wet behind the ears'. **1991** G. DE BEER *Informant, Port Nolloth (N. Cape)*, I don't like that club anymore: the teeny boppers and pipijollers have taken it over. **1993** A.L. HAYCOCK *Informant, Grahamstown* The .. disco .. has toned down. I am not sure whether it has closed for the evening (Pippie-jollers' bed-time) or whether they are just having a smoke break.

Hence (*nonce*) the back-formation **piepiejol** *n.*, see quot.

1989 M. BRAND in *Fair Lady* 25 Oct. 92 *Piepiejol*, joint where the young hang out.

piet-my-vrou /ˈpitmeɪfrəʊ/ *n.* Also **peit myn vrouw, piet-mein-vrow, piet mifrau, piet-mij(n)-vrouw, piet-myn vrouw, pit me frow, pit-me-wrou**, and with initial capital(s). [S. Afr. Du., onomatopoeic fr. the bird's three-note call.] The migratory red-chested cuckoo *Cuculus solitarius* of the Cuculidae; its call.

1790 tr. *F. Le Vaillant's Trav.* II. 311 He had scarcely killed the female, when the male began to pursue him with great fury, continually repeating *Pit-me-wrou, Pit-me-wrou!* It must be observed that these two words exactly represent the animal's cry. *c*1808 C. VON LINNÉ *System of Natural Hist.* VIII. 356 The male, uttering his call, seemed to pronounce distinctly these words, *piet, myn vrow*, meaning in Dutch, which the Hottentot understood very well, 'Peter, my wife.' **1835** A. STEEDMAN *Wanderings* I. 189 The *Piet-myn-vrouw*, a bird of which the Hottentots relate many amusing stories. **1856** R.E.E. WILMOT *Diary* (1984) 134, I must not forget the species [known] as '*the Piet mifrau*' from its singular note. **1867** E.L. LAYARD *Birds of S. Afr.* 130 *Piet-myn-Vrouw* of the Colonists ... This bird – which, from its singular cry, has acquired the name by which it is known to the colonists – is common in the Knysna district. **1905** W.L. SCLATER in Flint & Gilchrist *Science in S. Afr.* 141 The Red-chested Cuckoo (*C. solitarius*) called the 'Piet myn Vrouw' by the Dutch from its voice, which consists of three clear notes in the descending chromatic scale. **1912** *E. London Dispatch* 9 Oct. 4 The well-known call of *Piet-mijn-vrouw* was heard in the park in the evening of 7 October. **1930** N. STEVENSON *Farmers of Lekkerbat* 153 Somewhere near by the call of a *piet-mein-vrouw* could be heard quite clearly. **1956** P. BECKER *Sandy Tracks* 118 The three syllabled song of the 'piet-my-vrou', the elusive red-chested cuckoo, followed us as we entered an eroded path which meandered into the mountain. **1964** L.G. GREEN *Old Men Say* 164 Cape Town's favourite bird is the *piet-my-vrou*, a cuckoo which has become famous not for its plumage or its habits (which are reprehensible) but for its call. Spring is not regarded as a fact in the Cape Peninsula until someone has written to the newspapers claiming to have heard the first *piet-my-vrou*. **1970** [see MOSSIE sense 1]. **1972** *Cape Argus* 16 Sept., The piet-my-vrou (Cuculus solitarius) is the nearest relative of the European cuckoo to reach this corner of the African continent. His repetitious call, which gives him his name, is one of the most typical sounds of Africa. **1977** *Het Suid-Western* 12 Sept., Spring has arrived a week early. Its annual herald, the Piet-my-vrou, started calling on Sunday. **1971** K.B. NEWMAN *Birdlife in Sn Afr.* (1979) 178 The Red-chested Cuckoo, popularly known as the Piet-my-vrou, is a common and vociferous summer visitor to Southern Africa. Although very difficult to see it can be heard calling through most of the day and often at night too. **1982** *S. Afr. Panorama* Sept. 48 The *piet-my-vrou* arrives with the swallows. Its call is so monotonous that you may regret having heard this first cuckoo harbinger of Spring. **1991** T. BARON in *Sunday Times* 5 May 27 A passable imitation of the red-breasted cuckoo or *piet-my-vrou*.

pietshow var. PITSO.

pietsnot /ˈpitsnɔt/ *n.* [Afk., *Piet* Pete + *snot* nasal mucus; see first quot.] The creeping plant *Grielum humifusum* of the Rosaceae, bearing yellow flowers and having an edible root covered by a slimy film when peeled. Also **pietsnotjie** /-snɔɪki/ [see -IE].

1975 W. STEENKAMP *Land of Thirst King* 130 Other table-roots, as it were, that are available are the rather bitter kanna, which is boiled in goat's milk, and the tgoubee, otherwise known by the rather unpleasant nicknames of 'snotwortel' (snot root) or 'Piet Snot', the root of which has a slimy film on it when it has been peeled. **1975** *Argus* 17 Sept. 28 Pietsnot has a creeping habit and flowers of different shades of yellow, from very soft and creamy to a bright near-orange. **1987** *S. Afr. Panorama* Mar. 43 Stretches of sunny yellow *pietsnotjies* (*Grielum humifusum*). **1990** F. LE ROUX in *S. Afr. Panorama* Jan.-Feb. 88 The course at Springbok .. is a picture when the wild flowers bloom ... Pietsnot (*Grielum humifusum*) .. and gooses' eyes .. proliferate from tee to tee, and sporadically a quiver-tree (*Aloe dichotoma*) reigns imperiously over the carpet of flowers. **1991** J. COOPER in *Weekend Post* 5 Oct. 7 A bouquet of terracotta gazania, satiny flowers of *grielum humifusum* (pietsnot) and daisies abound in the Kamieskroom district.

piggyback *adj.* [Perh. an interpretation of Afk. *abba* (see ABBA), to carry 'piggyback', in the comb. *abbahart* piggy-back heart; or the Afk. may be derived fr. the Eng.: see first quot.] Of or pertaining to a surgical procedure in which a donor heart is implanted as a support or ancillary to the patient's heart (which is not removed).

First performed at Groote Schuur hospital, Cape Town, in 1977.

1978 *Argus* 19 Apr., The word abba ... has an interesting rebirth in the recent use of the term 'abbahart' in Afrikaans for the piggy-back heart operation. **1979** *Daily Dispatch* 5 Apr. 3 Professor Barnard used a baboon's heart for the first time in a 'piggy-back' operation .. in June 1977 as a last resort to save her life. **1979** *E. Prov. Herald* 19 June 3 Mr S— K— .. has died .. a little over two years after receiving a second heart in a 'piggy-back' operation ... He died last Thursday when both hearts stopped beating. **1980** *S. Afr. Digest* 14 Mar. 1 The 14-year-old schoolboy .. became the youngest person in South Africa to receive a new heart in a 'piggyback' transplant in January. **1981** *Ibid.* 9 Oct. 5 The 'piggy-back' or twin technique pioneered by Professor Chris Barnard. **1985** C. GROENEWALD in *S. Afr. Panorama* Aug. 37 Chris Barnard performed his first piggyback heart transplant after a friend's son died on the operating table because the transplanted heart refused to do its work ... Such a piggy-back heart transplant enables the patient to retain his own heart and to use the donor's heart as an aid.

pig-lily *n. obsolescent.* [tr. S. Afr. Du. *varklelie*, *vark* pig + *lelie* lily, see quot. 1883.] The arum lily *Zantedeschia aethiopica* of the Araceae, which grows profusely in damp places; *varkblaar*, *-blom*, see VARK sense 2.

[**1844** J. BACKHOUSE *Narr. of Visit* 73 By the sides of watercourses in the lower ground *Zante-deschia aethiopica*, grown in English greenhouses under the name of Arum and Lily of the Nile, was exhibiting its large white flowers abundantly. As swine are fond of its roots it is called in this country *Pig-root*.] **1848** C.J.F. BUNBURY *Jrnl of Res. at Cape of G.H.* 188 Calla (*Zantedeschia*) *Æthiopica* ... Commonly called at the Cape the Pig Lily. **1861** 'A LADY' *Life at Cape* (1963) 6 They .. especially smile at my passion for the 'arum' which grows in all the ditches under the title of 'pig-lily' and reaches an enormous size. **1883** M.A. CAREY-HOBSON *Farm in Karoo* 42 'Please bring me some of those "arums". What do the natives here call them?' ... 'They are commonly called pig-lilies. Why, I do not know – unless it be that pigs are very fond of the roots, and eat them voraciously. I have also thought that it might be on account of the similarity in the shape of the large single convoluted petal to a pig's ear.' **1887** A.B. ELLIS *S. Afr. Sketches* 61 Clusters of arum lilies, known to the Africander as 'pig lilies' whitened every gully. **1890** A. MARTIN *Home Life* 11 Large, pure white arums, or, as the colonists unromantically call them, 'pig-lilies'. **1906** H. RIDER HAGGARD *Benita* 78 Along the banks of the stream and around the borders of the lake the pig-lilies bloomed, a sheet of white. **1915** D. FAIRBRIDGE *Torch Bearer* 36 'Arums?' ... 'She means pig-lilies,' said Mrs. Roux with some contempt. 'Arums is their English name, but I prefer to call them pig-lilies.' **1918** S.H. SKAIFE *Animal Life* 119 The arum lily hawk moth is common wherever the pig-lily grows wild in this country. **1925** F.C. SLATER *Centenary Bk of S. Afr. Verse* 232 There is no true arum in South Africa. The plant meant is probably *Zantedeschia aethiopica*. Often found in immense numbers in damp places. It is usually called 'Arum Lily' or 'Pig Lily'. **1929** M. ALSTON *From Old Cape Homestead* 22 They dig them up for pigs! But don't you ever dare to call them *pig-lilies* in my hearing again. **1971** U. VAN DER SPUY *Wild Flowers of S. Afr. for Garden* 229 It [*sc. Zantedeschia aethiopica*] is said to have been given the common name of 'pig-lily' because in the south-western Cape, where it grows prolifically, pigs are said to relish the rootstock.

piicho var. PITSO.

pijp(i)e var. PYPIE.

pik /pək/ *n. colloq.* Shortened form of PIKKIE.

1970 E.G.B. HARDY *Informant, Bergvliet* Pik. A small child (from piccanin?). **1971** V. KELLY *Informant, Grahamstown*, I was fourteen when I went to Tech, a real little pik! **1974** in *Eng. Usage in Sn Afr.* Vol.5 No.1, 14 'A laitie' or 'a pik'. A small or young person. **1992** P. DOBSON *Informant, Cape Town* Pik/Pikkie. Little fellow.

pikienienie, pikinini, pikkanien varr. PICCANIN.

pikkie /ˈpəki, ˈpɪki/ *n. colloq.* [Afk., bantam; little chap, fr. dial. Du. *piek* 'chicken', later also 'small child'; or perh. rel. to PICCANIN.] A small person; a child; PIK. Occas. *transf.*, any small object.

Used either affectionately or with contempt.

1948 V.M. FITZROY *Cabbages & Cream* 192 The older boys were paid one-and-sixpence a week, and the pikkies, as they dubbed the little ones, a shilling. **1959** J. MEIRING *Candle in Wind* 38 But he's grown, eh, Kleinhansie? Last time I saw you, you were just a little pikkie, so high! **1970** K. NICOL *Informant, Durban* Ag, that little pikkie won't give you any trouble. (Someone small, or insignificant – usually denotes contempt – corruption of *piccanin?*). **1972** on Radio South Africa 10 Jan., They [*sc.* adolescents] don't want to mix with, if, I may use the term, pikkies – I think it's the right word to use for children of 11 or 12. **1975** *Friend* 11 Jan. 4 For the proud parents .. and the six little pikkies it has been a hectic year in which World newspapers carried front page stories of the multiple birth. **1982** D. BIGGS in *Weekend Argus* 18 Dec. 15 Pentax's little Auto 110 camera is a highly pedigreed 'pikkie'. **1987** P. SCHIRMER in *Personality* 26 Aug. 26 The *pikkies* see it happening, see their heroes punching and playing dirty rugby so they think it's OK for them to do the same. I saw it happen a couple of weeks ago when I went to watch an under-13 match. **1992** [see PIK].

pill *n. slang.* Also **pil.** [Transf. use of general Eng. slang *pill* cigarette.] Esp. in the Western Cape: ZOL *n.* sense 1 a.

1946 *Cape Times* 22 May, A shot of dagga is 'a pill' and dagga itself is sometimes known as 'boom'. **1971** *Ibid.* 3 July (Mag. Sect.) 4 The dagga pill is a three-out pill. I draw in quick and long into my body. **1974** *Het Suid-Western* 17 Oct. 1 He and the constable each then rolled a 'pill'. Orban started to smoke his. **1979** [see SKYF *n.*].

pillar *n.* [Eng. *pillar* (fig.) 'a fact or principle which is a main support or stay of something' (*OED*).] In the phr. ***pillar(s) of apartheid*** *hist.*, a name given to (any of) several Acts which were central to the administration of apartheid, esp. the POPULATION REGISTRATION ACT, the *Group Areas Act* (GROUP AREA *n. phr.* sense 2 a), and the Land Acts (see LAND ACT).

1989 *Reader's Digest Illust. Hist.* 376 The next pillar of apartheid was the Group Areas Act. **1989** [see APARTHEID sense 1 b]. **1991** *Weekly Mail* 24 May 15 The Abolition of Racially Based Land Measures Bill has been revised ... The other three Bills intended to bring down the last pillars of apartheid are still in place. **1991** on TV1, 6 June (News), The Population Registration Act will be relegated to history ... Other pillars of apartheid collapsed when the Group Areas Act and the two Land Acts were scrapped.

pimp *n. slang.* [Prob. fr. *impimpi.*] IMPIMPI.

Also used in this sense in *Austral.* and *N.Z. Eng.*

1984 *Drum* July 48 Shortly after he had been released from a police cell where he spent eight years for a series of crimes, he vowed revenge on those singled out as the 'pimps' who drove him to prison.

pimp *v. slang.* Also **piemp.** [Prob. fr. *impimpi* (see IMPIMPI).]

Also used in this sense in *Austral.* and *N.Z. Eng.* See also IMPIMPI.

1. *trans.* To betray (someone).

1979 M. MATSHOBA *Call Me Not a Man* 74 And 'strue, Mme Thandi. We might have been 'pimped'. You know, I don't trust that Sarah.

2. *intrans.* To inform (on someone).

1984 *E. Prov. Herald* 19 June 13, I can take care of myself and I know the rules. The worst you can do is piemp (squeal) on them. I haven't.

pinc-pinc /ˈpɪŋk ˈpɪŋk/ *n.* Also **pink pinkje.** [Echoic; see first quot.] Any of several small warblers of the Sylviidae, esp. *Cisticola textrix*; also called TINKTINKIE. Also *attrib.*

*c*1808 C. VON LINNÉ *System of Natural Hist.* VIII. 461 The *Pinc-pinc.* This is one of the smallest birds of Africa; in size and manners very like the wren .. in continual motion, .. uttering its note of *pinc-pinc, pinc-pinc, pinc-pinc*, the whole time. The children at the Cape call it the *pinc-pinc* from its note. **1868** J.G. WOOD *Homes without Hands* 217 The Pinc-pinc of Africa .. has a similar custom, constructing a supplementary roosting-place upon the nest. **1894** NEWTON *Dict. Birds, Pinc-pinc* (or rather 'Tinc-tinc'), the name which a South African bird .. has given itself from its ringing metallic cry. **1896** J. WOOD in *Scientific African* Mar. 76 The obtrusive 'pink-pinkje' (*D. Tetrix*) was also there. **1901** STARK & SCLATER *Birds of S. Afr.* II. The Pinc-pinc appears to be confined to the south western parts of the Colony ... The Pinc-pinc builds a regular Cisticoline, deep, purse-shaped nest, of dry grass and cobwebs lined with vegetable down. **1931** *Guide to Vertebrate Fauna of E. Cape Prov.* (Albany Museum) I. 109 *Cisticola ayresii* .. Little Pinc-pinc Warbler, Striped Grass-Warbler, Cloud Warbler. *Ibid.* 110 *Cisticola textrix mystica* .. Transvaal Pinc-pinc Warbler. **1973** J. COWDEN *For Love* 66 There are cisticolas that are: Fantail, .. Moustache, Pinc-pinc, Zulu Reed, .. right down to the Lazy Cisticola!

pincushion *n.* [See quot. 1977.] In full ***pincushion protea***: any of several indigenous shrubs of the genus *Leucospermum* of the Proteaceae, esp. *Leucospermum conocarpodendron* (the 'tree pincushion'), and *L. cordifolium.* See also KREUPELBOOM sense a, PROTEA sense 1 a.

1957 L.G. GREEN *Beyond City Lights* 214 Caledon has the rarest and choicest wildflowers; .. the coral-red pincushion protea. **1971** *Evening Post* 5 Jun. (Weekend Mag.) 5 The whole protea family thrives here, including .. the gay pin-cushion proteas. **1973** M.R. LEVYNS in *Std Encycl. of Sn Afr.* VIII. 574 *Pincushions*, Name applied to two species of *Leucospermum* (family *Proteaceae*) ... Pincushions ... Kreupelhout .. (*Leucospermum conocarpodendron.*) Large, much-branched shrub with soft hairs on the younger parts. **1977** E. PALMER *Field Guide to Trees* 98 *Leucospermum*, About 40 species, .. easily distinguished because of the leaves with notched tips, and the flowers .. with the styles protruding, in a roundish head resembling a pincushion — the basis of the common name 'pincushion' for members of the genus. **1987** T.F.J. VAN RENSBURG *Intro. to Fynbos* 16 The tree pincushion (*Leucospermum conocarpodendron* sub-species), with its curry-yellow flowers, often grows into an extremely large tree. There is also a large variety of .. pincushions (*Leucospermum* spp.). **1989** *Gardening Questions Answered* (Reader's Digest Assoc.) 347 *Pincushion, Leucospermum* .. Indigenous, evergreen shrubs with leaves similar to protea leaves and flower heads composed of tiny flowers in shades of yellow, orange and salmon pink. **1989** *Motorist* Aug. 21 If you think of the Cape, you think of proteas from the large pink and brown variety .. to the fragile and dainty pincushion protea. **1991** [see KREUPELHOUT].

pink pinkje var. PINC-PINC.

pinotage /ˈpɪnə(ʊ)tɑːʒ/ *n.* Also with initial capital. [Blend formed on the words *Pinot Noir* and HERMITAGE.]

1. A locally-developed red grape cultivar, a cross between the Pinot Noir and Cinsaut varieties. See also HERMITAGE.

1964 L.G. GREEN *Old Men Say* 142 Remember the name Pinotage if you want some of the best red wine the Cape can offer. About twenty years ago Professor C. J. Theron and the late Dr. A. I. Perold .. crossed the Hermitage and Pinot Noir grapes to produce a new type .. the Pinotage strain ... Up to then, all the Cape wine grapes had been grown from imported stock. Pinotage is a Cape product, designed as it were for the soil and climate. **1971** B. BIERMANN *Red Wine* 64 By crossing the imported shy-bearing Pinot with the generous native Hermitage, Professor Perold achieved a remarkable success; a cross-bred [*sic*] with staying power, exhibiting good characteristics from both parent stocks. Its name is Pinotage. This indigenous variety yields a silky wine, young and lively. **1977** *E. Prov. Herald* 9 Sept. 17 Just as the old Stellenbosch home was created of several cultures, so also was the Pinotage grape created by a marriage of two different grape types. The shy bearing Pinot Noir and the more generous Hermitage. **1978** *Signature* June, The Pinotage hybrid, cold fermentation and much else have put South African oenological and viticultural research to the front in World wine development. **1979** *S. Afr. Digest* May 11 *Pinotage* was first developed in Stellenbosch in 1928. Today about half the *pinotage* crop comes from the Stellenbosch area. **1982** *S. Afr. Panorama* Jan. 22 A decided exception is the Pinotage, a cross between the Pinot Noir of Burgundy and the Hermitage, the local name for the Cinsault of the Rhone valley.

2. Red wine made from this cultivar. Also *attrib.* See also CAPE WINE.

1964 [see sense 1]. **1966** H. BECK *Meet Cape Wines* 12 Someone with imagination thought how good it would be to have a vine as productive as the hermitage producing a wine grape of the quality of the pinot, so .. crossed the hermitage with the pinot, producing a new vine type giving a new wine now named pinotage. **1975** *S. Afr. Panorama* Mar. 36 There were three varieties — Cabernet, Shiraz and Pinotage, the country's best-known red wines. **1977** *E. Prov. Herald* 9 Sept. 17 Pinotage. A noble and mature red wine with a full body and characteristic nose. A wine cultivated and brought to perfect fruition in the Stellenbosch sun. **1979** *Fair Lady* 5 Dec. 117 Pinotage is a peculiarly South African wine, full with a slightly plummy, flowery bouquet and after-taste which makes it popular among those with a sweeter tooth. **1981** J. DOXAT *Indispensable Drinks Bk* 52 The strength and body of most South African Pinotage wines suggest that the grape takes more of its character from the Rhône than burgundy. **1990** S. RAPPOPORT in *Flying Springbok* July 20 When a pinotage was declared champion red wine of the 1959 vintage, the wine fraternity was taken totally by surprise. **1992** P. DEVEREUX in *Sunday Times* 29 Mar. (Mag. Sect.) 6 When properly aged for such a period (bottles lying on their sides in a cool dark place) Pinotage mellows to a velvety smoothness and great depth of ripe-grape flavour. Its aftertaste can seem never-ending. It can be one of the great wine experiences, yet Pinotage is often quite inexpensive to buy.

pioneer *n.* [Special sense of general Eng.] A member of the PIONEER COLUMN.

1890 V. MORIER in P. Gibbs *Hist. of BSAP* I. (1972) 20 Neither the Police nor the Pioneers are quite all we heard from the enthusiast in London. The Pioneers are exactly the same class of men as our troopers, chiefly miners thrown out of employment by the smash of the Johannesburg gold fields. **1891** M. COLQUHOUN in E.T. Jollie *Real Rhodesia* (1924) 305 It is expedient for the defence of Mashonaland that a certain number of ex-pioneers and prospectors under agreement with the British South Africa Company should be called upon to assist in the defence of Mashonaland. **1937** J. STEVENSON-HAMILTON *S. Afr. Eden* 289 He accompanied the pioneers to Rhodesia in 1890. **1970** T.V. BULPIN in *Outpost* 11 By the middle of June 1890, the Police and Pioneers were considered to be ready. **1970** S. HOSTE in *Ibid.* 18 This note was signed by Mahan, Suckling and Ogilvie, all of them ex-pioneers. **1972** P. GIBBS *Hist. of BSAP* I. Within the next two weeks the pioneers were disbanded, to fan out over the surrounding countryside in search of the farms and mining claims they had been promised as part of their contracts.

Pioneer Column *n. phr. Hist.* A force of settlers and police sent from South Africa in 1890 by Cecil Rhodes to occupy Mashonaland under the concession granted by Lobengula.

[**1923** B. RONAN *Forty S. Afr. Yrs* 202 When the British South African Company received its charter in 1889 steps were promptly taken to back up its authority by armed forces. The first instalment of these was the Pioneer Force, which occupied Mashonaland in 1890.] **1924** E.T. JOLLIE *Real Rhodesia* (1971) 14 The country had an almost fabulous reputation for mineral wealth before the pioneer column entered it owing to reports from the hunters and traders. **1947** C.R. PRANCE *Antic Mem.* 949 A man whose career reads like a fairy-tale. One of the pioneer column in the annexation of Rhodesia, he shared with youthful glee in that unprincipled raid on Portuguese Macequece, of which the curious may read the inside history in Kipling's story 'Judson and the Empire.' **1971** H. ZEEDERBERG *Veld Express* 137 Selous .. owed a great deal of his reputation to the fact that he had been chosen to guide the Pioneer Column. **1974** P. GIBBS *Hist. of BSAP* I. Land promised by Rhodes to the Fingoes who had gone up to Rhodesia with the pioneer column — the origin of the present Fingoe Location near Bulawayo today. **1976** *E. Prov. Herald* 4 Sept. 3 The Rhodesian Prime Minister, Mr Ian Smith, laid the first wreath at a ceremony in Salisbury's Cecil Square yesterday to mark the 86th anniversary of the founding of White settlement in Rhodesia with the arrival of the Pioneer Column on September 12, 1890. **1985** *S. Afr. Panorama* June 40 A Monument marking the departure point of the Pioneer Column which opened up Rhodesia. **1990** D. CAPEL in *Personality* 27 Aug. 12 RASA's Peninsula branch will commemorate the arrival of the Pioneer Column at its destination in 1890 with a wreath-laying ceremony at the Rhodes Memorial on 12 September.

pip *n.* [Special sense of Eng. *pip* the small seed of various fruits such as apples, pears, etc.; perh. influenced by Afk. *pit*, see PIT.]

1. The stone found in soft fruits such as peaches, plums, etc. Cf. PIT.

1933 J. JUTA *Look Out for Ostriches* 25 We did say our rhyme for prune stones, and loquat pips, so golden and brown and numerous. **1949** L.G. GREEN *In Land of Afternoon* 156 Fruit pips provide floors in the Cape ... It takes thousands of pips to cover even a rondavel floor, and the surface is liable to be slippery. **1958** [see DOLOS sense 1]. **1977** [see STELLASIE]. **1988** F. WILLIAMS *Cape Malay Cookbk* 62 Wash mangoes well, leave skin on and cut into 2 cm chunks, discarding pips. **1991** *Best of S. Afr. Short Stories* (Reader's Digest Assoc.) 110 The famous peach stone floors (now rare) required thousands of peach pips, which were set close together into moist clay.

2. In the n. phr. ***peach-pip floor*** [tr. Afk. *perskepitvloer*], in early Cape houses, a floor of closely-laid peach stones embedded evenly in a clay base; PEACH-STONE FLOOR.

1949 L.G. GREEN *In Land of Afternoon* 156 The peach-pip floor is still to be found on some farms. **1974** *S. Afr. Panorama* Sept. 37 One becomes acquainted with the lay-out of the kitchen two or three centuries ago, .. not forgetting the peach pip floor! **1983** *Cape Times* 10 Jan. 9 The Drostdy Museum in Swellendam .. has a fine collection of period furniture and glassware and an unusual peach-pip floor. **1986** [see OPSTAL].

pipe *n.* [Special senses of general Eng.]

1. *Mining* and *Geology.* [Special sense of Eng. *pipe* 'a vein of ore of a more or less cylindrical form' (*OED*); see quot. 1985.] A vertical, cylindrical mass of volcanic agglomerate in which diamonds occur. See also BLUE GROUND.

1873 E.J. DUNN in *Quart. Jrnl of Geol. Soc.* (1874) XXX. 54 The contents of these 'pipes' in the shale are the same in all cases, and show distinctly that they are of igneous origin. **1886** J. NOBLE *Cape of G.H.: Off. Handbk* 194 The strata .. where cut through by the vertical 'pipe,' have their edges turned sharply upwards, as by a pressure from below. **1889** H.A. BRYDEN *Kloof & Karroo* 201 [I] believe that like the Kimberley 'pipe,' — as diggers call it — the diamondiferous earth had been shot upwards funnel-wise from below. **1903** *Daily Chron.* (U.K.) 2 June 2 Diamonds .. only appear at the surface in places where they have shared in a volcanic upheaval. Hence they are found in what are technically known as pipes. **1920** F.C. CORNELL *Glamour of Prospecting* 89 In many places along our .. route .. we came across .. well-defined 'pipes' .. in which 'yellow' and 'blue' ground .. was disclosed in dry watercourses. **1920** R.H. LINDSEY-RENTON *Diary* (1979) 36 The diamonds are found in what is known as 'blue ground', the soil being of a colour which might by a stretch of imagination be called pale blue. This soil is found in 'pipes', that is a more or less circular area of ground stretching down, practically perpendicular, I believe, towards the centre of the earth. *a*1930 G. BAUMANN in Baumann & Bright *Lost Republic* (1940) 141 Two prospectors .. came and asked me to do a survey of the farm on which the vlei stood, as they had discovered a diamond pipe. **1941** C.W. DE KIEWIET *Hist. of S. Afr.* 92 Here on the veld were alluvial deposits too, but the greatest proportion of diamonds was found in the unique geological formation of pipes of blue ground running deep into the earth. **1968** S. TOLANSKY *Strategic Diamond* 26 Broadly speaking, diamonds occur in two kinds of deposits, namely in deep mines, in what are called 'pipes', and in alluvial deposits, once perhaps riverbeds, or even marine beds. **1971** *The 1820* Vol.43 No.11, 26 The alluvial diggings were soon overshadowed .. in 1870 and 1871 when the sites of five diamond-bearing volcanic pipes were disclosed — four of them in an area of less than five square miles that was to be Kimberley ... Diamonds to great depths were found in the pipes. **1985** A.J.A. JANSE in Glover & Harris *Kimberlite Occurrence & Origin* 24 The person who first introduced the term 'pipes' in print and who usually gets the credit for being the first to recognise the igneous origin of this peculiar kind of breccia in a matrix of gabbro, was the Australian geologist E.J. Dunn, who was at the time the Geological Survey geologist for the Cape Province.

2. *slang.* [Transf. use of general (orig. U.S.) Eng. slang *pipe* opium-pipe.]

a. A quantity of marijuana sufficient for smoking in a pipe; *dagga pipe* sense (*b*), see DAGGA *n.*² sense 3 b. Cf. BOTTLENECK sense a, STOP sense 1 a.

[**1967** *Drum* 27 Aug. 7 Pyp or bottelkop: Drinking-end of broken bottle with silver paper filter (healthier than chilam-pipe because it can be changed often).] **1970** *Forum* Vol.6 No.2, 20 How's the pipe? I tend to miss every joint, pipe, roach, cookie, roller, twist, cob, stick, grass-thing that's around. **1972** *Rhodeo* (Rhodes Univ.) 23 Mar. 4 Like Friday night starts with cracking a coupla' pipes, sinking a jack of Martell and splitting for the fuzz shop. **1972** *Argus* 1 Apr. 7 A young boy asked my daughter at Clifton the other day whether she liked 'the pipes'. She at first thought he meant bagpipes. Then she discovered he was inviting her to smoke dagga. **1987** S.A. BOTHA in *Frontline* Oct.-Nov. 11 You wanna zol, my bra? Here's a fat blade. Easy make two, three pipes out of this, my bra. **1991** A. BARKER in *Daily Dispatch* 8 Jan. 8 Unscrupulous dealers are supplying deadly fakes, disguised as the crude pills. 'Guys just keel over after a pipe. You say wow, what a rush, Then you see the guy is dead.'

b. With qualifying word: **white pipe**, also **wit pipe** /vət -/ [Afk. *wit* white], a quantity of marijuana and tobacco mixed with powdered methaqualone tablets; see also BUTTON sense a.

1981 *Rand Daily Mail* 21 May 1 Five men .. were making a 'white pipe' out of Mandrax and dagga. **1984** D. PINNOCK *Brotherhoods* 8 Here, undisturbed, the brothers can smoke 'white pipe' (a mixture of dagga, tobacco and mandrax) and 'rap'. **1985** *Drum* Dec. 26 He .. received money from time to time and was able to smoke 30 to 40 'white pipes' a day containing two 'buttons' (mandrax tablets). **1987** [see BOTTLENECK]. **1988** [see FULL]. **1993** J. WILHELM in *Sunday Times* 17 Oct. 15 Combined .. with Mandrax and smoked as a 'white pipe', it's [*sc.* marijuana is] positively destructive. **1994** A. DONALDSON in *Style* Oct. 43, I was 17 when I was first offered a white pipe (a Mandrax and dagga mixture).

pipijoller, pippie-joller varr. PIEPIEJOLLER.

pipperag var. PIEPERIG.

piri-piri see PERI-PERI.

pisang *n. obs.* Also **piesang**. [Malay, 'banana', absorbed into S. Afr. Eng. through S. Afr. Du. (later Afk. *piesang*). In the past also used elsewhere.]

1.a. The cultivated banana plant; its fruit.

1786 G. FORSTER tr. *A. Sparrman's Voy. to Cape of G.H.* I. 78 The *pisang* was to be met within his garden of a luxuriant growth, but was said not to produce fruit of so high a flavour as it does in its native country. **1790** tr. *F. Le Vaillant's Trav.* I. 34 The small banana, or *pisang*, has a bad taste. **1795** C.R. HOPSON tr. *C.P. Thunberg's Trav.* II. 283 The Pisang (*Musa Paradisiaca* or *Bananas*) would seldom blossom in the few gardens where it was cultivated, and never yielded any fruit that was perfectly ripe and high flavoured. **1809** J. MACKRILL Diary. 67 Pisang, Musa Paradisaica or Bananas. **1897** S.J. DU TOIT *Rhodesia: Past & Present* 184 Two Days without Food on the Pungwe — Subsisting on Pisangs (Bananas). **1906** D. DE V. HUGO *In Kerkhof* 4 'Yam Pilsie' .. owned the best cherries and pisangs (bananas) in our hunting ground. **1910** D. FAIRBRIDGE *That Which Hath Been* (1913) 141 He put in 1,162 orange, lemon and pummelo trees, ten pisangs, two olives, [etc.]. **1913** C. PETTMAN *Africanderisms* 375 *Pisang*, .. *Musa paradisaica* and *M. sapientum*. This word is not so common in South Africa as it seems to have been at one time, though it is still in use among the Dutch.

b. *comb. rare.* **pisang fig**, a banana.

1731 G. MEDLEY tr. *P. Kolb's Present State of Cape of G.H.* II. 87 The Figs in this Garden are .. all admirably sweet and good. The choicest are those they call *Pisang* Figs; and they are the largest. They grow upon a Plant, which as soon as it has brought 'em to Maturity, withers quite away.

2.a. STRELITZIA sense a.

1821 C.J. LATROBE *Jrnl of Visit* 48 Fences of the large aloe, and of cactus or Indian fig, are common. Of pisang we saw several large beds. *Ibid.* Glossary, *Pisang*, The sort growing wild in the Zuureveld, is Strelitzia reginae; that which grows in Plettenberg-bay, is Strelitzia augusta.

b. With distinguishing epithet: **geele pisang** /ˈxɪəl-/ [Afk., *geele* attrib. form of *geel* yellow], *Strelitzia regina*; **wild piesang** [see WILD], *S. alba*.

1913 C. PETTMAN *Africanderisms* 183 **Geele pisang**, .. *Strelitzia regina*. **1812** A. PLUMPTRE tr. *H. Lichtenstein's Trav. in Sn Afr.* I. 204 We crossed a stream called the Pisang-river: It has this name from the profusion of **wild Pisang**, as it is here called, *strelitzia alba*, that grows upon its banks. **1824** W.J. BURCHELL *Trav.* II. 258 The very close resemblance which exists between the *Strelitzia augusta* or *Wild Pisang* (Wild Plantain) of the Cape Colony, and the *Urania speciosa* of that island [*sc.* Madagascar]. **1939** J.F. BENSE *Dict. of Low-Dutch Element in Eng. Vocab.* 285 *Wild pisang*, the name given to a S. African allied plant, *Strelitzia augusta*.

pisgoed /ˈpəsxʊt, -xut/ *n.* [Afk., *pis* urine + *goed* matter, 'stuff'.]

1. The plant *Euphorbia genistoides* of the Euphorbiaceae, a cause of urethritis in livestock; PISGRAS. Also *attrib.*

1906 F. BLERSCH *Handbk of Agric.* 257 The following are some weeds of a poisonous character found on our pastures: Dronk gras .. , stink blaar .. , pisgoed (*Euphorbia*), steek gras .. [etc.]. **1913** C. PETTMAN *Africanderisms* 375 *Pisgoed, Euphorbia Genistoides, Linn.* So called because when eaten by castrated animals it produces severe urethritis, which unless treated in its early stages results in death. **1917** R. MARLOTH *Common Names* 67 *Pis'goed. Euphorbia erythrina, E. genistoides.* Injurious to oxen and kapaters. **1958** [see PISGRAS]. **1962** WATT & BREYER-BRANDWIJK *Medicinal & Poisonous Plants* 405 *Euphorbia genistoides* ... Experimental 'pisgoed' poisoning has been described but the names of the plants tested were unfortunately not mentioned.

2. *Pathology.* Any of several urinary diseases of livestock, esp. bladder stones and urethritis.

1954 MÖNNIG & VELDMAN *Handbk on Stock Diseases* 247 Various plants promote the formation of bladder calculi .. , thus causing urethral calculus (*pisgoed*). **1962** WATT & BREYER-BRANDWIJK *Medicinal & Poisonous Plants* 405 Steyn .. has proved that the urethritis in the sheep, known as 'pisgoed,' is an infective urethritis ... The symptoms of pisgoed are reddening and swelling of the prepuce, and matting of surrounding wool. **1976** MÖNNIG & VELDMAN *Handbk on Stock Diseases* 300 Urinary Calculi (Bladder Stones, Pisgoed). *Ibid.* 301 Another form of pisgoed consists of an inflammation of the tip of the sheath ... This form of pisgoed is infectious and there is reason to believe that wet kraals promote its occurrence.

pisgras *n. obs.* [S. Afr. Du., fr. Du. *pis* urine + *gras* grass.] PISGOED sense 1. Also Englished form **piss grass**.

1786 G. FORSTER tr. *A. Sparrman's Voy. to Cape of G.H.* I. 295 Here there is said to grow a herb, called by the colonists p– grass, and which .. is, probably, a species of *euphorbia*. This is said to be frequently eaten by young cattle .. , which thereby get a dysentery, or stoppage of urine, that often proves fatal. **1954** MÖNNIG & VELDMAN *Handbk on Stock Diseases* 248 Farmers in Clanwilliam, Laingsburg, Uniondale and other districts call certain Euphorbia species *pisgras* or *pisgoed* and they maintain that these plants do not cause the formation of calculi but only an inflammation of the urethra.

pit /pɪt, pət/ *n.* Pl. **-s**, ‖**pitte** /ˈpətə/. [Afk., pith, kernel, pip. Cf. U.S. Eng., and Brit. Eng. dial.] The stone of a stone-fruit; a pip; occas., an edible seed, esp. a pine-nut (see DENNEBOL). Cf. PIP sense 1.

1913 A. GLOSSOP *Barnes's S. Afr. Hsehold Guide* 185 Every apricot must be halved and the stone removed; the 'pits' (as the farming community call them here) being excellent fattening and hardening-up food for pigs. **1913** C. PETTMAN *Africanderisms* 375 *Pit*, .. This word is in common use in South Africa as a name for the stones of fruit. It is used with the same meaning in New York, and is a remnant there of the old Dutch occupation. **1916** [see PLATDAK]. **1919** M.M. STEYN *Diary* 32 When he asked, 'Who has been throwing orange pips about here?' we burst out laughing (fancy calling those things 'pips', we had always called them 'pitte'). To us it seemed sheer affectation to call them anything else. *c***1929** S. BLACK in S. Gray *Three Plays* (1984) 93 Van K: Will it do if I suck a peach-pit? .. Haywhotte: Yes, but don't swallow it. **1969** *Argus* 13 Dec., 'Pit,' according to the English dictionary, is a 'fruit stone.' It is also the Afrikaans word for 'pip.' This was a South African short story and the use of the word 'pit' lent an added South African flavour to it. **1977** *Pickstone's Catal.* 9 The fruit [*sc.* peach] is yellow to reddish yellow, the flesh is deep orange coloured right through to the pit.

pitcho var. PITSO.

piti var. IPITI.

pit me frow, pit-me-wrou varr. PIET-MY-VROU.

pitso /ˈpiːtʃʊ/ *n.* Also **pe(e)cho, peetcho, peetsho(e), pe(e)tso, pic(h)o, piet-show, piicho, pitcho, pitsho.** Pl. **-s, -es.** [Sotho.] Among Sotho-speakers: a traditional gathering or conference of (the leaders of) the people, usu. held in the village or the chief's meeting-place; those constituting this assembly. Also *transf.*, and *fig.* Cf. INDABA sense 1. See also KGOTLA sense 1.

1822 J. CAMPBELL *Trav. in S. Afr. Second Journey* I. 264 The other chief said they should come to the *peetso* all well powdered. **1824** W.J. BURCHELL *Trav.* II. 408 The *piicho* or assembly remained sitting in easy conversation for nearly an hour longer. *Ibid.* 534 This council or assembly of chieftains, is called a *píicho* (peecho). **1824** *Cape Chron.* in *S. Afr. Jrnl* I. 77 A very curious and interesting account of the debates that took place on this occasion at the Bechuana 'Piet-show', or *Parliament*, has been inserted in the newspapers both in this Colony and in Europe. **1846** R. MOFFAT *Missionary Labours* 66 His power [*sc.* the chief's] though very great, and in some instances despotic, is nevertheless controlled by the minor chiefs, who in their *pitchos* or *pitshos*, their parliament, or public meetings, use the greatest plainness of speech in exposing what they consider culpable or lax in his government. **1857** D. LIVINGSTONE *Missionary Trav.* 220 There was a large halo, about 20° in diameter, round the sun; thinking that the humidity of the atmosphere, which this indicated, might betoken rain, I asked him if his experience did not lead him to the same view. 'O no' replied he 'it is the Barimo (gods, or departed spirits), who have called a picho; don't you see they have the Lord (sun) in the centre?' **1866** [see LEKGOA]. *a***1873** J. BURROW *Trav. in Wilds* (1971) 22, I forgot to say anything about the Piet Show Moschesh ordered, at which Smith presented him with a medal and cloak from Government. **1892** *The Jrnl* 10 Sept. 3 The *Press* special at Pietersburg wires that Magato has called a pitso of every Induna who owes allegiance to him. **1906** *E. Prov. Herald* 12 Apr., A large Pitso was held on Monday by the paramount chief Letsie at Matsieng. **1913** V.R. MARKHAM *S. Afr. Scene* 33 The Resident Commissioner and small group of British officials have their headquarters at Maseru, and here the 'Pitso,' or Great Council of the Basutos, meets annually, when chiefs and people confer with the Imperial authorities about all matters of government. **1925** D. KIDD *Essential Kafir* 261 While the coast tribes usually make their chief an absolute despot, who rules by means of councillors, the mountain and inland tribes frequently exert great power over their chief by pitsoes, or public debates. **1953** LANHAM & MOPELI-PAULUS *Blanket Boy's Moon* 81 There are those who will rise in the pitso of the white man, and say: 'Why must we pay so many policemen if there is no crime?' **1968** A. FULTON *Dark Side of Mercy* 27 The Chief had summoned the men of the clan to the Khotla and opened the pitso by telling those assembled that the season had been poor, the crops bad, the cattle infertile. **1976** WEST & MORRIS *Abantu* 121 It was more usual for all matters of general concern to be aired at a *pitso*, a general meeting open to all adult men in the chiefdom and held in the *kgotla* of the chief. **1983** P. WARWICK *Black People & S. Afr. War* 65 At the pitso on 24 October he agreed, after weeks of opposition, to abide by the decision to collect the new rate of hut tax.

PK *n. colloq.* Also **P.K.** [Rhodesian (now Zimbabwean) Eng.] Initial letters of *piccanin(ny) kaya*, see PICCANIN *adj.* sense 2.

1966 I. VAUGHAN *These Were my Yesterdays* 151 'A baboon behind "picaninny kaiah" tried to scratch my tail.' Charles said, 'You must be mad, baboons don't do that.' Old man said, 'It did — I saw it run behind the P.K.' **1970** D. PROCTOR *Informant, Clarens (OFS)* P.K. WC, Toilet, lavatory. 'Where is the P.K. on this farm?' **1994** [see *piccanin(ny) kaya* (PICCANIN sense 2)].

plaas /plɑːs/ *n.* Formerly also **plaats.** Pl. **plaases, plase** /ˈplɑːsə/, and (formerly) **plaatzen.** [Afk., fr. Du. *plaats* farm, place, square.]

1.a. PLACE sense 1. Also *attrib.*

In modern usage, when consciously used instead of 'farm', 'plaas' may have derogatory or mocking overtones (see quots 1959 and 1988).

1834 T. PRINGLE *Afr. Sketches* 296 He possessed eleven *plaatzen*, or farm properties. **1868** W.R. THOMSON *Poems, Essays & Sketches* 157 They saddled their horses and rode off, leaving only his wife and a few old men and women on the 'plaats'. **1879** R.J. ATCHERLEY *Trip to Boerland* 70 As grazing land, it commands the highest price in the Transvaal, and lucky is the Boer to whom has been awarded a farm, or plaats on the High Veld. **1896** R. WALLACE *Farming Indust. of Cape Col.* 162 Every man had a *plaats*, which grew as much grain as he wanted, as many grapes as he cared to make into wine of a sort. **1927** *Outspan* 4 Mar. 9 He had driven twelve donkeys and a wagon laden with yellow peaches from the 'plaas' and intended to hawk the fruit in the streets. **1931** G. BEET *Grand Old Days* 18 An old gentleman .. insisted on taking two or three of our party across to his 'plaas' nearby, and introducing us to his charming grown-up daughters. **1959** J. MEIRING *Candle in Wind* 117 An older girl .. looked Lena up and down. 'Are you from the plaas?' she asked impudently. **1980** C. BARNARD in *Daily Dispatch* 15 Sept. 6 Every so often I take off my surgical mask, put away the scalpel, .. and head for the plaas to spend a few glorious days playing farmer. **1982** *Sunday Times* 19 Dec. 4 Many of today's achievers .. started out as barefoot boys on remote *plaases* in the platteland. Now, often still barefoot boys on the *plaas*, they unashamedly enjoy the status symbols. **1988** *Star* 1 June (Tonight) 14 Stateside he [*sc.* Paul Slabolepszy] hit the media roundabout for 10 hours a day ... 'I still felt like this oke from the plaas and there they were talking bigtime.' **1989** P. LEE in *Sunday Times* 26 Feb. (Mag. Sect.) 36 The bakkie is synonymous with the local farmer out on his plaas, battered veld hat with leopard skin strip keeping the blinding African sun from his eyes, and bags of mealies and his workers in the back. **1990** J. NAIDOO *Coolie Location* 99, I didn't want to run the risk of having beauty accompanied by naiveté. I didn't want a plaas girl for a lifelong companion.

b. *nonce.* ***meanwhile, back at the plaas*** [by analogy with *meanwhile, back at the ranch* in general Eng., orig. used in Western cowboy stories and films]: used to introduce a subsidiary plot, or a change of topic.

1990 *Style* June 53 Meanwhile, back at the *plaas* Marieke had a face-lift and so did her political party. Overnight we were confronted with a new South Africa and a new set of rules.

‖**c.** *comb.* **plaasboer** /-buːr/ [Afk., lit. 'farm-farmer'], BOER sense 1 a; **plaas koffie** /- kɔfi/ [Afk.], farm-style coffee; see also MOER KOFFIE; **plaasmeel** /-mɪəl/ [Afk., *meel* meal, flour], BOER MEAL; **plaasmeisie** /-meɪsi/ [Afk., *meisie* girl], BOEREMEISIE sense 1; **plaasmense** /-mensə, -mɛ̃sə/ [Afk., *mense* people], farm-people; **plaasseuntjie** /-siœŋki/ [Afk., *seun* boy + dim. suffix -IE], BOERESEUN; **plaasskool** /-skʊəl/ [Afk., *skool* school], FARM SCHOOL; also *attrib.*

1968 E.A. WALKER *Hist. of Sn Afr.* 86 The interests of these **plaas-boers** lay in their farms, each of which was a state in miniature, producing little more than was needed for the maintenance of its inhabitants. **1974** *Drum* 8 Apr. I don't want to change the running of this country because I'm no blerry politician, but just a plain plaas boer. **1978** *Daily Dispatch* 24 Nov. 9 As a sturdy product of the 'plaasboere' from Henneman, he made a faithful and conscientious policeman in his duty to enforce the law. **1980** *Farmer's Weekly* 2 July 68 Lady, 49, is looking for a *plaasboer* over 50. **1978** *Darling* 13 Sept. 28, I meet the country people in a farmhouse outside Worcester, in the gently green heart of grape-growing country ... There is **plaas koffie**, soft-centred home-made chocolate cake, sherry, biltong. **1955** L.G. GREEN *Karoo* 99 Any farmers' wife will tell you that this stone-ground flour, known as **plaasmeel**, rises more surely and produces tastier bread than the flour from a modern mill. **1987** *Sunday Times* 12 Apr. (Extra) 4 Mynie Grovê, who says she was reared as a **plaasmeisie**, wants Cape Town to become more aware of the talents beyond the Hex River. **1990** *Weekly Mail* 21 Dec. (Suppl.) 31 A mixed bunch of glamour girls and '*plaasmeisies*' reading Gramsci and misunderstanding each other. **1990** *Style* Feb. 30 The Bekkers .. are what you might call **plaasmense**, with perhaps a touch of brilliance. **1986** *Argus* 1 Mar. 15 His roots are in the Eastern Cape and beacuse he was a barefoot boy on the farm, his father a farm labourer, the **plaas-seuntjie**-makes-good tag is one with which he is often labelled. **1986** B. NASSON in Burman & Reynolds *Growing Up* 109 As one rural primary teacher has remarked: Look, if you're a **plaasskool** pupil, life can be very difficult. There is a genuine stigma attached to coming from a farm school, believe me.

2. *obs.* An enclosed courtyard; a square.

1862 LADY DUFF-GORDON *Lett. from Cape* (1925) 95 As I sat waiting for early prayers under the big oak trees in the Plaats (square), he came up. **1878** H.A. ROCHE *On Trek in Tvl* 138 Arrived in the Plaas, or square, in which their church is its most prominent, but by no means most beautiful object.

Hence (sense 1) **plaas** *adj.*, rural.

1985 A. GOLDSTUCK in *Frontline* Feb. 19 'Pasop!' Two arms, linked and jutting dangerously, swing inches from his nose. 'Kyk waar jy dans!' he shouts at the unconcerned young couple vanishing into the distance. The plaas-Travolta takes no notice.

plaasjapie /ˈplɑːsjɑːpi/ *n. colloq.* Also **plaasjaap(ie).** [Afk., *plaas* farm + *Japie* see JAPIE.] A yokel or country bumpkin. Also *attrib.*, and *fig.* See also JAPIE sense 3, MOEGOE. Cf. STADSJAPIE.

[**1949** L.G. GREEN *In Land of Afternoon* 178 'Plaas Japie' of the Malmesbury wheat belt is a character you can tell at a glance, the product of generations of labourers who have worked on the same farms and grown wise in the ways of the district.] **1959** J. MEIRING *Candle in Wind* 113, I must take my doek off ... It makes me look like a plaasjapie. **1978** L. SAMPSON in *Darling* 13 Sept. 29 Why do all you people think we're backward .. I mean, to you city people, we're just a lot of plaasjaaps. Farming is hard, man, that's what you don't understand. **1979** *Daily Dispatch* 6 Mar. 7 Strife between Robben island prisoners .. the Johannesburgers regarding the Pretorians as 'plaasjapies'. **1979** *Staffrider* Apr.-May 49 They were rude to a 'plaasjaapie' who had the nerve to come onto the black side of the station. **1984** *Fair Lady* 11 Jan. 107 She mocked me for being a 'country bumpkin' and '*plaasjaap* Sarel'. **1986** *Style* Dec. 41 Everything that went wrong with the country one blamed on the damn plaasjapies in power. **1987** B. KHUMALO in *Drum* Aug. 26 In the townships they call us *Plaas Japies, moegoes, zaos* and other derogatory terms. They seem to think that everything that is good is from the cities. **1988** M. BRITZ *Informant, Grahamstown* Their house (double-storey) is absolutely charming. Everything that opens and shuts, gadget and appliance-wise. I feel like a plaas japie. **1988** D. TURPIN in *Star Tonight* 20 May 16 To any charge that tastewise I am just a 'plaasjapie', I can only reply — 'a silly comment, for if a plaasjapie can enjoy good red beef, why not good red wine?'

plaatland var. PLATTELAND.

plaats var. PLAAS.

placaat /plə'kɑːt, pla-/ *n. hist.* Also **placaard, placa(a)rt, plakkaat.** Pl. **placa(a)ten, placaats.** [Du. *placaat* edict, 'placard'.]

a. An edict or proclamation, esp. as issued at the Cape of Good Hope during the rule of the Dutch East India Company.

[**1731** G. MEDLEY tr. *P. Kolb's Present State of Cape of G.H.* II. 66 There is a Placard, publish'd by the Government, Laying a heavy Fine upon such *Europeans* as shall knowingly retain in their flocks a rotten or scabby Sheep.] **1796** Van Ryneveld vs Brown & Spooner, 4 The Statutes, Ordinances, and Placarts which were in Force in this Government, shall be observed in their full Power and Validity. **1857** *Cape Monthly Mag.* II. Sept. 156 When the Governor and the other gentlemen had bartered abundantly, he declared the trade open; but after a little time, this was again forbidden by placaat. **1862** *Cape Stat.* 5 This Placaat, fixing the tariff of Stamp Duties on Public Instruments. **1907** T.R. SIM *Forests & Forest Flora* 43 From historical records and from the Placaats mentioned in Chapter X, it is evident that parts of the mountain range of the Cape Peninsula were originally sufficiently well wooded to yield commercial yellow-wood planks and other valuable timber. **1910** D. FAIRBRIDGE *That Which Hath Been* (1913) 212 During his Honour's government no *placaten*, ordinances, laws or statutes have been framed or issued by his Honour and the Council. **1926** P.W. LAIDLER *Tavern of Ocean* 14 One of the earliest *Placaats* or edicts of 1652 forbade any to roam more than a half-musket-shot away from the Fort ... This placaat also forbade the use of lights of any kind in the huts by night or by day. **1934** *Off. Yrbk of Union* (Union Office of Census & Statistics) 467 (Swart), The Debt Register was established by a Placaat, dated the 19th June, 1714, and every ledger that has been used in connection therewith has been preserved. **1946** L.G. GREEN *So Few Are Free* 13 The Council of the Dutch East India Company issued a 'Placaat' forbidding the importation of Malay slaves into the Cape. **1952** G.M. MILLS *First Ladies of Cape* 15 On recapture they had been condemned to work as slaves in irons for two years. One of the earliest placaats or edicts issued by Jan had decreed this punishment for deserters. **1968** E.A. WALKER *Hist. of Sn Afr.* 89 The Company had to issue a special *placaat* to secure a small shipload of wheat, rye, barley, wine and tallow for Holland. **1984** R.C. FISHER in Martin & Friedlaender *Hist. of Surveying & Land Tenure* I. 70 The community of free burghers were subject to the legislative Ordinances or Placaaten of the Governor of the Cape and those of higher authorities in the VOC hierarchy. **1987** *S. Afr. Panorama* Feb. 19 The first borders of the district were proclaimed in a 'plakkaat' (government notice) dated July 19, 1786, which was signed by the governor on August 30, 1786. **1989** *Reader's Digest Illust. Hist.* 57 In 1732 a placaat (proclamation) was published to express the Company's concern .. and also to announce that the annual sum payable for a leningplaats would henceforth be doubled.

b. An official notice for public posting or reading.

1920 R. JUTA *Tavern* 174 They are going to hang up the Plaacarten in the Heerengracht to-night — and — and — those awful things are going to be written on them. **1926** P.W. LAIDLER *Tavern of Ocean* 52 This was the centre of all official life, both social and work-a-day. From its raised steps placaats were read, and sentences on criminals promulgated. **1941** N. DEVITT *Celebrated S. Afr. Crimes* 5 The ex-sergeant, after posting the 'placaat' on the wall of the church building, rode off with his followers ... That evening a wind sprang up and the 'placaat,' loosened from its fastening, blew from the church wall across the furrow which skirted the churchyard. **1957** L.G. GREEN *Beyond City Lights* 190 Even at Stellenbosch the burghers tore down placaats and other orders so that they could plead ignorance of unpopular laws. **1969** I. VAUGHAN *Last of Sunlit Yrs* 50 De Kat, the place where the Burghers, two centuries ago, had pasted their placaats and read their announcements.

place *n.*[1] *?obs.* [Calque formed on Du. *plaats* (later Afk. *plaas*) farm.]

1. A farm; PLAAS sense 1 a.

1809 R. COLLINS in G.M. Theal *Rec. of Cape Col.* (1900) VII. 12 The stream called the Rugte Vallei is the supposed boundary between Hendrik Barnard's two places. *Ibid.* 20 A possibility of making a shorter and better road between the place of Stephanus Ferreira and the drostdy of Uitenhage than that which goes by the place of Petersen. **1812** A. PLUMPTRE tr. *H. Lichtenstein's Trav. in Sn Afr.* I. 18 We halted at .. the Government Place upon the Strand. [*Note*] *Place*, as thus used, signifies every spot cultivated and inhabited, or capable of being so. **1816** J. MACKRILL Diary. 123 My Route was thro' the Tarka wherein I found many very pretty places & capable of elegant Improvements. Almost every farm is supplied with its own fountain of the purest water. **1823** W.W. BIRD *State of Cape of G.H.* 101 They are the proprietors of the farms, or places as they call them. **1827** *Reports of Commissioners upon Finances at Cape of G.H.* II. 77 The church-rate .. consists of .. 6s. 6d. sterling per annum on farms or 'places' in the district. **1833** *Graham's Town Jrnl* 28 Feb. 3 Many of them never work their places, they ride every day to Graham's Town to tell and write bad things of the Hottentots. **1843** *Cape of G.H. Almanac & Annual Register* 345 Voorste Bosjesveld .. contains 17 places or farms, of which some are divided into smaller farms. **1860** J. SANDERSON in *Jrnl of Royal Geog. Soc.* XXX. 237 The path lay along the course of Liebenberg's Vley until I reached a farm or 'place' called Pretorius's Kloof. **1872** 'Y.' in *Cape Monthly Mag.* V. Sept. 183 When night came, far from any 'place,' he would be thankful for the comfort of a 'kaross'. **1899** 'S. ERASMUS' *Prinsloo* 74 A young Jewish smoucher broke his leg by falling down a shaft on Piet's place, and had to lie up at the farm for many weeks till the limb was well. **1908** F.C. SLATER *Sunburnt South* 139 He had recently met me at a neighbouring farm and, finding in me an attentive and admiring auditor, had cordially invited me to visit his 'place'. **1929** W.M. MACMILLAN *Bantu, Boer & Briton* 200 (Swart), A great number of the places they deserted are now used as cattle places by proprietors who do not reside upon them but leave them and their cattle in charge of freedmen, Bechuanas and Bushmen. **1931** F.C. SLATER *Secret Veld* 219 He had recently met me at a neighbouring farm, and, finding in me an attentive and admiring auditor, had cordially invited me to visit his 'place'. **1958** A. JACKSON *Trader on Veld* 49 Since our place covered 12,000 morgen — about 26,000 acres — we were able to farm on a large scale.

2. With distinguishing epithet (see quots): **cattle place** *obs.* [tr. Du. *veeplaas*]; **full place** *obs.*; **half place** *obs.*; **loan place**, see LOAN; **request place** *obs.*, see REQUEST sense 2; **tuin place** *obs.* [Du. *tuin* garden], a fruit farm.

1812 A. PLUMPTRE tr. *H. Lichtenstein's Trav. in Sn Afr.* I. 18 The estate of Mr. Kirsten, as well as several other neighbouring possessions, abounds with excellent pasture for horned cattle: they are for this reason distinguished by the appellation of **cattle places**. **1822** W.J. BURCHELL *Trav.* I. 248 This place is a permanent residence, and consequently possesses a better house than the temporary cattle-places we had hitherto seen in the Karro. **1827** W. SHAW Diary., Preached morning and afternoon at our Cattle place, there was good attendance. **1929** [see sense 1]. **1827** G. THOMPSON *Trav.* I. 65 The farms here, and indeed throughout all the frontier districts except Albany, are of the average extent of 6000 acres; this large extent only being considered a **full place**. *Ibid.* 102 The great ambition which the African colonists have to see all their children settled upon 'full places,' that is, farms of 6000 English acres in extent. **1809** R. COLLINS in G.M. Theal *Rec. of Cape Col.* (1900) VII. 13 It is generally considered as a **half place**, for which reason it has not hitherto been granted in loan. *a***1823** J. EWART *Jrnl* (1970) 78 The different farms in the Piquet berg are what the Boors call **tuin places** or garden farms, their principal produce consisting in fruit.

place *n.*[2] [Calqued on Afk. *plek* space, place.] Space, sufficient room.

1982 *Cape Times* 9 Jan. 2 The arrival of the police provided the finale — when a black man in the back of their vehicle was set free to make place for the white woman. **1984** *Drum* Jan. 25 Conditions are very bad here ... There is lack of sleeping place. **1985** *Frontline* Sept. 45 It would be more accurate to say the purpose of all South Africans of good intent include such elements as .. — having place to express ourselves within our culture.

plak /plak/ *v. colloq.* [Afk.]

1. *intrans. nonce.* To paint, plaster.

1966 I. VAUGHAN *These Were my Yesterdays* 25 He found a huge hole had burst open in his silk stocking. No time to get another or mend. What did you do I asked ... Says, 'Well my girl .. I just plakked all over the hole in my leg with ink.'

2. *trans.* To paste, stick, or glue (paper or any other material).

1970 M. VAN DEVENTER *Informant, Pietersburg* Just plak the two slices of bread together with butter. **1971** P. FREEDMAN 'The Traffic Cop'. (*lyrics*) First I scribbles out a ticket Tears it quickly out and lick it Then I plaks it on the car with all my might.

So **plakking** *vbl n.*

1946 T. MACDONALD *Ouma Smuts* 8 Through the years her children would hear her saying: 'I must get on with the "plakking"'(that is Afrikaans for pasting in cuttings).

plakkaat var. PLACAAT.

plakkerswet /'plakə(r)sˌvet/ *n. Hist. Law.* Also **plakkers' wet**, and with initial capital(s). Pl. **-wette(n)**. [Afk., *plakker* squatter + linking phoneme *-s-* + *wet* law.] See quot. 1899.

1899 J.P. FITZPATRICK *Tvl from Within* 102 No sooner had they located their tribe .. than an official came down to them, Plakkerswet in hand, and removed all except the five [families] allowed by law and distributed them among his friends and relations. *Ibid.* 427 The government is enforcing the 'plakkerswet', which forbids the locating of more than five families on one farm. **1929** W.M. MACMILLAN *Bantu, Boer & Briton* 178 (Swart), The new-fledged Volksraad passed the first of a long series of Plakkers' Wetten (Squatters' Laws), restricting the allowance of squatters on any one farm. **1934** C.P. SWART Supplement to Pettman. 137 *Plakkerswette*, .. The Natal Volksraad, in 1840, enacted that no farmer might keep more than five families of Native squatters on one farm ... This law has been incorporated, inter alia, into the Union Land Act of 1913. **1968** E.A. WALKER *Hist. of Sn Afr.* 276 As for the Zulus already in the country, the principle of the *Plakker's Wet* (squatter's law) had been laid down again and again. So that labour might be shared evenly, no one save the Commandant-General might have more than five native families living on his farm. *Ibid.* 351 In the Transvaal .. the principle of the *plakkers wet* was maintained in theory limiting the number of native families which might squat on any one farm.

plakkie /'plaki/ *n.* [Afk., *plak* to stick + -IE; see quot. 1966.] Usu. in the *pl.*

1. Any of several plants, esp. species of the genera *Cotyledon*, *Crassula* and *Kalanchoe*.

1917 R. MARLOTH *Common Names* 67 *Plakkies*, *Crassula portulacea*. **1938** *Press-cutting* in B. Van der Riet Letters. (Cory Library), There is another disease known as krimpzichte, or neto, affecting goats throughout the Karoo, but the cause of this is a Cotyledon (plakkies). **1929** *Farming in S. Afr.* Feb. 1279 Spineless Cactus, Botterboom (Cotyledon paniculata), Plakkies (Crassula portulacea), pumpkins or potatoes can be used in the place of prickly-pear. **1934** C.P. SWART Supplement to Pettman. 138 *Plakkies*, .. A shrub, the crassula portulacea, is so termed by the Dutch farmer. **1966**

C.A. SMITH *Common Names* 371 *Plakkie*, Assigned to a number of species of *Cotyledon, Crassula* and *Kalanchoe*, either from the sound produced by slapping the leaves against one another ... or from the fact that the leaves of several species, after being warmed and the skin removed, .. were applied to abscesses, sores etc. to draw out the pus. **1984** A. WANNENBURGH *Natural Wonder of Sn Afr.* 103 Growing in a small pocket of earth among the rocks, succulent plakkies derive their name from the fact that the leaves of certain species were used as dressings for drawing wounds. **1994** *Weekend Post* 19 Feb. (Leisure) 6 The use of plants to cure maladies is interesting, with this one coming hard on the heels of the recent recommendation of the leaves of *Cotyledon orbiculata* (commonly known as *plakkies*) and *Kalanchoe thyrsiflora* for calluses.

2. *rare.* SLIP-SLOP.

1970 T. KRIGE *Informant, Bloemfontein* In the midday heat of the summer sun I have to wear my plakkies on the beach to protect the soles of my feet from the heat. (Plakkies — rubber beach sandals or beach thongs.) **1971** M. COZIEN in *UCT Studies in Eng.* Feb. 29 Beach-thongs, sandles [*sic*] made of rubber .. have a great many names here — sloppies, slip-slops, plakkies, etc.

plan, maak 'n see MAAK *v.* sense 2.

plan, make a see MAKE.

platanna /pla'tanə, plə-, 'platanə/ *n.* Also **platan(a), plat anna, plathander, plotaner.** [ad. S. Afr. Du. *plathander* clawed toad, *plat* flat + *-hander* '-handed one'.] The clawed frog or toad, any of several species of the genus *Xenopus* of the Pipidae, including *X. laevis* (the 'common' platanna) and *X. gilli* (the 'Cape' platanna). Also *attrib.*

1856 R.E.E. WILMOT *Diary* (1984) 131 Below in the shallows is wading the common heron, and the tufted umber, with his strong powerful bill from which no frog or platana was ever known to escape. **1883** *Meteor* Oct. 3 Where once the merry, croaking frog made night musical and the graceful plotaners disported themselves in the crystal water. **1898** E. GLANVILLE in *Empire* 24 Sept. (Pettman), It's a platanna, one of them web-footed, flat-backed, smooth-skinned, yeller frogs, with a mouth that goes all round its neck. **1911** J.D.F. GILCHRIST *S. Afr. Zoology* 224 The .. Plathander (flat hand) or Clawed toad .. occurs in most pools of water. **1918** S.H. SKAIFE *Animal Life* 214 The *plathander* is a curious creature common all over the country, and flourishes in almost every pool ... It differs from the ordinary frog in having no tongue, and in possessing claws on three of the toes on each hind foot. **1939** —— *S. Afr. Nature Notes* 169 A few years ago workers in the Physiological Laboratories at the University of Cape Town showed that the platanna could be used in a simple and certain test for pregnancy, and nowadays gynaecologists make use of them for this purpose. **1945** MILLARD & ROBINSON (1965) (*title*) The Dissection of the Spiny Dogfish and the Platanna. **1950** W. ROSE *Reptiles & Amphibians* 27 The platanna is the only frog we have ever seen that is capable of jumping backwards and he can do this both in water and on land. **1958** I. VAUGHAN *Diary* 43 On the banks if you go quietly you can see the platans and lakavans and sometimes great awful crabs in holes in bank. **1963** S.H. SKAIFE *Naturalist Remembers* 132 The platanna frog, *Xenopus laevis*, is easily kept in captivity but the female will normally never lay eggs under such conditions. **1973** D. HEY on Radio South Africa 9 Oct., The platanna is used extensively in scientific research, and until recently in the diagnosis of early pregnancy. **1985** L. DELLATOLA in *S. Afr. Panorama* July 40 The Platanna is so named because it cannot sit up like other frogs. It also has no tongue and, presumably, no voice. **1989** PICKER & DE VILLIERS in *Afr. Wildlife* Vol.43 No.3, 141 When compared with other true frogs, platannas are seen to be large, powerful, and flattened, and lack the jumping skills so typical of the frogs and toads. **1989** *Weekend Argus* 4 Mar. (Our Living World) 6 The six endangered species are the geometric tortoise, Cape platanna, micro frog, and Table Mountain ghost frog — all found in the Cape Peninsula area — as well as Hewitt's ghost frog and Smith's dwarf chameleon.

‖**platdak** /'platdak/ *n.* [Afk., *plat* flat + *dak* roof.] A dwelling with a flat roof, often of corrugated iron. Also *attrib.*

[**1896** M.A. CAREY-HOBSON *At Home in Tvl* 455 The only alternative they had to the thatch was what they called a platt-huis, or flat-roofed house.] **1916** *Farmer's Weekly* 27 Dec. 1585 A 'white man's' residence and 'werf' has sprung up in the veld. 'Oom Koos's' old modest 'platdak', 'dirty werf', as well as his 'pit' (seedling) fruit trees are eclipsed. **1978** M. TLALI in *Staffrider* Vol.1 No.2, 55 If I can't get a proper builder to build me a house then I die in that zinc 'platdak' of mine. **1987** J. BARHILL in *Frontline* Mar. 20, I have a farm in Africa, at the foot of the Cashane hills .. where the sun beats relentlessly down on the platdak dwellings which are devoid of design and everything else that makes living easy.

platdoorn /'platdʊə(r)n/ *n.* Also **plattdoorn, platdoring.** [Afk., *plat* flat + *doorn* (later *doring*) a thorn.] The stemless plant *Arctopus echinatus* of the Apiaceae, with a root which contains an aromatic balsam (used medicinally), and flat-lying leaves which are covered with stellate sharp spines; SIEKETROOS.

1835 J.W.D. MOODIE *Ten Yrs* I. 233 The 'plat doorn' (*Arctopus echinatus*, Lin.) has long been known to some of the surgeons of the colony. [**1837** ECKLON & ZEYHER *Enumeratio Plantarum Africae* 354 Arctopus *echinatus* .. — Incolis: Plattdoorn.] **1913** C. PETTMAN *Africanderisms* 377 *Platdoorn*, .. This plant is also known among the Dutch as Ziekte troest .. ; a decoction is made from the root and used for all kinds of cutaneous eruptions. **1947** L.G. GREEN *Tavern of Seas* 199 The platdoorn, which grows well in low country, forms an ancient Hottentot decoction for skin troubles. **1966** C.A. SMITH *Common Names* 372 *Platdoring*, .. The much thickened root contains an aromatic balsam which was used medicinally at the Cape towards the close of the 17th century ... The acaulescent habit of the plant and the unisexual flowers, together with the spiny bladdery fruits, make it a singular plant in the South African species of Umbelliferae.

plathander var. PLATANNA.

platkop bagger see BAGGER sense 2.

platoon *n.* [Transf. use of general Eng. *platoon* a squad or set of people.] Used *attrib.* of schools or a schooling system in which two separate sets of teachers and pupils use the same school building, one set in the morning and one in the afternoon; occas., of a school or system in which classes use limited class-room space in turns on a rotational basis, being taught out of doors for the remainder of the school day.

1972 A.D. LAZARUS in *Std Encycl. of Sn Afr.* VI. 71 Education for Indians was transferred to central government control (Department of Indian Affairs) by Act 61 of 1965 ... There has been a considerable reduction in numbers of children in platoon schools (11 000 in 1970 and there should be none in the foreseeable future). **1974** G.K. NAIR in *Fiat Lux* Oct., This lack of school accommodation led to the introduction of 'platoon' classes as an emergency measure to accommodate more pupils ... While educationists acknowledge the fact that the platoon school system is both undesirable and educationally unsound, one must be mindful of its achievements in Indian Education. **1992** P. MAURICE in *Weekly Mail* 16 Apr. 14 The Etwatwa community on the East Rand plans to turn the government's double shift 'platoon' system on its head with its new 'two of everything' school, officially launched this week.

platoon *v. trans.* [fr. prec.] To apply the platoon system to a school. Hence **platooning** *vbl n.*

1974 G.K. NAIR in *Fiat Lux* Oct., It seldom happens that a school is fully platooned. **1987** W.A. STAUDE in *M.C.I. Newsletter* 10 June, It has been found necessary to platoon 14 schools (that is to say, to allow the staff and pupils of a destroyed school to use the buildings and facilities of an existing school in the afternoons). 'Platooning' is not an ideal solution because it brings administrative and other problems in its train. **1995** S. BENGHU on Radio South Africa 11 Jan. (Newswrap), We shall be platooning, and that way having double sessions.

platsak /'platsak/ *adj. colloq.* [Afk., *plat* flat + *sak* pocket.] Penniless, 'broke'.

1959 J. MEIRING *Candle in Wind* 85 Where do you think we are going to find food and money? We are platsak. [**1970** K. NICOL *Informant, Durban*, I can't go out tonight because I'm plat (broke).] **1982** FUGARD & DEVENISH *Marigolds in Aug.* 30 Emily: That man was only looking for work. Daan: Ja, but whose work was he looking for? .. Steal some of my jobs and then I sit platsak. **1985** E. WRIGHT in *Fair Lady* 4 Sept., I was platsak when the first few clients started trickling in. I spent most of my time crying. **1988** LAMPERT & FOURIE in *You* 21 Jan. 102 We have been inundated with visitors every year for the past 15 years — family, dropouts etc, etc .. Once again we are 'platsak'. We will get a huge electricity bill and telephone account. **1991** J. LEURS *Informant, Grahamstown* Thanks .. — I hope you have not been 'platsak' because of this!

plattdoorn var. PLATDOORN.

platteland /'platəlant/ *n.* and *adj.* Also **plaatland**, and with initial capital. [Afk., *platte* (combining form of *plat* flat) + *land* land.]

A. *n.*

a. The rural areas or country districts; cf. BACKVELD *n.* sense a.

1925 H.J. MANDELBROTE tr. *O.F. Mentzel's Descr. of Cape of G.H.* 143 Snakes and scorpions are fairly plentiful in the platteland, but are rarely met within Table Valley. **1933** C.J. UYS *In Era of Shepstone* 199 (Swart), Like a leaven the discontent spread from town to town — leaving the platteland unaffected. **1943** 'J. BURGER' *Black Man's Burden* 236 The main strength of the Nationalist Party lies in the *Platteland*, the rural areas. **1948** O. WALKER *Kaffirs Are Lively* 27 The old label 'Kaffir' .. is still commonly used in the 'Bible Belt' or Platteland (Flat land) which is predominantly Afrikaans-speaking. **1955** [see HUISBESOEK sense 1]. **1958** A. JACKSON *Trader on Veld* 20 The idea of leaving the comfort and relative sophistication of Port Elizabeth held no terrors for me .. when my Uncle mentioned that he might fix me up on the Platteland. **1961** T. MACDONALD *Tvl Story* 24 Better farming is also the key to stop the drift of the people from the platteland to the cities. **1963** B. MODISANE *Blame Me on Hist.* (1986) 90 The South African police force attracts into its ranks young Afrikaners recruited from the Platteland, rural areas. **1987** *Frontline* Mar. 13, I went to another dorpie. There was a Masonic Hotel there. I think it was the Masonic. They're all Masonic on the platteland, unless they're the Grand. **1990** *Weekend Post* 19 May 6 In a city one would go to a shop and buy music to suit your needs, but on the platteland I find that it's sometimes quicker just to compose something yourself.

b. With defining word: **deep platteland**, usu. in political contexts, those rural areas which are furthest from the cities and thus most conservative.

1971 *Daily Dispatch* 6 Sept. 6 They obviously .. think that 70 voters in the deep Platteland should have the same say as 115 voters in the city. **1972** U. KENNEY in *Evening Post* 6 May 12 Senator Horak, and others, want the party to forget the 'deep platteland', as Sen. Horak put it, and go all out for more support in the cities. **1976** *Sunday Times* 10 Oct. (Mag. Sect.) 4 The hazards of life in the deepest platteland. **1983** *S. Afr. Digest* 20 May 21 The problem facing the Prime Minister is that the deep platteland still has an unequal influence on parliamentary politics ... The rural vote is loaded to favour scattered farming communities.

B. *adj.*

a. Of or pertaining to the country districts. **b.** Rural, unsophisticated. Cf. BACKVELD *adj.*

1952 [see PLAY sense 1]. **1956** A. SAMPSON *Drum* 161 The young Afrikaner policeman coming to Johannesburg from a platteland farm, where his family may have been cut off from civilisation since the Great Trek, was in a situation not very different from the Zulu coming from his reserve. **1967** W.A. DE KLERK *White Wines* 20 'Welkom,' he said . . . And a welcome it was, expressed by a man whose basic *platteland* values were obviously as firmly extablished here as the fine vineyards which had produced a Cape wine of quality. **1971** *Sunday Times* 27 June 6 Even the platteland voter has become far more sophisticated. **1971** M. COOK in Baraitser & Obholzer *Cape Country Furn.* p.ix, There are several ways of looking at country, 'platteland', or traditional art of any sort. **1979** *Capetonian* July 4 A metropolitan city with a platteland night life does not make sense! **1980** E. PATEL *They Came at Dawn* 48 'Whats [*sic*] there my sweet haanetjie?' 'There you stupid plaatland skakes-speare [*sic*].' **1984** *Fair Lady* 25 Jan. 52 A *platteland* Fellini took Annari off to the abbatoir to film the carnage. **1985** *E. Prov. Herald* 21 Mar. 12 In certain platteland and black areas the enumeration had taken longer than expected because of the widespread rains. **1987** J. JOUBERT in *Style* July 103 Like most Platteland towns, Mossel Bay cannot hold on to its youth once they have left school. **1988** A. KENNY in *Frontline* Apr. 21 There is a conspicuous lack of Platteland courtesy. In the shops and pubs, words like 'asseblief' and 'thank you' are rare. **1988** V. KHUMALO in *Pace* May 17 AWB-type treatment outside a Hillbrow all-night grill . . . A platteland punch that felt like it came from the bowels of earth clipped his eye which promptly ballooned inside its socket. **1989** *ADA* No.7, 7 Namaqualand, so quintessentially platteland. **1990** R. GOOL *Cape Town Coolie* 2 'These people,' he said in a strong *Platteland* Afrikaans, 'are mad!' **1989** D. BRISCOE in *Motorist* 4th Quarter 4 Take time to walk the streets of Lady Grey . . . This is the platteland South Africa and a haven of commonsense tranquility. **1990** J. NAIDOO *Coolie Location* 118 Their faces were pumpkin-like, their *platteland* characteristics were unmistakable: glad-neck shirts, shorts, snub-nosed shoes with thick serrated rubber soles.

Hence **plattelander** *n.*, one from the rural areas; cf. *backvelder* (see BACKVELD *n.*).

1948 *Press Digest* No.3, 22 Generally speaking, the 'plattelander' knows what the Nationalist Party is and wants, while the city inhabitant does not know this. **1956** M. WIGHT in M. Rogers *Black Sash* 81 The Transvaal plattelander struck a true prophetic note, when away back in the 'twenties they opposed the women's vote. **1967** W.A. DE KLERK *White Wines* 87 He was one of the first of the *plattelanders* with a feudal background to break fully and dynamically into the 20th century. **1973** E. LE ROUX in S. Gray *Writers' Territory* 147 Paradoxically enough, there is a similarity between the plattelander and the inhabitant of a densely populated area. The end product of loneliness and reticence is the same. **1975** [see FARM *n.*]. **1985** *E. Prov. Herald* July 22 I'm a backvelder, a plattelander, a country bumpkin if you like.

play *v.* [Special senses of Eng. *play* to imitate, pretend, act.]

1. *trans.* and *intrans. **to play (for) white***, less frequently ***to play coloured***. Esp. under apartheid: to cross the colour bar by passing oneself off as a member of the white (or 'coloured') group. Hence **playing white** *vbl n. phr.* See also PLAYWHITE, VENSTER KIES. Cf. TRY.

1952 MANUEL & VAN DE HAER in *Drum* Aug. 6 It is the almost-white who, strangely enough, hates the Coloured and the Africans with a greater vehemence than the rabid racialists. It is these people who 'play white' who have added yet another problem to the already complicated colour problem of the country. *Ibid.* 7 In the Platteland dorps playing white is the easiest thing in the world if you have the slightest suspicion of a fair complexion and your hair has most of the offensive kink missing. **1953** 'AMPERBAAS' in *Ibid.* Apr. 6 Coming to Johannesburg from the Cape thirty years ago, I tried to find a job. There was none . . for a Coloured man. I didn't think of playing white then. **1953** G. MAGWAZA in *Ibid.* Dec. 42 His friends say Dale is playing Coloured — materially, it pays an African to play Coloured. **1963** K. MACKENZIE *Dragon to Kill* 103 It is a well known ploy: if you want to play white, you make your mother into your maid. **1974** A.P. BRINK *Looking on Darkness* 109 I'm not trying to play for white, Ma. I only want to be an actor. I don't care about the rest. **1983** N. MKELE in *Star* 10 Sept. 27 There are . . any number of Africans who play coloured because of the benefits that flow from being coloured . . . To escape the . . effects of these colour bars, coloureds have evolved the schizophrenic phenomenon called 'playing white' by those . . who are fair-skinned and blue-eyed enough to merge with the white group. **1988** E. MPHAHLELE *Renewal Time* 96 The white people who governed the country had long been worried about the large numbers of coloured Africans who were fair enough to want to play white, and of Africans who were fair enough to want to try for 'coloured'.

2. *trans.* In the phr. ***to play sport***, to take part in any sport or sports.

Not exclusively *S. Afr. Eng.*, but the standard usage in South Africa.

1970 *Grocott's Mail* 24 Nov. 4 (*advt*) Play Sport? There is a Sportsman's Insurance for you. **1973** *Sunday Times* 9 Dec. (Mag. Sect.) 10 The horrible phrase, 'playing sport' of which I am sorry to say some of our best newspapers are guilty. One can play cricket, rugby, tiddly-winks, or the piano; but what of other sports like yachting, motor-racing . . , mountaineering, even huntin' and fishin'? How can one possibly *play* athletics, for example? **1976** *Fair Lady* 21 July 163, I had polio when I was a child and . . I couldn't play sport. **1987** C. CLEARY in *Star* 24 Oct. (Weekend) 8 We played a lot of sport and attended church organised socials.

play-play *adj. colloq.* [Reduplication based on *play* to amuse oneself; dissimulate, pretend; prob. influenced by Afk. *speel-speel* (lit. 'play-play') 'with ease' or 'while playing'.] Simulated, fake, toy, make-believe.

See note at NOW-NOW.

1941 *Star* 1 Feb., Our gallant boys who have been bearing the real heat and burden of the day up north will return to find many of the play-play soldiers and base wallahs wearing what should be a badge of honour. **1982** *Fair Lady* 21 Apr. 47 She gives a play-play leer: 'What would you like me to open up and bare to you?!' **1987** *Sunday Times* 17 May (Mag. Sect.) 60 When I was in the film industry I was involved with play-play creation. Rocks were made from papier mâché, buildings, even whole villages, were constructed from wood, canvas and polystyrene. **1989** *Edgars Christmas Catal.* Dec., They're at the age when they want more than just a play-play watch.

Hence **play-play** *v. trans.*, to make believe, pretend; **play-play** *n.*, pretence.

1989 J. HOBBS *Thoughts in Makeshift Mortuary* 257, I could play-play I was a beach boy, complete with surfboard and dark shades. Most of them are much more tanned than me. **1993** I. VLADISLAVIĆ *Folly* 115, I really don't get this. Are you imagining things? Is it a case of play-play? Are you hallucinating?

playwhite *n.* [See PLAY sense 1.] During the apartheid era: a 'coloured' person who has succeeded in being accepted as a white person; *vensterkie*, see VENSTER KIES. Also *attrib.* See also PLAY sense 1, WHITE *n.* sense 2.

1952 MANUEL & VAN DE HAER in *Drum* Aug. 6 These 'Colourpeans,' as they have been dubbed, can never hope to fool their own people. They are easily recognised for what they are, but most Coloureds are not malicious and allow these 'Playwhites' to have things their own way. **1956** A. SAMPSON *Drum* 205 Harry was only one of thousands of 'playwhites', as they call the light-skinned Coloureds who 'pass for white' and break away from the Coloured world. *Ibid.* 210 Whites scorned playwhites, playwhites scorned Coloureds, Coloureds scorned natives, light Coloureds scorned dark Coloureds. **1963** K. MACKENZIE *Dragon to Kill* 137 He . . danced well and told her stories about the antics of the play-white Coloureds. **1975** *Drum* 22 Apr. 4 When offered a palace He said without malice, I'm not a play-White, I'm a muntu. **1976** A. SMALL in *Sunday Times* 10 Oct., The time has come for the Coloured man in the street, to decide once and for all whether he is going to align himself with Black consciousness or the play-White system . . . What about Black consciousness and the 'play-white' coloured? **1988** J. HEYNS in *Ibid.* 3 July (Extra) 2 The play-whites of Cape Town nonchalantly sauntered through the turnstiles in style . . . That was apartheid's finest hour. On stage were black-painted white faces entertaining white-painted brown faces.

Hence **play whitism** *n. phr.*

1976 *Drum* June, In the front rows the coloured kids converse with their white counterparts with no sham of play whitism. It is common . . to hear 'Hey whitey, move up one seat.'

‖**plein** /pleɪn/ *n.* [Du.] A square or open space; also used as an element in urban place names.

1815 *Afr. Court Calendar & Dir.*, Byl, David, Retailshop, 1, Boereplein. *Ibid.* Louwrie, Gesina, 7, Kerkplein. **1822** W.J. BURCHELL *Trav.* I. 73 It [*sc.* the Stadhuis] stands in the middle of the town, on one side of the square called Groente Plein, in which a daily market for vegetables is held. *a***1827** D. CARMICHAEL in W.J. Hooker *Botanical Misc.* (1831) II. 23 The Boeren Plein, or Hottentot Square, is situated in the upper part of the town. **1927** C.G. BOTHA *Social Life in Cape Col.* 68 The large *plein* or square in front of the church was the market place and the rendezvous of the farmers when they came to the village for business or to church. **1950** [see *Dopper Church* (DOPPER *n.* sense b)]. *a***1951** H.C. BOSMAN *Willemsdorp* (1977) 96 All that was left of Kruger Day were orange peels, and banana skins and pieces of paper littering the church *plein*. **1983** J.A. BROWN *White Locusts* 61 Someone was running across the *plein* from the postal shanty. *Ibid.* 270 Pretoria was hot and steamy as Rawlinson hitched his horses in the broad market *plein*. **1991** *Bulletin* (Centre for Science Dev.) Jan.-Feb., Many of Factreton's '*pleins*' (a circle of about 12 houses) have between two to three shebeens each.

plek /plek/ *n.* Pl. **-ke** /-kə/. [Afk. (cf. Eng. dial. *pleck*).] Place; position; home; 'joint'. Also dim. form **plekkie** [see -IE]. Now *colloq.*

1939 S. CLOETE *Watch for Dawn* 15 Magtig, it was his. For two hundred miles round this valley was known as Oom Frederik's Plek. **1958** — *Mask* 34 He was a truly skilful young man with his paints and he could hardly keep his eyes off the picture he had painted of the *plek*, the homestead. [**1973** *Drum* 22 Apr. 60 It is a law of this country that we all belong to different bantustans. Xhosas, Tswanas Zulus — everybody in sy plek.] **1979** *Daily Dispatch* 21 Sept. 16 Being an objective journalist I decided the only thing to do was to go to that other city that has seagulls . . and case the plek. **1984** *Frontline* Feb. 25 These ouens . . who . . make you come and watch their slide shows and everyone falls asleep while they're telling you about all the quaint little plekke overseas. *Ibid.* 26 There's lots of other things I'd like to tell you about this weird and amazing plekkie. *Ibid.* 27 He must up and off from his little shop . . to some plek the govt. figured was better for him. **1984** G. UNDERHILL in *Style* Nov. 106 This is the only plekkie, apart from Kirstenbosch, where you can get good teas.

plotaner var. PLATANNA.

plural *n.* Freq. with initial capital. [Derived from *Department of Plural Relations and Development*, a name given briefly (during 1978) to the Department of Bantu Affairs.] A joking or ironical term for a black person, mocking official terminology. Also *attrib.*

1978 *Sunday Times* 19 Feb. 14 If the old term 'Bantu' (to which the Government clung so obdurately for a generation) was offensive, the new term 'Plural' is hilarious. **1978** *Drum* June 2 Just imagine overseas readers of South African newspapers rolling on the floor in fits of laughter when they read something like 'The Dube hostel is built to accommodate 10 000 single male Plurals.' . . That which is not a Plural is a Singular. It is the Singulars who run the affairs of

Plurals in this country because the Singulars know what is good for the Plurals. **1978** *Sunday Times* 16 July 16 It's official. A Bantu is not a Plural – even though he may have some plural relations. Every Government Department has received a letter from the Secretary for Plural Relations which says: 'The Honourable the Minister of Plural Relations and Development has indicated that the word "plural" must please under no circumstances be used as a noun to mean "Bantu"'. **1978** 'PLURAL STAN' in *Drum* Aug. 2 Two Nationalist MP Singles have been invited ... And are these two men not the very people who have been running the affairs of us Plurals for 30 years because they know just what prescription to make for all Plural ills? **1978** *Staffrider* Vol.1 No.4, 32 News spread like wildfire. Every 'plural' was talking about it ... Every 'idle Bantu' gave it a thought. **1979** *E. Prov. Herald* 13 June 1 The bottle store in Port Elizabeth that put up a sign over the entrance for blacks which read 'Plurals – Plurale' came under attack in Parliament .. from a Nationalist ... He said this was a clear attempt to impugn the dignity of blacks. **1979** [see BAAS sense 3]. **1982** *Voice* 14 Feb. 4 Remember I used to be a native with a capital n, then I became a kaf .. (or was it kaf .. first now?) I grew into a bantu then rapidly into a plural. **1986** M.S. HLATSHWAYO in Bunn & Taylor *From S. Afr.* (1988) 298 Today you're called a Bantu, Tomorrow you're called a Communist Sometimes you're called a Native ... Sometimes you're called a Plural. **1987** S. VAN DER MERWE in *New Nation* 23 Apr. 11 Sent to 'native school' at the age of 10 ... Sent to the 'plural school' a few years later ... Enrolled at a Bantu school in the city.

Hence **pluralism** *n. nonce*, blackness.

1981 *Pace* Sept. 174 We'll be fed slabs of manna straight out of our 'nativism,' 'bantuism,' 'co-operativism,' 'pluralism' and all the other 'isms' laced up with this jumbled structure of separatism.

pluralstan see -STAN.

plus-minus *adv.* [The full written form of the spoken interpretation of ±, shorthand for 'more or less'; perh. reinforced by Afk. *plus-minus*; according to the *OED*, long obs. in Brit. Eng.] 'More or less', about, approximately; used of area, number, time, amount, age, etc.

*c***1970** C. DESMOND *Discarded People* 46 The extent of living quarters must be restricted to approximately 1/8th morgen (plus-minus 10,000 sq. ft.). **1971** *Evening Post* 27 Feb. 21, 125 Dorper and cross-bred Lambs (plus/minus six months). **1973** *Weekend Post* 6 Oct. 7 Bake in oven 425F for plus minus 10 minutes. **1975** 'BLOSSOM' in *Darling* 9 Apr. 95 The male spectators outnumber the female by plus-minus six to one. The ideal proportion. **1981** *Voice* 29 Apr. 7 Early in the day (plus-minus 8.30 am) on June 23. **1981** *Grocott's Mail* 28 Aug. 14 Young couple .. require accommodation urgently. Plus minus R120 per month. **1982** *Het Suid-Western* 29 Dec., Are you looking for a valuable piece of land adjacent to sea and river plus-minus 50 ha. **1984** *E. Prov. Herald* 9 Mar. 7 One longliner is capable of catching 300 tons of tuna in two weeks and I believe that there are plus-minus 100 operating along our east coast. **1988** *Pace* May 94, 1 chicken (plus minus 1,5 kg), salt and pepper. **1990** *Grocott's Mail* 5 Apr. 3 Both these erven .. are plus minus 500 metres from the sea. **1992** *Weekend Post* 20 June 9 He expected 'plus-minus 1 000 files' would eventually be forwarded for 'possible prosecution'.

pocket *n.* [Transf. use of Brit. Eng. *pocket* a sack or bag used chiefly for wool or hops.] A narrow sack, smaller than a BAG, in which agricultural produce (such as sugar, potatoes, and oranges) is sold; a measure for trading.

1892 *The Jrnl* 20 Sept. 1 (*advt*) 300 Pockets Sugar. **1944** H.C. BOSMAN in L. Abrahams *Cask of Jerepigo* (1972) 229 Close examination shows that the hessian in a sugar-pocket is of finer texture and better woven than that in a mealiebag. **1949** [see SCOTCH CART]. **1968** *Farmer's Weekly* 3 Jan. 97 Good-as-new Orange and Onion Pockets at very keen prices for large quantities. **1972** *Daily Dispatch* 23 Feb. 11 Five sugar pockets of dagga were found in the boot of the car he was driving. **1978** *Grocott's Mail* 14 Nov. 5 A spokesman for the Department has asked residents to bring their .. cats in orange pockets or net bags for safe handling. **1986** L.B. HALL in *Style* July 97 We stop for refreshments at a thatched tearoom where pockets of oranges hang from the rafters. **1987** *E. Prov. Herald* 30 May 4 (*advt*) Rathmead Farms Shops ... Pocket Patensie Potatoes 1st Grade ... R8,99. **1988** R. MCCREA in *Rusa Reporter* (Rhodes Univ.) 9 In the 1987 Academic Year residential students and staff consumed the following: .. 16 900 pockets of potatoes, [etc.]. **1990** *Weekend Post* 27 October 4 Consumers are paying the same price for 10kg pockets of potatoes as they paid for the larger 15kg pockets four months ago.

poco var. PHOKO.

podder var. PADDA.

poegaai /ˈpʊxaɪ/ *adj. slang.* Also **poegaaied**, **poeg-eye(d)**. [Afk., drunk; dog-tired, ad. Du. *pooien* to tipple, *pooier* tippler, or *po(e)chai, po(e)-ha(ai)* fuss, bother (Afk. *bohaai*).]

1. Tipsy, drunk.

1942 M.G. GILBERT *Informant, Cape Town* 21 June, Dear child, I can just imagine how beautifully poeg-eye he was last night! **1946** H.C. BOSMAN in L. Abrahams *Cask of Jerepigo* (1972) 200, I trust Mr Partridge will find colloquialisms like 'lawaai-water', 'poegaai' and 'Goewerment's hond' useful. **1946** C.P. WITTSTOCK in E. Partridge *Dict. of Slang*, Drunk: *rook-gat*, poegaai. **1960** C. HOOPER *Brief Authority* 225 Hell, man, .. let's get poegaaied. Have a drink, man; drown your troubles! **1970** A.L. RUSSELL *Informant, Johannesburg* Poeg-eyed. **1973** [see sense 2]. **1975** 'BLOSSOM' in *Darling* 29 Jan. 103, I had a ball that night – go-going on the table for this ring of chuckling ole dads in paper hats, most of them poegaai, all of them egging me on much better. **1991** V. WARREN *Informant, Alberton* We had to carry him home after the office party he was so poegaai. **1991** M.A. KARASSELLOS *Informant, Cape Town* After staying up all night she went to work feeling poeg-eyed. **1994** *Informant, Westminster (OFS)* He didn't know *what* he was doing – he was really poegaai.

2. Exhausted.

1970 V. JAQUES *Informant, Pietersburg* To be poeg(aai). To be very tired. **1973** BEETON & DORNER in *Eng. Usage in Sn Afr.* Vol.4 No.2, 36 *Poegaai*, .. exhausted, physically weary or semi-conscious because intoxicated. **1991** M.A. KARASSELLOS *Informant, Cape Town* Poeg-eye. Tired, exhausted.

poempelmoesje var. PAMPELMOESIE.

poendoe var. PUNDU.

poenskop /ˈpʊnzkɔp, ˈpʊnskɔp, ˈpuns-/ *n.* Also **poeskop**, and with initial capital. Pl. unchanged, or **-s**. [Afk., earlier S. Afr. Du. *poe(n)skop* a polled, hornless animal, or a type of fish, prob. ad. Du. *potskop, butskop* a species of dolphin or of fish, fr. *pots, buts* bump, boss + *kop* head; the spelling *poeskop* prob. arose through confusion with Du. *poeskop* 'cat-head'.]

1. A cow-elephant without tusks. Also *attrib.*

1860 A.W. DRAYSON *Sporting Scenes* 151 Of all things mind cow-elephants without tusks; they are not common, but if you do come across a 'poes-kop' like this, 'pas-op' (take care). **1971** E.C.G. MARAIS tr. *E.N. Marais's My Friends the Baboons* 109 Among gregarious animals there is usually a special leader ... Among elephants this special function is entrusted to a 'poenskop' cow (a cow without tusks).

2.a. Either of two species of seabream of the Sparidae, so called for the shape of their heads: **i.** The *red stumpnose* (see STUMPNOSE sense 2), *Chrysoblephus gibbiceps*. **ii.** The *black musselcracker* (see MUSSELCRACKER sense 2), *Cymatoceps nasutus*.

1887 *S.W. Silver & Co.'s Handbk to S. Afr.* 182 *Chrysophrys gibbiceps* ... Poeskop ... One of the choicest of colonial fishes. **1893** [see PAMPELMOESIE]. **1930** C.L. BIDEN *Sea-Angling Fishes* 263 Drew on the beach an enormous poenskop. The many children .. laughed .. loudly ... The great fish lay on its belly; the widely separated and staring eyes, the high forehead and broad head, the massive long nose depending below the thick lips, the stumpy protruding teeth .. reminded them of a familiar town figure. **1955** C. HORNE *Fisherman's Eldorado* 89 The poenskop is the fish which is also known as the stompkop, the black musselcracker and the black biskop in the Western Province. It is the black steenbras of the Eastern Province and the Wild Coast, the musselcracker of Natal. **1971** *E. Prov. Herald* 15 July 16 The South African records do contain a Musselcracker, but is is no. 719, which is our Poenskop. The Eastern Province records list it as a Poenskop. **1982** *S. Afr. Fishing* Apr.-May 10 Along Seaview, a lot of poeskop have been caught, but most of these fish are small and anglers should return them to the water alive. **1982** *E. Prov. Herald* 24 June 21 Also the big chaps are about – the poenskop and the musselcrackers – keeping company with the elf. **1990** M. HOLMES in *Ibid.* 14 Sept. 18 In those days the Natalians knew the poenskop as musselcracker. **1991** *Ibid.* 8 Mar. 18 Red Steenbras barely 15cm long, Red Roman even smaller, dozens of Poenskop under 2kg.

b. With distinguishing epithet: **blue poenskop**, the *black musselcracker* (see MUSSELCRACKER sense 2), *Cymatoceps nasutus*; **red poenskop**, the *red steenbras* (see STEENBRAS sense b), *Petrus rupestris*.

1981 *E. Prov. Herald* 25 March 6 There is great excitement in Plett angling circles. For the first time in many years **blue poenskop** have been caught in the bay ... Red poenskop have been caught .. lately but the blue variety have become a rarity. **1981** *Ibid.* 23 Apr. 11, I read a report .. from Plettenberg Bay about 'blue poenskop' and 'red poenskop' being caught down that way ... I had to telephone Jock Hunter, of Plettenberg Bay ... He told me the fish referred to were poenskop and red steenbras. **1981** [**red poenskop**: see both of the prec. quots].

poep /pʊp/ *n.* and *adj. Slang.* Also **poop**. [Afk.]

Not in polite use. Used also in *U.S. Eng.*, in the form 'poop' pronounced /puːp/.

A. *n.*

1. A breaking of wind; faeces; *fig.*, a derogatory term of reference to a person.

1969 A. FUGARD *People Are Living There* 13 He'll laugh at you you know. He'll tell me again I'm married to a poep. **1975** J. MCCLURE *Snake* (1981) 58 'Look, Doc, all I want to do is get this straight,' Kramer said. 'I'm too bloody busy to waste time on a poop.' **1977** — *Sunday Hangman* 105 Ja, we scared the poop out of him that time. **1984** A. DANGOR in *Staffrider* Vol.6 No.1, 17 Let Kakgat stay out there a while longer. Smell of his last poep isn't even gone yet. **1991** I.E.G. COLLETT *Informant, Pilgrim's Rest* The new boss has turned out to be a bit of a poep.

2. Used quasi-adverbially with intensifying force, usu. in the *comb.* **poep-scared** *adj.*, terrified.

1972 J. MCCLURE *Caterpillar Cop* (1974) 80 'He was very frightened, boss?' 'Poop scared. But he wouldn't tell me why.' **1974** C. HOPE on Radio South Africa 7 Sept. (Variations on Offside Rule), Groenbek must be poepscared, hey? **1975** J. MCCLURE *Snake* (1981) 85 Kramer smiled and said: 'I take my hat off to them then – at least *they* can't be so poop-scared of him.' **1976** 'BLOSSOM' in *Darling* 17 Mar., Talk about nipping straws .. never been so poep-scared in my whole entire life. **1983** J. DE RIDDER *Sad Laughter Mem.* 87 'This killing of Vicci has sure made me wonder.' 'I think it's made a lot of people wonder Tami boy. And .. it's made a lot of people poop-scared.' **1985** P. SLABOLEPSZY *Sat. Night at Palace* 69 He a bloody pusher. A dagga mert ... Gott, no wonder he's so poep-scared – they catch him for this it's life! *Ibid.* 79 *Poep-scared* – shit scared. **1989** *Frontline* Apr. 25 Lefty is saying 'Ag, you KPs, you're poep-scared of the kaffirs, that's why you want to chase them away.'

B. *adj.* Bad, unpleasant.

1970 A. VAN DEN BERG *Informant, Pretoria* My friend says she feels poep today (out of sorts, not well). **1991** I.E.G. COLLETT *Informant, Pilgrim's Rest* Poep. Unpleasant ... 'Well, what a poep deal that was.'

poep *v. intrans. Slang.* Also **poop.** [Afk.] Not in polite use. To break wind. Also used reflexively.

1963 A. FUGARD *Notebks* (1983) 84 Bean soup and how it makes him 'poep'. Now take a glass of Andrews Liver Salts immediately after a plate of bean soup to minimise the effect. **1969** — *Boesman & Lena* 8 Lena: I want somebody to listen. Boesman: To what ... When you *poep* it makes more sense. **1970** M.C. DUFFY *Informant, Durban* Poep. To make wind. **1978** P.-D. UYS in S. Gray *Theatre One* 130 I've decided I hate men, especially wholesome brawny men like Stephen. Screw screw screw and when you poep, the house falls down. **1984** A. DANGOR in *Staffrider* Vol.6 No.1, 17 'He's still going to poep himself to death,' said Seth the son-in-law who, emerging from the only bedroom, screwed his face in disgust at the smell. **1991** *Informant, Port Nolloth (N. Cape)* Poep (Break wind v. or n. Slang.) He poeped loudly in assembly.

Hence **poeping** *vbl n.*

1984 A. DANGOR in *Staffrider* Vol.6 No.1, 17 Poeping Forbidden.

poephol /ˈpʊp(h)ɔl, ˈpʊpɔːl/ *n.* [Afk.] An anus; *fig.*, a derogatory term for a stupid or unpleasant person. (Not in polite use, although used freely by some speakers of *S. Afr. Eng.* who are not aware of the word's literal meaning.)

1969 A. FUGARD *Boesman & Lena* 26 That tickey deposit heart of his is tight, like his *poephol* and his fist. **1978** S. ROBERTS in *New Classic* No.5, 23 So what's left? Just all us other poephols, what they call the man-in-the-street. **1985** P. SLABOLEPSZY *Sat. Night at Palace* 29 Those poephols at the post office — they not so stupid as they look. *Ibid.* 47 He doesn't own it, poephol. How can a kafir own a road-house? **1986** G. SILBER in *Style* Apr. 44 A thug .. threw a baseball bat at his head and called him a *poephol* because he had not managed to vault a wooden horse. **1988** *Informant, Grahamstown* The same review by some absolute poephol appeared in paper after paper. **1990** on M-Net TV 4 Nov. (Carte Blanche), All my patient wanted to learn to say was 'poephol' so that she could tell her doctor what he was. **1991** D. KRAMER on M-Net TV 3 Apr., Forty years to paint a ceiling. Why? Because he's a bloody poephol, man! **1991** G. DE BEER *Informant, Port Nolloth (N. Cape)* Poepole/poeppoll/poepholl. Idiot; literally (slang) arsehole. You poepoll!

poeskop var. POENSKOP.

poetie var. PUTI.

pofadder /ˈpɔfadə(r)/ *n.* Also **pof(f)-adder.** [Afk., fr. S. Afr. Du. *pof-adder* (see PUFF-ADDER).]

1. *obs.* PUFF-ADDER.

1812 A. PLUMPTRE tr. *H. Lichtenstein's Trav. in Sn Afr.* (1928) I. 35 It proved to be a *pof-adder*, as we believed, one of the most poisonous species that are found in this country. **1822** [see PUFF-ADDER]. **1849** A. SMITH *Illust. of Zoo. of S. Afr.: Reptilia* Appendix 21 *Echidna arietans*, .. Poff Adder of the Cape colonists. Individuals of this species have been observed in all the districts of Southern Africa.

2. *fig.* See quot.

1986 M. VAN WYK *Cooking the S. Afr. Way* 54 *Pofadder*, .. large intestines of sheep, liver, heart and kidney, cleaned and diced ... Clean intestine thoroughly. Combine liver, heart and kidneys with remaining ingredients and stuff mixture into intestine. Grill over coals.

poffertjie /ˈpɔfə(r)ki, -ci/ *n.* Also **poffartje, poffertje.** [Afk., ad. Du. *poffertje*, fr. Fr. *pouffer* to blow up.] A light fritter dusted with sugar.

1872 'Z.' in *Cape Monthly Mag.* V. Oct. 229 Shall we take offence if an English host .. set before our craving appetites the savoury 'bobotie,' and the dainty though untranslatable pumpkin 'poffartjes?' **1891** H.J. DUCKITT *Hilda's 'Where Is It?'* 196 'Poffertjes' is an old Dutch Pudding Recipe worth preserving. **1913** C. PETTMAN *Africanderisms* 378 *Pofferjes*, (F. pouf, pouffer, to blow up; Eng. puff, anything swollen and light, as puff-pastry, powder-puff.) Light spongy cakes, cooked in fat and coated with crushed or powdered sugar. **1927** [see OBLIETJIE]. **1930** M. RAUBENHEIMER *Tested S. Afr. Recipes* 46 Poffertjies. **1949** L.G. GREEN *In Land of Afternoon* 61 Jeanette van Duyn demonstrated the old Cape recipes ... She was able to bake a cake and prepare melktert and poffertjies for Queen Mary and her ladies-in-waiting. **1954** [see KLUITJIE sense 1 b]. **1955** J. HENDRIE *Ouma's Cookery Bk* 133 Poffertjies ... Drop by spoonfuls into a pot of deep, hot fat. Cook until brown and puffed up. **1968** K. MCMAGH *Dinner of Herbs* 15 No pofferjies were as light as those Fluerie had fried, no konfyt of green fig or watermelon had been as transparent. **1974** *E. Prov. Herald* 16 May, No matter that 'Les Beignets aux Ananas' is only a pynappel poffertjie in disguise, the guests were having none of it. **1977** *Fair Lady* 8 June (Suppl.) 6 Golden Poffertjies ... Take teaspoonfuls of the mixture ... cooking a few at a time until golden brown ... Sift drifts of icing sugar over top and serve hot.

‖**pofu** /ˈpɔ(ː)fʊ/ *n.* Also **po(o)ffo,** and with initial capital. [Venda *phofu* (pl. *dzipofu*), S. Sotho *phofu* (pl. *diphofu*), N. Sotho *nphohu* (pl. *diphohu*), seTswana *phohu*; cf. IMPOFU.] ELAND sense 1 a.

[**1785, 1789** see IMPOFU. **1839** W.C. HARRIS *Wild Sports* 376 *Boselaphus Oreas.* The Impoofo, Eland *of the Cape colonists.* Impoofo, or Pooffo of the Bechuana and Matabili. **1964** E.P. WALKER et al. *Mammals of World* II. 1419 Elands .. Impofu, Pofu, Siruwa (native names).]

pokaalie see quot. 1827 at BOKAAL.

pokkies /ˈpɔkis, -iːz/ *pl. n.* Also **pokjes.** [Afk., 'pox'.]

1. *Pathology.* ***The pokkies***: Smallpox.

1859 *Queenstown Free Press* 19 Oct. (Pettman), The Boers are .. withheld from coming from a fear of the *Pokkies*; the virulency of which is greatly exaggerated. **1871** J. MACKENZIE *Ten Yrs* (1971) 251 Small-pox again visited the colony ... We had difficulty in contradicting the story which was consequently spread by some Dutchmen who ... affirmed that the English missionaries had certainly the 'pokjes' in their party, for one waggon had been drawn aside from the rest! **1896** J. COLE *Reminisc.* 26 They cried out, 'But we are doctors come to vaccinate you and prevent you from getting the *pokkies*.' **1911** BLACKBURN & CADDELL *Secret Service* 103 The money left on a stone in payment remained there until a witch doctor had been called in to remove the 'pokkies' from the coins.

2. *comb.* **pokkiesblom** /-blɔm/ [Afk., *blom* flower; see quot. 1966], the shrub *Hermannia hyssopifolia*; AGTDAEGENEESBOS.

1950 M.M. KIDD *Wild Flowers* Pl.48, *Hermannia hyssopifolia L.* (*sterculiaceae*). Erect shrubs, 1–4 ft.: common in moist or sheltered places ... *Pokkiesblom.* **1966** C.A. SMITH *Common Names* 375 Pokkiesblom, *Hermannia hyssopifolia* (SW), see agtdaegeneesbossie; *H. althaeifolia* (sw): Both species were cultivated in Europe towards the close of the 18th century. The vernacular name is probably derived from the medicinal use of the plants, in the form of an aromatic tea, against syphilis (Afk.: pokkies). **1970** M.R. LEVYNS in *Std Encycl. of Sn Afr.* I. 252 *Agtdae-geneesbos. Pokkiesblom.* (*Hermannia hyssopifolia.*) Undershrub of the family *Sterculiaceae*, having rather small, wedge-shaped, short-haired leaves which are toothed near the tip. The flowers are borne in small clusters at the ends of short branches ... The plant is common in the coastal districts of the South-Western Cape Province. The dried leaves are sometimes used as a substitute for tea.

poko var. PHOKO.

pompelmoes, -mouse, -mus varr. PAMPELMOES.

pompelmoosje var. PAMPELMOESIE.

pompoen var. PAMPOEN.

pom-pom /ˈpɒmpɒm/ *n.* [Echoic; see quot. 1979.] The name given to the Maxim automatic quick-firing gun during the Anglo-Boer War of 1899–1902. Also *attrib.*, and *fig.*

'Pom-pom' is now in extended use worldwide for other weapons.

1899 *Daily News* 6 Dec. 5 Automatic guns, nicknamed pom-poms. *Ibid.* 26 Dec. 2 An automatic gun, which Tommy Atkins, with his aptitude for expressive phrases, promptly christened 'Pom! Pom!' [**1900** J.B. ATKINS *Relief of Ladysmith* 175 A volley from the Vickers-Maxim, with the 'pom-pom-pom' voice, like the sound of a postman rapping on the door of an empty house.] **1900** *Daily News* 5 Mar. 2 Near where the pom-pom gun was placed, is the over-flowing supply store. *Ibid.* 25 June 3 We secured a Hotchkiss gun, 500 rounds of pom-pom ammunition. **1901** E. WALLACE *Unofficial Despatches* 74 They are here in Matjesfontein, with their two spare horses and their Cape carts, with their native scouts and pom-poms. **1902** *Westminster Gaz.* (U.K.) 27 Jan. 1 The fact .. has never influenced him .. towards a modification of his verbal pom-poms. **1903** J.D. KESTELL *Through Shot & Flame* 59 Our Maxim Nordenfelts were the especial aversion of the British soldiers. We heard from some of them that were taken prisoners at Spion Kop that 'Hell clock' was the name that they gave our Pom-pom. **1937** R. KIPLING *Something of Myself* 160 Then pom-poms opened ... On soft ground they merely thudded. On rock-face the shell breaks up and yowls like a cat ... The pom-poms opened again at a bare rock-reef that gave the shells full value. **1943** F.H. ROSE *Kruger's Wagon* 18 There were, in addition to Long Tom, only two Krup guns, .. two pompoms and a few small guns here and there. **1957** D. GRINNELL-MILNE *Baden-Powell at Mafeking* 70 His miserable antiques the muzzle-loading 7-pounders were completely outranged by the enemy's high-velocity Krupp guns and even by the Vickers-Maxim 'pom-pom'. **1979** F. MYATT *19th C. Firearms* 194 Perhaps one of the oddest aspects of the South African War was the employment by the Boers of a number of guns made by Maxim-Nordenfelt. These were automatic guns of 1, 48 in (37 mm) calibre, firing an explosive shell of about 1 lb (.373 kg) weight, supplied to the Boers by the French. The guns were heartily disliked by the British who usually referred to them as 'pom-poms', a name probably first applied by the local natives as a result of their very characteristic sound in action.

pondakkie var. PONDOKKIE.

pondho(c)k var. PONDOK.

Pondo /ˈpɒndəʊ/ *n.* Also **Ponda, Mpondo** /m̩ˈpɔːndɔ/. Pl. unchanged, **-s, -es,** or **ama(m)-Pondo(s)**, occas. **Amaponda.** [Xhosa *amaMpondo* 'the people of Mpondo' (the founding chief); see also AMA-.]

1.a. A member of a Xhosa-speaking people of the Nguni group, from the northern half of the former Transkei (now part of the Eastern Province); GONAQUA sense 2; MAMBOOKIE; MBO sense 1. Also *attrib.* See also MPONDOMISE.

1824 BROWNLEE in G. Thompson *Trav.* (1827) I. 209 A tribe called Amaponda, who live on the coast to the eastward of the Tambookies. **1828** W. SHAW *Diary.* 29 June, The country is occupied by the Amapondo Nation, whose principal Chiefs are Fakoo and Umyaykie ... The Amaponda nation, of which we saw a few kraals near the Umtata, are easily distinguished from other nations, by the singular manner in which they dress their hair. **1835** A. STEEDMAN *Wanderings* I. 249 The Amapondo tribes, called Mambookies, whose territories extend from the Bashee to the River Umsikalia, about thirty miles beyond the St. John, or Zimvoobo River. **1836** R. GODLONTON *Introductory Remarks to Narr. of Irruption* 210 It will be seen that the Tambookies, or Amatembu and the Amaponda, or Mambookie tribes are both branches, in a direct line, of what the colonists usually term the great Kafir family. **1837** F. OWEN *Diary* (1926) 15 Faku, the chief of the Amapondas. **1838** *Ibid.* 120 The Amaponda country — Faku's tribe — beyond the Umzimvubu between Port Natal and Caffraria. **1847** 'A BENGALI' *Notes on Cape of G.H.* 23 The most powerful of all are the Caffres, composed of three great tribes, the Amakosoe [*sic*], the Tambookies, and the Amapondas. **1855** J.W. COLENSO *Ten Weeks in Natal* 124 The old chief, Faku, (of the Amampondo Kafirs,) when lately visited by Mr. Shepstone, granted him all his requests but one. **1871** C.M. YONGE *Pioneers & Founders* 258 The next tribes, the Amapondas, were scrupulously honest. **1872** *Wesleyan Missionary Reports* 79 Should peace continue a few years between the Pondo and Tembu tribes, we may calculate on this becoming the centre of a wide and extensive field of usefulness. **1882** C. DU VAL *With Show through Sn Afr.* I. 205 All went on smoothly until some Pondos, a tribe on the southern border .. converted a number of cattle belonging to the Boers into a movable feast. **1884** *Cape Law Jrnl* I. 223 These are the Amaxosa Kafirs, Fingoes, Tembus, Amampondo, Xesibes [etc.]. **1908** D. BLACKBURN *Leaven* 33 The native personal attendant .. complained that he was being molested and insulted by 'the kafirs'. He was a Pondo, an educated mission boy. **1949** M. WILSON in A.M. Duggan-Cronin *Bantu Tribes* III. 11 Up to the time of the famous chief Faku, who died in 1867, the Mpondo are said to have formed one tribe; then they divided under two of Faku's sons into independent sections, the Qaukeni and the Nyandeni. **1949** J. MOCKFORD *Golden Land* 118 Five main tribes inhabit the Transkei — the Xosa, Tembu, Baca, Pondo and Fingo. They occupy an area roughly the size of Switzerland and total, according to the 1946 census, 1,300,000. **1963** M. BENSON *Afr. Patriots* 104 Although thousands of Pondo had gone year after year to the mines, he [*sc.* Oliver Tambo] was the first to go to *boarding school* in the great city. **1964** N. NAKASA in J. Crwys-Williams *S. Afr. Despatches* (1989) 345, I am supposed to be a Pondo, but I don't even know the language of that tribe. **1968** F.G. BUTLER *Cape Charade* 9 If everybody who got drunk at New Year was sent to work on the road, the road would be past the Langkloof, past the Setlaars, past the Xhosas and past the Pondoes, right among the Zulus by now. **1976** *Family of Man* Vol.6, 80 The Pondo are one of the tribes living between the Indian Ocean and the Drakensberg Mountains ... The tribe is composed of a nucleus of 46 related clans which trace descent from a common ancestor, Mpondo. Many members of 21 other clans, unrelated to the descendants of Mpondo have subsequently accepted the authority if the paramount chief and have so become members of the Pondo. **1986** [see MPONDOMISE]. **1987** *E. Prov. Herald* 9 Oct. 9 Her father, President Botha Sigcau, was a paramount chief ... Chief Botha was King of the amaMpondo, which makes the premier a real princess. **1990** H. ALLAN in *Style* Oct. 61 No wonder the Zulus are asking 'Who is this jumped up Pondo?'

b. *comb.* **Pondoland**, see quot. 1973.

1913 G.E. CORY *Rise of S. Afr.* II. 230 A wave of bloodshed and destruction, which, beginning in faraway Zululand, spread in all directions until it reached Pondoland in the south, [etc.]. **1973** H. POTGIETER in *Std Encycl. of Sn Afr.* VIII. 651 *Pondoland*, .. Region on the Transkei coast between the Mtamvuna and Umtata Rivers, bordering on Natal in the north and divided by the Umzimvubu River into East and West Pondoland, each with its own chief. **1983** *Fair Lady* 2 Nov. 139 In Pondoland schoolchildren look after the cattle after classes.

2. The form of Xhosa spoken by the Pondo peoples.

1919 H.H. JOHNSTON *Compar. Study of Bantu & Semi-Bantu Lang.* I. 298 The [Xhosa] dialects include Feñgu, Baca and Pondω words. *Ibid.* 797 The divergent dialects of ?ōsa, such as Isi-pondω, Isi-ba¿a, Feñgu, &c.

3. A type of tobacco.

1941 C.W. DE KIEWIET *Hist. of S. Afr.* 251 Boer tobacco or the notorious 'Pondo' leaf which caused experienced smokers to blanch.

pondockie var. PONDOKKIE.

pondok /ˈpɔndɔk, ˈpɒndɒk/ *n.* Also **bondhoek**, **pandok**, **pondhock**, **pondhok**, **pondoek**, **pontok**. Pl. **-s**, or (formerly) **-ken**. [Afk. (also *pandok*), fr. Malay *pondok* hut, shed; school and lodgings for students of religion.

The word was used in Cape Town, at the beginning of the 19th century, of the reed huts occupied by slaves in the gardens of slave-masters' properties. The word occurs frequently in the records of the Court of Justice from this period, and moved into S. Afr. Du. and S. Afr. Eng. usage. (In modern Malaysia the *pondok* is a rural, resident, Islamic educational institution, conducted in reed huts.)]

A rough shelter, usu. a crude hut or shanty made of scraps of wood, cardboard, corrugated iron, etc.; loosely (often jokingly), a small house; PONDOKKIE sense 1.

1815 A. PLUMPTRE tr. *H. Lichtenstein's Trav. in Sn Afr.* (1930) II. 185 Near it stand six or eight *pandokken*, as they are called, a kind of huts made of reeds woven into a wooden frame, which are inhabited by the principal Bastard-Hottentots. **1818** C.I. LATROBE *Jrnl of Visit* 218 The present dwelling .. is a hovel, not much better than a Hottentot's bondhoek. **1832** *Graham's Town Jrnl* 6 Apr. 59 The State of Cape Town .. will suggest a remedy, namely .. to prohibit *pondhoks* being erected on any common or other public land within five miles of the town. **1843** J.C. CHASE *Cape of G.H.* 235 The Hottentots .. planted themselves at the outskirts of the country villages in small pondhoks, or huts, partly covered with old rags, decayed hides, sugar bags, and occasionally a little thatch. **1852** *Trial of Andries Botha* 60 Was it a house or a pandok? It was a house. **1888** *Cape Punch* 4 Apr. 203 You have liv'd for years here, darling, .. In this tidy little pondok ... Oft I think of the sasaaties, And the biltong that I ate; In this quaint and curious pondok Years ago when we first met. **1893** 'J.G.' in *Cape Illust. Mag.* Mar. 252 Cookery is an art, and it is not learnt in the pandok. **1920** F.C. CORNELL *Glamour of Prospecting* 112 The few miserable Hottentots occasionally to be found there, living in miserable pondhoeks of leaves and branches. **1960** J. COPE *Tame Ox* 221 Must I be a servant in the kitchen, are they going to make me live down in the location in a pondok? **1963** M. KAVANAGH *We Merry Peasants* 152 He had a wife and two small children in a temporary *pondok* of corrugated iron cardboard and flattened out paraffin tins at Nyanga township (temporary section). **1968** A. FUGARD *Notebks* (1983) 169 At Veeplaas Boesman got a job at the Zwartkops Salt Works. To begin with rented a small pondok — later built one of their own. **1973** *Cape Times* 9 June 11 Waiting lists of up to four years for City Council houses drive many people, some of them white-collar workers, to live in pondoks. **1987** M. POLAND *Train to Doringbult* 138 He glanced at Elsa and said, 'I thought that I might convert Koen's old *pandok* into a holiday cottage but Liz wants to build a new house altogether.' **1990** C. LAFFEATY *Far Forbidden Plains* 88 As they approached the farmhouse she saw that it was little more than a *pondok* built of wattle-and-daub, roofed with zinc.

pondokkie /pɔnˈdɔki, pɒnˈdɒki/ *n.* Also **pandokkie**, **pantokkie**, **pondakkie**, **pondockie**, **pondokie**. [PONDOK + -IE.] PONDOK. Also *attrib.*, and *fig.*, and *comb.* **pondokkie-dweller**.

1862 'A LADY' *Life at Cape* (1963) 71 To watch a black fellow smoking at the door of his pondockie is to envy him the supreme nonchalance with which he treats time, duty and space. **1899** *E. Prov. Herald* 4 Nov. (Pettman), The poor burghers are living in *pandokkies* on the outskirts of the town. **1936** C. BIRKBY *Thirstland Treks* 118, I saw children dying of typhus fever because their parents in the *pondokkie* huts, lacking water, were living in filth. **1950** D. REED *Somewhere S. of Suez* 163 A *pondokkie* is a shack built of pinewood, packing, flattened barrels, tin, or any available scraps of material. **1957** B. O'KEEFE *Gold without Glitter* 28 He told Scheepers to wait at the tent and went over to the grass pondokkies where the native loaders slept. **1960** J. COPE *Tame Ox* 84 Thousands of shanties and pondokkies grew overnight with the swiftness of a malignant fungus in the bush. *Ibid.* 86 The woodhawker himself was slouched asleep against his pondokkie wall. **1964** G. GORDON *Four People* 118 Some of the *pondokkies*, or shanties, consisted of no more than poles pointed drunkenly skywards and linked with sacking and ill-assorted scraps of wood and iron, small gaps being stuffed with cardboard and paper. **1966** L.G. BERGER *Where's Madam* 1 Couldn't decide whether to buy a 'character' home at enormous expense, or a pondokkie to hell and gone from town. **1973** *Cape Times* 10 May 3 More than 50 pondokkie-dwellers sat and stood around disconsolately yesterday ... The pondokkie people were being evicted. **1975** *Friend* 14 Mar. 5 These homelands, or more accurately, independent pondokkies, are going to turn into a time bomb poised to explode over a racialistic South Africa. **1976** *E. Prov. Herald* 19 Aug. 3 He told the people .. he would continue to work for the rejection of independence to the homeland. 'I see the Transkei as nothing but a "pondokkie" after October 26' he said. **1983** *E. Prov. Herald* 2 June, I bought a run-down pondokkie and Chelseafied it — it's my anchorage. **1987** *Scope* 9 Oct. 65 (*caption*) Barbra Streisand lives in this quaint little pondokkie. **1983** *Fair Lady* 16 Nov. 167 The years have passed and people find themselves still jampacked in the same rotting pondokkies, still without waterborne sewage and electricity. **1985** J. MAKUNGA in *Staffrider* Vol.6 No.2, 35 Bedraggled pondokkies, some made of flattened-out paraffin tins, others of old plywood and boards. For the most part they were sack-built by those luckless enough not to have found something better to build with. **1990** R. GOOL *Cape Town Coolie* 75 The other problem — the squatters, who have set up *pondokkies* or tin shacks on vacant land.

Pondomise(s), **-misi** varr. MPONDOMISE.

pont /pɒnt/ *n.* [Du., ferry-boat, pontoon (fr. L. *ponto* punt, pontoon, floating bridge, fr. *pons* bridge).]

1. A flat-bottomed ferry-boat for crossing rivers, worked on cables or ropes.

1775 F. MASSON in *Philosophical Trans. of Royal Soc.* LXVI. 279 Oct 6th, we came to the pont or ferry. **1827** G. THOMPSON *Trav.* II. 307 Ponts, or floating bridges, are used with great success on the Berg and Breede Rivers. **1835** A. STEEDMAN *Wanderings* I. 92 Bending our course .. to the Pont, a raft constructed for the purpose of conveying waggons across the river, and continuing our journey until past mid-night, we again *uitspanned*. **1856** R.E.E. WILMOT *Diary* (1984) 12 Not until an hour had been spent in trying to smoke in the cold wind did we see the pont emerge from the darkness and approach our bank. **1872** C.A. PAYTON *Diamond Diggings* 9 A little above the ferry is the 'pont', an immense flat-bottomed decked boat, for the conveyance of waggons and carts, with horses, mules, or oxen, when the river is so high that the ordinary passage by the 'drift', or ford .. is not practicable. **1886** G.A. FARINI *Through Kalahari Desert* 8 The coach was driven down to the *pont* (*Anglice*, ferry, or floating bridge) — a flat bottomed scow, attached by a pulley-block to a wire stretched tightly across the river. **1899**, **1936** [see DRIFT sense 1 a]. **1937** H. KLEIN *Stage Coach Dust* 20 The pont was so successful that it was used day and night, travellers preferring to pay the toll than go by the longer route. **1955** A. DELIUS *Young Trav.* 153 At a river crossing we came to where there were a whole lot of Bantu men singing in deep fine voices as they pulled a car across on a *pont* (ferry). **1957** L.G. GREEN *Beyond City Lights* 232 Many a wagon went into the stream, but that was not so serious. When a motor-car slips off the pont, the owner has a great deal more to worry about. One cannot really mourn the passing of the pont. **1961** T.V. BULPIN *White Whirlwind* 19 The pont held 100 men with their impedimenta. It was capable of three trips an hour. **1987** *Personality* 4 Nov. 29 'It's a question of developing a knack so that you know how to take the strain of the pulling chain and gauge the movement of the currents rather than brute strength that is needed to pull a pont successfully,' he tells me. **1991** M. HOLMES in *E. Prov. Herald* 17 May 27 Travel via Kei Mouth. The pont at the river mouth operates daily from dawn to dusk. It easily takes a vehicle and trailer or boat and saves several hours of travel.

2. *comb.* **pontman**, a ferryman.

1815 A. PLUMPTRE tr. *H. Lichtenstein's Trav. in Sn Afr.* II. 128 (Pettman), We stopped at the house of the ferry-man, or *pontman* as he is termed. **1931** G. BEET *Grand Old Days* 13 We succeeded in ingratiating ourselves with the overworked pontman so well that we had the pleasure of being ferried across .. hours before our turn! **1987** *Personality* 4 Nov. 30 He never learned to swim. 'It was something I just didn't think about when I applied for the job as pont man.'

Pontac /ˈpɒntæk/ n. Also **Ponta(c)k**, and with small initial. [Fr., a family name of the Médoc region, given to a sweet wine fr. that region; see quot. 1988.]

1. A sweet or dry red wine similar to port, made of the Pontac grape. Also *attrib*. See also CAPE WINE.

1812 A. PLUMPTRE tr. *H. Lichtenstein's Trav. in S. Afr.* I. 151 Du Toit gave us an excellent sort of wine, called here Pontac, a sweet deep-red wine, which is sold at the Cape at thirty dollars the hogshead. 1827 G. THOMPSON *Trav.* II. 285 The more distant farms above mentioned, produce the common wine, denominated Cape Madeira and Pontac. 1832 *Graham's Town Jrnl* 4 May 76 A small quantity of Pontack and sweet Muscadel, 5 years old, at 1Rd. 4sks. per gallon. 1843 *Cape of G.H. Almanac & Annual Register*, (advt) Old Cape Wines of superior quality consisting of Madeira, .. Pontac, equal and in many respects preferable to the Port wine generally imported into this country; sweet wines of very excellent quality and fine flavour, to wit: Pontac, Frontignac, Muscadel, etc. 1856 *Cape of G.H. Almanac & Annual Register* 68 Genuine Constantia Wines consisting of Pontac, Frontignac, White, Red which may be had either in bottle or cask. 1872 C.A. PAYTON *Diamond Diggings* 93 Cape wines, one of which, Pontac, a wine much resembling new port, is much affected up here, as it is believed to act as an astringent. 1880 E.F. SANDEMAN *Eight Months in Ox-Waggon* 14 The best known Cape wine is Pontac, resembling in taste and colour a rough-edged, strong port wine. 1880 [see S.W. Silver quot. at GREEN GRAPE]. 1911 M.S. EVANS *Black & White in S.E. Afr.* 226 One of the white boys had a bottle of Cape wine (pontac) in his possession. 1937 C.R. PRANCE *Tante Rebella's Saga* 213 She chattered in spate almost hysterically, and the bottle of Pontac which she produced in default of tea stimulated an artless and amazing tale. c1955 [see FRONTIGNAC]. 1968 C.J. ORFFER in D.J. Opperman *Spirit of Vine* 100 De Mist also indicated that the following wines were sent to the Netherlands in 1792 .. 1 leaguer Pontac price 176 guilders, 6 leaguers brandy price 528 Guilders. 1979 C. PAMA *Wine Estates of S. Afr.* 40 The two farms produced the famous red and white Constantia, natural sweet, muscadel wines, blended with Frontignac and Pontac wines. 1986 *S. Afr. Panorama* June 47 *Pontac*, an almost purple-black colour, is sweet and full-bodied and, if handled well, makes a valuable contribution to the blending of a good port.

2. A red grape imported from France during the 18th century.

1880 S.W. SILVER & Co.'s *Handbk to S. Afr.* 222 The only grape at the Cape which produces *red juice* is the Pontac. 1905 P.D. HAHN in Flint & Gilchrist *Science in S. Afr.* 415 The vines cultivated at the Cape for white wines were known as Steen, Green and Hanepot Grape, for red and dark wines Pontac, Frontignac and Muscadel Grape. c1911 [see HERMITAGE]. 1988 D. HUGHES et al. *Complete Bk of S. Afr. Wine* 108 Since the making of this Pontac coincided with the advent of the Hugenot immigration .. , it has been speculated that they may have brought cuttings of the vine with them, perhaps naming it after the famous Pontac family, who were important vineyard owners in the Médoc ... Pontac has now all but disappeared from the Cape's vineyards, only 39000 vines existing at present. 1990 *Excellence* Vol.6 No.2, 5 The best-known names are jerepigo, red or white muscadel and hanepoot, made from muscat d'alexandrie, muscat de frontignan, muscat de hambourg, but also from pinotage, pontac, tinta, chenin blanc, palomino.

pontok var. PONDOK.

pooffo var. POFU.

poola var. PULA.

poop n.¹ var. POEP n.

poop n.² *obs*. [Englished form of Zulu *impuphu* meal, flour.] PAP n. sense 1.

1899 G.H. RUSSELL *Under Sjambok* 176 In about an hour a man came .. and shoved in another of those wooden bowls containing mealie poop. 1913 C. PETTMAN *Africanderisms* 88 Poop, .. Mealie meal porridge is generally known by this name among the natives of Natal. c1929 L.P. BOWLER *Afr. Nights* 41 When the eggs and fowls failed to appear, I had to live as the Kafirs do at the kraals, on *poop*, a pap made from mealie meal.

poop v. var. POEP v.

poort /pʊə(r)t/ n. Also **port**, **po(o)rte**. [S. Afr. Du., pass, passage, fr. Du. *poort* gate.] A narrow pass or defile through mountains, particularly one cut by a stream or river; an element in place-names; NEK sense 2.

1796 E. HELME tr. F. *Le Vaillant's Trav.* II. 194 We issued from the mountains through a sort of passage, or defile, which is called the *Poort*. 1801 J. BARROW *Trav.* I. 109 The Poort may be considered as the entrance into Camdeboo. 1812 A. PLUMPTRE tr. *H. Lichtenstein's Trav. in Sn Afr.* (1928) I. 90 A pass between two little hills which unites two plains with each other, without any difficulties or unevenness of ground in the passage, is called by the colonists a *poort* (a door). 1822 W.J. BURCHELL *Trav.* I. 41 We entered an enormous fissure which divides the upper edge of the mountain: this opening is called the Poort, and, on each side, two lofty natural walls of rock .. contract it, towards the top, to a width just sufficient for a pathway. 1827 T. PHILIPPS *Scenes & Occurrences* 97 At the bottom of this steep descent, we had to go through what the Dutchmen call a *poort*; a chain of hills on either side, and room only for the road. 1835 A. STEEDMAN *Wanderings* I. 82 Among these hills are many quiet glens and vast ravines, from which are openings, or *poortes*, as they are here called, bounded on either side by overhanging cliffs. 1835 C.L. STRETCH *Journal*. 9 Apr., The 2nd Batt[n] was ordered to pass down the Port or ravine from which the Buffalo River takes its rise. 1847 J. BARROW *Reflect.* 178 The termination of the Snowy Mountains is somewhere about twelve miles to the north-east of the Compassberg, where a poort, or passage through the last ridge opens upon a plain, extending to the northward without a swell farther than the eye can command. 1850 R.G.G. CUMMING *Hunter's Life* I. 45 This poort, or mountain pass, the terror of waggon-drivers. 1866 E. WILSON *Reminisc.* 38 When we emerged from this kloof, or poort, we came to a very wide-spreading, open flat, — a peculiarity quite common in South Africa. 1877 R.M. BALLANTYNE *Settler & Savage* 142 The long line of emigrants had slowly defiled through the *poort*, or narrow gorge, of the mountains from which Baviaans River issues into the more open valley where it joins the Great Fish River. 1894 B. MITFORD *Renshawe Fanning's Quest* p.xxii, A poort is a pass or defile as distinct from a kloof. 1905 H. BOLUS in Flint & Gilchrist *Science in S. Afr.* 223 The Region is, broadly speaking, a vast shallow basin, which appears to have formed, in earlier ages, the bed of a large lake, which at length broke through the various 'poorts' of the southern mountain-range to the sea. 1910 A.B. LAMONT *Rural Reader* 4 Through passes or poorts in the mountains run the rivers. a1928 C. FULLER *Louis Trigardt's Trek* (1932) 68 Once through the poort, the junction of the spruit with the river is but a few hundred yards off. 1944 C. ROGERS in *S. Afr. Geog. Jrnl* Apr. 22 The Magaliesberg .. appears only as isolated blocks of quartzite in this region, so the river cuts no poort, but traverses the western end of the Bushveld Igneous Complex. 1949 L.G. GREEN *In Land of Afternoon* 21 A poort is different from a pass, for it is a passage through the mountains along the bed of a stream. 1967 W.A. DE KLERK *White Wines* 11 It was good to pause at the summit of the pass, where the river bursts through a narrow *poort* having through the ages eaten away the Warm Bokkeveld. 1979 T. GUTSCHE *There Was a Man* 154 The rest pushed and shoved their way along the escape route and through two narrow poorts .. until they reached a safe distance from the English onslaught. 1989 P.E. RAPER *Dict. of Sn Afr. Place Names* 220 Howison's Poort, .. Defile 8 km south of Grahamstown, in the Albany district. It was named after Captain Howison who constructed the road through the defile. 1990 *Frontline* Mar.-Apr. 20 A fairytale stream meanders through the kloof, and round each corner there's another stretch of poort ... Meiringspoort goes on and on, and you can marvel that Mr Meiring ever worked his way through this mighty gateway of God.

poor white n. phr. and adj. phr. Also **poor-white**. [Orig. U.S. Eng. (early 19th century).]
A. n. phr. Esp. *hist*.: a member of the most indigent section of the (Afrikaans-speaking) white population; see quot. 1922. Often in *pl*., used collectively. See also BYWONER sense 1, IGXAGXA sense 1.

1896 R. WALLACE *Farming Indust. of Cape Col.* 406 The so called 'poor whites' are chiefly the descendants of French protestant refugees, and .. of early Dutch settlers. The initial cause at work in reducing them to poverty, was the excessive subdivision of the land among the members of a family. 1908 J.H. DRUMMOND *Diary.* 28 Aug., The boy is a poor white and .. is very thin and his jacket sleeves are halfway down his arms. 1912 H.H. JUTA *Reminisc.* 148, I firmly believe that the evil and pernicious system of 'by-woonerschap' is more responsible for the manufacture of the poor white than anything else. 1913 V.R. MARKHAM *S. Afr. Scene* 301 The poor white in South Africa, as in America, is the peculiar product of a bi-coloured state, where manual labour is despised and vested entirely in the hands of the weaker black race. 1922 S.G. MILLIN *Adam's Rest* 42 In South Africa the term 'poor white' has a particular significance — a significance depending not entirely either on poverty or on whiteness ... A poor white belongs to a type characterised by dubious antecedents, dubious whiteness, dubious respectability, dubious earning capacity. 1925 P. SMITH *Little Karoo* (1936) 162 As the child of the poor-whites and as the mother of poor-whites she drifted for seventy years from farm to farm in the shiftless, thriftless labour of her class. 1932 *Star* 2 May 13 Poor Whites invade Durban — Lorry loads arriving weekly ... A big influx of poor whites into Durban very soon is predicted. 1939 R.F.A. HOERNLÉ *S. Afr. Native Policy* 92 Whilst literally millions of pounds have been spent on preventing Whites .. from becoming 'Poor Whites', and on preventing those who already are 'Poor Whites' from becoming poorer still .. , little attention has been given, and very little public money spent, on ameliorating the condition of poor non-Europeans. 1947 F.C. SLATER *Sel. Poems* 28 Defeated, dispirited poor-whites. 1948 H.V. MORTON *In Search of S. Afr.* 127 A native hut would be a palace compared with some of these awful shacks, which are the homes of 'Poor Whites'. This term, though not as contemptuous as the American 'White trash', is the South African equivalent, and denotes those people of European origin who have descended in the social and economic scale. 1949 A. KEPPEL-JONES *S. Afr.: Short Hist.* 177 Among these 'Poor Whites', for whom there seemed no place in South African society, hatred of the black race became more bitter than in other sections of the people. c1954 C.W. DE KIEWIET in *Virginian Quart. Rev.* Winter 182 The poor whites are the South African equivalent of the 'crackers' and 'mean whites' of the former slave states of America. 1955 W. ILLSLEY *Wagon on Fire* 174 They dismiss African workers and substitute poor-whites at four times their wages. 1974 *Rand Daily Mail* 28 Jan. 11 Poor Whites — Afrikaners divorced from their rural background and living in squalor under the alien conditions of urban life. 1977 F.G. BUTLER *Karoo Morning* 120 Poor-whites were a common enough sight in the Karoo in the early 'thirties. It is estimated that there were 300 000 of them at the time. 1986 *Cape Times* 3 Jan. 5 Shot in Johannesburg, the film showed whites .. queuing for food handouts. The commentator said: 'Poor whites are once again a political issue in South Africa.' ... Poor whites provided a fertile ground for the right-wing parties. 1987 R. MCGREGOR in *Leadership* Vol.6 No.3, 118 The poor whites were absorbed into the civil service which became their haven — the equivalent of a welfare state. Not only was every Afrikaner assured of a job, but of an inviolate job with benefits and perquisites which raised his standard of living in a very short period of time. 1988 A. KLAASTE in *Sunday Star* 22 May 11 The Afrikaners made many mistakes. The critical mistake was, while they built a strong Volk from the poor whites of the 1940s-50s, they forgot the rest of us. **1991** [see ROCKSPIDER].

B. *adj. phr.* Of or pertaining to poor whites.

1909 R.H. BRAND *Union of S. Afr.* 28 The growth of a poor white class which is too ignorant for any skilled trade and yet refuses to do 'Kaffir work' is an ominous sign. **1909** H.E.S. FREMANTLE *New Nation* 221 The poor white is the European who is permanently incapable of maintaining for himself and his family a standard of living which can be regarded as decent for white people. **1920** F.C. CORNELL *Glamour of Prospecting* 56 He was a most naive sort of old chap, typical of the degenerate 'poor white' trek Boer of these barren desolate and almost uninhabitable wastes. **1920** R.H. LINDSEY-RENTON *Diary* (1979) 22 We left Kirkwood at about nine o'clock, taking with us a young boy of the 'poor white' type to act as guide. **1926** S.G. MILLIN *S. Afr. from Within* 226 'The poor white' problem is one of pressing urgency. *c***1936** *S. & E. Afr. Yr Bk & Guide* 225 In the old Colony numbers have sunk to the 'poor white' level from losses incurred through drought and from the gradual deterioration of lands. **1978** *Sunday Times* 10 Aug. 15 The deplorable 'poor white' period of the post-depression Thirties. **1979** J. DRUMMOND *Patriots* 77 He'd been poor, the son of a poor-white farmer. **1988** J. SHARP in Boonzaier & Sharp *S. Afr. Keywords* 85 Nationalist insistence that the 'poor white' problem (the movement of impoverished Afrikaans-speakers from rural to urban areas) was caused solely by British depredations in the countryside during the war (implying that there were no earlier divisions amongst the *volk* itself).

Hence **poor whitedom** *n. phr.* (*rare*), **poor whiteism** *n. phr.*, the phenomenon of extreme poverty among white people.

1916 *Rand Daily Mail* 1 Nov. 4 Facts and figures which were of service to every student of poor whiteism in this land. **1934** N. DEVITT *Mem. of Magistrate* 202 One of the effects of poor white-ism is the resulting competition between this class and coloured people. **1936** C. BIRKBY *Thirstland Treks* 253 For a period these deserving people were to be thrown back into the pit of poor-whitedom. **1943** I. FRACK *S. Afr. Doctor* 106 The teaching of children solely through the medium of Afrikaans, with perfunctory attention to English .. ; the drumming into their heads of a narrow and rigid form of nationalism, is a contributory cause of poor whiteism. **1943** L. SOWDEN *Union of S. Afr.* 136 Poor whiteism is one of the sores of the South African economic system and, broadly speaking, is the result of the white man's reliance on the black man's labour. **1952** B. DAVIDSON *Report on Sn Afr.* 79 The sons and daughters of the *platteland* .. , saved by the growth of industry from 'poor-white-ism', have flocked into the towns. **1968** K. MCMAGH *Dinner of Herbs* 65 Her mother set great store by observing the proprieties, for she had seen families degenerate into poor-whiteism from having to live in houses with mud floors and unglazed windows. **1991** A. VAN WYK *Birth of New Afrikaner* 41 Poor-whiteism was misery: poor-blackism was even worse.

poosa var. PHUZA *n.*

pooti var. PUTI.

pootie var. IPITI.

popla /ˈpɔpla, ˈpɒplə/ *n. slang.* Also **poplar.** [Etym. unkn.] In urban (esp. township) slang: beer.

1977 P.C. VENTER *Soweto* 124 Say, 'Auntie, what about a popla?' That means you would like a beer. Or, 'A drop of moonshine, sister!' That will send her running for a tot of whisky. **1979** A.P. BRINK *Dry White Season* 252 It's a party, lanie .. the sort where you dance non-stop till you pass out. And then we bring you round with popla .. and there you go again. **1985** H. PRENDINI in *Style* Oct. 41 Sweet relief from these heavy pressures comes in the form of the 'phuza-cabin' or 'spot' (shebeen) where you drink 'ubrown' (brandy) or 'poplars' (beer) with your 'phuza-buddies' or any good guy you can call your 'bra'.

‖**poppie** /ˈpɔpi/ *n. colloq.* [Afk., *pop* doll + -IE.]

a. 'Doll', a term of endearment for a woman.

1975 'BLOSSOM' in *Darling* 26 Feb. 111 It's not violent even, it's *sport*, Bloss. There's a hang of a difference, poppie, Boxing's like a art, see. **1987** *Sunday Times* 1 Nov. 6 You have to wade through the admirers, buddies and adoring acquaintances who flock about her. 'Howzit poppie!' 'Hullow blom!' 'Ciao my babes!' **1987** M. POLAND *Train to Doringbult* 158 'Hello *poppie*,' Fanie yelled down the erratic line ... What's up, hey?' 'Just wanted to say Hi,' she said. **1989** J. HOBBS *Thoughts in Makeshift Mortuary* 294 He was smiling down at her ... 'I'll miss you too, poppie. You know that.'

b. *derog.* A doll-like woman.

1992 B. RONGE in *Sunday Times* 8 Mar. 14 Helene Truter, playing the pretentious Pretoria *poppie*, who shudders when she is served frozen fish and wilts at the sight of a tomato sauce bottle.

Hence **poppie** *adj. nonce*, 'dolled' up in an excessively feminine manner.

1989 J. ALLAN in *Sunday Times* 11 June To counteract the overall effect which was terribly Pretoria *poppie*, I defiantly added a pair of silver ear-rings the size of Ferrari hubcaps and a huge, mouldering suede bomber jacket.

population group *n. phr.* Also with initial capitals. [tr. Afk. *bevolkingsgroep.*] During the apartheid era, the official term for an 'ethnic group'.

*c***1967** *State of S. Afr. Yrbk 1967* 60 There are now four main population groups in the Republic, each consisting of two or more sub-divisions. **1971** [see UNISA]. **1973** *Govt Gaz.* Vol.93 No.3814, 19 Interested persons .. may .. submit memoranda to the Secretary of the Commission of Inquiry into Matters relating to the Coloured Population Group. **1980** D.B. COPLAN Urbanization of African Performing Arts. p.xi, Terms fall into several classes, the first including designations of sociocultural categories and 'population groups,' as they are termed in South Africa. **1982** [see GROUP AREA *n.* sense 2 a]. **1983** [see Govt Gaz. quot. at OWN AFFAIR sense 1]. **1989** E. REID in *Motorist* 4th Quarter 19 The park is open to people of all population groups. **1990** *Sash* Vol.33 No.1, 33 There is no legal provision with respect to opening government schools to all 'population groups'. **1994** [see HSRC].

Population Registration Act *n. phr. Hist.* An Act of Parliament which made it mandatory for every South African to be registered as a member of a particular ethnic group. See also *pillar(s) of apartheid* (PILLAR).

Promulgated in 1950, this legislation was repealed in June 1991.

1950 *Population Registration Act* in *Stat. of Union* 299 This Act shall be called the Population Registration Act, 1950. **1963** M. BENSON *Afr. Patriots* 164 The Population Registration Act .. defined the race of each individual and particularly hit the Coloured people. **1987** *Frontline* Feb. 5 Group Areas Act review? Is Mr H—joking? This Act is one of the Government's three non-negotiables: viz the Group Areas Act, the Population Registration Act and the Separate Amenities Act. **1991** *Sunday Times* 10 Feb. 21 The Population Registration Act is so loaded with evil symbolism — pencils in the hair, dividing families, the examination of finger nails, and all the foul rituals of race classification — that President De Klerk's promise to repeal it seems now to have been a major turning point.

Poqo /ˈpɔːkɔ, ˈpɔkɔ/ *n. hist.* [Xhosa, 'steadfast', 'standing alone'.] The military wing of the Pan-Africanist Congress (see PAC), operative during the early 1960s. Also *attrib.* See also APLA.

1960 *Flyer* (P.A.C.) in Karis & Carter *From Protest to Challenge* (1977) III. 560 The Pan Africanist Congress (Amafrika Poqo) Has A Message For The Downtrodden Black Masses Of Africa. **1963** M. BENSON *Afr. Patriots* 294 The social disruption caused by apartheid has ensured an upsurge of ugly gangsterism, menacing to black and white alike; taking terrible form in the Western Cape of POQO — 'We go it alone'. **1964** H.H.W. DE VILLIERS *Rivonia* 49 The Bashee River murders were perpetrated by members of Poqo, a terrorist organisation which is a resurrection of the banned Pan African Congress. **1968** J. LELYVELD in Cole & Flaherty *House of Bondage* 10 In Port Elizabeth .. fifty-six rural Africans were being tried en masse for belonging to a terrorist organization called Poqo (meaning 'only' or 'pure'). **1970** P.K. LEBALLO in *10th Anniversary of Sharpeville* (PAC) 1 With the growing strength of POQO, our military wing, the people of Azania are resolved to carry out armed struggle until fascist tyranny and U.S. led imperialism are totally wiped out. **1975** *E. Prov. Herald* 18 June 2 The so-called Poqo Act, the 90-day Act, .. legislation passed to deal with Poqo. **1977** *Rhodeo* (Rhodes Univ.) 30 Sept. 7 In the Transkei and the Eastern Cape, Poqo ('Ourselves Alone'), said to be the military arm of the PAC, blew up installations and attacked civilians. **1986** E.W. BÖHMER *Left Radical Movements in S. Afr. & Namibia 1900–1981* I. 589 From 1960 to 1963 South Africa was terrorised by the Poqo acts of terror ... During a press conference held on 24 March 1963, P.K. Leballo announced that Poqo was the militant wing of the PAC and that 150000 revolutionaries were ready to act on his command. **1986** P. MAYLAM *Hist. of Afr. People* 191 Poqo's strategy was based on the assumption that its acts of violence could escalate into a mass popular uprising that would overthrow white supremacy. **1990** *City Press* 4 Feb. 1 Justice Minister Kobie Coetsee published notices repealing the prohibition of the ANC, Umkhonto we Sizwe, the PAC, Poqo, and the South African Communist Party. **1991** O. MUSI in *Drum* Dec. (Then & Now) 58 The message was apparently not lost to .. the ANC and the PAC whose guerilla groups Umkhonto we Sizwe and the short-lived Poqo of the PAC began an intensive and costly campaign in lives and misery.

porpoise shark *n. phr.* [tr. Afk. *tornynhaai*, see TORNYNHAAI.] With distinguishing epithet designating a shark of the Isuridae: **great porpoise shark**, the great white shark *Carcharodon carcharias*; **blue porpoise shark**, the mako shark *Isurus mako*; JUMPING JACK. In both senses also called TORNYNHAAI.

1930 [see TORNYNHAAI]. **1947** K.H. BARNARD *Pict. Guide to S. Afr. Fishes* 13 Blue Porpoise Shark (*Isurus glaucus*), 15 ft. **1949** J.L.B. SMITH *Sea Fishes* 50 *Isurus glaucus ... Blue Pointer. Mako Shark. Snapper Shark. Blue Porpoise Shark.* **1957** [see JUMPING JACK].

Porra /ˈpɔra/ *n. Derog. slang.* Also with small initial. [See Toffoli quot., 1989.] An offensive name for one of Portuguese descent.

1975 *Informant, South West Africa (Namibia)* The Porra that we get our beer from has been shot. **1988** *E. Prov. Herald* 30 May 2 The .. article was intended to show that settlers of diverse origin had contributed to the country's progress and prosperity ... Bartholomew Diaz [did it] for the 'Porras'. **1988** C. ROBERTSON in *Star* 31 May 4 We call one another Kaaskoppe, Boere, Hotnots, Porras or *Seekaffers*, Yanks, Pommies or *Rooinekke*, [etc.]. **1989** *Frontline* March 26 I .. bought Winston, my boy, a half-dozen beers which he distributed amongst his colleagues. The Porras didn't like that. **1989** H.P. TOFFOLI in *Style* July 41 To the average South African in Blairgowrie a porra .. is a porra. Half the time the South African's not aware that the person he's referring to is actually Greek ... Porra is a swearword in Portuguese, what a labourer building a house says when he drops a brick on his foot. One theory claims the term was first used by upper class Portuguese to denote the lower orders, who were always shouting 'Porra!' Another theory claims the word comes from the lazy Afrikaans pronunciation 'Porregees'.

port(e) var. POORT.

Port Jackson *n. phr.* [The name of the harbour of Sydney, Australia.] In full ***Port Jackson willow***, formerly also ***Port Jacksons willow***: either of two species of acacia tree, *Acacia cyanophylla* or *A. longifolia* of the Leguminosae, introduced from Australia in 1847. Also *attrib.*

1857 'J.S.H.' in *Cape Monthly Mag.* I. May 267 That which, eight years ago, was a mass of drifting sand, is now covered with pyp grass and a luxuriant growth of Port Jackson willow. **1891** T.R. BEATTIE *Ride Through Transkei* 35 Port Jacksons willows are planted here and there near the house, and when the light strikes on them they add a tint of loveliness to the scene. **1902** *Trans. of S. Afr. Phil. Soc.* XI. 61 The value of Port Jackson bark on trees still standing .. is worth 6s. per acre. **1911** *Farmer's Weekly* 4 Oct. 139 Planting the Port Jackson willow on the higher ground .. has had the effect of preventing any further sand drifting. **1950** *Cape Times* 12 Dec. 9 Great masses of rooikrantz and Port Jackson willow grow to within a few feet of the houses. **1955** H.B. RYCROFT in *Jrnl of Botanical Soc.* XLI. 15 We hope to propagate the species of that area .. which today have been almost completely ousted by the spread of exotic weeds such as the Australian wattles, Port Jackson and Rooikrans. **1959** *Cape Times* 27 Mar. 1 A man was shot dead at Durbanville last night after a 400-yard police chase at dusk through thick Port Jackson bush. **1965** J. BENNETT *Hawk Alone* 118 He came back to Port Elizabeth, to the sea chopped by the south easter, even the interminable Port Jackson willows green after the Free State. **1966** C.A. SMITH *Common Names* 376 *Port Jackson Acacia*, .. Introduced from Australia as a useful sand binder on the Cape Flats and from there it spread. It proved an aggressive antagonist of the native flora when it spread further afield. **1972** PALMER & PITMAN *Trees of Sn Afr.* II. 731 Some Australian species, such as the aggressive and fast-spreading Port Jackson willow, Acacia cyanophylla Lindl., are cultivated in South Africa. **1974** A.P. BRINK *Looking on Darkness* 323 There were no trees apart from a thin lane of Port Jacksons serving as a wind-break. **1979** *E. Prov. Herald* 14 Nov. 3 The ubiquitous Port Jackson willow which is hated by many. **1980** E. JOUBERT *Poppie Nongena* 119 He cut Port Jackson branches and made palings to enclose the yard. **1986** J. DE WETTE in *Upstream* Summer 4 The mismatched trees of childhood .. the revenant silverleaf and pollen-caked Port Jackson. **1986** *E. Prov. Herald* 25 June 23 Have you noticed that the Australian wattles, which we call collectively Port Jackson Willow, seem to be disappearing from Port Elizabeth? **1987** *Fair Lady* 13 May 85 *Beaches*: It's a way of life. Some people spend entire days parked under the Port Jackson in the station wagon, drinking cane and listening to Bobby Angel. **1988** M. BRANCH *Explore Cape Flora* 42 *Port Jackson* wattles have straggly stems, yellow pompom flowers and black seed. Nothing grows beneath them.

post(al) stone see POST OFFICE STONE.

post-apartheid /ˌpəʊstəˈpɑːtheɪt/ *adj.* and *n.* [Eng. *post* after + APARTHEID.]

A. *adj.* Of or pertaining to a South Africa in which apartheid no longer exists.

1986 *E. Prov. Herald* 25 June 24 While disinvestment and sanctions might seem compelling .. the consequences of these punitive measures will exact a high price .., particularly in the post-apartheid society of the future. **1988** *R.S.A. Policy Review* (Bureau of Information) Vol.1 No.1, 25 As part of this change in style, the ANC drafted constitutional guidelines for a post-apartheid South Africa. **1990** T.M. NKOSI in *Tribute* Sept. 54 Any social order different from this one can be called 'new South Africa', but it may not necessarily be a post-apartheid social order. **1991** S. MACLEOD in *Time* 5 Aug. 11 The All-Party Conference .. where the major political groups, white and black, will decide how negotiations on a postapartheid constitution should proceed. *Ibid.* 12 The black leader .. clearly aspires to be South Africa's first postapartheid head of Government. **1993** *Weekend Post* 30 Oct. 4 Negotiators face a deadline of next Friday to agree on an interim constitution to carry the country through to a democratic post-apartheid era.

B. *n. nonce.* The time after apartheid.

1990 D. BECKETT in *Frontline* Sept. 30 He's moved into a whole new realm — beyond anti-apartheid, or post post-apartheid ... Joe's gone beyond the old story about how apartheid caused every ill, and 'post-apartheid ' is Nirvana.

post-matric /pəʊst məˈtrɪk/ *adj.* and *n.* [Eng. prefix *post-* after + MATRIC.]

A. *adj.* Of or pertaining to a thirteenth year of schooling, offered (usu. by a private school) as a preparation for tertiary education.

1987 *Grocott's Mail* 13 Nov. 11 A post-matric pupil at St. Andrew's College .. recently undertook an exciting rugby tour to Taiwan ... He decided to broaden his education before proceeding to university, coming to St. Andrew's for a post-matric year. **1988** Z. VENDEIRO in *Star* 26 Apr. 1 Post-matric courses popular at SA schools. A post-matric year of study, aimed primarily at preparing pupils for tertiary education, is being offered by an increasing number of private schools. **1992** S. MATTHEWSON in *Natal Mercury* 19 Dec. (Natal Results Suppl.) 4 Until now, the 'post-matric' year was the sole preserve of such private institutions as Hilton College, Michaelhouse, Kearsney College and St. Mary's Diocesan College ... Those entering the post-matric class must have been at school the previous year. **1994** *Weekend Post* 22 Oct. 11 Post-matric students enjoy the opportunity of participating in conventional sports as well as a wide range of extra-mural and cultural activities.

B. *n.*

1. A thirteenth year of schooling, after MATRICULATION.

1992 *Weekend Post* 22 Oct. 4 The concept of a 'post-matric' — a 13th year of schooling for pupils who want to prepare themselves better at university — is likely to become commonplace in Natal's 'government' in the next few years.

2. A student in the post-matriculation year of study; POST-MATRICULANT.

1994 *Informant, Grahamstown* How many post-matrics are we going to have next year? **1994** *Weekend Post* 22 Oct. 11 Woodridge offers wide choice for post-matrics.

post-matriculant *n.* [Eng. prefix *post* after + MATRICULANT.] POST-MATRIC *n.* sense 2.

1994 *Weekend Post* 22 Oct. 11 There are .. several societies and clubs at Woodridge, [in] which Post-Matriculants are encouraged to play a leading role.

post office stone *n. phr. Hist.* Any of several large inscribed stones under which early mariners calling at the Cape placed letters for collection by the crews of other passing ships. Also *attrib.*

[**1893** H.B. SIDWELL *Story of S. Afr.* 12 The captains hit upon the idea of leaving their letters stowed safely away beneath heavy stones, engraved with the vessel's name .. till the next ship that anchored in the bay took the mails away from this queer post-office to Europe or to India.] *c***1911** S. PLAYNE *Cape Col.* 65 Those interesting 'post-office stones', set up to indicate the spot on which were left letters by passing ships when calling at the Bay. **1926** P.W. LAIDLER *Tavern of Ocean* 4 Stones that acted as covers to the holes in which they hid their letters encased in cloth, oiled silk, or tarpaulin. The earliest of these 'post office stones', as they are called, bears a French inscription, .. probably recording the call of certain ships that left Dieppe in 1526. *Ibid.* 137 After the 'post office stone' period, postage was restricted to dispatches sent by the Company and conveyed on their ships to Holland or Batavia. *c***1936** *S. & E. Afr. Yr Bk & Guide* 146 Interesting post-office stones used at the beginning of the 17th century to call the attention of mariners to letters deposited beneath them. **1946** L.G. GREEN *So Few Are Free* 37 The navigators of the sixteenth century placed their letters, wrapped in tarpaulins, under the famous post office stones, in the hope that a ship homeward bound would find them. **1965** A. GORDON-BROWN *S. Afr. Heritage* I. 3 (*caption*) Early voyagers calling at the Cape before any settlement was established left letters under stones on which they inscribed particulars of their ship and voyage. The 'post office stones' above are dated 1614 and 1622. **1973** *S. Afr. Panorama* Aug. 48 A post office stone, built into the walls of the Castle, Cape Town, records the visits in 1607 and 1609 of the British ship, *Dragon*.

post-Soweto *adj.* [Eng. prefix *post* + *Soweto* see SOWETO.] Of or pertaining to a society (or period) transformed by the Soweto uprising of 1976. See also SOWETO sense 1.

1977 *Rhodeo* (Rhodes Univ.) 30 Sept. 4 Recent clashes on and around campus have focused attention on a development which is inevitable and indeed essential in a post-Soweto South Africa. **1977** *The 1820* Vol.50 No.12, 17 In 1961 .. we were in what could be termed the post-Sharpville period, whereas today commentators are inclined to speak of 'post-Soweto'.

pot-bread *n.* [tr. Afk. *potbrood.*] Bread baked in a closed cast-iron pot which is either buried in hot embers or placed over a fire; POTBROOD. Also *attrib.*

[**1883** E.L. PRICE Letter. 25 June, Jonas, our new cook, has never been on a journey before, and therefore does not understand the *pot-loaf* as we call it, wh. we bake on the road when our home bread has come to an end.] **1984** *Cape Times* 27 Oct., Detectives heard about another labourer in the area who regularly brought potbread to work. A piece of potbread was one of the clues found at the scene of the killing. **1986** *Ibid.* 16 Jan. 7 Worcester Farm Museum .. Pot bread baking, wheat milling in a water mill, coffee bean roasting, thong-curing [etc.]. **1986** M. VAN WYK *Cooking the S. Afr. Way* 96 Potbread (Potbrood) ... Place dough in pot and leave to rise to twice its original size. Place pot in ash of braai fire, heaping coals up around it. Bake, covered, for 45 minutes-1 hour. Heap coals on lid for last 15 minutes. **1989** H. GOOSEN in *S. Afr. Panorama* Feb. 17 Scrumptious rib of mutton with pot-bread and home-brewed coffee. **1990** M.M. HACKSLEY (tr. E. Van Heerden) in *Lynx* 189 Girlie broke some pot-bread for their supper and held out the tin of dripping for him to wipe his bread across it. **1991** *Farmer's Weekly* 25 Jan. 53 A heavy, flat-bottomed pot is ideal for cooking the most delicious potbread — either indoors in the oven or outdoors on smouldering coals.

potbrood /ˈpɔtbrʊət, -bruət/ *n.* [Afk., *pot* pot + *brood* bread.] POT-BREAD. Also *attrib.*

1913 C. PETTMAN *Africanderisms* 382 *Potbrood*, .. Bread baked in a pot. **1980** *Argus* 28 Aug. 12 'Potbrood' .. is cooked in a hole in the ground in which the fire is made and then raked out to provide an oven. It is a method used by frontier people in many parts of the world and which is still used by keen scouters and other outdoor enthusiasts. **1983** F. MATTHÉE in *Sunday Times* 18 Sept. (Mag. Sect.) 8 We want to bake '*potbrood*' on the premises, churn our own butter, make *konfyt* and pickles. **1985** *Fair Lady* 18 Sept. (Suppl.) 29 The sosaties .. served with crumbly mealie porridge or *potbrood*. **1986** C. KIRSTEIN *Best S. Afr. Braai Recipes* 80 Bread .. can be a traditionally South African 'cook-over-the-coals' bread such as 'roosterkoek' or 'potbrood'. *Ibid.* 82 Potbrood ... Knead the dough again, shape it into a round and place it in a well-greased flat cast-iron pot. **1989** *Sunday Times* 22 Jan. (Mag. Sect.) 49 Ester's Potbrood ... Place dough directly into well-greased, flat-bottomed potjie. Brush lid with oil and cover potjie ... Place potjie on a few well-burnt-down coals. Push some coals around potjie and place a few on the lid.

Potch /pɒtʃ/ *n.* Colloquial abbreviation of *Potchefstroom*, a town in the North-West Province; *transf.*, the university situated there. Also *attrib.*, and *comb.* **Potch-born** *adj.*

The full English name of the university is 'Potchefstroom University for Christian Higher Education'.

1978 *Sunday Times* 19 Mar. 18 Maties were first to break the ice, and Potch this week admitted a coloured student to its classrooms .. a darn sight more progress than there has been on the biggest of all Afrikaans campuses, Tukkies. **1983** *Star* 1 Mar. 2 Potch sex-party: two acquitted. **1986** *Style* Dec. 41 Potch is giving away six honorary doctorates. **1992** C. LEONARD in *Sunday Times* 16 Feb. 6 The young Potch-born Afrikaner keeps that distance.

pot dance *n. phr. Obs.* exc. *hist.* Also with initial capitals. [So called because of the use of the

ROMMELPOT in the musical accompaniment; but see also quot. 1987.] A dance performed in the past by the KHOIKHOI.

1830 MRS HODGSON in B. Shaw *Memorials* (1841) 254 My first visit to Buchnap presented my future charge to me in a truly pitiable state; for I found them engaged in what is called a *pot dance*. **1838** J.E. ALEXANDER *Exped. into Int.* II. 182 As our arrival at Niais commenced with a dance, so our sojourn there also ended with one. The pot-dance, which I had not yet seen, was performed. **1841** B. SHAW *Memorials* 26 The pot dance, in which rommel pots are made use of instead of reeds, is somewhat different and more general. **1987** B. LAU *Namibia in Jonker Afrikaner's Time* 16 Among the popular dances were those called the Pot Dance, and the Great Reed Dance. The former involved exclusively men ... A sheep was slaughtered as the men danced around the pot.

potjie /ˈpɔiki, ˈpuɪci/ *n.* [Afk., 'little pot' (see -IE).] A lidded, almost spherical cast-iron pot, made for use over an open fire; *kaffir pot (offensive)*, see KAFFIR *n.* sense 2 e; *three-legged (cooking) pot*, see THREE-LEGGED. Also *attrib.*, and *fig.*

1985 *Cape Times* 19 Aug., Have fun out of doors cooking the traditional way with a potjie. **1986** *E. Prov. Herald* 23 May 10 (*advt*) Potjie No. 2. Traditional 3 legged Cast Iron R25,99. **1986** C. KIRSTEIN *Best S. Afr. Braai Recipes* 84 Bring the milk, water and salt to the boil in a potjie over hot coals. **1987** *Weekend Post* 28 Nov. (Property Post) 11 The potjie is also widely used by the Malay population as well as the black nations in their traditional kraal environments ... The average potjie, being made of cast iron .., is subject to rusting, especially if left out on the coals overnight. **1989** H. GOOSEN in *S. Afr. Panorama* Feb. 17 Potjie cuisine is .. no novelty but dates back to the country's early history. *Ibid.* 19 The seafood potjie .. was a winner. **1989** I. JONES *Woman's World Cookbk* 61 An excellent vegetable potjie dish ... Lightly oil the potjie and layer the vegetables sprinkling each layer with the sauce. **1989** *Sunday Times* 17 Dec. 11 Chief ingredient in the Pik potjie is political savvy. Then there's tenacity, vigour, ambition. **1992** *Weekend Post* 8 Feb. (Leisure) 6, I received a *potjie* as a Christmas present, and I'm looking forward to entering the world of potjiekos cooking.

potjiekos /ˈpɔikikɔs, ˈpuɪci-/ *n.* [Afk., *potjie* (see prec.) + *kos* food.]

1. A stew cooked in a three-legged cast-iron pot over an open fire. Also *attrib.*

1985 L. SAMPSON in *Style* Feb. 100 'Come to dinner, we'll make potjiekos.' The word is rimmed with nostalgia and tradition ... The fact that it turns out to be rather a dreary stew is neither here nor there. **1985** M. DARKE in *Argus* 6 Apr. 7 Potjiekos is basically food cooked in a three-legged pot over an open fire, with the important distinction that it should never, never be stirred. **1986** [see GOGOG]. **1986** *S. Afr. Digest* 6 June [Cover], Hundreds of *potjiekos* (traditional stew) experts gathered to renew their faith in the old black pot. **1987** *Scope* 9 Oct. 14 I'm just about to stop to make a quick *potjiekos* under these *lekker* big coconut trees. **1987** *Daily Dispatch* 17 Oct. 2 It's a serious if tasty job judging a potjiekos competition. **1988** N. ABBOTT in *Personality* 27 June 38 Braaivleis has bowed to potjiekos. **1989** *Sunday Times* 22 Jan. (Mag. Sect.) 49 Potjiekos .. has been with us for centuries, but only recently has it gained wide popularity. **1992** [see POTJIE].

2. *fig.*

1989 *Sunday Times* 17 Dec. 11 Pik Botha is the potjiekos politician. Tough, homely, thoroughly indigenous, able to withstand massive heat. **1990** *E. Prov. Herald* 27 Feb. 9 An interesting new trio .. The Kerels, their music, described variously as *boerekos*-bop, *boere*-punk, or *potjiekos*-pop. **1990** *Style* May 40 He was an assimilated Afrikaner, a 'South African' rather than a Boer, proud to be just another ingredient in the spicy, colourful potjiekos of cultures and languages and races. **1991** G. SILBER in *Sunday Times* 20 Jan. (Mag. Sect.) 10 American-style Scratch 'n Break rhythms, spiced up with a potjiekos of indigenous textures and flavours, ranging from Mbaqanga to Boeremusiek .. to the Malay-accented jazz of Abdullah Ibrahim.

potleg *n. obs.* [See quot. 1913.] Pieces of cast iron used as bullets.

[**1888** D.C.F. MOODIE *Hist. of Battles & Adventures* II. 27 They used powder horns in those days, and long junks of lead or the legs of iron pots, and thus took a long time to load.] **1895** *Chambers's Jrnl* (U.K.) XII. 738 Ball or shot they rarely use, but prefer a handful of broken cast-iron potleg, which at close quarters makes a ghastly wound. **1900** *Longman's Mag.* (U.K.) Dec. 143 When the sergeant raised his officer, ragged potleg was whirring everywhere. **1911** P. GIBBON *Margaret Harding* 63 The 'pot-leg,' the Kafir bullets hammered out of cold iron, sang in the air like flutes, and made a wound when they struck that a man could put his fist into. **1913** C. PETTMAN *Africanderisms* 383 *Potlegs*, The pots used by the natives for cooking purposes are of cast iron, and stand upon three long thin legs. It was no uncommon thing in the earlier Kaffir wars for the natives to break these legs into pieces of a suitable size to use in their muzzle-loaders as bullets. [**1990** *Weekly Mail* 24 Aug. 1 The others use 'qwashas', home-made guns made from pipes. They use the legs from the three-legged (potjiekos) pots for bullets.]

potso-tsos var. BOTSOTSOS.

pou /pəʊ/ *n.* Forms: α. **p(h)ow, pou(w)**; β. **paauw, paou(w), paow, pauuw, pau(w), peau.** [S. Afr. Du. (later Afk.), transf. use of Du. *pauw* peacock.]

1. Any of several species of large bustard of the Otididae, esp.: **a.** The KORI, *Ardeotis kori*. **b.** *Neotis ludwigii*, 'Ludwig's bustard'. **c.** The *white-bellied korhaan* (see KORHAAN sense 1 b), *Eupodotis cafra*. **d.** *Neotis denhami*, 'Stanley's bustard'.

α. **1798** LADY A. BARNARD *Lett. to Henry Dundas* (1973) 135 We dined .. and had .. Johnnie's pow, stewed and then baked .. I never tasted any sort of game equal to it for delicacy and flavour. **1827** G. THOMPSON *Trav.* I. 96, I saw .. the pouw, which is a sort of large bustard, and very delicate eating. **1835** T.H. BOWKER Journal. 4 May, One of the riflemen Shot a pow for which Leslie gave him half a pound of baccy. **1856** R.E.E. WILMOT *Diary* (1984) 131 After some time the wild bustards or pouws, the magnificent secretary birds .. will oblige him to confess that South Africa yields to no country in the world for ornithological interest ... The wary pouw shows afar off in his strongly contrasting whites and browns. **1862** J.S. DOBIE *S. Afr. Jrnl* (1945) 25 Sept., Came upon some fine large bustards called by the Dutch paus (pows) and also some oribi. *c*1881 A. DOUGLASS *Ostrich Farming* 146 After some time it was discovered that the guinea-fowls, pows, corhans, fowls, and many of the small birds throughout the country had contracted the disease. **1892** *Daily News* 8 Mar. 5 Shooting in all two quagga, two koodoo, .. and a pow, .. an enormous bird, standing about 4ft. high, chiefly body. **1909** LADY S. WILSON *S. Afr. Mem.* 84 We now traversed a fine open grassy country, very desolate ... The only signs of life were various fine 'pows' .. or 'korans,' .. or a covey of guinea-fowl. **1959** *Cape Argus* 3 Jan. (Mag. Sect.) 8 Even the beginner in bird lore would not look for .. a pou in the Knysna forest. **1966** E. PALMER *Plains of Camdeboo* 33 Fanny's pot-roasted venison and pou, her van der Hum made of brandy, syrup and naartjie peel, her pickled peaches, .. are still remembered. **1975** W. STEENKAMP *Land of Thirst King* 135 A forbidden fruit one still finds in fair numbers in the North-West is the pou, or great bustard. The pou is a handsome bird and very good eating. There also happens to be a long-standing ban on hunting it.

β. **1800** G. YONGE in S.D. Naudé *Kaapse Plakkaatboek Deel V* (1950) 209 As pauws or wild peacocks are becoming extremely scarce, I do hereby order that till twelve months shall have expired .., none shall be killed or destroyed within one hundred miles of the Cape Town. **1837** 'N. POLSON' *Subaltern's Sick Leave* 118 There are many varieties of the korhaan and a few of the *paauw* or peacock as it is here called, being exactly the bustard of India. **1860** J. SANDERSON in *Jrnl of Royal Geog. Soc.* XXX. 239 We had no time to shoot a paauw or bustard, so dined off wildebeest-steaks and stew. **1872** C.A. PAYTON *Diamond Diggings* 39 The 'paauw', or Cape bustard, a fine large bird, the size of a turkey, with very strong wings, handsome plumage, and excellent eating. **1881** P. GILLMORE *Land of Boer* 245, I shot a pauw, a bird weighing over fifty pounds' weight; it is a member of the bustard family, and possesses beautiful plumage. **1898** W.C. SCULLY *Between Sun & Sand* Immense wild bustards, or, as they are called, 'paauws', come over from the Kalahari Desert in large flocks. **1915** W. EVELEIGH *S.W. Afr.* 76 There are several species of bustard, notable among them being the big Kori bustard, or Dutch pauuw, *Otis Kori*, which sometimes stands as high as 5 feet and weighs 40 pounds. **1939** S. CLOETE *Watch for Dawn* 39 To make this feast there had been a great killing: of oxen, .. of wildfowl, guineas, pauws, and pheasants. **1941** M. HIGHAM *Hsehold Cookery* 89 Paauws should be *skinned*, not plucked, as this removes an unpleasantly strong flavour. **1958** S. CLOETE *Mask* 186 He put up a giant pau, the great bustard that was common here. **1961** [see BUSHMANLAND sense 1]. **1967** O. WALKER *Hippo Poacher* 150 Tom moved off with the shot gun, and presently sighted some fine plump pauws, difficult birds to shoot but very tasty and full of meat. **1991** [see KORI].

2. With defining word: (all *obs.*) **bush pou**, KORI; **vlak(te)pou** /ˈflak(tə)-/ [Afk., *vlakte* plains], KORHAAN sense 1 a; **wild - or wilde pou** /ˈvəldə -/ [Afk., *wilde*; cf. WILD], KORI. See also GOMPOU.

β. **1907** J.P. FITZPATRICK *Jock of Bushveld* (1909) 336 There were plenty of birds — guinea-fowl, pheasant, partridge, knoorhaan and **bush pauw.** *c*1936 *S. & E. Afr. Yr Bk & Guide* 577 Birds are represented by two sorts of Bustards (gom paauw and **vlakte paauw**) three koorhaan, guinea fowl, two partridge, quail, dikkop *thick head*, geese, ducks and snipe. **1937** H. SAUER *Ex Afr.* 53 The gom paauw is the largest variety [of bustard], .. though in size he is closely approached by his cousin the vlak paauw. **1801** J. BARROW *Trav.* I. 139 A third which appeared to be by much the finest bird in South Africa .. called here the **wild pauw**, or wild peacock. **1822** W.J. BURCHELL *Trav.* I. 393 We shot a large bird of the bustard kind, which was called **Wilde Paauw** (Wild Peacock). **1834** T. PRINGLE *Afr. Sketches* 515 The Wilde Paauw (wild peacock) is a large species of Otis, about the size of the Norfolk bustard, and is esteemed the richest flavoured of all the African feathered game.

praat /prɑːt/ *v. colloq.* [Afk.]

a. *intrans.* To talk.

1920 R.Y. STORMBERG *Mrs Pieter de Bruyn* 69 Please will I praat bietje instead. **1972** P. O'BYRNE on Springbok Radio 1 Dec., I've been praating away to myself for the last twenty seconds; I forgot to switch on the mike.

b. *trans.* To speak (a language).

1977 *Sunday Times* 24 July 15 We should learn to praat die taal. **1984** *Rand Daily Mail* 9 Feb. 9 Praat Esperanto, my old China? **1984** *Pace* Oct. 174 Indians are going to talk-talk Indian. Coloureds are going to praat-praat coloured ... there'll be no African voice.

praiser *n.* Also with initial capital. [Special sense of general Eng.] IMBONGI sense 1.

1836 [see IMBONGI sense 1]. **1855** J.W. COLENSO *Ten Weeks in Natal* 107 The 'praisers' are rushing here and there, chattering, with foaming lips, the honours of their chief. *a*1873 J. BURROW *Trav. in Wilds* (1971) 74 The Chief never stirred without his 'praisers', namely, those men who did nothing but extol him until they fell foaming at the mouth like so many madmen. **1888** [see IMBONGI sense 1]. **1904** D. KIDD *Essential Kafir* 92 All chiefs keep a Court Praiser, whose business it is to go in front of the chief and sing his praises. **1913** [see IMBONGI sense 1]. **1937** G.P. LESTRADE in I. Schapera *Bantu-Speaking Tribes* 299 A praiser .. may .. alter the order .. of stanzas. **1953** LANHAM & MOPELI-PAULUS *Blanket Boy's Moon* 83 He was now a well-known man, both as a 'praiser' and as a merchant. **1968** T. COPE *Izibongo: Zulu Praise Poems* 26 When a man of distinction is rewarded for his services by the chief .. he .. establishes a great kraal and appoints a personal praiser, who will collect .. and perfect his praises, so that they constitute what we call a 'praise-poem'. **1983** *Rand Daily Mail* 26 May 9 The praiser's duty was to extol his chief and confound his enemies with a licence that had no regard for truth or even possibility.

predikant /prɪədəˈkant/ *n.* Also **predekant, predicant, predikaant.** Pl. **-s,** ‖**-e** /-ə/. [Afk., earlier Du., preacher, minister, fr. L. *praedicans, praedicantem,* pres. ppl. of *praedicare* to proclaim, to cry in public, in late and medieval L. 'to preach'. (In former times *predicant* was used also in Brit. Eng.).] **a.** A minister of a Dutch Reformed church; DOMINEE sense 2 a; LEERAAR. **b.** Used before a name, as a title; DOMINEE sense 2 b ii. Also *transf.*

1821 *Missionary Notices* 22 They are very respectful to me, and always honour me with the appellation which they give their own ministers, viz. 'Predicant.' **1833** *Cape of G.H. Lit. Gaz.* 1 Mar. 37 The *predicant,* who had unfortunately lent himself to the oppressions of the Company, now plied them with religious advice. **1835** G. CHAMPION *Jrnl* (1968) 13 We were at the Paarl on the occasion of choosing a precentor in the Dutch church. This like that of the Predikant (or preacher) is a salaried office & is for life. **1849** R. MOFFAT in *Daily News* (24 Feb. 1900) 6 They have a measure of religious knowledge culled from the Bible and their itinerant predikants. **1851** R. GRAY *Jrnl of Bishop's Visitation* II. 14 They cannot believe that a predikant would walk ... It is in vain to tell tham that our Lord and Master and His holy apostles walked ... They know that predikants don't walk. **1868** W.R. THOMSON *Poems, Essays & Sketches* 169 'The *juts* or the *predikant* said so,' forecloses all thought or argument. **1882** C.L. NORRIS-NEWMAN *With Boers in Tvl* 191 Next day being Sunday, service was held in the open air, and a sermon preached by a Dutch predikant. **1890** A. MARTIN *Home Life* 272 The *predikant* is a great man indeed throughout the widespread circle of his parishioners, and to offend him .. means to be boycotted. **1900** B. MITFORD *Aletta* 2 On one side of him sat 'Mynheer', as the local *predikant,* or minister, is commonly known among his flock. **1903** [see *Dopper Church* (DOPPER *n.*[1] sense b)]. **1915** D. FAIRBRIDGE *Torch Bearer* 308 The Cape huis-vrouw is a hospitable and generous soul, and the predikant of a district is at all times kept well supplied with the good things of this life by his flock. **1919** M. GREENLEES tr. *O.F. Mentzel's Life at Cape in Mid-18th C.* 68 He intended to call upon Predikant Beck, but he did not find him at home. **1926** R. CAMPBELL in *Voorslag* July 17, I believe that the power behind the universe is something better than an omnipotent old parson or predikant with a colour prejudice and a dirty puritanical mind. **1934** [see LANDDROST sense 2]. **1943** 'J. BURGER' *Black Man's Burden* 240 In the days of Milner and the Anglo-Boer war the *Predikante* (ministers) were the leaders of the Boers in their resistance against British rule, and they were cordially hated and reviled for their pains by Milner ... To-day, however, the Church is not united, and the *Predikante* firebrands lead a minority of the South African people in a crusade for Afrikaner independence. **1956** D. JACOBSON *Dance in Sun* 92 You've got no vices. You should have been a predikant. **1965** [see DOMINEE sense 2 a]. **1972** J. PACKER *Boomerang* 90 Ma, you talk like a predikant. In a minute you'll tell me to kneel down and pray for humility and courage! **1984** *Probe* Nov. 4 The United Congregation Church predikant. **1982** D. TUTU *Voice of One* 33 Woe betide the religious leader when he has the temerity to criticise a particular political status quo. He then runs the gauntlet of harsh criticism – for being a political predikant. **1990** R. STENGEL *January Sun* 65 The new MP, .. a quiet, scholarly former predikant, believes the present Nationalist government is preparing to give power away to the blacks.

Hence **predikantess** *n. nonce,* the wife of a predikant.

1920 R.Y. STORMBERG *Mrs Pieter de Bruyn* 20 Mrs Van Rooyen, the predikantess, is a sweet, beautiful character; her husband a rigid, uncompromising, pitiless latter-day Calvin.

‖**preekstoel** /ˈprɪəkstʊl/ *n.* [Afk. (ad. Du. *predikstoel*), *preek* preach + *stoel* chair.] A pulpit.

[**1812** A. PLUMPTRE tr. *H. Lichtenstein's Trav. in Sn Afr.* (1928) I. 207 A high and remarkable rock, which, on account of its resemblance to a pulpit, is called by the herdsmen the *Predikstoel.*] **1817** G. BARKER Journal. 31 Mar., Held no school, worked for the church, began a Preek Stoel. *Ibid.* 2 Apr., Finished the Preek Stoel today and occupied it in the evening. **1950** H.C. BOSMAN in L. Abrahams *Jurie Steyn's Post Office* (1971) 55 A preekstoel, the place where Dominee Welthagen was to stand. **1955** W. ILLSLEY *Wagon on Fire* 99 The deacons filed out of the vestry to occupy semi-circular pews on either side of the preek-stoel. They were followed by an elder who bore his Bible into the preek-stoel. [**1957** L.G. GREEN *Beyond City Lights* 18 Always I visit a natural pillar surrounded by water ... The cottage folk call it the Preekstoel. It stands up from the shallows like a stone exclamation mark, but it does also resemble a pulpit.] **1959** E. MPHAHLELE *Down Second Ave* (1965) 129 Pastor Paulen's disciplinary code under which he pronounced damnation from his preekstoel – pulpit – for sinners.

premier grand cru /ˌpremɪə grɑːŋ ˈcrʊ/ *n. phr.* Also with initial capitals. [Reordering of Fr., *premier cru* 'first growth' (used in general Eng. to designate a wine of the best quality) + *grand* great.] See quots 1993; GRAND CRU. See also CAPE WINE.

1981 *Signature* Jan. 9 Premier grand cru .. was conjured up to describe a certain type of wine and was devised by Bellingham ... In the South African context premier grand cru indicates a good quality dry white blended wine ... It seems that chenin blanc is the most popular cultivar used for our premier grand cru's, with certain exceptions where colombar is preferred. **1985** *Avenue* May 12 Many of our Premier Grand Crus mightn't be so popular if the public knew that under the fancy French hide a variety of very indifferent grape types. However erroneous the title Premier Grand Cru, it does sound a whole lot better than 'a blend of clairette blanche and groendruif'. **1988** D. HUGHES et al. *Complete Bk of S. Afr. Wine* 329 *Premier Grand Cru* .. This wine should be as dry as vinification techniques allow. *c***1993** J. PLATTER *S. Afr. Wine Guide* 15 *Premier Grand Cru,* Unlike in France, not an officially recognised rating in South Africa, simply a dry white. *Ibid.* 299 *Premier Grand Cru*: In local terms not a 'first great growth' but a style of wine – very dry, light-bodied, nearly always a blend.

prescribed area *n. phr. Hist.* See quot.

*c***1970** C. DESMOND *Discarded People* 13 *Prescribed Area,* An area prescribed in the Government Gazette; in practice any area which is considered to be a white area, but where a large number of Africans live and work.

President's Council *n. phr. Hist.*

Also abbrev., see PC *n.*[2].

a. A multi-racial body of 60 members (nominated as representatives of the various ethnic groups), created in 1980 to act as an advisory council for the State President. Also *attrib.*

1980 S. JENKINS in *Rand Daily Mail* 19 June 9 You see constitutional commissions, President's Councils, consultative procedures with blacks, the olive branch held out to Buthelezi, and so on, while at the same time you introduce tougher Terrorism Acts, or ban more people, or ruthlessly suppress demonstrations and marches, or introduce laws to control the Press. **1980** [see NON-BLACK *n.*]. **1981** *Rand Daily Mail* 27 May 12 The President's Council has been a non-starter, rejected by the official Opposition as well as representative coloured, Indian and Black leaders. **1981** *Daily Dispatch* 22 Sept. 4 Far-reaching powers, including the right to subpoena witnesses to testify before it, are to be conferred on the President's Council. **1981** *E. Prov. Herald* 13 Oct. 1 Labour backs leader's President's Council stand.

b. Under the TRICAMERAL constitution of 1983: a body of 60 members (of whom 25 were nominated and 35 elected) with certain legislative powers, such as the ratification of legislation.

The President's Council ceased to exist when the transitional Constitution came into effect in 1994.

1983 C.W. EGLIN in *Hansard* 16 May 7353 The President's Council, which alone can make a final and binding decision on matters of dispute between the three Houses, is dominated by the NP caucus and the NP's President. **1983** R.B. MILLER in *Ibid.* 16 May 7314 We would like to see a change in the formula for representation of elected members to the President's Council ... Instead of being elected by the majority of the House of Representatives and the House of Deputies, .. it would be preferable to have proportional representation in respect of the representation of the different parties. **1983** *Govt Gaz.* Vol.219 No.8914, 50 The President's Council shall at the request of the State President advise him on any matter referred to it by the State President for its advice, and may, in its discretion, advise him on any matter (excluding draft legislation) which, in its opinion, is of public interest. **1986** *E. Prov. Herald* 20 June 4 The President's Council met briefly yesterday ... President P W Botha is bound by the decision of the council, but since it has a built-in National Party majority, it is virtually certain to approve the Bills in the form approved by the white House of Assembly. **1987** G. CARPENTER *Intro. to S. Afr. Constit. Law* 317 The President's Council which was established in 1980 was a purely advisory body appointed entirely by the State President ... It was in essence nothing more or less than a permanent commission ... The President's Council constituted under the 1983 Constitution differs both in composition and in function. There are still 60 members, but only 25 of these are nominated by the State President. Ten of these so-called State President's nominees are .. appointed by opposition parties in the three houses ... The remaining fifteen members are appointed by the State President acting in conjunction with the executive. **1992** P. CULL in *Weekend Post* 24 Oct. 20 Dominated by the National Party there is little doubt the President's Council will obey its master's voice, and ensure that the legislation is signed and on the Statute Book in time.

Hence **President's Councillor** *n. phr.,* one serving on the President's Council.

1981 *Voice* 11 Oct. 15 Fringe benefits for President's Councillors include a pension scheme, accident insurance, transport facilities, parking and tax-free expense allowances. **1987** *E. Prov. Herald* 9 Oct. 8 Mr Colin Eglin admits the loss of two parliamentarians and a President's Councillor is a setback for the PFP.

Pretoria /prəˈtɔːrɪə/ *n.* [Named for the Voortrekker leader *Andries Pretorius* (1798–1853).] The name of the city (in Gauteng Province) which is the country's executive and administrative capital.

1. By metonymy: the Government. Also *attrib.* See also BOER sense 7.

Quot. 1899 refers to the government of the former Transvaal Republic.

1899 T. FROES *Expelled from Randt* 14 Peddling 'Peruvian' Jews were mulcted in sums from £10 downwards .. and compelled to contribute to the Pretoria war chest. **1913** M.M. CLEAVER *Young S. Afr.* 2 He was reported to Pretoria for having spoken unprofessionally of his Superiors in the Department. **1936** *Cambridge Hist. of Brit. Empire* VIII. 598 Pretoria accused Downing Street of putting forward new terms. **1944** [see KHAKI *n.* sense 1 a]. **1963** M. BENSON *Afr. Patriots* 128 The 4,000 'sat down and there were cat calls and threats. Then, acting on instructions from Pretoria (the Government), the police drew their batons and charged.' **1976** *Progress* Oct. 7 If the average company were run the way Pretoria has recently been managing the South African economy, it would have been insolvent long ago. **1979** *Cape Times* 1 Jan. 6 A Pretoria decision to shipwreck the UN plan in South West Africa .. would destroy any chance of a new understanding between South Africa and the West. **1982** [see BOER sense 7]. **1985** *Financial Mail* 18

Jan. 33 Is it not time that Pretoria stopped blaming the falling gold price and the weather for the country's economic ills? **1985** 'DE-KAFFIRNATED STAN' in *Drum* Sept., The wheels of Pretoria are trundling as ponderously as ever in the direction of phasing out discrimination. **1986** [see *Times* quot. at EMINENT PERSONS GROUP]. **1991** S. MACLEOD in *Time* 5 Aug. 10 As Pretoria quickly admitted, Inkatha and an allied labor union had received more than $600,000. The disclosure caused an uproar.

2. Special Comb. **Pretoria Minute**, an agreement published on 6 August 1990 by the National Party and the African National Congress after talks in Pretoria, including matters such as the suspension of the ANC's armed struggle, and an undertaking by the state to dismantle white minority domination, release political prisoners, and allow the repatriation of exiles; also *attrib.*

1990 *Sunday Times* 12 Aug. 7 We find the office abuzz. This is the first day of the Pretoria Minute and the first day after the suspension of the armed struggle. *Ibid.* 16 There is an unfortunate tendency to regard events such as the crafting of the Pretoria Minute as frozen moments in our history ... The Minute is only one stage in a long journey ... Dries van Heerden calls for the centrists in South Africa to take a stand against the demands of the extremists in the post-Pretoria Minute era. **1990** *New African* 13 Aug. 6 What does the Pretoria Minute really mean? How does it affect the struggle for liberation? **1990** *Weekly Mail* 14 Sept. 8 The expected return of 30 000–100 000 exiles in the wake of the Pretoria Minute. **1991** J. KANE-BERMAN in *Race Rel. News* (S.A.I.R.R.) Apr. 23 One can only express the hope, the prayer, that the various peace pacts hold: the Groote Schuur Minute, the Pretoria Minute, and .. the recent peace pact between the ANC and the Inkatha Freedom Party.

So **Pretorian** *n.*, a citizen of Pretoria; **Pretorian** *adj.*, of or pertaining to Pretoria, to the central government, or (*obs.*) to the government of the former Transvaal Republic.

1880 G.F. AUSTEN *Diary* (1981) 8 She carried the bundle triumphantly to its destination, no doubt much to the edification and amusement of the Pretorians. **1896** M.A. CAREY-HOBSON *At Home in Tvl* 431 Pilfering continually going on in the gardens of the Pretorian erfholders. **1900** 'ONE WHO WAS IN IT' *Kruger's Secret Service* 6 Mysterious talk of some movements to be initiated against the corruption and tyranny of the Pretorian oligarchy. **1975** *Sunday Times* 27 July 20 It has taken 10 years .. for Pretorians to reach such a pitch of righteous indignation .. and develop an un-Pretorian taste for protest. **1987** *Cosmopolitan* Dec. 210 Pretorians have a reputation for being dedicated 'ravers'. Many Johannesburgers drive the 50-odd km to party in Pretoria rather than in the Golden City.

Pretoriastroika /prəˈtɔːrɪəˌstrɔɪkə/ *n.* [Formed by analogy with Russian *perestroika* restructuring.] A term coined by journalists for the political change and accommodation initiated in South Africa in February 1990.

1990 *Sunday Times* 30 Sept. 22 The tentative move by the World Bank to become involved in some development projects in South Africa is one of the first visible pay-offs for Pretoriastroika. **1990** *Ibid.* 30 Dec. 1 Thanks to President de Klerk's commitment to Pretoriastroika, there will be no predicted bloody revolution in South Africa. **1990** *Weekly Mail* 21 Dec. (Suppl.) 17 This was the year of Pretoriastroika. Good intentions twinkled across the country. **1991** *Weekend Argus* 26 Jan. 1 Stunning events have gripped South Africa. Some people call it *Pretoriastroika* for it is a revolution of sorts – likened to the astounding changes and ferment which President Mikhail Gorbachev launched in the Soviet Union and elsewhere.

Pride of De Kaap /- də ˈkɑːp/ *n. phr.* [Named for the *De Kaap* valley, in the Lowveld; see quot. 1985.] The lowveld bauhinia, *Bauhinia galpinii* of the Leguminosae, a showy shrub or rambler bearing a profusion of red flowers.

1913 C. PETTMAN *Africanderisms* 385 Pride of de Kaap, *Bauhinia Galpini* ... A scrambling leguminous bush or climber, bearing a profusion of scarlet flowers, very common in the Kaap valley, Barberton, is known by this name. **1917** R. MARLOTH *Common Names* 68 *Pride of De Kaap, Bauhinia Galpinii*. A shrub with showy crimson flowers, easily cultivated. **1966** C.A. SMITH *Common Names* 377 *Pride-of-De Kaap*, A small arborescent shrub or occasionally a scrambler or a twiner on taller plants, with a profusion of large showy red flowers. Now frequently met in cultivation as a trellis or hedge plant. **1985** S. *Afr. Panorama* Dec. 15 Its common name, pride of De Kaap, refers to the subtropical De Kaap valley near Nelspruit in the Eastern Transvaal where it is most abundant. *B. galpinii* was named after Dr E. E. Galpin, formerly an amateur botanist of the Transvaal Bushveld ... The petals vary in colour from pale orange to flame red. **1991** H. HUTCHINGS in *Weekend Post* 16 Mar. (Leisure) 7 The *Bauhinia galpinii* .. has made a lovely showing this year. Commonly known as Pride of de Kaap, this species is found growing profusely in the Kaap valley near Barberton. It thrives in most parts of South Africa.

Pride of Table Mountain *n. phr.* [See quot. 1888.] The rare and beautiful red disa *Disa uniflora* of the Orchidaceae; its carmine flowers; *red disa*, see DISA sense b; also called DISA (sense a).

1869 R. NOBLE *Cape & its People* 261 Singly or in masses, the 'Pride of Table Mountain', fondly named so by Capeites, is a magnificent representative of Flora, and many are the pilgrimages made to her shrine on the top of the mountain during the flowering season. **1887** [see MOEDERKAPPIE]. **1888** H. BOLUS *Orchids of Cape Peninsula* (1918) 147 The colour of the side sepals is a brilliant carmine, the remaining parts blush-coloured, with delicate carmine veins on the inside of the back sepal, and bright orange tints on the upper part of the petals ... The name which has been given to it, the 'Pride of Table Mountain,' indicates the honour in which it is held. It is indeed the queen of terrestrial orchids in the Southern Hemisphere. **1913** [see DISA sense a]. **1925** F.C. SLATER *Shining River* 233 *Disa*, A genus of orchids widely spread in the more humid parts of South Africa. *Disa uniflora* is 'the pride of Table Mountain'. **1966** C.A. SMITH *Common Names* 378 *Pride-of-Table-Mountain, Disa uniflora* (Cape) ... Regarded as the finest flower on Table Mountain. **1970** *Personality* 24 Sept. 65 There are 20 species of disa but the best known is the red disa or 'The Pride of Table Mountain' ... It is the rarest and richest of all. **1981** S. *Afr. Panorama* Aug. 49 Of the 434 indigenous South African orchids, over 100 are Disa species. *Disa uniflora*, 'The Pride of Table Mountain', is the most beautiful of all. **1981** [see DISA sense a]. **1985** A. TREDGOLD *Bay between Mountains* 16 The Pride of Table Mountain, the red disa, finds its home there too in the False Bay mountains in damp shady places.

prime *n.* Ostrich-farming. [Perh. fr. Eng. *primary* (*wing-feather*), or absol. use of adj. (see quot. 1881).] A long, pure white feather of the highest quality, taken from the wing of a cock ostrich; WHITE *n.* sense 1. See also BLOOD, BYOCK, FEATHER sense a, WING.

[c**1881** A. DOUGLASS *Ostrich Farming* 80 The sorter will first take in hand the cock's quill feathers; these he will – feather by feather – sort first into heaps consisting of prime whites.] **1896** R. WALLACE *Farming Indust. of Cape Col.* 234 White primes and bloods, superior cut or light quills .. £6.10.0 to £9.10.0 per lb. **1910** A.B. LAMONT *Rural Reader* 144 First in importance come the white feathers on the wings. These fetch the best price, and are known as 'primes'. **1911** O. EVANS in S. Playne *Cape Col.* 55 The process of clipping consists merely of cutting first the long white feathers, known as 'primes', which grow in a single row on the wing. **1930** M.F. WORMSER Ostrich Industry. 11 The whites and feminas grow in a single row at the outside edge of the wing ... The primes or whites of the cock are of a superior quality to the feminas of the hen, the latter not being a pure white and often fringed with grey. **1956** P.J. BOTHA in *Farmer's Weekly* 14 Mar., The market for the aristocrat of feathers – wing 'primes' – is still in the doldrums. **1968** J. LE ROUX in F. Goldie *Ostrich Country* 57 Because one knows what primes were worth in the old days, one always hopes. **1973** D.J. MAREE in *Std Encycl. of Sn Afr.* VIII. 398 The highest price for selected primes (whites) recorded on the London market before 1914 was £112 per lb.

prison farm *n. phr.* [Eng.] A farm run by the Department of Correctional Services and worked by prisoners who are employed during working hours and confined under prison conditions at night.

Also *U.S. Eng.*

1953 A. MOGALE in *Drum* Apr. 36 The last time you heard from me I was doing compulsory labour on some prison farm. **1971** *Area Handbk for Rep. of S. Afr.* (American Univ., Washington) 720 In the 1960's the trend in new prison construction favored .. prison centres or complexes, each containing a reception center, a maximum security capability, and a prison farm. **1974** *Farmer's Weekly* 20 Mar. 25 This prison farm in the picturesque Cape rehabilitates its inmates using 'agricultural therapy' ... An environment has been created in the form of prison farms to provide a 'work climate' .. with the emphasis on training which can be utilised successfully after release. **1982** E. *Prov. Herald* 31 Dec. 3 The South African Prison Services and the South African Police remain silent on the probe into the death of three prisoners at the Barberton Prison Farm on Wednesday. **1983** *Daily Dispatch* 7 Sept. 2 A Barberton Prison Farm convict said yesterday that .. he had been beaten up by warders during the day. **1987** M. POLAND *Train to Doringbult* 127 'Nazambane?' 'The prison farm. Far away. You will work till the heat of the sun boils your blood.'

Prize Negro *n. phr. Obs. exc. hist.* Also with small initials. [Eng. *prize* taken in war + *Negro* African.] A black African from beyond South Africa's borders, who, having been rescued from a slave-ship, was 'released' at the Cape and indentured to a colonist as a labourer. See also APPRENTICE *n.*

1824 S. *Afr. Jrnl* I. 84 One hundred and eighty are slaves; fifteen are apprentices (or Prize Negroes); and four are Hottentots. **1827** *Reports of Commissioners upon Finances at Cape of G.H.* II. 75 The prize negroes indentured for fourteen years, may in general be considered to have been as great a source of profit to their masters as slaves. **1868** J. CHAPMAN *Trav.* II. 182 Their [*sc.* the people of Mazhanga's] language is .. very like that spoken by most of the prize negroes brought from the east coast to the Cape. c**1963** *Stellenbosch: Oldest Village in S. Afr.* (brochure) 8 The well-known D.R. Minister Meent Borcherds included in his memoirs a detailed description of the village as he knew it in 1825 .. the population .. consisting of 774 Christians, 144 Hottentots, 852 slaves, 22 prize negroes and 64 free blacks.

pro-apartheid /ˌprəʊəˈpɑːtheɪt/ *adj.* [Eng. *pro-* favouring, siding with + APARTHEID.] Supportive of apartheid.

1972 *Drum* 22 Mar. 14 Managing editor of the now defunct pro-apartheid magazine *Africa South*. **1978** *Sunday Times* 26 Mar. 6 Mr De G— was angered by a hostile reception on arrival from black students accusing France of being pro-apartheid. **1984** S. ZUNGU in *Pace* Oct. 63 President of the pro-apartheid African Foundation.

pro-Boer /prəʊˈbʊə, prəʊˈbuːr/ *adj.* and *n.* [Eng. *pro-* favouring, siding with + BOER.]

A. *adj.* Supportive of the Boer cause (esp. during the ANGLO-BOER WAR of 1899–1902).

1896 *Daily News* 22 Apr. 5 If it were indeed a necessity of the situation to be pro-Boer or pro-British then as Britons we should be for the British. **1909** H.E.S. FREMANTLE *New Nation* p.xvi, It would hardly be an exaggeration to say that we are all pro-British and all pro-Boer. **1939** M. RORKE *Melina Rorke* 250 The whole of

South Africa was molten with pro-English or pro-Boer sentiment, which might burst forth at any moment into a gigantic conflagration. **1955** D.L. HOBMAN *Olive Schreiner* 124 Even in England Lloyd-George had to be secretly hustled out of a side door of the Birmingham Town Hall in order to avoid the angry crowd after a pro-Boer speech. **1987** G. VINEY *Col. Houses* 144 Robinson had been 'unhelpful' and, worse, 'pro-Boer'. **1990** M. NICOL *Powers that Be* 109 The modest John Sainsbury, gold digger, pro-Boer sympathiser.

B. *n.* A supporter of the Boer cause.

1902 W.C. SCULLY *Harrow* 65 The Pro-Boers, who, be it remembered, did not label themselves – were they not treated under martial law with the same ignorant malignity that characterised the proceedings of the Inquisition? [**1922** J. GALSWORTHY *Forsyte Saga* 604 'Pro-Boer!' The word still rankled.] **1955** D.L. HOBMAN *Olive Schreiner* 123 Englishmen who took their side, pro-Boers, could not but appear as traitors in the eyes of their patriotic countrymen.

Hence **pro-Boerism** *n.*, support of the Boers.

1900 *Dundee Advertiser* (U.K.) 23 Aug. 4 Lord Rosslyn brings the novel charge of pro-Boerism against us.

proclaim *v. trans. Hist.* [Special sense of general Eng.] To designate (a defined area) as reserved exclusively for one particular ethnic group in terms of the *Group Areas Act* (see GROUP AREA *n. phr.* sense 2 a); ZONE. Usu. *passive*. See also REPROCLAIM, UNPROCLAIMED. Cf. DEPROCLAIM.

1953 *Off. Yrbk of Union 1950* (Bureau of Census & Statistics) 776 It may be mentioned expressly that no group area can be proclaimed anywhere until some time after the Act has been brought into operation. **1955** E. DE S. BRUNNER in *Pol. Science Quarterly* Sept. 375 A commission 'proclaims' an area for white or African or Asiatic. **1970** J. PACKER *Veronica* 12 The conversion had been cleverly accomplished when the area, which had till fairly recently been coloured, was proclaimed white. **1987** *New Nation* 25 June 5 The Group Areas Act is about to destroy one of South Africa's few remaining racially integrated communities, nearly 37 years after the hated Act was passed. Kleinskool, Port Elizabeth's only settlement of African and coloured residents, was this week proclaimed a coloured group area.

So **proclaimed** *ppl adj.*, designated for a particular ethnic group under the Group Areas Act; **proclamation** *n.*, such designation of an area.

1953 *Off. Yrbk of Union 1950* (Bureau of Census & Statistics) 777 *The defined area* is an area defined by proclamation. *Ibid.* 778 Interim measures which should .. lead up to the proclamation of group areas. **1963** WILSON & MAFEJE *Langa* 182 In 1926 the municipal area of Cape Town was declared a 'proclaimed area' in terms of section 12 of Act 21 of 1923. **1970** *Daily News* 1 June (*letter*), Those whose homes have not been proclaimed yet, dread proclamation. They fear the area will go White. **1971** *Evening Post* 5 June 6 The authorities, he said, had told him he could get only a temporary permit for her to be in the proclaimed area of Uitenhage. **1982** *Cape Times* 23 Dec. 3 As Crossroads is a 'non-proclaimed area', Dr Toms explained that he didn't need a permit to be in the area. **1989** *Reader's Digest Illust. Hist.* 371 In terms of this legislation farmers in 'proclaimed' areas could transform squatters into labour tenants and extend compulsory labour service from 90 to 180 days.

pro Deo /ˌprəʊ ˈdeɪəʊ/ *adv. phr.* and *adj. phr. Law.* [L., 'for God'.]

A. *adv. phr.* With reference to the legal representation of one accused of a capital offence and unable to afford counsel: with no charge, legal costs being paid by the State at the instruction of the court; loosely, (defending one) without the usual fee. Also *transf.*, referring to other services rendered without charge.

1919 M.M. STEYN *Diary* 280 We had a proper jury, usher, policeman, counsel for the prisoner, who, of course, was defended pro deo, and public prosecutor. **1948** A. PATON *Cry, Beloved Country* 123 Did you not hear him say he would take the case *pro deo*? .. It is Latin, and it means for God. So it will cost you nothing, or at least very little. **1957** B. O'KEEFE *Gold without Glitter* 86 The young counsel who defended him *pro deo* put up a determined defence. **1974** A.P. BRINK *Looking on Darkness* 11 'Did *they* hire you?' I asked. 'I've been appointed Pro Deo ...' 'I didn't ask for counsel.' 'But the law demands it ... It's a matter of procedure. I'm taking your case Pro Deo.' **1980** *Informant, Grahamstown* We [*sc.* medical practitioners] always treat the clergy pro deo. **1983** F.G. BUTLER *Bursting World* 111 Was it a difficult or an expensive operation? No, if I wanted to get myself into shape for the army he'd do it *pro Deo* or, correcting himself, *pro patria*. **1983** *Cape Times* 29 Dec. 1 The couple have been defended by counsel appointed *pro Deo*, all of whom were in court yesterday. **1987** M. POLAND *Train to Doringbult* 219 'Who's paying for this, by the way?' said Elizabeth ... 'No one. *Pro Deo*.' 'Who'd work *Pro Deo* in this day and age?' said Captain Olivier.

B. *adj. phr.* Of or pertaining to legal representation where the fee is paid by the State at the instruction of the court.

1962 A. FUGARD *Notebks* (1983) 50 Found him, feet up on his desk, reading a novel. He's been in practice for about four months and his only real cases have been *pro-deo*. **1974** A.P. BRINK *Looking on Darkness* 11 Some Pro Deo advocates regard their cases as a matter of routine and assume that they've lost before they've even started. **1979** *E. Prov. Herald* 6 Apr. 2 While junior counsel might be able to handle pro Deo murder cases, they would experience difficulties with complicated terrorism cases ... Senior members of the Bar had on occasions taken on pro Deo work. **1989** *E. Prov. Herald* 8 June 3 A murder trial was postponed for the third time this week yesterday when it was found that there was no pro Deo counsel available in Port Elizabeth or Grahamstown. **1992** *Natal Mercury* 25 Nov. 3 Mr A– V–, pro deo counsel for Mrs C–, asked that .. the Court should impose a sentence as 'light as possible'.

Prog /prɒg/ *n. colloq.* [Shortened form of PROGRESSIVE.] A member of the liberal-democratic Progressive Party (1959–1975) and its successors the Progressive Reform Party (see PRP) (1975–1977), the Progressive Federal Party (see PFP) (1977–89), and the Democratic Party (see DP *n.*[2]); anyone with similar views; PROGRESSIVE sense 3 b. Also *attrib.* passing into *adj.*, of or pertaining to these parties.

1966 *Argus* 27 Sept. 4 'Exclusion' will not kill Progs. **1969** *Rand Daily Mail* 20 Oct. 1 Progs will stand for 20 seats. **1970** *News/Check* 4 Sept. 9 He is fluent in both languages, something which cannot always be said for Prog and United Party candidates. **1972** *Sunday Times* 27 Feb. 4 A man stands as an Independent and then everybody sets out to prove that he's a crypto-Nat or a Prog in disguise. **1973** [see NAT *n.* sense a]. **1977** *Guardian Weekly* (U.K.) 11 Dec. 7 Liberal-minded South Africans cheered their favoured Progressive Federal Party .. the 'progs', as they are locally termed. **1980** *Rand Daily Mail* 14 Nov. 8 Does the Prog Party propose a federal constitution for South Africa? **1981** *Sunday Times* 22 Nov. 27 'Obie' .. talks of 'Prog gevaar' rather than 'swart gevaar'. **1983** *Frontline* May 36 In white SA, if a man is a Nat, say, then he's not a Prog. **1987** *Daily Dispatch* 22 Oct. 15 Mr Cronje said there were 'two types of Progs' – those who had genuine commitment to reach out to blacks and those who merely made overtures. **1990** G. FYSH in *Weekend Post* 5 May 11, I remember how the Nationalists not just rejected, but mocked everything the Progs were saying; how they assured them the whites would never accept their policies and that separation was the only way to go. **1991** K. OWEN in *Sunday Times* 8 Sept. 17 DP leader Zach de Beer says the Nationalist constitutional plan includes all the main ideas put forward in the past by his party and its predecessors. If so, I'm thankful I have never been a Prog.

Progressive *n. hist.* Also with small initials. [An element in the names of the parties or movements.]

1. A member of the Progressive Party of the Cape, which was formed in the late 1890s and became the Union Party in 1908. Also *attrib.*, of the party or its members. See also UNIONIST.

1898 A. MILNER in C. Headlam *Milner Papers* (1931) I. 277 A solid 'Progressive' Opposition of 38 or 39 would make the tenure of a Bond Ministry an extremely precarious one. **1898** P.A. MOLTENO *Sel. from Correspondence* (1981) 67 He is no real progressive, and all Garrett's talk is merely so much chaff to catch and use the progressives now that the Bond refuses to be used any more by Rhodes. **1904** G. SPRIGG in *Cape Times* 4 Dec., A considerable number of those who call themselves Progressives hampered us very much in the passage of that Bill. **1913** [see UNIONIST]. **1936** *Cambridge Hist. of Brit. Empire* 616 At the general election which followed early in 1904 the Progressives, under the leadership of Dr Jameson, were returned to power. **1983** C. SAUNDERS *Hist. Dict.* 140 In the 1898 election there were for the first time two well-defined parties, with colony-wide constituency organizations, opposing each other. After the election the Progressives formed the opposition, led by Sir Gordon Sprigg.

2. Usu. in *pl.*: Collectively, the members of the Progressive Association of the Transvaal, a political party representing the interests of the wealthier English-speaking residents of the Transvaal before Union.

1909 F. CANA *S. Afr. from Gt Trek to Union* 229 The intention of the Government to grant the Transvaal a Constitution was announced in Parliament on the 21st of July, and was followed by a great political activity among the Boers and the Progressives. **1909** R.H. BRAND *Union of S. Afr.* 120 The Progressives in the Cape and the Transvaal are the British parties. **1982** R. DE VILLIERS in *Cape Times* 13 Apr. 8 The Unionist Party, an amalgamation formed in 1910 and led by Jameson of the Transvaal Progressives, the Cape Unionists and the Orange River Constitutional Party.

3.a. In the phr. ***Progressive Group***, that group of United Party members of Parliament who broke away and formed the Progressive Party in 1959.

1961 H. OPPENHEIMER in A. Hocking *Oppenheimer & Son* (1973) 359 After careful consideration of the issues involved .. I find myself in general sympathy with the Progressive Group. **1971** *Progress* May 5 There had been talk of a split for a long time; the Press had even coined the term the 'Progressive Group' of the United Party.

b. PROG.

1977 *Daily Dispatch* 5 Oct. 1 All he is doing, in effect, is making the Progressives the official opposition – and spending R2 million of the taxpayers money in doing so. **1991** A. VAN WYK *Birth of New Afrikaner* 110 The very shape of things makes me see a vision of myself in a vast crowd ... former Nats and Saps, Progressives, DPs and perhaps a few CPs too; former haters of blacks, Afrikaner hairy-backs, Boer-Haters, British-haters, lovers of blacks.

pronk /prɔŋk, prɒŋk/ *n.* Pl. **-s**, or (formerly) **-en**. [Afk., transf. use of Du. *pronk* prank.] A leap, bound, or prance; the characteristic display of the springbok (see PRONK *v.* sense 2).

[**1889** H.A. BRYDEN *Kloof & Karroo* 226 The antelopes became disturbed, and began those extraordinary saltatory accomplishments ('pronken,' the Boers term them), from which they take their name. **1897** — *Nature & Sport* 197 Here .. is another band suddenly startled into a leaping fit – 'pronken' (pranks) the Boers well call these displays.] **1913** C. PETTMAN *Africanderisms* 386 When making these bounds, *pronken*, this white hair, which at other times is well-nigh hidden, is made to look like a large plume laid along the back. **1970** C. KINSLEY *Informant, Koegasbrug (N. Cape)* Pronk. Prancing of a horse or Springbok. **1972** *Daily Dispatch* 27 July 1 The Afrikaans name means the 'jumping buck' and this leap is part of a display known as 'pronk'. **1981** H. THESEN in *Outeniqualander* 25 June 9 More often, it is sheer speed and grace that leaves one silent with wonder; the wild joyous leaps and then the stiff legged bounce ending in that great, arched-neck bound, back crest flaring, the famous 'pronk' so characteristic but always so magnificent.

pronk *v.* [Afk. *pronk* to show off, make a display (fr. Du. *proncken*); (of a springbok) to leap.]

1. *comb. obs.* **pronkbok** [Afk., *bok* buck], SPRINGBOK sense 1 a.

1796 E. HELME tr. *F. Le Vaillant's Trav.* III. 29 (Pettman), The above name [*sc.* gazelle de parade] is one of those given to this antelope at the Cape of Good Hope, where the planters distinguish it by that of *pronkbock* (the goat which adorns itself). 1913 C. PETTMAN *Africanderisms* 386 *Pronk bok*, .. Another name for the Spring-bok ... The reference is to the peculiar bounds which this antelope is in the habit of making.

2. *intrans.* Of an antelope (usu. a springbok): to leap into the air with arched back and stiff legs.

1896 F.V. KIRBY *In Haunts of Wild Game* 49 He quickly settles down into a long 'rocking-horse' canter, or else goes 'pronking' away, as the Boers style it. 1915 *Chambers's Jrnl* (U.K.) Nov. 703 A whole troop of these antelopes are thus leaping .. 'pronking', or 'pranking', as the Boers call it. 1921 W.C. SCULLY *Harrow* 103 A few springboks were 'pronking' with strange antics, bounding hither and thither with sheer joy of life; their pure-white, erect, dorsal manes gleaming like snow. 1931 G. BEET *Grand Old Days* 15 What magnificent sights were the herds of tens of thousands of graceful springboks 'pronking,' as the Boers call it, in all directions. 1939 J.B. TAYLOR in F.G. Butler *When Boys Were Men* (1969) 259 Springbok, when disturbed, would invariably jump the road and then 'pronk', jumping high in the air and landing with all four feet bunched together. 1949 J. MOCKFORD *Golden Land* 213 Springboks, those *fleet* antelopes that leap high in the air arching their back, that is to say pronking, so that their short white mane and spine-protector gleam in the sun. 1955 L.G. GREEN *Karoo* 42 Suddenly huge groups of buck would take fright and begin 'pronking', with backs arched, in twenty-foot leaps. 1971 *Sunday Mail* (Brisbane) 10 June (Family Sect.) 6 The beautiful springbok .. gives a spectacular alarm signal ... It springs into the air, back arched, displaying a crest of pure white hairs. This is called 'pronking'. 1972 *Daily Dispatch* 22 July 4 The animal has a fan of longer white hairs on its back and when it is 'pronking' these stand up erect on the arched back. 1983 *Nat. Geog. Mag.* Mar. 375 Jumping for joy, a springbok 'pronks' in stiff-legged leaps, behaviour that sometimes signals alarm but also seems to express exuberance, often observed in the cool of evening or after a rainstorm. 1987 *You* 22 Oct. 56 The Springbok's name originates from his ability to leap high into the air. This is also known as pronking. When threatened, the animal leaps three to four metres into the air while simultaneously fanning open the long white hair on his back, very much like a Spanish fan. 1990 *Weekend Post* 24 Mar. 3 In the rural area of Theescombe, tame grysbok can be seen zig-zagging down a lawn in roan-coloured flashes or pronking over tall tufts of grass on impossibly dainty hooves. 1992 C. URQUHART in *Afr. Wildlife* Vol.46 No.6, 264 When disturbed this inquisitive and rather trusting antelope [*sc.* the oribi] .. gives a sharp whistle or sneeze, leaps up and runs off rapidly for a short distance, sometimes 'pronking' quite high into the air.

Hence (sense 2) **pronking** *vbl n.*

1925 S.C. CRONWRIGHT-SCHREINER *Migratory Springbucks* 17, I have never seen in any museum, not even in South Africa, a springbuck set up in the act of pronking, which is remarkable, because pronking is its most characteristic attitude.

Pro Nutro /prəʊ ˈnjuːtrəʊ/ *n.* The proprietory name of a nutritionally-balanced, high-protein powdered food, originally made as an affordable food for the poor and malnourished, but subsequently sold as a breakfast cereal.

1964 M.G. McCOY *Informant, Port Elizabeth* It [*sc.* the rabbit] is hopping about .. quite happily, & eating fantastic amounts of lettuce leaves & brown bread & Pro Nutro. 1970 *Survey of Race Rel.* (S.A.I.R.R.) 103 Pro Nutro and soup powder were made available to children and old people. 1971 *Daily News* 8 Mar. 10 Dr. Waldburger dedicated the whole of his life to finding a health-giving food for our non-White people. He came to South Africa to Hind Bros ... When at last 'Pro Nutro' was launched, his joy was unbounded. 1994 *Package information* For a high protein breakfast drink pour Pronutro into $\frac{1}{3}$ of a tall glass and top up with milk, stir and add sugar to taste.

‖**propvol** /ˈprɔpfɔl/ *adj. colloq.* [Afk., 'full to the stopper', *prop* stopper, plug + *vol* full.] Full (of), chock-full (of), stuffed (with).

1977 *Sunday Times* 8 July (Extra) 2 Take one naive South African ('propvol propaganda'), add a first overseas trip, and stir in a Communist country. 1987 M. MELAMU *Children of Twilight* 41 What can't you get the skepsels to do with their stomachs propvol? 1992 K. BERMAN in *Cue* 10 July 2 Strauss' text deals with contemporary theologies, ideologies and popular paths to redemption. And it is vicious. And propvol porno-perv high-priests and radical feminist lesbians on the rampage.

protea /ˈprəʊtɪə/ *n.* [Modern L. generic name, fr. *Proteus*, in Gk and Roman mythology a sea-god renowned for assuming many different shapes, an allusion to the great variety of forms of the various species.]

1.a. Any of a large variety of evergreen shrubs or small trees of the genus *Protea* of the Proteaceae, bearing cone-like flowers with prominent bracts; the generic name. Also *attrib.* See also BLUSHING BRIDE, PINCUSHION, SUGARBUSH.

The national flower of South Africa (but also native to Australia).

1753 CHAMBERS *Cycl. Suppl.*, *Protea*, in the Linnæan system of botany, a genus which takes in the lepidocarpodendron, and the hypophyllocarpodendron of Boerhaave. 1786 G. FORSTER tr. *A. Sparrman's Voy. to Cape of G.H.* I. 125 This *protea* is a shrub from two to four feet in height, which sometimes grows up undivided as straight as a rod, and at other times throws out two or three spiral branches. 1819 C. ABEL *Narr. of Journey* 286 The fine contrast afforded by the verdant slope of the Lion's Hill, and the silvery foliage of the dazzling *Proteas*. *a*1827 D. CARMICHAEL in W.J. Hooker *Botanical Misc.* (1831) II. 262 Next to the *Heaths* in variety and beauty, stand the *Proteas* ... Some have small flowers which attract the attention of no one except the Botanist; others at the elevation of a few inches, bear a blossom that exceeds in size the crown of a hat. 1850 R.G.G. CUMMING *Hunter's Life* I. 19 The splendid protea, whose sweets never fail to attract swarms of the insect tribes. 1853 F.P. FLEMING *Kaffraria* 36 The only shrub appearing in such localities being the Protea (*Grandiflora*), growing to about the height of eight or ten feet, and covered with its rich cuplike flowers of white and pale pink. 1878 T.J. LUCAS *Camp Life & Sport* 18 The stately fir, the home-looking oak .. are interspersed with the charming protea (Protea argentea) or silver tree of the colonists. 1901 L.H. BAILEY *Cycl. Amer. Hort.* III. 1438 Proteas are tender shrubs which are among the most attractive and characteristic plants of the Cape of Good Hope. 1925 F.C. SLATER *Centenary Bk of S. Afr. Verse* 236 Proteas are chiefly found in South-West Cape Colony, but some fine ones are found in south-east mountain ranges, and one is common in the Transvaal. 1955 A. DELIUS *Young Trav.* 112 Proteas .. were the National flower of South Africa. They were shaped rather like brandy goblets and contain a very sweet juice, which is why the Afrikaners call them suikerbossie, or sugar bush. 1961 PALMER & PITMAN *Trees of S. Afr.* 221 The Protea family is of special interest to botanists, some of whom see in it possible proof of a former close connection between South Africa and Australia, for this large family is abundantly represented in these two countries, and is more rarely found in other parts of the world. 1971 BARAITSER & OBHOLZER *Cape Country Furn.* 57 A striking feature in the construction of these chairs is the use of proteawood in the dwelling. 1976 W. HÉFER in *Optima* Vol.26 No.2, 46 Proteas dominate the indigenous growth on the mountain slope and include the creamy-white and the rarer coloured sugar bush, and, in one area, the beautiful blushing bride. 1987 T.F.J. VAN RENSBURG *Intro. to Fynbos* 11 The first protea to bloom overseas was a long-bud protea (*Protea aurea*), which flowered in Utrecht in 1794. 1989 *Gardening Questions Answered* (Reader's Digest Assoc.) 350 *Protea*, Famous genus of indigenous, evergreen shrubs with tough, leathery, oval, lance-shaped or needle-like leaves. The flowers are composed of tiny, white, pink or cream florets, often with dark tips, surrounded by showy, pink, rose, red, white, cream or green-yellow bracts. 1991 D.M. MOORE *Garden Earth* 196 The seeds of many proteas will germinate only after the heat of fire has cracked the hard seedcoat.

b. With distinguishing epithet: **giant protea**, *P. cynaroides*; **giant woolly-beard(ed) protea**, *P. barbigera*; **golden protea** *hist.*, *Mimetes stokei*; **king protea**, *P. cynaroides*; **Marloth protea**, *P. marlothii*; **mountain-rose protea**, *P. nana*; **pincushion protea**, see as a main entry; **snow protea**, *P. cryophila*.

1913 C. PETTMAN *Africanderisms* 187 **Giant protea**, *Protea cynaroides*, found on Table Mountain, not often flowering. 1977 *S. Afr. Panorama* May 30 The best-known and most magnificent of all is the King Protea, also known as the Giant Protea .. , the *Protea cynaroides L.* [1951 S. ELIOVSON *Flowering Shrubs & Trees* 114 *Protea barbigera* (**Giant Woolly-Beard**) is one of the most attractive Proteas, with its large, water-melon pink heads filled with white woolly hairs and a black centre]. 1957 L.G. GREEN *Beyond City Lights* 104 Mr. E.G. van der Merwe .. has been sowing the seeds of the rarer proteas in the mountains year after year for decades. Thanks to his efforts the giant woolly-bearded protea, with its soft white hairs and black centre, is being revived. 1959 — *These Wonders* 166 The famous and beautiful new **golden protea** .. was named Mimetes Stokei ... [It] was a silver bush growing up to eight feet, with a magnificent collection of crimson and orange blooms shot with silver in the head ... It is almost certain that the golden protea is now extinct. 1962 S. ELIOVSON *Discovering Wild Flowers in Sn Afr.* 50 Often the size of a dinner plate, the flower-head of the **King Protea** is the most spectacular of a large genus. 1977 [see quot. at *giant protea* above]. 1987 *S. Afr. Digest* 8 May 13 The national flower is the king protea, *Protea cynaroides*. 1957 L.G. GREEN *Beyond City Lights* 104 He [*sc.* Mr. E.G. van der Merwe] sows the **Marloth protea**, too, greenish-crimson when in flower; the slender, wine-coloured **'mountain-rose' protea** and the 'blushing bride'. 1987 T.F.J. VAN RENSBURG *Intro. to Fynbos* 17 The king of the dwarf and ground proteas must surely be the **snow protea** (*P. cryophila*), which is found only on certain high peaks in the Cedarberg.

2. Special Comb. **protea canary**, the bird *Serinus leucopterus*, which feeds on the seed and nectar of the protea.

1970 O.P.M. PROZESKY *Field Guide to Birds* 329 Rarer species ... **Protea Canary** (*Serinus leucopterus*). 1984 G.L. MACLEAN *Roberts' Birds of Sn Afr.* 784 *Protea Canary*, ... Habitat: Mainly Protea-covered mountain slopes ... Food: Seeds (of *Protea* ..); also nectar of *Protea*, *Halleria* and *Salvia*. 1987 T.F.J. VAN RENSBURG *Intro. to Fynbos* 48 We know most of the birds and know that only two endangered species are actually dependent on the fynbos for their survival. They are the protea canary .. and the Cape sugarbird.

Proto /ˈprəʊtəʊ/ *n.* Also with small initial.

1. The proprietory name of a breathing apparatus which filters out toxic gases and supplies oxygen to the wearer during underground rescue operations. Usu. *attrib.*

1932 WATERMEYER & HOFFENBERG *Witwatersrand Mining Practice*, Teams are organized and trained in the use of Proto Rescue apparatus and they are liable to be called to their own (or other) mine at any time. 1946 [see sense 2]. 1975 *Chambers Dict. of Science & Technology* 945 *Proto set* (*Mining*), Mine rescue equipment, weighing some 18 kg and incorporating an oxygen cylinder, breathing bag, and face mask, used for work in foul underground air. 1977 *Sunday Times* 30 Jan. (Mag. Sect.) 1 *Proto*, The name of a breathing apparatus which filters out toxic gases and supplies its wearer with oxygen in conditions of intense heat and bad air. **1983** *Mining Dict.* 202 Proto apparatus ... Proto mask.

2. Special Comb. Proto captain, the leader of the Proto team; **Proto man**, a member of a Proto team; **Proto team**, a team with special training in (underground) rescue procedures. Also *attrib.*

1983 *Mining Dict.* 202 Proto captain. **1972** *Mining Survey* Oct. 28 What is a **Proto man**? Taking his name from the breathing apparatus — his primary 'tool' — he is a highly skilled, self-disciplined member of a team that can be called upon at a moment's notice night or day, to go underground in an emergency and fight fire or save lives. **1946** C.B. JEPPE *Gold Mining on Witwatersrand* II., '**Proto' teams**, One or more fully trained Proto teams are maintained on most mines ... *Proto Team Equipment*, ... 5 sets of Proto rescue apparatus ... Canaries in small cages. **1960** *Rand Daily Mail* in J. Crwys-Williams *S. Afr. Despatches* (1989) 325 Nobody knows how many hundred yards of rock and debris separate them from the proto (rescue) teams who are working in two-hour shifts. **1976** *Citizen* 19 Dec. 2 Police and mine proto teams were last night digging through the rubble of a five-storey block of flats which collapsed when an earthquake struck Welkom yesterday. **1980** *Sunday Times* 3 Feb. (Mag. Sect.) 5 Proto teams went down. Wearing oxygen masks and working round the clock they tried to break through to the men. **1989** J. CRWYS-WILLIAMS *S. Afr. Despatches* 327 It was hope .. which kept everyone going, from the Proto teams clearing a passage at the rate of two metres every three hours, .. to the witchdoctor throwing bones in their midst. **1993** *E. Prov. Herald* 15 May 1 Specially trained proto teams are working against the clock in a search for the miners.

Province *n. colloq.* Ellipt. for WESTERN PROVINCE (sense c). Also *attrib.*

1969 N. LECK in J. Crwys-Williams *S. Afr. Despatches* (1989) 383 Their one-time supermen were crushed 28–9 by 'Tiny' Neethling's inspired band of Province cavaliers. **1990** *Weekend Post* 23 June 20 Transvaal beat Province 25–24. **1994** *Sunday Times* 31 July 29 Province put it all together and book final spot.

PRP *n. hist.* The initial letters of *Progressive Reform Party*, a liberal-democratic political party (1975–1977), formed by the merger of the Reform Party with the Progressive Party. Also *attrib.* See also PROG.

Members of the PRP later joined with former United Party members to form the Progressive Federal Party (see PFP).

1976 *E. Prov. Herald* 23 Aug. 2 PRP will advise .. tenants. **1977** *Sunday Times* 14 Aug. 14 Mr Schwarz's dance, if discordant to PRP ears, is in tune with a large slice of white South African opinion. **1977** *Argus* 27 Aug. 6 Johannes van Eeden, 20, chairman of the PRP student branch.

‖**pruimpie** /ˈprœɪmpi/ *n.* Also **pruimpje**. [Afk., *pruim* a quid of chewing tobacco + dim. suffix -IE.] A small quantity of tobacco, a quid.

1889 H.A. BRYDEN *Kloof & Karroo* 329 Even the Sunday school teachers .. had complained that there were so many quids (*pruimpjes*) and so much tobacco spittle on the floor, that they got quite a turn in their stomachs. **1913** C. PETTMAN *Africanderisms* 387 *Pruimpje*, .. A small quantity of tobacco for either chewing or smoking. **1968** K. MCMAGH *Dinner of Herbs* 115 There were rolls of Transvaal tobacco, for every farm hand expected and was given a weekly 'pruimpje' of the strong black stuff.

puddysticks, puttysticks *adj.* Also **pudsticks**. [Unknown; see Daily Dispatch quots (Oct. 1993) for various theories. Cf. colloq. Brit. Eng. *potty* easy.] In the language of children: very easy. Also the *abbrev.* forms **puds** /pʌds/, **putts, putty**.

Remembered in use in Grahamstown since the 1930s; also in Kimberley since c1940.

1992 P. DOBSON *Informant, Cape Town* Putty/Puttysticks. Easy (Children's slang). Adding one and one is putty. **1993** R. ROSS-THOMPSON in *Daily Dispatch* 30 Sept. 20 How would you manage if you had to nip flies and mosquitoes out of the air using a pair of long-nosed pliers or tweezers .. ? ... For European and lesser striped swallows it was puddy sticks. **1993** *Daily Dispatch* 18 Oct. 8 Puddy sticks ... I would say I first used it in my own vocabulary when at Selborne Primary in the 1950s ... It could be a speedy vocal derivation of 'putty'. Say putty fast and it becomes puddy. Now if I remember correctly, .. putty used to come in long sticks wrapped in oil proof paper. Maybe the kids thought of it as soft and easily manipulated. Putty was something to play with, to make into models ... It was probably before the discovery of plasticine too, which would have replaced it. **1993** *Ibid.* 27 Oct. 20 Puddy sticks, or puds .. is used by children of primary school age, and means easy ... Mrs Pits Hayes of Kwelera said she could trace the expression back to the 1930s when she was at primary school in Kimberley ... 'Putty sticks and dabbies — meaning "I want something" — was [*sic*] in common use at that time,' she said ... Mrs Marian Watts of Gonubie .. recalls the word 'putsy' being used widely in her 10 to 12-year-old days in Wales. That was also in the 1930s and it was said mostly by boys. East Londoner Charles Morris' offering seems to confirm that putsy came from Britain. He says it was a common word in Rhodesia .. in the 1945 to '50 era when a lot of British expatriates settled there. 'Kids bastardized it to "putts",' he said, meaning easy. Mr Hans Köhler .., who is from Saxony in Germany, says the word 'puddstock' was used by his parents who were born around the turn of the century. It was used when referring to politicians or girls who were 'a soft touch, or easy — with no backbone, a pushover'. **1993** I.A. WRIGHT *Informant, Grahamstown* Doing handstands is pudsticks! I can't think why I couldn't do it before! **1994** *Informant, Grahamstown* Puddysticks was just a normal word in the house. I knew it as a child in the 20's.

pufaro var. BAFARO.

puff-adder *n.* [tr. S. Afr. Du. *pof-adder*, fr. Du. *poffen* to puff + *adder* adder, viper; so named because when disturbed it inflates its body, making a blowing sound.] The poisonous snake *Bitis arietans arietans* of the Viperidae, with flat, spade-shaped head and rough, chevron-patterned skin in various combinations of pale grey, brown, and black; POFADDER sense 1. Also *attrib.*, and (rarely) with defining words denoting a particular type of puff-adder, **spotted dwarf puff-adder**.

1789 W. PATERSON *Narr. of Four Journeys* 164 The Puff-adder .. has its name from blowing itself up to near a foot in circumference. **1804** R. PERCIVAL *Acct of Cape of G.H.* 170 The puff-adder is often met with: it is so called from its swelling itself out to a great size when enraged .. it is nearly as thick at the tail as at the head. **1817** G. BARKER *Journal.* 14 Sept., This morning a puff adder was killed [by] dear brother U's garden gate .. ; these are counted the most dangerous of all the serpents in Africa. **1822** W.J. BURCHELL *Trav.* I. 469 It is well known in the colony .. by the name of the Pof-Adder (Puff Adder). Its venom is said to be most fatal, taking effect so rapidly as to leave the person who has the misfortune to be bitten, no chance of saving his life, but by instantly cutting out the flesh surrounding the wound. [**1834** W.H.B. WEBSTER *Narr. of Voy. to Sn Atlantic Ocean* 304 The puff, one of the viper tribe, is extremely dangerous; its bite killing a person in half an hour.] **1851** T. SHONE *Diary.* 10 Oct., The bitch Mow was this day bitten by a large Puff-adder. **1871** C. KINGSLEY *At Last: Christmas in W. Indies* p.ii, But who will call the Puff Adder of the Cape .. anything but ugly and horrible? **1890** A. MARTIN *Home Life* 255 Of all the Cape snakes the puff-adder is not only the deadliest, but by far the most to be feared. For, being of the same colour as the ground, it is extremely difficult to see: it is lazy, too, and will not take the trouble to get out of your way as every other snake does. **1901** E. HOBHOUSE *Report of Visit to Camps* 3 While we sat there a snake came in. They said it was a puff adder, very poisonous, so they all ran out, and I attacked the creature with my parasol. **1915** W. EVELEIGH *S.W. Afr.* 82 The puff-adder *Bitis arietans* .. is highly venomous and exceedingly dangerous, as it coils up and lies quite still in the open until touched or roused. **1931** F.C. SLATER *Secret Veld* 79 An ominous hiss at his feet revealed .. the puff-adder that lay across his path. **1947** L.G. GREEN *Tavern of Seas* 121 Puffadders bring forth their young alive; and even a tiny puffadder can inflict a terrifying bite. **1963** S. CLOETE *Rags of Glory* 483 As full of hate and anger as a puff adder is full of poison. **1972** A. SCHOLEFIELD *Wild Dog Running* 146 The fangs of a puff adder are the longest and most vicious of any snake in Southern Africa. **1987** T.F.J. VAN RENSBURG *Intro. to Fynbos* 49 The following species are listed as endangered species .. Spotted dwarf puff-adder (Hondeklip Bay). **1988** M. BRANCH *Explore Cape Flora* 37 Puff adder venom causes swelling and bruising ... Even if a bite is not lethal, it may take months to recover from it. **1994** M. ROBERTS tr. *J.A. Wahlberg's Trav. Jrnls 1838–56* 11 A large puff-adder was shot by K. Dreyer from his horse.

‖**pula** /ˈpuːla/ *int.* and *n.* Also **poola**. [Sotho and seTswana.] Rain.

A. *int.* Esp. among Sotho- and seTswana-speaking people: a greeting or salute; an invocation or blessing. See also KHOTSO.

1827 G. THOMPSON *Trav.* I. 180 Mattebe .. made the same movements with his assagai .. after which he waved the point towards the heavens, when all called out '*Poola!*' i.e. rain or a blessing. **1864** T. BAINES *Explor. in S.-W. Afr.* 436 His speech was greeted by cries of 'poola, poola' (rain, rain), a term synonymous in a dry country with refreshment or blessing. **1887** [see sense B 1]. **1918** H. MOORE *Land of Good Hope* 284 The royal salute, 'Pula, Pula,' echoed and re-echoed. **1934** *Star* 1 Mar. (Swart), When Prince George, at the end of his reply .. raised his hand and uttered the traditional Basuto salute 'Pula' which means rain, a wave of enthusiasm swept the .. council chamber. **1943** D. REITZ *No Outspan* 182 They stood respectfully, each man holding up his arm in salute crying 'Poola-poola' which in their language means 'rain-rain'. In a drought stricken country rain is like God to them so 'Poola' is their cry. **1952** *Drum* Apr. 23 'Pula! Pula!' 'Bayete! Bayete!' These are the cries that welcomed Queen Elizabeth II, then Princess Elizabeth, and the rest of the Royal Family wherever they met their loyal African subjects. **1953** [see KHOTSO]. *a*1968 D.C. THEMBA in E. Patel *World of Can Themba* (1985) 149 The sun was softly flushing the western sky with its gold when I closed the meeting with the words, 'Pula! Pula! (Rain! Rain!). **1979** *S. Afr. Panorama* Aug. 20 The Basotho salutations — '*Khotso*' (Peace) and '*Pula*' (Rain) — linger in one's memory long after one has returned home. **1979** *Fair Lady* 12 Sept. 23, I heard for the first time .. the meaningful traditional greeting 'pula' (rain) and the ululations, that strange yodel-call of the African women. **1990** *Frontline* Feb. 12 When Tlhabane finally took the floor, there was silence. As he talked, there were replies of 'Pula, pula,' which means literally 'rain' but figuratively 'prosperity'. **1991** M. KANTEY *All Tickets* 10 We cranked white water from the African desert. There [*sc.* in Botswana] the water was a blessing — Pula, they said as a greeting, meaning 'let it rain'.

B. *n.*

1. A cry of 'pula'.

1887 J.W. MATTHEWS *Incwadi Yami* 286 Basutos, be united to your chief ... Let the Fathers and the Sisters pray for .. rain, which is so much wanted. Pula.' In response to the royal speech a tremendous 'Pula' burst forth from all.

2. As a common noun.

1982 C. VAN WYK in Chapman & Dangor *Voices from Within* 199 Tonight it rains. Hitting hard against the rooftops. Thundering at the windowpanes ... But it rains until it stops. Pula! Pula! Pula!

pull *v. trans.* [Special sense of general Eng.] a. To draw (the winning number) as the banker in a game of FAH-FEE. **b.** In the v. phr. *to pull fah-fee*, to conduct a fah-fee game.

1952 'SKAPPIE' in *Drum* Sept. 6 He started writing out a new number saying, 'Today I want to pull No. 11'. 1956 L. LONGMORE in *S. Afr. Jrnl of Science* Vol.52 No.12, 278 The 'jumps', itching or twitching of the player's body indicate different numbers and they are regarded as very important indications as to what the Chinaman pulls ... Most Chinamen who pull Fahfee have in their clubs two or three runners who also run liquor for them. 1980 R. GOVENDER *Lahnee's Pleasure* 25 He comes here every afternoon to pull fahfee.

Hence **pull** *n.*, a draw; **pulling** *ppl adj.*

1956 L. LONGMORE in *S. Afr. Jrnl of Science* Vol.52 No.12, 275 The Chinese bankers .. leave their cars parked some distance from the 'pulling house' in order to avoid arrest. 1977 D. MULLER *Whitey* 56 The fah-fee runner moved about the tavern, paying the winners of the morning 'pull' and taking the evening bets for the ancient numbers game of dreams and symbolism.

pumplemus var. PAMPELMOES.

pundah /ˈpʊndə/ *n. Offensive. slang.* Also **punda**. [ad. PUNDU.] A demeaning term for a woman, or for women collectively; PUNDU sense b.

1986 *Informant, Durban* We're going out tonight to [catch] some pundah. 1989 *Informant, Port Elizabeth* That pundah up front, she drives really carefully. 1990 *Style* June 79 Darryl had turned to her and said 'Nice pundah.' She turned to face him ... 'You say what?' 'Um,' Darryl had stammered. 'Nice *hoender*. In this country, when we are pleased, we say, "Nice *hoender*".' 1991 H. DUGMORE in *Personality* 18 Mar. The word 'pundah' (a very rude word for 'chicks') will definitely be uttered by the real animals.

pundu /ˈpʊndu:/ *n. slang.* Also **poendoe**. [Xhosa *iimpundu* buttocks.] Esp. in the Eastern Cape: **a.** The buttocks; a buttock. **b.** *transf.* PUNDAH.

1970 *Informant, Grahamstown* She has a large pundu, that woman. 1970 S. SPARKS *Informant, Fort Beaufort* Don't sit on the cement child — your poendoes will get cold. 1991 J. OWEN *Informant, Pietermaritzburg* Pundu. Girl, woman. Look at that pundu.

pusa *n.* var. PHUZA *n.*

pusa *v.* var. PHUZA *v.*

put *v. trans. Colloq.* In the phr. *to put foot*, to use the accelerator on a motor vehicle; so (*fig.*), to 'get a move on', to hurry. Cf. *to tread tackie* (see TACKIE sense 1 c).

1981 L. & P. ROBERTSON-HOTZ in *Bloody Horse* Jan.-Feb. 32 Now we'd better put foot; we've only got a couple of hours before they discover we've escaped. 1989 T. BOTHA in *Style* June 108 A love story about the long open road, putting foot, fly-bitten caffies, *ver verlate vlaktes* as well as the art of sleep-driving at 120km/h. 1990 G. BETRIX on TV1, 21 Apr., They know that they [*sc.* show-jumpers] really have to put foot, so to speak, if they want to have a chance in the competition. 1991 M.J. SILVA *Informant, Grahamstown* I've got to meet him at the video shop. Come on Dad, put foot.

Putco /ˈpʌtkəʊ/ *n.* Also PUTCO. [Acronym formed on *Public Utility Transport Corporation*.] A large bus company transporting black commuters in the Transvaal provinces and in KwaZulu-Natal. Also *attrib.* See also *green mamba* sense (b), MAMBA sense 2.

1952 *Drum* July 33 About ten years ago, the PUTCO bought over the Alexandra bus route ... A month ago .. a well-known transport man .. sold his business to PUTCO, which runs some 27 routes on the Reef and in Pretoria. 1963 B. MODISANE *Blame Me on Hist.* (1986) 18 Our repertoire included games like .. stealing rides on horse-drawn trolleys, getting on and off whilst in motion, and the more proficient we became the more ambitious we got, graduating to the green Putco buses. 1977 P.C. VENTER *Soweto* 46 They were playing a new game called 'Soweto, Soweto'. 'How do you play that?' Moses asked. 'Easy,' came the reply, 'Sissy is a PUTCO bus and I'm setting her on fire'. 1978 *S. Afr. Panorama* Mar. 41 Putco conveys 96 000 commuters a day into Johannesburg from Soweto, Alexandra and Tembisa, while its suburban service inside Soweto carries 27 000 Blacks a day at 10c a trip. Putco conveys another 70 000 daily commuters into Springs and Boksburg from KwaThema and Vosloorus, and 13 000 more into Pretoria from Atteridgeville and Mamelodi on its outskirts. 1979 A.P. BRINK *Dry White Season* 41 In the streets the charred skeletons of Putco buses. 1983 [see AU]. 1984 *Frontline* Mar. 12 No matter how much Putco, or its Cape Town equivalent City Tramways, protest, many of their passengers view them as an extension of government, making substantial profits not least from the effects of the Group Areas Act. 1990 *Sash* Vol.33 No.1, 32 Until recently, bus companies mainly served racially defined groups: Public Utility Transport Corporation (Putco) buses carried Africans and 'coloureds'. 1994 [see AZIKHWELWA].

puti *n. obs.* Also **poetie, pooti**. [ad. seTswana *photi*.] The *common duiker* (see DUIKER sense 1 b), *Sylvicapra grimmia*.

[1835 A. SMITH *Diary* (1940) II. 204 The Baquas give the following names to animals ... duiker *pooti*.] 1857 D. LIVINGSTONE *Missionary Trav.* 56 Other animals, such as the düiker (*Cephalophus mergens*) or puti (of the Bechuanas) .. are .. able to subsist without water for many months at time living on the bulbs and tubers containing moisture. [1940 P.R. KIRBY *Diary of Dr Andrew Smith* II., The names, in modern spelling .. are as follows ... duiker *photi*.] 1941 A.G. BEE *Kalahari Camp Fires* (1943) 63 Khama's folk revered the 'poetie' or duiker (a small antelope very common and very cunning in South Africa).

puto, putopap varr. PUTU, PUTU PAP.

Putterie /ˈpʌtəri/ *n.* [Named for *Frans Putterie* (1880–1958), who developed the breed.] In full *Putterie pigeon*: a strain of racing pigeon first bred in 1937, and raced from 1942 onwards.

1961 F.J. KIPPEN in *S. Afr. Racing Pigeon/Posduif* 5 Any purebred Putterie pigeon mated to any other strain in our country will produce outstanding racing birds. 1981 *Durban & District Racing Pigeon Fed. Yr Bk* 98 The Silas Willis family of Old Putteries has been inbred since 1942 with the object of retaining the good qualities of this Super family of racing pigeon, always bearing in mind not to lose the will to win, super wing formation, firm bone structure, supple muscles, strong feathers, ability to breed champions, vitality and super health. 1991 *Philatelic Services Bulletin* No.8075, The most salient characteristics of the Putterie pigeon are the distinctive eyes, superb plumage, strong bone structure and the short curved appearance of the flight feathers.

putts, putty see PUDDYSTICKS.

puttysticks see PUDDYSTICKS.

putu /ˈpu:tu, ˈpʊtʊ/ *n.* Also **phut(h)u, puto, uphuthu**. [See PUTU PAP.] Maize-meal porridge, made in either of two ways: **a.** very stiff (see STYWE PAP), or, **b.** stirred into a dry, crumbly consistency; KRUMMELPAP. In both senses also called PAP *n.*, PUTU PAP. Cf. MEALIEPAP sense 1. Also *attrib.*

1952 H. DE LEEUW in Bosman & Bredell *Veld Trails & Pavements* 161 She dug the stirring stick into the thick mess of meal ... A lump of putu fell over the edge on to the mud floor. 1953 LANHAM & MOPELI-PAULUS *Blanket Boy's Moon* 6 To know how the Putu was spoiled, must one have been present at its cooking. 1956 J. CHATTERTON *Return of Drums* 12 The one pot contained a thin gruel ... The other contained putu — dry lumps of cooked mealie meal — on top of which was a piece of meat. 1961 T. MATSHIKIZA *Choc. for my Wife* 102 Ehe, the one who does not eat phutu, too bad! 1971 *Nat. Geog. Mag.* Dec. 746 Roast chicken and uphuthu, a kind of hominy that has been a staple Zulu dish for centuries. 1980 *Family Post* 9 Feb. 2 Bobby Lang notes that these days on the Rand it is the smart thing to serve phutu very stiff with the chops, boerewors and steak at braais instead of baked potatoes. However, braaied meat and phutu have been popular on white farms in many parts of South Africa for generations. 1990 R. MALAN *My Traitor's Heart* 150 As a child, she used to hang around the black cane-cutters' shacks, sharing the wild spinach and *putu* they cooked in iron pots on open fires.

putu pap /ˈpu:tu pap, ˈpʊtʊ -/ *n. phr.* Also **putopap**. [ad. Zulu *uphuthu* thick porridge (prob. rel. to ideophone *putu* of crumbling to pieces) + Afk. *pap* porridge.] PUTU.

a1931 S. BLACK in S. Gray *Three Plays* (1984) 165 Jan was the exception, a good boy. He only eats putupap. 1975 *Argus* 16 July 22 Write down .. all the things you see when you hear the word *breakfast*. The list might include dry bread and coffee, putu pap, oatmeal porridge, [etc.]. 1977 *S. Afr. Panorama* Oct. 3 'Putopap' (a tasty stiff porridge made from maize in a traditional manner) is a popular feature of South African 'vleisbraais'. 1978 J. BAULING *Walk in Shadows* 129 Stywe putu pap, made from meal, .. was the staple diet of some of the country's poorer indigenous inhabitants, but, ironically, a party treat for more recent settlers. 1986 [see KRUMMELPAP]. 1988 H. PRENDINI in *Style* June 105 Recently Wendy discovered putu pap. One of her trendy liberal friends served it at one of her braais.

puza, puzamandla varr. PHUZA *n.*, PHUZAMANDLA.

puzzle bush *n. phr.* [Eng., fr. the appearance of the interlaced branches.] The *deurmekaarbos* (see DEURMEKAAR sense 2), *Ehretia rigida*.

1980 C. LETTY *More Trees of S. Afr.* 46 The Puzzle Bush is found throughout South Africa ... A Puzzle Bush is an asset to a large garden; is drought and frost-resistant, but suckers easily. 1982 FOX & NORWOOD YOUNG *Food from Veld* 132 *Ehretia rigida* ... *Common names*: English — puzzle bush. 1987 [see *Cape lilac* sense (b) at CAPE sense 2 a].

PWV *n.* [Acronym formed on *Pretoria-Witwatersrand-Vaal* (Triangle).] The PWV:

a. A name for the area round the cities of Johannesburg and Pretoria, characterized by its industrial and economic activity and situated in the southern part of the former province of the Transvaal. Also *attrib.*

[c1979 L.M. MANGOPE *Place for All* 11 Our subcontinent's permanent economic pivot, the Pretoria-Witwatersrand-Vaal complex.] 1981 *Rand Daily Mail* 28 Mar. 1 The fight .. will be broadcast in the PWV area on Channel 702. 1983 *Financial Mail* 16 Sept. 25 Bombs in PWV. Three bombs explode in the PWV area, one at the Ciskeian government offices in Pretoria and the other two at power substations in Johannesburg northern suburbs. 1987 L. BOOMKER in *Conserva* Oct. 22 To the north of Pretoria lies the Magaliesberg Nature Area ... This mountainous landscape, close to the PWV urban area makes it an ideal wilderness retreat for city-dwellers. 1989 A. BERNSTEIN in *Optima* Vol.37 No.1, 18 The abolition of influx control has *not* resulted in mass migration to the PWV. 1990 R. STENGEL *January Sun* 76 The government's policy was to get industry to move away from the PWV Triangle (Pretoria, Witwatersrand, Vaal) to the rural areas near the homelands. 1991 *Spotlight* (S.A.I.R.R.) No.1 Mar. 5 The PWV (the 'triangle' comprising Pretoria, the Witwatersrand and the Vaal).

b. *hist.* From April to December 1994, the name of one of the nine provinces of South Africa (subsequently renamed GAUTENG). Also *attrib.*

1994 *Sunday Times* 25 Sept. 6 The PWV has passed only the first of three bills that comprise vital start-up legislation ... PWV Premier Tokyo Sexwale has enjoyed a very high media profile.

‖**pylstert** /ˈpeɪlstɛrt/ *n.* Also **pylstart, pylstort**. Pl. unchanged, **-e** /-ə/, or **-s**. [Afk. (earlier S. Afr. Du., fr. Du. *pijlstaart* ray, *pyl* arrow + *stert* tail).]

a. A species of eagle ray, prob. *Myliobatis aquila* of the Myliobatidae. **b.** Any of several species of stingray, esp. *Dasyatis pastinaca* of the Dasyatidae.

In Smith and Heemstra's *Smiths' Sea Fishes* (1986), the name 'eagleray' is used for *M. aquila*, and 'blue stingray' for *D. pastinaca*.

1821 C.I. Latrobe *Jrnl of Visit* 487 Mr. Duckett presented me with the tail of a pylstort, (arrow-tail,) a fish caught in Simon's-bay. The tail itself is slender, and about fourteen inches in length. From the upper part of its insertion into the body, proceed two sharp bones, serrated on both sides... Every tooth of this bony saw acts as a barb, and if once inserted, cannot be extracted without great laceration of the flesh. **1930** C.L. Biden *Sea-Angling Fishes* 294 They [sc. electric rays] don't grow as big as the sting-ray — the common pylstert. *Ibid.* 295, I saw scores of enormous pylstert slowly swimming into the unexplored alleys of the cave. **1947** K.H. Barnard *Pict. Guide to S. Afr. Fishes* 27 The Common Sting-Ray, Pylstart (*Dasybatis pastinacus*) is a European species found on the Agulhas Bank and as far as Natal. **1958** L.G. Green *S. Afr. Beachcomber* 99 Sting-rays or stingarees, the dreaded pylstert (arrow tail) of the Cape fishermen, have killed unsuspecting, bare-footed people who have stepped on them in shallow water.

pynstillende druppels see DRUPPELS sense b i.

pyp gras(s) /ˈpeɪpxras (-grɑːs)/ *n. ?obsolescent.* [Afk. (earlier *pijpgras*), *pyp* pipe + *gras* grass, (or Eng. *grass*); named for the pipe-like nature of the culms.] Either of two perennial grass species, *Ehrharta thunbergii* or *E. villosa*, which grow up to one and a half metres in height. Also *attrib.*

1854 P.L. Simmonds in *Pharmac. Jrnl* XIII. 421 Something must be sown with the berry [of the Myrica] to screen its shoot... Pyp grass seed should.. be prepared for the purpose. **1857** [see Port Jackson]. **1880** S.W. Silver & Co.'s *Handbk to S. Afr.*, Of indigenous grasses which may be usefully employed to arrest drifting sands none are better than the Pyp grass. **1917** R. Marloth *Common Names* 36 *Pijpgras, Ehrharta villosa.* **1966** C.A. Smith *Common Names* 379 *Pypgras, Ehrharta gigantea* .. and *E. villosa.*

pypie /ˈpeɪpi/ *n.* Also **papie, pijp(i)e, pypje.** [Afk. (earlier S. Afr. Du.), *pyp* pipe + dim. suffix -IE; see quot. 1973.] Any of various species of indigenous plants with tubular flowers, esp. species of GLADIOLUS, IXIA, and WATSONIA.

1907 A.R.E. Burton *Cape Col. Today* 250 *Watsonia*, One of the commonest plants we have. They are known locally as *pijpes.* **1912** *Cape Times* 14 Sept. 9 The pretty little pink or reddish *papie* (gladiolus villosus) is scattered over flat places. **1913** H. Tucker *Our Beautiful Peninsula* 70 Garden-gay with .. the pale blue and delicate rose of afrikanders and pypjes. **1917** R. Marloth *Common Names* 66 *Pijpe*, Used for many plants with tubular flowers, but especially for species of *Watsonia, Antholyza* and *Gladiolus.* **1924** D. Fairbridge *Gardens of S. Afr.* 122 The sweet-scented Afrikanders and Pypjes belong to the gladiolus family. **1928** *Jrnl of Botanical Soc.* XIV. 8 One's youthful memories of the Aandbloms, Painted Ladies, Papies and Afrikanders that marked the passing of the months. **1970** M. Muller *Cloud across Moon* 26, I combed the lower slopes of the peaks for pink pypies, the delicate pale pink gladioli Trina loved so much. **1973** Beeton & Dorner in *Eng. Usage in Sn Afr.* Vol.4 No.2, 38 *Pypie*, .. first applied to one or several species of *Gladiolus* or *Watsonia* wh[ich] resemble miniature, long-stemmed pipes; this is most pronounced when the base of the stem is held up & only one flower hangs down. **1981** L. Bolus in P. Dane *Great Houses of Constantia* 73 There was eager waiting for the first *pypies*, blue and pink.

python dance *n. phr.* Also with initial capitals. [So called because the dance is dedicated to the python (considered a symbol of fertility).] A dance performed by unmarried Venda girls during a period of initiation into womanhood; *domba dance,* see DOMBA sense 2.

1931 [see DOMBA sense 1]. **1970** B. Tyrrell in *Std Encycl. of Sn Afr.* II. 76 At night, linked arm to arm with a long line of fellow initiates, she dances the python dance, around a sacred fire, to the snake god of fertility. **1976** West & Morris *Abantu* 96 (caption) Caught up in the hypnotic beat of the drums, *domba* girls perform the 'python dance', their movements gradually gaining momentum. **1979** [see DOMBA sense 2]. **1987** [see DOMBA sense 1]. **1990** N.H.G. Jacobsen in *Fauna & Flora* No.47, 26 At a lake called Fundudzi, Venda maidens are performing the Python Dance in anticipation of the rain that is going to fall.

Q

‖**qaba** /ˈɬaba/ *n.* Also **iqaba**, and with initial capital. Pl. **amaqaba, -s.** [Xhosa and Zulu *iqaba,* heathen, uncultured or ignorant person: sing. prefix i- + *qaba* (pl. *amaqaba,* voc. *qaba*), prob. development of earlier Xhosa sense 'person who wears traditional dress consisting of a blanket reddened with ochre', fr. *qaba* (v.) paint, smear (cf. IQABANE). For notes on pl. forms, see AMA- and I-.] A person (usu. from a rural area) who adheres to traditional customs and beliefs. See also RED *n.*

1949 L. HUNTER *Afr. Dawn* 16 One of the first people to be converted was the Chief's mother and in order to distinguish herself from the *Amaqaba,* she put aside her red blankets and adopted European dress. *Ibid.* 17 He, who had once been a *Qaba,* was now a deacon of the church. 1962 W.D. HAMMOND-TOOKE *Bhaca Soc.* 64 Christians are called by pagans *amakholwa* (believers) .. while pagans are referred to as *amaqaba* (those smeared with red ochre). [1974 J. BROSTER in *S. Afr. Panorama* Dec. 38 Blacks who wear tribal beadwork and dress are called in Xhosa 'amaQaba', a name which signifies that they worship their ancestral spirits ... In everyday life those who adhere to this belief are recognised by the red ochre or clay which they apply to body, blankets and clothing.] 1976 *Daily Dispatch* 20 Aug. (Suppl.) 6 Amaqaba, the red-blankets, were a people of good discipline. 1987 *Pace* May 4 The mlungu missionaries came to darkest Africa to civilise the qabas. 1987 L. NKOSI *Mating Birds* 86 'She had a mouth painted red and she was smoking a cigarette. I said to her, are you not afraid your mouth will catch fire?' ... 'She said, shut your mouth, you pagan woman! That's what she said. She called me *iqaba*!'

qabane var. and pl. form of IQABANE.

‖**Qamata** /ɬaˈmaːta, kəˈmaːtə/ *n.* Also **Qamatha, Qhamata, uQamat(h)a.** [Xhosa *uQamata,* perh. fr. an unrecorded Khoikhoi word.] Esp. among Xhosa-speakers: TIXO.

1880 *Cape Monthly Mag.* III. 294 We considered that Qamata was the great spirit, .. as he, in our opinion, made the chiefs. 1905 W.H. TOOKE in Flint & Gilchrist *Science in S. Afr.* 88 Their [*sc.* the Xhosas'] word for God is Unkulunkulu, denoting the first man or progenitor; also Uhlanga and Itongo, the Great spirit. He is an ancestral deity from whom all men trace their origin. Other terms for God are Tixo and Qamata, the former certainly, the latter probably of Hottentot derivation. 1908 I.W. WAUCHOPE *Natives & their Missionaries* 21 The missionary .. came there suddenly and told them of the Qamata, whom they did not know although they used his name when they sneezed, and said 'Qamata, keep us, protect us and save us from the *Amagqwira*'. 1918 H. MOORE *Land of Good Hope* 117 Tixo bears other names, as Qamata, or Molimo. 1925 D. KIDD *Essential Kafir* 101 They never seem to offer any sacrifices to him, for they do not know his praise names; yet sometimes when they sneeze they will say 'Qamata, help me.' 1939 N.J. VAN WARMELO in A.M. Duggan-Cronin *Bantu Tribes* III. i. 16 The Nguni have a form of ancestor-worship as their common religion, while a belief in the existence of a Superior or supreme deity, called 'Unkulunkulu' by the Zulu and 'u Qamatha' by the Xhosa, exists side by side with it. 1978 *Bona* Oct. 81 Chief Sebe .. is .. a strong believer in the ancient traditions and customs of his people ... The Xhosa have always spoken of 'uQamata', the God above, the Uvoko, or the re-awakening. 1982 *Pace* Oct. 37 The Africans believed in one God. The Xhosa called Him *Qamata,* the Arabs called him *Allah,* the Zulu called Him *Mvelinqangi.* 1992 V. MAYEKISO in *Focus on Afr.* Vol.3 No.2, 52 'Qamata' is the supreme being whom even the probing thoughts of man dare not defile ... Man's knowledge is limited to the knowledge that 'Qamata' is the Protector, the Giver of blessings, and the Receiver of offerings.

qawali var. QUAWWALI.

qawwal var. QUAWWAL.

Qhamata var. QAMATA.

qhwasha var. QWASHA.

Qoranna var. KORANNA.

quaai var. KWAAI.

quagga /ˈkwaxa, kwɒxə/ *n.* Also **kwag(g)a,** and (formerly) **kwakka, quacha, quag(g)er, quag(g)ha, quaker, quakka, qwagga.** Pl. unchanged, **-s.** [S. Afr. Du. (prob. fr. Khoikhoi), onomatopoeic, named for the braying of the species; current in Xhosa as *iqwarha* quagga, Burchell's zebra, mountain zebra.]

1.a. Any of several zebras of the Equidae. **i.** The extinct *Equus quagga; mountain zebra* sense (*c*), see MOUNTAIN; *wild ass,* see WILD sense b. **ii.** Burchell's zebra, *E. burchelli; bont(e)quagga,* see sense 1 b below; *mountain zebra* sense (*b*), see MOUNTAIN. **iii.** The *mountain zebra* (sense *a*) see MOUNTAIN), *E. zebra zebra.* Also *attrib.*

In earlier times the distinctions between the different species were not always noted, but the name 'quagga' is now used primarily for the extinct *Equus quagga,* a zebra once found at the southern tip of Africa and now recognised, from genetic information, as a sub-species of *E. burchelli* (see quot. 1991).

[1776 F. MASSON in *Phil. Trans. of Royal Soc.* LXVI. 297 We saw numbers of wild animals, and in particular a variety of the Zebra, called by the Hottentots Opeagha.] 1786 G. FORSTER tr. A. *Sparrman's Voy. to Cape of G.H.* I. 223, I saw for the first time in my life, one of the animals called *quaggas* by the Hottentots and colonists. It is a species of wild horse, very like the *zebra.* 1790 PENNANT in W. Paterson *Narr. of Four Journeys* 17 The Quacha is striped like the former [*sc.* the Zebra] on the head and body, but with fewer lines. 1795 C.R. HOPSON tr. C.P. *Thunberg's Trav.* II. 84 Buffaloes, elephants, two-horned rhinoceroses, striped horses and asses, (Zebra, Quagga) and several kinds of goats. 1798 S.H. WILCOCKE tr. J.S. *Stavorinus's Voy. to E. Indies 1768-71* III. 4 The quagga (*equus quagga*); these animals can be tamed and broke in; Sparrman says he saw one driven in a team, with five horses, at the Cape. 1802 [see GNU]. 1806 J. BARROW *Trav.* I. 44 We were gratified with the sight of a small herd of the beautifully marked animal the zebra, and a great number of another species of wild horse, known in the colony by the Hottentot name of qua-cha. 1822 W.J. BURCHELL *Trav.* I. 138 This beautiful animal has been hitherto confounded by naturalists with the Zebra. When these were first described by modern writers, the Quakka was considered to be the female Zebra while both that and the true Zebra bore in common, among the colonists, the name of Quakka. *Ibid.* 386 Pits for ensnaring game were every where to be seen ... A line of large branches and limbs of trees, placed so closely together as not to be easily passed by any of the antelopes or kwakkas. 1827 [see *wild ass* (WILD sense b)]. 1834 T. PRINGLE *Afr. Sketches* 503 The cry of the Quagga (pronounced quagha, or quacha) is very different from that of either the horse or ass. 1838 [see *wild horse* (WILD sense b)]. 1846 [see LEKUKA]. 1860 A.W. DRAYSON *Sporting Scenes* 33 The Kaffir .. stood up to his full height, and .. told the commissioner .. that he was not a Hottentot: he here referred to the practice these men have of eating the quagga, or zebra. 1896 *Scientific African* Mar. 72 The Quagga is so named onomatopoetically [*sic*], the word being an imitation of the peculiar bark of the animal sounding like 'ouag-ga,' the last syllable being very much prolonged. 1897 H.A. BRYDEN *Nature & Sport* 273 The true quagga (*Equus quagga*) has already clean vanished from the great hunting-grounds of Southern Africa. 1920 E.H.L. SCHWARZ *Thirstland Redemption* 3 Near Dassie Klip .. he saw a number of quaggas, now extinct (unless the report be true, that there is a herd of them in the Kaokoveld, in the north of South West Africa). c1936 *S. & E. Afr. Yr Bk & Guide* 1077 The *Quagga* (*equus quagga*), which was perhaps a Southern variety of Burchell's Zebra, was only striped to the centre of the body. This beautiful animal has been exterminated, although, eighty years back, it was found in immense numbers on the plains of the O.F.S. 1948 A.C. WHITE *Call of Bushveld* 140 There were, at the beginning of the 19th century, thousands of quagga on the plains of South Africa. The last wild specimen is reported to have been shot at Aberdeen in the old Cape colony in 1858. The last quagga in the London Zoo died in 1872, while another in the Amsterdam Zoo died in August, 1883. 1957 L.G. GREEN *Beyond City Lights* 114 Veldkornet Frans van der Merwe .. was the owner of a tame quagga which he hoped to use for stud purposes to improve the local horses. 1975 *Motorist* May 34 Since the arrival of man at the Cape .. no fewer than three species of our fauna have completely disappeared — the genuine quagga which in earlier times roamed the plains of the present Karoo and Free State in vast numbers, the Cape lion and the blue antelope. 1976 D.M.B. PRESTON *Story of Frontier Town* 22 There is only one single quagga to be seen in South Africa and this is a stuffed foal in the Museum in Cape Town. 1979 *Daily Dispatch* 10 May 7 Two boys found guilty of malicious injury to property after shooting a Quagga at their local zoo .. worked weekends at the same zoo. 1990 *Farmer's Weekly* 8 June 86 (*advt*) Fifteenth annual sale of game — Werksplaas Tshipise. Game species: .. 15 Quagga. 1991 E. ABRAHAMS in *Sunday Times* 7 July 16 Research, which used dry muscle tissue and blood removed from the skins of stuffed quaggas in museums around the world, proved that the creatures were merely sub-species of the plains zebra which had adapted its colour to fit in with its dusty Karoo environment. **1993** *Sunday Times* 16 May 2 Reproduction history is to be made on Tuesday when South African scientists implant a zebra embryo into a horse in an attempt to revive the extinct quagga.

b. With defining word: **bergquagga** /bɜːg-, bɛ(r)x-, beəx-/ [Afk., *berg* mountain], the *mountain zebra* sense (a) (see MOUNTAIN), *Equus zebra zebra*; **bont(e)quagga** /ˈbɔnt(ə)-/, also (formerly) **bonti quagga**, [Afk., *bont* see BONT], *E. burchelli* (see sense 1 a ii above).

1970 J.F. PRINSLOO *Informant, Lüderitz (Namibia)* Bergquagga, a type of zebra found in the eastern Karoo, and should not be confused with the quagga that became extinct around 1870. **1972** *Daily Dispatch* 22 July 4 The old pioneers used 'quagga' rather loosely for the mountain zebra (bergkwagga), Burchell's zebra (bontquagga) and the quagga itself, so that it is difficult to say how far the range of the extinct species extended north. **1986** *Our Living World* 4th Quarter 1 The bergkwaggas are back! The threatened Cape mountain zebra has made a welcome return to the Cape Peninsula after an absence of 300 years. **1839** W.C. HARRIS *Wild Sports* 372 *Equus Burchelli.* Burchell's Zebra. **Bonti Quagga** of the Cape Colonists. **1846** J.C. BROWN tr. *T. Arbousset's Narr. of Explor. Tour to N.-E. of Col.* 87 Two distinct species of quaggas are found on this side of the Orange River, that which the dutch colonists call brown quagga .. and the speckled quagga. [*Note*] Bonte-Kwagga. **1852** [see *wildepaard* (WILDE sense b)]. *a*1875 T. BAINES *Jrnl of Res.* (1964) II. 53 A herd of forty of the handsome bont quaggas — *Equus burchelli* — stopped to gaze at the wagons. **1982** *S. Afr. Panorama* Nov. 8 The stripes of the mountain zebra are slightly different from those of the zebras found on the plains. The latter are sometimes called *bontkwagga* (variegated zebra). **1990** SKINNER & SMITHERS *Mammals of Sn Afr. Subregion* 719 The name quagga was applied to *E. burchelli* as well, although later *bontquagga* was used.

2. Special Comb. **quagga bok** *obs.* [S. Afr. Du. *bok* antelope], some unknown animal; **quagga moed** /-mut/ [Afk. *moed* courage], see quot. 1948!; **quagga quick** *obs.*, QUICK sense 1 a.

1835 A. SMITH *Diary* (1940) II. 79 **Quagga bok**: About the size of a spring bok; striped blackish and dull white down the sides. **1948** A.C. WHITE *Call of Bushveld* 146 In connection with zebras, men speak of 'zebra courage' or '**quagga-moed**'. This is used as a term to signify the kind of courage which draws nothing from experience. **1913** C. PETTMAN *Africanderisms* 388 **Quagga quick**, .. the name given to a species of grass that springs up in the Karoo veld after heavy rains.

Quaiquae var. KHOIKHOI.

quarri var. GUARRI.

quawwal /kaˈwɑːl/ *n.* Also **qawwal, quawal**, and with initial capital. [fr. Urdu, see next.]
1. One who sings QUAWWALI songs.

1969 ESSOP et al. *Challenge to 25 Natal Moolvies*, In Ahmedabad I met a *Majzoob* (God intoxicated Saint) named Ali Shah Bapoo and I joined his company, then I drank the '*pyala*' or the *cup of bestowal*, immediately after which the *miracle* happened — and from a *qawwal* (singer) a *mubal-ligh* was born. **1976** *Leader* 5 Mar. 4 (*caption*) The picture of quawal F. Khan .. was taken during the recital. **1984** *Post* 11 Apr. 8 The organisers .. have selected two artists who have had considerable experience as Quawwals in South Africa.

2. QUAWWALI.

1985 *Cape Times* 8 July, Whether the Indian Chamber in Parliament served any useful purpose ... 'Are our Parliamentary representatives .. contributing positively to a better South Africa, or are they just singing quawals while the country burns?' Post asked.

quawwali /kawaːli/ *n.* Also **qawali, qu(a)wali**, and with initial capital. [Urdu *qavvali*.] An Urdu devotional song (see quot. 1992); QUAWWAL sense 2. Also *attrib.*

1971 *Post* 8 Aug. 27 (*advt*) Quawali LP, India print, R4,50 ... Shandar Quawali Maqabla, Various Artists ... Local Print R3,75. **1972** *18th Anniversary Programme* (Women's Cultural Group, Durban), If the Women's Cultural Group has indulged in gourmet fare and uninhibited histrionics, .. it has also organized high brow symposiums, .. erudite Nushaeras and spell binding Quawwalis. **1976** *Leader* 5 Mar., In commemoration of the martyrdom of Hassan the grandson of the Prophet, .. a number of persons fell into a trance while listening to various quawali singers recanting the death of the Islamic luminary. **1984** *Post* 11 Apr. 8 Samad Shola, a name almost synonymous to Quawwali in South Africa. Samad Shola has been singing since he was 13 and acquired his taste for Quawwali singing from his late father. **1992** R. MESTHRIE *Lexicon of S. Afr. Indian Eng.* 39 Qawali, .. Spirited Urdu devotional song with musical accompaniment, performed by a small group of musicians.

quay vogel var. KWÊVOËL.

quedien, -dine varr. KWEDINI.

queen *n.*[1] Also **quean**. [Calque formed on Afk. *kween* barren cow.] A barren female mammal, particularly, a barren domestic cow. Also *attrib.*

1892 NICOLLS & EGLINGTON *Sportsman in S. Afr.* 61 Old [elephant] cows, and especially 'queens' (barren females), will be found more difficult to deal with than the bulls. [**1913** C. PETTMAN *Africanderisms* 287 Kween, .. A barren animal of any sort.] *c*1964 J. HOPE in *New S. Afr. Writing* 34, I glared with all the arrogance of my fifteen years — 'Good oxen! Quean cows, and a bob's worth of butchers' meat!' **1971** *Daily Dispatch* 16 Oct. 21, 5 Old cows, 4 trek oxen, 1 queen heifer, Shorthorn type.

queen *n.*[2] *colloq.* Ellipt. for *shebeen queen* (see SHEBEEN sense 2).

1948 A. PATON *Cry, Beloved Country* 35 She is one of the queens, the liquor sellers. *c*1948 H. TRACEY *Lalela Zulu* 62 There are many famous, or infamous, 'queens' of illicit bars in the Reef native townships. **1951** *Drum* Oct. 6 Shebeens are run sometimes by Queens, sometimes by men, the Queens in Malay Camp and Fordsburg are mostly Europeans, who employ Africans as their assistants to sell the liquor. **1969** [see AI-AI]. **1977** P.C. VENTER *Soweto* 121 The queens prefer to pay their house-rent six months in advance. Who needs a rent collector banging on the door when there are thirsty clients to be served? **1990** G. SLOVO *Ties of Blood* 618 She made her way through a Soweto in which rumours abounded: the shebeens had been raided and the queens fought back said one.

Queen's tears see TEAR.

quei var. KWAAI.

quela var. KWELA.

queur-boom var. KEURBOOM.

quick *n.* Also with initial capital. [Special sense of general Eng. *quick(-grass)* couch-grass; influenced by Afk. *kweek(gras)*, see KWEEK.] In full *quick grass*.

1. Any of several species of creeping grass of the Poaceae, esp. **a.** the sturdy and often troublesome couch-grass *Cynodon dactylon* (subfamily Chloridoideae); *common* - or *fine quick*, see sense 2; *quagga quick*, see QUAGGA sense 2; *small quick*, see sense 2; and **b.** BUFFALO GRASS (sense 1 b), *Stenotaphrum secundatum.* Cf. KWEEK sense a.

1838 J.E. ALEXANDER *Exped. into Int.* II. 89 Sometimes half way up to the knee in sand, and with our feet scorched with the heat, stung with the quick grass, and bruised with the baked clay, we reached the tent. **1841** J. COLLETT *Diary.* II. 30 Apr., All the quick Grass & much of the other destroyed by the Locust. **1896** R. WALLACE *Farming Indust. of Cape Col.* 100 The grass which forms the closest covering in the veld .. is the *small couch grass* or quick, of light cultivated soils — the dúb grass of India, *Cynodon dactylon*, .. called Bermuda grass in Australia. *Ibid.* 441 The *quick grass* .. gives a great deal of trouble while the work of ploughing progresses, if the implement be not of a shape which will overcome it. **1917** R. MARLOTH *Common Names* 53 Kweek, .. Employed now for several plants with a creeping rhizome, mostly troublesome weeds in lands and gardens. E[nglish]: 'Couch-grass, Quick'. **1931** E.P. PHILLIPS *Afr. Grasses* 79 Quick grass. *Cynodon Dactylon; C. incompletus; Stenotaphrum secundatum.* **1957** *Handbk for Farmers* (Dept of Agric.) II. 798 The soil should be thoroughly and carefully prepared .. to ensure that most perennial weeds, such as quick-grass (*Cynodon* spp.) are destroyed. **1969** E. ROUX *Grass: Story of Frankenwald* 161 The wild *Cynodon dactylon* .. is popularly known in South Africa as 'kweek' or 'quick', while to the Americans it is Bermuda grass or devil grass. **1973** F.J. VELDMAN in *Std Encycl. of Sn Afr.* VIII. 603 It is known that almost all quick-grasses (*Cynodon* spp.) .. may contain dangerous quantities of cyanogenetic glucosides under certain climatic conditions.

2. With distinguishing epithet designating a particular species of grass: **coarse quick**, BUFFALO GRASS (sense 1 b), *Stenotaphrum secundatum*; **common - or fine quick**, *Cynodon dactylon* (see sense 1 a); **grove quick**, BUFFALO GRASS (sense 1 b), *Stenotaphrum secundatum*; **Karoo quick (grass)**, see KAROO sense 3; **quagga quick**, see QUAGGA sense 2; **red quick**, *Transvaal kweekgras* (see TRANSVAAL), *Cynodon hirsutus*; **sand quick**, *Schmidtia pappophoroides* (subfamily Chlorodoideae); **seaside quick**, BUFFALO GRASS (sense 1 b), *Stenotaphrum secundatum*; **small quick**, *C. dactylon* (see sense 1 a); **Transvaal quick**, see TRANSVAAL.

1917 R. MARLOTH *Common Names* 53 Grove [quick], *Stenotaphrum glabrum*, also called **Coarse quick**, Coarse couch-grass, Buffalo-grass. **1935** J.W. MATHEWS in *Jrnl of Botanical Soc.* XXI. 11 Their [*sc.* imported seeds'] failure has been general, and back in the nineties of the last century the local grasses, Coarse Quick and, occasionally Fine Quick were being used. **1955** L.K.A. CHIPPINDALL in Chippindall et al. *Grasses & Pastures* 12 Well known examples of grasses that are cultivated extensively for .. these purposes are Kikuyu grass .. and **Common Quick** grass (*Cynodon dactylon* varieties). **1912** *S. Afr. Agric. Jrnl* Aug. 173 (Pettman), This idea [*sc.* that lamziekte is caused by eating wilted grass] seems to have originated among the Batlapings, some of whom associate the disease with the **fine quick** grass (*Cynodon incompletus*). **1935** J.W. MATHEWS in *Jrnl of Botanical Soc.* XXI. 12 The Bermuda grass is our Fine Quick (*Cynodon dactylon*), and is even more widely spread over the globe than the Coarse Quick. **1970** E.G.B. HARDY *Informant, Cape Town* Fine quick, coarse quick = names given to lawn grasses correctly called 'Kweek'. **1917** [**grove quick**: see quot. at *coarse quick* above]. **1991** G.E. GIBBS RUSSELL et al. *Grasses of Sn Afr.* 97 *Cynodon hirsutus.* **Red quick** grass. **1913** C. PETTMAN *Africanderisms* 424 **Sand quick**, A Bechuanaland name for *Schmidtia bulbosa*. **1918** J.W. BEWS *Grasses & Grasslands* 160 *Schmidtia bulbosa.* Sand Quick Grass. **1992** F.P. VAN OUDTSHOORN *Guide to Grasses* 201 *Schmidtia pappophoroides.* Sand Quick ... A tufted perennial, often with stolons and roots at the lower nodes. **1955** L.K.A. CHIPPINDALL in Chippindall et al. *Grasses & Pastures* 367 *Stenotaphrum* .. 1 species: *S. secundatum* ... A well known '**seaside quick** grass' that occurs in abundance above the beaches in numerous coastal districts. **1955** J.D. SCOTT et al. in *Ibid.* 543 On the deep sands of the sea-shore dunes, pioneer grasses are *Sporobolus virginicus* .., *Dactyloctenium australe* .., and *Stenotaphrum secundatum* (Seaside Quick). **1987** [see *buffel(s)gras* (BUFFEL sense 1 b)]. **1913** A. GLOSSOP *Barnes's S. Afr. Hsehold Guide* 316 *Grasses, Native*, In order of merit come 'Rooi' grass .., **small quick** grass (Indian doab grass), rib grass.

quickstertje *n. obs.* [Partially Englished form of S. Afr. Du. *kwikstertje*, fr. dim. form of Du. *kwikstaart* (see KWIKSTAART).] Any of several species of wagtail of the genus *Motacilla* of the Motacillidae, esp. the *Cape wagtail* (see CAPE sense 2 a), *M. capensis*; KWIKSTAART; QUICKY.

[**1900** STARK & SCLATER *Birds of S. Afr.* I. 259 *Motacilla capensis* ... 'Quick Stertje' of the Dutch.] **1905** W.L. SCLATER in Flint & Gilchrist *Science in S. Afr.* 139 The species most often seen is perhaps the little Cape Wagtail or Quickstertje (*Motacilla capensis*). **1913** C. PETTMAN *Africanderisms* 389 *Quick stertje* or *Quicky*, .. These friendly little wagtails are regarded everywhere with special favour. **1923** HAAGNER & IVY *Sketches* 15 The confiding little Quickstertje .. is too well-known to need any description.

quicky *n. colloq.* [Formed on QUICKSTERTJE + Eng. (informal) n.-forming suffix *-y*.] QUICKSTERTJE.

1909 A. HAAGNER in *Afr. Monthly* Vol.6 No.33, 270 On the bank are seen a pair of those confiding little birds the Quicky of the Colonial, or the Cape wagtail. **1913** [see QUICKSTERTJE]. **1923** HAAGNER & IVY *Sketches* 15 Our confiding little friends the Wagtails (*Motacilla*), locally called 'Quickies' or 'Quickstertjes', of which South Africa possesses seven species. **1994** D.J. JOYCE *Informant, Port Elizabeth* Watch – the quicky's coming in the back door to eat the crumbs on the floor. Don't move.

quitrent *n.* [Special senses of general Eng.] See also LOAN.

The meanings attached to this word varied considerably; it was often used loosely rather than in the strictly legal sense.

1. *Obs.* exc. *hist.* An annual rental (and subsequently a tax) calculated upon the estimated value of land occupied, and paid by a tenant farmer to secure a renewable tenancy.

1796 *Royal Proclamation* in G.W. Eybers *Sel. Constit. Doc.* (1918) 7 Our Will and Pleasure is That the Revenue derived from the Annual Quit Rent paid by the Persons holding Lands granted to them by the Dutch Government shall continue to be collected. **1801** H.C.D. MAYNIER in G.M. Theal *Rec. of Cape Col.* (1899) IV. 60 A considerable number .. have already .. paid their Quit Rents as usual and to enable them all to do so I have prolonged the usual time to one month. **1827** G. THOMPSON *Trav.* II. 157 The annual quit-rent is fixed at the inspection, and is generally from thirty to fifty rix-dollars, perhaps about one per cent of the estimated value. **1887** [see *kaffir tax* (KAFFIR *n.* sense 2 e)]. **1911** A.W. BARLOW in *Farmer's Weekly* 11 Oct. 154 In the Free State the natives pay in direct taxation more than double the amount derived from the quit-rent on farms. **1974** E. LANDSBERG in *Std Encycl. of Sn Afr.* X. 436 In the Transvaal and Orange Free State the quitrent became a land tax with an annual rate of 2s. per 100 morgen in the Orange Free State and a basic rate of 1s. 6d. per 100 morgen in the Transvaal.

2. *hist.*

a. A system of land tenure based on such an agreement; ERFPACHT. Also *attrib.*, and *fig.* See also LOAN.

1811 J.A. TRUTER in G.M. Theal *Rec. of Cape Col.* (1901) VIII. 106 Quitrent expires with the end of fifteen years, after which Government has a right again to take possession of the ground on payment of the mere Opstal, trees and buildings, without anything else. **1832** *Graham's Town Jrnl* 24 Aug. 135 On Saturday .. will be sold a Quit rent Farm, belonging to the Estate of the late William Thackery. **1843** J.C. CHASE *Cape of G.H.* 132 *Quit-rent*, By far the large majority of farms are held under quit-rent tenures ... The rent then determined can never be increased, although instances are not rare wherein the original assessment having .. found to be too highly rated, a reduction of the tax has been made. **1924** L.H. BRINKMAN *Glory of Backveld* 178 It is not yet thirty years that Prospect was surveyed by the Government and sold as a quitrent farm. **1938** C.G. BOTHA *Our S. Afr.* 26 Quitrent, introduced in 1732, gave occupancy on a lease for fifteen years, after which the contract had to be renewed. **1945** [see ERFPACHT]. *c*1960 J.M. DONALD in J.B. Bullock *Peddie* 28 The farms were granted on condition of personal occupation and under a quit-rent system. **1985** A. TREDGOLD *Bay between Mountains* 181 When the quit-rent system that had elapsed was re-introduced after the second British occupation, several farmers took advantage of it.

b. With defining word designating a particular type of land tenure: **perpetual quitrent**, a system of land-ownership created by the conversion of an ordinary quitrent tenancy into one maintained in perpetuity. Also *attrib.*, and *transf.*

1813 *Proclamation* in *Stat. Law of Cape of G.H.* (1862) 49 This perpetual quitrent shall, further, not be liable to any other burthens ... All applications for the conversion of loan lands into perpetual quitrent ... must be made within twelve months. **1825** A.G. BAIN in A.C. Partridge *Lives, Lett. & Diaries* (1971) 71, I believe the farms in Hex River are held in perpetual quitrent, consequently the government reserves the right of making roads where they think proper. **1832** *Graham's Town Jrnl* 20 Apr. 65 The whole of the Property belonging to said Estate, viz; The perpetual quit-rent Place *Tempe*, situated as aforesaid, measuring 3150 morgen. **1840** *Echo* 22 June 10 His Excellency Sir Rufane Shaw Donkin .. to .. bestow upon the undermentioned gentlemen who had been aiding and abetting His Excellency Lord Charles Henry Somerset in the year 1819, .. to expel 'Makana' and his hordes of Amakosa from the loyal city, the Eastern Province, to be held by them and their heirs lawfully begotten for ever, on perpetual quitrent. **1843** [see LOAN]. *c*1881 A. DOUGLASS *Ostrich Farming* 191 In 1813, seven years after the final establishment of the British Government in the colony .. Governor Sir John Cradock invited all possessors of 'loan places' to submit their claims and receive title-deeds for the land, to be known under the name of 'Perpetual Quitrent Tenure' ... 'Quitrent Tenure' .. only differs from 'Freehold' in that Government reserve their rights to precious stones, gold and silver, and the right of making and repairing roads, and of taking materials for that purpose without compensating the owner, together with the perpetual annual payment of £4 16s. **1936** *Cambridge Hist. of Brit. Empire* VIII. 766 Of land held under perpetual quitrent tenure there were only about 4000 Dutch acres in all. **1949** E. HELLMANN *Handbk on Race Rel.* 178 The system of tenure .. has been described as one of 'perpetual quitrent'. The land may not be mortgaged; it passes at the death of the owner to the next of kin as defined in Native law; and it may not be alienated except to another Native and with the government's consent.

3. *transf. Rare*, perh. *nonce*. A system whereby, if the owner of a mortgaged property cannot keep up his or her loan repayments, ownership of the mortgaged property is transferred to the mortgagee, who then charges the former owner rent for the use of the property. Used *attrib.*

1993 *Weekend Argus* 16 May 1 Banks offer new 'quitrent' scheme to owners in trouble. Under the 'quitrent' scheme, the 'rents' being paid for a home which was effectively repossessed would be less than the bond repayments.

quiver tree *n. phr.* [tr. S. Afr. Du. *kokerboom*.]

1. The KOKERBOOM (sense 1), *Aloe dichotoma*. Also *attrib.*

1789 in P. Cullinan *Robert Jacob Gordon* (1992) 18 *(caption)* Aloe Dichotoma, or Quiver Tree. **1790** W. PATERSON *Narr. of Four Journeys* 58 This plant [*sc. Aloe dichotoma*] is called the Koker Boem, or Quiver Tree; and has its name from the use to which it is commonly applied by the natives. **1806** J. BARROW *Trav.* I. 334 The largest I met with was about one hundred feet. It was called in the country the Kooker boom, or quiver tree. **1824** W.J. BURCHELL *Trav.* II. 199 The *quiver* is usually made of some thick hide .. ; but the natives more towards the western coast, frequently use the branches of the *Aloe dichotoma*, which is therefore called by the Hottentots and Colonists, *Koker-boom* or quiver-tree. **1838** J.E. ALEXANDER *Exped. into Int.* I. 56 We .. ascended .. the higher parts of the Kamiesberg, where we saw the strange koker boom, or quiver-tree, with its thick and silver-green trunk, hollow arms (from which the quivers are made), and leaves like those of the aloe. **1841** [see KOKERBOOM]. **1883** B. RIDSDALE *Scenes & Adventures in Great Namaqualand* 35 Vegetation scarce existed here .. and very occasionally a *koker boom*, or quiver tree. **1902** G.M. THEAL *Beginning of S. Afr. Hist.* 11 The arrows were carried in a quiver usually made of the bark of a species of euphorbia, which is still called by Europeans in South Africa the Kokerboom or quiver tree. **1920** [see KOKERBOOM]. **1961** O. LEVINSON *Ageless Land* 12 Weirdly decorative koker or quiver tree of the aloe family jabs its fingers at the pallid blue sky – fingers that are strange forked ramifications of its stem. **1989** A. STEVENS in *S. Afr. Panorama* 6 Feb. 46 The kokerboom is also known as the Quiver Tree because the bushmen would use a suitable branch from one as an arrow container ... The two open ends would be sealed with a flap of tanned skin. **1991** D.M. MOORE *Garden Earth* 203 The quiver tree (*Aloe dichotoma*) .. is a giant succulent member of the lily family ... The indigenous African San peoples used the soft branches as quivers for their arrows, from which the tree derives its name.

2. With distinguishing epithet designating a different species of aloe: **giant quivertree**, the *baster kokerboom* (see KOKERBOOM sense 2), *Aloe pillansii*.

1992 A. DE KLERK in *S. Afr. Panorama* Mar.-Apr. 76 Cornellskop .. in the Northwestern Cape is the home of the endangered giant quiver tree (*Aloe pillansi*), a rare sight on the desolate Richtersveld landscape.

Qung var. KUNG.

quwali var. QUAWWALI.

Qwabe /ˈɬwaːbe, ˈkwaːbe, -bi/ *pl. n.* Formerly also **Amaquabe, Amaquabi**. [See quot. 1978. For an explanation of *ama-* forms, see AMA-.] The members of a Zulu-speaking people settled in the northern regions of the province of KwaZulu-Natal. Also *attrib.*

As is the case with many names of peoples and groups in *S. Afr. Eng.*, this word has been found only in plural uses; however, it may be that it has also been used in unrecorded singular forms.

1836 R. GODLONTON *Introductory Remarks to Narr. of Irruption* 255 The neighbouring clans were thrown into commotion by a furious attack of the Amaquabi. **1895** H. RIDER HAGGARD *Nada* 17 The tribe of the Amaquabe. [**1978** A. ELLIOTT *Sons of Zulu* 15 Zulu's elder brother Qwabe .. gave his name to a large group of followers who today are one of the biggest clans in KwaZulu. Both clans pay ultimate allegiance to the Zulu king.] **1986** P. MAYLAM *Hist. of Afr. People* 26 The Qwabe were one among a number of independent lineages in the area. Early in the eighteenth century, during the reign of Kuzwayo, the Qwabe became increasingly powerful ... At the height of their power the Qwabe were also able to dominate the region west of the Ngoye. **1989** *Stanger Mail* 24 Feb. 14 In Mansomini .. women from the Qwabe tribe have won international and local recognition for making their sugar farms not only viable but very profitable.

qwasha /ˈɬwaːʃa, ˈkwɑʃə/ *n.* Also **qhwasha, qwash**. [Zulu ideophone, used of a crunching sound, as of movement in gravel; here prob. echoic (see quot. 1994).] In township Eng.: a home-made rifle.

1989 O. MUSI in *Drum* Apr. 36 One veteran policeman out there convinced his higher-ups to grant an amnesty to anyone who surrendered his 'Qhwasha' (that is the home-made rifle). There were no takers. **1989** *Weekly Mail* 5 May 6 Our only weapon is the *qwasha*, says Gadaffi, referring to the home-made guns that make up the armoury of the boys' army. 'Down in Moscow they make the best *qwashas*. A good one costs R120. Some take R1 bullets and others use the big bullets for a shotgun.' **1992** A. Sparks in *Guardian Weekly* 26 June 17 There are stolen revolvers and army rifles, clubs, spears and machetes, and a crude homemade zip gun called a qwash, produced from piping, rubber tubing and springs. **1994** P. Hawthorne in *Time* 19 Dec. 16 A homemade pistol called a 'quash' — from the explosive click it makes when fired.

qwela var. KWELA.

R

R *n.*[1] The written abbrev. of RAND sense 3 a.

1959 *Act 61* in *Stat. of Union* 702 The coinage units of the Union shall .. be the rand (abbreviated as R) and the cent (abbreviated as c). 1965 *S. Afr. in Sixties* (S. Afr. Foundation) 17 South Africa's Net National Income: Total at 1948 prices (mil. R). 1967 E. ROSENTHAL *Encycl. of Sn Afr.* 413 The word 'Rand' is derived from 'Witwatersrand', to emphasise its gold backing. The abbreviation is R (singular and plural) written before the numeral. c1970 C. DESMOND *Discarded People* 30 At Limehill they were given a plot, 50 yards by 50 yards, for which they pay R1 a year. 1992 [see *Getaway* quot. at GOGGA sense 1]. 1993 *Weekend Argus* 15 May 9 The replacement value of the bungalow only was 'conservatively' estimated at R400 000.

R /ɑː(r)/ *n.*[2] The eighteenth letter of the alphabet, combined with various numbers to denote military rifles of local manufacture.

a. *R1*: The name given to the Belgian automatic F.N. (7,62mm) assault rifle when manufactured locally. Also *attrib.*

1971 F.V. LATEGAN in *Std Encycl. of Sn Afr.* IV. 532 The .. series of 'short Lee Enfields' .. was partly replaced by the Belgian automatic F.N. (7.62 mm Cal.) in 1961, which shortly afterwards was manufactured as the R.1, the military rifle of the Republic of South Africa. 1986 S. SEPAMLA *Third Generation* 115 The number of policemen carrying *R1* rifles was enough to discourage the monkeying around one sometimes sees at such large gatherings. 1988 *Frontline* Feb. 27 The South African conscript is forced into one side of a civil war situation where he is seen by the South Africans and Namibians he faces from behind the R1 barrel as part of a force upholding apartheid. 1991 *Natal Witness* 27 Mar. 2 Police have arrested a white man armed with a R1-rifle and ammunition in Johannesburg's Alexandra township. 1992 C.M. KNOX tr. E. Van Heerden's *Mad Dog* 151 The Leader climbs out (the slap of palms against R-1s from the present-arms squad tells us that).

b. *R4*: A 5,56mm military assault rifle (see *Paratus* quot. 1979).

1979 *Paratus* May 1 The development of a new rifle, dictated by the needs of modern warfare. It is a 5, 56 mm rifle, known as the R4. Other specifications include: Weight – 4,3 kg, length – 970 mm (stock extended) 740 mm (stock folded); length of barrel – 460 mm. The rifle is gas-operated with a rotating bolt. Magazines: 35 rounds (standard). Cyclic rate of fire: 650 rounds a minute; maximum effective range: 600m. 1979 *Evening Post* 10 May 3 The new R4 assault rifle .. would replace the R1 rifle in particular fields only and not entirely. 1986 *Sunday Times* 16 Mar. 14 The R4 assault rifle .. is said to incorporate the best elements of the Israeli Galil and the Soviet AK-47, topped by improvements to suit local bush conditions. It is an addition to the R1 rifle and is of 5,56 mm calibre. 1991 N. MBATHA in *Pace* Feb. 41 Most taxi drivers are armed, not only with primitive weapons like knives, pangas or axes, but with increasingly sophisticated weapons like AK-47 and R4 rifles in some cases. 1992 *Natal Witness* 6 Nov. 3 Three of them had firearms — an AK47, an R1 and an R4.

c. *R5*: A 5.56mm assault rifle with folding stock, a short-barrelled version of the R4. Also *attrib.*

1986 G. CAWTHRA *Brutal Force* 256, 5,56mm R5 SA (Isr.) *Ibid.* 269 Short-barrelled version of the R4 used by the SA Air Force and for urban operations. 1988 M. NEL in *Personality* 18 July 12 Bruce puts on headphones, loads an R5 rifle and points it at a tin centimetres away from the muzzle. 1990 *Armed Forces* Nov. 24 (*caption*) Members of the Battalion bearing the R5 rifle with folding butt. 1993 *Sunday Times* 10 Oct. 7 Right-wingers, three of them national servicemen, made off with at least 20 R5 rifles, 20 shotguns and 30 South African-made Z88 9mm pistols.

raad /rɑːt, rɑːd/ *n.* Also with initial capital. [Du., council; cf. HEEMRAAD, *Kerk(e)raad* (see KERK sense 2), VOLKSRAAD.]

1. A board or council, particularly, *hist.*, the council of the Rehoboth Baster people (see REHOBOTH). See also BURGERRAAD sense 1.

1840 C.A. KINLOCH in *Echo* 9 Nov. 5 The Chief, with a look of incredulity, signified that the matter should be laid before the Council ... [It was] not until the evening of the 18th that the Raad could make up their minds. 1847 J. TINDALL *Jrnl* (1959) 101 The case was brought before the Raad who .. caused the Damara .. to be beaten wrongfully. 1856 C.J. ANDERSSON *Lake Ngami* 57 He laid his complaint before the chief of the tribe; and a 'raad', or counsel, was held. 1877 *Sel. Comm. Report on Mission to Damaraland* 110 Minutes of proceedings of meeting, at which were present Captain Jan Jonker Afrikaaner, the members of his Raad, and about 15 other natives. c1936 *S. & E. Afr. Yr Bk & Guide* 176 Until 1924 .. they [*sc.* the Basters] were ruled by a chief with the title of 'Captain,' supported by a Raad or Council partly hereditary and partly chosen every five years by the 'Burghers' of Rehoboth. 1973 J. COPE *Alley Cat* 126 The Raad, the village council, also meets there. 1973 M.L. MITCHELL in *Hansard* 8 Feb. 297 The Minister of Labour .. says that in no circumstances will he sit in the same 'raad' as a non-white. 1976 R. Ross *Adam Kok's Griquas* 41 From the beginnings of Griqua organisation, there had been a council, a *raad*, which aided and advised the *Kaptyn*, and acted as the legislative body for the Captaincy. 1987 B. LAU *Namibia* in *Jonker Afrikaner's Time* 46 The position of the chief and his 'raad', the leaders of the commando, was primarily based on their military skills in securing access to specific commodities like guns and horses or taxes and booty in cattle.

2. *hist.* [Shortened form of Afk. (earlier S. Afr. Du.) *Volksraad.*] VOLKSRAAD sense 1.

1851 R. GRAY *Jrnl of Bishop's Visitation* II. 25 These men have formed themselves into a Republic, and have their 'Raad' (Council). 1873 F. BOYLE *To Cape for Diamonds* 153 The gentlemen .. obtained their grant under solemn seal and bond of the Transvaal Parliament, or *raad*. 1888 *Cape Punch* 6 June, Those absurd old creatures the members of the Transvaal Raad. 1897 *E. Prov. Herald* 1 Mar., The Raad was prorogued this afternoon, and the President, in the course of his speech, indirectly referred to the constitutional crisis, saying the steps which were taken were for the well-being of the State. 1899 F.R.M. CLEAVER in M.M. Cleaver *Young S. Afr.* (1913) 27 The Raad will be asked to place the control of the police and detectives under the State Attorney. 1899 P.A. MOLTENO *Sel. from Correspondence* (1981) 102 One of the demands is equal rights for the English language in the Raads and Courts. 1903 D. BLACKBURN *Burgher Quixote* 236, I found myself at the door of the bar of the Transvaal Hotel, a place I rarely went into unless I wanted to see a member of the Raad or a Government official. a1930 G. BAUMANN in Baumann & Bright *Lost Republic* (1940) 160 The new laws .. were terribly mutilated in their passage through the Volksraad, the main culprits being the attorneys, of whom there were quite a number elected as members of the Raad. 1940 F.B. YOUNG *City of Gold* 209 Even when the Raad was not sitting he felt it his duty to stay in Pretoria and stand by the President. 1974 K. GRIFFITH *Thank God We Kept Flag Flying* p.xvii, On 7 September [1899] President Kruger said in the Raad, the Parliament in Pretoria, 'They have asked for my trousers, and I have given them; then for my coat, I have given that also; now they want my life, and that I cannot give.' 1994 M. ROBERTS tr. *J.A. Wahlberg's Trav. Jrnls 1838–56* 38 News that Pretoria has overthrown the Raad and chosen a new one.

3. *comb.* **raad huis** /-heɪs, -hœɪs/ *n. phr. Obs.*, also with initial capitals, [Afk., *huis* house], RAADSAAL.

1888 *Cape Punch* 29 Feb. 117 This S[tout] O[ld] F[armer] .. made a Bee line — B stands for Boer — to the corner of the Raad Huis. *Ibid.* 1 Aug. 39 A wagon stood in the great square, opposite the Raad Huis. 1921 H.J. MANDELBROTE tr. *O.F. Mentzel's Descr. of Cape of G.H.* I. 150 The Town and Stellenbosch had each a burger council and a 'raadhuis;' the latter also possessed a gaol.

Hence (*nonce*) **Raadist** *n.*, a member of a raad.

1899 *Grocott's Daily Mail* 12 July 2 The thousands of British Subjects in the Republic, who have .. furnished the handful of Raadists and the Executive with tens of thousands sterling per annum.

Raadsaal /ˈrɑːtsɑːl/ *n. hist.* Also **Raadzaal**. [Afk. (earlier S. Afr. Du. *raadzaal*), *raad* council + *saal* hall.] The council-chamber or parliament-house in which the legislative assemblies of the former Boer Republics sat; *raad huis*, see RAAD sense 3. Also *attrib.*

1893 *Brown's S. Afr.* 184 One of the first buildings erected in the town .. has been a Church, a Raad Zaal and a Court House. 1899 D.S.F.A. PHILLIPS *S. Afr. Recollections* 113, I went over to Pretoria next day and visited the Raadzaal .. and was accommodated with a seat. 1923 B. RONAN *Forty S. Afr. Yrs* 170 When the Volksraad was sitting President Kruger always drove down to the Raadzaal about eight o'clock in the morning, accompanied by an escort of mounted police or Staats Artillerie. 1933 C.J. UYS *In Era of Shepstone* 311 (Swart), His sketch of the interior of the Raadsaal or Volksraad chamber, reminds the reader of Dickens' description of an English bankruptcy court with its foul atmosphere and squalid appearance. 1948 H.V. MORTON *In Search of S. Afr.* 238 The harmony of Bloemfontein is in a great measure due to the buildings erected in the proper style for South Africa. The perfect little Raadsaal gave me great pleasure. 1955 A. DELIUS *Young Trav.* 57 The old Raadsaal, the Boer House of Parliament. 1972 *S. Afr. Panorama* Feb. 30 The Appeal Court, the Town Hall, the Fourth Raadsaal (last home of the parliament of the old 'Model Republiek' and present seat of the

Orange Free State Provincial Council). **1980** *Ibid.* Aug. 26 Some of the first newsreels ever filmed in South Africa showed top-hatted President Paul Kruger driving his State carriage to the Pretoria Raadzaal (Parliament), escorted by a body of smart 'Zarps' (cavalry police). **1989** *Sunday Times* 22 Oct. 28 Tuks have set an example for a local city council that seems to believe that the clock on the Raadsaal tower stood still in the 19th century.

raak /rɑːk/ *adj.* and *adv.* Also **rak**. [Afk., telling, effective, as in the expressions *dit is raak!* that (shot or blow) went home, *raakgooi* hit or strike (with a missile), and *raakskiet* hit (the mark), shoot straight; fr. Du. *raken* to hit, reach, touch.]
A. *adj.* On target, accurate.

1871 J. MACKENZIE *Ten Yrs* (1971) 147 Click went one man's gun — bang went Hendrik's, who shouted 'Dat's raak! — I've hit him!' **1913** C. PETTMAN *Africanderisms* 390 *Raak*, This word, sometimes corrupted into 'rock,' is in common use in the Midland Districts, in such expressions as : 'That's rak,' i.e. 'That is a hit,' when a missile, such as a bullet or stone, has hit the object aimed at.

B. *adv.* Accurately.

1883 M.A. CAREY-HOBSON *Farm in Karoo* 125 There he stood, the fine old fellow, with his trunk erect ... Just as I was all ready — I had taken such good aim that I knew I should shoot 'raak' — young Hans calls out — 'Hendrick! You musn't shoot.'

Hence **raak** *v.*, to hit a target.

1900 B. MITFORD *Aletta* 67 Nee, nee. It comes to the same thing, I tell you, and if you miss you can go on shooting until you raak. [**1913** C. PETTMAN *Africanderisms* 406 *Rock, To*, (D. *raken*, to hit, touch.) To hit with a missile; the word is also used by children for a hit when playing at marbles.]

raamakie var. RAMKIE.

rabbit *n. Prison* and *school slang.* [Rel. to Afk. *hasie* hare, but cf. also U.S. Eng. (homosexuals' slang) *rabbit* prostitute who sells sex to persons of his or her own sex.] HASIE sense 2.

1949 H.C. BOSMAN *Cold Stone Jug* (1969) 90 'And they also say you're a sodomite' ... 'They say you are some blue-coat's rabbit.' *Ibid.* 158, I was glad to have these little presents. But I was also embarrassed by his attentions. I was scared the warders and convicts would think I was homosexual, and that I was Pym's rabbit. **1974, 1984** [see HASIE sense 3]. **1984** *Informant, Tvl* The regular term of my school-days [for a homosexual] was rabbit and bunny boys — *hasie* is a new one to me.

rabekin /ˈræbəkɪn/ *n. Obs.* exc. *hist.* Also **rabouquin.** [ad. Pg. *rabequinha*, dim. form of *rabeca* fiddle, but denoting the Nama stringed instrument *ramgi-b*.] RAMKIE.

1790 tr. *F. Le Vaillant's Trav.* II. 107 *The rabouquin is a triangular* piece of board, with three strings made of intestines, supported by a bridge, which may be stretched at pleasure by means of pegs, like those our instruments in Europe; it is indeed nothing else than a guitar with three strings. **1795** C.R. HOPSON tr. *C.P. Thunberg's Trav.* (1773) II. 43 Rabekin is a musical instrument, something like a guitar, made of a calabash and a narrow board, with three or four strings, which may be stretched or relaxed at pleasure, by means of screws. On this instrument the Hottentots play with their fingers. [**1861** P.B. BORCHERDS *Auto-Biog. Mem.* 178 In the evenings the labourers .. indulged in gossip .. or listened to the music of the ramakienjo (an instrument with three strings stretched over a calabash, which acted like a sounding board).] **1970** P. OLIVER *Savannah Syncopators* 109 *Ramkie, remkie*, three- or four-stringed guitar related to the Portuguese *rabequinha* brought from Malabar to South Africa and developed by the Cape Hottentots. Also *rabekin, ramakienjo, raamakie, ramki*.

race classification see CLASSIFICATION.

race mera see quot. 1884 at RYSMIER.

raed vatje var. ROOIBAADJIE.

Raid *n. colloq.* Also with small initial. ***The Raid***: Ellipt. for *Jameson raid* (see JAMESON).

1913 C. PETTMAN *Africanderisms* 391 The armed invasion of the Transvaal Republic by the troops of the Chartered Company, under Dr. Jameson, on 29 December, 1895, is known throughout South Africa as 'The Raid'. **1924** L. COHEN *Reminisc. of Jhb.* 127 The Raid led to world political changes, and a great loss of British prestige abroad. **1936** R.J.M. GOOLD-ADAMS *S. Afr. To-Day & To-Morrow* 160 The last stage in the pursuit of the Voortrekkers, the climax of the Raid, the Boer War, the final annexation, all these were fired .. by the gold from a ridge in his own Transvaal. **1946** M.S. GEEN *Making of Union of S. Afr.* 130 The Raid even had repercussions in Europe. **1963** A. KEPPEL-JONES *S. Afr.: Short Hist.* In less than four years from the Raid the British Empire and the Republics were at war. **1977** *Dict. of S. Afr. Biography* III. 441 J[ameson] instructed by Rhodes had planned as well as led the Raid. **1989** *Reader's Digest Illust. Hist.* 237 The raid intensified the power struggle in the SAR between Boer and British.

rainbird *n.* [See quots. 1928 (sense 1) and 1913 (sense 2).]
1. The coucal *Centropus burchellii* of the Cuculidae; also called *vlei loerie* (see VLEI sense 2).

In G.L. Maclean's *Roberts' Birds of Sn Afr.* (1993), the name 'Burchell's coucal' is used for this species.

1906 'ROOIVLERK' in *E. London Dispatch* 4 Aug. 4 Of all the notes to be heard during a day at the Nahoon, I fancy those of the rain-bird: (one of our resident cuckoos) are the most strange. **1928** E.H.L. SCHWARZ *Kalahari & its Native Races* 100 There were any amount of Burchell's Kukels ... One nests every year in my garden in Grahamstown, and when it is going to rain, utters the curious trill just at sun-down. The Kaffirs call it the rain bird. **1980** J.O. OLIVER *Beginner's Guide to our Birds* 28 Their call is rather like water running out of a bottle, 'doo-doo-doo', repeated many times. This call is said by some to be heard before rain and Burchell's Coucal is often called 'The Rainbird'. **1983** D.A.C. MACLENNAN *Reckonings* 41 City of bells and birds: hornbills squeaking in the loquat tree their voices too absurd for such intrinsic dignity; a rainbird and his bottle bubbling down the scale. **1990** D.N.E. KAIN in *Weekend Post* 19 Jan. (Leisure) 1 All canoeists are familiar with the distinctive and rather mournful cry of the large brown rain bird (Burchell's coucal).

2. *rare.* The BROMVOËL, *Bucorvus leadbeateri*.

1913 C. PETTMAN *Africanderisms* 391 *Rain-bird*, In the Native Territories the Turkey buzzard — *Bucorax cafer* — is so named by the colonists, because in times of drought the natives try to drive these birds into the water to drown them, thinking thus to secure rain — the superstition being that while the body of the bird remains in the water the rain will continue.

rainbow *n.* [Special sense of general Eng., alluding to the colours of a rainbow.] Used *attrib.* in *fig.* senses, alluding to the country's many cultures: of or pertaining to the transformed non-racial South African society. Freq. in the collocations ***rainbow children, - nation, - people***.

1994 MRS MNGCONGO in *Grocott's Mail* 29 Apr. 2 Everyone can be happy because God helps all his rainbow children. **1994** B. RONGE in *Sunday Times* 5 June 19 They have placed it deftly in the context of South Africa's 'rainbow nation'. **1994** G. WILLOUGHBY in *Weekly Mail & Guardian* 17 June 42 What's available? A rainbow-nation's worth of colours and tastes. **1994** F. MABUSE-SUTTLE on CCV TV 21 Aug. (Top Level), We are the rainbow people. **1994** J. SHARP in *Democracy in Action* Vol.8 No.5, 12 Archbishop Desmond Tutu and others have referred to South Africa as a 'rainbow nation', enjoining us to celebrate our diversity. **1994** *Style* Oct. 10 Became a born-again South African when he returned .. to the rainbow nation after having lived in Toronto, Canada, for five years.

rain frog *n. phr.* [See quots 1937 and 1970.] Any of several species of burrowing frog of the genus *Breviceps* of the Microhylidae, esp. *B. verrucosus*; also called BLAASOP (sense 3). Now often with distinguishing epithet denoting a particular species of frog, see quots since 1979. See also DONDER PADDA sense b.

1929 W. ROSE *Veld & Vlei* 47 His other common name is 'Reen Padda' or 'Rain Frog,' which probably indicates a propensity to emerge from concealment at the advent of rain. **1937** *Guide to Vertebrate Fauna of E. Cape Prov.* (Albany Museum) II. 117 *Breviceps tympanifer* .. Rain Frog ... The cry is considered to foretell rain. **1970** C.A. DU TOIT in *Std Encycl. of Sn Afr.* I. 341 They are nocturnal and secretive, and are seldom seen except after heavy rains, when they are forced to the surface in large numbers; hence the other common name, 'reënpadda' or rain frog. **1979** PASSMORE & CARRUTHERS *S. Afr. Frogs* 20 *Terrestrial Development (a)* Species which construct nests in moss, under logs, etc., or in burrows. No aquatic larval stage. Parental care often evident, e.g. Rain Frogs. *Ibid.* 82 Rain Frogs. *Breviceps* ... Eleven species occur in South Africa. *Ibid.* 84 Plaintive Rain Frog, *Breviceps verrucosus*. *Ibid.* 88 Cape Rain Frog, *Breviceps gibbosus* [etc.]. **1990** N.H.G. JACOBSEN in *Fauna & Flora* No.47, 25 As the clouds gather and the earth becomes cool and moist, a shrill trilling call is heard. This belongs to the Soutpansberg rain frog *Breviceps sylvestris taeniatus*, calling because of the increase in humidity ... They are adapted to a terrestrial life, unable to swim. **1993** *Earthyear* (ed.5) Winter (Earthling) 27 Also found on Table Mountain .. is a frog that can't swim! It is the Cape rain frog or blaasop (*Breviceps gibbosus*) ... If an adult lands in water it blows itself up like a ping-pong ball with legs and floats until it reaches dry land. **1994** *Afr. Wildlife* Vol.48 No.4, 47 (advt) The Bushveld rain frog (*Breviceps adspersus*). It is one of about 12 species of rain frog occurring in southern Africa.

Rain Queen *n. phr.* Also with small initials. **a.** The hereditary queen of the Lobedu people, believed to have special medicinal skills and power over the elements, esp. the ability to bring rain; MODJADJI sense 2. Also *attrib.* **b.** Occas. used as a title, with the queen's name. See also LOBEDU.

1933 J. JUTA *Look Out for Ostriches* 97 The dark mysterious Rain Queen ... Mujaji is her name, and she is probably the last of the direct line of Rain Queens. **1937** B.H. DICKE *Bush Speaks* 40 The indunas living under the Rain-Queen did not hang back. They .. acknowledged Schiel as their chief ... That was too much for 'Her Who Must Be Obeyed.' **1943** E.J. & J.D. KRIGE (*title*) The Realm of a Rain-Queen. **1955** T.V. BULPIN *Storm over Tvl* 85 All these people .. lived in some awe of Mujaji, the renowned Rain Queen who lived with the loBedu people thirty miles north-east of Wolkberg, in a tribal home of magnificent splendour. **1959** L.G. GREEN *These Wonders* 33 For centuries the rain queen was expected, in her old age, to pass on her secrets to a daughter or younger woman, and then to commit ritual suicide by taking poison. Mujaji was prevailed upon by missionaries to break this savage tradition, and she died of old age. **1972** *Caravan* May 61 A special visit was arranged to the kraal of Mojaji, the Rain Queen. **1979** P. MILLER *Myths & Legends* 204 Modjadji: The Rain Queen ... In a land where rain is the harbinger of life and lack of it means death, the ability to control it by supernatural means is the most valuable of a magician's skills ... It is doubtful whether anyone other than the queen herself is in possession of her secrets. **1983** *S. Afr. Panorama* May 37 The mystique of the *Land of the Silver Mist* well serves the Rain Queen with her sacred grove of Modjadji palms, prehistoric cycad survivals from the age of giant reptiles. **1986** [see LOBEDU]. **1987** *Star* 2 Sept. 12 Molototsi Valley — the home of Modjadji, the legendary 'rain queen'. **1988** E. MAKWELA in *Pace* May 59 The amazing resident of Mothomeng Village, in the Lebowa area of Rain Queen Modjadji, still has a complete set of teeth at the age of 128.

rak var. RAAK.

ra'king var. RAMKIE.

ramenas /ˈram(ə)nas/ *n.* Also **ramnas, romines.** [Afk., ad. and transf. use of Du. *ram(m)enas* a name for the black radish.] Either of two plants of the Brassicaceae, the wild radish *Raphanus raphanistrum*, or (formerly) the wild mustard *Sinapis arvensis* (but see also quot. 1917).

1896 R. WALLACE *Farming Indust. of Cape Col.* 117 *Charlock*, wild mustard, or 'romines,' [*printed* romincs] *Sinapis arvensis, L.*, is a widely prevalent weed of the corn-fields of Cape Colony. **1913** C. PETTMAN *Africanderisms* 391 *Ramenas*, .. *Raphanus raphanistrum*. Wild mustard is known by this name in the Western Province. *Ibid.* 558 Wild ramenas .. *Gunnera perpensa, L.* A decoction of the root of this plant is used for dyspepsia. **1917** R. MARLOTH *Common Names* 69 *Ramenas*. In the S.W. the 'Jointed Charlock'. In the eastern Karoo *Aloe longistyla*, one of the small species. **1932** WATT & BREYER-BRANDWIJK *Medicinal & Poisonous Plants* 56 *Raphanus raphanistrum* L., an introduced species known as Charlock (jointed), Ramenas, Ramnas, and Knopherik, is used by Europeans in the treatment for gravel. **1950** *Cape Times* 8 Aug. 9 Weeds such as 'wilde ertjies', ramenas and sorrel, .. are regarded by farmers as their biggest enemies. **1953** *Ibid.* 20 May 8 The ramnas, the wild radish of the Cape .. is a weed of cultivation also introduced from Europe. **1966** C.A. SMITH *Common Names* 382 *Ram(e)nas, Raphanus raphanistrum* .. Introduced at the Cape during the very early days of the Settlement, and comparatively recently spread north in the Republic .. The seeds have been shown to be toxic.

ramese var. RAMMIES.

ramkie /ˈramki/ *n.* Also **raamakie, ra'king, ramkee, ramki, ramky, remkie.** [Nama *ramgi-b*, prob. ad. Pg. *rabequinha*, see RABEKIN.] A guitar-like instrument played particularly (in the past) by the KHOIKHOI peoples of the Cape, and consisting of three or four strings stretched along a board, at one end of which is a gourd resonator on which the bridge is placed; RABEKIN; RAMKIEKIE. Cf. GORAH.

1805 *Gleanings in Afr.* (anon.) 232 Others were busily employed in dancing to the music of the ramky, (as they call it,) and seemed highly delighted with their exertions. **1827** G. THOMPSON *Trav.* I. 391 In the evening we were entertained by a Bushwoman, in the service of Nel, playing on the *Raamakie*, — an instrument about forty inches long by five broad, and having the half of calabash affixed to the one end, with strings somewhat resembling those of a violin. With this instrument she produced a dull monotonous thrumming. **1835** J.W.D. MOODIE *Ten Yrs* I. 224, I have often listened with great pleasure to the wild and melancholy notes of the 'gorah' and 'ramkee'. *Ibid.* 226 The 'ramkee' is constructed on the same principle as the guitar, by stretching six strings along a flat piece of thin board, with the half of a gourd or 'calabash' at one end, over which a piece of dried skin is strained, on which the bridge is placed. **1934** P.R. KIRBY *Musical Instruments of Native Races* (1965) 249 Another stringed instrument, the name of which is familiar to most South Africans, is the *ramkie*. The name itself is full of interest, being derived, according to the best authorities, from the Portuguese *rabequinha* (cf. *cavaquinho*, a little guitar, or *machete*), which is equivalent to *rabeca pequena*, a little violin. The instrument itself shows traces of Portuguese influence, but throughout the years the name has gone through many changes. *Ibid.* 251 Borcherds, while he lived at Stellenbosch (1786–1801), heard the *ramakienjo*, as he called it, played by his father's slaves. *Ibid.* 255 Unquestionably the *ramkie* was borrowed directly or indirectly, by the natives of South Africa from the Portuguese, in all probability its prototype being the *machete*. The earliest true South African players were, in my opinion, the Hottentots, who passed the instrument on to the Bushmen on the one hand and to the Bantu on the other. **1936** J.A. ENGELBRECHT in D.B. Coplan, Urbanization of African Performing Arts. (1980) 56 Of the *ramkie*, the Bloemhof men stated that it belonged to those Hottentots who had lost their own language and had adopted Dutch. **1945** L.G. GREEN *Where Men Still Dream* 130 The thin music of a Hottentot 'ramkee', the empty circle of veld under the blue bowl of the sky. **1955** V. DE KOCK *Fun They Had* 53 Hottentots .. too loved to dance, .. and their music was provided by the ramkie, whose strains seemed to possess an almost magical power of setting them all in motion. **1960** J. COPE *Tame Ox* 38 The coloured folk sensed in their hearts the great tautness like the gut string of a ramkie tuned almost to breaking. **1961** L.E. VAN ONSELEN *Trekboer* 63 The ramkie .. is a box-like affair with a stick protruding from it ... It can be played with artistry and rhythm only by a Hottentot Bushman. **1969** J.M. WHITE *Land God Made in Anger* 41 There is everything here from .. the two-note whining of the Bushman ramkie to Schonberg and Karl Amadeus Hartmann. **1970** P. OLIVER *Savannah Syncopators* 109 *Ramkie, remkie*, three- or four-stringed guitar related to the Portuguese *rabequinha* brought from Malabar to South Africa and developed by the Cape Hottentots. Also *rabekin, ramakienjo, raamakie, ramki*. **1972** *Std Encycl. of Sn Afr.* V. 609 Besides stringed instruments, such as the *!goura* (gorah), the *!guba* and the *ramgyb* (ramkie), they [*sc.* the Hottentots] used a set of reed-pipes. **1980** D.B. COPLAN Urbanization of African Performing Arts. 46 The *igqongwe*, a Zulu ramkie. **1989** *Reader's Digest Illust. Hist.* 61 The four-stringed plucked *ramkie* was brought to the Cape by Malabar slaves.

‖**ramkiekie** /ˈramkiki/ *n.* Also **ramkietjie.** [Afk., *ramkie* see prec. + -IE.] RAMKIE.

1959 A. DELIUS *Last Division* 76 For, Masters, when affairs got tricky I'd tingle-tangle on my ou ramkietjie, And, true as Gord, you know, those Things Would come and dance round me in rings. **1989** F.G. BUTLER *Tales from Old Karoo* 176 James gave him a one gallon oil tin, and a plank, and lent him the tools to make a *ramkiekie* for himself.

rammies /ˈræmiːz/ *pl. n. Slang.* Also **ramese.** [Austral. Eng. (recorded from 1906 in the *Australian National Dict.*), prob. ad. *roundme's*, originally in the form *round the houses*, rhyming slang for *trousers*.] Trousers.

Still current in *S. Afr. Eng.*

1946 J.B. FISHER in E. Partridge *Dict. of Underworld* (1950) 554 *Ramese*, Trousers: South Africa: late C19–20. **1949** H.C. BOSMAN *Cold Stone Jug* (1969) 34 The name for a warder was a crew. You never heard any other name for him. Shoes they called daisies; trousers, rammies. *Ibid.* 35 Snowy Fisher comes out of the window all right, with half his rammies burnt off him, right into the arms to them two johns. **1961** *Personality* 16 May 27 Narrow trousers have ceased to be 'drain-pipes' and are now indentified .. as 'rammies'. **1970** S. SMUTS *Informant, Cape Town* Ma, have you sent my rammies to the cleaners? **1991** G. McCONNELL *Informant, Howick*, I wore my blue rammies (pants). You know, the ones I klepped (pinched) from Jack.

ramnas var. RAMENAS.

rampi, rampie /ˈrampi/ *n.* [Afk., 'sachet', fr. Malay *rampai* mixture; or fr. Hindu *Rampa* the name given to three heroes in Hindu mythology (A. Davids, 'Words the Cape slaves made' in *S. Afr. Jrnl of Linguistics* Vol.8 No.1, 1990).] In the Cape Muslim community:

a. A sachet filled with shredded orange-leaves which have been dipped in sweet-smelling oils, prepared on the prophet Muhammed's birthday.

1944 I.D. DU PLESSIS *Cape Malays* 14 On this occasion, the women go to the mosques on Saturday afternoon from two o'clock till sunset ... Here the afternoon is spent cutting up orange leaves, dipping them in costly, sweet-smelling oils, and tying them up in sachets (*Rampi's*, from the Malay *rampai*: a mixture). **1953** DU PLESSIS & LÜCKHOFF *Malay Quarter* 33 Small sachets of the leaves .. known as *rampi's*, from the Malay word *rampai*, meaning a mixture, .. give the popular name to the festival. **1970** HEARD & FAULL *Cookery in Sn Afr.* 586 The cut-up leaves were mixed with oils (some from Mecca) and then made into sachets (Rampi) which the men place in their breast pockets. **1971** *Argus* 5 June (Weekend Mag.) 1 The delicately perfumed 'rampies' were filled in brightly coloured paper sachets and after the ceremony, were distributed among everybody present. **1981** *Sunday Times* 12 July (Mag. Sect.) 1 The women gather at the mosque in the afternoon, dressed in their most colourful clothes, to cut the orange leaves and to prepare the so-called 'rampies'.

b. *comb.* **rampi-sny** /-sneɪ/, occas. **rampies-sny** [Afk., 'the cutting of rampies'], *Feast of the Orange Leaves* (see ORANGE LEAVES).

1953 DU PLESSIS & LÜCKHOFF *Malay Quarter* 31 Feast of the Orange Leaves. This is the most colourful and beautiful festival of the Muslim year. Popularly known as *rampi sny*, it is held in honour of Moulidu'n-Nabi, the birthday of the Prophet. **1970** *Cape Times* 18 May, They spent the afternoon till sunset cutting up orange leaves on small boards using special knives. The pieces were put on trays and sprinkled with rare oils. The practice is known as *rampi-sny*. **1971** *Argus* 5 June (Weekend Mag.) 1 Every medora was zealously stored away and used for special occasions such as weddings, baptisms and 'rampies-sny'.

rand /rænd, rant, rɒnt/ *n.* Formerly also **randt, rant(z), ront.** [Afk., fr. Du. *rand* edge, border.]

1.a. Pl. **-s**, ‖**-e** /-ə/, occas. (formerly) **rantzes.** A long (rocky) hillock; an area of high, sloping ground; cf. RANDJIE.

1839 J. COLLETT Diary. II. 27 May, Finished making New Kralls to day on Willow fountain rant. **1846** J.M. BOWKER *Speeches & Sel.* (1864) 223 The Kafirs mustered on the height where the attack was ... The whole of the rant was black with them and their horses. **1882** J. NIXON *Among Boers* 118 At the base .. were a multitude of stony rantzes. The term rantz .. is applied to the huge ridges .. which cross the veld in all directions, looking like railway embankments in the process of construction. **1882** S. HECKFORD *Lady Trader in Tvl* 361 Just as I got to the highest part of the randt, the wind and rain came whirling up. **1891** B. MITFORD *Romance of Cape Frontier* 23 He is standing on the top of the *randt* for a brief blow after his exertions. **1900** A.H. KEANE *Boer States* 22 We can here speak of 'rands', that is, ridges of moderate elevation, which, however, are sometimes high enough to form water-partings. **1947** H.C. BOSMAN *Mafeking Rd* (1969) 74, I shall never forget the scene .. in the early morning, when there were still shadows on the rante. **1968** *Farmer's Weekly* 3 Jan. 7 The veld consists of iron stone rante, vleis and sweet Karoo flats. **1980** A.J. BLIGNAUT *Dead End Rd* 91, I could hear the swishing of the grass fifty paces away as the leopard tiptoed on the rand.

b. A common element in place-names, e.g. *Fish River Rand, Randburg, Randfontein, Witwatersrand.*

[**1836** C.L. STRETCH Journal. 24 Feb., Descended the Fish river heights called by the Dutch 'Vis Rivier ront' and encamped at a stream.] **1839** [see sense a]. **1914** C. PETTMAN *Notes on S. Afr. Place Names* 32 Suikerbosch Rand. *Ibid.* Boschrand. **1989** P.E. RAPER *Dict. of Sn Afr. Place Names* 460 *Randfontein*, .. Gold-mining town some 24 km west of Johannesburg ... The name is Afrikaans and means 'ridge fountain', 'fountain on the edge'.

2. ***The Rand*** [short form of Afk. place name *Witwatersrand, wit* white + *watersrand* watershed, divide]: **a.** The gold fields, mining towns, and cities (including Johannesburg) situated along the Witwatersrand gold-reef, in the province of Gauteng. **b.** This gold-reef. Also *attrib.* In both senses also called *the Reef* (see REEF sense 2). See also RANDLORD.

1888 *Cape Punch* 7 Mar. 136 If you just take a trip up to the Randt you'd get a good property in no time. **1890** C. & A.P. WILSON-MOORE *Diggers' Doggerel* 28 Romeo Troilus Giddy McSmack, Surmised that 'a very consid'rable whack' Should be paid for his rights in this Government grant, 'The best Crushing spec,' he explained, 'on the Rand'. **1896** P.A. MOLTENO *Sel. from Correspondence* (1981) 11 What a foolish proposition was Chamberlain's home rule for the Rand — I'm much relieved that he stated he will not press it.

1900 H.C. HILLEGAS *Oom Paul's People* 5 A thousand miles from the Cape of Good Hope, are the gold mines of the Randt, richer than California and more valuable than the Klondike. **1900** H. BUTTERWORTH *Trav. Tales* 57 What is the Randt, or Rand? The gold mines of the deserts, a thousand miles north of the Cape of Good Hope, – an underground treasury. **1903** R. KIPLING *Five Nations* 198 I'd give the gold o'twenty Rands, (If it was mine) to set 'em free. **1917** S.T. PLAATJE *Native Life* 297 Senator General De la Rey .. was accidentally shot by a 'Rand' policemen on the night of September 15. **1940** F.B. YOUNG *City of Gold* 437 I'ld bet you ten thousand pounds to a farthing .. that before twenty years are gone, there'll be a quarter of a million people living on the Rand. **1941** C.W. DE KIEWIET *Hist. of S. Afr.* 127 Maybe new gold-fields as great as the Rand itself. *Ibid.* 130 The belief was strong that South Africa stood on the threshold of other Rands in the Transvaal and in the new lands between the Limpopo and the Zambesi. **1946** S. CLOETE *Afr. Portraits* 269 Kimberley had been the magnet which attracted the iron rails till the discovery of gold made the Rand the financial centre of Africa. **1951** *Drum* Oct. 9 Few people who know the facts can have serious doubts about the real causes of crime on the Rand. **1980** D.B. COPLAN Urbanization of African Performing Arts. 117 Most of the European missions followed their rural converts to the Rand (as the gold fields were called). **1985** V. MARTIN in *S. Afr. Panorama* Aug. 45 The *Sunday Times* wrote in its edition of January 23, 1910 – when Johannesburg was 24 years old – that the Rand was 'a place where people sit in five-guinea chairs and gaze at five shilling pictures'. **1987** C.T. MSIMANG in *S. Afr. Jrnl of Afr. Langs* Vol.7 No.3, 82 Tsotsitaal is a contact medium which developed when blacks of various ethnic groups were thrown together in the South African cities, especially on the Rand.

c. Special Comb. *hist.* **Rand Revolt**, the violent miners' strike of 1922, which was put down by government troops; **Rand Tram** [see quot. 1933], a railway-service linking Johannesburg with the towns of the east and west Rand.

1962 A.P. CARTWRIGHT *Gold Miners* 210 Forty years have passed since the '**Rand Revolt**' was suppressed but the historian still finds it hard to explain the sudden surge of violence that turned a dispute over wages and hours of work into civil war. **1977** BOUCH & HAINES in R.J. Bouch *Infantry in S. Afr. 1652–1976* 206 The Regiment [*sc.* Durban Light Infantry] played a crucial role in the suppression of the 1922 Rand Revolt. Called out on 10 March, it was rushed to Johannesburg and on the 12th relieved the police at Brixton ridge, taking 250 revolutionaries prisoner at bayonet point. **1983** J. CRONIN *Inside* 7 He was nine when his father came blacklisted home from the 1922 Rand Revolt. **1989** J. CRWYS-WILLIAMS *S. Afr. Despatches* 229 The 1922 Strike, or the Rand Revolt as it is more popularly known, was precipitated by the British government's announcement towards the close of 1921 that it intended returning to the gold standard at the parity enjoyed before the start of the 1918–24 conflict. **1926** M. NATHAN *S. Afr. from Within* 67 A concession was granted to the Netherland Railway Company to construct a line (then known as the '**Rand Tram**') between Springs, at the eastern end of the Reef, and Krugersdorp, at its western end. **1933** W.H.S. BELL *Bygone Days* 312 The company owned 717 miles of railway (including the Rand Tram). [*Note*] In the very early days of the Rand Tram – a railway extending from Johannesburg to Boksburg on the east and Krugersdorp on the west – the Boers were much averse to railways and in order to obtain Volksraad approval to the construction and working of the line, it was called a 'tramway'.

3.a. Often with initial capital. Pl. unchanged, or **-s**. The unit of decimal currency adopted in 1961, replacing the pound, and originally equivalent to ten shillings sterling; BUCK *n.*[3]; MAPHEPHA sense 1 a; R *n.*[1] Also *attrib.*

1959 [see R *n.*[1]]. **1961** *Times* (U.K.) 27 Jan. 19 There was a boom on the Johannesburg Stock Exchange last night ... The occasion was the second dress rehearsal for trading in rand and cents when decimalization overtakes South Africa on the second Tuesday of next month. **1961** *Star* 14 Feb. 1 The pronunciation of rand is still so fluid you could drown in it. It varied from rand (like hand) to runt, raint, rarnd and rent. Most people still say '10 bob'. **1970** J. MCINTOSH *Stonefish* 35 He let himself go out of control, spinning faster and faster, littering the sandbank with three thousand rand. **1973** *Sunday Times* 9 Dec. (Mag. Sect.) 10 With point or dash, *not comma*, fill The space on cheques to pay the bill, And always put into his hands Your grocer's cash in cents and *rands*. *c*1979 [see OWN]. **1982** *Daily Dispatch* 10 Mar. 1 The exchange rate of the rand slipped below $1 for the first time in history. **1986** *Sunday Star* 15 June 1 If tomorrow passes without serious trouble the rand will recover from its steep slide, say foreign-exchange dealers. **1989** B. RONGE in *Sunday Times* 20 Aug. (Mag. Sect.), Rands that are worth less than single-ply toilet-tissues and a balsa-wood economy. **1989** F.G. BUTLER *Tales from Old Karoo* 142 Anything over 100 000 is an impressive figure, except in bankrupt currencies, like the Rand. **1991** *E. Prov. Herald* 17 May 27 Make friends with the locals and for a few rand the hired help will lighten the load.

b. With qualifying word: **blocked rand** *hist.*, from 1961 to 1976, rands held in South Africa by non-residents, permitted to be invested only in particular types of securities, and not to be withdrawn from the country except under certain conditions (superseded by the *securities rand* system, see below); **commercial rand**, the rand at the ordinary foreign exchange rate, applicable to import and export transactions and to international trade by South African residents; **financial rand** *hist.*, (the unit of) investment currency for non-residents, used also by emigrants and immigrants for their settling-in allowances; FINRAND; **securities rand** *hist.*, the rand proceeds from the local sale and redemption of South African securities and other investments owned by non-residents. Also *attrib.* See also KRUGER sense 2 a.

1963 *Annual Econ. Report* (S. Afr. Reserve Bank) 38 The Treasury .. was replacing the 5 per cent five-year **blocked rand** bonds with new $3\frac{1}{4}$ per cent three-year bonds. **1986** R.M. GIDLOW in *Securities Markets* No.1 (3rd Quarter) 37 Blocked rand could .. be utilised to purchase quoted government, municipal and public utility stocks with a maturity of five years or more. **1988** P.J. MOHR et al. *Prac. Guide to S. Afr. Econ. Indicators* 22 This blocked rand arrangement was .. a form of exchange control. **1989** R.M. GIDLOW in *Econ. Focus* Nov., Two-tier exchange rate arrangements in South Africa originated .. in 1961 when the blocked rand system was introduced. **1982** *Growth* June 28 If the discount were falling because the financial rand was appreciating, instead of resulting from a decline in the **commercial rand**, the authorities would doubtless feel differently. **1986** R.M. GIDLOW in *Securities Markets* No.1 (3rd Quarter) 39 The existence of a discount on the financial rand may .. affect adversely the operation of leads and lags in the commercial rand market. **1986** *Sunday Star* 8 June 6 Long-term foreign holders of South African bonds are still entitled to receive their interest in commercial rands. **1988** P.J. MOHR et al. *Prac. Guide to S. Afr. Econ. Indicators* 22 The commercial rand applies to all international trade between South Africa and the rest of the world, i.e. to all transactions recorded in the current account of the balance of payments. **1989** *E. Prov. Herald* 16 Mar. 10 To abolish the financial rand now would simply mean that the country would lose much by way of foreign reserves, and moreover would have to accept a sharp depreciation of the commercial rand. **1993** *Financial Mail* 23 Apr. 63 The dual system of a financial and a commercial rand is an integral part of exchange control and was intended to bring foreign investment to SA through the discount offered on initial investments. **1980** *Ibid.* 16 Jan. 15 With the fantastic run in the gold price, the **financial rand** has increased sharply. **1981** *Rand Daily Mail* 4 Feb. 1 The 'financial' rand is currency sold abroad at a discount .. to encourage investment in South Africa. **1985** P. VAN NIEKERK in *Weekly Mail* 6 Sept. 5 The financial rand was reinstated .. to prevent capital flowing out of the country. **1985** N. BRUCE in *E. Prov. Herald* 2 Sept. 1 The local sale proceeds of shares by non-residents .. will have to be retained in South Africa as financial rand balances. **1986** R.M. GIDLOW in *Securities Markets* No.1 (3rd Quarter) 37 In January 1979 .. the financial rand market .. became accessible to non-resident investors for the purchase of a proprietor's interest in a business in South Africa, and not just listed securities. **1987** *Pretoria News* 18 June 5 International companies have been challenged to .. use their Financial Rands to buy housing for their employees. **1988** P.J. MOHR et al. *Prac. Guide to S. Afr. Econ. Indicators* 23 The financial rand rate is determined by non-residents' demand for and supply of South African assets. **1990** C. WILSON in *Independent* (U.K.) 12 Feb. 8 The financial rand, which trades at a discount to the commercial rand, .. is widely seen as a barometer of South Africa's economic health. **1991** *Flying Springbok* May 133 While no limit has been placed on the value of commercial property which may be purchased (via a South Africa-registered company) with financial rand, a change was announced in September 1990 in respect of the financial rand purchase of residential property. **1993** *Africa S. & E.* July 14 Without the protective cover provided by the financial rand mechanism, the effective level of foreign net disinvestment would .. undoubtedly have been higher. **1994** H. MARKS on Radio Algoa 30 Sept., The rumours about the abolition of the financial rand had the market in a tizz yesterday. **1977** *Rand Daily Mail* 18 June 5 The **securities rand** rate yesterday was 73 US cents buyers and 74,75c sellers. **1986** R.M. GIDLOW in *Securities Markets* No.1 (3rd Quarter) 37 Transfers of securities rand could take place directly from one securities rand account to another. **1988** P.J. MOHR et al. *Prac. Guide to S. Afr. Econ. Indicators* 23 The securities rand .. could only be used to buy shares and certain government securities and semi-gilts, often at a large discount relative to the commercial rand. **1993** J. POSTMAS on M-Net TV 14 Mar. (Carte Blanche), The so-called securities rand.

Hence (sense 2) **Randite** *n. obs.*, one from the Rand; (sense 1 a) **randsy** *adj. nonce*, hilly.

1882 J. NIXON *Among Boers* 267 We drove full tilt across a stony rantzy country, which neither delighted the eye, nor afforded ease to the back. **1923** B. RONAN *Forty S. Afr. Yrs* 175 The whole thing would look very shoddy to the present-day Randite. It was the golden youth of the Golden City, when its precocious vitality was exuberant. **1926** *E. Prov. Herald* 16 Jan. 12 Mutton for Randites.

randjie /ˈraɪŋki/ *n.* Also **randje**, **rankie**, **rantj(i)e**. [Afk., earlier S. Afr. Du. *rand(t)je*, dim. form of *rand* (see prec.).] A small ridge; a rise; cf. RAND sense 1 a. See also BULT, HOOGTE, KOPPIE.

*a*1878 J. MONTGOMERY *Reminisc.* (1981) 98, I saw some wagons drawn up; these had shortly before come through the river, and were outspanned on the randjie. **1889** [see SPITSKOP]. **1902** E. HOBHOUSE *Brunt of War* 285, I do wish you could stand on the randje and watch it [*sc.* the concentration camp] for a few minutes. Your thoughts seem to overwhelm you, and you have to turn away. **1914** L.H. BRINKMAN *Breath of Karroo* 17 Here and there a few kopjes relieved the monotony of the view, and every few miles, randjes, or low stony hills, stretched across the plains. **1917** A.W. CARTER *Informant, Ladybrand* 20 Aug., Seeheim Junction .. a dreadful place low down between randjes. On one of the ridges was an imposing building, the 'Hotel Bellevue'. **1924** G. BAUMANN in Baumann & Bright *Lost Republic* (1940) 107 The first inspection .. showed me a beacon well up in a niche in a 'rantje' (small range of hills). **1940** V. POHL *Bushveld Adventures* 17 The eye can still trace the well-worn path where it runs down the rantjie. **1949** M. LEIGH *Cross of Fire* 99 The track climbed the randjie on which we stood and petered down again into the darkness and the gloom towards Matzana's kraal. **1963** S. CLOETE *Rags of Glory* 389 They held kopje and rankie till they became untenable, and then slipped away on their veld-raised ponies. **1970** E. CHAPMAN *Informant, Bloemfontein* The farm house was built on a randjie overlooking the farm. **1984** *Fair Lady* 18 Apr. 84 Because he knew every *randjie* and every *kloof*, his men were in position and ready for action hours before anyone else.

Randlord /ˈrændlɔːd/ *n.* Often *derog.* [S. Afr. Eng. *Rand* (see RAND sense 2 a) + Eng. *lord*, after *landlord*; coined by the Brit. press.]

1. *hist.* A Johannesburg-based mining magnate or tycoon of the late 19th and early 20th centuries. Also *attrib.* See also RAND sense 2.

[**1904** *Daily Chron.* (U.K.) 21 Mar. 5 The Randlords' proposal really drives the British workman out of the Transvaal.] **1936** R.J.M. GOOLD-ADAMS *S. Afr. To-Day & To-Morrow* 54 The black man may go away to his kraal and die a premature death, but that — so the Randlords say — is not the fault of the mines in which he worked. **1955** L. HOTZ in Saron & Hotz *Jews in S. Afr.* 357 Among the leading figures from Kimberley who quickly assumed a commanding position on the goldfields, the so-called Randlords, were Barnato, the Joels, Alfred Beit, Albu, and Lionel Phillips. **1965** C. VAN HEYNINGEN *Orange Days* 69 The fine houses of the mining millionaires (the Rand Lords) and .. the shanties of the poor whites and African miners. **1970** B. ROBERTS *Churchills in Afr.* 143 'The Nineties', says a historian, 'were the high and palmy days of the great Randlords ... Johannesburg seemed nearer to London than any English town'. **1970** A. PARKER in *Personality* 8 Jan. 28 They were a swaggering lot, those Randlords of the 1890's .. adventurers, buccaneers, robust and red-blooded. **1974** *Sunday Times* 3 Nov. (Mag. Sect.) 7 Before the year 1925, .. it was comparatively easy for social-climbing millionaires from the colonies to buy a baronetcy from the British Government ... South Africa's Randlords were not slow to take advantage of what presently became a racket. **1979** T. PAKENHAM *Boer War* (1982) 46 Hohenheim, the suburban villa of Percy Fitzpatrick, a Cape-born Uitlander who worked for the great mining house of Wernher-Beit .. built in 'Randlords Gothic' .. commanded the hillside on which lay Johannesburg. *c*1985 M. KIRKWOOD in *Eng. Academy Rev.* 3 1 Time goes down on the Randlord town and street by street the decades fall in clouds of dust. **1986** *Frontline* June 19 It has taken the best part of a century for anything like the whole truth to dawn about the Randlords. They were rapacious, corrupt, and responsible for a significant proportion of both the world's wealth and its suffering in their lifetimes, and quite a bit in ours. **1987** *Weekly Mail* 10 July 7 This is the empire built by the Oppenheimer dynasty, started by the second generation Randlord, Sir Ernest Oppenheimer. **1990** K. OWEN in *Sunday Times* 3 Mar. 21 The top public servants, who live like Randlords (Pretoria-style: two Alsatians, a *broodboom* and a heart by-pass).

2. *transf.* Any wealthy or powerful Johannesburg person, esp. one linked with the mining-houses.

1975 *E. Prov. Herald* 18 Nov. 13 What evidence does he have for the claim that 'Randlords' are supporting Saan financially as a mouthpiece for the Progressive Reform Party? **1985** *Financial Mail* 18 Jan. 35 Nor last week was it the Rand Lords or Big Business that spoke out ... In their midst were the grassroots businessmen of the Afrikaans community from the Handelsinstituut (AHI). **1991** *Weekly Mail* 20 Dec. 32 Randlord ... Julian Ogilvie-Thompson, known as 'Jot' succeeded Gavin Relly as head of Anglo American.

rankie var. RANDJIE.

rant var. RAND.

rantjie var. RANDJIE.

rantz var. RAND.

Rapportryers /raˈpɔ(r)treɪə(r)z, -s/ *n.* [Afk., *rapport* despatch + *ryers* riders. See Stengel quot. 1990.] A service organization for Afrikaans men who are prominent in business and cultural affairs; as *pl.*, its members collectively. Also *attrib.*

1960 E.G. MALHERBE in H. Spottiswoode *S. Afr.: Rd Ahead* (1960) 148 The Voortrekkers hived off from the Boy Scouts, and the Noodhulpliga hived off from the Red Cross, and latterly the Rapportryers are going to break away from Rotary. **1970** *Cape Argus* 3 Oct. 4 A party which remains dominated by sectional organisations, the Broederbond and Rapportryers, both of which deny rights of membership to English-speaking South Africans. **1972** *Sunday Times* 8 Oct. 3 The Broederbond's concern about membership of the Rapportryers arises from the fact that the Rapportryers are one of the Bond's front organisations and can be said to be controlled and dominated by the Broederbond. **1973** [see FAK]. **1976** *E. Prov. Herald* 2 Oct. 6 The Rapportryers, an organisation of hard-core Afrikaner nationalists whose object in life is to uphold and promote Afrikanerdom. **1980** *Cape Times* 18 Jan. 7 The Federation of Rapportryers wants blacks excluded from any future constitutional development and believes that their needs are met through existing independent bantustan policy. **1981** *Sunday Times* 14 June (Mag. Sect.) 9 If .. Napier seems like the proverbial sleepy village, to its inhabitants it's a humming hive of activity. If it's not a Rapportryer evening, it's the Women's Agricultural Union afternoon. **1990** R. STENGEL *January Sun* 150 The Rapportryers, an organization of Afrikaner businessmen .. are a kind of training ground for the Broederbond ... In the Anglo-Boer War, there were thirty people who carried messages back and forth between commanders. They rode on horseback and 'rapportryer' is the word for the rider who carried these vital dispatches. The organization was founded to support business among Afrikaners. **1990** D. VAN HEERDEN in *Sunday Times* 17 June 12 The Broederbond .. tried gamely to prepare its membership elite for the new South Africa ... Its long-time front, the Rapportryers, diminished in influence as the rifts in Afrikanderdom grew bigger.

Rarabe var. RHARHABE.

ratel /ˈrɑːt(ə)l/ *n.* Also **rattel**, **rattle**, and with initial capital. [S. Afr. Du., etym. dubious; prob. rel. to Du. *raat* honeycomb; but perh. ad. Du. *ratel* rattle (see quot. 1835).]

1. The mammal *Mellivora capensis* of the Mustelidae; HONEY-BADGER; HONEY-RATEL.

In Skinner & Smithers's *Mammals of Sn Afr. Subregion* (1990), the name 'honey badger' is used for this species.

[**1731** G. MEDLEY tr. *P. Kolb's Present State of Cape of G.H.* II. 124 There is a Creature, pretty often seen in the *Cape*-Colonies; and which the People there call a *Rattle*-Mouse, tho' it has Little or Nothing of the Likeness of any Kind of Mouse seen in *Europe*. **1777** (tr. A. Sparrman) in *Phil. Trans. of Royal Soc.* (U.K.) LXVII. 43 Not only the Dutch and Hottentots, but likewise a species of quadruped, which the Dutch name a Ratel, are frequently conducted to wild bee-hives by this bird. [*Note*] Probably a new species of badger.] **1786** G. FORSTER tr. *A. Sparrman's Voy. to Cape of G.H.* II. 180 The *ratel*, a sort of weasel or badger, by nature destined to be the adversary of the bees, and the unwelcome visitor of their habitations, is likewise endued with a particular faculty for discovering and attacking them within their entrenchments. **1806** J. BARROW *Trav.* I. 293 Here .. is abundance of that species of viverra called the Ratel. **1827** T. PHILIPPS *Scenes & Occurrences* 51 When the bird has eaten the honey, the young bees are carefully closed up with stones to prevent the *ratel* from taking them out. **1835** J.W.D. MOODIE *Ten Yrs* II. 190 From its size, peculiar rattling cry, and general appearance, I at first thought it was a 'ratel' which is now well known to naturalists. **1862** C. ROSSETTI *Goblin M.* (1884) 13 Cat-like and rat-like, Ratel- and wombat-like. **1875** C.B. BISSET *Sport & War* 166 There is .. a small animal in South Africa, known there as the Rattle, a description of badger, which displays great intelligence in searching after wild honey. **1876** F. BOYLE *Savage Life* 12 For the sportsman, there were .. rattels. **1905** W.L. SCLATER in Flint & Gilchrist *Science in S. Afr.* 127 The Ratel (*Mellivora ratel*), renowed for its love of bees and honey though seldom seen, as it is strictly nocturnal, causes much annoyance to the Colonial apiarist, throwing over the hives and destroying the combs in its efforts to obtain its favourite food. **1911** D.B. HOOK *'Tis but Yesterday* 56 The ratel cares nothing for stings. Its hide is so loose that it is supposed to be able to turn round in its skin. **1947** J. STEVENSON-HAMILTON *Wild Life in S. Afr.* 242 The ratel does not hesitate to attack the most venomous species of snakes. **1951** L.G. GREEN *Grow Lovely* 146 A ratel is a vicious opponent, often more than a match for a pack of dogs. **1961** L. VAN DER POST *Heart of Hunter* 73 He gave me such a vivid picture of the ratel eating snakes that I saw it gobbling up tangles of serpents like spaghetti. **1975** H.B. COTT *Looking at Animals* 73 Ratels are said to trot unhurriedly with a long, swinging stride. **1980** D. PITCHER *Calabash Child* 60 Ratel loves honey dearly. He is greedy for honey and his thick fur protects him from the stings of bees. **1987** M. HOLMES in *Optima* Vol.35 No.4, 196 The ferocious ratel or honey-badger, .. is a musteline: cornered, it will emit a foul-smelling substance from the perineal gland. **1994** M. ROBERTS tr. *J.A. Wahlberg's Trav. Jrnls 1838–56* 42 The dogs find a Ratel; a terrific fight. After a quarter of an hour the Ratel was still perfectly fresh.

2. *transf. Military.* Usu. with initial capital. [Prob. alluding to the tough nature of the vehicle (rel. to the Afk. idiom *so taai soos 'n ratel* as tough as a honey-badger).] A six-wheeled armoured personnel-carrier and infantry combat-vehicle. Also *attrib.* See also BUFFEL sense 2.

1977 B. MARKS *Our S. Afr. Army* 32 *The Ratel*, This .. is probably the most respected vehicle in the whole defence force ... There is virtually no terrain through which it cannot travel. Even water up to the depth of 1.2 metres ... It has an incredible range of up to a thousand kilometres and can support its crew for two days. **1987** [see G sense a]. **1988** D. RICCI in *Frontline* Apr. 6 Fear-stricken English and Afrikaans voters have prostrated themselves before the chimaera of Ratel-based Nat 'security' instead of supporting the true security of open negotiations and rule of law. **1988** 'KNOCKESPOTCH' in *Frontline* Apr. 21 Oh send me I pray thee thy ratels and troops. Restore me to grace with thy military swoops. **1990** *Ibid.* Dec. 10 In vain did churchmen plead for peace, And diehards call for more police, The fighting simply wouldn't cease: He had to send in Ratels.

ratiep /raˈtip/ *n.* Also **ratieb**, **ratip**. [Afk., fr. Malay *ratib* a sacred formula acknowledging Allah.] In the Cape Muslim community: **a.** KHALIFA sense 1 b; **b.** the rhythmical recitation of a sacred formula during this sword-ritual. Also *attrib.*

1944 I.D. DU PLESSIS *Cape Malays* 90 *Chalifah* or *Khalifa* (Caliph) is the name of the central person conducting the ceremony; but in South Africa the word is often used for the ceremony itself, especially by the Europeans. The Malays use *ratiep* for the actual dance. **1969** *Drum* June 51 In between continuous chanting, prayer giving and mystic displays of ratiep — a form of self-assault with sharp instruments — tasty Malay food was served. **1970** *Personality* 27 Aug. 104 Eight-year old Moochietab Sallie is a ratieb dancer, the youngest in the troupe. During his dance, in front of thousands of wedding guests, he passed steel skewers through his ear lobes and tongue. **1977** *Family Radio & TV* 30 May 18 We see *maan keikers*, children going from house to house offering sweetmeats, and *ratip* which is a display of their strength of faith by the insertion of skewers through their flesh. **1977** *Argus* 13 Jan. 10 The ritual, called ratiep, is performed under the guidance of a spiritual leader known as a Khalifa. Enthusiasts say their only protection from certain death, is faith in their deity — Allah, and the ceremony cannot be performed without a Khalifa praying throughout. **1985** J. CLOETE in *S.-Easter* Oct.-Nov. 22 As a composer, I could respond to the repetitive drum accompaniment of the *ratiep*. **1989** C. CHAPMAN in *Edgars Club* Apr. 45 The dancers work themselves into a trance by means of a rhythm which is called *Ratiep*. This enables them to stick skewers through their cheeks and walk on burning coals, which is a demonstration of their faith.

ration *n.* [Special sense of general Eng. *ration* a (daily) allowance of food or other provisions, esp. as provided in the army.] Usu. in *pl.*: Food supplied to black or 'coloured' farm-workers and domestic servants as part of their wages, or in lieu thereof. Also *attrib.*

1821 G. BARKER Journal. 11 Aug., I was told by others that he has said he expected to receive Rations of food here & never thought to have been requested to herd cattle &c. **1835** T.H. BOWKER Journal. 25 May, The fingoes shufle each other in dealing their ration meat. **1892** *The Jrnl* 20 Sept. 1 (*advt*) Mealies, Kafir Corn, Ration Meal, Flour, Mealie Meal, Kafir Corn Meal, .. Transvaal and Boer Tobacco. **1944** C.R. PRANCE *Under Blue Roof* 107 Kafirs, fear-spurred at last to energy, ran to and fro with the milk-pails, their rations, and embers to start their fire. **1958** A. JACKSON *Trader on Veld* 45 The average labourer's pay was ten to twenty shillings cash per month, or in lieu thereof, one or two sheep or goats, plus a fixed quantity of rations. **1961** D. ROOKE *Lover for Estelle* 105 The servants were waiting at the back door for their rations ... Each servant got a basinful of mealie meal, a double handful of broad beans and two tablespoonsful of dripping every night; and as much skim milk as they wanted. **1973** *Weekend Post* 27 Oct. 17 The average annual payment, including rations, is R67 a servant. **1980** J. COCK *Maids & Madams* 34 A number of workers, 18 percent, received the same food as their employers, but the majority, 80 percent, received 'servants' rations' and one received both.

ratip var. RATIEP.

rat-pack *n. Army slang.* [Abbrev. of *ration pack.*] A food pack issued by the army to men on duty away from base camp. Also *transf.*, see quot. 1993.

1984 *Fair Lady* 14 Nov., 'There is only one thing I can't stand — those fleshy pink pork sausages that come out of a tin .. and the dog biscuits in our rat packs.' They take rat packs with them when they leave the base — one for each day they are away. **1985** S. VEAL in *Family Radio & TV* 1 Apr. 43 The food in the rat packs gave us plenty of energy and included little goodies like milk shakes and chocolate bars but after three days it was monotonous, to say the least. **1985** *Frontline* Aug. 54 We give him a ratpack (a seven day food supply, containing corned beef, chocolate bars, 'dog biscuits', etc). **1988** A. CAMPBELL in *Fair Lady* 27 Apr. 95 In his letters he was always moaning about the ratpacks (ration packs) they get. **1988** C. MITCHELL in *Personality* 6 June 12 The youngsters report for their two-year absence from civilian life, when short hair, 'rat packs,' early rising, PT and much floor scrubbing will become .. the alternative to a pretty easy and pampered lifestyle. **1990** C. SHERLOCK *Hyena Dawn* 209 Fortunately he had a rat-pack with enough food and water to last him for two days. **1993** E. BEATTIE in *Motorist* Mar. 12 The company was to rely heavily on army-style ration packs for meals, affectionately known as 'rat packs'.

rattel, rattle varr. RATEL.

RAU /raʊ/ *n.* [Acronym formed on *Rand Afrikaans University.*] An Afrikaans-medium university in Johannesburg.

1971 *Rand Daily Mail* 16 Mar. 20 Former Springbok rugby captain Dawie de Villiers .. puts Rand Afrikaans University students through their paces ... De Villiers, a lecturer at RAU, is one of five South Africans invited to attend the British Rugby Union centenary celebrations. **1981** *Ibid.* 1 June 1 The SRC at RAU said in a statement that it was 'no longer in favour of holding an intervarsity' against Wits. **1987** *E. Prov. Herald* 14 May 2 De Klerk for RAU ... Dr Willem de Klerk .. has accepted a full-time position at the Rand Afrikaans University. **1989** S. MIRNIS in *Sunday Times* 19 Mar. 29 Willemse, now at RAU, will develop into a major force, specially in crosscountry.

raw *adj. derog.* [Special application of the general Eng. senses of *raw*, 'uncultivated', 'uncivilized' (rarely used), or the more common 'inexperienced', 'untrained'.] Used of black Africans: **a.** From a traditional tribal or rural culture. Cf. RED *adj.* sense 2 b ii. **b.** Uneducated; unsophisticated; RED *adj.* sense 2 b iv. See also BLANKET sense a, RED-BLANKETED.

1866 E.L. PRICE *Jrnls* (1956) 200 My cook .. very civil and respectful, wh. is really all I care for, because the more thoroughly 'raw' or untaught the better for me. **1884** *Queenstown Free Press* 19 Feb., Selecting two of his smartest detectives, he directed them to assume the 'red clay' and blanket of the raw Kafir. **1890** *Cape Law Jrnl* VII. 225 Raw natives, or natives who have not come under the conflicting influences of civilisation. *c*1911 S. PLAYNE *Cape Col.* 39 In their 'raw' state especially the Kafirs are exceedingly superstitious, and have a firm belief in the power of witchcraft. **1925** D. KIDD *Essential Kafir* 18, I have travelled for many years among the raw Kafirs, and yet have been far less conscious of their nakedness in real life than when looking into shop windows of colonial towns, where photographs of Kafir nakedness .. are exposed to view. **1933** W.H.S. BELL *Bygone Days* 62 An instance of where a raw native, quite unaccustomed to the ways of civilization, did not get justice. **1949** L. HUNTER *Afr. Dawn* 161 They did not know that his visit to the mines had made him familiar with these things, but he was annoyed that they should think him so 'raw.' **1952** L.E. NEAME *White Man's Afr.* 46 The Natives in the Reserves consist mainly of raw, or 'red' tribesmen who are intensely conservative. **1953** D. JACOBSON *Long Way from London* 107 Paulus was a 'raw boy', as raw as a boy could possibly come. He was a muscular, moustached and bearded African, with pendulous ear-lobes showing the slits in which the tribal plugs had once hung. **1963** WILSON & MAFEJE *Langa* 14 Class differences are clearly evident in town .. the townsmen looking down on the migrants as uncivilized or 'raw'. **1973** *Cape Times* 13 Apr. 9 My other maid doesn't know Monday from Friday — she's raw, but reliable. **1976** M. THOLO in C. Hermer *Diary of Maria Tholo* (1980) 152 The Bhacas were very confident because they knew how to wield a kierie. They were still raw from the country. But they hadn't reckoned with the stones from the township people. **1979** D. SMUTS (tr. *E. Joubert's Swerfjare van Poppie Nongena*) in *Fair Lady* 9 May 120 He is not happy because he does not know the people in the country, he calls them the raw people.

Hence **rawness** *n.*

1957 D. JACOBSON *Through Wilderness* (1977) 25 There were enough Africans to be found .. who were more sophisticated than himself, and though they teased him for his 'rawness' .. ,they helped him too.

raybok var. RHEBOK.

RB *n. ?nonce.* Abbrev. of RUGGER-BUGGER.

1991 *Personality* 18 Mar. 14 You'll definitely find one or two RBs called Butch, Hammer or Vleis among this crew ... Everyone says 'yeh baw' a lot, and the word 'pundah' (a very rude word for 'chicks') will definitely be uttered by the real animals.

Rd *n. hist.* Also **RD, Rdl, Rxd.** The written abbrev. of RIX-DOLLAR.

1796 [see DROSTDY sense 1]. **1801** G. YONGE in G.M. Theal *Rec. of Cape Col.* (1898) III. 376 There was an Old Establishment for the Botanical Garden of 500 R.D. p. annum payable by the Civil Paymaster. **1810** J. MACKRILL Diary. 47 The only retail Wine House in Cape Town pays a License of 7300 Rd's. pr. Ann:-its privilege is exclusive. **1820** J. HANCOCK Diary. 51(a), You have taken 35 Rds more than you ought to have done. **1831** *Graham's Town Jrnl* 30 Dec. 2 We are glad to learn, that the collections made on those occasions, and at the General Meeting on Monday, amounts to Rds. 200. **1835** C.L. STRETCH Journal. 7 Feb., From the Commissariat it appears £6,000 had been expended for horses, and the daily expenditure to this period was 8,000RD^s. **1836** J. COLLETT Diary. I. 31 Aug., *Purchased* last evening M. Wessels Farm for Akerman for Rd 2500. **1971** R. RAVEN-HART *Cape G.H. 1652–1702* I. 520 *Rxd.*, Rixdollar, say 4s/2d: purchasing value say 35s. **1973** J. MEINTJES *Voortrekkers* 64 Says Cilliers ... 'I had property in slaves valued at Rds. 2,888, the price paid by myself. I received Rds. 500 in goods.'

RDP *n.* [Initial letters of *Reconstruction and Development Programme.*] The economic restructuring programme of the Government of National Unity, against which all expenditure and planning is tested. Also *transf.* See also GNU *n.*[2]

1994 R. RUMNEY in *Weekly Mail & Guardian* 8 July (Business Mail) B3, It is not surprising that the RDP has been embraced by so many different interest groups. It is symbolic enough to stand, like the new flag, for all things bright and beautiful. Few can doubt the RDP's stress on meeting basic needs, on achieving socio-economic goals which must lay the foundation stone for economic growth ... Development of the wasteland left by apartheid is a necessity. But redirecting spending within the Budget is also part of the RDP. **1994** *Grocott's Mail* 5 Aug. 2 Because the RDP was 'about removing unfair privilege and addressing the needs of the majority, not the advantaged minority, those with power and privilege would be a little reluctant.' ... The 'new system of standards' necessitated by the RDP was explained by Ms Cheryl Carolus. **1994** K. DAVIE in *Sunday Times* 11 Sept. 21 Thembalihle residents support this approach. They have worked out their own RDP which calls first for sites, then water and sewerage. They will in the meantime start building using the numerous bricklayers, plumbers, carpenters and plasterers among the residents. Next comes the electricity, then the tarred roads, and so on. **1994** C. ROBERTSON in *Ibid.* 25 Sept. 7 The bosom of a state department is the safest place to be when RDP-hungry eyes turn toward quango assets. **1994** W. HARTLEY in *Weekend Post* 26 Nov. 12 The Reconstruction and Development Programme — that's the expression on everybody's lips ... For the private sector it has become politically correct speak to mention the RDP to prove that you are on the side of the angels ... The RDP began its life as the election manifesto of the ANC. It was a compilation of election promises which would be implemented when the ANC came to power .. a necessary promise of socio-economic realignment in the new South Africa for a political party entering the fray of its first election struggle ... The reality is that the RDP is a political symbol designed to persuade voters that their hope of a better future is not misplaced ... The RDP is the promise that the cake will be resliced according to a new set of priorities.

Hence (*nonce*) **RDP** *v. trans.*, to bring (something) into line with the aims of the RDP.

1994 K. MKHIZE in *Natal Witness* 23 Dec. 8 *Sidelines* will be the archives of first-hand reporting of our history. Let the sponsors .. , a German foundation which is dedicated to promoting a liberal .. worldview, be thanked for its endeavor in RDPing our media.

reaction *n.* Used *attrib.* in the phrr. ***reaction police, reaction squad, reaction unit***, designating a police unit which specializes in the control of crowds and rioters, and which is on standby so that it can react quickly when summoned.

1982 *E. Prov. Herald* 2 Sept. 1 The reporter saw the morning convoy as it sped along Settlers Way, .. three reaction unit vans, three large police transporters and two buses. *Ibid.* 4 Dec. 1 The reaction squad had stormed the armoury after the gunman had fired his first shot. **1985** *Weekly Mail* 12 July 12 To some, the heightened presence of the SADF and the Riot Squad's reaction unit has become so much part of everyday life that it scarcely attracts attention. **1987** *Argus* 8 July 3 The former commander of the Bellville reaction unit .. has been relieved of his riot duties.

ream var. RIEM *n.*

rebel *adj.* and *n. Hist.* [Special sense of general Eng. *rebel* defiant; one who resists authority.]

A. *adj.* Always *attrib.* Of sporting fixtures: in defiance of the international sporting boycott of the country; freq. in the collocation ***rebel tour.***

1988 *E. Prov. Herald* 12 Feb. 4 Mayor urged to stop rebel match in PE. 1990 *Sunday Times* 14 Jan. 17 The position of the NSC is that the tour, being a 'rebel' tour, will jeopardise all chances of a 'normal' tour. 1990 *City Press* 17 June 13 John Robbie .. is a former rugby player who toured this country with the 'rebel' British Lions in 1980 before he decided to settle in South Africa after losing his job because of the tour. 1992 L. SEEFF in *Style* Oct. 112 Our chances of getting back into international cricket through the front door were precisely nothing. We were left no option but to go the route of rebel tours. 1994 P. KIRSTEN on TV1, 4 Jan., We've struggled a bit during the isolation period, the rebel tours.

B. *n.* One participating in a rebel tour.

1989 J. PERLMAN in *Weekly Mail* 1 Sept. 36 His keen pleasure at watching the Springboks for the first time in years seems diluted not a bit by the discord that has surrounded this tour. Rumours of rebels and rands, opposition at home – none of the storms .. have cast a single cloud over the Doc.

rebok var. REHBOK.

Recce /'reki/ *n. Military. colloq.* Also **Reccie**. [Abbrev. of *reconnaissance*, from the name of the unit.] The *Reconnaissance Commando Unit*, the First Parachute Battalion of the South African Defence Force; a member of this unit; in *pl.*, this unit or its members collectively. Also *attrib.*

1981 *Pretoria News* 26 Nov. 1 It is also believed the mercenary force included several members of the South African Recce Commandos. 1987 *Personality* 30 Sept. 13 Most people associate the Recces with a tough, hard, un-feeling bunch of soldiers, but Louis was a feeling person. 1987 G. EVANS in *Weekly Mail* 20 Nov. 7 This period came to an abrupt end on May 21 1985 when SADF 'Recce' Captain Wynand du Toit and his team were captured at the Cabinda oil installation. 1989 H. HAMANN in *Scope* 10 Mar. 56 They are the silent warriors .. , with an arm that can reach into any part of Africa and strike at any foe ... They survive by subterfuge and secrecy ... They are SADF's legendary Reconnaissance Commandos. The Recces. 1989 *Sunday Times* 19 Nov. 2 Col. Breytenbach served in the SADF with 1 Parachute Battalion, better known as the Reccies. 1991 R. LANDMAN in *Style* Nov. 82 Ndomeni was the ex-reccie who left the country and told the story of how he was kidnapped and tortured and forced to join the reccies. 1991 J. PAUW *In Heart of Whore* 174 The 'recces' can be described as South Africa's Special Air Services – highly trained specialists in unconventional warfare. *Ibid.* 261 Can we ever trust the politicians who devised and justified the 'total onslaught' ideology, the generals who unleashed crack 'recce' regiments on hapless populations and governments in Southern Africa. 1993 *Africa S. & E.* May 13 All had apparently earlier quit the South African Defence Force, from regiments like 32, 'Recce' and other so-called special forces.

re-classify *v. trans. Hist.* [Eng. *re-* again + CLASSIFY.] Usu. *passive.* In terms of the POPULATION REGISTRATION ACT of 1950: to have one's official ethnic designation changed, thus becoming a member of a different legally-defined ethnic group.

1970 *Daily News* 9 June, A Durban Coloured woman .. who was acquitted in January of contravening the Immorality Act with her White boyfriend, is still battling to be re-classified as a White. 1970 *Survey of Race Rel. 1969* (S.A.I.R.R.) 24 In many smaller towns .. there are few Coloured people ... An inter-departmental committee had completed an examination of the possibility of reclassifying such of these people as had become Africanized. 1980 C. HOPE *A Separate Development* (1983) 130 Joerie had got himself reclassified as a white man and was damn proud of his status. 1982 *Pace* June 41 According to statistics released in Parliament this year, more than 600 people were reclassified last year. Of these, 558 were Cape Coloureds who were reclassified white and 15 were whites who were reclassified Cape Coloured. 1990 D. BECKETT in *Frontline* Mar.-Apr. 33 Ahmed started off, by barroom consensus, as an Indian ... Somewhere in South Africa's maze of changing racial legalities he got himself reclassified as coloured. 1991 K. SWART in *Sunday Times* 17 Feb. 12 His brother, who was blond with blue eyes and fair skin was classified white and had to be reclassified coloured before he was allowed to write his matric exams at a coloured school.

Hence **re-classification** *n.*, the changing of a person's official ethnic designation from one legally-defined group to another. See also CLASSIFICATION.

1971 *Daily News* 24 Apr. 9 Wrote on his behalf to the Minister of the Interior asking for his re-classification as 'Malay'. 1973 *Sunday Times* 27 May 7 A number of Coloured people who have been living in Churchhaven for many years have made application for reclassification as Whites so that they can stay there. 1977 D. MULLER in *Quarry '77* 64 Perhaps she'll try for re-classification: that strange South African alchemy of forms and rubber stamps that would transmute her from a beautiful Coloured girl into a beautiful White one, from restrictions to freedom! 1982 *E. Prov. Herald* 29 Apr. 1 The Department of Internal Affairs has had specially trained people working overtime to handle the number of applications for racial reclassification. 1982 *Pace* June 40 Old Mr Mills, despite his pigmentation, is classified as a coloured – a Cape Coloured to be exact. And this because he wants to be. Mr Mills is one of the few whites in South Africa to apply successfully for re-classification.

Reconciliation, Day of see DAY OF RECONCILIATION.

recuse *v.* [Special sense of general Eng. *recuse* to reject, renounce (a person, his authority etc.); to object to as prejudiced.] Used reflexively:

1. *Law.* **a.** To disqualify oneself from office because of a conflict of interest. **b.** Of a court: to declare a conflict of interest (and thus an inability to reach a verdict).

Also a legal term in *U.S. Eng.*

1960 J.J.L. SISSON *S. Afr. Judicial Dict.* 669 *Recusation*, Once a court has recused itself it becomes *functus officio*, and cannot then record any verdict. 1968 G.I. RAFTESATH *Suppl. to Sisson's S. Afr. Judicial Dict.* 116 A magistrate who in his administrative capacity has become aware of all the facts which gave rise to a prosecution, and possibly gave instructions for, or at least approved of, the institution of the prosecution, cannot sit to hear the case, and should recuse himself.

2. *transf.* To absent oneself from a (committee) meeting for a period, because of a conflict of interest.

1994 on M-Net TV 19 June (Carte Blanche), The obligation to recuse oneself rests with the chairman. *Ibid.* Failing to recuse himself from council when his family interests were involved. *Ibid.*, I had sat in on a meeting 4 years ago when I should have recused myself.

So **recusation** *n.*, the act of recusing oneself or of being recused.

1943 in J.J.L. Sisson *S. Afr. Judicial Dict.* (1960) 669 The object of *recusation* in the Roman-Dutch law was a declinatory exception known to the Roman Law as the *exceptio judicis suspectii*. 1960 [see sense 1].

red *adj.* and *n.* [Special senses of general Eng.]

A. *adj.*

1. In the special collocations ***red beak***, and ***red bill*** [tr. Afk. *rooibekkie*], ROOIBEKKIE sense 1.

1795 [see ROOIBEKKIE sense 1]. 1822 W.J. BURCHELL *Trav.* I. 266 The *Roode-bekje* (Red beak), a small finch, .. is a very common bird. 1824, 1861 [see ROOIBEKKIE sense 1]. 1890 [see ROOIBEK]. 1923 HAAGNER & IVY *Sketches* 116 The Common Waxbill (*Estrilda astrild*), more widely known in South Africa as the Rooibekje (Red-bill), .. may be found in enormous flocks.

2. Of certain African peoples (formerly often in the offensive collocation ***red kaffir***):

a. *obs.* [tr. of a N. Sotho word: see TAMMAKA.] Usu. in *pl.*, and with initial capitals: Collectively, members of the TAMMAKA people.

1821 *Missionary Notices* June 201 To the N.E. of the above-mentioned place, (about four days' journey) there is a large and populous town, called by the natives Meribahwhey, inhabited by an extensive tribe, called the Tammakas, or Red Caffres. 1824 W.J. BURCHELL *Trav.* II. 532 The principal nations of which I could procure any account from the natives, were; – eastward from Litakun, the *Támm̃akas* or *Batámm̃akas*, (Red people) called by the Klaarwater Hottentots, *Roode Kaffers* (Red Caffres). 1846 R. MOFFAT *Missionary Labours* 4 From this class of people, the Tamahas, or Red people, as the etymology of the word imports, who are by the Griquas called Red Kafirs, arose.

b. [Referring to the red ochre traditionally used by Xhosa peoples to smear the body and clothing.] **i.** *obs.* XHOSA *adj.* sense 2. **ii.** Of a Xhosa: from a traditional rural and tribal culture; BLANKET sense a; RED BLANKET *adj. phr.* sense 1. Cf. RAW sense a. **iii.** *derog.* Heathen; RED BLANKET *adj. phr.* sense 1. **iv.** *derog.* RAW sense b; so the superlative form **reddest**. In these senses also RED-BLANKETED. Cf. SCHOOL *adj.* sense 1.

1835 A. STEEDMAN *Wanderings* II. 18 The red clay with which they are accustomed to besmear their bodies .. has .. obtained for them among earlier travellers the distinction of Red Caffers. This peculiar clay is found in the vicinity of the Fish River. 1855 G. BROWN *Personal Adventure* 167 When all the men had got back, both station people, red Caffres, and Hottentots, the station itself seemed converted into one vast shambles. 1877 R.M. BALLANTYNE *Settler & Savage* 417 Shouts and yells that would have done credit to the wildest tribe of reddest Kafirs in the land. 1878 A. AYLWARD *Tvl of Today* 376 These despised races are inflicting .. much more severe losses on the men now in the field than the Red Kafirs have done in the late war. 1882 C. DU VAL *With Show through Sn Afr.* I. 137, I saw for the first time a tribe known as Red Kaffirs, from a fashion they had been daubing not only their bodies and faces, but their garments and blankets, with a species of red clay or loam. 1891 T.R. BEATTIE *Ride through Transkei* 6, I have not yet spoken to a 'red' Kafir who does not confess to drinking kakulu of the national beverage. 1894 E. GLANVILLE *Fair Colonist* 145 'Mawoh!' exclaimed the others, and two or three seized their kerries, for they were red Kaffirs, and the blood of warriors was in their veins. 1908 F.C. SLATER *Sunburnt South* 45 He beheld a young red girl approaching. Now Moses, as a rule, looked upon red people with scorn and contempt, and unhesitatingly dubbed them 'ignorant heathen.' 1912 AYLIFF & WHITESIDE *Hist. of Abambo* 77 It cannot be doubted that the Christian Fingo is more progressive than his 'red' neighbour, more appreciative of education, and a more enterprising farmer. 1913 C. PETTMAN *Africanderisms* 239 Raw or Red Kaffir, the latter sometimes shortened to Reds, are designations applied to these people in their uncivilized condition; the epithet 'red' having reference to the red clay or ochre with which they smear themselves. 1925 D. KIDD *Essential Kafir* 30 Red ochre and oil are rubbed into the skin, and frequently the blanket. When this latter is done by a tribe the people are called Red Kafirs, or merely 'Reds'. 1925 F.C. SLATER *Centenary Bk of S. Afr. Verse* 234 *Kaffir*, A general name applied to members of the Bantu race; usually the Amaxosa or Red Kaffir is meant, in contrast to the Fingos, Zulus and Sechuanas. 1937 C. BIRKBY *Zulu Journey* 249 Well over half of the million blacks in the Territories to-day are 'Red Natives' – the South African phrase for the blanketed kafir who lives a primitive life in a hillside hut, sleeping on mats, rearing a few scrub cattle, living on mealies and sour milk. 1948 E. HELLMANN *Rooiyard* 103 Some women regard the custom [of offering beer to the ancestors] with contempt as being performed only by 'red' or 'blanket' Natives and not by educated Natives. 1948 O. WALKER *Kaffirs Are Lively* 42, 600,000 are classified as 'Red' or heathens. 1952 L.E. NEAME *White Man's Afr.* 46 The Natives in the Reserves consist mainly of raw, or 'red' tribesmen who are intensely conservative. 1955 J.B.

SHEPHARD *Land of Tikoloshe* 22 Most of the Red Africans whom we had met were well content with an occasional mess of wild spinach gathered casually from the veldt. **1961** P. MAYER *Townsman or Tribesman* 21 There are parts of Xhosa country where the Red-School 'problem' hardly arises, in a practical sense, because a whole rural location is either solidly Red or solidly School. **1970** M. TYACK *S. Afr.: Land of Challenge* 144 The Xhosa, among themselves, distinguish between tribally rooted persons, called the 'Red People,' and detribalized persons, called the 'School People'. Currently the 'Red People' still outnumber the 'School' group. **1980** J. COCK *Maids & Madams* 70 The 'Red' Xhosa wife spends several years in her mother-in-law's homestead doing all the domestic work under her direction. **1980** D.B. COPLAN Urbanization of African Performing Arts. 80 The policy of encapsulation, which made mission stations islands of acculturation in a traditional sea, led to the structured opposition of 'red' (traditional) and 'school' (Western educated) categories of Xhosa speakers in the towns of the Eastern Cape. **1986** P.A. MCALLISTER Xhosa Beer Drinks. 25 Like 'red' Xhosa in East London, the migrants .. cope with their situation largely by a kind of 'encapsulation' .. , one of the most important aspects of which is drinking together. **1993** *CSD Bulletin* (Centre for Science Dev.) July 19 Western education and Christianity have divided rural African villagers in the Transkei into 'school' people and conservative or 'red' people ... The social division into 'school' and 'red' is not an absolute distinction, but is best seen in terms of a continuum.

B. *n.* Often with initial capital. [Absol. uses of sense A 2 b.] Referring to the Xhosa: **a.** One who lives in a rural, traditional, tribal culture. **b.** A heathen. In both senses also called QABA, RED BLANKET *n. phr.*

1913 [see sense A 2 b]. **1925** [see Kidd quot. at sense A 2 b]. **1950** [see RED BLANKET sense 1]. **1958** I. VAUGHAN *Diary* 18 In this place we will see many kafirs called Reds becos they wear red clay blankets and beads. **1961** P. MAYER *Townsmen or Tribesmen* 28 There are others who manage to remain good Reds in spite of their education — especially women who after being schooled have married Red husbands. **1963** WILSON & MAFEJE *Langa* 17 A great many of them are 'school people' .. and in the country distinguish themselves from 'reds'. **1976** WEST & MORRIS *Abantu* 22 The 'Red' .. are the conservatives who cling to tradition and eschew the ways of the West, including their religion.

Hence (sense A 2 b) **redness** *n.*, resistance to change among the rural Xhosa.

1993 *CSD Bulletin* (Centre for Science Dev.) July 19 The 'redness' refers to an historical resistance to Western culture — in particular, to Western education and religion.

red alder *n. phr.* [tr. S. Afr. Du. *roode els*, later Afk. *rooi-els*.] ROOI-ELS.

1798 S.H. WILCOCKE tr. *J.S. Stavorinus's Voy. to E. Indies 1768–71* II. 79 *Buckuhout* .. ; *roode else*, or red alder. **1822** [see ROOI-ELS]. **1832** J.C. CHASE *Cape of G.H.* 160 Alder, red (Ronde Els). **1907** T.R. SIM *Forests & Forest Fauna* 21 Red Alder or Red Els. **1961** PALMER & PITMAN *Trees of S. Afr.* 192 The red alder is found in moist mountain forests throughout the country, often in association with the stinkwood and the real yellowwood. **1970** MORRIS & VAN AARDT in *Std Encycl. of Sn Afr.* II. 569 The indigenous timbers of South Africa, such as stinkwood .. and red alder, are too scarce and expensive to be regarded as structural timber now. **1972** *Evening Post* 19 Aug. 4 All that remained of the trees that must have grown there in former years were a few stumps of red alder and yellowwood.

red-bait *n.* [tr. Afk. *rooi aas*, *rooi* red + *aas* bait, carrion.] The large sea-squirt *Pyura stolonifera*, an ascidian used as bait by anglers; ROOI-AAS. Also *attrib.*

1895 *Agric. Jrnl* (Dept of Agric. Cape Col.) 912 The bait most used is crayfish, and 'rooiaas' (red bait) a species of Zoophyte. **1905** J.D.F. GILCHRIST in Flint & Gilchrist *Science in S. Afr.* 192 One of the features of the rocky parts of the coast line from Cape Point eastwards is the clusters of 'rooias' or 'red-bait'. **1913** [see ROOI-AAS]. **1930** C.L. BIDEN *Sea-Angling Fishes* 217 The name 'red-bait' is the English interpretation of the Dutch 'rooi aas'. **1938** J.S. DUNN *Sea Angling* 318 If the south west wind is lashing the sea with foam, on goes a piece of red-bait to a 3/O hook tied on gut, and a cast is made in the surf. **1955** C. HORNE *Fisherman's Eldorado* 13 Red bait, often the older the better, and white mussels were for long regarded as standard galjoen baits. **1958** L.G. GREEN *S. Afr. Beachcomber* 119 Now that I have converted you to dogfish, how about some redbait? This humble sea-squirt is not good company when old ... Fresh red bait, however, can be used as an ingredient in fish soup. **1975** *E. Prov. Herald* 30 Jan. 13 Muscle-crackers [*sic*] and red bait were found in tidal pools and in some places the rocks were stripped right to the low water line of red bait and other sea life. **1979** *Signature* Dec. 17 Cliffs and perpendicular rocks make it difficult for the red bait cutters to get down to the rocks at low tide without crossing his land ... What we really need are huge red bait 'colonies' where nothing but a hungry fish can snatch it from its base. **1982** KILBURN & RIPPEY *Sea Shells* 7 The large tunicate or ascidian *Pyura* — known to fishermen as 'red bait' or *nsenene*. **1988** 'IZAAK' in *E. Prov. Herald* 5 Mar. 8 Some anglers prefer slightly off redbait, particularly for galjoen. **1992** *Weekend Post* 1 Aug. 11 Shellfish life was abundant, redbait squirted on virtually every rock at spring low tides ... Redbait disappeared first.

red blanket *adj. phr.* and *n. phr.* [Alluding to the ochred blankets traditionally worn by the Xhosa people.]

A. *adj. phr.*

1. RED *adj.* senses 2 b ii and iii.

1937 B.J.F. LAUBSCHER *Sex, Custom & Psychopathology* 104 The wardrobe of a pagan or 'red-blanket' native woman is very limited. **1950** A.W. BURTON *Sparks from Border Anvil* 224 Proud, painted, heathen Xhosa women; the type known as 'red blanket Natives' or 'reds'. **1967** J.A. BROSTER (*title*) Red Blanket Valley. **1980** M. LIPTON in *Optima* Vol.29 No.2, 148 The stress placed by the Xhosa of Transkei and Ciskei on wider kinship ties, rather than on the husband-and-wife relationship, has facilitated adaptation to the frequent absences of the migrants; as has the resistance of the conservative 'red blanket' Xhosa to taking their families into the towns.

2. XHOSA *adj.* sense 2.

1982 A.P. BRINK *Chain of Voices* 145 The Boers were pushing from one side; and from across the river Hintsa's people, the Red Blanket Men, were pushing back. **1991** *Best of S. Afr. Short Stories* (Reader's Digest Assoc.) 79 The Xhosa have often been referred to as the 'Red Blanket People' because of their elegant blankets which used to be dyed with red ochre. Today they are often dyed with modern chemical dyes.

B. *n. phr. Rare.* [Absol. use of sense A 1.] RED *n.* See also BLANKET sense a.

1961 P. MAYER *Townsmen or Tribesmen* 255, I never bothered about the country practice .. because I thought the girls would look on me as a 'Red blanket'.

red-blanketed *ppl adj.* [See prec.] RED *adj.* sense 2 b.

1894 E. GLANVILLE *Fair Colonist* 89 A red-blanketed Kaffir squatted near the back door, and two native women, bare to the waist, sat near at hand. **1912** F. BANCROFT *Veldt Dwellers* 13 Jonas .. prided himself upon being a 'church-boy' — a peg higher in the social scale of a red-blanketed barbarian. **1947** F.C. SLATER *Sel. Poems* 29 The red-blanketed heathen .. killed the fattest ox and prepared a feast for the witch-doctor. **1955** J.B. SHEPHARD *Land of Tikoloshe* 4 Mbongo's patients were nearly all red-blanketed Africans, that is to say, pagans. **1970** G. WESTWOOD *Bright Wilderness* 91 Small groups of Africans .. were walking into town to do their shopping. They were the 'Pagan' kind, the red blanketed Africans. **1972** *Daily Dispatch* 8 Jan. 12 It is only the red blanketed Bantu who have not yet been spoiled by the White man's kind of worship who know and preach that only Qamata is their true God.

red-buck *n.* [tr. S. Afr. Du. *roodebok* (see ROOIBOK).] IMPALA sense 1 a.

1815 J. CAMPBELL *Trav. in S. Afr.* 484 The following are the number of creatures killed by our people during the journey ... Redbucks .. 6. **1824** [see ROOIBOK]. **1827** G. THOMPSON *Trav.* I. 201 On the banks of this stream I observed a species of antelope .. called by the Bechuanas *Paala*, and Mr. Burchell has described it under the name of the red buck. **1871** J. MACKENZIE *Ten Yrs* (1971) 173 The country on the other side, studded with large trees, in the shade of which I beheld the gnu and the zebra, the red-buck, [etc.]. **1883** —— *Day-Dawn in Dark Places* 97, I beheld the gnu and the zebra, the red-buck, the spring buck, and .. the lechwe, or water-buck. [**1887** A.A. ANDERSON *25 Yrs in Waggon* II. 91 They were, from his description, the rooi or red antelope, the size of our fallow-deer.] **1965** A. NICHOL *Truly Married Woman* 44 It was, after all, only a red-buck, an impalla, that they were afraid of. [**1979** HEARD & FAULL *Our Best Trad. Recipes* 53 Our own big game hunters favour the following for venison: eland, .. redbok and oribi.] **1994** M. ROBERTS tr. *J.A. Wahlberg's Trav. Jrnls 1838–56* 22 A young red-buck (sick) and various little birds.

red cat *n. phr.* [tr. S. Afr. Du. *roode kat*, later Afk. *rooikat*.] The ROOIKAT (sense 1), *Felis caracal*.

1731 G. MEDLEY tr. *P. Kolb's Present State of Cape of G.H.* II. 127 There are a few that are call'd Wild Red Cats. These have a streak of bright Red running along the Ridge of the Back, from the Neck to the Tail, and Losing its self in Gray and White on the sides. **1781** T. PENNANT *Hist. of Quadrupeds* II. 564 Wild Red Cat. **1887** A.A. ANDERSON *25 Yrs in Waggon* I. 273 As night advanced, the different wild animals began to move about, the red cat, a kind of panther, the wolf-jackals, and porcupine were very plentiful. **1970** S. SHARPE *Informant, Grahamstown* The red-cats have been getting my sheep.

red els *n. phr. Obs.* Also **red else**. [Part. tr. S. Afr. Du. *roode els*, later Afk. *rooi-els*.] ROOI-ELS.

1833 *S. Afr. Almanac & Dir.* 195 The other woods most in request, and found in Albany, are — Red and White Milk, Red and White Else, [etc.]. **1837** J.E. ALEXANDER *Narr. of Voy.* I. 347 Dutch wheels are made of three or four kinds of wood: namely, for the nave, yellow wood; for the spokes, assegai; and for the felloe, red els, or white pear. **1843** R. GODLONTON in J.C. Chase *Cape of G.H.* 48 The Cape mahogany, or stinkwood, is not found in Albany, but it produces several others, such as sneezewood, saffron, red-els, &c., which, when seasoned, are found to be excellent substitutes. **1880** *S.W. Silver & Co.'s Handbk to S. Afr.* 135 Red Els .. resembles red birch; is used for farm and waggon building purposes. **1907** T.R. SIM *Forests & Forest Flora* 217 Red Alder or Red Els. **1934** *Star* 17 Mar. (Swart), Next in favour for furniture are yellow-wood and red and white Els. **1936** E. ROSENTHAL *Old-Time Survivals* 11 Red pear, red els, white pear, and scores of other precious African timbers go to the making of the numerous characteristically-named sections of the conveyance.

red grass *n. phr.* [tr. Afk. *rooigras*.] ROOIGRAS.

1934 *Friend* 15 Mar. (Swart), Besides encouraging the growth of red-grass, the effects of any previous, differential grazing are neutralised by burning. **1948** E. ROSENTHAL *Afr. Switzerland* 128 The natural grasses of the mountains have their own Basuto names. Commonest of all is the Seboku type, known in English as 'red grass', estimated to grow on more than half the countryside. The old Boers called it 'Sweet veld'. **1952** B. DAVIDSON *Report on Sn Afr.* 208 The rich 'red-grass' of Basutoland was steadily worn down, and the containing soil eroded. **1955** J.H. WELLINGTON *Sn Afr.: Geog. Study* 276 Along the south coastal areas from Swellendam to Mossel Bay a century ago were large tracts of grassland occupied by the valuable red grass *Themada triandra*. **1963** POLLOCK & AGNEW *Hist. Geog.* 18 *Themeda triandra* or red grass is the climax over most of the plateau ... In the sixteenth century .. the High Veld consisted of waving grasslands of *Themeda triandra*, green in summer and coppery brown in winter. **1972** *Daily Dispatch* 11 Mar. 17 This property is divided into seven camps. It is well grassed with sweet red grass. **1982** *Grocott's Mail* 18 May 2 One could only .. wonder if posterity would ever be able to walk through waving red-grass or bushman grass. **1987** M. Poland *Train to Doringbult* 42 As children they had run .. , with the red grass bending to the wind, bush willows green by the *spruit*.

red-hot poker *n. phr.* [See quot. 1966.] Any of several indigenous plants of the Liliaceae bearing spikes of scarlet flowers, usu., any of several species of tall, perennial herb of the genus *Kniphofia* (esp. *K. uvaria*), but also *Aloe peglerae*. Also *attrib.*

1884 W. Miller *Dict. of Eng. Names of Plants*, Red-hot-poker-plant. **1887** 'F. Anstey' *Talking Horse* (1892) 216 The dahlias and 'red-hot pokers' and gladioli .. burnt with a sinister glow. **1899** *Pall Mall Gaz.* (U.K.) 11 Oct. 2 The clustered sunflowers and 'red-hot pokers', most gorgeous of September's old-fashioned blooms. **1906** B. Stoneman *Plants & their Ways* 186 *Kniphofia* ... A genus of handsome African plants with a short rootstock, long, narrow radicle, leaves and scapes bearing dense racemes of yellow or scarlet flowers. *K. alooides*, 'The Red Hot Poker' is the most familiar. [**1909** N. Paul *Child in Midst* 128 So it sat on that red poker and watched us, never dreaming that a cruel boy wanted to kill it just for fun.] *c***1936** M. Valbeck *Headlong from Heaven* 94 The long-stemmed red-hot-poker flowers pointing their tongues skywards. **1948** A. Paton *Cry, Beloved Country* 19 Here in their season grow the blue agapanthus, the wild watsonia, and the red-hot poker. **1965** J. Bennett *Hawk Alone* 89 The subaltern's grave was on the ridge where he had died, among the antheaps and prickly pear and red-hot poker flowers. **1966** C.A. Smith *Common Names* 385 *Red hot poker*, .. Commonly applied to a number of species of *Kniphofia* ... Flowers in more or less cylindric racemes, flame-coloured, aloe-like ... *Aloe peglerae* .. with a cylindric raceme of coral-red flowers ... The vernacular name was apparently first coined for *K. uvaria* in English gardens, and subsequently (probably) after 1820 applied to this species in the field from the suggestion of a glowing poker conveyed. **1971** *Argus* 13 May 20 Agapanthus and red hot pokers may soon be lifted and divided. **1988** M. Branch *Explore Cape Flora* 35 Look for Mystropetalon, an orange or maroon parasite the grows around proteas and looks a bit like a red hot poker flower. **1992** S. Johnson in *Afr. Wildlife* Vol.46 No.4, 178 Some plants such as aloes and red hot pokers, which have red flowers, are visited by *Meneris* but are not pollinated by the butterfly. **1993** [see GRASSVELD].

red-lipped *ppl adj.* [tr. Afk. *rooilip(slang)*, *rooi* red + *lip* lip(ped) (+ *slang* snake).] In the special collocations ***red-lipped herald***, **- *snake***: the HERALD, *Crotaphopeltis hotamboeia*.

1910 [see HERALD]. **1913** C. Pettman *Africanderisms* 395 *Red-lipped snake*, .. The upper lip of this snake is a bright red colour. **1937** [see NIGHT-ADDER]. **1947** [see HERALD]. **1962** V.F.M. Fitzsimons *Snakes of Sn Afr.* 187 One of best known and most widespread snakes in Africa. (Known as red-lipped snake over most of S.A. and as herald snake in E. Cape.) Back-fanged. **1966** [see HERALD]. **1967** S.M.A. Lowe *Hungry Veld* 102 Hope to God it's not a puff adder or a night adder ... I'll suck the bite for safety, but I think it is just a red lipped herald. **1970** [see HERALD].

redneck *n. obsolescent.* Often *derog.* Also with initial capital. [tr. Afk. *rooinek* (but see also quot. 1900).] ROOINEK.

1898 *Empire* 29 Jan. (Pettman), In South Africa, Englishmen, owing to their more rosy complexion, as compared with other white men living there, are jocosely spoken of as 'red necks' (rooi nek in Transvaal Dutch, roodnek in the Dutch of Holland). **1900** A.H. Keane *Boer States* p.xviii, Rooinek, 'Red-neck', in reference originally to some merinos introduced by an English farmer into the Free State, and marked with a red brand on the neck. These were spoken of as *red-necks* — an expression afterwards extended to the English themselves, and then as a term of contempt to the British troops in red uniform. **1921** *Chambers's Jrnl* (U.K.) Jan. 32, I was thinking of the efforts that that infernal rooinek (red-neck) of a son of yours is making to deprive me of my only child. **1936** R. Campbell *Mithraic Emblems* 111 To find a redneck cheap upon this day You do not need to wander far away. **1944** J. Mockford *Here Are S. Africans* 83 The South Africans — Dutch and British, Boer and Red-neck — were .. living a colonial and frontier life enriched by the manufactured products of mid-Victorian England. **1961** T. Matshikiza *Choc. for my Wife* 85 They called us boers that time when we were fighting with English Red Necks. **1972** J. McClure *Caterpillar Cop* (1974) 18 What's with this Red-neck? .. Another bloody English immigrant? **1979** J. Gratus *Jo'burgers* 14 His pale skin burnt red by the sun gave him away immediately as a 'redneck'; and .. his accent was English, not Dutch.

red oath *n. phr. Hist. colloq.* [Named for the red flashes worn during World War II by soldiers who had taken the oath.] The Africa Service Oath taken by volunteers from the Union Defence Force who were willing to serve anywhere in Africa for as long as World War II lasted. See also NEW OATH, RED TAB.

The oath was first taken on 29 March 1940.

1940 *Forum* 7 Sept. 3 Now the women must also take the red oath. Thus they will also have to wear the red tab. I hope our Afrikaans ladies will possess enough courage not to wear that monstrosity. **1953** A. Paton *Phalarope* (1963) 35 He took the red oath, which meant that he would go anywhere in Africa, and they gave him red flashes to put on his shoulders. But the red oath, to those who would not take it, meant only one thing, that the wearer of it was a Smuts man, a traitor to the language and struggle of the Afrikaner people, and a lickspittle of the British Empire and the English King. **1956** H. Van Rensburg *Their Paths Crossed Mine* 185 Many of them, especially the officers and instructors, had been in the Army and had been thrown out because they had refused to take the 'red oath'; the oath as volunteers for the anything but popular war. **1970** *Rand Daily Mail* 14 Nov. 9 Within only two years of joining .. [he] was awarded the Queen's Medal — the Commonwealth's V.C. for policemen. The award had its moments of irony, because Le Grange refused to sign the 'Red Oath' during the Second World War.

red roman see ROMAN.

red tab *n. phr. Hist. Military.* [See quot. 1946.] Usu. in *pl.*: The distinguishing flashes worn during World War II by one who had volunteered for service beyond South Africa's borders; *transf.*, the servicemen or servicewomen wearing these flashes. See also RED OATH.

1940 [see RED OATH]. **1941** *Star* 1 Feb., No self-respecting and honest man should put up red tabs until passed medically fit for active service anywhere in Africa and only after having completed all domestic arrangements for such service. **1941** C. Birkby *Springbok Victory* 111 Now men with red tabs on their shoulders had got to the country that had been their goal for six months. **1946** T. MacDonald *Ouma Smuts* 86 The Springboks and the women in the South African Army and Air Force Services wore red tabs, or the orange flash as it was called .. indicating that they had taken the oath to serve anywhere in Africa ... When the war ended in Africa .. the red tabs had to go to Italy, and they went. Ouma used to call the troops the 'anywhere boys'. **1951** O. Walker *Shapeless Flame* 217 A soldier with the red tabs of the South African Army. **1975** S. Roberts *Outside Life's Feast* 8 She picked out Dad among the line of soldiers walking from the plane .. , all of them in khaki and wearing red tabs on their shoulders. [**1976** J. McClure *Rogue Eagle* 39 Volunteering went into a second stage, with those willing to fight beyond their borders wearing a red flash on the shoulder ... The red flashes made them a prime target for the Ossewabrandwag.] **1983** F.G. Butler *Bursting World* 163 In terms of the oath they had taken they could be required to serve anywhere in Africa ... On the 26th January Parliament passed legislation authorising a new oath for service anywhere in the world. All who took it wore red tabs on their epaulettes. This drew visual attention to those who refused to take it and caused much bitterness. *Ibid.* 220 They .. took the goose along as a mascot and named him Egbert ... He'd been given red tabs to his wings. **1992** *Weekend Post* 14 Aug. 9 Taillard had refused to take the 'red tab' and had taken his discharge from the force.

red ticket *n. phr. Mining.* A certificate of fitness which is compulsory for all miners who work underground.

1958 R.E. Lighton *Out of Strong* 1 Yearly the underground man must pass the mine doctor to keep his red ticket. Without it he may no longer drop in clanging skip down mile-deep shaft. **1980** *Sunday Times* 30 Mar. 33 We are looking for men .. to appoint as Blind Hole Boring Operators. You should also be in possession of, or able to obtain, a Certificate of Fitness (Red Ticket) as issued by the Mine Workers' Medical Bureau for Occupational Diseases. **1988** *Personality* 17 Oct. 38 They have brought up four children, now all adults, and Odd even got a 'red ticket' certificate of health, which allowed him to work underground after they moved to Van-rhynsdorp in 1951 and he got a job on the nearby monazite mine.

redwater *n. Pathology.* [See quot. 1916.]

1. In full ***redwater fever***: a form of piroplasmosis, a highly contagious, febrile disease of cattle, caused by the blood parasite *Babesia bigemina* and transmitted by the BLUE TICK. Also *attrib.*, and *comb.* **redwater veld**, countryside in which the disease is endemic.

Different from *Brit. Eng.* 'red-water': see quot. 1896.

1873 *Queenstown Free Press* 15 July, The 'Red Water.' This dreadful cattle disease is said to be steadily but surely approaching the Colonial Frontier. **1880** [see LUNGSICK *n.*]. **1885** H. Rider Haggard *King Solomon's Mines* (1972) 42 This lot were thoroughly 'salted,' that is, they had worked all over South Africa, and so had become proof .. against red water, which so frequently destroys whole teams of oxen when they get on to strange 'veldt' (grass country). **1896** R. Wallace in C. Pettman *Africanderisms* (1913) 396 As it is understood in the Cape Colony, red water is not the non-contagious derangement known by the name in Great Britain, but is identical with the highly communicable disease called 'Texas fever' in the United States of America. **1897** 'F. Macnab' *On Veldt & Farm* 231 Some mystery appears to attach to the disease called red-water. On some farms it seems almost identical with the disease known by that name at home, but in many districts of Cape Colony and the Transvaal it assumes a severer form, and is believed to be the same as Texas fever in America. **1914** *Farmer's Annual* 125 The symptoms of Redwater are again inconclusive. General disturbance is obvious; the animal is dull and dejected, with staring coat and drooping ears. Appetite and rumination cease. **1916** *Farmer's Weekly* 20 Dec. 1494 The diagnostic symptom of redwater is passing of redwater — that is, blood-coloured or even coffee-coloured urine. Other symptoms are very like gallsickness. **1923** G.H. Nicholls *Bayete!* 265 Clean and infected cattle — infected with the dreaded redwater disease — rubbed shoulders together; and the result of years of careful dipping and isolation might be destroyed in a day. **1937** *Handbk for Farmers* (Dept of Agric. & Forestry) 502 Cattle that have lived for several generations in redwater areas become less susceptible to the disease than are freshly introduced cattle. **1955** J.B. Shephard *Land of Tikoloshe* 144 Many Africans .. do not connect the bont-tick, the red-legged tick, and all the other parasites which dipping helps to destroy, with East Coast fever and Red Water. **1968** [see FLY sense 2 a]. **1972** *Farmer's Weekly* 21 Apr. 60 The animals are used to virulent heartwater, redwater and gallsickness veld. **1978** *Daily Dispatch* 16 Aug. (Suppl.) 16 The blue tick is the main transmitting agent for anaplasmosis and redwater and therefore veterinarians are often required to make the difficult distinction between the very similar symptoms of both diseases. **1980** P. Schirmer *Concise Illust. S. Afr. Encycl.* 18 Redwater Fever; an acute cattle disease transmitted by the blue tick. **1991** *Farmer's Weekly* 5 Apr. 10 The Veterinary Reseach Institute at Onderstepoort has for many years produced an effective and reliable redwater vaccine to protect cattle against the disease. **1993** [see *gallsickness veld* (GALLSICKNESS sense 3)].

2. *obsolescent*. Bilharzia, a disease of human beings which is characterized by haematuria.

[**1887** J.W. MATTHEWS *Incwadi Yami* 15 The principal diseases of importance being dysentery, low malarial fever (bilio-remittent) and a peculiar form of *hæmaturia*, due to a parasite named the *Distoma hæmatobium*, introduced into the system by the drinking of impure water.] **1906** *Education Gaz.* Vol.6 No.11, 220 It appears that a very large proportion of the boys suffer from *redwater* as the result of bathing in the Buffalo River. No girl bathes there, and no girl suffers from the disease. **1957** S. Poss in *Pietersburg Eng. Medium School Mag.* Dec. 52 Bilharzia first originated in Egypt about 4,000 years ago, although people only started thinking about a cure in 1850, when nearly every child had the disease then known as 'Red Water'.

reebo(c)k var. RHEBOK.

reedbuck *n.* Also **reidbuck.** Pl. unchanged. [tr. S. Afr. Du. *rietbok*, see RIETBOK; see quot. 1834.]
1. The RIETBOK, *Redunca arundinum*. Also *attrib*.

In Skinner & Smithers's *Mammals of Sn Afr. Subregion* (1990), the name 'reedbuck' is used for this species.

1834 *Penny Cyclopaedia* 79 The reitbok .. or reedbuck, so called from its habits of frequenting the reedy banks and beds of dry water-courses. **1852** R.B. STRUTHERS *Hunting Jrnl* (1991) 7 Shot a fine large reed buck which was a most welcome addition to our commissariat. **1867** T. SHONE *Diary.* 27 May, Henry shot a reed Buck. **1884** 'E.V.C.' *Promised Land* 75, I loosed off at a reidbuck, rather far off, but I saw him wince to the shot. **1896** R. WARD *Rec. of Big Game* 134 The Reedbuck (Rietbok of the Boers) is much less common in South Africa than it used to be, and to get fairly into the country of this interesting and characteristic water antelope one has nowadays to travel far. **1900** W.L. SCLATER *Mammals of S. Afr.* I. 196 The reedbuck lives always in grassy or reedy valleys in the neighbourhood of streams and vleys ... When distressed, this buck gives vent to a loud characteristic whistle. *c*1936 *S. & E. Afr. Yr Bk & Guide* 1090 The *Reedbuck* (*cervicapra arundinum* ..) ... On the approach of danger the animal gives a shrill squeak, which is sometimes continued by the females, which bound forward and stop at intervals, thus giving the alarm to all game in the neighbourhood. **1940** V. POHL *Bushveld Adventures* 47 Eric shot a full-grown reedbuck ram whose weight must have been well over two hundred pounds. **1947** E.R. SEARY *S. Afr. Short Stories* Glossary, *Reedbuck*, .. an antelope which has its hiding place in reeds and long grass. It is about three feet in height at the shoulder. **1974** *E. Prov. Herald* 7 Sept. 6 There are fewer than 100 reedbuck left in the Cape. **1990** SKINNER & SMITHERS *Mammals of Sn Afr. Subregion* 704 Reedbuck are named from their characteristic association with vleis or reedbeds. **1991** J. SHEPHERD-SMITH in *Sunday Tribune* 19 May 5 Along the route reedbuck, .. waterbuck, kudu and red duiker can be seen grazing and browsing before skittishly running off to observe us from a safe distance.

2. With distinguishing epithet: **mountain reedbuck,** the antelope *Redunca fulvorufula* of the Bovidae, found mainly in hilly, mountainous, or rocky areas and characterized by its fawn to grey-coloured fur, white underparts and bushy tail; *mountain rhebuck,* see RHEBUCK sense 2; *red rhebok,* see RHEBOK sense 2; *red rhebuck,* see RHEBUCK sense 2; RHEBOK sense 1 b; RHEBUCK sense 1 b; ROEBUCK sense b.

1973 C.M. VAN DER WESTHUIZEN in *Std Encycl. of Sn Afr.* IX. Formerly also known as the red reebok .., the **mountain reedbuck** is distributed over .. mountainous regions. **1974** *E. Prov. Herald* 7 Sept. 6 The department estimates that there are roughly 20 000 springbok and 40 000 rooi ribbok (mountain reedbuck) .. mainly on private land. **1980** J. HANKS *Mammals* 28 Found in broken hilly country ... The mountain reedbuck is mainly a grazer, occasionally browsing. **1982** *S. Afr. Panorama* Aug. 29 At Umfolozi itself a population of 900 white rhinoceroses remain. In addition to these there are .. great numbers of impala, waterbuck, common and mountain reedbuck, nyala, kudu .. hyena, jackal and many smaller mammal species. **1990** *Weekend Post* 5 May 8 Red hartebees, mountain reedbuck, waterbuck, jackal, bushpig, vervet monkey, baboon and lynx.

reed-dance *n.* A traditional ceremonial dance accompanied by reed flutes, part of the culture of several African peoples.

[**1824** W.J. BURCHELL *Trav.* II. 411 When the dancers, who were all men, had tuned their reeds, they formed themselves into a ring ... The rings was drawn as closely together as their number would conveniently allow, but each person danced separate.] **1838** J.E. ALEXANDER *Exped. into Int.* I. 233 On the 20th February, the chief, according to Namaqua usage, presented me with six sheep, and gave me a grand reed dance. **1841** B. SHAW *Memorials* 25 The reed dance is carried on with high glee. A leader, bending forward his head, and at the same time stamping violently upon the ground to keep time, commences the performance. **1897** R.S.S. BADEN-POWELL *Matabele Campaign* 14 A native *reed-dance* was going on in the 'stadt' (as they call the native town). **1913** C. PETTMAN *Africanderisms* 397 Reed dance, ... A dance in vogue among the Bechuanas, in which each man blows upon a reed flute, or whistle of very small compass, two notes at most. The men dance in a circle stamping the time, while women move round the outside of the circle clapping their hands. **1987** *Royal Swazi Airways Tourist Guide* 3 When the 'Reed Dance' is performed in August-September colourfully dressed maidens gather reeds and dance before the Queen Mother at Lobamba. **1987** J. KHUMALO in *Pace* Nov. 158 Modern though Swaziland is, the tiny kingdom is steeped in tradition and no ceremony is more honoured than the annual reed dance. **1987** B. LAU *Namibia in Jonker Afrikaner's Time* 16 Among the popular dances were those called the Pot Dance and the Great Reed Dance. The former involved exclusively men, the latter apparently only women dancers while the men played the reeds ... These dances were probably shared by people on both sides of the Orange river. **1994** on TV1, 19 Sept. (News), Attending the Reed Dance of the Maidens at Nongoma on Saturday.

reef *n.* [Rel. to Austral. Eng. *reef* lode or vein of auriferous quartz, transf. use of general Eng. *reef* narrow ridge or chain of rocks lying at or near the surface of the water, fr. Du. or Low G. *rif* rib, ridge.]
1. *Geology*. In a mine, that rock which surrounds the lode or vein, but which is itself not gold- or diamond-bearing. Also *attrib*.

1872 C.A. PAYTON *Diamond Diggings* 25 There is a reef of rock and shale running round nearly all the rich tracts of ground. **1873** F. BOYLE *To Cape for Diamonds* 288 Climb the reef or rock at its nearer end, and look around. **1882** J. NIXON *Among Boers* 159 The diamondiferous area in each is rigidly marked out by the surrounding reef. **1886** J. NOBLE *Cape of G.H.: Off. Handbk* 188 The encasing rock of the Mine, or the 'Reef,' as the diggers called it, being exposed by the removal of the diamondiferous ground, began to disintegrate. **1893** T. REUNERT *Diamonds & Gold* 21 The surface shales and basalt surrounding the pipes are called 'Reef' ... The reef troubles .. more than once threatened to involve the whole mine in ruin. **1897** F.R. STATHAM *S. Afr. as It Is* 191 A heavy fall of 'reef' might stop the working of two or three companies at once. **1923** B. RONAN *Forty S. Afr. Yrs* 69 A company called, I think, the White Horse Syndicate .. had discovered a reef, suspected of being gold-bearing. **1933** W.H.S. BELL *Bygone Days* 131 The reef at surface was oxidised and of a reddish colour. **1946** S. CLOETE *Afr. Portraits* 183 Began to work what they knew to be a minor reef while they searched for the mother lode.

1959 L. LONGMORE *Dispossessed* 13 In an eighty-mile-long belt stretching east and west of Johannesburg lie the conglomerate 'reefs' of the Witwatersrand geological system. **1964** R. CRISP in *Best of S. Afr. Short Stories* (1991) 51 'I tell you it's gold! You think I can't tell the difference by now? ...' 'Well, I've never seen this amount in reef before' ... He made a careful selection of some of the more promising bits of reef and placed them in the curve of the share. **1972** S. LYNNE *Glittering Gold* 31 The reef is a layer of rock with rounded pebbles in beds of fine-grained rock.

2. Usu. with initial capital, **the Reef:** the Rand, see RAND sense 2. Also *attrib*.

1905 L. PHILLIPS *Tvl Problems* 49 Meetings took place along the Reef from Boksburg to Krugersdorp. **1908** *Rand Daily Mail* 11 Sept. 7 Recently gangs of natives — known as Amalaita — have been making their presence known to Europeans along the Reef. **1914** *Nongqai* No.5 July (Extra), There civil servants play .. snooker pool in company with them that labour deeply subterraneous on the Reef. **1926** M. NATHAN *S. Afr. from Within* 298 The gold mines, which lie along the 'Reef', extending for a distance of nearly 50 miles, from Randfontein to Springs. **1941** N. DEVITT *Celebrated S. Afr. Crimes* 120 Sergeant Martin coming to the bank went towards him as he rode down the main reef road. **1951** *Drum* Oct. 6 In proportion to population, there are twenty times as many murders on the Reef than in the U.S.A. **1953** LANHAM & MOPELI-PAULUS *Blanket Boy's Moon* 63 Makulu Baas arranged a big War Dance Competition in the compound at Msilikazi, at which all the Reef mines would be represented. **1956** M. ROGERS *Black Sash* 28 Brakpan, on the Reef. **1960** *Star* in J. Crwys-Williams *S. Afr. Despatches* (1989) 330 Today's heavy rain on the Reef reaches south only as far as Vereeniging. **1962** M. BRANDEL-SYRIER *Black Woman* 47, I believe in the new Townships, which have arisen next to the European towns all along the Reef. **1973** *Farmer's Weekly* 18 Apr. 107, I am a 45-year-old widower and would like to meet a widow living on the Reef or in the Pretoria area. **1976** J. VAN DER COLFF *Bible Route: Mozambique* 45, I planned to remain in LM for one week before returning to the Reef (the gold-belt in the Transvaal Province of South Africa). **1986** *E. Prov. Herald* 19 Aug. 9 Down at the coast or up on the reef. **1986** S. SEPAMLA *Third Generation* 4 There was a time when our grand-fathers worked on the Reef mines for long spells of time. **1987** C.T. MSIMANG in *S. Afr. Jrnl of Afr. Langs* VII. July 82 The wholesale influx of rural blacks to urban areas, especially the Reef. **1989** *Reader's Digest Illust. Hist.* 268 The Chamber of Mines found a ready supply of cost-efficient labour for the Reef gold mines.

reem var. RIEM *n.*

reem shoe var. REM SHOE.

reetbok var. RIETBOK.

reference book *n. phr. Hist.* [A term introduced by the 'Natives (Abolition of Passes and Co-ordination of Documents) Act' of 1952.] PASS sense 3. Also *attrib*.

1952 *Act* 67 in *Stat. of Union* 1013 To repeal the laws relating to the carrying of passes by natives; to provide for the issue of reference books to natives. **1955** *Report of Commission for Socio-Economic Dev. of Bantu Areas* (UG61-1955) 93 The movement of Bantu work-seekers and labourers is controlled by their having to carry a personal document, the reference book that may be compared to a passport. This system of issuing reference books has certain advantages over the former 'pass' system. **1960** *Natal Mercury* 4 Apr. 3 A 100-strong mob of natives pranced around a bonfire of reference books in Walmer last night. **1961** M.A. WALL *Dominee & Dom-Pas* 21 When the Reference Book unit first came to Lefurutse, it visited first the royal village, Dinokana. **1963** M. BENSON *Afr. Patriots* 221 Early in 1956 .. in Winburg in the Free State, many women were tricked into accepting passes — or reference books as the Government retitled them. **1966** [see DOMBOOK]. **1968** COLE & FLAHERTY *House of Bondage* 40 He calls this reference book his 'passport to existence'. Without it a black man is nothing. He cannot get a job, find housing, get married, or even pick up a parcel at the post office. He must have an employer's signature on his pass to prove he is working. **1973** *Cape Times* 18 Jan. 1 Chief Gatsha Buthelezi .. denounced reference books as symbols of oppression and the greatest cause of resentment between Whites and Africans. Waving his own passbook in the air, the Chief reminded the special session .. that he had been arrested several times for not carrying it. **1976** West & Morris *Abantu* 172 Today all Africans, by law, have to carry a reference book — the contentious 'Pass' — which must be produced on request and which contains details of the bearer's status in terms of residential rights, employment, tax payments and so on. **1980** J. Cock *Maids & Madams* 235 In 1952 the Natives (Abolition of passes and co-ordination of documents) Act introduced the 'reference book' which was to be issued to all Africans (men and women) and made it an offence not to possess one. **1986** P. Maylam *Hist. of Afr. People* 178 Two important measures were passed in 1952. One consolidated passes into a single reference book. **1986** *Rhodeo* (Rhodes Univ.) May 19 The reference book system as an influx control measure will be abolished and replaced by uniform identity documents issued to all races in South Africa. **1989** *Reader's Digest Illust. Hist.* 377 Verwoerd .. 'abolished' the Pass in favour of a consolidated document called a *Reference Book* .. 96 pages thick and standard green or brown issue. It had to be carried at all times by all Africans. **1990** *Weekend Post* 24 Feb. (Leisure) 4 The dream ended in '57, when 'reference books' (passes) were introduced for black women. Resistance to passes remained firm, and rude treatment by Native Affairs and local police was soon replaced by the systematic brutality of the police Mobile Unit and rank denial of the process of law by the Native Commissioner's court. **1993** [see dompas sense 1].

Reform *n. hist.*

a. ***Reform Committee***, also with small initials: A group (formed in 1895) of leading members of the so-called 'uitlander' community of the Transvaal Republic, initially with the aim of obtaining for the 'uitlanders' a greater say in the affairs of the Republic, but later aiming at the overthrow of President Kruger's government. Also *comb.* **Reform Committeeman**, Reformer. See also uitlander *n.* sense b.

1895 *Star* 31 Dec. 1 Reform Committee. Notice is hereby given that this Committee adheres to the National Union Manifesto, and reiterates its desire to *maintain the independence of the Republic.* **1900** H.C. Hillegas *Oom Paul's People* 79 When the news of the invasion reached Johannesburg the excitement became intensified. A reform committee of about one hundred persons was quickly formed, and into their hands was given the conduct of the revolution. **1900** 'One Who Was in It' *Kruger's Secret Service* 11 Let me make a remark of general significance with regard to the reform movement in Johannesburg. It was this stopping of business, this entire cessation of all decent means of earning a livelihood, that caused seventy per cent of the working class and professional population of Johannesburg to enrol themselves under the aegis of the Reform Committee. **1923** B. Ronan *Forty S. Afr. Yrs* 190 The rounding-up of the members of the Reform committee began on January 6, and as each well-known name was recorded a thrill of fearsome excitement passed through Johannesburg. **1926** M. Nathan *S. Afr. from Within* 77 The leaders did not take the general public into their confidence ... Instead, they formed a Reform Committee which sixty-four prominent citizens (many of whom were totally ignorant of the venture upon which they were embarking) were invited to join. **1933** W.H.S. Bell *Bygone Days* 209 That afternoon a further large batch of Reform Committeemen arrived, they had a stormy passage, especially at the hands of the burghers; their approach could be heard when they were some distance away and the great roar increased until it reached the prison gate. **1937** G.F. Gibson *Story of Imp. Light Horse* 15 In spite of the Jameson Raid, and the trial and sentence of the Reform Committee, the Uitlanders renewed their agitation — nothing could deter them from their purpose. **1979** J. Gratus *Jo'burgers* 204 What we want is a committee to organise it ... A Reform Committee. We want total reform of all the laws which prevent us from having a say in our own country. **1986** L. Capstickdale in *S. Afr. Panorama* Nov. 10 The so-called Reform Committee which had as its aim the overthrow of the Republican government in Pretoria .. imported guns into Johannesburg concealed in oil drums.

b. Used *attrib.*, designating persons, organizations, and actions associated with this group, as **Reform movement**, the initiatives taken in 1895 and 1896 by those 'uitlanders' supporting the Reform Committee to force political change in the Transvaal Republic, culminating in the *Jameson raid* (see Jameson).

1896 P.A. Molteno *Sel. from Correspondence* (1981) 31 The political atmosphere has been very much cleared by the action of the Transvaal Government in releasing the Reform Prisoners. **1897** F.R. Statham *S. Afr. as It Is* 299 The reform organisation was strictly confined within the walls of the Rand Club, the resort of speculators, financiers, brokers, and a certain percentage of professional men. **1899** J.P. Fitzpatrick *Tvl from Within* 291 All these things were among the causes which led to the Reform movement of 1895–6, and are not a consequence of that movement as they erroneously suppose. **1899** D.S.F.A. Phillips *S. Afr. Recollections* 63 Remember that those who started the Reform Movement in Johannesburg were, most of them, serious men with families — men who .. did not shut their eyes to the gravity of the undertaking. *Ibid.* 87 The Reform Movement in Johannesburg failed because, as some one put it to me at the time, 'they all wanted to be a little too clever'. **1933** W.H.S. Bell *Bygone Days* 187 He was concerned in the Reform Movement in the Transvaal in 1895, and adds 'with which he had no sympathy'.

Reformed *adj.* [tr. Afk. (and formerly Du.) *gereformeerde.*] Dutch Reformed.

Formerly used most commonly of the *Nederduitse Gereformeerde Kerk* (see NGK), 'Reformed' now usu. refers to the *Gereformeerde Kerk in Suid-Afrika* (see Gereformeerde).

1809 Afr. Court Calendar, Reformed Church. Wilhelm Buissinne Esq. Political Comissioner. **1827** A.J. Jardine *Fragment of Church Hist.* 10 The Rev. Messrs. Smith and Murray, Ministers of the Reformed Church .. in the Eastern Province of the settlement. **1882** J. Nixon *Among Boers* 130 The tenets of the Reformed Church are Calvinistic. **c1936** *S. & E. Afr. Yr Bk & Guide* 95 Smaller Dutch churches are (1) the Reformed Church of South Africa (2.73 per cent), based on the regulations of the Dordrecht Church Assembly of 1618–19, amended by the Synod of Utrecht of 1905. **1946** [see Hervormde]. **1975** *S. Afr. Panorama* Jan. 9 *(caption)* The spires of the Dutch Reformed and Reformed Churches tower above the skyline of Burgersdorp, the town where the Reformed Church was founded in 1860. **1991** A. Van Wyk *Birth of New Afrikaner* 109 He [*sc.* F.W. de Klerk] is a true Christian, belonging to the Reformed Church (*Gereformeerde Kerk*) which was also the church of .. Paul Kruger.

Reformer *n. hist.* Occas. with small initial. [Reform + Eng. agential suffix *-er.*] A member of the *Reform Committee* (see Reform sense a); *Reform Committeeman*, see Reform sense a.

1896 P.A. Molteno *Sel. from Correspondence* (1981) 31 The generosity of the Transvaal Executive in releasing the bulk of the Reformers ought to have an excellent effect. **1897** F.R. Statham *S. Afr. as It Is* 299 However anxious the reformers might be to exchange shots with some hostile force, and thus raise a plea for British intervention, there was no one to oblige them. **1899** J.P. Fitzpatrick *Tvl from Within* 263 The period of gaol life afforded the Reformers some opportunity of studying a department of the Transvaal Administration which they had not before realized to be so badly in need of reform. **1914** *Rand Daily Mail* 17 Dec. 1 If President Kruger's Government ought to have pulled the 'reformers' and those connected with the 'Jamieson [*sic*] Raid', against the 'wall', then General Botha would be wrong in making this appeal. **1924** L. Cohen *Reminisc. of Jhb.* 126 It has often been asked if the four Reformers condemned to death were ever in serious peril of being hanged. I should think at one time they were in a position of the greatest danger ... What saved the Reformers was Paul Kruger's horror of blood-guiltiness. **1926** M. Nathan *S. Afr. from Within* 14 In 1896 .. President Kruger commuted the death sentences of the leading 'Reformers' at Johannesburg. **1972** *Std Encycl. of Sn Afr.* VI. 181 Sixty of the Reformers were arrested and pleaded guilty to charges of high treason. **1989** J. Crwys-Williams *S. Afr. Despatches* 94 Younghusband kept himself aloof from the intrigue, but allowed himself to be persuaded by the Reformers, whose ardour towards the armed uprising in Johannesburg was cooling rapidly, to go to Cape Town, see Cecil Rhodes and persuade him to postpone the raid.

refugee camp *n. phr. Hist.* Also with initial capitals. concentration camp.

1900 *Bloemfontein Post* in W.S. Sutherland *S. Afr. Sketches* (1901) 84 There is certainly nothing unpleasant about the name of a 'camp' ... It is only when you attach the name 'refugee' to it that it sounds unpleasant ... No, a Refugee Camp is no joke, at least to the elders of the Orange River Colony band. **1901** *Grocott's Penny Mail* 17 Apr. 3 Troops were despatched to the farm and just punishment was inflicted on the women. They were sent to the refugee camp. **1902** E. Hobhouse *Brunt of War* 103, I have been out with a column, and it is sickening. We burn every farm we come to and bring the women and children to the Refugee Camps. **1901** Mrs Dickenson in E. Hobhouse *Brunt of War* 207 Refugee Camps is a misnomer; they are really prisons. **1902** D. Van Warmelo *On Commando* 134 Some men got messages from their wives imprisoned in refugee camps, bidding them to surrender for the sake of their wives, since fighting was of no avail and the country was already lost. [**1903** E.F. Knight *S. Afr. after War* 81 He wore a medal with the letters 'R.C.' and a number inscribed on it, which showed that he had accompanied the womenfolk to the refuge camp.] **1974** J.P. Brits *Diary of Nat. Scout* 55 From November 1900 the British established 'Refugee camps', in which Boer women and children were concentrated under appalling living conditions which resulted in the death of approximately 26 000.

registration certificate see certificate.

regmaker /ˈrexmɑːkə(r), ˈrɛx-/ *n.* Also **regmaaker.** [Afk., *reg* right + *maker* maker.] A drink, medication, or medicine taken to alleviate a hangover; a pick-me-up; regmakertjie. Also *transf.* See also *babalaasdop* (babalaas *n.* sense b).

1954 K. Cowin *Bushveld, Bananas & Bounty* 46 We asked why he was not wearing his hat, he said simply that it banged his head and he was very sick and needed a regmaker for the love of God. We told him to go and sleep it off. **1965** J. Bennett *Hawk Alone* 120 You haven't got a spot of anything, have you? I could do with a little regmaker ... It'd pull me right. **1972** *Cape Herald* 22 Sept. B1, The search for the ideal '*regmaker*' goes on ... A barman from Kensington says there is nothing better than a pint of cold beer as a much needed 'regmaker'. **1975** S. Roberts *Outside Life's Feast* 26, I hear him say in a slow begging voice Anna get me a *regmaker.* No Bill man it will start you off again. Have some more black coffee. But I am sick. Well regmakers won't make you better. **1979** *Daily Dispatch* 28 Feb. 13 Once or twice you've actually noticed his hands shaking as he poured a 'regmaker'. Poor devil, you thought, he can't take his drink without dreadful hangovers. **1982** *Daily News* 11 Nov. 25 So called magic potion .. to reduce the amount of alcohol in the blood stream. Somebody referred to it as a regmaker. Somebody else said, no nonsense, a regmaker couldn't be anything but more alcohol ... A regmaker comes after the babalaas. **1987** P. Wilhelm in *Optima* Vol.35 No.2, 65 His hobby is playing the fiddle and banjo in a local *Boereorkes*, which explains why [the photographer] found him in a bottle store at 8.30 a.m. on a Saturday. 'I need a *regmaker,*' he explained. **1987** A. Hogg in *Fair Lady* 17 Oct. 70 South Africa's overheated economy had a great icy bucket of water poured all over it: a *regmaker* that should make people feel better in the long run but right now hurts a great deal. **1992** C. Vineall in *Natal Mercury* 23 Nov. 18 You .. feel dreadful around 11.30am. That's when your hangover is really starting — and that's why the regmaker around noon .. seems to work. **1993** P. Dickson in *E. Prov. Herald* 21 Sept. 1 Sipping a *regmaker* and still severely shaken an hour after the blaze, Mr B— .. said it was the first accident in his home in the 40 years he had lived there.

regmakertjie /'rɛxmɑːkə(r)ki, 'rɛx-/ *n*. Also **regmaakertjie**. [Afk., *regmaker* (see prec.) + -IE.] REGMAKER.

1977 *Drum* Mar. 77, I just must have my night cap and a regmaakertjie first thing in the morn. **1978** K.M.C. Motsisi in M. Mutloatse *Casey & Co.* 95, I would wake up to prepare the morning meal .. heavily spiced bully beef with brown bread and, of course, a 'regmakertjie'.

‖**regte** /'rɛxtə, 'rɛxtə/ *adj*. [Afk.] Authentic, real; archetypal; 'dyed-in-the-wool'. Cf. EGTE.

1985 *Vula* Oct. 15 To quote a regte young jorler: 'The guilt makes them (white kids) search for a new identity.' **1985** *Cape Times* 25 Nov., Some good scenes in a 'regte' South African *bar* (as opposed to an English pub). **1986** *Style* Dec. 41 The regte boere ruled with an iron fist and God help anyone who thought otherwise. **1987** 'K. De Boer' in *Frontline* May 37 A regte plattelandse Oom picks me up. He's on his way to Sunday lunch with his children in Pietersburg and I'm welcome to travel along. **1987** [see BOEREKOS].

rehbo(c)k var. RHEBOK.

reh-buck, **reheebuck** varr. RHEBUCK.

Rehoboth /'rɪəbɒθ, 'rɪɔbɔt/ *n*. Also **Rehobother**, **Rehobothian**. [The name of a river, town, and district in Namibia (fr. the Biblical town, Hebrew *rehobhoth* wide places, space, room).] A member of a people (of mixed ethnic descent) orig. resident in the Cape colony but subsequently inhabiting the Rehoboth Gebiet in Namibia (see GEBIET); often *attrib.*, now usu. in the *n*. phr. *Rehoboth Baster* [see BASTER]; BASTARD sense 2; BASTER *n*. sense 2. See also KAPTEIN sense 2, RAAD sense 1.

*a*1867 C.J. Andersson *Notes of Trav.* (1875) 104 My next step was to order the Rehobothians, and a strong body of Damaras to follow me. **1926** [see GEBIET]. **1926** S.G. Millin *S. Africans* 198 Today self-governing half-caste tribes like the Bondelswarts and the Rehoboths still exist in South-West Africa. **1930** C.G. Seligman *Races of Afr.* (1939) 34 The old Hottentot population of the Cape has become largely absorbed by racial admixture with incoming Europeans and East Indian slaves, and has thus constituted the basis of the present .. 'Rehoboth' half-breeds. **1936** [see BASTER *n*. sense 2]. **1943** D. Reitz *No Outspan* 93 The Rehoboth half-breeds assisted us in the war and the Germans took heavy toll of them. **1960** *State of Union 1959–60* 430 The *Rehobothers* whose number is estimated at 8,900 are of mixed origin, having immigrated from the Cape. **1969** J.M. White *Land God Made in Anger* 196 This small group are not Rehobothers, but belong to the people called Cape Coloureds. **1970** *Survey of Race Rel.* (S.A.I.R.R.) 260 The Rehoboth Basters (or Rehobothers) are mainly descendants of unions between Afrikaner trekkers and Nama women. **1972** *Sunday Times* 12 Mar. 13 The Rehoboth Basters have formed a national convention through which they are making a united demand for independence. **1973** [see BASTARD *n*. sense 2]. **1980** S. Collett in *Optima* Vol.28 No.4, 194 The Coloureds and the Rehoboth Basters emigrated from the Cape province of South Africa in the last century. [**1987** *E. Prov. Herald* 15 June 9 Mr Matjila has tried to desegregate Namibia's schools, but thus far has been thwarted by the National Party and the conservative, mixed-race Rehoboth Basters Party.] **1990** *Weekend Post* 24 Mar. 4 The Afrikaner Weerstandbeweging (AWB) has crossed the race barrier to declare its solidarity with Namibia's independence-seeking 31 000-strong Rehoboth Baster people.

reibock var. RHEBOK.

reidbuck var. REEDBUCK.

reim *n*. var. RIEM *n*.

reim *v*. var. RIEM *v*.

reimpj(i)e, **reimpy** varr. RIEMPIE *n*.

reimschoen, **-schoon** varr. REMSKOEN.

reitboc, **-bok** varr. RIETBOK.

reitbuck var. RIETBUCK.

release *n*. *hist*. [Special sense of general Eng.; see next.] The scheduling of land for occupation by black people, in terms of the Native Trust and Land Act of 1936.

1936 R.J.M. Goold-Adams *S. Afr. To-Day & To-Morrow* 44 The Bill also provides for the 'release' of some 14,000,000 more acres to the natives over the whole Union. **1988** A. Fischer in Boonzaaier & Sharp *S. Afr. Keywords* 132 The Bantu Development Trust bought up large tracts of land which had been earmarked for 'release' (from white ownership to the reserves) by the 1936 Land Act.

Hence **release** *v. trans.*, to schedule (land) in this way.

1965 *S. Afr. in Sixties* (S. Afr. Foundation) 72 The Native Trust and Land Act of 1936 released a further 7,250,000 morgen for purchase by the South African Native Trust, or by African tribes or individuals. **1973** [see RELEASED AREA].

released area *n*. phr. [See quot. 1973.] An area of land set aside for occupation by black people, in terms of the Native Trust and Land Act of 1936.

1936 Act 18 in *Stat. of Union* 90 The areas defined .. shall, together with such land .. as may from time to time be acquired by and transferred to the Trust be released areas. **1936** R.J.M. Goold-Adams *S. Afr. To-Day & To-Morrow* 44 What of the Trust — a new name for the Union Government itself, which already has charge of crown-lands and administers 'released areas', having done so for many years? **1965** *S. Afr. in Sixties* (S. Afr. Foundation) 72 When the remaining Released Areas have been acquired by the Trust the Reserves will, according to the Tomlinson Commission, cover 13.7% of the Republic's surface. *c*1970 C. Desmond *Discarded People* 130 From Acornhoek to White River there is a huge tract of 'Released Area' (i.e. land which the 1936 Land Act prescribed should be added to the land set aside for African occupation by the 1913 Land Act). **1973** T. Bell *Indust. Decentral.* 3 The Native Trust was established in terms of the Act to purchase this land, known as 'released areas' (released, that is, from the provisions of the Natives Land Act of 1913) for African occupation. **1993** S. Collins in *Democracy in Action* 31 Aug. 27 Called 'Released Area number 33' by Pretoria, Inanda might have been included in KwaZulu but for the fact that some of the land was owned and inhabited by Indians.

relocate *v. trans.* [Special sense of general Eng. *relocate* move (to a different place).] RESETTLE. Usu. *passive.*

1968 Cole & Flaherty *House of Bondage* 52 A 'black spot' is an African township marked for obliteration because it occupies an area into which whites wish to expand ... It can literally be wiped off the map and its people relocated in Government-built housing projects in remote areas. **1986** R. Bhengu in *City Press* 2 Nov. (City Woman) p.vi, The people were forced out, relocated in dreary little townships. **1986** P. Maylam *Hist. of Afr. People* 175 The Surplus People Project has estimated that between 1960 and 1982 over three and a half million people have been relocated under the government's resettlement policy.

Hence **relocated** *ppl adj., resettled* (see RESETTLE); **relocation** *n.*, RESETTLEMENT sense 1; also *attrib*.

1968 Cole & Flaherty *House of Bondage* 52 Authority for relocation lies in the so-called Group Areas Act of 1950 ... Once an area is designated white, those disqualified by skin color from remaining there must move out ... A non-white reluctant to move is moved by force. *Ibid.* 86 The relocation housing in which more and more Africans now are living is modestly priced, but .. far too high for people living below subsistence. **1982** *E. Prov. Herald* 17 Sept. 9 To accelerate the removal of 'black spots' .. the Nationalist Government has decided to spend an extra R1 000-million on relocation schemes. **1986** *Weekly Mail* 21 Nov. 1 Monitoring groups claim the government is exploiting the fact that communities are in disarray .. to carry out long-planned relocations. **1987** *New Nation* 12 Feb. 4 'No to Qwa Qwa ..' reads the grafitti in Botshabelo. This is South Africa's largest relocation camp 50 kilometres east of Bloemfontein. **1987** *Weekly Mail* 3 Apr. 10 (*advt*) Patrick Harries: oral testimony and the history of the relocated Makuleke community.

rem var. RIEM *v*.

remkie var. RAMKIE.

removal *n*. [Special sense of general Eng. *removal* the act of moving (something or someone) to another place.] Often in the phr. *forced removal*. RESETTLEMENT sense 1. Also *attrib*.

[**1851** R.J. Garden Diary. I. (Killie Campbell Africana Library MS29081) 25 June, Mr Fynn, Duka and myself came to Umnini's kraal ... A short time back he and his people dwelt on the coast extending from the Bluff to the Umlazi river. The Government directed their removal when the Bishop of Cape Town, who was on a visit to Natal, remonstrated.] **1927** *Act* 38 in *Stat. of Union* 316 The Governor-General may .. whenever he deems it expedient in the general public interest, order the removal of any tribe or portion thereof or any Native from any place to any other place within the Union. **1956** *New Age* 5 July 5 The people of Albertynsville have been given a flat ultimatum ... Another of the Nationalist removal schemes is being carried out. **1963** M. Benson *Afr. Patriots* 146 There had been riots, with police firing on the crowd, during recent violent resistance to enforced removals of squatters. *c*1970 C. Desmond *Discarded People* 23 The lot of Africans in South Africa is a hard one at the best of times .. but it is greatly aggravated by removals. **1970** *Survey of Race Rel.* (S.A.I.R.R.) 44 At the end of 1968 there were 19 persons under removal orders issued by Chiefs. **1983** D. Tutu in J. Johnson *S. Afr. Speaks* 53 They must put an immediate stop to all population removals. **1984** R. Davies et al. *Struggle for S. Afr.* I. 208 Bantustan policy after 1960 gave rise to an accelerated programme of mass forced removals of Africans from the rural and urban areas of 'white' South Africa. **1986** P. Maylam *Hist. of Afr. People* 180 Urban segregation and relocation .. has added enormously to the number of those Africans who have been victims of forced removals and resettlement. **1987** *New Nation* 25 June 5 Both settlements .. face removals under the Group Areas Act. **1989** *Reader's Digest Illust. Hist.* 426 The policy remained in place for more than 25 years, during which time at least 3,5-million people were the victims of forced removals. **1991** *Race Rel. News* (S.A.I.R.R.) Vol.53 No.1, 1 He said its failure to address the special grievance of forced removal victims .. would have to be rectified.

remove *v. trans.* [Special sense of general Eng. *remove* (cf. prec.).] RESETTLE.

1913 Act 27 in *Stat. of Union* 442 No native resident on any farm in the Transvaal or Natal shall be liable .. to be removed from such farm .. if he or the head of his family is registered for taxation or other purposes in the department of Native Affairs as being resident on such farm. **1945** Act 25 in *Stat. of Union* 114 No location, native village or native hostel shall be removed .. without the consent of the Minister .., and upon such terms as to compensation .. as the Minister .. may direct. **1968** Cole & Flaherty *House of Bondage* 41 The Government .. may expel him from the city, even if he was born there and has a home, job, and family there. Such a man is 'removed' to the tribal district of his forbears, even though he .. has never lived in that district. **1983** A.C. BORAINE in *Hansard* 18 May 7282 From October 1980 to September 1981 62 White, 2583 Coloured and 1201 Indian families were removed. **1987** *New Nation* 10 Sept. 2 The municipality .. issued notices to residents threatening to remove them by force if they had not left the area by the end of this month.

rem shoe *n. phr. Wagon-making.* Also **reem shoe.** [Part. tr. Du. *remschoen.*] REMSKOEN sense 1.

1832 J. COLLETT Diary. I. 6 Jan., Reem shoe 2.0.0. **1974** A.P. CARTWRIGHT *By Waters of Letaba* 1 For years coaches and wagons slithered down the mountainside, their wheels locked in 'rem shoes' and all hands clinging to riems and thus acting as an additional brake during the downhill slide.

remskoen /ˈremskʊn, -skun/ *n.* Also **re(i)m-schoen, reimschoon, remscoan, ri(e)m-schoen.** Pl. **-skoene** /-skunə/. [Afk. (earlier Du. *remschoen*), *rem* to brake + *skoen* shoe.]

1. *hist. Wagon-making.* A brake-shoe or skid of iron or heavy timber, used on the rear wheels of a wagon prior to the invention of the screw-brake; LOCK-SHOE; REM SHOE. See also RIEM *v.* sense 1.

1816 G. BARKER Journal. 13 Feb., Some Hottentots persuaded us to cross it [*sc.* the river] immediately which we did my box was set upon the rim-schoem to keep it dry. **1822** W.J. BURCHELL *Trav.* I. 151 The remschoen (lock-shoe or skid), is a log of wood, generally about eight inches square, and nearly two feet long, having a groove in it to receive the felly of the wheel; and is furnished in front with a stout loop of twisted raw hide. **1835** A. STEEDMAN *Wanderings* I. 121 On regaining the track, we found the *reimschoon*, or iron slipper, which had fallen from the waggon, lying in the road. **1839** W.C. HARRIS *Wild Sports* 299 The perpendicular character of the bank rendered a *skid*, or as it is termed by the Colonists, a *remscoan*, necessary upon each hind wheel, in addition to the drag-chain. **1860** J. SANDERSON in *Jrnl of Royal Geog. Soc.* XXX. 239 Christmas-day we celebrated by dining *al fresco*, seated on stones, riemschoen (waggon-drags), and wildebeest skulls, which, turned up, make capital rocking chairs. **1866** *Cape Town Dir.* 117 Upon every wheel of every four wheeled vehicle not provided with a wooden shoe (remschoen) or an iron shoe not less than eight inches broad. **1872** *E. London Dispatch & Shipping & Mercantile Gaz.* 29 Oct. 3 All wagons not provided with a patent break or a reimschoen not less than eight inches in breadth, will be charged half the above rates in addition to the ordinary toll. **1892** *The Jrnl* 8 Sept. 1 Notice is hereby given that the Divisional Council has agreed to frame a Bye-Law .. forbidding the use of a 'Remschoen' on Public Roads in this Division under a penalty not exceeding £5.0.0. **1936** E. ROSENTHAL *Old-Time Survivals* 12 Previously the sole way of moderating its speed or of preventing the vehicle careering down a hill was to lock the wheels with a chain and place a so-called 'remskoen' or braking-shoe beneath the iron tyres, to prevent their being worn away. **1949** L.G. GREEN *In Land of Afternoon* 126 Voortrekker wagons were equipped with .. the remskoen instead of brakes. **1974** A.A. TELFORD in *Std Encycl. of Sn Afr.* 569 To brake the wagon on steep slopes a *remskoen* or skid, of timber or iron, was placed under the rear wheels ... The *remskoen* had gone out of use by this time; brake blocks acting on the rear wheels by means of a screw had been introduced in 1860. **1988** J. BURMAN in Smuts & Alberts *Forgotten Highway* 75, I was particularly struck by the wide band cut into steeply-sloping rock two feet high, presumably by the 'remskoene' (brakes) of descending wagons.

2. *fig.* Usu. *attrib.* (passing into *adj.*), often in the phr. ***remskoen party.*** An obscurantist or reactionary group or person.

1898 *Cape Argus* 2 Feb. 36, I am pleased to find that my frequent allusion to the backward element in the Legislative Council as a 'riemschoen' party has gone home. **1911** *E. Prov. Herald* 27 Oct., Those arguing against the Act were 'sukkelars', and formed a 'remschoen'. He [*sc.* General Botha] asked them to co-operate in making the Act a success. **1912** *E. London Dispatch* 2 May 5 *Riemschoen party*, The name applied a few years back to that party in Cape politics which appeared to be averse from progress; the word Riemschoen is applied in other directions with the same meaning, e.g. 'Riemschoen Districts'. **1919** M.M. STEYN *Diary* 266 My vote has always been for progress, whereas the 'remschoen' party's vote was always for keeping the country back. They set themselves against the Scab Act, Dipping and other measures that were for the good of the land. **1960** L.M. THOMPSON *Unification of S. Afr. 1902–10* 391 The remschoen (brake-shoe; obscurantist) element in the Transvaal was held in check by the enlightened non-racial leadership of General Botha's government. **1975** *Dict. of Eng. Usage in Sn Afr.* 146 *Remskoen* .. is .. used figuratively, for anyone who holds back progress hence the expression 'a remskoen party' in early Cape politics.

renoster var. RHINOSTER.

renosterbos var. RHENOSTERBOS.

renosterveld /rəˈnɔstə(r),felt/ *n.* Also with initial capital. [Afk., *renoster* rhinoceros + *veld* natural vegetation.] Countryside in which rhenosterbos *Elytropappus rhinocerotis* is the dominant vegetation; *rhenosterbosveld*, see RHENOSTERBOS sense 2.

1955 J.H. WELLINGTON *Sn Afr.: Geogr. Study* I. 275 At the lower hyetal limit of the Sclerophyll region, a fifth subdivision can be recognized, consisting of simple open communities often dominated by a single species. Of such communities the *renosterveld* is the commonest example. **1980** *S. Afr. Digest* 24 Oct. 11 It [*sc.* the geometric tortoise] was formerly found in a large part of the Western Cape, inhabiting low-lying areas of coastal fynbos and renosterveld. **1983** [see FYNBOS]. **1993** *Earthyear* (ed.5) Winter (Earthling) 25 *Renosterveld* is rich in a wide variety of species but with the evergreen fine-leaved shrub renosterbush dominating.

renostervoël var. RHENOSTERVOËL.

reproclaim *v. trans. Hist.* [See PROCLAIM.] In terms of the Group Areas Act of 1950: to change the restrictions which limit the occupation or use of an area to members of a particular ethnic group, so allowing occupation by a different ethnic group. Usu. *passive.* See also *Group Areas Act* (GROUP AREA sense 2 a), PROCLAIM.

1971 *Rand Daily Mail* 16 Feb., The Department of Planning has proposed that areas already proclaimed for Indian occupation in the town be deproclaimed and reproclaimed for White ownership and occupation. **1987** *Evening Post* 20 Jan. 3 Mr Terblanche said that if the area were reproclaimed existing white owners would be able to stay on, but any whites wanting to move in afterwards would require permits.

Republic Day *n. phr. Hist.* The 31st of May, an annual public holiday commemorating the creation of the Republic of South Africa in 1961. Also *attrib.*

Formerly called *Union Day* (see UNION sense 2 b). Scrapped as a public holiday from 1994.

*c*1965 *State of S. Afr. 1965* 107 Public Holidays ... Ascension Day, Republic Day (May 31), [etc.]. **1979** *Sunday Times* 27 May 1 No school under the Administration of Coloured Affairs will be forced to celebrate Republic Day on Wednesday, according to a spokesman for the administration. **1981** *Rand Daily Mail* 21 May 2 Republic Day should be spent pondering on the inequalities of opportunity and achievement of black and white in South Africa. **1981** *E. Prov. Herald* 28 May, Scores of arrests and detentions, school and university boycotts, protest meetings and Security Police raids were reported as the Republic Day celebrations neared their weekend climax. **1981** *Oppidan* (Rhodes University) 28 May 4 If you are planning to celebrate Republic Day, consider carefully what this means. Will the future not see Verwoerd .. only in a state museum of shame? **1986** P. LE ROUX in Burman & Reynolds *Growing Up* 191 The *volksfeeste* (folk festivals) — Republic Day, Kruger Day, and Day of the Covenant — interspersed with National Party *stryddae* (fêtes), attracted fewer participants every year. **1988** D. WEBSTER in *Star* 30 May 9 This Republic Day will be no different from that first one in 1961. Many white South Africans will celebrate again while their black countrymen remain sidelined by the numerous laws known collectively as 'apartheid'. **1990** R. STENGEL *January Sun* 46 On May 31, Republic Day, we were told to raise the flag. But I refused. Republic Day is no cause to celebrate. **1994** *E. Prov. Herald* 8 Sept. 1 A number of public holidays, including Sharpeville Day, Kruger Day and Republic Day, will be scrapped next year.

request *n. obs.* Also **rekwest.** [Du. *request* application (the modern form being *rekwest*).]

1. An application for a grant of land; the certificate serving as a title deed to land granted on 'request'.

1827 G. THOMPSON *Trav.* II. 157 A boor, upon discovering water on a sufficient quantity of unoccupied land, forwards, through the secretary of his district, what he terms a 'request' for a place, — that is, a memorial, asking for a grant of 6000 acres. **1912** *Diamond Fields Advertiser* 2 Sept. 7 (Pettman), On the purchase of these lands from the natives of the O.F.S. Government issued titles to those who had acquired them in the form of *requests* or 'certificates'. **1913** [see sense 2].

2. In the phrr. ***request farm, request place*** [tr. Du. *requestplaats* 'application farm', see PLACE *n.*[1]], a grant of land (not exceeding 3 000 morgen) for which any qualified burgher was allowed to make application.

Request farms were granted under Dutch rule at the Cape and later in the Orange Free State and South African Republic.

1827 *Reports of Commissioners upon Finances at Cape of G.H.* I. 43 The pursuits of the people to whom the occupation of tracts under the name of 'request places', has been granted by the magistrate of the district .. consist altogether of grazing sheep and cattle. **1831** *S. Afr. Almanac & Dir.* 197 The Rents hitherto received by the Colonial Government have not yet exceeded a third of the sum likely to accrue to the Revenue when the survey of the numerous 'Request Farms' now in progress shall have been completed and the occupiers put in possession of their title deeds. **1913** C. PETTMAN *Africanderisms* 398 *Request Farm*, In the early days in the Orange Free State and South African Republic, farms not exceeding 3 000 morgen were granted to applicants who signed their names in the Field Cornet's Register and undertook to remain permanently in the country. The application or 'rekwest' being registered the applicant could choose a vacant site, and at the next meeting of the Land Commission the grant would be confirmed. Farms granted thus were known as Request Farms.

reseintje var. ROSYNTJIE.

reserve *n. Obs.* exc. *hist.* Also with initial capital. [Prob. U.S. Eng., 'land set aside for North American Indian groups' (later *reservation*).] (An extensive area of) land set aside for occupation by black people under largely rural conditions; LOCATION sense 2; *Native area*, see NATIVE *n.* sense 1 c; *scheduled area*, see SCHEDULED. Formerly often in the offensive phr. ***Native reserve.*** Also freq. ***the reserves***, used collectively. See also HOMELAND sense 1, TRUST.

Although laws placing racially-based restrictions on land occupation have been repealed, the areas once so restricted are still referred to by some as 'reserves'.

1851 GODLONTON & IRVING *Narr. of Kaffir War 1850–1* 232 They fell upon two Fingo kraals in the 'Reserve' .. and completely destroyed them. **1852** M.B. HUDSON *S. Afr. Frontier Life* 255 He inhabits a part of what is termed 'the Native Reserve,' a district of territory lying between the Kraai River and the Orange River, and appropriated to the use of Natives. **1859** *Cape Town Weekly Mag.* 11 Feb. 39 Mr Austen, the superintendent of the Native Reserve in the Wittebergen, met field-cornet Olivier on Thursday last. **1903** E.F. KNIGHT *S. Afr. after War* 219 The Kaffirs have their huge reserves, always in the most fertile regions, where they can settle at will and pay no rent. **1912** AYLIFF & WHITESIDE *Hist. of Abambo* 76 In the Transkei, the Fingos live in 'Reserves', allotted to the sole occupation of Natives, with the exception of a few European traders, and in which farming offers them congenial employment. *c*1936 *S. & E. Afr. Yr Bk & Guide* 97 In some areas, particularly the Native Reserves in the old colony and western Free State, the damage done may prove irretrievable. **1936** R.J.M. GOOLD-ADAMS *S. Afr. To-Day & To-Morrow* 31 To segregate the black races from the white is the whole object of the formation of native reserves, 'released areas', non-native land-holding country and so forth. **1939** J.K. GODFREY in *Outspan* 24 Nov. 71 Today the Native in the reserve has arrived at the cross roads. The old and the new jostle cheek by cheek. **1941** *Bantu World* 15 Mar. 4 The ambition of the New African whether in urban areas or in the reserves, is to possess the good and higher things of civilisation. **1943** 'J. BURGER' *Black Man's Burden* 251 The result of segregation in South Africa is to turn the Reserves into national slums and the locations into urban slums. **1948** *Press Digest* No.13, 80 If apartheid were fully carried through and industries set up in the reserves, not only would the native market be lost to S.A., but industries in the reserves might also be able to produce more cheaply through paying lower wages than were being paid in the European areas. **1949** E. HELLMANN *Handbk on Race Rel.* 171 Under existing laws in South Africa the ownership of land by Africans is limited to the areas known as Native reserves .. and within them ownership in most cases is by tribal tenure and not by private title. **1950** [see GREAT TREK sense 2]. **1951** O. WALKER *Shapeless Flame* 272 The kraals of the native reserves lying close to the road. **1952** [see GEBIET]. *c*1954 C.W. DE KIEWIET in *Virginian Quarterly Rev.* Winter 34 Geographic apartheid might be more feasible if taken together the reserves could maintain the native population. **1955** E. DE S. BRUNNER in *Pol. Science Quarterly* Sept. 369 One step toward this goal should be the gradual extension of home rule to the Natives in the areas they now occupy, namely the Reserves, or, as some say, 'the Bantu Fatherland.' *Ibid.* 373 Some persons in the government hope to meet this problem by offering inducements .. and exerting pressures upon new industries to locate near the Reserves. **1960** D.P. DE V. GRAAFF *Policy of Ordered Advance* (handbill), It is futile to imagine that we can ever have total racial segregation as Dr. Verwoerd implies. We will always have a large settled, Native population in the White areas with no roots in the reserves. **1961** D. ROOKE *Lover for Estelle* 12 We arrived at the store which was on the edge of the Native Reserve. **1962** L.E. NEAME *Hist. of Apartheid* 74 In view of their possession of their own national home in the Reserves, Natives in the European areas can make no claim to political rights. **1963** WILSON & MAFEJE *Langa* 3 What drives men to town is poverty: they must earn or their families in the reserves go hungry. **1968** J. LELYVELD in Cole & Flaherty *House of Bondage* 8 Eventually — or so the theory of *apartheid*, at its most preposterous, holds, the entire urban black population will melt back into tribal reserves. **1968** COLE & FLAHERTY *House of Bondage* 98 There are three tribal colleges for blacks, administered by whites, and located only in the Bantustan reserves. *c*1970 [see SCHEDULED]. **1971** *Rand Daily Mail* 6 Mar. 10 All believe that the tribal reserves should be energetically developed. **1971** G. ROUTH in B. Sachs *Herman Charles Bosman* 265 The action took place partly in a Native reserve and partly in the nearby town. **1980** J. COCK *Maids & Madams* 309 Wolpe .. points to the fact that the extended family in the Reserve fulfils 'social security' functions necessary for the reproduction of the migrant work force. **1980** J. SHARP in Boonzaier & Sharp *S. Afr. Keywords* 92 The reserves in South Africa were long thought to provide employers, and in particular the mining industry,

with a source of cheap labour ... After the reserves had been formally proclaimed in 1913, mining capital certainly impressed upon Botha and Smuts's South African Party the importance of maintaining the reserves, and of seeing that they did not decline into absolute stagnation. **1990** *Conserva* Jan. 7 Since 1913, the first of the Land Acts which established the so-called 'Native Reserves', the whole pattern of rural agriculture has changed radically. **1990** R. STENGEL *January Sun* 27 Homeland is the term used by the government for what was once known as 'reserves' and 'Bantustans', supposedly sovereign countries which were created to accommodate all black South Africans and remove them from white urban areas.

resettle *v. trans.* [Prob. a back-formation from RESETTLEMENT.] To move (a person or community) from one area to another in terms of apartheid legislation; to compel (a person or community) by law to move from one area to another; RELOCATE; REMOVE. See also RESETTLEMENT.

1970 *Post* 18 Oct. 18 People belonging to other ethnic groups will be resettled in their respective homelands in future. **1977** *E. Prov. Herald* 29 Nov. 7 The ground near Addo will be used to resettle Africans at present under the jurisdiction of the management board. **1980** J. COCK *Maids & Madams* 313 There are no .. work opportunities other than building houses for the further 5000 people it is ultimately planned to resettle there. **1981** *Pace* Sept. 16 The Government is rumoured to have set itself 1985 as the year by which all black people — except those needed as workers in so-called 'white' South Africa — will have been nicely resettled in their respective homelands. **1987** *E. Prov. Herald* 18 Sept. 9 More than 126 000 families, more than 600 000 people, were resettled in terms of the Group Areas Act between 1950 and 1984, according to the constitutional committee of the President's Council. **1991** *Race Rel. News* (S.A.I.R.R.) Vol.53 No.1, 19 About 30 000 Africans were removed from the white urban areas and resettled.

Hence **resettled** *ppl adj.*, forcibly removed; *relocated*, see RELOCATE.

1971 *Seek* June 11 The M.U ... has channelled .. materials, sewing machines and household goods to centres where 'resettled' women struggle to keep alive themselves and their dependants. **1979** *Sunday Post* 12 July 1 The resettled people felt that no one was representing them. **1982** *E. Prov. Herald* 19 Apr. 7 Thousands of people may have to leave homes in which they have been born and bred, places where some families have existed for generations, to join the thousands more resettled people who have been on the move since 1974. **1988** *Ibid.* 24 June 6 E. Cape had most resettled blacks.

resettlement *n. hist.* [Special senses of general Eng.]
1. The forcible removal of individuals or communities from their place of residence, usu. into new, ethnically homogenous rural settlements; *relocation*, see RELOCATE; REMOVAL. Also *attrib.*

Most racially-based resettlements were carried out between 1960 and the mid 1980s, under the National Party government's policy of apartheid. However they have occurred since the 19th century, and have been provided for in law since the Land Act of 1913 (see quots 1913 and 1945 at REMOVE, and quot. 1927 at REMOVAL). See also BLACK SPOT, GROUP AREA *n. phr.* sense 1, HOMELAND sense 1.

1954 *Natives Resettlement Act* in *Stat. of Union* 139 There is hereby established a board to be known as the Natives Resettlement Board. **1963** B. MODISANE *Blame Me on Hist.* (1986) 105 We in Sophiatown resisted the removal and resettlement scheme. **1970** *Daily Dispatch* 23 Dec. Shot after shot of wretched, starving South African children appeared on Granada Television at peak viewing time last night, and effectively revealed some of the more shocking aspects of the Bantu resettlement policy. **1977** J. SIKAKANE *Window on Soweto* 10 They are women who, during the mass urban removals and resettlements,

were found to be without spouses. **1978** *S. Afr. Digest* 9 June 26 The Minister of Community Development .. said the resettlement of 277 Indian traders over the next three years would cost about R30-million. **1981** G.R. NAIDOO in *Sunday Times* 21 June 18 About 92 000 blacks from Natal's Ladysmith area will be forced out of their homes in a projected mass 're-settlement' move. **1981** *Voice* 12 August 1 Resettlement disrupted stable communities and broke up families as the head of the house was forced to become a migrant labourer. **1985** PLATZKY & WALKER *Surplus People* p.xviii, The resettlement policy is the cornerstone of the whole edifice of apartheid. **1987** *New Nation* 21 May 2 Despite PW Botha's May 6 claim that forced resettlements had been stopped, George municipal workers and police this week pulled down a house in Lawaaikamp, in the Cape ... The family is being forced to move to Sandkraal.

2. *Attrib.*, and *comb.* **resettlement area** or **resettlement camp**, the place to which resettled people are moved.

Such areas have usually consisted of vacant land sub-divided into plots provided with pit latrines, and sometimes with tents; water is provided via standpipes, each of which serves the residents of several plots.

1970 *Survey of Race Rel.* (S.A.I.R.R.) 126 The Rand Daily Mail featured a report on a resettlement area at Morsgat, called Madikwe .., where some 300 families .. had been moved. Most of them previously lived in huts or brick houses at quarries, where the men are employed. **1970** *Cape Times* 5 June, Black labour force units are tolerated .. while their superfluous appendages are removed .. and repatriated to resettlement camps. **1971** *Rand Daily Mail* 16 Feb., She left .. for Illingi African resettlement township. **1971** *Argus* 4 June, David Russell .. discloses the pitiful plight of Ciskeian resettlement camp families. **1971** *Daily Dispatch* 30 June, The Government has once again .. muffled a man who has exposed the awful realities of poverty, malnutrition and death in the ghettos, called resettlement areas, that smudge this wealthy land. **1972** *Cape Times* 1 May 5 Many potentially healthy children in the Dimbaza resettlement township .. die for want of the little food necessary to keep them alive. **1979** *Sunday Post* 8 July 1 A *Sunday Post* investigation of 10 resettlement camps in Natal and the Eastern Cape revealed that 'change' had certainly not reached the thousands of people existing there. We found malnutrition, sickness, unemployment and a general feeling of helplessness among the people restricted to these areas against their will. **1980** *E. Prov. Herald* 11 Oct. 5 The huge resettlement camps .. in the Whittlesea district .. have turned into vast rural slums. **1980** *Rand Daily Mail* 24 Nov. 1 When people first moved to the Vlaklaagte resettlement village, they thought they were going 'home'. **1987** *New Nation* 28 May 2 White residents living around Noordhoek have opposed the removal of squatters to the Khayelitsha resettlement area. **1988** P. WILHELM *Healing Process* 33 I've seen a resettlement camp ... It's worse than anything I've ever been told.

rest camp *n. phr.* A fenced enclosure in a game reserve in which accommodation is available for visitors; CAMP *n.*[1] sense 3 a. Also *attrib.*

1936 *Wonderful S. Afr.* 381 At intervals rest-camps are provided with rough comforts and means of protection, apart from the armed guard which is told off to act as guides. *c*1936 *S. & E. Afr. Yr Bk & Guide* 1065 Eight rest camps have been provided; visitors should bring with them their own food supplies, but catering is to be provided for later. **1944** 'TWEDE IN BEVEL' Piet Kolonel 190 Apart from the game in the reserve itself, and the extremely pleasant life of the Rest Camps, the country is magnificent. **1948** H. WOLHUTER *Mem. of Game Ranger* 223 The lions caught, killed and ate a kudu inside the Rest camp at Pretorius Kop! **1972** *Etosha Nat. Park* (brochure), The rest camps .. are .. ten miles .. from the gates where only primitive emergency facilities for overnighting are available. **1974** *S. Afr. Panorama* Jan. 35 The Game Reserve provides a rest-camp with a swimming bath and rondavels where visitors can spend the night. **1975** *E. Prov. Herald* 14 Jan. 1 An elderly lioness has taken up residence in the only ablution block of the rest camp in the Kalahari Gemsbok National Park. **1983** *Ibid.* 8 Sept. 14 Breakfast at another rest camp, more game spotting .. then out of the park for lunch at the scenic forestry settlement of Sabie.

restrict *v. trans.* [Special sense of general Eng. *restrict* 'to restrain by prohibition' (*OED*).] To constrain (a person or organization) by official order (setting out limited rights of movement, association, and communication) in terms of the Suppression of Communism Act of 1950, or the Internal Security Act of 1982. Usu. *passive.* So **restricted** *ppl adj.* Cf. BAN *v.*

Such limits were imposed by the National Party government on many political leaders and activists opposing apartheid.

1971 *Rand Daily Mail* 8 Mar. 3 Mr. Pelser .. told the 'Rand Daily Mail': 'Miss Naidoo is a restricted person.' **1988** *Weekly Mail* 3 June 2 The Detainees Parent's Support Committee .. was restricted on February 24 this year. **1990** M. KENTRIDGE *Unofficial War* 77 He said, '.. I'm a restricted person and so I am limited ... To be restricted is like living in a fish-bowl. You can see everything but you can do nothing.'

restriction *n.* [Special senses of general Eng.; cf. prec.]

1. BANNING.

1977 [see sense 2]. **1990** *Race Rel. Survey 1989–90* (S.A.I.R.R.) 725 The .. publicity secretary of the UDF .. said that the MDM, which did not have a constitution or a list of members, enabled anti-apartheid organisations to operate without fear of restriction or banning.

2. *comb.* **restriction order**, the official term for a BANNING ORDER.

1977 *Survey of Race Rel.* (S.A.I.R.R.) 102 'Restriction' or 'banning' orders are served on persons in terms of the Internal Security Amendment Act which replaced the Suppression of Communism Act. **1989** *New Nation* 9 Mar. 2 Lekoaletsoe was served with restriction orders last July, preventing him from taking part in the activities of the Soweto Civic Association, the Soweto Youth Congress and the Detainees Parents Support Committee. He is also prohibited from being in the company of more than 10 people and is house arrested between 6 pm and 5 am. **1991** J. PAUW *In Heart of Whore* 282, *1989 .. Christy Ntuli* Stabbed to death .. after reporting to Imbali police in terms of a restriction order imposed on him.

Rharhabe /xaˈxaːbe/ *n.* Also **Hahabee, Hahabi, Kakabi, Khakhabe, Rarabe**. Pl. unchanged, **ama-**, or **-s**. [Named for the Xhosa leader *Rharhabe* (*c*1722–1787).] **a.** A member of a major division of the Xhosa people, historically based in the central and southern parts of what is now the Eastern Cape; NGQIKA sense b. See also XHOSA *n.* sense 1 a. Cf. GCALEKA sense 1. **b.** *obs.* NGQIKA sense a (so called through confusion as to the composition and leadership of the two peoples). Also *attrib.*

Formed when Rharhabe and his brother Gcaleka quarrelled over the right to succession. Gcaleka won the battle, and Rharhabe and his followers moved south of the Kei River, leading to the division into Rharhabe and Gcaleka people and to the creation of the territories later known as Ciskei and Transkei; The Rharhabe later divided into the NDLAMBE and the NGQIKA (sense a).

[**1803** J.T. VAN DER KEMP in *Trans. of Missionary Soc.* I. 433 Chachabee, who governed this country .. about the year 1780.] **1809** R. COLLINS in G.M. Theal *Rec. of Cape Col.* (1900) VII. 20 His son Jalamba, finding his force unequal to a contest with the Hahabees, retired with his people into Agter Bruintjies Hoogte. **1829** [see NEUTRAL TERRITORY]. **1837** J.M. BOWKER *Speeches & Sel.* (1864) 39 We, the Fingo chiefs .. have thought fit to make this declaration .. that we, with the people residing under us, were never servants or dependants of the Amahahabi tribes of Kafirs on this side of the Kye river. **1841** B. SHAW *Memorials* 247 Do you hear now, you Amakakabi, (Slambie's tribe of Kaffirs), and you Gonakwebu, (Pato's tribe of Kaffirs). **1887** *S.W. Silver & Co.'s Handbk to S. Afr.* 44 In the meanwhile Hintsa, unable to hold out against the British troops, sues for peace .. giving his assistance in bringing the Rarabe chiefs to submission. **1920** S.M. MOLEMA *Bantu Past & Present* 72 In 1818 he joined Ndlambe in his fight against his nephew Ngqika, chief of the Amararabe people, who now called themselves Ama-Ngqika, after their chief. **1931** J.H. SOGA *Ama-Xosa* 7 About 1750, through internecine war, the right-hand house, the Ama-Rarabe or Gaikas, became independent of the great house of the Gcalekas. **1939** [see GCALEKA sense 1]. **1968** F.C. METROWICH *Frontier Flames* 1 It was with these Rarabes (or Gaikas as they were subsequently called) that the colonists had first come into contact and with whom most of the Kaffir Wars were directly concerned. **1972** *Daily Dispatch* 22 Feb. 2 An assurance that there was no danger or possibility of a split among the Rarabe tribe in the Ciskei was made by the chairman of Rarabe tribunal .. in a statement yesterday. **1978** *Bona* Oct. 18 The Tshawe clan of the Rarabe tribe in the Ciskei must be one of the few tribes in South Africa that has its own community centre. **1988** R. THORNTON in Boonzaier & Sharp *S. Afr. Keywords* 21 Sandile, paramount chief of the Xhosa-speaking Rharhabe.

rhebok /ˈriːbɔk, -bɒk/ *n.* Forms: α. **raybok, rebok, reebo(c)k, rehbo(c)k, reibock, rhe(a)bok, rhee-boc(k), rhy-bôk**; ‖β. **ribbok** /ˈrəbɔk/. Pl. unchanged, (occas.) **-s**. [S. Afr. Du. *rhebok*, transf. use of Du. *reebok* the male of the roe-deer *Capreolus capreolus*. (The modern Afk. form is *ribbok*, pl. *ribbokke* /bɔkə/.)]

1. Either of two species of antelope of the Bovidae, esp. *Pelea capreolus*. **a.** The small grey antelope *Pelea capreolus* with very long, narrow, pointed ears and soft, thick, greyish-brown hair; *grey rhebok*, see sense 2 below; *grey rhebuck*, see RHEBUCK sense 2; RHEBUCK sense 1 a; ROEBUCK sense a; *vaal rhebok* sense (*b*), see sense 2 below; *vaal rhebuck*, see RHEBUCK sense 2. **b.** *rare.* The *mountain reedbuck* (see REEDBUCK sense 2), *Redunca fulvorufula*.

α. **1776** F. MASSON in *Phil. Trans. of Royal Soc.* LXVI. 270, I spent a whole day .. hunting a sort of antelope called Ree Bock; but had no success. **1786** G. FORSTER tr. *A. Sparrman's Voy. to Cape of G.H.* II. 221 The *reebok* is a gregarious animal, two feet in height. The predominant colour of it is an ash-colour, somewhat resembling that of a hare, but a little inclining to red. **1796** C.R. HOPSON tr. *C.P. Thunberg's Trav.* II. 44 Reeboks, Rietboks (*Capra*) and Bonteboks .. frequented much these hilly and verdant fields. **1810** G. BARRINGTON *Acct of Voy.* 282 The ree-bok is the most remarkable; its size is that of the domestic goat, though much more elegantly made. The colour is a bluish grey; the belly and breast white; horns .. annulated or ringed about a third part of the length from the base. **1824** [see ROEBUCK]. **1834** T. PRINGLE *Afr. Sketches* 22 The Reebok (Antelope Capreolus or Villosa), abounding in .. the mountainous country around, is one of the smaller species of antelopes. **1837** 'N. POLSON' *Subaltern's Sick Leave* 119 Graceful rheebok bounding over the hill tops or up their sides; every now and then .. stamping with his slight forefoot and sending his peculiar whistle down the breeze. **1851** R.J. GARDEN Diary. I. (Killie Campbell Africana Library MS29081) 2 July, Game such as blue, red & bush bucks, Duikers and Reh-boks abound. **1862** LADY DUFF-GORDON *Lett. from Cape* (1925) 128, I have got a rhebok and a klipspringer skin for you. **1880** E.F. SANDEMAN *Eight Months in Ox-Waggon* 92 The others came down the hill, dragging between them a fine rhy-bok, about the size of a donkey, and not unlike it in colour and appearance. **1919** R.Y. STORMBERG *With Love from Gwenno* 61 We .. threw stones at dassies big as small bears; .. followed the spoor of rhebok; brought down partridges and rock doves. **1933** W.H.S. BELL *Bygone Days* 38 On one occasion we were looking for reibock on the hills; we loaded one barrel with buckshot and the other with a round bullet wrapped in a bit of greased rag. **1971** *Evening Post* 12 June 1 He already has springbok, eland, wild ostrich, rhebok and gemsbok roaming his farm and intends to add black wildebeest. **1987** B. MOODIE in *Motorist* 2nd Quarter 16 The reserve .. has antelope such as the duiker, steenbok, grysbok, rhebok and bontebok (about 400).

β. **1935** H.C. BOSMAN *Mafeking Rd* (1969) 86 He had disembowelled the ribbok. **1953** *Cape Argus* 25 Apr. 8 The animals include ribbok, grysbok, .. and one blue wildebeest. **1966** E. PALMER *Plains of Camdeboo* 124 'The skull is ribbok,' he said, 'and that's the tibia of a buffalo.'

2. With distinguishing epithet: **grey rhebok**, *Pelea capreolus* (see sense 1 a above); **red -** or **rooi rhebok** /rɔi-/, formerly also **roode -, rooye rhebok** [Afk. *rooi* (earlier S. Afr. Du. *roode*) red], the *mountain reedbuck* (see REEDBUCK sense 2), *Redunca fulvorufula*; **vaal rhebok** /fɑːl-/ [Du., *vaal* pale, grey, tawny], (*a*) *rare*, the BLEEKBOK; (*b*) *Pelea capreolus* (see sense 1 a above). Also *attrib.*

α. **1985** J. DEACON in *S. Afr. Panorama* Sept. 6 The Wilton people .. were specialised hunters of the **grey rhebok**. **1986** *S. Afr. Panorama* June 40 Grey rhebok grazed among silver thorn bushes. **1883** M.A. CAREY-HOBSON *Farm in Karoo* 149 Three beautiful light **red Rehbock's** (a species of wild antelope) darted past. *c***1936** *S. & E. Afr. Yr Bk & Guide* 1090 The Red Rhebok (*C. fulvorufula*; Dutch, *rooi reebok*). Sometimes, but erroneously, called the Lesser Reedbuck. **1974** *E. Prov. Herald* 25 May 4 He has many species of antelope including eland and red rheebok. [**rooi rhebok**: **1786** G. FORSTER tr. *A. Sparrman's Voy. to Cape of G.H.* I. 131 Some of the smaller kinds of antilopes, as *steenboks, klip-springers, rie-reeboks*, and boschboks, run without stopping, till they are out of the hunter's sight.] **1835** A. STEEDMAN *Wanderings* I. 176 We observed, at some little distance, several antelopes of the description called roode-rheebok, which were running up the mountain. **1835** A. SMITH *Diary* (1940) II. 111 A female rooye rheebok, head and greater part of neck dull rufous. **1896** R. WARD *Rec. of Big Game* 132 The Rooi (red) Rhebok is usually found in .. rough hilly country .. but prefers, as a rule, the lower slopes to the highest parts of the mountain. **1923** [see quot. at *vaal rhebok* below]. **1939** J.B. TAYLOR in F.G. Butler *When Boys Were Men* (1969) 259 The hills held vaal and rooi rhebok. **1957** *Cape Argus* 13 July 7, I have seen a rooi-rhebok ewe battling to save her kid from an eagle. **1990** G. HARESNAPE in M. Leveson *Firetalk* 31 As we near the peak, a fine rooi-rhebok runs up ahead of us. **1786** [**vaal rhebok**: see BLEEKBOK]. [**1824** W.J. BURCHELL *Trav.* (1953) II. 215 It is found in various parts of the Cape Colony, where it is known to the Boors and Hottentots, by the name of *Vaal Reebok* (Fallow Roebuck).] **1896** R. WARD *Rec. of Big Game* 130 Next to the Klipspringer, the Vaal Rhebok affords the best mountain-stalking in South Africa. **1923** *S. Afr.: Land of Outdoor Life* (S.A.R. & H.) 267 Both the vaal and rooi rhebok are found in nearly all high and isolated mountains and hills. **1939** [see quot. at *rooi rhebok* above]. **1982** *Flying Springbok* Sept. 89 The third area is closer to Greytown .. and the fourth .. in the Eastern Cape Province, for the bontebok, red lechwe, Vaal rhebok, black and white springbok and gemsbok. **1993** G. ETHERINGTON in *Weekend Post* 12 June (Leisure) 4 Eland, bontebok, vaal rhebok, all seemed to have come out for their evening meal.

β. **1948** A.C. WHITE *Call of Bushveld* 109 A **rooi ribbok** (formerly spelt rheebok) of average size weighed 75 lbs. **1974** [see *mountain reedbuck* (REEDBUCK sense 2)]. **1947** L.G. GREEN *Tavern of Seas* 154 You will find the surviving **vaal ribbok** only in South Africa. **1957** — *Beyond City Lights* 224 It is the land of partridges and hares, *vaal ribbok* and duiker. **1982** *E. Prov. Herald* 14 Dec. 7 The animals are steadily increasing and so far the count is 1 100 kudu, 45 eland, 50 buffalo, 40 springbok, 11 vaalribbok, [etc.].

rhebuck /ˈriːbʌk/ *n.* Also **rhee buck, reh-buck, reheebuck**. Pl. unchanged. [Englished form of S. Afr. Du. *rhebok*, see RHEBOK.]

1.a. The RHEBOK (sense 1 a), *Pelea capreolus*. **b.** The *mountain reedbuck* (see REEDBUCK sense 2), *Redunca fulvorufula*.

1839 W.C. HARRIS *Wild Sports* 384 *Redunca Capreolus.* The Rhee Buck. Rhee-bok of the Cape Colonists. **1860** A.W. DRAYSON *Sporting Scenes* 62 The reh-buck (Eleotragus villosus) ... Found in troops of from six to twelve, generally on the rocky hills. **1898** G. NICHOLSON *50 Yrs* 21 On and around this farm black gnus and springbuck grazed in thousands on the plains; among the mounts rhebuck and klipspringer were to be had. **1930** S.T. PLAATJE *Mhudi* (1975) 48 On the surrounding hills, bushbuck and rhebuck peeped through the tree stems from the distance. **1952** H. KLEIN *Land of Silver Mist* 115 Herds of rhebuck dashed away. **1960** U. KRIGE (tr. J. van Melle) in D. Wright *S. Afr. Stories* 131 There was hardly any game left; now and again a steenbok or duiker, .. a couple of rhebuck, a rietbok, nothing to speak of. **1986** *E. Tvl* (Satour) 16 Rhebuck inhabit the grassy highlands.

2. With distinguishing epithet: **grey rhebuck**, the RHEBOK (sense 1 a), *Pelea capreolus*; **mountain -, red -,** or **rooi rhebuck** /rɔi-/ [Afk. *rooi* red (attrib. form *rooie*)], the *mountain reedbuck* (see REEDBUCK sense 2), *Redunca fulvorufula*; **vaal rhebuck** /fɑːl-/, the RHEBOK (sense 1 a), *Pelea capreolus*. Also *attrib.*

1972 *S. Afr. Panorama* Jan. 19 On the plateau one finds **grey rhebuck** and oribi. **1980** J. HANKS *Mammals* 29 The grey rhebuck is frequently misidentified, and the most similar species is the mountain reedbuck. **1986** *Sunday Star* 9 Nov. (Trav. Suppl.) 2 Among a dozen species of antelope you may see grey rhebuck, unique to South Africa, high up on the plateau, if you should venture to those heights. **1987** T.F.J. VAN RENSBURG *Intro. to Fynbos* 52 Species that are still found abundantly in fynbos areas are the bontebok .. , grysbok, klipspringer, baboons, black-backed jackal, caracal and grey rhebuck. **1982** *E. Prov. Herald* 16 Sept. 11 **Mountain rhebuck** and kudu as well as a variety of smaller game. **1891** R. WARD *Sportsman's Handbk* 122 In Natal are found the Bushbuck .. and **Red Rhebuck.** **1971** *Grocott's Mail* 8 June 3 A red rheebuck ram and eight ewes .. have been released in the Thomas Baines Nature Reserve. **1987** T.F.J. VAN RENSBURG *Intro. to Fynbos* 52 Species that occur in limited numbers because they move from adjoining veld types are the bush-pig, kudu, red rhebuck, oribi, duiker, steenbok, bushbuck and blue duiker. **1839** W.C. HARRIS *Wild Sports* 224 The mountain range and its grassy environs, are the resort of six smaller species of antelope, hitherto unnoticed in these pages; viz., the klipspringer, rheebuck, **rooe rheebuck**, or nagor, ourebi, steenbuck, and duiker. *Ibid.* 384 *Redunca Lalandii.* The Nagor. Rooye Rhee-bok *of the Cape Colonists.* **1973** *E. Prov. Herald* 26 Sept. 4 The bag limits will be: Blesbuck two, rooirhebuck three, kudu two and springbuck four. **1912** W. WESTRUP *Land of To-Morrow* 163 If you're as handy with a rifle as you are with a shot gun, you ought to do well after **vaal rhebuck** in the mountains. **1952** H. KLEIN *Land of Silver Mist* 115 Suddenly Piet yelled 'N'Yama' — and two vaal-rhebucks broke cover immediately in front of us. **1993** *Earthyear* (ed.5) Winter (Earthling) 27 Table Mountain is unique ... There are still duiker, grysbok, vaal rhebuck.

rhee-boc, rheebok varr. RHEBOK.

rheim, rheimpy varr. RIEM *n.* , RIEMPIE *n.*

rhem var. RIEM *v.*

rhenosterbos /rəˈnɔstəbɔs/ *n.* Also **renosterbos(ch), rhenosterbosch, rhinosterbos(ch).** [S. Afr. Du., fr. Du. *rhenoster* rhinoceros + *bos(ch)* bush. The influence of mod. Afk. *renosterbos* is seen in the most recent quots.]

1. RHINOCEROS-BUSH. Also *attrib.*, and **rhenosterbosje, -bossie** [see BOSCHJE].

1812 A. PLUMPTRE tr. *H. Lichtenstein's Trav. in Sn Afr.* (1928) 173 We here found in abundance a plant which .. the colonists call .. *rhinosterbosjes*, because, they say, that in the time when the rhinoceros was an inhabitant of the country, it used to feed very much upon this plant. **1822** W.J. BURCHELL *Trav.* I. 101 A neat pale bushy shrub, of the height of three or four feet, called Rhenoster bosch (Rhinoceros bush) and said to have formerly been the food of the huge rhinoceros, till those animals fled before the colonists. *a***1827** D. CARMICHAEL in W.J. Hooker *Botanical Misc.* (1831) II. 56 The country .. is overrun with the heath-like shrub called the *Rhinoster bosch*, (Stoebe rhinocerotis), from under cover of which we startled numbers of Duyker antelopes. **1844** J. BACKHOUSE *Narr. of Visit* 511 The Rhinosterbos, *Rhinoceros-bush*, a low shrub, which is said to grow only on country which will produce wheat. **1861** LADY DUFF-GORDON *Lett. from Cape* (1925) 69 The whole *veld* (common) ... is covered with a low thin scrub, about eighteen inches high, called *rhenoster-bosch* — looking like meagre *arbor vitae* or pale juniper. **1872** E.J. DUNN in A.M.L. Robinson *Sel. Articles from Cape Monthly Mag.* (1978) 39 How much better it would be to see the 'Ruggens' covered with 'schaapbosch', instead of the worthless 'rhinoster bosch'. **1910** A.B. LAMONT *Rural Reader* 259 Rhenosterbos is one of our commonest bushes, being found all over the country. **1918** J.W. BEWS *Grasses & Grasslands* 95 In the South-Western region, the species which is usually dominant over great areas .. is the Rhenoster bosch, a composite (*Elytropappus rhinocerotis*). **1927** C.G. BOTHA *Social Life in Cape Col.* 103 The tops of branches of the rhenosterboschjes, .. when infused in wine or brandy gave a good stomachic bitters. **1941** C.W. DE KIEWIET *Hist. of. S. Afr.* 189 Tumbleweed, prickly pear, rhenosterbos, and jointed cactus invaded the territory of the edible grass and nutritious plants. **1957** L.G. GREEN *Beyond City Lights* 225 Within a brushwood fence, in a kraal covered inches deep with manure by the sheep, sheltered from the sun by a *renosterbos* roof, the tobacco plants flourish. **1961** M. COLE *S. Afr.* 541 Burning and overgrazing .. have destroyed many of the grasses and permitted the sway of the useless renosterbos (*Elytropappus rhinocerotis*), a low shrub whose leaves are impregnated with wax and are unpalatable to animals. **1964** L.G. GREEN *Old Men Say* 149 *Renosterbos*, gummy and resinous, to be infused with brandy; a tonic for dyspeptics. **1973** Y. BURGESS *Life to Live* 113 She says you can try some wildeals or renosterbos in a little brandy to make you strong. **1978** *Sunday Times* 5 Mar. 3 Just one teensy-weensy elephant peering at one over a renosterbossie. **1984** A. WANNENBURGH *Natural Wonder of Sn Afr.* 87 Here the most prevalent taller plants are the grey-green renosterbos and four species of protea, including the water white sugarbush. **1988** SMUTS & ALBERTS *Forgotten Highway* 24 At the southern entrance in the Cold Bokkeveld, the vegetation is not unlike that of Ceres, with the rhenosterbos (*Elytropappus rhinocerotis*) much in evidence. [**1993** see RENOSTERVELD.]

2. *comb.* **rhenosterbosveld** /-felt/ [Afk. *veld* (open) countryside], RENOSTERVELD.

1987 T.F.J. VAN RENSBURG *Intro. to Fynbos* 14 As indicated earlier, there are five veld types in the Cape Floral kingdom or Fynbos Biome: strandveld, coastal rhenosterbosveld, coastal fynbos, fynbos and false fynbos ... The soils on which strandveld and coastal rhenosterbosveld are found are fertile, neutral to alkaline and sometimes somewhat brackish. *Ibid.* 23 Coastal Rhenosterbosveld ... What strikes one about this veld type is the dominance of the evergreen fine-leaved shrub rhenosterbush (*Elytroppapus rhinocerotis*) and the characteristic wealth of spring flowers. [**1989** *Weekend Post* 7 Oct. 3 It was considered vital to conserve the Baviaanskloof because it was the meeting place of four major veld types — mountain fynbos, valley bushveld, Knysna forest and Cape grassveld. A fifth veld type, renosterbos, was found on the fringes.]

‖**rhenostervoël** /rəˈnɔstə(r),fuəl/ *n.* Also **renostervoël**, and (formerly) **rhenoster-, rhinaster vogel.** [S. Afr. Du., *rhenoster* rhinoceros (later Afk. *renoster*) + *vogel* (later Afk. *voël*) bird.] OXPECKER.

1822 W.J. BURCHELL *Trav.* I. 245 They distinguish also a Rhenoster-vogel and an Olifants vogel; but whatever might have been believed of these birds formerly, they are not now to be depended upon by the hunter, in search of these quadrupeds. [**1899** see RHINOCEROS BIRD.] **1990** C. LAFFEATY *Far Forbidden Plains* 356 'They are *renostervoëls*,' he said. 'Those red bills of theirs are searching out ticks on the hides of the cattle.'

rhiem var. RIEM *n.*

rhinoceros bird *n. phr.* Also **rhinoceros' bird.** [Prob. tr. S. Afr. Du. *rhenostervoël*, see prec.] OXPECKER. Also (*colloq.*) **rhino bird.**

1822 J. CAMPBELL *Trav. in S. Afr. Second Journey* I. 282 There is a brown bird, about the size of a thrush, called the rhinoceros' bird, from its perching upon these animals and picking off the bush-lice which fix on them. **1850** R.G.G. CUMMING *Hunter's Life* I. 344 Before I could reach the proper distance to fire, several rhinoceros-birds, by which he was attended, warned him of his impending danger by sticking their bills into his ear, and uttering their harsh, grating cry. **1897** SCHULZ & HAMMAR *New Africa* 130 On nearing the bush, the rising of some 'rhinoceros' (also known as '*tick*') birds, with their shrill, peculiar shriek, warned me that the beast was near. **1899** J.G. MILLAIS *Breath from Veldt* 95 (Swart), I should like to add a few notes from personal observation of the rhinoceros bird (or 'rhinaster vogel', as it is called by the Dutch), which to my mind is the most interesting bird I have ever seen. **1937** W.D. DE KOK tr. *E.N. Marais's Soul of White Ant* (1973) 54 In this country the rhinoceros-bird, which used to relieve the now vanished thick-skinned game of ticks, has undertaken the same office for the thinner-skinned domestic animals. **1947** J. STEVENSON-HAMILTON *Wild Life in S. Afr.* 47 The black rhinoceros .. is often accompanied by rhinoceros birds (*Buphaga*), which give the alarm on the approach of enemies. **1991** *Farmer's Weekly* 25 Jan. 20 (*advt*) By controlling the cursed ticks on cattle and game, highly toxic poisons also wiped out large numbers of the good old Rhino birds.

rhinoceros-bush *n.* [Prob. tr. S. Afr. Du. *rhenosterbos(ch)*, see RHENOSTERBOS; see quot. 1731.] The evergreen shrub *Elytropappus rhinocerotis* of the Asteraceae, with grey-blue, fine-leaved foliage and clusters of small, purple flowers; RHENOSTERBOS sense 1; RHINOSTER sense 2.

1731 G. MEDLEY tr. *P. Kolb's Present State of Cape of G.H.* 103 [The Rhinoceros] is not fond of Feeding on Grass, chusing rather Shrubs, Broom and Thistles. But the Delight of his Tooth is a Shrub, not much unlike the *Juniper*, but not of so fine a Scent, nor quite so prickly. The *Cape-Europeans* call it the *Rhinoceros-Bush.* **1786** G. FORSTER tr. *A. Sparrman's Voy. to Cape of G.H.* I. 251 The *rhinoceros*-bush (a species of *stoebe*) a dry shrub, which is otherwise used to thrive on barren tracts of land, now begins to encroach more and more on such places as have been thoroughly cleared and cultivated. **1801** J. BARROW *Trav.* I. 69 Two species of *seriphium*, called here the rhinoceros-bush, predominate. **1821** C.I. LATROBE *Jrnl of Visit* 55 Some of us rekindled the fire, keeping up a constant blaze, by feeding it with rhinoceros-bushes, a resinous shrub, with large roots, but easily pulled up. **1824** W.J. BURCHELL *Trav.* II. 126 The rhinoceros-bush grows abundantly on different parts of these mountains, and was the only fuel which I saw used at this house. **1839** W.C. HARRIS *Wild Sports* 30 Barely sufficient quantity of fuel, from a shrub called the rhinoceros bush, could be obtained for culinary purposes. **1976** *E. Prov. Herald* 21 Oct. 4 Invader plants that cause the greatest problem in the mountainous parts of the Eastern Karroo Region were the broom bush, taaibos or kraaibossie, Leucosidea, rhinoceros bush, resin bush and buffalo thorn. **1991** H. BRADFORD in *Cosmopolitan* Aug. 127 In addition to swallowing one cup of this cocktail three times a day, at night the pregnant woman was urged to find, strain, and drink a black-ant nest made in the rhinoceros-bush.

rhinoster /rəˈnɒstə/ *n.* Also **r(h)enoster, rhinaster, rhenosta.** [Englished form of S. Afr. Du. *rhenoster* (later Afk. *renoster*) rhinoceros.]

1. *obs.*

a. Either of two species of rhinoceros of the Rhinocerotidae, the white or square-lipped rhinoceros *Ceratotherium simum*, or the black or hook-lipped rhinoceros *Diceros bicornis* (now an endangered species).

1839 W.C. HARRIS *Wild Sports* 371 *Rhinoceros Africanus.* The African Rhinoceros. Rhinaster *of the Cape Colonists* ... *Rhinoceros Sinusus.* The White Rhinoceros. Witte Rhinaster *of the Cape Colonists.* **1844** J. BACKHOUSE *Narr. of Visit* 172 The common two-horned Rhinoceros, *Rhinoceros bicornis*, called *Rhinoster* by the Cape colonists, was formerly common throughout the country.

b. *comb.* **rhinoster bird**, OXPECKER.

1851 J.F. CHURCHILL Diary. (Killie Campbell Africana Library MS37) 29 June, Met with no wild animals during the day. Saw a few Rhinoster Birds with large Bills.

2. In full ***rhinoster bush***: RHINOCEROS-BUSH.

1851 R. GRAY *Jrnl of Bishop's Visitation* II. Unbroken, monotonous rhinoster bush. **1867** *Blue Bk for Col. 1866* JJ15, The rhenoster bush, since the introduction of sheep, has fearfully encroached on the pasturage, leaving no alternative but to burn it. **1896** R. WALLACE *Farming Indust. of Cape Col.* 81 The rhenoster bush has spread more widely and more quickly than exotic plants generally do, on account of it having been carried through the Colony by the brandy distilling Boers of old time, who used it as dunnage in packing the casks on their waggons. **1902** H.J. DUCKITT in M. Kuttel *Quadrilles & Konfyt* (1954) 17 There was the large oven (built into the kitchen), which took a cartload of wood to heat; by wood I mean 'rhenoster bush', which grows on the hills, and strange to say, wherever land has been under cultivation, in a few years it is covered with this bush, which makes excellent firewood. **1905** H. BOLUS in Flint & Gilchrist *Science in S. Afr.* 219 The constituents of the 'zuur-veld' (or sour-veld), as it is called by the colonists, are of a coarser character .. which are of little use to live-stock; just as they, and also the rhenoster-bush (*Elytropappus rhinocerotis*) and the Restioncaeae, are the great drawbacks of the grazing grounds in the South-west Region. **1913** D. FAIRBRIDGE *Piet of Italy* 131 Francesco followed him across the werf and up the grey rhinoster-clad hillside. *Ibid.* 137 He found himself passing through a gate which led to nowhere — or only to an expanse of stony veld covered with grey tufts of rhinoster. **1915** —— *Torch Bearer* 49 The fragrant scent of burning rhinoster-bush rose from a cottage chimney near by and floated in at the open window. **1917** R. MARLOTH *Common Names* 69 *Renosterbos* (*Rhenoster Bush*), *Elytropappus rhinocerotis* ... Mostly looked upon as a useless bush, which much impedes the farming operations, but on the Ruggens (Caledon distr.) it is in many cases the only fuel available for ovens and other domestic use. **1920** E.H.L. SCHWARZ *Thirstland Redemption* 19 We have in South Africa the example of the Rhenoster Bush, that is said to have sprung from a few plants brought to Simon's Town. **1928** N. STEVENSON *Afr. Harvest* 175 There was an overpowering smell of rhenosta bush. **1947** F.C. SLATER *Sel. Poems* 229 *Rhenoster*, A grey low bush (Elytropappus rhinocerotis), growing gregariously in South-West Cape Colony, but extending to Grahamstown on temporarily unused arable land and on overstocked pasturage — a great pest. **1969** I. VAUGHAN *These Were my Yesterdays* 48 Dawn of the next day had brought us out of the renoster bush of Swellendam and Robertson.

Rhodes grass *n. phr.* Also with small initial. [Named for *Cecil John Rhodes* (1853–1902); see quot. 1913.] The indigenous African grass *Chloris gayana* of the Poaceae, cultivated for pasturage and hay.

1913 C. PETTMAN *Africanderisms* 399 *Rhodes grass, Chloris Gayana, Kunth.* A native grass which was brought to the notice of the late Hon. Cecil Rhodes while on a visit to the Queenstown District, as a valuable fodder plant, and sent by him to his farm in the Matopos, is now generally known as Rhodes grass. **1929** J.W. BEWS *World's Grasses* 179 'Rhodes grass', a native of Africa .. is cultivated in the S.W. States of N. America, in Hawaii, and in Australia. **1937** *Handbk for Farmers* (Dept of Agric. & Forestry) 409 Rhodes grass .. is a sweet-veld grass, hence its establishment and persistence in sour-veld areas is not likely to prove successful. **1962** *New Scientist* (U.K.) 1 Mar. 487 Since the beginning of the century, when it was introduced into Australia from its native home in Africa, Rhodes grass (*Chloris gayana*) has become the dominant pasture species. **1991** D.M. MOORE *Garden Earth* 199 The Rhodes grass (*Chloris gayana*) is now an important pasture and hay grass in warm areas outside southern Africa.

Rhodesian lion dog see LION DOG.

Rhodesian ridgeback see RIDGEBACK.

Rhodie /ˈrəʊdi/ *n.* Often *derog. colloq.* [Formed on *Rhodesian* + Eng. (informal) n.-forming suffix *-ie*.] A white expatriate of the former Rhodesia; a white person from Zimbabwe (esp. one resentful of majority rule).

Used (since the renaming of the country in 1980) in contrast to *Zimbabwean*.

1983 *Rand Daily Mail* 16 Sept. 1 Detention without acquittal would remain in Zimbabwe as long as there were threats from 'South African destabilisation, bandits and old Rhodies who still try to carry on the war which ended at Lancaster House'. **1985** [see WHEN-WE]. **1988** *E. Prov. Herald* 27 Feb. 6 The SABC has hurtled into 20th century politics .. laying on a simulcast in English for the Rhodies on the Natal South Coast. **1990** *Weekly Mail* 28 Sept. 9 They were told that the skills they'd acquired abroad were urgently required by the new, non-racial nation now that the Rhodies' illegal government had been toppled ... Cynics and doom merchants are already muttering that .. there'll be the same migration out of South Africa, though where the brains draining away go could be a problem (as it is for Rhodies) — the southern tip of the continent being the end of the road. **1993** *Ibid.* 21 May 16 Not so long ago, Rhodies ruled the world ... But .. they had to give way, and they are not happy.

rhy-bôk var. RHEBOK.

ribbetjie /ˈrəbəki/ *n.* Also **ribitje**. [Afk.] Ribs (or 'rack') of lamb or mutton (see quot. 1970); chops. Also with defining word, as **braairibbetjie** /ˈbrai-/ [Afk., *braai* grill(ed)], barbecued ribs, **skaapribbetjie** /ˈskɑːp-/ [Afk., *skaap* sheep], mutton ribs. See also SOUTRIBBETJIE.

1916 *Farmer's Weekly* 27 Dec. 1585 The 'old style' man goes to town for 'Nachtmaal' every quarter, lives in his wagon while there, eats 'gebraaide ribbetje' or 'biltong' at the camp fire, and drinks his coffee out of his own kettle. **1935** P. SMITH *Platkops Children* 213 An' the picnic was saasaaties an' ribitjies cooked on the coals, an' coffee an' cookies. **1958** A. JACKSON *Trader on Veld* 23 Her range of culinary art was limited to serving us with 'braairibbetjie' (grilled mutton chops) without vegetables for breakfast, lunch and dinner. **1968** L.G. GREEN *Full Many Glorious Morning* 232 Richter and Frikkie had just finished their evening meal of *braairibbetjies* with potatoes baked in the embers. **1970** *Evening Post* 17 Oct. (Suppl.) 6 *Braairibbetjie*, This consists of 4–6lb of mutton or lamb. When the shoulder has been removed, the breast and ribs are cut and chopped down to the spine, just before the chops are reached. Keep the ribbetjie in one piece, but chop through the bones so as to cut it into convenient serving pieces when grilled. **1984** *Sunday Times* 7 Oct. (Lifestyle) 1 This [*sc.* Graaff-Reinet] is a typical platteland town, you know. We like our ribbetjies on the braai after church. **1985** T. BARON in *Frontline* Feb. 31 White mussels, they told us that night in the bar as Scotch Jan fed us skaapribbetjies. They taste better than limpets, even to a galjoen.

ribbok var. RHEBOK.

ride *v.* [Calque formed on Afk. *ry* drive, ride, convey.]

1. *trans.* **a.** To convey or transport (goods or substances). **b.** In the phr. ***to ride transport***, to work as a carrier; KURVEY. See also TRANSPORT-RIDER, TRANSPORT-RIDING.

Also *U.S. Eng.* in sense a.

1862 *Abstracts in Cape Stat.* p.vi, Prohibition against overworking cattle in riding wood, and thus rendering them unfit for the plough. **1866** E.L. PRICE *Jrnls* (1956) 218 Roger has had a very hard and busy time with the Dam-making. The soil proves too sandy — and he has been obliged to get Seidras to ride earth from other place[s] round about. **1870** *E. Prov. Herald* 9 Aug., First you sift your earth, and then sieve in water with the gravel on the table to be sorted ... Two casks of water will last you all day, and that will save riding earth all day. **1878** *Cape Parl. Papers* in R. Ross *Adam Kok's Griquas* (1976) 110 I also reaped 30 bags of mealies, selling them at 12s.; .. riding transport as work permits. **1880** *Alice Times* 30 Jan. It is a common thing to hear farmers .. complain that they have to ride water for household uses a distance of eight or ten miles. **1897** E. GLANVILLE *Tales from Veld* 26, I want you to 'ride' a load of wood to the house. **1905** P. GIBBON *Vrouw Grobelaar* 67 The man was clean mad, and, in spite of all we could do, .. he rode her to the dorp and married her there. **1911** —— *Margaret Harding* 61 When I was a young man I rode transport ... Then I travelled. **1913** [see *misrybol* (MIS sense 3)]. **1913** C. PETTMAN *Africanderisms* 400 *Ride, To* A common South African colloquialism uses this verb somewhat peculiarly, e.g. 'He is riding wood, forage, etc.' meaning 'He is carting wood, forage, etc.,' from one place to another. **1926** P. SMITH *Beadle* (1929) 115 Aalst Vlokman was at that time riding transport between Platkops dorp and Princestown village. **1929** J.G. VAN ALPHEN *Jan Venter* 44 One of the neighbours has put a fence across his road which we have been using for riding mealies to the railway siding for the last fifteen years. **1937** C.R. PRANCE *Tante Rebella's Saga* 125 The ox- and the donkey-wagon are almost obsolete, and with them has died out Jock's hope to make his poorer debtors ride transport to work off their debt. **1962** F.C. METROWICH *Scotty Smith* 166 De Jay must have been a complete fool, because .. he actually agreed to go transport riding with him. **1972** *Grocott's Mail* 15 Dec. 3 Farmers have to ride in feed. **1979** M. PARKES *Wheatlands* 84 He .. had the foresight to know that in times of drought, the prickly pear was an asset and very useful, not only to us, as neighbours rode loads of it to feed their animals.

2.a. *trans.* In the phr. ***to ride (someone) over***, to run (someone) over.

1978 *Darling* 19 July 12 An African has accused me of riding him over with the panel van I possessed at the time.

b. *trans.* To drive (a motor-vehicle).

1986 *Informant, Durban* You must see how he rides his car!

c. *intrans.* To travel.

1991 G. DE BEER *Informant, Port Nolloth (N. Cape)* Ride in (drive in/travel in): Let's ride in your car today.

Ride Safe *n. phr.* Also with small initials. The name of the voluntary organization co-ordinating assistance with free travel for national servicemen who are on leave (see quot. 1981). Usu. *attrib.* Cf. BELLERYNA.

1979 W. STEENKAMP in *Cape Times* 20 Jan., Project Ride Safe, the give-a-troopie-a-lift scheme, is now well under way ... Thanks to the Ride Safe scheme our troopies' hitch-hiking is rather better regulated ... If you see a garage displaying the red-and-yellow Ride Safe sign call in there in case there is a soldier waiting for a lift. **1979** *Grocott's Mail* 8 Feb. 1 Two Ride Safe pick-up points for homeward bound soldiers are planned for Grahamstown. **1979** *Paratus* Oct. (Suppl.) 1 The Ride Safe scheme for National Servicemen wishing to go home over weekends is working admirably well. However, some motorists fear an accident with a soldier in the car. **1981** *Rand Daily Mail* 29 Sept. 14 The 'ride safe' project was launched in 1978. This project, which is at present being expanded and improved, provides lifts for national servicemen, safe boarding along freeways, free sleeping accommodation in certain towns along the main routes, proper third party insurance and special luminous sashes to make them more visible at night. **1982** *E. Prov. Herald* 10 Nov. 10 If funds are needed to make the Ride-Safe telephone service more effective, why on earth should they come from the good-hearted women who do the job? **1985** *Cape Times* 30 Dec. 7 *Ride Safe*: Lifts for national servicemen.

ridgeback *n.* [See quots 1971 and 1991.] In full ***Rhodesian ridgeback***: (one of) a breed of large, muscular, smooth-coated dogs, brindled to pale brown in colour, with a ridge along the spine, formed by hair growing in the opposite direction to the rest of the coat; LION DOG. Also *attrib.*

1937 *Our Dogs* 10 Dec. 886 The belief that the Rhodesian Ridgeback is the direct result of crossing the old Cuban Bloodhound with the Hottentot Hunting Dog arose a considerable time ago ... The ridge in the breed .. is present in practically every Ridgeback puppy. **1945** L.G. GREEN *Where Men Still Dream* 167 The finest type of Bushman hunting dog, a light brown ridgeback mongrel with dark stripes and a trace of the greyhound in his appearance, is now verging on extinction. **1956** — *There's Secret Hid Away* 43 Ridgeback owners regard their dogs as true South Africans, the only pure-bred dogs that really belong to the country. **1965** J. BENNETT *Hawk Alone* 13 One morning the dogs – they had a cross-bred ridgeback and a boerboel – had put up a rooikat ... The ridgeback .. had been killed .. when it unwisely cornered a big yellow Cape Cobra in the feed store behind the house. **1971** D. MARAIS in *Std Encycl. of Sn Afr.* IV. 53 The Rhodesian ridgeback, or 'lion-dog', is a rather large dog weighing from 70 to 80 lb (32 to 36 kg). Ridgebacks differ from all other breeds in having the hair of the back pointing forward to form a characteristic ridge. Dogs with this ridging were first seen by the European settlers when they made contact with the Hottentot tribes. By cross-breeding between these Hottentot dogs and dogs imported from Europe the new breed was evolved ... Formerly these dogs were quite famous as hunting-dogs, but today they are mainly used as watchdogs and companions. **1977** P.C. VENTER *Soweto* 51 A ridgeback yawned and got up from the polished door step. **1980** *E. Prov. Herald* 29 Aug. 15 Dog lovers .. have steadfastly refused to consider changing the name of the Rhodesian Ridgeback since the birth of Zimbabwe ... A Johannesburg Ridgeback breeder .. said that the breed would remain Rhodesian Ridgebacks. **1991** *Philatelic Services Bulletin* No.8075, *Ridgeback Dog* ... It is thought that the Khoi brought the dogs with them during their migration southwards. The recent history of the breed begins with two dogs sold by the Reverend Charles Helm of Swellendam to the famous hunter Cornelius van Rooyen in 1874. This type of dog was first known as the Van Rooyen or lion dog (because of its hunting ability). In 1924 the Kennel Union of Southern Africa acknowledged the breed at the request of a group of Ridgeback enthusiasts from Bulawayo in the former Southern Rhodesia (now Zimbabwe) – hence the name Rhodesian Ridgeback.

riem /rim, ri:m/ *n.* Also **ream, reem, r(h)eim, rhiem, rim.** Pl. **-s**, or occas. **-e.** [Du., thong, strap.]

1.a. Esp. in the past, (a strip or thong of) raw-hide used as rope; RIEMPIE sense 1 b. **b.** RIEMPIE sense 1 a. **c.** *fig. rare.* A link or tie (see quot. 1974).

1817 G. BARKER Journal. 15 May, Began, with Piet Kampher, to make a plough. Oxen rims were also cut. **1820** T. PHILIPPS *Lett.* (1960) 56 He .. tied the Rhiem (made out of a Bullocks hide ..) to his knee and turned him out. **1822** W.J. BURCHELL *Trav.* I. 151 The reim (or halter), is a leathern thong about twelve feet in length, with a noose at one end, by which it is fixed round the ox's horns. It is used for holding and managing the animal, while yoking and unyoking. **1827** T. PHILIPPS *Scenes & Occurrences* 64 His horse is unsaddled, a thong made of a bullock's hide, called a *riem* is tied round his neck and fastened to his foreleg. **1836** A.F. GARDINER *Journey to Zoolu Country* 343 It was a severe labour for the poor oxen, requiring .. no less than three wheels to be locked as we descended on the other side, where it was necessary to apply reims to the sides, in order to keep them from falling over. **1837** 'N. POLSON' *Subaltern's Sick Leave* 131 The skin of the *wildebeest* or gnu when brayed, is used for *reims* or thongs to harness the oxen, and indeed for every purpose to which twine or string is usually applied in other countries. **1850** J.E. METHLEY *New Col. of Port Natal* 22 The oxen have reims or thongs of undressed skin tied round their horns and a native is required to lead the front pair. **1872** in A.M.L. Robinson *Sel. Articles from Cape Monthly Mag.* (1978) 280 He must rack his memory many times in vain for a good English equivalent for 'riem', that most invaluable adjunct in every journey. **1872** C.A. PAYTON *Diamond Diggings* 43 Some rope or one or two good strong rheims will also be required. Rope is very dear just now. Rheims about 2s.6d each in stores, but can be bought much cheaper in the market. **1880** E.F. SANDEMAN *Eight Months in Ox-Waggon* 130 A large stock of 'rims,' as lengths of prepared hide are called, and which entirely take the place of rope throughout the whole of South Africa. **1895** [see LEADER]. **1899** *Natal Agric. Jrnl* 31 Mar. 3 'Riem,' in the days before railways, was one of the commonest words in the Colony. It was indispensable for the handling of cattle and horses, and colonists when looking at a patched post-cart, a roughly-repaired wagon, or mended harness, would observe 'the whole colony is hung together with riems.' **1899** D.S.F.A. PHILLIPS *S. Afr. Recollections* 14 The furniture consisted of .. rude benches and chairs, with the seats made of riem (hide) instead of cane. **1905** G. BAUMANN in Baumann & Bright *Lost Republic* (1940) 245 The town of Reddersburg .. was laid out, and built upon, by farmers, who used an ordinary riem (raw-hide thong) as a chain or tape. **1935** P. SMITH *Platkop's Children* 76 Close by the dam was a tremendous oak-tree with riems hangin' down from it for makin' harness. **1944** J.J.L. SISSON *S. Afr. Judicial Dict.* (1960) 674 *Reim* is not a precise or accurate term. It is used looseley to cover any thing made from hide, and includes anything from a strip of raw hide to a hide rope which has been subjected to a considerable process of treatment and manufacture. **1968** K. MCMAGH *Dinner of Herbs* 30, I get the volk to drag away the carcasses and skin them. I make riems from the good skins. **1973** M.A. COOK *Cape Kitchen* 79 Pails were carried .. two at a time, hanging by rieme from a yoke. **1974** *E. Prov. Herald* 28 Jan. 11 The riem that was made fast 60 years ago was now being torn loose ... 'I don't know why we have to give up this land,' the headman said. 'I don't know why the Government wants us to tear the riem loose.' **1985** B. JOHNSON-BARKER *Wynboer* June 71 They said good day to Hendrik Terblans, who said nothing, but sat still on his chair of riem and white pear. **1994** M. ROBERTS tr. *J.A. Wahlberg's Trav. Jrnls 1838–56* 55 As we were driving down 'Skönhogten', the riem holding the chain broke, and in consequence the waggon came near to toppling over.

2. Parasynthetic derivatives (*adjs*): **riem-bottomed, riem-seated.**

1870 H.H. DUGMORE *Reminisc. of Albany Settler* 27 Weary enough to sleep soundly on their **reim-bottomed** kaatles. **1955** A. DELIUS *Young Trav.* 98 They .. arrived in a big dining-room with **riem-seated** chairs [*Note*] Riem seat – a seat made of criss-crossed leather thongs.

3. Special Comb. and *comb.* **Riemland**, hence **Riemlander**, see quots 1913; **riem-manufacturer** (objective).

1913 C. PETTMAN *Africanderisms* 400 **Riemland**, The name by which Kroonstad, a district of the Orange Free State, used to be known. *Ibid.* 401 *Riemlander*, A nickname jokingly applied to the people of the above district. **1974** *S. Afr. Panorama* May 28 There were more than enough hides for 'riems' .. hence the name 'Riemland'. Many of the early inhabitants made their living by selling riems. **1947** C.R. PRANCE *Antic Mem.* 100 Biltong specialists, **riem-manufacturers**, and 'head-hunting' sportsmen from the Rand.

riem *v. trans. Obs.* Also **r(e)im, r(h)em.** [Prob. from prec.; however the spelling-forms *rhem* and *rem* suggest that there was confusion between, or conflation of, S. Afr. Du. *rem* brake (see REMSKOEN) and *riem* thong (RIEM *n.*).]

1.a. To lock (a waggon-wheel) with chains or raw-hide thongs.

1835 A. STEEDMAN *Wanderings* I. 182 The banks being very steep, and the driver having objected to *rhem* the wheels, we descended with great rapidity into the bed of the river. **1850** R.G.G. CUMMING *Hunter's Life* I. 45 Having rheimed or secured the two hind wheels by means of the drag-chains. **1851** R. GRAY *Jrnl of Bishop's Visitation* II. 36 He said he did not dare 'reim' (lock) the wheel; and that if went down with it unlocked, all would roll into the precipice below. **1856** A.G. BAIN in J. Burman *Guide to Garden Route* (1973) 43 This road has been worn down in the course of ages by 'remming' (braking) at least two wheels of every wagon that descends it, into a deep channel from six to eight feet high. *a***1858** J. GOLDSWAIN *Chron.* (1946) I. 3 The drift was so narrow so that no one could go by the side of the Oxen and verey steep to go down to the water or cold we rim the wheal for if I had they Oxen wold have had to stop wile I had to on loos the wele. **1875** 'P.' in A.M.L. Robinson *Sel. Articles from Cape Monthly Mag.* (1978) 193 Although the wheels were reimed and skidded to the utmost the incline was so steep that it appeared a miracle that the whole wagon and its contents were not turned bodily over upon the oxen yoked to the disselboom. **1876** T. STUBBS Reminiscences. 21 Old Fancutt said Master I think as how we had better lock her (Meaning to reim the waggon), My Father Thought he could Keep them back. **1878** H.A. ROCHE *On Trek in Tvl* 276 John has bound it round with a good stout reim – 'to reim' is a verb peculiar to South Africa – I cannot but think the first stone .. will sever the hide, thick as it is. **1887** A.A. ANDERSON *25 Yrs in Waggon* I. 89 One road from this place goes down to the river through a fearful valley, it is necessary to 'riem' (tie) the four wheels of the waggon, otherwise it would go crash down into the precipice below, and then turn over and be smashed. **1934** B.I. BUCHANAN *Pioneer Days* 92 When .. he reached a short, rather steep dip he 'rimmed' (blocked by fastening a chain round the rim) both wheels on one side of the bus, with the inevitable result that the vessel promptly capsized.

b. *comb.* **riem-chain**, a chain used for locking the wheels of a wagon.

1860 W. SHAW *Story of my Mission* 352 An accident occurred to the riem chain, or wheel-lock, of one of the wagons, while running down the rocky bank to the stream.

2. To tie with a leather thong or 'riem' (see RIEM *n.* sense 1 a).

1852 H. WARD *Jasper Lyle* 111 'And so now .. I'll reim the prisoner.' 'Reim the prisoner?' said Ormsky ... 'Tie him to the wagon wheel, master,' answered May. **1878** T.J. LUCAS *Camp Life & Sport* 43 The oxen are 'reimed' together by the horns, and are inspanned in couples by means of a yoke of heavy wood, which rests horizontally upon their necks.

Hence **rieming** *vbl n.*, the locking of a wheel.

1878 H.A. ROCHE *On Trek in Tvl* 280 John's constant 'reiming' makes it just hold, but it is very shaky.

riempie /ˈrɪmpi, ˈri:mpi/ *n.* Also **reimpj(i)e, r(h)eimpy, ri(e)mpje, rim pey, rimpi(e), rimpy, rympie.** [Du. (and Afk.) *riem* leather thong, strap + -IE.]

1.a. (A thin strip of) worked leather, used esp. for thonging the backs and seats of chairs, settles, and other furniture, for shoe-laces, and as string; RIEM sense 1 b. Also *attrib.* (passing into *adj.*), and occas. *fig.* (see quot. 1852).

1850 N.J. MERRIMAN *Cape Jrnls* (1957) 110 I .. cut out a rimpie (small thong of leather), and mended my veldtschoons. *Ibid.* 146 Very luckily I had carried an awl and piece of bush buckskin for rimpies, as our shoes wanted frequent patching in so long a march. **1850** R.G.G. CUMMING *Hunter's Life* I. 384 A wide-awake hat, secured under my chin by 'rheimpys', or strips of dressed skin. **1852** *Trial of Andries Botha* 63 He brought a message to me from John Goliath, that he wanted me for the purpose of cutting me into *riempies* (strips). **1880** [see VOORSLAG sense 2]. **1880** E.F. SANDEMAN *Eight Months in Ox-Waggon* 130 Rimpey, a sort of skin string. **1885** [see SWARTWITPENS]. **1895** H. RIDER HAGGARD *Nada* 44 Slowly undoing the rimpis with which it was tied. **1896** R. WALLACE *Farming Indust. of Cape Col.* 439 Thongs, called 'rimpies', made from the fine soft skins of bucks, are extensively employed by people living on the veld for pointing whip lashes, mending harness, and for the common purpose for which twine is generally employed in more densely populated places. **1913** J.J. DOKE *Secret City* 36 Several farm-made chairs to match, thongs of leather – riempjes – crossing each other forming their seat, and fixed together with wooden nails. **1916** *Rand Daily Mail* 1 Nov., Oak Bookcase, .. 7 Solid Oak Chairs with Reimpje Seats; 2 Morris Chairs. **1919** M.C. BRUCE *Golden Vessel* 71 Riempje furniture is so typical of South Africa and so suitable. **1943** *Outspan* 20 Aug. 41 Oil-free Furniture Riempies in strips 6 feet long by 1/4 inch wide, 1/3 per strip. **1969** D. CHILD *Yesterday's Children* 40 Beds and chairs were home-made and were no more than rough wooden frames with *riempies* (strips of hide) stretched across. **1970** *Cape Times* 11 June, Boy Scouts tuck a piece of *riempie* under their chins, .. wound round the crown of their 'wide-awakes'. **1970** *Forum* Vol.6 No.2, 46 Heavy chairs of dark polished wood and with riempies strung across the seat and backrest. **1976** *Fair Lady* 21 July 119, I can never walk past a second-hand shop, .. spindle-turned chairs with *riempies* as limp as overcooked spaghetti. **1982** C. HOPE *Private Parts* 12 He put his feet upon the 'riempie' table and dozed. **1982** *Sunday Times* 10 Oct. (Mag. Sect.) 20 An ox-wagon bed – a stout wooden frame with a riempie base made of ox-hide thongs. **1987** J. KENCH *Cottage Furn.* 158 Riempies, a local speciality, are thongs cut from cowhide and woven to form simple but effective and hard-wearing seating for chairs, stools and benches.

b. RIEM sense 1 a.

1936 P.M. CLARK *Autobiog. of Old Drifter* 134 By the second evening we had a quantity of nice hides pegged out to dry. They were to be cut into *reimpjes* – hide strips that were a substitute for ropes and useful for many purposes. **1944** [see TOULEIER]. **1971** H. ZEEDERBERG *Veld Express* 165 The driver and his assistant cut down various saplings, and braced up the wheel with 'riempies'. These strips of leather were always carried in case of emergencies.

c. *rare*. By metonomy: a riempie chair.

1949 L.G. GREEN *In Land of Afternoon* 194, I believe that even the homely, straight-backed riempie, so typical of the Cape farmhouse, may be traced back to the Stuart chair. **1971** *Argus* 14 May 22, I don't have any aversion to using words like 'braaivleis', 'pondok', 'rondavel' and even 'riempie' – when I want to refer to a specific kind of chair – in the English I speak.

2. *comb.* Usu. with combining form (or plural) -*s*-. **riempie(s)bank** /-baŋk/ [Afk., *bank* bench, stool], a stool with thonged seat; **riempie bench, riempie(s) chair**, [prob. part. trr. Afk. *riempiebank* and *riempiestoel* respectively] simple, traditional Cape furniture with thonged seat (and, sometimes, back); **riempie(s)mat** /-mat/ [Afk., *mat* bottom, seat (of chair)], the woven seat or back of a piece of thonged furniture; **riempie-seat**, a seat of woven riempies; **riempieskoen** /-skʊn, -skun/ [Afk., *skoen* shoe], see quot. 1975; **riempiestoel** /-stʊl, -stul/, also **riempies-stoel** and calque (or part. tr.) **riempie stool**, pl. **-s** or **-stoele** [Afk. *stoel* chair], a riempie chair (or stool).

1947 H.C. BOSMAN *Mafeking Rd* (1969) 102, I went and sat next to her on the **riempies-bank** and took her hand. **1979** *E. Prov. Herald* 9 Sept. 17 The Cape-Dutch home ... The grandeur of Victorian crystal from England, the old Malay brasswork, the earthiness of the 'riempiesbank'. **1985** P. DIAMOND in *Style* Dec. 26 *Objets* African/Victorian, a riempiebank with Laura Ashley cushions. **1990** *Personality* 1 Jan. 42 Mynhardt took his Oom Schalk riempies-bank, his stone jug of mampoer, his Oom Schalk beard and moustache and soft felt hat and went on the road. **1920** R. JUTA *Tavern* 133 No carpets spoiled the red tiled floors. **Riempje benches**, carved and seated with thongs of hide, stood against the white walls. **1974** A.P. BRINK *Looking on Darkness* 240 When the hour struck, everybody would be present, some on *riempie* benches or rickety bentwood chairs. **1982** *S. Afr. Panorama* Mar. 32 Stinkwood display cabinets with copper metalwork, and a *riempie* (thonged) bench. **1983** M. DU PLESSIS *State of Fear* 75 The tall window opposite my bed, with the low *riempie* bench underneath it. **1990** *Grocott's Mail* 20 Mar. (Suppl.) 6 Oom Schalk Lourens in his veldskoene, with his riempie bench and peach brandy. **1915** D. FAIRBRIDGE *Torch Bearer* 27 A few comfortable chintz-seated or **reimpje chairs**. **1926** P. SMITH *Beadle* (1929) 66 In this room the Englishman now had his bed, his bath, his guns, two rimpje chairs, a yellow-wood table. **1950** H.C. BOSMAN in L. Abrahams *Jurie Steyn's Post Office* (1971) 95 This circumstance of our not feeling quite at ease manifested itself in the way that most of us sat on our riempies-chairs – just a little more stiffly than usual. **1977** J. PACKER *Dark Curtain* 55 The divan and two low *riempie* chairs had been ordered for her by the king. Straw-stuffed cushions with hand-woven covers hid the neat hide thongs of the wooden chairs. **1988** D. SAMUELSON in *Fair Lady* 16 Mar. 133 She pushed her riempie chair against the wall and felt the warmth of the afternoon sun. **1991** D. GALLOWAY in *Weekend Argus* 26 Jan. 18 Most of the old Cape furniture, from beds and dressers to kists and riempie chairs, was collected from second-hand shops and homes and restored. *a*1878 J. MONTGOMERY *Reminisc.* (1981) 87 Our furniture consisted of a wooden katel (bedstead), with a **riempie mat**, a mattress, a featherbed, pillows. **1973** *E. Prov. Herald* 24 Jan. 23 Pictures, Riempiesmat-chair, small cupboards. **1991** M. PRETORIUS in *Weekend Post* 9 Feb. (Leisure) 1 He wears dark trousers and a dark waistcoat with a watch chain, one end of which disappears into a pocket. His hands rest on the back of a riempiesmat chair. **1927** *Outspan* 18 Mar. 49 The four parents of the couple sat on **riempie-seat** chairs in a semi-circle. **1975** D.H. STRUTT *Clothing Fashions* 223 Shoes made without nails, the uppers sewn to the soles, were known as **riempieskoene**. **1989** *Reader's Digest Illust. Hist.* 114 The trekkers, dressed in traditional *dopper* coats (short coats buttoned from top to bottom), *kappies* (bonnets) and hand-made *riempieskoene* (leather thong shoes), set out in wagons. **1933** W. MACDONALD *Romance of Golden Rand* 72 Louw Geldenhuys, sitting on a **riempiestoel** in the little office. **1953** U. KRIGE *Dream & Desert* 75 Marta, sitting on her *riempiestoel* in front of the door leading to the kitchen. *a*1953 H.C. BOSMAN in L. Abrahams *Unto Dust* (1963) 122 A newly-appointed veld-kornet, looking important, seated on a riempies-stoel. **1965** M.G. ATMORE *Cape Furn.* 84 The cabriole leg form or 'riempie stool'. **1970** E. MUNDELL *Informant, Pearston (E. Cape)* All riempiestoels are rather uncomfortable. **1975** *E. Prov. Herald* 25 June 24 Stinkwood double Riempie Stool. **1985** L. SAMPSON in *Style* Feb. 101 They sat on riempie stools in the sun peeling potatoes.

3. Parasynthetic derivatives (*adjs*): **riempie-bottomed, riempie-laced, riempie-seated**, etc.

1939 [see RUSBANK sense 1]. **1952** G.M. MILLS *First Ladies of Cape* 41 Riempie-bottomed chairs. *a*1953 H.C. BOSMAN in L. Abrahams *Unto Dust* (1963) 38, I sat on the riempie-bottomed bench next to Mr Huysmans. **1959** M. W. SPILHAUS *Under Bright Sky* 101 She sought her doll, lying .. on a rympie-seated chair against the wall. **1968** G. CROUDACE *Silver Grass* 34 Unfurnished but for a wash-stand and a riempie-laced bed. **1973** *Evening Post* 14 July 19 Six riempie seated ladder back chairs. **1979** J. GRATUS *Jo'burgers* 21 Pienaar .. leaned back in his large, riempie-seated chair which groaned beneath his weight.

riempie /ˈrɪmpi, ˈrimpi/ *v. trans.* [fr. prec.] To weave a thong seat or panel for a piece of furniture.

1971 BARAITSER & OBHOLZER *Cape Country Furn.* 29 The seat is riempied with fine riempie in the pattern of caning. *Ibid.* 51 The front and back seat rails are riempied through vertical holes.

Hence **riempied** *ppl adj.*, **riemp(ie)ing** *vbl n.*

1971 BARAITSER & OBHOLZER *Cape Country Furn.* 9 Examination of the riempie wear shows that the riemping was done through horizontal holes and not vertical holes. *Ibid.* 51 In some of these chairs horizontal riemping is confined to the two lateral seat rails. **1987** J. KENCH *Cottage Furn.* 158 No nails, tacks or metal fasteners are used in riempieing, the thongs being secured by knots only ... Begin the weaving process by inserting the pointed end of the riempie up through the countersunk hole ... Stretch the riempie across the top of the frame to the opposite hole, inserting it from above and pulling it tight from below ... The riempie should be stretched as tightly as possible, with the smooth side uppermost ... Pass the riempie back across the frame ... Weave the second layer of riempies over and under the thongs of the first layer, once again using the awl as a peg to secure the riempie temporarily. No nails, tacks or metal fasteners are used in riempieing, the thongs being secured by knots only. **1991** F.G. BUTLER *Local Habitation* 284 All that they had lacked were the riempied seats and backs.

riemschoen var. REMSKOEN.

Riesling /ˈriːʒlɪŋ, ˈriːslɪŋ/ *n.* Also with small initial. [Named after the Rhine Riesling cultivar which it resembles in appearance.]

1. A variety of vine and grape originating in south-western France, where it is known as *Cruchen Blanc*; the white wine produced from this grape; *Cape Riesling*, see CAPE sense 2 a. See also CAPE WINE.

1980 J. PLATTER *Bk of S. Afr. Wines* 88 Different to the more recently imported Weisser Riesling of Germany, the S.A. riesling nonetheless is closely related to its German namesake. **1981** J. DOXAT *Indispensable Drinks Bk* 53 South African Riesling, not the true Rhine Riesling, is what is usually meant if the word Riesling *tout court* appears on a wine label. **1982** M. BEAZLEY *Hugh Johnson's Pocket Wine Bk* 173 South African Riesling makes some of the country's better white wines, but it is not the same as Rhine Riesling, which has only recently been planted in any quantity in S. Africa. **1988** D. HUGHES et al. *Complete Bk of S. Afr. Wine* 47 The South African Riesling was found to be unrelated to the German Riesling; instead it has been identified with the French vine, Cruchen Blanc.

2. With distinguishing epithet: **Weisser Riesling**, Rhine Riesling.

1980 J. PLATTER *Bk of S. Afr. Wines* 88 Weisser Riesling (Also referred to as 'true' or 'Rhine' riesling) is everything that is the 'South African' riesling, except more so; more aromatic, spicier, more complex, more subtle, more scented.

rietbok /ˈritbɔk/ *n.* Also **reetbok, reitboc, reitbok, ri(e)tbock**. Pl. unchanged, or **-s**. [S. Afr. Du., *riet* reed + *bok* antelope, goat; see quot. 1827.] The small antelope *Redunca arundinum*, having a bushy tail, fur of a colour from brown or buffy-grey to buffy-yellow, and (in the male) V-shaped, forward-curving, ridged horns; REEDBUCK sense 1, RIETBUCK. Also *attrib.*

In Skinner & Smithers's *Mammals of Sn Afr. Subregion* (1990), the name 'reedbuck' is used for this species.

[**1786** G. FORSTER tr. *A. Sparrman's Voy. to Cape of G.H.* II. 222 The *riet*, (or reed) *ree-bok*, I saw but once.] **1796** C.R. HOPSON tr. *C.P. Thunberg's Trav.* II. 44 Rietboks (*Capra*) and Bonteboks (*Capra scripta*) frequented much these hilly and verdant fields. **1801** G. SHAW *General Zoology* II. 348 The female Ritbock resembles the male in colour, but has no horns. **1827** G. THOMPSON *Trav.* I. 201 On the banks of this stream I observed a species of antelope, .. I believe, the same animal termed *Riet-bok* by the colonists, from its inhabiting the spots along the rivers overgrown with reeds and sedge. **1835** A. SMITH *Diary* (1940) II. 47 The core of the riet bok horns is slightly porous longitudinally, some fine holes, some larger, the finest towards centre where they are very numerous. **1843** J.C. CHASE *Cape of G.H.* 51 The rietbok .. and several others of the antelope tribe are often met with, though they are by no means numerous. **1860** A.W. DRAYSON *Sporting Scenes* 49 From his back I shot elands, hartebeest, reitbok, ourebis, steinbok, duikers, etc. **1877** R.M. BALLANTYNE *Settler & Savage* 154 From their lairs among the reeds and sedges of the river rushed the reitbok and wild hog. **1949** C. BULLOCK *Rina* 63 The riet-bok meat had .. been well cooked, and the Chief and I ceremoniously ate together, cementing a bond of friendship. **1951** A. ROBERTS *Mammals* 29 *Rietbok* ... This species is found either solitary or in family parties ... When alarmed they run off with .. 'a rocking-horse motion,' and in doing so flash their white tails as a warning, often at the same time uttering their whistling note. **1979** J. GRATUS *Jo'burgers* 45 He did not see the fields of ripened mealies nor the ponderous cattle nor even the timid rietbok that had strayed too far from its herd by one of the streams. **1989** L. BADENHORST in *Motorist* May 4 Within yards of our campsite a rietbok grazed on the bank of the river. **1994** M. ROBERTS tr. *J.A. Wahlberg's Trav. Jrnls 1838–56* 31 On the other side of the Umvoti saw 4 lion hunting a Rietbock.

rietbuck /ˈri(ː)tbʌk/ *n.* Formerly also **reit-buck**. Pl. **-s**, or unchanged. Englished form of RIETBOK.

1827 T. PHILIPPS *Scenes & Occurrences* 87 Before the day was over we had destroyed pheasants, partridges, orabees, riet bucks, bush bucks, [etc.]. **1832** *Graham's Town Jrnl* 13 July 112 The old denizens of the wilderness, Bush-bucks, Riet-bucks, and Bucks with every variety of prefix have disappeared. **1839** W.C. HARRIS *Wild Sports* 177, I strolled down the river with my rifle in search of riet-buck, of which some had been seen in the morning. **1860** A.W. DRAYSON *Sporting Scenes* 61 The reit-buck (Eleotragus reduncus): three feet high, nearly five feet in length; horns one foot long .. ears six inches long; colour ashy grey, white beneath; female smaller, but hornless, otherwise similar. **1898** G. NICHOLSON *50 Yrs* 124 A few bustards, both large and small, are to be had here and there, as are also duiker and steinbucks and now and again a reitbuck. **1902** D. HUTCHEON *Rinderpest* 3 The following antelopes are reported to have suffered most from Rinderpest. In the Northern Protectorate the eland, buffalo, gemsbuck, and rietbuck; and in the South Protectorate, the steinbuck, duiker, rhebuck, and koodoo. **1907** J.P. FITZPATRICK *Jock of Bushveld* (1909) 33 The rietbuck, scared by us, had gone ahead and was keenly on the watch for us and therefore not worth following. **1961** D. BEE *Children of Yesterday* 177 They dined on rietbuck steak and Hennessy brandy, by the light of an electric light bulb on a flex from the Bedford's battery.

rietdak /ˈritdak/ *n. Archit.* [Afk., *riet* reed + *dak* roof.] In full ***rietdak ceiling***: a ceiling of reeds (usu. 'Spanish reed') laid over wooden beams, common in Cape colonial houses.

1984 *Style* July, The perhaps unlikely-sounding combination of patterned slip-covers .. rietdak ceiling and inherited stinkwood. **1984** *S. Afr. Panorama* Jan. 33 The upper loft, which was used as an extra bedroom and as a study. In the original building it had a *rietdak* (reed ceiling). **1985** *Weekend Argus* 1 Nov. (Suppl.), Rietdak ceiling in sitting room over Yellowwood beams. Completely renovated. Consisting of voorkamer, large dining room, [etc.]. **1987** *Personality* 23 Dec. 68 The spectre which haunts the 130 year-old farmhouse with its metre-thick walls and *rietdak* ceilings. **1987** G. VINEY *Col. Houses* 18 The Cape Dutch interior — modest farmhouse *voorkamer* with casement windows, tiled floor, *rietdak* ceiling, yellowwood furniture and the provebial welcoming cup of coffee or tea.

right hand *n. phr.* and *adj. phr.* [fr. Xhosa and Zulu *owasekunene* 'the one of the right side', *owa-* the one of + linking phoneme *-s-* + adv. *ekunene* on the right.]

A. *n. phr.*

a. In traditional Xhosa society: the second most important branch of a (royal) family. **b.** In traditional Zulu society: the most important branch of a (royal) family.

*c*1847 H.H. DUGMORE in J. Maclean *Compendium of Kafir Laws* (1906) 11 At some specified period, the chief of a tribe, who, it is assumed, has a plurality of wives, assembles his relatives, with his principal officers and councillors, to decide as to the investment of two of his wives with the respective dignities of 'the great one' (*omkulu*), and 'the one of the right hand' (*owasekunene*). **1860** W. SHAW *Story of my Mission* 435 The ruling Chief in Council .. usually determines which of his wives shall be the mother of the great house of the clan, tribe, or nation .. ; and inferior positions are then assigned to the descendants of two other of the wives, under the denomination of the 'right hand' and the 'left hand' of the family, which designations are apparently taken from the relative situations occupied by the huts of these wives respectively. **1980** C. NKOSI in M. Mutloatse *Forced Landing* 11 King Somhlolo said we should not fight them. We should not spill even a drop of that foreign blood on this land. Indeed, long after he of the right hand had gone to join his forefathers.

B. *adj. phr.* Attributive, and *comb.*, as **right hand house, right hand son, right hand wife**. (Cf. GREAT.)

a. In traditional Xhosa society: of or pertaining to the second wife of a chief, her children, and their descendents (the 'right hand house'), who are second in influence and importance only to the family of the principal wife. **b.** In traditional Zulu society: of or pertaining to the most senior wife, her children, and their descendants. See also INKOSIKAZI sense 1.

*c*1847 H.H. DUGMORE in J. Maclean *Compendium of Kafir Laws* (1906) 14 Khili, being but a young man, has as yet formed no 'right hand house'. **1866** W.C. HOLDEN *Past & Future* 332 The other sons of the paramount chief take rank according to certain established usages, as before detailed, thus — after the 'Great House,' there is the 'Right Hand House' etc. **1882** [see GREAT]. **1887** J.W. MATTHEWS *Incwadi Yami* 38 The hut of the right-hand wife is placed to the right side, that of the left-hand wife to the left of that of the 'inkosikazi,' and of course they occupy the next position to that of the chief wife. **1887** *S.W. Silver & Co.'s Handbk to S. Afr.* 42 The old chief Ngqika died, leaving his 'great son', Sandili, a minor .. He [*sc.* Maqoma] now became chief of one tribe, as the 'right-hand son' of his father, and regent of another during his brother's minority. **1925** D. KIDD *Essential Kafir* 13 On the right-hand side of the great wife is the hut of the right-hand wife. **1945** N. DEVITT *People & Places* 112 A few days later the chief returned with his two great wives — the chief wife, and the wife of the right-hand hut. **1955** J.B. SHEPHARD *Land of Tikoloshe* 18 'Your wife?' I asked Mafuto. He nodded, grunted, and held up two fingers as sufficient indication that she was his second or Right-hand Wife. **1967** J.A. BROSTER *Red Blanket Valley* 9 The second wife has her hut on the right-hand side of the main hut, and is called 'right-hand wife'. **1978** A. ELLIOTT *Sons of Zulu* 169 The half of the establishment on his right is literally known as the Right-Hand Side and that on his left as the Left-Hand Side. This is .. a vital division of the kraal because by it the status of the wives in a polygamous marriage — and of their children — is decided. Those of the Right-Hand Side constitute the main house and those of the Left-Hand Side the supporting house. The *right* side carries the weight and the power and provides the future heir to lead the family. **1981** J.B. PEIRES *House of Phalo* 29 The second-ranking wife was known as the Right-Hand Wife and her son was the Right-Hand Son.

‖**rijksdaalder** /ˈreɪksdɑː(d)ə(r)/ *n. hist.* Also **riksd(a)aler, rixdaaler, ryksdaalder**. [Du., see RIX-DOLLAR.] **a.** RIX-DOLLAR. **b.** DOLLAR sense b. Also *attrib.*

1817 G. BARKER Journal. 18 June, I bought several things. Also a cow of him for 12 Rixdaalers. *a*1878 J. MONTGOMERY *Reminisc.* (1981) 56 The Colonel .. gave me a bundle of rixdaler notes, quite a large sum. **1914** L.H. BRINKMAN *Breath of Karroo* 146 The old Dutch ryksdaalder was equal to eighteenpence in English money, and was for many years the standard of reckoning; so much so that the term 'dollar' has survived in the Colony to this day to designate the sum of eighteenpence. **1919** M. GREENLEES tr. *O.F. Mentzel's Life at Cape in Mid-18th C.* 77 The occupiers have to pay to the Company a ground-rent of twenty-four rijksdaalders per annum. **1931** H.C. BOSMAN in V. Rosenberg *Almost Forgotten Stories* (1979) 13 She remembered that one night-dress she made. It was very fine stuff that cost a riks-daler a yard. **1934** C.P. SWART Supplement to Pettman. 145 Today the word riksdaler or daalder is used in S.A. to denote 1/6. **1968** K. MCMAGH *Dinner of Herbs* 60 The currency of that time was the 'rix-daler' ... The original silver coinage had been replaced by a paper rix-daler which had dropped in value.

rijst mier var. RYSMIER.

riks-daler, riksdaaler varr. RIJKSDAALDER.

riksdollar var. RIX-DOLLAR.

rim *n.* , **rim** *v.* varr. RIEM *n.*, RIEM *v.*

rimp(e)y, rimpi(e), rimpje varr. RIEMPIE *n.*

rim-schoen var. REMSKOEN.

rinderpest /ˈrɪndəpest/ *n. Pathology.* [Eng. fr. G., *Rind(er)* cattle + *Pest* fr. Lat. *pestis* plague.] A virulent, highly infectious disease affecting ruminant animals, esp. cattle; used with reference to the outbreak of the disease in South Africa in 1896: **a.** As a landmark of time, referred to esp. by illiterate people. **b.** *fig.* In expressions such as ***before the rinderpest*** and ***since the rinderpest***: 'a long time ago'; 'for a long time'.

1903 E.F. KNIGHT *S. Afr. after War* 315 Following the rinderpest and the Matabele rebellion came the recent three years' Boer War. **1958** [see VIERKLEUR]. **1961** O'BRIEN in *Pick of Punch* 60 His wife said that she was born in the year of the 'lindipesi,' meaning the great rinderpest epidemic among cattle in 1897. **1961** D. BEE *Children of Yesterday* 57 'Do you remember the Rinderpest?' 'Yes, Inkosi.' The old man thought. 'I was perhaps twenty-six.' The Sharp Knife wrote again — twenty-six in 1897. **1977** *Daily Dispatch* 29 Nov. 11, I have never yet voted NAT. Do they need my vote? No, they have been in power since the time of the rinderpest. **1979** *Voice* 1 Apr. 5 Frank was not sure when he was born but knows it was in Wakkerstroom, Natal. During the rinderpest epidemic he was already in his teens. **1980** A.G.T.K. MALIKONGWA in *Staffrider* Vol.3 No.1, 33 He was with me during that terrible year, the year of rinderpest. **1982** *Cape Times* 9 Oct. 11 Mrs Moses's mind is still clear and she can remember incidents in Venterstad — where she was born — before the Great Rinderpest disaster. **1984** B. JOHNSON-BARKER in *Wynboer* June 72 In the first place, there was no school; the building had been used as a source of firewood ever since the rinderpest and only the foundations remained. **1985** E. EUVRARD in *Sunday Times* 24 Nov. 15 If my memory serves me right, and the last time I had it was during the rinderpest, cuddles are nice but there is nothing like sex. **1987** *Frontline* Mar. 22 Far from the rioting crowds of Soweto .. , the life of Jonas on the farm goes on much as it did when his grandfather worked for the Oubaas at the time of the Rinderpest. **1987** J. OPENSHAW in *Star* 21 May 3 Some of us still remember the time before the rindepest [*sic*] when we didn't believe there had been a diamond rush .. , and, by the time we discovered the rumours were true, had missed our chance of becoming rich because the diamonds had run out. **1990** [see GOLDEN CITY].

ring *n.*[1] [Special sense of general Eng.] HEAD-RING.

1833 *Graham's Town Jrnl* 15 Aug. 3 This late Zoola attack on these tribes, was for the purpose of taking cattle to obtain the sinews, or Caffer thread, to sew rings on the heads of several of the junior Regiments. **1835** A. SMITH *Diary* (1940) II. 131 The old ring-kop was speaking ... This ring-kop was the person in charge of the party ... None of the others had rings. **1836** [see ISICOCO]. **1837** F. OWEN *Diary* (1926) 61 One whole regiment of .. young men, who have not a ring on their head, were summoned to exhibit their skill and energy in military exercises. **1855** J.W. COLENSO *Ten Weeks in Natal* 126 Many of the Kafirs now around us had the *ring* upon their head, which forms the peculiar distinction of a Zulu *married* man. The hair .. is first tied or stitched into a ring, made of sedge. Then having obtained .. a white gummy substance .. they roll it between their hands, until it becomes of sufficient length to be laid over the sedge ring, and completely cover the stitches. By the aid of grease and rubbing, the ring is made to take an excellent polish, and its upper surface .. has the appearance of solid leather. **1870** C. HAMILTON *Life & Sport in S.-E. Afr.* 13 The ring is considered a mark of honour and distinction; 'Indunas', or ministers or the chief, generally wear three or four. **1882** C. DU VAL *With Show through Sn Afr.* I. 246 A stalwart old party – with little clothing but the ring on his head which indicated matrimony. **1925** D. KIDD *Essential Kafir* 33 Only married men were allowed to wear this ring, and when once they are allowed to adopt it they feel important, for they are regarded as warriors of the nation and are consulted more or less in tribal concerns. **1937** C. BIRKBY *Zulu Journey* 121 His woolly hair had been worked into a ring with gum and beeswax as a sign of his standing among the tribe. **1960** G. LISTER *Reminisc.* 75 He was .. clad in a huge skin mantle and had a hard ring round his head and great ivory bangles on his arms.

Hence **ring** *v. trans.*, to bestow the head-ring upon (someone).

1967 E.M. SLATTER *My Leaves Are Green* 180 Then, for a reward, Mpande told me that I would be 'ringed', young though I was. And, then I had permission to marry.

ring *n.*² Also with initial capital. [Calque formed on Afk. *ring* 'circle', 'presbytery'.] The group of Dutch Reformed congregations forming a regional presbytery (see quot. 1934). See also RINGKOMMISSIE.

1934 C.P. SWART Supplement to Pettman. 144 *Ring*, .. The congregations of the D.R.C. are divided into Church Districts or Circles, as fixed from time to time by the Synod, to ensure regular working of Church administration. These Rings are equivalent to the Scotch Presbyteries. **1934** *Sunday Times* 18 Feb. (Swart), The Pretoria Ring of the Dutch Reformed Church .. has been in session during the past week. **1950** *Cape Times* 20 Sept. 16 The dominees of the Ring. **1970** *Sunday Times* 15 Nov. 5 Unfrocked Ds. asks court to set aside Ring's ruling. **1974** *Rand Daily Mail* 28 Jan. 3 He had lodged the complaint on orders from the Public Morals Commission of the Parow ring ... The congregation of Parow North .. falls under the jurisdiction of the Parow ring. **1990** *Sunday Times* 27 May 7 He has been suspended for three months by the NG Kerk Ring commission in Vanderbijlpark.

ring calse, ringculse, ringeaault varr. RINKHALS.

ringed *adj.* [fr. RING *n.*¹] Wearing a HEAD-RING; of an age or status such that one is allowed to wear such a ring. Also *comb.* **ringed-head**, RINGKOP sense a.

1850 [see KEHLA sense 1]. **1877** LADY BARKER *Yr's Hsekeeping* 120 When a chief or the induna of a kraal passes this way, I see him clad in a motley garb of old regimentals, with his bare 'ringed' head, riding a sorry nag. **1913** C. PETTMAN *Africanderisms* 403 Zulu men are distinguished from boys by a head-ring. The head is shaved all but a narrow strip quite round, the hair along this strip is worked up with gum, etc., into a black polished ring called isiCoco ... The sanction of the chief is required before a man can become a Kehla .. or 'ringed' man. **1930** S.T. PLAATJE *Mhudi* (1975) 131 Several 'ringed-heads' raised their voices on purpose that their words should reach the ears of the king. **1951** R. GRIFFITHS *Grey about Flame* 126 Warriors lounged in the yellow sunlight, flirting openly with the girls and paying no heed when M'Busi, a ringed Induna, stalked contemptuously among them. **1970** P.B. CLEMENTS in *Outpost* 45 Shortly after our arrival, an old 'ringed' induna from a neighbouring kraal came to us and told us that the impis had withdrawn and that a big 'white impi' was marching in our direction from the mission station about thirty miles away.

ringel-hals, ring(k)hals varr. RINKHALS.

‖**Ringkommissie** /'rəŋkɔ,misi/ *n.* [Afk., *ring* circle (see RING *n.*²) + *kommissie* commission.] The executive of a 'ring' (or regional presbytery) of Dutch Reformed churches. See also RING *n.*²

1857 in N.J. MERRIMAN *Cape Jrnls* (1957) 191 With the concurrence of the Kerkraad at Colesberg, the Ringkommissie of Graaff-Reinet decided .. to establish a new centre and church. **1970** *Sunday Times* 15 Nov. 5 Dominee A.J.H. S– this week asked .. the Windhoek Supreme Court to set aside the decision of the Ringkommissie of Keetmanshoop and the decision of the synod of the Dutch Reformed Church of October 10 last year when he was defrocked as Minister of Luderitz. [**1990** see RING *n.*²]

ringkop *n. obs.* [Afk., *ring* ring + *kop* head.] In traditional African societies: **a.** A man entitled to wear the HEAD-RING as a mark of seniority; *ringed-head*, see RINGED; RING-TOP sense a; also called KEHLA (sense 1). **b.** Occas., the HEAD-RING.

1835 A. SMITH *Diary* (1940) II. 72 Three persons arrived, one a ring-kop who was walking in front, and the two other boys about 16 and 17 years of age. [**1907** J.P. FITZPATRICK *Jock of Bushveld* (1909) Glossary, *Kehla*, .. a native of certain age and position entitled to wear the head ring. Dutch, *ring kop* – ring head.] **1910** J. BUCHAN *Prester John* (1961) 89 In such a man one would have looked for a *ring-kop*, but instead he had a mass of hair, .. long and curled like some popular musician. **1935** *Brit. S. Afr. Ann.* 35 Our principal native warrior, an old 'ringkop', promptly took up his quarters in a friendly tree.

ringmuur /'rəŋmy:r/ *n. Archit.* [Afk., circular wall, *ring* circle, ring + *muur* wall.] A white-washed ring-wall surrounding the homestead and outbuildings of a farm, characteristic of Cape Dutch country architecture. See also CAPE DUTCH *adj. phr.* sense 2 a, WERF sense 1.

1957 L.G. GREEN *Beyond City Lights* 164 Visser's Hok is the oldest farm in the Koeberg ... The present house bears the date 1768, but the *ringmuur*, the white wall enclosing about eighteen morgen round the homestead, must be much older. **1962** A.M. LOUW *20 Days* 25 Leafy twigs, scraps of paper and dry leaves were piled in the corners of the ringmuur. **1977** *Darling* 16 Mar. 36 Lanzerac's oak leaves, slave bell, lemon trees, ringmuur, vineyards, pine-clad mountain slopes. **1977** *S. Afr. Panorama* Aug. 33 The restoration of Boschendal .. includes the outbuildings and the entire area contained within the characteristic white-washed ringmuur (ringwall).

ring-top *n. nonce.* **a.** RINGKOP sense a. **b.** HEAD-RING.

1949 O. WALKER *Proud Zulu* (1951) 25 They were ring-tops – a senior regiment therefore, with leopard-skin collars round their necks and white shields. *Ibid.* 232 He kept his finger-nails long as a mark of aristocratic idleness and of course his ring-top of melted bee's-wax, symbol of Zulu manhood. *Ibid.* 313 His ring top, to touch which was a mortal insult, was cut off and put round Pita's neck. **1967** —— *Hippo Poacher* 115 When he saw Tom, the *kehla*, or ringtop, rejoiced, 'Today I will taste sugar again after so long a time.'

Hence **ring-topped** *adj.*

1949 O. WALKER *Proud Zulu* (1951) 182 Neither the Ulundi nor the Gqikazi divisions of the Zulu army had found real employment at Isandhlwana. They were ring-topped men all of them. *Ibid.* 216 'Now I am an old man,' he said shaking his ring-topped head.

rinkhals /'rəŋkals/ *n.* Forms: α. **ringel-hals, ringhals**; β. **ringeaault, ringkhals, rink(h)als**. Also with initial capital. Pl. unchanged, or **-es**. [Afk. *rinkhals*, earlier S. Afr. Du. *ringhals, rinkhals*, fr. Du. *ring* (earlier *rinc*) ring + *hals*, neck.]

1. The large venomous spitting-cobra *Hemachatus haemachatus* of the Elapidae, brown or black in colour and distinguished by one or two white rings round the neck; SPITTING SNAKE; SPURTING SNAKE; SPUUGSLANG. Also *attrib.* See also *Cape cobra* (CAPE sense 2 a).

α. **1793** C.R. HOPSON tr. *C.P. Thunberg's Trav.* I. 208 A colonist had been bitten in the foot .. by a serpent, of the species called Ringhals (or Ring-neck). **1834** T. PRINGLE *Afr. Sketches* 280 There are several species of snakes which have come under my own observation, such as .. the ringel-hals (ring-throat), with a variety of others which I have not seen. **1847** 'A BENGALI' *Notes on Cape of G.H.* 82 The 'schaap-stikker' or sheep-stifler; and the 'Ringel Hals' or Ring-throat, all venomous. **1860** J. SANDERSON in *Jrnl of Royal Geog. Soc.* XXX. 237 One of my drivers also killed a black snake, called the 'ringhals' or 'ringthroat', from two or three white bars under its throat: it measured about 4 feet in length, and is said to be very venomous. **1864** T. BAINES *Explor. in S.-W. Afr.* 449, I think the species is called 'ringhals' (or ringed throat) in the colony. **1897** E. GLANVILLE in E.R. Seary *S. Afr. Short Stories* (1947) 20, I killed a snake, a ringhals, yesterday morning back of the kraal, and in the evening when I went by there was a live ringhals coiled round the dead one. **1906** *Westminster Gaz.* (U.K.) 16 Jan. 4 A couple of Ring-hals snakes. **1915** W. EVELEIGH *S.W. Afr.* 82 The name 'ringhals' means 'ring-neck,' and has reference to the whitish band or bands across the throat. Not only has this reptile the power to inflict a deadly bite with its poison fangs – it is able to spit a stream of venom into the eyes of a person standing some feet away. *c*1936 *S. & E. Afr. Yr Bk & Guide* 1107 The ringhals or spitting snake is of allied genus, having the expanding hood and concentrated venom of the cobras with the ability to eject the contents of its poison glands in a fine spray for a distance of several feet. **1948** [see BAKKOP]. **1956** P. BECKER *Sandy Tracks* 121 A large 'ringhals', the dreaded white-necked cobra of the bushveld, lay basking in the radiance of the dazzling sun. **1989** V. OWENS in *Grocott's Mail* 20 Jan. 11 Snakes were a part of our lives and I imagine we saw one just about every day of our lives – lots of ringhals, few boomslang or Cape cobra and now and then a puffadder.

β. [**1836** A.F. GARDINER *Journey to Zoolu Country* 330, I saw a dark coloured, thick-bodied snake, about five feet long, with a wide flat head .. It is, I believe, of the species called by the Dutch the 'wrinkle snake'. **1844** W.N. IRWIN *Echoes of Past* (1927) 229, I was nearly bitten by Ring Calse (Dutch) a most venomous snake. **1880** E.F. SANDEMAN *Eight Months in Ox-Waggon* 74 Next morning .. we killed the first snake .. a long black fellow with a white ring round his neck, the Dutch name for which is Ringculse; but as it has a hood which it inflates when angry, it may probably be a variety of the Cobra di Capella.] **1911** *E. Prov. Herald* 1 Nov., The Rinkhals, so called because of a white narrow band across its throat. **1926** *Ibid.* 24 Feb. 10 Spying a plump rinkhals cobra, the Mfesi, hungry after its long journey, attacked with the object of making a hearty meal. **1933** J. JUTA *Look Out for Ostriches* 70 Of all the cobra family that inhabit Africa, the *rinkhals* is unique in that its scales are keeled, and that it produces its young alive. **1945** M. HONE *Sarah-Elizabeth* 20 The snake turned out to be a rinkals, a kind of African cobra, extremely poisonous. **1956** A.G. MCRAE *Hill Called Grazing* 47 The six-foot-long *Rinkhals* cobra, reared above its coils, hood flattened and tiny, evil head weaving. **1970** D.M. MCMASTER *Informant, Cathcart (E. Cape)* Rinkhals – which ought to be ringhals but is never pronounced that way. **1973** *Weekend Argus* 24 Feb. (Mag. Sect.) 6 Even if you manage to walk around all the puff adders, horned adders, mountain adders, .. Perinquey's adders, blacknecked cobras, rinkhals and busky-bellied water snakes, you still stand a chance of running slap into a barred spitting cobra. **1974** *Sunday Times* 10 Nov. (Mag. Sect.) 6 Cobras, rinkhalses and mambas have a lethal nerve-paralysing (neuro-toxic) poison. **1991** *Light Years* Vol.2 No.3, 8 Wear glasses or sunglasses since the rinkhals is a spitting snake, which aims for the eyes with deadly precision, causing intense pain and even blindness.

2. *obs.* In full ***ringhals kraai*** /-'krɑːɪ/ [Du. *kraai* crow, raven]: the white-necked raven *Corvus albicollis* of the Corvidae, black with a white band round the neck.

In this sense found only in the obs. form *ringhals.*

α. **1796** E. HELME tr. *F. Le Vaillant's Trav.* II. 34 Its .. plumage is black, but, having a white patch on the hinder part of the neck, it has thence, in the colonies, received the appellation of *ring-hals-kraai* (ring-neck crow). **1867** E.L. LAYARD *Birds of S. Afr.* 167 *Corvus Albicollis*, .. *Ringhals Kraai* of Colonists, lit. Ring-neck Crow. **1884** LAYARD & SHARPE *Birds of S. Afr.* 417 This large Raven, which goes by the name in the colony of the 'Ringhals' (Ring-neck), is abundant throughout the colony. **1897** H.A. BRYDEN *Nature & Sport* 62 The common crow in South Africa is not white, but black and white. There are two kinds both very familiar figures — one known to the colonists as the bonte kraai (pied crow) (Corvus scapulatus), and the other called the ringhals kraai (ring-neck crow) (Corvus albicollis), a big, bold fellow, constantly seen about the colonial roads and outspans. **1900** W.L. SCLATER *Mammals of S. Afr.* I. 11 The *Ring-hals* is usually resident in Cape Colony and Natal, and roosts all the year round in or near its nests. **1918** S.H. SKAIFE *Animal Life* 248 The common white necked raven, or *ringhals*, is well known all over the country. It feeds on carrion, small animals, and ticks.

risper var. RUSPER.

ritbock var. RIETBOK.

ritual *adj.* [Special sense of general Eng. *ritual* pertaining to rites.] Always *attrib.*, usu. in the special collocations ***ritual killing*** or **- *murder***: a murder carried out for the purpose of obtaining body parts to be used in the making of MUTI (sense2a); DIRETLO sense a; *medicine murder*, see MEDICINE sense 2; *muti killing* or *- murder*, see MUTI sense 5; ***ritual killer*** or **- *murderer***: one who perpetrates such a murder; *muti killer* or *- murderer*, see MUTI sense 5.

'Ritual murder' is sometimes considered a misnomer, since the preparation of muti made from human parts may or may not involve the performance of rites.

1949 J. MOCKFORD *Golden Land* 89 Of the nineteen cases of ritual murder which the police have taken to court since 1942, headmen or chiefs of one grade or another have been involved in every case but one. **1952** *Drum* Apr. 25 In Africa, the worst form that superstition takes is what is popularly known as Ritual Murder. Actually the murders are not part of a ritual, and they should really be called diretlo, or medicine murders ... Many people that Mr. Drum spoke to thought that the people at the bottom of ritual murders were the ngakas, or medicine men (or witch doctors, as corrupted by Europeans). **1953** R. CAMPBELL *Mamba's Precipice* 151 The alarm is out for Mahakaan, the skebanga who murdered the two cousins of Mpathla here to get medicine out of their bodies. He was chief of the Ninevite gang of ritual murderers. **1959** E. MPHAHLELE *Down Second Ave* (1965) 141 Alfred was murdered in an eastern Reef town in most mysterious and ugly circumstances which suggested ritual killing. **1968** A. FULTON *Dark Side of Mercy* 17 Our chiefs are educated men ... They are not likely to resort to ritual murder to fill the ancient medicine horns. **1974** *E. Prov. Herald* 28 Sept., Police are expected to offer a substantial reward for information leading to the arrest of a ritual-type killer on the Natal South Coast following the discovery of a fifth dismembered body. **1976** WEST & MORRIS *Abantu* 154 The potency of these medicines was largely owed to the use of parts of the human body, obtained through what has come to be known as 'ritual murder' — a highly emotive term that has excited much comment over the years. **1978** *Pace* Dec. 13 The Capital City has become a hotbed of ritual crime. **1982** *Daily Dispatch* 15 Apr. 3 A Venda deputy minister was sentenced in the Venda Supreme Court yesterday to death for the ritual murder of a school principal. **1983** *Drum* Apr. 20 This lush tropical country of mango and banana trees is the habitat of some of the sub-continent's worst ritual killers. An average of four ritual killing cases come to the courts every month. **1988** B. NTLEMO in *Frontline* Oct. 9 Although we are supposed to be living in a modern age, Venda is still behind ... Young people want to drag their leaders 'kicking and screaming' into the modern age where ritual murders will be unheard of. **1990** J. EVANS in A. Goldstuck *Rabbit in Thorn Tree* 61 Children and old people are usually the victims of ritual murders because they are the most vulnerable and accessible.

river digging *n. phr. Hist. Diamond-mining.* [Orig. U.S. Eng., as a gold-mining term.] Usu. in *pl.*: The mining operations associated with prospecting for diamonds near a river or stream; WET DIGGING. Cf. DRY DIGGING.

1876 F. BOYLE *Savage Life* 11 It was by no means unpleasant, this river, or wet, digging. **1881** E.E. FREWER tr. *E. Holub's Seven Yrs in S. Afr.* I. 60 The settlement at the river-diggings sprang up with a rapidity as marvellous as those of California. **1882** J. NIXON *Among Boers* 162 We had some idea of visiting the river diggings in the bed of the Vaal River, but we were told that they were almost entirely deserted. **1887** J.W. MATTHEWS *Incwadi Yami* 101 The river diggings having existed for some time, matters there had assumed more of a settled appearance than at the dry diggings. **1926** M. NATHAN *S. Afr. from Within* 198 The romantic interest in the stream [*sc.* the Vaal River] lies in the fact that from Krugersdorp downwards it is the centre of the 'river diggings'. The alluvial diamonds found along its course .. are of great purity and value ... The river diggings were worked before the 'New Rush' at Kimberley was discovered. **1931** G. BEET *Grand Old Days* 48 In order to distinguish between the two main digging areas, the one came to be known as the 'river' diggings, and the other the 'dry' diggings. *c*1936 *S. & E. Afr. Yr Bk & Guide* 366 For many years the *River* Diggings were confined to the river beds in the neighbourhood of the confluence of the Vaal and Orange Rivers, but since 1926 the *S.W. Transvaal* has been the centre of greatest activity. **1955** E. ROSENTHAL in Saron & Hotz *Jews in S. Afr.* 115 Apart from the development of Kimberley proper, many Jews continued to be active on the river diggings. **1983** [see DRY DIGGING]. **1985** [see WET DIGGING].

Hence **river digger** *n. phr.*

1904 J.L. SPENCER tr. *Bauer's Precious Stones* I. 185 The amalgamation of the 'dry diggings' to form the De Beers Consolidated Mines, has had the effect of increasing the number of river diggers. **1920** F.C. CORNELL *Glamour of Prospecting* 10 There were .. men of past experience — principally ex-'river-diggers'.

Riversdale foot *n. phr.* [Named for a town in the Western Cape, which was in turn named for *Harry Rivers* (1785–1861), resident magistrate and civil commissioner at Swellendam, 1826–1842.] See quot.

1971 BARAITSER & OBHOLZER *Cape Country Furn.* 264 Occasionally a strip of yellowwood is laid into the tapered feet .. but the most important of all are the so-called Riversdale feet. They are important because .. many of the cupboards with these feet are the best examples of Cape country furniture. The feet are wider than the conventional tapered leg and there are often three to support the [front of the] cupboard instead of the usual two. The middle foot is more decorative than functional ... Most of the cupboards with these feet were found in the Riversdale area and although they pre-date the founding of Riversdale in 1839, we have retained the name. The hallmark of the Riverdale foot is the combination of a horizontal line of block inlay with vertical strip inlay below it.

rivierganna see GANNA sense 2.

Rivonia /rɪˈvəʊnɪə/ *n.* [The name of a suburb to the north of Johannesburg.] Often *attrib.*, designating **a.** OPERATION MAYIBUYE (sense a); **b.** the police raid on Lilliesleaf Farm on the 11th of July 1963 which ended Operation Mayibuye, seventeen members of the 'national high command' being arrested, and, **c.** (usu. in the phr. ***Rivonia trial***), the lengthy trials for treason which followed. Also *transf.*

1964 H.H.W. DE VILLIERS (*title*) Rivonia. *Ibid.* (Back cover), The Rivonia Trial revealed a sinister plot by communist-inspired conspirators whose objectives were the overthrow of the South African Government by means of violence, guerilla warfare and bloody revolution. **1967** E. ROSENTHAL *Encycl. of Sn Afr.* 460 *Rivonia Trial*, Named after fashionable northern suburb of Johannesburg where in June and July 1963 quantities of equipment were found, designed for attempted civil war in South Africa. **1971** *Weekend Post* 6 Nov. 1 The liberal press in South Africa were busy trying to break down the Security Police to the ground and to create a new Rivonia. **1987** *New Nation* 23 July 2 Motsoaledi, a former organiser of the South African Congress of Trade Unions (Sactu), was sentenced to life imprisonment in the historical Rivonia trial. **1987** J.C. MOLL in *Dict. of S. Afr. Biography* V. 263 F[ischer] .. led the legal team for the accused in the Rivonia trial in 1963 when *Umkonto we Sizwe* planned to sabotage state property. **1989** *Sunday Times* 15 Oct. 7 The Rivonia raid was a major security coup ... The raid led to the famous Rivonia trial at which ANC leader Nelson Mandela, Sisulu and six others were sentenced to life imprisonment. **1990** R. MHLABA in *E. Prov. Herald* 18 Jan. 8, I was banned off and on until Rivonia. **1990** *E. Prov. Herald* 12 Feb. 8 On July 11, 1963, the police swooped on the Rivonia farm in Johannesburg and arrested most of the ANC's underground leadership. When the famous Rivonia trial was held, Mr Mandela was accused No 1. **1990** M. VAN WYK SMITH *Grounds of Contest* 99 In the early 60's .. massive security clamp-downs and several treason trials (notably Rivonia) effectively brought to an end most open resistance. **1992** *Drum* Jan. (Then & Now) 10 The first signs of the new militancy were evident in the reports on sabotage. The Rivonia trial ended in June 1964, and the leadership of both the ANC and the PAC was effectively silenced.

rixdaaler var. RIJKSDAALDER.

rix-dollar /ˈrɪksdɔlə/ *n. hist.* Also **riksdollar, rix doller**. [ad. Du. *rijksdaalder*, *rijks* imperial + *daalder* dollar. There is a range of forms between the fully Englished *rix-dollar* and the original Du. *rijksdaalder* (see RIJKSDAALDER), including *riks-* or *rix-daler*, *rixdaaler*, and *ryksdaalder*.] A unit of currency introduced at the Cape by the Dutch East India Company, initially a silver coin and later (from 1781) a paper note; DOLLAR sense a; RD; RIJKSDAALDER sense a. See also CAPE GUILDER, STIVER sense 1.

For the value of the rixdollar against the pound sterling, see quots 1827 and 1843. Although officially withdrawn in 1841, the unit continued in use long after this date. The rix-dollar was also used in other Dutch colonies such as Ceylon (Sri Lanka) and Batavia (Jakarta, Jawa).

1765 MRS KINDERSLEY *Lett.* (1777) 65 The custom is to pay a rix-dollar daily for each person's board and lodging, for which they are provided with everything. **1785** G. FORSTER tr. *A. Sparrman's Voy. to Cape of G.H.* I. 19 Board and lodging are paid for here as at the Cape, from one rix-dollar to one and a half a day. **1790** tr. *F. Le Vaillant's Trav.* I. 32 A rixdollar is about three shillings and nine pence sterling. **1798** S.H. WILCOCKE tr. *J.S. Stavorinus's Voy. to E. Indies 1768–71* I. 569 Accounts are kept here, just as at *Batavia*, in rixdollars of forty-eight stivers. At public sales, and likewise in retail, the prices are taken at Cape gilders of sixteen stivers each. **1824** W.J. BURCHELL *Trav.* II. 540 A Cape rix dollar .. is equal nominally to four shillings currency. **1827** G. THOMPSON *Trav.* II. 261 The colonial paper rix-dollar of the Cape, first issued by the Dutch East India Company in 1781, was declared to be equal to forty-eight full weighed pennies of Holland, (about 4s sterling), and which, under all its fluctuations, had generally been considered to be its *nominal* value. The value of the rix-dollar gradually sunk in exchange, till in the year 1825 it appears to have reached its lowest point of depression, viz. below 1s. 5d. **1832** *Graham's Town Jrnl* 20 July 115 By a Proclamation .. it is provided, that .. the *Rixdollar Notes* shall be gradually withdrawn from circulation, and be replaced by Promissory Notes, the value of which shall be expressed in *pounds sterling*. **1836** A.F. GARDINER *Journey to Zoolu Country* 397 For a repast, such as I have described, and even where a tough chop is added, although no charge is formally made, a rix dollar

(1s.6d.) is considered as a liberal equivalent. **1843** J.C. CHASE *Cape of G.H.* 188 The large majority of the inhabitants, especially in the country districts, still retain in their business calculations the nomenclature of the old paper money, called in some years back. This consists of the rix-dollar whose value has been fixed by the Home Government at one shilling and sixpence each, or thirteen one-third to a pound sterling. **1881** G.F. AUSTEN *Diary* (1981) 28 Persons guilty of the offence of entering the Krygsraad or other offices without doffing their hats .. are fined for disrespect, the fines varying from one shilling to – in one case – Thirty-seven pounds, ten shillings or Five hundred rix dollars. **1910** D. FAIRBRIDGE *That Which Hath Been* (1913) 181 They will not let you sell your wine retail, no, but they will compel you to sell it to them for twelve rix-dollars a leaguer. **1920** K.M. JEFFREYS tr. *Memorandum of Commissary J.A. de Mist* 279 The Rixdollar is an imaginary coin or so-called money of account, valued at 48 stuivers or ⅔ of a ducaton or driegulden; but at the time of the introduction of the paper currency in the year 1782, it was given a tangible form, since all the paper money was stamped with the denomination of Rixdollar. **1936** *Cambridge Hist. of Brit. Empire* VIII. 237 The rix-dollar .. had depreciated rapidly from 4s. to round about 1s. 6d. when, in the financial reorganisation following the resumption of specie payments by the Bank of England, the British Government proposed to make British silver current throughout the Empire. **1957** L.G. GREEN *Beyond City Lights* 60 He found that after half a century of British rule the country people still spoke of gulden, skellings, rix dollars and stuiwers, though the money they handled consisted of pounds, shillings and pence. **1968** K. MCMAGH *Dinner of Herbs* 39 The paper rixdollar had been devalued (it had originally been a silver coin worth 4/6 but was now a paper token only 1/6 (15c in value). **1989** *Reader's Digest Illust. Hist.* 45 Panic-stricken authorities were offering slaves a rix-dollar a day and food to watch over the sick and the dying.

roan *n.* Pl. unchanged, or -s. Ellipt. for ROAN ANTELOPE. Also *attrib.*

1895 J.G. MILLAIS *Breath from Veldt* (1899) 236 A pan under the mountain where many roans, .. and some giraffes, drank. **1900** W.L. SCLATER *Mammals of S. Afr.* I. 220 The roan was first recognized as a new antelope under the Sechuana name of Takhaitse. **1937** [see Cloete quot. at SWARTWITPENS]. **1976** J. HANKS *Mammals* 34 *Roan, Hippotragus equinus* ... Overall a light reddish brown or a light chestnut in colour, white below. **1979** ZALOUMIS & CROSS *Field Guide to Antelope* 46 Roans live in herds of between 5 and 30, usually led by a master bull. **1990** SKINNER & SMITHERS *Mammals of Sn Afr. Subregion* 673 Roan are very large antelope, surpassed in size only by the eland. *Ibid.* 675 The individual members of roan herds tend to space themselves out with distances of five to 10 m between them.

roan antelope *n. phr.* [Eng. *roan* (usu. of horses) 'having a coat in which the prevailing colour is thickly interspersed with some other' (*OED*) + *antelope*.] The large antelope *Hippotragus equinus* of the Bovidae, greyish-brown in colour, tinged with strawberry, with strong black and white markings on the face, and ridged horns curving evenly backward; BASTARD GEMSBOK; BLAUWBOK sense 1 b; ROAN.

1839 W.C. HARRIS *Wild Sports* 194 We descended into a valley, bent upon the destruction of a roan antelope. **1850** R.G.G. CUMMING *Hunter's Life* (1902) 83, I perceived a pair of the rare and beautiful roan antelope or bastard gemsbok warily approaching the fountain. **1866** [see BLAUWBOK sense 1 b]. **1895** J.G. MILLAIS *Breath from Veldt* (1899) 187 The roan antelope (*Hippotragus equinus*) at one time ranged from Cape Colony up to Central Africa. *c*1902 F.C. SELOUS in C.J. Cornish *Living Animals of World* I. 250 The larger and more handsomely marked *roan antelope* .. once had a more extensive range than any other antelope, as it was found in almost every part of Africa south of the Sahara. **1988** *Quagga* No.20, 19 As one of South Africa's three endangered mammals .. the *Roan Antelope* is of special concern to the Endangered Wildlife Trust. **1991** *Personality* 5 Aug. 29 Too many animals suffer and die for the supposedly humane alternative of game trading ... Species that easily succumb .. are springbok, nyala, reedbuck, bushbuck, red hartebeest, tsessebe and roan antelope.

roaster-cake *n. obs.* [Calqued on Afk. *roosterkoek*, see ROOSTERKOEK.] **a.** ASKOEK sense 1. **b.** ROOSTERKOEK sense a.

1883 O.E.A. SCHREINER *Story of Afr. Farm* 239 In the dining-room she had lighted a fire, and sat on the ground before it, turning the roaster-cakes that lay on the coals to bake. **1910** 'R. DEHAN' *Dop Doctor* 27 It lived on a little mealie pap and odd bits of roaster-cakes that were thrown to it as though it were a dog. **1947** E.R. SEARY *S. Afr. Short Stories* Glossary, *Roaster-cake*, (Roosterkoek in Afrikaans): girdle-cake; cake made on a gridiron.

roaster cookie *n. phr. Obs.* [Calqued on Afk. *roosterkoekie*, see ROOSTERKOEKIE.] ROOSTERKOEK sense a.

1937 B.H. DICKE *Bush Speaks* 79 He sported no bread; did not bother about making it or even roaster cookies. *Ibid.* 251 The trader .. sat by the fire and made roaster cookies, a tasty substitute for bread.

Robben Island /ˌrɒbən ˈaɪlənd/ *n. phr.* [Part. tr. Du. *Robben Eiland* (*robben* seals), the island in Table Bay formerly used as a leper-colony, an asylum, and, later, a place of detention for political prisoners.]

1. The prison on Robben Island, formerly used for the detention of political prisoners. Often used allusively as a symbol of imprisonment for political reasons; ISLAND. Also *attrib.* See also *Mandela University* (MANDELA).

[**1731** G. MEDLEY tr. *P. Kolb's Present State of Cape of G.H.* I. 108 This Hottentot .. was sent away to the *Robben* Island, where he died an Infidel. *Ibid.* II. 44 The Company's Servant was, for this Crime, banish'd to the *Robben*-Island for Life. **1833** *S. Afr. Almanac & Dir.* 204k, 1820. Dec. 25 The Caffer Prophet Lynx, with other Caffers, and the Hottentot-Chief David Stuurman, sent to Robben Island.] **1953** A. MOGALE in *Drum* May 31 I'll get you a few years on Robben Island – I know all about you and the joint in Cato Manor. **1969** M. BENSON *At Still Point* (1988) 17 'Grobelaar looks very horrible but he's not a bad fellow.' 'How could he say that when Grobelaar helped send him to Robben Island!' **1974** *E. Prov. Herald* 16 Dec., Robben Island was not introduced by the Afrikaners, it was here in the time of Lord Charles Somerset. **1976** *Drum* Sept. 2 I, Sipho Themba, graduate of Robben Island, say blackstan citizenship is just a four-letter word. **1977** *Weekend World* 17 July 51, I have never heard of a White man who has been to Robben Island. **1981** *Rand Daily Mail* 22 June 10 Bannings, detentions without trial and Robben Island are symptoms of this country's sickness. **1982** M.O. MTSHALI in Chapman & Dangor *Voices from Within* 76 He don't care for politics He don't go to church He knows Sobukwe he knows Mandela They're in Robben Island. **1983** *Rand Daily Mail* 11 Feb. 7 Robben Island graduates at the congress, all of whom were given .. 'an ovation and a hero's welcome'. **1986** *Style* Dec. 41 The only good bantus, commies, liberals and Engelse were dead ones. Any talk of multiracialism, in any form, got you 90 days or 180, or early retirement on Robben Island. **1987** *Frontline* Aug.-Sept. 18 'What is freedom?' asks Joe Khoza, who has spent 16 of his 50 years on Robben Island. 'We want to be free from oppression, but then what?' **1990** G. SLOVO *Ties of Blood* 611 They were going they said, to Robben Island: they were three of many: they were proud. **1992** D. BERESFORD in *Weekly Mail* 16 Apr. 25 She'd had fun telling her friends she was going overseas. She repeated the line to make sure we had the joke: 'Overseas, you see – overseas to Robben Island'. **1992** R. TYLER in *Pace* Aug. 46 We were all encouraged by the leadership to study – that is why it was known as the University of Robben Island. You got a complete political education there.

2. *comb.* **Robben Island slate**, a bluish stone quarried on Robben Island, used for paving and the construction of monuments.

[**1833** *S. Afr. Almanac & Dir.*, (advt) J. Fitzpatrick, Stone Mason and Monumental Letter Engraver, Dealer in Robben Island Stone.] **1951** L.G. GREEN *Grow Lovely* 35 Paving tiles were either Robben Island slate, or were brought from Holland or Batavia. **1963** R. LEWCOCK *Early 19th C. Archit.* 380 Robben Island 'slate', also called 'bluestone' was used for paving slabs, steps, kerbings, hearthstones and, under Somerset, for fireplace surrounds.

Hence **Robben Islander** *n. phr.*, one sentenced to imprisonment on Robben Island for political activities; *Islander*, see ISLAND.

1972 *Drum* 8 Dec. 55 He has little to eat – and, as an ex-Robben Islander, little chance of getting a job. **1987** *New Nation* 5 Nov. 7 That same year, Inkatha members broke up a meeting organised by activists in Hammarsdale to welcome former Robben Islanders. **1990** *Weekly Mail* 21 Sept. 7 There is also the complication of multiple levels of leadership; the returning ANC hierarchy, the internal ANC leadership, the UDF executive, .. the trade union leadership, the Communist Party leadership, the military commanders, the former Robben Islanders. **1994** *Weekly Mail & Guardian* 13 May 14 A former Robben Islander, Mhlaba is among the ANC's 'leadership which is unmatched by any political party on earth'.

robot /ˈrəʊbɒt, ˈrəʊbəʊ/ *n.* [A sense formerly found in Brit. Eng. but now obs.; fr. Czech *robota* forced labour, used by Karel Capek in his play *R.U.R.* (1920).] Automatic traffic-lights. Also *attrib.*, and occas. *fig.*

1930 *Star* 24 Jan., I think the success attained by the introduction of the robots is such that no motorist would like to see them removed. **1939** *Forum* 4 Feb. 35 The Daily Dispatch, East London, is critical of a proposal to fix robots in the town's streets. **1948** H.V. MORTON *In Search of S. Afr.* 17 Another word used in South Africa, but long discontinued in England, is robot for traffic lights. **1953** *Drum* Jan. 32 A lady carrying a big but empty shopping bag .. waited at the robot. We waited for the robot across the street. **1960** J.J.L. SISSON *S. Afr. Judicial Dict.* 869 There may be certain circumstances when a motorist is entitled to proceed against a robot. **1969** A. FUGARD *Boesman & Lena* 38 When the robot said 'Go' there at Berry's Corner I was nearly *bang in my broek*. **1970** *S. Afr. Panorama* Mar. 39 An automatic camera installed at a robot-controlled intersection .. records the date, time, number of seconds after the light turned red. **1971** *Argus* 12 May 14 A person who deliberately goes through a red robot, causing an accident which kills his own passenger or other folk on the road, is a murderer. **1973** *Star* 12 May 12 You espy the warning, painted in huge white letters on the road, *Caution: Robot.* If I was from Little Rock and didn't know that here we merely describe traffic lights thus, I'd tend to panic. **1980** *Family Post* 29 Nov. 2 Transkeian robots – straying cattle, sheep and goats, as well as pigs. **1982** *E. Prov. Herald* 9 June 7 During construction there will be single lane traffic, controlled by a robot system. **1985** H. PRENDINI in *Style* Oct. 39 We're still stuck behind that verdommde robot (which some older South Africans insist on calling a 'rowboh' in the mistaken belief that this Czech word is French or something). **1990** T. CARNIE in *Natal Mercury* 31 July 2 Jumping red robots has always been a problem, but we don't have the staff to man every intersection in the city. **1994** S. BOTHA in *Sidelines* Dec. 31 Waiting at a robot I caught the eye of a young blonde matron at the wheel of a BMW.

rock *n. Derog.* and *offensive. slang.* Ellipt. for ROCKSPIDER.

1970 G. FERREIRA *Informant, Pietersburg* That rock can't speak English. **1970** R. TANKARD *Informant, Pietersburg* Rock – an Afrikaner (short for rockspider). **1971** A. BRYANT *Informant, Tarkastad* Where we live there are a lot of rocks, so my dad made my brother have his hair cut as soon as he got back from varsity. **1974** S. ROBERTS in S. Gray *On Edge of World* 144 She really behaves like a rock at times ... She's helluva narrow-minded and suspicious you know, like a lot of Afrikaners. **1983** T. McAllen *Kyk Daar*, South Africa's superglue, Broederbond. Made from a secret formula. Even binds Rocks together. **1985** H. Prendini in *Style* Oct. 40 In the army .. Afrikaners are 'rocks' or 'pebbles'. **1990** R. Malan *My Traitor's Heart* 57 Most policemen .. were rocks, or Afrikaners, and rocks were not all that fond of soutpiels, especially those who worked for the disloyal English press. So the crime reporter slot usually went to someone like me, a rockspider who could speak the tongue. **1992** *Financial Mail* 13 Mar. 102 Nelson Mandela should also choose his words more carefully ... 'The path has been stony and many rocks lie in our way.' Is that any way to refer to Treurnicht, Terror'blanche and the rest? **1994** 'Crunchies United' in *Style* June 10 (*letter*) At last we knew someone in Style! If someone we knew had made Style, and that person nogal a rock, by implication we're moving in one helluva rockery.

rock *adj.* and *adv.* see RAAK.

rock *v. intrans.* [Special sense of general Eng. *rock* to stagger or sway along.] Usu. in the colloquial phrr. ***rock in, rock over, rock up***, to arrive in a casual way (unexpectedly, late, or inappropriately).

Usu. expressing disapproval.

1974 *Schoolgirl informant, Grahamstown* Communion this morning ... Real African time set-up here ... The service was at 7.30 and at eight o'clock the first person rocks up. **1975** 'Blossom' in *Darling* 12 Feb. 119 There by the camping site the day we rock in, it's 95 in the shade. **1975** *Ibid.* 12 Apr. 95 Seems he rocks over from Vredies to challenge the local pinball boks. **1979** *Ibid.* 16 May 131 When you rock inside there's these two more yooge settees covered with about a million cushuns. **1982** *Sunday Times* 6 June (Mag. Sect.), Like this taxi rocks up with two old toppies. **1984** J. Taylor 'Stuff'. (*lyrics*), I duly rocked up. **1991** D. Boswell *Informant, Giyani (N. Tvl)* Rock up. To arrive; turn up. There were gatecrashers at the party ... These guys were not invited; they simply rocked up and caused all sorts of havoc. **1992** on M-Net TV 13 Dec. (Carte Blanche), Even the two hospitals .. are tired of junkies rocking up. They OD, and then they rock up. **1993** *Ibid.* 3 May (Egoli), He rocks up after two years in Israel and gets a top job in Walco! **1994** M.J. Silva *Informant, Grahamstown* This one girl rocks up wearing a short leather skirt and a .. black lacy corset.

rock-cod *n.* Pl. unchanged, or **-s**. Any of a number of fishes of the family Serranidae, so called because they live mainly among rocks or coral.

1856 *Cape of G.H. Almanac & Annual Register* 283 Fish abound in the river and in the bay. The mullet rock cod and Cape Salmon, are most esteemed. **1891** R. Monteiro *Delagoa Bay* 151 The rock cod .. are especially good. **1930** C.L. Biden *Sea-Angling Fishes* 272 There are thirty kinds of rock-cod on the South African coast. **1949** J.L.B. Smith *Sea Fishes* 189 Family Serranidae. Rock-cods. Groupers. Garrupas ... All are excellent eating, many with delicate flesh, .. some are strikingly or beautifully coloured. **1963** *Rand Daily Mail* 17 May 23 A 4-lb rock cod tackled and swallowed a 4-ft green mamba. **1973** J.L.B. Smith in *Std Encycl. of Sn Afr.* IX. 387 *Rock Cods (Serranidae)* ... They live mostly among rocks and are fishes of warmer waters. In Southern African seas 40 species are known, ranging from tiny fishes to giants like the brindle bass. **1989** 'Jack the Fish' in *Stanger Mail* 3 Feb. 8 The ski-boats have been having a lean time recently ... Catches have been restricted to small salmon, grunter and rock-cod. **1990** M. Holmes in *E. Prov. Herald* 31 Aug. 26 A 3kg Catface Rockcod, a fish which normally makes one reef its home.

rock-fish *n. obs.* [tr. S. Afr. Du. *klipvisch*, see KLIPVIS.]

1. KLIPFISH sense 1. **2.** The HOTTENTOT (*n.* sense 2 b), *Pachymetopon blochii.*

1731 G. Medley tr. *P. Kolb's Present State of Cape of G.H.* I. 225 The *Hottentots* frequently take Abundance of a Sort of Fish, call'd Rock-Fish. These are Fish without Scales. *Ibid.* II. 207 There is a Sort of Fish at the *Cape* which the *Europeans* there call *Rock-Fish*, from their being mostly taken in Holes of Sea-Rocks, in which the tide leaves 'em. **1801** [see KLIPFISH sense 1]. [**1949** J.L.B. Smith *Sea Fishes* 355 *Ophthalmolophus helenae ... Klipfish. Klipvis. Rocky* ... Attains 4ins. From East London to the Bashee River, in shallow water under rocks.]

3. With qualifying word: **king rock-fish**, the KINGKLIP (sense 2), *Genypterus capensis.*

[**1801** J. Barrow *Trav.* I. 30 Another Blennius, called the King Rock-fish, is sometimes caught with the former.] **1843** J.C. Chase *Cape of G.H.* 169 Koning Klip Fish, King Rock Fish. Scarcer than the preceding [*sc.* klipfish], very considerably larger, and less delicate, but in much repute.

rock-goat *n. obs.* KLIPSPRINGER.

1731 G. Medley tr. *P. Kolb's Present State of Cape of G.H.* II. 116 The Rock-Goat is as well known in the *Cape-Countries* as he is in *Europe*; but the *Cape-Rock-Goat* is not near so large as the *European*. **1820** J. Campbell *Trav. in S. Afr. Second Journey* I. 29 The rock-goat .. had found its way to a place, which no human foot had ever yet trod. **1840** A.G. Campbell *Echo* 12 (Jeffreys), The rock-goat, .. he informed us, had found its way to a place which no human foot had ever trod. [**1866** J.W.D. Moodie *Soldier & Settler* Perceive the nimble 'klip springer', or Rock Antelope, gliding along the face of the inaccessible precipice as if by magic.]

rock lobster *n. phr.* [Transf. use of general Eng. name, which is applied esp. to the langouste *Palinurus vulgaris.*] CRAYFISH. Also *attrib.*

1953 *Sun* (Baltimore, U.S.A.) 9 Sept. 10 The name of the South African crawfish was changed by law to 'rock lobster'. **1960** J. Cope *Tame Ox* 163 He started with a rock-lobster boat in the Cape waters. **1970** G. Croudace *Scarlet Bikini* 73 'And no kreef,' Tony said, referring to the rock lobster. **1975** *Dict. of Eng. Usage in Sn Afr.* 149 *Rock lobster*, .. (*Jasus lalandii*) alt: Cape crayfish, spiny lobster S Afr sea crustacean of the fam[ily] *Palinuridae* to wh[ich] the crayfish belongs; flesh of this crustacean when frozen or canned for export. **1978** *S. Afr. Panorama* Feb. 45 Off Southern Africa there are three species of rock lobster of any commercial value. **1981** G. & M. Branch *Living Shores* 189 There are many species of rock lobster around the coast of southern Africa. *Jasus lalandii* .. is the common west coast species. On the south and east coasts live a host of *Panulirus* and *Palinurus* species. **1985** *Cape Times* 15 Nov. 13 Rock lobster season open. Today is the big day in the lives of the amateur rock lobster or kreef catchers. *c*1988 *S. Afr. 1987–8: Off. Yrbk* (Bureau for Info.) 382 The total wholesale value of rock lobster products was estimated at over R70-million in 1984/85. **1991** *Flying Springbok* May 99 The menu is quite breathtaking, with a repertoire that ranges from foie gras, Cape rock lobster tails on rice pilaff .. to lamb noisettes. **1991** B.J. Barker *Fairest Cape* 60 (*caption*) A rare (and expensive) delicacy is the Cape rock lobster (Jasus lalandii).

rockspider *n. slang.* A derogatory and offensive name for an Afrikaner; ROCK.

1970 *Informant, Cape Town* Those rockspiders look like they've come straight off the farm. **1973** *Star* 11 Apr. 3 A professor at the university .. took offence at the use of the word 'rock spider'. He gave the definition of 'rock spider' as a slang word for an Afrikaans person. **1973** *Cape Times* 4 May 3 The committee held that the terms 'rockspider' and 'hairyback' .. were .. grossly racialistic and grossly insulting overall to the Afrikaans community. **1980** C. Hope *A Separate Development* (1983) 112 He, being a good nationalist *rock-spider*, didn't like to think he was getting a reputation as a guy who gave strange natives a free snooze in his cars. **1985** P. Slabolepszy *Sat. Night at Palace* 19 Let the rock spiders go fight. It's their bladdy country. **1989** *Personality* 6 Feb. 21 English kids really used to hurt Afrikaans children a lot in the past, mocking us with names like 'plank' and 'rockspider'. **1990** [see CHRISTIAN-NATIONALISM]. **1991** F.G. Butler *Local Habitation* 256 The old portion of town — Settlers' Hill — was regarded as only fit for poor-whites, rock-spiders and an odd eccentric academic without social ambitions. **1992** [see DUTCHMAN sense 1 b].

roebuck *n. obsolescent.* Pl. **-s**, or unchanged. [Special sense of general Eng. *roebuck* the male of a roe-deer *Capreolus capreolus*; see quot. 1824.] **a.** The RHEBOK (sense 1 a), *Pelea capreolus.* **b.** The *mountain reedbuck* (see REEDBUCK sense 2), *Redunca fulvorufula.*

1731 G. Medley tr. *P. Kolb's Present State of Cape of G.H.* II. 114 Roebucks are seen in the *Cape*-Countries. They agree in every Particular with the Roe-bucks in *Europe*. **1824** W.J. Burchell *Trav.* II. 23 The name of *Gemsbok* belongs properly to the *Antilope rupicapra* of Europe, the *Chamois* of the Alps ... So also is the name of a common European animal, the *Reebok* or *Roebuck*, applied to two animals of another genus, and which are found only in Southern Africa. *a*1827 D. Carmichael in W.J. Hooker *Botanical Misc.* (1831) II. 47 *Roebucks* and *Duykers* were seen daily. **1827** T. Philipps *Scenes & Occurrences* 59 Fine roebucks, one of which we shot; they are covered with a very soft fur resembling that of rabbits. **1944** V. Pohl *Adventures of Boer Family* 11 There were roebuck in the *rantjies*.

roer /ruːr, rʊə/ *n.* [Du., long-barrelled gun.] **a.** *hist.* A large, heavy, long-barrelled flintlock musket similar to the type known elsewhere as the 'Brown Bess', used esp. for hunting; *elephant-gun*, see ELEPHANT; SANNA sense 1; SNAPHAAN. Cf. STERLOOP. See also BOBBEJAANBOUD, VOORLAAIER. **b.** *transf.* Any rifle or gun.

[**1801** in G.M. Theal *Rec. of Cape Col.* (1899) IV. 388 A lion .. had been mortally wounded by a snelroer (a firearm placed purposely in the ground to catch wild beasts).] **1824** *S. Afr. Jrnl* I. 26 Civilized man, — the possessor of the formidable *roer* or rifle. **1827** T. Philipps *Scenes & Occurrences* 210 On his shoulder he carried a large *roer* (or flintlock), and dangling by his side an enormous powder flask. **1834** T. Pringle *Afr. Sketches* 525 Roer signifies simply gun: but the term is more especially applied to the heavy long-barrelled guns used by the Boers for hunting elephants and other large game. **1834** *Makanna* (anon.) I. 188 That inseparable companion of a Dutch Boer, his 'roer', (or gun — and by the by, the weapon of that sort used by an 'Africanor' is no plaything, being of a make between a blunderbuss and a musket). [**1847** J. Barrow *Reflect.* 182 Our party of boors .. discharged a whole volley of their tremendously-large muskets, which they call *rooars* or *caveers*, into the herd, and killed or wounded five or six.] **1852** H. Ward *Jasper Lyle* 16 The dissertation between the old man and his son was amusing; the patriarch remarking that where the pistol might *wound six*, the *roer*, the long gun of the Boers, *must* kill all it aimed at. **1873** F. Boyle *To Cape for Diamonds* 18 The farmer's roer, a clumsy old rifle, but one to do desperate execution. **1878** T.J. Lucas *Camp Life & Sport* 106 They are excellent shots, and make nothing of bowling over a gnu or spring-buck at three hundred yards with their long 'roers,' or smooth bore guns. **1887** A.A. Anderson *25 Yrs in Waggon* I. 24 He once came on a lion asleep, and put his elephant 'roer' at his ear, when .. the bullet .. rolled down and dropped into the lion's ear. **1899** *Natal Agric. Jrnl* 31 Mar. 4 English colonists when speaking to natives in .. kitchen-kaffir, often use words such as .. 'roer' (the barrel of a gun) for fire-arms of all descriptions. **1908** J.M. Orpen *Reminisc.* (1964) 8 His formidable 'roer', a single-barrelled, smooth-bore gun, .. about five feet six inches long, with an eight to the pound round ball, and furnished with only one low back sight and an ivory front sight, or 'korel.' **1910** J. Buchan *Prester John* (1961) 117 All were armed with good rifles and bandoliers. There were none of your old roers and decrepit Enfields. **1937** F.B. Young *They Seek Country* 539 Jan carried his long-barrelled roer, an elephant-gun that fired a four-ounce bullet of lead and tin. **1944** J. Mockford *Here Are S. Africans* 65 Next in importance to the wagon itself was the Voortrekker's *roer*, his flintlock, which he kept .. ready to his hand, together with his powder horn and bullet pouches. **1949** L.G. Green *In Land of Afternoon* 206 Flintlock muskets were deadly enough to kill off most of the game ... These roers, with improvements, remained in use until 1859. **1979** M. MATSHOBA *Call Me Not a Man* 32 He raised the gun and shook it at us. 'Climb in,' he growled in Afrikaans. 'I'd like to see if this old *roer* can still spit fire. I ask you to give me a chance to try it, kaffers.' **1983** J.A. BROWN *White Locusts* 199 Our president blew his thumb off when his elephant *roer*, his great old musket, exploded.

c. *comb. obs.* **roer-drager** [Du. *drager* carrier], **roerdrawer**, a musket bearer.

1835 T.H. BOWKER Journal. 6 Sept., They say that the number of men with all their chiefs was very large, and that all the roerdrawers were here. **1838** *Graham's Town Jrnl* in J. Green *Kat River Settlement in 1851* (1853) 49 No Hottentot who was a '*roerdrager*' (musket bearer) should remain with the women and children, as they would all be required to fight. **1852** GODLONTON & IRVING *Narr. of Irruption* I. (Pettman), 170 Kreli was to have been with the Kaffir division, having a body guard of Kaffir (*roer-dragers*) musket bearers.

d. In the phrr. ***Boer and*** (or ***with***) ***his roer***, ***Boer en*** (or ***met***) ***sy roer*** [Afk. *en* and or *met* with + *sy* his], the archetype of the frontier Afrikaner.

1948 A. KEPPEL-JONES *When Smuts Goes* 60 The 'Boer with his roer' — his old muzzle-loader — meant security from the old attacks. **1965** D. MARAIS *Ag, Sis Man!*, (*caption*) *Opsaal Kêrels!* I don't mind boycotts and cancelled contracts, but when Wilson starts interfering with the *Boer* and his *roer* — that's too much! **1971** *Farmer's Weekly* 12 May 5 The new uniform is completely South African and even if it does not have any direct link-up with the keen-eyed, straight-shooting 'Boer en sy roer' it does have in it this element of basic simplicity. **1971** L.G. GREEN *Taste of S.-Easter* 56 'Die Boer en sy roer' suggests the traditional picture of the old warrior and hunter who seldom wasted a shot. **1972** *Daily Dispatch* 22 July 4 This was the roer that created a South African legend and the first image of that heroic figure Die Boer met sy roer.

roestekoek var. ROOSTERKOEK.

rofie var. ROOFIE.

roi-batje var. ROOIBAADJIE.

roibek, roibok varr. ROOIBEK, ROOIBOK.

roineck, roinek varr. ROOINECK, ROOINEK.

roker var. ROOKER.

rolbos /ˈrɔlbɔs/ *n.* Pl. **-se** /-sə/ [Afk., *rol* to roll + *bos* bush; see quot. 1966.] The small tumbleweed *Salsola kali* of the Chenopodiaceae.

[**1964** V. POHL *Dawn & After* 43 Far and near the dried skeletons of roll-bushes careered over the veld. These bushes were circular in form and very compactly interlaced, and in summer they flourished everywhere, but in winter they dried up and broke off at the root to be carried away by the wind.] **1966** C.A. SMITH *Common Names* 392 *Rolbos, Salsola Kali* ... The vernacular name is derived from the fact that the stems break off from the annual rootstock when drying off and roll over the veld in the wind. **1973** *Cape Times* 30 July 11 Piled up against the fences the up-rooted rol-bos (tumbleweed) — that strange round mass of ashen-grey twigs, weightless, powerless, driven hither and thither by the wind. **1974** *E. Prov. Herald* 9 Sept., On one farm a dense stand of rolbosse on 50 hectares of dryland easily carried 200 dorper ewes from lambing time until the lambs were weaned. **1989** F.G. BUTLER *Tales from Old Karoo* 201 With her came .. a teacher at the Training College who had .. red hair, which she never brushed; it sat like a dry rolbos all around her head.

Rolong var. BAROLONG.

roman *n.* Pl. unchanged, or **-s**. [Englished form of Afk. *rooiman*, see ROOIMAN.]

1. Often with initial capital. In full ***roman fish***: any of several red- or pink-coloured species of seabream of the Sparidae, esp. **a.** *Chrysoblephus laticeps*; DAGERAAD sense b; but also **b.** the DAGERAAD (sense a), *C. cristiceps*; and **c.** the SEVENTY-FOUR (sense a), *Polysteganus undulosus*. In all senses formerly also called ROOIMAN (sense 1). Also *attrib.*

Now commonly called 'red roman', but see quot. 1973. In Smith and Heemstra's *Smiths' Sea Fishes* (1986), 'roman' is used exclusively for *C. laticeps*.

1804 R. PERCIVAL *Acct of Cape of G.H.* 43 All kinds of fish peculiar to the Cape are found in this bay .. The most common is the Roman fish, so called from its being caught about the rock of that name; it is a deep rose colour and of the perch kind. **1806** J. BARROW *Trav.* II. 37 The Roman, a deep rose-coloured perch, is considered as the best fish in the colony. **a1823** J. EWART *Jrnl* (1970) 13 There is also one peculiar to Simons Bay called roman fish .. of the size and shape of the silver fish, and of a beautiful deep rose colour. **1831** *S. Afr. Almanac & Dir.* May, Fish in Season ... Snoek, Geelbek, Silverfish, Roman, Kabeljau. **1838** [see STUMPNOSE sense 1]. **1861** 'A LADY' *Life at Cape* (1963) 45, I there for the first time tasted a most delicate fish, called the 'seventy four' by some, and the 'Roman' by others, but which undoubtedly was as good as the best cod or turbot out of England. **1883** M.A. CAREY-HOBSON *Farm in Karoo* 87 'What fish have they there?' inquired Fred; 'the sea looks quite rose colour.' 'They are called Romans, sir, those that are so pink.' **1891** H.J. DUCKITT *Hilda's 'Where Is It?'* 79 At the Cape the best fish for pickling are 'Kabeljon,' [*sic*] 'Geelbeck,' 'Roman,' etc. **1913** C. PETTMAN *Africanderisms* 408 *Roman*, .. Chrysophrys cristiceps, Cuv. One of the prettiest and most delicious of the South African fishes. It has given its name to the Roman Rock in False Bay, in the neighbourhood of which the fish abounded. The name, which is a corruption of 'roodman,' 'rooiman,' has reference to the deep orange colour of the fish. **1949** J.L.B. SMITH *Sea Fishes* 272 *Chrysoblephus laticeps* (Cuvier) ... *Roman* or *Red Roman* (Cape). *Daggerhead* (Natal) ... Attains 18 ins. Occurs from the Cape to Mauritius. Favours rocky ground in deepish water ... Fresh from the water is a gorgeous creature. **1960** G. LISTER *Reminisc.* 21 One of the Dreyer boys dragged me out and just near me, in the same wave, they caught by hand a large Red Roman fish which was also being washed ashore. **1971** *Argus* 14 May 14 Standing on the bottom in 23m of water, John Hughes shot a roman of 4,1 kg — which is equal to the South African spearfishing record. **1973** *Farmer's Weekly* 18 Apr. 102 In the piping days of plenty, the red roman was not rated among the finest of fish. Its name is a corruption from 'rooi man' or red man. To refer to it as 'red' is, therefore, just a piece of tautology. **1983** *Cape Times* 9 July 11 When they did pick up a reef which produced a few red roman or stumpnose, .. hordes of small sharks and barbel devoured the entire catch. **1990** S. GRAY in *Staffrider* Vol.9 No.1, 50 Mounds of yellow rice, studded with whole abalones, Red Romans, bordered by mussels ... A Cape lobster on top. **1991** M. HOLMES in *E. Prov. Herald* 8 Mar. 18 Some of the largest Red Roman I have ever seen.

2. JAGSPINNEKOP. Rarely also with distinguishing epithet, **red roman**. Cf. ROOIMAN sense 2.

1905 F. PURCELL in Flint & Gilchrist *Science in S. Afr.* 178 The large nocturnal .. species of *Solpuga* .. are variously known .. by the name of *Romans, Jagd-spinnekoppen* (Hunting Spiders) or *Haarscheerders* (Hair cutters), and there is a current belief that they cut off the hair of a sleeping person at night. **1918, 1939** [see JAGSPINNEKOP]. **1979** *Grocott's Mail* 7 Sept. 5 Sun spiders, also known as solpugas, red romans or jagspinnekoppe are not spiders but belong to a related group, the Solifugae.

Roman-Dutch *adj.* [See quot. 1979.] Of or pertaining to a system of law based on that of ancient Rome, modified by that of Holland, and serving as the basis of South African law; usu. in the collocation ***Roman-Dutch law***, the system of law operating in South Africa (see quot. 1920).

1845 *Cape Stat.* 744 Ordinance for establishing the Roman-Dutch Law in and for the District of Natal. **1920** J. WESSELS in *S. Afr. Law Jrnl* No.37, 265 Roman Dutch law is not Roman law codified in Dutch nor is it Dutch law written in Latin. It is a system of law which was developed during the 16th and 17th centuries out of diverse legal elements. One of these elements was the Roman law ... Another element was the customary laws of Holland founded on old German customs, and a third was the statutory law in force in the Provinces of North and South Holland and West Friesland. **c1936** *S. & E. Afr. Yr Bk & Guide* 145 The fundamental difference between English Common Law and Roman Dutch would seem to be that whereas the former 'has broadened down from precedent to precedent,' the latter bases its ruling on principles of equity and common sense ... Curiously enough, something of the old Roman Dutch law of the Netherlands survives to-day only in the British dependencies of South Africa, Ceylon and, till 1916, in British Guiana. **1937** J. STEVENSON-HAMILTON *S. Afr. Eden* 213 Owing to the principle of inheritance embodied in the Roman-Dutch Law, many .. unoccupied farms had, in the course of years, become the property of a dozen or more owners, some of whom could not be found. **1948** O. WALKER *Kaffirs Are Lively* 170 An examination of Roman Dutch law, which is Common law in South Africa. **1958** H. WICHT *Rd below Me* 20 My grandfather was the youngest, but in accordance with Roman-Dutch law, all the sons inherited equally. **1971** *Jrnl of 1820 Settlers Memorial Assoc.* Nov. 22 Every man is presumed to know the law. So you had better know something about the everyday working of the Roman-Dutch law, which was planted here by the Hollanders and has survived although it was superseded in the parent country by the Code of Napoleon. **1979** W.J. HOSTEN et al. *Intro. to S. Afr. Law & Legal Theory* 180 He [*sc.* Simon van Leeuwen] was the first writer to refer to the existing Dutch law as Roman-Dutch law, and the designation is therefore attributable to him. **1986** P. MAYLAM *Hist. of Afr. People* 84 Criminal cases involving Africans outside the reserves were heard under Roman-Dutch law. **1989** M. MANLEY tr. *L.M. Oosthuizen's Media Policy & Ethics* 35 The principle of the welfare of the state community as the supreme law is solidly established in the Roman Dutch legal tradition of South Africa. **1989** *Reader's Digest Illust. Hist.* 394 The basis of law in South Africa is called Roman-Dutch Law, which means exactly what it says: a law based on ancient Rome modified by Dutch law introduced into the country by Jan van Riebeeck in 1652.

romines var. RAMENAS.

rommelpot /ˈrɔməlpɔt/ *n. hist.* Also **romelpot**. [Du., 'rumblepot' (used also of a friction drum of the Low Countries).] The colonial name given to a simple Khoikhoi drum, the *khais*; also called BAMBUS. See also POT DANCE.

1790 tr. *F. Le Vaillant's Trav.* II. 107 The *romelpot* is the most noisy of all the instruments ... It is formed of a piece of the trunk of a tree made hollow, over one of the ends of which is stretched a sheep's skin well tanned; on this the performer beats with his hands, or, to speak more accurately, with his fists, and sometimes even with a stick. **1841** B. SHAW *Memorials* 26 The pot dance, in which rommel pots are made use of instead of reeds. *Ibid.* 92 In their state of ignorance, they had often danced to the sound of the *rommel pot*, while the moon was walking in brightness. **1861** P.B. BORCHERDS *Auto-Biog. Mem.* 103 They [*sc.* the San] were enjoying themselves with playing their native music, produced by beating on a pot covered with skin, a rude drum known as the rommelpot. *Ibid.* 114 Amongst their instruments is one known by the colonists as the rommel-pot. It is simply a vessel covered with skin, and played like a drum. **1881** *Encycl. Brit.* XII. 311 The 'rommel-pot' was a kind of drum. **1934** P.R. KIRBY *Musical Instruments of Native Races* (1965) 12 The name *rommelpot* .. was that by which the colonist described the *Hottentot* drum. **1948** L.G. GREEN *To River's End* 153 They [*sc.* the San] do not seem to have had drums of their own, but they copied the Hottentot 'rommelpot' and called it a 'tam-tam'. **1976** A.P. BRINK *Instant in Wind* 213 They took out musical instruments and in the moonlight the reedflutes began their breathy shrill, accompanied by the sad monotony of the *ghoera* and the rumbling of the *rommelpot*. [**1980** D.B. COPLAN Urbanization of African Performing Arts. 45 The *ramkie* rapidly became a favorite with Cape Hottentots, who played on it the first blendings of Hottentot and European folk melodies. Other instruments included a Hottentot drum (*khais*; Dutch: *rommelpot*) and an imitation of the European bugle made of kelp and called the sea-weed trumpet. All three accompanied slave-Hottentot dances performed after the European fashion.]

rondavel /rɒn- rɔn'dɑːv(ə)l/ *n.* Also **rondabel**, **ronddavel**, **rond(d)awel**, **rondhavel**, **rondheuvel**. [Afk. *rondawel*, applied orig. to an African hut; etym. unkn.: perh. fr. *ronde* round + *wal* wall (or *rond* + *heuvel* hillock); or fr. Afk. *rond* round + Malay *dewala* wall; or fr. Pg. *roda* ring, wheel + *vallo* wall.]

a. A traditional circular African dwelling with a conical (generally thatched) roof; *transf.*, a circular building (usu. a single room) based on the design of an African hut but with additional features, used as guest-room, store-room, holiday cottage, etc. Also *attrib.* passing into *adj.*, and (occas.) *fig.* So (*nonce*) **longdavel** (see *Farmer's Weekly* quot. 1971), and **square-davel** (see quot. 1960).

*a***1875** T. BAINES *Jrnl of Res.* (1964) II. 282 Four thatched houses, a considerable number of huts — and rondheuvels, a kind of dwelling scarcely superior — and an immense kraal. *c***1892** J. WIDDICOMBE *14 Yrs in Basutoland* 84 Mr. Charles Bell had very kindly engaged a Mosuto .. to build us a round hut, or *rondavel*, as the whites usually call it. **1900** A.H. KEANE *Boer States* p.xviii, Rondabel, ronddawel, a round hut .. ; is now an outhouse detached from the dwelling, and is used as a kitchen. **1910** J. BUCHAN *Prester John* (1961) 37 Inanda's kraal was a cluster of kyas and rondavels, shaped in a half-moon. **1912** W. WESTRUP *Land of To-Morrow* 82 To one side were a couple of rondavels, or round sod huts, built in the native fashion and warmly thatched. **1922** S.G. MILLIN *Adam's Rest* 104 'Well, my idea is' said Miriam, 'to have rondavels. Four rondavels, joined together by a few feet of passage. Each rondavel a separate room with its own doors and windows. White, of course. And a thatched roof.' **1930** N. STEVENSON *Farmers of Lekkerbat* 17 The house .. was thatched as the native *rondawels* were with veld grass. **1931** *Nat. Geog. Mag.* Apr. 473 A peaceful mountain camp, with its .. group of rondavels, for that is what the Afrikaner calls his stone-walled thatched development of the native's circular hut. **1937** J. STEVENSON-HAMILTON *S. Afr. Eden* 16 Many *rondhavels*, or improved native huts, had been built. **1948** H.V. MORTON *In Search of S. Afr.* 123 A rondavel is a type of hut peculiar to South Africa, a circular, thatched European version of the Kaffir hut, fitted with windows. *Ibid.* 230 The rest camp at Hluhluwe stands upon the top of a hill. There are a number of circular white rondavels standing in lines upon grass, a welcome and cheering sight. **1948** E. ROSENTHAL *Afr. Switzerland* 16 A quaint little rondavel, one of those circular huts of brick with a roof of thatch that tell by their very appearance how white men have copied them from the Bantu hut. **1950** H. GIBBS *Twilight* 129 Here you will see Native kraals for the first time, little villages of rondavels, mud and straw and dung, circular in shape, with thatched roofs and an occasional rusty piece of corrugated iron, weighted down by squashes. **1949** L.G. GREEN *In Land of Afternoon* 156 The peach-pip floor is still to be found on some farms. It takes thousands of pips to cover even a rondavel floor. **1960** FILMER & JAMESON *Usutu* 97, I started to build two square-davels. **1965** K. THOMPSON *Richard's Way* 38 Jesse's thatched rondavel bedroom .. was still today exactly as it had been. **1967** J.A. BROSTER *Red Blanket Valley* 11 The house, a small thatched cottage, consisted of two rondavels linked by a rectangular passage leading into a kitchen and bathroom. There were two outside rondavels; one was a hut used for visitors, and the other served as a dairy. **1971** *Farmer's Weekly* May 25 'Red-Top' Steel Longdavels. **1971** N. GORDIMER *Guest of Honour* 43 He was back where he started, in the rondavel room at Roly Dando's. **1972** *Daily Dispatch* 25 Mar. 19 Well-constructed rondavel Dairy. **1975** RALLS & GORDON *Daughter of Yesterday* 19 A huge mimosa tree, .. so rounded inside as to form a 'rondavel'. **1979** M. MATSHOBA *Call Me Not a Man* 159 Below them there were picturesque villages of perfectly circular, thatched rondavels whitewashed for about a foot just below the edges of the thatch and around the windows and doors. **1982** *S. Afr. Panorama* Mar. 23 Their half-finished *rondavel* homestead. **1984** E. MPHAHLELE *Afrika my Music* 217 Eastern Cape Africans build on the tops of hills, something you rarely if ever see in the Transvaal ... These rondavel houses do not have wall enclosures like ours in the Transvaal. **1988** *S. Afr. Panorama* May 14 Accommodation for the hunter ranges from tents in the veld, to rustic lodges and luxurious rondavels, complete with air-conditioning, waiters and five-star cuisine. **1989** *Weekend Post* 25 Nov. (Leisure) 7 The veranda-ed rondavel shape of the building. **1990** R. STENGEL *January Sun* 39 When Afrikaners first encountered the black tribes of the highveld, they were intrigued by their round, hive-shaped huts ... The Afrikaners admired them and called them *rondawels*. In the 1930s, Life's grandfather fashioned many rondavels and thatched roofs for white houses in town. **1991** *Settler* Vol.65 No.1, The Pondos live in east-facing rondavel huts. The grey mud walls are decorated with white around the doors and windows. **1992** G. TEMPLETON in *Weekend Post* 8 Feb. (Leisure) 4 Each rondavel can accommodate two people comfortably and three at a pinch, but offers tranquillity disturbed only by the wind and sea.

b. *comb.* **rondavel-shaped**, **-style**, **-type**.

1987 G. VINEY *Col. Houses* 161 The two **rondavel-shaped** buildings .. were the cool-houses — one for meat, the other for vegetables and fruit. **1971** BEETON & DORNER in *Eng. Usage in Sn Afr.* Vol.2 No.2, 37 A **rondavel-style** cottage or house is a dwelling consisting of a number of rondavels linked with one another by means of short passages. **1974** *S. Afr. Panorama* Sept. 33 Picturesque **rondavel-type** houses each with their own 'lapa'. **1985** *Style* Oct. 54 In the Barnett Collection there is a picture of a grass-roofed rondavel-type house on the outskirts of Johannesburg before the turn of the century.

rondeganger var. RONDGANGER.

Ronderib /'rɔndərəb/ *n.* Also with small initial. [Afk., lit. 'round rib', see quot. 1934.] Now often in the phr. ***Ronderib Afrikander***. A variety of Afrikander sheep (see AFRIKANDER *n.* sense 7) raised where conditions favour animals with relatively high feeding requirements, and sometimes sub-divided into silky-haired (see BLINKHAAR *n.*[2]) and coarse-haired types; ROUND-RIBBED AFRIKANDER. Also *attrib.* See also VAN ROOY.

1934 C.P. SWART Supplement to Pettman. 145 *Ronderib*, .. A term applied to one of the two breeds of Afrikaner or fat-tailed sheep sprung from the old stock originally found in the Cape Province and Namaqualand. As the name denotes, this sheep has well-sprung ribs which distinguish it from the hardy Namaqua type found in the driest parts of South Africa which is rather flat-ribbed. **1934** *Farming in S. Afr.* Apr. 134 (Swart), Although there are two types of Ronderib, these distinct types are now-a-days only found in a few pure-bred stud flocks. **1937** *Handbk for Farmers* (Dept of Agric. & Forestry) 199 The ronderib is .. a hardy breed and thrives under semi-arid conditions ... Though distinctly heavier than the Persian, the Ronderib also may not be regarded as a desirable mutton breed for export purposes .. as .. there is an undesirable localization and abundance of fat. **1937** [see BLINKHAAR *n.*[2]]. **1953** [see VAN ROOY]. **1957** *Handbk for Farmers* (Dept of Agric.) III. 221 *The Ronderib Africander*, This breed was developed during the latter part of the 19th century from the broad-tailed sheep breeds which were in possession of the Cape Hottentots. **1974** *Farmer's Weekly* 20 Mar., (*advt*) Africanders For Sale ... Ronderib Blinkhaar Africander rams R30 and studs R75. Also young ewes ... The mothers of these sheep weigh up to 180 lb. live weight. **1988** T.J. LINDSAY *Shadow* (1990) The docking of tails of the Ronderib Afrikaaner sheep. **1990** *Grocott's Mail* 6 July 8 It seems that the fat-tailed Ronderib Afrikaner sheep can serve a useful purpose in raising the reproductive rate of Merino ewes.

rondganger /'rɔntxaŋə(r)/ *n. hist.* Also **rondeganger**. [Afk., fr. Du. *rondeganger* roundsman, watch.] See quot. 1887.

1873 'L.G.R.' in *Cape Monthly Mag.* VI. 211 In the guard-house are two soldiers placed called the 'Rondegangers,' who watch an hour-glass and take turns to reverse it when the sand is run out. **1887** *S.W. Silver & Co.'s Handbk to S. Afr.* 11 In the Castle there was an accurately manufactured sun-dial, and in the guard-house two soldiers, called 'Rondgangers,' whose sole duty it was to watch an hour-glass, and take turns to reverse it when the sand had run out. Then they had to ascend a small tower placed over the Castle-gate, and with a cudgel strike a bell weighing six hundred-weight as many blows as may denote the hour. **1919** M. GREENLEES tr. *O.F. Mentzel's Life at Cape in Mid-18th C.* 157 Owing to the violent winds that frequently rage at the Cape, no clock can be put up in the open, so the hours are struck by hand upon a bell that hangs in a little tower over the Castle gate. There are always two soldiers, 'rondgangers' as they are called, stationed in the guard-house to see to the ringing of the bell. **1926** P.W. LAIDLER *Tavern of Ocean* 52 During September, 1716, a 'rondeganger' or rounds man left the guard room to sound the hour as usual. The bell did not sound, nor did the man return. **1969** I. VAUGHAN *Last of Sunlit Yrs* 50 The old bell which tolled the hours, and where story has it, a rondganger hanged himself for love of a secunde's daughter, still hangs there.

rondhavel, **-heuvel** varr. RONDAVEL.

rondloper /'rɔntluəpə(r)/ *n. colloq.* Also **rondlooper**. [Afk., idler, loafer, vagrant, fr. *rondloop* to wander about.] A tramp or vagrant; one with wanderlust; a gad-about.

1863 *Queenstown Free Press* 3 Mar., The Kaffir when engaged had no pass whatever in his possession — he was, what I may term a, rond looper. *c***1870** J. MONTGOMERY *Reminisc.* (1981) 86 From this family, I chose my life partner, so I settled down and was no longer a rondlooper (tramp). **1899** G.H. RUSSELL *Under Sjambok* 101 What! do you mean the rondlooper (tramp) I was told had been near the store last night? **1917** S.T. PLAATJE *Native Life* 84 No wonder that Anna is so upset. I have been thinking that same rondloper (vagabond) from the towns had been trying to take her away. **1971** *Sunday Times* 7 Nov. (Mag. Sect.) 5, I got to know this country well when I was a child because my uncles and aunts were great rondlopers and holidaymakers and would pack up and go at the drop of a hat. **1980** *Capetonian* Jan. 26 Jus' cos I worked for a lotta masters and merrems doesn't mean to say I'se a rondloper wot cannot hold down a job. **1985** *Cape Times* 24 Aug., Yet such rondlopers .. were selected for the farcical Boks team chosen for a tour of South Africa, for goodness' sakes!

Hence back-formations **rondloop** *v. intrans.* (so **rondloping** *ppl adj.*) and **rondloop** *adj.*

1966 F.G. BUTLER *Take Root or Die* (1970) 61 My father says that, other things being equal, a man with a good safe job with the government is to be preferred to a saddler, or a 'rondloping smous'. **1976** *Het Suid-Western* 1 Sept., In spite of all the rubbish .. that has been written .. there have been no rondloop goggas and factions on this town council. **1977** S. ROBERTS in E. Pereira *Contemp. S. Afr. Plays* 232 Sieg: Is Dauw in Ma? Hester: No, he's out. Either at the Versters or rondloping with one of his tjommies.

rong /rɔŋ/ *n. Hist. Wagon-making.* Pl. **-e** /-ə/, (occas.) **-en**, or **-s**. [Afk., fr. S. Afr. Du.] A stanchion or metal upright on a wagon, holding the body in place on the chassis.

1822 W.J. BURCHELL *Trav.* I. 152 The sides resting on the skammels, lean against the rongs. **1833** *Graham's*

Town Jrnl 4 Apr. 2 The fatal wound seems to have been inflicted by the rong of a wagon, which caused an extensive fracture of the skull of the deceased. **1919** [see Gibson quot. at SCHAMMEL]. **1974** A.A. TELFORD in *Std Encycl. of Sn Afr.* X. 569 The body with side rails was simply lifted out from between the *ronge* (four metal uprights, one at each corner of the chassis) and replaced by a body with higher sides.

ront var. RAND.

roodbeckje, roode-bekje varr. ROOIBEKKIE.

roode-batje var. ROOIBAADJIE.

roodebec, -bek varr. ROOIBEK.

roodebok, roode els varr. ROOIBOK, ROOI-ELS.

roode haas *n. phr. Obs.* Also **rooihaas**. [S. Afr. Du., *roode* (later *rooi*) red + *haas* hare.] Either of two rock rabbits of the Leporidae, *Pronolagus rupestris* or *P. crassicandatus*.

[**1796** E. HELME tr. *F. Le Vaillant's Trav.* II. 166 (Jeffreys), This was a hare ... known there by the name of *roode-gat-haas* (the hare with the red anus).] **1844** J. BACKHOUSE *Narr. of Visit* 485 (Jeffreys), The Red Hare or *Roode Haas, Lepus rupestris*, is smaller than the Common Hare. **1905** W.L. SCLATER in Flint & Gilchrist *Science in S. Afr.* 134 The Hares, known as the Vlackte haas (*Lepus capensis*), Rhebok haas (*L. saxatilis*) and Roode haas (*L. crassicandatus*) .. are spread all over the country. **1918** S.H. SKAIFE *Animal Life* 254 The red hare, or *roode haas*, is smaller than the Cape Hare and redder in colour. It lives in small colonies on hill tops, and feeds on grass and shrubs. **1940** V. POHL *Bushveld Adventures* 27 He raced down the rantjie with the agility of a 'rooihaas'.

roodehout, roodekat(t), roode lavendel varr. ROOIHOUT, ROOIKAT, ROOILAVENTEL.

rood elze, roodhout, roodman varr. ROOI-ELS, ROOIHOUT, ROOIMAN.

Roof /ruːf/ *n.*[1] In the phr. *Roof of (South) Africa* [by analogy with general Eng. *roof of the world* the Himalayas], a name given to the highest southern African mountains, the Qathlamba of Lesotho and the Drakensberg of western KwaZulu-Natal; *transf.*, the Kingdom of Lesotho.

1912 *Cape Times* 28 Sept. 9 (Pettman), The Drakensberg range has been aptly called the Roof of Africa. **1948** E. ROSENTHAL *Afr. Switzerland* 27 Not until 1935 were the first tentative beginnings made at combating the washing-away of the soil in the sudden violent storms of the 'Roof of South Africa'. **1989** J. HOBBS *Thoughts in Makeshift Mortuary* 360 'If we go to Lesotho, maybe we can live in the mountains,' Rose said. 'They call it the Roof of Africa, don't they?'

roof /rʊəf/ *n.*[2] *Army slang.* [See ROOFIE.] ROOFIE.

1975 [see Picard quot. at ROOFIE]. **1980** *Armed Forces* May 9 Do not let us forget the Band Masters who at times I am sure are quite ready to have a nervous breakdown especially when the 'Roofs' arrive. **1986** *Uniform* 16 June 1 One of the 'roofs', Rfn P A Joubert, .. said the training was especially important for protection of local property.

roofie /ˈruəfi/ *n. Army slang.* Also **rofie**. [Etym. uncertain: perh. Afk. *roof* scab + -IE.] A newly-recruited national serviceman; ROOF *n.*[2] Also *attrib.*

1975 J.H. PICARD in *Eng. Usage in Sn Afr.* Vol.6 No.1, 36 The new recruits are called *roofies*, a *roof* becomes a *blougat*, when he is halfway through his course. **1975** *Scope* 10 Jan. 76 (*headline*) Attention roofies, blouies and oumanne, you will read this! **1977** G. HUGO in *Quarry '77* 91, I give them 'Hard Rains a Going to Fall'. And they don't really seem to dig the irony of it, just another mad roofie. **1980** *Sunday Times* 4 May (Mag. Sect.) 4 (*caption*) We love introducing the new intakes to the army with a 'rofie ride' from the station to the camp. **1986** [see OUMAN]. **1991** R. FRAGOSO *Informant, Pretoria* Roofie: .. Rookie. Somebody who has just started his army service, i.e. is doing basics. Army colloquialism.

rooge valk var. ROOIVALK sense 1.

rooi-aas /ˈrɔɪ ɑːs/ *n.* Also **rooias**. [Afk., *rooi* red + *aas* bait, carrion; see quot. 1916.] RED-BAIT.

1895 *Agric. Jrnl* (Dept of Agric. Cape Col.) 912 The bait most used is crayfish, and 'rooiaas' (red bait) a species of Zoophyte. **1905** H.E.B. BROOKING in *E. London Dispatch* 30 May, Of the baits available .. 'rooi-aas' .. is given the preference because .. far more are taken upon 'rooi-aas', and the fish bite upon it more freely. **1905** J.D.F. GILCHRIST in Flint & Gilchrist *Science in S. Afr.* 192 One of the features of the rocky parts of the coast line *from Cape Point eastwards* is the clusters of 'rooias' or 'red bait' (a large Ascidian) which cover the rocks. **1913** W.W. THOMPSON *Sea Fisheries of Cape Col.* 62 The 'red bait' (Polycarpa), or rooi-as, as it is locally known, is an Ascidian belonging to the order Tunicata or sea-squirts. **1918** S.H. SKAIFE *Animal Life* 197 All around the South African coast the so-called red-bait or *rooiaas*, is very commom. Anglers know it as a soft, red animal enclosed in a tough, protective coat of a dull green colour. **1923** *S. Afr.: Land of Outdoor Life* (S.A.R. & H.) 150 Typical winter fishing .. is confined to the conquest of the red stump-nose .. and the galjoen, principally on the ascidian known as rooiaas or red bait. **1930** [see RED-BAIT]. **1952** N. ORPEN in Bosman & Bredell *Veld Trails & Pavements* 147 He .. occasionally earned by collecting bait .. for a few regular anglers who came down to collect their rooi aas, mussels, or chokka from him before going back to the warmer side of the barren Cape of Good Hope. **1973** *Weekend Post* 3 Mar. 2 Fishermen from George .. recently made the observation that good old red bait, or 'rooi aas' might possibly be an aphrodisiac.

rooibaadjie /ˈrɔɪbaɪki, ˈrʊɪ-/ *n.* Also **raed vatje, roi-batje, roode-baatje, rooi baadje, -baatje, -baatjie, -baatye, -badgie, -badjie, -batjee, rooie batje, rori baajte**. [Afk. (earlier S. Afr. Du. *roode-baatje*), *rooi* red + *baadjie* (fr. Malay *badju*) jacket.]

1. *hist.* Usu. *derog.* 'Redcoat', a name for a British regular soldier, esp. during the 19th century. See also AMAJONI sense 1, KHAKI *n.* sense 1 a.

The name outlived the wearing of the distinctive red jackets, which had been replaced by the less visible khaki by the time of the Anglo-Boer War.

1848 H. WARD *Five Yrs in Kaffirland* I. 154 We rode out, keeping pretty close to the Cape Corps, the *Raed Vatjes*, or red jackets (as they term the British troops on the frontier). **1852** C. BARTER *Dorp & Veld* 171 (Pettman), The border colonist would have held his ground against the native, without the aid of a single *Roode-baatje* (red-coat). **1858** *Cape Monthly Mag.* IV. Sept. 149 It was only when a volley from the outskirts of the bush caused many of them to bite the dust that they perceived themselves to be partially surrounded by a party of 'rooi batjes.' **1884** B. ADAMS *Narr.* (1941) 176 As soon as they caught sight of us they raised the cry 'Rooi Badjies' — Red Coats — and away they went as fast as their legs would carry them. **1887** J.W. MATTHEWS *Incwadi Yami* 445 The Boers formed a supreme contempt of the 'Rori Baajtes.' **1888** tr. L.A.J. Délegorgue in J. Bird *Annals of Natal* I. 562 In December, 1839, the 'rooi-baatjes' weighed anchor, and had scarcely set sail, when a three-coloured flag was hoisted on the same staff that had lately borne the British ensign. **1904** H.A. BRYDEN *Hist. of S. Afr.* 211 (The Boers) don't seem to think very much of the foot-soldier, or 'rooi-baatje' .. for they say he cannot ride and he cannot shoot. **1911** BLACKBURN & CADDELL *Secret Service* 89 She said that Cetawayo had gained a great victory, and that the *rooie-batjes* (redcoats) lay upon the field of battle 'like winter leaves beneath a tree'. **1942** S. CLOETE *Hill of Doves* 116 Why, our men were soldiers, veterans of wars, when these Rooibaadjies were but children. **1955** B.B. BURNETT *Anglicans in Natal* 21 Freed from the presence of British rooibaatjies .. , the Boers settled down to enjoy the land which they had acquired. *c*1963 B.C. TAIT *Durban Story* 24 Captain Smith and his 'rooibaadjies' were kraaled in the Fort and there the Boers meant to starve them into surrender. **1971** *Daily Dispatch* 18 Dec., At that time Kipling's Private Thomas A. was the sturdy Victorian redcoat — ' .. a rooibaadjie' in South Africa.

2. *transf.* A red larval form of the brown locust *Locustana pardalina*; also called VOETGANGER (sense 1). Also *attrib.*

1858 H. CALDERWOOD *Caffres & Caffre Missions* 157 The young locusts .. are then partly red and partly black. The Dutch call them then *vootgangers* — that is, footmen, or goers on foot. Sometimes they are called *roibatjes* — that is, red-coats, in allusion to the soldiers. **1875** C.B. BISSET *Sport & War* 170 You see the very earth become alive with diminutive insects, .. increasing in size and becoming the colour of the brightest red. At this stage they are called Rooi baatyes. **1902** *Trans. of S. Afr. Phil. Soc.* XI. p.xlv, The young of the migratory one [*sc.* locust] are so gaily coloured as to have earned for them the local name of '*rooibatjes*', or redcoats. **1924** L.H. BRINKMAN *Glory of Backveld* 10 A newly-hatched locust .. is quite black, but after a few weeks its coat changes into a dull red colour, when it is known as a 'rooibaatje' (red coat). This coat the insect sheds when full grown and emerges as a winged locust of a khaki colour. **1972** A. LEA in *Std Encycl. of Sn Afr.* VII. 21 Young crowded hoppers would develop into typical phase *gregaria* 'rooibaadjies'. **1986** *S. Afr. Panorama* June 13 They [*sc.* brown locusts] 'go critical' and take flight after their sixth change of skin, at one stage assuming a menacing striped colour — the *rooibaadjie* or redcoat stage.

rooibeckie var. ROOIBEKKIE.

rooibek *n. obs.* Also **roibek, roodebec, roodebek, rooibeck**. [See ROOIBEKKIE.] ROOIBEKKIE sense 1.

1890 A. MARTIN *Home Life* 18 Another soft-voiced little singer is the *rooibeck*, or red-beak, a wee thing very like an avadavat. **1899** R.B. & J.D.S. WOODWARD *Natal Birds* 66 This bird (*V. principalis*) derives its name from its pretty wax-like red bill, which resembles that of the estrilda, and in common with them it is called *roibek*. **1900** A.C. STARK *Birds S. Afr.* I. 99 The 'Roodebec' may be found nearly everywhere in South Africa.

rooibekkie /ˈrɔɪbeki, ˈrʊɪbeki/ *n.* Also **roodbeckje, roode-bekje, rooibeckie, rooibekje**. [Afk., earlier S. Afr. Du. *roodebekje*, *roode* red + *bekje* little beak.]

1. Either of two birds with red beaks, the common waxbill *Estrilda astrild* of the Estrildidae, or the pin-tailed whydah *Vidua macroura* of the Viduidae; also called *red beak* (see RED *adj.* sense 1), ROOIBEK (also occas. with defining word, **king** - or **koning** /ˈkʊənəŋ/ **rooibekkie** [Afk. *koning* king]).

1795 C.R. HOPSON tr. *C.P. Thunberg's Trav.* I. 312 The *Loxia Astrild*, on account of its red beak, was called Rood-beckje, or *Red-beak*, and was found in great numbers in the farmers gardens. [**1824** W.J. BURCHELL *Trav.* II. 41 A number of very small finches, (*Loxia astrild*) frequented the bushes at this place ... This little bird is not peculiar to Southern Africa; it is very common at St. Helena ... It is known to the Dutch colonists by the appellation of *Roode-bekje* (Red-beak).] **1861** LADY DUFF-GORDON *Lett. from Cape* (1925) 60, I will try to bring home some cages of birds — Cape canaries and 'roode bekjes' (red bills), darling little things. **1868** J. CHAPMAN *Trav.* II. 17 We shot and skinned some birds, among which was a long-tailed finch (king rooi bekkie). **1910** D. FAIRBRIDGE *That Which Hath Been* (1913) 307 Nautilus shells, sun-dried peaches and apricots, ostrich eggs, watermelons, rooibekjes in little cages. **1923** HAAGNER & IVY *Sketches* 123 The sprightly little Pin-tailed Whydah (*Vidua serena*) is also a well-known figure in its pied plumage of black and white, long narrow tail, and pink bill. It is known to the boys as the Koning Rooibekje (King Red-bill). **1928** E.H.L. SCHWARZ *Kalahari & its Native Races* 114 The whole area was now one vast field of maize, long since harvested, but the *rooi beckies* — a tiny fawn bird with a red beak — stayed on, waiting for the next sowing. **1955** V. DE KOCK *Fun They Had* 31 We read of an occasion, when an old sportsman had caught a number of *rooibekkies.* **1967** S.M.A. LOWE *Hungry Veld* 90 Tiny rooibekkies with speckled grey feathers and bright red beaks were eating grass seeds. [**1970** A. FULTON *I Swear to Apollo* 19 'In Tshiyane', .. the name given to the little grey bird with the red bill that the Afrikaners called rooibekkie.] **1975** G.J. BROEKHUYSEN in *Std Encycl. of Sn Afr.* XI. 371 Among common species in Southern Africa are the swee waxbill .. and the common waxbill or rooi-bekkie (*Estrilda astrild*).

2. *obsolescent.* A variety of bean.

1930 *Farming in S. Afr.* Oct. 346 (Swart), Half coloured beans, e.g. 'Lappies and Rooi Bekkie' are being cultivated. These vary in shape, though they are mostly roundish. **1934** C.P. SWART Supplement to Pettman. 146 *Rooibekkie,* .. A variety of dry bean, so called because it has a red discoloration.

rooiblom *n. obs.* Also **rooibloem, rooi-bloom.** [Afk., *rooi* red + *blom* flower.] The WITCHWEED, *Striga asiatica.* Also *attrib.*, and occas. **rooibloemtje** [see -IE.]

1904 *Times* (U.K.) 25 July 12 Complaints .. were constantly being received .. of damage done .. to the mealie .. crop by .. rooi-bloom or witchweed. **1911** *E. London Dispatch* 13 Apr. 6 (Pettman), The plant disease ... is that known as witch-weed or *rooi-bloemtje.* **1912** *Dept of Agric. Report* (UG54–1912) 255 The investigation must be based upon a knowledge of the conditions of germination of the Rooibloem seed and by [*sic*] those affecting the penetration of the Mealie Root by the Rooibloem seedling. **1913** C. PETTMAN *Africanderisms* 411 *Rooibloem,* .. The parasitic *Striga lutea, Lour.*, which attaches itstelf to the roots of wild grasses and also to cultivated crops of the grass family, especially mealies; by absorbing the juice of the plant it prevents its maturing. **1939** S. CLOETE *Watch for Dawn* 97 She was like a weed that spread over the land; like the Rooiblom that was so beautiful, but which lived by sucking the sap from the mealies.

‖**rooibok** /ˈrɔɪbɔk/ *n.* Also **roibok, roodebok, rooyebok.** [Afk., *rooi* (earlier S. Afr. Du. *roode*) red + *bok* buck.] IMPALA sense 1 a.

1824 W.J. BURCHELL *Trav.* II. 215 One [antelope] is called *Paala* (Parla) by the Bichuanas, and is known by the name of *Roodebok* (Redbuck). **1835** A. SMITH *Diary* (1940) II. 239 The crocodile shot on Saturday had a rooyebok entire in its stomach. **1839** W.C. HARRIS *Wild Sports* 383 *Antilope Melampus.* The Pallah. Rooye-bok *of the Cape Colonists.* Pallah *of the Matabili and Bechuana.* **1874** A. EDGAR in *Friend* 4 June, I fired at a 'rooibok' a long way off, and of course missed him. **1887** *S.W. Silver & Co.'s Handbk to S. Afr.* 171 The pallah (Æpyceros melampus, Licht.) is found in Bechouanaland and on the eastern edge of the Kalihari, but seldom south of the Vaal River ... It is also called the roodebok. **1939** S. CLOETE *Watch for Dawn* 274 It was said that no man knew how high a rooibok could jump when pressed. **1941** A.G. BEE *Kalahari Camp Fires* (1943) 18 They rode out in search of things to shoot, and found the spoor of Rooibok or Impala. **1968** L.G. GREEN *Full Many Glorious Morning* 189 Palapye Road, named by an extinct tribe after the *rooibok*, was once the site of the 'post office tree' where Livingstone and other travellers left their letters. **1989** I. JONES *Woman's World Cookbk* 62 Choice fillet of rooibok — impala — is used for these marinated treats for the braai.

rooibos /ˈrɔɪbɔs/ *n.* Formerly also **rooibosch.** [Afk., *rooi* red + *bos* bush.]

1. In full ***rooibos tea*** [so named because the oxidized leaves are red in colour]:

a. The dried leaves of any of several shrubs of the genus *Aspalathus*; the tea made from an infusion of these leaves; ROOI TEA; also called BUSH TEA. Also *attrib.*

1911 *S. Afr. Jrnl of Science* VII. 374 The author described .. a *Borbonia*, the source of Cape 'rooibos' tea. **1919** *Dunell, Ebden & Co.'s Price List* 30 Tea .. Colonial ... Rooi Bosch. loose, in bags [per lb.] 8½d. **1958** A. JACKSON *Trader on Veld* 36 Rooibos (bush) tea was another popular line carried by the vrugtesmous, a very cheap and healthy herb from the Cedarberg and elsewhere, much used by our farmers in sickness and in health. **1973** *Personality* 26 Jan. 88 A few years ago Mrs Annekie Theron made the amazing discovery that Rooibosch tea alleviated milk allergies in infants. **1973** *S. Afr. Panorama* Apr. 15 Rooibos tea, also known as Rooi tea, Naald tea or Speld tea (Needle tea) and Koopmans tea (merchants tea) can be divided into four main groups: Rooi tea (Red tea), Swart tea (Black tea), Rooi-bruin tea (Red-brown tea) and the Vaal tea (Hottentot tea) type. **1980** *Sunday Times* 11 July 1 Hundreds of hardened rooibos drinkers in the City were aghast yesterday at the news that rooibos production was down to 50 per cent of demand. **1985** *Style* Dec. 139 The tea is very good and though there is only a choice between Indian and rooibos there are excellent plain or wholewheat scones. **1990** *Pace* May 117 Rooibos tea is a completely natural product with no additives or harmful sustances such as caffeine.

b. Any of several shrubs of the genus *Aspalathus*, cultivated for their leaves; ROOI TEA; also called BUSH TEA. Also *attrib.*

1949 L.G. GREEN *In Land of Afternoon* 52 Bush tea is often confused with buchu. It is, of course, an entirely different plant — a legume. You hear it called rooibos, heuning tee, stekel tee, boer tee. **1955** A. DELIUS *Young Trav.* 102 'This is bush-tea,' Frank told him. 'It's made from South African bushes called *rooibos*'. **1975** *Tvl Post* 25 Oct. 10 The Rooibos shrub is grown commercially in the Western Cape and is used to brew a tannin-free tea. It is also known as Bush tea and Heuning tee. **1982** K. SUTTON in *E. Prov. Herald* 24 Sept., He described rooibos as a plant 'you can make friends with and find it very much obliging'. **1984** A. WANNENBURGH *Natural Wonder of Sn Afr.* 72 The rooibos tea shrub, Aspalathus linearis, a legume with small yellow pea flowers that grows in the Cedarburg, has been domesticated for half a century and is widely used as a stimulant-free substitute for tea. **1987** T.F.J. VAN RENSBURG *Intro. to Fynbos* 30 Most South Africans know rooibos tea (*Aspalathus linearis*). **1989** *Farmer's Weekly* 13 Oct. 27 Fungal diseases of rooibos tea will devastate the whole industry unless producers modify their farming practices ... Rooibos-tea seeds are sown from February to March each year.

2. Either of two trees of the Combretaceae, *Combretum apiculatum* which bears red fruit and red or yellow winter foliage, or *C. erythrophyllum.* In both senses also called BUSH-WILLOW. Also *attrib.*

1932 WATT & BREYER-BRANDWIJK *Medicinal & Poisonous Plants* 128 The Zulus regard *Combretum erythrophyllum* Sond., Bush willow .. Rooibos .. as poisonous. **1958** S. CLOETE *Mask* 184 The veld changed. There were more trees — rooibos, seringa and vaalbos. **1961** PALMER & PITMAN *Trees of S. Afr.* 244 *Rooibos*, This is a small deciduous tree, sometimes a bush, common in the Transvaal bushveld. **1965** P. BARAGWANATH *Brave Remain* 142 It was rapidly becoming dark but they used a cattle track and by the time it petered out they were through the *hardekool* and into the *rooibos* trees which have no thorns. **1975** *S. Afr. Panorama* May 37 This is the domain of mopane, knobthorn, .. rooibos (red bush-willow). **1977** F.G. BUTLER *Karoo Morning* 89 Special suits of harness .. had been made for them from leather cured by old Langjan himself, who used pounded mesembrianthemum to remove the hair, and rooibos for tanning.

rooibuck *n. obs.* Also **roy-buck.** [Part. tr. Afk. *rooibok*, see ROOIBOK.] IMPALA sense 1 a. Also *attrib.*

1881 P. GILLMORE *Land of Boer* 241 He was a very successful sportsman, and as proof of his prowess presented me with half of a noble roy-buck (red) which he had shot in the morning. **1926** *Glasgow Herald* (U.K.) 31 Aug. 2 He had got a rooibuck (or impala) ram.

rooidoek /ˈrɔɪdʊk, -duk/ *n.* Pl. **-e** /-ə/. [Afk., *rooi* red + *doek* (head-)scarf, cloth.] Esp. in the townships of Johannesburg and surrounding areas: one of a band of (armed) men from a migrant workers' hostel, using for identification a red cloth attached to a weapon, or worn on the head, neck, or arm. Usu. in *pl.*, used collectively. See also HOSTEL sense 1 a, VIGILANTE. Cf. WITDOEK.

1990 *Weekly Mail* 14 Sept. 1 United Nations secretary general Perez de Cuellar has expressed serious concern about the role of security force members in the Reef violence as reports of collaboration between white men and Inkatha *rooidoeke* mounted this week ... Similar reports were received from Vosloorus township, where residents said police troop carriers had dropped off *rooidoeke* in the township when it was attacked on Tuesday night. **1990** 'HOGARTH' in *Sunday Times* 16 Dec. 20 He appeared on a public platform this week with Chief Mangosuthu Buthelezi to address an audience of armed men wearing red headbands. The sight of the two men together before the *rooidoeke* has been taken in the townships of the Transvaal as final, irrefutable proof of collusion between Inkatha and the police. **1991** L. KAUNDA in *Natal Witness* 28 Mar. (Echo) 1 Inkatha has also been accused of unleashing 'rooidoeke' (Reef hostel dwellers) on Reef township residents, which Inkatha has denied. **1991** *Sunday Times* 21 July 1 Did the police protect the 'impis' that attacked ANC supporters? Did the Casspirs guard the 'rooidoeke'?

rooi-els /ˈrɔɪ ɛls/ *n.* Formerly also **roode els, rood elze.** [S. Afr. Du. *roode* (later Afk. *rooi*) red + *els* alder.] The evergreen timber tree *Cunonia capensis* of the Cunoniaceae; the red-coloured wood of this tree; RED ALDER; RED ELS. See also ELS.

1801 J. BARROW *Trav.* I. 339 Roode els .. stands water well. [**1821** C.I. LATROBE *Jrnl of Visit* 559 Roth-els — *Cunonia Capensis.*] **1822** W.J. BURCHELL *Trav.* I. 143 Its colonial name is *Rood Elze* (Red Alder), although the tree has not .. the least resemblance to the Alder of Europe. **1913** C. PETTMAN *Africanderisms* 409 *Roode els,* .. *Cunonia capensis.* The flowers have a strong, sweet scent. **1932** *Farming in S. Afr.* July 128 (Swart), *Rooi Els* (*Cunonia capensis*), It occurs as a evergreen tree up to 50 ft. in height. **1948** *Cape Times* 5 Aug. 8 If trees must be planted, let them rather be the .. rooi els and other local forest trees. **1965** A. GORDON-BROWN *S. Afr. Heritage* II. 7 Other Cape woods used in old furniture, but seldom met with or recognized were olive wood, witte els, rooi els, camphor wood and pearwood. **1971** BARAITSER & OBHOLZER *Cape Country Furn.* 184 Early country cupboard of stinkwood, yellowwood and rooi-els showing canted corners and shaped apron. **1974** *Cape Times* 28 Sept. (Suppl.) 4 The indigenous woods — yellowwood, stinkwood, rooi-els, wit-els — are becoming more and more rare and costly. **1982** *S. Afr. Panorama* Feb. 20 Using indigenous woods such as stinkwood, yellow wood, tambotie, *wit els, rooi els* (white and red ash), mahogany, cedarwood and blackwood .. he also makes side tables, coffee tables, [etc.]. **1987** J. KENCH *Cottage Furn.* 20 Other local timbers used in tables included cedar, rooi-els and wit-els.

rooi-essenhout see ESSENHOUT sense b.

rooi ganna see GANNA sense 2.

‖**rooi gevaar** /ˈrɔɪ xəˈfɑː(r)/ *n. phr.* [Afk., 'red peril', *rooi* red + *gevaar* danger, peril; formed by analogy with SWART GEVAAR.] 'The red peril', communism; the political tactic of encouraging an unreasonable fear of communism; a communist. Also *attrib.* See also GEVAAR.

1972 *Cape Argus* 16 Sept. 9 Mr Pyper predicted the three 'emotional' fronts the National Party would employ were 'khakiegevaar, Swartgevaar, and rooigevaar'. **1981** *Daily Dispatch* 15 May 14 The 'rooi gevaar' is alive and well and living in Europe. The National Party's favourite scapegoat — when in trouble or doubt blame the communists — has its adherents in Britain and France as well. Two elections in the past week show, however, that the 'rooi gevaar' tactic is not a sure-fire guarantee of electoral success. **1987** 'K. DE BOER' in *Frontline* May 37 Even though I might be part of the rooi gevaar I remained an Afrikaner. **1990** *Sunday Times* 14 Oct. 22 Joe Slovo, the original *rooi gevaar*, debated freedom of religion with Professor John de Gruchy of UCT. **1991** D. CAPEL in

Personality 2 Sept. 20 'If the images are subliminal,' he said emphasising the if, 'the person or organisation responsible should be judged more harshly than any extreme terrorist group. Our minds have been screwed up by so many ideologies over the years, such as *die rooi gevaar* and *die Roomse gevaar.* Is technology now going to be used as well?' Blignaut asked.

rooigras /ˈrɔɪxras/ *n.* [Afk., *rooi* red + *gras* grass.] Any of several good pasture grasses of the Poaceae with a reddish tinge, esp. *Themeda triandra* but also species of *Cymbopogon* and *Hyparrhenia*; RED GRASS; ROOIGRASS. Also *attrib.*

[**1887** *S.W. Silver & Co.'s Handbk to S. Afr.* 158 There has .. been sent a specimen of pasture herb which, though not poisonous is said to be worthless. It is called Wilde rooi gras; this, though grass-like and called a grass, is a Trefoil or Clover, Trifolium angustifolium, the narrow-leaved trefoil.] **1906** [see SKAAPBOS]. **1916** *Farmer's Weekly* 20 Dec. 1519 Nothing in the world of veld food could beat 'rooigras' and 'Cynodon' for grass lands. **1929** J.W. BEWS *World's Grasses* 253 'Rooi gras' .. is a valuable forage grass. **1937** *Handbk for Farmers* (Dept of Agric. & Forestry) 159 A farmer .. having steekgras dominating his veld cannot follow the same system of grazing as the farmer who has rooigras dominant. **1950** *Cape Times* 30 Oct. 9 A.C. Erasmus scattered the first *rooigras* seeds in the .. bare land recently cleared. **1972** J.G. ANDERSON in *Std Encycl. of Sn Afr.* V. 320 A large number of species e.g. Guinea grass, .. rooigras, .. are important pasture grasses or are used as hay or silage. **1978** [see SWEET KAROO]. *c***1980** *S. Afr. 1979: Off. Yrbk* (Dept of Info.) 18 In the 'sweet' grassveld areas 'rooigras' (themeda) is the dominating grass, forming a dense sod in places. Where original 'rooigras' cover has been destroyed, less valuable species have taken over, e.g. 'steekgras'. **1987** *E. Prov. Herald* 24 Aug. 10 Rooigras needs undisturbed periods of about 90 days to recover from leaf removal after defoliation. **1990** R. MALAN *My Traitor's Heart* 288 She stopped occasionally to exclaim over a rare plant, or to point out a patch of rooigras, 'red grass'.

rooigrass /ˈrɔɪgrɑːs/ *n.* [Part. tr. Afk. *rooigras.*] ROOIGRAS.

1889 H.A. BRYDEN *Kloof & Karroo* 88 Much of the lower parts of these hills is clothed with rooi-grass. **1906** F. BLERSCH *Handbk of Agric.* 254 The best of the rooi grasses belongs to the genus *Anthistiria* it is closely related to the Australian kangaroo Grass, which is frequently recommended as a grass for pastures. **1907** T.R. SIM *Forests & Forest Flora* 37 The rushes have given place to rooi-grass. **1910** A.B. LAMONT *Rural Reader* 256 Rooi grass, with its open, spreading head, is one of the most valuable [native grasses], and takes its name from its red winter colour. *c***1911** S. PLAYNE *Cape Col.* 356 The veld is unrivalled for Angora goats .. the abundance of 'rooi' grass making it excellent for cattle. **1913** H. GLOSSOP *Barnes's S. Afr. Hsehold Guide* 316 In order of merit come 'Rooi' grass (similar, if not identical with the Australian Kangaroo grass), small quick grass, .. rib grass. **1933** W. MACDONALD *Romance of Golden Rand* 5 After toiling through the tall rooi grass, prickly thorns and the dense mimosa bush the Strubens finally arrived at the Hot Springs. **1966** C.A.W. GUGGISBERG *S.O.S. Rhino* 92 The dominant grass throughout the .. range of the southern white rhino is *Themeda triandra*, which stands quite high and is popularly known as 'rooigrass'.

rooihaas var. ROODE HAAS.

rooihout /ˈrɔɪhəʊt/ *n.* Formerly also **rood(e)-hout, roye-houtt.** [S. Afr. Du., *roode* (later Afk. *rooi*) red + *hout* timber.] Either of two trees of the Ochnaceae having red wood, *Ochna arborea* (also occas. called *Cape plane*), or *O. citropurpurea*; the wood of these trees. Also *attrib.*

1790 tr. *Le Vaillant's Trav.* II. 288 Another tree, called *Roye-houtt* (red wood) so named from its deep red colour, grows very thick. **1812** J.T. VAN DER KEMP *Acct of Caffraria* 63 There is a variety of timber, of which I will mention the names by which they are known in the Colony, viz. the geelhout, roodhout, .. and the gonjawood. **1896** E. CLAIRMONTE *Africander* 2 A flock of long-tailed mouse-birds .. would dash past to settle in a *rooihout* tree. **1913** C. PETTMAN *Africanderisms* 409 *Rooi hout,* .. *Ochna arborea,* one of the forest trees reserved by Government. **1973** *E. Prov. Herald* 28 May 13 No self-respecting woodcutter would have the handle of his axe made from any timber other than 'rooihout' (Cape plane) a reddish close grained wood from a tree which has bark like the garden guava and never reaches much more than 15 centimetres in diameter. **1973** J. VAHRMEIJER in *Std Encycl. of Sn Afr.* IX. 404 *Rooihout,* .. (*Ochna arborea*) ... The name rooihout is also applied to *Ochna atropurpurea.* **1977** E. PALMER *Field Guide to Trees* 220 *O. atropurpurea* Rooihout.

rooikat /ˈrɔɪkat/ *n.* Also **roodekat, roode katt, rooyekat.** [Afk., earlier S. Afr. Du. *roodekat*, fr. Du. *roode* red + *kat* cat.]

1. The caracal, *Felis caracal* of the Felidae, a fierce, lynx-like predator, esp. among sheep and poultry; RED CAT. Also *attrib.*

1786 G. FORSTER tr. *A. Sparrman's Voy. to Cape of G.H.* I. 150 There is another kind of cat, as it is called, the *roode kat*, the skin of which is in Africa universally supposed to possess a great medicinal power in the cure of lumbagos. **1796** C.R. HOPSON tr. *C.P. Thunberg's Trav.* II. 182 *Roode Katt* is the name here given to a kind of red lynx, with long locks of hair at the extremities of its ears, and the tip of its tail black. Pennant calls it a *Persian cat*, and Buffon *Caracal.* **1835** A. SMITH *Diary* (1940) II. 213, I am like an animal of the game kind with strong limbs like wood, legs like those of jackals, like those of (the) rooyecat. [**1890** A. MARTIN *Home Life* 217 Jackals, wild cats, lynxes — or, as the Dutch call them, *rooikats* — and numerous other four-legged free-booters pounce at night on those hens foolish enough to make their nests far from the comparative safety of the house.] **1905** W.L. SCLATER in Flint & Gilchrist *Science in S. Afr.* 126 The Caracal or Rooikat (*Felis caracal*) found throughout Southern Asia as well as Africa, approaches in some respect the Lynxes of the northern Hemisphere as regards its pencilled ears and the absence of the anterior upper premolar, but it has a long tail and no ruff round its neck. **1918** S.H. SKAIFE *Animal Life* 269 The caracal, or *rooi kat*, is widely distributed throughout South Africa, but is not common ... Although it is often called a lynx, it is not a true lynx, these only being found in the northern hemisphere. **1942** S. CLOETE *Hill of Doves* 622 The moths have got into my rooikat tails. **1958** [see SPOOR *v.* sense a]. **1958** A. JACKSON *Trader on Veld* 64 Of vermin, a large variety existed, especially the .. 'rooikat' (lynx). **1964** A. ROTHMANN *Elephant Shrew* 43 One day two tiny live rooikats were brought to the Museum. The rooikat's real name is *caracal* and it is also called *lynx* .. but nobody in South Africa seems to call it anything but rooikat. **1976** S. CLOETE *Canary Pie* 95 Augusta was slim, as clever as a rooikat. **1988** P. KINGWILL *Message of Black Eagle* 14 Daniel reported seeing the spoor of a big rooikat in Dam Camp on Monday and said he was going to set traps.

2. *transf.* With initial capital. An armoured combat-vehicle used by the South African (National) Defence Force.

1988 D.W. POTGIETER in *Sunday Times* 23 Oct. 21 The Rooikat, a new generation armoured combat vehicle .. is a formidable landmine-proof opponent, designed to take on nothing less than tanks. **1989** *Cape Times* 30 June, The new Rooikat, said to be one of the most advanced armoured cars anywhere. **1991** K. BENTLEY in *E. Prov. Herald* 21 Nov. 8 The ZA-35 is based on a slightly modified Rooikat (8 x 8) armoured car chassis. **1992** D.W. POTGIETER in *Sunday Times* 16 Aug. 10 The Rooikat, South Africa's much-vaunted armoured car, was launched in 1988 and had everything its designers planned — except a searchlight.

rooikrans /ˈrɔɪkrans/ *n.* Also **rooikrants, rooikrantz.** [Afk., *rooi* red + *krans* wreath, garland; named for its red seedstalk.] The invasive yellow-flowered tree *Acacia cyclops* of the Fabaceae. Also *attrib.*

1917 R. MARLOTH *Common Names* 71 Rooikrans, .. From Australia ... One of the Golden willows. **1920** *S. Afr. Smallholders' & Fruit Growers' Yr Bk* 175 Rooikrantz — A shrubby wattle useful for firewood. **1950** [see PORT JACKSON]. **1951** L.G. GREEN *Grow Lovely* 19 The great Melkbosch dune was halted as recently as 1936, after it had been zigzagged with marram grass and vygies and the rooikrantz seeds had germinated. **1955** [see PORT JACKSON]. **1963** A.M. LOUW *20 Days* 221 Silver trees supposed to be dying out. Too many cluster pines, rooikrans and wattle on the mountain these days. **1973** J. RABIE in S. Gray *Writers' Territory* 169 You take your saw and you go to cut down that dead rooikrants-tree you so often passed before. **1979** *E. Prov. Herald* 31 Oct. 13 One restaurant in Cape Town .. where meat will be grilled over open fires, bringing rooi kranz wood from his own farm. **1987** T.F.J. VAN RENSBURG *Intro. to Fynbos* 44 The following are the more important invader species in fynbos: .. Rooikrans *Acacia cyclops.* Imported from Australia in 1835 as an ornamental tree and later used for driftsand reclamation. **1992** *S. Afr. Panorama* Nov.-Dec. 8 Today two-thirds of the island are covered in exotic tree species such as rooikrans.

rooilaventel /ˌrɔɪləˈfent(ə)l, -la-/ *n.* Also **roode lavendel, rooi lavental, rooi leventel,** and with initial capital(s). [Afk., *rooi* (earlier *roode*) red + *laventel* lavender.] Tincture of lavender, a patent medicine; LAVENTEL. See also (*old*) *Dutch medicine* (DUTCH *adj.* sense 2).

1884 *B.G. Lennon & Co.'s Catal.* 65 Roode Lavendel, doz. 5s.0d. **1919** *Dunell, Ebden & Co.'s Price List* Oct. 20 Roode Lavendel 2/6. **1929** J.G. VAN ALPHEN *Jan Venter* 6 Particular Dutch patent medicines ... There was *Wit Dulcies* for indigestion, *Rooi Laventel* for fainting and headaches. **1931** [see DULSIES]. **1958** A. JACKSON *Trader on Veld* 30 To mention just a few of the favourites: Versterkde Druppels, Roode Lavendel, [etc.]. **1959** L. LONGMORE *Dispossessed* 157 Some educated mothers do not have faith in these doctors and use Afrikaans *druppels* to protect the baby, who is .. bathed in warm water containing drops of *rooi laventel* and entrance druppels which are considered to keep the baby strong and protect it from all dangers. **1972** N. SAPEIKA in *Std Encycl. of Sn Afr.* VII. 302 Rooilaventel (compound tincture of lavender). **1974** Y. BURGESS in S. Gray *On Edge of World* 23 She kept among other remedies, the *groenamare* for her cramps, .. and the *rooi laventel* for her heart. **1975** W. STEENKAMP *Land of Thirst King* 138 For many years the only formal medical help the average farmer possessed was what he called his 'apteek', or pharmacy, which consisted of a fitted tin trunk containing such time-honoured specifics as Hoffmann's Drops, a cough remedy known as 'Borstdruppels' (chest drops), .. 'Rooi Laventel' (lavender drops). **1988** D. SAMUELSON in *Fair Lady* 16 Mar. 125 Back in the kitchen, the child dutifully drank the glass of *rooi lavental* mixed by her grandmother. **1990** *You* 18 Oct. 34 The entire, natural GR Dutch Medicine range. The tried and tested Cape Dutch remedies like Jamaica Ginger, Rooi Lavental and Essence of life.

rooiman *n. obs.* Also **roodman, rooimann, rooman, rooy-mann,** and with initial capital. [S. Afr. Du. *roodeman*, later Afk. *rooiman, rooi* red + *man* man.]

1. ROMAN sense 1. Also *attrib.*

1790 tr. *F. Le Vaillant's Trav.* I. 32 Fish are very abundant at the Cape. Among those most esteemed, the principal are the *rooman*, a red fish found in the bay of Falso. **1798** S.H. WILCOCKE tr. *J.S. Stavorinus's Voy. to E. Indies 1768–71* I. 34 A kind of red fish, named *roomans* or *red men*, by the inhabitants of the Cape. *Ibid.* 560 The *Rooman*-fish .. is one of the most delicious that is caught; it is covered with light red scales. **1919** M. GREENLEES tr. *O.F. Mentzel's Life at Cape in Mid-18th C.* 81 The commonest kind of fish caught here is the so-called 'rooy-manns'. They retain their blood-red appearance even after they are boiled, and are about two feet long and proportionately heavy. *Ibid.* 101 There are days when steenbrass, rooimanns or galjoens cannot be had for love or money.

2. JAGSPINNEKOP. Cf. ROMAN sense 2.

1913 C. PETTMAN *Africanderisms* 412 *Rooiman,* .. A species of Solpuga found in the Karoo; it is a reddish colour and has claws not unlike those of a lobster. **1966** E. PALMER *Plains of Camdeboo* 233 On the farm we know .. the nocturnal species [of spiders] as Rooimans or Red Men, and of these latter I can neither think nor speak except in capitals.

rooineck /ˈrɔɪnek/ *n.* Often *derog.* Also **roineck.** [Part. tr. Afk. *rooinek.*] ROOINEK.

1918 C.G. CARTER *Informant, Westminster (OFS)* They seem very keen on getting out to S.A ... of course they think it is a snake ridden burnt up place, like all other rooi necks. **1933** W. MACDONALD *Romance of Golden Rand* 244 President Kruger .. rose heavily in his chair. 'I am going outside to speak to the rooinecks,' he said. [*Note*] Rooineck (redneck), nickname for an Englishman. **1969** VISCOUNT BUCKMASTER *Roundabout* 279 An English taxi-driver told me that he had lived for twenty years in Cape Town, only still to be called 'A bloody roineck', the name given to our troops in the Boer War.

rooinek /ˈrɔɪnek/ *n.* Also **roinek.** Pl. **-s**, occas. **-nekke** /-nekə, -nɛkə/. [Afk., *rooi* red + *nek* neck; see quots 1924 and 1945.] Esp. among Afrikaners (often *derog.*): an Englishman; an English-speaking South African; also used humorously and affectionately by English-speakers of themselves; REDNECK; ROOINECK; SOUTIE. Also *attrib.* See also KHAKI *n.* sense 1 b.

1891 J. KELLY *Coming Revolt of Eng. in Tvl* 6 Those were .. glorious times, when our gallant Burghers drove the *Rooi Neks* before them like sheep, and shot them down like rabbits. I was one of the stormers of Majuba. **1896** H.A. BRYDEN *Tales of S. Afr.* 210 Cornelis would open up, and yarn to me in a way that, until you know him well, the Boer seldom manifests to the *rooi-nek.* **1897** SCHULZ & HAMMAR *New Africa* 397 Rooi Nek, once a term of bantering endearment, has unfortunately lost its charm since it has been converted into a term of dislike by the Boers for the foreigner. **1899** 'S. ERASMUS' *Prinsloo* 14 One morning he was on the market with his waggon when two men – English Rooineks – came and said: 'Piet, do you want to make £15?' **1902** M'CORMICK in E. Hobhouse *Brunt of War* 97 We were the 'verdomte rooineks' (red-necks), and often they would say, 'You kill my father or brother at the war.' **1905** P. GIBBON *Vrouw Grobelaar* 39 He told us a story about a rooinek that bought a sheep, and the man gave him a dog in a sack, and he paid for it and went away, and we all laughed at it. **1913** C. PETTMAN *Africanderisms* 412 *Rooinek*, Originally a jocose Dutch name for an Englishman, subsequently used somewhat contemptuously, and occasionally preceded by a vigorous adjective. **1924** L.H. BRINKMAN *Glory of Backveld* 73 The word 'rooinek' (red-neck) is an epithet for 'Englishman,' due to the fact that, as a rule, an Englishman coming to South Africa, and unaccustomed to the hot, glaring sunshine, burns red in face, neck and hands. When a Boer addresses an Englishman by that epithet it is a sure sign that he is well disposed towards him and counts him as a friend, otherwise he would take no such liberties. **1928** L.P. GREENE *Adventure Omnibus* The Boer drew a revolver, which he levelled at Major's head. 'Hands up!' he growled in a harsh, gutteral voice. 'I say, Hands up, you verdoemte roinek!' **1945** N. DEVITT *People & Places* 144 The Englishman of the early 'eighties was dubbed 'Rooinek', because of the habit of the sundowner type of man to tramp the countryside humping his swag, wearing a cap which left his neck exposed to the hot sun. **1949** H.C. BOSMAN *Cold Stone Jug* (1969) 147 Of course no rooinek can make a living out of farming, unless they send him money every month from England. **1962** *Times* (U.K.) 6 Jan. 7 The [English] boys [at Sasolburg] were constantly taunted by school-mates as 'Pommie', 'Limey', and 'Rooinek'. **1963** S. CLOETE *Rags of Glory* 316 The Englishmen were sunburned, red as lobsters. They did not go brown like the Boers. That's why we call them rooineks – rednecks – Renata thought. **1972** *Daily Dispatch* 2 Feb. 6 That humour is full of nasty little racist jibes, which we South Africans have been listening to for the past 10 years, about Van der Merwe and the Rooinekke and 'a bantu'. **1973** *E. Prov. Herald* 8 Sept. 3 It's quite a thing being appointed commodore of a South African fleet, especially as I'm a rooinek. **1977** *Sunday Times* 7 Aug. (Mag. Sect.) 3, I mean, belonging to the minority white group, namely the English-speaking of the country, I'm only a 'rooinek' to the Afrikaner. **1983** F.G. BUTLER *Bursting World* 189 It was silly to refer to the people of South Africa, when there were clearly many peoples there – Afrikaners, and Zulus, and Pondos, and Rooineks. **1987** H. PRENDINI in *Style* Feb. 30 Typical of us unscrupulous rooinek reporters, I immediately jump to all sorts of subversive conclusions. **1992** M. CALITZ in *Weekend Post* 25 Apr. 13, I respectfully wonder whether your correspondent .. could be one of those 'rooineks' who have a paranoia about the English language.

rooi rhebok see RHEBOK sense b.

rooi rhebuck see RHEBUCK sense b.

rooi skimmel see SKIMMEL.

rooi steenbras see STEENBRAS sense b.

rooi tea /ˈrɔɪ tiː/ *n. phr.* [Afk. *rooi* red + Eng. *tea.*] ROOIBOS sense 1. Also *attrib.*

1968 *Farming in S. Afr.* July 17 Rooibos tea (*Aspalathus linegris*), or Rooitea as its improved descendant is known today, is a genuinely South African product. **1973** *S. Afr. Panorama* Apr. 14 Because Rooi tea is a perennial plant which adapts well to dry regions, it is continually being cultivated on a large scale ... The Nortier type is a selected and improved product of Rooibos tea, which produces a high and constant quality of rooi tea. **1982** *S. Afr. Jrnl of Science* Vol.78, 472 Rooi Tea Control Board, Clanwilliam.

rooivalk /ˈrɔɪfalk/ *n.* [Afk., earlier S. Afr. Du. *roodevalk, rooi* red + *valk* hawk, falcon.]

1. *obs.* Also **roode valk.** The rock kestrel *Falco tinnunculus* of the Falconidae, named for the deep red colour of its plumage.

*c*1808 C. VON LINNÉ *System of Natural Hist.* VIII. 74 *Mountain Kestrel*, This species is very common in the colony of the Cape, where it is called *roode valk* [*printed* rooge valk], red falcon, or *steen valk*, rock-falcon.

2. *Military.* Always with initial capital. A sophisticated combat helicopter with a very low vibration level, developed initially for the South African Air Force. Also *attrib.*

1991 *Natal Mercury* 2 Apr. 1 The Rooivalk was originally designed for the SAAF which needed a helicopter ground attack capability to counter Soviet equipment used by MPLA and Cuban forces in Angola. **1991** *E. Prov. Herald* 13 June 4 Rooivalk financing to continue ... Funding for the continued development of South Africa's tandem-seat Rooivalk combat helicopter is to be provided for at least the next 12 months. **1994** T. RALSTON in *Flying Springbok* Apr. 118 Just like a Rooivalk helicopter, it's a precision, high performance machine that links you to its soul.

rooker /ˈrʊəkə(r)/ *n. colloq.* Also **roker.** Ellipt. for DAGGA-ROOKER.

[**1946** C.P. WITTSTOCK in E. Partridge *Dict. of Underworld Slang* (1950) 563 A fine fellow: a reg rooker.] **1949** H.C. BOSMAN *Cold Stone Jug* (1969) 46, I got a thrill out of the thought that I was smoking dagga, and not out of the act ... But with the rookers it is different. *a*1951 —— *Willemsdorp* (1977) 81 The authorities might .. think as how I'm also a *roker.* That's what they calls among themselves a man that smokes it. **1967** *Drum* 27 Aug. 7 He is not yet a confirmed 'roker', having smoked the stuff about ten or twelve times, at random, over a period of three years. **1967** [see SKYF *n.*]. **1974** *Eng. Usage in Sn Afr.* Vol.5 No.1, 10 Here the common boop terms invariably have further significance for the *rokers* i.e. those who smoke *boom* (dagga – occasionally *weed* or *tree*). **1974** *Ibid.* [see STOP sense 1]. **1975** *Sunday Times* 9 Nov. 15 Then I saw the tattoo on her leg which she had shown me before she died. It read: 'Rookers don't sug,' which means 'dagga smokers don't worry'. **1977** D. MULLER *Whitey* 108 'Who are these people?' 'Outies, goffels, rookers. Old ones who have no place.' **1985** *Fair Lady* 6 Mar. 59, I started smoking with my sister and some of her friends and then began to mix with the rokers (dope smokers). **1985** [see STOP sense 1]. **1992** *South* 27 Feb. 7 When 10-year-old Ashley goes to the park, he doesn't spend time playing on the swings. Instead he huddles in a corner with the 'rookers'.

rooman var. ROOIMAN.

Roomse gevaar /ˌrʊəmsə xəˈfaː(r)/ *n. phr.* [Afk., 'the Roman peril', *Roomse* Roman + *gevaar* danger; prob. formed by analogy with SWART GEVAAR.]

In both senses, see also GEVAAR.

a. A derogatory reference to Roman Catholicism; also used ironically.

1965 *Informant, Grahamstown* So you're Anglican? I'm of the Roomse Gevaar. **1973** A. PATON *Apartheid & Archbishop* 47 The important N.G.K. journal, *Die Kerkbode*, to this day warns its readers against the *Roomse gevaar*, the 'Roman danger'. **1981** C. BARNARD in *Daily Dispatch* 9 Mar. 6 A few prejudices picked up in my youth .. were based mainly on dark warnings about the 'Roomse gevaar' (Romish danger).

b. An attitude of extreme prejudice towards the Roman Catholic Church. Also *attrib.*

1975 W. MARAIS in *Crozier* Nov. 1, I stood there with childhood memories of 'Roomse Gevaar' still echoing albeit softly, through my mind, with my arms linked .. with Catholic Pentecostals, Anglicans, nuns and laity. **1978** *TV Times* 14 May 3 This is a movie which may please the 'Roomse gevaar' campaigners. **1989** *Weekly Mail* 20 Oct. 33 The [Catholic] church's initial response was conciliatory, partly from fear of a government which .. espoused the *Roomse gevaar* mentality of the Dutch Reformed churches. **1991** [see ROOI GEVAAR].

rooster cake *n. phr. Obs.* Also **roster cake.** [Part. tr. Afk. *roosterkoek.*] ROOSTERKOEK sense a.

1871 E.J. DUGMORE Diary. 11 Our diet is principally coffee and tea, rooster cakes, porridge, rice and a little meat. **1896** M.A. CAREY-HOBSON *At Home in Tvl* 79 One day, Mrs. Herbert taught me how to make roster cakes (a roster means a gridiron).

roosterkoek /ˈrʊəstə(r)kʊk/ *n.* Also **roestekoek, roostekoek, rooster cock, roster-koek, roster-kook.** Pl. unchanged, or **-s.** [Afk., *rooster* grid (iron) + *koek* cake.]

a. A bread or dough cake, leavened or unleavened, baked on a grid-iron over a fire; ROASTER-CAKE sense b; ROASTER COOKIE; ROOSTER CAKE; ROOSTERKOEKIE. Cf. COOKIE.

*a*1878 J. MONTGOMERY *Reminisc.* (1981) 53 The old people were very dark, but they received me kindly, soon made a big rooster cock (griddle cake) and grilled some meat. **1880** O.E.A. SCHREINER in C. Clayton *Woman's Rose* (1986) 16 When she went to the house her mistress gave her a whole roosterkoek for her supper, and the mistress's daughter had stuck a rose in the cake. **1911** D.B. HOOK *'Tis but Yesterday* 16 Marie had everything in readiness – 'roosterkoek' (scones), coffee, biltong, which were all stored in the front wagon-box. **1913** W.C. SCULLY in F.G. Butler *When Boys Were Men* (1969) 250, I had brought in my pocket a lump of *roster-koek* (a lump of unleavened dough, flattened out and roasted on a gridiron). **1920** [see BILTONG sense 1]. **1936** C. BIRKBY *Thirstland Treks* 241 He ate .. *roosterkoek*, dampers made of sour dough, and over cups of the Afrikaners' black coffee he heard their tales of misfortune. **1941** A.G. BEE *Kalahari Camp Fires* (1943) 179 Taking a blanket, coffee, sugar .. 'rooster-koeks', meat, a shot gun, .. he followed. **1950** H. GERBER *Cape Cookery* 47 Both Vetkoek and Roosterkoek were made either with unleavened dough or with a dough leavened with suurdeeg. **1964** L.G. GREEN *Old Men Say* 133 These old aias .. are treated with great respect. They can bake .. *roosterkoek.* **1978** *Sunday Times* 5 Mar. (Mag. Sect.) 3 The women had made roosterkoek and soetsuurdeeg bread. Then they served homemade apricot jam. The wine, dry and tart, was made in the district. **1986** C. KIRSTEIN *Best S. Afr. Braai Recipes* 80 Bread .. can be a traditonally South African 'cook-over-the-coals' bread such as 'roosterkoek'. **1992** G. ETHERINGTON in *Weekend Post* 9 May (Leisure) 4 There was freshly baked brown bread and *roosterkoek*.

b. ASKOEK sense 1.

1900 B.M. HICKS *Cape as I Found It* 170 The coffee is the most delicious you ever tasted in your life — the roestekoeks, too, that have been roasting on the 'coals'. **1977** *Fair Lady* 8 June (Suppl.) 37 There's plenty for big beef eaters in braaivleis country, chops, homemade boerewors, sosaties, mealiepap and roosterkoek cooked in the ashes.

roosterkoekie *n. obs.* Also **rooster koekje, ro(o)ster-kookie.** [Afk. (earlier *roosterkoekje*), *roosterkoek* (see ROOSTERKOEK) + dim. suffix -IE.] ROOSTERKOEK sense a.

1870 *E. Prov. Herald* 2 Aug., I have tried my hand at baking 'rooster koekjes', and made a bucketful, which have turned out first-rate. **1883** J. EDWARDS *Reminisc.* 53, I had .. meal to fall back upon, with which to make 'rooster kookies,' that is, cakes without leaven, baked on the gridiron. **1913** C. PETTMAN *Africanderisms* 414 *Rooster koekjes*, .. Cakes of unleavened bread cooked on a gridiron over the coals of a wood fire. [**1913** *Bk of Recipes* (Diocesan School for Girls, Grahamstown) 59 *Roostje Cookies*, 1lb. flour. 1 heaped tablespoon baking powder. Mix with water into a soft dough. Roll out about $\frac{1}{2}$inch thick. Cut into squares and toast on a gridiron. Serve hot with plenty of butter.] **1920** F.C. CORNELL *Glamour of Prospecting* 51 Every few days I would bake a batch of 'roster kookies', little flat cakes made of the same meal with a little baking-powder to make this rise, and baked over the embers on a 'roster', or gridiron. **1937** H. KLEIN *Stage Coach Dust* 210 They filled their pockets with 'rooster koekies' (baked scones), .. and climbed the embankment to the great steel bridge.

rooster koekje, -kookie varr. ROOSTERKOEKIE.

rooti(e) var. ROTI.

rooyebok, rooyekat varr. ROOIBOK, ROOIKAT.

rooy-mann var. ROOIMAN.

rope *n. Derog.* and *offensive. slang.* [Fig. use of Eng. *rope* line or cord made of twisted strands; see quot. 1975.] A contemptuous and insulting name for an Afrikaner; occas., a coarse person.

1970 B. KIRK-COHEN *Informant, Pietersburg* Ropes. Afrikaners. **1972** on Radio South Africa 1 Apr. (Forces Favourites), To all the ropes in Bungalow 1a, don't worry about your girls, the corporals will take care of them. **1975** F.G. BUTLER *Informant, Grahamstown* Rope. An extreme case of a Rock Spider, but not necessarily Afrikaans speaking, in fact, most are English-speaking — thick, coarse, twisted, hairy and bitter. **1982** *Informant, Grahamstown* Rope. Afrikaans-speaking person. Derogatory (thick, twisted, hairy).

rori baajte var. ROOIBAADJIE.

rosindje var. ROSYNTJIE.

roster cake, roster kookie var. ROOSTER CAKE, ROOSTERKOEKIE.

roster-koek, -kook varr. ROOSTERKOEK.

‖**rosyntjie** /rə'seɪŋki/ *n.* Also **reseintje, rosindje, rosijnte, rozijntje, rozyntje.** [Afk., fr. Du. *rozijn* raisin + -IE.]

1.a. A raisin. **b.** Any of several small, raisin-like fruits, esp. the fruit of plants of *Grewia* spp., or of *Rhus lancea*. See also *kareebessie* (KAREE *n.*[2] sense 3), KRUISBESSIE.

1844 J. BACKHOUSE *Narr. of Visit* 548 An old woman kindly refreshed us with sour milk, and gave the people plenty of Rozyjntjes, *Little Raisins*. **1913** C. PETTMAN *Africanderisms* 415 *Rozijntjes*, .. The small fruit of *Grewia Cand., Sond.* **1981** *Fair Lady* 28 Jan. 3 (advt) Who wants a skin that looks like a 'rosyntjie'? **1987** B. LAU *Namibia in Jonker Afrikaner's Time* 63 To make brandy, a liquid was pressed from 'reseintje' berries (which had formerly been a staple foodstuff, being very nutritious).

2. *comb.* **rosyntjieboom** /-buəm/ [Afk., *boom* tree], the tree *Rhus popullifolia*, having fruits which, when ripe, resemble raisins; **rosyntjiebos** [Afk., *bos* bush], or part. tr. **rosyntjie bush** (occas. simply *rosyntjie*), either of two shrubs with raisin-like fruits (a) the MORETLWA, *Grewia flava*, or (b) *Rhus lancea* (see KAREE *n.*[2] sense 1 a i); **rosyntjiehout** (also **-houd**) [S. Afr. Du., *hout* wood], **-tree**, see *rosyntjieboom*.

1970 D. VAN ZYL *Informant, Postmasburg* The rosyntjieboom grows well in the Kalahari. [**1872** rosyntjiebos: E.J. DUNN in A.M.L. Robinson *Sel. Articles from Cape Monthly Mag.* (1978) 49 The islands are .. to a considerable extent covered with a dense jungle of willow, rosindje, .. and blue bush.] **1897** [see SWARTHAAK]. **1917** R. MARLOTH *Common Names* 71 Rosijntes'bos, .. *Grewia cana, G. flava.* The drupelets possess a little sweet pulp and resemble small currants. Used by the Natives for beer making. In some districts also species of *Rhus*, e.g. *R. viminalis.* **1955** L.G. GREEN *Karoo* 133 Then there is the rosyntjiebos or brandy-bush, often five feet high, with flowers like yellow stars and a fruit about the size of a pea. 'Mampoer brandy' is made by crushing this fruit, adding water so that it ferments and then distilling the mixture. **1968** *Farmer's Weekly* 3 Jan. 7 Grazing in good condition with Olienhout, vaalbos, rosyntjiebos, suurkaree and mixed grazing. **1944** H.C. BOSMAN in V. Rosenberg *Almost Forgotten Stories* (1979) 73 And the delicate green of the **rosyntjie bush** that grew just to the side of the school-building within convenient reach of the penknife of the Hollander schoolmaster, who went out and cut a number of thick but supple canes every morning just after the Bible lesson. [**1789** W. PATERSON *Narr. of Four Journeys* 113 The banks of the river produce lofty trees peculiar to this country, such as Mimosa, Salix, and a species of Rhus, called by the Dutch, **Rezyne Houd**.] **1934** P.R. KIRBY *Musical Instruments of Native Races* (1965) 154 They are made from tiny river-reeds, plugged with fibre, and tuned with thin twigs of *rosyntjehoed* (*Grewia caffra* ?), called by the Bushmen ≠*oū*. **1966** C.A. SMITH *Common Names* 403 *Rosyntjiehout*, .. The vernacular name was first recorded by Paterson (1779) as Rosynehoud and the name was no doubt derived from the ripe fruits which resemble raisins. **1870** R. RIDGILL in A.M.L. Robinson *Sel. Articles from Cape Monthly Mag.* (1978) 34 Most of its sacred hours were spent beneath the grateful shade of the thorn, willow, and **rozyntje trees** which border the river.

roti /'rɔti/ *n.* Formerly also **rooti(e)**. [Hindi and Urdu, 'bread'.]

1. Indian flat-bread or chupatti, cooked (unleavened) on a flat surface. Also *attrib.*, and *transf.*

Also used in W. Indian and Indian Eng.

1903 D. BLACKBURN *Burgher Quixote* 59 'Oh,' says he 'the whiskey is a great healer, and I am nearly well, and if I have some more of it, with some rooti and beef, I shall be all right.' **1961** L. MAYAT *Indian Delights* 126 Roti is unleavened bread made of either white flour or unsifted boermeal with a little shortening, but instead of being baked they were toasted over griddles until they were freckled gold. **1971** *Leader* 7 May 9, (advt) My roti's the best is good enough ... That's why I use only Bakers Homo Flour for my roti. **1978** *Voice* 8 Nov. 7A Pour a little of melted butter or margarine around the edge of the roti to prevent sticking. Flip over and brown on other side. **1986** F. KARODIA *Daughters of Twilight* 9 She was too hot, too bothered and too put out by what Yasmin had said. She fixed her attention on the roti dough. **1988** E. MPHAHLELE *Renewal Time* 101 As for Indians, they like their curry and rice and *roti* and money and mosques and temples too much to pretend they want us for next-door neighbours. **1990** E. DE LA HARPE in *Staffrider* Vol.9 No.2, 65, I am moved by dove-people proffering roti charity. **1992** G. RADOWSKY in *Weekly Mail* 24 Apr. 30 Her matchless salamies, rotis containing a choice of bean, mutton, mince or chicken curries, enjoy an almost religious following among local office workers, labourers and denizens of the nearby 'Malay quarter' of Bokaap.

2. *comb. slang.* Esp. among South Africans of Indian descent: **roti ou**, a Hindi-speaker. See also CHAR OU, OU *n.* sense 2 b.

1978 L. BARNES in *The 1820* Vol.51 No.12, 19 The Afrikaans word *ou* seems to have caught on in Natal just as much as in other parts of the country. There are chaar ous (Indians); roti ous (Hindi speakers) — this name is obviously derived from the fact that roti, a type of flat bread, was an important part of the diet of certain Hindi-speaking Indians. **1986** [see CHAR OU]. **1992** R. MESTHRIE *Lexicon of S. Afr. Indian Eng.* 116 *Roti-ou n.* A male of North Indian origin, in whose household *roti* .. is traditionally a favoured preparation.

roukoop var. ROUWKOOP.

round-ribbed Afrikander *n. phr.* [tr. of Afk. *ronderib Afrikander.*] RONDERIB. Also **round-rib Afrikander.**

1961 L.E. VAN ONSELEN *Trekboer* 138 The merino does not take kindly to this part of the country. The Trekboer has found it necessary to breed a bastardized version of the round-rib Afrikander and the Karakul. **1970** W.J. HUGO in *Std Encycl. of Sn Afr.* I. 182 These Hottentot sheep .. gradually evolved into two distinct types: one, a broad-tailed sheep of the Cape, later known as the Round-ribbed Africander; and the other, the Namaqua Sheep. **1975** [see VAN ROOY].

rouwkoop /'rɔukuəp/ *n. Law.* Also **roukoop.** [Du. *rouw* (Afk. *rou*) regret, mourning + *koop* purchase.] Money which, having been paid as a deposit, is forfeited if a sale falls through; money paid as compensation for a broken contract.

1934 C.P. SWART *Supplement to Pettman.* 147 *Rouwkoop*, .. Forfeit money. **1960** J.J.L. SISSON *S. Afr. Judicial Dict.* 703 *Rouwkoop*. May sometimes mean 'something given to break the bargain'. **1961** C.I. BELCHER *Norman's Law of Sale* 354 Where a sum .. given as a deposit in part payment of the purchase price can be clearly proved, in terms of the requirements laid down in the authorities, to be *arrha*, roukoop or earnest, it is forfeited to the vendor if the sale falls through due to default on the part of the purchaser and forms a portion of the purchase price if the sale goes through. **1977** *Sunday Times* 30 Oct. 1 On these grounds he could have made a claim of roukoop (forfeit of the deposit).

roy-buck var. ROOIBUCK.

roye-houtt var. ROOIHOUT.

rozijntje, rozyntje varr. ROSYNTJIE.

RSA *n.* [Initial letters of *Republic of South Africa.*] South Africa. Also *attrib.*, South African. Cf. SA *n.*[1]

[**1973** J.C. GOOSEN *S. Africa's Navy* 191 Until the Department of Transport's supply ship RSA was brought into service, most of the voyages were routine trips.] **1974** *S. Afr. Panorama* Nov. 41 The need for a single comprehensive and authoritative work of reference on the RSA has long been experienced. **1981** *Rand Daily Mail* 13 Apr. 3, 19-year-old Daniela D—, of Durban, was crowned Miss RSA at a glittering function in Cape Town on Saturday night. **1983** [see NATIONAL STATE sense 1]. **1984** D. BECKETT in *Frontline* Feb. 32 The 'RSA Government' had no real interest in the homelands until about five years ago. **1986** [see BOEREMUSIEK sense 2]. **1990** SCHEEPERS et al. in *Armed Forces* Nov. 12 The operational concept behind the light infantry is to have a rapidly deployable force that can be utilised from cross border strikes to acting as a binding force in case of a conventional attack on the RSA. **1991** T. SISSON *Just Nuisance* 150 Citizens of the RSA, from the Cape Peninsula, Johannesburg, Durban, Port Elizabeth, East London, and many other towns and cities of the Republic.

RSC *n.* Initial letters of *Regional Services Council*, a regional body created in terms of Act 109 of 1985 to represent all municipalities in a region, and to coordinate the provision of services. Also *attrib.*

1985 P. BELL in *Business Day* 15 May 6 Next in line are the Regional Services Councils (RSCs); the new super-councils of the third tier ... RSC chairmen will in turn by appointed by the Provincial Administrators, themselves Presidential appointees. **1986** P. CULL in *E. Prov. Herald* 24 Nov. 2 The PFP chairman .. stated that the RSCs were a new structure designed to co-opt groups and individuals, and extend apartheid in a more subtle and effective way. **1987** *New Nation* 2 Apr. 7 The RSCs are part of a sophisticated attempt to meet the demands for a non-racial democracy half-way. **1987** *Weekly Mail* 28 Aug. 10 Unlike the tri-racial parliament for whites, coloureds and Indians, RSCs do not exclude blacks. Nor are blacks nominated to serve on the RSCs, as they are in the reshaped provincial executives. But .. white paramountcy or control is built into the RSCs. **1988** *Race Rel. Survey 1987–8* (S.A.I.R.R.) 121 It was envisaged that the entire country would be divided into RSCs although the exact number to be established was not known. The proposal was that the Transvaal would have 12, the Cape 14 and the Orange Free State 10. **1993** *Sn Argus* 12 Aug. 1 Mud dumped by RSC threatens marine life.

rubber duck *n. phr. Colloq.* [Used also in Australian and U.S. Eng. (usu. as *rubber duckie*), but its origin is uncertain.] An inflatable flat-bottomed rubber dinghy, often motorized; DUCKIE *n.*[2] Also *attrib.*

1986 *Motorist* 3rd Quarter 14 The Tugela Challenge is thought to be the longest in the world for inflatables — 'rubber ducks'. **1989** L. GOODLIFF in *Weekend Post* 25 Nov. 6 This week is your last chance to win a rubber duck and accessories in our Weekend Post Kretz Marine win-a-boat competition. **1990** *Daily Dispatch* 10 Sept. 5 (*caption*) Lionel and Nadia Endersby .. watch the Gonubie rubber duck challenge on Saturday.

Hence **rubber ducker** *n. phr.*, the pilot of a rubber duck; a rubber duck enthusiast.

1994 R. OLIVIER in *E. Prov. Herald* 30 Aug. 3 The near-fatal injury of livesaver Wayne Willets, gashed on the head by a dingy at the mouth of the Swartkops River at the weekend, has rekindled the feud between rubber duckers and surfers over right of way ... The river mouth .. has been a bone of contention between surfers and rubber duckers for some time.

rubbish *n. colloq.* Pl. unchanged. [Special use of Brit. Eng. *rubbish* (used only as a noncount n.). In S. Afr. Eng., the word is used as though both sing. and pl.] An unsavoury character. Also *attrib.*

1941 'R. ROAMER' in *Bantu World* 15 Feb. 5 If this Jeremiah rubbish left me thinking I would starve, he was mistaken. **1961** M.A. WALL *Dominee & Dom-Pas* 20 The Chief Commissioner of Police will be here — I *hope* he will give us orders to shoot *dead* all these rubbish! **1971** J. MCCLURE *Steam Pig* (1973) 32 Truly artistic people — as opposed to the rubbish at the university — were so often the retiring sort. **1981** [see Sunday Times quot. at GEMORS sense b]. **1984** *Drum* July 22, I dug my fingernail into his arm and whispered, 'You are a rubbish. Keep your eyes on her face — not on her exposed thighs'. **1989** E. BREGIN *Kayaboeties* 35 She turned to Peter. 'And next time, you bladdy rubbish, *ask* before you swipe my new mattresses!' she bellowed, making us all jump. **1990** G. EVANS in *Weekly Mail* 27 Apr. (Suppl.) 6 As an only child living with his mother there was always the risk of me turning into either a 'nancy' or the biggest rubbish on two legs.

Rubicon *n.* [fr. general Eng. idiom 'to cross (or pass) the Rubicon' to take a decisive or final step; alluding to P.W. Botha's use of this expression in his speech.] Often in the phr. ***Rubicon speech.*** Used to allude to a speech made by President P.W. Botha in August 1985, in which he was expected to announce substantial reform in government racial policies, but failed to do so. Often used ironically. Also *attrib.*

1986 *Race Rel. Survey 1985* (S.A.I.R.R.) p.xxvii, The failure of the State President, Mr P W Botha, to live up to expectations that he would announce significant reforms in his August 'Rubicon' speech in Durban led to increased dissatisfaction with the government internationally and in business and opposition circles in South Africa. **1989** *Sunday Times* 31 Dec. 18 His [*sc.* Mr P.W. Botha's] Rubicon speech of 1985 knocked South Africa down to Third World status and made inevitable the imposition of far-reaching sanctions in 1986. **1990** *Weekly Mail* 2 Feb. 1 According to the NP source, .. Pik Botha was 'terrified of a Rubicon repeat' and wanted Nelson Mandela to be released on Monday January 29 — a move which the cabinet came close to accepting. **1990** A. BERRY in *Ibid.* 12 (*cartoon caption*) So cut out the *finger* business and any mention of taking Mandela across the *Rubicon!* **1990** B. RONGE in *Sunday Times* 16 Dec. (Mag. Sect.) 6 Connoisseurs of political catastrophe will surely get a subtle, arcane thrill out of owning the nail-clipper that groomed the fatal Botha finger that set us over the Rubicon and into social and economic chaos. **1991** [see GAPS]. **1991** A. VAN WYK *Birth of New Afrikaner* 100 P.W. Botha's so-called Rubicon speech .. was as unseemly and untimely an exhibition of *kragdadigheid* (power play) as a brawl at a prayer meeting. **1993** C. CROCKER in *Sunday Times* 16 May 25 This speech offered a welcome contrast to the Rubicon precedent. **1994** J. LANE in *Style* Oct. 22 It was the early eighties and PW Botha had not yet encountered the Rubicon. **1995** J. SMITH on Radio South Africa 12 Jan. (Newsbrief), The days of the Rubicon and the state of emergency — difficult days.

||**ruggens** /ˈrəxəns, ˈrœxəns/ *pl. n.* [Afk., fr. Du. *rug* back, down, ridge, saddle, spine + pl. suffix *-(g)ens*.] Downs; undulating hills.

Also used as an element in place-names, e.g. *Swartruggens.*

[**1862** LADY DUFF-GORDON *Lett. from Cape* (1925) 154 But the atmosphere here won't do after that of the 'Ruggens' as the Caledon line of country is called.] **1867** *Blue Bk for Col. 1866* JJ15, More rain fell during the last quarter than during some previous years, and on the ruggens rather than on the forest range. **1872** [see RHENOSTERBOS sense 1]. **1912** *S. Afr. Agric. Jrnl* July 35 (Pettman), In the Bredasdorp District ... the real lamziekte veld is said to lie between the dunes and the *ruggens.* The disease is not known in the *ruggens*, where the veld is sweet. *c***1936** *S. & E. Afr. Yr Bk & Guide* 37 *Rug*, pl. ruggens — undulating slopes, unirrigated hilly country. **1967** E. ROSENTHAL *Encycl. of Sn Afr.* 473 *Ruggens*, .. Literally backs or ridges. Closely packed hills in rolling country, which occurs in various parts of the Cape, including Caledon and Bredasdorp. They are usually fertile.

rugger-bugger *n. slang.* [Eng. *rugger* rugby + *bugger* (see note at BUGGER on the use of this word in S. Afr. Eng.] An aggressively masculine (young) male, fanatical about sport, enthusiastic about group drunkenness, chauvinistic towards women, and usually partial to all-male gatherings; BUGGER sense 1 a; RB. Also *attrib.* See also MAN *n.*[2] sense 1 a.

1970 *Forum* Vol.6 No.2, 59 Roared with laughter they did, foolishly as any rugger-buggers. **1975** *Fair Lady* 1 Oct. 67 The boy's father may have been, in local parlance, a ruggerbugger who did nothing more strenuous in the house than call for another beer. **1983** *Grocott's Mail* 18 Feb. 13 *Rugger-bugger*, .. (1) A person who wears shorts in Winter. (2) Person who adopts the 3-P's philosophy: pubcrawls, piss-ups and puking. (3) A term used by Lefties to label anyone who disagrees with them. (4) A Person who takes a rugby ball to bed. **1985** [see BUNGI]. **1989** J. HOBBS *Thoughts in Makeshift Mortuary* 145 The student body divided quite neatly into four factions: the studious, the rugger buggers, the social set and the lefties. **1990** T. SEALE in *Weekend Argus* 9 June 6 I'm sure that like many people on the periphery of the game I had a picture of rugby players as rugger-buggers, but they are really extraordinary people with political opinions that lean mainly towards the left of South African politics. **1991** *Personality* 18 Mar. 14 Lets get down to a bit of hard core rugger-bugger talk now as we 'ambush the pub and slaat a coupla pints over a bit of comm' (go to the pub and have a few beers and a chat).

Hence **rugger-bugger** *quasi-adj.*, of the life-style of rugger-buggers; **ruggerbuggerdom** *n.*, the state of being a ruggerbugger.

1983 *Grocott's Mail* 18 Feb., *The Vic*, (n.) Night-time haunt of those inclined towards ruggerbuggerdom with an aptitude for weaving between lamp-posts and trees late at night on foot. **1990** J. MICHELL in *Style* Nov. 62 At the top of our list, because it was recommended so often, is *The Cattleman* which, we were warned, is 'rather rugger bugger'.

ruiter *n. obs.* Also **ruyter.** [Afk., fr. Du. *ruyter.*] A horseman. Also *attrib.*

Used in *Brit. Eng.* 1579–1702 (*OED*).

1809 H. ALEXANDER in G.M. Theal *Rec. of Cape Col.* (1900) VI. 477 The landdrost shall have for his due assistance in his office a Clerk and two Police Ruyters to be paid by Government. **1809** R. COLLINS in *Ibid.* (1900) VII. 143 The mail was formerly carried by the messenger or the mounted police ruiter from the drostdy of Swellendam to the place of the veld commandant Petrus Lombard. **1947** C.R. PRANCE *Antic Mem.* 97 Some of the few horsemen still left in disguise as South African 'Ruiters'.

Ruiterwag /ˈreɪtəvax, ˈrœitərvax/ *n.* [Afk., *ruiter* horseman, cavalryman + *wag* (fr. Du. *wacht*) guard.] The junior wing of the BROEDERBOND (sense 1). Also *attrib.*

1972 *Sunday Times* 23 Apr. 3 Dr Treurnicht's election reflects the grave unease of conservative members in both the Broederbond and the Ruiterwag (junior wing of the Broederbond). **1974** *E. Prov. Herald* 17 Oct. 18 Bitterly hostile to the National Party, the Broederbond, the Ruiterwag, the Rapportryers and the Afrikaans Press. **1981** *Sunday Times* 15 Feb. 2 Made up of men in their twenties or early thirties, the Ruiterwag observes a strict code of secrecy. It is regarded as a kind of kindergarten to test the commitment of members to exclusive Afrikaner causes. **1985** *Ibid.* 3 Mar. 12 My name appeared in the list of Ruiterwag members published in the Sunday Times of February 3. **1990** *Ibid.* 15 July 2 His early career followed a path that should have taken him to the very top of the political heap — leader of the National Party youth movement, president of the Junior Rapportryers, president of the Ruiterwag (the youth wing of the Broederbond).

ruměela, ruměla varr. DUMELA.

rups see quot. 1786 at RUSPER.

rusbank /ˈrəsbaŋk, ˈrœsbaŋk/ *n.* Also **rus'-bank, rust-bank.** Pl. **-s, -e** /-ə/, and formerly **-en.** [Afk., *rus* (Du. *rust*) rest + *bank* bench.]

1. A long wooden settle with back and seat made usu. of woven leather thongs (see RIEMPIE *n.* sense 1 a), but also occas. of cane. Also *attrib.*

1868 W.R. THOMSON *Poems, Essays & Sketches* 167 With a waive [*sic*] of the hand in the direction of the *rustbank* — the sofa, or apology for it — at the other end of the room, she says '*Zit!*' **1882** J. NIXON *Among Boers* 202 You are requested to place yourself on the seat of honour or 'rustbank', which is a long seat, something like what is called the 'lang settle' in Yorkshire. **1894** E. GLANVILLE *Fair Colonist* 96 They went into a cool front room, plainly furnished with Madeira-made cane chairs for coolness, and a *rustbank*, or couch of thongs interwoven. **1902** W. DOWER *Early Annals of Kokstad* 25 The few very rough seats and the rust banken .. were occupied by the men, the women sat on the floor. **1910** D. FAIRBRIDGE *That Which Hath Been* (1913) 301 Caught sight of the worthy burgher, and crossing the room, sat down next to him on the *rust-bank.* **1910** *Ibid.* [see HUISVROU]. **1939** S. CLOETE *Watch for Dawn* 29 How alike all these Boer houses were. Each had the same rough, home-made riempie-seated rus-banks, the same beds, the same tables. **1948** H.C. BOSMAN in L. Abrahams *Unto Dust* (1963) 58 There am I sitting on the rusbank next to her, wearing my best clothes and my veldskoens rubbed smooth with sheep's fat. **1965** M.G. ATMORE *Cape Furn.* 77 At all times the rusbank has been a 'multiple chair' in which the form was copied from the single chair of the time. **1971** BARAITSER & OBHOLZER *Cape Country Furn.* 101 Although Cape country rusbanks are mainly similar in style to Cape chairs, the spindle chair and transitional Tulbagh chair have no complete counterpart in rusbanke. **1971** *Daily Dispatch* 8 Sept. 18 Old Rusbank-type Lounge Suite. **1987** G. VINEY *Col. Houses* 102 The stinkwood *rusbank* is Cape eighteenth-century.

2. *transf.* A brick or plaster seat built into the end of the verandah of a Cape Dutch house. See also STOEP sense 1 a.

1910 D. FAIRBRIDGE *That Which Hath Been* (1913) 229 Drowsily smoking on the brick *rust-bank* at the end of his high stoep. **1915** — *Torch Bearer* 157 The stoeps were paved with large red tiles or blue slates, and some of them were rounded off with gracefully carved rust-banks. **1935** P. SMITH *Platkop's Children* 76 After that was a long white house with a big stoep an' rus'-banks at each end.

‖**rusper** /ˈrəspə(r)/ *n.* Also **risper, ruspe**. [Afk., ad. Du. *rups* caterpillar.] Any of several caterpillars which are destructive to crops, esp. the American bollworm, *Heliothis armigera*, and the Karoo caterpillar (see KAROO sense 3), *Loxostege frustralis*.

[**1786** G. FORSTER tr. A. Sparrman's *Voy. to Cape of G.H.* II. 174 A worm with legs and feet, which was grey at top, but yellow under the belly, like *rups*, or caterpillars.] **1906** *E. London Dispatch* 26 June (Pettman), The caterpillars, which are very like the destructive *rispers* familiar to residents in the Karoo, have already killed a large number of trees in this neighbourhood. **1930** H.C. BOSMAN *Mafeking Rd* (1969) 64 We all shook hands and said it was good weather for the mealies if only the *ruspes* didn't eat them. **1974** *E. Prov. Herald* 16 Feb., There are areas where the Karoo bush has still not recovered from the long dry spells and attack from ruspers. **1980** [see KAALGAT sense 2]. **1980** A.J. BLIGNAUT *Dead End Rd* 95, I reckoned he should talk less about ruspes and more of my share of what they left behind to go into the bottle.

Russian *n.* and *adj.* [Unkn.; but see Venter quot. 1977.]

A. *n.* Usu. in *pl.*

1. *hist.* A member of a blanketed gang of Sotho men which terrorized townships in the Johannesburg area from the 1940s. Also *attrib.*

1951 *Drum* Oct. 8 A favourite device of the Russians is to use a woman to attract their victim. **1952** *Ibid.* May 37 Russians wear black blankets with white stripes and a white or black hat with an ostrich feather, and gaberdine trousers ... They carry sticks, which are hollow in the centre for screwing an axe, which they call a 're-inforcement.' ... Most Russians are Basutos but many other tribes are to be found among them. **1960** C. HOOPER *Brief Authority* 293 Worse than Russia-gangs. [*Note*] Gangs of Basuto, mostly in the urban areas round Johannesburg, who attacked Africans of other tribes, driving them from their homes, and popularly known as 'Russians'. *a*1968 [see FAMO sense 1]. **1971** [see sense B]. *a*1977 K.M.C. MOTSISI in M. Mutloatse *Casey & Co.* (1978) 103 To the south of Western Native Township vibrates Newclare, home of the faction fight-happy blanketed Basutos, known as 'Russians'. **1982** *Pace* Nov. 16 We .. fear the police and 'Russians'. If it is not the police who raid us we are attacked by the 'Russians' who drink our liquor and rape us. **1984** M. MTHETHWA in *Frontline* July 30 There is one name which brings cold fear to their spines. The name is 'Russians', but you do not have to travel as far as Russia to see these Russians. They are the blanket-clad Sotho men who carry decorated sticks, which they use with great dexterity and without any hesitation or regret. **1988** *Daily Dispatch* 29 July 23 'The Russians' are a gang of blanket-clad men who habitually carry knobkerries.

2. *transf.* In these townships: any Sotho person.

1974 *Sunday Times* 20 Oct. (Mag. Sect.), The South Sotho, known in Soweto as the 'Russians' because of their distinctive blanket dress, have built a reputation for wild parties. **1977** P.C. VENTER *Soweto* 184 He says my mother's parents were real Russians. That is what we call the South Sotho people, because of the way they wear their blankets. **1989** *Reader's Digest Illust. Hist.* 390 Evaton's desperately poor Basotho group — called the 'Russians'. **1990** M. MELAMU in *Lynx* 275 Hlalele was a member of a notorious gang of Basuto men who were known as the 'Russians'. It was not quite clear how they had acquired that name, but it had stuck to Basuto men working in Johannesburg ... We came to associate the name 'Russians' with violence. **1990** P. GARSON in *Weekly Mail* 8 Feb. 7 The ANC supporters allege .. that various black policemen living in Uptown have aligned themselves with Azapo and have recruited the Basothos or 'Russians' to protect them.

B. *adj.* *hist.* Of or pertaining to the Sotho gangs of the townships in the Johannesburg area.

1963 L.F. FREED *Crime in S. Afr.* 115 The way a Native goes 'Russian' is simple and yet disturbing. *Ibid.* 116 The 'Russian' movement started originally among the Rand Basuto — especially among the mine boys — somewhere about 1948, and it has been growing in strength ever since. **1971** *Post* 24 Oct. 2 Russian gang battle leaves 3 dead. Three men were shot dead and two others wounded at Delmore Station, East Rand when two rival gangs of blanketed 'Russians' fought it out yesterday.

Hence **Russianism** *n.*, the gangster lifestyle adopted by some of the Sotho youth; **Russianized** *adj.*, transformed into a 'Russian'.

1952 *Drum* May 39 Treat the Basuto well and fairly in all walks of life and you will put an end to Russianism. **1963** L.F. FREED *Crime in S. Afr.* 115 Natives who are normally quiet and peace-loving have been known to become 'Russianised' in an instant, once the order has been given by the gang leader.

ruyter var. RUITER.

Rxd var. RD.

ryksdaalder var. RIJKSDAALDER.

rympie var. RIEMPIE *n.*

rysmier /ˈreɪsmiːr/ *n.* Also **rijst mier**. Pl. **-e** /-ə/, and (formerly) **-en**. [Afk., *rys* (Du. *rijst*) rice + *mier* ant.] BUSHMAN RICE.

[*a*1884 E. WIGGILL in J.K. Larson, Talbots, Sweetnams & Wiggills. (1953) 22 These ants are about half an inch long. Their nests are underground, about the size of a bushel basket. Their nest is full of eggs, which the natives eat like rice; they call them 'Race Mera' (rice ant).] **1899** *Cape Argus Weekly* 27 Sept. 40 The officials .. would require a little elementary knowledge of natural history, so as to be able to distinguish between the genuine article [*sc.* locusts' eggs] and other things approaching it in likeness, such as rice-ants, or 'rijst mieren,' tampans, ticks, or Kafir-corn. **1913** C. PETTMAN *Africanderisms* 402 *Rijst mieren*, .. The bodies of the *Termites*, which are so named, are not unlike a grain of rice, while their eggs resemble it more closely still. **1955** L.G. GREEN *Karoo* 104 Having secured your *rysmiere*, throw them into lukewarm water and they will float. Other ants, which may be mixed with them but which are not so tasty, will sink. Dry the *rysmier* in the wind and grill in a frying pan. Keep the abundant fat which is given out, this is Namaqualand's most valued ointment for sores, bruises and burns. **1967** [see BUSHMAN RICE]. **1975** W. STEENKAMP *Land of Thirst King* 132 Veld food of rather a different kind can be found in the termites known colloquially as 'rysmiere' or rice-ants. This used to be a popular dish, and never mind what you are told by Namaqualanders of one race or another who have risen to higher station and conveniently forgotten the armies of rysmiere which have vanished down their gullets. **1979** HEARD & FAULL *Our Best Trad. Recipes* 38 Ants — Rysmiere ... How do you serve grilled ants? Spread them on bread and butter.

S

sa /sɑ/ *int.* Also **saa, sah, sar**. [Prob. fr. 17th C. Du. *sa* at him, come on (cf. Fr. *ca*, used (repetitively) to incite an opponent in fencing, and obs. Eng. *sessa*, used to rouse fighting dogs).] An exhortation used to urge dogs (or, less frequently, other animals or people) to attack; TSAA.

Often used repetitively.

1790 tr. F. *Le Vaillant's Trav.* I. 71, I had been told that .. I must not say *saa, saa*, for that word would render the beast furious, and that he would rush on the person that uttered it ... I .. repeated the word for a hundred times together, by the way of encouraging the dogs, and likewise to drive the beast from the thicket. **1899** G.H. RUSSELL *Under Sjambok* 86 He was still on the leash, and could hear their cries of 'sar, sar' (a South African term used to hiss on a dog). **1941** G.H. GALPIN *There Are No S. Africans* 361 In the midst of this morning disaffection, with the fear of fifth columnists lurking in every block of flats, the cry of 'Sa, sa' ('Catch him, catch him') was heard. **1946** S. CLOETE *Afr. Portraits* 41 He was asked if he would lead the Boers, and said, 'When I have a hunting dog, and I say "Sah," he attacks. I am not yet certain if the people are ready — if I say, "Sah," that they will fight'. **1969** A. FUGARD *Boesman & Lena* 39 Then they must run. It will chase you too. Sa! **1986** J. CONYNGHAM *Arrowing of Cane* 9 'Sa Brutus!' The boxer — he is too much his own to be called *my* — plunges into the bugweed from the dirt road. **1989** F.G. BUTLER *Tales from Old Karoo* 152 His two dogs did not come bouncing up to welcome Henry; they were waiting next to Stoffel, as if expecting to be sent into action on the word 'Sa!'

Hence **sa** *v. intrans.*, to go in to the attack.

1982 *Sunday Times* 19 Sept. 25 After I heard one of the men tell the dogs to 'sa!' they attacked me.

SA /es 'eɪ, 'es eɪ/ *n.*¹ and *adj.* Also **S.A.** [Initial letters of *South Africa(n)*.]

A. *n.* South Africa. Cf. RSA. Also *attrib.*

[**1864** *Notes & Queries* (U.K.) 6 Feb. 117 Cape Town, S.A. **1891** W.S. CHURCHILL in R.S. Churchill *Winston S. Churchill* (1967) I. 270 Mama has got a big map of S.A. on which she follows your route.] *c***1936** *S. & E. Afr. Yr Bk & Guide* 138 Central Government under the S.A. Act, 1909. **1983** A. GOLDSTUCK in *Frontline* Feb. 44 Many of SA's top band managers are also record company executives. **1983** [see PROG]. **1987** *Weekly Mail* 17 July 7 (*advt*) Ideal for: Journalists .. Academics .. SA watchers. **1993** on Radio Algoa 22 Sept., (*advt*) *You* [magazine] tells all about the love-affair that shocked S.A.!

B. *adj.*

1. SOUTH AFRICAN *adj. phr.*

*c***1936** *S. & E. Afr. Yr Bk & Guide* 46 A South African Students' Club was formed, in 1920, in London, to provide a social centre for all S.A. Students of European descent. **1961** L.C.F. TURNER et al. *War in Sn Oceans* 143 French and Malagasy troops surrendered a strong position .. after bombardment by the 16th S.A. Field Battery. **1977** C.L. VILJOEN in B. Marks *Our S. Afr. Army* 7 The SA Army will execute the task of landward defence with one aim only: to not only win every battle, but to win the war! **1987** *New Nation* 6 Aug. 1 The NUM has indicated that the strike could be the costliest and biggest in SA mining history.

2. Commonly used as a first element in special collocations: see SAA, SAAF, SABC, SABRA, SABS, SABTA, SACC, SACP, SACTU, SADF, SANDF, SANSCO, SANTA, SAP, SAPA, SAPS, SAR, SARB, SAS, SASO, SATOUR, SATS, SATV, SAWAS, SAYCO.

S.A. *n.*² *obs.* The written abbreviation of *Senior Advocate*, for a short time the name given to one who had 'taken silk'; now called SC. See also ADVOCATE.

1961 *Rand Daily Mail* 1 Dec. 3 Dr. P. Yutar, S.A., with him Mr. G.M. Israel, appeared for the appellant State. Mr. A. Mendelow, S.A., with him Mr. Gordon, appeared for .. the respondent.

saa *int.* var. SA *int.*

SAA /es eɪ 'eɪ/ *n.* Also **S.A.A.** [Initial letters of *South African Airways*.] The largest commercial airline, the national carrier. Also *attrib.* See also SATS.

1940 [see SAAF]. **1951** *Rand Daily Mail* 2 Nov. 9 Although statistics show that they are the lowest-paid airline men in the world, S.A.A. pilots have an international reputation for 'above the average' flying ability. **1958** *Ibid.* 4 Mar. 9 At the airport. Departures. S.A.A: To Durban 7.45. a.m. **1971** *Personality* 4 June 99, I rather think that SAA will lose the battle to have the new aircraft termed 747 or superjet rather than jumbo. **1984** *S. Afr. Panorama* Feb. 2 SAA was the first airline in the world to incorporate its automated reservations system into a single centralised computer. Its SAAFARI system (South African Airways Fully Automated Reservations Installation) incorporates not only all cities on SAA's domestic route network, but practically all stations worldwide. **1987** J. CLARKE *Like It Was* 105 In February 1934 .. the Government named the enterprise South African Airways ... S.A.A. then began operating the first regular over-the-border flights from Rand Airport as far north as Kisumu, Kenya. **1990** C. ROGERS in *Style* Oct. 70 When you come upon a load of men with Jumbo *boeps*, *trackies* and *takkies*, drip-dry and crimp, all clutching clutch bags, you're back in South Africa even before you put your feet on SAA.

Saab var. SAAP.

SAAF /es eɪ eɪ 'ef, sæf/ *n.* Also **S.A.A.F.** Initial letters of *South African Air Force*. Also *attrib.*

1940 *Star* 2 Mar. 12 The machines transferred from the S.A. to the S.A.A.F. are unsuited to our military requirements, being too large, too slow, too expensive and inadequately armed either for offence or defence. **1941** C. BIRKBY *Springbok Victory* 103 The troops on the ground saw the S.A.A.F. helping them throughout the operation. Our bombers came over early on Dingaan's Day and plastered El Wak. **1944** 'TWEDE IN BEVEL' *Piet Kolonel* 101 The sporting soldier-girl (transferred to the S.A.A.F., and unaccountably dressed in yachting clothes). **1945** S. DE WET *Shifty in Italy* 107, I .. was distracted by a young S.A.A.F. officer, a trifle merry. **1961** L.C.F. TURNER et al. *War in Sn Oceans* 100 The survivors from *Brandford City* .. wrote food and water in large letters on the beach, and on their second day a S.A.A.F. aircraft saw them and dropped its crew's emergency rations. **1979** *Paratus* Jan. 27 The SAAF also provides a valuable service to the Caprivi government when it provides aircraft to assist in game counting from the air. **1987** *S. Afr. Digest* 10 July 8 The inter-war history of the Union Defence Force was largely one of retrenchment and economy. In 1920, however, the South African Air Force (SAAF) was founded. **1990** *Sunday Times* 30 Sept. 13 The SAAF's Second World War Spitfire .. has changed hands again — this time fetching a whopping R2 587 000 at an auction in the United States.

saaidam /'saɪdam/ *n.* Formerly also **zaaidam**. Pl. **-me** /-mə/, **-s**. [Afk., *saai* sow + *dam* see DAM.] A basin of agricultural land enclosed by a low earth embankment which retains flood water for irrigation; occas., an embankment built for this purpose. Also *attrib.*

*c***1911** S. PLAYNE *Cape Col.* 678 The valley below the dam in the old days was utilised for cereal crops, the water being applied on the *zaai-dam* principle when the floods were out, and after a thorough soaking the crops were sown ... The other dam .. consists of an enormous depression through which the waters flow, advantage having been taken of the natural level to turn it into a huge *zaaidam*. **1925** R. DEAKIN *Southward Ho!* 79 The raising of crops with the help of *saaidams* .. would transform the scene. **1933** STAMP & JAMIESON *World* 227 In the Union there are four main ways of irrigating land ... (4) By the system of 'warping' or 'Zaaidams'. Flood water, rich in alluvium, is allowed to spread over the land, and the deposit of silt is then ploughed in. **1937** MARAIS & SIM in *Handbk for Farmers* (Dept of Agric. & Forestry) 704 The so-called 'saaidam' system is practised. Flood water is guided over level terraces surrounded by low walls, in which the water is allowed to stand and soak into the soil. When the soil has been sufficiently soaked the remaining water is guided on to a lower terrace. As soon as the soil is workable it is ploughed over and sown. The crop then often grows to maturity without further irrigation. **1955** L.G. GREEN *Karoo* 224 The saaidam is simply a low embankment thrown across a flat valley or plain to delay the flow of water and ensure sufficient moisture in the soil for the germination of a crop. **1961** M. COLE *S. Afr.* 129 The alluvial lands are divided by earth walls into basins or 'saaidams', which are irrigated in turn by the passing flood waters. **1972** L.G. GREEN *When Journey's Over* 58 Alluvial flats lend themselves to saaidam farming, an unpredictable yet tempting enterprise. **1972** D.F. KOKOT in *Std Encycl. of Sn Afr.* V. 445 There is considerable irrigation, including the unique system whereby flood-water is diverted into shallow basins, known as 'saaidamme'. **1975** *Std Encycl. of Sn Afr.* XI. 422 In the North-Western Cape wheat is grown on saaidams.

saaly var. SALIE.

saamie var. SARMIE.

saamsmelting var. SAMESMELTING.

Saan *n.*¹ var. SAN.

Saan /sɑːn/ *n.*² [Khoisan.] See quot. 1969. See also HEIKUM.

1969 J.M. WHITE *Land God Made in Anger* 225 Other groups in South West include the seldom-seen River

Bushmen, .. and the so-called Saan people. The latter are an ancient stock, taller and darker than the normal Bushman, who linger on in a small tribe called the Heikom. **1976** O. LEVINSON *Story of Namibia* 25 Only one tribe survived – the Hei//om (men who sleep in the bush) – generally incorrectly classed as Bushmen but who in fact are the last survivors of the Saan tribe.

Saap *n. obs.* Also **Saab**. [Khoisan.] A name used of themselves by the San people: see SAN sense 1.

1801 W. SOMERVILLE *Narr. of E. Cape Frontier* (1979) 74 A bosjesman has been seen ... They call themselves Saap – sometimes Canna. **1830, 1876** [see SAN sense 1].

saasaatie var. SOSATIE.

saasie var. SYSIE.

SABC /es eɪ biː ˈsiː/ *n.* Also **S.A.B.C.** Initial letters of *South African Broadcasting Corporation*, a statutory body established in 1936; AUCKLAND PARK. Also *attrib.*

1940 *Star* 2 Mar. 15 Another concert by the combined orchestras of the Johannesburg Symphony Society, African Consolidated Theatres and the S.A.B.C. will be relayed from the Colosseum Theatre on both the Johannesburg transmissions tomorrow. **1956** *S. Afr. Panorama* No.1, 25 The S.A.B.C. plans an extensive service for all our neighbours in Africa from the Cape to Cairo. **1961** D. MARAIS *Hey! Van der Merwe, (cartoon caption)* As you know, Van der Merwe, the Minister does not interfere in the affairs of the SABC, but he suggests that you cut out the sardonic laugh when you say 'Here is the news'. **1971** *Seek* June 8 What will television in South Africa be like? A depressing thought is that it will be directed by the SABC which is directed by Dr Piet Meyer, chairman of the Broederbond and a verkrampte. **1982** D. TUTU *Voice of One* 43 You are brainwashed by the South African Broadcasting Corporation (SABC) which constantly misleads you as it does its propaganda work for the Nationalist Party. **1987** K. CARLEAN in *Grocott's Mail* 31 Mar. 1 Answering a question on SABC coverage of the election, Mr Moorcroft said the National Party was using the corporation 'quite unashamedly' as a propaganda arm. **1988** G. SILBER in *Style* May 65 Since South Africans of all colours and creeds agree that the SABC test pattern is by far the most exciting thing on television, its adoption as a cross-cultural emblem in a country where no-one agrees on anything else is surely long overdue. **1990** *Weekend Mail* 13 July 9 Broadening the SABC from being the voice of the National party to being the voice of the South African people. **1992** *Natal Mercury* 3 Jan. 2 'The SABC appears to be simply proceeding with unilateral restructuring regardless of the political processes underway,' said the ANC. **1993** *Weekly Mail* 4 June 1 Despite the much-publicised 'openness' of the SABC board selection process, neither the government nor the selection panel will discuss their hours of intense horse-trading.

sa'bon(a) var. SAWUBONA.

Sabra /ˈsæbrə, ˈsabra/ *n.* Also **SABRA, S.A.B.R.A.** [Acronym formed on *South African Bureau of Racial Affairs.*] An organization established as a 'think-tank' on racial matters for the National Party (within the ideological framework of separate development). Also *attrib.*

1952 L.E. NEAME *White Man's Afr.* 60 Sabra – as it is called for short – has devoted a great deal of time and study to the problem. **1956** M. ROGERS *Black Sash* 140 The nature of S.A.B.R.A. – the South African Bureau of Racial Affairs – was examined and discussed. **1961** Z.J. DE BEER *Multi-racial S. Afr.* 32 Certain Nationalist intellectuals, mainly identified with a body called SABRA (South African Bureau for Racial Affairs), gave very strong support to the apartheid ideology .. on the basis that it would be complete partition. **1970** *Survey of Race Rel.* (S.A.I.R.R.) 14 Sabra has again pressed for a more speedy and radical programme of separate development than the Government envisages. **1973** [see FAK]. **1974** C.J. JOOSTE in *Std Encycl. of Sn Afr.* X. 91 *South African Bureau of Racial Affairs* (Sabra). Independent, non-profit-making organization established in 1948 with the twofold aim of promoting harmonious relations between the different peoples of South Africa, and their development in the political, economic and other spheres. The separate development of peoples is its declared policy and on that basis it seeks to promote peaceful co-existence in the subcontinent. **1974** *E. Prov. Herald* 20 July 2 Officials had tea or shook hands with Blacks in order to protect the white nation, the Director of Homelands .. said ... He assured 165 Afrikaner schoolchildren at the Sabra Youth Congress that it was not an infringement of apartheid – 'it's a sacrifice for the sake of the people'. **1987** *Race Rel. Survey 1986* (S.A.I.R.R.) 174 Professor Boshoff.. explained that while SABRA mirrored the traditional viewpoint and stand of the Afrikaner, anybody from another white group would be welcome in SABRA. **1989** *Reader's Digest Illust. Hist.* 491 *South African Bureau of Racial Affairs* (SABRA), NP 'think-tank' on racial affairs. **1990** D. CALDWELL in *Frontline* Sept. 24 Pleased by February's unbannings? Well, if the ANC got power, it would ban 'the NP, CP, AWB, HNP, Afrikanervolkswag, SABRA, [etc.]'.

SABS /es eɪ biː ˈes/ *n.* Initial letters of *South African Bureau of Standards*, a statutory body established in 1945 to standardize testing procedures in industry and commerce; freq. *attrib.*, esp. designating a mark displayed on manufactured goods which meet the required standards of the Bureau.

[**1953** *Off. Yrbk of Union 1950* (Bureau of Census & Statistics) 1024 The Standards Act No. 24 of 1945 ... An Act to promote the standardization of commodities, and the manufacture, production, processing or treatment of commodities, and for that purpose to establish a South African Bureau of Standards.] **1970** *News/Check* 15 May 3 Any product bearing the SABS label is sure to conform to high standards of safety and reliability. c**1980** *S. Afr. 1979: Off. Yrbk* (Dept of Info.) 523 The SABS is partly financed by parliamentary grant and partly by income earned by means of inspections and tests. **1987** *E. Prov. Herald* 2 June 5 Less ice, more prawns with new SABS rule. **1988** D. DANNHAUSER in *S. Afr. Panorama* Apr. 3 The South African Bureau of Standards (SABS) was established as a statutory body by Act 24 of 1945.

Sabta /ˈsæbtə/ *n.* Also **SABTA.** [Acronym formed on *South(ern) African Black Taxi Association.*] An organization formed in 1979 to represent the owners and drivers of 'minibus taxis' (see TAXI sense 1). Also *attrib.*

1985 *Race Rel. Survey 1984* (S.A.I.R.R.) 434 Both the Transvaal taxi association and its mother-body, SABTA, experienced internal conflict during the year. **1990** *E. Prov. Herald* 19 Jan. 2 A spokesman for the company confirmed that only 'about 15% to 20%' of Sabta's taxis were covered by it [*sc.* insurance]. Sabta represents more than 90% of all taxi owners in South Africa. **1991** N. MBATHA in *Pace* Feb. 39 Mike Ntlatleng of Sabta's public affairs office said ... 'The Katlehong taxi war started over a dispute about the routes between operators from the Germiston and District Taxi Association .. , a Sabta affiliate, and the Katlehong Taxi Association.' **1992** *Race Rel. Survey 1991–2* (S.A.I.R.R.) 366 SABTA, which was formed in 1979, claimed in May 1991 to have a total of 68 910 members and to enjoy about 58% of the black taxi market.

saca bona var. SAWUBONA.

sacaboola var. SAKABULA.

SACC /es eɪ siː ˈsiː/ *n.* Initial letters of *South African Council of Churches*, the name (since 1968) of an organization formed in 1936 to represent a number of (Protestant) churches, and concerned particularly with issues of social justice. Also *attrib.*

The SACC was formerly known as the Christian Council of South Africa. It is affiliated to the World Council of Churches.

1978 *Survey of Race Rel.* (S.A.I.R.R.) 196 The SACC's Division of Justice and Reconciliation urged that churches in SA and overseas cease further investment in SA unless the .. code of ethics .. be accepted. **1981** *Rand Daily Mail* 26 Feb. 1 SACC takes defiant stance. **1987** *South* 3 July 1 The debate followed a decision by the World Council of Churches in Lusaka last month – backed by an SACC delegation – that the use of force to overthrow apartheid is morally justified. **1991** *Weekly Mail* 24 May 3 It has now become clearer that the SACC initiative has been to try to convince De Klerk that his conference will not achieve its goals.

saccabula var. SAKABULA.

sachabona, sackaboni varr. SAWUBONA.

sack-milk *n. obs.* [See quot. 1913.] MAAS sense 1.

1786 G. FORSTER tr. *A. Sparrman's Voy. to Cape of G.H.* I. 239 We went to pay a visit to the community of Hottentots assembled on this spot, who received us very friendly, and invited us to drink some of their *sack-milk*. **1795** C.R. HOPSON tr. *C.P. Thunberg's Trav.* I. 197 Here we were refreshed, thirsty as we were, with Hottentots sack-milk, as it is called, which, perhaps, few travellers, unless urged by extreme thirst, will be able to prevail on themselves to taste. It is a very acid, cool, and refreshing milk. [**1828** W. SHAW Diary. 25 Feb., After all the cows had been milked, and the Milk, as usual poured into the leather sacks, we had a good opportunity while they waited for fermentation of the milk to hold Divine Service.] **1913** C. PETTMAN *Africanderisms* 417 *Sack milk*, .. The earlier colonial name for what is now known as Sour milk or Amasi ... It was commonly prepared in a bag made of the skin of a goat or sheep – hence the name.

SACP /es eɪ siː ˈpiː/ *n.* Also **S.A.C.P.** [Initial letters of *South African Communist Party.*] A political party formed (illegally) in 1953 as a successor to the Communist Party of South Africa (see CPSA *n.*[2]). Also *attrib.*

Unbanned in 1990, the SACP became part of the Government of National Unity in 1994.

1963 *Afr. Communist* No.3, 15 Like the A.N.C., we of the S.A.C.P ... regard as our 'immediate and foremost task' a united front of national liberation. **1971** *Ibid.* No.46, 77 Message of the South African Communist Party ... Delivered by J.B. Marks, Chairman of the S.A.C.P. **1977** J. SIKAKANE *Window on Soweto* 77 The leadership of such organisations as the ANC-SA, PAC and SACP (Communist Party) were either in jail or exile. **1983** *E. Prov. Herald* 26 Sept. 3 Top SACP man buried in London. **1986** [see FREEDOM CHARTER sense 1]. **1987** *Nusas Talks to the ANC (pamphlet)* 19 We were told that the SACP has been .. involved in the South African political struggle for 65 years since its formation in 1921. **1990** [see INSPAN *v.* sense 2]. **1991** *Sunday Times* 7 Apr. 20 Nor does the old ANC-SACP-Cosatu alliance look nearly as solid as it did.

Sactu /ˈsækt(j)uː/ *n. hist.* Also **SACTU, S.A.C.T.U.** [Acronym formed on *South African Congress of Trade Unions.*] A labour federation formed in 1955 as the trade union wing of the *Congress Alliance* (see CONGRESS sense 3). Also *attrib.*

Sactu's leadership operated from exile after the banning of the African National Congress in 1960. After the ANC was unbanned in 1990, Sactu was integrated into COSATU.

1959 M. HORRELL *Racialism & Trade Unions* 23 The *S.A. Congress of Trade Unions* (S.A.C.T.U), furthest to the left, .. had mixed, Coloured and African affiliated unions. **1963** M. BENSON *Afr. Patriots* 237 In mid-1957 .. Lutuli and the A.N.C. called for a stay-at-home on June 26 in protest against apartheid and in support of a S.A.C.T.U. call for £1 a day basic wage. **1966** *Survey of Race Rel. 1965* (S.A.I.R.R.) 238 The left-wing S.A. Congress of Trade Unions (Sactu) has, in the past, allied itself with the A.N.C. and other members of the (political) Congress Group ... The Security Police have continued to raid Sactu's offices from time to time. **1969** A. HEPPLE *S. Afr.: Workers under Apartheid* 71 Sactu became a consultative member of the Congress

Alliance ... By 1961, Sactu had 46 affiliated unions, representing 53,323 members, of whom 38,791 were Africans. **1980** LUCKHARDT & WALL *Organize or Starve!* 92 The aspirations of progressive trade unionists from all parts of South Africa were finally realized on 5 and 6 March 1955 in Johannesburg at the Inaugural Conference of SACTU. **1990** *Weekend Argus* 17 Feb. 4 He held posts in Sactu and has been outside the country since the '70s.

saddle *v. obs.* [Special uses of general Eng.]

1. In the phr. ***to saddle off*** [ad. OFF-SADDLE by the transposition of the two elements], OFF-SADDLE *v.*

a. *intrans.*

1835 T.H. BOWKER Journal. 19 Jan., Saddle off in the edge of the Bush lose the horses. **1839** W.C. HARRIS *Wild Sports* 329 The mention of 'Sillekat's land,' while it elicited an oath, and an exclamation of surprise, procured me also an invitation to 'saddle off'. **1913** C. PETTMAN *Africanderisms* 418 *Saddle off, To,* See Off-saddle.

b. *trans.*

1835 J.W.D. MOODIE *Ten Yrs* I. 65 He .. asked us if we would 'saddle off' our horses. **1871** J. MACKENZIE *Ten Yrs* (1971) 259 He had not met with any game, and after some hours' search, had saddled off his horse to let it graze for a few minutes before returning to the waggons. *c*1881 A. DOUGLASS *Ostrich Farming* 203 When travelling, if the horse is saddled off every two hours, even if only for a few minutes, to allow him to stale, and is not allowed to drink water whilst hot, he will seldom hurt in South Africa.

2. *intrans.* In the phr. ***to saddle up*** [ad. UPSADDLE by the transposition of the two elements], UPSADDLE sense 2.

Also used elsewhere. The general Eng. transitive sense 'to put a saddle on (a horse)' occurs widely in *S. Afr. Eng.*

1836 J. COLLETT Diary. I. 14 Feb., Having had heavy rains yesterday the Rivers began rising so that fearing I shd not cross I saddled up & rode off but was too late. **1849** E.D.H.E. NAPIER *Excursions in Sn Afr.* II. 12 When you wish to depart, your order is to 'saddle-up'. **1852** *Trial of Andries Botha* 24, I then saw some confusion where Boko was, and I saddled up, and went down into Fort Armstrong. **1882** C. DU VAL *With Show through Sn Afr.* I. 228 Accompanied by Fry, my comrade we 'saddled up' and left the capital of Natal at a little past the midnight hour. **1882** LADY F.C. DIXIE *In Land of Misfortune* 333 The order to saddle up and begin the homeward journey was given. **1925** D. KIDD *Essential Kafir* 9 After a short rest, we 'saddle up' and continue our journey.

Hence **saddling-up** *vbl n.*

1849 E.D.H.E. NAPIER *Excursions in Sn Afr.* II. 12 Another term of Colonial import is that of 'saddling-up,' and 'off-saddling.'

SADF /es eɪ diː ˈef, ˈsædəf/ *n. hist.* Also **S.A.D.F.** [Initial letters of *South African Defence Force.*] The collective name of the armed forces or their personnel. Also *attrib.* See also DEFENCE FORCE, and note at that entry.

[**1957** *Act 44* in *Stat. of Union* 530 The South African Defence Force shall consist of — (a) the Permanent Force; (b) the Citizen Force; and (c) Commandos.] **1971** *Std Encycl. of Sn Afr.* III. 601 The S.A.D.F. ... is subdivided into the South African Army, the South African Air Force and the South African Navy, known as the Arms of the Force. **1980** *S. Afr. 1980: Off. Yrbk* (Dept. of Foreign Affairs & Info.) 328 Non-Whites are not liable for compulsory military service but are employed in the SADF on a voluntary basis. **1984** *Daily Dispatch* 9 Oct. 1 The Minister of Law and Order .. announced last week that SADF forces would be used in a support role for the police in the black townships as a 'rationalisation' measure. **1987** F. VAN ZYL SLABBERT in *Leadership* Vol.6 No.3, 22 Riot and unrest led to the SADF moving from the 'border' into the townships supporting the police on a continual basis. The distinction between Police and Army became blurred and the role of the latter totally politicised. **1988** E. MCDONALD in *S. Afr. Panorama* May 8 Armscor supplies the SADF with almost 150 different types of ammunition, which vary from small hand rifles to enormous aircraft bombs. **1991** [see Pauw quot. at SECUROCRAT]. **1991** H. GRANGE in *Star* 1 Nov. 5 Failing to respond to call-up instructions has become an increasing problem for the SA Defence Force, according to SADF spokesmen. **1993** C. KHAN in *Africa S. & E.* Mar. 17 There is a very strong feeling among senior SADF officers .. that in a future defence force the core will be the SADF, with all other armed forces .. being absorbed into it. **1994** J. CONTRERAS in *Newsweek* 7 Nov. 14 Most of the instructors are former members of the South African Defense Force (SADF) who fought alongside UNITA guerrillas.

sadza /ˈsʌdzə/ *n.* Also **sadze, sudsa, sudza.** [Rhodesian (now Zimbabwean) Eng., fr. Shona.] STYWE PAP.

1949 C. BULLOCK *Rina* 224 Tell the carriers to clear out a sleeping-place for us in the big 'house'; then they can make their own camp and cook their sadza. **1950** *Cape Times* 3 June (Weekend Mag.) 2 Manaas had gorged himself with *sadza* and his little stomach was distended. **1962** F.C. METROWICH *Scotty Smith* 219 He told the driver to ask the Bushman if he would like some 'sadza'. This was a very stodgy mealie-meal porridge and there was a large three-legged pot of it. **1968** L.G. GREEN *Full Many Glorious Morning* 170 Of course the great indispensable food of Rhodesia is sadza. You don't know sadza? Maize, the kernel you had in your soup tonight. **1970** *Forum* Vol.6 No.2, 44 Better still was dipping balls of steaming grey sadza which you had rolled in one hand, (it had to be one hand to keep the other free) into a pot of gravy and meat. **1987** *Weekly Mail* 23 Oct. 19 In 1966 John Omer-Cooper published *The Zulu Aftermath*, .. a seminal work for its time, demonstrating to a prejudiced and complacent academic community that black South Africa did have a history of their own, and that they did not spend all the years before Van Riebeeck sitting around, eating *sadza*, and waiting for the whites to arrive. **1990** E. FOSTER in *E. Prov. Herald* 14 Sept. 8 *Sadze* .. is the local staple food. It is rather like a cross between wallpaper paste and playdough.

Saen var. SAN.

safari /səˈfɑːri/ *n.* [General Eng. (fr. Swahili), journey, expedition, fr. Arabic *safar* journey.] Used *attrib.* in Special Comb. (designating clothing): **safari jacket**, (*a*) *bush jacket*, see BUSH *n.*[1] sense 1 b; (*b*) latterly, the top half of a *safari suit*; **safari pants**, **- shorts**, (*a*) (khaki) shorts having pockets with buttoned flaps; (*b*) (latterly) the bottom half of a *safari suit*; **safari suit**, a light-weight informal working suit for men, consisting of a short-sleeved shirt with pockets, worn loosely over short or long trousers; also used allusively as a symbol of bad taste, or of bureaucracy; also *attrib.*; hence **safari-suited** *adj.*

1961 D. BEE *Children of Yesterday* 42 He was dressed in a **safari jacket** and khaki shorts and stockings and heavy brown shoes. **1985** *Sunday Times* 8 Sept. (Lifestyle) 3 In addition to the cameras and meters .. they wear turtle-neck sweaters, safari-jackets, jeans and running shoes. **1983** *Ibid.* 18 Sept. (Lifestyle) 1 He was 'perfectly properly dressed' to go to a party in his **safari pants** and army jacket. **1937** C. BIRKBY *Zulu Journey* 138 The tall, thin, rough man .. met me in khaki shorts and **safari shirt**. **1948** H.V. MORTON *In Search of S. Afr.* 231 Upon a parquet floor covered with lion and zebra skins stood Captain Potter, wearing a safari shirt and khaki trousers. **1988** G. SILBER in *Style* Apr. 33 He is wearing a sensible cotton safari shirt with matching shorts. **1988** [see GAMTAAL]. **1983** *Sunday Times* 28 Aug. (Mag. Sect.) 19 A man wearing only a pair of **safari shorts** sits on a bench. **1970** *Post* 15 Mar. 9 Oom Piet makes me — in my old **safari suit** — look like a refugee from the bush. **1972** *Star* 12 Dec. 26 White officials reach gratefully for safari suits. **1975** *Sunday Times* 5 Mar. 1 The safari-suited man who is so revved up that he can't easily unwind. **1975** S. ROBERTS *Outside Life's Feast* 86 It was wraggies hard to believe those men were policemen ... The older, fatter, man had worn a grey safari suit. **1982** *Staffrider* Vol.4 No.4, 18 He folded the paper and put it back in his safari suit jacket pocket. **1986** O. OBERHOLZER in *Volkskas* May 1 Went back to Pretoria to find a job. Saw many people in safari suits. **1987** *Frontline* Feb. 36 A crowd of pot-bellied, heavy-jowled, comb-in-sock, white-shoed, safari-suited, sideburned, Brylcreemed caricatures of white South Africa. **1988** S. LUPTON in *Weekend Argus* 19 Mar. 21 The safari-suited Transvaaler browsing on Greenmarket Square. **1989** D. KRAMER in *ADA* No.7, 8 Suddenly I saw myself standing on top of a dam wall wearing a safari suit and long socks, and looking like a Water Affairs civil engineer. **1989** P. LEE in *Sunday Times* 26 Feb. (Mag. Sect.) 36 Who needs the Leaning Tower Of Pisa .. when you've got absolute gems like .. any of the following: Tassies, safari suits, biltong, proteas and *Scope* magazine. **1990** M. KENTRIDGE *Unofficial War* 215 The security police were .. present in the form of a man in a safari suit a size too small. **1992** J. WILHELM in *Sunday Times* 16 Feb. 11 The Swiss are known for neutrality and the cuckoo clock. We came up with apartheid and the safari suit.

safe *adj.* and *int. Slang.* [Etym. uncertain; prob. an extension of the general Eng. sense 'free of danger'.]

A. *adj.* Good, worthy of approval or admiration.

1970 J. STODEL *Informant, Cape Town* Wow, that new dance is safe. (It's fabulous, wonderful, fantastic.) ... A safe band is playing at the jeet tonight. **1974** J. MATTHEWS *Park* (1983) 25 Orkas looked up at her and smiled. 'Jammie say yer my number forra five-titty,' Orkas said. 'Safe?' **1976** *Darling* 29 Sept., Give me a safe ensemble and a new hairstyle .. and I can slay the ou's with the rest of them. **1978** *Fair Lady* 29 Mar. 76 'Laid back' is in, sweet like a lemon, safe, uptight, lekker .. the thing to be. **1983** *Sunday Times* 31 July (Lifestyle) 4 We bleached our 'safe kuifs', put rouge on our cheeks and padding into our bras. **1991** L. HORNE *Informant, Benoni* 'That shirt with polka-dots is real safe!' he said. 'Cool' is frozen, dead, out.

B. *int.* An expression of approval or agreement.

1981 *Fair Lady* 9 Sept., A circle made with the forefinger and thumb and accompanied by a conspiratorial wink is obligatory when saying 'Safe, my mate!' This corresponds roughly to an Upper Cruster's 'Jolly good show' or a Middle Classer's 'Fantastic' or 'Ten out of ten, my friend.'

saffraan /saˈfraːn, səˈfrɑːn/ *n.* Also **saffran.** [S. Afr. Du. (fr. Du. *zaffraan*), saffron, yellow; named for its yellowish bark.] In full ***saffraanhout*** /-həʊt/ [S. Afr. Du. (Du. *hout* wood)]: any of several trees with yellowish bark, particularly two trees of the Celastraceae: **a.** The tall evergreen tree *Cassine crocea*, bearing clusters of greenish flowers followed by white fruit; its hard light-brown timber; SAFFRON. **b.** *Cassine papillosa*, also with defining word, **bastersaffraan** /ˈbastə(r)-/ [Afk., *baster* see BASTER *adj.*].

1819 C.G. CURTIS *Acct Col. Cape of G.H.* 72 Saffran Hout .. Close and hard. **1831** *S. Afr. Almanac & Dir.* 187 The other woods most in request, and found in Albany are .. Red and White Pear, Saffran. **1854** [see SAFFRON]. **1951** L.G. GREEN *Grow Lovely* 95 He points to a large pear tree, a Dutch saffraan, as the oldest inhabitant of the Cape Town gardens. **1957** —— *Beyond City Lights* 70 The Farm Bellingham .. has a sweet safraan pear tree planted about two centuries ago. **1966** C.A. SMITH *Common Names* 406 *Saffraanhout*, .. A tall forest tree .. with a whitish bark which is covered with a resinous crust of gamboge or saffron (Afr.: saffraan)-yellow and gives the vernacular name to the plant ... The wood is red, hard, finely close-grained, heavy, tough, and has been used for beams and planks and for furniture-making as well as for general wagon work ... Several other tree species are often referred to as *saffraanhout* because of a yellowish colour but generally with a qualitative prefix to distinguish them from *saffraanhout* ... Thus *bastersaffraanhout* and *Transvaalsaffraanhout*, the suffix word 'hout' being usually dropped. **1973** *E. Prov. Herald* 28 May 13 A typical wagon of the Great Trek period

saffron *n.* [tr. S. Afr. Du. *saffraan.*] In full *-wood, saffron tree*: SAFFRAAN sense a.

1843 J.C. CHASE *Cape of G.H.* 48 Stinkwood is not found in Albany, but it produces several others, such as sneezewood, saffron, red-els, &c, which, when seasoned, are found to be excellent substitutes. 1854 L. PAPPE *Silva Capensis* 11 Saffronwood; Saffraan-hout. Branches much spreading. 1961 PALMER & PITMAN *Trees of S. Afr.* 254 The large spreading saffron tree is found in coastal forests from Swellendam eastwards to Natal.

sage-wood *n.* [tr. Afk. *saliehout.*] *saliehout*, see SALIE sense 2.

1854 L. PAPPE *Silva Capensis* 31 Sage-wood ... Wood hard, tough, heavy. 1913 C. PETTMAN *Africanderisms* 418 Sage wood, Buddleia salviaefolia ... A strongly scented plant, a native of the Transvaal. 1917 R. MARLOTH *Common Names* 72 Sage wood. Buddleia salviifolia. Leaves resembling the garden sage. In some districts also *Tarchonanthus camphoratus*. 1932 WATT & BREYER-BRANDWIJK *Medicinal & Poisonous Plants* 140 Sagewood, Saliehout, .. is possibly used medicinally by the Hottentots. 1973 *Std Encycl. of Sn Afr.* IX. 458 The sagewood .. belongs to the rather heterogeneous family Loganiaceae.

sah var. SA *int.*

sahalahala var. SEHALAHALA.

sail *n.* [Calque formed on Du. *zeil, seil* tarpaulin, wagon tilt.]

1.a. TENT sense 1 a. **b.** A canvas sheet or tarpaulin; also *transf.*, nylon or plastic sheeting. Also *attrib.* See also BUCKSAIL, SKERM sense d.

1820 G. BARKER *Journal.* 19 Dec., Began to mend the sail of the waggon. 1850 J.D. LEWINS *Diary.* 3 Feb., Saw his son's wagon, which when new cost only £54/10/ complete, sail & all, without boxes at Cocroft's in Graham's Town. 1874 A.O. WOOD *Diary.*, We left Jacobsdal where we had a very heavy storm the sail Blowing in the air and I & Mr Winter holding on fast as we could. 1882 C. DU VAL *With Show through Sn Afr.* I. 235 Just in time to get under the sail-cover of the bullock waggon and dodge a severe thunderstorm that rattled over us. *Ibid.* 250 Canvas sails attached to the top of the waggon sides and pegged to the ground formed a tent of some capacity. 1883 M.A. CAREY-HOBSON *Farm in Karoo* 134 You'll get up into the back of the waggon, and I'll tie the sail down tight. I suppose you have made the beds already. 1907 J.P. FITZPATRICK *Jock of Bushveld* (1909) 423 Crouching under the waggon where I had crept down to lash the sail, I looked out at the deluge, hesitating whether to make a dash for my tent-waggon or remain there. 1913 A. GLOSSOP *Barnes's S. Afr. Hsehold Guide* 309 Take a sharp penknife or thin sail-needle, and .. pierce the skin. 1931 V. SAMPSON *Kom Binne* 262 Impromptu tents were made with canvas 'sails' let down the side of a waggon or stretched out on poles along it. 1951 J. WEDGEWOOD *Last of Radicals* 59 A sail spread on the square did for a dance floor, until Josiah ordered a wooden one from Durban and inaugurated it with a masked ball. 1979 *Farmer's Weekly* 11 Apr. 122 (*advt*) Sails & tents ... Pool cover. Black plastic, 6m by 12m. 1979 *Ibid.* 5 Nov. 147 (*advt*) Our sail material is ideal for hard work. 1987 *Grocott's Mail* 6 Oct. 2 The sail covering fully laden plastic crates broke loose from the side of a truck as it was negotiating the bend at the bottom of Southwell Road.

2. With distinguishing epithet: **car sail**, a protective (nylon or plastic) cover for a motor car; **tent sail** or **wagon sail**, (canvas used for) the tilt of a wagon; cf. *wagon-tent* (see TENT sense 1 b).

1968 *Farmer's Weekly* 3 Jan. 96 (*advt*) Protect your car. New Car Sails at factory prices; 9 x 12 at R6.60. 1832 *Graham's Town Jrnl* 27 July 118 The Undersigned .. has at present in his stores, Tent Sail, Navy blue Prints, Foolscap. 1895 H. RIDER HAGGARD *Nada* 2 Took refuge on the second wagon, drawing a tent-sail over them. 1858 T. SHONE *Diary.* 8 Jan., I finish'd Banks waggon sail, he paid me 7/6 for it. 1866 E.L. PRICE *Jrnls* (1956) 165 Drops of water .. inside the wagon-sail have been frozen into cakes of ice by the morning. 1919 *Dunell, Ebden & Co.'s Price List* Aug. 33 Wagon Sails, Green Proofed. 16 x 30, in bales of 6. 1932 *Grocott's Daily Mail* 13 Jan. 16 ft. Wagon with half tent, in good order, Wagon Sail, Trek Gear. 1947 H.C. BOSMAN *Mafeking Rd* 103, I was leaving early in the morning for Zeerust with a load of mealies and I wanted to borrow Krisjan's wagon-sail. 1976 A.P. BRINK *Instant in Wind* 17 The wind .. has blown steadily through the days, .. tugging the wagon sail from the plaited reeds of the bodywork and shredding it to bits.

Saint *n. obs.* [fr. CITY OF SAINTS.] A jocular name for an inhabitant of Grahamstown, a city in the Eastern Cape.

1888 *Cape Punch* 18 July 6 Friday .. brought up the Ballot and the looking-glass of Grahamstown, with the report and desires of another public meeting of the Saints. 1913 *E. London Dispatch* 14 Aug. 4 (Pettman), The older generation of Grahamstown's citizens regarded Mr. Sheffield's book ('The Story of the Settlement') as one which no loyal Saint should be without.

Saints, City of see CITY OF SAINTS.

saka bona var. SAWUBONA.

sakabula /ˌsækəˈbuːlə, sakə-/ *n.* Also **isakubula, sac(c)aboola, saccabula, sakaboola, sakabuli, sakabulla, sakubula**, and with initial capital. [ad. Zulu *isakabuli* widow bird.] The longtailed widow bird *Euplectes progne* of the Ploceidae; also called FLOP. Also *attrib.*

1877 LADY BARKER *Yr's Hsekeeping* 179 Lynx tails hung down like lappets on each side of her face which was over-shadowed and almost hidden by the profusion of sakabula feathers. 1885 H. RIDER HAGGARD *King Solomon's Mines* (1972) 127 They were all men of mature age, mostly veterans of about forty ... They wore upon their heads heavy black plumes of Sacaboola feathers, like those which adorned our guides. 1896 H.L. TANGYE *In New S. Afr.* 105 One of the most strange inhabitants of the Transvaal is a small black bird, the Sakabula. 1905 W.L. SCLATER in Flint & Gilchrist *Science in S. Afr.* 138 The Great-tailed Widow Bird (*Coliopasser procne*) .. is called 'Sakabuli' by the kafirs and often by the English, and has a tail sometimes reaching a length of 20 inches although the body of the bird only measures three or four. 1936 E.L. GILL *First Guide to S. Afr. Birds* 28 Sakabula, *Diatropura progne* ... The males in breeding dress, flying over the veld with their enormous tails streaming behind them, are a common sight in many parts of the country. 1937 S. CLOETE *Turning Wheels* 362 A saccabula, gorgeous in his black spring feathers, his wings blotched with red. 1949 J. MOCKFORD *Golden Land* 83 Uniformed in leopard skins and sakabula feathers, the feathers of the widow-bird. 1969 E. ROUX *Grass: Story of Frankenwald* 43 The sakabula will not breed except in long grass and does not flourish when open fields give place to cultivation, orchards and buildings ... The sakabula .. eats seeds only. 1973 *Weekend Post* 28 Apr. 3 The long-tailed, black widow birds, commonly known as sakabullas. 1980 J.O. OLIVER *Beginner's Guide to our Birds* 71 A familiar sight to everyone in the summer, is the male 'Sakabula' with his long, beautiful tail, flying over his territory.

Sakekamer /ˈsaːkəkaːməɹ/ *n.* [Afk., ellipt. for *Afrikaanse Sakekamer, Afrikaanse* attrib. form of *Afrikaans* (see AFRIKAANS *adj.*) + *sake* business + *kamer* chamber.] The chamber of commerce representing Afrikaans business interests in a given area. Also *attrib.*

Individual Sakekamers are usu. affiliated to the Afrikaanse Handelsinstituut (see AHI).

[1956 M. ROGERS *Black Sash* 125 Dr van Rhijn, Minister of Economic Affairs, .. arrived to address a meeting of the Afrikaanse Sakekamer.] 1972 *Sunday Times* 24 Sept. 16 The Bond has just as much right as the Sons of England or the Chamber of Industries or the Sakekamer to make representations to the Government. 1975 *Daily Dispatch* 31 Mar. 7 The Sakekamer is busy arranging a special course for the benefit of training black personnel. 1990 *Weekend Post* 15 Dec. 14 Alexandria Sakekamer members are angry that the consumer boycott is aimed at commerce when the complaint is with industry.

sakkie-sakkie /ˌsakiˈsaki/ *adj.* and *n. Music.* Also **sakkie-sakie**. [Afk., prob. echoic, representing the repetitive rhythm of the music.]

Sometimes used disparagingly.

A. *adj.* Descriptive of a simple, rhythmical style of BOEREMUSIEK (sense 1).

1970 L. DU TOIT *Informant, Bloemfontein* With all the pop music today, sakie-sakie music is not very popular with the younger set. 1980 *In the Clouds* (S. Afr. Airways) Dec. 9 This R5 million Spa in the Bushveld ... Piped sakkie/sakkie [sic] music, fish and chips, melted ice cream cones on the grass. 1983 A. BARON in *Cape Times* 9 Dec. 10 He .. does a tiekie draai with the constable to sakkie sakkie music. 1987 *Star* 27 Feb. 4 The Chip Chip band from Vryburg gave 'boeremusiek' a whole new meaning with its electronic instruments but the 'sakkie-sakkie lang-arm dans' will never change if the CP has its way. 1989 J. EVANS in *Personality* 29 May 15 As the *sakkie-sakkie* music drifts over the desert ..., bikes and cars limp in, their drivers looking haggard, frustrated and grubby. 1991 V. WARREN *Informant, Alberton* Tonight we are going to the Townhall to dance to real sakkie-sakkie music.

B. *n.* **a.** BOEREMUSIEK sense 1. **b.** A dance performed to this music. See also LANGARM *n.*, SKOFFEL *n.*[2] sense 1. Also *attrib.*

1982 *Album sleeve*, Gallo Recording Co. Also Hooked on Sakkie Sakkie. First National Sakkie Sakkie Boere Country Band. 1983 *E. Prov. Herald* 12 Jan. 6 For the sakkie-sakkie fans, Mandy Faiers enchanted the crowds with her performance of 'Hak hom Blokkies'. 1985 A. GOLDSTUCK in *Frontline* Feb. 21 Barry thinks of Cajun music as the American version of sakkie sakkie — using fiddles instead of guitars. 1985 [see SKOP *n.*[1] sense 1]. 1988 [see GAMTAAL]. 1990 R. STENGEL *January Sun* 186 They are extremely good dancers and do something called the sakkie-sakkie, which looks like a cross between a square dance and the hustle. The sakkie-sakkie is done in rows, and the dancing is regimented. 1990 P. FELDMAN in *Star* 11 Sept. (*Tonight*) 8 He has come up through the music ranks from sakkie-sakkie to punk to original Afrikaans rock, but based on a strong '60s vibe.

sako bona, sakubona varr. SAWUBONA.

salaam aleikum /saˌlɑːm əˈleɪkʊm/ *int. phr.* Also **salaam aleikoem, salaam-a-leikum, salam alaikoem**, and with initial capitals. [fr. Arabic *as-salam alay-kum* peace be with you, in use throughout the Muslim world.] Among Muslims: a greeting or benediction, 'peace be with you'.

1964 L.G. GREEN *Old Men Say* 60 Only a handful of Cape Malays now speak the language of their ancestors. 'Salam alaikoem' is often heard. 'Peace be with you.' 1977 D. MULLER *Whitey* 14 'Goodbye ... Thank you for all your wonderful kindness.' He went out, and .. caught her soft reply: 'Salaam aleikum, Paul.' 1980 A. DANGOR in M. Mutloatse *Forced Landing* 161, I offer you a smile, a gesture of brotherly love. But you regard me with suspicion. *Salaam-a-leikum* to you too. 1980 *Cape Times* 18 Oct. 6 He first greeted the person answering his knock (Salaam Aleikoem) then he said he had a message (Garbar) of the passing of someone, and gave the name of the deceased and said who his nearest relatives were.

sala kahle /ˌsala ˈɡɑːɬe/ *int. phr.* Also **sala gahle, sale gahle, slalla gooshley, tsala kahle**. [Zulu, *sala* stay, remain behind + *kahle*, see GASHLE; when addressing more than one person, the form used is *salani kahle*.] Esp. among Zulu-speakers: 'stay well', an expression of good wishes, offered on parting by one leaving to one staying behind; HLALA KAHLE; cf. STAY WELL. See also *hamba kahle* (HAMBA sense 2 a).

1855 G.H. Mason *Life with Zulus* 73 They approached the open door of the tent, and .. saluted us with 'Slalla gooshley,' literally (Rest in peace), after which .. they vanished. **1855** [see HAMBA sense 2 a]. [1930 S.T. Plaatje *Mhudi* (1975) 147, I am going into the wilderness and will not rest till I have found Mzilikazi. Sala kahle (farewell in Zulu), my .. sister.] 1940 F.B. Young *City of Gold* 359 The headman welcomed him and asked him to sit and drink beer with him. 'Sala kahle, Inkos — Stay in peace,' he said, with a formal dignity. **1951** [see INKOSAZANA]. 1952 H. Klein *Land of Silver Mist* 73 My son, I die happy ... May the spirits protect you and make you a great chief ... Sale Gahle. 1967 O. Walker *Hippo Poacher* 34 'You will not see me again. Sala gahle (Stay sweetly).' 'Hamba gahle (Go sweetly),' said Tom. 1975 S.S. Mekgoe *Lindiwe* (1978) 26 He is in Ward 21, Mdangeni Fort Hospital ... You say Ward 21. Thank you ... Salani kahle. 1978 *Voice* 11 Oct. 3A, 'You ladies are brave ... I'm glad you are going to stay ... Salani kahle (goodbye),' he said as he quickly disappeared. 1989 B. Ludman *Day of Kugel* 44 'If I go, and you stay, I say to you Sala kahle. That means "Stay well".' ... 'And what do I say?' 'You say Hamba kahle,' he said. 'That means "go well".' 1991 P. Slabolepszy *Braait Laaities.* 18 Sala kahle, Moira. I want to wish you Good Luck in all the things you do.

Hence **sala kahle** *n. phr.*, an utterance of the words 'sala kahle'.

1899 A. Werner *Captain of Locusts* 171 Nono was already off, throwing back a 'Sala kahle' over her shoulders.

salampore var. SALEMPORE.

Saldanha /sal'dɑːnə/ *n.* [fr. the original Pg. name for Table Bay, *Agoada de Saldanha* (named for *Antonio de Saldanha*, an admiral wounded there by Khoikhoi inhabitants in 1503); the name was transf. to the present Saldanha Bay by Joris van Spilbergen who mistakenly believed that he had reached Table Bay in 1601. In early English accounts 'Saldanha Bay' often refers to Table Bay.]

1. *hist.* [Named for *Agoada de Saldanha* (Table Bay).] Usu comb. **Saldanhaman, Saldania man**, or in derivatives formed in Du. or Eng.: **Saldanhar, Saldanhater, Saldania, Saldanier**.

a. A member of any of several clans of Khoikhoi living in the south-western Cape during the seventeenth century; in *pl.*, also a collective term for any or all of these clans; GORINGHAIQUA. Also *attrib.* See also GORACHOUQUA, KAAPMANS, KHOIKHOI.

1607 [see KAFFIR sense 2]. 1614 N. Downton in R. Raven-Hart *Before Van Riebeeck* (1967) 64 The Saldanians broughte vs downe some fewe cattell, which is formerlie we bought for copper, but .. theie alltogether desired brasse. 1643 P. Mundy in *Ibid.* 141 Theis that are hereabouts (by report) are of a baser Sort and live in feare of others called Saldania men, whoe are further in the Land. 1731 G. Medley tr. *P. Kolb's Present State of Cape of G.H.* I. 61 Bordering on the Gunjemans, Northward, is the Kochoqua Nation, call'd by Dapper, Saldanhaters. 1841 B. Shaw *Memorials* 7 By means of a Hottentot named Harry, who could speak a little English, Van Riebeeck obtained a supply of cattle from the natives called Saldanians. 1849 E.D.H.E. Napier *Excursions in Sn Afr.* I. 24 Another tribe .. inhabiting the neighbourhood of Saldanha Bay ... Between these 'Saldanhers' and the 'Strandloopers' there existed a deadly feud. These Saldanhers appear to have been a race much superior to that of the Strandloopers. 1861 P.B. Borcherds *Auto-Biog. Mem.* 270 They would keep away altogether and you would find yourselves deprived not only of daily barter with the Saldanhars, but also of the trade with all the other tribes before named. **1900** [see sense b]. 1913 C. Pettman *Africanderisms* 420 Saldanier, A Hottentot from the neighbourhood of Saldanha Bay was so called by the early Dutch colonists. **1952** [see GORINGHAIQUA]. 1961 L.E. Van Onselen *Trekboer* 106 The clans were named Namaquas, Saldanhas and Outeniquas to mention only three. They were a yellowish people, larger in stature than the Bushman and spoke a language of their own. 1972 J.P. van S. Bruwer in *Std Encycl. of Sn Afr.* V. 606 As soon as they arrived in South Africa the Portuguese, .. followed by the Dutch colonists in 1652, came into contact with a yellowish brown pastoral people at the Cape. The colonists at first called them Kaapmans and Saldanhars, but later on the name 'Hottentot' .. became firmly established. 1976 A.R. Wilcox *Sn Land* 155 The Saldanhars .. had a regular annual migration into South West Cape from the rather arid region to the north.

b. *transf.* A cattle trader of Khoikhoi or Xhosa origin (prob. so called because of the cattle trading carried on by the Khoikhoi people of sense a).

1846 J. Sutherland *Memoir* II. 589 The Saldanha-man .. come every year with innumerable cattle and sheep. 1900 A.H. Keane *Boer States* p.xviii, Saldaniers, originally the Hottentots of the grassy Saldanha Bay district, who had always plenty of cattle to sell to the Dutch East India Company's people; later, any native livestock dealers.

2. The name of present-day Saldanha Bay, used *attrib.* and in Special Comb., as **Saldanha man**, a fossil hominid belonging to an ancient form of *Homo sapiens*; **Saldanha skull**, the fragments of the skull found in 1955 by the archaeologists R. Singer and K. Jolly.

These fragments were found at Hopefield, near Saldanha Bay, about 100 km north of Cape Town.

1953 M.R. Drennan in *S. Afr. Jrnl Sci.* L. 8 (caption) Side view of the skull-cap of Saldanha Man ... The Saldanha skull is thus somewhat shorter .. than .. the Rhodesian skull. 1954 *Amer. Jrnl Physical Anthropol.* XII. 349 Fluorine tests also revealed that *Mesochoerus* and *Paleoloxodon* lived contemporaneously with Saldanha Man. 1959 J.D. Clark *Prehist. of S. Afr.* 83 Saldanha Man may .. be considered to be representative of the kind of 'proto-Australoid' individual who was responsible for the final expression of the Earlier Stone Age cultures in Southern Africa at the end of the Middle and beginning of the Upper Pleistocene. 1973 L.H. Wells in *Std Encycl. of Sn Afr.* IX. 473 Saldanha Man, Most widely current name for the fossil man found at the Elandsfontein site near Hopefield. Fragments of the skull were recovered by Keith Jolly, an archaeologist working on the site in association with Dr. Ronald Singer. 1973 B.J. Williams *Evolution & Human Origins* 184 The later find of the Saldanha skull provided another specimen almost identical to that of Rhodesian Man. 1985 G.T. Nurse et al. *Peoples of Sn Afr.* 42 There are morphological objections to seeing in the Broken Hill and Saldanha rhodesioid remains the ancestral common stock suggested by Tobias (1962a) and Brothwell (1963).

salee var. SALIE.

sale gahle var. SALA KAHLE.

salempore /ˈsæl(ə)mpɔː/ *n. obsolescent.* Also **salampore, salemporis**. [In general Eng. from the late 16th century, but perh. now obs.; perh. fr. *Salampur*, a city in the Nellore district of India. (Cf. 17th century Du. *salamporij*, 18th century Fr. *salempouri*.)]

1. A blue (often striped) cotton cloth, originally made at Nellore in India, and commonly worn in the past by African people. Also *attrib.*

The cloth was originally exported to the W. Indies for use by slaves.

1863 W.C. Baldwin *Afr. Hunting* 21 Paid them on arrival with brass wire and blue salempore, or calico. 1883 B. Mitford *Through Zulu Country* 189 On shelves against the walls are arranged blankets, Salampore, cloth [etc.]. 1921 H.J. Mandelbrote tr. *O.F. Mentzel's Descr. of Cape of G.H.* I. 143 He sells wholesale, by the piece, East Indian cotton goods such as chintz, calico, 'salemporis', .. as well as quilts and counterpanes lined with cotton wool and cotton yarns. 1949 O. Walker *Proud Zulu* (1951) 71 When Catherine heard of the new birth she got out a roll of salempore (native blanket cloth), thinking to send it down. 1961 T.V. Bulpin *White Whirlwind* 53 They took up blankets, Salampore cloth, brass wire, and other items which they traded for the fancy skins the Zulus use in their military costumes.

2. A garment made from salempore.

1948 O. Walker *Kaffirs Are Lively* 79 She was dressed only in a *salempore* — a striped cotton blanket tucked under the arms, which is almost universal among the Bavenda women.

‖**salie** /ˈsɑːli/ *n. obsolescent.* Also **sa(a)ly, salee, zalie**. [Du., the herb *Salvia officinalis* (sage).]

1. Any of numerous plants of the genus *Salvia* of the Lamiaceae; *wild sage* sense (a), see WILD sense a.

All these plants are considered to have medicinal value.

1796 E. Helme tr. *Le Vaillant's Trav. into Int.* III. 426 He assured me it [*sc.* the plant] was equally common in the colony and at the Cape, where it is known by the Dutch name of *saaly* (sage). 1847 'A Bengali' *Notes on Cape of G.H.* 15 Quinsy, for which the native cure is gargle and fermentations of 'Saaly' or sage, is bad on the frontier. **1913** [see sense 2]. 1917 R. Marloth *Common Names* 72 Salie (Sage). Species of Salvia. 1966 C.A. Smith *Common Names* 406 Salie, Generally used as a collective name for various native species of *Salvia* as the equivalent of *sage*, with a colour, habit, leaf-character or habitat prefix used for specific distinction. 1975 W. Steenkamp *Land of Thirst King* 140 There were many remedies for minor ailments which were effective to a greater or lesser degree. An infusion of leaves picked from the 'salie', or wild sage, was taken for common coughs and colds.

2. In full *saliehout* /-həʊt/ [Du. *hout* wood]: any of several shrubs or trees with ridged or corrugated leaves suggesting those of a Salvia, esp. *Buddleia salviifolia* of the Loganiaceae, with racemes of small, strongly perfumed, tubular, mauve flowers; the tough, hard wood of this tree; SAGE-WOOD. Used less frequently of *Tarchonanthus camphoratus* and *Brachylaena discolor* (see VAALBOS sense 1 b), and *Nuxia congesta* (family Loganiaceae). Also *attrib.*

1819 C.G. Curtis *Acct Colony Cape of G.H.* 72 Saly hout ... Hard and heavy. 1887 S.W. Silver & Co.'s *Handbk to S. Afr.* 130 In those [patches of forest] of Klein and Van Staden's rivers are found .. Salee (*Tarchonanthus camphoratus*). 1908 F.C. Slater *Sunburnt South* 11 Wild willows and feathery-flowered zalie trees grew in delightful profusion. 1913 C. Pettman *Africanderisms* 420 Salie, .. The numerous species of Salvia found in South Africa are known by this name among the Dutch; but beside these *Chilianthus olaceus, Brachylena elliptica, Tarchonanthus camphoratus* and *Buddleia salviaefolia*, all share this name with the true *Salviae* ... *Salie hout*, .. See Sage wood. 1944 C.R. Prance *Under Blue Roof* 81 The 'Salie' trees thick along the stream are blood-kin to the cemetery cypress. 1952 *Cape Times* 2 Aug. 9 Among indigenous trees, three are milkwood, salie and kafir plum. 1973 *Std Encycl. of Sn Afr.* IX. 459 Saliehout ... Tall, much-branched shrub .. with large, simple, opposite, grey-green leaves. **1974** [see VAALBOS].

salmon *n.* Ellipt. for CAPE SALMON (sense 1).

1955 C. Horne *Fisherman's Eldorado* 209 When an angler from Natal talks to one from the Cape about salmon, it is certain, unless the two have clearly established the identity of the fish under discussion, that the Natalian will have in mind the kob while the man from the Cape will be thinking about the geelbek.

salt *v.* Also **sault**. [Prob. special senses of Eng. *salt* to preserve, to cure.]

a. *trans.* To render (an animal) immune to disease by allowing it to suffer a disease, or by inoculation. Also *fig.* See also SALTED.

1864 T. Baines *Explor. in S.-W. Afr.* 418 He asked carefully 'whether the horse was salted' (i.e. acclimatised by having recovered from the horse sickness). 1878

P. GILLMORE *Great Thirst Land* 59 In purchasing cattle up the country, .. it is customary to obtain a guarantee that a horse is saulted, or an ox over the lung-sickness. **1898** *Cape of G.H. Agric. Jrnl* 9 Jan. 6 The expression *to salt a beast* means to render the animal immune to the disease, to immunize him. **1903** D. BLACKBURN *Burgher Quixote* 52 The young Burghers .. had learned to drink whiskey in Johannesburg and at Krugersdorp, and were thus poison-proof, being, so to speak, salted. **1911** J.F. PENTZ in *Farmer's Weekly* 11 Oct. (*letter*) 158 It is very clear that no cattle can be 'salted' for lam-gallziekte. **1929** J. STEVENSON-HAMILTON *Low-Veld* 18 A horse or mule 'salted', implies one which, having previously contracted the disease, is amongst the lucky 5 per cent or 6 per cent which survive. **1937** B.H. DICKE *Bush Speaks* 296 With the lung sickness they had found that, if an incision was made into the end of the animal's tail, and a piece of diseased lung was tied to the wound .., a mild form of the sickness manifested itself from which the animals easily recovered and .. such animals became immune to the contagion, became what was called 'salted'. **1940** F.B. YOUNG *City of Gold* 66 I'll give you eight yoke of oxen and guarantee they're all sound in hoof and limb and salted for lung-sickness. **1953** [see HORSE-SICKNESS]. **1974** A.P. CARTWRIGHT *By Waters of Letaba* 9 The horse sickness spelt death to any horse that had not been 'salted'. **1986** W. STEENKAMP *Blake's Woman* 87 He's broken to hunting .. and he's salted, which means he is immune to the horse-sickness.

b. *intrans.* Of an animal: to become immune to a disease by contracting it and surviving.

1882 S. HECKFORD *Lady Trader in Tvl* 57 It was very difficult to get horses, owing to the fact of the 'horse disease' being so very bad .. that very few horses ever 'salted', i.e. recovered from the disease. **1912** *S. Afr. Agric. Jrnl* July 54 All farmers agree that cattle which recover [from lamsiekte] do not *salt* from the disease, in other words, there is no immunity.

Hence **salting** *vbl n.*, immunizing.

1871 J. MACKENZIE *Ten Yrs* (1971) 262 Horses are now safe far to the north of this district: there is no annual return of the disease ... The 'salting' of the districts where the disease has thus become mitigated, does not stand good in the interior. **1899** 'S. ERASMUS' *Prinsloo* 39 These rascally Englanders ... gave out to Magato that they were doctors who could vaccinate, which is salting for the small-pox.

saltbush *n.* [fr. Austral. Eng. (1846), extended to include both indigenous plants and imported Australian species; named for its salty nature and habitat.]

a. Any of several species of the fodder plant *Atriplex* of the Chenopodiaceae which flourish in saline soil; SOUTBOS sense a; VAALBOS sense 2; *vaalbrak*, see VAAL sense 2; also called BRAKBOS. Also *attrib.*

Also *Austral.* and *U.S. Eng.*

1906 F. BLERSCH *Handbk of Agric.* 254 Other species of plants of considerable feeding value are *Atriplex capensis*, the Vaal boschje or South African Salt bush [etc.]. **1917** R. MARLOTH *Common Names* 72 *Salt-bush. Atriplex Halimus.* A valuable fodder-shrub of brackish Karoo lands. Several Australian species introduced, suitable in similar localities, e.g., *A. halimoides* and *A. semibaccata* (low spreading), also *A. nummularia* (tall). **1931** H.D. LEPPAN *Agric. Policy* 42 Where the [salt] concentration is slight, some of the more tolerant crops. e.g., sorghums, cotton and salt bushes may be grown. **1973** *Std Encycl. of Sn Afr.* IX. 480 Several species of *Atriplex* .. are known as saltbush. **1985** *Farmer's Weekly* 26 July 46 Almost all these farmers bought saltbush seed before leaving. **1991** F. MARTIN in *Ibid.* 25 Jan. 8 Establishing saltbush is a tiresome task as each plant must be planted by hand ... Sheep need to be 'taught' to eat saltbush. **1993** MILTON & DEAN in *Afr. Wildlife* Vol.47 No.1, 28 Perhaps their .. taste for such alien plants as .. saltbush (*Atriplex* spp.) ensures the future of leopard tortoises on Karoo rangeland.

b. With distinguishing epithet: **old man saltbush**, also **old man's -**, [Austral. Eng. *old man* (attrib.) 'of exceptional size, duration, or intensity'], the plant *Atriplex nummularia; oumansoutbos*, see SOUTBOS sense b. Also *attrib.*

1929 *Farming in S. Afr.* Sept. 294 (Swart), There is an ever-increasing demand for the seed of 'Old man Salt bush'. *c***1936** *S. & E. Afr. Yr Bk & Guide* 280 The saltbush 'Old Man' (*atriplex nummularia*) and the creeping saltbush, are of Australian origin. **1974** *S. Afr. Panorama* Dec. 4 To provide feed for his enormous flocks, the owner has successfully planted oumansoutbos (old man's salt bush) (Atriplex nummularia). **1985** *Farmer's Weekly* 26 July 46 The sales of old-man saltbush seed escalated during the first five months of this year. **1991** F. MARTIN in *Ibid.* 25 Jan. 8 He was introduced to old-man salt-bush (*Atriplex nummularia*) by pasture expert John Fair. It's the one crop that has remained immune to climatic factors.

salted *ppl adj.* Also **saulted.** [fr. SALT.] Of animals: immune to a disease after having survived an attack either contracted by normal contagion or artificially induced in a mild form.

1871 J. MACKENZIE *Ten Yrs* (1971) 261 A horse which has recovered from this sickness never gets it again, and, according to the colonial phrase, he is now a 'salted horse'. The term is used in certificates and other documents, and is taken to mean a horse which has recovered from the distemper. **1882** J. NIXON *Among Boers* 239 A saulted animal has always a more or less mangy appearance. **1905** D. HUTCHEON in Flint & Gilchrist *Science in S. Afr.* 345 One of his young animals developed a fatal attack of Biliary Fever after an innoculation with blood from a salted horse. **1917** [see STOCK-FAIR sense 1]. **1953** [see HORSE-SICKNESS]. **1979** T. GUTSCHE *There Was a Man* 108 'Salted' oxen from which to produce the serum were rare.

salt pan *n. phr.* [Calque formed on S. Afr. Du. *zoutpan* (later Afk. *soutpan*), *zout* salt + *pan*, see PAN. Used also in general Eng., primarily of man-made salt-works.] A salt lake; a natural depression in which a salt deposit is left after rain water has evaporated. In both senses also called PAN.

1786 G. FORSTER tr. *A. Sparrman's Voy. to Cape of G.H.* II. 14 About a mile and a half from the river, we met with the principal *Zout-pan*, or Salt-pan. By this name those places are distinguished, where there is a quantity of culinary salt produced. **1796** C.R. HOPSON tr. *C.P. Thunberg's Trav.* II. 6 The name of Salt-pans is given, in this country, to large collections of salt water. **1810** G. BARRINGTON *Acct of Voy.* 239 It was one of those salt-water lakes which abound in Southern Africa, where they are called *salt pans* by the Colonists. *a***1823** J. EWART *Jrnl* (1970) 71 These salt pans .. are merely pools of water .. which imbibing a portion of the saline matter with which the ground is strongly impregnated, deposit during the summer months when the water evaporates, a considerable quantity of fine white salt. **1835** A.G. BAIN in A. Steedman *Wanderings* II. 250 A periodical lake, having all the appearance of a salt-pan, but almost always without water. **1867** *Blue Bk for Col. 1866* FF12, There are two salt pans, from which salt is procured in large quantities. **1890** F. YOUNG *Winter Tour* 67, I walked to see those wonderful 'Salt Pans'. *Ibid.* 68 The salt and soda brine is perpetually oosing [*sic*] from the bottom, and is continually being scraped up with a sort of wooden scraper into heaps, where .. it becomes crystallised ... These Salt Pans are the property of the Transvaal Government. **1936** R.J.M. GOOLD-ADAMS *S. Afr. To-Day & To-Morrow* 28 East and west from the moisture laden kloofs of Natal to the dried up salt-pans and the withered bush of the Kalahari. **1958** A. JACKSON *Trader on Veld* 26 The brakish nature of the water .. turned large dams into veritable saltpans. **1991** O. OBERHOLZER in *Time* 29 July 28 (*advt*) I .. saw what I'd have to go through; the mountains of Lesotho, Zimbabwe, Caprivi, the Skeleton Coast, the Namib desert, and a whole lot of swamps, rivers and salt pans in between.

saltriem /ˈsɒltrim/ *n. derog.* Also **salt reim.** [Part. tr. Afk. *soutriem* salt thong, perh. a euphemism for *soutpiel* (see SOUTPIEL).] Esp. among Afrikaners: ROOINEK.

1883 O.E.A. SCHREINER *Story of Afr. Farm* 258 Without asking the price the Englishman had .. brought oxen worth ten pounds for sixteen. The Dutchman chuckled, for he had the 'Salt Reim's' money in the box under his bed. [**1970** J.F. PRINSLOO *Informant, Lüderitz (Namibia)* Sout-riem. A Britisher.]

saly var. SALIE.

sama var. TSAMMA.

samango /səˈmæŋgəʊ/ *n.* [Zulu *insimango*, prob. rel. to *isimanga* something surprising, *isimangamanga* something wondrous or beautiful; or perh. rel. to Pg. *samango* lazy man.] In full ***samango monkey***: either of two species of the forest monkey *Cercopithecus mitis* (or *albogularis*) of the Cercopithicidae: **a.** *C. m. labiatus*, with dark-brown face and shoulders, long white throat-hair extending upwards on each side like a collar, and sooty-grey saddle, occurring from the Eastern Cape northeastwards to the KwaZulu-Natal Midlands. **b.** *C. m. erythrarchus*, similar to *labiatus* but with yellowish saddle and reddish-brown lower back, occurring in the north-eastern parts of South Africa and in countries to the north.

1888 *Proc. Zool. Soc.* 564 The most notable additions during the month were:— .. the Small-clawed Otter .. the Samango Monkey. **1894** H.O. FORBES *Handbk Primates* II. 71 (*heading*) The Samango Guenon. **1919** F.W. FITZSIMONS *Natural Hist. of S. Afr.* I. 23 The Samango monkey inhabits the wooded gorges, kloofs, and dense forests on the eastern side of South Africa, and as far north as the East Coast. **1932** S. ZUCKERMAN *Soc. Life Monkeys & Apes* 185 Very near where the Samangos were seen, I came across a party of seven Vervet monkeys. **1934** C.P. SWART Supplement to Pettman. 149 *Samango*, The native name for a species of monkey, Cercopithecus labiatus, very common in Zululand where it inhabits the darkest and gloomiest recesses of the forests. **1972** *Std Encycl. of Sn Afr.* VII. 515 The African monkeys can be divided into two main groups, the guenon and the guereza monkeys. The majority of African tree-dwelling monkeys belong to the guenon group. *Ibid.* 516 To this group belong the vervet and samango monkeys of Southern Africa ... The Samango monkey (*C. mitis*) is darker in colour than the vervets. **1981** *Natal Bushveld (brochure)* 66 (Samango Monkey; South Africa, from Zululand to eastern Cape Province), dark green, underparts dirty white. **1988** *Stanger Mail* 23 Dec. 7 The Samango is a shy creature and seldom, if ever ventures out of the forest. The samango is being mistaken for the vervet which is the usual raider. **1988** D. WYLIE in *New Coin Poetry* Vol.24 No.2, 14 The *somangoes* have bitten the waxy rind from the moon and discarded its hard kernel on the hill. **1990** SKINNER & SMITHERS *Mammals of Sn Afr. Subregion* 162 Samango monkeys, which are much darker than vervets, have dark brown faces. The long hair on the throat is pure white and extends upwards on either side like a white collar. **1992** *S. Afr. Panorama* Mar.-Apr. 76 Scarce mammals such as the samango monkey .. and the blue duiker .. are also found on this site.

samareelboom *n. obs.* Also **sambrielboom.** [S. Afr. Du., *samareel*, *sambreel* umbrella, parasol, fr. Du. (as used in the E. Indies) *sombreel*, fr. Malay-Pg. *sumbrelu*, fr. Pg. *sombriero* 'that which shades', + Du. *boom* tree.] KIEPERSOL.

[**1837** ECKLON & ZEYHER *Enumeratio Plantarum Africae* 355 *Cussonia spicata* ... Incolis europaeis: Samareelboom, Nojesboom.] **1907** T.R. SIM *Forests & Forest Flora* 230 [W.H.] Harvey says:- 'Tree 15 feet high, with the aspect of a palm, called by the colonists *Samareelboom, Nojesboom*.' Samareel-boom means Umbrella-tree. **1917** R. MARLOTH *Common Names* 72 *Sambrielboom* (*Samareel*), *Cussonia spicata*. On account of the umbrella-like terminal tufts of leaves. Also other species. The huge fleshy roots edible.

sambal /'sæmbəl, 'sambal/ *n.* Also **sambol, zambal.** [Malay.]

1.a. A relish of Malay or Indonesian origin, made of the pulp of raw vegetables or fruit, pounded chilli, spices, and vinegar. **b.** Any of a variety of side-dishes served as an accompaniment to food. Cf. ATJAR.

Unassimilated in *Brit. Eng.*

1815 A. PLUMPTRE tr. *H. Lichtenstein's Trav. in Sn Afr.* (1930) II. 84 *Sambal* is a mixture of gherkins cut small, onions, anchovies, Cayenne pepper, and vinegar. **1862** 'A LADY' *Life at Cape* (1963) 98 They make a sort of 'chutnee' out of quinces, which they call '*sambal*', by slicing the fruit into a mortar, adding a pinch of salt and cayenne pepper, and a green chilly minced very fine, and then pounding the whole with a pestle till it is well bruised and reduced to a pulp. **1891** H.J. DUCKITT *Hilda's 'Where Is It?'* 199 Quince 'Sambal.' (A Green Chutney. Malay Recipe.) **1919** M.M. STEYN *Diary* 17 The older ones had soup meat in their plates with 'Zambal' (a relish composed of cucumber or apple or quince, rasped fine, with different sauces). **1944** I.D. DU PLESSIS *Cape Malays* 43 The spicy stew of meat and vegetables is enhanced by various *sambals* (condiments): sliced onion sprinkled with finely pounded chili, fresh grated quince mixed with pounded chili, and a highly seasoned sambal of mint leaves and chili pounded together and moistened with vinegar. **1950** H. GERBER *Cape Cookery* 126 Quince sambal (Malay): Peel a quince and grate it. Add a little salt and let the quince stand for an hour or two. Then squeeze out all the water and add to the fruit pulp some red vinegar and a chilli. **1964** L.G. GREEN *Old Men Say* 131 The modern Cape Malay sambal is a cool salad eaten with curry; but a strong condiment which included red pepper used to be known as a *sambal*. **1979** HEARD & FAULL *Our Best Trad. Recipes* 29 This has a curried flavour and is served with salads and sambals such as chutney, banana and sliced tomatoes sprinkled with finely chopped onion, shallots or chives. **1985** *S. Afr. Cookbk* (Reader's Digest Assoc.) 383 *Sambals*, Side dishes served with Indian or Malay dishes. **1988** F. WILLIAMS *Cape Malay Cookbk* 58 The word 'sambal' is Javanese in origin and means condiment. It is usually a highly seasoned relish of grated raw fruits or vegetables, squeezed dry, mixed with pounded chilli and moistened with vinegar or lemon juice. **1989** *Weekend Post* 2 Dec. (Leisure) 6 Sambals can include diced pawpaw, poppadoms, dessicated coconut, chutney, cucumbers in yoghurt, or sour cream, sliced bananas and sweet pickles.

‖**2.** Special Comb. **sambalbroek** /sam'balbruk/ [Afk., *broek* trousers], wide trousers.

1913 C. PETTMAN *Africanderisms* 422 **Sambalbroek**, .. A humorous name for the very wide trousers worn by the Malays. [**1972** L.G. GREEN *When Journey's Over* 121 One hundred Afrikaans words with clear Malayo-Portuguese origins ... Those .. included .. *sambalbroek* (wide trousers) [etc.].]

sambo(c)k, sam-bok varr. SJAMBOK *n.*

sambrielboom var. SAMAREELBOOM.

sambuc(k) var. SJAMBOK *n.*

‖**samesmelting** /'sɑːmə,smeltəŋ/ *n.* Also **saamsmelting.** [Afk., *saam* together + euphonic *-e-* + *smelting* coalition, fusion.] FUSION.

1934 C.P. SWART Supplement to Pettman. 150 *Samesmelting*, Amalgamation, fusion or union. Grammatically it is synonymous with 'vereniging', .. but politically it has acquired the meaning of indiscriminate mixture. **1934** *Star* 12 Feb. (Swart), Dr Van der Merwe in conclusion said, that he was confident there would be no samesmelting, but hereniging. **1934** *Friend* 15 Feb. (Swart), No unanimity was reached between the four organisations of the National Party in regard to their various decisions concerning fusion (samesmelting), union (vereniging), and reunion (hereniging). **1972** S. & B. STENT in A.P. Cartwright *Forthright Man* 168 South Africa's millenium has dawned. We know this because the archangels of Coalition have sounded their off-golden trumpets and .. have proclaimed the peace of Ons Saamsmelting, which passeth all understanding.

sammy *n. offensive.* Freq. with initial capital; formerly also **sami.** [ad. Tamil suffix *-samy* (fr. Sanskrit *swami* master), in Indian names such as *Ramasamy* and *Munsamy*.]

1. An insulting and racist term of address or reference to an Indian man. Also *attrib.*

[**1883** B. MITFORD *Through Zulu Country* 52 The picturesque dresses of the coolies lend colour to the variously clad throng of humanity, .. of which the Indian element forms no small part, for 'Ramsammy' is quite an institution in Natal.] **1906** *Indian Opinion* 7 July 456 The conductor roughly addressed him in the following terms: 'Hurry up, Sammy.' As may be supposed, the insult stung the complainant, Mr. Francis, into a retort that the conductor should not call him 'Sammy'. [**1913** C. PETTMAN *Africanderisms* 391 *Ramasammy*, (A corruption of *Ramaswami*, 'Lord Rama'). In Natal and the Cape this word is used as a generic name for Indian coolies.] *Ibid.* 423 *Sammy*, See *Ramasammy*, of which this is an abbreviation. **1927** M. DESAI tr. *M.K. Gandhi's Autobiog.* 110 '*Sami*' is a Tamil suffix occurring after many Tamil names, and is nothing else than the Sanskrit *Swami*, meaning a master. When .. an Indian resented being addressed as a '*sami*' and had enough wit in him, he would try to return the compliment in this wise: You may call me *sami*, but you forget that *sami* means a master. **1949** A. KEPPEL-JONES *When Smuts Goes* 18 The good people of Johannesburg were told that .. they would be jostled out of the parks and swimming-baths by 'Jim' and 'Sammy'. **1970** [see MARY sense 1]. **1972** J. MCCLURE *Caterpillar Cop* (1974) 112 'Brandy and telephone directory, Sammy.' The waiter's name was not Sammy, but his race has been divided by the whites into Sammy units and Mary units to facilitate friendly relationships. **1973** *E. Prov. Herald* 22 Sept. B2, Because 'Mariamma' was a common name among Indian women and 'Munsamy' among the men, they were referred to as 'Marys and Sammies'. This was considered to be insulting.

2. *transf.* An insulting generic name given to an Indian trader or hawker, particularly a vegetable-hawker.

1926 P.W. LAIDLER *Tavern of Ocean* 174 The Malay fish-hawker .. was disappearing, and now all the retail trade is in the hands of his fellow Moslem, the Indian, 'Sammy'. **1949** J. MOCKFORD *Golden Land* 179 Sammy's baskets balanced on the end of a bamboo pole, like the nests of a weaver bird, go bobbing along the streets and lanes of every township in Natal. **1953** LANHAM & MOPELI-PAULUS *Blanket Boy's Moon* 161 That Indian tribe .. the white man calls 'Sammies' .. whose members sell fruit and vegetables to the white women. **1968** [see MARY sense 1]. **1980** *Sunday Times* 16 Nov. 35 The man who sold us fruit was Sammy and the woman Mary. **1990** D. CHILD in *Settler* Nov.-Dec. 18 The Indian vegetable and fruit seller ... was known as a 'sammy', presumably because many Hindu surnames ended with the suffix 'samy'.

samoosa /sə'muːsə/ *n.* Also **samosa.** [Hindi.] A deep-fried triangular Indian pastry containing curried meat or vegetables. Also *attrib.*

Unassimilated in *Brit. Eng.* (found usu. in the form 'samosa' /sə'məʊsə/).

1961 Z. MAYAT *Indian Delights* p.xvi, The art of samoosa making should be a must for who-so-ever wishes to learn Indian cookery. **1963** A.M. LOUW *20 Days* 74 The odour of the curry dish .. raged through the house ... She was mixing the dough for samosas, punctuating the vigorous slaps and punches with an occasional grunt of: 'so ja!' **1974** *E. Prov. Herald* 3 Dec. 30 The galley at the Naval Gymnasium, Saldanha Bay, is often redolent with the spicy smell of fresh samoosas these days. **1979** HEARD & FAULL *Our Best Trad. Recipes* 60 The perfect samoosa is one that is a perfect triangle, and has no corner left gaping, not even the tiniest gap. **1986** SILBER & PRENDINI in *Style* Apr. 46 Man cannot live on nouvelle cuisine alone! Man needs the odd samoosa, dammit! **1987** L. BEAKE *Strollers* 38 Caught, by the police, at the café that sells the lekker samoosas. **1990** *Weekly Mail* 14 Sept. 7 As we sit around the fancy dinner table with its fancy chairs, .. we tuck into samoosas, biryani and roast served by a domestic worker. **1992** *Sunday Times* 13 Dec. 7 Over tea and samoosas, Indians were given a rundown on the party and what they hoped to achieve if they became Nats.

samp /sæmp/ *n. noncount.* [Extended use of U.S. Eng., 'coarsely-ground maize', fr. Algonquian *nasamp*, Narragansett *nasaump* 'softened by water' (applied to stews, cereal, and bouillon).] Coarsely ground maize kernels; the stiff 'porridge' made of these kernels; STAMP; STAMPED MEALIES. Also *attrib.* See also MNGQUSH(O).

A staple food for many.

1900 *Grocott's Penny Mail* 6 July 1 (*advt*) 30 Bags Bran, 50 Bags Samp. **1902** E. HOBHOUSE *Brunt of War* 117, ½lb. either meal, rice, samp or potatoes. **1916** *Farmer's Weekly* 20 Dec. 1454 (*advt*) Before placing your orders for Mealies, Kaffir Corn, Mealie Meal, Samp or Wheat or Meal elsewhere, .. ask Messrs. Freeman & Dersley .. to quote. **1955** W. ILLSLEY *Wagon on Fire* 187 He saw two little piccanins fighting with his master's dog for possession of a plate of scraps, meat and samp. **1963** B. MODISANE *Blame me on Hist.* (1986) 31 A dish of samp mealies — a sort of hominy dish — with meat followed by more tea. **1965** K. MACKENZIE *Deserter* 139 He scooped up some samp — squashed-together boiled mealies — from a bowl and pushed it into his mouth. **1972** *Grocott's Mail* 1 Feb. 3 The basic diet for many families has become samp and pumpkin, both having little nutritive value. **1979** Y. BURGESS *Say Little Mantra* 111 Old Boer recipes like bredies and sugar beans and yellow rice and stiff mealie meal porridge and boerewors and samp and sour milk. **1979** M. MATSHOBA *Call Me Not a Man* 43 The samp is part of our payment — we receive a bag as big as this one you're wearing plus ten rands every month's end. **1981** *Job Mava* (Ikwezi Players) in *Staffrider* Vol.3 No.4, 27 My wife, Noamen, was at home, cooking our samp and beans on the primus stove. **1988** K. BARRIS *Small Change* 75 He had one memory left of his childhood .. : a black, three-legged pot standing on the ground .. , a few cowpats smouldering, slowly cooking the samp all day long. **1991** A. VAN WYK *Birth of New Afrikaner* 44 We lived close to the .. *arbeidskoloniewinkel* (labour colony store) with its profusion of tickey's (three-pence) worth of salt, sugar, coffee or samp, to be paid for from the next harvest.

sampan var. TAMPAN.

San /sæn, san, sɑːn/ *n.* Also **Saan,** and (formerly) **Saen, Sana.** [Nama, 'collector (of food)'; a name given to this people by the Khoikhoi (see quot. 1988).]

1. A name originally given by the Khoikhoi to a member of an indigenous people of southern and south-western Africa, traditionally hunter-gatherers, now living mainly in the Kalahari regions of Angola, Botswana, and Namibia, in dwindling numbers; BOSJESMAN sense 1; BUSHMAN sense 1 a; HOUZOUANA; SAAP; SOA; cf. SONQUA. Also *attrib.* See also BUSH *adj.*[2], HEIKUM, KHOISAN sense 1, MASARWA.

In the early 1970s, academic and scientific writers preferred the term 'San' to 'Bushman', the latter being perceived as pejorative. However, 'San' is now believed by some to have been a derogatory word when used by the Khoikhoi, and 'Bushman' is again in use among scholars (see quot. 1993).

Latterly the supposed distinction (in culture, and often in language) between San and KHOIKHOI has come to be considered as spurious, and many writers now refer to these peoples collectively as 'the KHOISAN'.

1830 A. SMITH in *S. Afr. Quarterly Jrnl* I. 171 To this [division] the other tribes, as well as its own members, apply the name of *Saap* or *Saan*, and history describes a portion thereof under the appellation of Bushmen. **1853** F. GALTON *Narr. of Explorer in Tropical S. Afr.* 42 A savage loses his name, 'Saen,' which is the Hottentot word, as soon as he leaves his Bushman's life and joins one of the larger tribes .. ; and therefore when I say Oerlam, Hottentot or Bushman, the identically same yellow, flat-nosed, woolly-haired, clicking individual must be conjured up . . , but differing in dirt, squalor, and nakedness, according to the actual term employed. **1876** *Encycl. Brit.* IV. 575 Bushmen or Bosjesmans, so named by the British and Dutch colonists of the Cape, but calling themselves Saab or Saan are an aboriginal race of South Africa, allied in some respects to the Hottentots. **1881** T. HAHN *Tsuni-||Goam* 3 In the Nama language, one of the Khoikhoin idioms, the Bushmen are called Sa-n (com. pl.). The meaning of this term is not quite intelligible. **1905** W.H. TOOKE in Flint & Gilchrist *Science in S. Afr.* Aug. 17 The Hottentot name for the Bushman was San, Sonqua and Obiqua or robber. **1920** S.M. MOLEMA *Bantu Past & Present* 22 The Bushman race, or, as they termed themselves, the Sana. **1930, 1966** [see SONQUA]. **1977** R. ELPHICK *Kraal & Castle* 28 The word *San* could . . be exceedingly flexible in reference. It was applied not only to hunter-gatherers but to small-scale stock breeders like the Horisans and Sangomomkoa. **1980** D.B. COPLAN Urbanization of African Performing Arts. p.xi, 'Khoisan' refers to indigenes of so-called 'Hottentot' (Khoi) and 'Bushman' (San) stock. **1981** *Voice* 23 June 7 The Saan people in the Kalahari Desert have a different view of God. The Saan speak directly to their God, asking him for guidance through the moon. **1981** [see SONQUA]. **1988** H. ANGULA in B. Wood *Namibia 1884–1984* 103 The San do indeed now also call themselves by the name *San*, a word which originally meant hoarding, collecting fruits, digging roots and capturing animals. Anthropological studies tend to classify the San people with the Khoi-Khoi people in a *'Khoisan race'* . . . Anthropologists believe them to be descendants of a Late Stone Age people who roamed southern Africa at least 30,000 years ago . . . Nevertheless, the origin of the San people is a matter of controversy amongst notable scientific researchers. *Ibid.* 114 Informed estimates place the number of San now living in the Kalahari Sandveld regions of Botswana, Namibia and Southern Angola at above 55,000. The main San groups, found in the north-east of Namibia now include the *Heikum*, the *Kwankara*, the *Ovangola*, and the *Kung* or *!Khang*, who are the most numerous. **1990** E. HOLTZHAUSEN in *Sunday Times* 31 Mar. 15 David – 'I am a Bushman not a San' – and his tribe live on the Kagga Kamma game reserve, . . overlooking the barren, sandy scrubland of the Great Karoo. **1993** J.A. LOUW *Informant, Pretoria* Saan is a Khoi word meaning *collector* i.e. of food. It has a slightly pejorative meaning and the Bush people do not like it.

2. The group of languages or dialects spoken by this people; BOSJESMAN sense 2; BUSH *n.*[2]; BUSHMAN sense 2. Also *attrib.* See also KHOISAN sense 2.

Although Khoikhoi and San are said to be 'distinct language families', to the early colonists each appeared to be understood by speakers of the other. See also KHOIKHOI sense 2.

1883 R. CRUST *Mod. Langs. of Afr.* II. 442 Bleek was engaged busily working at his San Dictionary up to ten o'clock on the night of August 16, 1875, and he was suddenly called away the following morning. **1967** D.S. PARLETT *Short Dict. Lang.* 73 The Khoin or 'Click' languages . . comprising to the south Bushmen (San), to the north Hottentot (Nama) [etc.]. **1977** C.F. & F.M. VOEGELIN *Classification & Index World's Lang.* 201 South African Khoisan. Central . . . 36. San = Saan.

sancord /'sænkɔːd/ *n.* Also **sanchord.** [Unkn.; perh. ad. Malay *sangkor* bayonet (the spines of the Scorpaenidae inflict intensely painful stabs which, if deep, may be dangerous).] Either of two species of scorpionfish (Scorpaenidae): **a.** The JACOPEVER (sense 1 a), *Helicolenus dactylopterus.* **b.** The JACOPEVER (sense 1 c), *Trachyscorpia capensis.*

1887 *S.W. Silver & Co.'s Handbk to S. Afr.* 181 *Sebastes maculatus.* Sancord. A delicious fish, not very common. **1900** J.D.F. GILCHRIST *Hist. of Local Names of Cape Fish* 224 (Pettman), We have hitherto considered names for which derivations can be suggested . . There are a few, however, for which no plausible derivation can be discovered. These are bafaro, assous . . forfarin, sanchord. **1913** C. PETTMAN *Africanderisms* 423 *Sancord, Sebastes maculatus.* Known as the bastard Jakob Evertsen. **1949** J.L.B. SMITH *Sea Fishes* 369 *Helicolenus maculatus* (Cuvier). *Sancord. Jacopever* (West Coast) . . . Attains 15 ins. From Walfish Bay to Natal . . sometimes quite abundant in the trawl. Flesh palatable. **1951** L.G. GREEN *Grow Lovely* 90 It is possible that such mysterious names as bafaro, sancord, halfcord and kartonkel are really Malay names. **1972** — *When Journey's Over* 147 Season after season he offered the popeyed Jakob Evertsen or Jakopiver, the slender and delicious Sancord and the stout kabeljou. **1979** SNYMAN & KLARIE *Free from Sea* 33 *Jacobever,* Sancord . . . An attractive red fish with delicately-flavoured flesh, marketed in South Africa as Sea Bream.

sandalwood *n.* Also **sandle-wood.** [Transf. use of general Eng. *sandalwood* a name used of several species of trees of the genus *Santalum* with scented wood; see quot. 1961.] The TAMBOTIE (sense 1), *Spirostachys africana*; the wood of this tree. Also *attrib.* Occas. also with defining word, as **African -, Cape sandalwood.**

1850 R.G.G. CUMMING *Hunter's Life* II. 89 Here Mollyee climbed to the summit of a sandle-wood tree to try if he could see the elephants. **1864** T. BAINES *Explor. in S.-W. Afr.* 182 Within the last few days a small tree called sandal-wood has put forth its beautiful light yellow flowers, which droop most gracefully from its long and slender twigs. **1913** C. PETTMAN *Africanderisms* 423 *Sandalwood, Excaecaria africana.* The natives make necklaces and charms of the scented wood of this tree. **1961** PALMER & PITMAN *Trees of S. Afr.* 239 *Spirostachys Africanus, Tamboti,* sandalwood, jumping-bean tree. *Ibid.* 240 The wood has a permanent pleasant strong smell and so, in parts of the country, has been given the name of sandalwood. **1972** — *Trees of Sn Afr.* II. 1157 *Spirostachys africana,* . . Tamboti, Cape sandalwood. **1987** F. VON BREITENBACH *Nat. List of Indigenous Trees* 97 *Spirostachys africana,* . . Tamboti, African sandalwood, Jumping-bean tree.

sand-creeper *n. obs.* [tr. S. Afr. Du. *zandkruiper,* see SANDKRUIPER.] SANDKRUIPER sense 1.

1731 G. MEDLEY tr. *P. Kolb's Present State of Cape of G.H.* II. 203 There is a fish at the Cape, call'd the Sand-Creeper, from its keeping near sandy shores, and endeavouring to hide itself in the sand, when 'tis taken in the net. The Sand-Creeper is something like the Thornback above-describ'd: But 'tis thicker and longer.

SANDF /es eɪ en diː 'ef, 'sændəf/ *n.* Initial letters of *South African National Defence Force,* from 1994 the collective name of the armed forces. Also *attrib.* See also DEFENCE FORCE.

Formerly called the South African Defence Force (see SADF).

1994 W. GOLDMAN in *Grocott's Mail* 29 Apr. 1 Grahamstown-based South African National Defence Force (SANDF) officials knew the first multi-racial election went 'without a hitch' when they witnessed a cricket match at the same hotel where a bloody massacre took place just one year ago. **1994** *Weekend Post* 6 Aug. 8 The appointment of former SADF chief of staff Lt-Gen Pierre Steyn as Defence Secretary is a wise move. It remedies the failure to make him chief of the SANDF when the opportunity arose with the installation of the new government in May. **1994** *Sunday Times* 28 Aug. 1 Exhausted policemen . . traffic officers, SANDF soldiers and police reservists wrapped up the night's work at 4am yesterday. **1994** *Natal Witness* 23 Dec. 1 The fact that the king is being protected by the SANDF had brought 'worrying dimensions' to the king's 'alienation' from his people.

||**sandkruiper** /'santkrœɪpə(r)/ *n.* Also **sandkruper, zandkruiper.** [Afk., fr. Du. *zand* sand + *kruiper* creeper; see quot. 1731.]

1. Any of several species of marine fish of the family Rhinobatidae (guitarfishes); SAND-CREEPER.

1887 *S.W. Silver & Co.'s Handbk to S. Afr.* 185 *Rhinobatus annulatus* . . . Zand Kruiper . . . Flesh tender and delicate. [**1906** J.G. SCHEUCHZER tr. *E. Kaempfer's Hist. of Japan* I. 233 Jeso by the Dutch call'd Sandkruper, is a middling fish between a Smelt and an Eel.] **1913** C. PETTMAN *Africanderisms* 536 *Vioolvisch,* A species of sand shark, *Rhinobatus annulatus,* has received its name because of its fiddle-like shape. Called also *Zand-kruiper.* **1949** J.L.B. SMITH *Sea Fishes* 64 *Rhinobatos blochii . . . Rhinobatos obtusus . . . Sand Shark. Sandkruiper. Fiddlefish. Vioolvis . . . Rhinobatos annulatus . . . Sand Shark. Sandkruiper. Shovelnose. Fiddlefish. Vioolvis. Guitarfish.* **1971** R. RAVEN-HART *Cape G.H. 1652–1702* 521 Sandkruiper, *Rhinobatus sp.*

2. *obs.* A type of tortoise.

1911 *The State* Dec. 643 (Pettman), There were berg tortoises, and vlakte tortoises and zandkruipers and even water tortoises. **1913** C. PETTMAN *Africanderisms* 569 *Zand kruiper,* . . The name is also applied to a variety of tortoise.

sandle-wood var. SANDALWOOD.

sand-mole *n.* [tr. S. Afr. Du. *zandmol,* see ZAND-MOL.] The large subterranean rodent *Bathyergus suillus* of the Bathyergidae, which burrows in the coastal sand dunes of the Western Cape; BLESMOL sense b; *Cape dune molerat,* see MOLERAT sense 2; MOLERAT sense 1 a; ZAND-MOL.

1850 A. WHITE *Pop. Hist. Mammalia* 232 Another member of this family . . is also a native of South Africa: this is the Coast Rat or Sand-Mole (*Bathyergus maritimus*). **1905** W.L. SCLATER in Flint & Gilchrist *Science in S. Afr.* 134 To the family *Bathyergidae* belong the Rodent-Moles; there are seven or eight species described, the best known being the large Sand Mole (*Bathyergus maritimus*), which forms long burrows all over the sand-hills in the neighbourhood of Cape Town. **1912** [see ZAND-MOL]. **1913** C. PETTMAN *Africanderisms* 112 The Sand-mole, *Bathyergus maritimus,* is as large as a half-grown rabbit, it burrows in the sand of the Cape Flats and similar localities . . . Its food consists of bulbs and roots. **1918** S.H. SKAIFE *Animal Life* 255 The heaps of sand thrown up by the large sand mole are familiar sights on the Cape Flats, and in sandy districts around the coast. **1972** C.M. VAN DER WESTHUIZEN in *Std Encycl. of Sn Afr.* VII. 490 The largest mole-rat is the Cape sand-mole or dune mole (*Bathyergus*).

sandveld /'sændfelt, 'santfɛlt/ *n.* Also **zandveld,** and with initial capital. [Afk., earlier S. Afr. Du. *zandveld,* fr. Du. *zand* sand + *veld* terrain, (open) undeveloped countryside.]

1. Land characterized by dry, sandy soil. Also *attrib.*

[**1824** W.J. BURCHELL *Trav.* II. 242 The plains on the other side [of the Langeberg] are called by the name of *Zandveld.*] **1873** *Blue Bk for Col.* JJ3, Several hundred trees have been planted along the main road to Cape Town . . on 'Zandveld'. **1919** *S. Afr. Geog. Jrnl* III. 73 The Free State farmer in the early spring-time treks to the 'sand veld' with his stock. **1929** *Farming in S. Afr.* Apr. 43 (Swart), Soils which contain a fair amount of phosphate . . are found principally in the 'sandveld' area of the Malmesbury-Piquetberg districts. **1937** MARAIS & SIM in *Handbk for Farmers* 704 In the sandveld the production of a grain crop is not easy – the soil is a light sand, not particularly fertile. **1939** 'D. RAME' *Wine of Good Hope* I. 158 They left the last of the wheat and came to a queer sand-veld. **1944** M. OLDEVIG *Sunny Land* 51 The Kalahari, the waterless sandveld of Bechuanaland and South West Africa. **1949** [see CAKE]. **1953** D. LESSING *Five* 121 This . . was farming country, . . a pocket of good, dark, rich soil in the wastes of the light sandveld. **1964** *Listener* (U.K.) 6 Aug. 192 He plants the first rose on the burnt sandveld. **1985** *Weekend Argus* 30 Nov. (Suppl.) 6 If you are one of those amateur nature-lovers like me who has often heard the word 'sandveld' but never really known what it referred to, you now have a chance to make a proper acquaintance with this fascinating and increasingly rare veld type. **1991** J. HUNTLY in *Sunday Star* 16 Feb. (Weekend) 4 The camel-thorn is the common thorn-tree of the Kalahari Sandveld. **1993** [see SOUR FIG].

2. With initial capital, usu. *attrib.* in the Special Comb. **Sandveld chair** [so called because usu. made in the Sandveld, a region of the Western Cape named for its characteristic soil type], a country chair of simple design, made of indigenous woods, esp. LEMON WOOD.

1973 M.A. COOK *Cape Kitchen* 9 A low kitchen chair of the 'Sandveld' type. **1974** *S. Afr. Panorama* Mar. 42 It is just as if a small part of the South African veld has been captured in the 'Pierneef Room' .. with its Sandveld chairs of wild lemon wood with riempie seats. *Ibid.* 43 The 30 'Sandveld' chairs in the room .. are made of wild lemon wood, and no more than approximately 500 are still extant in South Africa. **1979** *Ibid.* Aug. 3 Today, many of these quaint cottages .. are holiday homes belonging to Cape Town people who have restored them with loving attention to detail, down to the original old Zandveld chairs, [etc.]. **1986** [see HARD VELD]. **1987** *Cape Times* 19 Dec. 3 (*advt*) Antique Oregon pine 8-seater table with turned legs, .. Sandveld riempie chair.

sangoma /sæŋ'gəumə, saŋ'gɔma/ *n.* Also **i(n)-sangoma, (i)songoma, sangome, umungoma,** and with initial capital. Pl. **-s**, ‖**izangoma**, or (rarely) **abangoma**. [Zulu *isangoma* (pl. *izangoma*) diviner, fr. *-ngoma* sacred song; the stem *-ngoma* is found in some other Sintu (Bantu) languages in the sense of 'drum'. Forms with *umu-* and *aba-* are derived from less-frequently used Zulu forms of the word (see UM- and ABA-). For notes on the use of sing. and pl. forms, see ISI- and IZI-.] Esp. among Zulu-speakers: a traditional healer or diviner who employs music, dance, and the throwing of bones to discover evil and diagnose disease; also used as a title. Also *attrib.*, and *comb.* **sangomaland** *nonce*, see quot. 1978. See also WITCHDOCTOR.

1870 H. CALLAWAY *Religious System of Amazulu* 280 The doctor of divination is called Isanusi, or Ibuda, or Inyanga, or Umungoma: for when people are inquiring of a diviner, they say, 'True, Umungoma.' [*Note*] *Umungoma*, a diviner, but an epithet of respect. Etymology unknown. **1893** J.F. INGRAM *Story of Gold Concession* 72 Further out amongst the cliffs, slinking leopards, stately lions, and ravening wolves waited continually to do the bidding of the great sangome (prophetess, or witch). **1895** H. RIDER HAGGARD *Nada* 53 Five of the bravest captains of the army had been smelt out by the Abangoma, the witch-finders, together with many others. **1905** R. PLANT *Zulu in Three Tenses* 21 An Isanusi or Isangoma, that is a diviner, would be called in to discover the cause of this persistent illness, and to suggest a remedy. **1930** H.A. CHILVERS *Seven Lost Trails of Afr.* 170 (Swart), Tshaka sent for an 'isangoma', or wise-woman, and invited her to smell-out the author of the blood-spilling. **1949** A. KEPPEL-JONES *When Smuts Goes* 255 While soldiers marched about the town .. the *izangoma* threw their bones and examined entrails in the ballroom of their hotel. **1969** *Drum* Aug. 45 She is a herbal healer, or sangoma, by profession, who has even treated patients 10,000 miles away in America. The astonishing thing .. is that she is a member of the United Baptist Church which she attends regularly. **1974** C.T. BINNS *Warrior People* 250 *Ngoma* is the Zulu for a drum, *isa* being merely the personal prefix. Thus, an *isa-Ngoma* is a person who drums, or, as applied to witch-finding, one who drums out the witch from the individual who is supposed to be possessed. **1975** *S. Afr. Panorama* Nov. 21 Sangoma training involves the learning of songs, special dances, drumming, the ingestion of emetics for purification, and the continual instruction of the Baba (teacher) as she watches her twasa (pupil) carefully, noting her particular spirit manifestation. **1978** *Pace* Dec. 12 'Mpapane,' said to be the most powerful sangoma in the Transvaal .. came in .. armed with bones, flywhisks, all the blessings from sangomaland. **1988** [see BULA]. **1988** *Weekly Mail* 12 Aug. 5 The company agreed .. to grant workers five days' paid sick-leave per annum if they produce a certificate from a sangoma, inyanga, herbalist or other healer. **1989** H.P. TOFFOLI in *Style* Dec. 94 Diagonal Street is where you buy: A) Blue chips from white brokers. B) Dried crocodile tails from your friendly local sangoma. C) A rolex that fell off a truck. **1990** R. MALAN *My Traitor's Heart* 349 There are several sangomas in the crowd, draped in beads and totems, with inflated pig bladders in their hair. **1992** S. CHETTY in *Sunday Times* 17 May 4 At least 80 percent of the black population consult sangomas instead of medical doctors, and the respect these traditional healers command will be invaluable in AIDS awareness. **1992** *Natal Witness* 9 Nov. 11 Pretorius .. is a sangoma, and woe betide anyone who calls him a witchdoctor.

sanibona, sanibonani var. SAWUBONA.

Sankwa var. SONQUA.

sanna /'sana, 'sanə/ *n.* Also with initial capital. [Afk., shortened form of the name *Susanna.*]

1. *hist.* ROER sense a.

1900 H. BLORE *Imp. Light Horseman* 214 You will all have heard of his skill with the rifle .. the old-fashioned Sanna (Susan), the flint-lock musket. **1950** H.C. BOSMAN in L. Abrahams *Bekkersdal Marathon* (1971) 19 Gunpowder and lead, and oil to make the springs of our old sannas work smoothly. **1955** L.G. GREEN *Karoo* 110 The father had his flintlock muzzle-loader with him, an old-fashioned 'Sanna'. **1963** A.M. LOUW *20 Days* 52 Here we are going about as usual this morning and not a gun in the house except Oupa's old sanna. **1971** *Std Encycl. of Sn Afr.* IV. 520 The true or French flint lock, known in South Africa as the 'snaphaan' or 'sanna', was .. an improved version of the Dutch snaphaan, in that the frizzen and pan cover were now one unit. **1972** D.W. KRÜGER in *Ibid.* VII. 399 Both the British troops and the burgher commandos used the flint-lock, which was in general use from about 1760 to 1840. This was the famous 'Brown Bess', the standard weapon during the American War of Independence and the Napoleonic Wars. In South Africa this muzzle-loader was known as the 'sanna' and was made famous by the Voortrekkers. **1975** W. STEENKAMP *Land of Thirst King* 58 A long smoothbore 'sanna' of the Voortrekker pattern, almost six feet long from the gaping muzzle with its ivory-tipped forestock to the deep-bellied butt. **1977** *S. Afr. Panorama* Feb. 40 In the case of the Voortrekkers .. their sannas (flint-lock rifles with frizzen pan) were part of their life .. not only for self-defence but also for food. **1989** *Reader's Digest Illust. Hist.* 116 The loading of the sanna (the name they gave to the muzzle-loading rifles they used) was a complicated procedure.

2. In full ***Sanna* 77**: a light semi-automatic machine-gun.

1978 *S. Afr. Digest* 29 Sept. 4 The Sanna 77, said to be the first fully South African-made, semi-automatic hand machine-gun, has been launched in Durban. **1979** *Farmer's Weekly* 21 Mar. 10 The latest in an increasingly long line of South African weaponry is the Sanna 77. It's a light, handy weapon designed with survival in mind. *Ibid.* 11 It's the lines of the Sanna 77 that provides [*sic*] that special interest, for this semi-automatic 9 mm Parabellum hand carbine is a light, handy weapon. *Ibid.* 12 The manufacturers of the Sanna maintain that the weapon — it's a fixed striker, blowback-operated gun — has an effective range of 300 m. **1986** M. GWALA in S. Ndaba *One Day in June* 61 Ideas more long-ranged than an FN rifle or a Sanna 77, and more absolute than a hippo, will always crop up and surpass those ideas born of repression.

Sansco /'sænskəu/ *n.* Acronym formed on *South African National Students' Congress*, the name, from December 1986, of the student organization formerly known as AZASO. Cf. COSAS.

The change of name from 'Azaso' to 'Sansco' was intended to prevent confusion with AZAPO and AZASM (of the black consciousness movement). See also quot. 1991 at SASO.

Sansco merged with NUSAS in 1991 under the name 'Sansco'.

1987 J. DOWSON in *Argus* 1 Sept. 11 Known until last December as the Azanian Students' Organisation (Azaso), Sansco, like Nusas, is a UDF affiliate and supports the principles contained in the Freedom Charter. **1989** *Race Rel. Survey 1988–9* 302 On 24 February 1988 the South African National Students' Congress (SANSCO) was banned ... A month prior to the banning, SANSCO had branches on 85 university, college and technikon campuses. **1991** *Rhodeo* (Rhodes Univ.) Apr. 9 The merger of the National Union of South African Students (NUSAS) and the South African National Students Congress (SANSCO) is particularly symbolic at Rhodes, because it was here that Steve Biko led the walk-out by black students from NUSAS in 1969.

Santa /'sæntə/ *n.* Also **SANTA, S.A.N.T.A.** Acronym formed on *South African National Tuberculosis Association*, a welfare organization established in 1947 to combat the spread of tuberculosis. Also *attrib.*

1952 B. DAVIDSON *Report on Sn Afr.* 195 The South African white T.B. rate, S.A.N.T.A. concluded, is 'dangerously high' — as indeed one might expect, given .. a steep rate of incidence among non-whites. **1955** J.B. SHEPHARD *Land of Tikoloshe* 156 There is a ray of hope in S.A.N.T.A. The South African National Tuberculosis Association is a private body which is setting out to raise a million pounds by public subscription. Part of the funds will be used to build suitable settlements where African T.B. patients can be segregated. **1967** E. ROSENTHAL *Encycl. of Sn Afr.* 521 SANTA .. receives substantial contributions from the Government, but is dependent to a large extent on the generosity of the public. **1971** *Daily Dispatch* 30 June 2 The need for more beds at the Santa Settlement at Fort Grey was emphasised by the treasurer of the local branch of Santa. **1973** *Evening Post* 16 July 2 Santa says its function is to prevent the disease spreading, provide treatment services, undertake research, assist with control measures, educate the public and provide social assistance for TB families. **1990** *Grocott's Mail* 19 June 6 Re-elected for another term as Chairman of the SANTA Bathurst District Branch.

santheit var. GESONDHEID.

sanuse, -nusi varr. ISANUSI.

SAP *n.*[1] Also **S.A.P, Sap.** [Initial letters of *South African Party.*]

1. /es eɪ 'piː/ *hist.* Any of several political groupings, but esp.: **a.** A party representing conciliation between white English- and Afrikaans-speaking people, founded in 1911 after Union by Generals Smuts and Botha, and fusing with the Nationalist Party in 1934 to form the United Party (see UP); *Nationalist Party* sense (*a*), see NATIONALIST *n.* sense c; see also UNIONIST, VOLK sense 3 a i. **b.** A short-lived party (from 1977 to 80) formed by a conservative group which broke away from the United Party. Also *attrib.*

1908 *Star* 3 Feb. 7 S.A.P. Leaders ... The South African Party .. is likely to be in power for years to come. **1920** [see Black quot. at sense 2]. **1927** *Star* 31 May 9 An S.A.P. victory in the Cape. Hopetown regained from the Nationalists. **1974** D.W. KRÜGER in *Std Encycl. of Sn Afr.* X. 103 At its inception the South African Party (S.A.P. for short) was representative of all the nation-minded sections of the population, English- as well as Afrikaans-speaking. **1978** *Daily Dispatch* 25 Jan. 1 Both men were leading figures in the old United Party before the breakaway last year to form the SAP with four other conservative MPs. **1989** *Reader's Digest Illust. Hist.* 346 In December 1984, after a long debate and acrimonious splits in both the NP and the SAP, the United South African National Party (later the United Party) came into being.

2. /sap, sæp; es eɪ 'piː/. Pl. **-s**, **Sappe** /'sapə/. **a.** *hist.* A member or supporter of the South African Party. **b.** *hist.* A (conservative) member or supporter of the United Party (see UP); see also

BLOEDSAP. **c.** *hist.* In *pl.*: The South African Party; the United Party; collectively, the members of either party. **d.** *transf.* Any conservative opposition politician. Also *attrib.*

Used chiefly as an acronym, freq. in contrast to 'Nat' (see NAT *n.* sense a).

1920 S. BLACK *Dorp* 9 The scornful word 'Sappers', which he knew to be a term of contempt applied by members of Hertzog's Party (the Nationalists) to all those of the Botha-Smuts element or 'SAP' (South African Party). **1920** R.Y. STORMBERG *Mrs Pieter de Bruyn* 20 Don't talk politics, or if you have to, be an S.A.P. to du Preez and Mr van Rooyen. **1926** [see NAT *n.* sense a]. **1933** J.C. SMUTS in J. Van der Poel *Sel. Smuts Papers* (1973) V. 567 It may be a case of Sap predominance, with a Nat prime minister with a small following of his own. **1943** I. FRACK *S. Afr. Doctor* 89 Complete disregard of politics on the part of a citizen rendered him liable to be regarded as a Sap. by the Nats. and as a Nat. by the Saps., incurring the displeasure of both and becoming a subject of endless gossip to the whole population. **1963** A. DELIUS *Day Natal Took Off* 8 An aspirant politician, a third generation Sap, bitter from having been for so many years on the losing side. **1972** *Daily Dispatch* 20 July 10 That silly Second World War those naughty Allies — and the Sappe — insisted on fighting. **1972** *Argus* 27 Nov. 23 The Broederbond — those extra streamlined super de-luxe Afrikaners, who do not just discriminate against the English, or the Jews, or the Sappe (U.P.), but against their fellow Afrikaners. **1975** *Sunday Times* 3 Aug. 19 People are born Nat or Sap and die that way. **1977** F.G. BUTLER *Karoo Morning* 99 Political humanity at this time was entirely white, and was divided into two species or races: Nats and Saps. Nats were all Afrikaans, Saps were mostly English, plus Jews, and some very brave Afrikaners. **1980** *Sunday Times* 3 Feb., My father .. often changed his politics and we went to Afrikaans schools when he was a Nat and to English schools when he was a Sap. **1981** *Ibid.* 14 June (Mag. Sect.) 9 It's an area that still thinks in terms of 'Nat' and 'Sap' ... 'Here the Progs don't stand much of a chance.' **1988** SMUTS & ALBERTS *Forgotten Highway* 131 The lawyer in Ceres was United Party — a Sap — and Pa was a Nat. **1990** [see Sunday Times quot. at NAT *n.* sense a]. **1991** A. VAN WYK *Birth of New Afrikaner* 56 At school we had gangs of pro-Germans and pro-British, corresponding closely to parental party-political affiliations. The Nats were pro-German and the Saps pro-British. The term Saps for the followers of the South African Party, formed in 1911, remained in existence for decades after its merger with the United Party. **1991** *Ibid.* [see BLOEDSAP]. **1991** [see ENGELSMAN sense 2].

SAP /es eɪ 'piː/ *n.*[2] *hist.* Also occas. **Sap** /sæp/. [Initial letters of *South African Police.*] The police force; a member or members of this force. Also *attrib.*

Renamed the South African Police Service (see SAPS) on 28 April 1994.

[**1912** *Act 14* in *Stat. of Union* 292 There shall be established .. a police force entitled the South African Police.] **1913** *Report of Commissioner of Police .. 1911* (UG62–1912), I hope that, under the S.A.P. Regulations, the practice of awarding marksman's badges will be continued. **1914** [see DEFENCE FORCE]. **1917** *The Jrnl* 26 Apr., The bayoneted platoon of the Port Elizabeth SAP marched in columns of four from the Court House. **1966** K.M.C. MOTSISI in *Golden City Post* 30 Jan. (Drum) 16 The Khakied ones with helmets and batons or bayonets are called Saps (South African Police). **1972** *Drum* 22 June 8 Ahead of a cloud of dust, came a convoy of SAP vehicles carrying a hundred policemen with dogs. **1979** *Citizen* 9 Apr. 2 In pitched battles, the SAP unit met up with the terrorists repeatedly in the most difficult terrain. *c*1980 *S. Afr. 1979: Off. Yrbk* (Dept of Info.) 316 The SAP is a national force and therefore the first line of defence in the event of internal unrest. **1983** W. STEENKAMP in *Leadership* Sept. 66 It is a safe bet that the SADF and the SAP combined would be able to maintain essential internal security, if not absolute peace, if the need arose. **1986** L.M. THEUNISSEN in *Hansard* 28 Apr. 4502 South Africa is deeply indebted to the SAP and cannot express enough thanks for the excellent services rendered by the Force to maintain law and order and internal security. **1988** H. GOOSEN in *S. Afr. Panorama* Nov. 2 The SAP was established on 1 April, 1913, when the four provincial police forces joined to form a more efficient national force. **1991** J. PAUW *In Heart of Whore* 106 It is important to remember that the SAP has for decades been misused as a political instrument by the National Party governments to maintain and uphold the apartheid system. **1992** C. WHITFIELD in *Natal Mercury* 23 Nov. 3 The Goldstone Commission will investigate all security forces allegedly involved in violence in South Africa ... These would include the SAP, the SADF, Umkhonto we Sizwe, Apla, the Kwazulu Police and certain security firms. **1994** H. NKHOMA in *Sidelines* Dec. 15 Here with the whole SAP surrounding him, he had escaped again.

Sapa /'sɑːpə/ *n.* Also **SAPA**. Acronym formed on *South African Press Association*, an organization formed in 1938 to gather news and disseminate it to members and subscribers in the news media. Also *attrib.*

1938 *Star* 1 July 8 Both men feared the new purge now being carried out in Russia. — SAPA-Reuter. [*Ibid.* 19 A new source of news appears in The Star today, the South African Press Association, which has absorbed Reuter's Press Agency in South Africa.] **1971** *Evening Post* 2 Jan. 3 A total of 67 assault cases have been reported to the Port Natal Division since Thursday night .. -(Sapa). **1980** *Rand Daily Mail* 11 Feb. 1 Sapa, quoting British sources, reports that the Governor .. has banned one of Mr Mugabe's top lieutenants .. from campaigning in the coming election. **1987** *New Nation* 22 Jan. 2 A Sapa report said the police had launched a massive dragnet.

SAPS /es eɪ piː 'es/ *n.* [Initial letters of *South African Police Service.*] The police service; a member of this force. Also *attrib.*

Before 1994 called the South African Police (see SAP *n.*[2]).

1994 S. GOVENDER in *Natal Mercury* 8 Aug. 3 SAPS spokesman Col Hamilton Ngidi said when the policemen, who were travelling in a Nyala armoured car, approached a suspected stolen car, the occupants opened fire ... The SAPS have opened dockets of attempted murder. **1994** A. DONALDSON in *Style* Oct. 43 He revealed that the SAPS were investigating the laundering of drug money in this country ... There's not an SAPS member who does not believe that the recent murderous spree on local police officers .. was instigated by organized crime. **1994** D. FERREIRA in *Natal Witness* 23 Dec. 2 (*advt*) Natal Command is here to serve the people of our province ... In this we must endeavour to assist the Provincial Government and the SAPS in making KwaZulu Natal a province we can all be proud of.

sar *int.* var. SA *int.*

SAR /ˌes eɪ 'ɑː(r)/ *n.*[1] *Hist. rare.* Initial letters of *South African Republic*: see ZAR.

1899 A. MILNER in C. Headlam *Milner Papers* (1931) 555 Saw Schreiner early this morning and told him about very acute stage of relations between us and S.A.R. and O.F.S. **1899** M. STEYN in *Volkstem* 9 Oct. 1 It would not be practicable to induce the Government of the S.A.R. to make or entertain proposals or suggestions unless .. the troops menacing their State are withdrawn further from their borders.

SAR /es eɪ 'ɑː(r)/ *n.*[2] *hist.* Also **S.A.R.** [Initial letters of *South African Railways.*] **a.** A state-owned organization responsible for a range of transport and other services: see quot. 1970. **b.** *colloq.* SPOORWEG. Also *attrib.* Also **SAR & H**, South African Railways and Harbours.

Established in 1910, the SAR was renamed the South African Transport Services in 1981 (see SATS) and 'Transnet' in 1990.

1911 A.W. BARLOW in *Farmer's Weekly* 11 Oct. 154 It would be interesting to know how much revenue the SAR receive from natives .. travelling by rail. **1938** *Report of Railways & Harbours Board* (UG41–1938), South African Airways (S.A.R. & H.) The rapid expansion of the activities of South African Airways .. was continued during the year under review. **1948** *We Fought the Miles* (S.A.R. & H.) 15 The work .. of the S.A.R. & H. Women's War Fund. **1956** D. JACOBSON *Dance in Sun* 145 Informed his sister that he was working for the S.A.R. in De Aar. **1963** A. FUGARD *Notebks* (1983) 84 Forced out of his home to take a job with the S.A.R. laying sleepers on the line to Graaff-Reinet. **1970** *Std Encycl. of Sn Afr.* IX. 221 The S.A.R. The term 'South African Railways' includes railways, harbours, airways and associated services such as the road transport services, oil pipelines, catering services, and the management of publicity and travel. The system is State-owned and administered and worked under the Ministry of Transport. **1971** *Evening Post* 4 Apr. 7 The SAR & H in Durban has just taken on 50 Africans as fork-lift drivers. **1972** *Daily Dispatch* 24 Jan. 10 South Africa is largely a socialist country with several socialistic manifestations — SAR and H, Iscor, Sasol and the state-controlled enterprises such as broadcasting and the XDC. **1980** M. LIPTON in *Optima* Vol.29 No.2, 91 Of 125 000 Blacks employed by South African Railways and Harbours (SAR), one-third were migrants. **1984** *Frontline* Feb. 25 Going .. to Cape Town on the SAR or whatever the Railways calls itself these days. **1991** M. KANTEY *All Tickets* 10 The train of my first twenty-eight years. The SAR & H — now the South African Transport Services — suburban line from Simon's Town to Cape Town and back again.

SARB /es eɪ ɑː(r) 'biː/ *n.* [Initial letters of *South African Rugby Board.*] A body formed in 1889 to co-ordinate the administration of rugby in South Africa. Also *attrib.*

1972 K. LOUW in *Sunday Times* 11 June 7 To talk of a rugby dictatorship is ridiculous. The game is run by the SARB, which consists of 20 unions, all of whom have a say. **1987** *E. Prov. Herald* 29 July 1 A majority of SARB delegates saw no purpose of staying within the rules of the IRB. **1990** M. SMIT in *Sunday Times* 16 Sept. 25 Meetings have been held between SABC's sport arm chief .. and SARB negotiators.

sardine *n.* [Calque formed on Afk. *sardyn.*]
1. Esp. on the east coast: the pilchard *Sardinops ocellatus* of the Clupeidae; SARDYN; SHAD sense 2.

In Smith and Heemstra's *Smiths' Sea Fishes* (1986), the name 'South African pilchard' is used for this species.

1913 C. PETTMAN *Africanderisms* 424 *Sardine*, .. a small species of herring — *Clupea ocellata* — very abundant on the coast at times. **1966** *Daily News* 12 Sept. 5 Feeding on the sardines are large numbers of garrick and shad. **1973** *E. Prov. Herald* 5 July 21 The 'sardines' are the same as the pilchards which are found in vast shoals off the West Coast ... The most acceptable theory of the origin of the Natal 'sardines' is that they are breakaway shoals of the West Coast concentrations which migrate round the Cape coast and up to Natal waters. **1981** *Ibid.* 9 July 9 In the south and south-east Cape .. the shoals of sardines (they are actually pilchards) pass our coast on their way north and are followed by shoals of game fish. **1990** *Weekend Post* 30 June (Leisure) 4 *S. ocellata* is the name given to the elusive shoals of sardines, little silver fish which tumble on to Natal and Transkei beaches during their (still mysterious) northward migration.

2. Special Comb. **sardine fever**, the excitement generated by the annual appearance inshore of these fish in large numbers; **sardine run**, the annual northward movement of these fish in huge shoals, esp. off the coast of KwaZulu-Natal, accompanied by predators and other fishes; also *fig.* (see quot. 1980).

1980 *S. Afr. Panorama* July 28 Every year in mid-winter South Africans along the South and North coasts of Natal are gripped by '**sardine fever**'. **1982** *Daily Dispatch* 25 June 1 Sardine fever hit the Port Edward area last night ... 'Sometimes I wish the sardine run never happened — it's absolute chaos.'

1984 *Natal Mercury* in *S. Afr. Digest* 13 July 24 Sardine fever! They came to the Natal South Coast with sacks and baskets, light trucks and cars ... The little fish were paying their yearly visit. **1990** *Sunday Times* 1 July 27 Every year she faces sardine fever with fear and trepidation. **1955** C. HORNE *Fisherman's Eldorado* 75 Katonkel .. the barracuda of Natal, fish which stir anglers on the Natal south coast to intense activity in the annual **sardine run**. **1957** S. SCHOEMAN *Strike!* 16 The annual 'sardine run' along the Pondoland and Natal South Coasts during June each year, is a typical example of the migratory habits of fishes towards and along our coasts. **1978** *Sunday Times* 2 July (Mag. Sect.) 3 Racing, sugar cane and the sardine run. Yes friends, it's your actual Durbs, somnolent in winter sunshine. **1980** *Rand Daily Mail* 5 Dec. 1 Within hours of schools closing for the Christmas holidays, Transvaal yesterday started their annual 'sardine run' to the country's coastal areas. **1981** *E. Prov. Herald* 9 July 9 The Natal sardine run which occurs every winter remains one of the world's unsolved natural mysteries and is a happening unique to South Africa. **1992** DUDLEY & CLIFF in *Afr. Wildlife* Vol.46 No.6, 258 Large numbers (several thousands) of bottlenose dolphins visit Natal waters from the south in association with the annual 'sardine run'. **1992** R. RUDDEN in *Sunday Times* 17 May 15 They [*sc.* the dolphins] were following the annual so-called sardine run (the fish are really pilchards) and became entangled in the nets before suffering slow and horrifying deaths. **1993** R. VAN DER ELST *Guide to Common Sea Fishes* 155 It [*sc.* the Cape yellowtail] is mainly an inhabitant of Atlantic waters, but each winter it follows the pilchard migrations, or 'sardine run', up the East Coast to Transkei and Natal.

sardyn *n. obs.* [S. Afr. Du.] SARDINE sense 1.

1837 *Moderator* 17 Jan. 2 The varieties of fish were striking; viz. the harder, smelt, .. the sardyn (sprat), in countless myriads, and even the sole. **1887** [see SHAD]. **1913** W.W. THOMPSON *Sea Fisheries of Cape Col.* 38 The herring (Clupea ocellata), known to fishermen as sardyn and almost identical with the true herring .. of Europe, was early identified by the settlers. [**1934** C.P. SWART Supplement to Pettman. 151 *Sardyn*, The Clupea ocellata was so called by the early Dutch colonists because the form and disposition of the fish brought to mind the European herring.]

Sarie /'sɑːri/ *n. hist.* Also **Sari**. [Acronym formed on *South African Record Industry*, the award having been initially sponsored by various members of this industry. The award was subsequently administered by Springbok Radio, when the letter *e* was added to the name (*Sarie* being a woman's name in Afk.), possibly to link it with the well-known Afrikaans song *Sarie Marais*.] Any of several awards presented annually in the past to local artists judged the year's best in various categories of music. Also *attrib.*

1972 *Evening Post* 14 Oct. 7 The list of past Sarie winners (it was Sari at one time) reads like a South African musical Who's Who ... Many up and coming young artists used a Sarie win as a springboard to launch their careers. This is the main purpose of Sarie — to find new South African talent. **1973** *Weekend Post* 30 June 2 The Springbok Sari awards are for the year's best recordings in various categories. Only South African artists are eligible. *c*1988 *S. Afr. 1987–8: Off. Yrbk* (Bureau for Info.) 726 The latest Springbok Radio Sarie awards went to Hotline (best song of the year).

sarmie /'sɑːmi/ *n. colloq.* Also **saamie**, **sarmy**. [Perh. ad. N. Eng. dial. *sarnie*, representing local pronunciation of the first element of *sandwich*; in S. Afr. Eng. *sandwich* is often pronounced 'samwidge'.] Esp. in the language of children: a sandwich.

1970 M. BURGER *Informant, Pietersburg*, I forgot to make sarmies for school. **1970** M.C. DUFFY *Informant, Durban* The children swop sarmies at break. **1975** 'BLOSSOM' in *Darling* 12 Mar., A delicacy known as the chip butty (sort of sarmy with chips in the middle). **1975** *Ibid.* 9 Apr. 95 Giant cooler-bags full of beer, cold drinks, packets of biltong and home-made salami sarmies like you never tasted. **1978** J. HOBBS *Darling Blossom* 170 Under the gumtree in the playground .. opsing each others' sarmies. I crave Lorna's marmite and she goes for my fish paste. [*Note*] Opsing — swopping. **1979** *Sunday Times* 23 Sept. (Mag. Sect.) 31 She's got the ladies in the show bringing in meals to eat between performances so they don't have to send out for boring old toasted saamies. **1986** V. COOKE et al. in S. Gray *Market Plays* 45 Every time I try to touch you — you just close off or you — you offer me sarmies or coffee or something. **1989** T. BOTHA in *Style* June 111 The soulfood of the long-distance driver. The valium of the N1. Padkos. Sarmies, biltong, beers, Cokes, chips, Nux bars and indigestion. **1990** M. VAN BILJON in *Your Family* Oct. 178 You must admit there's something about a soggy tomato sarmie that has no equal in haute cuisine. **1991** E. WILLIAMS *Informant, Cape Town* Jonathan's Ma makes super sarmies, you know, sandwiches with polony and tomato sauce and pickles and stuff like that. **1993** L. NICHOLLS in *Natal Mercury* 18 Mar. (Woman's Weekly) 1 The ever-starving 'hostels' — the farm children who were the rubbish dump for spoilt day-pupils who didn't like *their* 'sarmies'.

sarsapi var. SASSABY.

sarsartie var. SOSATIE.

SAS /'es ei es/ *n.* Also **S.A.S.** [Initial letters of *South African Ship*.] The official designation used before the names of vessels of the South African Navy.

In the past (1922–1952) preceded by the letters 'HM', abbrev. of 'His Majesty's'.

[**1952** *Govt Gaz.* 20 June 26 The Governor-General has been pleased .. to amend the Regulations for the South African Permanent Force as follows ... By the addition .. of the following:— 'Any reference in these regulations to "H.M.S.A. Ships" shall be deemed to read "S.A. Ships".'] **1971** *Argus* 13 May 19, I .. tuned into direct transmission from S.A.S. Tafelberg. **1981** *Rand Daily Mail* 15 May. 1 The frigate SAS Kruger .. stopped and two divers plunged into the sea to rescue the struggling ratings. **1984** *Cape Times* 9 Jan. 1 Bushfire crews drawn from naval units and the frigates SAS Pretorius and SAS Protea .. were involved. **1993** *Weekend Post* 20 Nov. 3 The current SAS Fleur was the first warship built in South Africa since the Second World War.

sasaartjie, **sasaatie**, **sasaatj(i)e**, **sasa(i)tie**, **sasart(j)ie** varr. SOSATIE.

Sasafrika /sas'aːfrika/ *n. ?nonce.* [Pronunciation-spelling of *South Africa*, prob. intended to represent the phonetics of the Sintu (Bantu) languages; coined by Buntu Mfenyana.] South Africa.

1980 [see ISIJITA]. **1981** B. MFENYANA in M. Mutloatse *Reconstruction* 298 Our discussion would not be complete if we left out Sjita-scamto: a creole with mainly Afrikaans, Sintu and English elements, used by 10–15 million people in Sasafrika alone.

Sash *n.* Ellipt. for BLACK SASH (sense b). Also *attrib.*

1955 *Friend* in M. Rogers *Black Sash* (1956) 65 When delegates assembled outside for a group photograph of the congress, the 'Sash' women were there to meet them again. **1963** M.G. MCCOY *Informant, Port Elizabeth*, I had to get to a Sash stand in front of the Stock Exchange so we shared a taxi down. **1980** *Rand Daily Mail* 2 Oct. 3 'Sash members who attended the inquest of Mr Steven Biko were horrified .. ,' Mrs Jill Wentzel, the Sash's vice-president, said yesterday. **1990** *Weekly Mail* 9 Mar. 7 Reform or not, the Sash still has plenty of work. **1992** *Black Sash Newsletter* Aug. 3 At the heart of the debate is different perceptions of what Sash's role is and should be in transition and in the future.

Hence **Sasher** *n.*, *Black Sasher* (see BLACK SASH).

1964 *Black Sash* Vol.8 No.1, 46 The attentions of the ubiquitous sashers appeared to embarrass the Ministers, who went to considerable lengths to avoid them. **1965** Z. HERRIES-BAIRD in *Black Sash* Vol.9 No.2, 21, I have never considered myself a particularly adequate Sasher. **1971** J. ROBERTSON *Liberalism in S. Afr.* 142 It rapidly became clear to the Sashers that the infringements of such rights .. was having its chief impact on the non-whites rather than the whites. **1980** *E. Prov. Herald* 13 June 3 Sashers to persevere. The Port Elizabeth branch of the Black Sash will continue to hold solitary placard protests.

sash *v. obs.* Also with initial capital. [fr. prec.] Of members of the Black Sash: **a.** *intrans.* To stand in silent protest wearing a black sash. **b.** *trans.* To confront (government officials) with such a demonstration. In both senses also *black sash v.* (see BLACK SASH).

1956 M. ROGERS *Black Sash* 125 Dr van Rhijn, Minister of Economic Affairs, was 'sashed' in Johannesburg when he arrived to address a meeting of the Afrikaanse Sakekamer. **1956** *Queenstown Daily Rep.* in *Ibid.* 169 This morning four members of the Queenstown branch of the Women's Defence of the Constitution League left by car on the first leg of their 'pilgrimage' — which will entail their stopping and 'Sashing' at many centres en route — to Cape Town. **1965** J.M. RICHEY in *Sash* Vol.9 No.2, 33 As Grahamstown is tucked away in a corner of the forgotten Eastern Province, the Black Sash there did not have many chances of 'sashing' Cabinet Ministers.

SASO /'sæsəʊ, 'sɑːsɔ/ *n.* Also **S.A.S.O.**, **Saso**. [Acronym formed on *South African Students' Organisation*.] A student movement espousing the BLACK CONSCIOUSNESS philosophy, formed in 1969 after black students left NUSAS. Also *attrib.*

Banned in 1977; the founding of AZASO in 1979 was seen by some as a move to reconstitute this organization under a different name.

1970 *Survey of Race Rel.* (S.A.I.R.R.) 226 At a meeting of students from the non-white universities and seminaries that was held in December 1968 it was decided that they would form a South African Student's Organization (S.A.S.O.). **1977** *Pamphlet, Rhodes Univ.* Oct. 20 Black student leaders saw SASO as the best way of gaining some form of self respect, confidence and unity among the divided black community. **1977** *Survey of Race Rel.* (S.A.I.R.R.) 22 Over the next few years many Saso members came to feel that they no longer needed or wanted the cooperation of Whites. **1984** R. DAVIES et al. *Struggle for S. Afr.* 303 SASO was formed by Black students previously affiliated to the National Union of South African Students (NUSAS), but who had grown tired of what they saw as the paternalism of its dominant liberalism and its major concern with issues affecting white students. **1990** *Weekly Mail* 21 Sept. 11 Saso, whose leadership included Steve Biko, Barney Pityana and Patrick Lekota, was influenced by the United States' civil rights movement and adopted the black consciousness ideology. **1991** *Rhodeo* (Rhodes Univ.) Apr. 9 Following the walk-out in 1969, black students formed the South African Students Organisation (SASO), which ascribed to the philosophy of black consiousness. However, with the emergence of non-racial politics and the Freedom Charter in the late 70's and 80's, SASO reformed as Azaso and then changed its name to SANSCO in 1986.

sassaby /'sæsəbi/ *n.* Also **sarsapi**, **sassabie**, **sassaby**, **sassa(y)be**, **sesayby**, **sessaby**. [ad. SeTswana *tshêsêbe*.] The TSESSEBE, *Damaliscus lunatus*.

[**1801** W. SOMERVILLE *Narr. of E. Cape Frontier* (1979) 160 We found an Antelope of a species unknown called in the Bootshooana language Sesayby and by the boors .. the bastard Hart-beest.] **1820** S. DANIELL *Sketches S. Afr.* 18 The Sasaybe is an Antelope .. found in the Booshwana country. **1839** W.C. HARRIS *Wild Sports* 378 The Sassayby. Bastard Hartebeest *of the Cape Colonists*. **1857** E.L. LAYARD in *Cape Monthly Mag.* II. July 57 The skin of a Sassaybi .. received from Natal. **1866** [see PALLAH]. **1880** E.F. SANDEMAN *Eight Months in Ox-Waggon* 259 The sarsapi .. is the fleetest, toughest and most enduring of all South African antelopes. **1891** R. WARD *Sportsman's Handbk* 123 In Zululand were to be found, a few years ago, Elephants .. Sassabies, [etc.]. **1900** W.L. SCLATER *Mammals of S. Afr.* I. 146 Both Kirby and Selous state that the sassaby is the fleetest, toughest and most enduring of all South African antelopes. **1925** F.C. SLATER *Centenary Bk of S. Afr. Verse* 237 *Sasseby*, A large antelope found in Southern Rhodesia and the low country of the Transvaal. Colour dark purplish red. Said to be the swiftest of our antelopes. *c***1936** *S. & E. Afr. Yr Bk & Guide* 1083 The *Sassaby* or *Tsesebe* .. in general appearance .. somewhat resembles the Cape hartebeest, but is a faster runner. **1948** A.C. WHITE *Call of Bushveld* 74 Sessaby I have never seen in a herd ... More often one comes across them in twos, threes and fours. **1974** *Std Encycl. of Sn Afr.* X. 640 The tsessebe .. , also known as the sassaby, .. is related to the hartebeest. **1978, 1980** [see TSESSEBE].

sassart(j)ie, sassatee, sassatie, sassatj(i)e, sassatye varr. SOSATIE.

Sassiqua's var. SUSEQUA.

sat /sat/ *adj. slang.* [Afk.] Satiated; worn out, exhausted.

1970 A. VAN DEN BERG *Informant, Pretoria*, I feel sat today .. from the party last night. **1977** D. MULLER *Whitey* 108, I can smell you've been drinking the blue-ocean, ou pellie. It makes your brain *lam*. You was asleep in the bathroom — *sat!* **1986** *Informant, Grahamstown* He laughed himself sat. **1991** K. SULLIVAN *Informant, Cape Town*, I felt sat after having played cards the whole night. **1991** G. DE BEER *Informant, Port Nolloth (N. Cape)* I'm sat. I couldn't eat another thing.

satansbos /ˈseɪtənzbɔs, ˈsɑːtansbɔs/ *n.* Also with initial capital. [Afk., *satans* Satan's + *bos* bush.] The plant *Solanum elaeagnifolium* of the Solanaceae, a noxious weed with a deep, spreading root system, introduced from the southern states of America.

[**1966** HENDERSON & ANDERSON *Common Weeds* 276 *Solanum elaeagnifolium* Cav. Silwerblaar Bitterappel; Satansbos ... Silverleaf Bitter Apple.] **1972** *Grocott's Mail* 22 Feb. 3 Assistance in the campaign against Satansbos had also been announced, yet unless drastic steps were taken against the weed, the country was likely to be on its way to an infestation like that of jointed cactus. **1975** *E. Prov. Herald* 18 Apr., Satansbos was introduced to South Africa in pig food which was fed to animals at Kendrew in 1925, and since then has spread to all four provinces and South West Africa. **1977** *Ibid.* 28 Nov. 4 He urges farmers to watch out for satansbos in the areas under irrigation. This weed can spread quickly and ruin irrigable land.

Satour /ˈsætʊə/ *n.* Also **SATOUR**. [Blend formed on *South African Tourist Corporation*.] A parastatal body formed in 1947 to promote and co-ordinate South African tourism.

The South African Tourism Corporation was renamed the South African Tourism Board when its composition was changed in 1983 (see quot. 1988).

1951 A. GORDON-BROWN *Yr Bk & Guide to Sn Afr.* 159 A new tourist promotional organisation, known as the South African Tourist Corporation, and sponsored by the Union Government, commenced activities in 1947 to develop tourist traffic to the Union. The Corporation is often referred to as 'Satour'. **1977** *S. Afr. Panorama* Dec. 19 The South African Tourist Corporation (SATOUR) has offices in all the world's leading capitals. **1987** *E. Prov. Herald* 19 May 1 Mr Gunter Dettweiler, director in international tourism promotion for the South African Tourism Board (Satour), was interviewed after the opening of the Indaba '87 Travel Market Expo in Durban. **1988** *S. Afr. Panorama* Jan. 33 Satour is a parastatal organisation which .. was established in 1983 through the amalgamation of the former Hotel Board, the South African Tourist Corporation and the Department of Commerce, Industry and Tourism. The main objective is to encourage tourism within and to South Africa and to improve tourist facilities in the country.

SATS /sæts/ *n. hist.* Also **Sats**. [Acronym formed on *South African Transport Services*.] A parastatal organization controlling the railways, road transport services, harbours, airports, and the national air carrier, South African Airways (see SAA). Cf. SAR *n.*[2] Also *attrib.*

In 1981, the former SAR (& H) was renamed 'SATS' in terms of the South African Transport Services Act; in 1990 the organization was privatized and renamed 'Transnet'.

1982 *E. Prov. Herald* 31 Dec. 2 Sats order of 50 locos to cost R47,5m. **1983** *S. Afr. Panorama* Apr. 2 South African Transport Services (SATS) has developed into a mammoth organisation with an annual expenditure approaching the seven thousand million rand mark. **1987** *S. Afr. Digest* 1 May 5 Sats officials finalised arrangements to fire the 16 000 striking workers who had failed to return to work. **1989** *E. Prov. Herald* 23 Feb. 5 Draft legislation has .. been tabled .. to provide for the creation of a private company, and for Sats to be divided into separate semi-independent business units. **1989** D. BRISCOE in *Motorist* Nov. 6 Well, it's not the Blue Train of course. Be prepared to share a SATS green bench in part of the guard's van. **1990** *Sunday Times* 18 Mar. 7 When Thulsee M— .. phoned Transnet — previously Sats — to book his trip, he was told he could not travel in the coach he picked as it was for whites only.

SATV /es eɪ tiː ˈviː/ *n.* A popular abbreviation of *South African television*, designating the service inaugurated by the South African Broadcasting Corporation on 5th January, 1976.

1978 *Evening Post* 5 Dec. 1 The nation is braced for further shocks today when first details of the report of the Erasmus Commission's inquiry into the Department of Information are made public at 11pm on SATV. **1980** *E. Prov. Herald* 1 May 1 Sapa reports that Mr Botha said the Government would issue instructions to SATV not to give prominent treatment to the activities of subversive and revolutionary elements. **1985** R. ISACOWITZ in *Financial Mail* 18 Oct. 73 SATV has done its bit to perpetuate the illusion of calm and to whitewash the nasty bits. **1989** *Sunday Times* 20 Aug. 2 SATV is gearing itself for the biggest broadcast exercise in its 13-year history with its coverage of election results on September 6 and 7.

satyagraha /satˈjɑːgraha, satjaˈgraha/ *n.* [Sanskrit, 'insistence on truth', *satya* truth + *agraha* firmness, perseverance.] Passive resistance as formulated by Mahatma Mohandas Gandhi. Also *attrib.*

Used in Eng. throughout the world. The satyagraha movement originated in South Africa in demonstrations led by Gandhi in 1906–7 (see quots 1928 and 1957).

1920 M.K. GANDHI *Non Co-Operation* (1921) 46 All the painful experience that I then gained did not in any way shake my belief in Satyagraha or in the possibility of that matchless force being utilised in India. **1928** V.G. DESAI tr. *M.K. Gandhi's Satyagraha in S. Afr.* 1 The Satyagraha struggle of the Indians in South Africa lasted eight years. The term Satyagraha was invented and employed in connection therewith. *Ibid.* 173 I .. began to call the Indian movement 'Satyagraha', that is to say, the Force which is born of truth and love or non-violence, and gave up the use of the phrase 'passive resistance'. **1950** H. GIBBS *Twilight* 116 At a meeting at the Empire Theatre, Johannesburg, at which the slim little lawyer presided, a large audience took the Satyagraha Oath, refusing to carry the compulsory passes introduced by the Transvaal Government, [etc.]. **1957** M.K. GANDHI *Autobiog.* 318, I could not for the life of me find out a new name [for 'passive resistance'], and therefore offered a nominal prize through *Indian Opinion* to the reader who made the best suggestion ... As a result Maganlal Gandhi coined the word 'Sadagraha' (Sat = truth, Agraha = firmness) and won the prize. But in order to make it clearer I changed the word to 'Satyagraha' which has since become current in Gujurati as a designation for the struggle. **1982** H. SEEDAT in *Sunday Times* 10 Apr. (Extra) 2 The beginning of what later became known as Satyagraha was Gandhi's unexpected discovery of the beauty and power of a pledge taken with God as witness, to suffer all the penalties of nonsubmission to a bad law. This was at a Mass Meeting held in Pretoria on the 11/9/1906. **1983** *S. Afr. Panorama* Jan. 30 It is not generally known that the world's first public demonstration of *satyagraha* — passive resistance — was led by Gandhi in Johannesburg in 1907. **1984** BHANA & PACHAI *Doc. Hist. of Indian S. Africans* 111 The energies of South African Indians, mobilised in the 1890s against growing anti-Indianism in various parts of South Africa, were channelled into a concentrated movement which aimed at eradicating the various disabilities from which Indians of all castes, classes and creeds suffered. The documents show the dramatic way in which the *satyagraha* campaign unfolded from 1906–1914. Gandhi .. explained *satyagraha* as 'soul force, pure and simple, a weapon for those in search of truth'. **1988** LABAND & HASWELL *Pietermaritzburg 1838–1988* 196 M.K. Gandhi, H. Kellenbach, Mr Glask and Mrs M. Polak, all leading figures in the Satyagraha (Passive Resistance) campaign. **1990** R. STENGEL *January Sun* 77 Gandhi, a young lawyer who arrived in South Africa in 1893, was then evolving his technique of *satyagraha*, which consisted of peaceful resistance to the government's restrictions on Indian residential and trading rights.

sa'ubona var. SAWUBONA.

sault, saulted varr. SALT, SALTED.

Saunqua var. SONQUA.

SAWAS /ˈsɑːwəz/ *n. hist.* Also **Sawas, S.A.W.A.S.** [Acronym formed on *South African Women's Auxiliary Services*.] A voluntary organization which attended to the welfare of military personnel during World War II, in particular arranging entertainment and private accommodation for those on leave; as *pl.*, members of this organization. Also *attrib.*

1942 *Star* 1 Oct. 3 There were nurses and members of the S.A.W.A.S. **1944** 'TWEDE IN BEVEL' *Piet Kolonel* 65 Halts at stations .. would see the platforms thronged with a .. crowd, hurrying to buy coffee and buns and fruit, or .. getting them free at the stalls of gallant S.A.W.A.S. **1945** S. DE WET *Shifty in Italy* 2, I was wearing my S.A.W.A.S. uniform, .. so of course she didn't realise I wasn't in one of the paid services and didn't want promotion. *Ibid.* 4 We were to have free travel, accommodation and rations, but no pay. S.A.W.A.S. have never been paid. *Ibid.* 5 On Friday the Durban S.A.W.A.S. gave a party for us. *Ibid.* 226 Nine S.A.W.A.S. were sent up as our replacements, after the war was over. **1963** S.H. SKAIFE *Naturalist Remembers* 141 My wife was in command of the Cape section of the South African Women's Auxiliary Services, a voluntary organization affectionately known to the men as 'Sawas'. **1979** MARTIN & ORPEN *S. Afr. at War* 288 The biggest uniformed women's organization directly supporting the war effort, yet not actually part of the UDF, was SAWAS ... Working voluntarily, without pay, SAWAS was running a variety of institutions. *Ibid.* 289 One of SAWAS's most widespread schemes .. was its hospitality scheme, under which its officers arranged private hospitality for servicemen on leave.

‖**sawubona** /ˌsa(w)ʊˈbɔ(ː)na/ *int.* and *n.* Also **sa'bon(a), sac(h)abona, sackaboni, saka bona, sakobona, sako bono, sakubona, sanibona(ni), sa'ubona, se'bona, zakubona.** [Zulu (earlier form *sakubona*, contraction of *siyakubona*), 'we see you' (pl. *sanibona(ni)* 'we see you all'). Most of the variant spellings arise from attempts by English-speakers to represent Zulu pronunciation.]

The sing. and pl. forms of the greeting are often used interchangeably by English-speakers.

A. *int.* Among Zulu-speakers: a polite greeting or salutation; DAKUBONA *int.*

1837 F. OWEN *Diary* (1926) 90 As soon as they reached the waggon where I was sitting, they ceased and saluted me in the usual way 'Säkubona Umfundis,' 'We see you Teacher.' **1850** J.E. METHLEY *New Col. of Port Natal* 46 When they meet any one, they give the usual salutation of 'Zaku bona Umgaan,' with a free and lively air. **1870** C. HAMILTON *Life & Sport in S.-E. Afr.* 241 A Kaffir will never pass the settler or stranger, if he likes his appearance, without the friendly greeting of 'sachabona inkosi', or 'hamba gooschly inkosi'. **1887** J.W. MATTHEWS *Incwadi Yami* 326 Seeing some wounded men accompanying the ambulances one Zulu .. shouted out 'Sakubona,' ('I see you', a form of greeting). **1908** D. BLACKBURN *Leaven* (1991), He went up boldly and said: 'Saku bona, baas. I want work and I am very hungry.' **1930** S.T. PLAATJE *Mhudi* (1975) 112 Behold, here comes Umpitimpiti, the one man in this city who has the freedom of the royal harem. 'Sakubona (good day), Mpitimpiti.' **1949** O. WALKER *Proud Zulu* (1951) 22 'Se'bona. I see you, child of Mister Dunn.' greeted Umbuyazi. c**1957** D. SWANSON *Highveld, Lowveld & Jungle* 9 The Zulu guard .. smiled widely ... 'Sakabona, inkosikas,' he greeted her in Zulu. 'Sakabona, Joseph. Is Baas Maclean in his office?' **1961** D. BEE *Children of Yesterday* 217 'Sabona, 'Kosi!' Johannes greeted him cheerfully. 'Sabona, Johannes!' It was the proper good morning. **1970** M. KUNENE *Zulu Poems* 12 When a Zulu greets, he says (even if he is alone) 'sawubona' meaning 'we see you', or more accurately, 'I on behalf of my family or community pay our respects to you.' He may even say 'sanibona' meaning 'I on behalf of my family pay our respects to you and your family.' **1971** *The 1820* Vol.43 No.12, 26 'Ha', I thought, 'let's hear what the Zulus have to say.' I went up to him. 'Sakubona kehla', I greeted him. **1977** P.C. VENTER *Soweto* 173 'Edward? Sanibonani.' Which means 'I see you' and doesn't really apply to a telephone conversation, but the Zulu language is old and not easily bent to modern technology's will. **1984** F. JAY in *Staffrider* Vol.6 No.1, 20, I raised my hand and murmured, '*Sawubona, umfaan*'. Didn't I know your name? **1990** P. CULLINAN in M. Leveson *Firetalk* 18 'Sa'bona, Barnabas, good afternoon.' 'Sa'bona, Muravukela. You have come in good time.' **1990** M. STANTON in *Estcourt High School Mag.* No.49, 46 We didn't speak the same language, but that didn't matter, we were friends. 'Sawubona Lindiwe', you'd say. 'Yes, sawubona Togo', I'd answer. **1993** *Natal Witness* 8 Apr. (Learn with Echo) 1 Hello, sawubona.

B. *n.* An utterance of this greeting; DAKUBONA *n.*

1877 LADY BARKER *Yr's Hsekeeping* 164 Every cowherd on the veldt has his 'sako bono', or good morning, as he passes one fern or grass-seed hunting in the early morning. **1907** J.P. FITZPATRICK *Jock of Bushveld* (1909) 404 As I passed he rose slowly and gave his 'Sakubona! Inkos!' with that curious controlled air. **1937** C. BIRKBY *Zulu Journey* 67, I walked around and smiled a greeting in answer to their polite 'Sa'bon,' which is the slurred way in which the Zulus say 'Sakubona — I see you.'

Sayco /ˈseɪkəʊ/ *n. hist.* Also **SAYCO**. [Acronym formed on *South African Youth Congress*.] A political organization launched in 1987, affiliated to the United Democratic Front (see UDF *n.*[2]) and accommodating members of banned student organizations (such as COSAS). Also *attrib.*

In 1991 Sayco was replaced by the ANC Youth League (see ANCYL).

1987 *New Nation* 2 Apr. 1 Not only has the Sayco launch brought together 1 200 congress members nationally, but also members of trade unions, student, community and political organisations. **1987** M. BADELA in *Weekly Mail* 3 Apr. 14 In its guiding principles, Sayco has formally adopted the ANC's guiding light, the Freedom Charter. **1987** *New Nation* 11 June 6 The SA Youth Congress (Sayco) — the largest UDF affiliate, with half a million members. **1990** *Sunday Times* 16 Sept. 2 Sayco, which is something of an over-arching body drawing membership from the Congress of South African Students and the South African National Students Congress, will dissolve once the Youth League is fully re-established inside the country. **1991** *Weekly Mail* 24 May 2 Mokaba enjoyed a meteoric rise within the anti-apartheid movement, culminating in his unanimous election as president of the South African Youth Congress (Sayco) in 1987 and his election to head the ANC Youth League at this year's re-launch.

SA Youth Day see SOUTH AFRICAN YOUTH DAY.

saysie var. SYSIE.

SB *n.* Also **S.B.** [Initial letters of *Special Branch*.] **1.** *colloq.* SPECIAL BRANCH. Also *attrib.*

1965 A. FUGARD *Notebks* (1983) 123 She .. has seldom kept a job for longer than a month because of the recurrent delusion that any new appointment in the office where she is working is a S.B. spy placed to keep an eye on her and Piet. **1969** M. BENSON *At Still Point* (1988) 70 Terror — yes, terror — not the ultimate as with Hitler and Stalin, though of course the S.B. are now adept at torture — I mean continual, massive, administrative terrorizing. **1969** *Post* 15 June 19 Her husband was arrested by S.B. cops for questioning. [**1977** *Daily Dispatch* 2 Feb., Neither the Ciskei nor the Transkei Essbees tailed me (to my knowledge).] **1978** A.P. BRINK *Rumours of Rain* 181 'You must help me to hide for a while. They're on my heels.' 'I don't understand.' 'The SB infiltrated one of their men into our organisation.' **1982** M. MZAMANE *Children of Soweto* 117 There are two guys in there, with dark glasses on, who must be SBs. They've been watching every movement in this street. **1984** *E. Prov. Herald* 6 Apr. 6 Chris G— is a great SB type putting the Bezuidenhout family through a third degree interrogation. **1986** S. SEPAMLA *Third Generation* 86 Sue brought the shocking news about Potlako escaping to Botswana because the SB were on his trail. **1993** [see NIS].

2. *Prison slang.* [A play on sense 1 and the initial letters of *shit bucket*.] A latrine bucket, as used in prison.

1977 J. SIKAKANE *Window on Soweto* 68 We could spend a week inside without any exercise, just the door opening three times a day to bring in the food and take out the shit bucket. We used to call these buckets SB's — the same name as we gave the Special Branch.

‖**sbali** /sˈbɑːli/ *n. colloq.* Also **s'bali**, **(u)sibali**. Pl. **oosibali**. [Xhosa *sibali*, ad. Afk. *swaer* brother-in-law.] Among speakers of the Sintu (Bantu) languages: an informal term of address or reference to a brother-in-law, (*rare*) a sister-in-law, or (loosely) any male friend. Cf. SWAER.

1963 WILSON & MAFEJE *Langa* 86 One term — *usibali* (from the Afrikaans 'swaer') has ousted the old terms for brother-in-law, and sister-in-law, *umlanya* and *umlanyakazi*, even in the country ... In traditional Xhosa custom a woman's brother would never have dreamt of going to a married sister's home when drunk, and thereby disgracing her in front of their brothers-in-law (oosibali). **1978** *Voice* 25 Nov. 2 That mean, late and unlamented sbali of hers had booby-trapped the box with grenades. **1982** *Pace* Nov. 47 And so, S'bali, the managing director .. went through one night's bout of Azapo nightmares and acted promptly. **1983** *Ibid.* Oct. 70 Yhu, sbali! Ever heard about this Soweto morning daily whose sub-editors are said to have a rather limited vocabulary. **1987** *Pace* Aug. 4 The people can share, but not wives sbali.

SBDC *n.* [Initial letters of *Small Business Development Corporation*.] A parastatal public company registered in February 1981, with the aim of aiding the growth of small business ventures in the private sector by making loans and providing technical assistance to entrepreneurs.

1987 *E. Prov. Herald* 23 June 10 Shebeen owners in the Port Elizabeth-Uitenhage area have the support of SA Breweries and the Small Business Development Corporation ... They have the confidence of both the breweries and the SBDC. **1988** *S. Afr. Panorama* Jan. 15 Ironically the SBDC has been deprived of American aid in terms of sanctions legislation. **1990** *Flying Springbok* July 89 The SBDC believes that the development of small business is essential to create jobs, maintain free enterprise, generate wealth and prosperity, provide healthy competition, enhance society, ensure innovation and creativity and to encourage grass-roots development. **1991** *Weekend Argus* 26 Jan. (Business) 3 SBDC flooded with course inquiries.

sbongi, **'sbongi** pl. forms of IMBONGI.

SC *n.* Also **S.C.** [Abbrev. of modern L. *Senior Consultus* (but mistakenly interpreted as the initial letters of *Senior Counsel*).] The designation *Senior Consultus*, granted to senior advocates of the Supreme Court. See also ADVOCATE, SENIOR COUNSEL.

Equivalent to the British designation 'Queen's (or King's) Counsel', 'SC' replaced 'QC', after a brief use of the term 'Senior Advocate' (see S.A. *n.*[2]), when South Africa became a republic in 1961; however, anyone granted the title of 'QC' before 1961 had the choice of retaining this title (see quot. 1979).

'SC' is used in both English and Afrikaans contexts.

1971 *Rand Daily Mail* 23 Feb. 7 Mr L. L—, S.C. appeared for Captain M-. **1972** *Std Encycl. of Sn Afr.* VI. 567 When an advocate considers that he has achieved sufficient status in his profession he may apply to the Minister of Justice for senior status ... The senior is entitled to place the distinctive letters S.C. (for *Senior Consultus*) behind his name. **1979** *E. Prov. Herald* 17 Mar. 1 The hearing of the application brought by Mr G. F. S— SC, and Mr A. J. L—, SC, lasted four days. One of the documents .. handed in by Mr H. S—, QC, was a copy of the judgement in a similar application. **1981** J.R. DU PLESSIS *Elementary Intro. to Study of S. Afr. Law* 1981 34 A senior advocate in this sense means an advocate who has 'taken silk', ie an advocate who has been officially designated a senior advocate; the letters SC (senior counsel) appear behind his name and he wears a silken gown in court. **1986** *Frontline* Mar. 20 Traditionally, it has not been a particularly easy task to get the best senior counsel to accept appointments to the judiciary — largely because a judge's income is but a fraction of the enormous earnings a leading SC commands. **1986** *Reader's Digest Family Guide to Law* 824 SC (*Senior Counsel* — strictly, *Consultus*, the Latin being acceptable to both official languages.) An advocate may be granted the status of senior counsel, or 'takes silk', because of the silk gown he will wear in court. Thereafter he or she takes only more serious or difficult cases, usually assisted by a junior counsel.

scale /skeɪl/ *n. colloq.* [Eng. (obs.), drinking bowl or cup (Du. *schaal*). The forms *sekale* (see quot. 1959) and *skaal* (see quot. 1977) represent this word's use in the Sintu (Bantu) languages and Afrikaans respectively.] Esp. in township Eng.: a large vessel for beer or other liquor, used in drinking establishments; a measure for drink.

1946 P. ABRAHAMS *Mine Boy* (1954) 36 Old Ma Plank sat over a huge vat in the yard and doled out scales of beer ... Xuma put the scale to his lips then passed it to Daddy. **1953** LANHAM & MOPELI-PAULUS *Blanket Boy's Moon* 274 Drink a scale of fine home-brewed kaffir beer with us. **1959** K.M.C. MOTSISI in M. Mutloatse *Casey & Co.* (1978) 33 They have to use both their hands to lift up the painted tin scales to their mouths each time they take a swig. [**1959** L. LONGMORE *Dispossessed* 142 The client is .. expected to buy a *sekale*, about a pint of illegally brewed liquor or beer.] *Ibid.* 227 He had to steal a packet of candles .. to give it away to a beer brewer for a scale of mbamba (about a pint of strong drink). **1968** [see MAIZA]. **1968** [see BEE-AH]. **1969** *Golden City Post* 6 Apr. 14 Chauke .. gave her R1 and told her to buy a scale of KB from Mathebula, who ran a shebeen and sold offal. **1970** *Drum* Oct. 8, I found myself firmly grasping a plastic scale. That's what they call them. I thought it was a pot plant ... The next minute I was shoving my scale under a tap from which oozed a fawn liquid with a familiar smell. [**1973** see SKOMFAAN]. [**1977** P.C. VENTER *Soweto* 124 Classy establishments .. serve anything from imported beer to Scotch whiskey. But don't ask for a skaal of Bantu beer.] **1978** C. MOTSISI in M. Mutloatse *Casey & Co.* 33 They have to use both their hands to lift up the painted tin scales to their mouths each time they take a swig. **1989** *Weekly Mail* 27 Oct. 26 Next to the tray stood two four-litre glass containers ('scales'), and a dozen beer quarts were placed under the table. **1990** M. MELAMU in *Lynx* 298 They supported each other as they staggered their unsteady way from their drinking spree. It cost a mere sixpence for a 'scale' of mqomboti in those days. **1992** [see UMQOMBOTHI].

scaly /ˈskeɪli/ *n.* Also **scaley, scalie**. [Absol. use Eng. *scaly* covered in scales.] The freshwater fish *Barbus natalensis* of the Cyprinidae; also called YELLOWFISH (sense a). Also *attrib.*

The name 'scaly' is used for this species in Skelton's *Complete Guide to Freshwater Fishes* (1993).

1938 *RAC Handbk* 365 'Scalies' are the local brand of indigenous fish, and in the waters around Maritzburg many big specimens are captured. There is no season for 'Scalie' fishing. **1947** K.H. BARNARD *Pict. Guide to S. Afr. Fishes* 56 The well known Scaley .. of Natal is a near relative of the Yellow-fish. **1970** *Daily News* 30 Oct., The best catch of scalies taken recently was 15 weighing 12.2kg (27lb) from Wagendrift Dam, near Estcourt. **1971** *Rand Daily Mail* 27 Mar. 23 An interesting observation last week was the presence of shoals of scalies in the Bushmans river. **1975** *Std Encycl. of Sn Afr.* XI. 563 The Natal scaly .. reaches 5 kg and is restricted to the Pongola system and the rivers of Natal.

scaly weaver see BAARDMAN sense 2.

scamt(h)o var. ISICAMTHO.

scandal *v. intrans.* [Prob. calqued on Afk. *skinder*, see SKINDER *v.*; also in general Eng., but arch. and dial.] To gossip, spread rumours.

1969 A. FUGARD *People Are Living There* 73 You don't protect me you know. You let them scandal about me. **1972** *Informant, Grahamstown* You can scandal to my own child about me, but don't expect her not to tell me.

scandal stories *pl. n. phr.* [Calqued on Afk. *skinderstories* gossip (*skinder* to gossip + *stories* stories).] *skinder stories*, see SKINDER *v.* sense 2.

1977 *Cape Times* 5 Feb. 1 Mr Vorster had rejected Dr W—'s recently published attacks, alleging that the .. chairman had not levelled constructive criticism but had indulged in 'scandal stories'. **1978** *Daily Dispatch* 22 Sept. 1 His withdrawal came after a report .. that he had been a victim of 'scandal stories' during the 'cat-and-dog' fight for the premiership. **1983** *Seek* Dec. 4 The evidence .. was one sided and weak ... The articles .. encourage the spread of scandal stories involving the country's military forces. **1984** *Fair Lady* 22 Feb. 134 Cruel scandal stories hinting at anorexia and fights .. could not be passed off as a joke.

scarpsticker var. SKAAPSTEKER.

scathamiya var. ISICATHAMIYA.

schaap var. SKAAP.

schaapboer see BOER sense 1 b.

schaapbos(ch)(je) var. SKAAPBOS.

schaap stecker, schaap-ste(e)ker, schaap-sti(c)ker varr. SKAAPSTEKER.

schaapwachter /ˈskɑːpˌvaxtə(r)/ *n.* Also **schaapwagter, skaapwachter, skaapwagter**. [Du. (later Afk. *skaapwagter*), *schaap* sheep + *wachter* guard.]

‖**1.** A shepherd.

1822 W.J. BURCHELL *Trav.* I. 236 A few slight instructions, from a *schaap-wagter* (shepherd) whom we met with were considered sufficient to enable us to take the proper direction. **1900** S.T. PLAATJE *Boer War Diary* (1973) 122 Surely those Transvaal Boers are abominable. I really do not think they are children of the same Dutchland as the inhabitants of the O.F.S. No wonder their President was a judge while Oom Paul was a 'schaapwachter'. **1958** A. JACKSON *Trader on Veld* 40 After the natives were directed to their particular portions of the farm, the boss and his sons spent most mornings on horseback watching the 'skaapwachters' (shepherds), and in the lambing season scouring the veld for stray ewes.

2. ?*obs.* [Various reasons are given for this name: see quots 1822, 1913, and 1937.] The bird *Oenanthe pileata* of the Turdidae. Often in dim. form **schaapwagtertj(i)e** [see -IE].

In G.L. Maclean's *Roberts' Birds of Sn Afr.* (1993), the name 'capped wheatear' is used for this species.

1822 W.J. BURCHELL *Trav.* I. 270 The Schaapwagtertje (the Little Shepherd), so called from its familiarity in approaching the Hottentots while tending their sheep, is a bird common in all the open country of this part of Africa. *a***1867** C.J. ANDERSSON *Notes on Birds of Damara Land* (1872) 108 The Dutch boors have given it the name of 'Schaap Wagter' or Shepherd; it has also the more local name of 'Nagtgaal' and 'Rossignol,' from a habit it is said to have of singing by night. **1867** E.L. LAYARD *Birds of S. Afr.* 103 *Schaapwachter* of Colonists (lit the Shepherd). He is a favourite with the farmer and the shepherd. **1897** H.A. BRYDEN *Nature & Sport* 60 A rather remarkable wheatear, the imitative wheatear (*Saxicola pileata*), well known in South Africa by its Dutch name 'schaap-wachter' — sheep-watcher ... Not content with a fair song of his own, he mimics almost every note he hears, and will imitate, not successfully, birds, dogs, sheep, goats and other creatures. He is a little afraid of man, and had apparently a natural fondness for sheep and other stock, for which reason the Boers gave him his colonial name. **1913** C. PETTMAN *Africanderisms* 426 *Schaapwachterje, Saxicola pileata*. This favourite among the birds is so styled because, possessing great powers of mimicry, it not only imitates other birds, but whistles exactly as the shepherd does when driving his sheep. **1923** HAAGNER & IVY *Sketches* 27 The Capped Wheatear (*S. pileata*) is the Schaap-wachter of the Dutch .. recognized by its rufous-brown back and broad black chest-band ... It is a tame, confiding bird and is fond of the neighbourhood of buildings and kraals. **1937** M. ALSTON *Wanderings* 61 The Dutch have several names for the capped wheat-ear. One is 'Schaapwachter' (shepherd) because of the birds predilection for cattle and sheep kraals.

schammel /ˈskɑ(ː)məl/ *n. Hist. Wagon-making.* Also **schamel, skammel**. [S. Afr. Du. (later Afk. *skamel*).] The base-frame of the undercarriage of a wagon.

1822 W.J. BURCHELL *Trav.* I. 150 On the top of each axletree lies a strong piece of timber, called the *skammel*, upon which the *buik plank* or bottom of the waggon rests. **1899** *Natal Agric. Jrnl* 31 Mar. 4 All the words in connection with trekking are of Dutch origin .. besides the parts of the wagon, such as 'draaibors,' 'voortang,' 'schammel,' etc. **1919** *Dunell, Ebden & Co.'s Price List* Aug. 34 (*captions*) Front schamel. Hind schamel. False schamel or short brake bar. **1919** J.Y. GIBSON in *S. Afr. Jrnl of Science* July 6 The upper rails of the sides, *leerboomen*, were curved upwards from about the second third ... The sides stood upon the schammels, and were supported outwardly by the *rongen*, or struts, which were tightly morticed into the projecting ends of these. **1958** S. CLOETE *Mask* 84 All these woods except for the bed were iron hard ... They were the working parts of the wagon — the wheels, the schamel and tongue or forecarriage as it were, which enabled the wagon to turn sharply.

schans /skans, skɑːns/ *n.* Also **schants, schan(t)z, schanze, skans**. Pl. **-es**, and (formerly) **-en**. [Du. (Afk. *skans*), redoubt, breastwork, defensive works (cf. 17th C. Eng. *sconce* small fort, earthwork).] A barricade or breastwork, usu. of stones and earth, used as cover from which to fire upon the enemy.

[**1801** DAMBERGER *Trav.* 8 (Pettman), The line-guard, also called the *schanz wache*, or foot guard.] **1848** J. TINDALL *Jrnl* (1959) 88 They heard a strange noise near one of the 'schansen,' forts so called but nothing more than a circle of stones piled 18 inches high and so loosely that the levelling of the musket frequently causes them to fall. **1868** *The Jrnl* 6 Mar. 3 Platberg was strongly fortified ... After breaking down the *schansen* there and at other places we crossed the Caledon. **1872** E.J. DUNN in A.M.L. Robinson *Sel. Articles from Cape Monthly Mag.* (1978) 50 Around are rocky kopjes, once the lurking-places of Korannas and Bushmen. Their *schantsen* still remain. **1880** *Times* (U.K.) 18 Oct. 4 Some of these paths are .. barred by lines of schanzes, or stone barricades. **1882** C. DU VAL *With Show through Sn Afr.* II. 96 They kept up a lively fusillade on the enemy above, tolerably secure behind their kraal-walls, schanzes, and stones. **1882** C.L. NORRIS-NEWMAN *With Boers in Tvl* 155 Boers erecting schanzes and earthworks on hill. **1900** H. BLORE *Imp. Light Horseman* 59 On a commanding peak of one chain .. the Boers had .. raised a schans, that is a redoubt of stones loosely piled upon each other, behind which they might shelter while shooting at an attacking force. **1913** C. PETTMAN *Africanderisms* 427 *Schanz*, .. A protection or defence made of stones, earth, thorn-bushes, etc. **1933** W. MACDONALD *Romance of Golden Rand* 174 It was strongly fortified. Huge stone schanzes blocked the tortuous pathways leading up the mountain-side. **1940** F.B. YOUNG *City of Gold* 192 It's a nasty position to attack, all rocks and schanzes; the Kaffirs will have plenty of cover from behind which to shoot. **1963** S. CLOETE *Rags of Glory* 228 Volley after volley came from Lee-Metfords in the stone schans twenty yards away. **1969** *Grocott's Mail* 28 Mar., There are still .. some signs of the schanzes, earthworks, hastily thrown up when General Smuts and his commandoes approached the district.

Hence **schans** *v. trans.*, to protect (a position) by means of defensive works.

1888 D.C.F. MOODIE *Hist. of Battles & Adventures* II. 185 The top of this mountain was about a mile long and about half a mile broad, and was also completely schanzed in every direction. **1901** *Contemp. Rev.* (U.K.) Dec. 888 The English had schanzed the long ridge for a long distance.

schapsticker var. SKAAPSTEKER.

scharem var. SKERM.

scheduled *adj. hist.* Also with initial capital. [Named for the *Schedule of Native Areas* which was appended to Act 27 of 1913.] Of land: reserved for the exclusive use of African people. Often in the phr. *scheduled area*: RESERVE.

1913 Act 27 in *Stat. of Union* 438 1.(1) From and after the commencement of this Act, land outside the scheduled native areas shall .. be subject to the following provisions, that is to say:- (a) a native shall not enter into any agreement or transaction for the purchase, hire, or other acquisition from a person other than a native, of any such land or of any rights therein, or servitude thereover. [*Ibid.*, Schedule of Native Areas. 1. Cape of Good Hope [etc.].] **1969** [see BLACK SPOT]. *c***1970** C. DESMOND *Discarded People* 11 All the former native reserves in the four provinces were set out in the Schedule to the Act, and are referred to as 'Scheduled Areas'. These areas are reserved solely for the occupation and ownership by the tribes in them. **1973** T. BELL *Indust. Decentral.* 2 The Natives Land Act of 1913 set aside areas, known as 'scheduled areas', which were to be reserved exclusively for occupation by Africans. **1974** DAVENPORT & HUNT *Right to Land* 42 This Act [sc. the Natives Land Act, No.27 of 1913] defined areas (referred to as the 'Scheduled Areas') outside which natives could not purchase land, and within which people other than the natives could not purchase land. **1985** PLATZKY & WALKER *Surplus People* 138 Those with title-deeds are assured of better treatment than those without; scheduled land cannot be cleared quite as easily as non-scheduled land.

schei var. SKEY.

scheit var. SKIET.

‖**schelling, skilling** /ˈʃelɪŋ, ˈskɪlɪŋ/ *n. hist.* Also **schilling, skelling**. [Du. *schelling*, Englished form *skilling*.] A small Dutch silver coin, current at the Cape during the 18th century and originally worth 6d sterling; the note which replaced this coin; SK. See also STIVER.

1691 BROWNE in R. Raven-Hart *Cape G.H. 1652–1702* II. 388 They value noe monie except it bee a skilling or a dubleke with which they buy brandie or tobacco from the Dutch. **1731** G. MEDLEY tr. *P. Kolb's Present State of Cape of G.H.* II. 8 At an Auction of Horses at the *Cape* in the year 1712, I saw three of those Horses .. sold for Eighteen *Dutch* Schellings. **1786** G. FORSTER tr. *A. Sparrman's Voy. to Cape of G.H.* II. 245 A number of these [wethers] .. they dispose of yearly, at the rate of from six schellings to a dollar the head, Dutch money. **1795** J.H. CRAIG in G.M. Theal *Rec. of Cape Col.* (1897) I. 278 A very considerable difficulty is experienced in the Province, for want of a smaller currency than a skilling (6d) which is at present the lowest in circulation. **1798** S.H. WILCOCKE tr. *J.S. Stavorinus's Voy. to E. Indies 1768–71* I. 569 The coins which are current in Holland, are equally so here ... Sesthalfs (pieces of 5 1/2 stivers) go for skillings (pieces of six stivers). **1806** D. BAIRD in G.M. Theal *Rec. of Cape Col.* (1899) V. 433 The Quarter Guilder is to pass for Six Stivers Currency, or be equal in value to the present Paper Skilling. **1822** W.J. BURCHELL *Trav.* I. 78 The only money in general circulation, is small printed and countersigned pieces of paper, bearing value from the trifling sum of one schelling, or sixpence currency, upwards to five hundred rix-dollars each. **1843** J.C. CHASE *Cape of G.H.* 188 The schelling, eight of which go to the rix-dollar, of the value of twopence farthing each. **1888** *Cape Punch* 21 Mar. 174 When the adjutant calls the roll of the Royal Irish Fusiliers, why is he like a Dutch miser? Because he's counting *in his skillings*. **1957** [see RIX-DOLLAR]. **1965** A. GORDON-BROWN *S. Afr. Heritage* IV. 7 An early Cape shopkeeper kept his account in rix-dollars, skillings and stuivers. **1986** J. & I. RUDNER (tr.) in V.S. Forbes *Capt Peter Thunberg 1772–5* 121 The coins current here .. from Europe .. which is here always termed the Fatherland (*Vaderland*), are ducatoons, schellings and doits (*Duyten*).

schel(lu)m var. SKELM.

schelpat var. SKILPAD.

scheme *v. trans. Slang.* Also **skeem**. [Special sense of general Eng.] To think or 'reckon' (something).

1970 B. HANSEN *Informant, Durban* You .. scheme you're a joller, hey. (You think you're just the guy, hey.) **1972** M. DEVELIN on Radio South Africa 25 Jan., That ou schemes he's like a mainman (that gentleman considers himself to be a big cog in a small machine). **1972** A. SCOBY on Radio South Africa 23 May, You scheme you'd do that? You'd graft, work? **1985** P. SLABOLEPSZY *Sat. Night at Palace* 26 What you scheme this is? A bloody party? *Ibid.* 79 *Scheme*, think, reckon, figure. **1985** *Vula* Oct. 15 She checks her stepfather's reaction, 'Bloody Kaffirs', and she skeems 'shame'. **1987** G. SILBER in *Style* Aug. 46 'Say you want to buy the Ferrari for R10, can you pay by cheque. What do you scheme?' The barman schemes nooit. He's not going to make a fool of himself. **1987** *Scope* 6 Nov. 36 Jimmy schemed that 'suicide by dynamite' would be a *kiff* idea. **1991** C.L. WARD *Informant, Cape Town* Scheme. Think, when implying planning or uncertainty. I scheme it'd be tomorrow. Scheme you can change my mind? **1991** G. DE BEER *Informant, Port Nolloth (N. Cape)*, I scheme it could work.

‖**schepel** /ˈskɪəp(ə)l/ *n. hist.* Also **schippel**, **ske(e)pel**, **skeppel**. Pl. **-s**, occas. **-en**. [Du. (later Afk. *skepel*).] **a.** A unit of capacity roughly equivalent to one third of a bushel, formerly used as a measure for grain, etc. **b.** In full ***skepelmaat*** /ˈskɪəp(ə)lˌmaːt/ [Afk., *maat* measure]: the box used for this measurement. Cf. MUID.

1806 J.M. SMYTH in G.M. Theal *Rec. of Cape Col.* (1900) VI. 47 Oats .. will be received at the rate of five skeepels or bushels. **1809** J. MACKRILL Diary. 66 A load of anything they call a Freight and their measure called Mudde/Muid contains Four Skeppels. **1815** *Ibid.* 118 The Dutch Schepel in Cape Town, Three Schepelen make two English Bushels. **1824** *S. Afr. Commercial Advertiser* 28 Jan. 30 Public Sale ... 396 Schepels of Coals and Coal Dust, in Lots of 36 Schepels each. **1833** *S. Afr. Almanack & Dir.* 41 Corn measure. 4 Schepels, equal to 1 Muid. 10 Muids, equal to 1 Load. **1866** *Cape Town Dir.* 118 Fees for assizing weights and measures ... For measuring every bushel or schepel. **1877** J. JEPPE *Tvl Bk Almanac & Dir.* (1976) 74 Schepels are about 3 imperial bushels and 11 schepels are about 1 quarter. A schepel is [1]4½ inches square by 8½ deep. **1912** W. WESTRUP *Land of To-Morrow* 94 A schippel is the box — any old box — we use as a measure when buying grain. *c*1963 B.C. TAIT *Durban Story* 124 Grain was measured out in schepels. The schepel was a square box of 14½ inches with a depth of 8½ inches and was lifted by means of handles on opposite sides. **1964** L.G. GREEN *Old Men Say*, Dutch weights and measures were also in everyday use; and some people were only able to think in terms of the 'ell,' the 'old gallon,' 'schepel' and 'muid.' **1971** BARAITSER & OBHOLZER *Cape Country Furn.* 259 Grain was portioned out by a wooden measure in the form of a 30 cms square, lidless box (skepelmaat) that held a quarter of a bag of grain.

‖**schepen** /ˈskɪəpən/ *n. Obs.* exc. *hist. Law.* Pl. **schepenen**. [Du., alderman, sheriff. Used formerly also in Brit. Eng. (in *OED* recorded between c.1481 and 1809).] At the Cape under Dutch rule: a Dutch alderman or petty magistrate.

1862 tr. *Est. of Debt Registry* in *Stat. Law of Cape of G.H.* 3 There hath hitherto remained unused and not adopted in practice in this Government the registration of Kusting Brieven, Obligations before Schepenen and Orphan Masters. *Ibid.* 27 In order to examine whether the 'Kusting Brieven', 'Schepenen' — orphan masters — and bank obligations .. are or are not duly registered. **1899** in G.M. Theal *Rec. of Cape Col.* V. 199 The deeds of mortgage shall be passed before two of the commissioners, and shall have the same power as those passed before schepenen or orphan-masters. **1960** J.J.L. SISSON *S. Afr. Judicial Dict.* 426 In Holland the registration took place before the schepenen of the district in which the land was situated ... The Registrar of Deeds therefore took the place of the Commissioners as these had taken the place of the schepenen.

schepsel var. SKEPSEL.

scherm var. SKERM.

schilling var. SCHELLING.

schilpad var. SKILPAD.

schim(m)el var. SKIMMEL.

schippel var. SCHEPEL.

schlenter /ˈʃlentə/ *adj.* and *n.* Also **s(h)lenter**. [Du. and Afk. *slenter* trick, knavery. The *-ch-* spelling probably reflects the influence of Yiddish in diamond mining during the 19th century.]

Used also in *Austral.* and *N.Z. Eng.* (perh. fr. *S. Afr. Eng.*).

A. *adj.*

1. Pretended; dishonest, crooked; inferior.

1891 A. DE BREMONT *Gentleman Digger* 99 'Of course,' whispers the seller who had pushed his way to the side of the buyer, 'this sale was only *schlenter*'. **1892** J.R. COUPER *Mixed Humanity* 384 Numerous were the offers to subscribe handsomely to the stakes in the event of the challenge being no 'schlenter' one. **1900** T. FROES *Kruger & Co.* 14 Messrs. Evans and Fursey .. were determined that no slur should remain upon them, so far as having supplied 'schlenter' goods to Pretoria was concerned. **1911** L. COHEN *Reminisc. of Kimberley* 50 Give him three suits of home-spun. The ones with the schlenter linings. **1957** B. O'KEEFE *Gold without Glitter* 123 If I thought the only way I could get around that Strydom dame .. was working a schlenter mine, I'd do it, too.

2. Of minerals offered for sale: fake or counterfeit.

1892 J.R. COUPER *Mixed Humanity* 265 A new branch of industry had started in Kimberley, the manufacture of 'schlenter' stones, a name given to diamonds made of glass. **1924** L. COHEN *Reminisc. of Jhb.* 165 Confidence men found customers in plenty for schlenter gold bricks and amalgam. **1932** *Zionist Record* 25 Our courts employ schlenter as a word requiring no further definition, in the sense of fake when applied to mineral products. **1937** H. KLEIN *Stage Coach Dust* 112 Schlenter diamonds, as the fakes were called, were manufactured in vast quantities in Germany, and being so like real diamonds were extremely useful to the individual digger to drop into the pans of their rotating washing machines to test the honesty of their native boys. **1974** *Sunday Times* 24 Nov. 4 What makes the event more gratifying still is the fact that they sold schlenter uranium. **1975** *Ibid.* 15 June 4 The Precious Jewels Club: Boys learn to tell the difference between genuine and schlenter diamonds. **1981** P. DALE *Great Houses of Constantia* 149 Thirteen bars of gold .. were in fact 'schlenter gold', which is brass mixed with other metals and gilded.

B. *n.*

1.a. A fake diamond.

1899 G.C. GRIFFITH *Knaves of Diamonds* 35 Good Lord, man, can't you see they're all schlenters? **1931** G. BEET *Grand Old Days* 60 This done, he secretly salted the claim with a big 'schlenter', or dud diamond. **1946** L.G. GREEN *So Few Are Free* 127 'Schlenters', bits of glass shaped roughly from bottle stoppers to resemble diamonds. They have none of the peculiar soapy feel of the genuine diamond, but they pass muster sometimes in a hurried deal at night. **1950** E. ROSENTHAL *Here Are Diamonds* 198 No South African word is more frequently used in fiction connected with the Diamond diggings than 'Schlenter,' for a fake stone, a word which seems to have come from the Yiddish. **1969** J.M. WHITE *Land God Made in Anger* 131 Schlenters, or slenters, are fake diamonds. The best Schlenters in South West are made from the marbles in the necks of the lemonade or mineral-water bottles that can be found in dozens at the old German diggings. **1985** W. SMITH *Burning Shore* 465 The quickest way is to dip it into a glass of water my dear. If it comes out wet, it's a schlenter. If it comes out dry, it's a diamond.

b. *rare.* Fake gold.

1911 BLACKBURN & CADDELL *Secret Service* 132 He had paid £400 for a brick of gilded lead worth at least, at Johannesburg rates, elevenpence per pound. The gold of this standard is known as 'Schlenter' on the Rand.

2. *transf.*

a. An illegal or dishonest scheme or action, a 'fiddle'; a confidence trick.

1980 *Rhodeo* (Rhodes Univ.) June, Swaggering round the hills he crooned 'A schlenter here, a schlenter there, schlenter schlenter everywhere'. **1981** *Sunday Times* 22 Feb. 22 No one is going to sell a pass law schlenter to the straight-talking Ben Mokaetle. **1988** *Star* 9 Jan. 1 An SAP spokesman confirmed that police in Pretoria were never short of complaints about 'schlenters' of all kinds. **1991** P. EDGECOMBE *Informant, Durban* Schlenter. Bad or shady deal or action.

b. A confidence-trickster. Also **schlent** *nonce*.

1987 *Student party invitation, Grahamstown* Hear ye all okes, schlents and other bra's of the house! A celebration .. will be held on Saturday 25 April. **1992** *Natal Mercury* 3 Aug. 6 The South African schlenter is immoral in business or personal dealings; the Aussie/Pommie counterpart lacks morals in more intimate activities.

schlenter /ˈʃlentə/ *v. trans. Slang.* Also (occas.) **schlent**. [fr. prec.] To wangle (something); to achieve (something) by devious, underhanded means.

1970 S.E. NATHAM *Informant, Cape Town* They told her she couldn't pay by cheque but somehow she schlentered it and came home with the goods. **1970** C.M. KNOX *Informant, Grahamstown*, I can always manage to schlent a car. **1982** *Star* 31 Mar., Schlenter — to organise something in an underhanded way, to pull strings.

Hence **schlenterer** *n.*, a devious, untrustworthy person.

1983 *Grocott's Mail* 18 Feb. 13 The Rhodes Dictionary ... *Schlenterer*, (n) Person who manipulates behind the scenes, usually used to describe the more devious student politicians.

schloep /ʃlʊp/ n. slang. Also **s(c)hloop**. [Prob. a rendering of the sucking sound made by children as a response to a class-mate's 'sucking up' to a teacher.] A toady or bootlicker.

1962 *Informant, Port Elizabeth* They think you're a schloep if you help the teacher with anything. 1980 C. HOPE *A Separate Development* (1983) 7 An open, honest, anxious guy who'd begun life as a class schloep, a toady, before he'd come over to us, the bad eggs of the class. 1985 [see GAT sense 1 b].

Hence **schloep** v. intrans., to toady, ingratiate oneself; **schloepy** adj., ingratiating.

1976 J. BECKER *Virgins* (1986) 41 Vicky Reed was the sort who went to chapel often and shlooped up to the teachers, but was mingy to the new little kids. 1978 'BLOSSOM' in *Darling* 15 Feb. 131 So I tune him (all shloepy), 'Ag keep yore shirt on, Bok-Bok man, what you take me for?'

schmeerlap var. SMEERLAP.

schmous var. SMOUS.

schoelpat var. SKILPAD.

schoff n. var. SKOF n.²

schoff v. var. SCOFF v.

schoffel var. SKOFFEL.

schoft var. SKOF n.²

school adj. Also with initial capital. [Special sense of general Eng.]

1. Of a black African: educated (formerly esp. at a mission school), westernized (in dress, behaviour, and language), and (usu.) Christian. See also KHOLWA. Cf. DRESSED.

1851 WILMOT in Godlonton & Irving *Narr. of Kaffir War of 1850–51* 508 Last night seven of the *School Kaffirs*, with their families, decamped. 1865 [see INTONJANE]. 1867 *Blue Bk for Col.* 1866 JJ40, The distress among the aged and school natives .. has been great. 1882 J. NIXON *Among Boers* 233 Rudolph .. was a School Kaffir, that is, he had been educated by some German missionaries. 1912 AYLIFF & WHITESIDE *Hist. of Abambo* 78 The school Kaffir professes to look down upon the 'red' who in his turn regards his professing Christian neighbour with dislike and suspicion. 1925 D. KIDD *Essential Kafir* 404 The school-kafir is frequently a very objectionable person. He is apt to suffer from self-conceit. 1955 J.B. SHEPHARD *Land of Tikoloshe* 14 Among school Africans the customary semi-circular arrangement of hut groups is giving way to straight rows. 1961 P. MAYER *Townsmen or Tribesmen* 21 'The difference between a Red man and myself', said a young School countryman, 'is that I wear clothes like White people's, as expensive as I can afford, while he is satisfied with old clothes ... He is illiterate whereas I can read and write ... A Red man attends sacrifices but I attend church.' 1970 M. TYACK *S. Afr.: Land of Challenge* 144 The Xhosa .. distinguish between tribally rooted persons, called the 'Red People,' and detribalized persons, called the 'School People'. 1980 D.B. COPLAN *Urbanization of African Performing Arts.* 80 The policy of encapsulation, which made mission stations islands of acculturation in a traditional sea, led to the structured opposition of 'red' (traditional) and 'school' (Western educated) categories of Xhosa speakers in the towns of the Eastern Cape. 1989 *Reader's Digest Illust. Hist.* 153 Simple economics .. played a crucial role in persuading many Xhosa that being 'red' (those choosing the traditional way of life) as opposed to 'school' (those opting for a European lifestyle) was, perhaps, a better option in the long run. 1993 *CSD Bulletin* (Centre for Science Dev.) July 19 Western education and Christianity have enabled rural African villagers in the Transkei into 'school' people and conservative or 'red' people ... The social division into 'school' and 'red' is not an absolute distinction, but is best seen in terms of a continuum.

2. Of a given name: of Western origin.

Many speakers of the Sintu (Bantu) languages in South Africa have two given names: one of African origin and one of Western origin.

1979 M. MATSHOBA *Call Me Not a Man* 118 Nothing embarrasses me like being called by that other name I got from church, and which was my 'school name'.

school v. intrans. [Special use of general Eng. *school* (trans.) to put or send (someone) to school, to educate (someone) at school.] Chiefly among speakers of the Sintu (Bantu) languages: to attend school.

Also *Indian Eng.*

a1968 D.C. THEMBA in E. Patel *World of Can Themba* (1985) 176 St Cyprian's, Sophiatown, where Dolly schooled. 1974 A. FUGARD *Statements* 27 Two are schooling. The other two stay at home with their mother. 1982 *Voice* 10 Jan. 3 Students will school only in the areas they live in. 1986 PRESTON-WHYTE & LOUW in Burman & Reynolds *Growing Up* 364 Grace, although schooling in the township, was regarded at Umzinyati as one of the young girls of the neighbourhood. 1987 *Drum* Aug. 75 The child is already schooling.

Hence **schooled** ppl adj., educated; **schooling** ppl adj., school-going.

1977 J. SIKAKANE *Window on Soweto* 21 My father is what I could describe as a typical schooled 'Johburger' at heart. 1990 H. VILAKAZI in *Tribute* Sept. 59 One of the .. roots .. was the encounter between people of this social class .. and the .. urbanised, schooling youth.

schotel var. SKOTTEL.

schreik, schrick, schrijk varr. SKRIK n.

schrik var. SKRIK v.

schut var. SKUT.

‖**schuur** /skɪʊə, skyːr, skiːr/ n. Also **skuur**. [Afk., fr. Du.] A barn, shed, or store for grain.

1861 P.B. BORCHERDS *Auto-Biog. Mem.* 5 The front stood, but the back part, commonly called the schuur (store), was burnt to the ground! [1919 M. GREENLEES tr. *O.F. Mentzel's Life at Cape in Mid-18th C.* Among the sergeants are reckoned the men in charge of the big battery called the Water-Kasteel .. and of the outpost called Schuur. 1926 P.W. LAIDLER *Tavern of Ocean* 18 The Company's corn lands around the Big Barn (Groot Schuur still retains its ancient name) produced heavy crops.] 1936 C. BIRKBY *Thirstland Treks* 243 The wheat stored in the main *schuur* was safe. 1987 G. VINEY *Col. Houses* 170 There was a house of the Cape Dutch period into which the original barn or *schuur* had been converted.

schwala var. TSHWALA.

schwempe var. SWEMPI.

scoff n.¹ var. SKOF n.²

scoff /skɒf/ n.² Also **skaf, skof(f)**. [fr. Du. *schoft* three hours' work, shift, quarter of a day; hence each of the day's meals; or fr. *schaften* to eat. (This sense does not exist in Afk.) See also folk etym. at quot. 1993.] Food; a meal. Also *attrib.*

Cf. Scot. Eng. 'scaff'.

1855 J.W. COLENSO *Ten Weeks in Natal* 54 The plate would be open; the *meat* and other *scoff* (food), which the Kafirs are so fond of, would be within his reach. a1862 J. AYLIFF *Jrnl of 'Harry Hastings'* (1963) 48, I had written down some sentences ... One was 'Is this good to eat?' and I found that Mr. Carnal had written it down 'good for skof'. 1877 LADY BARKER *Yr's Hsekeeping* 314 At last it became time for 'scoff', and they all retired to partake of that dainty. 1885 LADY BELLAIRS *Tvl at War* 170 The native messengers sent in that direction had to take with them as much *scoff* — biscuit and biltong in this case — as they could conveniently carry. 1901 R. RANKIN *Subaltern's Lett. to Wife* (1930) 100 Food, with the colonials, was always 'skoff', a malingerer was never anything but a 'skrimshanker'. 1908 D. BLACKBURN *Leaven* 193 Will you go to Johannesburg and work on a mine? Plenty puza, plenty skoff and five sovereigns a month. 1936 H.F. TREW *Botha Treks* 109 Our mess man .. instead of packing our extra mess stores in the scoff box, had filled it with packets of German black lead. 1949 H.C. BOSMAN *Cold Stone Jug* (1969) 133 Of course, you are used to having skoff in only the best hotels, where you tips the waiter ten bob. 1955 L.G. GREEN *Karoo* 96 Where does that familiar South African word 'skoff' come from? Some say it was brought on shore three centuries ago by Dutch sailors who spoke of 'schaften' — to take the noon meal. Others think it arose on the veld. The Afrikaans dictionary gives *skof* as the equivalent of lap, stage or trek. There would be food at the end of the *skof*, and skoff is the anglicised form. 1977 W. STEENKAMP in *Cape Times* 5 Dec. 13 Grubb Minor sank back into his seat, grumbling about lousy poets who didn't know that 'scoff' meant food where he, Grubb Minor, came [from]. 1990 *Weekend Mail* 13 July 5 What definitely is true is: woe unto the maid who eats an apple which little Thabo was to take in his skaf tin (lunch pack) to school. 1993 *Fly Paper* (S. Afr. Airforce Assoc.) Feb. 20 Scoff. You have most likely heard this word which is considered rather a vulgar term for food. Its origin is interesting. During the Anglo-Boer War the rations of bully beef and biscuits came from England, and when the boxes were sent off to the various units, they were consigned to the Senior Commissioned Officer which, when abbreviated, resulted in S.C.OFF, hence the troops associated it with food.

scoff /skɒf/ v. Also **schoff, skof**. [fr. Du. *schoften* to rest, break from work for a time; to have a meal; or fr. *schaften* to eat.

Used in general Eng. in this sense from the mid 19th C., at first prob. ad. *scaff* to beg for food (Scot. Eng., of obscure origin, perh. fr. Du. *schaften*), but latterly assoc. with S. Afr. Eng. *scoff*, see prec.]

a. intrans. To eat.

1798 LADY A. BARNARD *Lett. to Henry Dundas* (1973) 149 No invitation on such occasions is necessary from the farmer, — when a waggon stops at the door, he concludes of course that the passengers want to scoff (to eat), and the horses the same after they have rolled themselves. 1840 W. PITT *Cabin Boy* 151 To see them schoff as they call it, (I mean eat). 1855 G.H. MASON *Life with Zulus* 193 Surrounded with his choice viands, he would commence a war-song, or call for us to get up and 'scoff' (eat) *with him.* 1899 A. LOWTH *Daughter of Tvl* 191, I say, here come those three, still skoffing.

b. trans. To eat (something) voraciously; to feed upon (something).

1900 F.R.M. CLEAVER in M.M. Cleaver *Young S. Afr.* (1913) 73 The local horses come along and skoff that bush entirely and wax fat and rich. 1903 B. MITFORD *Veldt Vendetta* 122 Why the Kafirs'd have skoffed the whole span long before and started out to rake in more. 1931 F.C. SLATER *Secret Veld* 270 Well, when you got outside some of that, you felt as if you had scoffed the finest hotel-dinner that was ever cooked. 1941 A.G. BEE *Kalahari Camp Fires* (1943) 48 We still had a small stock of beautiful potatoes, and you should have seen how they skoffed them up. 1978 *Sunday Times* 24 Sept. (Mag. Sect.) 3 Pancakes should be eaten immediately, in relays, with people scoffing their first, or second, or third, all piping hot from the pan. 1980 A.J. BLIGNAUT *Dead End Rd* 96 You must be thinking of your Hottentot brothers who scoff bats and frogs and lizards as well.

scoffle var. SKOFFEL v.

scolly var. SKOLLY.

Scotch cart n. phr. Also with small initial. [Calqued on S. Afr. Du. *skotskar* (ad. G. *schuttkarren* tip cart).] A small, stout, springless, two-wheeled tip cart which is horse- or ox-drawn and used mainly for transporting rough materials such as refuse, gravel, or manure. Also *attrib.*

1845 *Cape of G.H. Almanac & Annual Register*, (advt) Best Scotch Carts and wheelbarrows made to order. 1871 J. MACKENZIE *Ten Yrs* (1971) 96 The following is a diamond-seeker's outfit, as given in a colonial paper: 'A Scotch cart; waggon axles; a long tom; three sheets of iron, .. tools, [etc.].' 1882 C. DU VAL *With Show through Sn Afr.* II. 191 He was the proud possessor of a two-wheeled vehicle, known colonially as a Scotch cart, though where the connection between it and 'Caledonia stern and wild' exists, I never could make out. **1894** E. GLANVILLE *Fair Colonist* 124 The vast pile of manure .. had been partially removed, and a couple of native boys were now returning .. with a Scotch cart for another load. **1909** LADY S. WILSON *S. Afr. Mem.* 311 We were .. accompanied by the (in Africa) familiar 'Scotch cart' ... This is a strong cart on two wheels, drawn by bullocks, and its usual pace is about two and a half miles an hour. It apparently possesses the delightful qualification of being able to travel on any road, no matter how rough, without breaking down or turning over. **1914** *Farmer's Annual* 96 A Scotch cart is very severe on the after-oxen when the brake is fast, going down hill. **1919** *Dunell, Ebden & Co.'s Price List* Aug. 35 Felloes ... Scotch Cart, White Pear, 2/8. **1937** B.H. DICKE *Bush Speaks* 305 A Scotch cart is a most uncomfortable conveyance to travel in. It is a springless, badly balanced box affair on two wheels, too short to lie down in. **1949** *Cape Argus* 14 May (Mag. Sect.) 2 At first a few skins were sent in from farms, then .. they began to arrive in sugar pockets .. and finally by the Scotch-cart load. **1967** E.M. SLATTER *My Leaves Are Green* 32 Standing between the tents were carts of all descriptions — post-carts, Cape carts, 'spiders', scotch carts, [etc.]. **1977** *Fair Lady* 16 Mar. 63 Two short .. television films about the war. One showed the aftermath of a landmine explosion on a scotch cart carrying little children. **1983** *Argus* 15 Feb., Mr Mkomo surprised residents of Plumtree by walking to the town from his village, 90 km away, towing a scotch-cart full of 'macimbi' (edible caterpillars).

Scotchman *n.* [Special sense of general Eng.; see quot. 1879.]

1. *Obs.* exc. *hist.* A florin.

1879 R.J. ATCHERLEY *Trip to Boerland* 55 In dealing with the Kafirs I frequently heard the term 'Scotchman' applied to a two-shilling piece: and upon enquiry was informed that an enterprising gentleman of that nationality having once passed a large number of florins to the Kafirs as half-crown pieces, the latter had ever since christened the florin 'Scotchman'. **1887** H. RIDER HAGGARD *Jess* (1901) 92 Jantje .. spat upon the 'Scotchman,' as the natives of that part of Africa call a two-shilling piece. **1911** P. GIBBON *Margaret Harding* 275 'Did he give any message?' 'No,' replied Fat Mary. 'Jus' stink-flowers, an' give me Scotchman.' 'Scotchman' is Kafir slang for a florin; it has for origin a myth reflecting on the probity of a great race. **1913** C. PETTMAN *Africanderisms* 433 *Scotchman*, .. Is said to have originated thus: a certain Scotchman employed a number of natives at half a crown a day, at the end of the engagement he palmed off upon the unsophisticated labourers a number of florins as half-crowns, it was not until they tried to pass them as half-crowns that they discovered how they had been 'had'. **1983** V.S. FORBES *Informant, Fish Hoek* A 'Scotchman' is a florin which the canny Scots are alleged to have passed off as half-crowns to gullible blacks. **1988** C.J. SKEAD *Informant, Port Elizabeth* What, when it's not a person from Scotland, is a Scotchman in South Africa? Answer: The name once used for a florin (two shilling piece) as used mostly in Natal and Zululand.

2. *obs.* An early form of SCOTSMAN.

1913 C. PETTMAN *Africanderisms* 434 *Scotchman, Dentex præorbitalis, Günther*, is known by this name in Natal.

scotsman *n.* Also with initial capital. [Unknown (but see quot. 1953).] The seabream *Polysteganus praeorbitalis* of the Sparidae; SCOTCHMAN sense 2.

The name 'scotsman' is used for this species in Smith and Heemstra's *Smiths' Sea Fishes* (1986).

1949 J.L.B. SMITH *Sea Fishes* 278 *Scotsman* ... Profile of head smoothly convex ... Attains 30 ins ... Found only in South Africa, from Algoa Bay to Beira, in deep water. **1953** B. FULLER *Call Back Yesterday* 107 One fish became 'The Scotsman' because it was slippery. **1957** S. SCHOEMAN *Strike!* 230 Scotsman. **1979** SNYMAN & KLARIE *Free from Sea* 48 *Scotsman*, Although not plentiful, this deepwater Caledonian is excellent eating. **1991** *Weekend Post* 6 April 4 Among the linefish species affected by the increased size limits, the most commonly caught are .. : Musselcracker .. , scotsman (30cm, 25cm), [etc.].

‖**scriba** /ˈskriːbə, ˈskriba/ *n.* [L., scribe, clerk.] The title given to the secretary of the synods of the Dutch Reformed churches.

1831 *S. Afr. Almanac & Dir.* 135 Synod of the Reformed Church ... Second Presbytery (meets at Swellendam) Rev. J. Casse President, Rev. C. Mol Scriba. **1843** *Ordinance for Repealing Church Regulations of 25 July, 1804* in *Stat. Law of Cape of G.H.* (1862) 619 There shall be a permanent scriba nominated by the general church assembly from among the ministers. The scriba shall be charged, — *a.* With the duties of scriba during the general church assembly and the meetings of the synodical commission. **1877** F. JEPPE *Tvl Bk Almanac & Dir.* (1976) 38 A 'Commission' consisting of the Chairman (Præses) and Secretary (Scriba) of the General Church meetings. [**1953** B. FULLER *Call Back Yesterday* 133 Mr Johan Naudé lives in a pleasant house not far from the Church, Bethlehem West, wherein he performs the duties of a scribe.] **1970** *E. Prov. Herald* 13 Oct. 4 It is becoming more a custom to appoint women as scribas of Dutch Reformed Churches.

scrick *n.* var. SKRIK *n.*

scrick *v.* , **scrik** varr. SKRIK *v.*

scuffle var. SKOFFEL *v.*

scuse-me var. EXCUSE-ME.

scut var. SKUT.

SDU /esdiːˈjuː/ *n.* [Initial letters of *self-defence unit*.] A name given to any of several vigilante units, originally formed to protect township communities, but subsequently falling into disrepute because of the lawlessness of their members; a member of such a unit. Also *attrib.*

1993 *Sunday Times* 4 Apr. 2 SDUs turning into monsters. In the early 90s the ANC looked to self-defence units to protect communities — today they are mostly renegade bands of criminals who barricade roads, rape women and hold up shop owners. The typical SDU member in the PWV area is .. a disgruntled returned Umkhonto we Sizwe member who has no money no status and years of accumulated grudges. **1993** C. HANI in *Weekly Mail* 8 Apr. 5 It's time nonpartisan control structures are found which introduce a genuine element of accountability into SDU activities. **1993** *City Press* 12 Dec. 1 A leading ANCYL and civic leader from Katlehong — who requested anonymity because SDU members have vowed to kill him — said the conflict was triggered by the SDU's quest for absolute power. **1994** H. NKHOMA in *Sidelines* Dec. 14, I realised they were not police, so they must be the SDU, the Self-Defence Units started by the ANC for the purpose their name implies, but now sometimes out of control, sometimes hand-in-glove with the police, and definitely shady. *Ibid.* 15 These guys were SDUs who had joined forces with the police.

sea bamboo *n. phr.* [tr. S. Afr. Du. *zeebamboes*, see SEEBAMBOES.] The giant kelp *Ecklonia maxima*; SEA TRUMPET; SEEBAMBOES.

1798 S.H. WILCOCKE tr. *J.S. Stavorinus's Voy. to E. Indies 1768–71* I. 25 On the 10th of November, we saw for the first time trumpets, or sea-bamboo, floating on the ocean. **1822** W.J. BURCHELL *Trav.* I. 28 The Dutch call this plant *Zee bambos* (sea bamboo), and boys after cutting its stalk to a convenient length when dry, sometimes amuse themselves in blowing it as a horn or trumpet. **1913** H. TUCKER *Our Beautiful Peninsula* 30 The great, glistening, brown sea-bamboos loll and sway in the smooth swell of the luminous green shallows. **1946** L.G. GREEN *So Few Are Free* 116 The place is called Bamboes Bay, because the sea bamboo is piled high on the beach after heavy gales. **1954** K.H. BARNARD *S. Afr. Shore-Life* 76 The Sea-bamboo .. has a stalk reaching 20 feet in length, crowned by a bunch of strap-shaped fronds. **1973** W.E. ISAAC in *Std Encycl. of Sn Afr.* IX. 562 The largest kelp of Southern Africa is the sea-trumpet or sea-bamboo (*Ecklonia maxima*), which commonly reaches lengths of over 6 metres. **1981** G. & M. BRANCH *Living Shores* 254 One of the local kelps ('sea bamboo', *Ecklonia maxima*) produced 10 000 spores per hour from each square centimetre of its fertile blades. **1982** KILBURN & RIPPEY *Sea Shells* 7 The giant kelp or sea bamboos .. of cold western Cape waters are well known as the habitat of the limpet. **1986** M. VAN WYK *Cooking the S. Afr. Way* 26 Perlemoen in sea bamboo.

sea-cat *n.* [tr. Du. *zeekat*, *zee* sea + *kat* cat. (The modern Afk. form is *seekat*, see SEEKAT.)] CATFISH sense 1. Also *attrib.*

1785 G. FORSTER tr. *A. Sparrman's Voy. to Cape of G.H.* I. 26 The *sepia loligo*, and the *sepia octopodia*, .. are known to our sailors by the name of black-fish and sea-cats. **1882** *Cape Quart. Rev.* Oct. 36 Even the sea cat responded to the hook. **1913** W.W. THOMPSON *Sea Fisheries of Cape Col.* 51 The octopus or sea-cat (Octopus horridus) appears to find a more congenial habitat on the rocky stretches of sea-board on the south and east coasts. **1926** P.W. LAIDLER *Tavern of Ocean* 77 Strange dishes appeared on the tables: stewed 'klip kos,' a large Venus-ear shellfish; sea-cat soup. **1930** C.L. BIDEN *Sea-Angling Fishes* 273 It's the surest sign of a sea-cat down below ... Ten to one the sea-cat shoots out from under the rock ... Be quick and gaff it .. and then you have bait for the day. **1939** A.P. CARTWRIGHT in *Outspan* 24 Nov. 79 On the coast of the Cape Peninsula they call an octopus a 'sea-cat'. **1957** S. SCHOEMAN *Strike!* 210 Bait supplies are plentiful, redbait, fish bait, seacat and mussels being the favourite baits used. **1973** *E. Prov. Herald* 28 Nov. 37 A whole mullet gleamed dully in the lantern light with half a big seacat, tentacles trailing enticingly. **1975** [see SIFFIE]. **1982** [see SEEKAT]. **1985** A. TREDGOLD *Bay between Mountains* 125 A triumph of the visit was to see a seacat swim ... Its lumpy shape became a comet, streaming across the tank, bulbous body in front and tentacles flying out behind.

sea-cow *n. Obs.* exc. *hist.* [Calque formed on S. Afr. Du. *zeekoe* (see ZEEKOE); see also quot. 1913.] **1.** The hippopotamus, *Hippopotamus amphibius* of the Hippopotamidae; ZEEKOE sense 1. Also *attrib.*

1688 G. TACHARD *Voy. to Siam* 74 In the great Rivers there is a Monstrous Creature which they call a Sea-cow, .. the Flesh, or to say better, the Lard of it is good to eat. **1731** G. MEDLEY tr. *P. Kolb's Present State of Cape of G.H.* II. 30 This Valley has its Name from an amphibious Creature, vulgarly call'd a Sea-Cow, and by the Learned, *Hippopotamus*. **1786** G. FORSTER tr. *A. Sparrman's Voy. to Cape of G.H.* II. 274 A sea-cow came out of the river, rushing upon us, with a hideous cry. *Ibid.* 291 Neither does it in the least resemble the ox; so it could be only the different stomachs of this animal, which could occasion it to be called *sea-cow*, at the Cape. **1806** J. BARROW *Trav.* I. 396 She had been cut .. with one of those infernal whips made from the hide of a rhinoceros or sea-cow. **1838** T. SHONE Diary. 4 Sept., Put some sea cow hide in pickle for sambucks. **1850** R.G.G. CUMMING *Hunter's Life* (1902) 93 An equally persuasive sea-cow jambok. **1860** W. SHAW *Story of my Mission* 383 Hippopotami, or, as the Colonists call them 'sea-cows,' were .. frequently met with in the Keiskamma and Fish Rivers. **1870** [see SPEK]. **1913** C. PETTMAN *Africanderisms* 434 *Sea-cow*, The latter half of the name appears to be a corruption of the Hottentot name of the animal *gao (with an initial palatal click) ... The Dutch word zee (sea, lake) would have to be prefixed to distinguish the animal from the ordinary cow. **1915** J.K. O'CONNOR *Afrikander Rebellion* 42 St. Lucia Bay, a lagoon, the home of the sea-cow. **1949** C. BULLOCK *Rina* 59 Two nostrils and a bovine eye appeared for a second, then were gone. It was one of the sea-cows, as the Afrikaners call them, blowing and taking breath. **1976** A. DELIUS *Border* 204 We came upon a sea-cow enjoying itself in a large pool in the local stream. **1982** *S. Afr. Panorama* Jan. 40 Van Riebeeck complained in his diary that he was kept awake in his tent all night by the 'roaring of many sea-cows .. and other wild animals.' **1994** M. ROBERTS tr. *J.A. Wahlberg's Trav. Jrnls 1838–56* 24 Two bullets went whistling at the same moment, and found their mark in the head of a young sea-cow.

2. *comb.* **sea-cow hole** [calqued on S. Afr. Du. *zeekoegat*], a deep river-pool frequented by hippopotamuses; *zeekoe gat*, see ZEEKOE sense 2.

1786 G. FORSTER tr. *A. Sparrman's Voy. to Cape of G.H.* II. 136 We now repaired to a *sea-cow* hole, (*zeekoe-gat*) near *Visch-rivier*, to look for the hippopotamus. **1795** C.R. HOPSON tr. *C.P. Thunberg's Trav.* II. 46 I .. rode plump into the river, till, in a moment, I sank with my horse into a large and deep sea-cow hole, up to my ears. **1810** G. BARRINGTON *Acct of Voy.* 226 By the side of the river there are a number of holes or pits, which the planters call the sea cow-holes, into which, as these creatures are amphibious, they generally retire in the day-time. **1829** C. ROSE *Four Yrs in Sn Afr.* 170 A deep part of the river, called, by the natives, a sea-cow-hole, where several of these huge animals then were. **1875** C.B. BISSET *Sport & War* 175 On their looking up this sea-cow hole, or expanse of water, they saw the spirit walking on the surface of the water.

sea-eagle *n. ?obs.* An early name for the FISH EAGLE, *Haliaetus vocifer.*

1731 G. MEDLEY tr. *P. Kolb's Present State of Cape of G.H.* II. 137 There is another Sort of Eagle about the *Cape*, which the Naturalists call *Haliœetus*: i.e. (as the Cape-Europeans call it) the *Sea-Eagle*. **1884** LAYARD & SHARPE *Birds of S. Afr.* 46 *Haliaetus vocifer.* African Sea-Eagle. **1903** STARK & SCLATER *Birds of S. Afr.* III. 310 *Sea Eagle*, .. Haliaëtus vocifer. *Ibid.* 311 *Distribution.-* .. Cape Colony .. ; Natal .. Transvaal. **1940** A. ROBERTS *Birds of S. Afr.* 58 *Cuncuma vocifer vocifer*, Cape Sea-Eagle.

sea trumpet *n. phr.* [So called because sometimes used as a horn; see quot. 1822 at SEA BAMBOO.] SEA BAMBOO.

[**1798** see SEA BAMBOO.] **1822** J. SMITH *Dict. Pop. Names Plants* 419 *Trumpet, Sea,* (*Ecklonia buccinalis*) a strong-growing seaweed of the Laminaria section of Algae. **1829** LOUDON *Encycl. Plants* (1836) 945 L[aminaria] buccinalis furnishes the singular vegetable production called the sea-trumpet. **1868** L. PAPPE *Florae Capensis* 45 The gigantic stems of the *Sea-trumpet* (*Ecklonia Buccinalis, Horn*). **1913** C. PETTMAN *Africanderisms* 434 *Sea Bamboo,* or *Trumpets, Eklonia buccinalis.* This large marine algae is thus designated in the Cape Peninsula. **1973** [see SEA BAMBOO].

sebilo var. SIBILO.

seboko *n. obs.* Also **siboko**. [S. Sotho and perh. obs. seTswana.] Among the Sotho and Tswana peoples: a totemic name (usu. that of an animal) which is common to all members of a clan or other grouping; the custom of using such a name and venerating the animal or object associated with it.

1902 G.M. THEAL *Beginning of S. Afr. Hist.* 47 The people of the interior .. hold in veneration the animal that their ancestors regarded as a possible embodied spirit. Most .. take their tribal names from it, thus the Bakwena are the crocodiles, the Bataung the lions, the Baphuti the little blue antelopes. Each terms the animal whose name it bears its *siboko*, and .. will not kill it or eat its flesh .. or come into contact with it in any way. **1909** [see MOFOKENG]. **1920** S.M. MOLEMA *Bantu Past & Present* 172 Among the Bechuana .. there was a .. custom known as seboko, by which each tribe venerated a certain animal or natural object. **1936** *Cambridge Hist. of Brit. Empire* VIII. 45 There was a wider system of grouping which cut across the limits of the tribes. The members of these larger groups .. had a common name, the *seboko*, which served as a ceremonial and laudatory form of address ... There were various taboos and observances, ritual songs and dances connected with the species of animal or object whose name was the *seboko* of a group.

se'bona var. SAWUBONA.

se-Chuana, **Sechuana**, **Sec(h)wana** varr. SETSWANA.

second tier see TIER.

Secretarius *n. obs.* Also with small initial. [Du., fr. medieval L.] The secretary to the Council of Policy at the Cape, under Dutch rule; the Dutch term for the Government Secretary during the first British occupation of the Cape, 1795–1803.

1798 LADY A. BARNARD in Lord Lindsay *Lives of Lindsays* (1849) III. 414 By her was Mynheer the 'Secretarius'. **1800** *Ibid.* III. 397 A number of boors also, who were beginning to get reconciled to the English government, came to wait on the 'Secretarius' and the Landrost, partly from curiosity, partly from policy. **1910** D. FAIRBRIDGE *That Which Hath Been* (1913) 22 'Our friend, Mynheer Grevenbroek, formerly Secretary to the Council of Policy,' said the elder van der Stel, beaming kindly on the meagre secretarius. **1924** — *Lady Anne Barnard* 76 Lady Anne beguiled her leisure, amongst her orange trees in the shade of her oaks, in writing charming letters to Macartney and other friends; even the busy Secretarius found time for long accounts of Cape affairs.

secretary *n.* [See quot. 1984.] In full ***secretary bird***, formerly ***secretaries bird***: the large raptor *Sagittarius serpentarius* (the sole species of the Sagittariidae), pale grey and black in colour, with long legs and tail, and crest-feathers which droop at the nape; SLANGVREETER.

1786 G. FORSTER tr. *A. Sparrman's Voy. to Cape of G.H.* I. 155, I have very frequently seen the *secretaries bird* both in its wild and tame state. **1795** C.R. HOPSON tr. *C.P. Thunberg's Trav.* I. 214 The *Secretary-bird*, which is a great destroyer of serpents, after having trod them under his feet, and beat them with his pinions, so that they cannot hurt him, devours them. **1797** *Encycl. Brit.* (ed.3) XVII. 236 Secretaries bird .. classed by Latham under the genus Vultur. *c*1808 C. VON LINNÉ *System of Natural Hist.* VIII. 20 The name of *secretaire*, or secretary, was afterwards given it [*sc.* the serpent-eater] by the Dutch, from comparing it with the office-clerks, who have a habit of sticking a pen behind their ear, to which this bird's tuft bears some resemblance. *a*1823 J. EWART *Jrnl* (1970) 64 We likewise saw several of the larger birds called secretarys ... Destroying them is prohibited by law, from their great use in destroying snakes. **1827** T. PHILIPPS *Scenes & Occurrences* 21 The secretary bird is held in very high estimation, and a penalty of five pounds enforced for destroying them. **1834** T. PRINGLE *Afr. Sketches* 278 Whether the secretary meet with a serpent or a tortoise, he invariably crushes it under the sole of his foot. **1838** J.E. ALEXANDER *Exped. into Int.* I. 123 A tall and beautiful secretary bird, with its blueish plumage, its 'black breeches and grey stockings,' and quills stuck behind its ear, marched along fearlessly and unharmed near the waggon. **1860** A.W. DRAYSON *Sporting Scenes* 271 The secretary bird is one of the greatest destroyers of snakes, and either is proof against their bites or is too active to be bitten. **1890** A. MARTIN *Home Life* 217 Secretary birds are sometimes taught to be very useful guardians of the poultry-yard, especially against aerial enemies. **1905** W.L. SCLATER in Flint & Gilchrist *Science in S. Afr.* 142 Many sportsmen would like to see the extinction of the Secretary bird encouraged, as it undoubtedly destroys numbers of the young partridges and hares. **1915** W. EVELEIGH *S.W. Afr.* 79 The Secretary bird .. with its curious crest of feathers, may sometimes be seen stalking .. among the low bush in search of a little animal or a young snake. **1951** T.V. BULPIN *Lost Trails of Low Veld* 267 The sedate Secretary Birds looking like preoccupied old men walking with their hands behind their backs. **1978** C.L. REITZ *Poisonous S. Afr. Snakes* 5 No animal is naturally completely immune to snakebite, although certain predators of snakes, such as .. the secretary bird (*Sagittarius spp*) .. have an increased resistance. **1984** G.L. MACLEAN *Roberts' Birds of Sn Afr.* 97 Name 'Secretarybird' said to derive from crest's resemblance to old time secretary's quill pens, but is actually Anglicized corruption of Arabic *saqr-et-tair*, meaning hunter-bird. **1989** J. HOBBS *Thoughts in Makeshift Mortuary* 219 He .. stalked about the campus in a black leather jacket and white polo-neck sweater looking like a secretary bird. **1994** [see FLATS sense a].

Section 10 *n. phr. Hist.* Also **Section Ten**. [Referring to sections of Acts so numbered.] **1.a.** Section 10.1 of the Natives (Urban Areas) Consolidation Act (No.25 of 1945 as amended), the law which formerly controlled and limited the rights of black people to live and work in urban areas; used allusively, with reference to the application of this law or to the rights granted in terms of it; *ten one*, see TEN sense a. Often *attrib.*, esp. in the phr. ***Section 10 rights***. **b.** Occas., one having Section 10 rights, a *Section Tenner* (see below). See also ILLEGAL, INFLUX CONTROL.

The Act was repealed in 1986.

[**1945** *Act 25* in *Stat. of Union* 130 Restriction of right of natives to enter an urban area for certain purposes. 10.(1) The Governor-General shall, if requested to do so by a resolution adopted by a duly constituted meeting of any urban local authority, by proclamation in the *Gazette*, declare that from and after a date to be specified therein no native shall enter the urban area under the jurisdiction of that urban local authority for the purpose of seeking or taking up employment or residing therein, otherwise than in accordance with conditions to be prescribed by the Governor-General in that proclamation.] **1963** M. BENSON *Afr. Patriots* 265, 'Endorsing out' was the Government's euphemism for driving out Africans from urban areas to reserves under the notorious Section 10 of the Urban Areas Act. No African might be in an urban area for more than seventy-two hours unless he or she had resided there for fifteen years or worked with the same employer for ten years, or had a discretionary permit to reside and work there. **1977** J. SIKAKANE *Window on Soweto* 43 A white labour official .. maintained that it was illegal to have been issued with a reference book in Natal for a Jo'burg Section Ten. **1979** *Pace* Sept. 84 If you were born in 1951 and your family removed from that area in 1952 only to return in 1979, we are afraid that you may have forfeited your Section 10 rights in Odendaalsrus. **1980** *Sunday Times* 2 Nov. 12 The 'insiders' are all those people — and their descendants — who currently hold the precious Section 10 rights enabling them to live and work in urban areas. **1982** [see DOMPASS]. **1982** *Pace* Nov. 74 He hanged himself ... Section Ten, you know? Influx Control. **1985** *Probe* Oct. 8 The .. controversial section 10 practice which has kept black people out of South Africa's cities, [seems] to be on the way out. **1986** P. MAYLAM *Hist. of Afr. People* 180 These unfortunates were the people who could be 'endorsed out' of urban areas for not possessing section 10 rights under the 1952 Native Laws Amendment Act (and its subsequent amendments). **1987** *Frontline* Feb. 13 A science graduate, a lecturer at a motor firm .. needed help getting the magical Section 10 rights of a permanent resident so that he could bring his wife and six-year-old daughter to live with him.

2. Section 10 of the Internal Security Act, which provides for detention without trial.

1982 *Staffrider* Vol.4 No.4, 41 If you persist with your activities in Wetonia I shall have no option but to lock you up under Section Ten, and you know what that means. **1987** A. KLAASTE in *Tribute* Feb.-Mar. 48 Mr M— and sundry other pillars of black society are spending several months in jail under Section 10 of the Internal Security Act (as it was then called).

Hence **Section Tenner** *n. phr.*, one with the right to live and work in a particular urban area in terms of this law (cf. sense 1 b above); *ten one*, see TEN sense b.

1977 J. SIKAKANE *Window on Soweto* 43, I was a Section Tenner, having been born in Soweto, and being the daughter of a man who also qualified.

Section 29 *n. phr. Hist.* Also with small initial. Section 29 of the Internal Security Act of 1982, in terms of which one could be detained for interrogation for an initial period of thirty days, extendable to six months on the order of the Minister of Police. Often *attrib.*, of or pertaining to such detention, or to a person so held.

In June 1991 an amendment to the Act reduced the maximum period of detention to ten days, extendable only on the order of a Supreme Court judge.

[1985 *Staffrider* Vol.6 No.2, 43 Johannes Rantete .. was detained under Section 29 of the Internal Security Act 1982.] **1987** *New Nation* 5 Mar. 3 (advt) Mr Mkhize .. was detained on January 6, and is being held under Section 29. **1990** *Weekend Post* 2 June 12 A Section 29 detainee died in prison yesterday in what police said appeared to be an act of suicide. **1990** *Weekly Mail* 14 Sept., The government is allowing the use — and abuse — of section 29 detention, even against senior ANC leaders.

Secunde /seˈkʊndə/ *n. hist.* Also **Secundu's, Secundus,** and with small initial. [Du., fr. L. *secundus* second.] The deputy governor (or second-in-command) at the Cape under the Dutch East India Company; also used as a title, with a name. Rarely, used *attrib.* in the phr. **Secunde Persoon** [Du. *persoon* person] (see quot. 1857).

1796 C.R. HOPSON tr. *C.P. Thunberg's Trav.* II. 40 It took its name from Mr Zwellingrebel, who was at that time vice-governor, or *Secundu's* (*Tweede*) at the Cape. **1843** *Ordinance for Repealing Church Reg.* in *Stat. Law of Cape of G.H.* (1862) 616 The meeting elects in the same manner, a secundus, who acts as assessor for the president, and in case of indisposition occupies his place. **1857** *Cape Monthly Mag.* II. Sept. 155 The honourable the 'Secunde Persoon,' Samuel Elzevier (the colonial secretary of the day) .. bore the treasure in triumph to the Governor's residence. **1858** 'F.' in *Ibid.* III. Mar. 149 Mr. Hemmy, the 'secundus,' .. was also a German, from Bremen. **1881** *Cape Monthly Mag.* IV. Jan. 3 For a long time the Secunde Cornelis de Cretzer had been the most active member of the Cape government. **1899** G.M. THEAL *Rec. of Cape Col.* V. 2 The late secunde — Johan Isaac Rhenius — was offered and accepted the office of receiver and treasurer general. **1910** D. FAIRBRIDGE *That Which Hath Been* (1913) 274 We are at the gates of Elsenburg and I see the Secunde waiting on the stoep to greet us. **1926** P.W. LAIDLER *Tavern of Ocean* 21 Up to August, 1653, Johan van Riebeeck was alone in command … There was no one to act as Commander's deputy in case of his illness. Convinced of his fitness, Van Riebeeck appointed the Junior Merchant Jacob Reyniersz to be 'Secunde'. *Ibid.* 28 Mrs. Fothergill, widow of Secunde Swellengrebel. **1949** M.W. SPILHAUS in A.C. Partridge *Lives, Lett. & Diaries* (1971) 17 The Secunde, — The Governor (Commander) at the Cape was chairman of the Administrative body the Council of Policy, with supreme judicial powers at the Station. In his absence the chair was taken by the commander of the garrison called the Secunde (i.e. second in charge). **1952** G.M. MILLS *First Ladies of Cape* 26 Contained the house of the Commander .., the Secunde's house and several others. *Ibid.* 53 So unpopular and so disliked by the colonists, ..[he] transferred the administration to the Secunde Rhenius three months after he had received his instructions. **1969** [see RONDGANGER]. **1987** G. VINEY *Col. Houses* 59 He was rich — probably very rich — after nine years as *Secunde,* for in the last days of Company rule official corruption reached a perfectly disgraceful level.

securities rand see RAND sense 3 b.

securocrat /səˈkjʊərəʊkræt/ *n.* [Blend of Eng. *security* + *bureaucrat.*] One who advocates the close involvement of military and police officers in government, and the extensive use of the security forces as a means of ensuring order; a military or police officer who has an influential position in the government. Also *attrib.* passing into *adj.*, of rule by a government dominated by such people.

Used particularly of the Nationalist government of South Africa in the mid-1980s, during the term of President P.W. Botha.

1989 *E. Prov. Herald* 7 Mar. 4 If the party wants the emergency relaxed while the securocrats (whom President Botha tends to attract) want it maintained, then maintained it will be. **1990** A. GOLDSTUCK *Rabbit in Thorn Tree* 33 At the height of PW Botha's 'securocrat' rule .. the various state security bodies were virtually given the run of the country. **1991** J. PAUW *In Heart of Whore* 122 The rise of the military can be traced back to 1978 when PW Botha, former Minister of Defence, became Prime Minister … The new Prime Minister began to use the military to fulfil functions which in normal circumstances should have been a police preserve. Moreover, the growing influence of the military was reflected in the numbers of SADF personnel now in positions of power as public decision-makers. South Africa was now to be governed largely by 'securocrats'. **1991** A. VAN WYK *Birth of New Afrikaner* 30 The crisis .. exposed the backstairs influence of .. the so-called securocrats, owing much to the power of General H.J. van den Bergh, head of the Bureau of State Security (*Boss*, counterpart of the American CIA ..) … Yet their new government headed by P.W. Botha was merely to replace the Police Big Chiefs with the Armed Forces and continue securocrat rule. **1992** P. CULL in *Weekend Post* 13 June 10 More suited to the securocrat days of P.W. Botha than the present.

‖**seebamboes** /ˈsɪəbamˌbus/ *n.* Formerly also **zee bamboes, zee-bambos.** [Afk. (earlier S. Afr. Du. *zeebamboes*), see *sea* + *bamboes* bamboo.] SEA BAMBOO.

1822 [see SEA BAMBOO]. **1913** C. PETTMAN *Africanderisms* 571 Zee bamboes, Ecklonia buccinalis; the name given to this algae by the Dutch. **1958** L.G. GREEN *S. Afr. Beachcomber* 133 Tough, dry stems of seebamboes are usually reduced to ashes. **1966** C.A. SMITH *Common Names* 412 Van Riebeeck in 1654 records that the Hottentots stored oil from stranded whales in the seebamboes.

‖**seekat** /ˈsɪəkat/ *n.* Formerly also **zee kat.** [Afk. (earlier Du. *zeekat*), see *sea* + *kat* cat.] CATFISH sense 1.

1913 C. PETTMAN *Africanderisms* 571 Zee kat, .. The octopus. **1958** L.G. GREEN *S. Afr. Beachcomber* 101 Last of these horrors lurking in Cape seas is the octopus or seekat. **1964** J. BENNETT *Mr Fisherman* (1967) 87 There was a good market for octopus, or *seekat* as they were called along the coast. **1982** KILBURN & RIPPEY *Sea Shells* 141 Several species of octopus occur on the Southern African shore, and are often found at low tide, hiding within submerged holes and crannies in the reef. From such retreats they are avidly dragged by bait-seeking fishermen, who know the octopus as the 'sea-cat' or 'seekat'.

seekoe(i) var. ZEEKOE.

seepganna see GANNA sense 2.

‖**seepkissie** /ˈsɪəpkəsi/ *n. hist.* [Afk., *seep* soap + *kis* box, case + dim. suffix -IE.] A soap-box (used in an Anglo-Boer War concentration camp as a coffin for a small child). See also CONCENTRATION CAMP.

1971 *Daily Dispatch* 20 May 9 Perhaps the key symbol in these people's minds was the tragic 'seepkissie' or small soapbox in which children who died in the concentration camps were buried. **1971** *Sunday Times* 14 Nov. (Mag. Sect.) 2 This was the pitiful era of the 'seepkissie' — the little soapbox which became a coffin for so many Boer children who died of enteric. **1976** S. GRAY in *Quarry '76* 122 It was your world took me over there was Oom Gert and the seepkissie and even the starved babies and hanging young patriots.

seer var. SIEUR.

sefanagalo var. FANAKALO.

sehalahala /sehalaˈhaːla/ *n.* Also **sahalahala, sohalahala.** [S. Sotho; special use of the Lesotho name for any of several shrubs, including *Eriocephalus punctulatus.*] The aromatic woody shrub *Eriocephalus punctulatus* of the Asteraceae, from which an essential oil is obtained for the perfume industry. Also *attrib.*

1957 A.A. MURRAY *Blanket* 58 A thick column of blue smoke rose steadily into the still air, charged with the smell of burning fat and cow dung and the sweet-smelling sehalahala bush. **1968** A. FULTON *Dark Side of Mercy* 15 There was no wood in the mountains; sohalahala and disu were the only sources of fuel. *Ibid.* 26 A chill wind whipped the sohalahala bushes into a frenzied dance. **1974** *S. Afr. Panorama* May 33 'Sahalahala' the Basuto of Lesotho call the grey shrub which grows high up against the slopes of their highland home … One of the only two naturally blue essential oils known to the world's perfume industry is extracted from 'Sahalahala' … Even Mr. de la Harpe, senior, could hardly have guessed then that 'sahalahala' oil would one day become a sought-after product on the world perfume market. *c*1976 H. FLATHER *Thaba Rau* 46 As there is neither peat nor timber at Thaba Rau we have had to improvise, and the answer to our problem is summed up in the simple word 'sehalahala' … He picked up a bunch of sehalahala. 'Seriously,' he said, 'that is how we heat the geyser — with this stuff'.

seisje var. SYSIE.

sekale var. SCALE.

self-governing *ppl adj. Hist.* [Special sense of general Eng. *self-governing* autonomous, independent; or tr. Afk. *selfregerende.*] Of or pertaining to the former ethnically-based territories (or 'homelands') within South Africa which enjoyed a limited form of self-government by legislative assembly, but which did not accept 'independence' under the policy of SEPARATE DEVELOPMENT. See also HOMELAND sense 1. Cf. INDEPENDENT.

The territories thus designated were re-incorporated into South Africa in 1994.

1978 *Survey of Race Rel.* (S.A.I.R.R.) 311 Transkei was granted independence on 26 October 1976 and BophuthaTswana became an independent state on 6 December 1977. All other homelands have self-governing status. **1980** *Survey of Race Rel. 1979* (S.A.I.R.R.) 299 Ciskei, Gazankulu, Lebowa, QwaQwa and KwaZulu were 'self-governing territories' in that they had duly constituted legislative assemblies which legislated for those territories in an increased number of areas of government. **1988** A. FISCHER in Boonzaaier & Sharp *S. Afr. Keywords* 131 Constitutionally, homelands were 'developed' from self-managing (*selfbesturende*) to self-governing (*selfregerende*) homelands, and from self-governing homelands to self-governing or independent 'national states'. **1992** D. BERESFORD in *Guardian Weekly* 11 Sept. 12 Six areas (Gazankulu, Lebowa, KwaNdebele, Qwaqwa and KwaZulu) are now designated as self-governing states.

sell-out *n.* [fr. general Eng. *sell out* to betray.] Esp. designating a (black) person perceived to be co-operating with apartheid: a collaborator, a betrayer of his or her people. Also *attrib.* See also IMPIMPI.

1960 Z.K. MATTHEWS in H. Spottiswoode *S. Afr.: Rd Ahead* 189 With the usual quota of quislings and 'sell-outs' to be found among all people, much can be done to keep vast sections of the population in a kind of mental dungeon. **1969** *Post* 25 May 2 'Sell-out' Chieftainess gets sack. **1974** A.P. BRINK *Looking on Darkness* 335 I'm White. But I'm revolting against everything White represents in this country, and so my sympathy lies with those who aren't White. It turns me into a sell-out and a traitor, since in our society every person is judged, and damned, by his relation to a particular group. **1976** [see UBC]. **1976** *E. Prov. Herald* 19 Oct. 13 He was invited to address Stellenbosch University, the first 'Coloured' selected .. and pressed ahead, in spite of the severest criticism from the 'Coloured leaders' of the day, who branded him 'a sell-out'. **1977** J. HOFFMAN in *Quarry '77* 56 By November the fact that we were comparatively untouched and healthy, while other schools were burnt out or invaded, would become a cause for reproach. Some of us would feel ourselves a college for sell-outs. **1979** M. MATSHOBA *Call Me Not a Man* 99 Sellouts seldom go around with familiar faces ... Wisdom says that any stranger may be a sellout. **1983** *Frontline* May 37 The 'sell-outs' .. who have made good through the white man's system, are so unpopular that they have to ride around in armoured cars. **1987** *Cosmopolitan* Aug. 192 The black musicians who joined Simon's triumphant tour were labelled sell-outs by some far-left organisations. But overseas, it was clear that 'sell-out' meant no seats available. **1988** N. MATHIANE in *Frontline* Apr.-May 12 What do you do when you are told to necklace an informer, and refusing implies you are condoning 'sell-outs' and therefore your home will be gutted? **1990** R. MALAN in *Cosmopolitan* Apr. 166 If you lived in Soweto, there were some things you dared not say for fear of being labelled a sellout. Sellouts did not live long. **1993** *Weekly Mail & Guardian* 13 Aug. 35 The man with the megaphone said: 'The DP says Helen Suzman has helped you. But what has she brought you? Not two cents. Blacks working for the DP are nothing but sell-outs.' **1994** *Ibid.* 16 Sept. 12 The targets of this new rough justice are no 'sell-outs' or *impimpis* — they are alleged criminals.

‖**selons** /sə'lɔns/ *n.* Also **Selon's**. [Afk., 'of Ceylon'.] In full ***selons-roos*** /-rʊəs/ [Afk., *roos* rose], ***selons-rose***: CEYLON ROSE.

1946 H.C. BOSMAN in L. Abrahams *Cask of Jerepigo* (1972) 170 The oleander — Selon's-roos it is called in Marico — at one time the most popular flowering tree in certain parts of the country. *a***1951** —— in L. Abrahams *Unto Dust* (1963) 133 That half-red flower, the selons-rose .. is the flower that a Marico girl most often pins in her hair to attract a lover. The selons-rose is also the flower that here, in the Marico, we customarily plant upon a grave.

‖**semels** /'sɪəm(ə)ls/ *n.* Formerly also **semmels**, **simmels**. [Afk., fr. Du. *zemelen*.]

1. Bran.

1833 S. KAY *Trav. & Researches* 503 A quantity of '*simmels*' (coarse bran) also lay on the ground. **1971** BARAITSER & OBHOLZER *Cape Country Furn.* 227 Storage chest or meelkis in Swellendam Museum with compartments for fynmeel, growwemeel and semels. **1989** M. ROBERTS *Herbs for Healing* 101 Constipation remedy .. 20ml bran (Digestive Bran — 'Semels').

2. *transf. Mining.* See quots 1871 and 1985.

1871 J. SHAW in *Cape Monthly Mag.* II. June 359 At Jagersfontein there is a substance of a singular character, which, from its appearance, has been named by the Boers *semmels* (bran). This is a fine clayey *dêbris* glistening with talc, and is undoubtedly the *detritus* from the talcose claystone or clayey schist. **1913** C. PETTMAN *Africanderisms* 436 *Semmels*, .. The Dutch have applied this term to a substance not unlike bran in appearance, found in the neighbourhood of Jagersfontein. **1985** A.J.A. JANSE in Glover & Harris *Kimberlite Occurrence & Origin* 23 The Boer diggers recognised that the stuff from the Dry Diggings was different from the alluvial muddy sand and gravel of the River Diggings and referred to the mud of the Dry Diggings as 'Zemelen' or 'Semmels' because the ubiquitous mica flakes reminded them of bran husks in meal.

Sendebele var. SINDEBELE.

‖**sendeling** /'sendələŋ/ *n.* Also **zendeling**, and with initial capital. [Afk., fr. Du. *zendeling*.] A missionary.

1838 J.E. ALEXANDER *Exped. into Int.* I. 76 'Where are all the Hottentots?' asked the zendeling. 'The Hottentots!' cried the farmer, 'you would not have them with us also?' **1955** A. DELIUS *Young Trav.* 108 The congregation was very devout and sang the hymns and psalms with great spirit in good, full voices, the *Sendeling* intoning for them.

‖**Sendingkerk** /'sendəŋkɛrk/ *n.* Also **Sendingskerk**. [Afk., *sending* mission + *kerk* church.] A short name for the *Nederduitse Gereformeerde Sendingkerk* (Dutch Reformed Mission Church), the branch of the Dutch Reformed Church founded for 'coloured' members.

See note at DUTCH REFORMED.

1974 *Sunday Times* 27 Oct. 15 Today there exists in South Africa the NG Sendingkerk (mission church) for Coloureds and the NG Church of Africa for Blacks. **1978** *Ibid.* 23 Apr. 15 The NGK family consists of four churches, divided along ethnic and racial lines: The white NGK, the 'coloured' Sendingkerk (mission church), the 'Indian' Reformed Church in Africa and the African Dutch Reformed Church in Africa (NGKA). **1982** *Reader* Dec. 9 The Nederduitse Gereformeerde Sendingkerk has joined the struggle against apartheid. The Sendingskerk is the Dutch Reformed Church (DRC) for the so called Coloured people. **1989** D. VAN HEERDEN in *Sunday Times* 5 Mar. 4 Led by the irrepressible Dr. Alan Boesak, the Sendingkerk, NGSK, has adopted its own credo — the Belhar Confession — in which it declared apartheid a sin against God. **1990** *Sunday Times* 14 Oct. 4 The Sendingkerk's adherence to the Belhar Confession — which declared apartheid a heresy.

Senior Certificate *n. phr.* Also with small initials. The formal name for MATRICULATION (sense 2). Also *attrib.*

1955 A. DELIUS *Young Trav.* 37 If you want to get a decent job of any sort, or go to a university, you've got to get your standard ten, that's matric. or senior certificate. **1963** S.H. SKAIFE *Naturalist Remembers* 59 Children began to take biology in the Junior Certificate, Senior Certificate and Matriculation examinations. **1970** *Daily Dispatch* 11 Dec. 6 Umtata's Hoërskool Transkei will be able to offer English higher to junior and senior certificate candidates next year.

Senior Counsel *n. phr.* Also with small initials. [tr. modern L. *Senior Consultus*.] SC; also used with a name, as a title.

1978 A.P. BRINK *Rumours of Rain* 107 He'd been elevated to Senior Counsel (no doubt in recompense for his performance in that particular case). **1981** [see SC]. **1984** *Daily Dispatch* 20 Jan. 1 Mr M.Z. Ngoqo, the presiding magistrate, .. said Mr Kirk had informed him he intended briefing Senior Counsel on the matter. **1986** [see quots at SC]. **1987** G. DAVIS in *Weekly Mail* 11 Sept. 3 Senior counsel L. D—, appearing for the displaced squatters, argued yesterday that it was every citizen's fundamental right under common law to have a say in his or her government. **1988** *Cape Times* 31 Aug. 9 Senior Counsel Mr J. S— was submitting argument on behalf on the SA State President in an application challenging the validity of a certificate issued in terms of Section 103 of the Defence Act.

separate development *n. phr. Hist.* [Either formed in S. Afr. Eng. fr. Eng. *separate* + *development*, or tr. Afk. official terminology, *aparte ontwikkeling*.] The National Party government's policy of creating a separate 'homeland' (intended to become a self-governing state) for each of the officially-defined black 'nations' in South Africa, reserving for whites, 'coloureds', and Indians the right to South African citizenship, and to permanent residence in 'white' areas of the country; often considered a euphemism for 'apartheid'. Also *attrib.* Cf. GRAND APARTHEID, *multinationalism* (see MULTINATIONAL). See also APARTHEID sense 1, HOMELAND sense 1, SEPARATE FREEDOMS.

Introduced in the 1950s, this policy was abandoned in the late 1980s.

1955 *Report of Commission for Socio-Economic Dev. of Bantu Areas* (UG61–1955) 105 Objections to the Policy of Separate Development. **1956** M. ROGERS *Black Sash* 142 The demarcation of the country into separate European and non-European areas for the twin purposes of residence and separate development involves a change so revolutionary as to be almost impossible in practice. **1962** *Sunday Times* in *S. Afr. Speaks* Feb. 4 The map shows the Transkei, *Homeland* of the Xhosa people who will attain self-rule in 1963 in terms of the policy of separate development. **1966** *Cape Argus* 8 Apr. 14 Nationalist speakers with an eye to doubts about Bantustans .. are now prone to claim that separate development is being more accepted abroad. **1970** *Rand Daily Mail* 14 Nov. 4 'With the Government's brand of separate development there is plenty of separation but not much development,' said Mr. Winchester. **1971** *Sunday Times* 9 May 12 The disclosure that, after 23 years of apartheid, there are more Africans in the White areas than in the Black, shows that the Nationalist policy of 'separate development' cannot be implemented. **1971** *Nat. Geog. Mag.* Sept. 773 'Why do you participate in the separate development scheme?' I asked. 'Because only within its framework can I help my people,' Chief Buthelezi replied. **1974** [see PARAMOUNT sense b]. **1977** [see NP sense 1]. **1980** A.P. BRINK *Mapmakers* (1983) 202 We have followed the semantic metamorphosis of 'apartheid' into 'separate development' into 'parallel development' into 'equal opportunity' into 'constellation of states' ... In an authoritarian society semantics is a very subtle game. **1985** PLATZKY & WALKER *Surplus People* 68 Chapter 5, which considers the shaping of the 'Separate Development policy' (as the Nationalists like to call apartheid), starts by tracing the increasingly sophisticated elaboration of the Group Areas and (especially) the bantustan programme after 1948. **1986** P. MAYLAM *Hist. of Afr. People* 170 The official ideology of the Nationalist government has been based on the theory of 'separate development' ... In terms of this theory South Africa's population is .. comprised of .. a whole set of ethnic minorities ... Each African group should be allotted its own 'homeland' where it can develop culturally, politically and economically along its own lines. **1991** F.G. BUTLER *Local Habitation* 200 Creon becomes Kroon, the leader of an (imaginary) Trek determined to establish an all-white republic on separate development lines like those of the ruling Nationalist Party.

separate freedoms *pl. n. phr.* In the terminology of apartheid: the privileges and rights which are extended to each ethnic group under the policy of SEPARATE DEVELOPMENT. Usu. used ironically.

1970 *Cape Times* 5 June 70 Thus Black 'labour force units' are tolerated in urban 'bachelor quarters' while their 'superfluous appendages' are removed to their 'dwelling units' and 'repatriated' to 'resettlement' camps' — all in the name of 'separate freedoms'. Homebreaking is, apparently, a dirty word; to be avoided at all costs. **1973** *Ibid.* 26 May 8 Mr S— P— has argued eloquently and with great sincerity in defence of the concept of separate freedoms. No one can deny the nobility of the conception nor, indeed, that it has had a wholesome educative effect on the entrenched attitudes of white *baaskap*. **1990** *Sunday Star* 11 Mar. 16 The Government can never run away from the fact that it went merrily ahead, against all advice to the contrary, with its hair-brained schemes about 'separate' freedoms.

Hence (*nonce*) **separate freedomite** *n. phr.*, a supporter of the concept of separate freedoms.

1973 *Post* 23 May 5 Separate 'Freedomites' have beautiful visions about Bantustans.

Sepedi /se'pe:di/ *n.* Also **se-Peli**. [Sotho *sePedi*, n. prefix *se-* + *Pedi* (or in Lesotho orthography *Peli*), see PEDI.] The language of the Pedi people; PEDI *n.* sense 2; also called *North(ern) Sotho*, see SOTHO sense 2 c. Also *attrib.*

SePedi is the dominant Northern Sotho language and, with Southern Sotho and seTswana, is one of the three main Sotho-Tswana languages. See also SOTHO sense 2.

1909 G.Y. LAGDEN *Basutos* II. 654 The leading dialect of the *Northern Sub-branch* is the *se-Peli*, and of the *Southern Sub-branch* the leading dialect is *se-Suto proper*. Both are reduced to writing ... The *se-Peli* is undoubtedly more primitive and pure. **1941** [see SETSWANA]. **1975** [see PEDI *n.* sense 1]. **1988** *Drum* Mar. 29 Had I not been told that he was Allie Otto, I would have given him the traditional Sepedi greeting — 'warra'.

seringa var. SYRINGA.

‖**sersant** /sɛr'sant/ *n.* Also with initial capital. [Afk.] Sergeant.

Used esp. to designate an Afrikaans-speaking police sergeant, or to allude to the predominance of Afrikaans-speakers in the police force.

1971 A. MENDELOW in *Convocation Commentary* (Univ. of Witwatersrand) Apr. 9 'Man', says Koos, 'when my sersant tells me to patrol these koppies, I patrol these blerrie koppies'. **1983** O. MUSI in *City Press* 28 Aug. 8 The good sersant was able to arrest Mrs Ngwenya and drop her at the local cop shop. **1987** M. MELAMU *Children of Twilight* 25 It was the Sersant who later told me what had ensued after I'd left. **1992** S. VOLLENHOVEN in *South* 27 Feb. 15 The naked Sersant from the narcotics squad says she was merely making a quick buck.

sesayby var. SASSABY.

‖**seshweshwe** /se'ʃwe(:)ʃwe/ *n.* Also **(i)sishweshwe, seseshwe, seshoeshoe, sheshwe,** and with initial capital. Pl. **-s**, or unchanged. [S. Sotho, n. prefix *se-* + *-shweshwe* (or *-shoeshoe*), 'of the people of Moshoeshoe (Moshesh)'. Forms with the n. prefix *isi-* prob. result from the writers' mistaken perception of the word as Xhosa or Zulu.] A short skirt made of *German print* (see GERMAN), and decorated with several rows of pin-tucks, worn esp. by Sotho women. Also *attrib.*

1973 *Daily Dispatch* 16 June 8 The Xhosa skirts or shweshes, worn by the women in the Ciskei and Transkei. **1973** *Drum* 8 Sept. 38 Muriel decided to modify the traditional Isishweshwe dresses and made them into maxi and midi dresses. **1974** *Ibid.* 8 Aug. 7 Mrs S— took to knitting jerseys, pullovers and baby clothes as well as [making] 'sishweshwe' — traditional Sotho dresses — to narrow the gap between income and financial need. **1982** *S. Afr. Panorama* Apr. 38 Long, voluminous cotton fabrics in red and blue Shangaan fashions with crowning turbans, vied with Sheshwe (Basotho) skirts inherited from 19th century German missionaries, a mode that has become an institution. **1986** *Learn & Teach* No.2, 14 She began to make 'Seshoeshoe' dresses at home. **1994** [see Weekly Mail & Guardian quot. at GERMAN].

Sesotho /se'su:tu/ *n.* Forms: α. **Sesuto, Se-Suto, Sesutu, Sisuto, Susuto**; β. **Sesotho, siSotho.** [fr. Sotho *seSotho*, n. class prefix *se-* + *Sotho*, see SOTHO.] **1.** *South(ern) Sotho*, see SOTHO sense 2 c. **2.** SOTHO sense 2 b. Also *attrib.*

For a time 'Sesotho' was used to designate all the Sotho languages. It is now officially used only of the southern Sotho languages (but in popular usage might refer to the northern languages as well).

α. **1846** J.C. BROWN tr. *T. Arbousset's Narr. of Explor. Tour to N.-E. of Col.* 251, I spoke Sesuto, a dialect which the chief of the place .. also understood. **1850** J.W. APPLEYARD *Kafir Lang.* 35 In the Sisuto dialect, several portions of the Old and New Testaments have been translated and published by the Missionaries of the Paris Society, besides a Hymn book. **1871** J. MACKENZIE *Ten Yrs* (1971) 492 They [*sc.* clicks] are found in other African languages, as in Zulu and Kaffir, and a few words in Sesuto. **1872** [see DUTCH *n.* sense 2 a]. **1894** F.A. BARKLY *Among Boers & Basutos* 109 By this time they could both speak Sesuto and 'Low' or 'Kitchen Dutch' (as it is called in those parts) well. **1908** *Rand Daily Mail* 11 Sept. 7 The gangs quickly gained adherents ... English words of command were discarded, and the language of the Amalaita became Sesuto. **1909** G.Y. LAGDEN *Basutos* 654 The contact with Zulu-speaking tribes has exercised a marked influence over *se-Suto*, making it softer and less guttural [than *se-Pedi*], and introducing into it the *click* sound, which is unknown to all other se-Chuana dialects. **1916** J. BUCHAN *Greenmantle* 120, I spoke rapidly in Sesutu, for I was afraid the captain might know Dutch. **1923** G.H. NICHOLLS *Bayete!* 75 All Nelson's followers seemed to speak English, though most of the conversation was carried on in Susuto, with here and there a slip into Zulu. **1942** [see MORENA sense 1 b]. **1948** A. PATON *Cry, Beloved Country* 103 Spoke to Mrs Lithebe in Sesutu, so that she withdrew. **1957** S.G. MILLIN in D. Wright *S. Afr. Stories* (1960) 152 Her name was Rosie and she was a Basuto from his parts in the Northern Transvaal ... Rosie and her sister .. knew English, Afrikaans and Zulu, no less than Sesuto, their own language. **1971** E.C.G. MARAIS tr. *E.N. Marais's My Friends the Baboons* 81 From the struggling mass there arose constant laughter, mingled with Sesutu curses of the grossest kind. **1991** O. MUSI in *Drum* Dec. 18 There are those whites who, because they have picked up a smattering of Zulu or say Sesuto, mostly consisting of vulgar expressions, portray themselves as 'experts on the Native'.

β. **1950** T.J. KRIEL *New Sesotho-English Dict.* Preface, Dr. Eiselen .. asked him .. to provide a Northern Sesotho-English Dictionary. **1953** LANHAM & MOPELI-PAULUS *Blanket Boy's Moon* 208, I am a Mosotho; I love Lesotho; I love my language Sesotho. **1960** J. COPE *Tame Ox* 85 His Sesotho Bible lay, carefully wrapped, in the bottom of his tin box and he felt its presence there like his father's voice, reproachful, full of distant music. *a***1968** D.C. THEMBA in E. Patel *World of Can Themba* (1985) 18 He spoke fluent Sesotho and believed he could pass for a Mosotho. **1979** [see JUNIOR CERTIFICATE]. **1980** D.B. COPLAN Urbanization of African Performing Arts. 214 For shebeen dancing, most Sotho migrants preferred neo-traditional styles such as focho ('disorder') played on the concertina and a homemade drum ... However, organists like Gashe blended Sesotho songs into the structure of marabi. **1984** N.S. NDEBELE in *Staffrider* Vol.6 No.1, 43 A lot of fiction in the African languages, Zulu or Sesotho, for example, is set in the rural areas.

sessaby var. SASSABY.

‖**Sestiger** /'sestəxə, 'sɛstəxər/ *n.* Also with small initial. [Afk., *sestig* sixty + suffix *-er* signifying 'belonging to'.] A member of a group of Afrikaans authors and poets of the 1960s who were innovative in both theme and technique, and were influenced esp. by French literature. Also *attrib.* Cf. DERTIGER.

1968 COPE & KRIGE *Penguin Bk of S. Afr. Verse* 17 The new generation of writers, loosely grouping themselves as the *Sestigers* (writers of the sixties) were responsible for significant developments in Afrikaans literature. **1969** *Sunday Times* 31 Aug. 19 The Sestiger movement petered out through lack of stimulus and appreciation (though it is known that several Sestiger books remain to this day unpublished). **1970** T.T. CLOETE in *Std Encycl. of Sn Afr.* I. 166 The movement of the 'Sestigers', by now consciously established with its magazine .. , paid particular attention to prose. **1973** *Weekend Post* 17 Feb. 9 Mr Jan Rabie, one of the 'sestiger' group of writers, said .. that any language that had the stigma of racialism had no future in a multiracial South Africa. **1975** *Sunday Times* 20 Apr. (Mag. Sect.) 14 The Sestigers were a group of young writers who deliberately challenged the local tradition of petty realism and helped break down the current taboos on sex and religion. **1977** *Weekend Post* 25 June 1 The names of leading Afrikaner academics .. have emerged in the trial of 'Sestiger' poet and author Breyten Breytenbach. **1981** V.A. FEBRUARY *Mind your Colour* 114 The white Afrikaner, who undergoes his cultural revolution under the name of 'Sestiger' .. must prove that Afrikaans is not synonymous with Afrikaner oppression and *baaskap* (overlordship/domination). **1988** K. BRYNARD in *Star* 28 May 11 Dr John Kannemeyer, literary historian, points out that the Sestigers applied their art in an international context — they experimented with and were influenced by new literary and philosophical forms such as surrealism and existentialism. **1990** *Sunday Times* 29 July 20 The Nasionale Pers is a formidable publishing house ... There was hardly an event of significance — be it a change of government, of policy or the emergence of a new literary movement like, say, the Sestigers — in which Naspers or its people were not intimately involved.

Sesuto, -tu varr. SESOTHO.

Seswati see SWATI sense 1.

Setebele var. SINDEBELE.

‖**seties** /'sɪətis/ *n.* [Afk., see quot. 1991.] An Afrikaner dance resembling the schottische.

1980 *E. Prov. Herald* 27 Oct. 13 There's Zoutspansberg Seties, Kliprivier Polka [etc.]. **1990** *Weekend Post* 8 Dec. 6 Couples on the floor danced the *seties*, the *vastrap*, and the *wals*. **1991** *S. Afr. Panorama* May-June 20 The *seties* resembles the European dance, the *'schottische'* .. which was corrupted in the boer tongue to *seties*.

setlaar /'setlɑ:(r)/ *n. Obs.* exc. *hist.* Also **setlar, settlaar,** and with initial capital. [S. Afr. Du.] SETTLER sense 2 a. Often *derog.*

Used to suggest the speech of South African Dutch and, later, Afrikaans people.

1846 A.G. BAIN *Jrnls* (1949) 199 Then to an Engels setlaar fool We had ourselves contracted. *a***1862** J. AYLIFF *Jrnl of 'Harry Hastings'* (1963) 55 The knavish Hottentots .. called out one to another 'aller mopstick' or something like that, 'Englis setlars!' **1885** L.H. MEURANT *60 Yrs Ago* 80 In ringing his brass plate at the commencement of a sale his stereotyped condition was — 'drie monts krediet for de Christemens — no krediet for de Settlaar.' **1968** F.G. BUTLER *Cape Charade* 9 If everybody who got drunk at New Year was sent to work on the road, the road would be past the Langkloof, past the Setlaars, past the Xhosas and past the Pondoes, right among the Zulus by now.

Setswana /ˌse'tʃwana, -'tswɑ:nə; ˌse'tswa(:)na, -'tswɑ:nə/ *n.* Forms: α. **se-Chuana, Sechuana, Sec(h)wana, Si(t)chuana**; β. **Setsoana, Setswana.** [SeTswana *seTswana*, n. prefix *se-* + *tswana* see MOTSWANA; the α forms perh. represent an obs. seTswana pronunciation of the word.] The language of the Tswana people, spoken mainly in the North West Province and in Botswana; BECHUANA sense 2; CHUANA sense 2; TSWANA sense 1. Also *attrib.*

Also occas. called *Western Sotho*. With North(ern) Sotho (or sePedi) and South(ern) Sotho (or seSotho), seTswana is one of the three main Sotho-Tswana languages. See also SOTHO sense 2.

α. **1824** W.J. BURCHELL *Trav.* II. 295 The Bachapins call this language the Sichuána. **1829** W. SHAW Diary. 16 May, His name .. in the Sichuan Language signifies a Battle Axe. **1835** A. SMITH *Diary* (1940) II. 39 Mr Moffat had a Dutch service in the morning, in the middle of the day an English service, and in the evening one in Sitchuana. **1835** D. LINDLEY in D.J. Kotze *Lett. of American Missionaries* (1950) 86 The Sitebeli is much the same with the Sichuana in its structure, many words are the same in both languages. **1841** W. SHAW in B. Shaw *Memorials* 263 The language spoken by the Baraputsi is not Sechuana but Kaffir, with a dialect like that of the Zuloos. **1857** D. LIVINGSTONE *Missionary Trav.* 201 The language of the Bechuanas is termed Sichuana. **1860** W. SHAW *Story of my Mission* 574 The Gospel is regularly preached within these Districts by the Wesleyan Missionaries in four different languages; vis., the English, Dutch, Kaffir, and Sechuana. **1871** J. MACKENZIE *Ten Yrs* (1971) 40 Most of the young missionaries had preached short sermons in Sechuana ... At that time there was no printed vocabulary, and practically no grammar on the language. **1896** H.A. BRYDEN *Tales of S. Afr.* 164 Much of their speech resembled the Sechuana and Basuto tongues. **1905** *Native Tribes of Tvl* 137 Sechuana is so closely allied to Sesuto, that it is sometimes difficult to discern to which of these languages certain dialects spoken in the Transvaal belong. **1909** [see SESOTHO]. **1918** H. MOORE *Land of Good Hope* 192 He became one of the chief authorities upon the Sechuana language, and mastered Baralong as well. **1928** E.H.L. SCHWARZ *Kalahari & its Native Races* 106 The Bakalahadi speak a debased Sechuana, so from that standpoint they have been regarded as the precursors of the whole Bechuana nation. **1930** S.T. PLAATJE *Mhudi* (1975) 63 Two of the Qoranna men could speak a few Sechuana words. **1951** H. DAVIES *Great S. Afr. Christians* 19 The man who first reduced Sechuana (the language of the Bechuana) to writing and then translated the whole of the Bible into this tongue. **1964** D. Varaday *Gara-Yaka* 108 When at a loss for a word he helped himself in Afrikaans, Chivenda, Sechwana, Zulu and Shangaan. **1965** J.D. Jones in *Setswana Dict.* (1982) p.vi, The Secwana language has several dialects.

β. **1941** E.H.S. Motlemekoane in *Bantu World* 25 Jan. (Suppl.) 1, I cannot see why Southern Suto, Setsoana and Sepedi should be considered unifiable, whereas Xhosa and Zulu aren't. **1953** A. Sandilands *Intro. to Tswana* p.x, When referring to the language by name, I have used, as of equal validity, both its forms – the long-established prefixal form 'Setswana', and the modern 'dehydrated' form 'Tswana', which has gained currency of recent years. **1965** J.D. Jones in *Setswana Dict.* (1982) p.iii, The preceding generation .. pioneered the study of the language, .. systematising their studies into the first Setswana grammars ... Setswana, in its beauty and subtlety, has exercised a great fascination on these men. **1979** [see Motswana]. **1990** *Weekly Mail* 11 May 6 Her many years of exile in Europe did not prevent her from addressing the people in impeccable Setswana.

settlaar var. setlaar.

settler *n.* [Special senses of general Eng.]

1. *obs.* Boer sense 2.

1731 G. Medley tr. *P. Kolb's Present State of Cape of G.H.* II. 76 There are but very few Settlers who have not, from their own Vineyards, a plentiful Provision of Wines for themselves. **1731** *Ibid.* [see Jacob Evertson sense 1]. **1799** W. Somerville *Narr. of E. Cape Frontier* (1979) 23 The present supplies of Bullocks and Sheep for the consumption of the Navy, Army, and the Settlers in the lower and western parts of the Colony. **1809** R. Collins in G.M. Theal *Rec. of Cape Col.* (1900) VII. 99 The wars that were at first waged against the kaffres were carried on exclusively by the settlers, who seem, whenever they have been unsuccesful, to have failed in a great degree from their having considered the recovery of stolen cattle as the principal object of hostility.

2. Often with initial capital.

a. A British settler, esp. one of a group of about 4 000 people located on the eastern frontier of the Cape of Good Hope in 1820; setlaar. Also *attrib.*

1821 G. Barker Journal. 2 Dec., Two settlers at morning worship & a Boer at the afternoon. **1823** [see heemraad sense 1]. **1833** *Graham's Town Jrnl* 11 Apr. 2 Peace was concluded with the Caffers in 1819; early next year the Settlers arrived. **1837** 'N. Polson' *Subaltern's Sick Leave* 111 The settlers, as the British immigrants are styled, .. have engrafted on the European stock several Afrikaander habits indigenous to the climate. **1851** Godlonton & Irving *Narr. of Kaffir War 1850–1* 5 The same year [*sc.* 1819] the British Parliament .. sent out 4,000 Emigrants of all classes ... Those Emigrants formed the Albany and Uitenhage original Settlers. **1863** E.L. Price *Jrnls* (1956) 134 The Mission work we do is but a wee bit when compared to all the drudgery, the toiling after the things wh. the Gentile's seek. We resemble the traders or *settlers* to a melancholy degree – and the holiest, purest, most devoted among us cannot help it. **1894** R.W. Murray *S. Afr. Reminisc.* 93 *The Zuid Afrikaan* was to the Dutch of the West precisely what *The Graham's Town Journal* was in Mr. Godlonton's time to the Settlers of the East. **1904** *Argus Christmas Annual* (Cape Colony Sect.) 25 Grahamstown, the beautiful old city of the settlers. **1913** C. Pettman *Africanderisms* 437 In 1820 a number of emigrants were brought out to South Africa under a scheme of State Aided Emigration, and were located principally in the district of Albany; these emigrants are spoken of throughout South Africa as *the* Settlers. **1947** F.C. Slater *Sel. Poems* 102 Yes, you are lauded in song, in legend, picture and story, Trekkers ... but what of the sturdy Settlers, Souls forgotten and lonely toilers who tarried behind. **1955** A. Delius *Young Trav.* 121 After the arrival of the settlers, English ideas of freedom began to work .. more actively. The original settlers were set down mostly around Grahamstown and between there and the sea. **1969** M. Benson *At Still Point* (1988) 92 Port Elizabeth on the Indian Ocean: I drove through the dock area, past the clock tower which commemorated the settlers .. past Queen Victoria, whites only on the benches around her plinth. **1976** A.R. Wilcox *Sn Land* 180 The Settlers came from all parts of the British Isles, 4000 in 1820 in organised parties and many more to follow in private parties or independent families or groups. **1983** *Grocott's Mail* 19 Apr. 1 Prices of Settler Cottages are soaring as they are becoming popular with young married couples. **1986** *Ibid.* 21 Oct. 7 Unique settler double storey home restored to perfection with beautiful yellowwood floors. **1989** *Style* Feb. 36 Right now we could do with a whole bag of Settler mythology to bolster up our national consciousness. It would sort out our identity problems. **1990** H. Allison in *Weekend Post* 22 Dec. 8 We are planning the official opening of our new premises and would like to invite a Settler grandchild as a guest of honour. **1990** *Style* June 127 A Disneyland of lovingly restored settler cottages, oodles of culture, temples of learning, more than one church for every week of the year, no industry and an overdose of Third-World poverty, Grahamstown is an anomaly in a country which specialises in anomalies. **1991** F.G. Butler *Local Habitation* 256 The epithet 'old' was the worst thing that could be said about a house in Grahamstown ... The time when early small buildings would be advertised by estate agents as 'charming Settler Cottages' was still some years ahead.

b. *comb.* **Settlers' Bible**, a nickname given to the *Graham's Town Journal*, a pro-Settler newspaper published from 1831 to 1919 (now incorporated in *Grocott's Mail*); **Settler's bread**, see quot.; **Settlers' City**, a nickname given to Grahamstown; **Settler country**, the district of Albany, Eastern Cape, between Grahamstown and the sea (but see also quot. 1982); **Settlers' Day** *hist.*, the first Monday in September, until 1980 observed as a public holiday commemorating the arrival of the British settlers of 1820.

1861 *Queenstown Free Press* 23 Oct. (Pettman), Time was when the **Settlers' Bible**, the 'Graham's Town Journal,' was *the* newspaper of the Colony. **1904** *Argus Christmas Annual* (Cape Colony Sect.) 5 The 'Grahamstown Journal' was known as the Settler's Bible, and it earned its title. It was the settler's literature .. , and it fought against the harsh decrees of autocratic governors. *a***1868** T. Stubbs Reminiscences. (1876) I. 24 We gave them a lot of **Settler's bread**, i.e. hard biscuit. **1947** F.C. Slater *Sel. Poems* 182 Grahamstown .. is generally spoken of as the 'City of Saints' because of its numerous churches, or as the **'Settlers' City'** owing to its connexion with the British settlers of 1820. *c***1960** J.B. Bullock *Peddie* Foreword, Each Settlers' Day is celebrated by an assembly of 1820 Settler descendants and friends to commemorate and mark some spot, in **Settler Country**, by erecting a natural stone pillar to which a bronze plaque is attached. **1982** F.G. Butler in *Grocott's Mail* 24 Aug. 3 Outside the town [*sc.* Grahamstown] lies the Settler Country: a number of smaller towns and villages, coastal resorts, a landscape rich in history, and two big city centres, Port Elizabeth and East London. **1988** S. Krige in *E. Prov. Herald* 6 Feb. 5 Built in the mid-19th century in the heart of Settler country, this complex of military and farm buildings serves as a reminder of the turbulent past on the Eastern Cape frontier. **1991** *Bulletin* (Centre for Science Dev.) Mar. 12 This eastern Cape university, at the heart of Settler country, has its main campus in Grahamstown and a division in East London. *c***1960** [**Settlers' Day**: see quot. at *Settler country* above.] **1970** *Daily News* 20 July, Visitors from all over South Africa, including many settler descendants, are expected to gather in Grahamstown on Settlers Day, September 7. **1980** *Govt Gaz.* Vol.180 No.7060, 3 The First Schedule to the principal Act is hereby amended .. by the deletion of the words 'Settlers' Day (first Monday in September)'.

3. *derog.* Esp. among members of the Pan Africanist Congress (see PAC):

a. Any white inhabitant of South Africa. Also *attrib.*

1970 D.M. Sibeko in *10th Anniversary of Sharpeville* (P.A.C.) 4 From its inception PAC followed the directive of President Sobukwe, to mobilise the African people for a showdown with the settler oppressors. **1991** *Rhodeo* (Rhodes Univ.) Apr. 5 Shoba pointed out that white people in South Africa were allowed to own twenty-seven separate firearms ... Shoba said so-called 'settlers' controlled 85 percent of the country's economically productive assets, and 95 percent of its personal wealth. **1991** A. Van Wyk *Birth of New Afrikaner* 115 Others .. say they would rather fight to the finish than accept majority rule. I am as strongly against them as against those who call me a 'settler' ('One settler, one bullet!') for the colour of my skin. **1993** S. Phama in *Daily News* 12 Jan. 15 The strategic objectives of national liberation have not been realised and so Apla still has a mission to liberate Azania. We say the situation there is settler colonialism.

b. In the slogan ***one settler, one bullet***: a parody of 'one man, one vote', used as a political rallying-cry.

1988 P. Lawrence in *Saturday Star* 9 July 11 Similar uncompromising attitudes may be maturing in the camps of the PAC army, the Azanian People's Liberation Army (Apla). Its recruits are reported to chant a chilling slogan: 'One settler, one bullet.' **1990** [see Azasm]. **1990** *Weekly Mail* 11 May 13 A familiar PAC slogan was 'One Settler, One Bullet'. But, says Desai: 'This slogan has no place in our organisation. It is not a serious proposition and is certainly not our policy'. **1991** B. Breytenbach in *Democracy in Action* Apr.-May 7 A spokeslady for the PAC explains their slogan of 'one settler, one bullet' thus: the PAC is a poor organisation and cannot afford more than one bullet per settler. But not all settlers are white, she also adds. **1991** [see sense a]. **1992** N. Mbatha in *Pace* Aug. 51 Johnson Phillip Mlambo cannot understand what all the fuss, surrounding the slogan 'One Settler, One Bullet', favoured by the PAC diehards, is all about. **1993** [see *toyi-toying* (toyi-toyi *v.*)].

c. See quot.

1991 L. Kaunda in *Natal Witness* 28 Mar. (Echo) 5 Asked to define a settler, PAC health secretary Dr Selva Saman said people of Western origin came to Africa and imposed a government on Africans. Anyone who sees himself or herself as part of that establishment, and does not see himself/herself as an African and part of the African constituency, is a settler.

‖**seun** /siœn/ *n.* [Afk., ad. Du. *zoon* son, boy.] A boy; a son; also used as a term of address. Cf. boereseun.

1913 A.B. Marchand *Dirk, S. African* (Swart), 4 'Well, you leave me to shut the gate, seun,' said the stranger. **1968** G. Croudace *Silver Grass* 28 The old man looked at him approvingly .. 'That's what I like to hear, my *seun*.' **1980** A. Paton *Towards Mountain* 154 The colour-bar has strongly influenced the Afrikaans language, and to some extent South African English also. A white girl is a *meisie*, a black girl is a *meid*. A white boy is a *seun*, a black boy is a *jong*. **1986** *Drum* Oct. 59 The fact that he is a true-blue Afrikaner 'seun' makes it even more interesting.

seur var. sieur.

Seventeen *n. hist.* Also **17**, **XVII**. Usu. in the n. phrr. ***Chamber of Seventeen***, ***Council of Seventeen***, and (occas.) ***Assembly of Seventeen*** [fr. Du. *Here Seventien* 'the Seventeen Lords' (see Here Seventien)]: the committee of seventeen directors of the Dutch East India Company, representing every state and almost every town in Holland; Here Seventien; Lords Seventeen. See also Company.

1858 W.S. Van Ryneveld in *Cape Monthly Mag.* III., There was .. a letter from the Chamber of XVII .. in which they .. command us to encourage the Colonists in .. the exports of grain to the mother country. **1877** J. Noble *S. Afr.* 8 The Assembly of Seventeen, who represented the East India Company. *Ibid.* 12 A despatch dated September 1701, from the Chamber of Seventeen, to the Cape Commander. **1893** H.B. SIDWELL *Story of S. Afr.* 9 The supreme governing power of the Company was exercised by a council of Directors, called, from the number of its members, the *Chamber of Seventeen.* **1909** C.D. HOPE *Our Place in Hist.* 24 The Chamber of Seventeen which ruled the Company was almost as national a body as the States-General of the Netherlands. **1913** D. FAIRBRIDGE *Piet of Italy* Glossary, *Seventeen*, The directors of the Dutch East India Company. **1920** K.M. JEFFREYS tr. *Memorandum of Commissary J.A. de Mist* 235 A petition sent to the Seventeen in Holland by the Cape Burghers in the year 1779. **1926** P.W. LAIDLER *Tavern of Ocean* 11 The instructions given to the Commander by the 'Seventeen' Directors of the Company were .. that a fort be built .. and named 'Good Hope.' *Ibid.* 33 Van Riebeeck received a letter from the Seventeen. **1952** G.M. MILLS *First Ladies of Cape* 34 What South Africa was to become was no longer entirely in the hands of the Council of Seventeen. **1976** W. HÉFER in *Optima* Vol.26 No.2, 46 The Chamber of Seventeen, which directed the affairs of the far-flung Dutch East India Company from Holland. **1982** [see HERE SEVENTIEN]. *c*1988 *S. Afr. 1987–8: Off. Yrbk* (Bureau for Info.) I. 23 Jan van Riebeeck .. was not sent by his powerful directors, the Council of Seventeen, to colonise or exploit.

seventy-four *n.* Also **74**. [See quot. 1902.] Either of two species of seabream of the Sparidae: **a.** *Polysteganus undulosus*, a large, colourful fish with blue, red, and golden-yellow stripes along its body; ROMAN sense 1 c. **b.** The *red steenbras* (see STEENBRAS sense b), *Petrus rupestris*. Also *attrib.*

In Smith and Heemstra's *Smiths' Sea Fishes* (1986), the name 'seventy-four' is used for *Polysteganus undulosus*.

1861 'A LADY' *Life at Cape* (1963) 45 A most delicate fish, called the 'seventy four' by some, and the 'Roman' by others, .. which undoubtedly was as good as the best cod or turbot out of England. **1875** 'J.P.C.' in *Cape Monthly Mag.* XI. July 25 Day by day I .. tasted all the edible treasures extracted from the depths of the seas, such as 'seventy-fours.' **1890** [see GALJOEN sense 1]. **1902** J.D.F. GILCHRIST in *Trans. of S. Afr. Philological Soc.* XI. iv. 221 (Pettman), The Seventy-four is charactised [*sic*] by several very distinct bright blue bands running along the body, not unlike the rows of guns of an ancient man-of-war, one carrying seventy-four guns being considered a well-equipped vessel in those days. **1913** C. PETTMAN *Africanderisms* 438 *Seventy-four, Dentex rupestris* ... A delicious table-fish; it has received its name, so tradition says, 'from its having been caught from a ship of the line of that number of guns, on dropping anchor in Simon's Bay'. **1923** *S. Afr.: Land of Outdoor Life* (S.A.R. & H.) 249 The tugs go further afield to the 'seventy-four' grounds ... The seventy four averages about 9 lbs, and is a strong fighter. **1949** J.L.B. SMITH *Sea Fishes* 278 *Polysteganus undulosus* (Regan) (*Dentex undulosus.*) *Seventy Four* ... Attains at least 40 ins. Found only in South Africa, from the Cape to Delagoa Bay, in deep water. At one time abundant .. this elegant fish has become scarce in recent years. The flesh is esteemed. **1955** C. HORNE *Fisherman's Eldorado* 89 The seventy-four, one of the very few South African fish with only one common name, is reputed by some to derive its name from the lines on its body, which are said to resemble rows of gun ports; by others to be named because the fish was first caught from a seventy-four gun warship. **1970** *Daily News* 12 July, Winter shoals of 'seventy-four' have now moved into Natal waters, commercial skippers making good hauls of these much prized table fish. **1980** *Daily Dispatch* 20 Aug. 8 Local ski-boats have had a rather lean time this past week ... One of the better catches made at the weekend was 100 kg of 74. **1988** A. BOWMAKER in *Stanger Mail* 9 Dec. 8 The delicious 74, once the staple fish of the South African hotel trade, has to all intents and purposes disappeared. **1990** D. JONES in *Sunday Times* 18 Nov. 7 Another endangered species, called seventy-four, is also being fished in vast quantities by his company.

seven year *n. phr.* [tr. Du. *zevenjaart(je)*, later Afk. *sewejaartjie*, see SEWEJAARTJIE.] Used *attrib.* in the phr. ***seven year(s') bloem*** /-blʊm/ [S. Afr. Du. *bloem* flower (pl. *-en*)], also ***seven year bloom, -flower***: EVERLASTING.

1847 [see EVERLASTING]. **1857** 'HORTULANUS' in *Cape Monthly Mag.* I. June 350 Of the order *Compositeæ Helichrysum* .. the well-known 'seven years' bloem,' or 'everlasting flowers,' are rarely seen in the Cape gardens, although so showy in appearance, and so often seen, in the dried state, in the parlours of the curious. **1883** M.A. CAREY-HOBSON *Farm in Karoo* 51 They found on the mountain a great variety of everlasting flowers; or, as Dollie called them, 'seven years' bloemen'. **1970** L. CROUDACE in J.W. Loubser *Africana Short Stories* 156 The wax-flowered sewe-jaartjies – the little seven year flowers as they call them in the ever-practical Afrikaans – .. spangled the mountains.

se voet /sə 'fʊt/ *int. colloq.* [Afk., possessive pronoun *se* his, her, their + *voet* foot; perh. fr. Eng. *my foot.*] 'My foot', an expression of derision or disbelief, challenging a statement or suggestion made by another.

1971 BEETON & DORNER in *Eng. Usage in Sn Afr.* Vol.2 No.1, 49 Good rugby player *se voet!* he didn't score a single goal. **1977** 'BLOSSOM' in *Darling* 18 July 123 Of course the ole man overhears ... 'Guilty conshence se voet' .. he says at the top of he's voice. **1980** A. DANGOR in M. Mutloatse *Forced Landing* 165 'Oh shut up. I told you I'm not moving, this is my home!' 'Home *se voet*! Look at it.' **1989** H. PRENDINI in *Style* Feb. 36 So we talk roots. The Afrikaner identity and the English lack of one. 'Identity se voet' turns out to be a common reaction. **1991** T. BARON in *Sunday Times* 5 May 27 'Oh my aching feet!' 'Aching feet, *se voet*' I was still being polite, you understand. **1992** A. HARBER in *Weekly Mail* 15 May 25 The authorities argue that the secret police network which we have shown to be connected to violence was a legitimate under-cover operation directed at arms smuggling. *Se voet*, we say.

sewejaartjie /ˌsɪəvə'jɑːrki/ *n.* Formerly also **zevenjaartje**. [Afk. (earlier Du. *zevenjaartje*), *sewe* seven + *jaar* year + dim. suffix -IE.] EVERLASTING.

[**1847** see EVERLASTING.] **1910** J. RUNCIE *Idylls by Two Oceans* 8 The eyes of the Zevenjaartjes Were full of the sun's white glare. **1945** F.C. SLATER *New Centenary Bk of S. Afr. Verse* 230 *Zevenzjaartjes*, Plants known as 'Everlastings'; species of *Helichrysum* and *Helipterum* (*Compositae*). **1949** L.G. GREEN *In Land of Afternoon* 72 An overwhelming majority favoured the sewejaartjie, the white everlasting that grows most abundantly on the mountain slopes round Elim. **1966** C.A. SMITH *Common Names* 415 *Sewejaartjie*, A general name for almost all species of *Helichrysum* and *Helipterum*, especially the more showy and larger-headed species. **1983** M. DU PLESSIS *State of Fear* 110 On the ride home through the reserve we saw sewejaartjies, the sheen on their papery flowers. **1986** *Motorist* 3rd Quarter 29 The everlasting flowers – called 'sewejaartjies' – have a shorter life in the unhospitable poort.

sgodongo var. SKEDONK.

sgomfaan var. SKOMFAAN.

shackland *n.* Chiefly in KwaZulu-Natal: an urban shack settlement, usu. erected very rapidly, and not officially proclaimed as a residential area; cf. *squatter camp* (see SQUATTER sense 3). Also *attrib.* See also INFORMAL sense 2 a.

1986 *Cape Times* 25 Jan. 1 Two days of bitter clashes between Zulus and Pondos has wiped out the sprawling shackland .. in the Umbogintwini area near Malakazi, south of Durban. **1986** PILLAY & HARRIS in *Sunday Times* 26 Jan. 2 A once-bustling shackland has disappeared, the houses burned to the ground and survivors fleeing ... The antagonism between the Zulu and Pondo tribes in these shackland settlements came to a head on Wednesday. **1986** C. MANN in *Frontline* June 17 Sunday's not the best of nights, the mist billowing down the shackland streets, in a country gone to the dogs. **1987** *E. Prov. Herald* 3 Oct. 1 Durban has 590 000 shackland homeless. **1990** W. BOTHA in *Frontline* Sept. 21, I hoped it would help me to know what is happening in Natal. But as I delved into shackland life and the power struggle, truth became elusive, and values entangled. **1994** R. MALAN in *Style* May 44 There are heavily armed soldiers on the bridges, and sentinels in towers on the freeway verge. They are there to protect people like me from those in the shacklands, and .. I am grateful. I would never dream of entering the squatter camps on a Saturday.

shad *n.* [Transf. uses of general Eng. *shad* a name used of any of several fish of the herring family.] In KwaZulu-Natal, either of two marine fishes: **1.** The ELF (sense a), *Pomatomus saltatrix*. **2.** The SARDINE (sense 1), *Sardinops ocellatus*.

1887 *S.W. Silver & Co.'s Handbk to S. Afr.* 185 *Clupea ocellata*. Shad, Sardyn. Used occasionally as pickled fish. **1905** *Natal Mercury Pictorial* 251 (Pettman), The photo this week is that of the fish known locally as the Shad. It arrived here in large shoals in August. **1913** C. PETTMAN *Africanderisms* 438 *Shad*, So called in Natal, this fish is known in the Cape Colony as the Elft. **1930** C.L. BIDEN *Sea-Angling Fishes* 34 At Natal the local name for the elf is 'shad'. **1947** K.H. BARNARD *Pict. Guide to S. Afr. Fishes* 108 The Elf (*Pomatomus saltatrix*) known in Natal as the shad (quite different of course from the true shad of the Herring family). **1970** *Daily News* 18 May, Weekend fishing along the Natal coast was patchy. Angling conditions were good .. but, except for a small shad south of Durban, few fish were caught. **1970** *Ibid.* 30 Oct., Shad should be biting at all the usual places north and south of Durban. **1972** [see STREPIE]. **1982** *E. Prov. Herald* 10 June 8 Natal anglers are incensed that the catching of elf (known as shad up there) is strictly controlled and yet no controls exist outside that province. **1987** R. NAYSMITH in *Ski Scene* Mar.-Apr. 13 Numerous shoals of bait fish have started returning to False Bay. These shoals .. have attracted many shad (elf). **1988** D.E. POLLOCK in *Conserva* Oct. 10 Several well-known angling-fish species such as *geelbek*, *shad* (elf) and *red steenbras* undertake eastward spawning migrations. **1992** *Natal Mercury* 3 Nov. 3 Commercial fishermen in Natal will be restricted to catching five shad, per person per day, once the open season starts on December 1, the Natal Parks Board announced yesterday.

Shaka Day /'ʃɑːkə 'deɪ/ *n. phr.* Also **Shaka's Day**. [After *uShaka* (*c*1778–1828), considered the founder of the Zulu nation.] The 24th of September, the anniversary of the death of Shaka, formerly kept as a public holiday in KwaZulu. Also *attrib.* See also HERITAGE DAY.

1987 L. DELLATOLA in *S. Afr. Panorama* May 27 On the 24th September every year, Shaka's Day celebrations are held at King Shaka's grave at Stanger. **1987** *New Nation* 23 July 9 Since 1970, Shaka Day has been a public holiday in kwaZulu. **1992** *Weekend Post* 26 Sept. 16 'Strenuous efforts have been made .. to prevent violence during the Shaka Day celebrations in KwaMashu,' the ANC said. **1993** *Africa S. & E.* May 15 Shaka fought against the occupation of our land by the whites. When we attend Shaka Day celebrations, we go as ANC members. **1994** [see HERITAGE DAY].

Shaka's Spear *n. phr. Hist.* [Loose tr. of Zulu *umkhonto* spear + *ka* of + *Shaka* (see prec.).] A short-lived Zulu political party, formed in June 1973.

1974 *E. Prov. Herald* 15 May 2 The Prime Minister is to be asked in Parliament to clear up allegations that Boss has been secretly funding Shaka's Spear, the Zulu opposition party. **1974** *Drum* 8 July 4 Shaka's Spear, a party which wants KwaZulu to be divided into a north and south zone, each with its own legislative assembly and chief minister. **1974** *Ibid.* 8 Aug. 24 Chief Gatsha Buthelezi and his five-member cabinet were all there at this meeting at Durban's Umlazi Stadium which had been called to 'finally expose' the activities of the opposition Shaka's Spear party and its alleged involvement with the Bureau of State Security (BOSS).

Shalambombo /ˌʃalamˈbɔːmbɔ/ *n. Obs.* exc. *hist.* [See quot.] An early form of FLAAITAAL.

1987 C.T. MSIMANG in *S. Afr. Jrnl of Afr. Langs* Vol.7 No.3, 82 The earliest form of Tsotsitaal, namely Shalambombo, was .. strictly a secret language. Unlike Tsotsitaal, the term Shalambombo is easy to explain. This is a compound word formed from two Zulu ideophones, *shala* (i.e. of shunning) and *mbo-mbo* (i.e. of covering over or turning upside-down).

shambo(c)k var. SJAMBOK *n.*

shame *int.* [Special sense of general Eng. *shame* an expression of disapproval; perh. influenced by Afk. expressions of sympathy or pity, see FOEITOG, SIESTOG.] An expression of sympathy or pity; an expression of pleasure or sentiment, esp. at something small or endearing. Freq. in the phr. ***ag shame*** [see AG], often used ironically. See also FOEITOG senses 3 and 4, SIESTOG.

1932 *Grocott's Daily Mail* 9 Jan. 3 During the address of our local dairy representatives .. I heard several murmurs of Oh! and Shame! and grant the statements were given in a manner that commanded much sympathy. **1941** M.G. GILBERT *Informant, Cape Town* 10 Nov., Shame, he seemed so touched at my having written that I'm doubly glad I sent him some food too! **1959** L. HERMAN in *Eng. Studies in Afr.* 243 Women and children on beholding something small and endearing, a kitten, a puppy, a baby, exclaim: Shame! an exclamation used in English only to express strong disapproval. **1965** K. MACKENZIE *Deserter* 29 'He is asleep,' said Sannie. 'Shame.' 'He has come a long way,' said his father. 'And he is wounded.' **1972** *Star* 15 Nov. 18 In South Africa one can actually carry on a conversation quite easily by using only four words: 'Shame,' 'Hey,' and 'Is it?' Try it sometime and see whether anybody notices. **1976** *Sunday Times* 14 Nov. 1 Oh, look, look ... those foals. Oh, shame, aren't they sweet. **1977** L. ABRAHAMS *Celibacy of Felix Greenspan* 159 She exclaimed, to herself, not to him, 'Auw, *shame*!' It was the reflex sympathy of a complete stranger. **1978** *Darling* 20 Dec. 34 We started a hundred-mile-an-hour sprint down the aisle ... And shame he cried when he gave me away and I cried also. **1978** K.C. ORAM in *Newsletter* (Grahamstown Cathedral) Nov.-Dec., You may sentimentalise Christmas, as if the sort of baby that was born would have won a baby-contest and you can say 'shame' (or 'shime') over the cradle. **1980** E.M. MACPHAIL in *Staffrider* Vol.3 No.1, Oh shame, the next one to read his poems has been told there isn't time. How disappointing for him. **1982** *Sunday Times* 31 May, *Shame*, .. to express joy, sorrow, pity, admiration etc etc: 'Shame, she looks so pretty in that frock.' **1984** *Cape Times* 16 Mar. (Funfinder), One night .. someone stabbed 'some poor guy, shame' in the parking area. **1988** H. PRENDINI in *Style* June 102 Ag, shame is the only possible reaction. **1989** [see Personality quot. at HAU]. **1989** T. BARON in *Sunday Times* 8 Oct. 22 Ag shame. The rigours of being posted to an emergent country in Darkest Africa. **1990** *Fair Lady* 6 June 160 A regular response from people who hear you are living in England is, 'Oh shame! That terrible climate.' **1990** *Weekend Mail* 14 Sept. 2 'We fed from the tables of the rich and we got all the educational facilities.' 'Ag shame ... While everybody else was having a wonderful time getting killed in Soweto.' **1991** *Personality* 6 May 24 Their idea is not novel at all. It's been done before. Ag shame. **1992** J. BOSHOFF in *Sunday Times* 6 Sept. 5 The teacher said .. he would probably die, but I looked at him and thought shame, he hasn't even had a life. **1993** A.L. HAYCOCK *Informant, Grahamstown* It's a bright sunny day here [*sc.* in London] (top temperature 20°C!!) ... The radio is now jamming 'English Country Garden' down my neck — this is what happens at the first bit of sunshine ... Shame.

Hence **shame** *n.*, an utterance of 'shame'.

1991 S. JOHNS in *Personality* 11 Mar. 98 It's 'Ag-shame' time again folks!

Shangaan /ʃaŋˈgaːn, ʃæŋˈgaːn/ *n.* Pl. usu. **-s**. Forms: *sing.* **Mshangaan, Shangaan**; *sing.* and *pl.* **Machangana, Shangana, Shangane**; *pl.* **Amachangana, amaShangaan, Amatshangane, Mashangana, MaShangane, Shangaans.** [Prob. named for the founding chief, *Soshangane*; but see also quot. 1905.]

1.a. A member of a people of Zulu and Tsonga origin, living mainly in the Northern and Eastern Transvaal, Gaza Province in southern Mozambique, and southern Zimbabwe; KNOBNEUS; KNOBNOSE; KNOPNEUS; MAGWAMBA; TONGA sense 1; TSONGA sense 1. Also *attrib.*, and *comb.* **Shangaan-Tsonga**. See also VATUA sense a.

1884 *Cape Law Jrnl* I. 223 The Amaxosa Kafirs, Fingoes, Tembus, Amampondo, .. Shangaans, Matabele, [etc.]. **1887** J.W. MATTHEWS *Incwadi Yami* 183 The native labour of the diamond fields .. includes nearly twenty different tribes such as Zulus, Swazees, Basutos, Shangaans, [etc.]. **1905** *Native Tribes of Tvl* 64 The name Shangaan is an abbreviation of Amachangana, meaning 'the destroyers' ... Ma-gwamba, a name by which they are often known, was given to the Shangaans by the Bavenda and Basuto peoples on account of their swearing by 'Gwamba,' who according to them was the first man created. They used to be called 'Knob-noses' from the custom of lacerating their faces, especially the nose. *Ibid.* 88 The Shangaans found in the eastern districts .. are mostly recent immigrants from Portuguese territory, having fled into the Transvaal after the defeat and capture of their chief Gungunyana by the Portuguese in 1896. **1910** J. BUCHAN *Prester John* (1961) 40 The countryside was crawling with natives, and great strings used to come through from Shangaan territory on the way to the Rand mines. **1937** J. STEVENSON-HAMILTON *S. Afr. Eden* 120 Among the Amatshangane the memory of the strict regimental system of the Zulus still lingered. *a***1951** H.C. BOSMAN *Willemsdorp* (1977) 55 Pieta .. was only a Bechuana, which wasn't much better than a Mshangaan. **1961** T.V. BULPIN *White Whirlwind* 140 The mountain was known to Europeans as the Mountain of Ghosts. Somewhere near its summit the Shangane tribe buried their chiefs in a secret cave. **1971** *Daily Dispatch* 4 Feb. 1 The territorial authorities of the .. Tswanas, the Venda, the North Sotho and the Machangana. **1975** H.P. JUNOD in *Std Encycl. of Sn Afr.* IX. 600 The characteristic tribal mark of the Shangana-Tsonga is the pierced ear-lobe ... The Shangana-Tsonga are a pastoral people, with a strong cattle complex ... In accordance with Government policy, the Transvaal Tsonga — called Machangana (Shangaans), their language being Tsonga — have been recognised as one of the eight Bantu peoples living in the Republic of South Africa. **1975** W.F. LYE *Andrew Smith's Jrnl 1834–6* 320 *maShangane* (also called Ngoni). Tribe composed of Tsonga and their Northern Nguni conquerors led by Soshangane when he fled from Shaka and the Zulu empire. **1976** WEST & MORRIS *Abantu* 109 A Tsonga maiden. Her people now live in Mocambique and the North-Eastern Transvaal. They derive the name 'Shangaan' from one of Shaka's lieutenants, Shoshangane, who conquered them in 1820–21 in the course of his flight from the Zulu despot. **1978** A. ELLIOTT *Sons of Zulu* 66 Soshangane .., the founder of the Shangane nation whose kingdom stretched from north of Maputo .. to the banks of the Zambezi River. **1984** D. BECKETT in *Frontline* Feb. 32 When Mashangane quit Natal, chased out by Shaka, he moved north and set up his Gaza empire. Mozambique's Gaza province is still populated largely by Shangaans. **1985** *Population census form, Rep. of S. Afr.* North Sotho .., Shangaan/Tsonga, South Ndebele .., South Sotho, [etc.]. **1988** G. SILBER in *Style* Apr. 38 The Shangaan tribal homeland of Gazankulu, on the western boundary of the Kruger National Park. **1990** *New African* 11 June 12 Black is beautiful was coined to unite Amazulu, Basotho, Mashangana, Indians, so-called 'Coloureds', etc.

b. Esp. among miners: a Mozambican member of this people.

1980 M. LIPTON in *Optima* Vol.29 No.2, 112 'Our Malawians' and 'our Shangaans' (Moçambicans), as the old-timers on the mines now nostalgically call them.

2. The language of the Shangaan people, including the South African and the Mozambican dialects. Cf. TSONGA sense 2.

1957 JUNOD & JACQUES *Wisdom of Tsonga-Shangana People* 11 The new standard Shangana-Tsonga orthography. **1959** B. BUNTING *Story Behind Non-White Press* 7 'Workers' Unity' .. reports trade union and political news in Zulu, Sesotho, Shangaan, Xosa, Afrikaans and English. **1971** *Rand Daily Mail* 28 July 7 Besides Afrikaans and English he speaks all the African languages in the Republic except Shangaan and Venda. **1971** *S. Afr. Panorama* Dec. 29 'Tzana' is the Machangana word for basket, and the name, Tzaneen, .. may have been derived from it. **1982** *Voice* 30 May 7 The album .. is in both English and Shangaan and boasts of tracks with gospel music and modernised church hymns that have been given an African cultural beat. **1985** *S. Afr. Panorama* Jan. 48 The Shangaan for *Hippotraginae* is *Mpala Mpala*.

shark net *n. phr.* A net suspended from buoys and positioned off-shore to protect bathers from shark attacks. Hence **shark netting** *n. phr.*, the material (now usu. flat braided polyethylene twine) from which the nets are made, and as *vbl n.*, the employment of shark nets.

Introduced in Australia in 1937, nets were first installed in South Africa in 1952. They do not form a continuous barrier, but reduce the shark population in the bathing area to such an extent that there is virtually no risk of attack.

1962 J. ALLEN in *Star* 16 Feb. 14 Another pointer to the massive population of the world's sharks is the evidence of the few hundred yards of shark nets erected off the South African coast at Durban for the protection of bathers. During the first year, ten years ago, 552 sharks became entangled. **1965** J. MALHERBE *Port Natal* 248 Today people bathe in safety along the whole stretch of bathing beaches .. thanks to the highly effective shark nets that have been installed along this stretch. **1970** *UCT Studies in Eng.* I. 33 The bracelets were originally made of shark netting. The surfer would dig his way out to the shark nets, cut himself a piece and tie it around his wrist. **1981** G. & M. BRANCH *Living Shores* 133 Shark nets act like giant gill nets, enmeshing the sharks ... The success of shark nets in reducing attack is proven beyond doubt. **1992** A. GIFFORD in *Afr. Wildlife* Vol.46 No.6, 252 Shark-netting, as practised off the Natal Coast .. is exacting a terrible toll on other marine animals as well. **1992** DUDLEY & CLIFF in *Afr. Wildlife* Vol.46 No.6, 255 There is .. no conclusive evidence that the shark-nets are fishing any species at a non-sustainable rate, although there is cause for concern about two species of dolphin. *Ibid.* 257 One of the most emotive issues related to shark-netting is the annual mortality of some 80 dolphins. **1994** N.B. WYNNE *Informant, Natal Sharks Board, Umhlanga Rocks* The first shark nets in South Africa were installed off Durban's South Beach in 1952.

Sharpeville *n.* [The name of a black township near Vanderbijlpark (Gauteng Province).]

1. The incident at Sharpeville police station, on the 21st of March 1960, during which 69 people were killed and 180 wounded by police at a Pan Africanist Congress gathering in protest against the pass laws; *transf.*, any similar confrontation. Also *attrib.*

1960 *News Chronicle* in J. Crwys-Williams *S. Afr. Despatches* (1989) 336 The coloured people's hospital at Barangwanath, Johannesburg, already filled with 140 victims of Sharpeville, is standing by for the arrival of a fully equipped 100-bed military field hospital. **1961** P. GINIEWSKI *Bantustans: Trek towards Future* 8 Sharpeville .. has become a symbol, and people think of it with sympathy, pity and hope, as well as resentment. And so we wait, expecting news of some new Sharpeville. **1970** D.M. SIBEKO in *10th Anniversary of Sharpeville* (P.A.C.), Since Sharpeville PAC has elevated the Azanian liberation struggle to greater heights. **1971** *Daily Dispatch* 26 Oct., Our Prime Minister, Mr.

B.J. Vorster, .. said there were known to be churchmen and academics who were planning 'another Sharpeville'. **1974** L.M. MANGOPE *Place for all* (*c*1979) 118 Since Sharpeville there has been a rapidly accelerating awareness in the Black ranks of this country. **1976** *Time* 28 June 19 South African black leaders had been warning the Pretoria government for months that unrest in Soweto could lead to another Sharpeville. **1985** *Drum* May 43 The loss of life was as tragic as it was avoidable. That it had to happen on March 21 made it even worse. For if anything, it scraped open old wounds of people who still remember Sharpeville. **1986** J. CONYNGHAM *Arrowing of Cane* 16 My father added shutters, ostensibly for greater coolness and privacy but .. I suspect that security was his motive. Simple calculation places them just after Sharpeville. **1986** S. SEPAMLA *Third Generation* 89 The happening came to be known as Sharpeville. It was so devastating that spectres of it remain in the country even to this day. **1986** P. MAYLAM *Hist. of Afr. People* 190 One effect of the post-Sharpeville crackdown was to break a commitment to non-violence that had been held dear by many African leaders. **1987** M. MELAMU *Children of Twilight* 26 How many more Sharpevilles and Sowetos were we going to have, before we all learned to live together in peace? **1988** A. KLAASTE in *Sunday Star* 22 May 11 Sharpeville happened on March 21. On exactly the same day 30 years later police shot people in a funeral procession in Langa, Uitenhage. **1990** P. CULLINAN in M. Leveson *Firetalk* 9 It was the time of the Republic, the post-Sharpeville recession. But somehow we did survive, and later, after a few years we came right. **1990** [see NECKLACING]. **1991** *Rhodeo* (Rhodes Univ.) Apr. 5 Sharpeville was the day the PAC freed the people from their fear of sacrifice. **1992** D. BERESFORD in *Guardian Weekly* 26 June 6 Mr Mandela announced the suspension of talks during a visit to Boipatong ... At a bigger rally later, Mr Mandela said: 'The negotiation process is completely in tatters.' The country was back in 'Sharpeville days,' he added. **1992** A. SPARKS in *Ibid.* 3 July 17, I was in the midst of the mini-Sharpeville that followed Mr de Klerk's visit to the township on June 20, when the police fired point-blank, without orders and without warning, into a crowd of about 3,000 people.

2. *comb.* **Sharpeville Day**, HEROES' DAY sense 1. Also *attrib.*

1969 M. BENSON *At Still Point* (1988) 43 Today is March 21. Sharpeville Day. **1987** G. DAVIS in *Weekly Mail* 31 July 4 It [*sc.* the University of Cape Town] wants workers to give up two public holidays in exchange for June 16 and Sharpeville Day on March 21. **1988** *New Nation* 17 Mar. 5 A major date in the anti-apartheid calendar — Sharpeville Day. **1989** *Weekly Mail* 17 Mar. 4 The 29th Anniversary of Sharpeville Day — marking the shooting by police of 69 pass protesters in March 1960 — will be commemorated by political and trade union organisations across South Africa. **1991** *E. Prov. Herald* 18 Mar. 2 The Azanian Peoples' Organisation has called for a 'stayaway' on March 21 to commemorate Sharpeville Day. **1991** L. MARTIN in *Ibid.* 2 Apr. 6, I look forward to holidays such as Sharpeville Day, Soweto Day, and Biko Day being recognised paid holidays. **1992** *Natal Witness* 30 Dec. 9 There might be objections to Youth Soweto day (June 16, named after the 1976 uprising) and Sharpeville Day (March 21) as public holidays 'because they are linked to oppression and resistance'. **1993** R. MCNEILL in *Sunday Times* 4 Apr. 19 *Ordinary People*, a documentary about last month's rival Sharpeville day rallies. **1994** *E. Prov. Herald* 8 Sept. 1 A number of public holidays, including Sharpeville Day, Kruger Day and Republic Day, will be scrapped next year.

shayile var. TJAILE *n.*

shebeen /ʃəˈbiːn/ *n.* [Transf. use of Anglo-Irish *shebeen*, modern Irish *sibín* (of obscure origin), a low public-house; see also Coplan quot. 1980.] **1.** A drinking establishment (usu. in a private home in a township) where liquor is sold or consumed; SPOT. Also *attrib.*

Formerly illegal, such establishments have, since 1980, been allowed to obtain licences and operate as 'taverns' (see TAVERN sense 2), but some are still unlicensed (see SMOKKELHUIS).

[**1873** *Cape Argus* 20 Mar. 2 The unlicensed beershops after the model of the Irish *shebeens* would thrive.] **1900** 'ONE WHO WAS IN IT' *Kruger's Secret Service* 135 In Fordsburg there was a shebeen kept by a certain Pulinski ... Pulinski took me inside, where I found the place to be full of Kaffirs. **1910** J. BUCHAN *Prester John* (1961) 93 In five minutes I had made the room stink like a shebeen. **1934** *Sunday Times* 7 Jan. (Swart), Native Shebeens in Parktown North, run by Coloured men in outbuildings of Europeans' houses, call for some explanation. **1956** A. SAMPSON *Drum* 68 Shebeens are illegal African drinking-places, where European liquor is sold at double prices. **1956** N. GORDIMER in D. Wright *S. Afr. Stories* (1960) 71 He had accompanied Jake to a shebeen in a coloured location, where it was illegal for a white man to be, as well as illegal for anyone at all to have a drink. **1966** *Post* 16 Jan. (Drum) 6 The safest way to survive the turbulent South African night was to spend it in a shebeen, where you met amiable people and where you could drink and listen to the music in peace .. until the cops came. **1968** J. LELYVELD in Cole & Flaherty *House of Bondage* 9 Most Africans prefer the illegal speakeasies known as shebeens, which operate out of parlors and backyards ... The talk at the shebeens is ironic and careful, habitually inexplicit. Politics is out. **1971** *Weekend Argus* 5 June (Mag.) 5 Urban slum-dwellers enjoying a Friday night shebeen party which suddenly erupts into a faction fight. **1977** D. MULLER *Whitey* 20 He was .. doomed .. to bum a few coins, to find a smokkelhuis and buy a bottle of cloudy shebeen wine. **1977** J. SIKAKANE *Window on Soweto* 27 Shebeens are the homes where the Sowetonians can go and buy liquor 'on tick' and drink after hours, rather than in the official municipal beerhalls. **1980** D.B. COPLAN Urbanization of African Performing Arts. 202 The institution later known as the shebeen dates back to the slaves of Dutch colonial times ... The word .. seems also to have originated in Cape Town in the early 20th century among immigrant Irish members of the city's police force ... These constables named the ubiquitous illegal non-White drinking houses *shebeens* (Gaelic: 'little shop'). Coloured and Xhosa people brought the term to the Transvaal, where female entrepreneurs had developed the shebeen into a fundamental urban African social institution in Johannesburg and other towns ... Women who made it a full-time occupation became 'shebeen queens'. **1980** *Times* (U.K.) 31 May 1 The South African Government, after years of battling to control illicit drinking dens, known as shebeens, in black townships, has conceded defeat and legalized them. **1982** *Drum* Nov. 56, I am not going to run a shebeen in my house even if its going to have a fancy name, like a Tavern. **1986** P. MAYLAM *Hist. of Afr. People* 150 Liquor formed a central part of a wider African working-class urban culture, often known as *marabi*. It was linked to prostitution .. and to the shebeen parties. **1988** *E. Prov. Herald* 31 Mar. 5 Only four shebeen owners from Port Elizabeth townships applied on Tuesday to trade legally. **1989** *Reader's Digest Illust. Hist.* 358 Police empty cars of illicit liquor after a raid on a shebeen. The drinking of illegally brewed beer and isiqataviku ('kill me quick') helped thousands of urban slum-dwellers to forget their drab existence. **1989** C. NAIDOO in *Sunday Times* 8 Oct. (Business Times) 3 Shebeens take 80% of the beer sold in SA. **1990** *New African* 4 June, The illegal pubs, popularly known today as shebeens, .. provided solace and serenity. **1991** *Best of S. Afr. Short Stories* (Reader's Digest Assoc.) 395 The shebeen has become such a feature of social life in the South African black townships that the Irish origin of the word (from Gaelic *sibín*, meaning poor-quality ale) is often forgotten. Although South African shebeens formerly sold illicit liquor (often home-brewed), these days they can be licensed.

2. Special Comb. **shebeen queen**, the female owner of a shebeen, a woman who sells illicit liquor; AUNTIE sense 2; QUEEN *n.*[2]; *skokiaan queen*, see SKOKIAAN sense 2. See also SHEBEENER. By analogy, **shebeen king**.

1941 'R. ROAMER' in *Bantu World* 29 Mar. 4 When the Police raided her mother's home and rudely called her mother 'Shebeen Queen' she thought they were honouring her [for] her great beauty. **1950** *Report of Commission to Inquire into Acts of Violence Committed by Natives at Krugersdorp* in L.F. Freed *Crime in S. Afr.* (1963) 130 Shebeens have now established themselves in strong competition with the municipal beerhalls. The shebeen queens resort to devious means to evade police detection, such as .. calling upon the tsotsi gangs for protection. **1952** 'SKAPPIE' in *Drum* Nov. 6 There is big money in illicit liquor. The shebeen queens are very wealthy. **1961** T. MATSHIKIZA *Choc. for my Wife* 93 The coloured shebeen queen at the counter is Jessica Davids, notorious for beating up cops, bail bonds and bootleggers. **1971** *Post* 4 Apr. 1 'Everything is just up man,' said one shebeen king — commenting on booze prices and not fines for a change. **1976** *E. Prov. Herald* 14 Oct. 3 The shebeen kings and queens in the Black townships .. are angry because of the raids on their shebeens. **1977** P.C. VENTER *Soweto* 120 Before the liquor laws were relaxed to allow blacks to buy alcohol, the shebeen queens brewed concoctions in their backyards; dangerous liquids like methylated spirits were mixed with the fermenting juices of dead animals and rotting plants to create potential killers. **1980** [see Coplan quot. at sense 1]. **1981** *Daily Dispatch* 15 Sept. 12 Although there are shebeen kings, they were out-numbered by shebeen queens ... Most men prefer to go and work rather than sit down and sell liquor. **1982** [see WOZA-WOZA]. **1982** *New Dawn* Aug. 16 The National Taverners Association is blazing a trail on behalf of shebeen kings and queens leading them along a route that will establish them as solid business people. **1984** *Cape Times* 6 Mar. 7 A shebeen queen was a mysterious, corrupt underworld figure who had considerable power. **1984** *Drum* July 44 While shebeen kings and queens are celebrating their licences, we regulars have retreated into quiet nooks to mourn the passing of an institution. **1990** A. MAIMANE in *Weekly Mail* 22 June (Suppl.) 2 Thousands of gallons of 'European liquor' were poured down African thoats every day to the delight of shebeen queens who charged double the legal prices they paid. **1990** R. STENGEL *January Sun* 103 Oukasie's most famous shebeen king is presently lying fast asleep across the hood of his bruised red Mercedes, which is parked in front of his house. **1994** *Weekly Mail & Guardian* 13 May 8 Even the miser of Orlando East, shebeen queen 'Ma Stompie', sold her beers at half-price.

Hence **shebeen** *v. intrans.*, to run a shebeen; to patronize a shebeen; **shebeening** *vbl n.*, the running of a shebeen; **shebeeny** *adj.*, of shebeens.

1897 *E. Prov. Herald* 17 Feb., Tom .. was brought before the magistrate on Monday morning charged with shebeening. **1900** 'ONE WHO WAS IN IT' *Kruger's Secret Service* 129 The methods employed by magistrates who wished to get off their accomplices accused of shebeening were somewhat as follows [etc.]. **1953** A. MOGALE in *Drum* Sept. 25 I'm going high-class shebeening tonight — in Doornfontein. **1955** D.C. TEMBA in J. Crwys-Williams *S. Afr. Despatches* (1989) 321 The swarming, cacophonous, strutting, brawling, vibrating life of Sophiatown that was .. was not all just shebeeny, smutty, illegal stuff. **1964** G. GORDON *Four People* 120 They're up to no good, some of those people — shebeening. **1975** *Friend* 10 May 3 He had started using his hands to repair radios and had done 'a little shebeening' as a sideline. **1989** *Weekend Argus* 11 Nov. 19 The day-to-day battles residents fight against inadequate recreational facilities, sandy pavements, shebeening, gangsterism and other problems. **1990** *Fair Lady* 28 Mar. 139 She smoked and drank into shebeeny nights, waiting.

shebeener /ʃəˈbiːnə/ *n.* [fr. SHEBEEN sense 1 + Eng. agential suffix *-er*.] The proprietor of a shebeen. See also *shebeen king* and *shebeen queen* (SHEBEEN sense 2), *taverner* (TAVERN).

Also used in *Scot.* and *Irish Eng.*

1900 'ONE WHO WAS IN IT' *Kruger's Secret Service* 137, I investigated the case of another shebeener, Zeinvitch, who had an illicit shop near the City and Suburban Mine. **1942** *Cape Times* 24 Dec. 7 The shebeeners of large townships naturally press for the abolition of municipal beer-halls. **1950** [see DOP *n.* sense 3 a]. **1952** *Drum* Dec. 20 Tsotsi stands for young ruffians .. Shebeeners for illegal liquor sellers. **1963** L.F. FREED *Crime in S. Afr.* 140 The 'skollies', the 'shebeeners', the gangsters, the thugs and the robbers. **1972** *Drum* 1 Jan. 22 Shebeeners were forced to cough up part of their profits plus whatever drinks the gang required for themselves. **1981** *Frontline* May 10 Traditionally, the shebeener has been a woman, probably because rural African custom required women to be the brewers of beer. **1982** [see SMALL TIME]. **1982** *New Dawn* Aug. 17 'Mooi Auntie' like almost every one of the shebeeners we visited, said the worst aspect of their business was the police raids and the admission of guilt fines. **1982** *Fair Lady* 1 Dec. 181 In spite of the government announcement in 1980 that shebeeners could apply for liquor licences, no licences have yet been granted, and it is still illegal to run a shebeen. **1988** VAN DER WAAL & SHARP in Boonzaier & Sharp *S. Afr. Keywords* 144 Because other drinking or health facilities are limited in the townships, shebeeners and herbalists are able to supply commodities and services which the workers need. **1991** *Natal Witness* 28 Mar. (Echo) 18 Shebeeners, buy in bulk and save. Come in and discuss our cheap rates.

sheepskin *n.* In full *sheepskin dance*: VASTRAP sense 2.

1934 C.P. SWART Supplement to Pettman. 154 *Sheepskin Dance*, .. A farm-dance is so designated in South Africa, as these functions were formerly held in sheds where sheep were shorn ... These social affairs are also known as Veldskoens, Vastraps (Tread-fasts) and Kop-en-Pootjies (Head and Trotters). **1961** D. ROOKE *Lover for Estelle* 76 It was the night of the Van Wyk's sheepskin dance. Mamma had made new dresses for all of us. **1970** L.G. GREEN *Giant in Hiding* 105 Weddings are occasions for the capers known as 'sheepskin dances' because they are held in the shearing-shed. **1970** S. MOORE *Informant, Port Elizabeth* The party on the farm was a proper old sheepskin! **1970** P.J. SILVA *Informant, Grahamstown* A sheepskin is the same thing as an 'opskud' — a boeremusiek dance.

sheep's tail fat *n. phr.* Also **sheeptail fat**. Fat rendered down from the tail of the *fat-tailed sheep* (see FAT-TAILED sense a) and used for culinary or other purposes; TAIL FAT. Also *ellipt.* **sheep's tail**, and *comb.* **sheep's tail fat honey**, see quot. 1912.

1785 G. FORSTER tr. *A. Sparrman's Voy. to Cape of G.H.* I. 298 He shewed himself a perfect master in the art, stewing it [*sc.* the bird] in a *quantum sufficit* of water, and a little *sheep's tail* fat. **1806** *Gleanings in Afr.* (anon.) 59 When they leave their master's house in the morning, they are provided with some bread, and *sheep's tail* to supply the place of butter. **1827** T. PHILIPPS *Scenes & Occurrences* 100 All the game of this country is so dry that it requires plenty of sheeps' tail fat ... Sheep's tail fat is useful for many purposes — lamp oil, frying fish; and salted and dried it eats like the best bacon ... The tail weighs in general from four to six pounds. **1829** C. ROSE *Four Yrs in Sn Afr.* 257 There was one dish that haunted me during the journey — an abominable mixture of Sheep's Tail-fat and sheep's head. **1838** J.E. ALEXANDER *Exped. into Int.* I. 16, I forced myself to eat of their dishes, swimming as they were in sheep's tail fat. *Ibid.* 28 The people are perhaps like African oaks — they soon come to maturity and soon decay ... That horrid sheep's tail fat clogs the wheels of the machine. **1849** E.D.H.E. NAPIER *Excursions in Sn Afr.* II. 14 A grand and substantial supper .. seasoned with sheep's-tail fat, and washed down with a 'soupje' (dram). **1859** 'AN OLD CAMPAIGNER' in *Cape Monthly Mag.* V. June 342 An old cracked pot held a vile greasy mixture, called sheep's tail fat, with which Tim imbued sundry thick slices of toasted bread. **1887** A.B. ELLIS *S. Afr. Sketches* 6 The usual way-side meal of greasy mutton-chops floating about in a liquid sea of sheep-tail fat. **1888** D.C.F. MOODIE *Hist. of Battles & Adventures* I. 215 They did not take kindly to mealie bread and pumpkin fritters, even when fried in sheepstail. **1891** H.J. DUCKITT *Hilda's 'Where Is It?'* 170 Rub the piggie all over with butter (or sheep-tail fat), and set it in a hot oven. **1899** G.H. RUSSELL *Under Sjambok* 188 The illuminations consisted of some half-a-dozen candles made from sheep-tail fat, and stuck at intervals round the wall. **1912** *S. Afr. Agric. Jrnl* June 790 (Pettman), An absolutely white honey .. it almost immediately solidifies to the consistency of vaseline. In this state no one would imagine it to be anything but pure lard. It is known amongst the Boers as Sheep tail fat honey. **1927** C.G. BOTHA *Social Life in Cape Col.* 57 In 1799 a gentleman recorded that the 'English cookery has in a great measure banished the delicious ragouts sent up in a sea of sheep's tail fat which usually was the sauce for every dish'. **1949** L.G. GREEN *In Land of Afternoon* 15 The people who were not Boers were Hottentots, and this servile race spoke kitchen Dutch, wore nothing but a skin kaross and rubbed themselves all over with sheep-tail fat and buchu. **1979** HEARD & FAULL *Our Best Trad. Recipes* 94 One of the chief cooking joys of our great-grandmothers and their great-grandmothers before them, was sheeptail fat. *Ibid.* 95 Sheeptail fat came in abundance from fat-tailed sheep. **1988** F. WILLIAMS *Cape Malay Cookbk* 83 Rille gebak: These rich sweetmeats, like heavy dough-nuts, are distinctively diamond shaped ... In the past, sheeptail fat would have been used instead of oil. **1989** J. CRWYS-WILLIAMS *S. Afr. Despatches* 20 *De Zuid-Afrikaan* .. (kindly referred to in *The African Journal* as 'the "Dutch drop" in the Literary Ocean — that chronicler of small beer and sheep's tail fat').

sheep-sticker *n.* [Calque formed on S. Afr. Du. *schaapsteker*, see SKAAPSTEKER.] SKAAPSTEKER. Also *attrib.*

[**1849** A. SMITH *Illust. of Zoo. of S. Afr.: Reptilia* Pl.56, The *Schaap Sticker* varies considerably in colour, and the markings differ in different individuals.] **1881** P. GILLMORE *Land of Boer* 147 Another species well known in the colony as the sheep-sticker, and pronounced to be very poisonous, .. I am inclined to believe innocuous. [**1910** see SKAAPSTEKER.] **1936** L.G. GREEN *Secret Afr.* 233 My movement disturbed a poisonous snake known as the skaapsteker (sheep-sticker). **1987** D. MATTHEE *Mulberry Forest* (1989) 314 If it was a sheep-sticker snake, I would be able to save him myself.

sheep-stinger *n. obs.* [tr. S. Afr. Du. *schaapsteker*, see SKAAPSTEKER.] SKAAPSTEKER.

1818, 1834, 1856 [see SKAAPSTEKER]. **1887** *Encycl. Brit.* XXII. 197 The second African snake of this family is the 'schapsticker' (Sheep Stinger), *Causus rhombeatus*. **1905** [see SKAAPSTEKER].

sheep-striker *n. rare.* [Calqued on Afk. *skaapsteker.*] SKAAPSTEKER.

*c*1936 *S. & E. Afr. Yr Bk & Guide* 1106 The principle representatives of this group [*sc.* back-fanged snakes] are the *boom-slang* or *tree snake*, .. and the *schaapsteker* (sheep-striker), .. to which the farmers erroneously attribute the death of many sheep.

sheila *n.* [Prob. transf. uses of Austral. and N.Z. Eng. *sheila* girl, woman.]

1. *obs. slang.* The girlfriend of a DUCKTAIL or TSOTSI.

1963 L.F. FREED *Crime in S. Afr.* 81 The ducktail girls are also known as 'quacktails', 'sheilahs', and 'pony-tails'. **1977** P.C. VENTER *Soweto* 40 A sheila is a tsotsi's girlfriend in more ways than one ... In the Chicago of the speak-easy days they would have called her a gangster's moll. She is the equivalent of a groupie, one of those bright-eyed and slack-mouthed girls who slavishly follow pop-singers.

2. *colloq.* With initial capital(s). [See quot. 1974.] In the phr. ***Sheila's day***, also ***Sheila-day***, esp. among domestic workers, Thursday, the day on which many women in domestic service are off duty, or have an afternoon off. Also *attrib.*

1974 in *Eng. Usage in Sn Afr.* Vol.5 No.1, 8 A woman is a *goose* .. or *sheila* (cf. in Soweto, Thursday is Sheila-day, day off for the nannies). **1980** M. MELAMU in M. Mutloatse *Forced Landing* 51 It's 'Sheila's Day' and Babsy gets a special dispensation from her lawyer boss to share the privilege of a day off with the Jo'-burg domestics. **1981** *Voice* 11 Oct. 15 'Make us workers' said the country's domestic workers at a big 'Sheila's Day' rally last weekend. **1985** H. PRENDINI in *Style* Oct. 41 Thursday is day off for domestics, therefore known as 'Sheilas' day'. That's when the 'Sheilas' get together with the other 'ousies' and 'cherries'. **1987** D. TUGWANA in *True Love* Mar. 42 Thursday afternoon, when by tradition domestic workers take off their uniforms and don their private casual clothes, has come to be known as 'Sheila's day'. *Ibid.* 44 The streets bustle with black women dressed in their 'Sheila's day' best, walking, talking, laughing, sharing jokes in groups on the pavements ... Those employers who can't afford the minimum wage will be asked to compromise by giving extra days off, over and above the traditional 'Sheila's day'.

shellhole *n.* [Fig. use of *shell-hole* a hole in the ground made by an exploding projectile.] A branch or unit of the MOTH organization of ex-servicemen and -women; DUG-OUT.

1962 E.W. TURPIN *Grahamstown: City of Settlers*, (*caption*) On the right is the first house built in Grahamstown and now used by the Makana Kop Shellhole of the M.O.T.H. organisation. **1966** *Survey of Race Rel. 1965* (S.A.I.R.R.) 305 Massed African choirs .. have presented the *Messiah* annually to segregated audiences in Johannesburg, under the sponsorship of the Desert Lily MOTH Shellhole. **1972** [see DUG-OUT]. **1980** *Daily Dispatch* 3 Dec. 2 Moth clubs involved are: the Lead-swingers Shellhole, Swartberg, assisted by the Tipperary Shellhole, [etc.]. **1983** L. CAPSTICKDALE in *S. Afr. Panorama* Dec. 19 The grand old MOTH order is still going strong, the dwindling membership of its Shellholes (units) of a few years back having received an infusion of new recruits. **1993** [see MOTH sense b]. **1994** G. O'NEILL in *Grocott's Mail* 22 July 4 (*letter*) My brother M.O.T.H.S. from the Makanaskop Shellhole.

Shembe /ˈʃe(ː)mbe/ *n.* [Named for *Isaiah Shembe* (*c*1867–1935), the church's founder, or for his son and successor *Johannes Galilee Shembe.*] A colloquial name for the ZIONIST church *iBandla lamaNazaretha* ('the Church of the Nazarene'), which broke away from the African Baptist Church in 1911, and blends Christian beliefs with traditional Zulu cultural and organizational practices. Also *attrib.*

Also known as the Nazareth Baptist Church or the Zulu Church of Nazareth, the church reveres its founder, Isaiah Shembe, as a saint who is believed to be present in spirit at the church's holy village of Ekuphakameni, near Durban. In the 1970s, after the death of its second leader, Isaiah Shembe's son Johannes Galilee Shembe, the church split into two factions, one led by a son and the other by a grandson of the founder.

1941 W.M.B. NHLAPO in *Bantu World* 1 Mar. 9, I have been fortunate to see two well-established churches; Shembe in Natal and Mahona in the Free State. All the other Zionist churches are but tiny and poor shadows of these two. *c***1966** *Standard Bank Pocket Guide to S. Afr.* 14 Shembe Festival. Held at Inanda about 12 miles from Durban on the week-end nearest July 25. **1970** *Daily News* 27 July 4 Several thousand men and women of the Zulu Christian Shembe sect gathered on the Inanda Hills from many parts of the country this week-end for their annual rain festival. The festival, the sixtieth to be held in Shembe history .., reached a dramatic climax .. when members .. danced for hours in the hot sun to the slow beat of drums ... The Shembe Church is one of about 6 000 separatist Christian churches scattered throughout the African continent. **1981** *Cape Times* 22 Dec. 2 The spokesman said the Shembe pilgrims would .. be warned against the dangers of cholera. **1982** *Pace* Nov. 100 The Church of Nazareth was held together by the unique personality of Galilee Shembe, so much so that it became known as 'Shembe's Church'. **1989** S. KAHN in *Weekly Mail* 3 Mar. 27 A friend is writing the songs, whose influence comes from *amahuba* (church music) done by the Shembe church deep in Zululand.

Hence **Shembeite** *n.*, a member of the Shembe church.

   1961 B.G.M. SUNDKLER *Bantu Prophets* 163 Shembeites often refuse to shake hands with other people. **1979** *Argus* 29 Dec. 2 At least two Shembeites died when more than 1 000 followers of the Rev A K Shembe, brandishing machine-guns and other firearms, ambushed a large group of pilgrims headed by the Rev Londa Shembe.

shepherd's tree *n. phr.* [So called because reputedly used for shade by shepherds.] The WITGAT (sense 1), *Boscia albitrunca*.

   1907 [see WITGAT sense 1]. **1914** *Farmer's Annual* 92 As specimens of the tuberous root variety, you will find such plants as Witgat-boom (Shepherd's Tree). **1955** L.G. GREEN *Karoo* 105 The shepherd's tree .. grows .. to a height of twenty feet, sometimes offering the only shade for miles. **1970** *S. Afr. Panorama* Nov., Witgat (Shepherd's tree) trees keep watch. **1990** CLINNING & FOURIE in *Fauna & Flora* No.47, 9 The northern woodlands .. are characterised by a number of species of tree: the shepherd's tree *Boscia albitrunca*, [etc.].

sheshwe var. SESHWESHWE.

shimiyana /ʃɪmɪˈjɑːn(ə)/ *n.* Also **isishimyana, isishishimeyane, isityimiyana, shim(a)yane, shimeya(na), shimiaan, shimya(a)n, simelane, sishimeyana.** [Zulu *isishimeyana*, intoxicating drink made from sugar-cane or treacle; A.T. Bryant (*Zulu-English Dictionary*, 1905) suggests that the Zulu word is an ad. of Eng. *machine*; but see also quot. 1948.] Esp. in KwaZulu-Natal: a home-brewed liquor of sugar (or treacle) and water, fermented in the sun. Cf. MBAMBA.

   1870 A.F. LINDLEY *After Ophir* 306 Shimyan and jwarlar were produced for our consumption, and we were invited to witness the usual dancing performances at the kraal after dark. **1891** *Natal Code of Native Law 19 of 1891* (Swart), Isityimiyana, An intoxicating liquor made of treacle or sugar mixed with water. **1900** J. ROBINSON *Life Time in S. Afr.* 307 'Shimyaan', a concoction of treacle and water allowed to ferment in the sun. This beverage was maddening in its effects, and the parent of much crime. **1906** H.C. CAMPBELL et al. *Col. of Natal Native Affairs Commission 1906-7* 25 The use of Isityimiyana was not very prevalent in Durban, but a great deal of methylated spirits was drunk by natives. **1948** E. HELLMANN *Rooiyard* 48 Babaton comes first in popularity, with *shimeya* or *shimeyani* as close second. Isiqataviki (kill-me-quick) is made to a much lesser degree ... *Isishishimeyane*, now usually contracted to *shimeya*, was first concocted by the workers in sugar cane fields. Its name is popularly conceived as onomatopoeic, suggesting the swaying gait of an intoxicated man. **1949** L. HUNTER *Afr. Dawn* 12 There, our sons learn to drink *isishimiyana*, which enters their brains like a maggot, making reasonable people act like madmen. **1950** [see BARBERTON sense 2]. **1961** T. MATSHIKIZA *Choc. for my Wife* 76 They plug you cockfull of Shimiyana. Some randy home brew mixed with brandy. **1963** L.F. FREED *Crime in S. Afr.* 204 Another kind of poison drink used by Natives is known as 'gabeen', and, like 'skokiaan' and shimyane', predisposes to crime. **1967** O. WALKER *Hippo Poacher* 25 Tom sat down while they shared a big clay pot full of *sishimeyana*, a very potent drink made from sugar cane. **1980** D.B. COPLAN *Urbanization of African Performing Arts.* 203 Noxious chemical mixtures such as *babaton, 'komfana, shimiyane, skokiaan,* and *isikilimikwiki* ('kill me quick'), and commercial European liquors. **1986** P. MAYLAM *Hist. of Afr. People* 150 Insanitary shacks, sheds and backyards, where women sold beer or more potent alcohol such as methylated spirits and isitshimiyane to African workers. **1989** O. MUSI in *Drum* Apr. 36 Shimeyane (that was their version of barberton).

ship *n. hist.* [Transf. use (or ad.) of general Eng. expressions.] Esp. in the phrr. *ship of the desert,* *ship of the plains, ship of the veld*: the ox-wagon.

   1878 T.J. LUCAS *Camp Life & Sport* 42 The Cape ox-waggon is quite an institution, and has been called, like a camel, the 'ship of the plains'. **1884** *Queenstown Free Press* 12 Feb., Our lady passengers .. we assisted into the 'cartel', a sort of arbour .., at the stern of this 'ship of the desert.' **1898** J.F. INGRAM *Story of Afr. City* 179 Ready for their journeys, stand the great trek-wagons, waiting but the order to start like 'ships of the desert' to the far-off lands of the Matabele and Mashona. [**1925** see BUCK-WAGON.] **1976** A.R. WILLCOX *Sn Land* 161 This ox-drawn vehicle was as much the ship of the veld as it became later the 'ship of the prairie' in America.

shlenter var. SCHLENTER *n.*

shloop var. SCHLOEP.

shoe var. SHU.

shongalolo, shongolala, shongululu varr. SONGOLOLO.

shoo var. SHU.

shottist *n.* [Perh. a blend of general Eng. *shootist* one skilled in shooting + *shot* (as in 'he is a good shot').] One skilled in shooting; one who competes in shooting competitions. Also *attrib.*

   1949 O. WALKER *Proud Zulu* (1951) 33 It was clear that his reputation as a fighter and shottist had been enhanced by the battle. *Ibid.* 270 Sibebu with his eager horsemanship, his keen fighting brain, his shottist prowess. **1951** *Natal Mercury* 19 Apr. 13 Durban shottist wins trophy. **1973** *E. Prov. Herald* 21 May 11 Leading South African shottists will take part in the Eastern Province smallbore championships to be held in East London on Saturday May 26. **1977** P. RICHARDSON in R.J. Bouch *Infantry in S. Afr. 1652–1976* 71 In German South West Africa he [sc. the South African soldier] retained these fighting abilities, being an expert shottist, a fine horseman .. , and a bold and self-reliant scout. **1985** *Grocott's Mail* 11 Oct. 16 Rhodes University shottists occupied the first four places of Class A at Saturday's Fort Beaufort Bisley shot at the Arthur Walters Range on the Rhodes campus. **1986** H. PRENDINI in *Style* Oct., X is arguing with another journalist whether the word 'shottist' is legitimate or some nasty American invention. 'It's nowhere in *my* Oxford' says X who's been calling them 'guns' or 'shots'. **1987** C. HOARE in *Pace* 43 Raffique won a trophy for best shottist with both the 9mm pistol and shot-gun. **1991** C. NEL in *Farmer's Weekly* 15 Feb. 36 The rifle stock is primarily a practical means for the shottist to hold the working parts .. in such a manner as to achieve the minimum of variation in bullet point-of-impact on the target.

shrimpi var. SWEMPI.

shu /ʃʊ, ʃu/ *int. colloq.* Also **shoe, shoo, shuee, sjoe.** [Prob. fr. Xhosa, Zulu, or S. Sotho *shu,* the use of the word being reinforced by the existence in Afk. of *s(j)oe* (in similar senses) fr. Du. dial. *soech, soeg, soe(c)k.* As used in Eng. by speakers of Sintu (Bantu) languages, prob. taken directly fr. Xhosa, Zulu, or S. Sotho.] An exclamation expressing a variety of emotions, esp. surprise, wonder, or relief.

   1979 'BLOSSOM' in *Darling* 16 May 131 Sjoe, that was close. **1986** *Pace* May 110 Sneak into stokvels of the kind I visited yesterday. Shu mfondini, your eyes catch sight of fat ugly aunties whose faces are daubed with an assortment of alcoholic graffiti. **1989** D. BRISTOW in *Weekly Mail* 21 Apr. 29 From the escarpment .. , Van der Stel is supposed to have looked out across the mirage-dancing plain .. and said to his underlings: 'Shoo manne, what a spektakel!' **1989** A. DONALDSON in *Style* Dec. 8 Well, *sjoe*, there's just no way to describe it, man.

shuluga var. UMSHOLOGU.

shu-shu /ˈʃʊʃʊ/ *adj. colloq.* [Xhosa *shushu*.]
a. Hot.

   [**1964** G. GORDON *Four People* 105 'Ushushu!' explained someone in the Xhosa idiom.] **1970** S. SPARKS *Informant*, Fort Beaufort It has been shu-shu today and we're sure to have rain after this heat. **1994** T. QUIRK on TV1, 2 Dec., It's shu-shu here at Sun City. **1994** M.G. McCOY *Informant*, Grahamstown Have a piece of chicken, David — careful, it's shu-shu.

b. Special collocation: **shushu broekies** *n. phr.* [see BROEKIES], a joking name for 'hot pants' or tight shorts for girls.

   1971 *Grocott's Mail* 23 Nov. 1 (*advt*) Hot-pants or Shu-shu broekies. Call them what you may but see our selection now.

Shutu var. SOTHO.

shwimpi var. SWEMPI.

sibali var. SBALI.

sibilo *n. obs.* Also **sebilo, sibillo.** [S. Sotho *sebilo*.] Powdered black micaceous or iron ore, used as a cosmetic by certain African peoples.

   1824 W.J. BURCHELL *Trav.* II. 256 The *sibilo* (sibeelo) is found. Hither all the surrounding nations repair for a supply of that ornamental and, in their eyes, valuable substance ... This *sibilo* is a shining, powdery iron-ore of a steel-grey or blueish lustre, and soft and greasy to the touch, its particles adhering to the hands or clothes. **1827** G. THOMPSON *Trav.* I. 166 Her hair is shaved in the Bechuana fashion, leaving a bunch on the crown of the head, which is anointed with grease and powdered well with *sibillo*, a shining mineral powder much in request at the court of the Matchlapees. **1839** W.C. HARRIS *Wild Sports* 51 Fat and grease of all kinds form their delight: their bodies and skin cloaks being also plentifully anointed with *sibilo*, a grey iron-ore sparkling like mica, procured from mines in the neighbourhood, which are visited from all parts of the country. **1846** R. MOFFAT *Missionary Labours* 66 The lower part of their hair is shaven off, and the upper part profusely bedaubed with a paste of butter and *sebilo*, black shining ochre.

siboko var. SEBOKO.

sibonga, -bongo varr. ISIBONGO.

sicathamiya, sichatamiya varr. ISICATHAMIYA.

Sichuana var. SETSWANA.

sick comforter *n. phr.* [tr. Afk. *sieketrooster.*] SIEKETROOSTER.

   1881 'G.M.T.' in *Cape Monthly Mag.* IV. May 269 There was no resident clergyman at the Cape. Services were occasionally held by the chaplains of ships, and a sermon was read every Sunday and on special occasions by the Sick Comforter. **1921** H.J. MANDELBROTE tr. *O.F. Mentzel's Descr. of Cape of G.H.* I. 113 Every evening after the lamps are lighted, a reader or sick-comforter, comes to the hospital and recites the evening prayers; all those who can do so must attend. **1927** C.G. BOTHA *Social Life in Cape Col.* 48 There were two classes of clergy which the Company provided. To the important stations clergymen or 'predikanten' were appointed, and to the smaller places men of a lower rank called sick-comforters or sick-visitors, 'ziekentroosters'. **1934** M.E. McKERRON *Hist. of Educ.* 15 The sick comforter (Siekentrooster) was the first type of teacher at the Cape. **1967** [see SIEKETROOSTER]. **1969** D. CHILD *Yesterday's Children* 14 He was the son of Willem Wijlant, the 'sick-comforter'. The baby's baptism had to be deferred until a *predikant* came ashore from a visiting Dutch ship.

sickness *n. Obs. Pathology. The sickness*: HORSE-SICKNESS.

   1833 *Graham's Town Jrnl* 13 June 2 The horses left by Barend's commando are dead of the sickness. **1844** J. BACKHOUSE *Narr. of Visit* 156 At daybreak, one of our horses exhibited symptoms of a fatal disease, called in this Colony, The Sickness. His eyelids were swollen, and the blood-vessels of his tongue and mouth were in a state of congestion.

siding *n.* [Special sense of general Eng. *siding* a short railway track at the side of the line, used for shunting.] A scheduled (and named) stop for goods and passenger trains, often in open country, where farming produce may be loaded, passengers taken on board, etc.

1911 J.W. SAUER in *Farmer's Weekly* 15 Mar. 10 So far as sidings are concerned, especially sidings where there is no staff on duty, I do not think it would be advisable to provide storage accommodation thereat. **1913** D. FAIRBRIDGE *Piet of Italy* 172 Pausing at Bosman's Siding to pick up a predikant in a white tie. **1916** *Farmer's Weekly* 20 Dec. 1454 (*advt*) For Sale. Boer Seed Oats Price 30s. per bag 153lb. delivered on rails Rooi Spruit Siding. **1919** R.Y. STORMBERG *With Love from Gwenno* 75 To-morrow I shall stand shivering at that old siding down the valley, waiting for the train to bear me away from this dear wretched old place. **1926** L.D. FLEMMING *Fun on Veld* (1928) 55 In this particular spot a railway train passes a little siding two miles away once every twenty-four hours. *Ibid.* 98, I wrote and told him I would be very glad if he would send me the plough to Backveld Siding. *c***1936** *S. & E. Afr. Yr Bk & Guide* 135 Land at about £300 per acre, inclusive of railway siding and water laid on. **1956** N. GORDIMER in *Best of S. Afr. Short Stories* (1991) 220 It was only the train that had stopped. Mrs Hansen lay and listened; they must be at some deserted siding, in the small hours. **1960** J. COPE *Tame Ox* 67 Voices were singing outside as she awoke, a gang of labourers loading bales of hides into a truck at the siding. **1979** T. GUTSCHE *There Was a Man* 35 No bush, no blade of grass – only rocks varied by slight eminences, sometimes a tiny dorp of corrugated iron shacks, sometimes only a deserted siding. **1989** D. BRISCOE in *Motorist* 4th Quarter 5 From Lady Grey the train goes forward to Melk Siding, then backward to Bamboeskloof Siding, then forward, backward in a zig-zag fashion, hugging the contours of the mountain all the way. **1990** A. CAMPBELL in *Fair Lady* 11 Apr. 56 Her childhood was passed in those small sooty railway sidings, with names like Karakuwisa .. developed round the mysterious iconography of South African Railways. **1991** J. WINTER tr. *P. Pieterse's Shadow of Eagle* 27 'That is Huntley siding,' he told her to ease the moment. He pointed down towards the small white signboard alongside the track.

sidwaba var. ISIDWABA.

sieckentrooster var. SIEKETROOSTER.

sieketroos /ˈsikətruəs/ *n.* Also **zieketroost, ziekte troest**. [Afk., fr. Du. *ziekentrooster*, see next.] The PLATDOORN, *Arctopus echinatus*.

1795 C.R. HOPSON tr. *C.P. Thunberg's Trav.* I. 234 The *Arctopus echinatus* (Zieke-troost) a low umbelliferous plant without stalk, and even with the surface of the ground, grew in common near the town. **1809** J. MACKRILL Diary. 56 Medical plants, Arctopus echinatus – Zieke-troost. **1913** [see PLATDOORN]. **1917** R. MARLOTH *Common Names* 91 *Ziekètroost, Arctopus echinatus.* A stemless dioecious umbellifer. The root contains an aromatic balsam. **1966** C.A. SMITH *Common Names* 416 *Sieketroos, Arctopus echinatus*, see *platdoring*. The vernacular name is derived from the medicinal value of the rootstock which was stated to bring comfort (Afr. troos) to the sick (Afr. siekte).

sieketrooster /ˈsikəˌtruəstə(r)/ *n. Obs. exc. hist.* Also **sieckentrooster, siekentrooster, ziekentrooster**. [Afk., fr. Du. *ziekentrooster* sick comforter, *zieken* the sick + *troos* solace + agential suffix -*(t)er*.] A minor clerical official in the service of the Dutch East India Company, whose function, as lay preacher, was to conduct services, visit the sick, and teach children; SICK COMFORTER; also called DOMINEE (sense 1). Cf. *oefening-holder* (see OEFENING sense 2).

1861 P.B. BORCHERDS *Auto-Biog. Mem.* 276 On the 17th April 1658, he commenced to arrange the keeping of a school for the male and female Angola slaves, in the morning and evening under a Catechist (Ziekentrooster). **1926** P.W. LAIDLER *Tavern of Ocean* 21 One of the settlement's minor officials, the 'Ziekentrooster,' was a peculiar mixture of lay preacher and parish visitor. *Ibid.* 75 Each evening when the lamps were lit the ziekentrooster or sick-visitor paid his call. **1927, 1934** [see SICK COMFORTER]. **1934** C.P. SWART Supplement to Pettman. 155 *Sieketrooster*, .. In the early days of the Cape comforters of the sick or sick-visitors, men of lower ecclesiastical rank, held offices similar to those of catechists in the English Church. They also instructed children and conducted religious services, but were not allowed to administer the sacraments. **1957** L.G. GREEN *Beyond City Lights* 45 Lombard was the sieketrooster of the Huguenots. **1967** E. ROSENTHAL *Encycl. of Sn Afr.* 384 The original settlers under Jan van Riebeeck in 1652 were accompanied by a 'Ziekentrooster' (sick comforter) who, not officially qualified, was expected to carry out certain ministrations. **1975** P.G.J. MEIRING in T. Sundermeier *Church & Nationalism* 57 The State appointed and remunerated the 'sieketroosters' and ministers. *Ibid.* 61 The very first school started in the Castle in Cape Town, in 1663 with 17 pupils (12 white and four slave children as well as one Hottentot boy) who were daily instructed by the church's sieketrooster. **1988** P.E. RAPER tr. *R.J. Gordon's Cape Trav. 1777–86* I. 52 Was present at a sermon which was delivered by a *sieketrooster*, a man who travels from place to place. **1990** C. LAFFEATY *Far Forbidden Plains* 39 Mamma was also what the Boers called a *Ziekentrooster* ... it meant 'Comforter of the Sick'.

sier var. SIEUR.

sies var. SIS *int.*

‖**siestog** /ˈsɪstɔx, ˈsistɔx/ *int. colloq.* Also **cis toch, sis tog**, and **siestorg**. [Afk., 'what a pity', 'poor thing', etc. (*sies* see SIS *int.* + *tog* see TOG).] An expression of sympathy, pity, or dismay; occas., an expression of disgust. See also SHAME.

1928 N. STEVENSON *Afr. Harvest* 87 She had a cunning heart and godless ways which drew you against your will, he thought. *Cis toch!* She made decent men sick. **1952** B.B. MYERS in *Silver Leaves* 34, I gazed at it all in wonder, And murmured 'Ag, sis tog man!' **1962** J. TAYLOR 'The Lift Girl's Lament'. (*lyrics*) Ag sis tog Marlene, what a hell of a job this is. **1972** R. MALAN *Ah Big Yaws* 45 Siestorg! An expression of either slobbering sympathy or almost complete indifference, depending on the tone of voice. See also *Shaayme!*, in conjunction with which it is most often used. **1975** *Fair Lady* 10 Dec. 2 (*advt*) Sies tog Dainty, says my ma. The fast furious city life must be taking it out of you, you've lost at least 10 kilograms. **1977** *Sunday Times* 29 May 16 Last Thursday South Africa celebrated .. 29 years of National Party rule. That means a whole, mature, generation that has known no other kind of government. Siestog. **1986** D. CASE *Love, David* 16 Oupa picked him up again. 'Siestog, man!' he exclaimed. 'Look here – he's only got three legs. One of his back legs is missing.' *Ibid.* 62 Siestog, and all those visitors must have made her feel nervous, the way she looked around her all the time. **1990** R. CRAIG in *Personality* 28 May 88 'Mommee! – the Aunty's sat on my choclit!' ... 'Ag, sis tog,' said an old man sympathetically. **1991** *Sunday Times* 7 Apr. 26 Most people agree, it was the Voortrekkers who invented the sport. I knew so little about it I had to ask: which is the *juk* and which is the *skei*? *Siestog*! Even a soutie shouldn't display such ignorance.

‖**sieur** /siœ(r)/ *n.* Also **seer, seur, sier**, and with initial capital. [fr. Afk. *seur*, ad. Du. *sinjeur* lord, master, rel. to F. *seigneur*.] 'Master', 'sir': a respectful form of address or reference to a superior; also used as a title, with a name, and occas. as a common noun. Cf. BAAS.

1812 A. PLUMPTRE tr. *H. Lichtenstein's Trav. in Sn Afr.* (1928) I. 118 There is this great distinction between them [*sc.* the Hottentots] and the slaves, that the former only address their master by the title of *Baas* (Master), while the slave addresses him as *Sieur* (Lord). *a***1875** T. BAINES *Jrnl of Res.* (1964) II. 21 The other begged for 'just one charge of powder, if you please, Sieur'. **1883** M.A. CAREY-HOBSON *Farm in Karoo* 96 'Ya, sieur,' came from a corner, the drunken servant unconsciously responding to the voice to which he was in the habit of yielding obedience. **1886** G.A. FARINI *Through Kalahari Desert* 163 He is a skellum lion, and the sieur must not go. **1894** E. GLANVILLE *Fair Colonist* 247 'John!' shouted Mr Gardner. 'Yah, sieur.' 'Here, this is your new Baas.' **1900** H. BLORE *Imp. Light Horseman* 168 '*Allewereld*, sieur' said Quguza admiringly, employing one of the Dutch expletives, 'if this be your skill then I need not fear.' **1921** H.J. MANDELBROTE tr. *O.F. Mentzel's Descr. of Cape of G.H.* I. 156 The more capable clerks sometimes drew up accounts for provisions supplied to ships at the request of the ship's book-keeper, styled *seur*. **1924** L. COHEN *Reminisc. of Jhb.* 138 Mr Rhodes turned his head upwards and commenced to survey the horizon .. which caused the Sieur Barnato, after a few desultory words of farewell, to wish him good-bye and turn his back. **1945** N. DEVITT *People & Places* 145 Those were the days when the Cape Coloured man learned politeness, and customarily addressed his White master as 'seur', from the French 'sieur.' **1961** L.E. VAN ONSELEN *Trekboer* 18 This 'Seer' they use to address Europeans, is as old as South Africa itself. It originated from the days of the Dutch East India Company. **1969** D. CHILD *Yesterday's Children* 60 As soon as he could speak, the child was taught to address his master as '*Sieur*', though the free Hottentots used the Dutch word '*Baas*'. **1977** *Fair Lady* 25 May 105 The old man appeared at the window, his smile showing three yellow teeth ... 'Rain, Seur.' Robert shot out of the lorry ... Seur Robert gives me a rand a week. **1983** F.G. BUTLER *Bursting World* 247 'Van Niekerk,' I say, 'Tell Seedman to bring the truck around as soon as he has finished his breakfast'. 'Ja, seer.' **1988** P. KINGWELL *Message of Black Eagle* 63 We must catch him, but also we must tell your Oom. Vusi must go quickly and tell Seer Pete.

siffie /ˈsəfi/ *n.* Also **ciphy**. [Afk., lit. 'little sieve'; so named for the row of holes round the edge of the shell.] Among anglers: the univalve shellfish *Haliotis sanguinea* of the Haliotidae, commonly used as bait.

1961 *Red Wing* (St. Andrew's College, Grahamstown) 13 Other shellfish in the forms of .. Venus ears (ciphy) and limpets are very numerous and plentiful. **1972** *Grocott's Mail* 15 Sept. 3 Bait collectors should remember that the limit for perlemoen (venus-ear) is five, for siffie 10, for armadillo (saddle-back) six, and for red-bait a cut off weight of 4 lbs. **1975** *E. Prov. Herald* 30 Oct. 41 The angler can take his choice from the following list and if the poenskop are feeding they will take one of them: crab, red bait, whole seacat, seacat tentacle, fish fillet, chokka, ollycrock and siffie (venus ear). **1976** *Bait Regulations* (Dept of Industries), Venus ear or siffie (Haliotis sanquinae [*sic*]). **1981** *Het Suid-Western* 22 Apr., No person shall catch for himself or any other person, purchase, convey, be in possession of more than the following species at any time or at any place: Alikreukel (10), Black Mussel (25), Bloodworm (5), Crab (2), Perlemoen for own use only, not to exceed (5) per day, .. Siffie (10), White mussel (50). **1982** KILBURN & RIPPEY *Sea Shells* 35 *Haliotis spadicea* ... A common species, known to fishermen as the 'siffie' (little sieve).

sijsje var. SYSIE.

silver *n.* Pl. -**s**, or unchanged. Ellipt. for SILVER-FISH (sense 1).

1960 J. COPE *Tame Ox* 40 The trawlers came in from the deep sea loaded .. with stock-fish, not to mention soles, silver, gurnet, kingklip, [etc.]. **1977** *Darling* 8 June 118 The best fish to ask for at the coast are the following: .. silvers or doppies, which tend to be full of bones but have a delicate flavour.

silver-fish *n.* [Named for its colour; cf. Du. *zilvervisch*.] Any of three species of marine and freshwater fish.

1. Either of two species of seabream, esp. **a.** the CARPENTER, *Argyrozona argyrozona*; and **b.** the *red steenbras* (see STEENBRAS sense b), *Petrus rupestris*. In both senses also called SILVER.

1731 G. MEDLEY tr. *P. Kolb's Present State of Cape of G.H.* 203 The fish at the *Cape*, call'd the Silver-fish, is of the shape of a Carp, and of the size of a Carp of a pound weight, and tastes not much unlike a carp. 'Tis a very white fish, adorn'd with several streaks, of a bright silver-colour. These silver-streaks appear like leaf-silver. **1806** J. BARROW *Trav.* II. 37 Another perch, called the Silver-fish, has one back fin, and tail bifid; .. with five longitudinal silver bands on each side. *a***1823** J. EWART *Jrnl* (1970) 13 Hottentot fish, a small fish .. covered with scales of a dirty brown colour, silver fish, something of the size and shape of the former, and of a bright silver colour. **1831** *S. Afr. Almanack & Dir.*, May. Fish in Season – Snoek, Geelbek, Silverfish, Roman, Kabeljau. **1861** 'A LADY' *Life at Cape* (1963) 3 It is a very pretty sight .. to .. watch the fleet of fishingboats coming to the anchorage after a hard day's toil at hooking snoek, silverfish, hottentot, stumpnose and geelbeck. **1891** H.J. DUCKITT *Hilda's 'Where Is It?'* 71 Put your fish (mackerel, or Cape 'silver-fish,' or young 'kabeljou' [*printed* kabeljon]) in a tin baking pan. **1913** C. PETTMAN *Africanderisms* 442 *Silver fish, Dentex argyrozona.* The Western province name of this fish, which shows, when fresh, a beautiful silver sheen, though the fish is a delicate pink. *Dentex rupestris* is known by this name in the Eastern Province. **1926** M. NATHAN *S. Afr. from Within* 204 The larger staple fish are silverfish, stumpnose, Cape Salmon, Kabeljauw (maigre) and stockfish (hake). **1951** L.G. GREEN *Grow Lovely* 91 The silver fish is not silver but red, and in earlier times was known as the goldfish. **1991** *Weekend Post* 6 Apr. 4 Size limits remain the same for .. silverfish (25cm), [etc.].

2. The freshwater fish *Barbus mattozi* of the Cyprinidae (yellowfishes and barbs).

Found in the Limpopo river system. In P. Skelton's *Freshwater Fishes* (1993), the name 'papermouth' is used for *B. mattozi.*

1892 NICOLLS & EGLINGTON *Sportsman in S. Afr.* 138 The Silver Fish. (May be caught up to 3 lbs in weight, and in shape resembles the Yellowtail. The colour is a bluish silver grey, with a pinkish tinge.) This fish is not met with in the rivers North of the Crocodile, and as an object from which sport can be derived, it deserves no special mention. It is not good eating. **1893** H.A. BRYDEN *Gun & Camera* 462 Speaking of the silver-fish, as they are called, there are numbers of them to be found, curiously enough, in a huge, rock-encircled tarn of very deep water about fifteen miles from Mafeking. **1945** H. GERBER *Fish Fare* 71 The best known freshwater fish are yellowfish, witvis, silverfish. **1971** BEETON & DORNER in *Eng. Usage in Sn Afr.* Vol.1 No.2, 52 *Silver fish,* .. Predatory fish with characteristic large mouth, thin lips & protruding lower jaw; known in the Limpopo system.

silver-leaf *n.* [Perh. tr. S. Afr. Du. *silwerblaaderen* silver tree, see quot. 1790. (The modern Afk. name is *silwerboom*).]

a. In full ***silver-leaf tree***: SILVER TREE.

[**1790** tr. *F. Le Vaillant's Trav.* I. 96 In the environs of Constantia and of *Niuwe-land*, is found that charming tree, called *silwer blaaderen*.] **1981** *S. Afr. Panorama* July 42 A cone of the silver leaf tree (*Leucadendron argenteum*). **1986** J. DE WETTE in *Upstream* Summer 4 The mismatched trees of childhood .. the revenant silverleaf and pollen-caked Port Jackson. **1990** R. GOOL *Cape Town Coolie* 99 A footpath .. wound past short, silver-leaf trees and sourfig grass to the beach.

b. A leaf of this tree, characterized by its silky, silvery down.

1988 M. BRANCH *Explore Cape Flora* 8 If you have ever stroked a silver leaf, kept one as a bookmark, or watched the silver tree glistening in the wind, you will understand why the Table Mountain silver trees are grown all over the world.

silver tree *n. phr.* [So named for its leaves, which are covered with fine silvery hairs.] The tree *Leucodendron argenteum* of the Proteaceae, indigenous to the Western Cape; *silver-leaf tree,* see SILVER-LEAF sense a; WITTEBOOM. Also *attrib.*

1731 G. MEDLEY tr. *P. Kolb's Present State of Cape of G.H.* II. 224 *Argyrodendros Africana* .. i.e. The Silver Tree. These trees are seen equally in the Vallies and on the Hills in the *Cape*-Countries. They are, particularly, much seen about *Constantia*. The Fruit is conical, like that of the Pine-Tree. **1786** G. FORSTER in *A. Sparrman's Voy. to Cape of G.H.* I. 32 The *protea argentea*, or the silver-tree, as it is called, exhibited the whole year through its glossy white, or silver gray leaves. **1795** C.R. HOPSON tr. *C.P. Thunberg's Trav.* I. 116 The seed-vessels of the silver-tree (*protea argentea*) serve for fuel. **1804** R. PERCIVAL *Acct of Cape of G.H.* 142 To add to the beauty of this place [*sc.* Constantia] there are groves of the silver-tree planted all round ... The leaves of the colour of that metal .. are as rich as satin to the touch. They may indeed be said to be every way similar to a grayish or bluish pearl-coloured plush velvet. *a***1823** J. EWART *Jrnl* (1970) 22 The most striking object in botany .. is the Silver-Tree (Protea Argentea) which is seen exuberantly clothing the least-rugged part of the Table Mountain (to which it is indigenous) .. with its downy and silver color'd foliage. **1832** C.S. STEWART *Visit to S. Seas in U.S. Ship Vincennes 1829–30* II. 325 The approach to the gate is through a grove of the silver tree, *protea argentea*, affording us full proof of the appropriateness of the name. The long-pointed leaves are thickly set on the branches .. covered with a fine white furze or down. **1857** D. LIVINGSTONE *Missionary Trav.* 283 A species of silver-tree of the Cape (Leucodendron argenteum) is found in abundance in these parts through which we have travelled. **1890** A. MARTIN *Home Life* 10 The silver tree .. is found only on Table Mountain. The long, pointed leaves seem made of the glossiest pale-grey satin. *c***1911** S. PLAYNE *Cape Col.* 49 The well-known Silver Trees, so called from the silvery appearance of their leaves, are only common to the Cape Peninsula. *c***1933** J. JUTA in A.C. Partridge *Lives, Lett. & Diaries* (1971) 151 The silver tree – the 'witteboomen' – circled the hilltop with a pointed crown of glistening silver. **1947** L.G. GREEN *Tavern of Seas* 119 Mercifully the silver trees were not seriously affected by the fire. Nowhere else in the world do these gracious and remarkable trees thrive as on Table Mountain, their stronghold and native home. **1961** PALMER & PITMAN *Trees of S. Afr.* 218 The silver tree of the Cape Peninsula, both in shape and colour, is one of the loveliest of our wild trees ... Its silver foliage makes it a conspicuous sight on the slopes of Table Mountain, where, hardier than its neighbours, it often stands in windy, dry positions. **1963** R. LEWCOCK *Early 19th C. Archit.* 79 A framework of Silvertree poles with infilling panels of nine-inch sunburnt brick. **1978** *Daily Dispatch* 25 Jan. 10 The beautiful Silvertree (Leucadendron argenteum) .. has been selected as the provincial tree of the Cape Province. **1989** *Gardening Questions Answered* (Reader's Digest Assoc.) 352 *Leucadendron argenteum* (Silver tree). Famous indigenous tree with blue-green, oval, pointed leaves covered with silky, silvery hairs. The male plants produce orange flower heads in summer – the female plants bear silvery cones. **1993** *Earthyear* (ed. 5) Winter (Earthling) 27 Table Mountain is unique ... Some of the plants, such as .. the silver tree (*Leucadendron argenteum*) grow nowhere else in the world.

simanje-manje /si'mandʒe'mandʒe/ *n. Music.* [Zulu *isimanje-manje*, lit. 'the "now" style', *isimanje* current custom, manner, style + *manje* now.] A style of popular music in which traditional or neo-traditional African (esp. Zulu) songs, played in a rapid tempo and set to MBAQANGA and marabi rhythms and instrumentation, are sung in the GROANING style, (usually) by a male singer, backed by a three- or four-woman chorus. Also *attrib.* Cf. MARABI sense 3, MGQASHIYO.

The style became popular in the 1960s.

1973 *Drum* 18 Jan. 18 My hobbies are dancing, soul music, simanjemanje music and soccer. **1980** D.B. COPLAN Urbanization of African Performing Arts. 379 [Rupert] Bopape built on .. vocal *mbaqanga* .. to create a new style called *simanje-manje* ... The new music, pioneered by Joyce Mokgatusi's Dark City Sisters and *kwela-mbaqanga* innovator Aaron Lerole, showed less American influence. It .. set traditional and neo-traditional songs to urban rhythms derived from *marabi* and *tsaba-tsaba*, and was played at a rapid tempo by backup groups consisting of three reed instruments plus electric bass, guitar, and drum-set. **1989** *Reader's Digest Illust. Hist.* 418 A new musical form was beginning to emerge, borrowing heavily from Zulu music, with the underlying rhythms of mbaqanga to give it commercial appeal. This was simanje-manje .. a melodious moving sound led by a deep-voiced bass that sounded like a goat.

Hence (*?nonce*) **simanje-manje** *adj.*, of the younger generation (cf. general Eng. 'the "now" generation').

1982 M. MZAMANE *Children of Soweto* 197 A general discourse on the *simanje-manje* generation, as they called them, followed.

simelane var. SHIMIYANA.

simlunga var. MLUNGU.

simmels var. SEMELS.

||**simpel** /'səmp(ə)l/ *adj.* [Afk.] Stupid, thick-headed; mentally retarded. See also DOF, DOM sense a.

1950 H.C. BOSMAN in S. Gray *Makapan's Caves* (1987) 119 People must have been a bit *simpel* in the head, in those old times that Oupa Beller was talking about if they thought anything about that sort of news. *a***1951** — in L. Abrahams *Unto Dust* (1963), She came of a Cape family of which quite a few members were known to be 'simpel'. [**1972** *E. Prov. Herald* 8 June 15 Where student activities were concerned, he said, he hoped Government members would stop using the 'simple' story that because taxpayers subsidised students, students should not be politically active.] **1984** B. JOHNSON-BARKER in *Wynboer* June 71 It was one thing to be simpel, but to be stupid was quite another.

Sindebele /sin'debele, sɪndə'beːli/ *n.* Also **isi-Ndebele, Sendebele, Setebele, Sitabele, Sitebeli, Sitibela.** [In the Nguni languages *isiNdebele*, sing. n. prefix *isi-* (denoting language or culture) + n. stem *Ndebele*, see NDEBELE.] The language spoken by the Ndebele people (see NDEBELE sense 1); NDEBELE sense 2. Also *attrib.*

1835 D. LINDLEY in D.J. Kotze *Lett. of American Missionaries* (1950) 86 The Sitebeli is much the same with the Sichuana in its structure, many words are the same in both languages, and many more so little changed in the Sitebeli as to be immediately known by one acquainted with Sichuana. **1836** A.E. WILSON in *Ibid.* 105 The Sitibela is the proper language of [the] Matebela. **1871** J. MACKENZIE *Ten Yrs* (1971) 338 Mr Sykes .. who is a .. student of the Zulu language, of which Setebele is a corruption, was availing himself of the opportunity of meeting with the chief's sons and other Zulus, to compare the language as spoken by them with that given in a Zulu lexicon. **1872** T.M. THOMAS *11 Yrs in Central S. Afr.* 194 The Isindebele (as the language of the Amandebele is called) .. is a dialect of the Zulu Kafir. **1913** J. O'NEIL (*title*) A grammar of the Sindebele dialect of Zulu. **1919** H.H. JOHNSTON *Comparative Study of Bantu & Semi-Bantu Lang.* I. 798 Tebele (Sin-debele) This dialect of the Matebele (Amandebele) Zulus. **1930** S.T. PLAATJE *Mhudi* (1975) 95 You must speak Setebele too? I would like to send you as a spy to Inzwinyani before we proceed to attack Mzilikazi. **1950** C. BULLOCK *Mashona & Matabele* 147, I should be the last to advocate the translation of our word God by the Shona word Mwai or the Sindebele word Mlimo. **1961** D. BEE *Children of Yesterday* 42 'You! Remove the hand!' he commanded sharply in Sindebele. *c***1988** *S. Afr. 1987–8: Off. Yrbk* (Bureau for Info.) 68 In the past the Ndebeles used mainly Zulu for their literary needs. Recently, however, isiNdebele became the fourth Nguni language to receive official recognition.

sinkens var. SINKINGS.

sinkhole *n.* [Transf. use of (chiefly) U.S. Eng. *sinkhole* 'a hole, cavern, or funnel-shaped cavity made in the earth by the action of water on the soil, rock, or underlying strata, and frequently forming the course of an underground stream' (*OED*).] A deep cavity in the ground caused by a sudden subsidence resulting from undermining (particularly in the gold fields of the Rand). Also *attrib.*

1970 *Rand Daily Mail* 16 Nov. 1 Families are preparing to evacuate eight houses .. because of the enormous sinkhole which appeared .. three weeks ago ... The new sinkhole, measuring 100 ft. by 70 ft. and about 70 ft. deep, appeared in pasture land near the East Driefontein mine ... It is continuing to cave in. **1971** *Personality* 8 Jan. 66 One of the events of the year was the death of Bank – the Transvaal town which had to be totally evacuated because of sinkholes. **1971** *Argus* 5 May 23 The photographs .. record .. the sinkhole menace on the West Witwatersrand. **1972** P. DRISCOLL *Wilby Conspiracy* 178 Sinkholes had become something of an object lesson in the mining engineer's handbook .. great, almost literally bottomless pits that opened without warning. **1977** *Sunday Times* 30 Oct. 7 Many of the stands could not be built on because of sinkhole danger.

sinkings /ˈsəŋkəŋs/ *n. Obs.* exc. *hist. Pathology.* Also **sinkens, zinkin(g)s.** [Afk. (earlier S. Afr. Du. *zinking(s)*), fr. Du. *zinking* an excessive flow of blood, serum, etc., to any part of the body.] Neuralgia; tooth-ache; rheumatism. See also *zinkingsdruppels* (DRUPPELS sense b i).

1823 W.W. BIRD *State of Cape of G.H.* 176 There is a rheumatic affection called the Sinkings, which shows in swellings, (lucus a non lucendo,) and is painful. **1832** *Graham's Town Jrnl* 12 Jan. 11 It gives me some satisfaction to find a clause in the regulations, which allows copious ablutions to such of [the Temperance Society's] members as may be troubled with the Cholic, the Sinkens, Low-spirits, and Nausia. **1835** J.W.D. MOODIE *Ten Yrs* II. 33 'What is the matter with your head?' I now asked him, perceiving that it was wrapped up in a piece of dirty flannel pinned under the chin. – 'Ach! mynheer, I am sorely troubled with the zinkins,' (a kind of rheumatism common in the colony,) answered my now defendant. **1838** J.E. ALEXANDER *Exped. into Int.* I. 64, I found Taylor laid up with severe pains in the face, called zinkins in the Cape, arising from cold. **1844** J. BACKHOUSE *Narr. of Visit* 84 The changeableness of the temperature in spring and autumn renders a kind of rheumatism common, which is here called 'sinkings'. **1859** *Argus* in V. De Kock *Fun They Had* (1955) 93 His under jaw is at once contracted and swollen painfully, and gives unmistakable indications that the noble animal is suffering from a severe attack of *zinkens*. **1861** P.B. BORCHERDS *Auto-Biog. Mem.* 140 The sudden variation of temperature .. is apt to produce .. tic doloureux, known in the colonial language by the name of 'zinkings'. **1866** *Cape Town Dir.*, (advt) Zinkings or Face-ache. Calf's Antifebrile Lotion is the speediest alleviator, 1s. 6d. per bottle. **1873** W.L. SAMMONS in A.M.L. Robinson *Sel. Articles from Cape Monthly Mag.* (1978) 261 The sufferer seemed to be for ages labouring under some unspeakable toothache, mumps, *zinkings* (? risings), or lockjaw. **1887** A.A. ANDERSON *25 Yrs in Waggon* I. 69 They are always getting what they call sinkings (neuralgia). **1913** C. PETTMAN *Africanderisms* 444 *Sinkings*, .. Toothache and neuralgia are often spoken of by this name, as is also an acute form of rheumatism. **1979** *Scope* 20 July 24 Her health was fine, Ouma said. She was only troubled by the 'sinkings' an obsolete Afrikaans word for neuralgia or rheumatic pains, which I had last heard mentioned as a child.

Sintu /ˈsɪntuː, ˈsiːntʊ/ *adj.* and *n.* Also **isintu.** [Formed on elements common to a number of Sintu languages: n. prefix *(i)si-* denoting language or culture + n. stem *-ntu* (African) person, as in Zulu *isintu* African language or culture, humankind.]

See note at BANTU.

A. *adj.* BANTU *adj.* sense 1.

1979 B. MFENYANA *Neo-Sintu: Dynamic Challenge* 1 Let us make a conscious effort to grow away from referring to the Sintu languages of sub-Saharan Africa as Bantu. The people insist that '*bathetha isiNtu*' [they speak Sintu], so there. The 'Bantu' habit may be old and infectious but it is far from correct. **1980** *Voice* 20 Aug. 14 There are Sintu languages in south, east, central and western Africa.

B. *n.* BANTU *n.* sense 2.

1979 [see sense A]. **1980** C. NKOSI in M. Mutloatse *Forced Landing* 13 This lambschild shall remind the nation of the oft-remembered but never used Isintu. **1983** H. MASHABELA in *Frontline* June 17 He who speaks *isingisi* [English] instead of *isintu* loathes his people and their language! .. We have *isintu* (our language).

sis /sɪs, səs/ *int.* Also **cess, ciss, sies, siss.** [ad. Afk. *sies* (which form is also used), perh. fr. Khoikhoi *(t)si*.] An ejaculation expressing disgust or contempt; an expression of disappointment or dismay. Cf. GA, SIESTOG, SKANDE *int.*

1862 A.W. DRAYSON *Tales at Outspan* 67, I have lost more cattle from the attacks of hyænas than I have from lions, or leopards, and as to sheep, *cess*, I've had nearly a whole flock worried by them. **1909** *Cape* 30 Apr. 6 Sis for her. She gave me nothing to eat but semalina and kofee. **1913** A.B. MARCHAND *Dirk, S. African* (Swart), Sis! it is all lies. **1916** S. BLACK in S. Gray *Three Plays* (1984) 233 Peace: Bone, remove the prisoner. Van K: I protest, ach sis wat sis. Peace: Sis, eh? Van K: Yes sis, I'm bally well fed up. *Ibid.* 234 Sis doesn't really mean anything at all. It's the same as foi toch. *a*1928 R.R.R. DHLOMO *Afr. Tragedy* 9 'Sis!' exclaimed a young girl fashionably dressed. 'Isn't he a coward !' **1941** M.G. GILBERT *Informant, Cape Town* 10 Nov. 4 [She] can't afford to come down. Sis, I wish we could get up a collection for her train ticket or something. **1959** E. MPHAHLELE *Down Second Ave* 78 One morning she had a quarrel with the 'woman next door' as she always called her. 'Sies!' grandmother hissed and spat at intervals to show her utter contempt. **1961** M.A. WALL *Dominee & Dom-Pas* 3 'Our Padre talks to kaffirs ... He invites them to his house, and offers them tea .. – he makes friends with them!' Then they said 'Sis!' and gave up going to church. **1962** J. TAYLOR 'Hennie Van Saracen'. (*lyrics*) Ag sis man, I'm telling you, the next thing that I knew I was issued with a uniform, boots and rifle too. **1970** M. DIKOBE Marabi Dance. 65 Sis, a man of your age and with a grown daughter still fights like a small boy. **1974** B. SIMON *Joburg, Sis!* 129 Sis. They walk around there with their long hair and their tight jeans and so bladdy filthy dirty man. **1977** L. ABRAHAMS *Celibacy of Felix Greenspan* 13 Very soon someone said, 'Sis, Felix has messed his pants!' 'I haven't ..' he muttered hopelessly ... 'Yes, you have!' 'Sis! Look! ' **1982** *Sunday Times* 31 May, '*Sis!*' – terminal disgust, but not only applied to something unpleasant that has been trodden in: 'Sis! Don't talk to your father like that!' **1991** P. SLABOLEPSZY Braait Laaities. 2 The floor – it's – it's very dirty. Sies! Look at this! Too terrible. **1992** *Weekly Mail* 6 Mar. 23 Sis, it's just not cricket. **1992** T.M. PEARSON *Informant, Knysna* 'Ach sis!' – a tremendously expressive saying – one can render the concept of really nauseating disgust by emphasising the 'ach *surrsss*!'

sis /səs/ *n.*[1] Also **sus.** [Afk., fr. Du. *sits* chintz.]

1. Chintz.

1958 A. JACKSON *Trader on Veld* 35 Paris fashion plates had not reached the 'Backveld,' dress materials being limited to the 'Dutch' and 'German' Blaudruck print, checked Ginghams, Kapje Sis (a light cotton dress material always with a very small pattern), used for making the Voortrekker kapje. **1975** D.H. STRUTT *Clothing Fashions* 221 For everyday wear the dress was made of a simple material, usually printed cotton or *sis* (chintz) with a small design, floral or checked or striped, in soft muted colours.

2. *German print*, see GERMAN.

1970 M. BRITZ *Informant, Grahamstown*, I used to buy yards and yards of sis for the native women on the farm – that's what they call that cheap print they all use. **1994** B. BOWIE in *Weekend Post* 9 Apr. (Leisure) 3 Women wearing *blaudruck* (blue-printed) cotton cloth came to East London .. in 1858 ... The long-lasting cotton was known as German print or 'sis'. It has a white design on a background of indigo (navy blue), chocolate-brown or red.

sis /sɪs/ *n.*[2] Also **sis'.** [Shortened form of SISI, or of Eng. *sister*.] Esp. in township Eng.: a courteous title for, or form of address to a woman. Cf. BRA sense 1, SISI sense 1.

1966 K.M.C. MOTSISI in *Drum* 30 Jan. 20, I turn around and recognise this non-voter as none other than Sis Well – the doll at whose wedding we sang. **1976** M. THOLO in C. Hermer *Diary of Maria Tholo* (1980) 15 One patient hissed, 'Hey, sis Maria,' and .. I realised I knew him. **1980** E. PATEL *They Came at Dawn* 10 Whitening cream lightens your skin sis .. but strusgod your soul will never turn white in the night. **1981** B. MFENYANA in M. Mutloatse *Reconstruction* 294 By the time he's through I've already downed four beeahs at Sis Nota's grog-house. **1986** M. RAMGOBIN *Waiting to Live* 116 Once I also thought that all the men in my life .. were different from one another. Sis, they are all the same. **1986** S. SEPAMLA *Third Generation* 1 Whenever Sis Vi arrived home from work my anger was roused. **1990** *Pace* May 11, I was merely trying to help, Sis' May.

sishimeyana var. SHIMIYANA.

sisi /ˈsɪsiː, ˈsi(ː)si/ *n.* Also **sissie, sissy,** and with initial capital. [ad. Afk. *sussie* sister.]

1. Sister. Cf. BHUTI, OUSIE, SIS *n.*[2], SISTER, SUSSIE, SUSTER.

a. In the form **sisi** /ˈsiːsi/, among speakers of Sintu (Bantu) languages: **i.** A courteous form of address to a woman (see quot. 1963). **ii.** A title, used with a name. **iii.** A common noun: a woman.

1963 A. FUGARD *Blood Knot* (1968) 103 Sister, Sissy, they say, for short. **1963** A.M. LOUW *20 Days* 232 He had called: 'Sisi, I am a man without a home. May I come into your house to shelter from the rain?' **1963** WILSON & MAFEJE *Langa* 88 *Sisi* (from the Afrikaans – 'sussie') without any possessive pronoun, is in general use as a polite form of address by a woman to a senior contemporary. It is used by a bride, for all her sisters-in-law over puberty, replacing 'mother-of-so-and-so' in address .. and in the country it is used by all unmarried girls in addressing young married women. **1973** *Drum* 22 Sept. 63 Why does this sisi sit like this when she sits for a photograph? **1976** R.E. PETENI *Hill of Fools* 14 'Why did those girls attack you, sisi?' 'I really don't know.' **1979** M. MATSHOBA *Call Me Not a Man* 111, I approached the tiny woman ... I immediately felt like offering her some kind of protection. 'Er, sorry, *sisi*,' I said to her. **1980** M. MZAMANE in M. Mutloatse *Forced Landing* 25 'I know you weren't chasing me away, Sisi,' I say, 'but I was already on my way out.' **1982** *Drum* July 114 Soweto singer, Sophia Mgcina is said to be on the verge of cracking the international market. Sis Sophie .. is now under the wings of Letta Mbulu and Miriam Makeba. **1989** J. HOBBS *Thoughts in Makeshift Mortuary* 89 This is Sister Quthing. Sisi – Mr Kimber. *Ibid.* 238 Don't forget, these people are crazy in the head about staying pure and unadulterated, Sisi.

b. *Offensive* to many. Usu. in the Englished forms **sissie** and **sissy** /ˈsɪsiː/. Esp. in the Eastern Cape: **i.** A term of address or reference to a black woman (often a domestic worker) whose name is unknown. **ii.** A common noun: a domestic worker.

Habitually used by students and schoolchildren in the Eastern Cape for domestic workers in universities and schools (the male equivalent being *boetie*, see BOETIE sense 4).

1971 *Poster, Rhodes Univ.* We need *you* to teach Sissies and waiters to write. **1976** *Rhodeo* (Rhodes Univ.) 29 Apr., Of the .. black staff a Grahamstown psychologist says the sissies have the roughest deal ... Two daily free meals provided for sissies. **1977** *Oppidan* (Rhodes Univ.) June, He does not like the way students treat the waitresses. 'There are continual screams of "sissie", "sissie" at meals. They don't even bother to find out the names.' **1979** *Daily Dispatch* 23 Mar. (Indaba) 1 The customer said she hated the way they were addressed by the woman, who refers to them as 'sissie'. **1980** J. COCK *Maids & Madams* 94 In Victorian England, servants were deliberately depersonalised and often called by standardised names ... In the Eastern Cape black women are generally called 'Sissy', which indicates something of the same depersonalisation mechanism at work. **1981** *Rhodeo*

(Rhodes Univ.) May, Other matters are now being investigated: the diet of the 'sissies', the salaries of black workers.

2. See quot. 1966.

1966 C.A. SMITH *Common Names* 417 *Sissie*, Several species of plants with umbellate or closely grouped flowers go by this vernacular name, which is perhaps a corruption of 'sussie' (little sister) in allusion to the groups of similar flowers. The various species are distinguished by some character or habitat prefix, e.g.: *Adenandra fragrans*, see *klipkissie*, a name sometimes also applied to *Lachenalia tricolor*..; *Erica ampullacea*, see *flask heath*; *Rochea jasminea*. 1984 A. WANNENBURGH *Natural Wonder of Sn Afr.* 76 Sissies, a member of the Penaeceae family endemic to the south-western Cape, has an even more restricted distribution range as it occurs only in the Cape Peninsula.

siSotho var. SESOTHO.

siss var. SIS *int.*

sissie *n.*[1], **sissy** varr. SISI.

sissie *n.*[2] var. SUSSIE.

sister *n.* [A translation of words used in Sintu (Bantu) languages for a blood sister, but also for a woman friend or acquaintance.] Esp. among speakers of Sintu (Bantu) languages: a courteous term of address or reference to a woman. Cf. SISI sense 1 a, SUSTER.

1902 G.M. THEAL *Beginning of S. Afr. Hist.* 37 This statement arose from their attaching the European meaning to the words sister and daughter, which when used by people of the Bantu race applied equally to cousins and nieces on the father's side. 1963 [see Fugard quot. at SISI sense 1 a]. 1977 P.C. VENTER *Soweto* 120 The shebeen queens are never married or young... They are always addressed as auntie or sister, with a note of deference. 1978 M.W. SEROTE *Behold Mama, Flowers* 40 Tell me what are all these brothers and these sisters doing in the streets frozen like that in these akward poses. 1978 A. ELLIOTT *Sons of Zulu* 167 In real life all the boys and girls of contemporary age belonging to the same clan regard each other as brothers and sisters and all the joint *parents* are their parents. They are called 'father' and 'mother' as readily as are those who bore them. 1990 *Weekend Mail* 13 July 5 In the old days, you did not need to know who someone bearing your name was or where he or she came from. Anyone who bore that name was your brother or sister.

sis tog var. SIESTOG.

Sisuto var. SESOTHO.

siSwati, **Siswati** varr. SWATI sense 1.

siSwazi var. SWAZI *n.* sense 2.

sit *v. intrans. Hist.* In the phr. *to sit up* [calqued on Afk. *opsit*, see OPSIT *v.*], to conduct a courtship by staying up for part of the night (with someone) by the light of a candle, the burning of which determined the duration of the suitor's visit; OPSIT *v.* See also OPSIT *n.*, OPSITKERS, OPSITTING, UPSITTING.

1878 H.A. ROCHE *On Trek in Tvl* 136 The question of questions is, whether she will 'sit up and keep company with him!' If she has consented to do this she has virtually consented to 'sit up' with him as long as they both shall live. 1883 O.E.A. SCHREINER *Story of Afr. Farm* 188 Tant Sannie took two candles out of the cupboard and held them up triumphantly ... 'He's asked for them' she said. 'Does he want them for his horse's .. back?' asked Gregory, new to up-country life. 'No,' said Tant' Sannie indignantly; 'he's going to sit-up!' 1913 J.J. DOKE *Secret City* 106 You are as good as any of them that come courting her, and better too! Ask for your candle like a man, and sit up with her. 1914 L.H. BRINKMAN *Breath of Karroo* 185 Should a young man wish to make advances to a young woman, he asks her to sit up with him, and if she wishes to encourage him, she consents. 1940 F.B. YOUNG *City of Gold* 140 It would certainly be exciting to 'sit up' with any young man and to be told, however clumsily, that he loved her. 1961 D. ROOKE *Lover for Estelle* 36 He had solemnly shown a candle which he carried in his pocket and said to Estelle that they should sit up together that night. 1965 K. MACKENZIE *Deserter* 32 After some years in which he did not see her, he was invited, not long before he left on commando, to come and 'sit up' with her. 1974 *Daily Dispatch* 29 Mar. (Suppl.) 12 You've been sitting up with Nellie an taking her to picnics, and to church, an car riding and nothing's come of it.

Hence **sitting up** *vbl n. phr.*, courting; (staying up for) an evening of courtship; also *attrib.*

1914 L.H. BRINKMAN *Breath of Karroo* 185 The Boer youth's idea of love-making is expressed in the term 'Sitting up'. 1937 H. SAUER *Ex Afr.* 26 On the second visit, the 'sitting up' period in the evening is somewhat more prolonged, but the young man does not finally commit himself yet, and it is only after several 'sittings up' that he puts the vital question. 1958 [see OPSITKERS].

Sitabele var. SINDEBELE.

Sitchuana var. SETSWANA.

Sitebeli, **Sitibela** varr. SINDEBELE.

‖**sitkamer** /'sətkɑːmə(r)/ *n.* Formerly also **sitkaamer**, **sitkomer**, **zit-kamer**. [Afk. (earlier *zitkamer*), *sit* + *kamer* room, chamber.] A sitting room, living room, or parlour; a public lounge.

1902 'INTELLIGENCE OFFICER' *On Heels of De Wet* 88 Those cushions you have on your front seat came out of the Nieuwjaarsfontein sitkomer [sic]. 1904 *Argus Christmas Annual* (Orange River Colony Sect.) 12 He saw his mother standing at the door of the zitkamer ... He went through the empty kitchen to the zit-kamer, empty too. 1908 F.C. SLATER *Sunburnt South* 12 The room into which he showed me was the *zit-kamer* or sitting-room; it was scrupulously neat and tidy. 1909 F. MASEY in *State* Vol.2 No.7, 67 In the 'zitkamer', .. there stands that commonly met feature the curio cabinet. 1912 F. BANCROFT *Veldt Dwellers* 31 It was smoke-room, bar room, and general zit-kamer combined. 1927 F.C. SLATER in *Outspan* 1 Apr. 5 The room into which he showed me was the zit-kamer or sitting-room; it was scrupulously neat and tidy. 1929 J.G. VAN ALPHEN *Jan Venter* 249 The *sitkamer* was packed with visitors. Coffee flowed. 1935 P. SMITH *Platkop's Children* 84 The sit-kamer is so beautiful you know, that Ou-ma Carel never lets the sun shine in it except for a little on Sundays. 1955 W. ROBERTSON *Blue Wagon* 3 Van Zyl and John .. entered the *sit-kamer*, as the general running of the place was called. 1956 A.G. MCRAE *Hill of Doves* 422 'Good Heavens! are you psychic or something?' Anne grinned 'Yah! That's us. Spooks in the sitkamer, spirits on our spoors.' 1964 J. MEINTJES *Manor House* 7 We entered a lounge on the right, the *sitkamer* — a large room with high ceiling on beams. 1964 M.G. MCCOY *Informant*, Port Elizabeth It'll make a lovely family room — keep my sitkamer tidy, for a change. 1971 J.A. BROWN *Return* 79 The door of the cuckoo clock in the *sitkamer* banged in and out.

situation *n. slang*. Pl. -**s**, ‖**ama-** /ˌama-/. [Special sense of general Eng. *situation*; see quots 1963, 1968, and 1982.] In township parlance: a derogatory name for an educated or professional black person, esp. one considered to be a social climber. Cf. EXCUSE-ME.

1963 B. MODISANE *Blame Me on Hist.* (1986) 94 The educated African is resented equally by the blacks because he speaks English, which is one of the symbols of white supremacy, he is resentfully called a Situation, something not belonging to either, but tactfully situated between white oppression and black rebellion. 1968 COLE & FLAHERTY *House of Bondage* 170 As far as they are able, middle-class African families will try to behave like Englishmen ... Such people choose their associations with care ... The tsotsis contemptuously call them 'situations,' because they try to reject all but the topmost social situation. 1977 J. SIKAKANE *Window on Soweto* 9 The ghetto dwellers generally refer to Dube Township as the home of 'Situations' because it is choice situated, or as the place of 'excuse me's' because the African intelligentsia residing there prefer speaking English. 1982 M. MZAMANE *Children of Soweto* 153 They were called *Ama-Situation* by township people because they were forever trying to situate themselves out of everyone else's social orbit. 1983 [see LARNEY *n.* sense 1 a]. 1984 *Natal Mercury* 8 June, There are also the 'situations'. A situation is a person who probably talks English all the time. He thinks he's fine. He is above the ordinary people. 1984 *Drum* Sept. 26 He was not like the hoity-toity, starchy teachers we called 'situations'.

Sixer *n.* Ellipt. for *District Sixer* (see DISTRICT SIX).

1979 *Voice* 4 Mar. 7 But I know something which all 'Sixers know. That old indominable spirit that was District Six will not rest.

Si-Xosa var. XHOSA.

‖**siyavuma** /siːaˈvʊːma/ *int.* Also **si ya vuma**, **siya vuma**, **vooma**. [In Nguni languages, first pers. pl. pref. *si* we + aux. with *-ya-* (forming definite present tense) + *vuma* assent, agree.] Among Xhosa- and Zulu-speaking people: 'we agree', the traditional response when a diviner's diagnosis meets with approval; also found in other contexts.

1875 D. LESLIE *Among Zulus* 79 He speaks, all stretching forward .., their eyes bent on the ground, and at every pause crying 'vooma' (we agree). 1891 T.R. BEATTIE *Pambaniso* 18 He is made aware when he has guessed wide of the mark by the attitude of those who are consulting him, for then they make no response whatever, but when he luckily mentions the 'thing' they strike their hands together, and shout '*Siyavuma!*' — we assent. 1899 A. WERNER *Captain of Locusts* 60 'Grandfather, are you coming to supper?' 'All right, lass — si ya vuma — you may bet Mr Graham's ready for it after listening to dry yarns all this time.' 1928 N. DEVITT *Blue Lizard* 109 The magician spoke to them short, sharp words, then paused and with each pause listened for the answering words 'si ya vuma'. 1934 C.P. SWART Supplement to Pettman. 156 *Si ya vuma*, .. The revelations of a witch-doctor are usually punctuated by a chorus of Natives who clap their hands and shout out these words whenever the oracle prophesies. 1972 *Daily Dispatch* 14 May 1 He spoke to his ancestors in a chanting tone and was greeted by cries of 'siyavuma' (we agree). 1976 WEST & MORRIS *Abantu* 20 After each one the audience claps and shouts 'Siya vuma!' (we agree) or 'Asiva' (we do not hear), if he is off the track. 1978 A.P. BRINK *Rumours of Rain* 44, I knew Charlie to be a born negotiator. He appeared to handle their barrage of questions with consummate skill ... He was applauded with a thundering: 'Siya vuma!' 1980 *Daily Dispatch* 10 Oct. (Indaba) 4 Modern man is as superstitious as his forefathers. 'Vumani, Siya vuma' cry the igquira with his audience. Halleluya, Amen to St so-and-so,' say the Christians in their beautiful buildings.

siyayinyova /ˌsiːajinˈjɔːva/ *int.* and *n.* Also **sayinyova**, **siya inyova**, **siyanyova**. [Zulu sentence, 'we are going to crush it', 'we are going to turn it upside down'.]

‖**A.** *int.* 'We are going to destroy': a slogan chanted at left-wing political marches and associated particularly with young political activists.

1985 *Drum* Dec. 30 Once pupils take up the battle cry 'Siya Inyova — We are spoiling for trouble' no one dare stand in their way. 1986 F. CHIKANE in Burman & Reynolds *Growing Up* 343 Nursery school children .. too have learned the language of *siyayinyova* (we will destroy), which is the popular slogan used by the youths when attacking what they call 'targets', meaning the buildings, vehicles, and individuals regarded as symbols of the apartheid regime and its forces. 1987 G. MHLOPE in *Best of S. Afr. Short Stories* (1991) 453 Young children who hardly understand what is really going on are also shouting the slogan 'Siyayinyova' which simply means 'We will destroy or disrupt'. *Ibid.* 454 They poured out of their classes ... They were shouting 'Siyayinyova!' at the tops of their little voices. They picked up rocks and bricks and started attacking buses, company delivery vans and police cars.

B. *n.* Pl. **-s**, **abo-**, or unchanged. [The pl. prefix *abo-* is fr. the Nguni languages.] A young activist, esp. one advocating or taking part in violent protest, or in the informal policing of a township. Cf. COMRADE.

1986 *True Love* Feb. 2 When people are not talking about 'abosayinyova', the talk in taxis, buses, trains and homes is about the randy gorilla. **1986** *Pace* May 4 Since the advent of the 'comrades' and 'siyayinyovas' housewives are forever beaming as they carry out their household duties. **1986** *Learn & Teach* No.5, 35 Do you think the siyayinyova's think I look smart. No, they think I look like a policeman. **1987** K. SOLE in *Eng. Academy Rev.* 4 Jan. 23 Parents begin to whisper ill of the siyayinyova, those purposeful young men he idolizes. **1988** Z.C. NDABA in *Staffrider* Vol.7 No.1, 20 Since they left school they have been associating with bad elements. They have even joined abo 'siyayinyova' ... He knew that the township would be buzzing with the 'comrades' singing and chanting in the streets and that if they found him there he would be doused with petrol and set alight. He had heard too many such stories since 'abo siyayinyova' had come to rule the township.

sjambok /ˈʃæmbɒk, ‖ʃamˈbɔk/ *n.* Also **chamboc(k)**, **chanbok**, **jamboc**, **jambok**, **samboc**, **sambo(c)k**, **sam-bok**, **sambuc(k)**, **s(c)hambok**, **shambock**, **sjamboc**, **sjambohk**. [S. Afr. Du. *tjambok*, *s(j)ambok* fr. Malay *tjambok*, *samboq*, ad. Urdu *chabuk* horsewhip.]

a. A heavy whip, formerly cut from rhinoceros or hippopotamus hide but now often made of plastic or rubber, used for driving animals or administering punishment. Also *attrib.* See also AFTER SJAMBOK, AGTEROS SJAMBOK, AGTER SJAMBOK.

1790 tr. *F. Le Vaillant's Trav.* I. 368 Next morning my people were employed in cutting to pieces the hide of the hippopotamus, to make what in the country are called *chanboc*. These are whips for flogging the oxen. **1801** W. SOMERVILLE *Narr. of E. Cape Frontier* (1979) 78 The Hide which is about two inches thick is used for whips, it is cut into proper lengths as broad as thick and when dried it is planed into the tapering shape of a jockey whip — and called a shamboc, too often an instrument of inhumanity in the hands of those who wield it. **1802** in G.M. Theal *Rec. of Cape Col.* (1899) IV. 325 He had received upwards of 36 strokes with a solid Sjambok. **1804** J. BARROW *Trav.* II. 96 One of those infernal whips .. known by the name of *sambocs*. **1812** A. PLUMPTRE tr. *H. Lichtenstein's Trav. in Sn Afr.* I. 98 The skin [of the rhinoceros] is the only thing valuable to the colonists to cut into strips for making the driving whips known here by the Malay name of *Schamboks*. **1816** G. BARKER Journal. 29 Jan., Another .. had been shamefully beaten, having large marks on her back from the Sambok. **1822** W.J. BURCHELL *Trav.* I. 86 The shambok, here mentioned, is a strip, three feet or more in length, of the hide either of a hippopotamus or of a rhinoceros, rounded to the thickness of a man's finger, and tapering to the top. *a*1827 D. CARMICHAEL in W.J. Hooker *Botanical Misc.* (1831) II. 34 Of the hide of the *Rhinoceros* and *Hippopotamus*, the boors manufacture a sort of horse-whip, known by the name of *Shambok*. **1834** T. PRINGLE *Afr. Sketches* 379 These sort of whips, which they call *sjambocs*, are most horrid instruments, being tough, pliant, and heavy almost as lead. **1840** *Echo* 20 July 7 He .. ordered me to lie down that he might chastise me, and I would not (because it was not, my countrymen, a common sambok in his hand, but a large new one). **1846** *Natal Witness* 7 Aug., Market Intelligence ... Shambocks, 15s. per dozen. **1849** N.J. MERRIMAN *Cape Jrnls* (1957) 40 The Sambuc is the common whip here, being a strip of the hide of a sea cow ... I shall keep it and take care of it (which means something very significant with a Sambuc, to wit much doctoring with cow dung and oil). **1853** F.P. FLEMING *Kaffraria* 47 In front of the cardell is the waggon-box, on which the driver sits, .. having at his side a 'jambok' .. a kind of long cutting whip, about three feet in length, composed of a strip of the skin of the hippopotamus, about two inches thick at the handle, and tapering to a point at its extremity. **1872** C.A. PAYTON *Diamond Diggings* 90 The driver, by dint of much yelling and whipping, and his sable assistants by running beside the bullocks and belabouring them with the terrible 'sjambok,' managed to overcome the constitutional slowness of these animals. **1908** D. BLACKBURN *Leaven* (1991) 24 Mr Betts took up the sjambok .. — a tapering rod of rhinoceros hide, tough and flexible as the gutta percha it resembled. **1910** D. FAIRBRIDGE *That Which Hath Been* (1913) 156 The baas beat him with the sjambok, mevrouw, until he thought he was dead, and they rode away and left him lying on the ground. **1916** *Farmer's Weekly* 20 Dec. 1458 (*advt*) Sjamboks — Achter Sjamboks 8s. 6d., Walking Sjamboks (curved handle) 8s. 6d., Riding Whips 3s. and 5s. **1956** A. SAMPSON *Drum* 40 At dawn on the Monday we were herded into the fields by black and white men, riding horses and carrying sjambohks. **1963** L.F. FREED *Crime in S. Afr.* 265 She gave me such a hiding with a sjambok that I could not go to work for some days. **1971** *Cape Times* 25 Mar. 2 A Coloured boy's hands were tied together after which he was hit with a plastic sjambok. **1974** *Sunday Times* 27 Oct. (Mag. Sect.) 2 The legkotla tries offenders and dispenses the rough justice of public floggings with a sjambok on Sunday mornings in Naledi township. **1977** J. HOBBS in *Quarry '77* 7 One night he beat the most recently pregnant of his daughters with the orange plastic *sjambok* he kept for the compound dogs. **1980** *Cape Times* 16 July 1 The police are using 'quirts' — short-handled riding-whips — and not sjamboks, to quell unrest in the Eastern Cape. **1985** K. OWEN in *Sunday Times* 15 Sept. 22 Every time a policeman looses a round of birdshot, or swings a quirt (or whatever we call sjamboks these days), he recruits another child to the cause. **1986** *E. Prov. Herald* 7 Apr. 2 Police Casspirs and SADF Buffels surrounded the Centenary Great Hall ... Rifles were cocked and some police carried orange sjamboks. **1986** *New African* May 10 A swollen eye, a lacerated lip and sjambok weals on his back. **1986** C. MANN in *Frontline* June 17 Bored, nervous, Pieter the soldier climbs forth, .. and .. with a sjambok of rubber, .. turns to confront with a swish and a grunt the chants of the children gathering in the shadows. **1992** J. PEARCE in *South* 27 Feb. 4 The police hit a person with a sjambok or the buckle of a belt and they swear at you.

b. *Fig.* and *transf.*, usu. *attrib.*, alluding to violent, aggressive, or threatening behaviour.

1898 G. NICHOLSON *50 Yrs* 169 Gibeonites, and black ones at that, generally had to put up with a good allowance of 'Sambok' treatment in those days. **1989** S. BILAC in *Personality* 10 Apr. 30 The government's uninspiring 'sjambok-and-carrot' approach to reform. **1991** F.G. BUTLER *Local Habitation* 233 The disastrous combination of corrupt intellectuals and the sjambok complex of the lower white. **1992** C.M. KNOX tr. *E. Van Heerden's Mad Dog* 5 From some farmers a man simply wouldn't take a job if he could possibly help it. These were the sjambok farmers, who gave you nothing but bokkems, mealie meal and trouble.

c. *comb.* (objective) **sjambok-carrying**, **sjambok-wielding** *ppl adjs.*

1952 *Drum* Mar. 7 At dawn .. we were herded into the fields by horse-riding, sjambok-carrying black and white men. **1989** A. DONALDSON in *Style* Aug. 96 A youth being whipped by sjambok-wielding men while others stood around laughing.

sjambok /ˈʃæmbɒk/ *v. trans.* Also **sjambook**. [fr. prec.] To strike or flog (someone or something) with a sjambok.

1853 *Natal Mercury* 6 Jan., He .. sjamboked them. **1853** R.B. STRUTHERS *Hunting Jrnl* (1991) 26 The rascal I sjambokked yesterday sent back the things he had stolen. **1881** *Blackwood's Mag.* (U.K.) Dec. 756 To associate or have anything to do with blacks, except to make them work, or *sjambook* them if they don't work hard is an unpardonable offence in a Boer's eyes. **1894** E. GLANVILLE *Fair Colonist* 116, I would cheerfully sjambok a stock-lifter until he dropped. **1900** F.R.M. CLEAVER in M.M. Cleaver *Young S. Afr.* (1913) 155, I personally felt as if I had been sjambokked all over and hung out to stiffen. **1900** R. KIPLING in J. Crwys-Williams *S. Afr. Despatches* (1989) 160 Suppose you had dismissed a servant, or got him sjamboked, and he saw you go out? He would wait for you to come back on a tired horse, and then ... You see? **1928** E.H.L. SCHWARZ *Kalahari & its Native Races* 85 On one occasion he jumped on the back of one of the traders, and sjamboked him. **1943** I. FRACK *S. Afr. Doctor* 63 Conscription of labour in the best Hitlerian manner, sjamboking the hide of the black to get the devil out of him and make him work better. **1962** L.E. NEAME *Hist. of Apartheid* 108 The labourers alleged that they were worked long hours with insufficient food and were sjambokked if they did not work fast enough. **1986** *Weekly Mail* 21 Nov. 2 A union official kneeled on the ground in front of the police ... The next moment a policeman was sjambokking him. **1993** *Daily News* 13 Jan. 1 She had been sjambokked several times because she was thought to have been involved in witchcraft.

Hence **sjambokker** *n.*, one who uses a sjambok; **sjambok(k)ing** *vbl n.*, a whipping with a sjambok (also *fig.*).

1899 G.H. RUSSELL *Under Sjambok* 247 True, I have given him many a sjamboking — so has my father; but I think he will help us for all that. **1908** D. BLACKBURN *I Came & Saw* 208 Your sjambokking of Sixpence gave me the idea for the Humanitarian Company. **1937** C.R. PRANCE *Tante Rebella's Saga* 60 He .. settled him the good old way with a good sjamboking. **1953** *Cape Times* 30 Mar. 1 A police investigation into the alleged sjambokking of two United Party canvassers ... The sjambokker came outside and hit .. Mr Eddy .. on the legs. **1980** *Listener* (U.K.) 17 Apr. 487 Lilford, landowner and power behind Smith and the Rhodesian Front, gave me a verbal sjambokking over the telephone. **1985** *Sunday Star* 27 Oct. 16 One thing is becoming clear: Police action, declaration of emergencies, sabre-rattling, water cannons and sjambokking will not halt the unrest. **1989** D. KRAMER in *ADA* No.7, 8 All the beatings and sjambokking and stuff going on in the Cape Flats.

sjita var. ISIJITA.

sjoe var. SHU.

Sk *n. obs.* Written abbrev. of *skilling*, see SCHELLING.

1824 *Albany Settlers 1824–1836* (Soc. for Relief of Distressed Settlers) (1836) 6 During the past year the sum of Rds. 2 767, 4 Sks. has been expended, partly in small donations of money and partly in the purchase of blankets and warm clothing. **1832** [see PONTAC sense 1].

skaal var. SCALE.

skaam /skɑːm/ *adj.* and *n. Slang.* [Afk. adj. (fr. n. *skaamte* shame, shyness).]

A. *adj.* Shy, embarrassed, bashful.

1970 V. YOUNG *Informant, Queenstown*, I feel skaam to meet those people (shy or ashamed.) **1976** *Darling* in J. Branford *Dict. of S. Afr. Eng.* (1987) 320 'Cut it out, man ..' Frik mutters, getting all skaam at the way she's performing .. 'Don't give us a hard time now, doll.' **1991** K. SULLIVAN *Informant, Cape Town*, I felt very skaam today — you really put me in the eyes.

B. *n.* Remorse, (sense of) shame.

1970 *Informant, Grahamstown* That little boy has no skaam. **1985** *Frontline* Aug. 54 Maybe we'll help him along with a bit of the rifle butt ... I feel no skaam.

skaap /skɑːp/ *n.* Also **schaap**. [Afk. *skaap* (earlier S. Afr. Du. *schaap*) sheep.]

‖**1.**

a. A sheep; mutton.

1882 C. DU VAL *With Show through Sn Afr.* I. 270 When you have filled his flesh-pots with the stew of the 'schaap', (sheep), his pipe with Boer tobacco, and poured him out a decoction he is pleased to call coffee, .. you have crowned his happiness in the present. **1886** G.A. FARINI *Through Kalahari Desert* 83 If we would buy a sheep and share it with him, he would give us another when he got home; to this we of course assented, and the *skaap* was soon bought, caught, and slaughtered. **1966** L.G. BERGER *Where's Madam* 149 Carmel was supposed to be a superb cook, but all the time I was there, we lived on skaap which appeared interminably. [**1980** *Daily Dispatch* 3 Dec. 2 Operation Skaap helps Durban needy. A record number of sheep are to be sent to Durban for distribution among the needy ... The custom, called Operation Skaap, was started by the late Moth Ebbo Bastard in Kokstad in 1946 and has been continued annually.]

b. *comb.* **skaaps poo(i)tjies** /-pɔikis/ [Afk., linking phoneme *-s-* + *pootjies* trotters], sheep's trotters; **skaapvleis** /-fleɪs/ [Afk., *vleis* meat], mutton.

1982 *Pace* June 60 Sheep's feet, **skaaps pooitjies**, amanqina .. call them what you will, they were once freely available as a cheap and tasty snack on the long way home from work ... There were no sellers of skaaps pooitjies at all in that crowded market place at Dube. **1882** C. DU VAL *With Show through Sn Afr.* I. 63 Dinner at a Dutch farmhouse, *en route* to the Diamond Fields, is a delightful simplicity, consisting chiefly of '**schaap fleish**' — (mutton) — eggs, brown-bread, and coffee.

2. *fig. derog.* Also **ska(a)pie** [see -IE].

a. (Latterly esp. in township slang) a simpleton; a country bumpkin; a fool.

1925 H.J. MANDELBROTE tr. *O.F. Mentzel's Descr. of Cape of G.H.* II. 97 The bystanders made fun of me, for I was the 'schaap', yet I explained that .. I had not done so badly. **1944** 'TWEDE IN BEVEL' *Piet Kolonel* 130 He was never noisy in enforcing discipline or giving orders; there was no shouting at or to his men. When irritated, he found the use of the word 'skaap' most effective. **1965** E. MPHAHLELE *Down Second Ave* 41, I had stopped worrying over being called *skapie* — sheep — I was told that's the label they stuck on to anybody fresh from the country. **1970** M. DIKOBE Marabi Dance. 108 Sepai is not a boy like the town ones. He is what we call 'scapie — sheep'. He won't allow me to go to the Social Centre or Bioscope. **1970** C.B. WOOD *Informant, Johannesburg* He's a real 'skaap' (stupid chap). **1976** *Citizen* 9 Dec. 7 Skaap — expression used to anger or wound person (e.g. 'Can't you talk proper yet, you skaap?'). **1978** A. AKHALWAYA in *Rand Daily Mail* 10 July 7 The 'lahnie' may think the 'lightie' is a 'sny' or a 'skapie' or a 'kabaab', but the lad is no bumpkin. **1978** L. BARNES in *The 1820* Vol.51 No.12, 19 If you want to call somebody a fool, you can take your pick from *kabab, skaberash, pookoo, garrak* and a host of others — all of them are 'right way skapies'. **1982** M. MZAMANE *Children of Soweto* 36 'He's not doing too badly for a country skaapie,' Monty said. [**1982** D. BIKITSHA in *Rand Daily Mail* 14 Oct. (Eve) 5 A fool, country bumpkin or yokel had a variety of titles [in 'isicamtho'] too: vossie, mogo, skappie, barrie, zeff, battersby, mommish zow or zao.] **1988** S. SOLE in *Style* Apr. 48 After I had the car, I phoned this Captain, told him he is a skapie (sheep). Jee was he cross for me. **1988** S. WOODGATE in *Star* 10 May 3 Johannesburg's controversial George Harrison statue was defaced at the weekend ... The word, 'skaap' (sheep), as well as two Stars of David were stencilled in white on the 13m-high monument.

b. An insulting name for an Afrikaner.

1981 [see HAIRYBACK]. **1992** E.M. MACPHAIL *Mrs Chud's Place* 15 Listen, Duif. I am called a *skaap. Ja*, and who called the French frogs, hey? Yes, and what about Yids and Huns?

skaapbos, skaapbossie /ˈskɑːpbɔs(i)/ *n.* Formerly also **schaapbosch(je), schaapbos(je)**. [Afk. (earlier S. Afr. Du. *schaapbosch, skaapboschje*), *skaap* sheep + *bos* bush (+ -IE).] Any type of *Karoo bush* (see KAROO sense 2) suitable for use as grazing for sheep.

1872 E.J. DUNN in A.M.L. Robinson *Sel. Articles from Cape Monthly Mag.* (1978) 39 Covering the ground is .. a tiny shrub, seldom attaining the height of one foot, called 'schaap bosch'. On this sheep and all kinds of cattle live and fatten, preferring it to grass or any other kind of vegetation. *Ibid.* 64 Fraserburg itself is rather a small village ... Round about grows the useful 'schaapbosch', on which the value of wool so much depends throughout this region. **1906** F. BLERSCH *Handbk of Agric.* 254 Though plants bearing common names such as rooi gras, Schaap boschje, karroo boschje, aar boschje, etc., convey the meaning of their being useful and valuable, it does not signify that they are botanically the same plant everywhere ... The valuable *schaap boschjes* belong to the *Pentzia* group. **1910** A.B. LAMONT *Rural Reader* 257 The schaapbos or good Karoo, is one of the best known of the smaller bushes. **1917** R. MARLOTH *Common Names* 72 *Schaap'bos, Pentzia virgata*. One of the most valuable fodder-shrublets of the Karoo (= Goed'karoo). In some districts the same name applies to *Felicia fascicularis*. **1937** *Handbk for Farmers* (Dept of Agric. & Forestry) 395 *Pentzia incana forma* (Goeie karo, skaapbossie) ... A variety of forms, differing considerably in appearance and palatability to stock. **1966** C.A. SMITH *Common Names* 418 *Skaapbossie*, Nowadays more frequently used as a general term for any fodder bush which is not only relished by sheep but also on which they fatten, and usually employed in certain districts with specific reference to only a few such species. **1977** *Fair Lady* 8 June (Suppl.) 23 Brenda Landman adds some 'Skaapbos' to her lamb. This is the bush the sheep eat which seems to give Karoo lamb that unique flavour. **1993** S. DIKENI in *House & Leisure* Nov. 42 The Karoo sun .. will whisper .. good morning .. on the breath of awakening *skaapbossies* and herbs.

skaapie see SKAAP sense 2.

skaapplaas /ˈskɑːplɑːs/ *n.* [Afk., lit. 'sheep farm'.] Either of two lawn grasses: **a.** The drought-resistant grass *Cenchrus ciliaris; blue buffalo grass*, see BUFFALO GRASS sense 2. **b.** *Eragrostis nindensis*. Also *attrib.*

1968 *Farmer's Weekly* 3 Jan. 91 *Skaapplaas*. The most sought after grass, usually in short supply, now available again. **1971** *Daily Dispatch* 22 Nov. 10 We've got a wide variety of lawn grasses in South Africa ... Florida, Elliot, Skaapplaas, Magennis, Royal Cape. **1973** *S. Afr. Garden & Home* Jan. 50 A Transvaal company specialising in turf uses skaapplaas, one of the finest of lawn grasses. **1975** *Ibid.* Mar. 13 How can I get rid of kweek from my skaapplaas lawn and my brickface pathways?

skaapribbetjie see RIBBETJIE.

skaapsteker /ˈskɑːpˌstɪəkə(r)/ *n.* Formerly also **scarpsticker, schaap stecker, schaap-ste(e)ker, schaapsti(c)ker, schapsticker**. [Afk., earlier S. Afr. Du. *schaapsteker, schaap* sheep + *steker* piercer, sticker; so called because reputed to attack sheep.] Any of several venomous (but unaggressive) snakes of the genus *Psammophyllax*, esp. *P. rhombeatus* and *P. tritaeniatus*, both greyish-brown with darker markings; SHEEP-STICKER; SHEEP-STINGER; SHEEP-STRIKER.

In B. Branch's *Field Guide to Snakes* (1988), the name spotted or rhombic skaapsteker is used for *P. rhombeatus*, and 'striped skaapsteker' for *P. tritaeniatus*.

1818 C.I. LATROBE *Jrnl of Visit* 353 Our good natured Hottentots, perceiving that I had begun to collect serpents, brought me several kinds, among which were the .. schaapsteker, (sheep stinger); and copra di capella. **1834** T. PRINGLE *Afr. Sketches* 280 There are several species of snakes .. such as the nacht-slang (night adder), the schaap-steeker (sheep-stinger), [etc.]. **1847** 'A BENGALI' *Notes on Cape of G.H.* 82 The 'schaap-stikker' or *sheep-stifler*; and the 'Ringel Hals' or *Ring-throat*, all venomous. **1856** C.J. ANDERSSON *Lake Ngami* 303 Different species of what the Dutch term 'schaap-steker,' or sheep-stinger .. are also occasionally met with. **1890** A. MARTIN *Home Life* 256 The *schaapsticker* .. has a wonderfully marked skin, the pretty and bright tints of which might well be utilized by some artistic designer of floor-cloths. **1905** W.L. SCLATER in Flint & Gilchrist *Science in S. Afr.* 147 Among the *Opisthoglypha*, the commonest forms are the so-called night adder .. and the Schaap-stikker or sheep stinger (*Trimerorohinus rhombeatus*), a handsome species with rhomboid brown markings on the back and sides. **1910** V.F.M. FITZSIMONS *Snakes of S. Afr.* 57 The farmer, or his herdman comes along, finds the dying sheep, and seeing Schaapstekers about, immediately concludes they are the guilty parties, hence the name Schaapsteker, which means sheep-sticker. **1939** *Outspan* 16 June 29 Back-fanged snakes, e.g. boomslang, herald snake or skaapstekers, have their fangs situated between the front and base of the upper jaw, also on either side, and in the back maxilliary bone. **1947** L.G. GREEN *Tavern of Seas* 121 You may meet a yellow cobra in a suburban garden, a skaapsteker in the backyard, a puffadder or boomslang in your path as you walk up the slopes of Table Mountain. **1971** *The 1820* Vol.43 No.10, 20 Skaapstekers and boomslangs are venomous, but they are back-fanged snakes and not aggressive, so we do not worry about them. **1973** *Std Encycl. of Sn Afr.* IX. 651 The name skaapsteker is quite misleading and unfortunate, as there is certainly no truth in the widespread belief that these snakes are in the habit of biting and killing sheep. **1985** *S.-Easter* Oct.-Nov. 35 My partner claims he spotted a snake (a Rhombic, or spotted Skaapsteker, he thinks it was), but I think he was just trying to speed up the pace.

skaapwachter, -wagter varr. SCHAAPWACHTER.

skabanga, skabenga varr. SKEBENGA.

skaf var. SCOFF *n.*[2]

skammel var. SCHAMMEL.

skandaal /skanˈdɑːl/ *n. colloq.* [Afk., scandal.] A scandal (and the consequent uproar) which is considered to be exaggerated or ultimately insignificant.

1986 *Fair Lady* 5 Mar. 61 An aristocrat whose background of high society *skandaal* is so stupendous that it surpasses everything that's ever happened on Dallas and Dynasty combined. **1990** *Personality* 4 June 7 The best is yet to come in *Loving* ... There's huge skok, skandaal and drama to come. **1990** J. EVANS in *Ibid.* 18 June 51 Along came this ditsy American adorned with plastic bangles, lace leggings and *skok! skandaal!* no shirt over her black bra! And singing about sex *nogal!* **1991** L. WILLIAMS on Radio South Africa 15 Mar. (Woman's World), Do you remember the skandaal when Elwyn Morris was the first woman to read the news? **1991** G. PINE-JAMES on TV1, 10 Sept., I'm not allowed to enter [the competition]. Can you imagine the skandaal if I won? It would be ridiculous. **1992** K. WILLIAMS in *South* 27 Feb. 23 No reports of I—'s arrogance could prepare me for the skandaal he caused in that quiet, little Woodstock Holiday Inn.

skande /ˈskandə/ *int.* and *n.* [Afk.]

A. *int.* Often in political contexts: 'disgraceful', an exclamation of disapproval or disgust; also used ironically. Cf. SIS *int.*

1973 *Argus* 12 Oct. 3 Amid calls of 'sies' and 'skande' he pointed out that Whites and non-Whites were forced to make use of the same changing rooms, showers and toilets. **1974** *Star* 30 Sept. 28 The expelled men have been accused of backing their own men for Cape party posts (skande!), raising money to help their campaign and talking to a hostile political correspondent. **1979** *Daily Dispatch* 22 Feb. 3 'It could only have been a political murder.' 'What do you know about it?' shouted one Nationalist Senator. 'Skande,' cried several others. **1980** *Sunday Times* 23 Nov. 29 Some of the older traditionalists .. insist that 'ware' (true) boeremusiek is not played with electric guitars, organs and drums. Skande! **1981** *Ibid.* 23 Aug. 6 Skande, if not actually sies! Permissiveness is having its way in the land. **1985** *S.-Easter* Aug.-Sept. 9 Probably because the conservationists weren't born yet, the house was demolished in 1935 to make way for a factory. *Skande.* **1988** *E. Prov. Herald* 13 Feb. 1 Amid a chorus of interjections and cries of 'skande' from government benches, Mr Van Eck said the Minister of Law and Order .. had 'the blood of detainees on his hands'. **1989** *Ibid.* 8 Feb. 1 Cries of 'skande,

skande' from opposition benches. **1992** G. ETHERINGTON in *Weekend Post* 2 May (Leisure) 1, I had unwittingly alienated most of the diners by the time the meal ended — thanks to cricket. This is not a game I generally follow (*skande*).

B. *n.*

1. A disgrace; a scandal.

1974 *Daily Dispatch* 26 Nov. 15 Their lack of manners was a 'disgrace,' a 'skande' and a slur on the French hosts. **1985** *Weekly Mail* 18 Oct. 9 The President was condemned as a traitor, and his new constitution as '*skande*' by the several thousand supporters of the far-right Volkswag movement. **1988** *Cape Times* 8 Aug. 2 It was an absolute 'skande' that black policemen took the fingerprints of white women, black hospital staff treated whites, and black children were allowed to mix with their white counterparts on sports fields, Conservative Party members said. **1990** *Weekend Post* 27 Oct. 1 It's the *skande* of Queenstown ... Women have been illegally exposing their midriffs at the city swimming bath for 44 years!

2. Scandal-mongering. Also *attrib.*

1985 J. THOMAS in *Fair Lady* 1 May 20 Boetie, lies and skande are punishable by 20 km pole PT and leopard crawl. **1991** S. BRITTEN in *Style* Nov. 108 All I had to go on were the *skande* articles in *You* magazine.

skans var. SCHANS.

skapie see SKAAP sense 2.

skarm var. SKERM.

‖**skat, skattie** /skat(i)/ *n.* [Afk. (see also -IE).] 'Darling', 'beloved', 'treasure': a term of endearment.

*c***1964** M. JABOUR in *New S. Afr. Writing* 21 You listen to Ouma, skat. Ouma won't tell you wrong. **1967** J. HOBBS in *Ibid.* IV. 65 He said to Magdalena, his wife, 'Skat,' he said, 'we will call it Scheepersdal, and so will our sons after us and our grandsons.' **1974** *Daily Dispatch* 28 May 22 (*cartoon*) No braaivleis, skat. **1982** [see COME sense 1]. **1985** *Cape Times* 3 Aug. (*cartoon*) Don't worry, Skattie, Bapetikosweti will stick with you through thick and thin. **1989** J. LECOAT in *Cosmopolitan* Apr. 34 One summer's day, her father came home early from work. 'I've found you a drum *skattie*,' he told her. 'You come down and see.' **1990** C. LEONARD in *Weekly Mail* 2 Nov. 29 'Yes, I'll have another brandy and Coke, skattie,' Bennie's wife says. **1990** G. SILBER in *Sunday Times* 16 Dec. (Mag. Sect.) 24 A no-holds-barred biography of the life and times of Evita Bezuidenhout, South Africa's Sacred Cow and Ambassadress to Bapetikosweti: what a wonderful idea, skatties! **1990** G. NEVILL in *Sunday Times* 30 Dec. 1 Don't be pessimistic, skatties.

skate *n. Derog. slang.* [Etym. dubious: perh. a narrowing of sense of the general Eng. *skate* mean or contemptible person (as in *cheap-skate*); or a Royal Navy name for a troublesome rating, 'a leave-breaker and "bad hat" generally' (E. Partridge, *Dict. of Slang*, 1967); or perh. fr. Afk. *skuit* (see Goldstuck quot., 1983).] A disreputable white male (from a working-class background) whose behaviour is uncouth, hedonistic, and irresponsible; GÉ sense 2.

1975 *Informant, Grahamstown* Skate. Difficult to define. Low class. Wear all the wrong things — don't know what goes, don't know how to behave. Usually four in a Cortina G.T. with G.T. stripes, fluff on the dash board and an orange on the aerial ... Behaviour rather than speech is the determinant. **1983** A. GOLDSTUCK in *Frontline* Oct. 58 This is the skuit (or skate, if you're saying it in English). In colloquial Afrikaans the word refers to excretion, but .. the people thus labelled consider it a term of endearment. Which says something about the skates ... They're South Africa's answer to the punks or the skinheads of Britain. Nihilists. *Ibid.* 61 The skate has his own dialect ... 'I got a graft, a cabbie, I got stukkies, booze, and I got zol. I tune you, mate, if I can get one mamba chow a day, I scheme life is kif' ... Freddie has vacant eyes, a happy brain, a pile of threatening letters from the SADF, a yen for anything punishable by law, and immense debts. In short, he is a fully qualified skate, able to operate anywhere on the East Rand ... Jonathan Handley .. has been making a study of the skate subculture ... 'The skate .. is unemployed, lives with his parents, and has no direction in life ... He isn't the rebel without a cause. He is no longer the romantic that the ducktail was.' **1983** *Cape Times* 9 Dec. 16 The 1950s skates .. knew their virility lay in their greased back hair. **1987** P. SLABOLEPSZY in *Style* May 100 They're not really 'skates'. There are a helluva lot of people who're like that out there and they've made a lot of money, and they're basically middle-class. **1989** M. BRAND in *Fair Lady* 25 Oct. 93 Danger: these buzz words have gone decidedly off ... *Kugel* (borderline case). *Moffie. Safe. Skate.* [etc.].

skattie see SKAT.

skayf var. SKYF.

skdonk var. SKEDONK.

skea var. SKEY.

skebenga /skəˈbeŋgə, skeˈbeːŋga/ *n.* Also **scabanga, skabanga, skabenga, skebengo, skebengu.** [ad. Zulu *isigebengu* bandit, plunderer, fr. *gebenga* live a plundering life, assault (someone).] A gangster, bandit, or robber; a scoundrel or rascal. Also *attrib.* Cf. AMALAITA, SPOILER.

1953 R. CAMPBELL *Mamba's Precipice* 15 1 The alarm is out for Mahakaan, the skebenga who murdered the two cousins of the Ninevite gang of ritual murderers. *Ibid.* 170 Like a trapped wolf, the *skebenga* died, knowing he was caught, but growling curses. [*Note*] Skebenga means foot-pad or bandit. **1962** J. TAYLOR 'Tsotsi Style'. (*lyrics*), I got no more food in my stomach Tell me what me to do The skebengas got all the money So I became a tsotsi too. **1964** G. CAMPBELL *Old Dusty* 89 These practices must not be confounded with those of the ordinary *skebenga*, the latter being merely a low-class thief and foot-pad who would rob his mother's hen-roost. **1970** *Informant, Durban* He will not stay at home alone as he fears that a skebenga may come. **1975** J. MCCLURE *Snake* (1981) 164 *Hau, hau, hau,* but he was a real *skabenga* when he was small, that one. **1978** L. BARNES in *The 1820* Vol.51 No.12, 19 Many Zulu words have crept into South African Indian English ... Some of the most commonly used are: *Skoten* (from *isikhoteni*) — a rogue, .. *skebengu* — thief, [etc.]. **1980** D.B. COPLAN *Urbanization of African Performing Arts.* 142 Following his apprenticeship as an accomplice of White criminals in Johannesburg, a Zulu houseboy, Jan Note, assumed leadership of a community of migrant contract deserters and landless laborers living as '*skebengos*' (Zulu: *izigebhengu*, 'bandits') in the hills south of the city ... Gradually these rural-based peasant marginals were joined by urban proletarians drawn from the informal sectors of the economy ... The gang made the transition to an urban-based, multi-ethnic underworld alliance ... The gang organized burglaries, robbery, prostitution, gambling, illicit liquor, and *dagga* smuggling throughout the southern Transvaal. **1982** *Sunday Times* 14 Nov. (Mag. Sect.) 10 There were pimps and bums ... There were scabangas and scruffs and sophisticates. **1988** W. BIZLEY in Laband & Haswell *Pietermaritzburg 1838–1988* 80 The serene life could take a violent turn, as on Sunday afternoons, when 'kitchen boys' formed gangs to have *skabenga* stick fights. **1994** A. LEVIN in *Style* Oct. 96 An over-friendly Skabanga in Seventies shades and a tatty woman's blazer.

skedonk /skəˈdɒŋk/ *n. colloq.* Also **sk(ie)donk, sgodongo.** [Unknown; prob. echoic (see quot. 1994); perh. fr. a Sintu (Bantu) language.] TJORRIE.

1970 M. WOLFAARDT *Informant, Stilfontein* That car is a real skdonk. **1987** *Style* Mar. 84, I can't start the car. It is an all-weather skedonk, a crock around the clock, a lemon for all seasons. **1990** P. MANTZEL *Informant, Pietermaritzburg* This guy comes along on a real skedonk of a bicycle. **1991** J. WARDEN in *Sunday Times* 28 July (Motoring) 3 Everybody just has to park in the street, whether it is a Rolls-Royce or a skedonk. **1992** M.D. PRENTICE *Informant, Durban* Skedonk. Old car. **1992** on M-Net TV 12 June (Egoli), 'I don't have a car.' 'Don't worry, my skedonk is quite willing and able.' **1993** S. GOODWIN in *Weekend Post* 14 Aug. 2 Nobody wants to insure a student's skedonk or mom's taxi. The risks are too high and the premiums too low. **1994** *Sunday Times* 1 May 15 *Isikorokoro*: What we'll all be driving if car prices continue to escalate, battered heaps also known as *sgodongo* — both words mimic the sound of engines failing to start.

skee var. SKEY.

skeef /skɪəf/ *adv.* and *adj. Slang.* [Afk., crooked, askew.]

A. *adv.* Disapprovingly. See also *to check (someone or something) skeef* (CHECK sense 1 b), *to tune (someone) skeef* (TUNE sense 2 a).

1969 A. FUGARD *Boesman & Lena* 11 Why you looking at me so *skeef*? **1983** G. SILBER in *Sunday Times* 28 Aug. (Mag. Sect.) 17 He slots a filter cigarette into his mouth. The wrong way round. The flame burns his fingers. He can see a man and a woman watching him. *Skeef.*

B. *adj.* Crooked, skew; ugly; disapproving.

1970 O.A. MCCANN *Informant, Johannesburg* He's got a skeef face (ugly). **1986** *Style* Nov. 140 My mouth is too small and my neus is skeef. **1970** A. PALMER *Informant, King William's Town* Your tie is skew/skeef (crooked). **1993** T. JARVIS on M-Net TV 21 June (Carte Blanche), People really think it's strange and you get skeef looks from all sides.

skeem var. SCHEME.

skeepel var. SCHEPEL.

skei var. SKEY.

skelling var. SCHELLING.

skelm /ˈskel(ə)m/ *n.* and *adj.* Also **schel(lu)m, skelem, skelim, skellam, skellum, skil(l)um.** Pl. **-s**, formerly also **-en.** [Afk., ad. Du. *schelm* (cf. the now archaic Brit. Eng. *skelm*, fr. Du. or G.). The forms ending in *-am, -em, -im,* or *-um* are pronunciation-spellings representing the added /ə/ in the S. Afr. Du. and Afk. pronunciation of *-lm*.]

A. *n.*

1. A rascal, rogue, scoundrel; sometimes used affectionately; occas. *fig.*, a danger, an evil.

1802 in G.M. Theal *Rec. of Cape Col.* (1899) IV. 328 They were obliged .. to give 12 firelocks to the Hottentot Claas Stuurman; which certainly instead of terrifying the Schelmen, served on the contrary very much to encourage them. **1827** T. PHILIPPS *Scenes & Occurrences* 39 Told the Caffer that .. he was a *schelm*. The Caffer flew into a violent passion, and said he was no *schelm*. **1836** C.L. STRETCH Journal. 4 July, He .. began rowing the company calling them alternately his children, Kinders, and Skellums. **1838** J.M. BOWKER *Speeches & Sel.* (1864) 73 He asked me if I thought Umkye clever. I said no; but that I thought him easily led away by schellums. **1860** A.W. DRAYSON *Sporting Scenes* 314 It is my belief that a thorough Cape 'schelm' would .. beat the best English swindler living. **1876** F. BOYLE *Savage Life* 274, I see dis here Riet, the skellum, rise twenty feet in half-hour, no? And in half-day I see him flood the veldt up to yonder hills! **1882** J. NIXON *Among Boers* 28 Generally speaking the Boers will not allow the natives even to be boys. They are 'schelms' i.e. rascals — the term applies to awkward oxen. **1900** B. MITFORD *Aletta* 52 At this man Colvin's neighbours looked askew. He had 'schelm' writ large all over his yellow personality, they declared. **1911** BLACKBURN & CADDELL *Secret Service* 309 A committee of three, which included young 'schelm' David van der Merwe, .. went to Germany to examine and study rifles and big guns. **1914** [see sense 2 below]. **1930** J. BUCHAN *Four Adventures* 168, I got into German Territory all right, and then a skellum of an officer came along, and commandeered all my mules. *a***1931** S. BLACK in S. Gray *Three Plays* (1984) 167 You don't know Goldenstein, hey? Ooh, today he's very rich but such a skelm! **1953** U. KRIGE *Dream & Desert* 43 You've a good mother, Jannie, and you're such a *skelm!* How's it possible? **1958** I. VAUGHAN *Diary* 3 He said Missie, I know you, you are the small skelm. You will run away .. and I will not find you soon. **1961** T. MACDONALD *Tvl Story* 93 'Don't you lock the door?' I asked. 'No,' he said. 'No skellem has a hope on earth to get in while the dogs are about.' **1971** [see **INTOMBI** sense 1]. **1975** S.S. MEKGOE *Lindiwe* (1978) 17 Sergeant: Where have all the skelms gone to? It has been very quiet for two whole weeks. 1st Constable: Yes Sarge, maybe tsotsis are repenting. **1978** M.J. MTSAKA *Not his Pride* 18, I never knew that all along I've been rearing and feeding a big skelm in my house who would one day rise up against me. **1986** S. SEPAMLA *Third Generation* 74 All communists are skelms, crooks I tell you. **1986** *1 000 Ways to Die* (N.U.M.) Sept. 24 Workers say that white miners do not do proper searches and inspections. They do not think about all the dangers ... 'If there is too much reef in the stope, the white miner forces us to work on — even if there are skelms in the reef.' **1990** J. NAIDOO *Coolie Location* 212 De Beer asked me one day if I was signing the passes of 'boys' who no longer worked for the Depot ... 'In future don't sign their passes. They're real skelems.' **1991** P. SLABOLEPSZY Braait Laaities. 16 There are sharks out there jong. White men can also be skelms. White men are sometimes the biggest skelms around.

2. A rogue animal; a bad-tempered, recalcitrant, or vicious creature.

1827 G. THOMPSON *Trav.* II. 385 Both the lion and saddle had disappeared, and nothing could be found but the horse's clean picked bones. Lucas said he could excuse the schelm for killing the horse .. but the felonious abstraction of the saddle .. raised his spleen mightily. **1850** N.J. MERRIMAN *Cape Jrnls* (1957) 146 Our horse from Burghersdorp .. was a real skelm (as the Dutch call a rascally man, or unmanageable horse). **1882** [see sense 1 above]. **1887** H. RIDER HAGGARD *Jess* 6, I am glad that you have killed the skellum (vicious beast). **1907** J.P. FITZPATRICK *Jock of Bushveld* (1909) 260 The natives told us it was quite useless to follow it up as it was a real schelm, and by that time would be miles away in some inaccessible krans. **1914** S.P. HYATT *Old Transport Rd* 213 A schelm is any noxious creature. As a rule the word is used for wild animals, from lions down to owls, but really it is equally applicable to Colonial politicians and their kind. **1937** [see **TREK** *v.* sense 1 a]. **1939** S. CLOETE *Watch for Dawn* 67 'I am not dead,' Kaspar said, having quieted his horse, 'and I do not think anything is broken .. but your horse is a skelm.' **1960** J. COPE in D. Wright *S. Afr. Stories* 55 'Hey, skelm!' He reeled in one of the lines and a long slender fish .. was swung on to the deck, snapping vicious jaws. **1968** S. CLOETE *Chetoko* (1976) 188 'I'll teach you,' he said. 'Ya, you damn lazy *skelm*.' He raised his whip and brought it down on Old Lucy's quarters.

3. As an abstract noun: see quots.

1990 R. STENGEL *January Sun* 50 There is some intangible, undefinable quality that they all seem to have. *Skelm* — it's a kind of dull-witted shrewdness. **1993** N. JARDINE *Informant, Grahamstown* 'He's looking for some skelm tonight' i.e. a sexual encounter.

B. *adj.*

1. Rascally, sly, villainous, wicked, evil.

1802 R. CURTIS in G.M. Theal *Rec. of Cape Col.* (1899) IV. 442 It being deemed impracticable to send a messenger to Algoa Bay by land, owing to the present hostile disposition of the Skellam Hottentots, .. I sent the *Euphrosyne* with the Dispatch. **1806** *Gleanings in Afr.* (anon.) 253 A military post has been established in this distant part of the country, as a check upon the boors, and a security against the incursions of the neighbouring Caffres, and *Schelm Hottentots*. **1829** C. ROSE *Four Yrs in Sn Afr.* 115, I joined a party of Schelm (robber) Hottentots and Kaffers, and we had horses, and arms, and we would attack the boors' houses. [**1855** G.H. MASON *Life with Zulus* 201 The two Zulus .. had .. become tolerably familiar with the coast Caffres (Fingoes), whom they described as Bonya-skellom Fingoe (rascally Fingoes).] **1920** F.C. CORNELL *Glamour of Prospecting* 88 The police would put him in *tronk* if he went there; no one was there but *schelm* Bushmen, cattle thieves. **1933** W.H.S. BELL *Bygone Days* 237 If Baas only knew what a schelm place it is Baas would never have come here. **1963** M. KAVANAGH *We Merry Peasants* 145 Those who would rather work down a mine .. than dig *skelm* grass roots under an open sky. **1964** J. BENNETT *Mr Fisherman* (1967) 8 'He's very *skelm*, that fish,' he said. 'I'll say,' said the young man, with feeling. **1973** J. COPE in S. Gray *Writers' Territory* 115 'My, but you good. The hotnots is skelm but you more skelm, mister' he said. 'Oh yes, I'm very skelm.' **1979** *Capetonian* May 9 Some skelm politician whose double vowels jump up and down .. when he lays down that syrupy Oxford Afrikaans that they manufacture in Pretoria. **1987** L. NKOSI *Mating Birds* 80 Mrs. Van Rooyen was found in the bathroom .. hanging by the belt of her dressing gown ... Van Rooyen burst into laughter. 'That *skellum* whore has gone and done it at last!' **1988** M. TLALI in *Staffrider* Vol.7 No. 3, 356 When you don't have cash I give you eggs and I know you come back and pay me. Everybody is so 'skelm'. **1989** *Weekly Mail* 13 Oct. 15 Spotted at a Jo'burg shopping hotbed, a *skelm* garment which pictured a palmy island and said: *Robben Island — Time Sharing*. **1990** [see **DRONK**].

2. Of an animal: bad-tempered, recalcitrant, vicious.

1827 T. PHILIPPS *Scenes & Occurrences* 151 Diederik .. determined on shooting it, declaring that no schelm beast should kill his horse. **1828** T. PRINGLE *Ephemerides* 114 'Tis his lair — 'tis his voice! — from your saddles alight, For the bold schelm-beast is preparing for fight. **1852** M.B. HUDSON *S. Afr. Frontier Life* 16 It was with our horses no easy affair, For we had in our drove a most skellum young mare That had never been broken or handled before. **1886** G.A. FARINI *Through Kalahari Desert* 163 He is a skellum lion, and the sieur must not go. The lion is bad-tempered, and will fight. **1911** L. COHEN *Reminisc. of Kimberley* 397 'Hi, skilum Pontac!' (crack) 'Ah! you verdompt England!' (crack, whack, bang) and poor England would plunge into the yoke mad with pain and terror. The most useless ox in a Dutchman's team is always named England — and suffers accordingly.

Hence **skelm** *adv.*, badly, cunningly.

1971 *Grocott's Mail* 3 Dec. 3 He says the Jan Bruin was there but he could not hook them. They were biting 'skelm,' probably wanting a different type of bait or needing to be coaxed.

skelpad, -pot varr. SKILPAD.

skep /skep/ *v. trans.* Also **schep**. [Afk., fr. Du. *scheppen*, in both senses.]

1.a. To serve (food); to scoop or ladle out (something).

[**1838** J.E. ALEXANDER *Exped. into Int.* I. 50 The farmer gave the order to 'Schenk een zoopjé' (pour out a dram), and then to 'Skep op,' (set the victuals on the table).] **1913** C. PETTMAN *Africanderisms* 428 *Schep*, .. To *schep* water is to dip it up with a small vessel into a larger one. *Opschep* is the order to dish up for the table. **1946** [see **SLUK** *n.*]. **1972** *Informant, Grahamstown* Can I help you skep out the food, Ma? **1977** F.G. BUTLER *Karoo Morning* 72 You must skep just the right lot of dagga on to your trowel, and throw it right, like this. **1991** *Informant, Johannesburg* My shoes are skepping sand.

b. *comb.* **skepnet** [Afk.], a landing-net or scoop-net (used when fishing).

1969 J.R. GRINDLEY *Riches of Sea* 74 Pilchards being scooped aboard by means of a skepnet or brailer from the net held alongside.

||**2.** To shape or create (something).

1989 *Sunday Times* 29 Oct. 28 A much more favourable *klimaat* is being *skepped* and Mr De Klerk and his .. Cabinet .. deserve praise.

skep(p)el var. SCHEPEL.

skepsel /ˈskeps(ə)l/ *n.* Formerly also **schepsel**. [Afk. (earlier S. Afr. Du., fr. Du. *schepsel* creature).] An offensive term for a black or 'coloured' person; also used as a form of address.

1844 J. BACKHOUSE *Narr. Visit to Mauritius & S. Afr.* 620 The coloured .. are generally styled Heathen, Schepsels, *Creatures*. **1871** [see **VOLK** sense 2]. **1896** M.A. CAREY-HOBSON *At Home in Tvl* 405, I believe God in his goodness put the black schepsels upon this earth that they might be hewers of wood and drawers of water to the white Christian menschen. **1898** W.C. SCULLY *Vendetta* 29 She called to the Hottentot, who .. had remained close at hand. 'Here, *schepsel*, — bring in a bottle of that honey from the front chest.' **1920** R.Y. STORMBERG *Mrs Pieter de Bruyn* 96 Swartz was called a Hottentot, a Shangaan, a skepsel and a few other elegant compliments, and being a full-blooded and very proud Basuto his eyes rolled at the insult. **1931** W.A. COTTON *Racial Segregation* 143 He was but echoing the complacent language of the backveld, where the African people are just *schepsels* (creatures). **1934** N. DEVITT *Mem. of Magistrate* 30 In regard to the native, he considered him as a 'schepsel' sent here for his special convenience. **1939** R.F.A. HOERNLÉ *S. Afr. Native Policy* 72 The Native to many Afrikaners was a *schepsel* ('creature') not wholly human; standing intermediate, as it were, between the game and the livestock, on the one side, and White humanity, on the other. **1943** 'J. BURGER' *Black Man's Burden* 67 The Boer farmer treats his workers in a kindly and tolerant fashion; he does not refer to them as 'bloody niggers', but as *skepsels*. **1967** L. MARQUARD in M. Marquard *Lett. from Boer Parsonage* 21 The location was about a mile from the end of Victoria Street ... The inhabitants were called kaffirs, or *volk*, or *schepsels* (creatures), none of these terms being regarded as terms of abuse or being intended in an unkindly or inhuman spirit. **1968** A. FULTON *Dark Side of Mercy* 108 The policeman .. shouted at the Basutos. 'O.K., skepsels, get back inside.' **1987** M. MELAMU *Children of Twilight* 41 It was all so different with his 'volk'. You had to feed them properly. And what can't you get the skepsels to do with the stomachs propvol. **1992** J. KHUMALO in *Pace* Sept. 34 God-forsaken black skepsels who spend their entire existence on the edge of life, wondering as to where their next meagre meal will come from.

skerm /skɛr(ə)m/ *n.* Also **scharem, scherm, skarm.** [Afk., fr. Du. *scherm* screen, protection.] A screen, barrier, or windbreak, usu. of (thorny) branches and brushwood, but sometimes of stones, earth, reeds, or animal skins, and taking various forms.

a. The simple (temporary) dwelling of nomadic (Khoisan) people; a rough sleeping-shelter for travellers.

1835 A. SMITH *Diary* (1940) II. 272 Have neither cattle nor chiefs, cut all the hair off, use red clay, have no fixed residences, make skerms under a bush. **1838** J.E. ALEXANDER *Exped. into Int.* I. 100 The Namaquas put up a scherm, or screen, for us of boughs and mats, and with a fire at our feet, we lay there comfortably. **1864** T. BAINES *Explor. in S.-W. Afr.* 78 Making a fire in a small *scherm* under a group of the largest 'wagt een beetje' (wait a bit) thorn trees I had ever seen. **1872** E.J. DUNN in A.M.L. Robinson *Sel. Articles from Cape Monthly Mag.* (1978) 62 The Bushmen scherms, made of stones, still remain, as well as the marks of the bullets on the rocks. **1885** H. RIDER HAGGARD *King Solomon's Mines* 53 We went to work to build a 'scherm' ... This is done by cutting a quantity of thorn bushes and laying them in the shape of a circular hedge. Then the space enclosed is smoothed, and dry tambouki grass, if obtainable, is made into a bed in the centre, and a fire or fires lighted. **1905** W.H. TOOKE in Flint & Gilchrist *Science in S. Afr.* 95 The home of the Bushman is the shady cover of a kameeldoorn, a rough 'scherm' of branches and skins on the lee side of a clump of bush, or a crevice or cave in the cliffs overlooking a stream. **1907** W.C. SCULLY *By Veldt & Kopje* 221 A small hut, or 'scherm,' constructed of bushes and fragments of skin, stood before us. It was not so much a hut as a kind of movable screen such as the Hottentots use. **1924** G. BAUMANN in Baumann & Bright *Lost Republic* (1940) 103 The Chief .. received me in his 'skerm' in the presence of some of his councillors and one interpreter. **1936** L.G. GREEN in *Best of S. Afr. Short Stories* (1991) 163 Deep in .. the Knysna forests you will find a race of white people more isolated than any other human beings in South Africa ... Years ago these People of the Forests dressed in skins and lived in *skerms* with only three walls. **1948** A.C. WHITE *Call of Bushveld* 17 Better even than a tent or reed hut, is the humble windbreak, with a bed of grass on mother earth, with only the stars above to light the camp, or skerm. **1961** T.V. BULPIN *White Whirlwind* 55 The three men surrounded their sleeping place with a barricade made of branches cut from thorn trees. Inside this 'scherm', as it was called, they made themselves comfortable for the night, with their horses tethered beside them. **1973** J. COPE *Alley Cat* 75 Pitjie's place was not a hut, it was merely a skerm, the rough grass and thorn-bush shelter open on one side and with its back to the wind. **1977** F.G. BUTLER *Karoo Morning* 203 Vagrant Hottentots and rare Bushmen sheltering behind a 'scherm' of ashbush; their flesh the colour of dust, they were desolate, resigned.

b. In the wild: a screen or hide for hunters and game-watchers; a protection from wild animals.

1838 J.E. ALEXANDER *Exped. into Int.* II. 210 Three of the party then made a scherm or screen of bushes opposite a pool, where they expected elephants or rhinoceroses to come and drink, and inside the scherm they dug up a hole, the better to conceal themselves. **1885** H. RIDER HAGGARD *King Solomon's Mines* 56 We seized our rifles, and slipping on our veldtschoons, .. ran out of the scherm. **1896** H.A. BRYDEN *Tales of S. Afr.* 159 Here there was good water: the camp could be rendered pretty impregnable by the help of a *scherm* of thorn-bushes. **1914** W.C. SCULLY *Lodges in Wilderness* 62 A few shrubs had to be pulled out of the ground and piled in the form of a low, circular fence enclosing a space about six feet in diameter. This is the 'scherm' or screen so often used by those who hunt in the desert. Within it the hunter lies prone, fully concealed from any approaching quarry. **1937** J. STEVENSON-HAMILTON *S. Afr. Eden* 16 The camp was encircled by a dense scherm, or thorn zeriba, as much to keep out dangerous wild animals as hostile human beings. **1939** S. CLOETE *Watch for Dawn* 266 The lions were a perpetual menace, necessitating the building of strong skerms each night. **1943** D. REITZ *No Outspan* 70 After sunset lion roared about our skerm. **1949** C. BULLOCK *Rina* 43 At each new camp it was necessary to build scherms for the donkeys, and for myself and the Natives. **1957** L.G. GREEN *Beyond City Lights* 201 They treated the Hollanders kindly, made a skerm to protect them from wild animals at night, put up a mat hut.

c. In an African village: an enclosing fence round a homestead.

1844 J. BACKHOUSE *Narr. of Visit* 42 (Jeffreys), There is much of a kind of shrubby Asparagus, which is used at Thaba Unchu, for making *skerms*, shelters, round the huts of the Baralongs. **1895** A.B. BALFOUR *1200 Miles in Waggon* 50 A scherm (sheltering fence) of reeds, about seven feet high in front, and forming a small courtyard at the entrance of the hut. **1970** P.B. CLEMENTS in *Outpost* 43 Napier reported that Wilson's party had passed through several scherms (enclosures) full of women, children and cattle.

d. *obs.* A large piece of canvas used as a shelter; see also SAIL sense 1 b.

1894 E. GLANVILLE *Fair Colonist* 219 All hands were intensely busy fixing the scherm or large canvas sheet drawn from the bottom rim of the outer wheels, up over the tent, and out for a space of twelve feet to two trees.

e. *hist.* A windbreak behind which cooking-fires were tended and food prepared.

1898 W.C. SCULLY *Between Sun & Sand* 28 Susannah came out of the mat-house and superintended the lighting of a fire by the Hottentot maid in the kitchen scherm. **1943** D. REITZ *No Outspan* 155 Presently we heard them [*sc.* the lions] above the pots and the pans in the smaller skerm in which we did our cooking. **1963** R. LEWCOCK *Early 19th C. Archit.* 137 In the small frontier farmhouses cooking was done in the open air, behind a simple screen shelter, or 'skerm'.

f. *obs.* A stockade to protect domestic livestock and to prevent animals from straying.

1909 LADY S. WILSON *S. Afr. Mem.* 312 Every evening our animals were put into a 'skerm', or high palisade, constructed of branches by the ubiquitous carriers with marvellous rapidity. **1924** E.T. JOLLIE *Real Rhodesia* (1971) 188 He knows exactly .. how to make a 'scherm' for the animals, where to build the fire and how to make up soft beds from the grass. **1928** L.P. GREENE *Adventure Omnibus* 99 Major and Jim set their camp in better order, building a scherm in which to put their mules at night. **1936** C. BIRKBY *Thirstland Treks* 283 Your camels or your donkeys might scream behind their *skerm* of thorn boughs in the night at the onslaught of lions.

skey /skeɪ/ *n.* Also **schei, skea, skee, skei**. Pl. -s, occas. **skeyes**, and (sense 2 only) **skeie** /ˈskeɪə/. [ad. S. Afr. Du. *skei*, fr. Du. *schei* tie piece, crossbar; sense 3 may be fr. Afk. *skei* to divide, part, split.]

1. *hist.* Each of a pair of notched wooden pegs or bars passing vertically through the end of an ox-yoke, being inserted one on either side of the neck of the ox and having the neck-strap (see STROP sense 1 a) linking them below; JUKSKEI sense 1; YOKE KEY; YOKESKEY sense 1.

1835 T.H. BOWKER Journal. 2 June, Some of the men make Yokes & Skees. **1850** R.G.G. CUMMING *Hunter's Life* (1902) 7 The yoke is placed on the back of the neck of the ox, with one of these skeys on either side. **1851** R.J. GARDEN Diary. I. (Killie Campbell Africana Library MS29081) 29 June, The yokes, skeyes, trek touw etc .. he has made him self. **1863** W.C. BALDWIN *Afr. Hunting* 103 From the beams hung .. old saddles, yokes, skeys, neckstraps, and all apparatus for wagoning. **1882** J. NIXON *Among Boers* 172 The yoke is kept from slipping sideways by wooden stays, or 'skeys', which are fastened under the throat by a small 'strop' of hide. **1895** A.B. BALFOUR *1200 Miles in Waggon* 72 At each end of it [*sc.* the yoke] .. is a pair of notched slips of wood called skeis, let into holes in the yokes at a sufficient distance apart for the neck of an ox to fit in between them. **1911** *Farmer's Weekly* 15 Mar. 5 (advt) Good strong hard wood skeys (Hewn, not sawn) at 2s. 6d. per dozen. **1947** H.C. BOSMAN *Mafeking Rd* (1969) 157 As we were also without skeis we had to fasten the necks of the oxen straight on to the yokes with strops. **1963** S. CLOETE *Rags of Glory* 404 Through these holes went the skeys – pieces of hard wood notched to take the leather strops or straps that passed under the ox's throat and were adjusted in the notches according to the size of the animal. **1973** *Farmer's Weekly* 30 May (Suppl.) 37 (*advt*) Skeys R3,60 doz. **1980** A.J. BLIGNAUT *Dead End Rd* 80 The leaders flung the yokes about on their necks and rattled the skeis. **1991** *Sunday Times* 7 Apr. 26 With nothing better to do in the evenings, when it was nice and cool and they had outspanned, they would remove the *skeis* from the *juks* so they could throw them at a stick they had stuck in the ground for this purpose.

2. A pin of the type thrown in the game of jukskei, orig. the wooden skey of a yoke, but now usu. a bottle-shaped rubber pin about 450mm long and weighing up to 1,8 kg; JUKSKEI sense 2 b.

1955 A. DELIUS *Young Trav.* 104 The *jukskei* pitch was pitted at both ends and softened by the fall of the *skeie*, which were made of wood and shaped not unlike Indian clubs ... The object was to throw a *skei* from one end to the other and to knock down the further wand. **1971** *Argus* 14 May 22 The monarch was King George VI and the picture of him lobbing a skei .. is on view at the South African Archives. **1972** D.A. KRÜGER in *Std Encycl. of Sn Afr.* VI. 246 Several types of skeys evolved .. - round, flat, double, Natalia, Olivier, bottle, rolling-pin and 'tap-root'; but the bottle-skey has proved to be the most effective. **1982** *S. Afr. Panorama* Sept. 29 The *skey* itself has changed considerably from the old bottle neck type, the triangular *skey* and rolling pin, to the present day composite *skey* with a maximum mass of 1,8 kg. **1991** *Sunday Times* 7 Apr. 26 These days the *skeis* are not made from wood ... Now the *skeis* are composed of some kind of rubber compound ... A set of two costs about R100.

3. A V-shaped notch, cut or punched in the ear of an ox or other farm animal as a means of identification. Also *attrib.*

1971 *Grocott's Mail* 28 May 1 One Red Ox with brown markings, swallow tail and skey right ear, hole in left ear. *Ibid.* 27 July 2 Jersey Cow, tip, skey and slit, left ear. **1971** *Daily Dispatch* 2 Sept. 11, 1 Ntsundu ox, R-E two skeys behind and swallow tail; L-E skey in front and skey behind; no brand. **1975** *Ibid.* 13 June 9 One She Goat right ear skey, left ear vent.

ski-boat /ˈskiːbəʊt/ *n.* [See quot. 1953.] Originally, a broad, flat-bottomed boat designed for offshore angling, with two water-tight holds and two outboard motors; loosely, any boat designed to take an outboard motor and be used at sea. Also *attrib.*

*c*1953 C. BIRKBY *In Sun I'm Rich* 38 A fleet of close on a hundred tiny craft .. surging along on the swells. Those were the ski-boats. An odd name, but then the ski-boat is an odd craft ... Durban dreamed up the ski-boat. *Ibid.* 39 Hayden Grey snapped his fingers one day in 1942. Why not, he thought, build bigger and stouter versions of the surf-skis? And .. why not power them with outboard motors? Soon he had planned, designed and built the first 'ski-boat' ... The ski-boat craze grew, unnoticed, in Natal. By the middle of 1951 there were a hundred of them. **1964** A. TREW *Smoke Island* 43 José brought the skiboat round and Andy recovered some of the lost line as he scrambled into the fighting-chair. **1971** *Daily News* 26 Feb. 8 The best reports of Natal 'cuda .. were excellent catches at the Aliwal Shoal by skiboats. **1979** *E. Prov. Herald* 15 Nov. 23 One of them, whose skiboat we were fishing from, put down a chokka dolley. **1983** [see Fairall quot. at LINEFISH]. **1991** *Leisure Books Catal.* Apr.-June 14 Read all about .. ski boat angling. **1993** *Argus* 12 Aug. 16 Anglers ranging from the casual weekend skiboat fraternity to professional snoek fishermen on commercial snoek boats. **1993** [see GEELBEK sense 1 a].

Hence **skiboater** *n.*, one who uses a skiboat for fishing.

*c*1953 C. BIRKBY *In Sun I'm Rich* 39 The ski-boaters usually fished in old khaki shorts or in bathing trunks. **1992** YELD & GUBB in *Afr. Wildlife* Vol.46 No.2, 203 There is a .. lack of .. evidence on .. the effect of ski-boaters, of which about 250 have commercial licences, as well as thousands of rock and surf anglers.

skiedonk var. SKEDONK.

skies var. EKSKUUS.

skiet *n.* var. SKUT.

skiet /skit/ *v.* Also **scheit, skit**. [Afk., to shoot (fr. Du. *schieten*).]

‖**1.** *intrans.* and *trans.* To shoot (someone or something).

1885 H. RIDER HAGGARD *King Solomon's Mines* 91 'Skit, Baas, skit!' .. whispered the Hottentot, throwing himself on his face. **1894** E. GLANVILLE *Fair Colonist* 115 'They will have buffalo meat to-morrow night.' 'Good, sir. Baas will surely skit one, and they are now fat.' **1912** F. BANCROFT *Veldt Dwellers* 32 You'll be sjamboked for a skulker, or *scheit* for a deserter if you try running away. *Ibid.* 282 As we round that *kopje* – at top speed, men – scheit! scheit! **1937** H. KLEIN *Stage Coach Dust* 160 Take steady aim .. and when I say 'skiet', let go. I will shoot the other. **1985** *Frontline* Aug. 54 When the terr is standing there with his AK pointing at you you can't say 'hey, now hold it hey' ... You've got to skiet him or he skiets you.

2. *intrans. slang.* See quot.

1950 E. PARTRIDGE *Dict. of Underworld Slang* 630 *Skiet*, To gamble with dice.

3. *trans.* and *intrans. Slang.* [Prob. fr. Afk. idiom. usage, *spek skiet* (lit. 'shoot bacon'), to tell lies, or *kaart skiet* 'to shoot a line', to deceive.] To fantasize, to imagine (something); to lie.

1970 G.E.Q. ABSOLOM *Informant, Germiston* It can be fun to skiet kaarte (talking [*sic*] nonsense). **1970** B. HANSEN *Informant, Durban* Don't skiet here. Don't tell lies ... You skiet you're a joller, hey. You think you're just the guy, hey. **1970** J. STODEL *Informant, Cape Town* Gee, she skits she's the ace. She thinks a lot of herself.

skiet en donder /'skit(ə)n 'donə(r)/ *n. phr.* and *adj. phr. Colloq.* Also **skiet and donder, skiet-en-donner, skiet 'n donder, skiet 'n donner.** [Afk., *skiet* shoot + *en* and + *donder* to thrash or beat up.]

In all senses also SKOP, SKIET, EN DONDER.

A. *n. phr.* 'Blood and thunder'; action entertainment; an action film or book.

1960 *Star* 22 Mar., Why Dr. Hertzog is Anti-TV. It would be all 'skiet en donder' — and fabulous fees. **1971** on Radio South Africa 13 July, Skiet en donder, blood and thunder, cloak and dagger — it's all the same thing. **1973** *Cape Times* 19 June 11 It's the organizer's task to bring the script to life. International intrigues, bloody *skiet en donder*, and dreamy romance are staged .. all as quickly, cheaply and smoothly as possible. **1976** *Drum* June 18 At these semi-blue shows 99 per cent of patronage are white. The blacks return with a change of programme — of the usual 'skiet 'n donder'. **1978** *Sunday Times* 21 May (Mag. Sect.) 2 It's just a good 'skiet en donder' — though my publisher tells me 'suspense thriller' is a more proper description. **1979** *Ibid.* 20 May 10 Without the good old 'skiet en donner', it's not much of a Western to me. **1985** A. MONTEATH in *Ibid.* 15 Sept. 20 They're in flight again .. in a movie not illogically called *Wild Geese II*. And a jolly good piece of *skiet-en-donner* it is too. **1991** *Daily Dispatch* 9 Feb. 8 Even if they did make films like that, they would not be shown in the four-wallers in East London, which have been suffering from a plague of skiet and donders. **1992** *Natal Witness* 9 Nov. 9 Now the film begins to become more complex and this is what raises it far above the popular conception of the Western as 'skiet 'n donner' into an examination of .. the film created-myth of the heroic West.

B. *adj. phr.*

1. Of or pertaining to action entertainment, particularly in films, but also in books.

1961 O. WALKER in *Star* 14 Nov. 13 The toga-and-tonsure school of drama is pretty active these days ... It has a slight start on the skiet-and-donder genus. **1972** E. ROSENTHAL *Meet Me at Carlton* 39 At the Carlton Bioscope, which lasted till comparatively modern times, generations of young Johannesburgers saw 'Skiet en Donder' pictures. **1979** *Sunday Times* 1 July 8, I could have done without scenes of torture ... This one you can safely miss. And that's advice from a confirmed skiet-en-donner fan. **1979** *Voice* 17 June 2 So John 'The Duke' Wayne, hero of many a 'skiet en donder' epic has at last bitten the dust. **1982** *Sunday Times* 15 Aug., Enjoy skiet 'n donner movies (Charles Bronson's a popular hero).

2. In real life: of or pertaining to violent or coercive action.

1973 *Sunday Times* 4 Feb. 4 The Government intend to resort to what are known as skiet-en-donder tactics. It .. has nothing further constructive to say. **1986** *Pace* May 110 Side-step the political skiet-en-donder daily dance in our ghettoes and with unseemly haste crawl into a shebeen. **1993** S. LAUFER in *Weekly Mail* 4 June 9 M— V— is anything but a *skiet-en-donner tannie*.

skiet-kommando see KOMMANDO sense 1 b.

skiet, skop, en donder var. SKOP, SKIET, EN DONDER.

skilling see SCHELLING.

skil(l)um var. SKELM.

skilpad /'skəlpat/ *n.* Also **schilpad, sch(o)elpat, skelpad, skel(l)pot, skilpot.** [Afk., fr. Du. *schilpad* tortoise, turtle (*schild* shield + *pad* toad).]

a. *?obs.* A tortoise. Also *fig.*

1844 J. BACKHOUSE *Narr. of Visit* 489 Tortoises of various species, are also numerous; their colonial name is Skilpot, which is a corruption of Schildpat, Shield-toad. **1862** 'A LADY' *Life at Cape* (1963) 107, I have had the tiny shells of the little 'schoelpats' .. slightly lacquered. They are used by some natives to hold money and snuff. **1863** LADY DUFF-GORDON in F. Galton *Vacation Tourists* (1864) III. 194 On the road I chased and captured a pair or remarkable swift and handsome little 'Schelpats'. That you may duly appreciate such a feat of valour and activity, I will inform you that their English name is 'tortoise'. **1896** E. GLANVILLE *Tales from Veld* 43 The skelpot he's got a head like a puff-adder. **1905** W.L. SCLATER in Flint & Gilchrist *Science in S. Afr.* 144 The Leopard Tortoise (*Testudo pardalis*) .. attains a length of about 2 to 3 feet ... This species .. are frequently to be seen wandering about on the Karroo and are often kept as pets by the farmers, who call them 'schild pad'. **1911** P. GIBBON *Margaret Harding* 260 She's got no more the spirit of a real lady than a cow has ... For two pins I'd tell her so, the old cross-eyed *skellpot*. **1931** F.C. SLATER *Secret Veld* 277 The 'skilpad' (tortoise) is the slowest of animals, well, the good Lord gave him a shell to protect him from the swift snakes. **1936** C. BIRKBY *Thirstland Treks* 68 He met a *skilpad*, a tortoise, and he had a game of races. **1938** F.C. SLATER *Trek* 7 Wagon on tented wagon, one by one, Drawn by slow-footed oxen, followed on, Lumbering like giant skilpads, slow and sure, In long procession.

b. *comb.* **skilpad beetle**, see quot. 1916; **skilpadbessie** /-besi/, formerly also **skildpad-besjie, skildpatbesje,** [Afk., *bessie* (earlier S. Afr. Du. *besje*) berry], DUINEBESSIE; **skilpadblom** /-blɔm/ [Afk., *blom* flower], the plant parasite *Hyobanche sanguinea* (see AARDROOS); **skilpadbos** /-bɔs/ [Afk., *bos* bush], any of several species of *Dorotheanthus*; also called VYGIE; **skilpadkos** /-kɔs/ [Afk., *kos* food], *skilpadblom* (see above); **skilpadtrek,** formerly also **schilpad trick** [Afk., *trek* pull; in earlier quots this word seems to have been interpreted as Eng. *trick* feat of dexterity or skill], see quot. 1913; also *attrib.*

1918 S.H. SKAIFE *Animal Life* 103 Many of them [*sc.* the chrysomelid beetles] closely resemble ladybirds .. ; others look something like a miniature tortoise and are popularly known as **schilpad beetles.** [**1837 skilpadbessie:** ECKLON & ZEYHER *Enumeratio Plantarum Africae* 29 *Mundia spinosa* ... 'Skildpadbesjes' cognitis, vescuntur incolae.] **1868** L. PAPPE *Florae Capensis* 2 The fruit .. is eaten by children and Hottentots who call them Skildpatbesjes. **1887** *S.W. Silver & Co.'s Handbk to S. Afr.* 139 Skildpad-besjies, though somewhat astringent in taste, are eaten by Hottentots and children. They are the fruit of the *Mundtia spinosa*, D.C., a decoction of the tops of the branches of which is used in atrophy, phthisis, &c. .. It grows abundantly on the downs. **1894** R. MARLOTH in *Trans. of S. Afr. Phil. Soc.* p.lxxxvi, Eatable berries occur, among others, on *Mundtia spinosa* (schildpad besjes), .. *Cissus Capensis* (wild grape), .. *Aberia Caffra* (Kei apple), [etc.]. **1913** [see DUINEBESSIE]. **1917** —— *Common Names* 73 *Schildpad bessie* = Duinebessie. **1966** C.A. SMITH *Common Names* 419 *Skilpadbessie*, .. Fruit a juicy, acidulous berry ... Formerly collected in quantity by the Cape Malays and hawked in the streets of Cape Town. **1971** L.G. GREEN *Taste of S.-Easter* 161 Amber honey from skilpadbessies on the dunes was good and Rawlins had tasted some with distinct herbal flavours. **1975** W. STEENKAMP *Land of Thirst King* 130 Two one-time favourites, the bokbessie (goat-berry) and skilpadbessie (tortoise-berry) grow on bushes. **1983** M. DU PLESSIS *State of Fear* 186 *Skilpadbessie*, The low, untidy bush with the small, translucent globes that hang and dip in amongst its spiky leaves. **1984** A. WANNENBURGH *Natural Wonder of Sn Afr.* 53 A parasite on the roots of bushy plants, the vivid **skilpadblom** was known as the inkblom in early colonial times because .. the flowers were used to make ink. **1913** C. PETTMAN *Africanderisms* 429 **Schilpad bos,** The name given in Namaqualand to a bush the seed-pods of which are not unlike a tortoise's head in shape. **1917** R. MARLOTH *Common Names* 73 *Schildpad bos, Zygophyllum Morgsana.* **1973** *E. Prov. Herald* 28 Feb. 4 In the dry sub-tropical route was found migration of the gifboom, melkbos (or spurge), honey locust, blackthorn and skilpadbos (or vygie). **1984** *Motorist* 3rd Quarter 25 Mesembryanthemums (vygies) provide almost translucent shades of shimmering colours. Skilpadbos (*Zygophyllum* species) have a strange affection for the sandy wastes. **1988** M. BRANCH *Explore Cape Flora* 34 The velvety *snail flower*, Hyobanche, has .. been given many interesting names ... The fleshy fruits are eaten by animals, especially tortoises, so it is also called **skilpadkos.** **1864** T. BAINES *Explor. in S.-W. Afr.* 386 Two of the drivers, Jan and Harry, performed the '**schildpat**' (tortoise) **trick**; i.e. a rein is passed round the neck of each, they then, with the bight passing between their legs, go on all-fours, and exert their strength in trying to run away with each other. **1913** C. PETTMAN *Africanderisms* 429 *Schilpad trick*, A game in which two boys fasten themselves together with a riem round the waist or neck, then turning their backs to each other and going upon all fours, the riem passing between their legs, each tries to pull the other, the one who succeeds in pulling his opponent after him, does the trick or trek. **1973** BEETON & DORNER in *Eng. Usage in Sn Afr.* Vol.4 No.2, 51 *Skilpad trek*, .. old Afrikaner game .. ; the attitude, manner of crawling & position is reminiscent of the movement of a tortoise .. hence the name. **1988** *Sunday Times* 3 July 22 There is to be a national boeresport championships ... Whoever emerges as the kennetjie winners, or skilpad-trek winners, will be *world* champions.

skimmel /'skəməl/ *adj.* and *n.* Also **schim(m)el.** [Afk., ad. Du. *schimmel* mildew; mottled; grey horse (fr. *schimmelen* to mildew, grow mouldy).]

A. *adj.*

1. Roan, grey, or dappled; often with defining words, as **bla(a)uw skimmel** *obs.* [Du., *blaauw* blue], or **blue skimmel,** blue roan or dapple grey; **rooi skimmel** /rɔɪ -/ [Afk., *rooi* red] or **red skimmel,** red- or strawberry roan; also *attrib.*

1832 *Graham's Town Jrnl* 10 Aug. 127, 1 red schimmel Ox, slit ear, marked 'E.D.' *Ibid.* 24 Aug. 135, 1 red and White Cow, .. 1 red schimmel Horse, sore back, 1 blue schimmel Mare. **1877** C. ANDREWS Reminiscences of Kafir War 1834–5. 5 We observed several horses grazing, in charge of a coloured boy riding a very nice red schimmel horse. **1877** T. BAINES *Gold Regions of S.-E. Afr.* 66 A 'blaauw-schimmel paard' is a dappled grey, and others are distinguished as red or brown, according to their colour. **1910** J. BUCHAN *Prester John* (1961) 99 An Afrikander stallion of the *blaauw-schimmel*, or blue-roan type. **1920** F.C. CORNELL *Glamour of Prospecting* 320 One of the natives had a horse I greatly coveted. It was nothing to look at, a shabby-looking little blue roan (blaauw schimmel) pony of about 14.2, but a perfect marvel for endurance .. and capable apparently of living on stones. **1958** A. JACKSON *Trader on Veld* 32 He specialized in 'rooi schimmel' (roan) and yellow horses. **1976** O. LEVINSON *Story of Namibia* 45 The story goes that Franke, who usually rode a 'Schimmel' or white horse, went off to reconnoitre upon his arrival at Omaruru.

2. *fig.* In the special collocation **skimmel day** [partial tr. Afk. *skimmeldag*], see quot.

1877 T. BAINES *Gold Regions of S.-E. Afr.* 66, I may as well explain that schimmel means mottled or dappled. Schimmel day is when the light clouds begin to be dappled with the tints of early dawn, but the word is generally used to imply the time of dawn, even though there are no clouds.

B. *n.* A grey, roan, or dappled horse. Also with defining words, as at sense A 1.

1849 E.D.H.E. NAPIER *Excursions in Sn Afr.* I. 295, I was as brusquely informed, that if I wanted to purchase the 'schimmel' (roan), I must return in the evening. **1852** C. BARTER *Dorp & Veld* 109 (Pettman), This feat was performed .. by one horse, a large grey or *schimmel*, the favourite colour in South Africa. **1852** A.W. COLE *Cape & Kafirs* 51 He rides a horse about fourteen hands high, which he calls a red-schimmel, but which you would term a roan. **1882** C. DU VAL *With Show through Sn Afr.* I. 156 An old 'blau schimmel', or steel-grey horse. *Ibid.* 163 We stayed two nights at Port Alfred, and on the second of these I bought another horse — a 'rooi schimmel' (red roan). **1899** *Natal Agric. Jrnl* 31 Mar. 4 'Schimmel,' a roan horse, although in Dictionary Dutch it means a grey horse. **1899** 'S. ERASMUS' *Prinsloo* 30 Who should ride up on Piet's own blue schimmel but 'Scotty' himself. **1899** A. WERNER *Captain of Locusts* 57 My schimmel was quite fresh still — I gave him a cut over the flanks and let him out to do his best. **1905** *Blackwood's Mag.* (U.K.) Sept. 393 Saddle the blue schimmel and ride hard after Baas Hartley. **1910** J. BUCHAN *Prester John* (1961) 182 The shock of my entering the saddle made the schimmel fling up his head violently, and the rope snapped. **1931** V. SAMPSON *Kom Binne* 146 They were fine animals, red roans, known as rooi-schimmel, the most hardy of horses for South African conditions, ponies in activity and endurance, hackneys in size, bone and make. **1939** S. CLOETE *Watch for Dawn* 152 Petrus clung to the mane of his skimmel, riding with his head bent. **1955** L.G. GREEN *Karoo* 79 Riding his little roan *skimmel* from Colesberg to Cape Town .. in less than six days. **1971** *Farmer's Weekly* 12 Mar. 104 Stud comprises some 20 animals including 8 tip-top Mares, 6 Fillies, etc., plus Vonk the sire (skimmel) who is producing true to type.

skinder /ˈskənə(r), ˈskɪnə(r)/ *n. colloq.* Also **skinner.** [fr. next.] Gossip; slanderous talk. Also *attrib.* Cf. SCANDAL STORIES.

1979 *Darling* 83, I think skinner is the nearest thing we've got to truth. Ooh, yes, and I love eavesdropping. **1981** *Pretoria News* 26 Nov. 2 In keeping with the topic of food, which permeates the portals of .. health and beauty hydro, where 'there's no dinner and lots of skinder,' this play is like a juicy sosatie strung on a skewer. **1982** *Rhodeo* (Rhodes Univ.) 6 Apr. 10 Political skinder. Reportage. **1985** C. BARNARD in *Cape Times* 2 Sept., Gossiping is as old as speech ... So it wasn't much of a surprise to overhear the latest *skinder* within minutes of sitting down at an international fashion show. **1989** J. SPARG in *Daily Dispatch* 13 July 3 The doings of the inhabitants of the Groot Marico are recounted by the simple, uncouth but lovable rogue Oom Schalk Louwrens — who isn't above the occasional 'skinner'. **1990** *Sunday Times* 4 Mar. 24 Skinder. There's a neat line in Steel Magnolias ... 'If you've got nothing good to say about anybody, come and sit with me'. **1990** J. ROSENTHAL *Wake Up Singing* 48 Someone will come and visit you and you can catch up on all the skinner.

skinder /ˈskənə, ˈskɪnə/ *v. intrans. Colloq.* Also **skinner.** [Afk., to slander, gossip, tattle. The combinations originated in Afk., formed on *skinder* v. (the Afk. n., 'gossip', being *skindery*).]
1. To gossip.

1942 M.G. GILBERT *Informant, Cape Town* 8 Feb. 1, I went up to her losieshuis at twelve, after I'd been at office — Had lunch, and sat sewing and skinnering till tea-time. **1959** J. MEIRING *Candle in Wind* 96 The women may discuss Lena and 'skinder' about her. But the men are silent. They keep their own thoughts. **1974** 'BLOSSOM' in *Darling* 8 May 91 Ouma as usual, is off *skindering* behind some bushes with her main mates. **1975** *Scope* 16 May 20 The poor fellow .. would spend an uncomfortable evening in the second row .. wondering what his wife and Mireille were skindering about. **1979** *Darling* 83, I love talking, .. and I'm a terrible gossip. In fact that's what the law in Parliament is all about — to stop me gossiping. I love skinnering. **1981** C. VAN WYK in *Bloody Horse* No.4, 59, I was standing on the first storey of the block of flats listening to the women cackle and skinder between the lines of washing below. **1988** M. NEL in *Personality* 25 Apr. 54 We may quarrel and 'skinner' (gossip) among ourselves, but when someone is in trouble everyone arrives to help. **1988** 'K. LEMMER' in *Weekly Mail* 2 Dec. 15 We're back in business, kêrels, so let's skinner! **1991** *Weekly Mail* 24 May 15 What he possessed was a common touch ... He could drink and skinner with the best of us and had a rough-diamond wit, which was given to barbed sideswipes.

2. *comb.* **skinderbek** /-bek, -bɛk/, pl. **-ke** /-kə/, [Afk., *bek* mouth], a scandalmonger; also *attrib.*; **skinder stories** /-stɔːriz, -stuəris/ [Eng. or Afk. *stories*], often in political contexts, malicious rumour, gossip; SCANDAL STORIES.

1959 J. MEIRING *Candle in Wind* 90 Perhaps that will teach you not to believe everything that old **skinderbek** says! **1976** S. LYNNE *Beloved Viking*, I can see madam isn't a skinder-bek and won't say bad things about another person. **1985** D. KRAMER in *Cosmopolitan* May 102 A rebellious boereseun whose name was causing fever blisters to break out on the lips of the local skinderbek association. **1987** *Sunday Times* 1 Mar. 17 It's amazing where gossiping on a stoep can get you these days. Those wonderful *skinderbekke* of TV's 'Kooperasie Stories' are making a bid for the big time. **1974** *Sunday Times* 6 Oct. 9 Kies said he was sick and tired of sensational '**skinderstories**' about his private life. **1978** *Ibid.* 1 Oct. 17 Dr Mulder's men remain scornful of the clinging stain of the Information debacle, calling it 'skinderstories'. **1979** *Daily Dispatch* 12 Dec. 1 She said she had beaten Nosipo because she had spread 'skinder stories' about her. **1980** *Ibid.* 24 Mar. 6 Later came Dr Wassenaar's book proving the material cost of apartheid (38 billion). 'Skinder-stories' said Mr Vorster in Parliament. **1989** D. WATTS on M-Net TV 29 Oct., Skinner-stories at the very highest level. **1990** *Weekend Mail* 13 July 5, I suppose that most of the *skinder*-stories about the habits of the middle-class blacks were fabrications by jealous people.

Hence **skinderer** *n.*, gossiper; **skindering** *vbl n.* and **skindering** *ppl adj.*, gossiping.

1980 *E. Prov. Herald* 1 Oct. 17 Defending the threat .. to sue anybody who came forward with unfounded allegations about the industry, Mr W— .. said Dr L— could not allow 'skinnering' to continue. **1981** *Sunday Times* 25 Oct. 20 After naughty 'skindering' between the two, brunette model Pat W— had slapped blonde model Jennifer G— .. in the mouth. **1982** *E. Prov. Herald* 31 Aug. 15 Who has not squirmed at that *skindering* in post office and *voorkamer*, .. at that canny tongue, that sharp ear. **1990** *Weekly Mail* 14 Sept. 7 Journalists are a skinnering lot, it's true, but this week quite a few of them will be hoping they weren't overheard. **1993** M. GLASER *Unquiet Love* 19, I *heard* the dismembering of at least five persons who had somehow got on the wrong side of the skinderers ... Ouma's voice was as raspy as a true skinderer's voice should be.

skipjack *n.* [Transf. uses of general Eng. *skipjack* a name most frequently used of the tuna *Katsuwonis pelamis*. (In U.S. Eng., the name is used of a variety of fishes.)] Any of several marine fishes (esp., as in general Eng. usage, *Katsuwonis pelamis*): **1.** The SPRINGER (sense 2 a), *Elops machnata*. **2.** The tuna *Katsuwonis pelamis* of the Scombridae; KATONKEL sense 2 a. **3.** The ELF (sense a), *Pomatomus saltatrix*.

In Smith and Heemstra's *Smiths' Sea Fishes* (1986), the name 'skipjack tuna' is used for *K. pelamis*.

1909 *E. London Dispatch* 3 Mar. 6 The 'Cape Salmon, ' Skipjack, 'Victoria trout', and other aliases. **1912** *Ibid.* 26 Sept. 4 The fish .. was a Saury pike, known here as a 'Greenback' and in some places as the *Skipper* or *Skipjack*, from its habit of jumping out of the water. It is fairly common hereabout and has often been known to leap into a 'grainer's' boat, attracted by the light. **1949** J.L.B. SMITH *Sea Fishes* 298 *Euthynnys pelamis* (Linnaeus) ... *Skipjack. Bonita. Watermelon* ... In all but the coldest seas, not often inshore .. only rarely taken in estuaries. **1973** *E. Prov. Herald* 1 Feb. 14 There appears to be lots of skipjack tunny around and deep sea men now are catching them only for bait to troll for marlin. **1978** *Sunday Times* 12 Mar. (Mag. Sect.) 8 Earlier we braaied a freshly-caught skipjack on the coals — and I spared a thought for those sad, hassle-ridden people in the Golden City. **1980** *Weekend Post* 13 Sept. (Suppl.) 6 Fishing to suit all tastes ... The best time for fishing in Port Alfred is from December to March, when cob, leervis, elft, skipjack, spotted grunter and white steenbras are plentiful.

skipper *n.* [Unknown; perh. rel. to Eng. *jumper.*] Esp. in township Eng.: a long-sleeved sweatshirt or tee-shirt, usu. of cotton-knit fabric.

1971 *Post* 26 June, Plain nylon doeks ... Men's knitted skippers, long sleeves, three buttons in front. **1973** *Drum* 8 May 11 Members of Youth for Christ .. were wearing skippers with a finger pointed upwards to a small cross with the legend: One Way. **1975** F. JOHENNESSE in *New Classic* No.1, 44 His striped skipper, awkward pants, heeled tackies. **1977** *World* 17 June 21 (*advt*) Bargain! With Free Ball ... Nylon Long sleeve skippers ... Goalie Skippers. **1980** M. MATSHOBA in M. Mutloatse *Forced Landing* 105 His Elmer skipper that was no longer its original white but brownish, and the flimsy dark trousers .. were worn without any thought of physical decoration, but only to cover the body. **1982** *Voice* 2 May 8 Calling all Hawkers! .. Factory prices! .. Skippers, Jerseys, Blankets. **1987** *E. Prov. Herald* 19 Aug. 1 The special constables .. were issued with one pair of boots, two overalls, one raincoat, and two skippers — but no shirts or warm coats. **1988** E. MAKWELA in *Pace* Sept. 51 The farmer bought him a pair of rubber shoes, a pair of trousers and a skipper as his salary for the whole year. **1990** O. MUSI in *Drum* May 26 My neighbour's little boy pestered his dad for a 'Viva' T-shirt. This long-suffering man pointed out to his son that he had been sharing his Cosatu skipper with him .. , but the kid .. did not want to wear it any longer as it was not, as he put it, 'skipa sa Mandela'.

skit *n.* var. SKUT.

skit *v.* var. SKIET.

skof *n.*[1] var. SCOFF *n.*[2]

skof /skɔf, skɒf/ *n.*[2] Also **schoff, s(c)hoft, scoff, skoff, skoft.** Pl. **-s**, occas. ‖**-te** /-tə/, and (formerly) **-ten.** [S. Afr. Du. *schoft* (later Afk. *skof*), stage of a journey, transf. use of Du. *schoft* three hours' work, shift, quarter of a day.]
1. A leg or stage of a journey; *obs.* exc. *hist.*, the distance or period of travel between outspans; the distance travelled by an ox-wagon in a day. Cf. SCOFF *n.*[2], TREK *n.* sense 3.

1785 G. FORSTER tr. *A. Sparrman's Voy. to Cape of G.H.* I. 132 Four such hours with a horse, or with eight oxen are reckoned to make one *skoft*. **1801** J. BARROW *Trav.* I. 55 Each day's journey is called a *skoff*; and the length of these is generally regulated by local circumstances, being from five to fifteen hours. **1821** C.I. LATROBE *Jrnl of Visit* 287 Mr Melville .. prevailed upon her to promise to let us have one spann in the morning, for a six-hours *skoff*, or half a day's journey. **1834** A. SMITH *Diary* (1939) I. 177 A man asked 120 Rds. to convey the articles from this to Graaff Reynet, a distance of 7 schoffs. **1861** P.B. BORCHERDS *Auto-Biog. Mem.* 80 We proceeded to a fountain called Gatarkomo, about a schoft (the common term for a day's journey) from the chief's residence. **1882** J. NIXON *Among Boers* 182 We tried three treks, or 'scoffs', daily, instead of two. **1895** R.H.S. CHURCHILL *Men, Mines & Animals* 134 We have done twenty-five miles from Silika in three 'skoffs', which is excellent trekking. [Note] *Skoff*, journey from outspan to outspan, or from meal to meal. **1914** L.H. BRINKMAN *Breath of Karroo* 108 The shorter the morning 'schoft' (as the Dutch term a stage), the better the animal will be able to work during the rest of the day. **1932** L. FOUCHE *Trigard's Trek 1837–8* p.xv, It became imperative to ascertain the value of Trigardt's unit, the length of a 'skof'. **1951** T.V. BULPIN *Lost Trails of Low Veld* 34 Each day, except Sunday, a stage of travel, a skof, was completed. **1969** A. FUGARD *Boesman & Lena* 2 That last *skof* was hard. Against the wind ... Heavier and heavier. Every step. **1973** J. MEINTJES *Voortrekkers* 51 The obstinate Jan Pretorius and his companions journeyed on for about a month, time being reckoned by day-treks or *skofte*.

2. *transf.* A stage in the game of jukskei (see JUKSKEI sense 2 a).

1991 *Sunday Times* 7 Apr. 26 In Thursday's 'Test' the Bokke and the Rest were locked on 22-all in the first *skof*. When the Bokke chucked the peg down by accident the three points took them over 23 for a 'bust' and they had to start all over again, trailing 0–22 ... You must understand that to win a *skof*, which is worth five points, you first have to score 23 points, exactly.

skof *v.* var. SCOFF *v.*

skoff *n.*[1] var. SCOFF *n.*[2]

skoff *n.*[2] var. SKOF *n.*[2]

skoffel /'skɔf(ə)l/ *n.*[1] Also **scoffel**, and (formerly) **schoffel**. [Afk. (fr. Du. *schoffel*).] A hoe. Also *attrib.*

1913 C. PETTMAN *Africanderisms* 431 *Schoffel*, .. A hoe; a weeding tool. **1963** M. KAVANAGH *We Merry Peasants* 110 Those who are interested should ask themselves whether they are prepared to take a *skoffel* — a hoe — and work with the labourers. **1966** I. VAUGHAN *These Were my Yesterdays* 122 Moses brings a 'Scoffel girl' to cut down long grass.

‖**skoffel** /'skɔf(ə)l/ *n.*[2] [Afk., fr. Du. *schoffelen, schuffelen* to shuffle.]

1. A dance of any kind, but esp. SAKKIE-SAKKIE (*n.* sense b).

1946 A. NASH in E. Partridge *Dict. of Underworld Slang* (1950) 632 Dance: Skoffel (scuffle-shuffle). **1980** *Sunday Times* 23 Nov. 29 It was time to grab partners for a final 'skoffel' around the studio, to the combined music of two bands.

2. *comb.* **skoffel jazz**, BOEREMUSIEK sense 1.

1990 *Weekend Post* 8 Dec. 6 Some young South Africans today scoff at it [*sc.* boeremusiek]. They call it sakkie-sakkie. Young Afrikaans-speaking people of a 'worldly' persuasion call it *langarm musiek* or 'Skoffel jazz'.

skoffel /'skɔf(ə)l, 'skɒf(ə)l/ *v.* Formerly also **schoffel, scoffle, scuffle**. [Afk., fr. Du. *schoffelen*.]

Commonly used in the farming community.

a. *intrans.* To work with a hoe.

1882 S. HECKFORD *Lady Trader in Tvl* 78 He .. had the right to order the women to weed or to scoffle, as it is called here, giving them a basket of peaches in return. **1893** A. SMITH *Short Papers on S. Afr. Subjects* 42 The flowering of the wild chestnut .. and the ripening of the fruit on the Kaffir plum, show that it is time [to] scuffle. **1894** E. GLANVILLE *Fair Colonist* 115 Keep the men well to their work ploughing and scoffling in the mealie-fields. **1916** L.D. FLEMMING *Fool on Veld* (1933) 88 Hadn't we dug, and blown up, and schoffeled and pummelled and picked for weeks trying to remove prehistoric deposits. **1963** M. KAVANAGH *We Merry Peasants* 147 James had been *skoffeling* (hoeing) in the vegetable garden after rain when snails in the Cape invade as armies. **1976** *Darling* 3 Mar. 67 She .. hates working in the vegetable patch. 'I can't take a hoe and *skoffel*.' **1989** I. VLADISLAVIC *Missing Persons* 1 The garden was veld ... The way to get the grass out is to attack the roots. You can't skoffel with a spade — it grows back. You have to work a fork in around each tuft, loosen the earth, stick a hose-pipe in among the roots, turn it on full-blast, blow the soil away.

b. *trans.* To weed (a piece of land) with a hoe.

1908 F.C. SLATER *Sunburnt South* 142, I swallowed the dop as I worked and kept steadily on. And, .. in three days I *skoffeled* a 'land' of potatoes which had taken my wife and three of my sons a week to do the previous year. **1949** C. BULLOCK *Rina* 226 In a little time they came back with bundles of long, dry grass; and, having skoffled my chosen spot in the open, laid down my bed with a ceremonious foot-log at the end of it. **1991** [see KOSMOS].

Hence **skoffeler** *n.*, one who hoes; a mechanical cultivator (also *attrib.*); **skoffeling** *vbl n.*, also **scoffling**, hoeing.

1904 *E. London Dispatch* 16 Sept. 4 In the native lands, where the owner cannot rise to a 75, the scoffler is busy with the hoe. **1913** C. PETTMAN *Africanderisms* 431 *Schoffler*, One who clears the ground by 'schoffeling'. **1948** O. WALKER *Kaffirs Are Lively* 47 The rest is the woman's sphere — the planting, the *skoffeling* or hoeing, the weeding and the harvesting. **1954** K. COWIN *Bushveld, Bananas & Bounty* 178 Burrweed sprang up so thick and fast on the dry land that hand scoffling was impossible, and we had to plough the land again and the cotton with it. **1972** *Daily Dispatch* 17 May 15, 8 scoffler oxen, 6 baby beef. **1973** *E. Prov. Herald* 30 May 19, 1 3-point Linkage Scoffler; 1 Plough. **1993** L. GRANT in *Weekend Post* 13 Nov. 4 There was a great demand for mules for ploughing and skoffeling at the moment.

skoft var. SKOF *n.*[2]

skokiaan /'skɔkiɑːn, skɔk'jɑːn/ *n.* [Unknown; perh. fr. Zulu *isikokeyana* a small enclosure, with reference to the common practice of hiding containers of illicit liquor in holes in the ground; or fr. Xhosa *koka* make drunk.]

1.a. An illicit home-brewed liquor made primarily of yeast, sugar, and water. Also *attrib.*, and *comb.* (objective) **skokiaan-seller**. Cf. MBAMBA, SKOMFAAN.

1908 *Rand Daily Mail* 11 Sept. 7 Furnish the wherewithal to purchase chali or skokeyana (native intoxicants). **1926** *E. Prov. Herald* 7 Jan. 8 The greatest difficulty the police have to deal with .. is .. the prevention of the brewing and drinking of skokiaan and gwebu. *a*1928 R.R.R. DHLOMO *Afr. Tragedy* 8 She approached an innocent looking ash-heap; and, after casting hurried glances round, dug quickly, and brought to the surface a small can full of Skokiaan. **1943** 'J. BURGER' *Black Man's Burden* 100 In many cases Europeans are behind both the illicit drink traffic and the brewing of 'skokiaan'. **1948** E. HELLMANN *Rooiyard* 48 Four shilling's worth of yeast and one shilling's worth of sugar are the quantities commonly used to make two gallons of *skokiaan*. **1946** P. ABRAHAMS *Mine Boy* (1954) 165 Black policemen dug up two drums of skokiaan. They poured the foul-smelling, well-loved liquid down the drain. **1959** *Drum* Jan. 27 Skokiaan: Made of yeast, lukewarm water, sugar and oats. Like other drinks fermented overnight, can be very damaging to the system. **1959** E. MPHAHLELE *Down Second Ave* (1965) 74 Grand mother did not allow anyone to brew *Skokiaan* because it made the sturdiest of men violently drunk. *Skokiaan* is a drink made by beating compressed yeast in warm water and leaving it to ferment. It's deadly, but there are deadlier brews. **1975** *Friend* 25 June 4 A 37-year-old White mother of nine submitted .. that she brewed 50 litres of sifted skokiaan (an illicit brew) in an attempt to get her alcoholic husband 'off other liquor.' **1977** I. MARGO in *Quarry '77* 161 'No Christmas this Christmas,' grins a skokiaan-seller. **1979** J. GRATUS *Jo'burgers* 263 Miz Bessie brewed her skokiaan from water, yeast, stale bread, over-ripe fruit, a few choice decaying leaves of lettuce or cabbage, plenty of sugar, whatever pure spirit she could buy, and just a dash of commercial carbide to give the brew that extra kick. **1980** *Rand Daily Mail* 7 Oct. 5 Skokiaan is a witches' brew of tartaric powder, yeast, and a rather eerie imagination. **1980** [see MBAMBA]. **1982** [see *Sunday Times* quot. at FACTION sense a]. **1986** P.A. MCALLISTER Xhosa Beer Drinks. 41 Some of the illegal urban brews of the time [*sc.* 1938] (*isikokiyana*, etc.) .. were much more potent because of the ingredients (carbide, brown bread, and suchlike) that went into them. **1989** [see MARABI sense 1]. **1990** *Fair Lady* 28 Mar. 136 The home-brewed spirit 'skokiaan', a swig of which Aunt Sal said could knock your head right across the nation.

b. See quot.

1963 L.F. FREED *Crime in S. Afr.* 204 'Isikoivane' ('skokiaan') appears to be a general term used for all drinks other than the traditional beer sold in municipal beer halls. But these drinks are sheer poison in that they are mixed with blue stone (copper sulphate), tobacco juice, dagga, methylated spirits, snakes, carbide, rats, beetles — anything to give a kick and a bite.

2. *comb.* **skokiaan queen**, a woman who brews and sells illicit liquor; cf. *shebeen queen* (see SHEBEEN sense 2).

1936 WILLIAMS & MAY *I Am Black* 175 The white men call me a skokiaan queen. **1946** P. ABRAHAMS *Mine Boy* (1954) 232 He said the only way to stop Skokiaan Queens is to make bars for black people. **1950** C. BULLOCK *Mashona & Matabele* 219 Skokiaan queens defy the law, and the vile concoctions they sell sap the moral resistance of their customers and destroy decent behaviour. **1959** L. LONGMORE *Dispossessed* 211 The brewer or skokiaan queen simply supervises, keeps an eye on the business and sits around chatting to customers who, if they want credit, appeal to her. **1962** M. BRANDEL-SYRIER *Black Woman* 87 There is always the possibility of readmission for the repentant sinner, whether the unmarried mother, the adulteress, or the Skokiaan queen. **1970** HEARD & FAULL *Cookery in Sn Afr.* 479 We don't hear too much about the skokiaan queens reigning in 'madam's' backyard these days. **1979** J. GRATUS *Jo'burgers* 261 She established herself as the unrivalled leader of the skokiaan queens. Those who attempted to dispute this found their supply of drink poured out on the roadway and their hovels on fire. **1981** *Frontline* May 10 In the days when 'white man's liquor' was prohibited to blacks, shebeens .. served up some pretty rough concoctions (the famous days of the skokiaan queens). **1990** G. SLOVO *Ties of Blood* 143 Many was the night he spent drinking in the homes of the *skokiaan* queens and never had he had a hangover such as this.

skolly /'skɔli, 'skɒli/ *n. colloq.* Also **scolly, skollie**. [Afk., prob. ad. Du. *schoelje* a rogue, scavenger (see quot. 1963); but perh. ad. *skorriemorrie* rascal, riffraff, fr. Yiddish *soyrerumoyre* rogue, hoodlum; see also quot. 1980.] **a.** Esp. in Cape Town: a 'coloured' street hoodlum or petty criminal, often a member of a gang. Formerly also in the phr. ***skolly boy***. **b.** *transf.* Any thug or hooligan. Also *attrib.* Cf. TSOTSI sense 1.

1934 *Cape Argus* 8 Jan. 10 The accused .. were actually several degrees lower than the average 'scolly-boy' who commits most of the crimes of violence and theft in the Peninsula. **1943** 'J. BURGER' *Black Man's Burden* 85 In Cape Town the so-called 'Skolly gangs' are a public menace, rendering many parts of the town unsafe for European women at night. **1949** [see MUNTU sense 1]. **1950** D. REED *Somewhere S. of Suez* 163 The dens of District Six, where the police go in pairs and only if they must; that is where the *skollies* live, the roughs and hoodlums. **1963** L.F. FREED *Crime in S. Afr.* 139 The name 'skollie' comes from the old Dutch 'schoelje', meaning 'scavenger'. Dutch sea-captains shouted 'schoelje' at the seagulls which swooped to snatch up ships' offal from the waters of Table Bay. Early Cape settlers shouted the same word at Coloured vagrants who snatched at their refuse dumps or begged in the streets. **1966** VAN HEYNINGEN & BERTHOUD *Uys Krige* 143 A skolly boy of Cape Town's District Six. **1967** *Drum* 7 May 4 A skollie may get a few years' imprisonment for a stabbing and is then set free on the community. **1970** *Daily Dispatch* 13 Oct. 2 How often are these Pretoria skollies apprehended by the police? **1973** *Argus* 19 Apr. 5 Unemployment among Coloured youths was said to be the main cause of the 'skolly menace' and anti-social elements among the community. **1974** *To the Point* 12 July 41 She is degraded by her skollie-husband. **1980** A.S.A. EAST in *Cape Times* 22 Feb. 8, I was .. surprised to read of the origin of the word 'skolly' as described by Mr Manuel (Cape Times, February 16), in that he avers that it is derived from the word to 'skol'. Certain researchers aver that the derivation of the word comes from the English 'scullery boy'. This was later corrupted to 'skolly boy'. The 'scullery boy' was a very low form of humanity .. , and it was believed that this was the true source of the name. **1981** *Sunday Times* 10 May 6 These people presumably wouldn't mind sitting next to a white skollie, or object to a black man driving them in a taxi. **1981** *Voice* 17 June 14 Elsies River .. has the highest crime rate in the Cape .. with skollies (young gang members) terrorizing the community. **1982** *Ibid.* 30 May, Can you imagine what could happen if it were people of colour who had done that ... It looks like white[s] don't qualify as skollies though. **1984** *Grocott's Mail* 19 Oct. 11 Let the Police keep up the good work ... The Government should not give in to skollies and educated trouble-makers. **1985** [see LARNEY *n.* sense 1 a]. **1986** *Cape Times* 25 Feb., Some of the force used was so serious that a person could only describe it as the actions of *skollies* (rogues) in police uniforms. **1989** *Sunday Times* 31 Dec. 5 The fiery forward lost his cool when a player called him a 'skollie'. **1991** H.P. TOFFOLI in *Style* Nov. 88 As for the Cape Town girls, it's tough

... There are all those hooting, whistling skollies around. You can't bare too much. Not like the girls in Sunnyside, who only have inhibited boereseuntjies to contend with. **1993** M. Mzonqwana in *Democracy in Action* Vol.7 No.5, 32 Skollies or tsotsis take advantage of any situation. It is a most convenient thing for them to be able to blame their actions on apartheid! **1994** *Style* Oct. 30 Pin-stripers queued to sip from tin mugs, street skollies saved up the entrance fee.

Hence **skolly** *v. intrans. nonce*, to scavenge; **skollydom** *n.*, the condition or activity of a skolly; **skollyism** *n.*, the way of life of a skolly.

1949 *Cape Times* 10 Sept. 8 The cure for skollydom is not mollycoddling. **1954** R. St John *Through Malan's Afr.* 32 Experts say that dagga is one of the least harmful of the narcotics, and yet in District 6 it leads to the shebeens and skollyism. **1964** P. Clarke in R. Rive *Modern Afr. Prose* 97 We and the other schoolboys called them 'skollyboys' because they were always 'skollying' for something to eat.

skomfaan /sgɔm'fɑːn/ *n.* Also **sgomfaan**, **skomfana**. [ad. Zulu *isigomfane*, formed on *gomfa* bend, crouch, stoop.] In township slang: a potent illicitly-brewed alcoholic drink (see quot. 1987). Also *comb.* (objective) **skomfaan-drinker**. Cf. SKOKIAAN.

1969 *Post* 16 Feb., Mrs Selina M— travels all the way from Zone 3 in Meadowlands for her regular fruit can of 'sgomfaan'. **1973** P. Clarke in *Contrast 32* Vol.8 No.4, 27 One of the *skomfaan*-drinkers .. asked her to give him a rag to wipe off a spoon he had used .. in the jam-tin *skaal* out of which he had been drinking *skomfaan*. **1980** D.B. Coplan Urbanization of African Performing Arts. 203 Shebeen owners .. could vary their products to suit individual tastes, offering traditional maize and sorghum beer, noxious chemical mixtures such as *babaton*, *'skomfana*, *'shimiyane*, *skokiaan*, and *isikilimikwiki* ('kill me quick'), and commercial European liquors. **1982** *Pace* May 34 All the illegal concoctions being brewed by domestic servants in their quarters — skomfaan, mbamba, skokiaan, barberton, what have you. *Ibid.* 103 It was the time of prohibition and the liquor laws, and good wives would help make ends meet by brewing 'Skomfana'. **1987** M. Melamu *Children of Twilight* 163 Mma-Lekwete's special brew called *skomfaan*, a curious mixture of such incredible ingredients as methylated spirits, used dynamite, malt and various other odds and ends reputed to give the much desired 'kick' to the concoction.

skop /skɔp/ *n.*[1] [Afk., 'kick'.]

1. *slang.* A party, a 'thrash'; in the expression ***to give it a good skop***, to celebrate energetically.

1961 L.E. Van Onselen *Trekboer* 58 'I cannot stay long,', I said. 'Oh, but you will stay for the "skop". Karnallie! Tell him to stay for the "skop".' **1985** *Sn Suburbs Tatler* 25 July, Everybody .. comes down from the hills for the weekly *skop* ... If you've never experienced *sakkie-sakkie* before, don't miss the disco at Paternoster. **1990** A. Rice in *Frontline* Dec. 15 Sadly, I never made it to the jol at Camden Lock, so I can't tell you how many of London's South African emigres responded ... But .. I'll bet that those who did go .. gave it a good skop that night.

2. *colloq.*

a. A kick.

1975 'Blossom' in *Darling* 12 Apr. 95 One more skop, this time from behind, and he's out for the count with yores truly snarling back down the M1 for home sweet home. **1977** *Sunday Times* 30 Nov. (Mag. Sect.) 8 At this spot a giraffe once kicked a warthog a distance of 78 yards. This is a world record for giraffes — and warthogs. It was a big skop. **1983** *Fair Lady* 19 Oct. 45 At Sun City the critics were so thrilled to give me a *skop* in the pants. **1984** *E. Prov. Herald* 9 June 5 (*advt*) Skop a goal with these low prices.

b. *fig.* The 'kick' of alcohol; alcohol itself.

1982 D. Kramer *Bakgat* (*record cover*) We drank dop with a skop. **1983** *Daily Dispatch* 25 Feb. 22 For decades lovers of the ultimate in undiluted 'skop' watched despairingly as distillers grew fewer. **1987** *Sunday Times* 12 Apr., Hey, stop taking the skop out of our dop!

skop /skɔp/ *n.*[2] *slang.* [Prob. a contraction of Afk. *se kop* as in *skaap se kop* sheep's head.] In township Eng.: SMILEY.

1991 *Black Market Report* 2 Dec. 3 *Skop* is said to derive from the Afrikaans words, 'skaap kop' ... Skop is the head of a sheep or cow or goat. **1994** *Sunday Times* 23 Jan. 28 (*advt*) Smilies (also known as skop) is one of the best known, best loved delicacies in the township ... Soccer on Saturday wouldn't be the same without a newspaper wrapped smilie on your lap.

skop /skɔp/ *v. slang.* [Afk., to kick.]

1.a. *intrans.* To kick; also *fig.*, to enjoy oneself, let one's hair down; cf. OPSKOP.

Reduplication (as in quot. 1929) is a common phenomenon in *S. Afr. Eng.*; see note at NOW-NOW for further examples.

*c*1929 S. Black in S. Gray *Three Plays* (1984) Frikkie: You want to fight? Smith: I don't mind. Frikkie: Fair play or skopskop? **1973** *Star* 9 June 12 Skop man. Skop. Skop. **1985** A. Goldstuck in *Frontline* 21 They are all here to 'skop 'n bietjie' with the family. They've come to enjoy themselves, and, wragtig, nothing's going to stop them.

b. *trans.* To kick (something). Also *fig.*

1975 'Blossom' in *Darling* 12 Apr. 95 They even got steel toecaps, in case the cow you milking takes a step forward, then you jis skop her right back, see. **1985** P. Slabolepszy *Sat. Night at Palace* 57 They going to skop me out? I want to see it. I want to see anybody try to kick me out. *Ibid.* 58 He tunes me, ja that's why they skopped me out of Iscor. **1988** *Fair Lady* 22 June (Suppl.) 20 You've got a room where you can just *skop* off your shoes and be yourself.

2. In phrr.: ***skop die blik(kie)*** /ˌskɔp di 'blək(i)/ [Afk., 'kick the tin', *die* the + *blik* tin (+ -IE)], a children's game of hide and seek (called 'Lerky' or 'Urkey' in *Brit. Eng.*) in which a tin is the den and any player able to kick it and shout '*Skop die blik!*' frees those already blocked; ***to skop it***, to die, to 'kick the bucket'; ***to skop lawaai*** [Afk., *lawaai* disturbance, racket], to have a (rowdy) good time (see also LAWAAI).

*c*1966 M. Jabour in *New S. Afr. Writing* 93 Doctor says as soon as your leg is strong enough you'll be able to do everything. Even play Skop die Blik. **1971** *Informant, Grahamstown* Ma we want to go to the Eksteens to play skop-die-blik. **1972** *Drum* 8 Apr., We are not out to skop lawaai .. we wore expensive clothes and moved around with pretty dolls. **1985** P. Slabolepszy *Sat. Night at Palace* 49 Like say — some ou's going to kick the bucket and now you going to take him his oxygen cylinder before he actually skops it. **1987** P. Jooste in *Fair Lady* 25 Nov. 139 Children played *skop die blikkie* in the street and got together impromptu cricket games. **1990** J. Rosenthal *Wake Up Singing* 26 The church hall enveloped in a haze of dust from the early morning games of soccer and 'skop die blik' going on round it. **1991** R. Greenblo in *Farmer's Weekly* 25 Jan. 54 Stories for Joan were not Winnie the Pooh, Tigger and Piglet, but South African songs .. and recollections of games like *skop-die-blik* and *bok-bok* which her mother had played many years before.

skop, skiet, en donder /ˌskɔp ˌskit(ə)n 'dɔnə(r)/ *n. phr.* and *adj. phr. Colloq.* Also **skiet, skop, en donder; skop, skiet and donner**; etc. [Afk., *skop* kick + *skiet* shoot + *en* and + *donder* beat up.]

A. *n. phr.* SKIET EN DONDER *n. phr.*

1970 W.J. Hardman *Informant, Swaziland* The film we saw last night was all skop, skiet en donner. **1978** *Family Radio & TV* 27 Mar. 36 For a really good read, give me *skop, skiet en donder.* **1978** J. Rabie in *Cape Times* 2 Aug. 6 Recently Jan Harmse .. astonished the Afrikaans literary scene with 'Zap-Zap', the raciest, most satirical *skop-skiet-en-donner* to hit our market. **1986** *Uniform* 16 June 7 Gung-ho skop, skiet and donner — but this time it goes too far. **1986** *Frontline* June 31 'Ag, it was the first black movie ... Things have changed nowadays. The blacks fight with the white man, they knock him down, they even kill him.' But don't get the wrong idea. Van der Merwe is talking skiet, skop en donder, not politics. **1988** J. Bunke in *Windhoek Advertiser* (Namibia) 25 Nov. 5 'The Secret of my Success.' This is a nice refreshing change from the usual 'Skiet, Skop en Donner.' **1990** *Sunday Times* 1 Apr. 10 Will he write another book? 'Yes ... Perhaps a skop-skiet-and-donder on illegal ivory trade in Namibia or Zimbabwe.' **1990** *Grocott's Mail* 29 June 6 For droolers of skop, skiet and donner Chuck Norris provides thrills and spills in Braddock: Missing in Action II.

B. *adj. phr.*

1. SKIET EN DONDER *adj. phr.* sense 1.

1972 *Family Radio & TV* 10 Jan., Sean Connery seems quite happy to have stepped back into his old role — even if it is of the skop-skiet-and-donder sort. **1985** *Scope* Apr. 5 Ask stars of *skop-skiet-en-donder* TV shows about the violence and they usually softsoap it. [**1987** G. Silber in *Style* June 26 The black movie sausage-machine annually churns out hundreds of skop, skiet, and phata-phata flicks.] **1989** *Reader's Digest Illust. Hist.* 7 We may not have our lordly declaration of independence, but we have action, deviousness, and enough characters to fill a library of *skop-skiet-en-donder* novels. **1989** *Weekly Mail* 20 Oct. 30 They are an interesting mixture of *skiet, skop 'n donner* films .. ; serious local films; and others which fit into neither category. **1989** *Ibid.* 3 Nov. 28 Patrick Swayze stars in this 'skop, skiet en donner' number .. about a bar-room bouncer hired to clean up a rural night club.

2. SKIET EN DONDER *adj. phr.* sense 2.

1987 *Weekly Mail* 1 May 3 Skop, skiet en donner election.

skorokoro /skɔrɔ'kɔrɔ/ *n. colloq.* Also **isikorokoro**, **skorrokoro**. [SeTswana, old car; perh. echoic (see quot. 1994); or ad. *makgôrôkgôrô* a cramped jumble, or *segologolo* old, antique.] TJORRIE.

1986 R. Bhengu in *City Woman* 2 Nov. p.vi, Those stickers were meant to distinguish a skorokoro from a 'target' ... One posh car even had a sticker that reads 'I love Mshenguville'. Do I need to mention that the driver was white? **1987** *Frontline* Aug.-Sept. 36 In middle-class Parkview nobody raises an eyebrow if the lady of the house drives a beat-up old Beetle, but in Diepkloof Extension it is infra-dig to drive isikorokoro. **1987** *Drive On* Sept. 9 Don't let your car turn into a skorokoro! **1988** *Pace* Mar. 117, I was resigning myself to keeping my old skorokoro on the road by whatever means until it finally gives up the ghost. **1989** *Bumper sticker, Grahamstown* This car is not a skorokoro. **1991** C. Van Ulmenstein in *Weekend Argus* 12 Jan. 5 'Skorokoro' is the name for old vehicles, a term which was used in an advertising campaign by Sasol. **1991** F. Anthony *Journey* 31 Many years back the vehicle had been a beige Mazda ... It now retained only the global aspect of its origin ... The whole vehicle fitted the description *Skorrokoro* (used) which was the term of the region. **1991** O. Ericksson in *Weekend Post* 16 Nov. (Leisure) 4 She called the bakkie a skorokoro, but Vusi told himself this would be the best bakkie ever made. **1994** *Sunday Times* 1 May 15 *Isikorokoro*: What we'll all be driving if car prices continue to escalate, battered heaps also known as *sgodongo* — both words mimic the sound of engines failing to start.

skottel /'skɔt(ə)l/ *n.* Also **schotel**, **skottle**. [Afk. (fr. Du. *schotel*).]

1. A bowl or basin. Cf. BLIKSKOTTEL sense 1.

1913 C. Pettman *Africanderisms* 432 Schotel, (D. *schotel*, a dish; Lat. *scutella*; cf. Eng. *scuttle*). A dish whether of earthenware or tin. **1978** *Fair Lady* 19 July 172 If you find someone with his entrails beside him, place them in a *skottel* or even your skirt and transport them together. **1980** A.J. Blignaut *Dead End Rd* 100 Tjaart was sitting on a camp-stool at the fire with a skottel of hot snake bones on his lap. **1992** M.G. Gilbert *Informant, Ladybrand* The Anglican Church is giving us a morning tea tomorrow ... One puts 20c into a skottle — and everyone eats too much and many can't go to lunch afterwards!

2. In full ***skottel-braai*** /-braɪ/ [see BRAAI *n.* sense 2 a], or ***skottel-skaar*** /-skɑ:(r)/ [Afk., *skaar* plough-disc; so called for a perceived resemblance]: the proprietory name for a large, shallow, concave disc which is similar to a wok but not as deep, which is used as a cooking-surface over a gas cooker, for outdoor cooking; used loosely of any similar appliance; *gas braai*, see BRAAI *n.* sense 2 b. Also *attrib.*

1984 *Sunday Tribune* 22 July (Today) 4 The idea of food free and fresh from the sea is widely appealing ... The editor may now relax — with not a braai grid or even a skottel in sight. **1987** *Scope* 10 Apr. 30 A 'skottelbraai' breakfast on the deserted beach. **1988** *You* 17 Nov. 54 (*advt*) Skottelskaar: Plough share gas braai. Stand permits steady placement on table. Even flame distribution. **1988** *Advertising Leaflet* (Cadac), Mini Skottel. Combines the portability of the Mini with the unique 'plough disc' cooking method. **1989** S. JOHNSON in *Laughing Stock* Sept.-Oct. 12 Knots of hopelessly-addicted new wave braaiers gape and finger price tags ... The 'Skottelskaar' also attracted attention, with its unforgiveably curvaceous lines and tripod base. **1990** *Weekend Post* 25 Mar. (Suppl.), As advertised on TV: Cadac skottelskaar braai. **1990** E. COELHO in *Sunday Times* 12 Aug. 9 Everywhere people are dusting off their skottel-braais, bringing out the coolerbags, buying surplus bottles of suntan lotion, and ironing those Bermuda shorts. **1992** *Weekend Post* 2 May (Property Post) 25 The spray-on grease-cutter will help keep skottels clean after a braai. **1992** C.S. VAN DER GAAST in *Weekend Argus* 23 May (People) 3 He is .. likely to bat one of his green peppers — straight into the skottel, which sometimes accompanies them on Sunday walks up Lion's Head ... 'We love cooking outdoors.' **1994** *Grocott's Mail* 28 Oct. 13 (*advt*) Deluxe vendor's trolley ... Contains Bain Marie and Skottel skaar facilities.

skraal /skrɑ:l/ *adj.* [Afk., thin; flimsy, meagre.] **1.** *colloq.* Thin, scrawny, 'skinny'. Also *fig.*, meagre.

1970 *Informant, Grahamstown* The little boy is skraal and fair-haired. **1978** A.M. SMITH in *Contrast No.46* 44 He's hang of a skraal and his hair's only short, hey. **1981** L. & P. ROBERTSON-HOTZ in *Bloody Horse* No.3, 37 Two skraal, yellow dogs rushed out and started barking. **1991** J. SILVA *Informant, Grahamstown* She's very skraal, with a dark brown bob. **1991** K. SULLIVAN *Informant, Cape Town* My bank balance is skraal this month (meagre).

2. *slang.* Hungry.

1970 M. BENNETT *Informant, Krugersdorp* Skraal. Hungry. **1978** L. BARNES in *The 1820* Vol.51 No.12, 19 If somebody says *I'm skraal*, he probably does not mean he is thin, as one would expect, but rather that he is hungry. **1986** — in *Eng. Usage in Sn Afr.* Vol.17 No.2, 2 *I'm skraal* — 'I'm hungry'. **1991** K. SULLIVAN *Informant, Cape Town*, I am feeling a bit skraal — haven't eaten the whole day.

skrik /skrək/ *n. colloq.* Also **schreik, sc(h)rick, schrijk, skrick.** [Afk., fr. Du. *schrick* fear, terror.] **1.** A fright; used esp. in the phrr. ***to get a skrik, to have a skrik, to give*** (*someone*) ***a skrik***, and (*slang*) ***to catch a skrik.***

1887 A.A. ANDERSON *25 Yrs in Waggon* I. 21 The waggon had been gone half-an-hour when they heard the rattling of wheels in a manner which made them think that the oxen must have had a 'scrick' (scare) from a lion. **1896** H.A. BRYDEN *Tales of S. Afr.* 68 It gave me a very nasty schrijk at the time. **1901** T.R. ADLAM in M. Fraser *Jhb. Pioneer Jrnls 1888–1909* (1985) 94 A small card nailed above the knocker incribed thus: 'Jules Matern, Bertha Schrink' (followed by names of six coolies). This gave me a 'skrick'. Who was Bertha S. and were the coolies living in my house? **1903** D. BLACKBURN *Burgher Quixote* 243 For a moment I got a great schrick, thinking he might be dead, and that they had come to arrest me. **1913** C. PETTMAN *Africanderisms* 432 *Schrik*, .. A start, a fright. The word is in common use, both as a noun and as a verb, all over South Africa. **1913** J.J. DOKE *Secret City* 255 How you do frighten me. You gave me quite a schrik. **1943** F.H. ROSE *Kruger's Wagon* 139 Next moment I experience what we Dutch call a 'skrik'. But it was more than a mere start: it was a shock so sudden and overwhelming that ... I was completely unprepared for it. **1946** S. CLOETE *Afr. Portraits* 322 He certainly — to use a Boer word — gave them all a good 'skrik' — a fright. **1957** B. O'KEEFE *Gold without Glitter* 124 A bloody great snake ... Hell I got a skrik. **1969** A. FUGARD *Boesman & Lena* 7 Remember that night the water came up so high? When we woke up *pap nat* ...? You got such a *skrik* you ran the wrong way. **1976** 'BLOSSOM' in *Darling* 4 Feb. 87 Hang but it only gives you a skrik when yore old folks start to talk like they've had you in chunks. **1984** *Frontline* May 39 The SABC got a hang of a skrik from all the stories about how Bop was buying the best shows from abroad ... It saw its audience and its advertising revenue going for a ball of chalk. **1985** *Cape Times* 2 Sept., Nobody was actually hurt, but my dog got a helluver *skrik* and hid under the bed. **1986** [see VINT]. **1989** [see ANGLIKAANS]. **1990** *Frontline* Jan. 23 'You are bold, Mr Botha' the young man said 'And your thinking's become most verlig. But we're not at all sure what goes on in your head And it gives us one hell of a skrik'. **1993** *Pace* July 56 'Sorry,' Peppy said, 'I didn't mean to give you a *skrik*.' 'Me get a fright?' Tom shook his head and laughed.

2. ***the skriks***: 'the shivers'; an attack or feeling of anxiety, fear, or apprehension.

1967 J. MCINTOSH in *New S. Afr. Writing* No.4, 123 Some prints arrived from Johannesburg that really gave me the *skriks*, and made me shiver. **1975** 'BLOSSOM' in *Darling* 12 Feb. 119 'Who, me?' I tune him, meantime feeling the skriks running up and down my spine. **1977** *E. Prov. Herald* 29 Nov. 2 The Nationalists care all right about which party becomes the official Opposition, it gives them the skriks (shivers) to think it will be the PFP.

skrik /skrək/ *v. colloq.* Also **schrik, scri(c)k, skreck.** [Afk., fr. Du. *verschrikken* to scare.]

a. *intrans.* To become frightened, to start.

*c*1881 A. DOUGLASS *Ostrich Farming* 61 The great secret is to take things quietly, and never to gallop after a bird; when he 'scricks' and runs away, if you can cut him off and turn him, well and good. *Ibid.* 189 Even if the dogs do not chase the birds .. the birds will 'scrik' from them at night, and many are thus killed or injured. **1895** H. RIDER HAGGARD *Nada* 2 The oxen had 'skrecked' in a mob. **1913** [see SKRIK *n.* sense 1]. [**1916** S. BLACK in S. Gray *Three Plays* (1984) 190 He's not afraid of the chief! Aapie! — lekker ga schrik, ne!] **1982** FUGARD & DEVENISH *Marigolds in Aug.* 44 Daan: .. You skrik easy. Milton: You gave me a fright.

b. *trans.* ?*obs.* To frighten (someone).

1892 *The Jrnl* 10 Sept. 3 The Britstown Era comes out with a deep dark headline .. '*The dread messenger*' ... The Era should be more careful about 'Schrikking' folks.

skuif var. SKYF.

skut /skət, skɪt/ *n. obsolescent.* Also **sc(h)ut, ski(e)t.** [Afk. (earlier S. Afr. Du.), ellipt. form of Du. *schutkraal*, see SKUTKRAAL.]

1. A (municipal) pound for the control of stray animals; SKUTKRAAL.

1849 J.D. LEWINS Diary. 76 Sent Fengou to the schut with a horse of A. Ridgard's, I believe. **1882** C. DU VAL *With Show through Sn Afr.* I. 245 Having overhauled him and interrogated him as to his intention, I received for answer the words 'Hamba schut', which my limited knowledge of the Zulu language and Cape Dutch told me meant he was driving them to 'the Pound', a receptacle for strayed cattle. **1892** *The Jrnl* 31 Mar. 4 'Klaas' ... 'Ja, baas,' 'Take these cattle to the skit at once.' 'Maar baas —' 'Don't 'baas' me, take them off.' **1899** *Natal Agric. Jrnl* 31 Mar. 4 'Skit,' in South African, and 'schuthok' in European-Dutch, is always used by the English speakers when addressing kafirs on matters dealing with the useful, yet frequently harassing, institution of civilisation, the stock pound. **1913** C. PETTMAN *Africanderisms* 433 *Schut*, .. The common name in South Africa for what is known in England as the 'pound'; an enclosure for strayed animals. It is often spelled and generally pronounced 'Skit'. **1958** A. JACKSON *Trader on Veld* 41 Stock was often sent by angry farmers to the skut (pound), and only released on payment of a fee of so much per head. **1970** A. PALMER *Informant, King William's Town* We sent the cattle to the skiet (pound).

‖**2.** *comb.* **skutgeld** /-xɛlt/ [Afk., *geld* money], the fee payable upon redemption of an impounded animal; **skuthok** /-hɔk/ [Afk. (earlier S. Afr. Du. *schuthok*), *hok* see HOK], an enclosure at a pound; also Englished form **skut hock.**

1958 A. JACKSON *Trader on Veld* 32 As his neighbours made their pocket money from **'schutgeld'** (pound fees) by catching his stock trespassing on their farms, Rooi was advised to sell one thousand of his horses to provide the wherewithall for the cost of fencing. **1852** A. SCOTT in Godlonton & Irving *Narr. of Kaffir War of 1850–51–52* 253 The party off-saddled here, .. stowed away a part of the unbroken furniture in the **schut hocks** around the dwelling, .. saddled up and rode down to Mr. Temple Nourse's farm. [**1899** see sense 1.]

skutkraal *n. obs.* Also **schutkraal, skitkraal, skuit kraal.** [S. Afr. Du., fr. Du. *schutkraal*, *schut* screen, fence, partition (cf. *schutten* to impound, fence) + *kraal*, see KRAAL sense 3 a.] SKUT sense 1.

1827 G. THOMPSON *Trav.* II. 45 On calling for the horses I had engaged, found they had been put in the skut-kraal or pound. **1832** *Graham's Town Jrnl* 12 Oct. 160 On the following morning the horse was missed; about a month after saw the horse in the Scut-Kraal in Uitenhage. **1836** *Abstract of Proceedings in Albany Settlers 1824–1836* (Soc. for Relief of Distressed Settlers) 75 He also lost 23 oxen at Somerset .. but being put in the Schutkraal and he not having the means of paying the expenses upon them, they were sold. **1839** T. SHONE Diary. 2 May, Outspand in front of Mr Festare House for the night and put our oxen in the Skitkraal for safety during the night. **1850** N.J. MERRIMAN *Cape Jrnls* (1957) 135 We clapped our panniers on the new steed, and trudged on to Bloemfontein, intending when we arrived to deposit the animal in the skuit kraal (pound). [**1899** G. RUSSELL *Hist. of Old Durban* 151 A cherished institution of the Boers, by whom it is known throughout South Africa as the *Schut kraal.*]

skuur var. SCHUUR.

'skuus var. EKSKUUS.

skyf /skeɪf/ *n. slang.* Also **skayf, skuif.** Pl. usu. -**s**, occas. **skuiwe, skywe** /ˈskeɪvə/. [ad. Afk. *skuif* a pull on a pipe, a puff of smoke, fr. Du. *schuiven* to smoke.] **a.** ZOL *n.* sense 1 a. **b.** ZOL *n.* sense 3. Also dim. form **skyfie** [see -IE].

1946 C.P. WITTSTOCK in E. Partridge *Dict. of Underworld Slang* (1950) 399 Dagga .. : laughing skuif, boom, etc. [**1963** see GOOI sense 1 a.] **1967** *Drum* 28 Aug. 7 This roker did not touch liquor at all. What did he get out of smoking dagga? 'It kept me calm and even-tempered ... I couldn't go to sleep at night unless I had a good few skuifs ... If I didn't smoke it, I would fight too much. But when I caught a skuif, I didn't feel like fighting.' **1974** *Eng. Usage in Sn Afr.* Vol.5 No.1, 10 Tobacco is *snout* ... *Skuif* is a cigarette — sometimes also *laugh, spill* or *zoll*. Most *skuiwe* are hand-rolled from *pipe-snout*. *Ibid.* 11 To the ordinary smoker, a *stop* .. means sufficient *snout* to roll a *skuif*. **1977** *Family Radio & TV* 23 Jan. 19 Cigarettes are an extravagance far beyond their almost non-existent means, so they buy cheap pipe-tobacco and roll it in newspaper to make *skyfs*. **1979** *Cape Times* 1 Dec. 11 Smoking dagga green is mostly for the beginner and soon he becomes addicted to smoking his 'skuif' or 'pil' white. (The term white indicates that mandrax tablets ground to a fine white powder have been sprinkled onto the smoker's green dagga.) **1982** J. ALLAN in *Sunday Times* 6 June (Mag. Sect.), The taxi-driver oke (he's got one of those custom-bent *skyfs* like hanging from his lower lip) is taking his cherrie .. for a 'hoddog' and chips. **1985** H. PRENDINI in *Style*

Oct. 39 Student slang .. tends to be more entertaining and imaginative and less deliberately vulgar than southern suburbs jol talk. Students .. 'swaai a zephyr', or get 'goofed' on a 'skyf' (smoke dagga) before .. 'zonking out' (going to sleep). **1987** *Frontline* Oct.-Nov. 11 Bumming pinches of tobacco to make himself skywe. **1990** R. GOOL *Cape Town Coolie* 60, I was just pulling your legs. Take it easy. Sweet. You got a *skayf*? **1990** C. LEONARD in *Weekly Mail* 2 Nov. 29 One of them, a big 'oke' with a moustache, cap, bright orange string vest and lime green bermudas, drags deeply on a dagga cigarette ... His friend, giggling, takes the 'skyf' and follows his example.

skyf /skeɪf/ *v.* [fr. prec.]

a. *trans.* To smoke (a cigarette or reefer).

1971 *Cape Times* 3 July (Mag. Sect.) 4 Boon makes us a lekker zol of B.B. tobacco .. and we skuif it down to a slimy half-inch butt.

b. *intrans.* To smoke.

1977 D. MULLER *Whitey* 16 The shaven heads were thrust forward. 'Skyf,' they said, 'Smoke!' **1985** [see Vula quot. at JOL *n.* sense 1]. **1991** G. DE BEER *Informant, Port Nolloth (N. Cape)* You skyf too much.

‖**slaap** /'slɑːp/ *v. intrans.* In the phr. ***slaap gerust*** /- xə'rəst/ [Du., *slaap* sleep + *gerust* peacefully; the modern Afk. form is *slaap gerus*]: a good-night greeting, 'sleep well'.

1829 C. ROSE *Four Yrs in Sn Afr.* 257 Having completed our supper, were shown to our room, where Hendrick left us with the wish slaap-gerust — sound sleep. **1908** F.C. SLATER *Sunburnt South* 25 Well, good-night, *slaap gerust*. **1910** D. FAIRBRIDGE *That Which Hath Been* (1913) 240 *Slaap gerust*. If you want a zoopje there is Van der Hum on the table yonder and a bottle of old dop. **1951** H. DAVIES *Great S. Afr. Christians* 7 At the conclusion of the service each person shook his neighbour's hand and said, *Slaap gerust!*

slaap-kamer /'slɑːpkɑːmə(r)/ *n. obs.* [Du., *slaap* sleep + *kamer* room, chamber.] A bedroom.

1834 T. PRINGLE *Afr. Sketches* 294 On retiring to rest I was conducted to a *slaap-kamer*, containing three good curtained bedsteads, furnished with two, three, or four feather-beds each. **1841** B. SHAW *Memorials* 64 We were about to prepare the wagon for our night's rest, but found the slaap kamer (bedroom) in such confusion .. that we were constrained to desist from our purpose, and .. we were soon asleep in a less agreeable place. [**1935** P. SMITH *Platkop's Children* 77 Our father he went to the sleep-kamer where there is a great big feather-bed an' a little one as well.]

slag /slax/ *v.* Also **slacht**. [Afk., fr. Du. *slachten* to slaughter.]

a. *trans.* To slaughter (an animal); *rare*, to kill (someone) in battle.

1850 J.D. LEWINS Diary. 8 July, Slachting sheep at Scott's & William's. *a***1931** S. BLACK in S. Gray *Three Plays* (1984) 165 Katoo: Helena Joubert never had no family ... Samuel: Never? Not even a little brother? Katoo: Ah yes, but he was slagged by the Zulus, when Helena was jus' a little girl. **1970** I. PALMER *Informant, Grahamstown* We will have to slag a sheep next week because we are having visitors. **1985** *Learn & Teach* No.3, 33 Grandma slags a chicken. **1990** J. ROSENTHAL *Wake Up Singing* 39 'They call her Tannie Wessels.' 'Yeah, I'll bet they do,' grinned Theo. 'She could "slag" an ox by the look of her!'

b. *intrans.* To provide meat by slaughtering.

1972 'M.S.' *Informant, Graaff-Reinet* The farming community here use 'slag' quite commonly in this 'Anglikaans' that is spoken on the farms. They use it in all tenses too — pronounced the Afrikaans way to boot. 'Have you slagged yet?' the farmer's wife enquires re the weekly killing of the sheep for domestic use. 'No, I am slagging this afternoon', replies her husband. **1991** on TV1, 24 Apr. (Big Time), We slag here, we make boerewors so long it stretch from here to Johannesburg.

So **slag**, **slagtery** /'slaxtəreɪ/ *ns* (perh. *obs.*), slaughter.

1836 J.M. BOWKER *Speeches & Sel.* (1864) 10 Pato said to Colonel Somerset, he had heard .. that the Colonel Smith's last great meeting was to be the time of a great 'slag', and that all the big wigs and friendly chiefs were to be knocked on the head. **1948** A.C. WHITE *Call of Bushveld* 183 A shooting party .. rolled up with tents and with the whole bloody paraphernalia for 'slagtery'. Haulage equipment had been provided to drag animals on to a motor lorry as soon as they were shot.

slagter *n. obs.* Also **slaghter**. [S. Afr. Du., fr. Du. *slachter*.]

a. A butcher.

1822 [see *slagter's brief* at sense b]. *a***1878** J. MONTGOMERY *Reminisc.* (1981) 90 The slagter bills were printed on a half sheet of foolscap, and had a neat border round them — the slagter binding all his movable and immovable property, and his wife and children, to fulfil the payment. An open space was left for his agent to fill in the number of sheep or cattle and the amount purchased.

b. *comb.* **slagter bill**, **slagter's brief** /-brif/ [see BRIEF], a butcher's note of purchase; **slagter's knecht** /-knɛxt/ [see KNECHT], a butcher's agent (see quot. 1822).

*a***1878** [**slagter bill**: see sense a]. **1822** W.J. BURCHELL *Trav.* I. 201 The farm of Pieter Jacobs .. was visited at this time by a *slagter's knegt* (butcher's man), for the purpose of purchasing a large number of sheep. A slagter's knegt is a person commissioned by a butcher in Cape Town to travel into the grazing districts, and buy up the number of sheep or oxen he may require for which the man pays the *grazier*, not in money, but in small notes of hand, called **Slagter's brief**, previously signed by his employer, and the validity of which is certified at the Fiscal's office. **1822** [**slagter's knecht**: see quot. at *slagter's brief* above]. **1824** W.J. BURCHELL *Trav.* II. 19 Not even the butcher's man, or *slagters knegt*, ever made his appearance at this distant farm; although the owner possessed a flock of not less that four thousand sheep. *Ibid.* 178 The place we were in .. was now used only for the accommodation of 'slagter's knegts' and visitors. **1861** P.B. BORCHERDS *Auto-Biog. Mem.* 56 Most of their sheep were disposed of on their farms to butchers' itinerant servants .. generally Germans or other foreigners, and commonly known as slaghter's knechts.

slalla gooshley var. SALA KAHLE.

slamaaier /sla'maɪə(r)/ *n.* Also **slamaier**, **slameier**. [Afk., blend of *Islam* and *Maleier* Malay.] Esp. among Afrikaans-speakers:

1. *obs.* A member of the Cape Muslim community; cf. SLAMS *n.*

1913 C. PETTMAN *Africanderisms* 448 *Slamaier*, (This word seems to have originated in a confusion of the two words *Islam* and *Maleier*.) A term applied to a Malay, a follower of Mahomet. **1934** A.J. BARNOUW *Lang. & Race Problems* 28 A colourful element is added to this half-breed population of the city by the Mohammedan Malayans, Slameier or Slamsen, as they are called by the Dutch. *Ibid.* 29 The Slameiers' Carnival which they celebrate on January 2, has long remained the most picturesque survival of eighteenth century Capetown life.

2. In the Cape Muslim community: one who deals in the supernatural; cf. DOEKUM, SLAMS *n.* See also GOËLERY, *Malay magic* (MALAY *n.* sense 3).

1943 I. FRACK *S. Afr. Doctor* 126 The magic workers or Slamaaiers .. had reduced quackery to the very finest of arts ... I arrived at the farm in the early evening, in time to see the whole family gathered in a corner of the kraal, listening to a weird collection of incantations by the slamaaier. **1975** *Sunday Tribune* 27 July 3 A spiritualist, a bishop, a Catholic priest, a Malay slamaaier, a group of Jehovah's Witnesses and a Scientologist are keeping a close watch on the situation. **1975** *Het Suid-Western* 30 July, The Port Elizabeth slamaaier whom the 'ghost family' consulted and who gave them several 'jumats', tiny parcels wrapped in silver paper and brown cotton, has now asked them to send him a black fowl to be slaughtered as a sacrifice.

Slambie *n. obs.* Also **(T)'Slambi**, **T'Slambie**. [Englished pronunciation-spelling of Xhosa n. stem *-Ndlambe* (as found in the name *ama-Ndlambe*).] A member of the NDLAMBE people. Also *attrib.*

1835 C.L. STRETCH Journal. 23 This sad and disgraceful act of the Commission, which final caused the murder of Landdrost Stockenstrom .. in 1811, and the ruin of the Slambie Tribe in 1817. **1837** J.M. BOWKER *Speeches & Sel.* (1864) 44 On the 10th instant, Umala, and ten other chiefs of the Slambi tribe, brought to me thirty-nine head of cattle. **1846** J. MACLEAN in *Imp. Blue Bks* Command Paper 786–1847, 110 The T'Slambies would never join any party against the Government. **1846** *Ibid.* [see GAIKA]. **1852** M.B. HUDSON *S. Afr. Frontier Life* 43 He referred to a meeting of Slambies he'd had. **1853** F.P. FLEMING *Kaffraria* 24 They were divided into two distinctive bodies of the Gaikas and the T'Slambies. **1864** J.M. BOWKER *Speeches & Sel.* p.vi, He was continued in office as Diplomatic Agent with the 'Slambi and Congo tribes. **1877** C. ANDREWS Reminiscences of Kafir War 1834–5. 24 Three Hottentots who had been with the T'Slambie tribe gave themselves up.

‖**Slams** /slams/ *n.* Also with small initial. [Afk., fr. *slamse* (see next) or formed on *Islam* Islam.] A Cape Muslim person; particularly, one who deals in the supernatural. Cf. SLAMAAIER.

1966 I.D. DU PLESSIS *Poltergeists* 9 On occasion an appeal has been made by a distressed family to send a 'Slams' (wrongly used in South Africa for 'Cape Malay') to deal with startling events which seem to be due to supernatural causes. **1974** A.P. BRINK *Looking on Darkness* 112 'I tole you, I put money away fo' you, Joseph.' 'Yes, Ma.' 'The hospittul took some of it en' the blerry Slams took some of it, but I got a bietjie fo' you.' **1974** Y. BURGESS in S. Gray *On Edge of World*, She went to pee in the veld and that Slams followed her and buried a live bullfrog there and then she couldn't pee any more.

Slamse /'slamsə/ *adj.* Also with small initial. [Afk., contracted form of *Islaamse* Islamic.] Of or pertaining to the Cape Muslim people; in special collocations (now *obs.*), as **Slamseman** [Afk., *man* man], a Muslim man; **Slamsemeisje** [Afk., *meisje* obs. form of *meisie* girl], a Muslim girl or woman.

1913 D. FAIRBRIDGE *Piet of Italy* 71 If our Piet marries other than a Slamsemeisje he may become even such as Da'ood who cares nothing for the Faith. *Ibid.* 291 It is good to make the Hadj ... Now must every Slamseman go, to meet there men from Sham, from .. Marokish .. and to hear much talk. *Ibid.* 314 Make me a Christian, eh? I, who am a slamsemeisje and the wife of Da'ood! **1971** L.G. GREEN *Taste of S.-Easter* 154 All the good old Cape cookery books cry out for coriander; in blatjang and peach pickle, slamse wors and buriyani.

slangbos /'slaŋbɔs/ *n.* Formerly also **slange bosch**. [Afk., *slang* snake + *bos* bush.] A name given to any of several shrubs, esp. the rigid, spiny shrub *Lycium kraussii* (family Solanaceae), the dwarf shrub *Elytropappus glandulosus* (family Asteraceae), or any of several species of the genus *Stoebe*. Also **slangbossie** [see -IE].

1795 C.R. HOPSON tr. *C.P. Thunberg's Trav.* I. 268 The *Slange bosch* (*Seriphium*) which grew here, was said, when made into a decoction, to expel worms. **1809** J. MACKRILL Diary. 67 Slange Bosch, Seraphium, expels Worms. **1917** R. MARLOTH *Common Names* 75 *Slangbos, Stoebe cinera, Elytropappus glandulosus.* Favourable hiding places of snakes. Often employed by mountaineers and campers as bedding. In Karoo applied to *Crassula lycopodioides* ([slang]bossie). **1949** L.G. GREEN *In Land of Afternoon* 36 Those who can climb no more remember their mattresses of slangbos, the grey bush that makes the finest of all open air beds. **1966** C.A. SMITH *Common Names* 422 *Slangbos* ... *Lycium kraussii* ... *Elytropappus scaber* .. the plant mentioned by Thunberg (1773) as 'Seriphium,' .. used as an antidote for snakebite, and not really from its being a favourite hiding place for snakes, as Marloth suggests. **1987** T.F.J. Van Rensburg *Introduction to Fynbos* 17 Slangbos or 'kooigoed' (*Stoebe* spp.) are conspicuous amongst wagon trees on unstable scree slopes. **1988** M. Branch *Explore Cape Flora* 22 Spittle bugs on small leafed slangbos.

slangen-vrechter, slangenvreeter varr. SLANGVREETER.

slangkop /ˈslaŋkɔp/ *n.* [Afk., *slang* snake + *kop* head (see quot. 1966).] Any of several species of plant of the Liliaceae and Amaryllidaceae which are highly poisonous to livestock. Also *attrib.* See also GIFBOL.

1896 R. Wallace *Farming Indust. of Cape Col.* 96 One species of tulp, under the name of 'slangkop' (snake head), or poison onion, *Ornithoglossum glaucum*, Sal., which comes up in September and disappears in December, is particularly prevalent and destructive in the vicinity of Mafeking. **1905** D. Hutcheon in Flint & Gilchrist *Science in S. Afr.* 355 'Slangkop,' *Ornithoglossum glaucum Sallisb.* — This is another bulbous plant which is found over a large area of South Africa. When eaten by stock, it produces similar effects to those produced by 'Tulp,' more especially on sheep who eat it readily when young. **1911** [see GIFBOL]. **1929** J. Stevenson-Hamilton *Low Veld* 19 Cattle are subject to a variety of ills, mainly due to ticks, and those animals not indigenous to the Low-Veld are often fatally poisoned by a weed known as slangkop, from its resemblance to a snake's head. **1929** *Handbk for Farmers* (Dept of Agric.) 201 We distinguish between the Transvaal Slangkop (*Urginea Burkei*), the Natal slangkop (*Urginea macrocentra*), and the Cape slangkop (*Ornithoglossum glaucum*). **1930** *Outspan* 31 Oct. 69 'Chincherinchee,' which often finds its way into forage, 'gifblaar,' the various 'tulps' and 'slangkops,' are all responsible at different seasons and in different areas for considerable mortality among stock. **1937** *Handbk for Farmers* (Dept of Agric. & Forestry) 453 Slangkop Group of Plants (*Liliaceae and Amaryllidaceae*). **1936** W.B. Humphreys in *Hansard* 10 Mar. 1007 This poisonous plant, which is coarsely called vermeerbos, covers a vast area, a greater area than prickly pear or jointed cactus, slangkop or gifblaar. **1966** C.A. Smith *Common Names* 423 Slangkop, The name most generally heard for *Ornithoglossum viride, Urginea burkei* and *U. macrocentra*, all highly toxic to stock ... They are usually referred to as slangkop .. from some resemblance of the inflorescence as it rises from the bulb to a snake's head. **1989** F.G. Butler *Tales from Old Karoo* 81 The poisonous tulp after which the farm was named was not in bloom, but the slangkop was — dozens of yellow racemes on long stalks like cobras' heads, swaying. **1989** J. du P. Bothma *Game Ranch Management* 189 Springbok proved to be the most resistant to slangkop poisoning of all animals tested.

slangmeester /ˈslaŋˌmɪəstə(r)/ *n. Obs.* exc. *hist.* [S. Afr. Du., *slang* snake + *meester* master.] One (esp. among the Khoisan) who is expert in the handling of snakes and the treatment of snake-bites.

1827 G. Thompson *Trav.* I. 399 Among the Bushmen are found individuals called *slang-meesters* (serpent-masters). **1828** T. Pringle *Ephemerides* 174 Several of the most respectable Dutch colonists assured me .. that there are to be found among the wandering Bushmen persons whom they term Slang-Meesters, who actually possess the power of charming the fiercest serpents, and of readily curing their bite. **1837** J.E. Alexander *Narr. of Voy.* I. 344 The 'slang meester' then seized the neck firmly: when immediately the snake coiled itself in agony round his right arm. **1955** L.G. Green *Karoo* 183 It would be more difficult to find a genuine slangmeester nowadays than any of the snakes I have mentioned. Some of the old Karoo Hottentots undoubtedly possessed the art of proofing themselves against all sorts of poisons, especially snake venom. I would not say that the last slangmeester or gifdokter has passed on, for as recently as 1928, the late Dr. P.W. Laidler found an extremely clever one practicing in Namaqualand. **1973** Y. Burgess *Life to Live* 12 Witbooi could only reply that he had done his best, that he was not, nor had he ever made himself out to be, a slangmeester.

slangvreeter *n. obs.* Also **slangen-vrechter, slangenvreeter.** [S. Afr. Du. *slangvreter*, fr. Du. *slangen* snakes + *vreter* eater.] The SECRETARY, *Sagittarius serpentarius.*

1786 G. Forster tr. *A. Sparrman's Voy. to Cape of G.H.* I. 154 The Hottentots give it a name most suitable to its nature, *viz.* as translated into Dutch, *slangen-vreeter*, (or serpent-eater). **1796** E. Helme tr. *F. Le Vaillant's Trav.* II. 244 (Jeffreys), The secretary is known in the colonies both by the name *secretaris*, and by that of *slangvreeter*. *c***1808** C. von Linné *System of Natural Hist.* VIII. 20 Kolbe has confounded it with the pelican; for the name of *slang-vreeter*, serpent-eater, which he applies to the pelican, is the only appellation by which this bird is known, both by the Hottentots and the Dutch colonists. The name of *secretaire*, or secretary, was afterwards given it by the Dutch. **1847** 'A Bengali' *Notes on Cape of G.H.* 80 The 'Secretary bird' called by the colonists '*slangen-vrechter*,' or serpent-eater, is common in the interior. **1867** E.L. Layard *Birds of S. Afr.* 33 *Serpentarius Reptilivorus. .. Le Mangeur de Serpents* .. ; Secretary Bird; *Slangvreter* of Colonists. **1897** H.A. Bryden *Nature & Sport* 53 The curious secretary bird (Sagittarius secretarius, the 'Slang vreeter' — snake-killer — of the Boers), that puzzle to scientists, still stalks the veldt with ludicrous solemnity. **1913** C. Pettman *Africanderisms* 449 *Slang vreeter*, .. The Dutch name for the Secretary bird.

slap /slap/ *adj.* Also **slup.** [Afk., dangling; weak, flabby; flexible.]

1. *slang.* Feeble, lacking energy; ineffectual; disorganized, sloppy; lacking in discipline; flabby, limp, slack; (esp. of food) runny, soft.

1970 K. Nicol *Informant, Durban* Only a very slap mackie could live in a pigsty of a room like this. **1970** *Informant, Grahamstown* That horse is slap, he can barely go faster than a jog. [**1972** M. Van Biljon in *Star* 16 June 6 Members of the Cabinet .. are gradually exchanging those long slap limousines that used to make parliamentary parking look like an undertakers' convention.] **1973** K. Dawe *Informant, Grahamstown*, I really hated that school — one could only call it 'slap'. [**1978** *Informant, OFS* His nickname at school was Slap, because he was so casual and easygoing.] **1982** *Sunday Times* 15 Aug. 3 It was while she was at this ad agency that the idea of 'The Kugel Book' was born — although it took her three years to write because she was 'very *slap*'. **1984** *Informant, Johannesburg* If the organization's slap the results are slap and that's all there is to it. **1985** *Fair Lady* 3 Apr. 139 If it rains or there is what the locals call a 'slap' mist, the flowers might not open at all. **1991** on TV1, 24 Apr. (Big Time), The people are complaining the pap is too slap. **1991** P. Buck *Informant, Johannesburg* I'm sorry that this is such a 'slap' communication, but I look forward to hearing from you. **1993** A.L. Haycock *Informant, Grahamstown* He brought chips .. — crisp outside and slap inside.

2. Special collocations. **slap chip** *colloq.*, usu. in *pl.*, hot fried potato chips (distinguishing these from 'chips', the *S. Afr. Eng.* term for potato crisps), often referring to chips fried until they are cooked but not crisp; **slapgat** /ˈslapxat/ *slang* [see quot. 1973], not in polite use, (as *adj.*) useless, lazy, slovenly, undisciplined; (as *n.*) a lazy or undisciplined person.

1972 R. Malan *Ah Big Yaws* 17 Several *Dry-fin* [drive-in] restaurants cunningly distinguish between these [*sc.* crisps] and the French-fried potato chips by referring to the latter as *Long chups* or **Slup chups.** **1982** [see VERLEP]. **1986** D. Wilson in *Argus* 1 Jan. 2 Antoinette let out a joyous shriek like an early-morning seagull discovering some discarded *slap* chips outside a roadhouse. **1988** *Flying Springbok* Oct. 141 These days, it is perfectly possible to plan a holiday that actually avoids the lunchtime *slap* chips and burgers of wayside cafés. **1988** *Weekly Mail* 18 Oct. 19 James .. with his celebrated Portuguese cafe ... 'You want one packet of Chesterfield, slap chips, what you want?' **1989** B. Ronge in *Sunday Times* 9 Apr. (Mag. Sect.) 9, I once starved myself all day to do justice to an immensely chi-chi repast prepared by a visiting French chef ... After the meal .. I fled straight to the nearest Bimbo's where I bought a large packet of hot, *slap* chips drenched in vinegar. **1990** C. Fluxman on TV1, 17 Oct. (Good Morning South Africa), There's nothing like a delicious burger with onions and slap chips. **1991** *Fair Lady* 27 Mar. 49 Final proof that the royals are human — Heinz Tomato Ketchup features on their list of warrants. For the Queen Mother's burgers? The Queen's hot dogs? Di's slap chips? **1991** *Sunday Times* 2 June (Mag. Sect.) 37 It was one of those small little Portuguese supermarkets ... You could buy old eggs, old fish in batter, the usual *slap* chips, a toasted whatever. Or you could go for peri-peri chicken. **1993** M. Schofield in *Cape Librarian* Mar. 38 A plate of 'slap' chips and tomato sauce and coffee stylishly served in styrofoam cups. **1994** [see GOOI sense 1 b]. **1970** S.E. Natham *Informant, Cape Town* **Slapgat.** Untidy (crude). **1973** Beeton & Dorner in *Eng. Usage in Sn Afr.* Vol.4 No.2, 51 *Slapgat*, adj .. lit: slack hole. Vulgar expression wh[ich] refers to a useless person. **1974** *Informant, Grahamstown* Mrs S— said in class this morning that we were the most slapgat school she'd ever been in. **1985** P. Slabolepszy *Sat. Night at Palace* 11 Vince: Katz!? What about him? Forsie: He's a slapgat.

Hence **slapheid** *n.* [Afk., abstract n.-forming suffix *-heid* -ness], looseness, sloppiness.

1978 *Darling* 20 Dec. 33 She shambles across the room .. and throws herself into a chair, arms dangling. There is a familiar *slapheid* about her actions which doesn't quite level with the new-look.

slaphakskeentjies /ˈslapˈhakskɪənkis/ *n.* Also **slaphaksteentjies.** Pl. unchanged. [Afk., *slap* see SLAP + *hakskeen* heel (Du. *hak* heel + *scheen* shin) + dim. suffix -IE + pl. *-s*.]

a. *pl. n.* Onions cooked in a sauce, served as a salad.

1977 *Fair Lady* 8 June (Suppl.) 38 Slaphakskeentjies (Weak heels — boiled onions with egg sauce). **1978** [see FUNERAL RICE]. **1990** *Style* July 18 A buffet of hors d'oeuvres made up of dishes which sing with the robust flavours of traditional Cape food: smoked snoek and moskonfyt, fragrant pickled fish, marinated mushrooms, mussels and calamari — and slaphaksteentjies, those delicious little baked onions.

b. *noncount.* Onion salad.

1978 M. Van Biljon in *Sunday Times* 24 Dec. (Mag. Sect.) 1 Salads, beetroot, tomato .. and 'slaphakskeentjies' which, for those who don't know, is a salad of small onions in a sweet-sour sauce. **1981** S.J.A. De Villiers *Cook & Enjoy It* (1991) 289 Cooked onion salad ('slaphakskeentjies') ... Serve hot as a vegetable or cold as a salad. **1986** M. Van Wyk *Cooking the S. Afr. Way* 35 Onion Salad (Slaphakskeentjies).

slasto /ˈslæstəʊ/ *n.* Also with initial capital. [Blend of Eng. *slate* + *stone*.] The proprietory name of a slate-like shale used (often in irregularly-shaped pieces) for flooring and tiling; applied loosely to any similar material. Also *attrib.*

1970 *Informant, Krugersdorp* Slasto. Large flat slabs of shale. **1986** *Cape Times* 15 Feb. (Weekend Homefinder) 1 A face brick home in Constantia's picturesque Strawberry Lane ... Windows: Wood framed. Flooring: Carpeting and golden Slasto tile. **1986** *Style* June 78 The hallway has a spiral staircase entirely covered in slasto. **1988** *Fair Lady* 22 June (Suppl.) 19 The room .. was very dark with a wooden ceiling, plywood panelling, a slasto fireplace and an ugly metal window. **1988** H. Prendini in *Style* June 102 We're talking Blairgowrie, Westdene, Mondeor. The land of the slasto patio, the curlicued burglar guard, the avo dip. **1993** I. Vladislavić *Folly* 135 It was a cute miniature, complete with .. a fibreglass swimming-pool with Slasto surround and a Kreepy Krauly.

slave bell *n. phr.* A large bell hung between two white-washed pillars, or in a tall white-washed arch, used in the past to summon slaves and mark certain times of the day, as the beginning and end of work periods. Also *attrib.*

1926 P.W. LAIDLER *Tavern of Ocean* 203 Behind .. are traces of terracing indicating former vineyards. Among the oaks stood the slave-bell, and from one tree hung a pair of scales, dated 1756. *c***1937** C.E. PEERS *Our Land* 8 Reminiscent of by-gone days the slave bell still survives on many of the old Cape farms. **1946** T. MACDONALD *Ouma Smuts* 14 The old slave bells by the farmhouses were still rung to bring the coloured folk to work and to end the labour of their days, but all were now free men. **1949** J. MOCKFORD *Golden Land* 47 The dominant farmhouse was usually flanked by the wine cellar, the slave quarters and the stables, and these, together with carefully treated adjuncts such as slave bell towers, pigeon houses and enclosing walls, formed a complex. **1975** *E. Prov. Herald* 4 Dec. 24 Legend says that if the slave bell is tolled on New Year's Eve the ghost will ride again. **1977** [see RINGMUUR]. **1982** A.P. BRINK *Chain of Voices* 302 When the slave bell is rung in the morning he has to fall in just like us .., although he's neither slave nor Hottentot and can come and go as he wishes. **1990** *Weekend Argus* 10 Feb. (Weekender) 4 The Oranje Zight homestead was surrounded by outbuildings, including slave quarters and an impressive slave bell.

slave chair *n. phr.* An antique kitchen chair of simple design, purported to have been made or used by slaves at the Cape.

1946 H.C. BOSMAN in L. Abrahams *Cask of Jerepigo* (1972) 183 It was an old Cape chair with dowelling-pins less than an eighth of an inch in diameter, and the mortise and tenon joints as solid as when the chair was constructed over a century ago ... I read, on the dealer's tag .., these words, 'Old Cape Slave Chair'. **1963** W. FEHR *Treasures at Castle of Good Hope* 264 The utility chairs made of stinkwood or yellowwood with solid square legs but attractively styled wooden backs are usually referred to as Slave chairs denoting that many of these were made by slaves, particularly on farms. **1971** BARAITSER & OBHOLZER *Cape Country Furn.* p.xv, What is the attraction of a low worn-away kitchen chair (commonly called a slave-chair: but how many slaves had shoes that could have produced the characteristic wearing-away of the front rail?). **1971** L.G. GREEN *Taste of S.-Easter* 49 The so-called 'slave chairs', made on farms, have riempies, as cane was not easily available in the country. **1973** M.A. COOK *Cape Kitchen* 67 Chairs .. were also apt to be extremely old but were definitely kitchen chairs ... Dealers usually call these chairs 'slave chairs', but this name is purely a flight of fancy and was designed to create an aura of romance.

slecht(e) var. SLEG.

‖**sleep** /sliəp/ *v. trans.* Also **slepe**, **slip(e)**. [Afk., fr. Du. *slepen*.] To drag (someone or something).

1838 J.E. ALEXANDER *Exped. into Int.* II. 211 He was seized by a lion, he called in vain for help, and was slipped off among the reeds. *a***1858** J. GOLDSWAIN *Chron.* I. (1946) 75 Thear apread to be serfishent blood for a Ox but they Kaffers had sleped him into a bead of rushes. *Ibid.* II. 33 They Kaffers had sliped him along the ground and rocks. **1969** A. FUGARD *Boesman & Lena* 6 It's *me*, that thing you *sleep* along the roads. **1970** L.A. HOPKINS *Informant, Cape Town* Don't sleep that thing along the floor. [**1985** *S. Afr. Digest* 30 Aug. 778 South African English is indeed a unique genre of its own ... It did bring home the numerous linguistic oddities in a cross-culture where a dress becomes a *drag* and a drag becomes a *sleep*.]

Hence **sleper** *n.*, an implement which is dragged over the veld to clear bush. Also *attrib.*

1934 *Farming in S. Afr.* Dec. 371 (Swart), Where the veld is fairly level, farmers in this area use, today, an implement known locally as a 'sleper' which, by being dragged through a patch, uproots the bushes. **1934** C.P. SWART Supplement to Pettman. 159 *Sleper*, .. A home-made drag employed by farmers to eradicate undesirable vegetation by uprooting and cutting it up. The frame of this instrument is usually made of steel rails and the cutters are fashioned out of old wagon-springs. Two or three applications of the sleper method serve to keep the veld clean.

Sleepy Hollow *n. phr. Colloq.* [Special sense of general Eng. *Sleepy Hollow* any place with a soporific atmosphere, or characterized by torpidity.] A nickname given to the city of Pietermaritzburg, in KwaZulu-Natal. Also *attrib.* See also MARITZBURG.

1949 O. WALKER *Proud Zulu* (1951) 139 Never had such an array of V.C.'s, C.B.'s, and titles descended in scarlet and gold upon 'Sleepy Hollow' as the little rustic, Dutch-gabled capital of Maritzburg was known. **1988** K. MKHIZE in *Frontline* Mar. 11 Blood River at Sleepy Hollow. No one has ever been interested in Maritzburg. People have called us 'Sleepy Hollow'. Now we are suddenly in the spotlight. **1994** E. NAIDU in *Natal on Sat.* 8 Jan. 11 Party-time in the Sleepy Hollow. It's party time in Pietermaritzburg, and the Natal capital seems hell-bent on shrugging off its 'Sleepy Hollow' tag ... Cynics had better note – 'Sleepy Hollow' is wide awake.

sleg /slex, slɛx/ *adj.* Formerly also **slecht**. [Afk.] Bad, poor; wicked.

1900 B. MITFORD *Aletta* 34 We would soon show him whether we young ones are so *sleg*! **1900** S.T. PLAATJE *Boer War Diary* (1973) 91 Snyman had gone up country to fight Plumer as his Dutch opponents were very 'slecht' and generally good for nothing. [**1913** J.J. DOKE *Secret City* 280 'How many men have you got?' 'Drie honderd,' said the man, 'but most of them are sick, baaija slecht,' and he spat reflectively into the fire.]

Hence **sleg** *adv.* (*slang*), unpleasantly, badly.

1962 G. SMITH *Informant, Johannesburg* Don't jerry me squint or I'll chat you sleg with my charmies [*sc.* eyes].

‖**Slegs vir Blankes** /ˈslɛxs fər blaŋkəs, ˈslɛxs fə-/ *adj. phr.* Also **Slegs Blankes**. [Afk., *slegs* only + *vir* for + *blankes* white people.] Only for whites; cf. BLANKES ALLEEN. Usu. *attrib.* See also BLANKE.

In the past this was the Afrikaans wording on racially-restrictive signs; the phr. was subsequently used allusively of institutions or structures perceived to be subject to the influence of apartheid.

1956 A. SAMPSON *Drum* 85 At every turning were the signs *Slegs vir Blankes, Nie Blankes*, sorting the two races like an infallible machine, and sending them separate ways. **1973** *Time* 15 Oct. 26 Elevators may still carry 'Slegs vir blankes' (Reserved for whites) signs, but the rule is ignored. **1975** *Sunday Times* 21 Sept. 20 It's just no use pretending to the delegate from Verkeerdevlei that the law hasn't changed .. and then expect him to nod comprehendingly when you whip the 'Slegs vir Blankes' sign off the Sannieshof post office. **1982** *Ibid.* 5 Sept. (Mag. Sect.) 29 Beside me on the old, wooden *Slegs Blankes* bench are a pair of feet which lead to dirty grey socks. **1986** *Style* Dec. 41 The Mayor of Bloemfontein stopped Eartha Kitt singing in the Slegs Blankes town hall. **1987** 'K. DE BOER' in *Frontline* Oct.-Nov. 42 What was my surprise to find no 'slegs blankes' or even 'slegs boere' notices. **1992** 'K. LEMMER' in *Weekly Mail* 16 Apr. 24 Vaal rugby's still 'slegs blankes'.

slenter var. SCHLENTER *n.*

slepe var. SLEEP.

slim /sləm/ *adj.* Usu. *derog.* Also **slimme**. [Du., clever; wily.]

Introduced from Dutch into *Brit. Eng.* during the 17th century, and during the 19th century reinforced by *S. Afr. Eng.* usage.

1. Clever, shrewd; sly, cunning, crafty, underhand, wily. So also the comparative forms **slimmer**, **slimmest**.

[**1806** J. BARROW *Trav.* II. 100 A man, who in his dealings can cheat his neighbour, is considered as a slim mensch, a clever fellow.] **1836** C.L. STRETCH Journal. 4 July, One observed the Col. was a heathen, another that he was very slim and others that he was a devil that escaped from the herd of swine. **1866** E. WILSON *Reminisc.* 89 It would appear that Schlangani had carried on thieving for years, with the greatest impunity, – he being, according to colonial parlance, very 'slim'. **1872** in A.M.L. Robinson *Sel. Articles from Cape Monthly Mag.* (1978) 283 Of all the 'bywohners' hanging on to the skirts of the language there is only one to which we have a decided aversion – to wit, that symbol of Oily-Gammon-Iago-Judas-Iscariotism, 'slim'. We confess we hate the word, and .. that off-coloured cleverness, that masked fair-seeming roguery, which its glib snake-like sound so aptly represents. **1887** A.A. ANDERSON *25 Yrs in Waggon* II. 120 It is necessary to be very slim, as it is called here, that is very sharp and clever in stalking your game. **1891** [see TRONK sense a]. **1897** H. RAYMOND *B.I. Barnato* 29, I have always found that I was as good a hand at buying and selling as most people I came across, and my experiences with the slimme Dutch farmers on the Kimberley market were sometimes very queer. [*Note*] A Cape-Dutch word in general use in S.A., signifying sly, cunning, with a propensity for cheating. The nearest English equivalent is perhaps 'knavish'. **1908** —— *Leaven* 268 Gambling? He's a demon at it ... He is very smart; about the 'slimmest' kafir in the compound. **1910** J. BUCHAN *Prester John* (1961) 39 The Dutch about here are a slim lot, and the Kaffirs are slimmer. Trust no man, that's my motto. **1910** D. FAIRBRIDGE *That Which Hath Been* (1913) 201 Have a care, mynheer, they are very *slim*, the men who pull the strings of this agitation. **1929** J.G. VAN ALPHEN *Jan Venter* 200 When anyone suggested that he had been a bit *slim* in a deal, he would shrug his shoulders and say, 'Vel, look how we haf been persecuted'. **1937** H. KLEIN *Stage Coach Dust* 125 We have been up all night spooring him amongst the rocks on the kopje; he was slimmer than a dassie (a rock rabbit). **1940** F.B. YOUNG *City of Gold* 188 Paul Kruger's too slim to run the risk of having anything he has said recorded in black and white. *Ibid.* 452 Oom Paul is slimmer than you think, Andries. **1984** J. SCOTT in *Cape Times* 18 Feb. 11 'The wording is very *slim*,' admitted Dr. Helgaard van Rensburg of Mossel Bay. 'It could just as well have come out of a National Party publication.' **1993** *Ibid.* 25 Feb. 11 Having put the Chinese in their place, Mr Stofberg turned his attention to the 'very *slim* Jewish community'. It caused an uproar.

2. In nicknames, with a first name, with (grudging) admiration:

a. ***Slim Piet***: The Anglo-Boer War General, Petrus Jacobus Joubert.

1900 H. BLORE *Imp. Light Horseman* 251 The last was a thick-set, dark-complexioned man, with a broad face .. which bore no trace of that sagacity which had earned for him the sobriquet of 'Slim Piet Joubert'. **1911** L. COHEN *Reminisc. of Kimberley* 303 Joubert was known all his life as 'Slim Piet', and .. he could drive a bargain with the acumen of a Scotchman and the intelligence of an Israelite. **1923** B. RONAN *Forty S. Afr. Yrs* 173 The Executive of the Transvaal was composed of men whose names afterwards became historical .. Commandant-General P.J. Joubert ('Slim Piet'). **1937** B.H. DICKE *Bush Speaks* 45 Just imagine the position in which 'Slim Piet' found himself. 'Slim' (crafty) Piet, they called him, the commandant general, because his political moves surpassed his generalship; his plausible tongue, his sword.

b. ***Slim Jan(nie)***: Field-Marshal Jan Smuts.

1926 S.G. MILLIN *S. Africans* 131 'Slim Jannie' the people call him; and by that they mean many things – some not flattering. **1946** T. MACDONALD *Ouma Smuts* 7 His political enemies use the term in its definition of craftiness or slyness, but some of his friends also called him 'Slim Jannie' to stress his cleverness or astuteness. **1955** A. DELIUS *Young Trav.* 93 'Of course, the "brei" is the only thing that I and Slim Jannie have in common,' said Oom Thys and laughed uproariously ... Oom Thys was a nationalist and .. he was still very annoyed about being outsmarted by 'Clever Jannie' – as Smuts was known to many of his own people. **1970** *Cape Times* 16 May (Mag. Sect.) 2 To many he was 'Slim Jannie,' whose reasonable phrases masked a ruthlessness that revealed itself in the *platskiet-politiek* of the 1922 Rand Revolt, Bulhoek and the Bondelswart rebellion. **1970** *Daily News* 29 May, He was known among his Boer comrades-at-arms as 'Slim Jannie' ... 'Slim' as they used it, simply meant 'clever', and not .. 'cunning or crafty'. **1977** D. MULLER *Whitey* 89 He fixed his eyes on the photograph of J.C. Smuts ... He found that the unsmiling eyes of Slim Jan held a chilly light.

Hence **slimness** *n.*, craftiness, cunning.

1899 'S. ERASMUS' *Prinsloo* 76 He found that his partner used his great slimness rather for himself than for him. **1911** *Farmer's Weekly* 29 Mar. 11, I could tell some amusing anecdotes with regard to sheep stealing and the slimness of the native thief. **1930** J. BUCHAN *Four Adventures* 179 We do not understand slimness in this land. If you are honest you will be rewarded, but if you dare to play a double game you will be shot like dogs. **1946** S. CLOETE *Afr. Portraits* 283 The Boer understood this double standard as little as the British understood the Boer 'slimness,' which is its equivalent. No slavery, said the British. Then they took a man's land, imposed a head tax on him, and forced him to work.

slinger /'slɪŋə/ *n.* [Unknown (but see quot. 1953).] The seabream *Chrysoblephus puniceus* of the Sparidae.

The name 'slinger' is used for this species in Smith and Heemstra's *Smiths' Sea Fishes* (1986).

1905 *E. London Dispatch* 21 Nov. 3 Catching ten fish all 'slingers' totalling 35 lbs. weight, in under two hours. **1949** J.L.B. SMITH *Sea Fishes* 272 *Chrysoblephus puniceus* ... *Slinger* (Natal and Mozambique). *Wara-Wara* (French Colonies) ... Found only on the east coast of Africa, in deepish water. Most abundant off Mozambique ... Smaller numbers plentiful off Durban, odd migrants reach East London, very young fishes sometimes found at Knysna. **1953** B. FULLER *Call Back Yesterday* 107 One afternoon yet another variety, hitherto unnamed, appeared on deck ... Alex .. shouted, 'Oh, never mind the names; just sling 'em aboard'. Whereupon the fish concerned became 'The Slinger', a name which it has retained. **1984** *E. Prov. Herald* 10 May 21 Research into line fish ... There will be comprehensive life histories of kob, elf .. leervis, slinger, dageraad, .. among others. **1991** *Weekend Post* 6 Apr. 4 Size limits remain the same for .. slinger (25cm).

slip(e) var. SLEEP.

slip-slop *n. colloq.* [Perh. fr. general Eng. *slip-slop* to move with a flapping sound; or ad. general Eng. *flip-flop*, perh. influenced by Afk. *slof* easy slipper; or named for the slip-on nature of the sandal, and its loose fit.] A slip-on beach sandal consisting of a thick rubber sole with a V-shaped thong, attached to it on either side of the instep and between the first and second toes; PLAKKIE sense 2; SLOP. Also *attrib.*

1970 M. WEITZMAN *Informant, Johannesburg* A type of rubber sandal. She is wearing blue slip slops. **1971** [see PLAKKIE sense 2]. **1976** 'BLOSSOM' in *Darling* 4 Feb. 87 One slip-slop. I lost the other one on South Beach when we was down at Durbs last. **1976** J. MCCLURE *Rogue Eagle* 31 Knotted blouse, blue jeans and slip-slop sandals. **1981** *E. Prov. Herald* 3 Mar. 11 At the end of last year we had .. one tiny pre-school-size girl's white shoe; and one slip-slop. **1987** G. STUART in *New Coin Poetry* June 23 My feet in slip-slops were smelling from the sweat and the car was filled with screaming kids. **1989** J. HOBBS *Thoughts in Makeshift Mortuary* 224 I'd go bananas if I had to share my house with a pair of slip-slops. **1990** *Personality* 27 Aug. 12 Whenwe women .. wear cotton print dresses and slip-slops and will never be seen having a chiboolie at the bar with the men. **1991** M. KANTEY *All Tickets* 43 Some students get off .. and I start thinking how their different clothes start to lose their idiosyncracy and take on a kind of uniform: cotton print, Afrika and leather for new agers; T-shirts, shorts and slip-slops for would-be technocrats; fashion and gold for the marriageable.

sloot /slu:t, sluət/ *n.* Forms: α. **sloat, sloet, sloot, slote**; β. **sluit.** [S. Afr. Du., later Afk. (fr. Du. *sloot* ditch). The form *sluit* is perh. a pronunciation-spelling on the analogy of *fruit*; but it has also been suggested that it is a confusion between *sloot* and SPRUIT (the latter being occas. pronounced /spru:t/).]

1. Esp. during the 19th century: a narrow water-channel constructed for the flood-irrigation of gardens or farm-lands; FURROW; WATER-FURROW. See also LEAD.

α. **1818** C.I. LATROBE *Jrnl of Visit* 187 It has .. water in abundance, brought by a *slote*, or canal, from a considerable distance. **1844** J. BACKHOUSE *Narr. of Visit* 216 He had formed a dam in the Tyamie River, and had cut a waterditch or *sloat*, by which a considerable piece of ground was irrigated. **1852** A. ESSEX in A. Rabone *Rec. of Pioneer Family* (1966) 33 The Sunday's River, a stream which you can generally walk across .., the greater part of the water being dammed up and led through the town in open gutters called sloots so as to irrigate the gardens and furnish the inhabitants with water for domestic purposes. **1852** C. BARTER *Dorp & Veld* 33 Going on one dark night to a friend's house, and keeping in the middle of the road to avoid the *sloots*, I stumbled over .. a large black ox. **1861** LADY DUFF-GORDON *Lett. from Cape* (1925) 69 There is no water but what runs down the streets in the *sloot*, a paved channel, which brings the water from the mountains and supplies the houses and gardens. **1880** E.F. SANDEMAN *Eight Months in Ox-Waggon* 38 The noisy .. croaking of innumerable frogs in all the sloots running along each side of the streets. **1921** H.F. MANDELBROTE tr. *O.F. Mentzel's Descr. of Cape of G.H.* I. 119 The garden is advantageously situated for watering purposes ... Each flower or vegetable bed is surrounded by sloots and water-furrows. **1965** C. VAN HEYNINGEN *Orange Days* 26 The water that ran past the house .. was in an open sloot, not cemented out. Besides being used for household purposes it was also used for watering the garden.

β. **1857** W. ATMORE in *Cape Monthly Mag.* II. Sept. 130 Referring again to the sketch, the dotted lines represent the right of passage water-sluits. **1867** *Blue Bk for Col. 1866* JJ41, The water of the Cogman's River has been led into the farm 'Karpad' by means of a long drain or sluit, built by the side of the bed of the river, almost entirely of stone. **1882** C. DU VAL *With Show through Sn Afr.* I. 273 The dropping into two or three sluits on the way home had the effect of often restoring sobriety to an intoxicated brain, and the skipping over the furrows formed an invigorating exercise. **1898** J.F. INGRAM *Story of Afr. City* 66 The system of water supply established by the original Dutch settlers was that of open watercourses called 'sluits', by means of which the supply was led through the streets. **1902** W.C. SCULLY *Harrow* 3 Not a sound would be audible except the murmurous cadences of the water running down the 'sluits' on either side. These sluits are paved with round, water-worn stones and, except in rainy or very windy weather, keep the water crystal-clear. **1910** J. RUNCIE *Idylls by Two Oceans* 80 A man came out of a house while I was sitting by a sluit, Wynberg way. **1934** B.I. BUCHANAN *Pioneer Days* 15 Until 1887 the town was supplied with water from the Dorp Spruit, led in open sluits along the edge of the streets ... The sluits, often shrouded in grass, were veritable man traps for the unwary pedestrian. **1953** U. KRIGE *Dream & Desert* 90 Soon he had turned into Dorpstraat, the long oak-shadowed street leading out of the town. On either side the water sang in the sluits. **1975** *Het Suid-Western* 30 Jan., A determined fight is being put up by Mrs. Olive van der S— to save the picturesque little sluit with running water that flows down the side of Caledon Street before it is closed in by the municipality – and replaced by an underground pipe.

2. A ditch; a gully eroded by water; cf. DONGA. Also (rarely) *fig.* (see quot. 1974).

α. **1850** J.D. LEWINS Diary. 5 Aug., Dug some holes in sloot on hill opposite house for willows, also some in vley watercourse, to be planted towards sun-down. **1873** F. BOYLE *To Cape for Diamonds*, The leading horses were observed, or felt, to take a flying leap. Investigation showed them to have cleared a sloot some five feet deep which ran across the veldt. **1883** O.E.A. SCHREINER *Story of Afr. Farm* 234 What it could not swallow ran off in mad rivulets to the great 'sloot,' that now foamed like an angry river across the flat. **1914** L.H. BRINKMAN *Breath of Karroo* 233 The undertaking would be too hazardous, owing to the number of sloots and hollows traversing the road, which would soon be in flood and impassable. **1932** *Grocott's Daily Mail* 31 Mar. 4 The larger sloots have been dammed by means of rubble walls reinforced with wire-netting. **1949** J. MOCKFORD *Golden Land* 214 If a sloot (gully) is come to, so wide and deep that the bucks cannot leap over or go through it, the front ranks are forced in until it is levelled up with their bodies, when the mass marches over and continues its irresistible way. **1958** I. VAUGHAN *Diary* 6 There is .. a big sloot at the back side of houses which has not water except when it rains. **1971** *Star* 18 Sept. 12 Water is already running quite strongly in the sloots and veld pitfalls are completely disguised by the snow. **1990** *Grocott's Mail* 6 July 8 He has telephoned the Provincial Roads Inspector in Port Elizabeth. Since then potholes and sloots had been filled.

β. **1851** J.F. CHURCHILL Diary. (Killie Campbell Africana Library MS37) 21 Oct., Rode out by the road but across country over sluits & stony ground. **1857** 'C.' in *Cape Monthly Mag.* I. June 374 Through the rivers, across the sluits, Over the mountains and into the spruits, As fast as can drag it the half-fed brutes, Away like a flash of lightning it shoots. So merrily goes the post-cart. **1863** W.C. BALDWIN *Afr. Hunting* 30 On coming into a mud sluit .. the sudden check of the wagon threw me off. **1872** E.J. DUNN in A.M.L. Robinson *Sel. Articles from Cape Monthly Mag.* (1978) 58 How many ages must have elapsed while this great sluit was being eroded! Below the fall is a huge channel cut in solid hard gneiss for a depth of about 200 feet, a width of 600 or 700 feet, and three or four miles long. **1881** *Meteor* 25 July 1 If the Town Council do not do something to the sluit in African Street, near the residence of Mr. S. Bax, there will be a serious accident to someone. **1910** *Rand Daily Mail* 10 May 3 It is absolutely necessary that farmers should understand the enormous damage done by these sluits or dongas. *c*1911 E. GLANVILLE in S. Playne *Cape Col.* 661 The wind strips off the top dressing, the summer floods wash the silt into the sluits, and millions of tons of good soil are rushed off into the sea. **1926** P.W. LAIDLER *Tavern of Ocean* 55 Very soon the trampling of oxen, the rutting of wheels, and the erosive action of strong winds and rain on the bared ground caused sluits and holes which were dangerous to traffic. **1963** S. CLOETE *Rags of Glory* 284 Veld paths ran like streams. Sluits became rivers. **1973** C. HALLACK in *Weekend Post* 31 Mar. 2 One old dame dressed in the usual black frock with a small sluit amidships, where the strings of her apron marked the half-way boundary of her baggy form. **1977** F.G. BUTLER *Karoo Morning* 112 Innumerable globules of water. Gutters, runnels, sluits, dongas, rivers, receive the fluid which has cut and carved them, which is cutting and carving them now. **1980** E. JOUBERT *Poppie Nongena* 206 The whole Mdantsane was sluits everywhere that overflowed when it rained.

Hence (sense 2) **slooting** *n.* (*obs.*), soil erosion caused by water.

1910 A.B. LAMONT *Rural Reader* 265 The evils of sluiting might be decreased by planting trees on mountain slopes and on bare karoo. **1932** *Grocott's Daily Mail* 31 Mar. 4 Deviating the stormwater on to hard formation to prevent slooting.

slop *n.* Short for SLIP-SLOP.

1970 J. LENTON *Informant, Orkney* Go and put on your slops (thongs or open-toed sandals). **1989** *Stanger Mail* 3 Feb. 7 Don't wear 'slops' on your first day [in the army]. You will have to run a lot, so wear a good pair of takkies or comfortable running shoes.

slote, sluit varr. SLOOT.

sluk /slək/ *n. slang.* Also **sluck.** [Afk., as next.] A gulp, mouthful, swig, or 'slurp'. Also *fig.*

1946 *Cape Times* in E. Partridge *Dict. of Underworld Slang* (1950) 630 *Skep a sluk*, to take a drink. **1972** R. MALAN *Ah Big Jaws* 47 'Gimmie a sluck ivyaw Pipsie, mehn [*sc.* of your Pepsi, man].' **1975** 'BLOSSOM' in *Darling* 12 Feb. 119 Trying to catch a sluk of yore cane and Coke as the sun sinks slowly into the Valley of a Thousand Hills. **1975** *Ibid.* 26 Feb. 111 A tiekiedraai coming out the loudspeakers and all around us the crowd shifting and muttering and taking sluks out the half-jacks .. in they back pockets. **1976** J. MCCLURE *Rogue Eagle* 129 As peach brandy goes, this is among the best *sluks* I've ever tasted. **1977** C. HOPE in S. Gray *Theatre Two* (1981) 51 Bo-Bo (*offers can*): Have a sluk. Jimmie: Nay, I already drowned a nip of voddies. **1981** C. BARNARD in *Daily Dispatch* 19 Oct. 8 After the meal we went back for another sluk of culture at the British Museum, sated with boere asparagi. **1986** G. SILBER in *Style* Sept. 88 'Okay,' he claps, rising from the chair with a last sluk of tea from a paper cup. **1990** P. O'BYRNE on Radio South Africa, Nov., Must take a breath and a sluk.

sluk *v. slang.* [Afk., fr. Du. *slikken* to swallow.] **a.** *trans.* To swallow, swig, or gulp (something). Also *fig.*

1970 *Informant, Grahamstown* She sluks everything I say. (Believes). **1972** A. SCOBY on Radio South Africa 23 May, Here — have a drink. Hey, hey, don't sluk the lot! **1981** B. PODLASHUK in *Sunday Times* 8 Nov. (Mag. Sect.) 1? You only get the full appreciation and enhancement of wine if you drink it in moderation. If you 'sluk' it down, its function is not fulfilled. **1985** T. BARON in *Frontline* Feb. 30 'Cheers. Down the hatch.' We slukked down a few.

b. *intrans.* To drink.

1975 'BLOSSOM' in *Darling* 9 Apr. 95 And round each of these there's a swarm of okies waving spanners and slukking out of cans and giving last-minute advice.

slup var. SLAP.

||**slymstok** /'sleɪmstɔk/ *n.* Pl. **-stokke** /-stɔkə/. [Afk., *slym* slime + *stok* rod-like stick.] Any of several plants of the Liliaceae with a juicy, edible peduncle: **a.** Either of two species of the genus *Albuca, A. canadensis* or *A. altissimus.* **b.** *Bulbine praemorsa.* In both senses *comb.* **slymstokuintjie** /-ˌeɪŋki/ [Afk., *uintjie* bulb].

1917 R. MARLOTH *Common Names* 75 *Slijmstok (-'uintje). Albuca minor, A. major,* etc. Children eat the basal portion of the flowering stalk. According to Thunberg the white portion is used for quenching the thirst. Also *Bulbine praemorsa.* **1966** C.A. SMITH *Common Names* 424 *Slymstok (-uintjie),* Bulbous plants ... The basal portion of the peduncle is eaten by children ... In all three species the vernacular name is derived from the copious secretion of mucilage .. from the lower end of the rod-like peduncle .. as well as from the scales of the bulb .. when broken. **1975** W. STEENKAMP *Land of Thirst King* 130 There are two kinds of stapelia the old people used to eat, and others known to me only by their colloquial names: the 'bokhorinkies' .. and the 'slymstok', or slimy stem, a lily variety of which the stem exudes a sweet slimy juice when chewed. **1975** *Argus* 17 Sept. 28 Another treat for children in a pre-lollipop era were slymstokke, slimy long, green shoots, a little thicker than one's thumb, sweet and juicy. 'Nothing like slymstokke on a hot day.'

slyt /sleɪt/ *adj. Sheep-farming.* [fr. Afk. *slyt* to wear out, *slyting* attrition, wear.] Of sheep: 'broken-mouthed', having worn-down or missing teeth, i.e. mature or old. So **slyting** *vbl n.*, in the same sense.

In describing the ages of sheep the terms 'two-tooth', 'four-tooth', 'six-tooth', 'eight-tooth', and 'slyt' are used.

1970 W. JACOBS *Informant, Bloemfontein* The rams for sale are from two teeth to slyting. **1972** *Daily Dispatch* 20 May 17 (*advt*) 250 'Slyt' sheep. **1973** *Farmer's Weekly* 18 Apr. (Suppl.) 13 (*advt*) Merino ewes full mouth-slyt. **1973** *Weekend Post* 7 July 19 (*advt*) 15 Registered Slyt Ewes. **1987** *Grocott's Mail* 13 Feb. 10 (*advt*) 150 Slyt Ewes.

smaak /smɑːk/ *v. trans. Slang.* Also **smaka, smark.** [Afk.] To fancy, relish, like, be keen on (something or someone).

1963 L.F. FREED *Crime in S. Afr.* 75 They [*sc.* the ducktails] employed an argot which was peculiarly their own, and to know which was to have the pass-word to their twilight world ... 'I don't smaak that' meant I don't like that! **1970** W. HUMPHRIES in *Forum* Vol.6 No.2, 28 Ya, she's not so bad, but I smaak the ones with their padding a little lower. **1975** 'BLOSSOM' in *Darling* 9 Apr. 95 If there's one thing I only smaak on a Saturday arvey, it's a session at the off-road racing there by Syringa Spa. **1980** R. GOVENDER *Lahnee's Pleasure* 31 Watch it — you're getting too personal, the both of you. If you don't smaak the man's company, say so. **1981** *E. Prov. Herald* 28 Apr. 7 Todayze kidds .. like got no kulchur and smaak essayes fulla bludden gutts. **1981** B. MFENYANA in M. Mutloatse *Reconstruction* 295 Since this is an exploratory and experimental essay, we don't smaka to turn the reader off .. with strings of dates, tone markers, references, statistics and other technicalities. **1984** *Frontline* May 40, I didn't smaak so much that for lots of the larnies this was a lekker sideshow and a source of light relief. **1985** P. SLABOLEPSZY *Sat. Night at Palace* 79 Smark, keen (to be keen on someone, something). **1992** S. GUTKNECHT in *Sunday Times* 19 Apr. (Mag. Sect.) 28 Afterwards we'll zap round to your pad on my boney. Park off till we get there. Then we can catch a couple of dops and hit the jol. You smaak?

Hence (*nonce*) **smaaksome** *adj.* [Eng. adj.-forming suffix *-some*], tasty, delicious.

1978 *E. Prov. Herald* 2 Dec. 2 Smaaksome braai ... After years of practice they're pretty smart at turning out smaaksome grub, these Lions and their ladies.

small claims court *n. phr. Law.* Also with initial capitals. A court which deals speedily with claims not exceeding R1 500, and in which claimants present their own cases; PEOPLE'S COURT sense 2. Also *attrib.*

Established by Act 61 of 1984.

1983 *E. Prov. Herald* 24 Oct. 12 With the introduction of a Small Claims or People's Court .. Justice ought to be within the reach of everybody. **1986** *Natal Convocation News* (Univ. of Natal) 17 The Republic of South Africa acquired the mechanism to establish Small Claims Courts in August of 1985. They were established in response to public clamour and pressure from the organised legal profession. Today Small Claims Courts are operating successfully in many centres ... The Small Claims Court is a peoples [*sic*] Court .. designed to provide cheap and speedy settlement of small disputes. **1986** *E. Prov. Herald* 4 June 3 Mr. Justice Zietsman reserved judgment on the granting of a final order to stay proceedings in a Small Claims Court case. **1987** *Ibid.* 27 Apr. 6 Top representatives of South Africa's legal profession met .. to discuss proposals to .. bring it [*sc.* civil litigation] closer to the man in the street along the lines of the highly successful Small Claims Courts. **1988** *New Nation* 17 Mar. (Learning Nation) 2 The Small Claims Court has been called 'the little people's court' because ordinary, working people can go there to fight for their rights. **1991** *SAPA* 21 Jan., A Klapmuts chicken farmer has been ordered by a Paarl small claims court to pay back R271,20 to a Durbanville man who had unknowingly bought 21 de-beaked hens from him.

small time *adj. phr. Slang.* [fr. (mainly U.S.) theatrical slang *small-time* second-rate, small-scale.] In urban (esp. township) Eng.: of or pertaining to the lowest type of township drinking establishment or shebeen. Often in the collocation **small time joint.** See also SHEBEEN sense 1.

1973 P. BECKER in *The 1820* Vol.46 No.7, 32 The lowest class shebeens, known in some townships as Small Time Joints, are patronized by rough-necks and ne'er-do-wells. **1977** P.C. VENTER *Soweto* 124 Bantu beer .. is considered a cheap drink fit only for cheap shebeens, those Small Time Joints where they add water to the beer to make it last longer. **1982** *Voice* 10 Jan. 3 Though several 'Big Time' and 'Small Time' shebeeners did not want to be identified, they expressed certain fears over the procedure of legalisation. **1983** *Pace* Dec. 152 The 'small time joints', patronised by .. tsotsi gangs .. and 'hesh girls' .. seldom carry stocks of the better-known brands of liquor.

smark var. SMAAK.

smasher *n. Obs.* exc. *hist.* [Prob. transf. use of general Eng. slang *smasher* anything uncommon or unusual, esp. anything exceptionally large or excellent.] In full ***smasher hat***: a soft felt hat with a wide brim; a slouched hat.

1891 E. GLANVILLE *Fossicker* 156 The Dutchmen stared at him from under the brims of their felt 'smashers'. **1892** J.R. COUPER *Mixed Humanity* 4 A wide-awake, called in South Africa a smasher. **1899** G.H. RUSSELL *Under Sjambok* 107 The men .. are content to put a piece of crape round the arm and smasher hat. **1913** C. PETTMAN *Africanderisms* 451 *Smasher,* A soft felt hat with a broad brim, made familiar to the people in England first by the Rhodesian troops at the Jubilee festivities, 1887. **1921** W.C. SCULLY *Harrow* 116 As the force withdrew, seven Boers stood up on the crests of seven respective koppies several hundred yards apart from each other and waved their smasher hats in sarcastic farewell. **1937** J. STEVENSON-HAMILTON *S. Afr. Eden* 168 His clothes consisted merely of a pair of lion-skin breeches, self-made, a very inadequate shirt, and a smasher hat. **1972** P. GIBBS *Hist. of BSAP* I. 136 [During the Jameson Raid] the RMP wore .. grey felt 'smasher' hats — as they were known — the broad brim pinned up on the left side and the crown of the hat wrapped round with a blue puggaree with white spots.

smaus, smauser varr. SMOUS, SMOUSER.

smear *v. trans. Hist.* [tr. Afk. *smeer* to smear, plaster, fr. Du. *smeren* to grease, lubricate.] To spread or treat (floors or walls) with any of several mixtures containing cow dung. See also MIS sense 2.

1816 J. MACKRILL Diary. 129 To clean the House they besmear the floor with cow dung, so that literally to make a house in Africa clean, you have only to cover it with manure. **1835** W.B. BOYCE in A. Steedman *Wanderings* II. 276 Sent for in great haste to her husband's kraal, and had gone immediately .. though engaged at the time in smearing Mrs. Painton's house. **1839** W.C. HARRIS *Wild Sports* 143 The space was smeared with a mixture of mud and cow-dung, resembling that used in all parts of India for similar purposes. **1849** J.D. LEWINS Diary. 15 Sept., Had the hall & bedroom smeared today & everything cleaned up. **1879** [see DAGHA *n.* sense a]. **1900** E.E.K. LOWNDES *Every-Day Life* 96 You could never guess what a South African carpet is! .. The Kaffir girl goes out with a pail or tin, and fills it with the dried cow-dung which is lying plentifully about. This she lays in a heap on the floor, pours water over it, and mixes it up with her hands till it is like thick batter. Then she spreads or 'smears' it over the floor by a peculiar scraping of the mass along with the side of the hand. **1911** L. COHEN *Reminisc. of Kimberley* 399 When the size of Buckingham Palace was explained to a gray-beard, he .. expressed his undying opinion that it must take a day at least to smear the floors with cow-dung. **1933** W.H.S. BELL *Bygone Days* 127 The floor .. had been freshly smeared with cow-dung mixed with blood. **1949** L. HUNTER *Afr. Dawn* 7 A third was mixing cow dung and water to the right consistency for smearing the floors of the huts. **1956** U. LONG *Jrnls of Elizabeth Lees Price 1854–1883* 516 They .. will sleep in the wagons while the house is aired, cleaned and 'smeared'. **1973** [see MIS sense 2]. **1976** G. & G. FAGAN in *Optima* Vol.26 No.2, 75 Clay floors, smeared with dung once a week, were common at the Cape till the end of the 19th century. **1977** F.G. BUTLER *Karoo Morning* 38 Dan .. was sure that all his guests would sleep comfortably enough on the mis-vloer, which had been smeared with cow-dung the day before 'to fix the fleas'.

Hence **smeared** *ppl adj.*, **smearing** *vbl n.*

1855 J.W. Colenso *Ten Weeks in Natal* 97 There was no time for the usual smearing of the floor with cowdung, which is a great specific against vermin. 1870 R. Ridgill in A.M.L. Robinson *Sel. Articles from Cape Monthly Mag.* (1978) 22 No man could be more ignorant of the way in which inspanning, outspanning, smearing, and other strange operations would have to be performed. 1883 E.L. Price *Letter*. 25 June, When we go home, wh. will be the day after tomorrow perhaps, we shall have a great house-cleaning — smearing and airing — for it needs all. 1912 W. Westrup *Land of To-Morrow* 101 The floor was of the usual smeared earth. 1973 M.A. Cook *Cape Kitchen* 20 Smearing was repeated as often as was necessary, and was usually carried out in large swirling traditional patterns.

‖**smeerlap** /ˈsmɪə(r)lap/ *n*. Obsolescent. *slang*. Also **schmeerlap, smeerlop**. [Du., fr. *smeren* to grease + *lap* clout, rag.] A term of abuse: 'blackguard', 'cad'.

1853 J. Green *Kat River Settlement 1851* 46 Jan Groepe and Albert Groepe designated their father an 'old wash vrouw' and a 'Smeerlap'. 1864 [see DONDER *int*.]. 1899 *Cape Times* 25 Oct. 22 (Pettman), No, my friend, give your burgher rights to Hollanders and other schmeerlaps, but not for me, thanks. 1920 S. Black *Dorp* 5 'When an Afrikander's turned khaki like that .. he's not a brother-in-law, he's a smeerlap' (blackguard). 1943 *Week-End News & Sunday Mag*. 20 Mar. 4 'I tink jou smeerlops is torking troo de bak orf julle neks!' I tole dem. [1988 A. Sher *Middlepost* 270 Since when do you play with Hottnot smear-rags? You don't play with them.]

smell *v*. [tr. of the Nguni word *nuka*; cf. ISANUSI.] Usu. in the phr. *to smell out*. In traditional African medicine:
a. *trans*. To detect or discover (an evil-doer or source of misfortune) by supernatural means. See also UMHLAHLO, WITCHDOCTOR.

1836 C.L. Stretch *Journal*. 254 After some time spent in smelling the invalid, the articles in the hut, *c* the Doctor declares such a one is the witch. 1847 *Natal Witness* 1 Jan. 1 This murder was committed under the influence of a superstition .. that persons possess the power of injuring others by means of Witchcrafts; and that such persons may be 'smelt out', or discovered, by certain pretenders to such skill, called 'Witch Doctors'. 1855 N.J. Merriman *Cape Jrnls* (1957) 215 They were then assembled .. to determine who it was that in their language should be 'smelt out' and 'eaten up' for this supposed offence. 1867 S. Turner in D. Child *Portrait of Pioneer* (1980) 70, I found that old Machingela .. had been 'smelt out' as cattle had died at the kraals near him. 1875 C.B. Bisset *Sport & War* 41 This she-devil or witch doctor, first commenced to smell out the bewitching matter. 1891 T.R. Beattie *Pambaniso* 14 In the language of the Kaffirs he was 'smelt out' for his evil practices, and punishment must follow. 1907 W.C. Scully *By Veldt & Kopje* 21 We came here to look upon the killing of Gungubele, who was 'smelt out' for having bewitched his elder brother. 1925 D. Kidd *Essential Kafir* 22 Nothing is easier than to get a witch doctor to 'smell out' an old hag who makes herself objectionable. 1939 N.J. Van Warmelo in A.M. Duggan-Cronin *Bantu Tribes* III. 33 If the diviner 'smelt out' someone as having caused illness, .. this person would have to be removed by some means, possibly with torture, and frequently by being thrown over a cliff. 1943 I. Frack *S. Afr. Doctor* 126 Primed previously by his assistant, he intimated that he 'smelled' some evil spirits, who were directly responsible for his host's eye-ache, back-ache, or stomach-ache. 1976 D.M.B. Preston *Story of Frontier Town* 40 The Chief's witchdoctor would 'smell out' an evildoer, whereupon the wretched man, guilty or not, would be killed and all his cattle would be taken to the Chief — a very profitable arrangement! 1980 A.G.T.K. Malikongwa in *Staffrider* Vol.3 No.1, 35 Doctors don't betray. They use bones to smell witches. Some see them through water contained in small, round, charmed calabashes. 1991 *Settler* Vol.65 No.1, The shield is used for dancing and the tail switch of a cow for smelling out spirits.
b. *intrans. rare*. To perform the ritual by which an evil influence is identified.

1959 L. Longmore *Dispossessed* 176 Africans have lost confidence in all European doctors who ask for histories of illnesses and the painful areas of the body. They want the doctor to 'smell out'.
Hence **smeller out** *n. phr.*, ISANUSI.

1837 F. Owen *Diary* (1926) 58 They are not even afraid of the 'smellers out'. 1885 H. Rider Haggard *King Solomon's Mines* 122 So says Gagool, the wise woman, the smeller out of witches. 1905 *Native Tribes of Tvl* 126 The professional 'smeller-out' (i.e., discoverer of persons who by a power obtained from demons are supposed to bewitch others, thereby causing sickness, death or disaster) naturally enjoys great power in a tribe. 1954 G. Magwaza in *Drum* Jan. 49 The smellers out were 'D- boys' who wanted everybody to follow the 'D- line'.

smelling *vbl n.* and *ppl adj*. [fr. prec.] In full **smelling-out**.
A. *vbl n*.
1. In traditional African medicine: the detection of evil (by one trained to discern it by supernatural means). See also ISANUSI.

1857 J. Shooter *Kafirs of Natal* 175, I could not help smiling at them, and at their solicitude to know the result of her 'smelling.' 1867 S. Turner in D. Child *Portrait of Pioneer* (1980) 62 It would not suit people given to fainting to be present at the smelling-out of a witch and the consequent butcher's work afterwards. 1890 Mhlakwapalwa in *Cape Law Jrnl* VII. 226 Although 'smelling-out' is not permitted by Government, we still firmly believe in the existence of witchcraft, and further that the witch-doctor or *Sanuse* has the power of divining those who are guilty of practising it. 1912 Ayliff & Whiteside *Hist. of Abambo* 79 Belief in the power of witchcraft .. is as strongly rooted in the minds of the people as ever; although smelling out cannot be practised as openly as formerly. 1949 J. Mockford *Golden Land* 106 There is no appeal against the witch-doctor's smelling out.
2. UMHLAHLO sense a.

1895 H. Rider Haggard *Nada* 60 There will be a smelling out, but a smelling out of a new sort, for he and you shall be the witch-finders, and at that smelling out he will give to death all those whom he fears. 1923 G.H. Nicholls *Bayete!* 11 We will have a grand smelling out tomorrow; the rattle of the bones — the vumisa, piff — Balumbata food for jackals. 1936 Williams & May *I Am Black* 43 Twice he had witnessed a smelling-out by a witch-doctor. 1951 T.V. Bulpin *Lost Trails of Low Veld* 262 Witch-doctors .. use it .. for signifying the victim at the end of a smelling-out. 1969 I. Vaughan *Last of Sunlit Yrs* 145 A Vomese (smelling out) was in progress.
B. *ppl adj*. Of or pertaining to the detection of evil, or the ceremony at which this is done.

1929 J. Stevenson-Hamilton *Low-Veld* 221 For 'smelling out' purposes it is nowadays usual for witch doctors to invoke the assistance of 'the bones'. 1937 B.J.F. Laubscher *Sex, Custom & Psychopathology* 62 The 'smelling out' ceremony is still in use in the Transkei territory ... The word 'smelling' is symbolic of bad behaviour. If a native's ways are wrong, they say 'he smells', or *ukunuka*. 1971 *Drum* Feb. 4 These smelling-out guys have a reputation for following their noses to the wrong directions. 1974 C.T. Binns *Warrior People* 33 The izAngoma at all 'smelling out' ceremonies used to daub themselves all over with both red and white powders.

smiley *n. slang*. Also **smilie**. [Prob. so called because of the appearance of the mouth on the cooked head.] Esp. in township Eng.: the head of a sheep or goat (or less often of a cow), cleaned, sometimes halved, and stewed or grilled with or without the brain and tongue; SKOP *n*.[2]

1990 J. Cullum in *Weekend Post* 18 Aug. 7 At the entrance to Njoli square, half a stewed goat's head (known as a "Smiley") costs R2,50. 1991 on TV1, 24 Apr. (Big Time), 'What is smiley?' 'Half sheep's head, with tongue sticking right out, and big smile.' 1994 [see SKOP *n*.[2]]. 1994 E. Badenhorst in *Flying Springbok* June 9 The only spanner in our spokes was very kind 'gift' Iyavaya decided to bestow on us — a 'smiley'. This is local slang for a grilled sheep's head — apparently a local township speciality. 1994 G. Jezi *Informant, Grahamstown* You put the whole smiley on a drievoet and burn off all the hair, you wash it with a stone and hot water until it's clean, clean. You take an axe and chop it in half to get the brain and the tongue out. Then you cook the smiley and the tongue in a pot for about three hours.

smokkel /ˈsmɔk(ə)l/ *v. slang*. [Afk., to deal in illicit goods, smuggle.]
1. *trans. rare*. To get the better of, confuse (someone or something).

1946 *Cape Times* in E. Partridge *Dict. of Underworld Slang* (1950) 646 *Smokkel the peace*, To infringe the law. 1990 *Style* June 113 Bumstead immediately arranged the three worst degenerates he could find .. to act as guides on the trip. One group, he points out, would definitely have 'smokkeled the other group's heads', thus providing a source of 'neverending amusement' to see who came out on top.
2.a. *intrans*. To do illicit business, to 'deal'. See also SMOKKELHUIS.

1973 *Informant, George* They say they smokkel in that house down there, so there's coming and going all the time. 1977 D. Muller *Whitey* 44 'We know you. We know that you smokkel here!' the cop snapped, at length. 'We know that these skolly bastards gather here and buy wine!'
b. *trans*. To sell (illicit drugs).

1983 *Informant, Cape Town* Henry says Philip's smokkeling dagga as well as hooch.
Hence **smokkelaar** *n*., a smuggler or dealer in illicit liquor; **smokkeling** *vbl n*. (also *attrib*.).

1977 D. Muller *Whitey* 32 The back gate remained closed, for there was a lull in the smokkeling business. By this time the legal bottle-stores would be open, and the 'mailers' — the runners from shebeens big and small — would be at the counters, buying supplies for the long-week-end-thirst. Ibid. 84 When he died he left nothing ... I had three little children and I had to feed them, so I turned to smokkeling. 1985 *Argus* 24 Aug. 1 This was part of a three-year battle between the Kapedi gang and a rival group of 'smokkelaars'.

‖**smokkelhuis** /ˈsmɔk(ə)lhœɪs, -hœɪs/ *n*. Pl. **-e** /-ə/. [Afk., *smokkel* see prec. + *huis* house.] A SHEBEEN (sense 1), esp. one operating illegally; SMOKKIE.

1950 E. Partridge *Dict. of Underworld Slang* 646 *Smokkelhuis* is the Afrikaans equivalent of S. African *shebeen*. 1977 D. Muller *Whitey* 23 It was a lulu of a shebeen — a jolly old smokkelhuis of five-star rating! 1977 *E. Prov. Herald* 4 May 18 The madam of the 'smokkelhuis', La Residence Stilhuis, the international mother figure of the underworld, kind and generous and yet hard as a 50c piece. 1980 *Cape Times* 12 Sept. 4 'Smokkelhuise' (shebeens) were warned not to sell drugs and other items in competition with the gang. 1987 P. Jooste in *Fair Lady* 25 Nov. 142 Gus-Seep found him drunk in the street outside The Buildings, a well known *smokkelhuis* close to the railwayline, where seamen came and went.

smokkie /ˈsmɔki/ *n. slang*. [Formed on prec. + Eng. (informal) n.-forming suffix *-ie*.] SMOKKELHUIS.

1977 D. Muller *Whitey* 21 You seem to be suffering, ou Whitey ... Maggy Aap's piss, I suppose. That's a bad smokkie. They never wash their bottles. 1990 *Weekend Argus* 29 Sept. 3 Death is etched on the face of the thin adolescent fingering the 'lemmetjie' (blade) in his pocket. It's scrawled across the gang that has swaggered out of the 'smokkie' (shebeen).

smoor /smʊə(r)/ *adj*. and *n*. [Afk., fr. *smoor* to stew, smother.]

A. *adj.* SMOORED. Usu. in the collocations ***smoorfish*** or ***smoorvis*** /-fəs/ [Afk., *vis* fish], a traditional Malay dish containing gently braised fish, also ***smoorsnoek*** /-snuk/ [Afk., *snoek* see SNOEK *n.*], this dish, made from snoek (see SNOEK *n.* senses 1, 2, and 3).

1902 H.J. DUCKITT *Hilda's Diary of Cape Hsekeeper* 65, I am often asked for the recipe for smoorfish, so I will write down once for all the way we ourselves do it. *a***1905** — *Bk of Recipes* (1966) 45 Smoorvis, an old Malay speciality, is an excellent dish for luncheon. Tomatoes, if in season, may be added to it. **1954** [see KLUITJIE sense 1 b]. **1973** [see STOCKFISH]. **1979** HEARD & FAULL *Our Best Trad. Recipes* 22 Smoorvis or gesmoorde vis, the traditional Voortrekker recipe probably came from the East with the Malays. **1979** SNYMAN & KLARIE *Free from Sea* 116 Smoorvis ... This delicious dish is traditionally made with smoked snoek but any dry, smoked fish could be used. **1984** *Fair Lady* 18 Apr. 201 Lunch with the family (smoorsnoek, salad, ice cream and fruit, white wine). **1985** A. TREDGOLD *Bay between Mountains* 101 Whatever other food may be available on the coast, fish has remained the favourite, particularly smoorvis. **1988** F. WILLIAMS *Cape Malay Cookbk* 34 Serve with Smoor tomato and onion and mashed potato. **1989** *Weekend Post* 14 Oct. 6 Dried salted snoek is used for the traditional *smoorsnoek*, which originated along the West Coast.

B. *n.* A braised dish; a stew. Also with distinguishing epithet, as **snoek smoor** (cf. *smoorsnoek* at sense A).

1941 FOUCHÉ & CURREY *Hsecraft for Primary Schools* 8 Snoek Smoor. Dried snoek, 2 or 3 onions, 1 chilli, water for boiling, 1 oz. fat, boiled rice. **1950** H. GERBER *Cape Cookery* 75 Snoek Smoor with Sugar Beans (Malay). Proceed as indicated for snoek smoor, but add, instead of potatoes, presoaked and parboiled sugar beans. **1984** *Flying Springbok* May 31 The cuisine of this restaurant is .. enriched by indigenous Cape dishes such as babotie, pickled fish, the aromatic bredies and smoors of the Cape Malays.

||**smoor** *v. trans.* and *intrans.* [Afk.] To braise or stew (meat or fish); (of meat) to stew or simmer.

1891 H.J. DUCKITT *Hilda's 'Where Is It?'* p.ix, Fry the onion with the meat, a light brown ('smoor,' as the Cape cooks say). This must be done rather quickly. **1913** D. FAIRBRIDGE *Piet of Italy* 115 Brown your onions well, let the meat smoor gently at the side of the fire or bake it in a pot. **1913** C. PETTMAN *Africanderisms* 453 *Smoor*, .. As used in South Africa this word means 'to stew'. **1945** H. GERBER *Fish Fare* 56 Smoor in pan till the fish is brown and tender; serve piping hot.

smoored /smʊə(r)d/ *ppl adj.* [Englished form of Afk. *gesmoorde* braised (usu. of steak).] Braised, stewed; SMOOR *adj.* Usu. in the collocations ***smoored fish, smoored snoek.***

1890 A.G. HEWITT *Cape Cookery* 6 Smoored Kreeft. Boil the kreeft first. **1913** A. GLOSSOP *Barnes's S. Afr. Hsehold Guide* 52 Smoored snoek. [**1919** M.M. STEYN *Diary* 54 George, .. was lying fast asleep .. ; dreaming, probably, of 'Gesmoorde visch' and 'Kreef kerrie', and other dainty Cape dishes that he so well knew how to prepare. **1979** see Heard & Faull quot. at SMOOR *adj.*] **1988** F. WILLIAMS *Cape Malay Cookbk* 22 Smoored Fish with Tomatoes. Another quick and easy economical dish. **1989** I. JONES *Woman's World Cookbk* 49 Try smoked angelfish for a variation of this casserole, which is a different approach to 'smoored' snoek.

smouch *n. obs.* Also **smoutch**. [Special sense of obs. general Eng. *smouch* (ad. Du. *smous*) a derog. word for a Jew (many itinerant traders having been Jewish).] SMOUS *n.*

1839 W.C. HARRIS *Wild Sports* 63 Traders, or *smouches*, as they are called by the colonists, constantly visit Latakoo and its neighbourhood. **1849** E.D.H.E. NAPIER *Excursions in Sn Afr.* II. 391, I dare say .. you have heard that I have turned a regular 'smoutch,' the Colonial term for trader. **1863** T. SHONE Diary. 14 Oct., Mr & Mrs Crout, Smouch, Stopt all night. I bought from them 2 Shirts paid 7/- for them. **1867** *Ibid.* 19 Aug., Bought from a Smouch, a box of wax Matches, a Quire foolscap paper.

smouch *v. intrans. Obs.* exc. *hist.* [fr. SMOUCH *n.*] SMOUS *v.* sense 1. So **smoucher** *n.*, SMOUS *n.*; **smouching** *vbl n.*, SMOUSING, or haggling.

1823 W.W. BIRD *State of Cape of G.H.* 148 Smouching, which here is an appropriate word, meaning buying an article, and selling it again at profit, is practiced by all the Cape-Dutch, except a few of the highest class. **1899** 'S. ERASMUS' *Prinsloo* 74 A young Jewish smoucher broke his leg by falling down a shaft on Piet's place. **1920** R. JUTA *Tavern* 56 They found a word for the legitimized bargaining – 'smouching' mostly indulged in by the women. **1926** P.W. LAIDLER *Tavern of Ocean* 98 They were much given to 'smouching' or 'smousing' – buying articles from the stores and selling them again at a profit. **1968** K. MCMAGH *Dinner of Herbs* 31 The smous was almost without exception a Jew, a trader who had his beginnings in the custom of smouching or smousing in the early days at the Cape.

smous /smɔʊs, smaʊs/ *n.* Also **schmous, smaus, smouse.** Pl. **smouses, smouse** /smɔʊsə/, rarely **schmousen.** [S. Afr. Du., hawker, pedlar, transf. use of Du. *smous* 'Jew, usurer, supposed to be the same word as G. dialect *schmus* talk, patter' (*OED*); cf. Yiddish *s(c)hmooz(e)* heart-to-heart talk, fr. Hebrew *schmuos* '(originally) "things heard"; (in time) "rumors", "idle talk".' (L. Rosten, *The joys of Yiddish* 1968).

The obs. spellings 'smaus' and 'smouse' suggest that /-aʊ-/ was a common pronunciation in the past.]
Esp. during the 19th century: a (Jewish) itinerant trader; a peddler; a hawker; SMOUCH *n.*; SMOUSER. Also *attrib.* See also *togt-ganger* (TOGT *n.* sense 1 b).

1796 E. HELME tr. *F. Le Vaillant's Trav.* I. 55 There is at the Cape a species of old-clothes men .. who from their enormous profits and the extortion they practice have obtained the name of Capse-*Smouse*, or Cape Jews. **1806** J. BARROW *Trav.* II. 331 His load .. may consist of fifteen hundred weight of butter and soap, for which he is glad to get from the retail dealers at the Cape, whom he calls Smaus or Jew, sixpence a pound. **1827** G. THOMPSON *Trav.* II. 136 Brandy (the only luxury besides tobacco in which the poorer boors indulge) is purchased from *smouses*, or hawkers, who traverse the remotest skirts of the Colony with waggon-loads of this detestable beverage. **1832** *Graham's Town Jrnl* 74 That useful and industrious class of people the *Smouses*, to whose spirit of enterprize this town is maily indebted for its rapid rise. **1864** T. BAINES *Explor. in S.-W. Afr.* 75 The chief Jan Jonken came to visit us, and .. complained that all the 'Smouses' hurried past as fast as possible, so that if the Hottentots wanted clothing or other goods they had to run after the wagons. **1872** E.J. DUNN in A.M.L. Robinson *Sel. Articles from Cape Monthly Mag.* (1978) 58 Under a handsome spreading camel-thorn tree is pitched a very tiny tent. Within is a 'smous' with his wares. **1882** C. DU VAL *With Show through Sn Afr.* I. 272 The wily 'smouse' or pedlar .. still in a minor degree glories in the successful manner in which he is able to best the 'Mynheers' in the matter of buying and selling, swap and barter, profit and loss. **1900** B. MITFORD *Aletta* 21 They saw no one month in month out, save an occasional Boer passer-by, or a travelling *smaus*, or feather-buyer, usually of a tolerably low type of Jew – and therefore, socially, no acquisition. **1919** J.Y. GIBSON in *S. Afr. Jrnl of Science* July 3 Until late in the 19th century the 'smous,' or itinerant trader was a common visitant, carrying his wares in a Kap-tent wagon to remote habitations of trekkers and settlers. **1925** H.J. MANDELBROTE tr. *O.F. Mentzel's Descr. of Cape of G.H.* II. 75 Voyagers .. are sometimes badly 'stung' in their dealings with rascally sailors and .. are apt to classify all Cape inhabitants as 'schmousen,' or even rogues. [*Note*] Hawkers or pedlars. **1930** J. BUCHAN *Four Adventures* 261, I met a Peruvian Smouse and sold him my clothes and bought from him these. [*Note*] Peter meant a Polish-Jew pedlar. **1937** C.R. PRANCE *Tante Rebella's Saga* I. 272 The smous could always be relied on to bring a good pack of news or lies, but he would not open it until business in the contents of his other packs had been encouraging. **1937** H. SAUER *Ex Afr.* 12 The arrival of the *smous* on a Boer farm always created a little excitement. The *smous* was a sort of travelling merchant, who went all over South Africa, visiting nearly every farmstead. **1944** J. MOCKFORD *Here Are S. Africans* 64 Concertinas and mouth-organs were brought to the outspans by far-travelling pedlars or *smouse*, as they were called. **1949** L.G. GREEN *In Land of Afternoon* 142 Another duty of the smous was to bring news of the outside world. **1949** O. WALKER *Proud Zulu* (1951) 31 He knew John had been in the wrong, but he was not prepared to be told so by a bunch of traders whom he despised as glorified peddlers and 'smouses'. **1956** S.D. NEUMARK *S. Afr. Frontier* (1956) 145 The smous is known to have played an important part in the frontier economy during the time of the Great Trek (in the 1830's). It was usual for him to come to the remote farms with two or three wagonloads of wares containing articles of clothing, groceries, and most other things required by the colonists. **1968** K. MCMAGH *Dinner of Herbs* 32 As the population grew and the settlers moved further afield the smous followed and took to the road, bearing his pack on his back until such time as his profits enabled him to afford first a cart and horses and later a wagon and oxen. **1976** *Het Suid-Western* 26 May 1 George Flip S—, a fish smous of Boekenhout Street, George. **1977** *S. Afr. Panorama* Mar. 25 An important facet of Jewish life was found outside the main centres. Now part of history is the figure of the 'smous' or travelling salesman, who was often the farmer's only contact with the outside world. **1980** *Daily Dispatch* 23 Aug. 3 He left school at the age of 13! At that age, Willie took employment with a travelling pedlar (smouse) and went with him from farm to farm and so earned his first wages. **1980** B. SETUKE in M. Mutloatse *Forced Landing* 64 The only people, other than the train-gang, who have free passage between one coach and the next, are the smouses, who .. are a force to be reckoned with. **1984** S. GRAY *Three Plays* 134 (*Enter Abraham Goldenstein, aged about forty; dirty, unkempt and bearded like many a smous dealer*) ... Jacob: .. I never sell my farm to a Jewish smous! **1984** M. MTHETHWA in *Frontline* July 29 Smouses – self-appointed train hawkers – are .. found in almost every train. **1991** I. BERELOWITZ in *Weekend Argus* 26 Jan. (Weekender) 2 He began his business career as a smous, a Jewish itinerant trader in the Western Cape, travelling by horse and cart and selling mainly articles required by farmers. **1992** *Natal Mercury* 2 Nov. 7 A thorough knowledge of merchandise – a 'feel for the goods' – is known in the retail industry as the key to success. Trevor K— .. has that 'smous' instinct. **1993** A. BRISTOWE in *Business Day* 25 Feb. 6 Milton Sahin .. says the image of the smous and pioneer Jewish trader and his relationship with the Afrikaner farmer has been glorified and mythologised.

smous *v.* Also **smouse, smouth.** [fr. prec.]
1. *intrans.* To be engaged in intinerant trading; to peddle; to solicit business (esp. in a demeaning manner); SMOUCH *v.*

1839 T. SHONE Diary. 4 May, We met John a coming back, he was going a smouthing. *a***1862** J. AYLIFF *Jrnl of 'Harry Hastings'* (1963) 77 You want to stop there to trade, or I should say *smouse*, for that's the Dutch word for trade. **1887** *S.W. Silver & Co.'s Handbk to S. Afr.* 35 They reared flocks, grew wool, went 'smousing,' and made themselves merchants. **1911** D.B. HOOK *'Tis but Yesterday* 16 Jan Hofmeyr had migrated from under the shadow of Table Mountain in 1820 .. and moved north by slow degrees, trading or smousing, following the business of a hawker. **1912** W. WESTRUP *Land of To-Morrow* 212 He has the sauce to come smousing around to me for an order ... He didn't get an order. **1955** D. ABELSON in Saron & Hotz *Jews in S. Afr.* 341 Max Rose started life at the Cape in the traditional way by *smousing*, but soon gave that up, and .. opened a shop at Zoar. **1968** D.R. EDGECOMBE Letters of Hannah Dennison. 235 He had opened a shop in Graaff-Reinet in 1824 and 'smoused' about the country. By 1836 he had established a shop in Colesberg. **1972** Beeton & Dorner in *Eng. Usage in Sn Afr.* Vol.3 No.1, 6 *Smous*, .. as v = to dispose of goods in an undignified manner. **1973** *Caravan* July 21 During the evening's friendly circle at Beaufort West Guy was fined for 'smousing' on a public road. **1977** F.G. Butler *Karoo Morning* 132 He loaded the Whippet up with samples of butter paper and stationery, and albums of H.M.V. records, plus an older child as gate-opener, and went smousing among the richer farmers. **1985** D. Bikitsha in *Sunday Times* 1 Sept. 4 Until now, we have been in the habit of smousing, drinking, pick-pocketing, preaching, and generally enjoying ourselves on trains.

2. *trans.* To obtain (something) in a questionable way.

1977 *Het Suid-Western* 21 Dec., They wanted to sell us the pictures they had smoused during the rescue – and that at the world's most inflated prices.

3. *intrans.* ?*nonce.* To search for bargains.

1991 F.G. Butler *Local Habitation* 190 Not only did we visit the local auctioneer's sales rooms regularly, but we broke our car journeys to Cape Town or elsewhere to smouse around second-hand and antique shops in towns and dorps en route.

smouser /smɘʊsɘ, 'smɘʊzɘ, 'smaʊzɘ/ *n. obsolescent.* Also **smauser, smouzer.** [smous *v.* + Eng. agential suffix *-er.*] smous *n.*

1887 A.A. Anderson *25 Yrs in Waggon* I. 40 The people .. wanted to know what I was doing in the country, as I did not handel (trade), and was not a smouser, the term applied to those who went about the country in waggons to sell and buy. **1899** G.H. Russell *Under Sjambok* 46 Can you not see that I am a smouzer? (trader). **1900** O. Osborne *In Land of Boers* 82 Since there has been such a demand in the country the last few years for financiers and company promoters, the smausers have disappeared wonderfully. **1905** P. Gibbon *Vrouw Grobelaar* 146 He was a smouser (pedlar) ... He sold thimbles and pills and hymnbooks ... I remember a Scotch smouser, who was called Peter Piper. **1912** W. Westrup *Land of To-Morrow* 116 The coolie smouser – the Indian who peddles goods all over the country and has no office or store expenses. **1924** L. Cohen *Reminisc. of Jhb.* 25 Drunken loafers, thirsty fossickers, .. ruined gamblers, cunning smousers, a bushel of toffs from Poland. **1977** F.G. Butler *Karoo Morning* 18 Oh! such watches! .. Smousers sell them ... I was shown one, a wretched Geneva watch in metal-gilt case. **1985** D. Bikitsha in *Sunday Times* 1 Sept. 4 Will God's lighter-skinned creatures tolerate the piercing whistles of the smousers as they tread up and down the coaches plying their trade of nail-clippers, shoelaces, fruit, combs, mirrors and hankies?

smousing /'smɘʊsɪŋ, ?'smaʊzɪŋ/ *vbl n.* [fr. smous *v.*] Peddling; itinerant trading; illicit trading or smuggling; also called *smouching*, see smouch *v.* Also *attrib.*

1856 J. & M. Churchill *Merchant Family in Natal* (1979) 79 We were about a week in trading amongst the farmers, and for the first time I saw what 'smousing' was. **1876** T. Stubbs Reminiscences. I. 51 Having given up Kurveying – I thought a Smousing trip might pay, I got a waggon load of goods from W.R. Thompson at 6 Months Credit, and started. **1880** *S.W. Silver & Co.'s Handbk to S. Afr.* 227 The traffic still goes on, for ostrich-farming has not, as yet, made interior *smousing* unprofitable. The departure of a great trader with his train of, perhaps, half-a-dozen waggons, all of them gaily painted and cosily covered in with snow-white canvas, is an event in some Cape towns. **1886** G.A. Farini *Through Kalahari Desert* 328 They have large farms now and thousands of sheep and cattle, and I might have been like them, but I fancied *smousing* (trading), and in two years I lost all I had. **1897** 'F. Macnab' *On Veldt & Farm* 271 Smuggling, or, as the kaffirs term it 'smousing', in brandy was carried on. **1926, 1968** [see smouch *v.*]. **1968** J.T. McNish *Rd to Eldorado* 15 Schalk van Niekerk .. a poor farmer, at times reduced to setting out on what was then known as a 'smousing' trip to make ends meet. **1984** M. Mthethwa in *Frontline* July 29 Smousing is an illegal practice and, consequently, gives practitioners a false bravado in that they defy the law in their own backyard.

smouth var. smous *v.*

smouzer var. smouser.

‖**snaaks** /snɑːks/ *adj. colloq.* Also (attrib. only) **snaakse** /'snɑːksɘ/. [Afk.] Odd, peculiar.

1913 C. Pettman *Africanderisms* 454 *Snaaks*, .. Droll, strange, peculiar. **1921** W.C. Scully *Harrow* 96 'Snaakse kêrel,' .. would be the comment of his hearers. **1961** [see ou *n.* sense 2 a]. **1973** M. Philip *Caravan Caravel* 64 Yesterday, when it was nearly dark, I knew there was something *snaaks* about the bushes. **1984** 'Dan' in *Frontline* Feb. 24 Man, these Capey ouens are very snaaks. They're otherwise. **1984** *Ibid.* 27 All of a sudden I got this like snaakse lump in my throat. **1984** *Frontline* May 38 They've made it [*sc.* free enterprise] into a sort of religion and even put it into the constitution ... But that is .. snaaks, since the govt ous were quite a bunch of socialists back in the olden days when P.W. Botha still had lots of hair. **1984** 'Dan' in *Ibid.* 39 Koos you can pick up this Bop radio sommer easily, even by accident, and when you do it sounds very snaaks.

snaphaan /'snaphɑːn/ *n. hist.* [Du. 'snapping cock', *snap* snapping + *haan* cock, perh. because the action of the hammer resembled a cock pecking.

Found in 17th century English (in this sense as well as others) as *snaphance* or *-haunce.*]

roer sense a.

1905 W.S.J. Sellick *Uitenhage Past & Present* p.v, Every morning, after prayers and coffee, the first thing that occupied attention was the *snap-haan*, or as it later grew to be called, baviaan bout. **1913** C. Pettman *Africanderisms* 456 *Snap haan*, .. An earlier name for the old-fashioned muzzle-loading musket, subsequently known as the Babiaan bout. **1937** F.B. Young *They Seek a Country* 531 He loaded his snaphaan with slugs, and saw that the flint was clean and the priming in order. **1947** F.C. Slater *Sel. Poems* 159 The foe leapt up, advanced; at this To earth the trekkers sprang, Their steady snaphaans rang! **1968** G. Croudace *Black Rose* 13 She saw a Hottentot in a skin cloak, ancient *snaphaans* over his shoulder, assegaai raised in his right hand. **1971** R. Raven-Hart *Cape G.H. 1652–1702* 516 In the snaphaan the pan-cover protecting the priming was arranged to slide back as the hammer fell, in the flint lock the blow of the flint moved the cover by striking on a part of it. **1971** F.V. Lategan in *Std Encycl. of Sn Afr.* IV. 518 In South Africa during the 17th century the matchlock and the wheel-lock were replaced by the Dutch 'snaphaan' ... This weapon was superseded in turn by the true flint-lock gun ... The term 'snaphaan' and its variants were used by the Voortrekkers to describe the true or French flint-lock. In his description of the Battle of Blood River, Preller .. refers to the small arms used by the Boers during the fight as snaphaan and elephant gun. Outside South Africa also the term 'snaphaan' was used to refer to any fire-arm requiring a flint and steel ignition. *Ibid.* 520 The true or French flint-lock, known in South Africa as the 'snaphaan' or 'sanna', was .. an improved version of the Dutch snaphaan. **1977** F.G. Butler *Karoo Morning* 117 He put the old voorlaaier to his shoulder, and pulled the trigger. Nothing happened. The flint had fallen out of the old snaphaan.

snees(e)wood var. sneezewood.

sneeze machine *n. phr.* Also **sneezing machine.** A cannon-like device used for spraying tear-gas; sneezer.

1977 *Drum* Aug. 25 Again the clash of white and black sides erupted in violence. A sneezing machine had to be called in as missiles flew into the field five minutes from the end of play. **1979** *Survey of Race Rel. 1978* (S.A.I.R.R.) 75 At White City, Jabavu, the police used the sneeze machine to stop youths from stoning a Putco bus. **1981** *Rand Daily Mail* 17 June 1 The 'sneeze machine' was used, and police said 10 rubber bullets were fired. **1984** *E. Prov. Herald* 24 Sept. 1 Hundreds covered their faces and ran away as palls of tear smoke from a sneeze machine on the back of a police van engulfed the camp. **1985** *Cape Times* 3 Dec., A Middleburg policeman .. told a magistrate .. yesterday that he ordered a sneeze machine moved from the vicinity of a cemetery where an unrest victim was being buried. **1986** *Ibid.* 17 Mar., Casspirs, Buffels, sneeze machines and police vans cordoned off the townships.

sneezer *n.* sneeze machine. Also *attrib.*

1977 *World* 17 June 3 Reef demos are broken up by sneezer cannon. **1983** *Drum* Aug. 7 Although initially peaceful, the chanting turned uglier at the sight of the 'Sneezer' which came spewing teargas.

sneezewood *n.* Also **snees(e)wood, sneize wood.** [tr. S. Afr. Du. *nieshout*, see nieshout; see also quot. 1853.] The exceptionally hard and durable timber of the tree *Ptaeroxylon obliquum* of the Ptaeroxylaceae; this tree; nieshout. Also *attrib.*

1823 J. Ayliff Journal. 18 We found a good supply of dry sneesewood. **1827** T. Philipps *Scenes & Occurrences* 79 Furniture here, I am told, is generally made from sneeze wood, which admits a very high polish. **1834** T. Pringle *Afr. Sketches* 219 A saffron-coloured timber, called sneeze-wood, from the effect of its pungent scent when newly cut. **1853** F.P. Fleming *Kaffraria* 36 The Iron-wood (*Sideroxylon*) is also much used, and likewise the Sneeze-wood, locally so-called, from the pungent perfume of the sawdust, similar to that of strong snuff. **1887** *S.W. Silver & Co.'s Handbk to S. Afr.* 352 The Sneeze-wood is a very hard and durable timber, excellent for piles, sleepers, lintels, and other engineering purposes where strength and lasting properties are required. **1897** S.C. Cronwright-Schreiner in F. Goldie *Ostrich Country* (1968) 16, I have seen an ostrich, at great speed, run against a sneeze-wood pole .. four inches in diameter at its thinnest end, which was broken off just where it emerged from the ground. **1910** A.B. Lamont *Rural Reader* 261 Sneezewood is one of the hardest of trees, and grows to a great height. *c*1936 *S. & E. Afr. Yr Bk & Guide* 320 The valuable Stinkwood .. occurs rarely in the forests of the Eastern Province, while the latter contain much Sneezewood (*Ptaeroxylon utile*), one of the most durable timbers known. **1961** Palmer & Pitman *Trees of S. Afr.* 281 *Sneezewood*, This remarkable wood is widely known for its almost imperishable properties as timber. **1971** *Grocott's Mail* 27 July 2 Sneezewood is too hard for nails, so the steps .. are kept in place by pegs. **1981** J.B. Peires *House of Phalo* 6 Well-trodden footpaths guided him through dense woods of mimosa trees, punctuated with .. sneeze-wood, the toughest of them all, which was hardened in fire to provide a substitute for iron. **1990** *Weekend Post* 11 Aug. (Leisure) 4 Africa's contribution lies in its ferns and indigenous woods, among them yellowwood .. sneezewood and wild lemon.

snelskrif /'snelskrɘf/ *n.* [Afk., *snel* rapid + *skrif* writing, script.] A system of shorthand for the Afrikaans language. Also *attrib.*

1949 *Cape Argus* 16 Apr. 11 (*advt*) Take a rapid course .. in book-keeping, Afrikaans, snelskrif, shorthand, [etc.]. **1952** *Cape Times* 2 Aug. 9 Typists who qualify for shorthand and *snelskrif* tests. **1971** on Radio South Africa 23 Oct., Preference will be given to ladies with snelskrif and/or shorthand. **1972** *Grocott's Mail* 1 Sept. 2 Bilingualism, shorthand, snelskrif, typing .. are all essential. **1988** *Cape Times* 3 Nov. 3 Papers written yesterday were needlework, metalwork, snelskrif and woodwork.

snijsel(s) var. snysels.

snoek /snʊk, snuk/ *n.* Also **snook.** Pl. unchanged, or (less commonly) **-s.** [S. Afr. Du., transf. use of Du. *snoek* a name for the European pike *Esox lucius.*] Any of several large marine fishes:

1. Most commonly, the snake mackerel *Thyrsites atun* of the Gempylidae, a common food-fish, often eaten smoked, or salted and dried. **2.** Either of two species of barracuda of the Sphyraenidae: **a.** *Sphyraena flavicauda*. **b.** *S. jello*. **3.** The KATONKEL (sense 2 d), *Scomberomorus plurilineatus*. Also *attrib.*

In Smith and Heemstra's *Smiths' Sea Fishes* (1986), the name 'snoek' is used for *T. atun*; the name *yellowtail barracuda* is used for *S. flavicauda*, and *pickhandle barracuda* for *S. jello*.

1797 LADY A. BARNARD in Lord Lindsay *Lives of Lindsays* (1849) III. 388 The fish called *snook* .. when salted and dried, was one of the best fish at the Cape. **1804** J. BARROW *Trav.* II. 300 Two kinds of fish, the *Hottentot* and the *Snook*, are split open, salted, and dried in the sun in large quantities. *a***1823** J. EWART *Jrnl* (1970) 13 Snoek, a long oily fish which being caught in great quantities and consequently cheap, forms the principal food of the slaves. **1827** G. THOMPSON *Trav.* II. 68 Some [fish] are said to measure six or seven feet in length, being probably of a sort known at Cape Town by the name of snook or pike. **1843** J.C. CHASE *Cape of G.H.* 169 Snoek: The most favourite food of the colonists. **1847** 'A BENGALI' *Notes on Cape of G.H.* 70 Snooks, the grand Cape stape, and which are dried in millions for foreign markets, are greasy, scaleless horrors, .. and are sold by the *yard* for a mere trifle. **1872** C.A. PAYTON *Diamond Diggings* 75 The snook is a fish shaped something like a pike, only rather longer, and in skin and colour something like a dusky mackerel. It has a huge mouth and terrible teeth, the bite of which is said to be poisonous. **1888** *Cape Punch* 14 Mar. 151 Brandy is cheap, retail'd at a price That will keep you a fortnight on snoek and boiled rice. **1891** H.J. DUCKITT *Hilda's 'Where Is It?'* 127 Boiled *snook* or cabeljon [*sic*], if at the Cape, or any white fish will do. **1910** D. FAIRBRIDGE *That Which Hath Been* (1913) 17 An old Malay fisherman, carrying his baskets of snoek and *kabeljaauw* suspended from a thick bamboo which rested on his bent shoulders. **1913** —— *Piet of Italy* 47 Trailing the snoek-lines over the stern of Hadje Magmoet's boat in False Bay. **1931** *Times Lit. Suppl.* (U.K.) 16 Apr. 301 The snoek .. is not a pike .. but a distant cousin of the mackerel. *c***1936** *S. & E. Afr. Yr Bk & Guide* 347 The most valuable fish .. on the South African Coast are the sole, silver-fish, snoek (barracouta), [etc.]. **1951** S. VAN H. TULLEKEN *Prac. Cookery Bk* 87 Snoek is a godsend to people living on farms or too far away from places where fresh fish is procurable. **1971** *Drum* Apr. 8 He was sipping Vodka (what else?) and stripping a dried snoekhead of its flesh. **1981** *Sunday Times* 12 July (Mag. Sect.) 1 Kebaabs with yellow rice, snoek masala with masala chips. **1988** C. NORMAN in *S. Afr. Panorama* Dec. 40 Cape snoek .. , a long and toothy creature whose oak-smoked flesh is one of the great traditional delicacies of South Africa. **1989** I. JONES *Woman's World Cookbk* 19 Smoked Angelfish or Snoek Pâté ... A Cape favourite.

4. With qualifying word: **China snoek**, a juvenile snoek; **smoorsnoek**, see SMOOR *adj.*

1950 *Cape Argus* 28 Oct. (Mag. Sect.) 3 **China snoek** .. have thicker bodies and shorter heads than the large snoek. The scientists refuse to recognize the China snoek as a different species. **1957** S. SCHOEMAN *Strike!* 117 The so-called 'China snoek', those undersized snoek which are found in Table bay docks during August to October and in False Bay during November-January.

5. *comb.* **snoek boat**, a boat of a type commonly used for snoek fishing; **Snoek Derby**, an annual competition for the largest snoek caught; **snoek horn** *hist.*, a horn sounded to announce the transporting, through the streets of Cape Town, of the first snoek catch of the year; cf. FISH HORN; **snoek pekelaar** /-ˈpɪəkəlɑː(r)/ [Afk. *pekelaar* salted fish], pickled snoek, or snoek cut into strips, salted, and dried; **snoek smoor**, see SMOOR *n.*

1963 K. MACKENZIE *Dragon to Kill* 86 My father went out with the **snoek boats** from Hout Bay early this morning. **1976** *S. Afr. Panorama* April 39 Tourists may see a snoek-boat chugging. **1982** *Argus* 22 Oct. (Suppl.) 3 (*advt*) *Snoek Boat.* 4,8 m Sachal, fibreglass with two 8 l Yamaha's ... Steering console, trailer, radio, echo. **1981** *Cape Times* 27 June 7 The organizers of the Multana **Snoek Derby** — the third — are now overjoyed that the winter snoek have put in an appearance off Hout Bay. **1982** *S. Afr. Digest* 3 Sept. 1 When women boat anglers were excluded from the male-only Snoek Derby at Hout Bay, they protested so strongly that the sponsors had to change their minds. **1965** K. THOMPSON *Richard's Way* 61 A high, winding **snoek-horn** began to call down the street. A horse-drawn cart came trotting by fast. **1986** P. JOOSTE in *Fair Lady* 22 Jan. 108 The first snoek catch was trumpeted through the streets by the snoek horn. **1890** A.G. HEWITT *Cape Cookery* 11 **Snoek Pekelaar.** Have the snoek cut into mootjes. **1902** H.J. DUCKITT *Hilda's Diary of Cape Hsekeeper* 142 Snoek pekelaar is the name we give to fillets of snoek slightly salted and sun-dried. **1919** M.M. STEYN *Diary* 253 We sent them a keg of 'snoek pekelaar' (salted or pickled snoek), which was worth having, as fresh fish was out of the question. **1958** L.G. GREEN *S. Afr. Beachcomber* 113 Snoek pekelaar consists of slices of the fish placed in layers in a jar of saltpetre, salt, sugar, coriander seeds and bay leaves. It will keep for months.

snoek /snʊk, snuk/ *v. intrans.* [fr. prec.] To fish for snoek. Hence **snoeker** *n.*, one who fishes for snoek; **snoeking** *vbl n.*, snoek-fishing; also *attrib.*

1913 W.W. THOMPSON *Sea Fisheries of Cape Col.* 50 It is a pretty sight to watch a fleet of fishing boats snoeking under sail. *c***1937** *Our Land* (United Tobacco Co.) 1 During the snoeking season this corner of the Cape Town docks is a scene of great activity and the snoekers recall the old sailing days. **1935** L.G. GREEN *Great Afr. Mysteries* (1937) 137 The total catch by all the snoeking vessels often amounts to a million fish. **1942** *Off. Yr Bk of Union 1941* (Union Office of Census & Statistics) 769 'Snoeking' is still one of the most important branches of the Cape fishing industry. **1952** L.G. GREEN *Lords of Last Frontier* 299 Snoeking, a trade that has prospered here for forty years, keeps a grand fleet of small craft in commission. **1959** *Cape Times* 5 May 2 Snoeker found ringed bird ... While snoeking at St. Helena Bay, John Mentor .. found a dead black sea-duiker. **1981** *Ibid.* 12 Sept. 3 Spawning season hits Cape snoeking. Snoeking in Cape waters has now come to a virtual standstill.

snoep /snʊp, snup/ *adj. colloq.* Also **shnoep**. [Afk., greedy, grasping (fr. Du. *snoepen* to eat sweets stealthily, to enjoy forbidden things in secret).] Stingy, miserly, mean.

1966 *Informant, Grahamstown* He's so horribly snoep that he makes two 35c bottles of wine do a dinner party for twelve. **1970** E. MUNDELL *Informant, Pearston (E. Cape)* Don't be so snoep with your sweets (greedy, selfish). **1971** *Informant, Grahamstown* Oh! Here it is, I couldn't find it. Penny's so snoep with the paper — she's written it on the back! **1975** 'BLOSSOM' in *Darling* 9 July 95 Try and pick up some free samples .. only the make-up folks is getting hang of a snoep like everybody else these days. **1975** S. ROBERTS *Outside Life's Feast* 55 'Look, I've only got a few cartridges with me and I need them.' 'Jesus, how snoep can you get!' **1977** *Darling* 18 July 123 Maybe its on account of I'm born snoep .. but I only gotta see those big red *Sale* signs outside a shop and I go into orbit. **1977** S. ROBERTS in E. Pereira *Contemp. S. Afr. Plays* 244 My God, but I hate a snoep person!

So **snoep** *n.*, a stingy person.

1994 L. LÜNSCHE *Informant, Johannesburg* I'm such a shnoep. I don't want to dip into my savings to buy the computer.

snook var. SNOEK.

Snor City /snɔr ˈsɪti/ *n. phr. Colloq.* [Afk. *snor* moustache + Eng. *city*; named for the supposed preponderance of men wearing moustaches in Pretoria.] A nickname given to the city of Pretoria.

1987 *Cosmopolitan* Dec. 168 Other aliases are Snor City (there's a 'total onsnort' of moustachioed men), and Spark Plug (NGK) Country. 'Pretoria,' said a retired clerk living in Irene, 'is Sodom and Gomorrah in a cloak of respectability.' **1990** *Weekly Mail* 4 May 23 When the police .. start shouting at the dogs through loudhailers in the roof, the associations with Snor City, our capital, will send extra shivers down a Johannesburger's back. **1993** N. JOHNSTON on CCV TV 8 Apr. (Toyota Top 20), The tour comes to an end in good old Snor City — Pretoria.

snort sick, - sickte varr. SNOTSIEKTE.

snot and tears *n. phr. Slang.* [tr. Afk. *snot en trane.*] SNOT EN TRANE.

1969 A. FUGARD *Boesman & Lena* 36 The women and children sitting there with their *snot* and tears. The *pondoks* falling. **1979** A.P. BRINK *Dry White Season* 88 Shorty never was a talkative sort. But that day it was proper spring cleaning ... Snot and tears. About life in jail.

snot en trane /ˈsnɔt (ə)n ˈtrɑːnə, ˈsnɒt- / *n. phr. Slang.* Also **snot and trane**. [Afk., *snot* snot, nasal mucus + *en* and + *trane* tears.] 'Snot and tears', symbolizing misery, or maudlin or sentimental behaviour; SNOT AND TEARS. Often *attrib.*

1970 M. BRONSLOW *Informant, Cape Town* She was crying snot and trane (crocodile tears). **1971** G. MASSYN *Informant, Grahamstown*, Needless to say I was all snot and trane last night when Mommy had left. **1972** *Cape Times* 25 Mar. 5 Nerina Ferreira .. plays a *snot-en-trane* prima donna gone to seed. **1972** *Sunday Times* 24 Sept. 19 We must get away from the traditional 'snot and trane' and capture realism in Afrikaans theatre. **1978** *Speak* Vol.1 No.5, 41 Our cinematic myths are empty, superficial, mindless, still at the 'snot en trane' stage. **1979** *Daily Dispatch* 13 Feb. 2 All the snot en trane of last week's no-confidence debate gave way yesterday to an afternoon of amicable agreement on a whole list of vital issues. **1981** *Ibid.* 10 Mar. 7 There must be more of a future for us all than eternal snot en trane, presuming we don't cease upon the midnight first. **1985** *Fair Lady* 20 Feb. 47 Tears and triumphs, passion and shame, snot en trane. **1988** *E. Prov. Herald* 13 Feb. 1 A heightened sense of momentous poignancy delicately tinged by a pinch of 'Snot and/or Trane'. **1990** J. HOBBS in *New Contrast* Winter 70 It doesn't quite pass the first-few-pages test with its rather slow, traditional *snot-en-trane* start.

‖**snotsiekte** /ˈsnɔtsiktə/ *n. Pathology.* Also **snort sick(te)**, **snotziekte**. [S. Afr. Du., fr. Du. *snot* nasal mucus + *ziekte* disease.] Any of several catarrhal diseases affecting livestock (see quot. 1914).

[**1850** R.G.G. CUMMING *Hunter's Life* II. 362 A horrible and very fatal illness, called by the Boers 'snot sickness,' which cattle are very liable to from pasturing on ground frequented by black wildebeests.] *a***1875** T. BAINES *Jrnl of Res.* (1964) II. 34 Mr. Francis .. complained that his cattle were dying daily of an epidemic disease that produces blindness and subsequently death ... This is called here the snort sickte and is generally regarded as incurable, but McCabe has found a decoction of wild olive leaves, used hot as a wash, very effective if applied in time. *Ibid.* 39 An ox .. had died during the night, of the 'snort sick'. **1912** *Agric. Jrnl of Cape of G.H.* Jan. 139 (Pettman), The term *snotziekte* does not describe any particular or specific disease; it is a term applied when excessive mucous discharge is observed to run from the nose, such discharge being seen in different diseases, in different species of animals, and is due to many different causes. **1914** *Farmer's Annual* 205 The term 'snotziekte' is applied by the average farmer to any disease of animals in which there is a pronounced mucous discharge from the nostrils, such as is seen in glanders, strangles, influenza, inflammation of the lungs, or a severe cold in equines, or in cattle suffering from tuberculosis, ordinary cold, or the presence of some foreign body, such as a nail, piece of wire, or pin in their lungs. **1925** *E. Prov. Herald* 27 July 10 Many years ago when game was plentiful, it was observed .. that a peculiar disease which they called snotsiekte .. broke out among their cattle in contact with wildebeeste. **1979** T. GUTSCHE *There Was a Man* 369 J.B. Quinlan dealt with an aspect of bovine Contagious Abortion and

R.W.M. Mettam .. with 'Snotziekte', a sporadic cattle disease. **1989** J. du P. Bothma *Game Ranch Management* 625 Snotsiekte or malignant catarrh is a problem common to all large warm-blooded ungulates. **1991** *Personality* 5 Aug. 31 Buyers of black and blue wildebeest and buffalo have to be registered as a control on *snotsiekte* and corridor disease respectively.

||**snysels** /ˈsneɪs(ə)ls/ *n.* Also **snijsel(s)**. [Afk., cuttings, slices, noodles, fr. *sny* cut.] **a.** Home-made noodle pasta, cut into strips. **b.** In full ***melk snysels***, a traditional pudding made of noodles cooked in milk, sugar and cinnamon; MELKKOS.

1913 C. Pettman *Africanderisms* 457 *Snijsel*, .. A preparation of flour somewhat like macaroni, cut into short lengths and used to thicken soup, etc. **1930** M. Raubenheimer *Tested S. Afr. Recipes* 81 Snijsels. Homemade Maccaroni [*sic*] ... Beat egg up with the water and stir it into the flour. Mix well and knead into a very stiff dough ... Allow the 'Snijsels' to dry off slightly, but it may be used at once. **1934** *Cape Argus* 5 Jan. (Swart), 'Melk Snysels' is a popular supper dish. **1934** C.P. Swart Supplement to Pettman. 115 *Melk-Snysels*, .. A popular Cape milk food is so called, its chief ingredient being dough cuttings resembling macaroni. **1939** S. Cloete *Watch for Dawn* 283 How fond the children had been of her snysels! ... Flour mixed with well-beaten egg till it was stiff dough; a little salt. Then you had to roll the paste, lifting it as you rolled ... You rolled it like a carpet and then you cut it length-wise into strips ... And melk snysels, cooked with milk, sugar, and cinnamon! **1974** *Sunday Times* 3 Mar. (Mag. Sect.) 7 Our own South African dishes — things like sosaties, the real bredies ... And those delicious onions with a sour sauce, melk snysels, koeksisters. **1989** I. Jones *Woman's World Cookbk* 96 Snysels (Milk Noodles) ... A traditional Cape Dutch dessert, in which homemade ribbon noodles are cooked in milk and served with cinnamon or nutmeg — snysels were a favourite supper dish for children. **1990** [see MELKKOS].

Soa *n. obs.* SAN sense 1.

1857 *Cape Monthly Mag.* II. Sept. 183 A small and rapidly vanishing division of the Gariepine or Hottentot race is the Soa or Bushman.

soap bush *n. phr.* Any of several species of shrubby plant formerly used for making soap. See also GANNA.

1838 J.E. Alexander *Exped. into Int.* I. 83, I found his three fresh and strapping daughters boiling soap, prepared with fat and the branches of the soap-bush. **1913** C. Pettman *Africanderisms* 459 *Soap bush*, .. This name is also applied to Noltea africana; after macerating the saponaceous leaves of this bush the natives use them for washing. [**1934** C.P. Swart Supplement to Pettman. 160 *Soap Plant*, .. Helinus ovatus, a climbing plant used in soap-making, is so called in the Eastern Province.] **1987** M. Poland *Train to Doringbult* 63 The afternoon light was harsh. Even the soap bushes were withered, casting short, dry shadows.

sobo-sobo var. UMSOBOSOBO.

Sobukwe /sɔˈbʊ(ː)kwe, səˈbu(ː)-/ *n. hist.* [The surname of *Robert Sobukwe* (1926–1978), Pan-Africanist Congress leader; so called because the clause was introduced specifically as a means of keeping Sobukwe in prison after his three-year prison term ended in May, 1963.] In the phrr. ***Sobukwe Bill, Sobukwe Clause***, the General Law Amendment Act of 1963 (in particular Clause 4 of this Act) which amended the Suppression of Communism Act of 1950 which provided for the continued detention of sentenced political prisoners after their prison terms had ended, if the Minister of Justice deemed them likely to promote communism on their release.

The clause was not invoked after Robert Sobukwe's release from prison in 1969. After 1976, the Internal Security Amendment Act provided for the detention of anyone who, in the opinion of the Minister, was engaging in acts which subverted state security or public order.

1971 *Post* 14 Mar. 9 He was due to leave prison ... The Government rushed through a new law ... Sobukwe stayed in jail and the new law became known as the 'Sobukwe clause.' **1972** *Drum* 22 Nov. 5 After he had finished his three-year sentence a Bill — The Sobukwe Bill the Press called it — was rushed through Parliament and The Prof was held on Robben Island for another six years. **1977** *Survey of Race Rel.* (S.A.I.R.R.) 45 The so-called 'Sobukwe clause' .. provided that if the Minister was satisfied that any person serving a sentence .. under any of the security laws was likely .. to promote .. communism .., the Minister might direct that this person should be detained in custody .. for a stated period. **1990** *City Press* 4 Mar. 9 The government rushed a special bill through Parliament known as the 'Sobukwe Clause' and he was not released.

soega var. SUKA.

soek /sʊk, suk/ *v. intrans. Slang.* [Afk., seek, look for.] **1.** To look for trouble. **2.** To look (for something).

1970 K. Nicol *Informant, Durban* If you're going to soek here, you'll get hurt. **1986** *Style* June 86 It's people who think if you're naked you must be *soeking* for sex who create perverts in society. **1986** *Informant, East London* Don't soek for trouble.

soeka var. SUKA.

Soekor /ˈsukɔː/ *n.* [Acronym formed on Afk. *Suidelike Olie Eksplorasiekorporasie* 'Southern Oil Exploration Corporation' (a play on Afk. *soek* seek, search for).] A parastatal corporation established in 1965 to prospect for oil. Also *attrib.*

1971 *S. Afr. Panorama* July 43 The search by the Southern Oil Exploration Corporation (Soekor) is going on without interruption. **1973** *Weekend Post* 19 May (Mag. Sect.) 1 Since the South African Government established the Southern Oil Exploration Corporation (Soekor) in 1965, the search for oil within the Republic has gone on relentlessly. **1985** *E. Prov. Herald* 1 Mar. 1 The first major crude oil strike in more than a decade of oil exploration in South Africa has been made off Mossel Bay, the South African Oil Exploration Corporation, Soekor, announced yesterday. **1986** *Sunday Star* 13 July (Review) 26 Soekor comes of age this year, but the R600 million its 21-year oil search has cost will be recouped from just one year of the Mossel Bay gas flow. **1989** *Weekend Post* 14 Oct. (Leisure) 7 A Soekor oil/gas rig on the Agulhas Bank near Mossel Bay.

soemaar var. SOMMER.

soepie, soepje varr. SOPIE.

soesatie var. SOSATIE.

soetdoring /ˈsutˌdʊərəŋ/ *n.* Formerly also **zoetdoorn**. [Afk. (earlier Du. *zoetdoorn*), *soet* sweet + *doring* thorn.]

1. The SWEET THORN, *Acacia karroo*. Also *attrib.*

*a***1912** *S. Afr. Agric. Jrnl* June 790 (Pettman), The only compensation seems to be afforded by the *zoetdoorn* (one of the *Acacias*). These trees started flowering early in the season. *a***1951** H.C. Bosman *Willemsdorp* (1977) 87 All around there was just African bush, soet-dorings and moepels. **1972** *S. Afr. Panorama* May 29 Australian blue grass, silver wattle and indigenous soetdoring trees. **1976** V. Rosenberg *Sunflower* 35 It was a vast dust bowl studded with the whole panoply of thorn-trees, from the haak-en-steek to the apiesdoring, the kameeldoring and the widespread soetdoring. **1990** M. Smit in *Sunday Times* 2 Dec. 27 The wise among us sat at breakfast in the shade of mopani and soetdoring. **1992** *Weekend Post* 6 June (Leisure) 7 *Acacia karroo, sweet thorn, soetdoring.* The principal tree of the Karoo regions, it appears in different sizes ranging from shrub to large spreading tree.

2. *comb.* **soetdoring-veld** *obs.* [Afk. *veld* uncultivated country], grassland upon which soetdoring shrubs or trees have appeared.

1914 *Agric. Jrnl of Union* in E.N. Marais *Rd to Waterberg* 23 It was attempted to start growth by damping and shading two hundred clumps of sweet grass of different varieties growing on zoetdoorn-veld.

soete-koekie var. SOETKOEKIE.

soetes /ˈsutəs, ˈsutis/ *n. colloq.* [Afk., 'sweet ones'.] Sweet fortified wine.

1977 D. Muller *Whitey* 63 If you'd do just one last little thing for me — if you'll just get me a bottle of soetes, and then lock me in here. **1986** D. Case *Love, David* 45 He would then go to the back door and shout 'Beer!' or 'Soetes!' or something like that. One of the women would appear and hand him whatever it was that he wanted. **1988** O. Oberholzer *Ariesfontein to Zuurfontein*, Millie Beukes had been sitting there in the sun sipping 'soetes' all day. Since early morning, his wife wasn't speaking to him any more. **1990** *Excellence* Vol.6 No.2, 7 Soetes can and should be drunk at any time. **1991** *Daily Dispatch* 1 Mar. 10 We refer .. to the family of fortified wines or 'soetes' which include sherry, port, muscadel and hanepoot.

soetjes *adv. obs.* Also **sootjes, su(i)tjes**. [Afk., obs. form of *soetjies*.] Softly, gently, quietly.

[**1885** H. Rider Haggard *King Solomon's Mines* 9 It's a stiff place, and I feel as though I were bogged up to the axle. But 'sutjes, sutjes,' as the Boers say (I'm sure I don't know how they spell it), softly does it.] **1894** [see *Durbanite* (DURBAN)]. **1898** E. Glanville *Kloof Bride* 275 Suitjes, baas, suitjes. If we miss the spoor we lose time and all. **1913** C. Pettman *Africanderisms* 459 *Soetjes*, (D. *zoetjes*, softly, gently.) Gently, slowly.

soetkoekie /ˈsutkuki/ *n.* Formerly also **soete-koekie, soet koek, soet-koekje, zoete-koekie, zoetenkoekje, zoetkoekie**. [Afk. (earlier S. Afr. Du. *zoetekoekje*), *soet* sweet + *koek* cake + dim. suffix -IE.] A traditional spiced biscuit. Also part. tr. **soet-cookie**. See also KOEKIE sense 1.

1891 H.J. Duckitt *Hilda's 'Where Is It?'* 243 Tea Cakes ('Zoete Koekies'). (Very old Dutch Recipe ..). **1899** 'A Housewife of the Colony' *Col. Hsehold Guide* 93 Soet Koek, (Dutch) Three lbs flour, $1\frac{1}{2}$ lbs sugar, ground cinnamon, cloves, nutmeg and ginger. **1910** D. Fairbridge *That Which Hath Been* (1913) 113 Juffvrouw wanted very bad to help hand *zoete-koekies*. **1915** [see OBLIETJIE]. **1930** N. Stevenson *Farmers of Lekkerbat* 78 They drank weak coffee out of large tin mugs, and ate rich cakes made of fat and treacle. These soetkoekies reminded Uncle Eloff of his youth. **1955** V.M. Fitzroy *Dark Bright Land* 243 The boer's wife .. patted Martinus's shoulder and slipped a soet-koekje into his hand, and said he had better call her Tant' Alida. **1959** M.W. Spilhaus *Under Bright Sky* 123 She approached with a plate of *soete-koekies*. **1963** A.M. Louw *20 Days* 10 He helped himself to plenty of cream and sugar and several soetkoekies from the mahogany biscuit barrel. **1972** S. Lynne *Glittering Gold* 147 The tea was delicious, the biscuits crisp home-made soetkoekies, the same little sweet biscuits that once again reminded Nerina of her childhood. **1973** *Fair Lady* 7 Mar. 23 With visions of my Voortrekker ancestors embarking on hazardous journeys with tinfuls of 'mebos', biltong, and 'soet-koekies', I scratched through my recipe book. Obligingly it yielded a recipe for real 'Zoetenkoekjes'. **1989** Z. Roos in *Sunday Times* 3 Dec. (Mag. Sect.) 78 The fragrance of *soetkoekies* baking in ouma's Aga is one of the most evocative memories of my childhood.

||**soetriet** /ˈsutrit/ *n.* [Afk.] IMFE.

[**1925** see PHOKO.] **1927** *Farming in S. Afr.* Dec. 505 (Swart), Grain sorghums .. have as yet not received much attention from our grain farmers, chiefly because kaffircorn and soetriet are considered Native crops. **1934** C.P. Swart Supplement to Pettman. 161 *Soetriet*, .. The common name of the saccharine Sorghum, much cultivated by Natives ... Its chief value is its ability to withstand drought. All Natives and many Europeans relish the stalks, which have a sweet flavour. **1964** V. Pohl *Dawn & After* 22 Soet riet, the indigenous type of sugar-cane, was to us what ice-cream is to the modern child. **1968** *Farmer's Weekly*

3 Jan. 90 Haakdoring Soetriet .. 6c lb. **1972** *Ibid.* 21 Apr. 75 Haakdoring Soetriet, per 91kg R12,00.

soet suurdeeg see SUURDEEG.

Sofasonke /ˌsɔ(ː)faˈsɔ(ː)ŋke, ˌsɔ(ː)fə-/ *hist.* [Zulu sentence, lit. 'we shall all die together'.] **a.** A slogan coined by James Mpanza when he founded an illegal but successful squatter settlement near Orlando station, Johannesburg, in March, 1944; also *attrib.*, designating the settlement and associations or activities connected with it. **b.** Used as Mpanza's nickname, and as the name of the political party which he and his followers established.

1958 A. SAMPSON *Treason Cage* 72 In April 1944, .. a crowd of thousands .. living in the tents and hessian shelters of Orlando location .. made a well-disciplined trek to a nearby plot of empty municipal land, and squatted there ... They were led by .. James Mpanza, who adopted the slogan '*Sofasonke*' – 'we all die together' – for his bold operation ... The municipality accepted the new shanty town. **1963** M. BENSON *Afr. Patriots* 113 Mpanza's slogan, Sofasonke, 'we all die together', became his nickname. **1977** J. SIKAKANE *Window on Soweto* 13 In the latter years Shantytownians had their own law courts known as the 'Sofasonke Courts' named after Sofasonke Mpanza .. who led them into setting up the squatter settlement. **1989** *Reader's Digest Illust. Hist.* 356 The main attraction of the *Sofasonke* camp was the protection it offered its vulnerable inhabitants.

sohalahala var. SEHALAHALA.

||**sokkiejol** /ˈsɔki jɔl, -ˌdʒɔl/ *n. colloq.* Also **sokkiesjol.** Pl. **-s, -jolle** /-jɔlə, -dʒɔlə/. [Afk., *sokkie* little sock + *jol* jollification.] Esp. among young Afrikaans-speakers, a discotheque or party. Also *attrib.*

1983 *Sunday Times* 18 Sept. (Mag. Sect.) 33 They go to '*sokkiejols*' together. **1985** *Cape Times* 23 July, 'Sokkie jolle' culture ... An Ll B student at the Rand Afrikaans University .. said the young Afrikaner woman no longer took part in folk dancing, but lived in the 'spirit of a new cultural idiom', which included rugby, music, reading and 'sokkie-jolle'. **1986** *Sunday Times* 10 Aug., They left the drive-in and went to a sokkiesjol (boere disco) at the Island hall – a dance-hall on an island in the middle of a nearby dam. [**1987** *Fair Lady* Feb. 18 The Hotel (where they have sokkies in the disco on Saturday nights sometimes – what a jol).]

solder /ˈsɔldə(r)/ *n. Archit.* Formerly also **zolder.** [Afk., fr. Du. *zolder.*] A loft or attic; cf. BRANDSOLDER sense 2.

1862 LADY DUFF-GORDON in F. Galton *Vacation Tourists* (1864) III. 159 There is a yard behind, and a staircase up to the zolder or loft, under the thatch ... There are no ceilings; the floor of the zolder is made of yellow wood, and, resting on beams, forms the ceiling of my room. **1891** H. RABONE in A. Rabone *Rec. of Pioneer Family* (1966) 95 Dear Harrie and I slept in the great zolder, and a larger or more airy bedroom few people have had. **1891** J.P. LEGG in *Cape Illust. Mag.* I. 96 In our houses we should find it hard to do without our 'solder.' **1913** W.C. SCULLY *Further Reminisc.* 46 This [*sc.* the coffin] was kept upstairs in the 'solder', where it was used as a receptacle for 'biltong' and dried peaches. **1945** N. DEVITT in *Outspan* 27 July 51 All self-respecting heads of Boer families would have their coffins ready against the day. It was usually kept in the 'solder' or loft. **1977** N. OKES in *Quarry '77* 136 There in the eerie unaccustomed brightness illuminating the voorhuis, she saw that the whole central gable had collapsed, bringing parts of the solder with it. **1987** G. VINEY *Col. Houses* 34 There was an amount of wheat and rye in the *solder.*

soldier *n.* [Prob. transf. use of general Eng. *soldier* a name used of any of several deep-water fish (perh. a translation of the former L. specific name *miles*).] The seabream *Cheimerius nufar* of the Sparidae.

In Smith and Heemstra's *Smiths' Sea Fishes* (1986), the name 'santer' is used for this species.

1913 C. PETTMAN *Africanderisms* 459 Soldier, (1) *Dentex miles* is so named in Natal. **1949** J.L.B. SMITH *Sea Fishes* 277 *Cheimerius nufar* ... *Wittevis* (Cape). *Sonvis. Sunfish* ... *Soldier* (Natal). *Rubalo.* **1970** *Albany Mercury* 29 Jan., It is seldom that a soldier is caught from the surf. **1970** *Daily News* 5 Oct., Most boats reported good catches of salmon, soldiers, slinger and rock-cod. **1971** *Grocott's Mail* 28 May 3 Mrs. E. Birch took both the ladies' awards with a soldier of 0,963 kg, another unusual fish and decidedly a deep sea species. **1972** *Ibid.* 11 Feb. 3 Caught a soldier of 1.25 kg. using a pilchard and a 9/0 hook. **1993** R. VAN DER ELST *Guide to Common Sea Fishes* 338 *Cheimerius nufar* ... *Common names* Worldwide – santer, soldier.

soldoedie /sɔlˈdudi/ *n. Army slang.* [Afk., blend of *soldaat* soldier + *doedie* 'popsy', lass.] An army nickname for a member of the Women's Army College in George, Cape Province; BOTHA'S BABE. Also *attrib.*

1975 *Evening Post* 30 Jan. 5 'Soldoedies' start to train today ... Girls will arrive by train and by car from many parts of South Africa and South West Africa today when this year's 152 hand-picked 'soldoedies' begin their 10-month training at the Civil Defence College. **1975** *Het Suid-Western* 30 Jan., Already soldoedies have completed their training at the college. **1981** [see BELLERYNA]. **1981** *Het Suid-Western* 9 Oct., Getting ready for the big Soldoedie parade tomorrow. **1985** *Financial Mail* 30 Aug. 151 The girls' understandable apprehension at becoming volunteer *soldoedies* expresses itself in very different ways.

so long *adv. phr.* [Calque formed on Afk. *solank*, with the same sense.] Meanwhile, for the time being.

1893 A. SUTHERLAND in *Cape Illust. Mag.* Apr. 267 'Oh it doesn't matter in the least,' Ida hastened to interrupt. 'I can go on with my book so long.' **1900** B. MITFORD *Aletta* 45 Take the reins, so long. There are a couple of fine pauw. Think we can get any nearer? **1900** *Ibid.* [see TAKKIE *n.*[2]]. **1909** *George & Knysna Herald* 28 July 4 He has got what you call confirmation of de lungs, en de Dokter say he mus go by de O-spital, so long. **1915** D. FAIRBRIDGE *Torch Bearer* 82 'That's a fine pair of horses that you are driving.' Pleasure beamed from every pore of Jan's face. 'Ja, baing mooi,' he said enthusiastically. 'I mean veree nice. They belong to my auntee who is in Cape Town so long.' **1920** S. BLACK *Dorp* 54 'Is your sister home, Maggie?' asked Klaas ... 'Oh yes, Anita's inside.' 'Won't she come out on the stoep so long?' **1970** K.S. DEWAR *Informant, Randburg* He says he will come just now. Will you sit down, so long? **1975** *Darling* 25 June 111 She wants me to go right now ... mind the shop so long, you hear? **1982** A.P. BRINK *Chain of Voices* 428 'Why the hell didn't you think of it before?' 'Sorry, Baas. But I can go back and get them. You can ride home so long.'

sommer /ˈsɔmə/ *adv. colloq.* Formerly also **soemaar, soma, so maar, soma(a)r, somer, somma(ar).** [Afk. *sommer, somaar* simply, just, for no specific reason, fr. Du. *zomaar.*] 'Just', 'simply', 'only'; for no specific reason, 'because'; without more ado. Also used redundantly in the phr. ***just sommer.*** Cf. MAAR *adv.* sense 2, MOSSIE(S).

1786 G. FORSTER tr. *A. Sparrman's Voy. to Cape of G.H.* II. 19 When we propounded this difficulty to them, they gave us no other answer than, *So maar, Baas! This is our way, Master!* **1835** T.H. BOWKER Journal. 12 May, Bowkers party gone out on patrole *somer* heard from the third Division, they have been shooting some Kafirs, & taking Cattle & Goats. [**1850** R.G.G. CUMMING *Hunter's Life* I. 27 The Dutch word *somar* .. is also a word to which I think I could challenge the most learned schoolmaster in the Colony to attach any definite meaning. It is used by both Boers and Hottentots in almost every sentence; it is an answer to every question; and its meanings are endless.] **1866** E.L. PRICE *Jrnls* (1956) 213, I have soma short-coated the little maid to-day Jeanie, and she reminds me of my sweet Moffat – so wee and light. **1916** S. BLACK in S. Gray *Three Plays* (1984) 237 Man: Why are you here alone ... Van K: I'm waiting soemaar to go out on bail ... No man, no – volstrekt nie, jong! Man: What's that? Why do you say I'm young? Van K: No, it's soemaar an expression. Man: Don't you speak English? Van K: Man, that's English, man. **1920** —— *Dorp* 174 'Ach, Oom Kaspar, can't I go back to look for my pipe and put it somaar in the box?' 'Nay, kerel, they won't let you go again inside the ballot-box.' *c***1929** [see ALLEMAGTIG]. **1948** V.M. FITZROY *Cabbages & Cream* 42 Dahlia unfolded a touching tale of a young son who had nowhere to live 'and can sommaar sleep in Aaron's room if missis will only be so kine, and he will do any sorter work that missis wants'. **1963** A.M. LOUW *20 Days* 212, I got such a fright, .. I sommer ran out in my night-clothes. **1963** K. MACKENZIE *Dragon to Kill* 57 'You want them to just sommer stand there and be stoned to death?' asked Jan Marais. **1969** A. FUGARD *Boesman & Lena* 15 Sannie who? Sommer Sannie Somebody. **1970** A. FULTON *I Swear to Apollo* 229 'Man,' he said to himself. 'It somer doesn't make sense.' **1976** [see DOPPIE sense 3]. **1977** P.-D. UYS *Paradise Is Closing Down* 136 We had no fridge or stove; somaar a ou tin with cold water for the milk. **1978** *Voice* 29 Nov. 2A, People never learn – they somer throw caution to the winds when it comes to weddings. **1979** *Sunday Times* 22 Apr. (Mag. Sect.) 5 The third International Film Festival to be held in Cape Town promises to be a visual delight for the fans who know the difference between just sommer movies and the cinema as art. **1984** 'DAN' in *Frontline* Feb. 27 The Capeys worry about relations between the larnies and the bushies. The darkies don't feature. They are sommer a fact of life, like mosquitos or income tax. **1984** *Frontline* May 39 These are meant to be independent states' stations, but actually they are sommer advertising tricks to make money from the same white listeners who used to think that the name of broadcasting was Springbok. **1985** P. SLABOLEPSZY *Sat. Night at Palace* 37 Delicate wafer. Tiny ripples for artistic effect. I mean, this isn't just sommer a chip any more – it's a bladdy twentieth-century work of art! **1986** D. CASE *Love, David* 110 'I would rescue it, but, I would not keep it.' 'Why not?' I asked curiously. 'Sommer,' David said. **1986** R. MORRIS in *Style* Nov. 130 Cape Point Nature Reserve makes for a great day's entertainment ... Once in you can picnic, swim, fish or just *sommer* look around. **1987** L. BEAKE *Strollers* 32 'Let's go to the Parade.' 'What for?' ... 'Sommer.' **1988** E. PLATTER in *Style* June 65 *Cycling glasses*: Not goggles, *sommer* sunglasses, but the trendy cyclist will not settle for anything less than a R190 pair of Oakleys from the States. **1990** H. DE ZITTER in *Ibid.* May 88, I used to just sommer sit there, waiting for the horses to come by, a prime target for ticks and tick-bite fever. **1991** P. SLABOLEPSZY Braait Laaities. 29 What are you going to do if these blokes have just sommer disappeared? **1994** L. MACKENZIE on Radio South Africa 6 May, You can sommer hug any Vaalie you like.

songololo, tshongololo /ˌsɔŋgɔˈlɔlɔ, ʃɔŋ-, ˌtʃɔŋ-/ *n.* Forms: α. **songalolo, songolola, songololo;** β. **chongololo, shongalolo, shongolala, shongululu, tjongololo, tshongololo.** [Xhosa *i-songololo*, Zulu *i-shongololo* (fr. *ukus(h)onga* to roll up).]

1. Any of several species of millipede of the Diplopoda (esp. *Julus terrestris*) which have hard shiny exterior armour, and which curl up into a pinwheel-shaped coil when disturbed.

α. **1913** C. PETTMAN *Africanderisms* 461 *Songalolo*, .. *Julus terrestris* bears this name in the Eastern Province; it refers to its habit of curling up into a coil when disturbed. **1913** J.J. DOKE *Secret City* 149 The songololo, pursuing its even path with the steady movement of a thousand feet. **1947** F.C. SLATER *Sel. Poems* 8 The grass curls up and withers – Curls, as a songololo curls At the touch of a careless foot. **1947** *Kowie Announcer* 21 Oct. 5 Our remark the other day about rain and Songololas (the correct local native name) has brought in the following: – 'When Songololas climb the wall, Rain must soon begin to fall'. **1956** A.G. MCRAE *Hill Called Grazing* 84 The anxious scanning of roots for signs of damage by eelworm or the songololo centipede. [1969 F.G. Butler *When Boys Were Men* 119 'Thousand-leg insects' is a direct translation of Afrikaans *duisendpoot* i.e. millepede, probably the large variety found in the eastern Cape called *songololo* by Africans.] 1972 on *Radio South Africa* 9 Feb., In one month flat kitty had cleared the place of rats — it was still lousy with snakes and scorpions and songololos, but no rats. 1977 M. Van Biljon in *Sunday Times* 1 May (Mag. Sect.), A songololo is .. a millipede with a hard shiny exterior armour .. a plague in Tamboerskloof where after the first rains they have marched in their serried ranks down the mountain, into nooks and crannies, crevices, baths, curtains, up walls, down paintings, into cupboards. 1989 T. Botha in *Style* June 112 Songololos loll in the way of my tyres. 1990 *Style* Feb. 52 Imagine .. you're so hungry you're prepared to eat songololos! 1991 *Ibid.* Apr. 102 We share it [sc. the shower room] with the fattest, most colourful songololo we've ever seen.

β. 1951 W.T. Miller *Wild Life of Sn Afr.* (Chapter 74), A tjongololo .. in danger .. winds itself into a stiff coil and trusts the strength of its armour-plated shell ... Common on the veld are little heaps of dried-out, grey and empty rings that were once the burnished armour of a tjongololo. 1977 *Sunday Times* 22 May 9 The children tickled her .. and tried to scare her with creepy-crawlies ... 'They apple-pied beds and landed me with frogs and tshongololos.' 1988 T.J. Lindsay *Shadow* (1990) 266 She saw a chongololo, a millipede. 1990 D. Capel in *Personality* 276 Aug. 13 They have their own peculiar brand of bug, called 'chongololos' which eat the tobacco crop. 1992 T. Carnie in *Natal Mercury* 9 Nov. 7 We were shown the waterhole where Dingiswayo's sister was killed by a crocodile ... why some shongalolos have lime green stripes ... and the gobandlovu tree, with its famed aphrodisiac properties.

2. *fig.* See quots.

α. 1977 *Fair Lady* 17 Aug. 107 Xhosa women call the coiled intra uterine contraceptive device songololo – millipede! 1991 P. Mullineux *Informant*, Grahamstown She told us to bring a songololo of boerewors.

β. 1963 M. Kavanagh *We Merry Peasants* 149 James was ready to take his chance on getting on the *shongolala* (creepy-crawly) train home. 1987 *Sunday Times* 17 May (Mag. Sect.) 8 Barbie kugel with plastic hair, shongululu eyelashes, and lips thick with strawberry sherbet.

songoma var. SANGOMA.

Sonqua /ˈsɔŋkwa, ˈsɒŋkwə/ *pl. n. Hist.* Also **Sankwa, S(a)unqua, Songua, Sonquas.** [Khoikhoi, var. of *Sanqua*, *San* (see SAN) + pl. suffix *-qua*.] (The) members of the SAN (sense 1) people.

As is the case with many names of peoples and groups in S. Afr. Eng., 'Sonqua' has been found only in plural uses; however, it may be that it has also been used in unrecorded singular forms.

1688 G. Tachard *Voy. to Siam* 68 The first Nation in the language of the country, is called *Sonquas*. The Europeans call those people Hottentots ... There is not one Nation who besides their own Natives have not also *Sonquas* in their Militia. 1930 I. Schapera *KhoiSan Peoples* 31 The Bushmen do not appear to have any general or collective names for themselves ... The Hottentots term them all *San*. The meaning of this word is uncertain, but Hahn interprets it as 'aborigines, or settlers proper'. The names *Sunqua, Saunqua, Sonqua*, etc. by which the Bushmen are often referred to in the early records of the Cape, are merely verbal variations of its masc. plur. form Sa(n)-qua. 1966 J.P. van S. Bruwer *S.W. Afr.: Disputed Land* 19 These roaming pastoralists [the Nama] referred to themselves as Khoi-Khoi or 'people of people' to distinguish themselves from the Bushmen, whom they called the San or Sankwa, and the Dama indicated as Daman or Black People. 1981 Newton-King & Malherbe *Khoikhoi Rebellion* 1 The hunter-gatherers, though their languages were sometimes mutually unintelligible, were collectively called San or Sonqua by the pastoralists.

soopee, -pie varr. SOPIE.

Soosequas var. SUSEQUA.

sootjes var. SOETJES.

sopie /ˈsʊəpi/ *n.* Also (esp. formerly) **soepie, soepje, soopee, soopie, so(o)pje, sopi, soupé, soupee, soupi(e), soupje, soupk(i)e, sup(j)e, suppe(e), suppie, suppy, zoepie, zoopje, zoupie.** [Afk., fr. Du. *zoopje* a little glass, fr. *zuipen* to tipple or drink.] A drink, esp. of spirits; a dram; a sip or small quantity of alcoholic drink. Also *attrib.* Cf. DOP *n.* sense 3 a.

Quot. 1980 refers to the *tot* system (see TOT *n.*² sense 2).

[1696 W. Mountagu *Holland* 38 The common Dutch are satisfied with a sopie of Brandy-Wine.] 1790 tr. F. Le Vaillant's *Trav.* I. 92 Those who enter a house are always presented with a *sopi*, that is to say, a glass of rack or gin, or rather of French brandy. 1798 Lady A. Barnard *Lett. to Henry Dundas* (1973) 181 The Boers from the Country .. generally come to pay their respects at the castle at seven 'o clock in the morning and always have their Sopi of Gin with me while I am at breakfast. 1804 R. Percival *Acct of Cape of G.H.* 254 Sit in the porch for an hour or two with a pipe in their mouths, and a slave by their side holding a glass and a small decanter of gin from which the master every now and then takes his soupkie or glass. 1827 G. Thompson *Trav.* I. 270 He pressed me to take a *soopie* with him, to which I willingly agreed, as the night was very chilly, but asked for water to mix with the brandy. 1832 *Graham's Town Jrnl* 18 Oct. 167, I did not see deceased drink any brandy on that day, she does take her *soopie*, but never so much as to cause her to fall on the ground, or make a noise. 1840 C.A. Kinloch in *Echo* 26 Oct. 4 An English trader, from Graham's Town .. informed them that we were three poor Indian Gentlemen travelling for amusement, and the whole affair was most satisfactorily explained by the aid of the Snuff-box and a soopee of the real Cognac. 1847 J. Barrow *Reflect.* 183 Our very devout boors prepared themselves for the enterprise by singing three or four hymns ... , and drinking each a sopie, or glass of Cape brandy. 1852 H. Ward *Jasper Lyle* 3 Major Frankfort .. solaced himself and his friend moderately with a *sopie* (dram) from the flask stuck in his leather waist-belt. 1863 T. Shone *Diary* 30 Apr., I went to J. Knights, got my Dinner, and a suppe of gin. 1868 W.R. Thomson *Poems, Essays & Sketches* 167 You will have to drink one or two [cups] for every hour you stay, varied now and then, mayhap, with a soepie from your host. 1875 [see GESONDHEID]. 1882 C. Du Val *With Show through Sn Afr.* I. 272 The ice having thus been broken, it required only the application of the flask of brandy to create a complete thaw, and a proffered 'soupje' was at once accepted. 1908 [see CAPE BRANDY]. 1910 D. Fairbridge *That Which Hath Been* (1913) 240 If you want a *zoopje* there is Van der Hum on the table yonder and a bottle of old dop. 1913 C. Pettman *Africanderisms* 461 The quantity of spirit which goes to make a soopje is variable, one man's soopje would be another man's overthrow. 1958 A. Jackson *Trader on Veld* 44 Although the average farmer was fond of his 'sopie' (spot), alcoholic excesses were unknown. 1968 F.C. Metrowich *Frontier Flames* 99 After being sufficiently primed with innumerable sopies Gaika would also fling off his blanket and join vigorously in the fun. 1976 A. Delius *Border* 225 Soon we were all, ladies as well as the gentlemen, prevailed upon to try a glass — and those who didn't try a second 'soepie' were declared guilty of insulting this distant relative of Oom Roer. 1979 Heard & Faull *Our Best Trad. Recipes* 18 In mid-18th century Cape Town it was customary for the gentry to take a sopie (small glass of gin or brandy) before breakfast. 1980 A. Paton *Towards Mountain* 117 Part of the remuneration of the farm workers is the 'sopie,' the draught of sour inferior wine that is given to them three or four times a day ... The sopie has been condemned by generation after generation of social workers, teachers, and ministers of religion.

soppies /ˈsɔpis, ˈsɔpiːz/ *n. slang.* Also with initial capital. [Etym. unknown.] BIO-CAFÉ.

1970 J. Stodel *Informant*, Cape Town There's a double feature showing at the soppies (tearoom bioscope). 1972 M. Develin on *Radio South Africa* 25 Jan., Like the other day I checked a mission scopes by the local soppies. (The other day I viewed an outstanding film at the local biocafé.) 1981 *Sunday Times* 10 May (Mag. Sect.) 7 Nobody who has never sat in a darkened Soppies (or cinema tea-room, as the larney-er ones liked to be called) will ever understand their appeal. I don't know about Cape Town's Soppies, but the ones in Durbs have all been replaced with discount stores now, and the ones in Joeys will soon be naught but a happy memory.

sopvleis /ˈsɔpfleɪs/ *n. Music.* [Afk., lit. 'soup meat'.] In the Cape Malay community: a movement in square-dancing; the type of music to which it is performed. Also *attrib.* See also KLOPSE sense 2.

1952 *Drum* Dec. 19 Square leader Dale Quaker .. and members of his Square Club are here seen enjoying a 'Sopvleis' .. the movement where opposite formations of the square advance to the centre and back. 1973 *Contrast* 32 Vol.8 No.4, 24 The band is playing the *sopvleis* part of the square dance. 1987 [see E. Prov. Herald quot. at KLOPSE sense 2]. 1987 *New Nation* 3 Dec. 11 Simply called 'Mac and the Genuines' it is a combination of moppies and sopvleis (klopse-lingo for humorous and serious music, respectively).

sorba-sorba var. UMSOBOSOBO.

sore-eye flower *n. phr.* [According to C.A. Smith (1966), 'derived from a popular tradition that long staring at the inflorescence or flower .. produces sore eyes'; but see also quot. 1917.] Any of several plants of the Amaryllidaceae: **a.** Any of several species of *Brunsvigia*; see also CANDELABRA sense 1. **b.** *Boophane disticha*; also called GIFBOL. **c.** NERINE. **d.** The KNYSNA LILY (sense a), *Cyrtanthus obliquus*. **e.** Any of several species of *Ammocharis*. Also *ellipt.*, **sore-eye**.

1910 *E. London Dispatch* 27 May 5 (Pettman), A large *Cyrtanthus* or *sore-eye flower* (though why so called we have yet to learn). 1917 R. Marloth *Common Names* 76 *Sore-eye flower*, Numerous Amaryllidaceae bear this name, owing to the irritation of the eyes, caused by the pollen, e.g. *Brunsvigia gigantea, Buphane ciliaris* etc. 1953 J. Hoyle *Some Flowers* 2 Sore-eye, *Buphone disticha* — Amaryllidaceae. This plant is often confused with the Fireball (*Haemanthus*). *Ibid.* 3 The Flowers of Sore-eye are larger, and much fewer, than those of the Fireball. 1961 *Redwing* (St Andrew's College, Grahamstown) 3 On the banks of a certain stream a scattering of 'sore-eye' flowers grew (ammocharis coranica). 1966 C.A. Smith *Common Names* 429 *Sore-eye flower*, *Brunsvigia orientalis* ... , Perhaps also other species enumerated under *Seeroogblom*. 1975 J.M. Gibson *Wild Flowers of Natal* 13 *Boophane disticha* .. (Sore Eye Flower). I had to hurry drawing this flower because my eyes were so sore. 1982 A. Moriarty *Outeniqua Tsitsikamma* 46 *Boophane disticha, Sore-eye Flower, Seeroogblom*. 1982 [see KNYSNA LILY sense a].

sorghum *n.* [In general Eng. use, but of local significance. (In S. Afr. Eng., perh. applied to a wider variety of species than in general Eng.).] **1.** Any of several species of *Sorghum*, esp. the widely cultivated Indian millet *S. bicolor* (or *S. vulgare*), the grain of which is ground to make porridge, and sprouted to make beer; MABELA sense a. Also *attrib.* See also IMFE, MTOMBO sense 1 a.

'Sorghum' is increasingly the preferred term as the offensive word 'kaffir' in the name KAFFIRCORN is avoided.

a1915 H.W. Struben in A.C. Partridge *Lives, Lett., & Diaries* (1971) 129 We kept our horses in good fettle on cut buffalo grass and 'sorghum' (Kaffir corn). 1936 *Cambridge Hist. of Brit. Empire* VIII. 769 The variety of sorghum known as Kaffir corn is .. apparently indigenous to South Africa, .. and the basis for the brewing of Kaffir beer. **1985** *Cape Times* 10 Oct., Later they bought an adjacent farm, .. using the women's sorghum – 'kaffircorn', they still call it – which sold at the time for nearly £4 a bag.

2. In full ***sorghum beer***: TSHWALA sense a. Also *attrib.*

'Sorghum beer' is increasingly the preferred (urban) term as the offensive KAFFIR BEER is avoided.

1975 *Friend* 11 June 1 In a bitter blow to thousands of African beer drinkers, the Government has authorised a massive $33\frac{1}{3}$ percent increase in the retail price of sorghum (Ijuba) beer. **1978** A. ELLIOTT *Sons of Zulu* 73 Zulu custom is that, for most ceremonies, the host supplies the meat – a goat or ox or whatever he can afford – and a measure of sorghum beer. **1979** *E. Prov. Herald* 6 Apr. (Indaba) 5 Sorghum beer was not jabulani a member was told in the national Assembly here ... The sale of sorghum beer had not been prohibited in Transkei as it was included in the definition of liquor in the Liquor Act. **1980** M. LIPTON in *Optima* Vol.29 No.2, 161 The problem was exacerbated by a switch from traditional sorghum beer, which is nutritious, has a low alcohol content, and is drunk in large quantities, to more expensive, potent and less nutritious (but widely advertised) 'European' spirits. **1981** *Time* 7 Dec. (Liquor), The black man has traditionally and for centuries been a sorghum beer drinker. **1987** *Frontline* Aug.-Sept. 9 Coated fibreboard cartons for milk, sorghum beer and fruit juices. **1987** *S. Afr. Panorama* Oct. 8 The Sorghum Beer Amendment Act of 1987 paved the way for privatisation of the sorghum beer industry. **1990** D. STANLEY in *Frontline* Sept. 12 Outside the claustrophobic hostel atmosphere, the sun is beating down on a different scene: a mad market. Youths lounge around, swigging sorghum. **1990** M. KENTRIDGE *Unofficial War* 86 A reporter .. found .. a group of Inkatha men sitting around drinking sorghum beer. They were armed with sticks and knobkerries.

3. *derog. rare.* A black person.

1978 *Drum* Apr. 2 There was a time they referred to us as sorghums in Pretoria. This was after they had changed kaffir corn and kaffir beer to sorghum corn and sorghum beer.

sort *v. Diamond-mining.* [Special sense of general Eng. *sort* to separate or distinguish (from something else).] To search diamondiferous ground (by hand) for diamonds; also in the phrr. ***to sort dry, to dry-sort***, in the same sense.

a. *intrans.*

1873 F. BOYLE *To Cape for Diamonds* 111 Lonely little camps occurred, consisting perhaps of a family waggon with two or three gipsy tents around, .. mostly occupied by boers, who carry their stuff home for wives and children to 'sort' ... Screened from the merciless sun by an old umbrella, sits the master of the claim, 'sorting'. **1873** *Ibid.* [see ERF sense c]. **1976** B. ROBERTS *Kimberley* 44 One of his African labourers told him that there was talk in the camp of a solitary white man working 'out there', .. 'dry-sorting and finding diamonds every day'.

b. *trans.*

1873 [see sense a]. **1882** J. NIXON *Among Boers* 163 At first the diamondiferous soil was sorted 'dry', a system which allowed many valuable stones to escape the eye of the sorter; now all sorting is done with the aid of water. **1893** T. REUNERT *Diamonds & Gold* 56 In the very early days of the Fields, when water was scarce and costly, the diamonds were won by 'dry-sorting' the pulverised ground, and the resulting 'debris', scattered over a large area of the townships, has since been nearly all washed with more or less profit by the workers. **1913** [see *sortings* (SORTING)].

Hence **sorter** *n.*, one who performs this task.

1873 F. BOYLE *To Cape for Diamonds* 127 When nothing is left but the dry little lumps like fine gravel, and the diamonds, he unhooks the sieve and carries its contents to a neighbouring table on which it is poured before the panting sorter. **1876** —— *Savage Life* 14 A bucket of 'stuff' is poured upon the boards. The sorter grasps a 'scrape' of iron, .. with this he rakes towards him a double handful of the shingle. **1913** [see *sortings* (SORTING)].

sorting *vbl n. Diamond-mining.* [As prec.]

1.a. The process of searching diamondiferous ground (by hand) for diamonds. Also *attrib.*

1871 J. MACKENZIE *Ten Yrs* (1971) 95 After the washing has been performed the 'sorting' process begins. A rude table has been constructed upon which the pebbles are placed. The novice performs the sorting slowly and carefully; but the experienced worker .. goes through the operation with great rapidity. **1882** [see SORT sense b]. **1977** [see sense b].

b. With qualifying word: **dry-sorting**, see quot. 1913; also *attrib.*

1913 C. PETTMAN *Africanderisms* 156 *Dry sorting*, .. The earliest and most primitive method of searching for diamonds adopted at the Diamond Fields. It consisted in passing the diamondiferous ground through a succession of hand-sieves, and then passing the residuum over a sorting table. **1919** M.M. STEYN *Diary* 173 In 1917 I pulled down the building and had the ground, which I had carted there for a floor in 1872, washed, and found £160 value of diamonds! That shows how diamonds were thrown away in the old 'dry-sorting' days!

2. *comb.* **sorting table**, a table or board on which the final stage of sorting diamondiferous gravel is performed; see also GREASE TABLE.

1872 C.A. PAYTON *Diamond Diggings* 8 The gravel being thus thoroughly cleansed by this double process of sifting and washing, the large stones in the top sieve are hastily glanced over, .. and the other sieve or sieves are taken out, and the contents emptied on to the '**sorting table**,' which is an ordinary table of deal, with or without legs, or a smooth sheet of iron or other inexpensive metal ... Diamonds .. show out brilliantly, and can very seldom be missed on a sorting table. **1873** F. BOYLE *To Cape for Diamonds* 79 Here and there is a 'canteen' of dirty canvas, or a plank-built 'store' ... But such habitations are rare. Rarer still is the 'sorting table.' **1876** —— *Savage Life* 13 The topmost box is emptied, after a glance that assures the digger there is no monstrous diamond among the stones. The next box, of smaller pebbles, is examined very much more carefully, for in it will be found any gem over twenty carats or so. This looked over and thrown away, the contents of the last box are poured into a bucket, and carried to the 'sorting table.' **1887** J.W. MATTHEWS *Incwadi Yami* 176 It may be as well to briefly describe the 'sorting table'. The top of a packing case balanced on a heap of gravel often had to serve this purpose in the early days of the river diggings, and beside it the digger knelt, crouched or sat. **1891** R. SMITH *Great Gold Lands* 72 When he is satisfied that the heavier contents had been separated from the lighter stones, he deftly turns over the sieve on to a flat board termed a 'sorting table'. **1893** T. REUNERT *Diamonds & Gold* 58 The heavy deposit, with the diamonds, passes through the screens into pointed boxes below, whence it is drawn off at the lowest point of the box and taken to the sorting tables. **1896** M.A. CAREY-HOBSON *At Home in Tvl* 231 Whenever I was called away and had to leave my sorting-table to a servant, I felt sure that the illicit diamond buyers had more of my diamonds than I had. **1931** G. BEET *Grand Old Days* 84 The sorting tables had .. to be placed out on the veld, but as near the Kopje as possible. These places afterwards came to be known as 'depositing floors'. **1968** J.T. MCNISH *Rd to Eldorado* 240 The gravel left behind .. was tipped out upon a sorting table and treated in the usual way when searching for diamonds. **1977** *S. Afr. Panorama* Aug. 18 Built with windows on one side only and tilted so that no direct sunlight ever strikes the sorting tables, Harry Oppenheimer House accommodates some sophisticated equipment for the sorting of diamonds. **1981** *Daily Dispatch* 25 June 1 He had removed a bucket of washed gravel from the pulsator sieve without paying much attention to what he was doing. At the sorting table he poured out the contents of the bucket. With a 'sudden shock' he noticed a diamond the size of a R1 coin.

Hence **sortings** *n. noncount*, the residue of diamondiferous ground remaining after the sorting process.

1873 F. BOYLE *To Cape for Diamonds* 111 The mounds of sortings are now close by thronged with busy men, black and white. **1913** C. PETTMAN *Africanderisms* 462 *Sortings*, .. The refuse material after it has undergone the above process. Occasionally a small diamond would be over-looked by the 'sorter'; the 'sortings' were eagerly 're-sorted' by others in the hope of finding some such overlooked stone.

sosatie /səˈsɑːti/ *n.* Also **sa(a)saatie, sa(r)sartie, sasa(a)rtjie, sasaatj(i)e, sasaitie, sassart(j)ie, sassatee, sas(s)atie, sassatj(i)e, sassatye, soesatie, sosaartjie, sosati, sosatje, sozatie.** [Afk. (earlier S. Afr. Du. *sasaatje*), fr. Javanese *sesate* skewered meat.]

1.a. Cubes of curried or spiced meat grilled on a skewer, sometimes alternated with onions, dried fruit, or fat; a kebab. Also *attrib.*, and *fig.*

1833 *Cape of G.H. Lit. Gaz.* 2 Sept. 138 (Pettman), *Sasaitie*, or cabobs, is really no despicable eating. [**1882** C. DU VAL *With Show through Sn Afr.* I. 50 An ingenious youth who had lately returned from 'the front' was cooking at a gipsy fire what the Dutch call 'sasaatjies' – chunks of meat broiled on bits of wood, and flavoured with curry-powder.] **1885** L.H. MEURANT *60 Yrs Ago* 29 There existed in those days what were termed 'Sasaatje and Rice' houses, places where a favourite Dutch dish called 'Sasaatjes' was served in the evenings ... Two sassatjes (diamond-shaped inch-sized pieces of mutton, curried and about half a dozen stuck upon a bamboo skewer, and then roasted upon a gridiron) .. were served for a 'Kwartje' .. a piece of stout, blue black paper money. **1890** A.G. HEWITT *Cape Cookery* 18 To cook the sassatees stick the pieces of meat fat and lean alternately, on wooden skewers, and broil them over a charcoal fire. **1891** H.J. DUCKITT *Hilda's 'Where Is It?'* 214 Roast the skewered meat (sasaties) on a *gridiron* heated on wood coals, and serve with the sauce. **1910** *S. Afr. 'Inquire Within'* (Cape Times) 46 Sasaties. Cut a leg of mutton into small inch-long pieces and put in fat in between. **1928** N. STEVENSON *Afr. Harvest* 279 For dinner, that day, Susie made *sasarties*, a sort of curried meat, pierced through with a skewer. **1935** P. SMITH *Platkop's Children* 213 An' the picnic was saasaaties an' ribitjes cooked on the coals, an' coffee an' cookies an' thin's. **1947** L.G. GREEN *Tavern of Seas* 65 Some say you must use two sorts of meat, mutton and pork for the genuine sosaties or kabobs of the Cape. Miss Duckitt cut squares from a leg of mutton, soaked in onion, lemon, brown sugar, milk, tamarinds, curry powder and garlic. Next day they would be skewered (on the traditional bamboo sticks) and grilled over a wood fire. **1948** H.V. MORTON *In Search of S. Afr.* 293 Sosaties – another Malay word .. can be as simple as veal or mutton cutlets sprinkled with curry powder and roasted on a skewer over a clear wood fire, or as complex as pieces of mutton or pork soaked in wine and vinegar, spiced with coriander, tumeric [*sic*], pepper, tamarind, and grilled in the same way .. a more ambitious version of kébab. **1953** [see VOLKSPELE]. **1967** S.M.A. LOWE *Hungry Veld* 96 The Aunts normally prepared sosaties with spiced meat, threaded on willow sticks, interspersed with chunks of fatty bacon. **1968** K. MCMAGH *Dinner of Herbs* 83 The men made the fires that would die down to give the 'coals' on which to grill .. skewered sasaaties lying ready in immense basins of delectable curry sauce. **1977** [see DONNER *v.* sense 1]. **1981** *Flying Springbok* Sept. 54 *Sosaties* is another dish we have inherited from those slave women who knew exactly what to do in the kitchen to preserve foods in a hot climate. Sosaties .. consists of cubed and marinated meat (usually mutton and pork) speared on to freshly cut sticks and grilled over glowing coals. **1989** I. JONES *Woman's World Cookbk* 83 Ostrich Fillet Sosaties in the pan ... These superb sosaties/kebabs are not for the braai.

b. *comb.* **sosatie stick**, a fine wooden skewer on which pieces of meat are grilled.

1982 *Pretoria News* 24 Nov. (Suppl.) 16 We stock an enormous range of kitchenware, from Sosatie sticks to non-stick bakeware. **1990** *Weekly Mail* 22 June 5, I had to buy two dozen sosatie sticks.

2. The dwarf succulent *Crassula rupestris* of the Crassulaceae, with masses of small pink-white flowers in dense clusters.

1966 C.A. SMITH *Common Names* 429 *Sosaties(-bossie), Crassula rupestris* ... The vernacular name is derived from the resemblance of the arrangement of the leaves along the branches to a Cape delicacy (sosaties). **1992** *S. Afr. Garden & Home* Dec. 104 Botanic name: *Crassula rupestris*. Common name: Concertina plant, *sosaties*.

Sotho /ˈsutu/ *n.* Formerly also **Ceuta, Shutu, Sutho, Suthu, Suto, Sutu.** [fr. Sotho *Mosotho* (see MOSOTHO), and *seSotho* the language of the Sotho; the n. stem *-Sotho* may be fr. the adj. stem *sootho* brown, or fr. the name of the *Usutu* river (see quot. 1978 at sense 1 a).

In Sotho orthography, the letter *o* in the n. stem *-Sotho* represents a vowel sound between /o/ and /u/. This is often interpreted by Eng.-speakers as /u/, hence the apparent discrepancy between the S. Afr. Eng. orthography and pronunciation of this word, and the frequent use of the letter *u* in earlier texts. A similar pattern is found in the word MOSOTHO.]

I. People.

1. Pl. **-s.**

a. Esp. in academic texts: a member of any of several linguistically and culturally related African peoples constituting the large group which includes the Basotho, Lobedu, Pedi, and Tswana; also called SOTHO-TSWANA. **b.** Esp. in popular use, or with reference to (former) official ethnic categories: a member of one of the *Southern Sotho* or *Northern Sotho* peoples (see sense 1 c below), as opposed to those of the Tswana (or *Western Sotho*) group. Also *attrib.* See also MOSOTHO.

Sotho people live mainly in Botswana and Lesotho, and (in South Africa) in the (former) Transvaal and parts of the Orange Free State.

1827 T. PHILIPPS *Scenes & Occurrences* 34 All that can be ascertained is, that they belonged to the *Ceuta* tribe, a very formidable, but very distant nation. **1937** B.H. DICKE *Bush Speaks* 42 In Majate's country Schiel rallied all the Magwamba still there ... The following day not a single Suto could be found on the plains which had been gone through with a fine comb. **1965** [see PEDI *n.* sense 2]. *a***1968** D.C. THEMBA in E. Patel *World of Can Themba* (1985) 117 The different tribes are separated. There is a building for the Sotho group, a set of buildings for the Nguni (Zulu, Xhosa, Swazi) group, another for the Venda-Shangaan group. **1970** B. DAVIDSON *Old Afr.* 223 The Sotho are thought to have gone south over the river into what is now the Transvaal in the middle of the fifteenth century, or thereabouts. **1974** [see sense 1 c below]. **1976** WEST & MORRIS *Abantu* 8 The Sotho comprise about 28% of the South African black population. *Ibid.* 133 The word Sotho simply means 'black people', which raises the interesting questions: how and why did they receive this name — and from whom? **1977** T.R.H. DAVENPORT *S. Afr.: Mod. Hist.* 7 The area of Sotho dominance between the Drakensberg, the Kalahari and the Limpopo was apparently occupied by two further settler waves. **1978** *Reader's Digest Illust. Guide to Sn Afr.* 298 It was the Nguni people from the east coast who called them all the Suthu ('dark brown people'), not because of their colour, but because they were first encountered when they were living in the valley of the Usutu River in Swaziland. **1980** LYE & MURRAY *Transformations* 25 The generic name, Sotho, which is widely adopted today, is accepted by all but a few of the Western Tswana clans and derives from their own language. 'BaSotho' translates from their language as 'Black People'. **1984** *S. Afr. Panorama* Feb. 43 These men .. are drawn from .. Southern Africa's Black peoples, ranging from the Tswanas in the west to the Sotho, Shangaan, Zulu and Xhosa groups in the east. **1985** [see PAP *n.* sense 1]. **1986** P. MAYLAM *Hist. of Afr. People* 20 In the twentieth century the vast majority of African people south of the Limpopo have come to be classified under one of two broad generic labels — Nguni or Sotho. **1987** P. CULL in *E. Prov. Herald* 1 May 4 In Natal and the Orange Free State .. the major black groups were Zulus and Sothos respectively ... It might be possible to divide the Cape into the Eastern Cape with Xhosas, Western Cape also with Xhosas and Northern Cape with Tswanas.

c. With distinguishing epithet: **North(ern) Sotho**, a member of a group comprised of the Pedi and Lobedu peoples; see also LOBEDU, PEDI *n.* sense 1; **South(ern) Sotho**, MOSOTHO; **Western Sotho**, TSWANA sense 2 a. Also *attrib.*

1971 *Daily Dispatch* 4 Feb. 1 The Minister .. had had consultations with the territorial authorities of .. the South Sotho, the Tswanas, the Venda, the **North Sotho** and the Machangana. **1974** W.W.M. EISELEN in *Std Encycl. of Sn Afr.* X. 64 The Western Sotho are generally known as the Tswana. The other two sub-divisions of the Sotho group both lay claim to the name 'Sotho', for which reason they are distinguished as Northern and Southern Sotho. *c***1980** *S. Afr. 1979: Off. Yrbk* (Dept of Info.) 84 The North Sotho speaks the language of the Pedi, spoken by 20 million people in the eastern, north-eastern and north-western Transvaal. **1980** D.B. COPLAN Urbanization of African Performing Arts. 207 Whatever its origins as a term, *marabi* was a product of the Johannesburg slumyards and could not have emerged in the small, predominantly Northern Sotho location of Marabastad. **1989** *Reader's Digest Illust. Hist.* 66 The principal group among the northern Sotho were the Pedi, a branch of the iron-working 'Kgatla people. **1973** *Drum* 8 Mar. 35, I am a **Southern Sotho**, who would like to have male and female penpals to correspond with. **1976** [see West & Morris β quot. at MOSOTHO]. *c***1980** *S. Afr. 1979: Off. Yrbk* (Dept of Info.) 84 The South Sotho of South Africa and those of the Lesotho kingdom share a common origin. They speak the same language and share other cultural characteristics. The Basotho of Lesotho are, however, the nucleus of the South Sotho people. **1983** *Survey of Race Rel. 1982* (S.A.I.R.R.) 403 The Commissioner-General of the South Sotho .. stated that Qwa Qwa could never become a viable economic state. **1989** *Reader's Digest Illust. Hist.* 66 The country now known as Lesotho has probably been occupied by the southern Sotho people, called the Basotho, since the 16th century. **1974** W.W.M. EISELEN in *Std Encycl. of Sn Afr.* X. 64 The Northern and the **Western Sotho** have remained separate groups ... The Western Sotho are generally known as Tswana. **1989** *Reader's Digest Illust. Hist.* 67 The basis of western Sotho society was the family, of which several went to make up a ward, under the authority of a hereditary headman.

II. Language.

2.a. Any language of the *Southern Sotho* or *Northern Sotho* groups (see sense 2 c below). Also *comb.* (objective) **Sotho-speaking** *ppl adj.*

1928 *Africa* I. 481 In reality there are two main branches of this group, Chwana spoken in Bechwanaland and the Western Transvaal, and Suto with its main dialects. **1941** 'R. ROAMER' in *Bantu World* 25 Jan. 4 In Xhosa and Sutho it urged us to 'come in our thousands and fight .. low wages and discriminating laws'. **1959** B. BUNTING in *New Age* Dec. 6 Published in Xosa, Sotho and Zulu, the journal is packed with picture stories of 'society' Africans who have 'made good'. **1968** *Drum* Sept. 36, I managed even to get a neatly typewritten letter on how he was converted to this religion. It is in Sotho. **1976** J. BECKER *Virgins* (1986) 11 Susan explained in Sotho, and reported; 'She say she has no papers, Mam, but she has worked on the farm at home as washgirl.' **1979** W. EBERSOHN *Lonely Place* 12 Two black policemen .. leaning against a wall and talking softly in Sotho. **1983** *Drum* June 89, I will only reply to letters with photos please. You can write to me in either Sotho or English. **1987** *New Nation* 12 Feb. 4 As a result of Bophuthatswana's independence in 1977, the Tswana authorities refused their Sotho-speaking neighbours work permits, residential rights and mother-tongue instruction in schools under their control.

b. Any of the group of languages spoken by the Sotho and Tswana peoples; these languages as a group; SESOTHO sense 2. Also *attrib.*, and *comb.* (objective) **Sotho-speaking** *ppl adj.* See also SOTHO-TSWANA.

1950 H. GIBBS *Twilight* 33 Divided into groups, forming the South African Bantu languages, the south-eastern groups have five group languages, Nguni, Sotho, Venda, Tonga, and Inhambane, among which fusion has occurred, producing in the Nguni groups, Xosa and Zulu; in the Sotho group, Southern and Northern Sotho and Tswana; in the Tonga group, Ronga, Tonga and Tswa; in the Inhambane group, Chopi and Tonga; and in the Venda group a language which is homogenous. **1961** R.A. PAROZ *Sn Sotho-Eng. Dict.* p.i, Eugene Casalis, it is true, did very soon write a book on Sotho grammar (Etudes sur la Langue Sechuana, 1841) but no systematic list of words was added in the book. **1974** W.W.M. EISELEN in *Std Encycl. of Sn Afr.* X. 72 The Western Sotho are a sub-group of the Sotho-speaking Bantu peoples of Southern Africa and comprise over 50 tribes, collectively known in anthropological literature as the Tswana. **1977** T.R.H. DAVENPORT *S. Afr.: Mod. Hist.* 7 The original Sotho speakers are not easy to identify. Among the first were the Fokeng. **1990** R. STENGEL *January Sun* 38 The Tswana are a Sotho-speaking people of small, patrilineal communities who migrated into central South Africa in the fifteenth century.

c. With distinguishing epithet designating a particular sub-division of the Sotho language group: **North(ern) Sotho**, the group of Sotho dialects spoken in the northern parts of South Africa; see also SEPEDI; **South(ern) Sotho**, the group of Sotho dialects spoken in Lesotho and the Orange Free State; SESOTHO sense 1; see also sense 2 a above.

The three major Sotho languages are sePedi, Southern Sotho, and seTswana (see SETSWANA).

1961 R.A. PAROZ *Sn Sotho-Eng. Dict.* p.v, The seventh edition, *Southern Sotho-English Dictionary*, thus called in order to distinguish it clearly from other books dealing with **Northern** or Transvaal **Sotho**, appeared in 1950. **1973** *Drum* 22 May 31, I would like girls not older than 22, and letters can be written in English, Zulu, North Sotho or Tsonga. **1961** R.A. PAROZ *Sn Sotho-Eng. Dict.* p.i, When the first Europeans made contact with Mosheshoe and his tribe, about the year 1833, the language which is now called **Southern Sotho** or Basutoland Sotho had not been reduced to writing yet. **1984** P. DICKENS in *Jrnl of Afr. Lang. & Ling.* Vol.6 No.2, 110 Let us look at Southern Sotho, a language spoken in an area adjacent to the Tswana region.

Sotho-Tswana /ˈsuːtuˈtswɑːna, -nə/ *pl. n.* Also **Sotho-Chwana.** [SOTHO + TSWANA.] Collectively, the southern, northern, and western Sotho peoples; their languages. Also *attrib.* See also SOTHO senses 1 a and 2 b, and TSWANA.

The term 'Sotho-Tswana' is used primarily in academic contexts.

1930 *Bantu Studies* IV. 211 They may be still more widespread, at least among the Sotho-Tswana tribes. [**1941** E.N. MSUTHWANA in *Bantu World* 1 Feb. 5 The 'ea' and 'oa' which were used in seSuthu-Choana, have now been replaced by the 'ya' and 'wa' as is employed in the Zulu-Xhosa languages.] **1950** T.J. KRIEL *New Sesotho-Eng. Dict.* Preface, The editor is convinced that, with patience and tact, the whole cluster of Sotho-Chwana languages can be merged into one unified Sesotho language for the Union of South Africa. **1977** T.R.H. DAVENPORT *S. Afr.: Mod. Hist.* 6 Four main groups are normally distinguished where the Bantu-speakers south of the Limpopo are concerned. These were the Venda themselves, the Sotho-Tswana, the Ngieri and the Tsonga. **1980** LYE & MURRAY *Transformations* 12 The Sotho Tswana as defined in this book, however, comprise speakers of the Tswana and Southern Sotho languages only. *Ibid.* 20 The term Sotho-Tswana is often used to define people's identity, either by insiders who claim it or by outsiders who impose it. *c***1980** *S. Afr. 1979: Off. Yrbk* (Dept of Info.) 83 The traditional territories of the Sotho-Tswana group are situated on the central plateau of Southern Africa and include the present independent states of Botswana, Bophuthatswana and Lesotho.

soupé, soupee, soupi(e), soupje, soupke varr. SOPIE.

sour *adj.* [tr. Du. *zuur.* The dial. use in general Eng. emphasizes palatability; in S. Afr. Eng. the word refers to nutritional value: animals will eat sour grass, but become thin or ill.]

1. *?obs.*

a. Of vegetation: coarse and lacking in nutritional value, esp. during winter. **b.** Of land: bearing such vegetation. Cf. SWEET.

1786 G. FORSTER tr. *A. Sparrman's Voy. to Cape of G.H.* II. 77 The district round about, was of the kind called *Sour.* **1821** *S. Afr. Jrnl* (1824) I. 18 The herbage though abundant was almost universally of the description called *sour*; but varying very much in quality and appearance in different soils and situations. **1835** J.W.D. MOODIE *Ten Yrs* II. 37 The pasturage along the banks of the Kromme river is everywhere of that coarse description which is distinguished by the term 'sour' by the colonists. **1837** 'N. POLSON' *Subaltern's Sick Leave* 115 In some parts the grass is of a sour kind on which cattle bred in sweet pastures do not thrive, but beasts bred on it fatten and do well. **1860** W. SHAW *Story of my Mission* 403 The best grazing districts .. are at a distance from the sea: the grass near the coast, being constantly fed by the heavy dews which prevail in that region, becomes long, coarse, and 'sour'. **1867** *Blue Bk for Col. 1866* JJ44, During .. drought farmers take their stock to Fort Fordyce, where there is usually abundance of grass, though of the kind called '*sour*'. **1905** [see SWEET sense 1].

2. *comb.* **sour-field(s)** *obs.* [calque formed on S. Afr. Du. *zuurveld*, see ZUURVELD], *sourveld* (see below); **sour grass**, also with initial capitals, grass lacking in nutrition; also *attrib.*; see also KOPERDRAAD; **sourveld**, formerly also **sour veldt** [part. tr. S. Afr. Du. *zuurveld*], land (usu. in areas of relatively high rainfall) on which the dominant vegetation is sour grass; the vegetation on such land; ZUURVELD sense a; also *attrib.*; cf. *sweetveld* (see SWEET sense 2).

1786 G. FORSTER tr. *A. Sparrman's Voy. to Cape of G.H.* I. 249 What are termed by the colonists *Zuure-velden*, or **Sour-fields**, are such as lie somewhat higher and cooler than the shore. **1812** A. PLUMPTRE tr. *H. Lichtenstein's Trav. in Sn Afr.* (1928) I. 63 The name of *sour-fields* is given to such lands as are a mixture of sand and loam, and only produce spontaneously a coarse rushy kind of grass. **1853** F.P. FLEMING *Kaffraria* 99 In many parts, what is called the 'Zureveldt' or sour-field, preponderated, which the cattle will not touch. **1801** J. BARROW *Trav.* I. 110 That division of the district called the *Zuureveldt*, or **Sour Grass** plains. **1809** R. COLLINS in G.M. Theal *Rec. of Cape Col.* (1900) VII. 126 Beyond the Kranz River, the country opens near the sea, and presents a plain of coppice and sour grasses, .. in some places affording tolerable pasturage for horned cattle. **1852** M.B. HUDSON *S. Afr. Frontier Life* 236 About Graham's Town and Lower Albany is 'the Zuurveld or Sour Grass Country'. **1861** J.M. BOWKER *Speeches & Sel.* (1864) 102 There we lost it, the sour grass being too long and thick to admit of our seeing it further. **1937** *Handbk for Farmers* (Dept of Agric. & Forestry) 398 The soil is sour and here the vegetation tends more to that of the heath, protea and inedible sour grass and rush type. **1948** [see *sweetveld* (SWEET sense 2)]. **1968** *Farmer's Weekly* 3 Jan. 92 (advt) Farm. 170 Morgen sour grass veld. **1863** J.S. DOBIE *S. Afr. Jrnl* (1945) 76 On across the Little Tugela .. over rank **sour-veldt** grass. **1887** J.C. BROWN *Crown Forests* 67 There is a vulgar prejudice against sour veldt, which will disappear when its more enduring qualities are better appreciated. **1892** R.H.S. CHURCHILL *Men, Mines & Animals* 197 The whole veldt .. is what is called 'sour veldt' (that is, coarse, hard, dry grass), distasteful to the animals, especially to oxen, perfectly unnourishing. **1897** 'F. MACNAB' *On Veldt & Farm* 114, I have found a change from sweet veldt to sour veldt for a week, and then back again to the sweet veld, to be very beneficial to cattle. **1910** A.B. LAMONT *Rural Reader* 253 Sour veld .. is found on poor, dry, sandy soils that lack certain minerals — especially lime. **1937** *Handbk for Farmers* (Dept of Agric. & Forestry) 396 The results obtained apply only to sour veld regions. **1947** C.R. PRANCE *Antic Mem.* 124 Nobody farmed them now; there was no water and only sour veld. **1970** *Farmer's Weekly* 16 Dec. 48 The natural grazing is usually sour veld of low quality. **1981** J.B. PEIRES *House of Phalo* 9 Sourveld, which predominated .., provided excellent grazing in summer but lost most of its nutritional value after about four months. **1983** *S. Afr. Panorama* Apr. [Back cover], The .. geometric tortoise .. is endemic to the South-western Cape and can only exist in sour veld. **1986** *Farmer's Weekly* 13 June 19 Reasonable palatability may extend into winter even in sourveld areas.

sour fig *n. phr.* [tr. Afk. *suurvy.*] Any of several species of succulent creeping plant of the genus *Carpobrotus* of the Aizoaceae, esp. *C. edulis*, *C. acinaciformis*, and *C. muirii*, common on the coast and on sandy flats; the sour fruits of these plants, used for jams and preserves; SUURVY. Also *attrib.* See also *Hottentot('s) fig* (HOTTENTOT *n.* sense 6 a).

1890 A.G. HEWITT *Cape Cookery* 67 Sour Fig (Zuur Vijgen) Konfyt. Soak the figs in water till they peel easily. **1891** H.J. DUCKITT *Hilda's 'Where Is It?'* 176 Preserve ('Hottentot Fig,' or 'Sour Fig') ... (The Hottentot Fig is the fruit of a kind of mesembryanthemum which grows wild at the Cape.) **1894** R. MARLOTH in *Trans. of S. Afr. Phil. Soc.* p.lxxxiv, *Mesembryanthemum edule* (sour fig). *a*1905 H.J. DUCKITT in M. Kuttel *Bk of Recipes* (1966) 89 Preserve, Hottentot Fig or Sour Fig. **1913** H. TUCKER *Our Beautiful Peninsula* 75 Long, many-fingered fronds of sour-fig, uplifting flowers like yellow paint brushes. *a*1949 [see GOCUM]. **1957** L.G. GREEN *Beyond City Lights* 225 Figs and sour-figs are both fruits of the *strandveld*. Sour-fig jam made there is probably the most typical dish of the dune world. *c*1968 J. HOBBS in *New S. Afr. Writing* 116 Her English daisies .. were being overpowered by vigorous red cannas and a blaze of creeping sour figs. **1973** *Argus* 13 Apr. 4 In the Duine, the arid part of the Southern Cape coast .. where almost nothing grows except thatch reed, farmers are turning more and more to the cultivation of sour figs. **1976** A.P. BRINK *Instant in Wind* 27 Smells of cinnamon and buchu and salted fish and dried fruit, of wild sour-figs and tanned hides. **1982** *S. Afr. Panorama* May 38 There were three meat courses, starting with fried porcupine and herb stuffing, pickled mushrooms, and sour figs. **1989** C.M. KNOX in *Motorist* May 36 Sunday afternoon picnickers gathering sour figs from the juicy plants. **1990** R. GOOL *Cape Town Coolie* 44 Bowls of kossiters, mebos, sourfigs and other sweetmeats. *Ibid.* 114 An Indian shopkeeper .. began to eat sourfigs spitting uneaten ends into the gutter. **1993** *Flying Springbok* Apr. 126 An extraordinary range of wild veld plants and herbs, wild sour figs — and the Sandveld sugar pumpkin.

sour milk *n. phr.* MAAS sense 1.

1838 F. OWEN *Diary* (1926) 101 He asked .. whether we wanted food, and at my request sent for the common beverage 'amas' or sour milk, a great refreshment in these warm climes. **1860** A.W. DRAYSON *Sporting Scenes* 227, I stayed seven days at the kraal; after the third day I had no bread or biscuit, but merely rotated Indian corn and meat, with the amasi and ubisi (sour and sweet milk). **1878** T.J. LUCAS *Camp Life & Sport* 93 They are vegetarians, living almost entirely on Kaffir corn and sour milk left to ferment in skins until it becomes thick, despising it when sweet as unfit for grown men. **1897** F.W. SYKES *With Plumer in Matabeleland* 104 Calabashes containing Kaffir beer, sour milk (amasi), or mutton fat rendered down. **1978** [see MAAS sense 1]. **1980** *S. Afr. Digest* 16 May 16 This porridge is the favourite of the Zulu, Swazi and Xhosa people who traditionally served it with sour milk (amasi) or wild green vegetable stew.

sousboontjies /ˈsəʊsbʊɪŋkis, -kiz/ *pl. n.* [Afk., *sous* sauce + *boon* bean + -IE + pl. -*s*.] A dish of dried sugar beans cooked in a sweet-sour sauce and served hot or cold. Also *attrib.* See also SUGAR BEAN.

1946 *Food & Cookery* (Dept of Agric.) 115 'Sousboontjies'. **1970** *Evening Post* 17 Oct. (Mag. Sect.) 3 Sousboontjies (sweet and sour dried beans). 2 cups dried sugar beans (brown flecked dried beans), ½ cup sugar, ¼ cup vinegar, salt ... Serve with venison or roast mutton. **1970** A. THERON *More S. Afr. Deep Freezing* 173 Sousboontjies. This is sometimes called bean salad, but I should say that sweet and sour beans would describe it better. **1971** *Post* 6 June 2 She made her own soap, candles, butter, cream, bread, sousboontjiebredies. **1972** *Evening Post* 26 Aug. 5 Have you ever eaten rice, bredie awash with gravy, mashed pumpkin, sousboontjies and slaphaakskeentjies with your fingers? **1979** HEARD & FAULL *Our Best Trad. Recipes* 80 Sousboontjies can be served hot or cold and can be kept in the fridge for a long time ... Sousboontjies and yellow rice are a must for a typical Afrikaans meal. **1981** *Fair Lady* 9 Oct. 178 The table was laden with every traditional dish imaginable: .. smoked snoek, bobotie, sosaties .. yellow raisin rice, *sousboontjies*, .. atchar, .. sambals. **1983** [see GEELRYS]. **1989** F.G. BUTLER *Tales from Old Karoo* 94 The food was excellent, of the flavoursome but fattening kind he used to long for in Europe. Particularly the sousboontjies and the sweet potatoes.

souskluitjies /ˈsəʊsˌkleɪkis, -ˌklœɪkis/ *pl. n.* [Afk., *sous* sauce + *kluitjie* dumpling.] A dessert of sweet dumplings in cinnamon and butter sauce. See also KLUITJIE.

1934 C.P. SWART Supplement to Pettman. 162 *Souskluitjies*, .. A very popular South African dessert, sweetened dumplings served with cinnamon and butter sauce. **1939** S. CLOETE *Watch for Dawn* 279 She thought of .. souskluitjies, of curries, of preserves and konfyts. **1951** S. VAN H. TULLEKEN *Prac. Cookery Bk* 234 *Souskluitjies* or *Dumplings* ... Have some more cinnamon and sugar mixed at the table to serve with dumplings. **1969** *Sunday Times* 23 Nov. (Suppl.), 'Souskluitjies' (sweet dumplings) ... Drop teaspoonfuls in rapidly boiling water. Close tightly and cook slowly for 15 minutes. **1977** *Fair Lady* 8 June (Suppl.) 4 Souskluitjies ... Sauce: 250 ml water from saucepan in which the 'kluitjies' were prepared; .. Makes 20 'kluitjies'. **1979** HEARD & FAULL *Our Best Trad. Recipes* 75 Souskluitjies. Traditional Sweet Dumplings. **1989** I. JONES *Woman's World Cookbk* 105 Old Fashioned Sweet Dumplings (*souskluitjies*) ... Cinnamon flavoured dumplings, a Dutch favourite from the South African past. **1992** G. ETHERINGTON in *Weekend Post* 9 May (Leisure) 4 It was followed by *souskluitjies* (I don't know how to translate that) and coffee.

‖**soustannie** /ˈsəʊsˌtɑni/ *n. colloq.* [Afk., lit. 'sauce-auntie', *sous* sauce + *tannie* 'auntie'.] A derogatory name for a fat (Afrikaans) woman. See also TANNIE.

1970 M. BENNETT *Informant, Krugersdorp* Soustannie. Fat woman. **1989** M. LOCHER *Informant, Pietermaritzburg* We used to tease him at school that he'd one day land up with a real fat Afrikaans soustannie. Well, true's Bob, that's exactly what he married now. **1989** 'K. DE BOER' in *Frontline* May 38 That grande dame of Afrikaans journalism (and definitely *not* a soustannie).

‖**soutbos** /ˈsəʊtbɔs/ *n.* Formerly also **zoutbos, zoute bosch.** [Afk., fr. Du. *zout* salt + *bosch* bush.]

a. SALTBUSH sense a.

1878 *Trans. of S. Afr. Phil. Soc.* I. 24 (Pettman), Here we find .. several kinds of 'air-plants,' 'canne doet's,' or aloes, and the *Zoute bosche.* **1936** C. BIRKBY *Thirstland Treks* 118 The sun blisters the *driedoorn* and the *soutbos* that battle to keep alive in the desert.

b. With qualifying word: **oumansoutbos** /əʊman-/ *rare* [Afk., *ou* old + *man* man], *old man saltbush* (see SALTBUSH sense b).

1974 [see SALTBUSH sense b].

South African *adj. phr.* and *n. phr.*

A. *adj. phr.*

1. Before 1910: Of or pertaining to southern Africa or its inhabitants. **2.** Between 1910 and 1961: Of or pertaining to the Union of South

Africa or its inhabitants. **3.** After 1961: Of or pertaining to the Republic of South Africa or its inhabitants; SA *adj.*

1824 *S. Afr. Jrnl* I. 29 Poor Gert Schepers, a Vee Boer of the Cradock District, was less fortunate in an encounter with a South African lion. 1827 A.J. JARDINE *Fragment of Church Hist.* 40 There are those who would dwell on certain defects in the character of the South African people. 1837 J.E. ALEXANDER *Narr. of Voy.* I. 341 We .. saw a noble and extensive South African landscape. 1843 J.C. CHASE *Cape of G.H.* 231 The luxury of this free mode of life .. and the palpable manifestations of power, render a South African waggon trip enviable. 1848 H. WARD *Five Yrs in Kaffirland* I. 173 A South African morning is incomparably beautiful. 1857 *Cape Monthly Mag.* II. Oct. 200, I entered upon the free .. life of a South African colonist. 1861 W.A. NEWMAN in J.S. Mayson *Malays of Capetown* 25 A man (whether Dutch or English, Malay or South African) marrying in the colony without an *ante-nuptial contract*, immediately creates a partnership between himself and his wife. 1871 J. MACKENZIE *Ten Yrs* (1971) 310 This South African despot .. seemed to be possessed of tender feelings. 1915 J.K. O'CONNOR *Afrikander Rebellion* 116 The spirit of parochialism must be deleted, and in its place must grow a united South African spirit. 1930 L. BARNES *Caliban in Afr.* 108 When the Dutchman speaks of the South African nation ... he means the Dutch plus so many British perverts to the Dutch point of view as they can muster. 1934 B.I. BUCHANAN *Pioneer Days* 29 Very comfortable we found the South African ox-wagon. 1949 J. ROSE INNES in F.G. Butler *When Boys Were Men* (1969) 268 'The South African spirit', as understood by those who extol it, implies a view on the Native question which I cannot share. 1964 G. GORDON *Four People* 304 Ignoring the South African 'way of life', groups of Africans ... so far from respectfully making way for whites to pass, in some cases even pushed them off the pavements. 1970 *Cape Times* 4 June, I trust that .. he will concentrate on the differences in policy which divide his party from mine, rather than hurling round hollow adjectives like .. 'un-South African'. 1971 *S. Afr. Panorama* July 23 The house is typically South African. 1974 *E. Prov. Herald* 28 Sept., 'The established South African way of life,' was yesterday given as the reason for the Government's refusal to allow sexually mixed university residences. 1976 *Sunday Times* 1 Aug. 15 Afrikaans schools in general are more attuned to the so-called South African way of life, namely, rugby, Chevrolet and braaivleis .. than to inculcating in young people culture development. 1976 V. ROSENBERG *Sunflower* 228 We .. find ourselves at the .. crossroads in respect of South African literature. 1980 C. HERMER *Diary of Maria Tholo* 5 The Tholos 'belonged' to the Ciskei — and on independence of that homeland they automatically lost their South African citizenship. 1985 *Frontline* Sept. 17 Some die particularly South African deaths — stepping on a landmine, burned by a mob, or at the receiving end of 'rubber bullets and birdshot.' 1987 C. HOPE *Hottentot Room* 155 Mona's voice was one which gives to the South African accent, already suspect for flat monotonous vowels and droning pronunciation, its rather dull reputation. 1989 P. CULL in *E. Prov. Herald* 7 Feb. 7 The ANC .. was .. 'as South African as any of us here,' the deputy-leader of the Labour Party .. said yesterday.

4. In the special collocation *South African English*: **a.** Those varieties of English spoken by South Africans. **b.** *The South African English* (*pl.*): South African English-speakers collectively; see also ESSA.

1909 J.W. WESSELS in *State* Dec. 702 Do you .. believe that there will be in the remote future a type of English known as South African English? 1967 W. BRANFORD *Elements of Eng.* 51 Within South African English, for instance, there are now both RP and non-RP dialects ... I shall occasionally abbreviate South African English as SAE. [1976 V. ROSENBERG *Sunflower* 228 Writing in English in this country, are we going to write English or are we going to write South African?] 1981 A. PATON in *Optima* Vol.30 No.2, 86 It is interesting to note that the South African English have never called themselves a nation. 1986 N.

WRENCH in *Style* Dec. 53 His outburst on *Midweek* .. added a new word to South African English.

B. *n. phr.*

1. Before 1910: An inhabitant of southern Africa. **2.** Between 1910 and 1961: A citizen or inhabitant of the Union of South Africa. **3.** Since 1961: A citizen or inhabitant of the Republic of South Africa. See also SA *n.*[1]

1867 *Cape Town Mail & Advertiser* in L. Lloyd *Notes of Trav.* (1969) 332 Mr Andersson, though a Swede by birth, was half an Englishman by blood, and quite a South African by adoption. 1871 J. MACKENZIE *Ten Yrs* (1971) p.v, That part .. describes the results of the past contact of Europeans with South Africans. 1891 O.E.A. SCHREINER *Thoughts on S. Afr.* (1923) 45 The South African in Europe hardly knows whether to admire or to scorn the smooth, gentle-flowing streams between their green banks. 1893 *Cape Illust. Mag.* Vol.4 No.10, 368 We are to all intents and purposes no longer Englishmen or Dutchmen, but South Africans, with common aims and common interests. 1903 D. BLACKBURN *Burgher Quixote* 5 If I appear to put great weight on my good descent, it is .. for the .. reason that I am writing not only for South Africans, but for uninformed Englanders. 1912 F. BANCROFT *Veldt Dwellers* 120 You're an English South African, but a Transvaler. 1936 L.G. GREEN in *Best of S. Afr. Short Stories* (1991) 167 It is good for city-dwelling South Africans to enter this green world of the forests. c1949 *Survey of Race Rel. 1948–9* (S.A.I.R.R.) 4 The Coloured .. have always regarded themselves as South Africans with aspirations to a full development of life here. 1957 JUNOD & JACQUES *Wisdom of Tsonga-Shangana People* 12 If this book can help South Africans of European descent and South Africans of Bantu descent to understand .. that Man finds his own humanity in the relations and contacts he has with other men, the .. aim .. will have been fulfilled. 1963 B. MODISANE *Blame Me on Hist.* (1986) 55 We seldom report the death of a South African, we speak of a dead African, a dead Indian, a dead Coloured, a dead European. 1978 *Financial Mail* 14 Apr. 105 A few months ago Plural Relations Minister Connie Mulder confirmed that the aim of the bantustan policy was that ultimately there would be no black South Africans. 1985 R. GOTKIN in *Style* Apr. 34 (*letter*) As a child it was always traumatic to be on the beach while hundreds of fellow South Africans had to remain on the landing above. 1987 *Weekly Mail* 28 Aug. 11 Their next village will be incorporated into Bophutatswana, making the Mogopa people non-South Africans. 1991 *Sunday Times* 14 July (Extra) 8 Now that the Population Registration Act is gone Mrs Robertson wants to see a single, non-racial welfare department ... 'They are all South Africans now and parity is the answer ...'

4. *Absol.* uses of the *adj.*

Quot. 1930 refers to shares on the stock market.

1930 *Economist* (U.K.) 8 Nov. 866 South Africans remained firm. 1969 *Guardian* (U.K.) 24 Oct. 9 You will need some medium-dry sherry ... You could go for a good South African at about £1.

5. *nonce.* A hypothetical language common to all South Africans.

1990 R. VAN TONDER in *Frontline* Sept. 27 Nobody can speak 'South African'. There is no such language or culture and never has been.

Hence **South Africana** *n. phr. nonce,* artefacts which are characteristically South African (cf. AFRICANA); **South Africanize** *v. phr. trans.*, to make (something) South African in nature; **South Africanness** *n. phr.*, the quality of being South African.

1985 *Cape Times* 25 Nov., A lovely tongue-in-cheek look at South Africana, of which Van's home is the epitome: Springbok trophies (two nogal!) at the entrance, fur-on-the-dashboard cars and veldskoens. 1990 *Weekly Mail* 22 June (Suppl.) 7 The white man in Africa must earn his right to belong ... Botha .. at first imagines it requires only that he succeed in denying his South Africanness. 1990 *Ibid.* 29 June 5 The new state, first of all to attenuate the legacy of structural apartheid, and then to valorise our South

Africanness by orchestrating and blending our diversities, will have to be strong. 1990 *Sunday Times* 30 Sept. 18 They use the tune, the refrain and the idea of the song, South Africanising the words with not too much wit or invention.

South African cedar *n. phr. Obs.* The YELLOWWOOD (sense 2 c), *Podocarpus elongatus*.

1828 T. PRINGLE *Ephemerides* 101 The yellow-wood tree (podocarpus elongata) is termed by some writers the South African cedar. 1831 P. GAUGAIN *Diary.* 88 Yellow Wood Tree, Podocarpus Elongata, or South African Cedar. 1913 C. PETTMAN *Africanderisms* 569 Yellow wood, .. One of the most useful of the indigenous trees .. ; it is sometimes called South African cedar.

South African Dutch *n. phr.* and *adj. phr. Obs. exc. hist.*

A. *n. phr.*

1. The dialect of Dutch which developed in South Africa among Dutch settlers and their descendants, and which came to be known as 'Afrikaans'. Cf. DUTCH *n.* sense 2 a. Also *attrib.* See also AFRIKAANS *n.*

First formalized as a written language in the 1870s.

1871 J. MACKENZIE *Ten Yrs* (1971) 7, I had followed only too strictly the rules given in the Grammar, from which South African Dutch has considerably departed ... Dutchmen fresh from Holland are sometimes misunderstood, and their language mistaken for German. 1919 M.C. BRUCE *Golden Vessel* 10 The roll of the South African Dutch 'r' .. must be rubbed off. 1939 J.F. BENSE *Dict. of Low-Dutch Element in Eng. Vocab.* 171 This South African Dutch word .. does not occur in the Dutch of the Netherlands. 1970 *Life* 19 Jan. 49 The horns of the hartebeest ('hart' or 'stag' beast in South African Dutch) are unlike those of any other animal.

2. *The South African Dutch* (*pl.*): The white South Africans whose ancestors were predominantly from the Netherlands (and from France), and who spoke Dutch (and subsequently Afrikaans). Also *attrib.* Cf. *The Cape Dutch* (see CAPE DUTCH *n. phr.* sense 1). See also AFRIKANER *n.* sense 2 a.

1926 P. SMITH *Beadle* (1929) 11 She had .. that astonishing fairness of skin which is sometimes found among the South African Dutch. 1936 R.J.M. GOOLD-ADAMS *S. Afr. To-Day & To-Morrow* 4 The South African Dutch belong essentially to South Africa.

B. *adj. phr.* DUTCH *adj.* sense 1.

1936 E. ROSENTHAL *Old-Time Survivals* 20 'Braaivleisaand', or 'Roast Meat Evening': An old South African Dutch custom. 1974 D. ROOKE *Margaretha de la Porte* 23 The De La Portes called themselves South African Dutch although the roots of the family lay in France: they were descended from Huguenots.

South Africanism *n. phr.* [SOUTH AFRICAN *adj.* + Eng. *n.*-forming suffix *-ism*.]

1. A linguistic feature typical of, or particular to, South Africa; see quot. 1989. Cf. AFRIKANERISM sense 3.

1896 'S. CUMBERLAND' *What I think of S. Afr.* 39 They — to use a South Africanism — were high old times for those with luck as well as those with enterprise. 1971 [see JISLAAIK]. 1972 [see ANGLIKAANS]. 1972 *Daily Dispatch* 14 Feb. 9 Some may find themselves adding more colourful South Africanisms to their glossary such as 'Kaffirs,' 'coolies' or 'coon'. 1973 *Cape Times* 19 June 12 An astonished visitor .. wrote .. describing her first collision with what, as far as I know, is a South Africanism, the unorthodox use of the exclamation 'Shame!' 1979 *Voice* 17 June 11 Fatima Dike .. lards her text with South Africanism [sic] effectively — that is, using several languages. 1980 *E. Prov. Herald* 16 Sept. 11 Multilingual South Africanisms like 'ag' and 'doek', 'muti' and 'kwedine'. 1989 D. GOLD in *Dictionaries* (Dict. Soc. of N. Amer.) No.11, 242 A South Africanism could be defined as .. a usage which arose in South African English (and not in any other variety of English). 1992 S. GUTKNECHT *Sunday Times* 19 Apr. (Mag. Sect.) 28 The search is on for more typical South Africanisms to join the ranks of indigenous words and phrases in common use throughout the English-speaking world. **1994** [see MAN *int.*].

2. A distinctively South African quality; overarching and inclusive 'South Africanness'; a broad patriotism or sense of belonging to South African society.

1955 T.B. DAVIE *Hoernlé Mem. Lecture 1955* 30 The early stages of a restored South Africanism having been prepared in the infant and primary schools and carried forward into the high schools, what can be done to further this aim at the university level? **1963** K. MACKENZIE *Dragon to Kill* 71 His father, coming out from England in 1932, had taken to South Africanism with the enthusiasm of a convert and had swiftly learnt enough Afrikaans to speak it insultingly badly. **1970** *Cape Times* 27 May, It is this latter quality which Professor Haarhoff sees as the foundation of Smuts's belief in a bilingual South Africanism. **1972** *Sunday Times* 21 May 31 Recent surveys done by a newspaper among Stellenbosch students on the issue of South Africanism. These revealed that young Afrikaners, by a large majority, regarded themselves as South Africans first. **1973** *Evening Post* 1 Dec. 11 He takes a strictly neutral line, and his compassion, warmth and broad South Africanism are an example to all of us. **1988** E. VOSLOO in *Femina* May 143 A broader South Africanism was emerging in which a Xhosa said with as much pride as an Afrikaner or and English-speaker: 'I'm a South African.' **1990** J. REDDY *Varsity Voice* Apr. 3 Broad South Africanism implies, firstly, a recognition that there *are* differences in cultures, and secondly, that there is a common loyalty to the country. **1990** *E. Prov. Herald* 17 Aug. 6 This is the time for political leaders to show true South Africanism and persuade those warring elements to make their peace and help forge a united nation. **1993** H. TYSON *Editors under Fire* 11 Those newspapers which supported a 'broad South Africanism' were attacked from both sides — from the reactionary government for being unpatriotic, and from the radicals for supporting 'The System'.

South African War *n. phr.* ANGLO-BOER WAR sense 1.

A term preferred by some as more representative of all involved than is 'Anglo-Boer War' (see quot. 1986).

1915 J.K. O'CONNOR *Afrikander Rebellion* 114 At the termination of the South African War, those rebels of the Cape Colony who had joined the Republican forces were disenfranchised for a period of years. *c*1937 *Our Land* (United Tobacco Co.), Long Cecil, Kimberley. The famous gun made in Kimberley and used during the siege in the South African War. **1950** H. GIBBS *Twilight* 21 It is 1899. War has flared up north of the Orange River, the South Africa War. *Ibid.* 116 The South African War, the event known to Afrikaners as the 'War of Liberation' and to Britons as 'the Boer war'. **1952** B. DAVIDSON *Report on Sn Afr.* 149 Frustration from years in the wilderness, traditions which had not forgotten or forgiven the rapacious shamelessness of the Jameson Raid and the South African War. **1971** *Sunday Times* 28 Nov. 3 Cigarette cards .. were a feature of the *fin-de-siecle* years and extremely popular during the South African War. **1986** P. MAYLAM *Hist. of Afr. People* 137 The widely used label, 'Anglo-Boer War', has recently been rejected as misleading. Warwick has thoroughly examined the involvement of blacks in the war and has accordingly suggested it should be called the 'South African War'. Blacks were not only active participants in the struggle, they also endured much of its suffering and were greatly affected by its outcome. **1990** *Weekend Post* 5 May (Leisure) 7 A decade from now we'll be marking the centenary of the South African War.

South African Youth Day *n. phr. Soweto Day*, see SOWETO sense 3. Also **SA Youth Day**, and *attrib.*

1986 *City Press* 8 June 1 Le Grange banned: All gatherings to commemorate South African Youth Day, the 10th anniversary of the 1976 Soweto uprising. **1987** *New Nation* 4 June 3 The UDF will also commemorate June 16 as South African Youth Day 'in honour of the gallant young people of our country'. **1987** *Ibid.* 11 June 1 Significant dates .. are June 12 (the anniversary of the emergency), June 16 (SA Youth Day) and June 26 (Freedom Charter Day). **1987** M. BADELA in *Weekly Mail* 19 June 1 Sisulu's surprise message .. was delivered by General and Allied Workers Union president .. to nearly 1 000 people at a South African Youth Day commemoration service. **1988** *New Nation* 30 June 30 On June 16 we commemorated South African Youth Day and International Day of Solidarity by remembering Hector Peterson and all the youths who have fallen or are in detention because they have sought a free and just society. **1990** *New African* 9 July 3 She said despite the observance of South African Youth Day (June 16), the shooting of her daughter was unprovoked because there had been neither violence nor any action that might warrant the SADF action.

South West *n. phr.* A colloquial shortening of *South West Africa* (now Namibia). Also *attrib.*

1944 'TWEDE IN BEVEL' *Piet Kolonel* [Dedication], The boredom and monotony of these long months in the Union and in South West, the soul-destroying task of guarding Italian prisoners of war. *Ibid.* 22 We would collect bottles and snacks, and eat South West biltong. *a*1951 H.C. BOSMAN *Willemsdorp* (1977) 27 If it's real class detective work you want, there's a Bushman I came across in South West. **1970** *Daily News* 10 June, He's just made a fortune in South-West. He sold his civil engineering group, the largest in South West .. in one of the biggest take-overs in the territory's history. **1970** *News/Check* 24 July 31 The Kaokoveld is also the haven of at least three unique animals — the mountain zebra, the black-faced impala and the South West elephant. **1977** S. STANDER *Flight from Hunter* 66 She .. soon learnt to imitate their speech. But it was still German with a South-West accent. **1978** A.P. BRINK *Rumours of Rain* 253 A small collection of semi-precious stones from South West. **1988** *E. Prov. Herald* 20 July 12 Today will tell whether the Government has decided to begin the long process of handing over South West Africa ... The need to shed the burden of South West is obvious ... South West swallows money both to administer and to defend. Its continued occupation invites world opprobrium and its defence costs lives.

Hence **South Wester** *n. phr.*, an inhabitant or citizen of South West Africa (now Namibia).

1944 'TWEDE IN BEVEL' *Piet Kolonel* 172 You can give me South Westers every time. **1979** *Daily Dispatch* 18 Oct. 7 There would be a 40 per cent increase in the number of South Westers doing operational duties next year. **1983** *Sunday Times* 13 Feb. 14 Thousands of politically disillusioned Southwesters .. have forged new lives in the fertile valleys of the Western Cape. **1990** J.G. DAVIS *Land God Made in Anger* 235 Roger elaborated: 'All South Africans, which includes South Westers up [to] 1984 when they got limited local self government, have to carry the so-called Book-of-Life.'

soutie /'səʊti/ *n. slang.* [Afk., *sout* (short for *soutpiel*, see SOUTPIEL) salt + -IE.] ROOINEK. Also *attrib.*

1946 C.A. SMITH in P. Beale *Partridge's Dict. of Slang* (1984), *Soutie*, English sailor, soldier or, above all, airman serving in S. Africa.: S. African: 1939+. **1972** P. DRISCOLL *Wilby Conspiracy* 191 So tell me, *soutie*, if she warned you why didn't you get out of this flat? *Ibid.* 192 You're no good to me without a memory, *soutie*, in fact you're an embarrassment, walking around like this when you should be locked up for *dondering* policemen. **1977** W. STEENKAMP in *Cape Times* 5 Dec. 13 A good South African of fairly recent 'soutie' origin. **1978** *Star* 29 Aug., If you wear corduroys from America in Zeerust then everybody seems to know that you are a soutie before you open your mouth ... The butcher is .. smiling to himself in that funny way they smile at souties in Zeerust. In Mafeking they are more used to the English. There was a time when the only people in Mafeking were souties and their servants ... In that new place called Mmabatho .. Zulus and souties can sit together for supper at the same table and they do not even wash the knives and forks separately. **1979** *Sunday Times* 9 Sept. (Mag. Sect.) 4 As in most Karoo towns, the South African War is still being fought on the cricket and rugby fields ... At our stock sales and annual shows the 'Souties' and 'Vaalseuns' still vie for superiority. **1986** *Ibid.* 16 Mar. (Business Times) 2 Last week we highlighted the awkward situation in which Barclays stands — like a 'soutie', with one foot in South Africa and the other in the UK. **1986** S. SMITH in *Style* Nov. 52 Typical *souties* ('a man who has one foot in South Africa and the other across the sea in England, suffering a gentle dousing in consequence' as the *Observer* laboriously explained) arrive with just over £2 000 and the addresses of a few old South African friends and the odd English cousin. **1989** J. SCOTT *Daily Dispatch* 11 Apr. 5 The Speaker called him to order when he announced: 'We are not a soutie party.' **1991** [see SIESTOG].

soutpiel /'səʊtpil/ *n. derog.* Pl. **-e** /-ə/, **-s.** [Afk., *sout* salt + *piel* penis; see quot. 1983.] Not in polite use. ROOINEK.

The word SOUTIE is considered more acceptable than 'soutpiel'.

1972 P. DRISCOLL *Wilby Conspiracy* 191 What does she want with Bushmen and bolsheviks and a kaffir-loving *soutpiel* like you? .. You know what does *soutpiel* mean? No? That's what we call an Englishman. Saltprick. **1976** A. DELIUS in *Times Lit. Suppl.* (U.K.) 21 May 446 A variety of names conveying racial or social contempt ... *momparas, backvelders, plaasjapies, Kaffers, rooineks, kafferboeties*, though not that striking soubriquet for an Englishman, *sout piel*. **1983** *Frontline* May 54 These are the true Soutpiele — one foot in SA and one foot in Britain and another extremity dangling in the salt waters of the Mediterranean. **1986** *Rhodeo* (Rhodes Univ.) May 6 I was living amongst fellow Christians — yet all I heard was their racist attitudes, with constant use of terms 'koelies', 'kaffirs', 'jews', and 'soutpiele'. **1986** *Weekly Mail* 18 Apr. 18 A hairy-back and a *rooinek*, a *boer* and a *soutpiel*, a dumb Dutchman and a *donnerse* Engelsman. **1990** R. MALAN *My Traitor's Heart* 57 Most English South Africans had some Afrikaans, but their accents betrayed them as soutpiels — 'salt dicks'. A soutpiel was an Englishman with one foot in South Africa and the other in England — a straddle so broad that his cock dangled in the sea. Most policemen, on the other hand, were rocks, or Afrikaners, and rocks were not all that fond of soutpiels.

soutribbetjie /'səʊtˌrəbəki/ *n.* Formerly also **zout(e) ribbetje.** [Afk., *sout* salt + *ribbetjie* chop, rib.] Salted mutton ribs, grilled on an open fire. See also RIBBETJIE.

1890 A.G. HEWITT *Cape Cookery* 16 Zoute Ribbetje. A fore-quarter of mutton, remove the neck and shoulder, and crack ribs across. **1900** F.R.M. CLEAVER in M.M. Cleaver *Young S. Afr.* (1913) 63 The pen does not fit deftly to the finger of the scribe, since that yesterday Gert used it to spit a zout-ribbetje upon. [**1935** P. SMITH *Platkop's Children* 91 Boers .. roastin' their salt ribitjes an' makin' their coffee on fires outside.] **1950** H. GERBER *Cape Cookery* 94 Soutribbetjie. Take ribs of mutton and salt them well. **1968** G. CROUDACE *Silver Grass* 217 She left him on the stoep, sipping his peach-brandy, while she prepared supper; freshly-baked bread, soutribbetjies — the salted ribs of mutton — and sweet potatoes. **1971** L.G. GREEN *Taste of S.-Easter* 88 Her meat and poultry section started with pot-roasting and went on to the traditional hoenderpastei, soutribbetjie and bobotie. **1975** *S. Afr. Panorama* Dec. 20 One can almost savour the aroma of this South African-style braaivleis (barbecue) with soutribbetjie (salted ribs of lamb ..) and sosaties (kebabs) with roosterkoek. **1977** *Fair Lady* 8 June (Suppl.) 23 'Soutribbetjie.' 1,4 kg — 1,8 kg rib of lamb; 10 g brown sugar; 225 g salt; 2 ml saltpetre. **1986** M. VAN WYK *Cooking the S. Afr. Way* 62 Salted Rib (Soutribbetjie) ... Combine sugar, salt, saltpetre, coriander, cloves and vinegar. Rub well into meat. Place in .. container and refrigerate for 2 days. Remove and hang in a cool, airy place to dry. Grill rib until done to taste. **1990** *10 Ways to Save Money on Red Meat* (Meat Board) 7 Beef, lamb or pork ribs can make an entire meal — *Lamb* soutribbetjies, portion with a glaze, cured portions with a barbeque sauce. **1991**

Leisure Books Catal. Apr.-June 19 Recipes are included, such as biltong quiche, biltong potbread, .. soutribbetjie, [etc.] .. Traditional SA fare at its very best.

‖**so waar** /sʊəˈvɑː(r)/ *int.* [Afk.] 'Really', 'truly'; used for emphasis.

1969 A. Fugard *Boesman & Lena* 17 Lena: Don't joke. I'll walk tonight. *So waar.* Boesman: Go! Goodbye darling. **1974** *Farmer's Weekly* 4 Dec. 83 Don't you worry. Dan will find the water if it's there. And, Oom Karel silently added, if you call me 'my dear fellow' once more, sowaar I might just do something. **1977** P.-D. Uys *Paradise Is Closing Down* 175 Do you have a hard stomach? *(they keep firm eye contact as she prods his stomach)* Sowaar, a nice hard stomach. **1985** E. Bergman in *Fair Lady* 27 Nov. 80 If she tints her hair once more, *so waar* it will all fall out. *Ibid.* 83 *So waar,* I felt like the girl in the ad, all soft colours and wistful and dreamy. **1987** S. Roberts *Jacks in Corners* 82 But it's true, *so waar,* it's true, Joos did see me being born.

Sowetan /səˈwe(ː)t(ə)n/ *n.* Formerly also **Sowetoan.** [Formed on Soweto + Eng. suffix *-an* (forming adjectives which are often used as nouns).] A resident of Soweto; one born in Soweto; Sowetonian.

1974 *Sunday Times* 27 Oct. (Mag. Sect.) 2 A 10 per cent poll would suggest that most Sowetans were either wholly apathetic or boycotted the elections entirely. **1977** *Time* 10 Jan. 25 Even the usual small pleasures have been denied to many Sowetoans this Christmas. The township is in un-official mourning. **1978** *Time* 26 June 21 The housing is a better offer than Sowetans have experienced up to now. **1982** *Drum* Jan. 61 Soweto 9 am. That rare breed of young men who don't even know what an employer looks like but whose shoes cost more than the average Sowetan's monthly income. **1984** M. Mthethwa in *Frontline* July 28 Such incidents have long been to Sowetans what vanilla is to ice cream — common. **1990** *Independent* (U.K.) 10 Feb. (Mag. Sect.) 34 Nothing reveals more eloquently the essentially bourgeois aspirations of average Sowetans than the fixation they have on weddings.

Soweto /səˈwe(ː)təʊ, sɔˈwe(ː)tu, sə-/ *n.* [Acronym formed on *South Western Townships,* an early name for this area.] The name of a conglomeration of townships to the south-west of Johannesburg. See also Sowhereto.

1. (An allusive reference to) a series of uprisings by black schoolchildren in 1976 which began in these townships and spread round South Africa, being characterized by violent clashes with the police which led to many deaths; also *transf.,* any political demonstration or uprising which ends in violence and deaths. See also post-Soweto.

[**1963** *Star* 20 Aug., The name of Soweto for Johannesburg's spreading complex of African townships to the south-west of the city has been firmly accepted by the Johannesburg City Council and is already in general use ... Soweto .. has found favour with the Africans because it does not specially favour the language of any tribe. **1968** J. Lelyveld in Cole & Flaherty *House of Bondage* 8 Soweto is not a Zulu or Xhosa word standing for something like Harmony or the name of some great black leader. It is simply an amalgam of the words South Western Townships.] **1976** A.P. Brink *Mapmakers* (1983) 147 Already it is evident that 'Soweto' represents not just a moment of transition like Sharpeville: it is an effective watershed. Life in South Africa will never again be the same. **1976** I. Hamilton in *New Statesman* (U.K.) 10 Sept. 352 Now that Soweto has happened, the solidarity between the generations is genuinely impassioned. **1976** M. Tholo in C. Hermer *Diary of Maria Tholo* (1980) 10 Cape Town is no longer the only quiet place in the country. We have Soweto with us. **1977** *Daily Dispatch* 17 Aug. 6 Internally, ten years ago, Soweto had not happened. Black conciousness and black power were phrases that had no meaning to most South Africans. *Ibid.* 14 Sept. 1 In 1960 we witnessed Sharpeville. In 1976 we witnessed a brutal and devastating Soweto. **1978** *Washington Star* (U.S.) 1 Sept. 9 If you've seen reports of the riots and confrontations you know what to expect, but this show tries to go beyond the Sowetos for an overview of what's involved. **1987** [see Sharpeville sense 1]. **1990** *Varsity Voice* Apr. 9 Annually we hear calls to make this day or that day a holiday. The predominant dates that come to mind are the following: *21 March (Sharpeville), 16 June (Soweto).*

2. *fig.* The archetype of a South African township.

1980 *Rand Daily Mail* 31 Oct. 1, 20 Sowetos needed before year 2000. **1985** *Sunday Times* 29 Sept. 12 The CP propaganda is focusing on the 'second Soweto' envisaged by the Department of Constitutional Development. **1986** R. Bhengu in *City Post* 2 Nov. (Suppl.) p.vi, We have no business to be in the Sowetos of this country — let alone love them.

3. Special Comb. **Soweto Day**, the 16th of June, the anniversary of the start of the uprising by Soweto schoolchildren in 1976, kept, esp. among left-wing political groups, as a day of mourning commemorating those who died in the struggle against apartheid; June 16 (sense b); National Youth Day; South African Youth Day; Youth Day. Also *attrib.*

1977 *Rand Daily Mail* 16 June 2 Vigils, pickets, church services and demonstrations are planned today in Britain and many European centres to commemorate **'Soweto Day'**. **1986** *Financial Mail* 13 June 36 Confrontation is probable because of the country-wide ban placed on meetings in June to commemorate Soweto Day and Freedom Charter Day. **1990** *City Press* 17 June 1 It was tense, but quiet, in most of Natal with many people apparently having resisted the Soweto Day stayaway call and reporting for work. **1990** A. Goldstuck *Rabbit in Thorn Tree* 188 It was called the 'Pretoria virus', or 'June 16th virus', and it .. is designed to go off on Soweto Day. **1992** *Guardian Weekly* (U.K.) 3 July 7 His organisation's [*sc.* the ANC's] plan to unseat the recalcitrant apartheid regime .. was to begin with a series of Soweto Day marches ... When the ANC responds with peaceful mass action, such as Soweto Day rallies, the government cynically tries to pin the blame for continued violence on it. **1993** *Newsletter* (Black Sash) 29 June 1 We wonder why the Boipatong attack should have happened on June 17th — the day after the commemoration of 1976's Soweto Day.

Sowetonian *n. obsolescent.* [Formed on Soweto + Eng. n.-forming suffix *-ian* denoting 'a resident of (a place)'.] Sowetan.

1974 *Drum* 8 Mar. 7 Sowetonians, Swazis, White Jo'burgers, Indians, Coloured, all in their finest clothes, mixed happily. **1976** *Time* 5 July 13 Hundreds of distraught Sowetonians last week began the grim task of identifying and claiming the bodies of their loved ones. **1977** J. Sikakane *Window on Soweto* 72 From the minute a Sowetonian starts looking for a job he is faced with the cruel reality that as an African he is only wanted as a cheap labour tool by the white economy.

Sowhereto /səʊˈweətu/ *n.* A punning or cynical name for Soweto.

1977 J. Sikakane *Window on Soweto* 8 Soweto (jocularly called by its inhabitants 'so-where-to') is the largest single modern ghetto in Africa. **1977** P.C. Venter *Soweto* 115 They shouldn't call this place Soweto! .. They should call it 'Sowhereto'. I don't know where I'm going, that's for sure.

sozatie var. sosatie.

spaan var. span *v.*

spaansch spek, spaan-spek varr. spanspek.

‖**spaansriet** /ˈspɑːnsrit/ *n.* Also **spaansche riet, spaanse riet, spansriet,** and with initial capital(s). [Afk. (earlier S. Afr. Du. *Spaansche riet*), *Spaans* Spanish + *riet* reed.] The Spanish reed, *Arundo donax.*

1824 W.J. Burchell *Trav.* (1953) II. 77 The ceilings of the rooms were formed of a reed, called by the colonists *Spaansche riet* (Spanish reed). **1919** M.M. Steyn *Diary* 23 For rods, we used the common 'spansriet' (common cane) which grew in many gardens, or the famous 'Vanderlandsch bamboes', but the former slender cane broke very easily. [**1971** Baraitser & Obholzer *Cape Country Furn.* 247 In Europe four-poster beds gave warmth and privacy, but at the Cape there was an additional advantage in that the cloth canopy protected the sleeper from the grit that sifted down from the riet ceiling and clay brandsolder.] **1973** M.A. Cook *Cape Kitchen* 19 Reed ceilings were mostly made of thick spaansriet.

spadona /spəˈdəʊnə/ *n. Ostrich-farming.* Also **spadone.** [fr. It. *spadone* large sword; see quot. 1896.] An imperfectly developed feather taken from a young ostrich in its first year. Also short form **spad.** See also chick.

1877 J. De Mosenthal *Ostriches & Ostrich Farming* 226 Spadones. White and Light femina. *c*1881 A. Douglass *Ostrich Farming* 91, 15 oz. light Spadona .. 5 oz. femina Spadona. **1896** R. Wallace *Farming Indust. of Cape Col.* 235 'Spadonas' refers to the imperfectly developed first year's crop from young birds. These feathers are pointed like a sword, hence the name. **1908** J.E. Duerden in *Agric. Jrnl of Cape of G.H.* XXXIII. 789 The size of the adult plume is not determined by that of the spadona. **1909** *Ibid.* XXXIV. 518 Chick feathers .. taper towards their tip in a spear-like manner, hence their name of *spadona. Ibid.* 524 The first or chick wing-quills, clipped at about six months, are much smaller and more tapering than those produced later, and receive the special name of spadonas. **1910** A.B. Lamont *Rural Reader* 142 The feathers of young birds are called 'spadonas', from an Italian word meaning sword-shaped. **1930** M.F. Wormser Ostrich Industry. 10 Spadonas are the only feathers of commercial value on the chick. **1932** *Grocott's Daily Mail* 14 Jan. 3 Spadonas: white and light, 7/6 to 9/6; coloured, 4/- to 6/-. **1968** F. Goldie *Ostrich Country* 20 Chick feathers, called spadonas or spads, are not nearly as valuable as those of later clippings. **1973** D.J. Maree in *Std Encycl. of Sn Afr.* VIII. 398 The first feathers .. taken off the chick at the age of six to eight months .. are known in the trade as 'spadonas'.

span /spæn/ *n.*[1] Formerly also **spann.** Pl. **-s,** or (rarely) unchanged. [Du., team, pair of draught animals, fr. *spannen* to unite, fasten.]

1. A team of oxen or other draught animals, consisting of two or more yoked pairs; *transf.* (*rare*), the harness or other equipment for a span of draught animals (see quot. 1849).

1806 J. Barrow *Trav.* I. 3 Such a carriage is commonly drawn by a team, or span as it is termed in the colony, of ten or twelve oxen. **1812** A. Plumptre tr. *H. Lichtenstein's Trav. in Sn Afr.* (1928) I. 192 The strength of the oxen was so much exhausted by the exertions they had been obliged to make in the midst of a hot sun, that they could not get on the rest of the way without a double *Spann.* **1822** W.J. Burchell *Trav.* I. 134 Mr Mong, the Boode, had informed me that proper oxen might be obtained in the Bokkeveld, at the price of three hundred rix dollars for a span (a team). **1837** F. Owen *Diary* (1926) 11 Great difficulty was experienced in ascending the opposite bank, one span of oxen being obliged to help the other. **1849** J.D. Lewins Diary. 30 See and get fm. Kew the span of wagon riems he has for sale. **1851** T. Shone Diary. 15 Oct., This day Thurston return'd home to procure more cattle for his waggon, the kaffers having stolen 9 of his span. **1861** Lady Duff-Gordon *Lett. from Cape* (1925) 33 The teams of mules (I beg pardon, spans) would delight you — eight, ten, twelve, even sixteen sleek, handsome beasts. **1879** R.J. Atcherley *Trip to Boerland* 47 A full span of oxen consists of about sixteen or eighteen, yoked together in pairs along a chain called the Trektouw. **1882** C. Du Val *With Show through Sn Afr.* II. 40 To each of these waggons was attached a span of probably not less than sixteen oxen, yoked in pairs. **1896** R. Wallace *Farming Indust. of Cape Col.* 269 Sixteen is the usual number of a span of oxen, though on very heavy roads twenty may be yoked together. **1907** W.C. SCULLY *By Veldt & Kopje* 270 The convoy included eight wagons and sixteen spans of oxen. **1926** P.W. LAIDLER *Tavern of Ocean* 138 Post wagons left the Cape for Stellenbosch every Wednesday and Saturday at five a.m. in summer and seven a.m. in winter, each drawn by a span of twelve to sixteen oxen. **1941** C.W. DE KIEWIET *Hist. of S. Afr.* 250 As long as a span of powerful Afrikander oxen was considered a valuable possession, there was less room for select dairy cattle. **1961** T. MACDONALD *Tvl Story* 48, I grew mealies, ploughing with two spans of donkeys and an ox. **1972** L.G. GREEN *When Journey's Over* 50 There is little rest for the weary voorloper from the time he rounds up his scattered span in the morning to the inspanning, the outspanning, the grazing and watering of the team at night. **1979** A. GORDON-BROWN *Settler's Press* 15 He set out from Grahamstown with three wagons and six span of oxen with trade goods (£700) presumably supplied by local merchants. **1994** M. ROBERTS tr. *J.A. Wahlberg's Trav. Jrnls 1838–56* 55 When the oxen arrive, Oosthuizen offers me his own span.

2. *transf.* A team or work-gang of prisoners or reformatory inmates; any team, gang, or group.

1893 C.A. GOADE in *Cape Illust. Mag.* May 313 Let me explain that all the Convicts are divided into 'spans' of about 50 men each. Each span has a separate ward and is superintended by an overseer. **1900** F.R.M. CLEAVER in M.M. Cleaver *Young S. Afr.* (1913) 75, I suppose the old span in the Specials (police) is getting less and less as they are drafted off to the front from time to time. **1913** *Nongqai* 12 Nov. 46 These 'spans' .. help to maintain themselves (owing to being let out on payment), thereby becoming .. a less burden to the State than others .. where improvements in roads, etc., are performed gratis. **1939** M. RORKE *Melina Rorke* 82 The African wagon is a huge affair with buck-rail bed, eight feet wide by sixteen feet long .. and three span of oxen. **1948** O. WALKER *Kaffirs Are Lively* 171 Most of them .. join the gaol-gangs which can be hired out by the 'span', like oxen, to private persons and public bodies anxious to use a bit of cheap labour. **1949** H.C. BOSMAN *Cold Stone Jug* (1969) 70, I was informed that I had been given a change of labour. 'What span, sir?' I asked of the head-warder who imparted this information to me. **1953** *Drum* Jan. 14 Boys of 10 and 11 years have threatened grown-ups ... 'Be careful, mister. I'll bust you, my span's Crimson League.' **1954** H. NXUMALO in J. Crwys-Williams *S. Afr. Despatches* (1989) 316 After breakfast we were divided into many work spans (parties). I spent my first day with a span cutting grass, pulling out weeds with my hands and pushing wheelbarrows. **1969** A. PATON *Kontakion* 88 When all the boys had paraded with their spans, they were counted. If the count proved correct, the two gates were opened and the spans marched out to work on the reformatory farm. **1974** B. HEAD in S. Gray *On Edge of World* 71 This particular work span was known as Span One. It was composed of ten men and they were all political prisoners. **1976** *Sunday Times* 10 Oct. 6 One man in the group worked in a span outside the prison and another was a cleaner in the hospital. **1980** A.J. BLIGNAUT *Dead End Rd* 79 Would be like asking his span of labourers to pay for a gift, or pansela as they called it. **1980** A. PATON *Towards Mountain* 145 Each boy paraded with his own *span* ... Afrikaans was the language of the reformatory.

3. *fig. slang.* Esp. in the language of children: a lot, very much.

1960 [see LEKKER *adj.* sense 1 a]. **1963** M.E. MCCOY *Informant, Port Elizabeth* I've found myself a real honey of a vanity case for my birthday. So if Ma agrees, I'll get it, it's R7.50, rather a span, that's the snag! **1965** S. DEDERICK *Tickey* 43 It's the most beautiful dress I've ever seen in all my life. Thank you! Thanks a span! **1970** A. VAN DER BERG *Informant, Pretoria* Span, very much, a lot. Thanks a span for the lovely gift. That man has spans of kids. **1975** 'BLOSSOM' in *Darling* 26 Feb. 111 In the middle there's this like platform all set up with ropes and floodlights and a span more folks packed around on folding chairs ... Killer Katz's got a tattooed blonde laying across he's chest too what undulates every time he flexes he's muscles. She gets a span of titters. **1976** *Ibid.* 4 Feb. 87 One love-letter .. ending off *Spans of kisses, yores for ever.* **1980** R. GOVENDER *Lahnee's Pleasure* 29 Sunny: Plenty of dames too, huh? Johnny: Span. **1981** *Sunday Times* 19 Apr. 4 Although we will miss the Cape a span, it is important we operate from Johannesburg. **1981** [see STOP sense 2].

span /spæn/ *n.*[2] [Du. *spanne* (or general Eng. *span*), the distance from the tip of the thumb to the tip of the little finger when the hand is fully extended, or the equivalent length, averaging 9 inches.] A length of rolled tobacco of approximately 20 to 23 cms (8 to 9 inches).

1824 W.J. BURCHELL *Trav.* II. 49 Among the boors, these [rolls of tobacco] are sold by the pound: but to the Hottentots, they are more commonly meted out by the span of about eight inches .. ; and bargains among the latter are most frequently made for a certain number of *spans of tobacco.* **1925** H.J. MANDELBROTE tr. *O.F. Mentzel's Descr. of Cape of G.H.* I. 84 Every slave or Hottentot must be given a weekly dole of a span of tobacco to get any work out of him. This forms their most cherished comfort. **1955** W. ILLSLEY *Wagon on Fire* 62 When their purchases were completed, each member of the family pressed forward to the counter to receive the customary 'pasella'; a span of thick twist tobacco for the man, .. and for each child a handful of sweets. **1980** A.J. BLIGNAUT *Dead End Rd* 17 He gave me a span of tobacco off his Magaliesberg roll this morning.

span /spæn/ *v.* Also **spaan**. [fr. Du. *spannen* to fix or fasten, to draw tight, to join.]

Also borrowed directly into general Eng. (*c*1550) from Flemish, Du., or Low G. (meaning 'to harness or yoke'), being reinforced by *S. Afr. Eng.*

1.a. *intrans. obs.* Of draught-oxen: to feed after having been unyoked.

1815 J. CAMPBELL *Trav. in S. Afr.* 64 To take the oxen from the waggon in order to feed, is, to *outspan* .. : oxen feeding on a journey are said to be *spaning*: the place where they feed is called a *spaning-place.*

b. *trans.* INSPAN sense 1 b.

1838 T. SHONE Diary. 24 Sept., We span'd the Oxen and plowed part of Lamas. **1838** D. MOODIE (tr. *J. van Riebeeck's Jrnl) Record* I. 33 Meanwhile we prepared the apparatus for *spanning* oxen before the wagon. **1858** SIMMONDS *Dict. of Trade, Span,* .. to attach draught cattle to a wagon. **1873** F. BOYLE *To Cape for Diamonds* 299 Spanned the leader to the pole, and put another alongside ... Spanned them this fashion – that fashion – every fashion that harmonical progression would allow. **1913** C. PETTMAN *Africanderisms* 463 *Span, To,* .. To yoke or harness animals to a vehicle. 'To inspan' is now more commonly used. **1958** S. CLOETE *Mask* 132 They were lucky that it had not rained because they might have had to double-span the wagons to get them through the drifts. **1984** *Fair Lady* 14 Nov. 166 He went to the bottom camp to fetch his donkeys, spanned them to Titus's cart that had been washed and scrubbed, and then led them to the lawn.

2. In the phr. ***to span in***:

a. *trans.* INSPAN sense 1 b. Also *fig.*

1815 G. BARKER Journal. 28 Aug., About 5 o' clock all were spanned in and an attempt made to proceed, but before we had gone 10 rods my waggon was overturned with me and my wife both in. **1825** J. AYLIFF Journal. 45 Excuse my not Enlarging as the waggon is spaand in. **1846** J.M. BOWKER *Speeches & Sel.* (1864) 251 Half the oxen that are here can scarcely trail their own carcases, .. to span them in is quite out of the question. **1857** R. GRAY *Jrnl of Visitation* 65 Ordering the horses .. not to be spanned in for an hour. **1868** W.R. THOMSON *Poems, Essays & Sketches* 185 A South African wagon is the greatest institution ever set a-going in this country ... I must go and span mine in, for I must be in town before morning. **1882** O.E.A. SCHREINER Diamond Fields. 98 January made two holes in a box, and she spanned the goat into it. For a short way the goat would pull very well. **1892** *Grocott's Penny Mail* 12 Jan. 3 The 'baas' wanted his wagon spanned in, but no oxen appeared. **1894** *Westminster Gaz.* (U.K.) 11 Sept. 8 One day he spanned-in his mules .. and leisurely trekked to the widow's homestead.

b. *intrans.* INSPAN sense 1 a.

1818 G. BARKER Journal. 1 Sept., Spanned in again at sun set & arrived about midnight in the Colony. **1837** F. OWEN *Diary* (1926) 21 We spanned in earlier than usual and hoped to make a good days' journey before any rain. *a*1867 C.J. ANDERSSON *Notes of Trav.* (1875) 18 Span in and go back the way you came. *c*1929 L.P. BOWLER *Afr. Nights* 116, I did span in, and continued my journey.

c. *trans. fig.* INSPAN sense 2.

1882 C. DU VAL *With Show through Sn Afr.* I. 118 'Span in' all the spare Kaffirs available to carry seats and for platform building.

3. In the phr. ***to span out***:

a. *intrans.* OUTSPAN *v.* sense 1 a.

1816 [see OUTSPAN *v.* sense 1 a]. **1826** [see TANG]. **1835** A.G. BAIN in A. Steedman *Wanderings* II. 242 We accompanied the waggons to the place where they intended spanning-out. **1876** T. STUBBS Reminiscences. I. 49 She was Kilt and murdered. W[e] had to span out in the river. **1958** I. VAUGHAN *Diary* 8 The waggons all span out at the outspan place. The drivers chase the oxen to the dam to drink water then let them eat on the comonage.

b. *intrans.* OUTSPAN *v.* sense 2 a.

1816 G. BARKER Journal. 2 Mar., Spanned out about mid-day, at Sunday's river, for refreshment & worship. **1821** *Ibid.* 19 Feb., Spanned out at night, between Bushmans river and Sweet milk fountain. **1836** A.F. GARDINER *Journey to Zoolu Country* 151 Last night the driver of the waggon .. shot a panther close to my hut. They had spanned out in the road for the night. **1838** T. SHONE Diary. 17 July, Left home with the waggon for Town, span'd out at Cooper's place. **1850** J.D. LEWINS Diary. 17 May, Dale & Ezra Ridgard spanned out.

Hence **spanning-out** *ppl adj.*

1924 L. COHEN *Reminisc. of Jhb.* 18 Patronising .. a bed in a spanning-out farmhouse.

Spanish reed *n. phr.* [tr. S. Afr. Du. *spaansche riet.*] The grass *Arundo donax* of the Poaceae (subfamily Arundinoideae), with slender bamboo-like canes which in the past were used in Cape houses, being laid across beams to form ceilings; SPAANSRIET.

Introduced as a garden plant from south Europe in about 1660, the reed was found throughout the colony by 1800.

[**1821** C.J. LATROBE *Jrnl of Visit* Glossary, *Spanish Riet, Arundo donax.*] **1824** W.J. BURCHELL *Trav.* II. 172 Near the house, were the largest 'Spanish reeds' which I had observed in any part of the colony. **1845** J. COLLETT Diary. II. 19 July, Began cutting our Spanish Reeds & replanting fence. **1850** J.D. LEWINS Diary. 78 My bottom land beginning to look like a meadow. Must get about January some Spanish reeds to plant. **1933** W.H.S. BELL *Bygone Days* 35 Among the miscellaneous imported plants were ginger, arrowroot, New Zealand flax, Spanish reeds, bamboos, coffee, and many others. **1976** G. & G. FAGAN in *Optima* Vol.26 No.2, 81 The ceiling .. no longer existed and there were no records describing what he had used. In all probability it was made of *Arundo donax* (Spanish reed) which had been imported before 1700 and which was growing profusely on most farms by 1800. These were commonly used for 'rietplafonne' or reed ceilings. **1977** F.G. BUTLER *Karoo Morning* 14 Adam figs, and Spanish reeds, and lucerne patches shimmering with butterflies.

Spanish Spec(k) *n.* [Calque formed on Du. *Spaansche spek*, see SPANSPEK.] SPANSPEK.

1863 T. SHONE Diary. 11 Feb. We had some fine melons and Spanish Spec to eat Very fine ones. **1971** R. RAVEN-HART (tr. E. Hesse) *Cape G.H. 1652–1702* II. 227 They observed no measure of diet, but drank all too much wine, and ate too much Spanish Speck and water-lemons [*sic*], and thus fell into a mortal sickness.

spanspek, **sponspek** /span'spek, spɒn-/ *n.* Also **spaansch spek**, **spaanspek**, **spanspeck**, **sponspeck**, and with initial capital(s). [Afk. (earlier S. Afr. Du.), ad. Du. *Spaansche spek* 'Spanish bacon', the name in the West Indies for a type of melon (*Van Dale Groot Woordeboek der Nederlandse Taal*, 1859); see also quots 1913 and 1972; and the following:

'It seems that Sir Harry Smith [the Governor of the Cape Colony] .. liked his British breakfast of ham and eggs every morning. But his Spanish wife, Lady Juana Smith, preferred musk-melon ... Lady Juana's Hottentot maids .. considered musk-melon for breakfast rather peculiar, while "spek" for breakfast was O.K. with them. So they .. called Lady Juana's breakfast "Spaans spek", meaning "Spanish ham".' (A. Theron, *More S. Afr. Deep-Freezing*, 1970, p.173).]

The musk melon or sweet melon *Cucumis mels* of the Cucurbitaceae, round in shape, with succulent pinkish-gold flesh and a hard, textured skin; SPANISH SPEC(K). Also *attrib.*

[**1731** G. MEDLEY tr. *P. Kolb's Present State of Cape of G.H.* II. 277 *Melo Hispanicus* i.e. The *Spanish* or Musk-Melon. The Musk-Melons, produc'd at the *Cape*, are as good as Those produc'd in *Spain*. The *Cape-Europeans* call 'em *Spanish* Bacon.] **1849** J.D. LEWINS Diary. 14 Put in a small row of spanspecks and five of wheat. **1857** R.J. MULLINS Diary. 24 Mr Reynolds and I caught two boys in the garden – we caught them, and Reynolds gave them a good thrashing for they had 9 sponspeks and 2 watermelons! **1886** G.A. FARINI *Through Kalahari Desert* 61 Mr. Barlett came and asked if I would like to buy any musk-melons (*sponspeck*), figs, pomegranates, or mealies. **1900** A.W. CARTER *Informant, Ladybrand* 8 Mar. 4 Mr Pohl came out and asked us to join them at dinner which we did not refuse – wound up with a fine Spaansch Spek. **1913** C. PETTMAN *Africanderisms* 463 *Spaanspek*, .. The sweet or musk melon, apparently known to the Dutch through the Spaniards. It is called 'spek' from the bacon-like colour of the fruit when cut. **1913** J.J. DOKE *Secret City* 78 In their season the ground was cumbered by water-melons and spanspeks. **1916** *Farmer's Weekly* 20 Dec. 1543 (*advt*) Sow Them and Make Money!! .. Winter Sponspek, Melons all winter, 1s.6d. ounce. **1941** *Star* 9 Jan. 7 A few days ago I sold spanspek to a hawker at sixpence each and found him a little later selling the same fruit at 2s each. **1944** J. MOCKFORD *Here Are S. Africans* 45 And there were always dishes piled with fruit on the table – peaches, *nartjies* or tangerines, pears, grapes, *pompelmoes* or grapefruit, *spanspek* or muskmelon. **1965** E. MPHAHLELE *Down Second Ave* 82 We met at the river .. with a good haul of oranges, sponspecks, carrots, tomatoes, bananas and other items. **1972** L. VAN DER POST *Story like Wind* 233 The wonderful yellow melons they grew so successfully .. a melon called 'span-spek' (Spanham), a name which Ouma had maintained was a contraction of Spanish-ham, being eaten as an horsd'oeuvres with ham. **1975** *Cape Times* 13 Jan. 2 Spanspek price in UK may drop. **1981** *Signature* Apr. 15 No fruit grown in South Africa has improved in recent years more impressively than our beloved spanspek, sometimes called the cantaloupe. **1990** *Weekend Post* 17 Feb. (Leisure) 6 Peeled and served ice-cold, prickly pears are delicious, and, combined with watermelons or spanspek or in a fruit salad, they are gourmet fare.

spansriet var. SPAANSRIET.

sparaxis /spə'ræksɪs/ *n.* Also with initial capital. Pl. unchanged. [Modern L. (1805), fr. Gk *sparassein* to tear, lacerate.] A genus of iridaceous plant, species of which are grown for their flowers, which are multi-hued, often with black or yellow centres; a plant or bulb of this genus; also called BOTTERBLOM. See also IXIA.

1829 *Loudon Encycl.* Pl.40. **1841** DUNCAN *Hist. Guernsey* 557 The innumerable species of ixia, sparaxis, and other cognate genera of Cape bulbs. **1852** G.W. JOHNSON *Cottage Gardeners' Dict.* 517 The true Ixias are known from *Sparaxis* by not having, like it, a jagged sheath. **1856** R.E.E. WILMOT *Diary* (1984) 33, I came suddenly upon a lustrous patch of *Sparaxis pendula* both purple and white and soon filled my hands with what I never hoped to see in flower again. *Ibid.* 35 A spacious hollow .. clothed with damp ferns .. and rich in bouquets of *sparaxis*. **1906** B. STONEMAN *Plants & their Ways* 194 *Sparaxis*. Perianth regular, with a short, funnel-shaped tube. Bracts papery, deeply fringed or lacerated. **1917** R. MARLOTH *Common Names* 45 *Kalossie*, .. several species of *Ixia* ... *Wit* – *Sparaxis grandiflora* var. *Liliago*. **1928** *Jrnl of Botanical Soc.* XIV. 7 Many of our 'bulbous' plants may be considered safely established in cultivation. The number is steadily increasing – more especially in the case of the family, *Iridaceae*, whose *Sparaxis*, *Tritonia*, *Ixia*, are acknowledged favourites. **1963** M.G. MCCOY *Informant, Port Elizabeth* We had a long walk in Settlers' Park, all the Namaqualands are out, & the sparaxis & bobbejantjies. **1988** M. BRANCH *Explore Cape Flora* 14 Botterblom sparaxis grows in marshy areas. **1989** *Reader's Digest Gardening Questions Answered* 353 *Sparaxis*. Brightly coloured, indigenous, spring flowering bulbs with narrow, stiff, sword-shaped leaves and stems of multicoloured, six-petalled flowers, often with black or yellow centres, in a wide range of colours. There are many hybrids. **1994** *E. Prov. Herald* 26 Mar. 9 Sparaxis: Small, on thin stems, the bulbs produce multicoloured blooms. **1994** [see Wasserfall quot. at FREESIA].

Sparm *n. Obs.* exc. *hist.* [See quot. 1970.] HONEY-GUIDE.

1853 F.P. FLEMING *Kaffraria* 74 One of the most remarkable of the birds of this country .. is the Kaffrarian Honey-bird, or Sparm (*Cuculus Indicator*). **1970** V.S. FORBES *Informant, Grahamstown* In my opinion Sparm must derive from the fact that this bird is called after the Swedish naturalist who first described it, hence it is known as Sparrman's Honeyguide or the Honeyguide of Sparrman. In the latter version the preposition *of* could have been mistaken for the Dutch word meaning *or*, thus resulting in the Honeyguide *or* Sparrman, the latter becoming contracted to Sparm.

spaza /'spɑːzə, 'spa(ː)za/ *n.* Also **sphaza**. [fr. township slang *spaza* (adj.) 'camouflaged', 'dummy' (see Ngwenya quot. 1989); ultimate origin unknown.] In full ***spaza shop***: a small informal store in a township, often run from a private home. Also *attrib.* See also *informal sector* (INFORMAL sense 1).

In the past spazas, being illegal, were usu. operated clandestinely.

1988 *Natal Mercury* 22 Dec. 2 The proliferation of 'spaza' or camouflage grocery shops in township homes .. was evidence that more blacks were becoming self-employed ... About 240 spaza stores were opening .. around the country .. every month. **1989** K. NGWENYA in *Drum* Feb. 6 Spaza is a [*sic*] township parlance for camouflage or dummy. The word describes the way traders were forced to operate underground because they usually broke all rules and regulations ... The typical spaza today consists of a section of a private house that has been converted into a grocery store. **1989** *ADA* No.7, 49 This spaza sells printers' paper overruns bought from a factory in Paarden Eiland and sold for 50c a roll ... Many of the grocery store oriented spazas even have accurately copied Coke or Pepsi signs. **1989** [see FORMAL sense 1 a]. **1989** *Sunday Times* 5 Nov. (Business Times) 3 Natbev is developing solar-powered coolers for spazas in even the humblest squatter camps. **1990** A. MAIMANE in *Weekly Mail* 2 Nov. 10 Free-market capitalism is practised by hawkers, shebeen queens, spaza shopowners and other 'informal' businesses. **1990** [see FORMAL sense 1 b]. **1991** C. VON ULMENSTEIN in *Weekend Argus* 26 Jan. (Business) 5 Sphaza shops have become an established link in the retail chain. **1991** S. BROKENSHA in *Cosmopolitan* Aug. 44 Originally discouraged by the authorities, the spaza shops (informal shops in the townships) have become big business. **1992** *Academic Standard* Apr. 4 Throughout the settlement little 'spaza' shops have sprung up selling household commodities. **1992** B. KELLER in *Scope* 13 Nov. 88 Meadowlands has several fruit stands and a score of wardrobe-sized general stores, called *spazas*. **1994** *Sunday Times* 15 May 9 Free enterprise in the form of a spaza or house-shop. **1994** A. Boso in *E. Prov. Herald* 26 Aug. 10 Florence Ulana .. a lone spaza (house-shop) owner supplying the mushrooming squatter settlement. **1994** *Sunday Times* 18 Sept. 9 A Chinese woman .. runs a spaza shop from her garage.

Spear of the Nation *n. phr.* [tr. Xhosa *Umkhonto* spear + *we* of + *Sizwe* nation, the official name of the ANC's military wing.] UMKHONTO WE SIZWE.

1963 H. TUCKER in *Hansard* 7 June 7528 Then there is .. the A.N.C., and its militant wing, the Spear of the Nation. **1964** H.H.W DE VILLIERS *Rivonia* 80 Umkhonto we Sizwe (The Spear of the Nation), was formed under the auspices of the National Liberation Movement. **1986** M. PICARDIE in S. Gray *Market Plays* 81 If ever there is any suggestion of the Spear of the Nation .. contacting you .. I'm personally going to get you inside. **1990** J. CONTRERAS in *Newsweek* 1 Oct. 33 The Congress's fighting arm – Spear of the Nation – has never been a serious military threat.

spec boom var. SPEKBOOM.

special *n. hist.* Also with initial capital. In full ***special pass***: PASS sense 2.

*a***1928** R.R.R. DHLOMO *Afr. Tragedy* 14 'Hey – wena. Special!' ... He fumbled in his coat pockets as if he were looking for his special Pass. **1928** N. DEVITT *Blue Lizard* 116 Particularly was he light-hearted when he had received a 'special' from the missus to go to church. **1934** C.P. SWART Supplement to Pettman. 163 Special passes are necessary if the Natives wish to remain in town after 9 p.m. *c***1948** H. TRACEY *Lalela Zulu* 54 Forward ... Onward .. to Marshall Square! 'Produce your special pass!' **1948** E. HELLMANN *Rooiyard* 17 The Native who slips out without a 'special' or the Native who has to return home in an inebriated condition after a convivial beer drink is well aware that the shorter the distance he has to travel the more he minimises the danger of meeting a policeman on his beat. **1953** LANHAM & MOPELI-PAULUS *Blanket Boy's Moon* 278 Should Africans desire to use the streets of the city late at night, then must they obtain Special Passes from their white men employers. **1963** L.F. FREED *Crime in S. Afr.* 111 If they went into town without a special they could be arrested. **1980** L. CALLINICOS *People's Hist. of S. Afr.* I. 42 A 'special pass' had to be carried when a worker left his employer's premises even for a few hours. **1990** J. NAIDOO *Coolie Location* 212 I'd seen my uncles on the market sign passes and sometimes provide specials, but I had no practical sense of what they implied. **1990** R. STENGEL *January Sun* 70 Ras routinely arrested people for pass violations. 'If he found you in town after nine without a "special" (a signed pass from one's employer),' Life recalls, 'he would arrest you.'

Special Branch *n. phr. Hist.* Also with small initials. [fr. Brit. Eng.] The security division of the police force; *colloq.* (pl. unchanged), a member of this section; BRANCH; SB. Also *attrib.*

The Special Branch dealt with political matters.

1953 A. MOGALE in *Drum* Apr. 36 'What's in it for me, Mister Chief-of-the-Special-Branch?' I asked him. **1956** [see FREEDOM CHARTER sense 1]. **1958** A. FUGARD *Dimetos & Two Early Plays* (1977) 157 You got to watch him. Because if you don't, he'll report you as well. Yes, he will ... He'll report you to the Special Branch. **1962** A.J. LUTHULI *Let my People Go* 192 All the way to Tambo's home we had a guard of honour of Special Branch cars. **1963** K. MACKENZIE *Dragon to Kill* 39 He could .. see a sprinkling of white special branch policemen sitting near the door. **1969** M. BENSON *At Still Point* (1988) 101 A young man, sober-faced, .. adjusted the white-tabbed collar of his Prosecutor's robes ... The others were obviously Special Branch. *Ibid.* 152 From the court came the escort, surrounding Makhana, followed by a group of Special Branch. *Ibid.* 228 The corridors clattered with uniformed police. The handful of spectators entered the galleries of a court bristling with Special Branch. **1977** *Daily Dispatch* 17 Nov. 1 In a day punctuated with angry exchanges in the court, it was also revealed that: The Special Branch considered it was not bound by statute law. **1977** S. KENTRIDGE in *E. Prov. Herald* 18 Nov. 17, I don't think your worship has heard any criticism of the special branch or of the Security Police except for .. those who were concerned with Biko. **1980** J. COCK *Maids & Madams* 164, I hope I'm not going to have the Special Branch after me (nervous laughter). **1982** M. MZAMANE *Children of Soweto* 27 After being pulled in several times by the Special Branch he decided to flee the country and died in exile. **1985** in PLATSKY & WALKER *Surplus People* 256 One day I was in the office. There came a special branch. He threatened me, asking me, he was a black. **1986** F. KARODIA *Daughters of Twilight* 85 A few weeks later we read in the *Sunday Times* that Solly K–, arrested by the Special Branch a week earlier, had jumped to his death from the sixth floor of the building. **1991** F.G. BUTLER *Local Habitation* 189 With touching care for the safety of the régime the Special Branch used to keep a kindly eye on High Corner, taking down the numbers of cars parked outside.

speck var. SPEK.

speckboom, -baum varr. SPEKBOOM.

speckvreter var. SPEKVRETER.

speering var. SPIERING.

spek /spek, spɛk/ *n.* [Du., pork(-fat), bacon.] **a.** *hist.* Hippopotamus fat; *zeekoe spek*, see ZEEKOE sense 2. **b.** Pork or bacon fat. Also Englished form **speck**, and *attrib.*

Found in *U.S. Eng.* as 'speck'.

[**1688** see SPEKBOOM sense 1.] **1838** J.E. ALEXANDER *Exped. into Int.* I. 110 The natives .. quickly dispatch them with their javelins, and make merry over the rich spek, or fat under the skin. **1856** C.J. ANDERSSON *Lake Ngami* 517 The flesh of the hippopotamus is highly esteemed, .. and the fat ('spek,' as it is termed by the colonists) is very excellent. **1870** R. RIDGILL in A.M.L. Robinson *Sel. Articles from Cape Monthly Mag.* (1978) 34 Astonishment at our escape was mingled with anxiety to pursue the monster, which I forbade, tempting as the idea of sea-cow steaks and *spek* might be. **1968** L.G. GREEN *Full Many Glorious Morning* 17 Only in South Africa will you find boerewors on the menu; that highly-spiced sausage with its blend of beef and pork, cubes of *spek*, coriander, ground cloves and nutmeg. *Ibid.* 82 One hippo killed in winter often provided two hundred pounds of delicious fat or spek and in the wilds this was used as a substitute for butter. **1972** *Sunday Times* 6 Feb. (Mag. Sect.) 16 Lard the meat with speck strips. **1973** M.A. COOK *Cape Kitchen* 108 All the chopped meat (pork was by far the most commonly used) had to be mixed with fresh pork fat (spek). **1975** *Drum* 22 Apr. 57 Lard beef with strips of speck. **1977** *Fair Lady* 8 June (Suppl.) 23 Mock Venison. 1kg of mutton; 125g spek (pork fat) ... Cut spek into strips, garlic into slivers and lard meat using both. **1978** *Drum* 22 Mar. 57 For an outstanding flavour lard hump with strips of speck and raisins. **1980** *Meat Board Focus* Dec. 10 Fry spek in a heavy based suacepan until crisp. Remove and reserve. Saute onions in remaining fat. Arrange beans and crisp spek in layers in the saucepan. **1989** I. JONES *Woman's World Cookbk* 86 Roast Leg of Venison. This recipe uses the usual lardings of spek. **1991** *Weekend Post* 4 May (Leisure) 6 Venison is a dry meat and should be well larded with spek or bacon fat.

spekboom /ˈspekbʊəm, ˈspɛk-/ *n.* Also **speckbaum, spec(k)boom, spe(c)k-boom, spek-boem.** [S. Afr. Du., fr. Du. *spek* blubber, pork fat + *boom* tree.]

1. The succulent shrub or small tree *Portulacaria afra* of the Portulacaceae, a valuable fodder plant in times of drought, with fleshy leaves and small pink to lilac flowers; *elephant's food*, see ELEPHANT. Also *attrib.*

[**1688** G. TACHARD *Voy. to Siam* 51 High and thick Hedges, of a kind of Laurel, which they call *Speck*, always green, and pretty like to the Filaria.] **1823** in *Albany Settlers 1824–1836* (1836) 20 For six days Mrs. B. and six children were reduced to live on *speckboom*, which they gathered in the woods, and a little milk. *a***1827** D. CARMICHAEL in W.J. Hooker *Botanical Misc.* (1831) II. 261 The *Speckboom* (*Portulacaria Afra*) is common in the eastern parts of the colony, but does not grow in the vicinity of the Cape ... The leaves are small, cuneiform, fleshy, and of an agreeably acid taste. **1828** T. PRINGLE *Ephemerides* 104 There the spekboom spreads its bowers Of light-green leaves and lilac flowers. **1835** A. STEEDMAN *Wanderings* I. 67 We .. obtained a partial alleviation of our thirst by roasting some branches of the spekboom, *Portucalaria Afra*, which had a juicy, pungent flavour. **1843** *Cape of G.H. Almanac & Annual Register* 446 The high lands .. are in general thickly clothed with bush, chiefly speckboom and other succulent shrubs on which cattle, and sheep, and goats readily browse. **1844** J.M. BOWKER *Speeches & Sel.* (1864) 135 Dried spek-boom branches have equal qualifications with old cordage for excellent brown paper manufacture. **1851** R. GRAY *Jrnl of Bishop's Visitation* II. 171, I saw here .. the spekboom tree or shrub in full flower ... The flower is of a delicate pink, and reminds me more of the heliotrope than of any other. **1871** J. MCKAY *Reminisc.* 156 The path was lined on both sides abundantly with spek-boom, a kind of succulent sour plant tree, and the hunger of the men was so intense that they could not be restrained from eating the acid leaves of this bush. **1896** R. WALLACE *Farming Indust. of Cape Col.* 88 A fleshy, rounded-leaved, scrubby soft-wooded tree or bush, .. a very valuable food plant for sheep, cattle and even horses .. the spekboom is a bush which recovers rapidly from the injury done by too close browsing by stock, if a season's respite be granted to it. **1907** T.R. SIM *Forests & Forest Flora* 5 When the Spekboom is in flower its bright rosy colour pervades the scene; at all other times the landscape is dull and sombre, desolate and monotonous; the secluded resort of the Koodoo, the Buffalo, and the Elephant. **1939** [see NABOOM]. **1951** N.L. KING *Tree-Planting* 70 *Portulacaria afra (Spekboom)*, .. An inhabitant of scrub in hot dry localities in eastern Cape, Natal and Zululand. Makes a neat compact hedge, if clipped frequently. **1961** PALMER & PITMAN *Trees of S. Afr.* 323 Spekboom. *Portulacaria Afra.* This small juicy-leaved tree or bush is one of the most outstanding of all our many fodder trees. It is found in abundance in the drier parts of the Eastern Province and on Karroo koppies. **1971** L.G. GREEN *Taste of S.-Easter* 161 It was the spekboom or elephant's food, an evergreen shrub flowering in early summer, that provided an enormous honey flow. **1982** *E. Prov. Herald* 16 Sept. 11 The vegetation in the park, mainly spekboom, sneezewood, karoo boerboom and guarri .. is so nutritious that it supports three times the number of elephants found in any equivalent area in Africa. **1985** *Style* Oct. 89 Halali, which huddles at the foot of a spekboom-fringed hill, Etosha's highest point. **1990** M.M. HACKSLEY (tr. E. van Heerden) in *Lynx* 201 You stand high on the roof of the world, among hot ironstone and spekboom shrubs. **1992** T. VAN RENSBURG in *S. Afr. Panorama* Mar.-Apr. 8 In the Richtersveld to the north, the quiver tree (*Aloe dichotoma*) and the elephant's trunk (*Pachypodium namaquanum*) are the most typical, with the many species of aloe and the spekboom (*Portulacaria afra*) most typical of the Little Karoo.

2. *comb.* **spekboomveld** /-felt, -fɛlt/ [Afk., *veld* open undeveloped countryside], see quot.

1987 T.F.J. VAN RENSBURG *Intro. to Fynbos* 24 The following .. veld types are mainly found adjoining fynbos areas: .. Spekboomveld (dense shrubs dominated by the porkbush *Portulacaria afra*). From Calitzdorp to Graaff-Reinet.

spekvreter *n. obs.* Also **speckvreter.** [S. Afr. Du., fr. Du. *spek* fat, bacon + *vreter* eater; see quot. 1867.] The familiar chat *Ceromela familiaris* of the Turdidae; also called DAGBREKER.

1867 E.L. LAYARD *Birds of S. Afr.* 107 *Speckvreter* of Colonists. A pair or two frequent every farm-house in the colony, and are accused of picking the grease out of the cart-wheels; hence their colonial name. Dr. A. Smith, in Zool. of S. A., says it differs from Le Vaillant's bird. **1908** HAAGNER & IVY *Sketches* 19 The Familiar Chat (*S. familiaris*), the Spekvreter (Bacon-eater) of the Boers, .. is fairly well distributed throughout South Africa. **1937** M. ALSTON *Wanderings* 145 A familiar chat had built its nest ... In Rhodesia it is known as the 'house-bird' ... The Dutch call it the speck-vreter (fat-eater) because it has often been seen eating the grease from wagon wheels.

spens see DISPENS.

sperrgebiet /ˈʃpeə(r)gəˌbit/ *n.* Also **sperregebiet**, and (freq.) with initial capital. [G., forbidden territory, fr. *sperren* to close, bar + *Gebiet* area, territory.] The area of the Namibian coast between Lüderitz and the Orange River, where diamonds were found in 1908 and to which the German Government (and subsequently the South African authorities) allowed only restricted access. Also *attrib.*

1926 M. NATHAN *S. Afr. from Within* 46 In April 1908, diamonds were discovered in the desert sand near Lüderitzbucht ... The German Government ordered the closing of the area which had not been pegged off by companies. This area, known as Sperrgebiet, and believed to be of great value, was also closed to prospecting by the succeeding British Administration. The sperrgebiet extends from Lüderitzbucht to the Orange river. **1936** L.G. GREEN *Secret Afr.* 99 The guards were withdrawn from the diamond-fields of Luderitzbucht when the Germans retreated inland, and one foreigner slipped into the 'Sperrgebiet,' collected a parcel worth £80,000, and escaped with it. **1945** L.G. GREEN *Where Men Still Dream* 159 Dramatic discoveries are sometimes made in the Namib Desert and the forbidden 'Sperrgebiet'—or coastal diamond areas near Luderitzbucht. **1957** C. BIRKBY *Airman Lost in Afr.* 55 Two men .. had found an immensely rich pocket of diamonds in the sperrgebiet. **1967** E. ROSENTHAL *Encycl. of Sn Afr.* 527 *Sperrgebiet*, Zone in South West Africa, mainly along the coast, access to which was prohibited without special permission, owing to its wealth in diamonds. The Sperrgebiet was established during the German régime, and has been maintained since then by the South African Government. **1968** G. CROUDACE *Black Rose* 67 The whole coastline south to the Orange River mouth to be *sperregebiet* – forbidden territory. **1971** *Std Encycl. of Sn Afr.* IV. 25 The 'Sperrgebiet' was proclaimed in Sept. 1908, when the Imperial government in Berlin gave sole right to prospect and recover diamonds in the area to the Deutsche Diamanten Gesellschaft. **1978** E.L. WILLIAMS in *Optima* Vol.27 No.4, 86 When it became apparent that this harsh, inhospitable place held diamonds it was named the *Sperrgebiet*, the forbidden region, and sealed off by the German colonial administration of the time, thus adding a man-made sense of secrecy to its natural isolation. **1985** *S. Afr. Panorama* Nov. 45 Alexander was privileged to be allowed access to the *Sperrgebiet* by the De Beers Diamond Mining Company in the early 1980s. The area has been prohibited for all but a few mining personnel since the *Sperrgebiet* Decree of 1909. **1993** G. WILLIAMSON in *Afr. Wildlife* Vol.47 No.2, 52 The Sperrgebiet lies in the south-western corner of Namibia, comprising the southernmost portion of the great Namib Desert. It is about 220 kilometres long, roughly rectangular in shape, and wedged between the rugged Atlantic coast and the base of the high inland escarpment.

sphaza var. SPAZA.

spider *n.* [See quot. 1974.] A light carriage with a high body and four disproportionately large and slender wheels; occas., a dog-cart. Also *attrib.*

1873 F. BOYLE *To Cape for Diamonds* 238 Concluded an arrangement with Mr Martin for the use of his spider cart and two horses, in exchange for my rifle and smooth-bore gun ... Mr Martin .. sent me up the spider fully equipped at 5.30 a.m. **1879** *Daily News* 21 Aug. 5, I don't know how often that 'spider' and I rolled over together into the mud. **1881** *E. London Dispatch & Frontier Advertiser* 15 Jan. 2 On Monday a pair of horses .. bolted with a spider from the Episcopal Church at Kei Road and made a complete smash of the vehicle. **1883** O.E.A. SCHREINER *Story of Afr. Farm* 257 At the farmhouses where he stopped the 'ooms' and 'tantes' remembered clearly the spider with its four grey horses. **1897** J.P. Fitzpatrick *Outspan* 103 The leaders shied violently to the off, the spider swung down the slope, slid a little, poised for a moment on two wheels, and turned slowly over on its side. **1900** *Grocott's Penny Mail* 6 July 1 Double-seated Spider, almost new. **1915** D. Fairbridge *Torch Bearer* 216 'What about an ambulance, Mr le Sueur?' 'We could only get a spider — there are no closed carriages in Vredendorp.' **1934** B.I. Buchanan *Pioneer Days* 71 Considerably later began the importation of American single and double seated buggies, here rechristened 'spiders'. **1949** O. Walker *Proud Zulu* (1951) 225 A featherweight but strong American spider which could get him down to the Bay in two days easily. **1967** [see Scotch cart]. **1969** A.A. Telford *Jhb.: Some Sketches* 44 Another favourite, often seen among the wagons, carts and buggies, was the 'Spider' with its light body slung on four large slender wheels. **1971** H. Zeederberg *Veld Express* 101 The 'spider' was certainly a luxurious vehicle. The four wheels were higher than the conventional type to enable it to negotiate the rivers and drifts more comfortably. **1974** A.A. Telford in *Std Encycl. of Sn Afr.* 571 The more popular type of four-wheeled vehicle, both with the farmer and the townsman, was the American buggy, one of several vehicles commonly called a 'spider' in South Africa. Very slender large wheels supporting a small light body suggested a spider in appearance .. Two to six passengers could be carried. The four-wheeled dogcart with passengers sitting back to back was also called a spider. **1982** *S. Afr. Panorama* Nov. 33 Socialites drove in their 'spiders' to attend London theatrical productions in the Masonic Hall. **1991** B. MacKenzie (tr. F.P. Van den Heever) in *Best of S. Afr. Short Stories* 59, I pulled the old spider carriage out of the clump of reeds where our Oubaas had hidden it from the tommies.

spiering *n. obs.* Also **speering**. [S. Afr. Du., transf. use of Du. *spiering* a name used to designate a different species of fish; see Thompson quot. 1913.] The silverside, *Atherina breviceps* of the Atherinidae, a small, translucent estuarine and marine fish; assous. Also *attrib.*

Often used as bait. In Smith and Heemstra's *Smiths' Sea Fishes* (1986), the name 'Cape silverside' is used for this species.

1804 R. Percival *Acct of Cape of G.H.* 44 The speering eel, a small fish, with white clear shining spots. **1806** J. Barrow *Trav.* II. 38 The Speering, a species of *Antherina*, is a small transparent fish with a broad band. **1843** J.C. Chase *Cape of G.H.* 169 Speering, an Antherina. Similar to Smelt but not very plentiful. **1913** W.W. Thompson *Sea Fisheries of Cape Col.* 58 (Swart), Elft and spiering .. are very similar in appearance to their Dutch counterparts, although not scientifically related to them. **1913** C. Pettman *Africanderisms* 466 *Spiering*, .. a fish not unlike the English smelt.

sping slang see quot. **1883** at spuugslang.

spirting snake var. spurting snake.

spitskool /ˈspətskʊəl/ *n.* [Afk., *spits* pointed peak + *kool* cabbage.] See quot. 1934; spitskop sense 2.

1898 Smith Bros. *Horticulture* 19 The best varieties [of cabbage] for our climate are, Colonial Spitskool, Brunswick Short Stem, Three Star, [etc.]. **1934** C.P. Swart Supplement to Pettman. 163 Spitskool, .. A South African cabbage with large, solid, conical-shaped hearts.

spitskop /ˈspətskɔp/ *n.* Also **spitzkop**. [Afk., fr. Du. *spits* (G. *spitz*) pointed peak + *kop(je)* head ('hill' in S. Afr. Du.).]

1. ?*obs.* A sharply pointed or conical hill. Also **spitskopje** [see -ie], and *attrib.*

1872 J.L. Babe *S. Afr. Diamond Fields* 103 When the traveler [sic] passes through the Free State by Fauresmith, he has the tabular mountains and spitzkops, so common and all-prevailing in South Africa. **1889** *Argus Annual & S. Afr. Dir.* 849 Stony hills and knolls — known locally as *randjies* and *spitskops*. **1905** G.W. Stow *Native Races of S. Afr.* 396 The headquarters of 'Kousopp were at the two spitzkopjes to the left of the 'Gumaap. **1908** M.C. Bruce *New Tvl* 4 A flat-topped mountain and its inevitable companion a cone-shaped spitz-kop, and over all burns a hot blue sky. **1920** F.C. Cornell *Glamour of Prospecting* 188 On the horizon, westward, a jagged line of fantastic-looking peaks show faintly blue in the shimmering heat, prominent among them being the two pointed spitz kopjes which mark the spot where the Molopo joins the Orange. [**1931** V. Sampson *Kom Binne* 144 A conical hill, like a bell tent in shape, called by the Dutch a spitzkop.] **1937** A.H. Goodwin in I. Schapera *Bantu-Speaking Tribes* 33 The flat-topped and 'spitzkop' hills so typical of the Karroo country and other parts.

2. *transf.* spitskool.

1968 *Farmer's Weekly* 3 Jan. 91 (advt) Cabbage Plants. Spitskop; Cauliflower, Southern Cross, 30 cents 100.

spitting snake *n. phr. Obs.* [tr. S. Afr. Du. *spuugslang*, see spuugslang.] The rinkhals (sense 1), *Hemachatus haemachatus*.

1789, 1849, 1883 [see spuugslang]. **1887** *Encycl. Brit.* XXII. 197 One [genus] *Sepedon haemachates* .. or 'Ring-Neck Snake', shares with the cobra a third Dutch name, that of 'spuw slang' (Spitting Snake). *c*1936 [see rinkhals sense 1].

spitzkop var. spitskop.

splint *n. Diamond-trade.* [Special sense of general Eng. *splint* splinter of wood or stone.] A fractured or broken fragment of diamond. See also melee.

1872 C.J. Rhodes in B. Williams *Cecil Rhodes* (1921) 29 You must not .. think that every diamond one finds is a beauty, the great proportion are nothing but splints. **1887** J.W. Matthews *Incwadi Yami* 415 Faithfully carrying out their master's bequests, and never robbing him of a single splint. **1903** W. Catelle *Precious Stones* 79 Beyond the small pieces resulting from cleavages, other fragments are saved which cannot be cut to jewels. Some of these are called 'splints', and are used for mechanical purposes or ground to powder. **1913** C. Pettman *Africanderisms* 466 *Splint*, The term applied on the Diamond Fields to a fractured diamond. **1973** Beeton & Dorner in *Eng. Usage in Sn Afr.* Vol.4 No.2, Splint, .. a fractured diamond.

spoew-slang var. spuugslang.

spog /spɔx/ *v. intrans. Colloq.* Also **spogh**. [Afk., earlier S. Afr. Du. *spochen*, fr. Du. *spochten* (var. *pochen*) boast, brag.] To boast, brag, or show off.

1870 H.H. Dugmore *Reminisc. of Albany Settler* 33 There were many handsome, high-fed horses on the commando .. and many a youth 'spogh'd' dashingly enough upon them at starting. **1913** C. Pettman *Africanderisms* 467 *Spogh, To* .. To show off, to make a display. **1958** A. Jackson *Trader on Veld* 33 On a Saturday afternoon .. the young man would arrive from a neighbouring farm .. mounted on a prancing horse, on which he would proceed to 'spog', or show off in front of the abode of the girl. **1970** D.J. Olivier *Informant, Johannesburg* He is 'spogging' now, but at one time he could not afford to buy a 'stert-riempie'. **1970** *Informant, Pietersburg* He spogs about his new bike.

spoiler *n. Obsolescent. slang.* [fr. *the Spoilers* a gang operating in Alexandra township, Johannesburg, during the 1940s and '50s (see quot. 1952).] In urban (esp. township) Eng.: a troublemaker; one who terrorizes law-abiding persons. Cf. skebenga, tsotsi sense 1.

[**1952** *Drum* May 40 The Spoilers take their name from a gangster film, and their operations are centred around the Pimville and Moroka areas ... Spoilers dare not come to town during the day.] **1963** Wilson & Mafeje *Langa* 22 The *townees* or *tsotsis* are also called '*location boys*', '*ooclever*', bright boys, and *spoilers*, after a gang which terrorized Alexandra Township in Johannesburg. **1963** A.M. Louw *20 Days* 95 Only last night Eunice, the wife of a Xhosa policeman .. had told of the way the spoilers had dragged out their furniture and burnt everything, even her husband's uniforms. *Ibid.* 235 He was told that there had been clashes with the police .., that the police had gone now and that the 'spoilers' were more active than ever. **1964** G. Gordon *Four People* 218 'Why do they call them "spoilers"? ..' Philemon was puzzled at her ignorance. The meaning of the word seemed so obvious. 'They spoil your pass, Madam. They tear it, or burn it, or throw it away.' *Ibid.* 237 'Spoilers,' he said. 'That's what they call these damn agitators. Tomorrow you'll see we won't get any newspapers.'

spong-siekte var. sponssiekte.

sponspe(c)k var. spanspek.

sponssiekte /ˈspɔnsiktə/ *n. Pathology.* Also **spongsi(e)kte**, **sponse-ziekte**, **sponsiekte**, **spons-siekte**, **sponsziekte**, **spon zickte**. [S. Afr. Du., *spons* sponge + *ziekte* (later Afk. *siekte*) disease.] A disease of livestock resulting in a high fever and spongy swellings in the muscles of one or more quarters.

In general Eng. called 'quarter evil', this disease is caused by a bacillus.

1790 tr. F. Le Vaillant's *Trav.* II. 80 The *spong-sikte*, a terrible scourge among horned cattle, and very alarming ... It is a kind of leprosy, that may be communicated in an instant; and the flesh of such animals as are attacked by it, swells in an extraordinary manner, and grows spongy and livid. **1795** C.R. Hopson tr. C.P. Thunberg's *Trav.* I. 151 The spongy sickness (*sponsziekte*) begins in this manner; first a foot swells, and then by degrees the whole body. **1809** J. Mackrill *Diary.* 61 Sponsziekte, Spongy Sickness, probably caused by the Bite of a Viper. **1863** *Queenstown Free Press* 3 Feb., Mr Wynand Bezuidenhout has cured 'sponseziekte' among calves, and lung-sickness among cattle. [*c*1881 A. Douglass *Ostrich Farming* 204 In the Cape Colony .. the three main diseases are lung-sickness (pleuro-pneumonia), fall-sickness, and spon-sickness (quarter evil).] **1914** *Farmer's Annual* 118 Black Quarter, Quarter Evil or Sponsziekte. These names and several others, such as quarter ill and black leg, are used for another disease attacking cattle, and occasionally sheep and goats. It is caused by the presence of an organism known as the Bacillus Sarcophysematos, or Bacillus Chauvaei. **1916** *Farmer's Weekly* 20 Dec. 1489 The following vaccines are obtainable ... Black Quarter in Cattle, also known as Quarter Evil or Sponsziekte. **1944** [see galsiekte sense 1 a]. **1968** *Farmer's Weekly* 3 Jan. 85 Recently immunised against heartwater, red water, gallsickness, anthrax, sponsiekte, botulism. **1979** T. Gutsche *There Was a Man* 50 Theiler abandoned the farrier project for an attack on 'Sponsziekte' or Black Quarter Evil, an historic cattle disease then prevalent in the Transvaal and recently conquered by a vaccine devised in Europe.

spoog slang var. spuugslang.

spook /spʊk/ *n.* [Special senses of general Eng. *spook* ghost, apparition, spectre, which originated in U.S. Eng. (fr. Du.) and is widely used also in S. Afr. Eng. (reinforced by S. Afr. Du. and Afk. *spook*).]

1. *fig.* Esp. in political contexts: a scare-story; a spectre, a bogey; a fear. Also *attrib.* See also gogga sense 2 a.

1939 J.C. Smuts *Plans for Better World* (1942) 225 General Hertzog .. is resurrecting from the grave an old and very dead corpse — the so-called British jingo ... I thought that he and Hoggenheimer and a number of other 'spooks' had disappeared ... Let us drop this racial talk, this nonsense about 'spooks' and 'goggas'. **1972** *Sunday Times* 21 May 16 If this spook is to be the basis of political debate — 'You hate me, therefore I now hate you' — what is to become of South Africa? **1982** *Rhodeo* (Rhodes Univ.) 6 Apr. 11 One of the things that frightened me the most was the security police. So I decided to take all the spooks out of the dark corners ... All those right-wing things. **1982** S. Sepamla in Chapman & Dangor *Voices from Within* 127 The myths attending your name have been spooks in the minds of many. **1985** H. Pienaar in *Frontline* Dec. 23 The CP never had so many factors in their favour as in this round of by-elections. That they failed indicates in my view that the far-right spook will stay a spook for a long time yet.

2. *Military.* Usu. pronounced /spʊək/. An armoured vehicle used to detect mines. See also BUFFEL sense 2, SPOOK *v.* sense 2.

1978 *Sunday Times* 2 Apr. 15 Its own special mine detecting vehicle ('die spook') for use in the operational area.

3. In the intrans. v. phr. ***to spook loop*** /- luəp/ [Afk., *loop* walk], to creep unseen.

1979 *National Serviceman, Informant* We had to spook loop round the outside of the whole camp without getting seen.

4. *slang.* A fright.

1986 *Crux* Aug. 43 Well, these Israelites only catch a big spook — like they were all too chicken to take this ou on.

‖**5.** *comb.* **spookdorp** /ˈspʊəkdɔrp, -dɔːp/ [Afk., *spook* ghost + *dorp* town], a ghost town; **spookhuis** /ˈspʊəkheɪs/ [Afk., *spook* ghost + *huis* house], a haunted house.

1975 *Het Suid-Western* 4 June, Mossel Bay down yonder .. really does seem to be getting nearer to the day when it will become a **spookdorp**. **1983** *Pace* Oct. 70 More than 22 families have turned their backs on the house and prefer to linger on the long waiting list for houses — but not the '**spook huis**'. They say pots, beds, wardrobes and what-have-you fly around the house. **1987** J. VAN DER MERWE in *Pretoria News* 22 June 3 A new complex on the site of the famous Erasmus 'Spookhuis' next to the Delmas highway. **1990** *Frontline* Mar.-Apr. 12 A haunted house? I think he's joking. But no; he pinpoints the spookhuis, soberly, and says to be sure to be gone by dark.

spook /spʊk, spuək/ *v.* [Afk.]

1.a. *intrans.* Of a place: to be haunted.

1873 *Cape Monthly Mag.* VII. 292 It is a very common thing for it to be said that at some particular spot on a road, generally a dark, lonely drift, or near a place where a murder has been committed, that it 'spooks.' **1929** J.G. VAN ALPHEN *Jan Venter* 265, I do believe that the thief must be a *spook*. Does it *spook* on your farm?

b. *trans.* To haunt (a person or place); to frighten (someone).

Also in *U.S. Eng.*

1883 O.E.A. SCHREINER *Story of Afr. Farm* 12 Three nights ago she hears a rustling and a grunting behind the pantry door, and knew it was your father coming to 'spook' her. **1939** J.F. BENSE *Dict. of Low-Dutch Element in Eng. Vocab.* 542 *Spook* vb. 1883 ... From the earliest record in N.E.D. — see quot. 1883 — it seems to have its origin in South Africa. **1965** C. VAN HEYNINGEN *Orange Days* 244 Unless they came, I would die from working alone in the garden as I was now old, and then I could come back and 'spook' them. **1977** F.G. BUTLER *Karoo Morning* 244 One night he begged me to come to his room because he was being frightened by noises. He was being spooked. **1980** *Cape Times* 16 Jan. 11 Spooking the baddies out of the troop. **1982** *Ibid.* 23 Dec. 3 No arrests had been made, but residents felt 'threatened and spooked' by the police presence. **1984** *Sunday Times* 1 Apr. 3 Widow spooked by her husband's 'ghost' for 20c ... She said her dead husband's ghost kept pestering her for 20c. **1986** D. CASE *Love, David* 92, I woke up feeling very frightened in the dark night. I had goosebumps all over me and thought that Stumpy had come to 'spook' me. **1990** *Sunday Times* 12 Aug. 5 Ghosts aren't spooking us, says graveyard Jan.

2. *trans. Army slang.* To clear (an area) of mines. See also SPOOK *n.* sense 2.

1979 *National Serviceman, Informant,* I tell you they kla you on if you ride on a road that hasn't been spooked.

Hence (sense 1 a) **spooked** *ppl adj.*, haunted; afraid.

1931 G. BEET *Grand Old Days* 87 The natives came to believe that the place was 'spooked,' or haunted.

spoor /spuə(r)/ *n.* Formerly also **spor(e)**, **spur**. [Du.]

1.a. Pl. **-s**, or unchanged. In *pl.*: Footprints or tracks. **b.** *noncount.* The trace or trail left by a person or animal. Also in the phr. ***on spoor***, following a trail.

1823 in T. PRINGLE *Some Account of Eng. Settlers in Albany* (1824) 84 Soon afterwards the *spoor* (footprints) of three Caffers was discovered, and of course we then knew where they went. **1824** *S. Afr. Jrnl* I. 27 A lion, having carried off a heifer of two years old, was followed on the *spoor* or track for fully five hours. **1832** *Graham's Town Jrnl* 1 June 91 He followed the *spoor* of a naked foot for about half an hour, and came up with the prisoner, upon whom these articles, witness' property, were found. **1835** A. SMITH *Diary* (1940) II. 34 Spoors of many lions along the road. **1837** 'N. POLSON' *Subaltern's Sick Leave* 136 He became aware of a lion following his *spoor*, that is taking up his trail of footsteps, a common habit of the lion when hungry. **1844** J. BACKHOUSE *Narr. of Visit* 223 This evening two of our horses have strayed ... As the country was bushy, it was needful to trace them by their footprints. This, indeed, is the common mode of finding cattle in South Africa: it is called 'following the spoor'. **1845** J.M. BOWKER *Speeches & Sel.* (1864) 154 Not only can the farmer follow the spoor through Kaffirland, but he can recover his cattle there at any time, if he can identify them. **1851** T. SHONE *Diary.* 28 Feb., The young men went thro the Kap river and could find no Kaffer spors. **1852** M.B. HUDSON *S. Afr. Frontier Life* 174 News .. Was brought by patrol who had been out on spoor In pursuit of some cattle. *a***1858** J. GOLDSWAIN *Chron.* II. 62 We fell in with the spur of meney more Cattle and a number of Kaffer spurs. **1862** E.L. PRICE *Jrnls* (1956) 90 He had chased Elands till falling in with his brother's *spoor*, who had evidently been on foot and wandering, he augured ill for him and giving up Elands chased *him* — the Bushman accompanying him. **1895** A.B. BALFOUR *1200 Miles in Waggon* 105 Another day he wounded a magnificent koodoo bull, but could not follow its spoor (footprints). **1896** H.A. BRYDEN *Tales of S. Afr.* 15 We did find spoor of a man and donkey to the north-east. **1907** J.P. FITZPATRICK *Jock of Bushveld* (1909) 139, I hunted for Koodoo spoor; there was none to be seen but on an old molehill there was a single print of a dog's foot. **1913** J.J. DOKE *Secret City* 94, I called Klaas to the front and told him to hunt carefully and pick up the spoors. **1925** D. KIDD *Essential Kafir* 288 A Bushman is so used to follow a spoor through the bush that he will tell that an animal has passed by that way recently, his judgement being based on the slightest bending of twigs or displacement of stones. *a***1936** E.N. MARAIS *Soul of Ape* (1973) 126 Heavy rain had fallen, destroying every vestige of spoor. **1958** R.E. LIGHTON *Out of Strong* 8, I read the spoor as the white man reads the black marks on the paper. **1966** F.G. BUTLER *Take Root or Die* (1970) 71 Cattle spoors, naked human footprints, and signs of a struggle. **1990** J. HEALE *Scowler's Luck* 45 He might as well make a point of identifying the human spoor as well from now on, especially since he hadn't spotted any decent animal tracks yet. **1994** M. ROBERTS tr. *J.A. Wahlberg's Trav. Jrnls 1838–56* 68 Spoor of rhinoceros etc.

c. *transf.* The track of a wagon or motor vehicle. Often with defining word, as **motor-spoor** or **wagon-spoor**.

1856 R.E.E. WILMOT *Diary* (1984) 12 From Adcocks we were directed to follow the waggon spoors, in pursuance of which direction we struck off to the right. *a***1858** J. GOLDSWAIN *Chron.* I. 38 Found a Wagon spur wich I followed untill it lead me into a Wagon road. **1874** 'P.' in A.M.L. Robinson *Sel. Articles from Cape Monthly Mag.* (1978) 174 We found, to our chagrin, that we had lost our road ... However, as we saw the spoor of our wagon was still ahead, we deemed it advisable to overtake our heavy baggage. **1879** C.L. NORRIS-NEWMAN in J. Crwys-Williams *S. Afr. Despatches* (1989) 52 One thing we had observed coming along the road was the fresh spoor of a wagon or two. **1920** F.C. CORNELL *Glamour of Prospecting* 132 Not far from this water-hole we came upon the first trace of man we had seen for many days, a faint old waggon-spoor in the sand. **1925** D. KIDD *Essential Kafir* 4 When they had previously noticed the spoor of the waggons in the sand they at once decided that these could only have been caused by animals, for they had never seen any spoor marks except those left by animals. **1944** 'TWEDE IN BEVEL' *Piet Kolonel* 61, I had followed a Trojan car .. and had watched with interest the crooked and waving spoor peculiar to Trojans struggling through sand with their narrow track. **1952** L.G. GREEN *Lords of Last Frontier* 31 Byleveld can tell the age of a motor-spoor at a glance. *c***1963** [see WATERBOOM sense 2].

d. *fig.*

1852 M.B. HUDSON *S. Afr. Frontier Life* 218 His household affairs .. No longer depend on the Hottentot vrouw; All marks of her spoor from the room are effaced. **1950** R.K. COPE in B. Sachs *S. Afr. Opinion: Trek Anthology* (1971) 186 It is on the less inspired productions of the period that the present generation turns an inquiring eye. The spoors of overrated early writers of Afrikaans literature are found to be a hindrance. **1977** P.C. VENTER *Soweto* 231 If you browse through the dailies, the spoor of violence is there.

2. With distinguishing epithet: **blood spoor**, also (occas.) **bloed spoor** /ˈblʊt -/ [Afk., *bloed* blood], the blood traces left by a wounded person or animal; **dew spoor**, see quots; **hand spoor**, see quot. 1980.

1826 A.G. BAIN *Jrnls* (1949) 119 The Bushmen traced the '**Bloed Spoor**' a great way down the river, but the bleeding monster had got into another Zeekoegat. **1835** T.H. BOWKER Journal. 6 Feb., Five traces seen in the Morning no blood spoors this time. **1862** *Queenstown Free Press* 16 Sept. (Pettman), A native man .. came somewhat suddenly upon the two wolves. He .. shot both. The *blood spoor* was traced a considerable distance. *a***1875** T. BAINES *Jrnl of Res.* (1964) II. 219 We found his blood-spoor on the rock where he had passed. **1898** G. NICHOLSON *50 Yrs* 211 Animals of certain size (say up to three hundred-weight) do not afford sufficient resistance to projectiles to cause an expansion of the bullet, and therefore make but a small external wound, in consequence of which little or no 'blood spoor' is visible generally, to enable or encourage a man to follow up wounded game. **1907** J.P. FITZPATRICK *Jock of Bushveld* (1909) 285 There was nothing for it but to hark back to the last blood spoor and, by following it up, find out what had happened. **1930** *Outspan* 31 Oct. 15 His shot had been a poor one and for hours afterwards he had followed the blood spoor amongst the low, scrub-clad hills. **1936** H.F. TREW *Botha Treks* 113 We found the boxes of explosives .. together with a good deal of blood spoor. **1968** S. CLOETE *Chetoko* 17 He came to where the man had abandoned his hunt. It had been a big buck — an eland, as he had thought — and he followed the blood spoor. **1970** E. CRABBE in *Outpost* (1970) 223 In late April 1968, Leon and his new handler were dropped to track a blood spoor after security forces had engaged a group of terrorists. **1972** *Sunday Times* 24 Sept. 5 Disappeared near the Ellis Park railway station leaving a trail of blood in the streets. But neither the blood spoor nor tracker dogs led to his hideout. *a***1858** J. GOLDSWAIN *Chron.* II. 75 They must have gon over verey erley in the Morning as the prent of thear feet on the grass is waat is caled a **due spoor**. *Ibid.* 128 Mr Thomas left quite late at Night and the Kaffers spoors was what his caled a dewspoor — that is wile the dew is falling it can plainly be known. **1980** E. JOUBERT *Poppie Nongena* 27 We like to smear the floors of our house ... We make patterns in the wet dung, down on our knees with the palms of our hands, drawing wide circles with great sweeps away from our bodies and back again. We Xhosa people call these patterns indima or hand spoor.

3. *comb.* **spoor-boy** *obs.* [see BOY], a tracker; **spoor law** *obs.* exc. *hist.*, a regulation, promulgated in 1816 by Lord Charles Somerset (and repealed in 1836), which gave frontier farmers the right to follow the spoor of stolen cattle beyond the boundary of the Cape Colony, and to demand compensation from the village nearest to the spoor; (objective) **spoor-tracker** *n.*, **spoor-tracking** *ppl adj.*, **spoor-watching** *vbl n.*

1959 L.G. Green *These Wonders* 14 One of Martin's **spoor-boys** could follow elephant across a wide expanse of hard rock. **1929** W.M. Macmillan *Bantu, Boer & Briton* 56 (Swart), The **Spoor Law** is described in a memo. drafted by Mr (now Sir) W.E. Stanford, in 1882. **1936** *Cambridge Hist. of Brit. Empire* VIII. 306 In spite of the 'spoor law' .. colonists certainly continued to be subject to devastating cattle raids. **1937** C. Birkby *Zulu Journey* 251 The famous 'spoor law'. If the spoor of a stolen beast is tracked to any native location, the people of the place must take up the trail and either trace the missing beast or compensate the owner; the 'spoor law' often cuts the Gordian knot of detecting the real culprit. **1937** B.F.J. Laubscher *Sex, Custom & Psychopathology* 313 When the early Colonial Government found how difficult it was to recover property, or live stock stolen from the colonists by the natives, they introduced the 'Spoor Law' based on this principle of collective responsibility in native custom. **1907** W.C. Scully *By Veldt & Kopje* 88 Old Gezwindt, a Hottentot celebrated all over the countryside for his skill as a **spoor-tracker**. **1985** *S.-Easter* Oct.-Nov. 52 Everything you hear about the **spoor-tracking** qualities of those Red Indians is absolutely true. **1989** *Weekend Post* 11 Nov. (Leisure) 4 At least half of the route is on a jeep track and when the soil is smooth and damp after rain this makes an ideal area for **spoor-watching**.

spoor /spʊə(r)/ *v.* Also **spure**. [fr. Du. *sporen* to track, or fr. prec.]

a. *trans.* To track (animals, people, or vehicles).

1850 R.G.G. Cumming *Hunter's Life* p.xxi, He could not see those [elephants] we were spooring. *a*1858 J. Goldswain *Chron.* II. 62 We spured them for about two Miles. *Ibid.* 123 His Excellency [Sir H. Smith] then said: how was it that you cannot spoor them? **1863** W.C. Baldwin *Afr. Hunting* 122 We spoored them beautifully into a dense thicket. **1937** [see slim sense 1]. **1937** C.R. Prance *Tante Rebella's Saga* 148 With no Colonel to keep him up to the mark while she was out lion-shooting or spooring a stray beast, Aladdin's Slave degenerated on kafir beer laced with the Colonel's own Very Special Scotch, till house-keeping became a farce. **1958** S. Cloete *Mask* 63 He lived alone, hunted jackals, rooikats and other vermin, killing an occasional buck to eat and waiting till his master sent for him to go hunting or spoor lost cattle. **1963** — *Chetoko* 17 Taking the spear .. he set off to spoor the man.

b. *intrans.* To follow a trail or spoor; to track; (*nonce*) to lead towards (something).

1872 E.J. Dunn in A.M.L. Robinson *Sel. Articles from Cape Monthly Mag.* (1978) 55 There is not one, but many carts, and which is the real one? Luckily, at this juncture he fell in with the track and this 'spoored' up to his own identical vehicle. **1896** R.S.S. Baden-Powell *Matabele Campaign* p.iv, One .. who can ride and spoor and can take charge of the horses. **1939** P. Louw in *Outspan* 6 Oct. 31 A big male lion was shot dead recently in the act of seizing a dog in broad daylight. At the time the dog was spooring fifty yards ahead of his master in the long grass. **1970** *Cape Times* 14 May, Spoored 4 days. When the farmer realized she was feeding cubs, Mr. Bristow tracked her spoor for four days to find the litter nearly dead from starvation.

Hence **spoorer** *n.*, a tracker; **spooring** *vbl n.* and *ppl adj.*, tracking, also *attrib.*

1850 R.G.G. Cumming *Hunter's Life* p.xv, I had great faith in the spooring powers of the Bamangwato men. **1856** F.P. Fleming *Sn Afr.* 368 After about an hour's search and 'spooring,' we at length came upon its object. **1860** A.W. Drayson *Sporting Scenes* 50 By these kaffirs I was taught the art of spooring; my lessons were learned over the print of some buck's foot on the bent-down blade of a bit of grass. **1863** W.C. Baldwin *Afr. Hunting* 259, I followed silently in the rear of the spoorers. **1878** P. Gillmore *Great Thirst Land* 434 At length .. I saw the spoorer stop, look back, and wave his hand. **1885** H. Rider Haggard *King Solomon's Mines* 45 Ventvögel I had known before; he was one of the most perfect 'spoorers' (game-trackers) I ever had to do with, and tough as whip-cord. **1948** A.C. White *Call of Bushveld* 172 Spooring is the most highly skilled 'profession' of the bushveld. **1949** C. Bullock *Rina* 80 Sooner or later he would be found with good spooring, probably sooner than later, and he would be dangerous. **1964** V. Pohl *Dawn & After* 128 His spooring abilities exceeded those of primitive peoples anywhere. **1971** [see go-away sense 2].

‖**spoorweg** /ˈspuə(r)vɛx/ *n.* [Afk., *spoor* track + *weg* way.] The railway system; SAR *n.*² sense b. Also *attrib.*

1881 F.R. Statham *Blacks, Boers & Brit.* 68 Truly the 'spoorweg' is a great institution. **1920** F.C. Cornell *Glamour of Prospecting* 66 The advent of a rare stranger – especially if he looked a townsman and an 'Engelsman' – usually gave raise to some faint hope that at length the spoorweg (railway) was coming, or roads were to be made, or a mine opened, or some kind of Gouvermentse werk to be started to benefit the country at long last. **1987** O. Musi in *Drum* May 47 Not so long ago when reporters used to use public transport .. the prudent ones among us would buy season tickets for the spoorweg. **1987** D. Von Tonder in *New Nation* 22 Oct. 17 Hannetjie, who has a 'spoorweg mentality', is at the centre of these poems, which depict a smug acceptance of the South African situation. **1990** *City Press* 11 Feb. 8 He .. adds that the spoorweg, too, will be off-track adding that in these essential services they enjoy many supporters. So if you don't hear trains trundling around that day .. know that the call has gone out to Die Volk.

spor(e) var. spoor *n.*

sporrie /ˈspɒri, ˈspɔri/ *n.* Also **sporries**, and (formerly) **spurrie**. Pl. unchanged. [Afk., fr. Du. *spurrie*.] Any of several species of wild flax, *Heliophila* of the Brassicaceae, which bear small white or blue flowers.

Imported as a fodder plant by Jan van Riebeeck during the 17th century.

Found in general Eng. as 'spurry'.

1731 G. Medley tr. *P. Kolb's Present State of Cape of G.H.* II. 71 There is an Herb at the *Cape* the *Europeans* there call *Spurrie*, which grows very thick in a great many Places ... It grows about Half a Foot high; and bears a great Number of White Flowers, which are follow'd by several *Capsulae*, containing each a Quantity of very small Seed. When the Sun smites the *spurrie* very hotly, the *capsulae* open. [*Ibid.* 272 Spurry was brought to the *Cape* from Holland; and some was brought from Batavia.] **1917** R. Marloth *Common Names* 76 *Sporrie, Spergula arvensis.* Cultivated as fodder-plant, sometimes a garden weed. **1975** *S. Afr. Panorama* Sept. 32 Hundreds of tourists flock to the area. On warm sunny days they can be seen rambling through fields of vivid Namaqualand daisies, white and blue 'sporrie' (Heliophila sp.), buttercup yellow and orange daisies, exquisite vygies, 'hongerblomme', [etc.]. **1986** *Personality* 3 Nov. 32 A patch of delicate white sporries makes a perfect backdrop to the furry grey coat of a young donkey. **1987** S. Eliovson in *Flying Springbok* Aug. 97 Another dainty sky-blue flower, *Heliophila*, meaning sun-loving, comes into flower quickly. Its common name is sporries or wild flax. White sporries lie in vast tracts like snowdrifts on the Kamiesberg mountains near Leliefontein.

spot *n.* [Prob. ellipt. for Eng. *nightspot* club; or transf. use of *spot* a drink.] In township slang: shebeen sense 1. Also *attrib.*

1976 M. Tholo in C. Hermer *Diary of Maria Tholo* (1980) 99 One man arrived .. soused. Everybody jumped up and asked, 'Where did you get wet?' I mean especially on Sunday, and when the children thought they had wiped out liquor. So he just laughed and said, 'I am not telling because I don't want my spot uncovered.' **1979** M. Matshoba *Call Me Not a Man*, They went to this particular 'spot' which was run by a cute sister .. and bought with ten rand notes. **1981** *Frontline* May 12 With a little financial help from some friends, like the big liquor companies, a newspaper appears monthly. (It's called eSpotini, At The Spot. 'Spot' is a nickname for a shebeen.) **1982** M. Mzamane *Children of Soweto* 80 Molly herself .. ran a spot (which is our euphemism for a drinking joint) at her house. **1982** *Voice* 24 Jan., At Timmy's spot ... Just then Timmy the spot owner walks in. **1982** *New Dawn* Aug. 16 New Dawn set out meeting shebeen owners. You have to get out there to meet the people behind the 'spots' and their clients to understand that shebeens are actually mild palliatives for .. the people. **1982** *Fair Lady* 1 Dec. 183 The NTA (National Taverners' Association) claims to have an affiliation of more than 6 000 shebeeners throughout the country and brings out a newspaper called eSpontini – 'On the Spot' ('Spot' being township slang for a shebeen). **1983** *Pace* Dec. 152 Two types of shebeens. First is the 'big-time' spot run by a full-time owner (usually male) ... Next are the small-time shebeens, usually run by females to augment their husband's meagre wages. **1987** *Learn & Teach* No.3, 36 Try not to drink too much liquor ... Stay away from the 'spot' for a while. **1989** *E. Prov. Herald* 11 Jan. 2 Mr Q– died .. after he allegedly attempted to escape while pointing out 'spots' in Sebokeng township.

sprew /spruː/ *n.* Also **spreeu(w)**, **spreu(w)**, **sprieu**, **sprue**. [Englished form of Du. *spreeuw* thrush. (The modern Afk. form is *spreeu*.)]

Although there is a great deal of uncertainty among English-speakers as to the spelling of this word, 'sprew' is the form which occurs most frequently.

1. Any of several starlings of the Sturnidae, esp. **a.** *Spreo bicolor*; **b.** *Sturnus vulgaris*; and **c.** any of the glossy starlings of the genus *Lamprotornis*.

In G.L. Maclean's *Roberts' Birds of Sn Afr.* (1993), the name 'pied starling' is used for *Spreo bicolor*, and 'European starling' for *Sturnus vulgaris*.

1795 C.R. Hopson tr. *C.P. Thunberg's Trav.* II. 48 A kind of *Corvus*, (or crow) called *Spreuw*, was found both here and in several other places in great plenty. **1801** J. Barrow *Trav.* I. 29 Turtle doves, a thrush called the Sprew, and the Fiscal bird, the *Lanius collaris*, frequent the gardens near the town. *a*1823 J. Ewart *Jrnl* (1970) 81 There are .. here great numbers of ring doves, sprews, and other larger birds, which do great damage among the fruit trees. **1827** T. Philipps *Scenes & Occurrences* 68, I particularly remarked two sprews of a dark though glossy green, that, when they met the sun's rays were of exquisite beauty. **1838** T. Shone Diary. 20 Oct., This day I began by cutting up the weeds .. and shooting of a Sprew and another bird. *Ibid.* 31 Nov., This evening the children brought home four young spreus. **1899** B. Mitford *Weird of Deadly Hollow* 161 A cloud of spreeuws fluttered on sheeny wing, making flash after flash of blue light, their long-drawn piping whistle echoing melodiously from the overhanging crags. **1906** W.S. Johnson *Orangia* 17 Some of the spreeuws, or starlings, destroy much fruit. **1923** Haagner & Ivy *Sketches* 82 First in order of classification comes the Spreeuw, or Pied Starling (*Spreo bicolor*), which is very common throughout South Africa. **1924** D. Fairbridge *Gardens of S. Afr.* 99 The handsome red spreeu has a bad character as a fruit-eater, but the brown and white variety lives on insects – chiefly ticks. **1929** F.C. Slater *Sel. Poems* (1947) 117 Bald-headed vultures and the burnished sprew. [*Note*] Sprew = Green sprew or spreeuw (starling family), a bird of brilliant plumage. **1939** S. Cloete *Watch for Dawn* 106 A spreeu dug its beak into some half-dried dung for the fly-worms that were in it. *c*1963 B.C. Tait *Durban Story* This beautiful and natural park where blue-black sprews flash above incredibly green lawns. **1982** J. Krige in *Staffrider* Vol.5 No.2, 20 A sprieu chattered away. **1983** *Evening Post* 26 Mar. 7 A garden full of exotic (foreign) plants may be colourful and attractive but its bird life will be mainly sprews (European starlings) and European sparrows. **1986** J. Conyngham *Arrowing of Cane* 85 A swarm of spreeus wings noisily overhead. **1987** M. Poland *Train to Doringbult* 172 At ten to two the children flew out of the house like sprews migrating.

2. With distinguishing epithet: **green sprew**, *Lamprotornis nitens* of the Sturnidae; **red-winged sprew**, *Onychognathus morio* of the Sturnidae; **witgat sprew** /ˈvətxat-/ [Afk., *wit* white + *gat* hole, vent], *Spreo bicolor* of the Sturnidae; **yellow sprew**, (*?obs.*), in the Eastern Cape, *Oriolus larvatus* of the Oriolidae (more commonly called *black-headed oriole*).

[**1822** W.J. BURCHELL *Trav.* I. 318 The beautiful Groene spreeuw (Green Thrush).] **1853** F.P. FLEMING *Kaffraria* 72 The **Green**, or Purple, **Sprew** is .. a most beautiful and common resident in the Mimosa bush. **1856** R.E.E. WILMOT *Diary* (1984) 133, I must now mention one of the conspicuous birds of the Eastern Province viz. the green sprue ... The first sight of a flock of these superb creatures with their glowing iridescent green and purple plumage and bright yellow eyes, is a thing to remember. **1923** HAAGNER & IVY *Sketches* 153 A common member of this family is the Red-shouldered Glossy Starling (*Lamprocolius phoenicopterus*), commonly known as the Green Spreeuw in the Eastern portion of the Cape Province ... The true Green Spreeuw is confined to Cape Province, it being replaced in the Transvaal and Natal by a smaller subspecies (*L. p. bispecularis*). **1925** F.C. SLATER *Centenary Bk of S. Afr. Verse* 236 Many species [of sprew] occur in South Africa; the Green Spreeuw, a beautiful bird of brilliant plumage, is common in bush districts. **1929** [see sense 1]. **1965** J. BENNETT *Hawk Alone* 67 He kept the Winchester .. for knocking off the **red-winged spreeuws** which fouled the rainwater tanks. **1821** C.I. LATROBE *Jrnl of Visit* Glossary, **Wittegat Spreuw**, *Turdus morio of Linnæus*. **1913** C. PETTMAN *Africanderisms* 563 *Witgat spreeuw*, .. *Spreo bicolor*. **1961** *Redwing* (St Andrew's College, Grahamstown) 20 In the Autumn of 1956 our garden was cluttered up with 'Witgatspreeus'. **1971** BEETON & DORNER in *Eng. Usage in Sn Afr.* Vol.2 No.2, 10 *Pied starling* .. alt: witgatspreeu. **1853** F.P. FLEMING *Kaffraria* 72 Another Kaffrarian bird is the Oriole bird (*Oriolus Galbula*), generally known locally as the Golden, or **Yellow, Sprew**. **1909** A. HAAGNER in *Afr. Monthly* Vol.6 No.33, 269 We may hear the beautiful flute-like notes of the Black-headed Oriole (*Oriolus larvatus*), locally known as the Yellow Spreeuw, and catch a glimpse of its robust figure in yellow and green coat, and black head. **1913** C. PETTMAN *Africanderisms* 568 *Yellow spreeuw*, In some parts of the Eastern Province *Oriolus larvatus* is known by this name. (Albany.) **1923** HAAGNER & IVY *Sketches* 156 The last member of the family is the Black-headed Oriole .. fairly common in the Albany and Bathurst Divisions of the Cape Province, where it is often known as the Yellow Spreeuw.

spring adder *n. phr. Obs.* An unidentified species of snake found at the Cape.

1790 W. PATERSON *Narr. of Four Journeys* 164 The Spring Adder is a very dangerous but uncommon snake; it is jet black, with white spots, from three to four feet long, and proportionately thick. **1804** R. PERCIVAL *Acct of Cape of G.H.* 170 The spring adder derives its name from springing backwards at its object. Its spring not a little resembles those of a tumbler exhibiting his feats of activity. In size it is small, from two to three feet in length but very dangerous. **1819** G.M. KEITH *Voy.* 70 The spring adder, very dangerous, but not common ... Jet black with white spots.

springbok /ˈsprɪŋbɒk, -bʌk/ *n.* Pl. unchanged, **-s**, occas. **-ken**. Also **spring-boc(k)**. [S. Afr. Du., fr. Du. *springen* to jump + *bok* antelope; see quot. 1810.]

I. The animal.

1.a. The gazelle *Antidorcas marsupialis* of the Bovidae, in colour cinnamon-brown, dark reddish-brown, and white, having long narrow ears, ribbed lyre-shaped horns, and a dorsal fan of long white hairs, and characterized by the high and graceful leaps into the air which it makes when excited or disturbed; *pronkbok*, see PRONK *v.* sense 1; SPRINGBUCK; SPRINGER sense 1. Also *attrib.* See also HOUBOK, *trekbok* (TREK sense 12 b).

South Africa's national animal.

1775 *Phil. Trans. of Royal Soc.* (U.K.) LXVI. 283 We saw some herds of the spring bocks, a species of antelope. **1777** G. FORSTER *Voy. round World* I. 84 The *spring-bock*, a beautiful species, named A. pygargus by Pallas, live in vast herds in the interior parts of Africa. **1786** — tr. *A. Sparrman's Voy. to Cape of G.H.* II. 83 This animal, which is called by the colonists *spring-bok*, a term in the Dutch language signifying the *leaping* or *bounding* goat. **1795** C.R. HOPSON tr. *C.P. Thunberg's Trav.* II. 23 The leaping goats (*Springboks*) .. do a great deal of mischief in the wheat-fields. **1810** G. BARRINGTON *Acct of Voy.* 277 The spring-bok is an animal so swift, and with such an elasticity of muscle to facilitate the act of leaping, that the Dutch have given it a name indicative of its motions. **1838** J.E. ALEXANDER *Exped. into Int.* I. 163, I always found plenty of springboks on the plain ... Of light and airy form and delicate proportions, its general colour is cinnamon on the back, and the breast and belly white. **1875** C.B. BISSET *Sport & War* 202 The spring-bok is considered the best eating antelope. **1884** B. ADAMS *Narr.* (1941) 214 During the morning we came across a drove of springbok. In my opinion they are the prettiest species of the deer I ever saw. **1919** M.M. STEYN *Diary* 274 She loaded Osche and myself with almost more than we could carry .. including a lot of Springbok biltong. **1934** B.I. BUCHANAN *Pioneer Days* 33 With wondering admiration, we watched some springbok speed across the veld, clearing trees in their marvellous leaps. **1973** *Farmer's Weekly* 9 May 9 Springbok, which a decade ago ranged the plains in herds of thousands, are now limited to small groups and individuals on a few farms. **1983** *Nat. Geog. Mag.* Mar. 375 The favorite prey of cheetahs, springbok are among the world's fastest animals, reaching top speeds of more than 40 miles an hour. **1990** W. SMITH *Golden Fox* 224 Mingled with the flocks of merino sheep were vast herds of springbok. These graceful little antelope danced upon the plains like puffs of wind-driven dust. Their delicate bodies were pale cinnamon slashed with bars of chocolate and blazing white.

b. *transf. Prison slang.* Alluding to 'jumping' (slang for 'escaping'): an escapee from prison.

1987 S.A. BOTHA in *Frontline* Oct.-Nov. 15 *Springbok*, escaper.

II. *transf.* Used as a national symbol.

2. Now always with initial capital. Pl. **-s**; when used collectively, freq. ***the Springboks***.

a. An amateur sportsman or sportswoman selected to represent South Africa; BOK sense 3 b; used collectively, a South African sporting team, esp. the national rugby team; cf. *the green and gold* (see GREEN AND GOLD *n. phr.* sense b). Also *attrib.*

1906 *S. Afr. News Weekly* 3 Oct. 1 A crowd of 9,000 .. accorded the springboks a great reception as they walked on the field. **1908** M.C. BRUCE *New Tvl* 35 'They may not be able to teach us anything,' wrote an English sporting paper of the Springboks before they had reached England, 'but they will be content to learn from us.' *c***1911** P.W. DAY in S. Playne *Cape Col.* 393 When the next visiting team came, in 1903, of the 3 test matches, 1 was won by the South Africans at Newlands, and 2 were drawn ... The South African Rugby players then first became known as the Springboks. **1932** *Grocott's Daily Mail* 2 Jan. 3 It cannot be said that many English rugby critics strongly favour England's chance against the Springboks on Saturday. **1943** I. FRACK *S. Afr. Doctor* 77 The names of at least 20 Springboks are mentioned who have represented this country on the field of sport. **1948** O. MEDWORTH in J. Crwys-Williams *S. Afr. Despatches* (1989) 294 Never have I seen a crowd at a cricket match so charged with excitement ... Had the Springboks held their catches, then who knows, they might have been the ones cheered to victory. *a***1951** H.C. BOSMAN *Willemsdorp* (1977) 18 Jack Brummer had never got as far as wearing a Springbok jersey, but he had several times played for his Province. **1960** *Natal Mercury* 6 Apr. 1 Springboks face hostility in U.K. The South African cricket tourists are likely to face a demonstration at London Airport. **1966** VAN HEYNINGEN & BERTHOUD *Uys Krige* 16 The performance of the Springbok teams is almost a barometer of national self-confidence. **1971** *Daily Dispatch* 17 May 12 According to his party's policy no South African non-White chosen to represent South Africa .. can ever be called a Springbok. According to Mr. Waring, the term 'Springbok' is reserved for Whites only. **1979** *S. Afr. Digest* 13 July 19 Springbok colours have been awarded to four South African motor sportsmen. **1982** *Diamond Fields Advertiser* 4 Dec. 8 A Springbok aerobatic pilot died on Thursday when his biplane plummetted to the ground during practice for the South African Acrobatic Championship. **1987** L. NKOSI *Mating Birds* 114 At one corner of the shop .. two big-shouldered, red-faced Springbok types were arguing about the respective merits of two Rugby players. *c***1988** *S. Afr. 1987–8: Off. Yrbk* (Bureau for Info.) 675 The management decided on the name 'Springbokken' at the request of the London Press which suggested the South Africans should have a name. **1990** 'T. COBBLEIGH' in *Sunday Times* 16 Dec. 21 The four brainy and burly South Africans who helped Oxford overwhelm Cambridge .. this week are the latest in a long and noble Springbok contribution to Oxford sport. **1992** F. KEATING in *Guardian Weekly* (U.K.) 9 Oct. 31 Rugby is spiritually entwined in the very soul of white South Africa ... Clothed in their vestments of green and gold the Springboks are religious icons and totems to the faith. **1992** *Guardian Weekly* 13 Nov. 31 England remain favourites to beat the tourists at Twickenham but any hint of complacency on their part will have been dispelled by the Springboks' strong, stylish performance.

b. *Obs.* exc. *hist.* A nickname for a South African soldier during the two world wars; collectively, the Union Defence Force (see UDF *n.*[1]). Also *attrib.* Cf. BOKKIE sense 3.

1916 *Daily Mail* (U.K.) in J. Crwys-Williams *S. Afr. Despatches* (1989) 218 The South Africans .. waited till the Germans were close up. The Springboks then hurled themselves on the Germans, whom they fiercely attacked with rifle and bomb, driving them back in a panic. **1918** *Star* 10 July, The home-coming. Springboks arrive at Park Station. Invalided survivors of Delville Wood arrive. **1925** FRASER & GIBBONS *Soldier & Sailor Words, Springboks, The,* The South African contingent in the War. From their badge, the Colonial emblem of a springbok antelope. **1941** [see OUTSPAN *v.* sense 2]. **1942** *Grocott's Daily Mail* 3 July 2 Missing Springboks. We report with regret that .. local men up North are missing. **1942** *Ibid.* 6 July 3 The Springboks are still in great heart and are .. hitting out against Rommel's shell-worn panzers. **1943** 'J. BURGER' *Black Man's Burden* 236 The Springboks (Union troops) are spoken of as the successors to the pioneer Voortrekkers. **1946** T. MACDONALD *Ouma Smuts* 83 These people had been frantic at the idea that the black man should be recruited for the Springbok army. **1991** F.G. BUTLER *Local Habitation* 7 A captain of Royal Army Supply Corps, who had served in Italy cried, 'Hullow, Springbok, you look lost.'

3. *hist.* Ellipt. for *Springbok Radio*, a commercial radio station of the South African Broadcasting Corporation, operating from May 1950 until the mid-1980s. Also *attrib.*

1967 M.G. GILBERT *Informant, Westminster (OFS)* They .. are writing to the Mercury & will also broadcast thanks over Springbok. **1971** J. MCCLURE *Steam Pig* (1973) 97 Not so busy you can't listen to serials on Springbok, hey? **1971** *Weekend Post* 27 Feb. (Mag. Sect.) 9 Half-a-million listeners who tune in every Saturday night at nine to .. Springbok's top comedy show, 'Men from the Ministry'. **1972** *Ibid.* 23 Sept. 2 The news that there is to be no advertising on TV is a welcome relief ... I wish someone could afford to subsidise Springbok too. **1973** [see SARIE]. **1975** 'BLOSSOM' in *Darling* 26 Feb. 111 Sitting there by the house Saturday nights jis listening to Springbok and thinking how everybody else is out enjoying theyselfs. **1985** *Frontline* May 39 White listeners who used to think that the name of broadcasting was Springbok.

4. In the phr. ***Springbok Scout***: from 1961 the name given to a 'Queen's Scout'.

1970 F.N. GLOVER in *Std Encycl. of Sn Afr.* II. 478 What was a Queen's Scout .. is now a Springbok Scout. **1985** *S. Afr. Panorama* Sept. 16 South Africa once had king or queen scout badges for boys who had achieved high levels of expertise. Today, there are Springbok scouts.

5. The springbok symbol, used on badges, insignia, etc. Also *attrib.* Cf. BOKKIE sense 3.

[**1925** see sense 2 b.] **1973** D.H. CRAVEN in *Std Encycl. of Sn Afr.* IX. 427 In 1906 a team was sent to the United Kingdom under the captaincy of Paul Roos ... On this tour the name 'Springbok', as a sobriquet for the South African team, originated, as well as the Springbok emblem as badge on the jersey. **1979** *S. Afr. Panorama* Dec. 1 On one of every 42 Boeing 747 jets in the world, SAA's emblem, the 'Flying Springbok', can be seen. **1991** *Sunday Times* 10 Feb. 23 There is no doubt that the question of our national sporting emblem will be discussed. Should the leaping Springbok remain in pride of place or should it be replaced ... Deshi Baktawer, *SA Goalkeeper*: 'The Springbok is a symbol of excellence in the world of sport. If I went to my father and told him I'd gained Springbok colours, I'm sure he'd be very proud.' **1991** *South News* 14 Nov. 6 A national nervous breakdown over the retirement of the springbok for national service. **1991** P. HAWTHORNE in *Time* 25 Nov. 54 The sporting springbok was replaced by a deliberately neutral flag, but the symbol will not disappear completely. South African rugby and cricket sides are unlikely ever to be known by any other name. **1992** F. KEATING in *Guardian Weekly* 9 Oct. 31 At least the white, black, and coloured rugby unions are one and the Springbok blazer badge is now decorated with a wreath of protea flowers indicating 'peace and hope'. **1992** E. GRIFFITHS in *Sunday Times* 16 Aug. 30 No more does the Springbok leap across our beating heart. Today, it tramples through a flowerbed of proteas. **1992** E. JAYIYA in *Pace* Sept. 23 About half an hour before the match a huge, beaming, white man appeared in the crowd waving a large ANC-flag with a springbok on [it].

springbuck /ˈsprɪŋbʌk/ *n.* [Englished form of S. Afr. Du. *springbok*.] SPRINGBOK sense 1 a. Also *attrib.*

1776 F. MASSON in *Phil. Trans. of Royal Soc.* LXVI. 311 They informed us, they had seen great flocks of the spring bucks. **1795** [see DUIKERBOK]. **1798** B. STOUT *Narr. of Loss of Ship 'Hercules'* 82 We frequently perceived .. such droves of that species of deer which the farmers call spring buck, that we supposed one flock alone could not contain less than from twelve to fourteen thousand. **1822** W.J. BURCHELL *Trav.* I. 290 The variety of names by which it has been this antelope's fate to be called by different writers, is rather remarkable. But Springbok by the Dutch, and Springbuck by the English inhabitants of the Cape, is the common appellation. **1824** *Ibid.* II. 109 The *springbucks* were far the most numerous, and, like flocks of sheep, completely covered several parts of the plain ... It was only occasionally, that they took those remarkable leaps which have been the origin of the name. **1829** C. ROSE *Four Yrs in Sn Afr.* 204 The beautiful spring-buck, with its bounding motion — spreading the snowy fur of its back, as it flies with a speed that laughs at the hunter. **1837** J.E. ALEXANDER *Narr. of Voy.* I. 351 An elegant springbuck or two appeared near the road; and, as with fairy-bound they cleared obstacles, showed large patches of white among their light brown skins. **1845** J. COLLETT Diary. II. 20 Aug., Caught about 30 young spring Bucks to day with our young Grey hounds. **1857** D. LIVINGSTONE *Missionary Trav.* 103 Before we came to the Orange River we saw the last portion of a migration of springbucks (Gazella euchore, or tsépe). They came from the great Kalahari Desert, and, when first seen after crossing the colonial boundary, are said to often exceed forty thousand in number. **1887** H. RIDER HAGGARD *Jess* p.x, A couple of dozen or so of graceful yellow springbuck. **1895** J.G. MILLAIS *Breath from Veldt* 23 The most .. successful springbuck shooter of Beaufort West. **1896** R. WARD *Rec. of Big Game* 163 There are few better forms of rifle practice than stalking the fleet and wary Springbuck upon the great plains on which it loves to feed and disport itself. **1900** W.L. SCLATER *Mammals of S. Afr.* I. 212 Springbucks are always found on the open dry plain so characteristic of the central and western parts of the Colony. **1926** P. SMITH *Beadle* (1929) 63 Jumping from tables and chairs in a series of leaps and bounds terrifying to behold and meant to represent the agility of a spring-buck. *c***1936** *S. & E. Afr. Yr Bk & Guide* 1091 The Springbuck (*a. euchore*; Dutch, *springbok*) ... A most graceful animal and the only gazelle found in South Africa. **1973** *E. Prov. Herald* 26 Sept. 4 The bag limits will be: Blesbuck two, rooirhebuck three, kudu two and springbuck four. **1974** [see E. Prov. Herald quot. at FARM *v.*].

springer /ˈsprɪŋə/ *n.* Pl. unchanged, or **-s**. [S. Afr. Du., fr. Du. *springer* leaper, fr. *springen* to leap.]

1. *obs.* In full ***springer antelope***: SPRINGBOK sense 1 a.

1781 T. PENNANT *Hist. of Quadrupeds* I. 82 The Springer Antelope .. weighs about 50 pounds, and is rather lesser than a roebuck. **1785** G. FORSTER tr. *A. Sparrman's Voy. to Cape of G.H.* II. 285 This tract of country .. harboured a considerable number of *springers, quaggas*, and *hartbeests*. **1829** E. GRIFFITH tr. *Cuvier* IV. 208 The Springer Antelope .. is the largest of a small subordinate group ... The Springer resembles the Dorcas of nomenclators, but is nearly a third larger in size.

2. Any of several species of marine fish noted for their ability to leap out of the water (but particularly *Elops machnata*). **a.** *Elops machnata* of the Elopidae; CAPE SALMON sense 2; SKIPJACK sense 1. **b.** HARDER. **c.** The sandfish *Gonorhynchus gonorhynchus* of the Gonorhynchidae.

In Smith and Heemstra's *Smiths' Sea Fishes* (1986), the name 'ladyfish' is used for *E. machnata*, and 'beaked sandfish' for *G. gonorhynchus*.

1786 G. FORSTER tr. *A. Sparrman's Voy. to Cape of G.H.* II. 285 In some of the rivers .. there is not a fish to be seen; and in others only a few *bastard springers*, as they are called, (*cyprinus gonorynchus*), which are scarcely as big as a common herring. **1797** LADY A. BARNARD in A.C. Partridge *Lives, Lett. & Diaries* (1971) 24 The lake is famous for a fish called the springer, the very best fish I ever tasted in all my life, the most delicate and the fattest. **1804** R. PERCIVAL *Acct of Cape of G.H.* 44 The springer, a flat fish, of a heavy, fat, luscious quality, particularly well adapted for the palate of a Dutchman. **1823** [see KARPER]. **1827** T. PHILIPPS *Scenes & Occurrences* 49 The fish caught here are principally of the mullet species ... The best is the springer so called from his frequently springing many yards out of the water. **1838** J.E. ALEXANDER *Exped. into Int.* I. 116 So much wild fowl at the mouth of the Orange, plenty of excellent fish; as 'springer' and 'harder,' for the seine. **1860** A.W. DRAYSON *Sporting Scenes* 303 There is a fish called a 'springer' that makes tremendous leaps out of the water after insects, and would give capital sport. **1887** *S.W. Silver & Co.'s Handbk to S. Afr.* 185 *Mugil multilineatus, Springer*, A species of mullet found in the bays and rivers of the colony. Good table fish. Commonly salted or smoked for exportation. **1913** W.C. SCULLY *Further Reminisc.* 245 To me the most enjoyable sport was that obtained at night by following the shoals of 'springers' in a boat with a lighted lantern hung over the prow. **1937** C. BIRKBY *Zulu Journey* 149 Their nickname is 'springer,' of course; and they do spring too. You don't need a rod at St Lucia when the mullet come in — in a day 30 or 40 are liable to leap right into your boat. **1953** R. CAMPBELL *Mamba's Precipice* 73 'Look, it's a springer,' cried Michael, as a beautiful white fish leapt from the water flinging the trace and the sinker and the hook away with a great jerk of his head as it somersaulted back, free, into the water. **1969** J.R. GRINDLEY *Riches of Sea* 81 Mullet or springer (mugil tricuspidens) one of the several species of mugil which are common in estuaries. **1977** *E. Prov. Herald* 13 Oct. 15 In our boyhood my brothers and I caught dozens of big springers (mullet) in the Gamtoos River by getting them to jump into a boat. **1982** *Grocott's Mail* 27 July 10 A freshwater springer — Trachystoma Euronotus — caught by local angler Errol Hall. **1985** *S. Afr. Panorama* July 31 These lakes are the typical habitat of large mullet, or springer, which is a fine eating fish and traditionally sought after by local residents.

3. SPRINKAAN sense 1.

1934 *Star* 12 Feb. (Swart), As the farm on which the springers have made their appearance is untenanted, the full extent of the hatchings is not yet known.

springhaan var. SPRINKAAN.

springhaas /ˈsprəŋhɑːs/ *n.* Pl. unchanged, **-hase** /-hɑːsə/, or (formerly) **-hasen**. [S. Afr. Du., fr. Du. *spring* jump(ing) + *haas* hare.] The large nocturnal rodent *Pedetes capensis*, the sole species of the Pedetidae, with long hind legs which make possible its kangaroo-like bounds; *berghaas*, see BERG sense 1 b ii; SPRINGHARE. Also *attrib.*

1786 G. FORSTER tr. *A. Sparrman's Voy. to Cape of G.H.* II. 194 By the colonists it is called *berg-haas*, or *spring-haas*, (the mountain or bounding hare) and lives upon roots and other vegetables. **1796** [see *berghaas* (BERG sense 1 b ii)]. **1822** [see SPRINGHARE]. **1834** T. PRINGLE *Afr. Sketches* 277 The *spring-haas*, leaping-hare, or Cape jerboa .. an animal which .. burrows in the earth. **1837** J.E. ALEXANDER *Narr. of Voy.* I. 347 One of the party shot a *spring-haas*, or jumping hare, formed like the kangaroo with very short fore-legs and long hind ones. **1861** P.B. BORCHERDS *Auto-Biog. Mem.* 64 The spring haas or jerboa basked and showed its white breast in the moonlight nights. **1890** A. MARTIN *Home Life* 225 Most uncanny of all the hares is the *springhaas*. This creature, with disproportionately long hind-legs and kangaroo-like mode of progression, is never seen in the day-time, and can only be shot on moonlight nights. **1901** W.L. SCLATER *Mammals of S. Afr.* II. 83 The springhaas is found both in the plains and in mountainous country ... It progresses, when pressed, by great bounds in similar fashion to a kangaroo. **1906** W.S. JOHNSON *Orangia* 16 The springhaas, which jumps like a kangaroo, but is really one of the rat tribe, with bushy tail and pleasant face. **1911** *Farmer's Weekly* 4 Oct. 120, I have done a great deal of springhaas shooting with gun and bull's-eye lantern. **1911** *Ibid.* 11 Oct. 161 Can you tell me the easiest way for [*sic*] getting rid of birds, field rats and springhaas, destroying crops, by poisoning or otherwise? **1954** P. ABRAHAMS *Tell Freedom* 226 Sometimes we set traps for *Springhaas*. **1990** SKINNER & SMITHERS *Mammals of Sn Afr. Subregion* 200 Springhaas are neither related ancestrally nor collaterally to other rodents and .. their pre-Miocene history is a mystery ... The name *springhaas* was first applied by the early Dutch settlers and has been translated into English as springhare which is unfortunate as hares belong to another family, the Leporidae.

springhare /ˈsprɪŋhɛə/ *n.* Pl. **-s**; occas. unchanged. [Calque formed on S. Afr. Du. (later Afk.) *springhaas*.] SPRINGHAAS. Also *attrib.*

1822 W.J. BURCHELL *Trav.* I. 343 Besides the holes of the aardvark, those of the Springhaas (Springhare), .. were very frequent. **1889** F. GALTON *Trav. in S. Afr.* 172 A pleasant moonlight evening was spent on much smaller game — the spring hare as the Dutch call it. It is a creature about two feet long, shaped like a kangaroo in body and tail, but very different head; it burrows and lives in a hole all day, but at night frisks about and grazes. **1899** *Std & Diggers' News* 16 Sept. 4 A farmer, near Riverton, was out springhare shooting on Wednesday night, with a friend. **1911** *Farmer's Weekly* 4 Oct. 120 The spring hare always jump sideways towards the light with the result that only one eye is visible. **1920** R.Y. STORMBERG *Mrs Pieter de Bruyn* 71 Springhares are causing some trouble. They break into the garden and lands at night and cause ruinous havoc. **1923** *S. Afr: Land of Outdoor Life* (S.A.R. & H.) 268 Springhares are numerous, but as they are nocturnal animals it is only possible to shoot them at night time with the aid of an ordinary bull's-eye lantern or acetylene lamp. **1926** L.D. FLEMMING

Fun on Veld (1928) 251 A 'spring hare' is a small hopping animal not unlike a miniature kangaroo, which does a lot of damage to crops. *c*1936 [see BLES-MOLE]. **1940** V. POHL *Bushveld Adventures* 34 Scores of spring hares, at the mercy of natives and dogs, scampered from their burrows as the water overflowed the river banks till a vast sea was formed on either side of the main stream. **1951** A. ROBERTS *Mammals* 349 Spring Hares .. are rodents belonging to an ancient group, distantly related to the Cave Rats on the one hand and the Dassie Rats on the other. **1964** N. GORDIMER in C. Millar *16 Stories* 83 Small glowing points jumped about; it looked as if .. someone was throwing cigarette butts away in the dark ... They were the eyes of spring-hares, who had a big warren just there. **1990** C. LAFFEATY *Far Forbidden Plains* 145 Monotony sometimes relieved by a springhare leaping in the air in front of their path as it dashed to safety. **1991** K. URQUHART in *Weekend Post* 16 Mar. (Leisure) 1 If luck was on their side they would see about 20 different nocturnal animals .. including bushpig, Cape and spring hares, porcupine, antbear, [etc.].

‖**sprinkaan** /ˈsprəŋkɑːn/ *n.* Also **springhaan**, **springkaan**. Pl. **springkane** /ˈsprəŋkɑnə/, and (formerly) **springhaane**. [Afk., fr. Du. *sprinkhaan*, *sprink* jump, leap + (obs.) *haan* singing creature.]

1. A locust; SPRINGER sense 3. See also VOETGANGER sense 1.

[**1835** A. STEEDMAN *Wanderings* I. 125 An immense swarm of young locusts, covering the ground .. sprang with great agility, deriving from this circumstance the Dutch name of Spring-kaan.] **1872** in A.M.L. Robinson *Sel. Articles from Cape Monthly Mag.* (1978) 282 We shall lend a hand to drive out the 'springhaane', but we shall resign ourselves to the irrepressible 'voetgangers'. **1913** C. PETTMAN *Africanderisms* 469 *Springhaan*, .. A common name in South Africa for all varieties of *Locustidae*. **1958** *Pietersburg Eng. Medium School Mag.* Dec. 32 No doubt the 'scourge of Tanganyika' – the agile sprinkaan [*printed* sprikaan] - .. will soon be in rapid retreat. **1982** *Sunday Times* 21 Mar. 44 The Boers always said that the British would have to shoot three bullets for every one they shot, but when the English came they left like springkane (locusts).

2. *comb.* **sprinkaanbos** /-bɔs/ *n.* [Afk., *bos* bush], either of two poisonous plants of the Asteraceae, *Senecio burchellii* or *S. ilicifolius*; **sprinkaan Senecio**, *Senecio ilicifolius* (see prec.); **sprinkaanvoël** /-ˌfuəl/, formerly also **springhaan vogel**, [Afk. *voël*, Du. *vogel* bird], LOCUST-BIRD.

1934 C.P. SWART Supplement to Pettman. 165 **Sprinkaanbos**, .. The popular name of a Senecio plant that is often the cause of bread-poisoning. **1934** *Farming in S. Afr.* Feb. 46 (Swart), Every mill in which grain is milled for human consumption shall be provided with efficient sieving and winnowing appliances, so as completely to remove the seeds of Senecio (Sprinkaanbos). **1957** *Handbk for Farmers* (Dept of Agric.) III. 464 Certain poisonous plants, such as 'sprinkaanbos', cause severe constipation and loss of appetite, and so may indirectly cause domsiekte. **1974** M.R. LEVYNS in *Std Encycl. of Sn Afr.* X. 235 *Sprinkaanbos*. (*Senecio ilicifolius; S. burchellii.*) In the Riversdale district the same name is given to both these species of the family *Compositae*. **1988** J. MUNDAY *Poisonous Plants in S. Afr. Gardens & Parks* 37 Humans have been poisoned in this country by ingesting the indigenous species, S. burchellii and S. ilicifolius (both known as 'Sprinkaanbos'). **1966** HENDERSON & ANDERSON *Common Weeds* 392 *Senecio ilicifolius L*, .. **Sprinkaan Senecio** ... An indigenous species that was proclaimed a noxious weed because of the poisonous properties that it imparts to flour made from wheat containing parts of the *Senecio* plant as an impurity. **1824** *S. Afr. Jrnl* I. 71 We have not got a good description of the South African **springhaan vogel**, further than that it is rather larger than the mountain swallow, and spotted. **1828** T. PRINGLE *Ephemerides* 177 If they [*sc.* locusts] happen to be accompanied, or rather pursued, by the birds, called by the African farmer *springhaan vogels*, .. the prospect is less appalling, since these birds .. subsist on them alone. **1839** W.C. HARRIS *Wild Sports* 81 Prodigious swarms of locusts .. were followed by such dense flights of birds as almost to darken the air. The *springhaan-vogel*, as the latter is called by the colonists, is about the size of a swallow. **1877** R.M. BALLANTYNE *Settler & Savage* 254 Locust-swarms are followed by a little bird – named *springhaan-vogel* or locust-bird – which comes in such dense flocks as almost to darken the air. These locust-birds are about the size of a swallow, with numerous speckles like a starling. **1923** HAAGNER & IVY *Sketches* 10 The *true* Locust Bird, or Klein Springhaan Vogel, is the celebrated Wattled Starling. **1959** L.G. GREEN *These Wonders* 175 Farmers know that the sprinkaanvoel can be relied upon to clear the veld of locusts and other unwelcome insects.

sproot var. SPRUIT.

sprout *n. obs.* [Calqued on Du. *spruit*, see SPRUIT.] SPRUIT sense a.

The *OED* contains one example of this word from *U.S. Eng.* (1794), probably also a result of Dutch influence.

1833 *Graham's Town Jrnl* 12 Sept. 2 The expectations .. of the quiet removal of the Caffer chief T'jalie, from the sprouts of the Mancanzana, have been fully realized. **1842** J. COLLETT Diary. II. 11 Oct., River running sufficient to fill two sp[r]outs. **1852** M.B. HUDSON *S. Afr. Frontier Life* 254 An abundant supply of water from a sprout of the Konap.

sprue var. SPREW.

spruit /spreɪt, sprœɪt, spruːt/ *n.* Also **sproot**. [Du. (later Afk.), 'offshoot'.]

a. A small stream or watercourse, usu. containing little or no water except in the rainy season; SPROUT. Also *attrib.*

1832 *Graham's Town Jrnl* 13 Apr. 62 They were joined by Lieut. Warden and his party .. who had been ordered to come over the back of the mountains and rendezvous at the *spruits* of the Keiskamma. **1843** J.C. CHASE *Cape of G.H.* 149 From this source are fed numerous streams, or spruits, as they are called, which enable the agriculturist, by means of irrigation, to counteract the summer's drought. **1860** J. SANDERSON in *Jrnl of Royal Geog. Soc.* XXX. 236 After crossing three small spruits or streams, the road to Bloemfontein enters a pass on the skirts of the Wittebergen. **1878** H.A. ROCHE *On Trek in Tvl* 71 We have crossed at least twenty-two spruits, wet and dry. **1882** [see *wet erf* (ERF sense b)]. **1899** *Natal Agric. Jrnl* 31 Mar. 3 'Spruit,' meaning in Dutch to issue, and in South African Dutch stream or streamlet, has become a thoroughly accepted word in South African English. **1903** E.F. KNIGHT *S. Afr. after War* 274 Most of the .. crops had been destroyed by the drought, the spruits were dry, and there was no water in the dams of the deserted farms. **1911** L. KNOBLAUCH in *Farmer's Weekly* 18 Oct. 194 There existed across this flat from the mountain, a natural drain or spruit, which carried the drainage from the mountains directly into the River Zonder End stream. **1918** C. GARSTIN *Sunshine Settlers* 205 We splashed across a sproot, that coursed like a dirty gutter. **1923** G.H. NICHOLLS *Bayete!* 157 All your spoors were plainly marked in the spruit bed. **1934** B.I. BUCHANAN *Pioneer Days* 99 The steady rain swelled all streams, so that spruits were converted into rivers, and rivers became torrents. **1942** S. CLOETE *Hill of Doves* 51 The water in the spruit was very low: lower, Stoffel had said yesterday, than he ever remembered it. **1961** T. MACDONALD *Tvl Story* 131 Often, suddenly, you come across a spruit (with water even in winter). **1968** S. CLOETE *Chetoko* 70 A dry spruit ran across the road. **1974** *The 1820* Vol.47 No.2, 25 He noticed the influence American and Australian diggers were having on that corner of Africa – where else in Africa are krantzes, spruits and dongas called anything else except in the Eastern Transvaal where a spruit had become a creek when there was water in it or a gulch when it was dry. **1991** *Best of S. Afr. Short Stories* (Reader's Digest Assoc.) 277 There are many words for watercourses of varying size and flow ... A *spruit* is a tributary feeding a larger stream, and for much of the year usually has a dry bed.

b. An element in place names.

1850 N.J. MERRIMAN *Cape Jrnls* (1957) 135 We found ourselves, just after sundown, at Carl Spruit (a small stream), about ten miles this side of Bloemfontein. **1867** *Blue Bk for Col. 1866* FF19, The Stormberg Spruit and other streams abound in barbel, white, and yellow fish, which are excellent food. **1882** C. DU VAL *With Show through Sn Afr.* I. 255 By the evening we reached a tributary rivulet known as the Sand Spruit – a term usually applied to small watercourses running to river-beds. But 'spruit' as it was, we found about six feet of water in the drift. **1900** W.S. CHURCHILL *London to Ladysmith* 413 The iron bridge across the Onderbrook Spruit had to be crossed. **1903** E.F. KNIGHT *S. Afr. after War* 283 The British position was a strong one, having the steep Selous Spruit on one side of it and a donga on the other. **1949** O. WALKER *Proud Zulu* (1951) 208 From the hidden depression of the unseen Ulundi spruit rose a mass of Sibebu's Mandhlokazi who came on firing raggedly. **1988** O. OBERHOLZER *Ariesfontein to Zuurfontein*, This idea came to me – a pictorial journey from Ariesfontein to Zuurfontein. Sure, I admit, it could have been place names ending in 'spruit' or 'kraal' or 'berg'.

spugslang, **spuig-slang**, **spungh-slange**, **spung-slang** varr. SPUUGSLANG.

spur var. SPOOR *n.*

spure var. SPOOR *v.*

spurrie var. SPORRIE.

spurting snake *n. phr. Obs.* Also **spirting snake**. [tr. S. Afr. Du. *spuugslang*, see SPUUGSLANG.] The RINKHALS (sense 1), *Hemachatus haemachatus.*

1812, **1834** [see SPUUGSLANG].

spuugslang *n. obs.* Also **spoew-slang**, **spoog slang**, **spu(i)gslang**, **spung(h) slange**, **spuugh-slange**, **spuw slang**, etc. [S. Afr. Du., *spuug* (Afk. *spoeg*), fr. Du. *spugen* to spit, + *slang* snake.] The RINKHALS (sense 1), *Hemachatus haemachatus.*

1789 W. PATERSON *Narr. of Four Journeys* 165 The Spoog Slang, or Spitting Snake, has been mentioned to me by the inhabitants of the country, who say it will throw its poison to the distance of several yards. **1812** A. PLUMPTRE tr. *H. Lichtenstein's Trav. in Sn Afr.* (1928) I. 95 A very rare sort of serpent, called here the *spugslang* (the spurting snake) .. is from three to four feet long, of a black colour, and .. when attacked it will spurt out its venom. **1834** T. PRINGLE *Afr. Sketches* 280 Another species of serpent .. is about three feet in length ... Its peculiar property is the faculty it possesses of spouting its venom in the face of an assailant ... From this singular faculty, it is called by the Cape colonists the spuig-slang, or spirting-snake. **1849** A. SMITH *Illust. of Zoo. of S. Afr.: Reptilia* Pl.21, The latter [*sc.* colour variety C] is known throughout the Cape colony by the name of *Spuugh-slang* (spitting snake), and is so called from the power it is supposed to possess of ejecting poison to a distance. [**1883** M.A. CAREY-HOBSON *Farm in Karoo* 145 It was of the kind called by the coloured people, 'Sping Slang' (Spitting Snake), which, when it is angered, raises itself and runs at its enemy; and the natives say that directly it gets the opportunity, it ejects a quantity of poison right into the eye of the being who has irritated it.] **1886** G.A. FARINI *Through Kalahari Desert* 367 While walking ahead of the waggons I saw a fullgrown capell or *spungh slange*, lying under a bank. **1911** *Encycl. Brit.* XXV. 299 It shares with the cobra a third Dutch name, that of 'spuw slang' (spitting snake). **1923** R. KIPLING *Land & Sea Tales* 34 He gave us half-a-crown for a spuugh-slange – a kind of snake. **1931** R.L. DITMARS *Snakes of World* 172 Another name [for the rinkhals] is Spoew-slang, applied from the reptile's 'spitting' its poison.

square-davel see RONDAVEL.

square-face *n. Obs.* exc. *hist.* [See quot. 1880.] Esp. among the diamond prospectors of the 19th century: an imported Dutch gin. Also *attrib.*

1879 FORBES in *Daily News* 13 June 5 That potent fluid that goes by the endearing name of 'Square-face', and that in reality is the rankest of schiedam. 1880 E.F. SANDEMAN *Eight Months in Ox-Waggon* 97 The only gin in use is the Schiedam, sold in square green glass bottles, and generally known as square-face or square-rigger. 1882 C. DU VAL *With Show through Sn Afr.* II. 177 Messiers the Canteen keepers .. were nimbly pocketing the shillings of their defenders in exchange for 'Cape Smoke', 'Natal Rum', and 'square-face'. 1887 A.A. ANDERSON *25 Yrs in Waggon* II. 207 Each member had to undergo fresh baptism in the way of a souse in a large bath .. and pay his footing in the way of a certain quantity of brandy or square face (gin). 1897 J.P. FITZPATRICK *Outspan* 109 They passed the door showing the rough gin-case counter, backed by shelves laded with 'square face'. 1897 [see WINKEL]. 1911 L. COHEN *Reminisc. of Kimberley* 391 Perceiving some 'square face' (gin) on his table, I, much against the medico's learned advice, drank the lot — and recovered. 1924 — *Reminisc. of Jhb.* 28 Of course, there was floating about any amount of cape smoke, square face, dop brandy. 1937 H. KLEIN *Stage Coach Dust* 32 No miner was considered a pukka old-timer until he had a wall of empty 'square-face' gin bottles around his tent. 1955 T.V. BULPIN *Storm over Tvl* 63 There was a good deal of arguing, a certain amount of indulgence in 'creature comforts' — you have all heard of square face gin — and a good deal more arguing. c1963 B.C. TAIT *Durban Story* 58 A popular drink was Dutch gin, at first known as 'Geneva' or 'Hollands', but later as 'Square face', no doubt from the square flasks in which it arrived from Holland packed in red and green cases. 1971 H. ZEEDERBERG *Veld Express* 166 He alleged that the driver .. had fallen asleep .. and that his African assistant had taken advantage of the fact by producing a bottle of 'Squareface', and taking copious draughts from it.

squat *v. intrans.* [Special sense of general Eng. *squat* 'to settle upon new, uncultivated, or unoccupied land without any legal title and without the payment of rent' (*OED*).]
1. Of a black person in a rural area: to live on white-owned land as a labour-tenant or rent-paying tenant.

1936 *Cambridge Hist. of Brit. Empire* VIII. 803 Agricultural labour is of two types, wage-earners paid in cash or partly or wholly in kind, and labour-tenants, giving service for the privilege of 'squatting' with their families.

2. To live in a self-built shack (either as a rent-paying tenant or with no authorization) on land which one does not own or which is in an area in which one does not have a legal right to live.

1986 M. BADELA in *City Press* 20 Apr. 2 Judge Kroon said the families were 'squatting' on white land bordering the Langa township. 1988 F. KHASHANE in *Pace* May 39 While bureaucrats bungle, squatters squat and vandals vandalise, our .. sports stars of the future .. waste their talents in the back yards and wastelands of Soweto.
Hence **squatting** *vbl n.*

1949 E. HELLMANN *Handbk on Race Rel.* 248 The City Council .. declared that it would not have its hand forced by lawlessness, knowing .. that capitulation would be an invitation to organize further squatting. 1990 G. SLOVO *Ties of Blood* 151 He was a squatter and squatting was an offence.

squatter *n.* [Special senses of general Eng. *squatter*]
1. *hist.* A black person living on white-owned farm land; in law, a black man living on such land but not employed by the white farmer. Also *attrib.* Cf. BYWONER.

In many cases the black communities considered to be 'squatters' were the earliest inhabitants of the land in question.

1936 *Act 18 in Stat. of Union* 120 There shall be paid by the owner in respect of each squatter to the native commissioner a licence fee. *Ibid.* 140 'Squatter' means, in relation to land .. , a native male .. residing thereon, if such native is neither a servant nor a labour tenant as herein defined. 1949 O. WALKER *Proud Zulu* (1951) 95 The squatters on the farms taken up by the Boers were chary about giving their labour, and still more chary about paying taxes. 1980 *Rand Daily Mail* 24 Nov. 13 The helplessness of black farm workers is crowned by official policy .. : the moment a farmhand becomes 'unproductive' he is defined as a 'squatter' liable to removal to a 'homeland'. 1983 D. BOUTALL in *E. Prov. Herald* 28 Apr. 1 Trying to solve the squatter problem in the rural areas .. was like trying to sweep up leaves on a windy day, the council's chief engineer .. said yesterday.

2.a. A (black) person living in a shack settlement which occupies an area (usu. in or near a town) which is either not officially proclaimed as a residential area or (*hist.*) is set aside for the use of a racial group to which the person does not belong. **b.** A (black) person who occupies a self-built shack on land owned by somebody else (sometimes paying rent). Also *attrib.* Cf. stand-owner (see STAND sense 2).

1949 E. HELLMANN *Handbk on Race Rel.* 248 An area of land four miles from Orlando at Jabavu, where the squatters were permitted to put up temporary shelters. 1954 *Bantu World* 15 May 1 The squatters had been throwing dirt into the spaces between the closely packed shanties. 1982 *Cape Times* 29 Jan. 2 A group of Nyanga squatters will appear in .. Court today charged with being in the Cape Town area for more than 72 hours without a permit. 1985 PLATZKY & WALKER *Surplus People* p.xiv, Squatters, The official use of the term is far broader .. and it may be used to describe any black person whose presence on a particular piece of land is not approved of by the authorities, regardless of the nature of the agreement between the occupant and the landowner. It has been used to describe people living on white-owned land, on black-owned land, both within and without the bantustans, on tribal land and on state land. 1987 *Weekly Mail* 12 June 15 The Crossroads complex, a focal point of squatter resistance to the state, no longer exists. 1990 M. KENTRIDGE *Unofficial War* 84 Trust Feed is a township occupied in freehold by about fifty landowning families who let their land to tenants and squatters.

3. *comb.* **squatter camp**, also **squatters' camp**, a shanty town of self-built dwellings; cf. SHACKLAND.

1954 *Bantu World* 15 May 1, I visited the ruins of the Vierfontein squatters' camp which had been burned down by the police in a dawn raid. 1970 J.H. COETZEE in *Std Encycl. of Sn Afr.* II. 141 Attention was also given to .. residential segregation. That objective was realised in part by providing more and better housing .. and by demolishing squatters' camps and slums. 1985 *S. Afr. Panorama* Apr. 1 Khayelitsha is a Xhosa word meaning 'new home'. It is the new home for the inhabitants of the Crossroads squatter camp. 1992 G. EVANS in *Weekly Mail* 16 Apr. 2 Winnie may remain popular in squatter camps and other communities faced with repression.

SRC *n.* [Initial letters of *Students' Representative Council.*] The elected committee representing students at universities, colleges, and some schools. Also *attrib.*

1921 *Cathartic* (Univ. of Cape Town) Sept. 4 We believe that the recent protest on the part of the S.R.C. to the Maatie University .. has caused considerable criticism in 'Varsity circles. 1970 *Cape Times* 5 June, The University of Cape Town SRC unanimously decided to bring the UCT inter-varsity cheer-leader .. before a disciplinary committee of the SRC. 1981 *Rand Daily Mail* 30 June 4 The SRC used the only available constitutional means — refusing to accept Mr C—'s apologies for missing two SRC meetings — to expel him. 1984 *Daily Dispatch* 10 Oct. 1 Until now, the government has refused to accept the institution of SRCs at secondary schools. 1987 [see KLOPJAG]. 1988 *Weekend Argus* 19 Mar. 12 Matie SRC chairman, Mr Francois Beukman, said the move to open all residences was a positive step forward. 1990 J. ROSENTHAL *Wake Up Singing* 65 It is clear that the Security Police know who is on the SRC and that they are looking for all of them. 1994 M. HUMPHREYS *Informant, Grahamstown* As I am sure you are aware, the SRC has adopted along with its principles of non-racism, non-sexism and democracy, the principle of non-homophobia.

's'strue's Bob var. (*as*) *true as Bob* (see TRUE sense b).

staad var. STAT.

staaldruppels see DRUPPELS sense b ii.

staart-riem var. STERTRIEM.

staat var. STAT.

‖**Staatsamptenaar** /ˈstɑːtsˌam(p)tənɑː(r)/ *n.* Also with small initial. Pl. **-amptenare** /-ˌam(p)tənɑːrə/. [Afk., *staats* combining form of *staat* state, government + *amptenaar* official.] A civil servant; a government official. Usu. used ironically, drawing attention to the predominance of Afrikaans-speakers in the civil service.

1971 *Cape Times* 3 July 10 There was an assemblage of Staatsamptenare to take statements, but on surveying the damage to the car, there was a sense of relief that the taxpayer is so rich. 1975 *Daily Dispatch* 31 May 6 The title Staatsamptenaar has taken on a new dimension. It was always a grand-sounding title, of course. 1990 M. VENABLES in *Weekly Mail* 5 Oct. (Weekend Mail) 5 Oct. 15 Having exhausted the Roomsegevaar, Rooigevaar, Swartgevaar and even Moffiegevaar, two earnest staatsamptenare .. work themselves into a near-orgasmic frenzy, dreaming up bloodcurdling descriptions of mass orgies.

staats huis var. STADTHUIS.

stad var. STAT.

stad-house, **stadhuis** varr. STADT-HOUSE, STADTHUIS.

stadsjapie /ˈstatsjɑːpi/ *n. colloq.* [Afk., *stads*-combining form of *stad* city + *japie* see JAPIE (formed by analogy with PLAASJAPIE).] A city-dweller; one ignorant of country ways. Cf. PLAASJAPIE.

1970 A. PALMER *Informant, King William's Town* Stadsjapies know nothing about the country. 1980 C. MARAIS *Rand Daily Mail* 7 Oct. 5 'Why do you stadsjapies (city boys) come out here at this time of year?' Tant Mart queried from under her Voortrekker sunbonnet. 1988 D. HUGHES et al. *Complete Bk of S. Afr. Wine* 61 This is not a world which is often seen or penetrated by the *stadsjapies*, the city folk who flock to the winelands in the golden height of summer.

stadt var. STAT.

stadt-house *n. obs.* Also **stad-house**, and with initial capital. [Part. tr. S. Afr. Du. *stadhuis*, see STADTHUIS.] A town hall or city hall; particularly, the Old Town House in Cape Town, formerly the seat of the Burgher Senate; STADTHUIS.

Used also in other Dutch colonies.

1731 G. MEDLEY tr. *P. Kolb's Present State of Cape of G.H.* II. 41 The next Day the *Ceylonian* brought the dead Lion in a Cart to the Guild- or Stadt-house of Stellenbosch. 1795 in G.M. Theal *Rec. of Cape Col.* (1897) I. 249 The Stadt House was allotted to the guard, each captain in his turn for two months attending to the mounting of guard. 1804 R. PERCIVAL *Acct of Cape of G.H.* 110 The high court of Justice is held in the Stadthouse, and the burghers also assemble there to consider questions relative to the regulation of the town. 1805 R. SEMPLE *Walks & Sketches* 17 The Stadthouse is a clumsy building of red stone, in the market square, about the centre of the town. Here the burghers of the Cape assemble on particular occasions, though it be now but seldom used. 1823 W.W. BIRD *State of Cape of G.H.* 159 In case of fire, even of a chimney, the bell of the stad-house and all the church bells are tolled.

stadthuis *n. obs.* Also **staats huis, stadhuis, stadt-huis,** and with initial capital. [S. Afr. Du. (fr. Du.) *stadhuis*.] STADT-HOUSE.

1822 W.J. BURCHELL *Trav.* I. 73 The Stadhuis, or Burgher Senate-house, is a large, handsome building, appropriated to the transacting of public business of a civic nature. It stands in the middle of the town, on one side of the square called Groente Plein, in which a daily market for vegetables is held. 1841 B. SHAW *Memorials* 14 The public buildings of this metropolis are the castle, barracks, stadt-huis, custom house, commercial exchange, town jail, and the colonial offices. 1851 H. WARD *Cape & Kaffirs* 3 The public edifices [of Cape Town] numerous and substantial, including the Government House, the Stadthuis, or Municipality, several handsome churches, an exchange, and an observatory. 1882 C. DU VAL *With Show through Sn Afr.* I. 137 Righteous wrath at the temerity exhibited by any outsider in venturing to question the excellence of the arrangements of the 'Staats Huis', or town hall. 1883 M.A. CAREY-HOBSON *Farm in Karoo* 274 The Dutch Church is the finest as well as the oldest public building in the place, unless, it may be, the Drosdtdy, or 'Stadt-huis.'

staff *adv. slang.* [See STAFFRIDER.] In urban (esp. township) Eng., in the v. phr. *to ride staff,* or (occas.) *to play staff:* to ride without paying on a train (or bus), often clinging to the sides, or riding on the roof; STAFFRIDE. See also STAFFRIDER, WASHING.

1978 *Staffrider* Vol.1 No.1 Editorial, A staffrider is, let's face it, a skelm of sorts ... He is part of the present phase of our common history, riding 'staff' on the fast and dangerous trains. 1979 in *Ibid.* Vol.2 No.1, 45 At sunrise he rode staff on buses. In summer he braved rains and thunderstorms. 1980 *Voice* 20 Aug. 2 Neither shall a staff rider ride staff on the top of the white section of the train. 1980 M. KIRKWOOD in *Eng. in Afr.* Vol.7 No.2, 23 A staffrider is somebody who rides 'staff' on the fast and dangerous trains that come in from the townships to the city, hanging on to the sides of the coaches, climbing on the roof, harassing the passengers. A mobile disreputable bearer of tidings. 1982 *Pace* Apr. 72 There are those who will go one up, 'ride staff' then go on to climb on top of the moving train and do dangerous balancing acts on top of the coach as the train hurtles at speeds of up to 90km per hour. 1985 J. MAKUNGA in *Staffrider* Vol.6 No.2, 35 He knew that Vuyo didn't have one [sc. a ticket] and rode the trains from Randfontein to Springs 'staff' with disgusting effrontery. 1988 M. KIRKWOOD in *Ten Yrs of Staffrider* 1 The A[utomobile] A[ssociation] has its offices there now, and probably even lists among its members some of those who ten years ago were 'riding staff'. 1989 *Weekly Mail* 13 Oct. 9 They thought I was playing staff, and wanted to arrest me, but later one of them understood.

staffride *v. intrans. Slang.* [See STAFFRIDER.] *to ride staff,* see STAFF.

[1962 W.S. MANQUPU in *Star* 22 Feb. 14 [In the argot of the townships] 'staff' means to board a train in motion.] 1979 *Daily Dispatch* 10 Feb. 6 For many it is a way of life .. to staffride between Soweto and Johannesburg. For too many the bravado ends in death.

staffrider *n. slang.* [Prob. referring to the pole (or 'staff') in the doorway of a railway carriage, to which those who board a train at the last minute must cling if (as often) there is insufficient room in the carriage for them to go inside; see also quot. 1962 at STAFFRIDE.]
1. Esp. in township Eng.: one who rides (a suburban train) without paying, often hanging onto the outside of a coach or riding on the roof. See also STAFF.

1977 P.C. VENTER *Soweto* 81 Clinging to the side of a fast train is dangerous — but not dangerous enough for some of the 'staff riders'. There are those who prefer to travel on the roof of a train ... The mortality rate of so-called staff riders is high. 1979 *Sunday Times* 28 Oct. 21 Trains rumble into stations, stuffed with humanity, freeloaders on the running boards and staffriders on the roofs. The staffriders don't always make it — some are electrocuted on overhead wires. 1980 B. SETUKE in M. Mutloatse *Forced Landing* 59 The 'staffriders' .. jump into the train while it is still in motion to secure themselves a place before anybody else ever sets his foot on the train. *Ibid.* 64 The only people other than the train-gang who have free passage between one coach and the next, are the smouses ... These smouses are indeed the most breath-taking 'staffriders' of them all. 1982 *Pace* Apr. 72 It may be fun. But some staffriders have died horrific deaths. Ask any Soweto train commuter ... Stories abound of staffriders who have been electrocuted whilst they did their balancing act on top of the moving train coaches. 1989 in *Weekly Mail* 13 Oct. 9 'I am not a staffrider, but I became one that night' ... Kukeba later struggled to convince the policemen at the station that he was escaping from thugs.
2. *fig.* A 'chancer'; a daredevil.

1980 N. MONTANA in *Staffrider* Vol.3 No.1, 14 He sheds a handful of lovers. He finds them to be either superficial or immature. 'Parasites and staff-riders!' he thinks aloud. 1980 M. KIRKWOOD in *Eng. in Afr.* Vol.7 No.2, 23 A suitable title for the magazine ... Somebody .. had suggested the word 'staffrider' ... It incorporated the notion of a daredevil, somebody who would go a little bit further than most.

staffriding *vbl n. Slang.* [See STAFFRIDER.] Esp. in township Eng.: the action of clinging to the outside of a suburban train (or bus) in order to obtain a free ride. Cf. STAFF.

1980 B. SETUKE in M. Mutloatse *Forced Landing* 64 They thought this [sc. introducing sliding doors] would reduce the number of train deaths caused by 'staffriding'. 1984 M. MTHETHWA in *Frontline* July 28 A knee-high lad executes acrobatic tricks in the dangerous art of staff-riding.

stamfrucht var. STAMVRUG.

stamp /stæmp/ *n. noncount.* [Ellipt. for Afk. *stampmielies,* stamp crush(ed) + *mielies* maize; or fr. STAMP v.] In full **stamp mielies** /-miːliːz, 'stamp milis/, also occas. **-mealies** [see MEALIE]: SAMP.

1923 *S. Afr. Pioneer* Dec. 143 All partook freely of the feast of meat and stamp. 1952 L.G. GREEN *Lords of Last Frontier* 79 We now live well and keep strong on stamp mealies from Oorlog's place. 1973 D.A.C. MACLENNAN in *Bolt* No.7, 6 They have, between them, two saucepans, some jam tins and a few small cloth bags of food, stamp-mielies, coffee and sugar. 1976 J. MCCLURE *Rogue Eagle* 112 The price of mealie *stamp* in Maseru. 1977 *E. Prov. Herald* 18 Nov. 10 The Xhosas on the farms .. kept their milk in calabashes and left it to sour. This was a staple diet for the family together with their stamp mielies and beans. 1987 G. DAVIS in *Weekly Mail* 5 June 3 The family's staple diet was 'sweet water, bread and stamp mielies'. 1991 D. QOLOZA in *Weekly Mail* 12 Mar. 8 Tonight we'll go and make a camp in the bush and then we'll go and look for bread, rice, porridge and stamp mielies that people throw into their rubbish bins.

stamp *v. trans. Obs.* [Afk.; also formerly found in Brit. Eng. in this sense, but obs. since 1764, according to the *OED*.] To pound or crush (maize kernels).

1883 O.E.A. SCHREINER *Story of Afr. Farm* 19 Two, who stamped mealies in a wooden block, held the great stampers in their hands. 1910 [see STAMPED MEALIES]. c1937 *Our Land* (United Tobacco Co.) 27 'Stamping Mealies.' This primitive method of crushing mealies is still practised in the native kraals throughout South Africa. [1948 O. WALKER *Kaffirs Are Lively* 79 More often than not it is the sound of women 'stomping' the mealies — that is, crushing them into a powder with big pestles in hollowed tree-trunks.]
So **stamped** *ppl adj.* (see also STAMPED MEALIES); **stamping** *vbl n.*

1795 C.R. HOPSON tr. *C.P. Thunberg's Trav.* IV. 85 Before the husk can be separated from the pure grain, a second threshing, or stamping is necessary. 1852 T. SHONE *Diary.* 27 Sept., For dinner we have a small Bit of dry'd pork fried With some stampt corn And pompkin. 1948 E. HELLMANN *Rooiyard* 10 The purchase of ready-prepared mealie meal and ready-stamped mealies.

stampblock *n.* [Calqued on Afk. *stampblok,* see next.] A wooden mortar (usu. made of a hollowed-out tree-trunk), in which grain is crushed with a wooden pestle; STAMPBLOK.

1864 T. SHONE *Diary.* 19 May, Henry made a stamp block for India corn. 1883 O.E.A. SCHREINER *Story of Afr. Farm* 21 The new-comer fixed his eyes pensively on the stamp-block. 1913 C. PETTMAN *Africanderisms* 472 *Stampblock,* The wooden mortar in which grain stamping is done. 1923 W.C. SCULLY *Daniel Vananda* 107 Vardy .. sat down on a mealie-stampblock which lay prone close to the mat. [1949 L. HUNTER *Afr. Dawn* 6 Fowls .. pecked at the grains of mealies falling from the stamping block.] 1956 F.G. BUTLER *Dove Returns* 79 Visit us, and you'll find gold pumpkins stacked Along the outhouse wall, and a stamp-block for mealies Near the kitchen door. 1958 S. CLOETE *Mask* 239 Caught between the two like mealies in a stamp block, we will make an end. 1965 A. GORDON-BROWN *S. Afr. Heritage* I. 31 In the kitchen ... were .. a stamp-block for crushing mealies, a mortar for grinding coffee. 1968 K. MCMAGH *Dinner of Herbs* 106 Father managed to lay hands on a 'stamp-block', the genuine egg-cup-shaped hollowed-out tree-trunk mortar with the wooden pestle used by the natives to pound their grain.

‖**stampblok** /'stampblɔk/ *n.* Pl. **-blokke** /-blɔkə/. Also with initial capital. [Afk., *stamp* pound, crush + *blok* block.] STAMPBLOCK.

1966 C.A. SMITH *Common Names* 342 Natives use the wood for 'Stampblokke' in which they pound grain and it seldom cracks. 1970 A.J. DU PREEZ *Informant, Misgund* (W. Cape) Stampblok. A round block of wood approx 30" × 10", hollowed out at the top, used for crushing mealies. 1971 BARAITSER & OBHOLZER *Cape Country Furn.* 261 A more primitive method of milling grain was by crushing the grain in a Stampblok, a large wooden mortar with a pestle that looks very similar to the more recent Transvaal African ones, but can often be distinguished from them by the presence of a metal hoop around the upper rim.

stamped mealies *n. phr.* Also **stampt melies.** [tr. Afk. *stampmielies,* see STAMP *n.*] SAMP.

1853 R.B. STRUTHERS *Hunting Jrnl* (1991) 33 Got a dinner of hippopotamus, Buck, Ducks & Geese, Izinthulu & stamped mealies being our only vegetables. 1858 T. SHONE *Diary.* 20 May, Breakfast: stampt melies. 1890 A. MARTIN *Home Life* 228 The crop which best pays cultivation in that arid soil is Indian corn ... The nicest way of preparing it is in the form called 'stamped mealies'. 1894 E. GLANVILLE *Fair Colonist* 217 They breakfasted off the remaining ostrich egg, stamped mealies boiled in milk, coffee, and the sweetest of brown bread. 1910 A.B. LAMONT *Rural Reader* 189 'Stamped mealies' — that is, mealies from which the outer husk has been removed — are made by stamping the grain with a heavy wooden stick in a large bowl. 1937 C.R. PRANCE *Tante Rebella's Saga* 82 Oom Fanie and his family had just asked a blessing on their supper of pumpkin and stamped mealies. 1949 L. HUNTER *Afr. Dawn* 102 She bustled about preparing the evening meal, but she was sorry that she had only stamped mealies and beans to offer her son and their guest. 1966 I. VAUGHAN *These Were my Yesterdays* 49, I eat mostly stamped mealies and grilled chops. 1980 E. JOUBERT *Poppie Nongena* 190 He ate the food she placed in front of him, the steam rising from the stamped mealies and dried beans.

stampkoring /ˈstampˌkʊərəŋ, ˈstæmp-/ *n. noncount.* [Afk., *stamp* crush(ed) + *koring* wheat, corn.]

1. Crushed wheat.

1972 L.G. GREEN *When Journey's Over* 70 He described a special corn, the *langkoring* (also known as *stampkoring*) that is pounded with a wooden stamp, then boiled and served with milk and sugar.

2. Whole wheat kernels, used as a substitute for rice. Also *attrib.*

1979 HEARD & FAULL *Our Best Trad. Recipes* 75 Stampkoring has always been an important food in Southern Africa; the whole wheat kernels have been used for sweet puddings and boiled as an accompaniment to putu for generations. **1984** *Sunday Times* 4 Mar. (Lifestyle) 9 Stampkoring Salad. Also known as 'weetrice', this is a nutty grain ... If not steamed, it can be stodgy. **1986** M. VAN BILJON in *Style* Apr. 112, I have a particular fondness for the tomato bredie served with *stampkoring*.

‖**stamvader** /ˈstamfɑːdə(r)/ *n.* [Afk., *stam* clan, tribe (lit. 'stem') + *vader* father.] The founder or progenitor of a family; the first member of a particular family to have arrived in South Africa.

1957 L.G. GREEN *Beyond City Lights* 43 Charles Marais, first owner of the farm and *stamvader* of the large Marais family, was stoned to death by the Hottentots. **1971** BARAITSER & OBHOLZER *Cape Country Furn.* 145 He was a grandson of the 'stamvader', Johann Nikolaus Stassen. **1973** M. BRITZ *Informant, Grahamstown* Our particular stamvader was Dr. John Murray who founded the theological seminary in Stellenbosch. **1990** W. STEENKAMP in *Frontline* Dec. 19, I do not yield one inch of my African-ness to, say, a Xhosa, whose people marched southwards some while before my senior white stamvader presented his copper wire to buy cattle from my Khoi ancestors.

stamvrug /ˈstamfrəx, -frœx/ *n.* Also **stamfrucht, stam-vruchte, stamvrugte.** [Afk., fr. Du. *stam* stem + *vrucht* fruit (pl. *vruchte*); see quot. 1913.] The wild plum tree *Bequaertiodendron magalismontanum* of the Sapotaceae, which bears its fruit on its stem; the fruit of this tree; also called *wild plum* (sense (c) see WILD sense a). Also *attrib.*

1887 *S.W. Silver & Co.'s Handbk to S. Afr.* 140 The Wild Kastanie, or Wild Chestnut, is the fruit of the *Calodendron Capense*; the Wild Medlar is that of *Vangueria infausta*; the Stamfrucht appears to be the same. **1913** C. PETTMAN *Africanderisms* 473 *Stam-vruchte*, .. The fruit of *Chrysophyllum magalis-montanum, Sond.*; an edible berry common on the kopjes around Johannesburg, Pretoria, Barberton, etc. so called because its flowers and fruits are borne on very short stalks on the thick stem of the shrub, and not at the ends of the twigs. It has a pleasantly acid flavour. **1929** J. STEVENSON-HAMILTON *Low-Veld* 47 Umnumbela (*Chrysophyllum megalismontanum*), the stamvrugte of the Boers, sometimes grows into a large tree with predicellate flowers: large berries, which make excellent vinegar, grow on the stem. *a***1936** E.N. MARAIS *Rd to Waterberg* (1972) 89 There is the wild fig, the wild grape, the *stamvrug* (wild plum), [etc.]. **1958** R.E. LIGHTON *Out of Strong* 239 Glossy green and more golden beneath than the calendula, the stamvrugte leaves were shrivelled and dead. **1961** PALMER & PITMAN *Trees of S. Afr.* 140 The stamvrug, which bears one of the best of our native fruits, is widely distributed from tropical Africa to Natal. **1977** *S. Afr. Panorama* Apr. 48 The gnarled old silver-green and copper leafed stamvrug trees — Beqaertiodendron magalismontanum — which twisted up out of cracks in nature's much-sculpted rocks had cherry-red fruit on the stems. **1987** F. VAN BREITENBACK in *Conserva* June 11 Some of the most common and decorative bushveld trees are stubbornly refusing artificial propagation — such as .. Transvaal milkplum or 'stamvrug' (*Bequaertiodendron magalismontanum*). **1991** *Ornamental Trees & Shrubs of Afr. Calendar, Bequaertiodendron magalismontanum* or 'Stamvrug' needs no introduction to hikers in the Magaliesberg who probably relish the fruit — but have to compete with other primates for this delicacy.

-stan /stɑːn, stæn/ *suffix.* [Suffix found in Hindi (in the form *-sthān*) and other Indo-Aryan languages, meaning 'place', 'country', and added to the name of a people to form the name of a state (e.g. *Pakistan*); in S. Afr. Eng. first used in BANTUSTAN, prob. modelled on *Hindustan*; later S. Afr. uses were in turn modelled on *bantustan*.]

Esp. during the apartheid era, used usu. to deride the homeland policy of the National Party government, or to satirize the tendency towards separation in South African society. Added (freq. *nonce*) to the name of a people or group to create the name of their putative or proposed national state; added satirically to any word to illustrate the (effects of the) policies of apartheid, or to expose the ideas of conservative (white) people: **bantustan**, see as a main entry; **Blackstan** [coined by Stan Motjuwadi of *Drum* magazine], also *attrib.*, or **bundustan** [see BUNDU; a reference to the remote locality of many of the 'homelands'], a satirical name for a HOMELAND (sense 1); **casinostan** [a reference to the fact that casinos were allowed in the 'homelands', but not in South Africa]; **Catholicstan**; **Colouredstan** [see COLOURED]; **Griquastan** [see GRIQUA]; **homostan** [formed on *homosexual*]; **Kalaharistan** [named for the *Kalahari* desert]; **Mlungustan** [coined by *Drum* magazine; see MLUNGU], a satirical name for 'white' South Africa; **multistan**, see quot. 1974; **pluralstan** [coined by Stan Motjuwadi of *Drum* magazine; see PLURAL], see *Blackstan*; **Tsongastan** [see TSONGA]; **Tswanastan** [see TSWANA sense 2]; **Vendastan** [see VENDA sense 1 a]; **Verkramptstan** [see VERKRAMP] or **Voortrekkerstan** [see VOORTREKKER], jocular names for a 'homeland' for conservative Afrikaners; **Whitestan**, see *Mlungustan*; **Xhosastan** [see XHOSA]; **Zulustan** [see ZULU].

1975 *Drum* 8 Nov. 2 The **Blackstan** bookies are already making brisk business taking bets as just to who of the Blackstan leaders is going to accept an invite for the occasion. **1982** *Voice* 24 Jan. 4 The whole sham of **bundustans**. **1987** C. HOPE *Hottentot Room* 96 It had become clear .. that their country was violently torn, increasingly Balkanised into pseudo-states, principalities, Bantustans, **casinostans**, reserves. *c***1970** C. DESMOND *Discarded People* 31 The people from Alva and Amakhasi Roman Catholic Missions were put into the promised **'Catholicstan'** at Uitval. **1971** *Sunday Times* 28 Mar. 5 The long-simmering row .. over Coloured policy — whether the two-million Coloureds should be treated as 'partners' of the Whites, or herded into a **Colouredstan** — has flared up finally with .. a Coloured leader's plan for a fully-fledged Coloured Republic in South Africa. **1974** *E. Prov. Herald* 9 Aug. 6 Descendants of the Griqualand leader Adam Kok are demanding 1000 square miles of fertile farmland near Kokstad to form the nucleus of the country's first Colouredstan ... White farmers in the district are up in arms over the proposed **'Griquastan'**. **1970** *Post* 6 Dec. 20 They want their own **Homostan** where they can do what they like. **1989** K. OWEN *E. Prov. Herald* 13 Mar. 6 The right-wingers like Carel Boshoff, trying desperately to establish a utopion **Kalaharistan** for an endangered Afrikaner species. **1985** *Drum* July 24 **Mlungustan** is Mlungustan. Pluralstan is Pluralstan .. and never the twain shall meet. **1974** *Evening Post* 20 Aug. 6 **Multistan** .. means setting aside a portion of the country in which racial laws are repealed thus giving South Africa a region within its own borders which resembles other multi-racial societies. **1985** *Drum* June 31, I made a beeline to the hut of the Oracle of **Pluralstan**, Old Dabula. *c***1970** C. DESMOND *Discarded People* 144 The Tswanastan belies the idea of a nation-state ... But the Vendastan and **Tsongastan** make the idea of creating a viable nation-state even less plausible. **1985** PLATZKY & WALKER *Surplus People* 127 At that stage there was no thought of a separate 'Tsongastan'. *c***1970** [**Tswanastan, Vendastan**: see quot. at *Tsongastan* (above)]. **1972** *Sunday Times* 5 Nov. (Mag. Sect.) 2 **Verkramptstan** ... I suggest that a small corner of the Free State be set aside for those countrymen who cannot stomach it [*sc.* mixed sport]. **1977** *Financial Mail* Vol.65 No.8, 669 **Voortrekkerstan**, and all that. There is growing talk of partition. **1960** E.G. MALHERBE in H. Spottiswoode *S. Afr.: Rd Ahead* 145 However much we may cut it up into 'Bantustans' and **'Whitestans'**, South Africa will have to remain an interlinked economic and political unity. **1972** *Sunday Times* 2 Sept. (Mag. Sect.) 4 Among the Blacks the Government have created two **Xhosastans**, a Zulustan, Vendastan, etc ... Why do the Government not have an Afrikanerstan, and an Englishstan, a Frenchstan, Jewishstan, Germanstan, etc? **1970** *Daily News* 26 May, No mention is made in the regulations of the position of urban Zulus and whether or not they would have a stake in the **Zulustan**.

Hence **stan** *n. rare*, HOMELAND sense 1; also *attrib.*; **-stania** [+ Eng. n.-forming suffix *-ia*], suffix added to a noun to form a place name, as *Bantustania* (see BANTUSTAN); so **-stanian** [+ Eng. n. and adj.-forming suffix *-ian*], suffix used to form nouns and adjectives, as *Bantustanian* (see BANTUSTAN), **Blackstanian**, **mlungustanian**, **pluralstanian**, etc.

1970 A.G. EBRAHIM in *10th Anniversary of Sharpeville* (P.A.C.) 9 The fascist authorities in South Africa have systematically herded the vast majority of the people into so-called 'stans' which are made up of the 13% arid and semi-arid areas of South Africa. **1972** *Daily Dispatch* 26 July 14 The 'go-it-alone attitude' of which the stan system is a typical example was introduced by whites. **1973** *Drum* 22 May 60 Like I said mlungustanians do not believe in doing things that way. **1974** *Ibid.* 22 Sept. 2 The mlungus were at it again discussing in Parliament us Blackstanians. **1977** 'BLACK STAN' in *Drum* July 2 We Blackstanians have a long history of being taken for a ride right down the years we have been burdened with dummy bodies, supposedly to represent us. **1978** S. MOTJUWADI in *Drum* Aug. 2 Two Pluralstanians of very high standing are invited to a conference in West Germany. They would like to attend because this conference is vital to us Pluralstanians and Singularstanians here. **1981** *Drum* 120 Why should Pluralstanians be required to sing Die Stem when they are not regarded as South African citizens? **1983** *Ibid.* Jan. 40 Never trust a mlungu. Bedevilling for a young pluralstanian mind. **1986** *Ibid.* Dec. 14 Mlungu and pluralstanian can pray together in a church. **1987** *Ibid.* Oct. 92 There is a faded photograph showing some unknown pluralstanian signing a document with some mlungus.

stan *n.* see -STAN.

stand *n.* [Perh. fr. Afk. *standplaas* (Du. *standplaats*) 'standing place', plot of land, or a broader use of general Eng. *stand* industrial site.]

1.a. *Hist. Mining.* In terms of the Gold Law of the South African Republic, Law No.21 of 1896: a plot of land for residential purposes, either containing no gold, or on which prospecting was not allowed; STANDPLAATS. **b.** In general use: a plot of land, a site; cf. ERF sense a. Also *attrib.*, and occas. with distinguishing epithet.

1893 T. REUNERT *Diamonds & Gold* 155 *Stands*, The lots of ground into which a town on a proclaimed field is divided are called 'Stands', or, in Dutch, *Standplaatsen*. They are usually granted for ninety-nine years, subject to a monthly licence of seven shillings and sixpence. **1895** *Star* 19 Dec., Sale of Splendidly situated Stands Rosettenville with mineral rights. **1896** MÉLIOT *Eng.-Fr. Dict. Terms Finance* etc. 222 In the Transvaal, a stand is a portion of any land measuring 150 × 150 feet, sold or let. **1896** *Gold Law of S. Afr. Republic* (Law No.21 of 1896) 68 Prospecting and digging is forbidden on or in towns, villages, stand townships, .. *erven* stands, locations, village grounds, gardens, .. machine stands .. and other such places as the Mining Commissioner may point out. **1899** [see NIKS sense 1]. **1910** in *Stat. Law of Tvl 1839–1910* I. 233 Claims and stands are not fixed property. **1919** M.C. BRUCE *Golden Vessel* 61 If you have had to buy a stand facing south and you do not want your principal rooms to face that way, exercise a little ingenuity and turn 'the house round'. **1926** M. NATHAN *S. Afr. from Within* 64 A township named Johannesburg was proclaimed, and 'stands' or building lots were surveyed. **1936** E. ROSENTHAL *Old-Time Survivals* 34 Originally, in the 'seventies, on the alluvial goldfields of Pilgim's Rest and Lydenburg, every miner was granted his claim ... When he worked in the river, washing his precious metal, he needed a place on which to deposit his tools and on which to pitch his tent ... Consequently the Diggers' Commission arranged that he could hire a plot of ground which contained no gold, and this was called a 'stand'. **1950** D. REED *Somewhere S. of Suez* 48 When Johannesburg was taking shape 'corner stands' were much sought and therefore most valuable. **1963** L.F. FREED *Crime in S. Afr.* 109 The sizes of the stands are 140 feet by 80 feet, of which there are 2,185, and also 140 feet by 50 feet, of which there are 340. **1977** C.J. CLAASSEN *Dict. of Legal Words & Phrases* IV. 118 *Stand*, A plot of ground ... *Standplaats*, A term used in the Gold Law of the South African Republic signifying a stand. **1989** *Sunday Times* 10 Dec. (Mag. Sect.) 26 The record price of R40 000 was recorded for a 25 morgen stand on the seafront. **1991** F.G. BUTLER *Local Habitation* 126 We think someone might buy it for the stand – it's a prize site .. on the corner of High and Somerset Streets.

2. *comb.* **stand licence** *Hist. Law*, (*a*) a rental paid to secure a trading site for a month at a time; (*b*) under the Transvaal Gold Law, a monthly fee paid to maintain leasehold rights to a site; (objective) **stand-owner**, esp. in township Eng., the owner of a plot of land; cf. SQUATTER sense 2.

1873 F. BOYLE *To Cape for Diamonds* 320 **Stand licences**, or shop sites, are charged there £2 or £3 per month, according as they have a frontage of 50 or 100 feet. **1933** W.H.S. BELL *Bygone Days* 125 Many years after, the holder was permitted to obtain a freehold title to Government stands on very easy terms, without any further payment of stand licenses. **1960** J.J.L. SISSON *S. Afr. Judicial Dict.* 757 *Stand Licence*, a monthly licence payable under the Transvaal Gold Law in respect of a stand. **1977** C.J. CLAASSEN *Dict. of Legal Words & Phrases* IV. 118 *Stand Licence*, A monthly licence payable under the Transvaal Gold Law in respect of a stand. **1962** M. BRANDEL-SYRIER *Black Woman* 46 She may now be a '**stand-owner**' or live in her own-built, middle-class home. **1968** *Drum* Sept. 44 Matthews decided to use his vigilantes as a gang to rob and extort money from businessmen and stand-owners in the township.

standplaats *n. Obs. Law.* [S. Afr. Du., *stand* stand(ing) + *plaats* place.] In the law of the old South African (or Transvaal) Republic: STAND sense 1 a. Also *attrib.*

[**1893** see STAND sense 1]. **1899** 'S. ERASMUS' *Prinsloo* 117, I did you a great wrong over that stand plaatsen sale, and I want to show you that I am sorry. **1977** C.J. CLAASSEN *Dict. of Legal Words & Phrases* IV. 118 *Standplaats*, A term used in the Gold Law of the South African Republic signifying a stand.

Stanley crane *n. phr.* Perh. *obsolescent.* [Named for *E.G. Stanley* (later Lord Stanley, Earl of Derby), British Secretary of State for War and the Colonies during the periods 1833–1834 and 1841–1845.] The BLUE CRANE, *Anthropoides paradisea*.

1856 R.E.E. WILMOT *Diary* (1984) 133 First of all come the indescribably graceful and beautiful kind called after Lord Derby '*the Stanley crane*'. The plumage is a pale lavender grey with white cheeks and long black wing coverts streaming behind until they mingle with the tail. **1867** E.L. LAYARD *Birds of S. Afr.* 303 The 'Stanley' or 'Blue' Crane is not abundant in any locality. **1899** [see Woodward quot. at BLUE CRANE]. **1923** HAAGNER & IVY *Sketches* 210 The Blue or Stanley Crane .. is a much commoner and better-known species [than the Wattled Crane]. **1931** *Guide to Vertebrate Fauna of E. Cape Prov.* (Albany Museum) I. 240 *Tetrapteryx paradisea* .. Blue Crane, Stanley C[rane] ... Frequent grain-lands and open country generally ... Confined to South Africa. **1963** S.H. SKAIFE *Naturalist Remembers* 165 Not long ago it was officially announced that the blue Stanley crane had been chosen as our national bird. **1966** E. PALMER *Plains of Camdeboo* 187 Our blue crane is also known as the Stanley crane. It belongs only to South Africa. **1970** O.P.M. PROZESKY *Field Guide to Birds* 161 Stanley or Blue Crane. Long, curving ornamental secondaries black.

start *n. slang.* [Etym. unknown; perh. orig. a transf. use of the general Eng. phr. *a start* help given towards entering on a course of action.] Money.

1970 M. BENNETT *Informant, Krugersdorp* Start. Money. **1970** K.M. BRAND *Informant, East London* I'll ask my old lady for some start to buy a new tyre. **1975** C. HOPE in *Bolt* No.12, 5 How's it ou china, ou bebops, ou maat – Ek se, major, can you battle us some start? **1985** [see GOOI sense 1 a]. **1991** A. KUTTNER *Informant, Johannesburg* Start means money. Origin unknown. 'Can you believe it, I came all the way to buy some pots and I didn't bring any start.' **1992** M.D. PRENTICE *Informant, Durban* Start. Money.

stat /stat/ *n.* Also **sta(a)d, staat, stadt.** [Afk., ad. Du. *stad* city.] A black settlement.

1. A traditional rural village or town: KRAAL *n.* sense 1 a.

1896 *Daily News* 28 Dec. 5 The principal Stadt is in flames. **1897** R.S.S. BADEN-POWELL *Matabeleland Campaign* 14 A native 'reed-dance' was going on in the 'stadt', as they call the native town. **1897** 'F. MACNAB' *On Veldt & Farm* 126 The journey is 618 miles from Mafeking to the chief's staat on Lake N'Gami. **1899** *Mafeking Mail* 1 Nov., The Colonel Commanding having made a careful inspection of the defences of the town and the native stadt, is now of opinion that no forces that the Boers are likely to bring against us could possibly affect an entrance at any point. **1905** W.H. TOOKE in Flint & Gilchrist *Science in S. Afr.* 91 These houses are not clustered in little groups like the kraals of the Kafirs, but form large towns or 'stads,' .. such as Kolobeng, Shoshong, Palachwe. **1913** *Stat. of Union* 446 The Governor-General may make regulations for preventing the overcrowding of huts and other dwellings in the stadts, native villages and settlements. **1929** D. REITZ *Commando* 130 Our first day's trek brought us to the big native stad of a local chief named Koos X. *a***1936** E.N. MARAIS *Soul of Ape* (1973) 95 The visit of a trader to a stat was invariably followed by numerous deaths directly due to acute alcohol-poisoning. **1941** A.G. BEE *Kalahari Camp Fires* (1943) 63 This is the only native stad (town or village) of any size on the southern side of the river until one arrives at Segomi's Stad thirty miles north of Lake N'Gami. **1942** S. CLOETE *Hill of Doves* Glossary, *Stad*, Village, town, or collection of native huts. **1948** O. WALKER *Kaffirs Are Lively* 79 Far more primitive were the one or two *stads*, or main kraals, of Bavenda chiefs like Rasengane. **1948** H.C. BOSMAN in L. Abrahams *Unto Dust* (1963) 52 During the rest of the time that he remained head of the tribe, he would not allow a white man to enter his stat again. **1950** C. BULLOCK *Mashona & Matabele* 200 The enormous aggregations known as 'stats' in Bechuanaland. **1973** [see HARTEBEEST *adj.*].

2. An urban settlement: TOWNSHIP sense 2 a.

Almost invariably referring to the settlement on the outskirts of Mafikeng.

1909 LADY S. WILSON *S. Afr. Mem.* 98 The fine stand made by the natives when the Boers attacked their stadt, adjacent to the town. **1920** S.M. MOLEMA *Bantu Past & Present* 283 On May 13th the young Boer leader was right in the town of Mafeking with 300 men. He had effected entry by marching up the bed of the Molopo River .. , which runs through the native staadt. **1935** R.S. GODLEY *Khaki & Blue* 73 This attack was pressed home with great determination, the native staad just on the outskirts of the town .. being captured. **1949** E. HELLMANN *Handbk on Race Rel.* 535 At Mafeking 200 Natives were enrolled to assist in the defence of the Native *stad* which was in the danger zone of the defences. **1957** D. GRINNELL-MILNE *Baden-Powell at Mafeking* 27 A valuable prize: with its railway material and workshops, its well-filled stores, its cattle, its cash in the bank and its nearby native *stad*. **1968** L.G. GREEN *Full Many Glorious Morning* 191 Mafeking .. once a frontier settlement round a market square .. is now a flourishing town and railway depot with the Baralong *stad* a mile away. [**1987** *Star* 5 Sept. 11 Snowy de Witt was told .. that Casper was living in the *kaffer stat* with his wife Naledi and their little girl.]

state attorney *n. phr.* [tr. Afk. *staatsprokureur*; cf. ATTORNEY.]

1. *hist.* With initial capitals. In the old Boer Republics: the state legal advisor, a position equivalent to that of Minister of Justice.

1877 F. JEPPE *Tvl Bk Almanac & Dir.* (1976) 46 State Attorney – Dr. W.J. Leyds. £1,200. **1897** F.R. STATHAM *S. Afr. as It Is* 306 It had not been sufficiently born in mind that Mr. Justice Gregorowski, who previously held the post of State-Attorney in the Orange Free State, is a member of the English Bar. **1899** *Volkstem* 5 Oct. 1 Judge Herzog, Judge Stuart and ex-State Attorney De Villiers have left for the front. **1902** E. HOBHOUSE *Brunt of War* 312 Nothing can more fitly close this slight outline of the tale of the women's sufferings than the passages which follow, culled from the Report of General J.C. Smuts, late State Attorney. **1946** T. MACDONALD *Ouma Smuts* 29 It was a Godsend when her husband at the age of twenty-eight was appointed State Attorney by President Kruger, and she was glad to leave the mining town and find sanctuary in Pretoria. **1974** K. GRIFFITH *Thank God We Kept Flag Flying* 19 In Pretoria, the capital of the Transvaal, President Kruger, ably advised by the young State Attorney, Jan Smuts, noted Queen Victoria's proclamation summoning the British Parliament and calling out the British Army's reserves.

2. An attorney employed by the government to protect its interests in any legal issue that may arise.

1956 *Act 3* in *Stat. of Union* 13 'State Attorney' means the officer appointed under paragraph (*a*) of sub-section (2) of section *two* of the State Attorney Act, 1925 (Act No. 25 of 1925). **1981** W.A. JOUBERT *Law of S. Afr.* XIV. 408 The functions of the office of the state attorney and of its branches are the performance in any court or in any part of the Republic of such work on behalf of the government of the Republic as is by law, practice or custom performed by attorneys, notaries and conveyancers or by parliamentary agents. **1985** H. HAMMANN in *Sunday Times* 6 Oct. 2 The decision to condone certain procedural actions by the applicant was taken by council and the instructing State Attorney. **1989** *Cape Times* 4 Sept. 7 Evidence is being led by advocate Mr E Bertelsmann, briefed by the state attorney for the liquidators.

State President *n. phr. Hist.* [tr. S. Afr. Du. *Staatspresident*.]

1. From 1866 to 1901, the name given to the executive heads of state in the Boer Republics of the Orange Free State and the Transvaal.

1877 F. JEPPE *Tvl Bk Almanac & Dir.* (1976) 37 This Court is appointed by the State President and Executive Council whenever there is a certain number of civil or criminal cases on the roll. **1887** *George & Knysna Herald* 29 Aug. 3 The Free State Volksraad ... A resolution expressing the feeling of grief and sorrow at the death of the universally-beloved and honoured State President, Sir John Brand, was unanimously carried by the Volksraad. **1897** in C. Headlam *Milner Papers* (1931) I. 204 S.J.P. Kruger, State President of the South African Republic ... M.T. Steyn, State President of the Orange Free State. **1900** in E. HOBHOUSE *Brunt of War* (1902) 5 From State President Orange Free State, and State President of the South African Republic. **1933** W.H.S. BELL *Bygone Days* 302 The safe-conduct was granted and .. the Acting State President and the members of the Transvaal Government entered the British lines at Balmoral on the Delagoa Bay line of railway. **1985** *S. Afr. Panorama* June 17 The Witwatersrand Agricultural Society was founded in 1894 and the following year Paul Kruger,

State President of the then 'Zuid-Afrikaanse Republiek', opened the first three-day show in Johannesburg.

2. From 1961 to 1983, the constitutional head of state of the Republic of South Africa, without executive powers; also as a title, used with a name.

1961 *Act 32* in *Stat. of Rep. of S. Afr.* 415 The State President shall in addition as head of the State have such powers and functions as were immediately prior to the commencement of this Act possessed by the Queen by way of prerogative. **1966** [see 90-DAY sense a]. **1970** *News/Check* 15 May 5 Former State President C.R. Swart is at present working on a book of his political memoirs. **1970** *Book of Common Prayer .. for use in the Church of the Province of South Africa* 234 And grant unto the State President and all that are set in authority over us, that they may truly and impartially minister justice to the removing of wickedness and vice, and to the maintenance of order and right living. **1982** [see OOM sense 1 a]. **1983** *Daily Dispatch* 18 Oct. 2 Shortly after the start of a 21-cannon salute as the State President arrived, a huge banner proclaiming a No-vote unfolded barely 50 m behind the President.

3. The ceremonial (and sometimes also executive) head of state of a HOMELAND.

1976 *Bona* Oct. 29 The Paramount Chief of Eastern Pondoland .. has been tipped to be the first state president when Transkei is granted its independence. **1983** *Daily Dispatch* 13 Apr., Umtata. The usual pomp and pageantry will mark the opening of the fourth session of the second Parliament by the State President, paramount Chief Kaiser Matanzima, here today. **1988** *Cape Times* 4 Jan. 2 Umtata ... The executive power of the government would be vested in the state president, acting on the advice of the military council at all times.

4. Under the South African constitution as amended in 1983: the executive head of state; also used as a title, with a name.

In the interim constitution of 1994, the title 'President' is used.

1983 *Act 110* in *Stat. of Republic of S. Afr.* 1305 If any electoral college removes the State President from office .. it shall forthwith proceed to elect a State President. **1983** [see Govt Gaz. quot. at OWN AFFAIR sense 1]. **1987** [see GREEN BEAN]. **1987** [see OPERATIONAL AREA]. **1988** [see NIS]. **1989** *E. Prov. Herald* 14 Sept. 4 National Party leader Mr F W de Klerk is scheduled to become South Africa's second Executive State President. **1989** A. DUNN in *Pretoria News* 20 Sept. 1 State President F W de Klerk today used his first words in office for an appeal to all South Africans to help him and his government break through to peace. **1993** J. SCOTT in *Cape Times* 25 Feb. 11 Mr Van der Merwe .. painted a picture of .. evil-doers overrunning South Africa while the State President shuffled his cabinet.

Hence **State Presidency** *n. phr.*, the office of State President.

1980 *Rand Daily Mail* 29 Aug. 1 Mr Muller — then also Minister of Transport and a leading candidate for the State Presidency. **1982** *E. Prov. Herald* 28 June 2 About 100-million coins celebrating the premiership and state presidency of Mr Vorster had been minted for circulation this year.

States *n. Military slang.* [Transf. use of U.S. Eng. *the States* the United States of America, hence meaning 'home' when used by soldiers serving abroad; but see quot. 1981.]

1. ***The States***: South Africa, home.

1977 *National Serviceman, Informant* 'Hell I can't wait to get back to the States.' .. 'Had a letter from the States today.' **1981** *E. Prov. Herald* 4 Mar. 12 If a crisis arises in the family back in 'the States' it is treated as an emergency. The affectionate name for the Republic has its origins in the Orange Free State, I understand. **1984** *Fair Lady* 14 Nov. 133 They are reluctant to talk, far preferring to tell you what they'll do when they get back to the States — as everyone from the most wet-behind-the-ears private to the rugged and weatherbeaten commanding officer, calls South Africa. **1988** *Personality* 7 Nov. 27 Sooner or later everyone goes back to live in 'the States' (armyspeak for the Republic). **1989** P. KENNY in *Sunday Times* 25 June 11 For the South African troops it was back to the 'States' (South Africa).

2. *comb.* **Stateside** *adv.* [transf. use of U.S. Eng. *Stateside* in the United States of America, prob. a contraction of *States side*], in South Africa, at home.

1980 M. VAN BILJON in *Sunday Times* 12 Oct. (Mag. Sect.) 5 There's some aggro about the attitudes at home ('**Stateside**') ... 'The Israelis who fight go home as heroes. What do they feel for us Stateside when we get back?' ... Stateside, we need to reassess our attitudes.

stay *v. intrans. Colloq.* [Prob. reinforced by Afk. *bly* stay, live.] To live, reside.

Used also in *Indian, Scottish,* and *U.S. (regional) Eng.*

1908 J.H. DRUMMOND Diary. 3 Her daughter stays in P.E. and studies the violin. *a***1915** *Mod.* (Cape Colony: communicated), Englishman: Who lived in that house last? Colonial: Oh, Mr. Brown stayed there. **1949** H.C. BOSMAN *Cold Stone Jug* (1969) 21 The only times I've ever walked about looking for a whore it was in the other end of the town from where he stays. **1959** A. FULLERTON *Yellow Ford* 45 'Would you care to stay round here man?' I had not caught on, at first, to her meaning: the verb 'stay' is used in South Africa when in England we'd say 'live'. **1969** *Daily Dispatch* 30 Sept., The date for the funeral has been provisionally set for Saturday this week at Buntingville, where they stayed. **1972** *Evening Post* 10 June 5 'I haven't seen Romolo since he left South Africa with my father in 1905,' said Mario S- .. who stays in Thornhill, near Port Elizabeth. **1973** [see SUNDOWNER sense 1]. **1979** M. MATSHOBA *Call Me Not a Man* 115 The generation gap. I bridged it by telling her exactly where I stay in Mzimhlope and who my people are. **1988** [see Mkhize quot. at IQABANE]. **1989** J. HOBBS *Thoughts in Makeshift Mortuary* 171 Ma stays by the house. My older sister Violet .. and the four kids moved back. They stay in the garage. **1991** G. ZWIRN in *Settler* Vol.65 No.2, 10 *To stay.* 'Where do you stay?' was .. the first question put to me on arrival in South Africa. Since I was staying neither at a hotel, boarding-house or hostel, I was at first non-plussed for an answer. Then the penny dropped: what the speaker was asking me was merely 'Where do you live?' **1991** *Sunday Times* 31 Aug. (Extra) 3 Mr Gert H–, 30 years old and now staying in Kuils River after the tractor tragedy that left him hospitalised.

stay well /ˈsteɪ ˌwel/ *int. phr.* [tr. of Sintu (Bantu) expressions for 'goodbye', such as Xhosa *hlala kakuhle*, Sotho *sala hantle*, Zulu *sala kahle* (see SALA KAHLE).] An expression of good wishes, spoken on parting by one leaving to one staying behind; cf. SALA KAHLE. See also GO WELL.

In the past invariably used by writers to suggest dialogue in the Nguni or Sotho languages, but now in general use in *S. Afr. Eng.*

1948 A. PATON *Cry, Beloved Country* 17 Go well, my child. Stay well, umfundisi. Stay well, mother. Go well, my child. **1952** F.J. EDMONSTONE *Where Mists Still Linger* 54 'Stay well, my friend,' he said. 'Will we see you at work in the morning?' ... 'I will be at work,' said my father. 'Go well.' **1961** [see GO WELL]. **1965** J. NGUGI *River Between* (1970) 55 'Go in peace. These hills from the ancient times have seen strange things.' 'Stay well. Remain in peace.' **1983** N.S. NDEBELE *Fools* 265 The boy .. curtsied when I placed the orange in his hands 'Stay well,' he said as he walked out. **1991** S. DACOMBE on Radio South Africa 3 Feb., This is Sandy Dacombe in Pretoria saying 'stay well', and thanks for joining me.

steakie var. STUKKIE.

‖**steeg** /stɪəx/ *n.* [Du.] An alley or lane between buildings. Also *attrib.*

A feature of early Cape Town, reflected still in street names.

[**1815** *Afr. Court Calendar & Dir.*, Abrahams, Johannes, Fisherman, 1, Harder Steeg. Alexander, Carel Lodewyk, Boatman, 2, Harder Steeg.] **1926** P.W. LAIDLER *Tavern of Ocean* 185 It became usual in the days of thatched roofs to leave little four-foot passages between the houses to allow of the overhang and drip of the thatch. This resulted in numerous lanes and alleys, for which at one time the town was famous. Koffie Steeg remains in its translated form of Coffee Lane. **1951** L.G. GREEN *Grow Lovely* 63 In the old town the houses usually had lanes between them four feet in width ... Such a lane was called a 'steeg' and the 'steeg' names were often picturesque. Off Waterkant .. one found Dopper Steeg, Crabbe Steeg, Mossel Steeg, Klipfish Lane and Lelie Steeg. **1971** — *Taste of S.-Easter* 141 When you glance into a cobbled steeg filled with washing you move back two centuries.

steekbos /ˈstɪəkbɔs/ *n.* [Afk., *steek* puncture, prick, stab + *bos* bush.] Any of several plants characterized by sharply-pointed leaves or flowers which are capable of puncturing the skin, esp. *Cliffortia ruscifolia* of the Rosaceae.

1917 R. MARLOTH *Common Names* 77 *Steekbos, Cliffortia ruscifolia.* One of the most common shrubs of the south-western districts. Leaves rigid and sharp-pointed. Also other shrubs with such leaves, and Argemone mexicana. **1934** C.P. SWART Supplement to Pettman. 166 *Steekbos,* The common name of a shrub, metalasia muricata, which spreads rapidly and in a year or two renders large tracts of country useless for sheep farming as it develops a very dense growth, which soon suppresses other useful grasses and bushes. Its flower is prickly, hence the name. **1966** C.A. SMITH *Common Names* 435 So far it would appear that the term Steekbos is expressly applied only to such plants which, owing to their abundance and social habit, are capable of being a source of irritation to persons coming into contact with them. **1973** M.A. COOK *Cape Kitchen* 107 As the branches burnt away, more and more were pushed in, as well as billets of wood, stumps of bushes and so on: renosterbos (*Elytropappus rhinocertis*) and steekbos (*Cliffortia ruscifolia*) were favourites for this purpose.

steekgras /ˈstɪəkxras/ *n.* [Afk., *steek* to prick, stab + *gras* grass.] A general term for grasses (family Poaceae) which are characterized by sharp awns which cling to wool, fabric, etc.: **a.** Any of several species of *Aristida* (sub-family Arundinoideae); see also BUSHMAN GRASS. **b.** *Heteropogon contortus* (sub-family Andropogonodae); ASSEGAI *n.* sense 3. In both senses also called STICK-GRASS. Also *attrib.*, and (*obs.*) part. tr. **steekgrass**.

1893 W. SPILHAUS in J. Noble *Illust. Off. Handbk of Cape & S. Afr.* 314 A year or two ago the Colony was troubled with a particularly obnoxious seed, that of the 'steekgrass' (*Andropogon contortus*, Ness, and *Aristida congesta*, R. and T.). **1896** R. WALLACE *Farming Indust. of Cape Col.* 99 'Steek-grass' is the colonial name applied to a number of species of the natural order Gramineae, having long sharp awns attached to their seeds, by which they adhere to the wool of sheep. **1906** F. BLERSCH *Handbk of Agric.* 258 The burr weed .., steek gras, thorny mesembryanthemum, .. karroo thorn .. become injurious by their getting into and spoiling wool and hair, though the steek gras (*Aristida* and *Andropogon*) and the mimosa at times form valuable food. **1910** A.B. LAMONT *Rural Reader* 257 Steek grass is one of the most troublesome grasses. **1913** C. PETTMAN *Africanderisms* 474 *Steekgras, .. Aristida barbicollis* ... The seeds of this grass have sharp barbed awns attached to them by which they cling to the wool of sheep, work their way through the skin, and set up considerable irritation. *Andropogon contortus* .. is also a steekgras, but is not the common one. **1918** J.W. BEWS *Grasses & Grasslands* 114 *A. congesta* (Steek gras) is dominant over immense stretches of primitive Veld in the Free State. **1955** [see BOESMANGRAS]. **1958** R.E. LIGHTON *Out of Strong* 62 If I wear socks the sharp grass seeds, like those of the steekgras, stick into them. When I walk I must stop to pull them out where they hurt me. **1975** [see STICK-GRASS]. **1986**

Farmer's Weekly 25 July 14 In the legume pastures again the steekgras grasses increased. **1987** J. MUNDAY *Grasses, Grains & Conservation* 32 Steekgras, any species of *Aristida*.

||**steeks** /stɪəks/ *adj.* Also **steuks, sticks.** [Afk., fr. Du. *steegs.*] Usu. of horses: obstinate, inclined to jib.

It appears that this word is being interpreted by non-Afrikaans speakers as a plural noun in many of the quots.

1882 C. DU VAL *With Show through Sn Afr.* I. 115 Every hill resolved itself into a battle with the horses; there being one or two 'sticks' amongst the team. **1887** J. MACKINNON *S. Afr. Traits* 163 There we stand at the bottom of a steep hill, struggling with our horses, who have taken it into their heads not to move an inch further – they have become 'steeks,' as the Boers say. **1893** F.C. SELOUS *Trav. & Adventure* 157 He was a big powerful animal and wonderfully steady shooting horse, but liable to become sulky and refuse to run at his best pace – a phase of temper recognised by the Transvaal Boers, and described by them by the word 'steeks,' – and when in this mood spurring was simply wasted upon him. **1902** C. WARREN *On Veldt in Seventies* 92 The horses of this country are mostly 'sticks,' *i.e.*, they get sulky, at times, and will not move when they are put into a cart. **1924** S.G. MILLIN *God's Step-Children* 164 He turned round to Edith and said. 'The horses are steuks, Little Missis' ... Most of her recollections of driving were connected with horses bewitched into an immobility that was only varied by a plunging resistance to any forward impulse, while the native drivers plaintively remarked that the horses were steuks again. **1970** B.C. MARITZ *Informant, Port Elizabeth* That horse of yours will have to be ridden as he is getting steeks.

steembras var. STEENBRAS.

steen /stɪən, stiːn/ *n.* Often with initial capital. [S. Afr. Du., ellipt. for *steendruiven*, *steen* stone + *druiven* grapes.]

Used interchangeably with the word STEIN by some.

1. In full ***steen wine***: a wine made from steen grapes (see sense 2); cf. STEIN sense 1. Also *attrib.* See also CAPE WINE.

1798 S.H. WILCOCKE tr. *J.S. Stavorinus's Voy. to E. Indies 1768–71* I. 545 Next to the genuine constantia, the wines called muscadel, and *steen*-wine are esteemed the best. **1804** R. PERCIVAL *Acct of Cape of G.H.* 188 The Steen wine has a sparkling quality and tartish taste, something like Vin de Grave, but much inferior in flavour. **1806** *Gleanings in Afr.* (anon.) 224 The Steen wine made here is of a superior quality. **1832** *Graham's Town Jrnl* 24 Aug. 135 Old Rough Pontac, Steen, and other Cape Wines. **1920** K.M. JEFFREYS tr. *Memorandum of Commissary J.A. de Mist* 204 *The Cape grapes*, .. produce .. various other kinds of very healthy and delicious wines, known under the names of Cape Madeira, .. steen wine, vintint and others. **1968** C.J. ORFFER in D.J. Opperman *Spirit of Vine* 100 The memorandum drawn up by De Mist in Holland in 1802 contained the following significant wine data: Cape grapes produced, apart from the world-famous *Constantia* wine, other and delicious [wines] under the names: *Cape Madeira, Cape Malaga, medicinal wines, Steen wine, Vintint*, [etc.]. **1975** *E. Prov. Herald* 20 Feb. 2 Experts say that except for the Steen, all have tremendous potential for improvement if laid down for a number of years. **1986, 1988** [see STEIN sense 1].

2. A common white grape, the French 'Chenin Blanc' cultivar; the vine producing this grape; STEIN sense 2. Also *attrib.*

1887 *S.W. Silver & Co.'s Handbk to S. Afr.* 222 A pale, light wine, with a sub-acid, grateful flavour, somewhat resembling Hock, may be made from the Steen grape (with a small addition of Green grape). **1902** [see HANEPOOT sense 1]. **1905** [see PONTAC sense 2]. *a***1918** *Off. Yr Bk 1916–17* 439 (Swart), Wine-making – Green Grape, Hanepoot, Hermitage, Steen etc. **1966** H. BECK *Meet Cape Wines* 11 The stein (or steen) was rapidly approaching the position it holds today of being one of the most valuable of our table wine grapes. **1972** M.S. LEROUX in *Std Encycl. of Sn Afr.* 306 Van Riebeeck's first modest vintage, pressed on 2 Feb., 1659, consisted mainly of the crop gathered from two-year-old Muscadel vines and another white variety of round grape which could have been Steen or 'White French' grapes. **1979** *S. Afr. Digest* May 11 The most common white cultivar, the Steen (or *Chenin Blanc*), varies widely from the full and robust to the off dry and light, as it is grown widely throughout the Cape and illustrates the result of different climatic and soil conditions on a cultivar. **1980** J. PLATTER *Book of S. Afr. Wines* 65 Stein, Semi-sweet white usually a blend and often confused with steen, a grape variety, though most stein style wines are made at least partly from steen grapes. **1982** [see LATE HARVEST sense 2]. **1988** D. HUGHES et al. *Complete Bk of S. Afr. Wine* 96 Chenin Blanc, or Steen. For years this cultivar was known as Steen in South Africa and was believed to be unique to the Cape. In 1965 .. it was established that the Steen cultivar was identical to the French variety, Chenin Blanc – since then, both names have been recognised.

steenbok /ˈstɪənbɔk, -bɒk/ *n.* Also **ste(e)nbock, steinbok.** Pl. unchanged, **-s**, or (formerly) **-bokken.** [S. Afr. Du., transf. use of Du. *steenbok*, *steen* stone + *bok* buck, a name for *Capra ibex*. The form *steinbok* is perh. based on the misconception that the word is of German origin.] The small antelope *Raphicerus campestris* of the Bovidae, reddish-brown in colour (sometimes with a silvery sheen), and with large ears and straight horns; STEENBOKKIE; STEENBUCK; STEMBUCK; STONEBUCK. Also *attrib.* See also BLEEKBOK.

1775 F. MASSON in *Phil. Trans. of Royal Soc.* LXVI. 277 We found many curious plants, and shot several animals, as steenbocken, hares, partridges. **1786** G. FORSTER tr. *A. Sparrman's Voy. to Cape of G.H.* II. 223 The animals called by the colonists *steen-bok, grys-bok, duyker-bok*, and *klipspringer*, are about two feet high, being probably of the *gazel* kind, and are not uncommon near the Cape ... My piece was .. loaded with what they call *steen-bok* shot, or shot about the size of a common pea. **1795** C.R. HOPSON tr. *C.P. Thunberg's Trav.* II. 11 This species .. called *steenboks*, were reported to hide their heads, in the idea that nobody can see them. **1801** [see ORIBI]. **1810** G. BARRINGTON *Acct of Voy.* 157 The Steenbok, formerly the most numerous of the antelope tribe, is now nearly extirpated from the neighbourhood of the Cape, though still numerous beyond the isthmus. **1822** W.J. BURCHELL *Trav.* I. 281 Philip .. brought home a Steenbok, the meat of which was very good-tasted. **1838** J.E. ALEXANDER *Exped. into Int.* I. 13 The steenbok (or stone buck), of which the boors were now usually in pursuit, is a small but very graceful antelope, three feet and a half in length .. about one foot eight inches high. **1882** C. DU VAL *With Show through Sn Afr.* I. 159 A sack made of steinbok-skins, gaily emblazoned with strips of thong, beads, etc. **1900** W.L. SCLATER *Mammals of S. Afr.* I. 174 The Steenbok ... Form slim and slender; general colour a rufous brown, often with a light silvery sheen. **1918** C. GARSTIN *Sunshine Settlers* 176 A steenbok arose, and headed straight into the sun-blaze, flying over the dewy grass and through the scrub like a red flame. **1951** A. ROBERTS *Mammals* 339 Steenbok .. lies in hiding amongst even short grass, so flat on the ground that it may not be noticed until it suddenly darts off at surprising speed. **1963** S. CLOETE *Rags of Glory* 207 Little, big-eared steenboks .. nibbled away the night. **1974** *E. Prov. Herald* 13 Sept. 4 A house-trained steenbok kid which liked to be cuddled before being tucked up in bed for the night. **1980** J. HANKS *Mammals* 23 Steenbok. *Raphicerys campestris* ... Usually seen in light woodland where it browses and grazes. Shoulder height about 50 cm. **1992** J. FEELY in *Afr. Wildlife* Vol.46 No.4, 157 Some if not most of the fossil specimens of *Raphicerus* found at archaeological sites in the 'Berg are more likely to be grysbok than steenbok (*R. campestris*).

steenbokkie /ˈstɪənbɔki/ *n.* [Afk., *steenbok* see prec. + -IE.] STEENBOK.

1944 H.C. BOSMAN in L. Abrahams *Cask of Jerepigo* (1972) 157 The bush was populated with koodoos and cows and duikers and steenbokkies and oxen [etc.]. **1973** J. RABIE in S. Gray *Writers' Territory* 173 Quite a number of duikers and steenbokkies in the thickets between us and Hawston. **1985** *Weekend Argus* 30 Nov. (Suppl.) 6, I saw numerous small buck, mostly steenbokkies but also other duiker. **1985** T. BARON in *Frontline* Feb. 31 In some parts of the country a steenbokkie is protected.

steenbras /ˈstɪənbras, -brɑːs/ *n.* Also **ste(e)mbras, steenbrasen, steen brass, steenbras(s)em, steenbrazen, steinbrase, stem brass, stienbrass.** Pl. unchanged, or (formerly) **-braesem, -brassam, -brassen.** [Transf. use of Du. *steenbras*, *steen* stone + *brasem* bream (a name given to *Sparus saxatilis*).]

a. Any of several marine fishes, esp. either of two species of seabream of the Sparidae, *Petrus rupestris* (see *red steenbras*, sense b below), or *Lithognathus lithognathus* (see *white steenbras* sense (a), sense b below). Also *attrib.*

The first quot. refers to New Guinea.

[**1625** S. PURCHAS *Hachluytus Posthymus* (1905) II. 278 Sixe great Canoas followed us, (and yet we saw no men on land) bringing dried fish, (which wee tooke to be Steenbrasses). **1731** G. MEDLEY tr. *P. Kolb's Present State of Cape of G.H.* II. 203 The sea about the Cape is well stocked with a sort of fish the Cape-Europeans call *Stone*-Brassen; and the Cape-Europeans take great numbers of 'em.] **1790** tr. *F. Le Vaillant's Trav.* I. 32 Fish are very abundant at the Cape. Among those most esteemed, the principal are the *rooman*, .. the *steenbraasen*, the *stompneus*, and some others. **1790** W. PATERSON *Narr. of Four Journeys* 8 About noon we came to the mouth of the Stienbrassam River, which takes its name from a species of fish, called Stienbrassam. **1801** R. SEMPLE *Walks & Sketches* (1805) 124 We supped upon a fine large Steinbrass fish, and went soon to rest. *a***1823** J. EWART *Jrnl* (1970) 13 Stienbrass, similar in shape and size to the salmon. **1823** [see JACOB EVERTSON sense 1]. **1890** [see GALJOEN sense 1]. **1892** NICOLLS & EGLINGTON *Sportsman in S. Afr.* 141 The Steen Brass (Dentex rupestris). (Some have been caught weighing up to 70 lbs. General colour, variegated, clouded irregularly with ultramarine blue, oil green, and lavender purple; profile of head, irregular; a large bulge over the eyes.) **1913** W.W. THOMPSON *Sea Fisheries of Cape Col.* 58 The steenbras was supposed to be a bream, even in Percival's Voyages (1786–1801) it is designated 'la brême de roche'. **1930** C.L. BIDEN *Sea-Angling Fishes* 156 All local anglers and fishermen use the word 'steenbras' which is Dutch for 'stonebream'. The Afrikaans name is 'rooisteenbras' (.. the approximate pronunciation .. is 'roy-stĕ'm-bräss)'. *Ibid.* 159 Old anglers are of opinion that the young steenbras is the most gorgeously painted fish of all at the Cape, even allowing for the brilliance of such others as the dageraad .. and red stumpnose. **1930** M. RAUBENHEIMER *Tested S. Afr. Recipes* 112 The best fish for pickling is either Geelbek, Snoek, Kabeljaauw or Steenbras. **1950** M. MASSON *Birds of Passage* 121 Vendor and buyer alike haggled over the merits of Hottentot, Hake, Evert, Kingclipfish, Steenbrazen and Stompneus. **1977** *E. Prov. Herald* 17 Nov. 15 Many estuary fishermen believe steenbras and grunter blow burrowing baits, mainly prawns, out of the beds to feed on them. **1981** *Ibid.* 23 Apr. 11 The name 'steenbras' is probably the most abused name in the whole of our fish nomenclature ... Species called steenbras in various parts are only distantly related, some not at all. **1982** *S. Afr. Panorama* May 29 The picturesque fisherman's cottages have long gone, but some seine netters remain, still catching mullet, yellowtail, *galjoen* and *steenbras* in the old-fashioned way. **1992** V. KABALIN in *Afr. Wildlife* Vol.46 No.2, 201 No ill effect on the sustainable stock in the Bay of yellowtail, kob, baartman, elf and steenbras.

b. With distinguishing epithet: **bank steenbras** [Eng. *bank* shelving elevation in the sea], either of two species of marine fish, (*a*) the *red steenbras* (see below); (*b*) the fingerfin *Chirodactylus grandis* of the Cheilodactylidae; TIGERFISH sense 2 a; **black steenbras**, the *black musselcracker* (see MUSSELCRACKER sense 2), *Cymatoceps nasutus*; **bronze -**, **copper -**, or (more commonly) **red steenbras**, the seabream *Petrus rupestris*, a fine game fish reaching over two metres in length and varying in colour from golden yellow to bronze and red; COPPER; *red poenskop*, see POENSKOP sense 2 b; SEVENTY-FOUR sense b; SILVER-FISH sense 1 b; **river steenbras**, *bank steenbras* sense (*b*), see above; **rooi steenbras** /ˈrɔɪ-/, [Afk. (earlier *roode steenbrassem*), *rooi* red], *red steenbras* (see above); **sand steenbras**, the BONTROK, *Lithognathus mormyrus*; **silver steenbras**, the east coast name for the *white musselcracker* (see MUSSELCRACKER sense 2), *Sparodon durbanensis*; **white steenbras**, either of two species of seabream, (*a*) *Lithognathus lithognathus*, which reaches up to two metres in length and is considered a fine game fish; MUSSELCRACKER sense 1 a (also called MUSSEL CRUSHER); (*b*) less frequently, the *white musselcracker* (see MUSSELCRACKER sense 2), *Sparodon durbanensis*; **yellow steenbras**, in KwaZulu-Natal, a name for the *red steenbras* (see above).

In Smith and Heemstra's *Smiths' Sea Fishes* (1986), the name 'bank steenbras' is used for *Chirodactylus grandis*, 'red steenbras' for *Petrus rupestris*, 'sand steenbras' for *Lithognathus mormyrus*, and 'white steenbras' for *Lithognathus lithognathus*.

1902 J.D.F. GILCHRIST in *Trans. of S. Afr. Philological Soc.* XI. iv. 230 Rooi Steenbras, Roode Steenbrasem (Pappe), Red Steenbras, **Bank Steenbras** .. *Dentex rupestris*. **1905** [see TIGERFISH sense 2]. **1971** *Argus* 14 May 14 At Anvil Rock, Brian Clark, John Hughes and Arthur Ridge found the reef alive with 5 kg bank steenbras and red roman. **1930** C.L. BIDEN *Sea-Angling Fishes* 257 *Pagrus nasutus* .. East London — **Black Steenbras. 1971** *Daily Dispatch* 2 June 15 J. Opperman, one black steenbras 13,5 kg. **1989** A. SPARG in *Ski-Boat* Jan.-Feb. 35 The two best black steenbras (poenskop) of the tournament .. weighed 28 and 25,5 kg. **1981** *E. Prov. Herald* 23 Apr. 11 There is the red steenbras, a name used right around the coast except in Natal where it is a **bronze** or **copper steenbras**. **1988** C. NORMAN in *S. Afr. Panorama* Dec. 41 In the eastern Cape the copper steenbras (*Petrus rupestris*) and .. musselcracker .. are prized trophies. **1990** D. JONES in *Sunday Times* 18 Nov. 7 A lucrative operation at Coffee Bay .. is threatening the last known breeding ground of the red or copper steenbras. **1801** J. BARROW *Trav.* I. 30 The **red** and the white **Steenbrassems**, or Stonebreams, two species, or perhaps varieties only, of perches. **1831** *S. Afr. Almanac & Dir.* January ... Fish in Season ... Harder, red Steenbrassem, [etc.]. **1843** [see quot. at *white steenbras* below]. **1880** [see KLIPFISH sense 1]. **1902** [see quot. at *bank steenbras* above]. *c*1936 *S. & E. Afr. Yr Bk & Guide* 1108 The steenbras, red and white, which may be caught with a 20-foot rod from the rocks around the Cape Peninsula, runs up to 70 lbs. in weight. **1949** J.L.B. SMITH *Sea Fishes* 277 *Petrus rupestris* ... *Red or Rooi Steenbras* (Cape). *Yellow Steenbras* (Natal) ... Attains over 6 ft. in length and .. 150 lbs. Found only in South Africa. **1973** *Farmer's Weekly* 18 Apr. 102 The red steenbras is seldom caught weighing over 120 pounds. **1981** *E. Prov. Herald* 23 Apr. 11, I read a report .. from Plettenberg Bay about 'blue poenskop' and 'red poenskop' being caught down that way ... I had to telephone Jock Hunter, of Plettenberg Bay ... He told me the fish referred to were poenskop and red steenbras. **1988** D.E. POLLOCK in *Conserva* Oct. 10 Red steenbras undertake eastward spawning migrations. **1991** *Weekend Post* 30 Mar. 2 (*caption*) Craig Saunders .. holds a 40,6kg Red Steenbras which he caught from a boat off Noordhoek. **1902** J.D.F. GILCHRIST in *Trans. of S. Afr. Philological Soc.* IX. 231 Tiger-fish, or **River Steenbras** (E. London). **1902** [**rooi steenbras**: see quot. at *bank steenbras* above]. **1913** C. PETTMAN *Africanderisms* 413 *Rooi steenbras*, A much esteemed Cape fish. [**1930** see Biden quot. at sense a.] **1949** [see quot. at *red steenbras* above]. **1993** R. VAN DER ELST *Guide to Common Sea Fishes* 352 It is adept at camouflage, for the darker crossbars marking its flanks blend with the ripple marks that .. pattern the .. sandy sea-bed ... Thus the **sand steenbras** remains inconspicuous even when present in fair numbers. **1971** *Daily Dispatch* 2 June 15 One **silver steenbras** of 7,7 kg on light tackle. **1979** SNYMAN & KLARIE *Free from Sea* 38 *Musselcracker*, .. Steenbras/Silver Steenbras. **1990** [see STOMPKOP]. **1993** *Grocott's Mail* 17 Sept. 13 Athol Waters and his son Vivian caught hottentot and a silver steenbras aggregating 12,0 kilograms in the Kleinemond area. **1801** [**white steenbras**: see quot. at *red steenbras* above]. **1843** J.C. CHASE *Cape of G.H.* 169 Steenbras, red and white. Very good. **1902** J.D.F. GILCHRIST in *Trans. of S. Afr. Philological Soc.* XI. 231 Steenbras, Steenbrasen (Castelnau), Steenbraesem (Riebeck's Journal), White Steenbras, Kaapse Blaauwe Steenbras (Pappe) ... *Pagellus lithognathus*. **1905** [see MUSSELCRACKER sense 1]. **1930** C.L. BIDEN *Sea-Angling Fishes* 257 *Sparus durbanensis* ... East London — White Steenbras. **1970** *Argus* 30 July 8 White steenbras of up to 9 kg have been taken on prawn and worm. **1979** SNYMAN & KLARIE *Free from Sea* 56 *White Steenbras*, .. Highly prized angling fish, delicately flavoured, and the white flesh has large flakes when cooked. **1989** I. JONES *Woman's World Cookbk* 41 Fish Vinaigrette ... Use a firm white fish such as .. white steenbras or white stumpnose. **1992** [see DASSIE sense 2]. **1949** [**yellow steenbras**: see quot. at *red steenbras* above]. **1979** SNYMAN & KLARIE *Free from Sea* 44 *Red Steenbras*, Yellow Steenbras /-Steenbras.

steenbuck /ˈstɪənbʌk/ *n.* Also **steinbuck**. [Part. tr. S. Afr. Du. *steenbok*.] STEENBOK. Also *attrib.*

1839 W.C. HARRIS *Wild Sports* 224 Six smaller species of antelope .. viz., the klipspringer, rheebuck, rooe rheebuck, or nagor, ourebi, steenbuck, and duiker. **1854** R.B. STRUTHERS *Hunting Jrnl* (1991) 48 Shot a Steenbuck (Iqina). **1860** A.W. DRAYSON *Sporting Scenes* 60 The steinbuck (Oreotragus tragulus): about twenty one inches high, and about three feet in length; horns four inches long, .. slender and pointed; colour brownish-red, with belly white. **1881** P. GILLMORE *Land of Boer* 191 In these little covers the stein-buck and diker-buck find a shelter. **1896** R. WARD *Rec. of Big Game* 114 The Steinbuck has the faculty of being able to exist for long periods without water. In the very heart of the most waterless recesses of the Kalahari both this animal and the duiker are extremely numerous. **1939** *Outspan* 29 Dec. 31 Remembered once seeing a steenbuck trapped by fire. **1944** J. MOCKFORD *Here Are S. Africans* 21 Antelopes, from the great eland to the small steenbuck, .. grazed and frolicked behind the mountains. **1968** S. CLOETE *Chetoko* 12 Sometimes he .. came with a duiker, or a steenbuck, gutted, hanging over his shoulder. **1970** E. MUNDELL *Informant, Pearston* (*E. Cape*) Do you like steenbuck biltong? **1987** *You* 3 Sept. 104 Small game like duiker and steenbuck.

steentjie /ˈstɪəŋki/ *n.* Formerly also **steenje**. [Afk., *steen* stone + dim. suffix -IE.]

1. Either of two small species of seabream of the Sparidae: **a.** *Spondyliosoma emarginatum*, a fish commonly used as bait; DASSIE sense 2 b. **b.** Less frequently, the STREPIE, *Sarpa salpa*.

In Smith and Heemstra's *Smiths' Sea Fishes* (1986), the name 'steentjie' is used for *Spondyliosoma emarginatum*.

1893 H.A. BRYDEN *Gun & Camera* 448 We caught also at this time .. steenje, another small fish which we cut up principally for bait. **1913** C. PETTMAN *Africanderisms* 474 *Steenje*, .. *Cantharus emarginatus*. **1930** C.L. BIDEN *Sea-Angling Fishes* 166 The men .. caught many steentjies which were scaled and pulped with a baton and baited whole on the big lines. **1949** J.L.B. SMITH *Sea Fishes* 276 *Spondyliosoma Emarginatum* ... *Steentjie* ... Found only in South Africa from Saldanha Bay round to Madagascar, abundant at times. Enters estuaries, and is found even at 30 fathoms near rocky ground. Excellent bait, normally too small to be of any significance as a food-fish. **1954** K.H. BARNARD *S. Afr. Shore Life* 58 The Hottentot and Steentjie have bands of numerous small teeth and are mainly vegetarian. **1971** L.G. GREEN *Taste of S.-Easter* 186 The 'small fish time' that lasted eight months, when they could only expect to bring harders, steentjies and other such fish back to the beach. **1993** R. VAN DER ELST *Informant, Durban* A number of small or unsized species, including the sand-soldier .. , the pinky .. and the steentjie (*Spondyliosoma emarginatum*).

‖**2.** *rare.* A diamond: KLIP *n.* sense 2.

1957 D. JACOBSON *Price of Diamonds* 76 Gottlieb .. asked if he knew of the people who bought and sold the *steenjies* — the little stones — but Amos laughed and said in Afrikaans that the *steenjies* were dangerous stuff and he did not like them.

steertriem var. STERTRIEM.

stein /staɪn/ *n.* Also **steine**, and with initial capital. [Unknown; perh. alteration of STEEN, or fr. G. *Steinwein* a dry white wine produced in the Steinmantel vineyards near Würzburg, Bavaria.]

Used interchangeably with the word STEEN by some.

1. In full ***stein wine***: a style of blended, semi-sweet, fruity, white wine, often containing steen grapes; cf. STEEN sense 1. Also *attrib.* See also CAPE WINE.

1797 LADY A. BARNARD *S. Afr. Century Ago* (1910) 115 'Lord bless me, what fine wine this is!' said he; 'I have not tasted a glass such as this since I came here.' I then found, on asking, that it was Steine wine, a cheap Cape wine, which Mr. Barnard had not liked, and had ordered for common use in the household. **1844** J.S. LITTLE *S. Afr: Sketch Bk* I. 111 These gentlemen produce, beside the brand Constantia, Pontac — (the only wine which owes its red colour to the pulp and juice of the grape, the other purple wines were so tinted by allowing the skins to remain during fermentation) — Red Constantia, Frontignac, White Constantia, dry Sherry, Stein Wine, and Hock. **1966** H. BECK *Meet Cape Wines* 45 Of the white wines those which are most in the public eye are the rieslings and the steins ... The tendency today is to develop the rieslings into dry wines and the steins into semi-sweet, but that is merely a tendency. There are a number of semi-sweet rieslings and some dry steins. **1973** BEETON & DORNER in *Eng. Usage in Sn Afr.* Vol.4 No.2, 55 *Stein*, .. Semi-sweet S Afr wine produced fr the grapes of vines orig introduced fr Germany. **1977** *Fair Lady* 8 June, Serve with .. Stein, a fragrant, smooth, semi-sweet white wine. **1980** [see STEEN sense 2]. **1982** *S. Afr. Panorama* Jan. 22 Stein wines are generally light and delicate, combining the delicacy of Riesling with the soft dryness of Sancerre. **1982** M. BEAZLEY *Hugh Johnson's Pocket Wine Bk* 174 *Stein*, Name used for any medium dry white wine. **1986** *Style* Mar. 22 Thoughts of making wine in any but the German way were hygenically filtered out, and the entire industry was regimented into a boom of stainless steel tanks. Even fermentation wasn't allowed to do its thing but had to be, as in Germany, cold. Little wonder Stein and Steen became interchangeable ... White wine rules, OK. **1988** D. HUGHES et al. *Complete Bk of S. Afr. Wine* 330 *Stein*, Should not be confused with the cultivar Steen and its wine, though Steen, otherwise known as Chenin Blanc, is normally the basis of the local Stein wines. The name applies specifically to the style in which the wine is made, being semi-sweet .. , and with a fruity flavour.

2. STEEN sense 2. Also *attrib.*

1952 C.L. LEIPOLDT *300 Yrs Cape Wine* 204 Stein, another old and favourite variety, .. is very susceptible to oidium, but makes a far better wine than Green Grape. **1966** [see STEEN sense 2]. **1969** *Entertaining with Wine* (K.W.V.) 11 White table wines from the Cape are dry, semi-dry or semi-sweet ... They are made chiefly from Riesling, Stein, .. and Clairette Blanche grapes. *c*1970 *Pickstone's Catal.*, *Chenel* (Stein x St Emilion). This cross was made at Elsenburg and a very good quality white table wine is made from it. It is very similar to Stein in all respects except that the bunches are larger, it ripens a little later and does much better in the hotter inland wine growing areas. **1975** *S. Afr. Panorama* Mar., South Africa has types of grape which are peculiar to this country ... In the field of white wines, Stein is a mutation, possibly, of a Sauvignon Blanc, and, like Pinotage, grows

steinbok var. STEENBOK.

steinbrase var. STEENBRAS.

stekkie var. STUKKIE.

stel /stel, stɛl/ n. Also **stell**, **still**. [S. Afr. Du., fr. Du. *stelle* place, position. 'The meaning .. is derived from the plan .. of placing traps, or setting spring-guns, for the destruction of beasts of prey; the meaning has been transferred from the place to the trap itself.' (C. Pettman, *Africanderisms*, 1913).]

1. *obs.* A trap for wild animals; a spring-gun.

1801 J. BARROW *Trav.* I. 360 The animal had been shot through the body by a *stell-roar* (trap-gun, set by a Hottentot. 1852 C. BARTER *Dorp & Veld* 116 As soon as he [*sc.* the wolf] has seized the bait .., he tightens the string, releases the trigger, and if the *stel* is properly set, receives the bullet in his head. 1894 W.C. BALDWIN *Afr. Hunting* 377 The lions had killed two zebras .., and I set a stell (spring-gun) for them by the remains of one of the zebras. *Ibid.* 381 The Masaras set these spears (stells) for rhinoceros and other game. 1895 J.G. MILLAIS *Breath from Veldt* (1899) 264 A 'still' .. is formed by two rifles fixed to trees or posts.

2. *transf.* A trap used in witchcraft.

1957 L.G. GREEN *Beyond City Lights* 79 Sometimes you may still come across a *stel* put out in the path of an intended victim of witchcraft. The *stel* is a circle, drawn on the earth, with a nail or some other object in the centre. If the victim puts his foot within the circle then he is bewitched. Ignorant people who believe in *toondery* are indeed seriously influenced.

Stellalander /ˈstelələndə, -landər/ n. hist. [Afk. *Stellaland*, L. *stella* star + Afk. *land* country + Eng. (or Afk.) suffix -*er* denoting 'belonging to'. Stellaland was so named because a comet appeared during the year in which the republic was founded.] A citizen of the miniature republic of Stellaland (1882–1885) situated in what is now the North-West Province, round its capital, Vryburg. Also *attrib.*

1968 E.A. WALKER *Hist. of Sn Afr.* 400 He induced the Stellalanders to submit to Cape rule provided their lands were assured to them.

stellasie /steˈlɑːsi, stɛ-/ n. Also **stellassee**, **stellasi**. [Afk., fr. Du. *stellage* scaffolding, fr. *stellen* to place.] A framework or rack for drying meat, fish, fruit, or tobacco.

1882 S. HECKFORD *Lady Trader in Tvl* 145 Parties of Kaffir girls used to come .. to pull the fruit and spread it on things made of wood and reeds, called stellassees, that look something like stretchers. *Ibid.* 162 Peculiar sort of yellow peach — a fruit unknown in England but common in Italy — had yet to be dried, and I was hard at work gathering it in, and spreading it on the stellassees. 1913 C. PETTMAN *Africanderisms* 475 Stellasi, (D. *Stellage*, a scaffolding, platform.) Low platforms, generally made of open reedwork, upon which fruit is dried: a somewhat similar arrangement for the protection of young tobacco plants is also known by the same name. 1951 L.G. GREEN *Grow Lovely* 92 The fish are threaded through the eyes and hung in large bunches for a fortnight or more on a wooden framework or stellasie. 1955 — *Karoo* 126 Almost everyone in South Africa has tasted ostrich biltong ... Mile after mile of this biltong may be seen drying on the frames and wires called *stellasies* near Oudtshoorn. 1960 J. COPE *Tame Ox* 175 There were long wooden frames of fish-drying stellasies with the bunches of silver doppies and flecked yellow-tail and snoek out in the sun and salt. 1977 F.G. BUTLER *Karoo Morning* 45 Nearby .. Caspar Jafta was making 'stellasies' out of reeds — trays on which de-pipped peaches and apricots were spread to dry in the sun. 1985 A. TREDGOLD *Bay between Mountains* 131 The old Muizenberg, of simple houses, trek nets, booths for pickling fish, .. stellasies on which harders and other fish swung drying in the sun and wind had almost disappeared.

Stellenbosch /ˈstelənbɒʃ/ v. trans. Military slang. Also with small initial. [Name of a town in the Western Cape which was far from military action during the Anglo-Boer War; see Daily Telegraph quot. 1900.] Esp. during the ANGLO-BOER WAR: to relegate (an incompetent officer) to a position in which little harm could be done. Also *transf.*, and *fig.*

a. passive.

1900 R. KIPLING in *Daily Express* 16 June 4 'After all', said one cheerily .. 'what does it matter, old man? You're bound to be Stellenbosched in three days?' 1900 *Daily Telegraph* (U.K.) 2 Oct. 6, I heard .. that he had been 'Stellenbosched' ... I must inform the uninitiated that Stellenbosch .. was formerly the place selected for command by officers who had failed in Kaffir wars; and to be 'Stellenbosched' is the equivalent of being superseded without formal disgrace. 1901 W.E. CAIRNES *Army from Within* 59 In fact they are more probably 'stellenbosched' to the depot owing to an absence of any special qualifications. 1901 J. RALPH *War's Brighter Side* 106 To say that a man had been *Stellenbosched* was but the ordinary polite mode of mentioning what might otherwise have had to be said in many harsher words. 1902 C.R. DE WET *Three Yrs War* 256 This veldkornet was shortly afterwards 'Stellenbosched'. 1921 W.C. SCULLY *Harrow* 16 This officer .. was, shortly after the first of the raiding Boers from the north crossed the border of the district, 'Stellenbosched'. 1937 G.F. GIBSON *Story of Imp. Light Horse* 243 Much to our joy, Barton has been Stellenbosched (a term frequently used in those days, meaning that a certain officer had been relieved of his command) as he has treated us shamefully. 1976 *E. Prov. Herald* 17 Apr. 6 While some poor generals were being Stellenbosched, banks were burning in the free State, among them the Vrede branch of the old National Bank of the OFS. 1991 D. LIVINGSTONE *Littoral Zone* 58 The storm fumbles, folds its podium: Down in the mouth, gets Stellenbosched south, booted on its journey by the dawn.

b. active.

1900 *Daily Telegraph* (U.K.) 20 Oct. 7 It is a gross injustice to Stellenbosch any doctor because some nurse does not get her own way, and has influence in high quarters. 1913 *Times Lit. Suppl.* (U.K.) 24 July 309 Take the phrase 'to Stellenbosch,' a household word during the war for the shelving of an incompetent officer. 1975 J.H. PICARD in *Eng. Usage in Sn Afr.* Vol.6 No.1, 35 The British military tradition in South Africa is very old. To 'Stellenbosch' an officer, that is to transfer him to a less responsible appointment where he would be out of harm's way, is a typical example.

Hence **Stellenbosch** n. (alluding to the verbal usage).

1903 R. KIPLING *Five Nations* 196 We were sugared about by the old men ... That 'amper an' 'inder an' scold men For fear o' Stellenbosch! 1921 W.C. SCULLY *Harrow* 18 He was now a man marked down for transfer to Stellenbosch upon the first feasible pretext.

Stem /stem/ n. [Afk., 'voice', ellipt. for *Die Stem van Suid-Afrika* 'The Voice of South Africa,' the name of a patriotic song written in Afk. by C.J. Langenhoven and set to music by M.L. de Villiers.] *Die Stem* /di -/, *the Stem*: From 1938 to 1960, one of two official national anthems, with 'God save the King (or Queen)'; from 1961, the sole official national anthem; from 1994, one of two national anthems, with NKOSI SIKELEL' (IAFRIKA).

[1934 A.J. BARNOUW *Lang. & Race Problems* 57 By Die Stem van Suid-Afrika he [*sc.* Langenhoven] will remain alive to later generations, for .. his voice has become the voice of his people.] 1939 *Star* 4 Feb. 12 Dr Malan .. is the first in the field with a request that 'Die Stem' shall be the one and only national anthem of the country. 1944 'TWEDE IN BEVEL' *Piet Kolonel* 52 Wilfred played the 'Stem,' and 'God Save the King,' and then again came over to ask whether he should play all the National anthems over and over again. 1952 *Rand Daily Mail* 5 Apr. 1 'Die Stem': English translation issued. 1956 M. ROGERS *Black Sash* 34 All stood to join in singing 'Die Stem' in both languages. 1957 *Cape Times* 3 Apr., In a blaze of naval pageantry 143 years of British occupation of Simonstown came to an end yesterday as the Union Jack was lowered and a Royal Marine band played 'The Queen'. Then .. the national flag was hoisted .. as the South African Navy band struck up *Die Stem*. 1972 *Sunday Times* 14 May 14 We were endowed with two flags and two anthems. The Union Jack and 'The King' were mainly associated with the English section, and the Union Flag and 'Die Stem' with the Afrikaans section ... In 1938 the newly established United Party under the Prime Ministership of Gen. Hertzog, gave official recognition to Die Stem. 1973 *Star* 8 June 13 Somehow Afrikaans schools always seem to emphasise things like flag-hoisting and singing 'Die Stem'. 1981 [see NKOSI SIKELEL' (IAFRIKA)]. 1991 *E. Prov. Herald* 16 May 1 Die Stem had political connotations and .. it should either be dropped or sung with *Nkosi Sikelel' iAfrika*. 1991 F. KEATING in *Guardian Weekly* 9 Oct. 31 The appalling double-cross of the ANC when the hated anthem Die Stem was played in the 'comeback' Test at Ellis Park.

stembras, **stem brass** varr. STEENBRAS.

stembuck n. obsolescent. Also **stembok**. [Englished form of S. Afr. Du. *steenbok*.] The STEENBOK, *Raphiceros campestris*.

1851 T. SHONE *Diary.* 27 Aug., Jack shot a stem buck. a1867 C.J. ANDERSSON *Notes of Trav.* (1875) 199 Sent Hans and Kamoja out in search of game. The former brought in a stembuck only; Kamoja ditto. 1897 J.P. FITZPATRICK *Outspan* 34 Towards sundown two of us strolled on ahead, taking guns in hopes of picking up a guinea-fowl, or a stembuck, or some other small game. 1907 — *Jock of Bushveld* (1909) 172 The herdboy came in one afternoon to say that there was a stembuck feeding among the oxen. 1917 A.W. CARTER *Informant, Ladybrand* 11 Sept., There are lots of little birds visible & occasional Koorhans and Stembuck. 1939 J.E. TAYLOR in F.G. Butler *When Boys Were Men* (1969) 259 In the grass country which begins at the Modder River, oribi, duiker, and stembok could be 'walked up' and killed by the score. 1963 D. JACOBSON *Through Wilderness* (1977) 44 It was dead when we came to it, a little stembuck, in height not much taller than a fair-sized dog, but slender in the shoulders, haunches and muzzle; most slender in the legs.

‖**stemvee** /ˈstemfiə/ n. [Afk., *stem* vote, voting + *vee* cattle.] Those whose vote is relied upon (by a political party), but whose views are not considered in decision-making.

1934 C.P. SWART *Supplement to Pettman.* 167 *Stemvee*, Voting fodder; back-benchers whose duties in parliament are confined to voting on, and not discussing, the measures brought forward. 1943 I. FRACK *S. Afr. Doctor* 115 These 'educated' men and women forget the depressed social state of their brethren and only look upon them as 'stemvee' — voting cattle, who are useful in furthering their insular ideas. 1988 *Sunday Times* 10 Apr. 18 A backlash is building up among English-speaking South Africans. Taken for granted by President Botha — treated as mere *stemvee* even though they provided more than 40 percent of the votes that returned him to office .. — many people are beginning to flex the political muscles which they are only beginning to sense they have.

sten bock var. STEENBOK.

‖**sterk** /stɛrk/ adj. [Afk.; the form *sterrek* reflects the word's use in Fanakalo.] Strong, powerful.

Latterly, common in *colloq.* speech (pronounced /stɜːk/), used particularly of strongly-built people.

1864 J.S. DOBIE *S. Afr. Jrnl* (1945) 174 The psalmody in the evening .. was so 'sterk' as to be nearly overpowering! **1899** 'S. ERASMUS' *Prinsloo* 29 'Scotty' was a sterk kerel, and had no fear of Landdrost, but preferred to steal their horses above everybody's. **1911** L. COHEN *Reminisc. of Kimberley* 388 The ragged groom regarded me with some admiration as having performed a gastronomic feat which he would like to emulate, the tousle-haired wench muttered, 'I was (being) sterk' (strong), the concerned hostess said 'I ought to see the doctor'. **1913** J.J. DOKE *Secret City* 256 Wait, there's a good soul, until you are quite strong, baaija sterk. [**1939** C. DELBRIDGE in *Outspan* 20 Oct. 71 The Baas hit you 'maningi sterrek' Nkos.]

sterkte /'stɛrktə/ *n. colloq.* [Afk., lit. 'strength'.] Used as an interjection: 'courage', 'more power to your arm'.

1978 J. HOBBS *Informant, Johannesburg* Sterkte ou maat. All things must pass. **1982** *Evening Post* 2 Nov. 3 Dr Slabbert's toast to the Government was '*sterkte*, and healthy power-sharing'. **1990** A. RICE in *Frontline* Dec. 15 The toast is immediately mine — sterkte ou maat. **1991** D. HALL-GREEN on TV1, 28 Nov. (Good Morning South Africa), May I wish you — and you'll need lots of it — sterkte.

sterloop /'stɛrlʊəp/ *n.* [Du., *ster* star + *loop* barrel; see quot. 1957.] A smooth-bore flintlock musket made by Scholefield of Birmingham, in use from about 1820; *rare*, the barrel of this gun, which was decorated with a star. Also *attrib.* Cf. ROER sense a.

1957 G. TYLDEN in *Africana Notes & News* Vol.12 No.6, 204 The *sterloop*, very popular in the O.F.S .. so called from a twelve pointed star about 2 inches across stamped on top of the barrel about a foot from the muzzle. *Ibid.* 217 *Sterloop*, the muzzleloading flint and percussion guns by Scholefield, later Scholefield, Goodman & Sons of Birmingham, from 1820 onwards. **1969** F.G. BUTLER *When Boys Were Men* 180 *Sterloper* or *Sterloop*: literally 'star-barrel'. A muzzle-loading gun made during the first quarter of the 19th century. It had a calibre of .75", known as musket bore. A star stamp on the barrel gave this gun its name. The maker was Joshua Scholefield of Birmingham. **1971** L.G. GREEN *Taste of S.-Easter* 56 Frederik Botha was celebrated for his sterloop rifles, a favourite flint and percussion muzzle-loader used by the Voortrekkers. **1972** *Daily Dispatch* 22 July 4 By the middle of the 19th century the greatest damage to the game herds of the plains was being done by the famous sterloop — a smooth-bore flintlock of about 1842 manufactured in Birmingham with the much prized star mark on the barrel. **1973** J. MEINTJES *Voortrekkers* 107 The Voortrekker gun was generally called a *Sanna*, a popular type being the *Sterloop*, so called after a twelve-pointed star about a foot from the muzzle. **1990** *Caption, 1820 Settlers' Memorial Museum (Grahamstown)* A typical 'bobbejaanbout sterloop' smooth-bore with a 45" barrel ... 'Sterloop' referred to the star engraved around the front or back sight of these weapons. **1991** *Best of S. Afr. Short Stories* (Reader's Digest Assoc.) 12 The average Boer frontiersman would not own a weapon without a *sterloop* (star barrel) and the tradition was passed down to his sons and grandsons.

sterretjie /'sterəki, 'stɛrəki/ *n.* Formerly also **sterrentjie, sterrethe.** [Afk., 'little star', *ster* star + dim. suffix -IE.]

1. Any of several species of flowering plant of the Amaryllidaceae.

[**1810** G. BARRINGTON *Acct of Voy.* 341 The soil here is further distinguished, by the star-flower with its regular radiated corolla.] **1917** R. MARLOTH *Common Names* 77 *Sterretje*. Several kinds of flowers, particularly species of *Curculigo* as *C. plicata*, and *Hypoxis*, as *H. stellata*. **1966** C.A. SMITH *Common Names* 438 *Sterretjie*, A general term for a number of species of Amaryllidaceae with cormous rootstocks, grasslike leaves and the perianth segments arranged in a star-like manner. **1984** A. WANNENBURGH *Natural Wonder of Sn Afr.* 122 Like many other members of the Amaryllidaceae family, these cormous plants with grass-like leaves and six-petalled pink flowers are known as sterretjies, 'little stars'.

2. The sea-gull *Larus hartlaubii* of the Laridae, common on the Western Cape and Namibian coasts.

In G.L. Maclean's *Roberts' Birds of Sn Afr.* (1993), the name 'Hartlaub's gull' is used for this species.

1955 C. HORNE *Fisherman's Eldorado* 12 Sterrentjies and malagas, their immaculate plumage shining, dived for their prey, or rested in great flocks, gorged and exhausted. **1971** R. RAVEN-HART *Cape G.H. 1652–1702* 133 Those which are called Starling-Gulls ('Stahr-Moebigen', perhaps Sterretje) are smaller. **1977** *E. Prov. Herald* 17 Nov. 15 Often when the sterretjies are flitting over the surface there are penguins in the area ... But I know some men who ignore sterretjies (terns). They claim that sterretjies working do not necessarily mean anything. **1982** *S. Afr. Digest* 8 Jan. 24 Up to a few years ago the Hartlaub's gull, or sterretjie as it is better known, bred in seclusion on Robben Island. But as more and more open fill refuse dumps sprang up around the city the gull's food supply .. increased, and so did their numbers. **1983** *E. Prov. Herald* 13 Jan. 13 There are two schools of thought among deep sea anglers. One believes that terns (sterretjies) are the best guides to feeding tunny. The other school believes that working gannets (malgas) are the surer indication. **1987** R. NAYSMITH in *Ski Scene* Mar.-Apr. 13 These shoals of summer game fish have been relatively easy to find with the 'sterretjies' (terns) and Malgas gulls ever present to feed on a rising bait shoal.

3. The GEOMETRIC TORTOISE, *Psammobates geometricus*.

1985 [see SUURPOOTJIE]. **1989** E. BAARD in *Afr. Wildlife* Vol.43 No.4, 179 Call it what you will — geometric tortoise, *suurpootjie, kransie, sterretjie* — all of these names are used to refer to one of the world's rarest tortoise species, *Psammobates geometricus*.

stertriem /'stɛrtrim/ *n.* Formerly also **staartriem, steertriem.** [Afk. (earlier S. Afr. Du. *staartriem*, transf. use of Du. *staartriem* crupper), *stert* tail + *riem* thong.] A loin-cloth of soft leather, traditionally worn in rural society by Sotho men. Cf. MUTSHA.

[**1822** W.J. BURCHELL *Trav.* I. 397 From the hinder part of the belt, is suspended a piece of leather, seldom so long as twelve inches, including the strap by which it hangs ... When speaking in Dutch, they call this a *Staart-riem*, which in English may be expressed by the word *Tail-piece*.] **a1875** T. BAINES *Jrnl of Res.* (1964) II. 44 His uniform consisted of an old hat, two strings of beads, a rather limited kaross .. and the usual 'staart riem', or exceedingly scanty Kafir breeches. **1905** G.W. STOW *Native Races of S. Afr.* 266 Here we find in the Ovaherero a tribe of men wearing the staart-riem. **1910** J. ANGOVE *In Early Days* 69 Though perhaps clad (if the term may be used) in a *staart riem* only, they managed to conceal diamonds about their persons. **1937** B.H. DICKE *Bush Speaks* 329 The trader had taken the owner of the kraal for a Mosuto because he wore a 'steertriem' (sesibe), a kind of extravagantly abbreviated bathing slip made of skin, the male attire of the Basuto ... However, the gentleman .. was .. a Movenda. The Bavenda also wear the steertriem. **1940** BAUMANN & BRIGHT *Lost Republic* 223 When I was a boy your father was my gun-carrier in a 'stert riem' (loincloth), and was content with 'kaboe' mealies. **1951** H.C. BOSMAN in L. Abrahams *Bekkersdal Marathon* (1971) 165 I'd feel that I was walking with nothing more than a stert-riem on, in the hereafter ... Isn't that a scream, the thought of me wearing a stert-riem. **1953** LANHAM & MOPELI-PAULUS *Blanket Boy's Moon* 16 Proud in their wearing of the stertreim — sign of manhood — these young boys, clad in their tribal clothes of well-trimmed, round-cut goatskins, play about on the grassy banks of the stream. **1980** A.J. BLIGNAUT *Dead End Rd* 98, I pulled a handful and began plaiting a hat, thinking the brown they were turning would go well with my new stertriem of springbok hide. **1988** M. TLALI in *Staffrider* Vol.7 No.3, 358 During the week we wore 'litsheha' (stertriems) and the usual Basotho 'mekhahla' (leather blanket) over them. Every male person wore these.

steuks var. STEEKS.

steuve ziekt var. STYFSIEKTE.

stick *n. Military slang.* [Prob. transf. use of general Eng. *stick* a collective name for a group of parachutists jumping in quick succession (see quot. 1977).] In the army: a small fighting unit.

[**1977** B. MARKS *Our S. Afr. Army* 37 Trainee paratroopers have been divided into small groups of approximately twelve known as sticks. The reason for such small groups is to enable the troops to receive personal attention from instructors.] **1978** *Daily Dispatch* 25 Sept. 1 Most of them had left the previous night and a few sticks (small fighting units) stayed behind to mop up. **1978** E. DIBB in *Fair Lady* 25 Oct. 108 Ben Salmin and his stick of men were striking camp ... Frans's next job was to bring in the other members of his stick — Gardiner, Sanders, and Graves — and let them know where to meet Ben Salmin. **1982** *Sunday Times* 21 Mar. 21 Early the next morning we hit Swapo. They were not expecting an attack and we received no fire as we dropped a stick of troops. **1982** *E. Prov. Herald* 3 May 5 With a scream from the twin jet engines of the 'chopper' we were away. Riding with us were a 'stick' of soldiers from the air base's reaction force, which is on standby day and night. **1990** D. GORDON in *Sunday Times* 10 June 3 The R4-million movie shows an army patrol disintegrating under combat pressure and guilt over a shooting incident. The 'stick' of eight soldiers annihilate a village of black women and children and shoot the witchdoctor.

stick-fight *n.* A traditional martial game among black youths (in rural areas), involving two fighters, each wielding two sticks, the right-hand for attack and the left-hand for defence. See also FIGHTING STICK sense 1.

[**1731** G. MEDLEY tr. *P. Kolb's Present State of Cape of G.H.* I. 292 They frequently exercise themselves in Mock-Fights. And at these Mock-Fights I have frequently beheld 'em with inexpressible Pleasure ... These Disputes are chiefly maintain'd with *Kirri*-Sticks, *Rackum*-Sticks and Stones.] **1882** C. DU VAL *With Show through Sn Afr.* I. 159 He and his comrade, the gentleman in the woollen shirt, executed a little stick fight for our edification, which was amusing. **1971** *Daily Dispatch* 11 May 11 A stick fight .. broke out at a circumcision party in Xobo Locations near here. **1979** *Daily Dispatch* 28 Feb. 3 The editor .. is lucky he wasn't challenged to a stick fight. **1979** C. ENDFIELD *Zulu Dawn* 37 The headless hardwood *assegai* that he would use for this stick-fight. **1987** J. JADI *Informant, Grahamstown* A stick-fight is a game or exercise for boys before they go to initiation school. They use two sticks each, one for defence and one for attack ... Stick-fights rarely take place in urban areas.

Hence **stick-fight** *v. intrans.*, **stick-fighter** *n.*, **stick-fighting** *vbl n.*; also *attrib.*

1903 *Ilanga* 9 Oct. 4 Various games indulged in by the boys such as 'Ubedu' .. , stick-fighting with the 'insema', foot-racing and similar pastimes. **1972** *Drum* 8 Aug. 20 As I see it, the Xhosas will romp home with all the gold medals for stick-fighting. **1979** C. ENDFIELD *Zulu Dawn* 37 All were certain that it would be a classic stick-fighting (in performance of which, as in knowledge, all Zulus excelled) ... Though stick-fighting was regarded merely as training for truly mortal contest with the flat-bladed, stabbing *assegai*, as well as to test courage under duress of pain, at this level of skill and antagonism it could easily cripple, or damage permanently or, with some frequency, end fatally. **1987** J. JADI *Informant, Grahamstown* When big men stick-fight, they use one kierie each, and it is serious. **1988** F. KHASHANE in *Pace* June 154 John Sepheko first showed his boxing ability as a stick-fighter. **1988** *Learning Nation* Vol.1 No.4, 1 The main way that boys competed with one another was through stick-fighting ... The fights were controlled by strict rules of conduct to ensure that no one was badly injured and that only youths of equal strength fought one another ... Stick-fighting .. helped to teach youth the values of courage, the importance of justice and respect for the rules. **1991** G. SILBER *Sunday Times* 23 June (Mag. Sect.) 35 A Xhosa stick-fighting song.

stick-grass *n.* [Calque formed on S. Afr. Du. *steekgras.*] STEEKGRAS.

1838 J.E. ALEXANDER *Exped. into Int.* I. 237 The Boschmans have a peculiar mode of fishing .. ; they make conical baskets of stick grass, which is as thick and hard as quills. **1844** J. BACKHOUSE *Narr. of Visit* 540 The cows could get little but a scanty supply of rigid herbage, called here Stickgrass, and which is a shrubby, gramineous plant. [**1897** 'F. MACNAB' *On Veldt & Farm* 73 They [*sc.* thorns] are very injurious to the fleeces of sheep and Angora goat, as is also a grass called 'sticky grass' from the small splinters which work their way into the wool.] **1916** *Farmer's Weekly* 27 Dec. 1594 We all know that stick grass and Merinos do not agree. **1971** *Golden Fleece* (S. Afr. Wool Board) June (Suppl.) 8 Pioneer Stage: *Aristida curvata* – Stickgrass. **1975** W.J. MORRIS in *Std Encycl. of Sn Afr.* XI. 382 Stick-grass or steekgras (*Aristida congesta*) is a biennial pioneer grass.

sticks var. STEEKS.

stienbrass var. STEENBRAS.

stiff-sickness *n.* [tr. Afk. *styfsiekte.*]
1. *Pathology.* STYFSIEKTE sense 1.

1886 G.A. FARINI *Through Kalahari Desert* 64 We have sickness among the flocks and herds to contend with. First, the *lung ziekt*, or lung-sickness, and then the *steuve ziekt*, or stiff-sickness – the latter a very curious plague, which appeared only a few years ago. The cattle get stiff in their forequarters, till after a few days they cannot walk, and gradually dwindle away and starve to death. **1894** E. GLANVILLE *Fair Colonist* 231 'You have lost fifteen head of cattle.' 'The lung-sickness carried off nine, stiff-sickness killed four, and two were stolen.' **1905** D. HUTCHEON in Flint & Gilchrist *Science in S. Afr.* 360 Osteomalacia or Stijfziekte and Lamziekte. This is a disease which is characterised by a gradual softening of the bones .., accompanied by a highly vascular condition of the articular extremities of the bones of the limbs, causing acute lameness, which is locally called 'Stiffsickness'. **1912** [see STYFSIEKTE sense 2]. **1954** MÖNNIG & VELDMAN *Handbk on Stock Diseases* 227 Several forms of stiffsickness occur in cattle and should be differentiated from one another ... 1. Three-day stiffsickness (also called three-day sickness) – see Virus Diseases. 2. Stiffsickness due to phosphorus deficiency – see Metabolic Diseases. 3. Stiffsickness caused by the stiffsickness plant. **1968** K. MCMAGH *Dinner of Herbs* 2 His milk cows all have stiff sickness. **1978** *S. Afr. Panorama* May 37 After the bones were cleared away and the cattle fed with fresh bonemeal, the incidence of paralysis dropped and there was a spectacular improvement in the cattle's productivity. The meal also cured 'stywesiekte' (stiff sickness) which was related to rickets. **1979** T. GUTSCHE *There Was a Man* 21 Visiting Griqualand West in 1884, he had satisfied himself that both Lamziekte and Stijfziekte (Stiff Sickness) were due to defective nutrition.

2. *comb.* **stiff-sickness bush**, also **-plant**, the *styfsiektebossie* (see STYFSIEKTE sense 2), *Crotalaria burkeana*.

1954 MÖNNIG & VELDMAN *Handbk on Stock Diseases* 67 Three-day sickness should be differentiated from true stiffsickness (phosphate deficiency), stiffsickness bush (crotalaria) poisoning, diplodia (mealie fungus) poisoning, laminitis, etc. *Ibid.* 228 Stiffsickness caused by the stiffsickness plant (rattle bush, *Crotalaria burkeana*).

stiffy *n.* [Named for the rigidity of the plastic in which it is encased, as opposed to the flexible casing of the larger disk or 'floppy'.] A $3\frac{1}{2}$ inch (9 cm) computer diskette, contained in a rigid casing. Also *attrib.*

1993 *Weekly Mail* 18 June (Suppl.) 8 As a profession it is only lawyers who will still giggle hysterically when confronted with computer speak such as 'stiffy' and 'floppy'. **1993** *Sunday Times* 10 Oct. (Business Times) 3 (*caption*) Conversion software: Butch R–'s company puts proselytism on a stiffy. **1994** *Weekly Mail* 18 Mar. 20 (*advt*) When ordering the PC version please specify 3.5 (stiffy) or 5.25 (floppy). **1994** C. MULLER *Informant, Grahamstown* I'll just boot it from your stiffy drive so that we can see whether you can connect to the network.

stiftziehte, **stijfsiekte**, **-ziekte** varr. STYFSIEKTE.

still var. STEL.

stinka var. STINKER.

stinkblaar /ˈstəŋkblɑː(r)/ *n.* Pl. **-blare** /-blɑːrə/. [S. Afr. Du., fr. Du. *stinken* to stink + *blaar* leaf.] Any of several annual herb-like weeds of the genus *Datura* of the Solanaceae, including *D. stramonium*, *D. metel*, and *D. ferox*, of rank growth and foetid smell, bearing trumpet-shaped mauve flowers and thorny fruit containing highly poisonous seeds (see MALPITTE). Also *attrib.*

The source of the drug Stramonium.

1835 C.L. STRETCH Journal., The same parties taking advantage of the Native Ignorance sold the Seed of the Stremoniacie or 'Stink blaar' for Coarse gun powder. **1881** *Alice Times* 14 Jan., When the children came indoors they both had a peculiar frightened expression, with bright scarlet faces, dilated pupils and great heat of skin ... I found lying on the ground fragments of the capsules of the seed-vessel of the Stramonium, or Stink-blaar, as it is called. **1896** R. WALLACE *Farming Indust. of Cape Col.* 117 The stramonium just mentioned, 'stink blaar', *Datura tatula*, L., grows a large fruit capsule. If eaten freely it brings on paralysis in young ostriches ... The juice of the leaf is used as a remedy for sore eyes in sheep. **1913** C. PETTMAN *Africanderisms* 478 *Stink blaar, Datura stramonium, Linn.* This plant has an exceedingly disagreeable smell. **1916** S. BLACK in S. Gray *Three Plays* (1984) 196 Van Slaap: We'll strike! Van K: We'll put stinkblare in his office. **1925** L.D. FLEMMING *Crop of Chaff* 23, I had systematically been killing a plant that was worth a small fortune. 'Stinkblaar' was a most valuable drug ... Stinkblaar leaves, dried and bagged – were being asked for by all the leading druggists in the world, and paid for at so much per ounce. **1948** *George & Knysna Herald* 14 May 5 Stinkblaar or Thorn Apple (also known as Malpitte) occurring in many parts of the country as a noxious weed, possesses dangerous poisonous properties. **1949** L.G. GREEN *In Land of Afternoon* 51 Some asthmatics claim they have found relief by smoking dried Stinkblaar (Datura Stramonium) leaves. This is a weed which must be treated with respect, however, for two seeds are enough to kill a child and three may finish an adult. **1966** C.A. SMITH *Common Names* 438 *Stinkblaar*, .. Esteemed as a remedy for asthma and for this purpose the dried leaves are smoked in a pipe. The freshly warmed leaves or the vapours from an infusion are used as a sedative in cases of neuralgia, rheumatic or other pains and, in the form of poultices, are also applied to cancerous ulcers, and, rolled up into little pellets, are employed .. to ease earache. **1976** *E. Prov. Herald* 8 Sept., The plant *Datura stramonium*, otherwise known as thorn-apple or jimsonweed (or stinkblaar) has large white or violet trumpet-shaped flowers which bloom at night, and a hard-spiked date-shaped fruit. **1988** P. JOHNSTONE in *Personality* 25 July 32 There stood a miniature forest of stinkblaar seedlings. 'Darned poisonous,' she said.

stink-cat *n. obs.* [So called because of the foul-smelling fluid emitted from the animal's anal glands when it feels threatened.] The MUISHOND (sense 1 a i), *Ictonyx striatus*.

1834 W.H.B. WEBSTER *Narr. of Voy. to Sn Atlantic Ocean* 296 It is said that there is good shooting on the top of the Table Mountain, as it abounds in rock rabbits and baboons, besides stink-cats, probably no very desirable game after all. **1899** H. RIDER HAGGARD *Swallow* 50, I have shammed dead like a stink-cat when dogs are about. **1913** C. PETTMAN *Africanderisms* 478 *Stink cat, Zorilla striata.* This by no means pretty name is sometimes given to the Muishond.

stinker *n. Hist. slang.* Also **stinka**. [Special sense of general Eng. *stinker* something which stinks, something repugnant because of its unendurable nature.] Esp. in township parlance: a contemptuous name for a PASS (sense 3). Also *attrib.*

1977 J. SIKAKANE *Window on Soweto* 5 The men feel the inside pocket of their jackets, just to make sure that the 'stinker' or pass book is safely tucked in or else it means being picked up by the police. **1979** A.P. BRINK *Dry White Season* 84 Man needs a *stinka*, he comes straight to you. 'A *stinka*?' Gleeful, perhaps not without disdain, Stanley stared at him, then laughed again. 'A reference book, man. A *domboek*. A pass.' **1981** *Voice* 27 May 2 He takes him back into the kwela-kwela, which is devouring all other gentlemen who have forgotten their stinkers at home that quiet and sunny Sunday. **1982** *Staffrider* Vol.4 No.4, 4 The door is kicked down And a torch shines in our faces The command: 'Permit, Baba Permit'. I produce my 'Stinker'. **1983** O. MUSI in *City Press* 6 Nov. 7 The next few guys appear for not having 'stinkas' – the hated dompas. **1985** D. BIKITSHA in *Sunday Times* 15 Sept. 6 We refer to reference books as 'stinker', 'nzangan', 'nzenga', 'dompas' or 'lankof'. Different regions have their own original names, but a 'stinker' remains one from Guguletu township in Cape Town to Dube townships in Soweto ... It stinks. **1986** *Drum* Aug. 55 My colleagues' books were in order and one look at my terrified face showed that I was in stinka-trouble. **1986** *Pace* Aug. 4 So they say the stinker is gone, mzala. Me, I'll try to forget the many weekends I spent in jail for 'failure to produce' and other stinker offences. **1987** *New Nation* 9 July 7 'Hamba Dompas' ... The title of the play was later used by the South African government during the phasing out of 'stinka' or 'ndzangana' as the passbook is called. **1987** *Pace* Nov. 14 The old stinker is an embarrassment to this supposedly verlig Government and .. the repeal of the pass and influx laws was a hefty stride for them.

‖**stinkhout** /ˈstəŋkhəʊt/ *n.* Formerly also **stink-houtt**. [S. Afr. Du., fr. Du. *stink* stink(ing) + *hout* wood.]
a. STINKWOOD sense a. Also *attrib.*

1790 tr. *F. Le Vaillant's Trav.* II. 239, I observed here many trees of the same kind as those I had met with in the country of Auteniqua: the *stink-houtt*, or stinking wood, abounded in every quarter. **1795** C.R. HOPSON tr. *C.P. Thunberg's Trav.* I. 169 Stink-hout (Stinkwood) .. is used for making writing-desks and chests of drawers. *Ibid.* II. 110 Of the *Stinkhout* there are two sorts, the white and the brown. **1798** S.H. WILCOCKE tr. *J.S. Stavorinus's Voy. to E. Indies 1768–71* II. 79 *Stinkhout*, or stinkwood, which is a beautiful brown wood, like *walnuttree-wood*; household furniture of all kinds is made of it; it is susceptible of the finest polish. **1809** J. MACKRILL Diary. 58 Stink hout, like the Walnut tree. [**1812** A. PLUMPTRE tr. *H. Lichtenstein's Trav. in Sn Afr.* (1928) I. 188 Large oaks, sumachs, and a tree that is called here *Stinkholz* called by Thunberg *ilex crocea*, but it seems not yet systematically classed.] **1834** T. PRINGLE *Afr. Sketches* 219, I observed .. iron-wood, stinkhout (laurus bullata), .. and many other woods prized for their useful qualities. **1847** J. BARROW *Reflect.* 162 *Stink-hout* takes its name from an offensive odour which it exhales while green. **1887** *S.W. Silver & Co.'s Handbk to S. Afr.* 128 'How many stinkhout trees of three feet diameter have you?' Not a man in the colony can tell whether there are a thousand or a hundred thousand. **1986** *Sunday Times* 7 Sept. 7 The sexual antics of the Matie lovers in the sanctimonious privacy of the 'stinkhout ossewa'.

b. With distinguishing epithet: **Camdeboo stinkhout** (*obs.*), or **wit stinkhout** [Afk., *wit* white], *Camdeboo stinkwood* (see STINKWOOD sense b); also *attrib.*

1852 M.B. HUDSON *S. Afr. Frontier Life* 34 Ensconsed in a corner at foot of the rock Is the **Camdeboo Stinkhout.** **1971** BARAITSER & OBHOLZER *Cape Country Furn.* 220 Early **'wit stinkhout'** wakis with tapered sides, a voorkis. **1984** [see *Camdeboo stinkwood* (STINKWOOD sense b)].

stinking wood *n. phr. Obs.* [tr. S. Afr. Du. *stinkhout* (see STINKHOUT).] STINKWOOD sense a.

1790 tr. *F. Le Vaillant's Trav.* I. 211 They might .. cut down a certain tree, called *stinking wood*, and export it to Europe, where it would undoubtedly soon be preferred to every other kind employed by cabinet-makers. **1804** R. PERCIVAL *Acct of Cape of G.H.* 148 The stink hout or stinking wood is so called from its offensive smell when cut green; but when well seasoned is reckoned the best for building at the Cape. **1810** G. BARRINGTON *Acct of Voy.* 326 *Stinkhout*, or stinking wood, takes its name from an offensive excrementitious odour, that it exhales while green. *a***1823** J. EWART *Jrnl* (1970) 63 The stink or stinking wood, so called from an unpleasant smell it emitts when green .. , being very hard, and close grain'd, is used for furniture, implements of farming, &c.

stinkkruid /ˈstəŋkreɪt, -krœɪt/ *n.* Formerly also **stink kruit, stinkkruyd.** [Afk., *stink* stink(ing) + *kruid* (medicinal) herb.] Any of several species of shrubby aromatic annual herb, esp. *Penzia suffruticosa*, used medicinally for a variety of ailments.

[**1837** ECKLON & ZEYHER *Emuneratio Plantarum Africae* 367 *Anthospermum spermacoceum* ... Olanta subsiceata olet ova putrida, quamobrem ab incolis, stinkkruyd, Poepgras denominatur.] **1896** R. WALLACE *Farming Indust. of Cape Col.* 222 Young birds are sometimes poisoned by eating 'stink kruid,' but old ones are more wary and avoid it. **1911** *Farmer's Weekly* 18 Oct. 196 When walking with the chicks, teach them to eat various kinds of herbs ... Pretend you are an ostrich, by picking at the plant with your hand. Be careful not to swallow any, as some of these bushes do not taste nice! – 'Stink-kruit', for instance! **1933** *Farming in S. Afr.* 190 Stinkkruid and a weedy species of 'saltbush' are of general occurrence. **1966** C.A. SMITH *Common Names* 440 *Stinkkruid, Pentzia suffruticosa* ... A bushy aromatic annual herb .. said to impart a bitter flavour to the milk of cows grazing on the plants. The vernacular name in all cases is an allusion to the marked scent of the bruised plant. **1981** *S. Afr. Panorama* Nov. 49 Among the daisies are *stinkkruid, gansogiebos, rapuisbos, hongerblom* and the bitter *gousblom*.

stinkwood *n.* [tr. of S. Afr. Du. *stinkhout*, fr. Du. *stink* smell(ing) + *hout* wood; see quot. 1731.]
a. The protected indigenous tree *Ocotea bullata* of the Lauraceae, prized for its timber (in full ***stinkwood tree***); the finely-grained, dark, heavy wood of this tree; *African oak*, see AFRICAN *adj.*[1] sense 1 b i; *Cape mahogany* sense (*b*), also *Cape walnut* sense (*a*), see CAPE sense 2 a; STINKHOUT sense a; STINKING WOOD. Also *attrib.*

A prized wood in furniture, particularly when used in combination with yellowwood.

1731 G. MEDLEY tr. *P. Kolb's Present State of Cape of G.H.* II 260 The Stink-Wood Tree grows to the Size of an Oak. The leaves are of the Breadth of Three fingers. 'Tis call'd *Stink*-Wood, because it has a filthy Scent. While it is under the Tool, it sends out so nauseous a Stench, that the Workman can hardly endure it. But, after some Time, the Stench goes quite off. **1798** LADY A. BARNARD in Lord Lindsay *Lives of Lindsays* (1849) III. 438, I was told of charming woods where the greatest variety of choice timber was to be found – stink-wood, ebony or black-wood, satin-wood, [etc.]. **1802** *Cape Town Gaz.* 16 Aug. 2 Stink wood planks, 2 inches, 4 Sch. per foot. **1815** G. BARKER Journal. 10 Sept., Spent the sabath at a farm house that was forsaken by its owner & a number of the people belonging to Bethelsdorp .. were cutting Stink-wood at a small distance. **1832** *Graham's Town Jrnl* 16 Feb. 29 (*advt*) On Saturday next .. will be Sold, in front of the Magistrate's Office ... 6 new Cane bottomed stink wood Chairs, a Mahogany Writing Desk. **1843** [see *Cape mahogany* (CAPE sense 2 a)]. **1849** N.J. MERRIMAN *Cape Jrnls* (1957) 21 The pulpit and reading pew are constructed mainly of stink wood with some beading of sneeze-wood, which has a handsome appearance. **1868** W.H. HARVEY *Genera of S. Afr. Plants* 328 *O. bullata*, Nees, which yields the well-known 'Stinkwood' of cabinet makers, is the only Cape species. **1887** *S.W. Silver & Co.'s Handbk to S. Afr.* 351 The Stink-wood, sometimes called Cape mahogany, or rather Cape walnut, which latter timber it much resembles, is a most useful and elegant wood for furniture uses when properly seasoned. **1891** R. SMITH *Great Gold Lands* 179 Perhaps it may be useful to say what the timber-yielding plants of Natal are. The best known are yellow-wood, a species of yew (*Podocarpus elongata*); .. stink-wood, a laurel (*Laurus bullata*), [etc.]. **1910** [see ESSENWOOD]. **1927** C.G. BOTHA *Social Life in Cape Col.* 51 Early in the eighteenth century mention is made of stinkwood and yellow-wood chairs, tables and bedsteads ... The two most common indigenous woods were stinkwood and yellow-wood. **1949** L.G. GREEN *In Land of Afternoon* 193 You have to stand in a sawmill to smell the powerful stinkwood odour. Fetid when freshly cut, the smell soon becomes aromatic and finally vanishes. **1952** G.M. MILLS *First Ladies of Cape* 42 Cupboards, built into the walls, were usually framed by stinkwood and yellow-wood doors which contained silver key-plates. **1970** *The 1820* June 7 Growing on the slopes of the Outeniquas are the magnificent giant yellow-wood trees, some as old as 1500 years, intermingling with the hard, beautifully grained, but unpleasant smelling stinkwoods. **1977** *E. Prov. Herald* 3 Mar. 6 Sneezewood was nearly wiped .. and stinkwood came even closer to extinction ... Intensive cutting was stopped in time and the species are regenerating, though very slowly. **1977** *Het Suid-Western* 19 Oct., Records toppled once again at the indigenous timber auctions ... J— Brothers of Knysna paid R3 700 a cubic metre for prime stinkwood, beating last year's record by R100 and establishing conclusively that stinkwood is the most expensive timber in the world. **1979** *Sunday Tribune* 3 June 23 The slaughter of Stinkwood trees had to be checked nearly 100 years ago and the tree has for a long time been totally protected. Only windfall timber may be sold. **1981** *Fair Lady* 23 Sept. 172 A yellowwood armoire with inlaid patterns in stinkwood and with an unusual pediment, shows an English influence. **1991** S. WELZ in *Light Yrs* Feb. 11 A Cape stinkwood and beefwood armoire, dating from the second half of the 18th century.

b. With distinguishing epithet: **bastard stinkwood** [see BASTER *adj.*], the protected tree *Ocotea kenyensis* of the Lauraceae, found in the northern and eastern regions of the country; **black stinkwood**, *Ocotea bullata* (see sense a above); **Camdeboo stinkwood** /ˈkæmdəˌbuː -/ [named for a region between Graaff-Reinet and Aberdeen, in the Karoo; Khoikhoi *kam* green + *deboo* unknown, perh. 'pool in river' or 'hollow'], the tree *Celtis africana* of the Ulmaceae; its wood; CAMDEBOO; *Camdeboo stinkhout*, see STINKHOUT sense b; *wit stinkhout*, see STINKHOUT sense b; **cannibal stinkwood** *obs.* [see quot. 1913], *Camdeboo stinkwood* (see above); **red stinkwood**, the tree *Prunus africana* of the Rosaceae; **white stinkwood**, *Camdeboo stinkwood* (see above). Also *attrib.*

1983 K.C. PALGRAVE *Trees of Sn Afr.* 176 *Ocotea kenyensis* ... **Bastard stinkwood.** **1990** *Flora & Fauna* No.47, 10 The upper parts of the Hanglip forests contain some fine specimens of the bastard stinkwood *Ocotea kenyensis*. These differ from the stinkwood .. in that they lack the conspicuous blisters or bullae on the upper surface of the leaves ... They also lack the distinctive but offensive smell of the stinkwood. **1916** *Farmer's Weekly* 20 Dec. 1456 Yokes, all stapled and rivetted, genuine **Black Stinkwood.** **1917** R. MARLOTH *Common Names* 78 *Stinkhout*, The most familiar kind, called Black stinkwood, is *Ocotea bullata* (Knysna, etc.). Much esteemed for furniture. *c***1936** *S. & E. Afr. Yr Bk & Guide* 320 Black Stinkwood or Laurel. A furniture wood. **1961** PALMER & PITMAN *Trees of S. Afr.* 129 The black stinkwood, or stinkwood .. is a large evergreen tree found in most of the high forests .. and at its best in the Knysna forests ... It is a tall straight tree, 60 to 90 feet high. **1979** *Sunday Tribune* 3 June 23 South Africa's first total survey of indigenous forests on private land has disclosed that Natal's remaining black stinkwoods have been almost totally destroyed by the depredations of muti hunters. **1980** *E. Prov. Herald* 18 June 11 The Green Heritage Committee has chosen the Black Stinkwood as Tree of the Year for 1980. **1896** R. WALLACE *Farming Indust. of Cape Col.* 132 Celtis rhamnifolia, Pres ... **Camdeboo Stinkwood.** **1917** R. MARLOTH *Common Names* 17 *Camdeboo stinkwood, Celtis Kraussiana*. A tree frequent in wooded ravines and the forests of the coast. **1949, 1961** [see quots at *white stinkwood* below]. **1966** A. FUGARD *Notebks* (1983) 135 Unspoiled indigenous bush – massive yellow-woods and Cape fig trees growing beside a little river, Camdeboo stinkwoods, wild gardenias. **1984** *S. Afr. Panorama* Feb. 38 A beautiful indigenous tree used to line city streets is the White, or Camdeboo, Stinkwood (witstinkhout), *Celtis africana*. It is not related to the well-known Stinkwood (*Ocotea bullata*). **1988** *Farmer's Weekly* 1 Jan. 17 The camps have natural shelter and shade from olive wood and camdeboo stinkwood trees. **1859** R.J. MANN *Col. of Natal* 156 There is a variety of this wood, known under the name of the '**Cannibal stink-wood**' which is of a light colour, woolly and porous. **1877** LADY BARKER *Yr's Hsekeeping* 325 For what rhyme or reason, what sense or satire can there be in such a name as 'Cannibal Stinkwood'? – applied too to a graceful, handsome tree, whose bark gives out an aromatic though pungent perfume. **1913** C. PETTMAN *Africanderisms* 107 *Cannibal stinkwood, Celtis Kraussiana.* The first part of this name appears to be a corruption of Camdeboo .. ; it is applied to a variety of stinkwood, the wood of which is woolly, porous, and useless to the cabinet-maker. **1913** *Ibid.* 395 **Red stinkwood**, *Pygeum africanum*. A fine tree known for many years by this name, but only recently botanically identified. **1917** R. MARLOTH *Common Names* 78 The most familiar kind, called *Black stinkwood*, is *Ocotea bullata* ... The *Red* - is *Pygeum africanum* (East, forests), and the *Camdeboo* - or *White* -, *Celtis Kraussiana*. **1951** N.L. KING *Tree-Planting in S. Afr.* 70 *Pygeum africanum* (*Bitter almond or red stinkwood*), A large and extremely handsome tree with dense glossy foliage. **1961** PALMER & PITMAN *Trees of S. Afr.* 145 The red stinkwood, which closely resembles its imported relation, the Portugal laurel, .. is a handsome, evergreen tree and under good conditions grows to a height of 80 feet with a stem diameter of 3 feet. **1990** [see LEMON WOOD]. **1949** L.G. GREEN *In Land of Afternoon* 193 **White stinkwood**, or Camdeboo stinkwood, also has an offensive odour; otherwise the white and black stinkwood have nothing in common. **1950** [see ESSENHOUT]. **1961** PALMER & PITMAN *Trees of S. Afr.* 201 The white or Camdebo stinkwood is one of the most widely distributed of all our native trees ... It varies tremendously .. in growth and form depending on the conditions under which it grows. **1975** *E. Prov. Herald* 21 May 22 White or Camdeboo Stinkwood could be the tree of the future. It is an attractive, deciduous tree that can be grown in almost every part of the country. **1984** [see quot. at *Camdeboo stinkwood* above]. **1993** *Weekend Argus* 14 Aug. 7 *White Stinkwood*, The indigenous white stinkwood (Celtis africana) is a 12m high, spreading shade tree.

stiver, stuiver /ˈstaɪvə/ *n. hist.* Also **stuiwer, st(u)yver.** [Du. *stuiver*, of obscure origin.]

Not exclusively *S. Afr. Eng.*

1. The smallest monetary unit in use at the Cape under the Dutch East India Company, being the sixth part of a SCHELLING (or skilling) and the forty-eighth part of a RIX-DOLLAR, roughly equivalent to a half-penny sterling. See also DUBBELTJE *n.*[2] sense 1.

1697 W. DAMPIER in R. Raven-Hart *Cape G.H. 1652–1702* (1971) 382 A Flask of Wine which holds 3 quarts will cost 18 stivers, for so much I paid for it. **1786** G. FORSTER tr. *A. Sparrman's Voy. to Cape of G.H.* I. 245 This quantity [of butter] is carried to the Cape in one or two journies, and is sold at the rate of from three to six stivers a pound. **1795** [see DUBBELTJE *n.*[2] sense 1]. **1798** S.M. WILCOCKE tr. *J.S. Stavorinus's Voy. to E. Indies 1768–71* II. 84 The .. solid gum .. is packed in wooden boxes .. and is sold at the *Cape* for three and four stivers per pound. **1806** D. BAIRD in *Cape Town Gaz.*

& Advertiser, I .. direct that these Penny Pieces are henceforth to pass current in this Settlement for two stivers currency, or the third part of a Paper Skilling. **1822** W.J. BURCHELL *Trav.* I. 79 Six stuivers are equal to one schelling, and eight schellings to one rix-dollar or four shillings currency; but the value of this currency is excessively reduced by the rate of exchange, which, in 1810, was 33 per cent. in favour of England; and has, since that time, gradually risen to above 120. **1832** *Graham's Town Jrnl* 6 Apr. 59 This puts many a good vrouw on the fidgets, some of whom have nearly a dozen small bags of different sorts of choice dried fruits for sale, and stivers are objects of consequence to them. **1833** *S. Afr. Almanac & Dir.* 42 Accounts are kept either in Pounds, Shillings, Pence, and Farthings, or Rix Dollars, Skillings, and Stivers. 1 Stiver equal to $\frac{3}{8}$ of a Penny. 6 Stivers equal to $2\frac{1}{4}$ Pence, or 1 Skilling. 8 Skillings equal to 18 Pence, or 1 Rix-dollar. **1925** [see DUBBELTJE *n.*[2] sense 1]. *c***1936** *S. & E. Afr. Yr Bk & Guide* 1023 The old Cape Dutch Coinage consisted of the Rix dollar, 4s.; the Gulden, 1s. 4d.; the schilling, 6d.; and the stuiver, 1d. **1951** L.G. GREEN *Grow Lovely* 85 There the settlers grumbled at the price of eland or hartebeest and paid three stivers a pound for mutton when they could get it. A dressed penguin could be had for a stiver. **1957** [see RIX-DOLLAR]. **1968** K. MCMAGH *Dinner of Herbs* 5 The smallest urchin with no more than a 'stuiwer' clasped in his damp grubby little paw could find something to buy. **1972** [see DUBBELTJE *n.*[2] sense 2]. **1976** A.R. WILLCOX *Sn Land* 153 From the first the Directors of the Company, who counted every stuiver, complained about the 'overwhelming expenditure' in maintaining the station. **1981** *Flying Springbok* Dec. 55 The first postal 'stamping' of letters in the Cape came into operation on 2 March 1792. The stamp indicated that 6 stuivers had been paid to the 'Vereenigde Nederlandsche Oost-Indische Compagnie' for the conveyance of the letter.

2. *fig.* A little; a small amount; something of little value.

1822 W.J. BURCHELL *Trav.* I. 248 The weather being a little chilly, the mother, in the true colonial style, observed that, down in the Karro, it was only a stuyver cold, but that we should find a ducatoon cold, up in the Roggeveld. **1883** O.E.A. SCHREINER *Story of Afr. Farm* 77 'That boy Waldo', said Bonaparte, rubbing his toes, 'took himself off coolly this morning as soon as the waggon came, and has not done a stiver of work all day'. **1910** D. FAIRBRIDGE *That Which Hath Been* (1913) 170 There are many at home who regard this Colony as an expensive superfluity, and who would rather see it fall into the hands of France to-morrow than vote a stiver for its defence. **1972** A. SCHOLEFIELD *Wild Dog Running* 101 Oh, aye, the crop. I suppose you'll have a few *stuivers* in your purse then, but that's no living, m'dear.

stock-fair *n.* [Eng. *stock* livestock + *fair* periodical gathering of buyers and sellers.]

1. A livestock auction and farmers' gathering held in a country district. Also *attrib.*

1892 *The Jrnl* 20 Sept. 1, October Stock Fair. **1917** *Grocott's Penny Mail* 23 Apr. 1 Grahamstown Stock Fair: 16 Salted Tollies, 16 Trek Oxen, 20 Donkey Geldings. **1948** *George & Knysna Herald* 4 June 3 Monthly Stock Fair, Summary of entries to date: 355 Prime Boer Goats. **1966** I. VAUGHAN *These Were my Yesterdays* 47 Last Stock Fair Day in Beaufort, Jehu bet Ou Broer he would race him with his horses, Duke and Gift, against his Ford to the Kroomie Hotel, and beat him. **1970** V. ROSENBERG *Sunflower* 15 Regular stock fairs brought the farmers to town more frequently than had the old Nagmaal gatherings. **1971** *Grocott's Mail* 4 June 4 My next stock fair at Alexandria will be held at the New Municipal Pens, Alexandria. **1977** *Fair Lady* 25 May 188 Our next Berlin stock fair will be held on Monday, August 2, at 11 a.m. **1990** [see STOKVEL sense 1].

2. *transf.* An earlier form of STOKVEL (now *obs.*). Also *attrib.*

1948 E. HELLMANN *Rooiyard* 43 Commercialised beer-brewing has given rise to an institution known as the 'stockfair', which can be roughly defined as a mutual benefit society. Stockfair is primarily a women's society, although men have infrequently tried to adopt it. The stockfair has two functions: to assist in disposing of any surplus beer which has remained unsold during the week-end, and to act as a kind of savings society. **1963** A.M. LOUW *20 Days* 100 Tonight we will have our stockfele — stockfair, beer drinker's meeting — in peace. **1965** E. MPHAHLELE *Down Second Ave* 124 Marabastad life: .. Sunday afternoon 'stock-fair' parties where clubs entertained themselves after pooling their wages to give to each member in turn.

stockfel(e), stockfell varr. STOKVEL.

stockfish *n.* Also **stokfish**. Pl. unchanged. [Calque formed on Du. *stokvis* (see STOKVIS).

In general Eng., the name *stockfish* has long been used for the cod and other similar fish cured by drying in the air without salt.]

The hake *Merluccius capensis* of the Merlucciidae, an important food-fish; STOKVIS. Also *attrib.*

In Smith and Heemstra's *Smiths' Sea Fishes* (1986), the name 'shallow-water hake' is used for this species.

1823 W.W. BIRD *State of Cape of G.H.* 159 The .. hake or stockfish, the king klipfish, the steen brazen .. are all of excellent quality. **1834** [see KINGKLIP]. **1847** 'A BENGALI' *Notes on Cape of G.H.* 69 It is all cheap enough but the 'sole', and that unfortunately is the best eating. Stock fish is the next, and like cod. **1853** L. PAPPE *Edible Fishes of Cape of G.H.* 31 The cured or dried Cape Stok-fish is an excellent dish. **1905** J.D.F. GILCHRIST in Flint & Gilchrist *Science in S. Afr.* 193 The familiar Stock-fish .. and the Maasbanker .. are examples from the group of fishes illustrating identity of Cape and European forms. **1913** C. PETTMAN *Africanderisms* 479 *Stock-fish, Merlucius vulgaris*, known at Port Elizabeth as the Hake. **1926** M. NATHAN *S. Afr. from Within* 204 The larger staple fish are silverfish, stumpnose, Cape Salmon, .. and stockfish (hake). **1930** C.L. BIDEN *Sea-Angling Fishes* 108 The fresh European cod is called 'Kabeljaauw' by Netherlandic and German people and the dried or salted cod is called stockfish. The South African stockfish (*Merluccius capensis*) bears a stronger resemblance than our kabeljou to the North Sea cod. **1942** *Off. Yrbk of Union 1941* (Union Office of Census & Statistics) 770 The stockfish is the same as the Hake of European seas. **1945** H. GERBER *Fish Fare* 60 Stockfish is plentiful and widely known. Its soft, white meat is easily digestible. **1949** J.L.B. SMITH *Sea Fishes* 139 *Merluccius capensis ... Stockfish ...* In greatest abundance on our west coast, and extends, but is progressively scarcer, eastwards to or just beyond East London ... The Stockfish is commercially the most important single species .. , being taken in great quantity by trawl ... Our species is very like the European Hake. **1955** C. HORNE *Fisherman's Eldorado* 188 Cape Town docks .. draw many anglers each winter ... They hope to catch kabeljou, .. white stumpnose, stockfish, mackerel and maasbanker. **1969** J.R. GRINDLEY *Riches of Sea* 71 The main trawled fish is the South African hake or stockfish, Merluccius capensis, which may grow up to 48 inches, but those caught today are usually 12 to 30 inches long. **1973** *Farmer's Weekly* 18 Apr. 100 Stockfish, or hake .. is most obliging. You can do almost anything with it — fry, boil, bake or make into fish cakes or fish pies. It is too soft for pickling or the making of smoorvis. **1975** *Financial Mail* 11 Apr. 112 The company called on a local white fish trawling company to buy kreef bait (which consists largely of stockfish and kingklip heads). **1983** *S. Afr. Panorama* Jan. 10 Trawler fishing .. is aimed particularly at the catching of stockfish, kingklip, sole, kabeljou, snoek, and some less important species.

stockvel(d), stockvelt varr. STOKVEL.

stoep /stuːp, stʊp/ *n.* Also **stoop, stoup, stupe**. [S. Afr. Du., fr. Du. *stoep* step, porch, small paved elevation in front of a house.]

1. *Archit.*

a. In Cape Dutch buildings: a raised (paved) platform or terrace running the whole length of the front of a house, often with a seat at each end (see RUSBANK sense 2). **b.** In general use: a verandah or porch, whether open, covered, or enclosed. Also *attrib.*

1797 LADY A. BARNARD *S. Afr. Century Ago* (1910) 57 As for the young Dutchmen, I saw hardly any; the young ones prefer smoking their pipes on the *stoep*. **1804** R. PERCIVAL *Acct of Cape of G.H.* 116 Many of the houses have .. in front a neat porch or stoop as the Dutch call it, raised a few steps from the ground and running the whole length of the house. They are enclosed with a parapet or wall three or four feet high, and have a seat or bench at each end. **1820** G. BARKER Journal. 11 Feb., Filled the Stoop with ground ... Began to put up the short pailing before the door & to render the stoop more agreeable. **1822** W.J. BURCHELL *Trav.* I. 71 In front of each house .. is a paved platform, usually eight or ten feet wide, and raised, commonly, from two to four feet above the level of the street ... This platform is called the Stoep (step); and here the inhabitants frequently walk or sit, in the cool of the evening. *Ibid.* 159 Brought out chairs, and remained sitting on the 'stupe' .. the rest of the day. *a***1827** D. CARMICHAEL in W.J. Hooker *Botanical Misc.* (1831) II. 21 These stoops are a great annoyance to the public, occupying an unreasonable proportion of the large streets, and reducing the smaller ones to mere lanes. **1833** *S. Afr. Almanac & Dir.*, (*advt*) Ornamental Iron Railing, for Stoeps and fronts of Houses. **1837** J.E. ALEXANDER *Narr. of Voy.* I. 326 In the evening, the family parties of the respectable classes enjoyed themselves walking slowly about the raised *stoep*, or terrace, in front of their houses. **1852** A.W. COLE *Cape & Kafirs* 25 The houses are all stuccoed; many of them have trees in front of them, and all of them a terrace or *stoep*, as the Dutch call it, with a seat at each end. **1879** E.L. PRICE *Jrnls* (1956) 303 It is not a *verandah* on which we sit, it is a stoep. Do you remember the old Kuruman stoep without [a] roof — with the seat at the end and the steps down & the syringa trees in front? **1882** S. HECKFORD *Lady Trader in Tvl* 70 A raised 'stoop' .. was covered by an iron verandah, and ended in two small rooms, one used as a visitor's room, the other as a lumber room. **1899** R. DEVEREUX *Side Lights* 34 The *stoep* bears about the same relation to the Africander as his *café* does to the Frenchman. There he transacts his business, and distracts his leisure: there he smokes, drinks, loves, and sometimes dies. Not even the jerriest builder would dream of dispensing with it. **1910** D. FAIRBRIDGE *That Which Hath Been* (1913) 106 A wide stoep, paved with large red tiles, ran entirely round the building, under the green-shuttered windows, with a curved white-plastered seat at each corner. **1918** H. MOORE *Land of Good Hope* 23 The farmer is content with a plain square building of rough-baked bricks, or mud, with a verandah or 'stoep', upon which he sits in the evening for his pipe and coffee. **1926** P.W. LAIDLER *Tavern of Ocean* 59 A very ornamental centre gable, and a stoep seat at right angles to the wall. *a***1936** *S. & E. Afr. Yr Bk & Guide* 37 Stoep, platform in front of house. **1947** O. WALKER in *Vandag* Apr. 25 The saurian torpor of a Bushveld farm stoep. **1956** D. JACOBSON *Dance in Sun* 14 It was called the 'Mirredal Hotel', on a painted sheet-metal poster above the roof of the stoep. **1960** D. MULLER *Art Past & Present* 109 The uncovered or 'trellised' stoep, with its built-in seats at either end, formed a charming feature of the Cape Dutch house. **1963** A. FUGARD *Notebks* (1983) 104 Little semi-detached houses, some derelict .. ; young girls leaning on stoeps chewing bubble-gum. **1964** M.G. MCCOY *Informant, Port Elizabeth* Four bedrooms & a gorgeous enclosed east-facing wide stoep, plus a front stoep. **1971** *E. Prov. Herald* 30 Apr. 7 Four only Steel-Frame Chairs, suitable for Stoep or Garden use. **1971** *Het Suid-Western* 14 May 9 Wrought iron porch or stoep lanterns. **1973** *E. Prov. Herald* 4 July 27 Two shell back wooden Stoep Chairs. **1982** *Fair Lady* 27 Jan. 141 He spent his days lying on an old leather couch on the front stoep, watching the passers-by. **1990** *Afr. Wildlife* Sept.-Oct. 257 The Tokai Manor House is a fine example of his work, with its round stoep pillars and its rectangular gable.

2. *comb.* **stoep-farmer**, a farmer who is considered to be a *stoepsitter*; cf. *cheque-book farmer* (see CHEQUE-BOOK); **stoepkamer** /-kɑːmə(r)/ [Afk., *kamer* room], a room built into one end of a covered verandah; also *attrib.*; **stoep plant**, a pot-plant decorating a verandah; **stoep room**, *stoepkamer* (see above); **stoepsitter** /-sətə(r), sɪtə/ [Afk., *sitter* sitter], one who habitually sits on a stoep; an idler, one who gives others instructions and avoids work; hence **stoep-sitting** *ppl adj.*

1948 O. WALKER *Kaffirs Are Lively* 102 The laziest men I've seen in this country are the **stoep-farmers** and the boss-boys. **1963** R. LEWCOCK *Early 19th C. Archit.* 171 It [*sc.* the house] is today preserved in a form substantially like that of the plan .., the main difference being that the **stoepkamer** walls are not splayed outwards as shown on the plan. **1985** *Informant, George* Changing the stoepkamer into a kitchen has revolutionized my life. **1916** L.D. FLEMMING *Fool on Veld* (1933) 115 The heat had .. shrivelled up my **stoep plants** to a gasping mass. **1961** D. BEE *Children of Yesterday* 231 The solid, wide-veranda'd house with its mass of stoep plants. **1968** S. CLOETE *Chetoko* 111 She attended to her stoep plants. **1974** *E. Prov. Herald* 8 May 21 A pineapple can make an attractive stoep plant and even yield fruit when grown in a pot. **1880** H.M. PRICHARD *Friends & Foes* 122 Two very miniature **stoeprooms** as they are called at the Cape. (Small rooms stolen out of each end of the verandah.) **1913** C. PETTMAN *Africanderisms* 480 *Stoep rooms*, .. Rooms built as wings to a house, but with entrance and exit opening on to the 'stoep' only; sometimes they were merely the 'stoep' ends walled off. **1978** A.P. BRINK *Rumours of Rain* 334 We boys would be instructed to stay in the stoep rooms until four, the curtains drawn to shut out the world outside. **1934** C.P. SWART Supplement to Pettman. 168 **Stoepsitter**, .. A sluggard or lazy person; sometimes humorously applied by townsmen to farmers, who used to spend much of their time on the stoep, drinking their favourite beverage, coffee. **1948** O. WALKER *Kaffirs Are Lively* 92 They don't work. They're stoep-sitters, coffee-tipplers and pipe-spitters. **1955** L.G. GREEN *Karoo* 14 In the villages knowing *stoepsitters* left their benches to gather round the car and jeer at our 'Cape to Bulawayo' banner. **1972** *Evening Post* 9 Sept. 3 One of the devices in the play is a chorus of three old men, 'stoepsitters', who represent the traditional small-town community and comment on the main action. **1900** C.R. PRANCE *Antic Mem.* 130 There he remains in memory well over forty years, an abiding object-lesson in the folly of newspaper-prattle about the '**stoep-sitting** farmer' and his distaste for 'Kaffir work'.

Hence (*nonce*) **bestoeped** *adj.*, possessing a stoep; **stoeping** *n.*, sitting on a stoep.

1901 E. WALLACE *Unofficial Despatches* 16 Cool old Dutch homesteads, bestoeped and beflowered, peep out from a dozen gardens. **1948** H.V. MORTON *In Search of S. Afr.* 286 Stoeping can become almost a profession, certainly a calling. The spell of the stoep is tremendous. Once you have your own seat there, it is difficult to be anywhere else.

stofie var. STOOFIE.

stoker /'stʊəkə(r)/ *n.* [Afk.] One who distills spirits in a small still (or KETTLE). See also STOOK. See also *mampoerstoker* (MAMPOER sense 2).

1977 *Family Radio & TV* 19 Sept., All the stokers swear to its [*sc.* naloop's] medicinal value. **1981** *E. Prov. Herald* 18 Mar., Witblits — that legendary liquor whose kick is said to make an angry mule's best effort feel like a love tap — is alive and well and being distilled in full public view at Worcester ... Veteran stoker Mr X .. was on hand to see to the production of yesterday's batch. **1983** A. SPARKS in J. Crwys-Williams *S. Afr. Despatches* (1989) 445 Saturday's decision was occasioned by the decision of the mampoer-makers, or *stokers* as they are called, to form themselves into a guild appropriate to their new status. *Ibid.* 446 Dominee Daniel J— .. quoted from Genesis to warn the assembled stokers of the evils of liquor.

stokfel var. STOKVEL.

stokfish var. STOCKFISH.

stokkie /'stɔki/ *n.*[1] Also **stokie**. [Formed on STOKVEL + Eng. (informal) n.-forming suffix *-ie* (or -IE).] A colloquial short form of STOKVEL.

1974 M.V. MOTSISI in *Drum* 8 Mar. 29 Tells me to join him at his pal's place who is having a stockvel ... We all go ... Before we can drink, some non-voter whose house and stokkie this turns out to be, comes out of the bedroom. **1977** *E. Prov. Herald* 14 Oct. 6 The existence of the 'stokies' which had mushroomed all over the townships was indicative of the community's desire for better entertainment ... At the 'stokies' music is played, and there is plenty to eat and drink. **1979** *Voice* 24 Jan. 3A, Stokvels or 'stokies' are not only a money-saving device, they are also a [*sic*] tremendous social value to people. That is where we meet, in a relaxed atmosphere. **1987** *Learn & Teach* No.1, 47, I must just play along. As long as I'm not very late for the stokkie. **1991** T. WA MOLAKENG in *Weekly Mail* 28 Mar. 15 The law doesn't give a bean about stokkies; there is no legislation that governs them ... Stokkies today aim at less sepulchral purposes than funeral expenses. Some members swop money in order to start up business ventures.

stokkie /'stɔki/ *n.*[2] [Afk., *stok* stick + -IE.] A stick; in the wine industry, the woody stem of a vine (used as new stock when rooted).

1976 V. ROSENBERG *Sunflower* 36 The location of water was .. usually conducted with the aid of a water-divining 'stokkie' which was believed to twist downwards at the point where water was to be found. **1990** *You* 20 Dec. 85 When everyone settles down to a braai, the Capies point out that mealie cobs or charcoal can't be half as good as grapevine *stokkies*. **1995** J. MCNAUGHT *Informant, Fransch Hoek* In this heat the stokkies are all dying.

stokvel /'stɒkfel, 'stɔkfel/ *n.* Also **stockfel(e)**, **stockfell**, **sto(c)kveld**, **stockvel(t)**, **stokfel**. [ad. S. Afr. Eng. *stockfair*; see quot. 1990 (sense 1) and quot. 1962 (sense 2). It appears that the Africanized pronunciation of *stock-fair*, /(i)stɔkfeːle/, resulted in the modern spelling because of a misconception that the word's origins lay in Afk.] Esp. in township Eng.:

In all senses also called STOCK-FAIR (sense 2), STOKKIE *n.*[1]

1.a. A savings or investment society to which members regularly contribute an agreed amount, receiving a lump-sum payment either in turn, or in times of need. **b.** A similar society formed to share the cost of holding regular parties which at the same time generate profits for the hosts. **c.** Collectively, the members of such societies. Also *attrib.*

1946 P. ABRAHAMS *Mine Boy* (1954) 74 'Who were those women'? Xuma asked ... 'They are the Stockvelt. They are all women who sell beer. And if one is arrested they all come together and collect money among themselves and bail out the arrested one.' **1951** *Drum* Nov. 10 A contributory factor to the success of these hooch merchants are the stockfel parties, parties when the guests pay for the liquor. **1954** P. ABRAHAMS *Tell Freedom* 118 *Stockveld* is the trade union of the women who deal in illicit liquor. Each pays a weekly contribution. The total amount thus collected is given to a different member each week. **1959** L. LONGMORE *Dispossessed* 183 There are other groups capable of organizing intimate personal relations and controlling individual behaviour, among these .. *tsotsi* gangs, stockfels, manyano societies, separatist sects and such like. **1962** M. BRANDEL-SYRIER *Black Woman* 17 The '*Stockfel*' type of organization .. is a form of organized mutual assistance based on the rule of reciprocity. The origin of the word 'Stockfel' is unknown, but this form of organization occurs in many variations, and under a great many different names; also amongst men, but the women form the main membership. *Ibid.* 78 The name Stockfel has become associated with things 'primitive' and 'backward' and 'drink and all that'. **1973** *The 1820* Vol.46 No.6, 19 In *Stokvel* much of the success depends not only on the flow of liquids and food, but also the liquidity of money ... In contrast to the 'Tiekie-Line' parties which attract predominantly female 'followers', 'Big-Time' *Stokvel* has a special lure for males ... The amount spent by members at any one party must be reciprocated by the host as the *Stokvel* gatherings rotate. **1981** *Voice* Aug. (Reader) 5 They decided to use the Stokvel way to buy their machines. Every month they each put in R20,00. This made R80,00. One of them bought a machine ... Each person had a turn ... The Stokvel way is better than the Lay-by way. **1989** M. BRAND in *Fair Lady* 25 Oct. 92 *Stokvels*, party syndicates that organise township jols. **1990** A.K. LUKHELE *Stokvels in S. Afr.* 4 The term 'stokvel' comes from the rotating cattle auctions or 'stock-fairs' of English settlers in the Eastern Cape during the early nineteenth century. Black farmers and labourers who attended these stock-fairs exchanged ideas and gambled whatever resources they had ... The discovery of the Main Reef triggered a gold rush ... Some of the Cape blacks brought the stokvel concept with them. **1991** T. WA MOLAKENG in *Weekly Mail* 28 Mar. 15 The concept of the stokvel, an informal savings scheme, is as old as the urbanisation of the black population ... There are more than 800,000 stokvel groups in the country, says Lukhele, president of the National Stokvel Association of South Africa. **1991** *Sunday Times* 26 May (Business Times) 1 The money will be lent at a fixed interest rate repayable over five years. The loan will be secured by the 'stokfel system' — individuals contribute to a group deposit. **1991** *Ibid.* 22 Sept. 19 Avoid the financial stress of paying for your own parties by joining a *stokvel*. Groups of buddies contribute to a monthly fund — proceeds of which are handed to the stokvel host of the day. **1992** *Tribute* Feb., (*advt*) Helping each other. Such an important part of belonging to a burial society, savings club or stokvel. **1993** *Financial Mail* 23 Apr. 63 Stokvels, the traditional savings outlets for the underprivileged, still have many supporters — indeed, formal financial institutions encourage the stokvels.

2. A social gathering or party, held at each stokvel member's home in turn. Also *attrib.*

1962 A.M. LOUW *20 Days* 100 Tonight we will have our stockfele — stockfair, beer drinker's meeting — in peace. **1977** P.C. VENTER *Soweto* 184 A Stokvel was a dance session which started on a Friday in the townships and ended on the Sunday afternoon. **1977** M. MZAMANE in *New Classic* No.4, 26 It is possible to have .. an inspired wake or Zionist service throughout the night, next-door left; and a rowdy stockvel-cum-gumbagumba, next-door right. **1978** [see MARABI sense 2]. **1979** A.P. BRINK *Dry White Season* 252 Why don't you come with me this Friday, then we'll have a solid stokvel right through to Sunday night ... It's a party, lanie .., the sort where you dance non-stop till you pass out. **1982** *Pace* Apr. 15 We have had a problem of gigs and 'stockfels' going on in the township, where these youngsters drink for the whole weekend, sometimes the whole week. **1987** *Learn & Teach* No.2, 7 There were stokvels every weekend. Sometimes the police raided and people who made 'umqombothi' were arrested. **1988** B. NTLEMO in *Frontline* Apr.-May 8 He enjoyed the company of women with whom he could go to stokvels or casinos.

Hence **stokveler** *n.* [Eng. agential suffix *-er*], a member of a stokvel.

1989 *Weekly Mail* 27 Oct. 26 The stokvelers changed from talking to singing.

||**stokvis** /'stɔkfəs/ *n.* Formerly also **stokvisch**. [Afk. (earlier S. Afr. Du. *stokvisch*) fr. Du. transf. use of *stokvis* a name applied to the European hake; according to some sources, the name (lit. 'stick fish') arose because that fish was dried on sticks.] The STOCKFISH, *Merluccius capensis*.

1887 *S. Afr.* 185 *Gadus Merlucius*. Stokvisch, Hake. Its flesh delicate, resembling haddock. **1890** A.G. HEWITT *Cape Cookery* 1 Boiled stokvisch. Have the fish carefully cleaned; the head is never eaten ... Fried Stokvisch. The tail half is best for frying. **1982** *E. Prov. Herald* 14 Dec. 19 Some of the most popular table fish .. include .. geelbek, stokvis, poenskop and more.

stomp /stɔmp/ adj. [Du.] Of distinguishing marks cut into the ears of livestock: blunt, cropped.

1833 *Graham's Town Jrnl* 14 Feb. 1, 1 black Ox, left ear square behind, right ear stomp and slit. 1833 *Ibid.* 11 Apr. 1, 1 black Ox, right ear stomp and square, left ear square behind. 1979 M. PARKES *Wheatlands* 31 They will go in time to my goat ranch, Tierbosch, and I will keep that stomp ear mark to remind me, should I get the blues, how much I have to be thankful for, in the shape of good friends. 1982 *Grocott's Mail* 21 May 1 The C.I.A. of Grahamstown wish to obtain information about the following: 5 strayed angora goats ... Description is as follows. One has a bell around neck, earmarks, left ear 'stomp' at bottom, 'halfmoon' at top.

stomp v. var. STAMP v.

stompie /'stɔmpi/ n. colloq. [Afk., *stomp* stump + -IE.]

1.a. A cigarette or cigar butt; a half-smoked cigarette, kept for later use; ENTJIE sense a. Also *fig.* (rare), a small, worthless remnant.

1947 L. ABRAHAMS in B. Sachs *Herman Charles Bosman* (1971) 235 'Izaks! Izaks! come here!' This to a skinny, sullen-looking boy wearing blue, patch-seated pants, smoking greedily a crushed 'stompie.' 'My baas?' He stubbed out the 'stompie' on the kerb. 1949 H.C. BOSMAN *Cold Stone Jug* (1969) 47 You held it to your lips with a needle, because the stompie wasn't long enough to be held in your fingers. 1950 E. PARTRIDGE *Dict. of Underworld Slang* 691 *Stompie*, a cigarette butt: S. Africa. 1951 — in L. Abrahams *Makapan's Caves* (1987) 134 Everybody thinks that the lawyer did it, because the cigar *stompie* the police found in the garden. 1959 J. MEIRING *Candle in Wind* 3 The fisherman .. lounged irritably and restlessly on their rickety beds, smoking their pipes or 'stompies', and gazing out at the smoke-blackened ceilings. 1965 J. BENNETT *Hawk Alone* 199 That stompie would have started a fire. Bush's pretty dry around here. 1969 A. FUGARD *Boesman & Lena* 36 The whiteman stopped the bulldozer and smoked a cigarette ... He threw me the *stompie*. 1975 S. ROBERTS *Outside Life's Feast* 27, I must get outside because the stink of stale brandy and piss and old stompies will not let me breathe. 1976 [see *flat-boy* (BOY sense 1 b)]. 1980 A. PATON *Towards Mountain* 34 He would come back into class .. smelling powerfully of tobacco smoke. The smell was made worse by his habit of keeping stompies in his pocket, a stompie being a cigarette not fully smoked, then stubbed out, and stored away for future use. 1985 D. KRAMER in *Cosmopolitan* May 102 That lipstick-stained stompie was a treasure I kept hidden in a matchbox under a stone in our garden. 1987 S.A. BOTHA in *Frontline* Oct.-Nov. 14 Can't you see we're just stompies in an ashtray and that one day some mother is going to kill a big fat burning cigar right on your head? 1992 R. CUTLER in *Sunday Times* 17 May 15 The thing that irritates me most .. is an open ashtray ... You're having a wonderful gourmet dinner, then suddenly there is this hideous sight of the curled-up stompies killing the bouquet of the Chardonnay. 1993 *Pace* July 54 He found a *stompie* and lit up, cupping his hands around the flame.

b. (In *pl.*) In the idiomatic expression *to pick up stompies* [cf. Brit. Eng. *to pick up fag-ends*]: to break into a conversation, having heard only the tail-end of a story or discussion.

1970 *Informant, Grahamstown* Don't pick up stompies and you won't burn your fingers. 1970 *Informant, Grahamstown* The little girl picked up a stompie during the conversation. (Something not for her ears.) 1991 *Informant, Durban* Three days ago he heard Marie skinnering to her maat ... She told him not to pick up stompies. 1993 N. JARDINE *Informant, Grahamstown* 'Picking up stompies' i.e. joining a conversation in ignorance of the subject being discussed.

c. *comb.* **stompie throw** *nonce* [formed by analogy with gen. Eng. *stone's throw*], a short distance.

1986 *Style* Feb., 'Luckily,' — he gestures out of the window — 'the library is a *stompie* throw away from my office.'

2. A stump or end (of a candle, vine, etc.); ENTJIE sense b.

1966 I. VAUGHAN *These Were my Yesterdays* 78 Eat food in the huge diningroom by only light that did not fail. Go to bed with two candle stompies 'cookie' found in scullery. 1989 E. PLATTER in *Style* Aug. 106 A fire (and for a Cape Master of Wine .. vine stompies are the most appropriate fuel) must be made before the crayfish can be steamed.

stompkop /'stɔmpkɔp/ n. [Afk., *stomp* blunt + *kop* head.] Esp. along the Western Cape coast, either of two species of seabream of the Sparidae: **a.** The *black musselcracker* (see MUSSELCRACKER sense 2), *Cymatoceps nasutus*. **b.** The *white musselcracker* (see MUSSELCRACKER sense 2), *Sparodon durbanensis*; also with defining word, **sand stompkop**.

1948 *George & Knysna Herald* 7 May 5 It is understood a red steenbras and a stompkop were caught at Heralds Bay recently. Galjoen time is approaching: the popular attraction is red bait. 1949 [see Smith quot. at MUSSELCRACKER sense 1]. 1955 [see POENSKOP sense 2 a]. 1955 [see MUSSELCRACKER sense 1]. 1990 M. HOLMES in *E. Prov. Herald* 14 Sept. 18 In the Western Cape they knew the musselcracker as white biskop, while Tsitsikamma anglers called them perdetand or stompkop. The Border fishermen called them silver steenbras.

stompneus /'stɔmpnœs/ n. [S. Afr. Du., fr. Du. *stomp* blunt + *neus* snout, nose.]

a. STUMPNOSE sense 1.

1790 tr. F. *Le Vaillant's Trav.* I. 32 Fish are very abundant at the Cape. Among those most esteemed, the principal are the rooman, .. the steenbraasen, the stompneus, and some others. 1823 [see JACOB EVERTSON sense 1]. 1890 A.G. HEWITT *Cape Cookery* 4 Three stompneus make a good dish. 1937 C. BIRKBY *Zulu Journey* 149 Silver bream (they call it stompneus in the Cape). 1985 A. TREDGOLD *Bay between Mountains* 195 The fishing boats come racing in with their catch ... Silverfish, geelbek, stompneus.

b. With distinguishing epithet: **red stompneus**, the *red stumpnose* (see STUMPNOSE sense 2), *Chrysoblephus gibbiceps*; **white stompneus**, *white stumpnose* (see STUMPNOSE sense 2).

1823 W.W. BIRD *State of Cape of G.H.* 159 It is a remarkable circumstance, that the **red stompneus** rarely, and the red roman never, (though the chief fish of Simon's Bay), pass the Cape point into the waters of Table Bay. 1843 J.C. CHASE *Cape of G.H.* 169 Stomp neus, red and white. A most delicious fish. [1893 see red stompneus (STUMPNOSE sense 2).] c1936 *S. & E. Afr. Yr Bk & Guide* 347 The most valuable fish .. are the sole, silver-fish, .. red and white stompneus, 16 lbs. [etc.]. 1843, c1936 [**white stompneus**: see quot. at *red stompneus* above]. 1945 H. GERBER *Fish Fare* 61 White stompneus .. is inclined to be bony ... Red stompneus .. is very nice for boiling. 1953 *Cape Times* 4 Mar. 2 Kabeljou, yellowtail, white stompneus and stockfish were all caught in Hermanus.

stone n. [Special sense of general Eng. *stone* precious stone.] A diamond weighing one carat or more; loosely, any diamond; KLIP n. sense 2. See also CLEAVAGE.

1887 A.B. ELLIS *S. Afr. Sketches* 133 Well; last night from my tent there was taken A small packet of stones — just a few. 1888 *Cape Punch* 14 Mar. 155 'Kimberley,' he said ... 'The only canopy above it the blue sky of heaven, in which at night the stars shone like regular genuine "stones".' 1891 E. GLANVILLE *Fossicker* 292 The cooling mud has closed around the 'stones,' taking the impress of every angle and facet. 1897 J.P. FITZPATRICK *Outspan* 193 'Where's your claim?' 'Going to-morrow!' The youngest shook his head and smiled faintly ... 'Have you found any stones?' 1899 G.C. GRIFFITH *Knaves of Diamonds* 67 They know I've got stones from Ridley, but they don't know what stones — see? 1920 F.C. CORNELL *Glamour of Prospecting* 3 The finder of these small stones was again a transport rider, who had been working in German South-West Africa, and had brought back a small phial full of these tiny stones, which he said could be had for the picking any where in the sand near a certain bay he knew of. *Ibid.* 15 Now, this seemed a perfectly God-sent opportunity for locating the 'big stones' we all felt certain existed, and we set about getting in stores for the trip at once. a1931 S. BLACK in S. Gray *Three Plays* (1984) 167 Jacob: The doctor said I've got maar a stone inside. Samuel: A stone — how many carats? 1939 M. RORKE *Melina Rorke* 57 We were supposed to sell any diamond so discovered to the De Beers Company, which scrupulously paid the highest market value of each stone, so that it mightn't fall into the hands of the I.D.B. 1957 D. JACOBSON *Price of Diamonds* 14 A crazy fellow, Gottlieb thought, bringing a box of little stones and talking for half an hour. 1967 E.M. SLATTER *My Leaves Are Green* 44 When the illicit diamond buyers arrived they began bribing the boys to conceal the diamonds they found while digging, and to bring the stones to them. 1971 *Std Encycl. of Sn Afr.* IV. 20 The first stones were found in a substance near the surface known as 'yellow ground' ... Before long the secret of treatment stood revealed: to allow the blue ground to weather by exposure to the atmosphere before being searched for stones. 1972 *S. Afr. Panorama* Dec. 27 'Stones' are usually over one carat (a carat being 200 milligrams). Anything smaller falls in the 'melee' category.

stonebuck n. *obs.* [tr. S. Afr. Du. *steenbok*.] The STEENBOK, *Raphiceros campestris*.

In general English, 'stonebuck' is a name given to the ibex.

1822 W.J. BURCHELL *Trav.* I. Speelman brought home a Steenbok (Stone-buck) he had shot on the rocky plain .. a little antelope, of nearly the same size as the Duyker, but of a lighter and reddish color, having the under part of the body white. 1824 *Ibid.* II. 15 We traversed a very extensive plain ... Stonebucks here and there starting up, bounded over it and were soon out of sight. 1838 [see STEENBOK]. 1855 J. OGILVIE *Imperial Dict.* (Suppl.), *Stone-buck*, the steinbok, .. an animal of the antelope kind.

‖**stoof** /stʊəf/ n. *hist.* [Du.] KOMFOOR sense b.

1910 D. FAIRBRIDGE *That Which Hath Been* (1913) 192 A slave hastened in from the kitchen with a fresh shovelful of burning charcoal to replenish the *stoof* under his feet. 1934 *Cape Argus* 21 June (Swart), On a chilly night in those old houses, if there were no fire-places built into the room, a 'stoof' used to be produced for heating purposes.

stoofie /stʊəfi/ n. *hist.* Also **stofie**, **stoofje**. [Afk. (fr. Du. *stoofje*), *stoof* foot-warmer + -IE.] KOMFOOR sense b.

1905 O.E.A. SCHREINER in C. Clayton *Woman's Rose* (1986) 105 He would sit on the stofie at his grandmother's feet and lean his head against her knees. 1927 C.G. BOTHA *Social Life in Cape Col.* 50 A third [slave] brought the 'stoofje' or footwarmer. The latter was a box-like footstool, one side open and the top perforated. A chafing dish with warm coals was placed underneath. 1952 G.M. MILLS *First Ladies of Cape* 41 The *stofie* a small hollow wooden stool, in which charcoal was burnt to warm the feet. 1965 M.G. ATMORE *Cape Furn.* 85 The brass komvoors or stoofjes used in Holland in the first half of the 18th century. 1968 K. MCMAGH *Dinner of Herbs* 14 It had been the custom for elderly folk to have a couple of slaves precede them to church, one carrying a 'stoofie', a padded metal-lined footstool containing glowing charcoal when it was winter.

stook /stʊək/ v. *intrans.* [Afk.] To distil spirits. See also STOKER.

1977 *Family Radio & TV* 19 Sept. 51 Often the licence and the still have been in the family for close on a century. 'I stook because my pa and oupa did before me,' says Skilly P— of Besemkop near Calitzdorp.

Hence **stoking** /'stʊəkɪŋ/ vbl n., distilling.

1990 M. Shafto in *Weekend Argus* 9 June 11 The liberalising of the law on mampoer stoking. 1990 *Ibid.* [see MAMPOER sense 1].

stoop var. STOEP.

stop /stɔp/ *n. slang.* [Transf. use of Afk. *stop* a plug or fill of tobacco.] Esp. among marijuana-smokers:

1.a. A quantity of marijuana sufficient to roll a cigarette or fill a pipe; *boomstop*, see BOOM *n.* sense 2. Occas. **stoppie** [see -IE]. Cf. PIPE sense 2 a, ZOL *n.* sense 1 b. **b.** A marijuana cigarette: ZOL *n.* sense 1 a.

1949 H.C. Bosman *Cold Stone Jug* (1969) 44 Dagga was smuggled into the prison in various ways, and the price for it was high, a single stoppie of dagga being reckoned as the equivalent of twenty doppies (or a whole week's ration) of tobacco. 1974 *Eng. Usage in Sn Afr.* Vol.5 No.1, 11 To the ordinary smoker a *stop* (Afrikaans pronunciation) means a fill for a pipe or sufficient .. to roll a *skuif*: to the *roker, stop* means *boom-stop*. These *stops* – or rather the boom for the stop .. come in varying parcels. 1974 J. Matthews *Park* 22 Jammie turned to his companion. 'Eyes, gif him de udder stop. We get more dagga at de Alabama.' 1979 *Cape Times* 1 Dec. 11 As an introduction, a stolen item such as a radio or tape recorder is offered to the gang leader for a 'button, knoop or stop, se geld' (money for dagga). 1985 P. Slabolepszy *Sat. Night at Palace* 69 Hey, what's this? Stoppe!? You a bloody rooker, chief? Gott, there's enough boom here to – .. How much you make on the quiet, chief?

2. Marijuana: DAGGA *n.*[2] sense 1.

1952 'Mr Drum' in *Drum* Sept. 12 Derived from Hottentot Dachab, it [*sc.* dagga] is known in the slang as 'garnja,' .. 'stops,' 'boom,' [etc.]. 1967 *Drum* 27 Aug. 7 He pauses to recall the pleasant moments of his most recent encounter with 'stop'. 'You know, I'm seriously thinking of giving up the booze and hitting the weed full-time' ... Aardpyp (earth-pipe): Four to six foot length of steel tubing with the stop packed in at one end; you pull while lying flat on your stomach. 1975 *Daily Dispatch* 27 Mar. (Suppl.) 10 Mr B– offered him 'stop' for sale. 'I asked "what stop"' ... Mr B– told him it was the 'stop' in zolls. Mr M– said that he did not want any stop in zolls but would rather buy it in a large quantity. 1977 *Sunday Times* 1 May 7 They are regular dagga smokers and know a number of places to buy 'stop'. 1981 L. & P. Robertson-Hotz in *Bloody Horse* No.3, 36 Nearby there was a span of stop, I remember, fields of the stuff ... We just perch there, smoke some stop, slap away mosquitos.

stormjaer /ˈstɔːmjɑː(r), ˈstɔrmjɑːr/ *n.* Also **storm jager**. [Afk., *storm* storm + *jaer* (earlier *jager*) hunter.]

1. Usu. in *pl.*: Dumplings fried in fat, or baked in the embers of a fire, made often by travellers as a substitute for bread. See also MAAGBOM. Cf. ASKOEK sense 1, VETKOEK.

1900 F.R.M. Cleaver in M.M. Cleaver *Young S. Afr.* (1913) 39 In looking for writing material I remember that I have used my writing paper for wrapping up 'stormjagers' (cakes fried in fat), and that owing to grease it will no longer retain the impression of ink. 1900 *Ibid.* [see PANNEKOEK]. 1902 [see MAAGBOM]. 1913 C. Pettman *Africanderisms* 481 *Stormjagers*, Dumplings cooked in fat; they can be quickly prepared, and are often made by men living in the veld. The name and the thing were both well known before De Wet's men prepared them. 1955 L.G. Green *Karoo* 99 There is also a type of *asbrood*, a mixture of meal and water and soda baked in cakes in the campfire embers, known as *stormjaers* (dumplings). 1956 P. Becker *Sandy Tracks* 90 There had been mutton, vegetables, milk, and 'stormjaers', wholesome flour cakes, baked in the ash of the camp fire. 1963 S. Cloete *Rags of Glory* 41 Moolman taught the boys how to cook the flour they drew in boiling fat. These delicacies were known as *stormjagers* or *maagbommen*, that is to say, storm hunters because they were rapidly cooked, or stomach bombs, owing to their effect of the digestion. 1975 W. Steenkamp *Land of Thirst King* 126 The most basic item in the Namaqualander's larder is the so-called 'stormjaer', a kind of dumpling which was often used as a substitute for fresh bread when the farmers went out hunting or were summoned for a commando expedition.

2. *hist.* Usu. with initial capital. A member of the military wing of the Ossewa Brandwag (see OB *n.*[1]). Freq. used collectively in the plural. Also *attrib.*

1942 D.F. Malan in *Hansard* 2 Feb. 1328 They had never before heard of such an inner circle. They never knew that there were Stormjaers. 1948 O. Walker *Kaffirs Are Lively* 153 The Ossewa Brandwag – Oxwagon Sentinel – movement and its inner core of Stormjaers – fighters. 1956 H. Van Rensburg *Their Paths Crossed Mine* 160 The ferment of activism in the O.B. was the Stormjaer element – the S.J.s, as they were commonly called. 1972 *Sunday Times* 3 Dec. 4 He would start his speech with 'Broeders, friends, warriors, rapportryers, verraaiers, stormjaers, ruiterwagte and front-line soldiers who fight shoulder to shoulder with me in the battle for survival'. 1973 *Std Encycl. of Sn Afr.* VII. 396 Besides the Ossewa-Brandwag, and associated with it by a common commanding officer in the person of the Commandant-General, there developed a smaller and more activist organisation of youthful adventurers known as the Stormjaers ('Storm troops'). 1976 *E. Prov. Herald* 1 Dec. 9 Under Van Rensburg, a former UDF brigadier and Administrator of the Free State, it became dangerous, its Stormjaers prepared to sabotage, kill and steal in order to gain their objective. 1977 T.R.H. Davenport *S. Afr.: Mod. Hist.* 236 The OB already had an elite body of Stormjaers whose potential danger to public security had led Smuts to order the general surrender of rifles. 1979 *Daily Dispatch* 21 Mar. 1 An Ossewabrandwag general and leader of the organisation's military wing, the Stormjaers. 1979 *Sunday Times* 28 Oct. 13 Major Diedrick's special squad .. captured vital documents which gave a full list of all members of the OB's military 'Stormjaer' wing and their plans to take over the country. 1989 *Weekend Post* 28 Oct. 2 The hard core of the Ossewa Brandwag – the anti-Semitic Stormjaers modelled on the Nazi stormtroopers.

Stormvalk /ˈstɔːmfalk, ˈstɔrm-/ *n.* Pl. **-e** /-ə/. [Afk., *storm* to charge, storm + *valk* falcon.] Usu. in *pl.*, used collectively: the members of a motorcycle brigade of the Afrikaner Weerstandbeweging (see AWB), formed in 1981.

1981 *Sunday Times* 23 Aug. 21 We do have a special motorcycle unit, the Stormvalke, and a marching unit, called the Blitskommando. And we also have the Jeugkommando, from whom we select our potential leadership talent ... His Blitskommando and Stormvalke will wear black-shirted uniforms, reminiscent of fascist Germany and Italy in the Thirties. 1982 *E. Prov. Herald* 7 Apr. 11 Barely 10 months ago the AWB launched its 'stormvalke', a motorcycle brigade, and its 'stormkommando', a unit created to 'maintain law and order' at its meetings and to ensure that none were disrupted. 1985 A. Goldstuck in *Weekly Mail* 2 Aug. 7 We expect a hall packed with rabid frothing farmers ... We expect the *stormvalke* ... We get a pair of puffed-up, sweating functionaries, preceded up the aisle by an aroma of brandy. 1986 J. Mills in *Style* Sept. 8 To find a blackshirt brigand among the usual socialite, gourmet, and field-and-stream profferings, blew many an elegant reader's mind. I wonder how your readers will have .. reacted to the intrusion of the Stormvalk Supreme himself ..? 1990 *Sunday Times* 10 June 8 The Boerekommandos .. are the latest in a long list of failed attempts by the AWB to get a militant wing off the ground. Their predecessors were the Stormvalke and Aquila.

stormwater *n.* Used *attrib.* in Special Comb. **stormwater drain** or **-pipe**, a large cement pipe or cemented trench constructed (esp. in urban areas) to carry rainwater off roads; **stormwater drainage**, this system of drainage, or the infrastructure required for this system.

1965 A. Fugard *Notebks* (1983) 123 She would never have reached her destination on foot that day ... She said she knew it and would have slept in one of the **stormwater drains**. 1971 *Cape Times* 3 July (Mag. Sect.) 1 To its credit, the Council has also energetically tackled the provision of basic services – gravel roads, stormwater drains and night soil removals in the slum parts. 1974 *Barkly East Reporter* 3 Dec. 2 No stormwater drains are dug beside the sidewalks and the surface is left rough. 1979 *Daily Dispatch* 17 Apr. 9 (*caption*) Police carry the body of Jose J– who was drowned while playing in a Johannesburg stormwater drain with friends. 1980 C. Hope *A Separate Development* (1983) 97 The municipal sweepers will come along with brooms and hoses and wash your blood and guts down the stormwater drains so the whole place is tidy again for the next day. 1982 *Grocott's Mail* 25 June 1 Why did they tar over the old cobbled stormwater drains instead of repairing the cobbles. 1986 *Ibid.* 14 Mar. 3 Improvements will include laying drains, storm-water drains and water reticulation. 1994 *Weekly Mail & Guardian* 16 Sept. 26 The problem is caused by heavy development and huge new stormwater pipes installed upstream, which the council allowed despite warnings of severe flooding. 1979 *Quarterly Newsletter* (George Municipality) 24 Sept. 1 **Stormwater Drainage** – Again. The rather unusual downpour on Saturday, 15 September 1979, has again highlighted the necessity of an effective stormwater drainage system. 1982 *Sunday Times* 5 Dec. (Mag. Sect.) 4 The services also had to be accommodated under the sidewalks .. and there had to be provision for stormwater drainage. 1986 *Sowetan* 24 Sept. 7 He said the council will also embark on the following projects: Improve the water pressure and distribution of water in the township; Upgrade roads; Improve stormwater drainage [etc.].

stoup var. STOEP.

stove *n. obs.* [Calque formed on Du. *stoof* foot-warmer.] KOMFOOR sense b.

Rarely, found also in *Brit. Eng.* in this sense.

1810 G. Barrington *Acct of Voy.* 182 They generally .. make use of small stoves to warm their feet on. 1868 W.R. Thomson *Poems, Essays & Sketches* 167 At the bare little table .. sits the *huisvrouw*, with her feet on a stove. 1883 O.E.A. Schreiner *Story of Afr. Farm* 5 She sat on a chair in the great front room, with her feet on a wooden stove. *Ibid.* 199 May I not bring you a stove, Miss Lyndall, to put your feet on?

straand wolf var. STRANDWOLF.

straight *n.* [Perh. transf. sense of U.S. slang *straight* unadulterated whisky, very strong whisky.] In township slang: a 750 ml (formerly one-quart) bottle of liquor. Cf. HALF-JACK.

1958 K.M.C. Motsisi in M. Mutloatse *Casey & Co.* (1978) 16 Now here I am .. wondering when Kid Hangover is going to throw another midnite party .. so's he can pay me back the three quid I loaned him so's I can pay Aunt Peggy for the 'straights' I got on tick the month before. 1959 L. Longmore *Dispossessed* 222 African women who buy large quantities of liquor from dealers and traders .. may not sell a whole bottle of brandy or gin but measure out tots for 2s. 6d., nips for 5s., half-jacks for 10s., or a straight (a full bottle) for £1 or 30s. 1965 K.M.C. Motsisi in *Drum* Dec. 11 As the party started getting real hot I saw Kid G. trying to make off with a straight of mahog. *a*1968 D.C. Themba in E. Patel *World of Can Themba* (1985) 79 Boet Mike said, 'Straight.' And they brought a bottle of brandy that looked like guilty blood. 1975 *Drum* 22 Apr. 13 Men like him, who never had the opportunity to own a straight of whisky, .. never had three good meals in one day. 1990 [see MAHOG]. 1994 H. Masekela on TV1, 16 Nov. (People of South), A full bottle was a straight, then there was a three-quarter, and a half was a half-jack, and then there was a nip.

straightrun *n. noncount.* [Unknown.] In full ***straightrun mealie-meal***: unrefined, coarsely ground maize meal.

1968 *Farmer's Weekly* 3 Jan. 89 Yellow Crushed Maize at R3.99. White Straightrun Mealie-meal R3.49 per 180lb. bag. 1972 *Fair Lady* 19 Apr. 11 Recently, the Maize Board brought out a book .. which has several appetising recipes for straight-run mealie meal, their name for unrefined mealie meal. **1994** N.J.D. GRUE *Informant, Grahamstown* A stabled horse would get lucerne (or teff), and then (three times a day) 1 kg straightrun, 1 kg bran, germ meal, bone meal, coarse salt – all mixed with water ... Straightrun is a high carbohydrate feed. You ask for it at the Roller Mills.

‖**strandjut** /'strantjət/ *n.* [S. Afr. Du., fr. Du. *strand* beach + *jut(ter)* thief, wrecker.] The STRANDWOLF, *Hyaena brunnea.*

1869 'E.L.L.' in *S. Afr. Mag.* III. No.9, 596 From Mr. Flashman, Queen's Town, the skin of a strandjut (*Hyæna fusca*). **1900** W.L. SCLATER *Mammals of S. Afr.* I. 85 Hyaena brunnea. *Vernacular Names*: Strand Jut or Strand Wolf of the Colonists. **1988** A. HALL-MARTIN et al. *Kaokoveld* 31 This is the preserve of the brown hyaena, which lives up to its traditional name of *strandjut*, patrolling the beaches and seal colonies for carrion.

strandloper /'strantluəpə(r)/ *n.* Formerly also **strandlooper.** [Transf. use of Du. *strandlooper*, fr. *strand* beach + *looper* walker, runner (used of various birds throughout the world).]

1. *obs.* Any of several coastal plovers of the Charadriidae; STRANDLOPERTJIE.

[**1731** G. MEDLEY tr. *P. Kolb's Present State of Cape of G.H.* II. 157 The *Dutch* call this Bird *Strand Loper*, i.e. Shore-Courser. She is frequently seen about the *Cape*.] **1884** LAYARD & SHARPE *Birds of S. Afr.* 662 This pretty little Plover, the *Strand-looper* of the colonists, is common throughout the colony. **1923** HAAGNER & IVY *Sketches* 257 The little Three-banded Plover (*Charadrius tricollaris*) is called the Strand-looper (Shore-runner) in most parts of the country, and is found almost everywhere within our limits.

2.a. *hist.* With initial capital. Usu. in *pl.*, often used collectively: originally, (the) members of those Stone Age communities of Khoisan fisher-gatherers living in former times on the shores of Table Bay, and subsisting on plants, shellfish, etc.; subsequently, (the) members of any of several similar (nomadic) communities on the Western Cape and Namibian coasts; GORINGHAIKONA; WATERMAN. Also *attrib.* See also KAAPMANS.

'Strandloper' denotes those sharing a common mode of life rather than a common ethnic identity.

Used in general Eng. by archaeologists to denote any prehistoric people who were nomadic about coastal areas or inland shores.

1838 D. MOODIE (tr. *J. van Riebeeck's Jrnl*) *Record* I. 16 In the evening some of the Saldania Ottentoos came to the Fort ... These two *Saldaniers* were much bolder and livelier men than the *Strandlopers* who daily live with us, but still having the same language and clothing. **1846** J. SUTHERLAND *Memoir* II. 29 For a little tobacco the Strandlopers will always fetch firewood for the cooks. **1849** E.D.H.E. NAPIER *Excursions in Sn Afr.* I. 19 On his arrival, Van Riebeck found the shores of Table Bay frequented by a small tribe of these all but naked savages ... By the Dutch these wretched beings were first called 'Strandloopers,' or frequenters of the shore. **1905** W.H. TOOKE in Flint & Gilchrist *Science in S. Afr.* 97 The spear heads and pottery found in the sand dunes around Table and Algoa Bays are probably the manufacture of the Hottentot 'strandloopers'. **1913** [see WATERMAN]. **1930** I. SCHAPERA *KhoiSan Peoples* 29 The term 'Strandlooper' (coast ranger), applied by several writers on the prehistory of South Africa to the people associated with the kitchen middens found along the south and west coasts of the Cape, should be abandoned, as the latent implication that these people form a distinct racial group is not justified. For the most part they were merely Bushmen who took to the seashore, so that we have to deal with a particular mode of life rather than with a particular people. *c***1936** *S. & E. Afr. Yr Bk & Guide* 448 The recumbent skeletons of two indigenous adults, probably Strand-Loopers. **1937** C. BIRKBY *Zulu Journey* 150 There are kitchen middens of early strandlopers on the beach, well worth digging over if you are interested in primitive man. **1943** 'J. BURGER' *Black Man's Burden* 12 The first aborigines with whom the Dutch officials came into contact were the Hottentots ... At the coast were the *Strandlopers* (Beachcombers). **1958** S. CLOETE *Mask* 40 Sometimes he wished he could always live like .. a strandlooper or trek-Boer – a masterless, homeless wanderer. **1961** L.E. VAN ONSELEN *Trekboer* 106 Along the coasts roamed the Strandlopers, existing on shellfish and the washed up remains of whales. They lived in caves and middens and were closer relations to the Hottentot than the Bushmen. **1963** A. FUGARD *Notebks* (1983) 107 Went into a couple of Strandloper caves ... They stank of darkness and fear. **1974** *Motorist* Nov. 12 At the river mouth there is an interesting archaeological excavation of a Strandloper scrapheap where fine examples of and information about this find may be seen. **1975** *E. Prov. Herald* 4 Aug. 4 A skeleton believed to be that of a Strandloper Hottentot, who was buried in the traditional seated position with legs drawn up and hands placed across the knees, has been unearthed near Sedgefield. **1976** A.R. WILLCOX *Sn Land* 112 Living on or near the coast there were hunter-gatherers (*strandlopers* to South Africans). **1977** R. ELPHICK *Kraal & Castle* 24 'Strandloper' (i.e. Beachranger) .. referred to the fisher-scavenger folk of Table Bay and later, by extension, to many other coastal peoples. *Ibid.* 29 Early Dutch officials stated that the Strandlopers (or Goringhaicona), a scavenging people on the Cape Peninsula, spoke the same language as the neighbouring Goringhaiqua, a cattle-keeping Khoikoi group. **1981** *Flying Springbok* Sept. 46 From impoverished Hottentots, Bushmen, Damaras and occasional shipwreck survivors emerged the proletariat of the Skeleton Coast – the Strandloper. **1982** *E. Prov. Herald* 14 Dec. 7 Here there is much evidence of Strandloper habitation. **1989** *Reader's Digest Illust. Hist.* 43 The Strandlopers – as they came to be called – were the outcasts of Khoikhoi society. They .. were bound together not by kinship, but rather by common misfortune. **1993** *Weekend Post* 15 May (Leisure) 5 Middens – large rubbish heaps where the Late Stone Age folk (Strandlopers) discarded their shells .. can be seen.

b. *transf.* One who walks along the shore; a beachcomber.

1939 S. CLOETE *Watch for Dawn* 46 Where will you go then ... There is one place left. There is the sea. Our children becoming a nation of strand-loopers, eaters of shellfish. **1939** *Outspan* 6 Oct. 37 Hiking and Beach-Combing with Modern South African Strandlopers. **1952** *Chambers's Jrnl* (U.K.) Feb. 87 The man turned out to be a strandlooper – a coloured beachcomber, one who shared the food of the gulls. **1978** F. CHISHOLM in *Cape Times* 31 July 4 Beach combing, were it possible off the barren coast between South West Africa and Angola, might be marvellously lucrative for some lucky *strandloper*. **1987** D. BRISCOE in *Motorist* 2nd Quarter 4 Those tides which are so important to fishermen are equally vital for other 'strandlopers' – those who have a touch of conchology .. running through their veins.

Hence **strandloop** *v. intrans.*, see quot. 1928.

1928 E.H.L. SCHWARZ *Kalahari & its Native Races* 148 The question of the Strandlooper and their [*sic*] relationship to the Bushmen does not come within the scope of the present description; my own impression is that all natives 'strand loop', i.e., go to the seaside, Bushmen, Hottentots and Bantu.

‖**strandlopertjie** /'strantluəpə(r)ki/ *n.* Formerly also **strandloopertje.** [Afk., fr. Du. *strandlooper* (see prec.) + dim. suffix -IE.] STRANDLOPER sense 1.

1905 J. DU PLESSIS *1000 Miles in Heart of Afr.* 137 On the river you see .. the nimble *strandloopertje* (plover), [etc.]. **1972** *Evening Post* 9 Sept. 2 They seem to be as contented as any ostrich could wish to be, except that they find the little sandplovers (strandlopertjies) on the farm a nuisance. These little birds dart at them frequently, either to tease them or to try to chase them away. **1980** *E. Prov. Herald* 13 Dec. 6 Birds which live along the shore feeding on small creatures on and in the sand .. go by such names as sanderlings, sandpipers, sandplovers, snipes and curlews ... I call them by their attractive Afrikaans name of strandlopertjies.

strandveld /'strændfelt, 'strantfɛld/ *n.* Also with initial capital. [Afk., *strand* coast, beach + *veld* terrain.] A name given to the coastal terrain near Bredasdorp, Western Cape, the southernmost point of Africa; hence, any coastal land characterized by loose, sandy soil and semi-succulent vegetation. Often *attrib.*, passing into *adj.*

1880 *Trans. of S. Afr. Phil. Soc.* I. iii. 196 The variety is usually termed the 'Strandveldt' (sea-coast) locust. **1884** LAYARD & SHARPE *Birds of S. Afr.* 47 Mr. John Van der Byl's farm, Nacht-wacht, in the Strandveldt. **1887** *S.W. Silver & Co.'s Handbk to S. Afr.* 511 Bredasdorp. A Division formerly included in the Division of Caledon ... It lies along the coast E. of Caledon, in the country formerly called the Strandvelt. **1912** *S. Afr. Agric. Jrnl* July 35 In the Bredasdorp district it [*sc.* lamziekte] occurs on the flats of the strand veld. **1953** *Cape Times* 3 Apr. 2 Bredasdorp ... Mr Hennie Geldenhuys has .. killed two lynx which marauded farms in the strandveld area of the district in the summer. **1957** L.G. GREEN *Beyond City Lights* 224 Swellendam's forgotten world is the *strandveld*, the dune country down towards the sea. **1975** J.P.H. ACOCKS *Veld Types* 75 *Strandveld*, The vegetation of the lower parts of the sandy western coastal plains ... It has two variations: (a) A dense, dwarf semi-succulent scrub .. ; (b) the Strandveld proper, an open, semi-succulent scrub of fynbos form and intermediate between the Coastal Fynbos and the Succulent Karoo. **1975** W.M. MACMILLAN *My S. Afr. Yrs* 140 There is a scrub- or strand-veld, and a rather more favourable belt of middle-velt below the Karoo escarpment. **1977** *E. Prov. Herald* 29 Nov. 13 The reserve will provide for the preservation of wild life and vegetation, particularly of endangered types such as the strandveld and coastal macchia. **1983** [see FYNBOS]. **1985** *Weekend Argus* 30 Nov. (Suppl.) 6 A private farm on the West Coast has opened three hiking trails through natural strandveld vegetation. **1987** T.F.J. VAN RENSBURG *Intro. to Fynbos* 14 Strandveld includes a number of succulents and thorny plants and the soils on which strandveld and coastal rhenosterbosveld are formed are fertile, neutral to alkaline and sometimes somewhat brackish. **1990** *Staffrider* Vol.9 No.1, 84 Enraged gale lording at ground level, come to pleat the strandveld – forcing brown shrubbery down into prayer.

strandwolf /'strantvɔlf, 'strændwʊlf/ *n.* Also **straand wolf, straand wulf, stront(e) wolf, stronte woolfe.** Pl. **-wolwe** /-vɔlvə/, **-wolves.** [S. Afr. Du. (fr. Du.), *strand* coast, beach + *wolf* wolf (pl. *wolwe*); or Eng. *strand* beach + *wolf* (pl. *wolves*).] The brown hyaena *Hyaena brunnea* which scavenges along the sea shore; STRANDJUT; also called WOLF (*n.*[1]).

1786 G. FORSTER tr. *A. Sparrman's Voy. to Cape of G.H.* I. 165 Two other voracious animals of this kind are found in Africa, which are distinguished by the names of *mountain-wolf* and *strand-wolf* ... The *mountain-wolf* is of a greyish cast, but the *strand-wolf* blackish with a grey head. **1796** E. HELME tr. *F. Le Vaillant's Trav. into Int.* III. 67 The second [type of hyaena] is called *strand-wolf* (shore wolf). **1810** G. BARRINGTON *Acct of Voy.* 272 There are two kinds [of wolf]: the first is spotted, and .. called by the Colonists tiger-wolf: the other is the strand-wolf. **1835** A. STEEDMAN *Wanderings* 112 From its peculiar habit of frequenting the sea-coast, the Dutch Colonists have given this animal the name of '*Straand wolf*,' to distinguish it from the tiger wolf, or spotted hyaena, and the Aard wolf, or *Proteles* of zoologists, which are found throughout the Colony. **1846** H.H. METHUEN *Life in Wilderness* 126 There are two kinds of hyæna in South Africa – the spotted one, tiger-wolf of the colonists, is commonest and fiercest: the striped, or strand wolf, is not so large or bold. [*Note*] *Hyæna villasa.* **1871** [see TIGER-WOLF]. **1878** T.J. LUCAS *Camp Life & Sport* 237 Besides the spotted and striped, there is the strand or stront wolf (the aard or earth wolf of the colonists), another kind of hyena, whose fur is of a reddish tint. **1881** P. GILLMORE *Land of Boer* 205 There is a very pretty little hyena to be found up in these localities, called by the natives 'aard-wolf,' and by the colonists 'strand wolf'; it is about the size of a jackal, [and] possesses a bright fawn-coloured coat, handsomely marked with black lines. **1920** F.C. CORNELL *Glamour of Prospecting* 19 Their spoors and those of the stronte woolfe, or brown hyena, were .. to be seen along the desolate shore, where these creatures probably picked up a precarious living from the dead fish occasionally stranded there. **1958** S. CLOETE *Mask* 44 These great hyenas are called beach or strand wolves by Boers because they tended to roam along the coastal shores looking for dead fish, or birds or bodies washed up by the waves. **1968** G. CROUDACE *Black Rose* 19 He could imagine his father, weak, exhausted, falling asleep at last beneath a rock and the strandwolf sneaking up on him, snatching one cowardly bite at his throat. **1987** T.F.J. VAN RENSBURG *Intro. to Fynbos* 51 Brown hyena (strandwolves) are still found in the Groendal Wilderness Area.

straws, nipping see NIP.

streepdassie /ˈstrɪəpdasi/ *n.* [Afk., *streep* stripe + *dassie* (see DASSIE sense 2).] The ZEBRA, *Diplodus cervinus hottentotus*.

[**1906** H.E.B. BROOKING in *E. London Dispatch* 26 June 3 'Sargus cervinus' .. also called 'wilde paard', 'striped dasje', and 'five-fingers.'] **1934** C.P. SWART Supplement to Pettman. 169 *Streepdassie*, .. The Diplodus cervinus is so called on account of the well-defined stripes running across the body of the fish, which for the same reason is called Zebra in Natal. **1949** J.L.B. SMITH *Sea Fishes* 269 *Diplodus trifasciatus* ... *Streepdassie. Wildeperd* (Cape). *Bontrok* (Knysna). *Zebra* (General).

streepie, streepje varr. STREPIE.

street committee *n. phr.* Also with initial capitals. An elected body consisting of residents of a township street, falling under the control of a CIVIC, and carrying out the tasks of local government. Also *attrib.* See also PEOPLE'S COURT sense 3.

The street committees perform the duties of the former township municipalities, which collapsed during the 1980s (having been widely perceived as illegitimate apartheid structures).

1986 *Race Rel. Survey 1985* (S.A.I.R.R.) 531 The unrest led to the collapse of black local government structures in many areas. The development of alternative structures of government by residents emerged .. and took the form of street committees, area committees, and 'people's courts'. **1986** *Grocott's Mail* 2 May 1 Street committees — recently set up in every street in the townships as an alternative form of local government. **1986** [see PEOPLE'S COURT sense 3]. **1986** A. SPARKS in *Cape Times* 18 Dec. 12 An extensive network of community organizations has sprung up in the townships in recent years — action committees, street committees, civic associations and student groups. Backed by the trade unions and co-ordinated by national political organizations like the United Democratic Front and Azapo, they have developed into a shadow civic administration in the black areas. **1987** *Race Rel. Survey 1986* (S.A.I.R.R.) 131 A further component of ANC strategy is the creation of alternative structures of government to replace official structures such as black town councils and community councils. One such structure is the street committee. **1987** [see quot. at *Mandela Plan* (MANDELA)]. **1987** *Weekly Mail* 17 July 4 Each ward in the area, it is alleged, was divided into street committees with a 'street captain' as the leader. **1988** *Now Everyone Is Afraid* (Catholic Inst. for Internat. Rel.) 6 Communities developed their own structures to take over the running of the townships. Street committees were set up to organise basic services and to represent residents on co-ordinating structures. **1989** B. SOKUTU in *E. Prov. Herald* 26 Oct. 8 A street committee consisted of seven people, and seven streets usually formed an area committee, depending on the size of the area. **1989** N. MATHIANE in *Frontline* Mar. 9 She was prominent in street committee work and it is widely believed that her committee had aroused jealousies among others who believed that her street was meant to be part of their territory. **1990** R. MALAN in *Cosmopolitan* Apr. 163 A UDF street committee ordered her to produce her grandson; when she failed to comply, she was killed. **1991** M. ALEXANDER on M-Net TV, 10 Mar. (Carte Blanche), In Alexandra a network of street committees or small people's courts report upward to the civic association. **1993** *Sunday Times* 31 Oct. 7 We have excellent intelligence. We are plugged into the street committees and area committees .. and we know everything.

strelitzia /strəˈlɪtzɪə, -sɪə/ *n.* Also **strelitza**, and with initial capital. [Named for *Countess von Mecklenburg-Strelitz*, queen of George III.] **a.** Any of several perennial plants of the genus *Strelitzia* (family Strelitziaceae), esp. *S. reginae* and *S. alba*, with long, rigid leaves, and stiff flowers of orange, yellow, and purple; PISANG sense 2 a. **b.** Its flower. See also CRANE FLOWER, *wild banana* (WILD sense a).

1789 W. AITON *Hortus Kewensis* I. 285 Strelitzia ... Canna-leav'd Strelitzia. Nat. of the Cape of Good Hope. **1795** C.R. HOPSON tr. *C.P. Thunberg's Trav.* I. 191 The *Strelitsia*, with its yellow flowers and blue *nectarium*, grew near this spot, and was one of the most beautiful plants, of which the bulbs were procured to send to Europe. **1797** J. BARROW in D. Fairbridge *Lady Anne Barnard* (1924) 50, I found a new Strelitzia, a curious plant which will be a very acceptable thing in England. I sent half a dozen bulbs by the Hope. **1815** J. MACKRILL Diary. 103 The seed .. so much like that of the Strelizia is it the same? **1836** A.F. GARDINER *Journey to Zoolu Country* 17 We slept well under the shade of some strelitza trees (very similar to wild bananas). **1847** J. BARROW *Reflect.* 160, I observed, at a little distance, a whole line of strelitzias in full flower, which, on approaching, I was pleased to find were not of the species reginae, but a new species (at least in England), with pointed instead of spoon-shaped leaves, and from six to ten feet long. **1971** *S. Afr. Panorama* Aug. 19 Flower arrangements display South African flora such as the tangerine-and-blue strelitzia. **1986** M. RAMGOBIN *Waiting to Live* 7 They saw the hundreds upon hundreds of strelitzia plants with their pointed buds. Most were still half-opened. **1987** *E. Prov. Herald* 29 Apr. 10 The new Uitenhage logo depicts a Cape house and strelitzia, a plant which grows from the Tsitsikamma Forest to Natal. **1989** H.P. TOFFOLI in *Style* Jan. 57 Those puny little strelitzias in the hot-house at Kew Gardens always bring lumps to the throats of homesick South Africans.

strepie /ˈstrɪəpi/ *n.* Also **streepie**, and (formerly) **streepje**. [Afk., 'little striped one', *streep* stripe + dim. suffix -IE.] The seabream *Sarpa salpa* of the Sparidae, a small fish (with gold and silver stripes) which is often used by anglers as bait; BAMBOO FISH; BAMVOOSIE; KARANTEEN sense 1 c; MOOI NOOITJE; *Natal -, silver -*, or *striped karanteen*, see KARANTEEN sense 2; STEENTJIE sense 1 b. Also *attrib.*

The name 'strepie' is used for this species in Smith and Heemstra's *Smiths' Sea Fishes* (1986).

1913 W.W. THOMPSON *Sea Fisheries of Cape Col.* 61 The pretty little bamboo-fish of the Cape is also known as stink-fish, and is the mooi nooitje of Hermanus and Struis Bay, the streepje of the Knysna and the silver karanteen of Natal. **1949** J.L.B. SMITH *Sea Fishes* 274 *Sarpa Salpa* (Linnaeùs) ... *Bamboo, Mooi Nooitje* (Cape). *Streepie* (Knysna) ... *Striped Karanteen, Bamboo Fish* (Natal) ... Body neatly oval and plump ... Abundant in most rocky areas, is said to occur right round Africa ... A beautiful shapely fish, one of the best baits. **1957** S. SCHOEMAN *Strike!* 89 The strepie, with its beautiful gold and silver colouring, is the favourite prey of the elf. **1968** [see KARANTEEN sense 1]. **1971** *E. Prov. Herald* 15 July 16 The Eastern Cape bamvoosie (derived from Bamboo fish) is known in Natal as the Karanteen and in other parts as the streepie. **1972** *Grocott's Mail* 28 Jan. 3 Denis Butler .. played havoc with the shad down there. Using .. a strepie fillet he accounted for 96. **1974** *Farmer's Weekly* 14 Dec. 111, I hear that some *geelbek* .. have been caught in the deep water towards the end of the pier. If there's any about these live *strepies* should tempt them to feed. **1975** [see BLACKTAIL]. **1989** *Weekend Post* 23 Dec. 5 Prof Hecht said signs of complete recovery of the estuary created by the marina walls were very encouraging. 'We have already found samples of marine fish such as butterfly fish, the *strepie* and zebra in the canals themselves.'

strews Guard var. (*as*) *true as God* (see TRUE sense a).

strijkgeld var. STRYKGELD.

stroes (God) var. (*as*) *true as God* (see TRUE sense a).

stroller *n. slang.* [Special sense of (Scot.) Eng. *stroller* vagrant, itinerant beggar.] A homeless young urban vagrant, a street child; cf. MALALAPIPE.

1986 W. SCHARF et al. in Burman & Reynolds *Growing Up* 262 A stroller is someone who don't sleep by his house — he sleeps in the street. He don't eat by his house — he eats by the bins. A stroller is someone who thinks he is free ... It's a nice name for us. **1987** L. BEAKE *Strollers* 35 Gangs didn't bother strollers — not unless strollers did something unacceptable, that is. *Ibid.* 79 The things they normally picked strollers up for, like spitting or loitering, or putting your feet on a bench or begging. Man, they could even pick you up for just *being* there. **1987** *Personality* 16 Dec. 77 Cape Town's twilight children who call themselves Strollers. **1987** L. BUTLER in *Fair Lady* 30 Sept. 6 Waysel, a Hillbrow stroller, obviously no more than a malnourished 10 year old, told us he was 17 ... The only certain thing in his hand-to-mouth existence was how to spell his own name. **1989** *Femina* Oct. 74 In this country there are estimated to be about 9 000 children living on the streets of our cities ... 'Strollers' they're called and some are as young as four. **1992** *South* 27 Feb. 3 At a traffic light a little stroller taps on my car window in the drizzle, cupping his hands in a begging gesture.

Hence **stroll** *v. intrans.*, to live as a vagrant; so **strolling** *vbl n.*, this way of life.

1987 L. BEAKE *Strollers* 6 'Strolling's,' he paused, looking for the right word, 'like free. Yes, man, freedom's what it's all about. I been going now for years. My folks don't mind. One less mouth, my Da always says.' *Ibid.* 7 'You'll find us when you change your mind,' he said cheerfully. 'Town's where I most often stroll.' Then he was gone. *Ibid.* 9 He knew .. that to stroll meant to stay out of sight and out of trouble.

stronte wolf var. STRANDWOLF.

strooidak /ˈstrʊɪdak/ *n.* [Afk., *strooi* straw + *dak* roof.] Special Comb. ***Strooidak church, Strooidakkerk*** /kɛrk/ [Afk., *kerk* church], the early 19th century thatched Dutch Reformed Church at Paarl, Western Cape.

1957 L.G. GREEN *Beyond City Lights* 43 A much finer church was built at Paarl, to be followed early last century by the beloved *strooidak* (thatched roof) church. **1978** *Reader's Digest Illust. Guide to Sn Afr.* 74 Many of Paarl's ancient buildings remain. Among these is the Dutch Reformed Strooidakkerk ('thatched church'). Built in 1805, it is the oldest church still in use in South Africa. **1979** *S. Afr. Panorama* Sept. 49 A larger organ for the 'Strooidak' (thatched roof) church in Paarl with 26 registers, 56 notes and 1 800 pipes. **1980** *Sunday Times* 9 Mar. (Mag. Sect.) 5 An old lady, who had years ago, been a member of the famous strooidakkerk until she was moved to her 'own' area. **1984** *S. Afr. Digest* 15 June 14 The *Strooidakkerk* (thatched roof church) is Cape-Dutch architecture. **1987** *Frontline* Mar. 5 A few days after the 'Free the Children Vigil' in St. George's Cathedral Cape Town, the State President and Cabinet and white residents of Paarl gathered in the Strooidak Church to dedicate to God the 300 years of white settlement in the Berg river valley.

strools var. STRUIS.

strop /strɒp, strɔp/ *n.*[1] Pl. **-s, stroppe** /strɔpə/. [Afk., fr. Du. *strop* noose, *stropje* small strap, loop, or cord.]

Formerly used in *Brit. Eng.* (fr. Old Eng.), but obs. since the 18th century.

1.a. The leather strap (on a yoke) which was fastened under the throat of a draught animal; NECKSTRAP; NEKSTROP. **b.** Any leather strap. Also **stroppie** [see -IE].

1846 *Natal Witness* 3 July, Market Intelligence ... 10 Strops, 4s. 6d. **1882** J. NIXON *Among Boers* 172 The yoke is kept from slipping sideways by wooden stays, or 'skeys', which are fastened under the throat by a small 'strop' of hide. **1899** *Natal Agric. Jrnl* 31 Mar. 5 Dutch words such as 'aasvogel,' .. 'ringhals,' 'strop,' 'stoep,' 'pas op,' etc ... We believe that we have placed on record all the agricultural words of South African Dutch now in use among English colonists at the end of the present century, and likely to retain their vitality during the next. **1900** B. MITFORD *Aletta* 35 If I returned a second time without having shot a buck I was allowed some dinner, but first of all I got plenty of 'strop'. **1916** *Farmer's Weekly* 20 Dec. 1458 (*advt*) For Sale, Bushbuck Skins, ready brayed for cutting voorslags, riems, strops, whips, sjamboks. *Ibid.* 27 Dec. 1564 We have a full stock of: Game Reims, Game Neck Strops, Game Whip Lashes, Game Voorslags, [etc.]. **1920** R. JUTA *Tavern* 12 A dirty unladylike enough proceeding calculated to draw Tante Petronelle's wrath – if not the stroppie (strap). **1925** L.D. FLEMMING *Crop of Chaff* 3 A native boy is despatched hot-afoot for the oxen. Another boy oils the wheels and pours water over them to tighten up the spokes – riems and strops are hurriedly dealt out. **1947** H.C. BOSMAN *Mafeking Rd* (1969) 157 As we were .. without skeis we had to fasten the necks of the oxen straight on to the yokes with strops, and several of the oxen got strangled. **1963** S. CLOETE *Rags of Glory* 404 Through these holes went the skeys – pieces of hard wood notched to take the leather strops or straps that passed under the ox's throat and were adjusted in the notches according to the size of the animal. **1970** *Informant, Grahamstown* He used a stroppie to mend the halter (a small piece of hide or leather). **1973** *Farmer's Weekly* 13 June (Suppl.) 39 (*advt*) Boermaak Riems 10 ft. R5,00; cheaper quality R3,60; Strops R3,00; Agterslaags R1,35; Voorslaags 86c doz., Skeys R3,60 doz.; Skey Yokes R4,50. **1977** F.G. BUTLER *Karoo Morning* 117 What's a strop ... Man, it's a thick thong that hooks into the notches of the jukskeis under the ox's neck. It keeps the yoke in place. Now the best skin for stroppe comes from the skin of the old aardvark – very tough.

2. *comb.* **Strop Bill** *hist.*, a bill proposed in 1890: see quot. 1936.

1936 S.G. MILLIN *Rhodes* (1936) 227 The Strop Bill was a Bill empowering magistrates, in certain master and servant cases, to impose the lash (hence 'strop'). Not only Rhodes, but Hofmeyr, supported the Bill. The Bill did not become law. **1946** S. CLOETE *Afr. Portraits* 281 His first act as Prime Minister was to support the Strop Bill ... This was a bill which would allow magistrates to impose the lash upon recalcitrant Kaffirs. **1955** D.L. HOBMAN *Olive Schreiner* 49 She disapproved of his [*sc.* Rhodes's] policy and her anger against him was aroused when, as Prime Minister in the Cape Parliament, he voted in favour of the 'Strop Bill'; this measure permitted the infliction of lashes on natives for minor offences. **1980** *E. Prov. Herald* 13 May 3 He tried to push through Parliament the Strop Bill, which allowed for flogging of black labourers.

strop /strɒp/ *n.*[2] *slang.* [Perh. fr. prec. (see quot. 1900 sense 1, and sense 2); or back-formation on general Eng. *stroppy* obstreperous.] Trouble; 'back-chat'; uncooperative behaviour. See also *to gooi strop* (GOOI sense 2).

1985 P. SLABOLEPSZY *Sat. Night at Palace* 13 And on top of it this ou chops me as I go past. So because I want to stuff him up, Carstens has a big shit from the bench. Says I mustn't cause strop. **1987** P. POLLOCK in *Personality* 15 June 53 'These born-again women are much better than ordinary wives, they give you less strop,' I told them.

'strue as Bob, 'strue's Bob, etc. varr. (*as*) *true as Bob* (see TRUE sense b).

'strue as God, 'strue's God, etc. varr. (*as*) *true as God* (see TRUE sense a).

struis /strœɪs/ *n.* Also **strois**. [Afk., contraction of *strooi huis*, *strooi* straw + *huis* house.] A thatched hut built in traditional African style; *transf.*, the home of a black (farm) labourer (so called whether thatched or not).

1913 C. PETTMAN *Africanderisms* 484 *Struis*, A not infrequent contraction in the Transvaal of *strohuis* [*sic*], a straw-house. **1919** M.M. STEYN *Diary* 131 Upon some kopje about a mile away, the shepherd would erect a small reed house ('struis' – short for 'strooi huis' – straw house,) and for three weeks or as long as the eggs were being hatched, he would remain watching the nest. **1970** *Informant, Grahamstown* Jonas lives in the struis on the hill. (Native hut). **1971** M. BRITZ *Informant, Grahamstown* He went to fetch the boy ... While he was down at the struis I was pacing up and down. **1975** *Dict. of Eng. Usage in Sn Afr.* 169 *Strois*, .. alt: struis. Afr[ican] hut; the word is a contraction of 'strooi-huis' (straw house) in ref. to the thatched roof.

struse Bob var. (*as*) *true as Bob* (see TRUE sense b).

stryddag /ˈstreɪ(t)dax/ *n.* Also **strydag**. Pl. **-s, -dae** /-dɑːə/. [Afk., *stryd* struggle, conflict + *dag* day.] A rally held by an Afrikaner political organization; *transf.*, any political rally.

1950 *Cape Times* 26 July 1 Mr. C.R. Swart, Minister of Justice, told a Nationalist Party stryddag here yesterday that he was not prepared to reintroduce public hanging. **1961** *Ibid.* 11 Jan. 1 In Britain he will be able to give the moderately-phrased versions of *apartheid* far more expertly and convincingly than in heated debates in Parliament or during *stryddae* in the platteland. **1963** M. BENSON *Afr. Patriots* 146 J.G. Strijdom, Nationalist leader, significantly chose Bethal for a Stryddag (struggle day), when he announced that the white man should always be master .. in public life in South Africa. **1972** *Daily Dispatch* 14 Apr. 10 The day of the big stryddag is over. Those large crowds will never again drive across the veld to hear emotional appeals to the blood. **1975** *Sunday Times* 13 Apr. 4 Bring me there a bottle of 1973 Scharzberg. You know, man, the kind we knock back at a stryddag in the Waterberg at a Herstigte rally. **1978** *Pace* Dec. 51 On Sunday, Chief Buthelezi is going to put on his Inkatha uniform and address an all-black *stryddag* in Soweto. **1980** *Voice* 20 Aug. 2 As an old traveller on the South African Railways I have always been amused by the fact that the higher-ups .. seem to become deaf when one points out that they make more money out of black commuters than they will ever make in a life-time of strydags. **1986** P. LE ROUX in Burman & Reynolds *Growing Up* 191 The *volksfeeste* (folk festivals) – Republic Day, Kruger Day, and Day of the Covenant – interspersed with National Party *stryddae* (fêtes), attracted fewer participants every year.

stryd duur voort, die see DIE STRYD DUUR VOORT.

strykgeld /ˈstreɪkxɛlt/ *n. Obs.* exc. *hist.* Formerly also **strijkgeld**. [S. Afr. Du., transf. use of Du. *strijkgeld* premium.] See quot. 1927.

A term used in the Dutch method of auctioneering. See also AFSLAG, OPSLAG sense 2.

1823 W.W. BIRD *State of Cape of G.H.* 42 To encourage these speculators to go on bidding, money sometimes to the amount of more than one thousand rix-dollars is given to the individual who bids the largest sum on the advance, and this is called the strykgeld. [**1839** *S. Afr. Commercial Advertiser* 11 Sept., Thursday Morning, 18th September Two Hire Houses Situate in Vrede Street, St Johns Street. Liberal Stryk-money will be given on the landed property.] **1839** *Ibid.* 18 Sept., The House is in a thorough state of repair, with every requisite for a genteel family; .. Liberal Strykgeld will be given. Vendue Officer, Stellenbosch. **1873** *Cape Monthly Mag.* VI. 209 A fundus (landed property) is .. always sold twice, once by public proclamation or by the rise to the highest bidder (who receives ten or twelve or more ducats as *strijkgeld*, as he seldom cares to remain the purchaser ..), and then by the fall. **1913** G.E. CORY *Rise of S. Afr.* II. 254 This premium was the *strijkgeld* or reward to the man who bid highest without, most probably, any intention of buying. *Ibid.* 255 The highest upward bidder received a certain percentage of the value of the property sold and this was called the *strijkgeld*. **1927** C.G. BOTHA *Social Life in Cape Col.* 99 The method of selling immovables at such sales differed somewhat to that of other countries. The property was first of all sold by *opslag*, advance bidding, and then put up again and sold by *afslag*, or downward bidding. The bidder in the first instance did not intend to make the purchase, but rather to increase the final sum. For this service, he received a bonus, or, as it was called, *strykgeld* ... Advertisements of sales invariably stated that 'liberal *strykgeld*' would be given, which naturally tended to bring many to the sale and also enhanced the purchase price. **1965** [see OPSLAG sense 2].

stuckvat var. STUKVAT.

stuiver, -wer varr. STIVER.

stuk /stək/ *n.* Pl. **-ke** /-kə/. [Afk., piece, bit.]

1. *obs. slang.* STUKKIE sense 1.

1946 J.B. FISHER in E. Partridge *Dict. of Underworld Slang* (1950) 700 *Stuk*, A fast girl; S. Africa.

2. A piece (of something); STUKKIE sense 2.

[**1933** W. MACDONALD *Romance of Golden Rand* 144 Nourse put down his name with Jan Meyer for a block of thirty-four (stukke grond) claims.] **1971** A. SCHOLEFIELD *Young Masters*, 'Fish!' the tramp said in disgust as he opened the padkos ... Want a stuk, Pauline?' **1984** *Frontline* Feb. 27 I've got this picture in my mind of some govt. ou coming round to this Nanabhai with a stuk of paper to tell him he must up and off from his little shop .. to some plek the govt. figured was better for him. **1984** *Ibid.* May 39 Koos, what the govt ous say is that .. this Bop is a separate country all of its own, being a stuk of the West Transvaal there by Rustenberg and a stuk of the North Transvaal there by Warmbaths and a stuk of the Free State there by Thabanchu and a few other stukke around and about. **1989** R. SLADEN *Informant, Cape Town* There's somehow still nothing that compares with a good stuk of biltong.

stukkie /ˈstəki, ˈsteki/ *n.* Also **stekkie**. [Afk., (small) piece, bit (*stuk* piece + -IE).]

1. *slang.* An offensive term for a woman (viewed as a sexual object); a girlfriend; STUK sense 1.

1970 J.R. BENNETT *Informant, Krugersdorp* How old is your stukkie? **1978** L. BARNES in *The 1820* Vol.51 No.12, 19 *She's a kif chick*. That means of course that *she's a sleek stukkie*, or for you squares, she's an attractive girl. **1983** A. GOLDSTUCK in *Frontline* Oct. 61 'Sure I'm functioning,' he says. 'I got a graft, a cabbie, I got stukkies, booze, and I got zol.' **1986** *Informant, Durban* Brian's going out with a new stukkie now. **1987** *Scope* 6 Nov. 36 We sell it to them and they give us each a yacht with drugs, booze and *stukkies*. [**1990** R. GOOL *Cape Town Coolie* 59 'Ow's all those Cape Town *steakies*?] **1992** M.D. PRENTICE *Informant, Durban* Stukkie. Pretty girl. **1993** *'Jimbo' programme insert, Napac* Stekkie. Girl, Girlfriend.

‖**2.** *attrib.* STUK sense 2.

1970 *Cape Argus* 3 Oct. 11 We have a trout stream and we grow our own vegetables. As a South African I had to have my own 'stukkie grond'. **1989** P. LEE in *Sunday Times* 26 Feb. (Mag. Sect.) 36 Consider the humble Vellie. Originally crudely crafted from a stukkie vel and net 'n bietjie leather, the velskoen has become one of the country's greatest treasures.

stukvat *n. obs.* Also **stu(c)k-vat**. [S. Afr. Du., fr. Du. *stuk vat*.] A large wine- or brandy-vat, holding 24 ankers (192 imperial gallons or 888 litres). Also *attrib.* See also ANKER.

1824 *S. Afr. Commercial Advertiser* 14 Jan. 23 Waggons, Draughthorses, .. Stuckvats, Leaguers, Casks, *c* **1829** *Govt Gaz.* 23 Jan. 8 Six fine new six-and-a-half Leaguer

Stuckvats, made of blue Staves; common Stuckvats, Leaguers, Pipes, and smaller fustage. **1831** *S. Afr. Almanac & Dir.*, (*advt*) Has continually on sale Stuckvat Staves and Teakwood do., large and small Iron Hoops. **1832** *Graham's Town Jrnl* 13 Apr. 61 P. Heugh & Co. having sold their premises in the Town, will sell, on Tuesday next .. Without Reserve, the remainder of their Stock, consisting of ... Stukvat Staves, Teakwood Planks, cane, empty bottles. **1877** LADY BARKER *Yr's Hsekeeping* 16 It is in the long corridor beyond this that the 'Stuck-Vats' live, — puncheons which hold easily some thousand gallons or so. **1887** *Silver & Co.'s Handbk to S. Afr.* 224 The wine is racked into a fresh stuckvat whenever it is wished to check fermentation. **1894** G. PAYNE in H. Beck *Meet Cape Wines* (1966) 16 In the majority of cellars I visited it would be impossible to make good wine ... The cellars are dirty .. and stukvats anything but clean. **1910** D. FAIRBRIDGE *That Which Hath Been* (1913) 107 The long, white wine-house with its rows of massive oak stukvats bound with iron. **1915** —— *Torch Bearer* 186 Their deep and lofty cellars were filled with gigantic oak stuk-vats, the mighty casks into which the pressed grape-juice from the neighbouring farms was poured, to be treated and blended and issued to a thirsty South Africa as Hermitage or Sauvignon Blanc. **1936** L.G. GREEN *Secret Afr.* 175 Six of the wine casks still in use at Alphen were there in 1708 ... Some of the oak *stukvats* used as fermenting vats were made by slaves on the farm.

stump *n.* [Ellipt. form of STUMPNOSE.]
a. STUMPNOSE sense 1.

1949 J.L.B. SMITH *Sea Fishes* 272 *Chrysoblephus gibbiceps ... Red Stumpnose ... Stump* (Eastern Cape). **1977** *Daily Dispatch* 17 Aug. 11 Fair catches of copper steenbras and stumps were made.

b. With distinguishing epithet: **red stump**, *red stumpnose* (see STUMPNOSE sense 2); **white stump**, *white stumpnose* (see STUMPNOSE sense 2).

1957 S. SCHOEMAN *Strike!* 36 The **red stump** is generally regarded as a very astute and intelligent fish. **1971** *Argus* 14 May 14 Derek Hammond found shoals of red stump in deep water off Platbank. **1987** R. NAYSMITH in *Ski Scene* Mar.-Apr. 13 Reports of good catches of .. **white stump** have been made.

stumpnose *n.* [tr. S. Afr. Du. *stompneus*, see STOMPNEUS.]
1. Any of several species of seabream (family Sparidae): **a.** (see *red stumpnose*, sense 2 below). **b.** (see *white stumpnose*, sense 2 below). In both senses also called STOMPNEUS (sense a), STUMP (sense a).

1838 J.E. ALEXANDER *Exped. into Int.* I. 88 Excellent fish are to be procured here; such as the delicious Roman fish, Hottentot, 'Jacob Fever,' .. stump nose, and clip fish. **1878** T.J. LUCAS *Camp Life & Sport* 30 The harbour abounds in fish, amongst which 'Stumpnose,' 'Seventy-four,' .. and other strangely named but well flavoured fish are pre-eminent. **1913** D. FAIRBRIDGE *Piet of Italy* 12 The fishcarts were well on their way to Wynberg, the drivers' horns .. bringing every good housewife running to her gate to secure fresh elf or stumpnose. **1926** M. NATHAN *S. Afr. from Within* 204 The larger staple fish are silverfish, stumpnose, [etc.] **1970** *S. Afr. Panorama* June, There are actually quite a number of fish suitable for making bokkems ... We concentrate on haarder, stumpnose, steenbras, elf (shad) and 'doppies' (small silver fish). Bokkems are also often made from marsbanker. **1990** *Our Living World* 11 Mar. 4 Angling favourites such as white steenbras and stumpnose.

2. With distinguishing epithet: **red stumpnose**, *Chrysoblephus gibbiceps*; LUCY; MISS LUCY; POENSKOP sense 2 a i; *red stompneus*, see STOMPNEUS sense b; *red stump*, see STUMP sense b; **white stumpnose**, any of several species of the genus *Rhabdosargus*, esp. *R. globiceps*; FLATTY sense 1; *white stompneus*, see STOMPNEUS sense b; *white stump*, see STUMP sense b.

In Smith and Heemstra's *Smiths' Sea Fishes* (1986), the name 'Cape stumpnose' is used for *R. holubi*, 'Natal stumpnose' for *R. sarba*, 'red stumpnose' for *C. gibbiceps*, and 'white stumpnose' for *R. globiceps*.

1831 *S. Afr. Almanac & Dir.*, January .. Fish in Season. Hottentot, **red Stumpnose**, [etc.]. **1872** C.A. PAYTON *Diamond Diggings*, Having refreshed ourselves at a funny Dutch inn, we returned to Cape Town with a good appetite for dinner, at which we had a very excellent fish called 'red stumpnose!' **1893** H.A. BRYDEN *Gun & Camera* 448 Presently some bigger fish made themselves felt; these were the rooi stompneus (red stump-nose), a big, heavy-shouldered fish, vividly striped in red and silver. **1930** C.L. BIDEN *Sea-Angling Fishes* 169 Little bands of anglers, not aware of the original names, have given 'pet' names to this fish ... The red stumpnose is known as 'Lucy' by many anglers at East London and Port Elizabeth, Michael or Mighel at Knysna. **1977** *Darling* 8 June 118 The stumpnose family make excellent steaming fish, and always remind me of my dear late grandmother, who was very choosy .. and considered that a piece of steamed red stumpnose was the only kind of fish really beneficial to her delicate digestion, while the rest of the family were messily gnawing away at harder heads. **1984** *Daily Dispatch* 6 Nov. 13 Sustained catches .. had resulted in serious depletion of the stocks of species such as .. red stumpnose. **1880** 'C.W.' in *Cape Monthly Mag.* II. Mar. 162 As fast as I could haul them in, came up bouncing fat Hottentot fish, varied now and then by a grand **white stumpnose**. **1955** C. HORNE *Fisherman's Eldorado* 23 When warm water comes to False Bay white stumpnose leave the shallows and do not return till the following winter. **1969** J.R. GRINDLEY *Riches of Sea* 81 Other common estuarine fish — the white stumpnose .. and the white steenbras .. are carnivores and feed mainly on the little crustaceans in the mud banks. **1981** *Argus* 29 Jan. 9 Elf and white stumpnose have been extremely scarce this summer. **1992** YELD & GUBB in *Afr. Wildlife* Vol.46 No.2, 201 'Angling' species such as white steenbras, yellowtail, elf, kob, white stumpnose, dassie and belman.

stumptail *n.* [tr. S. Afr. Du. *stompstertje, stomp* stump(y) + *stertje* little tail.] The CROMBEC, *Sylvietta refuscens*.

[**1884, 1901** see CROMBEC.] **1908** HAAGNER & IVY *Sketches* 80 The Crombec (*Sylviella rufescens*), known to the farmers as the Stomp-stertje (Stump-tail), is ash-grey above and tawny-buff below. **1937** [see CROMBEC]. **1955** MACKWORTH-PRAED & GRANT *Birds E. & N.E. Afr.* II. 423 *Crombecs or Stump-tails*, .. Called Crombecs by the early Dutch settlers in South Africa because of their curved bills. **1962** [see CROMBEC]. **1970** G.J. BROEKHUYSEN in *Std Encycl. of Sn Afr.* II. 343 Sylviidae. Another very large family, which includes many birds commonly known as warblers ... Among them are .. the krombek or stumptail (*Sylvietta refuscens*), [etc.].

stupe var. STOEP.

styfsiekte /ˈsteɪfsiktə/ *n.* Also **steuve ziekt, stiftziehte, stijfsiekte, stijfziekte, styf(f)-ziekte, stywesiekte, styweziekte**. [Afk., earlier S. Afr. Du. *stijfziekte* (*stijf* stiff + *ziekte* disease).]
1. *Pathology.* Any of a variety of diseases of cattle and sheep causing partial or complete paralysis, particularly: **a.** Poisoning by the plant *Crotalaria burkeana* of the Leguminosae. **b.** The result of phosphate deficiency. **c.** THREE DAYS' SICKNESS. In these senses also called STIFF-SICKNESS (sense 1).

[**1863** *Queenstown Free Press* 3 Feb., Appoplexy [*sic*] in sheep ... This sickness is known to be very fatal among sheep, and is what the Dutch usually call 'Styff-ziekte,' for after a few fits the animal always died.] **1886** [see STIFF-SICKNESS sense 1]. **1897** 'F. MACNAB' *On Veldt & Farm* 230 Another mysterious complaint is stiftziehte, which appears to be the same as .. lumziehte, or paralysis, in the colony. **1905** D. HUTCHEON in Flint & Gilchrist *Science in S. Afr.* 352 Acute Rheumatism — 'Stijfsiekte' in Sheep .. is characterised by acute inflammation of the sheaths of the tendons and capsular ligaments of the joints of all four limbs. **1907** T.R. SIM *Forests & Forest Flora* 202 In this Colony the genera Crotalaria, Lessertia, Indigofera, and Tephrosia are under suspicion of producing the leguminous poisoning of cattle known locally as 'stijfziekte.' **1911** *Agric. Jrnl of Union* Feb. 13 (Pettman), The above facts appear to me to indicate that the diseased condition termed *stijfziekte* is due to defective nutrition of the bones of the affected animal, and that this arises from the absence of a sufficiency of phosphates in the vegetation upon which the animal feeds. **1916** *Farmer's Weekly* 20 Dec. 1498 Styfziekte is a distinct trouble from gallamziekte. It is a disease of the bones and joints .. not nearly so serious. **1937** *Handbk for Farmers* (Dept of Agric. & Forestry) 480 Two kinds of stywesiekte are recognized, namely the so-called aphosphorosis .. and the stywesiekte caused by ingestion of the plant *Crotalaria burkeana* (Klappers). **1978, 1979** [see STIFF-SICKNESS sense 1].

2. *comb.* **styfsiektebossie**, also **-boschje, -bosje** /-ˌbɔsi/ [Afk., *bossie* fr. Du. *bos(ch)je* small bush], the plant *Crotalaria burkeana*, causing leguminous poisoning in cattle; DRONKGRAS sense c; *stiff-sickness bush*, see STIFF-SICKNESS sense 2.

1912 *S. Afr. Agric. Jrnl* June 780 (Pettman), The *cause* of this stiff-sickness had been experimentally established by feeding of the so-called **stijfziekte boschje** (*Crotolaria burkeana*). **1917** R. MARLOTH *Common Names* 77 *Stijf'ziekte'bos. Crotalaria Burkeana* (Tr.). **1966** C.A. SMITH *Common Names* 443 *Styfsiektebossie, Crotalaria burkeana* ... Cattle eating the plants develop a disease known as styfsiekte (stiffsickness) marked by an abnormal growth of the hoofs ... The vernacular name appears to have been used as far back as about 1880. **1979** T. GUTSCHE *There Was a Man* 244 The Transvaal farmers had long ascribed it [*sc.* the disease] to the stijfziekte bosje, a tough little plant with hard bean-pods.

styver var. STIVER.

stywe pap /ˈsteɪvə pap/ *n.* [Afk., *stywe* attrib. form of *styf* stiff + *pap* porridge.] Firm maize-meal porridge, often eaten with meat; PUTU sense a; SADZA. See also MEALIEPAP sense 1.

1968 *Fair Lady* 30 Oct. (Suppl.) 6 Mieliepap for every taste. Have you tried it with meat and gravy? A real old-time South African favourite, this — perfect at braais. Make the firm 'Stywe pap' or the dry and crumbly 'Krummelpap'. **1973** *Ibid.* 8 Aug. 193 'Stywe' pap with honey, butter and milk. Try it with porridge and crumbly pap too. **1974** *E. Prov. Herald* 6 May 9 They were served with stiff porridge (*stywepap*). But then, when we were in the bundu on a safari, everything was served with *stywepap* — even mopani worms. **1975** *Darling* 1 Oct. 31 The only other necessary ingredients for a braaivleis are salads, fly swatters, and boiled potatoes with butter. Mealies .. are nice too. If you must have stywe pap, give your guests a choice of bread too. **1976** *Farmer's Weekly* 28 Jan. 92 When a woman turned a man weak at the knees, his brains were about as much use as a plate of cold stywepap. **1976** V. ROSENBERG *Sunflower* 213 The menu in the Bosman-Vorster camp comprised braai chops, 'stywepap' and 'vetkoek' all washed down with claret from the large bottle. The 'stywepap' was Herman's sacred charge. **1979** *Capetonian* May 9 If your ancestors had the bad taste to trek over the Orange River, that's toughies on you, my unwanted bed fellows from the land of stywepap and mampoer! **1986** *Cape Times* 16 May 11 Surely *stywepap* is *stywepap*, not 'stiff mealie meal porridge'. **1990** [see THREE-LEGGED].

styweziekte var. STYFSIEKTE.

Suazi var. SWAZI.

Sub A *n. phr.* [Ellipt. for *Sub-standard A.*] A name given in many educational systems to the first year of formal schooling, being (with SUB B) one of the two 'Sub-Standards'; a member of a Sub A class. Also *attrib.*

In KwaZulu-Natal called 'Class 1'. [*a*1950 Remembered in use in Port Elizabeth.]

1974 *S. Afr. Panorama* Jan. 39 The little ones of Sub A and B are elephants here — during the physical training class! **1978** *E. Prov. Herald* 14 Feb. 5, 6 000 new black Sub As expected. **1979** M. MATSHOBA *Call Me Not a Man* p.vii, At seven I entered 'Sub-A' in a Salvation Army school in Orlando East ... After 'Sub-B' I was shuttled to Mzimhlope Primary School for Standard I. **1979** *Sunday Times* 8 July (Extra) 3, I sent my child there [*sc.* to a non-racial school] from Sub A and as such I cannot see any problem. At that age children will mix, irrespective of race. **1981** *Fair Lady* 1 July 108 Of the 2 184 pupils 831 are in Sub A (some are 16 years old), though this is not unusual in rural areas where on average more than half the pupils are in the first two years of school. **1988** *Pace* Dec. 21 Even a Sub A pupil could have written better than headmaster M—. **1991** *E. Prov. Herald* 20 June 1 Since Sub A, the boy had been 'difficult'.

Sub B *n. phr.* [Ellipt. for *Sub-standard B.*] A name given in many educational systems to the second year of formal schooling (see prec.); a member of a Sub B class. Also *attrib.*

In KwaZulu-Natal called 'Class 2'. [*a*1950 Remembered in use in Port Elizabeth.]

1974, 1979 [see SUB A]. **1985** *E. Prov. Herald* 27 Feb. 1 A Sub B pupil at Grey Junior School. **1985** *Fair Lady* 1 May 7 For two or three years, Sub A and Sub B could become multi-racial in government schools and then gradually higher standards could also become multi-racial. **1987** *Daily Dispatch* 6 May 10 Do you have a card for a Sub B teacher who cracked up?

sub-drostdy /ˈsʌbˌdrɒsti, ˌsʌbdrɔsˈdeɪ/ *n. hist.* Formerly also **sub-droastdie**. [Eng. *sub* subsidiary, secondary + DROSTDY.] A secondary magisterial district or office within a DROSTDY (sense 1).

1827 *Reports of Commissioners upon Finances at Cape of G.H.* I. 18 It has been found necessary to establish Sub-Droastdies, differing in no respect from the constitution of the larger divisions. **1827** G. THOMPSON *Trav.* I. 272 Beaufort was created a sub-drostdy only a few years ago, and the village which had arisen in consequence of the establishment of the provincial magistracy, contains about thirty houses. **1835** A. STEEDMAN *Wanderings* I. 105 The district of Graaff Reinet, of which Beaufort is a *subdrostdy*, covers an extent of country containing more than fifty thousand square miles. **1963** R. LEWCOCK *Early 19th C. Archit.* 223 The *Cape Gazette* of 14 February 1825 announced the dissolution of the sub-drostdy of Cradock and its removal to 'Bruintjes Hooghte on the spot heretofore known as the Somerset Farm'.

subsidiengeld see GELD sense b.

sudsa, sudza varr. SADZA.

sugar baron *n. phr.* A nickname given to a farmer (in KwaZulu-Natal) who has made his fortune from sugar cane. Also *attrib.*

1937 C. BIRKBY *Zulu Journey* 155 Now you are in the land of the sugar barons, the old families famous throughout Natal as pioneers of planting and milling. Great wealth has been won from these silver-green fields that flash by below. **1951** O. WALKER *Shapeless Flame* 191 We are all masters of men here, whether one has a few borrowed pounds in one's pocket, like me, or a sugar baron of which this town has a few. **1978** *Sunday Times* 5 Mar. 12 Even sugar barons have to tighten their belts at the end of the month, it seems. **1982** *Daily News* 21 Apr. 1 A member of one of Natal's best-known sugar baron families. **1982** *Pace* Nov. 218 Stanger .. is the commercial centre of one of the richest farming communities in the world, built to serve the needs of the sugar barons and their employees. **1991** J. MCCLURE *Song Dog* 63 Natal farmers driving Rolls Royces ... What did Grantham himself get out of this unusual liaison of the cop and the sugar baron?

sugar bean *n. phr.* Usu. in *pl.*: The dried beans, reddish and mottled in colour, of a hybrid of *Phaseolus vulgaris* of the Fabaceae, a staple food for many. Also *attrib.*

1916 *Farmer's Weekly* 20 Dec. 1454 For Sale. Seed Beans, large White Butter, Round Sugar and Yellow; also Soya Beans. **1923** LEPPAN & BOSMAN *Field Crops in S. Afr.* 324 The rate of planting varies with the size of the bean; .. 30 to 40 lbs. of sugar, and 50 to 60 lbs. of white kidney beans will be found to be the right quantity to plant per acre. *Ibid.* 325 Beans belonging to the sugar group are those in greatest demand and fetch the highest prices. **1946** *Food & Cookery* (Dept of Agric.) 114 Dried Beans. The following varieties are included — (1) the cheap kidney bean and white haricot bean; (2) the more expensive sugar bean, lima and butter bean; (3) the soybean. **1950** [see SMOOR *n.*]. **1973** P.A. WHITNEY *Blue Fire* 60 It was hard to swallow, and sugar beans, cooked with meat and served over rice, tasted as flat as her spirits. **1975** *Daily Dispatch* 27 Mar. (Suppl.) 8 (*advt*) 1 Kg coffee beans .. 1 Kg yellow beans .. 5 Kg fowls food ... 1 Kg sugar beans. **1975** *E. Prov. Herald* 5 July 9 What most of the women had in common were their purchases of .. 2,5 kilogram packets of mealie meal, samp, flour and sugar, 250 grams of coffee, large or small packets of sugar beans, [etc.]. **1979** A.P. BRINK *Dry White Season* 255 One really needed space to do justice to Susan's turkey and leg of lamb and topside, yellow rice with raisins, peas, sweet-potatoes with cinnamon, stewed fruit, sugarbeans and the salads. **1979** [see Burgess quot. at SAMP]. **1981** *Pace* Sept. 168 Add the meat stock, salt and sugar beans and cook lightly till tender. **1982** *Grocott's Mail* 18 May 3 Floor prices for four types of dry beans were announced by the Manager of the Dry Bean Board .. recently. The prices per ton for second grade beans are: large white kidney beans R570, speckled sugar beans R715, yellow haricot R570 and brown haricot R550. **1988** F. WILLIAMS *Cape Malay Cookbk* 95 In the past, this [funeral meal] would have been wortel en ertjie bredie or sugar bean bredie, but nowadays mutton curry served with rice .. has taken preference.

sugarbird *n.* [tr. S. Afr. Du., transf. use of Du. *suikervogel* humming bird (*suiker* sugar + *vogel* bird).]

1. Either of two species of bird of the Promeropidae, *Promerops cafer* or *P. gurneyi*, in colour brown, white, and rufous, and with long tails and long, slender, curved beaks; SUNBIRD.

In G.L. Maclean's *Roberts' Birds of Sn Afr.* (1993), the name 'Cape sugarbird' is used for *P. cafer*, and 'Gurney's sugarbird' for *P. gurneyi*. These two species together constitute the family Promeropidae.

1798 LADY A. BARNARD in Lord Lindsay *Lives of Lindsays* (1849) III. 408, I began to collect my Cape trifles for my friends at home, — some beautiful loories, .. some plumes of the sugar-bird's tail, which is long and elegantly formed at the season of the year. **1804** R. PERCIVAL *Acct of Cape of G.H.* 101 The sugar bird appears here with a very large bill, and the tongue extending a great way out of its mouth, yet not thicker than a knitting needle. This instrument these birds thrust into the flowers and extracts the sweets. **1834** [see BOKMAKIERIE]. **1905** W.L. SCLATER in Flint & Gilchrist *Science in S. Afr.* 139 The longtailed Sugar birds (*Promerops*), two species of which are generally recognised, form a distinct family, the range of which is confined to South Africa. *c*1911 S. PLAYNE *Cape Col.* 549 A bird which is peculiar to South Africa is the Longtailed Sugar Bird, two distinct species of which have been recognised ... The Cape Longtailed Sugar Bird (*Promerops cafer*) is very common about the slopes of Table Mountain. **1923** HAAGNER & IVY *Sketches* 18 The Sugar-Birds, called Zuiker-vogels by the Boers — a name shared by the Sunbirds — are also real friends of the farmer, for although subsisting largely on nectar sucked from the flowers of protea bushes and other blooms, they feed extensively on various insects. **1936** E.L. GILL *First Guide to S. Afr. Birds* 37 The Natal Sugarbird, *Promerops gurneyi* .. has a shorter tail than the Cape species and is much redder on the crown, throat and breast. **1965** H. STOKES *What Bird Is That?* 63 Sugarbird (Long-Tailed) ... This decorative bird is peculiar to South Africa. Wherever there are Protea bushes, you are likely to see this distinctive bird. **1968** G. CROUDACE *Silver Grass* 64 Sugar birds broke their dancing flight above the proteas only to plunge their beaks into the sweet heart of the blooms. **1976** W. HÉFER in *Optima* Vol.26 No.2, 46 The home of .. the Cape francolin; .. the long-tailed sugar bird; and the malachite sunbird. **1983** K.B. NEWMAN *Newman's Birds* 388 Gurney's Sugarbird *Promerops gurneyi* ... Occurs on eastern mountain slopes where proteas or aloes are flowering ... Cape Sugarbird ... The song is a series of jumbled metallic, grating churring notes. **1986** *Weekend Argus* 9 Aug. (Suppl.) 4 Brightly coloured sunbirds (orange-breasted, malachite and lesser double-collared) and the Cape sugarbird are common. **1992** D.M. RICHARDSON in *Afr. Wildlife* Vol.46 No.2, 210 Starlings feed enthusiastically on the nectar of the shrub *Protea repens*, much to the annoyance of the native Cape sugarbirds.

2. *obs.* Any of several species of sunbird: HONEY-SUCKER sense 2. Also *attrib.*

See note at SUNBIRD.

1810 G. BARRINGTON *Acct of Voy.* 298 The little sugar bird is another wonder of nature .. with a long sickle-shaped bill. **1822** [see SUIKERBOS]. **1822** W.J. BURCHELL *Trav.* I. 245 A beautiful green Sugar-bird frequented the thorn-trees, and in splendid plumage surpassed all the other birds of the place. **1827** T. PHILIPPS *Scenes & Occurrences* 69 The sugar bird, of a dark green, hangs pendant by its legs, and never leaves the tree until the flowers fade. **1828** T. PRINGLE *Ephemerides* 104 Gorgeous erythrina shakes Its coral tufts above the brakes, Brilliant as the glancing plumes Of sugar-birds, among its blooms. **1850** J.E. METHLEY *New Col. of Port Natal* 30 A brilliant-hued family of sugar birds, (nectarinae) which flutter like insects round the blossoms and flowers. **1856** R.E.E. WILMOT *Diary* (1984) 131 The gay sugar birds in their coats of burnished green. **1861** LADY DUFF-GORDON *Lett. from Cape* (1925) 66 The sugar-birds .. are the humming birds of Africa. **1878** T.J. LUCAS *Camp Life & Sport* 83 Several varieties of sugar bird, a species allied to the humming birds or 'hovers' .. were constantly to be seen flying restlessly over the aloe blossom. **1897** H.A. BRYDEN *Nature & Sport* 59 The sunbirds, or sugar-birds as the Cape colonists call them, .. are .. famous for their brilliant colouring and the gorgeous metallic sheen of their plumage. **1906** B. STONEMAN *Plants & their Ways* 136 There flashed quite close to me one of those animated streaks of God's brightest colours that we call sugar-birds. **1923** [see SUIKERBEKJE].

sugarbush *n.* Formerly also **sugar-bosch**. [tr. S. Afr. Du. *zuiker bosch*, fr. Du. *zuiker* sugar + *bosch* bush (see quot. 1823).] **a.** The flowering shrub *Protea repens* of the Proteaceae; TULP-BOOM. **b.** Any protea. In both senses also called SUGAR TREE, SUIKERBOS. Also *attrib.* See also PROTEA sense 1 a.

1821 C.I. LATROBE *Jrnl of Visit* 367 Wageboom is frequent, and in other places, the sugar-bush, being now in full flower, adorned the slopes of the hills, with great splendor. *a*1823 J. EWART *Jrnl* (1970) 14 The Protea of Linn[aeus], called by the colonists the sugar bush, from the quantity of sweet juices the large and beautiful flowers contain, which they often extract and use as a substitute for that article. **1838** J.E. ALEXANDER *Exped. into Int.* I. 25 Here there were broad green leaves encircling the purple flowers of the protea mellifera, or sugar-bush of the Cape. **1856** R.E.E. WILMOT *Diary* (1984) 114 The sugar bush (P. mellifera) was in profusion of flower. **1857** 'J.S.H.' in *Cape Monthly Mag.* I. May 268 The native plant which has grown most luxuriantly of all in the sands, is the sugar-bush — Protea myrtales ... Sugar bushes, and Port Jackson willow, .. thrive well. **1862** 'A LADY' *Life at Cape* (1963) 89 When we left the dear old soul .. promised to send me some sugar-bush syrup as a cure for cough and relaxed throat for my little girls. *a*1875 T. BAINES *Jrnl of Res.* (1964) II. 257 On the height we had now attained, the sugar-bush, or protea, .. was expanding its crimson cones into lighter but still beautifully coloured flowers. **1893** J.G. WOOD *Through Matabeleland* 41 The protea (sugar bush) and the wild citron grow here. **1897** [see WAGONBOOM]. **1900** E.E.K. LOWNDES *Every-Day Life* 34 Dotted with bushes of varying colour and appearance, .. the sugar bush, or protea, being conspicuous. **1906** B. STONEMAN *Plants & their Ways* 209 The involucres of *P. mellifera* (the Sugar Bush) are often half filled with honey in the early spring. **1917** R. MARLOTH *Common Names* 78 *Sugar bush*, The most frequent species of *Protea* employed for the manufacture of a syrup (bossies stroop) is *P. mellifera*. **1926** P.W. LAIDLER *Tavern of Ocean* 94 The beautiful silver-tree was used for fuel, and sugar-bush was planted to replace it. **1931** F.C. SLATER *Secret Veld* 146 Surrounded by rugged hills mottled with light grey rocks and dotted with glossy-leaved sugar-bush. **1965** S. ELIOVSON *S. Afr. Wild Flowers for Garden* 265 *P. mellifera* ... True Sugarbush .. This is the *Sugar-bush* that was used by the first Cape colonists who collected the nectar. **1970** M. MULLER *Cloud across Moon* 239 The masses of white and pink sugar bushes were covered with newly opened sticky, stiff flowers. **1976** W. HÉFER in *Optima* Vol.26 No.2, 46 Proteas dominate the indigenous growth on the mountain slope and include the creamy-white and the rarer coloured sugar bush, and, in one area, the beautiful blushing bride. **1984** *S. Afr. Panorama* July 48 Members of the well-known family Proteaceae (popularly known as sugar bushes). **1986** *Conserva* Oct. 24 *Protea caffra* Common sugarbush ... *Protea repens* True Sugarbush. **1987** T.F.J. VAN RENSBURG *Intro. to Fynbos* 10 The flower-bud of a blue sugar-bush (*Protea neriifolia*). *Ibid.* 16 There is .. a large variety of sugarbushes (*Protea* spp.). **1993** *Grocott's Mail* 6 Aug. 10 Protea obtusifolia, Bredasdorp Sugarbush. Protea Repens, Sugarbush.

sugarmummy *n. slang.* [Formed by analogy with U.S. Eng. *sugar daddy*.] In urban (usu. township) Eng.: a wealthy middle-aged (white) woman who spends money freely on a younger man in return for his companionship or intimacy.

1986 W. SCHÄRF et al. in Burman & Reynolds *Growing Up* 279 In June 1984 .. there was a lot more talk among the boys about 'bunnies' (white men) and 'sugarmummies' (white women) than occurred a year later. This is partially attributable to the international AIDS scare. **1992** M. MTHETHWA in *Pace* Sept. 74 Joe's taste in women varies — from sugar mummies (elderly women who keep toyboys for sexual pleasure and shower them with money and expensive gifts in return) to '16 Valves' — sexy schoolgirls. **1993** J. LENAKE *Informant, Pretoria* 'Sugarmummy' is used because many men die early and women have relationships with younger men.

sugar tree *n. phr. Obs.* SUGARBUSH.

1797 LADY A. BARNARD *S. Afr. Century Ago* (1910) 67 We had first to scramble up the side of a pretty perpendicular cascade .. the sides of which were shaded with myrtles, sugar trees, and geraniums. **1797** *Ibid.* [see BOSSIESTROOP]. **1797** — in Lord Lindsay *Lives of Lindsays* (1849) III. 384 The silver-tree .. and the sugar-tree, which was covered in beautiful pink flowers with black seeds — when the flowers are boiled they produce a syrup as rich as honey. **1801** J. BARROW *Trav.* I. 61 Of these, .. the mellifera, called here sugar-tree, from the great quantity of saccharine juice contained in the bottom of its vase-shaped flowers. **1874** 'P.' in A.M.L. Robinson *Sel. Articles from Cape Monthly Mag.* (1978) 179 The sweet-scented mimosa bush .. gave place to the 'sugar tree' (protea), a small shrub-like tree, devoid of much foliage, and useful only as fuel.

sugga var. SUKA.

suikerbekje *n. obs.* [S. Afr. Du., fr. Du. *suiker* sugar + *bekje* little mouth.] Any of several species of sunbird: HONEY-SUCKER sense 2.

1810 G. BARRINGTON *Acct of Voy.* 302 The honey bird, unknown in Europe .. the inngwinngwe, (by the Colonists called suikerbekje). **1913** J.J. DOKE *Secret City* 14 Little birds, particularly green-clad suikerbekjes, flitted in the sunshine. [**1923** HAAGNER & IVY *Sketches* 124 The next group of Architects is the Sunbirds (family *Nectarinidæ*), sometimes called Sugar-birds, and Zuikerbekjes (Sugar-mouths) by the Boers.]

suikerbos /ˈsœɪkə(r)bɔs, ˈseɪkəbɔs/ *n.* Formerly also **suikerbosch, suiker-bosje, zuiker-bosch, zuyker-bosch.** [Afk., earlier S. Afr. Du. *zuikerbosch*, fr. Du. *zuiker* sugar + *bos(ch)* bush.] SUGARBUSH. Also *attrib.*, and **suikerbossie** [see -IE].

[**1795** see TULP-BOOM.] **1821** C.I. LATROBE *Jrnl of Visit* Glossary, Zuyker-bosch — *Protea mellifera*. **1822** W.J. BURCHELL *Trav.* I. 18 The delicate Humming-birds .. are .. called by the Dutch colonists *Suiker-vogels* (sugar birds), from having been observed .. to feed principally on the honey of the flowers of the *Suiker-bosch* (sugar-bush). **1852** C. BARTER *Dorp & Veld* 74 We came upon knolls covered with the evergreen Suiker bos a graceful shrub. **1887** A.A. ANDERSON *25 Yrs in Waggon* I. 210 The fine flat-topped Kameel doorn is very common, palms, baobab, .. zuiker-bosch, acacia. **1893** 'AFRICANUS' in *Cape Illust. Mag.* July 418 [The mountain protea] is of the same family as the suiker-bosje, but does not seem to have the sweet juice. **1937** S. CLOETE *Turning Wheels* 104 As he rode past a clump of soikerbos [*sic*] a duiker sprang out, and .. made for a clump of heavy thorn scrub fifty yards away. **1952** *Cape Times* 4 Sept. 5 The five dozen selected proteas include .. two varieties of the furry suikerbos type. **1961** *Red Wing* (St Andrew's College, Grahamstown) 5 About the only plants that flourished here were the suikerbos, handsome and great in their surroundings. **1971** *Argus* 10 July 5 Now is the time to see all those lovely Proteas and suikerbossies in full bloom. **1974** A.P. CARTWRIGHT *By Waters of Letaba* 14 Where the suikerbos grew there was no malaria, they said, but below this level, where it was too warm for proteas to flourish .. , there lay the danger. **1977** *Fair Lady* 12 Oct. 14 The protea has about 130 species. These include what is known as the 'King Protea' (*P cynaroides*), South Africa's national flower, and the ubiquitous *suikerbossie* (*P repens*). **1980** *Afr. Wildlife* Vol.34 No.4, 30 Bossiestroop from the suikerbos (*P. repens*) was a cough mixture found in all self-respecting medicine chests about 100 years ago.

suip /sœɪp, seɪp/ *v. intrans. Slang.* [Afk., to drink (used of an animal; not polite when used of a person).] To drink (immoderately), to 'swill'. See also GESUIP.

1972 *Argus* 9 Dec. 17 'This is the land of rape and suip,' he says. 'Murder's the national sport around here.' **1989** M. BRAND in *Fair Lady* 25 Oct. 92 Suip — drink.

Hence **suiper** *n.*, a heavy drinker, a drunkard.

1984 *E. Prov. Herald* 12 Mar. 5 Our macho brothers across the sea in Australia .. have as much of a palate for the hops and malt as the most hardened South African 'suiper'.

suitjes var. SOETJES.

suka /ˈsʊga, ˈsʊka, ˈsuːkə/ *v. intrans.* Also **soega, soeka, sugga.** [In the Nguni languages, 'get up', 'go away'.] Used in the imperative, mainly among speakers of the Nguni languages:
a. As an insulting dismissal: 'get away', 'scram'. Hence (occas.) **suka** *n.*, an utterance of this word. Cf. HAMBA sense 1.

1833 *Graham's Town Jrnl* 16 May 2 He called out to the Caffer *suka*, an expression of great contempt, as if driving away a dog; the man not moving, he repeated his '*suka*'. **1949** C. BULLOCK *Rina* 219 'Suka!' I shouted, .. as I stepped threateningly towards him with my rifle half raised to my shoulder. *c*1955 M. HUME *Sawdust Heaven* 64 Waving her arms at Sidawana, she directed him to leave. 'Suka!' she cried shrilly. 'Go away!' **1970** *Informant, Grahamstown* Suka. Same as 'voetsak'. **1970** H. KUPER *Witch in my Heart* 21 Ai suka! Be off! **1979** *E. Prov. Herald* 9 Aug. 9 The Xhosas repeatedly shouted: *Gha suka! Gha suka!* The troops .. supposed the blacks were shouting the name of the river. Actually, of course, what they were really shouting was 'Buzz off', or 'Voetsek'. **1994** on M-Net TV 6 Oct. (The Schoolmaster), Suka! Leave.

b. As an interjection: An expression of surprise, disbelief, reproof, or disgust: 'get away', 'I don't believe you', 'go on'.

1979 F. DIKE *First S. African* 7 Hayi suka, I'm asking you, what's wrong with that? **1979** M. MATSHOBA *Call Me Not a Man* 154 'Suka, woman!' returned one who seemed to care little about woman's views. 'You would never be able to start and support families without *amadoda*. What makes you think that you're the more responsible parties?' **1980** C. NKOSI in M. Mutloatse *Forced Landing* 16 Nkambule regained his feet and ran ... But *suka*, the man behind him was closing in again fast. **1982** *Voice* 10 Jan. 13 'We'll see about that.' 'Awu suka! You're being jealous.' **1983** *Drum* Dec. 62 The girls in the salon shouted, 'Hayi, soega! Go away. You cannot tell us that story. Not you, Louisa.' **1985** P. SLABOLEPSZY *Sat. Night at Palace* 74 Forsie: You stabbed him. It *was* you, man. Jesus —. September: Hai sugga! **1989** J. HOBBS *Thoughts in Makeshift Mortuary* 328 We tried reason, and where did it get us? .. Our leaders in jail, our people divided ... Reason, suka! **1990** 'P.W.' in *Weekly Mail Review of Bks* Apr.-May, As a young man, one of his first plans against apartheid was .. to spray paint a huge slogan reading 'I'm black and I'm proud' ... His maid .. contemptuously shakes her head and says 'Ah, Suka' (get lost). **1991** [see HAAI]. **1993** [see TOYI-TOYI *v.* sense 2].

sukkel /ˈsək(ə)l/ *v. intrans.* [Afk., to struggle, to live poorly.]
1. *colloq.* To struggle, to have difficulty (with someone or something).

1912 F. BANCROFT *Veldt Dwellers* 201 Toch! .. I can tell you girls it's we poor women who've got to sit at home and *sukkel* for men's pleasure. **1963** M.E. MCCOY *Informant, Port Elizabeth* We have been sukkeling with your tape. We all freeze up the sec the thing is switched on. **1969** A. FUGARD *Boesman & Lena* 6 Sukkel along! The dogs want to bite but you can't look down. **1970** E. MUNDELL *Informant, Pearston (E. Cape)*, I haven't sukkeled with any dress like I have with this one (had difficulties). **1970** F. PHILIP *Informant, Johannesburg*, I suppose we've all had to sukkel sometime in life, I know I have. **1973** D.A.C. MACLENNAN in *Bolt* No.7, 8 Every night you lie there and sukkel with things you'd like to forget. **1976** 'BLOSSOM' in *Darling* 4 Feb. 87 After sukkeling with that lot I am only pooped hey so I will tune you chow for now, fans. **1978** T. COUZENS in *Speak* July-Aug. 13, I have sukkeled around to try to work out what is meant by 'popular culture'. It seems to be generally what is regarded as 'low' culture as distinct from 'high' culture. **1979** F. DIKE *First S. African* 4 Maybe he thinks I'm going to sukkel to sell this jacket. But he forgets, this location is full of moegoes. **1980** R. BONNKE in *New Vision* Vol.5 No.4, 8 It [*sc.* evangelism without the Holy Spirit] is like a body without the heart, and it is like a car without the engine. You sukkel and sukkel and sukkel ... and nothing happens! **1984** *Frontline* May 40 Koos, you know how when English-speaking ous are sukkeling to speak in Afrikaans, .. they .. sommer pronounce it an Afrikaans-sounding way and hope for the best. **1991** *Natal Mercury* 1 Apr. 1 Although you sukkel for about a whole hour to find parking it's worth the trouble. **1994** *Informant, Grahamstown* A lot of their lines are out of order. You sukkel like anything — you get through or you don't.

2. *slang.* To look for trouble, to create trouble, to annoy (someone) on purpose.

1970 K. NICOL *Informant, Durban* If you're going to sukkel here, you'll get hurt. (Look for trouble, look for a fight). **1972** BEETON & DORNER in *Eng. Usage in Sn Afr.* Vol.3 No.1, 26 *Sukkel*, .. 'annoy, interfere with', eg 'Don't *sukkel* with me'. **1985** *Frontline* Dec. 23 But from behind .. his crossed arms he gives me a moenie sukkel look when I ask for the names of CP supporters who went back to the National Party. **1986** B. SIMON in S. Gray *Market Plays* 113, I pay twenty-five rand for this flat .. so don't go sukkeling around the caretaker like that. You don't sukkel with anybody like that.

So (sense 2) **sukkelaar** /-ɑː(r)/ *n.* [Afk.], a trouble-maker.

1911 *E. Prov. Herald* 27 Oct., Those arguing against the Act were 'sukkelars', and formed a 'remschoen'. He [*sc.* General Botha] asked them to co-operate in making the Act a success.

Sullivan *n.* [Named for *Leon H. Sullivan* (b. 1923), U.S. businessman and Baptist minister, who proposed the code in 1977.] *Attrib.*, usu. in the phr. ***Sullivan principles***, designating a code of practice relating to the employment of staff by U.S. companies operating in South Africa,

sunbird *n. obs.* [Transf. use of general Eng. *sunbird*, a name for any bird of the Nectariniidae family.] SUGARBIRD sense 1.

As in general Eng., the name 'sunbird' is widely used in *S. Afr. Eng.* of any of several small birds of the Nectariniidae (see HONEY-SUCKER sense 2).

1866 J. LEYLAND *Adventures* 3, I also succeeded in killing a few common Sun-birds (Promerops Caffir) violet-headed Sun-birds, (Nectarinia Violacea,) Green Sugar-birds, (Nectarinia Fermosa,) also a few thrushes, yellow and black.

Sun City *n. phr. Prison slang.* [A joking transf. use of the proprietary name of a luxury hotel complex situated near the town of Rustenburg (North-West Province).] A nickname for Diepkloof prison (Gauteng Province). Cf. BLUE SKY, OUBAAS sense 5.

1987 S.A. BOTHA in *Frontline* Oct.-Nov. 9 Don't you worry, my broer, this isn't boep. Wait until you get to Central. Oh yes, my broer then you'll check what's potting. You'll beg them to come back here to Sun City. **1990** *City Press* 4 Feb. 6, I am sorry to tell you that the last time I saw Bessie she was once more on the move — this time in a kwela-kwela destined for an enforced holiday at 'Sun City' ... The official handle for her new premises is Johannesburg Jail — the tronk on Soweto's doorstep. **1990** *New Nation* 16 Mar. 1 More than 250 warders and staff refused to continue performing their duties at the Bloemfontein Prison yesterday in protest against similar grievances that sparked off the 'Sun City' sit-in. **1993** *Sunday Times* 4 Apr. 1 The ease with which the 16 prisoners escaped from Diepkloof Prison has left many questions unanswered ... Prison officials say they cannot recall a similar escape. Only one prisoner got out of 'Sun City' last year.

Sunday house *n. phr.* [tr. S. Afr. Du. *Zodaghuis*.] A house in town which is used by a country family during their visits to attend church; CHURCH HOUSE; *kerkhuis*, see KERK sense 2; *nagmaalhuis*, see NAGMAAL sense 3; TUISHUIS; ZONDAGSHUIS.

[**1851** R. GRAY *Jrnl of Bishop's Visitation* 11 Many of the Dutch farmers have built small houses for themselves, which they occupy during the 'nacht maal' (communion), and occasionally when they come in on a Sunday.] **1876** *Cape Argus* 19 Oct. 3 Large family residences, which are known in this place as 'Sunday houses', being used only on Sundays by families who come in from country farms to the Sunday services. **1929** W.M. MACMILLAN *Bantu, Boer & Briton* 300 (Swart), On this assumption, the Volksraad had promised burghers an erf for a 'Sunday house', to be used on visits to markets and Nachtmaal. **1967** [see ZONDAGSHUIS]. **1967** C. DE VILLIERS in M. Booysen *More Tales from S. Afr.* 243 The Sunday houses are gradually being abandoned — the ease of the motor-car making the long outspan for the horse-drawn Cape Cart no longer a necessity. **1975** *S. Afr. Panorama* Sept. 37 A few private houses with their verandahs bordering the street. In the old days, they were 'little Sunday houses' where the farmers stayed when they came into town for 'Nagmaal' (communion services).

sundowner *n.* [A colonial usage, perh. originating in West Africa (see quot. 1909).]
1. A drink taken in the early evening; a pre-dinner cocktail. Also *attrib.*

[**1909** *Daily Chron.* (U.K.) 20 Oct. 6 The 'sundowner' refreshment of the West African late afternoon.] **1922** *Chambers's Jrnl* (U.K.) 359 As a rule he did not even take the almost universal 'sundowner' for he felt that he could not afford to spend his very meagre profits on luxuries. **1937** G.F. GIBSON *Story of Imp. Light Horse* 215 The A.D.C., with a touch of military genius, said .. : 'I think, Sir, it is about time for a "sundowner!"' The General judicially agreed. The A.D.C. then produced a flask from his saddle wallet, which he offered to the General. **1947** C.R. PRANCE *Antic Mem.* 81 Over sundowners, it was arranged that after an early breakfast Chips should meet the Vet. at Oom Philip's stable. **1953** D. JACOBSON *Long Way from London* 33 When Bridget came home from work, there was a sundowner; sherry for the women, whisky and soda for the father. **1959** L. LONGMORE *Dispossessed* 223 Africans have observed the function of European liquor in the life of the average white man. They see him enjoy a 'sundowner' with a few friends; they see them go into bars together. **1961** T. MATSHIKIZA *Choc. for my Wife* 32 When you're big, and you've done your work, then pour yourself a sundowner. But never a sun-drowner, my lad. **1968** L.G. GREEN *Full Many Glorious Morning* 165 This sundowner habit of ours goes back to the early days ... All the Pioneers believed that whisky kept the fever away and we observe the legend. **1973** *Drum* 8 Oct. 19 After a hard day's work friends who stay in different townships .. would like to have a little chat over a sundowner before going their ways. Just how petty it is that they are not allowed to do this! **1985** *S. Afr. Panorama* Jan. 47 As dusk falls, the ranger .. invites guests to stretch their legs and enjoy a sundowner and *sosaties* (kebabs).

2. *obsolescent.* An evening cocktail party. Also *attrib.*

1944 'TWEDE IN BEVEL' *Piet Kolonel* 105 It will always be memorable that Mr. and Mrs. Ferdie Ballot threw open the doors of their house and cellar to all the officers of the Battalion on the occasion of a sundowner. **1956** H. VAN RENSBURG *Their Paths Crossed Mine* 154, I called the Brigade Staff together (including members who had not been on the invitation list to the possible sun-downer of the evening before) and said that I felt we should understand each other. **1962** *Pretoria News* 9 Nov. 9 The war raged on, much to the delight of our sundowner guests. **1972** *Caravan* May 61 Ras .. celebrated his birthday and invited all to a sundowner. **1973** *Cape Argus* 24 Feb. (Mag. Sect.) 2 Bearing in mind some rather tart remarks made at last night's sundowner party, he made the forthright statement: 'Mrs Smith very bad.'

Sunqua var. SONQUA.

sun-under *n. ?obs.* [Calque formed on Afk. *sononder*, shortened form of *sonsondergang*, fr. Du. *zonsondergang*.] Sunset.

[**1850** R.G.G. CUMMING *Hunter's Life* II. 204 (Jeffreys), I had got into a .. custom of allowing the cattle to feed about the waggons long after the sun was under.] **1891** E. GLANVILLE *Fossicker* 94, I would .. creep on after him from sun up to sun under. **1913** C. PETTMAN *Africanderisms* 486 Sun under, The moment of sun-set. **1915** J.K. O'CONNOR *Afrikander Rebellion* 103 They may be found on the river diggings, starving, working from sun-up to sun-under, searching for the stones.

supje, sup(p)e, suppee, suppie, suppy varr. SOPIE.

suring /'syrən/ *n.* Also **surings** (retaining singular force), and **zuring**. [Afk., ad. Du. *zuring* sorrel.] Any of several species of plant with an acidulous sap, esp. species of *Oxalis* (sorrel) and *Rumex* (dock).

1870 H.H. DUGMORE *Reminisc. of Albany Settler* (1958) 27 The young bucks had to dress in sheepskin. If .. they could afford to sport cuffs and facings of jackal's or tiger's fur, .. they might then calculate on making quite a sensation among the fair sex; especially if the *Zuring* had done its Saturday duty, and had given the proper bright yellow to the 'crackers'. **1900** F.R.M. CLEAVER in M.M. Cleaver *Young S. Afr.* (1913) 154 We hunted among the rocks for zuring (sorrel), which we chewed for the rest of the day. **1913** C. PETTMAN *Africanderisms* 575 *Zuring*, .. Various species of *Oxalideæ* are so termed by the Dutch; the leaves were used to clean and stain the 'Crackers' .. which the colonists of earlier days wore. **1917** R. MARLOTH *Common Names* 92 *Zuring*, A number of plants with acidulous sap, most of them either species of *Rumex* (dock) or of *Oxalis* (sorrel). **1947** T.M. SALTER in *Jrnl of Bot. Soc. of S. Afr.* XXXIII. 9 Out of over 200 species of South African *Oxalis* (Surings) 32 occur in the Cape Peninsula. **1972** A.A. TELFORD *Yesterday's Dress* 96 The settlers called their homemade sheepskin trousers, 'crackers' from the noise they produced with the slightest movement of the wearer. They stained them a bright yellow with the leaves of the 'zuring' (the sorrel plant). **1973** M.A. COOK *Cape Kitchen* 109 Herbs were either picked and used fresh (parsley, mint, sorrel or suring, and fennel), or else hung up in cotton bags. **1975** W. STEENKAMP *Land of Thirst King* 129 A variety of sorrel commonly known as 'surings' boiled in milk provided a favourite breakfast food. **1986** *Grocott's Mail* 1 July 6 *Oxalis* — an indigenous suring or sorrel — was also used to colour sheepskin clothing yellow. The British Settlers of 1820 adopted the practice happily. **1989** I. JONES *Woman's World Cookbk* 57 In Cape dishes sorrel ('suring') means the leaves of the yellow oxalis that blooms in autumn and winter. **1990** *Weekend Argus* 10 Feb. (Weekender) 4 Peach and plum trees scattered blossoms over the surings (sorrel) which we loved to gather and suck.

sus *n.*[1] var. SIS *n.*[1]

‖**Sus** /səs, sœs/ *n.*[2] [Afk., short form of *suster* (see SUSTER).] 'Sister', used as a title, with a first name. **1973** Y. BURGESS *Life to Live* 162 He shook hands with Nel formally, called her 'Sus Nel' in the old manner and asked how long she would be staying. **1979** A.P. BRINK *Dry White Season* 174 'They covered Gordon's name with dirt,' Emily persisted calmly, staring straight ahead, as if she hadn't heard what he'd said. 'Aren't you afraid, Sus Emily?' the old priest reproached her.

Susequa /suː'sɛkwə/ *pl. n. Obs. exc. hist.* Also **Sassiqua's**, **Soosequas**, **Sussaquas**, **Sussiqua's**. [Khoikhoi.] Collectively, the members of a Khoi group living on the western Cape coast during the 17th century. Also *attrib.*

As is the case with many names of peoples and groups in *S. Afr. Eng.*, this word has been found only in plural uses; however, it may be that it has also been used in unrecorded singular forms.

1731 G. MEDLEY tr. P. Kolb's *Present State of Cape of G.H.* I. 289 It is the Custom of the lesser *Namaquas*, with their Allies the *Sussaquas* and *Udiquas*, to continue fighting till News runs in the Armies that they have lost abundantly more Men than the Enemy. **1795** C.R. HOPSON tr. C.P. Thunberg's *Trav.* I. 306 In continuing my journey to the northward, and Saldanha Bay, I visited the Sussaquas Hottentots, some of whom were still remaining. **1862** *Abstracts in Cape Statutes* p.xviii, Mention of the Soosequas, Heesequas, Ubiquas, Griquas and Namaquas. **1972** [see ODIQUA].

‖**sussie** /'səsi, 'sœsi/ *n.* Also **sisi**, **sissie**. [Afk., *sus* short form of *suster* + dim. suffix -IE.] A little sister; also used as a form of address. Cf. SISI, SUSTER.

1867 E.L. PRICE *Jrnls* (1956) 253 'Tis the ruling principle of every action, I think — love for the 'vrow & kinderen' — 'the man & the kinderen' — 'the buttie & Sisi'. **1966** J. TAYLOR 'Mommy I'd Like to Be'. (lyrics) Daddy, stop the car, There's still another sixty miles of tar, And sussie and me can't last that far, Ag, please man, stop the car. *Ibid.* Sussie, I chaff I'll win, Win my bet to make you grin, With a blade of grass I'll tickle your chin. **1977** [see *Sunday Times* quot. at

OUMA sense 2]. **1978** L. BARNES in *The 1820* Vol.51 No.12, 19 A large number of Afrikaans words are in common use [in Natal English] — *broer, sussie, swaer, tannie* — although the latter usually refers to an older woman rather than an aunt. **1986** M. PICARDIE in *S. Gray Market Plays* 94, I was the youngest, you see. My boeties and sussies were all at school.

Sussiqua's var. SUSEQUA.

‖**suster** /'səstə(r), 'sœstər/ *n.* [Afk.] Sister; esp. among Afrikaans-speakers, an affectionate or respectful form of address or reference to a sister, or to any woman; also **sustertjie** /'səstərki, 'sœs-/ [see -IE]. Cf. OU SIS, SISI, SISTER, SUSSIE.

1944 'TWEDE IN BEVEL' *Piet Kolonel* 11 Fate doomed him to a biblical argument with the old lady, while they, or better still I, were conferring with 'Suster'. **1979** *Fair Lady* 9 May 120 My sustertjie, said Mosie, I don't like these riots either ... My sustertjie, I can't help it, there's something in my heart that says: At last. **1980** *Sunday Times* 14 Sept. 11 They are descendants of the black Voortrekkers. And even though they struggle to eke out an existence they are an independent, proud and happy people, at peace with their white neighbours. In the quaint manner of the old-timers they address each other as 'neef', 'niggie' or 'suster'.

Susuto var. SESOTHO.

Sut(h)o, Sut(h)u varr. SOTHO.

sutjes var. SOETJES.

suurdeeg /'sy:rdɪəx/ *n.* Formerly also *zuurdeeg*. [Afk.] Yeast or leaven, made in various ways; bread made with this leaven. Usu. with distinguishing epithet: **soet suurdeeg**, formerly also *zoet zuurdeeg*, /'sut -/ [Afk., *soet* (earlier S. Afr. Du. *zoet*) sweet], home-made salt rising leaven (see quot. 1941); also *attrib.*; **suur suurdeeg** /'sy:r -/, formerly also *zuur zuurdeeg* [Afk., *suur* (earlier S. Afr. Du. *zuur*) sour], sour dough leavening made with a piece of dough from the last baking (see quot. 1923).

1923 S. VAN H. TULLEKEN *Prac. Cookery Bk* 4 (Swart), Sour Dough Yeast (Zuur Zuurdeeg). Take an earthenware saucepan; pour in 3 cups of boiling water; add 1¾ tablespoons of salt; sprinkle unsifted boermeal over to thickness of about an inch ..; cover with a tight-fitting lid and leave in a warm place to rise overnight ... Keep a small piece of dough of the last baking. **1934** *Star* 9 Apr., (Swart), It all depends whether you want a very light rusk made from compressed yeast, or a more substantial one made from Soet Suurdeeg. **1941** FOUCHÉ & CURREY *Hsecraft for Primary Schools* 33 Soet Suurdeeg (Salt Rising Yeast). Put 1 tablespoon salt into a warm basin, add 1 cup cold water and 2 cups boiling water. Stir in enough boer meal to make a batter and sprinkle meal over the top. Cover well and leave in a warm place overnight. Bread with soet zuurdeeg is kneaded with the yeast, shaped and allowed to rise only once. **1950** H. GERBER *Cape Cookery* 47 Suurdeeg (Yeast). Take 1½ large breakfast cups of boiling water and a breakfast cup of cold water, a little salt and enough flour to make a thick paste ... Cover the dish with a warm cloth .. by the side of a fire until it sours ... Both Vetkoek and Roosterkoek were made either with unleavened dough or with a dough leavened with suurdeeg. **1951** S. VAN H. TULLEKEN *Prac. Cookery Bk* 12 Make yeast in the morning, using 2 yeast cakes, .. or 'zoet zuurdeeg'. **1955** V.M. FITZROY *Dark Bright Land* 315 The bread was *suurdeeg*, the heavy coarse loaf of the backveld farmhouse, made with fermented meal and to those who have not been brought up on it, an acquired taste. **1971** L.G. GREEN *Taste of S.-Easter* 90, I do not know whether the soetsuurdeeg recipe for brown bread has been used at Buckingham Palace yet. **1971** C. SMUTS *Informant, Grahamstown* Suurdeeg, the old-fashioned yeast they use on the farms still. **1978** *Sunday Times* 5 Mar. (Mag. Sect.) 3 The woman had made roosterkoek and soetsuurdeeg bread. **1978** *Ibid.* 7 May 12 There's a whole story to breadmaking with hops or soet suurdeeg, and I love it. In the country, housewives take it for granted that you make your own bread ... There is another dough called Suur Suurdeeg — Sour Dough Ferment — and this to my mind is even more delicious, rather reminiscent of rye bread, which is slightly sour. **1980** *Ibid.* 9 Mar. (Mag. Sect.) 5 She .. taught him to bake bread — he's still a dab hand at kneading soetsuurdeeg-brood. **1980** *Argus* 28 Aug. 12 In the old days the bread would have been made, with 'soet suurdeeg', a yeast started by fermenting raisins then adding a little flour, sugar and salt to luke-warm water and leaving it until the raisins floated to the surface and the mixture bubbled. **1988** ADAMS & SUTTNER *William Str.* 28 The men who did the baking .. were good men ... We went to buy the suurdeeg from them — they kept this yeast in a big tin, it was always bubbling, and they ladled it in a mug for us, a penny a mug.

suurkaree see KAREE *n.*² sense 2.

suurpootjie /'sy:rpuɪki/ *n.* [Afk., *suur* sour + *poot* foot + -IE.] The GEOMETRIC TORTOISE, *Psammobates geometricus*. Also *attrib.*

1977 *Cape Times* 17 Jan. 8 The rarest tortoise in mainland Africa is the geometric tortoise of the south-west Cape ... The *suurpootjie*, as it is more commonly called, is about 150 mm long, and each scale is marked with yellow stripes on a black background. **1978** Dept of Nature & Environmental Conservation: *Director's Report No. 34* 38 Eensaamheid Tortoise Reserve. This reserve was established to protect the suurpootjie (geometric) tortoise's habitat against further inroads by agricultural operations. **1985** *S. Afr. Panorama* Mar. 48 The geometric tortoise, *Psammobates geometricus*, often referred to as the *suurpootjie*, *kransie* or *sterretjie-skilpad* by local farmers, has the smallest distribution range of all the species confined to the restricted winter rainfall region of the south-western Cape Province.

suur suurdeeg see SUURDEEG.

suurveld(t) var. ZUURVELD.

suurvy /'sy:rfeɪ/ *n.* Formerly also *zuurvijg* (pl. *suurvijgen*). [Afk. (earlier S. Afr. Du. *zuurvijg*), *suur* sour + *vy* fig.] SOUR FIG. Also (occas.) **suurvygie** /-feɪxi/ [see -IE].

1890 [see SOUR FIG]. **1966** C.A. SMITH *Common Names* 448 Suurvy, *Carpobrotus acinaciformis* ... When the rind of the fruit hardens, the fruits are picked and sold, or the fruits are gathered just before the rind hardens and the rind removed and the contents boiled into a jam. **1980** *Sunday Times* 5 Oct., The .. sour fig, .. suurvy, as we call it, is not listed in 'A Geographical Atlas of World Weeds' nor is it on the list of South African weeds ... Both the fruit and leaf of this plant have been widely used medicinally. **1981** *S. Afr. Panorama* 5 Oct. 14 To the *vygie* family belong the *donkiebos*, *sandlaai*, *suurvygie* and *varkiesknol*, the latter a delicacy for porcupines that uproot the juicy bulb. **1985** *Fair Lady* 3 Apr. 137 The .. flashy dayglo hues of the mesems — bokbaais, lampranthus, suurvy and drosanthus — look their best against a clear background and an open sky.

swaer /swa:(r)/ *n.* Also **swaar**, and (formerly) **zwaarger**. [Afk., fr. Du. *zwager* brother-in-law.]
a. Brother-in-law; used as a term of address, and as a title, with a name. Cf. SBALI sense a.

1844 C. DENNISON in R. Edgecombe, *Letters of Hannah Dennison*. (1968) 200 [Written to his brother-in-law] Good Morning Old Swaar .. I hope you are all quite well. **1886** G.A. FARINI *Through Kalahari Desert* 317, I went with Jan and his *swaar* (brother-in-law) to the top of the hill. **1896** M.A. CAREY-HOBSON *At Home in Tvl* 317, I felt as if I couldn't stay fightin' against my own people like that, and so I told Zwaarger Piet, I'd come home and mind the farm, but fight I wouldn't. **1973** *E. Prov. Herald* 20 Dec. 20 David, dearly loved son and *swaer* — so brave and courageous, missed and deeply mourned.

b. *colloq.* Often in the phr. **ou swaer** /əʊ -/ [Afk. *ou* old]. A form of address between men, equivalent to 'old chap'. Cf. SBALI sense c.

1970 A.H. NEWEY *Informant, Stutterheim* Good morning, ou swaer. (Literally, brother-in-law. Greeting between men, originating in Queenstown district.) **1972** BEETON & DORNER in *Eng. Usage in Sn Afr.* Vol.3 No.1, *Swaer*, .. Afk equiv[alent] of 'brother-in-law'; 'ou swaer' is used coll[oquially] in the sense of 'old chap', eg 'Good morning, *ou swaer*, how are you today?' **1977** N. OKES in *Quarry* '77 141 'Ou swaer' he said .. 'They tell me you are now a famous man ... Nou kom, ou swaer, there's a vatjie in the lorry. It's high time for a drink.' **1978** [see SUSSIE]. **1988** M. MZAMANE in *Staffrider* Vol.6 No.3, 35 Please, Sabelo, my *swaer*, what shall we say when we get home? **1990** S. JACOBS in *Ibid.* Vol.9 No.2, 25 So tell me, ou swaer, what's missing? **1992** *Grocott's Mail* 8 Sept. 4 A Lower Albany farmer's description of driving the latest model of luxury car: 'Quiet, you say? Look 'ere, swaer, this car's as quiet as a mouse wearing tackies!' **1994** on Radio Algoa 27 July, (advt) 'How was that? 'No, fine, swaer, I think you looked great.'

Swakara /swəˈkɑ:rə/ *n.* [Acronym formed on *South West Africa(n) Karakul*.] A proprietory name for Persian lamb skins ('karakul') produced for the fur trade in Namibia (formerly South West Africa). Also *attrib.*

1966 *Fur Rev.* May 13 Selective breeding has improved the .. qualities of S.W.A. Persian Lambskins and brought about a changeover .. to a flat glossy pelt. In order to spread .. the extended range of S.W. African merchandise, a publicity agent has [come] up with the clever catchword '*Swakara*'. **1970** *News/Check* 15 May 25 So 1970 will see a great deal of karakul, or swakara as the South West African product is more often called. But mink is still the best seller. **1971** *Daily Dispatch* 7 Apr., The soft design of this midnight blue Swakara coat is enhanced with a wide border of snow white mink. **1971** *Rand Daily Mail* 13 May 7 A sure winner for the Durban July — complete Swakara ensemble consisting of Hot Pants, battledress top, midi gilet and wide-brimmed hat. **1973** *Evening Post* 16 July 8 Karakul, now internationally designated as Swakara, has turned South West Africa into a viable economic entity and many farmers into wealthy men. **1977** *S. Afr. Panorama* Oct. 10 Swakara, diamonds and venison all have one thing in common — they are part of South Africa's traditional way of life and have grown into world-wide industries. **1981** *Ibid.* Dec. 6 Karakul sheep whose Persian lamb skins are known commercially as *Swakara*. More than R12-million worth of karakul skins are traded annually on the London pelts market.

Swans *n.* Also SWANS. Acronym formed on *South African Women's Auxiliary Naval Service*, denoting this unit, or its members collectively; without the -s, a member of this unit. Also *attrib.*

1973 A.M. McGREGOR in *Std Encycl. of Sn Afr.* VIII. 116 The Swans .. enabled many young men who had been on shore jobs to be drafted to sea. **1974** *E. Prov. Herald* 23 May, For the girls, naval cadets from the new training base in Simonstown, this is their first official sea-going voyage as ratings .. or Swans to put it more correctly. **1976** *Suidwestelike Herald* 24 Dec. 5 Desiree left the navy .. where she was an Able Swan in the Telecommunication Department at Fish Hoek. **1979** MARTIN & ORPEN *S. Afr. at War* 287 On 9 October 1943 the SWANS was established with a total establishment of 281 ... There was only one SWAN officer allowed.

swart aasvoel see AASVOEL sense b.

swartganna see GANNA sense 2.

swart gevaar /ˌswart xəˈfa:(r), ˌswa:t -/ *n. phr.* [Afk., *swart* black + *gevaar* danger, peril.]

In both senses also called BLACK PERIL (sense 2). See also GEVAAR.

1. A perceived threat posed by black people to whites; black people collectively; *black danger*, see BLACK *adj.* sense 1 d; ?*nonce*, a black person. Also *attrib.*

1939 R.S.A. HOERNLÉ *S. Afr. Native Policy* 1 To protect White South Africa against 'the Native Danger' — die *donker gevaar* or *die swart gevaar* – is .. the simple pole towards which the needle of Native Policy steadily points. **1960** C. Hooper *Brief Authority* 226 His actual experience of real Africans – the nanny who carried him, the companions who played with him, the 'boy' who worked in the garden – had in no way modified his fears of the Peril, the Swart Gevaar. **1971** *Daily Dispatch* 16 Sept. 8 The Dean said: 'I believe apartheid is a doctrine based on one of the great emotions, fear, the "swart gevaar".' **1973** *Newsweek* 15 Oct. 16 Once again, the great white hope has triumphed over *die swart gevaar* (the black danger). **1977** *World* 13 Oct. 3 Only a Nationalist landslide .. could hold back the 'swart gevaar'. (Black menace). **1978** P.-D. Uys in S. Gray *Theatre One* 157 Anna: .. So what did the Swart Gevaar take? Mouse: Everything. My writing paper, my perfume, my spare pair of glasses. **1979** M. Matshoba *Call Me Not a Man* 124 Where were the haters then? Doubtlessly barricaded in their hatred and waiting, shotguns in readiness, for a *swart gevaar* onslaught on their identity and civilization. **1982** *E. Prov. Herald* 17 July 4 Afrikaners believed and white politicians pronounced that blacks were dangerous – the swart gevaar. **1983** *Pace* Oct. 20 A black guy .. seeing his white girlfriend off at the station .. was rudely reminded that he was in South Africa by a bunch of white toughies. But such incidents are becoming a thing of the past as 'swart gevaar' takes over. **1991** J. Pauw *In Heart of Whore* 220 He had believed he was fighting for a just cause 'against ANC terrorists, communists and the *swart gevaar* (black peril)'. **1992** S. Macleod in *Time* 9 Mar. 27 The A.W.B. has .. at the root of its militancy .. what it terms the swart gevaar, or black threat.

2. A political slogan introduced in the elections of 1929 (see *To the Point* quot. 1974), referring to the threat of whites being swamped by the black majority; any political tactic evoking fear and prejudice. Also *attrib.*

1948 P.V.G. Van der Byl in *Hansard* 20 Jan. 111 By their ineptitude as an Opposition they have become our best friends: In a pathetic attempt to get into power they have dropped Republicanism and adopted the Swart Gevaar. **1970** *Daily News* 16 Oct. 5 The Government has returned to the old tactics of 'swart gevaar'. **1971** *Sunday Times* 14 Nov. 14 'Swart gevaar' propaganda, a luxury South Africa can no longer afford if it ever could afford it. **1973** *Cape Times* 13 June 12 There is a widespread feeling in the Republic that a halt must be called to the sterile politics of *Boerehaat* and *swart gevaar.* **1974** *Daily Dispatch* 26 July 14 Functioning in terms of the old politics, which amounted to a contest to see who could scare the electorate most successfully with swart gevaar. **1974** *To the Point* 29 Apr. 28 It was the late Oswald Pirow who introduced the well-known propaganda slogan, the *Swart Gevaar* (Black Peril) as a trump card in the election of 1929 when the first Nationalist Government was caught in the worldwide depression of the time. Ironically, this *Swart Gevaar*, though in a somewhat different form, is still with us as an election issue. **1977** F.G. Butler *Karoo Morning* 111 In the early 'thirties, in the shadow of the 'swart gevaar' election, during the depression when blacks and whites were competing for the same pick-and-shovel jobs, she would have the priest in charge of the black Anglican parish .. to tea. **1981** *Weekend Post* 9 May 1 While some Ministers took a verligte line in their speeches, others reverted to 'swartgevaar' tactics. **1982** *Sunday Times* 28 Feb. 46 A petition is circulating at present in Secunda suggesting that a curfew be imposed at night on the black population ... But a curfew tends to support the 'swartgevaar' neurosis, and does not distinguish between the guilty and the innocent. **1983** S. Motjuwadi in *Drum* Apr. 16 When the Nats got into power in 1948 they did so on the 'swaart gevaar' ticket. **1991** S. Sole in *Sunday Tribune* 19 May 8 The CP .. have been using the 'swart gevaar' scare tactics that served the Government so well for so long.

swarthaak /ˈswarthɑːk/ *n.* Formerly also **zwarthaak.** [Afk., *swart* (earlier Du. *zwart*) black + *haak* hook, thorn.] HAAKDORING sense 1. Also *attrib.*

1897 S.J. Du Toit *Rhodesia: Past & Present* 32 We passed through a calcareous strip of country .. with various kinds of sweet grass and small shrubs, varied with very good large bush and trees, as 'knoppiesdoorn,' 'vaalbrach,' 'rozyntjes'-bosch,' 'Zwarthaak,' 'noem-noem,' 'quarri,' &c. **1917** R. Marloth *Common Names* 93 *Zwarthaak.* **1944** H.C. Bosman in L. Abrahams *Cask of Jerepigo* (1972) 157 Then there was the bush. Thorn-trees. Withaaks and kameeldorings. The kremetart-boom. Swarthaak and blinkblaar and wag-'n-bietjie. **1972** *S. Afr. Garden & Home* Oct. 33 Sitting on the branches of a *swarthaak* tree is a pair of pririt flycatchers. **1973** [see GEVAAR]. **1978** A.P. Brink *Rumours of Rain* 302 On the farm .. there had also been a row of old Griqua graves in the open veld among the *swarthaak* thorn-trees, far from the house.

Swartland /ˈswartlant/ *n.* Formerly also **Zwartland.** [Afk., earlier S. Afr. Du. *Zwartland*, fr. Du. *zwart* black + *land* country; see quots 1934 and 1986.] The wheat-growing area round Malmesbury, Western Cape. Also *attrib.* passing into *adj.*, of or pertaining to the Malmesbury region.

'Swartland' was the official name of this region from the early 18th century until 1829.

1822 W.J. Burchell *Trav.* I. 232 An umbelliferous plant, probably a *Seseli*, was called by the Hottentots, *Anýs-wortel* (Anise-root) the root of which was said to be eatable; but it is entirely different from the Anyswortel of Zwartland. **1931** *Farming in S. Afr.* 221 (Swart), The Swartland farmers keep on an average 55,84 per cent of their cultivated land as fallow and old lands. **1934** C.P. Swart Supplement to Pettman. 171 *Swartland*, The Malmesbury district was originally so called on account of the black soil found there. **1936** E. Rosenthal *Old-Time Survivals* 23 The district of Malmesbury, near the Mother City, is to this day known as 'Zwartland' to crowds of South Africans, who prefer a name that has been superseded in the official gazetteers for more than a century. **1949** L.G. Green *In Land of Afternoon* 131 It was early in the eighteenth century that the Swartland grain farmers started breeding mules. **1972** *Cape Times* 19 Apr. 2 Because of better feed, better fertilizers, and better calculation, the grainlands of the Swartland are producing more organic matter than can be incorporated into the soil between sowing seasons. **1977** *Sunday Times* 14 Aug. (Mag. Sect.) 3 Showing beneath the gentle, courteous manner is the rigid disciplinarian, the stickler for detail that brought the boy from the Swartland, born out of sight of the sea, to his present position. **1978** *Sunday Times* 19 Feb. 8 She laughs and says in the rich Swartland accent she makes so much her own: 'And then I enjoy living here by the sea so much that I don't really want to go anywhere else!' **1982** *Grocott's Mail* 27 Aug. 13 Despite a mildew outbreak in this year's wheat crop in the Swartland being relatively heavy in comparison to past years, farmers need not worry. **1985** J. Cloete in *S.-Easter* Oct.-Nov. 30 A gastronomic introduction to Swartland *boerekos* – offal, milktart and sosaties. **1986** *Style* July 94 It is called the Swartland because of the charcoal-coloured bush, the kanna bush, that used to grow abundantly in these parts. **1992** C. Curzon in *Motorist* Aug. 6 The first part of the route from Cape Town takes you through the bread basket of South Africa. The Swartland (black land), as it is known, turns to a golden sea of wheat during the spring.

Hence **Swartlander** *n.*, an inhabitant of the Swartland.

1972 *Cape Times* 19 Apr. 2 To prevent the building from deteriorating, Dr. Leon Goldman, of Cape Town (an old Swartlander) .. has purchased the building and has given it to the Malmesbury Municipality. **1985** J. Cloete in *S.-Easter* Oct.-Nov. 29 As the Swartlanders used to say, the children 'ate letters,' and the more letters they ate, the more learned they became.

swart varkie /ˌswart ˈfarki/ *n. phr. Hist.* [Afk., *swart* black + *varkie* piglet (perh. ad. *vaatjie* firkin; cf. 16th C. Du. *vercken* firkin, pig); see also VAATJIE.] A twenty-litre black plastic container for wine. Also *attrib.*

1980 *Cape Times* 28 Mar. 2 Varkie's days are numbered. The Minister .. yesterday asked wine producers and dealers to take immediate steps to phase out the notorious 'swartvarkie' 20l wine container ... Although he did not intend proceeding with legislation to ban the 'swart varkie' .. he agreed the container should disappear. **1981** *Daily Dispatch* 19 Feb. 9 The government was accused yesterday of breaking faith by failing to stop the sale of 20 litre '*swart varkie*' wine containers this year ... 'I am sure that, if the Minister stopped pandering to the liquor industry and started considering the devastating effects the "*swart varkies*" are causing, he would stop the sale of these containers forthwith.' **1984** W. Steenkamp in *Cape Times* 18 Aug., Commemorate the 'swartvarkie' – that 25l. demijohn of fond memory in which dedicated vaaljapie men used to buy their tipple.

‖**swartwitpens** /ˌswartˈwətpens, -pẽs/ *n. obsolescent.* Also **swart-vet-pens, swart-witpense, swartwitpenz, zwart-wit-pens.** [Afk. (earlier Du. *zwartwitpens*), *swart* black + *wit* white + *pens* belly, paunch; see quot. 1913.] The HARRIS BUCK, *Hippotragus niger.*

1869 T. Baines *Diary* (1946) I. 137 We saw a fine troop of *Zwart-wit-pens* .. or Harris bucks. **1880** E.F. Sandeman *Eight Months in Ox-Waggon* 254 We rode along .. hoping to find a koodoo or perhaps a swartwitpense feeding on the luxuriant grass growing under the shade of the trees. **1885** H. Rider Haggard *King Solomon's Mines* 25 He groped in his shirt and brought out what I thought was a Boer tobacco pouch of the skin of the Swart-vet-pens (sable antelope). It was fastened with a little strip of hide, what we call a rimpi. **1897** H.A. Bryden *Nature & Sport* 209 A European would make little of that spoor; but Hans Botha sees at a glance that a troop of Zwart-wit-pens (sable antelope), big, long-horned beasts, has after drinking at the river, passed that way but half-an-hour since. **1913** C. Pettman *Africanderisms* 579 *Zwart-wit-pens*, .. The name refers to the black and white markings on the under part of the animal, lit. 'black and white belly'. **1937** S. Cloete *Turning Wheels* 45 Large numbers of buffalo, wildebeeste, koodoo, roibok, eland, roan and swartwitpenz were dragged in every day by the tired oxen. **1939** [see HARRIS BUCK]. **1951** *Cape Argus* 8 Dec. 4 He and Conroy spotted a fine buck – a swartwitpens. **1958** S. Cloete *Mask* 135 Not only lions and tigers were dangerous. The greater buck like the swart witpens or sable with horns like scimitars were dangerous when wounded.

Swasi var. SWAZI.

Swati /ˈswɑːti/ *n.* [SiSwati: fr. either *siSwati* the siSwati language, or *emaSwati* (the) Swazis (sing. *liSwati*), both formed on the name of *umSwati*, a leader who consolidated the Swazi peoples during the 1840s.]

SWAZI (the Zulu name for this people and their language) is the usual form in *S. Afr. Eng.*

1. Usu. **siSwati** /sɪˈswɑːti, si-/ [siSwati n. class prefix *si-*], also **Seswati, Siswati**: SWAZI *n.* sense 2. Also *attrib.*

1975 *Std Encycl. of Sn Afr.* X. 372 The Swazi language (siSwati) is typically Bantu, and is related to Zulu and Xhosa. **1976** P. Schachter in *Studies in Afr. Linguistics* Nov. (Suppl. 6) 211 Like other Southern Bantu languages, siSwati has a class of consonants with a special affinity for low tone. **1979** *S. Afr. Panorama* May 16 The name Swazi is derived from that of King Mswati, or Mswazi, and the language spoken by the Swazi is called siSwati. **1983** *S. Afr. Digest* 20 May 8 Raised in Mbabane and schooled at Waterford, he regards English as his first language. Joint second come French, German and Seswati. **1986** *True Love* June 27 Please reply with photos and try to write in English or Swati. **1987** *Drum* May 14 After the service, .. the Reverend Barnabas Mndebele presented Prince Charles with a Siswati Bible. **1990** P. Cullinan in M. Leveson *Firetalk* 10 'Who are you?' I asked him in siSwati.

2. *rare.* Pl. **amaSwati.** [In siSwati the pl. prefix is *ema-* (the form *ama-* being Zulu).] In *pl.*: The Swazis (see SWAZI *n.* sense 1 a). Also *attrib.*

1977 *World* 28 Sept. 7 The Soweto tycoon appointed chief of the Amaswati on the Witwatersrand last week ... Among the Amaswati chiefs present were: Paramount Chief Jakonia Tshabalala and the Swazi chief of the Orange Free State, Chief Paulos Tshabalala.

Swazi /'swa(:)zi, 'swɑ:zi, 'swɒzi/ *n.* and *adj.* Formerly also **Suazi, Swasi, Swazie.** [Prob. fr. Zulu *amaSwazi* (the) Swazis (sing. *iSwazi*), ad. siSwati *emaSwati* (sing. *liSwati*), and *isiSwazi* the language of the Swazis, ad. siSwati *siSwati*, see SWATI sense 1; or the forms with *-zi* may represent an obs. pronunciation used among Swazis. The Zulu forms are the forms most commonly used in S. Afr. Eng.]

A. *n.*

1. Pl. unchanged, **-s**, or **ama-**.

a. A member of a predominantly Nguni people living mainly in the Kingdom of Swaziland but also in the Eastern Transvaal; see also SWATI sense 2. **b.** Any citizen of the Kingdom of Swaziland.

1846 *Natal Witness* 16 Oct. 1 The Pongola River, the boundary between the Zoolahs and the Amaswazi. **1857** J. SHOOTER *Kafirs of Natal* 591 The Amaswazi partially shave their heads. **1880** *Volkstem* 2 Jan. 2 Sir Garnet Wolseley declared that the Swazies carried out the duties for which they were employed to his entire satisfaction. **1881** *Pretoria Convention* in S.W. Eybers *Sel. Constit. Doc.* (1918) 461 The independence of the Swazis, within the boundary line of Swaziland, as indicated in the first Article of this Convention, will be fully recognised. **1882** J. NIXON *Among Boers* 98 Dingaan did not long survive his defeat. His brother Panda revolted against him, and forced him to take shelter among the Amaswazi. **1884** *Cape Law Jrnl* I. 223 These are the Amaxosa Kafirs, Fingoes, Tembus, Amampondo, Xesibes, Zulus, Bayeiye, Baloquazi, Shangaans, Matabele, Amatonga or Batoka, Amasuazi, Interior Basuto tribes and those in the Transvaal Territory and Colonial Basutos. **1897** F.R. STATHAM *S. Afr. as It Is* 17 They are .. separated by differences of race and by ancient hatreds ... Zulus would never make common cause with Swazies, and neither Swazies nor Zulus would ever act in concert with Basutos. **1901** *Natives of S. Afr.* (S. Afr. Native Races Committee) 143 The Amaswazi and the people from the Portuguese territory above Delagoa Bay. **1901** [see TONGA sense 1]. **1905** *Native Tribes of Tvl* 132 The Swazis dress after the style of the Zulus of Zululand, wearing the skin 'moocha'. **1920** S.M. MOLEMA *Bantu Past & Present* 89 Ama-Swazi (or Swazis) are a small tribe occupying the country north-west of the Zulu country. **1926** M. NATHAN *S. Afr. from Within* 53 The Swazis .. are a Bantu people, predominantly Nguni in culture and language. **1953** LANHAM & MOPELI-PAULUS *Blanket Boy's Moon* 211 As the motor car approached the land of the Amaswazi, the tobacco lands, the orange groves, the fields of sugar cane, gave way to a country of bush. **1978** *E. Prov. Herald* 12 Apr. 8 The Swazi are a proud race yet they are inherently courteous and have a basic sense of humour. **1982** *Sunday Times* 18 July 24 If the Swazis – a foreign nation – can be helped to form a greater Swaziland, why not Xhosas for a greater Xhosaland. **1983** *Pace* Oct. 173 *(caption)* Young white Swazi.

2. The language of the Swazi people; SWATI sense 1. Also (occas.) **Siswazi.**

1905 *Native Tribes of Tvl* 136 The language of the Swazis, called Siswazi is merely a dialect of the Zulu tongue. *c*1948 H. TRACEY *Lalela Zulu* 6 The land of the Baca is in the southern part of Natal where they speak a dialect which is akin to Swazi. **1954** C.M. DOKE *Sn Bantu Languages* 91 Swazi has not been used as a literary form, educational work in Swaziland being through the medium of Zulu. **1982** *Sunday Times* 30 May 3 Even though his tribe spoke Swazi and for decades many of them had intermarried with Swazis, this did not mean that they regarded Swaziland as having any overlordship in the area.

3. *rare.* A switch or whip.

1947 F.C. SLATER *Sel. Poems* 77 An irate father would greet them, Stinging their shrinking rumps with strokes of his well-known 'swazi, 'Swazi that bites like a bug and stings like an angry hornet.

B. *adj.*

1. Of, pertaining to, or characteristic of the Swazi people.

1847 J. BOSHOF in *S. Afr. Archival Rec.: Rec. of Natal Executive Council* (1960) I. 208 The numerous Amaswazi tribe is already nearing from the Pongola and beyond it, and settling in the Klipriver division in considerable numbers. **1852** R.B. STRUTHERS *Hunting Jrnl* (1991) 6 Several young men arrived from the army which had been fighting with the Amaswazi tribe who live over the Umpongolo River. **1859** *Cape Town Weekly Mag.* 21 Jan. 15 They bring the news of their defeat by some three or four Amaswasi chiefs. **1880** *Volkstem* 2 Jan. 2 When a renegade Swazie chief – we believe his name was Mapothla – was taken prisoner the Swazie General ordered some of his men to seize him. **1908** J.M. ORPEN *Reminisc.* (1964) 272 Moshesh told me that Wietzie had been out on commando to the north against a Swazi chief, Namandhla ka Impisi. **1943** D. REITZ *No Outspan* 70 No European lived in this country and we encountered only wandering Swazi cattlemen. **1985** *Fair Lady* 16 Oct. 60 My sister Zeni married into the Swazi royal family. **1991** *Settler* Vol.65 No.1, He normally carries his hand mirror and the typical Swazi stick, which has a fluted knob.

2. Special collocation. **Swazi print**, a boldly-coloured cotton print.

1971 *Drum* Mar. 6 Irene's top and skirt are made up of Swazi print – a new material designed in Swaziland and doing nicely in the colour fashion stakes.

swee /swi:/ *n.* Also **swi(e)**. [Onomatopoeic, imitative of the bird's call.] In full ***swee waxbill***: the bird *Estrilda melanotis* of the Estrildidae.

1908 HAAGNER & IVY *Sketches* 68 The Swee Waxbill (*E[strilda] dufresnii*) is the best known species in the South-eastern Province of Cape Colony. **1913** C. PETTMAN *Africanderisms* 487 *Swee,* .. *Estrilda dufresnii.* It owes its popular name to its cry of 'swee-swee'. **1913** J.J. DOKE *Secret City* 78 In the thicket of quince behind the summerhouse the Cape robin, the tintinkje, the spotted rooikop, and the more fragile swi built their nests. **1931** *Guide to Vertebrate Fauna of E. Cape Prov.* (Albany Museum) I. 71 *Coccopygia melanotis* ... Yellow-bellied Waxbill, Swee Waxbill ... Young birds go about in small flocks. **1937** M. ALSTON *Wanderings* 96 These other beautiful little birds .., the Dufresne or 'Swee' (from the sound they make) waxbills .. are grey and olive green, black and scarlet. **1967** W.R. SIEGFRIED *Some Protected Birds* Pl.161, *Swie Waxbill,* A widely distributed bird, gregarious and a seed eater. **1975** [see ROOIBEKKIE sense 1]. **1993** G.L. MACLEAN *Roberts' Birds of Sn Afr.* 757 *Swee Waxbill* .. *Estrilda melanotis. Ibid.* 758 *East African Swee* ... Size very small; sexes alike; similar to ♀ Swee Waxbill.

sweet *adj.* [Prob. tr. Du. *zoet.*]

1. *?obs.*

a. Of vegetation: nutritious, and suitable for year-round use as pasture. **b.** Of land: bearing such vegetation. Cf. SOUR sense 1.

1786 G. FORSTER tr. *A. Sparrman's Voy. to Cape of G.H.* I. 345 This tract of land seems to come under the character I have given of the *Sweet* grass-fields and plains towards the shore. **1835** J.W.D. MOODIE *Ten Yrs* II. 37 The pasturage .. was tender and sweet, which showed that the soil was naturally fruitful. **1852** [see VELD sense 3 a]. **1896** R. WALLACE *Farming Indust. of Cape Col.* 58 The veld lying between the first and second chain of mountains is generally 'sweet', and the country excellent for live-stock. **1905** E.A. NOBBS in Flint & Gilchrist *Science in S. Afr.* 383 The two phrases 'sweet' and 'sour,' as applied to our natural pasture land, have no connection with the usual English acceptation of the words. 'Sweet' implies rich land producing nutritious food whether natural or cultivated.

2. Special collocations. **sweet-field(s)** *n. obs.*, *sweetveld* (see below); **sweet grass** *n. phr.*, nutritious grass (see quot. 1913); also *attrib.*;

sweetveld /-felt, fɛlt/ *n.*, formerly also **sweet-feldt, sweetveldt,** and with initial capital, [prob. part. tr. Du. *zoeteveld*], land providing nutritious grazing; the vegetation on such land; also *attrib.*; cf. *sourveld* (see SOUR sense 2); see also MIXED VELD.

1786 G. FORSTER tr. *A. Sparrman's Voy. to Cape of G.H.* I. 250 By the **Sweet-fields** (*Zoete-velden*) are meant such places as do not correspond to the descriptions given above of the *Zuure* and *Carrow-veld.* **1812** A. PLUMPTRE tr. *H. Lichtenstein's Trav. in Sn Afr.* (1928) I. 63 The most fertile parts where the fine grass is produced are called .. *sweet-fields.* **1809** R. COLLINS in G.M. Theal *Rec. of Cape Col.* (1900) VII. 20 That part .. lying west of Storm Berg is, in general, flat, and composed of a rich vegetable mould, producing what the farmers call **sweet grass** in the utmost luxuriance. **1832** *Graham's Town Jrnl* 22 June 101 *(advt)* For Sale ... A Valuable Farm .., in extent 1,700 morgen, two thirds of which is sweet grass. **1838** W.B. BOYCE *Notes on S. Afr. Affairs* 186 Men should be sent from .. the sweet-grass and karoo farms. **1842** R. GODLONTON *Sketches of E. Districts* 44 The greatest part of the District .. is covered with a thick sward of grass, principally of that kind designated by the colonists 'sweet grass'. **1856** [see GEBROKEN VELD]. **1913** C. PETTMAN *Africanderisms* 487 *Sweet Grass,* The food plants growing on rich alluvial soil or on land of good quality are succulent and nourishing, this is termed 'Sweet veld' or 'Sweet grass'. **1960** W. PLOMER in D. Wright *S. Afr. Stories* 179 An aromatic smell of burning sweet-grass sometimes drifted through the air. **1972** *Grocott's Mail* 17 Nov. 2 The veld consists of sweet grass and bush-veld. **1850** R.G.G. CUMMING *Hunter's Life* (1902) 10 Those from about the frontiers of the colony, or any-where beyond the Orange River, are termed **'Sweet-feldt'** oxen. **1871** W.G. ATHERSTONE in A.M.L. Robinson *Sel. Articles from Cape Monthly Mag.* (1978) 83 Zuurveldt may be made sweet veldt, by energy and industry; I have seen it done. **1881** *Cape Monthly Mag.* IV. May 306 A good deal of the ground is sweet veldt, and therefore very valuable. Oxen and sheep seem to thrive in large numbers. **1896** R. WALLACE *Farming Indust. of Cape Col.* 82 Animals brought from sweet veld suffer from what is termed veld sickness which results from insufficient nutrition and the hard and irritating nature of the food consumed. **1910** A.B. LAMONT *Rural Reader* 253 Sweet veld is found on good land that gets plenty of rain, and is so called because the grasses growing on it are sweet and juicy, and well liked by stock. **1913** [see quot. at *sweet grass* above]. **1930** *Friend* 25 Aug. 12 *(advt)* The farm is fenced and divided into eight camps; Grazing – Excellent sweet veld. **1937** *Handbk for Farmers* (Dept of Agric. & Forestry) 381 The types of grass found in the Sweetveld maintain their feed value after maturity and to a large extent even after they have been frosted. **1948** E. ROSENTHAL *Afr. Switzerland* 128 Commonest of all is .. 'red grass', estimated to grow on more than half the countryside. The old Boers called it 'Sweet Veld,' to distinguish it from the dreaded 'Sour Grass'. **1957** *Handbk for Farmers* (Dept of Agric.) II. 620 The most distinctive characteristic of sweetveld is that it retains a comparatively high nutritive value through all stages of growth. **1968** *Farmer's Weekly* 3 Jan. 92 *(advt)* Suitable for dairy or cattle farm. Sweet veld. **1970** [see KRAAL *n.* sense 3 d]. **1981** J.B. PEIRES *House of Phalo* 9 Sweetveld remained nutritious throughout the year but it was very fragile, and it was believed .. that an excess caused consumption in cattle. **1992** *Weekend Post* 17 Oct. (Leisure) 5 The sweetveld savannah plains which surround Etosha Pan, on the Kalahari Beds, contain a myriad of game and other life forms. **1992** [see MIXED VELD].

sweet cane *n. phr. Obsolescent.* [See quot. 1966.] IMFE.

1822 J. CAMPBELL *Trav. in S. Afr. Second Journey* I. 226 A constant succession of fresh visitants arrived, several of whom brought us presents of sweet cane. **1828** W. SHAW Diary. 26 Feb., Before we left one of the men, said he should like to give me some sweet cane, to chew. **1832** *Graham's Town Jrnl* 8 June 94 During the last season were produced on the settlement 450 muids of wheat .. besides large quantities of Caffercorn, potatoes, pumpkins, sweet cane, and many other edibles of a minor character. **1840** J. CAMPBELL *Journey to Lattakoo* 96 Several brought us presents of sweet cane. **1966** C.A. SMITH *Common Names* 452 *Sweet cane*, The vernacular name was first recorded by Backhouse (1838), most probably as a literal translation of soetriet.

sweet Karoo /ˌswiːt kəˈruː/ *n. phr.* [tr. Afk. *soet* sweet + *Karoo* (see KAROO).] Land on which the *Karoo* bush (see KAROO sense 2) is found; this bush. Also *attrib.*

    1896 R. WALLACE *Farming Indust. of Cape Col.* 16 The country to the west of **De Aar** .. is genuine sweet Karoo, forming excellent pasture for sheep, goats, and ostriches. **1968** *Farmer's Weekly* 3 Jan. 7 The veld consists of iron stone rante, vleis and sweet karoo flats. **1972** *Ibid.* 21 Apr. 76 13 excellent camps with water, outstanding sweet karoo grazing carrying 1 200 sheep. **1978** *Daily Dispatch* 17 Aug. 3 The farm is 1 978 ha of mountain veld with good mixed bushveld, thorn trees and sweet Karoo with rooigras.

sweet thorn *n. phr.* [tr. Afk. *soetdoring*; see quot. 1992.] The shrub or small tree *Acacia karroo* of the Fabaceae, with long, straight, glossy-white paired thorns, and small, golden-yellow, fluffy flowers; DORINGHOUT; *Karoo thorn*, see KAROO sense 3; SOETDORING sense 1; also called DORINGBOOM. Also *attrib.*

    1970 S. STANDER in *Farmer's Weekly* 16 Dec. 50 Among the sweet-thorns which lined the river, a dove sang low. **1986** *S. Afr. Panorama* July 29 Native sweetthorn trees are in full leaf. **1987** T.F.J. VAN RENSBURG *Intro. to Fynbos* 24 River valleys usually contain dense sweet thorn (*Acacia karroo*). **1988** J. DEACON in *S. Afr. Panorama* May 46 One of the lower slopes .. is densely wooded with yellow-flowering sweetthorns. **1990** CLINNING & FOURIE in *Fauna & Flora* No.47, 11 The common hook thorn *Acacia caffra*, sweet thorn *Acacia karoo* and umbrella thorn *Acacia tortillis* are the dominant species. **1991** *Best of S. Afr. Short Stories* (Reader's Digest Assoc.) 254 The sweet thorn, which has balled flowers, occurs almost everywhere and is the best known species [of acacia] in South Africa. **1992** D.M.C. FOURIE in *Philatelic Services Bulletin* No.61, Sweet thorn is considered to be an indicator of sweet veld, but its common name refers to the sweet-scented flowers which attract masses of bees and other insects.

swempi /ˈswempi/ *n.* Also **s(ch)wempe, shrimpi, shwimpi, swempie.** [fr. Zulu *inswempe* (perh. introduced into S. Afr. Eng. via Afk. *swempie*).] The francolin *Francolinus coqui* of the Phasianidae, with yellowish head and heavily-barred black-and-white belly; *bush-partridge* sense (a), see PARTRIDGE sense b; occas., the call of this bird.

    1906 *Blackwood's Mag.* (U.K.) Sept. 396 Partridges, namaquas, and 'shrimpies' (a little partridge — a great delicacy) .. were to be found everywhere. **1909** *S. Afr. Field* 30 July 141 Coquifrancolin, generally known as the *Swempi* from the Zulu name, but corrupted into *Shrimpi* by some. **1912** *Queenstown Rep.* 10 July 7 (Pettman), I was riding with the front line of the advance guard near Zeerust, when a covey of *shwimpi* were flushed three or four times. **1937** [see PHEASANT sense a]. **1948** A.C. WHITE *Call of Bushveld* 230 Swempis, to my mind, make the most delicious meal of all the game birds … One bird provides a nice meal for one person. **1970** O.P.M. PROZESKY *Field Guide to Birds* 86 *Francolinus coqui* … The smallest of the partridges, usually found in small coveys … Voice. A loud penetrating 'Kwee-kit, kwee-kit' or 'Swem-pi, swem-pi', can be heard throughout the day. **1971** *Evening Post* 12 June (Weekend Mag.) 1 Among the indigenous types he breeds he particularly likes the little greywing partridge known in the Eastern Province as the 'swempie'.

swi(e) *var.* SWEE.

syringa /səˈrɪŋɡə/ *n.* Also **seringa.** [Transf. use of Eng. *syringa* a name used of trees of the genus *Philadelphus* (mock-orange).]

a. In full *syringa tree*: the shade tree *Melia azedarach* of the Meliaceae, bearing small, sweetly-scented lilac blossoms in clusters, and ochre-coloured poisonous round berries; *Cape lilac* sense (a), see CAPE sense 2 a.

    Introduced from India, the syringa was first recorded at the Cape in 1800.

    1852 C. BARTER *Dorp & Veld* 103 (Pettman), The watercourses .. along which we had sown the seeds of the *seringa*-boom. **1859** R.J. MANN *Col. of Natal* 109 Seringa-trees (a species of lilac) are planted along the sides of the streets. **1864** 'A LADY' *Life at Natal* (1972) 20 In West-street an effort has been made to run a brick footway or pavement on either side, and .. seringa trees have been planted along the outer edge. **1893** G. NICHOLSON in *Cape Illust. Mag.* Jan. 167 Surrounded beyond by a curve of the Klip River, was the little town, the houses showing through the masses of syringa foliage. **1900** H. BLORE *Imp. Light Horseman* 96 In the seringa trees outside, one after another, the cicadas set up their shrill, incessant song. **1960** W. PLOMER in D. Wright *S. Afr. Stories* 186 At times the wind brought a hint of the perfume of a hidden syringa. **1967** E.M. SLATTER *My Leaves Are Green* 1 In Pietermaritzburg a bloom of purple lay across the syringa trees. **1985** D. KRAMER in *Cosmopolitan* May 102 On Friday after school I'd climb into the highest branches of the syringa tree and wait trembling with anticipation. **1989** *Grocott's Mail* 17 Feb. 4 Poisonous trees like syringas.

b. With distinguishing epithet: **red syringa**, *Burkea africana* of the Fabaceae; **white syringa**, *Kirkia acuminata* of the Simaroubaceae; **wild syringa**, see *red syringa* (see above).

    These are deciduous trees of the hot, low-lying areas of the northern interior.

    1961 PALMER & PITMAN *Trees of S. Afr.* 171 The wild seringa is found from the Transvaal bushveld northwards to Abyssinia and Nigeria. It is a very common tree of the sandy areas of the dry open bushveld where it grows as a small tree of 8 to 20 feet high. **1988** A. HALL-MARTIN et al. *Kaokoveld* 12 The vegetation of the northeastern escarpment zone .. contains many species of plants that are .. representative of the eastern mesic flora. Among the latter categories are the baobab (*Adansonia digitata*) .. white syringa, jakkalsbessie .. and the marula (*Sclerocarya birrea*). **1990** CLINNING & FOURIE in *Fauna & Flora* No.47, 9 Here the dominant trees are the magnificent red syringa *Burkea africana*. **1993** *Grocott's Mail* 6 Aug. 9 Kirkia acuminata, White Syringa.

‖**sysie** /ˈseɪsi/ *n.* Also **saasie, saysie, seisje, sijsje, syssie.** [Afk., ad. and transf. use of Du. *sijsje* linnet, siskin.]

a. Any of numerous species of song-birds of the genus *Serinus* of the Fringillidae. See also *berg canary* (BERG sense 1 b ii), *Cape canary* (CAPE sense 2 a).

    1861 'A LADY' *Life at Cape* (1963) 28 There is a yellow and brown finch, called the saasie which runs up and down a limited scale with much sweetness and expression, but the singing is soft and subdued, and, as it were, lisped out. **1910** D. FAIRBRIDGE *That Which Hath Been* (1913) 53 They had left Stellenbosch at an hour when even the sparrows and seisjes were still sleeping, long before the false dawn had whitened the eastern sky. **1913** C. PETTMAN *Africanderisms* 442 *Sijsie*, .. The name appears to be onomatopoetic [*sic*] in its origin, and to be connected to the Dutch *sissen*, to hiss. **1924** D. FAIRBRIDGE *Gardens of S. Afr.* 99 The Turtle-dove feeds largely on the seeds of weeds, so do all the Seisjes – those sweet singers of the veld.

b. With distinguishing epithet: **dik-bek sysie** *obs.* [Afk., *dik* thick + *bek* beak], the canary *Serinus albogularis*; also occas. called **berg sysie** (see quot. 1923); **geel sysie** *obs.* [Afk., *geel* yellow], the BULLY, *S. sulphuratus*; **klein sysie** *obs.* [Afk., *klein* small, lesser], the yellow canary *S. flaviventris*.

    1913 C. PETTMAN *Africanderisms* 144 **Dik-bek sysie**, .. *Serinus albigularis*. **1923** HAAGNER & IVY *Sketches* 146 A vastly different bird is the sombre-plumaged White-throated Seedeater (*S. albigularis*) called 'Dik-bek Seisje' or 'Berg-seisje' by the Colonial boys. It is of an ashy-brown colour streaked on the back with darker brown. **1908** *Ibid.* 84 The Large Yellow Seedeater (*Serinus sulphuratus*), the 'Geel-seisje' and 'Bully' of the Colonial boys, and its smaller congeners, the Kleine seisjes (*S. flaviventris* and *S. marshalli*) make handsome cage birds in their greenish-yellow and bright golden yellow colours. **1958** I. VAUGHAN *Diary* 52 We put them in a big cage in the garden where they all sing. They are cape canareys, blackheads and geel sysies. **1900** STARK & SCLATER *Birds of S. Afr.* I. 171 Although not such a favourite cage-bird as the 'Cape Canarie', the 'Kleine Seisje' is by no means a despicable songster. **1908** [see quot. at *geel sysie* above].

T

taaibos /ˈtaɪbɔs/ *n.* Also **taaibosch, ta(a)ybosch**. [Afk. fr. S. Afr. Du., fr. Du. *taai* tough + *bosch* bush.] Any of several species of shrubs or trees with strong, pliable branches and tough bark, esp. any of several shrubby species of *Rhus* (family Anacardiaceae) and *Passerina* (family Thymelaeaceae); the timber of this tree. Also *attrib.*

1821 C.I. LATROBE *Jrnl of Visit* 559 *Taaibosch*, a species of Rhus, of which genus several bear the name of Taaibosch. [1824 W.J. BURCHELL *Trav.* II. 234 *Taaibosch* (Tough-bush) is a Dutch name given to several species of *Rhus*.] 1833 *S. Afr. Almanac & Dir.* p.xlviii, One of the Cape sumachs (Taaybosch) has been recommended for culture. 1834 *Cape of G.H. Lit. Gaz.* Mar. 41 It is not unlikely that the extract may be procured in larger quantities from the wattle, if the tree is treated as recommended for the colonial *Taybosch.* (Rhus lucida.) 1906 B. STONEMAN *Plants & their Ways* 31 Tannin is excellent for preserving leather, and so the beautiful *Protea cynaroides* .. and *Rhus lucida* (Taai bosch) are destroyed for this substance which was intended for their protection. 1937 C.R. PRANCE *Tante Rebella's Saga* 131 With prehistoric tools he split a log of 'taaibos,' one of the toughest timbers known. 1948 *Cape Times* 5 Aug. 8 The safer and more effective plants are reeds and many-stemmed shrubs, such as taaibos. 1964 L.G. GREEN *Old Men Say* 104 Genadendal .. initiated the famous Madeira chairs, and sold their taaibos versions at ten shillings apiece. 1966 C.A. SMITH *Common Names* 454 *Taaibos*, A name generally given to several species with a tough .. bark, but more especially to *Passerina filiformis*. 1974 B. DE WINTER in *Std Encycl. of Sn Afr.* X. 396 *Taaibos*, Name generally applied to plants with tough branches and bark, such as *Passerina vulgaris* .. but particularly to shrubby *Rhus* species. 1989 F.G. BUTLER *Tales from Old Karoo* 34 He cut a fork from an old taaibos.

taak haar(er) var. TAKHAAR.

taal /tɑːl/ *n.* [Afk., language, speech.]
1. Also with initial capital(s). Usu. *die taal* /di -/ [Afk., *die* the], **the taal**.
a. AFRIKAANS *n.* Also *attrib.*

1888 *Cape Punch* 18 Jan. 23 Said the people of Paarl, Who spoke the old Taal, 'Let us invite our dear Mr. Varley' ... With the people of Paarl did he parley. 1893 *S. Afr. Methodist* 24 Dec. 307 As a rule, the Dutch-speaking colonist has but one string to his bow ... They know no language but the taal. 1893 'M' in *Cape Illust. Mag.* Aug. 443 This is the section which honestly imagines that a *patois* like the taal is eventually to prevail against the inroads of the Anglo-Saxon tongue. 1896 PURVIS & BIGGS *S. Afr.* 29 The term Boer .. is roughly applied in South Africa as descriptive of all Whites who speak the taal — a language which has been evolved by the Dutch colonists, and which is of very limited vocabulary, containing only a few hundred words — as their familiary medium of intercourse. The taal is of Dutch foundation, but with a few other European, Malay and Native terms embodied. 1896 'S. CUMBERLAND' *What I Think of S. Afr.* 154 The Boer taal is not pretty at its best; in its harshness, it makes one feel thirsty. 1898 *Johannesburg Star* 4 June, Sundry clever and humorous volumes of taal-verse. 1900 *Spectator* (U.K.) 6 Oct. 460 One of the first results .. was to establish the Taal, the Cape patois, as the official language. 1901 W.S. SUTHERLAND *S. Afr. Sketches* 46, I have put the verse into some kind of English from the original Taal, and of course all poetry loses in translation. 1903 [see CAPE DUTCH *n. phr.* sense 2]. 1905 *Star* 2 Oct. 6 When his Excellency says, 'Let the medium be the taal if the child is a Boer', he does not mean, we take it, that each school is to be split up into two distinct sections. 1908 M.C. BRUCE *New Tvl* 11 The Dutch element includes both well-to-do and cultivated Dutch and the poor and ignorant. The better class speak English perfectly, but in their homes they talk the taal always. 1909 O.E.A. SCHREINER *Closer Union* (1960) 24 The white race consists mainly of two varieties, or rather mixed European descent, but both largely Teutonic, and though partly divided at the present moment by traditions and the use of two forms of speech, the Taal and the English, they are so essentially one in blood and character that within two generations they will be inextricably blended by inter-marriage and common interests. 1910 J. RUNCIE *Idylls by Two Oceans* 51 He yelled for Jantje in the taal, for Rachel in Yiddish, and to me as he passed in convoluted English. 1911 L. COHEN *Reminisc. of Kimberley* 393 The mother tongue [*sc.* Dutch] had merged itself into what is called the Taal, a medley of Dutch, Kaffir and Hottentot words, a linguistic compound enough to drive a *savant* crazy. 1911 *E. Prov. Herald* 9 Dec., He disagreed with the present movement for the study of the Taal in preference to the Dutch language proper with its fine literature. 1911 P. GIBBON *Margaret Harding* 78 'Koos' is the Taal for cousin, you know; it's a sort of familiar address. 1913 D. FAIRBRIDGE *Piet of Italy* 100 Gamaliah .. was explaining in voluble Taal to Hadje Omar. 1914 S.P. HYATT *Old Transport Rd* 92 The Taal, the horrible jargon of the Cape Dutch. 1914 W.C. SCULLY *Lodges in Wilderness* 187 He spoke in High Dutch, before which my homely 'taal' faltered, abashed. 1928 [see UNION]. 1930 J. BUCHAN *Four Adventures* 178 The newcomer .. started questioning Peter in the taal. 1943 'J. BURGER' *Black Man's Burden* 241 Afrikaans is still spoken of slightingly as an inferior language, as 'kitchen-Dutch', as the'taal', by people who ought to know better. 1955 G. SARON in Saron & Hotz *Jews in S. Afr.* 189 Sammy Marks .. spoke the 'taal' fluently, and this counted with Kruger. 1963 A. DELIUS *Day Natal Took Off* 4 We finally got used to calling the Dutch Afrikaners, and even learning a few words in the Taal ourselves. 1973 J. MEINTJES *Voortrekkers* 19 Speech was conditioned by environment to such an extent that a new language began to evolve, then simply called the *Taal* (the language), or Cape Dutch, and much later Afrikaans. 1976 *Sunday Times* 22 Aug. (Mag. Sect.) 5 No matter how often you might speak English, .. the heart is truly stirred only by the cadences of the taal. 1978 *Speak* Vol.1 No.5, 55 Language is felt to be a political issue in South Africa. One thinks of the taal and Soweto. 1981 *Rand Daily Mail* 25 Mar. 23 Swazi schools to teach the 'taal'. Swaziland's Parliament has approved in principle a recommendation by the Minister of Education .. that Afrikaans be taught in the country's schools. 1988 'K. DE BOER' in *Frontline* Oct.-Nov. 42 Another taal truth was established: when deciding whether something should be one or two words the rule was very simple: one concept, one word. 1991 A. VAN WYK *Birth of New Afrikaner* 24 It was Language Year, commemorating the formation a century before of *Die Genootskap van Regte Afrikaners* .. which first set out to formalise Afrikaans as a language separate from Dutch. Once more we were bombarded with *taal* doings ... My reaction to this overdose of *taal* propaganda was identical to the way I closed my mind to the anti-communist campaign in the 1960s.
b. FLAAITAAL.

1956 T. MAKIWANE in *New Age* 19 July 6 The various groupings ... Somebody speaking English there — teachers — then one or two other smaller groups often hostile to the former, speaking in their own language (the taal) stressing every word in loudest tones, are the 'boys' (Tsotsis). 1962 W.S. MANQUPU in *Star* 22 Feb. 14 The very name 'tsotsi' had its birth as a result of a film, shown in 1946 (though by this time 'Die Taal' had long been flourishing) ... 'Die Taal' still flourishes, and grows, at places such as Meadowlands and Diepkloof. 1979 C. VAN DER MERWE in *Frontline* Dec. 17 Dutch swears by Flytaal ... He's known .. as the brabisa manoja, the mhlophe who knows the taal. 1988 [see TOWNSHIP sense 2]. 1990 P. ALEXANDER in *Weekly Mail* 5 Oct. (Weekend Mail) 14 Dialogue is in the form of *die taal* 'which is neither English, Afrikaans nor ethnic'. This makes it difficult for most whites and foreigners to follow.

‖**2.**
a. Language.

1944 'TWEDE IN BEVEL' *Piet Kolonel* 35 Afrikaans was the home taal of the majority, but the language of the regiment was English and Afrikaans on alternate days. 1957 D. GRINNELL-MILNE *Baden-Powell at Mafeking* 172 Speaking but a few hundred words of a *taal* that was neither German nor Dutch. 1969 A. FUGARD *Boesman & Lena* 20 Sit and rest ... How do say that in the kaffir *taal*? 1972 *Cape Times* 10 Mar. 5 Any more taals tossed into the translation arena would have escalated the number of permutations possible. 1972 [see EINA *n.* sense 2]. 1979 J. GRATUS *Jo'burgers* You'd better learn the taal of my friend. It's called English. 1980 *Fair Lady* 19 Nov. 384 Stumbling along in some strange *taal*, poking fun at each other's bad (language) habits. 1982 *Pace* Apr. 15 These youngsters communicate in their own lingo ... It is a quick-shifting 'taal' that alarms parents. 1992 J. RAPHAELY in *Femina* June 6 If you are tone-deaf you can't sing in tune in your own *taal*, let alone any other.
b. With defining word: **moedertaal** /ˈmʊdə(r)-, ˈmuːdə(r)-/ [Afk., *moeder* mother], 'mother-tongue' (meaning Afrikaans); also *attrib.*

1957 L.G. GREEN *Beyond City Lights* 36 G.W.A. van der Lingen, the Dutch Reformed Church minister at Paarl, later to become prominent in the *moedertaal* struggle. 1990 *Sunday Times* 11 Feb. (Mag. Sect.) 11 Feb. 34 Until such time as their own private school brand of education is available in the *moedertaal*, Afrikaans parents who choose English-medium education for their children will continue to make a sacrifice.

‖**3.** *Comb.* and *Special Comb.* (in sense 1 a): **Taal-beweging** /-bəˌviəxən/ [Afk., *beweging* movement], either of two language movements, the first for the recognition of Afrikaans as a written language (1875-1900), and the second for the acceptance of Afrikaans as an official language (1915–1925); **Taalbond** /-bɔnt/ [Afk., ellipt. for *Suid Afrikaanse Taalbond* South African Language Society], (*a*) a society formed in 1890 to strengthen and encourage the use of Dutch (and later Afrikaans); also *attrib.*; (*b*) *ellipt.*, the national examinations set by this body, known as the *Higher Taalbond, Lower Taalbond* and *Voorbereidende (Preparatory) Taalbond* (examinations); **taalfees** /-fɪəs/ [Afk., *fees* festival, feast], a language festival celebrating a hundred years of the Afrikaans language, held on the 14th of August 1975; **taalmonument** /-ˌmɔny'ment/, a monument to the Afrikaans language, particularly that near Paarl; **taal-speaker** *obs.*, an Afrikaans-speaker; **taalstryd** /-streɪt/ [Afk., *stryd* struggle, battle], 'language struggle', esp. the struggle to advance the status of the Afrikaans language; hence **taalstryder**, one active in this movement; **taaltoets** [Afk., *toets* test], a test of proficiency in both official languages, obligatory for all hotel employees.

1970 T. HATTINGH *Informant, Bloemfontein* **Taalbeweging** – the name for the first Afrikaans language-movement. **1975** *Sunday Times* 17 Aug. 14 On its hundredth birthday, Afrikaans finds its future uncertain .. As it stands on the threshold of a new era it is in the throes of a Derde Taalbeweging, facing challenges as great as those which confronted the Genootskap van Regte Afrikaners. **1987** W.A. DE KLERK in *Ibid.* 25 Jan. 32, 1876: The Taalbeweging. **1892** *Cape Illust. Mag.* Nov. 90 What .. gave rise to the word Kameahs, .. is a problem I leave to .. a Select Committee of the **Taal Bond**. **1893** *Ibid.* Vol.4 No.10, 370 The crass ignorance of the Taal-Bond. **1921** *E. Prov. Herald* 15 Jan. 3 The following are the official results of the Taalbond examination. **1932** *Grocott's Daily Mail* 12 Jan. 2 The passes in the Lower Taalbond Examination .. are as follows. **1941** *Bantu World* 15 Feb. 15 Preference will be given to an applicant .. who has passed Matric Afrikaans or the Hoer Taalbond. **1966** T.R.H. DAVENPORT *Afrikaner Bond* 140 In October 1890 the Taalbond was inaugurated, to propagate the Dutch language and culture in schools. **1974** J.R. OLIVIER in *Std Encycl. of Sn Afr.* X. 396 The Taalbond had its origin in a language conference held in Cape Town on 1 Nov. 1890. It aimed at improving the knowledge of what it called the 'language of the people' (Dutch) and developing a national sentiment ... The civil service accepted the certificates of the Taalbond as proof of competence in the Dutch (later Afrikaans) language. **1975** *Sunday Times* 17 Aug. 14 It must learn, this language of Africa, to speak to Africa in words that it will accept. If it does – and few who know its vitality will doubt that it can – this week's **Taalfees** will mark not the end of one chapter, but the beginning of another. **1971** *Daily Dispatch* 31 Aug. (Suppl.) 7 The first '**taalmonument**' (language monument) for the Afrikaans (Dutch) language was founded here and it can rightly be said that the first Afrikaans language movement was inspired by Burgerdorp. **1982** *Sunday Times* 18 July 24 Why on earth do supermarkets stick price labels on everything with a glue that could stick the Taal Monument together if it broke in two? **1896** PURVIS & BIGGS *S. Afr.* 94 The Transvaal **taal-speaker**. **1975** *Sunday Times* 17 Aug. 14 In a year which marks those triumphs, Afrikaans is once again racked by a **taalstryd**. Once again academics are prophesying its demise, once again it is under stress. **1990** S. DE WAAL in *Weekly Mail* 23 Feb. (Suppl.) 9 He is concerned with *Taalstryd* (linguistic struggle), harking back to the days when Afrikaans fought for its identity and its survival. **1980** N. FERREIRA *Story of Afrikaner* 136 The Afrikaner nation was born when his language was born, when an early **taalstryder** exclaimed: 'Ons skryf soos ons praat.' [We write as we speak.] **1972** *Het Suid-Western* 14 Dec. 19 Recently .. became the first hotel employee .. to pass her '**taal toets**'. Now she has a certificate to prove that she can say 'boerewors' in both official languages.

taaybosch var. TAAIBOS.

table *n.* Also with initial capital. [Special use of general Eng. *table* flat elevated tract of land.] ***The table***: Table Mountain, overlooking Cape Town; the flat surface along the top of this mountain. Formerly also called ***the Table land***.

1607 in R. Raven-Hart *Before Van Riebeeck* (1967) 35 We brought parte of the table to the northward of the sugar lofe still opening it more and more and having given the outmost point on our starborde syde .. a good birth wee stode in So.E. and So. with the high land on wch is the table. **1612** T. BEST in *Ibid.* 57 We and the Sallomon in the morneing stod in with the land, and sawe both the Seugar Loaffe and the Table. **1634** P. MUNDY in *Ibid.* 142 This hill is never uncovered with Clouds but in verie faire weather. Soe that it is an infallible rule That when the Table is Covered there succeedes dirt and raine, and contrarywise when it is uncovered. **1655** E. TERRY *Voy. to E.-India* (1777) 13 A mighty hill, (called from its form, the Table); close by which there is another hill, .. called by passengers, the Sugar-loaf. **1688** G. TACHARD *Voy. to Siam* I. 43 We made the Table Land first, and it is called by that Name because the Top of it is very flat, and much resembles a Table. *Ibid.* II. 64 They have .. huge great Apes that comes [*sic*] sometimes in Troops down from the *Table-land* into the Gardens of private Persons. **1731** G. MEDLEY tr. *P. Kolb's Present State of Cape of G.H.* II. 14 'Tis an usual Saying among Sailors approaching the *Cape*, as soon as they discover this cloud, *The Table is cover'd*, or *The Cloth is laid on the Table*; intimating, that they must prepare immediately for a Storm. **1773** P. CARTERET in J. Hawkesworth *Acct of Voy.* 441 At day-break on the 28th we made the Table Land of the Cape of Good Hope, and the same evening anchored in the bay. **1780** in I. Munro *Narr. of Milit. Operations on Coromandel Coast* (1789) 7 When this [sheet of fog] appears, the natives say 'the devil has covered his table,' as it is an infallible sign of an approaching gale of wind from the land. **1925** H.J. MANDELBROTE tr. *O.F. Mentzel's Descr. of Cape of G.H.* II. 144 The wind is ushered in by a white cloud which covers the whole summit of the mountain. Its appearance causes seafaring men to mutter 'we must hurry, the table is laid' – a signal for either hastening back to their ship or scurrying on land. **1973** P.A. WHITNEY *Blue Fire* 113 It [*sc.* the cloud] spread out in a layer of white over the entire table, drifting a little way down the sides so that it looked as if a tablecloth had been spread evenly over the flat top of the mountain. **1979** M. MATSHOBA *Call Me Not a Man* 110 The top of the Table was covered in clouds. 'They call that cloud the tablecloth.' **1990** P.T. PIENAAR *Informant, Grahamstown* There are always wisps of cloud seemingly waiting to lay the Table.

table-cloth *n.* [Fig. use of general Eng.] The layer of cloud which often covers the top of Table Mountain and cascades down its slopes. Also *attrib.*

1634, 1731 [see TABLE.] **1764** MRS KINDERSLEY *Lett.* (1777) 58 The Table-land .. before a gale of wind, is always covered with a thick cloud, which the people call the devil's table-cloth. **1791** *Encycl. Brit.* VII. 16 The Table Land or Mountain is sometimes suddenly capped with a white cloud, by some called 'the spreading of the Table-cloth'. **1797** LADY A. BARNARD *Lett. to Henry Dundas* (1973) 37 Table Mountain over which a white damask table cloth had been spread half way down shewd its broad face and smiled. **1804** R. PERCIVAL *Acct of Cape of G.H.* 129 It is a common observation with the Dutch to say .. 'that the Devil is going to dinner and he has laid the cloth on Table Mountain.' **1829** C. ROSE *Four Yrs in Sn Afr.* 7 The table-cloth on the Table Mountain, and the South-east wind that it denotes. **1834** W.H.B. WEBSTER *Narr. of Voy. to Sn Atlantic Ocean* 322 There is a remarkable circumstance connected with the south-east wind at Cape Town, viz. the dense mantle of vapour which rests upon Table Mountain, and rushes over its precipitous sides like a cataract .. This peculiar appearance is called by the inhabitants the Table-cloth. **1852** A.W. COLE *Cape & Kafirs* 24 A great white cloud is approaching us – 'the devil's table-cloth' by all that is fearful! **1882** C. DU VAL *With Show through Sn Afr.* I. 50 Stealing over the top of Table Mountain was a white filmy vapour, known as the 'table-cloth', the certain precursor of the 'south-easter.' **1898** *E. Prov. Herald* 2 Aug., A Real Table-Cloth. The weather has been very boisterous .. snow fell heavily on Table Mountain. The ridges of the face of the mountain are covered with hail and presents a pretty sight. **1905** *Addresses & Papers* (Brit. & S. Afr. Assoc. Agric. Science) I. 287 (Pettman), South-easters are three kinds .. (1) 'Table Cloth' south-easters (2) 'Blind' south-easters (3) Black south-easters. **1926** P.W. LAIDLER *Tavern of Ocean* 193 An ever-tumbling cataract of cloud that never succeeds in reaching the city below – a phenomenon which the English named 'the table-cloth,' but which was likened by the French to a white powdered wig, 'la perruque'. **1944** J. MOCKFORD *Here Are S. Africans* 45 The legend grew that .. a retired pirate .. had smoked for many days in competition with a sulphurous stranger on Devil's Peak, smoked until the stranger collapsed, smoked until Table Mountain was covered by its famous cloudy tablecloth. **1963** K. MACKENZIE *Dragon to Kill* 88 Table Mountain was covered with its tablecloth of cloud. **1971** *Argus* 24 July 9 Cape Town has two tablecloths – a natural white cloth of cloud resting on the top of Table Mountain, and a dark spread of man-made smoke suspended low over the harbour area. **1979** [see TABLE]. **1991** A. JAY on Radio 5, 9 May, There's a tablecloth on the mountain, and all us Vaalies are going ape. **1993** C. EDEN in *Food & Home* Aug. 138 Seagulls wheeling in the wide blue bowl of the sky, the South-Easter nudging the tablecloth over Table Mountain.

tackey var. TAKKIE *n.*[2]

tackie, takkie /'tæki/ *n.* Also **tack(e)y, teckie, tekkie**. [Etym. uncertain: perh. fr. general Eng. *tacky* sticky, or Scot. Eng. dial. *tacky* cheap, rubbishy (but see also quot. 1987, sense 1 a). The common spelling *takkie* reflects a perception that the word is Afk. in origin; the spellings *teckie* and *tekkie* reflect Afk. or marked S. Afr. Eng. pronunciation.]

1.a. A rubber-soled canvas shoe; *transf.*, a sports shoe or running shoe. Also *attrib.*, and *fig.*

Similar shoes are elsewhere called 'plimsolls' or 'sandshoes' (esp. in *Brit. Eng.*), and 'sneakers' (esp. in *U.S. Eng.*).

1913 C. PETTMAN *Africanderisms* 491 *Tackies*, In the border towns of the Eastern Province this is the name given to rubber-soled sand-shoes. **1924** *Ann. Mountain Club S. Afr.* No.27, 46 Ye who scale with ropes and 'tackies' Cliffs of awe-inspiring grandeur. **1941** *Bantu World* 22 Feb. 8 The constant wearing of tackies is not good .. for the rubber soles do not allow the feet to perspire freely. **1947** H.C. BOSMAN in L. Abrahams *Cask of Jerepigo* (1972) 236 And he looked quite all right, too, in his dinner-jacket and black trousers and carrying a tray. But his tackies, reinforced with string and newspapers, formed the subject of a good deal of ill-natured gossip in the dining saloon. **1955** D. JACOBSON *Trap* 20 He wore canvas *takkies* on his feet, his toes poking through the ends. **1958** I. VAUGHAN *Diary* 60 We all have to wear blue pleeted [*sic*] skirts and blouses and white tackies on the feet and drill with wood dumb bells and broom sticks. **1966** L.G. BERGER *Where's Madam* 73 They come along when they hear there's a job going. Looking meek and downcast in their ragged T-shirts and scuffing their dirty, laceless tackies in the dust. **1978** A. ELLIOTT *Sons of Zulu* 69 Another line which is sold, mostly to the girls, is sparkling white sand-shoes – or tackies ('teckies') as they call them. **1987** M. GREEN in *Sunday Star* 6 Dec. (Review) 2, I mentioned that the new Oxford dictionary of South African English did not give a derivation for tackie (tennis shoe) and speculated that it might come from the Latin taceo, to be silent. Wharrie .. writes: 'It is a word used in Scotland to mean poor quality, rubbishy. Before World War 2 tennis shoes were imported into South Africa from Japan. They were very badly made and fell apart in no time and soon became known as tackies among the then fairly large Scottish community.' **1990** I. VUSI in *Drum* Dec. 39 If you dared turn up in tekkies and faded jeans, you might be led to a bathroom where you'll [*sic*] be rinsed and then dolled up in a pair of pants and shoes, two sizes too big. **1993** M. OOSTERBROEK in *Daily News* 11 Jan. 7 Even six-year-olds knew the difference between R150 no-name brand tackies and R400 Nikes.

b. *comb.* **tackie-deep** *adv.*, ankle-deep; **tackie gauntlet, - parade**, army slang for an unofficial punishment in which a recruit has to run the gauntlet, while being beaten with tackies; **tackie squad**, a collective nickname for (*a*) plainclothes policemen who patrol wearing running shoes, or (*b*) an intelligence unit of the Defence Force.

1977 *Daily Dispatch* 9 Nov. 1 Soweto policemen yesterday stood **tackie-deep** in flowing white beer froth that bubbled up like soap suds as they poured 1 700 dozen bottles of beer down police drains. **1976** *Cape Times* 29 Dec. 3 A national serviceman .. died after running a '**tackie gauntlet**' twice in one week 'to sharpen him up'. **1978** *Daily Dispatch* 18 July 2 A national serviceman .. died .. after he had undergone 'three or four unofficial **tackie parades**'. **1991** *Weekend Argus* 31 Aug. 14 A **Tackie Squad** — plainclothes policemen who wear running shoes and casual clothes — have already proven successful in fighting crime in the city centre. **1991** J. PAUW *In Heart of Whore* 178 A mysterious SADF intelligence unit known as the 'tekkie squad', presumably because its members wore civilian clothes. **1993** *E. Prov. Herald* 6 Oct. 4 Members of .. the 'takkie squad' have arrested 15 suspects this past week.

c. *colloq.* In idiomatic expressions: ***a piece of old tackie***, a 'piece of cake', an easy task; ***on a tackie-string*** (*nonce*), on a shoe-string, cheaply; ***to tread tackie***, to accelerate, to drive; cf. *to put foot* (see PUT).

1976 'BLOSSOM' in *Darling* 7 July 103 It's a piece of ole takkie chatting up ou's at pop festivals. **1977** C. HOPE in S. Gray *Theatre Two* (1981) Zip zap and we're in! Piece of old tackie, man. No grief. **1979** W. STEENKAMP in *Cape Times* 18 Dec. 2 Getting the news of the Zimbabwe Rhodesian ceasefire to the Patriotic Front guerillas might well make Paul Revere's famous midnight ride look like a piece of old tackie. **1987** J. SCOTT in *E. Prov. Herald* 25 July 4 Let's face it, channel swimming is a piece of old tackie compared to walking into the ocean from a beach that has not been allocated to your particular race group. **1989** H. MARTIN in *Daily Dispatch* 13 May 8 By the time they finally trod tackie on the road out, a full week had gone by. **1990** G. HORNING in *Style* June 102 *Style for me means*: Dressing to be myself, on a takkie-string. **1991** *Sunday Times* 8 Sept. 10 Looks like a piece of old takkie, tossing a magazine together. **1992** *Weekend Post* 4 Jan. 1, I was a bit apprehensive when I first started .. but now it's a piece of old tackie. **1993** on M-Net TV 29 Oct. (Egoli) 'Sounds dangerous!' 'Aah — piece of old tackie.'

2. *fig.* A tyre; with defining word, **fat tackie**, a broad, well-ridged tyre, as used for racing or beach-driving. Also *attrib.*

1971 *Informant, Grahamstown*, I hear about fat tackies every day of my life from that car-mad son of mine. [**1972** *Daily Dispatch* 3 Oct. 15 (*advt*) Super Premium radial is the safest tyre Dunlop ever built. Squat and square, it hangs onto corners. And sticks in the wet like a big fat sticky tacky.] **1972** *Informant, Grahamstown* Ma, look at the size of the tackies on that lorry. **1974** *Daily Dispatch* 30 Oct. 1 'Tackies' is used not to describe tennis shoes but car tyres. **1976** *Darling* 29 Sept. 61 He will announce that he fits Fat Tackies Radials .., although everyone can see his car is fitted with tatty old cross-plys like everybody else. **1982** *Sunday Times* 25 Apr. 26 All we need is some fur on the dashboard, an orange on the aerial and a set of 'fat takkies'. **1987** H. HAMANN in *Frontline* Apr. 22 All it is is a thin tin can with fat takkies at the rear and ludicrously scrawny front wheels. A state-of-the-art soap box cart. **1988** G. SILBER in *Style* Apr. 41 There are uniformed security wardens riding around on fat-takkie bicycles. **1989** *Sunday Times* 8 Oct. (Mag. Sect.) 52 The 'Maid Marian' of the '80s drives her 4x4 pickup, fitted with fat takkies, to a clearing in the forest. **1992** J. DAWES on Radio South Africa 30 May (Wheelbase), Driven on very fat Goodfellow tackies.

Hence **tackie** *v. intrans. slang*, to accelerate, speed.

1992 M.D. PRENTICE *Informant, Durban* Let's takkie (accelerate a car).

tagahti var. TAGATI *v.*

tagalash var. TOKOLOSHE.

tagati /təˈgɑːti, ‖taˈgati/ *n.* and *adj.* [ad. Xhosa and Zulu *umthakathi* wizard (pl. *abathakathi*), fr. *thakatha* practice witchcraft.] Among the Nguni peoples:

A. *n.* Pl. usu. unchanged or **aba-**, occas. **-s**. Forms: *sing.* **m'tagat, mtagati, mtakati, mtakiti, tagata, tagate, takata, togate, (um)-takati, (um)thakathi, umtigati**; *sing.* and *pl.* **amatagati, (um)tagati**; *pl.* **abatagati, abathakathi, amatikati, (m)takatis, mthakathi, umtagarties, umtugartie**.

1. A witch or wizard; a practitioner of evil magic; an evil-doer. See also WITCHDOCTOR.

1836 A.F. GARDINER *Journey to Zoolu Country* 263 The alleged Umtakati (bewitcher) is already in confinement. **1836** N. ISAACS *Trav.* (1937) II. 49 He said he only wanted one [*sc.* a musket] for himself to frighten away the Umtagarties. [*Note*] Witches — people not fit to live, or evil-doers. **1850** J.E. METHLEY *New Col. of Port Natal* 75 Many of them had .. witch charms of roots, &c, hanging round their necks, in order to prevent any evil influence being exercised over them by their *Tagate* or witch doctor. **1852** R.J. GARDEN Diary. I. (Killie Campbell Africana Library MS29081) 21 Apr., An Umtakati is one who casts spells upon people or people's cattle & is supposed to have power over wild beasts & be on intimate and friendly terms with serpents. **1852** R.B. STRUTHERS *Hunting Jrnl* (1991) 14 A man & his wife were murdered by their own son ... On asking why he killed them they said they were 'Amatagati'. **1854** *Ibid.* 41 He goes to an Inyanga or Isanusi (a witch doctor or diviner) and gets him .. to accuse his father of being a 'takati' or evil-doer — (this is a word not easily translated, may mean a witch or wizard — a poisoner etc.) and he is killed shortly. **1866** W.C. HOLDEN *Past & Future* 287 At a certain kraal, some one is suspected of being an umtakati, that is, 'evil doer,' or 'witch'. **1887** J.W. MATTHEWS *Incwadi Yami* 46 According to primitive native law, an 'Umtagati' caught in the act of placing, during the night time, at his intended victim's kraal, charms or medicines with the supposed object of causing death or injury, could be siezed and killed in the most cruel manner. **1893** B.M. ATHELING in *Cape Illust. Mag.* Jan. 158, I had the usual contempt for witchdoctors (Umtagati). **1898** B. MITFORD *Induna's Wife* 75 It is not good among us for a man to have a name for dealings with abatagati. **1911** BLACKBURN & CADDELL *Secret Service* 66 Tell him, Mr Interpreter, .. that the Government employs a whole staff of 'abatagati,' who know what you thieves are doing. **1948** E. HELLMANN *Rooiyard* 105 He maintains .. that the European doctor is powerless to combat an illness which is due to 'poisoning' by an *umthakathi*. **1966** A.T. BRYANT *Zulu Medicine* 17 The only form of contractible disease for which an *umThakathi* is not held to be responsible is that .. agglomeration of ailments .. combined under the generic term *umKhulane*, which may be roughly described as 'fevers'. **1967** O. WALKER *Hippo Poacher* 8 Zulu lore about *mtakatis*, or wizards. **1974** C.T. BINNS *Warrior People* 228 Amongst all Bantu witchcraft is .. regarded as abhorrent, fearsome, devilish, evil. It is the work of demons, .. *abaThakathi*, wizards, witches, and .. a menace to society that must be fought against and stamped out. **1980** M. MATSHOBA in M. Mutloatse *Forced Landing* 118 The African way of entering the company of others is for the newcomer to announce himself by greeting first. It is the '*umthakathi*' (wizard) who arrives unseen.

2. *noncount.* In the *sing.* forms (and *sing.* and *pl.* forms) listed above; also **ubutagati, ubuthakathi, ukutakata** [forms with *ubu-* are fr. Zulu *ubuthakatha* witchcraft, forms with *uku-* are fr. Zulu vbl n. *ukuthakatha* the practice of witchcraft]: witchcraft.

1852 H. FYNN in J. Bird *Annals of Natal* (1888) I. 107 'Tagata' includes every species of crime committed by the Kafir. **1860** A.W. DRAYSON *Sporting Scenes* 308, I managed to make them comprehend that by the stars and sun we understood our position; they could not quite make out the system, and seemed to think that there must be Takata (witchcraft) about it. **1899** A. WERNER *Captain of Locusts* 120 It seemed doubtful now whether he had been visited with a sudden madness, or whether he was only meditating some transcendant stroke of ubutagati. **1908** D. BLACKBURN *Leaven* 154 The mothers meeting dissolved with a jerk ... The mothers rushed off the veranda yelling 'Tagata! Tagata!' (Witchcraft!). **1929** J. STEVENSON-HAMILTON *Low-Veld* 229 All natives wear amulets against takati, such as pieces of tree root, small bones, .. or other portions of wild animals. **1937** C. BIRKBY *Zulu Journey* 232 A grey-bearded native who spoke to me of mtagati, the magic of the place. **1949** P.J. PRETORIUS *Jungle Man* 74, I didn't kill a single hippo that day — .. was it tagati — black magic? **1954** A. SEGAL *Jhb. Friday* 12 He handled the receiver as though it smacked of tagati, of magic. **1957** B. FRASER *Sunshine & Lamplight* 115 There is ukutakata (magic) in this bracelet. **1977** *S. Afr. Panorama* Oct. 23 Medicine men who practiced 'tagati,' or black magic, were condemned ... It is 'tagati' which has been responsible for hundreds of cases of malpractices in making 'muti' (medicine) using weird ingredients, including parts of the human body. **1981** *Bona* Jan. 45 Why will this beast not be scared off? Is this tagati? **1987** *Pace* Oct. 4 He decided to settle in this ubuthakathi-riddled continent.

3. A spirit (usu. evil). Cf. BOLOYI.

1892 A. SUTHERLAND in *Cape Illust. Mag.* Vol.3 No.4, 134 Respect for the *Umtagati*, or evil spirit, which he was fully persuaded lurked in my miserable body. **1899** G.H. RUSSELL *Under Sjambok* 82, I come to drink the water of the Tagati (spirit), that my wounded shoulder may get better. **1952** H. KLEIN *Land of Silver Mist* 180 When I mentioned the baboons Neremondo said nervously, 'They are tagati! The spirits of the dead come back to earth.'

B. *adj.* Forms: **(m)tagati, (m)takati, thakhatha, umtagati.** [Transf. use of the S. Afr. Eng. n.; Xhosa and Zulu do not have an adjective corresponding in form to the noun *umthakathi*.] Bewitched, under supernatural influence; magical.

1885 H. RIDER HAGGARD *King Solomon's Mines* 34 They had not allowed for the expansion caused by the fizz in the wine, and .. rolled about .. calling out that the good liquor was 'tagati' (bewitched). **1898** B. MITFORD *Induna's Wife* 10 Strange *tagati* beings are about in the darkness — half-men, half-beast. **1907** J.P. FITZPATRICK *Jock of Bushveld* (1909) 381 Niggers said I was 'takati': asked for some of my medicine. *Ibid.* 447 Rooiland is mad. Umtagati! Bewitched! **1933** W. MACDONALD *Romance of Golden Rand* 18, I see it is a tagati (magic) stone. I will give you a hundred sheep for it. **1937** C. BIRKBY *Zulu Journey* 58 Many places near Mahlabatini are mtagati, mostly because they have been the scenes of violence and bloodshed. **1937** C.R. PRANCE *Tante Rebella's Saga* 53 He .. would not have dared to open it [*sc.* the bottle] .., in case it might be 'tagati' which is what you people call 'bewitched'. **1945** S. NORTON in *Outspan* 3 Aug. 49 Kaffir-corn .. which the native farm-hands declared to be 'tagati' at first because the birds would not touch it. **1949** C. BULLOCK *Rina* 28, I was lucky to get back alive and well. Man! It's *tagati* there — uncanny. Black with witchcraft and queer things at night. **1976** S. CLOETE *Chetoko* 180 The horse is *tagati*, bewitched, and talks like a man.

tagati /təˈgɑːti, ‖taˈgati/ *v.* Also **tagahti, takata, takati, thakatha.** [ad. *thakatha* (common to several Nguni languages); forms with *-i* reflect the influence of the Nguni noun forms: see TAGATI *n.*]

1. *intrans.* To practice witchcraft; to deal in charms and poisons for the working of evil.

1866 W.C. HOLDEN *Past & Future* 123 This cutting up of dead people looks as if they knew how to 'takata' (use witchcraft).
2. *trans.*
a. To bewitch (someone).
1866 W.C. HOLDEN *Past & Future* (1963) 291 A report was soon circulated in the clan, that he had takatied, or 'ill wished', the people, as his cattle and gardens were so fat and productive, and theirs so very poor. 1948 E. HELLMANN *Rooiyard* 47 The prosperous brewer is continually subject to the fear that some less successful competitor will *thakatha* her and cause her to lose her beer-custom.
b. *passive.* To be named as a witch or wizard.
1939 H. KLEIN in *Outspan* 3 Nov. 27 He was accused by the witchdoctor of poisoning her. He knew the consequences of the accusation and before being 'tagatied' and killed in cold blood he fled from the kraal.
Hence **tagatied** *ppl adj.*, bewitched.
1913 C. PETTMAN *Africanderisms* 491 *Tagatied*, .. An anglicized form of the Kaffir word meaning to bewitch, to ill-wish. 1974 C. MELVILLE *Informant* Tagahtied. Bewitched.

tagga var. DAGGA *n.*²

tail *n. Ostrich-farming.* [Ellipt. for *tail-feather.*] A short feather taken from the tail of an ostrich; BOO. See also BLACK BUTT, FEATHER sense a.
c1881 A. DOUGLASS *Ostrich Farming* 80 The only feathers the grower should wash are old feathers that have got soiled and .. occasionally tails that are heavy with mud. 1886 NATHAN, ANDRADE & WILSON in *S. Afr. Exhib.* 408 White Tails — The best parcels of these were in Messrs P. & P. Rabie's exhibit. 1890 A. MARTIN *Home Life* 109 T— arranged prime whites, blacks, tails, feminas, chicken feathers .. according to length, colour, and quality. 1909 J.E. DUERDEN in *Agric. Jrnl of Cape of G.H.* XXXIV. 524 *Tails or Boos*, .. are the tail quills, being white, or white and brown in the cock, and light or dark in the hen. c1911 S. PLAYNE *Cape Col.* 323 A first prize was won for cock's tails at Middelburg. 1930 M.F. WORMSER *Ostrich Industry.* 21 Some signs of shortness in the supply of blacks, drabs and tails are shown. 1955 G. ASCHMAN in Saron & Hotz *Jews in S. Afr.* 130 The names of all the different types of feathers .. bodies, tails .. broken tails, bloods.

tail fat *n. phr. Obs.* Ellipt. for SHEEP'S TAIL FAT.
1890 A.G. HEWITT *Cape Cookery* 6 Cut it into small pieces and put into a saucepan with some onions browned in tail fat. 1936 M. HIGHAM *Hsehold Cookery* (1939) 291 Take four pounds fat. Scraps will do, but if bought specially, use a mixture of two pounds mutton suet to two pounds tail fat. 1937 [see BOEREWORS sense 1].

tailor bird *n. phr. Obs.* Also **taylor bird.** [See quot. 1827.] The warbler *Camaroptera brachyura brachyura* of the Sylviidae.
In G.L. Maclean's *Roberts' Birds of Sn Afr.* (1993), the name 'green-backed bleating warbler' is used for this species.
1827 T. PHILIPPS *Scenes & Occurrences* 69 The taylor bird when making its nest hangs from the tree; the female supplies him with long grass with which he actually sews the nest, inserting his head as a needle and pulling it out again until his threading is used. 1899 R.B. & J.D.S. WOODWARD *Natal Birds* 29 (Pettman), When we discovered the nest of this little Warbler we christened it the *Tailor bird*. It well earns this title from its skill in the art of sewing. 1913 C. PETTMAN *Africanderisms* 491 Tailor bird, The Grahamstown name of *Camaroptera olivacea*. The name refers to the neat way in which this bird stitches the neighbouring leaves with fibres and cobwebs to its neatly made nest. 1923 HAAGNER & IVY *Sketches* 138 First of all comes the Green-backed Bush-Warbler (*Camaroptera olivacea*), or Tailor-Bird, as it is appropriately called in Grahamstown. It is olive-green on the upper parts, except the crown of the head, which is grey.

takata *n.*, **takata** *v.* varr. TAGATI *n.*, TAGATI *v.*

takati var. TAGATI.

takhaar /ˈtakhɑː(r)/ *n. derog.* Also **taak haar(er), takhar, takkard, tokkara.** Pl. -s, occas. -hare, -hara. /-hɑːrə/, or (formerly) **takharen.** [Afk., *tak* branch + *haar* hair.] **a.** *hist.* An Afrikaner rustic or backwoodsman, usu. wearing his hair long (sometimes for religious reasons), and often of an unkempt appearance. Also *attrib.* passing into *adj.*, esp. in the collocation *takhaar Boer.*
b. *backvelder*, see BACKVELD. Also *attrib.*, and *transf.* (see quot. 1971).
1899 G.H. RUSSELL *Under Sjambok* 45 Their unkempt hair hung down on to their shoulders, for they were what colonials call 'taak haarers,' or 'doppers'. 1900 *Grocott's Penny Mail* 9 July 4 Many of these back country 'takhaaren' had never seen a train when the war broke out. 1903 D. BLACKBURN *Burgher Quixote* 287 Although Paul had once been a Taakhaar Boer and a Dopper, he had long ceased to be one, cutting his hair twice a-year so that he might not be thought one. 1910 J. BUCHAN *Prester John* (1961) 32 When he is with the natives, or it may be the *taakhaars*, or it may be something else. 1925 P. SMITH *Little Karoo* (1936) 15 His lank dust-coloured hair, fading with age instead of turning grey, and worn long like a Tak-Haar Boer's from the Transvaal, gave him a wild and unkempt look. 1937 H.C. ARMSTRONG *Grey Steel* 20 They had grown .. into unkempt, difficult people, uneducated takhara. 1946 V. POHL *Adventures of Boer Family* 17 A middle-aged Boer of the old Paul Kruger type (a *Takhaar* some would have called him). 1951 J. WEDGEWOOD *Last of Radicals* 13 The other interview was with Schalk Meyer. They rudely called him a 'dopper' and a 'takkard'. 1961 L.E. VAN ONSELEN *Trekboer* 51 Roaming around Bushmanland, I met one Trekboer after another ... They would say earnestly: 'Cousin! if you want to see real wild folk, then go onto the Knersvlakte. Here you will find the genuine takhare.' 1971 *Rand Daily Mail* 25 May 11 Commentator Gerhard Viviers (well known for his scathing comments on British 'takhare'). 1972 *Het Suid-Western* 16 Mar. 2 Those .. outbursts of violence that would be more apt in the context of a political meeting of takhare in the deep north. 1985 GARDNER & CHAPMAN in *Voorslag* 1–3 34 *Takhaar*, literally 'branch-hair' (Afrikaans); contemptuous term for a backveld Afrikaner.

takiti var. TAGATI *n.*

takkie *n.*¹ var. TACKIE.

‖**takkie** /ˈtaki/ *n.*² *obsolescent.* Also **tackey.** [Afk., *tak* bough, branch + dim. suffix -IE.] A small branch or twig. Also *fig.*, and occas. **tack.**
1890 A. MARTIN *Home Life* 111 It is impossible to walk about the camps unless armed with a weapon of defence called a 'tackey'. This is simply a long and stout branch of mimosa, with thorns all left on at the end. 1896 MACOWAN & PILLANS *Manual of Prac. Orchard-Work at Cape* 16 Upon the top of this pebble-bed it is customary to put a layer of brush-wood or *takkies*, well battened down. 1900 B. MITFORD *Aletta* 140 'Here, Gert. Give me the *tack*!' he said. 'That old brute is properly *kwaai*!' ... 'I think he will leave us alone, so long, Gert,' said Colvin, panting .. for even the thorn-tack means of defence requires some skill and physical effort .. against a full-grown and thoroughly savage male ostrich. [1946 V. POHL *Adventures of Boer Family* 10 Frederick, who because of his small stature had earned the nickname of *Takkie* (a small branch) never looked for trouble, and was more minded to pour oil on troubled waters.] 1971 *Informant, Grahamstown* Haven't we got some takkies to get this fire going?

Tamahas var. TAMMAKA.

tamaledjie, -etj(i)e, -ichie varr. TAMELETJIE.

tamatiebredie see BREDIE sense b.

Tambo var. TEMBU.

Tambookie /tæmˈbʊki/ *n.* and *adj.* Also **Tambo(e)kie, Tambooki, Tambouchi, Tambouki, Tambuckee, Tambu(c)ki, Tambuk(k)ie, Tambuqui, Tembookie, Tembuki**, and occas. with small initial. Pl. -s, or unchanged. [Prob. Englished form of S. Afr. Du. *Temboetje* or *Temboekie* (*Temboe* Tembu + dim. suffix -IE).] Esp. during the 18th and 19th centuries:
A. *n.*
1. *obsolescent.*
a. TEMBU *n.* sense 1 a. Occas. (nonce), the language of the Tambookies (see quot. 1942).
1786 G. FORSTER tr. *A. Sparrman's Voy. to Cape of G.H.* II. 147 On the other side of *Zomo* dwells another nation, who, by the Snese-Hottentots, are called *Tambukis*. 1790 tr. *F. Le Vaillant's Trav.* II. 164 He intended to visit the *Tambouchis*, a nation bordering on Caffraria, with whom they carried on a trade for iron and arms. 1795 C.R. HOPSON tr. *C.P. Thunberg's Trav.* II. 94 These Caffres, a few years before, had murdered *Heupnaer* and some of his company, who .. had travelled into the country of the Caffres and Tambukki. 1812 A. PLUMPTRE tr. *H. Lichtenstein's Trav. in Sn Afr.* (1928) I. 298 The first tribe after crossing the river Basseh is the Tambuckis, or Mathimbas; they are somewhat lower in stature than the Koossas, but their language is exactly the same. 1824 [see PONDO sense 1 a]. 1825 G. BARKER *Journal.* 26 July, The Revd Mr Wright of Wynberg came in off a journey to the Tamboekies. 1834 J.C. CHASE in A. Steedman *Wanderings* (1835) II. 200 The Tamboekie, or Amaytymbæ, is mild even to timidity. 1837 J.E. ALEXANDER *Narr. of Voy.* I. 366 The so-called Kaffirs are divided into three great nations: the Amakosas, or the people of a chief Kosa, extending from the Keiskamma to the Bashee; the Amatembus, or Tamboekies, between the upper Kye and Umtata; and the Amapondas, or people of the elephants' tooth. 1846 I.J. SMITH *Informant, Fort Beaufort* 20 Apr., From your communication and what Mr Bonatz writes, the Tamboekies I think certainly will ally themselves to the Gaikas. 1852 M.B. HUDSON *S. Afr. Frontier Life* p.vii, 'Amatembus' or Tamboekies; another branch of the Kafir race, considered the most royal in blood, and from whom, by intermarriage, the Amakosae head chiefs must, according to kafir law, be descended. 1877 R.M. BALLANTYNE *Settler & Savage* 316 The Fetcani, or Mantatee hordes ... precipitated themselves on the Tamboekies, and afterwards on the Galekas, threatening to extirpate these Kafirs altogether, or to drive them into the colony as supplicants and beggars. 1880 *Grahamstown Penny Mail* 28 Dec. 3 A gentleman who has spent many years among the Tamboekies and Pondomise. 1936 *Cambridge Hist. of Brit. Empire* VIII. 303 The Tembus, generally known at the time as 'Tamboekies'. 1942 *Star* 3 Nov. 6 Old assertions of Afrikaans being picked up from the Hottentots who spoke tomboekie .. were .. biased ignorance. 1972 [see FETCANI sense 1]. 1977 F.G. BUTLER *Karoo Morning* 89 A Xhosa .. bore the badge of being Tambukie (Tembu): the third finger of his right hand was short of the final nail section. Tambukies are thus deprived in infancy, for mysterious reasons.
b. *comb.* **Tambookieland** *obs.*, Tembuland (see TEMBU *n.* sense 1 b).
1835 T.H. BOWKER *Journal.* 5 May, The Missionarys & traders arrive this evening from Tambokie land. 1840 *Echo* 6 July 7 Marching into Tamboekie-land on the glorious day of — (I don't exactly remember, Mr. Editor). 1846 H.F. FYNN in *Imp. Blue Bks Command Paper* 786-1847, 91 Their period of service having expired, they returned to Tamboekieland. 1877 J. NOBLE *S. Afr.* 312 The Transkei, Tamboekieland, Idutywa, and Griqualand East districts, .. are also ruled by colonial magistrates, and the people regard themselves as British subjects. 1913 G.E. CORY *Rise of S. Afr.* II. 236 Tamboekieland, that is, the regions about the sources of the Zwart and White Kei Rivers, including the present districts of Queenstown, Glen Grey, St. Mark's, Xalanga, Cathcart, with perhaps Wodehouse and the Elliot Slang River.
2. In full *Tambookie grass* (also with small initial): any of several species of tall, reed-like grasses used for thatching, esp. those of the genera *Cymbopogon*, *Hyparrhenia*, and *Miscanthidium*; TAMBOTIE sense 2. See also DEKGRAS, DEKRIET.

1837 J. Kirkman in F. Owen *Diary* (1926) 158 The mother and child had hidden under the long Tambookie grass. **1855** G.H. Mason *Life with Zulus* 174 In the absence of thatch (Tambookie grass) we determined on using *flags* for that purpose. **1868** J. Chapman *Trav.* II. 456 The Tambuki-grass, a handsome grass, growing to a height of 6 or 8 feet, is always held to be an indication of good soil, and is itself considered to yield the best material for thatching. **1879** R.J. Atcherley *Trip to Boerland* 74 The grass, which just here was of a long and reedy variety, known as tambooki, caught fire, and .. speedily grew into a conflagration of enormous proportions. **1885** [see SKERM sense a]. **1907** J.P. Fitzpatrick *Jock of Bushveld* (1909) 279 The tambookie grass in these parts has a stem thicker than a lead pencil, more like young bamboo than grass. **1913** L. Lyster *Ballads of Veld-Land* 138 Where the 'Tambookie' waved wickedly red, 'Mehla-ka-Zulu' his warriors led. **1929** J. Stevenson-Hamilton *Low-Veld* 56 A height of about two feet is usual .. though the rank spear or tambookie grass .. with its needle sharp and barbed seeds, which penetrate and work through the thickest garments, reaches about five feet. **1933** W. Macdonald *Romance of Golden Rand* 46 A small company of troopers could be seen moving cautiously and watchfully through the tall tambookie grass. *c*1936 *S. & E. Afr. Yr Bk & Guide* 841 *Tambuki Grass*, So many varieties of grass are so designated that the name has ceased to have any accurate significance ... In 1916, two concessions to cut 'tambuki' in the Pungwe River were granted, which .. should produce nearly 40,000 tons of dried grass per annum. *a*1951 H.C. Bosman in L. Abrahams *Unto Dust* (1963) 119 Her hair was bleached the yellow of tamboekie grass in winter. **1958** R.E. Lighton *Out of Strong* 100 Drifts of tambooki grass grew tall as marsh reeds. **1966** C.A. Smith *Common Names* 456 *Tambotigras*, The vernacular name is in error for tambukigras, arising from the confusion with the prefix 'Tamboti' in tambotiboom. **1980** A.J. Blignaut *Dead End Rd* 26 At that time you could shoot an arrow into someone who had misused you, then crouch in the tambukie grass and watch the poison at work for you. **1981** J.B. Peires *House of Phalo* 6 Emerging from the woods, he might pass through long stretches of open plain covered with long qungu ('Tambooki') grass, so high that it hid a man completely. *c*1985 P. Sacks in *Eng. Academy Rev.* 3 24 Through a gate into the sweet tambookie grass, its reed-like spears lining the path.

3. *rare.* TAMBOTIE sense 1.

1858 Simmonds *Dict. of Trade, Tambookie-wood*, a hard handsome furniture-wood: when powdered it is used by the Zulus of Africa as an emetic.

4. In full ***tambookie thorn***: the small tree *Erythrina acanthocarpa* of the Fabaceae, bearing sharp thorns and showy scarlet flowers; occas., *E. humeana*; the very light, soft wood of this tree.

1893 S. Schonland *Informant, Grahamstown* 11 Mar., I have sent according to your request a nice piece of Tambookie pith to Mr. Lawrence Hamilton. **1907** *Afr. Monthly* Oct. 542 Another species to mention is the .. Tambookie thorn. This one is peculiar in the possession of an underground growth thick as a man's thigh composed of the lightest pith. **1913** C. Pettman *Africanderisms* 493 *Tambookie thorn*, .. *Erythrina acanthocarpa* is known by this name in the neighbourhood of Queenstown. **1917** R. Marloth *Common Names* 79 *Tambookie thorn, Erythrina acanthocarpa*. (Eastern C.P.). Spiny, the flowers showy. **1966** C.A. Smith *Common Names* 456 About 1860 Mrs Barber, who first recorded the English name as tambukithorn, writes that the succulent underground 'root,' is extremely light when dry, and in this state is sometimes made into light summer hats. **1972** I.C. Verdoorn in *Std Encycl. of Sn Afr.* VI. 264 Unlike its better-known relatives, its scarlet flowers are not clustered but borne in long, rather loose, tapering spikes. Owing to its smaller size, the tree [*Erythrina humei*] is also known as 'small Kaffirboom', or as tambuki-thorn; the latter name is also applied to *E. acanthocarpa*. **1981** *S. Afr. Garden & Home* June 116 Erythrina acanthocarpa, Tambookie thorn, is a spectacular shrub, bearing its flowers on bare branches.

B. *adj. obsolescent.* TEMBU *adj.*

1801 W. Somerville *Narr. of E. Cape Frontier* (1979) 37 We saw three of Guykas wives, .. the last of Tambooki origin, an overgrown corpulent young woman was said to cost five hundred bullocks. **1809** R. Collins in G.M. Theal *Rec. of Cape Col.* (1900) VII. 20 We could not see Grey's River .. but .. it comes from the south-east, and probably has its source in the Tambookie mountains. **1827** G. Thompson *Trav.* I. 67 The Tambookie tribe of Caffers, .. who have for some time lived close upon this frontier along the banks of the river Zwart-Kei, have hitherto conducted themselves in the most quiet and inoffensive manner. **1836** R. Godlonton *Introductory Remarks to Narr. of Irruption* 210 *Sandilli*, the youngest son of the late chief Gaika, being by a Tambookie woman of high rank, is acknowledged to take precedence. **1840** *Echo* 6 July 8 The memorable Tambookie commando. **1870** H.H. Dugmore *Reminisc. of Albany Settler* 31 In the year 1828, a savage and very formidable horde .. entered the Tembuki country from the north-east, having skirted the Kwahlamba mountains. **1908** J.M. Orpen *Reminisc.* (1964) 54 A number of Tambookie children, who had been enslaved, would be released. **1977** [see sense A 1 a]. **1979** A. Gordon-Brown *Settlers' Press* 20 Robert Bruce was a Grahamstown-born poet who died when very young from fever when on active service during the Tamboekie war in 1877. **1987** K. Sutton in *E. Prov. Herald* 6 June 5 The worst blizzards were thought to have been in September 1853, when many Tambookie people perished.

tambotie /tam'bʊti, tæm'bu:ti, -'bəʊti/ *n.* Also **ntomboti, tamboetie, tamboote, tambooti(e), tambouti(e), tambuti, (um)tamboti, umtomboti,** and with initial capital. [Xhosa and Zulu *umthombothi* poison tree (see quot. 1966).]

1. In full ***tambotie tree***: the deciduous tree *Spirostachys africana* of the Euphorbiaceae, with scented, durable wood and caustic sap; the timber of this tree; JUMPING BEAN sense 2 a; SANDALWOOD; TAMBOOKIE *n.* sense 3. Also *attrib.*

1852 J.S. Christopher *Natal* 32 The yellow, assegai, iron .. and Tamboote wood grow in abundance. **1871** J. Mackenzie *Ten Yrs* 460 The tall and resinous tambootie tree, which I selected for beams and rafters, was easily split. **1887** A.A. Anderson *25 Yrs in Waggon* I. 42 Some of the most valuable [timber trees] are ... Witgatboom, Tambootie. **1913** C. Pettman *Africanderisms* 522 *Umtamboti*, .. *Excoecaria africana*. The sap of this tree is very virulent; a drop in the eye has been known to cause blindness. **1936** E.C. Llewellyn *Influence of Low Dutch* 165 *Tambouki-grass and Tambouki-wood*, .. so named because they grow in Tembu-land; .. another form of the word, Tambooti, shows the use of the diminutive *-tje*. **1945** N. Devitt *People & Places* 116 Along the banks of the Umsimvubu grows a tree known as the umtomboti. It produces a handsome, mahogany coloured, scented wood. It is made into necklaces by the Pondos. **1950** H.C. Bosman in L. Abrahams *Unto Dust* (1963) 43 Inside were tamboetie wood trestles for the coffins. **1961** [see APPELBLAAR]. [**1966** C.A. Smith *Common Names* 464 *Tombotieboom*, ... The vernacular prefix 'tombotie', is corrupted from the original native name 'um Thomboti', which refers to the caustic properties of the sap and means 'a poison tree'.] **1970** B. Davidson *Old Afr.* 213 Fragments of drainage timber recovered .. have yielded dates between AD 591 and AD 702 ... The wood in question is of *tambootie*, a tree of great longevity. **1980** *Fiat Lux* May 13 Traditionally, tambuti was used by the Zulus in the construction of their huts. Tambuti huts were staked into the ground. **1991** *Style* Apr. 102 Use only ironwood for your camp fire. Some wood, like Ntomboti, known as tambotie, can make you very sick.

2. In full ***tambotie grass***: TAMBOOKIE *n.* sense 2. Also *attrib.*

1866 T. Geast *S. Afr. Diaries* 42, I observed that almost every stem of the long tambootie grass had a silken filament flying from it. **1880** E.F. Sandeman *Eight Months in Ox-Waggon* 304 My bed of soft aromatic tambooti-grass felt more comfortable and grateful than any feather bed ever did before. **1893** J.F. Ingram *Story of Gold Concession* 142, I .. left my blood on the tall blades of the tambootie grass. **1905** Pearson & Pardy in Flint & Gilchrist *Science in S. Afr.* 432 'Tambootie grass' land is excellent for cane. **1939** *Outspan* 29 Dec. 31 Tambootie grass at the height of six feet, as dense as a forest, quite dry, was burning fiercely. **1948** O. Walker *Kaffirs Are Lively*, The tall tambootie grass. **1966** [see TAMBOOKIE *n.* sense 2]. **1987** D. Kenmuir *Tusks & Talisman* 48 A dull, crackling roar rose from the valley below, tambuti grass feeding the fire in an orgy of destruction.

Tambouchi, -bouki, -buckee, -bu(c)ki, -buk(k)ie, -buqui varr. TAMBOOKIE.

tameletjie /ˌtamə'le(i)ki/ *n.* Also **tamaledjie, tamaletj(i)e, tamalichie, tamelet(t)je, tamelijtje, tammeletj(i)e, tammelijtje, tomelah, tommelaitje, tommelatche, tommelykie, Tommy Larche.** [Afk., perh. ad. Du. *tabletje* tablet, lozenge, flat cake of chocolate, sugar, etc.]

1. A hard toffee, sometimes containing pine nuts or almonds. Also *attrib.*, and *fig.*

1838 T. Shone Diary. 6 Aug., In the evening I made the children some tommelatche as a treat on my birthday. **1862** *Ibid.* 18 June, Made some Tommy Larche for the children. *Ibid.* 17 July, Mrs K. gave me a bason of sugar, to make Tomelah. **1874** *Cape Argus* 24 Nov. 4 She .. had a decided penchant for ginger-beer and *tamalichies*. **1891** H.J. Duckitt *Hilda's 'Where Is It?'* 237 'Tameletties.' (A favourite Cape Sweet.) **1919** M.M. Steyn *Diary* 48 He .. was a general favourite .. with us youngsters, who received many a sixpence from him for the purchase of tameletjes, a species of toffee dear to South African boys. **1926** P. Smith *Beadle* (1929) 181 Jantje brought with him, secreted about his person, a horrible sticky mess of almond tommelaitjes. **1945** N. Devitt *People & Places* 15 Favourite old Cape Dutch confections were tameletjes, a sweet flavoured with naartje peel. **1947** [see DENNEBOL]. **1953** *Cape Argus* 28 Feb. (Mag. Sect.) 3 Under a large oak in the main avenue sat a friendly, fat Coloured Woman selling sweets — the 'Tammeletje Woman' we called her. **1968** K. McMagh *Dinner of Herbs* 4 On display .. stood rows and rows of tamaletjies, each in its white paper shell with corners neatly pinched, each and every one richly encrusted with almonds — price: one penny each. **1970** E. Mundell *Informant, Pearston (E. Cape)* The jam cooked for too long and is tameletjie now. **1974** *Cape Times* 12 Jan. (Weekend Mag.) 7 The highlight of our excursions was the tameletjies, a delicious sweet made with butter, brown sugar, syrup, vinegar and water, and the addition of the [dennebol] pips, which my elder sister made for us. **1988** F. Williams *Cape Malay Cookbk* 7 Sweetmeats, like syrupy koeksisters and crunchy tameletjies.

2. MEBOS sense b.

1970 S. Sparks *Informant, Fort Beaufort* Minced fruit and sugar dried in the sun is known as Tamaledjie. **1970** C. Kinsley *Informant, Koegasbrug (N. Cape)* Tammeletjie. Minced fruit dried and then rolled. **1972** Beeton & Dorner in *Eng. Usage in Sn Afr.* Vol.3 No.1, 32 *Tameletjie*, .. flat slab of dried fruit or a kind of toffee made of butter and sugar. **1976** *S. Afr. Panorama* May 26 The women-folk get busy preserving, conserving and making dried fruit (tameletjie) and supervise the liqueurs.

Tammaka *n. obs.* Also **Batammaka, Tamaha.** [Prob. rel. to N. Sotho adj. stem *-thamakga* 'red with a white back' (used of cattle).] Usu. in *pl.*: Collectively, the members of a people of the Tswana group.

1821 *Missionary Notices* June 201 To the N.E. of the above-mentioned place, (about four days' journey) there is a large and populous town, called by the natives Meribahwhey, inhabited by and extensive tribe, called the Tammakas, or Red Caffres. **1824** W.J. Burchell *Trav.* II. 532 The principal nations of which I could procure any account from the natives, were; — eastward from Litakun, the *Tămmăkas* or *Batámmăkas*, (Red people) called by the Klaarwater Hottentots, *Roode Kaffers* (Red Caffres). **1846** R. Moffat *Missionary Labours* 4 From this class of people, the Tamahas, or

tampan /'tæmpæn/ *n*. Also **sampan, tampaan, tan pan**. [Prob. ad. Xhosa *intaphane*, or seTswana *letsipane* or *ditampane* (the latter perh. borrowed back from Afk.).] In full **tampan tick**: any of several ticks of the Argasidae: **a.** *Ornithodorus moubata*, a parasite of humans, carrying African relapsing fever; occas. with distinguishing epithet, **eyeless tampan**. **b.** A parasite of poultry, *Argas persicus*; FOWL TICK. **c.** *Ornithodorus savignyi*, which preys on cattle; occas. with distinguishing epithet, **sand-tampan**. Also *attrib*.

1857 D. LIVINGSTONE *Missionary Trav*. 176, I dreaded the 'Tampans', so common in old huts. 1873 F. BOYLE *To Cape for Diamonds* 256, I have fought with ticks in Borneo; fleas in Egypt; and l–e in Sardinia. These are nought. The tampan will give them half his armoury of daggers, and beat them badly. In shape he is flat, about the size of a threepenny piece and under. He has many legs. His courage approaches ferocity, and his vengeance is terrible. 1880 P. GILLMORE *On Duty* 295 Bitten all over by 'tampans,' an insect synonymous to the 'jigger' of the West Indies. 1898 W.C. SCULLY *Between Sun & Sand* 8 Woe betide the exhausted hunter who seeks the deceitful shade of these trees, for the ground beneath is full of the dreaded 'sampans', which bury themselves in the flesh and cause serious injury. 1914, 1929 [see FOWL TICK]. 1944 [see GALSIEKTE sense 1 a]. 1946 [see FOWL TICK]. 1958 A. JACKSON *Trader on Veld* 65 This [kameeldoring] is prolific in the desert and carries many nests of society birds, not to mention the tampaan tick, the size of a healthy bug, which descends upon you if you make your resting place under the tree. 1974 B. SMIT in *Std Encycl. of Sn Afr*. X. 503 True tampan, (*Ornithodorus moubata*.) Mainly a parasite of man and a serious danger because it transmits a deadly disease, African relapsing fever ... Its common name is eyeless tampan, and it should not be confused with the fowltick. It should also not be confused with the sand-tampan ... , which has recently become a great problem as a parasite of cattle ... This sand-tampan has not yet been proved to transmit a definite disease, but it causes much loss of condition and death by sucking blood from the animals. 1977 F.G. BUTLER *Karoo Morning* 177 She suddenly exclaimed, scratching her legs — 'It's fleas! Or tan pans!' — and leapt out of reach.

tang /tan/ *n. Obs. exc. hist. Wagon-making*. [S. Afr. Du., ellipt. for *achtertang*.] AGTERTANG.

1826 A.G. BAIN *Jrnls* (1949) 17 The hind *tang* (as the Dutch call it) of Mr. B.'s waggon having broken, we were compelled to span out within a mile of Mayase's bush where we intended to have gone to night. 1835 A. SMITH *Diary* (1940) II. 177 The tang of the wagon was finished early this morning and the wagon was repaired and packed by midday. 1974 J.M. COETZEE *Dusklands* 126 The rest of the day was spent in replacing the pole ... How lucky that the socket (*tang*) was not damaged. 1979 M. PARKES *Wheatlands* 76, 1 Scotch Cart £10. 0.0 ... 1 Tang for 5.0.

tankee var. DANKIE.

‖**tannie** /'tani/ *n*. Also with initial capital. [Afk., 'auntie', the familiar form of *tante* aunt.] 'Auntie', not necessarily referring to a blood relation. See also AUNTIE, TANTE, OOM, OOMPIE.

Usu. used to represent the idiom of Afrikaans-speakers.

1. A form of address: TANTE sense 3.

Sometimes substituted for the second person pronoun 'you', reflecting the respectful third-person form of address in Afrikaans. (see quot. 1988).

1958 R. COLLINS *Four-Coloured Flag* 16 'Good afternoon, Tannie,' he mumbled, from a distance of twenty feet. 1969 I. VAUGHAN *Last of Sunlit Yrs* 78 'Tannie', says the boy who has been listening to our conversation, 'I know them all well, I will guide you.' 1978 *Sunday Times* 3 Sept. (Mag. Sect.) 3 The nurses zipped in and out — thank heavens, only one calling me tannie. 1979 *Ibid*. 19 Aug. 6, I reacted sharply when a young man in a dry-cleaning shop addressed me as 'tannie'. I pointed out that we were not related, and that 'mevrou' would be just fine by me ... 'I was just being polite,' he said, obviously hurt. 1987 L. BEAKE *Strollers* 41 'Dankie, Tannie,' they said dutifully when they had shared the water. 'Dankie, Madam,' she corrected them mildly. 1988 A. CAMPBELL in *Fair Lady* 27 Apr. 96 Does *tannie* know Montagu pass? 1990 C. HURRY in *Style* June 101, I knew I was grown up when a teenager called me *tannie*.

2. TANTE sense 1 a. Also *fig*.

[1926 P. SMITH *Beadle* (1929) 151 What was this that Tan' Coba was saying?] c1967 J. HOBBS in *New S. Afr. Writing* No.4, 68 Tannie Lydia Vermaak, the postmistress, cowered behind her row of maidenhair ferns. 1973 *Weekend Argus* 26 May 4 It was Tannie Swart — a stout, forthright woman in her sixties — who caused a stir at the protest meeting. 1981 *Sunday Times* 28 Feb. 1 He welcomed Oom Albert Basson, his wife, simply known as Tannie, and Oom Pieter Theron and Tannie Johanna. 1983 *Sunday Times* 18 Sept. 3 After a night in the cells Mr van der M— told Mr C— the next day: 'It was I who killed Tannie Christine.' 1988 G. SILBER in *Style* Apr. 41 The ladies who have been preparing the salads for the braai .. try hard to look awestruck ... 'It's a very nice one, Hugh,' says Tannie Marie. 1990 J. ROSENTHAL *Wake Up Singing* 39 'She's nice,' she said indicating the ward sister. 'They call her Tannie Wessels.' 1990 *Weekend Mail* 13 July 9 Tannie SABC is still a vengeful old bag, you know.

3. A common noun.

a. *derog*. A narrow-minded, straight-laced (Afrikaans) woman.

1960 C. HOOPER *Brief Authority* 87 We still have to remind ourselves that we did not actually witness the reaction of a Zeerust tannie to the Spectacle of Sheila among the kindergarten at the Rectory tap. 1968 M. DOYLE *Impala* 97 The Indians .. were .. industrious, secular, sincerely religious. That's more than you could say for this clutch of plump 'tannies', fanning their faces with rugby programmes. 1978 *Voice* 11 Oct. 2 In a certain East Rand town which shall remain nameless, some verkrampte tannies are condemning discos on the grounds that they lead their daughters astray — overlooking the fact that the daughters never walked the straight and narrow in the first place. 1982 *Voice* 23 May, A group of tannies in some dorpie (I can't remember the name) went up in arms against the mini during a particularly bad season for farmers. 1988 P. ANDERSON in *Staffrider* Vol.7 No.1, 44 The tannies In their special church hats, Crying (The dried-up sanctimonious cows). 1990 D. VAN HEERDEN in *Sunday Times* 10 June 8 Most Afrikaner Volkswag tannies won't wear khaki and swastika outfits.

b. TANTE sense 2 b. Cf. AUNTIE sense 1 a.

1961 D. BEE *Children of Yesterday* 157 The old ooms and tannies of Katerina .. tell me I need a wife. 1979 *Sunday Times* 18 Nov. 6 He walked up to the counter and asked the tannie for a cold drink. 1983 *S. Afr. Panorama* Sept. 14 The old President summoned her in from the rain. 'Go around to the back,' he instructed, and the *tannie* (Mrs Kruger) will clean you up.'

c. TANTE sense 2 a.

1986 M. PICARDIE in *S. Gray Market Plays* 84 Tannie used to cook and clean the flat and tell me stories of the old days in the Transvaal and the Great Trek and the Kaffir Wars. 1987 C. SAWYER in *Style* Feb. 90 Extended families complete with tannies and domestic servants.

tan pan var. TAMPAN.

‖**Tante** /'tantə/ *n*. Also **Tant'**, **Tant(a)**, **Tantie**, and with small initial. [Du.] 'Aunt', used particularly of Afrikaner women, and not necessarily of a blood-relation. See also AUNTIE, OOM, TANNIE.

Usu. used to represent the idiom of Afrikaans-speakers.

1. A title, with a name.

a. A respectful and affectionate title for an older woman; TANNIE sense 2.

1841 B. SHAW *Memorials* 288 The children .. were quite delighted with *Tante Eve*, .. as they always addressed her, and she became a great favourite among them. 1870 H.H. DUGMORE *Reminisc. of Albany Settler* 22 Powers of persuasion had to be employed with oude Tanta Nieukerk, as she sat by the ever-simmering brass kettle, or with Oom Dederik, as he puffed away. 1887 F.E. COLENSO Letter. 6 Jan., Irma should have a blue frock too .. & so she shall when Tanta Nelly comes on the scene again. 1914 L.H. BRINKMAN *Breath of Karroo* 14 To the whole countryside she was known as 'Tante Let.' No one would ever have dreamed of calling her 'Mrs. Uijs,' and had anybody done so, she would have put him down as 'uppish.' 1920 R.Y. STORMBERG *Mrs Pieter de Bruyn* 75 It was the jolliest little home-coming, and we had a merry evening at Tante Cornelia's. 1940 F.B. YOUNG *City of Gold* 267 My father's always 'Oom Jan,' though mother calls him the 'ou baas,' and she's *Tante Lisbet*. 1958 [see BOEREBESKUIT]. c1965 [see State of S. Afr. quot. at OOM sense 1 a]. 1977 *Sunday Times* 31 Jul. (Mag. Sect.) 9 The Afrikaner woman in the city has lost the total sense of identity she once had. This included, in the rural life, an ouma in the background, Tant Sannie down the road ready with recipes or advice on childbirth. 1987 J. VAN DER MERWE in *Pretoria News* 15 June 3 Tant Tiena brews a formidable peach.

b. Special Comb. **Tante Sannie** *obs*., an affectionate name given to the wife of President Paul Kruger; also **Tant' Sann**.

1913 M.C. JACKSON *Soldier's Diary* 54 Everything was there: Tante Sannie's best silk-dress, all the clocks .. and fittings untouched. 1924 L. COHEN *Reminisc. of Jhb*. 127 What saved the Reformers was Paul Kruger's horror of blood-guiltiness, and perhaps the beneficent influence of that kindly, homely 'Tante Sanne' — the name by which Mrs. Kruger was affectionately known in Pretoria. 1946 S. CLOETE *Afr. Portraits* 265 The President's wife, 'Tante Sanna,' was a housewife. *Ibid*. 405 Kruger, who waited for his end patiently, more than ready to welcome it. Was not his wife waiting for him? His old Tant' Sann whom he called Ouma?

c. A title for an aunt (a blood relation).

1915 J.K. O'CONNOR *Afrikander Rebellion* 30 Photos of relatives were shown them, with the information: .. this is your Tante Sara and your poor little neef Koos, whom the English murdered. 1969 M. BENSON *At Still Point* (1988) 125 And then there was Tante Annetjie, my father's sister. 1976 A. DELIUS *Border* 320 That wrinkled, garrulous and ancient great aunt 'Ou Tante Gilsa', took my announcement of Sikki's employment with some scepticism. 1986 M. PICARDIE in *S. Gray Market Plays* 84 My unmarried Tant Marie from Turffontein used to come in and look after me if my ma and pa were both at work during [the] school day.

2. A common noun.

a. An aunt (a blood-relation); also used as if a proper name, without an article; TANNIE sense 3 c.

1845 S. DENNISON in D.R. Edgecombe, *Letters of Hannah Dennison*. (1968) 205 How are all the Salem maids pray give my love to Miss Gush and Mrs G and remember me kindly to your good Tant. 1896 M.A. CAREY-HOBSON *At Home in Tvl* 312 It was Colonel and Mrs. Herbert who came to see and thank Tanta. 1944 C.R. PRANCE *Under Blue Roof* 135 Tante had to make her own candles on the farm, scraping and cherishing every scrap of fat. 1961 T. MACDONALD *Tvl Story* 19 It was 'Tante' who did the buying of the corduroys ... To 'Tante' .. was entrusted the purchasing of almost everything she required. She ruled the roost in those days. 1973 E. LEROUX in S. Gray *Writers' Territory* 143 Grandsons and granddaughters from the city in the uniform of the teenager .. bend to kiss Tante, the unknown blood relative, on the down of her upper lip.

b. An Afrikaans woman older than the speaker; TANNIE sense 3 b.

1868 [see NEEF sense 1]. 1872 in A.M.L. Robinson *Sel. Articles from Cape Monthly Mag*. (1978) 283 Our beloved 'tantas'. 1883 O.E.A. SCHREINER *Story of Afr. Farm* 197 The arriving heavy freight of massive Tantes and comely daughters. **1900** B. MITFORD *Aletta* 37 Performing for the benefit of some old-fashioned and highly orthodox old Tanta who deemed all secular music an invention of Satan for the snaring of souls. **1913** J.J. DOKE *Secret City* 67 Here am I, bored to death, and obliged to waste a whole morning for you to bring coffee and rusks to a Dutch tante, and flirt with a great fool like that. **1937** C.R. PRANCE *Under Blue Roof* 63 Each homestead on a circuit has its own special call, with a list of all the bell-signals, so that every Tante on the line knows at once, if, for instance, someone has important things to say to Tant' Emmerentia Platvoetplaats, and the broadcasting of important tidings is simplicity itself. **1943** I. FRACK *S. Afr. Doctor* 120 All the old Tantes present described in the hearing of the patient how this one had died from 'Inflamasie' and how he had looked in his shroud. **1969** *Personality* 5 June, Always there is the contrast between past and present .. the austere black dress of the old tante and the bright miniwear of a visiting granddaughter. [**1990** see KAPPIE KOMMANDO].

3. A respectful form of address to any woman older than the speaker; AUNTIE sense 1 b; TANNIE sense 1.

1878 H.A. ROCHE *On Trek in Tvl* 141 The young folks call their seniors 'Oom' and 'Tanta', uncle and aunt, and the seniors, their juniors 'cousin.' [**1880** see OOM sense 2.] **1900** H. BLORE *Imp. Light Horseman* 162 If a Boer were to be presented at Court he'd offer to shake hands with Queen Victoria, and address her as 'Tante.' All women to whom one wishes to pay respect are called 'Tante', and all men 'Oom.' **1914** L.H. BRINKMAN *Breath of Karroo* 14 The words 'tante', meaning 'aunt,' and 'oom,' meaning 'uncle,' are still used by the young Dutch as a mark of respect when addressing their elders. [**1931** V. SAMPSON *Kom Binne* 263 The older men were usually addressed by the younger as 'Oom' (Uncle) and the older women as 'Tante' (Aunt).] **1940** F.B. YOUNG *City of Gold* 383 'I hear that chap Struben's found gold at Wilgespruit, tanta' he said. **1964** S. CLOETE in C. Millar *16 Stories* 114 He went up to a big fat woman and said, '*Tante* (auntie), this little girl is hungry. Will you give us some food?' **1990** W. SMITH *Golden Fox* 147 'We know that she is a patriot .. but I can't promise anything for Michael, Tantie.' Lothar used the respectful term of address which meant more than simply 'Aunt'.

‖**tarentaal** /ˌtar(ə)nˈtɑːl, ˌtæ-/ *n.* Also **tarantal, tarentall.** Pl. unchanged, **-s**, or ‖**tarentale** /-ˈtɑlə/. [Afk.; acc. to Boshoff & Nienaber (*Afrikaanse Etimologieë*, 1967) ad. S. Afr. Du. *Terra-Natal(vogel)* 'land of Natal (bird)', fr. L. *terra* land + NATAL (+ Du. *vogel* bird), or *Ternataals(ch)e (hoender)* (Du. *hoender* chicken).] Either of two species of guineafowl of the Numididae, *Numida meleagris* or *Guttera pucherani*.

In G.L. Maclean's *Roberts' Birds of Sn Afr.* (1993), the name 'helmeted guineafowl' is used for *N. meleagris*, and 'crested guineafowl' for *G. pucherani*.

[**1822** W.J. BURCHELL *Trav.* I. 364 The missionaries have a few domestic fowls .. and Guinea hens or Pintadoes, which are called by the quaint name of *Jan Tadentaal.* **1827** T. PHILIPPS *Scenes & Occurrences* 99 The dogs .. soon sprung ten guinea fowl, exactly like those now bred in Europe, called here, by the Hottentots *tarentalls.* **1906** W.L. SCLATER *Birds S. Afr.* IV. 228 Crowned Guinea-fowl ... 'Tarantal' of Dutch.] **1912** *Northern News* 27 Aug. (Pettman), It is rather interesting to note that there are two names for the guinea-fowl living side by side, 'Poulepetate' and 'Tarentaal,' apparently of Indian origin. **1948** H.V. MORTON *In Search of S. Afr.* 282 We would walk over the veld watching the guinea-fowl, the tarentaal, pour away into the mealies as if on rails. **1953** U. KRIGE *Dream & Desert* 187 Great Oupa, whose ear was so acute he could hear from the front stoep the call of a tarentaal against the ridge, slowly opened his eyes. **1963** M. KAVANAGH *We Merry Peasants* 127, I have in my fowl run a pair of guinea fowl and I travelled many miles by car to purchase another pair from another country dealer. No sooner had these been introduced to my pair when the trouble began — those 'tarentale' .. obviously derive their origin from South America and not South Africa! **1976** *Het Suid-Western* 8 Sept., The Hunting Season for guinea fowls (tarentaal) will be from April 1 to July 31. **1982** E.M. MACPHAIL *Falling Upstairs* 19 Her father said 'I'll take a couple of tarentaal for the boys before we start back'.

target *n. slang.* [Special sense of general Eng.] Esp. among township activists: something (or someone) considered to be a symbol of apartheid, and against which (or whom) violence or other criminal acts are consequently thought justifiable; esp., any motor vehicle thought to belong to a white-owned company.

1986 F. KHASHANE in *Pace* May 16 Take .. the hijacking of cars. It started .. with youths forcing motorists to transport them to funerals, but .. developed into a .. crime racket when the thugs took over. They branded any car believed to belong to a white company a 'target'. After two Pace cars were hijacked as 'targets', one was burnt and the other was recovered damaged. **1986** [see SKOROKORO]. **1986** F. CHIKANE in Burman & Reynolds *Growing Up* 343 *Siyayinyova* .. is the popular slogan used by the youths when attacking what they call 'targets', meaning the buildings, vehicles, and individuals regarded as symbols of the apartheid regime and its forces. **1988** N. MATHIANE in *Frontline* Apr.-May 12 At the height of 'comrade mania', my sister was stopped by youths for driving a 'target' meaning a car belonging to a white company. It was forcefully taken away from her. **1988** S. MBOKANE in *Fair Lady* 20 July 79 Not all white people are targets (township slang for whites who are targetted for attack) because every person is unique.

tassal /ˈtasal, ˈtasəl/ *n. Obs.* exc. *hist.* Also **tasa(a)l, tassall, tassel.** [Afk. *tasal*, earlier S. Afr. Du. *tasaal*, ad. Pg. *tassalho* a large slice or piece of food.] **a.** BILTONG sense 1. **b.** Dried pickled meat; occas. also *comb.*, **tassalvleis** /-fleɪs/ [Afk., *vleis* (earlier S. Afr. Du. *vleesch*) meat]. In both senses also called TASSELTJIES.

[**1826** A.G. BAIN *Jrnls* (1949) 25 Our first work this morning was to cut up the flesh of the two elands into what is called by the Dutch *Tasaal Vleesch.*] **1891** H.J. DUCKITT *Hilda's 'Where Is It?'* 246 'Tassal' is an old-fashioned up-country way of curing meat in the open air popular with travellers. *a***1905** — in M. Kuttel *Bk of Recipes* (1966) 135 Tassal ... (Now known as biltong). **1913** C. PETTMAN *Africanderisms* 494 *Tassal*, Meat cured and dried in the open air by an old-fashioned method adopted by hunters and travellers up country. **1945** N. DEVITT *People & Places* 16 Biltong, or, as the old Cape Dutch people called it, 'tassal'. **1971** L.G. GREEN *Taste of S.-Easter* 90, I believe Van Riebeeck's pickled meat recipe tasaalvleis is still followed in the country. **1979** [see TASSELTJIES].

tasseltjies /ˈtas(ə)lkis/ *n.* Also **tassalletjies** /taˈsaləkis/. [Afk., *tassal* (see prec.) + -IE + pl. -*s*.] TASSAL.

1955 L.G. GREEN *Karoo* 104 There is a .. dish called tassalletjies which is made differently in almost every Cape district. I place it in the biltong class because some cooks dry the meat in the wind after it has been laid in vinegar. The strips of preserved meat hang from the rafters in the loft, like biltong, until they are required. Then they are grilled on the coals. **1979** HEARD & FAULL *Our Best Trad. Recipes* 55 An exclusively South African product is .. biltong — the same word in English and Afrikaans, although in old books tassel or tasseltjies is used (from the Portuguese tassalho); but strictly speaking tasseltjies means pickled meats.

Tassies /ˈtæsiːz, ˈta-/ *n. colloq.* Shortened form of the proprietory names of any of several red wines, particularly *Tassenberg*, but also *Taskelder* and *Tasheimer*; applied loosely to other popular red wines (see quots 1981 and 1983). Also *attrib.*

All the proprietory names include the name of Adam Tas, a burgher arrested by the Governor in 1706 for circulating a petition.

1978 *Darling* 19 July, ½ bottle good red wine (Tassies will do). **1979** *Capetonian* July 19 South Africans can tart up their Tassies during cold Boland winters by making mulled wine or hot wine punches. **1981** *S. Afr. Digest* 31 July 12 *Tassies*, as it is affectionately known, is back with its old label. A combination of the names of Adam Tas and Papegaaiberg, *Tassenberg* has become a legend in its own time ... SFW has decided to bring back *Tassies* in its old livery. **1981** *Sunday Times* 13 Dec. (Mag. Sect.) 1 They only appear at lunch time to consume their entire weight in boerewors and potato salad. They down another couple of beers, while their wives drink Tassies out of plastic mugs. **1983** D. HUGHES et al. *Complete Bk of S. Afr. Wine*, In other wine ranges the name of Adam Tas is remembered .. as Tasheimer, Oom Tas, Taskelder & Tassenberg, to the extend that 'Tassies' has gone into the vernacular. [**1987** see OBIES.] **1989** [see SAFARI]. **1990** S. NICHOLS in *Style* Nov. 82 Cheap and cheerful parties, with Tassies and lasagne, limp salad and loud music, .. fondly remembered by everyone over 40. **1993** D. BIGGS in *Rhodent* 23 Have you ever heard a plonk drinker recommending a particular vintage of Tassies or Taverna? *Ibid.* 24 *Mature*, What an old Tassies drinker likes to think he is.

‖**tata** /ˈtaːta/ *n.* Also **tat', utata.** [Xhosa *utata.*] Esp. among speakers of Xhosa: 'father', 'daddy'. Cf. BABA *n.*[2]

a. A respectful form of address to a father, a paternal uncle, or any older man.

1963 WILSON & MAFEJE *Langa* 87 A girl will use *tata*, the equivalent of the more familiar 'daddy', rather than 'father', and *tata* is used in the extended sense by both men and women, for father's brothers and senior men, but not *bawo* as it was traditionally. *Ibid.* 88 Others use *tata*, whereas *bawo* used to be a common form of address to an elderly man. **1976** R.L. PETENI *Hill of Fools* 18 'You are not telling us the story clearly, Zuziwe,' interrupted her father. 'Try to give us a detailed account of the assault.' 'Excuse me, tata, my mind is confused.' **1979** F. DIKE *First S. African* 16 Hayi tata I'm reading the paper and I clean forgot that mama should have been home long ago. **1987** N. MATHIANE in *Frontline* Apr. 19 Winnie halts the noise by calling the old man to order, saying once more in a very soft manner, 'Tata, you must never call these children a gang'. **1992** J. MYBURGH in *Weekend Argus* 22 Feb. 5 They call him 'Tata' (Xhosa for father), but when he 'makes us cross, we call him Comrade President'.

b. A respectful form of reference to a father or an older man; also used before a name, as a title, sometimes in the construction **tata-ka-**, 'father of'.

1973 A.C. JORDAN in *Best of S. Afr. Short Stories* (1991) 37 No! We can't do that. *Tata* will beat us! **1976** R.L. PETENI *Hill of Fools* 29 'Where's your father? And where's Duma?' 'We left them at tata Dakada's home.' **1977** *Daily Dispatch* 7 Oct. (Indaba) 1 Tata (Mr. Motau) stood up and as he got to the steps leading to the inside room a man in camouflage uniform got through the window ... 'The men stood there as the dog dragged Tata across the floor.' **1979** D. SMUTS (tr. *E. Joubert's Swerfjare van Poppie Nongena*) in *Fair Lady* 9 May 112 All night long they prayed and sang hymns and comforted her for the death of tata-ka-Bonsile. **1980** E. JOUBERT *Poppie Nongena* 216 My tata let me know that he is waiting for me; he is old now. **1987** M. MOSOTHO in *Tribute* Feb.-Mar. 16 There was this American senator .. who saw *utata*. He was shocked when he met him and tried to introduce himself only to find that my father knew him. **1990** *City Press* 11 Mar. 7 Mangope .. recently referred sarcastically to bo-Tat'uMandela, Tat'uSisulu etc, as 'Mabinditi', a derogatory name for old convicts.

Taung /taʊŋ/ *n.* [Sotho and seTswana, 'place of the lion', *tau* lion + locative suffix *-ng*.]

1. Pl. unchanged, or **Bataung** [see BA-]. Usu. in *pl.*: Collectively, the members of a Tswana clan of the Orange Free State and Lesotho. Also *attrib.* See also TSWANA sense 2 a.

1905 W.H. TOOKE in Flint & Gilchrist *Science in S. Afr.* 92 The ba-Taung or 'lion' people .. are now practically dispersed, a small remnant still remaining in Herschel ... The ba-Tlapi or fish-folk under Mahura, Manloroane and his son Molala, are now in the Taung Reserve. **1909** G.Y. LAGDEN *Basutos* I. 20 The Bataung were more given to pastoral habits than to fighting and were notorious for border-thieving, a propensity which led them and the Basuto in later years into serious trouble with other tribes as well as with the Boers who became their neighbours in the Orange Free State. **1951** W.S. MATSIE in *Drum* Apr. 12 Other tribes began to spring up in the Country either by breaking away from the older and larger tribes or by coming into the sheltered safety of Basutoland from the troubled world outside. Thus the Bafarutse, Bataung, .. and the Makhoakhoa came about. **1970** J. WALTON in *Std Encycl. of Sn Afr.* II. 194 Certain tribes, such as the Tlokwa in the north, the Bataung between Mohale's Hoek and Mafeteng .. have continued to maintain their tribal identity. **1986** P. MAYLAM *Hist. of Afr. People* 56 The Taung were another southern Sotho community to gain prominence during the *difaqane*. Their ruler, Moletsane, emerged as one of the most powerful Sotho leaders during the early 1820s ... In the early years of the *difaqane* the Taung moved across the Vaal and became engaged in attacks on various Tswana chiefdoms, notably the Seleka-Rolong.

2. Also **Taungs**. [The name of a town.] Usu. *attrib.*, esp. in the phrr. ***Taung baby, - child, - skull***, etc., designating the remains of a fossil hominid discovered at Taung in the northern Cape Province in 1924.

1925 *Nature* 28 Mar. 469 A certain amount of criticism has been levelled at Prof. Dart's nomenclature of the Taungs skull. It is generally felt that the name Australopithecus is an unpleasing hybrid as well as etymologically incorrect. **1931** A. KEITH *New Discoveries Antiquity Man* 61 How does the brain development of the Taungs skull fit into the human scheme of growth? **1957** K.P. OAKLEY in *Third Pan-African Congress on Prehistory* 156 The Taung skull, generally regarded as the oldest of the known Australopithecines, belongs .. to a dry period following a pluvial phase. **1966** F.C. HOWELL *Early Man* 49 The Taung baby is hominoid rather than ape-like .. Its jaws are shorter and more lightly made than those of an ape, and its skull lacks the characteristic bony ridges that denote large muscles. **1974** *E. Prov. Herald* 8 Aug. 10 Boskop man was alive and well and living in southern Africa more than 20 000 years ago but was a youngster when compared .. in particular the Taung child discovered in 1924. **1989** *Reader's Digest Illust. Hist.* 15 The Taung baby, so named because the state of development of its teeth revealed that it had died at the age of three or four years, had walked upright, almost like man. **1990** on TV1, 20 July (Origins), What did surprise Dart was the reaction of the scientific community to his claim that Taung was an ancestor.

tausa /ˈtaʊzə, ˈtɔːzə/ *n. Prison slang.* Also **tauza**. [Etym. unknown; perh. rel. to Zulu *thosa* fry, toss, alluding to the jumping actions of the prisoners.] The full body inspection which is imposed upon prisoners to detect the hiding of forbidden objects or substances; a sequence of actions performed by prisoners during this inspection (see quot. 1954). Also *attrib.*

1954 A. MAIMANE in *Drum* Mar., Prisoners are made to strip naked and then to jump up in the air, clapping their hands, opening their mouths, and then turning around. That is known as *Tausa* or as the *Zulu dance*. **1956** A. SAMPSON *Drum* 175 We heard many stories of beatings, bad food, filthy cells, and a humiliating 'tausa dance' which prisoners performed naked when they were searched for tobacco. **1971** *Drum* Apr. 34 (*caption*) The late Henry Nxumalo went to jail to investigate jail conditions and we carried a photograph — which is no longer permitted — of the 'tauza'. **1991** O. MUSI in *Drum* Dec. (Then and Now) 56 The notorious 'tausa' in the prisons whereby convicts were stripped naked and anally inspected for contraband like dagga.

tausa /ˈtaʊzə, ˈtɔːzə/ *v. intrans.* [As prec.] To perform a 'dance' as required of prisoners during a full body inspection.

1954 H. NXUMALO in J. Crwys-Williams *S. Afr. Despatches* (1989) 316 We returned to the jail at 4. We were ordered to undress and 'tausa,' a common routine of undressing prisoners when they return from work searching their clothes, their mouths, armpits and rectum for hidden articles. **1965** R.H.L. STRACHAN in *Rand Daily Mail* 30 June 4, I was sent first to the Port Elizabeth North End Prison ... Searching was most undignified. The man puts his hand anywhere on your body. At times I was made to 'tausa'.

tavern *n.* [Special senses of general Eng. *tavern* inn.]

1. ***Tavern of the Seas***, or occas. ***Tavern of the East***: Cape Town, so called because of its traditional role as a refreshment-station for sailors on their voyages to and from the East; occas., District Six, one of the municipal districts of Cape Town.

1920 K.M. JEFFREYS tr. *Memorandum of Commissary J.A. de Mist* 168 The Cape was nothing more than 'The Tavern of the East,' on the 'Highway of the Sea'. *Ibid.* 196 All of them are equally interested in retaining the right to refresh themselves at this tavern of the high seas. **1920** R. JUTA *Tavern* 28 Those rich merchants of the Tavern of the Seas, the Receivers of the host of the East, the Harbour of the Flotsam and Jetsam of the two great Oceans. **1947** L.G. GREEN *Tavern of Seas* 21 She was white and dignified with her awnings spread under the South African sun and her anchor down in the mud of the 'Tavern of the Seas'. **1955** A. DELIUS *Young Trav.* 86 Cape Town is supposed to be more interested in good cooking than anywhere else in the Union ... It was known as the Tavern of the Seas once. Sailors used to drop in here for a change from the salt-pork and maggots. **1959** F.G. BUTLER in *Bk of S. Afr. Verse* (1963) 141 English, Dutch and Portuguese Sick of biscuits and sodden cheese Put in at the Tavern of the Seas. [*Note*] The Tavern of the Seas: nickname for Cape Town. **1964** L.G. GREEN *Old Men Say* 15 A coffee house for the business men who sold meat and vegetables to the ship that called at the 'Tavern of the Seas.' **1971** *Personality* 5 Mar. 21 The Cape of Good Hope was known internationally in the early days as the Tavern of the Seas ... Jan van Riebeeck's station had always been intended as a refreshment station and what better refreshment could a sailor find than liquor? **1989** *Reader's Digest Illust. Hist.* 60 The tavern of the seas ... The basis of Cape Town's economy was its situation between two 'trade routes': that is, agricultural produce was brought from the rural interior and sold to ships in port. **1990** *Staffrider* Vol.9 No.1, 44 District Six, the slum known to white Capetonians somewhat romantically as the Tavern of the Seven Seas. **1990** *Light Years* Feb. 1 Cape Town is becoming once again the Tavern of the Seas. **1992** *Natal Witness* 4 Jan. 2 Cape Town, known to many seafarers as the tavern of the seas, will host the third stopover of a new round-the-world yacht race in March next year.

2. A legal, licensed SHEBEEN (sense 1). Also *attrib.*

1981 *Frontline* May 12 The shebeeners organisation, which had its genesis a few years before, changed its name to the Soweto Tavern Association ... (Its members opted for 'tavern' instead of 'shebeen' to show their willingness to move away from illegality and, .. to add 'some tone'). **1985** *Probe* July 13 If you had a licence you ran a tavern and if not you belonged to the old days of prohibition and remained a shebeen. But tavern licences have to be given back .. for renewal. **1987** S. MOLRATH in *City Press* 15 Feb. 3 'Mississippi' and 'Madraai', longtime 'illegal' shebeen kings, were recently given 'conditional authority' by the Liquor Board to open taverns and sell liquor on their premises. **1990** [see CAFÉ DE MOVE-ON].

Hence (sense 2) **taverner** *n.*, the proprietor of a tavern; also called SHEBEENER.

1984 *City Press* 17 June, The National Taverners' Association has .. said they will close shebeens on this historic day [*sc.* June 16]. **1987** P. DEVEREUX in *Style* Mar. 24 Super-consultant Colin Hall .. addressed the National Taverners Association (shebeeners) in 1982 with the opening: 'Mr President, Mr Chairman, Mr Master of Ceremonies, distinguished guests, hoodlums, crooks and fellow spivs'. **1989** S. KUMALO in *City Press* 19 Feb. 9 A local taverner told *City Press* .. 'since these conservatives took over the town, we have decided to hit back in the only legal way we can'. **1990** *Weekly Mail* 28 Sept. 9 The loudest complaints were from taverners concerned about the fortune their shebeens will lose when customers have to be home by 9pm.

taxi *n.* [Special sense of general Eng. *taxi* a vehicle which transports passengers to a requested destination for a metered fare (in which sense the word is also used in S. Afr. Eng.).]

1. Often with defining words, as ***black taxi, kombi taxi, minibus taxi***, to distinguish this type of vehicle from a metered taxi: a light vehicle, now usu. a sixteen-seater minibus, which transports passengers on a fixed route for a set fare (as does a bus), but does not operate to a time-table; *kombi taxi*, see KOMBI sense 2; KWELA-KWELA sense 2. Also *attrib.* See also MARY DECKER sense b, SABTA, ZOLA BUDD sense b.

Such taxis operate on both urban and long-distance routes. This kind of service was probably introduced in the 1950s; until the late 1970s the vehicle used was normally a large motor car, and relatively few were in service. Estimates now put the number of taxis at anywhere between 50 000 and 100 000.

1973 *E. Prov. Herald* 27 Mar. 1 Many of the Black spectators arrived two hours before the match — brought in by a massive convoy of hired buses and pirate taxis. **1983** *Commission of Inquiry into Bus Passenger Transport* (RP50–1983) 24 The 'taxi industry' .. consists of the ordinary legal taxi .. , the legal kombi-type taxi that is normally used as a minibus and the pirate taxi that is in most cases a kombi-type of vehicle and used illegally. *Ibid.* 25 In the Soweto area, 694 ordinary sedan cars and 881 eight-seater vehicles are .. registered as taxis. In addition, 181 cars and 164 kombi-type vehicles are registered for use in .. Johannesburg and Soweto ... The number of unauthorized 'taxis' operating in these areas is estimated to be 3 600 to 4 000. **1984** *Frontline* Mar. 13 Rival wings of the Black Taxi Association fight each other in court. **1987** *Christian Science Monitor* (U.S.A.) 10 Mar. 12 Each morning .. about 500,000 Sowetans board trains, buses, or one of some 4,000 privately run mini-bus 'taxis' into Johannesburg. **1987** *Personality* 30 Sept. 39 Experts .. estimate that about 80 percent of all minibus taxis are run by pirate operators. **1989** A. DONALDSON in *Style* Aug. 98 By mid-1988 it was widely held that the booming black taxi business had saved the country's motor industry ... The industry .. is huge: Investment in black taxis is estimated at R3 000-million ... Turnover is said to be around R2 000-million a year. And you can probably double that figure if you include pirate taxis. **1990** C. MCCAUL *No Easy Ride* p.v, Some 625 000 African commuters travel to work in taxis every day.

2. *comb.* **taxi war**, a violent feud between groups of minibus-taxi operators over the right to use a taxi route or taxi rank.

1979 *Daily Dispatch* 6 Apr. 1 Taxi war blamed after man in mask kills ... Taxi owner .. could have been shot dead in a new taxi war ... A war is raging between licensed taxi drivers and pirate taxis. Trouble is believed to have flared when licensed drivers decided to operate between Mdantsane and King William's Town and in the rural areas in the Zwelitsha district. Pirate taxis have been operating on the same route. **1990** M. MALUNGA in *Weekly Mail* 8 June 9 The spate of taxi wars, in which dozens of people have been killed, is rooted in work conditions, say drivers. **1991** M. MBATHA in *Pace* Feb. 39 In February and March 1990, a taxi war in Katlehong on the East rand enveloped the whole community in factional violence, leaving up to 50 people dead ... During

1988 and 1989 there were also serious taxi wars in Alexandra ... 10 people died in clashes between the Alexandra Taxi Association and a rival taxi group. **1992** M. MTSHEKETSHE in *South* 27 Feb. 3 The search for a solution to the Western Cape's tragic taxi war has been widened.

taybosch var. TAAIBOS.

taylor bird var. TAILOR BIRD.

TBVC *n. hist.* Also **TVBC**. [Initial letters of *Transkei, Bophuthatswana, Venda*, and *Ciskei*, in the order in which they became 'independent'.] A collective name for the former 'independent' black states of Transkei, Bophuthatswana, Venda, and Ciskei, which were created out of South African territory. Usu. *attrib.*, often in the phr. ***TBVC state***. See also HOMELAND sense 1, INDEPENDENT.

1985 *Cape Times* 12 Sept., Citizens of the TBVC countries — Transkei, Bophuthatswana, Ciskei and Venda — are to have their South African citizenship restored. **1986** *Rhodeo* (Rhodes Univ.) May 19 Under the Aliens' Act, people from the TVBC states can be arrested as 'illegal foreigners' if attempting to settle in the republic. **1987** J. DEACON in *S. Afr. Panorama* July 14 Since the bank is strictly apolitical its activities are being studied with interest by countries outside the SATBVC ambit like Lesotho, Swaziland and Malawi. **1987** W.R. DOERNER in *Time* 12 Oct. 10 The nominally independent homelands — Transkei, Venda, Bophuthatswana and Ciskei — are collectively known in South Africa as the TVBC states. **1988** *E. Prov. Herald* 10 Mar. 1 The financial state of the 'independent' TBVC states is now so disastrous that the Government has had to intervene, guaranteeing loans from commercial banks. **1990** *Evening Post* 2 Feb. 3 There had recently been an 'interesting debate' about whether the TBVC countries should be re-incorporated into South Africa. **1992** *Weekend Post* 17 Oct. 3 Come and stay in sunny TBVC. **1993** *Star* 22 July 1 Mechanisms are already in place to integrate the ANC military wing, TBVC state armies, and Inkatha and Afrikaner Weerstandsbeweging units into the SA Defence Force.

tcherrie var. CHERRY.

Tea Meeting *n. phr. Hist.*

a. A social gathering of the members of a church or other organization, esp. a gathering organized for fund-raising purposes.

1842 J. COLLETT Diary. II. 24 Feb., Remained .. behind to attend Tea Meeting. **1844** W. HOWARD Note Book. 8 Feb., Annual Tea Meeting of the Port Elizabeth Total Abstinence Society. **1870** J. COLLETT Diary. 24 Oct., Attended Tea Meeting at the opening of New School Room. **1980** D.B. COPLAN Urbanization of African Performing Arts. 175 The term 'tea-meeting' originated with the church-oriented social affairs of British settlers in the eastern Cape.

b. A party or other social occasion, esp. an all-night entertainment held in a township.

[**1900** P. HARGREAVES in W.G. Mills, Role of African Clergy in Reorientation of Xhosa Society. (1975) 75 The young people are giving increased trouble by the vices and follies they run after with greediness. They are introducing night Tea-parties under the pretence of helping Church Funds.] **1980** D.B. COPLAN Urbanization of African Performing Arts. 175 In the *Cape Standard* for January 11, 1866 .. a White observer praised an African church choir performance in Graaff-Reinet ... He notes that while all attending were not converts, they all enjoyed the 'tea-meeting'. During the latter third of the 19th century, both rural and urban church communities held tea-meetings on Saturday nights, sponsored in rotation by individual members of the church women's group (*manyano*). Liquor was not served ... All-night tea-meetings were extremely popular among Cape Africans at the turn of the century ... Tea-meetings characterized early urbanization, involving a fusion of economic and social activities parallel to that involved in traditional work-for-beer parties. *Ibid.* 176 Government officials and missionaries were disturbed by the expansion of 'tea-meetings' to cover a variety of African entertainments in the towns.

tear /tɪə/ *n.* In the phr. ***tears of the Queen***, also ***Queen's tears*** [tr. Zulu *izinyembezi sikakhwini* tears of the Queen (perh. an allusion to British losses during the wars with the Zulus)], strong drink, usu. gin or brandy.

1949 O. WALKER *Proud Zulu* (1951) 116 He gave them glasses of gin (which the Zulus called 'the queen's tears'), for it was a chilly night. **1956** J. CHATTERTON *Return of Drums* 133 He waddled forward unsteadily, his big belly protruding before him. 'He is drunk, Nkosana,' Silas whispered. 'He has been drinking "The Tears of the Queen"!' **1970** H. KUPER *Witch in my Heart* 39 Better give him Tears of the Queen of England. Have you tasted it yet boy? *Ibid.* 40 Tears of the Queen of England! The White people call it brandy. It looks like golden water and after half a jack you are sweet all over. **1979** C. ENDFIELD *Zulu Dawn* 88 The bugler boy handed over the rectangular gin bottle — the drink the Zulus called the Queen's tears. **1986** S. HENDERSON in *Optima* Vol.34 No.4, 198 A giant Swiss mercenary, an orphan, Corporal Schiess, who, *faute de mieux*, had taken the 'Queen's shilling', had drunk of the 'Queen's tears'.

tearoom *n.* Also **T-room**. [Special sense of general Eng. *tearoom* a room in which tea is served.]

1. CAFÉ.

1951 A. GORDON-BROWN *Yr Bk & Guide to Sn Afr.* 607 *Alicedale*, .. Hotel, white population 148, is an important railway junction with Tea Room. **1951** *Natal Mercury* 5 Apr. 2 A beautifully fitted up Tearoom and General Dealer on main road. **1959** G. & N. GORDON tr. *F.A. Venter's Dark Pilgrim* 134 The police have often visited him here, but on the surface there is nothing wrong with a 'tea room'. **1963** M.G. MCCOY *Informant, Port Elizabeth* It's a nice place for a short visit, they've got ablution blocks now, and lots of taps and bins and braai places .., plus a tearoom for odd stores. **1972** BEETON & DORNER in *Eng. Usage in Sn Afr.* Vol.3 No.1, 32 Tearoom in G[reat] B[ritain] is a *room* where tea is served, whereas in S. Afr. it can be the section set aside for serving light refreshments in a café or Greek shop wh[ich] also sells groceries, confectionery, etc. **1972** *Evening Post* 10 June 9 The railway station was at the end of the main street with a restaurant-cum-tea room next door. **1976** *Personality* 22 Feb. (TV & Radio) 6, I told the girl in our local tearoom I wanted 40 cigarettes of a brand I named. **1977** *Daily Dispatch* 19 Nov. 8 When I was a girl of 17, the crowd in the office were doing their nuts about a fortune teller who was operating from a tearoom nearby. (Shows how long ago it was, who's ever heard of a tearoom in this generation?) **1987** *E. Prov. Herald* 3 Jan. 1 They started chanting ANC songs before ransacking a tea-room. **1990** R. GOOL *Cape Town Coolie* 30 He entered the tea-room, really an old-fashioned *winkel*.

2. *comb.* **tearoom bio(scope)**, **tearoom cinema**: BIO-CAFÉ.

1976 V. ROSENBERG *Sunflower* 29 Herman also whiled away many hours at the local **T-room bioscopes**. **1977** *Sunday Times* 2 Oct. (TV Times) 9 Most of the Saturday evening films .. would hardly have made it on the **tea room bio** circuit. **1978** T. OLSEN in *Cape Times* 21 July 1 An Epping schoolboy .. went into a coma from a suspected drug overdose in a City **tearoom cinema** yesterday.

tea-water *n. obs.* [Calque formed on Afk. *tee-water* tea, transf. sense of Du. *theewater* water for tea.] An infusion of tea.

Also found (but only rarely) in obs. *Scot. Eng.* and *Brit. Eng.* dial. usage.

1827 T. PHILIPPS *Scenes & Occurrences* 19 The waggons had all outspanned; the boors were quietly taking their favourite beverage, tea-water as they call it, and their Hottentots were sitting round the fire. **1827** G. THOMPSON *Trav.* I. 83 The mistress of the house, with a tea-urn and chafing-dish before her, dealing out every now and then *tea-water*, or coffee, and elevating her sharp shrill voice occasionally to keeep the dilatory slaves and Hottentots at their duty. **1838** J.E. ALEXANDER *Exped. into Int.* II. 120 Every one was on his feet in a moment; the meat dish was upset, and the precious 'tea-water' spilt in the sand, in the hurry to scramble up the rocks. **1852** H. WARD *Jasper Lyle* 10 One, less shy than the rest, came forward and ventured to offer the 'tea-water'. *a***1862** J. AYLIFF *Jrnl of 'Harry Hastings'* (1963) 77 You go in again when the farmer's wife sends you bason of tea (or they call it 'tea-water'). **1883** M.A. CAREY-HOBSON *Farm in Karoo* 182 The old Juffrouw was pouring out some tea at a small side-table — 'tea-water' she called it. [**1902** H.J. DUCKITT *Hilda's Diary of Cape Hsekeeper* 190 The quaint little 'Kommitje Tee-water' (little cup of tea), with its pink-and-white flower that looks as though it were made of china.] **1912** *E. London Dispatch* 26 July 6 Making sure the sheep-tail fat and tea-water had not been forgotton, lit his pipe, mounted, and set off with a light heart upon a journey of hundreds of miles. **1937** [see BRANDEWYN sense 1].

Teba /ˈteːbə/ *n.* Also **TEBA**. [Initial letters of *The Employment Bureau of Africa*, so named in 1977 in order to create an acronym corresponding with *KwaTeba*, a long-standing nickname for the NRC (Native Recruiting Corporation) among speakers of the Nguni languages, formed on the common Nguni locative prefix *kwa-* the place of + *Teba* ad. *Taberer* (H.M. *Taberer* was manager of the NRC from its establishment until his death in 1932).] An agency which recruits labour for the mining industry and co-ordinates the payment of migrant workers' salaries to their families; WENELA sense b.

Formed in 1977 by the merger of the Native Recruiting Corporation (see N.R.C. *n.*[1]) and the WNLA.

1947 *Monitor* 21 Mar. 21 A great organization exists, the Native Recruiting Corporation, known to the Africans as 'Kwa Teba' (after H. M. Taberer, who was for many years its chief organiser). This body acts under the control of the Chamber of Mines. **1978** *Survey of Race Rel.* (S.A.I.R.R.) 259 As from January 1, 1977, WENELA and the Native Recruiting Corporation merged to form the Employment Bureau of Africa Ltd. (TEBA). Approximately R100m was paid out in savings or remittances by TEBA in home territories during the year. **1980** M. LIPTON in *Optima* Vol.29 No.2, 176 The compilation of a skills register by TEBA would aid re-absorption into jobs at home. **1991** *S. Afr. Panorama* Jan.-Feb. 32 The Chamber of Mines .. accounts for most of the gold, uranium, coal, platinum and diamonds produced. Its 'family' includes an employment bureau, Teba.

Tebele var. MATABELE.

tebello /teˈbe(ː)lɔ/ *n.* [fr. Tswana *tebeló* a watching.] Among speakers of the Sintu (Bantu) languages: a wake. Also *attrib.*

1963 B. MODISANE *Blame Me on Hist.* (1986) 28 They sat around the room in a circle, night and day, and sang through the requiem hymnals, the sad songs of the tebello, the wake, which most of the mourners knew off by heart. **1974** *Drum* 8 July 58 He tells me that it is Friday which is a big day for tebellos in this man's town. Now he tells me he is sad on account none of his tebello contacts has got in touch with him to tell him at what place a tebello will be taking place. **1985** *Voice* 1 Apr. 2 Next time you want to .. hold a 'tebello' .. better have a quiet friendly word with your neighbour first.

technikon /ˈteknikɒn/ *n.* Also **technicon**, and with initial capital. [Noun formed on neut. of Gk *technikos* pertaining to skills.] Any of several institutions offering technical and vocational education at a tertiary level. Also *attrib.*

In forming the name of a particular institution, 'Technikon' is placed either before or after a proper name, e.g. 'Technikon Witwatersrand', 'Technikon Natal', 'Cape Technikon'. Formerly known as 'College for Advanced Technical Education' (see CATE).

1979 *Evening Post* 10 May 2 Professor Daniel P. Veldman, .. who has been a member of the Technikon council for about six years, will take over as director of the Technikon. **1979** *Sunday Times* 27 May (Business Times) 22 (*advt*) Technikon Natal formerly Natal College for Advanced Technical Education. *Ibid.* Closing date for Applications ... Cape Technikon. **1980** *Impact* Aug. 4 Mr Oppenheimer said all universities, technikons and training colleges should be opened on proper conditions to students of all races. **1983** *S. Afr. 1983: Off. Yrbk* (Dept of Foreign Affairs & Info.) 686 The technikons are autonomous institutions and provide training at tertiary or post-Senior Certificate level. The training, which involves the integration of theory and practice, is offered parallel to but separate from that offered by universities. **1983** G.V.N. VILJOEN in *Hansard* 8 Aug. 10773 We shall provide for the inclusion of spokesmen for Black universities and Black technikons on the Universities and Technikons Advisory Council. **1983** [see CATE]. **1992** *New Nation* 7 Aug. 9 Part of the role of universities .. will be to debunk the myth that technikon education is inferior to university education. **1992** *Pace* Sept. 66 A technikon education is essentially a co-operative education programme between the technikon, on one hand, and trade, industry and commerce on the other ... Technikon qualifications are held in high regard by employers.

teckie var. TACKIE.

tecoma /tə'kəʊmə/ *n.* [A former generic name of the plant (see quot. 1973), fr. modern L. (Jussieu 1789), ad. Aztec *tecomaxochitl*, mistakenly supposed by Jussieu to be the name of a species of the genus to which he gave this name (but really the native name of *Solandra guttata* of the Solanaceae).] The indigenous shrub *Tecomaria capensis* of the Bignoniaceae, bearing yellow or orange honeysuckle-like blooms, and commonly used as a hedge-plant; *Cape honeysuckle, - trumpet flower*, see CAPE sense 2 a. Also *attrib.*

1928 F.C. SLATER *Sel. Poems* (1947) 50 Now in dim woods, tecoma Her tapers lights, Like veld-fires twinkling nightly On distant heights. [*Note*] Native flowering shrub. **1956** *Cape Times* 1 Mar. 8 Manitoka and tecoma hedges. **1966** C.A. SMITH *Common Names* 458 *Tecoma, Tecomaria capensis* ... The vernacular name is an old generic name by which the species is known in gardens and which is transferred to the wild plants. [**1973** M.R. LEVYNS in *Std Encycl. of Sn Afr.* IX. 25 The Cape honeysuckle (*Tecomaria capensis*) .. has smaller flowers ... At one time it was included in the American genus *Tecoma*, but for many years it has been placed in a separate genus *Tecomaria*.] **1987** *E. Prov. Herald* 6 June 6 Indigenous plants are hard to get, excepting easy and popular things like agapanthus, strelitzia, vygies, and tecoma. **1987** M. POLAND *Train to Doringbult* 123 A picket fence, a hedge of *tecoma*, so choked with smoke it is dying slowly over years.

teegoedbalie see BALIE sense b.

tegwaan /'tegwɑːn/ *n.* Also **tegwan(e)**, **tegwani**, **t(h)ekwane**, **U-Tekwan**. [Xhosa and Zulu *uthekwane*.] The HAMMERKOP, *Scopus umbretta*.

1937 C. BIRKBY *Zulu Journey* 134 The friendly *tegwane* knows perfectly well that the Zulus think him *mtagati*; it brings bad luck on a hunter to kill one. [**1939** *Outspan* 26 May 84 While the Bantu trust and hold faith in various animals, there are certain birds which to them are abhorrent. Among these is the U-Tekwan, hammer-headed shadow bird .. the hammerkop.] **1952** H. KLEIN *Land of Silver Mist* 30 John .. clutched my arm ... 'Go careful baas, tegwaan.' And there, flying down the road in front of the car, was a tegwaan. Determined to disprove John's theory once and for all, I drove with exceptional care. **1958** R. COLLINS *Impassioned Wind* 48 A large dark bird, probably a hamerkop, flared upwards .. and drifted away into the night. 'There's a tegwaan' observed Jessica, using the Zulu name. **1959** L. LONGMORE *Dispossessed* 229 He believes that if he destroys the nest of *thekwane* he would bring death upon himself. *Thekwane*, on finding his nest destroyed, would become so cross that he would express his wrath by fetching lightning for his destruction. [**1967** J.A. BROSTER *Red Blanket Valley* 54 In hushed voices they told me of a mysterious bird which feeds on frogs and tadpoles. It has great powers of magic, but if left alone is harmless. In Xhosa it is called *u-thekwane*, in English, Hammerhead or Umber.] **1967** J. DRUMMOND *Saboteurs* 51 You can't put a marriage together all anyhow, like a Tegwan's nest. This is no marriage you have here, it's a mess. **1968** R. GRIFFITHS *Man of River* 134, I am Tegwani, the hammerkop .. the brown river bird, whose nest is so strong that only an axe or fire can harm it. **1987** M. POLAND *Train to Doringbult* 14 He knew *Thekwane*, the gaunt-winged *hamerkop*, relic of a pterodactyl, an ancient bird that wades in *vleis* and sees the destinies of men reflected from the sky. **1990** *Afr. Wildlife* Vol.44 No.5, 302 Hamerkops, better known as tegwaans in our home.

Tegwini /te'gwiːn(i)/ *n. colloq.* Also **Tegwen**, **Tegwin**. [ad. Zulu *eThekwini* in, to, or from Durban, lit. 'at the bay' (locative form of *itheku* enclosed bay, harbour).] The city of DURBAN; see also quot. 1978.

1898 B. MITFORD *Induna's Wife* 154 'I have a mind to send to the white people at Tegwini,' said the King. 'They are my friends, but not this new race. It may be that they will aid me to get rid of these Amabuna.' [*Note*] Durban. Lit.: 'The Bay.' **1928** N. DEVITT *Blue Lizard* 171 They reached the town (which he had heard certain Zulus .. call 'Tegwin'). **1968** K. MCMAGH *Dinner of Herbs* 101 So I drink ... tell him many stories. He not been to Tegwen (Durban) ... never see the sea ... the big ships and the horses that the white men like to make run races. **1978** L. BARNES in *The 1820* Vol.51 No.12, 19 Many Zulu words have crept into South African Indian English ... *Tegwini*, the Zulu name for Durban, is used in the general sense of 'town', *I'm going to Tegwini* means I'm going to town or the central part of Durban, although it can sometimes mean the Market area. **1992** R. MESTHRIE *Lexicon of S. Afr. Indian Eng.* 119 *Tegwin*, .. Durban. Also S[outh] A[frican] E[nglish] slang.

tekkie var. TACKIE.

Tembookie, -buki varr. TAMBOOKIE.

Tembu /'te(ː)mbuː/ *n.* and *adj.* Also **Tambo**, **Tembé**, **Tembo(o)**, **Thembu**, **Tembou**, **Tymbæ**. Pl. unchanged, **-s**, **Aba-**, **Ama-**, or occas. **Amatembus**. [Xhosa *Thembu*. For an explanation of pl. forms, see AMA-.]

A. *n.*

1.a. A member of a Xhosa-speaking people which moved southwards and westwards from what is now KwaZulu-Natal (probably during the 16th century), and became established in present-day *Tembuland* (see sense b), in the Transkei; a member of one division of this people, occas. called the *Emigrant Tembu*, who fled before invading peoples and settled round the sources of the Swart and White Kei rivers (the present-day Queenstown district of the Eastern Cape), being removed in 1852 to the Glen Grey district, in western Transkei; occas., the form of Xhosa spoken by this people (see quot. 1838); TAMBOOKIE *n.* sense 1 a.

The Tembu people consists of eight chiefdoms.

1809 R. COLLINS in G.M. Theal *Rec. of Cape Col.* (1900) VII. 20 The Tambookie people .. are known to their neighbours by the names Temboo and Tenjain. **1828** T. PRINGLE *Ephemerides* 196 The Country of the Amatymbæ, or Tambookie Caffers. **1828** W. SHAW in A. Steedman *Wanderings* (1835) II. 262 There are four entirely distinct nations, who all speak the Caffer language, and occupy a belt of beautiful country, extending along the coast from the Colony to Port Natal. The Amakosa, commonly called Caffers; the Amatembo, called Tambookies; the Amabambo, called Mambookies; and the Amaponda. **1838** J.E. ALEXANDER *Exped. into Int.* II. 166 The Amakosa and Tembé languages .. are different dialects of the same language. **1838** R. HADDY in B. Shaw *Memorials* (1841) 244 Clarkebury .. has afforded much pleasure to those who have watched the introduction and establishment of Christianity among the Abatembu. **1838** J.E. ALEXANDER *Exped. into Int.* II. 166 It will be seen how little similarity there is between the Damara and Namaqua languages, and again how much they differ from the Amakosa and Tembe languages, which last are different dialects of the same language. *c*1847 H.H. DUGMORE in J. Maclean *Compendium of Kafir Laws* (1906) 8 The Abatembu formerly occupied the whole of the country between the Bashee and the Umtata; but .. nearly the whole tribe has migrated to the country watered by the upper branches of the Kei. **1852** M.B. HUDSON *S. Afr. Frontier Life* p.vii, Macomo .. attacked and murdered some 'Amatembus' or Tambookies; another branch of the Kafir race, considered the most royal in blood, and from whom, by intermarriage, the Amakosae head chiefs must, according to Kafir law, be descended. **1853** F.P. FLEMING *Kaffraria* 121 These people belong to the second subdivision of the first Great branch of the Kaffir nation – namely, the Abatembu, under the chieftainship of Umtitata. **1866** W.C. HOLDEN *Past & Future* 142 According to the annexed table, it will be seen that the Abatembu, or Tembookie tribe, is paramount, being the oldest or great stock of the tree. **1871** J. MACKENZIE *Ten Yrs* (1971) 484 The oldest, or parent tribe, the Abatembu or Tembookies, treasures in its memory, as many as eighteen chiefs – taking us back, according to recent computation, to about A.D. 1400. **1880** *Grocott's Penny Mail* 24 Dec. (Suppl.) 1 Fighting was over at 5 p.m. the Tembus being beating [*sic*] off at all points. **1901** *Natives of S. Afr.* (S. Afr. Native Races Committee) 48 Dalindyebo, paramount chief of the Thembus, .. inoculated his cattle against rinderpest in 1897, in obedience to the Government. **1912** AYLIFF & WHITESIDE *Hist. of Abambo* 4 Madikana and his people .. were attacked by a combined force of the Tembus and Xosas. **1936** *Cambridge Hist. of Brit. Empire* VIII. 303 From about 1820 onwards waves of refugees, who were at the same time raiders, began to appear: for example the Bacas and the Fetcani or Fingos, or new migrations like that of the Tembus, generally known at the time as 'Tambookies'. **1949** J. MOCKFORD *Golden Land* 118 Five main tribes inhabit the Transkei – the Xosa, Tembu, Baca, Pondo and Fingo. They occupy an area roughly the size of Switzerland and total, according to the 1946 census, 1,300,000. **1967** J.A. BROSTER *Red Blanket Valley* 4 The Thembu, one of the chief tribes of the Transkei, were never conquered: they asked the European traders to settle. Later they accepted European administration, and gave allegiance to Queen Victoria. They are proud and dignified people and have always lived in friendship with us. **1979** *Sunday Post* 26 Apr. 1 The King of the Tembus, Chief Sabata Dalindyebo. **1981** J.B. PEIRES *House of Phalo* 43 In most recorded royal marriages, the Great Wife was a Thembu, from the nation with which the Xhosa was most often in contact. **1986** P. MAYLAM *Hist. of Afr. People* 96 In 1830 .. there were three main groupings, loosely defined, among the southern Nguni. In the south-west were the Xhosa ... In the north-east the Mpondo chiefdom .. was dominant. The Thembu occupied the central region, albeit somewhat uneasily. **1990** *Newsweek* 19 Feb. 24 When he [*sc.* Mandela] was 10 years old his father died; an uncle, the paramount chief of the Tembus, assumed responsibility for his education.

b. *comb.* **Tembu Church**, an independent church which broke away from the Methodist Church in the Transkei in 1884, under the leadership of the Rev. Nehemiah Tile; **Tembuland**, the area occupied by the Tembu people: (*a*) the uplands of the south-western Transkei (in the Eastern Cape Province), between the Kei and Umtata rivers; (*b*) *hist.*, an extensive area in the division of Queenstown in the Eastern Cape Province; in both senses formerly called *Tambookieland* (see TAMBOOKIE *n.* sense 1 b).

1893 *S. Afr. Methodist* 25 Mar. 137 The Tile following – known as the **Tembu Church** – was about to become an inconvenience to others. The Wesleyan body acted at once ... They resolved that a body of their Native men of wisdom should deal with the matter.

1961 B.G.M. SUNDKLER *Bantu Prophets* 38 As Tile was criticized by a European missionary because of his strong Tembu-nationalistic sympathies, he left the [Wesleyan Mission] church in 1882. Two years later he formed the 'Tembu Church', with Ngangelizwe, the Chief of the Tembu, as its visible head. **1986** P. MAYLAM *Hist. of Afr. People* 161 African independent churches in South Africa date back to the 1880's when the Thembu Church was founded in the Transkei by a Wesleyan minister, Nehemiah Tile. **1937** B.J.F. LAUBSCHER *Sex, Custom & Psychopathology* 210 Since most of my field-work was done in **Tembuland**, I shall confine myself to my personal observations and investigations among the Tembus. **1975** *Ethnic Composition of Ciskei & Transkei* (Dept of Bantu Admin., Ethnological Publ. No.53) He was buried beside the Msana, a tributary of the Bashee River in the Umtata District in the present Thembuland. **1977** T.R.H. DAVENPORT *S. Afr.: Mod. Hist.* 99 The gradual incorporation in the Colony of the Transkei between 1879 and 1894: Fingoland, Idutywa and Griqualand East in 1879, Port St Johns in 1894, Thembuland, Gcalekaland and Bomvanaland in 1885, [etc.]. **1989** *Reader's Digest Illust. Hist.* 285 The first [independent church] breakaway occurred in 1884 in Tembuland in the Eastern Cape. **1989** J.B. PEIRES *Dead Will Arise* 274 Fadana had been chased into the 'Tambookie Location' along with all his neighbours after the War of Mlanjeni. He was living the quiet life of a minor chief .. when Nongqawuse's prophecies were heard in Thembuland.

2. *obs.* With small initial. A type of bead used for trading. Also *attrib.*

1832 J. COLLETT Diary. I. 24 May, 63lb Tambo beads @ 2/-. **1832** *Graham's Town Jrnl* 24 Aug. 138 He exchanges it [*sc.* ivory] principally for beads. In April 1832, he preferred blood red and rose colored ones, but in the absence of such, he would accept the white tembos, when not too small, and also the dark-blue.

B. *adj.* Of or pertaining to the Tembu people; TAMBOOKIE *adj.*

1827 G. THOMPSON *Trav.* I. 349 A Tambookie Caffer is termed Tymba or Tembu, while the tribe collectively is called Amatymbae. **1835** A. STEEDMAN *Wanderings* I. 261 The indolent habits of the Amakosa and Amatembou tribes, who leave the cultivation of their lands entirely to the female part of the community, while the men lead a pastoral life in attending their cattle. **1843** J.C. CHASE *Cape of G.H.* 32 The country of the Amatembu or Tambookie tribes. **1851** R.J. GARDEN Diary. I. (Killie Campbell Africana Library MS29081) 30 June, By birth he is a Tambookie or one of the Amatembu Tribe. **1860** W. SHAW *Story of my Mission* 498 The respective great Chiefs of the Amampondo, Abatembu, and Amaxosa natives. **1872** *Wesleyan Missionary Reports* 79 Should peace continue a few years between the Ponda and Tembu tribes, we may calculate on this becoming the centre of a wide and extensive field of usefulness. **1934** D.D.T. JABAVU in *Lovedale Sol-Fa Leaflet No.17* 4 The late Enoch Sontonga (of the Mpinga clan among the Tembu tribes) was a teacher in one of the Methodist Mission Schools. **1976** R.L. PETENI *Hill of Fools* 2 The river is not safe. Thembu boys sometimes cross over to our side. **1987** *Learn & Teach* No.5, 1 Nelson Mandela was born on 18 July 1918 in the village of Qunu, near Umtata in the Transkei. His father, Henry Mgadla Mandela, was a chief of the Tembu people. **1990** *City Press* 11 Feb. 6 He [*sc.* Mandela] is looked upon by his Aba-Tembu tribesmen as a political messiah who will come back one day to liberate them.

ten *n.* [Ellipt. for SECTION 10.] In the phrr. *ten one* (written *10/1* or *10(1)*), *ten one a* (or *10(1)a*), etc.: **a.** SECTION 10 sense 1 a. **b.** *Section Tenner*, see SECTION 10. Also *attrib.*

1979 F. DIKE *First S. African* 10 Move out of Langa, but why, I'm a 10/1, and so are my parents. I qualify here. **1982** *Voice* 20 June 6 Is it true that I cannot get a 10(1)a qualification at Bloemfontein as I have no proof that I was born there?

tent *n.* [Calqued on Du. *tent* tilt.]

1.a. The tilt or canopy of a wagon, consisting of canvas over a hooped wooden framework; SAIL sense 1 a. Also *attrib.*

1820 G. BARKER Journal. 22 Nov., Repaired the tent sail of the waggon. **1832** *Graham's Town Jrnl* 27 July 118 The Undersigned .. has at present in his Stores, Tent Sail, Navy blue Prints, Foolscap. **1846** *Natal Witness* 24 July 2 Each wagon to be furnished with a good Tent. **1861** T. SHONE Diary. 3 Apr., Henry and his men were making a tent, for his new waggon. *a***1867** C.J. ANDERSSON *Notes of Trav.* (1875) 42 A large waggon-camp had been espied; .. the white tent covering of the vehicles could be distinctly perceived. **1871** J. MACKENZIE *Ten Yrs* (1971) 62 There is but a rotten and rickety waggon, whose tent is broken and its sail torn. **1878** T.J. LUCAS *Camp Life & Sport* 42 It [*sc.* the waggon] is covered with a strong canvas tent or tilt stretched upon a framework of bamboo. **1882** C. DU VAL *With Show through Sn Afr.* I. 105 A springless ill-covered bullock-waggon, whose 'tent' is so dilapidated that to prevent being wet through in the night we had to open our umbrellas. **1884** 'E.V.C.' *Promised Land* 9 'Very good', we agreed, and gave a contented glance at the strong canvas-covered tilt, or tent, as it is called in South Africa, that covered the stern end of the wagon. **1890** A. MARTIN *Home Life* 70 No Pullman car ever offered more luxurious sleeping accommodation than does the *kartel*, a large, strong framework of wood .. suspended inside the tent of the waggon. **1892** *The Jrnl* 9 July 1, 1 Large Tent Cart and 1 Buggy. **1893** F.C. SELOUS *Trav. & Adventure* 24 My waggon .. on the hinder part of which stood a tilt or tent where I slept. **1907** W.C. SCULLY *By Veldt & Kopje* 93 The 'tents' were of the whitest canvas. **1919** J.Y. GIBSON in *S. Afr. Jrnl of Science* July 6 The *boogen*, or tent bows, arched between *standers*, or standards, which were fastened on the outer sides of the leer-boomen. **1932** *Grocott's Daily Mail* 13 Jan. 1, 16ft. Wagon with half tent, in good order, Wagon Sail, Trek Gear. **1949** H.C. BOSMAN *Mafeking Rd* (1969) 146 There was so much stuff on the wagon that the tent had to be taken off to get everything on. **1969** F. GOLDIE *River of Gold* 81 Now and then Sam would climb up on top of the tent sail to get a wider view. **1974** A.A. TELFORD in *Std Encycl. of Sn Afr.* X. 569 Hunters favoured the buck-wagon with a half-tent because ivory and hides needed little protection and the tent provided better sleeping accommodation and shelter for perishable articles. **1986** W. STEENKAMP *Blake's Woman* 96 Mr Penton's wagon .. was hoisted on board .. its canvas tilt — or 'tent', as Cape people called it — rolled up and put below.

b. With defining word, in the same sense: **wagon-tent**; cf. *tent sail* (see SAIL sense 2).

1839 W.C. HARRIS *Wild Sports* 116 Large trees overhung the way, and threatened the destruction of the waggon tents. **1839** T. SHONE Diary. 30 Oct., Washed my waggon tent. **1845** *Cape of G.H. Almanac & Annual Register*, (advt) Wm. Thomas Sailmaker . . . 30-inch Canvas for Wagontents and Horse-cribs. **1866** T. SHONE Diary. 26 Sept., Henry is making A Waggon tent, the Waggon as gone to the sea side. **1871** J. MACKENZIE *Ten Yrs* (1971) 11 We fastened down the sails at both ends of our waggon, adjusted our little table, which was suspended from the side of the waggon-tent, and lighting our candle, spent the evening in reading or in conversation. **1872** T. BAINES in *S. Afr. Panorama* (Oct. 1971) 29 We breakfasted at Witklip, so called from a great quartz rock that looms like a wagon tent in the distance and at noon halted by a reedy pool. **1883** *Meteor* Nov. 1 The masculine portion of the party disdained to take advantage of the shade afforded by the wagon-tent. **1926** P. SMITH *Beadle* (1929) 59 The women wore stiffly starched plain white sun-bonnets, like miniature wagon-tents. **1947** H.C. BOSMAN *Mafeking Rd* (1969) 29 Inside the wagon-tent sat the women and children, listening to the rain pelting against the canvas. **1949** L.G. GREEN *In Land of Afternoon* 144 He slept on the familiar katel under the wagon tent. *c***1978** *Report No.34* (Dept of Nature & Environ. Conservation) 98 The wooden frame-work of a wagon tent, which will be used on one of the wagon exhibits. **1980** A.J. BLIGNAUT *Dead End Rd* 98 He watched me as I raked the embers over it near a leg of the tripod; then he lay down in the wagon-tent to snore.

2. *rare.* Ellipt. for TENT-WAGON.

1853 T. SHONE Diary. 7 Nov., This day Young Reiken And R'd Wright took a Tent load of forage from Henry's.

Hence (sense 1 a) **tent** *v. trans.*, to equip (a wagon) with a tilt; **tented** *adj.*, equipped with a tilt.

1852 M.B. HUDSON *S. Afr. Frontier Life* 67 The white-tented wagon round which were collecting the flocks of the homeless. **1926** W. PLOMER in *Voorslag* Vol.1 No.2, 45 They all climbed up into the tented waggon. **1946** S. CLOETE *Afr. Portraits* 34 Others were tented living wagons, the rear half-filled by a big kartel or bed that ran from rail to rail within it. **1955** A. DELIUS *Young Trav.* 66 A large tented wagon was kept in one of the University's halls in memory of the Voortrekkers. **1974** A.A. TELFORD in *Std Encycl. of Sn Afr.* X. 568 This small vehicle, .. tented throughout its length, was not only a means of transport but also a home and, on occasion, a fortress. **1989** B. GODBOLD Autobiography. 1 A full tented wagon, rather like the wagons of the Voortrekkers .. was my first real home.

tent-wagon *n.* ?*obs.* [Du. *tent* tilt + Eng. *wagon.*] A covered wagon; TENT sense 2.

1819 C.G. CURTIS *Acct Colony Cape of G.H.* 118 A light tent-waggon, drawn by six or eight horses, constitutes the carriage of the wine boor. **1854** T. SHONE Diary. 4 Feb., Henry came From Graham's Town With his tent Waggon and began to load up Potatoes and onions and Pomkins. **1894** E. GLANVILLE *Fair Colonist* 219 A large tent-waggon, drawn by a span of sixteen oxen, drew up at Orange Grove. **1907** [see SAIL sense 1]. **1913** C. PETTMAN *Africanderisms* 495 *Tent wagon*, A wagon part or whole of which is covered with a frame upon which canvas is stretched. **1936** P.M. CLARK *Autobiog. of Old Drifter* 56 The organizer of the trip .. was able to borrow ten mules and a light tent wagon. **1955** V. DE KOCK *Fun They Had* 102 A great lumbering tent-wagon, drawn by sixteen oxen.

terr /tɜː/ *n.* Also **ter.** [Rhodesian military slang, abbrev. of *terrorist.*]

1. *Army slang.* A derogatory term for a guerilla soldier; TERRO; TERRY. Also *attrib.*

1978 [see sense 2]. **1980** *Sunday Times* 12 Oct. (Mag. Sect.) 5 Not because I think the Swapo terr is a black man with a weapon he can't handle. He's good, with good weapons. **1982** *Voice* 30 May, Maybe these ouens really are trying to rid the country of 'commies' and 'terrs'. But they should know better that change in this country cannot come overnight, and that violence is a big no, no in any Christian country. **1983** *Star* 27 Sept. 18 A long way this, from the idea of galloping in and zapping a few terrs. This is real .. the true background of those simple .. news items which start 'Defence Headquarters in Pretoria announces ..' **1985** H. PRENDINI in *Style* Oct. 40 In the army .. Terrorists are 'terrs', Afrikaners are 'rocks' or 'pebbles'. **1985** *Frontline* Aug. 54 It was drummed into us that what we were there for was to moer the terrs. You feel nothing. **1985** *Ibid.* [see SKIET sense 1]. **1989** H. HAMANN in *Scope* 24 Mar. 59 The kind of dude who picked his teeth with a bowie knife and wore a string of terr ears around his neck.

2. *fig.* Abbrev. of *terrorist from the North* (see TERRORIST).

1978 *Sunday Times* 9 Apr. 1 Seen any terrs lately? Not the abandoned-parcel-time-bomb types, but the Lowveld .. inhabitants who desecrate the Kruger Park.

territorial authority *n. phr. Hist.* Under the Bantu Authorities Act of 1951: the government of a semi-autonomous area set aside for occupation by black people; the area governed by this authority.

In terms of the Act, black government was to be in three tiers: TRIBAL AUTHORITY, 'regional authority', and 'territorial authority', the last being the most powerful. All fell under the ultimate control of the white government. Some of the areas governed by territorial authorities were later developed into 'self-governing' homelands, the territorial authorities becoming (or being replaced by) legislative assemblies. See also HOMELAND sense 1.

1951 *Bantu Authorities Act* in *Stat. of Union* 1154 The Governor-General may .. in respect of any two or more areas for which regional authorities have been established, establish a Bantu territorial authority ... The chairman and the members of a territorial authority shall be elected or selected .. from amongst the members of the regional authorities. **1968** *Post* 17 Nov. 7 Amid much pomp and ceremony the Ciskei Territorial Authority was born at Zwelitsha, near King William's Town, this week. **1971** *Rand Daily Mail* 28 July 5 Mr. Mutsila said Vendas with higher standards of education had been removed from the Venda Territorial Authority. **1980** *Report of Ciskei Commission* 143 In 1961 the Ciskei graduated to a territorial authority.

terro /ˈterəʊ/ *n.* [Abbrev. of *terrorist.*] TERR sense 1.

1979 *Citizen* 9 Apr. 2 Terros fire on town. **1986** *Ibid.* 23 Apr. 2 Terro's arms cache. **1988** G. SILBER in *Style* June 46 The crew .. takes turns to interrogate the terro — .. ag, black man. **1989** *E. Prov. Herald* 6 Apr. 2 The beards are coming back ... The more terros there are, the longer the hair. When the terros go, so does the hair. **1994** *Weekly Mail & Guardian* 16 Sept. 2 Comic terros never die ... The photo-comic hero is still waging his one-man war against the likes of the evil Major Cuba.

terrorist *n. colloq.* [A play on the similarity in sound between *terrorist* and *tourist.*] In the phr. ***terrorist from the North***, a derogatory name for a tourist from the Transvaal provinces visiting the coastal regions of the Western Cape or KwaZulu-Natal; TERR sense 2. See also KY'DAAR.

1981 *Informant, George* Well summer's coming. We'll be inundated with terrorists from the north. **1982** *Cape Times* 21 Dec. 17 In Natal and the Eastern Cape they had a different name for .. tourists. Its 'K'daars' as in 'Kyk daar?' ... It's a far more affectionate name than the more usual terrorists from the north.

terry *n.* [Formed on *terrorist* + Eng. (informal) n.-forming suffix *-y.*] TERR sense 1.

1975 *Sunday Times* 10 Aug. 16 One day the 'terries' will depart, the army will pack up .. and South Africa will be left with yet another homeland. **1976** *Bike S. Afr.* Oct., Terry-bashing in lekker ol' Rhodeesha. **1988** J. FERGUSON in *New Nation* 14 Jan. 10 He'll come back to go a-hunting For the Terries in the backyard .. Bang Bang!!

tessie /ˈtesi/ *n.* [Afk.] **a.** KOMFOOR sense a. **b.** A small fire-pan of iron or copper for holding the coals in a komfoor.

1949 L.G. GREEN *In Land of Afternoon* 203 There, too, is a noteworthy silver tessie, lined with copper and designed to hold the charcoal embers from which smokers lit their pipes. **1955** V.M. FITZROY *Dark Bright Land* 92 The impeccable tessies and salvers, snuff-boxes and muffineers that came out of the silversmith's dark little lairs. **1965** A. GORDON-BROWN *S. Afr. Heritage* II. 17 As Cape silversmiths were mainly engaged in making articles for domestic needs, their largest output was of spoons and forks (flatware) ... There were many other articles, all of them rare, such as sugar and sweet dishes, tessies, salvers, Bible clasps [etc.]. *Ibid.* 18 Cape Silver Smoker's Tessie (to contain live coals for lighting pipes). **1965** M.G. ATMORE *Cape Furn.* 85 The charcoal container or tessie was inserted either through a gap left in one side or by removing the perforated top .. of the box. **1971** BARAITSER & OBHOLZER *Cape Country Furn.* 265 The only way of keeping warm .. was to sit with one's feet resting on a foot warmer .. A small wooden box, generally square .. held a pan or tessie of glowing charcoal. **1972** *Informant, Stellenbosch Museum* The tessie or kolebakkie is the small dish into which the glowing coals or embers are actually placed ... The tessie is then put into a voetstofie or konfoor ... Most voetstofies and konfore found today are without their tessies ... The tessie used on the table .. was often made of silver .. mounted on a wooden base, and always had a shallow copper lining in the bottom to protect the silver from the heat. **1973** M.A. COOK *Cape Kitchen* 63 Inside the brass konfoor was a slightly smaller tessie, which was made of semispherical copper .. or of thin straight-sided sheet-iron ... This inner tessie was the actual receptacle for the 'live coal'. **1977** N. OKES in *Quarry '77* 137 She broke matches into .. the old Cape silver tessie she used as an ashtray.

Test *n.* Also with small initial. [Extended sense of general Eng. *test* an international cricket match.] In full ***test match***: an international match in any sport or game.

Now used widely in this sense in other Eng.-speaking countries.

1924 *Times* (U.K.) 15 Aug. 5 The British team for the first Rugby Football Test Match on Saturday will be selected [in South Africa]. **1933** M. NICHOLLS in I.D. Difford *Hist. of S. Afr. Rugby Football* 335 We won this fourth Test match by 13 points to 5, and squared the rubber. *Ibid.* 336 In the first Test we won 16 scrums to their 36. **1934** *Week-End Advertiser* 12 May (Swart), The Afrikaans expression, 'Papbroek', is not without its significance in test match rugby, especially on one's initial appearance. **1971** *Rand Daily Mail* 4 Sept. 24 A series of diving Tests have been arranged against Rhodesia. **1993** A.C. PARKER in *Daily News* 5 Jan. 13 Craven, who captained South Africa in the three-test series against Sam Walker's British Isles team in 1938, played only 13 of his 16 tests at scrumhalf.

tetse var. TSETSE.

t'geitje var. GEITJIE.

t'goerra var. GORAH.

t'gokum var. GOCUM.

thakatha var. TAGATI *v.*

thakathi var. TAGATI *n.*

thakhatha var. TAGATI *adj.*

thank you *int. phr.* [Special sense of general Eng., influenced by S. Afr. Du. *dank u*, later Afk. *dankie*, fr. Du. *bedanken* to decline, refuse.] A polite refusal: DANKIE sense 2. So as *n. phr.*, an utterance of this phrase.

1833 J.C. CHASE in *S. Afr. Almanac & Dir.* 92 One thing more .. is to be recommended; if he value his meals, — .. never when invited to eat, reply with a genteel thank ye, (dank u) as that piece of politeness is understood throughout the colony as a negative, the disagreeable consequences of which the writer of this has more than once found to his cost. **1837** 'N. POLSON' *Subaltern's Sick Leave* 104 Travellers must avoid .. 'thank ye' .. The latter is always taken as a refusal (*Dank u*); as indeed it is in every language but English. This English mode of using 'thank you' is now becoming so well known on the continent of Europe, that is is no usual thing for a foreigner on making any offer and being thanked for it, to ask .. 'Merci oui?' or 'Merci non?'. **1906** A.H. WATKINS *From Farm to Forum* 17 There dawned upon my memory the story of the Englishman in France who would say 'merci' when offered refreshment till he nearly died of hunger, and I came to the conclusion that 'Thank you' being literally translated into Dutch idiom meant 'No thank you'. **1913** C. PETTMAN *Africanderisms* 496 *Thank you*, In the Dutch-speaking districts of South Africa the Englishman needs to be careful how he uses this phrase, since to the Dutch it conveys the meaning of 'No, thank you'. **1971** *Personality* 19 Feb., 'Will you eat with us?' asked the farmer. 'Thank you,' said Chase politely. 'Oh? A pity you are not hungry,' retorted the farmer. 'Excuse us while the family eats and we will talk afterwards.' It was in this salutary fashion that Mr Chase learnt to reply to a farmer's invitation with the words 'Yes, please,' and not 'Thank you' — the latter being the accepted way of voicing a polite refusal. **1973** *Drum* 8 Oct. 14 When anyone asked him to have a meal, he would say: 'Thank you I have eaten.' But his friends knew that he was starving.

thekwane var. TEGWAAN.

theleweni /ˌteleˈweːni/ *n. derog.* Also with initial capital. [Zulu *itheleweni, utheleweni* 'one who pours (people) over a cliff'; one who is guilty of violence towards other people (pl. *otheleweni*); n. prefixes *i-, u-, o-* + *thela* pour + *eweni* locative form of *iwa* cliff, precipice.] An insulting name for a member or supporter of *Inkatha* (see INKATHA sense 2), used as a taunt. Also *attrib.*

1989 *Natal Witness* 30 Mar. (Witness Echo) 1 Teachers .. will have to teach the KwaZulu-prescribed ubuntu-botho syllabus ... Opponents say .. it is biased in favour of Inkatha. A teacher .. said they had been told .. to resume teaching the subject. ' ... The children will brand me a theleweni (Inkatha supporter).' **1989** *Frontline* Apr. 12 Everybody said that the oTheleweni were identified by the carrying of sticks and guns. **1990** *Clarion Call* Vol.1, 9 There have .. been examples of Theleweni groups dissociating themselves from Inkatha youth groups. **1990** M. KENTRIDGE *Unofficial War* 21 The comrades have coined a range of insulting terms for their Inkatha enemies. The most widely used, and the one most likely to provoke a state of rage in the person thus labelled, is *theleweni*, meaning 'the one who pours us over a cliff'.

Thembu var. TEMBU.

the moer in see MOER *n.*[2] sense 2.

thick milk *n. phr. Obs.* [Calqued on S. Afr. Du. *dikmelk* curds and whey, clabber milk.] MAAS sense 1. Also *attrib.*

1826 A.G. BAIN *Jrnls* (1949) 56 Large wooden dishes containing a mess something like Scotch porridge, but made of Caffre Corn boiled in thick milk. **1852** R.J. GARDEN Diary. I. (Killie Campbell Africana Library MS29081) 17 Apr., Some Intombis came from the other kraal, viz: those who had brought the milk, the preceding evening, bringing sweet and thick milk and Caffir beer ... A stranger (Caffir) won't eat thick milk (Amasa) at a strange kraal, as it degrades him in the eyes of the maidens, it being considered womens' food. **1867** E.L. PRICE *Jrnls* (1956) 256, I am writing in the most awful din — a rabble of women all round me selling sweet-reed, mealies, thick-milk &c. **1881** *Ibid.* 463 Thick milk was brought on. Very rich and stiff, & cheesy — but *very* sour! **1891** H.J. DUCKITT *Hilda's 'Where Is It?'* 77 Mix well with the flour a pinch of salt, half a teaspoonful of carbonate of soda, a little pounded ginger, about a cupful of thick milk. **1897** J.P. FITZPATRICK *Outspan* 14 We were jogging along doing our thirty miles a day, living on old mealies roasted on a bit of tin, and an occasional fowl .. helped down by bowls of amazi — thick milk, you know. **1907** [see NATIVE *adj.* sense 1]. **1947** F.C. SLATER *Sel. Poems* 82 *Amoss* or *Amase* — thick milk usually kept in calabashes. **1951** S. VAN H. TULLEKEN *Prac. Cookery Bk* 274 Thick Milk Soap. 10 lbs thick milk, 2lbs fat, 1lb caustic soda, 1 bottle water. Put thick milk over a fire, and just as it begins to boil, remove it, and pour it gently on to a sieve, and let it drain very thoroughly — the drier the better.

thickoloshe var. TOKOLOSHE.

Thiko var. TIXO.

thikolosh(e) var. TOKOLOSHE.

third-class *n. hist.* Also **3rd class**. During the apartheid era, a euphemism for the segregated facilities for black commuters on trains. Also *attrib.* (sometimes meaning 'black').

1977 *Sunday Times* 24 July 15 Our railway compartment, whether Native third class, ditto second class or first class coupe, cramped as these accommodations were, became a veritable salon. **1977** J. SIKAKANE *Window on Soweto*, (*caption*) Black commuters travel 3rd class. **1990** *Frontline* Mar.-Apr. 10, I gird my loins for the right to travel third class, which I do not expect the conductor to lightly let a white family do ... All the white applicants are allocated to bunks with no difficulty. Then there is one person left, the only coloured. 'Nothing,' says the conductor, 'but you can travel third'. **1993** P. MCMAGH in *Weekend Argus* 14 Aug. 17 You are swept towards them [*sc.* the turnstiles] by the river of third-class commuters.

third force *n. phr.* Also with initial capitals. [Special sense of general Eng. *third force* 'a political party or parties standing between two extreme or opposing parties' (*OED*).] A group (or groups) of unknown composition (and the existence of which has not been proved), thought by some to have carried out murders and other acts of violence in order to sow discord, esp. among those left-wing groups mainly representing blacks, by creating the impression that these acts had been perpetrated by followers of rival groups. Also *attrib.*, passing into *adj.*

Many believe that such a force was formed by right-wing extremists who were members (or former members) of the security forces of South Africa and of the 'homelands'; others suggest that it was formed by left-wing extremists who believed that blacks should seize power by force rather than through negotiation with the Nationalist government, which was in power when rumours of the force's existence first arose. Some claim that the third force is still active.

1985 *Probe* July 27 Is there a third force fanning the divisions in Port Elizabeth's townships where .. a senseless black-on-black war .. is turning the clock back on the struggle? ... Many are convinced that the intensified violence directed at the Azanian Peoples Organisation .. and the United Democratic Front .. is the work of this third force. Both groups have raised the existence of this reactionary force. **1990** H. GRANGE in *Star* 11 Sept. 2 While police are probing a possible 'third force' instigating violence, township residents .. allege that whites — wearing balaclavas with blackened faces — have been shooting randomly at people from minibuses. **1990** *Weekly Mail* 28 Sept. He's done it again with his unlikely allegation that the 'Third Force' behind the violence on the Reef may be a group of ANC dissidents. This claim has been reiterated by President FW de Klerk, though he qualified this by saying white rightwing elements could also be the culprits. **1990** R. AINSLIE in *Weekly Mail* 12 Oct. 3, I think Nelson Mandela's 'Third Force' theory makes a lot of sense. **1992** *Sunday Times* 26 Apr. 24 The Trust Feed case has proved true, at least in this instance, the frequent accusation that the police acted, in pursuance of policy, as a 'Third Force' to stimulate violent conflict betwee the ANC-UDF forces and other black people. **1992** *Grahamstown Voice* July 3 He didn't believe there was one third force, 'but many third forces'. **1993** *Africa S. & E.* July 8 Small groups with a penchant for violence, assassination and 'third-force' type activity. **1994** *Weekly Mail & Guardian* 13 May 3 Reservations surfaced on the Nats' willingness to root out the 'third force' inside the security forces.

third tier see TIER.

Thirst *n. obs.* [Shortened form of THIRSTLAND.] **a.** An extensive arid region, stretching roughly from the Northern Transvaal through Botswana to eastern Namibia. **b.** THIRSTLAND sense 1.

1887 A.A. ANDERSON *25 Yrs in Waggon* I. Another part of the desert is thick bush, and very scarce of water in the dry season, and is a part of what is called thirst land (thirst) from the dryness of the country, and where the trek Boers suffered so much in their journey to the westward in 1877. **1892** NICOLLS & EGLINGTON *Sportsman in S. Afr.* 22 In hunting game in the 'thirst' the cart .. should be filled with water, and a start made the previous evening. **1913** C. PETTMAN *Africanderisms* 497 *Thirst* or *Thirst-land*, (1) A large area nearly or quite devoid of water is so designated. (2) More definitely it is applied to the territory lying between Mafeking and Palapye in Bechuanaland, which has to depend chiefly upon pits for a very meagre supply of very poor water.

Thirstland *n. phr.* Also with small initial. [tr. Afk. *Dorsland*, see DORSLAND.]

1. Any large arid area or desert; THIRST sense b. Also *fig.*

1892 NICOLLS & EGLINGTON *Sportsman in S. Afr.* 22 The chief drawback attending the hunting of the Giraffe, Eland, and Gemsbuck is the difficulty of watering the shooting horses regularly in the thirstlands frequented by these animals. **1898** [see TSAMMA]. **1908** J. WELLS *Stewart of Lovedale* 182 Stewart skirted without crossing the Karoo and great Thirstland of unbelief. **1913** [see THIRST]. **1978** A.P. BRINK *Rumours of Rain* 130 On the few excruciating expeditions into the thirstland we found some melon-like objects, but we were too scared to try them in case they were poisonous. **1985** *S. Afr. Panorama* Oct. 41 Oases are found in deserts or semi-deserts, so where is the basic fertility of this vast thirstland [*sc.* the Karoo]? **1989** *Sunday Times* 5 Nov. 22 Namibia is not the sort of territory that lends itself to social engineering ... From Ondangua in the north to Warmbad in the south, it is one of the most bleak and inhospitable pieces of real estate in the world ... Grand election promises and high sounding ideologies do not wash in the thirstland.

2. *Hist. Attrib.* and *comb.*: **Thirstland Boer** or **-pioneer**, *Dorsland trekker* (see DORSLAND); **Thirstland Trek**, *Dorsland Trek* (see DORSLAND); **Thirstland Trekker**, *Dorsland Trekker* (see DORSLAND).

1936 E. ROSENTHAL *Old-Time Survivals* 23 For persons wishing to to study the pioneer in his least 'modernised' environment, a visit to the descendants of the 'Thirstland Boers' can be recommended. **1936** L.G. GREEN *Secret Afr.* 106 In his youth Oorlog joined the Boers, the famous Thirstland trekkers, who opened up the hinterland of Angola last century. **1943** [see ANGOLA BOER]. **1945** N. DEVITT *People & Places* 104 It is the duty of posterity not to forget these Thirstland pioneers who are busy turning the Kalahari into a livable area. **1961** O. LEVINSON *Ageless Land* 101 Boers first entered South West towards the end of the eighteen-seventies. These were the people of the ill-fated Thirstland Trek. They had left their well-established homes in the Western Transvaal, to cross the Kalahari Thirstland and the fever marshes of the Okavango, trekking westward in their search for the 'Land of Rest'. **1961** L.E. VAN ONSELEN *Trekboer* 39 Uncle Andries asked me a number of times about people who lived 'north of here' ... It dawned on me eventually that he was referring to the thirst-land trekkers who crossed the Kalahari. **1966** J.P. VAN S. BRUWER *S.W. Afr.: Disputed Land* 29 During the second half of the 19th century a group of people called the Thirstland Trekkers left the Transvaal .. and moved north through Bechuanaland. **1974** *E. Prov. Herald* 5 Nov., A four-cent postage stamp to commemorate the Thirstland (Dorsland) Trek, which began 100 years ago from the Transvaal .. will be issued in South West Africa on November 13. **1976** CUBITT & RICHTER *South West*, Years ago that incorrigible Afrikaner band of Thirstland Trekkers settled temporarily in their endless search for Utopia. **1979** *Scope* July 26 My father ... was known as Thomas Thom, having adopted the name of the family he was trekking with during the great Thirstland Trek. **1987** D. HAARHOFF in *Eng. Academy Rev.* 4 27 Oorlog was connected to the black van der Merwe's who accompanied the Thirstland trekkers into Angola.

thisthelboon, thistleboom varr. DISSELBOOM.

Thixo var. TIXO.

Thlaping var. BATLHAPING.

thokoloshe, -los(h)i varr. TOKOLOSHE.

thomba /'tɔːmba, 'tɔmbə/ *n.* Also **(uku-)tomba**. [Zulu, 'reach puberty'.] Among Zulus: a ceremony performed to mark the transition from childhood to adolescence or adulthood; this transition itself, puberty. Also *attrib.*

1936 E.J. KRIGE *Social System of Zulus* 87 The attainment of physical maturity .. is made the occasion for an important ceremony, called the *Thomba*. The girl's puberty ceremony is sometimes called *uDwa*, but the use of this word is rapidly dying out. *Ibid.* 95 General feasting ensues for the rest of the *Thomba* period. **1955** E.A. RITTER *Shaka Zulu* 8 Two or three years after having reached the period of sexual maturity, uku-tomba — which occurs with the Zulus anywhere between the age of fourteen and a half and nineteen years — the boy moved up another rung on the scholastic ladder. **1978** A. ELLIOTT *Sons of Zulu* 142 There is a definite intention in the puberty ceremony (*thomba*) to reinforce the boy as a person and bring him closer to his ancestral spirits. **1987** L. NKOSI *Mating Birds* 43, I was fourteen .. , a boy looking much older .. but as yet to undergo the *thomba* initiation ceremony. **1988** *New Nation* 30 June (Learning Nation) 1 When boys were between the age of 12 and 14 they underwent a puberty ceremony known as the 'thomba'.

Thonga var. TONGA.

thorn *n.* [Shortened form of THORN-TREE.] DORINGBOOM. Also *attrib.*

1821 G. BARKER Journal. 11 Sept., Began to cut down thorns to fence my wheat land, the cattle being every day in it. **1835** T.H. BOWKER Journal. 5 June, Chopping the thorns down near the watering place, making a new horse kraal. **1839** J. COLLETT Accounts. II. 12 June, Exceeding mild Winter Thorns not as yet lost all their leaves. **1976** S. CLOETE *Chetoko* 158 The thorns are in bloom now ... In her mind Helen saw the little fluffy yellow balls of the thorn flowers and smelled them.

thorn bush *n. phr.* [Special sense of general Eng.] DORINGBOOM.

1810 G. BARRINGTON *Acct of Voy.* 273 The poor man had a very narrow escape, by hiding himself in a thorn-bush. **1835** T.H. BOWKER Journal., Considerable progress made towards the fort, it is made square with a kraal in the midle, and the whole surrounded by a hedge of thorn Bushes fifty Yards from the breast work. **1926** M. NATHAN *S. Afr. from Within* 205 From this part onwards to the Albany coast, the scenery is unattractive, and the prevailing vegetation is thorn-bush; but from Port-Alfred (Kowie) eastwards the vegetation is more abundant. **1941** C. BIRKBY *Springbok Victory* 7 A desert as grim as the worst parts of the Kalahari and Bushmanland. Vast stretches of its yellow sands are covered with thornbush 20 feet high. **1956** D. JACOBSON *Dance in Sun* 205 A thorn-bush grew between the rocks and gave not only some concealment, but also threw a necessary shade where we lay. **1964** A. ROTHMANN *Elephant Shrew* 33 There are miles and miles of bush, a dense, impenetrable mass of num-num, thorn bushes, 'taaibos', gnarled ghwarrie trees, 'boerboon' with its showy red flowers and flat pods and above all elephant's food or 'spekboom.' **1972** J. PACKER *Boomerang* 21 Everywhere, the thorn-bushes spread a drift of feathery yellow flowers pervading the brittle air of the veld with their soft sweet fragrance. **1978** *Daily Dispatch* 16 Aug. (Suppl.) 7 Thorn bush (Ocacia [*sic*] Karoo) encroachment has become a nightmare and curse to most farmers in the Eastern Cape and Border. **1991** *Weekend Post* 5 Jan. 11 The invading thorn bush (*Acacia karoo*) 'took over' vast areas of valuable farm land and became impenetrable if not checked.

thorn-tree *n.* [Special sense of general Eng., or tr. S. Afr. Du. *doornboom* (see DORINGBOOM).] DORINGBOOM. Also *attrib.*

1786 G. FORSTER tr. *A. Sparrman's Voy. to Cape of G.H.* II. 139 This tract of country was thinly covered with thorn-trees (*mimosa nilotica*,) which shaded the ground and kept it cool. **1798** LADY A. BARNARD in Lord Lindsay *Lives of Lindsays* (1849) III. 440, I plucked from the great thorn-trees some of their prickles, of which I send you a few; they exactly resemble the horns of the cattle. I hear the plant has found its way to Kew Gardens, and is there called the cuckold-tree. **1806** J. BARROW *Trav.* I. 40 The banks were skirted by a thicket of the doorn boom, or thorn tree, a species of mimosa. **1850** R.G.G. CUMMING *Hunter's Life* I. 60 A clump of tangled thorn-trees. **1877** R.M. BALLANTYNE *Settler & Savage* 250 The usually phlegmatic Conrad defended another weak point, while his at other times amiable spouse stood near him making fearful and frequent raids upon the foe with the branch of a thorn-tree. **1887** A.A. ANDERSON *25 Yrs in Waggon* II. 157 Several thorn-trees grow within the enclosure, under which the waggon stood. **1897** J.P. FITZPATRICK *Outspan* 35 In the direction indicated, partly hidden by the scant foliage of a thorn-tree, a man was sitting on a yellow portmanteau reading a book. **1944** H.C. Bosman in L. Abrahams *Cask of Jerepigo* (1972) 112 The sunbaked vlakte and the thorn-tree and South Africa. **1956** D. Jacobson *Dance in Sun* 8 The sun seemed to have seized the land, sucking all strength from the thorn trees, and the earth, and our own bodies. **1975** S. Roberts *Outside Life's Feast* 53 The sand of the uneven path leading from the house to the yard was also yellow, and the stench from the chicken hoks was awful. Ann stared across the fields and the open veld patterned purple with thorn trees. **1982** Fox & Norwood Young *Food from Veld* 198 *Acacia erioloba* .. *Common names*: English .. *thorn tree* ... *Acacia karroo* .. *Common names*: English .. *thorn tree*. **1985** *Style* Oct. 92 So begins our odyssey .. days spent traversing a kaleidoscopic landscape of semi-arid vegetation dotted with acacia, mopane, boabab [*sic*] and thorn trees. **1991** *Dict. of Horticulture* (Dept. of Nat. Educ.) 378 *Thorn trees*, (*Acacia* spp.): doringbome.

thornveld /'θɔːnfelt, -fɛlt/ *n.* Formerly also **thorn veldt**. [Eng. *thorn* + Afk. *veld* (see VELD sense 2 c).] Land on which thorny trees and bushes are the predominant vegetation.

1878 A. Aylward *Tvl of Today* 246 Four young men, all Africanders, nearly lost their lives in the Speckboom thornveld. **1907** T.R. Sim *Forests & Forest Flora* 4 Thorn-veldt .. produces park-like scenery and yields valuable fuel. **1926** M. Nathan *S. Afr. from Within* 209 This 'Thorn Veld' is interspersed with grassy tracts, and towards Natal and Zululand forests are met with. **1961** D. Rooke *Lover for Estelle* 6 The thornveld was like a park, with flat-topped trees scattered over the grassy plain. **1967** D. Edwards *Plant-Ecological Survey of Tugela River Basin* 201 This Thorn Veld has extended over large areas of former *Themeda-Hyparrhenia* Grassland. **1975** J.P.H. Acocks *Veld Types* 13 The veld today is more or less open thornveld with numerous and extensive patches of forest. **1980** *Farmer's Weekly* 30 July 67 Properly run, Boer-goats can be a paying proposition on the thorn veld. **1987** *Pace* Oct. 167 The sun set over the thornveld like a big molten globe of burnished red. **1991** D.M. Moore *Garden Earth* 197 In the thornveld many of the trees have small leaves, which reduce the potential loss of water through evaporation.

thornwood *n.* [THORN + Eng. *wood* timber.] **a.** The wood of any of a number of species of trees or shrubs of the Mimosaceae, esp. of the genus *Acacia*. **b.** A tree of any of these species. **c.** Such trees collectively. Also *attrib.* See also DORINGHOUT.

1801 Truter & Somerville in G.M. Theal *Rec. of Cape Col.* (1899) IV. 407 We had the necessary thornwood cut for beams, longwaggons, yokes, &c. **1850** R.G.G. Cumming *Hunter's Life* (1902) 147 Reducing with adzes a thornwood tree, which was to serve as a beam. **1863** W.C. Baldwin *Afr. Hunting* 148 A beautiful country of dense thornwood. **1987** *Grocott's Mail* 6 Feb. 8 (*advt*) Thornwood and Kraal manure.

three days' sickness *n. phr. Pathology.* Also **three day sickness**. [See quot. 1909.] A short-lived viral disease of cattle which is characterized by muscular pain and stiffness; STYFSIEKTE sense 1 c. Also **three days' disease**, **three-day stiffness**.

1909 *Cape of G.H. Agric. Jrnl* Aug. 145 (Pettman), The scientific term, Ephemeral fever, as well as the lay term *Three days' sickness*, are both somewhat appropriate, as in the great majority of cases the disease quickly runs its course and all acute symptoms have disappeared at the end of three days. **1913** C. Pettman *Africanderisms* 497 *Three days' sickness*, A sickness of short duration affecting cattle; it is sometimes called Stijfziekte. **1937** S. Cloete *Turning Wheels* 143 Three day sickness, which as a rule animals recover from if left alone, meant abandoning beasts since there was no time to wait for them to recover. **1954** [see STIFF-SICKNESS sense 1]. **1954** [see STIFF-SICKNESS sense 2]. **1970** *Cape Times* 27 May, She checks the cattle out of their pens and looks for signs of heart-water, gall sickness or three-day stiffness. **1974** *E. Prov. Herald* 27 Feb. 4 Diseases like blue tongue, red water, gall sickness, three days' disease and horse sickness, which are carried by insects or ticks, would probably occur fairly wide-spread this year because of the rain.

three-legged *ppl adj.* In the phrr. ***three-legged (cooking) pot***, or (*offensive*) ***three-legged kaffir-pot***: POTJIE. See also DRIEVOET *adj.*

1864 T. Baines *Explor. in S.-W. Afr.* 362 It is commonly said that a Scotsman, a Dutch cheese and Newcastle grindstone are all over the world, but I feel sure that a cast-iron three-legged pot penetrates as far as any of the trio. **1902** J.H.M. Abbott *Tommy Cornstalk* 28 A few Kaffir transport-drivers .. are boiling their 'mealie-pap' in three-legged pots. **1925** D. Kidd *Essential Kafir* 198 The load contained a sleeping-mat, a blanket, a roll of tobacco, and a few trinkets; and perched on the top of the bundle was a three-legged pot — representing an entire kitchen and scullery — while a few awkwardly-shaped calabashes were tied to the bundle by homemade grass string. **1979** Heard & Faull *Our Best Trad. Recipes* 87 The very first oven wasn't an oven at all, it was the ubiquitous iron pot used all over the world from the earliest times for stewing, and with a lid on, for baking anything over an open fire. Even bread was baked in the three-legged (kaffir) pot. **1980** E. Joubert *Poppie Nongena* 15 My ouma never used a Primus-stove, she did her cooking outside in three-legged cooking-pots over an open fire. **1982** [see MNGQUSH(O)]. **1986** M. Ramgobin *Waiting to Live* 134 The people who had come from near and far would have to be fed. Huge three-legged pots were filled with crushed mealies. **1989** [see MEALIE-MEAL sense 1]. **1990** F. Bates in *Style* Oct. 76 A three-legged pot of stywe pap bubbled and plopped on the hob. **1993** S. Gray in *Weekly Mail & Guardian* 5 Nov. 48 A little yellow brak put its head into the three-legged kaffir-pot bubbling with potjiekos. **1994** [see PAP *n.* sense 1].

three star *n. phr. Slang.* Also **three stars**, and with initial capitals. In full ***three star knife***. In urban (esp. township) Eng.: the proprietory name of a folding knife of German manufacture, having a curved handle ornamented with three stars. Also *attrib.* See also OKAPI.

A favoured weapon of township gangsters.

1952 *Drum* May 40 Apart from the Three Star and the 'Banana' knives, they also carry fire-arms of a dangerous kind. **1953** *Ibid.* May 41 N—, a member of the Koreans, challenged his leader, S—, in 'Three Star' (knife) fights all over the township. [**1953** A. Mogale in *Drum* 25 Joe 'Three Star' Mokwena who's very handy at slitting defenseless throats.] **1963** B. Modisane *Blame Me on Hist.* (1986) 77 My daughter will learn that there is no such thing as brotherhood; there are no neighbours, there are only enemies who carry Three-Star knives in the locations and Saracen armed trucks in the white camp. **1963** L.F. Freed *Crime in S. Afr.* 110 One of the leaders became involved in a 'Three Star' fight, that is a knife fight. *a***1968** D.C. Themba in E. Patel *World of Can Themba* (1985) 100 He sat there on the storm water drain with his mournful face, sharpening gratingly on the concrete his Three Star jack-knife which from some hazy movie memory he called his 'gurkha'. **1981** M. Tlali in *Rand Daily Mail* 7 May (Eve) 7 He .. confronts her with an ugly-looking 'three-star' knife and threatens her with death. **1982** M. Mzamane *Children of Soweto* 85 Various mobile stores soon emerged all over the townships and did a roaring business in three-star knives, baby browns, knuckle-dusters. **1988** R.S. Makhaya in *Staffrider* Vol.7 No.1, 74, I eased the kitchen door open My three stars Okapi knife open.

threethorn *n. obs.* [tr. S. Afr. Du. *driedoring*.] DRIEDORING. Also *attrib.*

1824 W.J. Burchell *Trav.* II. 41 We continued our journey across the mountain, and descended to an extensive plain covered with *threethorn* shrubs. **1886** G.A. Farini *Through Kalahari Desert* 133 With this understanding with myself, I lay down and was soon fast asleep under a three-thorn bush.

throw *v. trans.* [Special uses of general Eng.]

1. [Calqued on Afk. *gooi* (*iemand*) *met* (*iets*), lit. 'throw (someone) with (something)', resulting in the replacement of the standard Eng. '*throw* + obj. (thing thrown) + *at* + person or thing hit' with the construction '*throw* + obj. (person or thing hit) + *with* + thing thrown'.] In the phr. ***to throw*** (***someone***) ***with*** (***something***), to throw (something) at (someone); occas. ***to throw*** (***someone***), see quot. 1908.

Less common among first-language speakers of English than among those who speak English as a second language.

[**1851** T. Shone Diary. 24 June, This evening .. the young lads and lasses were playing about Henry's Hut throwing at one or the other with sods or anything else they could lay hold of.] **1872** in A.M.L. Robinson *Sel. Articles from Cape Monthly Mag.* (1978) 280 We often hear such expressions as 'by the house', .. 'throwing with a stone' [etc]. **1888** *Cape Punch* 18 Apr. 23 Translate into English: .. He threw me with a stone .., I never did it. **1891** J.P. Legg in *Cape Illust. Mag.* I. 95 It is superfluous to mention that horror of the teacher of English 'he threw me with a stone.' **1892** *The Jrnl* 16 Jan. 3 He retreated a little way and picked up stones, saying he would throw her dead with stones. **1894** E. Glanville *Fair Colonist* 229 'Little boy,' said Ada, sweetly, 'I whipped you once. Do you remember why?' 'Because I throwed you with plumpips.' 'Well, it is worse to "throw me with" words.' **1908** J.H. Drummond Diary. 27 Oct., While I was bowling a boy threw me against the knee. **1913** C. Pettman *Africanderisms* 498 *Throw with, To*, This is another form of expression common in the Midland Districts, and also due to the influence of Dutch: e.g. 'He threw me with a stone,' 'He threw me over the hedge with a rock'. The omission of the preposition makes the sentence, to English ears, a very curious one. **1919** [see WITH]. **1964** *Drum* Nov. 19 The living are throwing me with things. I know, I know .. but it is dangerous, they will kill me. **1972** R. Malan *Ah Big Yaws* 51 *Thrawwim withers tone* [throw him with a stone] ... Other people may encourage their compatriots to do damage by throwing things (stones, bottles or insults) *at* someone else. In South Africa, apparently, it's the *victim* who is thrown, together with the missile. Another alarming prospect .. is the cry common among schoolboys .. 'Thrawwim onnis het!' [throw him on his head]. **1974** [see NAARTJIE *n.* sense 1 b]. **1974** B. Simon *Joburg, Sis!* 106 The other day she was chasing her little brother because he threw her with a stone. **1987** *Informant, Grahamstown* Did you hear some woman threw PW with a rotten tomato? **1990** *Sunday Times* 11 Feb. 12 The Naboomspruit Recorder's headline of the incident .. read: 'Mike Gatting — Demos throw him with a stone'.

2. In the phr. ***to throw*** (***the***) ***bones*** (or occas. *- dolosse*), to cast a collection of divining bones and other objects down, and, from their pattern and positions, to foretell the future or divine the cause of a difficulty or an illness; BULA. See also BONE sense 2, DOLOS sense 1, WITCH-DOCTOR.

*a***1878** J. Montgomery *Reminisc.* (1981) 103 Others threw their bones and augured that there was nothing to fear. **1904** D. Kidd *Essential Kafir* 179 At a given signal they both throw the bones down to the ground, and the doctor very carefully examines the way in which the bones lie. **1914** S.P. Hyatt *Old Transport Rd* 160 The witch-doctor .. by throwing the bones, is always able to discover when the ghost of the departed calls for meat. **1930** S.T. Plaatje *Mhudi* (1975) 120 A few months later, Mzilikazi called his magicians together and asked the principal national wizard to throw bones, and communicate any omens he could divine. **1935** H.C. Bosman *Mafeking Rd* (1969) 72 They had heard that this witch-doctor was very good at throwing the bones. **1937** C. Birkby *Zulu Journey* 103 The witch-doctor gave Professor Kirby a horoscope — but asked for the traditional shilling before throwing the 'bones'. **1949** A. Keppel-Jones *When Smuts Goes* 255 The izangoma threw their bones and examined entrails in the ballroom of their hotel. **1969** *Drum* Aug. 46 If I pray and wait for God's Word, I cannot charge. So I throw the bones, and the people know they must pay me for it. **1976** B. Head in *Quarry*

'76 21 I'll throw the bones for you ... The bones will help me to see the one who is injuring your life. *Ibid.* Throwing the bones is cheaper than the medicine. It costs one rand. **1987** *Personality* 21 Oct. 12 Monica is a traditional Zulu 'witchdoctor' who throws the bones (African fortune-telling) and assists in diagnosing people's ailments. **1990** G. COETZEE in *S. Afr. Panorama* Jan.-Feb. 14 They [*sc.* hawkers] peddle fruit, vegetables and flowers, shine shoes, .. wash motor cars, .. throw the bones and provide herbs and remedies.

thuishuis var. TUISHUIS.

thula var. TULA.

thwala var. TWALA *v.*

thwasa /'twɑːsə, 'twaːsa/ *n.* and *adj.* Also **twasa, ukuthwasa.** [Xhosa and Zulu, become possessed by a spirit; undergo initiation as a diviner; undergo renewal.]

A. *n.* The process or period during which an initiate studying to be a diviner or traditional doctor develops the powers of a medium; the psychological manifestations of a calling to become a diviner; *transf.*, the person so affected.

1860 W. SHAW *Story of my Mission* 447 The proper practitioners, or .. the native Priests of the higher grade, are initiated into their office by a peculiar process, called *ukutwasa* ... The word which expressed this initiatory process, *ukutwasa*, means 're-newal', and is the same that is used for the first appearance of the new moon. *Ibid.* 448 Whenever they [*sc.* the 'priests'] are satisfied that the individual is really in a state of *ukutwasa*, and that he is no pretender or impostor, they finally admit him to their order. **1866** W.C. HOLDEN *Past & Future* 286 Having gone through these outward preparations, he experiences an inward change, real or imaginary, expressed by the term, ukutwasa, which signifies 'change of the moon'. Thenceforth, he is a new man, and holds intercourse with spiritual beings. This description applies, with some variations, to all the Kaffir races. **1907** W.C. SCULLY *By Veldt & Kopje* 82 The members of his family became uneasy and held anxious consultations over his unsatisfactory state. Eventually they came to the conclusion that he was undergoing the preliminary mental and moral disturbances incidental to the 'twasa' or spiritual change which comes over those who possess the vocation for witch-doctorship. **1937** B.J.F. LAUBSCHER *Sex, Custom & Psychopathology* 31 The *ukutwasa* is the period of psychic abnormality which a person must experience before the full development of mediumistic powers. **1955** J.B. SHEPHARD *Land of Tikoloshe* 84 Ukuthwasa, as the Africans call this state of mind, is something that I must leave to the psychiatrists to explain. All I can say is that it is accompanied by strange hallucinations, hysteria, and often lycanthropy, and is recognized by the Bantu tribes as a normal preliminary to becoming a full-blown witch doctor. **1962** W.D. HAMMOND-TOOKE *Bhaca Soc.*, The diviner's cult is esoteric and open only to the few who have received the 'call' and become ill with *thwasa*; the herbalist's calling is open to all who have the necessary diligence to learn the many medicines and who apprentice themselves to a master. **1975** *S. Afr. Panorama* Nov. 21 The animal is slaughtered, the bladder taken, its contents drunk by the twasa and the inflated bladder tied into her hair.

B. *adj.* Of or pertaining to the state of psychic sensitivity or abnormality experienced by one suited to the profession of SANGOMA; (of a person) predisposed to such a state, or in such a state.

1937 B.J.F. LAUBSCHER *Sex, Custom & Psychopathology* 35 He claims that the true *ukutwasa* states are rare and that many so-called *ukutwasa* conditions are loss of senses, which may be due to witchcraft or mild *ukutwasa* states not properly treated. **1954** W.D. HAMMOND-TOOKE in A.M. Duggan-Cronin *Bantu Tribes* III. v. 39 *Isangoma* are called to their profession by the dreams in which an ancestor shows them the medicines they should use. Initiation is preceded by a period of sickness when the novice is said to be *ukuthwasa*. **1980** E. JOUBERT *Poppie Nongena* 275 Your husband's grandma was thwasa, as a child I knew I was thwasa and must do the work. You are thwasa too, said the old woman, but you fight against it. Thwasa means to be able to talk to the ancestors, the izinyanya, thwasa is to have ears for words which others cannot hear. **1984** *S. Afr. Panorama* Dec. 43 Once the *thwasa* person has reached a certain level of healing, a series of ceremonies takes place over an extended period. The highlight is a four-day ceremony, at the end of which an ox is slaughtered, and the 'graduate' receives a white blanket to wear around his shoulders, as well as an assegaai and other emblems to indicate his status as a qualified *iggira*.

Hence **thwasa** *v. intrans.*, to undergo the spiritual initiation into the profession of 'sangoma'.

1987 *Pace* Aug. 10 The black girl sharing a house or flat with her white hubby is soon called upon to 'thwasa' (called by the spirits to become sangoma). The spirits will prick and hammer her in her sleep and in her social jaunts.

TIC /tiː aɪ 'siː/ *n.* [Initial letters of *Transvaal Indian Congress*.] An organization working for the political rights and social welfare of people of Indian descent living in the former province of Transvaal. Also *attrib.* Cf. CONGRESS sense 1.

1983 *Daily Dispatch* 2 May 9 The TIC traces its origins back to the formation by Mahatma Gandhi of the Transvaal British Indian Association in 1902 and was later a key member of the Congress Alliance during the passive resistance campaign of 1952. **1985** [see NIC]. **1987** A. AKHALWAYA in *Weekly Mail* 17 July 2 The TIC secretary .. yesterday said his organisation had collected affidavits from people 'who have been duped into casting special votes.' **1987** S. MEMELA in *City Press* 23 Aug. 2 The TIC has mobilised people to oppose the tricameral parliamentary system since its inception in 1984, and it has urged the community not to participate in any activities linked to the political status quo. **1988** *Sunday Times* 31 May 16 The TIC has also predicted that the tricameral constitution was a recipe for greater polarisation.

tic-bird var. TICK-BIRD.

ticcy var. TICKEY.

tick-bird *n.* Also **tic-bird.** [Perh. tr. Afk. *bosluisvoël* (bush)tick bird.]

1. The cattle egret, *Bubulcus ibis* of the Ardeidae, often seen near (or perching upon) grazing cattle or game.

Despite its name, the bird feeds mainly upon grasshoppers, caterpillars, earthworms, and frogs.

1863 W.C. BALDWIN *Afr. Hunting* 389, I was much amused by watching the tick birds trying to alarm an old white rhinoceros. **1899** H. RIDER HAGGARD *Swallow* 101, I remember .. the tic-bird that came and sat near you. **1939** S. CLOETE *Watch for Dawn* 366 The light flashed on some white wings as a flock of tick-birds flew past in the distance ... Where there were tick-birds there was water. **1949** J. MOCKFORD *Golden Land* 224 One lone sable, with far-curving scimitar-like horns, knelt in the shallow water ... On his shoulders and rump two tick-birds rummaged his chocolate-dark hair with their beaks. **1953** D. ROOKE *S. Afr. Twins* 25 Tickbirds, flying up from the donkeys' backs, cried out shrilly. **1961** *Red Wing* (St Andrew's College, Grahamstown) 33 The egrets, or tick-birds as most people call them, are the main form of bird life on the island. **1973** *S. Afr. Panorama* May 14 The beak of a tick-bird is long and strong — capable of gripping and disposing of a mouse. **1987** *Personality* 15 June 57 Most South Africans refer to cattle egrets as 'tick-birds'.

2. *obs. rare.* OXPECKER.

1905 W.L. SCLATER in Flint & Gilchrist *Science in S. Afr.* 137 Among the Starlings or Spreuws .. are the curious Oxpeckers, also called Tick birds (*Bulphaga africana*). **1907** J.P. FITZPATRICK *Jock of Bushveld* (1909) Glossary, *Tick, or Rhinoceros, Bird*, the 'ox-pecker' (*Buphaga Africana*).

tick-bite fever *n. phr. Pathology.* A common tick-borne typhus fever caused by the eubacterium *Rickettsia conori*, producing general lassitude, headache, and fever, and transmitted to people by the bite of esp. the red-legged tick *Rhipicephalus appendicularus* and the BONT TICK *Amblyomma hebraeum*, both of the Ixodidae. Cf. BILIARY FEVER.

1955 A.C. CHANDLER *Intro. to Parasitology* 569 The principal forms of tick-borne rickettsial disease are: .. spotted fever in North and South America .. ; boutonneuse fever around the Mediterranean and the same or a very closely related disease known as tick typhus or tick-bite fever in tropical South Africa, central Asia [etc.]. **1971** [see BONT-LEGGED TICK]. **1974** in *Std Encycl. of Sn Afr.* X. 499 *Tick-Bite Fever*, A typhus fever, widespread in South Africa, which is transmitted to man through the bite of a number of species of ticks. The disease has an incubation period of 6–7 days between the infecting bite and the onset of general symptoms. **1974** *Dorland's Illust. Medical Dict.* 1360 *Rickettsia*, .. *R. conorii*, the etiolic agent of boutonneuse fever .. , and possibly also Indian tick typhus, Kenya typhus, and South African tick-bite fever; transmitted by *Rhipicephalus* and *Hyemaphysalis*, *Amyblomma* [*sic*] and *Ixodes* ticks. **1989** F. OOSTHUIZEN *Informant, Grahamstown* You have the classic symptoms of tick-bite fever — and there's the bite! **1990** [see SOMMER]. **1991** J.B. WALKER in *Onderstepoort Jrnl of Vet. Research* Vol.58 No.2, 82 Both *A*[*mblyomma*] *hebraeum* and *A. variegatum* can transmit *Rickettsia conori*, which causes human tick-bite fever (tick-borne typhus).

tickelosh, tic(k)oloshe varr. TOKOLOSHE.

tickets *pl. n. Slang.* [Idiomatic use of general Eng. *ticket*.] 'Curtains', the end; cf. *finish and klaar* (see KLAAR *adj.* sense 4 b).

1966 S. CLOUTS *One Life* 54 It was luck but it was bad luck, maaster. I am Hotknife of Capricorn an she was in de Crab sir. It was tiekets. **1974** A.P. BRINK *Looking on Darkness* 327 'What are we going to live on if we appeal?' 'It's tickets anyway,' said Lucy. 'I can't take it any longer ... This time it's finish' en' klaar.' **1984** *Sunday Times* 29 Jan. (Mag. Sect.) 10 Debbie checks the man's pupils and pulse. *Ah ... I think he's dead. Tickets.* **1986** L. SAMPSON in *Style* May 10 He points again to the photograph album, 'There's the one time Chief Justice of the Cape. If you ever got in front of him it was tickets.' **1994** T. QUIRK on TV1, 12 Dec., I think that is tickets for New Zealand.

tickey /'tɪkiː/ *n.* Also **ticcy, tickie, ticky, ti(e)kie, tikkie.** [Etym. disputed.

Pettman's theory that the word comes fr. Pg. *pataca* a colonial coin, or Fr. *patac* 'small coin' (via the French Huguenots) is neither phonetically nor semantically likely. M.D.W. Jeffreys, in 'Tickey: Origin of the Word' (*Africana Notes & News*, Vol.10), points out that *pataca* was derived fr. Arabic *bataka* dollar, piece of eight (a coin of high value), while the Fr. *pataque* referred to coins in circulation in Turkey, Egypt, Algeria, and Brazil. The Malay *tiga* 'three' is also unlikely, as by the 19th century, when the coin was introduced, the influence of Malay was no longer strong.

Boshoff and Nienaber suggest *Brit. Eng.* dialect *ticky* 'small' as a possible origin (*Afrikaanse Etimologieë*, 1967). Both Xhosa and Zulu use *itiki* for the coin, described by lexicographers as being borrowed from *S. Afr. Eng.*, but it is possible that *itiki* was in fact a rendering in the Nguni languages of a Du. or Eng. word, such as Du. *stukje* 'little bit', or Eng. *ticket* (see quot. 1912), or even *threepence* (*i-tiki-peni* becoming *u-no-tiki* and then *itiki*, according to some, and recorded by Pettman). Jeffreys refers to Portuguese Angola, where the universal currency, a brass rod worth about 3d., was known as *ntaku*, but decides upon the Hindu *taka* (a stamped silver coin) as the origin of *itiki* in the Nguni languages of the east coast (whence it came into *S. Afr. Eng.* usage). Jeffreys claims that other words for money in African languages have similar origins (Swahili *pesa* fr. Hindi *pice*, Zulu *upeni* a three-penny piece, fr. Hindi and Sanskrit *pana*), and that Zulu *mali* (money) is from Arabic *malah* (wealth, money), all resulting from early trading contact.]

I. The name of a coin.

1.a. The standard name for the small silver three-penny piece (withdrawn from circulation in 1961). Also *attrib.*

Often used as a symbol of insignificant worth, lack of money (cf. 'not a penny'), a very small amount of money (cf. 'every last cent'), or small gain: see also *fig.* senses below.

[**1855** R.J. MULLINS Diary. 13 May, The Kafirs do not understand the value of anything except 3d. bits. It is very expensive work, for they will take nothing below 'Tick', as they call it, whereas some time ago they wanted 1d. for everything because it was 'in-kulu' (large) money.] **1871** *Cape Argus* 26 Aug. 2 The Fields have not proved themselves worthy of 'The Golden Dream,' in which so many indulged, but yet they really might do more than descend to the vulgar *tickey.* **1872** C.A. PAYTON *Diamond Diggings* 128 Coppers are altogether unknown on the diggings; the three-penny-piece, known as the 'ticky' is still in currency, but there is a considerable scarcity of these small coins. **1879** MRS HUTCHINSON *In Tents in Tvl* 91 Three-penny bits are the lowest coins which are in general circulation here ... They are in great request among the Kaffirs, who call them 'ticcys'. **1888** *Cape Punch* 25 Apr. 43 Spillikins has sent us the following astonishing bill of costs: Lamed ass .. 10 bob. Lamed wife .. tickey. Lamed self .. 7/6. **1893** [see DOLLAR]. **1894** C.E. FINLASON *A Nobody in Mashonaland* 87 When I saw them they were playing 'tickey' nap. [*Note*] An African term for a threepenny piece. **1899** 'S. ERASMUS' *Prinsloo* 121 A full explanation of every tickie that may be missing. **1900** B. MITFORD *Aletta* 57 His life would not be worth a tickey. They would shoot him. **1903** *Westminster Gaz.* (U.K.) 25 July 2 In purchasing-power the 'tickey' [of Johannesburg] is certainly not more than equal to the penny of London. In many cases its value is less than a halfpenny. **1912** *New Eng. Dict.* X., *Ticky*, .. Residents of Cape Colony, whose memory goes back to *c*1850, state that they have known 'ticky' all their lives. The prevalent notion is that the word was first used by the Caffres or other native labourers; it is at present in Sesuto (the Basuto lang.), *teke* ... But it is believed to have been a native imitation of some Dutch or Eng. word; e.g. of Cape Dutch *stukje* 'little piece, little bit', .. and imitated by the natives .. , according to others, of Eng. *ticket*, it being explained that on an occasion when a large body of natives were employed on a public work, they were, for want of small silver coin, paid with tickets for 3d., which were taken in payment by the provision stores, and redeemed at that rate by the authorities. Other statements or conjectures (e.g. that *tikki* was an attempt to say 'little') have been offered in the *Cape Times*, etc., Apr. to June 1912, but nothing in the form of evidence has been adduced. **1919** M.C. BRUCE *Golden Vessel* 15 Threepence is threepence, and not a 'tickey,' which is supposed to have originated in a Kaffir's attempt at saying threepence, still the word is so much used that if you say in a Johannesburg tramcar, 'I want a threepenny ticket,' the conductor will not understand you, and you will have to translate it into the African 'tickey', which is not literate to say the least. **1928** J.W.N. MOLLER *What Every Housewife Should Know* 103 Put a tickey's worth of liquid ammonia into a pint bottle. **1932** G.B. SHAW *Adventures of Black Girl* 42, I do conjuring tricks for them; and .. they only throw me coppers and sometimes tickeys. *c*1936 *S. & E. Afr. Yr Bk & Guide* 1022 The local term 'tikkie' (probably derived from the Malay 'Tiga' = 3, or perhaps from the Malay 'pat-aca' = doit) frequently heard, represents 3d. **1939** F.B. YOUNG *City of Gold* 482 Can you .. swear honest you're any better off now .. than you was in them days when every tickey counted? **1948** H.V. MORTON *In Search of S. Afr.* 45 Before I set foot in South Africa I had never heard the word 'tickey'. It is the South African name for a threepenny bit. It is almost impossible to live through a day anywhere in the Union without hearing this strange word mentioned. **1953** A. MOGALE in *Drum* May 30, I don't come tickey-a-dozen. I'm awfully expensive. **1955** W. ILLSLEY *Wagon on Fire* 29 'It's God's trufe, Oom Frikkie, I don't make freppence a gallon on the stuff' ... 'None of that nonsense, Ikay, .. You'd sell your soul for a tickey'. **1956** A.G. MCRAE *Hill Called Grazing* 46, I thought ruefully of the five shillings I'd paid him, all in *tickies* and pennies. **1963** *Rand Daily Mail* 11 May 1 Thousands of South Africans — housewives, motorists, telephone-users and trade unionists among them — are opposed to the Government plan to abolish the traditional 'tickey' ($2\frac{1}{2}$ c). **1963** S. CLOETE *Rags of Glory* 326, I have nothing to give you. I have no money. Not a tickey. **1965** S. DEDERICK *Tickey* 19 'Half a sixpence ...' she said. 'Half a five-cent piece. It's the same. It makes, it makes — one tickey.' **1970** S. MOORE *Informant, Port Elizabeth* When I was a child I could buy a tickey's worth of sweets in brown paper expertly rolled into a cone-shaped container called a kardoesie. **1973** *Cape Times* 18 June 7, I love the word 'bioscope'. It is essentially South African. I hope it does not disappear like the 'tickey' which was a part of our heritage. **1980** A. FUGARD *Tsotsi* 36 There was only an old man in the shop buying a tickey plug of chew tobacco. **1983** [see VELD POND]. **1985** *Cape Times* 23 Sept. 9 Just about every cartoon character I could remember from the old days of the tickey bioscope. **1989** B. COURTENAY *Power of One* 124 'You eat something, you hear. Here's a ticky to buy a cool drink,' he said handing me tiny silver coin. **1989** B. RONGE in *Flying Springbok* Nov. 13 Do you remember tickeys? Did you know the amount of precious metal they contained was worth more than a one rand coin today? Think of that and tremble. **1990** *Weekend Argus* 17 Feb. 16 Gold Burgerpond 1874, rare genuine Sammy Marks gold tickey 1898, gold Kruger Rands. **1990** *Pace* May 184 It was a case of taximen fighting over unwilling passengers. For a tiekie-and-a-halfpenny, the powderkeg for a territorial war was detonated. **1992** *Motorist* Aug. 15 Travel on a tickey ... In these deregulation days, it's a price free-for-all. **1993** *Business Day* 25 June (Suppl.) 1, 1931 Tickey.

b. With distinguishing epithet: **long tickey** *fig. colloq.*, a device (usu. a coin on a thread) used in a public telephone box in order to make calls without paying; *tickey-wire*, see sense 5 a.

1975 *Het Suid-Western* 13 Mar., Found guilty .. for telephoning with a '**long tickey**' from a public telephone booth. He .. pleaded guilty to using .. a 'long tickey'. The 'long tickey' exhibited in court was a ten cent coin suspended from a cotton thread which was attached with a piece of cellotape. **1975** *E. Prov. Herald* 17 Mar. 6 Fined R45 (or 90 days) last week by a George magistrate who found him guilty of fraud for using a 'long tickey' to make a call from a public telephone booth.

2. *hist.* In full ***tickey beer***: a beer (costing 3d. a bottle) produced in the past in Cape Town.

1888 *Cape Punch* 15 Feb. 88 What is the most appropriate drink for an undertaker who trades on credit? — Why, Tickey Bier. **1891** J.P. LEGG in *Cape Illust. Mag.* I. 96 'Tickey Beer,' with various names of liqueurs are well known, such as Van der Hum. **1910** J. RUNCIE *Idylls by Two Oceans* 177 Given a shilling, can a bag of Kat River, a bottle of tickey, and a full meal go into it? *Ibid.* 179 He went into a public-house and called for beer — generous tickey. **1911** P. GIBBON *Margaret Harding* 173 Off to the station on my tootsies and take train back to the land of ticky (threepenny) beer and Y.M.C.A.'s. **1928** N. STEVENSON *Afr. Harvest* 197 The men were celebrating their master's wedding with Cape brandy and *tickey* beer. **1947** L.G. GREEN *Tavern of Seas* 13 Only the middle-aged will remember the 'tickey beer' of wistful memory. Breweries supplied it in bulk, and it was bottled by the bar proprietors. It actually cost threepence for a large bottle. **1964** in L.G. Green *Old Men Say* 59 Just before de barrel, murrer, I was drinking tickey beer, But I took too much, dear murrer, So to home I could not steer. **1985** A. TREDGOLD *Bay between Mountains* 161 The strong south-easter buffeting under Elsie's Peak dusted sand into our tickey beer. **1987** W. STEENKAMP *Blockhouse* 8 I've had a guts-full ... Nothin' to drink but bloody awful tickey beer or a glass of dop that takes the linen off your guts.

II. Figurative senses.

3. Designating that which is inexpensive. Often *attrib.*, passing into *adj.*

1873 *Standard & Mail* 9 Sept. 4 Men and women who are so partial to three-penny bits as the current Sunday coin .. 'tickey' religionists ... The great multitude of ordinary men and women one meets in the street are of the 'tickey' Christian class. **1931** K. LINDSAY *'Neath Sn Cross* 40 Oh, those! .. Most of them are only 'ticky' spectators ... On some South African stations they charge a ticky for a platform ticket. A lot of people come to watch the trains in out of sheer idle curiosity. It's a cheap form of entertainment, see? **1992** T. TISANI in *Cue* 4 July 9 The audience is taken on a quick flight back to the pulsating township music of the fifties and sixties. The cast .. of genuine artists .. is complemented by young men who ably portray in movement and style what it must have been like to attend those tickey shows.

4. Alluding to the size of the tickey.

a. Denoting small physical size. **i.** A nickname given to small people.

1911 L. COHEN *Reminisc. of Kimberley* 64 As for 'Tickey' Erlich, he'd hardly been conceived, much less invented. **1916** [see OUPA sense 1]. **1965** S. DEDERICK *Tickey* 19 'Oh, Rebeccah, is that why I'm called Tickey?' 'Dat was the name I give you. I jes' said to Merrem, let's call her Tickey, she's so small.' **1970** W. MALCOLM *Informant, Kabwe (Zambia)* Tickey — nickname given to small person. **1971** *Argus* 10 May 23 Full credit must go to former Durban jockey 'Tickey' C—. **1971** *Sunday Times* 14 Nov. (Mag. Sect.) 8 Their most famous clowns were Tony Francisco and (in recent years) 'Tickey'.

ii. In the adj. phrr. ***two bricks and a tickey high, half a brick and a tickey high***, etc.: very small, very young; short of stature.

1970 *Cape Times* 30 May, In the days when he was two bricks and a tickey high .. a tickey was his reward for every furry digger caught. **1970** M. WEITZMAN *Informant, Johannesburg* He is two bricks and a tickey high. **1975** *Darling* 26 Feb. 111 Inside there's this tiny little ou half a brick and a tickey high, with a smashed nose and curled-over ears. **1976** *Ibid.* 9 June 74 He laughs. 'I called it Mr Brian because the staff at Riviera have been calling me "Mr Brian" since I was two bricks and a tickey high.' **1986** *Black Ace* Dec. 11 He may only be a tickey high to his boss, Solly Mogare's driver, but pint-sized Lungi Bohlela proved a wizard when reading the nap on the greens. **1989** *Cape Times* Sept., I have been travelling to and from Namaqualand since I was shorter than two bricks and a pre-decimalization tickey. **1990** *People* 22 Nov. 14 Since he was a brick and a tickey tall, wildlife has been his passion. **1990** *Weekend Post* 1 Dec. (advt) 7 The fact that Napoleon was only two bricks and a tickey high didn't stop him from getting a foothold in much of the civilized world.

b. Referring to a small surface area. In the adj. phr. or adv. phr. ***(turn) on a tickey*** [perh. tr. Afk. *tiekiedraai* (see quot. 1980)], in a small area or circle; accurate(ly); *transf.*, in a short time, rapidly.

1971 *Informant, Grahamstown* I've learned to turn the wheelchair on a tickey. **1976** D. TAYLOR in *Reader's Digest* Aug. (1977) 226 In boats that could touch 100 km/h and turn on a tickey, I learned how to handle the newly caught animals [*sc.* dolphins]. **1977** *Sunday Times* 20 Oct. 5 The power-assisted brakes, disks on all four wheels, stop the car — and it's big — on a tickey. [**1980** D.B. COPLAN Urbanization of African Performing Arts. 440 Glossary, *Tickey Draai*, (Afrikaans, 'turn on a tickey' — a threepence), A Coloured-Afrikaans dance derived from Cape square dancing in which couples turn rapidly around in one spot.] **1991** M. O'SHEA *Informant, Kokstad* He could turn his car on a tickey. **1992** D. RICHARDSON on TV1, 1 Apr., He was so accurate — when he bowled that last over he was on a tickey. **1992** J. VAN DER HORST in *Sunday Times* 23 Aug. (Business Times) 2 This market can turn on a tickey .. and the cost of missing the opportunity when the market does rally is much higher.

III.

5. Special Combinations.

Many of these terms are still in use despite the disappearance of the coin, the change in currency, and the rise in prices.

a. (from sense 1) **tickeyaand** /-ɑːnt/ [Afk. *aand* evening], a small-scale fund-raising venture in which entrance to an event or game, or the price of something to eat, was formerly a tickey; **tickey-box**, see as a main entry; **tickey-diver**, one who dives for coins to entertain tourists; **tickey-draai**, see as a main entry; **tickey-drive** or **tickey evening**, see *tickeyaand*; **tickey-I-do**, a dice game; **tickey-wire**, *long tickey* (see sense 1 c).

1934 *Friend* 9 Feb. (Swart), On Friday night a '**tickey-aand**' was held to augment the funds of the local branch of the Voortrekkers. **1970** S. SPARKS *Informant, Fort Beaufort* The school held a tiekieaand to raise funds for sports equipment. (Evening's entertainment where you pay a 3d to enter for different competitions — outdated now because of metric system but widely used by English-speaking people in the Karoo and other Afrikaans areas.) **1971** *E. Prov. Herald* 13 Oct., Members of the Dutch Reformed Church of the Tsitsikamma held a five cent function (Tiekieaand) in the church hall .. various games which were much enjoyed by young and old were played. **1956** *S. African's Holiday & Trav. Guide* 69 The liners .. call regularly [at the Cape Verde Islands], and the islands' boatmen-traders and '**tickey-divers**' swim out to welcome them. **1973** BEETON & DORNER in *Eng. Usage in Sn Afr.* Vol.4 No.2, 62 **Tickey drive**, .. Evening's entertainment at wh[ich] participants paid threepence to enter an event or game. **1948** E. ROSENTHAL *Afr. Switzerland* 82 A photograph of the formal presentation of the result of a '**Tickey Evening**' in 1939. It was in aid of the South African Governor-General's National War Fund, and the flat charge for every stake threepence. **1956** [see HOSTEL sense 2]. **1972** K.C. ORAM *Informant, Grahamstown* Cake sales, a bridge drive, a tickey-evening, or whatever you call it nowadays. **1986** *Poster, Grahamstown* Victoria Girls' High tickey evening. **1975** S. SEPAMLA in *New Classic* No.1, 11 In street-corners it is '**tickey-I-do**', you know the game of dice. **1970** K.M. BRAND *Informant, East London* **Tickey-wire.** A device used to evade putting a coin in the slot of a public phone booth.

b. (from sense 3) **tickey bazaar**, a general store carrying a range of cheap goods; **tickey-line** *n.* [prob. fr. the name given to a cheap line of sweets], esp. in the townships, anything cheap, particularly an 'easy' woman or a cheap prostitute; any small-scale organization, as a SHEBEEN (sense 1), STOKVEL (sense 1 a), etc.; as *adj.*, cheap, small-scale, poorly-funded; **tickey-shop**, see *tickey bazaar*; **tickey-snatching**, on the stock-market, small-time profit-taking, used esp. of small investors buying few shares and selling at the first rise in price; also *attrib.*; so **tickey-snatcher**, a stock-broker dealing in small numbers of shares; a small investor; a mean person, a 'skinflint'.

*c*1929 S. BLACK in S. Gray *Three Plays* (1984) 109 Gwen: .. I suppose you're in commercial life? Camelia: Well, I was cashier in a **tickey bazaar**. **1977** F.G. BUTLER *Karoo Morning* 28 He did assure me that if I behaved myself, he would take me to Hyam's Tickey Bazaar .. and buy me a present. **1964** *Drum* Nov. 36 Zel: .. These are people who have a very high choice in women and to find a woman who would suit their choice, it would be very Hard. Drum: You mean you can't plant a '**tickey line**' in their ranks? **1973** *The 1820* Vol.46 No.6, 19 Stokvel groups range in importance from what is commonly called the 'Tiekie-Line' type, where membership fees are small, to the 'Big-time' and 'Who's Who' kind where, as the names suggest, only top-crust names adorn the lists, and fees are known to range from upwards R10 a head. **1973** *Ibid.* [see STOKVEL sense 1]. **1974** *Drum* 22 May 55 Kid Windsor Castle decides that we should go to a 'Tickeyline' stokvel which is taking place not far away and he is a member of this club. **1977** P.C. VENTER *Soweto* 182 The Tickey-lines were, as the nickname implies, cheap prostitutes who knew how it felt to be the underdog. *a*1977 K.M.C. MOTSISI in M. Mutloatse *Casey & Co.* (1978) 76 Thomas had been trying to avoid Sponono ever since he realised he was in love with Mita. 'Ja, Thomas, you tickeyline,' Sponono said. Thomas looked up at his old flame, nodded his head and said, 'Hiya, Spo.' **1984** C. MATHIANE in *Staffrider* Vol.6 No.1, 31 'Ja,' said the woman, 'you think I am a ticky-line. You leave me sleeping at the hotel and you rush to your high society wife.' **1985** 'BLACK ACE' in *Drum* Oct. 4 Tickey line soccer ... Although they are by no means the only teams hard hit by recession, Orlando Pirates and Moroko Swallows Ltd seem to be the worst off. **1992** J. THOM *Informant, Springs* In White society, Tickey-line seems to me to refer to cheap sweets when used by English speakers, and cheap women when used in Afrikaans. **1959** M.W. SPILHAUS *Under Bright Sky* 128 You cannot get him out of a bazaar, or what we in our day used to call a '**tickey shop**'. **1924** L. COHEN *Reminisc. of Jhb.* 82 Barney .. asked how the — I dare sell my own shares, and that if I wanted three hundred threepenny bits, why didn't I ask him to give me them, and not go **tickey-snatching** like a blasted (noun substantive). **1970** F.G. BUTLER *Informant, Grahamstown* Tickey-snatcher. Cheese-parer. **1974** D. ROOKE *Margaretha de la Porte* 100, I bought shares, to sell again on the first rise: tickey-snatching, Father called it. **1978** *Cape Times* 10 Apr., The tickey-snatching lives of middle-class respectability. **1979** J. GRATUS *Jo'burgers* 201 Avoiding the main stockbrokers .. , George stopped at the offices of some of the jobbers, the 'tickey-snatchers' who dealt in small quantities of shares.

c. (from sense 4 a) **tickey-stock**, on the stock-exchange, the stock of a small company or group.

1991 *Sunday Times* 3 Mar. (Business Times) 2 **Tickey-stock** Royal takes a place in the guinea seats. Unsung Royal Corporation has one of the lowest profiles yet the highest success rate of any public company ... On value for money Royal group shares have the potential to grow at a faster rate than the bigger boys.

tickey-box *n. colloq.* [TICKEY sense 1 a + Eng. *box*; prob. by synecdoche (see quot. 1963), named for the box, attached to the public telephone, in which coins were deposited. See also quot. 1993.] A public telephone.

[**1963** L.F. FREED *Crime in S. Afr.* 150 On the Witwatersrand, the raiding of tickey boxes in telephone booths .. costs the Post Office more than £5 500 a year.] **1976** *E. Prov. Herald* 8 June 3 Miss Renee S— .. was apparently allowed to fix the telephones. 'I just go off in my bakkie on my own looking for all those tickey boxes you can't find.' **1982** [see BOKKIE sense 1]. **1985** P. SLABOLEPSZY *Sat. Night at Palace* 11 Forsie: .. (*Spotting the public phone*) Come on — there's a tickey box. Go phone. **1988** *Daily Dispatch* 5 Aug. 4 The name [tickey] lives on of course. It used to be the price of a telephone call and a public telephone is still called a tickey box. **1989** J. HOBBS *Thoughts in Makeshift Mortuary* 34 I'll run down to the tickey box and phone Dr Van Coller. **1991** L. HOWARD *Informant, Port Elizabeth* The phone inside rang and when one of the ladies answered it, she called my friend, telling him to hurry as the call was from someone in a tickey box. **1992** J. THOM *Informant, Springs*, I have never heard the term tickey-phone, it was always tickey-box. **1993** H. TYSON *Editors under Fire* 9 The man-on-the-run hung on to the end of a telephone in a public booth — known in South Africa in those days as 'a tickey box' because it accepted only the tiny silver threepenny coin of that name and because public booths sometimes felt that tiny. **1994** on M-Net TV 15 Apr. (Egoli), Are tickey-boxes hard to come by in deepest darkest Africa?

tickey-draai /ˈtɪkidraɪ/ *n.* Also **ti(e)kiedraai, tikkiedraai.** [Part. tr. Afk. *tiekiedraai, tiekie* see TICKEY + *draai* turn, twirl.]

1.a. A fast dance-movement derived from Cape square-dancing, in which couples link hands and spin round on one spot on their toes, leaning away from each other; a dance including this movement. Also *attrib.*, and *transf.* See also VASTRAP *n.* sense 1 a.

1929 J.G. VAN ALPHEN *Jan Venter* 251 An occasional rollicking set of dancers in which couples indulged in the 'tickey-*draai*', i.e. a rapid top-like spinning in one spot. **1934** C.P. SWART Supplement to Pettman. 176 *Tikiedraai*, In dancing, to turn on one's toes like a tickey that is spun round. The term is also applied to dancing picnic dances. **1936** E. ROSENTHAL *Old-Time Survivals* 28 The 'tikkie-draai' or 'three-penny turn' is one of the vigorous, uproarious steps favoured from the old days. **1938** *George & Knysna Herald* 19 Oct. 1 Give me a good old tickey-draai every time. **1952** *Drum* Dec. 18 The 'Tikkie Draai' .. where a single couple swing at the centre of the ring while the other dancers clap hands in rhythm ... The 'tikkie draai' (making sixty revolutions with your partner for a minute without getting dizzy!). **1959** A. DELIUS *Last Division* 76 It was like the annual Moffies' dance Where a zoo and a mad-house take their chance Stomping around up there on high Letting it go in a tickey draai. **1970** M. HOBSON *Informant, Tzaneen* It is fun to see the ostrich chicks doing the 'tiekie-draai'. **1972** N. HENSHILWOOD *Cape Childhood* 56 There were vigorous tickiedraais, gay moments when a man swung his partner round and round on one spot. **1974** D. ROOKE *Margaretha de la Porte* 15 The child in the centre had to choose a partner and then whirl, holding on by the tips of hooked fingers — this was called the tickey draai. **1975** [see SLUK *n.*]. **1980** D.B. COPLAN Urbanization of African Performing Arts. 208 Many African musicians had absorbed Afrikaans styles such as *vastrap* while serving in Afrikaans households in the country ... They enjoyed playing *tickey draai*, adding African melody to Afrikaans rhythms and chord structure. *Tickey draai* was played on solo guitar at first, but by the mid-1920's small Coloured-Xhosa string and concertina bands were also performing it for private African concerts called 'socials.' *Ibid.* 440 *Tickey Draai*, A Coloured-Afrikaans dance derived from Cape square dancing in which couples turn rapidly around in one spot. **1983** *Daily Dispatch* 7 Mar. 1 By evening time, it was tiekiedraai and boerewors time. **1987** C.L. KGAPHOLA in *Staffrider* Vol.6 No.4, 48 Leave your Molotov cocktail at home and join in the tikkie draai.

b. *fig.* Interaction; fast movement; spinning. Also *attrib.*

1975 *Drum* 8 Aug. 1 For their tickey-draai 200 verkramptes got together at Verwoerdburg. **1982** *Voice* 21 Mar. 4 The new Dr Ja-Nee leftwing (of a rightwing) is bound to end up in lots of tikkie-draais and other political dances in the Broederbond, Afrikaans-Ja Baas Pers, business et al. **1983** *Sunday Times* 31 July (Mag. Sect.) 26 Much of modern life consists of learning to hitchhike through the material advances of our age, an endless *tiekiedraai* with technology. **1989** *Ibid.* 29 Oct. 28 The Broederbond's political *tiekie-draai* act to improve its image, showing a bit of ankle here and there.

2. *Music.* The fast, rhythmical music played to accompany this dance; DRAAI sense 2. Also *attrib.*

1949 E. HELLMANN *Handbk on Race Rel.* 620 The coloured people at the Cape have for so long reflected the culture of their European progenitors that no indigenous music of theirs now exists, their principal contribution to the art being the instrumental idiom of the 'tickey-draai' since they and the Malays, during the epoch of slavery, provided most of the dance music for their European overlords. **1963** A. FUGARD *Blood Knot* (1968) 94 He could do a vastrap, that man, non-stop, on all strings, at once. He knew the lot. Polka, tickey-draai, opskud en uitkap, ek sê ... that was jollification for you. **1976** *Sunday Times* 11 July 20 At an impromptu performance .. the happy centenarian danced for about 10 minutes while playing a 'tiekkie draai' on his mouth organ. **1978** J. BAULING *Walk in Shadows* 129 One of their guests, an Afrikaans farmer, had brought his accordion and was providing some rollicking tiekie-draai and volkspele music. **1980** D.B. COPLAN Urbanization of African Performing Arts. 54 In Kimberley .. Coloured guitarists perfected the Cape style called *tickey draai* (Afrikaans: 'turn on a tickey' ..) ... Coloured performers brought *tickey* *draai* playing and dancing to other towns in the Eastern Cape. *Ibid.* 208 *Tickey draai* was played on solo guitar at first, but by the mid-1920's small Coloured-Xhosa string and concertina bands were also performing it. *Ibid.* 441 *Tickey Draai*, .. A guitar style popular between 1880 and 1930, used to accompany this [*sc.* the tickeydraai] and other black dances in the Eastern Cape, Kimberley, and Johannesburg. **1981** *Sunday Times* 15 Mar. 21 A concertina tikkiedraai going on all night in the dining room just below. **1990** *Weekend Post* 19 May (Leisure) 5 A musical diet ranging from bebop and marabi to vastrap and tiekiedraai.

Hence **tickey-draai** *v. intrans.*, to dance the tickey-draai; **tickey-draaing** *vbl n.*, spinning and whirling.

1966 I. VAUGHAN *These Were my Yesterdays* 112 Swinging himself and his partner wildly around in his own idea of the Charleston with much 'tickey-draaing'! **1985** *Drum* July 24 Wine is flowing freely as they tickiedraai to the twanging of guitars. **1994** *Weekly Mail & Guardian* 13 May 9 One black woman .. started twirling around wildly ... 'Where did you learn to *tiekiedraai* so good?' a bystander asked. 'In my *boerestaat!*' she laughed back.

tick-tock *n. ?obs.* Also **tik-tok**. [fr. Afk. *toktokkie*.] TOK-TOKKIE sense 2 a.

1911 *State* Dec. 586 (Pettman), The evening generally starts with the pleasant game known as *tick-tock* ... The game is a simple one and is played somewhat as follows; You .. select a window the light in which betokens life behind the drawn blind ... A trusted member of your force .. must .. securely pin to the wooden frame, between the panes, one end of a stout thread. The thread is then pulled taut like a violin string, and a piece of resin is gently rubbed along it. The weird noise that this simple process causes to be heard by those inside the window is something that must be experienced to be believed. **1970** S. SPARKS *Informant, Fort Beaufort* We played tik-tok on old Mrs. Brown's front door. (A game played at night by children who steal up to front doors, knock and run off before they're caught.)

tiekie var. TICKEY.

tiekiedraai var. TICKEY-DRAAI.

tier /tɪə/ *n.* [Special use of general Eng. *tier* rank, grade, stratum.] In phrases designating levels of government: ***first tier***, central or national government; ***second tier***, regional government; ***third tier***, local government. Also *attrib.*

1980 *E. Prov. Herald* 2 Nov. 1 South West Africa's ruling Democratic Turnhalle Alliance almost made a clean sweep of the territory's second tier elections. **1983** *Financial Mail* 16 Sept. 52 The question of third-tier (municipal) rule still has to be clarified. **1985** P. BELL in *Business Day* 15 May 6 The legislative power of the provincial, second tier of government has been removed. *Ibid.* Next in line are the Regional Services Councils (RSCs); the new super-councils of the third tier. **1986** *Sunday Times* 7 Sept. 2 A National Statutory Council and a Council of State aimed at bringing blacks into a consultative role on first-tier level. **1988** P. CULL in *Evening Post* 24 Feb. 1 The restrictions placed on Cosatu effectively seemed aimed at halting any attempt to disrupt the third-tier elections scheduled for October.

tiffy *n. Military slang.* Also **tiffie**. [Transf. uses of Brit. Eng. *tiffy* an engine room artisan (Royal Navy slang, from late 1890s).]

1. In the defence forces, a member of the Technical Services Corps, a mechanic.

1975 J.H. PICARD in *Eng. Usage in Sn Afr.* Vol.6 (May) 37 In the workshops some of the technicians or *tiffies* may feel *sterk* about their girl-friends at home. **1975** *Scope* 10 Jan., So you've finished .. cleaning your gatt, squaring off your bed, .. pushing beat .. bribing a tiffy to fix your cab. **1977** *Sunday Times* 7 Aug. (TV Suppl.) 1 Other stories they have lined up for the series concern the 'tiffies' (army slang for mechanics, believed to be derived from the British army term, 'artificers'). **1979** *Grocott's Mail* 19 June 3 Sgt. Major Fred Hattingh who was well known as the 'boss of the tiffies' joined the Permanent Force in 1954. He was stationed at 6 SAI for most of his 24 years of service. **1985** *Cape Times* 18 Dec., The Technical Services Corps 'tiffies' can make anything run. **1989** *You* 6 Apr. 7 Everybody wants to be drivers, tiffies, medics and so on, and nobody wants to be a chef.

2. Used loosely, with defining words to designate men with particular occupations in the forces: **kop-tiffy** /ˈkɔp-/ [Afk. *kop* head], a psychiatrist, **people-tiffy** or **pill-tiffy**, a doctor or medical official; **pot-tiffy**, an army cook; **soul-tiffy**, a chaplain, **teeth-tiffy**, a dentist, etc.

1978 A.P. BRINK *Rumours of Rain* 318 When church parade was called the Sunday morning ... There was a new soul-tiffy to do the job for us. You know, we used to call the mechanics 'tiffies', so the doctor was a 'cock-tiffy' and the chaplain a 'soul-tiffy'. **1979** *Sunday Times* 12 Aug. 7 Hey pot-tiffie. Lez trek to the cuca shop. **1984** *Cape Times* 18 July, All hope is not yet gone for SADF medical and dental officers who have lost out on the recent 12 percent pay hike for national servicemen ... 'An investigation into the remuneration of all Citizen Force members .. is still in progress' ... In other words, the people tiffies must vasbyt. **1988** W. STEENKAMP in *Ibid.* 6 Apr., The 'tears tiffie' virtually went around drumming up business. The result was a rash of welfare problems among people who had not given it a thought before then. As a cultural note, let me add that in the SADF psychiatrists are sometimes referred to as 'kop-tiffies', or head mechanics. This is in line with similar terms like 'people tiffies' (doctors), 'bedpan tiffies' (medical orderlies) and 'teeth tiffies' (dentists). **1988** *Cape Times* 25 June 19 They should have strekked one of the gun-tiffies, who is a total vuil uil.

tiger *n. Obs.* exc. *hist.* Also **tigre**, **tijger**, **tyger**. [Transf. use of general Eng. *tiger* a name for the Asian mammal *Panthera tigris*.]

1. [Influenced by Du. *tijger* tiger, leopard.] The leopard, *Panthera pardus* of the Felidae; *African tiger*, see AFRICAN *adj.*[1] sense 1 b i; *berg-tiger*, see BERG sense 1 b ii; *Cape tiger*, see CAPE sense 2 a. Also *attrib.* See also LION AND TYGER. Cf. TIGER-CAT.

1655 E. TERRY *Voy. to E.-India* (1777) 15 This remotest part of Africa is very mountainous, over-run with wild beasts, as lions, tigers, wolves, and many other beasts of prey. **1688** G. TACHARD *Voy. to Siam* II. 64 They have there also Civit-cats, many Wildcats, Lyons and Tygers which have very pretty skins and especially huge great Apes that comes sometimes in Troops down from the *Table-land* into the Gardens of private Persons. **1696** J. OVINGTON *Voy. to Suratt* 283 Tygers and Lions are very numerous, and so bold, that they range sometimes within Gun-shot of the Fort. **1731** G. MEDLEY tr. *P. Kolb's Present State of Cape of G.H.* I. 64 The Dutch officer .. planted Out-Guards in the proper Places, for a Defence against the Lions, Tigers, and other fierce and ravenous Beasts, abounding in this territory. **1786** G. FORSTER tr. *A. Sparrman's Voy. to Cape of G.H.* I. 269 The *tigers*, or more properly *leopards*, (for they seem rather to belong to that species) are not so easily extirpated. **1798** B. STOUT *Narr. of Loss of Ship 'Hercules'* p.xxxiii, They frequently encounter the lion, the rhinoceros, the hippopotamus, the buffalo, the hyaena, the panther or the tiger. **1801** W. SOMERVILLE *Narr. of E. Cape Frontier* (1979) 30 The dress of both sexes is composed of bullock hides – and those of the Captains or people of rank, of Tiger skin. **1827** T. PHILIPPS *Scenes & Occurrences* 18 It was very large and the skin was beautifully marked. The Dutch call them tigers, but we were informed that there is no tiger in the Colony, and this certainly was a leopard. **1836** A.F. GARDINER *Journey to Zoolu Country* 123 Some men bearing a dead leopard. There are three kinds of this species in the country, all included by the Dutch and the colonists under the general name of Tiger, although that animal is here unknown. **1841** B. SHAW *Memorials* 305 The tigers of South Africa, differing but little from the leopards, are small when compared with the Royal Bengal tigers, but they are numerous, and exceedingly troublesome to the farmers. **1847** 'A BENGALI' *Notes on Cape of G.H.* 77 The Cape people are continually talking about 'Tigers', but there are no such animals on the continent, and they *mean* leopards or panthers. **1851** J.F. CHURCHILL Diary. (Killie Campbell Africana Library MS37) 21 Nov., Two of our fellow Colonists have died of wounds from the Panther or Tiger as it is called here. **1865** T. SHONE Diary. 7 Oct., Henry and Meers went a Tigre hunting. **1872** C.A. PAYTON *Diamond Diggings* 82 In the dusk, coming up a gully, .. I almost stumbled on to a leopard, or 'tiger' as they call it here, which had apparently caught some small beast and was growling over it. **1883** M.A. CAREY-HOBSON *Farm in Karoo* 218 One of the tiger traps had been set by George and Allan on their way up to the cattle. **1890** A. MARTIN *Home Life* 237 Although the elephant and lion are now no longer found in the Karroo, there still remain a good number of leopards, or, as the colonists, in calm defiance of natural history, persist in calling them, 'tigers'. **1898** *The Jrnl* 2 Apr. 2 Two horrified hunters strolling on the Beach near the Nahoon River Mouth saw a huge tiger spring from the bush at a buck. **1900** O. OSBORNE *In Land of Boers* 43 There is almost unlimited sport to be had in South Africa .. , and even as far south as the fairly well populated Cape districts, leopards – miscalled tigers – zebras, quaggas, wild cats, baboons, and jackals are still to be found. **1911** *Farmer's Weekly* 18 Oct. 193 We can to-day produce more tiger and leopard skins in our homes than the whole of the rest of the Kuruman district. We have destroyed them on our farms. **1936** E. ROSENTHAL *Old-Time Survivals* 36 Many a South African, following his grandfather's custom, still calls a leopard a 'tiger'. **1941** A.G. BEE *Kalahari Camp Fires* (1943) 21 Leopards, which are called tigers in South Africa, did much harm to native stock. **1953** R. CAMPBELL *Mamba's Precipice* 131 'Well, what do you make of that?' said Willem. 'I tell you it's a *tiger* for sure and not a ratel, nor an otter, nor an ant-bear.' [*Note*] 'Tiger' is the common South African word for a leopard. **1970** G. WESTWOOD *Bright Wilderness* 93 There had been lions and elephant in these parts then, and the leopard that in the old days they had called 'tygers'. **1989** B. GODBOLD Autobiography. 30 Leopards were always referred to as 'tigers', the Dutch custom, hence 'Tiger Flats'.

2. Ellipt. for:

a. The TIGERFISH (sense 2 b), *Pomadasys commersonnii.*

1930 C.L. BIDEN *Sea-Angling Fishes* 241 The fish resembles the white steenbras and the grunter (the Port Elizabeth 'tiger' ..) in frequenting shallows where freshets run into the sea. **1979** [see KNORHAAN sense 2].

b. The TIGERFISH (sense 1), *Hydrocynus vittatus.*

1971 *Personality* 5 Mar. 16 The barbel, often too large to lift from the water, break the monotony and strain of the fighting tigers. **1973** *E. Prov. Herald* 1 Mar. 4 Heaviest edible (rivers). D.O. Jones, tiger, 3,7kg.

tiger-cat *n. obsolescent.* Also **tyger-cat**. [Formed on S. Afr. Du. *tyger-bosch-kat* 'tiger-bush-cat'.] The serval *Felis serval* of the Felidae, with small head, long legs and neck, large ears, and an off-white to golden-yellow coat patterned with black spots and bars. See also *wild cat* (WILD sense b). Cf. TIGER sense 1.

The name is also used of other species throughout the world.

[**1786** G. FORSTER tr. *A. Sparrman's Voy. to Cape of G.H.* I. 151 They have a third cat in Africa, which, in its motions and attitudes, is like our common cat, and is called at the Cape the *tyger-kat*, and the *tyger bosch-kat*. **1790** tr. *F. Le Vaillant's Trav.* I. 79 Another species, called by the Dutch *luypar*, or leopard of the French; and a third species, still smaller, called the *cat tyger*, and by Buffon the *osselot*.] **1797** J. BARROW in D. Fairbridge *Lady Anne Barnard* (1924) 52 Twenty and thirty different sorts of Antelopes, Tygers, Tyger-cats, and in short more kinds of beasts than ever entered Noah's Ark are daily scampering about the plains of Africa. **1810** G. BARRINGTON *Acct of Voy.* 247 The skin of the tyger-cat is used by the women as pocket handkerchiefs. *a***1823** J. Ewart *Jrnl* (1970) 39 A considerable traffic might .. be carried on in ox hides either dried or salted, to which may be added the skins of the leopard, panther and tyger cat. **1835** A. Steedman *Wanderings* I. 327 Leopards and tiger-cats were frequently seen in this part of the country. **1867** S. Turner in D. Child *Portrait of Pioneer* (1980) 66 It was either a tiger or large tiger-cat, as the cock, which happened to be roosting on the tree instead of in the hen-house, was bitten quite through the neck. **1871** J. Mackenzie *Ten Yrs* (1971) 43 But now for the case itself, which was the bite of the South African tiger or tiger-cat. **1884** 'E.V.C.' *Promised Land* 93 On one occasion, we had been more than usually successful, and bagged two bucks, a great many birds and a large bush tiger cat. **1907** J.P. Fitzpatrick *Jock of Bushveld* (1909) 245 Once they killed a tiger-cat ... They were tugging and tearing at the lifeless black and white body. **1912** *Queenstown Free Press* 29 July (Pettman), The wild cat or tiger-cat, as it is generally called, the mshlosi of the natives, is, I believe, irreclaimable. **1925** H.F. Mandelbrote tr. *O.F. Mentzel's Descr. of Cape of G.H.* II. 61 Their caps look handsome and imposing; the back is of blue kersey and the front of tiger skin – or alleged tiger skin; more probably it is made of the skin of the tiger-cat, an animal found locally. **1936** L.G. Green *Secret Afr.* 192 Leopards and tiger cats prowl in search of food. **1945** —— *Where Men Still Dream* 185 The native who risks his life with a blunderbuss is happy to receive half the amount for the skin. Tiger cats, striped like Bengal tigers, red cats, wild cats and jackals are usually hunted with dogs and finished with knobkerries. **1971** *S. Afr. Panorama* Jan. 38 The skin of a serval (tiger cat) was hung from the shoulders of the Chief Councillor.

tigerfish *n.* [Named for its rapacity.]
1. The freshwater characin *Hydrocynus vittatus* of the Characidae, a ferociously predatory fish considered good angling; TIGER sense 2 b.

In P. Skelton's *Complete Guide to Freshwater Fishes* (1993), the name 'tigerfish' is used for *H. vittatus.*

1893 F.C. Selous *Trav. & Adventure* 303 Burnett .. caught a fine tiger-fish. **1894** *Saturday Rev.* 24 Nov. 563 In fly-fishing .. the chief quarry, the 'tiger-fish', ran to $8\frac{1}{2}$ lbs., and afforded nearly as good sport as salmon. **1902** [see *river steenbras* (STEENBRAS sense b)]. **1905** *Addresses & Papers* (Brit. & S. Afr. Assoc. Agric. Science) I. 365 (Pettman), As to fish, the king of rivers is no doubt the tiger-fish, whose huge teeth, long and sharp as needles, placed outside his mouth, and fitted into sockets, in the opposite jaw, have truly formidable appearance and make him a dangerous enemy indeed to those of the finny tribe with whom he comes in contact. **1929** J. Stevenson-Hamilton *Low-Veld* 128 The usual feeding time of tiger-fish is during the two or three hours following sunrise, and again for a couple of hours before sunset. **1969** R.A. Jubb *Freshwater Fishes* 78 A few words of warning – where there are tiger-fish there are usually crocodiles – keep away from the teeth of both however small they may be. **1971** *Personality* 5 Mar. 16 The fighting tiger fish and the fresh water bream commit mass suicide on the bait or spinner. **1971** *Daily Dispatch* 2 June 15 Rhodesia's premier fishing contest, the Kariba International tiger fish tournament, is expected to draw more than 1 000 competitors from all over Southern Africa. **1974** *Sunday Times* 8 Dec. (Mag. Sect.), Even the tiger-fishing addicts behave with decorum on the serene waters.

2. Any of three species of marine fish: **a.** The *bank steenbras* (sense (*b*) see STEENBRAS sense b), *Chirodactylus grandis.* **b.** The spotted grunter *Pomadasys commersonnii* of the Haemulidae, characterized by its numerous black spots; TIGER sense 2 a; also called KNORHAAN (sense 2 b). **c.** The thornfish *Terapon jarbua* of the Teraponidae, a silvery fish with black or dark brown stripes.

In Smith and Heemstra's *Smiths' Sea Fishes* (1986), the name 'spotted grunter' is used for *P. commersonnii,* and 'thornfish' for *T. jarbua.*

1905 H.E.B. Brooking in *E. London Dispatch* 31 Oct. 6, I notice under the heading of 'Remarks,' upon the bank steenbrass, tiger-fish or river steenbras, the following:- 'Abundant all through the year, Black transverse stripes, .. thick lips and grunts when caught.' **1949** J.L.B. Smith *Sea Fishes* 183 *Therapon jarbua ... Tigerfish.* Pest of St Lucia ... Widespread .. , reaches as far south as Port Alfred, normally plentiful in estuaries north of the Kei, extends to almost fresh water.

tiger snake *n. phr.* [So called because its stripes are reminiscent of those on a tiger: see quot. 1974.] The slightly venomous colubrid snake *Telescopus semiannulatus semiannulatus*; also with defining word, **eastern tiger snake.**

1910 F.W. Fitzsimons *Snakes of Sn Afr.* 54 *Tiger Snake,* Average length 2 feet to 2 feet 6 inches. **1929** J. Stevenson-Hamilton *Low-Veld* 122 Among them may be noted the tiger snake (Tarbophis semiannulatus), which is often discovered living among a colony of weaver birds at nesting time, presumably preying mainly on their young. **1947** —— *Wild Life in S. Afr.* 330 The tiger snake .. is a yellowish snake spotted with brown. **1950** W. Rose *Reptiles and Amphibians* 280 The Tiger Snake, *Tarbophis semiannulatus* .. , is yellow-brown above with numerous dark bands, white belly ... It eats lizards ... It also seizes roosting birds. **1974** V.F.M. Fitzsimons in *Std Encycl. of Sn Afr.* X. 504 *Tiger-snake,* A slightly poisonous member of the back-fanged group of snakes of the family *Colubridae,* which is conspicuously marked throughout its length with alternate black and yellow to reddish brown cross-bands. **1987** Patterson & Bannister *Reptiles of Sn Afr.* 81 *Eastern Tiger Snake,* .. An irascible species, it bites at the least provocation, even after years in captivity, but its venom is mild and of no consequence to humans. **1988** B. Branch *Field Guide to Snakes* 86 *Eastern Tiger Snake, Telescopus semiannulatus* ... When first encountered, they will strike readily and often.

tiger-wolf *n. obs.* Also **tyger-wolf.** [tr. S. Afr. Du., fr. Du. *tijger* tiger, leopard + *wolf* hyaena; see quot. 1810.] The hyaena *Crocuta crocuta* of the Hyaenidae, off-white with dark brown irregular spots, powerful forequarters, and a broad, massive head with dark brown or nearly black muzzle and rounded ears. See also WOLF *n.*[1]

1731 G. Medley tr. *P. Kolb's Present State of Cape of G.H.* II. 107 With Regard to the *Tiger-Wolf,* Authors upon Animals are strangely divided and mistaken ... My own Account of the *Tiger-wolf* is this. He is of the Size of an ordinary Sheep-dog, or somewhat Larger. His Head is broad, like that of an English Bull-Dog. **1786** G. Forster tr. *A. Sparrman's Voy. to Cape of G.H.* I. 158 The *tyger-wolf* is a much more common beast of prey ... This is that hitherto unknown animal, which Mr. Pennant .. has briefly described and given a drawing of, by the name of the spotted *hyena.* **1795** C.R. Hopson tr. *C.P. Thunberg's Trav.* II. 57 In the morning, we found that the cattle had been pursued by the tyger-wolf (*Hyaena maculata*). **1810** G. Barrington *Acct of Voy.* 272 Of the latter [*sc.* the wolf] there are two kinds: the first is spotted, and on that account, called by the Colonists tiger-wolf: the other is the strand-wolf. **1827** G. Thompson *Trav.* II. 12 We .. seized our guns and ran to the rescue of the remaining horse, and found him beset in a corner of the thicket by a ferocious tiger-wolf (*hyaena crocuta,*) who was attempting to break in upon him. **1834** T. Pringle *Afr. Sketches* 267 Of all the beasts of prey .. that inhabit South Africa, the common spotted hyaena (*Hyaena crocuta*) called by the colonists the *tiger-wolf,* is the most voracious and destructive to flocks. **1846** H.H. Methuen *Life in Wilderness* 126 There are two kinds of hyæna in South Africa – the spotted one, tiger-wolf of the colonists, is commonest and fiercest. [*Note*] *Hyæna crocuta.* **1861** P.B. Borcherds *Auto-Biog. Mem.* 83 Soon after dark the report of a gun being heard, we found a tiger-wolf, or spotted hyena, had been killed. **1871** J. McKay *Reminisc.* 22 There is the hyena (wolf of the colonists), of which there are different species, such as the aarde-wolf, the tiger-wolf, striped hyena, and the strand-wolf or maned jackal. **1900** W.L. Sclater *Mammals of S. Afr.* I. 87 *Hyaena crocuta. Vernacular Names:* Tyger Wolf, or simply Wolf of the Colonists. **1915** W. Eveleigh *S.W. Afr.* 73 Among the enemies of the stock farmer are several species of jackals; the powerful spotted hyena, *H. crocuta,* the Dutch tiger-wolf, [etc.]. [**1920** F.C. Cornell *Glamour of Prospecting* 181 Probably a hyena had taken it, for both the stronte wolf and the tijger wolf are common in these mountains.]

tigoloshi var. TOKOLOSHE.

tigre, tijger varr. TIGER.

tikaloshi, tikilosh(e) varr. TOKOLOSHE.

tik(k)ie var. TICKEY.

tik(k)iedraai var. TICKEY-DRAAI.

tikolosh(e), tikiloshi varr. TOKOLOSHE.

Tikquoa var. TIXO.

tik-tok var. TICK-TOCK.

tin *n. colloq.* [Special sense of general Eng.] Corrugated iron, used either for roofing, or for the walls of houses. Also *attrib.* See also BLIK-HUIS, ZINC.

1897 R.S.S. Baden-Powell *Matabele Campaign* 10 (Pettman), Into Mafeking? Well, there's a little tin (corrugated iron) house and a goods' shed to form the station. **1897** E. Edwards *Journey through S. Afr.* 48 (Jeffreys), Kimberley struck me as a very peculiarly built town, being chiefly composed of buildings into whose construction corrugated iron largely entered; .. it would not be out of place to refer to Kimberley as a 'tin town'. **1913** C. Pettman *Africanderisms* 503 *Tin house,* A house the exterior of which is composed entirely of corrugated iron. **1949** [see BLIK-HUIS]. **1964** M.G. McCoy *Informant, Port Elizabeth* He, if you please, feels humiliated at having to live under a tin roof. **1969** M.W. Spilhaus *Doorstep-Baby* 115 It's a big sprawling house with a tin roof – corrugated iron, you know. We call them tin roofs. **1991** *Frontline* May 5 They see a person staying in a tin house, they take chances by taking for granted that the home is not well-protected traditionally.

tinc-tinc var. TINKTINKIE.

ting /tɪŋ/ *n.* [fr. SeTswana *leting.*] Thick, sour, fermented maize-meal porridge.

1980 *Rand Daily Mail* 8 May (Eve) 2 Huge tripods of traditional 'ting' (sour porridge), samp and other goodies. **1988** *Mother Love* June 29 Cook offal in 2 litres water until nearly tender ... Serve on pap, ting or rice. **1991** *Black Market Report* 2 Dec. 1 Have you heard of chakalaka, skop and pap, mogudu, seshabo, or ting? *Ibid.* 2 Not all black people eat the same kind of mealie meal porridge. *Ting* is the Tswana word for *their* type of mealie meal dish which is fermented ... How to make ting: 'Take five cups mealie meal. Pour boiling water. Put aside for three days. Then you can use it.'

tinktinkie /təŋ(k)ˈtəŋki, tɪŋ(k)ˈtɪŋki/ *n.* Also **tinc-tinc, ting-ting, tingtingatje, ting-tinkie, tinktinki, tink-tinky, tintinkie, tintinkje.** [Afk., echoic.] Any of numerous species of cisticolas (grass warblers) of the Sylviidae, small birds with distinctive calls; TINKY. See also PINC-PINC.

1874 J.M. Orpen in *Folklore* (1919) XXX. 146 Another bird called tinktinki, quinqininyq in Bushman. [**1884** Layard & Sharpe *Birds of S. Afr.* 279 This little species .. is called *Ting-ting* by the Dutch colonists.] **1894** [see PINC-PINC]. **1908** F.C. Slater *Sunburnt South* 186 The little mouse-coloured tinktinkie, which as you know is the smallest of all birds, is a most mischievous little creature. **1913** J.J. Doke *Secret City* 78 In the thicket of quince behind the summerhouse the Cape robin, the tintinkje, the spotted rooikop, and the more fragile swi built their nests. **1924** D. Fairbridge *Gardens of S. Afr.* 98 The Grass Warbler, the perky Tingtingatje, is equally useful, being mainly an insect feeder. **1929** F.C. Slater *Sel. Poems* (1947) 117 Tiny tinktinkies famed in nursery story. **1940** Baumann &

BRIGHT *Lost Republic* 234 There is a sweet little bird called a ting-tinkie. He is so small that you could put three, or even four, into your small pocket; his colour is bright green, and he has big round eyes. **1956** A.G. McRAE *Hill Called Grazing* 24 Big birds and small birds, from huge vultures .. to the tiniest tink-tinkies piping their thin little reeds of song. **1973** *Evening Post* 28 Apr. 3 The variety is overwhelming – from the tiniest tintinkie, honey bird or king fisher to the awesome albatross and the ungainly ostrich.

tinky /ˈtɪŋki/ *n.* Short form of TINKTINKIE.

1899 FITZSIMONS in R.B & J.D.S. Woodward *Natal Birds* 30 The boys call it [*sc. Cisticola terrestris*] the little 'Tinky,' from its cry of 'tink, tink, tink'. **1931** *Guide to Vertebrate Fauna of E. Cape Prov.* (Albany Museum) I. 110 The clappering noise made by the tinky .. is one of the best known sounds of the open treeless veld. **1973** J. COWDEN *For Love* 66 Another visitor was a Tinkie, quite at home in eagle landscape where he achieved fame and his South African name ... We laughed at this impudent miniature as he brightly reminded us of the story himself, of how he bested the eagle to become King Tinkie.

tinterintie var. CHINCHERINCHEE.

tintinkie, -tinkje varr. TINKTINKIE.

tintirintie var. CHINCHERINCHEE.

tiptol *n. obs.* Pl. **-s**, or **-tolle**. [Afk., bulbul; see quots 1912 and 1937.] Any of several species of bulbul (*Pycnonotus*) of the Pycnonotidae. See also TOPPIE *n.*[1]

1908 HAAGNER & IVY *Sketches* 52 These birds [*sc.* bulbuls] are of a general dark brown colour above and are known by various 'local' or vernacular names, such as 'Tiptol' in the Eastern Cape, 'Geelgat' or 'Kuifkop' of the Dutch, 'Topknot' or 'Blackhead' in Natal. It is also occasionally called the 'Blackcap'. **1912** *E. London Dispatch* 9 Aug. 3 (Pettman), [*Pycnotus layardi*] Known to the colonists as 'Tiptol,' and to the natives as 'Kwebula'. Both of these names .. are attempts to produce the bird's song. **1913** C. PETTMAN *Africanderisms* 503 *Tiptol or Tiptolitje*, Birds of the genus *Pycnonotus* are so called. **1937** M. ALSTON *Wanderings* 97 The black-capped bulbuls, known familiarly as 'toppies' or 'tiptols' or 'top-knots' because of their black-crested heads.

tisselboom var. DISSELBOOM.

titihoya /tɪtiˈhɔjə/ *n.* Pl. **-s**, ||**ama-** /ama-/. [Zulu, echoic.] In KwaZulu-Natal: the black-winged plover *Stephanibyx melanopterus* of the Charadriidae; the cry of this bird.

1948 A. PATON *Cry, Beloved Country* 13 The forlorn crying of titihoya, one of the birds of the veld. **1954** F.J. EDMONSTONE *Thorny Harvest* 12 The plaintive cries of the *titihoya* came drifting across the veld. **1969** A. PATON *Kontakion* 20 Many a time I walked over the hills .. sometimes in a world of mist, through grass and bracken, .. hearing the titihoya. **1978** McLACHLAN & LIVERSIDGE *Roberts Birds of S. Afr.* 174 Black-winged Plover *Stephanibyx melanopterus* ... Voice: Has a fine vocabulary of curses and varied pitch and intensity rising to high screams, 'che-che-che-cherek' and 'titihoya'. **1980** A. PATON *Towards Mountain* 86 Much of the beauty of the Ixopo countryside has gone, because the grass and bracken and rolling hills and the rich farms have in large part given way to endless plantations of gums and wattle and pine, and the titihoya does not cry there anymore.

Tixo /ˈtiːǁɔ/ *n.* Also **Tikquoa, Tuiqua, Uteco, (u)Thico (u)Thixo, Utika, Uti'ko, Utiko, Utixo.** [Xhosa *uThixo* God, fr. Khoikhoi *Tixwa* or *Tiqua*, see quots 1803 and 1827.] Used first among the Khoikhoi, and subsequently among Xhosa-speakers (the word having been adopted by missionaries): the traditional Supreme Being; the Christian God; also used as a mode of address in prayer, and as an interjection; QAMATA. Cf. MODIMO, UMVELINQANGI, UNKULUNKULU. See also UHLANGA.

1731 G. MEDLEY tr. *P. Kolb's Present State of Cape of G.H.* I. 29 The *Hottentots* say ... That they [*sc.* their First Parents] were sent into their Country by God himself, whom they call *Tikquoa.* **1803** J.T. VAN DER KEMP in *Trans. of Missionary Soc.* I. 432 A decisive proof .. with respect to the atheism of the Caffres, is, that they have no word in their language to express the Deity, .. calling him *Thixo*, which is a corruption of *Thuike*, the name by which God is called in the language of the Hottentots, literally signifying one who induces pain. **1812** A. PLUMPTRE tr. *H. Lichtenstein's Trav. in Sn Afr.* (1928) I. 253 They [*sc.* the Xhosa people] believe in the existence of a great Being who created the world, but in their own language .. they have no name by which he is called: they have therefore adopted one from the Gonaaquas, who call him Thiko. **1827** J. BROWNLEE in G. Thompson *Trav.* II. 352 The Caffers believe in a Supreme Being, to whom they give the appellation of Uhlanga (Supreme), or frequently the Hottentot name Utika (Beautiful). **1834** T. PRINGLE *Afr. Sketches* 502 Utiko, a term now in general use among many of the South African tribes for the Supreme Being, is derived from the Hottentot word 'Tiko', which is said literally to signify 'The Beautiful'. It has been adopted by the missionaries to denote the true God. **1846** R. MOFFAT *Missionary Labours* 68 The Hottentot word *Uti'ko* is now used by all the frontier (Kafir) tribes to denote the Christian's God. **1849** E.D.H.E. NAPIER *Excursions in Sn Afr.* II. 53 He said he was sent by Uteka, the Great Spirit, to avenge their wrongs. **1860** W. SHAW *Story of my Mission* 451 After long and careful consideration, the Missionaries have generally concurred in the adoption of the word *Utixo* as the name for God; and throughout the Colony to beyond the Umzimvubu River no other meaning is attached to this word by the Kaffirs. **1905** W.H. TOOKE in Flint & Gilchrist *Science in S. Afr.* 88 The Kafirs .. believe also in the spirits of the dead ... Their word for God is Unkulunkulu, denoting the first man or progenitor; also Uhlanga and Itongo, the Great Spirit ... Other terms for God are Tixo and Qamata. **1918** H. MOORE *Land of Good Hope* 117 Some tribes .. say that Tixo (a Hottentot word) made Unkulunkulu. **1925** D. KIDD *Essential Kafir* 104 One myth runs thus: Teco, or Tixo, made three kinds of men, namely, Hottentots, Kafirs, and white men. **1948** A. PATON *Cry, Beloved Country* 30 It would be truer to say, he said, that she has many husbands. Kumalo said, *Tixo! Tixo! Ibid.* 213 He prays, Tixo, we give thanks to Thee for Thy unending mercy. Tixo give us rain, we beseech Thee. **1949** [see Hunter quot. at UMFUNDISI]. **1952** S. BAVA in *Drum* Jan. 23 M'bolekwa was horrified. 'God! Tixo!' he gasped. **1963** A.M. LOUW *20 Days* 95 The Xhosa umfundisi had said a thing she had remembered. 'uThico is the big salt bag and we are the little salt bags. When we are empty we must go to Him to be filled again.' **1973** *Drum* 8 May 24 A rhino does not only charge. It takes its time and knows just when to charge, and when it does, hoo, Tixo. **1980** M. MATSHOBA in M. Mutloatse *Forced Landing* 119 You defend *abeLungu* by saying they do not know? Now, my boy, tell me this: is this – the way we live, all of us blacks – our rightful legacy from the ancestors, or from Tixo who made heaven and earth. **1983** *Pace* Oct. 70 The shock of shocks is that the two men are buddies, thixo! *Ibid.* 174 Tshini Mfondini! .. Another woman broke in ... 'au, au, au, Thixo!' and got into the graveyard act of feigning a faint. **1990** [see IGQIRA].

||**tjaile** /ˈtʃaɪlə, tʃaˈiːla/ *n.* Also **chaile, chiela, chihele, shayile, tjhaile, tjila, tshaile.** [See TJAILE *v.*] In full ***tjaile time***: 'knocking-off time', the end of a working day; the signal given to mark this time.

1937 H. KLEIN *Stage Coach Dust* 121 It was a very down-hearted cavalcade of technicians that moved off at 'chiela' time (knocking-off time). **1970** H.M. MUSMECI *Informant, Port Elizabeth* Thank goodness it is tjila time, and we can stop working. **1980** A.J. BLIGNAUT *Dead End Rd* 70 He called the chihele a little early and left for the tent. **1980** O. MUSI in M. Mutloatse *Forced Landing* 180 It is a wise man who tells his boss that, much as he would dearly love to stay on after *shayile* time, he dare not for fear of breaking the curfew laws. **1983** *Pace* Dec. 114 You yourself told me never to let anyone into the factory once after tshaile. **1988** K. MOEKETSI in *Staffrider* Vol.7 No.3, 367 We would play 'Saduva' when we know it's chaile – closing time. **1992** on M-Net TV 9 Nov. (Egoli), This place is like a circus today. How long before tjaile time?

||**tjaile** /ˈtʃaɪlə, tʃaˈiːla/ *v. intrans.* Also **chi(e)la, tjaila.** [ad. of Xhosa *-tshayile*, Zulu *-shayile*, or Tswana *-chaile* (perfective forms of the verbs *tshaya, shaya* and *chaya* finish, complete) finished.] To stop work, particularly at the end of the day; as a signal, 'stop work'.

1970 *Informant, Pietersburg* Tjaile. Finish up with work. **1970** M. BENNETT *Informant, Krugersdorp* Chiela. Down tools, finish work for the day. **1972** BEETON & DORNER in *Eng. Usage in Sn Afr.* Vol.3 No.1, 37 *Tjaila*, .. to stop working, either for the lunch break or at the end of the working day. **1990** R. MALAN *My Traitor's Heart* 32 At one o'clock, my uncle shouted, 'chila', African for knock off.

tjaloa var. TSHWALA.

tjarra var. CHARRA.

tjerrie var. CHERRY.

tjienkerientjee var. CHINCHERINCHEE.

tjila var. TJAILE *n.*

tjoalla var. TSHWALA.

tjoepstil /ˈtʃʊpstəl/ *adj. colloq.* [Afk., fr. Hindi *chup, choop* silence (perh. via Malay) + Afk. *stil* silent, quiet.] Absolutely silent.

1979 *Sunday Times* 29 July 16 Tjoepstil! One of South Africa's top businessmen gained the distinction this week of rendering the voluble Jesse Jackson momentarily speechless. **1980** *Ibid.* 9 Mar. 2 Where are the MPs – .. men of influence, leaders in their respective communities, faithful followers of P.W. Botha? The reply: 'Tjoepstil (silent), in the Cape.' **1982** D. KRAMER *Short Back & Sides* 22 Call me a crunchie And I'll take you outside. I'll show you just how The crunch is applied. Then you'll keep ... tjoepstil. **1985** *Vula* Oct. 21 How can they expect Beyers/Boesak/Tutuhulle to keep tjoepstil when the very fires of hell are now burning in our backyards? **1990** *Femina* June 70 Mark remembers his childhood as one in which children had to be tjoepstil.

tjommie var. CHOMMIE.

tjongololo var. SONGOLOLO.

tjoone var. TUNE.

tjorrie /ˈtʃɔri/ *n. colloq.* Also **chorrie, tjor(r).** [Afk. *tjor(rie).*] A dilapidated motor car or other vehicle; a 'jalopy'; SKEDONK; SKOROKORO. Also *transf.*

1961 D. BEE *Children of Yesterday* 91 That old tjorrie goes very well and I've always liked a V8. **1970** *Daily Dispatch* 10 Dec. 16 (*caption*) But, dear, I'm sure we parked the old chorrie right here. **1973** D.A.C. MACLENNAN in *Bolt* No.7, 22 Breakfast with my cat, get into the old chorrie and drive off to school. **1975** *Sunday Times* 21 Sept. 20 Any tjorrie tied together with faith, hope and bits of string can get through the safety checks on this road, provided it's driven by a White. **1977** *Het Suid-Western* 4 Oct., These dealers get their prices for these tjorrs. For instance, a little Fiat Nuova 500 that sounds like a sewing machine. **1982** *Cape Times* 11 Oct., I went straight to town and bought Pikkie the finest kite I could find ... Within days .. Pikkie was again flying his old *tjorrie* with the rag tail and knotted snoek line. **1983** G. SILBER in *Sunday Times* 28 Aug. (Mag. Sect.) 17 You drive in the gate, which is guarded by this snarling, grey concrete panther, and you park your tjorrie there under the trees. **1990** *Informant, Grahamstown* So .. this is your old chorrie, is it?

tjwala var. TSHWALA.

TLC *n.* [Initial letters of *Transitional Local Council.*] In the transformation of apartheid structures: a body, representative of all former ethnically-based municipalities in a city or town, which is responsible for civic functions until a single non-racial municipality is elected.

1994 *Grocott's Mail* 19 July (Coastal News) 1 The Amalgamation Agreement which is to be signed by Port Alfred's T.L.C. has as yet not been signed .. The Agreement has been studied by the Forum and agreed to in principle, but the omission of a clause dealing with the taking over by the T.L.C. of the R18 million debt of the township is to be rectified before the Agreement is signed. 1994 K. Paton in *Weekend Post* 21 May 7 Jeffreys Bay is following hot on the heels of Port Elizabeth and seems likely to become the second Eastern Cape town to have its transitional local council (TLC) approved.

Tlhaping var. BATLHAPING.

Tlokwa /'tɬɔkwa/ *n.* Also **Ba(c)klokwa, Bac(k)loqua, Batlokua, Botlokoa.** [Sotho *moTlokwa* a member of this people (pl. *baTlokwa*).] A member of a people of the Southern Sotho group. See also MANTATEE. Also *attrib.*

[1835 A. SMITH *Diary* (1940) II. 74 He told us that towards the sources of the Liqua .. were now Manatees, a bad class of people. They were called Matok.] 1835 *Ibid.* 142 Saw two men who said they were Backloqua and that their tribe lived a little to the eastward of where we found Masalacatzie. *Ibid.* 170 Found here a Backloqua. 1841 [see MANTATEE]. 1846 J.C. BROWN tr. T. Arbousset's *Narr. of Explor. Tour to N.-E. of Col.* 31 They were formerly called Batlokuas; from regard to her [*sc.* the queen], they have taken the name of Mantetis. 1905 *Native Tribes of Tvl* 25 The Batlokwa have the reputation of being skilled workers in copper and wire, of which they make bracelets and other ornaments. 1912 AYLIFF & WHITESIDE *Hist. of Abambo* 9 Motsholi was afraid, fled over the Drakensberg, and sought refuge with the Batlokoa, who treated him with kindness, and gave him land on which to reside. 1951 W.S. MATSIE in *Afr. Drum* Apr. 12 Other tribes began to spring up in the country either by breaking away from the older and larger tribes or by coming into the sheltered safety of Basutoland from the troubled world outside. Thus the .. Batlokoa .. came about. 1971 *Nat. Geog. Mag.* June 745 The king agreed, on condition that the Boers bring back Zulu cattle stolen by the Tlokwas, a neighboring tribe. 1986 P. MAYLAM *Hist. of Afr. People* 57 The *Tlokwa* had been the first victims of the Nguni invasions across the Drakensberg. Forced to abandon their territorial base after the Hlubi attack, the Tlokwa led a semi-nomadic existence during the turmoil of the *difaqane*. 1986 N. GARDINER in *S. Afr. Panorama* Sept. 25 Blacks of the Batlokua tribe .. kept cattle and planted crops. However, when Chaka rose to power in Natal, Zulus crossed the mountains and clashed with the Batlokua. This .. drove the tribe west to Ficksburg. 1990 *Motorist* 2nd Quarter, Chief Koos Mota of the Tlokwa tribe was granted a portion of Witsieshoek.

t'nenta var. NENTA.

toa-grass *n. obs.* [ad. San *doa, dhoa* grass + Eng. grass.] TWA-GRASS. Also (occas.) **towa.**

1883 B. RIDSDALE *Scenes & Adventures in Great Namaqualand* 79 The vast plains of Great Namaqualand, covered with the strong and high *towa*, or Bushman grass. 1897 [see TWA-GRASS]. 1914 W.C. SCULLY *Lodges in Wilderness* 21 Heavy-headed shocks of 'toa' grass, yellow or light green in hue, according to the more or less scanty rainfall. 1918 J.W. BEWS *Grasses & Grasslands* 153 *A. brevifolia*, English Toa Grass, Dutch T'waa Gras. 1920 F.C. CORNELL *Glamour of Prospecting* 246 We lit fires of dry *toa* grass. 1929 J.W. BEWS *World's Grasses* 211 *A. brevifolia*, 'Toa grass,' is a suffrutescent, very xerophytic species which covers wide areas of desert, or rather does not cover them, but is often almost the only plant to be found on them. 1949 K.L. SIMMS *Sun-Drenched Veld* 10 Tufts of toa grass.

toch *n.* and *adj.* var. TOGT.

toch *adv.* var. of TOG.

tock-tockie var. TOK-TOKKIE.

toding var. TOERING.

toe /'tu/ *adj. colloq.* [Afk., lit. 'closed'.] Impenetrably stupid, 'dense', 'thick'.

1970 E.J. LE ROUX *Informant, Bellville* If someone is 'toe' he's really dumb. 1970 A. LOMBARD *Informant, Grahamstown* Don't you catch the joke? Don't be toe. 1971 L. ROBERTSON *Informant, Grahamstown* This girl is so toe, man, that she never gives me any messages. I don't even let her answer the telephone if I'm out. 1978 *Het Suid-Western* 18 Jan., Today another precept holds and fairly makes you sob: 'Who me? You must be toe ou pêl, Not me! It's not my job.'

toeding var. TOERING.

toe maar *adv. phr. Colloq.* [Afk.] An interjection used to comfort or console: 'there there'; 'never mind'.

Often used by writers to suggest the idiom of Afk. speech.

[1943 I. FRACK *S. Afr. Doctor*, The husband simply said to me: 'Toe maar, loop' (Alright, you can go).] 1959 J. MEIRING *Candle in Wind* 64 'Toe-maar, ou Maggie!' she said, 'don't cry; don't worry.' 1966 VAN HEYNINGEN & BERTHOUD *Uys Krige* 146 When the farmer stops dead in his conversational tracks, I just say: Toe maar, Oom, it's nothing, go on ... don't let me interrupt you.' 1968 F.G. BUTLER *Cape Charade* 11 Toemaar, my skat, dis somaar a nine months stretch on a nine mile stretch of road. 1973 J. COPE *Alley Cat* 18 'Toe maar!' the mother soothed her, drawing out the words lovingly. 'Come here, April. Let me do your hair.' 1973 E. *Prov. Herald* 12 June 9 This is a different noise. Toe maar Boetie, we'll have to strip it down again. 1979 *Daily Dispatch* 23 May 11 'The government stands almost powerless before the press,' he explained ... 'Toe maar, we will protect you,' promised Mr Horace van Rensburg.

toenadering /'tu,nɑ:d(ə)rəŋ/ *vbl n.* [Afk., fr. *toenader* to approach, meet halfway.] Rapprochement, esp. between political parties.

1920 S. BLACK *Dorp* 187 All Oakley saw in any toenadering (coming together) of the bickering factions, was a trick to deprive King George and his heirs of their legitimate ownership of the country discovered by Bartholomew Diaz and settled by Jan van Riebeek. 1926 [see NAT *n.* sense a]. 1947 *Forum* 3 May 3 The whole question of toenadering with the English-speaking section has .. been .. an apple of discord in the Nationalist-Afrikaner Party circles. 1957 *Cape Times* 18 June 8 He must draw a large Nationalist vote if he is to win those English-speaking people who want White toenadering. 1973 E. *Prov. Herald* 16 June 8 As the session drew to a close .. everyone was fiercely denying 'toenadering', or should I rather use the new 'in' term 'consensus'. 1977 *Ibid.* 29 May 11 Dr Hertzog found himself in a political wilderness, because at a time of concerted 'toenadering' between the two groups he preached Afrikaner exclusivity. 1986 *Personality* 1 Sept. 34 Though Pickard .. would welcome .. a coming together of English- and Afrikaans-speaking South Africans, he believes the process of toenadering still has a long way to go. 1992 D. TUTU on TV1, 30 Apr. (Good Morning South Africa), So many working for the toenadering — this rapprochement. 1994 M. VAN WYK SMITH in *Albany Democrat* No.1, July 4 The ANC opposed federalism, the Nats let it slide in the interests of toenadering.

toer var. TOOR.

‖**toering** /'turəŋ/ *n.* Also **toding, toeding, toudang, tudong.** [Afk., ad. Malay *tudong* (now *tudung*) covering, lid (perh. influenced by Afk. *toring* tower).] A wide-brimmed conical straw hat worn (in the past) by Cape Malay people, usu. over a small crimson turban or headcloth.

1855 J.S. MAYSON *Malays of Capetown* 10 The coloured cap, the *tudong* or hat, and the sandals of wood, formerly formed part of the national dress; but being adopted by Mahometan converts of every class, are now regarded as badges of a common faith. 1909 *Cape* 25 June 9 There was .. the toeding (sometimes called toering), a conical, wide-brimmed hat of plaited straw. 1910 D. FAIRBRIDGE *That Which Hath Been* (1913) 52 The *toudang* of the old Malay coachmen is still to be seen at the Cape, but is fast disappearing before the fez, most senseless of head-coverings in a sunny climate. 1913 C. PETTMAN *Africanderisms* 504 *Toering*, (Mal. *tudung*), an umbrella hat, or a hat with a very broad brim; the word seems to have been affected in South Africa by the Dutch word *toren*, a tower, steeple.) 1949 E. HELLMANN *Handbk on Race Rel.* 595 A coachman wearing the toering, the traditional conical straw hat. 1953 DU PLESSIS & LÜCKHOFF *Malay Quarter* 60 In 1860 Malay dress was a compromise between Eastern and Western costume. The *toering* (*tudong*), a conical cane hat, was still being worn. 1969 M.W. SPILHAUS *Doorstep-Baby* 113 One of the hansom-cabs driven by a Malay, his head wrapped in a crimson cloth with a conical straw hat (called a *tudong*) perched on the top of it. 1972 A.A. TELFORD *Yesterday's Dress* 139 The men all kept their shaven heads warm with bright cotton kerchiefs, wearing over them a pagoda-shaped cane hat called a 'toering'. 1980 A. DAVIDS *Mosques of Bo-Kaap* 7 The conical straw hat, called the 'Toding', .. was the typical headgear of the nineteenth century Cape Muslims.

tog *n.* and *adj.* var. TOGT.

tog /tɔx/ *adv. colloq.* Also **toch.** [Afk., fr. Du. *toch* yet, still.] An (often phatic) interpolation or intensifier.

1. 'Indeed', 'really', 'still', 'after all'. See also SIESTOG, FOEITOG.

1883 M.A. CAREY-HOBSON *Farm in Karoo* 115 Piet, ever too ready to yield to temptation and get into trouble, but, the trouble once removed, as merry and as light-hearted as a cricket, took up the bundle and said, 'Oh, my dear master! Thank you! thank you, "toch"!' 1896 — *At Home in Tvl* 213 'Ach! the poor dear creature,' said the kind-hearted woman, in Dutch, soothing her as she would a child. 'Ach toch, mynheer! What is it that you have told the poor thing to excite her grief in this manner?' 1900 M. MARQUARD *Lett. from Boer Parsonage* (1967) 57 This morning at breakfast Murray sighed 'I wish the war were over', — 'why' asked his mother 'the tea is toch so bitter'! 1920 S. BLACK *Dorp* 228, I was toch so sorry to miss the sermon last night; I hear it was splendid. 1920 [see NIGGIE]. 1930 *Outspan* 25 July 63 'You have not changed so much after all these years,' said Alida enviously. 'I toch have grown so stout.' 1974 A.P. BRINK *Looking on Darkness* 234 When at last we were allowed to drive on again, he rubbed his hands together and bowed: 'Thanks, my Baas tog, the Lord will bless and protect you.' 1982 [see MOENIE sense 2].

2. Suggesting urgency or impatience: 'please', 'do please'.

1900 H. BLORE *Imp. Light Horseman* 306 'Ach, misses, my misses, my lieve misses toch,' sobbed the terrified woman, incapable of connected speech. 1912 F. BANCROFT *Veldt Dwellers* 127 'Ma, Ma! wake up, toch!' ... With a .. snore ending in a terrific snort, Tante Jacoba at last opened her little, faded blue eyes. 'Wake up, toch, Ma,' repeated her daughter, impatiently. 1913 [see ASSEBLIEF]. 1915 D. FAIRBRIDGE *Torch Bearer* 130 Here we are at my house — but come in, toch. 1935 P. SMITH *Platkop's Children* 152 Presently Katisje met another ayah an' stood showin' her the perambulator. An' the other ayah said How wonderful it was, an' did Katisje think she might jes toch push it a little? 1980 E. PATEL *They Came at Dawn* 9 Howsit Mister Black .. I am Miss White ... Let's jingle jangle but no tingle tangle. Tog please man?

togate var. TAGATI *n.*

togolosh var. TOKOLOSHE.

togt /tɔxt/ *n.* and *adj.* Also **toch, tog.** [Afk. (now *tog*), fr. Du. *tocht* expedition, journey.]

A. *n.*

1. *hist.*

a. A trading expedition or venture. Often in the phr. **on togt**, on such an expedition. Also *attrib.*

[**1821** C.I. LATROBE *Jrnl of Visit* 375 The master of the house .. was about to set off .. on a trip .. to dispose of it [*sc.* arrack] in barter ... They call this going *op de tocht.*] **1860** *Queenstown Free Press* 8 Feb., Horses have been discovered amongst those of 'smouses' who were returning to the upper districts after a somewhat successful *togt.* **1862** LADY DUFF-GORDON *Lett. from Cape* (1925) 114 He has made a fortune by 'going on togt', as thus: He charters two waggons ... The waggons he fills with cotton, hardware, etc., etc. – an ambulatory village 'shop' – and goes about fifteen miles a day .. swapping baftas (calico), punjums (loose trousers), and voerschitz (cotton gown-pieces) .. against oxen and sheep. *Ibid.* 127, I have just bought eight splendid ostrich feathers for £1 of my old 'togt' friend. **1883** M.A. CAREY-HOBSON *Farm in Karoo* 154, I had a fine crop this year and so I thought I had better take both the waggons and go on 'Toch,' and I have sold them very well. [**1957** L.G. GREEN *Beyond City Lights* 222 Half the village was making wagons while the other half was away on *togry* selling the wagons in the republics.] **1963** POLLOCK & AGNEW *Hist. Geog.* 64 Farmers living in the Lang Kloof went on long trading trips, known as togts, to obtain salt from Swartkops River and to trade with the Bantu and Hottentots.

b. *comb.* **togt-ganger**, also **togganger** [Du., *gang* go + personif. suffix *-er*], an adventurer; a travelling trader; also called SMOUS.

1854 H. LYNAR in *Cape of G.H. Annexures* 20 In the case of a togtganger, who was lately convicted of selling guns without a licence, it appeared in evidence that his wagons were more like travelling canteens than anything else. **1879** *Cape Monthly Mag.* XVIII. Feb. 88 For a long time he used to accompany the togtgangers (hawkers or traders). **1896** R. WALLACE *Farming Indust. of Cape Col.* 91 The plant [*sc.* prickly pear] was first spread in the Colony by transport riders or togt-gangers. **1957** L.G. GREEN *Beyond City Lights* 31 In slack times the clever speculators known as *toggangers* would drive out of Paarl with cavalcades of carts and wagons.

2. A casual labourer; casual labour. Also *attrib.*

Quot. 1948 (*Report of Native Laws Commission*) may be an example of *adj.* usage.

1901 A.R.R. TURNBULL *Tales from Natal* 120 The black devils .. so often put us about by deserting – without even the possibility of our being able to obtain togt even. **1939** [see sense B]. **1948** *Report of Native Laws Commission 1946–8* 37 Migrant labour tends to be casual and to produce less and earn less than stable labour. The supply of such labour is often badly adjusted to the demand ... In Durban it is .. a characteristic of so-called togt or daily labour. **1948** O. WALKER *Kaffirs Are Lively* 172 A Native is required to carry on his person .. one or more of the following documents .. A receipt for togt (casual labour) licence. **1969** *Receipt, Grahamstown Municipality* The togt licence or document of registration.

B. *adj.* Casual; hired by the day.

1898 *Port Elizabeth Telegraph* (Weekly ed.) 2 Sept., A Chinaman refused to supply a small quantity of bread and sugar to a togt boy on Saturday. **1907** *Col. of Natal Native Affairs Commission 1906–7* 36 Togt natives complained of not being able to earn sufficient money, and in many cases they were unable to work more than three days a week. **1923** G.H. NICHOLLS *Bayete!* 266 In Durban, the togt boys, and the native employees of large corporations, left their barracks at the same hour as their countrymen surged out of the mining compounds of Johannesburg. **1939** *Report of Railways & Harbours Board* (UG21–1939) 16 The wages of 'togts' and 'togt indunas' at the Point, Durban, should be increased by 6d. per day. **1951** *Cape Argus* 5 Jan 5 Durban harbour had been crippled by a shortage of rail trucks and togt (casual) labour ... A compound capable of housing up to 1,000 togt labourers should be set aside for this purpose. **1960** J.L.L. SISSON *S. Afr. Judicial Dict.* 121 *Casual labourer*, in terms of Native Pass Laws, is synonymous with the term togt labourer. **1961** D. BEE *Children of Yesterday* 69 For these jobs he .. hired an occasional 'togt-boy' – daily paid labourer – on his own account. **1968** K. MCMAGH *Dinner of Herbs* 101, I very hungry, I looking for work. Is there work, togt work nearby? **1972** J. MCCLURE *Caterpillar Cop* (1974) 139 He had slunk up to the door .. and informed the maid he was a *togt* boy. She .. said there were no odd jobs going. **1977** T.R.H. DAVENPORT *S. Afr.: Mod. Hist.* 355 An open compound system could be used for the control of casual ('togt') labourers. **1983** P. WARWICK *Black People & S. Afr. War* 144 Discontent prevailed, too, among togt labourers at the docks in Durban (i.e. those workers hired and paid on a daily basis). **1986** J. CONYNGHAM *Arrowing of Cane* 60, I scan the surrounding expanse of cane – the togt gang must weed there.

toi-toi *n.*, **toi-toi** *v.* varr. TOYI-TOYI *n.*, TOYI-TOYI *v.*

tokaloshi, **tokelosche**, **tokilosi** varr. TOKOLOSHE.

tokkara var. TAKHAAR.

tokkelok /ˈtɔkəlɔk, ˈtɒkəlɒk/ *n. slang.* [Unkn.; perh. influenced by Afk. *teologies* theological; or perh. fr. Gk *tokos* birth + *logos* discourse (see quot. 1934).] A nickname given to theological students at Stellenbosch University. Also (at Rhodes University) *abbrev.* **toc** or **tok** /tɒk/.

1934 C.P. SWART Supplement to Pettman. 176 *Tokkelok* (G. tokos, birth; logos, discourse.) A term humorously applied to theological students at Stellenbosch who are reputed to contemplate and discuss matrimony when the end of their course is in sight. **1971** *Rhodeo* (Rhodes Univ.) 13 May 2 This could be construed as a plot to take over the presidency – for what it's worth .. and after all, why not? .. they've had Tocs as President before. **1972** O. FRANKLIN *Informant, Grahamstown* 'What do they call the theological students at Stellenbosch?' 'Tokkeloks.' **1983** F.G. BUTLER *Bursting World* 151 When I mentioned E.G. Malherbe, Mrs Satchwell said: 'But I know him. His father and my mother were tokkeloks (theology students) together at Stellenbosch.'

tokoloshe, **tikoloshe** /ˈtɔkɔlɔʃ(e), ˈtɔkəlɔʃ, ˈtɔkəlɔs, ˈtɪkəlɒʃ ˈtikɔlɔʃ(e)/ *n.* Also **tagalash**, **thickoloshe**, **thikolosh(e)** **thokoloshe**, **thokolos(h)i**, **tickelosh**, **tic(k)oloshe**, **tigoloshi**, **tikaloshi**, **tikilosh(e)**, **tikolosh(i)**, **togolosh**, **tokaloshi**, **tokelosche**, **tokilosi**, **tokolosh(i)**, **ut(h)ikoloshe**, **utokoloshe**, and with initial capital. [Zulu *utokoloshe*, Xhosa *uthikoloshe*, Sotho *thökölösi*, *t(h)ikoloshi*.]

1. In African folklore, a mischievous and lascivious hairy water-sprite or goblin; HILI. Also *attrib.*, and (occas.) *fig.* (see quot. 1989).

1833 S. KAY *Trav. & Researches* 339 Tikaloshi also is much more frequently and familiarly talked about than amongst the more southern tribes. **1860** W. SHAW *Story of my Mission* 445 The people universally believe that .. bad persons may enter into league with wolves, baboons, jackals, and particularly with an imaginary amphibious creature .. called by the Border Kaffirs *utikoloshe.* **1894** E. GLANVILLE *Fair Colonist* 82 Tikoloshe is supposed to be an evil spirit which takes the shape of a small man. **1911** *Daily Dispatch* 24 Nov. 7 One might be dragged into the watery den of the *tikolosh.* **1918** H. MOORE *Land of Good Hope* 42 There is a widespread belief in a 'bogey man' called Tickelosh. **1931** F.C. SLATER *Secret Veld* 60 In early youth Tuta had been familiar with many old Bantu traditions and superstitions relating to Hili or Tikoloshe. Though invariably spoken of in the singular, Hili are regarded as plural, for they are said to be a race of faun-like, dwarfish male creatures – half men, half beast – who dwell in deep pools and among the reeds and rushes along the banks of flowing rivers. **1937** B.F.J. LAUBSCHER *Sex, Custom & Psychopathology* 8 The best-known and the most common of the mythical figures in the traditional beliefs of the people is the *Tikoloshe*, who is said to be a mischievous little fellow with aggressive sexual proclivities. **1949** E. HELLMANN *Handbk on Race Rel.* 561 Most widely believed in amongst many Nguni tribes is thikoloshe, a small hairy being with baboon-like face, having the form of a man but reaching no higher than man's knee. **1967** S.M.A. LOWE *Hungry Veld* 43 Incidents in the daily life of the native people, that could not be easily explained, were usually ascribed to the crafty work of the 'Utokoloshe'. **1968** *Drum* Sept. 42 At his trial Msomi confessed to all the murders and rapes but swore to high heaven that he was forced by a tikoloshi to do the deeds. **1971** *Post* 7 Mar. 11 Soon a huge crowd gathered threatening to stone the hag because she was a tokoloshe. **1976** WEST & MORRIS *Abantu* 20 *Uthikoloshe*, believed to be a short, hairy person of about knee-height with one buttock and a penis so long that it was carried over one shoulder. **1986** *City Press* 20 Apr. 8 (*advt*) Lucky charms, business problems, sores, .. nightmares, tokoloshe problems, bladder, kidney and heart ailments. **1989** S. BARBER in *E. Prov. Herald* 7 Mar. 4 He is possessed by that most prevalent of Washington tokoloshes, the desire for re-election. **1990** J. KNAPPERT *Aquarian Guide to Afr. Mythology* 241 A *tikoloshe* is a hairy monster, no taller than a baboon ... Although it once lived only in the rivers of the Transkei, it has since been seen in Natal and even in the city of Johannesburg.

2. *slang.* A derogatory name for a policeman.

1972 P. DRISCOLL *Wilby Conspiracy* 55 'You got a good chance of going all up the line to the death block at Pretoria Central. And if you don't, the *ore* will make you wish you had.' 'Who?' 'The ears. The jacks. The *tokoloshes*. The police,' Shack explained patiently.

Hence **tokolosh** *v. trans.*, to curse or bewitch (something); so **tokoloshed** *ppl adj.*, cursed, bewitched.

1963 M. KAVANAGH *We Merry Peasants* 59 The man .. had been disabled, .. and given a chance to rest unmolested while he nursed his 'tokoloshed' arm. **1988** *Informant, Seven Fountains* Do you know if the farm has been tokoloshed?

tok-tokkie /tɔkˈtɔki, tɒkˈtɒki/ *n.* Also **tock-tockie**, and (formerly) **toktokje**. [Afk. *toktokkie*, *tok-tok* fr. Du. *tokken* to tap, knock softly, fr. *tok* a tap, rap (prob. onomatopoeic) + -IE.]

1.a. Any of several tapping beetles of the Tenebrionidae, esp. *Dichtha cubica.* Also shortened form **tok**, and *attrib.*

[**1893** W.C. SCULLY *Between Sun & Sand* 37 (Pettman), Quaint beetles crawled out from under the stones and beat their soft *tok-tok-tok* – on the ground, signalling to prospective mates.] **1907** J.P. FITZPATRICK *Jock of Bushveld* (1909) 292 At my feet a pair of tock tockie beetles, hump backed and bandy legged, came toiling slowly and earnestly along. **1913** J.J. DOKE *Secret City* 149 That lazy toktokje, caught out after a long night's carouse, lumbered along trailing a shadow after it. **1948** V.M. FITZROY *Cabbages & Cream* 200 She knows just how to execute tok-tokkie beetles. **1952** L.G. GREEN *Lords of Last Frontier* 34 Koch is .. the world's leading authority on the desert beetles called tenebrionidae – or 'tok-tokkies', in South Africa. **1958** I. VAUGHAN *Diary* 8 There are tok tokkies .. the knocking kind of beetle. One day I had two toks in my room ... In the night .. the toks got out and started to walk, the wives looking for the husbands which were mixed up ... The husbands stands still and knock with his stumick on the ground and the wives knock back. **1974** B. SMIT in *Std Encycl. of Sn Afr.* X. 519 The true toktokkies or tapping beetles belong to the genera *Psammodes* and *Molurini.* Their bodies are almost spherical and as hard as nuts. **1980** *E. Prov. Herald* 24 Mar. 8 The toktokkie season is upon us again. All over the Eastern Cape these clumsy, dull black or brown beetles are blundering around the countryside in search of mates. **1986** SCHOLTZ & HOLM *Insects* 258 The often very stout, globular species of these groups [*sc.* the subtribes Phanerotomeina and Molurina] are known in South Africa as toktokkies because of the rapid tapping sound they produce when striking the abdomen on the ground. **1991** F.G. BUTLER *Local Habitation* 183, I remember an enchanted day on the Grobler's Kloof road, stopping the car to watch – and listen to – tok-tokkie beetles. **1993** *Weekend Post* 24 Oct. (Leisure) 7 The common 'toktokkie' beetles .. have shiny brown bodies with a rough and darker-coloured thorax section. They are called toktokkies because they tap their abdomen on the ground which, it is believed, attracts the females in the mating season.

b. *transf.* A simple toy made of a cotton reel with an elastic band threaded through the central hole, held in place by a match-stick at either end, and wound tightly, so that the reel is propelled forwards by the protruding ends of the match-sticks as the elastic band unwinds. Also *attrib.*

1969 *Informant, Grahamstown* Ma, it's tok tokkie season, can I have a cotton reel – a big one? **1971** *Informant, Grahamstown* The toktokkie craze is on again and all the cotton reels are plastic and no good. **1975** LEVICK & MULLINS *'Prep' Story* 147 It might be interesting to list the Prep crazes: .. Woer-woer, Toktokkie, [etc.].

2.a. Any of several children's games which involve tricking unsuspecting victims, particularly the game of knocking on doors and running away; TICK-TOCK.

1913 C. PETTMAN *Africanderisms* 505 *Tok-tokje* .. is the name of a boy's trick – a bullet is fastened by a piece of thread which is passed through a door-knocker and pulled from the other side of the street so that it knocks at the door. It has its variants. **1972** BEETON & DORNER in *Eng. Usage in Sn Afr.* Vol.3 No.1, 38 *Toktokkie*, .. schoolboys' game of knocking at doors and running [a]way. **1982** D. KRAMER *Short Back & Sides* 8 It was there .. that we played golf on the rugby field and tok-tokkie on hot summer nights. **1984** *Daily Dispatch* 16 Mar. 16 A man .. shot dead a school-boy playing toktokkie .. after he and two friends had rung the doorbell .. late at night and then hidden in the garden. **1987** *Fair Lady* Mar. 7 My teenage son plays *toktokkie* and cricket with our neighbours' maid.

b. *transf.* The name given to a fund-raising campaign for the National Cancer Association; the volunteers who knock on doors for this campaign. Also *attrib.*

1978 *Het Suid-Western* 22 Feb., Official tok-tokkie will be played in George next month when 150 women start knocking on doors to collect money for the National Cancer Association. **1979** *Ibid.* 10 Aug., This is the second time the National Cancer Association has played tok-tokkie in George. Last year R2 500 was collected. **1983** *S. Afr. Digest* 12 Aug. 3 A nation-wide *Toktokkie* campaign by the National Cancer Association .. is aimed at distributing educational pamphlets and collecting funds. **1989** *Grocott's Mail* 29 Mar. 1 Some 40 000 volunteers, or 'Toktokkies' as they are known, will be visiting homes throughout the country .. in an attempt to raise a target of R4-million.

tola var. TULA.

tolbos /ˈtɔlbɔs/ *n.* Formerly also **toll-bosch**. [Afk. (earlier S. Afr. Du. *tol bosch*), *tol* spinning top (referring to the shape of the cones or fruit) + *bos* bush.] Any of several shrubs or small trees bearing cones or cone-shaped fruit, including *Diospyros dichrophylla* of the ebony family (Ebenaceae), and any of several species of the genus *Leucadendron* of the Proteaceae.

1907 T.R. SIM *Forests & Forest Flora* 39 There is a belt of sea-bush .., then dense scrub forests .., and sparse clumps or single trees of Mimosa .. and Toll-bosch (Royena pubescens, W.) on the higher ground. **1913** C. PETTMAN *Africanderisms* 506 *Toll bosch*, (1) *Royena pubescens*. (2) *Leucadendron* species are so called. **1990** B. NIXON in *Weekend Post* 3 Nov. (Leisure) 3 Paths led us to .. mountain fynbos, featuring the shining yellow of tolbos (Leucadendron sp.). **1990** H. HUTCHINGS in *Ibid.* 23 Feb. (Leisure) 7 A good subject for difficult spots is *Diospyros dichrophylla*, more commonly known as tolbos or monkey apple. **1991** *Splash* Vol.4, 21 You will have travelled through false fynbos comprised of low-lying shrubs such as sugar bush, heath, 'tolbos' mountain cedars and buchu.

tollie /ˈtɔli/ *n.* Also **tolly**. [Afk., fr. Xhosa and Zulu *ithole* a (male or female) calf of a certain age, usu. one which has started developing horns or which has a younger sibling.] **a.** A young ox. **b.** A young bull-calf. Also *attrib.*

1900 *Grocott's Penny Mail* 2 July 1 (*advt*) 24 Tollies. *c***1911** S. PLAYNE *Cape Col.* 211 Tollies of nine months command a ready sale. **1916** *Farmer's Weekly* 20 Dec. 1451 Slaughter Oxen, Bulls, Cows, Heifers, and Tollies for sale. **1937** S. CLOETE *Turning Wheels* 64, I am tired of being played with like a tollie at the end of a rein running round and round. **1947** F.C. SLATER *Sel. Poems* 26 Tollie = a steer: a South African word derived from *etola* (Xhosa) = a calf. **1964** V. POHL *Dawn & After* 58 It was the sight of Eric driving along a young bull calf, or tolly .. which he had trained to pull a small sledge. **1970** J. WOODIN *Informant, Cape Town* Tollie. A young steer (Xhosa). **1971** *Evening Post* 27 Feb. 21 (*advt*) 12 Mateable Hereford Type Heifers; 33 Hereford X Type Tollies, 12–16 months old. **1971** *Grocott's Mail* 16 Apr. 1 Anyone requiring well-bred Tollies and Heifers should not miss this sale. *Ibid.* 26 Nov. 1 Dark Brown Bull Tollie. **1973** *E. Prov. Herald* 11 Apr., (*advt*) Annual tollie and breeding stock sale will be held in Adelaide. **1980** *Daily Dispatch* 26 Sept. 16 A neighbour and friend wanted to sell him a number of young tollies at R50 each at a time when cattle prices were at a low level. **1986** [see NKONE]. **1987** M. POLAND *Train to Doringbult* 109 She ran as wild as a *tollie* on the hills. **1994** *Grocott's Mail* 21 Oct. 8 Oxen & young cattle, Quality Tollies & Heifers, Store Cattle and Trade heifers. The cattle run on virulent Redwater Heartwater veld.

‖**tolofiya** /tɔlɔˈfijə, -ˈfiːja/ *n.* Also **itolofiya, tolofia**. [Xhosa *itolofiya*, ad. Afk. *dorrevy* (obs.); cf. TURKSVY.] TURKISH FIG. Also *attrib.*

1970 A. PALMER *Informant, King William's Town* Tolofia are my favourite (prickly pear). **1971** *Informant, Grahamstown* You just throw your tolofiya and watermelon skins out of the window – disgusting. **1976** *E. Prov. Herald* 11 Feb. 13 There is big business in the unfriendly little itolofiya, to use the Xhosa name. *Ibid.* 13 (*caption*) Katie .. knows a good itolofiya when she sees one. **1976** R.L. PETENI *Hill of Fools* 47 He concluded the feast with ripe, golden tolofiya fruit. *Ibid.* 75 Ntabeni wallked daily up and down the path .. hoping to meet Zuziwe and offer a doctored tolofiya fruit he carried in a small tin.

tomba var. THOMBA.

tombazaan, -besan, -bozane varr. INTOMBAZANA.

tomelah var. TAMELETJIE.

tommelaitje, tommelatche, tommelykie, Tommy Larche varr. TAMELETJIE.

tondel var. TONTEL.

Tonga /ˈtɒŋgə, ˈtɔŋga/ *n.* Also **Thonga**. [Either fr. an early form of a Tsonga word for this people, or fr. Zulu *iThonga* (pl. *amaThonga*), *umThonga* (pl. *abaThonga*) a member of this people (perh. earlier meaning 'blacksmith', 'metal-worker', or the source of this meaning, the Tonga being at one stage noted for their metal-working skills). For an explanation of pl. forms, see ABA- and AMA-.]

1. Pl. **-s, ama-, ba-**, or **amaTongas** (always with initial or medial capital). SHANGAAN sense 1 a. Also *attrib.*

1852 *Natal Mercury* 25 Nov., The property of the Amatongas, together with the ivory of the traders, were seized by Panda. **1852** R.B. STRUTHERS *Hunting Jrnl* (1991) 9 We were joined by a trader .. from the Amatonga country which lies N.E. from the Zulu country, leading to Delagoa Bay. **1856** *Ibid.* 98 The Amatongas say they often think when they go into Delagoa – whether any of the young slaves they see are their children or relations. **1872** *Cape Monthly Mag.* IV. Feb. 117 The Tonga does not own a single head of cattle. **1875** D. LESLIE *Among Zulus* 242 There are different tribes of Amatonga (*Itonga* the person, *Amatonga* the people – a general name for all the tribes thereabouts) in this country under different chiefs. **1877** F. JEPPE *Tvl Bk Almanac & Dir.* (1976) 29 A line along the Lobombo to the Pongola, and from this river to Zungin's Nek, and thence to Rorke's Drift on the Buffalo River, divides the Transvaal from the Amatonga and Zulu Tribes. **1884** *Cape Law Jrnl* I. 223 These are the Amaxosa Kafirs, Fingoes, Tembus, Ama-mpondo, Xesibes, Zulus, Bayeiye, Baloquazi, Shangaans, Matabele, Amatonga or Batoka, Amasuazi, Interior Basuto tribes and those in the Transvaal Territory and Colonial Basutos. **1897** J. BRYCE *Impressions of S. Afr.* 375 The Tongas of the east coast. **1901** R. RANKIN *Subaltern's Lett. to Wife* (1930) 97 The Swazis and the Amatongas are the Amorites and the Hittites over again. **1902** G.M. THEAL *Beginning of S. Afr. Hist.* 211 South of the Sabi river lived a tribe named the Batonga, whose outposts extended beyond Cape Correntes. **1937** J. STEVENSON-HAMILTON *S. Afr. Eden* 119 Strong mutual mistrust between people belonging to different clans of the Bathonga, to say nothing of the feeling between all members of that tribe and the Swazis. **1940** [see TSONGA sense 1]. **1949** O. WALKER *Proud Zulu* (1951) 47 The land of the mild amaTonga people who paid tribute to the Zulus and whom the Zulus spoke of contemptuously as 'dogs'. **1964** G. CAMPBELL *Old Dusty* 34 Be glad that you are an umLunga and not a one-time Zulu who has now become a snuff-pounder for the amaTonga. **1982** *E. Prov. Herald* 24 June, The vast majority of people in the area were Tembe-Thongas or Zulus, except in the west where there were equal proportions of Zulus, Thongas and Swazi. **1985** PLATZKY & WALKER *Surplus People* 92 When the Land Act of 1913 confirmed that the land was Crown land for eventual occupation by whites, there was again no complaint from the Tongas as they were not told of the loss of their land. **1991** MERRETT & BUTCHER *Robert Struthers's Hunting Jrnl* 9 *Amatonga* was the name used by the Zulu, and borrowed by the British, to refer to all the African groups between St. Lucia and Delagoa Bay.

2. TSONGA sense 2.

1941 *Bantu World* 29 Mar. 5 The Thonga language is a Bantu language spoken by the people living in Zoutpansberg, Lydenberg, Waterberg, Pietersberg and Pretoria districts ... Today .. we are instructed to write Thonga in a very different way. **1950** H. GIBBS *Twilight* 33 The south-eastern groups have five group languages, Nguni, Sotho, Venda, Tonga, and Inhambane, among which fusion has occurred, producing .. in the Tonga group, Ronga, Tonga and Tswa.

tong-sikte, tongziekte varr. TUNG-ZIEKTE.

tontel /ˈtɔntəl/ *n.* Also **tondel, tunde(r)l**. [Afk., fr. Du. *tondel* tinder.] 'Tinder', an element in the names of plants whose dry, woolly leaves were used in the past as tinder: **tontelblaar** /-blaːr/ [Afk., *blaar* leaf], **tontelblad** /-blat/ [Afk., *blad* leaf], **tontelbloem** /-blum/ [Afk., *bloem* flower], **tontelboom** /-buəm/ [Afk., *boom* tree], **tontelbos** /bɔs/ [Afk., *bos* bush, shrub], all names for *Hermas gigentea* of the Apiaceae; **tonteldoek** /-duk, -dʊk/ [Afk., *doek* head-scarf], *Arctotis acaulis* of the Asteraceae.

[**1837** ECKLON & ZEYHER *Enumeratio Plantarum Africae* 2256 *Hermas gigantea* ... – Incolis: Tundel-Bloom.] **1856** L. PAPPE in *Cape of G.H. Almanac & Annual Register* 343 Hermas gigantea Lin. (Umbelliferae). The thick, white woolly integument of this plant, when dried, serves the natives for tinder, and the women prepare from its radical leaves very curious fancy articles of hosiery, such as knitting bags, gloves, stockings, caps etc. The plant which grows on the mountains near Tulbagh is known as the Tinder-bush (Tondel-blad). **1868** W.H. HARVEY *Genera of S. Afr. Plants* 146 The wool of *H. gigantea* (*Tundelboom*) is used for tinder. **1906** B. STONEMAN *Plants & their Ways* 81 *Hermas gigantea*, the 'Tontel-bloom,' has the lower leaves well protected by a dense hairy covering on both sides; as they get older, and their leaves become firmer, they are less in need of protection, and the hair is easily brushed off. **1913** C. PETTMAN *Africanderisms* 506 A plant – *Hermas gigentea* [*sic*] – the dry, woolly leaves of which are sometimes used as tinder. It is sometimes called 'Tondel-boom,' though it is only a low herb. **1917** R. MARLOTH *Common Names* 82 *Tondelblaar, Hermas gigantea*. The large basal leaves are covered with a layer of white felt on the underside; when dried and properly prepared they are used for tinderboxes and as a dressing for wounds, like lint (Clanwilliam), etc. Some other plants are sometimes employed in a similar way, e.g., *Arctotis acaulis* (Tondeldoek). **1945** L.G. GREEN *Where Men Still Dream* 136 The Tontelboom has a dense hairy covering of lower leaves, used as tinder by old travellers. **1966** C.A. SMITH *Common Names* 465 Thunberg, who in 1772, gave the name as 'Tondelboom' for the species evidently gave an erroneous rendering, as the plants are not trees. **1988** SMUTS & ALBERTS *Forgotten Highway* 65 The Forgotten Highway has a forgotten grave. At the roadside in the shadow of the Paardeberg, and veiled by the nodding cotton-padded 'tontelbos', there stands a foot-high headstone.

too *adv.* Esp. among speakers of the Sintu (Bantu) languages: used as an intensifier, esp. in the phr. ***too much***, 'very', 'very much', 'very well', 'a lot (of)'.

1966 L.G. BERGER *Where's Madam* 160 'Can you paint too?' I asked him. 'Yes Ma'am.' 'Can you lay bricks?' 'Too much Ma'am.' **1975** *E. Prov. Herald* 5 July 9 We buy chicken and meat only once every two weeks. We get a big chicken, R1 beef and some boerewors. The children like it too much. **1979** A.P. BRINK *Dry White Season* 85 'And you met Gordon long ago?' 'Too much. When Jonathan was just so high.' He held out his hand, a foot or two from the floor. **1982** *E. Prov. Herald* 18 Mar., Miss Priscilla K–, who was five months pregnant .. , said yesterday: 'I feel too sad about it. We needed that baby'. **1982** *Drum* Mar. 32, I do not know what my future shall be, because my father hates me too much. **1982** *Voice* 11 July 6 He loves me too much and I love him too. **1991** *Informant, Grahamstown* 'One coffee please — with too much milk.' 'Not too much milk?' 'No, too much milk.' **1992** *Informant, Grahamstown* Yesterday night — it was too much cold. In Grahamstown it's not too much cold this winter. **1992** *Scope* 13 Nov. 84 An eloquent township obituary: 'He was just a quiet somebody. He was not too much violent.'

toola var. TULA.

toor /tʊə(r)/ *v. trans.* and *intrans.* Also **to(e)r**, **to(o)ver**. [Afk., fr. Du. *toueren*.]

a. To bewitch (someone or something), to cast a spell. See also TOWENAAR.

1912 F. BANCROFT *Veldt Dwellers* 5 Little baas, .. ask me not to touch the water-rat; for, as thou knowest, his mother is a witch, and would *tor* the house of my father so that all therein should die the death. **1934** *Sunday Times* 1 Apr., The Prosecutor: 'Did you believe this witchcraft?' 'Yes, she told me I had been "toored!"' **1950** V. DE KOCK *Those in Bondage* 127 A man .. had the reputation of being able to 'tover' (bewitch) ... Any individual accredited with this power was never *persona grata* with the authorities. **1959** J. MEIRING *Candle in Wind* 58 'Just so long as you "too:" me, I do not care. So be quick, old Tembela, and toor me now.' The witchdoctor studied his client with interest. 'And how must I toor you?' he wheezed. 'Toor me so that the police cannot catch me again.' **1970** C.B. WOOD *Informant, Johannesburg* I'll toor you (put a spell on someone). **1987** *Pace* Oct. 4 The bad luck makhulu baas .. walks with a limp because of a mysterious accident. And .. the baas is forever pointing a finger at his 'boy', saying he did toor him no matter what.

b. *comb.* **toor-doctor** or **toordokter** /-dɔktər/ [Afk., *dokter* doctor], a healer who relies on supernatural methods; **toorgoed** /-xut/ [Afk., *goed* stuff], accessories or material believed to be a source of magic.

1959 J. MEIRING *Candle in Wind* 56 Am I not a **toor-doctor**, my Baas? *Ibid.* 58 A man's life might hang on a thread, but the little toor-doctor only wanted to make sure that there was money in the bag. Only money could buy his wonderful magic. **1987** M. MOSIMANE in *Pace* July 54 There are whites who say I am doing satan's work because they belive that if you're a sangoma you're a witch. That is why they call sangomas and nyangas 'toor-doktors' (witchdoctors). But that is wrong because the job of the sangomas is to do good and give health. **1892** *The Jrnl* 24 Sept. 2 They had something in their possession which had bewitched her ... They beat them with switches, demanding all the time that they should produce the **toorgoed**. **1934** *Cape Argus* 27 Jan. (Swart), This labourer has been to a witchdoctor and obtained toergoed to bewitch you. **1980** A.J. BLIGNAUT *Dead End Rd* 75 'What did they, the toorgoed, say?' he asked. I told him they spoke of aasvoëls in the sky.

Hence **toordery** /ˈtʊə(r)dəreɪ/ *n.* [Afk.], magic, sorcery.

1957 L.G. GREEN *Beyond City Lights* 68 Some members of his congregation believed in witchcraft ... Even today ministers have sometimes to deal with *toordery* among white people. *Ibid.* 79 *Toordery*, and *goëlery*, the old magic of the Hottentots and Malays, has not vanished from the Western Province ... Ignorant people who believe in *toordery* are indeed seriously influenced.

Toorvenaar var. TOWENAAR.

toot *n. slang.* [Prob. ad. Italian *tutti* all.] In the phr. ***the whole toot***, everything, every last bit, the whole lot.

1979 L.S. WRIGHT *Informant, Grahamstown*, I paid for the license, the organ, the use of the church, the whole toot. **1982** *Sunday Times* 31 May, He arrived with his wife, his mother — the whole toot. **1992** A. MURPHY in *Style* Nov. 96, I do flowers for weddings, social events, the whole toot.

toover var. TOOR.

top-knot *n. obs.* [Named for the crest of feathers on its head; see quot. 1899.] TOPPIE *n.*[1]

1899 R.B. & J.D.S. WOODWARD *Natal Birds* 20 This [*sc. Pycnonotus layardi*] is one of our commonest birds, popularly called the 'Top-knot' from its black crest. **1908** [see TIPTOL]. **1913** C. PETTMAN *Africanderisms* 507 *Top-knot* or *Toppie*, .. *Pycnonotus layardi*. **1923** [see BLACKHEAD sense 1 a]. **1937** [see TOPPIE *n.*[1]].

toppie /ˈtɒpi/ *n.*[1] [Formed on TOP-KNOT + Eng. (informal) n.-forming suffix *-ie*; see quot. 1937.] Either of two species of bulbul of the Pycnonotidae with black or dark brown heads and crests, *Pycnonotus capensis* and *P. barbatus*; TOP-KNOT; also called TIPTOL. See also BLACKHEAD sense 1 a.

In G.L. Maclean's *Roberts' Birds of Sn Afr.* (1993), the name 'Cape bulbul' is used for *P. capensis*, and 'black-eyed bulbul' for *P. barbatus*.

1899 G. RUSSELL *Hist. of Old Durban* 176 Doves cooed, and 'Toppies' answered each other obtrusively. **1913** [see TOP-KNOT]. **1936** E.L. GILL *First Guide to S. Afr. Birds* 71 Toppie, blackcap bulbul, layard's bulbul; *Pycnonotus tricolor layardi* ... The Toppie is the one with the widest range, from the Eastern Cape Province through Natal and the Transvaal to Rhodesia and Nyasaland. **1937** M. ALSTON *Wanderings* 97 The black-capped bulbuls, known familiarly as 'toppies' or 'tiptols' or 'top-knots' because of their black-crested heads. **1940** A. ROBERTS *Birds of S. Afr.* 225 Cape Bulbul, or Toppie .. is not such a common bird as the Layard's Bulbul found further east, but has the same lively manner and habit of whistling ... It feeds on berries and fruit. **1953** J.M. WINTERBOTTOM *Common Birds of S.-E.* 22 The Scrub Bulbul is .. about the same size as the Toppie (*Pycnonotus barbatus*). **1964** D. VARADAY *Gara-Yaha* 126 His best friends became the Toppies, the conical-helmeted small dark birds that disclose the presence of snakes. **1972** PALMER & PITMAN *Trees of Sn Afr.* II. 1401 These fruits .. are .. eaten by many species of birds such as Green Pigeons, toppies, barbets and guineafowl. **1981** P. GINN *Birds Afield* 89 The bulbuls fall naturally into two groups: the toppies, with their black heads and yellow vents, and the forest or bush species which are generally a greenish or yellowish colour. **1989** M. GINN in *Rhodos* (Rhodes Univ.) Nov. 5 The odd false alarm caused by our resident Cape Robin and the ubiquitous and vaguely similar 'Toppie'.

toppie /ˈtɒpi, ˈtɔpi/ *n.*[2] *slang.* Also **itopi, topie**. [Perh. fr. Zulu ideophone *thopi*, of growing sparsely, as in *ukuthi thophi* 'to be sparse', used of thinning hair (among other things); or fr. Hindi *topi* hat, pith-helmet (see quot. 1963), via the Nguni languages (see quots 1963).] A middle-aged or elderly man; a father; loosely, a 'chap' or 'fellow'. Also with defining word: **old toppie, ou toppie** (in *pl.* referring to both sexes, 'old people', 'parents'), and shortened form **old top**.

1963 [see LARNEY *n.* sense 1 a]. [**1963** WILSON & MAFEJE *Langa* 28 The middle-aged and elderly type known as *amatopi* from topi, the pith sun-helmet worn by an earlier generation of Europeans ... The *amatopi* proper are over 45. *Ibid.* 163 R was still kicking him when an elderly man, an *itopi*, appeared.] **1966** *Drum* 30 Jan. 20 'Members only', says a certain toppie with grey hair. **1970** *Post* 15 Mar. 9 Oom Piet makes me — in my old safari suit — look like a refugee from the bush. He's such an elegant topie. **1970** J.R. BENNETT *Informant, Krugersdorp* My old Topie bought a new car (father, old man). **1974** J. MATTHEWS *Park* (1983) 44 De ole toppies is in for drunk, an' so de two party boys. De lighty issa moffie mobster. **1976** [see WOES]. **1978** L. BARNES in *The 1820* Vol.51 No.12, 19 [In S. Afr. Indian English] *The kêrel* usually means 'my father', 'my old man'. He is also referred to as the 'old toppie' or the 'old ballie'. **1979** F. DIKE *First S. African* 12 How can he live at the hostels taking all that shit from those topies there? **1979** *Sunday Times* 21 Oct. (Mag. Sect.) 1 *Old top* means either a parent, or someone who is past it. **1980** S. ROBERTS in *Bloody Horse* No.2, 55 Grandpa Bezuidenhout was turning eighty-nine, and Ruff begged to be allowed to arrange the candles on the huge cake baked for the old toppie. **1982** *Sunday Times* 6 June (Mag. Sect.), Like this taxi rocks up with two old toppies. I quickly suss that the taxi-driver oke .. is taking his cherrie (some ancient bird with ringlets) for a 'hoddog' and chips. **1982** D. KRAMER *Short Back & Sides* 46 All the old toppies .. Used to get pissed out of their heads And their wives had to drive them home. **1986** *Weekly Mail* 18 Apr. 19, I tell you we couldn't move for the air-conditioned coach loads of toppies buying roast peanuts. **1987** O. MUSI in *Drum* June 58 A far-sighted topi who also happens to be a member of the Rotterdam City Council .. strongly suggested that the Council buy and run its own brothel. **1990** J. NAIDOO *Coolie Location* 129 All you have to do is to get one of the boys working for your toppie to come to the shop .. with the receipt and the outstanding amount in cash. **1990** C. LEONARD in *Weekly Mail* 2 Nov. 28 It is a family occasion, with the ou toppies, ma, pa, ouboet and the kids listening to the music and braaing under the eucalyptus tree.

tor var. TOOR.

Torch Commando *n. phr. Hist.* [See quot. 1967.] A militant organization formed in 1951 to oppose the National Party government, esp. in its attempts to disenfranchise 'coloured' voters. Also *attrib.* Hence *colloq.* **Torchie** *n.* [Eng. (informal) n.-forming suffix *-ie*], a member of this organization.

Led by world war veterans, the organization was active until 1953.

1951 *Sun* (Baltimore, U.S.A.) 9 Nov. 13 South Africa's Torch Commando, an organization of war veterans pledged to uphold the Dominion Constitution, is building up into a potent opposition to Prime Minister Daniel F. Malan's Nationalist Government. **1952** *Star* 3 May 1 In a statement by the National executive of the Torch Commando today, the Prime Minister, Dr. Malan, was asked on what grounds he had made the 'damaging allegations against the Torch Commando and its leaders' in his speech .. last night. **1953** *Rand Daily Mail* 14 May 1 A hint that the Torch Commando might be remobilised on an all-party basis to fight the Senate Bill was given yesterday by Mr John Wilson, one of the 'big-five' of the leadership. **1956** G.F. VAN L. FRONEMAN in M. Rogers *Black Sash* 86 The Torch Commando, .. hailed as the determined, resolute, brave and incorruptible defender of our Constitution, a movement to save South Africa out of the bloody talons of these desecrators, the National Party. **1958** G. CARTER *Politics of Inequality* 304 Beginning with a knot of people at the time when the Nationalists decided to take the Coloured off the common roll .. the Torch Commando included nearly a quarter of a million members at its height late in 1952. **1967** E. ROSENTHAL *Encycl. of Sn Afr.* 563 It took its name from torches carried by participants in its spectacular early processions. The objects of the Torch Commando were largely those of the United Party. Its activities came to an end about 1953. **1974** *Std Encycl. of Sn Afr.* X. 525 Before the formation of the Torch Commando, as it was popularly called, other attempts were made to organise ex-servicemen into opposition movements. **1989** *Reader's Digest Illust. Hist.* 394 It was the activities of the War Veterans' Torch Commando – with its massed torchlight rallies – that grabbed the headlines in 1951. *Ibid.* 395 Ex-Battle of Britain fighter ace 'Sailor' Malan was one of the main organisers of the Torch Commando. **1991** A. VAN WYK *Birth of New Afrikaner* 72 The Torchies were a vociferous and near-militant English-dominated pressure group which rapidly gained mass support ... Torch Commando meetings almost automatically turned rowdy, with fisticuffs the rule rather than the exception. **1993** P. BELL in *Leadership* Vol.12 No.2, 82 The Torch Commando in Natal directed its appeal, not at the preservation of coloured voting rights as elsewhere in the country, but at the preservation of English political power and culture in the province.

‖**tornynhaai** /tɔ(r)ˈneɪnhaɪ/ *n.* Pl. **-haaie** /-haɪə/. [Afk., *tornyn* porpoise + *haai* shark.] PORPOISE SHARK.

1930 C.L. BIDEN *Sea-Angling Fishes* 44 He trolled too deep and struck an enormous shark (*Carcharodon carcharias*, the great white shark of the North Atlantic, or what is known by Cape fishermen as 'groot tornynhaai' = great porpoise shark). *Ibid.* 147 The mako shark (*Isuropsis mako*) is the same as the South African blue tornynhaai. **1957** [see JUMPING JACK].

tot /tɒt/ *n.*[1] *Offensive. colloq. rare.* [Shortened form of HOTTENTOT.] **1.** KHOIKHOI sense 1. **2.** COLOURED *n.* sense a.

1835 T.H. BOWKER Journal. 19 Apr., Some tots that joined the Kafirs at Mahoney come back to us. *Ibid.* 14 Aug., Fatigues Sweeping place, building huts for the Married tots. **1978** J. BRANFORD *Dict. of S. Afr. Eng.* 258 *Totty*, .. A mode of reference to a *Hottentot* .. still heard occ. as '*tot*', now regarded as offensive.

tot *n.*[2] [Special uses of general Eng. *tot* a small measure of drink, a dram.]

1. *hist.* ***The tot***: The measure of wine (usu. much more than a tot) supplied several times a day to a labourer in part payment of his wages. Also *attrib.*

[**1916** L.D. FLEMMING *Fool on Veld* (1933) 48 He predicts that the general cry, For labour that cannot be got, Will be instantly silenced if I Give my niggers a regular 'tot'.] **1926** *E. Prov. Herald* 23 Feb. 7 Did honorary members think that the wine farmer was such a fool as to give the tot to his labourer to make him drunk and incapable of work? **1952** 'MR DRUM' in *Drum* June 7 Farmers say that the tot makes workers work better, and that they can't do without it ... Many of the men who get the tot were born in 'tot' families, and have never known life without tots. Life on the vineyards revolves round the tot. **1952** *Drum* June 8 (*caption*) Young children work on the vineyards, and often take the tot from an early age. **1952** F. MARQUARD in *Ibid.* 8 The whole system should be abolished ... The tot is poison to the brain: it deprives people of a clear mind.

2. *comb.* and Special Comb. **tot-sodden** *adj.*; **tot system** *hist.*, the custom whereby labourers, esp. those employed on vineyards (or 'wine farms'), were paid part of their wages in wine; *dop system*, see DOP *n.* sense 3 c; also *transf.*; **tot-time**.

1952 'MR DRUM' in *Drum* June 8 The husband's **tot-sodden** existence is shown all too clearly by the grim bareness of the rooms – often with no furniture at all. [**1896 tot system**: R. WALLACE *Farming Indust. of Cape Col.* 403 The pernicious custom of giving a daily allowance of wine, a custom similar to that of supplying beer to the labourer in the South of England.] **1926** *E. Prov. Herald* 12 Feb. 7 Liquor Bill Under Fire – Evils of the Tot System. *c***1936** M. VALBECK *Headlong from Heaven* 229 The 'tot' system, whereby in many parts of the Western Province the farm labourer was kept stimulated with a ration of up to two pints of cheap wine daily. **1952** *Drum* June 7 The most surprising thing about the tot system is that it is perfectly legal. **1956** A. SAMPSON *Drum* 52 We published a series of articles by Mr Drum on labour conditions in South Africa. One was about the 'tot system' in the vineyards of the Cape, where Coloured workers are paid partly in tots of wine, and live in a haze of semi-drunkenness. **1963** M. KAVANAGH *We Merry Peasants* 86 Under the prevalent tot system initiated in the wine farming areas of the Western Cape, each working man – including any teen-ager not at school – receives a ration of five-plus condensed milk tins of wine every day. **1972** *Argus* 10 Aug. 3 The Coloured Representative Council has called for the abolition of the tot system on farms. **1973** *Ibid.* 14 Apr. 13 Most farmers who still apply the tot system argue they will lose their labour if they stop it ... Some of the side effects of the tot system are alcoholism of epidemic proportions, a high assault rate, and an abysmally low standard of living. **1974** *Sunday Times* 24 Feb. 14 Asked whether he made use of the tot system, Mr de J– said: 'I'll be quite frank. I give them a little wine in the morning and two bottles each during the day because I like to keep them happy.' **1981** V.A. FEBRUARY *Mind your Colour* 201 The 'tot system' is one whereby 'coloured' farm-hands are rewarded right through the day with tots of wine or brandy presumably to keep up productivity. It also keeps the poor worker in a constant state of inebriation and makes him a willing partner to his own degradation. **1987** *South* 27 July 1 Workers at a toy factory in Philippi are on the tot system ... The workers are recruited from farms in the surrounding area where the outlawed tot system is still a common practice. **1990** 'T. EQUINUS' in *Weekly Mail* 2 Nov. 54 He says he will pay us according to the Tot System – half a dozen crates of Fosters for the weekend and a free stomach pump every fortnight. **1952** 'MR DRUM' in *Drum* June 8 At work they are apathetic and half-dazed, watching the farmhouse and slackening off when it gets near **tot-time**.

total onslaught *n. phr.* [tr. Afk. *totale aanslag.*] **a.** *hist.* A perceived campaign by foreign (esp. communist) countries and South African left-wing movements against the Nationalist government and its policies, believed to be aimed at weakening South Africa through offensives in the military, economic, psychological, social, political, and cultural spheres; ONSLAUGHT; TOTAL STRATEGY sense a. Also *attrib.*

The perceived threat of 'total onslaught' formed the basis of (and stated justification for) the government's policies in many areas from about 1973 until the late 1980s.

[**1977** M. MALAN in J. Pauw *In Heart of Whore* (1991) 120 South Africa has for a long time been subjected to a total and protracted revolutionary onslaught.] **1978** tr. N. Diederichs in *Hansard* 27 Jan. 9 The Republic of South Africa continues to be the target of a total onslaught being made on it on the political, economic, psychological, security and other fronts in an attempt to force it to abandon its present system of government. **1981** *Argus* 29 Jan. 5 He .. claimed that the Press was .. unknowingly helping in a total onslaught by the forces of Marxism. **1981** *Rand Daily Mail* 10 Feb. 8 Swart gevaar, world hostility, now 'total onslaught' – these are the slogans that have frightened the electorate into uncritical endorsement of the Government. **1983** *Sunday Times* 30 Jan. 29 Rising unemployment, economic recession, a tough budget, the shopworn total onslaught theme .. , all will feature in the political passing parade. **1985** [see *Sunday Times* quot. at NÊ]. **1988** [see OSSEWA sense 2 b]. **1990** *Sunday Times* 11 Mar. 7 Gen. Magnus André de Merindol Malan .. the youngest ever Chief of the Defence Force and later its political head ... His lasting legacy has been the dogma of the total onslaught – to be countered by a total strategy – which permeated South African political life throughout the 80s. It has been said that he learned it from the French, with whose forces he served briefly in Algeria in the early '60s. **1990** *Ibid.* 18 Mar. 23 Mythology number one, which the South African whites called 'the total onslaught' theory. **1990** P. VALE in *Weekly Mail* 27 Apr. 5 Although intellectually vulgar, the total onslaught was stunningly effective in determining public policy in South Africa for more than a decade. **1990** *Weekend Argus* 29 Sept. 17 The security establishment must be made to shed its aggressive and even belligerent image of the 'total onslaught' era. **1991** C. LONG on TV1, 10 Mar. (Agenda), South Africa is well on the way towards establishing full diplomatic relations with the Soviet Union. Whatever happened to the total onslaught? **1991** D. CAPEL in *Personality* 2 Sept. 18 Those were the dark old days of total onslaught, when die groot krokodil was just waiting to gaps you if you put a foot out of line – or into his Rubicon. **1993** *Sunday Times* 10 Oct. 20 Like some restless Frankenstein monster, the old National Party – the party of PW Botha, and cold-hearted Jimmy Kruger, and the total onslaught – came lumbering back to life this week: violent, ruthless, inept.

b. *Transf.* and *fig.*, often *joc.*, or used ironically.

1981 *Rand Daily Mail* 14 Mar. 9 Will this total onslaught never cease? Now some bigots and cynics have actually dared to attack the suave and diplomatic Mr Pik Botha. They have carped at a calm and measured statement in which Mr Botha advised the West German president of the UN General Assembly to 'come out and fight like a man, you scaredy-cat, and sucks to you'. **1982** *E. Prov. Herald* 10 Nov. 11 The total onslaught has reached Kinkelbos ... It could, however, be worse, the culprits are porcupines. The quilly creatures have caused havoc in Mr W Muscott's .. pineapple land. **1982** *Cape Times* 24 Dec. 11 One total onslaught not in dispute during 1982 was the one on the pocket. Inflation continued to soar. **1983** *Drum* Jan. 24 Afra's Cheryl Walker says the Government has .. underestimated the degree of resistance it is likely to meet. 'They would need a total onslaught to achieve it.' ... Dr Koornhof has, publicly, at least, been putting a nicer image to relocation. **1986** *E. Prov. Herald* 5 May 8 At least one truly South African value is safe from Total Onslaught ... Parliament has agreed to make mincemeat of anyone who tries to tamper with the quality of our boerewors. **1987** *New Nation* 12 Feb. 6 With the emergency came a total onslaught on the media and on the image of the African National Congress. **1989** G. SILBER in *Sunday Times* 30 Apr. 17 Hiding behind subversive pseudonyms, yelling inciteful slogans – *Hou 'n party, bou ons nasie, met die nuwe dans sensasie!* – the *Voëlvry* brigade are the total onslaught with a rock 'n roll backbeat.

total strategy *n. phr. Hist.* [tr. Afk. *totale strategie.*]

a. TOTAL ONSLAUGHT sense a.

1973 P.W. BOTHA in *White Paper on Defence* (Dept of Defence) 1 A country's policy structure comprises three basic elements – internal policy, foreign policy, and defence policy ... These .. must .. be closely co-ordinated and integrated; and this is of vital importance, particularly in the present international climate which is typified by total strategy and which obliges us to face the onslaughts of monolithic organizations which are in absolute control of all the means available to their states. **1987** *E. Prov. Herald* 19 May 6 Those sanctioneers with consciences .. see it as a palliative for what they are wreaking with sanctions. The rest proclaim it part of their total strategy of isolating South Africa. **1988** T.L. SMITH in *Frontline* May 34 They see sanctions as part only of a total strategy (perhaps P W Botha is right, it is a 'total onslaught').

b. The co-ordinated plans and efforts, from about 1973 until the late 1980s, of various National Party government departments, public service bodies, quasi-government institutions, and covert organizations to counter this perceived threat. Also *attrib.*

1975 P.W. BOTHA in *White Paper on Defence* (Dept of Defence) 3 All countries must muster all their activities – political, economic, diplomatic and military – for their defence. This .. is the meaning of 'total strategy'. **1980** *Rand Daily Mail* 2 Dec. 1 The chairman of the Southern Transvaal branch of the National Education Union of South Africa said the Human Sciences Research Council's education inquiry was clearly part of the Government's 'total strategy.' **1983** *Daily Dispatch* 8 Feb. 2 The government's 'total strategy' for 'total onslaught' was nothing more than an attempt to exert total control over every area of life in South Africa, Dr Alex Boraine, MP, said. **1987** *New Nation* 10 Dec. 7 The government's 'total strategy' included the economic coercion of neighbouring states. **1989** *Reader's Digest Illust. Hist.* 453 The plan conceived by the Afrikaner capitalists and their military allies was called 'Total Strategy'. Its aim was basically twofold: to improve and expand the African middle class as a counter to the radical activists in the townships; and the removal of the African National Congress .. from South Africa's borders by creating a 'constellation' of southern African states .. to replace the crumbled buffer of colonial powers. **1990** *Weekend Argus* 29 Sept. 17 He [*sc.* President F.W. de Klerk] can no longer afford to delay .. steps to remove the repressive instruments of his predecessor's discredited 'total strategy' system from his administration. **1993** *Africa S. & E.* July 14 The South African economy has a distinct anti-export bias. It is, essentially, inward-looking – an inheritance from the 'fortress South Africa' ideology of the Total Strategy period.

||**totsiens** /'tɔt'sins/ *int. colloq.* Also **tot siens.** [Afk., *tot* until + *siens* see(ing).]
a. An informal expression used on parting: 'till we meet again', 'be seeing you', 'au revoir'.

1937 C.R. PRANCE *Tante Rebella's Saga* 175 Oom Koos thanked his visitor .. bade him 'tot siens' and farewell. **1944** 'TWEDE IN BEVEL' *Piet Kolonel* 176 Those who were going up to South West, I should be seeing in the train, so that Totsiens was easy to say. **1951** O. WALKER *Shapeless Flame* 240 Let me get out here ... Let me feel Africa under my feet for the last few yards ... Shall we say tot siens, in the vernacular? **1958** S. CLOETE *Mask* 194 The group of men waved and shouted, 'Good luck and tot siens, Jong. We shall soon be with you'. **1963** A. DELIUS *Day Natal Took Off* 72 This is, then, not good-bye, only totsiens. **1964** J. MEINTJES *Manor House* 16 He turned to me. 'I'll come and fetch you quite soon. *Tot siens*.' **1968** G. CROUDACE *Black Rose* 64 'Ja, kleinbaas, that's what it is: Tot siens, tot siens.' Farewell was so final: far better to say 'Be seeing you'. **1974** G. JENKINS *Bridge of Magpies* 131 'So long.' Captain Miki found two more English words. He seemed to know what they meant too. '*Totsiens*' – which means no more than *au revoir*, I meant to be back. **1978** *E. Prov. Herald* 26 Jan. 8 The 'goodbye' .. was really 'totsiens' for she is expected to visit EP Command regularly after her retirement. **1988** D. HIRSON in Bunn & Taylor *From S. Afr.* 100 Mevrou Duplessis in an orange polka-dot apron waves Totsiens to them from the front door. **1990** W. SMITH *Golden Fox* 142, 'I must go now, I have another function to attend.' He turned back to Isabella. '*Totsiens*, Doctor Courtenay, until we meet again.'

b. *fig.* 'Goodbye (to something)', signalling finality.

1972 *Sunday Times* 30 Apr. 1 Earlier he said 'totsiens' with a straight right. **1972** *Ibid.* 25 June (Mag. Sect.), Totsiens to a reputation. **1973** F. CHISHOLM in *Cape Times* 5 May 7 The Wynberg interchange means *totsiens*, among many places, to the gracious old Cape homestead on the main road, La Plaisance. **1981** M. VAN BILJON in *Sunday Times* 14 June 9 Tennis is no longer the great social occasion older inhabitants remember. 'It's this TV,' said one. 'It means "totsiens vrinne" [friends].' **1985** *Financial Mail* 9 Aug. (Suppl.) 16 Totsiens to the train. Not too long ago passenger trains reigned supreme. **1987** *Daily Dispatch* 14 Feb. 18 It's goodbye Graeme and totsiens Kim. **1992** P.-D. UYS in *South* 27 Feb. 24 Goodbye to maths, biology, geography. Totsiens Shakespeare, Goethe, Shaw.

Hence (sense a) **totsiens** *n.*, an utterance of this expression.

1988 *Personality* 6 June 62 A smile on your face and a friendly 'tot siens'.

tottie /'tɒti/ *n. Obsolescent. offensive. colloq.* Also **tottee, totty**, and with initial capital. [Formed on HOTTENTOT + Eng. (informal) n.-forming suffix *-ie* (or *-y*); cf. HOTTIE.]
1. *hist.* A derogatory or affectionate form of address or reference to a KHOIKHOI (*n.* sense 1). Also *attrib.*

1832 *Graham's Town Jrnl* 20 Apr. 67 Poor Tottee must bear the blame, he is always the rogue; and yet Tottee was living all over the country when the English came. **1835** T.H. BOWKER Journal. 27 Sept., The totties dancing to the sound of their Calabash fiddles & &. **1848** H. WARD *Five Yrs in Kaffirland* I. 287 Those gallant little Totties are an untiring, determined band. How little do we know in England of the smartness and courage of the Hottentot! **1856** R.E.E. WILMOT *Diary* (1984) 37 On asking him if it was true that many Kaffirs in female attire were found, he said 'No, I saw one Totty boy of about 15 years who tried the dodge but a burgher saw him'. **1863** J.S. DOBIE *S. Afr. Jrnl* (1945) 121 A great many well dressed 'Tottie' girls flaming about in their crinolines. **1868** W.R. THOMSON *Poems, Essays & Sketches* p.xxv, I am now as popular, not with 'Totties' alone, but with English, Dutch, and coloured people, as a member well can be in such a mixed constituency. **1876** F. BOYLE *Savage Life* 283 'What is it, Totty?' somebody asked ... 'Horses – go quick – stop now!' muttered the Totty. **1879** T.J. LUCAS *Zulus & Brit. Frontiers* 88 When I first joined the regiment, the Hottentots, or 'Tottys,' as we called them for abbreviation['s] sake, were habited in leather pantaloons. **1883** *Good News in Afr.* 110 The Hottentots are a miserable little race, sometimes called 'Totties' in contempt. **1887** [see Ellis quot. at FORE-LOUPER]. **1898** G. NICHOLSON *50 Yrs* 24 They might easily have been saved from extinction by appropriate legislation, but the anti-slavery enthusiasts insisted on drastic treatment, and the poor 'Tottie' succumbed to a full dose of freedom, administered without timely preparation. **1934** N. DEVITT *Mem. of Magistrate* 216 The Hottentot is a curious creature. He has some of the attributes of his white master ... The 'Tottie' has also at times a weird humour. **1968** F.C. METROWICH *Frontier Flames* 225 His Hottentot servant .. was a Private in the Cape Mounted Rifles ... Many a time the poor 'Totty' was ordered punishment for the faults of his master. **1976** A. DELIUS *Border* 185 An argument between an officer of the 55th and Captain Aitchison of the Cape Mounted Rifles. This officer had made some slighting remark about the value of the Totties as soldiers, and Captain Aitchison said by God he would rather have Totties at his back in this sort of war than any great clumsy clanking red dragoon.

2.a. A derogatory or affectionate term for one who is not white, particularly a 'coloured' person. See also COLOURED *n.* sense a.

1900 O. OSBORNE *In Land of Boers* 41 The Malays and 'Totties' were quite a new thing in humanity to us. **1955** A. DELIUS *Young Trav.* 36 Good lord, we wouldn't play with Totties! .. Black people and Coloured people aren't allowed to mix with the white people. *Ibid.* 50 What a little democrat you are, Paul! .. Always ready with some bad old name like Kaffir or Nigger or Tottie for the Bantu. **1964** G. CAMPBELL *Old Dusty* 14 No other society than the mongrel dog and a few fowls and an occasional Cape Tottie.

b. *comb.* **tottie pink**, *coolie pink* (see COOLIE sense 2).

1970 E.G.B. HARDY *Informant, Cape Town* Totty pink, coolie pink – puce or magenta. Later rendered respectable and fashionable by Schiaparelli as 'shocking pink'. **1972** *Informant, Grahamstown*, I had a shocking pink dress for a ball some years ago and asked the girl in the chemist's for a lipstick to match and asked her for a sort of totty pink – she nearly had a fit.

3. *rare.* HOTTENTOT *n.* sense 2.

1905 [see HOTTENTOT *n.* sense 2].

tou /təʊ/ *n.* Also **to(u)w.** [Du. *touw* (later Afk. *tou*); cf. Eng. *tow*.]
1. Rope; a rope or thong, esp. one by which a team of oxen is led. See also TOULEIER, TREKTOU sense a, VOORTOU.

1824 G. BARKER Journal. 23 Feb., Could not procure Duplicates of the cirtificates of pension, as Major Somerset was absent from home, nor did I receive payment for the tow for the same reason. **a1858** J. GOLDSWAIN *Chron.* (1946) I. 66 They leaders was forst to lay hold of the toe and they drivers had to walk to keep the Oxen [from] turning round as the Storm was beating in the frunt of the Oxen. **1914** *Farmer's Annual* 43 The filthy hands of the milkers from grasping dirty sticks and span tows. **1928** N. DEVITT *Blue Lizard* 125 The latter was to throw the head riem – the touw, as transport riders call it – on to the horns of the front oxen as they entered the water. **1937** H. SAUER *Ex Afr.* 124 The *voorloper* – the native who watches the oxen while feeding and takes the 'tow' on difficult or congested portions of the road. **1938** F.C. SLATER *Trek* 43 O'er stones and scrub we'll rattle and rub – So stretch the touw, and on we'll go. **1941** A.G. BEE *Kalahari Camp Fires* (1943) 71 The youngster hung on to them and tried to drag them back when suddenly we heard him shriek as the lion snatched him away from the 'touw' (leading thong) round the oxen's horns. **1948** H. WOLHUTER *Mem. of Game Ranger* 9, I would assist him with the herding of the oxen; cook his food; take the tow (the leading 'riem' attached to the heads of the two front oxen so that the team could be led when necessary).

2. With defining word: **bush tou**, MONKEY-ROPE.

1832 *Graham's Town Jrnl* 12 Oct. 162 Prisoner had a rope made of 'bush touw,' which he put round the neck of the hottentot and strangled him.

3. *comb.* **toutrek** /'təʊtrek/ [Afk., *trek* pull], 'tug-of-war', a popular game at BOERESPORT gatherings.

1970 *Argus* 24 Dec. 21 There will be the toutrek (tug-o'-war) and kussingslaan (cushion fights on greased poles). **1990** [see VOLKSPELE].

toudang var. TOERING.

toula var. TULA.

touleier /'təʊleɪə(r)/ *n.* [Afk., *tou* rope + *leier* leader.] VOORLOPER sense 1. Also *fig.*

1933 W. MACDONALD *Romance of Golden Rand* 8 Several of the natives deserted so that Fred Struben had to take the place of the touleier and lead a team of sixteen bullocks all the way to Pretoria for over four hundred miles. **1938** *Star* 1 Dec. 15 Elderly women in voluminous skirts and poke bonnets eagerly seized the thongs to act as 'touleiers' suiting their steps to the pace of the ox. **1944** J. MOCKFORD *Here Are S. Africans* 65 A *touleier*, perhaps the driver's son, perhaps a Hottentot or Kafir piccanin, sometimes led the team by a rawhide *riempie* whose ends were fastened round the horns of the two front oxen. **1955** L.G. GREEN *Karoo* 35 By the time he was twenty-one he had a wife and three children, two coloured shepherds and a Bushman *touleier* to lead the oxen and find the way from one water-hole or vlei to the next. **1968** M. DOYLE *Impala* 6 The Shangaan had worked as a *touleier*, or leader of an ox-wagon team, at Pilgrim's Rest when the diggings still flourished. **1971** H. ZEEDERBERG *Veld Express* 173 When they reached the Poort, Washington climbed down to act as a 'touleier' through the channel. **1977** L. ABRAHAMS *Celibacy of Felix Greenspan* 18 There was a ragged little black touleier, and a dusty looking white boy up front holding a whip. **1980** A.J. BLIGNAUT *Dead End Rd* 75 Nic Keet went to the nearest huts early the next morning and hired another touleier. **1990** *Weekend Post* 5 May 10 Mr C– believed it was time the coloured people advanced beyond the *touleier* stage. A *touleier mos* just led the oxen with a rope in his hands. If the coloured people stuck with F W de Klerk and his power-sharing, they would remain *touleiers*.

touw var. TOU.

tover var. TOOR.

tow var. TOU.

towa-grass var. TOA-GRASS.

‖**towenaar** /ˈtʊəvənɑː(r)/ *n.* Also **toorvenaar**. [Afk.] A miracle-worker; a magician. See also TOOR.

1924 S.G. MILLIN *God's Step-Children* 21 When it came to the more mysterious diseases, they still had greater faith in the efficacy of their own witchcraft. The Korannas, indeed, were called the Toorvenaars, or Wizards — and, in addition, many of them had taken to wife the relicts of the Bushmen they killed whenever they had the opportunity, and these, too, had brought with them a great tradition of magic. **1959** L.G. GREEN *These Wonders* 52 Hendrik Spoorbek was the most famous miracle worker of Afrikaans folklore, a towenaar as they say in the country. **1973** J. COPE *Alley Cat* 82 He was a *towenaar*, a keeper of magic. **1984** A. DANGOR in *Staffrider* Vol.6 No.1, 16 They spoke of it as a miracle, called him a sorcerer, a *towenaar*. And regarded him with awe and fear.

township *n.* [Special senses of Brit. Eng. *township* 'each of the local divisions of, or districts comprised in, a large original parish (etc.)' (*OED*).]

1. [Prob. fr. *Austral.* and *N.Z. Eng.* 'a site laid out prospectively for a town' (from 1802) (*OED*).] A site laid out by a local authority for a new suburb; an area of land to be subdivided and sold by developers as freehold residential or industrial plots.

Quots 1929 and 1934 might belong at sense 2 a.

1929 *Workers' Herald* 7 Sept. 4 The Township of Sophiatown, one of the suburbs of the City of Johannesburg, is being severely exercised by the Proclamation issued by the Governor-General under the Natives (Urban Areas) Act, declaring the Township as one of many where Natives are not allowed to reside except those who own plots of ground. **1934** *Lovedale Sol-Fa Leaflet No.17* 4 When the Bantu Township of Nancefield or Klipspruit (eleven miles West of Johannesburg) was first settled as a Suburb of the Rand Municipality, the late Enoch Sontonga .. was a teacher in one of the Methodist Mission Schools. **1937** C.R. PRANCE *Tante Rebella's Saga* 140 The tide of progress should enable Oom Sandy to float Suikerboswoestyn as a township and health-resort, and so to get away with enough 'unearned increment' to provide for his old age. **1971** *Daily Dispatch* 4 June (Suppl.) 5 Why have the council planned a new industrial township east of the town and situated on an area some 800 ha in extent? **1971** *Grocott's Mail* 2 June 3 Four camps have been made available for grazing in the area to be developed as an industrial township. **1971** *Daily Dispatch* 22 May 13 The purchase price was to be R50 000, payable in cash enabling him to establish a township in Stafford Hills, East London. **1982** *E. Prov. Herald* 29 Dec. (Suppl.), Proclaimed township with insurance guarantee covering Tarred roads. Water. Electricity.

2.a. [fr. sense 1; see quots 1929 and 1934 above.] A suburb or city developed near a 'white' urban area for occupation by black African people only (see quot. 1980); *Bantoedorp*, see BANTOE sense 2; LOCATION sense 3 a; STAT sense 2. See also *black-belt* (BLACK *adj.* sense 1 d) **b.** Less frequently, a residential area for 'coloured' people. Also *attrib.*

1941 W.M.B. NHLAPO in *Bantu World* 1 Mar. 9 Most of the townships (except Pimville) now have some form of street lighting. **1946** P. ABRAHAMS *Mine Boy* (1954) 98 This side of the township had mostly Coloured people. The other side was where the native people were. **1951** *Drum* Nov. 10 Nearly every location and township has these [stokvel] clubs where weekend debauchery has a lot to do with the large numbers of murders and assaults. **1953** LANHAM & MOPELI-PAULUS *Blanket Boy's Moon* 33 'Is the Moruti staying in Johannesburg?' 'Yes, I stay at Orlando township — that big location we are now approaching.' **1956** T. MAKIWANE in *New Age* 30 Aug. 6 Full time entertainers .. who were built up on the rough boards in the African townships and locations before the audiences who make township jazz what it is. **1963** WILSON & MAFEJE *Langa* 1 Langa is a township on the periphery of the city, very poor by comparison with most of the suburbs, and reserved for occupation by black Africans, most of them Xhosa-speaking. **1964** *Drum* Nov. 47 From Edenvale and Kempton Park some 20,000 Africans have been resettled in Thembisa — probably the largest single township in the Republic. **1966** K.M.C. MOTSISI in *Post* 30 Jan. (Drum) 16 There are the Municipal cops who the township wits call Black Jacks, so called because of their black uniform. **1968** J. LELYVELD in Cole & Flaherty *House of Bondage* 8 For a white South African the real risk of entering a township is something more terrible .. than the remote chance that he may be assaulted … Seeing black South Africans in their sprawling encampments could, just possibly, raise one or two questions about the set of principles that decrees this lopsided form of social organization. **1971** *Sunday Times* 14 Nov. (Mag. Sect.) 5 Last year he wrote 'Qundeni' a contemporary play about township life. **1973** *Sunday Times* 18 Feb. (Mag. Sect.) 3 How many White South Africans have ever set foot inside a township, or have counted the hours workers spend going to and from work. **1976** J. BECKER *Virgins* 10 Ashley had two wives, one at home in the country and one in the township. His township wife, Matilda, came sometimes on a Sunday and sat in the kitchen talking. **1977** B.L. LESHOAI in E. Pereira *Contemp. S. Afr. Plays* 257 A single bedroom-kitchen type of township room. **1977** *E. Prov. Herald* 29 Nov. 3 There are an estimated 40 000 Africans living in Grahamstown's townships. **1980** D.B. COPLAN *Urbanization of African Performing Arts.* 348 The S.A.B.C. .. increased cultural communication among diverse groups, exposing urban Africans to traditional music and migrants to 'township jazz'. *Ibid.* 441 *Township,* The current official term for urban residential areas where Africans are authorized to rent houses built by the government, subject to the Group Areas Act of 1950. Replaces the obsolete 'location' and does not apply to freehold or slum areas. **1982** *Staffrider* Vol.5 No.1, 34 In his novel *To Every Birth its Blood* he has captured that most elusive of creatures, the urban slum neighbourhood, that unique present-day South African anomaly, the township. **1982** *Star* 11 Nov. (Tonight) 4 It is 'tsotsi taal' which is more established, that has the aura of the brimming township lifestyle. **1982** *Times* (U.K.) 1 Dec. 1 More than 2,000 blacks have been arrested over the past months in Cape Town's 'townships' for breach of the pass laws which control the movement of blacks throughout South Africa. c**1985** J. CRONIN in *Eng. Academy Rev.* 3 34 This poem closely resembles the rhythmic qualities of contemporary 'township' music in South Africa. **1985** J. THOMAS in *Fair Lady* 3 Apr. 152 The quick, high-stepping, intensely rhythmic, familiar winding-out of the township beat. **1985** *E. Prov. Herald* 30 Oct. 12 Abroad the trend towards disinvestment and punitive sanctions will accelerate — a prospect which will encourage the township radicals to believe that they are winning. **1987** *Sowetan* 5 May 2 Soul Brothers elevated the show with their township sounds. **1987** NELM *News* (Nat. Eng. Lit. Museum) May 1 Black poets sought to assert their identity by recovering a sense of cultural continuity with the heroic, pre-colonial past .. while at the same time valorising the township sub-culture of their experience. **1987** *Cosmopolitan* Aug. 192 As the song threatened to end, the audience would whirl their hand in the air — township jive for 'rewind' — and the band would begin the song again. **1987** *New Nation* 1 Oct. 11 'How would you describe the theatre you're trying to develop?' 'I've always said it's township theatre, not protest theatre.' **1988** *1820 Foundation Annual Review* 3 The language of Chaucer, Shakespeare, Milton and Keats is likely .. to take a few knocks from 'township taal' and 'metro' slang. **1989** *Weekly Mail* 20 Oct. 31 Smal Ndaba and the Sibikwa Players' *So Where To?* is an interesting example of the dominant tropes of the genre now called 'township theatre'. **1990** *Weekend Argus* 17 Feb. 14 Two dance shows opened last week … The varied programme .. is a fascinating fusion of African, township and contemporary styles. **1990** *Drum* May 28 The sight of a white living in a township still raises a few eyebrows. **1990** M. KENTRIDGE *Unofficial War* 48 Clusters of township houses, four-room cinder-block constructions with corrugated iron roofs. **1991** R. RIORDAN in *Crux* Feb. 5 Your first two plays, *No-Good Friday* and *Nongogo* .. were 'township' plays .. scripted around and for black amateur casts. **1991** *Weekly Mail* 15 Mar. 1 The White Paper .. granted freehold ownership to 1,3-million township households. **1991** D. TUTU in *Sunday Times* 26 May 2 We are losing our self-respect; demonstrated, it seems to me most graphically, by the horrible extent of dumping and littering in our townships. **1992** *Weekly Mail* 24 Apr. 32 Through his works .. he [sc. George Pemba] has become .. the 'grandfather of township art'.

c. In *pl.*: **The townships**, collectively, the urban black residential areas of South Africa; *transf.,* the people of the townships.

1973 *Argus* 1 June 8 Life of fear in the townships. **1982** D. TUTU *Voice of One* 72 The Pass Laws are designed to keep the black population 'in their place', by .. restricting them to the 'homelands' or to the Townships. **1983** *Fair Lady* 2 Nov. 137 Amampondo, the Cape-based band that has burst on to the South African music scene, rallying the townships and bringing .. audiences to their feet. **1986** N.C. CHARTON *Informant,* Grahamstown Every young black leader is in prison; in the townships anarchy reigns; to live there is pure hell. **1987** N.S. NDEBELE in *Eng. Academy Rev.* 4 Jan. 10 Relations of power within the African family, particularly in the townships, appear to have undergone a tremendous transformation. **1987** *Drum* Mar. 48 A highly successful model a graceful hostess and the toast of the townships. **1988** J. LE MAY in *Inside S. Afr.* May 14 Growing criticism of the use of the troops in the townships. **1988** *Frontline* Oct. 31 From the point of view of the black person in the townships, none of the political movements are achieving. **1989** *Weekly Mail* 3 Nov. 2 We are doing our best to restore peace and calm to the townships. **1990** *Sash* Vol.33 No.1, 24 The idea of whites marching into the townships to show their rejection of apartheid, and their desire to work with those on the receiving end of it … , came originally from University of Port Elizabeth academics. **1991** *Economist* (U.K.) 18 May 13 South Africa's black politics is dominated by the people of the townships, the hideous dormitory suburbs into which millions of people migrated in the apartheid years. **1993** *Cape Times* 10 Aug. 6 We wept for *all* the violence in the land — almost all of which has been much closer to her than it has to me. That is, *in the townships.*

toyi-toyi /ˈtɔɪtɔɪ/ *n.* Also **toi-toi**, ‖**itoyi-toyi**. [Etym. obscure: prob. introduced into S. Afr. by ANC exiles returning from military training in Zimbabwe, where it is found in both Ndebele (see last quot. 1993) and Shona. The original source language is unknown.

A similar-sounding invocation, *Tayi* (one of the traditional titles accorded to the supreme being) was used by the Xhosa during the 19th century: 'They [sc. the Xhosa] advanced almost to the muzzles of the British guns … Some of them, shouting "Tayi! Tayi!" as they ran — the word they had been taught by Nxele to use as a charm against all manner of evil — actually reached the cannon.' (B. Maclennan, *A Proper Degree of Terror,* 1986, p.193, writing of the frontier war of 1818–19).

The etymology suggested in quot. 1988 is unsubstantiated, although many ANC cadres underwent military training in eastern European countries. See also quot. 1990 (*Sunday Times*), which is prob. an example of folk etymology.]

1. A quasi-military dance-step characterized by high-stepping movements, performed either on the spot or while moving slowly forwards, usu. by participants in (predominantly black) protest gatherings or marches, and accompanied by chanting, singing, and the shouting of slogans. Also *attrib.,* and occas. shortened form **toyi**.

Adapted from a training exercise performed in military camps by ANC guerillas.

1985 *Probe* Oct. 20 The crowd changed tune from the freedom songs and the 'toyitoyi' war cries to 'mayitshe' (let it burn) ushering in a new element. *Ibid.* Nov. 24 This was some kind of new revelation .. for whites — more especially the performance of the war-cry or emotive dance, 'itoyi-toyi' by the youths. **1986** *Evening Post* 21 Mar. 3 People sang freedom songs honouring Nelson Mandela and Oliver Tambo, and danced the 'toyi-toyi'. **1986** *E. Prov. Herald* 12 May 1 Brig. Schnetler's conditions included that toyi-toyi dancing not be allowed ... He explained that toyi-toyi dancing was a war dance which was used in the townships to incite crowds. **1988** P. BANESHIK in *Sunday Star* 7 Aug., The words [toi-toi] were a simple verbalisation of the sound made by people of Eastern European cultures when spitting ('Ptui-ptui!') to ward off the 'evil eye'. Since many ballet dancers and ballet conventions stem from those climes, the expression became common among dancers when wishing fellows good luck. (Similar to the other theatrical 'good luck' wish: 'Break a leg!') ... 'Toyi toyi' is the name of a form of black protest dance, in which phalanxes of protesters chant while prancing forward and punching the air with the right fist in rhythm with the chant. **1990** *Weekly Mail* 11 May 13 The PAC has produced few substitutes to the songs, *toyi-toyis* and other symbols of the ANC. **1990** R. MALAN *My Traitor's Heart* 141 They were dancing the toi, the township war dance, running on the spot, their feet thundering in unison. **1990** *Sunday Times* 18 Feb. 21 My UDF source said: 'The toyi-toyi was introduced to townships .. by trained ANC infiltrators from up north. It simply means toying — or practising — the military drill. In the guerilla training camps it is performed with military precision and discipline, but locally it has evolved as a dance aimed at pepping up the mood of militant youths.' **1990** M. KENTRIDGE *Unofficial War* 24 The toyi-toyi is particularly associated with the *amaqabane*, but Inkatha members use it as well, the two forms being distinguished by the slogans shouted. **1991** A. KLAASTE in *Race Rel. News* (S.A.I.R.R.) Apr. 13 The toyi-toyi .. this trance-like, almost zombie-like chant and shuffle. **1991** P. STOREY in *Star* 1 Nov. 13 The toyi-toyi, and the often insulting songs which go with it, is an invitation to mob hysteria. Its association with some of the worst political violence in the past makes it a liability. **1993** J. MALULEKE in *Drum* Aug. 32 The toyi-toyi was first performed inside South Africa in a rudimentary fashion in 1979 during the launch of Cosas. *Ibid.* 33 The toyi-toyi has moved from its purpose as a physical training exercise in the emaGojini [mountains] to the dynamic freedom dance of the 90s ... The toyi-toyi, according to [Mkhululi] Dliwayo, means in Ndebele 'moving forward while remaining in one place'.

2. *Transf.* and *fig.*

1987 M.G. WHISSON in *RUSA Reporter* (Rhodes Univ.) June 10 I must confess that the thought of seeing G— .. performing a Tyrolean toyi toyi .. is appealing. **1989** *Sunday Times* 13 Aug. 16 Perhaps the [reform] situation is best described as a boere toyi-toyi — one can see there is movement, but it is difficult to make out where it is all going.

toyi-toyi /ˈtɔɪtɔɪ/ *v. intrans.* Also **toi-toi**. [fr. prec.]
1. To perform the toyi-toyi. Occas. *trans.* (see McGibbon quot., 1988).

1987 *New Nation* 6 Aug. 19 As soon as the Buffels were out of sight, small crowds of youths started to toi-toi down the street singing: 'I am a guerilla.' **1988** *Weekly Mail* 29 Apr. 1 When the accused were brought back to court yesterday they were singing and *toyi-toyi-ing*. **1988** C. MCGIBBON in *Sunday Star* 22 May 2 As news of his death became known residents toi-toied their jubilation in the shanty streets. **1990** *Weekly Mail* 2 Mar. 22 What .. was the scene like at the Market Theatre tonight? Was it business as usual there too, or were they *toyi-toying* in the aisles? **1990** *Weekend Mail* 13 July 11 Richard Cock, conductor of the SABC choirs, was last week seen *toyi-toying* up and down the stage of the Pretoria State Theatre .. in an uncontrollable spirit of unison with the music. **1990** M. KENTRIDGE *Unofficial War* 116 The coffin is shouldered and carried out of the church. The guard of honour runs before it toyi-toying. **1993** H. GWALA in *Natal Witness* 13 Apr. 1 There are many blacks who are pro-apartheid, like Inkatha supporters who toyi-toyied in Imbali hostel chanting 'where is Chris Hani, he is in the mortuary'. **1993** J. MALULEKE in *Drum* Aug. 33 Just to hear 30,000 guerillas toyi-toying in the heat of the emaGojini, knees beating their chests, arms high-up in the air holding AK-47's, .. was a moving experience. **1993** W. HARTLEY in *Weekend Post* 13 Nov. 6 The image of Afrikaner Weerstandbeweging 'heavies' toyi-toyiing in the aisles to break up an African National Congress meeting .. has had me chortling all week.

2. *fig.* and punning.

1990 *Natal Mercury* 31 July 1 I'm glad both parties are still ready to negotiate. After all, it takes two to toyi-toyi. **1990** *Weekend Mail* 5 Oct. 14 Clever wordplay, leaving audiences in tears of laughter, is one of Mutloatse's strongest points — 'I've been toyi-toying with the idea.' **1993** J. HOBBS in *Sunday Times* 7 Nov. 15, I am hopeful that these good omens are the first stirrings of a future where Africa will toyi-toyi on to the world stage singing, 'You thought we were finished? Suka!'

Hence **toyi-toying** *vbl n.*, also **toyi-toyiing**, performance of the toyi-toyi; also as *attrib.*, performing the toyi-toyi.

1989 *Weekly Mail* 13 Oct. 4 *Toyi-toyi-ing* youths at a snap rally called by the Mass Democratic Movement in Athlone were repeatedly dispersed by police. **1990** *Personality* 4 June 27 Were police acting legitimately to save lives and property, or did they mistake toyi-toying for a threatening mob and spark the violence they were meant to prevent? **1990** *Style* Nov. 61 We're seeing choreography that includes anything from gumboot dancing to toyi-toying. **1993** *Weekly Mail & Guardian* 13 Aug. 35 The toyi-toyiing youths entered the stadium at a trot, chanting first 'One settler, one bullet,' followed by a rumbling 'We can run and shoot at the same time'.

track *n.*, **trac(k)** *v.* varr. TREK *n.*, TREK *v.*

tracktoe, trac(k)tow, tracto(e) varr. TREKTOU.

trak, traktow varr. TREK *v.*, TREKTOU.

tramp *v. trans.* [General Eng. *tramp*, influenced by Du. *trappen* to tread, to thresh (grain), or *trappelen* to trample, or *uittrappen* to crush underfoot.]
1. Often in the phr. ***to tramp out***.
a. *Obs.* exc. *hist.*
i. To thresh (grain), using horses or, occas., oxen; TRAP. Hence **tramping** *vbl n.*, threshing.

1851 T. SHONE Diary. 4 Mar., Henry and Jack and Billy on the farm with some horses tramping out oats for seed. **1851** H. JAMES in F.C. Metrowich *Valiant but Once* (1956) 215 Twenty-two of the horses had been kept here in the hopes of being able to tramp out the corn which was lying on the field — but the whole were carried off by the enemy the day after we 'trekked' to Post Retief. **1857** P.B. BORCHERDS in *Cape Monthly Mag.* I. May 323 By the colonial system of tramping out the corn with horses, and depending on the wind for cleaning it, fifty muids of wheat will require, on the average, six days. **1864** T. SHONE Diary. 7 Jan., This day was fine. Tramping Out oats with the horses. *Ibid.* 29 June, G. Shone tramping of oats. **1865** *Ibid.* 22 Nov., This day was fine, Henry was Tramping out Barley with the Oxen. **1867** *Blue Bk for Col.* 1866 JJ4, The wheat has not yet been tramped out. *Ibid.* JJ20, Owing to the rust having appeared both in the wheat and oats, and to some of the farmers having already tramped their wheat; it is feared that the latter will rise again to a high price. *Ibid.* JJ41, Two or three thrashing-machines are in use in the division, but the old system of tramping seems to find the greatest favour among the farmer. **1882** S. HECKFORD *Lady Trader in Tvl* 347, I do not think that this Boer would have hired me his oxen had it not been for the persuasions of his goodnatured wife .. for they, and all the young cattle, were being used for tramping out the corn.

ii. Special collocation. **tramp floor** [tr. S. Afr. Du. *trapvloer*], threshing floor.

1832 *Graham's Town Jrnl* 18 Oct. 168 Prisoner found the stick a little way from the further end of the house between the tramp floor; .. it was a forked stick, with which corn is tossed up in the tramp floor. [**1842** J. COLLETT Diary. II. 26 Nov., Brot our two first Loads of Corn to the trap floor to day.] **1862** T. SHONE Diary. 24 Mar., Henry brought a load of wheat to the tramp floar. **1896** R. WALLACE *Farming Indust. of Cape Col.* 472 The earlier custom still in use in most districts is the treading out of grain on the tramp floor or threshing floor, the work being done, not by cattle as in India, but by horses trotting round at a good pace. **1934** C.P. SWART Supplement to Pettman. 178 *Tramp Floor,* The Anglicised form of the Afr. 'trapvloer', a threshing floor. Before the advent of the threshing machine, horses or oxen were employed to tread out the grain on ground floors, specially prepared for this purpose. **1969** D. CHILD *Yesterday's Children* 38 On the wheat farms the children loved to watch the threshing, when the harvested grain was trodden by horses' hooves on a circular 'tramp-floor' hardened with a mixture of cow-dung and powdered antheap and surrounded by a low wall.

b. To overgraze (pasture or veld).

1916 L.D. FLEMMING *Fool on Veld* (1933) 61 A bee more or less does not matter; they do not tramp out your veld. **1937** *Handbk for Farmers* (Dept of Agric. & Forestry), Another result of the old system of farming was overstocking and tramping out the veld, erosion of the soil and a general tendency towards degeneration of the most valuable species of karoo bush, while 'opslag' vegetation increased. **1971** *Grocott's Mail* 27 July 3 The ground is valuable if it is properly run, but now it just gets tramped out. Outspans are really out-of-date.

2. Esp. in the Eastern Cape: to run (someone or something) over with a vehicle; often *passive*.

1913 C. PETTMAN *Africanderisms* 508 *Tramp*, .. A curious use of this word prevails in many parts of South Africa, which appears to be due to the influence of the Cape Dutch word *trap*, to ride or drive over; e.g. an ox that has been run over by a railway train is said to have been 'tramped' by the train; a gate that has been smashed by a passing wagon is said to have been 'tramped' by the wagon. **1969** *Informant, Grahamstown* I've shut the cat in the girls' bedroom because I don't want him to get tramped by the cars. **1970** D.M. MCMASTER *Informant, Cathcart (E. Cape)* The sheep was tramped by a car and is dead. This word used meaning 'to run over' is anathema to purists, but is is certainly in common use and very expressive. **1971** *Informant, Grahamstown* 'That pup is always running around.' 'Yes, I'm afraid of the traffic.' 'Yes, he'll get tramped.' **1975** *Darling* 3 Sept. 103 Pa's never been the same since .. Uncle Max gets tramped by that car outside Carsten's place. **1977** on Radio South Africa 24 Jan., The person who tramped [the cat] didn't even have the decency to stop. **1986** A. JACOT-GUILLARMOD *Informant, Grahamstown* Not seen in print but often heard in Eastern Cape: He was tramped by a car (from Afrikaans). **1989** *Informant, Grahamstown* There were no cars there, so she wouldn't get tramped. **1992** D. LANDMAN *Informant, Grahamstown* He tramped the guy who was holding on to the passenger side window.

Hence (sense 1 b) **tramped** *ppl adj.*, overgrazed.

1974 *E. Prov. Herald* 2 Dec. 4 Tramped hard soil prevented growth and litter accumulation must be built up so that rainfall will infiltrate into the ground.

transitional Tulbagh chair see TULBAGH.

Trans-Karoo /ˌtrɑːnskəˈruː/ *n.* [Eng. prefix *trans-* across + KAROO sense 1 a.] In full ***Trans-Karoo Express***: an express train which runs between Cape Town and Johannesburg five times a week. Also *attrib.*

1970 B. ZURNAMER *Locomotives of S. Afr. Railways* 80 Such famous trains as the Union Express, the Union Limited and the forerunner to the Trans-Karoo, the Cape-Johannesburg Express. **1979** *S. Afr. Railways & Harbours Handbk* 95 The Trans-Karoo Express operates daily, except Mondays and Wednesdays, in both directions between Cape Town, Johannesburg and Pretoria. It covers a distance of 1 608 km in a total journey of 29½ hours (27½ to Johannesburg). **1987** *E. Prov. Herald* 13 Feb. 1 A long story about the ballet teacher with 24 pieces of luggage who unexpectedly joined him and wife in their compartment in the TransKaroo as the train was about to pull out of Johannesburg. **1988** N. PATTERSON in *Cape Times* 11 Jan. 7 A Trans-Karoo train ticket, one way is also R230 (first class) or R163 (second class) ... When I travelled on the Trans-Karoo this month, there were many third-class carriages, packed with black people. **1990** *Frontline* Mar. 10 When the Trans-Karoo trundles in at 9.20, the station is packed. *Ibid.* 12 I'm sharing a Trans-Karoo compartment with a prison warder, a soldier, a German tourist and a matric boy from De Aar. **1991** *Best of S. Afr. Short Stories* (Reader's Digest Assoc.) 221 Running on days when the Blue Train is not scheduled, the Trans Karoo Express follows the same route ... It provides a comfortable and fairly fast link between Johannedburg and Cape Town.

Transkei /ˈtrɑːnskaɪ, trɑːnsˈkaɪ/ *adj.* [fr. the n. *Transkei*, Eng. prefix *trans-* over, across + *Kei* the name of a river (ad. of the Khoikhoi name, a word meaning 'sand').] TRANSKEIAN *adj.*

The name 'Transkei' is used of an area along the eastern seaboard of South Africa, situated between the Kei river and the province of KwaZulu-Natal, and has represented, at different times: (a) the territory beyond the eastern boundary of the Cape Colony (the Kei river forming the boundary between the Colony and this area from 1847 to 1877), also known as 'Kaffraria' (see KAFFRARIAN) or *Kaffirland* (see KAFFIR *n.* sense 1 d); (b) by 1885: a region of the Cape Colony (subsequently the Cape Province); (c) from 1976–1994: the Republic of Transkei, a Xhosa 'homeland'; (d) from 1994: a region of the province of the Eastern Cape.

Some of the uses below might more properly be considered instances of the noun used attributively.

1899 *Daily News* 10 Oct. 7 The Pondos and the other Transkei tribes are not absolutely to be relied on. *c***1929** L.P. BOWLER *Afr. Nights* 39 Makanna or Lynx, a Transkei chief. **1962** L. GANDAR in J. Crwys-Williams *S. Afr. Despatches* (1989) 340 If I were asked to state at what point I believed the forward approaches of disaster came into view, I would say it was the Government's announcement of its Transkei independence plan. **1971** *Rand Daily Mail* 31 May 6 The Transkei Bill was enacted and a fully-fledged Bantustan was born. **1977** [see TRANSKEIAN *n.*]. **1980** E. JOUBERT *Poppie Nongena* 299 They always hammer this homeland story: And if you're not Transkei, you're Ciskei by force. Even we who are city-born. **1990** G. ALLEN in *E. Prov. Herald* 19 Jan. 3 The Transkei military leader, Major-General Bantu Holomisa, .. said Transkei relations with South Africa were cordial.

Transkeian /trɑːnsˈkaɪən, træns-/ *n.* and *adj.* [TRANSKEI + Eng. adj.- and n.-forming suffix *-an*.]

See note at TRANSKEI.

A. *n.* An inhabitant or citizen of the Transkei.

1847 H.G. SMITH in *Imp. Blue Bks* Command Paper 969–1848, 25 I have made no mention of the Trans-Keians, 'Kreili' and 'Bokoo,' with them I have yet to deal. **1968** *Post* 7 Apr. 7 Why can't the rich Transkeians help them instead of showing off with their money by buying up land? **1976** *Weekend Argus* 9 Oct. 13 Many Transkeians feel they have not been sufficiently consulted or involved in the planning and preparations for independence. **1977** *Daily Dispatch* 14 Feb. 1 Transkei's Coloured community have pledged their loyalty to the Transkei Government and asked that they be regarded as Transkeians – not as Coloureds. **1988** *South* 21 July 3 Workers are being subjected to massive delays as Ciskei roadblocks continue to stop all traffic entering Mdantsane to search for Transkeians. **1990** D. JONES in *Sunday Times* 18 Nov. 7 Young Transkeians were ferrying crayfish to Mr F—'s factory – even though the crayfish season is officially closed.

B. *adj.* Of or pertaining to the Transkei; TRANSKEI.

1848 H.G. SMITH in *Imp. Blue Bks* Command Paper 1056–1849, 14 The friendly feeling of the distant trans-Keian chief Faku, is sufficiently shown. **1879** *Whitaker's Almanack* 259 The Transkeian territories stretch from the Kei to Natal. **1891** T.R. BEATTIE *Ride through Transkei* 51 The Statistical Register is an excellent authority to refer to. It will show some startling facts in regard to the progress and capabilities of the Transkeian territories. **1898** *Whitaker's Almanack* 515 (Principal events) Incorporation of all the Transkeian territories, except part of Pondoland, with the Colony, completed 1885; annexation of Pondoland 1894. **1962** [see GREAT]. **1970** *Daily Dispatch* 19 Aug. (Suppl.), The factory has .. a Transkeian accountant who is an articled clerk and studying for his certificate of theory. **1976** *Weekend Argus* 9 Oct. 13 Those Africans who do not want Transkeian citizenship and refuse or neglect to take it out will be unable to obtain passports to travel. **1976** *Financial Mail* 22 Oct. 1 On Tuesday .. the first Homeland, Transkei (it dropped the definite article some months ago), gets its independence. While Umtata, its capital, celebrates noisily, other countries will be looking on from a disapproving distance. Transkeian independence is seen by them as the offspring of apartheid and a mere ruse to side-step the problem of political rights for SA's urban Blacks. **1986** P. MAYLAM *Hist. of Afr. People* 137 African recruits, mainly Mfengu and Thembu, were called up to protect the Transkeian frontier against Boer invasion. **1990** D. JONES in *Sunday Times* 18 Nov. 7 An out-dated Transkeian law has left local nature conservation officials powerless.

Trans-Oranje Express see ORANGE EXPRESS.

transport driver *n. phr. Hist.* [Prob. an interpretation of Afk. *transportryer*, see TRANSPORT-RIDER.] TRANSPORT-RIDER.

1881 E.E. FREWER tr. *E. Holub's Seven Yrs in S. Afr.* I. 186 Close beside us were two other waggons belonging to a Transvaal 'transport-driver,' who came to have a talk with us. **1886** G.A. FARINI *Through Kalahari Desert* 4 Huge heavy-winged *aasvogels*, or vultures, making riot among the carcases of the horses and oxen that fairly strew the tracks used by the transport-drivers. **1926** P. SMITH *Beadle* (1929) 280 The old transport-driver drew her hand into his and looked down upon her with that tender and compassionate smile. *a***1951** H.C. BOSMAN in L. Abrahams *Unto Dust* (1963) 117 They knew that a young and attractive girl like Johanna Greyling would not have to wear out much shoe-leather in getting to Kimberley, transport-drivers being what they were. **1961** L.E. VAN ONSELEN *Trekboer* 20 In the days of the waggon teams rolling across the veld, the transport driver covered about 20 miles between sunrise and sunset. **1971** H. ZEEDERBERG *Veld Express* 100 The party left for Eytings early the following morning. This was a wayside halt for transport drivers, and named after the owner of the hotel-cum-store.

transport-rider *n. hist.* [Prob. tr. Afk. *transportryer*, *transport* transport, carriage, conveyance + *ryer* rider, driver.] A carrier of goods by wagon; KARWEIER; KURVEYOR; TRANSPORT DRIVER. See also *to ride transport* (RIDE sense 1 b).

1850 R.G.G. CUMMING *Hunter's Life* (1902) 10 The Dutchmen along their road being very unfriendly and inhospitable to the English transport-riders. **1871** 'R.M.R.' in *Cape Monthly Mag.* III. Dec. 373 The Company .. created a class of transport-riders, and made it worth their while to engage in the transport of copper ore from the mines to the sea-port. **1873** F. BOYLE *To Cape for Diamonds* 248 A black transport rider, going homeward with his team, came in at ten o'clock the other night, drenched to the skin. **1882** J. NIXON *Among Boers*, The transport rider learns which are the best grasses, how to distinguish signs of water, what soil suits cattle and what sheep or ostriches. **1896** R. WALLACE *Farming Indust. of Cape Col.* 247 The tsetse fly .. is the fatal pest which destroys the horses of big-game hunters, and the oxen of up-country transport riders. **1912** W. WESTRUP *Land of To-Morrow* 347 You may have heard that my second wife .. has eloped with a Dutch transport rider? **1924** E.T. JOLLIE *Real Rhodesia* (1971) 131 The transport rider is essentially a South African type, for no other country has either the special conditions which called him into being or the particular breed of man who could endure the life. **1937** C. BIRKBY *Zulu Journey* 190 He became a transport-rider working between Natal and the diamond fields of Kimberley. **1940** F.B. YOUNG *City of Gold* 45 The destruction of bullocks by the disease had pushed up transport rates, so that a single journey of five hundred miles from the coast to Kimberley brought more than a hundred pounds to the transport rider's pocket. **1958** A. JACKSON *Trader on Veld* 37 Whether with donkeys or with oxen, one class of the community usually did fairly well, and that was the transport rider, whose grandsons and great-grandsons are today doing a very similar, though easier and faster job with motor-trucks and lorries. **1968** K. MCMAGH *Dinner of Herbs* 27 All roads led to Kimberley in the early eighteen-seventies, when transport riders made good money transporting machinery and other goods to the bustling diamond town before the coming of the railway. **1977** F.G. BUTLER *Karoo Morning* 200 Father sought out Mr Gunning, one of the last transport riders, whose three ancient wagons rested among the pepper trees on the river bank, and whose thirty-six donkeys grazed on the commonage. **1980** *S. Afr. Panorama* Dec. 44 Lonely mounds marked the end of the road for the luckless hunters or transport riders who had succumbed to malaria. **1983** *Ibid.* Apr. 18 Transport riders plying their trade between Durban and Johannesburg took tree seed with them to plant in spots where they outspanned for the night. **1991** *Style* Nov. 67 His father – alternately a teacher, transport rider and miner.

transport-riding *vbl n. Hist.* [Prob. tr. Afk. *transport ry* the carrying or conveyance of goods.] The conveyance of goods by wagon; KURVEYING. Also *attrib.* See also *to ride transport* (RIDE sense 1 b).

1871 'R.M.R.' in *Cape Monthly Mag.* III. Dec. 372 In the Western districts, transport-riding has been followed generally by a poor class of men. **1878** A. AYLWARD *Tvl of Today* 35 The Englishman swaps (chops) and exchanges, engages in transport-riding, obtains cattle he cares little how or where, and may at any moment be the cause of great loss to his neighbours by contaminating their herds with lung sickness and worse diseases. **1882** J. NIXON *Among Boers* 308 The best pursuit for a young would-be farmer to take on reaching the country is 'transport riding', or carrying goods. A little capital is required for the purchase of the necessary spans of oxen and waggons, but it pays very good interest on the outlay. **1896** R. WALLACE *Farming Indust. of Cape Col.* 32 Of the *farmers* .. the most successful are those who stuck to farming, and did not divide their attention by going in for 'transport-riding.' **1900** H. RIDER HAGGARD *Black Heart* p.i, Transport-riding – that is, in carrying goods on ox-waggons from Durban or Maritzburg to various points in the interior. **1910** A.B. LAMONT *Rural Reader* 92 Transport riding .. is a cheap and suitable method of sending goods to places that are at some distance from the railway. **1940** F.B. YOUNG *City of Gold* 9 Money could be had for the asking by any man who possessed a bullock-wagon and cared to go transport-riding, dragging fuel and farm-produce and goods through the sand-belt to Kimberley. **1946** E. ROSENTHAL *General De Wet* 16 A large percentage of the Orange Free Staters were soon occupied in the most characteristic of old South African industries, known as 'transport riding'. **1980** *S. Afr. Panorama* Dec. 44 Their other neighbour was Mr Hall's old transport-riding friend, Sir Percy Fitzpatrick of *Jock of the Bushveld* fame. **1986** KALLAWAY & PEARSON *Johannesburg* 4 Transport riding continued until railways to all the ports of the Cape, Delagoa Bay, and Durban had been completed. **1988** *E. Prov. Herald* 27 Feb. 7 The Malayan kris (dagger) with which, while transport riding and hunting in the 1830s, he fought off a lion.

transport wagon *n. phr. Hist.* [Prob. tr. Afk. *transportwa*.] A large, heavy vehicle with low sides, used for the conveyance of goods and drawn usu. by a team of between fourteen and eighteen oxen.

1866 J. LEYLAND *Adventures* II., I travelled by a Dutch transport waggon. **1873** F. BOYLE *To Cape for Diamonds* 55 The tranport waggon is a gigantic van, with low wooden sides and a flat roof of canvas supported on iron stanchions. **1912** AYLIFF & WHITESIDE *Hist. of Abambo* 33 At daylight, the crossing of the river commenced. First, came a long line of transport wagons. **1926** P. SMITH *Beadle* (1929) 267 Made his living by driving a wool-and-transport wagon between the townships of Cortes. **1936** in N. Rouillard *Matabele Thompson* 46, I found myself at no great distance from a transport waggon, laden with goods intended for a trader in the north. **1958** A. JACKSON *Trader on Veld* 25 Draghoender was on the main road to Kenhardt, Upington and the whole hinterland, so that traffic by transport wagons both ways was quite brisk. **1974** A.A. TELFORD in *Std Encycl. of Sn Afr.* X. 569 *Buck- and transport-wagon.* Larger wagons were built after the Great Trek to explore the interior. They were constructed on traditional lines but were more lavishly fitted out, sometimes partitioned into two compartments, and equipped with side-boxes, gun-racks, folding stools and chairs, water and meat barrels, windows, curtains and lamps ... A large buck- or transport-wagon was usually from 5,5 to 6,7 metres long, and 1,5 to 2 metres wide, with either a half-tent covering the rearmost third of its length, or no tent at all, and it could carry between 2300 and 3200 kg.

Transvaal /ˌtrɑnsˈvɑːl, -ˈfɑːl/ *n.* [Eng. prefix *trans-* across + *Vaal*, the name of the river forming part of the area's southern border (Afk. *vaal* grey).] The former name of an area north of the Vaal River, used *attrib.* or *comb.* to designate anyone or anything from this area; found particularly in plant names, as **Transvaal bottle-brush**, see BOTTLEBRUSH; **Transvaal daisy**, *Barberton daisy* (see BARBERTON sense 1 a); **Transvaal ebony**, JAKKALSBESSIE sense a; **Transvaal kweek(gras)** [see KWEEK], or **Transvaal quick** [see QUICK], the grass *Cynodon hirsutus; red quick*, see QUICK sense 2; **Transvaal teak**, KIAAT; **Transvaal tobacco**, **Transvaal tulp**, etc. Also abbrev. form **Tvl**.

The Transvaal was formerly an independent republic (known as the *Transvaal Republic* or *South African Republic*), and subsequently the northernmost province of South Africa, before being divided in 1994 into the provinces of the Northern Transvaal, Eastern Transvaal, PWV (subsequently renamed Gauteng), and part of the North West Province.

1852 J.F. CHURCHILL Diary. (Killie Campbell Africana Library MS37) May, One of the Leaders of the Transvaal Dutch comes down to regain his farms. **1857** D. LIVINGSTONE *Missionary Trav.* 106 Sir George Cathcart .. entered into a treaty with the Transvaal Boers. **1882** S. HECKFORD *Lady Trader in Tvl* 235 Mr Felman was a Boer from the old colony, his wife a Transvaal Boer. **1892** J.E. RITCHIE *Brighter S. Afr.* 50 In Adderly Street I saw some Transvaal tobacco in a window. **1900** B. MITFORD *Aletta* 34 You smoke Transvaal tobacco then? **1901** *Gardener* 12 Jan. 1049 The Transvaal Daisy .. has been a bright patch for a long time ... The large flame-coloured flowers .. are a particularly fine sight. **1904** *Tvl Agric. Jrnl* Oct. 185 The Transvaal kweekgras is shorter and more of a surface grass than the Bermuda grass. **1913** M.M. CLEAVER *Young S. Afr.* 2, I disliked .. the acceptance of the Transvaal Burgher Right. **1913** C. PETTMAN *Africanderisms* 510 *Transvaal tobacco*, Tobacco grown in the Transvaal is very mild, and .. is generally preferred to any other. **1917** R. MARLOTH *Common Names* 83 *Tulp* (tulip). Several poisonous Irids: *Homeria collina*, the Geel (yellow) - ; .. *H. pallida*, the *Transvaal* -. *Moraea polystachya*, the Blauw - of the Karoo, etc. **1919** *Dunell, Ebden & Co.'s Price List* Aug. 32 *Tobacco*, Transvaal ... Guaranteed best Magaliesberg. **1921** W.C. SCULLY *Harrow* 7 The artful suggestio falsi .. that the Transvaal Boer .. had .. developed into a brutal robber. **1929** *Handbk for Farmers* (Dept of Agric.) 199 (*captions*), Cape Blue Tulp. Transvaal Yellow Tulp. **1935** J.W. MATHEWS in *Jrnl of Botanical Soc.* XXI. 13 In a publication on Lawns and Lawnmaking, by the Division of Botany, it says of the Regte Kweek (Cape Province) *Cynodon incompletus*: 'A surface creeping grass of the coastal districts of the Cape that resembles very much the Transvaal Kweek (*Cynodon hirsutus*), but is less hairy and a deeper green in colour'. **1949** [see JAKKALSBESSIE]. **1961** PALMER & PITMAN *Trees of S. Afr.* 311 *Gardenia spatulifolia*, often known as the Transvaal gardenia, is a small tree up to about 15 feet. **1969** N. LECK in J. Crwys-Williams *S. Afr. Despatches* (1989) 383 Cock-a-hoop Transvaal supporters gave them no chance of victory. **1968** [see PRUIMPIE]. **1969** T.H. EVERETT *Living Trees of World* 285 A fine African member of the genus [*Diospyros*] is the jakkalsbessie, West African ebony or Transvaal ebony (*D. mespiliformis*), which becomes 70 feet tall with a trunk diameter of 3 feet. **1971** J.A. BROWN *Return* 42 Cameron had .. coarse, dry Transvaal tobacco that crackled in the bowl. **1971** BARAITSER & OBHOLZER *Cape Country Furn.* 279 Kiaat is also known as blood wood, Transvaal teak and Kehatenhout. **1991** G.E. GIBBS RUSSELL et al. *Grasses of Sn Afr.* 97 *Cynodon transvaalensis* Transvaal quick grass. **1993** *Grocott's Mail* 6 Aug. 9 Greyia Radlkoferi, Tvl Bottlebrush.

Hence **Transvaalian** /ˌtrɑnsˈvɑːlɪən/ *adj. obs.*, of or pertaining to the Transvaal; **Transvaalite** *n.*, *Geology*, a mineral consisting mainly of black oxide of cobalt, resulting from the alteration of cobalt arsenide, found near Middelburg (Eastern Transvaal); and as *adj.*, of the Transvaal (however, quot. 1873 could reflect a noun usage); **Transvaler** *n.*, also **Transvaaler** /ˌtrɑnsˈvɑːlə/, one born or resident in the Transvaal; see also the often derogatory terms VAALIE, VAALPENS (sense 2 b).

1873 F. BOYLE *To Cape for Diamonds* 77 He complains bitterly of the meddlesome and greedy nation of the Free State against its neighbours, Kaffir and Transvaalite. **1880** *Grocott's Penny Mail* 28 Dec. 3 We sympathize with the Dutch .. in the distress into which they are plunged by the madness of their Transvaalian countrymen. **1887** H. RIDER HAGGARD *Jess* p.x, You going to show us Transvaalers how to do it, eh? **1890** MACGHIE & CLARK in *Engin. & Min. Jrnl.* (N.Y.) L. 96 Transvaalite. **1899** *Daily News* 19 Dec. 3 The position of Britishers under the Transvaalian oligarchy would .. become absolutely unbearable. **1903** E.F. KNIGHT *S. Afr. after War* 60, I told them that .. we Transvaalers for our part had had our bellyful of war and wanted no more of it. **1950** H.C. BOSMAN in S. Gray *Makapan's Caves* (1987) 139, I am, after all, a Transvaler. **1987** *Informant, George* Please drive carefully — especially you Transvalers.

trap /trap/ *v. trans. Obs.* [Du. *trappen*, see TRAMP.] TRAMP sense 1 a i; also in the phr. ***to trap out*** (grain).

1842 J. COLLETT Diary. II. 5 Dec., Again Trapped out another floor of Barley. **1845** *Ibid.* 14 Nov., Commenced Trapping at Waterkloof our last stack of Corn.

trapbalie see BALIE sense b.

Treason Trial *n. phr. Hist.* Also with small initials. A series of judicial hearings which took place from December 1956 to March 1961, after a charge of high treason had been brought against a number of left-wing political figures accused of committing or promoting politically-motivated sabotage; any one of these hearings, esp. the final trial of the thirty accused.

Of 156 people arrested in this connection during December 1956, 91 were charged, but only 30 were tried. During the trial, one of the accused died and one fled the country; the others were acquitted, and charges against the remaining 61 were dropped.

1956 *Rand Daily Mail* 20 Dec. 1 (*caption*) An African musician and leader conducts his waiting people in songs, hymns and anthems as they demonstrate outside the Drill Hall during yesterday's treason trials. **1957** E.S. SACHS in Forman & Sachs *S. Afr. Treason Trial* 215 This book has been written jointly by Lionel Forman, accused no. 83 in the mass Treason Trial now proceeding in Johannesburg, and myself. **1957** *Secretarial Report* (A.N.C. Youth League, Transvaal) in Karis & Carter *From Protest to Challenge* (1977) III. 407 We earnestly appeal to the Youth that wherever they are, they must of necessity focus the attention of the people on the Treason Trials. **1961** *Rand Daily Mail* 30 Mar. 1 The 28 accused in the treason trial were all acquitted at Pretoria yesterday by Mr. Justice Rumpff. *Ibid.* 27 July 8 With the decision of the Acting Attorney-General of the Transvaal to take no further action against the persons accused in the treason case, one of the most unfortunate episodes ever in South Africa has come to an end. The Treason Trial, 1956–1961, has been a sorry affair right from the start. **1963** M. BENSON *Afr. Patriots* 237 In mid-1957 .. Lutuli and the A.N.C. called for a stay-at-home ... It was a daring act when they were tied up in the Treason Trial and unable to take any direct part in the organizing. **1977** J. SIKAKANE *Window on Soweto* 41 One event .. always in my mind is the day in 1958 which I helped my grandfather prepare a dinner for the Natal ANC members who were in the Treason Trial. **1990** R. STENGEL *January Sun* 45 My schooldays were in the aftermath of the treason trial. There was a great amount of fear.

treck *n.* var. TREK *n.*

treck *v.* var. TREK *v.*

trecker var. TREKKER.

trecktouw, treck-tow varr. TREKTOU.

tree /ˈtrɪə/ *v.* In the phr. ***to tree aan*** /- ɑːn/ [Afk. *tree aan*, *tree* pace, step, stride + *aan* in, on], used mainly in army parlance:

a. *intrans.* To fall in, form up into line; to report for duty.

1981 *Fair Lady* 29 July 125 The only time you are ever able to relax and not worry about being screamed at by a corporal, or about whistles blowing and having to *tree aan* in two minutes flat, is when you go to bed at night. **1986** J. WHYLE in S. Gray *Market Plays* 168 Ricky: .. How you handling it, troep? ... Shaun: Well after studying English literature it's pretty weird learning how to kill people you know. Ricky: Sure. Clown: Tree aan! *Susan, Ricky and Shaun fall in a line.*

b. *trans.* To engage the help of (someone).

1984 W. STEENKAMP in *Cape Times* 1 Feb., Tree aan the padre! If a padre is not willing to intercede for a man or give him a hearing, he is no good. I must say I have come across very few padres of this stamp.

tree fuchsia see NOTSUNG.

tree of knowledge *n. phr.* Also with initial capitals. [Transf. sense of general Eng. *tree of knowledge* a figurative or symbolic expression of knowledge in general, comprising all its 'branches'.] DAGGA *n.*[2] sense 1.

1946 *Cape Times* (23 May) in E. Partridge *Dict. of Underworld* 740 Tree of knowledge [*sc.* dagga]. **1949** H.C. BOSMAN *Cold Stone Jug* (1969) 51 They say that the best way to smoke dagga is to draw it through water in a hole made on the ground, in a 'grond-aar', like the Bushman smokes it. You kneel down on the ground and pull at a reed. There seems to be something peculiarly fitting in this posture: making low obeisance to the Tree of Knowledge. **1949, 1952** [see BOOM *n.* sense 1]. **1982** D. BIKITSHA in *Rand Daily Mail* 14 Oct. 5 Take dagga for example. it has so many names ... It has over the years been called: 'Tree of Knowledge', [etc.].

tree-snake *n.* [tr. S. Afr. Du. *boomslang.*] BOOMSLANG.

[**1731** G. MEDLEY tr. *P. Kolb's Present State of Cape of G.H.* II. 163 The *Tree-serpent*, This serpent is so call'd on Account of her being seen mostly in Trees.] **1804** [see BOOMSLANG]. **1812** A. PLUMPTRE tr. *H. Lichtenstein's Trav. in Sn Afr.* (1928) I. 160 The colonists called it the tree-snake (*Boa canina*), a species which is very adroit at climbing. **1841** B. SHAW *Memorials* 310 Of several kinds of snakes .. one only is considered as innoxious. This is the *boomslang* or tree-snake, so called from its being found coiled round the branches of trees. **1936** L.G. GREEN in *Best of S. Afr.*

Short Stories (1991) 168 He walked into the forester's office one day with a tree snake, six feet long, over his shoulder. **1962** V.F.M. FITZSIMONS *Snakes of Sn Afr.* 196 Alternative names: green, brown, black, Cape or back-fanged tree-snake. **1987** R. PATTERSON *Reptiles* 83 *Boomslang or Tree Snake* .. Measuring 1 – 1,5 m in length, the Boomslang appears in a number of different colour variations. **1991** *Best of S. Afr. Short Stories* (Reader's Digest Assoc.) 168 The 'man who played with snakes' must have been quick to have caught a boomslang or tree snake (*Dispholidus typus*) which can move like a flash through the trees.

trek /trek/ *n.* Formerly also **track, treck, trekk.** Pl. **-s**, occas. **-ke** /-kə/. [Du., the basic sense being 'an act of pulling'; in most cases the transfer of sense occurred not in Eng., but in Du. or Afk., fr. which languages the new senses were assimilated into Eng.]

1. *obs.* The team of oxen pulling a wagon.

[**1833** see quot. at *trek ox* (sense 12 a below).] **1838** J.E. ALEXANDER *Exped. into Int.* II. 215 Stick to the trek (or line of pack oxen) and the trek will stick to you.

2. *hist.* In the phr. ***on (the) trek***, in the process of travelling or migrating by wagon; on the road.

1846 J.M. BOWKER *Speeches & Sel.* (1864) 222 Here we are on trek. **1873** F. BOYLE *To Cape for Diamonds* 258 We came upon a family of Griquas on the trek, moving towards Klipdrift, with their herds. **1878** A. AYLWARD *Tvl of Today* 17 They are still on 'trek;' and few, indeed, are there who are not ready at a moment's notice to hurl themselves once more into the desert in search of brighter and happier homes. **1882** C. DU VAL *With Show through Sn Afr.* I. 101 We started at sunrise .. 'on the trekk' for Bloemfontein. **1896** M.A. CAREY-HOBSON *At Home in Tvl* 83 They have been with the old Dutch people a long time; but you had better make sure of them as you return, or they will be off on the trek. **1931** W.A. COTTON *Racial Segregation* 63 Oppressive conditions on the farms .. send on trek great numbers of squatters, labour tenants, and farm labourers, with their families. **1949** L.G. GREEN *In Land of Afternoon* 127 On trek, the women and children .. slept inside the wagon. **1951** J. SACHS in B. Sachs *Herman Charles Bosman* (1971) 142 There is all of South Africa in that little book .. ; its ox-waggons on trek, its witch-doctors, [etc.].

3. A leg of a journey; *hist.*, the distance travelled by ox-wagon between halts (or 'outspans'). Cf. SKOF *n.*² sense 1.

1849 E.D.H.E. NAPIER *Excursions in Sn Afr.* II. 1 First day's 'trek' in Lower Albany. [*Note*] A Dutch term, generally pronounced 'track,' meaning a journey. **1878** H.A. ROCHE *On Trek in Tvl* 262 The men are not over-pleased at our having to lose one trek today. **1882** S. HECKFORD *Lady Trader in Tvl* 55 It is better even with tired oxen to make them take their waggon through the river at the end of a trek. **1897** J.P. FITZPATRICK *Outspan* 87 In order to pass the house in mid-trek they made their morning off-saddle below the Berg. **1910** A.B. LAMONT *Rural Reader* 92 Each trek thus lasts about four hours. **1945** N. DEVITT *People & Places* 40 'Trek' .. may connote a period of time, a day's trek for instance. **1951** L.G. GREEN *Grow Lovely* 205 'So oud soos die Kaapse wapad' is a saying that indicates the age of this route ... Burchell .. called this trek a nightmare. **1964** V. POHL *Dawn & After* 63 We had about two treks before us and .. we had nothing whatever to eat.

4. A relocation or exodus: **a.** *hist.* The relocation of a large group of people from one area to another, the move usu. being made by ox-wagon, and being prompted by political discontent or economic hardship. See also *Dorsland Trek* (DORSLAND); GREAT TREK. **b.** Latterly, any relocation, including a temporary move, as for the purpose of working for some months in a distant town. Also *attrib.*

1852 M.B. HUDSON *S. Afr. Frontier Life* 3 The time for such a trek was approaching us fast. **1871** J. MACKENZIE *Ten Yrs* (1971) 64 A party among them advocated a 'trek' or removal to a district in Namaqualand. **1893** J.F. INGRAM *Story of Gold Concession* 235 He and his family took part in the 'trek' or exodus, of Boers. **1955** L. MARQUARD *Story of S. Afr.* 189 The diamond and gold treks had begun with the ox and had drawn railways in their wake. **1971** M. BOWEN in *Sunday Times* 17 Oct. (Mag. Sect.) 21 The trek to Cowes has meant a rapid growth of sailing houses. **1973** J. MEINTJES *Voortrekkers* 57 The trek habit .. had got into the blood. **1980** M. MATSHOBA in M. Mutloatse *Forced Landing* 103 The hostel is .. the home of some twenty thousand migrant labourers from all parts of Southern Africa, some of whom begin the trek as far away as Malawi and Zambia. **1988** F. HEYDENRYCH in *Cape Times* 8 Oct. 13 Chips are down for a high-tech trek to Cape's 'Silicon Valley'. **1990** *Sunday Times* 2 Dec. 25 (*letter*) Why can't the government decide to let parliament sit only in Pretoria and end the trek to Cape Town every six months? **1992** C.M. KNOX tr. *E. Van Heerden's Mad Dog* 5 Trek groups rested at the side of the road.

5. A journey or trip: **a.** Usu. *hist.*, a long trip by ox-wagon. **b.** Any journey, esp. a long or arduous one, or one involving travel in the wilds; journeying.

1856 R.E.E. WILMOT *Diary* (1984) 36 Our host being on the eve of a trek we soon took our departure. **1875** C.B. BISSET *Sport & War* 228 It took Currie and myself back to the wonderful trek we had with the Prince in 1860 ... This trek was through the interior of South Africa. **1895** A.B. BALFOUR *1200 Miles in Waggon* 69 We have actually begun our waggon trek at last. **1918** C. GARSTIN *Sunshine Settlers* 154 You've got a long trek home, come to my place for a shake-down, unless you prefer dossing in the scrub. **1920** F.C. CORNELL *Glamour of Prospecting* 49 He did not live on the property, but a good two days' trek away. **1924** E.T. JOLLIE *Real Rhodesia* (1971) 126 The Dutch holiday custom of a trek on the veld or a camping party. **1939** M. RORKE *Melina Rorke* 121 The trail that we were following would converge in about two days' trek with the regular route. **1949** L.G. GREEN *In Land of Afternoon* 137 He always spent his holiday camping, and when he retired he had already planned his gigantic trek. It cost him about £10 a month, and he saw more of the Union's byways than others see in a lifetime. **1951** J. WEDGEWOOD *Last of Radicals* 57 He and his family arrived after a three-day trek from Middleburg, in six wagons and an old ambulance. **1966** L.G. BERGER *Where's Madam* 47 Once in three months he would gather his witnesses and make the hopeless trek. **1968** K. MCMAGH *Dinner of Herbs* 28 Kimberley was only a single day's trek distant. **1985** *E. Prov. Herald* 18 Mar. 2 Freed hostages describe trek through Angola. **1990** *Sunday Times* 3 June 14 The former South African pop group leader is packing his bags for a dream trek across America on his supercharged 1500cc motorbike. **1993** A. PUTTER in *Weekly Mail & Guardian* 22 Oct. 46 Discussion at last year's Grahamstown Festival about the South African National Gallery's small contribution to the visual component of the annual cultural trek.

6. *Obs.* exc. *hist.* A group of travellers; an expedition party; a wagon train, including the travellers, their goods and livestock, and their wagons and draught animals (usu. oxen). Cf. TREKKIE.

*a***1867** C.J. ANDERSSON *Notes of Trav.* (1875) 87 We were treacherously attacked by overwhelming numbers, just as the 'trek' had got into a narrow part of the road. **1898** G. NICHOLSON *50 Yrs* 100 A numerous Boer 'trek' passed through the country some fourteen years ago. **1931** H.C. BOSMAN *Mafeking Rd* (1969) 150 The youngest person in our trek was Koos Steyn's daughter Jemima ... Webber sold his wagon and went with Koos Steyn's trek. **1973** J. MEINTJES *Voortrekkers* 65 This party was now enormous and they had to split into smaller treks on account of all their livestock and the problems of grazing. **1976** A.P. BRINK *Instant in Wind* 25 Perhaps we'll find a farmhouse or a trek on the way.

7. *colloq.* Goods and chattels; possessions.

*a***1867** C.J. ANDERSSON *Notes of Trav.* (1875) 273 The Totties (Hottentots) had just left the mountain with their 'treck', with a view of coming here. **1970** MRS BERRINGTON *Informant, Jansenville* We are fetching the new boys' trek in the bakkie. **1976** A.P. BRINK *Instant in Wind* 16 She is surrounded by the remains of her trek, the relics representing in this wilderness the achievements of her civilization. **1984** *Informant, N. Tvl*, I was at the new flat waiting for Joy's trek to arrive.

8. *fig.* Hard work, a 'long haul'; mental or spiritual endeavour.

1882 C. DU VAL *With Show through Sn Afr.* I. 66 She is a very big woman; in fact, it is a good 'trekk' to go fairly round her, and I fancy she is well able to hold her own against most people. **1895** J.G. MILLAIS *Breath from Veldt* 123 From the sun-parched wilderness of Africa to art criticism is a big trek. **1936** R.J.M. GOOLD-ADAMS *S. Afr. To-Day & To-Morrow* 24 South Africa's newest and best trek of all, the trek to real conciliation of the white races. **1946** T. MACDONALD *Ouma Smuts* 23 Sometimes she wondered if her man would become a great poet ... He was concerned with the trek of mankind. **1948** O. WALKER *Kaffirs Are Lively* 140 Such men .. indulged in a few mental or physical treks away from the colour problem. **1972** K. TAYLOR on Radio South Africa 6 June, Now let's go back to our childhood days. For some of you it will only be a little hop – for me it'll be a long trek backwards. **1978** A. ESSOP *Hajji* 20 Man's life on earth is a phantasmagoric trek to nowhere. **1980** *Het Suid-Western* 23 July, We had to start on the long uphill trek to raise funds from the government. **1987** *Weekly Mail* 22 May 23 An unsettling trek through the sense of unbelonging.

9. A migration of animals. Also *attrib.* See also sense 12 b below.

1902 C.J. CORNISH *Naturalist on Thames* 67 The first [birds] to begin the 'trek' down the river are the early broods of water-wagtails. **1913** W.C. SCULLY *Further Reminisc.* 231 It was my fortune in 1892 to witness the last great 'trek,' as the annual migration of spring-bucks from east to west across the desert is termed. *c***1936** *S. & E. Afr. Yr Bk & Guide* 1092 The great herds .. were thought to have become a thing of the past, but during 1898 enormous 'treks' occurred in the north-west and north of the Cape Province. **1968** *Farmer's Weekly* 1 Mar. 50, I recall, as a small boy, hearing first-hand reports of the 'springbok treks'. **1973** *Cape Times* 27 Jan. (Weekend Mag.) 10 Spectacular but ecologically unsound occurrences as the Great Flamingo Trek in 1971. **1973** *Cape Times* 30 June 11 In 1896, he saw the tail end of one of the great springbok migrations ... The treks were usually followed by lion, leopards, hyenas, jackals, and vultures to pick out the eyes of the dying. **1985** *Custos* Sept. 7 The lack of water and food probably served as a trigger mechanism to initiate the trek movement of the game. **1990** *Weekend Post* 30 June (Leisure) 4 Natal-type sardines are found in the Cape East Coast water – until they begin their unusual trek.

10. Of fishing: (a haul of fish caught by) the act of hauling in from the shore a trek net which has been cast in the sea. See also sense 12 c below.

1930 C.L. BIDEN *Sea-Angling Fishes* 274 The first net brought out 90,000 bamboo-fish! The man responsible for that 'trek' deserved to be knighted. **1972** N. HENSHILWOOD *Cape Childhood* 60 Sometimes, if we were lucky, there might be a trek, when the fishermen pulled in their nets and we were allowed to keep them. **1973** *Cape Times* 13 Jan. (Weekend Mag.) 2 (*caption*) Last trek of the day.

11. *hist.* ***The Trek***: GREAT TREK sense 1. Also *attrib.*

1941 C.W. DE KIEWIET *Hist. of S. Afr.* 182 Average exports .. in the five years following the Trek had soared. *c***1967** J. HOBBS in *New S. Afr. Writing* 65 Oupa Hannes Scheepers received a grant of land from Louis Trichardt himself as a reward .. on the Trek up from the Cape. **1973** J. MEINTJES *Voortrekkers* 42 They are two important men in Trek history. **1983** F.E.O'B. GELDENHUYS in *Optima* Vol.31 No.3, 153 The official governing bodies of the DRC in Cape Province were very much opposed to the Trek. **1987** S. FRIEDMAN in *Weekly*

Mail 10 July 12 This suggests that the Trek celebrations will have something in common with other Nat-CP battles.

12. Special Comb.

a. Combinations related to ox wagons and to the oxen which pull them (see sense 1): **trek cattle**, draught cattle; **trek chain**, TREKTOU sense b; **trek gear** or **trekgoed** /-xut/ [Afk. *goed* goods, things], the equipment (such as yokes and chains) used in harnessing draught animals for wagon travel; **trekos** /-ɔs/ [Afk., *os* ox], or **trek ox**, (*a*) a draught ox; (*b*) *fig.*, tough meat; also *attrib.*; **trek wagon**, an ox wagon; a large, sturdily-built covered wagon used for long journeys.

*a*1867 C.J. ANDERSSON *Notes of Trav.* (1875), I was now enabled .. to collect the scattered **trek-cattle**, *c*, which were now inspanned. **1900** *Daily News* 6 Apr. 3 The local supply of trek cattle .. from the farms of the Boers. **1928** E.H.L. SCHWARZ *Kalahari & its Native Races* 55 The sand was trampled by the feet of thousands of trek cattle that had come here to drink. **1859** R.J. MANN *Col. of Natal* 207 The **trek-chain**, or hide-rope, (trek-tow) runs along between each pair of the oxen. **1878** H.A. ROCHE *On Trek in Tvl* 332 Our oxen were free, walking off a yard or two with our .. trek chain. **1895** [see DISSELBOOM]. **1918** C. GARSTIN *Sunshine Settlers* 48 The sixteen long-horned oxen .. strained on the trek-chain. **1937** S. CLOETE *Turning Wheels* 33 At night the working oxen were tied to their gear and the trek-chains anchored to each other. **1952** H. KLEIN *Land of Silver Mist* 29 The team strained at the trek-chain and soon had car and caravan on the hilltop. **1977** F.G. BUTLER *Karoo Morning* 11 She expressed a keen longing to experience a trek by ox-wagon .. the huge patient beasts, the straining of trek chain, the rifle-cracking whips, the intimate campfire. **1884** 'E.V.C.' *Promised Land* 39 Back we all climbed to the wagon, and carefully examined the **trek gear** before inspanning. **1914** L.H. BRINKMAN *Breath of Karroo* 48 Gijs was to come over with his trek-gear and oxen and fetch du Plessis's buck-waggon. **1931** O. LETCHER *Afr. Unveiled* 103 The oxen began to pick up their weary heads and to strain more heavily on the trek gear. **1942** S. CLOETE *Hill of Doves* Glossary, Trek gear: ox yokes, harness, chains, etc. **1971** *Daily Dispatch* 23 Oct. 24 (*advt*) Trek gear and many more items. **1979** *Farmer's Weekly* 21 Mar. 107 (*advt*) Trek Gear, etc. **1912** *Queenstown Rep.* 27 Jan. 5 (Pettman), These accidents especially as far as **trekgoed** is concerned always happen when they are least expected. **1922** J.G. FRASER in F.G. Butler *When Boys Were Men* (1969) 207 The *disselboom* or pole, to which the *trekgoed* or drawing gear was attached. **1941** A.G. BEE *Kalahari Camp Fires* (1943) 269 Try to disentangle them .. , and you will save the 'trek-goed' (hauling gear) as well as the oxen. **1968** J.T. MCNISH *Rd to Eldorado* 112 The unskilled diggers assisted the driver .. to disentangle the yoked animals and remove the 'trekgoed' to the river bank where it was properly aligned again. **1972** *Grocott's Mail* 17 Nov. 2 (*advt*) Dexter Tractor 3 000 .. ; Trekgoed. **1972** L.G. GREEN *When Journey's Over* 134. I place meat as the greatest of all foodstuffs. Not all meat of course. Not the **trekos** or the *hoender* that has to be roasted in a pot until it falls apart and comes out devoid of flavour. **1833** *Graham's Town Jrnl* 7 Mar. 1 On the same day will also be offered, Thirty fine **Track Oxen**. **1850** R.G.G. CUMMING *Hunter's Life* I. 220, I purchased .. several .. trek-oxen. **1867** S. TURNER in D. Child *Portrait of Pioneer* (1980) 63 The next night they pulled down a trek-ox close to the wagon. **1879** R.J. ATCHERLEY *Trip to Boerland* 48 When in fair condition and inoculated for lung-sickness, the trek-ox will cost about £8, and a good waggon may be purchased for £100. **1882** C.L. NORRIS-NEWMAN *With Boers in Tvl* 190 Forty oxen being killed daily in the camp, there was a profusion of good beef, all good and fat, and not like the trek ox 'Tommy Atkins' had to put up with. **1896** H.A. BRYDEN *Tales of S. Afr.* 230 Lying at their yokes, chewing peacefully the cud, the great trek oxen rested. **1905** P. GIBBON *Vrouw Grobelaar* 15 A great hulking fellow, with the strength of a trek-ox. **1906** H. RIDER HAGGARD *Benita* 249 Benita could swallow no food; she was weary of that sun-dried trek-ox. **1929** J.G. VAN ALPHEN *Jan Venter* 71 He looked as tired as a wheeler trek-ox at an outspan. **1938** F.C. SLATER *Trek* 3, I leave .. and make my pilgrimage, At trek-ox pace. **1948** V.M. FITZROY *Cabbages & Cream* 124 One day Shilling gave Christopher a trek-ox horn. It was a huge thing, like a drinking horn out of a Norse saga. **1961** L.E. VAN ONSELEN *Trekboer* 82 One old Trekboer said to me that when the trek oxen drink, they raise their eyes to Heaven in thanksgiving to their Maker. **1967** E.M. SLATTER *My Leaves Are Green* 6 Venison would make a change from the eternal 'trek-ox' which was 'Maritzburg's staple meat supply.' **1970** 'R.C.G.' in *Outpost* 140 The first war was won on bread and jam and tea, and who shall say how much crime was stamped out on tea and trek ox? **1971** H. ZEEDERBERG *Veld Express* 234 Another 2,509 Australians were loaded on to the heavy transport wagons drawn by Africander trek oxen. **1976** A.R. WILCOX *Sn Land* 177 One by one, stricken by *nagana*, the trek-oxen dropped. **1979** T. PAKENHAM *Boer War* (1982) 263 Now, with the Sunday lunch of 'T.O.' (trek-ox) and hard biscuits, the hard truth. **1985** *S. Afr. Panorama* Oct. 43 Villages were cut off from the world whenever drought prevented trek oxen from getting through. **1898** J.F. INGRAM *Story of Afr. City* 179 The finishing and painting department is encountered, where .. stand the great **trek-wagons**, waiting but the order to start like 'ships of the desert' to the far-off lands of the Matabele and Mashona. **1908** [see NAGMAAL sense 1]. **1936** E. ROSENTHAL *Old-Time Survivals* 6 Perhaps the proudest possession of the National Museum at Pretoria is the original trek-wagon of President Paul Kruger. **1948** H.V. MORTON *In Search of S. Afr.* 83 The African trek wagon was really a caravan in which people lived as they travelled. **1969** D. CHILD *Yesterday's Children* 101 The trek-wagon was a sturdy vehicle whose body was long in proportion to its breadth. It had four heavy wheels shod with iron, and a canvas canopy stretched over semi-circular hoops. **1988** J. BOEKKOOI in *Weekend Argus* 3 Sept. 5 They don't build trek-wagons like they used to.

b. Combinations related to travel or to the nomadic or migratory movements of people or animals: **trek boer** /- buə, - bur/, pl. **-s**, and (formerly) **-en**, [Afk., *boer* farmer] *hist.*, (*a*) a nomadic farmer, (*b*) VOORTREKKER *n.* sense 1; also *attrib.*; **trekbok** /-bɔk/ [Afk. *bok* antelope] or part. tr. **trekbuck**, a springbok which is part of a large migrating herd; (usu. in *pl.* form **trekbokken**) a collective term for the herd or the migration; see also SPRINGBOK sense 1 a; cf. HOUBOK; **trek farmer**, *trek boer* sense (*a*) (see above); **trek fever** or **trekgees** /-xɪəs/, earlier **trekgeest** [Afk., *gees* (Du. *geest*) spirit], restlessness, wanderlust, a longing for open spaces and the outdoor life; **trekpad** /-pat/ [Afk., *pad* path, roadway], an established route used by people trekking by wagon; **trek pass** [Eng. *pass* note of authorization]; in rural areas, a written document given to an employee on dismissal or departure, entitling him or her to seek other employment; **trek-path**, (*a*) a rural servitude; the right to herd animals across privately-owned land en route from one grazing area to another; also *attrib.*; (*b*) an established animal track; **trek-weary** *adj.*

1835 A. STEEDMAN *Wanderings* II. 53 We met a **Trek Boor**, with his cattle. **1837** J.M. BOWKER *Speeches & Sel.* (1864) 56 We met with .. springboks and trek-boeren. **1857** F.W. REITZ in *Cape Monthly Mag.* II. Oct. 198 There is a wide difference between our 'trek-boer' and the Canadian or United States backwoodsman. **1871** J. MACKENZIE *Ten Yrs* (1971) 14 'Trek-boers,' wandering farmers, .. live in their waggon and tent, and shift about from place to place with their flocks and herds. Many of these people never possess houses, but pass their whole life in this nomadic manner. **1882** C. DU VAL *With Show through Sn Afr.* I. 106 Abolition of slavery was the primary cause of the movement of these 'trekk Boers', and dissatisfaction generally with the subsequent native policy of the British Government aided it. **1898** W.C. SCULLY *Between Sun & Sand* 2 Bushmanland is .. intermittently inhabited by a nomadic population of Europeans of Dutch descent, who are known as 'Trek-Boers'. **1902** D. VAN WARMELO *On Commando* 74 It was a journey difficult even for a trek Boer, and more than difficult for a large commando. **1920** F.C. CORNELL *Glamour of Prospecting* 54 He had expected to find trek boeren at some old water-pits. **1941** C.W. DE KIEWIET *Hist. of S. Afr.* 17 The trekboers .. left the current of European life ... Though they never became true nomads, the mark of nomadism was upon them. **1958** A. JACKSON *Trader on Veld* 31 It was the happy hunting ground of the Trek Boer, moving from place to place with all his livestock, wherever the grazing was good. **1961** [see quot. at *trek-path* below]. **1971** BARAITSER & OBHOLZER *Cape Country Furn.* 97 In 1835 Bell sketched the inside of a trek boer tent. **1987** *Investing Today (pamphlet)*, This colourless tangy fruit spirit made in the traditional copper still of the old trekboer days. **1990** *Sunday Times* 8 July 18 The Trekboers, that much-romanticised group which 'tamed' the South African interior, were, like their American cowboy counterparts, a pretty untamed lot themselves. **1824** *S. Afr. Jrnl* I. 72 On the approach of the **Trek-Bokken** or migrating spring-boks, the grazier makes up his mind to look for pasturage for his flocks elsewhere. **1827** G. THOMPSON *Trav.* II. 40 The destructive trek-bokken or migratory springboks, pressed by the long droughts, occasionally inundate the northern parts of the Colony. **1839** W.C. HARRIS *Wild Sports* 33 The trek bokken, as the occasional immigration .. of countless swarms of these antelopes is called by the colonists. **1860** A.W. DRAYSON *Sporting Scenes* 159 They said that in the great 'trek-boken', or journey of the springbok, the numbers were inconceivable; that they destroyed all the grass, leaving the plain like a vast cattle-fold. **1875** C.B. BISSET *Sport & War* 197 The trek-boks were as much dreaded by the farmers as the locusts ... During the time of drought in the interior .. these trek-boks migrate southward, devouring every blade of grass before them. **1889** H.A. BRYDEN *Kloof & Karroo* 233 During this last great trek bokken, he killed with buck-shot no less than five bok at one shot. **1922** J.G. FRASER in F.G. Butler *When Boys Were Men* (1969) 212 It took about three days before the whole of the trekbokken had passed, and it left our country looking as if a fire had passed over it. **1941** N. DEVITT *Celebrated S. Afr. Crimes* 18 Wants and worries were few, unless perhaps the fear of drought, .. or that the trek-bokken should come, those herds of nomadic spring-bokken which move in their thousands across the countryside, trampling all before them. **1955** L.G. GREEN *Karoo* 44 Karoo farmers last century firmly believed in two varieties of springbok — the lean *trekbok* and the fatter *houbok* (about fifteen pounds heavier), which remained in one area. **1972** A. SCHOLEFIELD *Wild Dog Running* 105 Herds of springbuck, the 'trekbokken' as they were called, stretching from one horizon to the next. **1981** H. THESEN in *Outeniqualander* 25 June 9 This is a microcosm of the ancient sound of the 'trek bok' on the move, millions strong, trampling all before them in a sometimes suicidal search for new grazing for their burgeoning numbers. **1985** *S. Afr. Panorama* Oct. 43 'The **trekbuck** are coming; it will be death to stay in this river bed.' ... Soon a drumming sound .. and a cloud of dust warned that thousands of leaping springbok were being funnelled in his direction. **1912** *E. London Dispatch* 1 May 5 (Pettman), The desirability of amending the railway tariff for trek-sheep to enable **trek farmers** to avail themselves of the railway when moving stock to winter pasture. **1966** E. PALMER *Plains of Camdeboo* 128 The mountain bush had housed the first trek-farmers in hard and stormy weather. **1987** I. CLAASSEN in *S. Afr. Panorama* Aug. 22 It is sparsely populated by Coloureds and Namas, of whom many are trek-farmers with large herds of goats. **1897** J.P. FITZPATRICK *Outspan* 3 When .. this instinct, feeling, craving .. awakens, as it perdiodically does, it becomes a madness, and they call it **trek-fever**, and then .. 'You must trek or burst!' **1913** C. PETTMAN *Africanderisms* 513 *Trek fever*, The insatiable longing which possesses the man who has once yielded himself to the spirit of wandering and adventure in the vast areas of the sub-continent is thus designated. **1943** D. REITZ *No Outspan* 106 Here .. in 1878 they had built a church, their trek-fever temporarily stilled. **1953** D. ROOKE *S. Afr. Twins* 55 Trek fever started .. when a man turned his eyes toward the horizon and began to speculate what lay beyond. The next thing was to go and find out. **1904** H.A. BRYDEN *Hist. of S. Afr.* 65 The '**trek-geest**' — the spirit of wandering — stirred within them. The more discontented and masterful .. determined to sell their farms, quit the Cape Colony, .. and seek new homes and wide farms in the dim and unknown regions beyond the Orange River. **1936** *Cambridge Hist. of Brit. Empire* VIII. 530 Kruger's policy of expansion was entirely consonant with his countrymen's ever-present *trekgeest*, the desire to trek with guns and waggons to new lands in the 'vast spaces washed with sun' which beckoned them onwards into the Great Continent. **1941** C.W. DE KIEWIET *Hist. of S. Afr.* 47 The old trekgeest, the spirit of the open veld, of greener grass beyond the horizon. **1968** G. CROUDACE *Silver Grass* 26 Driven by *trekgees* — the restless fever that afflicted the Afrikaner trekkers at the sight of their neighbour's smoke — he had crossed the Kalahari Desert from the Transvaal. **1973** J. MEINTJES *Voortrekkers* 43 Louis even as a boy developed the *trekgees* and he was to wander far and wide. **1989** *Reader's Digest Illust. Hist.* 57 To tempt families to settle permanently, he proposed that .. a burgher might convert 50 hectares of his leningplaats to freehold property ... On those who had succumbed to the *trekgees* (wanderlust) this new offer had no effect. **1937** S. CLOETE *Turning Wheels* 11 The bends in the old **trek pad**, that so many followed later, were due to Herman van der Berg. Due to his signalling the voorlopers to the right or left, away from a tree stump or an ant-bear hole. **1952** H. KLEIN *Land of Silver Mist* 108 A cry that now .. takes me back .. to that first moment when I knew that I had found that 'somewhere' waiting for me on my trek pad. **1963** S. CLOETE *Rags of Glory* 33 The great *trekpad* was dotted with the graves of men and the bones of the stock that had died by the thousand on the way. **1926** W.A. COTTON *Race Problem* 77 The '**trek pass**' absolution of our British and Dutch farmers. **1931** H.C. BOSMAN in V. Rosenberg *Almost Forgotten Stories* (1979) 33 Francina wrote out all the trekpasses and made all the kaffirs clear off the farm. **1939** R.F.A. HOERNLÉ *S. Afr. Native Policy* 83 Those who were unwilling to renew their contracts on the new terms, were offered only a 'trek-pass,' entitling them to seek a position on another farm in the district. **1986** J. BALOYI *Learn & Teach* No.2, 36 Country people live better than town people because they can stay with their families in the same house. Nobody can ask them about 'trek-passes'. **1889** *Divisional Council Act in Stat. of Cape of G.H. 1652–1905* (1906) 2745 The words path or track shall not be taken to mean **trekpaths** lawfully used in certain districts of the Colony. **1929** J.G. VAN ALPHEN *Jan Venter* 47 He says he is no longer going to have his land cut up by roads and trek-paths. **1936** *Cape Argus* 18 Mar. 13 The trek-path controversy has led many men to fence their farms. **1945** G. WILLE *Principles of S. Afr. Law* 204 Trek-path, *trek pad*; the right of driving cattle, including large flocks of sheep, across the land of another. **1961** L.E. VAN ONSELEN *Trekboer* 45 The man who lives along the trekpath should realize his good fortune in owning a fixed property and a solidly built house. He should not look down upon the less fortunate Trekboer. **1968** S. STANDER *Horse*, A thousand animals .. moved down the ancient trek-path. **1977** — *Flight from Hunter* 38 They are trek-paths. The animals often go right across the pan, making their own paths. **1939** M. RORKE *Melina Rorke* 100 Thinking it too dangerous to risk a solitary crossing with **trek-weary** oxen, he had decided to turn back.

c. Combinations related to fishing (see sense 10): **trek boat**, a boat used in *trek fishing* (see below); **trek fisherman**, one who fishes using a *trek net* (see below); TREKKER sense 2; **trek fishing** vbl n., the act or practice of fishing with a *trek net*; also attrib.; TREKKING vbl n. sense 3; **trek net**, a seine net: a large fishing net, weighted at one end and fitted with floats on the other so that it hangs vertically in the water, usu. dropped from a boat and hauled in from the shore; also attrib.; hence **trek netter**, *trek fisherman* (see above).

1985 *S.-Easter* Oct.-Nov. 23 (advt) Dine in an antique **Trek Boat**. **1992** YELD & GUBB in *Afr. Wildlife* Vol.46 No.2, 200 Trek-boats have operated in the bay for well over a century. **1968** *Drum* Sept. 38 Osman 'Oesie' Mohammed, a 40-year-old **trek-fisherman**, is indeed a big man. **1973** *Farmer's Weekly* 18 Apr. 102 It [sc. the harder] is generally caught from the beaches in the nets of the trek fishermen. **1989** *Our Living World* Aug. 6 Nan .. watched trek fishermen catching dolphins in nets in Hout Bay. **1992** YELD & GUBB in *Afr. Wildlife* Vol.46 No.2, 200 There have been consistent catches of a number of different species by trek-fishermen over the years. **1970** *Cape Argus* 24 Dec. 2 Another crew member .. had gone along, to assist them with the **trek fishing**. **1983** *Cape Times* 5 Jan. 11 Cancellation of some trek-fishing licences has begun in terms of the government's tough new conservation policies. **1991** B.J. BARKER *Fairest Cape* 47 (caption) On the long, white beach at Fish Hoek, trek-fishing boats are drawn up on the sands. **1913** W.W. THOMPSON *Sea Fisheries of Cape Col.* 46 The seine, or '**trek-net**', has from the very earliest period of the European occupation of the country been the type of net generally adopted. **1934** C.P. SWART *Supplement to Pettman* 179 *Trek-net*, A seine is so called by S.A. fishermen, whose method is to set the nets near the shore and wait for the fish to come in, when the net and its catch are drawn on to the beach. **1964** L.G. GREEN *Old Men Say* 90 Poet's Corner in Woodstock was originally Fisherman's Corner because so many of the treknet brethren lived there. **1970** *Argus* 24 Dec. 2 They had cast trek nets in the surf about 50 yards from the beach. **1987** *Sunday Times* 15 Feb. (Mag. Sect.) 61 A dolphin-catching outfit had dragged ashore 200 dolphins in a trek net to select a couple for sale to South Africa's dolphinaria. **1947** [**trek-netter**: see JOSEPH]. **1956** J.L.B. SMITH *Old Fourlegs* 9, I lived with the coastal trek-netters. **1973** *Argus* 12 Jan. 20 (caption) This Bluefin Tunny of over 200kg was dragged ashore by trek netters at Fish Hoek .. , indicative of how close inshore these giant fish come. **1983** *Cape Times* 31 Dec. 9 The trek-netters at Glencairn took a shoal of about 300 big fish. **1993** *Southern Argus* 12 Aug. 4, I would like to reply to Mr Petty's letter, which accuses me of being .. unfairly biased against the trek netters.

d. Special Combination related to the underlying sense of 'trek' in Du. and Afk. (a tug, a pulling action): **treksaw**, a two-handled crosscut saw, operated by two people alternately pushing and pulling.

1972 *Daily Dispatch* 4 March 18 (advt) **Trek Saws**; Jacks; [etc.]. **1973** *E. Prov. Herald* 28 May 13 A large hole in the ground under the log and a double-handled treksaw pushed and pulled by two men, one down in the hole and the other above.

trek /trek/ v. Formerly also trac(k), trak, treck. [Du., imperative of *trekken*; many of the later senses are derived fr. Afk. *trek*. The central sense of the word in both Du. and Afk. is 'to pull'; see further notes at TREK n.]

1. Of draught animals.

a. intrans. To pull; often used as an order to animals to begin pulling, or to pull more strongly; LOOP sense 1 a.

1820 T. PHILIPPS *Lett.* (1960) 74 He carries his Mutton and dried beef and bread and his blanket in a large chest on which he sits to drive, and .. jogs on contentedly, now and then calling out 'Trac, Trac'. **1841** [see LOOP sense 1 a]. **1848** T. SMITH in *Wesleyan-Methodist Mag.* IV.ii. 1106 The patient oxen, .. strove with all their might to **trek**, (pull.) *a*1862 J. AYLIFF *Jrnl of 'Harry Hastings'* (1963) 50 The driver of the waggon gave his long whip a terrible swing shouting 'trak!' **1862** 'A LADY' *Life at Cape* (1963) 86 The morning air would be rent with the shrill cries of 'Bosman! Coburg! Englishman! Witfoot! trek, trek'. **1896** M.A. CAREY-HOBSON *At Home in Tvl* 286 The word 'Trek' was uttered; the patient bullocks moved on. **1908** J.M. ORPEN *Reminisc.* (1964) 11, I shall just say 'Trek,' gently, and you will see they will all set themselves steadily to the yokes and pull the wagon out. **1934** B.I. BUCHANAN *Pioneer Days* 31 Mr. Williams shouted 'trek,' and clapped his long whip, the oxen strained at the yokes, and we were under way. **1937** F.B. YOUNG *They Seek a Country* 162 'Trek, you devils,' he thundered.' ... Trek, you lazy troop of mares!' **1977** F.G. BUTLER *Karoo Morning* 90 Tembile would act as voorloper, Neville would work the whip and Godfrey the brake. 'Trek!' shouted Neville, and we would be off.

b. trans. To pull (a vehicle).

1863 W.C. BALDWIN *Afr. Hunting* 152 My oxen could not possibly trek my wagon through the heavy sands in their present condition. **1880** E.L. PRICE *Jrnls* (1956) 405 They remind me of Papa's young oxen when we have a span of them 'trekking' the wagon. **1893** H.M. DOUGHTY *Wherry in Wendish* 53 A farm horse .. trekked us for four or five miles.

2. intrans. To travel.

a. *hist.* To undertake a long or arduous journey by ox-wagon (often in convoy or with a large party). Also *fig.*

1835 T.H. BOWKER *Journal.* 25 Sept., Making ready for to track have got no horses. **1838** J. COLLETT *Diary.* I. 27 June Tracked to day with my Family to Grahams Town in consequence of rumours about war. **1852** M.B. HUDSON *S. Afr. Frontier Life* 69 Trek! Trek! then my muse; from our weary travel, Such scenes as may please with thy aid I'll unravel, All the picnicking pleasures attending on treks, I have found disappear as the novelty slacks. **1852** N.J. MERRIMAN *Cape Jrnls* (1957) 195 We .. 'trekked' up the Fish River and a very trying pull it was to the oxen and their drivers. **1885** LADY BELLAIRS *Tvl at War* 9 During the period for Nachtmaal, .. the farmers from the outlying districts *trekked* in to Pretoria with their families. **1900** A.C. DOYLE *Great Boer War* (1902) 621 Viljoen's force trekking north towards the line came upon this detachment. **1908** J.M. ORPEN *Reminisc.* (1964) 251 Makapaan .. invaded the Transvaal so that the people were compelled to trek into laagers. **1925** P. SMITH *Little Karoo* (1936) 9 The favourite way for the English colonists was to trek first to Mossel Bay and then to take ship. **1941** C. BIRKBY *Springbok Victory* 153 He commandeered a donkey and trekked back through the bush. **1951** J. WEDGEWOOD *Last of Radicals* 53, I was .. trekking along north of the Vaal between Vereeniging and Villiersdorp thinking what a ripping morning it was. **1955** A. DELIUS *Young Trav.* 46 It's a long way from some of the native mine-workers' homes to the mines, and great numbers of them trek all the way back after they've worked a year or so and earned sufficient money. **1984** *E. Prov. Herald* 6 Apr. 1 Thousands trek to coast as long weekend begins. **1990** S. JOHNSON in *Independent* (U.K.) 12 Feb. 8 Crowds will trek any distance to be at the homecoming.

b. To undertake a long or arduous walk; to hike.

1962 F.C. METROWICH *Scotty Smith* 23 He managed to escape and trekked across the veld on foot. **1983** *Sunday Times* 9 Oct. 19 Thousands of black townsfolk braved icy winds to trek to the summit of an unnamed desolate hill. **1987** *Argus* 15 Jan. 1 He hopes to go trekking in the Kalahari in April.

c. To undertake an onerous or inconvenient trip, esp. one which the traveller believes could have been avoided.

1971 *Drum* Aug. 35 Isaac and Rejoice have been trekking to Johannesburg almost every weekend to do their wedding shopping. **1972** *Cape Times* 10 Mar. 8 Each time there is a new issue of stamps we have to trek into Cape Town to procure a 'first-day cover.' **1987** *E. Prov. Herald* 19 May 3 Port Elizabethans are having to trek back and forth between the Traffic Department in Sidwell and the Receiver of Revenue in Central in order to equip themselves with the necessary credentials for driving a car. **1992** C. GLYN in *Natal Mercury* 30 Dec. 8 If John or I want to bath, we have to trek to one of the other couple's farmhouses.

3. intrans. To leave an area.

a. To relocate, to leave in order to settle elsewhere, formerly esp. as part of a larger exodus or movement of people.

1837 J.M. BOWKER *Speeches & Sel.* (1864) 57 Those boers .. complained bitterly of the manner in which he has deceived them, and wished that they had trekked sooner, before the Kafirs had left them so little to trek with. **1850** N.J. MERRIMAN *Cape Jrnls* (1957) 142, I soon began to meet Boers and their families trekking, i.e. quitting their farms, with their flocks and herds. **1850** J.D. LEWINS *Diary.* 20 Oct., He tells me Dods Pringle's people were insisting on leaving him. In Zwagershoek the Kafirs are all trecking. *a*1858 J. GOLDSWAIN *Chron.* (1949) II. 149 They had lost a great meney sheep thrue leveing thear homes — but what was they to do if they had not Tracked? **1882** C.L. NORRIS-NEWMAN *With Boers in Tvl* 3 Owing to the steady increase in their flocks, the scarcity of water and constant droughts, it became necessary for these pastoral patriarchs to 'trek' still further away. **1899** 'S. ERASMUS' *Prinsloo* 1 The original Edict of Nantes served upon Jacobus Piet Prinsloo the Huguenot, compelling him to trek to South Africa, exists to this day. **1926** P. SMITH *Beadle* (1929) 38 When the colony fell into the hands of the English it was to preserve this Heaven-granted sense of nationality that many Dutchmen, in succeeding generations, trekked still further north into unknown country with their wives and their families, their flocks and their herds, their Bibles and their guns. **1946** S. CLOETE *Afr. Portraits* 27 It was part of the restless Boer nature to trek anyway as soon as any place became over-populated, or the game was killed off, or the seasons were bad. **1949** L.G. GREEN *In Land of Afternoon* 93 They decided to trek to Tanganyika, where some friends had already settled. **1953** A. PATON *Phalarope* 20 They had trekked from the British Government with its officials and its missionaries and its laws. **1968** K. MCMAGH *Dinner of Herbs* 63 Each succeeding generation .. trekked even further with their families, their wagons, their slaves, their flocks and herds seeking land. **1980** E. *Prov. Herald* 3 Sept. 2 Zimbabwe sees another 1 644 trek. **1980** *Oudtshoorn Courant & Het Suid-Western* 9 Apr., Why I'm trekking from Mossel Bay. **1980** N. FERREIRA *Story of Afrikaner* 29 His father said he had had enough and decided to trek once more. **1990** *New African* 18 June 13, I trekked to Johannesburg in 1962 at the age of 22 and got a job as a pianist at the Dorkay House.

b. In the phr. *to trek out,* (esp. in a military context) to strike camp and leave an area, to pull out.

1852 M.B. HUDSON *S. Afr. Frontier Life* 152 The mass of rebels .. had trekked out, And had gone towards Kafirland. **1900** A.W. CARTER *Informant, Ladybrand* 24 Jan. 3 There was a report that the English were trekking out. **1960** U. KRIGE (tr. J. van Melle) in D. Wright *S. Afr. Stories* 129 Load, and round up the oxen; trek out; trek home.

c. To go away, make off, move off.

1863 LADY DUFF-GORDON in F. Galton *Vacation Tourists* (1864) III. 163 One rich old Boer got three lunches, and then 'trekked' (made off) without paying at all. **1876** T. STUBBS *Reminiscences.* 88 They had not heard any firing at Bowkers Camp — for some time, .. they must have been beaten — or had treked. **1885** H. RIDER HAGGARD *King Solomon's Mines* (1972) 73 'And now,' said Sir Henry, 'trek.' So we started. **1901** P.J. DU TOIT *Diary* (1974) 40 At sunset we trekked, not knowing whither. **1937** G.F. GIBSON *Story of Imp. Light Horse* 132 General Lucas Meyer had gone back to the Transvaal and .. the Free Staters around Ladysmith were trekking. **1963** S. CLOETE *Rags of Glory* 29 Get your horses, *kêrels*. We are trekking.

4. *intrans.* Of undomesticated animals: to move in large groups, esp. in seasonal migrations.

1850 R.G.G. CUMMING *Hunter's Life* (1902) We came upon an immense, compact herd of several thousand 'trekking' springboks. **1895** J.G. MILLAIS *Breath from Veldt* 25 The springbuck .. were beginning to trek backwards and forwards uneasily. **1937** J. STEVENSON-HAMILTON *S. Afr. Eden* 195 The isolated patches of hoppers .. join up and commence to trek. **1951** L.G. GREEN *Grow Lovely* 156 There was a panic-stricken exodus of rats from the city. They trekked through the sewers in thousands and out on to the beaches. **1972** *Daily Dispatch* 29 July 4 The herds were enormous, but they trekked about and could not stay in any area longer than the water supply lasted. **1976** A.P. BRINK *Instant in Wind* 187 The flood of brown bodies continues undiminished … 'But where are they going?' she asks … 'They just trek like this.' **1989** E. *Prov. Herald* 18 Nov. 10 An odd thing about terrapins, Dr Skead said, was that they trekked about. He had often seen them trekking across the veld.

5. *intrans.* To travel constantly from place to place; to live a nomadic life.

*c*1851 H. JAMES in F.C. Metrowich *Valiant but Once* (1956) 215 Buzby 'trekked' with this stock .. , guarding them day and night, enduring every privation for nine months. **1886** G.A. FARINI *Through Kalahari* 100 They had .. some 5000 sheep, 800 cattle, and 1000 goats, with which they wandered over the country … For the last seven years they had been 'trekking' from Carnarvon. **1930** N. STEVENSON *Farmers of Lekkerbat* 234 She met Rijk Martinus who, with his big horse and dog, was returning from native territory where he had been *trekking* for a month. *a*1943 W. WESTRUP in A.D. Dodd *Anthology of Short Stories* (*a*1958) 68, I bin trekking by myself for most o' them fifty years I spoke of. **1958** S. CLOETE *Mask* 21 My plan is to trek about seeing the world and painting as I go. **1971** *Rand Daily Mail* 29 June 13 When the holiday seasons are really booming, they trek from one hotel to another. **1978** A.P. BRINK *Rumours of Rain* 210 He moved to a frontier district and became a stock farmer, which meant that he had to spend his life trekking this way and that, his wanderings determined by available pasture, the onslaught of Bushmen or predators, and rumours of rain.

6. Of farmers and livestock.

a. *intrans.* To move from one grazing area to another, usu. for seasonal grazing.

1867 *Blue Bk for Col.* 1866 JJ15, Were it not for this dam, the owner would have to trek with all his stock. **1893** E. NICHOLSON in *Cape Illust. Mag.* Vol.4 No.6, 206 The sheep could not *trek* until there was grass in the Free State. **1911** *Farmer's Weekly* 11 Oct. 171 Many of the sheep farmers in the northern districts of Natal, who have for generations past been accustomed to 'trek' to the Free State and Transvaal for the summer grazing are .. now keeping their flocks in Natal. **1948** H. WOLHUTER *Mem. of Game Ranger* 12 We met some trek-boers who were trekking down to the winter veld with their sheep and cattle. **1953** U. KRIGE *Dream & Desert* 107 In times of drought he would trek with his sheep to find pasture.

b. *trans.* To move (livestock) from one place of grazing to another.

1972 J.D. KEET in *Daily Dispatch* 6 May 10 Long ago .. farmers trekked their sheep from the Free State to the better winter grazing of the Natal lowveld. **1979** T. GUTSCHE *There Was a Man* 212 They .. hid their animals and trekked them secretly or at night.

7. *trans.* To cover (ground, a distance, or a specific route).

1890 F. YOUNG *Winter Tour S. Afr.* 128 The ground which I have myself treked. **1912** A.W. HODSON (title) *Trekking the Great Thirst.* **1937** C.R. PRANCE *Tante Rebella's Saga* 101 He with his countless retinue must 'trek the Great Thirst' of nearly a hundred miles to Bloemfontein.

8. Fishing.

a. *intrans.* To fish using a *trek* net (see TREK *n.* sense 12 c) cast from a boat and pulled in from shore with the catch.

1934 *Sunday Times* 24 June, Local fisherfolk had been trekking for their fish. **1985** A. TREDGOLD *Bay between Mountains* 204 Not all trek licences are held by professional fishermen; some have been given to men who trek as a sideline or just for sport.

b. *trans.* To catch (fish) in this way.

1960 J. COPE *Tame Ox* 170 How could you explain her wanting to come and trek fish with a boat-load of rough men?

‖**9.** *intrans.* To draw, to infuse (as tea-leaves, etc., in liquid). See also TREKSEL.

1945 N. DEVITT *People & Places* 140 We speak of leaving tea leaves to trek in the teapot, or of buchu leaves to trek in the brandy bottle.

‖**10.** *intrans.* and *trans.* To pull (something).

1985 J. SCOTT in *Sunday Times* 5 May 4, I pulled up and down repeatedly, for good measure, I also trekked … At the bottom is a row of knobs, each one for a different type of chocolate. I pulled and trekked them all. Once again I tried the coin return.

trekker /ˈtrekə/ *n.* Formerly also **trecker**. [Afk., or formed in S. Afr. Eng.: TREK *v.* + n.-forming suffix *-er*.]

A further sense of 'trekker', not used in *S. Afr. Eng.* but found in *U.S.* and *Brit. Eng.*, is 'a hiker; one participating in a recreational walk or pony-ride'.

1.a. *hist.* Also with initial capital. VOORTREKKER *n.* sense 1. Also *attrib.* **b.** *transf.* One who is part of a migration of a people or large group; see also *Dorsland trekker* (DORSLAND).

1846 *Natal Witness* 26 June 2 What is the distance .. at which these 'trekkers' have chosen to place themselves? **1851** R. GRAY *Jrnl of Bishop's Visitation* II. 27 Only a few of the latest trekkers have a friendly feeling towards the English Government. **1892** *The Jrnl* 10 Sept. 2 It is said that even a son of President Kruger will join the trekkers. **1900** H.C. HILLEGAS *Oom Paul's People* 219 In their dealings with the Boers the British have invariably assumed the role of aristocrats, and have looked upon and treated the 'trekkers' as sans-culottes. **1919** J.Y. GIBSON in *S. Afr. Jrnl of Science* July 3 The 'smous,' or itinerant trader, was a common visitant, carrying his wares in the Kap-tent wagon to the remote habitations of trekkers and settlers. **1933** W.H.S. BELL *Bygone Days* 111 The party .. took with them about 30,000 sheep and several hundred horses and oxen, which the trekkers had obtained by barter. **1941** C.W. DE KIEWIET *Hist. of S. Afr.* 23 The Dutch were not the first trekkers in South Africa … The Bantu whom the advancing huntsmen first met at an early moment in the eighteenth century were the country's original trekkers. **1945** 'J. BURGER' *Black Man's Burden* 19 The trekkers complained of the suppression of their language and institutions; of the lack of protection on the frontier; of the unfair way in which the liberation of the slaves had been carried out; of the unjustifiable odium which missionaries and other prejudiced persons had cast upon them. **1951** R. GRIFFITHS *Grey about Flame* 98 Sometimes the warriors surprised a column of trekkers before they could form their laager. **1972** *S. Afr. Panorama* Mar. 27 Many hundreds of spectators were clad in typical Trekker costumes of the early nineteenth century period. **1973** *Sunday Times* 9 Dec. (Mag. Sect.) 5 Many Coloureds … trekked to .. the Cape Flats, but unlike other trekkers before them there was no promised land. **1975** A. PATON in T. Sundermeier *Church & Nationalism* 46 The seeds of future conflict between British authority and a nascent trekker nationalism were already to be discerned. **1988** *Sunday Star* 5 June 2 In the old days, the days of the Trekkers, mampoer was made from wild fruits. **1990** *Frontline* Mar.-Apr. 20 Farms like the Trekkers thought farms should be, where you can't see the smoke of the neighbour's chimney. **1990** *Sunday Times* 21 Oct. 11 Olifantshoek is seen by the trekkers as their Pretoria. **1991** P. HAWTHORNE in *Time* 20 May 8 Says Boshoff, the new trekkers 'will make the desert bloom'.

2. *trek fisherman,* see TREK *n.* sense 12 c.

1985 A. TREDGOLD *Bay between Mountains* 204 At night .. the trekkers cannot see what fish are about and how many small ones they are netting. **1988** *Weekend Argus* 19 Mar. 14 (*letter*) Selfish trekkers … No sooner do the weather and surf conditions become right for the fish to move inshore, than along come the trek nets which indiscriminately take everything out before you can take the rod from your attic.

trekkie /ˈtreki/ *n.* [Afk., *trek* (see TREK *n.*) + dim. suffix -IE.] A small party of persons travelling by ox wagon. Cf. TREK *n.* sense 6. Also *attrib.*, and *transf.*, a migratory bird.

'Trekkie' in *U.S.* and *Brit. Eng.* is 'an admirer of the U.S. science fiction television programme *Star Trek*; hence, a space-traveller; one interested (trivially) in space travel.' (*OED*, second ed.). This sense is not generally known in South Africa.

1888 J. Bird (tr. D.P. Bezuidenhout) *Annals of Natal* I. 367 A small 'trekkie' (party of emigrants) had preceded us. **1937** F.B. Young *They Seek a Country* 413 At each farm .. the *trekkie* halted and one or two of the men rode over to pay their respects. **1953** J. Collin-Smith *Locusts & Wild Honey* I. 10 We had inspanned the sixteen oxen, and the wagon wheels had turned, and the little trekkie had started away. **1959** J. Packer *High Roof* 193 Swallows swooped and twittered, gathering for their seasonal migration. How many of the winged trekkies would get through? **1985** *Sunday Times* 1 Sept. (Mag. Sect.) 12 Once a year he, and about 100 friends sold on the 'trekkie' lifestyle, would rekindle the pioneering past by spending five days trundling through the Agatha Mountains on the old transport road.

trekking /ˈtrekɪŋ/ *ppl adj.* and *vbl n.* [trek *v.* + Eng. participial suffix *-ing*.]

'Trekking' has developed further senses beyond South Africa's borders; these will be found in general dictionaries of English.

A. *ppl adj.*

1. Of animals, moving in a seasonal migration.

1850 R.G.G. Cumming *Hunter's Life* (1902) 28 We came upon an immense, compact herd of several thousand 'trekking' springboks.

2. Nomadic; moving constantly from place to place as required by the availability of grazing and water.

1852 N.J. Merriman *Cape Jrnls* (1957) 187 He was .. among the earliest of the trekking farmers, and had his sheep now on a place between Somerset and Graaff Reinet.

3. Emigrating; pioneering; of or pertaining to the Voortrekkers (see voortrekker *n.* sense 1).

1926 M. Nathan *S. Afr. from Within* 226 There has been a revival of the trekking spirit. **1931** W.A. Cotton *Racial Segregation* 133, I think that the trekking days are done for our South Africans. **1988** J. Boekkooi in *Frontline* Oct. 23 Cape Afrikaners .. stayed behind in comfort, .. talking English with the imperialists, while their trekking cousins braved lions and crocodiles.

B. *vbl n.*

1. The act or practice of migrating, or of living a nomadic life.

*a*1858 J. Goldswain *Chron.* (1949) II. 120 Meney of them his preparing for Tracking and sume of them are already gon. **1882** J. Nixon *Among Boers* 92 The Boers were no strangers to 'trekking'. Years before the English occupation they had been in the habit of emigrating beyond the pale of their government whenever they were displeased with it. **1908** M.C. Bruce *New Tvl* 35 The Dutchman's life has consisted chiefly of war and trekking. **1960** J.J.L. Sisson *S. Afr. Judicial Dict.* 814 Trekking, in relation to the Transkeian Pass Laws, does not apply only to permanent removal but includes also temporary movement.

2. The act or practice of travelling (*hist.* by ox wagon), esp. over a long distance. Also *attrib.*, and *fig.*

1871 J. Mackenzie *Ten Yrs* (1971) 64 Everybody was making preparations for the journey. 'Trekking' is quite a South African institution. **1899** B. Mitford *Weird of Deadly Hollow* 203 Surely there are half a hundred roads to heaven, and it's each man's business to hit off the one which seems to him to promise the easiest trekking. **1899** [see trektou]. **1910** A.B. Lamont *Rural Reader* 92 The trekking is usually done by night. **1939** M. Rorke *Melina Rorke* 117 After delightful days of easy trekking it was a blow to find that the Sabi River was a raging torrent. **1975** D.H. Strutt *Clothing Fashions* 139 Those farmers that lived within trekking distance of Cape Town .. saw the clothes worn by the Kaapstad folk. **1987** *Fair Lady* 18 Feb. 92 The .. years of trekking to Pring every weekend seem insignificant.

3. *trek fishing*, see trek *n.* sense 12 c. Also *attrib.*

1913 W.W. Thompson *Sea Fisheries of Cape Col.* 46 At Struis Bay, Keimouth and similar stations 'trekking' is practically the only mode of fishing carried on. **1960** J. Cope *Tame Ox* 169 He was waiting for two serving men and the wine steward to make up his boat-crew for the trekking. **1988** D. Fryer in *Weekend Argus* 19 Mar. 14 (*letter*) I fully endorse what the conservationists have to say about the appalling yellowtail trekking. **1992** Yeld & Gubb in *Afr. Wildlife* Vol.46 No.2, 201 There are just seven trekking teams still operating in False Bay.

4. In full *pony trekking*: cross-country horse-riding, esp. as a holiday excursion.

This sense possibly originated outside South Africa.

[**1968** *Punch* 14 Aug. 234 While some of the ponies probably would be kept in any case .. the majority are now kept principally for the revenue from trekking.] **1972** *Sunday Times* 13 Aug. (Mag. Sect.) 30 The start of a day's pony trekking. **1974** *S. Afr. Panorama* Jan. 23 Holidaymakers often like to base themselves at a comfortable mountain resort and then make day-trips to more hazardous ground, or go pony-trekking along a mountain trail.

treksel /ˈtrɛks(ə)l/ *n. obsolescent.* Also **trexel**. [Du.] A quantity of a commodity, as tea or coffee, from which a brew is prepared by infusion. See also trek *v.* sense 9.

1850 R.G.G. Cumming *Hunter's Life* (1911) 120 They are .. great beggars, generally commencing by soliciting 'trexels,' a trexel being a pound of tea or coffee. **1853** *Graham's Town Jrnl* 12 Mar. 3 They .. begged a treksel of coffee and went to their waggons. **1864** T. Baines *Explor. in S.-W. Afr.* 51, I sent back 'Treksels,' which .. means pounds (more or less) of tea, coffee, and sugar, done up in handkerchiefs, as a compliment to their chief. **1871** J. Mackenzie *Ten Yrs* (1971) 63, I have been often asked for a 'soepje' or dram by Griquas whose 'places' I was passing; and when my driver whispered that I was a missionary, nothing daunted, the beggar would then substitute the request for a 'treksel' or 'single infusion' of tea or coffee. **1877** *Sel. Comm. Report on Mission to Damaraland* p.xv, Jan Lambert said, if we but ask for a 'treksel' of coffee, you whites go back and complain of our ill treatment. **1945** N. Devitt *People & Places* 140 We speak of a 'treksel' — a small dose or quantity of a substance capable of infusion.

trektou /ˈtrektəu, ˈtrɛk-/ *n.* Usu. *hist.* Also **trac(k)toe, tra(c)ktow, tracto(w), treck-tow, trekto(u)w**, and as two words. Pl. **-s**, and (rarely) **-towen**. [Afk. (earlier Du. *trektouw*), *trek* see trek *n.* + *touw* rope, cord, twine; it is not clear whether forms in *-tow* arose through transliteration or through translation.] **a.** A trace or drawrope made of twisted or plaited rawhide thongs and used in drawing a wagon, being attached to the yokes of the draught animals and to the pole. See also tou sense 1. **b.** *transf.* A chain used for the same purpose; *trek chain*, see trek *n.* sense 12 a. Also *attrib.*

1817 G. Barker Journal. 16 May, Had a Buffaloo's hide cut to make a Trek tow. **1822** W.J. Burchell *Trav.* I. 151 The trektouw (draw rope or trace), is a long rope made of twisted thongs of raw hide, made fast by a hook to the staple at the end of the pole, and having iron rings attached to it at proper distances, into which rings the yokes are hooked. **1835** A. Smith *Diary* (1940) II. 32 The crocodile sometimes takes off tractoes and the iron rings have been found in the stomachs of some that have been killed. *Ibid.* 309 Wagons with trak tow rims etc. complete. **1836** A.F. Gardiner *Journey to Zoolu Country* 319 The baggage waggon sunk to the axles in the mud; twice the tractow was broken in the endeavour to urge it forward. **1850** J.E. Methley *New Col. of Port Natal* 22 A span of twelve or fourteen oxen .. are attached by yokes fastened on the neck to a long chain or treck-tow, which is made fast to the dissel-boom. **1864** S. Turner in D. Child *Portrait of Pioneer* (1980) 7 The trektouw or rope made of hide by which the oxen pull the wagon broke, and the wagon ran back off the road. **1872** [see *inspanning* (inspan *v.*)]. **1878** H.A. Roche *On Trek in Tvl* 185 A thump from impatient fists .. makes him clatter the trek-tow chain. **1899** *Natal Agric. Jrnl* 31 Mar. 4 All words in connection with trekking are of Dutch origin, 'trektouw,' the long hide rope or chain of modern days on which the oxen pull. **1910** J. Angove in J. Mockford *Here Are S. Africans* (1944) 91, I would .. have been able to buy a brand new buck-wagon, new yokes and a wire trek-tow! **1939** S. Cloete *Watch for Dawn* 300 The oxen .. were put in. The trek-tous slipped over their backs and strained tight as they came into line. **1955** L.G. Green *Karoo* 115 One great advantage of the raw hide *trektou* is that it does not attract lightning. **1969** T. Montgomery in F.G. Butler *When Boys Were Men* 183 The axles were made of wood and our trek towen of riems tied together, which were very apt to break especially in wet weather. **1977** F.G. Butler *Karoo Morning* 117 This fellow had a problem. How to connect the trek tow to the aardvark's tail? **1994** M. Roberts tr. *J.A. Wahlberg's Trav. Jrnls 1838–56* 55 Hans Joubert cheats me over the trektouw. *Ibid.* 59 Trektouw riem eaten by a dog, who paid for his prank with his life.

trexel var. treksel.

tribal authority *n. phr. Hist.* A body consisting of local chiefs and headmen, the lowest of the three tiers of government in a 'homeland'. See also homeland sense 1.

Established by the Bantu Authorities Act, No. 68 of 1951. See also the note at territorial authority.

1951 *Act 68* in *Stat. of Union* 1154 'Tribal authority' means a Bantu territorial authority. *Ibid.* 1158 A tribal authority shall .. generally administer the affairs of the tribe and communities in respect of which it has been established. **1961** *Off. Yrbk of Union 1960* (Bureau of Census & Statistics) 332 In terms of paragraph (c) of sub-section (1) of section *nine* of the *Bantu Authorities Act*, 1951 (Act No. 68 of 1951), the proceeds of .. levies, where they are applicable to tribes of communities in respect of which tribal authorities have been established, shall be paid into the treasury of such authorities. *c*1970 C. Desmond *Discarded People* 225 Many, including officials of the Tribal Authority, have recently built very big houses in the 'locations' so obviously they do not believe they are going to be moved. **1986** P. Maylam *Hist. of Afr. People* 167 The bottom tier was to comprise a Tribal Authority consisting of local chiefs and headmen. In the middle was the Regional Authority, which overlay two or more Tribal Authorities and drew upon the membership of the latter. **1987** *New Nation* 23 July 1 Lebowa tribal chiefs are demanding a 'vigilante levy' from residents to finance a shadowy terror campaign against villagers. The tribal authorities this week issued notices to hundreds of families .. demanding a total of more than R70 per household.

tribal college *n. phr. Hist.* During the apartheid era, a university located in an ethnic 'homeland' for the exclusive use of students belonging to that ethnic group; loosely, any university for a particular ethnic group; also called *bush college* (see bush *adj.*[1] sense 2). See also homeland sense 1.

1962 L.E. Neame *Hist. of Apartheid* 140 The National Union of Students, representing the English-speaking students, declared the proposal that 'tribal colleges' would not be able to search for the truth as their foundation rested on 'a belief in the racial inferiority of the Africans'. **1968** [see bantustan sense 2]. **1974** *Drum* 8 Aug. 63 (*letter*) I ask your readers to give me the names of schools I can go to after passing J.C. where I can specialize with the first three subjects together with shorthand and typing. I am not keen on Phapama, Tawana and Mopeli Tribal College. **1986** *Sowetan* 25 Apr. 4 Black students had no say in the making of these tribal colleges and separate institutions of learning. **1991** A. Van Wyk *Birth of New Afrikaner* 15 It was as a verligte that I parted with journalism in 1969 to join the Department of History at the University College for Indians on Salisbury Island in Durban harbour ... Small wonder that I was annoyed when I learned that fellow Nats were sneering at us for working at a 'tribal college'.

tricam /ˈtraɪkæm/ *adj.* and *n. Hist. colloq.* [Abbrev. of TRICAMERAL.]

A. *adj.* TRICAMERAL *adj.*

1989 *Stanger Mail* 11 Aug. 4 This conference of Tasa reaffirms its resolution of 1984, wherein it rejected the introduction of the tricam system of Govt.

B. *n.* TRICAMERAL *n.*

1989 *Sunday Times* 31 Dec. 18 Constitutions are supposed to regulate political conflict – tricam simply exacerbated it.

tricameral *adj.* and *n. Hist.* [Eng. prefix *tri-* three + *cameral* 'of the chamber', both orig. fr. L.]

A. *adj.* Of or pertaining to the parliamentary system (1983–1994) in which the legislature consisted of three ethnically-based houses; also used allusively of anything related in some way to this parliament or its activities; TRICAM *adj.* Also *transf.*, meaning 'racist' or 'divided'. See also *House of Assembly* (HOUSE sense 1 c), *House of Delegates* (HOUSE sense 2), *House of Representatives* (HOUSE sense 3), MINISTERS' COUNCIL, OWN AFFAIR, PRESIDENT'S COUNCIL sense b.

1984 *Daily Dispatch* 21 June 3 Powers and privileges are to be extended to members of the coloured and Indian chambers in the new tricameral Parliament. **1985** *Sunday Times* 15 Sept. 14 President Botha created the tricameral Parliament and thereby insulted 70 percent of South Africa's people by leaving the blacks out. **1985** PLATZKY & WALKER *Surplus People* p.xxix, The new tri-cameral parliamentary system became a reality in 1985 as a result of the implementation of the new 1984 constitution. **1986** R. SEGAL in *New Statesman* (U.K.) 28 Mar. 19 South Africa's tricameral parliament .. excludes the black majority, while purveying ersatz representation for Coloured and Indian in separate annexes to the white house. **1987** M. BADELA in *Weekly Mail* 10 July 3 A tricameral *no* from the UDF leaders. **1987** *New Nation* 1 Oct. 12 They have been living in tents provided by the red cross, despite promises of permanent housing by tricameral MPs. *Ibid.* 22 Oct. 11 A fair number of Indians and coloured people will tell you that they refused to be party to the tricameral joke. **1989** *Reader's Digest Illust. Hist.* 481 Under the new tricameral system .. the Bills bogged down in the coloured and Indian houses. **1989** *Sunday Times* 31 Dec. 3 An extra parliament will be added to our existing tricameral system. This will .. change the name of Parliament to the Quadriplegic System of Democratic Government. **1990** *Weekly Mail* 2 Mar. 22 We still have a tricameral television service. **1990** *South* 22 Mar. 13 His tricameral explanation of the sticky and soet koeksister of the title: 'Singular yet plural, individual yet united, all nicely covered with the golden syrup of democracy.' **1991** *Weekend Post* 1 June 8 The spectre of black domination and the end of the tricameral gravy train.

B. *n. nonce.* The tricameral parliament or parliamentary system; TRICAM *n.*

1991 *Weekend Post* 1 June 8 A 'permanence' beyond the tricameral.

tril(l) visch var. DRILVIS.

Tripartite Alliance *n. phr.* Also with small initials. A political grouping made up of the African National Congress (see ANC *n.*[1]), the South African Communist Party (see SACP), and COSATU. Also *attrib.*

1992 *Grocott's Mail* 15 Sept. 1 An ANC-led Tripartite Alliance march. **1992** *Weekend Post* 19 Sept. 1 Many of the participants in the large mid-week tripartite alliance marches in Port Elizabeth are unemployed people who hope liberation will bring jobs. **1993** *Sunday Times* 12 Dec. 2 Internal problems .. were identified as a major threat to the Tripartite Alliance. **1994** *Grocott's Mail* 19 Aug. 2 The Tripartite Alliance (ANC, Cosatu and the South African Communist Party) will convene a general meeting .. on Sunday.

triple, trippel varr. TRIPPLE *n.*

‖**trippelaar** /ˈtrəpəlɑː(r)/ *n.* [Du., *trippel* (see TRIPPLE *n.*) + agential suffix *-aar.*] *trippler*, see TRIPPLE *v.*

[**1852** C. BARTER *Dorp & Veld* 37 (Pettman), Those who possess this accomplishment to perfection are in high estimation among the Dutch, who call them *trippelaars.*] **1858** W. IRONS *Settler's Guide to Cape of G.H. & Natal* 159 The performances of 'pasgangers' and 'trippelaars,' in former days, are probably lost to history. **1900** S.T. PLAATJE *Boer War Diary* (1973) 88 He is a good horse and 'takes the Bun' as a trippelaar, but is slow – most piteously slow. **1971** *Farmer's Weekly* 11 Aug. 112 Chestnut gelding 15 hands. 9 Years, trippelaar can carry 240 lb easily.

tripple /ˈtrɪp(ə)l/ *n.* Also **triple, trippel.** [(Englished form of) S. Afr. Du. *trippel(en)* (fr. Du. *trippen* to trip, skip).] A horse's gait in which both left and then both right legs move together, similar to the amble.

1860 A.W. DRAYSON *Sporting Scenes* 67 His action .. is peculiar; he rarely walks, his mode of progression being a sort of tripple, at which he travels at about six or seven miles an hour: trotting is not admired by the Boers. **1880** P. GILLMORE *On Duty* 296 A slow tripple – a pace similar to what is designated 'racking' in North America. **1882** W.R. LUDLOW *Zululand & Cetewayo* 12 The usual pace of colonial horses is the triple, just between a walk and a trot. **1889** H.A. BRYDEN *Kloof & Karroo* 14 The triple is a sort of shuffling canter on three legs, peculiar to the Cape, and a horse that possesses it commands a higher price than its fellows. **1901** *Field* 9 Mar. 322 The 'tripple' is between a fast walk and a slow trot. **1910** D. FAIRBRIDGE *That Which Hath Been* (1913) 269 Frans and Joan rode at a gentle 'tripple', for the first night of their journey was to be spent at Elsenberg .. no great distance from Parel Vallei. **1944** J. MOCKFORD *Here Are S. Africans* 66 He schooled his pony to pace the *tripple* – an easy gait, a smooth-flowing lope – which tired neither of them. **1946** S. CLOETE *Afr. Portraits* 60 Each time they are off-saddled, the Boers let them roll, which they say rests them by relieving the stiffness that comes from carrying a heavy man at the canter or triple for long periods. This triple corresponds more or less to the American pace, the horse moving both near and then both off feet together, instead of alternately. **1967** S.M.A. LOWE *Hungry Veld* 87 The horses responded to the mood of their masters ... By sensitivity to the feel of the guiding hands and the stiffness of the limbs of the rider, they knew they were required to break into a quick tripple. **1977** F.G. BUTLER *Karoo Morning* 91 This horse was best for a long canter, that for a tripple. **1986** W. STEENKAMP *Blake's Woman* 112 A smooth gait which .. was called a 'trippel' and was favoured by the Boers. **1989** J. HOBBS *Thoughts in Makeshift Mortuary* 297 The three horsemen .. pass Gordon riding at a fast triple. **1991** *Best of S. Afr. Short Stories* (Reader's Digest Assoc.) 104 The 'trippel' or 'tripple' .. is a smooth, easy gait that is one of the least tiring for both horse and rider.

tripple /ˈtrɪp(ə)l/ *v. intrans.* Also **triple.** [See prec.] Of a horse: to move at the 'tripple' pace.

1888 *Cape Punch* 6 June 125 *(caption)* A Horse Study. (The Stud Horses). Old Farmer: 'My! But will they tripple!' **1899** G.H. RUSSELL *Under Sjambok* 49 Getting into their saddles, slowly trippled away (a kind of run, neither gallop, canter or trot), in the direction from which they had first arrived. **1900** S.T. PLAATJE *Boer War Diary* (1973) 90 He was trippeling very fast and as he is loath to turn quickly he ran plump into the wire fence. **1900** J.B. ATKINS *Relief of Ladysmith* 80 A scarcely intermitted line of Boers moved from left to right on their ponies, jogging, trotting, or trippling. **1903** *Longman's Mag.* Dec. 151 That easy hand canter usual in such Free State horses as do not tripple. **1931** F.C. SLATER in *Best of S. Afr. Short Stories* (1991) 104 That old grey mare .. was a splendid piece of stuff. People used to laugh when they saw me *trippling* along on her. **1971** *Farmer's Weekly* 11 Aug. 112 Four year old gelding ... Quiet to ride but willing. Can tripple. **1991** *Weekend Post* 13 Apr. (Leisure) 1, I once heard him talk .. about a horse .. that could tripple. I didn't know what he meant.

So **trippler** *n.*, a horse which is able to tripple; TRIPPELAAR; **trippling** *vbl n.* and *ppl adj.*

1852 A.W. COLE *Cape & Kafirs* 259 Since that event [he] had only ambled about on a 'trippler' warranted not to shy. **1875** C.B. BISSET *Sport & War* 192 It was a grey, trippler, one of those rare horses of the Cape which amble along and carry you as if you were sitting in a chair. **1901** *Field* 9 Mar. 322 The Boer never rides his horse at the trot, but at a quick walk or canter, and a step peculiar to the country and called 'trippling', or, as we should style it, ambling. **1905** *Blackwood's Mag.* (U.K.) Oct. 526 He could still hear the trippling patter of the other rider. **1910** A.B. LAMONT *Rural Reader* 68 A horse that has good qualities of wind and limb, and is a good pacer or 'trippler', is preferred as a riding horse by our farmers. **1924** L. COHEN *Reminisc. of Jhb.* 50 Oom Piet .. saddled his best trippler, and hurried into Johannesburg. **1937** C.R. PRANCE *Tante Rebella's Saga* 67 Oom Betje came out .. ready to ride his 'trippler' Swartbooi from the Cape to Cairo for a sufficient bet. **1950** D. REED *Somewhere S. of Suez* 221 For the present the Basuto remains a free man and proud. He is a figure of dignity in his blanket and plaited straw hat, on his tripling pony. **1958** S. CLOETE *Mask* 182 Only the shuffle of the trippling horses' unshod hoofs broke the stillness of Africa. **1963** —— *Rags of Glory* 145, I got good ones, real Boer ponies. Two tripplers. All about fifteen hands. **1966** I. VAUGHAN *These Were my Yesterdays* 49, I will buy you a nice little trippling horse and you can learn to drive the Buick. **1991** *Best of S. Afr. Short Stories* (Reader's Digest Assoc.) 104 A trippling horse moves both left legs and both right legs alternately, unlike the more bumpy trot, when diagonally opposite legs move together. **1991** *Weekend Post* 13 Apr. (Leisure) 1 Trippling is not a natural gait.

troepie var. TROOPIE.

trommel /ˈtrɔm(ə)l/ *n.* [Afk., box, tin.]

1. A tin trunk or storage box, esp. a medicine chest (see also HUIS-APOTHEEK), or the trunk in which a soldier stores his possessions. Also (occas.) dim. form **trommeltjie** [see -IE.]

1926 P. SMITH *Beadle* (1929) 49 Andrina carried a small, square, gaily painted tin canister, called a 'trommeltje', with padlock and key attached. In the trommeltje, in which the rusks were to be put, were little red cinnamon cakes for the miller's children. **1958** E.H. BURROWS *Hist. of Medicine* 190 Each household had its own medicine-chest or *trommel*, usually the ready-made *huis-apotheek* of the Cape Town chemists. **1975** J.H. PICARD in *Eng. Usage in Sn Afr.* Vol.6 No.1, A tin trunk is a trommel and the mess tray or 'dixy' is a varkpan. **1980** *Sunday Times* 18 May, *(caption)* No, sonny, you're not meant to keep your teddy bear in your trommel. **1982** *Sunday Times* 29 Aug. (Mag. Sect.) 29 What's three extra meals for 10 people? She simply digs deeper into her 'trommel'. **1987** *Fair Lady* 21 Jan. 144 Welcome to .. the eclectic English/Afrikaans language of survival that's armyspeak ... With two brothers, there was no way to avoid it. *Troopies, trommels* and the *lieut* infiltrated their English. **1989** [see quot. at *(old) Dutch medicine* (DUTCH *adj.* sense 2)]. **1992** H. HURWITZ *Informant, Johannesburg*, I have seen pictures of trommels of Dutch medicines used in the 2nd Anglo-Boer War. **1994** *House & Leisure* Jan. 121 A yellow metal *trommel* R199 at Oregon Cottage and Antiques.

2. *Mining.* [Perh. fr. U.S. Eng. (ad. G. *trommel* drum), reinforced by Afk.] A cylindrical screen or sieve.

*c*1936 *S. & E. Afr. Yr Bk & Guide* 395 The broken ore from the shaft is screened by steel gratings known as grizzlies, the portion passing through being sent direct to the stamp mill. The remainder is delivered into revolving trommels, where it is washed and is then discharged on to revolving tables or travelling belts for sorting. **1984** D.B. BOSMAN et al. *Bilingual Dict.* 537 *Trommel*, .. revolving screen, trommel *(mining)*.

tronk /trɔŋk, trɒŋk/ *n.* Formerly also **tronck.** [S. Afr. Du. (possibly in earlier use in other Du. colonies), perh. ad. Pg. *tronco* trunk, stock (of a tree), the stocks, by extension 'prison' (the etym. given in *OED*), or ad. Buganese and Sunda (a dialect of Bali) *tarunka* prison.

Mansvelt (in his *Idioticon*, 1884) suggests that the word might be derived fr. Fr. *tronc* a box, or fr. Persian *turang* a prison. Pettman (1913) suggests Malay *trungku* 'to imprison' as the source, and Bense (1939) agrees, referring to quot. 1693 below, and suggesting that 'the word was borrowed by the Dutch from Malay in the form *trunk*, and introduced, not only into the Eng. colonies on the Coromandel Coast, .. but also into South Africa at the time of van Riebeeck. The form may then have become *tronk* under the influence of the above-mentioned Ptg. or Fr. words, if not under that of European Du. *tronk* in the sense of L. *truncus*' (i.e. tree trunk). While the Malay word for 'prison' is *panjara*, in Buganese and Sunda *tarunka* is used, and 'the word *tronk* could thus have come into Afrikaans through the Buganese or Balian slaves' (Achmat Davids, 'Words the Cape slaves made', *S. Afr. Jrnl of Linguistics*, Vol.8 No.1, 1990).]

a. *colloq.* Prison; TRUNK. Also *attrib.*

[**1693** *Govt Rec. Fort St. George (Madras)*, The justices .. committed him to the Custody of the Tailliars in the Trunke, but on the 21 September last, he made his escape by breaking through the Prison wall.] **1798** LADY A. BARNARD in Lord Lindsay *Lives of Lindsays* (1849) III. 475 The cow .. had offended the laws by walking on the parade, the consequence of which was, like other caitiffs, she was put in the Tronck. **1803** S.E. HUDSON *Diary 1803–6* (Cape Archives, A609–4), One man, a Slave to an Englishman at Cape Town, has been guilty of numberless crimes. This had brought him once or twice to the Scafford [*sic*] where he had been publickly Flogged and several times privately punished in the Tronk. **1805** R. SEMPLE *Walks & Sketches* 11 Close to the water's edge yonder is the prison, used chiefly for slaves, and called here the Tronk. **1824** J. BARRY in G.M. Theal *Rec. of Cape Col.* (1903) XVII. 245 On the evening of the 6th I visited the Tronk .. and in a Dungeon of that place found Jacob Elliott with his thigh fractured. **1834** T. PRINGLE *Afr. Sketches* 301 The drostdy *tronk*, or gaol, which I visited more than once, .. was an interesting though deplorable scene. **1846** *Natal Witness* 7 Nov. 3 He .. was so violent, that if I could have got assistance, I would have sent him to the Tronk. **1853** T. SHONE Diary. 15 Apr., This morning The Police took all Henry's servants to the tronk for Stealing of Mr Banks India Corn. **1866** E. WILSON *Reminisc.* 140 Arresting a Native without a proper pass in his possession, or taking a drunken Hottentot to the tronk in a wheelbarrow, are, for the most part, the respective duties of the Frontier Armed and Mounted Police and the town police. **1870** [see PASS sense 1]. **1882** J. NIXON *Among Boers* 126 If a black man were to enter a white church, he would probably be taken off to the 'tronk', or jail, for his unheard-of presumption. **1891** J.P. LEGG in *Cape Illust. Mag.* I. 96 A 'slim' fellow often finds himself out done in 'verneukerij,' and ends perhaps in the 'tronk,' a word which is shouldering out gradually the English word 'jail.' **1900** F.R.M. CLEAVER in M.M. Cleaver *Young S. Afr.* (1913) 171, I myself am keeping in good condition, though at first the reaction from outdoor life to the inactivity of tronk told upon me considerably. **1905** *Blackwood's Mag.* (U.K.) Sept. 389 You shall be caught. You shall go to tronk. **1910** L.D. FLEMMING *Settler's Scribblings* (1921) 88, I found myself in prison — commonly called the 'tronk'. **1911** BLACKBURN & CADDELL *Secret Service* 76 Say you are guilty and get off with a month in tronk. It's not bad in our tronk. **1930** J. BUCHAN *Four Adventures* 258 I .. know something about the inside of prisons. You may build them like great castles, or they may be like a back-veld *tronk*, only mud and corrugated iron. **1959** J. PACKER *High Roof* 61 Coloured boys and White girls, it don't do here. You finish up in the tronk! [**1970** H. KUPER *Witch in my Heart* 70 *Tronk* is the Afrikaans word for gaol and more commonly used by Africans in the towns, who associate gaol with the Afrikaans-speaking police.] **1976** S. CLOETE *Chetoko* 113 'The police,' he said. '*Ja*, they'd throw my Missus into the tronk for giving an old man a drink because he is black.' **1977** D. MULLER *Whitey* 35 To steal a chicken is nothing. To steal a bottle of brandy from a bar is tronk business. **1988** *Saturday Star* 28 May 36 The Immorality Act (*remember?*) would encourage the fuzz to .. watch through curtains ajar and test the warmth of the bedsheets before clapping the loving sinners into the nearest tronk.

‖**b.** *comb.* **tronkvoël** /-fʊəl/ [Afk., *voël* bird], 'gaolbird'; **tronk volk** /- fɔlk/ [Afk., *volk* people], former prison inmates.

1973 *Contrast 32* Vol.8 No.4, 23 He looked like .. a thug, a real **tronkvoël**. **1987** *Drum* Dec. 27 Mbeki may be a tronkvoël, but he's in the illustrious company of Kwame Nkrumah, Jomo Kenyatta, Robert Mugabe, Kenneth Kaunda and others. **1824** W.J. BURCHELL *Trav.* II. 159 It may .. sometimes occur, that among these **tronk volk** (jail-people), there may be good and deserving Hottentots, as well as worthless. **1839** W.C. HARRIS *Wild Sports* 25 Nearly all of these being *tronk volk*, or in other words, discharged criminals, no agreement less binding .. would have answered our purpose. **1937** F.B. YOUNG *They Seek a Country* 408 Missionary boys perhaps, but *tronk-volk*, jail-birds for certain.

T-room var. TEAROOM.

troopie *n. colloq.* Also **troepie**. [Prob. fr. Rhodesian (Zimbabwean) Eng., ad. *trooper*.] A private soldier, esp. a national serviceman. Also *attrib.*

1972 J.H. PICARD in *Eng. Usage in Sn Afr.* Vol.6 No.1, Some of the troepies with particularly dirty habits .. receive the title *vuilgat* ... Of course some 'troepies' are impatient for their period of service to end. **1977** *Rand Daily Mail* 13 Jan., Man, us troepies is sommer bangled. Any troepie will tell you that the drie-streep korporaal met 'n volume control who sent that Jimmy vuiluil to Durban Beach after he was bangled in the varkpen is a koptoe ou. Gobbledegook? By no means. It is the lingua franca of the Defence Force. **1979** *Daily Dispatch* 21 Mar. 10 If one man in a platoon did not pull his weight then all the men suffered, .. and they soon 'encouraged' the tardy troopie to do his bit. **1980** *Sunday Times* 14 Dec. 17 Troopies come marching home on Friday. Friday is D-Day — Demobilisation Day — for thousands of young men. **1980** *Cape Times* 17 Jan. 2 It's hard to believe it in sweltering January, but a troopie's best friend is his greatcoat — with his steel trunk and his pillow next on the list. **1981** *Fair Lady* 8 Apr. 7 We live in a small town which has been a camp for basic training for thousands of troepies over the years. **1981** [see BELLERYNA]. **1982** *Grocott's Mail* 8 Oct. 2 For new troopies at Grahamstown's 6 SA Infantry Battalion, last week was their first pass after 12 weeks of basic training. **1987** [see TROMMEL]. **1989** [see GYPPO *n.*]. **1989** *Daily Dispatch* 21 Apr. 4 Troopie suicides high. **1992** *Weekly Mail* 6 Mar. 30 Any troepie who shows reticence or queasiness is branded a 'moffie'.

tropsluiter /ˈtrɔpsleɪtə, ˈtrɔpslœɪtər/ *n. hist.* [Afk., professional mourner, fr. Du. *trop* crowd, multitude + *sluiten* to close + agential suffix *-er*.] One hired to walk at the end of a funeral procession, thus extending its length. See also HUILEBALK.

1926 P.W. LAIDLER *Tavern of Ocean* 157 Funerals were pageants not soon forgotten. Professional mourners — 'huilbaken,' as they were called — accompanied the coffin and were paid to weep copiously. For eighteen pence a head 'tropsluiters' or extra individuals to lengthen the procession, in number according to the rank of the deceased, could be obtained. **1927** C.G. BOTHA *Social Life in Cape Col.* 65 There was also another class of paid mourners called 'tropsluiters,' who had to follow in pairs at the rear of the procession. **1952** G.M. MILLS *First Ladies of Cape* 76 The huilbalken were distinct from the tropsluiters who were merely employed to lengthen the procession. The tropsluiters always changed places with one another as they walked in the procession, because of the superstition that the last person following the deceased, would be the first to die. **1965** A. GORDON-BROWN *S. Afr. Heritage* III. 10 Funerals were accompanied at one time by professional mourners .. and others, 'Tropsluiters', were paid merely to walk in pairs to lengthen the procession.

true *adj.* In interjectional phrases.

a. (*as*) ***true as God***, also **strews Guard**, **stroes God**, **s'true's -**, **'strue's -**, **strues -**, **struse God**, **strusgod**, **true's God** [tr. obsolescent Afk. expression *so waar as God*]: 'really', truly'; used to emphasize the truth of an assertion. Occas. shortened to **s'trues**.

1946 P. ABRAHAMS *Mine Boy* (1954) 73 It is so, sister, 's true's God. **1948** E. HELLMANN *Rooiyard* 79 If my daughter get a baby before her time, true as God, I'll kill her. **1954** J. WILES *Moon to Play With* 228 Ag, *nee*, .. man, but you say the funniest things, 'strue as God. **1956** A. SAMPSON *Drum* 85 There's no difference really, man; true's God! They both want the same thing: they both want apartheid! **1957** D. JACOBSON *Price of Diamonds* 5 One said that his wife was in Johannesburg and as true as God he was going to see her; another that he had been offered a good job and as true as God he was going to start working again. **1959** [see RAMKIEKIE]. **1963** A. FUGARD *Blood Knot* (1968) 157 Morris: Really? Zach: S'true's God. **1971** J. MCCLURE *Steam Pig* (1973) 33 True's God, me not doing anything bad by that side! **1976** M. MELAMU in *New Classic* No.3, 9 Me, I'll run away from this place, *'strues God*, then I'll see who her punch-bag will be. **1980** A. DANGOR in M. Mutloatse *Forced Landing* 159 The glass showcase filled with cheap ornaments purchased on the Parade. 'Stroes merram, real bone china!' **1982** [see AIKONA *int.*]. **1990** M.M. HACKSLEY (tr. E. Van Heerden) in *Lynx* 186 He'd .. heard that the Lord had ridden on a donkey, but it wasn't .. a Karroo donkey, 'struesgod it wasn't. **1993** S. DIKENI in *Cape Times* 21 Aug. (Top of the Times) 17 The nation drinks from Sunday to Sunday non-stop. 'Strue's God, the Lord can punish me.

b. With euphemistic substitution. (*as*) ***true as Bob***, also **'s'strue's Bob**, **'strue as Bob**, **'strue's Bob**, **struse Bob**, etc., in the same sense.

1971 *Informant, Grahamstown* Then I'm resigning, 'strue as Bob. **1973** on Radio South Africa 22 Mar. (Take a Chance), As true as Bob, I nearly went right through the windscreen. **1975** 'BLOSSOM' in *Darling* 12 Feb. 119 One thing about January in Durbs — I dunno why everybody doesn't melt, s'true's bob. Talk about the yoomidity. **1981** *Fair Lady* 9 Sept., Ah dunno what Ah'd do iff itt was Gawie end me. Struse bob. Ah don't. **1989** [see Locher quot. at SOUSTANNIE]. **1990** *Style* July 62 'But it's — true as Bob — just like that with my relatives. They're all rich and high up and they wanted f—all to do with me.' **1992** C.M. KNOX tr. *E. Van Heerden's Mad Dog* 137 'Are they very rich?' ... 'Yes. Their house is as big as the school.' 'You lie.' 'Strue's Bob, just as big.' **1994** on Radio Algoa 19 Aug., (*advt*) 'You lie!' 'True's Bob!'

Truidjie-roer-my-nie /ˌtreɪki ˈruːr meɪ ni, ˈtrœɪki-/ *n.* Also **Truitjie-**, **Truytje-**, **-roer-mij-niet**. [Afk., *Truidjie* familiar or affectionate form of *Gertruida* Gertrude + *roer-my-nie* 'touch-me-not', by folk-etymology fr. Du. *kruidje-roer-mij-niet*.] KRUIDJIE-ROER-MY-NIE.

[**1896** see KRUIDJIE-ROER-MY-NIE.] **1913** C. PETTMAN *Africanderisms* 407 *Roer-mij-niet* or *Truitje roer-mij-niet*, .. This appellation is given (1) to two plants whose leaves when touched emit a very unpleasant odour — *Melianthus major* and *M. camosus*, *Vehl.*; and (2) to a very thorny plant the spines of which do more than suggest caution. **1924** D. FAIRBRIDGE *Gardens of S. Afr.* 154 Everyone at the Cape is familiar with the long spikes of red-brown flowers and the glaucous leaves of the Melianthus comosus, though they probably know it better under its Dutch name of *Truytje, roer mij niet* — Gertrude, touch me not. **1949** [see KRUIDJIE-ROER-MY-NIE].

trunk *n. obs.* [Englished form of S. Afr. Du. *tronk*.] TRONK sense a.

[**1732** T. PHILIPS in A. Churchill *Collection of Voy. & Trav.* VI. 215 (Gold Coast) Our factory .. stands low near the marshes ... Within is a long yard .. also a storehouse, a trunk for slaves.] **1799** in G.M. Theal *Rec. of Cape Col.* (1898) II. 322 If any Slaves shall be found in the street after dark without a Lanthern .. they shall be lodged in the Trunk. **1816** R.B. FISHER

Importance of Cape of G.H. 139 By the laws of the Colony, a master or mistress is forbid to punish a slave, but must send him to the trunk or jail for punishment, by the fiscal or his men. **1821** W. SHAW Diary. 28 Oct., Preached to the prisoners about twelve in number, at the Trunk or prison. *a***1827** D. CARMICHAEL in W.J. Hooker *Botanical Misc.* (1831) II. 33 The culprit shall be sent to the common trunk or prison, where he receives a certain number of stripes, according to the nature of his offence. **1835** T.H. BOWKER Journal. 18 Oct., One woman put in the trunk, let out and put in [a]gain. **1840** J. HARE in *Imp. Blue Bks* Command Paper 424–1851, 52 He [*sc.* Tyali] asked how it happened that the prisoners confined in our trunk, and at hard labour in our streets, were all Hottentots and black people. **1851** T. SHONE Diary. 25 Oct., In the afternoon Old Bradshaw order'd the Constables to take me in charge, my nights lodging was In the Trunk. *a***1858** J. GOLDSWAIN *Chron.* (1946) I. 27 On they forth day late we rived at Uitenhage Trunk ware we ware deposeted in averey little sell: hear we ware fead with Bread Beaf and water. **1880** [see LOCATION sense 3 a]. **1928** L.P. GREENE *Adventure Omnibus* 53 He was caught .. and sent to trunk – for my sake he was punished.

Trust *n. hist.* [Special sense of general Eng.] Ellipt. for *South African Development Trust* (or, formerly, *South African Native Trust, - Bantu Trust*), an authority established by Act 18 of 1936 to purchase land with which to create (exclusively) black settlement areas. Often *attrib.*, as ***Trust area, Trust land, Trust tenure***, etc. See also HERTZOG BILLS, RESERVE.

1936 *Act 18* in *Stat. of Union* 92 A corporate body, to be called the South African Native Trust, hereinafter referred to as the Trust, is hereby constituted ... There shall be vested in the Trust .. all Crown land which has been reserved or set aside for the occupation of natives; .. all Crown land within the scheduled native areas, and all Crown land within the released areas. **1949** ELTON MILLS & WILSON in Davenport & Hunt *Right to Land* (1974) 52 The average arable holding over which a domestic family averaging 7,2 members has effective rights of cultivation is .. $3\frac{1}{2}$ acres on Trust land ... The policy of the Administration is to give as many families as possible a little land, and the holdings are smallest where Administrative control is greatest, on Trust and communal land. *c***1970** C. DESMOND *Discarded People* 129 In about 1960 the farm was bought by the Bantu Trust ... The rest of it was replanned on the usual Trust Farm lines, which meant that the people who were scattered over the farm had to demolish their houses, move to the allocated residential sites and build new houses. **1974** DAVENPORT & HUNT *Right to Land* 51 The extension of Trust tenure throughout the Union, 1936. **1985** PLATZKY & WALKER *Surplus People* p.xi *Trust land*, Land purchased by the State in terms of the 1936 land legislation and administered by the SANT/SADT. *Ibid.* 89 The Development Trust and Land Act of that same year [*sc.* 1936] completed the package deal ... It established the South African Native Trust (later the Bantu Trust, still later the Development Trust). This Trust was empowered to see that all the released land was acquired and to adminster that land. It became the registered owner of almost all the reserves. *Ibid.* 116 In the early 1960s the first and most notorious of apartheid's relocation camps began to appear on remote stretches of Trust land. **1988** *E. Prov. Herald* 10 Mar. 7 The government yesterday scrapped a large number of restrictions affecting black businessmen in trust areas and paved the way for full property rights for people in these areas.

try *v. intrans.* [Special sense of general Eng.] In the phr. ***to try for white***, and (less frequently) ***to try for black, to try for coloured***, to attempt to pass oneself off as a white (or black or coloured) person in order to gain the privileges and advantages of belonging to that ethnic group; cf. PLAY sense 1. Also *attrib.*, and *fig.*

[**1948** O. WALKER *Kaffirs Are Lively* 131 It is any wonder that the number of young Coloured people who 'try *vir Europeane*' (as they put it) is a considerable factor in population trends?] **1951** L.G. GREEN *Grow Lovely*, In the United States they call it 'crossing the line'. The phrase in Cape Town is 'trying for white' ... Success .. carries its own penalties. It means, often enough, the loss of family and friends. All the dark-skinned ones must be left behind, passed in the street without a word of greeting. **1962** D. MARAIS *I Got a Licence*, (*caption*) If Bantu bars are going to be open an hour later now's the time to try for Black. **1964** G. GORDON *Four People* 58 'She is so light skinned,' said Katie, 'why doesn't she try for Coloured? Then she wouldn't need a pass.' *c***1968** J. PAUW in *New S. Afr. Writing* 54 She was Coloured. She was one of hundreds he knew, who had tried for white and got away with it. **1970** *Daily Dispatch* 30 Jan. 14, I decided that the tribal terrier would have to Try for White ... After a visit to the vet for various injections .. , his mange spots disappeared and his coat glowed with health. **1975** *Sunday Times* 23 Sept. (Mag. Sect.) 5 Ellen L— has fought bitterness and anger for most of her life. Descended from a Jewish grandfather and a Xhosa grandmother, her fair skin and pale eyes early on put her in a 'try for white' situation. **1987** C. RICKARD in *Weekly Mail* 3 Apr. 6 McBride 'tried for white' at one stage, and after being rejected and humiliated, took on 'an African identity'.

Hence **try-for-white** *n.*, one who tries for white.

1989 J. HOBBS *Thoughts in Makeshift Mortuary* 202 She hasn't cut us dead like most of the other try-for-whites do when they make it to the other side.

tsaa *int. obs.* Also **tza**. [See SA *int.*] SA *int.*

[**1821** C.I. LATROBE *Jrnl of Visit* 254 Mr. Fereira .. encouraged the dogs by the usual cry of *Zaza, Zaza*.] **1833** S. KAY *Trav. & Researches* 492 'Show us the enemy, and cry tza!' (Tza is the cry used to encourage a dog to attack.) **1899** J.P. FITZPATRICK *Tvl from Within* 275 It was very well to punish the dogs, but what was to happen to the owner of the dogs, who stood by urging them on and crying 'Tsaa!'? **1913** C. PETTMAN *Africanderisms* 516 *Tsaa!*, (Kaf. *uku Tsatsa*, to run quickly, to make speed). The common South African expression when urging a dog to attack.

tsaba-tsaba /ˈtsaːba ˈtsaːba, ˈtsɑːbə ˈtsɑːbə/ *n.* [fr. Zulu *tsaba* (v.) separate; see sense b.] **a.** *Music.* A style of dance music popular in the 1940s, combining traditional African melody and rhythm, particularly those of FOCHO, with jazz and Latin-American dance rhythms. **b.** The dance performed to the accompaniment of this music, in which two dancers repeatedly approach each other and (often at the shout of 'Tsaba' from a watcher) move apart again without having touched. **c.** A shout of 'tsaba'. Also shortened form **tsaba**, and *attrib.*

1941 W.M.B. NHLAPO in *Bantu World* 15 Mar. 9 The Jazz Maniacs were regarded as a 'marabi' or 'Tsaba-Tsaba' band ... They were fine and at one time outstanding exponents of hotcha strains. **1941** —— in D.B. Coplan, Urbanization of African Performing Arts. (1980) 334 Everyone spoke of Tsaba Tsaba ... Everybody sang it ... Some dance bands played it; it had the spirit of Africa in it. Regardless of the torrents of scathing abuse, it swept the country ... It (Tsaba) is an indispensable part of our musical and dance culture. **1972** A.A. MENSAH in *Ibid.* 332 A male and female danced towards each other, shaking the knees in what is sometimes described as a 'rubber-legged' style; pelvic movement was also emphasized in addition to footwork. Just before the couple made contact a shout of the word 'Tsaba!' was given and they danced backwards to their starting points. **1980** D.B. COPLAN Urbanization of African Performing Arts. 334 The literate professionals who specialized in American swing generally considered themselves both socially and culturally superior to the tsaba-tsaba audience. *Ibid.* 335 In 1947, August Musurugwa composed his classic *tsaba* dance tune, *Skokiaan* ... It became an international success, topping the American Hit Parade in 1954. **1989** *Reader's Digest Illust. Hist.* 416 The jive of New York mixed with traditional African dance steps to produce the *tsaba-tsaba*, a wildly energetic dance that inspired local composers to create music to fit the whirling feet.

tsala kahle var. SALA KAHLE.

tsamma /ˈtsama, ˈtsɑmə/ *n.* Also **(t')sama, tsama, tsame, t(')samma.** [Nama *tsamas* watermelon.] In full ***tsamma melon***: the trailing plant *Citrullus lanatus* of the Cucurbitaceae; its round, fleshy melon; BITTER APPLE sense 1; BITTER-MELON; BITTER WATERMELON; (*offensive*) *kaffir melon, - watermelon*, see KAFFIR *n.* sense 2 e; KARKOER; MAKATANE; *wild melon, - watermelon*, see WILD sense a.

The tsamma occurs mainly in the Kalahari desert, but also in Botswana, the Northern Transvaal, and the North West Province.

1886 G.A. FARINI *Through Kalahari Desert*, Here also we came across the first sama I had seen. This plant is invaluable to both man and beast on the desert. It is the 'wild water melon,' .. and serves both as food and drink for human beings as well as cattle and horses, its fleshy body contains a quantity of watery juice, and its seeds a considerable proportion of oil. It yields two crops in the year ... The ripened fruit will lie for a year without decaying, provided there is not rain. **1898** G. NICHOLSON *50 Yrs* 92 These melons are called by the natives 'tsamma,' and are about the size of a round Dutch cheese. The flavour is insipid, and the water which the traveller obtains from them by cutting them up and simmering them in a pot over a slow fire is rather flat, but sweet and wholesome. *Ibid.* 93 The 'Thirst Land' .. is known to have been occasionally (in tsamma season) traversed by native hunting parties. **1899** [see KORANNA sense 1]. **1915** W. EVELEIGH *S.W. Afr.* 67 That typical product of the Kalahari desert, the tsama melon *Citrullus vulgaris*, is found. Both man and beast rejoice in this juicy melon. In its raw state it has remarkable thirst-quenching properties, and when cooked it is a satisfying food. The seeds are oily and very fattening. [**1937** H. KLEIN *Stage Coach Dust* 150 Desert treasure: wild water melons, worth their weight in gold, called by the natives t'sama. These melons grow in the desert after a rainy season and store precious water.] **1941** A.G. BEE *Kalahari Camp Fires* (1943) 129 Millions of wild melons (samas) scattered over the veld. **1945** L.G. GREEN *Where Men Still Dream* 173 All the animals, from the elephant and lion down to the desert mice, flourish on the speckled green melon. T'samma, roasted in the camp fire and then cooled, quenches the Bushman's thirst. **1961** L.E. VAN ONSELEN *Trekboer* 117 The tsamma is the most important vegetable growth. This melon-like, watery squash is the desert's gift to the thirsty traveller. Stock can be maintained on its fleshy pulp in severe droughts. **1977** *Family Radio & TV* 6 June 18 In the Kalahari Desert .. I show viewers how a tsamma melon, growing in profusion, is cut open and the juice squeezed out. It's like a miniature waterfall. **1985** *Custos* Sept. 8 A tsamma is a trailing plant, the fruit of which looks like a watermelon and is the size of a spanspek ... Bushman hunters .. depend largely on tsammas for their water needs. By cutting the tsamma in half and slicing the fleshy part in thin shreds they squeeze enough water out to fulful their needs. **1989** *Personality* 6 Feb. 46 The tsamma melon is bitter to taste but it supplies essential moisture for animals in the desert. **1992** *Getaway* Apr. 41 The tsamma, 90 per cent of which consists of water, has thick walls which trap the moisture inside and last throughout the dry season.

ts(c)hokka var. CHOKKA.

tschwala var. TSHWALA.

tseiran var. TZEIRAN.

tsessebe /ˈtsesəbi/ *n.* Also **tsesebe, tsessabi, tsessêbe, tsesseby, tssess(e)be.** Pl. unchanged, or **-s.** [SeTswana *tshêsêbe*.] The large antelope *Damaliscus lunatus* of the Bovidae, reddish-brown in colour, and noted for its speed of movement; *bastard hartebeast*, see HARTEBEAST sense b; *bastard hartebeest*, see HARTEBEEST *n.* sense b; SASSABY; formerly also called HARTEBEAST (sense a), HARTEBEEST (*n.* sense a).

[**1801** in G.M. Theal *Rec. of Cape Col.* (1899) IV. 392 Saw an unknown antelope called by the Boetshoeanas Tsietsebee.] **1857** D. LIVINGSTONE *Missionary Trav.* 26 Zebras, giraffes, tsessébes, kamas or hartebeests. *Ibid.* 66 When the annual inundation begins .. antelopes such as the springbuck and tsessebe (Acronotus lunata) are swept down by its rushing waters. **1896** H.L. TANGYE *In New S. Afr.* 245 A large herd of tssessebe have been seen. **1907** W.C. SCULLY *By Veldt & Kopje* 206 Just before camping at sundown the boy shot a tsessabi, the flesh of which is among the very best the wilderness affords. **1910** J. BUCHAN *Prester John* (1961) 99 'Home with you,' I said. 'Home, old man, as if you were running down a tsessebe.' **1929** J. STEVENSON-HAMILTON *Low-Veld* 91 Tsessebe in the plains, and impala in the bush, both rely upon their speed. **1936** C. BIRKBY *Thirstland Treks* 297 The old hunter spoke .. of the *tsesebe's* rich purple coat. **1951** A. ROBERTS *Mammals* 287 *Tsessebe* ... When alarmed it travels at a fast lumbering gallop and can keep up this pace for suprising distances. **1978** *S. Afr. Digest* 29 Sept. 17 The Tsessebe, or Sassaby antelope, has returned to Natal after an absence of about 80 years. The *Conservationist* reports these antelopes are the fleetest of all African antelopes. **1980** J. HANKS *Mammals* 37 *Tsessebe* (Sassaby) *Damaliscus lunatus* ... Overall colour from reddish-chestnut to chocolate brown. Shoulder height about 120 cm. **1992** *S. Afr. Panorama* Mar.-Apr. 52 Tsessebe (*Damaliscus lunatus lunatus*).

tsetse /ˈtsetsi/ *n.* Also **tetse, tse-tse, tsetsi, tzetze.** [SeTswana *tsètsè* (see quot. 1846).] In full ***tsetse-fly***:

1. The tropical fly *Glossina morsitans* of the Tabanidae, which by its bite transmits sleeping-sickness to man, and the often fatal NAGANA to horses, cattle, and other domesticated animals; FLY sense 1. Also applied to other species of *Glossina*. Also *attrib.*, and *comb.* (instrumental), as **tsetse-bitten, tsetse-borne, tsetse-conveyed** *adjs.*

[**1846** J.C. BROWN tr. *T. Arbousset's Narr. of Explor. Tour to N.-E. of Col.* 181 Bitten by an insect, very numerous there, called *fly-flea* in Sechuana (*ntsintsi-a-tsetse*) on account of its bite.] **1849** E.D.H.E. NAPIER *Excursions in Sn Afr.* II. 396 Horses were killed either by lions or horse sickness, and the fly called 'tzetze'. All his oxen were killed by this insect. **1850** R.G.G. CUMMING *Hunter's Life* II. 215 They [*sc.* the black people] also told me that I should lose all my cattle by the fly called 'Tsetse'. **1851** D. LIVINGSTONE *Jrnl* (1960) 64 Several Englishmen have lost all their cattle horses & dogs by being led into a Tsetse district. **1853** *Ibid.* 139 There is only one small strip of Tsetse country to hinder one going westward. **1857** — *Missionary Trav.* 75 Tsetse, or Glossina Morsitans, .. is much larger than the common house-fly, and .. of .. brown colour ... It is well known that the bite of this poisonous insect is certain death to the ox, horse and dog. The mule, ass and goat enjoy the same immunity from the tsetse as man and the game. **1871** J. MACKENZIE *Ten Yrs* (1971) 203 Nothing could save the tsetse-bitten oxen from certain death. **1878** A. AYLWARD *Tvl of Today* 228 It has been asserted by many writers that the tsetse-fly is not fatal to donkeys and mules. I know contrary to be the fact. **1882** C. DU VAL *With Show through Sn Afr.* I. 266 The 'Tsetse fly', a little insect .. whose bite, but a trifling annoyance to man, is a death-warrant to stock of all kinds. **1887** A.A. ANDERSON *25 Yrs in Wag-gon* II. 29 Extensive districts are infested with the tsetse fly, where a traveller cannot go in with horses or oxen, for one single bite is death. **1893** F.C. SELOUS *Trav. & Adventure* 55 The tse-tse fly swarmed along the River Kadzi, and was a great pest, keeping one in a perpetual state of irritation all day long. **1906** H. RIDER HAGGARD *Benita* p.x, Tetse-bitten cattle. *Ibid.* 101 We can take .. the horses with us, and sell them in the north of the Transvaal .. before we get into the tetse-fly belt. **1917** *Nature* 18 Oct. 127 Tsetse-conveyed sleepingsickness. **1918** S.H. SKAIFE *Animal Life* 140 The well-known tsetse-flies, of which several species occur in the tropical regions of Africa, belong to the same family as the house-fly and the blow-fly. **1925** *Times* (U.K.) 29 Dec. 11 It was believed that wild game .. formed a permanent reservoir from which tsetses could convey 'nagana' to domestic stock. **1936** E. HEMINGWAY *Green Hills of Afr.* 108 It was a hot place to camp ... Everywhere were tsetse flies, swarming around you, biting hard on your neck, through your shirt, on arms, and behind the ears. **1945** L.G. GREEN *Where Men Still Dream* 102 We have our laboratories, the trypanosome has been isolated, drugs have been produced to protect men against the sting of the tsetse. Yet thousands still die. **1952** H. KLEIN *Land of Silver Mist* 123 Tsetse fly was bad in the lowveld ... A good salted pony was worth £60 or more. **1965** *New Scientist* (U.K.) 26 Aug. 504 Wild game don't suffer from nagana, the tsetse-borne trypanosome disease that disastrously affects domestic cattle. **1966** *Cape Argus* 19 Sept. 14 Mr. S— must have been bitten by an infected tsetse fly while on safari. **1977** *Daily Dispatch* 18 Aug. (Suppl.) 2 Africa would be able to supply the world with meat if only one little insect could be eradicated, the tsetse fly (Glossina morsitans). **1980** *S. Afr. Panorama* Dec. 44 The old wagon trails were strewn with the bones of trek oxen pulled down by the dreaded tsetse fly. **1983** J.A. BROWN *White Locusts* 121 We lose animals and transport riders. It's tsetse country. **1987** *Fair Lady* 18 Feb. 149 Viv has her mandatory brandy-and-soda to ward off any marauding tsetse flies.

2. *transf.*

a. *Pathology.* NAGANA. Also *comb.* (instrumental), as **tsetse-haunted, tsetse-poisoned, tsetse-stricken,** *ppl adjs.*

1857 D. LIVINGSTONE *Missionary Trav.* 591 We had travelled very slowly, the tsetse-stricken oxen being now unable to go two miles an hour. *a*1875 T. BAINES *Jrnl of Res.* (1964) II. 117 Here, some of the Kafirs caught the Tsetse, or fly. **1882** J. NIXON *Among Boers* 257 The malaria and tsetse-haunted flats round Delagoa Bay. **1906** H. RIDER HAGGARD *Benita* p.x, Hard, tetse-poisoned flesh. **1936** H.C. BOSMAN *Mafeking Rd* (1969) 9 That's the trouble with these low-lying districts, like the Marico and the Waterberg: there is too much horse-sickness and tsetse-fly here. **1952** L.G. GREEN *Lords of Last Frontier* 22 He experienced all the vicissitudes of the pioneer life ... Tsetse carried off his oxen. **1977** *Argus* 3 July 16 They were breeding them [*sc.* zebra-donkey crosses] commercially because of their immunity to tsetse.

b. *obs.* Country infested by the tsetse-fly; FLY sense 2 b.

1877 T. BAINES *Gold Regions of S.-E. Afr.* 41 We followed it till the herd escaped into the Tsetse Fly.

tshaile var. TJAILE *n.*

Tshangane var. SHANGAAN.

‖**tshila** /ˈtʃiːla/ *n.* Also **ukutshila.** [Xhosa *tshila* spin; perform the initiation dance. The form with *uku-* reflects the Xhosa infinitive prefix, used also to form verbal nouns.] A traditional exhibition dance performed by Xhosa initiates to manhood (ABAKWETHA), consisting of vigorous backward and forward movements of the pelvis and performed, as a test of endurance, to rhythmical beats on a dried ox-hide; KWETHA DANCE. So **tshila** *v.*, to perform this dance.

1937 B.J.F. LAUBSCHER *Sex, Custom & Psychopathology* 128 At each of their family kraals the *abakweta* have to *tshila*. On these occasions they dance the actual *Tshila* dance as follows ... While the *abakweta* perform these *Tshila* dances taught them by the *amakankata* the others toss coins to them. **1952** H. KLEIN *Land of Silver Mist* 48 The abaKweta are distinguished by their fantastic dress ... All exposed parts of the body are caked with white clay and thus attired they perform the dance known as the ukutshila .. one of the few relics of barbarism openly practised by South African tribes. **1978** *Voice* 15 Nov. 8 In most cases at the eve of their pass out the Abakhwetha perform a competition dance which is known as 'Ukutshila and Ukuyeyezela' (spin and chant).

tshisa var. CHEESA.

tshisa-nyama var. CHESANYAMA.

Tshivenda var. VENDA *n.* sense 2.

tshongololo var. SONGOLOLO.

tshwala /ˈtʃwɑːlə, ˈtʃwaːla/ *n.* Forms: α. **chali, chaloa, chuala, chu(a)llah, chwala, joila, jowalla, jwarlar, schwala, tjaloa, tjoalla, tjwala, ts(c)hwala, tswala, tyalla, tyalli, t(y)wala (')twyala;** β. **itywala, outchualla, outchuella, utshuala, utshwala, uTyala, utyal(l)a, utyalwa, utywala.** [Zulu *utshwala*, Xhosa *utywala* (formerly *utyalwa*); however, in some quots the writers may be using the Sotho synonyms (see JOALA).]

a. A thick home-brewed beer made traditionally among African people from fermented sorghum millet and water; any commercially-prepared equivalent; *African beer*, see AFRICAN *adj.*[1] sense 2 b; BOJALWA sense 2 a; IJUBA sense b; JABULA; JABULANI sense b; JOALA; MTOMBO sense 1 b; NDAMBULA; *sorghum beer*, see SORGHUM sense 2. See also LETING, MABELA, UMQOMBOTHI. **b.** A similar beer made of maize; cf. MAHEWU, MAIZA. In these senses also called BANTU BEER or KAFFIR BEER (sense a), both of which are offensive, and KB.

α. **1803** J.T. VAN DER KEMP in *Trans. of Missionary Soc.* I. 438 The Caffree corn is, as I think, a kind of millet, but grows from seven to ten feet high ... The corn .. is eaten boiled .. ; they likewise malt it, after which it is boiled, and the decoction fermented. This drink they call *tjaloa*. **1834** T. PRINGLE *Afr. Sketches* 509 Of the millet beer or ale the Caffers have two kinds, the common sort termed *chaloa*, and the stronger *inguya*. The millet (Sorghum) is first carefully malted, afterwards boiled in large earthern pots, and then regularly fermented. **1835** G. CHAMPION in J. Bird *Annals of Natal* (1888) I. 206 The twyala, or common beer of the country, made from Kafir corn, or Indian corn, fermented in water, is brought to the king daily. **1855** G.H. MASON *Life with Zulus* 153, I found them sitting under the shade of their craals or of mimosa bushes, taking snuff, drinking 'Joila' (Caffre beer), or smoking the root of a species of wild hemp that grows in great profusion all over the colony. **1860** D.L.W. STAINBANK Diary. (Killie Campbell Africana Library KCM8680) 19 July, I saw Masingua and drank some 'Schwala' for the first time — being very thirsty. I liked it very much. **1862** J.S. DOBIE *S. Afr. Jrnl* (1945) 21 A gourd full of sour drink called 'jowalla'. **1870** A.F. LINDLEY *After Ophir* 306 *Shimyan* and *jwarlar* were produced for our consumption. **1897** F.W. SYKES *With Plumer in Matabeleland* 256 Laden with offerings of grain, Kaffir beer (tshwala), freshly killed meat, and other useful produce, the credulous natives approach the mystic site. **1899** G.H. RUSSELL *Under Sjambok* 240 The man of this land can also abide here, eat my food, and drink my čhuala, but I do not say that he is welcome. **1908** [see SKOKIAAN sense 1 a]. **1930** S.T. PLAATJE *Mhudi* (1975) 46 The tshwala .. is brewed with the grain from Tsauana's corn-bins. **1941** in A.M. Duggan-Cronin *Bantu Tribes* III. Pl.150, *Tshwala*, beer, the favourite food of the Swazi, takes over a week to make, and goes through many complicated stages. **1952** H. KLEIN *Land of Silver Mist* 75, I called my young men. They were full with 'twyala and knew not what they were doing. **1972** *S. Afr. Panorama* Nov. 36 'Tshwala', the beer brewed by the Bantu, is more than a mere social drink. The traditional village brew is extremely nutritious and is considered a national foodstuff. **1976** A. DELIUS *Border* 183 'This beer, this tyalli,' he cries, holding up half a calabash full. **1981** *Voice* 18 Feb. 2 The amount of tshwala guzzled during the Xmas periods .. could fill the Vaal Dam. **1990** *Fair Lady* 28 Mar. 138 *Twala*. It's the stuff they give to black mineworkers. A kind of non-alcoholic beer, rich in vitamin B. **1990** R. MALAN *My Traitor's Heart* 227 Someone would press a bowl of bitter tshwala beer into my hands. **1994** M. ROBERTS tr. *J.A. Wahlberg's Trav. Jrnls 1838–56* 50 In the evening they drank Tjoalla (Kaffer drink, intoxicating).

β. **1836** A.F. GARDINER *Journey to Zoolu Country* 30 A large bowl of outchualla (native beer) was sent to my hut by order of Dingaan. **1839** W.C. HARRIS *Wild Sports* 133 A whole calabash of the native malt liquor. This detestable beverage, which is denominated *outchualla*, is of a whitish colour, frothy, and produced from fermented Kafir corn. **1850** J.E. METHLEY *New Col. of Port Natal* 77 They .. offered us outchuella, or native beer, a white liquid of acid taste, extracted from Kaffir corn, and fermented, of which they are very fond, and not unfrequently get intoxicated upon it. **1852** C. BARTER *Dorp & Veld* 217 (Pettman), Utshuala, a fermented liquor made from the grain of the amabele, or Kaffir-corn. **1855** J.W. COLENSO *Ten Weeks in Natal* 103 Two large pots of uTyala were then brought in ... It is a sort of beer, made of millet or Indian corn – looks like yeast, and tastes like a mixture of yeast and cider. **1855** R.B. STRUTHERS *Hunting Jrnl* (1991) 90 My hunters had .. been .. shooting game and drinking Itywala (beer) and abusing the people. **1860** W. SHAW *Story of my Mission* 458 About harvest time .. there is a supply of fresh corn to make fermented liquor called utyalwa, (kaffir beer). **1866** W.C. HOLDEN *Past & Future* 278 Drinking utyalla or beer .. being rather reserved for .. festival occasions, than used as a common every-day beverage ... Utyalla is made from the amabele or Kaffir Corn; and being long boiled in large beer-making pots, inbeza, and subjected to fermentation, it becomes intoxicating, acquires a sour taste, and is much liked by the people. **1878** T.J. LUCAS *Camp Life & Sport* 103 The Zulus make a kind of beer called 'outchualla,' which is strong and not unpalatable. This is prepared by the women, who make quite a secret of the process. **1909** N. PAUL *Child in Midst* 198 The women fill huge gourds with utywala or Kafir beer. **1935** R.S. GODLEY *Khaki & Blue* 113 The amount of alcohol contained in 'utywala' is very small. **1955** J.B. SHEPHARD *Land of Tikoloshe* 110 Utywala, the other kind of Kaffir beer, is also a nourishing food but, because it is made with grain which has sprouted, it is much more potent than Marewu. **1962** A.J. LUTHULI *Let my People Go* 57, I myself encouraged the healthy brewing of *utshwala*, corn beer. **1967** S.M.A. LOWE *Hungry Veld* 145 Ukhambas of utywala (native beer) were handed round. **1979** M. MATSHOBA *Call Me Not a Man* 153 She bears the children and brings them up while you drink *utshwala* and sleep with concubines. **1986** P.A. MCALLISTER Xhosa Beer Drinks. 41 Apart from the common *utywala* (Xhosa), *utshwala* (Zulu) or *bjalwa* (Sotho), made in earlier times almost exclusively from sorghum but nowadays mainly from maize, a variety of similar but non-alcoholic beverages were made. **1988** P. DU PLOOY *Informant, Pietermaritzburg* The origins of shebeens lie in the gathering of men at the homestead to drink *utshwala* brewed by women.

c. *rare.* Loosely, any liquor; BOJALWA sense 2 b; also called BANTU BEER (*offensive*), KB.

α. **1962** J. TAYLOR 'Tsotsi Style'. (*lyrics*) Me busy making money mighty fast, Selling the white man's tshwala. **1964** G. GORDON *Four People* 109 What would you do, if you were a Native like us? How would you get your *tywala*?

β. **1945** F.C. SLATER *New Centenary Bk of S. Afr. Verse* 230 *Utywala*, Xhosa for Kaffir beer; the term is also applied to spirits.

T'Slambi, T'Slambie(s) varr. SLAMBIE.

Tsonga /'tsɔŋga/ *n.* [See TONGA.]

1. SHANGAAN sense 1 a; cf. TONGA sense 1.

1940 A.A. JACQUES in *Bantu Studies* XIV. 259 It should be noted that it is not correct to spell the name of this people [*sc.* the Shangana-Tsonga] *Tonga* or *Thonga* ... Since the recent decisions taken by the Tsonga Language Board concerning orthography, there should be no difficulty in adopting the form *Tsonga*. **1970** M. WILSON *1000 Yrs before Van Riebeeck* 5 The Tsonga .. sought much of their food in river estuaries and lagoons, lacing the mouth of each river with fish traps. **1975** *S. Afr. Panorama* Oct. 22 Gazankulu, the Homeland of the Shangaan and Tsonga located in the North eastern Transvaal. **1976** WEST & MORRIS *Abantu* 105 The Tsonga, although not members of the Nguni family, were considerably influenced by the Zulu ... In the 19th century we know that the Tsonga were living in scattered units in the border area between Natal and Mocambique. **1985** PLATZKY & WALKER *Surplus People* p.xxx, There have been serious fights between Tsonga and Sotho over the Gazankulu/Lebowa borders. **1990** *Weekend Post* 6 Oct. (Leisure) 4 He met his death at the hands of a Shangean [*sic*] (Tsonga) warrior.

2. The language of the Shangaan people, esp. the dialect spoken in South Africa; TONGA sense 2. Cf. SHANGAAN sense 2.

1970 *Std Encycl. of Sn Afr.* II. 106 The Tsonga group is also often called the Shangana group. These languages are spoken by the descendents of the Zulu chief Shoshangana. *Ibid.* 306 The first portions of the Scripture in Tsonga .. appeared in 1883. **1971** *S. Afr. Panorama* Dec. 1 The complete Bible is already available in .. North and South Sotho, Tswana, Central Tswana, Venda, Xhosa, Zulu, Tsonga and the South West African Ndonga and also Nama. **1973** *Drum* 22 May 31 (*letter*) I would like girls not older than 22, and letters can be written in English, Zulu, North Sotho or Tsonga. **1973** M. HORRELL *Afr. Homelands* 60 Gazankulu was declared a self-governing territory within the Republic ... Its seat of Government is Giyani, and Tsonga is recognised as an additional official language. **1985** PLATZKY & WALKER *Surplus People* 125 For most South Africans, Gazankulu is barely known. For nearly one million Tsonga-speaking people, it is the bantustan they are tied to by apartheid policies. **1993** *Weekend Post* 9 Oct. 9 Sadly, .. multilingualism, including North and South Sotho, Swazi, Tsonga, Tswana, [etc.] .. is out.

Tsongastan see -STAN.

tsoro /'tsɔrɔ/ *n.* [Shona (Zimbabwe).] MORABARABA. Also *attrib.*

[**1958** A. DELIUS in R.M. Macnab *Poets in S. Afr.* 33 And in our cities under sunset's bloodshot eye, absorbed beyond the passing feet, Small gamblers play at tsolo on the kerb.] **1966** J. FARRANT *Mashonaland Martyr* 167 They played 'Tsoro' with small stones in prepared hollows of earth. **1968** L.G. GREEN *Full Many Glorious Morning* 49 You can watch a game of *tsoro* or African draughts near the city centre. **1990** *Personality* 5 Feb. 47 Around his waist, waking or sleeping, was slung his green canvas bag – full of his very own Tsoro pebbles, and when he squatted in the red dust to place them in the Tsoro game, Aie! How they gleamed in the sun!

tsotsi /'tsɔtsi/ *n.* Also **tsotsie**. [Origin uncertain; widely believed to be a Sotho corruption of *zoot suit*, see quots 1956, 1962, and 1980; C.T. Msimang (1987, in *S. Afr. Jrnl of Afr. Langs* Vol.7 No.3, p.82) writes 'The origin of the term *tsotsi* is not known ... Although the term has a Sotho phonemic structure, it is not a Sotho lexical item'. See also quots 1938.]

1.a. *hist.* Esp. during the 1940s and 1950s, a young black gangster or hoodlum who affected a particular style of language and flashy dress; PANTSULA sense 1 b. **b.** Loosely, a (young) black urban criminal. **c.** Used affectionately or contemptuously: a bad (young) man. Also *attrib.*, and *transf.* See also BOY sense 2 a, *location boy* (LOCATION sense 3 c). Cf. AMALAITA, CLEVER, COMTSOTSI, DUCKTAIL, SHEILA sense 2, SKOLLY, SPOILER.

[**1938** *Star* 1 June 16 Alleged to be members of the 'Ishotsi' gang, with aims of robbing and murdering natives. **1938** *Rand Daily Mail* 3 June 6 The accused were members of the 'Ishotsi' gang, .. composed for the specific purpose of robbery.] **1949** *Cape Argus* 20 July 8 (*heading*) Tsotsi gangs who hate Bantu students. **1949** *Cape Times* 10 Sept. 8 The 'Tsotsi' may be distinguished by his exceedingly narrow trousers which hardly reach his shoes, or else by his 'zoot suit'. **1950** *Report of Commission to Enquire into Acts of Violence Committed by Natives at Krugersdorp* (UG47–1950) in L.F. Freed *Crime in S. Afr.* (1963) 130 The shebeen queens resort to devious means to evade police detection, such as .. calling upon the tsotsi gangs for protection. **1954** *Star* in L.F. Freed *Crime in S. Afr.* (1963) 78 Young men roaming the city streets .. selling liquor to natives, smoking dagga, and accosting passers-by, .. the White tsotsis of Johannesburg ... European hooligans, known to the police as 'White tsotsis', terrorize people in the central area. **1956** T. HUDDLESTONE *Nought for your Comfort* 81 *'Tsotsi'*— .. familiar enough to have become a term of abuse when applied by a European to an educated African, a term of contempt tinged with fear when used by one African boy of another ... Every country in its large cities has its 'cosh-boys', its 'wise-guys', its 'gangsters,' its 'Teddys'. And the 'tsotsi,' the real genuine 'tsotsi,' is all of these ... The origin of the name is interesting, for it is a corruption of 'Zoot Suit,' and the 'tsotsi,' like the Teddy-boy, is supposedly characterised by the cut of his clothes. **1959** L. LONGMORE *Dispossessed* 317 Ntsotsi is a word denotating the notorious young thieves, murderers and terrorists, so commonly found in the locations, going around in well-organized gangs with a terminology of their own and whose main weapon is a large knife. I have used the now generally accepted form of the word: tsotsi. **1962** W.S. MANQUPU in *Star* 22 Feb. 14 The very name 'tsotsi' had its birth as a result of a film, shown in 1946 .. the all Negro 'Stormy Weather,' in which the cast wore stovepipe trousers .. and .. wide-brimmed hats. This type of dress became the vogue on the Reef, and the Sotho gave these youngsters the name 'tsotsis' ('tsotsi' being a Sotho word for stove-pipe trousers). **1963** L.F. FREED *Crime in S. Afr.* 126 A 'tsotsi' is one who follows 'the way of life of the sharp trousers', that is, trousers with legs narrowed at the bottom. **1963** WILSON & MAFEJE *Langa* 14 Within the category of townsmen an important distinction is made between the *tsotsi* set, who are violent and boisterous, and the respectable, 'decent people', of which the educated section forms the middle class. **1976** WEST & MORRIS *Abantu* 179 Crime is a major problem, and Soweto can claim the dubious distinction of being one of the most dangerous places in the entire country, where gangs and the delinquent *tsotsis* (hooligans) flourish. **1977** P.C. VENTER *Soweto* 146 Men's fashions saw the birth of a new, sleeker pair of trousers. The legs were tapered like stovepipes, tight in the crotch and even tighter around the ankles. In black townships and shanty towns the male youths immediately accepted the new fashion, and called it tsotsi trousers. **1980** D.B. COPLAN Urbanization of African Performing Arts. 350 The term *tsotsi* .. was an urban African pronunciation of 'zoot suit'. It indicated their orientation toward American popular culture, relative economic success, and flashy dress as a symbol of urban sophistication. *Ibid.* 442 *Tsotsi* .. suggested a clever, streetwise petty criminal or hustler, flashily dressed in urban American fashion. Today it applies broadly to any young, potentially violent African urban criminal. **1984** N.S. NDEBELE in *Staffrider* Vol.6 No.1, 45 Tsotsi violence. **1990** *Diversions* Vol.1 No.6, 8 Avoid a crooks tour – watch out for overseas tsotsies. **1990** M. KENTRIDGE *Unofficial War* 66 The *comtsotsis* .. preyed on commuters and mugged workers on pay-day much like *tsotsis* (gangsters) ... The difference was that they explained that their actions formed part of a political strategy. **1993** *Daily Dispatch* 14 Oct. 1 The PAC last night distanced itself from the violence .. and blamed it on 'tsotsi' (criminal) elements. **1993** [see LOST GENERATION].

2. *comb.* **tsotsi-taal** /-tɑːl/, also with initial capital, [Afk. *taal* language], FLAAITAAL. Also *attrib.*

The name 'tsotsi-taal' is seen as *derog.* by some, the terms FLAAITAAL or ISICAMTHO being preferred. Tsotsi-taal originated in the townships around Johannesburg, becoming particularly well-established in the 1950s. Spoken at first mainly by criminals, partly as a means of avoiding being understood by others within earshot, it has since come to be used more widely, esp. by young people, among whom it has more recently come to be called 'isicamtho' or 'scamtho'.

[**1951** *Drum* Nov. 10 To speak broken Afrikaans is one of the methods by which tsotsis identify each other, but each group has its own common vocabulary in the presence of strangers. **1956** A. SAMPSON *Drum* 101 As I sat down, between Bill and Can, I heard a murmur behind me of 'Laanis,' the *tsotsi* word for white men.] **1976** *Rand Daily Mail* 21 Apr. 5 Ordinary young men and women .. delight in chatting in any Black language or a Black language mixed with 'street' Afrikaans, commonly known as 'Tsotsi taal'.

1979 C. VAN DER MERWE in *Frontline* Dec. 17 If you know what's good for you, you'd better not call it tsotsi-taal. It's actually Flytaal, and proud of it. **1980** D.B. COPLAN Urbanization of African Performing Arts. 350 A new anti-social persona, *tsotsi* .. spoke .. *flytaal* or *mensetaal*, which by the late 40's had become known more widely as *tsotsitaal*. *Ibid.* 442 *Tsotsitaal* (*Flytaal; Mensetaal*), The Afrikaans-based urban African proletarian dialect, spoken by all urban African proletarians up until the 1960's, but especially by young juvenile delinquents, some of whom spoke no other language. **1982** D. BIKITSHA in *Rand Daily Mail* 14 Oct. (Eve) 5 Where fanagalo is gross, heavy and uncouth, tsotsi taal is smooth, facile and poetic ... With the little bit of schooling one had, the relation of certain tsotsi taal words to other world languages became obvious. **1982** M. MZAMANE *Children of Soweto* 6 In our street dialect, called tsotsi-taal, the lingua franca of black youth in South Africa .. we violated every known grammatical construction. **1982** *Pace* Oct. 49 Because Soweto is a melting pot of nations, languages tend to lose their individual purity, to merge with one another to reform as the vibrant tsotsitaal. **1983** *Natal Mercury* 8 June, Go to a doctor and tell him in tsotsi-taal that you need a certificate to say that you've been sick. If he's a 'bra' he'll knock off a certificate and say: 'Hier's hy, my bra.' But if he's a 'situation' he'll say: 'Hey, hey, I can't do that.' **1986** T. THOKA in *Eng. Usage in Sn Afr.* Vol.17 No.2, 19 Today, tsotsie-taal has become a street dialect, and is not confined to thugs. **1986** *Ibid.* [see MARABI sense 3]. **1987** C.T. MSIMANG in *S. Afr. Jrnl of Afr. Langs* Vol.7 No.3, 82 Tsotsitaal is a contact medium which developed when blacks of various ethnic groups were thrown together in the South African cities, especially on the Rand ... Tsotsitaal is also known as Flaaitaal. **1987** K. SOLE in Bunn & Taylor *From S. Afr.* (1988) 255 The tsotsitaal patois endemic to the townships. **1990** L. KAUNDA in M. Kentridge *Unofficial War* 24 If you speak Zulu you are Inkatha, but the *amaqabane* speak *tsotsi taal* (English, Afrikaans, some Zulu, some slang words from God knows where). **1990** A. MAIMANE in *Tribute* Sept. 32 That was the style of the Fifties. Right now I wouldn't want to write like that .. semi-sleek American, *tsotsi taal* style of writing. **1990** [see TUNE sense 2 d]. **1993** L. MADIKANE in *Weekly Mail & Guardian* 22 Oct. 17 As for going to the township to speak 'tsotsi taal': forget it pal. I will never be caught mouthing such linguistic vulgarity. **1993** [see ISICAMTHO]. **1994** H. MASEKELA on TV1, 16 Nov. (People of South), I have been thinking of making an album in tsotsi-taal and calling it 'Heita-daar'.

Hence **tsotsi-ism, tsotsism** *ns*, the tsotsi lifestyle and behaviour.

1952 T. MATSHIKIZA in *Drum* Apr. 15 A more ruthless condemnation of the menace of Tsotsi-ism. **1952** B. DAVIDSON *Rep. on Sn Afr.* 121 The conditions out of which have grown such strange and horrible manifestations of maladjustment as *tsotsi*-ism. **1959** L. LONGMORE *Dispossessed* 191 *Tsotsism* is spreading in a community which is socially ripe for it, where juvenile delinquency has become inevitable. **1977** P.C. VENTER *Soweto* 146 In his study on the history of tsotsism, Stanley Sikakane described the origin of the problem. **1980** D.B. COPLAN Urbanization of African Performing Arts. 357 Their targets were the location police .., *tsotsism* .., and physical conditions in the African areas.

tswala var. TSHWALA.

Tswana /ˈtswɑːnə, ˈtswana/ *n.* [fr. seTswana *baTswana*, see MOTSWANA.]

See also SOTHO-TSWANA.

1. SETSWANA. Also *comb.* (objective), **Tswana-speaking** *ppl adj.*

1937 *Bantu Studies* XI. 137 The orthography set out in the present pamphlet represents the latest result of a prolonged series of efforts made .. by the Education Departments .. to arrive at a uniform orthography of Tswana. **1948** M. GUTHRIE *Classification of Bantu Lang.* 68 In Tswana the verbal has the extra suffix – ŋ. **1953** [see β quot. at SETSWANA]. **1960** C. HOOPER *Brief Authority* 251 A number of the pamphlets appeared in the village. Written in Tswana, they implied that everybody who continued to patronise the white merchant might expect death by lightning. **1973** *Drum* 18 Jan. 19, I would like a photograph with the first letter and promise to answer all. I'm conversant in English, Ndebele, Sotho, Tswana, Shona. **1973** N. GORDIMER in *London Mag.* (U.K.) Feb.-Mar. 92 Out of the cheerful exchanges in the Tswana language there comes suddenly, in English, the authentic tone of Gaborone: 'I give it three years, and I buzz off.' **1981** *S. Afr. Panorama* Dec. 17 The Tswana Bible is the first complete Bible to have been published in a language of Africa south of the Sahara. **1981** *Bona* Jan. 12 (*advt*) Our news broadcasts in Tswana and English will be straight, no-nonsense reports ... Tune in to Radio Bophuthatswana. **1983** *Sunday Times* 3 July 6 The wedding took place at the magistrate's court in Hysterkrand, with the couple taking their vows in Afrikaans and Tswana. **1984** *Staffrider* Vol.6 No.1, 33 The village of Phokeng is the heartland of the Tswana-speaking Bafokeng people. **1988** [see sense 2 a].

2.a. Pl. unchanged, or **-s**. A member of a major group of western Sotho peoples living in the interior of southern Africa, and including the Bamangwato, Batlharo, Fokeng, Kwena, Ngwaketse, Rolong, Taung, and Thlaping peoples; BECHUANA sense 1 b; CHUANA sense 1 b; MOTSWANA sense a; *Western Sotho*, see SOTHO sense 1 c. Also *attrib.*, passing into *adj.*, of or pertaining to these peoples.

See the note at BECHUANA sense 1.

1949 I. SCHAPERA in M. Fortes *Social Structure* 104 In contrast to most other Bantu-speaking peoples of southern Africa, the Tswana tribes of the Bechuanaland Protectorate have remarkably few marriage prohibitions. **1957** C.G. SELIGMAN *Races of Afr.* (1939) 120 The Sotho .. includes the .. Tswana .. of Botswana and western Transvaal. **1965** *Fiat Lux* Mar. 8 In 1959 and 1960 .. 4 new University Colleges for the non-white communities were created — one for the Zulu nation, one for the Tswana and Northern Sotho, one for the coloured and one for the Indian People. **1970** B. DAVIDSON *Old Afr.* 37 It was a constantly recurring feature in Tswana history for a tribe to secede under a discontented member of the ruling family and to move to a new locality. **1971** *Rand Daily Mail* 5 Mar. 1 New Homeland. South Africa's 1.7-million Tswanas will become a self-ruling people with their own Parliament before the end of the year. **1973** M. HORRELL *Afr. Homelands* 97 Tswana tribesmen have, traditionally, not offered themselves in large numbers for employment as mine labourers. **1976** WEST & MORRIS *Abantu* 119 The Tswana are Sotho and live scattered over a very wide area extending beyond the Northern Cape Province and Transvaal into the Republic of Botswana. Ancestors of these Western Sotho peoples are believed to have entered the area in three main waves from the north. *c*1980 *S. Afr. 1979: Off. Yrbk* (Dept of Info.) 84 The 1,3 million Tswanas living in South Africa as well as the Tswanas living in the Republic of Bophuthatswana are closely related to the 600 000 people of the Republic of Botswana. **1980** LYE & MURRAY *Transformations* 98 In 1976 there were over two million Tswana of South African origin ... But only 736 000 of them (35 per cent) were resident in their 'homeland' of BophuthaTswana. **1988** S. MOLAKENG in *Frontline* Apr.-May 20 One man told me that Bop is tribal, only for Tswanas. 'We are made to pay money .. for schools but these schools only teach Tswana. Here, the Tswanas are in the minority.' **1990** R. STENGEL *January Sun* 38 The Tswana are a Sotho-speaking people of small, patrilineal communities who migrated into central South Africa in the fifteenth century ... In the nineteenth century, the Tswana were buffeted by the *Difaqane*, .. a series of bloody conflicts among the black tribes. **1993** *Africa S. & E.* July 8 Matthews, himself a Tswana, said the Zulus were predominant in South Africa.

b. *comb.* **Tswanaland**, see quot. 1974; cf. BOP sense 1.

1974 *Std Encycl. of Sn Afr.* X. 646 *Tswanaland*, Various territories within the borders of the Republic of South Africa, traditionally inhabited by the Tswana tribes spread in disparate units over parts of the Western Transvaal and Northern Cape, as well as a small area within the Orange Free State, and which, taken together, form the self-governing 'homeland' Tswanaland or, in the Tswana language, Bophuthatswana. *Ibid.* 647 In May 1971 Tswanaland became the first Bantu 'homeland' in the Republic of South Africa after the Transkei to receive a legislative assembly ... On 1 June 1972 the areas .. were declared a self-governing territory.

3. *hist. rare.* Only *attrib.*, of or pertaining to the former 'homeland' of BophuthaTswana.

1983 *Survey of Race Rel. 1982* (S.A.I.R.R.) 459 Only those people who were Tswana citizens or who were prepared to take out Tswana citizenship could share in the area's development.

Hence (*nonce*) **Tswanaize** *v. trans.*, to cause (something) to become Tswana in character.

1971 *Post* 28 Mar. 7 The Public Service of the TTA could not be speedily Tswanaised because there was a shortage of experienced Tswana manpower.

Tswanastan see -STAN.

Tucsa /ˈtʌksə/ *n. hist.* Also **TUCSA**. [Acronym formed on *Trade Union Council of South Africa*.] A federation of trade unions, formed in 1954 and dissolved in 1986. Also *attrib.*

By 1983 Tucsa was by far the largest union federation in the country, but subsequently shrank in size.

1966 *Survey of Race Rel. 1965* (S.A.I.R.R.) 238 Tucsa appears to maintain more careful membership records than do some of the other bodies ... During 1965 Tucsa has concerned itself increasingly with African workers. **1969** A. HEPPLE *S. Afr.: Workers under Apartheid* 67 The Trade Union Council of South Africa (Tucsa) was born in 1954 as a combination of unions to oppose the government's move .. to interfere with trade union freedom ... Individual members of Tucsa's executive made various attempts to force the issue of African membership but the body as a whole preferred to avoid it. *Ibid.* 68 A few small African trade unions which maintained some liaison with Tucsa unions, joined together to form the Federation of Free African Trade Unions. **1970** *Rand Daily Mail* 28 Sept. 11 Give Non-Whites rate for job, says Tucsa. **1979** R.M. IMRIE *Wealth of People* 130 Tucsa .. now has a membership in the region of 240 000, of which roughly 30 per cent are Whites, 60 per cent Coloureds and Indians and 10 per cent Africans. **1987** *Race Rel. Survey 1986* (S.A.I.R.R.) I. 239 In his presidential address on 2 December — when TUCSA's dissolution was announced — Mr Robbie Botha attacked the government, the emerging black unions, and the 25 unions that had disaffiliated from TUCSA in the last three years, blaming them all for the organization's demise.

tuc-tuc var. TUK-TUK.

tudong var. TOERING.

tuin place see PLACE *n.*[1] sense 2.

Tuiqua var. TIXO.

||**tuishuis** /ˈtœɪshœɪs/ *n.* Also (formerly) **thuishuis**. Pl. **-huise** /-hœɪsə/. [Afk., *tuis* home + *huis* house.] SUNDAY HOUSE. Also dim. form **tuishuisie** [see -IE] (pl. **-s**).

1913 A.B. MARCHAND *Dirk, S. African* 284 (Swart), The thuishuis was let to strangers. **1934** C.P. SWART Supplement to Pettman. 179 *Tuishuis*, The town-house kept by certain farmers and used by them only on those occasions when they visit the town; also known as Church House or Sunday House. **1970** E. MUNDELL *Informant, Pearston (E. Cape)* Most farmers have tuishuise in town (town-houses). **1984** C.M. KNOX in *Fair Lady* 25 Jan. 51 The old furniture was banished to the *tuishuis* (town house) .. the children stayed there during the week with a surrogate aunt and attended the village school .. returning to the farm every weekend. **1992** *Weekend Post* 17 Oct. 3 One of the nine Market Street *tuishuisies* she restored.

Tukkie /ˈtʌki/ *n. colloq.* [Afk., *Tuk* (see TUKS) + -IE.]

1. A student or alumnus of the University of Pretoria. Also *attrib.*, from or of this university.

1970 H.M. MUSMECI *Informant, Port Elizabeth* Tukkie. Students' expression for a student – past or present – from Pretoria University. **1973** *Star* 8 June 13 Stefan (a former Tukkie who started working as an engineer recently). **1974** *Sunday Times* 1 Sept. 15 Tukkie prof's topsy-turvey world. **1978** *Sunday Times* 24 Sept. 16 Pik is a Tukkie. **1979** *E. Prov. Herald* 10 Mar. 12 Two bright new stars burst onto the South African golfing scene at Humewood yesterday. The one is an 18-year-old Johannesburg schoolboy ... The other a young Tukkie from Pretoria, Louis Norval. **1982** [see TUKS]. **1987** *S. Afr. Panorama* May 43 In spite of his 78 years, the former Tukkie (student of the University of Pretoria) still has plenty of go. **1990** *Sunday Times* 4 Mar. 27 They kept out wave after wave of Tukkie jerseys for 28 minutes in the second half.

2. In *pl.*, sometimes used with singular construction. The University of Pretoria; (the members of) its sports teams, particularly its rugby team. Also *attrib.* See also TUKS.

1971 *Rand Daily Mail* 24 May 16 On Saturday Tukkies illustrated that they might be one of the leading club teams in South Africa as they hammered Pretoria, the Northern Transvaal champions, 30–3. **1973** *Star* 14 June 10 Tukkies Honour Medical Pioneers ... Pretoria University is to honour two founders of its medical faculty. **1973** *Weekend Argus* 16 June 8 The North-South confrontation became even more marked at Coetzenburg last Saturday when Tukkies were drubbed 14–3 by Maties. **1977** H.D.K. VAN DER MERWE in *Hansard* 20–24 June, Of course, we often have our differences. For example, he thinks the Maties are a better team than the Tukkies. **1978** [see POTCH]. **1984** *Pretoria News* 1 Feb. 1 Tukkies Rag celebrations are going to be a sober affair this year – and that's official. **1992** *Cape Times* 20 May 9 Stellenbosch has its oaks, Tukkies has its jacarandas.

Tuks /tʌks, ‖tœks/ *n.* [Afk., formed on *T.U.C.*, abbrev. of *Transvaal University College*, the institution's name until 1930.] The University of Pretoria; (treated as *pl.*) the students of this university. Also *attrib.* See also TUKKIE.

[**1927** *Star* 30 May 14 The following teams will represent Rand University in the inter-varsity matches against T.U.C., tomorrow.] **1971** *Rand Daily Mail* 26 July 5 Tuks veto exchange ... The Students' Representative Council of the University of Pretoria has rejected a plan for a multiracial student exchange programme. **1972** *Cape Times* 26 July 1 Rugby Tuks may play Maties. **1973** *Star* 8 June 13 When you first visited the Tuks campus, did you immediately recognise it as an Afrikaans university? **1978** *Sunday Times* 21 May 1 Tuks' hero was rangy fullback Pierre Edwards. **1982** *S. Afr. Panorama* Sept. 36 The arts and science departments were established at a branch of the Transvaal University College in Pretoria. This was the origin of the University of Pretoria; to this day the university is familiarly referred to as TUCS, and its students as 'Tukkies'. **1991** A. VAN WYK *Birth of New Afrikaner* 25 F.A. van Jaarsveld .. had promised me .. that at Tuks I would meet the cream of the Afrikaner youth. **1992** *Cape Times* 20 May 9 'Ag, have you never heard of Tuks?' asked a CP member, referring to Pretoria University.

tuk-tuk /ˈtʌktʌk/ *n.* Also **tuc-tuc**, and with initial capital. [Thai, echoic, for the sound made by the vehicle's two-stroke engine.] A three-wheeled taxi, being an adapted scooter, with covered seating for two or three passengers. Also *attrib.*

Similar vehicles are used in South and South-East Asia. Fleets were introduced first in Durban and later in Cape Town.

1988 *Daily News* 11 July 4 With its 'Tuk-tuks' and 'Mynahs', Durban is getting to grips with the transport needs of the eighties. **1988** J. SCOTT in *City Express* 18 Aug. 2 The introduction of scooter cabs (or Tuk Tuks, as someone has named them) .. will teach Capetonians to be hagglers. **1990** J. MICHELL in *Style* Nov. 54 Tuk-tuk taxis are the new thing, and one zips around in the back of these three-wheelers at far less than the price of a regular cab. **1990** *Sunday Times* 2 Dec. (Mag. Sect.) 40 Enjoy the surf and sand, ride on the tuc-tucs, paraglide and jetski off Addington Beach.

tula /ˈtuːlə, ˈtʊla/ *v. intrans.* Also **thula, to(o)la, toula**. [fr. the Nguni languages, in which it has the form *thula*.] Usu. *imp.* 'Be quiet'; 'hush'; 'shut up'.

1884 'E.V.C.' *Promised Land* 85 Nugget was undoubtedly getting the worst of it, we quickly dressed and jumping out of the wagon, shouted 'Toula, Toula,' meaning 'dry up'. **1899** G.H. RUSSELL *Under Sjambok* 81 'Toola!' (silence) I hissed, as I thrust my revolver barrel within an inch of his face. **1908** D. BLACKBURN *Leaven* 138 A burst of hysterical laughter .. brought the warder to the door shouting 'Tula!' (Silence!) **1930** S.T. PLAATJE *Mhudi* (1975) 47 Several voices already interjected, Tula (keep quiet), for the crowd had heard enough. **1952** F.J. EDMONSTONE *Where Mists Still Linger* 14 Even we smaller ones would be told to 'Tula' if we spoke out of turn. **1964** G. GORDON *Four People* 116 'Thula!' shouted Gus, truning round quickly and then as if to show the attendant – in case he did not understand the Xhosa word – where his own sympathies lay, followed it up with the English equivalent, 'Shut up!' **1971** *The 1820* Vol.43 No.10, 11 English as she is spoke – Toola = Belt up! [**1976** R.L. PETENI *Hill of Fools* 21 'Mamtolo, thula!' said Dakada sharply. 'I'm handling this.'] **1980** A. FUGARD *Tsotsi* 41 The baby .. was crying again ... He went to the bed and bending low over the puffed-up knob of a head shouted: 'Tula!' and then a second time, much louder, shaking the mattress with his hands. **1990** *Pace* May 2 Thula, come duze and listen to this juicy one. **1992** J. RAPHAELY in *Femina* June 6 Nothing will stop a mother singing to her children ... But as soon as they leave the *tula tula baba* stage the unmusical mama would be well advised to revert to the spoken word.

Tulbagh /ˈtʊlbax, ˈtəlbax/ *n.* [The reason for the name is obscure; see Baraitser & Obholzer quot., 1971.] Of a style of furniture: usu. *attrib.*, esp. in the phr. ***Tulbagh chair***, designating an ornate wooden chair with a back consisting of an oval (caned) splat or lozenge supported between 'barley-sugar'-turned uprights, and with box-shaped stretchers. Also with defining word, ***transitional Tulbagh (chair)***, any of several simplified versions of the Tulbagh chair, with straight-sided back panel (or plain vertical splats), and square legs and posts.

1965 M.G. ATMORE *Cape Furn.* 62 Many examples of the type [of chair] which developed at the Cape into the so-called 'Tulbagh' chair .. are known from England, Flanders, Holland, France and Germany ... In North America .. the closest parallel with the later Colonial 'Tulbagh' form is to be found. *Ibid.* 65 We left the Transitional Tulbagh type at the stage where it had been simplified to an overall rectangular form with square section legs and box stretcher and back formed from two plain vertical slats, supported between straight rails and enclosed by plain back posts. **1965** A. GORDON-BROWN *S. Afr. Heritage* II. 8 (*caption*) Small Baroque Stinkwood Table with Beefwood centre, Stinkwood 'Tulbagh' Chair. **1967** D. GODFREY *Antiques & Bygones* 15 In chairs the spindle-back type fetched between R30 and R60; traditional Tulbagh, R40 to R50; [etc.]. *a***1968** *Stellenbosch: Oldest Village in S. Afr. (pamphlet)* 20 The 'transitional Tulbagh chair' with its shaped back dates from c.1750 and its turned legs match those of the table. **1971** BARAITSER & OBHOLZER *Cape Country Furn.* p.x, A few 'Tulbagh' chairs were doubtless made, but probably not many, for it is a fairly elaborate type. Why .. is it called a Tulbagh chair? The name seems to be recent and not traditional. Certainly it has nothing to do with the place of that name. On the other hand, if it has been called after Governor Ryk Tulbagh (1715 to 1771), then it looks like an attempt to date it. But such a date is obviously too late. **1971** L.G. GREEN *Taste of S.-Easter* 49 There were .. the old diningroom chairs known as 'Tulbagh chairs' with square legs. **1974** *S. Afr. Panorama* Dec. 21 An antique Tulbagh chair of the 18th century. **1975** *Cape Times* 7 Jan. 8, R2 000 was paid for a pair of antique Dutch high-backed hall chairs. These cane-back chairs are a prototype of the variations of the 'Tulbagh chair'. **1975** *Wine: Guide for Young People* (K.W.V.) 69 An 18th Century Tulbagh chair of stinkwood. **1985** *Cape Times* 12 Dec., A set of eight Tulbagh-style riempie dining chairs. **1987** J. KENCH *Cottage Furn.* 32 Local variants [of Dutch chairs] included the sturdy Tulbagh chair with its box stretchers, and the so-called Transitional Tulbagh chair.

tulip *n. obs.* [Calque formed on S. Afr. Du. *tulp*.] TULP.

1731 G. MEDLEY tr. *P. Kolb's Present State of Cape of G.H.* II. 239 African *Hæmanthus*, call'd the *Tulip* of the *Cape of Good Hope*. **1844** J. BACKHOUSE *Narr. of Visit* 276 The species of *Moroea*, known in the country by the name of Tulip or Tulpe, which is very destructive to cattle. **1874** A. EDGAR in *Friend* 23 Apr., We lost 200 head of cattle through eating the tulip. **1885** H. RIDER HAGGARD *King Solomon's Mines* 51 Only twelve oxen remained to us out of the beautiful span of twenty ... three had died from eating the poisonous herb called 'tulip.' Five more sickened from this cause, but we managed to cure them with doses of an infusion made by boiling down the tulip leaves. **1903** E.F. KNIGHT *S. Afr. after War* 321 The tsetse fly and the poisonous tulip killed off the traveller's cattle. **1907** J.M. WOOD *Handbk to Flora of Natal* 128 The tubers of some species of *Moræa* are said to be poisonous, and the leaves are called by the Dutch and Colonists 'Tulp' or 'Tulip.' **1929** *Handbk for Farmers* (Dept of Agric.) 199 The tulips contain a strong heart poison, an alkaloid.

tulp /təlp, tœlp/ *n.* Pl. unchanged, or **-s**. [S. Afr. Du., transf. use of Du. *tulp* tulip.]

1. Any of several species of bulbous plant of the genera *Moraea* and *Homeria* of the Iridaceae, highly toxic to livestock and with tulip-like flowers; TULIP. Freq. with distinguishing epithet (see quot. 1966), as **blou-** /ˈbləʊ-/ [Afk.] or **blue-tulp, Cape (blue) tulp, geel-** /ˈxɪəl-/ [Afk.] or **yellowtulp**, *Transvaal (blue) tulp* (see TRANSVAAL). Also *attrib.*, and occas. **tulpie** [see -IE]. See also *black-gallsickness* (GALLSICKNESS sense 2).

1835 T.H. BOWKER Journal. 10 May, Lots of Bullocks sick with eating Tulp. **1837** J.E. ALEXANDER *Narr. of Voy.* II. 157 There is a blaauw tulp, or pale blue *Moræa*, which .. the cattle devour, with fatal effect. **1839** T. SHONE Diary. 29 Apr., The oxen have been eating of tulp, they are very loose. *a***1858** J. GOLDSWAIN *Chron.* (1947) I. 110 The tulp: this poisoned plant springs up so thick amung the grass and when a few inches Eigh thoues that do not know it wold think that it was leeks but it will sum times grow from two to two half feet Eigh and bears a light blue flower: Cattle that is acustumed to it when grazen and bites a blade of it off with the grass will let it fall out of thear mouths: it as a verey strong smel and it is a verey unplesent tast. **1877** *Alice Times* 25 May, He admits that a large number of oxen have died, but he attributes it to the fact that careless kurveyors have allowed their oxen to partake of tulp and poisonous weeds growing in vleys along the roadside. **1905** D. HUTCHEON in Flint & Gilchrist *Science in S. Afr.* 354 The different species of 'Cape Tulp,' *Moraea polystachya, M. polyanthos, M. collina* and *M. tenius*. **1907** W.C. SCULLY *By Veldt & Kopje* 232 Within three days all my team except four were dead. The ridge was covered with the dreaded 'tulp,' which is deadly poison to all cattle. **1917** R. MARLOTH *Common Names* 83 *Tulp* (tulip). Several poisonous Irids: *Homeria collina*, the *Geel* (yellow) - ; *H. aurantiaca* and *H. miniata*, the *Rooi* (red) -, both frequent in the south western Cape Prov.; *H. pallida*, the *Transvaal* -. *Moraea polystachya*, the *Blauw* - of the Karoo, etc. **1929** *Handbk for Farmers* (Dept of Agric.) 199 (*caption*) Cape Blue Tulp. *Ibid.* (*caption*) Transvaal Yellow Tulp. **1930** O.R. THOMPSON *Voice in Veldt* 60 The Iris was misnamed 'Tulp' by the early Dutch after their national flower 'the Tulip'. **1930**

[see GIFBLAAR]. **1957** [see quot. at *gousiektebossie* (GOUSIEKTE sense 2)]. **1966** C.A. SMITH *Common Names* 470 The specific differentiation is effected locally by the use of colour prefixes such as *bloutulp, geeltulp, rooitulp*. More recently, through plant and veterinary toxicological literature, provincial names coupled with or without the colour prefix, have also crept into use, such as *Kaapse bloutulp, Transvaalbloutulp, Transvaalgeeltulp*. **1972** BEETON & DORNER in *Eng. Usage in Sn Afr.* Vol.3 No.1, 45 *Tulp*, .. Name applied to a variety of irids .. eg bloutulp, geeltulp, kaapsebloutulp, rooitulp, Traansvaal-bloutulp, etc. **1973** *E. Prov. Herald* 18 Apr. 34 Evening Primrose and early blue Tulp. **1973** *Grocott's Mail* 19 June 3 An abundance of the highly poisonous tulp plant (Moraea edulis) in the Grahamstown district could mean stock losses for unsuspecting farmers. **1977** F.G. BUTLER *Karoo Morning* 241 There were seasons when the veld was .. glorified and transformed by flowers; when .. the 'tulp' came out in such abundance as to turn the grey flats into purple lakes. **1979** *E. Prov. Herald* 18 May 1 The tulp, a bulbous plant with a blue flower, usually grew at times when there was not much other greenery around. **1983** M. DU PLESSIS *State of Fear* 176 The fine, translucent bells of the *tulpies*. **1988** M. BRANCH *Explore Cape Flora* 38 Watsonias, pink march lilies, orchids and tulps flower later.

2. *comb.* **tulp-infested** *ppl adj.*; **tulp-poisoning** *vbl n.*

1975 *Farmer's Weekly* 10 Dec. 37 Sheep avoid **tulp-infested** pastures. **1966** C.A. SMITH *Common Names* 471 While **tulp-poisoning** is seldom now heard of in humans, the plants are annually responsible for heavy losses among stock.

tulp-boom *n. obs.* [S. Afr. Du., fr. Du. *tulp* tulip + *boom* tree.] The SUGARBUSH (sense a), *Protea repens*.

1795 C.R. HOPSON tr. *C.P. Thunberg's Trav.* I. 292 The *Protea mellifera* (**Tulp-boom** and *Zuyker-boom*) contains in its calyx a sweet juice. **1913** C. PETTMAN *Africanderisms* 519 *Tulpboom*, .. *Protea mellifera*.

tumbee, tumbi varr. INTOMBI.

tuna var. INDUNA.

tunde(r)l var. TONTEL.

tune *v. slang.* Also **choon, chune, tjoone.** [Transf. uses of general Eng. *tune* to set, to adjust, to put into alignment.]

1. *trans.*

a. *obs.* To hit or thrash (someone).

1946 C.P. WITTSTOCK in E. Partridge *Dict. of Underworld* (1950) 394 To hit a man .. to tune him, label him. **1946** A. NASH in *Ibid.* 394 To hit hard: Tune him, label him full of dents.

b. *fig.* To 'give it a bash', to enjoy life.

1982 *Pace* May 158 They used to 'tune' it in the olden days around Vrededorp alias Fidas.

2. Senses related to the underlying sense of 'to talk' or 'to tell'.

a. *trans.* In the phrr. ***to tune (someone) grief, to tune (someone) skeef*** [see SKEEF *adv.*], to give (someone) trouble, to abuse (someone) verbally; to complain.

1972 *Rhodeo* (Rhodes Univ.) 23 Mar. 5 We're a minority group and these cats tune us skeef. **1976** 'BLOSSOM' in *Darling* 4 Feb. 87 She never tunes me grief like that before. **1985** *Style* Oct. 36 'What's your case tcherrie?' 'So how *many* chicks you got?' 'You tuning me grief!' **1985** *Ibid.* [see GAAN].

b. *trans.* To tell (someone something), to relate (something to someone). Cf. CHAFF sense 2 b.

1976 [see SUKKEL sense 1]. **1979** *Informant, Grahamstown* So I must tune my aunt she sends me another postal order. **1981** L.P. ROBERTSON-HOTZ in *Bloody Horse* No.3, 33 Five minutes later he was back, this time with a bit of a bulge under his shirt. 'Ah,' he chuned us, 'it's good to have a gat again.' **1982** *Pace* May 158 Lekker, we sommer tune you everything. We jus' firs' go get a couple of beers and park by the lake. **1982** *Ibid.* [see LARNEY *n.* sense 1 a]. **1983** A. GOLDSTUCK in *Frontline* Oct. 61, I tune you, mate, if I can get one mamba chow a day, I scheme life is kif. **1983** *Cape Times* 9 Dec. 16 David 'the ou' (as opposed to Kramer 'the muso') starts tuning you lank Boland stories about his youth and his observations of life in suburbia. **1985** P. SLABOLEPSZY *Sat. Night at Palace* 58 Just because I come home a bit stoned, he tries to lock me out of the house. He tunes me, ja that's why they skopped me out of Iscor. I mean hell, man, when I met him he was a bigger rooker than I was! **1986** [see JOL *v.* sense 1]. **1987** *Scope* 20 Nov. 43 This is a mad move, isn't it now? See what I tuned you?

c. *trans.* To have (someone) on, to spin (someone) a yarn.

1983 *Sunday Times* 18 Sept. (Lifestyle) 1 No man, I'm not tuning you. I always wear my party gear when I feel like a pick-me-up.

d. *intrans.* and *trans.* To say; to speak to (someone). Cf. CHAFF sense 2 a.

1985 P. SLABOLEPSZY *Sat. Night at Palace* 13 He tunes: .. 'Don't take shit from the ref, man — hit him!' **1987** D.J. GRANT in *Frontline* June 16 'Two!' he says. You tune, 'It's seventy [cents] to Algoa, man. That's one Rand forty.' **1987** *Scope* 6 Nov. 4 Hey, *ek sê* bros, what I'm trying to tune is that we scheme this is a *kiff* issue, and we hope you *smaak* it. **1990** R. MALAN *My Traitor's Heart* 53 Black dope dealers were suspicious of whites, so you had to tune them in tsotsi-taal, the half-Afrikaans patois of the streets. **1993** *'Jimbo' programme insert, Napac* Tjoone. Speak.

e. *trans.* CHAFF sense 3.

1990 *Frontline* Mar.-Apr. 12 The warder .. spruces up and leaves to choon chicks. We see him no more.

tung-ziekte *n. Obs. Pathology.* Also **tong-sikte, tongziekte.** [S. Afr. Du. *tongziekte, tong* tongue + *ziekte* sickness.] BLUE TONGUE sense a.

1790 tr. *F. Le Vaillant's Trav.* II. 79 Another disease, the *tong-sikte*, is a prodigious swelling of the tongue, which then fills the whole mouth and throat; and the animal is every moment in danger of being choaked. **1795** C.R. HOPSON tr. *C.P. Thunberg's Trav.* I. 209 The *Tung-ziekte* is a disease of the cattle, in which vesicles or bladders break out on the tongue. **1798** [see KLAUWZIEKTE]. **1809** J. MACKRILL Diary. 64 Tungziekte, A disease of Cattle, vesicles break out on the Tongue and discharge ichorous matter the farmers cure it by rubbing the Tongue with Salt.

turf *n.* [Calque formed on Du. *turf* peat.] In full ***turf soil***: a greasy black noritic soil which is heavy, clayey, and fertile. Also *attrib.*, and *comb.* ‖**turfgrond** /-xrɔnt/ [Afk., *grond* soil, ground], or with defining word, **black turf**, in the same sense.

1929 *Handbk for Farmers* (Dept of Agric.) 297 There are all types of soils ranging from gravels to very heavy clays. Some of these contain as much as 50 per cent. of clay, as for example the Black Turfs. *Ibid.* 301 Black and red turfs [are] characteristic. **1932** *Farming in S. Afr.* May 50 (Swart), Only certain wheat soils in the Transvaal, particularly these belonging to the group commonly known as 'black turf' require potash for optimum yields. **1937** *Handbk for Farmers* (Dept of Agric. & Forestry) 733 Soils having a high silt content, such as heavy clay loams and black noritic turf soils. *Ibid.* 737 Wheat is cultivated on black clayey soil (turf), heavy red loam and also on sandy soils. **1947** C.R. PRANCE *Antic Mem.* 88 Addis must saddle-up and ride 'forthwith' in the dark through wilderness, a matter of fifty miles of blind bush including several miles of gluey 'turf' to Wachtenbeetje Drift. *Ibid.* 100 All patrols had now to be done by native Constables on foot or bicycle, so far as a push-bike can be carried or conjured in summer through black 'turf' soil. **1950** H.C. BOSMAN in L. Abrahams *Jurie Steyn's Post Office* (1971) 44 He had seen Johnny Coen .. busy scraping some of the worst turf soil off his veldskoens ... taking all the trouble .. to get the turf soil off his face. 'If he was coming here to see us, well, he wouldn't care how much black turf there was on his face.' **1950** — in L. Abrahams *Unto Dust* (1963) 178 It was muddy in the turf lands, and there was no firewood there, but we all said that we did not mind ... The mud of the turf lands was good enough for us, we said. *Ibid.* 179 We saw .. that what she had in the pot was black earth. It was wet and almost like turf soil. *a*1951 — in *Ibid.* 138 It was said that he was now even trying to find diamonds in the turfgrond on his farm. **1977** L. ABRAHAMS *Celibacy of Felix Greenspan* 64 He had to sit on the broken black turf of a ploughed furrow, that was like sharp stones. **1985** *S. Afr. Panorama* May 42 The soil at Medunsa is acidic turf, and desert plants have not yet adapted to it.

turkey buzzard *n. phr.* Freq. with initial capitals. [Transf. use of general Eng. *turkey-buzzard* a name for the vulture *Cathartes aura* of Central and South America.] The BROMVOËL, *Bucorvus leadbeateri*.

1853 F.P. FLEMING *Kaffraria* 71 The Broem Vogel, so called from the curious noise it makes, somewhat like a double repetition 'Broem Broem,' is the .. Turkey Buzzard or Turkey Vulture. **1899** R.B. & J.D.S. WOODWARD *Natal Birds* 97 (Pettman), This is a ground bird and not generally recognized as a 'Hornbill,' being known amongst colonists as the *Turkey Buzzard*. **1913** C. PETTMAN *Africanderisms* 91 *Brom vogel*, .. *Bucorax cafer* — the Turkey Buzzard. **1931** *Guide to Vertebrate Fauna of E. Cape Prov.* (Albany Museum) I. 153 *Bucorvus cafer* .. Ground Hornbill (Turkey Buzzard, Wild Turkey) ... Throat naked and wattled, the bare skin on throat and around eyes being red. **1983** K.B. NEWMAN *Newman's Birds* 445 Turkey Buzzard. Erroneous name for Ground Hornbill.

Turkish fig *n. phr. Obs.* [tr. S. Afr. Du. *Turksvij*, fr. Du. *Turks* Turkish + *vij* fig.] The fruit of any of several species of *Opuntia* (prickly pear) of the Cactaceae, esp. *O. vulgaris*; TOLOFIYA; TURKSVY. Also **Turk's fig.**

1844 J. BACKHOUSE *Narr. of Visit* 123 An orange-flowered *Opuntia*, which seems to be naturalized here, and is called Turkish-fig, is common in some sandy grounds. **1874** A. EDGAR in *Friend* 26 Feb., Here were a great many 'Turk's figs', and hearing that they were good eating, I got myself into grief by grabbing at a lot of them, but as quickly dropped them again, and could scarcely get their confounded little thorns out of my hands for a week after. **1902** D. VAN WARMELO *On Commando* 98 The old kraal walls and the peach-trees and 'Turkish figs', (prickly pears), overgrown by wild trees and an occasional earthen vessel, were the remains of the Kaffir city. *a*1951 H.C. BOSMAN *Willemsdorp* (1977) 88 A prickly pear, broad-leafed and steadfast: Turkish fig was the name the Boers gave to it.

‖**turksvy** /ˈtɜːksfeɪ, ˈtərksfeɪ/ *n.* Formerly also **turksvij.** Pl. **-vye** /-feɪə/. [Afk. (earlier S. Afr. Du. *turksvij*), see prec.] TURKISH FIG.

1913 C. PETTMAN *Africanderisms* 519 *Turksvij*, .. The Cape Dutch name for the Prickly pear. **1970** H.M. MUSMECI *Informant, Port Elizabeth* These turksvye are delicious (prickly pears). **1972** L.G. GREEN *When Journey's Over* 44 My coloured wagon crews gathered herbs and other veld medicines: *turksvye* for sores, wild garlic for many ailments, grilled Hottentot fig for earache. **1990** *Weekend Post* 14 Apr. 4 The common name of the prickly pear is Indian fig and the Afrikaans name is turksvy.

turlington /ˈtɜːlɪŋtən/ *n.* Also with initial capital. [Etym. unknown; perh. a proprietory name.] Friar's Balsam (compound tincture of benzoin), used as an application for ulcers and wounds, inhaled, or used as an expectorant.

1919 *Dunell, Ebden & Co.'s Price List* Oct. 20 Turlington, Per doz. 3/6. **1949** L.G. GREEN *In Land of Afternoon* 44 When Turlington is no longer in demand. **1972** N. SAPEIKA in *Std Encycl. of Sn Afr.* VII. 302 A list of these traditional remedies and the corresponding modern equivalents is given in the *South African Medical Journal* of 1 June 1957. It includes .. turlington (compound tincture of benzoin — Friar's balsam), [etc.]. **1973** S. STANDER tr. *A.P. Brink's Brandy in S. Afr.* 168 Another recipe which gives free rein to the imagination by avoiding any mention of measurements is a mixture of turlington, brandy and honey. **1989** D. SMUTS *Folk Remedies* 27 Coughing and asthma (*chronic*): Make a syrup ... Now add 2–4 lbs honey, 2 little bottles bitrate of tar, .. 3 little bottles turlington, 1 little bottle glycerine.

turpentine tree *n. phr.* [tr. Afk. *terpentynboom*, named for the turpentine-like smell of the leaves when crushed.] The *mopani tree* (see MOPANI sense 1 a), *Colophospermum mopane*.

1913 C. PETTMAN *Africanderisms* 519 *Turpentine tree*, Another Transvaal name for *Copaifera mopane, Kirk.* **1934** C.P. SWART Supplement to Pettman. 120 *Mopane*, .. The turpentine tree. **1970** A. SILLERY *Std Encycl. of Sn Afr.* II. 222 Outside the forest region, the turpentine tree or mopane .. covers a large area in the north and north-east. **1987** F. VON BREITENBACH *Nat. List of Indigenous Trees* 63 Mopane, Butterfly Tree, Turpentine Tree, Rhodesian Ironwood.

TVBC see TBVC.

Tvl see TRANSVAAL.

twa-grass, twa-gras /ˈtwɑ(:) grɑ:s, -xras/ *n.* Also **dwa-grass, twaa-grass.** [Afk. *twa(gras)*, ad. San *doa, dhoa* grass + Eng. *grass* or Afk. *gras*.] Any of several species of grass of the genera *Aristida* and *Stipagrostis* (esp. *S. brevifolia*) of the sub-family Arundinoideae (family Poaceae); TOA-GRASS; also called BUSHMAN GRASS.

1857 A. WYLEY *Rep. Min. Struct. Namaqualand* 44 Twa-grass .. grows from two to three feet in height, from a small bushy base. When it is green, oxen, horses, and sheep all thrive upon it. **1896** R. WALLACE *Farming Indust. of Cape Col.* 100 A species of Aristida, 'twa-gras', is the most abundant grass .. in the Kalahari region and in the upper region of the Karoo. **1897** EDMONDS & MARLOTH *Elementary Botany* 185 Dwa-grass or Toa-grass. **1906** F. BLERSCH *Handbk of Agric.* 256 *Aristida vestita*, the twa gras. **1913** W.C. SCULLY *Further Reminisc.* 217 Bushmanland was like an illimitable field of waving corn, the yellow shooks of 'twa' grass covering it continuously for thousands of square miles. **1913** C. PETTMAN *Africanderisms* 99 *Bushman grass* or *'Dwa grass'*. **1915** W. EVELEIGH *S.W. Afr.* 68 The Twa-gras, or Bushman grass of the Karroo, *Aristida brevifolia* ... Even when dry this grass retains its nourishing properties. **1932** [see BOESMANGRAS]. **1945** L.G. GREEN *Where Men Still Dream* 120 North-West roads, lined with bushman grass, the 'twaa grass' that crackles in the wind. [**1974** J.M. COETZEE *Dusklands* 123 When Bushmen first saw the grass which we call *Aristida brevifolia* and spoke among themselves and found that it was unknown and called it Twaa, was there not an unspoken botanical order among them in which *Twaa* now found a place?] **1983** P.S. RABIE tr. *Nienaber & Raper's Hottentot Place Names* 97 'Dwa grass' (a species of *Aristida*, e.g. *A. ciliata*, popularly called 'bushman grass').

twak /twak/ *n.* [Afk., contraction of *tabak* tobacco; (fig.) nonsense, rubbish.]

‖**1.** Tobacco.

1844 J. BACKHOUSE *Narr. of Visit* 240 We were frequently met by Caffers who came running .. extending their hands .. , calling out 'Bassella,' which signifies A present, to this they generally added 'Towak' or made signs that they wanted tobacco. **1963** *Informant, Wolmaransstad (North-West Prov.)* If I have the convicts to work for me I always buy them fat cracklings, coffee and twak — but the twak's what they always ask for and what they like best. **1974** J. MATTHEWS *Park* (1983) 40 'If yer gimme a smoke, I take ye case on.' 'Der prisoner hef no right to hef twak,' Jonas commanded. 'Orderly, take away his twak.' **1979** *Star* 17 Jan., When .. the first rains this year turn out to be a hailstorm that flattens the *twak* then it is time .. to discuss some of the big changes that are happening in the Marico ... A man must just sit .. and use up the winter quota of irrigation water for the *twak* that has already been flattened by the hail. **1980** C. HOPE *A Separate Development* (1983) 16 Bags of Magaliesberg pipe tobacco, dark, greasy and pungent, which I bought to empty out the twak and keep my marbles in. **1988** G. LATTER in *Staffrider* Vol.7 No.3, 110 Old Hennie would be sitting comfortably smoking his pipe and *twak*.

2. *slang.* Rubbish, nonsense, 'rot'.

a. As *int.*

1953 U. KRIGE *Dream & Desert* 86 'Don't forget, a third of that bat's mine!' 'Twak!' Pieter snorted. 'Just try and bluff us with that one.' **1970** Y. WINTERS *Informant, Kimberley* Twak, that's not what happened! — nonsense. **1983** *Sunday Times* 18 Dec. (Mag. Sect.) 10 Bull. Lies. Who says? Ag, twak. **1990** on TV1, 4 Apr. (The Game), 'I'm going home.' 'Twak! I'm buying you a beer.'

b. As a common noun.

1972 *Informant, Karoo* Honestly I know I wrote a helluva lot of twak — I knew I'd fail. **1979** T. GUTSCHE *There Was a Man* 210 Talk of ticks was twak (nonsense). **1982** M. MUTLOATSE in *Voice* 24 Apr., Loud and Clear dares Baas .. to repeat the 'twak' about detained leaders being terrorists outside court. **1990** *Grocott's Mail* 13 Feb. 5 (*letter*) While his erstwhile cronies support him, all that Mr de Klerk has to say may be considered as twak. **1991** P. SLABOLEPSZY *Braait Laaities*. 8 Do I have to sit here listening to you talk twak all night?

twala *n.*[1] var. TSHWALA.

twala, ukutwala /(ʊkʊ)ˈtwɑ:lə, (ʊgʊ)ˈtwa(:)la/ *n.*[2] Also **ukuthwala.** [See TWALA *v.*] Esp. in traditional Xhosa society: the abduction of a young woman for the purpose of marriage. Also *attrib.*

1931 F.C. SLATER *Secret Veld* 312 *Uku twala* .. is a secret carrying-away custom practised amongst those natives of South Africa still in a state of heathenism. A man becomes enamoured of a damsel, and, along with accomplices, awaits a favourable opportunity and carries her off by force, shoulderhigh, or on horseback. If he succeeds in reaching his homestead with her, her friends are appraised of her whereabouts, and she is sent for by them. She is then delivered up, together with *lobola* cattle. **1937** B.J.F. LAUBSCHER *Sex, Custom & Psychopathology* 16 She was married, much against her will, for twenty head of cattle, by means of *ukutwala* (kidnapping by consent of parents). She fought and struggled but was beaten and carried off by her kidnappers. *Ibid.* 193 The *lobola* fee has already been settled prior to the actual kidnapping, but an extra cow must now be paid for the audacity to kidnap the girl, even after they have all agreed that the marriage should be an *Ukutwala*. **1948** O. WALKER *Kaffirs Are Lively* 114 Some are concerned with tribal customs such as *twala* — marriage abduction — and its side-issues *teleka* and *ngena*. **1955** J.B. SHEPHARD *Land of Tikoloshe* 49 Another custom is called Twala, a euphemism for abduction; curiously it is often connived at by the people most intimately concerned for, in a sense, it is regarded as a form of marriage. **1961** P. MAYER *Townsmen or Tribesmen* 264 *Ukuthwala* procedure consists of the man's representatives abducting the girl and installing her at his home, where she is required to perform the duties of a wife ... Just as in more ceremonious marriages, the *ukuthwala* bride is being transferred from one homestead and group of kin to another. **1963** [see TWALA *v.*]. **1970** A. FULTON *I Swear to Apollo* 258 The Xhosa have a very fine custom. If a fellow fancies a girl he simply steals her and carries her off to his hut. They call it ukuthwala. **1971** *Daily Dispatch* 13 Feb. 2 The accused was never consulted before arrangements for her 'twala' were made ... she was very unhappy with her husband.

twala /ˈtwɑ:lə, ˈtwa(:)la/ *v. trans.* Also **thwala.** [Xhosa *thwala* carry off, abduct.] Esp. in traditional Xhosa society: to abduct (a girl or young woman) by force, often with the consent of her guardians, for the purpose of marriage.

1908 F.C. SLATER *Sunburnt South* 58 'What are you doing with the girl?' he asked. 'Don't you see we are carrying (*twala*) her,' said the stout man. 'I want her for my second wife.' **1961** P. MAYER *Townsmen or Tribesmen* 239 Parents can privately authorize a suitor's kin to *thwala* their daughter, that is, take her by suprise somewhere in the bush and carry her off by force to the suitor's home, where she will be made to put on the clothes and insignia of a newly married wife. *Ibid.* 240 Next day four men *thwala*'d her as she was drawing water. **1963** WILSON & MAFEJE *Langa* 47 It shocked even the pagans, both because Christians do not ordinarily practice [*sic*] *twala* marriage, and no man had ever been known to *twala* two women at the same time. **1971** *Daily Dispatch* 13 Feb. 2 Pleading mitigation her council, Adv. J— asked the court to be lenient because Noranga was forced by her parents to marry a man she did not love. She was 'twalaed' (abducted ..).

twasa var. THWASA.

Tweede Nuwejaar /ˈtwɪədə ˌnyvəja:(r)/ *n. phr.* Also **Tweede Nuwe Jaar, Tweedenuwejaar,** and with small initials. [Afk., *tweede* second + *nuwe* new + *jaar* year.] The second of January, observed as a public holiday in Cape Town and other areas (esp. of the Western Cape).

1947 *Cape Times* 30 Dec. 14 The Coons are ready for the New Year — and tweede nuwejaar — that extra holiday which is taken only in the Cape. **1953** *Ibid.* 1 Jan. 1 There will be no issue of the *Cape Times* tomorrow January 2 (*Tweedenuwejaar*). **1971** *Argus* 5 June 1 The 'Tweedenuwejaar' saw the troupes with shields and trophies cavorting through the streets followed by enthusiastic supporters. **1977** *Het Suid-Western* 6 Apr. 1 Shops in George will not open on Easter Saturday. But this is likely to be the last year that shops in the Cape are forced to close on Easter Saturday and Tweede Nuwe Jaar. **1978** *Argus* 29 Dec. 3 Normal editions of The Argus will be published on Tuesday January 2, Tweede Nuwejaar. **1981** *Cape Times* 28 Dec. 9 New Year's Day and Tweede Nuwejaar hours are also 8.30am until 1pm. **1981** *Ibid.* 31 Dec. 2 Cape Town will observe the traditional Tweede Nuwejaar and no shops in the Cape Town, Bellville, Goodwood, Parow or Pinelands municipal area will be open on Saturday. **1986** *Fair Lady* 22 Jan. 108 The New Year and Tweede Nuwejaar were joyously heralded by the Coons and the whole town came out to watch. **1988** [see *Coon Carnival* (COON sense 2)]. **1989** *Flying Springbok* Sept. 29 Colourful and noisy, 'Tweede Nuwejaar' is a party that has the Coons preparing their costumes and *passies* for months in advance. **1993** *Weekend Argus* 2 Jan. (Suppl.) 23 It used to be that when the rest of the country was going back to work on January 2, Cape Town was still wildly partying its way into the new year. This tradition, *Tweede Nuwejaar*, ranks alongside Table Mountain as an essential element of the Mother-City ... However, typically, other South African cities .. have plagiarised the *Tweede Nuwejaar* concept, attempting to replicate its totally *los* atmosphere in their own environs.

tweetalig /twɪəˈtɑ:ləx(ə)/ *adj.* Also (*attrib.*) **tweetalige** /twɪəˈtɑ:ləxə/ [Afk., *twee* two + *taal* language + adj. suffix *-ig* (attrib. form *-ige*).] BILINGUAL.

1973 *Cape Times* 21 June 7 This wall chart, attractive .. and tweetalig nogal, is to be distributed to all hospitals. **1980** *Fair Lady* 19 Nov. 384 It sounds ridiculous .. but it worked, we worked and we all came out more *tweetalig* than we went in. **1986** *Sunday Times* 12 Oct. 12 The SABC's new bilingual TV programmes are a smash hit — with an overwhelming 84 percent of TV1's white viewership giving a tweetalige thumbs-up. **1990** *Weekly Mail* 21 Dec. (Suppl.) 31 Tweetalig is tops ... The most exciting new indigenous theatre .. plays written in Afrikaans and English. **1992** J. RAPHAELY in *Femina* June 6, I can visualize myself giving a brilliant *tweetalige* speech. **1993** *Weekly Mail & Guardian* 10 Dec. 6 Soon your Coke and Fanta and even your beers will no longer be *tweetalig*. This week, South African Breweries and Amalgamated Beverage Industries .. decided to can Afrikaans on their products.

twenty-six *n. colloq.* Usu. written **26.** [See quot. 1992.] A member of a gang originating within the St Albans prison in Port Elizabeth, but also operating in other prisons, and beyond the prisons. Also *attrib.*

1984 *E. Prov. Herald* 19 June 13 The deadly rivalry between the 26s and the 28s, the big and brutal prison gangs with tentacles in jails throughout South

Africa, sucked 'The Hangman' inexorably into its maelstrom of violence, prison rape, homosexuality and dagga smoking ... At the peak of their orgy of butchery .. those in the coloured areas were subjected to a savage rule of violence. **1987** S.A. BOTHA in *Frontline* Oct.-Nov. 14 Ten to one he's a 26 — a member of a loosely bound gang of dedicated robbers. **1992** J. NEL in *E. Prov. Herald* 21 Nov. 4 The '26 gang' was formed when certain prisoners became unhappy with the '28s' habit of taking 'wyfies' (homosexual partners) ... All four accused had voluntarily joined the '26 gang'.

Two Oceans *n. phr.* A marathon which includes stretches on both the Atlantic Ocean and the Indian Ocean coasts of the Cape Peninsula. Also *attrib.*

First run in 1969.

1988 M. BRANCH *Explore Cape Flora* 44 The opening rush to their annual plant sale .. has been likened to the Two Oceans Marathon. **1992** G. EVANS in *Weekly Mail* 16 Apr. 29 Despite the lure of the Comrades, this year's Two Oceans has one of the strongest fields in the race's history. **1992** I. MORAKE in *Sunday Times* 17 May 26, I could have gone faster in the Two Oceans, but I was doing everything with the Comrades in mind. **1993** *Weekend Post* 20 Mar. 6 Albert Mahlahla .. will not only be running the Comrades, but also the Two Oceans in Cape Town on April 10. A veteran aged 40, he .. will tackle his fifth Two Oceans and his seventh Comrades.

twyala, twyala, tyalla, tyalli varr. TSHWALA.

tyger, tyger-cat varr. TIGER, TIGER-CAT.

‖**tyhini** /ˈcʰiːni, ˈtʃiːni/ *int.* Also **hienie, tshini**. [Xhosa.] Among Xhosa-speakers: an exclamation of surprise, disbelief, shock, dismay, or indignation.

1979 F. DIKE *First S. African* 13 Hayi tyhini, we can't let him get away with this. **1981** *Job Mava* (Ikhwezi Players) in *Staffrider* Vol.3 No.4, 23 Zizamele: Tyhini Tixo. Weren't you insured? Job: No. I trusted to luck. **1982** *E. Prov. Herald* 29 Apr. 13 The poor lad rushed to safety with cries of *Ai, ai* ... *Yoo* ... *Kwakhu!* and *Tyhini!* **1983** *Pace* Oct. 174 Tshini Mfondini! a woman screamed. Another woman broke in ... 'au, au, au, Thixo!' **1986** [see INKOSIKAZI sense 2].

Tymba var. TEMBU.

tywala var. TSHWALA.

tza var. TSAA.

tzeiran *n. obs.* Also **tseiran**. [Transf. use of Eng. dzeren, tzeiran a name given to the Mongolian gazelle *Procapra gutturosa*.] The BLAUWBOK (sense 1 a), *Hippotragus leucophaeus*.

1786 G. FORSTER tr. *A. Sparrman's Voy. to Cape of G.H.* II. 86 The *koba's* horns, as well as those of the *tzeiran* .. are .. too large ever to have belonged to this gazel. **1790** tr. *F. Le Vaillant's Trav.* I. 131 This antelope has been described by Pennant under the name of the *blue antelope*, by Buffon under that of the *tseiran*. **1796** C.R. HOPSON tr. *C.P. Thunberg's Trav.* II. 113 In this tract resided the Blue goat, as it is called, (*Blauwe bok, Tseiran, Capra leucophoea*).

tzetze var. TSETSE.

U

Uba /ˈuːbə, ˀjuːbə/ *n. hist.* [See quot. 1905.] A hardy variety of sugar cane cultivated extensively in Kwa-Zulu-Natal from the 1880s to the mid-20th century. Also *attrib.*

Introduced from India by sugar-farmer and businessman Daniel de Pass.

1905 PEARSON & PARDY in Flint & Gilchrist *Science in S. Afr.* 431 They have .. been supplanted by a variety called *Uba* — a name, it is said, formed of the only three letters remaining legible on a damaged label attached to the variety on its first arrival in the country. 1937 *Handbk for Farmers* (Dept of Agric. & Forestry) II. 691 From the beginning of the century until a few years ago, there was practically only one variety grown, e.g. [*sic*] Uba. This cane was introduced from India in 1884-85 and was found to be eminently suited to the somewhat erratic climate and soil conditions of the Natal sugar belt ... Uba did not prove an ideal milling cane, its crushing costs being high ... Efforts have been made to introduce suitable varieties with the aim of gradually replacing Uba. 1957 *Handbk for Farmers* (Dept of Agric.) 268 For many years the only cane that could profitably be cultivated was the Uba variety, which was resistant to the diseases of cane known in South Africa. This cane is now rarely cultivated. 1971 M. ARKIN in *Std Encycl. of Sn Afr.* III. 646 From India he [*sc.* Daniel de Pass] introduced the disease-resistant Uba variety of cane.

uBangalala var. BANGALALA.

UBC *n. hist.* Also **U.B.C.** [Initial letters of *Urban Bantu Council.*] An elected body responsible, during the apartheid era, for the administration of an urban black township. See also USELESS BOYS' CLUB.

Replaced by community councils (see COMMUNITY COUNCIL).

[1961 *Act 79* in *Stat. of Republic of S. Afr.*, Urban Bantu Councils Act.] 1968 *Drum* Sept. 25 After all the promises of what U.B.C. would mean to us, what has it actually meant? Has it given Soweto residents some form of self-rule .. ? 1970 T.W. KHAMBULE in *Post* 28 June 11 The UBC has no powers of any kind, there is nothing they can achieve in any direction because they have no form of autonomy. 1971 *Drum* May 51 The UBC has been called a bunch of emasculated bulls. 1976 *Weekend World* 12 Sept. 9 Since the township unrest more and more people have been calling the UBC a body of 'sell-outs' ... Allegations were made against certain UBC members in a civic action. 1978 *Survey of Race Rel.* (S.A.I.R.R.) 402 A statement issued by students said that since its inception the UBC had achieved nothing for the people of Soweto ... Student leaders visited individual UBC members urging them to resign. 1982 *Grahamstown Voice* Sept. 2 'The government is using us as stooges', said Mr Z—, who was on the old UBC, is on the present Council, and intends standing in the next elections.

Ubiqua /uˈbiːkwə/ *n. Obs. exc. hist.* Also **Obiqua**. [Khoikhoi.] A member of a San group living at or near the Cape of Good Hope in the 17th century.

1688 G. TACHARD *Voy. to Siam* 74 The third Nation are the Ubiquas. They are by Profession Robbers, and rob the Africans as well as strangers. Though they are not able to send five hundred Men into the Field, yet it is not easie to root them out, because they retreat into inaccessible Mountains. 1846 J. SUTHERLAND *Memoir* II. 589 About the promontory of Africa, they [*sc.* the 'Bosjeman'] called themselves, and were called by others, Obiquas, Souquas; and they had, doubtless, other denominations in parts farther inland. 1862 [see SUSEQUA]. 1977 R. ELPHICK *Kraal & Castle* 24 As for *Ubiqua*, Theal argued that it meant 'murderer,' a plausible explanation which has, however, been rejected on linguistic grounds by L.F. Maingard.

ubootie var. UBUTI.

ubukwetha /ˌubuˈkweːta/ *n.* Also **ubukhwetha**, **ubukweta**. [Xhosa, the seclusion period, and the place of seclusion, for initiates to manhood.] ABAKWETHA sense 2.

1856 J.C. WARNER in J. MacLean *Compendium of Kafir Laws* (1906) 95 [The] state of initiation is called 'ubukweta,' the boys themselves being termed 'abakweta.' 1891 T.R. BEATTIE *Pambaniso* 215 A Kaffir male who has not been circumcised is regarded as a boy, even though he be a full-grown man. The rite is known as *Ubukweta*, and those who are undergoing it are called *Abakweta*. The term *Ubukweta* or circumcision begins generally in December and lasts for six or eight months. During this period the *Abakweta* are isolated in huts by themselves, and a man is appointed to attend to them and look after their wants. 1905 W.H. TOOKE in Flint & Gilchrist *Science in S. Afr.* 88 Circumcision, as in nearly all South African Bantu, is practised with elaborate rites. It is called ubukweta, and the corresponding rite among the girls intonjane. 1964 G. GORDON *Four People* 80 Although they still cling to their tribal customs like *ubukhwetha*, the School- and Church-people did not daub their bodies with yellow ochre or drape themselves in blankets like the ignorant pagans.

ubulunga /ˌubuˈluŋga, -gə/ *n.* Also **ubulungu**. [Xhosa, n. prefix *ubu-* + *-lunga* make right or good.] In traditional Xhosa society:

1. Either of two heifers, one given by a man to his bride, and one given to her by her father, sacred beasts which may not be slaughtered and from the tail-brushes of which necklets are made for the use of members of the family. Also *attrib.*

1897 W.C. SCULLY in E.R. Seary *S. Afr. Short Stories* (1947) 31 All she wore in the way of clothing was a small apron of strung beads, unless a necklet of charms hung on hairs from the tail of the ubulunga cow can be counted as such. 1923 W.C. SCULLY *Daniel Vananda* 111 When the boy was born, a cow — the best of the herd — was assigned to him as the 'ubulungu' — the 'doer of good'. 1961 H.F. SAMPSON *White-Faced Huts* 15 A large stone .. rolled down and fatally injured an ox ... It was one of the 'ubulungu' cattle of Mandobe ... She .. said that he would have to pay compensation. 1989 *Greater Dict. of Xhosa* III. 735 The *ubulunga beast*, When a young man sets up his own home .. he .. sets aside one heifer as *inkomo yobulunga*, the ceremonial cow ... Should a member of the family fall ill and the trouble be regarded as having emanated from his ancestors, hairs will be plucked from the tail-brush of one of these animals to make the prescribed necklace ... When a bride goes to her new home, her father presents her with a heifer which will become the progenitress of her own strain of *ubulunga* cattle from which hairs will be plucked .. when the cause of their illness originates from her mother's ancestors ... When an *ubulunga* beast becomes old, it is nursed and kept alive as long as possible.

2. A necklet made of hairs from the ubulunga animal, a means of establishing communication with the ancestors, esp. when the wearer is ill or is to become a diviner. Also *attrib.*

1978 A.P. BRINK *Rumours of Rain* 297 You received .. an *ubulunga* for your neck, made from the tail hairs of a pregnant cow. 1989 *Greater Dict. of Xhosa* III. 735 The *ubulunga necklet* .. is .. made of the tail-brush hairs of the *ubulunga* ox or cow ... The hairs (about 10-12 cm long) spread out in all directions over the chest, shoulders and back. The necklet establishes contact with the ancestral spirits and thus ensures good health ... A diviner also wears an *ubulunga* necklet ... The neophyte wears the necklet continuously until he is fully trained as it establishes contact between him and the ancestors.

ubuntu /uˈbu(:)ntu/ *n.* Also **buntu**, **uBuntu**, and with initial capital. [Xhosa and Zulu, 'humanity', 'goodness'; formed on the noun stem *-ntu*, used to form words related to humans.]

a. Human-heartedness, compassion; the qualities embodying the values and virtues of essential humanity, or of Africanness; BOTHO sense a. Also *attrib.*

1926 G. CALLAWAY *Fellowship of Veld* 25 To the Native the qualities which go to make up ubuntu, the qualities which make an umntu (person), are largely social. 1953 G.H. CALPIN *S. Afr. Way of Life* 56 To the Bantu the Europeans, probably because of their materialistic outlook, lack the essential quality of human beings, which is best conveyed by the Zulu word 'Ubuntu.' 1978 *Rhodeo* (Rhodes Univ.) 15 Sept. 7 Steven Bantu Biko, founder member of SASO and the black consciousness movement .. The man of 'ubuntu' — humanness and togetherness. 1982 M. MZAMANE *Children of Soweto* 153 Bra P. possessed that rare quality Africans call *ubuntu* or *botho*, which is the sum total of human values as Africans understand them. 1983 *Fair Lady* 5 Oct. 12 In some black areas it's the second, third or fourth year of drought. What keeps the people going is *buntu*, an almost untranslatable word meaning caring, compassion, love. 1986 J. LEATT in *Leadership* Vol.5 No.4, 38 Even black 'reformist' groups such as Inkatha advocate 'welfare capitalism' — 'Capitalism with *siza* and *ubuntu*,' two Zulu words which can be translated as 'capitalism with a human face'. 1991 D. TUTU in *Sunday Times* 26 May 2 It seems to me that we in the black community have lost our sense of *ubuntu* — our humanness, caring, hospitality, our sense of connectedness, our sense that my humanity is bound up in your humanity. 1993 *Act 200* in *Govt Gaz.* Vol.343 No.15466, 180 There is a need for understanding but not for vengeance, a need for reparation but not for retaliation, a need for ubuntu but not for victimisation. **1994** J. THOMSON in *Weekend Post* 1 Jan. 7 Add 'shalom' and 'truth' to *ubuntu* – and with these three words .. perhaps .. the unborn's right to life will no longer be disputed. **1994** K. MKHIZE in *Natal Witness* 28 Dec. 8 Trust is the main axle in the wheel of Ubuntu.

b. *comb.* **ubuntu-botho** [Xhosa and Zulu *ubuntu* + Sotho *botho*, both words having the same sense], 'human-heartedness'; the name given to a non-examination subject in KwaZulu schools. Also *attrib.*

1987 KING G. ZWELITHINI in *S. Afr. Panorama* May 24 We Black people of South Africa regard Ubuntu, or Botho in Sotho, as our highest ideal. Ubuntu/Botho is almost synonomous [*sic*] with humanism. **1987** *Frontline* May 27 Whatever anyone thinks of Inkatha, you have to respect their efforts to include Sotho terms in their symbols ... The ideology course in KwaZulu schools is called Ubuntu-Botho – again both languages. **1989** L. KAUNDA in *Natal Witness* 30 Mar. (Echo) 1 Teachers at KwaZulu-run schools in Sweetwaters and other parts of Edenvale are apprehensive that they have to teach the KwaZulu-prescribed ubuntu-botho syllabus. Dubbed the 'Inkatha' subject by scholars, this non-examinable course has generated a lot of controversy ever since it was established. **1990** F. KHUMALO in *Weekly Mail* 4 May 11 At local schools children are being taught Zulu and *Ubuntu/Botho* – Zulu nationalism as seen through the eyes of Inkatha. **1990** M. KENTRIDGE *Unofficial War* 104 Inkatha keeps a tight hold on education ... Ubuntu Botho, a subject devoted to the values and philosophies of the organisation, forms an integral part of the syllabus. **1991** D. MATTERA in *Pace* Feb. 32, I write to encourage compassion, empathy and humanism (ubuntu/botho) ... I believe I am a humanist poet.

Hence (*nonce*) **ubuntuize** *v. trans.*, to infuse (something) with the qualities of ubuntu; **ubuntuism** *n.*, the philosophy of ubuntu.

1988 L.J. SEBIDI in *Sunday Times* 27 Nov., Put differently, ubuntu is some kind of humanism – African humanism. Shall we call it ubuntuism for lack of a more appropriate word? **1994** K. MKHIZE in *Natal Witness* 28 Dec. 8 Is it possible to decommercialise Christmas and Ubuntuise it for mankind?

ubutagati, ubuthakathi varr. TAGATI *n.* sense 2.

‖**ubuti** /ʊˈbʊ(ː)ti/ *n.* Also **booti, ubootie, ubute.** [Xhosa *ubuthi* bewitching charm.] In traditional Nguni (and esp. Xhosa) society: any charm or bewitching matter believed to exert an evil influence.

1828 W. SHAW Diary. Mar., She entered the cattle kraal, and dug with her spear in a small hole; but said the Ubootie (bewitching matter) is not here, it has been removed. **1833** *Graham's Town Jrnl* 8 Aug. 3 If I have bewitched the man, and was not at home at the time the beast was slaughtered, 'who' gave me the 'Ubute?' (bewitching stuff). **1835** A. STEEDMAN *Wanderings* I. 41 The woman produced a bag of ubootie, or bewitching matter, which appeared to have been hidden there in a pool of water. **1835** W.B. BOYCE in A. Steedman *Wanderings* II. 282 He mentioned the report of Mr. Shepstone having sent his men on horseback to plant booti (bewitching matter) upon his place. **1860** W. SHAW *Story of my Mission* 462 He is seized and tormented, with a view to compel him to confess his deeds, and to discover the ubuti, (bewitching matter or charm) that its evil influence may be destroyed. **1866** W.C. HOLDEN *Past & Future* 284 Besides these poisons, which produce universal distrust and suspicion, there is what is called *ubuti*, or 'bewitching matter;' which is supposed to be, or actually is, deposited in some secret place in the hut or cattlefold, and by which, in connexion with supernatural agency, some dire calamity is believed to be inflicted upon the person, or family, or kraal. **1956** [see UMHLAHLO].

uclever var. CLEVER.

UCT *n.* Initial letters of *University of Cape Town*. Also *attrib.* See also IKEY.

1970 *Daily Dispatch* 10 June 1 He could not submit his MA thesis .. on which he had been working at UCT since the beginning of this year. **1981** *E. Prov. Herald* 9 Oct. 3 UCT students lands R7 000 scholarship to study abroad ... At UCT he has served as vice-president and treasurer of the Student's Representative Council. **1983** [see OORBELIGTE]. **1987** *E. Prov. Herald* 28 Apr. 1 The UCT Vice-Chancellor, Dr Stuart Saunders, tried to negotiate with police but students demanded that the police leave. **1987** *Citizen* 6 May 3 In solidarity with those calling for democratic change and an end to violence, senate resolves to recommend to council that UCT be closed on May 6.

U.D.F. *n.*[1] *hist.* Also **UDF.** Initial letters of *Union Defence Forces*, the name, from 1912 to 1957, of the South African armed forces. Also *attrib.*

See note at DEFENCE FORCE.

1939 G. MAKEPEACE in *Outspan* 10 Nov. 9 Men between the ages of 17 and 60 who are not members of any other portion of the U.D.F. are National Reservists. **1944** 'TWEDE IN BEVEL' *Piet Kolonel* 62 The Battalion moved over such frequent and tremendous distances in 1941, that we became the most travelled unit of the U.D.F. **1945** S. DE WET *Shifty in Italy* Intro., When a senior officer from the Union or Cairo went on a tour of inspection to Italy, his trip was called, in U.D.F. slang, a 'shifty tour' or a 'shifty'. **1948** [see BUSH CART]. **1963** L.F. FREED *Crime in S. Afr.* 153 In spite of the vigilance of U.D.F. artillerymen, pilferers have been stripping lead, copper and electrical fittings from the installations. **1980** R. DALE in *Jrnl of Mod. Afr. Studies* Vol.18 No.1, 60 For the most part, the offensive combat role of the U.D.F. retained the distinction between blacks and whites practised in South Africa – namely, that only the latter served as combatants. **1981** ORPEN & MARTIN *Salute Sappers* I. 283 Lt. White had been detached to U.D.F. Headquarters in Cairo on 16 March. **1990** *Bulletin* (Centre for Science Dev.) Nov. 3 There was both strong opposition to, as well as voices in favour of black South Africans joining the Union Defence Force (UDF) during the Second World War. **1993** *Sunday Times* 11 July 17 A Nazi agent .. had been appointed a UDF instructor.

UDF *n.*[2] Initial letters of *United Democratic Front*, a grouping of Charterist anti-apartheid organizations, launched in 1983 and dissolved after the unbanning of the African National Congress in 1990; a branch of this organization. Also *attrib.* See also SAYCO.

1983 A. HARBER in *Rand Daily Mail* 30 July 2 Leaders of opposition groups .. are meeting .. to discuss the launching of a nationwide United Democratic Front (UDF) ... The national body would bring together the regional UDFs that have sprung up in different parts of the country ... The UDF was originally suggested by Dr Allan Boesak .. in January. Since then UDFs have been formed in the Transvaal, .. in Natal, .. in the Eastern and Western Cape. **1983** *Drum* Aug. 6 The UDF is comprised of organisations which adhere to the principles laid down in the Freedom Charter. **1983** *Pace* Oct. 6 The United Democratic Front (UDF) was launched last month. The UDF, .. an infallible powerblock against the government's proposed constitutional reform. **1985** *SASPU National* Vol.6 No.2, 3 The Soweto homes of UDF treason trialists, youth and student activists have been petrol bombed. **1988** *Now Everyone Is Afraid* (Catholic Inst. for Internat. Rel.) 5 The UDF led a boycott of the 1984 constitutional reforms and community council elections. **1989** *Race Rel. Survey 1988–9* (S.A.I.R.R.) 705 The United Democratic Front (UDF) was launched on 20 August 1983 and claimed to have 900 affiliated organisations with 3m members. **1989** [see IQABANE]. **1990** M. KENTRIDGE *Unofficial War* 7 On 24 February 1988, the UDF was effectively banned. The organisation was only unbanned in February 1990, having fought for two years underground. *Ibid.* 8 Both the UDF and COSATU are part of the MDM – in many respects the term MDM was first used in the context of the effective banning of the UDF and COSATU. **1990** R. MALAN *My Traitor's Heart* 249 In the early eighties, the ANC moved to reestablish an above-ground presence inside South Africa. This presence ultimately took the form of the UDF, .. which .. cleaved faithfully to the ANC line. **1993** *Sunday Times* 12 Dec. 24 Among those who will have to decide whether to include Mrs Mandela, will be former UDF leaders.

UDI /juː diː ˈaɪ/ *n.* [Initial letters of *Unilateral Declaration of Independence*, first used of Prime Minister Ian Smith's declaration of Rhodesian independence, on 11 November 1965.] **a.** *transf.* Any unilateral declaration of political independence. **b.** *fig.* Any move to self-sufficiency without consultation or mutual agreement.

[**1965** *Time* 5 Nov. 41 Wilson turned to another tack: subtle (and not-so-subtle) hints of the dangers of U.D.I. If Rhodesians felt they could break with Britain and escape hardships, they were wrong.] **1978** *E. Prov. Herald* 26 Feb. 1 A report expected today .. and a Cabinet meeting tomorrow could finally decide whether South Africa will go it alone with a South West Africa UDI. **1979** *Drum* Feb. 24 They all decided to stay on, but declared an editorial UDI saying that the editorial department and the editorial department alone would dictate editorial policy. **1979** A. KUMALO in *Ibid.* Mar. 17 He tried to salvage the situation by allowing us to declare editorial UDI; that we were to decide policy and call the tune without any interference. **1979** *Capetonian* May 8 In consultation with .. Capeys of all races and provenances whose hearts are in the right place, namely Milnerton Racecourse .. , I hereby announce our intention of declaring UDI. **1979** *Sunday Tribune* 3 June 30 Last year, in what amounted to a UDI, Chief Hadebe declared himself a monarch and petitioned the Government with a demand for a separate homeland, saying that he wanted nothing more to do with KwaZulu. **1981** *Rand Daily Mail* 30 June 1 South Africa will not allow a UDI in SWA 'by giving full executive powers to the Ministers' Council.' **1985** *Style* Apr. 32 Mr Joe Rabinowitz, a city councillor, mooted the idea of Sea Point declaring UDI. **1988** *Cape Times* 25 Mar. 1 Savimbi declares UDI.

Udiqua's var. ODIQUA.

UDW *n.* [Initial letters of *University of Durban Westville*.] A university established (originally, only for those of Indian descent) in 1961.

1992 *Academic Standard* Apr. 9 The Rector .. spelt out the challenge and constraints facing UDW and re-affirmed his commitment to the ideals of consultation and democratic participation.

ugologo var. GOLOGO.

ugubu /ʊˈgʊ(ː)bʊ/ *n.* Also **(i)gubu, ugubhu.** [Zulu *ugubhu*.] A single-stringed Zulu musical bow with a gourd resonator.

1866 W.C. HOLDEN *Past & Future* 271 The only attempt at an instrument that I have seen is the gubu. This consists of a calabash attached to a bow with a string of buck's skin: they beat the calabash with a rod, and it makes a monotonous, vibrating sound, without meaning or charm. **1906** E. CLAIRMONTE *Africander* 189 Their chief instrument, called a *gubu*, which is something like a one-string banjo with an empty gourd for a drum. **1925** D. KIDD *Essential Kafir* 333 The chief instrument in general use (called an Igubu) is made from a long stick which is bent like a bow by a string; the stick is fastened to a round gourd; the gourd is placed on the breast, and acts as a sounding-board. When the string is struck with a piece of reed the instrument gives out a sort of 'ting, ting, ting' sound which is most monotonous. **1949** O. WALKER *Proud Zulu* (1951) 59 She carried an uGubu, a stringed bow with a calabash attached as a resonator, the calabash pressed against her slim shoulder, the stick used for striking the bow to produce a rhythmic accompaniment, held lightly in her other hand. **1971** *Nat. Geog. Mag.* Dec. 745 (*caption*) Visitor from the city makes himself at home, strumming an ugubu while his host's wives prepare the evening meal. **1980** D.B. COPLAN Urbanization of African Performing Arts. 72 Gourd-resonated bows, such as the Zulu *ugubu* and its cognates .. supply bass ostinato while leaving the performer's mouth free for solo vocalization. **1984** *Daily Dispatch* 29 June 11 The Zulu gourd-bow 'ugubhu' .. is the classic Zulu instrument for solo song accompaniment.

uhili var. HILI.

uhlanga *n. obs.* Also **u-hlanga, Ut(h)langa.** [Zulu *uhlanga* reed, original stem, stock, ancestry; the word has been found in similar senses in Xhosa, and some uses may be derived from Xhosa *umhlanga* first ancestor.] Among Xhosa- and Zulu-speakers: the reed clump or primal source of being from which the first human ancestor is said to have emerged; the traditional supreme being. See also UNKULUNKULU sense 1.

1827 G. THOMPSON *Trav.* II. 352 The Caffers believe in a Supreme Being, to whom they give the appellation of Uhlanga (Supreme). **1828** T. PRINGLE *Ephemerides* 180 He told them that he was sent by Uhlanga, the Great Spirit, to avenge their wrongs. **1829** C. ROSE *Four Yrs in Sn Afr.* 145 When the kraal is struck by lightning, the site is either deserted, or an ox burnt on the spot, or buried beneath it, as an offering to the incensed spirit of the kraal, or to Uhlanga, the spirit of thunder. **1841** B. SHAW *Memorials* 41 Of a Divine Being, (whom they call Uhlanga or Supreme,) they have some distinct notion. **1846** R. MOFFAT *Missionary Labours* 68 Uhlanga is also used by the Kafirs to denote a Supreme Being. **1857** J. SHOOTER *Kafirs of Natal* 159 The Kafirs of Natal and the Zulu-country have preserved the tradition of a Being whom they call the Great-Great and the First Appearer or Exister ... Creation was effected by splitting a reed, when the first man and other things issued from the cleft ... *U-hlanga* signifies origin as well as reed. **1875** D. LESLIE *Among Zulus* 148 The first man, who they say 'tore them out of the reeds,' *Uhlanga*, literally, 'reed', they use for 'custom'. **1870** H. CALLAWAY *Religious System of Amazulu* 2 Uthlanga is a reed, strictly speaking, one which is capable of 'stooling', throwing out offsets. It thus comes, metaphorically, to mean a source of being. **1925** D. KIDD *Essential Kafir* 101 Brownlee tells us that Uthlanga simply means supreme, and that Utixo means beautiful.

‖**uilbaard** /'œɪlbɑː(r)t/ *n.* [Afk., *uil* owl + *baard* beard.] A beard worn as a fringe round the face, with cheeks and mouth clean-shaven.

1972 A.A. TELFORD *Yesterday's Dress* 121 Judging from old portraits, it would seem that numbers of Voortrekkers were unshaven, with full beards and moustaches. Some, however, shaved the area of the cheeks and mouth, leaving a growth under the chin known as an 'uilbaard'. **1975** D.H. STRUTT *Clothing Fashions* 217 Those who did shave removed the moustache and all the hair on the face, leaving a fringe right round it from sideburn to sideburn and under the chin. This was the *uilbaard* (owl beard).

uintjie /'eɪŋki, 'œɪŋki/ *n.* Also **aju(i)ntje, inchie, intje, oenkje, ointjie, uintje, untjie, uy(e)ntje, uynt(j)ie.** [fr. Du. *ajuintje* little onion.]

1.a. Any of numerous edible bulbs, esp. the corms of certain plants of the Iridaceae, including species of *Moraea* (esp. *Moraea edulis*), *Gladiolus*, and *Babiana*, and species of *Aponogeton* (of the Aponogetonaceae). Also *attrib.* See also GLADIOLUS, TULP.

1786 G. FORSTER tr. *A. Sparrman's Voy. to Cape of G.H.* I. 148 Among these [bulbous plants] I now could number several different varieties of *irises*. The roots, or more properly the bulbs of these, it is common here to roast in the ashes and eat: they are called *uynties*, and have nearly the same taste with potatoes. **1802** TRUTER & SOMERVILLE in G.M. Theal *Rec. of Cape Col.* (1899) IV. 419 They had .. nothing to eat but roots of uyntjes which they had digged from under the ground, and of which they had yet a provision in their pockets, which they shewed us. **1818** S.N. EATON Journal. 47 Besides the vegetables common in England, I have seen several new to me — one called Uintjes (pronounced oontches), resembling much the chestnut in flavour .. called Hottentot Bread, grows wild, with a yellow flower somewhat like a small daffodil. **1822** W.J. BURCHELL *Trav.* I. 417 At the same time, a present of *uyentjes*. This is a colonial name in very general use, and is applied to several kinds of small eatable bulbs. None of those in question were larger than a hazle-nut, and were cased in several thin brown husks. **a1827** D. CARMICHAEL in W.J. Hooker *Botanical Misc.* (1831) II. 265 With infinite labour they dig the root of a species of *Antholyza* ... The produce of half an hour's toil, which they call *Untjie*, does not exceed the bulk of a chestnut. **1856** L. PAPPE in *Cape of G.H. Almanac & Annual Register* 343 The mealy bulbs, commonly known as Uintjes (bulbs), are nourishing and somewhat approach chestnuts in taste. **1872** E.J. DUNN in A.M.L. Robinson *Sel. Articles from Cape Monthly Mag.* (1978) 54 The principal varieties consumed by them are two kinds of 'camberoo' and 'uintjes'. **1886** G.A. FARINI *Through Kalahari Desert* 138 Knowing that the *inchies* (roots) were generally good to eat before they were in flower, I searched for some, and tried to eat them raw; but they were so unpalatable that I had to make a little fire and cook them in the hot sand. **1911** D.B. HOOK *'Tis but Yesterday* 57 Wholesome little roots and bulbs — called 'intjes' — which Marie used as a tooth powder in order to whiten her beautiful teeth. **1913** C. PETTMAN *Africanderisms* 524 The bulbous roots of these plants, not unlike the chestnut in flavour, were an important article of food in the early days of the Colony, both among the Hottentots and the slaves, and even now, at the proper season, they are gathered in considerable quantities by the coloured and poorer classes of the Western Province. **1936** C. BIRKBY *Thirstland Treks* 317 When game is scarce they are content to loaf while their women gather *veldkos* or dig up *ointjie* bulbs to be baked in hot ashes. **1955** L.G. GREEN *Karoo* 103 Many varieties of *uintjies* (edible bulbs) are found in the karoo. Some are eaten raw, others stewed with meat ... Certain *uintjies* taste like chestnuts and make a strong soup. **1969** J.M. WHITE *Land God Made in Anger* 229 Tsi roots and *ointjie* bulbs are two of the delicacies for which a Bushman woman, accompanied by her children will grub around with the aid of her sharpened digging-stick. **1975** W. STEENKAMP *Land of Thirst King* 129 Many shelves of that vast storehouse are filled with edible bulbs of one variety or another, all known by the generic name of 'uintjie'.

b. *comb. obs.* **uintjies-tyd,** also (formerly) **uyntjes-tijd,** [Afk., *tyd* fr. Du. *tijd* time], the time when uintjies are in season.

[**1786** G. FORSTER tr. *A. Sparrman's Voy. to Cape of G.H.* I. 148 The Hottentots .. use the word *uynties* .. for the reckoning of time; always beginning the new year, whenever the uynties push out of the ground, and marking their age and other events by the number of times in which, in a certain period, this vegetable has made its appearance.] **1801** J. BARROW *Trav.* I. 159 The season of the year is usually indicated by being so many moons before or after uyntjes tyd, or the time that the roots of the *iris edulis* are in season. **1841** B. SHAW *Memorials* 26 The season of the year is generally indicated by its being so many moons before or after *uyntjies tyd*, or the time that the roots which they are accustomed to eat are in season. **1913** C. PETTMAN *Africanderisms* 525 *Uyntjes-tyd*, The time when these various roots were in season. How much these plants were esteemed and the large place they occupied in the domestic economy of the slaves and poorer classes, may be inferred from their making the *uyntjes-tijd* a point from to which to reckon.

2.a. The sedge plant *Cyperus rotundus* of the Cyperaceae, which produces strings of very small bulbs. **b.** The onion weed *Nothoscordum inodorum* of the Liliaceae, a common garden weed.

1958 R.E. LIGHTON *Out of Strong* 78 And our house, Johann? Shame! It will fall in. The black jacks, khaki weed and uintjies will choke our garden. **1973** *S. Afr. Garden & Home* Sept. 19 My neighbour's garden was covered in uintjies, but we eradicated them within a year. **1974** *Daily Dispatch* 18 May 4, I see that a preparation is being advertised for eradicating 'Uintjes' in lawns. I have not yet heard of any success with it. **1976** *E. Prov. Herald* 13 Oct. 11 Spray your lawn with new Basagran. Strong, fast-acting Bassagran quickly controls 'uintjies' (yellow nutgrass). **1991** *Weekend Post* 26 Jan. (Leisure) 7 Onion weed, or uintjies, are a constant source of irritation to many gardeners ... *Nothoscordum inodorum* is a stubborn pest. **1993** *Ibid.* 1 May (Leisure) 7 Every now and then I get a call from a rather desperate reader asking how to get rid of onion weeds (uintjies).

‖**uitlander** /'eɪtlandə, 'œɪtlandə(r)/ *n.* and *adj.* [Afk., lit. 'outlander'.]

A. *n.*

a. A foreigner or alien. **b.** *hist.* Often with initial capital. In the old Transvaal Republic during the years leading up to the South African War: one who was not Afrikaans and who therefore was not accepted as a 'burgher' or citizen. Also *fig.* In both senses also called OUTLANDER. Cf. BURGHER sense 4.

1871 J. MACKENZIE *Ten Yrs* (1971) 459 If Englishmen were once in numbers to the north of the restless Dutchmen, the latter would give up their search for the Land of Canaan, and be content with their present residences. In their northward movement they always complain of the increasing 'uitlanders,' or foreigners coming from the South. **1888** *Cape Punch* 1 Aug. 47 Me a simple Caper At whom uitlanders sneer. **1893** 'M' in *Cape Illust. Mag.* Apr. 287 Taxation has been made to fall lightly on the Boer and heavily on the 'uitlander'. **1896** *Argus* 2 Jan. 4 We confidently believe that the sentiment and sympathy of this Colony is on the side of the uitlander — who has only taken up arms as a last resort. **1899** 'S. ERASMUS' *Prinsloo* p.v, I take the opportunity to show how the presence of the Hollander and Uitlander in the Transvaal has ruined the character of the Afrikander. **1900** H. BUTTERWORTH *Trav. Tales* 57 Who are the Uitlanders? They are the outsiders, for the most part; people who expect to get rich in the country and to leave it. **1924** L. COHEN *Reminisc. of Jhb.* 74 Kruger was an impracticable person, fully determined to grant no privileges to the Uitlanders, who, he was certain, had it in their minds to filch his country ... Kruger never attempted to hide his opinion of the newcomers, no matter their nationality. **1924** D. FAIRBRIDGE *Gardens of S. Afr.* 99 The Starling .. is still an uitlander in South Africa. **1934** N. DEVITT *Mem. of Magistrate* 18 The fact that the British section, the Uitlanders, had no voice in the governing of the country, whilst paying most of the taxes was a political grievance, and a predisposing cause of the second Anglo-Boer War. **1936** R.J.M. GOOLD-ADAMS *S. Afr. To-Day & To-Morrow* 25 The rest of us, the rest of the people in South Africa to-day, both black and white, are interlopers — 'uitlanders', Paul Kruger might have called them. **1949** H. GIBBS *Twilight* 168 Boer attitude towards the British, the Uitlanders, hardens. **1952** B. DAVIDSON *Report on Sn Afr.* 180 The authentic sense of frustration and pent-up anger which the Boers felt, and their descendants still feel, against the *Uitlanders*, the foreigners, who somehow managed to take their 'liberties' away from them. **1961** [see OUMA sense 1]. **1962** L.E. NEAME *Hist. of Apartheid* 84 The Asian is regarded as an alien, a foreigner, an 'uitlander', a temporary sojourner in a foreign land who cannot claim rights of citizenship in that country. **1972** *Daily Dispatch* 19 June 12 The urbanised African .. is being treated far worse than Paul Kruger ever treated the Uitlanders. **1978** *Sunday Times* 28 May 15 Mines, industry and commerce were pioneered and run by so-called 'uitlanders' and the civil service by Hollanders. *Ibid.* 12 Nov. 3 Being a mere uitlander, I confess that I didn't understand half the recipes. **1980** *S. Afr. Panorama* Aug. 13 Pilgrim's Rest was the country's first big gold mining town, and it was in this region that the Transvaal Boers and Uitlanders (foreigners) first met in large numbers. **1986** L. CAPSTICKDALE in *S. Afr. Panorama* Nov. 10 Champions of the rights of the Uitlanders (as the foreign element in Johannesburg was called), the Reform Committee imported guns into Johannesburg concealed in oil drums. **1992** P. O'BYRNE in *Sunday Times* 16 Aug. 16 For many years I was a victim — an unabsorbed *uitlander* in a place where loyalties lay among the National Party. **1992** C. STUART in *Afr. Wildlife* Vol.46 No.6, 279 This [hybridisation] has serious implications for pure Cape buffalo stocks ... The most important factor to consider .. is the long-term genetic implication for the mingling of these 'uitlanders' with the local pure stock.

B. *adj.*

1. Of or pertaining to those resident in the Transvaal Republic but not accepted as its citizens.

1895 *Star* 21 Dec. 1 There is an uitlander population of more than 100 000 in the Transvaal, a large proportion being adult males who probably outnumber the burghers in the proportion of two to one. **1900** H. BLORE *Imp. Light Horseman* 14 A demand on the part of the burghers that .. the uitlander women and children should be transferred to the open vehicles. **1910** *Rand Daily Mail* 31 May 7 Through participation in the uitlander agitation he was compelled to leave the Rand before the outbreak of hostilities.

2. Foreign, alien.

1965 K. MACKENZIE *Deserter* 56 He had a way of swinging his head to get the hair back off his face which had always seemed to Japie a particularly *uitlander* sort of habit. **1973** *Star* 12 July 21 More than a hint of the uitlander mentality hovered at the back of the minds of most immigrants. **1975** *Weekend Post* 28 June 9 There are many greedy uitlander dealers there who think they're going to make a killing in South African wine.

Hence (by back-formation) **Uitland** *n.* nonce, foreign countries, 'abroad'.

1890 C. & A.P. WILSON-MOORE *Diggers' Doggerel* 40 Men from Uitland, Dutchman, Sheeney.

uitspan /ˈeɪtspæn, ˈœɪtspɑn/ *n.* [Du., see OUTSPAN *v.*] In full ***uitspan place***: OUTSPAN *n.* sense 1.

1801 in G.M. Theal *Rec. of Cape Col.* (1899) IV. 361 Unyoked at noon the oxen to graze, and in the afternoon being again put to the waggons, we went from this so called uitspan place. **1809** H. ALEXANDER in *Ibid.* (1900) VI. 473 What customary Uitspan places (places for unyoking Cattle) are in the Cape District. **1822** [see OUTSPAN *n.* sense 1]. **1823** W.W. BIRD *State of Cape of G.H.* 99 Without other rest than for an hour or two, at the public halting-places, called the Uitspan. **1830** *Cape Lit. Gaz.* 16 June 2 Things varied as we reached our first uit-span place. **1835** A. STEEDMAN *Wanderings* I. 91 It was our intention to have reached Pampoen kraal as our first *uitspan*-place. **1872** [see UITSPAN *v.*]. **1891** W. SELWYN *Cape Carols* 11 The evening 'uitspan' near a stream. **1902** [see HOOGE VELD]. **1910** L.D. FLEMMING *Settler's Scribblings* (1921) 61 Fitz Hyphen Jones strode swiftly through the 'uitspans'. **1949** L.G. GREEN *In Land of Afternoon* 13 All who lit uitspan fires and slept in their wagons beside the old Cape roads. *Ibid.* 17 Many villages formed themselves round an *uitspan* or store. **1951** — *Grow Lovely* 69 Farmers .. used as their uitspan a large open space called De Plein van De Kaap.

uitspan *v. obs.* [Du.; see OUTSPAN *v.*]

1. *intrans.* OUTSPAN *v.* sense 2 a.

1819 G. BARKER *Journal.* 23 Jan., Uitspanned in the Quaggers vlakte this evening. **1820** W. SHAW *Diary.* 5 June, Here we uitspan'd as it is termed i.e. the oxen were turned out to graze in the valley and its surrounding hills — while we employed ourselves in cutting wood, making a fire — and preparing food. **1829** C. ROSE *Four Yrs in Sn Afr.* 156 A Kaffer returned to his own country from Cape Town .. told his tale to the dark group around him, describing the wonders of a ship, which he called 'a waggon that moved upon the waters, and that never uitspan'd' (unyoked). **1833** *Graham's Town Jrnl* 20 June 2 Having *uitspanned* at the latter river the party proceeded out in different directions in quest of game. **1835** [see PONT sense 1]. **1872** 'Z.' in *Cape Monthly Mag.* V. Oct. 230 We shall be ready enough not only to 'inspan' or 'uitspan' according to circumstances, but we shall order our driver, when the horses are flagging and stomachs importunate, to look out for a nice 'uitspan'. c**1936** *S. & E. Afr. Yr Bk & Guide* 37 The following Afrikaans words are in general use throughout the country .. Uitspan, to unharness, to halt [etc.].

2. *trans.* OUTSPAN *v.* sense 1 b.

1882 C. DU VAL *With Show through Sn Afr.* I. 60 Some wonderful words have been manufactured in Southern Africa .. 'Inspan', and its reverse, 'Outspan' — or, to be more correct, 'Uitspan' — simply means the harnessing or yoking in of any draught animal or team, and the unyoking. **1891** W. SELWYN *Cape Carols* 2 How grateful the halt near the bush-margined stream where 'uitspanned,' our hungry and sweltering team lave their hot dusty hoofs.

uitvalgrond /ˈeɪtfɑlˌxrɔnt, ˈœɪt-/ *n. Law.* [Afk., *uitval* fall out, disagree + *grond* ground.] See quot. 1925. See also INKRUIP PLAAS.

1905 *Transvaal Law Reports, Supreme Court* 1904 709 Pieces of *uitval grond* between farms were to be sold by auction, when they could not be more profitably let. **1925** W.H.S. BELL *S. Afr. Legal Dict.* 562 *Uitval grond*, .. small pieces of land remaining over between surveyed or unsurveyed farms. **1943** L. SOWDEN *Union of S. Afr.* 128 Johannesburg was first laid out on a triangular piece of *uitvalgrond* — a piece of no man's land that no man, till then, had wanted. **1960** J.J.L. SISSON *S. Afr. Judicial Dict.* 820 *Uitval grond*, Small pieces of land remaining over between surveyed or unsurveyed farms. **1962** A.P. CARTWRIGHT *Gold Miners* 225 Nineteen miles to the east of Johannesburg lay Benoni ... The story goes that Rissik had the greatest difficulty in deciding where the boundaries of this *uitvalgrond* (literally an odd piece of ground surrounded by farms) fell. To mark the trouble it had given him he called it after Rachel's son whom she named Benoni, the 'son of my sorrow'. **1967** E. ROSENTHAL *Encycl. of Sn Afr.* 577 The most famous piece of Uitvalgrond was the farm Randjeslaagte on which the city of Johannesburg was laid out. **1978** *Sunday Times* 12 Nov. (Mag. Sect.) 9 The unoccupied uitvalgrond was the obvious choice of the staatsraad for the site of the proposed new town on the goldfields. [**1988** J. SCOTT in *Cape Times* 5 Dec. 6 It [sc. the town of Boksburg] was built on what was called, in the 19th century, 'uitvalgrond' because everybody who went there had a fall-out over what side of the hole people of colour were allowed to stand.] **1990** C. LAFFEATY *Far Forbidden Plains* 90 There is a piece of land between the van Tonder farm and Jakkalsdrif which both of them claim, and because neither will give way it has become *uitvalgrond*.

ukhamba var. KAMBA.

ukhehla var. KEHLA.

‖**ukubuyisa** /ʊkʊbʊˈjiːsɑ/ *n.* [Zulu, lit. 'to call back'; to retrieve.] Among Zulus: a traditional ceremony performed a year after a death, to call back the departed spirit and integrate it into the community of ancestral guardian spirits.

1955 E.A. RITTER *Shaka Zulu* 57 A platoon of warriors guarded the grave .., and day and night this watch was kept for many moons, until the ukubuyisa (bringing back the spirit) ceremony had been performed. **1974** C.T. BINNS *Warrior People* 75 A deeply-ingrained custom amongst the Zulus, and one of the strongest pillars of their belief down to the present day, is the ukuBuyisa ceremony, or the Bringing Back of the Spirit of their Ancestor into the kraal of his descendants or, under modern conditions, into the home of his family where henceforward he would reside as its guardian angel. **1981** M. KUNENE *Anthem of Decades* p.xix, The emphasis of the Zulu belief is on the continuity of life. After death, the spirit has to outgrow its period of infancy. At the end of a year, it is integrated into the community of all the guardian spirits (ukubuyisa — The feast of return). **1988** I. DARBY in Laband & Haswell *Pietermaritzburg 1838–1988* 166 By means of the ancestors, community was maintained. The ceremony of *imbeleko* which followed the birth of a child gave it personhood and identity. Likewise after death *ukubuyisa* ensured that the deceased was accepted by the ancestors. **1990** J. KNAPPERT *Aquarian Guide to Afr. Mythology* 40 The Zulu used to institute a special ceremony called *ukubuyisa* 'to bring back', hoping to induce the spirit of a venerated chief or a helpful and dependable father to take up his residence in his own village again, about a year after his death.

ukugiya var. GIYA *n.*

ukuhlonipha var. HLONIPHA *n.*

‖**ukulobola** /ˌʊkʊlɔˈbɔːla, ˌʊgʊ-/ *n.* [Xhosa and Zulu, vbl n. prefix *uku-* + *lobola* see LOBOLA *v.*] LOBOLA *n.* sense 1. Also *attrib.*

1855 J.W. COLENSO *Ten Weeks in Natal* 138 A Kafir, going to marry, usually pays a number of cows to the father of the bride. This is called ukuLobola. **1887** J.W. MATTHEWS *Incwadi Yami* 37 Ukulobola, or the practice of giving cattle to the father or guardian of a girl or widow, on her marriage, by her husband, is one of the oldest laws among the natives of South Africa. **1906** *Question of Colour* 65 There is one widespread custom in South Africa known as 'ukulobola', which must be realised in considering marriage customs. **1951** H. DAVIES *Great S. Afr. Christians* 48 He believed .. that the *uku-lobola* custom (or marriage-dowry of cattle) should be continued. **1962** W.D. HAMMOND-TOOKE *Bhaca Soc.* 132 The above descriptions of the marriage ceremonies of the Bhaca have shown the important part played by the handing over of cattle in these proceedings. The verb ukulobola is used to express this action. **1985** P. McALLISTER *Informant, Grahamstown* Ukulobola in its broad sense refers to the process of negotiating the exchange and size of the bridewealth, in its narrower sense it may be translated as 'to give bridewealth/dowry'.

‖**ukumetsha** /ˌʊkʊˈmɛːtʃa, ˌʊgʊ-/ *n.* Also **metsha**. [Xhosa, vbl n. prefix *uku-* + v. stem *metsha* have such intercourse.] Among Xhosa people: a form of sexual play (esp. among courting adolescents) in which the genitals are brought together (sometimes through a cloth barrier), but in which penetration does not take place.

A traditionally-accepted practice for unmarried couples which may also be practised by married couples as a form of contraception.

1933 I. SCHAPERA *Early Cape Hottentots* 197 The custom to which reference is made here is possibly that known to the AmaXhosa as *ukumetsha*, a form of unconsummated sexual intercourse practised by unmarried boys and girls. **1937** B.J.F. LAUBSCHER *Sex, Custom & Psychopathology* 79 The word *metsha* denotes courtship as well as a form of pseudo-sexual intercourse. **1976** *Daily Dispatch* 20 Aug. 6 Ukumetsha has .. been replaced by 'ukudyola'. This verb .. means anything from a kiss to living together. **1980** J. COCK *Maids & Madams* 276 Traditional rural people had their own contraceptive methods, especially ukumetsha. **1989** *Greater Dict. of Xhosa* 731 Ukumetsha, Traditionally of a boy or young unmarried man and a girl: engage in sexual play that did not involve penetration or contact of the sex organs.

Hence (rare) **metsha** *v. intrans.*

1937 B.J.F. LAUBSCHER *Sex, Custom & Psychopathology* 80 Schizophrenic patients frequently declare they never metsha'd ... The girls *metsha* with their lovers. *Ibid.* 82 Where she *metshas* with more than one man and pregnancy results, she will find it difficult to prove paternity.

ukumkani var. UMKUMKANI.

ukutakata var. TAGATI *n.* sense 2.

ukuthwala var. TWALA *n.*[2]

uku-tomba var. THOMBA.

ukutshila var. TSHILA.

ukutwala see TWALA *n.*[2]

ukutwasa var. THWASA.

um-, umu- /ʊm(ʊ)/ *pref.* A Xhosa and Zulu singular noun prefix, found in some words originating in these languages. Cf. I-.

For examples, see MLUNGU, UMFAAN. In Xhosa and Zulu, the plural of words beginning *um-* or *umu-* is formed by replacing the prefix with *aba-* or *abe-*, or with *imi-* ; in *S. Afr. Eng.* this pattern is not always observed, and the plural is sometimes formed by the addition of English pl. *-s* to the singular form. See also ABA-, ABE-.

umabalane var. MABALANE.

umantshingelani var. MANTSHINGILANE.

Umanyano var. MANYANO.

umatsha var. MUTSHA.

umatungulu var. AMATUNGULU.

umbhanselo var. BONSELLA.

Umbo var. MBO.

umbrella thorn *n. phr.* [So named for its wide-spreading crown.] The HAAK-EN-STEEK (sense a), *Acacia tortilis*. Also *attrib.*

1913 C. PETTMAN *Africanderisms* 521 *Umbrella thorn, Acacia spirocarpa* .. is so named in the Transvaal. **1988** A. HALL-MARTIN et al. *Kaokoveld* 12 Umbrella thorns (*Acacia tortilis*) with a mean height of 12 metres are co-dominant with tall mopane trees. **1990** [see SWEET THORN]. **1992** *S. Afr. Panorama* Mar. 120 The lordly nyala come down to drink from dense surrounding woods with their characteristic umbrella thorn and candelabra trees. **1993** *Getaway* Nov. 76 The spreading crowns of umbrella thorn trees *Acacia tortilis* perhaps best represent the archetypal image of the African savanna.

umbrella-tree *n.* [Named for its umbrella-shaped crown; perh. at first a literal tr. of Afk. *kiepersol*.] KIEPERSOL. Also *attrib.*

1951 N.L. KING *Tree-Planting* 67 *Cussonia paniculata (um-Senge or umbrella tree)*, A small tree with large leaves crowded together at the ends of the branches. Widespread at high altitudes. **1972** B. SMIT in *Std Encycl. of Sn Afr.* VII. 575 The umbrella-tree emperor-moth .. feeds on the 'kiepersol' or umbrella-tree. *c*1986 *Eng. Alive '86* 54 With the back of his hand, John would wipe his mouth and drain the beer from his can and, always, each would tell one story in the heat of the day under an umbrella-tree.

umconto var. UMKHONTO.

umdodie var. INDODA.

umdoni /ʌmˈdəʊnɪ, ʊmˈdɔːni/ *n.* Also with initial capital. [Zulu.] The tree *Syzygium cordatum* of the Myrtaceae, usu. found near water, which bears edible berries and provides durable wood; WATERBOOM sense 1. Also *attrib.*

1854 R.B. STRUTHERS *Hunting Jrnl* (1991) 40 Dying shirts a brown dry grass colour with the bark of the Waterboom (Umdoni). *Ibid.* 64 Troubled with Diarrhoea — took Infus (Umdoni) Waterboom bark, which quickly relieved me. **1951** N.L. KING *Tree-Planting in S. Afr.* 71 *Syzygium cordatum (um Doni or um Swi)*, A picturesque, medium-sized tree with a large, spreading crown. **1967** S.M.A. LOWE *Hungry Veld* 93 Birds of every description were chattering furiously in a large umdoni tree. **1983** K.C. PALGRAVE *Trees of Sn Afr.* 690 *Umdoni*, A medium sized tree 8 to 15 m in height, but sometimes flowering as a dwarf shrub ... *Flowers*: creamy-white to pinkish, the stamens being .. about 2 to 2,5 cm in diameter in dense heads up to 10 cm in diameter at the ends of the branches. **1986** [see *purple-crested loerie* (LOERIE sense 1 b)].

‖**umdudo** /ʊmˈduːdɔ, ʊmduːdɔ/ *n.* [Xhosa.] A dance at a traditional Xhosa wedding ceremony, indicating acceptance of the bride by her parents-in-law; the marriage ceremony.

1891 T.R. BEATTIE *Pambaniso* 54 The dance on an occasion of marriage is known by the name of *Umdudo.* **1902** G.M. THEAL Beginning of S. Afr. Hist. 70 Among these people the whole of the marriage ceremonies are included in the term *umdudo.* **1978** M.J. MTSAKA *Not his Pride* 29 Meko: But you're a liar, this occasion was never called a wedding day. I was already a big boy then, it was called *umdudo.* Palamente: All that you've just shown to us tells us of *umdudo*; and *umdudo* is the traditional wedding ceremony. **1988** M. MXOTWA in *Daily Dispatch* 17 Dec., A group of specially chosen men and women danced the umdudo — an indication of the acceptance of the bride by her in-laws. **1989** *Greater Dict. of Xhosa* 730 An *uduli* for which an animal has been slaughtered and an *umdudo* [which] has been held is regarded as proof that there has been a marriage.

umfaan /ʊmˈfɑːn, ˈʌmfɑːn/ *n.* Also **mfana, oomfa(a)n, umfan(a), umfane.** Pl. **-s, abafana, bafana.** [ad. Zulu *umfana* (pl. *abafana*, and vocative forms, sing. *mfana*, pl. *bafana*) boy, designating a male child from babyhood to young manhood. For notes on the varying pl. forms used, see M-, UM-, ABA-.]

1. Usu. in the forms **mfana** or **umfana** /(ʊ)mˈfana/ (pl. **(a)bafana**). Among Zulu-speaking people: a young man who has gone through initiation but is not yet married. Also used (often loosely) as a form of address.

1852 C. BARTER *Dorp & Veld* 213 The Kaffir *umfane* (boy) when he becomes an *indola* (man), shaves his head and *sews* into the scalp a circular coronet of reeds. **1928** N. DEVITT *Blue Lizard* 35 'Hau' he cried in his anguish. 'Abafana! Go and fetch the oxen.' **1937** B.J.F. LAUBSCHER *Sex, Custom & Psychopathology* 10 The *Abafana* and girls slept with the bridal couple in the honeymoon hut. **1939** N.J. VAN WARMELO in A.M. Duggan-Cronin *Bantu Tribes* III. 32 They are now young men (abafana), who will shortly look out for wives; having secured them, they become amadodana and finally, family men, amadoda. **1949** L. HUNTER *Afr. Dawn* 37 'How old are you *umfana*?' he asked. 'I am seventeen,' replied Mayeza. **1961** T. MATSHIKIZA *Choc. for my Wife* 101 The constant customers told us, 'Hey, bafana, wash hands.' **1963** WILSON & MAFEJE *Langa* 155 The conflict was between a newly circumcised young man (*ikrwala*) and another young but more senior man (*umfana*) ... The *umfana* reported the matter to one of the older men. **1967** J.A. BROSTER *Red Blanket Valley* 143 The amakrwala were known as abafana (singular umfana) or initiated youths. **1968** M. DOYLE *Impala* 135 Men who were full *umfaans* and *madalas*. **1968** [see PAP *n.* sense 1]. **1976** M. THOLO in C. Hermer *Diary of Maria Tholo* (1980), Most of the participants were quite young, about 12 to 15. They weren't the abafana. [*Note*] Older boys, who, traditionally would have been circumcised but not yet married (Xhosa). In the city, circumcision is often delayed but the term would refer to boys in the age group 16–22. **1979** M. MATSHOBA *Call Me Not a Man* 65, I reckon you're awed by your newly acquired fatherhood status, *mfana.* **1993** *Sowetan* 22 Jan. 8 Listen here, mfana. If you want to get drunk and go wild you must go somewhere else.

2. Pl. usu. **-s.** *Offensive.* Esp. in Natal: a male servant (of any age) employed in domestic service; cf. BOY sense 1.

1878 H.A. ROCHE *On Trek in Tvl* 21 Jim the Kafir, Sam the Coolie, or Tom the little Oomfaan, — all equally 'Boys'. *Ibid.* 39 Your wife .. if she be so lucky as to have floors at all, will make that lazy 'Jim' or that provoking '*Oomfan*' clean them for her. **1911** M.S. EVANS *Black & White in S.E. Afr.* 156 The last evidence of poverty of a family in South East Africa would be the inability to employ the ubiquitous umfaan to sweep, to wash, to tend the baby. **1913** C. PETTMAN *Africanderisms* 521 *Umfaan*, The term is applied in Natal to the Zulu boys who are employed by the Colonists to look after small children; indeed, in some parts of the 'Garden Colony' the word has almost become the equivalent of the English word 'nurse'. **1968** K. MCMAGH *Dinner of Herbs* 166 We .. suffered a succession of umfaans .. who were .. as bad as Lena except for the fact that they were not allowed into the bedrooms. **1972** BEETON & DORNER in *Eng. Usage in Sn Afr.* Vol.3 No.1, 47 *Umfaan*, .. In Natal, a junior male servant employed to care for small children or perform general work. **1973** *S. Afr. Garden & Home* Sept. 58 The umfaan is getting quite a lot of exercise trotting from one hose to another, and old Johannes is wandering around .. searching for weeds. **1975** D.H. STRUTT *Clothing Fashions* 349 A Durban mother dressed her young African *umfaan* very much as as she dressed her sons. **1980** A. PATON *Towards Mountain* 16, I have a vague recollection that you could engage an *umfana*, a boy, for five or ten shillings a month. **1986** M. RAMGOBIN *Waiting to Live* 22 'Umfaans' — clothed in short pants and thick white shirts edged with red. [*Note*] Umfaans (from Zulu *umfana*: boy): derogatory kitchen Zulu as used by whites; umfaan = black man of any age = 'boy'.

3. Pl. usu. **-s.** A young black boy; a youth. Cf. KWEDINI. Also (rarely) *attrib.*

1879 R.J. ATCHERLEY *Trip to Boerland* 102 A little Kafir boy, or *umfana*, may prig sugar, and a larger one may surreptitiously abstract rum if he can, but this he does not look upon as stealing. **1902** E. HOBHOUSE *Brunt of War* 241 The drivers and leaders are natives, many umfaans who have never driven before. **1907** *Zululand Times* 18 Jan., Some cattle in charge of a small umfana were near the Inseleni River when two lions .. gave chase. **1937** C. BIRKBY *Zulu Journey* 280 A Pondo umfaan, a youngster who scarcely came up to my elbow. **1940** *Star* 21 Mar. 7 Umfaans who pestered motorists to look after their cars in the streets were described as a nuisance. **1946** S. CLOETE *Afr. Portraits* 254 The men with Wilson were young, almost boys. 'These are but boys,' the Matabele said,'and if umfaans — children — can fight like this, what will we do when the bearded men come to avenge them?' **1953** LANHAM & MOPELI-PAULUS *Blanket Boy's Moon* 178 He heard one umfaan newsvendor call to another. **1956** J. CHATTERTON *Return of Drums* 123 Men seldom herded their cattle or took them to the dipping tank since that was the work of the umfaans. **1964** G. CAMPBELL *Old Dusty* 24, I awoke one morning to find that my natives, with the exception of one small umfaan, had disappeared. **1976** J. MCCLURE *Rogue Eagle* 21 Did the *umfaans* teach you to make oxen with it [*sc.* clay]? **1986** J. CONYNGHAM *Arrowing of Cane* 46 My guide, an umfaan who is apprenticed to the sangoma. **1990** *Weekend Post* 19 Jan. (Leisure) 3 Mischievous *umfaans* still hunt for souvenirs.

umfazi /ʊmˈfɑːzi/ *n.* Also **mfazi, umfase, umfasi, umfaz, umfaze, um Fazi,** and with initial capital. Pl. **(a)bafazi, -s,** and occas. **abafazis.** [Xhosa and Zulu *umfazi* (pl. *abafazi*, vocative forms, sing. *mfazi*, pl. *bafazi*). For notes on pl. forms, see UM-, ABA-, M-.] **a.** A married woman; a wife. **b.** Any (esp. black) woman. Also a form of address.

1833 S. KAY in A. Steedman *Wanderings* I. (1835) 45 In conversation the Caffer frequently classes his *umfaz* (or wife) and *ingegu* (or pack-horse) together. **1836** A.F. GARDINER *Journey to Zoolu Country* 97 An unmarried woman is called Intomebi, A married woman, without children, Umfaz. A married woman, with children, Eneena. **1855** G.H. MASON *Life with Zulus* 148 An old 'Umfaze' (Caffre wife) hastened to fetch a dish of new milk. **1855** J.W. COLENSO *Ten Weeks in Natal* 168 When she was in a room, she was very much like any other *um Fazi*; but when she came out among her people, then he saw that she was Queen of them all. **1860** A.W. DRAYSON *Sporting Scenes* 19 The hard work that an umfazi, or wife, has to perform very soon spoils her girlish figure and appearance, and she then becomes a haggard, wrinkled, repulsive old witch. **1876** T. STUBBS Reminiscences. II. 29 Just as my men were in the act of firing, they called Umfasi we then saw they were Women. **1882** C. DU VAL *With Show through Sn Afr.* II. 195 Klaus .. was going to work at the 'Diamant Veld' for the purpose of making sufficient money to enable him to buy cattle, to be bartered in turn for an additional 'umfase' (wife) or two. **1906** *E. Prov. Herald* 7 Apr., The local natives .. declare the white men to be a lot of old women (Umfazies), for they have no guns. **1968** K. MCMAGH *Dinner of Herbs* 101 His umfazi make very good beer. So I drink with Songololo and I tell him many stories. **1971** [see INDODA sense 1]. **1972** *Drum* 8 Apr. 19 We were out looking for fun with our bafazi's. **1972** *Fair Lady* 14 June 95 The umfazis had been organised into a chain to wet the sacks ... To the right was a small stream and the umfazis were running to it. **1978** J. HEYNS in *Sunday Times* 16 Apr. (Extra) 3 Bewildered and frustrated we read: Zulu Men Only, Indian Women Only,

Blankes Alleenlik, Coloured or European Descent Only, Abafazis and Amadodas ... By the time you found your own WC you had had that singular problem. **1979** M. MATSHOBA *Call Me Not a Man* 160 It's you that's drunk. Coming all the way from eRawutini (Johannesburg) to shepherd *umfazi* for a month and then leave her for a whole year or more. **1990** C. LAFFEATY *Far Forbidden Plains* 245 She find .. English soldier. She become his *mfazi* — his woman — and stay with him. **1993** *Sowetan* 22 Jan. 8 'I've been working hard helping my children study for their exams.' 'Mfazi, you want to produce doctors and lawyers!'

umfundisi /ʊmfʊnˈdiːs(i)/ *n.* Also **mfundisi, M'fundis, mfundizi, (um)fundees, (um)fundis, umfundise**, and with initial capital. Pl. **(a)bafundis(i)**, and (occas.) unchanged. [Xhosa and Zulu, a teacher (pl. *abafundisi*, vocative *mfundisi*).] Among speakers of Xhosa and Zulu: a priest or minister; a teacher; also (occas.) a term of address; MORUTI.

1825 W. SHAW in C. Sadler *Never a Young Man* (1967) 64 On my saying that the Caffres knew me to be a 'Fundis' (teacher) and why should a minister carry arms? Katongo said that might be, but he was not certain that if we fell in with any elephants they would recognise me as a 'Fundis'. **1833** S. KAY *Trav. & Researches* 73 Never have we been safe; but the *Umfundis* shall be our bush. **1835** A. STEEDMAN *Wanderings* I. 51 These '*Abafundis*' (Missionaries) have brought a thing into the land worth more than ten wives. **1837** F. OWEN *Diary* (1926) 44 On his asking them what they had learned they replied, we don't know what we have learned this morning, for the Umfundis (teacher) sent us away so soon. **1854** J.W. COLENSO *Ten Weeks in Natal* (1855) 53 One sheet of paper .. he had filled with figures of common things around him, .. while I was talking with his *umFundise* (teacher). **1860** W. SHAW *Story of my Mission* 471 He said that since he had been at the Mission Station, he had seen it was a very good thing to have *abafundis* or 'teachers' among them. **1863** J.S. DOBIE *S. Afr. Jrnl* (1945) 78 Called at a kraal and got enlightened on road to the umfundisi (missionary). **1871** J. MACKENZIE *Ten Yrs* (1971) 315 This person .. predicted to Tshaka that .. a white man called an 'umfundisi' (missionary) would make his appearance and ask permission from Tshaka to build a house in his country, that he might teach them the 'Great Word'. **1898** B. MITFORD *Induna's Wife* 151 So, Umfundisi, .. I think the people of Zulu prefer the god they know to the one whom thou and such as thee would teach them to worship. **1923** *Other Lands* Oct. 19 Their dear old *Umfundise* was the Moderator-elect. **1931** F.C. SLATER *Secret Veld* 65 'Did you hear a noise,' he asked ... 'No Umfundisi!' she replied, 'I heard nothing.' **1949** L. HUNTER *Afr. Dawn* 14 Not long after the coming of the *Mfundisi* (Missionary) they had all been converted and were married in the church ... This *Mfundisi* had built a large hut in which he told the people about *Dali* — the Creator — .. but the *Mfundisi* called him *Tixo*. **1949** O. WALKER *Proud Zulu* (1951) 80 The Amabunu seek our land, and our labour. The umfundisi — missionaries, they tell us about love. **1955** J.B. SHEPHARD *Land of Tikoloshe* 25 The Mfundisi, the African Minister. **1964** G. GORDON *Four People* 407 A neatly dressed young Xhosa, wearing a clerical collar, walked down the street and smilingly raised his hat as he passed them ... She found herself joining the chorus of respectful greeting that went out from the queue. 'M'fundis!' **1976** A. DELIUS *Border* 195 A group of children came to the edge of the field to stare at the Fundees and his 'umlungu' companion and wave. **1978** B.J. MOTAUNG in *Staffrider* Vol.1 No.2, 23 The people listen like they do to 'Mfundisi' at the Old school yard where they attend church. **1980** *Voice* 29 Oct. 13 A staunch anti-apartheid moruti .. who .. became a roving mfundisi-ambassador of a newly-born 'national state'. **1983** *Pace* Oct. 83 For six weeks .. I had the opportunity to don the mfundisi's garb in and around Durban townships. I have never been afforded the respect that I experienced .. behind that white dog collar. **1987** O. PROZESKY *Wrath of Lamb* 30 The white doctors and the white *abafundisi* or church ministers. **1990** O. MUSI in *City Press* 4 Mar. 6 There are too many churches, too many Bafundisi and too many Archbishops.

umhlahlo /ʊmˈɬaːɬɔ/ *n.* [Xhosa.] Among the Xhosa peoples: **a.** A traditional ceremony during which evil-doers are discovered, named, and punished; SMELLING *vbl n.* sense 2. **b.** The special singing and dancing performed at this ceremony. See also SMELL.

1828 W. SHAW Diary. 23 Mar., It appears that Pato's counsellors have now resolved upon .. going through the ceremonies of what they call Umhlahlo, in order that the wise woman may explicitly name the persons, who have bewitched Pato & his son. **1835** W.B. BOYCE in A. Steedman *Wanderings* II. 277 The messengers brought word that the brother-in-law of the sick girl, in the absence of Jama, the father .. had held an umhlahlo, that is a witch-dance, in order to find out the person guilty of bewitching the sick girl, and the stepmother was accused, and was in confinement. **1866** W.C. HOLDEN *Past & Future* 309 He does not hesitate to declare that Sorcerers are exerting an evil influence, to prevent the rain from falling; and recommends the chief to have the umhlahlo, or ceremony of 'smelling out', performed ... Sometimes the rainmaker himself names them; in which case the umhlahlo is dispensed with. **1891** T.R. BEATTIE *Pambaniso* 25 This was a dance that could only be performed by the doctor alone when engaged in smelling out, and was known by the name of *umhlahlo*. **1937** B.J.F. LAUBSCHER *Sex, Custom & Psychopathology* 99 The preparations include hand-clapping, dancing and the singing of a special song called *Umhlahlo*. **1956** F.C. METROWICH *Valiant but Once* 179 The superstitious tribesmen found it impossible to believe that a man of his rank and position could possibly have died a natural death. They therefore demanded that there should be an umhlahlo (a smelling-out) and that the Fingo witchdoctor .. should indicate who had bewitched the chief and where the ubuti (bewitching-matter) had been hidden.

u-mizi var. UMZI.

umkandhlu var. INKUNDLA.

umkhonto /umˈkɔntɔ/ *n.* Also **umconto, umkonto**. [Xhosa and Zulu.]

‖**1.** ASSEGAI sense 1 a.

1827 G. THOMPSON *Trav.* II. 413 They charge with a single umconto, or spear. **1836** A.F. GARDINER *Journey to Zoolu Country* 103 On a hunting expedition, or making a journey, .. a single umkonto, with one or two straight sticks, is all they require. **1839** W.C. HARRIS *Wild Sports* 355 Their principal weapon is a short spear, or assegai, termed *umkonto*, which is not thrown, .. but used for stabbing, for which purpose they rush in at once upon their opponents. **1849** E.D.H.E. NAPIER *Excursions in Sn Afr.* II. 82 Until the late introduction of fire-arms, the 'umk'honto' (or, as we term it, the assegai) and the 'kierie' were the only weapons used by the Kaffirs. **1860** A.W. DRAYSON *Sporting Scenes* 18 An assagy is called umkonto. **1898** B. MITFORD *Induna's Wife* 118 Now Jambula .. made mock of our Zulu casting-spears. The broad-headed *umkonto* — ah, that, he said, was good for its own purpose. **1961** D. BEE *Children of Yesterday* 213 Johannes wore a foot-long sheath-knife in his belt and leaning against the jeep was his short, heavy umkonto — the traditional Zulu stabbing assegai. **1963** A.M. LOUW *20 Days* 120 Hunger is good, for it makes the anger sharp as the umkonto — spear.

2. Always with initial capital. A short form of UMKHONTO WE SIZWE. Also *attrib.*

1964 H.H.W. DE VILLIERS *Rivonia* (Biogr. Appendix), His reason for not joining Umkhonto was that the National Executive of the A.N.C. thought it inadvisable that both he and Mandela should join. **1989** [see OPERATION MAYIBUYE]. **1989** *Sunday Times* 15 Oct. 4 Umkhonto (the ANC's armed wing). **1991** R. BEZUIDENHOUT in J. Pauw *In Heart of Whore* 266 In Lusaka .. I was kept under house arrest with other Umkhonto guerillas. **1993** *Africa S. & E.* Mar. 17 The government has insisted that Umkhonto must first be disbanded and its members apply individually to join the SADF.

Umkhonto we Sizwe /ʊmˈkɔntɔ we ˈsiːzwe/ *n. phr.* Also **Mkhonto -, Umkontho -, Umkonto we Sizwe.** [Xhosa, lit. 'the Spear of the Nation'.] The military wing of the African National Congress; MK; SPEAR OF THE NATION; UMKHONTO sense 2. See also ANC *n.*[1]. Also *attrib.*

1961 *Umkonto We Sizwe* 6 Dec. 1 Units of Umkonto We Sizwe today carried out planned attacks against Government installations. **1963** *People Accept Challenge of Nationalists* Mar. 3 Umkhonto we Sizwe, as the military wing to our struggle is also guided by the same principal [*sic*] of acting only on the bases of a scientific analysis of the objective conditions. **1971** *Post* 25 July 2 Ex chief Albert Lutuli was head of the ANC, Robert Sobukwe led the new PAC. Umkonto we Sizwe and Poqo were more militant wings. **1977** *Rhodeo* (Rhodes Univ.) 30 Sept. 7 Nelson Mandela of the ANC ran its military arm, known as Umkonto We Sizwe ('Spear of the Nation'). **1985** *Financial Mail* 2 Aug. 46 Anticipating the banning of the ANC, Mandela ... helped form Umkonto we Sizwe (Spear of the Nation), the ANC's military wing that started a sabotage campaign in December 1961. The ANC and PAC were banned in 1960. **1986** P. MAYLAM *Hist. of Afr. People* 190 The ANC did not officially abandon its non-violent strategy, but it did spawn a new organisation, *Umkonto we Sizwe* (The Spear of the Nation), which would engage in acts of sabotage without harm to life. **1991** G. MCINTOSH in *Sunday Times* 13 Jan. 16 Umkhonto we Sizwe soldiers will probably only require minimal retraining. **1992** *Guardian Weekly* (U.K.) 13 Nov. 10 He [*sc.* Nelson Mandela] issued .. a strong rebuke to extremists within the ANC, declaring that any members of the military wing, Umkhonto we Sizwe (MK), who engaged in 'acts of terror' automatically disqualified themselves from membership.

Umkhosi /ʊmˈkɔːsi/ *n.* Also **Umkosi**. [Zulu.] A festival kept by certain Nguni peoples, esp. Zulus, to celebrate the first harvest of a new season; cf. INGCUBHE. Also *attrib.* See also LETSEMMA.

1887 J.W. MATTHEWS *Incwadi Yami* 39 The Umkosi, or dance of first fruits, a festival before the celebration of which, at the chief's kraal, the first fruits of the season cannot be eaten. **1949** O. WALKER *Proud Zulu* (1951) 63 'Wasn't there a dust-up at the Umkosi, First-Fruits ceremony this year?' **1955** E.A. RITTER *Shaka Zulu* 155 He had .. held the annual little Umkosi, or first-fruits festival ... The little Umkosi had been held as usual at the full moon about Christmas. **1979** C. ENDFIELD *Zulu Dawn* 29 The excess of rain .. had delayed the crops. The Great King had decided that the *umKhosi*, the ingathering of the warriors for the First Fruits Ceremony, would not be delayed because of nature's intransigence. **1991** B. KING in *Sunday Tribune* 19 May 9 Bishop Colenso .. was told .. that at the great annual Umkhosi (first fruits) ceremony .. the regiments only carried sticks ... 'The Umkhosi lasts one day only, all the regiments dancing before the king. No weapons are carried at the Umkhosi for fear of accidents.'

umkhuhlu /ʊmˈkʊːɬʊ, ʊmˈkuːɬu/ *n.* Pl. **imikhuhlu**. [Zulu.] The *Natal mahogany* sense (*a*) (see NATAL sense b), *Trichilia emetica*.

1907 T.R. SIM *Forests & Forset Flora* 10 The kinds which have been worked to any extent are, viz. — Sneezewood, Real Yellow-wood, Outeniqua Yellow-wood, *Faurea arborea* under the name of Beukenhout, Flat Crown .. Umkuhlu, Umzimbeet, and in smaller quantity Assegai, Hard Pear, .. Umtenenenda, Impunzito, and several others. **1926** R. CAMPBELL in *Voorslag* (1985) 65 He carved his last sonnet on a big Umkuhla tree in Durban which is still standing but the letters are almost illegible. **1967** S.M.A. LOWE *Hungry Veld* 113 The .. party sat silently in the shade of a Mkhuhlu tree. **1983** *Daily Dispatch* 12 Mar. 3 To the right a bright green-foliaged resident, an umkhulu (Natal mahogany) tree stands tall and proud. **1987** L. CAPSTICKDALE in *S. Afr. Panorama* Aug. 47 At her death on 27 September, 1965, Killie's ashes were scattered, at her request, beneath an *umkhuhlu* tree in the garden which she loved so well.

umk(h)wetha var. ABAKWETHA.

umkonto var. UMKHONTO.

Umkosi var. UMKHOSI.

Umkulunkulu var. UNKULUNKULU.

umkumkani *n. obs.* Also **ukumkani**. [Xhosa *ukumkani*.] PARAMOUNT sense a. Also *transf.*

  1835 A. STEEDMAN *Wanderings* I. 247 The Amakosa tribe, whose 'Umkumkani' or sovereign, is Hintza, extend from the colony to the mouth of the Bashee river. *Ibid.* 255 The Umkumkani is usually a lineal descendant from the first great patriarchal chieftain of the tribe, and the title of *Inkose enkulu* is enjoyed exclusively by himself: all his male descendants are called Inkosi by birthright; but their power depends in a great degree upon their popularity, the people being at liberty to attach themselves to whichsoever of the sons their inclination may lead them to prefer. 1855 J.W. COLENSO *Ten Weeks in Natal* 100 Now He is living in Heaven, though we cannot see Him, and He is the Lord of us all, — the Umkumkani, Supreme King, Whose Kingdom ruleth over all; and we must obey Him, and try to please Him in all things. 1860 W. SHAW *Story of my Mission* 433 The Chief, who is the lineal representative for the time being of the great family, is regarded as the head of the nation, and called Ukumkani, which is equivalent to King, or paramount Chief. 1870 C. HAMILTON *Life & Sport in S.-E. Afr.* 58 The villages are each under the control of one petty Chieftain ... These, again, are subject to the sole authority of the 'umkumkani,' or great chief.

umlabalaba /om,laba'laba/ *n.* Also **mlaba-laba**, **umlambalala**, **umrabaraba**. [Zulu.] MORABARABA. Also *attrib.*

  1976 *Sunday Times* 10 Oct. 6, I often found prisoners squatting in a circle outside their cells. This could be an innocent gathering for an umlabalaba game. 1979 C. ENDFIELD *Zulu Dawn* 283 *Mlaba-Laba* is played with great skill and rapidity by its Zulu practitioners. Boards are of several designs depending on the regions where *Mlaba-laba* is played ... The game is structurally the same as a medieval European game called Nine-man Morris. 1981 [see MORABARABA]. 1982 *Signature* Sept. 21 Baines missed very little ... Such interludes as 'three men playing a game with pebbles which they deposited in small holes' .. and he went on to describe the game undoubtedly the one as seen on streets (and on TV3) as umlambalala. 1983 S. JACOBS in *City Press* 9 Oct. 3 The Mlabalaba game programme should be scrapped ... We're living in the 20th century, not the stone age. 1985 W.O. KA MTETWA in *Staffrider* Vol.6 No.2, 44 During dinner time a handful of men would gather under an oak tree to play umrabaraba.

umlunga, **umlungo**, **umlungu** *varr.* MLUNGU.

umlungi *pl.* form of MLUNGU.

umngqushu var. MNGQUSH(O).

umntu var. MUNTU.

‖**umnumzana** /,omnom'za:na, -za:nə/ *n.* Also **mnumzana**, **umnumxana**, **(um)numzan**, **(um)numzane**. Pl. **abanumzana**. [Xhosa and Zulu *umnumzana* (pl. *abanumzana*), Siswati *umnumzane* (pl. *abanumzane*).]

1.a. *hist.* In traditional Nguni society: (the title of) a lesser chief, usu. the headman of a village. See also INDUNA sense 1 a.

  1835 A. STEEDMAN *Wanderings* I. 257 Independently of these hereditary Chiefs, every village or kraal has its master, who is called the '*Umnumxana*.' 1835 [see INDUNA sense 1 a]. 1875 D. LESLIE *Among Zulus* 28 After leaving Chingwair, I saw Nobeta, the fattest Umnumzana I had yet seen in the Zulu country. 1955 E.A. RITTER *Shaka Zulu* 2 A number of kraals, in any one clan .. was .. grouped together .. and placed under the supervision of a local headman, unumzana, who functioned at once as a petty magistrate and a Member of Parliament possessing authority to adjust all minor disputes and acting as the voice and ears of his people.

b. The owner of a house; the head of a household.

  1857 J. SHOOTER *Kafirs of Natal* 15 This [house], at the head of the kraal, and a little larger than the rest, is for the *umnumzana*, a compound word signifying the owner of a place. 1979 M. MATSHOBA *Call Me Not a Man* 3 'Where's the owner of the house?' asked the first one in a gruff voice ... 'Are you the *mnumzane*, you?'

c. An employer.

  1980 *Voice* 23 Jul. 2 Where they sleep, where they come from (homeland), whether they have families or not, what they eat or wear, is none of the mnumzana's business.

d. A person of some status, wealth, or importance.

  1984 S. ZUNGU in *Pace* Oct. 64 Amasi is the food of 'abanumzane' (honourable gentlemen) ... In the past .. abanumzane used to enjoy amasi with umcaba (corn which is first cooked and then ground).

2.a. 'Sir', a respectful form of address. Cf. MORENA sense 1 a.

  1949 O. WALKER *Proud Zulu* (1951) 33 He sensed a feeling of deliberate respect along the footpaths as they stood aside, and with right arm raised to say: 'Nkosi' 'Chief' or 'Mnumzana' 'important person.' 1951 J.J. MKWANAZI in *Natal Mercury* 20 Apr. 20 (*letter*) I am sure that most of your readers will agree with me that the name, Sir, doesn't mean a European or Native but a respect only. In our language it means Mnumzana. 1956 J. CHATTERTON *Return of Drums* 5 The young Tribal Policeman turned to the tall Induna. 'Mnumzane,' he said, 'the thing that we knew would come has come.' 1963 K. MACKENZIE *Dragon to Kill* 102 The old African family retainer .. went to the Boer War with Grandpa and now goes round saying, 'Go well, child,' and 'Stay well, umnumzana', and breaking into Zulu proverbs. 1980 M. MATSHOBA in M. Mutloatse *Forced Landing* 111 Before I could say thanks: 'Say, *mnumzane*, have you got a cigarette on you?' 1982 *Voice* 5 Aug. 2 There was this guy who wanted to be classified 'Tswana'. He wrote a long letter to the Department of Bantu Administration ... The letter said: 'Greetings Mnumzane, my name is Muziwakhe M—.'

b. 'Mr', a respectful title used before a proper name; also used ironically.

  1952 F.J. EDMONSTONE *Where Mists Still Linger* 26 We always used to say that when Umnumzana Utomu died, his spirit would remain on the farm and in his lands to protect them from the doings of the evil ones. 1973 *Drum* 8 Mar. 53 The mbongis are out in their colourful dresses dancing and singing, shouting 'Bayete' to Mnumzana Vorster. 1974 *Ibid.* 8 Apr. 32 'This,' he points to the biggest bone of the lot, 'is Umnumzana Nationalist'.

umpakati /,ompa'ga:ti, ,ompə'ga:ti/ *n.* Pl. usu. **amapakati**. Forms: *sing.* **amapagate**, **iphakathi**, **umpagate**; *sing.* and *pl.* **amapakati**, **(um)pakati**; *pl.* **amapagati**, **amapakate**, **amapakatie**, **amapakati**, **mapakathi**, **pacati**, **pagaki**, **pagate**, **pagatees**, **pagati**, **umpugarties**. Also with initial capital. [Xhosa and Zulu *umphakathi*, also *iphakathi* councillor (pl. *amaphakathi*), n. prefix UM- (or I-) + *phakathi* inside, within. For notes on *sing.* and *pl.* forms, see AMA-, I-, UM-.] In traditional Nguni societies: **a.** A member of the council, or inner circle of advisers, of a chief; HEEMRAAD sense 3; cf. INDUNA (sense 1 a). **b.** Such a council; collectively, its members. Also *fig.*

  1803 J.T. VAN DER KEMP in *Trans. of Missionary Soc.* I. 436 He [*sc.* Ngqika] has his counsellors (*pagati*) who inform him of the sentiments of his people, and his Captains admonish him with great freedom and fidelity, when he abuses his authority. 1823 W. SHAW in C. Sadler *Never a Young Man* (1967) 54, I was obliged to ask the chief to appoint one of his men as a sort of sentry or police officer. This was readily granted, and an old umpagate .. with great good-will and a few hard strokes .. soon dispersed the crowd. 1833 *Graham's Town Jrnl* 4 Apr. 2 A demand has been made to the Amapakate (or Counsel) of Hintza, for prompt attention to the late circumstances. 1834 T. PRINGLE *Afr. Sketches* 225 One of his counsellors (*amapagati*) instantly suggested that the opportunity which now presented itself for striking a decisive blow was too good to be lost. 1848 [see CISKEIAN *adj.*]. 1851 R. GRAY *Jrnl of Bishop's Visitation* II. 157 Kama has sent one of his Pacati to his brother Pato to entreat him to have nothing to do with the prophet or with war. 1858 *Cape Monthly Mag.* IV. Sept. 165 This council, the members of which are called *Amapakati* (literally, 'middle ones'), is composed of commoners, who, by their courage in war, or their skill in debate on public questions .. have acquired great popular influence, and are thus qualified either to sustain or control the power of the chiefs. 1866 W.C. HOLDEN *Past & Future* 333 Next to the Royal family in order and office are the amapakati; or, Great Council of the Nation. The members of this council are persons of the greatest intelligence and influence, selected from different parts of the tribe, some of whom are always at the 'great place', and the whole may be called on great state occasions. 1870 C. HAMILTON *Life & Sport in S.-E. Afr.* 191 The shrewdness of the 'Amapakati', or Kaffir advocate. 1901 H. SMITH *Autobiog.* II. 75 If he is very rich, the chief and his *pagati*, or councillors, are satisfied with 'eating him up' (the native expression for having all one's property confiscated under an accusation of witchcraft). 1937 F.B. YOUNG *They Seek a Country* 515 Never in all my life have I seen a finer body of men than the older warriors — the Umpakati, they call them. 1939 [see INKUNDLA sense 2]. 1956 F.C. METROWICH *Valiant but Once* 17 This intelligence having been brought to a chief .. one of his counsellors (*pagati*) instantly suggested that the opportunity which now presented itself for striking a decisive blow was too good to be lost. 1968 —— *Frontier Flames* 113 He proved to be a political capture of some importance. On being interrogated he admitted that he was an amapakati (councillor) of the Galeka Paramount Chief. 1976 A. DELIUS *Border* 96 Those men in the middle are the councillors, the Amapakati ... They're arguing now to see what sort of bargain they can make not to give up the Chief. 1979 M. MATSHOBA *Call Me Not a Man* 172 His had been a warrior's body when he fought the frontier wars in the prime of his life. It was these wars which had won him promotion to *iphakathi* to the paramount chief. 1991 F.G. BUTLER *Local Habitation* 162 The high priest would rise and try to convince the disbelieving worshippers that he and his *amapagati* had indeed secured the best beast available.

umpugarties *pl.* form of UMPAKATI.

umpundulu var. IMPUNDULU.

‖**umqombothi** /,(o)mtom'bɔ:ti/ *n.* Also **mqombot(h)i**, **umqombhothi**, **umqomboti**. [Xhosa.] Among Xhosa-speakers: TSHWALA sense a; a non-alcoholic beer. Also *attrib.*

  1948 E. HELLMANN *Rooiyard* 47 In Rooiyard, *utywala* is regarded as a generic name for beer of all kinds, while pure kafir-corn beer is termed *mqombothi*. 1972 *Daily Dispatch* 4 Aug. 2 Mdantsane residents may brew mqomboti (African beer) in unlimited quantities provided it was for home consumption and not for sale. 1978 *Ibid.* 27 June 1 Afraid we can no longer afford bottled liquor — will you try a can of homemade marewu, or would you prefer mqombothi? 1980 *E. Prov. Herald* 16 May 4 On another occasion I was introduced to African beer, umqombothi. The stuff was bitter and brown and I wondered what people enjoyed as their Adam's apples went up and down. 1980 E. JOUBERT *Poppie Nongena* 111 He worked over the sandy soil with ash from the fire and with mqombothi bran which she begged off beer-making people as manure was scarce. 1986 P.A. McALLISTER *Xhosa Beer Drinks.* 41 Apart from the common *utywala* (Xhosa), *utshwala* (Zulu) and *bjalwa* (Sotho), .. a variety of similar but non-alcoholic beverages were made. These include .. umqombothi (Xhosa), unmature beer with no alcoholic content and *mabudu* or *mapoto* (Lovedu) which is light beer. 1987 [see STOKVEL sense 2]. 1987 *Rhodeo* (Rhodes Univ.) Apr. 4 Umqomboti, made from a fermented mixture of maize meal, sorgum, sprouted mealies and water, was served in large communal tins which were passed around. **1990** M. Melamu in *Lynx* 309 It took just one scale of 'mqombothi' to thaw and finally melt the ice. **1992** M. Mthethwa in *Pace* 37 They're drinking; lifting 'scales' of umqombothi, taking giant gulps and passing it to the next man.

umrabaraba var. UMLABALABA.

‖**umshologu** /ʊmʃɔ'lɔːgʊ/ *n.* Formerly also **shuluga**. Pl. **imishologu**. [Xhosa.] Among Xhosa-speakers: an ancestral spirit, believed to be either helpful or evil, depending on how it is treated. See also ITONGO.

1827 J. Brownlee in T. Pringle *Ephemerides* (1828) 186 The Caffers believe in a Supreme Being, to whom they give the appellation of *Uhlanga* (Supreme,) ... The spirit they call *Shuluga*. **1842** R. Godlonton *Sketches of E. Districts* 230 The name given by the frontier tribes to signify a being of the invisible world, is umshologu, and by the back tribes umnyanya. Both of these words have the same signification, namely, the spirits of departed friends; which they profess to believe are often sent to minister to them; and hence in great emergencies they frequently invoke their aid. **1866** [see ISITUTA]. **1866** W.C. Holden *Past & Future* 293 This girl .. professed to hear strange and superhuman sounds beneath her feet, which were interpreted by the prophet to signify that the imishologu were holding council; the result of which was, solemn and peremptory instructions from the region of ghosts, that the people must destroy their cattle and their corn. **1891** T.R. Beattie *Pambaniso* 221 Sacrifices were made to the *Imishologu*, or ghosts of ancestors, who, it was supposed, might have taken offence at neglect. **1907** W.C. Scully *By Veldt & Kopje* 297 A few of the bolder spirits, .. steal along .. taking cover .. and listening fearfully lest the restless 'imishologu' — the spirits of the wicked ones who have died violently — should be unseasonably awake. **1923** — *Daniel Vananda* 48 The Natives believe that when the generation of gases cause a dead body to swell, a spiritual entity — an 'umshologu' is in process of gestation, and if this is permitted to develop until it makes its escape through the decayed tissues, it will have attained conscious individuality and may revenge itself on the slayer. **1947** E.R. Seary *S. Afr. Short Stories* Glossary, *Imishologu*, (Bantu): ancestral spirit, ghost, which needs to be propitiated. **1950** A.W. Burton *Sparks from Border Anvil* 178 The 'ghost' or 'umshologu' of the greatest Chief must never be offended nor frustrated. **1975** F.G. Butler *Informant, Grahamstown* My maid .. says there is no difference between isinyanya and imishologu. Both are 'the old people'. It is only on second thoughts that she added 'the dead people'.

umsi var. UMZI.

umsimbiti var. UMZIMBEET.

umsobosobo /(ʊ)mˌsɔbɔ'sɔbɔ/ *n.* Also **msobosobo**, **sobo-sobo**, **sorba-sorba**, **(u)msobo**. [Xhosa and Zulu *umsobo, umsobosobo* nightshade plant, nightshade fruit.

Fox & Norwood Young (*Food from the Veld*, 1982, p. 356) state that in Zulu *umsobo* is the tree and *umsobosobo* the berry, while in Xhosa these words are interchangeable. Doke & Vilakazi's *Zulu-Eng. Dict.* (1964) does not make this distinction. McLaren's *New Concise Xhosa-Eng. Dict.* (1975) claims that in Xhosa *umsobosobo* is the fruit.]

a. Either of two nightshade plants of the Solanaceae, *Solanum nigrum* and *S. retroflexum*. **b.** The berries of these plants, poisonous when green but edible when ripe. Also *attrib*.

There is some confusion over the identification of this plant: 'Jacot Guillarmod [in *Sartryck ur Botaniska Notiser* vol. 119 fasc.2, 1966] considers that the *Solanum nigrum* of southern Africa consists of several different species or varieties, none or only one of which may be the *Solanum nigrum* of the northern hemisphere.' (Fox & Norwood Young p.347.) See also quot. 1977.

1909 *E. London Dispatch* 24 July 5 In South Africa where it is a very common weed [it is] known to most people by its native name, 'Umsobosobo.' **1911** *Ibid.* 10 Nov. 6 (Pettman), Mention may be made of the well-known weed common in old lands, *Umsobosobo* (*S. nigrum*). In the old country it is undoubtedly poisonous, but here in South Africa its little black berries are eaten with impunity and are even made into jam. **1913** C. Pettman *Africanderisms* 458 *Sobosobo*, .. The fruit of *Solanum nigrum*, Linn. *Ibid.* 522 *Umsobosobo*, (Kaf. *um Sobo*.) The name given by the natives to the fruit of *Solanum nigrum*. **1937** B.J.F. Laubscher *Sex, Custom & Psychopathology* 82 A herb called *Msobosobo* (cabbage) is tabooed in the diet of women. **1967** S.M.A. Lowe *Hungry Veld* 94 'Peter, umsobo-sobo!' Lucy exclaimed, pointing to a thick mass of small plants, each smothered in tiny black berries. **1971** L.G. Green *Taste of S.-Easter* 89 An early Natal cookery book has recipes for egg-plant cutlets, .. and msobo jam made with wild blackberries found in the mealie fields. **1972** *Farmer's Weekly* 21 Apr. 29 A correspondent asks about 'Sorba-Sorba'. From the name and the description, the plant is a species of *Solanum* but one which belongs to a complex of closely related species, some of which are poisonous and some of which are edible. This complex of species includes the European species *Solanum nigrum*, Black or Garden Nightshade. **1977** *Ibid.* 23 Nov. 81 Professor of Bantu Languages, D.T. Cole at the University of the Witwatersrand points out that the correct name is *umsobo* (pl *imisobo*) and that it is a Zulu word although the same name is used for the plant in Xhosa. The actual botanical name is a little more confusing, but it is generally thought that it is *Solanum retroflexum* and not *S. nigrum L. S. retroflexum* is thought to be indigenous to the warmer areas of South Africa whereas *S. nigrum* is of European origin.

umtagarties pl. form of TAGATI *n.*

umtagati *n.* var. and pl. form of TAGATI *n.*

umtagati *adj.* var. TAGATI *adj.*

umtakati var. TAGATI *n.*

umtamboti, **umtomboti** varr. TAMBOTIE.

umtcha var. MUTSHA.

umthakathi, **umtigati** varr. TAGATI *n.*

umtugartie pl. form of TAGATI *n.*

‖**umtwana** /ʊm'twana/ *n.* Also **m(n)twana**, **ntwana**. [Zulu and Xhosa *umntwana*, child, small child, offspring; (in Zulu only) prince, member of the royal family; the dim. form of Zulu *umuntu*, Xhosa *umntu* person.]

1. A prince; a child of the royal house; also a form of address.

1949 O. Walker *Proud Zulu* (1951) 125 Heralds ran to the wide-flung concord telling them that the umtwana was now veritably a man and king. **1967** — *Hippo Poacher* 4 In those days of the eighteen-eighties John was at the zenith of his power, and u-Tom, along with many brothers and sisters, was addressed as *Umtwana*, child of the royal house. **1985** *Fair Lady* 6 Feb. 78 The singers and dancers run before the Mtwana (Infanta or Prince) Buthelezi. **1987** *New Nation* 23 July 9 It is because he [*sc.* Buthelezi] is a prince — he is addressed as 'mntwana' — and because his ancestors were prime ministers to Zulu kings that he says he should be leader of the Zulus, leader of the kwaZulu and president of Inkatha.

2. A young fellow; also an affectionate form of address, 'kid'.

1961 T. Matshikiza *Choc. for my Wife* 58 'Hey, how is it, man? I hear you came running out?' 'Man, how are you, man? Agh Man.' 'Ntwana, man I'm okay, man.' **1980** C. Nkosi in M. Mutloatse *Forced Landing* 12 This umtwana shall but revel in revealing off-beat, creative, original graffiti sugar-coated with sweet nothings. **1986** S. Sepamla *Third Generation* 40 'I don't know the details but mom was brought home by the system.' 'Hey umtwana, this is serious business.' **1988** *Pace* Apr. 7 The doctor took a liking to this lightie who became his great buddy. Senyaka takes it up:

'GG liked this "ntwana" with his trendy bellbottomed trousers.'

umu- see UM-.

umungoma var. SANGOMA.

umuti var. MUTI.

umutsha, **umutya** varr. MUTSHA.

umuzi see UMZI.

‖**umvelinqangi** /ʊmˌveli'nǃaŋgi/ *n.* Also **mvelangqangi**, **umvelingqangi**, **(u)mvelingqangi**, **umvel'nqanki**, and with initial or medial capital. [Xhosa and Zulu, firstborn, the first to appear, the creator, fr. *vela* appear, come forth + *-qangi* nominal stem indicating priority.] The original being, the first to appear; used among Xhosa- and Zulu-speakers as a praise-name or term of address for the traditional supreme being and for the Christian God. Cf. TIXO, UNKULUNKULU.

1855 J.W. Colenso *Ten Weeks in Natal* 59 The true words for the Deity in the Kafir language — at least in all this part of Africa — are *umKulunkulu*, literally, the Great-Great One = The Almighty, and *umVelinqange* — literally, the First Comer-Out = The First Essence, or rather, Existence. *Ibid.* 238 The savage tribes .. appeared .. to attach very just notions to the names umKulunkulu and umVelinqange. **1925** D. Kidd *Essential Kafir* 101 Umvelinqangi, whose name is said to mean 'One who made his appearance,' is also said to be the same as Umkulunkulu. **1974** C.T. Binns *Warrior People* 76 The word uMvelinqangi was used by Shaka himself ... Its literal meaning is The First Appearer, The First to Emerge, The First to Exist, hence The Creator. It is usually associated with the word uNkulunkulu which signifies The First Ancestor or The Great Father of all the Spirits of the Zulu Ancestors. *Ibid.* 77 The Zulus regarded uNkulunkulu as a *man* but, though he derives his origin from uMvelinqangi, the attributes of a deity are never ascribed to him. **1978** A. Elliott *Sons of Zulu* 97 Mvelinqangi whose name literally means 'the-one-who-emerged-first'. He is the Creator of all things and the source of all blessings such as sunshine and rain and children. **1979** M. Matshoba *Call Me Not a Man* 170 The people have placed greater faith in witchcraft than in uMvelinqangi, amathongo and themselves to reverse the conquest. **1987** M. Poland *Train to Doringbult* 28 The Lord of the Sky, *Mvelangqangi*, has his herds, way above.

umzi, **umuzi** /'ʊmzi, ʊ'muːzi/ *n.* Also **u-mizi**, **umsi**. Also with medial capital. [Xhosa *umzi*, Zulu and Ndebele *umuzi*.] In Xhosa, Zulu, and Ndebele society: a village; a group of dwellings under one headman; cf. KRAAL *n.* senses 1 a and 2 a.

1835 A. Steedman *Wanderings* I. 17 Such is the avidity with which the natives of Cafferland importune those who visit their umzis or villages, for presents of beads, .. that a traveller must never fail to provide himself with a considerable quantity. **1860** A.W. Drayson *Sporting Scenes* 18 Kraal is a Dutch term, and means an inclosure for animals. I fancy that they call the Kaffirs' residences by this name to indicate their contempt for the people; the Kaffirs call their villages 'umsi'. **1970** A. Fulton *I Swear to Apollo* 47 The doctor's jeep .. pulled up in a great cloud of dust in the inkundla between the cattle-kraal and the huts of Debe's u-mizi. **1986** N. Dubow in *Leadership* Vol.5 No.4, 114 The architectural constituents of the Ndebele art, starting with its total application to the compound (kraal or *umzi*). **1988** J. Smith *Streams to Rivers* 16 A Pondo *umzi* in Natal. **1988** *Eva* Sept. 58 The Zulu village or uMuzi.

umzimbeet, **umzimbit(h)i** /ˌʊmzɪm'biːt(i), ˌʌm-/ *n.* Also **msimbithi**, **umsimbiti**, **umzimbete**, **umzimbeti**, **umzimbiet**, **umzimbit(i)**, **zimboti**. [Xhosa and Zulu *umsimbithi*.] The tree *Millettia grandis* of the Leguminosae; its hard and durable timber; *Natal ebony*, see NATAL sense b. Also *attrib.* Also called IRONWOOD (sense a).

1850 N.J. MERRIMAN *Cape Jrnls* (1957) 92 With Bible and prayer-book under one arm, and in the other hand my long umzinbili nob kerie. **1851** [see *Natal ebony* (NATAL sense b)]. **1859** [see IRONWOOD sense a]. **1870** C. HAMILTON *Life & Sport in S.-E. Afr.* 6 The wheels are made of the famous Natal wood called 'umsimbiti' or ironwood, from its strength and durability. **1902** G.S. BOULGER *Wood* 335 Umzimbit ... Known also as White Ironwood. **1912** *E. London Dispatch* 10 July 9 (Pettman), The flames of the fire died down and the embers of the *zimboti* wood glowed dull red. **1921** W.C. SCULLY *Harrow* 54 His stick was of 'umzimbeet', long strong and heavy. **1923** — *Daniel Vananda* 145 Old Songelwa's 'umzimbiet' club, and his single assegai, were not forgotten. **1950** [see ESSENHOUT]. **1955** E.A. RITTER *Shaka Zulu* 237 He only carried a little spear with a short handle of dark-red wood made from a freak-coloured umsimbiti or ironwood (milletia caffra). **1964** G. CAMPBELL *Old Dusty* 2 Our tents were pitched in a sylvan glade carpeted with deep, lush grass and surrounded by magnificent umzimbiti trees. **1968** K. MCMAGH *Dinner of Herbs* 22 And such sticks too! Cut from choice 'umzimbete', so hard that it is rightly named 'iron wood', they were decorated with cunningly wrought copper. **1972** *E. Prov. Herald* 12 Jan. 12 Many South Africans know the wood of Umzimbeet (which word is a corruption of the Xhosa and Zulu umSimbithi, meaning ironwood). Until its use was protectively stopped, it was the favourite wood for the tribal craft of making walking-sticks and knobkieries. **1976** R.L. PETENI *Hill of Fools* 19 Old Langa stood up, took his black, oiled msimbithi stick, and called on Duma, Mlenzana and Zuziwe to go with him to Ntombi's home.

unban *v. trans. Hist.* [Eng., *un-* prefix expressing reversal + *ban* (see BAN *v.*).] Usu. *passive.* Of a person or organization: to be released from the restrictions stipulated in a BANNING ORDER.

1973 *Drum* 22 Jan. 2 She has just been unbanned after being restricted to Orlando in Soweto for 4018 days. **1986** M. HLANGANI in *E. Prov. Herald* 10 Apr. 2 The recently unbanned vice-president of the United Democratic Front in the Eastern Cape .. was taken from his home at 5 am and questioned by Security Police for seven hours yesterday. **1989** *E. Prov. Herald* 9 Nov. 1 The Congress of South African Students (Cosas) was also unbanned.

uncivilized labour *n. phr. Obs.* exc. *hist. Derog.* and *offensive.* The labour provided by black people. Cf. CIVILIZED LABOUR.

1924 *Prime Minister's Circular No.5* in E. Hellmann *Handbk on Race Rel.* (1949) 152 Uncivilized labour .. [is] the labour rendered by persons whose aim is restricted to the bare requirements of the necessities of life as understood among barbarous and undeveloped peoples. **1949** *Survey of Race Rel. 1948–9* (S.A.I.R.R.) 32 In all Government Departments, except Native Affairs and the Railways and Harbours, 'civilized' labour is to be substituted for that which might be regarded as 'uncivilized'. **1969** A. HEPPLE *S. Afr.: Workers under Apartheid* 45 The so-called 'civilised labour' policy .. was first applied .. when the Nationalist-Labour government of the day instructed state departments and provincial authorities to employ 'civilised' labour instead of 'uncivilised' labour, i.e. to employ whites and not Africans in unskilled jobs.

uncle *n. colloq.* [Special senses of general Eng., influenced by Afk. *oom,* see OOM.]

1.a. A title, with a name: OOM sense 1 a.

1822 [see OOM sense 1 a]. **1880** E.L. PRICE *Jrnls* (1956) 409 'So,' said this pretty damsel, 'Om Price will find this little girl very wild. He must be strict with her' — and the little girl looked merrily into Uncle Price's face.

b. A respectful or friendly form of address to a man who is not a blood relation, esp. one older than the speaker; sometimes used in the (Afrikaans) respectful third person form (see quot. 1979). Cf. OOM sense 2

1873 F. BOYLE *To Cape for Diamonds* 368 We met a dingy old farmer going to his work on Bultfontein. 'Good morning, uncle!' said Mr. Fry. 'Good morning, brother!' returned the Boer. **1900** H. BLORE *Imp. Light Horseman* 77 'Allemachting! little uncle,' exclaimed the clerk in surprise. 'I did not know there was a Boer here.' **1902** D. VAN WARMELO *On Commando* 127 An old man galloped towards us ... I asked him, 'Uncle, are you sure that our lager is in the hands of the khakies?' to which he answered, 'Nephew, I saw with my own eyes how they rode up to the waggons and made all our people "hands up!"' **1933** W. MACDONALD *Romance of Golden Rand* 232 'Uncle,' I said, addressing Harry Struben, 'here is the gold we got from crushing the conglomerates'. **1968** *Post* 4 Feb. 7 Why do all Indians in Maritzburg address everybody no matter how young they are, as 'Uncle' or 'Aunty'? **1979** W. EBERSOHN *Lonely Place* 190 'Is Uncle sure Uncle knows what Uncle is doing?' the boy asked. 'Uncle couldn't be surer,' Yudel said. **1980** R. GOVENDER *Lahnee's Pleasure* 13 You must not stop him from school like this, Uncle. He seems an intelligent child. **1983** [see OOM sense 2].

2. As a common noun: OOM sense 3.

1883 O.E.A. SCHREINER *Story of Afr. Farm* 137 Some day, sooner or later, these graves will open, and those Boer-uncles with their wives walk about here in red sand. **1958** R.E. LIGHTON *Out of Strong* 181 'André has a clay ox the piccanin made for him. Show the uncle, André.' **1971** *Post* 28 Feb. 13 He thinks I'm a square of an Uncle who's not with it. *Ibid.* 28 Mar. 22 I'm not dying or going to Alcatraz, the place where they keep naughty uncles. **1973** Y. BURGESS *Life to Live* 111 When Bettie asked why 'the uncle' was always shouting, Nel could only say that he was a very sick uncle and could not help it. **1975** *E. Prov. Herald* 7 Aug. 17, I grabbed the uncle and tried to pull him off, but could not move him. The train was getting closer. **1978** A.P. BRINK *Rumours of Rain* 318 When church parade was called the Sunday morning ... There was a new soultiffy to do the job for us .. this .. elderly uncle with glasses. **1978** [see Brink quot. at OUTA sense 3]. **1980** N. FERREIRA *Story of Afrikaner* 39 My favourite piece was .. based on the character of a half-witted uncle who was the only true Christian I knew. **1984** *Sunday Times* 18 Nov. (Lifestyle) 1 A seven year old rape victim .. did not really know what had happened to her, only that some uncle had hurt her. **1993** in *Sunday Times* 31 Oct. 31 We are not pumpkins like the fat uncles running around in the AWB.

understel var. ONDERSTEL.

ungoobo var. INGUBO.

Union *n. hist.* [Special senses of general Eng. *union* the action of uniting into one political body.]

1. The creation of the legislative confederacy of the South African state, by the South Africa Act of 1909.

1908 J.C. SMUTS *What They Said* (1971) 222 The political status of the natives is no doubt a very important matter, but vastly more important is the Union of South Africa. **1909** *State* July 4 Till the last few days there was but little enthusiasm in Natal for the cause of South African Union. **1910** *Rand Daily Mail* 31 May 5 The Act of Union comes into force today and South Africa takes her place as the latest great Confederation within the Empire. **1933** [see DUTCH *n.* sense 1]. **1988** J. SHARP in Boonzaier & Sharp *S. Afr. Keywords* 88 After Union, mining capital and progressive agriculture (the alliance between 'maize' and 'gold') dominated national politics. **1990** *Frontline* Mar.-Apr. 20 Back at Union, South Africa had about twice as many blacks as whites. **1992** *Natal Mercury* 25 Nov. 8 The Mercury ... was .. after Union a fighter for Natal's provincial rights.

2.a. Ellipt. for *Union of South Africa*: the South African state as a legislative confederacy; the territory of this state. Also *attrib.*

1909 in R.H. Brand *Union of S. Afr.* 142 The words 'the Union' shall be taken to mean the Union of South Africa as constituted under this Act. **1928** V.G. DESAI tr. *M.K. Gandhi's Satyagraha in S. Afr.* 28 After the formation of the Union, Taal or Dutch and English are officially treated on a footing of equality throughout South Africa. **1928** E.A. WALKER *Hist. of S. Afr.* 561 Beyond sending a few men to Nyasaland and Northern Rhodesia, the Union had been unable to despatch troops far afield till the Hun had been driven from the gate. **1929** [see GIFAPPEL sense 1]. **1936** F.S. MALAN in *Cambridge Hist. of Brit. Empire* VIII. 659 The expression 'colour bar' as used in the Union means the exclusion of the natives from any skilled or semi-skilled work. **1939** J.C. SMUTS in *Hansard* 4 Sept. 29 It is in the interest of the Union that its relations with the German Reich should be severed. **1946** T. MACDONALD *Ouma Smuts* 36 Racialism is still the most deadly of all poisons which sap the energies of the Union. **1967** M.S. GEEN *Making of Union of S. Afr.* 251 In 1957 the Union flag was made the sole national flag of South Africa. **1977** T.R.H. DAVENPORT *S. Afr.: Mod. Hist.* 289 The Union became the Republic of South Africa on 31 May [1961] and its membership of the Commonwealth therefore ceased forthwith. **1980** A. PATON *Towards Mountain* 54 The franchise could be amended or abolished by a two-thirds majority of a joint sitting of both houses of the new Union parliament. Thus the Union came into being.

b. *comb.* **Union Day**, the 31st of May, observed as a public holiday from 1910 (and renamed REPUBLIC DAY in 1961); **Union Loan Certificate** *hist.*, a security issued by the Union Government to raise funds, maturing after five years at a low interest rate.

1925 *Off. Yrbk of Union 1910–24* (Union Office of Census & Statistics) 310 The following are the statutory public holidays as prescribed in Act No. 3 of 1910: New Year's Day .. **Union Day** (31st May), [etc.]. **1961** *Off. Yrbk of Union 1960* (Bureau of Census & Statistics) 196 [information repeated]. **1919** *Act 20* in *Stat. of Union* 120 In addition to the methods specified in the principal Act for the raising of money by the Governor-General, he is hereby empowered .. to issue securities to be called **'Union loan certificates'** ... A Union loan certificate — (a) shall have on its face the amount thereof and the date of maturity. (b) shall be issued at a discount. (c) shall be repaid at its face value upon maturity which shall not be more than five years from the date of issue; and (d) shall in no case be for an amount exceeding five hundred pounds. **1933** *Act 29* in *Ibid.* 204 The control, management, issue and repayment of Union Loan certificates issued on or after the first day of June, 1932, shall be vested in and entrusted to the Postmaster-General. **1977** F.G. BUTLER *Karoo Morning* 166 Fifteen shillings would buy a Union Loan Certificate, which would mature into a pound in due course.

Unionist *n. hist.* A member of the Union Party, a political party which favoured a federal union in South Africa. Also *attrib.*, of the party or its members.

Known as the 'Progressive Party' until 1908, the Union Party was absorbed into the South African Party in 1920. See also PROGRESSIVE sense 1, SAP *n.*[1] sense 1 a.

1911 [see NATIONALIST *n.* sense a]. **1913** V.R. MARKHAM *S. Afr. Scene* 213 The Unionists — for so the old Progressives now call themselves — are in the main the British party. **1926** M. NATHAN *S. Afr. from Within* 173 General Smuts entered into an alliance with the Unionists. **1960** L.M. THOMPSON *Unification of S. Afr. 1902–10* 23 The Liberals were no less anxious than the Unionists to preserve the British Empire. **1975** D.W. KRÜGER in *Std Encycl. of Sn Afr.* XI. 76 In the 1910 election 37 Unionists were returned to Parliament, forming the Opposition. **1982** [see PROGRESSIVE sense 2].

Unisa /juːˈniːsə/ *n.* Also **UNISA.** [Acronym formed on *University of South Africa.*] A national university based in Pretoria, which teaches by correspondence and short-attendance courses. Also *attrib.*

1971 *Rand Daily Mail* 29 Jan., New posts at Unisa ... A record number of new academic appointments has been made by the University of South Africa. **1971** S.

Afr. Panorama Sept. 3 While numbers of South Africans evade the cold at warmer leisure resorts during the month of July, thousands of students from all population groups congregate in Pretoria to attend the annual vacation school of the University of South Africa (Unisa). *c*1976 H. FLATHER *Thaba Rau* 57 'No, I'm studying. Correspondence course' ... 'Who with?', she asked. 'An overseas college?' 'No, here in South Africa. Pretoria. The University. Unisa they call themselves.' 1982 M. MZAMANE *Children of Soweto* 9 Did you know he completed his B.A. by correspondence under UNISA in fifteen years? 1988 C. NEL in *Inside S. Afr.* Feb. 14 There has been massive research on how to change black attitudes, knowledge and perception of business, with .. Unisa, the HSRC and others all focusing on blacks as if the problem in South Africa were somehow a black problem. 1989 D. VAN HEERDEN in *Sunday Times* 11 They are Unisa sociology professor A— .., [etc.]. 1994 *Weekend Post* 22 Oct. 10 The entry qualifications for a Unisa degree is matric exemption and at least three D symbols.

Unity Movement see NEUM.

unkoes var. ENKOSI *int.*

‖**Unkulunkulu** /ʊŋˌkʊlʊŋˈkuːlu/ *n.* Also **Nkulunkulu, Oukoolukoolu, (U)mkulunkulu**. [Xhosa and Zulu, 'great one', 'God'.]

1. In traditional Zulu society: the first being; the supreme being. Cf. TIXO, UHLANGA, UMVELINQANGI.

1836 A.F. GARDINER *Journey to Zoolu Country* 314 They acknowledge .. a traditionary account of a Supreme Being, whom they called Oukoolukoolu (literally the Great-Great), but knew nothing further respecting him. 1852 H. FYNN in J. Bird *Annals of Natal* (1988) I. 105 Some few Kafirs may be found who state their belief that Umkulunkulu (the Great Great), shook the reeds with a strong wind, and there came from them the first man and woman. 1855 [see UMVELINQANGI]. 1857 W.H.I. BLEEK in *Cape Monthly Mag.* I. May 291 The inhlamvu say: 'Umkulunkulu arose from beneath, he came out of the reed; he created all nations, all living animals, and all things on earth.' [*Note*] The spiritual world appears to the Zulu to be beneath. Reed is said to signify origin, beginning. 1870 H. CALLAWAY *Religious System of Amazulu* 17 The unkulunkulu *par excellence*, the first man, is nowhere worshipped. 1895 H. RIDER HAGGARD *Nada* 14 The exact spiritual position held in the Zulu mind by the Umkulunkulu — the Old — Old — the Great — Great — the Lord of Heaven — is a more vexed question. 1910 J. BUCHAN *Prester John* (1961) 81 He told them .. that he was the Umkulunkulu, the incarnated spirit of Prester John. 1934 N. DEVITT *Mem. of Magistrate* 213 The true South African black is not nearly as much of an unbeliever as some other dark-skinned people. He believes in an unseen Power above. The Great Mighty One. The M'Kulukulu, as the Zulus say. 1952 H. KLEIN *Land of Silver Mist* 72 It was not the umlungu's god, as the missionaries said, who controlled the destinies of all men. It was Nkulunkulu, the Great One, the Spirit of all the Great Ones long departed ... Nkulunkulu was more powerful and omnipresent than the puny god of the umlungu. 1967 O. WALKER *Hippo Poacher* 112 At the back of Bantu religion was the idea of a Great One, Umkulunkulu, who had brought men and all things living out of the earth — or was it out of the split reed? But Unkulunkulu was a shadowy personage, a kind of Father Adam rather than God the Creator. 1974 [see UMVELINQANGI]. 1980 M. MATSHOBA in M. Mutloatse *Forced Landing* 120 Man was created by Nkulunkulu so that he might avail himself of that which *umhlaba* (earth) was made to give.

2. Among Zulu-speaking Christians: God; cf. TIXO, UMVELINQANGI.

1936 WILLIAMS & MAY *I Am Black* 95 Samson .. took one trunk in his left hand and one in his right, and calling out to Umkulunkulu to avenge himself for the loss of his eyes, strained himself against the trunks, and with a mighty heave pulled down the great hut, so that everyone inside the hut and on the roof was killed. 1937 C. BIRKBY *Zulu Journey* 82 Even those [Zulus] who are Christian today and believe in 'Nkulunkulu', the greatest of the great, still live in awe of strange demons and departed spirits. [1963 P. HINCHLIFF *Anglican Church* 67 In the eastern Cape missionaries had .. used 'Thixo' for 'God', a word which had very few prior associations. Colenso determined to use the Zulu 'Unkulunkulu', the name already used for the Creator ... There was considerable opposition but Colenso's view triumphed and the word has now presumably acquired Christian associations.] 1975 [see IMBIZO].

unproclaimed *ppl adj. Hist.* [Special sense of general Eng., fr. PROCLAIM.] Of an area: not set aside in terms of the Group Areas Act for the exclusive use of one racial group; UNZONED. See also PROCLAIM.

1970 T.R.H. DAVENPORT *Informant, Grahamstown* In Grahamstown there are now therefore white areas, coloured areas and unproclaimed areas.

unsalted *adj.* [Eng. prefix *un-* not + S. Afr. Eng. SALTED.] Of animals: not rendered immune to disease. Cf. SALTED.

1879 R.J. ATCHERLEY *Trip to Boerland* 209 An 'unsalted' horse may die on the road, scores of miles from any human habitation, and leave the ill-starred traveller to carry himself and saddle as best he can. 1968 S. STANDER *Horse* 34 Nagana is almost always fatal to unsalted horses.

untjie var. UINTJIE.

unwisselled /ʌnˈvəsəld/ *ppl adj. Sheep-farming.* [Eng. prefix *un-* not + *wisselled* adj. formed on WISSEL.] Of a lamb or kid: not yet of the age at which second teeth are cut.

1969 *Grocott's Mail* 28 Mar., (*advt*) Merino hamels — unwisselled to 6 tooth — well grown and in good condition. 1989 *Ibid.* 4 Aug. 4 (*advt*) 30 Unwisselled Kids.

unzoned *ppl adj.* [Special sense of general Eng., fr. ZONE.] UNPROCLAIMED.

1966 *Survey of Race Rel.* 1965 (S.A.I.R.R.) 184 The racially mixed, and as yet unzoned, areas of District Six, Woodstock, and Salt River.

UP /juː ˈpiː/ *n. hist.* [Initial letters of *United Party* (earlier *United South African Party*).] A political party formed in 1934 by the merger of the National Party (see NP) and the South African Party (see SAP *n.*[1]). Also *attrib*. See also FUSION.

The UP was the governing party from its formation until 1948; it was the official Opposition from 1948 until 1977, when it was dissolved. In 1977 some former members joined with the Progressive Reform Party to form the Progressive Federal Party (see PFP), while others formed the NRP.

1938 *George & Knysna Herald* 19 Oct. 4 Malanites gain Marico ... Nationalist gain from U.P. 1943 *Cape Times* 29 July 4 The first election result to arrive at this office last evening was Major Piet van der Byl's at Bredasdorp — a smashing U.P. victory. 1950 H. GIBBS *Twilight* 139 Mr. J.G. Strauss .. became acting leader of the UP during General Smuts' absence abroad in 1949. 1970 *Daily News* 3 June Debate on Swing to U.P. 1977 *Cape Times* 29 June 1 UP to form new party today ... At least nine UP members voted against the decision to dissolve. 1986 *Style* Mar. 43, I remember during the referendum of 1959 or 1960 .. tearing off UP posters.

uphuthu var. PUTU.

up North *adv. phr.* and *n. phr. Hist.* During or with reference to World War II:

A. *adv. phr.* In the North African theatre of war, especially Egypt.

1941 *Star* 1 Feb., Our gallant boys who have been bearing the real heat and burden of the day up north will return to find many of the play-play soldiers and base wallahs wearing what should be a badge of honour. 1941 *George & Knysna Herald* 20 Aug. 4 The George branch of the S.A.W.A.S. want to show their appreciation of what our own George boys have done and are doing up North by sending them a small parcel three times a year. 1942 [see SPRINGBOK sense 2 b]. 1946 T. MACDONALD *Ouma Smuts* 9 Her love for her 'boys and girls' made her take two trips by air 'up north' to Egypt. 1963 M. BENSON *Afr. Patriots* 98 He spoke about 'our men' who were 'dying up North', who were helping to take North Africa and Madagascar. 1978 *Pace* Dec. 61 South African Bantu make excellent soldiers, you know? We had some of them Up North during the War. 1987 *Grocott's Mail* 9 June 3 During the war she raised funds, knitted socks and sent parcels 'Up North'. 1992 in *Natal Mercury* 27 Aug. 7 A fully equipped surgical ambulance which was inscribed: 'To the Allied Forces from the Children of Durban' .. was used 'up north'.

B. *n. phr.* This theatre of war.

1943 L. SOWDEN *Union of S. Afr.* 264 'Up North,' meaning the fighting fronts, has been an everyday expression. 1944 'TWEDE IN BEVEL' *Piet Kolonel* 179 He had flown down to the Union from up North, owing to the news of his wife's serious illness. 1977 L. ABRAHAMS *Celibacy of Felix Greenspan* 55 They were worrying about Hitler and up North. 1987 O. MUSI in *Drum* Dec. 32 These were the guys who had returned from Up North.

Uppie /ˈʌpi/ *n. colloq.* [Formed on *U.P.E.* the initial letters of *University of Port Elizabeth* + Eng. (informal) *n.*-forming suffix *-ie*.] A student of the University of Port Elizabeth; in *pl.*, a sports team representing this university.

1973 *Evening Post* 19 May 26 Rhodes kicked off with Uppies facing a weak sun. 1974 *E. Prov. Herald* 2 July 25 Uppies u-20 trouce Wits. The University of Port Elizabeth got off to a good start in the SA Universities under-20 rugby tournament .. yesterday, when they beat Wits 28-6. 1988 M. DERRY in *Ibid.* 11 Aug. 1 The Uppies have had to replace three players in their XV to take on Rhodes in the annual intervarsity rugby clash. 1993 *Weekend Post* 10 Apr. 3 PE students to help SAP at E. Cape trouble spots. Uppies put on army standby.

upright yellowwood *n. phr.* [Calqued on Afk. *opregte geelhout, opregte* genuine, true + *geelhout*, see GEELHOUT. See also second quot. 1934.] The YELLOWWOOD (sense 2 b), *Podocarpus latifolius*; the wood of this tree. See also YELLOWWOOD sense 1.

1887 S.W. SILVER & CO.'s *Handbk to S. Afr.* 133 The Upright Yellow-wood is scarce compared with either of those trees [*sc.* the common yellowwood and the black ironwood]. 1887 J.C. BROWN *Crown Forests* 237 Timber Valued Standing. Per cubic foot. Upright Yellowwood, £0 0s.3d. Outeniqua, £0 0s. 1d. 1904 D.E. HUTCHINGS in *Agric. Jrnl of Cape of G.H.* 3 Upright Yellow-wood is a smaller, more tapering tree with a broader leaf, rougher bark, and slightly harder timber than Outeniqua Yellow-wood. 1909 *George & Knysna Herald* 4 Aug. 1 The Sleepers shall be supplied from the timber felled during the Government Felling Season for 1909, of the following descriptions: Upright Yellowwood, Outeniqua Yellowwood, White Els, Hard Pear and Saffraan. 1934 *Star* 17 Mar. (Swart), It [*sc.* the yellowwood] is plentiful in the forests in several varieties, but the two almost exclusively used are the Outeniqua and the Upright. 1934 C.P. SWART *Supplement to Pettman.* 181 *Upright Yellow Wood*, This well-known Knysna wood owes its English name to a mistranslation. To distinguish it from the Outeniqua, the old-time Dutch foresters called it 'Die Opregte' or genuine yellow-wood. This was literally translated 'Upright' and Upright it has been ever since, though lately (probably since the mistake has been recognised) it has been called Real Yellow-wood. 1951 N.L. KING *Tree-Planting* 70 *Podocarpus latifolius* (Upright or real Yellowwood). 1954 U. VAN DER SPUY *Ornamental Shrubs & Trees* 189 *P. latifolius* (real or upright yellowwood) is the yellowwood which produced timber much used in cabinet-making, and for floors, ceilings and doors in the early days of the Cape.

upsaddle *v. obs.* [Calque formed on Du. *opzadelen* to saddle (a horse).]

1. *trans.* To saddle and mount (a horse). Cf. OFF-SADDLE *v.* sense 2.

1834 T.H. BOWKER *Journal.* 28 Dec., Before we could up saddle the horses word came in that the kafirs were taking the cattle. **1855** G. Brown *Personal Adventure* 52, I got my horse quickly caught and upsaddled, resolved to make home with all speed. **1860** A.W. Drayson *Sporting Scenes* 68 When the traveller is again ready, the animal is again up-saddled, and the journey continued.

2. *intrans.* To mount and prepare to ride off; *to saddle up*, see SADDLE sense 2. Cf. OFF-SADDLE sense 1. See also OPSAAL sense 1.

1838 T. Shone *Diary.* 24 Dec., When about nine o'clock we up saddle to make a start. **1838** in W.B. Boyce *Notes on S. Afr. Affairs* 148 Dingaan .. inveigled them within an enclosure .. just as they were up-saddling to depart. **1887** H. Rider Haggard *Jess* p.xxx, At midday they offsaddled their horses for an hour ... Then they upsaddled and went on. **1905** P. Gibbon *Vrouw Grobelaar* 39 It was late and dark before he up-saddled to go away. **1946** E. Rosenthal *General De Wet* 59 Leaping out of bed, Christiaan roared out: 'Upsaddle, everybody!' and within an hour the whole camp had been shifted miles across the veld. **1953** B. Fuller *Call Back Yesterday* 24 High Dutch, 'Opzadel', meaning to upsaddle.

3. *intrans. nonce.* Of a horse: to be readied for a journey.

1856 R.E.E. Wilmot *Diary* (1984) 41 While the horses were up saddling, Bartley and I rode down to .. *Alice*.

Hence **up-saddling** *ppl adj*.

1953 B. Fuller *Call Back Yesterday* 24 Upon this old up-saddling ground the town of Pietersburg was founded.

upsitting *vbl n. Obs.* [Calque formed on Afk. *opsitting*, see OPSITTING.] The old Afrikaner custom of courting a girl by sitting alone with her after her parents have gone to bed, for as long as it takes for a candle to burn down; OPSITTING. See also OPSIT *n.*, SIT.

1863 W.C. Baldwin *Afr. Hunting* 165 Two upsittings have been going on, at opposite corners of a large room. **1883** O.E.A. Schreiner *Story of Afr. Farm* 185 Tant' Sannie holds an upsitting, and Gregory writes a letter. **1896** *Westminster Gaz.* (U.K.) 20 Jan. 3 The nocturnal courting or 'upsitting'. **1924** L.H. Brinkman *Glory of Backveld* 25 Living on lonely farms, deprived of all pleasures and amusements, it is only natural that the Boer girl's fancy should turn to thoughts of .. love-making, up-sitting and an early marriage.

upstall *n. obs.* Also **upstal**. [Englished form of Du. *opstal*.] OPSTAL.

1801 J. Barrow *Trav.* I. 84 The buildings, .. the vineyards and fruit groves planted, called the upstals, were saleable like any other property, and the lease continued to the purchaser. **1806** G.M. Theal *Rec. of Cape Col.* (1899) V. 409 General State of the Revenues at the Cape of Good Hope ... 14. Duty on Sales of Upstalls of Loan Lands.

uQamat(h)a var. QAMATA.

urlam var. OORLAM.

Useless Boys' Club *n. phr. Hist.* In Soweto: a derogatory nickname for the Soweto Urban Bantu Council (see UBC).

1977 P.C. Venter *Soweto* 37 The teenagers have had it with waiting, man. Most of the older people are Uncle Toms ... Take the Urban Bantu Council. We call them the Useless Boys Club. **1987** P. Laurence in *Weekly Mail* 24 Dec. 3 Soweto's Urban Bantu Council — dubbed the 'Useless Boys' Club' by black activists.

usibali var. SBALI.

Usutu /ʊˈsuːtʊ, uˈsuːtu/ *int.* and *pl. n.* Also **Usuthu**, **Usuto**, and with small initial. [Zulu *uSuthu* the Zulu Royal House; see 1982 quot. at sense B.] The name of the Zulu royal clan.

‖**A.** *int.* Used among Zulus as a battle-cry.

1879 S. Turner in D. Child *Portrait of Pioneer* (1980) 97, I was out looking for some lost horses, and heard the Zulu war-cry 'Usutu!' **1893** J.F. Ingram *Story of Gold Concession* When all were placed, we got the word to charge, which we did, yelling 'Usutu!' **1913** L. Lyster *Ballads of Veld-Land* 79 Hark to the fierce 'Usutu!' Death comes with that dread shout. **1923** G.H. Nicholls *Bayete!* 171 Then from all round came the hoarse war-cry: 'Usutu! Usutu! Usutu!' **1937** C. Birkby *Zulu Journey* 75 Usibepu's Men of Great Might were a little too much for Cetywayo's warriors, even though they stormed down with their old war-cry 'U-su-tu!' **1967** E.M. Slatter *My Leaves Are Green* 106 They ran towards us, plumes waving, assegais rattling on their shields, leaping into the air and screaming their war-cry — 'Usutu! Usutu!' **1973** *Time* 19 Feb. 15 A crowd of 200 was dispersed by police with tear gas after the demonstrators had brandished clubs and chanted '*Usutu*!', a traditional Zulu war cry. **1985** *Weekly Mail* 16 Aug. 9 On Friday they saw an angry mob of about 300 'impi' shouting '*usuthu*', an old tribal warcry meaning power. **1993** G. McIntosh in *Sunday Times* 20 June 23 Many slogans are exclusive. The cry of 'Amathembu' will be supported by Transkeian Xhosas; 'Kom Boere' by Afrikaners and 'Usuthu' by Zulu warriors.

B. *pl. n.* Also **Usut(h)us**. Those associated with the Zulu royal house. Also *attrib*.

1904 H.A. Bryden *Hist. of S. Afr.* 197 The Usutus — the King's party — were attacked by two powerful chiefs. **1926** M. Nathan *S. Afr. from Within* 37 The adherents of Cetewayo, the Usuto. **1937** C. Birkby *Zulu Journey* 75 The usutu turned round and fled. **1949** J. Mockford *Golden Land* 203 Installed as Chief of the Usutu section of the Zulu people in August 1948, when he was twenty-five and owned two wives. **1961** T.V. Bulpin *White Whirlwind* 79 Cetshwayo's personal following were traditionally known as the Usuto. *Ibid.* 97 The Usutu faction showed signs of resuming their active hostility as soon as the crops had been reaped and men were free to fight and travel on the dry earth. **1982** *Pace* 16 June, The Usutu are the traditional royal clan of the Zulu. It's very interesting to learn where the name came from. Apparently Cetshwayo, in his younger days, raided across the Drakensberg and came back with some Sotho cattle. The Zulu cattle were very small, but these were huge things which had been bred by the Basotho, so the clan became known as the Usutu. **1983** *Ibid.* Dec. 48 It was ... the year of Inkatha and the year of Usutu. But most of all it was the year of Gatsha Buthelezi.

utata var. TATA.

Uteco var. TIXO.

U-Tekwan, **uthekwane** varr. TEGWAAN.

uthikoloshe var. TOKOLOSHE.

uThixo var. TIXO.

Uthlanga var. UHLANGA.

Utika, **Utiko** varr. TIXO.

utikoloshe var. TOKOLOSHE.

Utixo var. TIXO.

utlanga var. UHLANGA.

utokoloshe var. TOKOLOSHE.

utshuala, **utshwala**, **uTyala**, **utyalla**, **utyalwa**, **utywala** varr. TSHWALA.

UWC *n.* Also **U.W.C.** Initial letters of *University of the Western Cape*, a university established in Bellville in 1960.

Originally established to serve the 'coloured' population, UWC was at first an affiliated college of the University of South Africa, but became autonomous in 1970.

*c***1977** *S. Afr. 1976: Off. Yrbk* (Dept of Info.) 702 Facilities offered at the UWC bring university education within the reach of a growing number of Coloured students. **1978** *Sunday Times* 29 Oct. (Extra) 3 Prof R E van der Ross, rector, said that UWC had started a Department of Geology two years ago. **1980** C. Hermer *Diary of Maria Tholo* 7 Concerted protest at U.W.C. started at the end of July. **1987** C. Gutuza in *South* 9 July 5 Jenny is now a student at UWC.

Uwusa /uˈwuːsə, ʊˈwʊːsa/ *n.* Also **UWUSA**. Acronym formed on *United Workers' Union of South Africa*, a trade union formed in 1986 by the Inkatha movement, in opposition to COSATU. Also *attrib*.

1986 P. Van Niekerk in *New Statesman* (U.K.) 9 May 6 In Durban some 70,000 Inkatha supporters attended the launch of UWUSA, which espouses the principles of free enterprise and anti-sanctions. **1990** L. Kaunda in M. Kentridge *Unofficial War* 23 Inkatha people wear khaki, or sometimes UWUSA T-shirts. **1992** *Race Rel. Survey 1991-2* (S.A.I.R.R.) p.cii, In July 1991 *The Weekly Mail* published secret government documents showing that UWUSA had received R1,5m from the government. The documents described the union as a secret project under the joint control of the security police and the KwaZulu administration. **1992** *Natal Witness* 9 Nov. 7 Uwusa wants leader out ... According to Uwusa's chief negotiator, Butch Jantjes, the call was made at a .. shop stewards' meeting.

uyentje, **uyntjie** varr. UINTJIE.

Uys var. ACE.

V

‖**vaal** /fɑːl/ *adj.* Formerly also **fahl**. [Du.]
1. Pale; grey, fawn, tawny.

1821 [see quot. at *vaalblaar* (sense 2 below)]. *1886* G.A. FARINI *Through Kalahari Desert* 316 Straight to that *vaal koppje* (grey hill), and there off-saddle for a bit. *1919* J.Y. GIBSON in *S. Afr. Jrnl of Science* July 4 Common names were .. *Vaaltyn* (or possibly *Vaaltuijn*, 'Fallow garden') for a *vaal* or dun-coloured beast. *1939* P. Louw in *Outspan* 6 Oct. 29 Another fallacy cherished by many South Africans concerns the so-called types of lion. They speak derogatively of the vaal or dun-coloured animal as inferior to the black-maned breed. *1948* [see BITTER KAROO]. *1970* D. VAN SCHOOR *Informant, Kleinbrakrivier* After the heavy rain the river water has a vaal colour. *1972* A.A. TELFORD *Yesterday's Dress* 119 For everyday use clothes were made of coarser and stronger material; usually moleskin, and they were brown, vaal, and pale yellow.

2. Special collocations. **vaalblaar** *obs.* [S. Afr. Du., *blaar* leaf], the plant *Aloe striata*; **vaalboom** /-buəm/ [Afk., *boom* tree], the evergreen tree *Terminalia sericea* of the Combretaceae; MOGONONO; **vaalbrak** /-brak/ [Afk., *brak* salty], SALTBUSH sense a; **vaaldoring** /-duərəŋ/ [Afk., *doring* thorn], the thorn tree *Acacia haematoxylon*; also called CAMEL-THORN; also *attrib.*; **vaalhaai** /-haɪ/ [Afk., *haai* shark], the tope *Galeorhinus galeus*; also *attrib.*; **vaal korhaan**, see KORHAAN sense 1 b; **vaal rhebok**, see RHEBOK sense 2; **vaal rhebuck**, see RHEBUCK sense 2.

1821 C.I. LATROBE *Jrnl of Visit* 64 The waste produces some beautiful plants, .. particularly .. the *Fahlblar*, a species of aloe, the leaves of which are round, of a pale blue colour. *1926* *Farming in S. Afr.* Sept. 199 (Swart), It is common on hillsides and on flat ground, especially in localities where **Vaalboom** grows. *1961* PALMER & PITMAN *Trees of S. Afr.* 250 The graceful silver-grey foliage of the vaalboom is one of the loveliest features of the sandy areas of the Transvaal bushveld. *1971* B. DE WINTER in *Std Encycl. of Sn Afr.* III. 342 (caption) *Vaalboom* (Terminalia Sericea) in the Bushveld. *1897* [vaalbrak: see SWARTHAAK]. *1932* *Farming in S. Afr.* Apr. 5 (Swart), Vaalbrak was one of the plants sampled. *1971* J.P. BOTHA in *Std Encycl. of Sn Afr.* IV. 602 The different ganna species .., vaalbrak (*Atriplex capensis*) and rivier-draaibos .. are examples of plants with an exceptionally high nutritional value that are found in the Karoo. *1970* *S. Afr. Panorama* Nov. 70 The wide savannahs where Kameeldoring (camel-thorn tree), **Vaaldoring** and Witgat (Shepherd's tree) trees keep watch, have not shrunk. *1947* K.H. BARNARD *Pict. Guide to S. Afr. Fishes* 10 **Vaal-haai**, .. This medium-sized (6 feet) cosmopolitan shark has recently become of considerable economic importance in South Africa for the extraction of vitamins from its liver-oil. *1958* *Cape Argus* 14 June 13 The vaalhaai .. grows to about 6 ft. and is harmless to man. *1969* J.R. GRINDLEY *Riches of Sea* 99 The vaalhaai, (Galeorhinus galeus), is caught commercially, particularly in the Cape between Gansbaai and Cape Town. *1982* *E. Prov. Herald* 15 July 3 Shark biltong is made from the vaalhaai and the ratelhaai sharks caught off Gansbaai.

vaalbos /ˈfɑːlbɔs/ *n.* Formerly also **vaalbosch(je)**. [Afk., *vaal* grey + *bos* (earlier *bosch*, see BOSCHJE) bush.] Any of several drought-resistant small trees or shrubs. **1.** Either of two species of the Asteraceae with greyish-green, hairy leaves and an aromatic smell: **a.** *Tarchonanthus camphoratus*; *wild sage* sense (b), see WILD sense a; **b.** *Brachylaena discolor*; also called *saliehout* (see SALIE sense 2). **2.** SALTBUSH sense a. In both senses also called VAAL BUSH.

1855 *Queenstown Free Press* 6 Oct. (Pettman), This tract of country, which is covered as far as the eye can see by a short bush called *Vaal bosch*, is, however, a good grass veldt. *1906* [see SALTBUSH sense a]. *1910* J. ANGOVE *In Early Days* 16 The only vegetation of the kopjes is the Vaalbosch and haakdoorn, which grows profusely, covering miles of country. *1913* A. GLOSSOP *Barnes's S. Afr. Hsehold Guide* 316 Salt Bush, Try for brak ground both the Australian and Colonial 'Vaal boschje.' *1937* S. CLOETE *Turning Wheels* 17 An old wildebeeste bull that had been sleeping in the shade of a vaal-bos sprang up under his horse's feet. *1958* R.E. LIGHTON *Out of Strong* 232 The olive hues of the vaalbos were fading into powdery silver. *1961* PALMER & PITMAN *Trees of S. Afr.* 325 The Vaalbos is an important small tree or shrub in the dry western parts of the country where it is one of the chief fodder trees. *1968* [see ROSYNTJIE sense 2]. *1971* *S. Afr. Panorama* Feb. 19 People say they enjoy life in Sishen, where not so long ago the bare ground sustained only *vaalbos*. *1974* *Weekend Post* 2 Nov. 12 Commonly seen in coastal gardens is Brachylema discolor, sometimes known as 'Vaalbos' or 'salie'. *1986* *S. Afr. Panorama* June 11 At the farm Rita Green drove us to the site through thick clumps of *vaalbos* (low nutritious silvery bushes).

vaal bush /ˈfɑːlbʊʃ/ *n. phr.* [Part. tr. Afk. *vaalbos*.] VAALBOS. Also *attrib.*

1873 A.F. LINDLEY *Adamantia* 4 Its soil, nourishing .. a few straggling bushes of a low, utterly burnt-up appearance, known as 'Vaal bush.' *1887* A.A. ANDERSON *25 Yrs in Waggon* I. 71 Vaal bush .. is in full bloom at this season of the year, giving a pleasant perfume, the leaves also being strongly scented, and when boiled in water are sometimes used for tea. *1897* 'F. MACNAB' *On Veldt & Farm* 73 The material used was the Vaal bush blossom, most cleverly woven. *1930* S.T. PLAATJE *Mhudi* (1975) 37 Moving along the Vaalbush overlooking the gully .. I noticed two men walking in the hollow gully bottom near the foot of the koppie. *1932* G.C. & S.B. HOBSON in E.R. Seary *S. Afr. Short Stories* (1947) 150 The shack appeared pitifully shabby — eight sheets of corrugated iron black with smoke, fitted together in fours, the back part covered with vaalbush. *1969* J. MEINTJES *Sword in Sand* 46 A screen of mimosa- and vaalbushes being placed a few feet in front of the pits, .. to conceal the entrenched riflemen from view.

Vaalie /ˈvɑːli/ *n. colloq.* Also **Valie**. [Formed on TRANSVAAL + Eng. n.-forming suffix *-ie* denoting an inhabitant of a place.] A (derogatory) name for an inhabitant of the region formerly known as the Transvaal; VAALJAPIE sense 2. Also *attrib.* See also KY'DAAR, *Transvaler* (TRANSVAAL), VAALPENS sense 2 b, VENTER sense 2.

1976 E. TOWNSEND *Informant, Grahamstown* What faithful Cape Tonian does not feel an irrational pang of enmity towards the so called 'Valie' who annexes Clifton Beach in the December/January period. *1989* S. SOLE in *Sunday Tribune* 1 Jan. 2 Up-country visitors can be forgiven for getting that unwanted feeling when they spy their first 'Vaalies go home' graffiti. *1989* P. QUINTON in *Cape Times* 12 Jan. 7 (letter) After being born a Vaalie and living in Cape Town for 19 years, I am now a confirmed Capetonian. *1990* F. DOWNES *Informant, Cape Town*, I got so sunburnt. I had a Vaalie tan. *1993* *E. Prov. Herald* 4 Sept. 5 Hugh travelled with kind friends, Vaalie style — five up and the skottel braai, potjie and the beers bouncing along behind in the Venter trailer. *1994* 'T. COBBLEIGH' in *Sunday Times* 2 Jan. 19 To all you Vaalies sitting shoulder-to-shoulder on the beaches at Camps Bay, .. or being ripped off by porters, taxi-drivers and ice-cream vendors, I say: *Don't hurry back.*

‖**vaaljapie** /ˈfɑːljɑːpi/ *n.* Also **vaal japie**, and with initial capital(s). [Afk., *vaal* grey + *japie* see JAPIE.]
1.a. Any rough new wine (often of an indeterminate colour) produced privately on farms; any inferior wine. Also *attrib.*

1945 *Cape Times* 21 May, What I say is 'Come quick, go quick,' and Vaal Japie is my best friend. *1949* L.G. GREEN *In Land of Afternoon* 59 Young wine, not matured but about six months old, is known as Vaaljapie ... It takes its name from its tawny colour though some varieties are red. *1959* [see JEREPIGO]. *1963* M. KAVANAGH *We Merry Peasants* 78 We went inside to enjoy again a midnight feast .. and were content with *vaaljapie*, our *vin ordinaire*, with the added sparkle of soda water bubbles. *1964* J. MEINTJES *Manor House* 16 She began to chat to the lad about their wines and about *vaaljapie* (a crude type of new wine). *1979* *Daily Dispatch* 12 Oct. (Indaba) 7 Brandy became too expensive .. and blacks, eventually, had to settle for Vaal Japie. The wine subsequently attained a tattered image — the beverage of the skollies. *1986* E. TERRE' BLANCHE in *Style* July 47 The tricameral parliament is like a tripod. One leg is planted on a samoosa, another on a vaaljapie bottle, and the third is lifted in the air, pointed towards America. *1990* R. MALAN *My Traitor's Heart* 26 The brown shepherds would be lined up in the courtyard, tin beakers in their hands, waiting for their 'tot' — their daily ration of vaaljapie, a crude white wine.

b. Rough home-distilled brandy. Also *attrib.*

1970 *Informant, Krugersdorp* Vaaljapie. Home made brandy. *1974* G. JENKINS *Bridge of Magpies* 40 It sounds like a vaaljapie (brandy) yarn to me.

2. *transf.* Always with initial capital: VAALIE.

1992 A. WEBB *Informant, Grahamstown*, I come from the Eastern Transvaal. I'm a real Transvaal. *1992* I. BYTEL *Informant, Port Alfred*, I come from Klerksdorp in the western Transvaal. I'm a Vaaljapie.

Vaalpens /ˈfɑːlpens/ *n.* Also **Vaalpans**, and (in *attrib.* use) with small initial. Pl. unchanged, **-pense** /-pensə/, or (formerly) **-pensen**. With small initial in *attrib.* use.

1. *hist.* [Afk., *vaal* grey + *pens* belly, paunch (see quots 1897 and 1905).] A member of the KGALAGADI people. Also *attrib.*

1871 J. MACKENZIE *Ten Yrs* (1971) 53 Their fellow-countrymen to the south .. sometimes call them 'Vaalpensen', which is the Dutch for Bakalahari, the ill-favoured and lean vassals of the Bechuanas. **1887** A.A. ANDERSON *25 Yrs in Waggon* I. 107 Their cattle-posts away in the bush, where the stock is looked after .. are in charge of their slaves called Vaalpans [*sic*]. **1897** SCHULZ & HAMMAR *New Africa* 71 A remarkable irregular white blotchiness of the skin on the natives' abdomens, found explanation in the fact that the natives, during the cold nights on which they slept out without clothing, built themselves little oblong frameworks of green wood, sixteen inches high, on top of which they made fires. Sleeping under this for warmth, the burning embers often fell through the framework on to their naked skins, raising blisters which, when healed, left the affected part white or grey. It is from this circumstance .. that the Boers have humorously nicknamed the tribes living west of the Transvaal 'Vaalpense,' or 'grey bellies.' **1905** *Native Tribes of Tvl* 70 The Vaalpens. This name (signifying 'Dusty-bellies,' and given them by the Boers owing to their colour, caused, it is said, by their habit of crawling along the ground when stalking game) is applied to a few families of wandering aboriginal Bushmen who still survive in the remotest parts of the Waterberg and Blauwberg districts. **1916** *E. Prov. Herald* 28 Sept. 3 The Vaalpens reported that one of our oxen had been mauled ... We saddled up and with three Vaalpens soon found where the lion had caught the ox. **1920** S.M. MOLEMA *Bantu Past & Present* 36 Bakalahari (or Bakhalagadi) called Balala (i.e. vassals) by the Bechuana and Vaalpens (or Fallow Bellies) by the Dutch. *a***1936** E.N. MARAIS *Soul of Ape* (1973) 70 We had an opportunity here in Waterberg of examining just such a case of 'homing' in a descendant of the so-called 'vaalpens pygmies' that at one time inhabited the Bushveld of the northern Transvaal. **1947** G.C. & S.B. HOBSON in E.R. Seary *S. Afr. Short Stories* 153 When at length the wind dropped the road had become completely obliterated. Only a Vaalpens would now succeed in keeping the direction to Bushmanswell. **1979** T. GUTSCHE *There Was a Man* 93 'The low Vaalpense' as Soga called the residual Bushmen (the Bakalahari) – 'human vultures' who by instinct found dead animals and bore off infected meat in all directions.

2. *colloq.* [Perh. a play on sense 1 and the name of the *Vaal River*, the southern boundary of the Transvaal.] A derogatory term for:

a. An Afrikaner.

1899 *E. Prov. Herald* 6 Dec. 3 A South African Dutchman writes us a somewhat bitter letter ... He writes as a Dutch Afrikander, a *Vaalpens* in fact. **1974** *Informant, Grahamstown* We have also coined nicknames for ourselves 'the rooineks,' the Afrikaners being 'vaalpense' or the Germans 'plat-koppe'. **1979** *Capetonian* May 9 'My ancestors *could* read!' I hear an indignant *Vaalpens* shouting from the back row ... If there's one thing I hate more than an illiterate stirrer of *stywepap*, then it's a gatecrasher in *velskoene*.

b. *Transvaler*, see TRANSVAAL.

1934, 1945 [see BLIKOOR]. **1947** E.R. SEARY *S. Afr. Short Stories* Glossary, *Vaalpens*, .. nickname for a Transvaler. **1993** G. MCINTOSH in *Sunday Times* 20 June 23 'Amabhunu' can have the hint of a 'smear' in it rather as the words 'Vaalpens' (Transvaler), 'soutie' (white English-speaking South African) and 'hairy-back' (Afrikaner) have.

Vaal Triangle *n. phr.* [Named for the *Vaal* river, which flows through the centre of the 'triangle' formed by the three cities.] The highly industrialized area of what was formerly called the southern Transvaal (now Gauteng) and the northern Free State, being largely enclosed within an imaginary figure formed by lines joining the cities of Vereeniging, Vanderbijlpark, and Sasolburg. Also *attrib.*

1971 *S. Afr. Panorama* July 46 The Vaal Triangle, straddling part of the southern Transvaal and the northern Orange Free State, is formed by Vereeniging, Vanderbijlpark and Sasolburg which comprise its three corners. **1984** S. SELLO in *Drum* Nov. 46 The mass burial of seven victims of the Vaal Triangle upheavals. **1988** J.R. RATSHITANGA in *Staffrider* Vol.7 No.2, 49 Hear me O martyrs of Sharpeville and Soweto And you all of the smouldering Vaal Triangle. **1992** J. CONTRERAS in *Newsweek* 20 July 32 Throughout the 1980s the ANC vowed to make the townships ungovernable, and the anarchy reigning in Sebokeng and other townships in the Vaal triangle today is fulfilment of that pledge. **1993** *Natal Mercury* 1 Jan. 2 Mr Scott-Wilson said blacks living in the Vaal Triangle were 'dramatically more pessimistic .. than those living in Pretoria'.

vaatdock, -doek varr. VADOEK.

vaatjie /ˈfaɪki/ *n.* Also **vatjie**, and (formerly) **faatche, fachey, fadje, fagie, fatje, feiky, fikey, vaatche, vaatje, vaitje.** [Afk. (earlier S. Afr. Du. *vaatje*), *vat* water carrier + dim. suffix -IE.]

1.a. A small wooden cask or keg.

1835 A. STEEDMAN *Wanderings* II. 19 Klaas, the driver of my own waggon, an ardent lover of the juice of the grape, was even lamenting that I had not emptied the wine *vaatche* at the last fountain, and substituted water, which had now become to him as well as to the rest far the most precious liquid. *c***1838** A.G. BAIN *Jrnls* (1949) 197 Ons drained his vatjes dry man. **1850** R.G.G. CUMMING *Hunter's Life* I. 7 The .. general stores which I carried with me were as follows: .. 2 large 'fagie' or water-casks, [etc.]. **1850** J.D. LEWINS Diary. 20 Jan., Sent Umdingi to Whitehead's Kaarhoek for a feiky price 9/. **1871** J. MCKAY *Reminisc.* 8 The soldier acts as the beast of burden, having been supplied with a large wooden vessel, by soldiers called 'fadje', or keg, capable of holding about half a gallon; and in this he had to carry with him what water he thought necessary. *a***1873** J. BURROW *Trav. in Wilds* (1971) 14 Everyone found himself thirsty, and was of course calling loudly for water. The cart and wagon were searched, but none was forthcoming, the *faatche* or cask having been .. left behind. **1881** P. GILLMORE *Land of Boer* 333 Although Ruby has had a considerable portion of the water in my fachey, there are still remaining in it a couple of gallons, whereas the guide's driver's and foreloper's has long been empty. **1896** H.A. BRYDEN *Tales of S. Afr.* 135, I will take a *vatje*, fill it, and ride back as fast as possible. You have enough water to last till evening to-morrow. [*Note*] A 'little vat' or hand-barrel, holding about two gallons, usually slung by an iron handle under the wagon. **1909** *Chambers's Jrnl* (U.K.) Dec. 28 Some Congo brandy and a *vatje* of water. **1954** M. KUTTEL *Quadrilles & Konfyt* 51 A *vatjie* of butter. **1968** L.G. GREEN *Full Many Glorious Morning* 234 We gave up part of a *vaatjie* of red wine and soaked it [*sc.* the boar's head] and then roasted it in front of a huge fire. **1977** [see SWAER sense b].

b. With distinguishing epithet: **water vaatjie** *obsolescent* [Afk. *watervaatjie* (or part. tr.)], a water-barrel, part of the furniture of a wagon.

1873 in A.M.L. Robinson *Sel. Articles from Cape Monthly Mag.* (1978) 116 A little fountain was discovered, which was a perfect godsend, as we were parched with thirst, and the *watervatje* was dry. *a***1875** T. BAINES *Jrnl of Res.* (1964) II. 218 My first application was to Gordon's water-vatje, and I had hardly recovered my breath before we were looking over the hill into the kloof on the other side. **1891** in J. KELLY *Coming Revolt of Eng. in Tvl*, (advt) E. & W. Crooks, Coopers, Port Elizabeth (Established 1845) Have always on hand a large Stock of Coopers' Ware, viz.: – Churns, Water Vaatjes, Butter Tubs. **1891** E. GLANVILLE *Fossicker* 166 One of the three rose up .. took a final pull at the water 'fikey' and stretched himself on the bare ground. **1911** D.B. HOOK *'Tis but Yesterday* 6 Mr Jameson sitting smoking on the 'water vatje'. **1922** J.G. FRASER in F.G. Butler *When Boys Were Men* (1969) 208 Under the wagon a *water-vaatje* or water-cask would also be hung. **1949** L.G. GREEN *In Land of Afternoon* 127 Watervaatjies swung from hooks beneath the wagon, with the cooking-pots, gridirons and tarpot for greasing the axles.

2. *transf.*

a. A tin canteen, shouldered as part of a soldier's equipment. **b.** A two-litre wine-bottle; also called CAN. Also *attrib.*

1896 M.A. CAREY-HOBSON *At Home in Tvl* 315 Come, Meester, and take a sip out of my tin fatje. [*Note*] Tin fatje – a small canteen slung across the shoulders. **1991** A. FUGARD *Informant, Grahamstown* A vaatjie of Tassenberg between the two of us.

‖**vabond** /ˈfɑːbɔnt/ *n.* [Afk., ad. Du. *vagebond* vagrant, vagabond.] A rascal; also used ironically or affectionately.

1959 J. MEIRING *Candle in Wind* 56 The policeman laughed. 'All right, you old va'bond! You can have the whole five pounds.' **1968** M. MULLER *Green Peaches Ripen* 30 'Go on!' she shouted, her voice rising. 'You get away from her, you *vabond! Voetsak!*' **1970** —— *Cloud across Moon* 48 Her immense body seemed to swell like a toad's. 'Don't you look at me like that, you dirty vabond! Who you thinks you is?' **1982** S. MOTJUWADI in *Voice* 10 Jan. 11 They threatened the African foreman of the farm saying that they knew that there was another 'vabond' with cameras in the fields. **1993** *Weekly Mail & Guardian* 23 Dec. 9 Vera S– .. had to use a shoe to fight off a large rat that had 'robbed' a money box ... 'I wasn't actually cross with the vabond,' she said. 'Shame, he was probably just hungry.'

vaboom var. WABOOM.

vach-an-bechie, vacht am beechie, vacht-een-bidgte, vacht een bietjie varr. WAG-'N-BIETJIE.

Vaderland /ˈfɑːdə(r)lant/ *adj.*, *int.*, and *n.* Also **Faderland**, and with small initial. [Du., 'fatherland'.]

A. *adj. Obs.* exc. *hist.* Of one of the FATHERLAND breeds of cattle.

1824 *S. Afr. Commercial Advertiser* 14 Jan. 23 Waggons, Draughthorses, .. Milch Cows of the Vaderland breed, and 2 fine Bulls of the same. **1827** [see FATHERLAND]. **1833** *Graham's Town Jrnl* 1 The Stock consists of 95 Cows, Bullocks and Calves, .. 2 *Vaderland* Bulls, and two Horses. **1837** [see AFRIKANDER *n.* sense 4]. **1839** W.C. HARRIS *Wild Sports* 7 We also became the proprietors of a comfortable travelling waggon, .. and a span .. of twelve tough little *Faderland* oxen. **1913** C. PETTMAN *Africanderisms* 527 *Vaderland*, .. The term applied to cattle imported from Holland in the early days, and to their progeny. **1975** W.F. LYE *Andrew Smith's Jrnl 1836–6* Glossary, *Vaderland cattle*, Term referring to the cattle brought from Europe, as distinct from the indigenous type.

‖**B.** *int.* An exclamation of dismay or astonishment.

1868 W.R. THOMSON *Poems, Essays & Sketches* 127 The characteristic, seemingly meaningless expletive, 'Vaderland' – which I dare say most of my readers have heard uttered by the South African boer in moments of excitement.

‖**C.** *n.* ***the Vaderland***: 'the fatherland', South Africa. See also (*for*) *Volk and Vaderland* (VOLK sense 3 c).

1900 F.R.M. CLEAVER in M.M. Cleaver *Young S. Afr.* (1913) 177, I had the misfortune to be compelled to retire from the lists of those still actively engaged in the defence of the Vaderland. **1973** *Sunday Times* 9 Dec. (Mag. Sect.) 10 Let us ridicule the hypocrisy of politicians who .. broadcast an SOS for unity in the interests of the 'Vaderland'. **1976** VAN TONDER in *Weekend Post* 15 May 4 You bloody immigrant, pack your bags and go home. The Vaderland doesn't need people like you.

‖**vadoek** /ˈfaduk, ˈfɑːdʊk/ *n.* Also **fad(d)ock, feodhook, vaatdock, va(a)tdoek.** [Afk., ad. Du. *vaatdoek.*]

1. *obs.* A damp rag used at table as a communal napkin; JAMMERLAPPIE.

*a***1827** D. CARMICHAEL in W.J. Hooker *Botanical Misc.* (1831) II. 55 Each cover is furnished with a white napkin; but the duty of its office is executed by a deputy, the *vaatdock*, (dish-clout) which circulates from hand to hand, and from mouth to mouth. **1887** A.A. ANDERSON *25 Yrs in Waggon* I. 59 The old Boer got up from his chair, went to the bowl and began to rub his hands, then his face, wiping them with this rag, which I afterwards found out was called a feodhook.

2. A cloth for wiping up spills, cleaning surfaces, etc.; a tea-towel or dish-cloth. Also *attrib.*

1880 P. GILLMORE *On Duty* 151 An old lady waited at table with a clout in her hand, which, I believe is designated by these people a 'faddock.' **1913** C. PETTMAN *Africanderisms* 527 *Vaatdoek*, .. A common clout used for the thousand and one things that a damp cloth is needed for in a kitchen. [**1977** F.G. BUTLER *Karoo Morning* 99 To call the Union Jack a 'rooi spinnekop' was definitely cleverer, but was it more, or less, insulting than the 'die rooi vadoek'?] **1982** J. JACKSON *Informant, Grahamstown* Let me come in and help you. I could easily wield a vadoek or something.

3. *comb.* **vadoek plant**, see quot.

1978 *Garden & Home* Aug. 26 The 'vadoek' plant is a loofah, botanical name Luffa cylindrica .. sometimes called Egyptian cucumber. The long cylindrical fruits are used for sponges or for scrubbing pots when the outer covering has been removed.

vai var. WAAI.

vaitje var. VAATJIE.

Valie var. VAALIE.

valley *n. Obs.* exc. *hist.* Also **valey**. [Calque formed on S. Afr. Du. *vlei*, ad. Du. *vallei* a flat area through which a river flows.]

a. VLEI sense 1.

1795 C.R. HOPSON tr. *C.P. Thunberg's Trav.* II. p.xii, A *Valley* is nothing more than a rivulet, which is sometimes overgrown with rushes, and is broad in some places, and narrow in others. *Ibid.* 2 The whole country was covered with sand and downs, and abounded in swamps (*valley*), which having been filled with water during the winter, now began to produce fine pasturage for the cattle. **1801** J. BARROW *Trav.* I. 69 A lake called the *Vogel Valley* or the Bird Lake: The word *valley*, in the colony, implies either a lake or a swamp. **1822** W.J. BURCHELL *Trav.* I. 519 This word Valley is a Dutch word of most extensive use in the Cape Colony, and can seldom be translated by the English word Valley ... It should, therefore, be considered, not as an English, but as a colonial, term, its proper pronunciation being as if written faly, with the a sounded very faintly and indistinctly, and a strong accent on the y. *Ibid.* 538 We .. soon came to a large and very long valley, or lake, in a part of the road where, in September, no traces of any thing of the kind were to be seen. *a*1827 D. CARMICHAEL in W.J. Hooker *Botanical Misc.* (1831) II. 52 This valley, or rather plain, is a tract of marshy ground, three miles in extent, overgrown with reeds, rushes, and other aquatic plants. [**1834** T. PRINGLE *Afr. Sketches* 272 As they could not conveniently get within shot of the game without crossing part of the *valei* or marsh, .. they agreed to leave their steeds in charge of their Hottentots.] **1905** P.D. HAHN in Flint & Gilchrist *Science in S. Afr.* 417 The wine grown on hills is of a much superior quality to the product obtained from vineyards in the valleys – 'vleys,' where the wine thrives in a rich alluvial soil. **1994** M. ROBERTS tr. *J.A. Wahlberg's Trav. Jrnls 1838–56* 9 In a little Valey were a great crowd of *Totanana* and a *Fringa* [two species of wader].

b. *comb.* **valley-ground**, *vlei ground* (see VLEI sense 2).

1812 A. PLUMPTRE tr. *H. Lichtenstein's Trav. in Sn Afr.* I. Very few horned cattle are kept, from the want of what is called valley-ground; by this is meant a moist soil, composed of clay and sand.

Van /væn/ *n.* [Ellipt. for the Afk. surname *Van der Merwe*.]

1. VAN DER MERWE sense 1 a.

1978 *Fair Lady* 25 Oct. 116 'Fellow here didn't get the punch line.' He turned round and continued ... 'So next time Van sees the vet.' **1993** C. VINEALL in *Weekend Mercury* 27 Feb. (Suppl.) 20 Van bought in lambs in large quantities, dyed them, and made a fortune selling them as novelties.

2. VAN DER MERWE sense 2.

1988 H. MARTIN in *Daily Dispatch* 25 June 14, I see that bank bloke's a bit worried that the old Vans in the street are spending too much.

Van der Hum /ˌvæn də ˈhʌm/ *n. phr.* Formerly also **Van der Humm**, **Van Der Hums**, **Van Hum**, **Vanrhum**, and with small initial(s). [Etym. unknown; perh. a personal name (see quot. 1984).] A brandy-based liqueur, flavoured with naartjie peel and spices. Also *attrib.* See also NAARTJIE sense 1 a.

1861 'A LADY' *Life at Cape* (1963) 31 Mrs M— .. has even promised to show me how to brew liqueurs, and distil 'vanrhum', – the latter a most aromatic and powerful *elixir vitae.* **1891** H.J. DUCKITT *Hilda's 'Where Is It?'*, Liqueur (Vanderhum). (Old Recipe. Cape *Spécialité.*) ... Add one wineglass of best rum to *every* bottle of Vanderhum. The rum mellows the mixture. **1891** [see TICKEY sense 2]. **1893** R. KIPLING *Many Inventions* 330 Judson's best Vanderhum, which is Cape brandy ten years in the bottle, flavoured with orange-peel and spices. **1908** M.C. BRUCE *New Tvl* 79 In Cape Colony .. are produced .. many kinds of liqueur, of which Van der Hum, made from the naartje, is the best. **1934** N. DEVITT *Mem. of Magistrate* 12 One could picture the old aristocrat seated on the stoep with his wife and family sipping their afternoon 'soopjes' of Van der Hum, a luscious Cape liqueur. **1947** [see NAARTJIE *n.* sense 1 a]. **1968** W.E.G. LOUW in D.J. Opperman *Spirit of Vine* 325 There is only one local liquer which has obtained anything like international fame, which it certainly deserves because of its exceptional combination of flavours. I refer to our *Van der Hum.* **1984** *Daily Dispatch* 2 July 6 Van der Hum was appreciated by the early colonists of the Cape ... Some attribute the name to an old Dutch sea captain who developed a strong affinity for the liqueur, while others say the derivation literally is 'From Mr H'm'. Folklore has it that various characters .. laid claim to the liqueur's discovery and .. to avoid unpleasantness .. a decision was made to distribute the honours equally. And how better to do that than 'Mr H'm'! **1993** E. BADENHORST in *Flying Springbok* Apr. 117 Chocolate *potjie* pots filled with a Van der Hum mousse.

Van der Merwe /ˌfan də ˈmɛrvə, ˌvæn də ˈmɜːvə/ *n.* [A common Afk. surname.]

1.a. The surname of a stereotypical Afrikaans figure, the subject of numerous jokes and stories; VAN sense 1. Also (written abbrev.) **v.d. Merwe**. Also *attrib.*

1970 J.S.T. FLETCHER in *Outpost* 281 The lieutenant had always been the butt of strings of 'Van der Merwe' jokes – stories which he always managed to cap. **1975** *E. Prov. Herald* 2 July 17 The South African social scene has not been the same since Van der Merwe first lumbered on to it about a decade ago ... Anecdotes about him are swopped from boardroom to boudoir. **1977** *Sunday Times* 7 Aug. 3 These little jokes (ever heard the one about the Scotsman, the Irishman and the skeleton? – and what about v.d. Merwe?). **1978** P.-D. UYS in S. Gray *Theatre One* 141 He was so Afrikaans ... He .. spoke English like a Van der Merwe joke – 'Ag no sis man Anna sis.' **1989** *Style* Feb. 44 This theory has it that when Van Riebeeck landed he found Hottentots speaking Afrikaans. (No, this is not a Van der Merwe joke.) **1990** [see Stengel quot. at BILINGUAL].

b. In the facetious nonce phrr. ***the real Van der Merwe***, 'the real McCoy'; ***to meet one's Van der Merwe***, to meet one's Waterloo.

1975 *E. Prov. Herald* 21 May 16 The condensed end product is of course the real Van der Merwe. **1988** M.M. CARLIN in *Frontline* Apr.-May 16 I've seen photos of some of them [*sc.* ANC members] looking remarkably comb-in-the-sock; or perhaps it was the Mao jacket taken to extremes, and finally meeting its van der Merwe.

2. *transf.* A nickname for the Afrikaans man-in-the-street; VAN sense 2.

1990 *Style* July 45 It doesn't matter whether you treat your domestic worker better than Van der Merwe next door. **1992** J. KANI on TV1, 20 Mar., The time has come for me and Van der Merwe to look at ourselves and laugh, to look at the past and say 'Weren't we *stupid*?' **1993** [see VASTRAP *v.*].

vandue var. VENDUE.

Van Hum, **Vanrhum** varr. VAN DER HUM.

Van Riebeeck Day *n. phr. Hist.* [Named for *Jan van Riebeeck*, founder of the first colonial settlement at the Cape.] The 6th of April, from 1952 until 1973 observed as a public holiday commemorating the establishment of the first European settlement at the Cape. See also FOUNDERS' DAY.

1952 *Act 5* in *Stat. of Union* 39 First Schedule ... Van Riebeeck Day (sixth day of April). **1963** M. BENSON *Afr. Patriots* 173 Formalities; then the proposal was put; mass protests on April 6, 1952, Van Riebeeck Day, when white South Africans would celebrate 300 years of white rule. Unless the government repealed six particular unjust laws, passive resistance would be launched to defy those laws. **1973** *Govt Gaz.* Vol.95 No.3892, 2 The First Schedule to the Public Holidays Act, 1952, is hereby amended .. by the deletion of the words 'Van Riebeeck Day (sixth day of April)'.

Van Rooy /fan ˈrɔɪ/ *n. phr.* [See quot. 1975.] A locally-bred non-woolled sheep: see quots 1953 and 1975. Also *attrib.* See also *Blackhead Persian* (BLACKHEAD sense 2), RONDERIB.

1953 *S. Afr. Stockbreeder & Farmer Ref. Bk* 231 The Van Rooy is a new breed developed recently out of crossings between the Ronderib Afrikaner, the Rambouillet Merino and the Blackhead Persian. Being somewhat similar in type to the Blackhead Persian, it is sometimes referred to, although erroneously, as the White Persian. The Van Rooy breeders formed their association in 1948 ... Both the Blackhead Persian and Van Rooy have short, fat tails with a greater preponderance of subcutaneous fat, particularly on the rump. **1957** *Handbk for Farmers* (Dept of Agric.) III. 221 *The Van Rooy* was evolved by .. Senator J.C. van Rooy in about 1920. **1975** W.J. HUGO in *Std Encycl. of Sn Afr.* XI. 171 *Van Rooy Sheep*, Sheep of the fat-tailed and fat-rump type. In 1919 Senator J.C. van Rooy, of Koppieskraal, Bethulie, began the development of the Van Rooy sheep as it is known today, when he mated the round-ribbed Afrikander with Rambouillet ewes ... After 40 years, breeders of the Van Rooy sheep (sometimes incorrectly termed the Van Rooy Persian) have succeeded in developing a heavy, strong sheep with a good, compact tail and a better distribution of fat than the round-ribbed Afrikander has. The Van Rooy sheep is found chiefly in the North-Western Cape, particularly in broken veld on the Orange River.

‖**vark** /fark/ *n.* Pl. **-e** /-ə/. [Afk., pig.]

1. *colloq.* A pig; now usu. *transf.*, a term of abuse; a contemptuous term for a policeman.

[*a*1931 S. BLACK in S. Gray *Three Plays* (1984) 147 Helena: .. He claims he has found lots of gold on it. Katoo: Gold! Jou vark!] **1958** I. VAUGHAN *Diary* 47 It was a long church, when we came home Ellen said The vark has got out of its hok and is eating in Masters potatoes. **1975** S. ROBERTS *Outside Life's Feast* 88 'Bladdy vark!' she said bitterly. 'Rubbish, that's what you are.' She started sobbing and left the kitchen to stumble in her slippered feet to the bedroom. **1977** D. MULLER *Whitey* 65 Don't go into the voorkamer; that old vark will get you drinking again. **1979** [see ORE]. **1986** D. CASE *Love, David* 41 There is only one thing that he really loves and that is his bottle. The vark has a cheek to tell you that!

2. *comb.* **varkblaar** /-blɑː(r)/ *obs.* [Afk., *blaar* leaf], or **varkblom** /-blɔm/ [Afk., *blom* flower], the PIG-LILY, *Zantedeschia aethiopica*; **varkbos** *obs.* [Afk., *bos* bush], the plant *Helichrysum pentzioides* of the Asteraceae; **varkoortjies** *obs.* [Afk., *oor* ear + dim. suffix -IE + pl. *-s*], the medicinal plant *Centella asiatica*.

1821 C.I. LATROBE *Jrnl of Visit* Glossary, **Farkblar**, (*pig-leaf*), *Calla Ethiopica*. **1929** M. ALSTON *From Old Cape*

Homestead 22 'These pig-lilies — ' 'These what?' 'Piglilies — Varkenbiaar.' 1947 L.G. GREEN Tavern of Seas 199 The medicine chest of the Cape Flats is not without virtue ... For rheumatism there is **varkblom**, which must be heated before being applied to the skin. 1973 Y. BURGESS Life to Live 17 As Tolkie became paralysed, Boesman applied hot poultices of varkblom and cold poultices of buchu. 1934 Friend 4 July (Swart), Bushes which really were a stand-by to the farmer were the kerrie or **varkbos** and the grannat or daggabossie. 1934 C.P. SWART Supplement to Pettman. 183 Varkbos, .. the popular name of a drought resistant plant, Helichrysum pentzioides. 1977 Daily Dispatch 22 Aug. 6 Listing some of the medicine plants found in these parts, the writer names — among them — besembos, boetebos, .. wildekleur, **varkoortjies** and babalasbos.

varkpan /ˈfɑːk-ˈfarkpan/ n. Army slang. Pl. **-s, -panne** /-panə/. [Afk., vark pig + pan dish, pan.] A compartmentalized metal meal-tray, used in army canteens.
1971 Informant, Grahamstown Varkpan. Tin pan divided into compartments, in which the troops get their food. 1975 Scope 10 Jan. 76 OK, so you've finished complaining about the chow .. polishing your area, washing your varkpan. 1975 J.H. PICARD in Eng. Usage in Sn Afr. Vol.6 No.1, A tin trunk is a trommel and the mess tray or 'dixy' is a varkpan. 1979 W. STEENKAMP in Cape Times 5 May 7 Rifleman Snooks says as he lines up with his 'varkpan' to get his graze: Go for it, man, go for it. 1984 Fair Lady 14 Nov. 136 The troops line up outside their canteens, 'varkpan' and 'pikstels' in hand and queue to help themselves. 1986 DE VILLIERS in Uniform 16 June 1 They were divided into platoons, got up before daybreak, stood in queues to get food, ate out of 'varkpanne'; and jumped when the instructors spoke.

vasbyt /ˈfasbəit/ v. intrans. Orig. army slang; now colloq. [Afk., lit. 'bite hard', 'seize with the jaws', (vas firm(ly), fast + byt bite).] To bite the bullet, be stoical, endure; usu. imp., an encouragement to keep up one's spirits while on national military service. Now in extended use (usu. imp.) as a general exhortation: 'hang on', 'hold out', 'keep going'. Cf. hou moed (see HOU). See also MIN DAE.
1970 Informant, Grahamstown 'Vas byt' seems to be the 'In' word this year; does it mean 'hold tight, hang on?' 1972 [see OUMAN]. 1973 Informant, Grahamstown I've only got another 164 more days to vasbyt through. 1978 S. Afr. Panorama Jan. 10 The concept 'vasbyt' (keep going) has been incorporated into the new army language. 1979 Sunday Times 3 June 16 Vasbyt! The countries which survive the energy shortage of the coming decade will be those that muster the honesty to face reality and the will to deal with it. 1981 Fair Lady 8 Apr., I see them off at the station, and like all of you mothers, I am expected to vasbyt and hold back my tears. 1981 Rand Daily Mail 13 Oct. 1 Vasbyt on Fate ... Lance-Corporal Hugo Truter .. survived — against all the odds. 1984 B. GUNSENHAUSER in Ibid. 27 June 7 The army has long used the phrase vasbyt, which roughly translated means Be Strong. 1984 [see TIFFY sense 2]. 1986 [see HUISTOE]. 1987 M. MOSIMANE in Pace July 53 Because I had told myself that I wanted to be a sangoma I said 'vasbyt'. I'm thankful that my wife and children stood by me. Hence **vasbyt** n., an exhortation to endure; a spoken or written use of the word 'vasbyt'; stoical or cheerful endurance; and adj., dogged, stoical; **vasbyter** n. [Afk. or Eng. agential suffix -er], one who is stoical, one who endures; **vasbyting** ppl adj., stoical, showing endurance; and vbl n., endurance.
1972 Sunday Times 12 Mar. (Mag. Sect.) 1 Another vasbyting character had gone down in Parabat legend as the man who, after he had won his wings, asked whether he could buy his 'marble'. Ibid. 5 Agony of the Vasbyters. 1978 F. JOHENNESSE in Staffrider Vol.1 No.3, 20, I tire of this army life this tasteless food These uniform days and messages of vasbyt. 1981 Cape Times 13 Nov. 4 The documentary 'A Measure of Pain' — Vasbyt letters to his folks at home from a South African PoW. 1982 E. Prov. Herald 7 July 3 For them this was the taste of national service — the two years of 'vasbyt' of which they had heard so much. And the beginning of things new and military. 1985 Cape Times 7 Aug., A man is called up for three months and .. is plonked down for 30 days' vasbyting amid the dust and cold and/or heat. 1987 Personality 30 Sept. 12 Louis exhibited none of the tough, vasbyt characteristics which the public (possibly incorrectly) have come to associate with the parabats and Recces. 1989 H.P. TOFFOLI in Style Dec. 54 Half the house was burnt, but the family stayed on in Australia. It's what South Africans call vasbyt. 1990 'HOGARTH' in Sunday Times 28 Oct. 26 Here is a message .. from the 350 000-odd recipients of messages over the last quarter of a century: thanks for the vasbyt. [1994 T. SEXWALE on M-Net TV (Carte Blanche) 11 Dec., Keep at it all the time — 'vasbyt' as they say in Afrikaans.]

vastrap /ˈfastrap/ n. Also **vastrappe, vast-trap**. [Afk., vas (fr. Du. vast) firm(ly) + trap tread.]
1.a. A fast dance similar to the quickstep, danced (in the Afrikaans community) to the accompaniment of a type of BOEREMUSIEK (sense 1). Also **vastrappie** [see -IE], and attrib. See also TICKEY-DRAAI sense 1 a.
1913 E. London Dispatch 3 Jan. 5 The vast-trap was performed by a number of nondescript characters who provided much amusement by their antics. a1920 O.E.A. SCHREINER From Man to Man (1926) 360 Then she paused and began a reel. 'This is the "vastrap",' she said ... 'It's what the Hottentots dance.' 1957 Cape Times 17 Jan. 7 Rock and roll has affiliations with our own vastraps and tiekiedraais to which Coloured bands used to thrum the beat. 1959 J. MEIRING Candle in Wind 38 Rosie .. was dancing a vastrap; her partner was swinging her arm vigorously up and down like a pump-handle, as he propelled her around the small kitchen. 1969 A. FUGARD Boesman & Lena 12 Lena's still got a vastrap in her old legs. You want to dance Boesman. Not too late to learn. 1980 E. Prov. Herald 22 Nov. 5 When disco dancing is long forgotten, the old-time vastrappies and polkas will live on. 1984 Sunday Times 1 Jan. 11 Jawellnofine. Move over Kavalier — Jarman is going to be a big hit in the vastrappie stakes. 1991 S. Afr. Panorama May-June 20 The sparkling vastrap .. is reminiscent of the two step or foxtrot. 1994 [see LANGARM n.].
b. Music. The style of music played to accompany this dance; a piece of music in this style. Also attrib.
1920 R.Y. STORMBERG Mrs Pieter de Bruyn 94 Dirk Erasmus wheezed out a vas-trap on his concertina. 1935 H.C. BOSMAN Mafeking Rd (1969) 36 No Bushveld dance was complete without Manie Kruger's concertina. When he played a vastrap you couldn't keep your feet still. 1944 M. DE B. NESBITT Rd to Avalon 14 The band is playing a lively 'vastrap'. 1970 L.G. GREEN Giant in Hiding 105 You remember the candle light, the vastrap music. 1979 Fair Lady 28 Mar. 73 We listened to the music of the sertao: sometimes it has a Mexican lilt, at other times it's not unlike boeremusiek, with a spirited vastrap on the accordion. 1980 D.B. COPLAN Urbanization of African Performing Arts. 75 The latter [sc. the Basotho] were by no means immune to the Afrikaans vastrap rhythms. 1989 [see MARABI sense 1].
2. A country dancing-party; SHEEPSKIN; VELDSKOEN n. sense 2 a. Cf. OPSKOP sense a.
1945 Outspan 20 July 37 When he went back to the U.S.A. he said that he would come back if we could guarantee to fix him a real 'vastrap'. 1949 L.G. GREEN In Land of Afternoon 167 A country dance is often referred to as a vastrap or a velskoen ... Many tunes heard at a vastrap are nameless, for they are composed on the farms by the players themselves. 1980 A.J. BLIGNAUT Dead End Rd 94 He's gay when it's played on the concertina at a vastrap.

vastrap v. intrans. [See prec.] To dance the vastrap.
1974 E. Prov. Herald 16 May, The guests .. vastrapped across the concrete to the strains of 'Sarie Marais'. 1990 Sunday Times 8 Apr. 6 'My goodness, I love Big Daddy,' announces Gera L— .. flushed from vastrapping. 1993 Ibid. 13 June 20 (caption) Hold it Van der Merwe, when we go on mass action we will vastrap, not toyi-toyi!

‖**vat** /fat/ v. [Afk., take, get, seize.]
1. intrans. In urban, esp. township, Eng.: in the colloquial phr. **to vat en sit** [see VAT EN SIT n.], to live as husband and wife in a common-law marriage.
[1926 P.W. LAIDLER Tavern of Ocean 95 In the words of the modern person of colour, wives were somarso gevat, taken anyhow.] 1952 Drum Nov. 11 Only 5% of some 65,000 families in a local emergency camp were actually married. The rest just 'vat en sit,' bilingual for 'take and sit,' to get a shelter or some other convenience, and then quit when they've had it. 1959 L. LONGMORE Dispossessed 32 A girl who is foolish enough to agree to live with a man, as man and wife, known as vat en sit 'just take and sit', or 'keep', hoping that eventually he will decide to marry her, is entertaining false hopes. Ibid. 69 One informant remarked that any man who wants to be free from worries ought to live long should never enter into a marriage contract with any woman, but instead he should just 'keep' a woman or vat en sit (as it is expressed in vulgar colloquialism).
2. trans. In the phrase **vat jou goed en trek** [fr. the name of an Afk. folk song Vat jou goed en trek, Ferreira take your belongings and go, Ferreira], take your things and be gone; be off with you; good riddance. Hence **to vat one's goed and trek**, to leave, to take one's belongings and leave.
1974 Daily Dispatch 2 Dec. 10 For those members who don't contribute ..., to those members who walk out before the end of the meetings and to those who don't even attend meetings, all I can say is vat jou goed en trek. 1989 Sunday Times 30 Apr. 22 Vat jou goed en Trek. The massive Mobil disinvestment must be a cause for serious thought among the departing American oil giant's 2 800 employees in South Africa. 1989 J. DOWSON in Argus 17 Nov. (Tonight) 11 He's looking as sparkling as an Omo-white shirt and grinning as sweetly as a koeksister. The stubble of yore has vat-ed its goed and trekked.
3. trans. In the colloquial phr. **vat hom** /ˈfat (h)ɔm/ [Afk., get him, get it (a command to a dog, but also an exhortation to a rugby-player, etc.)], 'get him', 'go for it': an expression of approval or encouragement, as shouted (often with a name following) to a participant in sport or to a person attempting something daunting; sometimes used ironically, often representing Afrikaans speech.
1980 Cape Times 16 May 3 Years ago we had 'Vat hom Dawie' — and now we have 'Hey Morné', warning the current Springbok captain that the Boks had better donner the Lions. 1981 Fair Lady 25 Feb. 220 (advt) If Farmer Brown chickens were people, they'd all be Springboks (vat him Maudie) they're so fit. 1990 Style Feb. 49 Well, say I, whether the forces are heavenly or not, let them be with us. Vat hom, Flaffie! 1991 Weekly Mail 20 Dec. 19 The only locally made condom, elegantly entitled 'Crepe de Chine' instead of 'Voortrekker Mark 1' or 'Vat hom, Fluffie' is an option if you're into penetrating that market.

vatdoek var. VADOEK.

vat en sit /ˌfat ən ˈsət/ adj. phr. and n. phr. Colloq. Also **vat-'n-sit**. [Afk., 'stay put', vat take + en and + sit sit.] In urban (esp. township) Eng.:
A. adj. phr. Of a relationship between a man and a woman: common-law, unsolemnized, 'live-in'; of a person: in such a relationship; of an attitude or opinion: favouring such a relationship.
1959 L. LONGMORE Dispossessed 32 There inevitably comes the day when he fancies someone else and tries to get rid of his vat en sit woman. 1974 K.M.C. MOTSISI in Drum 8 Mar. 29 He will tell anybody .. that vat en sit marriages have been blessed by the gods seeing as the Little Woman will never nag you or

threaten to institute divorce proceedings. **1978** — in M. Mutloatse *Casey & Co.* 47 Kid Conscience, the guy who decided to marry his 'vat en sit' girl after a donkey's age. **1978** S. MHLONGO in *Staffrider* Vol.1 No.2, 10 Marriage counsellors and lobola instalments are customs rotting in the garbage since the willing patriots of the new idealism became authoritative here, with the 'vat en sit' stance to the fore.

B. *n. phr.* An unsolemnized or common-law marriage; a marriage undertaken without attention to custom. See also *to vat en sit* (VAT sense 1).

1977 J. SIKAKANE *Window on Soweto* 17 They had developed a system, dubbed 'vat en sit', meaning practically 'let's marry on our own without conforming to family tradition and the church'. **1979** *Voice* 25 Mar. 7 In South Africa these loose unions .. are laconically referred to as 'vat en sit' ... People who are involved in Vat-en-sit seem to have less problems than us legally married ones. **1984** M. DIKOBE in *Staffrider* Vol.6 No.1, 33 In Doornfontein there were few who had married in any form. It was 'vat en sit'. **1988** *Pace* June 4 Townships in the Kwa-Zulu capital of Ulundi are known for four things: vat-en-sits, early marriages, alcoholism and kwaai wives.

vatj(i)e var. VAATJIE.

Vatua /ˈvɑːtwə, -wa/ *pl. n. Hist.* Also **Bratwah, Vatwah(s)**. [A name once given to the Zulus by peoples living to the north of them.] **a.** (The) members of a group of Nguni people who, in the early 19th century, lived in what is now the northern part of KwaZulu-Natal, and who migrated, as a result of the MFECANE, to the area around Delagoa Bay (at Maputo), later becoming a part of the Shangaan people (see SHANGAAN sense 1 a). **b.** (The) members of the Zulu people. Also *attrib.*

As is the case with many names of peoples and groups in *S. Afr. Eng.*, this word has been found only in plural uses; however, it may be that it has also been used in unrecorded singular forms.

While those who migrated northwards did not form part of the Zulu people as unified by Shaka, they were from the same branch of the Nguni as the Zulus, and seem to have been identified with the Zulus by the peoples in the Delagoa Bay area. See also ZULU *n.* sense 1 a.

1823 W. THRELFALL in G. Thompson *Trav.* (1827) I. 356 A powerful tribe, called the Vatwahs, have lately overrun many of the little states in the vicinity of Delagoa Bay ... They are originally from the country adjoining to the sources of the Mapoota River, and the mountains west of the English River ... For two or three years past, the devastations of the Vatwahs have been like those of a swarm of locusts throughout all the adjoining country. **1823** — in T. Cheeseman *Story of William Threlfall* (1910) 39 Saw several of the Bratwah nation. **1827** G. THOMPSON *Trav.* I. 355 From the frontier of the Amapondæ (or Hambona Caffers) on the southwest, as far as the river Mapoota and Delagoa Bay on the north .., the whole country is now under the sway of one formidable tribe, governed by a chief named Chaka. This man, originally the sovereign of an obscure but warlike people, called Zoolas, or Vatwahs, has, within the last eight or nine years, conquered or extirpated the whole of the native tribes from Delagoa Bay to Hambona. **1832** J.C. CHASE in *Graham's Town Jrnl* 8 June 96 John Cane .. was despatched by Chaka, the Sovereign of the Zoolah or Vatwah Nation, to the Colony. **1841** B. SHAW *Memorials* 50 The warlike tribe called the Zuloos, or Vatwahs, is found to the northward of the Kaffirs. **1902** G.M. THEAL *Beginning of S. Afr. Hist.* 431 Captain Owen described the conquering clans, whom he termed Vatwahs, as a martial people. **1972** E. AXELSON in *Std Encycl. of Sn Afr.* VII. 612 A Nguni clan under Soshanga (also known as Manukuza) had fled northwards from Shaka about 1819, and within a decade its chief had become paramount over the region between the Lebombo Mountains and the Zambezi. In 1834 these Vatua people attacked Lourenço Marques.

Vavenda pl. form of VENDA.

v.d. Merwe var. VAN DER MERWE.

vechtgeneraal var. VEGGENERAAL.

vee /fɪə/ *n.* Also **vei, vieh, vij**. [Du., cattle.]
1. *obs.* Livestock, esp. sheep and goats.

1836 J. COLLETT Diary. I. 6 Dec., Set off this Morning up the Country to Purchase Vee for Slaughter. **1852** C. BARTER *Dorp & Veld* 215 (Pettman), After the arrival of Mr. McCabe with his *vee*, the Kaffir labourers .. made a feast on two of their master's fattest sheep. **1877** *Sel. Comm. Report on Mission to Damaraland* 57, I was not unwilling to .. let them have a place for their vee and cattle. **1913** C. PETTMAN *Africanderisms* 529 *Vee*, Cattle, but more frequently small stock, as sheep and goats, as distinct from *beesten*, cattle.

2. *comb.* **vee-boer** /-buːr, -bʊə(r)/ [S. Afr. Du., *boer* farmer], (*a*) *obs.* a cattle farmer; (*b*) *hist.*, an early Dutch settler given permission to farm cattle in an area remote from the settlement at the Cape of Good Hope; **vee kraal** /- krɑːl/ *obs.* [S. Afr. Du., *kraal* enclosure, shelter], a shelter for livestock; a *vee place*; **vee place** *obs.* [part. tr. S. Afr. Du. *veeplaats* (*plaats* place) or Afk. *veeplaas* (*plaas* farm)], an outpost or part of a farm at which livestock was kept when a change of grazing was required; **vee post** *obs.*, *vee place*.

1824 *S. Afr. Jrnl* I. 29 Poor Gert Schepers, a **Vee Boer** of the Cradock District, was less fortunate in an encounter with a South African lion. **1835** A. STEEDMAN *Wanderings* I. 146 We met with one of those graziers called by the Dutch a Vei Boor, who was removing with his flocks from the winter-veld to his summer residence. **1843** *Chambers's Jrnl* (U.K.) in J.M. Bowker *Speeches & Sel.* (1864) 117 The vee boers, far removed from the seat of authority and civilisation, have always been troublesome subjects. *c***1885** M. REID (*title*) The Vee-boers: a Tale of Adventure in Southern Africa. **1912** [see *schaapboer* (BOER sense 1 b)]. **1928** E.A. WALKER *Hist. of S. Afr.* 62 Long before the end of the seventeenth century, the frontier *veeboer* was in the process of becoming the *trekboer*. **1940** F.B. YOUNG *City of Gold* 545 Janse recognized among the prison-guard the *Vee Boer*, Trichard, who had given him his liberty after the fight at Bronkhorst Spruit. **1944** J. MOCKFORD *Here Are S. Africans* 39 The free burghers, the vee-Boers, rapidly acquired qualities unknown to the sedate residents of Table Valley. **1965** M.G. ATMORE *Cape Furn.* 55 As a result of the shortage of cattle for the Company, the third type came into being, the 'veeboere', on the outer perimeter of the wheat and wine farming belt. *Ibid.* 56 Thus arose the 'veeboere', each tenant on some 6,000 acres of land. **1841** J.M. BOWKER *Speeches & Sel.* (1864) 102 A brother of Botman's .. stopped at our **vee kraal** begging goats. **1894** B. MITFORD *Renshaw Fanning's Quest* 96 To look for half a dozen wretched sheep .., riding back by the vij-kraal to count Umsapu's flock. **1913** J.J. DOKE *Secret City* 23 I, Piet Retief, had ridden back from the Vee Kraal at the close of a hot afternoon. **1931** V. SAMPSON *Kom Binne* 267 Ian had gone off to the vee-kraal. **1818** G. BARKER Journal. 3 Jan., Did a little in the garden & numbered the people at the **Vee-place**. **1838** J. COLLETT Diary. I. 28 Aug., *Tracked* to day to the Vee Place with Wether Flock. **1851** GODLONTON & IRVING *Narr. of Kaffir War 1850–51* 123 As the crisis approached, it was deemed prudent to bring in the flocks and herds from the 'vee-places' or out-stations. **1876** T. STUBBS Reminiscences. 39 We arrived at the Vee place and found a lot more Dutchmen .. there. **1887** A.A. ANDERSON *25 Yrs in Waggon* II. 107 They have their cattle-posts away in the bush, where the stock is looked after ... These **'vieh-posts'** are in charge of their slaves. **1931** V. SAMPSON *Kom Binne* 67 This was the house flock and .. they had another at the vee-post, which was a kraal around the hill, in charge of the separate herd, the object of the division being to distribute the good veld between the two flocks.

veggeneraal /ˈfɛxˌxenəˈrɑːl/ *n. hist.* Also **vecht-generaal**, and with initial capital. [Afk., earlier *vecht-generaal*, fr. Du. *vecht-* fight- (n. used only in comb., fr. *vechten* to fight) + *generaal* general.] 'Combat general': the commanding officer of a division of the Boer army during the Anglo-Boer War; also used as a title.

[**1900** H.C. HILLEGAS *With Boer Forces* 91 The head of the army was the Commandant-General ... Directly under his authority were the Assistant Commandant-Generals, five of whom were appointed by the Volksraad a short time before the beginning of hostilities. Then in rank were those who were called Vecht-Generals, or fighting generals ... Then followed the Commandants, the leaders of the field-cornets of one district whose rank was about that of colonels.] **1902** C.R. DE WET *Three Yrs War* 35 Up to the 9th of December I had only been a Vice-Commandant, but on the morning of that day I received a telegram from States-President Steyn, asking me to go to the Western frontier as Vechtgeneraal. **1933** W.H.S. BELL *Bygone Days* 279 He was .. appointed Vecht-generaal of General Meyer's commando. **1937** C.R. PRANCE *Tante Rebella's Saga* 136 Willem Noordeveld, the Field-Cornet and the pre-destined 'Veg-Generaal' of the Bobbejaansburg commando. **1940** F.B. YOUNG *City of Gold* 201 *Veggeneraal* Smit rallied them. **1969** J. MEINTJES *Sword in Sand* 36 Cronje readily appointed him a veggeneraal (the equivalent of a Free State commandant, or a brigadier). **1977** O.J.O. FERREIRA in *Dict. of S. Afr. Biog.* III. 206 He .. was offered the rank of 'veggeneraal' (combat general). **1986** *Grocott's Mail* 4 June 11 On 9 December 1899, President Steyn of the Orange Free State, appointed him to the rank of *Vecht-Generaal* — Fighting General.

vehltschoon var. VELDSKOEN.

vei var. VEE.

veilgoed var. VUILGOED.

vel-broeks *pl. n. Obs.* Also **veldt-broeks**. [fr. Afk. *velbroek* (*vel* skin + *broek* trousers) + Eng. pl. *-s*; see also quot. 1913.] Leather or skin trousers. Cf. CRACKERS.

[**1846** *Natal Witness* 4 Dec. 2 Last seen with vel trousers, striped shirt, velveteen jacket, veld shoes, and Manilla hat on.] **1889** H.A. BRYDEN *Kloof & Karroo* 287 Many a good hunting story could the old man tell, and amongst them was one in which the *veld-broeks* played an important part. **1913** C. PETTMAN *Africanderisms* 530 *Vel-broeks*, .. Leather or skin trousers were much worn in the earlier days of the Colony, and were known among the settlers of 1820 and their descendants as 'Crackers'. The spelling 'veldt-broeks' in the quotation suggests a mistaken etymology. **1917** S.T. PLAATJE *Native Life* 109 Hides and skins were .. collected from the tribesmen, and their tanners were set to work to assist in making veldschoens (shoes), and velbroeks (skin trousers), and karosses (sheepskin rugs) for the tattered and footsore Boers and their children.

veld /felt, fɛlt/ *n.* Forms: α. **felt, veld, velt**. β. **feldt, veldt**. [Du. *veld* (formerly also written *veldt*) field, battle-field.]

1. *noncount. obs.* The area or (collectively) areas in which military operations are taking place, 'the field'; *rare* except in *comb.*, as in the former military and civil titles of persons who, while not necessarily permanent soldiers, were officers-designate, holding positions of authority in the field in times of war, and carrying out certain administrative duties in peacetime: see VELD COMMANDANT, VELD CORNET, *veld-corporal* (see sense 5), VELD-KORNET, VELDWAGTMEESTER.

α. **1785** [see *veld-corporal* at sense 5]. **1902** D. VAN WARMELO *On Commando* 40 Cowards and traitors remained behind, and the willing ones went to the veld. *Ibid.* 171 There was not much left to commandeer, unless we deprived the women whose husbands were in the veld of the necessities of life.

2. Open, undeveloped countryside.
a. i. *noncount.* Uncultivated and undeveloped land with relatively open natural vegetation, esp. open grassland or scrubland, but ranging from semi-desert terrain to savannah in which

grass and scrub are closely interspersed with trees; FIELD sense 1. See also BUSH *n.*[1] sense 3.

α. **1835** A. STEEDMAN *Wanderings* I. 71 We reached Fort Wiltshire late in the evening and .. retired to rest with very different feelings from those which we had entertained the previous evening in the *Veld.* **1856** R.E.E. WILMOT *Diary* (1984) 12 At last after leaving hills, and riding over flats and felt .. for some time came to a stand. **1887** *S.W. Silver & Co.'s Handbk to S. Afr.* 35 The Government had to support with measured rations the people who had been dropped on the veld. **1900** A.W. CARTER *Informant, Ladybrand* 8 Mar. 15 The Boers .. were scattered in small klompies over the veld. **1921** W.C. SCULLY *Harrow* 13 Having but some hundreds of miles of open, more or less barren 'veld' between it and the Orange Rivier, the little town was a tempting bait. **1954** *Bantu World* 15 May 1 They slept around fires in the open veld. **1971** *Post* 7 Mar. 12 A Soweto stockdealer .. knifed him, bound him with wire, locked him in the boot of a car, and took him to the veld. **1987** F. KRÜGER in *Weekly Mail* 12 June 30 The sign which directs you to 'Embassies' .. stands in the veld pointing to nowhere. **1991** C. SMITH in *Sunday Times* 22 Sept. 29 The bridge is .. in scrubby veld next to the main road.

β. **1802** TRUTER & SOMERVILLE in G.M. Theal *Rec. of Cape Col.* (1899) IV. 397 He was of the opinion that .. the veldt between this and Roggeveld and the fountains were too dry .. for the number of cattle of the expedition, and before we had copious rains there could not be sufficient water in that veldt. **1850** N.J. MERRIMAN *Cape Jrnls* (1957) 131 Our horse broke away .. galloping over the veldt, scattering my kit in different directions. **1862** 'A LADY' *Life at Cape* (1963) 98 In September, .. the hedges would be full of roses, and the veldt blazing with bulbs. **1876** T. STUBBS Reminiscences. I. 77 On Saturdays we generally went for a Hunt .. , I never had happier days than with them out in the Veldt. **1885** H. RIDER HAGGARD *King Solomon's Mines* 63 To the right was a scattered native settlement .. , and beyond it great tracts of waving 'veldt' covered with tall grass, over which herds of the smaller game were wandering. **1903** E.F. KNIGHT *S. Afr. after War* 53 Irrigation .. would make vast tracts of now barren veldt blossom like the rose. *Ibid.* 79 The rolling, treeless, and bushless brown veldt, which glowed like dull gold in the sunset. **1967** J.A. BROSTER *Red Blanket Valley* 3 When firewood is unprocurable cattle dung is collected and burned — thus further denuding the already impoverished veldt. **1990** R. GOOL *Cape Town Coolie* 165 Valleys of rolling caneland .. , knolls of dry open veldt with aloes, wattles, and thorntrees bristling above dense nests of subtropical jungle.

ii. *rare.* Pl. **-s**, **-e** /-ə/. A piece or stretch of uncultivated land; an enclosed but uncultivated field.

α. **1987** *New Nation* 23 July 3 The Hlongwane brothers were .. found dead in a veld. **1990** G. SLOVO *Ties of Blood* 81 They'd stood in the midst of an open veld and looked at the land which was once theirs.

β. **1900** H. BUTTERWORTH *Trav. Tales* 15 They wished to know about the great valleys, or veldts, that they expected to visit. **1989** D. DAY *Encycl. of Vanished Species* 191 The savannahs and veldte of Africa.

b. *Attrib.*, as ***veld fire*** (cf. *bushfire*, see BUSH *n.*[1] sense 1 b), ***-flower***, ***-grass***, ***-koppie***.

α. **1882** C. DU VAL *With Show through Sn Afr.* I. 62 In certain seasons .. the 'Veld' flowers in countless numbers burst into bloom, and substitute for their lack of perfume the richness of their variegated hues. **1911** J.A. DREYER in *Farmer's Weekly* 11 Oct. 157 (*letter*) For the whole of that summer these horses lived entirely on the veld grass. **1948** H.C. BOSMAN in L. Abrahams *Unto Dust* (1963) 109 Girls .. carry in the fragrance of romance with a red veld-flower in their hair. **1957** D. JACOBSON *Price of Diamonds* 16 The mines and the mine-dumps receded far across the veld, to become indistinguishable from the veld koppies on the horizon. **1966** L.G. BERGER *Where's Madam* 50 The veld grass by August is waist high. **1985** [see FIRE LILY]. **1989** J. HOBBS *Thoughts in Makeshift Mortuary* 78 The rocks began where the veld grass ended. **1992** T. VAN RENSBURG in *S. Afr. Panorama* Mar.-Apr. 14 Fynbos products such as .. veld flowers and thatching-reed are harvested.

β. **1976** N. ASHFORD in J. Crwys-Williams *S. Afr. Despatches* (1989) 414 Violence and rioting spread across the Rand like a veldt fire today.

c. With distinguishing epithet, denoting a characteristic feature of an area (such as a common animal species, altitude, etc.): see AGTERVELD, BACKVELD, BOKKEVELD, HIGHVELD, HOOGE VELD, LOWVELD, MIDDLEVELD.

d. In the phr. ***veld and vlei verse***, see quot. 1986.

α. **1986** D. ADEY et al. *Companion to S. Afr. Eng. Lit.* 204 *Veld and vlei verse*, A derogatory appellation for a considerable quantity of nineteenth (and early twentieth century) SA verse, the subject of which is the veld — usually evoked in sentimental Victorian-romantic rhythms and tones. Roy Campbell bitingly satirized the tendency of so many colonial poetasters to hymn the mystery of the wide outdoors in his poem 'A Veld Eclogue: The Pioneers'. **1991** M. CHAPMAN in *Embambiswaneni* No.10, 72 A late 19th Century South African tradition of what he [*sc.* Roy Campbell] scornfully called 'veld and vlei' verse (that is, sentimental hymns to the mystery of the veld).

3. *noncount.*

a. Natural uncultivated vegetation used as pasture; the vegetation (as described at sense 2 a i) on such land. See also *veld camp* at sense 5.

α. **1850** J.D. LEWINS Diary. 1 Mar., No lambs in velt. **1852** M.B. HUDSON *S. Afr. Frontier Life* 13 The greensward around us .. resembles the pasture of Albion's down: For this veld the Colonial expression is 'sweet'. **1867** *Blue Bk for Col. 1866* JJ46, The crops and veld have recovered from the ravages of the locusts .. , so that many who despaired of raising any produce have been able to reap a moderate harvest. **1925** L.D. FLEMMING *Crop of Chaff* 47 If your veld should happen to be long and your neighbour's veld is very short his cattle poke their heads .. through the wires and eat away all the veld within their reach. *c*1936 *S. & E. Afr. Yr Bk & Guide* 650 Grazing land round Aliwal North is fairly good and veld sells from 60s. to 80s. a morgen. **1948** A. PATON *Cry, Beloved Country* 269 *Veld*, .. Means open grass country. Or it may mean the grass itself, as when a farmer looks down at his feet, and says, this veld is poor. **1960** J.J.L. SISSON *S. Afr. Judicial Dict.* 838 By veld is generally understood the uncultivated and unoccupied portion of land as distinct from the portion which is cultivated, occupied and built upon. It is that part of open and uncultivated land over which cattle and sheep and other stock are turned for grazing purposes. **1973** *E. Prov. Herald* 11 Apr. 4 Following good rains .. the veld has made a remarkable recovery. **1981** [see NGUNI *n.* sense 3]. **1991** J. GLEN-LEARY in *Farmer's Weekly* 25 Jan. 29 The fodder supply by natural veld and/or cultivated pastures must be synchronised to fulfil the needs of the animals during the various stages of production, reproduction and growth. **1993** J. THOMAS in *House & Leisure* Nov. 50 The veld was hacked into bristly fairways, with odd little patches of kikuyu greens hosting embedded jam tins.

β. **1876** T. STUBBS Reminiscences. I. 91 As the Veldt was completely done, they asked me to help them to remove to another farm. **1897** [see FRIESLAND]. **1900** F.D. BAILLIE *Mafeking Diary* 135 The veldt all round looked fresh, green and undulating. **1903** E.F. KNIGHT *S. Afr. after War* 37 These great trekking flocks and herds coming through their farms were eating up all their veldt.

b. *Attrib.*, as ***veld green***, ***- management***, ***- rehabilitation***, ***veld-type***.

α. **1965** *Farmer's Weekly* 8 Dec. 8 Child of poor veld management, bitterbush is also the forerunner of approaching desert. *Ibid.* 33 Creeping salt bush .. is a hardy and valuable plant for veld rehabilitation on alkaline soils. **1971** *Ibid.* 12 May 431 Veld conditions are often poor .. ; lambs are weaned on poor veld (Karoo). **1973** *S. Afr. Panorama* Aug. 23 The most recent [map], made in 1953, shows 70 different veld types. **1974** *Personality* 12 July 34 Troop-carriers .. , all painted dull veld green, were made available. **1990** W.R. TARBOTON in *Flora & Fauna* No.47, 2 These mist forests fall within the Adcocks veld-type known as 'north-eastern mountain sourveld'. **1993** *Weekend Post* 22 May 4 Border farmers face a bleak winter with hardly any veld reserves.

c. An element in the names of terrain types, with distinguishing epithet denoting the dominant soil or plant type, or a characteristic of the vegetation: see BONTVELD, BOSVELD, BUSHVELD, GEBROKEN VELD, GRASSVELD, HARD VELD, MIXED VELD, RENOSTERVELD, SANDVELD, *sourveld* (SOUR sense 2), STRANDVELD, *sweetveld* (SWEET sense 2), THORNVELD, ZUURVELD.

4. *noncount. transf.* 'The country', rural areas or rural society, with characteristic atmosphere and lifestyle. Also *comb.* **veld-bred**, and (*nonce*) **veld-tipped** *adjs*, and *fig.* See also BACKVELD *n.* sense a.

α. **1881** P. GILLMORE *Land of Boer* 34 He was .. accustomed .. to velt-life. **1905** P. GIBBON *Vrouw Grobelaar* 84 She was of good veld-bred fighting stock. **1934** H.C. BOSMAN *Mafeking Rd* (1969) 135, I have known people who sit .. and dream about the veld .. , and start believing in what they call the soul of the veld, until .. the veld means a different thing to them from what it does to me. **1934** N. DEVITT *Mem. of Magistrate* 21, I shook the veld dust from my feet and went to live in Johannesburg. **1955** D.L. HOBMAN *Olive Schreiner* 3 This stocky little South African from the veld. **1970** *Daily News* 30 Nov., Dr. Steytler, essentially a man of the veld and an Afrikaner to the core. **1985** *Style* Oct. 68 Take to the African bush .. dressed for adventure ... Bush hats, long khaki socks and brogues to keep feet firmly on the veld. **1990** *Sunday Times* 27 May (Mag. Sect.) 20 The 22nd novel to pour from his veld-tipped pen.

5. *comb.* **veld burning** *vbl n. phr.*, the setting of controlled fires in the veld to encourage new plant growth, or to kill off unwanted species; see also BURN; **veld camp** [see CAMP *n.*[2] sense b], an area of natural vegetation enclosed as pasture; see also sense 3 a above; **veld-corporal** *obs.*, in the 18th century, the chief military officer of a Dutch-occupied region; **veld-craft**, practically useful knowledge of the veld, applied in such areas as path-finding, the use of plants, the tracking of animals, and the exploitation of terrain to one's advantage in warfare; **veld fever** *rare* (?*nonce*), a longing to be in the veld; **veldkool** /-kʊəl/, also **veldskool** [Afk., fr. Du. *kool* cabbage], any of several species of edible wild plant; *hotnotskool*, see HOTNOT sense 4; see also *Hottentot's cabbage* (HOTTENTOT *n.* sense 6 a); **veld management**, the controlled use of veld in order to prevent its deterioriation through overgrazing, the encroachment of exotic plant species, or other cause; **veld remedy**, a cure which makes use of natural products found in the veld; **veld school**, a camp for children held in the veld and including lectures and practical instruction on nature conservation and other topics (alleged by some to have been used by the National Party government for purposes of political indoctrination); **veld sickness** *Pathology*, a potentially fatal disease of livestock resulting from malnutrition, and occurring particularly when animals raised in a sweetveld area are moved to sourveld pastures; **veld(s)man** /-man/ [Afk.], a person knowledgeable in *veld-craft* (see above) or delighting in life in the veld; **veld sore** *Pathology*, an ulcerous skin eruption apparently caused or aggravated by dietary deficiencies and dry, dusty climatic conditions; cf. *Natal sore* (see NATAL sense a).

1856 R.E.E. WILMOT *Diary* (1984) 39 Near Grahamstown, at a **veld burning**, I saw full 300 [locust birds] in attendance on the flames. **1911** *Farmer's Weekly* 4

Oct. 117 (*letter*) We have been exhorted .. not to indulge in the wasteful practice of veld burning. **1936** W.B. HUMPHREYS in *Hansard* 10 Mar. 1008 There are two methods of eradication, one by veld-burning, which nobody will recommend, and the other is pulling it up by hand. **1949** L.G. GREEN *In Land of Afternoon* 176 Rhenosterbos .. defies eradication. Veld burning only encourages it. **1953** J.J. MORRIS in *S. Afr. Stockbreeder & Farmer* 61 Of all veld treatment practices, veld burning is surely the one which has caused most controversies for all times ... The policy of the Department of Agriculture is not to condemn veld burning altogether as this practice .. is sometimes very necessary. **1973** *Cape Times* 6 June 9 The flush of grass following veld burning .. is particularly attractive to blesbok. **1982** *S. Afr. Panorama* Feb. 14 Another long-term Ukulinga research project is concerned with veld burning ... Burning can be of benefit to humid grasslands, with red grass .. doing well under such conditions. **1992** RICHARDSON & VAN WILGEN in *Afr. Wildlife* Vol.46 No.4, 160 The 1923 report of the Drought Investigation Commission expressed the opinion that veld-burning was harmful. **1972** *Grocott's Mail* 3 Mar. 4 There are .. nine **veld camps**, all with permanent spring water. **1972** *Daily Dispatch* 11 Mar. 17 (*advt*) Camps and Grazing: Six land camps and four veld camps. **1785** G. FORSTER tr. *A. Sparrman's Voy. to Cape of G.H.* II. 144 The *land-drost* has appointed one of the farmers, with the title of **veld-corporal**, to command in these wars. **1893** 'HARLEY' in *Cape Illust. Mag.* June 378 Jack, who was famous .. for his knowledge of what for want of a better term we must call **veldt-craft**, acted as guide. **1910** J. BUCHAN *Prester John* (1961) 43 By and by I learned something of veld-craft: I learned how to follow spoor, how to allow for the wind, and stalk under cover. **1929** D. REITZ *Commando* 176 My knowledge of veld-craft brought our party safely through to the Vaal River. **1946** T. MACDONALD *Ouma Smuts* 37 The Boers, masters of veld-craft, were unerring thorns in the sides of the British Army. They would come suddenly out of the mist, attack, and vanish like shadows. **1964** V. POHL *Dawn & After* 149 Mosillikaas .., whose unrivalled veldcraft and wonderful constitution enabled him to live happily and comfortably under conditions that no white man could have endured .., had succumbed to Spanish influenza. **1899** D.S.F.A. PHILLIPS *S. Afr. Recollections* 9 '**Veld Fever**' is a malady, a longing indescribable which comes over many South Africans who have lived much on the veld, and about the month of April many people feel it in full force. **1971** L.G. GREEN *Taste of S.-Easter* 82 During .. May and June they picked the flower buds of the wild cabbage, the **veldskool**, that makes a fine bredie and a still more wonderful creamed puree. **1987** *S. Afr. Panorama* Jan. [Back cover], Flower lovers can taste a specially delicious local bredie (stew) made from *veldkool* (*Anthericum* spp.). **1937** *Handbk for Farmers* (Dept of Agric. & Forestry) 634 The Department is .. establishing research stations for the investigation of .. proper **veld management**, veld burning, pasture establishment, [etc.]. **1972** *Farmer's Weekly* 21 Apr. 70 (*advt*) They should have had practical experience of silage and hay making, veld management and all aspects of cattle management. **1992** RICHARDSON & VAN WILGEN in *Afr. Wildlife* Vol.46 No.4, 160 The policy of fire suppression was maintained until the late 1960s, when it became evident from results of research on veld management in fynbos that .. fire was necessary to *prevent* the extinction of certain species. **1956** F.C. METROWICH *Valiant but Once* 222 Bisset tried an old **veld remedy**. He stuffed the wound with cobwebs and in this way succeeded in partially stopping the bleeding. **1973** *Cape Times* 1 June 5 As a medicine it is interesting ... Like other veld remedies you have people who swear by them .. and others who swear at them. **1981** *Rand Daily Mail* 6 Mar. 8 (*letter*) We are a group of girls who attended the **veld school** camp ... We certainly felt that the camp was not a 'Hitler Youth Programme' ... At no time was any idea or doctrine forced on us. **1983** *Sunday Express* 19 June, Syllabi, textbooks, teacher training and promotional opportunities, veld schools and open universities have all been manipulated in the interests of Afrikaner Nationalist domination. **1990** A. GOLDSTUCK *Rabbit in Thorn Tree* 120 At the notorious Veld Schools .. 'youth preparedness' was the banner under which children were told that pop music and blue jeans were weapons of the communist onslaught. **1993** *Natal Mercury* 8 Apr. 9 Several ideas were put forward to save the village from demolition ... Turning it into an orphanage, a veldschool, low-income housing, [etc.]. **1896** R. WALLACE *Farming Indust. of Cape Col.* 82 Animals brought from sweet veld suffer from what is termed **veld sickness**, which results from insufficient nutrition and the hard and irritating nature of the food consumed. **1905** D. HUTCHEON in Flint & Gilchrist *Science in S. Afr.* 343 Dr. Edington .. proposes to group Horse sickness, Heartwater and Veld-sickness (Coast Gallsickness) under the generic name of 'South African Fever,' having Equine, Bovine and Caprine varieties. **1979** T. GUTSCHE *There Was a Man* 189 Edington .. asserted that the fatal epidemic was a combination of Red Water and Veld Sickness. **1895** J.G. MILLAIS *Breath from Veldt* (1899) 286 Tace .. liked to parade himself as an old **Veldtsman**. **1914** E.N. MARAIS *Road to Waterberg* (1972), My companion — an old hunter and clever veldman — pointed out an interesting fact: all day long every sounder of pigs was followed by a regular retinue of other animals. **1949** C. BULLOCK *Rina* 80, I fancied myself as a veldsman, but as trackers these natives left me standing. **1961** T. MACDONALD *Tvl Story* 22 The college 'veldsmen' say that the prospects for heavy horse and donkey breeding are not too rosy. **1972** S. & B. STENT in A.P. Cartwright *Forthright Man* 31 Vere met .. F.C. Selous, the famous hunter, guide and veldsman. **1897** F.W. SYKES *With Plumer in Matabeleland* 107 Throughout the campaign the constant 'meat and meal' diet, without the wholesome addition of vegetables, caused even the healthiest to break out in '**veldt sores**'. **1910** *Rand Daily Mail* 31 May 5 (*advt*) Zam-Buk cures .. festering sores, veld-sores and all skin diseases. **1915** O.S. ORMSBY *Pract. Treatment Diseases of Skin* 360 As distinguished from the Natal sore, which was chiefly found in the lower part of that country, the veldt sore was most abundant in the high, barren table-lands. **1941** C. BIRKBY *Springbok Victory* 173 Most of the Springboks had bandages on arms and legs to cover veld sores and festering spots, the inevitable result of the strenuous life they were leading on tinned rations. **1981** *Daily Dispatch* 12 Aug. 10 Dr Wollheim .. found himself teaching in schools for underprivileged children: 'I found I could not teach children with caries .. and veld sores.'

veld a beast var. WILDEBEAST.

veldbaroe see BAROE sense b.

veldchoon var. VELDSKOEN.

veld combas, veldcombers varr. VELKOMBERS.

veld commandant /ˈfelt kɒmənˌdant/ *n. phr. Hist.* Also **veldt commandant**. [S. Afr. Du., fr. Du. *veld* field (of battle) + *commandant*, see COMMANDANT.] COMMANDANT sense 1.

1799 F.R. BRESLER in G.M. Theal *Rec. of Cape Col.* (1898) II. 392, I furnished to all the Veldwachtmeesters and Veld Commandants a certain quantity of Gunpowder and Shot in order to enable them to maintain good order in their several Districts. **1802** F. DUNDAS in S.D. Naudé *Kaapse Plakkaatboek Deel V* (1950) 277, I do hereby require all the Heemraaden, Veld Commandants, Veld Cornets and others severally & respectively inhabitants of the district of Graaf-Reinet to pay due attention and implicit obedience to the said Major Sherlock. **1824** W.J. BURCHELL *Trav.* II. 119 They wear no uniform, but are divided into squadrons under the command of a *veld commandant*, who is also a boor, nominated by the government, and who at all times retains that title, and with it, a rank superior to that of *veldcornet*. **1827** G. THOMPSON *Trav.* I. 389 The Veld-Commandant, whose place I had now reached, I found to be a man of great substance as a stock farmer. **1971** [see FIELD COMMANDANT].

veld cornet /ˈfelt kɔːnət/ *n. phr. Hist.* Also **feld(t) cornet**, and with initial capital. [Part. tr. S. Afr. Du. *veld kornet*, see VELD-KORNET.] FIELD CORNET sense 1. Also *attrib.*

1806 *Cape Town Gaz. & Afr. Advertiser* 1 Feb., I do hereby order all Farmers or others, in possession of Horses procured from the Batavian Dragoons .. to give up the same forthwith, to the nearest Landdrosts, or Veld Cornets. **1822** [see VELD CORNETCY]. *a***1823** J. EWART *Jrnl* (1970) 41 This magistrate has a petty officer, called a feldt cornet, in every different division of the district, whose duty is to look into all crimes and abuses committed within his ward. **1827** [see PASS sense 1]. **1846** J.C. BROWN tr. *T. Arbousset's Narr. of Explor. Tour to N.-E. of Col.* 350 He went to the drinking place of a veldcornet, a kind of country magistrate. **1877** J. NOBLE *S. Afr.* 17 The 'veld-cornets' chosen from amongst the most respectable of the inhabitants .. were vested with the power .. to collect a force. **1886** G.A. FARINI *Through Kalahari Desert* 105 Outside the huts stood the proprietor, a fine looking, goodnatured old man .., holding the office of 'veldt cornet,' a kind of magistrate among the Bastards. **1900** M. MARQUARD *Lett. from Boer Parsonage* (1967) 72 The veldcornet entered and was evidently much annoyed at his presumption, calling him away. **1908** M.C. BRUCE *New Tvl* 20 Then began the dismissal of British civil servants and the reintroduction of the old Feld Cornet system. **1914** *Rand Daily Mail* 21 Dec., One rebel .. was killed, Veld Cornet Adam Bezuidenhout and two others being captured. *a***1930** G. BAUMANN in Baumann & Bright *Lost Republic* (1940) 167 When war was declared and the commandos called up for field service, the old elected Commandants took command of their different districts, with veldcornets as seconds in command. **1951** J. WEDGEWOOD *Last of Radicals* 61 They habitually move at a gallop .., Barend Smit, J.P. and ex-Veldtcornet, with a flying Cape Cart wildly challenging me to a .. race. **1962** F.C. METROWICH *Scotty Smith* 45 There was a police post under a veldcornet and half a dozen men. **1982** *Sunday Times* 16 May, Shortly after the fall of Bloemfontein, his elder brother, a chief veld cornet, came to get him.

veld cornetcy /ˈfelt ˌkɔːnətsi/ *n. phr. Obs.* exc. *hist.* [VELD CORNET + Eng. n.-forming suffix *-cy*.] FIELD CORNETCY sense 1.

1822 W.J. BURCHELL *Trav.* I. 76 Each district is subdivided into a number of Veld-cornetcies, in which the duty of the Veld-cornet, (or Field-cornet), is to put in execution all orders from the landdrost, to whom he is more immediately accountable. **1827** G. THOMPSON *Trav.* I. 370 A party of about 300 men made an irruption into the Tarka Veld-Cornetcy in 1824, and carried off some cattle. **1834** A. SMITH *Diary* (1939) I. 64 They [sc. wagons] drew up in different situations; generally those of a Veld Cornetcy or a particular part of the country assembled together. **1843** J.C. CHASE *Cape of G.H.* 109 The several districts are further sub-divided into veldt (or field) cornetcies, over which a veldt (field) cornet, a petty magistrate of great service, exercises authority, arranging all minor disputes occurring in his neighbourhood, and acting as a higher sort of constable or custos rotulorum. **1969** J. MEINTJES *Sword in Sand* 30 Every district was divided into veldcornetcies. Each zone chose a veldcornet and the veldcornets elected a commandant.

veld cornetship *n. phr. Obs.* [VELD CORNET + Eng. n.-forming suffix *-ship*.] FIELD CORNETCY sense 1.

1809 R. COLLINS in G.M. Theal *Rec. of Cape Col.* (1900) VII. 137 It would, perhaps, be only necessary strictly to enjoin the several landdrosts to issue such orders in each particular veld cornetship as might prevent the extinction of any species. **1810** J.G. CUYLER in G.E. Cory *Rise of S. Afr.* (1910) I. 222 I .. request you will impress the same upon the inhabitants of your Veld-Cornetship.

veld cos(t) var. VELDKOS.

veldebeest var. WILDEBEEST.

velder beast var. WILDEBEAST.

veld-kornet /ˌfeltkɔ(r)ˈnet/ *n. hist.* [S. Afr. Du., fr. Du. *veld* field (of battle) + *kornet* a military rank.]

1. FIELD CORNET sense 1. Also used as a title. See also VELDWAGTMEESTER.

1879 R.J. ATCHERLEY *Trip to Boerland* 130 His property and description were given to the nearest veldkornet, and he was interred the following afternoon. **1902** D. VAN WARMELO *On Commando* 114 Veld-Kornet Klaasen ordered his men to off-saddle and give the horses a rest. **1935** H.C. BOSMAN *Mafeking Rd* (1969) 48 Our veld-kornet told us that the burghers from our part had been ordered to join the big commando that was lying at Mafeking. We had to go and shoot a man there called Baden-Powell. **1951** H. DAVIES *Great S. Afr. Christians* 156 Although he had been wrongfully imprisoned by the Transvaal Government, he willingly came to its aid, as a peace-maker between the *veldkornet* Joubert and Makhatan. **1962** A.P. CARTWRIGHT *Gold Miners* 58 The man who was sent to report on the validity of these grazing rights was Johannes Petrus Meyer, the *veld-kornet* of the Klip River district. This means that he was a farmer in that district who acted as the Government's representative in his particular area under instruction from the *landdrost*. **1968** [see VELDWAGTMEESTER]. **1988** D. HUGHES et al. *Complete Bk of S. Afr. Wine* 132 As early as 1716 .. there were vines on the farm, 60 000 of them, according to the records of the *Veldkornet* who acted as tax-collector that year.

2. FIELD CORNET sense 2.

1986 *Sunday Star* 8 June 6 'Yes,' says ex-veldkornet Wilhelm K–, 'in 1939 there was fire, brimstone and talk of Volk and Vaderland. There was also much bitterness and hatred'.

veldkornetcy /ˈfelt͵kɔːnətsi/ *n. hist.* [VELDKORNET + Eng. n.-forming suffix *-cy*.] FIELD CORNETCY sense 1.

1972 *Evening Post* 19 Feb. (Weekend Mag.) 2 By 1800 there were at least 2 000 Whites living in the veldkornetcy of Achter Bruintjes Hoochte, which was by then the eastern section of the Graaff-Reinet landdrostdy.

veldkos /ˈfeltkɔs/ *n.* Formerly also **veldcos(t)**, **veldkost**. Pl. unchanged, or **-kosse** /kɔsə/. [Afk., earlier S. Afr. Du. *veldkost*, fr. Du. *veld* countryside + *kost* food.] Food gathered from the countryside, particularly bulbs and tubers, but also other plant foods, insects, grubs, and small game. Also *attrib.*

1831 *S. Afr. Almanac & Dir.* 235 There were families who literally had nothing but 'Veld Kost' to live upon until a crop was raised. **1834** T. PRINGLE *Afr. Sketches* 82 Veld-kost, literally *country-food*, is the term used for the wild roots and bulbs eaten by the Bushmen, and also by the Colonial Hottentots, on occasions of emergency. **1852** J. TINDALL *Jrnl* (1959) 163 They are living on 'veld kost' .. and we have no food to entertain them. *a***1867** C.J. ANDERSSON *Notes of Trav.* (1875) 101 We had been without any animal food for some days, and had been chiefly subsisting on 'veldt cost', i.e., on such roots as the soil yielded. **1898** W.C. SCULLY *Vendetta* 181 The vicinity proved to be rich in 'veldkost,' which is the name by which the edible bulbs and tubers with which the desert sometimes abounds, are known by. **1913** C. PETTMAN *Africanderisms* 531 *Veld kost*, Bulbs and other roots found in the veld, indeed anything that can be picked up in the veld and used as food. **1928** E.H.L. SCHWARZ *Kalahari & its Native Races* 147 A Bushman .. is a relic from prehistoric times, living as primeval man lived, by the chase and on *veld cos* — roots, wild fruits, such as the tsama melon and naras cucumber, resin from the yellow-wood trees, mushrooms, ant's eggs (Bushman rice), grubs, caterpillars, and so forth. **1936** [see UINTJIE sense 1 a]. **1960** L. MARSHALL in *Africa* Vol.30 No.4, 338 The band is characterized by the organization of rights to veldkos areas and water-holes. **1975** *Afr. Wildlife* Vol.29 No.4, The 'mermaids' of the seafarers of old .. also need urgent protection ... And our marsh roses and cycads, our stone-plants and 'veldkosse'. **1986** Y. VAN WYK *Practical Bk of Herbs* 17 Their initial poverty, and the hardships and drought they endured, hastened the settlers' recourse to 'veldkos' that included bush tea, wild grapes ..., wild celery .., pies of 'elephant's food' .., and that old standby, sorrel. **1987** W. STEENKAMP *Blockhouse* 23 We had taken to eating veldkos, roots and tubers that we knew would not poison us.

veld pond /ˈfelt pɔnt/ *n. phr.* Pl. **- ponde** /-pɔndə/. [Afk., fr. Du. *veld* field (of battle) + *pond* pound.] A gold coin minted in 1902 in Pilgrim's Rest, Transvaal, during the Anglo-Boer War; FIELD POUND.

Less than a thousand of these coins were minted; they are now very rare and much sought after by collectors.

1933 *Friend* 27 Apr. (Swart), In 'The Outspan' of March there appeared a story of the Kruger coinage, in the course of which the writer referred to the 'veld ponde'. **1957** B. O'KEEFE *Gold without Glitter* 17 Potgieter, Gert and Piet Uys laboured at transferring the gold bars and bags of *veld-ponde* from the bullion boxes. **1962** A.P. CARTWRIGHT *Gold Miners* 132 At Pilgrim's Rest they made dies and minted some eight hundred gold sovereigns, known as *veld ponde* because they were made in the field. **1973** *Sunday Times* 27 May 6 The story of the Veldponde begins with the era of the broken and embattled Transvaal. **1980** *E. Prov. Herald* 16 Apr. 9 One of the rarest and most valuable coins in the world, a ZAR veldpond minted in 1902. **1983** *Gold Jrnl* Vol.4 No.18, 5 The quality of some of the coins, in particular .. one of the Veld ponde and the Sammy Marks gold tickey, is peerless.

veldschoen, -schoon varr. VELDSKOEN.

Veldschoendrager, Veld-scoondrawer var. VELDSKOENDRAER.

veld shoe /ˈfelt ʃuː/ *n. phr.* [Part. tr. S. Afr. Du. *veldschoen*.] VELDSKOEN *n.* sense 1.

1835 T.H. BOWKER Journal. 22 Apr., Bought leather for felt shoes. **1846** *Natal Witness* 18 Sept. 3 The Fingoe shield must have been .. far more savory .. than the veld-shoes, which the traveller Thompson informs us he ate. *a***1867** C.J. ANDERSSON *Notes of Trav.* (1875) 298 He was dressed in .. 'veld' shoes. **1896** *Argus* 2 Jan. 1 (*advt*) Solid leather H.S. Veldt Shoes. **1901** W.S. SUTHERLAND *S. Afr. Sketches* 48 Even now I feel a shaking in my number twelve veldtshoes. **1972** *Vereeniging & Vanderbijlpark News* 14 Apr., (*advt*) Men's veld shoes — Available in all colours.

veldskoen, velskoen /ˈfeltskʊn, felskʊn, -skun/ *n.* and *adj.* Forms: α. **feldtchoen, feldtschoon, feltchoon, -scoon, -shoon, vehltschoon, veldchoon, -s(c)hoen, -schoon, -skoen, veldtsc(h)oen, -schoon, -shun, veltschoon**; β. **felchoon, fell-, velschoen, -schoon, -skoen**. Pl. **-s, -e** /-ə/, or unchanged, also (formerly) **-en**. [Afk., *veldskoen*, earlier Du. *veldschoen* shoe for outdoor wear, 'country shoe' (*veld* open country + *schoen* shoe); or *velskoen*, earlier S. Afr. Du. *velschoen* hide shoe, fr. Du. *vel* hide, skin + *schoen* shoe. One of these early forms was probably a corruption of the other.

It is not known whether *veldschoen* or *velschoen* is the earlier form; however, *veldschoen* is found in Dutch from as early as 1676 (designating similar shoes from other parts of the world), and some early descriptions state that the Khoikhoi wore these shoes when walking on rough veld. *Veldskoen* thus seems a more probable first form than the ostensibly more logical *velschoen*, which has not been found in Dutch elsewhere.]

A. *n.*

1.a. *hist.* A shoe or ankle boot similar to a moccasin, made of rough (often untanned) hide stitched with leather thongs, and having a soft sole, the whole shoe often consisting of a single piece of hide laced or sewn above. **b.** In recent times, a shoe with uppers made of such hide but with a thicker sole, usu. of leather or rubber; VELLIE. Also *attrib.* In both senses also called FIELD SHOE, VELD SHOE.

A style of footwear made by the Khoikhoi at the Cape and later adopted by settlers.

α. **1822** W.J. BURCHELL *Trav.* I. 214 The Hottentots .. took off the hide, which they cut in small pieces, for the purpose of making *velschoen* (hide shoes). [*Note*] Or, as some pronounce it, *Veld-schoen* (Country-shoes). *a***1827** D. CARMICHAEL in W.J. Hooker *Botanical Misc.* (1831) II. 277 The ox-hide .. is made into .. *feldtschoon* for himself and his family. **1829** C. ROSE *Four Yrs in Sn Afr.* 243, I have been obliged to eat the veldtschoon (untanned leather shoes) from my feet. **1834** T. PRINGLE *Afr. Sketches* 178 A sort of sandals .. are in common use, called *veld-schoenen* (country shoes), the fashion of which was, I believe, originally borrowed from the Hottentots. They are made of raw bullock's hide, with an upperleather of dressed sheep or goatskin. **1849** N.J. MERRIMAN *Cape Jrnls* (1957) 73 He made me a pair of veldt schoons, shoes worn by the Hottentots and Dutch Boers. **1850** J.D. LEWINS Diary. 17 June, Fengou has not got the veldschoen but he has brought the gate. **1856** T. SHONE Diary. 20 May, This day I made a feltchoon boot for Henry. **1860** A.W. DRAYSON *Sporting Scenes* 174 The 'veld schoens' (field shoes), similar to those worn by the Dutch boers, are much better than boots, as they are comfortable, soft, easy, and very silent. **1863** LADY DUFF-GORDON in F. Galton *Vacation Tourists* (1864) III. 163 The shoemaker .. is making a pair of 'Veldschoen' for you ... They are what the rough boers and Hottentots wear, buffhide barbarously tanned and shaped, and as soft as woollen socks. **1878** H.A. ROCHE *On Trek in Tvl* 139 His unaccustomed feet are stuffed into stiff, shinyleather boots, instead of his dear old, easy-going 'Veldtschoons' of home manufacture. **1883** M.A. CAREY-HOBSON *Farm in Karoo* 183 The Boers generally make their own shoes for using at home. Veldt schoens or fell schoens they call them, and very comfortable things they are. **1886** G.A. FARINI *Through Kalahari Desert* 202 The giraffe skin is the most valuable, the thick parts, off the back and neck, being cut into strips for soles of boots, called *veldt schoons*, which the natives make themselves. **1890** A. MARTIN *Home Life* 97 There is nothing so serviceable as the country-made *veldschoon*. **1906** H. RIDER HAGGARD *Benita* 226 His soft veld-schoons, or hide shoes, had made no noise. **1920** F.C. CORNELL *Glamour of Prospecting* 147 Our veldtschoens .. had to be cobbled every day with fragments of rimpi. **1931** H.C. BOSMAN *Mafeking Rd* (1969) 146 He was dressed .. in shirt and trousers and veldskoens ... But .. we saw that he had got socks on. Therefore we knew that he was an Englishman. **1939** F.B. YOUNG *City of Gold* 94 The rocky road had torn his *veldskoene* to shreds. **1944** J. MOCKFORD *Here Are S. Africans* 60 Their unstockinged feet protected by handsewn veldschoens, the equivalent of Canadian moccasins. **1958** S. CLOETE *Mask* 181 In leather clothes, their bare feet in veldschoen — homemade leather shoes. **1971** *Farmer's Weekly* 12 May 123 (*advt*) Game Leather Shoes (Veldskoene). Strong Kuduleather uppers, Feathercrepe soles. **1992** *Sunday Times* 6 Sept. 5 Veldskoen factory owner .. Hennie du Plessis.

β. **1822** [see α quot.]. **1837** 'N. POLSON' *Subaltern's Sick Leave* 131 The skin is used to make bags for grain, and the thick skin at the back of the hock for soles to the native sandals or *velschoon*. **1844** J. BACKHOUSE *Narr. of Visit* 490 We got some shoes made of undressed leather, and sewed with slender thongs of the same: these are called Vel Schoenen, *Skin-shoes*. **1851** T. SHONE Diary. 22 Apr., Jack was making himself a pair of Felchoons or rawhyde shoes. **1864** T. BAINES *Explor. in S.-W. Afr.* 76 Both had short skin petticoats .. and velschoens [*printed* belschoens] more clumsily made than I have seen at Windhock. **1870** H.H. DUGMORE *Reminisc. of Albany Settler* 17 Velschoen usurped the place of Wellingtons in many quarters. **1883** [see α quot.]. **1883** O.E.A. SCHREINER *Story of Afr. Farm* 97 The heavy shuffling of the well-known 'velschoens' could be clearly heard. **1896** [see FIELD SHOE]. **1913** C. PETTMAN *Africanderisms* 531 *Veld schoen*, This appears to be a corruption, now .. in general use, of *velschoen*, a skin shoe. Originally these shoes were cut out of raw, undried hide and fitted to the foot in a single piece; now the soles and uppers are cut separately and sewn together in a rough and ready fashion; but clumsy as they look, nothing could be more easy and comfortable for the feet when walking about the farm. The idea was borrowed from the Hottentots who seem to have adopted this method of protecting their feet before the advent of Europeans. **1936** E. ROSENTHAL *Old-Time Survivals* 25 Velskoene are shaped exactly as they were in the 18th century, and for that matter as they were in the 17th. A piece of carefully-softened hide is cut into a shape to suit the wearer, and is then sewn. **1949** L.G. GREEN *In Land of Afternoon* 138 He always carried .. two pairs of the velskoen type for the veld. **1958** R.E. LIGHTON *Out of Strong* 62 Look at socks. When I work I am better with just my velskoens. **1965** J. BENNETT *Hawk Alone* 13 He was wearing scuffed down velskoens without socks. **1975** S. ROBERTS *Outside Life's Feast* 54 Her brothers .. wore old jeans, clumsy jerseys and velskoens. **1984** *Cape Times* 2 Aug., Kramer told Zola that the red velskoens would come in handy for 'very long distances.' **1986** *Flying Springbok* Sept. 86 The only authentic *velskoen* factory. **1990** *E. Prov. Herald* 27 Feb. 9 People .. tap their *velskoens* in time. **1993** *Sunday Times* 10 Oct. (Business Times) 10 They work with the same moulds used six generations ago, making the original velskoen for R68 a pair.

2. *fig.*
a. VASTRAP sense 2.

α. **1934** C.P. SWART *Supplement to Pettman.* 154 *Sheepskin Dance,* .. A farm-dance is so designated in South Africa ... These social affairs are also known as Veldskoens, Vastraps (Tread-fasts) and Kop-en-Pootjies (Head and Trotters).

β. **1949** L.G. GREEN *In Land of Afternoon* 167 A country dance is often referred to as a vastrap or a velskoen.

b. *rare.* In the expression *to make veldskoens*, see quot.

β. **1958** A. JACKSON *Trader on Veld* 29 An increase in the family warranted .. a long trip ... Because the father, waiting for the happy event, would while away his time by making velschoens, this .. excursion was called 'making velschoens'.

c. Used allusively, as a symbol of conservative attitudes or values, or of toughness or aggression.

α. **1976** *Sunday Times* 15 Aug., The fact that the HNP lost the election to the Nats .. confirms that the Marico has outgrown its veldskoens. **1990** A. WOOD in *Top Forty* July 30 Edi Niederlander's tough 'jeans 'n veldskoen' image.

β. **1989** D. MULLANY in *Scope* 21 Apr. 4 That kamikaze, freeway-death-wish, velskoen-to-the-floor, crash-and-burn cretin known as the South African Motorist.

B. *adj.* Of or pertaining to the stereotypical wearers of veldskoens, esp. Afrikaners and farmers; conservative or reactionary.

α. **1881** *E. London Dispatch* 12 Jan. 3 We trust that the Executive will .. make short work of this attempt to re-establish the unutterable nuisance of a veldschoen republic. **1911** *Farmer's Weekly* 15 Mar. 16 The period of evolution and progress is taking the place of the 'veldschoen-remschoen' policy.

β. **1937** C.R. PRANCE *Tante Rebella's Saga* 101 A real 'hostile Baw', tall and bearded, a 'veldskoen' bitterender to the life. **1974** *Sunday Times* 6 Oct. 8 The day of the 'velskoen' mentality is past.

Hence **veldskoened** *adj.*, wearing veldskoens.

1929 J.G. VAN ALPHEN *Jan Venter* 251 Klaas, the fiddler, led the music, tapping the floor with a roomy veldskoened foot. **1977** [see *Vrystater* (VRYSTAAT)]. **1990** *Sunday Times* 4 Mar., Comfortably clad in a pair of old blue trousers and a short-sleeved, open-necked shirt, one veldskoened foot resting on his knee.

Veldskoendraer /ˈfeltskʊnˌdrɑə(r)/ *n. hist.* Also **Veldschoendrager**, **Veld-scoondrawer**, **Velskoendra(g)er**. [Afk. (earlier S. Afr. Du. *veldschoendrager*), *veldskoen* see VELDSKOEN + *draer* wearer] The colonial name for a member of the Hawobe subdivision of the Nama people, living during the nineteenth century in the far south of what is now Namibia. Also *attrib.*

1841 J. TINDALL *Jrnl* (1959) 24, I prepared to trek to the Velskoen Dragers. **1877** *Sel. Comm. Report on Mission to Damaraland* 94 Name of Tribe .. Hobobes or Velschoendragers. *Ibid.* p.xix, Forbes, a trader, came within the boundaries of the Veldschoendragers, and nearly died by thirst. **1887** A.A. ANDERSON *25 Yrs in Waggon* I. 256 The inhabitants are of various tribes, called the Namaquas, Veld-scoondrawers, [etc.]. **1928** H. VEDDER in *Native Tribes of S.W. Afr.* 115 Hawoben whose tribal name should be translated into 'Veldschoendragers' under which name they are referred to frequently in literature. **1958** A. JACKSON *Trader on Veld* 56 Witbooi .. and his small army were feared by the other tribes .., including .. Hans Arissimab of the Veldschoendrager Hottentots. **1961** O. LEVINSON *Ageless Land* 26 The missionary brothers, Albrecht, were the first to acquire a sound knowledge of the tribes around Warmbad and the Orange River. They left accounts of .. the Veldskoendraers. **1974** J.P. VAN S. BRUWER in *Std Encycl. of Sn Afr.* X. 156 The Hawobe or Velskoendraers lived in the region south of present-day Keetmanshoop.

veldt var. VELD.

veldt-broeks var. VEL-BROEKS.

veldt combass, veldt-kombaars, veldt kombarse varr. VELKOMBERS.

veldtschoen, -schoon, -scoen, -shun varr. VELDSKOEN.

veldwagtmeester /ˈfeltˌvagtmɪəstə(r)/ *n. hist.* Also **feld wag(h)t meester**, **veldtwagt(e)meester**, **veld valkt meester**, **veldwachtmeester**, **veldwaght(er)meester**, **veldwagmeester**, and with initial capital(s). [S. Afr. Du., fr. Du. *veldwacht* field patrol, country guard, *veld* (battle)-field + *wacht* a military unit + *meester* master.] A colonial peace-officer at the Cape, whose duties included measuring land by pacing, assisting the Magistrate with military duties in times of war, and settling land disputes.

Subsequently given extended powers under the new name of VELD-KORNET (sense 1).

*c*1795 W.S. VAN RYNEVELD in G.M. Theal *Rec. of Cape Col.* (1897) I. 252 Veld Wagtmeesters were those persons appointed by the Landdrost and the College of Burgher Officers to execute some functions belonging strictly to the Magistrate or other persons whose duty it is to preserve good order in a certain part of the district. **1797** EARL MACARTNEY in S.D. Naudé *Kaapse Plakkaatboek Deel V* (1950) 100 The 'Veldwachtmeesters' of the Cape district are to be proposed by the Burgher Senate and to be appointed by the Government ... In the first place they are in the country districts to maintain public peace and good order among the inhabitants. **1801** [see BAAKEN sense 1]. **1877** T. BAINES *Gold Regions of S.-E. Afr.* 72 Not many years ago their own surveyor general was mobbed for using a theodolite in the streets of Potchefstroom instead of stepping off the distance like the Veld-Valkt meester of the good old times. **1890** J. MACDONALD *Light in Afr.* 4 There were no surveyors nor surveyor's implements in the country, and the 'official pacer,' or *Veldt wagt meester*, could take an extra long step when measuring for a friend or favourite. **1904** H.A. BRYDEN *Hist. of S. Afr.* 36 The quantity of land upon a Government farm, according to the old Dutch custom, consisted in the distance covered in one hour's walk across it. The Veld-waght-meester, or peace officer, was usually called in to pace the distance in dispute. **1927** C.G. BOTHA *Social Life in Cape Col.* 72 The Field Cornet, formerly known as a 'Veldwagter' or 'Veldwagmeester' (Field Guard), undertook duties of a judicial and civil nature and in time of war acted in a military capacity. **1936** *Cambridge Hist. of Brit. Empire* VIII. 194 This step was followed by a codification of the functions of the Landdrost and his heemraden together with an important extension of the civil functions of the *veld wachtmeester*, now renamed *veld kornet*, whose relation to the central authority became analogous to that of the Tudor justice of the peace. **1968** E.A. WALKER *Hist. of Sn Afr.* 135 The *veldwachtmeester* had accumulated civil in addition to his military duties. All these duties were now regularized and his name changed to *veldkornet*. **1981** NEWTON-KING & MALHERBE *Khoikhoi Rebellion* 7 Other measures were unofficial, but were often given tacit sanction by *veldwachtmeesters* and landdrosts — deserters, when recaptured, were savagely beaten and sometimes put in irons. **1988** P.E. RAPER tr. *R.J. Gordon's Cape Trav. 1777–86* I. 81 This Koerikei called to the veldtwagtemeester Van der Merwe .. while standing on a cliff.

‖**velkombers** /ˈfelkɔmbɛrs, -kɔmbeəs ˈfɛl-/ *n. obsolescent.* Formerly also **feldt comberse, veld combas, veldcombers, veldt combass, veldt-kombaars, veldt kombarse, velkomba(a)rs, velkomers.** [Afk., fr. Du. *vel* skin, hide + *kombaars* (ship's) blanket. There was formerly some confusion among English speakers over the similar-sounding *vel* and *veld* countryside, field (cf. VELDSKOEN).] KAROSS sense 1.

1822 W.J. BURCHELL *Trav.* I. 360 Three on the right, beating a large *vel-kombáars* (or sheepskin coverlet), a frequent and very necessary operation. **1832** *Graham's Town Jrnl* 18 May 80(b), On Saturday, the 26th May, on account of William Henry Bond, one Silver Watch, one volume of a Family Bible, one Velkombaars. **1852** N.J. MERRIMAN *Cape Jrnls* (1957) 186, I was compelled, though my horse was thin and poor, to ride with the post till I overtook the wagon, as they had my veldt kombarse, or blanket, with them. **1862** 'A LADY' *Life at Cape* (1963) 105 The veldt-kombaars or sheep-skin rug .. is made of little squares of lamb skin. **1862** LADY DUFF-GORDON *Lett. from Cape* (1925) 157, I have a glorious 'Velkombaars' for you, a blanket of nine Damara sheep-skins, sewn by the Damaras, and dressed so that moths and fleas won't stay near them. **1870** 'JNO.' in *Cape Monthly Mag.* II. 179 (Pettman), Wrapped in a thick *velkombars* (sheepskin covering) we were not long in wooing 'tired nature's sweet restorer — balmy sleep'. **1878** T.J. LUCAS *Camp Life & Sport* 137 The clothing consisted of a huge feather mattress, not always of the sweetest kind, and a feldt 'comberse,' or quilt, made of a blanket sewn up in a sheet of cotton print, and, apparently, never washed. **1922** J.G. FRASER in F.G. Butler *When Boys Were Men* (1969) 212 He and his elder were sleeping together under their *velkombaars* (sheepskin blanket). **1955** L.G. GREEN *Karoo* 66 Colin Fraser .. was asleep one night under his velkombers (sheepskin blanket).

vellie /ˈfeli/ *n. colloq.* [Formed on VELDSKOEN + Eng. (informal) n.-forming suffix *-ie*.] VELDSKOEN sense 1 b.

1971 *Informant,* Grahamstown My brother always calls them vellies. **1980** *Sunday Times* 2 Mar. 13 His grandfather .. towered seven foot two inches above his no. 13 'vellies'. **1986** *Sunday Star* 23 Nov. (Timeout) 2 Don your 'vellies' for the premiere of 'Jock of the Bushveld'. **1989** P. LEE in *Sunday Times* 26 Feb. (Mag. Sect.) 36 Consider the humble Vellie ... Everyone .. can claim at least one tatty pair of vellies to their credit. **1993** *Weekend Post* 26 June 7 (advt) Just like any fine vellie, it's well ventilated.

velschoen, -schoon, -skoen varr. VELDSKOEN.

Velskoendra(g)er var. VELDSKOENDRAER.

velt var. VELD.

veltschoon var. VELDSKOEN.

Venda /ˈvendə, ‖ˈveːndə/ *n. and adj.* Pl. usu. unchanged, **-s**, **Bavenda.** Forms: *sing.* **Movenda, Muvenda**; *sing.* and *pl.* **Venda**; *pl.* **Bavenda, Bawenda, HaVenda, Mavenda, Vendas, V(h)avenda.** [A Venda n. stem found in such words as *Muvenda* a member of the Venda people (pl. *Vhavenda*), *Tshivenda* the Venda language, *Venda* the area inhabited by the Venda. The origin of the stem is not known.]

A. *n.*

1.a. A member of an African people living mainly in the Soutpansberg region of the Northern Transvaal. Also *attrib.*

1892 W.L. DISTANT *Naturalist in Tvl* 107 The Mavenda Kafirs are a branch of the Makatese, and closely allied to the Basutos. **1905** *Native Tribes of Tvl* 60 There are remnants of a tribe called Balemba among the Bawenda. **1908** *Jrnl of Afr. Society* VII. 412 Venda. Spoken by the Bavenda in North Transvaal. **1913** H.A. JUNOD *Life of S. Afr. Tribe* I. 18 They are called Magwamba by the Venda and Bvesha. **1954** C.M. DOKE *Sn Bantu Languages* 154 Linguistically the Venda share features both with the Shona group to the north of them and with the Sotho. **1966** F.G. BUTLER *S. of Zambesi* 30 Only the Venda possessed a drum of their fathers carried countless leagues from a land of gleaming lakes, a land of forests and fruits, innumerable moons ago. **1976** WEST & MORRIS *Abantu* 89 The Venda are a relatively small group of some 400 000 who live in the region of the Soutspansberg in the Northern Transvaal. **1977** *Financial Mail* 1 July 33 For example, 68% of Vendas actually live there — the highest figure of all the Bantustans. **1982** [see NGOMA n.²]. **1990** [see sense B].

b. comb. Vendaland, the area occupied by the Venda people; **Vendastan**, see -STAN.

An area in the northern part of the former Transvaal was intended as a 'homeland' for Vendas; granted a form of self-government in 1973, it became the Republic of Venda in 1979. The area was re-incorporated into South Africa in 1994. See also TBVC.

1971 *S. Afr. Panorama* Nov. 11 In Vendaland the 'watchdogs had been tied up' — the Venda way of assuring their honoured guests that they were welcome. **1979** *Drum* Jan. 31 Vendaland will become independent soon.

2. Also **Chivenda**, **Tshivenda**. The language of the Venda people, being one of the Sintu (Bantu) languages. Also *attrib.*

1908 [see sense 1 a]. **1939** *Outspan* 24 Nov. 93 The letter was written in Tshivenda. **1950** H. GIBBS *Twilight* 34 The south-eastern groups have five group languages, Nguni, Sotho, Venda, Tonga, and Inhambane. **1971** *Daily News* 4 Mar. 11 If we do come with an act saying we want Venda to be the official language of Vendaland, they would have voted against it, too. *c***1980** *S. Afr. 1979: Off. Yrbk* (Dept of Info.) 85 Their language, Chivenda, is related to languages found in Zimbabwe. **1993** *Weekend Post* 9 Oct. 9 If this letter is anything to go by, multi-lingualism, including North and South Sotho, Swazi, Tsonga, Tswana, Venda, [etc.] .. is out.

B. *adj.* Of or pertaining to the Venda.

1913 H.A. JUNOD *Life of S. Afr. Tribe* II. 327 There is a third tradition relating to the first man, but it has .. been borrowed from the Venda or Pedi tribes. **1921** *S. Afr. Jrnl of Science* Apr. 208 All these Venda clans (and the Malemba also) speak of their mountain. **1928** G.P. LESTRADE in A.M. Duggan-Cronin *Bantu Tribes* I. 17 Venda life .. revolves round the chief. **1937** B.H. DICKE *Bush Speaks* 143 She was a Movenda girl. **1951** T.V. BULPIN *Lost Trails of Low Veld* 62 Relations between Schoeman and the Vavenda people .. had .. been reasonably pleasant. **1953** B. FULLER *Call Back Yesterday* 14 The Bavenda hut tax should have yielded about £25,000 a year at that time. **1975** *Drum* Dec. 29 Your parents have followed Venda custom by choosing your wife for you. **1980** D.B. COPLAN *Urbanization of African Performing Arts.* 187 The Pedi .. patterned their *dinaka* flutes after the Venda *motaba*. **1987** E. *Prov. Herald* 4 June 13 Fest to show Vhavenda sculpture. **1990** A. GOLDMAN in *Motorist* 4th Quarter 4 Before the HaVenda people moved down from East Africa, the Bushmen lived in this part of the world. They were driven out by the aggressive HaVenda.

Vendastan see -STAN.

venditie var. VENDUSIE.

vendue /ˈvendjuː/ *n. Obs. exc. hist.* Also **vandue**, **vendu**. [S. Afr. Du., fr. Du. *vendu* (obs. *vendue*, fr. older Fr.).]

1. A public auction; VENDUSIE. Also *attrib.*

Also found in *U.S. Eng.* (from 1686) and *W. Indian Eng.*

1802 [see quot. at *venduemaster* (sense 2 below)]. **1822** W.J. BURCHELL *Trav.* I. 79 Vendues or auctions happen daily, and often several a day. **1827** in *Stat. Law of Cape of G.H.* (1862) 95 *(title)* Ordinance for abolishing the Office of Vendues and for imposing certain Duties on Licences to be taken out by all persons acting as Auctioneers and on Property sold by Auction. **1832** *Graham's Town Jrnl* 8 June 93 At the same time and place will also be sold, a quantity of Drapery and Piece Goods, Coffee, Sugar, Rice, and other articles, usually sold at Vendues. *a***1862** J. AYLIFF *Jrnl of 'Harry Hastings'* (1963) 83, I was struck with the sound of something like the beating of a tin dish, so said I, 'What is that?' 'O', said the taylor, 'that is the vendue notice.' 'Vendue', said I, 'what is that then?' 'Well, I think,' said he 'it is what you call in English auction'. **1892** *The Jrnl* 9 July 2 All overdue vendue accounts must be paid at once. **1927** [see VENDUSIE]. **1950** M. MASSON *Birds of Passage* 68 Vendues were the vogue. Ladies attending them returned home with a variety of treasures. **1972** A. SCHOLEFIELD *Wild Dog Running* 103 The crowd .. followed the vendue master from pen to pen while he sold off wethers and hoggets.

2. comb. venduebrief /-brif/ [Afk., *brief* letter (earlier, 'letter of administration')], a detailed account of goods bought by an individual at an auction; **venduemaster** [part. tr. S. Afr. Du. *vendumeester* (*meester* master)], the superintendent of auctions in a district; hence **venduemastership** *n.*, the position or duties of the venduemaster; **vendue note**, **-roll** *n. phrr.*, *venduebrief*.

1927 C.G. BOTHA *Social Life in Cape Col.* 99 Purchasers were allowed six weeks' credit, and received from the auctioneer a '**Vendubrief**' or specified account of the goods bought. **1802** TRUTER & SOMERVILLE in G.M. Theal *Rec. of Cape Col.* (1899) IV. 434 The expenses .. have been duly paid by the **venduemaster** Mr. Matthiessen. **1813** *Prohibition of Purchase at Sales by Auctioneers* in *Stat. Law of Cape of G.H.* (1862) 51 The Vendue clerks .. shall not be allowed to bid for any goods put up by them to sale ... The Vendue masters .. shall not themselves come forward at the sale .. to make any purchase. **1827** *Reports of Commissioners upon Finances at Cape of G.H.* II. 19 They frequently unite with their office that of Vendue-master, or Superintendent of Auction Sales in the district. **1861** P.B. BORCHERDS *Auto-Biog. Mem.* 297 The government determined that the Venduemastership should not remain attached to the situation of the secretary of Stellenbosch but be separated, and my old friend, Mr Wege, resolved to be venduemaster. **1955** V.M. FITZROY *Dark Bright Land* 120 When Major Pigot was Vendue Master he lodged the complaint not once but several times. **1844** [**vendue note**: see quot. at *vendue roll* below]. **1823** W.W. BIRD *State of Cape of G.H.* 45 The **vendue rolls** are readily taken in payment by every one, and are the only description of paper currency besides the rix-dollars that has full credit throughout the country. **1827** *Reports of Commissioners upon Finances at Cape of G.H.* II. 83 At the conclusion of each sale accounts are prepared in the vendue office, called 'vendue rolls'. **1844** *Ordinance for Regulating Sales by Auction* in *Stat. Law of Cape of G.H.* (1862) 673 The recovery of any duties imposed by virtue of the said ordinance or of any sum or sums of money due upon vendue notes or rolls.

‖**vendusie** /fenˈdisi/ *n. obsolescent.* Also **fandisi**, **venditie**, **vendutie**. [Afk., ad. Du. *vendutie*.] VENDUE sense 1. Also *attrib.*

1800 LADY A. BARNARD in D. Fairbridge *Lady Anne Barnard* (1924) 237 The female Blake pockets all she can get, and has such a hoard now of presents I think she must make a Vendutie of to realize. **1806** J. BARROW *Trav.* II. 101 The good woman .. dresses for a vendutie or public sale. *a***1823** J. EWART *Jrnl* (1970) 25 The females, if not engaged at home, attend the venduties or public sales, which they are extremely partial to, and where they are as busy trying to overreach each other in small matters as their husbands are in greater ones. **1823** W.W. BIRD in V. De Kock *Fun They Had* (1955) 168 An auction in the country .. is an important event ... The ladies repair to the venditie, dressed as for a gay assembly. **1912** W. WESTRUP *Land of To-Morrow* 343 The natives .. who were all wellknown to him, were treated with such liberality that they frequently almost forgot to ask for a pasella. He explained cheerfully that it was the fandisi — the sale week — and knowing the correct prices for everything as they did, they privately thought he was quite mad. **1927** C.G. BOTHA *Social Life in Cape Col.* 98 The people were noted for their passion for public auctions. In the country, particularly on a farm, the entertainment covered free meals ... The hot meals frequently included a dish of yellow rice and raisins ... This rice in course of time, was known as 'Vendutie rys,' or 'Vendue rice.' **1938** — *Our S. Afr.* 169 In South Africa the sale of goods by auction or 'vendusie' has prevailed from early times.

‖**venster kies**, **venstertjies kyk** /ˈfenstə(r)kis (keik)/ *n. phr.* [ad. Afk. *venstertjies (kyk)* (to look at) little windows (see quot. 1981); but sometimes interpreted by Eng.-speakers as *venster* window + *kies* choose.] 'Looking at windows', 'choosing the window': the avoidance of contact with 'coloured' people by one who is 'playing white' (see PLAY sense 1).

1951 L.G. GREEN *Grow Lovely* 174 'Venster kies' — choosing the window. That is the fate of the successful ones, to gaze intently into shop windows as the darker skinned brothers and sisters go by. **1981** V.A. FEBRUARY *Mind your Colour* 198 Since colour plays such an important role in South Africa, some 'coloureds' often try to cross the colour line and pass themselves off as whites. They are generally referred to as 'play-whites' or people who are 'trying for white'. This is a term known as 'venstertjies kyk' (lit. looking in the windows, pretending to window shop). This happens when coloured friends or relatives see other 'coloureds' approaching who are 'play-whites'. They pretend to do window shopping in order not to embarrass the person(s) or relative(s) in question.

Hence **vensterkie** /ˈfenstə(r)ki/ *n.*, PLAYWHITE.

1956 A. SAMPSON *Drum* 206 At Ma Parker's they were always telling stories about playwhites and their tricks. How they powder their faces to lighten them, use irons to straighten their hair, avoid sunshine, always wear a hat to hide their hair. How they're called Vensterkies, or 'window men', because when they see their old Coloured friends they stare into a shop window.

Venter /ˈfentə(r)/ *n.* [Named for the founder of the company, *Jasper Venter.*]

1. The proprietary name of a particular make of small trailer, suitable for towing behind a motor car; also applied loosely to any small trailer.

1989 *Sunday Times* 20 Aug. (Mag. Sect.) 40 Jasper's trailers are so famous .. that his surname's become a generic. In the same way people talk about Band-Aid .. for plasters .., say Venter to most South Africans and they'll think .. Trailer. **1990** L. MORGAN *Informant*, Grahamstown There was this chap coming down the road, towing his Venter.

2. *transf.* See quot. 1991. See also VAALIE.

1991 C. BARRETT in *Weekend Post* 5 Jan. 7 They were the 'Vaalies' (holidaymakers from the Transvaal), or 'Venters' as they have come to be known because of the proliferation of Venter trailers on the .. holiday run.

‖**verdom** /fə(r)ˈdɔm/ *int.* Also **verdam**, **verdompt**. [Afk., fr. Du. *verdoem* to damn.] An expletive, 'damn'.

[**1911** P. GIBBON *Margaret Harding* 212 'Come in and eat,' he bade gloomily. *'Gott verdam* — come and eat.'] **1960** J. COPE *Tame Ox* 144 'The spirits talked, the ox is his ...' 'Verdom!' Franz swore. **1974** K. GRIFFITH *Thank God We Kept Flag Flying* 4 'Verdompt!' rejoined the Boer. 'It would take us three months to kill them all.' **1985** *Drum* June 31 'We would not have what the newspapers call South Africa's race problems, the biggest problem the country has?' I chipped in naively. 'Verdom. Sphukuphuku', Dabula spat again.

Hence **verdom** *v. intrans.*, to use the expletive 'verdom', found as **verdoming** *vbl n.*

1899 G. LACY *Pictures of Trav., Sport & Adventure* 403 All got safely ashore, where the *verdoming* and *Almagtiging* was enough to make one's hair stand on end.

‖**verdomde** /fə(r)ˈdɔMdə/ *adj.* and *adv.* Also **verdoem, verdoemd(e), verdoemed, verdoemte, verdomd(e), verdomdte, verdommde, verdom(m)ed, verdommt(e), verdomnde, verdom(p)t(e), verdonde, voerdommde.** [Afk., fr. Du. *verdoemd.*]

A. *adj.* Damned, accursed. So the superlative form **verdomste** [Afk.].

Quot. 1838 might belong at VERDOM.

1838 J.E. ALEXANDER *Exped. into Int.* I. 73 Ver doem de government! it presses us in every way. **1850** R.G.G. CUMMING *Hunter's Life* I. 53, I overheard him remark to three other gruff-looking Boers who stood beside him that I was 'a verdomd' Englishman. **1864** [see DONDER *int.*]. **1873** F. BOYLE *To Cape for Diamonds* 187 He says there is a spot upon his farm where the gems lie thick as pebbles, but no verdomt digger shall come near. **1878** T.J. LUCAS *Camp Life & Sport* 232 Ah, you verdomde beast! you'll pitch me off in front of a lion, will you? Take that! **1910** 'R. DEHAN' *Dop Doctor* 90 (Swart), He was no Baas of mine verdoemde rooinek! **1910** D. FAIRBRIDGE *That Which Hath Been* (1913) 125 This verdoemde Governor is obstinate on this point. **1924** S.G. MILLIN *God's Step-Children* 96 'That will teach you to speak to White girls,' he said. 'Verdomde Bastaard.' **1930** J. BUCHAN *Four Adventures* 161, I shall know all about Africa, and be panting to get another whack at the *verdommt rooinek.* **1952** *Drum* Aug. 7 One never knows whom one speaks to nowadays — it is either an Englishman or a Jew; or (horror of horrors) a verdomde Baster! **1963** [see DOMPASS]. **1985** H. PRENDINI in *Style* Oct. 39 We're still stuck behind that verdommde robot. **1987** [see KLEURLING sense 1]. **1990** G. SLOVO *Ties of Blood* 563 '*Verdomde kommies,*' he shouted. 'What are you trying to do? Get me into trouble?'

B. *adv.* An intensifier: 'damned'.

1960 C. HOOPER *Brief Authority* 91 'Let me tell you this, you verdomde insolent blackskin.' **1976** S. CLOETE *Canary Pie* 96 Very good, then I will agree it is an ugly horse. A verdomde ugly horse. But a verdomde good one.

verdompt var. VERDOM.

‖**verdringing** /fərˈdrəŋəŋ/ *n.* [Afk.] Overcrowding; a term used by the former Nationalist Party government and others in warning that the abolition of apartheid would lead to the overcrowding of facilities. Used ironically.

1982 *Voice* 24 Jan. 4 It's what Dr Piet 'Promises' Koornhof calls 'verdringing'. Well, let's say it straight out: if Blacks did choose to use the pools . . , there would be 'verdringing'. Why? Because there are not enough pools for blacks. **1983** *Frontline* May 25 One of the massive shadowy ogres in White mythology goes by the name of 'verdringing'. **1992** 'HOGARTH' in *Sunday Times* 17 May 24 A . . World Bank report . . estimates that 40 percent of the land within a 10km radius of central Johannesburg is vacant. So much for *verdringing.*

verft var. WERF.

vergunning /fə(r)ˈxənəŋ/ *n. Obs.* exc. *hist. Law.* Pl. **-s**, formerly **-en.** [Afk., fr. Du. *vergunnen* grant permission, allow, permit + n.-forming suffix *-ing.*] Under the Transvaal Gold Law: one of sixty preference claims granted to the owner of a farm, to be assigned to persons of his or her choice prior to the land's proclamation as a public diggings. See also MIJNPACHT.

1895 *Gold Law of S. Afr. Republic* 14 He who possesses a written *vergunning* from the owner of a private farm or piece of ground, to prospect on his ground, shall obtain the requisite prospecting licence . . from the Landdrost of the district. **1901** D.M. WILSON *Behind Scenes in Tvl* 165 The number of *Vergunnings* that a farm owner could give away had often been a matter of dispute, but between the decision to proclaim Witfontein and the publication of that intention in the official gazette, the High Court had given an important judgment which once and for all settled the number of *Vergunnings* at sixty. **1913** C. PETTMAN *Africanderisms* 534 *Vergunning,* The Transvaal Gold Law permitted the owner of a farm, which had been proclaimed as a gold-field, to assign to his friends a certain number of claims, which were known as Vergunnings or preference claims. **1940** [see MIJNPACHT]. **1960** J.J.L. SISSON *S. Afr. Judicial Dict.* 840 *Vergunning,* (pl. vergunningen), a written permission granted by the owner of a farm or land in the Transvaal, to a person, authorising such person under s.43 of the Transvaal Gold Law, No. 15 of 1898 (now repealed) to peg out claims on the owner's farm or land prior to its proclamation as a public diggings.

verkijker var. VERKYKER.

verkramp /fə(r)ˈkramp/ *adj.* [Afk., 'extremely conservative' (lit. 'cramped'; the predicative form in Afk.; cf. VERKRAMPTE).] **a.** *hist.* Of or pertaining to those members of the National Party who supported the rigid application of apartheid laws. **b.** Conservative; bigoted. So the comparative form **verkramper**, and the superlative form **verkrampest**. In both senses also VERKRAMPTE *adj.* See also OUT-VERKRAMP. Cf. VERLIG.

1969 J. MERVIS in *Sunday Times* 24 Aug. 25 On a very strict, narrow interpretation, my guess is that most Nationalists are verkramp. But some are more verkramper, and others are most verkrampest. **1975** *Sunday Times* 28 Sept. 4 The secret of his [*sc.* the Cabinet Minister's] success is that he can see two sides to a question — the verkramp and the super-verkramp. **1975** *Friend* 10 July 6 Which is South Africa's most conservative (verkramp, if you like) city? Most often the accusing finger is pointed at either Pretoria or Bloemfontein. **1977** *Drum* Sept. 47 He believed that this Act was enacted to protect the ignorant and biased Afrikaner . . the verkramp type who saw illusionary 'swart gevaar' in 'Would you like your daughter to marry a black man' kind of propaganda. **1982** *S. Afr. Digest* 3 Sept. 4 Dr De Klerk . . was responsible, in 1966, . . for coining the terms 'verlig' and 'verkramp' to brand the enlightened and conservative elements. **1986** P. MOORCRAFT in *Frontline* June 26 Such an outcome might satisfy both verlig and verkramp sentiments in South Africa. **1987** *Cosmopolitan* Dec. 168 We have a jol in Pretoria . . . But only because we go to what I think is the only spot in this whole verkramp city: Club Equusite, the gay nightclub downtown.

verkrampte /fə(r)ˈkramp(tə)/ *n.* and *adj.* [Afk., 'extremely conservative' (the attrib. and n. form of *verkramp,* see prec.). Coined by W. de Klerk.]

A. *n.* **a.** *hist.* A member of the National Party with very rigid and conservative views, esp. in matters of racial segregation; in *pl.*, collectively, the right wing of the party. **b.** *transf.* One who is regarded as conservative or narrow-minded in politics, religion, social attitudes, etc.; a bigot. Also *attrib.* Cf. VERLIGTE *n.*

1967 *Race Rel. News* (S.A.I.R.R.) Sept. 7 The verligtes-verkramptes controversy must have raised in many minds the hope of a change of outlook in influential South African circles. **1969** [see VERLIGTE *n.*]. **1969** *Sunday Times* 31 Aug. 19 Things are certainly hotting up inside the Nationalist Party. The right-wing (hereinafter called the verkramptes . .) are a growing threat to Mr. Vorster and his supporters (hereinafter referred to, for want of a better word, as the verligtes). [**1969** *Times* (U.K.) 18 Sept. 9 The Army and its political directors have come in for much criticism . . from Unionist *verkramptes,* for apparent irresolution in bringing down the barricades.] **1970** [see VERLIGTE *n.*]. **1972** *Sunday Times* 5 Mar. 3 A gulf is developing between the party's verligtes and verkramptes over whether the party should close or open their ranks to ensure survival. **1978** *Daily Dispatch* 17 Oct. 8 As they are used in South Africa by the English language press they mean . . that a 'verkrampte' is a conservative realist devoted to his country and a 'verligte' is a liberal devoted to God knows what. **1979** *Indaba* 9 Nov. 7 Long before she arrived in South Africa and sent the verkramptes in a dizzy spell, the promoter Quibell Brothers, were worried about Millie's sexy acts. **1987** 'DEKAFFIRNATED STAN' in *Drum* Apr. 33 The Pretoria verkrampte's fear of being with us in the dark for hours reminds one of the old joke about the sun never setting in the British Empire because God could not trust them in the dark. **1988, 1990** [see VERLIGTE *n.*]. **1990** *Frontline* Jan. 29 You can make a tick on your sightseeing list for having met a definite 100% traditional verkrampte if you find people saying: Every white man can take ten kaffirs with him.

B. *adj.* VERKRAMP.

1968 *Green Bay Tree (pamphlet)* p.xiv, The most *verkrampte* Nationalist politicians are frightened of liberal foreign propaganda appearing on their screens. **1972** *Argus* 16 Sept. 2 I'm conservative, not verkrampte. **1977** *E. Prov. Herald* 18 Nov. 3 A judge ruled that it was potentially actionable for a man to be called 'verkrampt'. **1977** *Sunday Times* 27 Nov. 2 A triumph for verkrampte Nationalists in the Transvaal and a humiliating defeat for those so-called verligtes who believe they can reform the NP from within. **1980** N. FERREIRA *Story of Afrikaner* 115 There was a ruthless power struggle beneath the surface between *verligte* and *verkrampte* forces. **1981** *Observer* (U.K.) 5 Apr. 11 Like most black African Muslims, Edvis favours a liberal interpretation of the Koran, being *verligte* rather than *verkrampte* in that regard. **1983** *Evening Post* 11 May 6 The gravest error he could make now would be for him to halt his reform plans to try to woo back verkrampte voters. **1987** 'K. DE BOER' in *Frontline* Mar. 36 Challenged the ultra-verkrampte Transvaalse Onderwysersunie's rejection of mixed school sport. **1993** C. LOUW in *Weekly Mail* 8 Apr. 15 President FW de Klerk managed to change his public image overnight from a 'verkrampte' cabinet minister to that of an international statesman.

Hence (*nonce*) **verkramptedom** *n.*, ultra-conservatism, bigotry; **verkramptologist** *n.*, see quot. 1971.

1971 *Cape Times* 22 July 6 For budding verkramptologists the past few weeks have been heavy going. Students of the Nationalist ideological conflict on Coloured policy were having a tough enough time when published statements were not being denied before the ink was dry. **1990** *Frontline* Jan. 29 There are other proofs of verkramptedom, more common among white society overall, but overseas visitors seldom come across them.

verkramptheid /fə(r)ˈkrampthеɪt/ *n.* [Afk., *verkramp* see VERKRAMP + linking phoneme *-t-* + abstract n.-forming suffix *-heid* -hood.] Ultra-conservatism, esp. in attitudes to race; bigotry. Cf. VERLIGTHEID.

1969 S. UYS in J. Crwys-Williams *S. Afr. Despatches* (1989) 396 He [*sc.* Hertzog] appears to be under the impression that there is an essential 'verkramptheid' in Afrikanerdom. **1970** *Daily News* 25 May, Mr. Vorster must know as well as anybody that verkramptheid is far from dead in South Africa. **1972** *Daily Dispatch* 3 June 10 It is not only at the black and English-speaking universities that the government is having problems. At its own Afrikaans-speaking and Afrikaans controlled universities students are moving away from the narrow confines of verkramptheid. **1972** *Sunday Times* 24 Sept. 9 The atmosphere in Pretoria, when it comes to having women pouring drinks from behind the bar, is so fouled up with prejudice, bigotry and verkramptheid that you just cannot breathe. **1975** [see Friend quot. at OUDSTRYDER]. **1977** [see ASB]. **1987** 'K. DE BOER' in *Frontline* Apr. 36, I may be a romantic, but I believe that those loyal members of the HNP are the aristocrats of verkramptheid. **1988** E. VOSLOO in *Femina* Apr. 5 Say the word 'Afrikaner' and many an English-speaker thinks of *beskuit, koeksusters* and *verkramptheid.* No matter that *ware boere* have been known to live for years in Spain, speak five European languages fluently and be truly dedicated anarchists.

‖**verkyker** /ˈfɛːrkeɪkə(r), ˈfeəkeɪkə/ *n.* Also **verkijker.** [Afk. *vêrkyker* telescope; (pl.) binoculars (*vêr* far + *kyker* looker).] In *pl.*: Binoculars. Also *fig.*

1937 G.F. GIBSON *Story of Imp. Light Horse* 180 'What have you done with your field glasses?' ... 'Don't know!' was the reply; 'I certainly had verkijkers; they must have dropped while I was racing away.' **1980** *Voice* 29 Oct. 2 A member of the group told me that he had used his verkykers from the 50th floor of a Johannesburg hotel. And that there in Soweto some 20-km away, he had observed some 1,5 million smiling Bantus. **1983** V. MGOYOYO in *Drum* June 23 If all Afrikaners would pick up their verkykers and have a good look at our situation .., I am dead sure South Africa would be God's playground instead of the Devil's. **1985** *Weekly Mail* 28 June 15 Some 60 000 biltong-munching rugby fans packed their lunch hampers, a little liquid refreshment and a pair of *verkykers*, and trooped off to watch the Match of the Day at Pretoria's sunny Loftus Versfeld last Saturday.

||**verlep** /fə(r)ˈlep/ *adj. colloq.* Also **verlept**. [Afk.] Faded, wilted. Also *fig.*

1971 M.E. GREENBLO *Informant, Cape Town* The poor chicken – what she didn't do to it! By the time she'd finished cleaning it it was verlep. **1971** *Informant, Grahamstown* You started off with great vigour but at the end you sounded – well, all I can say is, 'verlep'. **1973** M.G. MCCOY *Informant, Port Elizabeth* I've made marmalade! June bought me Rex Union oranges ... They were a bit verlep so I added some of your lemons & it has jelled beautifully. **1978** P. BRANFORD *Informant, Grahamstown* The lettuces don't look edible – they're pretty verlep. **1982** I.H. KLEVANSKY *Kugel Book* 7 Doll, the steak looks terrible tonight. Ja, and what about those slup chips? The salads look a bit verlept too! **1990** C. MAXWELL *Informant, Grahamstown* The carnation is getting a bit verlep so now I have to hang it upside down to dry. **1991** K. SULLIVAN *Informant, Cape Town* My plants are all verlep after the heat today.

verlig /fə(r)ˈləx/ *adj.* [Afk., 'enlightened' (the predicative form; cf. VERLIGTE).] Usu. in the context of politics, particularly on issues of race: open-minded, enlightened, progressive; VERLIGTE *adj.* Cf. VERKRAMP.

1969 J. MERVIS in *Sunday Times* 24 Aug. 25 The odd thing about the whole affair is that the word 'verlig' should become an embarrassment to Nationalists ... There must be few countries where it is an insult to be called 'enlightened'. **1970** *Daily News* 12 May, Given the limited options available .. Mr. Vorster has been reasonably verlig – even kragdadig – in reshuffling his Cabinet. **1970** *Ibid.* 12 July, We are not as permissive as Natal, where one can even watch professional football on a Sunday, but much more verlig than the Free State, where God help you if they catch you fishing on the wrong side of the Vaal. **1971** *Daily Dispatch* 6 Sept. 6 Slowly but inevitably .. White South Africa is becoming more modern and in a sense more 'verlig'. **1975** *Drum* 22 Apr. 2, I hear everybody talking about Mr Vorster's verlig turn and his detente. **1982** J. DEGENAAR in *E. Prov. Herald* 30 June 2 The distinction between verlig and verkramp is valid within the limited world of Afrikaner politics, but meaningless when the dynamic presence of the black man is taken into account. **1986** P. MOORCROFT in *Frontline* June 26 Such an outcome might satisfy both verlig and verkramp sentiments in South Africa. Some of the costs of defending South West could be invested in reforms at home, as well as building up new, more defensible military lines along the Orange. **1991** G. EVANS in *Weekly Mail* 20 Dec. (Suppl.) 11 The DP .. found itself squeezed by an increasingly *verlig* NP on the one side, and to a lesser extent by a less radical ANC on the other.

verligte /fə(r)ˈləxtə/ *n.* and *adj.* [Afk., 'enlightened' (the attrib. and n. form of *verlig*, see prec.; cf. VERLIG). Coined by W. de Klerk.]

A. *n.* **a.** *hist.* A member of the National Party who supported the reform of discriminatory racial laws. **b.** *transf.* One who is regarded as enlightened in political, social, religious, etc., matters; a reformer or progressive. Cf. OORBELIGTE. Cf. VERKRAMPTE *n.*

1967 [see VERKRAMPTE *n.*]. **1969** *Manchester Guardian Weekly* (U.K.) 24 July 14 If the *verkramptes* of Louis Stoffberg and Dr Herzog win the day against Mr Vorster's *verligtes* and their good neighbour policy towards black Africa, it will be a useful gain for Peking. **1969** S. UYS in J. Crwys-Williams *S. Afr. Despatches* (1989) 396 If one looks at the Nationalist Party's parliamentary caucus, .. one sees that it is composed of verkramptes .., semi-verkramptes, semi-verligtes and verligtes. These are polarities, rather than two clear-cut groups. **1970** *News/Check* 29 May 9 People who later on were to become known as verligtes sided with *Silbersteins*, the verkramptes summed up the book as sinful. **1972** [see VERKRAMPTE *n.*]. **1977** *Rand Daily Mail* 5 Nov. 1 Natie F– is a disillusioned verligte ... He believed the only way to get urgently needed change was to join the Nationalists and try to work for it from within their ranks. **1979** W. EBERSOHN *Lonely Place* 25 You know of his father's political stance, don't you? He's a *verligte*. He has the reputation of being a balanced man. **1981** [see VERKRAMPTE *n.*]. [**1988** A. FOSTER-CARTER in D.S.G. Goodman *Communism & Reform in E. Asia* 75 Attitudes to South Korea constitute one touchstone of a divide between verkramptes and verligtes, diehards and reformers in Pyongyang.] **1990** *Frontline* Jan. 29 The verligtes are the most underrated of South Africans. Nobody admits to taking them seriously. The verkramptes think they're liberals in disguise; the liberals think they're verkramptes in disguise; and to the blacks, all whites look the same anyway. **1991** K. VAN DER MERWE in *Weekly Mail* 24 May 7 You must never forget that De Klerk was elected to the presidency because the conservatives were stronger than the *verligtes* and they voted him in.

B. *adj.* VERLIG *adj.*

1968 *Economist* (U.K.) 17 Aug. 32 The real object was to strengthen Mr Vorster in the ideological dispute that has arisen within his party between the *verligte* ('enlightened') wing and the *verkramptes* (that is, literally, the cramped ones). **1970** *Cape Times* 19 May, Mr Vorster intends pursuing a strong outward and *verligte* line. **1970** *Evening Post* 8 June, In the victory of the verligte (or 'enlightened') strain in Afrikaner thinking, particularly in foreign policy, some observers have claimed to detect that South Africa is shedding the laager mentality. **1970** *News/Check* 24 July 10 Botha scored his victory by way of an ultra-verligte approach, thus proving that verligtheid can be sold at the polls. **1970** *Ibid.* 4 Sept. 5 Piet Cillie, super-verligte editor of Die Burger. **1971** *Sunday Times* 4 Apr. 3 We in the Progressive Party must be prepared to discuss the future of South Africa with verligte South Africans, no matter what party they support today. **1972** *Time* 1 May 22 The Afrikaner-dominated National Party .. lost eight seats in the 1970 election and faces continuing tension between its moderate verligte (enlightened) and archconservative verkrampte (narrow-minded) wings. **1977** *S. Afr. Panorama* May 27 Although a notoriously conservative constituency, Mr Botha fought – and won – the seat on a 'verligte' ticket. **1980** N. FERREIRA *Story of Afrikaner* 115, I realised that there was a ruthless power struggle beneath the surface between verligte and verkrampte forces. **1982** M. MZAMANE *Children of Soweto* 26 The University's Rector, an Afrikaner of liberal inclinations and verligte views, explained .. that he'd personally stake his whole career in defence of the student's freedom of thought and expression. **1990** *Weekly Mail* 21 Dec. (Suppl.) 19 Outspoken *verligte* MP Albert Nothnagel, the man who made the mistake of saying 'let's talk to the ANC' .. was punished by exile to the South African embassy in Holland. **1993** K. OWEN in *Sunday Times* 20 June 22 It fell to the embattled editors of SAAN to precipitate the crisis that brought PW Botha, then in a reform-minded, *verligte* mode, to power.

verligtheid /fə(r)ˈləxtheɪt/ *n.* [Afk., *verligt(e)* enlightened (see VERLIG) + *-heid* -ness.] Esp. in the context of politics: enlightenment; the state of being enlightened; open-mindedness or liberalism, esp. in political and racial matters. Cf. VERKRAMPTHEID.

1970 *News/Check* 15 May 9 A reformist verligtheid implies a moving into a modern ethic, reflecting the new circumstances of all South Africa. **1972** *Argus* 10 Aug. 13 The loudest message from the Cape National Party's congress this week is that the party's biggest enemy is not verligtheid, verkramptheid, sinister subversive forces or even the United Party. It is apathy. **1974** *Sunday Times* 6 Oct. 14 The diehards wish to capitalise on Government verligtheid and encourage a rightwing backlash. **1986** *Ibid.* 19 Oct. 30 Succeeding, as he does, predecessors who were either alarmingly right-of-centre or simply bland, his energy, scholarship and verligtheid should help the church to catch up with the contemporary world. **1989** *Weekly Mail* 27 Oct. 1 The future of mass protest and of government *verligtheid* could depend on Sunday afternoon's 'welcome home' rally for the seven released African National Congress leaders.

vermeerbos, -bossie /fə(r)ˈmɪə(r)bɔs(i)/ *n.* Formerly also **vomeer bosch(je)**, **vomeerbos(sie)**, **vormeer bosch**. [Afk., earlier S. Afr. Du. *vomeer bosch(je)*, fr. Du. *vomeren* to vomit + *bosch(je)* see BOSCHJE.] Any of several varieties of the extremely toxic plant species *Geigeria* (esp. *G. africana*), causing prussic acid poisoning in sheep and goats, resulting in violent vomiting; *vermeersiektebossie*, see VERMEERSIEKTE sense 2.

1871 [see VERMEERSIEKTE sense 1]. **1905** *Cape of G.H. Agric. Jrnl* 716 (Pettman), I am sending you a small plant known as the *Vomeer bosch*, which I imagine must be an irritant poison, for it causes sheep to vomit very severely, which ultimately, as a rule, results in death. **1905** D. HUTCHEON in Flint & Gilchrist *Science in S. Afr.* 357 Vomeersiekte .. is generally attributed by the farmers to the action of the plant known as the 'Vomeerboschje' (*Geigeria passerinoides*). **1917** R. MARLOTH *Common Names* 87 *Vomeerbossie. Geigeria passerinoides.* A half-woody, depressed perennial of the drier districts. Poisonous (cumulative). **1930** *Outspan* 31 Oct. 69, I have it on good authority that in years of drought the losses in certain Karroo areas due to vermeerbossie alone are enormous. **1936** W.B. HUMPHREYS in *Hansard* 10 Mar. 1007 The Government should take steps immediately to assist farmers to eradicate the poisonous herb known as 'vermeerbos', which has spread at an alarming rate ... This poisonous plant .. covers a vast area ... Vermeerbos is a small insignificant plant which flourishes particularly in drought seasons ... Twenty-five years ago the herb was almost unknown ... It contains prussic acid and gives rise to prussic acid poisoning, an accumulation of poison. **1937** *Handbk for Farmers* (Dept of Agric. & Forestry) 441 Such heavy losses as the farmers in Griqualand West experienced in 1930, have never been known before ... These [early rains] caused the 'vermeerbossie' to grow, whereas the cold weather suppressed the growth of the remainder of the edible vegetation. **1966** C.A. SMITH *Common Names* 483 *Vermeerbossie*, A name applied to several species of *Geigeria*, from the vomiting (Afr.: vermeer) produced in sheep and goats browsing on the plants ... This is the original vermeerbossie of the central Karoo, where vermeersiekte was first recorded in 1871 ... Careful observers state that the plants are most toxic when growing in the dwarf state on limestone soils. **1971** *Golden Fleece* (S. Afr. Wool Board) June 8 Geigeria afrikana – vermeerbos. **1975** M.R. LEVYNS in *Std Encycl. of Sn Afr.* XI. 214 *Vermeerbos*, (*Geigeria africana* = *G. passerinoides*.) Small, short-stemmed perennial belonging to the family *Compositae* ... This plant is the cause of the serious 'vomiting sickness' (vermeersiek) in cattle, sheep and goats.

vermeersiekte /fə(r)ˈmɪə(r)ˌsiktə/ *n.* Also **vermeersiek**, **vomeersiekte**, **vomeer ziekte**. [Afk., earlier S. Afr. Du. *vomeerziekte* fr. Du. *vomeren* to vomit + *ziekte* sickness. In Afk., *vermeer* and *vomeer* are variant forms of the same word.]

1. *Pathology.* A potentially fatal illness in livestock, esp. sheep and goats, characterized by vomiting, bloating, stiffness, or paralysis, or all of these, and caused by the eating of bushes of the genus *Geigeria*. Also *attrib.*

1871 *Queenstown Free Press* 19 Dec., We learn .. of a new disease now prevalent among sheep ... The farmers call it *vomeer ziekte*, or vomiting disease ... It is attributed by the farmers to the eating of a small kind of 'tussock grass' (called by them *vormeer bosch*) when in flower. **1905** D. HUTCHEON in Flint & Gilchrist *Science in S. Afr.* 357 Vomeersiekte or Vomit Sickness of Sheep. This peculiar disease is due to the functional derangement of the stomach or of the nervous centre which regulates the spasmodic movements involved in the act of vomition. It is more or less prevalent in the western and north-western Karoo districts. **1929** *Handbk for Farmers* (Dept of Agric.) 203 Vermeersiekte only appears in dry years when there is little or no other edible vegetation ... Sheep and goats are mostly susceptible to vermeersiekte, cattle less so. Farmers in the vermeersiekte areas are well acquainted with the responsible bush. **1975** [see VERMEERBOS]. **1979** T. GUTSCHE *There Was a Man* 18 An urgent call from Victoria West to deal with the ancient 'Vomeerziekte' found him convalescent at the coast.

2. *comb.* **vermeersiektebossie** /-bɔsi/ *n.* [Afk., *bossie* (*bos* bush + -IE)], VERMEERBOS.

1929 *Handbk for Farmers* (Dept of Agric.) 203 Many Free State and Transvaal farms are practically covered with vermeersiektebossie. **1957** [see GEELDIKKOP].

verneuk /fə(r)'nju:k, fə(r)'niœk, fə'nu:k/ *v. trans. Slang.* Also **ferneuk, vernoek, vinook.** [Afk., fr. Du. *verneuken* (not in polite use).] To deceive; to cheat, swindle.

1871 W.G. ATHERSTONE in *Cape Monthly Mag.* III. July 46 How Hendrik enjoyed *verneuking* the Boer! [**1888** *Cape Punch* 13 June 139 Der Groot Gelt Vernuking Golt Mining Gompany was der soundest venture in der vorlt 'of its kind'.] **1899** 'S. ERASMUS' *Prinsloo* 4 Had I been able to cypher and read writing as the old teacher wishes, I should not have been verneuked by so many Rooineks. **1909** R. CULLUM *Compact* 213 He has vinooked the Kaffir chiefs into granting large concessions. **1915** *Rand Daily Mail* 1 Mar., The farmers, recognising .. that they have no friends, and no redress, merely shrung their shoulders, and scrap-heap the new separators, patent churns, etc. the Government and National Union 'verneuked' them into buying. **1937** S. CLOETE *Turning Wheels* 253 'Ach', she sighed, 'to think that Gert Kleinhouse, whose nose I used to wipe with a lappie, has verneuked me out of a lovely little pig'. **1963** K. MACKENZIE *Dragon to Kill* 101 'This story,' he said, 'would be of a South African farm, of course, deep in the Marico country perhaps and full of comic Bosman Afrikaners *verneuking* each other in dead-pan self-righteousness'. **1965** J. BENNETT *Hawk Alone* 191 'Don't let them verneuk you, Mr Vance,' said Harry Mulder. 'These gooses are damn slim, man. You got to watch them.' **1972** *Informant, Grahamstown* Please write down the weight and price per lb. of the meat so that my maid can see that I am not verneuking her. **1976** S. CLOETE *Canary Pie* 99 The boys and spans of oxen were just a ruse to draw them off and *verneuk* them.

Hence **verneuker** *n.* [Afk.], a swindler; **verneukering** *vbl n.* (*rare*), swindling, deceiving; **verneukery** /fə(r)'niœkə,reı, fə(r)'nju:kəri, fənu:kəri/ *n.*, also **verneukerie, verneukerij,** [Afk.], a deception or swindle; see also BOER VERNEUKER.

1891 J.P. LEGG in *Cape Illust. Mag.* I. 96 A 'slim' fellow often finds himself out done in 'verneukerij.' **1896** *Westminster Gaz.* (U.K.) 4 July 8 We women of South Africa despise such maudlin *verneukery*. **1900** J. ROBINSON *Life Time S. Afr.* 185 Hence arose the practice of 'verneukering' – by which buyer and seller each sought to get the better of each other. **1901** J. STUART *Pictures of War* 95 Of course these flags of truce are merely exhibited by Boers as a piece of *verneukerie* – a swindle. **1911** *E. London Dispatch* 23 Nov. 5 (Pettman), The assistant librarian from the British Museum testified that *verneuker* meant swindler. It was never used in polite society before a lady. **1915** D. FAIRBRIDGE *Torch Bearer* 233 Andries Brink looked at him in contempt. 'That is all the doctor's *verneukerij* (swindling). When did Dr. Lange ever stick a needle into people to cure them of sore throat?' **1924** L. COHEN *Reminisc. of Jhb.* 43 Heaven has sent thee, O Son of Palestine, into a Land of Promise, the inhabitants of which happy valley regard it as a distinction to be decently plundered, and where rogues and *verneukers* must surely prosper. *Ibid.* 96 A German share-dealer .. waxed exceedingly wroth; he had lost a sovereign. 'What is this verneukery?' he exclaimed angrily. **1940** F.B. YOUNG *City of Gold* 26 That slim verneuker lawyer played each of them off against the other and tricked them out of their claims. **1956** M. ROGERS *Black Sash* 185 'Nor did it provide any special protection against "verneukery" (cheating). In fact, such a protection is impossible,' she said. **1963** K. MACKENZIE *Dragon to Kill* 182 He looked unflusterable, the big policeman, and also much too trustworthy for any suggestions of *verneukery* to make any progress. **1983** J.A. BROWN *White Locusts* 105 The Rand's been built on a bluff so far, stock market *verneukerij*, as the Dutchmen say. **1984** *Drum* July 22, I have saved your good money from buying useless cream. The man is a verneuker.

Verreaux's eagle /'verəʊz ,i:g(ə)l/ *n. phr.* [Named for French naturalist *Jules Verreaux* (1807–73), or his father, *Edouard Verreaux*.] The BLACK EAGLE, *Aquila verreauxii*.

[**1830** R. PLESSON *Centurie Zool.* 105 L'Aigle Verreaux. *Aquila Verreauxii*, Less. L'oiseau que M. Verreaux, voyager naturaliste qui explore en ce moment l'extrémité australe d'Afrique, vient d'adresser à son père à Paris, est sans contredit un des aigles les plus remarquables.] **1867** E.L. LAYARD *Birds of S. Afr.* 11 Verreaux's eagle is not uncommon throughout the colony, wherever rocky precipitous mountains are to be found. **1903** STARK & SCLATER *Birds of S. Afr.* III. 293 Verreaux's Eagle is found in the highlands of Abyssinia and Shoa and reappears in South Africa. **1931** R.C. BOLSTER *Land & Sea Birds* 100 The other Eagles are birds of powerful flight and are determined killers, the great size of Verreaux's and Martial Eagles enabling them to attack prey as big as goats, sickly sheep, and some species of buck. **1955** [see DASSIEVANGER]. **1983** K.B. NEWMAN *Newman's Birds* 168 *Black eagle* (Verreaux's eagle). **1984** G.L. MACLEAN *Roberts' Birds of Sn Afr.* 117 *Black Eagle* (Verreaux's Eagle) .. *Aquila verreauxii*.

versterkdruppels /fə(r)'stɛrk,drəp(ə)lz, -əls/ *n.* Also **versterkende druppels, - droppels.** Pl. unchanged. [Afk., lit. 'strengthening drops', *versterk* to strengthen, fortify + *druppels* drops.] **a.** *noncount.* A liquid patent medicine used for the treatment of a range of ailments including heart-complaints and nervous tension, and taken in the form of drops mixed with another liquid. **b.** *pl.* Drops of this medicine. See also DRUPPELS.

1919 *Dunell, Ebden & Co.'s Price List* Oct. 20 Versterk Droppels 3/6. [**1937** C.R. PRANCE *Tante Rebella's Saga* 185 She and Christiaan had tried truly everything. They had both taken 'Strength-Drops' from the Home-Medicine chest.] **1949** L.G. GREEN *In Land of Afternoon* 44 It will be a transformed countryside indeed when the last bottle of 'Versterk Druppels' is sold. **1958** E.H. BURROWS *Hist. of Medicine* 191 *Versterk(ende) droppels* (lit. Strengthening Drops): used as a tonic for persons 'run down', nervous or with general debility – a few drops in a goblet of wine. **1963** A.M. LOUW *20 Days* 260 'Calm yourself, my old husband,' said old Susanna, handing him a small glass of wine and versterkdruppels. **1969** *Post* 16 Feb., Brighten your life with .. Versterkdruppels. The most trusted name in Dutch Medicines. **1974** Y. BURGESS in S. Gray *On Edge of World* 23 The triangular wall-cabinet where she kept, among other remedies, the *groenamare* for her cramps, the *versterkdruppels* for her nerves, and the *rooi laventel* for her heart. **1989** D. SMUTS *Folk Remedies* 22 *Childlessness*, .. 1 bottle old port wine, .. 1 small bottle versterkdruppels, 1 small bottle phosphorine ... This person I know of hadn't even finished the bottle .. before she conceived. **1991** [see quot. at *krampdruppels* (DRUPPELS sense b i)].

ver verlaate vlaktes see VLAKTE sense 1 b.

vervet /'vɜ:vət/ *n.* [fr. Fr. specific name *Cercopithèque vervet*.] In full ***vervet monkey***: the common monkey *Cercopithecus aethiops* of the Cercopithecidae, grizzled grey in colour, with black face surrounded by a white ruff, and black paws.

1884 *Imperial Dict.* **1893** R. LYDEKKER *Royal Natural Hist.* I. 97 Still better known than the malbrouck is the South African vervet monkey ... The fur of the vervet is of a greyish-green colour. **1932** [see SAMANGO]. *a***1936** E.N. MARAIS *Soul of Ape* (1973) 99 We tried the effects of the continued administration of alcohol on the following animals: vervet monkey (*Cercopithecus aethiops pygerythrus*), .. and klipspringer (*Oreotragus saltator*). **1967** E. ROSENTHAL *Encycl. of Sn Afr.* 594 *Vervet monkey*, Timid but cunning, it runs in troops and is a menace to crops of all kinds. **1972** [see SAMANGO]. **1984** G. VERDAL in *Style* Nov. 152 The fish eagle's cry, the solitude of deserted beaches, sun-warmed dunes, troops of chattering vervet monkeys. **1988** A. HALL-MARTIN et al. *Kaokoveld* 30 Vervet monkeys, which are more arboreal than baboons, are able to survive only in areas of riverine thicket and trees and close to water. Consequently, vervets have not been recorded [in Kaokoland] except along the upper Kunene and its tributaries last of the Baynes Mountains, and on the upper reaches of the Hoarusib east of the escarpment. **1988** C. & T. STUART *Field Guide to Mammals* 76 Vervet monkey, *Cercopithecus aethiops*. The face is short-haired and black, with a rim of white hair across the forehead and down the side of the cheeks ... The adult male has a distinctive bright blue scrotum. **1988** *Stanger Mail* 23 Dec. 7 The samango is being mistaken for the vervet which is the usual raider. People make mistakes and shoot the samango. The samango is much darker and furrier than the vervet. **1990** *Farmer's Weekly* 8 June 41 Species available to hunters today include .. spotted hyaena, baboon, vervet monkey and dassie. **1990** [see SAMANGO].

Verwoerdian /fə(r)'vʊ(r)dıən, -tıən/ *adj.* [Formed on the surname of former Prime Minister *H.F. Verwoerd* (1901–1966).] Of or pertaining to apartheid on a grand scale (particularly that including geographically-based segregation through massive social engineering), as propounded esp. by H.F. Verwoerd, and put into practice by the Nationalist government from the 1950s to the 1980s. See also GRAND APARTHEID.

Verwoerd, as Minister of Native Affairs from 1950 to 1958, and Prime Minister from 1958 to 1966, was the architect of the 'homeland' system (see HOMELAND sense 1).

1973 *Cape Times* 26 May 8 The Verwoerdian notion of South African nationhood as the 'White nation' can hardly command whole-hearted acceptance. **1980** *Rand Daily Mail* 2 Dec. 1 The days of Verwoerdian dreams of apartheid are over, Chief Gatsha Buthelezi told the Sunday Times .. Businessman of the Year banquet last night. **1987** *Daily Dispatch* 6 May 10 There is no country with stricter apartheid customs than India. Although it is not based on colour it is just as humiliating as Verwoerdian apartheid. **1989** [see quot. at *grootapartheid* (APARTHEID sense 1 b)]. **1992** A. HEARD in *Weekly Mail* 24 Apr. 23 Those were the days of revealed Verwoerdian certitude. **1993** *Weekend Post* 12 June 8 The Verwoerdian dream is being dismantled piece by painful piece.

Hence **Verwoerdianism** *n.*, rigid and extreme segregationist thinking.

1989 S. JOHNSON in *Weekly Mail* 1 Sept. 7 Treurnicht's address was state-of-the-art – as opposed to vintage – CP Verwoerdianism.

vetderm see DERM sense b.

vetkoek /'fetkʊk, -kuk/ *n.* Pl. unchanged, **-s**, or **-koeke** /-kʊkə/. [Afk., *vet* fat + *koek* cake.] **a.** A small unsweetened cake of deep-fried dough; FAT CAKE; FAT COOK; VETKOEKIE. **b.** *noncount.* Deep-fried unsweetened dough. Cf. MAAGBOM, STORMJAER sense 1.

1900 M. MARQUARD *Lett. from Boer Parsonage* (1967) 75 Yesterday Eva bought 12/-worth of meal (two buckets) and baked half of it into bread & 'vet koek'. 1902 D. VAN WARMELO *On Commando* 106 We were busy all evening baking vet-koek (a kind of scone fried in lard), as we had received the order to be ready to leave the following morning at one o'clock and to take provisions sufficient for two days. 1903 [see AUNTIE sense 1 b]. 1950 H. GERBER *Cape Cookery* 47 Both Vetkoek and Roosterkoek were made either with unleavened dough or with a dough leavened with suurdeeg ... Vetkoek ... Fry the rolls in deep hot fat. 1969 *Personality* 5 June, Always there is the contrast between past and present .. vetkoek and frozen foods. 1975 *Sunday Times* 19 Oct. (Mag. Sect.) 5 A typical meal would include *vetkoek*, the instant bread made by the Voortrekkers who had neither time to allow the dough to rise nor ovens for baking (it is made of wheat flour and yeast and is deep-fried). 1976 [see PANNEKOEK]. 1976 M. THOLO in C. Hermer *Diary of Maria Tholo* (1980) 58 Grace arrived with the heaviest looking vetkoeke. 1979 *Sunday Times* 29 July (Mag. Sect.) 3 The vetkoek should have a good golden colour all over. 1979 HEARD & FAULL *Our Best Trad. Recipes* 95 'Vetkoek' remains a favourite with South Africans today ... It is generally eaten instead of bread and is served with jam or syrup. 1980 A. FUGARD *Tsotsi* 57 A few of them had stayed behind to buy a tin of hot coffee and a vetkoek from the old woman on the corner. 1987 *Frontline* Aug.-Sept. 28 Agony Aunties lurking, with flabby open arms and gently clucking tongues and hearts of purest vetkoek. 1990 *S. Afr. Consumer* 4th Quarter 18 The first batch of vetkoek which was started in cold oil baked beautifully. 1994 [see MAHEWU].

vetkoekie /ˈfetkʊki/ *n.* [Afk., *vetkoek* (see VETKOEK) + -IE.] VETKOEK sense a.

1958 A. JACKSON *Trader on Veld* 44, I also recall .. 'mosbolletjes' (small aniseed cakes), 'melk tert' (milk tart), 'vet koekies' (a type of doughnut), and many other specialities of the old South African kitchen. 1986 S. SEPAMLA *Third Generation* 11, I wake up in the early morning, make fire, fry *vetkoekies*, push the hand-cart to the factories.

vetkousie /ˈfetkəʊsi, ˈfɛt-/ *n.* [Afk., *vet* fat + *kous* sock + -IE; see quot. 1966.] The edible succulent plant *Carpanthea pomeridiana* of the Aizoaceae.

1890 A.G. HEWITT *Cape Cookery* 30 Almost any vegetable may be made into a Brédé. Pumpkin, water eeintjes, vet kousies, tomatoes, [etc.]. 1966 C.A. SMITH *Common Names* 484 Vetkousie, Carpanthea pomeridiana ... A small annual. Leaves in a radical rosette, flat, more or less spathulate, fleshy; flowers solitary, pedunculed, golden yellow ... The young plants were formerly used as a salad. The vernacular name is a part corruption and a part translation of the Hottentot name. 1974 *Motorist* Aug. 35 No less imaginative were the names of some of the flowers — vetkousies, weeskindertjies, aandblommetjies and duikerwortel. 1983 M.M. KIDD *Cape Peninsula* 156 *Carpanthea pomeridiana*. Mesembryanthemaceae. *Vetkousie*. Sprawling annual .. common in sand.

vet ou var. WIT OU.

Vhalovedu pl. form of LOBEDU.

Vhavenda pl. form of VENDA.

vieh var. VEE.

Vierkleur /ˈfiːrklœr, ˈfiəklɪə/ *n.* Occas. with small initial. Pl. -s, occas. -e /-ə/. [Afk., *vier* four + *kleur* colour]. The flag of the old Transvaal (or South African) Republic, 1857-77 and 1881-1902, having three horizontal stripes of red, white, and blue, and a vertical stripe of green on the left-hand side; *rare*, the flag of the Orange Free State Republic (see Weekend Post quot. 1993). Also *attrib*.

1899 S.T. PLAATJE *Boer War Diary* (1973) 25 The missionary .. had the 'Vierkleur' waving over his dwellinghouse. 1900 B. MITFORD *Aletta* 40 When I return it will be with our conquering forces to help plant the 'Vierkleur' over our new Republic. 1915 D. FAIRBRIDGE *Torch Bearer* 130 We shall live under the Vierkleur, Mynheer, the good old flag of the Transvaal Republic, which will float all over South Africa some day, it all goes well. 1924 L. COHEN *Reminisc. of Jhb.* 119 He was killed, I believe, in the last Boer War, fighting for the *Vierkleur*. 1929 D. REITZ *Commando* 23 On the left of the track stood a large marquee over which floated the vierkleur flag of the Transvaal, indicating General Joubert's headquarters. 1936 *Cambridge Hist. of Brit. Empire* VIII. 509 The hope of young Afrikanerism to see the Vierkleur 'waving from Table Bay to the Zambesi' was publicly expressed. 1937 H. KLEIN *Stage Coach Dust* 203 As each draft marched out of camp, amidst much waving of the Vierkleur (the old Transvaal flag), their comrades cheered them on with patriotic and other songs. 1947 H.C. BOSMAN *Mafeking Rd* (1969) 52 We returned to our farms, relieved that the war was over, but with heavy hearts at the thought .. that over the Transvaal the Vierkleur would not wave again. 1958 A. JACKSON *Trader on Veld* 68 Rinderpest .. raced down from somewhere near the Equator, .. not caring whether the oxen that died lived under the Union or the Vierkleur. 1962 *Natal Mercury* 12 June, The South African flag consisted of the Transvaal Vierkleur, the Orange Free State flag and the Union Jack. 1977 [see NAT *n.* sense a]. 1982 *E. Prov. Herald* 1 June 4 Mr Marais was led into the meeting under the historic Wonderboom by a column of youths waving Vierkleurs. 1988 'K. DE BOER' in *Frontline* Apr. 26 Lots of Vierkleure and AWB flags waved about in fervour. 1993 *Sunday Times* 25 Apr. 21 The AWB's single-storey headquarters, bedecked with Transvaal Vierkleurs and guarded by khaki-clad guards bristling with beards and guns. 1993 *Weekend Post* 20 Nov. 13 (letter) None of the flags from which our present national flag is derived — the Dutch, the two Vierkleurs or the Union Jack — can be said to represent the majority of South Africans.

vies /fis/ *adj.* Also **fies**. [Afk. (fr. Du. *vies* dirty, nasty).] Furiously angry.

1916 S. BLACK in S. Gray *Three Plays* (1984) 207 Van K: I picked up a paper and read the advert, 'Strongly recommended to colonials, quiet, Christian home ...' The last place I lived in made me absolutely fies. Mrs H: Fish? Van K: No, fies — fed up! c1929 — in *Ibid.* 100 Sophie: This is your demn fault. Frikkie: My fault? Sophie: Yes, .. I'm blooming vies for you. 1969 A. FUGARD *Boesman & Lena* 12 This time I'm laughing, and you ... ! Vies! You don't like it when somebody else laughs. 1970 J.L. COUSINS *Informant, Vryburg* Why do you look so vies? 1989 *Weekend Argus* 25 Nov. 21 I get the hell in — not cross but in Afrikaans *vies*. 1990 *Frontline* Jan. 9 The doctor .. was vies. He said that he had been to the hotel. He had also phoned them to warn them that he isn't white. They had said that's fine, no problem.

Vietas var. FIETAS.

vigenbosch var. VYGEBOSCH.

vigilante *n.* and *adj.* [Special sense of general Eng.]

A. *n.* A member of an organised group of armed men, espousing conservative political views and formed with the expressed aim of disciplining 'comrades', working against activist groups, and controlling townships. See also A-TEAM, COMRADE, FATHERS, IBUTHO sense 2, MBOKODO, ROOIDOEK, WITDOEK.

1985 *Cape Times* 3 Jan. 1 A New Year raid by Ndebele vigilantes into the largely Pedi-speaking Moutse district north-east of Pretoria. 1985 *SASPU National* Vol.6 No.2, 6 Students constantly fear assassination as vigilantes .. have murdered and petrol bombed many who demand a better education. 1987 *E. Prov. Herald* 5 Sept. 1 Our children are growing up frightened of the police and vigilantes who are always questioning our children about their fathers. 1987 *Leadership* Vol.6 No.3, 58 Fire-bombing, shooting and necklacing by militant activists and vigilantes of their political opponents, the violence and counter-violence of the security forces. 1988 *Now Everyone Is Afraid* (Catholic Inst. for Internat. Rel.) 67 During 1987 armies of more than 1 000 vigilantes fought against 'comrades' in KwaNobuhle as well as Crossroads and KTC. 1989 *Reader's Digest Illust. Hist.* 479 The excesses of kangaroo courts and summary murders of people alleged to be 'collaborators' led to a reaction — and the emergence of the 'vigilantes', conservative groups who wanted a return to the old order in the townships. 1990 M. KENTRIDGE *Unofficial War* 9 The armed Inkatha members .. are known as vigilantes both by themselves and by their detractors ... Vigilantes are organised, violent groups of men who espouse conservative political views and are committed to the destruction of all progressive organisations and individuals. These vigilantes act either in collusion with the police or on their own, with the police apparently turning a blind eye ... In describing themselves as vigilantes, however, Inkatha members mean that they are merely sober citizens, forced, on those occasions when police protection proves inadequate, to defend themselves against attacks by radicals. Of the two definitions, the first is more widespread. 1992 R. LYSTER in *Natal Mercury* 25 Nov. 8 There is a continuous, low intensity war taking place .. between the Kwazulu police and Inkatha-based vigilantes on the one hand, and on the other any person or entity which represents a threat or challenge to the legitimacy of the KwaZulu government.

B. *adj.* Of or pertaining to such a group.

1987 *E. Prov. Herald* 19 Jan. 1 Two people died in an outbreak of vigilante violence in Port Elizabeth African townships at the weekend. Township sources reported a witch-hunt of supporters of the United Democratic Front. 1987 *New Nation* 12 Feb. 1 Attacks by vigilante groups on anti-apartheid activists — often described in the pro-government media as 'black-on-black violence' — have increased dramatically since the declaration of the state of emergency. 1987 *Ibid.* 9 Apr. 2 It appeared police were not prepared to check vigilante activities in the township. 1990 M. KENTRIDGE *Unofficial War* 9 Vigilante leaders are drawn from a variety of sources: Inkatha members with a particular penchant and talent for combat; .. chiefs of rural areas and their indunas, or headmen.

Hence **vigilantism** *n.*, also **vigilanteeism**, the attitudes and actions of vigilantes.

1987 *Weekly Mail* 7 Aug. 11 Township vigilantism and tough action against rent boycotters or squatters. 1990 *New African* 25 June 10 (letter) It is common knowledge that vigilanteeism has always been backed by the apartheid regime as it .. adds another brutal form of their defence strategies or assault tactics in a bid to crush the might of the progressive forces.

vij var. VEE.

vijg(i)e, **vijgen** varr. VYGIE.

vildemaakeon var. *wildemakou* (see WILDE sense b).

vilderbeeste var. WILDEBEEST.

vilge maccow var. *wildemakou* (see WILDE sense b).

vingerpol /ˈfəŋə(r)pɔl, ˈfiŋəpɔl/ *n.* Also **vingerpoll**. [Afk., *vinger* finger + *pol* tuft, tussock.] Any of several species of *Euphorbia* which have finger-like succulent branches, esp. *E. caput-medusae* (found in the Cape Peninsula), and *E. esculenta* (found in the Karoo). Also Englished forms **fingerpo(h)l**, **finger-pole**, **finger-poll**.

1883 M.A. CAREY-HOBSON *Farm in Karoo* 196 'Here is another very curious plant, circle within circle of things like fingers.' 'That is just what it is called,' said Frank. 'Finger-pole'; it has a very large white juicy root ... We dig it up out of the earth, and the moment it is exposed the cattle and sheep eat it with avidity. 1889 H.A. BRYDEN *Kloof & Karroo* 258 Spent and foundered oxen .. when fed with fingerpoll, regained vitality. 1890 A. MARTIN *Home Life* 58 Another of our many eccentric-looking plants, the *finger-poll*, is also used in very dry seasons to feed cattle. 1898 [see NOORSDORING]. c1911 P. WEYER in S. Playne *Cape Col.*

175 'Fingerpohl' .. is looked upon as being exceedingly nutritious for all kinds of ruminating stock, and, indeed, for ostriches ... It gives a very large tap-root which, in its raw state, can be eaten by human beings. **1913** C. PETTMAN *Africanderisms* 536 *Vingerpol*, .. *Euphorbia caput-medusæ*. A plant with a bunch of finger-like growths; it is common in most parts of the Karoo. **1917** R. MARLOTH *Common Names* 86 *Vingerpol*, Unarmed species of *Euphorbia* of the section Meduseae, e.g., *E. Caput medusae* (Lionshead near C.T.) and *E. esculenta*, the latter a valuable and drought-resisting nutritious stockfood (Jansenville). **1966** C.A. SMITH *Common Names* 84 *Vingerpol, Euphorbia caput-medusae*. **1973** O.H. SPOHR tr. *F. Krauss's Trav. Jrnl* 82 This plant 'fingerbollen', 'Fingerpol' appears only outwardly to be an Euphorbia caputmedusae, but belongs actually to the section Euphorbia pseudomedusae, and is described as Euphorbia esculenta Marloth.

vingertrek /ˈfəŋə(r)trek/ *n.* [Afk., *vinger* finger + *trek* pull, haul.] A tug-of-war game in which the two players link little fingers and pull in opposite directions; FINGER-TREK.

1955 V. DE KOCK *Fun They Had* 65 The children of South Africa, like those elsewhere, have always played all manner of singing, dancing and marching games, leap-frog, hide and seek, *vinger trek*, and prisoner's base, for which no equipment is needed. **1970** N. CONWAY *Informant, Salisbury (Harare, Zimbabwe)* Jukskei and vingertrek are popular boeresports.

vink /fɪŋk, fəŋk/ *n.* [S. Afr. Du., fr. Du., 'finch'.] **a.** FINK sense a.

1834 A. SMITH *Diary* (1940) II. 143 The black bird with red bill like the vink generally keeps company with the buffaloes. **1910** D. FAIRBRIDGE *That Which Hath Been* (1913) 30 Yellow vinks shrieked and jabbered on their hanging nests. **1925** F.C. SLATER *Centenary Bk of S. Afr. Verse* 235 The bird referred to in the text is evidently a weaver-bird, locally known as Vink. **1933** J. JUTA *Look Out for Ostriches* 160 The vinks whose beautifully woven nests hung from the reeds, or were suspended far out over the water. **1958** I. VAUGHAN *Diary* 43 At this drift the willos [*sic*] are very big so big you can swing right over the water. The water is very deep here. Vinks nests hang all over the river. They look like little baskets. **1958** *Cape Times* 15 July 8 Vinks feed on many kinds of tiny parasites and insects. **1965** J. BENNETT *Hawk Alone* 142 In the early morning there were always birds in the garden, drab mousebirds, .. bright spreeuws, .. noisy weaver birds, the yellow vinks. **1977** F.G. BUTLER *Karoo Morning* 90 We would all change direction .. into the reeds to rifle the vinks' nests; then back to our clothes.

b. With distinguishing epithet: **red vink** *obs.*, the red bishop bird *Euplectes orix; blood fink*, see FINK sense b.

1834 A. SMITH *Diary* (1939) I. 168 Red Vink and Caffer Vink common among the streams.

vinkel /ˈfəŋk(ə)l, ˈfɪŋk(ə)l/ *n.* Also **finkel**, occas. **vinkels**, and (formerly) **fenkel**. [Afk., ad. Du. *venkel* fennel.]

1. The fleshy, aromatic root of *Chamarea capensis* (family Apiaceae); usu. *comb.* **vinkelbol** /-bɔl/ [Afk., *bol* bulb], **vinkelwortel** /-ˌvɔrtəl, -vɔːt(ə)l/ [Afk., *wortel* root (see quot. 1966)], in the same sense.

1790 tr. *F. Le Vaillant's Trav.* II. 85, I found an equal relief in two other roots of the size of one's finger, but exceedingly long ... They are to be met with in the colonies, where they are known, one under the name of *anys-wortel*, and the other under that of *vinkel-wortel*. [**1837** ECKLON & ZEYHER *Enumeratio Plantarum Africae* 346 *Chamarea capensis* ... Incolis: 'Fenkel-wortel.'] **1868** W.H. HARVEY *Genera of S. Afr. Plants* 139 *C[arum] Capense*, Sond., our only species, has a fleshy aromatic root (*Fenkel-wortel*), a branching stem. **1913** C. PETTMAN *Africanderisms* 168 *Fenkel wortel*, .. The fleshy, aromatic roots of *Carum Capense, Sond.* **1924** L.H. BRINKMAN *Glory of Backveld* 53 Soon she had several beds planted with kanibro, barrol, gaap, nqom, vleiroots and finkel. All these are delicacies highly prized by the natives, and even Europeans enjoy eating them, especially finkel, which is a sweet, deliciously-flavoured root, pure white and resembling a long white radish. **1966** C.A. SMITH *Common Names* 484 *Vinkelbol, Chamerea (Carum) capensis*. Rootstock an aromatic tuber, often more or less cylindric-oblong or bulbous-based, with a somewhat cylindric neck ... The tuber has an aromatic taste, suggestive of fennel ... Both Europeans and Hottentots formerly dug up the tubers which were used medicinally.

2. The bushy, erect, annual herb *Foeniculum vulgare* (fennel), with a flavour similar to aniseed.

1913 C. PETTMAN *Africanderisms* 534 *Venkel*, .. *Foeniculum officinale*, known in England as Sweet fennel. **1947** L.G. GREEN *Tavern of Seas* 199 Vinkel, another famous shrub, is guaranteed to keep fleas away if you place a branch under your bed. **1966** C.A. SMITH *Common Names* 484 *Vinkel(bossie), Foeniculum vulgare* ... Formerly .. the fruits were used as a flavouring for cakes, buns etc. and are frequently chewed by children on account of the aromatic taste. **1972** L.G. GREEN *When Journey's Over* 142 When he went out after the rare showers and collected *vinkel* and *geelwortel* it reminded him of his childhood. **1977** *S. Afr. Panorama* Oct. 12 The green salads comprised interesting things like fennell (better known in South Africa as 'vinkel' – 'vinkel en koljander'), endive, coss and American spinach. **1988** SMUTS & ALBERTS *Forgotten Highway* 184 *Vinkels* (fennel), again, gives you a flat leaf, like this, and white food like a root, down into the ground, it's sweet as honey.

vinook var. VERNEUK.

vint /vɪnt, vənt/ *v. intrans. Slang.* [Englished form of *wind*, fr. Afk. *windgat* (see WINDGAT).] To drive fast or recklessly; also *fig.*

1986 *Crux* Aug. 43 No trouble – David vints over and lops this oke's head off. Too much, the Philistines only catch a big skrik and pull out, sharp like! **1994** *Informant, Grahamstown* Look at him, vinting about on his motor-bike!

viooltjie /fiˈʊəlki/ *n.* Also **viooltje**. [S. Afr. Du. *viooltje* fr. Du. *viool* violin + dim. suffix -IE, named for the noise produced by the stalks when they are rubbed together (see quot. 1913).] Any of several plants which produce a noise when their stems rub together, esp. species of *Lachenalia* and *Ornithogalum*. See also CHINCHERINCHEE.

1904 [see CHINCHERINCHEE]. **1913** C. PETTMAN *Africanderisms* 536 *Viooltjes*, .. *Ornithogalum thyrsoides*. The name is also applied throughout the Western Districts to the many species of *Lachenalia*. It refers to the squeaking noise which children produce by drawing the flower stalks of these plants across one another, and also to the manner in which the noise is produced. **1964** [see KALKOENTJIE sense 2]. **1973** J. RABIE in S. Gray *Writers' Territory* 169 In July and August the first wild flowers already steal the show. First the rosy viooltjie. **1975** A.A. MAUVE in *Std Encycl. of Sn Afr.* XI. 249 The name 'viooltjie' is sometimes wrongly applied to some bulbous Cape plants belonging to the lily family .., viz the genera *Lachenalia* and *Ornithogalum*.

vittkut var. WITGAT.

Viva /ˈvi(ː)və, ˈvi(ː)va/ *int.* Also with small initial. [It., Sp. and Pg., but in S. Afr. Eng. prob. fr. Pg., as used in Angola and Mozambique.] 'Long live', used as a greeting, exclamation, or salute at left-wing political rallies; loosely, in any context, a cry of celebration or triumph. See also AMANDLA.

1985 *Probe* Nov. 29 God helps those who help themselves. We can cry with Lawrence and say 'Viva La word of Almighty God'! and still remain far from liberation. **1986** *Daily Dispatch* 25 Mar. 9 When a large group of youths bearing the ANC flag ran into the stadium a roar went up from a crowd, who began chanting 'viva, viva'. **1987** *Frontline* Feb. 40 A big man yells: 'Viva African National Congress, Viva!' 'Viva!' replies the crowd. 'Viva South African Communist Party, Viva!' shouts the big man. 'Viva!' echoes forth from the crowd. **1988** *Learn & Teach* No.1, 13 Viva! The long, hard struggle against skin lightening creams is over! **1993** *Weekly Mail & Guardian* 13 Aug. 35 A woman took the microphone and started shouting slogans: 'Viva ANC viva! Viva local government viva! Viva MK viva!'

Hence **viva** *n.*, a cry of 'viva'.

1987 *Frontline* May 10 Feeling no need for a dose of Amandlas and Vivas, and assurances of the imminent demise of minority rule, I turn homeward. **1989** *Sunday Times* 15 Oct. 4 A clergyman chanted a litany of 'Vivas', and even said: 'Viva petrol bomb.'

vlaakte var. VLAKTE.

vlaat *n. obs.* [ad. Du. *vlakte*, prob. influenced by Eng. *flat*.] VLAKTE sense 1 a.

1835 A. STEEDMAN *Wanderings* I. 85, I enjoyed my ride before breakfast across the Quagger *vlaats*, whence I proceeded to the Sunday River. **1853** F.P. FLEMING *Kaffraria* 50 As each driver may select his own path, these are often very numerous, and sometimes, on the plains or 'Vlaats,' where the roads cross over them, perhaps ten or twelve roadways diverge to the right and left. *Ibid.* 73 The finches are very beautiful little tenants of the 'vlaats' being generally of a black or dark purple colour.

vlacke Vark var. VLAKVARK.

vlackte var. VLAKTE.

vlakpou see POU sense 2.

vlakte /ˈflaktə/ *n.* Formerly also **vlaakte**, **vlackte**. Pl. **-s**, formerly **vlakten(s)**. [Du.]

1.a. An open plain; an extent of flat country; VLAAT. Also *attrib.*

1786 G. FORSTER tr. *A. Sparrman's Voy. to Cape of G.H.* II. 222 The *vlaksteen-bok* was the name given at Agter Bruntjes-hoogte to animals (probably of the gazel kind) two feet in height, which used, in some sort, to herd together on the *vlaktens*, or plains. **1844** [see VLAKVARK]. **1852** C. BARTER *Dorp & Veld* 82 The plains, or *vlakten*, occupy more than two-thirds of the whole extent of the Sovereignty. **1911** *State* Dec. 643 (Pettman), There were berg tortoises and vlakte tortoises. **1934** *Cape Argus* 20 Jan. (Swart), In another case Constable du Preez followed the spoor of a donkey cart for many miles into the vlakte. **1947** H.C. BOSMAN *Mafeking Rd* (1969) 77 Everywhere, except for a number of lonely graves on hillside and vlakte, things were as they had been before Shepstone came. **1972** *Daily Dispatch* 22 July 4 The taxidermist has given the quagga herds of the South African vlaktes a certain fading, mouldy immortality. **1972** *Ibid.* 29 July 4 Two years later, Captain Cornwallis Harris .. crossed the same vlaktes, the prairies of South Africa. **1979** *Sunday Times* 15 July 16 He was remembering the way springbok on the Kalahari vlaktes grow restless before a coming storm, and slowly begin moving out of their territory into new and unknown fields. **1984** *Fair Lady* 30 May 176 The Free State *vlaktes* hang grittily on to their heart of the country status – although you don't actually live there unless you're a mealie magnate, they provide an inimitably earthy start to any curriculum vitae. **1985** *Ibid.* 3 Apr. 139 Taking of cuttings or collecting of seed in the wild or in public gardens is strictly prohibited and even in the vlaktes of Namaqualand you are not alone – there's a man from Flora and Fauna behind every kokerboom.

‖**b.** In the phr. ***ver verlate vlaktes*** /ˌfɛːr fərˌlɑːtə ˈflaktəs/ [Afk., *ver* far, *verlate* deserted], 'the far, deserted plains', a phrase from *Die Stem van Suid-Afrika* (see STEM). Usu. used ironically.

1988 H. PRENDINI in *Style* June 102 The cuisine of the Trekkers, with its roots in the ver verlate vlaktes and the kreun van ossewa. **1989** T. BOTHA in *Ibid.* June 108 A love story about the long open road, putting foot, fly-bitten caffies, *ver verlate vlaktes*.

2. *comb.* Esp. as an element in the names of animals: **vlaksteenbok**, **vlaktebok**, or **vlakte steenbok** *obs.* /-bɔk, -stɪənbɔk/ [see STEENBOK], BLEEKBOK; **vlakte haas** /-hɑːs/, also **vlakhaas**, [Afk. *haas* hare], the *Cape hare* (see CAPE sense 2 a), *Lepus capensis*; **vlakte vark**, see VLAKVARK; **vlakte veld** /-felt/ [see VELD], plains country.

1786 [vlaksteenbok: see sense 1]. **1900** [vlaktebok: see BLEEKBOK]. **1839** [**vlakte steenbok**: see BLEEKBOK]. **1844** J. BACKHOUSE *Narr. of Visit* 485 The Cape Hare or **Vlaakte Haas**, Lepus capensis is a smaller species inhabiting the open country. **1905** W.L. SCLATER in *Science in S. Afr.* 134 The Hares, known as the Vlackte haas (*Lepus capensis*), Rhebok haas (*L. saxatilis*) and Roode haas (*L. crassicandatus*) .. are spread all over the country. **1977** F.G. BUTLER *Karoo Morning* 131 Apart from the occasional loping light of a springhare's eye on the side of the road, or a vlakhaas frozen momentarily in the beam, we saw nothing. **1972** *Daily Dispatch* Jan., Grazing consists of a third berg veld and two thirds **vlakte veld**.

vlaktepou see POU sense 2.

vlakvark /'flakfark, -fɑːk/ *n.* Also (formerly) **fleck-vark, vlaaght-vark, vlack(t)e-vark, vlakte vark, vlakte verk, vleck vark.** Pl. unchanged, formerly **-varken.** [Afk., *vlak* (fr. *vlakte* plain, flat ground) + *vark* pig.] The warthog *Phacochoerus aethiopicus* of the Suidae.

1835 A. SMITH *Diary* (1940) II. 84 Botha shot yesterday a vlak vark. **1844** J. BACKHOUSE *Narr. of Visit* 213 The Vlackte Vark, *Pig of the Plains*, .. has a large head, a large fleshy protuberance behind each eye, and a warty excrescence on each side of the muzzle. **1860** A.W. DRAYSON *Sporting Scenes* 127 Towards evening, we had a brilliant affair with an old wild boar (the vleck vark), his wife and children. **1874** A. EDGAR in *Friend* 4 June, I saw today innumerable 'vlakvarken' scudding away with their tails locked right upward, like poles ... I believe they are very good eating. *a***1875** T. BAINES *Jrnl of Res.* (1964) II. 110 The animal .. breaking away over the plains, in the shape of a fine Vlakte Verk. Incited by the hope of pork for supper, I gave chase. **1879** R.J. ATCHERLEY *Trip to Boerland* 231 Here I shot a vlaaght-vark. **1881** P. GILLMORE *Land of Boer* 229 This animal was one of that species — which the Boers call fleck-vark. **1916** J.M. ORPEN *Reminisc.* (1964) 305 Presently I shot a 'vlak vark' (wart hog), and told my after-rider to stop beside it till the wagon came along. **1968** L.G. GREEN *Full Many Glorious Morning* 228 'The *vlakvark* or warthog,' Frikkie continued .. 'is the ugliest animal on earth, worse than a baboon or a rhinoceros. Black and naked, it has sharp tusks up to a foot long, whiskers and horrifying warts on its cheeks.' **1986** *Sunday Star* 8 June 5 It wasn't the vlakvark, nor the orkes, that had brought more than 2 000 to an open field on a smallholding in Potchefstroom last Friday. **1994** M. ROBERTS tr. *J.A. Wahlberg's Trav. Jrnls 1838–56* 63 Try in vain to get near 2 Vlakvark.

vlam /flam/ *n. slang.* Also **flam.** [Afk., lit. 'flame'.]

a. BLUE TRAIN sense 2.

1977 *Family Radio & TV* 23 Jan. 19 They brought out their own liquor: methylated spirits variously termed juice, mix or *vlam*. Of all the outies I met, only one, Willem, did not drink *vlam* ... One bottle might kill a man who isn't used to it. **1977** D. MULLER *Whitey* 70 He had another shot of vlam for good measure, then gave his mouth a good scouring with the toothbrush. *Ibid.* 108, I can see you don't remember nothing. It's the vlam. I can smell you've been drinking the blue-ocean, ou pellie. **1982** *Sunday Times* 16 May (Mag. Sect.) 1 A younger 'outie' joins the congregation, bearing a bottle of 'flam' (methylated spirits). All the 'outies' eagerly partake of the 'Blue Train' ... Once the 'flam' is speedily downed, eyes become even more red-rimmed.

b. *comb.* (objective) **vlam-drinker.**

1977 *Family Radio & TV* 23 Jan. 19 *Vlam*-drinkers invite blindness as well as the severe liver and intestinal damage that afflicts alcholics. **1977** D. MULLER *Whitey* 70 A vlam-drinker exudes the distinct odour of a veteran primus stove.

vlea var. VLEI.

vleck var. VLEK.

vleckvark var. VLAKVARK.

vleesch var. VLEIS.

vlei /fleɪ/ *n.* Also **flae(y), flay, flea, fleh, fley, vlea, vley.** Pl. **-s** /fleɪz/, or occas. ‖**vleie** /'fleɪə/. [S. Afr. Du. and Afk., reduced form of Du. *vallei* valley.]
1. A shallow natural pool of water; low-lying, marshy ground, covered with water during the rainy season; VALLEY sense a. Cf. PAN sense b. Also *attrib.*

1802 TRUTER & SOMERVILLE in G.M. Theal *Rec. of Cape Col.* (1899) IV. 369 We afterwards passed two other vleis or ponds about two hours distant one from another, and the water was in both of the same quality as in the first. **1824** *S. Afr. Jrnl* I. 73 The immense desert tracts .. are .. interspersed with stagnant pools, and 'vleys', or natural reservoirs of brakish water, which, however bad, satisfies the game. **1832** *Graham's Town Jrnl* 24 Aug. 136 During or soon after the fall of rain, *fleys* occur close to the road. **1848** H. WARD *Five Yrs in Kaffirland* I. 101 The Dragoon, on his arrival, must be taught frontier geography concerning kloofs, valleys, flays, short cuts, friendly or hostile kraals, &c. **1853** F.P. FLEMING *Kaffraria* 38 Vast plains, covered with grass and wild flowers, and here and there dotted with *'vleys'* (or large ponds of water). *a***1858** J. GOLDSWAIN *Chron.* I. (1946) 87 Neer the twentieth Mile Stone ware thear ware two large flaes of water. **1863** W.C. BALDWIN *Afr. Hunting* 226 We found the vley, where we fully expected water, dried up. **1871** J. MCKAY *Reminisc.* 11 Having come to a small pond or vley, the water in it was so thick that the men had to keep their teeth closed to act as strainers. **1886** G.A. FARINI *Through Kalahari Desert* 62 When at last we were off, the route lay along the edge of a *vley* or marsh. **1896** H.A. BRYDEN *Tales of S. Afr.* 13 He stayed for a week, and he was for ever talking of a wonderful *vlei* he had discovered. [*Note*] Pronounced *flay*. A vlei is the Dutch name for a shallow lake. **1906** H. RIDER HAGGARD *Benita* 67 Up slopes and down slopes, .. across half-dried vleis that in the wet season were ponds. **1912** W. WESTRUP *Land of To-Morrow* 155 There are a good many ducks in that big vlei below my place, and we ought to have some sport. **1926** P.W. LAIDLER *Tavern of Ocean* 6 At the foot of Lion's Head was a large vlei or marsh, where geese, ducks, and other wild water-fowl abounded ... The lion and the rhinoceros roamed around and in the vleis hippopotami sported. *c***1936** *S. & E. Afr. Yr Bk & Guide* 97 There are many shallow pans or vleis generally attributed to wind erosion, which receive drainage in times of heavy rainfall and are sometimes erroneously termed 'lakes'. **1948** V.M. FITZROY *Cabbages & Cream* 1 A lawn is bounded by a vineyard, and a row of Lombardy poplars, and beyond, the low-lying land we call the vlei which is green with barley in winter and in summer is a tapestry of vegetable rows. **1959** L.G. GREEN *These Wonders* 91 Along the Kalahari edge, especially in South West African territory, are so-called 'talking vleis', little ponds left after the rare rains. Some gurgle and rumble, the strength of the sound ranging from a whisper or a moan to a shriek. **1972** *S. Afr. Garden & Home* Oct. 34 The Malachite Kingfisher which is found throughout the streams and *vleie* of South Africa. **1982** *S. Afr. Panorama* Jan. 39 To regard a natural vlei not as an obstacle to be drained and reclaimed or as a convenient dumping site .. , but rather as a unique habitat for many forms of wildlife is a measure of civilisation. **1993** J. THOMAS in *House & Leisure* Nov. 50 A tranquil vlei, that had a strange colour and smelled funny, added to the suburb's rural character.

2. *comb.* **vleibos(sie)** /-bɔs(i)/ [Afk., *bos* bush (+ dim. suffix -IE)], any of several plants which grow om marshy ground or above underground water; cf. AARBOSSIE; **vlei grass**, any of several marsh grasses, esp. *Echinochloa holubii*; **vlei ground** or **vlei land**, marshland; *valley-ground*, see VALLEY sense b; **vlei lily**, any of several plants of the Amaryllidaceae, including *Galtonia princeps, Crinum spp.*, and *Nerine frithii*; **vlei loerie** /- luːri, -lʊəri/ [Afk., *loerie* see LOERIE], any of several species of coucal of the Cuculidae, esp. *Centropus superciliosus*; see also RAINBIRD sense 1; **vlei muis** *obs.* [Afk., *muis* mouse], the speckled dark brown mouse *Otomys irroratus*, favouring marshy localities; **vlei tea**, also **vleitee** /-tɪə/ [Afk. *vleitee*], the plant *Cyclopia maculata*; its leaves, infused as a tea; see also HONEY TEA; **vleiveld** /-felt/ [Afk., *veld* terrain], *vlei ground* (see above).

1963 S.H. SKAIFE *Naturalist Remembers* 108 A swampy patch covered with a dense growth of the plants farmers call **vleibossies** and which are known to science as *Berzelia lanuginosa*. As they only grow where there is permanent water in the soil these plants are a reliable indication of an underground spring. **1966** C.A. SMITH *Common Names* 485 *Vleibos, cliffortia strobilifera* .. , *Hertia pallens* .. , *Senecio lanceus*. **1913** C. PETTMAN *Africanderisms* 160 *Eastern Province* **Vlei Grass**, *Eragrostis lehmanniana, Nees.* **1968** *Farmer's Weekly* 3 Jan. 9 Approximately 120 morgen vleigrass is cut annually to provide hay for 400/500 cattle. **1972** *Ibid.* 21 Apr. 77 Excellent red and vlei grass grazing with carrying capacity 1 500–2 000 sheep and 200 head of cattle. **1981** *Grocott's Mail* 11 Dec. 2 A grass indigenous to South Africa, red vleigrass, has outyielded a number of comparable summer-growing species in trials in northern New Zealand. [**1812** **vlei ground**: see VALLEY sense b.] **1907** J.P. FITZPATRICK *Jock of Bushveld* (1909) 319 Only a little way off we came into dry vlei ground where there were few trees and the grass stood about waist high. **1937** *Handbk for Farmers* (Dept of Agric. & Forestry) 380 In vlei ground and also frequently as a pioneer grass in both sour and sweet veld, 'thatch grass' .. is often dominant. **1948** V.M. FITZROY *Cabbages & Cream* 153 They say he's rented that bit of **vlei land** down the road, that we never see anyone working on. Who is he? **1940** J.C.F. HOPKINS et al. *Common Veld Flowers* 40 The **Vlei Lily** can be arranged with considerable decorative effect in bowls or low vases. **1953** J. HOYLE *Some Flowers* 3 Vlei Lily ... This handsome lily-like plant lives in damp places .. and has an enormous bulb which is easily transplanted. **1984** *Daily Dispatch* 30 Aug. 22 Vlei lilies 'wetting their toes in the river's ripples'. **1856** R.E.E. WILMOT *Diary* (1984) 134 The curious tribe of *coucals* here called **vley lory** is not common ... They are all first cousins of the cuckoos. **1864** T. BAINES *Explor. in S-W. Afr.* 391, I shot one of the loosely-feathered birds called in the colony *Vlei Lories*, or Reed Hawks. **1908** 'AL FRESCO' in *E. London Dispatch* 4 Dec. 4 The 'vlei-lourie' perhaps better known hereabouts as the 'rain-bird,' the natives regarding it as a weather prophet. **1923** HAAGNER & IVY *Sketches* 59 The Vlei-Louries — as the name implies — are fond of hunting the bush along rivers and vleis. **1937** M. ALSTON *Wanderings* 105 Another bird .. that we heard continually was the vlei lourie or 'rain cuckoo'. This interesting and odd-looking bird loves long reeds. [**1953** J.M. WINTERBOTTOM *Common Birds of S.-E.* 11 The Vlei Loerie, as is called in Afrikaans, inhabits reed-beds and riverside scrub.] **1973** *Weekend Post* 28 Apr. 4 The vlei louries, the bokmakieries, the tit babblers and the Diederick cuckoo. **1901** W.L. SCLATER *Mammals of S. Afr.* III. 26 Vley otomys: otomys irroratus. Vernacular Names: **Vley Muis** of the Colonists. **1913** C. PETTMAN *Africanderisms* 537 *Vlei muis*, .. *Otomys irroratus*; so named because its habitat is generally in marshy localities near water. *Ibid.* 538 **Vlei thee**, .. The name given in the Riversdale District to *Cyclopia tenuifolia, Lehm.* **1979** HEARD & FAULL *Our Best Trad. Recipes* 19 Coffee and tea being imported luxuries we are not surprised to read of the many substitutes for coffee or of the popularity of *vlei* and bush tea. **1994** *Weekend Post* 26 Nov. 11 *Cyclopia subternata*, also called bush tea or *vleitee*. **1968** *Farmer's Weekly* 3 Jan. 9 This farm is well known for its high carrying capacity and **vleiveldt**.

‖**vleis** /fleɪs/ *n.* Formerly also **vleesch.** [Afk.] Meat. See also BRAAIVLEIS sense 2, *pap en* (or *and*) *vleis* (PAP sense 2).

[**1899** G.H. RUSSELL *Under Sjambok* 160 'You have the vleis (meat) van zee winkel last night steal,' he said.] **1920** F.C. CORNELL *Glamour of Prospecting* 220 As Klaas Fredericks had taken every goat and sheep with him, we could no longer give our labourers the vleesch they insisted upon, except by going far afield and bringing back an occasional buck. **1973** *Sunday Times* 15 Apr. 21 He flashed that infectious grin. 'The food was quite different from my daily diet of vleis and mieliepap.' **1990** *Style* June 113 Obviously, on the stress seminars it's low cholesterol, healthier stuff ... But, on your rock 'n roll weekends it's all *vleis* and *boerewors*.

vleisbalie see BALIE sense b.

‖**vleisbraai** /ˈfleɪsbraɪ/ *n.* Pl. **-s**, **-braaie** /-braɪə/. [Afk., lit. 'meat-grilling', *vleis* meat + *braai* to grill.] BRAAI *n.* sense 1 a. Also *attrib.*

1950 D. REED *Somewhere S. of Suez*, I went to a Vleisbraai, or barbecue, a picnic beneath the moon where chops and sausages were grilled over an open wood fire. **1970** D. VAN RENSBURG *Informant, Manaba Beach (KwaZulu-Natal)* Let's have a 'vleisbraai' tonight ... (Barbecue). Not 'braaivleis'. You eat braaivleis as a product of a 'Vleisbraai'. **1971** *Het Suid-Western* 13 May, There will be community singing and a vleisbraai until 7 p.m. **1973** M.A. COOK *Cape Kitchen* 108 They were in fact, exactly like the embers used for a vleisbraai at the present day. **1973** *E. Prov. Herald* 7 Feb., The Oudtshoorn Golf Club has invited the Free State vleisbraai champions Vrede as well as the Boland champions Montagu to compete on March 24 in a Vleisbraai competition against local braaiers. **1974** *S. Afr. Panorama* Aug. 21 The 'vleisbraai' (barbecue), a traditional and popular part of the South African way of life. **1977** [see PUTU PAP]. **1989** *Frontline* Dec. 11 It has been a month of political vleisbraaie, melktert, and koeksisters after meetings.

vlek /flek, flɛk/ *v. trans.* Also **vleck**. [Afk., fr. Du. *vlekken* to cleave, split open.] To gut, clean, or open out (a fish or a carcase); to cut (meat) into strips; FLECK.

1838 J.E. ALEXANDER *Exped. into Int.* II. 6 Many of the people were employed during the remainder of the 30th of March in *vleking* or cutting the meat of the game we had killed into thin flaps or steaks, and hanging it on the bushes to dry. *Ibid.* 127 All night a party remained by it to cut and 'vlek' the meat, for carrying off a quantity of it; and the young rhinoceros alarmed them by coming close to them in the night to look for its mother. [**1976** *Sunday Times* 2 May 6 Next day there's a strong smell of fish frying and in the window a great gevlekte snoek.] **1983** *Sunday Times* 6 Mar. (Mag. Sect.) 16 The snoek, vlecked, which is the fishmonger's job, is placed in a baking pan, dotted with butter. **1986** C. KIRSTEIN *Best S. Afr. Braai Recipes* 11 Some fish, particularly snoek, yellowtail, haarders and galjoen, can be 'vlekked' (cut open so that the flesh, still attached to the back bone, opens out flat). **1989** I. PAARMAN in *Femina* Feb. 99 Medium-large prawns, vlekked open, deveined and lightly salted with sea salt. **1991** *E. Prov. Herald* 15 Nov. 21 We either use them [*sc.* 'gorries'] whole or 'vlek' them open and remove the backbone.

Hence **vlekking** *vbl n.*, *flecking* (see FLECK).

1986 C. KIRSTEIN *Best S. Afr. Braai Recipes* 11 'Vlekking' and salting.

vley var. VLEI.

vlier /ˈflɪə(r)/ *n.* [Afk., ad. Du. *vlier* elder tree.] The evergreen tree *Nuxia floribunda* of the Loganiaceae, bearing sprays of tiny cream-coloured, sweetly-scented flowers.

In F. von Breitenbach's *Nat. List of Indigenous Trees* (1987), the name 'forest elder' is used for this species.

1887 J.C. BROWN *Crown Forests* 237 Timber Valued Standing. Per cubic foot £ s. d. Red Pear, ... 0 0 3 ... Vlier, ... 0 0 1. **1907** T.R. SIM *Forests & Forest Flora* 6 Black stinkwood (Ocotea bullata) and Vlier (Nuxia floribunda) are well known examples of Rus, as also the Palmiet (Prionum palmita). **1913** C. PETTMAN *Africanderisms* 538 *Vlier*, .. *Nuxia floribunda*, a handsome tree with small, white, scented flowers; it is known as the Wild peach in the neighbourhood of St. Johns. **1951** N.L. KING *Tree-Planting* 69 *Lachnopylis (Nuxia) floribunda (Vlier)*, A large, evergreen tree which bears masses of scented, white flowers towards the end of winter or spring. **1961** PALMER & PITMAN *Trees of S. Afr.* 295 The vlier, as *Nuxia Floribunda* is commonly called, is a handsome evergreen tree, and a lovely sight in winter when it is covered in bunches of tiny, cream-coloured sweet-scented flowers which resemble those of the true elder. It is found in the Midland forests and is fairly common in the forests of the Eastern Province and Natal. **1976** *Cape Times* 24 Sept. (Weekend Mag.) 9 There is a second yellowwood about 20 ft. hight, and a *Nuxia floribundia* (vlier), about 20 ft. high which, when I was there, was smothered in its off-white froth of flowers. **1991** H. HUTCHINGS in *Weekend Post* 23 Feb. (Leisure) 7 Another good flowering tree .. is *Nuxia floribunda* (vlier) ... It has a fairly straight trunk and spreading branches.

vlijtje var. FLUITJIE.

VOC /viː əʊ ˈsiː/ *n. hist.* Also **V.O.C.** [Initial letters of Du. *Vereenigde Oost-Indische Compagnie* 'United East India Company'.]

1. The monogram of the Dutch East India Company (used in the past on silver, porcelain, coins, etc.). Often *attrib.*

[**1786** G. FORSTER tr. *A. Sparrman's Voy. to Cape of G.H.* I. 222 This place, which I have marked in the map with the letters OVC interwoven with each other, or the Dutch company's mark, is the residence of a *landrost*.] **1910** D. FAIRBRIDGE *That Which Hath Been* (1913) 35 The arms of Amsterdam, Delft, Middelburg, Hoorn and Enkhuysen over the entrance flanked by the entwined V.O.C. of the Dutch East India Company and surmounted by the lion of Holland. **1926** P.W. LAIDLER *Tavern of Ocean* 50 Over the gateway, sculptured in stone, are the arms of Amsterdam, Delft, Zeeland, Hoorn, and Enckhuisen, the combination of whose chambers formed the Dutch East India Company, and whose monogram, the intertwined V.O.C. (for Vereenigde Oost-Indische Compagnie), is to be seen above the capitals. **1945** N. DEVITT *People & Places* 23 In the case of the Dutch East India Company the famous V.O.C. monogram was always in evidence. **1949** L.G. GREEN *In Land of Afternoon* 185 Oak chests and kists bearing the VOC monogram. **1971** BARAITSER & OBHOLZER *Cape Country Furn.* 267 The monogram V.O.C. denoted the possessions of the 'Vereenigde Oost Indiese Compagnie'. **1973** *S. Afr. Panorama* Oct. 18 A resolution by the Here XVII, dated February 28, 1603, stipulating that the VOC mark had to be used on all articles belonging to the Dutch East India Company. **1975** *Wine: Guide for Young People* (K.W.V.) 69 The so-called V.O.C. (.. Dutch East India Company) glassware. **1981** P. DANE *Great Houses of Constantia* 26 Hand-hewn beams in heavy teak, stamped with the letters, 'V.O.C.' **1988** D. HUGHES et al. *Complete Bk of S. Afr. Wine* 18 The VOC monogram is found as the central decoration to much of the Company's glass and chinaware.

2. *hist.* COMPANY. Also *attrib.*

1953 DU PLESSIS & LÜCKHOFF *Malay Quarter* 19 Since the liquidation of the old V.O.C. the Cape Malays were denied cultural or intellectual links with Indonesia. **1965** M.G. ATMORE *Cape Furn.* 54 From 1652 to 1657 the small colony was entirely composed of company servants busy with establishing rudimentary buildings and cultivating vegetables and other provisions for the V.O.C. ships. **1971** *S. Afr. Panorama* May 9 Commander Jan van Riebeeck, a ship's doctor employed by the V.O.C. (Dutch East India Company) ... The Company felt that the establishment of an independent farming community close to the settlement would save the V.O.C. a considerable sum of money. **1977** R.J. HAINES in R.J. Bouch *Infantry in S. Afr. 1652–1976* 1 The garrison was kept well below its necessary strength as the VOC hoped that the burger militia could substitute for regular troops. **1984** R.C. FISHER in Martin & Friedlaender *Hist. of Surveying & Land Tenure* I. 63 He had to be a trusted and responsible servant of the VOC.

voëlvry /ˈfʊəlfreɪ/ *adj. hist.* Formerly also **vogel vry**. [Afk., fr. Du. *vogelvrij* outlawed, *vogel* bird + *vrij* free, not subject to restrictions.] Of an outlaw: fair game, legally liable to be shot on sight.

*a*1875 T. BAINES *Jrnl of Res.* (1964) II. 157 Both McCabe and myself were reported to be 'Vogel Vry' — as free as a bird, i.e. for any one to shoot at. **1908** J.M. ORPEN *Reminisc.* (1964) 54 One Michiel Horn, somewhere Kroonstad way, considering him 'vogel vry,' i.e., bird-free, or outlawed, lay in wait for him and shot him dead. **1924** G. BAUMANN in Baumann & Bright *Lost Republic* (1940) 121 E. had been declared an outlaw — 'Vogelvry' ('as free as a bird', meaning that anyone could shoot him at sight as if he were a bird). **1972** J.A. NEL *Informant, Grahamstown* During the Boer War he was declared voël-vry by proclamation, which means he had to be shot on sight. **1986** H. VISSER in *Frontline* Dec. 34 My great grandfather was declared voëlvry by the British — to be shot on sight.

voerchitz /ˈfuːrsəts, -ʃəts/ *n. Obs.* exc. *hist.* Also **forcet(s)**, **voerces**, **voerchits**, **voerschitz**, **voersits**, **voorchits**, **vo(o)rchitz**, **vorcet(s)**, **vorsect**. [ad. S. Afr. Du. *voersis, voersies*, fr. Du. *voeren* to line + *sits* chintz.] **a.** *noncount.* A printed cotton fabric imported during the 19th century and sold usu. in 'gown-pieces' (dress-lengths). **b.** Pl. unchanged, or **voerchitzen**. A length of this fabric. Also *attrib.* See also *German print* (GERMAN).

1831 *S. Afr. Almanac & Dir.*, Bleached and unbleached linen, India and other Voorchits, Muslins, Cambric. **1832** *Graham's Town Jrnl* 27 June 104 For Sale ... English and India Voerchitz. **1833** *Graham's Town Jrnl* 7 Mar. 1 Just Received, and for Sale at very reduced prices ... Fine and coarse Voerchits. **1841** *Cape of G.H. Almanac & Annual Register* 387 Who among us does not remember the frontier boer of 1820, barefoot and clad in sheepskins, his wife covered (not dressed) in voerchitz. **1846** in A.G. Bain *Jrnls* (1949) 201 When drest up in my voersits pak, What hearts will then be undone, Should I but show my face or back, Among the beaux of London. **1851** J.F. CHURCHILL Diary. (Killie Campbell Africana Library MS37) 13–17 May, Business pretty brisk at Maritzburg with the Overberg Traders ... Today 17th cleared out of Blue Moleskins, White Calico & Voerchits. **1863** *Queenstown Free Press* 24 Feb., They charge 7s 6d for a voerchitz. [*a*1868 J. AYLIFF *Jrnl of 'Harry Hastings'* (1963) 82 For this sum, Mr. Thomas took half hide pole leathers Rds. 13. a piece of gown stuff called by the Dutch 'fusser' for Rds. 8.] **1868** J. CHAPMAN *Trav.* I. 10 Orleans and alpaca cloths, voerschits, and other articles of clothing .. generally meet the requirements of the market. **1896** M.A. CAREY-HOBSON *At Home in Tvl* 335 He .. had been doing a good business, both with Boers and English farmers — taking their farm produce .. and supplying in return coffee, tea, sugar, and calicoes, moleskin for the men's wear, and baftas and voerchitz (prints) for the women. **1920** K.M. JEFFREYS tr. *Memorandum of Commissary J.A. de Mist* 244 Voerchitzen, ginghams, and all sorts of coarse calicoes, bleached and unbleached. **1956** V.M. FITZROY *Dark Bright Land* 63 The women in voerchitz and coarse cotton stuffs from India.

voerdommde var. VERDOMDE.

voerlooper var. VOORLOPER.

voersla(a)g var. VOORSLAG.

Voertrekker var. VOORTREKKER.

voertsak, **voertsek**, **voessek** varr. VOETSAK.

voetebalie see BALIE sense b.

voetganger /ˈfʊtxaŋə(r)/ *n.* [S. Afr. Du., fr. Du. *voet* foot + *ganger* one who goes.]

1. A hopper, or locust in its immature wingless stage; FOOTGANGER sense 1; VOETLOPER sense 1. Also *attrib.* See also ROOIBAADJIE sense 2, SPRINKAAN sense 1.

1824 *S. Afr. Jrnl* I. 70 The flying locusts are .. less dreaded in this colony, than those which have not quite reached that stage of maturity, and are .. vulgarly called 'voetgangers'. **1834** T. PRINGLE *Afr. Sketches* 354 The flying locusts .. are less dreaded by the farmers than the larvae, devoid of wings — vulgarly called by the colonists *voetgangers* (foot-goers). **1882**

The Jrnl 27 Sept. 3 Young locusts in the wingless stage locally known as 'voetgangers'. [**1896** R. WALLACE *Farming Indust. of Cape Col.* 490 These immature wingless forms, called 'voetgangers', or pedestrians, by the Boers, .. frequently hop in the direction of the north whence the parent swarms came, and in vast numbers cross rivers and overcome all ordinary obstacles met with in their course.] **1901** *Grocott's Penny Mail* 9 Jan. 3 Notwithstanding the many remedies which are said to have been discovered .. for the extermination of voetgangers, the locust is not yet extinct. **1913** J.J. DOKE *Secret City* 119 The locusts, the voetgangers, came in their countless millions, tinging the whole country with their ruddy hue, and making the Karroo a hopping, hopeless desolation. **1924** L.H. BRINKMAN *Glory of Backveld* 10 From the time of hatching out it takes several weeks before a young locust develops wings, and while in that state its only mode of locomotion is short, quick hops. It is then known by the name of 'voetganger' (tramp). **1936** R. CAMPBELL *Mithraic Emblems* 79 See there, and there it gnaws, the Rust-Voetganger of the coming swarm. **1966** E. PALMER *Plains of Camdeboo* 244 All the world turns out to devour the voetgangers ... When the first voetganger column appeared, our domestic fowls went berserk. **1981** *Daily Dispatch* 4 Nov. 3 Motorists arriving here report several swarms of voetganger locusts between Graaff-Reinet and Pearston. **1983** *Govt Gaz.* Vol.214 No.8661, 8 A user of land shall forthwith notify the nearest available magistrate, justice of the peace, police officer or officer of the department if flying locusts or voetgangers have appeared on the land concerned, [etc.].

‖**2.** A person who goes on foot.

a. *hist.* An infantryman; FOOTGANGER sense 2.

1900 P.J. DU TOIT *Diary* (1974) 10 A man is just relating how they looted cattle a few days ago. He says 'a battery of 200 voetgangers' attacked them. **1902** C.R. DE WET *Three Yrs War* 410 They knew that not only would they have to be *voetgangers*, but also that if they were captured they would be very severely punished by the English.

b. *rare.* A pedestrian; one who walks; VOETLOPER sense 2.

1911 P. GIBBON *Margaret Harding* 133 'If a man had been meant for a *voetganger*' (a walker) — he watched the effect of the Dutch word on the Boer — 'he'd have been made with four feet.' **1981** *E. Prov. Herald* 4 May 12, I would want to license all voetgangers (those who go on foot), commonly known as pedestrians. It must be made clear at the outset that I am one of the most active voetgangers, preferring to walk rather than to drive a car.

c. *rare.* A tramp.

1928 L.P. GREENE *Adventure Omnibus* 640 We would have to go on foot, become voet gangers, or stay at one place and grow fat. 'I had not thought of that, Bass', he admitted. 'We are no voet gangers, we two.' **1949** L.G. GREEN *In Land of Afternoon* 144 In some ways the voetganger of a century ago fared better than the modern tramp who rides in limousines and covers a thousand miles a week.

‖**voetjie-voetjie** /ˌfuɪkiˈfuɪki, ˌfʊtsi-ˈfʊtsi, ˌfʊtʃi ˈfʊtʃi/ *n. colloq.* Also **foochie-foochie**, **footchy footchy**, **voetsie-voetsie**. [Afk., reduplication of *voet* foot + -IE.] A clandestine (usu. amorous) mutual touching of feet, usually under a table; FOOTSIE-FOOTSIE. Also *fig.*, flirtation.

See note on reduplication in *S. Afr. Eng.* at NOW-NOW.

1916 S. BLACK in S. Gray *Three Plays* (1984) 211 We've a fine little game in the Cape Colony that we call footchy footchy. **1930** N. STEVENSON *Farmers of Lekkerbat* 94 The farmers and their guests did not play cards nor did they dance but they amused themselves in various hilarious ways. The dressmaker from the village recited, Marina Loubser sang, and they played 'Blind Man's Bluff,' *'Voetjie-Voetjie'*, [etc.]. **1971** *Rand Daily Mail* 30 Mar. 2 A boy and a girl had each kicked off a shoe and the girl's foot was resting on the boy's ... What is illustrated is nothing more that what is commonly known in this country as voetjie-voetjie. **1971** *Het Suid-Western* 1 Apr., A boy and a girl had each kicked off one shoe and they were playing the delightful South African dinner-table game known as 'voetjie-voetjie'. **1975** *Darling* 9 Apr. 95 Playing footchie-footchie in a mud bath beats making mud-pies any day. **1978** G.B. DICKASON *Cornish Immigrants to S. Afr.* 76 *To fooch*, a pretence at doing a job, playful contact, maybe the origin of footchy-footchy (in South Africa today voetsie-voetsie). **1989** C. DERBY-LEWIS in *Frontline* Aug. 13 CP count will be much higher than 75 if government's voetjie-voetjie with ANC increases.

‖**voetloper** *n. obs.* Also **voet-looper**. [Afk., *voet* foot + *loper* walker, messenger.]

1. VOETGANGER sense 1.

1900 A.H. KEANE *Boer States* 59 (Swart), Such young broods the Boers expressively call footlopers (footrunners) and those on the wing sprinkaans. **1934** C.P. SWART Supplement to Pettman. 185 *Voetlopers*, .. Wingless locusts, more commonly known as voetgangers or hoppers.

2. *rare.* VOETGANGER sense 2 b.

1902 J.H.M. ABBOTT *Tommy Cornstalk* 10 As the Boer despises a *'Voet-looper'* so is Tommy Cornstalk ashamed to be seen walking.

voetsak /ˈfʊtsæk/ *n.* Also **feusack**, etc. [fr. next.]

1. An utterance of the word 'voetsak'. Also *fig.*

1881 P. GILLMORE *Land of Boer* 106 Imp, with his confounded feusack and a sjambok, hustled the dogs out from under the wagon. **1973** *E. Prov. Herald* 27 Mar. 17 He .. spat out some delectable Arabic swear words, including a 'voetsak' he'd collected from his nice Johannesburg-Cape Town mates. **1986** *Drum* Aug. 155, I pay a silent requiem and give a mighty voertsek to a document known in the Pretoria files as NIN 1890222. **1990** J. NAIDOO *Coolie Location* 153, I mean she's really a civilized chick. You know, .. no blerrys, no voetseks, [etc.].

2. *colloq.* Esp. in the phrr. ***the year voetsak*** and ***19-voetsak***: very long ago, 'the year dot'; an indeterminate time.

1971 *Informant, Grahamstown* 'Have you ever been to Intervarsity?' 'Yes of course, but that was in the year voetsak.' **1973** *Informant, Grahamstown* The clothes! We're going back to the nineteen voetsaks! **1973** *Daily Dispatch* 16 June 9 At least twice a week I get phone calls asking who won the world racing championship in 19-voetsak. **1987** *E. Prov. Herald* 5 Nov. 12 Just imagine. The year is nineteen-voetsek or, perhaps, two-thousand-and-voetsek. **1991** J. RIST *Informant, Grahamstown* We're also strong Methodists — we go back to voetsak, you know.

voetsak /ˈfʊtsæk, ˈfu(r)tsek/ *v. colloq.* Also **feusach**, **feusack**, **foetsek**, **voertsak**, **voe(r)tsek**, **voessek**, **voetsac(k)**, **voetzaak**, **voetzac**, **voortsec**, **voortzuk**, **vootsac**, **vootsek**, **vortsak**. [S. Afr. Du. *voe(r)tsek*, contraction of Du. *voort seg ik*, be off I say.]

In all senses also FOOTSACK.

1. *intrans.* An interjection or imperative.

a. Go away, 'scram', 'get lost': a rough command, as spoken to a dog or (with either insulting or humorous intent) to a person. Cf. HAMBA sense 1, LOOP sense 1 b.

1837 J.E. ALEXANDER *Narr. of Voy.* I. 351 Dogs attacked us as we approached; but on the cry of *'voortzuk!'* from the master, followed by a stone, they left us. **1899** *Natal Agric. Jrnl* 31 Mar. 4 'Voetsek,' according to Cape, or 'footsack,' according to Natal newspaper spelling, is an expression that soon attracts the attention of new-comers. It means 'forth say I,' an abbreviation of 'voort zeg ik,' and is exclusively applied to dogs. **1908** D. BLACKBURN *Leaven* 258 'Can't understand a damn word I say; but I'll learn him. Voetzak, you —!' He gave the boy a helpful kick down the embankment. **1911** L. COHEN *Reminisc. of Kimberley* 380 When I shouted I wanted to buy something, he cautiously opened the top part wide enough to show his carrot nose, and cried, 'Voetsak!' which is a highly expressive Dutch word meaning 'slip off'. [**1916** L.D. FLEMMING *Fool on Veld* (1933) 5 It is a well known fact that all the dogs in the Free State are called 'Voetzak' and that when you call them they run away.] **1930** N. STEVENSON *Farmers of Lekkerbat* 16 If he saw that one of them was resting he would shout angrily: 'Why are you idling there, you rascals?' Or if it was a woman he would cry 'Voertsek!' **1956** A. SAMPSON *Drum* 159 The English just use long words and big talk, isn't it? Segregation — ah, democracy — ah, civilised men ... The Dutchmen just say 'you blerry Kaffir, you voetsak!' They both mean the same; but with the Dutchmen you know where you are, man! Give me the Nats!' **1963** A. FUGARD *Blood Knot* (1968) 172 Zach: Voertsek. Morris: Yes, Voertsek off. We don't want you. Zach: Bugger off. **1976** M. THOLO in C. Hermer *Diary of Maria Tholo* (1980) 110 You could hear that the maid was getting impatient with them. 'Eat your breakfast or voetsak out of here.' **1988** *Now Everyone Is Afraid* (Catholic Inst. for Internat. Rel.) 85 The police took them to fetch the body of the dead man and then dropped them at a taxi rank and said: *O.K., voetsek, fuck off, go home.* [**1993** *Cape Times* 25 Feb. 1 One of the men pulled a pistol from his belt saying 'jy voetsek' before shooting.]

b. An exclamation or expletive, expressing rejection or disgust.

1949 O. WALKER *Wanton City* 74 What's White civilization in South Africa? .. Social inhibitions imported from Europe? Broken accents from the world's ghettos? Fooie! Voetsak. **1974** *Drum* 22 Apr. 25 Hamba. Voetsek. Haikona. Blast it all. **1982** N.S. NDEBELE in *Staffrider* Vol.1 No.2, 'Voetsek!' the woman cursed suddenly. **1990** A. WAGENAAR in *Personality* 21 May 23 You thought South African prices were going through the roof. R30 000 for a Toyota. *Eina!* R150 000 for a Merc. *Voertsek!*

2. Indicative or infinitive.

a. *trans. rare.* To chase (something) away.

1897 E. GLANVILLE *Tales from Veld* 227, I jes' drop in t' ask you *voetsack* all the dogs outer the place 'fore I bring him in.

b. *intrans.* To go, clear out, 'push off', esp. on another's orders.

1920 [see HAMBA sense 1]. **1951** H.C. BOSMAN in L. Abrahams *Jurie Steyn's Post Office* (1971) 155 Although I didn't say anything to him, .. when I was going out of the store, he called out to me, all the same, to voetsek. **1978** *Daily Dispatch* 17 July 6 But if you are wellwrapped in your fur or leather jacket and munching a hamburger or chicken pie while carrying the banner I shall tell you to Voertsek. **1986** R. CONSTANTINE in *New Coin Poetry* Dec. 16 No-one else approached her, so no-one made them voetsek. **1990** G. SLOVO *Ties of Blood* 255 Instead of telling the government to voetsak they roll over and concede without a fight.

voetsie-voetsie var. VOETJIE-VOETJIE.

voetstoets var. VOETSTOOTS.

voetstofie /ˈfʊtstʊəfi/ *n. hist.* [Afk., *voet* foot + *stoof* stove, warmer + dim. suffix -IE.] KOMFOOR sense b. Also (without dim. suffix) **voetstoof**.

1934 *Cape Argus* 21 June (Swart), Another method of heating a room in those days if a 'voetstoof' were not available, was to set a large pan containing coals on the floor. **1971** BARAITSER & OBHOLZER *Cape Country Furn.* 265 The hot air from the coals rose through the perforated top of the box. These holes were sometimes plain, but more often they were heart or flower-shaped, creating a delightful pattern on the top of the Voetstofie. **1987** J. KENCH *Cottage Furn.* 71 That favoured Dutch item, the voetstofie.

voetstoots /ˈfʊtstʊəts, -stuːts, -stʊts/ *adv.* and *adj. Law.* Also **voetstoets**, **voetstoot**. [Afk., formed on Du. *met de voet te stoten* to push with the foot.]

A. *adv.* Of sale and purchase: as it stands, without warranty; at the buyer's risk. Also *fig.*

1934 C.P. SWART Supplement to Pettman. 186 *Voetstoots*, .. A Roman Dutch legal term signifying the sale of property without warranty. **1945** WILLE & MILLIN *Mercantile Law of S. Afr.* 163 Where a thing is sold *voetstoots* the buyer must take it with all defects and vices. The seller warrants nothing. **1961** C.I. BELCHER

Norman's Law of Sale & Purchase in S. Afr. 272 Where the article is sold *Voet Stoets* the seller on his side cannot complain if the article turns out better than either party thought. **1979** *Sunday Times* 29 Apr. (Mag. Sect.) 3 I'm not saying that I'm 100 percent for school uniforms voetstoets. **1982** *Ibid.* 28 Feb. (Mag. Sect.) 1 At the end of the month, the Rhoodies move 'voetstoets' to America where Eschel, Jnr, is poised to enter Princeton University. **1990** M. FASSLER in *Fair Lady* 21 Nov. 81 Committed bachelors that we once were, we've taken each other voetstoots. **1993** *Weekend Post* 6 Nov. (Business Post) 7 The property is sold 'voetstoots' as it stands, subject to all servitudes and conditions specified in the title deed. **1993** L. AUPIAIS in *Femina* Aug. 184 A home .. sort of adopted us. It came voetstoots with an albino squirrel and a nine-year-old black mongrel named Snoopy.

B. *adj.* Unguaranteed, 'as is'.

1971 *Argus* 5 June (Property) 2 A so-called 'Voetstoets' clause does not protect the seller against fraud or the non-disclosure of a material defect. **1986** C. KAGAN in *Style* Apr. 146 Auctions are voetstoots deals, and the owner has no recourse in the event of serious latent defects. **1987** *Style* Mar. 44 The days of 'voetstoots' bloodstock buying are over. **1991** J. WALKER in *Sunday Times* 14 July (Business) 2 USKO firmed this week after the R50-million voetstoots sale of its steel division to Iscor.

voetzaak, -zac varr. VOETSAK.

vogel vry var. VOËLVRY.

volk /fɔlk/ *n.* Also with initial capital. Pl. unchanged, or **volke** /-fɔlkə/. [Du. and Afk.]

1.a. As *pl.*: People; members of a particular group, or citizens of a country.

1827 T. PHILIPPS *Scenes & Occurrences* 20 They style themselves Africaners, and distinguish all those who come from even any part of Europe as Vaderland Volk, or Fatherland people. **1880** HUDSON in Lady Bellairs *Tvl at War* (1885) 424 Mr Paul Kruger appeared nervous, and very anxious that I should keep out of sight of the 'volk' (people) as much as possible. **1987** *Frontline* Feb. 5 The English-speaking Volk should tell the Government what it can do with its attempts to foster 'white unity'.

b. Pl. **-e**. A people, a nation.

[**1731** G. MEDLEY tr. *P. Kolb's Present State of Cape of G.H.* I. 26 The people far up the country, on the appearance of strangers are us'd to say in Dutch, wat volk i.e. What People.] **1928** [see COLONY]. **1939** R.F.A. HOERNLÉ *S. Afr. Native Policy* 72 The Afrikaners (or Cape Dutch, or Boers), a new people, or *volk*, which has grown out of the fusion of Dutch, French, German, English and Scotch elements. **1958** S. CLOETE *Mask* 213 'If there are such [men],' he spat in the dust, 'we are no longer a people, a volk, a race designated by God to bring civilisation to this savage land'. **1971** *Sunday Times* 1 Apr. 15 There we were — the United Party was out to destroy the 'identity' of every volk in South Africa. **1977** *E. Prov. Herald* 6 Feb. 10 [Louis] Botha saw that even if peace were made the Afrikaner would continue to exist as a volk and that future planning would be possible. **1986** E. TERRE'BLANCHE in *Style* July 49 You cannot have a right to land unless you belong to a volk. The English-speakers are not a volk. **1987** [see sense 3 b]. **1988** R. THORNTON in Boonzaier & Sharp *S. Afr. Keywords* 18 The assertion of cultural differences distinctive of different 'peoples' or *volke*. **1990** *Daily Dispatch* 19 July 15 Within partitionist groups there was agreement that no volk could maintain its own values without a geographic power base. **1992** *Financial Mail* 13 Mar. 25 Remember when the Nats had a policy to give each *volk* its own territory? **1993** *Sunday Times* 23 May 23 They celebrate .. the Voortrekker leaders as their heroes. But this .. builds only a parochial volk, not a nation.

2. As *pl.*: Among Afrikaans-speakers: 'coloured' or black farm-workers; rural coloured people; *folks*, see FOLK sense a. Cf. VOLKIES.

1871 J. MACKENZIE *Ten Yrs* (1971) 65 'Volk' is used by them [*sc.* Dutch colonists] of all coloured people, and never of white persons ... The Griquas sought a place where they might again become 'menschen' and cease to be 'volk' and 'schepsels' (creatures). **1878** A. AYLWARD *Tvl of Today* 201 It is rare indeed for a family of farmers to visit the townships without buying some little present or another to gladden the hearts of their 'volk'. **1900** B. MITFORD *Aletta* 79 Come this way. My *volk* will see to your horse. **1900** in M. MARQUARD *Lett. from Boer Parsonage* (1967) 74 Eva found a Bethulie native among their 'volk' whom she brought here. **1913** A.B. MARCHAND *Dirk, S. African* 9 (Swart), Adoons, one of the coloured volk, almost fell over him and thereby spilt a goodly quantity from two steaming buckets of milk fresh from the cattle kraal. **1939** J.S. MARAIS *Cape Coloured People* 5 In the western Cape a farmer calls his labourers his 'volk' — the same word that Adam Tas used for his slaves. **1941** C. BIRKBY *Springbok Victory* 47 The South Africans, with their benevolent outlook on all natives as being just the same homely 'volk' as their black people in the Union, were kindly towards the Turkana. **1963** A.M. LOUW *20 Days* 77 'You know you're not allowed to have "volk" in your bedroom.' ... She had spoken of 'volk' — the collective name for Coloured farm labourers as though a Coloured man could never be anything else. [**1967** see SKEPSEL]. **1968** M. MULLER *Green Peaches Ripen* 13 The *volk*, (coloured labourers and their families) dressed in their best, standing at the foot of the wide steps. **1974** A. SMALL in S. Gray *On Edge of World* 182 He had to be up every morning at just a little past five, for that was when Baas Giel though his *volk* (labourers) should start moving. **1980** *Rand Daily Mail* 7 Oct. 5 On weekends we give our volk (farmhands) a cup of mampoer. Then we drink it ourselves, of course, at braais and the like. **1987** M. MELAMU *Children of Twilight* 41 It was all so different with his 'volk'. You had to feed them properly ... Mealie pap and sour milk, with the occasional offal which he knew the blacks liked so much.

3. Denoting the Afrikaner people.

a. *Obs.* exc. *hist.* ***Het Volk*** /het ˈfɔlk/ [S. Afr. Du. *het* the], 'The People'.

i. The name of a political party, founded by Generals L. Botha and J.C. Smuts in 1905, which merged with other groups to form the *Suid Afrikaansche Nasionale Party* (see SAP *n.*[1] sense 1 a) after Union in 1910. Also *attrib.*

1905 *Star* 2 Oct. 6 In marked contrast to the active propaganda of the Head Committee of 'Het Volk' we have the almost studied silence of the largest section of the community on the subject of education. **1908** *Indian Opinion* 18 Apr. 171 The recent Het Volk Congress in Pretoria. **1909** F. CANA *S. Afr. from Great Trek to Union* 229 The Boer leaders .. in January, 1905, formally adopted as the name of their organization Het Volk ('the people'). This society .. was in effect a racial organization which sought to regain through the ballot boxes the power lost at Vereeniging. **1916** E.H. SPENDER *General Botha* 171 Early in 1905, two great Reform organisations were founded with the sole object of securing responsible government — 'Het Volk', in the Transvaal; and 'Oranje Unie' in the Orange Colony. **1934** G.G. MUNNIK *Mem. of Senator* 236 A congress was called which led to the establishment of one united political party which afterwards became 'Het Volk' and then merged into what is today the great and powerful Nationalist Party. **1946** M.S. GEEN *Making of Union of S. Afr.* 153 General Louis Botha had formed Het Volk in the Transvaal pledged to a policy of conciliation and self-government. **1960** L.M. THOMPSON *Unification of S. Afr. 1902–10* 21 Within a very short time branches of Het Volk were established in every village in the Transvaal. **1979** T. PAKENHAM *Boer War* (1982) 575 Milner lost the support of the mass of the British Uitlanders; their political representatives formed an alliance with the emergent pan-Afrikaner party (Het Volk) of Botha and Smuts. **1989** *Reader's Digest Illust. Hist.* 270 By the time Botha and Smuts had established *Het Volk* as a political association in January 1905, they had begun to formulate a policy of reconciliation with Britain.

ii. As *pl.*: The citizens of a Boer republic. Cf. sense 3 b.

1926 M. NATHAN *S. Afr. from Within* 22 If any measure of importance was to be taken, a meeting of Het volk (the people) was summoned to sanction it. **1929** H.A. CHILVERS *Out of Crucible* 81 Kruger was .. the more determined .. to grant the 'Uitlander' neither the vote nor any other privilege lest the grip of 'het Volk' (the people) be relaxed from the land. **1941** C.W. DE KIEWIET *Hist. of S. Afr.* 131 The term *Het Volk*, or *The People*, had changed its loose connotation to mean more precisely the people to whom the Transvaal was a fatherland. **1968** E.A. WALKER *Hist. of Sn Afr.* 204 At Thaba Nchu, 'Het Volk' (the People) elected Maritz, a man of some education and legal experience as Landdrost.

b. Usu. ***the volk*** or ***die volk*** /di -/ [Afk., *die* the]. The (members of the) Afrikaner group or 'nation'; FOLK sense b. Cf. AFRIKANERDOM sense 1, BOERENASIE sense 1, BOEREVOLK sense 1. Also *attrib.* See also MENS *n.* sense 1 a.

1948 *Press Digest* No.1, 8 Die Volksblad thought it essential that a knowledge of Bantu history, tradition, customs and language be acquired by school children and eventually, in consequence, by the volk as a whole. **1949** *Blueprint for Blackout* (Educ. League) (*pamphlet*) 5 Nothing may become law if the people object to it. We are the people! We are die Volk! All of us, not only 12 per cent., 40 per cent., or even 60 per cent. We are all *die Volk*, that mysterious entity upon which the demagogues are constantly calling. **1958** G. CARTER *Politics of Inequality* 253 These [Broederbond] members are organized in small units of about 20 persons all over the Union, each group a cross-section of the *volk* in its vicinity. **1960** C. HOOPER *Brief Authority* 54 To look at you one would say that you were unimpeachably white, a member of the master race, though not the *volk*. **1971** *Informant, Grahamstown* Die volk. Afrikaners. I beg your pardon, Afrikaner Nationalists. **1981** *Sunday Times* 13 Dec. 45 We all know who 'Die Volk' are — they are those whites living in South Africa who refer to themselves as Afrikaners. **1982** *Drum* July 78 The PWs, Fanies and Piks, the blue-blooded scions of the Botha tree, have distinguished themselves among die Volk. **1984** J. SCOTT in *Cape Times* 31 Mar. 11 Is this the way in which the *volk* fathers should behave, by drinking in the morning? **1986** *Weekend Argus* 9 Aug. 13 Institutions like the Federasie van Afrikaanse Kultuurvereeninge [*sic*], the church and the various 'volk' get-togethers are all subjects of political wrangling. **1987** G. SILBER in *Frontline* Mar. 9 Once the Boerestaat is re-established .. it will be populated by the volk (three million to begin with) and depopulated of all extraneous volke. **1988** A. NOTHNAGEL in *Inside S. Afr.* June 12 Psychologically we have relinquished the following strongly-held myths: That the Afrikaner was a nation 'chosen by God'; That the Afrikaner nation, the 'volk', was more important that the South African nation [etc.]. **1989** W. EBERSOHN in *Cosmopolitan* Apr. 198 At one time Afrikanerdom was a by-word for unity. But lately there has been dissension in the ranks of the *volk*. **1992** *Scope* 13 Nov. 67 This is just the kind of violent inter-volk action that would unite the rightists. **1993** *Natal Witness* 13 Apr. 3 Rudolph said the weapons he had stolen in 1990 had been distributed to 'the volk (nation) which had been unarmed and still stood defenceless against the onslaught of those who wanted to take our land'.

‖**c.** Phrases. ***the*** (or ***die***) ***volk daar buite*** [Afk. *die volk daar buite*, *die* the + *volk* people + *daar buite* 'out there'], the Afrikaner electorate; ***(for) Volk and Vaderland***, (for) people and country; see also VADERLAND *n.*

1970 *Argus* 30 Jan. 11 While the nation watches Parliament with more than usual interest during the short pre-election session, its members will be watching **'die volk daar buite'** with even closer interest. **1973** *Weekend Argus* 21 Apr. 5 Certainly the Sap-Nat battle has been a long and wearing one, but .. differences .. are .. great among the volk daarbuite among whom MPs are currently taking the pulse. **1975** *Sunday Times* 21 Sept. 20 Political leaders have had a tough time telling it like it's not to the volk daarbuite at the Free State congress. **1980** *Rand Daily Mail* 23 Aug. 7 It is no use being verligte, a reformist, if you do not have a power base, and the power base, in the final reckoning, must be *die volk daar buite*. **1985** *Evening Post* 1 Feb. 5 Gazing beyond 'die volk daar buite'. **1991** M. Kantey *All Tickets* 22 Pimply Lenins, Fanons, and Guevaras, plotting the sudden overthrow of Volk and Vaderland. **1991** J. Pauw *In Heart of Whore* 13 The former policeman .. had killed and maimed supporters of the ANC 'for Volk and Vaderland, for my wife and my children and my mother and my father'. *Ibid.* 100 The '90-day Act' .. created a sub-culture in the police force that encouraged policemen to act mercilessly in their struggle against communism and in the protection of Volk and Vaderland.

‖**4.** *comb.* (Always in the Afk. combining form **volks-**.) **volksbeweging** /-bəˌvɪəxəŋ/ [Afk., *beweging* movement], a people's movement; **volkseie** /-eɪə/ [Afk., *eie* own], national or 'folk' ethos; **volksfees** /-fɪəs/, pl. **-te** /-tə/, [Afk., *fees* feast, festival], people's or 'national' festival; **volksidentiteit** /-identiˈteɪt/ [Afk., *identiteit* identity], cultural identity; **volkskongres** /-kɔŋˌxres/ [Afk., *kongres* congress], a national congress of Afrikaans-speaking people; **volksleër** /-lɪər/ [Afk., *leër* army], a 'people's army'; a name often given to right-wing private armies or paramilitary groups; **volksleier** /-leɪə(r)/ [Afk., *leier* leader], a popular leader of the Afrikaans people; **volksvreemd** /-frɪəmt/ *adj.*, also (*attrib.*) **volksvreemde** /-də/, [Afk., *vreemd* strange, alien (attrib. form *vreemde*)], alien to the people and their interests; **volkswil** /-vəl/ [Afk., *wil* will], the will of the people, the 'national will'.

1980 *Sunday Times* 16 Mar. 15 If, in the first flush of enthusiasm and conviction, the Nationalists (seen as a **volksbeweging** rather than as a political party) could not make separatism work, they certainly cannot do so now. **1982** *S. Afr. Digest* 26 Mar. 17 The verkrampte hoopla that accompanied its [*sc.* the new party's] creation may give an impression .. that organised bigotry is a viable volksbeweging. **1987** *Pretoria News* 18 June 5 The government was being challenged by a 'volksbeweging' (a nationalist movement) similar to the one that led to the creation of the Republic in 1961. **1960** E.H. Brookes in H. Spottiswoode *S. Afr.: Rd Ahead* 38 A valuable half-truth is included in the doctrine of the **volkseie**, the national ethos — that each 'national' group has something of its own to contribute to humanity. **1989** *Personality* 6 Feb. 20 There are other Afrikaners who favour the pragmatic approach. To try and preserve the volkseie (national identity) they are busy negotiating right and centre. **1978** *Sunday Times* 5 Mar. 13 Young city Afrikaners prefer pop music to volkspele, says a survey ... **Volksfeeste** don't appeal to them. **1986** P. Le Roux in Burman & Reynolds *Growing Up* 191 The *volksfeeste* (folk festivals) — Republic Day, Kruger Day, and Day of the Covenant — interspersed with National Party *stryddae* (fêtes), attracted fewer participants every year. **1990** C. Leonard in *Weekly Mail* 12 Oct. 1 A different sort of boerefees was held: non-racial, with no speeches, no praise for Kruger ... It was the Afrikaanse Demokratie's version of volksfees. **1975** T. Sundermeier *Church & Nationalism* 146 They do not see themselves as a 'volk' and have no desire to be propelled into becoming a separate nation based on **volksidentiteit**. **1976** *Drum* Sept. 27 Afrikaner nationalism operated on a model of *volksnasionalisme* which assumes and demands that all other people in South Africa, and especially the different black groups, should have a racial-ethnic *volksidentiteit* which should be developed separately. **1984** *Frontline* Mar. 43 The KP, indeed, has stolen the clothes of the original Nats. It appeals to the same instincts as Dr Malan did in the 40s, volksidentiteit. **1943** 'J. Burger' *Black Man's Burden* 240 In September 1939 a so-called **Volkskongres** was held to discuss economic questions as they touched the Afrikaner. **1968** *Post* 17 Nov. 7 'Die Transvaler', stepped up its campaign for a 'volkskongres' to debate the Bantustan situation. **1974** *Sunday Times* 15 Sept. 6 The two-day verkrampte Volkskongres .. will discuss the 'Dangers of liberalism' and .. will be held in Pretoria at the end of the month. **1982** M. Feinstein in *E. Prov. Herald* 22 Mar. 2 The Afrikaans education 'volkskongres' has dealt what could be the death blow to hopes for a single Ministry of Education for all races in South Africa. **1991** G. Evans in *Weekly Mail* 20 Dec. (Suppl.) 11 A campaign of mass action culminating in the Volkskongres in May met with only limited success. **1990** *Sunday Times* 27 May 3 Leading the horse cavalcade was the supreme commander of the Boer **Volksleer**. **1990** *Ibid.* 10 June 8 Mr Maritz claims to lead the Brandwag Volksleër — not to be confused with the AWB's Boerekommandos, the Boereleër or the SA Volksleër. **1991** G. McIntosh in *Ibid.* 13 Jan. 16 A volunteer and professional SADF could easily become sectional, whereas a conscripted citizen force, or people's army, or *volksleër*, could not become that. **1970** *Daily News* 16 Oct. 11 (*letter*) The great Dr. Verwoerd is considered by the faithful to be the most wonderful **volksleier** and generally the ablest politician that this country has ever produced. **1972** *Het Suid-Western* 17 Feb. 2 Perhaps the inner significance of the 'bohaai' is that there is a rising sense of panic abroad in South Africa today among 'volksleiers' who have clearly and irremediably lost their grip on the minds and hearts of young people. **1991** A. Van Wyk *Birth of New Afrikaner* 48 This theme was always embroidered in secular speeches by a few select *volksleiers*, respected individuals free to roam the wide expanse of our history, with special reference to what the Afrikaner had endured at the hands of black and Briton. **1949** A. Keppel-Jones *When Smuts Goes* 4 The Nationalists .. soon made it clear that foreign — uitheemse, **volksvreemde** — elements would not be welcome. **1971** *Rand Daily Mail* 16 Mar. 5 Charges that Round Table was 'Engels' and 'Volksvreemd'. **1972** *Sunday Times* 5 Nov. 18 A startling story of the Broederbond fight against 'volksvreemde' organisations. **1986** *E. Prov. Herald* 11 Nov. 8 Any Afrikaner who does not support the NP or one of its derivatives, the CP or HNP, becomes 'volks vreemd' and suffers in many cases from social ostracism from his own 'volk'. **1987** 'K. De Boer' in *Frontline* Mar. 36 Looking at the Special Day calendar of volksvreemde events forced down our throats, the most unwanted must surely be Valentine's Day. **1988** *Star* 28 May 11 To the Afrikaner establishment they were as alien and 'volksvreemd' (foreign) as the Beatles. **1948** *Cape Argus* 2 Dec. 1 The numerical question apparently no longer applies, and it is now just a question of '**volkswil**' and the support of the people. **1955** R. Foley in M. Rogers *Black Sash* (1956) 116 A Party which has claimed, until now, that its leaders are the heaven-sent interpreters of the *volkswil* — the people's will! **1956** *Cape Times* in *Ibid.* 265 If in a nation the united voice of the enrolled voters is an expression of the volkswil, then the volkswil is not behind the Government, but is deeply divided. **1960** C. Hooper *Brief Authority* 224 A country where God's Will and Volkswil are scarcely distinguishable in public utterances. **1975** W.R.G. Branford in *E. Prov. Herald* 14 Aug., If Afrikaans is a model of successful language planning, this is only because as far as the Afrikaner population was concerned, language planning and the volkswil have, on the whole, mutually reinforced one another. **1977** T.R.H. Davenport *S. Afr.: Mod. Hist.* 66 So concerned were the Rustenburg law-makers to preserve the authority of the Volkswil that they insisted on .. a minimum period of three months between the first tabling of a measure and its enactment, so as to ensure that the public had plenty of time to react. **1978** *Sunday Times* 24 Sept. 16 History will never forgive those 170-odd men if they do not take account of national opinion, the *volkswil*, in making their selection.

volkies /ˈfɔlkiːz, ˈfɔlkis/ *pl. n. Colloq.* [Afk., *volk* people + -ie + pl. suffix *-s*.] A patronizing term used collectively of 'coloured' farm-labourers. Cf. volk sense 2.

1949 L.G. Green *In Land of Afternoon* 179 These old volkies think nothing of starting out at four on a winter morning to reach the lands and their ploughs at daybreak. **1964** J. Meintjes *Manor House* 28 The *volkies* (Coloured families living and working on the farms) donned their Sunday-best, white trousers and finery, and .. sang hymns to the lilting strains of guitars and concertinas. **1973** *Argus* 14 Apr. 13 The veil of romantic myth which surrounds the 'volkies,' the picture of the sturdy-limbed peasant living healthily off the land. **1975** *Cape Times* 19 July 7 Days he was hard at it on his plaas with crops, tractor and complications with the Volkies. **1988** A. Dangor in *Staffrider* Vol.7 No.3, 89 Don't any of you volkies try and do anything by yourselves, understand? .. I want no more trouble on my farm. **1991** A. Van Wyk *Birth of New Afrikaner* 46 On the big day we joined the *volkies* (blacks) and entered our chips with my father ... The *volkies* came from nowhere and everywhere. They moved about in teams, .. cutting wheat wherever their labour was required.

Volk raad var. Volksraad.

Volksie /ˈfɔlksi/ *n. colloq.* [Formed on tradename *Volkswagen* + Eng. (informal) n.-forming suffix *-ie*.] A Volkswagen motor vehicle, esp. a Beetle. Also *attrib.*

1962 *Capricorn High School Mag.* 24 He drove up in a Blue 'Volksie' And she did stand and gape. **1977** *World* 17 June 21 (*advt*) Volksie Spares Centre for all your Volkswagen Spares. **1984** *Sunday Times* 8 July (Lifestyle) 9 Dampies .. and Jenny Ball .. are stranded on the motorway in their Volksie. **1991** O. Oberholzer in *Time* 29 July 28 (*advt*) When it arrived, the Synchro Bus looked just like a normal Volksie Bus. **1992** C.M. Knox tr. *E. Van Heerden's Mad Dog* 113 You with your yellow cane ... Your yellow Volksie in front of the school building.

volkslied /ˈfɔlkslit/ *n.* Also with initial capital. [Afk., *volk* people, folk + linking phoneme *-s-* + *lied* song.]

1.a. The national anthem of the former Transvaal Republic, '*Kent gij dat volk*' ('Do you know that people'). ‖**b.** Among Afrikaners: any national anthem.

1898 C. Rae *Malaboch* 217 *Volkslied*, The Transvaal National Anthem. **1900** 'One Who Was in It' *Kruger's Secret Service* 34 It was impossible to play either the Volksleid or the English National Anthem, because of the violent antipathies which these melodies excited ... If the Volksleid was played the anti-Boer element of the audience immediately created such a disturbance that the orchestra was drowned. **1900** B. Mitford *Aletta* 8 The whole assembly struck up the 'Volkslied', the national hymn of the Transvaal. **1901** W.S. Sutherland *S. Afr. Sketches* 61 The commencement of the Boer War was a critical time for Volkslieds. The Transvaal has a capital one. **1910** *Rand Daily Mail* 1 Nov. 8 Kaffir impis are approaching .. but are driven off with slaughter. The defenders jubilantly hoist the Vierkleur and sing the 'Volkslied' as a conclusion to the episode. **1921** *E. Prov. Herald* 18 Jan., The singing of the Volkslied and a vote of thanks to General Hertzog closed the meeting. **1929** D. Reitz *Commando* 29 During this time the cheering and the singing of the Volkslied were continuous. **1933** W.H.S. Bell *Bygone Days* 195 The market is lifeless; no business and everything politics. The 'Volkslied' and 'God Save the Queen' were loudly cheered in the theatre. *a*1951 H.C. Bosman *Willemsdorp* (1977) 96 The horse commando fired a volley into the air. The crowd struck up the old Transvaal Volkslied. **1953** B. Fuller *Call Back Yesterday* 38 She ran to a piano and began playing the Free State Volkslied. **1965** J. Malherbe *Port Natal* 146 The Boer President .. stepped on to the platform escorted by Sir Charles Mitchell, and stood in attention while .. the band played 'God save the Queen', and the Transvaal Volkslied. **1974** K. Griffith *Thank God We Kept Flag Flying* 43 The Boer sergeant .. played a series of National Anthems, including both 'God Save the Queen' and the 'Transvaal Volkslied'. **1985** *Argus* 24 Aug., The delegates whipped up spirits as they sang the old songs — Oranje, Blanje, Blou, the Transvaal Volkslied, and .. Sarie Marais.

2. Usu. **volksliedjie** [see -ie]: a folk song. Cf. boereliedjie.

1949 O. Walker *Wanton City* 198 Gus Swann switched suddenly from an experiment in Afrikaans volkslied to 'Colonel Bogey'. **1971** L.G. Green *Taste of S.-Easter* 4 High and silvery notes went forth into the heavens and Yussuf was away in a volksliedjie or Italian aria. **1994** *Weekend Post* 1 Jan. 6 Radio Pretoria

.. has become a leading torch-bearer for the right wing, broadcasting hours of *volksliedjies*.

volkspele /ˈfɔlkspɪələ/ *pl. n.* [Afk., *volk* folk, people + *spele* games, play.] Afrikaans folk-dances, created during the 1930s but usu. performed in traditional Voortrekker dress; see quots 1973 and 1986. Also *attrib.*

1949 *Cape Times* 24 Sept. 9 There would be volkspele demonstrations, recitations and singing. **1953** *Ibid.* 21 Mar. 3 These [South African recipes] are destined for Holland, where they will be needed to prepare *braaivleis* and *sasaties* when the South African *volkspele* team visits Culemborg and holds a *braaivleisaand* there. **1960** C. HOOPER *Brief Authority* 382 As long as volkspele and rugby offer escape and God defends the white. **1973** J. BOUWS in *Std Encycl. of Sn Afr.* VIII. 9 The revival of folk-dancing under the name of 'volkspele' began at Boshof under S. Henri Pellissier, modelled upon the Swedish folk-dances. The adoption of definite rules for the execution of movements and steps and of special garb to be worn ensured uniformity at mass displays on the occasion of national festivals .., but departed from the unpretentious 19th-century traditional folk-dances. **1986** P. LE ROUX in Burman & Reynolds *Growing Up* 190 Probably the most artificial cultural creation ever to see the light of day was *volkspele* (folk dances). Gustav Preller selected the less erotic movements from European folk dances, coordinated these with Afrikaans songs, and hey presto – we had our own folk dances! **1990** *Sunday Times* 3 June 4 They were too busy eating, discussing the volkspele, toutrek and SAP helicopter displays and buying Janita Claasen posters.

Hence **volkspeler** *n.*, one who performs volkspele.

1953 *Cape Times* 17 Apr. 9 The group of volkspelers will sail on an oversea tour in to-day's mailship. **1974** *S. Afr. Panorama* Nov. 19 The National Council for Folk Singing and Dancing chose 36 'volkspelers' (folk dancers) from different 'laers' (laagers) to accompany the overseas dancers and perform with them.

Volksraad /ˈfɔlksrɑːt, -rɑːd/ *n. hist.* Also **Folksraad, Volk raad.** [Afk., *volk* (Afrikaner) people + linking phoneme *-s-* + *raad* council, senate.]

1.a. The legislative assembly of any of the former Boer republics. **b.** *rare.* The *House of Assembly*, see HOUSE sense 1 a. In both senses also called RAAD (sense 2).

1841 in G.W. Eybers *Sel. Constit. Doc.* (1918) 165 In this Law or Regulation none the least alteration, addition or deduction shall be made .. without the consent of at least two-thirds of the Volks Raad, or Legislative Council. *a***1843** H. CLOETE in J. Bird *Annals of Natal* (1888) I. 387 The district was divided into twelve .. wards, from each of which the names of two .. persons were .. sent in, forming a council of twenty-four members, in which were vested all the combined, supreme, executive, legislative and judicial powers. This elective Council or Volksraad was required to assemble here (at Pietermaritzburg) every three months. **1847** in H. Ward *Cape & Kaffirs* (1851) 7 A spot has been selected by the late Volks Raad, for a town on the Sunday's River. **1852** C. BARTER *Dorp & Veld* 194 A resolution of the *Volksraad*, that no additional natives should be allowed to take up their residence within the colony. **1877** F. JEPPE *Tvl Bk Almanac & Dir.* (1976) 35 The legislative power of the State is vested in the Volksraad. **1887** A. DOUGLASS *Despotism in British Bechuanaland* 12 The 'lawfully adopted' here refers to laws that may be passed by the Volksraad of Stellaland. **1900** H.C. HILLEGAS *Oom Paul's People* 47 The Boer leader, Commandant-General Pretorius, .. had been chosen by the first 'Volksraad' – a governing body elected while the journey from Cape Colony to Natal was being made. **1937** C. BIRKBY *Zulu Journey* 202 Among all the Parliaments which have ever sat, the most comic and the most pathetic must surely have been the Griqua Volksraad. **1951** H. DAVIES *Great S. Afr. Christians* 45 The People's Council ('Volksraad') was set up by the Trekkers on Bushman's Ridge, now renamed Pietermaritzburg, in October of 1938. **1988** B.P.J. ERASMUS in *S. Afr. Panorama* Dec. 12 Relief came in June 1842 and a month later the *Volksraad* agreed to accept British rule. The following year Natal was annexed by Britain. **1990** D. BOSHOFF in *Ibid.* Jan.-Feb. 8 On 6 May 1889 President Paul Kruger laid the cornerstone of the Raadsaal. One year later the Volksraad met for the first time in the incomplete building. It was decided to provide for a second Volksraad for the so-called 'uitlanders' (foreigners).

‖**2.** *comb.* In Afrikaans combining form **Volksraadsbesluit** /-bəˌslœɪt/ [Afk., *besluit* resolution], a decree of the Volksraad; **Volksraadslid** /-lət/, pl. **-lede** /-lɪədə/ (formerly **-leden**), [Afk., *lid* member], a member of the Volksraad.

1977 *S. Afr. Panorama* Aug. 34 The judges claimed the testing right .. by declaring a **Volksraadsbesluit** null and void on the ground that it was legislation passed in a manner not authorised by the constitution. *c***1900** in M. MARQUARD *Lett. from Boer Parsonage* (1967) 93 To the **Volksraadsleden**, de Wet 't was who spoke Ere the Free State go down there are crowns to be broke. **1980** *Cape Times* 29 Mar. 8 The numbers, including ex-Volksraadslede and top officials, who poured into the Protectorates seeking refuge from their own people.

volkstaat /ˈfɔlkstɑːt/ *n.* [Afk., *volk* (Afrikaner) people + *staat* state.] BOERESTAAT. Also *attrib.*, and *transf.*

1987 L. WROUGHTON in *Pretoria News* 15 June 6 Terre-'Blanche demands 'Volkstaat' for his people. **1989** P. DICKSON in *Evening Post* 7 Mar. 6 When asked just how he intended to remove the country's black population from his white *volkstaat* ideal, an angry Mr Terre'-Blanche said he was 'certainly not going to ask them'. **1991** A. KENNY in *Frontline* Dec. 13 When I reproach AWB-supporters over the contradiction between the theory of an all-white Volkstaat where whites will do their own dirty work and the present reality of blacks doing all their dirty work for them, they are quite honest about it. 'Yes, that's a problem.' **1993** *Business Day* 19 July 4 The real danger is that Buthelezi is intent on a Zulu volkstaat. **1994** F. BRIDGLAND in *Weekly Telegraph* (U.K) 23 Mar. (Plus) p.iv, The AWB .. simply does not have the brain power, self-discipline or military skills to sustain the kind of prolonged uprising necessary to obtain a *volkstaat* by martial means.

Volkwyn /ˈfɔlkveɪn/ *n.* Also with small initial. [See quot. 1971.] In full ***Volkwyn chair***: a style of chair characterized by an ornamental turned rail on the back, placed above the two rails which join the uprights.

1971 BARAITSER & OBHOLZER *Cape Country Furn.* 70 Three late Regency chairs named Volkwyn chairs after the family of carpenters who made them. **1979** *S. Afr. Garden & Home* Dec., The yellow-wood table in the dining-room was made from wood salvaged from a home that was to be demolished. The volkwyn chairs, however, are antique. **1982** *Het Suid-Western* 29 Dec., When today one finds a riempiebank, a Volkwyn chair .. in these farflung districts, one can be pretty sure that they were brought there from George. **1984** *Furniture manufacturer's catal., George* Jan. 2, Chairs .. Volkwyn.

vomeerbos(sie) var. VERMEERBOS.

vomeersiekte, -ziekte varr. VERMEERSIEKTE.

vooma(h) see WOEMA.

‖**voorbok** /ˈfʊə(r)bɔk/ *n.* Pl. **-bokke** /-bɔkə/. [Afk., *voor* in front + *bok* goat.] A goat used as a bell-wether to lead a flock of sheep. Also *fig.*, a leader; a ringleader. See also VOORLOPER sense 2.

1913 C. PETTMAN *Africanderisms* 540 *Voorbok*, .. A goat – Kapater .. – is generally used on South African sheep farms, instead of a bell-wether as in England. **1947** *Cape Argus* 29 Mar. 6 Many English-speaking South Africans regarded him as a man wielding a moderating influence upon racial politics. Why then should he not be useful as a bell-wether ('voorbok') leading United Party sheep into the Herenigde kraal? **1951** *Cape Times* 15 Aug. 2 A delivery van ran into a flock of sheep .., killing 25 sheep and the voorbok. **1972** *Daily Dispatch* 6 May 10 Each flock was led by a goat, the voorbok. The sheep, silly creatures as they are, would never cross a river or enter a gate unless led by the more clever voorbok. **1976** *Cape Times* 21 Sept. 2 A 14-year-old schoolboy, who according to a bus conductor, was the 'voorbok' of a stoning incident in Wynberg on September 16, was found guilty of inciting others to public violence. **1976** *Het Suid-Western* 17 Nov., 'Riots voorbok' is jailed for 18 months ... The woman was described as one of the voorbokke of the riots and incited children to throw stones at white people's cars.

voorchitz var. VOERCHITZ.

voorhuis /ˈfʊə(r)heɪs, -hœɪs/ *n. Archit.* Formerly also **voorhuys, vorhaus, vorhuis.** [Afk., fr. Du.] The front room or entrance hall of a traditional Cape Dutch house, used as a reception room or parlour and separated from the dining area (or AGTERHUIS) by a wooden screen; FOREHOUSE; FORE HUIS; VOORKAMER sense a.

1821 C.I. LATROBE *Jrnl of Visit* 326 It was a poor cottage, no better than a Hottentot's house; but the vorhaus or hall, was large enough to contain a pretty numerous company of rebels. **1822** W.J. BURCHELL *Trav.* I. 118 All retired to rest; some to a mat on the floor in the *voorhuis* (entrance-room or hall), which is a large room used for general purposes, and occupying the middle and principal part of the ground-floor. **1834** T. PRINGLE *Afr. Sketches* 175 The house was divided into three apartments; the one in which we were seated (called the *voorhuis*) opened immediately from the open air, and is the apartment in which the family always sit, eat, and receive visitors. **1861** 'A LADY' *Life at Cape* (1963) 23 Where we should place a mere passage, the colonial builders have put a voorhuis – that is to say, a passage and room thrown into one, so as to make the dining-hall the coolest of chambers. **1896** M.A. CAREY-HOBSON *At Home in Tvl* 322 The party were soon seated together in the large voorhuis or entrance sitting-room, drinking the never-failing tea that, according to South African custom, is always served immediately after the arrival of visitors. **1910** D. FAIRBRIDGE *That Which Hath Been* (1913) 106 The voorhuis, or entrance hall, was divided from the dining-hall by a pierced teak screen of exquisite workmanship. **1925** H.J. MANDELBROTE tr. *O.F. Mentzel's Descr. of Cape of G.H.* II. 112 You enter into a voorhuis – a broad corridor, furnished with chairs and tables. This is the usual reception room. It leads on to a larger room which serves as a dining room. **1955** L.G. GREEN *Karoo* 89 You walk up stone steps to the stoep with its original iron railings and enter the *klein voorhuis* (hall) with the *groot voorhuis*, used as a dining room, straight ahead of you. **1960** M. MULLER *Art Past & Present* 111 The teak screen with glass panels which divides the voorhuis from the dining-room is a typical example of Eastern influence. **1971** C. DE BOSDARI *Cape Dutch Houses & Farms* 23 The entrance-hall or Voorhuis, is often divided from the main reception-room by a screen. **1987** G. VINEY *Col. Houses* 34 The inventory .. describes a three-roomed house and kitchen of the humblest sort: a *voorhuys* which was evidently also used as a dining-room, with two rooms on either side. **1991** *Best of S. Afr. Short Stories* (Reader's Digest Assoc.) 147 In early Cape-Dutch designs, the front door .. opened directly into a large room called the *voorhuis* or *voorkamer* (front room). A wooden screen provided privacy in the rear part of the room which became known as the *agterkamer* (back room) or the *achterhuis*.

voorkamer /ˈfʊə(r)kɑːmə(r)/ *n. Archit.* [Du., *voor* front + *kamer* chamber.] **a.** VOORHUIS. **b.** Any front room. Also *fig.*, and part. tr. **fore-kamer**.

1827 G. THOMPSON *Trav.* I. 49, I slept this night in the outer apartment (voorkamer) or sitting-room of the house, which was without a door. **1834** *Makanna* (anon.) II. 41 However rugged on the outside, the voorkamer of an Africander's has that within which may attract. **1896** *Cape Argus* 2 Jan. 5 The flash entered at the front doorway, and the shock was felt by all the occupants of the *voorkamer*, fourteen in number. **1900** D.S.F.A. PHILLIPS *S. Afr. Recollections* 14 The house consisted of the voorkamer, or hall, from which the kitchen and bedrooms .. led. **1926** [see AGTERHUIS]. **1937** H. SAUER *Ex Afr.* 28 We were then invited into the house, into the 'voorkamer,' or universal sitting-room, dining-room, and reception-room combined. **1952** G.M. MILLS *First Ladies of Cape* 42 Approached through the front door was the voorkamer or front room, on either side of which were sleeping apartments. Beyond the voorkamer was the achterhuis or back room. **1963** [see AGTERKAMER]. **1974** *Sunday Times* 20 Oct. (Mag. Sect.) 3 An enormous russet-toned bathroom was divided into voor and agter kamer featuring twin hand basins, bidet, loo, a bath in the far distance, and a shower in outer space. **1976** [see AGTERKAMER]. **1983** F. DE VILLIERS in *Sunday Times* 11 Sept. 35 If English-speakers do not believe that the end of that bad old world is nigh, neither yet do many Nationalists who are trying against the odds to keep the old home intact, even as they invite English-speaking South Africa into the voorkamer. **1984** [see BOERBOK]. **1987** [see AGTERKAMER]. **1991** [see VOORHUIS].

voorkis /ˈfʊə(r)kəs/ *n. hist.* Also **voorkisse**, **voorkist**. [Afk., earlier S. Afr. Du. *voorkist*, from Du. *voor* front, fore + *kist* chest.] A storage chest, traditionally used as the driver's seat on a trek-wagon. Also dim. form **voorkissie** [see -IE]. See also WAKIS.

1852 C. BARTER *Dorp & Veld* 17 (Pettman), A second wagon rolled up, on the *voorkist* of which I at once recognized our man. **1868** [see HOT *adj.*]. **1872** in A.M.L. Robinson *Sel. Articles from Cape Monthly Mag.* (1978) 229 What plight should we be in if we had not 'riems' and 'voorkist' and 'katel?' **1897** H.A. BRYDEN *Nature & Sport* 200 On a July morning in the South African veldt two hunters stand, just after sunrise, upon the voor-kist (fore-box) of one of their wagons, and, leaning upon the tilt, scan eagerly the great plains around them. **1902** H.J. DUCKITT in M. Kuttel *Quadrilles & Konfyt* (1954) 18 The goodies were packed in the box which formed the front seat of the wagon (*voorkissie*). **1906** H. RIDER HAGGARD *Benita* 63 One morning Benita .. thrust aside the curtain and seated herself upon the voorkisse, or driving-box. **1922** [see AGTERKIS]. [**1936** C. BIRKBY *Thirstland Treks* 292, I stood upon the forechest of my wagon for nearly two hours, lost in wonder.] **1948**, **1971** [see AGTERKIS]. **1991** *Best of S. Afr. Short Stories* (Reader's Digest Assoc.) 200 The *wakis* proper was made for its special function on the trek wagon. A *voorkis*, designed for the front of the wagon .. usually had a sloped front and sides ... The *agterkis* for the back of the wagon was smaller and square.

‖**voorlaaier** /ˈfʊə(r)laɪə(r)/ *n. hist.* Also **voorlaier**. [Afk., *voor* front + *laaier* loader.] A muzzle-loader. Also *attrib.* See also ROER sense a.

1934 *Sunday Times* 15 Apr. (Swart), One gun appears to be an old muzzle-loader 'voorlaaier', of home-made type. **1949** L.G. GREEN *In Land of Afternoon* 206 Tower muskets, horse-pistols, duelling pistols, fearsome elephant guns, pronk voorlaaier and panslaner .. you will find them all in the country museums. **1951** H.C. BOSMAN in L. Abrahams *Jurie Steyn's Post Office* (1971) 85 The percussion cap came in, to take the place of the flintlock that the old Boers used in their voorlaaiers. **1975** D.H. STRUTT *Clothing Fashions* 217 Besides the ever-necessary *voorlaaier* gun, powder horn and bandolier, the Voortrekker man carried a snuff-box. **1975** [see KNOPKIERIE]. **1977** [see SNAPHAAN]. **1987** O. MUSI in *Drum* Nov. 93 Now lest you hot-headed types reach for your voorlaiers or 'necklaces' – depending on your political persuasion or your mental age – let me hasten to add that my plea is to leave 'Oom Paul' where he is in Phirara's Church Square. **1993** G. DOMINY in *Natal Witness* 31 Dec. 8 Assegais rattled at Isandlwana; voorlaaiers were brandished and khaki-clad figures fulminated at the Voortrekker Monument and Blood River.

‖**Voorlezer** /ˈfʊərlɪəsə(r)/ *n. hist.* Also **Voorleezer**, and with small initial. [S. Afr. Du., 'reader' (Afk. *voorleser*), fr. *voorlezen* to read aloud.] DOMINEE sense 1.

1833 *Graham's Town Jrnl* 30 May 3 Pray can you inform me if a certain of my brethern [*sic*] is *again* elevated to the dignity of a Reverend ... It grieved me sore to have seen him a few years back, after his return from Latta-kooing, performing the duties of a *Voorlezer*. **1927** C.G. BOTHA *Social Life in Cape Col.* 43 The clerk, or 'voorleezer,' known as the Dominie, opened by giving out a psalm sung to the accompaniment of an organ. *Ibid.* 73 The village school was in charge of the Voorlezer or Parish Clerk who instructed the youth in reading, writing and arithmetic, the psalms and church catechism. **1934** M.E. MCKERRON *Hist. of Educ.* 136 (Swart), Fairly soon the terms voorlezer (reader) and voorzanger (precentor) creep into the records. **1968** F.C. METROWICH *Frontier Flames* 125 In the small towns and villages the Voorlezer or Parish Clerk, clad in a dignified black coat, waistcoat, breeches and long stockings, was also the local schoolteacher.

voorloop /ˈfʊərlʊəp/ *n. rare.* See quot. Cf. NALOOP.

1913 C. PETTMAN *Africanderisms* 541 *Voorloop*, .. In distilling brandy the first to make its appearance is known as the *voorloop*.

voorloop /ˈfʊərlʊəp/ *v. intrans. Rare.* [Back-formation from VOORLOPER.] To lead a team of oxen; FORE-LOUP.

1913 C. PETTMAN *Africanderisms* 541 *Voorloop*, .. To lead a span of oxen by means of the 'touw' fastened to the horns of the front pair. **1969** F. GOLDIE *River of Gold* 80 He called Tom and handed the leading riem to him, for it had been decided that Tom would voorloop for a while ... 'I go to voorloop,' he said smiling.

voorloper /ˈfʊə(r)ˌlʊəpə(r)/ *n.* Also **voerlooper**, **voorloeper**, **voor-loopa**, **vo(o)rlooper**, **voorlouper**. [Afk., earlier S. Afr. Du., fr. Du. *voor* front, fore + *looper* walker.]

1. *hist.* The person (usu. a young boy) who walks with the foremost pair of a team of draught oxen in order to guide them; FORE-LOUPER; LEADER; TOULEIER.

1837 J.E. ALEXANDER *Narr. of Voy.* I. 323 A long wagon would pass .., drawn by a span of ten or fourteen oxen under the guidance of a *voorlooper*, a brown boy, holding occasionally a small rope attached to the horns of the leading bullocks. **1847** 'A BENGALI' *Notes on Cape of G.H.* 76 A little Hottentot boy or 'voor-loopa' usually leads the first pair [of oxen]. **1852** C. BARTER *Dorp & Veld* 49 Our driver and leader, or voor looper, were both Hottentots. **1868** T. STUBBS Men I Have Known. 6 It was more like the clothing of some of our Voorloopers – Elbows, Knees and Bucksies bare, rich and rare were the gems he didn't wear. **1885** H. RIDER HAGGARD *King Solomon's Mines* 16 A wagon, with a driver, a voorlooper, and a Kafir hunter. **1909** LADY S. WILSON *S. Afr. Mem.* 14, I have been told that President Kruger was on this historical trek, a Voor-loper, or little boy that guides the leading oxen. **1914** S.P. HYATT *Old Transport Rd* 23, I engaged an alleged driver .. and a piccanin as voorloeper. **1924** [see VOORTREKKER *adj.*]. **1936** [see LEADER]. **1972** L.G. GREEN *When Journey's Over* 50 There is little rest for the weary voorloper from the time he rounds up his scattered span in the morning to the inspanning, the outspanning, the grazing and watering of the team at night. **1983** *Rand Daily Mail* 26 May 9 This fixes Ndongeni as between eight and 12 years old, the usual age for a 'voorlooper'. **1990** *Weekend Post* 5 May 10 As everybody knows, a *voorloper* is practically white man's work. A *voorloper* also walks ahead of the oxen, but he doesn't have to hold a rope.

2. *Transf.* and *fig.* One who goes ahead, a forerunner, in various specific senses, as: a pioneer; VOORTREKKER *n.* sense 1; a scout, moving ahead of the main body of troops; an animal leading a flock (see also VOORBOK); the leader of a Cape Malay carnival troupe; a small diamond found before one of substantial size is discovered.

1878 A. AYLWARD *Tvl of Today* 18 The Boers coming from the Cape Colony naturally sought in their new homes the peculiar features that have made the old ones pleasant ... These the 'Voorloopers' did not find on the Highveld. **1903** R. KIPLING *Five Nations* 181 Only a wave of our troopers, Only our flanks swinging past, Only a dozen voorloopers, Only we've learned it at last! **1910** A.B. LAMONT *Rural Reader* 127 One or two native goats called *voorloopers*, are frequently put among sheep to act as leaders and to bring the flock back to the kraal at night. **1950** E. ROSENTHAL *Here Are Diamonds* 198 Contrasting pleasantly with the 'Schlenter' stone is the 'Voorloper,' which does not here stand, as usual, for the small native boy leading the first ox of a span, but is the small stone which precedes a big one, lower down in the claim. **1951** L.G. GREEN *Grow Lovely* 192 Each troupe has its voorloper, a prancing drum-major swinging the staff of office and leading the musicians. **1955** —— *Karoo* 36 He could see a front line of buck at least three miles long, but he could not estimate the depth. Ahead of the main body were swift voorlopers, moving along as though they were leading the army. **1971** *Argus* 5 June (Weekend Mag.) 1 The 'Voorlopers' amused us with their acrobatic prancing through the streets. **1990** *Weekend Post* 5 May 10 If the Conservative Party ever gains power, the coloured people of South Africa can look forward to being *voorlopers*. This enticing prospect was held out .. yesterday.

‖**vooros** /ˈfʊə(r)ɔs/ *n.* Pl. **-osse** /-ɔsə/, and (formerly) **-ossen**. [Afk., *voor* fore, front + *os* ox.] FRONT OX. Cf. AGTEROS.

[**1868** see HOT.] **1896** R. WALLACE *Farming Indust. of Cape Col.* 269 The 'voor-ossen' and 'achter-ossen', or the first and last pair, being picked specimens, used to be worth in the good old early days as much as £16 each. **1937** H. SAUER *Ex Afr.* 191 Next in importance to the *achter-os*, or wheeler, comes the *voor-os*, or leader, who also is expected to be a cut above the ordinary middle ox member of the team ... The *voor-os* is expected to act the part of friend, philosopher, and guide to the rest of the team. **1977** F.G. BUTLER *Karoo Morning* 90 Having managed to inspan the two agterosse after half an hour's battle, we would turn our attention to the voorosse; but by the time these were under control the agterosse had wriggled free or broken their traces or tied themselves and the harness into inextricable knots.

voorshlag var. VOORSLAG.

voorskot /ˈfʊə(r)skɔt/ *n.* Pl. **-skotte** /-skɔtə/ [Afk., fr. *voorskiet* to lend, to advance (money).] An advance payment made to a farmer for a crop, wool-clip, etc., calculated at a predetermined fixed price per kilogram. Also *attrib.*, and *transf.* See also AGTERSKOT, MIDDELSKOT.

1948 *Cape Times* 22 Nov. 14 The Land Bank had fixed the *voorskot* price for first grade lucerne at 3s. for 100 lb. **1957** *Handbk for Farmers* (Dept of Agric.) I. 215 The Board employs agents, specially appointed for the purpose, to purchase kaffir corn from producers on its behalf at fixed 'voorskot' prices. **1961** *Cape Times* 15 Feb. 9 A figure of R50m. is being mentioned as a *voorskot* for Bantu homelands. **1970** S.S. BRAND in *Std Encycl. of Sn Afr.* I. 223 The product may again be sold only to the control board, but the price producers are paid, usually in the form of an advance (*voorskot*), and a final payment (*agterskot*) depends on the average price realised by the control board for all sales from the pool into which individual producers deliver their produce. **1972** *E. Prov. Herald* 9 Mar. 19 A one-channel marketing system with the board the sole marketing authority is a certainty. So is a 'voorskot-agterskot' payment system to farmers for their clips. **1976** *Daily Dispatch* 21 Aug. 9 Fixing the voorskot as closely as possible to the expected realisation price is an extremely difficult and responsible task. **1977** *Farmer's Weekly* 23 Nov. 119 The season's buckwheat crop has now been disposed of for export, .. and farmers have now received middle and agterskots which when added to the voorskot have shown them an excellent return. **1984** *Grocott's Mail* 17 Apr. 23 Voorskotte will be paid on winter deliveries. **1989** *E. Prov. Herald* 4 Mar. 1 Wool producers are to get an increased advance payment (voorskot) for the second time this season. The average voorskot price on merino wool will be increased 15%.

voorslag /ˈfʊə(r)slax/ *n.* Formerly also **forslat, voersla(a)g, voorshlag, voor slach.** [S. Afr. Du. (later Afk.), fr. Du. *voor* front + *slag* lash (of a whip).]

1. A fine strip of antelope hide forming the end of a whiplash; FORESLOCK. Cf. AGTERSLAG.

1833 *Graham's Town Jrnl* 4 Apr. 3 He .. took his whip and in endeavouring to frighten them began using the 'voor slach' of the whip; finding this ineffectual, he took the butt end of the whip stick. **1852** C. BARTER *Dorp & Veld* 43 Putting a new *voorslag* (lash) to the wagon-whip, that its smack might be clear and loud. **1883** M.A. CAREY-HOBSON *Farm in Karoo* 71 Wild deer skin, prepared and softened by much manipulation for cutting into narrow thongs to be used as whip-lashes or 'voerslaags'. **1907** J.P. FITZPATRICK *Jock of Bushveld* (1909) 226 They used to say he could kill a fly on the front ox or on the toe of his own boot with the voorslag of his big whip. **1916** [see STROP *n.*[1] sense 1]. **1919** M.M. STEYN *Diary* 49 Deftly catch the 'voorslag' as the lash coiled back, by a turn of the wrist, round the whiphandle! **1925** S.G. CRONWRIGHT-SCHREINER in F.C. Slater *Centenary Bk of S. Afr. Verse* 62 Let the voorslag's crack resound ... Let the Whip with its lightning crack Startle the buck from its lair in the kloof. **1937** H. SAUER *Ex Afr.* 193 The long lash ends in two shorter pieces, tapering to points and called the *achter-slag* and the *voor-slag*, the latter being the terminal section of the whip ... When a whip is properly handled, the *achter-slag*, and even more the *voor-slag*, inflicts the punishment on the victim and produces the rolling and cracking sound which can be heard at a distance of several miles. **1944** J. MOCKFORD *Here Are S. Africans* 65 The driver wielded a gigantic whip — a long bamboo, tapering like a fishing rod from thick base to slender tip, to which was laced a still longer rawhide thong ending in a spliced on *voorslag* or lash. **1948** V.M. FITZROY *Cabbages & Cream* 159 It was the voorslag at the end [of the whip], so we learned, that was responsible for that glorious resounding crack, like a shot from a gun. **1968** G. CROUDACE *Silver Grass* 152 The lash whipped back its lace-thin *voorslag*, flicking a droplet of blood on to Jeremy's cheek. **1973** [see AGTERSLAG]. **1986** W. STEENKAMP *Blake's Woman* 130 Although she had not handled a wagon-whip for years it did exactly what she required of it. The 'voorslag', or popper, snaked out at Blake's chest. **1991** [see AGTERSLAG].

2. *noncount.* Fine whip-cord of antelope skin used for making voorslags. Also *attrib.*

1870 *E. Prov. Herald* 5 Apr., A number of voerslag skins and sjamboks realized moderate prices. **1880** E.F. SANDEMAN *Eight Months in Ox-Waggon* 42 Supplies of rims, rim pey and forslat. *Ibid.* 130 Forslat, thin strips of skin used for the whip-lashes, and which the drivers wear out every two or three days. **1881** F.R. STATHAM *Blacks, Boers & Brit.* 197 Patched here with strips of hide — what the Dutchman calls 'voorslag' — there with string. **1907** J.P. FITZPATRICK *Jock of Bushveld* (1909) 449 It was wealth to him to have the riems and voorslag, the odd yokes and strops and waggon tools. **1913** C. PETTMAN *Africanderisms* 246 A karoo plant .. the fleshy, juicy leaves of which are used in the preparation of skins for karosses, voorslag, and other uses. **1914** S.P. HYATT *Old Transport Rd* 272 Voorshlag .. was a most paying thing to make. **1920** F.C. CORNELL *Glamour of Prospecting* 273 Soon the sole began to part company with the upper. And he had left his voorslag at Aar Pan. Luckily I had some fancy native wire-work .. which, unravelled, served to keep sole and upper together. **1932** *Grocott's Daily Mail* 9 Jan. 3, I definitely remember having bought a few shoe laces in place of the usual 'voorslag'. **1958** A. JACKSON *Trader on Veld* 56 Riems, of gemsbok skins, and voorslag (whipcord) of koodoo skins.

voorspan *n. obs.* Also **vorspann.** [S. Afr. Du., fr. Du. *voor* fore, front + *span* team.] A fresh team of draught-animals supplied by farmers free of charge, as required, to those travelling on government service. Also *attrib.*

1801 J. BARROW *Trav.* I. 358 For the better convenience of those who travelled on the public service, government imposed a kind of tax on the farmers, by obliging them to furnish *Voorspans*, or gratuitous teams of oxen, whenever they should be demanded. **1812** A. PLUMPTRE tr. *H. Lichtenstein's Trav. in Sn Afr.* (1928) I. 222 Amid a pouring and continued rain we pursued our way till we arrived at the above-mentioned farm, where we met the Field-cornet Ignatius Müller, with a new *vorspann*. **1821** C.I. LATROBE *Jrnl of Visit* 270 He made an apology, by explaining how he was continually harrassed by orders for Vorspann, caring for the transport of the military and their baggage, and put to the inconvenience of sending his men up and down the country. **1822** W.J. BURCHELL *Trav.* I. 183 This gentleman anticipated my wants, by proposing, as the passage of the Hex-river Kloof, and the ascent of the Roggeveld mountain would greatly exhaust the strength of my own oxen, that he might issue orders for a voor-span (relay of oxen) to meet me at those places. *Ibid.* 200 A boor, who had received orders to furnish the next voorspans, sent in the morning to enquire when they would be wanted. **1847** J. BARROW *Reflect.* 202, I shall start forthwith, with your permission, and avail myself of the privilege of taking *voorspan* oxen or cattle, supplied by the farmers, from station to station, for the service of Government free from charge.

voorstel /ˈfʊə(r)stel/ *n. Wagon-making.* [S. Afr. Du., fr. Du. *voor* front + *stel* short form of *wagenstel* lower framework of a wagon.] The front part of the lower framework of a wagon, to which one end of the pole (or DISSELBOOM) is attached; FORESTELL. Cf. AGTERSTEL. See also ONDERSTEL.

1822 [see AGTERSTEL]. **1833** S. KAY *Trav. & Researches* 298 Before reaching the plain .. the bolt that goes through the *voor-stel* and shaft broke. **1913** C. PETTMAN *Africanderisms* 541 *Voorstel*, The part of the wagon which receives the disselboom.

voortang /ˈfʊə(r)taŋ/ *n. Wagon-making.* [Afk., fr. S. Afr. Du. *voor* fore, front + *tang* pair of tongs.] A shaped wooden block connecting the perch-pole (or LONG-WAGON) and shaft (or DISSELBOOM) of an ox-wagon; FORE-TONGUE. Cf. AGTERTANG.

1899 *Natal Agric. Jrnl* 31 Mar. 4 All words in connection with trekking are of Dutch origin ... besides the parts of the wagon, such as 'draaibord,' 'voortang,' 'schammel,' etc. *a*1928 C. FULLER *Trigardt's Trek* (1932) 101 When part way down, the voortang broke in the axle. **1934** C.P. SWART Supplement to Pettman. 187 *Voortang*, The wooden block passing from the long-wagon through the axle-bed to the shaft of the ox-wagon, connecting the long-wagon and the shaft. **1958, 1977** [see AGTERTANG].

voort, die stryd duur see DIE STRYD DUUR VOORT.

voortou /ˈfʊə(r)təʊ/ *n.* [Afk., earlier S. Afr. Du. *voortouw*, fr. Du. *voor* fore, front + *touw* rope.] The short rope or thong by which a team of oxen is led; FORE-TOW; also called TOU (sense 1).

1822 W.J. BURCHELL *Trav.* I. 174, I obtained .. a voortouw (fore-rope) or short trektouw, which .. would be required occasionally to hook on at the end of the draw-rope, whenever it was necessary to employ a larger team than ten or twelve oxen. **1968** K. MCMAGH *Dinner of Herbs* 8 Her father had himself taken the 'voor-touw' — the thong looped around the horns of the leading oxen, and led the span to keep it upon its course.

‖**voortrek** /ˈfʊə(r)trek/ *n.* Also with initial capital. [Afk., back formation fr. next.] GREAT TREK sense 1.

1972 *S. Afr. Panorama* Mar. 27 This is the true significance of Blood River — South Africa's most hallowed spot. The victory won there made the Voortrekkers conscious of their strength ... It ensured the success of the *voortrek*. **1980** *Ibid.* Sept. 16 The Voortrek, a central episode in South Africa's rich historic past, was one of the great feats of human courage.

Voortrekker /ˈfʊə(r)trekə(r)/ *adj.* and *n.* Also **Voertrekker, Voortreker,** and Englished forms **Fore-tracker, -trek(k)er,** often with small initial. [Afk., fr. Du. *voor* advance, fore + *trekken* to travel, migrate, + agential suffix *-er*.]

A. *adj.* Of or pertaining to the Voortrekkers (see sense B 1).

Some quots might reflect attributive uses of the noun.

1872 *Queenstown Free Press* 27 Sept. (Pettman), Oom Koos will probably once again be our voortrekker leader. **1882** C.L. NORRIS-NEWMAN *With Boers in Tvl* 77 The large majority of the Volksraad were of the old 'Voortrekker' stamp, and did not in any way wish to again come under British rule. **1895** J.G. MILLAIS *Breath from Veldt* (1899) 61 The 'voor-trekker' Dutchmen. **1899** A. WERNER *Captain of Locusts* 34 He was possessed to the full of the old voortrekker spirit, and loathed the sight of the smoke from a neighbour's chimney. **1924** L. COHEN *Reminisc. of Jhb.* 69 The old man, soured by memories of the Great Trek period, could not forget those boyish days of bitter hardship, when to escape from the sight of the Rooinek, the *Voor*-trekker Boers — he a *Voor*-looper amongst them — penetrated far north .. in search of a magic region where they could live their simple lives in their own way. **1934** B.I. BUCHANAN *Pioneer Days* 3 During the long arduous trek from the Cape the Voortrekker women had stood behind parked wagons, loading the guns with which their men must repulse the Native impis. **1941** C.W. DE KIEWIET *Hist. of S. Afr.* 52 Like the Fathers of the American Constitution, the Voortrekker leaders came to be considered the founders of modern South Africa. **1943** 'J. BURGER' *Black Man's Burden* 239 The revival of Voortrekker beards, dress, games, songs, and dances [etc.] .. were part of a gigantic Nationalist campaign for political purposes. **1960** G. LISTER *Reminisc.* 4 An old-fashioned Voortrekker type waggon with dished wheels. **1963** B. MODISANE *Blame Me on Hist.* (1986) 17 Like America, South Africa has a frontier or voortrekker mentality, a primitive throw-back to the pioneering era. **1971** *Sunday Times* 19 Dec. 5 Traditional Voortrekker costumes were seen everywhere mingling with safari suits and mini dresses. **1981** *S. Afr. Panorama* July 46 The finest private collection of old Cape Dutch and Voortrekker-period furniture in South Africa. **1990** *Sunday Times* 11 Feb. 3 The irate band, in traditional Voortrekker dress, claimed .. Afrikaner culture was being eroded.

B. *n.*

1. *hist.* A member of one of numerous groups of Dutch-speaking people who migrated by wagon from the Cape Colony into the interior from 1836 onwards, in order to live beyond the boundaries of British rule; EMIGRANT *n.*; *emigrant Boer*, see EMIGRANT *adj.*; *Great Trekker*, see GREAT TREK; *trek boer* sense (*b*), see TREK *n.* sense 12 b; TREKKER sense 1 a; also called VOORLOPER (sense 2).

1873 F. BOYLE *To Cape for Diamonds* 32 We now come to that great epoch of South African history — the exodus of the Voor-trekers, or Fore-trackers. **1876** *Cape Monthly Mag.* XIII. Sept. 180 (*title*) The Journal of a Voor-Trekker. **1881** *E. London Daily Dispatch & Frontier Advertiser* 26 Jan. (Suppl.) 2 The President of the discontented farmers .. is one of the 'voortrekkers,' or original emigrants from the Old Colony, who trecked north to the Vaal river. **1882** C. DU VAL *With Show through Sn Afr.* I. 203 Through the parched plains of what is now the Orange Free State, over the snow-clad mountains of the Drakensburg .. came the dauntless 'Voortrekkers', with their waggons, their cattle, their 'vrouws', their 'kinderen', and their household belongings. **1893** F.C. SELOUS *Trav. & Adventure* 7 From the lips of some of the old 'voortrekkers' I heard the story of the wrongs they suffered under the British administration of the Cape Colony, which, culminating in the emancipation of the slaves, .. plunged the whole country into grief and dismay.

1900 H.C. HILLEGAS *Oom Paul's People* 37 The first 'trekking' party, or the 'Voortrekkers,' consisted of about two hundred persons under the leadership of Andries Hendrik Potgieter. 1926 G.E. CORY *Diary of Francis Owen* 145 Not only were there many sufferers in the far away Colesberg, but even the Boer voortrekkers in Natal were smitten. c1936 *S. & E. Afr. Yr Bk & Guide* 225 The voortrekkers, although they were always known as Boers or farmers, .. were, in the first instance, mainly hunters, eating the game they shot and trading the skins and horns. 1943 'J. BURGER' *Black Man's Burden* 19 The Voortrekkers envisaged an independent republican State with plenty of land and no nonsense about equality between black and white. 1955 D.L. HOBMAN *Olive Schreiner* 112 These voortrekkers or pioneers moved in ox-wagons which were their homes, and also served as encampments whenever they had to defend themselves against tribal attacks. 1973 J. MEINTJES *Voortrekkers* 13 The emigrants .. never referred to themselves as Voortrekkers — that came much later — but as emigrant farmers. 1987 *Fair Lady* 18 Feb. 103 (*letter*) I've had a decent education (even if it was full of Praise-the-Voortrekkers). 1988 *Star* 21 Jan. 9 Voortrekkers saw the execution of Piet Retief as an act of utmost treachery on the part of Dingaan, whereas Zulus saw voortrekkers as scheming land-grabbers who were out to rob them of their land. 1992 P.-D. UYS in *South* 27 Feb. 24 If everything we reject as Eurocentric ends up on the floor, we will have more mountains to cross than those damn Voortrekkers who started all the trouble.

2. *Transf.*, and *fig.*

a. A member of an Afrikaner youth movement similar to the Boy Scouts and Girl Guides; in *pl.*, this movement; its members collectively. Also *attrib.*

1932 *Grocott's Daily Mail* 5 Apr. 2 A resolution 'that full support be given to the Voortrekker movement, which should seriously be considered to replace the cadet movement,' was referred back to the committee. 1934 A.J. BARNOUW *Lang. & Race Problems* 50 This scheme of racial segregation of youth is extended to outside activities. Young Afrikaners are being urged to join the Voortrekkers movement, which has been organized by Mr. J. de V. Hees of Bloemfontein as a Nationalist rival of the Boy Scouts. 1946 *Forum* 7 Dec. 4 Dr. K.W. Heese .. explained at a Voortrekker (Boy Scout) function at Worcester that he had everywhere noticed a slackening in enthusiasm and interest. 1960 E.G. MALHERBE in H. Spottiswoode *S. Afr.: Rd Ahead* 148 The *Voortrekkers* hived off from the Boy Scouts, and the *Noodhulpliga* hived off from the Red Cross, and latterly the *Rapportryers* are going to break away from Rotary. 1975 *Daily Dispatch* 30 Apr. 14 An appeal to Boy Scouts, Voortrekkers and the schools to assist in the work of clearing the countryside and farms of the cruel devices poachers use. 1981 *Rand Daily Mail* 29 Sept. 14, I note that the 50th anniversary of the Voortrekker movement is to be marked by the issue of a special postage stamp. In the Western world this country is, as far as I know, the only one, apart from the Boy Scout movement .., which has a parallel, but politically and racially oriented, youth movement. 1982 P. LE ROUX in Burman & Reynolds *Growing Up* 189, I was nonplussed when an English friend proclaimed that Voortrekkers (the Afrikaner Nationalist answer to the Boy Scout movement) were similar to the Hitler Youth movement. 1987 *Sunday Times* 23 Aug. 2 According to our constitution, no Voortrekker is allowed to attend any kind of political gathering in uniform. 1988 SPIEGEL & BOONZAIER in Boonzaier & Sharp *S. Afr. Keywords* 55 Somewhat ironically, the 'traditional' British Boy Scouts were used as the model for the Voortrekker youth movement, established during the Depression years. 1993 [see GREAT TREK sense 2].

b. A pioneer.

1949 J.S. FRANKLIN *This Union* 211 It is sheer accident that the 'Voortrekkers' of the seas and oceans of the world were Portuguese, Spaniards, Hollanders and Englishmen. 1951 H. DAVIES *Great S. Afr. Christians* 40 There is no reason why this Voortrekker of God's Kingdom should not be widely honoured. *Ibid.* 48 He was a Voortrekker of the Spirit. 1968 *Green Bay Tree* (*pamphlet*) p.xxiii, Today's Afrikaner 'industrial voortrekkers', driving in Mercedes instead of ox-wagons. 1980 *Sunday Times* 14 Sept. 11 They are descendants of the black Voortrekkers. 1987 *Rhodeo* (Rhodes Univ.) May 2 To UDF supporters on the campuses we say: History is on your side. You are the new Voortrekkers with integrity and vision to build bridges into the future.

Hence **voortrekking** *adj.*

1873 F. BOYLE *To Cape for Diamonds* 115 These foretreking tradesmen. 1965 W. PLOMER *Turbott Wolfe* 74 Aucampstroom was an outpost of the voortrekking Dutch.

voortsec, -zuk *varr.* VOETSAK.

‖**voorwaarts** /'fʊə(r)vɑː(r)ts/ *adv.* Also **vorwärts, vorwartz**. [Afk.] 'Forward'; usu. an order to march.

[1882 C. DU VAL *With Show through Sn Afr.* I. 110 'Vorwartz'! was the motto of sturdy old Blucher, and adopting the saying of the Prussian general, again we started 'on the trekk' through Southern Africa.] 1900 W.S. CHURCHILL *London to Ladysmith* 257 Dundonald reflected, reflected again, and finally resolved. *Vorwärts*! So on we went accordingly. 1947 H.C. BOSMAN *Mafeking Rd* (1969) 75 'Voorwaarts, burghers,' came the veld-kornet's order, and we cantered down the road in two's.

vootsac, -sek *varr.* VOETSAK.

vorcet(s), vorchitz *varr.* VOERCHITZ.

vorhaus, -huis *varr.* VOORHUIS.

vorlooper *var.* VOORLOPER.

vormeer bosch *var.* VERMEERBOS.

vorsect *var.* VOERCHITZ.

vorspann *var.* VOORSPAN.

vortsak *var.* VOETSAK.

vorwärts, -wartz *varr.* VOORWAARTS.

Vow, Day of the see DAY OF THE VOW.

vrachter *adv. obs.* [ad. Afk. *wragtig* (see WRAGTIG) or *wragtie* (see WRAGTIE).] WRAGTIG.

1899 'S. ERASMUS' *Prinsloo* 50 Vrachter, Landdrost, you are right. 1911 L. COHEN *Reminisc. of Kimberley* 36 'One hundred and thirty pounds is your lowest price?' 'Yes, that's so, vrachter' (truly), emphatically cried the Dutchman. 1920 S. BLACK *Dorp* 178 But, Uncle, I didn't vote 'Sapper' ... Vrachter, Oom, that's true, so help me God! 1924 L. COHEN *Reminisc. of Jhb.* 19 You have besalt all right *vrachter* (truly).

vrau, vraw *varr.* VROU.

vrek /frek/ *v. intrans. Colloq.* [Afk., 'die' (of animals), ad. Du. *verrekken* to disjoint, strain; or ad. G. *verrecken* to die (not in polite use).] Of animals, or (sometimes contemptuously) of people: to die. Also *fig.*, and Englished form **freck**.

1913 C. PETTMAN *Africanderisms* 542 *Vrek*, .. To die, especially of animals; when used of men it is suggestive of contempt. c1929 S. BLACK in S. Gray *Three Plays* (1984) 104 A Johnny who called him Hay-Whotte .. Cashed a crowd of dud cheques, Well, I hope that he vreks, Such a blighter deserves to be shot. 1966 VAN HEYNINGEN & BERTHOUD *Uys Krige* 119 Koos .. speaks with neither awe nor self-pity of his own coming death: he is going to 'vrek,' the same process that a dog or an ox goes through. 1971 J. FISCHER *Informant, Grahamstown*, I kicked the engine and it went brrrmm and then vrekked. 1973 J. COPE *Alley Cat* 163 'Where's your mother live?' 'She frecked out ... must be two weeks ago.' 'Died?' 'I said so, didn't I?' 1973 *Farmer's Weekly* 11 July 49 'Our stock .. are "vrekking" like flies' Mr David Hobson told congress. 1977 *Het Suid-Western* 30 Nov., A plastic pool to hold a two-metre shark? .. The unhappy shark .. has vrekked after its ordeal. 1980 C. HOPE *A Separate Development* (1983) 140 With Molefe you pay or vrek. End of story! 1987 *Frontline* Mar. 35 A R3 000 bull on its side, foaming at the mouth and legs thrashing as it vreks from Heartwater. 1988 A. DANGOR in Bunn & Taylor *From S. Afr.* 199 'Muriel has murdered Jan April and Clarence Meyer' ... 'Stroes God? Vrek! Right there in the dust!' 1990 *Personality* 15 Jan. 17 English goes from bad to worse as .. Prince Charles rewrites Shakespeare — and Hamlet *vreks*.

vrij *var.* VRY.

vrijburger *var.* VRYBURGER.

vrijer *var.* VRYER.

vrijerij *var.* VRYERY.

vroetel /'frut(ə)l/ *v. intrans. Colloq.* [Afk.] To fidget, fuss, or wriggle.

1966 E. PALMER *Plains of Camdeboo* 144 'What do you think I saw with my own eyes' he would end triumphantly, 'but the two tips of the lions' tails fighting one another, *vroetel*, *vroetel*, *vroetel* in a little-little dust no higher than a Karoo bush!' 1970 H.M. MUSMECI *Informant, Port Elizabeth* Please sit still and don't vroetel like that (fidget). 1970 P.J. ROSE *Informant, Pietermaritzburg* Vroetel. To fuss around. 1971 G. WESTCOTT *Informant, Grahamstown*, I haven't got time to go on vroeteling with the hymns — let's do the anthem.

vrot /frɒt, frɔt/ *adj. colloq.* Also **frot**. [Afk., ad. Du. *verrotten* to rot.]

1. *fig.*

a. Rotten, no good, useless.

1910 C. MEREDITH *Peggy* 89 Sis, man, don't be such a vrot thing; look on the bright side of things, and tell your creditors to go to the devil. c1929 S. BLACK in S. Gray *Three Plays* (1984) 95 The government is absolutely vrot, rotten ... They talk about stopping our morning tea. 1975 *Fair Lady* 24 Dec. 14 There are girls in the school long-jump and swimming teams. 'Only because the guys are vrot this year', one of the boys said. 1979 *Sunday Times* 8 July, No, look, things may be a bit vrot here in Joeys so long, but we don't want to stop living, not yet, anyway. 1988 A. CAMPBELL in *Fair Lady* 27 Apr. 96 He told my father that he had given him a *vrot* pig. 1989 F.G. BUTLER *Tales from Old Karoo* 146 That husband of hers .. now there was a rotten man. Not bad or wicked. Simply *vrot*. 1990 J. NAIDOO *Coolie Location* 185 Dr Fannemeyer told me, in the presence of six other students, that my lesson was *frot*. In fact, he didn't allow me to finish. 1991 P. SLABOLEPSZY *Braait Laaities*. 16 You trying to tell me the man who sold you your *vrot* watch was a *nice* man? 1994 A. LEVIN in *Sunday Times* 9 Oct. (Mag. Sect.) 8 The *vrot* lefties, those hanging around for the image or the aspirations, quickly downgraded in the grand scheme of things: from lefties to leftovers.

b. Drunk.

1991 G. MURRAY *Informant, Alberton* He got vrot on too much beer and wine. (Drunk.) 1991 I.E.G. COLLETT *Informant, Pilgrim's Rest* Vrot, frot: Properly drunk. 'Those two were absolutely frot last night.'

2. Esp. of organic matter: rotting, putrid.

1939 S. CLOETE *Watch for Dawn* 44 What are the charges against me? That I broke a stick over Booy's head. It was a rotten stick, vrot, or it would not have broken. 1969 A. FUGARD *Boesman & Lena* 2 Vrot! This piece of world is rotten. Put down your foot and you're in it up to your knee. 1970 D.A.C. MACLENNAN in *Dawn Wind*., Like a lot of vrot oranges with names and numbers stamped on 'em. 1975 S. ROBERTS *Outside Life's Feast* 102 Watch it, Horace, you old fool. You're going to tumble! .. Leave that one, Horace, it's vrot! 1977 *Sunday Times* 7 Aug. (Mag. Sect.) 3 When my son of six was called a 'rooinek' by an Afrikaans boy of 14 his mother couldn't take it when my kid replied 'Afrikaner vrot banana.' 1980 *Daily Dispatch* 28 Mar. 13 He recalled that Mr Hendrik Schoeman, Minister of Agriculture, had once called him a hyena because he was always allegedly looking for vrot meat. 1985 T. BARON in *Frontline* Feb. 30 Smoked over an open fire it takes a long time for boerewors to go vrot. 1989 *Informant, Grahamstown*, I don't know, perhaps some people like vrot pineapple. 1991 G. DE BEER *Informant, Port Nolloth* (N. Cape) These bananas are vrot, we can't eat them. **1994** C.M. SILVA *Informant, Margate* Only shell of Bldg. wasn't rotten or 'frot' as the workmen said.

3. *comb. Pathology.* **vrot maag**, also (formerly) **verrot maag** /- mɑːx/, [Afk., *maag* stomach, crop], in ostriches: an inflammation of the stomach, caused by a worm.

1913 C. PETTMAN *Africanderisms* 535 *Verrot maag*, .. A disease affecting ostriches — an inflamed condition of the stomach with a secretion of a jelly-like mucus due to the presence of a Palisade worm. **1976** S. LYNNE *Beloved Viking*, The men were discussing the merits of certain medicine for vrotmaag. Philippa had just been reading about this scourge amongst ostrich chicks, so she listened with interest.

So **vrot** *v. intrans.*, to rot.

1890 J.F. SEWELL *Private Diary* (1983) 118 Kitty began to vituperate & wished the boat would *vrot* & she would take her girl away from me etc. etc. **1994** J. MCNAUGHT *Informant, Fransch Hoek* The plums aren't worth anything. It'd be better just to let them vrot on the trees.

vrotpootjie(s) /ˈfrɔtpʊiki(z), -ci(s), ˈfrɒt-/ *n. Pathology.* Formerly also **vrotpootje(s)**. [Afk., *vrot* (fr. Du. *verrot*) rotten, putrid + *poot* hoof, paw + dim. suffix -IE (+ pl. suffix *-s*).] Either of two plant ailments: **a.** A virulent root disease of wheat and other grain, caused by the fungi *Dermatophora necatrix* and *D. glomerata*. **b.** Eel-worm or root gall worm in other food-crops.

1898 *Cape of G.H. Agric. Jrnl* Aug. 213 (Pettman), The disease is commonly called in the Colony *vrot pootje* .. and in very sandy soil is due to a fungus, *Dermatophora necatrix, Hartw.*, and *D. glomerata, Viala.* **1913** C. PETTMAN *Africanderisms* 542 *Vrotpootjes*, .. A disease which attacks the roots of beans, potatoes, and other vegetables. **1958** R.E. LIGHTON *Out of Strong* 109 Mealies so tall you can't see the ostriches, and for the Receiver of Revenue rust in the tobacco, vrotpootjie in the groundnuts, hail in the citrus. **1975** *Dict. of Eng. Usage in Sn Afr.*, *Vrotpootjies*, .. Plant disease caused by a minute worm wh[ich] is known in the Transvaal as the 'eel worm' (*Anguillulidae*) & in the Cape Province as the 'root gall worm'. **1979** *Farmer's Weekly* 21 Mar. 20 In certain .. major producing areas, *vrot pootjie*, or 'take-all', has become the greatest single menace to wheat. *Ibid. (captions)* Vrotpootjie symptoms showing the characteristic blacking of the stem bases ... Close-up of vrotpootjie symptoms showing white heads among green heads.

vrou /frəʊ/ *n.* Formerly also **frau(w), frou, vrau, vraw, vro(u)w**. [Afk. (fr. Du. *vrouw*), woman, wife, mistress.] A (Dutch) woman; a wife; the mistress of a household; cf. HUISVROU. See also BOEREVROU, MEVROU.

1.a. A common noun.

1785 E. BRITTLE in V. De Kock *Fun They Had* (1955) 48 The vrouws, in a minuet, solemnly prance ... Mynheer, in cotillion, .. flounders about. **1797** LADY A. BARNARD *S. Afr. Century Ago* (1910) 123 The *vrow* sat like Charity tormented by a legion of devils. **1798** [see MAN *n.*[1]]. **1804** R. PERCIVAL *Acct of Cape of G.H.* 51 Besides being very handsomely paid for board and lodging, Mynheer expects over and above a present of some valuable Asiatic or European article for the Vrow his wife. **1824** W.J. BURCHELL *Trav.* II. 177 Its inhabitants were, the *baas*, and his *vrouw* (wife) and son, .. and two or three female servants, all Hottentots. **1832** [see STIVER sense 1]. **1838** J.E. ALEXANDER *Exped. into Int.* I. 130 The vrows and meisjes were .. at work day and night at the farm-houses below the mountain, preparing biltong or dried meat, and baking bread for their men. **1849** N.J. MERRIMAN *Cape Jrnls* (1957), I soon .. got on better terms with this family, .. by giving my blue spectacles to the vrou, who I observed had weak eyes. **1852** M.B. HUDSON *S. Afr. Frontier Life* 209 The washing is done by a Hottentot vrouw. **1859** H. RABONE in A. Rabone *Rec. of Pioneer Family* (1966) 119 A conversation with my wash *vrouw*. **1867** E.L. PRICE *Jrnls* (1956) 249 Roger used to measure off & take doses of medicine to the old vrow & have them refused as too nauseous or not suitable. **1871** J. MCKAY *Reminisc.* 207 The Hottentot or Kafir vrouw is the worker of the household. **1877** R.M. BALLANTYNE *Settler & Savage* 28 Myneer Marais' vrouw, a good-looking, fat, and motherly woman verging on forty. **1881** [see BOERESS]. **1890** A. MARTIN *Home Life* 138 The more highly the good vrouw wishes to honour you, the more .. she over-sweetens your cup of tea or coffee. **1903** D. BLACKBURN *Burgher Quixote* 31 It was less suffering to fight Rooineks against my conscience that to be physicked by all the vrouws in the dorp. **1908** [see KWAAI sense 1 a]. **1911** L. COHEN *Reminisc. of Kimberley* 304, I have often noticed the ponderous vrouws, those prototypes of Rubens's mountains of flesh .. wipe the chairs with their aprons after we had risen from them. **1924** S.G. MILLIN *God's Step-Children* 8 Tall, flat-faced, flat-roofed white houses, with open sun stoeps in front, on which stout Dutch vrouws .. sat drinking coffee with their cavaliers. **1936** R.J.M. GOOLD-ADAMS *S. Afr. To-Day & To-Morrow* 12 Their homely 'vrouws', each of whom considers it her natural duty to bring into the world as many children as she can. **1949** [see APPRENTICE *n.*]. **1963** in O. DOUGHTY *Early Diamond Days* 133 A Dutch boy brings some excellent sausages made by a good old *frouw* — his mother. **1970** *Daily Dispatch* 30 Jan. 14 And now youse can do me a favour. Cancel the policy on my vrou quickly! **1982** *Sunday Times* 21 Feb. 2 The Voortrekker's vrou and the Yorkshire farmer's wife and the Italian mamma all created a cuisine out of what was available. **1993** *Natal Mercury* 26 Mar. (TV Guide) 8 Whenever she came to a farm .. the owner had conveniently departed .., leaving his vrou or, in one case, the family tutor, to entertain her ladyship.

b. A title, with a surname: 'Mrs'.

1798 LADY A. BARNARD *S. Afr. Century Ago* (1910) 174 Vrow Van Rhenin lighted the fire and cooked the fish. **1862** LADY DUFF-GORDON *Lett. from Cape* (1925) 94 Vrouw Reits was as black as coal, but so pretty! **1876** F. BOYLE *Savage Life* 7 Vrouw Jacobs interfered, confiscating the stone of contention. *Ibid.* 201 We got to the cottage, the door of which, as usual, stood open, and by the fireplace sat Frow Groethode. **1905** P. GIBBON *Vrouw Grobelaar* 20 At times, and in certain matters, Vrouw Grobelaar would display a ready acumen. **1911** — *Margaret Harding* 211 You have been good, very good, to the Vrouw du Preez. **1970** M. DONOVAN in J.W. Loubser *Africana Short Stories* 56 The two young men followed their host into the parlour, and were introduced to portly vrou De Beer.

c. A form of address used by a husband to his wife.

1823 W.W. BIRD *State of Cape of G.H.* 74 An inclination to marriage cannot be more clearly ascertained than [in] the universal custom of calling each other man and vrouw, (in English, husband and wife). **1910** D. FAIRBRIDGE *That Which Hath Been* (1913) 184 'All has gone well, vrouw,' he cried. 'Let us have some Schiedam to drive out the wet and you shall hear.' **1929** J.G. VAN ALPHEN *Jan Venter* 49 Just give one cup to Venter, *vrou*. He is the new policeman. **1949** H.C. BOSMAN *Cold Stone Jug* (1969) 103 'Vrou', he said, 'the coffee is weak.' **1968** K. MCMAGH *Dinner of Herbs* 29 But where, I ask you, vrou, where is a poor devil like me to lay my hands on a hundred pounds? **1977** F.G. BUTLER *Karoo Morning* 42 One day he had staggered into the voorkamer, pale as a sheet, and said to his wife, 'Vrou, I've just seen the most terrible thing'.

2. *fig. Army slang.* As a common noun: a serviceman's rifle.

1979 *Ex-serviceman, Informant* Your vrou had to go with you — even to the pub — everywhere except the shower, and if you dropped it you had to kiss it better — you're wedded to the .. thing.

vry /freɪ/ *v. colloq.* Formerly also **fraai, fray, frey, vrij**. [Afk.]

1. *intrans.* To engage in erotic caressing. Also *fig.*

1887 A. TROLLOPE in J. Mackinnon *S. Afr. Traits* 118 They are very great at making love or 'freying,' as they call it. **1970** S. SMUTS *Informant, Cape Town* The two lovers sat and vryed in the corner. **1975** *Sunday Times* 20 Apr. 16 The truth .. is that people who play (or vry?) together, stay together. **1980** *Daily Dispatch* 27 Feb. 13 The question of the day — Who was busy vry-ing with whom? Nobody would have initially thought that Mr Chris R— was vry-ing with the NRP. On the contrary, he appeared to be fascinated by the courship between the NRP and the PFP, and wondered if a wedding was in the offing. **1983** *Cape Times* 9 Dec. 16 Who else can get away with describing .. 'vrying' with Sannie van der Spuy on the grass of the Bloemfontein public swimming bath? **1985** P. SLABOLEPSZY *Sat. Night at Palace* 40, I was gripping this chick ... Her folks were out and we were fraying much better.

2. *trans.* To court or woo (someone).

1899 G.H. RUSSELL *Under Sjambok* 77, I think the Landrost was fraaing (courting) the young woman we saw tonight, but she did not seem very pleased about it. **1958** A. JACKSON *Trader on Veld* 33 He had come to 'vry' (court) the young 'nooi' (daughter of the house). **1983** G. SILBER in *Sunday Times* 28 Aug. (Mag. Sect.) 19 Horse is reclining on a garden bench .. *vrying* his blonde peach and watching the talent show with his left eye. **1984** S. GRAY *Three Plays* 163, I wonder who's vrying her now. I wonder who's learning her how.

Hence **vry** *n.*, also **vrytjie** [Afk., see -IE], **vrying** *vbl n.*, VRYERY.

1925 L.D. FLEMMING *Crop of Chaff* 117 You put on a suit and a hat, and there you were .., all ready for the fray — or vrij. **1924** G. BAUMANN in Baumann & Bright *Lost Republic* (1940) 115 Saturday evening was the time the young farmer did his courting — 'vrying'. **1975** S. ROBERTS *Outside Life's Feast* 90 It's lekker to live a bit; to have a few drinks and a little vrytjie. **1990** *Personality* 13 Aug. 23 He became upset and said it didn't look as if I was interested in *vrying*.

vryburger /ˈfreɪbɜːgə, ˈ-bərgər/ *n. hist.* Also **vrijburgher**, and with initial capital. [Afk. (fr. Du. *vrijburgher*), *vry* free + *burger* citizen, inhabitant.] FREE BURGHER. Also *attrib.*

1955 L.G. GREEN *Beyond City Lights* 164 The *vryburgers* with their farms of sixty morgen were the frontiersmen of the day, and had to promise that they would remain on their farms for twenty years. **1977** B. MARKS *Our S. Afr. Army* 11 The Commando organization dates back to the Vryburgers in 1657. **1989** *Leisure* 30 Dec. 4 Its early development .. was essential to the conquest of the interior as carried out first by explorers and then by vrijburger farmers.

vryer /ˈfreɪə(r)/ *n.* Formerly also **vrijer**. [Afk.] A lover or sweetheart. Also *fig.*

1882 J. NIXON *Among Boers* 214, I have often been curious to how the young vrijer, or lover, manages to make known to the fair one his wish to 'opzit', or sit up, for the purpose of courting. **1883** O.E.A. SCHREINER *Story of Afr. Farm* 163 She herself contemplated marriage within the year with one or other of her numerous 'vrijers' and she suggested that the weddings might take place together. **1963** A.M. LOUW *20 Days* 91 Above her bed were two framed postcard-size pictures: one of a stout Coloured woman dressed in country Sunday best; the other of a young Coloured man ... He said: 'Your mother and your vryer — your sweetheart?' **1965** C. VAN HEYNINGEN *Orange Days* 54 He offered himself to be Ada's vryer (sweetheart). **1980** J. SCOTT in *Daily Dispatch* 27 Feb. 13 He saw the PFP as a threat to his own romantic inclinations. Far from being a flower girl at somebody else's wedding. He was a vryer in his own right ... It was at this point that Mr P— miraculously switched, like Mr R—, from accuser to vryer. **1982** C. HOPE *Private Parts* 73 Parking lots and Sundry vryers' hideaways from the Union Buildings to the Fountains.

‖**vryery** /ˈfreɪəreɪ/ *n.* Formerly also **vrijerij**. [Afk.] Wooing, love-making; *vry*, see *n.* at VRY *v.* Also *fig.*

1920 S. BLACK *Dorp* 96 If Anita said so it was all right. Vrijerij (courting) was to Van Ryn a clear, cut-and-dried business — no subtleties, no finesse, no bashfulness. **1980** *Daily Dispatch* 27 Feb. 13 A veteran front bencher whose stream of old-style vituperation has his .. colleagues in fits, spent most of his speech

vryheidsoorlog /ˈfrɛɪhɛɪtsˌʊə(r)lɔx/ n. [Afk., *vryheid* freedom + linking phoneme -s- + *oorlog* war.] A term used (generally among Afrikaners) for any of several wars against British forces, particularly the ANGLO-BOER WAR. Also *fig.*

1973 *E. Prov. Herald* 31 May 7 We in South Africa have another 'vryheidsoorlog' to fight — not against the cruel might of Britain, but against the selfishness which dominates our hearts and our laws. 1977 *Sunday Times* 6 Feb. 10, I believe he [sc. the Afrikaner] stands .. before a coming and unavoidable war, this time the third vryheidsoorlog — and he stands alone. 1988 G. CROUDACE *Secret of Rock* 77 'My great-grandfather sent his son to St. Gregs before the Tweede Vryheidsoorlog.' He glanced shyly at Neville as he gave the Afrikaans name for the Anglo-Boer War.

Vrystaat /ˈfrɛɪstɑːt/ int. and n. [Afk., ellipt. for *Oranje Vrystaat* the Orange Free State, a Boer republic during the 19th century, from 1910 one of the four provinces of South Africa, and since 1994 one of the country's nine provinces.]
A. *int.* Used as an (often ironical) exclamation of exaltation, triumph, approbation, or encouragement; a rallying call. Hence **Vrystaat** *n.*, a cry of 'Vrystaat!'; *attrib.*, enthusiastically South African.

1961 *Rand Daily Mail* 31 May 1 On the square several hundred young people sang folk songs and cheered lustily as a bearded veteran was hoisted shoulder high to wave a South African flag and shout 'vrystaat'. 1964 D. MARAIS in *Cape Times* 25 July, (*cartoon caption*) He's a French supporter. 'L'etat libre' is their way of saying 'Vrystaat!' 1970 *Cape Times* 16 May, Varsity's curvaceous champagne queen in a mini-minidress .. should whip up the whistles and the lusty V-R-Y-S-T-A-A-T-S. 1974 *Sunday Times* 1 Dec. (Mag. Sect.) 14 The one word we could use to express our triumphant delight: 'Vrystaat!' 1977 *Ibid.* 14 Aug. 3 A few scattered wolf whistles and hesitant shouts of 'Vrystaat' greeted a couple of the more daring dance steps but, otherwise, the girls battled for a response from the audience. 1978 A.P. BRINK *Rumours of Rain* 327 Until that moment we'd been speaking English; but as he raised his glass he said: 'Vrystaat!' 'Don't tell me you come from South Africa?' I said. 1990 G. SLOVO *Ties of Blood* 232 'Vrystaat! Vrystaat!' — the Nats' rallying cry ... 'We won! We won!' they shouted. 1990 *Sunday Times* 30 Dec. 1 Remember, the future is certain. It is the past that's unpredictable. Amandla/Vrystaat! 1991 G. SILBER in *Ibid.* 13 Jan. (Mag. Sect.) 20 Following the unconditional lifting of the Sports Boycott .. a combined Springbok rugby, cricket, soccer, hockey, wrestling, jukskei, karate, and water polo team will take on any ten teams .. and beat the smithereens out of them. Vrystaat! And Viva, too. 1991 *Sunday Times* 14 July (Mag. Sect.) 36 He .. has provided countless South Africans, and a few *Vrystaat* enclaves abroad, with many hours of pleasure and kinship. 1993 G. MCINTOSH in *Ibid.* 20 June 23 'Vrystaat' is probably the best-known South African slogan.

B. *n.* FREE STATE *n. phr.* Also *attrib.*

1969 I. VAUGHAN *Last of Sunlit Yrs* 101 He .. says, 'when I was a boy the Vrystaat was not like this'. 1971 *Personality* 2 Feb. 23 What else is there to do in the good old Vrystaat on Sundays? 1975 *Sunday Times* 20 Apr. 11 We all come from 'the conquered territory' — Oom Jim, Nico and myself. Vrystaat-power. 1978 *Voice* 11 Oct. 1 A young White woman and her Black lover recently hiked through South Africa together and were given lifts by Vrystaat farmers, a Nationalist supporter, [etc.]. 1982 M. MZAMANE *Children of Soweto* 26 We passed round to our members everything we read with the glee of Vrystaat Boers peddling round copies of *Playboy*. 1989 *Style* Dec. 151 Exposed to all the laagerisms of any Vrystaat Afrikaner boy.
Hence **Vrystater** *n.*, one from the Orange Free State.

1900 P.J. DU TOIT *Diary* (1974) 19 *Prisoners* .. 16 Vrystaters. 1948 O. WALKER *Kaffirs Are Lively* 70 Like the rest of the farming community, the Vrystaters do not connect inefficiency with low wages. 1969 I. VAUGHAN *Last of Sunlit Yrs* 101 He tells me he is an old 'Vrystaater', and his people before him. 1973 *Cape Times* 29 Jan. 11 The 'Vrystaaters' are assured of a good fight when they travel to Montagu in August. 1977 *Sunday Times* 27 Feb. 15 The veldskoened Vrystaters of Vrede. 1990 *E. Prov. Herald* 16 May (Food & Wine Suppl.), Although a 'Vrystater', Ross completed his high school education at SACS in Cape Town.

vuga var. VUKA.

vuilgoed /ˈfɛɪlxʊt, ˈfœɪlxʊt/ n. Also **veilgoed**. [Afk., *vuil* filthy + *goed* things.]
1. Filth, rubbish; also an insulting form of address or reference.

1917 S.T. PLAATJE *Native Life* 82 Instilling in Anna's mind all kinds of silly notions, about town flirts and black dandies, .. and similar vuilgoed (rubbish). 1924 S.G. MILLIN *God's Step-Children* 94 'Vuilgoed!' he shouted, and his voice was only a rushing in his own ears. 'Filth!' a1931 S. BLACK in S. Gray *Three Plays* (1984) 169 You'se the man who stole the farm — clear out of my house ... Vuilgoed! 1955 L. SOWDEN *Crooked Bluegum* 13 Only Izak Lotter grumbled about having such *vuilgoed* — such scum — about the house. 1956 H. BLOOM *Episode* 255 Both those black *vuilgoed* can buy up you or me and half the whole damn town if they want to. 1977 *Daily Dispatch* 15 Sept. 1 After standing silently .. they walked down the aisle .. of the Pretoria City Hall to cries of 'Sies' and 'Veilgoed'. 1979 J. GRATUS *Jo'burgers* 67 'Vuilgoed! — Filth!' he spat at him, 'You steal my claim. You don't deserve to live.' 1981 C. BARNARD in *Daily Dispatch* 6 July 6 The 'vuilgoed' and the 'robbies' [sc. rubbish] and 'sinkdak' that covered your children's heads and cost you a week's pay from the scrapyard, the wooden plank you stole from the construction site. 1982 J. SCOTT in *Cape Times* 17 Apr. 9 Mr S— repeated his claim that Mr F— was a *vuilgoed*, refused to withdraw it, and was ordered out of the chamber.

2. *Diamond-mining.* Overburden.

1950 E. ROSENTHAL *Here Are Diamonds* 198 Much of the digger's ingenuity has been bestowed on geological and mineralogical subjects. Hence we find such references as 'Concertina Rock' .. [etc.]. 'Vuilgoed', or overburden, expressively signifies 'dirt' in Afrikaans.

vuka /ˈvʊ(ː)ka, ˈvʊ(ː)ga/ v. intrans. Also **vuga**. [Xhosa and Zulu.] To wake up; usu. *imperative*. Also *fig.*

1911 D.B. HOOK *'Tis but Yesterday* 120 The bush seemed swarming with beaters, who plunged demon-like into the hidden recesses of the deepest kloofs and thickets, accompanied by yelping dogs, and the call of 'Vuka!' (wake up). 1947 F.C. SLATER *Sel. Poems* 58 (title) 'Vuka!' 1961 D. BEE *Children of Yesterday* 265 'Vuka! Vuka! Vukani! Wake up! Vuka-a-ani — bo!' 1964 G. GORDON *Four People* 68 Vuka! S'you think we've got all bloody day and night? 1978 L. BARNES in *The 1820* Vol.51 No.12, 19 Many Zulu words have crept into South African Indian English ... Some of the most commonly used are: *Skoten* (from *isikhoteni*) — a rogue, .. *vuga* — awake, *skats, skatools* (*isicathulo*) shoes, [etc.]. 1980 *Daily Dispatch* 27 Oct. 8 Dear Bennie, Ever since you advised Bonus Bond-holders to 'Vuka' (Wake up) we have watched the draw very carefully and, believe it or not, one of our numbers came up again, this time for R300.

vyacht um bige var. WAG-'N-BIETJIE.

vy(e) var. WAAI.

vygebosch *n. obs.* Formerly also **fei-bosch**, **vigenbosch**, **vygebosch**. Pl. **-bosse** /-bɔsə/, or (formerly) **-bosches**. [S. Afr. Du., fr. Du. *vijg* fig + linking phoneme -e- + *bosch* bush. (The modern Afk. form is *vyebos*.)] VYGIE.

1795 C.R. HOPSON tr. C.P. Thunberg's *Trav.* II. 35 The field was here of the Carrow kind, and the sheep were said to feed on those succulent plants, the Mesembryanthemums. 1890 A. MARTIN *Home Life* 48 The *fei-bosch* is another of our commonest and most useful plants. 1892 *The Jrnl* 9 July 1 The Veld consists of the much-sought-after Karoo, Vygebosch, Granaat, Brakbosch, with Mimosas in the Valley, and Pruim and Spekboom on the hills. 1914 *Farmer's Annual* 92 Vigenbosch (Mesembryanthemum). [1988 LE ROUX & SCHELPE *Namaqualand* 21 Many vyebosse of the Mesembryanthemaceae like *Ruschia* .., *Leipoldtia* .. and *Drosanthemum*.]

vygie /ˈfɛɪxi/ n. Formerly also **vijg(i)e**, **vijgen**. [Afk., 'little fig', *vyg* abbrev. of S. Afr. Du. *vygebosch* (see prec.) + dim. suffix -IE.] Any of several species of succulent flowering plants of the Mesembryanthemaceae, esp. of the genera *Mesembryanthemum, Lampranthus, Stoeberia,* and *Dorotheanthus;* MESEM; VYGEBOSCH. Also *attrib.* See also BOKBAAI VYGIE, *skilpadbos* (SKILPAD sense b).

1924 D. FAIRBRIDGE *Gardens of S. Afr.* 105 At Kew every weed of the veld seemed to be in blossom in the houses — all labelled with long Latin names which gave them an air of distinction and set them apart from our homely 'Vygies' and 'Buchus'. 1927 [see BRAKBOS]. 1928 [see MESEM]. 1931 *Farming in S. Afr.* 393 (Swart), Strange to say, the mineral and feeding-stuff analyses of a vygie give no clue to its probable palatability. 1948 H.V. MORTON *In Search of S. Afr.* 117 The best mutton in South Africa is raised on the small moisture-holding vygies of the Little Karoo and the Great Karoo. 1951 L.G. GREEN *Grow Lovely* 19 The *vygies!* Neon colours, staring from the petals with the authority of Pharaoh's glance .. acres of *vygies* so close together that you do not dare to walk among them. 1968 M. MULLER *Green Peaches Ripen* 37 The banks of the white sand-dunes were bejewelled with glittering *vygies*. 1975 *S. Afr. Panorama* Sept. 32 The majority of the 3 000 recognised vygie (mesembryanthemum) species occur in Namaqualand. 1981 D. COURT *Succulent Flora of Sn Afr.* 31 There's no doubt that the 'vygies' are responsible for the brightest and glossiest patches of the South African veld. 1990 *Weekend Mail* 14 Sept. 6 I .. have a soft spot for vygies. My garden sports .. one with obscenely bright pink flowers and another with luminous orange blooms. 1993 *Weekend Post* 2 Oct. 7 Small yellow and orange vygie plants.

vywer /ˈfɛɪvə(r)/ n. hist. [Afk., fr. Du. *vijver* pond.] A coastal pond or tidal trap, first used for inshore fishing by Stone Age peoples.

1959 J.D. CLARK *Prehist. of S. Afr.* 131 At various points ranging for over a thousand miles of coast are enclosures and dams known as *vywers*. Some .. are still in use and are or were ground-baited ... It seems probable that this method of inshore fishing dates back to these times ... The 'Mermaid' scene from a painted rock shelter at Ezeljachtspoort .. may well represent a fishing group at one of these *vywers*. 1992 YELD & GUBB in *Afr. Wildlife* Vol.46 No.2, 200 At some point in their ancient history they [sc. the Strandlopers] stumbled on the idea of building tidal fish traps, or vywers as they later came to be known.

W

waaboom var. WABOOM.

waacht var. WAG.

waacht-een-bietje, **waacht-en-beeche,** **waaght een beetji** varr. WAG-'N-BIETJIE.

waai /vaɪ/ *v. intrans. Slang.* Also **vai**. [Afk., prob. a fig. use of the basic sense 'to blow'; it has also been suggested that the word is ad. Pg. *vai* (a form of *ir* go).] To go, leave. Also Englished forms **vy, vye**.

1970 *Informant, Krugersdorp* Let's *waai* to the cafe. 1978 A. AKHALWAYA in *Rand Daily Mail* 10 July 7 There's spans of ous vying around with gonies ... The kerel will tension me up if I vy pozzie too late ... The timer's vied with the suitcase. 1980 E. PATEL *They Came at Dawn* 9 Haanetjie dresesup ..'n waai's to a chrismiss party. 1986 *Informant, East London* Let's waai before he gets back. 1987 [see LAS]. 1987 *Scope* 20 Nov. 39 We must *waai* from this pozzie! 1991 I.E.G. COLLETT *Informant, Pilgrim's Rest* Waai. Leave, get going, as in 'Its late, lets waai'. 1991 G. DE BEER *Informant, Port Nolloth (N. Cape)* Let's waai (vai), the music is far too loud. 1993 'Jimbo' programme insert, *Napac* Vye. Go.

waapenschauw var. WAPENSKOU.

waare var. WARE.

waater uyntie, - uyntje varr. WATERUINTJIE.

waboom /'vɑːbʊəm/ *n.* Also **vaboom, waaboom,** and (formerly) **wagenboom**. [S. Afr. Du. *wagenboom,* later Afk. *waboom* (*wa* wagon + *boom* tree); see quot. 1822 (sense b)].
a. In full *waboomhout* /-hɔʊt/ [Afk. *hout* wood]: the timber of any of several species of *Protea* (of the family Proteaceae), esp. the reddish wood of *Protea nitida*; WAGON WOOD. Also *attrib.*

1790 tr. F. *Le Vaillant's Trav.* I. 255 A few paltry woods, which had some resemblance to that named *Wage-Boom*. 1957 L.G. GREEN *Beyond City Lights* 89 They started a fire of *waboomhout* for comfort. Ibid. 149 The wood has a beautiful grain, and a floor of waboom blocks is a grand sight. 1967 W.A. DE KLERK *White Wines* 29 A bubbling tea billy over a *waboom* fire. 1971 BARAITSER & OBHOLZER *Cape Country Furn.* 268 Old household utensils of every sort are very common in the Sandveld and it is not unusual to find them still in use, particularly botterbakke of waboom, stampkarrings and teak vats. 1973 [see BOTTERBAK]. 1975 *S. Afr. Panorama* July 12 Indigenous waboomhout (wagon wood) was used for the roof beams and window frames.

b. Any of several species of *Protea,* esp. *P. nitida,* which grows up to 7m in height and bears pale yellow flowers; WAGONBOOM; WAGON TREE. Also *attrib.*

1795 C.R. HOPSON tr. *C.P. Thunberg's Trav.* II. 24 Near the mountains are sometimes seen a few low and scattered trees of the Protea grandiflora species (*Waageboom*). 1822 W.J. BURCHELL *Trav.* I. 123 We passed some large trees of Wagenboom (Protea grandiflora), so called by the colonists because the wood of it has been found suitable for making the fellies of wagon-wheels. It is reddish, and has a very pretty, reticulated grain. 1873 J.W. DAWSON *Earth & Man* 258 Cone-like fruits belonging to the Proteaceae (.. wagenbooms, etc.). 1906 B. STONEMAN *Plants & their Ways* 31 Tannin is excellent for preserving leather .. and so the beautiful *Protea cynaroides* (Wagen boom), [etc.] are destroyed for this substance. 1907 T.R. SIM *Forests & Forest Flora* 6 The whole country has, not very long ago, been Protea-veldt, the Sugarbush and the Wagenboom (or Vaboom) growing to considerable size. 1917 R. MARLOTH *Common Names* 87 *Waa'boom* (Wagen -). 1946 [see KREUPELBOS]. 1961 PALMER & PITMAN *Trees of S. Afr.* 220 The waboom is one of the tallest of the genus *Protea* and is found in dry rocky parts of the Cape, often with a trunk a foot or more in diameter. It has handsome, very blue foliage, oval leaves and large pale yellow flowers 2 to 4 inches in diameter, rather like a stiff, round shaving brush. 1976 W. HÉFER in *Optima* Vol.26 No.2, 46 Among the big Proteas are the wabooms or wagon trees, so called because their exceptionally hard wood was used for brake blocks, and the sledges on which the early pioneers of the Great Trek pulled their wagons .. over the mountains of the interior. 1982 *S. Afr. Panorama* May 39 In 1816 Latrobe .. recorded that when his supply of ink was finished he continued his diary 'with ink made from the leaves of the Wagenboom'. This was Protea arborea. 1988 P.E. RAPER tr. *R.J. Gordon's Cape Trav. 1777–86* I. 162 The mountains and ridges bore *wagenbomen* leucadendrons. 1989 *Weekend Post* 11 Nov. (Leisure) 4 Waboomberg .. was named for the waboom (*Protea nitida*), one of the tallest of the protea family.

wach een bitjes, wach en beetgen varr. WAG-'N-BIETJIE.

wacht var. WAG.

wacht-a-beetje, **wacht-e-beetje,** **wacht een beetje,** **wacht-een-beetye,** **wacht-eenbiche,** **wacht-een-bietj(i)e,** **wacht-en-beetje,** **wacht-en-bietje,** **wacht-n-bitje,** **wacht'nbietje** varr. WAG-'N-BIETJIE.

‖**waenhuis** /'vɑː(ə)nhœɪs, -heɪs/ *n.* [Afk., *waen* (fr. Du. *wagen*) wagon + *huis* house.] A coach house; a wagon house.

1967 M.M. HACKSLEY *Informant, Grahamstown* There is the Waenhuis as well as the three flats, of course, and together the four rentals will pay the monthly instalments. 1979 *Weekend Post* 10 Mar. (Family Post) 7 The old 'waenhuis' (Wagon house) on the side of the house was converted into a study and linked to the home. 1988 D. HUGHES et al. *Complete Bk of S. Afr. Wine* 218 The *Waenhuis* (now a gift shop). 1992 [see JONKERSHUIS].

‖**wag** /vax/ *v. intrans.* Also **wa(a)cht**. [Afk. *wag,* earlier *wacht* to wait.] In the interjectional phr. **wag 'n bietjie** /'vax ə ˌbɪki/ [Afk., see WAG-'N-BIETJIE], wait a bit; 'hang on'; 'not so fast'.

1895 *S. Afr. Balloons* 5 Some of the knowing ones said 'Wacht en bitje'! It is not a fault of the material but a flaw in the workmanship. 1913 J.J. DOKE *Secret City* 65 'Ach, Miss Atherstone,' interpolated Mrs Van Renan, holding up her hand, 'wacht een bietje! I forgot to say, of course'. 1939 M. RORKE *Melina Rorke* 148 With fortunes to be made on food and liquor the big Dutch merchants laughed at the idea of carrying tables and chairs, beds and bureaux. 'Waacht-eenbietjen!' ('Wait a little! One day when we have time!') they would say. [1955 D.L. HOBMAN *Olive Schreiner* 111 We would say to you in the words of the wise dead President of the Free State, which have become the symbol of South Africa, *Wacht een bietje, alles zal recht kom.* (Wait a little, all will come right.)] 1972 *Cape Times* 7 Dec. 1 Bilingualism in hotels: Wag 'n bietjie ... The Minister .. has extended .. the period within which receptionists and telephonists of licensed hotels are required to show proof that they are bilingual. 1989 *Sunday Times* 15 Jan. 9 (advt) Stoffel slammed on brakes. 'Wag 'n bietjie!' ... He turned around. 'This I got to check.'

wag-'bietjie, wag en bitje, wagenbietjie varr. WAG-'N-BIETJIE.

wagenboom var. WABOOM.

wag-'n-bietjie /'vaxəˌbiki, -ˌbici, 'vɒxəbɪki/ *n.* Also **vach-an-bechie, vacht am beechie, vachteen-bidgte, vachten een bietjie, vyacht um bige, waacht-een-bietje, waacht-en-beeche, waaght een beetji, waag 'n bikkie, wach een bitjes, wach en beetgen, wacht-a-beetje, wacht e(en) beetje, wacht-een-beetye, wacht-een-biche, wacht-een-bietj(i)e, wacht-een-bietje, wacht-enbietje, wacht'nbietjie, wacht-n-bitje, wag-'bietjie, wagenbietjie, wag en bitje, wag-'nbietje, wag-n-bietjie, waght-en-betjee, wagteen-betjie, wagt een beetji(e), wagt-eenb(e)itje, wagteen bitye, wagten beitjes, wakt e(e)n b(e)etje, wart-een-bitche.** [Afk., earlier S. Afr. Du. *wacht-een-beetje,* fr. Du. *wacht* wait + *een* a + *beetje* little bit, little while; see quot. 1785.] Any of numerous species of shrub having strong (usu. curved) thorns, esp. species of asparagus and acacia; a thorn from one of these shrubs; WAIT-A-BIT; WAIT-A-WHILE. Also *attrib.* See also *buffalo thorn* (BUFFALO sense 2), CAT-THORN, HAAKDORING sense 1, HAAK-EN-STEEK.

1785 G. FORSTER tr. A. *Sparrman's Voy. to Cape of G.H.* I. 236 A new species of *callophyllum;* which from its catching .. fast hold of the traveller with its hooked prickles .. is commonly called here *wakt een betje,* or *wait a bit.* 1795 C.R. HOPSON tr. *C.P. Thunberg's Trav.* I. 244 The *Asparagus Capensis,* with its recurved thorns, tore their clothes and retarded their passage, for which reason it has received from the inhabitants the name of *Wakt en beetje,* Stop a bit. 1812 A. PLUMPTRE tr. *H. Lichtenstein's Trav. in Sn Afr.* (1928) I. 188 Many sorts of asparagus were also among the plants which we had to break through; these are called by the colonists *wagt een beetje* (wait a little). 1827 G. THOMPSON *Trav.* I. 137 A thorny shrub (*acacia detinens*) well known in the Colony by the name of *wagt een bitje* (wait a bit), the prickles of which being shaped like hooks, there is no getting loose from them when they catch hold of one's clothes. 1866 E. WILSON *Reminisc.* 38 We came across a thick, thorny bush, well known by the name of 'Wacht-een-beetje', which, being interpreted, means 'Wait-a-while'. 1878 T.J. LUCAS *Camp Life & Sport* 44 The 'vacht een bietjie', or 'wait a bit', is .. furnished with sharp curved thorns pointing different ways alternately. Well does it deserve its title; .. the thorns are like so many fish hooks, and you come out from the encounter with your clothing torn to shreds. **1896** M.A. Carey-Hobson *At Home in Tvl* 91 The Acacia detinens noted for its curious hooked thorns, .. won from the first unfortunate Dutch hunters the appropriate name of waaght een beetji, or 'Wait-a-while' thorns. **1900** [see HAAK-EN-STEEK]. **1910** D. Fairbridge *That Which Hath Been* (1913) 153 Dacha ran through the wacht-een-beetje bushes and mimosas, tearing himself against the thorns. **1913** [see HAAKDORING sense 2]. **1944** H.C. Bosman in L. Abrahams *Cask of Jerepigo* (1972) 157 Then there was the bush ... Swarthaak and blinkbaar and wag-'n-bietjie. **1948** [see HAAKDORING sense 1]. **1956** F.C. Metrowich *Valiant but Once* 100 The troops .. had .. to struggle through a dense wag-'n-bietjie thicket which considerably hampered their progress. **1967** O. Walker *Hippo Poacher* 36 It was a thorny place with the long, bodkin-like, white *wag-'n-bietjie* (wait-a-bit) stabbing at their clothes. **1971** *The 1820* Vol.43 No.11, 26 Many of you will know the thorn with the very colourful Afrikaans name — the 'Wag-'n' Bietjie' thorn, the thorn that catches in your clothes and says 'wait a bit'. **1980** A.J. Blignaut *Dead End Rd* 97 As far as the eye could see .. there was sand, with a wag-'n-bietjie here and there doing its best to look like a tree.

wagonboom *n. obs.* [Part. tr. S. Afr. Du. *wagenboom*, see WABOOM.] WABOOM sense b.

1797 Lady A. Barnard in Lord Lindsay *Lives of Lindsays* (1849) III. 384 Each side .. was clothed with the waggombomb [*sic*], with its bright yellow flowers. **1880** A.H. Swinton *Insect Variety* 267 The .. Eocene flora .. shows fruits of .. Australian banksias, silver-trees, wagonbooms. **1897** S.J. Du Toit *Rhodesia: Past & Present* 126 This region cannot be unhealthy, for the 'sugar-bosch' and 'waggon-boom' grow everywhere.

wagon-tent see TENT sense b.

wagon tree *n. phr.* [tr. S. Afr. Du. *wagenboom*, see WABOOM.] WABOOM sense b.

1822 W.J. Burchell *Trav.* I. 123 (*heading*) The Waggon-tree. [**1963** Pollock & Agnew *Hist. Geog.* 108 The *Protea grandiflora* .. is popularly known as *waboom* (wagon tree) in Afrikaans.] **1976** [see WABOOM sense b]. **1987** T.F.J. Van Rensburg *Intro. to Fynbos* 16 The wagon tree, often better known by its Afrikaans name 'waboom' .. has silvery leaves. *Ibid.* 17 Slangbos or 'kooigoed' (*Stoebe* spp.) are conspicuous amongst wagon trees on unstable scree slopes. **1989** *Afr. Wildlife* Vol.43 No.3, 159 (*advt*) Only one .. achieves true tree status — the 'waboom' or wagon-tree *Protea nitida*.

wagon wood *n. phr. Obs.* WABOOM sense a.

1832 *Graham's Town Jrnl* 8 June 93 For Sale That well known property, the *Cap River Farm*, in extent 2,456 Morgen, abounding in Wagon-wood and other Timber. **1847** *Military Reports* in H. Ward *Cape & Kaffirs* (1851) 4 In a few localities valuable waggon-wood is obtained. **1856** *Cape of G.H. Almanac & Annual Register* 62 (*advt*) A great variety of English and Swedish Iron, Wagon wood, Stinkwood, Deals and Boards. **1880** *Grocott's Daily Mail* 28 Dec. 2 Cut Wagonwood, at least six months old.

wagt-een-beetje, wagt een beetji(e), wagt-een-b(e)itje, wagteen bitye, wagten beitjes varr. WAG-'N-BIETJIE.

wait-a-bit *n.* [tr. Afk. *wag-'n-bietjie*, earlier S. Afr. Du. *wacht-een-beetje*, see WAG-'N-BIETJIE.] In full ***wait-a-bit thorn***, or (*obs.*) ***wait-a-bit bush***: WAG-'N-BIETJIE. Also *attrib.*

1785 [see WAG-'N-BIETJIE]. **1857** D. Livingstone *Missionary Trav.* 61 The adjacent country is all covered with low thorny scrub, with grass, and, here and there, clumps of the 'wait-a-bit thorn', or Acacia Detinens. **1866** J. Leyland *Adventures* 120 The name given to the wait-a-bit thorn is very expressive and appropriate. In form it much resembles a small hook. It is the worst kind of bush for tearing anything it comes in contact with. **1871** J. McKay *Reminisc.* 140 Torn and scratched by 'wait-a-bit' thorns, tripped and half strangled by parasitical monkey-rope, the company tore away through the treacherous bush. **1886** G.A. Farini *Through Kalahari Desert* 170 The wait-a-bit thorns disputed my progress, and I was forced to wriggle through, snake-like, on my stomach. **1899** R.B. & J.D.S. Woodward *Natal Birds* 37 A favourite haunt of theirs is the 'Wait-a-bit' hedges, in the centre of which they [*sc.* the birds] often rest utterly out of reach. **1909** Lady S. Wilson *S. Afr. Mem.* 308 Round the edge of these groups .. lies slyly hidden the 'wait-a-bit' bush, according to the literal translation from the Dutch, whose thorny entanglements no one can gauge unless fairly caught. [*Note*] Wacht-een-bietze. **1929** J. Stevenson-Hamilton *Low-Veld* 50 Of all those coming under the embracive title of 'wait-a-bit', the worst to my mind is the umkaiya (Acacia apallens). **1940** J. Buchan *Memory* 119 You climb through bare foothills where the only vegetation is the wait-a-bit thorn. **1964** G. Campbell *Old Dusty* 50 Barbed wire and fish hooks are like velvet compared with the wait-a-bit thorn. **1972** A. Scholefield *Wild Dog Running* 69 Several wagoners had hacked their own paths through the wait-a-bit thorn.

wait-a-while *n. obs.* [Eng. interpretation of Afk. *wag-'n-bietjie*.] WAG-'N-BIETJIE.

1863 W.C. Baldwin *Afr. Hunting* 239 The Kaffirs throw in the most virulent 'wait-a-while' thorn branches into the pits, to prevent the oxen from trampling. **1896** M.A. Carey-Hobson *At Home in Tvl* 91 The Acacia detinens noted for its curious hooked thorns, .. won from the first unfortunate Dutch hunters the appropriate name of waaght een beetji, or 'Wait-a-while' thorns.

wakis /'vɑːkəs/ *n.* Also **wakist, wakus**. Pl. **wakiste** /-ˌkəstə/, **wakists**, or (rarely) **wakises**. [Afk., *wa* wagon + *kis* chest.] A chest made for use on a wagon; a similar chest made for use in the home. See also AGTERKIS, KIST, VOORKIS.

1953 U. Krige *Dream & Desert* 178 Great Oupa with Francina, his favourite grandchild, seated on the wakis beside him, drove off .. on his thousand-mile trek to the Transvaal. **1965** M.G. Atmore *Cape Furn.* 217 It is assumed that these wakiste were carried by the Voortrekkers and if so, they could not have been more suitable with their strength, maximum storage area and usefulness as seats or tables. **1971** Baraitser & Obholzer *Cape Country Furn.* 230A, Because wakiste are used frequently as seats, both on the wagon and in the home, the paint on the lid wears off, revealing the sheen of the yellowwood. **1973** [see DOEMELA-KLONTJIE]. **1974** *E. Prov. Herald* 24 May 31 A dealer in indigenous antiques warned .. that certain shady dealers were buying up wakiste (wagon boxes) and using the wood of one to make four fake wakiste. **1981** *Fair Lady* 29 July 111 A Picasso jug looks perfectly at home on an old *wakis*. **1991** S. Welz in *Light Yrs* Feb. 11 Many *wakiste* would have been painted by their original owners. **1991** *Best of S. Afr. Short Stories* (Reader's Digest Assoc.) 200 Many of the old chests called *wakiste* today were, in fact, designed for home use.

wakt een be(e)tje, - en beetje varr. WAG-'N-BIETJIE.

wapenskou /'vɑːp(ə)nskəʊ/ *n. ?hist.* Also **waapenschauw, wapens(c)haw, wapenschouw**. [Afk., fr. Du. *wapenschouwing*, *wapen* weapon + *schouwing* inspection, review.] A military review, often including manoeuvres and shooting contests.

In some older forms also *Scot. Eng.*

1899 *Daily News* (U.K.) 23 June 5 The Boers never drill, and .. the scene witnessed was probably an ordinary season's wapenshaw. **1905** *Cape Times Christmas No.* 13 A yearly Wapenschaw. **1905** P. Gibbon *Vrouw Grobelaar* 221 When her brothers, having drunk too much at a waapenschauw, wished to make a quarrel quickly, they called their man a coward. **1926** P.W. Laidler *Tavern of Ocean* 43 The captain of an English ship .. went ashore .. to dine. First they attended a 'wapenshaw' of soldiers and burghers, who carried out their evolutions to the best of their power, and 'caused great surprise to our English friends, who beheld a fine garrison and the formidable power we could command should an enemy arrive'. **1934** C.P. Swart Supplement to Pettman. 190 *Wapenskou*, A military review; formerly very common when district rifle associations were flourishing, cf Scotch wapenshaw. **1946** V. Pohl *Adventures of Boer Family* 7 Soon there were gathered here a large number of farmer-soldiers .. , looking much as if they were attending a *wapenschouw* (military review), their dress and arms as we used to see on those occasions. **1963** S.H. Skaife *Naturalist Remembers* 62 A *wapenskou* was held there by the Defence Force on a public holiday. **1983** J.A. Brown *White Locusts* 193 The Magato campaign was no more than a *wapenschouw*, a try-out for the gunners.

Wardmaster *n. Obs.* exc. *hist.* Also with small initial. [tr. Du. *wijkmeester*, see WYKMEESTER.] An unpaid civic official responsible for the administration and policing of a town ward (see quot. 1975); WYKMASTER; WYKMEESTER.

1809 *Afr. Court Calendar, Wardmasters. Cape Town. Ward, No. 1.* Edzard Adolph Grimbeck. Johannes Gerrit Munnik. **1819** *Ibid.* 67 The office of Wardmaster is absolutely necessary to the internal well-being of the Town. **1926** P.W. Laidler *Tavern of Ocean* 106 For each ward two respectable burghers were appointed as ward-masters. **1975** C.G. Henning *Graaff-Reinet* 66 The functions of the Ward-Masters (or *Wykmeesters*) were clearly defined: to keep a register of names and occupants of houses; to make a note of any foreigners who entered the ward; to report any irregularities; to counteract any illicit sale of liquor and gambling dens; to guard against fire; to keep waterfurrows and sluices in good condition; to guard against dirt and filth in the streets .. to see that '*niemand zal vermogen Gaten in de Straaten te maaken ten einde de Klei tot bouwen noodzakelijk er uit te halen*'. In return for his services, for which he received no salary, he was exempt from certain taxes and not liable to burgher duty.

ware /'vɑːrə/ *adj.* Formerly also **waare**. [Afk., attrib. form of Afk. and Du. *waar* true.] Usu. with reference to an Afrikaner, to a member of an Afrikaans-dominated political party, or to a South African: true, loyal, genuine; *nonce*, truly South African (see quot. 1992).

1840 *Echo* 31 Aug. 9 (*letter*) It is a good thing .. *when rogues fall out, &c.* — ('Waare Afrikaan'.) **1943** 'J. Burger' *Black Man's Burden* 239 The 'ware Afrikaner' (true Afrikaner) must refuse to speak English in private or in public, and the Nationalist Press conducts .. heresy hunts against .. officials who speak English only. **1952** G. Van de Haer in *Drum* Aug. 7 A burly 'ware' Afrikaner .. expressed his pleasure at hearing his taal spoken. **1970** *Sunday Times* 15 Nov. 8 They believed they were acting as 'ware' South Africans. **1971** *The 1820* Vol.43 No.10, 11 The purists will thump us on the ear, but there can be no denying the satisfaction a stranger gets when he can say this instead of that in the manner of a 'ware' (true) South African. **1972** *Drum* 8 Dec. 9, I am a 'ware' Nationalist. **1973** *Cape Times* 30 July 1, I'm a ware boermeisie, I love porridge. **1978** *Sunday Times* 30 Apr. 12 Mrs Odendaal is now preparing to go to Israel to live on a kibbutz ... It will be a far cry from .. her 'ware' Afrikaans family background. **1979** *Daily Dispatch* 21 Mar. 10 An image of Afrikanderdom that is no longer nurtured in the hearts of the average urban Afrikaner who, like Van Zyl Slabbert and Japie Basson of the PFP, both 'ware' Afrikaners, reject that image. **1989** P. Lee in *Sunday Times* 26 Feb. (Mag. Sect.) 36 We're talking about treasures as in potjiekos, witblitz, braaivleis and boerewors. *Ware* treasures which originated in South Africa, but are appreciated throughout the world. **1991** *Weekly Mail* 24 May 12 It's tough enough for a .. *ware* Afrikaner .. to be selected as a parliamentary candidate. **1992** J. Khumalo in *Pace* Sept. 19 These images are peculiar to South Africa and the a capella dudes are obviously *ware laaities*.

warlord *n.* [Transf. sense of general Eng. *warlord* a military commander; in China, a military commander ruling a region independently of the government.] The leader of an armed group of men who, through the use of force, control an area, esp. a section of a township or an informal urban settlement, dictating the (political) activities of the inhabitants of the area, and demanding rent and service.

1989 GQUBULE & KOCH in *Weekly Mail* 5 May 6 At Inanda on the outskirts of Durban, Inkatha 'warlords' are now fighting each other for control over the shanty towns of the region. **1990** M. KENTRIDGE *Unofficial War* 9 Vigilante leaders are drawn from a variety of sources ... These Inkatha leaders are known as warlords because they command armies of men and exact allegiance and obedience on roughly feudal lines: in return for military loyalty the warlords provide their men with money, food, drink and some political assistance such as the granting of licences and the favourable allocation of land. **1991** P. STOREY in *Star* 1 Nov. 13 The IFP could nail a couple of the warlords who are walking free, boasting of the murders they have committed, and hand them over to justice. **1993** *Weekly Mail & Guardian* 13 Aug. 9 Even though he leads the IFP southern Natal delegation .. he has a reputation of being a 'warlord' and his commitment to peace has been frequently questioned.

War of the Axe *n. phr. Hist.* [So called because the war began when British forces invaded Xhosa territory, after a patrol (sent to arrest a Xhosa man suspected of stealing an axe) had been ambushed; see quot. 1888.] A war on the eastern frontier between Xhosa and British forces, lasting from March 1846 to December 1847. See also *Frontier war* (FRONTIER sense b).

Also known as the Seventh Frontier War.

1888 H.B. SIDWELL *Story of S. Afr.* 100 *The War of the Axe*, One of Sandilli's tribe was arrested for stealing an axe, and sent to Graham's Town to be tried ... A band of Kafir warriors burst from the dense bush .. and overpowered the escort. **1912** AYLIFF & WHITESIDE *Hist. of Abambo* 17 The brother of Matiwana was living near Fort Beaufort, and took an important part in the defence of the town when attacked by the Hottentots in the war of the Axe. **1987** G. VINEY *Col. Houses* 113 By the outbreak of the Seventh Frontier War ('The War of the Axe') he already had immense stock in hand. **1991** F.G. BUTLER *Local Habitation* 268 This was the road down which .. Collett had sent his wool to Port Elizabeth during the War of the Axe.

wart-een-bitche var. WAG-'N-BIETJIE.

wash *v. trans.* [Special senses of general Eng.] In the phrr. ***to wash (one's) spear, to wash (one's) assegai*** [tr. Zulu *geza* or *hlamba*, as found in the phrases *geza imikhonto, hlamba imikhonto*, lit. 'wash spears', carry out a ceremonial cleansing (as after a period of mourning) by hunting or by slaughtering cattle; so, blood (oneself) in battle, cleanse oneself after killing in battle]: to mark the end of a period of mourning by slaughtering cattle or going on a hunt; (of a soldier) to blood oneself in battle; to perform a cleansing ceremony after killing in battle; less freq. ***to wash the spears*** (of soldiers), to send (soldiers, etc.) to battle, esp. for the first time, or on a large-scale hunt, often as part of a ceremony (e.g. to mark the end of a period of national mourning).

1878 H.A. ROCHE *On Trek in Tvl* 119 This chief .. craves nothing more eagerly than to wash the spears of the young men of his nation. **1897** F.R. STATHAM *S. Afr. as It Is* 20 Cetwayo .. was .. anxious for peace ... The very request which has been so often quoted as testifying to his ferocious nature is really evidence the other way. That request was for permission for his regiment to 'wash their spears' in the blood of their old hereditary enemies the Swazies. **1912** AYLIFF & WHITESIDE *Hist. of Abambo* 64 It is probable that Kreli did not himself desire war, but his young warriors were eager to wash their spears, and spurned all restraint. **1933** W. MACDONALD *Romance of Golden Rand* 173 Many .. Swazi warriors had washed their spears .. against the Bapedi tribe in the first Sekukuni campaign. **1934** B.I. BUCHANAN *Pioneer Days* 119 He had forbidden his young men to marry until they had 'washed their assegais in blood'. **1956** F.C. METROWICH *Valiant but Once* 186 We wage war only against men ... We do not wash our assegais in the blood of .. women .. or .. children. **1961** T.V. BULPIN *White Whirlwind* 129 In normal Zulu custom, the ending of royal mourning must be marked by some raid, or at least a mighty hunt so that the warriors can purge themselves of the evil effects of a monarch's death by washing their spears in blood. **1971** *Nat. Geog. Mag.* 6 Dec. 751 The Zulu regiments suddenly appeared — 20,000 strong — and swooped in to 'wash their spears' in the blood of the invaders, slaughtering some 1,300 of them. **1979** C. ENDFIELD *Zulu Dawn* 46, I have earned my *isi-Coco* slaying enemies of Cetshwayo — ask whose stabbing spear was washed in the blood of the Swazi King.

Hence **washing** *vbl n.*, in the phrr. ***the washing of the spear(s), the washing of spears***, the blooding of a soldier or regiment; bloodshed, esp. in warfare; a cleansing ceremony which follows such bloodshed.

1949 O. WALKER *Proud Zulu* (1951) 14 Maidens demanded that the men obtain the king's favour by valour and the right to marry them. The 'washing of spears' was ancient custom ... The Swazi 'dogs' in the north were the favoured target. **1978** A. ELLIOTT *Sons of Zulu* 46 The 'Wiping of the Axe' or the 'Washing of the Spear' ceremony .. is the cleansing ceremony for a returning warrior who has killed someone in battle. **1983** *City Press* 6 Nov. 6 The slaughter of students at Ongoye ... We wonder what the majority of Inkatha members feel about this 'washing of the spears' by .. brainwashed militants.

washing *n. noncount. Obs.* [Fig. use of general Eng. *washing* washed clothes.] In township Eng.: see quot. See also STAFF.

1968 COLE & FLAHERTY *House of Bondage* 60 Within seconds the cars are full ... Dozens of others have crowded onto the couplings between the cars or cling to precarious hand- and footholds on the outside. 'Washing' they call it. For when a train goes by at speed these passengers look like clothes hanging on a washline. It is no exaggeration to say that this wash hangs on for dear life.

waterbalie see BALIE sense b.

waterblom /ˈvɑːtə(r)blɔm/ *n. rare.* Formerly also **water bloem**. Pl. **-blomme** /-blɔmə/, or (formerly) **-bloemen**. [See WATERBLOMMETJIE.] **a.** WATERBLOMMETJIE sense a. **b.** A dish made from this plant. Also *attrib.*

1913 C. PETTMAN *Africanderisms* 546 *Water bloemen, Aponogeton distachyon L.* A common table dish in some parts of the Western Province, is so named in the Riversdale District. **1983** *Sunday Times* 18 Sept. (Mag. Sect.) 8 No longer can your *waterblom* aficionado curl a superior lip at the up-country ignoramus who has never tasted the steamed Cape water-lilies flavoured with sorrel and a scraping of nutmeg ... *Waterblomme* are harvested by hand.

waterblommetjie /ˈvɑːtə(r)ˌblɔməki, -ci/ *n.* [Afk., lit. 'little water flower', *water* water + *blom* flower + dim. suffix -IE.]

a. The edible water plant *Aponogeton distachyos* of the Aponogetonaceae, which occurs naturally in the Western Cape during the spring, and is prized in cooking; BLOMMETJIE sense 2; *Cape pondweed*, see CAPE sense 2 a; WATERBLOM (sense a); WATERUINTJIE sense a. Also *attrib.*

1950 [see sense b]. **1964** L.G. GREEN *Old Men Say* 122, I used to see the coloured women picking the *waterblommetjies* in the Diep River. **1975** *S. Afr. Panorama* Dec. 18 Waterblommetjie (Aponogeton distachys) — water-flowers — are found on the marshes of the Cape Flats. **1980** *Fair Lady* 7 May 195 When fresh waterblommetjies appeared on the shelves of our village co-op I couldn't wait to get my fork into them. **1983** *Sunday Times* 18 Sept. (Mag. Sect.) 8 The restaurant .. has a variety of *waterblommetjie* dishes on its menu. **1993** *Flying Springbok* Apr. 121 Blanch one kilogram of waterblommetjies in boiling salted water. **1994** G. BISSEKER in *Weekend Post* 8 Jan. (Leisure) 6 Waterblommetjies fulfil the function of a vegetable in bredie, but their taste is rather bland.

b. *comb.* **waterblommetjie bredie** /-ˌbriːdi, -ˌbrɪədi/ [Afk., *bredie* see BREDIE], a stew of meat and waterblommetjies; *wateruintjie bredie*, see WATERUINTJIE sense b.

1950 H. GERBER *Cape Cookery* 87 Wateruintjie (Waterblommetjie) Bredie. 2 soup plates of waterblommeties (Aponogeton), plucked from their stalks. **1971** *Argus* 29 June, Cape waterblommetjie bredie ... 1 to $1\frac{1}{2}$ kg mutton chops, or thick rib; 2 medium onions, sliced; 2 big bunches of waterblommetjies picked when blooms are open; [etc.]. **1975** [see *hotnotskoolbredie* (HOTNOT sense 4)]. **1980** *Fair Lady* 7 May 195 In the Cape, however, just mention that waterblommetjie bredie is a con, a disappointment, even (like some I have tasted) a disaster and people start wondering about your forebears, your passport and your eligibility for the voters' roll. **1986** [see *tamatiebredie* (BREDIE sense b)]. **1990** M. VAN BILJON in *Your Family* Oct. 178 Our national food is neither *waterblommetjie-bredie* nor *braaivleis*; it's tomato sandwiches or frikkadels.

waterbok *n. obs.* [S. Afr. Du., fr. Du. *water* water + *bok* antelope.] WATERBUCK.

1835 A. SMITH *Diary* (1940) II. 99 A male waterbok shot this morning. **1887** A.A. ANDERSON *25 Yrs in Waggon* I. 121 One afternoon I took my rifle for a ramble round in the thick bush veldt to look for a waterbok.

waterboom /ˈvɑːtə(r)bʊəm/ *n. obsolescent.* Pl. **-bome** /-bʊəmə/. [S. Afr. Du., fr. Du. *water* water + *boom* tree.]

1. The UMDONI, *Syzygium cordatum*. Also *attrib.*

1854 [see UMDONI]. **1907** J.M. WOOD *Handbk to Flora of Natal* 49 Our only useful species is *Eugenia cordata*, the well-known 'Waterboom,' the timber of which is valuable for building purposes, etc. **1949** C. BULLOCK *Rina* 38 In its bed, palms mingled with waterbome.

2. The shrub or tree *Mimusops caffra* of the Sapotaceae, found on the east coast; also called *red milkwood* (see MILK sense 2). Also *attrib.*

1899 G. RUSSELL *Hist. of Old Durban* 116 Two large red milkwood or 'waterboom' trees formed a natural archway. *c*1963 B.C. TAIT *Durban Story* 84 The wagon spoor .. passed under the lovely natural arch formed by two majestic red milkwood or 'waterboom' trees.

waterbuck *n.* [Calqued on S. Afr. Du. *waterbok*, see WATERBOK.] The antelope *Kobus ellipsiprymnus* of the Bovidae, found usu. in the vicinity of marshes and rivers, and characterized by a prominent white ring on the hindquarters; WATERBOK. Also *attrib.*

1839 W.C. HARRIS *Wild Sports* 186, I believe .. that I am the only European that ever shot a water buck. This noble antelope is about the size of an ass and of somewhat browner colour. **1852** R.B. STRUTHERS *Hunting Jrnl* (1991) 19 Saw a fine waterbuck in the lake cooling itself. *a*1867 C.J. ANDERSSON *Notes of Trav.* (1875) 326 Axel succeeded in knocking over a large male water-buck (*Aigocerus Ellipsiprymnus*), probably an adult. **1891** R. WARD *Sportsman's Handbk* 123 In Zululand were to be found, a few years ago, .. Waterbucks. **1923** [see NAGANA]. *c*1936 *S. & E. Afr. Yr Bk & Guide* 1088 *The Common Waterbuck*, Height about 3 feet 9 inches; colour, brown to roan with white bands on either side of rump. **1949** J. MOCKFORD *Golden Land* 224 A furrow led from the pool along the sandy bed of the dry river, and .. I came upon a dead waterbuck, dumped in a ravine as if in a larder. **1961** T.V. BULPIN *White Whirlwind* 288 One of the troopers had shot a water buck cow. **1967** E. ROSENTHAL *Encycl. of Sn Afr.* 606 A Waterbuck stands about four feet at the shoulder. It has great powers of survival and will defend itself in midstream with its long, twisted horns. **1990** *Farmer's Weekly* 8 June 41 Species available to hunters today include .. waterbuck.

water (e)eintje, - euntjie *varr.* WATERUINTJIE.

water-finder *n.* [So named because it is often found growing above artesian streams.] AARBOSSIE.

1896, 1913, 1975 [see AARBOSSIE].

water-furrow *n.* [Prob. tr. S. Afr. Du. *watervoor*, although *water-furrow* has been used in Eng. elsewhere, meaning a drainage furrow.] SLOOT sense 1.

1832 *Graham's Town Jrnl* 20 July 116 The many thousand yards of water furrows, many of which are cut through huge solid rocks. **1849** J.D. LEWINS Diary. 5 Oct., Fence at waterfurrow down. **1862** 'A LADY' *Life at Cape* (1963) 84 The streets are .. kept cool and clean by water-furrows, full of clear sparkling water from the river. **1884** 'E.V.C.' *Promised Land* 33 From this river numerous and quickly running streams are led through the town, each street having its water furrow, or furrows, as the case may be, running along one or both sides of it. **1908** M.C. BRUCE *New Tvl* 2 Charming little towns they look, with their .. streets bordered by water-furrows and trees. **1921** H.J. MANDELBROTE tr. *O.F. Mentzel's Descr. of Cape of G.H.* I. 135 Between the big plain .. and the houses .. there is a water furrow lined with masonry and provided with several sluices. **1940** V. POHL *Bushveld Adventures* 31 Dinnaar had reached the water furrow, but instead of clearing it at a bound .. , he came to a sudden stop. **1955** L.G. GREEN *Karoo* 85 'When I was a boy the water furrows were much wider and deeper,' Muller recalled. **1969** F. GOLDIE *River of Gold* 11 The water furrows on either side of the street .. were often frozen in the morning. **1976** V. ROSENBURG *Sunflower* 13 The dirt streets were flanked by water furrows. **1993** *Weekend Post* 14 Aug. (Leisure) 4 Wide-open gravel streets with water-furrows flanking them .. carry the .. city-dweller back to a different era.

Waterman *n. hist.* Pl. **-men, -mans.** [Prob. attrib. use of Eng. *water*, applied to persons who live near water and who depend on food sources found in water (cf. general Eng. *waterman* mariner, seaman); or fr. S. Afr. Du. (which derivation would explain the pl. forms ending with *-mans*).] STRANDLOPER sense 2 a.

1639 W. BAYLEY in R. Raven-Hart *Before Van Riebeeck* (1967) 146 We sent our shallopp to *Penguin Iland* to carry *Thomas* with whom we lefte our lettres with the Rest of his family of watermen therre to resyde the whole number Consisting of 20 p[er]sons menn, weomen and Children. **1847** J. SUTHERLAND *Orig. Matter Contained in Sutherland's Mem.* 589 Three tribes of people, similar in dress and manners. First, the Strandloopers or Waterman, who lived on muscles [*sic*] which they found on the rocks, and on roots. **1913** W.W. THOMPSON *Sea Fisheries of Cape Col.* 33 The Strandloopers, or Watermen, comparatively few in numbers .. eked out a more or less precarious existence roaming the shores of the bays, fishing after a fashion, and ever on the look-out for edible flotsam and jetsam. **1967** R. RAVEN-HART (tr. J.A. von Mandelslo) *Before Van Riebeeck* 152 Some .. live very miserably by the waterside ... They live on herbs, roots and fishes ... They are called the *Watermen*, because they live by the shore. **1968** E.A. WALKER *Hist. of Sn Afr.* 36 The 'Watermans' had killed the herdboy, David Jansen, and stolen forty-four head of Company's cattle.

wateruintjie /ˈvɑːtərˌœɪŋki, -ˌeɪŋki/ *n.* Also **waater uyntie, waater uyntje, water e(e)intje, water euntjie, water uintje, water untjie, water uy(e)ntje, water-uyentjie.** [S. Afr. Du., *water* water + *uintjie* fr. Du. *ajuintje* little onion.] **a.** WATERBLOMMETJIE sense a. Also *attrib.*

1795 C.R. HOPSON tr. *C.P. Thunberg's Trav.* I. 156 The *aponogeton distachyon* (*waater uynties*, or *water lilies*) grew in many places, in shallow puddles of water, very plentifully, and from its white flowers that floated on the water, exhaled a most fragrant odour. **1809** J. MACKRILL Diary. 62 Aponogeton distachyon Heptandria Tetragynia, (Waater uynties or water Lilies). **1822** W.J. BURCHELL *Trav.* I. 51 There grows a plant called Water-uyentjies, the root of which, when roasted, is much eaten by the slaves and Hottentots. The heads of the flowers, boiled, make a dish which may, in taste and appearance, be compared to spinach. **1856** L. PAPPE in *Cape of G.H. Almanac & Annual Register* 341 The root of this waterplant (Wateruintjies, water onions) when roasted is very palatable, and somewhat resembles the chestnut in taste. Its flowers which are highly scented, are eaten as spinage and used as pickles. **1868** W.H. HARVEY *Genera of S. Afr. Plants* 386 About 3 species, dispersed; *A. distachyon* (Water Uintjes) is the commonest. **1890** A.G. HEWITT *Cape Cookery* 30 Almost any vegetable may be made into a Brédé. Pumpkin, water eeintjes, vet kousies, tomatoes, [etc.]. **1894** R. MARLOTH in *Trans. of S. Afr. Phil. Soc.* p.lxxx, *Aponogeton distachyon* ('water-uintjes'). **1910** R. JUTA *Cape Peninsula* 115 The Malays gather the flower, 'water-eintje', and curry it or stew it into a thick soup. **1947** L.G. GREEN *Tavern of Seas* 197 Princess vlei is an oval basin .. famous for the water-uintjies its banks produce when submerged in the winter ... These wild vegetables of the veld, braised with fat and with wine and spices added, make one of the finest bredies. **1962** *Bokmakierie* June 2 The nests were floating nests more or less anchored between the floating wateruintjie leaves. The nest material consisted of the stems of wateruintjies. **1971** *Post* 6 June (Home Post) 2 She made her own .. cake wateruintjie. **1981** *S. Afr. Panorama* Dec. 21 He .. refers to it as a *wateruintjie* (water onion), and gives a few recipes varying from *bredie* (stew) to soufflés.

b. *comb.* **wateruintjie bredie** /-ˌbriːdi, -ˌbrɪədi/ [Afk., *bredie* see BREDIE], *waterblommetjie bredie*, see WATERBLOMMETJIE sense b.

1950 [see WATERBLOMMETJIE sense a]. **1964** L.G. GREEN *Old Men Say* 122 One could hardly expect to find a *wateruintjie bredie* at a State banquet. **1973** H. BECK in *Farmer's Weekly* 25 Apr. 101 A recipe which probably dates back to Hottentot times is wateruintjiebredie. **1978** *Daily Dispatch* 26 July 11 Fair-goers can taste some of these traditional dishes, including wateruintjiebredie.

water-wyzer *n. obs.* Also **waterwyser.** [S. Afr. Du., fr. Du. *water* water + *wijzer* indicator.] A dowser or water diviner.

1801 J. BARROW *Trav.* I. 376 The first had taken up the profession of a *water-wyzer* or discoverer of water. **1897** 'F. MACNAB' *On Veldt & Farm* 194 Certain persons .. style themselves 'Water Wyzers.' **1955** L.G. GREEN *Karoo* 178 Every district in the Karoo has its *waterwyser*, the diviner or dowser.

watsonia /wɒtˈsəʊnɪə/ *n.* Also with initial capital. Pl. **-s,** or unchanged. [Modern L., fr. the name of *William Watson* (1715–87), Scottish naturalist, + n.-forming suffix *-ia*.] Any of several species of indigenous bulbous plants of the genus *Watsonia* (family Iridaceae), having sword-shaped leaves and tall spikes of tubular flowers in shades of red, pink, salmon, orange, yellow, and white; also called PYPIE. Also *attrib.*

1801 *Curtis's Bot. Mag.* 1787–1844 XV. 533 (*heading*) Aletris-like Watsonia. **1843** M. EDGEWORTH *Lett. from Eng.* (1971) 595 The most beautiful flowers .. Gladiolis and red and white Watsonia. **1856** R.E.E. WILMOT *Diary* (1984) 14 The watsonias which have been *the* common flower for the last 3 months in George invariably catch my eye as I pass. **1906** B. STONEMAN *Plants & their Ways* 197 *Watsonia*, The flowers often live in moist places. **1913** [see PAINTED LADY]. **1916** *Farmer's Weekly* 20 Dec. 1454 For Sale — White Watsonia Bulbs (Watsonia Ardernie), price 2/- per dozen. *c*1933 J. JUTA in A.C. Partridge *Lives, Lett. & Diaries* (1971) 162 *Watsonias* ... The plant grows from corms and has sword-like leaves and masses of pink, magenta, white or orange flowers, resembling gladioli. **1948** A. PATON *Cry, Beloved Country* 19 Here in their season grow the blue agapanthus, the wild watsonia, and the red-hot poker. **1960** G. LISTER *Reminisc.* 58, I could gather .. pale pink Watsonias and white bearded orchids. **1982** *Flying Springbok* Sept. 22 A breathtaking show of mountain wild-flowers such as proteas, watsonias and ericas, filled the hall adjoining the church with the fragrance of the mountains. **1992** G. TEMPLETON in *Weekend Post* 8 Feb. (Leisure) 4 Watsonias, gladioli, [etc.] provide a touch of summer colour.

wau *int. obs.* Also **whau, wow.** [ad. Zulu *wawu* or *wo*.] An exclamation expressing wonder, dismay, despair, or regret. Cf. HAU. So **wau** *v. intrans.*, to exclaim 'wau'.

1887 J.W. MATTHEWS *Incwadi Yami* 326 This sight was enough .. to make all the Zulus stop work and 'wau' with curiosity. **1895** H. RIDER HAGGARD *Nada* 35 Wow! my father, of those two regiments not one escaped. **1898** B. MITFORD *Induna's Wife* 6 When the greater troubles which beset a man .. beset him no longer, does he not at once look around to see what troubles he can create for himself? *Whau!* I am old. I have seen. **1907** W.C. SCULLY *By Veldt & Kopje* 253 *Wau*, but it is hard for an old man who has owned cattle all his life to look every day into an empty kraal. **1925** D. KIDD *Essential Kafir* 38 They have many very expressive exclamations, such as 'Yo!' when they wish to show contempt, 'Hau!' when they show surprise, 'Wow!' and many other similar utterances.

wax-berry *n.* **a.** The fruit of the plant *Myrica cordifolia* of the Myricaceae, characterized by a powdery coating which, when boiled off, yields a wax which was used in the past for polishes and candles. **b.** This plant; BERRY WAX sense b; WAX SHRUB. Also *attrib.*

The name 'wax-berry' is also used of a species of *Myrica* found in North America.

[**1801** J. BARROW *Trav.* I. 19 In most of the sandy flats are found in great abundance two varieties of the *Myrica cerifera*, or wax plant, from the berries of which is procurable, by simple boiling, a firm pure wax.] **1821** C.I. LATROBE *Jrnl of Visit* 494 In other parts .. the waxberry-bush has found shelter. **1835** J.W.D. MOODIE *Ten Yrs* II. 197, I occasionally employed my people at spare times in gathering wax-berries. **1856** L. PAPPE in *Cape of G.H. Almanac & Annual Register* 344 The ripe drupes of this hardy bush (the Waxberry Myrtle), are covered with a white coat, and yield a superior kind of vegetable wax, which by mere boiling and straining is readily procured. **1897** E. GLANVILLE *Tales from Veld* 100 I .. found him peacefully employed boiling down wax berries for the manufacture of candles. **1906** B. STONEMAN *Plants & their Ways* 207 *Myricaceae* ... *Myrica*, the wax berry plant .. is the only genus. **1917** R. MARLOTH *Common Names* 89 *Wax berry, Myrica Cordifolia.* A shrub frequent among the sand dunes of the southern coast districts ... The fruit is a hard drupe, covered with a layer of whitish wax; this is obtained by treating the berries with boiling water; exported as 'berry wax'. **1926** P.W. LAIDLER *Tavern of Ocean* 197 Wax-berry shrubs grew abundantly. **1955** V.M. FITZROY *Dark Bright Land* 115 John has another manufacture in hand — wax-berries for candles ... It's green, quite a dark green, and brittle. **1975** M.R. LEVYNS in *Std Encycl. of Sn Afr.* XI. 371 *Waxberry, Wax myrtle. Wasbessie. Glashout.* (*Myrica cordifolia.*) Common plant on sand flats and coastal dunes in the southern part of the Cape Province, belonging to the family *Myricaceae.* **1987** T.F.J. VAN RENSBURG *Intro. to Fynbos* 22 Sprawling plants such as .. the waxberry (*Myrica cordifolia*) also occur.

wax shrub *n. phr. Obs.* WAX-BERRY sense b.

1798 S.H. WILCOCKE tr. *J.S. Stavorinus's Voy. to E. Indies 1768–71* The wax-shrubs (*myrica querifolia*, and *cordifolia*) afford a substance resembling bees'-wax. **1809** J. MACKRILL Diary. 56 Myrica cordifolia Wax shrub, Hottentots eat it.

Wee Bill *n. phr.* [Formed by analogy with OLD BILL.] The title given to a deputy leader in the Memorable Order of the Tin Hats (see MOTH sense a), an ex-serviceman's organization. See also OLD BILL.

1979 *Daily Dispatch* 15 Mar. 3 Moths elected Mr MacEwan, the former Wee Bill, as the new Old Bill. Mr Fraser Finlaison was elected the new Wee Bill.

Weeskamer /ˈvɪəskɑːmə(r)/ *n. hist.* [Du., *wees* orphan + *kamer* chamber.] ORPHAN CHAMBER.

1806 J. BARROW *Trav.* I. 362 His crime .. was an act of forgery on orphan property committed to the care of a constituted board in the Cape called the Weeskamer, or chamber of managing the effects of minors and orphans. *a***1823** [see ORPHAN CHAMBER]. **1832** *Graham's Town Jrnl* 5 Oct. 156 By the mass of the community the '*Weeskamer*' has been considered as a perfect institution. **1957** L.G. GREEN *Beyond City Lights* 107 The president of the *Weeskamer* threatened to drive him away from his office with a stick. **1984** *Sunday Times* 15 July (Business Times) 17 In 1673 the Dutch East India Company established a Weeskamer (orphan chamber) at the Cape to administer deceased estates and look after the interests of orphans and others under legal disability. The Weeskamer was abolished in 1833. **1993** *Business Day* 27 May (Centenaries) 16, BOE [*sc.* Board of Executors] was formed to replace the old Dutch Weeskamer.

weeskindertjies /ˈvɪəsˌkəndə(r)kis, -kiːz/ *n.* Also **wees'kinners**. Pl. unchanged. [Afk., *weeskinders* lit. 'orphans' (nick-name of plant) + dim. suffix -IE, perh. so named because the flowers appear isolated at the end of a long stem.] Any of several species of plant of the Iridaceae, esp. *Ixia scillaris* varr. *scillaris* and *subundulata*, bearing a spike of small pink flowers in spring. See also IXIA.

1917 R. MARLOTH *Common Names* 89 *Wees'kinners. Tritonia undulata* and *T. scillaris* (Tulbagh). Also *Nemesia affinis*, etc. **1970** M.R. LEVYNS in *Std Encycl. of Sn Afr.* I. 221 *Agretjie. Weeskindertjies* (*Ixia scillaris* = *Tritonia scillaris*.) A small but attractive plant of the family *Iridaceae*, widespread in the coastal strip of the Western Cape Province from Namaqualand southwards. **1974** *Motorist* Aug. 35 No less imaginative were the names of some of the flowers — vetkousies, weeskindertjies, aandblommetjies and duikerwortel. **1990** C. LAFFEATY *Far Forbidden Plains* 243 Those *weeskindertjies* may look pretty, but even the livestock won't eat them.

Weisser Riesling see RIESLING sense 2.

wena /ˈwe(ː)nə, ˈweːna/ *pronoun.* [Second person sing. pronoun common to the Nguni and Sotho-Tswana groups of languages.] Esp. among speakers of Nguni and Sotho languages: 'you'.

*c***1928** R.R.R. DHLOMO *Afr. Tragedy* 14 A cool voice addressed him, from the shadows. 'Hey — wena. Special!' Robert turned round and faced two stalwart Zulu policemen. **1979** F. DIKE *First S. African* 7 Hey listen wena, if I want to see Rooi I know where to find him. **1982** M. MZAMANE *Children of Soweto* 114 'Hey, *wena*,' his mother shouted after him, 'don't forget what I just told you ...' **1987** *Pace* Aug. 4 The people can share, but not wives sbali. Or wena, what do you say? **1990** M. MELAMU in *Lynx* 291 'Wena, Oupa and your big mouth,' Boy-boy warned.

Wenela /wəˈneːlə, weˈneːla/ *n.* [Acronym formed on WNLA.] **a.** WNLA. **b.** Occas., that organization's successor, TEBA. Also *attrib.*

1961 *Off. Yrbk of Union 1960* (Bureau for Census & Statistics) 525 In 1958 .. 96,318 Bantu used the airlift, known as Wenela Air Services. **1962** A.P. CARTWRIGHT *Gold Miners* 217 (*caption*) A 'Wenela' launch picks up potential mine workers. *Ibid.* 221 The letters W.N.L.A. have become 'Wenela' to all the tribes north of the Limpopo ... Wenela delivers cash allotments to wives and even provides letter writers and stamps. **1986** A.T. QABULA in Bunn & Taylor *From S. Afr.* (1988) 281, I went to Wenela to get recruited for the mines. [*Note*] The Employment Bureau of Africa.

wenkommando see KOMMANDO sense 1 b.

werf /vɛrf/ *n.* Also **verft, werft, wherf**. Pl. **-s**, occas. **werven** /vɛrvən/, **werwe** /vɛrvə/. [Older and dial. Du. *werf(t)* yard, raised ground on which a house is built.]

1. A farm homestead and its immediate environs; a farmyard. Also *attrib.*, and *fig.*

1818 C.I. LATROBE *Jrnl of Visit* 191 We .. took leave, pitched the tent on the werft, and kindled a fire. **1822** W.J. BURCHELL *Trav.* I. 238 On the werf, as the space immediately surrounding a colonist's dwelling, is termed, was a very large sheep-fold. **1841** B. SHAW *Memorials* 158, I am sure you will be long, for a woman *is a werf*, (village) and cannot easily be moved. **1859** W.G. ATHERSTONE in *Cape Monthly Mag.* V. Apr. 204 You lead your horse down the .. road, and are deafened by the usual canine salutation of a boer's werf. **1889** F. GALTON *Trav. in S. Afr.* 21 He was a huge, gaunt beast, miserably thin, and had a dog of Stewartson's in his inside, which he had snapped up on the werft the night before. **1896** M.A. CAREY-HOBSON *At Home in Tvl* 355 There were several houses on the verft or homestead, each inhabited by a married son or daughter of the family. **1915** D. FAIRBRIDGE *Torch Bearer* 261 He .. walked across the werf to the horses .. , and rode away. **1927** C.G. BOTHA *Social Life in Cape Col.* 82 On the corn farms the houses .. had a number of outbuildings on the 'werf' or yard. **1953** U. KRIGE *Dream & Desert* 175 Often carrying him on her back about the house or outside on the wide, sloping *werf*. **1967** H. FRANSEN *Stellenbosch Museum* 38 In .. Jonkershoek Valley lies *Lanzerac*, an example of a homestead with its forecourt surrounded by outbuildings and werf wall. **1968** — in D.J. Opperman *Spirit of Vine* 199 No *werf* (or farmyard) in the wine-producing districts of the Western Cape is complete without its gabled cellar-structure next to the homestead itself. *Ibid.* 207 Other farm complexes with enclosed *werwe* are *Uitkyk* .. and *Vredenhof*. **1987** G. VINEY *Col. Houses* 52 The farm buildings enclosed the *werf*.

2. In the context of traditional African societies: **a.** KRAAL *n.* sense 2 a. **b.** The temporary settlement of a nomadic group.

1852 J. TINDALL *Jrnl* (1959) 164 At the chief's werf. **1853** F. GALTON *Narr. of Explorer in Tropical S. Afr.* (1889) 60 We arrived at our guide's werft in the afternoon, and I was thoroughly fatigued. *Ibid.* 63 We arrived at the chief's werft, and I liked its situation and effect very much. **1861** C.J. ANDERSSON *Okavango River* 179 Five minutes further walk brought us to a werft consisting of between twenty and thirty huts. **1887** A.A. ANDERSON *25 Yrs in Waggon* I. 245 There is a hill .. with many wherfs of Bushmen. **1928** H. VEDDER in *Native Tribes of S.W. Afr.* 180 The 'werf' or village .. only includes a community of these who are family relatives. **1952** L.G. GREEN *Lords of Last Frontier* 6 He wanted his garrison to serve as a buffer between the Hereroes at Okahandja and the Hottentot werft of Hendrik Witbooi at Hoornkrans. **1969** J.M. WHITE *Land God Made in Anger* 228 Occasionally the Bushman *werf* or dwelling site will consist of a few flimsy *scherms* built of grass and interwoven branches. **1971** J.A. BROWN *Return* 35 The cattle were on the move back to all the werfs along the river.

3. By metonymy: the inhabitants of a werf.

1877 W.C. PALGRAVE *Damaraland* p.ix, The whole werft, about ten in number, came to the waggon. **1977** N. OKES in *Quarry '77* 138 Early on Saturday morning the horses and their riders departed to Rawsonville and at once the werf began to stir.

werven, werwe pl. forms of WERF.

Western Province *n. phr.* An informal name given to: **a.** The western districts of the Cape Colony. **b.** From 1910, the western districts of the Cape Province. **c.** A sports team representing these districts; PROVINCE. Also *attrib.*

Part of the province of the Western Cape from April 1994.

1843 J.C. CHASE *Cape of G.H.* p.v, The compiler has chiefly directed attention to the Eastern Province as an Immigration field. It must not, however, be considered that he wished to overlook, or cast into shade, the great capabilities of the Western Province for the same purpose ... He .. leaves the merits of the Western Province to be described and enlarged upon by one of its own residents. **1897** G.A. PARKER *S. Afr. Sports* 63 The competing [rugby] teams were: Western Province (holders), Transvaal, Griqualand West, Eastern Province, Border, and Natal. **1913** C. PETTMAN *Africanderisms* 120 *Chinkering ching, Ornithogalum thyrsoides.* The popular name of this plant in the Western Province. *Ibid.* 391 *Ramenas*, .. Wild mustard is known by this name in the Western Province. **1945** [see NATUURLIK]. **1949** [see CHINK]. **1955** C. HORNE *Fisherman's Eldorado* 8 The first few casts were sufficient to prove casual observation wrong, for yellowtail .. had been replaced by the Western Province katonkel, always to be distinguished from the Eastern Province katonkel which is the barracuda of Natal and a much bigger fish than the katonkel found in False Bay. **1969** N. LECK in J. Crwys-Williams *S. Afr. Despatches* (1989) 383 Muller and manager Dave Stewart led their Western Province rugby team into Johannesburg on Friday. **1978** [see DWAAL *n.*]. **1994** *Sunday Times* 31 July 29 Western Province finally put things together and whipped up a handsome victory yesterday.

wet /vet/ *n. Hist. Law.* Also with initial capital. [Afk.] A law passed by the legislative assembly of any of the former Boer republics. Cf. BESLUIT.

1936 *Cambridge Hist. of Brit. Empire* VIII. 574 At the end of a long test case .. Chief Justice Kotze .. denied the power of the Volksraad to alter existing law by resolution or by any means other than the slow and cumbrous progress of act (*wet*). **1949** J.S. FRANKLIN *This Union* 197 Some years ago .. the Department of Justice persuaded Parliament to pass a Bill repealing a number of obsolete and irrelevant Free State statutes. This particular 'Wet', a legacy of the old Republican days, was left untouched. **1968** E.A. WALKER *Hist. of Sn Afr.* 463 The Volksraad had legislated both by *wet* (statute), a process with occupied at least three months, and by *besluit* (resolution), a method which entailed no delay whatever.

wet digging *vbl n. phr. Hist. Diamond-mining.* [Orig. U.S. Eng., as a gold-mining term.] RIVER-DIGGING.

1876 F. BOYLE *Savage Life* 11 It was by no means unpleasant, this river, or wet, digging. *Ibid.* 14, I feel sure that an old hand rarely lets a diamond pass at the 'wet digging,' and scarcely ever at the 'dry.' **1985** A.J.A. JANSE in Glover & Harris *Kimberlite Occurrence & Origin* 21 These two mud quarries became the two famous diamond pipe mines Bultfontein and Dutoitspan. They were removed from any obvious rivers or streams so people referred to them as the Dry Diggings in contrast to the alluvial River, or Wet, Diggings.

wetie var. WIETIE.

whau var. WAU.

when-we /ˈwenwiː/ *n. colloq.* Also with initial capital(s). [So called because such people characteristically introduce comments with the words 'When we were in ..'.] A derogatory term for a resident of South Africa who formerly lived in another African country, esp. Zimbabwe (formerly Rhodesia); used esp. of one who retains a strong nostalgia for his or her former country. Hence *transf.*, a derogatory term for one who speaks of any place or occasion with what is seen as excessive nostalgia. Also *attrib.*

1985 *Grocott's Mail* 18 June (Coastal News) 1 Great interest has been expressed in the recent paragraph about 'Rhodesians Worldwide' ... Coastal Rhodies are ringing up and calling in, and it is intended to compile a local list, to put people in touch with each other, not as pathetic 'Whenwe' groups but for mutual help and interest. **1986** *Style* Feb. 62 What is a Reborn When-We? A Returned Rhodesian who's now nostalgic for South Africa. **1989** A. DONALDSON in *Ibid.* Dec. 8 Thanks to Amnesty International's Human Rights Now World Tour, the new wave of 'Whenwes' are with us — and they're every bit as painful as the first lot ... 'When we were in Harare ... y'know, Tracey Chapman/Bruce Springsteen/Sting/the vibe .. was just like so amazing, y'know ...' **1990** Y. DUFF in *Settler* Vol.64 No.6, 23 If you wish to touch a raw nerve with most Rhodesians try calling them a When-we.

This term, coined initially to describe people who left Kenya was successively applied to residents of Northern Rhodesia and finally in the 1970s to nostalgic ex-Rhodesians. **1990** [see SLIP-SLOP]. **1992** *Natal Mercury* 2 Nov. 7 The 'whenwes' who want to go home.

wherf var. WERF.

white *n.* and *adj.* Also with initial capital. [Special senses of general Eng.]

A. *n.*

1. *Ostrich-farming.* [Absol. use of general Eng. *white* 'of the colour of snow or milk' (*OED*).] PRIME.

*c*1881 A. DOUGLASS *Ostrich Farming* 81 Sort first into heaps consisting of prime whites, first whites, second whites, tipped whites. **1890** A. MARTIN *Home Life* 103 A large and magnificent bunch of wing-feathers, the finest and longest of 'prime whites'. **1896** [see FEMINA]. **1909** J.E. DUERDEN in *Agric. Jrnl of Cape of G.H.* XXXIV. 523 *Whites* .. include nearly all the wing-quills of the cock bird, both primaries and secondaries, and number about 24 from each wing. They are the most valuable of all the feathers, and are pure white, any admixture of black or grey placing them in a different class. *c*1911 S. PLAYNE *Cape Col.* 721 Ounceman has the record of yielding the heaviest plucking of 'whites' in the country, the return actually weighing 14 oz. **1930**, **1973** [see PRIME].

2. *hist.* [Special sense of general Eng. *white* one of light skin colour, one of European descent.] Designating a person:

a. During the apartheid era: one classified as belonging to the 'white' group, esp. in terms of the Population Registration Act (see quot. 1950 at sense B 1 a). See also CLASSIFY, NON-WHITE *n.*, PLAYWHITE.

1966 *Survey of Race Rel. 1965* (S.A.I.R.R.) 112 Japanese people in South Africa are classified as 'Other Asiatics' under the Population Registration Act, but as Whites under the Group Areas Act. **1970** *Survey of Race Rel.* (S.A.I.R.R.) 25 She and her parents and grandmother have always lived as whites, and have white identity cards.

b. Special Comb. **white-on-black** *adj.*, of or pertaining to racially motivated aggression perpetrated by a white person or persons against a black person or persons; cf. *black-on-black* (see BLACK *n.* sense 1 d); **whites only** *adj. phr. Hist.*, alluding to the wording on signs erected at places reserved for the use of white people; used *attrib.* in designating such signs, places so reserved, or activities restricted to white people.

1989 *City Press* 19 Feb. 9 **White on black** violence. **1992** *Sunday Times* 9 Feb. 18 A spate of 'retaliatory' white-on-black attacks also took place. **1973** *E. Prov. Herald* 27 Mar. 1 The **Whites only** signs had disappeared. **1986** R.J. COTTON *Ag, Man* 26 We .. are basking on the whites-only shores. **1989** *Sunday Star* 26 Feb. (Review Suppl.) 12 For those who believe a stopover in Louis Trichardt is a whites-only affair, there's light at the end of the tunnel. **1990** G. SLOVO *Ties of Blood*, This is a whites-only facility. If you want to catch a train you must wait outside. **1991** M. KANTEY *All Tickets* 10, I began .. within a four-coach *Whites Only* section of an eight-coach electric-driven train. **1992** W. KNOWLER in *Weekend Mercury* 4 Jan. 6 How about recycling those 'whites only' signs and turning them into bins on poles? **1992** S. MACLEOD in *Time* 9 Mar. 26 The growing strength of the .. Conservative Party has forced President F.W. de Klerk to hold a whites-only referendum. **1992** S. MEMELA in *Pace* Sept. 176 Every now and then I visit my childhood friends .. living in the formerly whites-only Northern Suburbs.

B. *adj.*

I. Of ethnicity.

1. [Special senses of general Eng. *white* of light skin colour, of European descent.] During the apartheid era:

a. *hist.* Of an individual: classified as a 'white person' in terms of the Population Registration Act (see quot. 1950). See also CLASSIFY, HONORARY WHITE.

1950 *Act 30* in *Stat. of Union* 277 'White person' means a person who in appearance obviously is, or who is generally accepted as a white person, but does not include a person who, although in appearance obviously a white person, is generally accepted as a coloured person. *Ibid.* 279 Every person whose name is included in the register shall be classified by the Director as a white person, a coloured person or a native, as the case may be. **1952** P. ABRAHAMS in *Drum* July 11 He had known a Coloured man who had been white nearly all his life, who had fought in the last war as a white officer, who had had a world of white friends — and then became a Coloured man quite suddenly. **1966** *Survey of Race Rel. 1965* (S.A.I.R.R.) 112 Mr W— had a 'White' birth certificate and identity card, but admitted when questioned that his mother was Coloured ... His wife was originally classified as White but officials later changed her classification to Coloured. **1970** *Survey of Race Rel.* (S.A.I.R.R.) 19 The Minister of the Interior said that a person could not be classified as white unless both his parents were so classified. **1977** *Ibid.* 33 The Secretary for the Interior altered the race classification of the following number of persons .. White to Cape Coloured 14, Cape Coloured to White 24, [etc.]. **1985** *Race Rel. Survey 1984* (S.A.I.R.R.) 186 Race classification ... White to Coloured 4, Coloured to white 462 ... White to Chinese 4, [etc.]. *Ibid.* His wife, who had a fair skin, would qualify for a white classification.

b. *hist.* Reserved by law for those classified as 'white'; usu. *attrib.*, as ***white area***, ***- beach***, ***- job***, ***- liquor***, ***- school***, ***- taxi***, etc.

1957 D. JACOBSON *Price of Diamonds* 90 This was true of the white and coloured areas alone, for the natives lived in locations. **1961** D. MARAIS *Hey! Van der Merwe*, (*caption*) *They'll* be able to buy White liquor. But will you and I be able to buy skokiaan .. ? **1961** *Star* 22 Nov. 1 Japanese .. may buy houses in White areas and own ground there, they may use all White amenities, including transport and liquor. This was confirmed by Government officials in Pretoria today. **1963** A.M. LOUW *20 Days* 80 Now I hear that this whole street will be proclaimed White. **1968** J. LELYVELD in Cole & Flaherty *House of Bondage* 8 The Government considers Soweto a .. social aberration in what has now been declared a 'white area'. **1970** [see PRESCRIBED AREA]. **1970** *Daily News* 9 June, The Minister of Labour's decision to allow increased use of Coloureds in 'White' jobs is obviously welcome. **1972** *Daily Dispatch* 17 Feb. 1 Taking into consideration the time factor involved in negotiations to buy white land, .. final consolidation could be as far away as ten years. **1972** J. SCOTT in J. Crwys-Williams *S. Afr. Despatches* (1989) 407 Come back along the platform to the point where the black coaches end and the white ones begin. **1975** *Daily Dispatch* 13 June 10 No signs indicating whether the restaurants are 'black' or 'white' are displayed. **1977** F.G. BUTLER *Karoo Morning* 204 To the south of the white town was an area with indeterminate frontiers ... Here lived the Coloureds. **1982** *E. Prov. Herald* 14 June 1 Early on Saturday morning a delegation of Fingos watched and listened as Parliament put the final seal on its plans to turn white 4800 hectares of land which had for 140 years been home to the Fingos. **1986** W. BAKER in *Style* July 88 In 'white' areas there are 'coloured' people renting houses or even owning them by proxy arrangements with sympathetic 'whites'. **1986** M. RAMGOBIN *Waiting to Live* 114 This is a white taxi ... I am not here for your kaffir girls! **1987** *E. Prov. Herald* 25 July 4 His announcement that he would again swim off a white beach was an attempt to steal the limelight ... Were Mr Hendrickse to bathe his body in white seawater .. he would .. attract greater international attention than any number of Channel swimmers. **1987** B. ORPEN in *E. Prov. Herald* 18 May 2 Margaret will speak at .. the white school in the afternoon. **1987** *Pretoria News* 17 June 5 The government turned away all 148 blacks who applied to study at 'white' agricultural colleges in 1986. **1987** [see OFF-SALES]. **1991** *Weekend Argus* 26 Jan. 14 There was a haphazard retreat from grand apartheid, with the granting of leasehold, and eventually freehold, property rights to blacks in 'white' areas.

c. *Offensive* and *derog.* Impudent, presumptuous; cf. CHEEKY. Often as an aggressive and racist warning given to a black person, ***don't get white (with me)***; sometimes used in contexts (e.g. of an animal) in which the offensively racist origin of the sense has been lost.

1978 A.P. BRINK *Rumours of Rain* 247 It's a real problem. They're getting too white, is what I say. **1978** *Informant, Grahamstown* She cheeked me — hell she's white, that one. **1988** S.A. BOTHA in *Frontline* Apr.-May 24 'I tjaaf you, the peckies are getting white these days ... You can't trust them', said Don. **1988** 'K. LEMMER' in *Weekly Mail* 9 Dec. 19 Said journalist's .. kitten leapt into said Flo's lap ... Barked Flo: '*Hey!* Don't get white with me, kitten.' The feline was a Red Burmese. **1989** M. NICOL *Powers that Be* 62 Who should he engage as gardener but a no-good layabout .. the whitest kaffir he'd ever come across. Besides, this white kaffir had talked a hole in Mondling's head. **1990** *Sunday Times* 13 May 13 Her 16-year-old brother .. was threatened with a gun and told: 'Don't be smart and get white with us' when he protested about the search.

d. Special collocations and phrases. ***white by night*** *adj. phr. Hist.*, (of a municipal policy or regulation) having the aim of keeping black people out of an area after dark or after a certain hour, esp. by the imposition of a curfew; (of a town or area) falling under such a regulation or policy; (of actions) resulting from such a policy or aimed at enforcing such regulations; freq. *attrib.*; ***White South Africa***, a collective term designating (*a*) those areas of South Africa which, during the apartheid era, were reserved for occupation by whites; (*b*) white South Africans collectively; (*c*) the cultural and social milieux and values of such people; ***white spot*** *hist.* [formed by analogy with BLACK SPOT], a white-occupied area surrounded by black-occupied areas; cf. BLACK SPOT; collectively, the inhabitants of such an area; also *attrib.*

*c*1970 C. DESMOND *Discarded People* 165 The vacated houses are now being used as hostels for domestic servants, since Pietersburg is '**White by night**'. **1970** *Post* 15 Mar. 9 Friday 13th was doubly unlucky for Germiston's domestics — it was the start of the 'exodus' into Natalspruit at night as the 'Germiston White by Night' policy came into effect. **1970** *Rand Daily Mail* 12 Nov. 14 Africans are not only expected to grin and bear the hardships brought on by apartheid, but they are .. expected to help finance the policy as well ... The 'White-by-night' programme is another harsh illustration of this. **1971** *Daily News* 17 Apr. 4 The new White suburbs will not allow servants to live-in so as to conform with the White-by-Night policy so beloved by verkramptes. **1978** B.J. MOTAUNG in *Staffrider* Vol.1 No.2, 22 The women sing about their children, who have turned moles in West Deep Levels and Owls in the white-by-night Johannesburg. **1989** *City Press* 19 Feb. 9 White-by-night beatings: we will not take it! **1988** *Benoni Homefinder & Advertiser* 1 June 1 No permit is required for occupation by domestic employees of a legal occupier of the premises, with the provision that such an area has *not* been declared 'White by Night'. **1989** *City Press* 19 Feb. 9 The CP council might reintroduce white-by-night regulations – curfews on blacks. **1926** R. CAMPBELL in *Voorslag* July 16 You people get an ideal like '**White South Africa**' tied to your noses and then you can't see anything else. **1968** J. LELYVELD in Cole & Flaherty *House of Bondage* 14 The last thing white South Africa is prepared to see black South Africa have is a voice. **1973** *Weekend Post* 27 Oct. 17 The Government has now in effect accepted the permanence of Africans in 'White' South Africa. **1977** [see AGTERRYER sense 2]. **1982** D. TUTU *Voice of One* 108 Whites .. say that blacks have no claim to political representation in 'white' South Africa. *Ibid.* 109 It will mean a declension in the very high standard of living that white

South Africa enjoys. **1992** F. KEATING in *Guardian Weekly* 9 Oct. 31 Rugby is spiritually entwined in the very soul of white South Africa. **1992** P. HAWTHORNE in *Time* 21 Sept. 37 Blacks .. would be permitted to work in white South Africa only as temporary residents. **1952** *Drum* Mar. 25 (*caption*) Where Black Meets White: A Street Corner in the Western Areas, where a **White Spot** (right) adjoins a Black Spot (left). **1955** *Rand Daily Mail* 11 May 11 'White spot' plan: Commerce Support for Meeting. **1960** J.H. COETZEE in H. Spottiswoode *S. Afr.: Rd Ahead* 70 Consider the reaction of the Transkeian White spots against Bantu self-rule. **1966** *Survey of Race Rel. 1965* (S.A.I.R.R.) 201 Smaller townships are being laid out beside 'White spot' towns, such as Eshowe (Sundimbili and Gezinsela), Umzimkulu (Bisi), Babanango (Mphungamhope), Empangeni (Ngwelezana), and others. **1973** *Star* 10 May 26 'White spots' problem. Can a 'nation' like Transkei make sense while its capital, Umtata, remains firmly White? .. It's a problem of 'White spots'. **1976** *Sunday Times* 10 Oct. 19 The cafe is a White spot within a Black spot (a Black-zoned part of Umtata) within a White spot (Umtata itself) within a Black spot (the Transkei) within a White spot (the Republic) within a Black spot (the African continent). **1990** *Varsity Voice* Apr. 15 It's a 'white spot' with full representation in the South African Parliament.

II. General. [Special uses of general Eng. *white* 'of the colour of snow or milk' (*OED*), light-coloured.]

2. Special collocations. **white button**, a badge worn by 'bitter-enders' during the closing months of the South African War, 1900–1902; see also BITTER-ENDER; **white els, -else** /ˈwaɪtels/, also with initial capitals, [part. tr. S. Afr. Du. *witte els*, see WIT ELS], (*a*) WIT ELS; also *attrib.*; (*b*) with defining word, **water white els**, *Brachylaena neriifolia*; **White French**, see as a main entry; **white lightning** [tr. Afk. *witblits* (see WITBLITS); cf. U.S. *white lightning* illicitly distilled whisky], WITBLITS sense b; **white pear**, the evergreen tree *Apodytes dimidiata* subsp. *dimidiata* (family Icacinaceae); the wood of this tree; **white pipe**, see PIPE sense 2 b; **white sore throat** *Pathology* [calque formed on Afk. *witseerkeel* diphtheria, *wit* white + *seer* sore + *keel* throat], diphtheria; **White Train** [so named for the colour of its livery], a special train used for ceremonial and state occasions; also *fig.*

1903 E.F. KNIGHT *S. Afr. after War* 112 These men .. took to wearing 'the **white button**' on the left breasts — the badge that distinguishes those who fought to the end from those who surrendered or were taken prisoner. *Ibid.* 200 Here many ex-burghers were still wearing the white button to show that they were among those that held out to the end. **1790** W. PATERSON *Narr. of Four Journeys* 34, I found myself by the White Else River, which takes its name from a tree, called by the Dutch, **White Else**. **1833** *S. Afr. Almanac & Dir.* 195 The other woods most in request, and found in Albany, are .. Red and White Else [etc.]. **1887** J.C. BROWN *Crown Forests* 122 White Els ... Requires from 30 to 50 years before useful; it is used for boat-building, for waggon sides, and chests. **1973** *E. Prov. Herald* 13 (*advt*) One White Els Chest. **1987** T.F.J. VAN RENSBURG *Intro. to Fynbos* 16 Another typical riverbank species is the water white els (*Brachylaena neriifolia*), with its bushy grey-green foliage. [**1934 white lightning**: see WITBLITS.] **1972** J. MCCLURE *Caterpillar Cop* (1974) 85 It's bloody dangerous when a kaffir gets filled up on white-lightning! **1977** *Family Radio & TV* 19 Sept. 51 As the fires were lit under the clay-sealed copper stills, the call would go out, 'The cow is giving milk.' And those in the know would arrive carrying milk-cans to collect their white lightning. **1988** D. HUGHES et al. *Complete Bk of S. Afr. Wine* 332 Witblits, Otherwise known as Dop, White Lightning, Boerblits, Cape Smoke, or Kaapse Smaak. **1831** *S. Afr. Almanac & Dir.* 187 The other woods most in request, and found in Albany are .. Red and **White Pear**, Saffran. **1837** J.E. ALEXANDER *Narr. of Voy.* I. 347 Dutch wheels are made of three or four kinds of wood; .. for the fellow, red els, or white pear. **1887** J.C. BROWN *Crown Forests* 122 *White Pear*, Grows from seed, and shoots from the stump; of slow growth, and must be 20 or 30 years old to be useful for waggon-wood. **1907** J.M. WOOD *Handbk to Flora of Natal* 31 *Apodytes dimidiata* is the well-known 'White Pear,' its wood being extensively used for felloes, etc. **1913** H. TUCKER *Our Beautiful Peninsula* 5 Hillside forests of yellow-wood, white pear and other native timber trees. **1919** *Dunell, Ebden & Co.'s Price List* Aug. 35 Felloes ... Scotch Cart, White Pear, 2/8. **1936** E. ROSENTHAL *Old-Time Survivals* 10 Red pear, red els, white pear, and scores of other precious African timbers go to the making .. of the conveyance. **1955** A. DELIUS *Young Trav.* 114 Other trees are white pears, assegai, [etc.]. **1971** BARAITSER & OBHOLZER *Cape Country Furn.* 63 Its loose inset seat .. is made of pearwood, that is the wood of the white pear. **1994** S. HOWELL in *Weekend Post* 1 Jan. 2 Mr Howell appealed to anyone who could help the museum with suitable hardwood — such as white pear and ironwood — .. to contact him. **1866** *Cape Town Dir.* 173 It was found that **white sore throat** had set in, and she became decidedly worse. **1891** H.J. DUCKITT *Hilda's 'Where Is It?'* 99 For White Sore Throat. Take half an ounce of chloride of potash, dissolved in a quart bottle of water. One tablespoonful three times a day. **1913** A. GLOSSOP *Barnes's S. Afr. Hsehold Guide* 238 A splendid gargle, especially if there is any indication of what is called a white sore throat .. is prepared from the 'Goonah' plant. **1915** D. FAIRBRIDGE *Torch Bearer* 178 'It may be diphtheria,' she said ... 'My cook .. sent to say that her two children were ill with white sore throats.' **1965** K. MACKENZIE *Deserter*, Gert and Marietjie had fallen sick with the white sore throat. **1937** C.R. PRANCE *Tante Rebella's Saga* 101 The great man must go .. to Kimberley by the best approximation to a '**White Train**' that the old Cape Government Railways could provide. **1947** *Rand Daily Mail* 15 Feb. 8 Mr. J.J. Kruger in the cab of the locomotive which will take the White Train, bearing the Royal Family, from Cape Town. **1974** *Rhodeo* (Rhodes Univ.) 5 Sept. 6 The White train coasted down the hill past my house and even I gave it a wave which was returned with the best of royal humour by a steward in the dining car. **1980** *Daily Dispatch* 18 Mar. 9 Mr Heunis confessed that the White Train had gone to the big station in the sky. 'I'm afraid it no longer exists'. **1981** *Sunday Times* 27 Sept. 30 That Boeing, Presidents, VIPs .. and Cabinet Ministers, for the use of, will soon take to the air. A sort of airborne White Train which was so unceremoniously pensioned off. **1984** *Daily Dispatch* 16 Mar. 1 The White Train .. is to form a central part of the signing of the pact. **1988** R. GORDON in Laband & Haswell *Pietermaritzburg 1838–1988* 95 For almost three months the White Train was his home.

white-eye *n.* [Either fr. Austral. Eng., or tr. Afk. *witogie*, see WITOGIE; see also quot. 1900.] Either of two species of small bird belonging to the genus *Zosterops* of the Zosteropidae, with white rings around the eyes, and predominantly green plumage; WITOGIE.

Also *Austral. Eng.*

1867 E.L. LAYARD *Birds of S. Afr.* 116 The 'white-eye' is common throughout the whole of the country. **1900** STARK & SCLATER *Birds of S. Afr.* I. 298 Zosteropidae. The 'White-eyes,' so-called from the conspicuous ring of white feathers which encircles the eyes of the majority of the species, are birds of small size and very uniform style of coloration. **1903** A.F. TROTTER *Old Cape Col.* 216 Little white eyes, greenish in colour, with white circles round each eye. **1936** E.L. GILL *First Guide to S. Afr. Birds* 41 This is the white-eye of the Western Province, abundant from Cape Town to about Port Elizabeth, beyond which the white eyes have more yellow on the forehead and are known as the sub-species *atmorii*, characteristic of the Eastern Province. **1971** *Personality* 2 Apr. 25 Birds had made themselves at home in the garden — brilliant sunbirds of several kinds, chattering white-eyes, finches, robins and thrushes. **1987** *Fair Lady* 18 Feb. 147 A small yellow-green White Eye is perched in a tangle of twigs within arm's reach.

White French *n. phr.* Also with small initials. FRENCH GRAPE. Also *attrib.*

*c***1911** P.D. HAHN in S. Playne *Cape Col.* 174 Many vineyards with Pontac, red and white Muscatel, Haanepot, and Frontignac have been replanted with Hermitage, Cabernet de Sauvignon, white French, and Green Grape. **1972** [see STEEN sense 2]. **1988** D. HUGHES et al. *Complete Bk of S. Afr. Wine* 97 Palomino, or White French .. one of the oldest known to have been grown at the Cape. In the local vineyards it was traditionally known as White French, or Fransdruif, but was identified by Perold in 1926 not with a French grape but with one of the famous sherry cultivars of Spain, Palomino Fino.

white kaffir /waɪt ˈkæfə/ *n. phr. Offensive.* [General Eng. *white* of light skin colour, of European descent + KAFFIR *n.* sense 2 b.]

1. A derogatory and racist term for a white person who is perceived as ill-bred, or for one who has become assimilated into a black community, or who associates with black people. Also *attrib.*

1846 *Natal Witness* 31 July, One of the white caffers have [*sic*] been taken into custody on suspicion. **1870** C. HAMILTON *Life & Sport in S.-E. Afr.* 264 In my opinion the Dutch Boer is little else than a White Kaffir. **1897** J.P. FITZPATRICK *Outspan* 27 You can't imagine — my surprise when I found that my naked white Kaffir sailor-friend, Sebougwaan, was the man of the hour. **1903** E.F. KNIGHT *S. Afr. after War* 154 They dub the British who adopt the local custom 'white Kaffirs'. **1908** D. BLACKBURN *Leaven* 38 'He educated a kafir girl and married her. That's the result.' Betts indicated the huts ... 'He's a white kafir now, with plenty of time on his hands for educating his nigger family.' **1926** S.G. MILLIN *S. Africans* 209 (Swart), In the old days men, thrusting their ancestry, their traditions .. completely behind them, became what people sometimes call in South Africa 'white Kaffirs'. **1949** C. BULLOCK *Rina* 91 Sailors who were shipwrecked or had deserted from their ships had sometimes sought refuge in African kraals and become 'white kaffirs'. **1955** W. ILLSLEY *Wagon on Fire* 88 If he appeared familiar and friendly with the Africans, the white people dubbed him a white kaffir, a destroyer of white prestige, and ostracized him from their social life. **1974** D. ROOKE *Margaretha de la Porte* 212 'You white kaffir', I said in his ear. 'I'm sure you are the one who gave her too much to drink.' **1976** S. CLOETE *Chetoko* 150 Trelawney's his name .. and he's a white Kaffir ... He's gone native. **1990** *New African* 18 June 7 About 10 white rightwing men .. yelled out 'white kaffir' to white members of the march.

2. A racist term for an African albino.

1934 C.P. SWART Supplement to Pettman. 191 *White Kaffir*, An albino. **1966** L.G. BERGER *Where's Madam* 164 He and his charwoman wife had between them bred three 'white Kaffirs' — albino natives with white hair, pink eyes, white freckled skin, yet unmistakable native features. **1974** *Informant, Grahamstown* Look at that — a white kaffir — an albino. **1980** C. HOPE *A Separate Development* (1983) 93 Lets just say I'm some kind of kaffir, and leave it at that ... Skin's the problem. Say a *white kaffir*, then.

Whitestan see -STAN.

whithaat var. WITGAT.

whitletomb see quot. 1799 at WITTEBOOM.

whitte haat var. WITGAT.

whittle boom see quot. 1806 at WITTEBOOM.

‖**wietie** /ˈwiːti, ˈwɪti/ *v. slang.* Also **wetie, witty.** [Isicamtho, perh. fr. Afk. *weet jy* or *weet u* (do) you know.] **a.** *intrans.* To talk. **b.** *trans.* To tell (something to someone), to speak (a language or argot).

[*a***1977** K.M.C. MOTSISI in M. Mutloatse *Casey & Co.* (1978) 68 This is nonsense wat die juveniles maak. Ek wietie jou.] **1980** *Cape Times* 11 Sept. Glossary of Gang Slang ... Wetie — tell something. **1982** D. BIKITSHA in

Rand Daily Mail 14 Oct. (Eve) 5 To speak or 'witty' tsotsi taal as the lingo goes is an art.

Hence **wietie** *n.*, township argot.

1993 M. KA HARVEY in *Weekly Mail* 23 Dec. 15 'Tsotsi taal' (mainly spoken in Meadowlands and Rockville), 'isicamtho' (spoken by the youth), 'jive lingo' .. and pristine 'wietie', directly from Sophiatown.

wigat var. WITGAT.

Wijkmeester var. WYKMEESTER.

wild *adj.* [Eng., referring to the similarity between a familiar European species and an unfamiliar African species.] Special collocations.

a. In the names of plants: **wild almond**, **wild chestnut** sense (a), see below; **wild apricot**, any of several small trees or shrubs, (a) any of several species of *Dovyalis* of the Flacourtiaceae, esp. *D. caffra*; see also **Kei apple** (KEI sense 1); (b) any of several species of *Diospyros* of the Ebenaceae; see also JAKKALSBESSIE; **wild banana**, either of two species of plant of the genus *Strelitzia*, *S. alba* or *S. reginae*, bearing stiff flowers of orange, yellow, and purple; also called STRELITZIA; **wild celery**, the BLISTER BUSH, *Peucedanum galbanum*; **wild chestnut**, either of two indigenous flowering trees with spreading branches and pink or lilac blossom, (a) *Brabejum stellatifolium* of the Proteaceae; **wild almond**; (b) *Calodendrum capense* of the Rutaceae; Cape chestnut, see CAPE sense 2 a; the fruit of these trees; **wild fig (tree)** [tr. Afk. *wildevijg, -vy*], any of several species of tree of the genus *Ficus*; **wild gardenia**, KERSHOUT sense 2; **wild garlic**, the *wilde knoflok* (see WILDE sense a), *Tulbaghia alliacea*; **wild grape**, see as a main entry; **wild kapok** [tr. Afk. *wildekapok*], the soft cotton-like hairs encasing the seeds of either of two plants, *Asclepias fruticosa* of the Asclepiadaceae (also called MELKBOS sense 1 a i), or *Ipomoea albivenia* of the Convolvulaceae; cf. KAPOK sense 1; **wild melon**, TSAMMA; **wild olive**, OLIENHOUT sense a; also *attrib.*; **wild orange** ?*obs.*, any of several small trees belonging to the genus *Strychnos* of the Loganiaceae (esp. *Strychnos pungens*), bearing fruit with edible pulp; see also KLAPPER *n.*[1] sense 1; **wild pear**, (a) the small deciduous tree *Dombeya rotundifolia* of the Sterculiaceae (cacao family); the wood of this tree; also called *wild plum* (sense (d), see below); (b) any of several trees of the Ochnaceae, esp. *Ochna pulchra*; **wild pisang**, see PISANG sense 2 b; **wild plum**, any of several trees bearing plum-like fruits, esp. (a) *Harpephyllum caffrum*; formerly also called *kaffir plum* (see KAFFIR *n.* sense 2 e); its fruit; (b) *Pappea capensis* of the Sapindaceae, valued for the shade and sustenance it offers in arid areas; its fruit; (c) *Bequaertiodendron magalismontum*; also called STAMVRUG; the fruit of this tree; (d) the *wild pear* (sense (a), see above), *Dombeya rotundifolia*; the fruit of this tree; (c) the AMATUNGULU, *Carissa macrocarpa*; (f) the MORETLWA, *Grewia flava*; **wild pomegranate**, (a) the moisture-loving shrub *Burchellia bubalina* of the Rubiaceae; (b) any of several species of *Rhigozum* of the Bignoniaceae, esp. the small twiggy tree *R. obovatum*; **wild sage** [see quot. 1966], (a) SALIE sense 1; (b) the VAALBOS (sense 1 a), *Tarchonanthus camphoratus*; **wild spinach**, MOROGO; **wild watermelon**, TSAMMA; **wild wormwood**, the *wilde als* (see WILDE sense a), *Artemisia afra*.

1731 G. MEDLEY tr. *P. Kolb's Present State of Cape of G.H.* I. 202 One Sort of Fruit they eat is call'd the **Wild** or the *African Almond*. They boil those Almonds twice or thrice in fresh Water, and then lay them in the Sun to dry. **1790** tr. *F. Le Vaillant's Trav.* II. 241, I have .. often met with the wild almond tree, *wilde-amandel*, the narrow leaves and fruit of which .. differed only in the reddish brown colour of the husk. **1887** *S.W. Silver & Co.'s Handbk to S. Afr.* 139 The Wilde Amandel, Wild Almond, is the fruit of *Brabeium Stellatifolium* ... It is a stone-fruit, clothed with a velvety coat, and has received its popular name from its striking resemblance to an almond. **1906** B. STONEMAN *Plants & their Ways* 210 *Brabeium*, (Kaffir Chestnut or Wild Almond) ... The almond-like fruits, when roasted, make a good substitute for cocoa, though they are poisonous if eaten raw. **1961** PALMER & PITMAN *Trees of S. Afr.* 216 The wild almond has the distinction of being the first indigenous tree to be cultivated in South Africa. **1790** W. PATERSON *Narr. of Four Journeys* 126 In this plain grows .. a beautiful shrub, called the **Wild Apricot**. **1913** C. PETTMAN *Africanderisms* 553 *Wild apricot, Dovyalis tristis.* **1972** PALMER & PITMAN *Trees of Sn Afr.* III. 1561 *Dovyalis caffra* .. Kei apple, Dingaan's apricot, wild apricot ... Although this is primarily a species occurring from the eastern Cape to the Transkei .. it is also recorded from Natal, Zululand, and .. from the central, eastern and northern Transvaal. *Ibid.* 1565 *Dovyalis rotundifolia* .. Wild Apricot. *Ibid.* 1567 *Dovyalis rhamnoides* .. Cape cranberry, wild apricot. *Ibid.* 1786 *Diospyros* ... In the Republic about 16 species grow as trees ... The early colonists called some species wild apricots. **1987** F. VON BREITENBACH *Nat. List of Indigenous Trees* 139 *Dovyalis caffra* .. Kei apple, Wild Apricot, Dingaan's Apricot. *Ibid.* 140 *Dovyalis zeyheri* .. Wild Apricot. **1991** *Philatelic Services Bulletin* No.8075, *Dovyalis caffra* ... The most common species of *Dovyalis* in Bophuthatswana is *D. zeyheri*, the wild apricot, but the Kei-apple also occurs in this area. **1836** A.F. GARDINER *Journey to Zoolu Country* 17 We slept well under the shade of some strelitzia trees (very similar to **wild bananas**).] **1917** R. MARLOTH *Common Names* 8 Banana, Wild -, of the coast districts, is not a *Musa*, but *Strelitzia augusta*. c**1963** B.C. TAIT *Durban Story* 83 Clumps of wild date-palms and wild bananas, with here and there a wild fig tree, grew among the scrub and Amatungula, coarse grass and rushes. **1986** J. CONYNGHAM *Arrowing of Cane* 23, I scan the slope of cane, palms, amatungulu and wild bananas. **1903** *Mountain Club Annual* (Cape Town) 24 (Pettman), The other day a friend of mine had a more than usual dose of blistering ... The awkward feature of this danger is that one does not notice any effect on the hand until about thirty of forty hours after one has touched the plant. Its name is Bubon, or if any one prefers the colonial name '**Wild celery**'. **1917, 1932** [see BLISTER BUSH]. **1970** M.R. LEVYNS in *Std Encycl. of Sn Afr.* II. 365 *Blister-bush*, Wild celery ... The dried leaves have been used medicinally for the treatment of dropsy. The home of the plant is on the mountains of the South-Western Cape Province. **1986** Y. VAN WYK *Practical Bk of Herbs* 17 Their initial poverty, and the hardship and droughts they endured, hastened the settlers' recourse to 'veldkos' that included .. wild celery (*Peucedanum* sp.). **1795** C.R. HOPSON tr. *C.P. Thunberg's Trav.* I. 129 The Hottentots eat the fruit of the brabeium stellatum, a large shrub that grows near brooks and rivulets, called *wilde castanien* (**wild chestnuts**) and sometimes used by the country people instead of coffee. **1809** J. MACKRILL *Diary.* 64 Calodendrum, Wild Chesnut [*sic*], is a lofty tree bearing flowers filled with a sweet nectar which attracts numerous butterflies. **1868** J. CHAPMAN *Trav.* II. 450 The Wild Chestnut .. well deserving its name for its exquisitely-pencilled delicate pink flowers. **1887** [see STAMVRUG]. **1909** *E. London Dispatch* 3 July 5 The beautiful lilac flowers of the wild chestnut are opening two or three months before their time. **1961** PALMER & PITMAN *Trees of S. Afr.* 269 The wild chestnut is found in forests and forest scrub from the Cape Province through Natal to the Transvaal, and northwards through Rhodesia and Abyssinia. **1972** *S. Afr. Garden & Home* Oct. 145 Among these trees are flowering wild chestnuts with pale lilac blossoms. **1731** [wild fig: see quot. at *wild sage* below]. **1827** [see MONKEY-ROPE]. **1853** F. GALTON *Narr. of Explorer in Tropical S. Afr.* 63 Along the ravines a few wild fig-trees grew. **1912** *E. London Dispatch* 12 Apr. 7 (Pettman), It is very seldom that the Cape chestnut and the Wild fig become altogether devoid of leaves. **1953** *Cape Argus* 25 Feb. 9 Eighty trees, including jakkalsbessie, geelhout, wild fig, .. have been planted along Table Bay boulevard. c**1963** [see quot. at *wild banana* above]. **1966** C.A. SMITH *Common Names* 508 *Wild fig* (tree), Various species of *Ficus* .., see *wildevy(e)(boom)*. The vernacular name was first applied to *F. capensis* and subsequently to *F. natalensis* by the Dutch-speaking colonists. **1972** M.R. LEVYNS in *Std Encycl. of Sn Afr.* VI. 370 Other common names of *R. capensis* are candlewood and **wild gardenia**. **1974** SKINNER & YATES *Our Trees* 41 *Rothmannia capensis*, Aapsekos, wild gardenia. **1975** C. LETTY *Trees of S. Afr.* 46 Wild Gardenia .. *Rothmannia capensis*. The three species of Rothmannia in South Africa are wide-spread. Named by the great Swedish plant collector Carl Thunberg, they were later taken into the Gardenia group, but after more than a century, in 1958, were given back the original name. The Wild Gardenia was first discovered at the Cape. **1984** R.J. POYNTON *Characteristics & Uses of Sel. Trees* 86 *Rothmannia capensis* .. Wild Gardenia. **1989** B. COURTENAY *Power of One* 153 The pale yellow blossoms of wild gardenia. **1991** *Ornamental Trees & Shrubs of Afr. Calendar*, This attractive glossy leaved wild gardenia occurs naturally from Grahamstown to Kosi Bay ... Sweetly scented flowers are followed by interesting, hard, grey, knob-like fruits which, in the wild, are eaten by large animals. **1795, 1809** [wild garlic: see quots at *wilde knoflok* (WILDE sense a)]. **1966** C.A. SMITH *Common Names* 508 *Wild garlic*, .. The vernacular name is derived from the garlic-like scent of the broken leaves and bulb scales. [**1913** C. PETTMAN *Africanderisms* 555 *Wild cotton* or *Wilde kapok*, *Asclepias fruticosa*, Linn., and other species are known as 'Wild cotton'. In Natal and Portuguese East Africa, this name has been given to *Ipomoea albivenia*.] **1990** *Staffrider* Vol.9 No.1, 85 Behind their jangled key-closed doors I may not touch her, fingers meeting soft as wild kapok against the glass. **1894** R. MARLOTH in *Trans. of S. Afr. Phil. Soc.* p.lxxx, Our common **wild-melon** (*Citrullus vulgaris*). **1920** F.C. CORNELL *Glamour of Prospecting* 88 Bushmen still wandered there, .. living on the tsamma (or wild melon). **1974** B. DE WINTER in *Std Encycl. of Sn Afr.* X. 640 Tsamma. Wild melon. Bitter melon. **1975** *Motorist* Feb. 36 In the rolling sand dunes of the Kalahari .. tsamas (wild melon) .. abound. **1731** G. MEDLEY tr. *P. Kolb's Present State of Cape of G.H.* II. 243 *Olea Africana humilis sylvestris*, folio duro, subtus incano. i.e. Dwarf African **Wild Olive**, with a hard Leaf, white on the underside. **1828** T. PRINGLE *Ephemerides* 113 By the wild-olive brake where the wolf has his den. **1856** R.E.E. WILMOT *Diary* (1984) 84 The road sides lined with jessamine, wild olive, and strelitzias. **1879** E.L. PRICE *Jrnls* (1956) 349 There are a good many wild-olives & camelthorns. **1905** D.E. HUTCHINS in *Flint & Gilchrist Science in S. Afr.* 392 The common 'Wild Olive' furnishes a good fencing post. **1907** [see HAAKDORING]. **1936** [see KAREE *n.*[2] sense 1 a i]. **1951** N.L. KING *Tree-Planting* 69 *Olea africana* (*verrucosa*) (Wild Olive), .. Very hardy. **1961** PALMER & PITMAN *Trees of S. Afr.* 301 The wild olive, with its dense, round crown and grey-green foliage, is a familiar sight in the Karroo, the north-west Cape, Bechuanaland, and the Free State, where it is one of the most common trees. **1970** *S. Afr. Panorama* Sept. 40 The wood of the wild olive-tree is extremely hard and can only be used for making furniture when it is hundreds of years old. **1972** [see DROOG-MY-KEEL]. **1988** [see OLIENHOUT]. **1989** J. HOBBS *Thoughts in Makeshift Mortuary* 74 Scrubby bushes, aloes and a single wild olive tree were the only plants that found a root-hold in the eruption of sandstone rocks. **1895** A.B. BALFOUR *1200 Miles in Waggon* 110 There were .. figs, **wild oranges** (I measured one: it was 13½ inches in circumference, and as hard as a cricket ball). **1913** C. PETTMAN *Africanderisms* 352 *Orange, Wild, See* Kaffir Orange. **1921** T.R. SIM *Native Timbers* 120 *Strychnos pungens* .. Wild Orange. **1932** WATT & BREYER-BRANDWIJK *Medicinal & Poisonous Plants* 140 The pulp of the fruit of *Strychnos pungens* Solered., Wild orange, Kaffir orange, Klapper. **1961** PALMER & PITMAN *Trees of S. Afr.* 227 The **wild pear** is a small deciduous tree growing up to 20 feet in height with hairy leaves, round in outline, and usually a rough brownish-black bark. **1990** *Weekend Post* 14 July (Leisure) 4 He makes it [*sc.* furniture] to order from popular woods like .. wild pear. **1907** T.R. SIM *Forests & Forest Flora* 145 (Pettman), In Transvaal .. it [*sc. Dombeya rotundifolia*] is known as **Wild plum** on account of the similarity of the flowering bush to a plum tree. **1913** C. Pettman *Africanderisms* 559 *Wild plum*, The handsome edible fruit of *Ximenia caffra, Sond.*, of a bright plum colour; it is very acid but of a pleasant flavour and is common in the Transvaal and Natal ... *Wild plum*, The Transvaal name for *Dombeya rotundifolia*. **1972** Palmer & Pitman *Trees of Sn Afr.* I. 283 The kernels of the small red fruits of the wild plum, *Pappea capensis*, are very rich in sweetly-scented oil which farmers' wives once used for soap, farmers for greasing their guns, and Hottentots for anointing their skin. *Ibid.* II. 1474 *Dombeya rotundifolia* ... Wild pear, wild plum. *Ibid.* III. 1714 *Bequaertiodendron magalismontanum* ... Stamvrug, wild plum. **1982** Fox & Norwood Young *Food from Veld* 54 Here are some of the plants reported to us as being resorted to when the usual foods become exhausted: .. *Carissa macrocarpa* — wild plum. *Ibid.* 155 *Garcinia livingstonei* ... Common names: English — *Lowveld mangosteen*, wild plum. *Ibid.* 351 *Grewia flava* ... Common names: English — *brandy bush, raisin tree, wild plum*. **1989** *Gardening Questions Answered* (Reader's Digest Assoc.) 356 *Wild Plum*, .. *Harpephyllum caffrum* (Wild plum). Quick-growing, indigenous, evergreen tree with glossy leaves composed of small leaflets. In early summer, it bears small, green-white flowers, which are followed by purple-red, plum-shaped fruits. **1992** *Weekend Post* 12 Dec. 10 Five indigenous wild plum trees chopped down in Bird Street were removed because they were dangerous to passers-by. **1994** G. Bisseker in *Ibid.* 12 Nov. (Leisure) 6 The popular *Harpephyllum caffrum* (Transkei wild plum), formerly known as kaffir plum. **1910** *E. London Dispatch* 27 May 5 (Pettman), Chief of which are the *Burchellia* (**wild pomegranate**). **1951** N.L. King *Tree-Planting* 66 *Burchellia bulbalina (capensis)* (*Wild pomegranate*), A handsome shrub widely distributed in moist forests from south-western Cape to Natal. Bears bright red flowers in profusion. Best suited to moist localities where frosts are not severe. Grows best in partial shade. **1966** E. Palmer *Plains of Camdeboo* 155 Springbuck have always loved the Karoo. They have grown sleek on the .. wild pomegranates of the koppies. **1977** —— *Field Guide to Trees* 285 *Rhigozum*, Four Southern African species, three sometimes small twiggy trees ... All species browsed, thus often kept to shrub size. Commonly called wild pomegranate or wildegranaat. **1731** G. Medley tr. *P. Kolb's Present State of Cape of G.H.* I. 309 They take .. the Powders or Infusions of but a very few Things; namely, **Wild Sage**, *Wild Figs* and *Fig-leaves, Buchu*, [etc.]. **1866** Lindley & Moore *Treasury of Bot.*, Wild Sage, a name in the Cape colony for *Tarchonanthus camphoratus*. **1913** C. Pettman *Africanderisms* 560 *Wild sage*, .. *Salvia africana, L.* **1966** C.A. Smith *Common Names* 510 *Wild sage*, A general name for several species of *Salvia* ... The vernacular name is in allusion to the resemblance of the native species to the European sage (*S. officinalis*). **1946** [**wild spinach**: see morogo sense a]. **1955** A. Delius *Young Trav.* 142 They don't eat much beyond mealie-meal, wild spinach and milk, with, say, meat about twice a month. **1967** [see intombi sense 1]. **1988** E. Mphahlele *Renewal Time* 164 At Easter time so many of us went home .. to eat chicken and sour milk and *morogo* — wild spinach. **1989** D. Baloyi in *Our Living World* 2nd Quarter 7 Morogo (wild spinach) was much distasteful on my tongue. **1990** R. Malan *My Traitor's Heart* 150 As a child, she used to hang around the cane-cutters' shacks, sharing the wild spinach and *putu* they cooked in iron pots on open fires. **1886, 1937** [**wild watermelon**: see tsamma]. **1991** D.M. Moore *Garden Earth* 198 The wild watermelon, or '*tsamma*' melon (*Citrullus lanatus*). **1822, 1987** [**wild wormwood**: see *wilde als* (wilde sense 1)].

b. In the names of animals: **wild ass** *obs.* [perh. tr. S. Afr. Du. *wilde ezel*], the quagga (sense 1 a i), *Equus quagga*; **wild cat**, any of several small predatory felines of the Felidae, esp. *Felis lybica*; see also tiger-cat; **wild dog**, the mammal *Lycaon pictus* of the Canidae; *Cape hunting dog*, see Cape sense 2 a; **wild horse** *obs.* [prob. tr. S. Afr. Du. *wildepaard*, see wilde sense b], any of several species of zebra, esp. the *mountain zebra* (sense (*a*) see mountain), *Equus zebra zebra*.

[**1688 wild ass**: G. Tachard *Voy. to Siam* II. 65 As for the Asses, they are of all colours, they have a long blew list on the back that reaches from head to tail, and the rest of the body like the horse, full of pretty broad streaks, blew, yellow, green, black and white, all very lively.] **1697** W. Dampier *New Voy. round World* I. 533 There is a very beautiful sort of wild Ass in this Country, whose body is curiously striped with equal lists of white and black: the stripes coming from the ridge of his Back. **1731** G. Medley tr. *P. Kolb's Present State of Cape of G.H.* II. 113 The *Cape* Wild Ass is one of the most beautiful Animals that ever I beheld. His Size is that of an ordinary Saddle-Horse ... There runs on the Ridge of his Back, from the Mane to the Tail, a black Streak. From this black Streak there run down, on each Side of him, a great many Streaks of various Colours, meeting under his Belly in so many Circles. Some of these circling Streaks are white, some yellow, and some of Chestnut-Colour. **1786** G. Forster tr. *A. Sparrman's Voy. to Cape of G.H.* I., I have seen *buffaloes* and *wild asses* (*quagga*) sometimes make a stand in the same manner. **1827** G. Thompson *Trav.* II. 139 Hunting the wild game, to save the consumption of their flocks, and feeding their Hottentot or Bushmen servants, with the flesh of the Quagha, or wild ass. **1828** T. Pringle *Ephemerides* 88 The mighty rhinoceros wallows at will In the vlei where the wild-ass is drinking his fill. **1839** W.C. Harris *Wild Sports* 55 Small troops of striped quaggas or wild asses, and of brindled gnoos .. enlivened the scene. **1844** [see *mountain zebra* (mountain)]. **1821** G. Barker Journal. 11 July, A **wild cat** got into the hen house last night & killed a hen. **1827** G. Thompson *Trav.* I. 162 We met about a hundred Bechuanas of the Karriharri tribe, on their way to Griqua Town to barter mantles of wild-cat and jackal skins, for beads, buttons, &c. **1860** T. Shone Diary. 6 Nov., The wild cat eat a hen and 14 Eggs. *a***1867** C.J. Andersson *Notes of Trav.* (1875) 162 A visit from a lion was, on the whole, a rare event; but leopards, chetahs [*sic*], lynxes (generally known as wild cats), paid frequent visits to the sheep-folds. *Ibid.* 187 The wild cat (*Felus Catus*) was common in the neighbourhood of Otjimbingue. **1910** C. Meredith *Peggy* 45 Peggy noticed that he had the skin of a wild cat, which he had found in the hills and killed. **1912, 1945** [see tiger-cat]. **1966** E. Palmer *Plains of Camdeboo* 223 All the quick, sharp-toothed creatures of the veld such as mongoose, meerkat, honey-badger, wild cat [etc.]. **1971** [see *kaffir cat* (kaffir *n.* sense 2 e ii)]. **1990** Skinner & Smithers *Mammals of Sn Afr. Subregion* 411 The African wild cat, *F. lybica*, differs from the European wild cat, *F. silvestris*, but there is still some disagreement about the genetic basis for this. **1731** G. Medley tr. *P. Kolb's Present State of Cape of G.H.* II. 65 Among the Cattle .. , the Wild Beasts, as Lions, Tigers, and **Wild Dogs** &c, make sometimes great Depredations. **1786** G. Forster tr. *A. Sparrman's Voy. to Cape of G.H.* I. 157 These wild dogs are some of the most pernicious beasts of prey. **1821** C.I. Latrobe *Jrnl of Visit* 124 The wild-dogs go in packs, are very bold and mischievous, and will attack oxen, horses and sheep, in spite of watch-men and dogs. **1833** *Graham's Town Jrnl* 4 July 2 Wild animals .. have increased .. greatly within the last few years — particularly the *Wolf* and *Wild Dog*. **1849** J.D. Lewins Diary. 11 The wild dogs have broken in upon us. Killed two cows & reduced a bull to the neuter gender. **1878** A. Aylward *Tvl of Today* 244 Wild dogs are dangerous when met in troops, being, I believe, the only African animal that wilfully and unnecessarily seeks an encounter with man. **1908** J.M. Orpen *Reminisc.* (1964) 30 The jackals, wolves (i.e., hyenas) and wild dogs were very numerous and troublesome. **1966** I. Vaughan *These Were my Yesterdays* 151 Wild dogs, looking like small wolves chased them in cart and horses. **1976** A. Delius *Border* 69 One went down fighting, bucking, charging to the last against a pack of wild dogs. **1981** *Sunday Times* 12 July 27 The Cape wild dog .. was plentiful in the area earlier this century but the last ones were shot out about 30 years ago after they were declared vermin. **1988** *Quagga* No.20, 19 As one of South Africa's three endangered mammals (with *Riverine Rabbit* and *Wild Dog*), the *Roan Antelope* is of special concern. **1990** [see *Cape hunting dog* (Cape sense 2 a)]. **1786, 1806** [**wild horse**: see quagga]. **1834** T. Pringle *Afr. Sketches* 14 The buffalo bendeth to my yoke, The wild-horse to my rein. **1838** J.E. Alexander *Exped. into Int.* I. 215 The wild horse, zebra, and quagga, nearly resemble each other: the first is striped all over; .. its feet are hard and compact, for its resort is the stony mountains. **1841** B. Shaw *Memorials* 316 The zebra is beautifully striped with dark bands on every part of its body except the legs, which are white, and is usually seen on the extensive plains. Very similar in appearance are the wild horse and the quagga.

wilde /ˈvəldə/ *adj.* [Du. and Afk., attrib. form of *wild* wild; cf. wild.] Special collocations.

a. In the names of plants: **wilde als** /- ˈals/, formerly also **wilde alsem, wilde alsies** [Afk., earlier S. Afr. Du. *wilde alsem*, fr. Du. *alsem* wormwood], the aromatic bushy shrub *Artemisia afra* of the Asteraceae, similar to the European wormwood, used medicinally and as a base for perfume; *wild wormwood*, see wild sense a; also *attrib.*; **wilde dagga**, see dagga *n.*[2] sense 2; **wilde knoflok** /-ˌknɔflɔk/, also - **knofflock**, - **knof(f)look** [Afk., fr. Du. *wilde knoflook* (*knoflook* garlic)], the plant *Tulbaghia alliacea* of the Liliaceae, the bulb of which smells strongly of garlic; *wild garlic*, see wild sense a.

1786 G. Forster tr. *A. Sparrman's Voy. to Cape of G.H.* II. 143 Having .. during the oppression on the chest, the swoonings, or the difficulty of respiration with which they were seized, been persuaded by me to take a cup or two of it [*sc.* brandy], especially when the virtues of it were heightened by **wilde alsies** (a kind of wormwood) being infused in it, .. their joy can hardly be conceived. **1822** W.J. Burchell *Trav.* I. 480 As soon as it began to heal, I employed a wash made of a strong decoction of the leaves of *Wilde-alsem* (Wild Wormwood.) **1910** *E. London Dispatch* 29 July 3 (Pettman), The *Wildeals* bush is .. well known to the Boers as a restorative. **1947** L.G. Green *Tavern of Seas* 199 Wilde als is a wormwood bush with a great reputation for restoring lost appetites. **1973** Y. Burgess *Life to Live* 113, I asked Rensie what you can do about your tubes .. , and she says you can try some wildeals or renoster-bos in a little brandy to make you strong. **1978** *Daily Dispatch* 11 Nov. 2 Farmers know it as 'wildeals' (wormwood) and the Amatola Mountains are its natural habitat. **1987** T.F.J. van Rensburg *Intro. to Fynbos* 31 Wild wormwood (wilde als) .. is one of the traditional frontier medicines. **1795** C.R. Hopson tr. *C.P. Thunberg's Trav.* I. 156 The *tulbaghia alliacea* (**wilde knofflook**, or wild garlic) the root of which smells very strong of garlic, was reported to be a charm for serpents. **1809** J. Mackrill Diary. 62 Tulbaghia Alliacea, (wilde Knofflock — or wild Garlic, a charm for Serpents). **1913** C. Pettman *Africanderisms* 557 *Wilde knoflook*, This bulb, which smells like garlic, is boiled in milk and used as a vermifuge. **1947** L.G. Green *Tavern of Seas* 199 The wilde knoflook, which smells like garlic, saved many lives during the 1918 influenza epidemic. **1973** Y. Burgess *Life to Live* 29 When the supply of domestic garlic was exhausted, they gathered the wild variety — the 'wilde knoflok'.

b. In the names of animals: ‖**wildemakou** /-məˌkəu, -maˌkəu/ (formerly also **vildemaakeou, vilge maccow**) [S. Afr. Du., *makou* perh. ad. Eng. *muscovy duck*; or fr. *Macao* the name of a (former) Portuguese territory in south China], the spurwinged goose *Plectropterus gambensis* of the Anatidae; **wildepaard** *obs.*, also **wilde-paerd** (pl. **-en**) [Du., *paard* horse], (*a*) usu. hyphenated, or as two words: any of several species of zebra, esp. the *mountain zebra* (sense (*a*), see mountain), *Equus zebra zebra;* (*b*) usu. as one word: an earlier form of **wildeperd** [Afk., *perd* horse], the zebra fish, *Diplodus cervinus hottentotus*.

1856 F.P. Fleming *Sn Afr.* 396 The most remarkable [wild duck] of which, is the '**Vildemaakeou**,' [*printed* Vildemaakeon] or spurwinged goose. **1886** P. Gillmore *Hunter's Arcadia* 59 'See bass, *vilge maccow*;' but it took a great deal of patient staring before we could detect what our man evidently saw. [1923 HAAGNER & IVY *Sketches* 245 The Spur-winged Goose (*Plactropterus gambensis*), known to the Boers as the Wilde Makaauw (wild Muscovy) is glossy black with metallic reflections.] **1977** *S. Afr. Panorama* Oct. 27 The spur-winged goose whose common name is 'wildemakou'. [**wilde paard**: sense (*a*)] **1786** G. FORSTER tr. *A. Sparrman's Voy. to Cape of G.H.* I. 130 I .. saw .. whole troops of wild *zebras*, called by the colonists *wilde paarden*, or wild horses. **1796** E. HELME tr. *F. Le Vaillant's Trav. into Int.* III. 34 At the Cape .. the quagga [is known] under that [name] of *wilde-paerd* (the wild horse). **1824** W.J. BURCHELL *Trav.* II. 272 A large mixed herd of *wilde-paards* (Wild Horses) .. appeared ... A *wilde-paard* (*Equus montanus*), or *quakka*, as it was oftener called, was shot. **1852** C. BARTER *Dorp & Veld* 112 (Pettman), There are in South Africa three varieties of the genus *Equus*, the true Zebra or *Wilde paard*; Burchell's zebra or the bonte quagga; and the quagga properly so called. **1873** W.G. ATHERSTONE in A.M.L. Robinson *Sel. Articles from Cape Monthly Mag.* (1978) 100 *Here* the *wilde paard* still roams at large. **1947** E.E. MOSSOP tr. *Jrnls of Brink & Rhenius* 49 We saw on the plains great herds of divers species of game such as rhinosceri, giraffes, buffaloes, witte wilde paarden, ezels, quaggas, kudus, Gemsboks, hartebeestes. [**wilde paard**: sense (*b*)]. **1906** [see STREEPDASSIE]. **1913** W.W. THOMPSON *Sea Fisheries of Cape Col.* 60 A well-shaped fish with zebra-like cross bars of blackish-brown is the wildepaard (zebra). **1930** C.L. BIDEN *Sea-Angling Fishes* 237 *Zebra fish*, The **Wildeperd** ... Port Elizabeth – Striped dassie, Five-finger, Zebra ... In addition to the sharp contrast of black and white bars, a dull golden colour often appears over the whole body. **1945** H. GERBER *Fish Fare* 62 Zebrafish or Wildeperd .. looks something like a white stompneus, but has very distinctive stripes. **1971** *Argus* 14 May 14 Dassie, wildeperd and galjoen were .. taken .. with 5.4kg breaking strain line and light sinkers. **1975** [see JOHN BROWN]. **1979** SNYMAN & KLARIE *Free from Sea* 57 It is a rare and exciting fish to catch ... Anglers often speak of 'their' wildeperd as having been something special! **1993** BENNETT & ATTWOOD in *Earthyear* Winter 35 The populations of .. wildeperd .. have recovered.

wildebeast *n. obs.* Also **veld a beast**, **velder beast**. [Englished form of S. Afr. Du. (later Afk.) *wildebeest*.] WILDEBEEST sense a.

[**1801** J. BARROW *Trav.* I. 259 The *gnoo* or *wild beast*, as it is called by the Dutch.] **1835** A. STEEDMAN *Wanderings* II. 11 The people .. were shouting '*Veld a beast*,' and .. I found that a herd of gnus had joined the oxen. **1875** C.B. BISSET *Sport & War* 210 The wildebeast is a most ferocious-looking animal. **1877** S.W. WOOD Letter. (Private collection, M.W. Wood) 30 Aug., It is a few large Bucks such as Gemsbuck and velder Beast.

wildebeest /ˈvəldəbɪəs(t), ˈvɪl-/ *n.* Also **veldebeest**, **vilderbeeste**, **wildebees**, **wildebe(e)ste**, **wilderbeest**. Pl. **-s**, **-beeste** /-ˌbɪəstə/. [S. Afr. Du., fr. Du. *wilde* (combining form of *wild* wild) + *beest* beast, referring to the animal either as an undomesticated bovine, or an untamable animal. (The modern Afk. form is *wildebees*.)]

a. Either of two species of southern African antelope belonging to the genus *Connochaetes* of the Bovidae, *C. gnou* (see *black wildebeest*, sense b below) and *C. taurinus* (see *blue wildebeest*, sense b below); GNU *n.*[1] sense a; WILDEBEAST. Also *attrib.*

1821 [see GNU]. **1824** W.J. BURCHELL *Trav.* II. 109 A very extensive open plain, abounding .. in wild animals; among which were .. many *wilde-beests* or *gnues*. **1843** *Cape of G.H. Almanac & Annual Register* 462 The gnu or wildebeest ... Forming the link which connects the ox tribe with the antelope, it partakes in some degree of the character of both. **1851** R. GRAY *Jrnl of Bishop's Visitation* II. 27 He .. often found that all the eatables they could produce were a little wilde-beest flesh. **1866** [see GNU *n.*[1] sense b]. **1866** E. WILSON *Reminisc.* 38 Wildebestes also abound on .. these large plains. **1878** H.A. ROCHE *On Trek in Tvl* 271 Bless-bok, reit-bok, rhe-bok, wilderbeest, and the graceful little spring-bok or antelope – I believe we have seen them all. **1882** S. HECKFORD *Lady Trader in Tvl* 263 A large herd of wilde-beests .. was a magnificent sight to see .. bounding through the bush, with their tails flying, the bulls tossing their long black manes. **1895** H. RIDER HAGGARD *Nada* 57 In the left hand of each was the tail of a vilderbeeste. **1934** B.I. BUCHANAN *Pioneer Days* 145 The wildebeeste always have a bull in front, and he gives the alarm at the approach of man. **1967** O. WALKER *Hippo Poacher* 102 Harry was .. known to have trained a span of wildebeeste to pull a wagon. **1975** *S. Afr. Panorama* Nov. 34 'Lions,' they called back. 'Just killed a wildebeest; it's lying in that dip'. **1987** *You* Sept. 104 Game includes .. wildebees.

b. With distinguishing epithet, designating one or other of these two species: ‖**bastaard wildebeest**, see *blue wildebeest*; **black wildebeest**, *Connochaetes gnou; black gnu, white-tailed gnu*, see GNU *n.*[1] sense b; *white-tailed wildebeest*; **blue wildebeest**, ‖**blouwildebeest** /bləʊ-/, also (formerly) ‖**blauw wilde beest**, [Afk., *blou* (earlier Du. *blauw*) blue], *C. taurinus; bastaard wildebeest; brindled gnu*, see GNU *n.*[1] sense b; KOKOON; **white-tailed wildebeest**, see *black wildebeest*.

1824 W.J. BURCHELL *Trav.* II. 278 The Mixed Hottentots have given it the name of **Bastaard Wildebeest**. **1866** J. LEYLAND *Adventures* 15 We shot a number of .. blue and **black Wildebeests**. **1891** R. WARD *Sportsman's Handbk* 123 In the open plains of the Orange Free State and the Transvaal, herds of .. Black wildebeests .. are still to be met with, but their numbers are becoming less and their range more circumscribed. **1976** J. HANKS *Mammals* 39 *Black Wildebeest*, .. Overall colour from black to dark brown, with a long tail that is mostly white. **1987** *Conserva* Apr. 5 The bloubok and the quagga were wiped out, and only the creation of game reserves prevented such species as the .. black wildebeest .. from a similar fate. **1839** W.C. HARRIS *Wild Sports* 375 The Brindled Gnoo. **Blauw Wilde Beest** *of the Cape Colonists*. **1970** *S. Afr. Panorama* Nov., One encounters a great number of **blouwildebeest**. **1866** [**blue wildebeest**: see quot. at *black wildebeest* above]. **1897** H.A. BRYDEN *Nature & Sport* 201 Brindled gnu they are called in Europe, in South Africa invariably blue wildebeest. **1925** *E. Prov. Herald* 6 July 7 The Prince of Wales, in the course of a perfect day in the bush, shot a blue wildebeeste. **1964** L.G. GREEN *Old Men Say* 162 Blue wildebees roamed the Cape Peninsula thousands of years ago. **1976** J. HANKS *Mammals* 38 *Blue Wildebeest*, .. Overall colour a dark silver grey, with a variable number of vertical darker bands on the foreparts. **1983**, **1990** [see *brindled gnu* (GNU *n.*[1] sense b)]. **1990** [**white-tailed wildebeest**: see *white-tailed gnu* (GNU *n.*[1] sense b)].

wilde pou see POU sense 2.

wilderbeest var. WILDEBEEST.

wild grape *n. phr.* Any of several shrubs or small trees which resemble vines or bear edible, grape-like fruits:

1. Any of several species of Vitaceae (the grapevine family): **a.** Any of several plants of the genus *Rhoicissus*, esp. *R. tomentosa*; see also DROOG-MY-KEEL sense 1 a. **b.** *Ampelocissus africana*. **c.** *Cyphostemma cirrhosum*; DROOG-MY-KEEL sense 1 b. **2.** *Lannea edulis* of the Anacardiaceae.

1790 tr. *F. Le Vaillant's Trav.* II. 244, I speak here of the fruit of a particular species of these plants, which is called the wild grape, on account of the great resemblance which its leaves have to those of the vine. [**1827** see MONKEY-ROPE.] **1843** [see GUARRI sense b]. **1892** 'KAMEAHS' in *Cape Illust. Mag.* Nov. 91 Those black, spherical berries, hanging all over the trees to the very tops like bead embroidery on a green dress, are Wild Grapes. They make a most delicious preserve. **1894** [see SKILPAD sense b]. **1913** C. PETTMAN *Africanderisms* 559 *Wild grapes*, The fruit of *Rhoicissus capensis* .. , which makes a preserve like black currants in flavour. **1917** [see DROOG-MY-KEEL]. **1932** WATT & BREYER-BRANDWIJK *Medicinal & Poisonous Plants* 108 A cold infusion of the root of *Lannea edulis* .. Wild grape, .. is used by the Lemba for treating diarrhoea. **1975** J.M. GIBSON *Wild Flowers of Natal* 62 *Rhoicissus tridentata* .. (Wild Grape) ... The fruits .. are like raisins but make the mouth exceedingly dry. **1982** FOX & NORWOOD YOUNG *Food from Veld* 40 Scramblers, herbaceous bushes or 'underground trees' such as the wild grape (*Lannea edulis*). *Ibid.* 366 This [*sc. R. tomentosa*] is one of the best of the wild grapes ... *Rhoicissus rhomboidea*, Common name in English is 'wild grapes' ... A vigorous wild grape. *Ibid.* 368 *Cyphostemma rhodesiae* .. Common name in English, *wild grape*. **1986** Y. VAN WYK *Practical Book of Herbs* 17 *Rhoicissus tomentosa* Wild Grape .. Jam and syrup, used by 1820 Settlers. **1989** B. COURTENAY *Power of One* 155 Tall old yellow wood trees, the branches draped with beard lichen and the vines of wild grape. **1993** *Grocott's Mail* 6 Aug. 10 Rhoicissus Tomentosa .. Common Forest Wild Grape.

wild pou see POU sense 2.

wilgat var. WITGAT.

windgat /ˈvəntxat/ *n.* and *adj. Colloq.* Pl. **-gatte** /-xatə/. [Afk., a braggart, transf. use of Du. *windgat* a hole made by wind or through which wind blows.]

Cf. VINT.

A. *n.* A braggart, windbag, or show-off, used esp. of motor-car drivers who show off in a reckless fashion. See also VINT.

1987 H. HAMANN in *Frontline* Apr. 23 What sort of person gets caught up in drag racing? 'The windgatte,' answers Mick van R– immediately. **1989** J. EVANS in *Personality* 9 Oct. 22 The difference between a rally driver and a *windgat* was played out in slow-motion horror when two spectators walked straight in front of a car travelling at galeforce speed. **1991** *Sunday Times* 8 Sept. 15 James Whyle makes the role of the local *windgat* showing off in his metallic plum van with deep-pile carpeting, both plausibly dangerous and attractive.

B. *adj.* Cocky, full of oneself.

1987 *Informant, Port Elizabeth*, I haven't seen Paul for years. Is he still so windgat? **1991** T. BARON in *Sunday Times* 17 Mar. 30 'Hell, I won the fight ...' Mitchell .. wasn't being *windgat* at all. He was just stating the facts, as he saw them.

Windy City *n. phr. Colloq.* [Alluding to its prevailing south-easterly wind.] PE.

1989 *Fair Lady* 20 Dec. 16 One of Port Elizabeth's best loved restaurants .. offers carefully prepared meals and a cosy atmosphere steeped in the Windy City's past. **1990** B. DEACON in *Weekend Post* 17 Nov. 10 Can one really still call PE the Friendly City? I disagree. Call it Windy City by all means, but PE has lost its claim to be the Friendly City.

wine farmer *n. phr.* [tr. *wine boer* (see BOER sense 1 b), fr. S. Afr. Du. *wynboer*.] A farmer who produces grapes for wine-making, and who may also make wine; *wine boer*, see BOER sense 1 b. So **wine farm** *n. phr.*, a vineyard; cf. ESTATE sense 2; **wine farming** *vbl n.*

1827 *Reports of Commissioners upon Finances at Cape of G.H.* II. 81 The practical inconvenience that has resulted to the wine farmer of being prohibited from disposing of a smaller quantity of wine than a half aum, or nineteen gallons, without the pagter's licence, has led to certain exemptions being granted. **1884** *Act 18* in *Stat. of Cape of G.H.* (1887) I. 1035 Wine farmer means a farmer who cultivates vines on land in his own occupation and who produces wine from grapes grown on such vines. **1920** K.M. JEFFREYS tr. *Memorandum of Commissary J.A. de Mist* 176 The desperate wine-farmer had .. been seen knocking the pegs out of his barrels, and allowing the precious wine to run to waste. **1923** O.E.A. SCHREINER in *Cape Times* 18 Aug. 3 The sinking valley with its sprinkling of wine farms. **1924** F.E.M. YOUNG (*title*) The Wine Farm. **1926** *E. Prov. Herald* 23 Feb. 7 Did honorary members think that the wine farmer was such a fool as to give the tot to his labourer to make him drunk and incapable of work? **1965** [see VEE sense 2]. **1967** W.A. DE KLERK *White Wines* 102 Successful wine farming begins here.

Ibid. 110 These older wine farms have an appeal that every wine lover understands. **1971** B. BIERMANN *Red Wine* 11 Since some poets give of their best in exile, some writers on wine may well be frustrated wine farmers. *Ibid.* 104 Professor Perold suggested .. that Uitkyk should rather be developed as a wine farm. **1981** P. DANE *Great Houses of Constantia* 129 When Dirk Gysbert Cloete owned 'Klein Constantia' it was not an imposing establishment, but a simple wine farm. **1992** on Radio South Africa 15 May, Cape Wine farmers have launched their second invasion of the English market. **1992** *Argus* 3 Sept. 11 The Meerlust estate .. is a national monument ... Numerous sales of Cape wine farms to foreigners had caused waves in the industry.

wine of origin *n. phr.* Also with initial capitals. An official designation which appears on some wine-bottle labels, indicating that the wine has been certified as originating from a recognized region or estate and (often) as being of a certain cultivar and vintage; usu. *attrib.*, used esp. to designate the official seal attached to bottles of such wine, or the (legislation which introduced the) system of certification; also *absol.*, a wine so certified.

1972 *Govt Gaz.* Vol.84 No.3569, 2 I, Dirk Cornelis Hermanus Uys, Minister of Agriculture .., hereby .. authorize the sale in or export from the Republic of any wine specified in .. the .. Schedule opposite the name of any .. area .. under the name of that area .., subject to the following conditions, namely — (i) if such name is used in conjunction with either the expression 'wine of origin' or .. 'wine of origin superior', any such expression is shown in the same type and size of print as such name .. (iii) .. application was made to the .. Board for a .. certificate to the effect that .. such wine .. has been produced from vines in the area concerned .. and such a certificate has been issued. **1979** C. PAMA *Wine Estates of S. Afr.* p.ix, The wine areas of the Cape are defined by the Wine of Origin legislation which came into effect on 1 September 1973. This legislation established the well-known wine seal, awarded by the South African Wine and Spirit Board. **1980** *S. Afr. Panorama* Dec. 49 Since the establishment of the wine-of-origin system, Cape wine farmers have earned high praise for the quality of their estate wines. **1988** D. HUGHES et al. *Complete Bk of S. Afr. Wine* 113 The Wine of Origin Seal is the aspect of the Wine of Origin legislation most familiar to the 'wine buyer in the street' ... Its purpose is to provide a guarantee of those aspects of the wine related to the Origin concept. These are the area of Origin, the vintage year, the cultivar, and whether or not the farm concerned has Estate status.

wine route *n. phr.* A touring route comprising numerous vineyards (or wine farms) which are within easy driving distance of each other and are open to the public for wine-tasting, tours, and the sale of wine; such farms collectively; an area in which such a route may be followed. Also *attrib.*

Suggested routes are shown on maps distributed by the wine industry, but the term is also applied to any devised or improvised route.

1971 *Rand Daily Mail* 28 July 17 A trip along what has become known as 'the wine route' is an almost unrivalled experience. **1988** D. HUGHES et al. *Complete Bk of S. Afr. Wine* 38 The early 1970s .. saw the introduction of one of the most popular innovations of recent years. This was the Stellenbosch Wine Route .. which was opened in April, 1971 and which now includes .. 13 .. Wine Estates. **1989** P. DEVEREUX in *Style* Dec. 22 According to Captour, last year's top attraction in the Cape was the cableway ... Third came 'the Wine Route'. **1992** *E. Prov. Herald* 30 June 10 There will also be a .. *trattoria* serving the passing wine-route trade.

wing *n. Ostrich-farming.* [Ellipt. for Eng. *wing-feather.*] A feather from the wing of an ostrich. See also FEATHER sense a, FEMINA, ONDERBAATJIE, PRIME.

*c*1881 A. DOUGLASS *Ostrich Farming* 80 Whilst plucking, the cocks' wings, the hens' wings .. have been kept separate. **1902** *Agric. Jrnl of Cape of G.H.* XX. 721 Wings £0.0.6d — £0.1s.0. **1930** M.F. WORMSER Ostrich Industry. 14 Feathers would be sold on a basis of £5 per lb. for fair average wings, and 15/- per lb. for average body feathers. **1956** P.J. BOTHA in F. Goldie *Ostrich Country* (1968) 56 There is always the hope that wings will again one day find a price level commensurate with their importance in the eyes of the breeder.

winkel /ˈwɪŋk(ə)l, ˈvəŋ-/ *n.* Also **winkle**. [Du., shop.] **a.** GENERAL DEALER sense 1 b. **b.** *hist. rare.* A travelling store. Also *attrib.*, and occas. *fig.*

1827 G. THOMPSON *Trav.* I. 61 The village contains a couple of small retail shops, or *winkels* as they are called. **1832** *Graham's Town Jrnl* 28 Sept. 153 It is mortifying to compare the degree of commercial enterprize of our *currency colonists* with that of the same class in New South Wales, the sons of the *scamps* who were sent there 140 years after Riebeek opened Jan Compagnie's winkel at the Cape! **1839** W.C. HARRIS *Wild Sports* 331 We lost not a moment in opening a *winkel*, or shop. **1855** [see quot. at *winkler* below]. **1855** N.J. MERRIMAN *Cape Jrnls* (1957) 221 Kreli himself was absent having gone .. to settle a dispute between two English or Scotch traders .. as to which had the prior right to the winkel or shop. **1878** T.J. LUCAS *Camp Life & Sport* 211 The wooden stores, or 'Winkels,' belonging to the general merchants. **1882** C. DU VAL *With Show through Sn Afr.* I. 185 We would get to a 'winkel' (shop) about an hour and a half from the town. **1897** E. GLANVILLE in E.R. Seary *S. Afr. Short Stories* (1947) 20 We were talking about snakes at the little roadside winkle — a composite shop, where you could buy moist black sugar, tinned butter, imported; tinned milk, also imported; cotton, prints, boots, 'square face', tobacco, dates, nails, gunpowder, cans, ribbons, tallow candles, and the Family Herald. **1908** *Cape* 28 Feb. 15 At the door to the winkel the proprietor stands in his shirt-sleeves. **1926** P. SMITH *Beadle* (1929) 14 He had built for himself and his grandmother the little 'winkel' in which they now lived. Here they sold prints and calicoes, bags of coffee-beans, rice, sugar, salt, spades and buckets, cooking-pots, kettles, gridirons, combs and mouth-organs, sweets, snuff and many patent medicines. **1937** C.R. PRANCE *Tante Rebella's Saga* 22 It was fully forty miles from one backveld 'winkel' to the next, where one can buy tinned milk with sardines and 'bully-beef' and perhaps some Home-Remedies warranted to cure everything except sudden death. **1942** S. CLOETE *Hill of Doves* 7 It would be wonderful to have real shoes from the winkel. **1960** G. LISTER *Reminisc.* 4 There were no bakers near us, and only one little winkel, as the shop was called. There one could buy almost anything from a needle to a plough. **1973** *Sunday Times* 14 Oct. (Mag. Sect.) 3 When I went into a dorp winkel .. did I throw hysterics because the woman in the shop could not speak a word of English? [**1990** *Weekend Post* 17 Mar. (Leisure) 3 'Go and hear there by Venter se winkel if they got any culture,' shouted the ever-obliging Marie.] **1990** R. GOOL *Cape Town Coolie* 30 He entered the tea-room, really an old-fashioned *winkel*.

Hence **winkler** *n.* [Eng. agential suffix *-er*], a shop-keeper; WINKELIER.

1840 *Echo* 22 June 8 A person from the country placed his son with a *winkler*, not a hundred miles from Graham's Town ... A lady came into the store. **1855** W.R. KING *Campaigning in Kaffirland* 138 'Winkel waggons' had come out to the camp, and the 'winklers,' or private traders, sold everything they had. **1871** J. MCKAY *Reminisc.* 21 Grabbing men called winklers, were charging one shilling per pound for meat, flour, sugar, salt, and similar necessaries. **1900** B. MITFORD *Aletta* 183 It was all very well twenty years ago .. to call him Oom Paul. But now the old man is rather sick of it. Only think, every dirty little Jew 'winkler' calling him 'Oom'. **1911** L. COHEN *Reminisc. of Kimberley* 213 He hurried back to the Boer winkler in a rage, and said: 'What do you mean? In your blessed barrel there are pebbles at the bottom, and coffee on the top.'

winkelhaak /ˈvəŋk(ə)lˌhaːk, ˈwɪŋk(ə)lhɑːk/ *n.*, passing into *adj.* Also **winklehaak**. [Afk., 'L-shaped tear', e.g. in cloth.] An identifying mark cut on the ears of sheep and cattle and taking the form of a three-cornered tear.

1878 *Bedford Advertiser* 13 July 1 Young black heifer .. right ear winklehaak in front. **1881** *Alice Times* 14 Jan. In the Municipal Pound, at Seymour, ... will be sold .. 1 Red Ox white hairs about head ... right ear winkelhaak, left ear do. **1934** C.P. SWART Supplement to Pettman. 193 *Winkelhaak*, An ear-mark on sheep and cattle cut in the form of a three-cornered tear is so called by South African farmers. **1980** A.J. BLIGNAUT *Dead End Rd* 49 They all carry my mark in their ears: a half moon in front of a winklaak at the back in the right ear.

‖**winkelier** /ˌvəŋkəˈliːr/ *n.* [Du.] *winkler*, see WINKEL.

1832 [see NEGOTIE sense 1]. **1952** G.M. MILLS *First Ladies of Cape* 11 At the Company's warehouse .. she could purchase from the Winkelier all that she required for her immediate needs. **1955** G. ASCHMAN in Saron & Hotz *Jews in S. Afr.* 129 There are many stories told of the hospitality of the farmers to the early Jewish *winkelier, handelaar* or *smous*.

winkle var. WINKEL.

winkommando see KOMMANDO sense 1 b.

wissel /ˈvəs(ə)l/ *v. intrans. Sheep-farming.* [Afk., to shed or cut teeth, fr. Du. *van tanden wisselen* lit. 'to exchange teeth,' to cut second teeth.] Of lambs or kids: to cut second teeth in the place of milk teeth. Hence **wissel** *adj.*, **wisselling** *ppl adj.*, of the age at which second teeth are cut. See also UNWISSELLED.

1968 *Farmer's Weekly* 3 Jan. 9 (advt) 6 tooth to full mouth Hamels; .. 100 'Wissel' Hamels. **1970** R. VAN DER MERWE *Informant, Beaufort West* Wissel/Wisseling ... To change ... Referring to a sheep at the stage when it is losing its milk teeth, and the two permanent incisors appear. e.g. For Sale: 500 Merino Ewes. Age wisseling to two teeth. **1971** M. BRITZ *Informant, Grahamstown* Lambs usually wissel at five months. **1972** *Grocott's Mail* 3 Mar. 4 (advt) 306 Wissel Lambs 600 Weaned Lambs. **1975** *Ibid.* 22 Apr. 4 (advt) 190 Wissel Kapaters.

witblits /ˈvətbləts/ *n.* Also **witblitz**, and with initial capital. [Afk., *wit* white + *blits* lightning.] **a.** MAMPOER. **b.** A colourless raw spirit, usu. (illicitly) home-distilled from grape by-products after the grapes have been pressed for wine-making, but sometimes made from the fermented juice of other fruits; BLITS; *white lightning*, see WHITE *adj.* sense 2. Cf. DOP *n.* sense 2 a i, WITHOND. Also *attrib.*

1934 *Sunday Times* 8 Apr. (Swart), 'Wit blits' (white lightning) was the name given to peach brandy in the Johannesburg Magistrate's Court yesterday. **1936** C. BIRKBY *Thirstland Treks* 225 A bottle of .. the harsh home-distilled brandy nicknamed *wit blits* or chain lightning. **1948** *Cape Times* 21 July 16 In cases of snake-bite people on the platteland have always run for the witblitz. **1963** J. PACKER *Home from Sea* 172 His thoughts, combined with the effects of the witblitz, seemed to pain him. **1966** *Economist* (U.K.) 12 Mar. 1044 Coloured people are drinking less, particularly the favoured types of plonk known affectionately as *witblitz* .. and *skokiaan*. **1971** L.G. GREEN *Taste of S.-Easter* 204 Some farmers made witblitz, others matured the sort of brandy that became liquid sunshine. **1980** *Rand Daily Mail* 7 Oct. 5 Mampoer, witblits and skokiaan — if you've ever stayed on a country farm you'll have heard of this evil trio of home-brewed liquors. Mampoer comes from peaches, witblits from grapes, and skokiaan is a witches' brew of tartaric powder, yeast, and a rather eerie imagination. **1983** *S. Afr. Panorama* Apr. 22 *Witblitz* is made from fermented grapes, apples, peaches, pears, apricots or plums, each with its own distinctive flavour and a high alcohol content. **1988** D. HUGHES et al. *Complete Bk of S. Afr. Wine* 332 Witblits was a rough local brandy which was made by distilling the wet mash of skins and pips left at the bottom of the tank when the fermented must had been run off. **1991** *Personality* 6 May 24 A few slugs of mampoer (also known as *witblits* (white lightning) ..). **1992** [see BOEREMEISIE sense 2].

Hence **witblits** *adj. nonce*, fast, speedy.

1992 *Weekly Mail* 6 Mar. 2 Along the trail with a witblitz FW.

witchdoctor *n.* [An application of the older (now obs.) general Eng. *witchdoctor* 'one who professes to cure disease and to counteract witchcraft by magic arts' (*OED*).] A traditional African healer or diviner, esp. one dealing with afflictions thought to be caused by spirit possession or witchcraft; one dealing with physical ailments, a herbalist; one casting either good or evil spells, a sorcerer. See also DOCTOR sense 1 a, ESEMKOFU, GOGO *n.*[1], HERBALIST, IGQIRA *n.*[2], IGQWIRA, INYANGA sense 1, ISANUSI, ITOLA, IXHWELE, MOLOI, NGAKA, SANGOMA, *to smell out* (SMELL), TAGATI *n.*, *to throw (the) bones* (THROW sense 2).

Now used also in general English. The term has been applied to persons of both benevolent and malevolent intent and actions; as a result, and because 'witchdoctor' has acquired derogatory connotations, anthropologists now prefer the terms 'diviner' and 'traditional healer' for those whose intentions are benevolent.

[**1731** G. MEDLEY tr. *P. Kolb's Present State of Cape of G.H.* I. 138 They believe that it is in the Power of their Wizzards or Witches to *lay* a Spirit, and for ever prevent its Appearing or being troublesome.] **1827** G. THOMPSON *Trav.* II. 351 Disease, especially if of any unusual description, is commonly ascribed to sorcery. A witch-doctor is immediately sent for, and these imposters never fail to encourage such belief. **1835** A. STEEDMAN *Wanderings* I. 38 The people are constantly kept in the most humiliating dread of the 'Witch Doctor,' who panders to the avarice of a despot, and enriches himself by the blood of his tribe. **1852** [see INYANGA sense 1]. **1878** T.J. LUCAS *Camp Life & Sport* 104 The witch doctor is all powerful here, as elsewhere in South Africa. He has unlimited power, the lives of innocent persons often being sacrificed to his cupidity or malice. **1905** *Native Tribes of Tvl* 126 There are several classes of witch-doctors, some being specialists in 'rain-making', some in 'smelling out' or witch-finding; and some having an intimate knowledge of herbal remedies and poisons. The greatest 'doctors' usually have some skill in all these arts. **1925** D. KIDD *Essential Kafir* 41 The witch-doctors are often consulted by relations who wish to get some medicine which will counteract the influence of the missionary, who is supposed often to act on people by magic. **1937** C. BIRKBY *Zulu Journey* 102 The Swazis worship strange gods, whom in times of scarcity .. they find it necessary to propitiate. Then the witch-doctors demand a 'buck' — their grim euphemism for a human being — to be slain in sacrifice. **1959** L. LONGMORE *Dispossessed* 324 A witchdoctor is a person who detects witches (and sorcerers) and protects people from them. He is, therefore, recognised as a public benefactor, not an enemy. **1968** [see IDLOZI]. **1976** WEST & MORRIS *Abantu* 11 'Witchdoctor' now carries so many connotations and the word has become so coloured by exaggeration that it should perhaps be discarded in favour of the more accurate term 'diviner': but it simply means one who doctors against witches. **1978** [see IGQIRA *n.*[2]]. **1983** J. SONO in *Daily Dispatch* 7 March 1 The local belief is that if one owned the hand of a white man — after being treated by a witchdoctor — one would never have to work again. **1990** R. MALAN *My Traitor's Heart* 185 Most of Soweto's dashing professional soccer teams had a witch doctor .. throwing the bones to ensure victory, and its business tycoons hired diviners to advise them on deals. **1992** [see Natal Witness quot. at SANGOMA].

Hence **witchdoctoring** *vbl n.*, **witch doctress** *n. phr.*

1912 AYLIFF & WHITESIDE *Hist. of Abambo* 65 The Gcalekas appeared led by a famous witch doctress. **1982** *Pace* Feb. 13 Father Alfred Dlamini, of Peddie, where the six youths died said: ' ... Any ministry which goes with witchdoctoring or sorcery is not the healing ministry of the Lord.'

witchweed *n.* The small, red-flowering weed *Striga asiatica* of the Scrophulariaceae, a destructive parasite which attacks the roots of maize and other grasses; ISONA; *Matabele flower*, see MATABELE sense 2; ROOIBLOM.

1904 *Times* (U.K.) 25 July 12 Complaints .. were constantly being received .. of damage done .. to the mealie .. crop by .. rooi-bloom or witchweed. **1907** [see ISONA]. **1911** [see ROOIBLOM]. **1917** [see ISONA]. **1966** C.A. SMITH *Common Names* 513 *Witchweed*, .. The vernacular name is commonly used in Natal, and is derived from the original Zulu 'Isona', meaning the little red flower that bewitches the mealies. **1975** M.R. LEVYNS in *Std Encycl. of Sn Afr.* XI. 470 *Witchweed*, .. The parasite attaches itself to the roots of its host by means of suckers and weakens it.

witdoek /ˈvə(t)dʊk, ˈvɪt-, -duk/ *n.* Pl. **-doeke** /-dʊkə/. [Afk., *wit* white + *doek* (head-)scarf, cloth. The term seems first to have arisen in Afk. during a period of violent political upheaval in 1976 (see Cole quot., 1987).] One of a conservative group of (armed) men in the townships of the Western Cape, using for identification a white cloth worn on the head, neck, or arm, or attached to a weapon. Usu. in *pl.*, used collectively. Also *attrib.* See also FATHERS, VIGILANTE. Cf. ROOIDOEK.

In the mid-1980s, used specifically of vigilantes from a group campaigning against squatters and left-wing activists in the vicinity of the Crossroads settlement near Cape Town; later applied more widely.

[**1976** M. THOLO in C. Hermer *Diary of Maria Tholo* (1980) 177 We .. spotted a group of youngsters sitting on the pavement. The one said, 'Hey, look. In those bushes there are a group of white-doeks. We're waiting for them.'] **1986** *Cape Times* 26 Mar., Mr Mdini said about 300 'witdoeke' there were told .. to wear white strips of cloth around their heads 'so we could know each other'. **1986** *E. Prov. Herald* 10 June 5 A recent Supreme Court interdict restraining police, soldiers and 'witdoeke' from participating in or permitting unlawful attacks on people or property in the KTC squatter community. **1987** *Learn & Teach* No.1, 38 In Cape Town .. the 'witdoeke' fought with the 'comrades' and 20 000 houses were burnt down. **1987** J. COLE *Crossroads* 83 A significant feature of the April [1983] conflict was that the men who participated as part of what was called 'Ngxobongwana's army', wore white bits of cloth to identify themselves. This was the first appearance of what would become known as 'witdoeke' in Old Crossroads. This phenomenon was not new to Cape Town. Migrants wore them during the conflict between hostel dwellers and township youth in 1976. **1990** *Tribute* Apr. 40 In 1986 Mhlawuli, along with thousands of others, had her home burned to the ground by 'witdoek' vigilantes. **1993** [see FATHERS]. **1994** C. LOUW in *Weekly Mail & Guardian* 4 Feb. 2 Alleged collusion between the police and the Witdoeke in fighting ANC-aligned 'comrades' led to the complete demolition of huge living areas on the Cape Flats.

witdulsies see DULSIES.

wit els /ˈvətɛls, ˈvɪtels/ *n. phr.* Also **witte els**, **witte elze**. [Afk. (earlier S. Afr. Du. *witte els*), *wit* white + *els* alder.] The evergreen tree *Platylophus trifoliatus* of the wild alder family (the Cunoniaceae), found in forests and on river banks in the Western Cape; the wood of this tree; *white els* sense (*a*), see WHITE *adj.* sense 2. See also ELS.

1822 W.J. BURCHELL *Trav.* I. 143 The name of *Witte Elze* (White Alder) is applied to another tree (*Weinmannia trifoliata*) which naturally grows in the same kind of places as the common Alder. **1887** J.C. BROWN *Crown Forests* 237 Timber valued standing. Per cubic foot ... Witte Els. **1907** T.R. SIM *Forests & Forest Flora* 12 Witte Els (Platylophus trifoliatus) and Coal Wood (Lachnostylis capensis) are endemic to this [*sc.* the Midland] Conservancy. **1934** C.P. SWART Supplement to Pettman. 194 *Wit Els*, A tree growing in the Knysna forest that has a local reputation for being a good furniture timber. The wood has an indefinite brownish-yellowish colour with little or no figure. **1965** A. GORDON-BROWN *S. Afr. Heritage* II. 7 Other Cape woods used in old furniture .. were olive wood, witte els, [etc.]. **1974** *Sunday Times* 28 Sept. (Suppl.) 4 The indigenous woods — yellowwood, stinkwood, rooi-els, wit-els — are becoming more and more rare and costly. **1987** J. KENCH *Cottage Furn.* 20 Local timbers used in tables included cedar, rooi-els and wit-els.

witgat /ˈvətxat/ *n.* Formerly also **vittkut**, **whit(te) haat**, **wi(l)gat**, **witte-gat**. [S. Afr. Du., fr. Du. *wit* (or combining form *witte*) white + *gat*, perh. ad. Khoikhoi *kaa/kchaa* drink (cf. Afk. *gat*, *gaat* coffee make from the roots of this tree); but often understood as Afk. *gat* hole.]

1. In full ***witgat tree***, **witgat boom** /- bʊəm/ [S. Afr. Du., *boom* tree]: the evergreen tree *Boscia albitrunca* of the Capparaceae, with white trunk and dense foliage; SHEPHERD'S TREE. Also *attrib.*

1824 W.J. BURCHELL *Trav.* II. 18 A number of scattered trees, distinguished .. by the color of their trunks, which appeared at a little distance as if they had been whitewashed. From this singular character, they have gained the name of *Wit-gat boom*. **1826** A.G. BAIN *Jrnls* (1949) 39 We resumed our journey .. with much difficulty, it being so very thickly overgrown with brushwood, *Wagt en Beetjis* camelthorn and *Wit gat* trees. [**1834** T. PRINGLE *Afr. Sketches* 514 The tree .. is termed by the Dutch-African colonists the witte-gat boom (white-bark tree).] **1886** G.A. FARINI *Through Kalahari Desert* 111 Kert pointed out a *whithaat boom* (white ass tree). **1907** *E. London Dispatch* 16 Aug. (Pettman), The root of the wit-gat or shepherd's tree are other favourite foods [of the porcupine]. **1958** A. JACKSON *Trader on Veld* 24 The poorer people roasted the root of a tree called 'Witgatboom', and ground it for coffee or at least added it to the Rio to make it last longer. **1969** D. CHILD *Yesterday's Children* 133 The little grave was dug under a *witgatboom*, a tree conspicuous because of its white trunk. **1976** V. ROSENBERG *Sunflower* 35 There were .. groves of tambotie trees .. , and the witgat with its rambling trunk structure and mushroom top whose roots yielded an ersatz type of coffee. **1992** C. NORMAN in *Sunday Times* 20 Sept. (Mag. Sect.) 31 *Witgat* trees growing out of solid stone cast pools of shade.

2. *comb.* **witgat coffee**, **witgatkoffie** /-ˌkɔfi/ [Afk.], a hot beverage made from the roasted and ground roots of the witgat tree.

1958 R.E. LIGHTON *Out of Strong* 67 Labuschagne drank the rotten **witgat coffee**. **1961** L.E. VAN ONSELEN *Trekboer* 57 It tasted like the hot breath of a dragon with halitosis ... The coffee was 'wit-gat' coffee made from the root of a tree. **1955** L.G. GREEN *Karoo* 105 Until you become used to it, **witgatkoffie** often acts as a purgative. **1974** J.M. COETZEE *Dusklands* 99 We lived .. on roots and on nestlings ... I made *witgatkoffie* and enjoyed it.

with *adv. colloq.* [Prob. influenced by Afk. *saam* together with, along, as in *kom saam* come along.] Along, with me, with us, etc.; used *absol.*, as 'Are you coming with?'

1909 *George & Knysna Herald* 22 Dec. 4 Never mind, come with. **1913** C. PETTMAN *Africanderisms* 563 *With*, It is employed without the substantive which it should govern, e.g. 'Can I come with?' ('you' being omitted). 'Are they going with?' ('us,' 'you,' or 'them,' being omitted). This appears to be entirely due to the influence of the Cape Dutch word *sam*, together. **1919** M.C. BRUCE *Golden Vessel* 14 'I threw him with a stone' is preposterous and a direct translation from the Dutch, and 'He asked me to come with' is another. **1962** A. DELIUS (tr. D.J. Opperman) in *Afk. Poems with Eng. Translations* 269 Three outas from the bleak Karoo saw the star, believed the angel true, took knobsticks and three bundles with and set forth along a jackal path. 1972 *Drum* 8 Apr. 13, I told the police to take my husband with. 1975 'BLOSSOM' in *Darling* 12 Apr. 95 'Hey!' he bellows. 'You scheme to come with or not, poppie?' 1987 M.A. DE M. MALAN in *Hansard* 9 June 115, I did take a fishing rod with and I did some pleasant fishing. 1993 A.L. HAYCOCK *Informant, Grahamstown*, I laughed and laughed. You should have been here! I should have taken you with.

withaak /'vətɑːk/ *n*. [Afk., fr. Du. *wit* white + *haak* hook, barb.] In full **withaak tree**: the thorn tree *Acacia erubescens* of the Fabaceae, bearing hooked white thorns. Also *attrib*.

1935 H.C. BOSMAN *Mafeking Rd* (1969) 21, I thought the cattle might be there because it is shady under those withaak trees, and there is soft grass that is very pleasant to sit on. *Ibid*. 24 In the shade of the withaak, the leopard and I lay down together. 1951 N.L. KING *Tree-Planting* 65 *Acacia litakunensis* (Withaak). 1974 D.J. LOUW in *Std Encycl. of Sn Afr.* X. 150 The withaak (*Acacia erubescens*) is found in the more mountainous parts of the Khomas-Hochland. 1980 A.J. BLIGNAUT *Dead End Rd* 80 Scattered withaak trees .. cleaved to the veld. 1985 *Sunday Times* 11 Aug. (Lifestyle) 5, I loll in the shade of the *withaak*.

withond /'vəthɔnt/ *n*. Also with initial capital. [Afk., *wit* white + *hond* dog.] A colourless brandy-like spirit similar to WITBLITS (sense b), distilled privately (and sometimes illegally) in the Cape farming districts. Also *attrib*.

1955 L.G. GREEN *Karoo* 84 Years ago the great local drink .. was *withond*, a colourless dop brandy which held its own valiantly against any *witblits* made in other districts. For a quarter of a century it has been illegal to distil *withond*. 1975 *E. Prov. Herald* 21 May 16 Mampoer has never been everyone's cup of tea of course, and .. many .. have never been quite sure .. how it differs from other potions such as Ireland's poteen, Western Cape witblits, Eastern Cape withond, [etc.]. 1979 M. PARKES *Wheatlands* 25 Brandy was made in Graaff Reinet for nearly a century, often in small back-street distilleries which produced the infamous fiery 'Withond' brandy. 1987 D.W. POTGIETER in *Sunday Times* 12 Apr. 7 Grapes are used for making witblits (also known as withond).

witmense /'vətmɛ(ː)nsə/ *pl. n*. Colloq. Also with initial capital. [Afk., *wit* white + *mense* people.] White people; often used ironically, alluding to the Afrikaans terminology of apartheid.

1976 *Post* 13 June 4 The poor madame was fed up. What, Darkies in the same line as Wit mense? 1980 *Staffrider* Vol.3 No.4, 11, I was about to sit and talk to the 'witmense' about life in general. 1991 M. KANTEY *All Tickets* 82 We use the same carriage for both witmense and .. swartmense, you see.

witogie /'vətʊəxi/ *n*. Also **witoog**, and (formerly) **witteoogje**. [S. Afr. Du., fr. Du. *wit* white + *oog* eye + dim. suffix -IE.] WHITE-EYE.

c1808 C. VON LINNÉ *System of Natural Hist*. VIII. 455 The *White-eyed Warbler* ... The Dutch at the Cape, and the Hottentot settlers, call it *glass-oog*, glass-eye, or *wit-oog*, white-eye. 1867 E.L. LAYARD *Birds of S. Afr.* 116 *Zosterops Capensis* ... *Witteoogje*, lit. white eye; and *Glasoogje*, lit. glass eye. [1913 C. PETTMAN *Africanderisms* 564 *Witte oogie*, ... *Zosterops capensis*. A common name among the Dutch for this small bird, anglicized into 'white eye'.] 1963 M. KAVANAGH *We Merry Peasants* 110 She finds time to see that the field mice and the birds, especially the tiny *witogies* have for their own use a fruit-laden pomegranate tree in the lush garden. 1970 [see MUISVOËL]. 1974 P. CLARKE in S. Gray *On Edge of World* 35 Witoogies, hiding in trees and hedges, little white eyes showing.

wit ou /'vɛt əʊ, 'vət -/ *n. phr*. Colloq. Also **vet ou**. [Afk., *wit* white + *ou*, see OU *n*.] Esp. among people of Indian origin in KwaZulu-Natal: a white person; often in *pl*., used collectively. See also OU *n*. sense 2 b.

1978 A. AKHALWAYA in *Rand Daily Mail* 10 July 7 The Natal pronunciation of Afrikaans words such as 'wit' and 'pik' come out [*sic*] as 'vet' and 'pek'. And our main ou, who is also a 'chaar ou' (Indian), has friends of all races — 'vet ous' (whites) 'pek ous' (blacks) and 'bruin ous' (coloureds). 1978 L. BARNES in *The 1820* Vol.51 No.12, 19 The Afrikaans word *ou* seems to have caught on in Natal just as much as in other parts of the country. There are *chaar ous* .. ; *wit ous* (pronounced 'vet'), [etc.]. 1980 R. GOVENDER *Lahnee's Pleasure* 9 Don't make so much noise. The wit ous are laughing at us. 1992 R. MESTHRIE *Lexicon of S. Afr. Indian Eng.* 120 *Vet-ou*, .. A white-man.

Wits /vəts, vɪts/ *n*. [Abbrev. of *Witwatersrand*, see RAND sense 2.] In full **Wits University**: the University of the Witwatersrand, which is situated in Johannesburg; sometimes treated as *pl.*, a sports team or other group representing the university. Also *attrib*.

1927 *Star* 30 May 14 Intervarsity Rugby ... Wits Wins Stirring Game. 1939 R. DICKIE-CLARKE in *Outspan* 27 Oct. 49 That little lawn in front of Men's Residence at 'Wits' is a place for crazy ideas. 1944 H.C. BOSMAN in L. Abrahams *Cask of Jerepigo* (1972) 112 Then there is Wits. I was a student at the Witwatersrand University in the early days. 1971 *Evening Post* 3 Nov. 1 There are indications that Wits students are planning a mass protest meeting on the campus. 1972 *Cape Times* 26 July 1 There is still a possibility that Wits and Tuks will meet in other sports. 1978 *Darling* 13 Sept. 102 The flat is within walking distance of Wits University. 1986 *Style* Dec. 41 Maties consider themselves a little left of Wits. 1987 [see AFRICANIZE]. 1992 *Natal Mercury* 25 Nov. 23 Wits University virtually assured themselves of fourth spot when they drew .. with Cape Town Spurs in their .. soccer match. 1993 R. CHARLTON in *Sunday Times* 10 Oct. 20 South African universities like Wits have developed an international standing. 1994 M. MBATHA in *Ibid*. 9 Jan. 18 Wits has developed good programmes specifically tailored for mining.

Hence **Witsie** /'vətsi, 'vɪtsi/ *n.-* forming suffix *-ie*], a student or alumnus of this University.

1981 *Rand Daily Mail* 18 June (Eve Suppl.) 2 The trip was organised .. by .. an ex-Witsie. 1987 [see IKEY].

witteboom /'vətəbʊəm, 'vɪt-/ *n*. Pl. **-bome** /-bʊəmə/, and (formerly) **-boomen**. [S. Afr. Du., fr. Du. *witte* combining form of *wit* white + *boom* tree.] The SILVER TREE, *Leucodendron argenteum*.

[1799 LADY A. BARNARD *S. Afr. a Century Ago* (1925) 83 Her Ladyship .. is soon to present the Regiment with their colours, in which the Whitletomb [*sic*] (native of this country) is happily blended and united with the Royal Oak.] 1801 J. BARROW *Trav.* I. 18 The Protea argentea, the *witteboom*, or silver tree of the Dutch. [1806 *Gleanings in Afr.* (anon.) 32 The silvertree, which, I believe, is peculiar to the Cape, is so named from its beautiful white foliage; it is generally known by the name of the Whittle Boom.] 1818 C.I. LATROBE *Jrnl of Visit* 35 The foot .. of .. Table-mountain is well clothed with witteboom (protea argentea). 1822 W.J. BURCHELL *Trav.* I. 61 Numerous plantations of large Witteboom, or Silver trees. 1857 'HORTULANUS' in *Cape Monthly Mag.* II. Sept. 175 Observe the silver-tree, or *witte-boom* of Table Mountain. 1910 R. JUTA *Cape Peninsula* 62 The firs, or pines, who came here last, are creeping, .. higher and higher ... Year by year the brave little witteboom (white trees) are driven before this strong green army of invaders. 1927 C.G. BOTHA *Social Life in Cape Col.* 85 Witteboomen .. is the name of the well known silver trees found in the Cape Peninsula. 1972 PALMER & PITMAN *Trees of Sn Afr.* I. 493 Witteboom .. is believed to grow naturally only in the Cape Peninsula.

witte dulsies see DULSIES.

witte els, **- elze** var. WIT ELS.

witte-gat var. WITGAT.

witteoogje var. WITOGIE.

witty var. WIETIE.

WNLA *n*. Also **W.N.L.A**. [Initial letters of *Witwatersrand Native Labour Association*.] An organization established in 1902 by the Chamber of Mines with the aim of recruiting mine labourers from northern Botswana, Mozambique, Malawi, and other African countries north of the Limpopo River (see quot. 1972); WENELA sense a. Also *attrib*.

On 1 January 1977 the WNLA merged with the Native Recruiting Corporation (see N.R.C. *n*.[1]) to form TEBA.

1903 *Tvl Leader* in *Ilanga* 5 June 3 He received a reply from the manager of the W.N.L.A ... The number of natives employed on the mines which were members of the association .. was .. 59,280. 1942 [see N.R.C. *n*.[1]]. 1951 *Off. Yrbk of Union 1949* (Union Office of Census & Statistics) 920 The majority of natives engaged by the W.N.L.A., contract to remain on the mines for twelve months .. , but thereafter the natives are under the obligation to return to their homes. The W.N.L.A. engaged 124,000 natives during 1949. 1963 A.P. CARTWRIGHT *Gold Miners* 216 Between them the W.N.L.A. and the N.R.C. now bring some four-hundred thousand natives to the mines every year. 1968 COLE & FLAHERTY *House of Bondage* 22 We were picked up by a Chamber of Mines official and driven to the WNLA depot. 1972 W.P. KIRSTEN in *Std Encycl. of Sn Afr.* VII. 442 The W.N.L.A. recruits Bantu labourers in Mozambique and in certain areas north of latitude 22° south, particularly Malawi, Northern Botswana and Barotseland. The W.N.L.A. also engages Bantu from Angola and Tanzania ... The N.R.C. obtains labour from South Africa, Swaziland, Lesotho and that part of Botswana south of latitude 22° south. 1986 KALLAWAY & PEARSON *Johannesburg* 11 The WNLA secured a monopoly on labour recruitment for the mines.

woema /'vʊmə, -mɑ/ *n. colloq*. [Afk., prob. orig. an interjection, imitative of the sound of a motor or an explosion; cf. U.S. Eng. *voom*.] Energy, power, verve. So **woema** *int*. Also Englished form **vooma(h)**.

1971 *Rand Daily Mail* (Suppl.) 6 Mar. (advt) Woema! Let your car come alive ... It'll save you money. And at the same time give you something really new. Woema! 1987 *City Press* 25 Oct. 24 New Ford Laser has added woema. 1987 *Scope* 20 Nov. 85 Verve and voomah. 1989 *Personality* 26 June 77 Why .. does David Kramer's music sound like a TV commercial .. with .. not enough *woema* in the *goema*? 1989 'HOGARTH' in *Sunday Times* 27 Aug. 24 They shone in contrast to a National Party turned feckless and without vooma.

woer-woer /'vurvur/ *n*. Also **woere-woere**, **woer-woor**. [Afk., ultimately fr. an echoic Khoikhoi word formerly found in Nama as *borob*, representing the whirring or humming sound made by this toy; similar words, derived fr. Khoikhoi and designating either this toy, or bull-roarers, have been found in several Sintu (Bantu) languages, and the word may have came into Afk. via one of these.] A toy consisting of a disc, button, or other flat object with a cord threaded through two holes near the centre and tied to make a closed loop, so that when the cord on either side of the disk is alternately pulled taut and relaxed by the hands, the object spins back and forth, making a whirring or humming sound.

In southern Africa the toy was prob. first made and used among Khoikhoi or San peoples.

1934 C.P. SWART *Supplement to Pettman*. 195 *Woer-Woer*, The onomatopoetic name of a well known boys' toy, consisting of a thinly cut piece of wood which is tied to a string and rotated. It makes a whirring sound, hence the name. 1949 H.C. BOSMAN *Cold Stone Jug* (1969) 62 You hold one end of the looped string between your teeth and the other end caught in your bent thumb, and you set the wheel a-spinning, like an Afrikaans child's 'woer-woer', and you bring the piece of stone into contact with the spinning steel wheel .. with the tinderbox in such a position as to catch the sparks that shoot off. **1957** B. O'KEEFE *Gold without Glitter* 106 Hold one end of the string in your teeth man and spin the button like a woere-woere. **1975** LEVICK & MULLINS *'Prep' Story* 148 'One of your able assistants has rightly removed from the possession of my son John David, a blackened and almost circular piece of wood with two perforations which enable it to be revolved by torsion ... I should appreciate its return.' ... The Professor got the woer-woer back!

woes /vʊs/ *adj. slang.* [Afk., wild, savage, angry.] Of people: angry. Of natural surroundings: wild.

1975 'BLOSSOM' in *Darling* 28 May 95 The crawl home is one big happy jol ... The only woes faces is those what's hung over. **1976** *Ibid.* 4 Feb. 87 Hang but I'm only woes too. Jis because you live at home the old tops think they got a right to run yore life for you. **1983** *Sunday Times* 12 June 38 Jan P— has Witbank woes after 'not watching' his Currie Cup champions being shovelled out of the Lion Cup. **1988** 'K. DE BOER' in *Frontline* Jan. 28 The historic voyage of Bartholmeo Diaz around the Cape that was woes en leeg (except for a couple of hundred thousand people of local colour and a million or so head of game ..). **1992** on Radio 5, 22 Dec., He was helluva woes.

wokhai var. HOKAAI.

wolf /wʊlf/ *n.*[1] *hist.* [Transf. sense of general Eng.] Any of several mammals bearing some resemblance to the wolf of the northern hemisphere, particularly the southern African hyaenas (but in some contexts, probably the aardwolf or the wild dog). See also AARDWOLF, STRANDWOLF, TIGER-WOLF.

[**1596** T. JOHNSON *Cornucopiae* B4, A certaine Wolfe called Hyena.] **1655** E. TERRY *Voy. to E.-India* (1777) 15 This remotest part of Africa is very mountainous, over-run with wild beasts, as lions, tigers, wolves, and many other beasts of prey. **1731** G. MEDLEY tr. *P. Kolb's Present State of Cape of G.H.* II. 107 There are two Sorts of Wolves in the *Cape*-Countries; one agreeing in every particular with the Wolves in *Europe*; the other are very different, and are call'd *Tiger*-Wolves. **1786** G. FORSTER tr. *A. Sparrman's Voy. to Cape of G.H.* I. 163 These wolves are to be found almost every dark night about the shambles at the Cape where they devour the offals of bones, skin, &c. **1804** R. PERCIVAL *Acct of Cape of G.H.* 76 Tigers hyenas wolves and jackals infest the neighbouring hills, and frequently come down at night to devour the cattle. **1812** A. PLUMPTRE tr. *H. Lichtenstein's Trav. in Sn Afr.* (1928) II. 15 The spotted hyena, *hyæna crocuta*, is here called simply the wolf. **1824** W.J. BURCHELL *Trav.* II. 277 During the night the hyenas, or wolves as they are usually called by the Boors and Hottentots, had devoured the flesh. **1836** N. ISAACS *Trav.* (1937) II., We were greatly concerned about our horses .. and .. feared that they might become a repast for the wolves, hyenas, panthers, leopards and other beasts which are extremely numerous through the whole of this part of the country. **1852** C. BARTER *Dorp & Veld* 117 (Pettman), As I have used the term *wolf* so frequently, it is right I should inform the reader that the animal properly so called does not exist in South Africa. **1881** P. GILLMORE *Land of Boer* 195 The wolves (hyenas) were destroying their cattle wholesale. **1926** P.W. LAIDLER *Tavern of Ocean* 97 Trap guns were commonly used for the destruction of .. wolves, leopards and lions, of which only the former two were now found around the Cape. **1969** F.G. BUTLER *When Boys Were Men* 24 Wolves: probably spotted or laughing hyenas (*Crocuta crocuta*). Usually scavengers, they are seldom known to have attacked healthy wild animals, but sometimes domestic animals. Alternatively the 'wolves' might be Cape hunting dogs (*Lycaon pictus*), which frequently attacked animals much larger than themselves, tearing strips out of them on the run. **1975** W. STEENKAMP *Land of Thirst King* 164 The first Dutch settlers tacked the name 'wolf' to the various hyaenas they encountered.

‖**wolf** /vɔlf/ *n.*[2] Also **woolf.** [S. Afr. Du. *wolf* hyaena (combining form *wolwe-*).] Used *attrib.* in combinations: **wolf gif** /-xəf/ (and formerly **-gift**), also **wolwegif** /ˈvɔlvəˌxəf/, [S. Afr. Du., *gif(t)* poison], poison used to kill hyaenas and jackals; a plant from which such poison is made; **wolf hok** /-hɔk/ [Afk., *hok* pen], **wolf huis** /-hœɪs/, also **wolvehuis** /ˈvɔlvəhœɪs/, [Du., *huis* house], a small building used as a trap for hyaenas and jackals; occas. in dim. form **wolfhuisie** /-hœɪs(i)/ [see -IE].

1790 W. PATERSON *Narr. of Four Journeys* 171 A small shrubby plant, producing a nut, called by the Dutch, **Woolf Gift**, or Wolf Poison, which they use for poisoning Hyenas. **1993** S. DIKENI in *House & Leisure* Nov. 43 Meat fell out of the sky and those who ate it .. were rescued from death with milk, and were made to throw up meat poisoned with *wolwegif.* **1985** B. JOHNSON-BARKER in *Wynboer* Feb. 63 That little stone building .. was actually a **wolf-hok** that his pa had built for trapping jakkalse and things many years ago. **1904** W.S.J. SELLICK *Uitenhage Past & Present* p.iv, At fixed intervals .. can still be seen little buildings, in the shape of a domestic oven, and .. they were **wolf-huizen** (wolf-houses) built by the old trekkers. **1912** *E. London Dispatch* 29 July 6 They .. built a *wolvehuis* to trap hyenas. **1957** L.G. GREEN *Beyond City Lights* 165 The old *wolfhuisie*, baited with a live sheep, last caught a hyena in 1819, but it still remains on the farm as a museum-piece.

wonder *n.* [Special senses of general Eng.]
1. ***Wonder of the Waste, Wonder of the Wilderness***: NARAS.

1915 W. EVELEIGH *S.W. Afr.* 56 The curious Naras, *Acanthosicyos horrida*, has been well termed the 'Wonder of the Waste,' for this scrubby, leafless member of the order *Cucurbitacea* spreads over the sand dunes in dense straggling masses, defying all the sandstorms that threaten to bury it. **1969** J.M. WHITE *Land God Made in Anger* 107 Naras, known as the 'Wonder of the Wilderness' pokes itself out of the sand in the shape of a half-buried coil of barbed wire. It has no leaves, but wicked two-inch thorns. From it sprouts a green fruit, the size of a man's fist which is kept alive by a tap root going down forty or fifty feet. **1976** O. LEVINSON *Story of Namibia* 3 The wind blows over the dry river-bed of the Kuiseb and the straggling patches of thorny bush, called Naras or 'Wonder of the Waste'.

2. Special Comb. **wonderbox**, also with initial capital, a cardboard or wooden box containing a polystyrene-filled bag or other insulating material, into which a pot of hot, partially-cooked food may be placed so that the cooking process is completed over a long period without further application of heat. Also *attrib.*

Intended to provide a safe and fuel-efficient means of cooking for the poor.

1985 *Fair Lady* 6 Feb. 82 Abby sets off .. loaded .. with .. the trappings of her role as health educator – soya beans, demonstration kits, cooking pots, wonder boxes. **1986** *Style* June 90 The Wonderbox Women ... The core symbol of WFP's brand of down-home pacifism is a thing called the Wonderbox ... The Wonderbox is sold for R15 to those who can afford it; others are shown how to make their own using readily-available materials. **1989** A.L. SARZIN in *Femina* Dec. 79 Both women worked with .. Women for Peace, selling 'Wonderboxes' in Johannesburg.

wonderboom /ˈvɔn(d)ə(r)bʊəm/ *n.* [Afk., *wonder* marvel, wonder + *boom* tree; named for one unusual specimen of the species near Pretoria, estimated to be approximately 1 000 years old, branches of which have drooped to the ground and taken root over an area about 50m in diameter.] In full ***wonderboom fig***: the fig tree *Ficus salicifolia*, found mainly in the Northern Transvaal and Zimbabwe.

[**1896** 'S. CUMBERLAND' *What I Think of S. Afr.* 156 Outside the Raadzaal, Pretoria has nothing .. to show, except the *wonderboom* (wonder tree).] **1929** J. STEVENSON-HAMILTON *Low-Veld* 43 The well-known wonderboom (Ficus pretoriae) on a hill outside Pretoria, is an example. **1961** PALMER & PITMAN *Trees of S. Afr.* 207 *Ficus pretoriae ... Wonderboom ...* This Species is a spreading, usually evergreen tree, growing up to 70 feet in height and found in Natal, in various parts of the Transvaal, and northwards into tropical Africa. To this species belongs the famous Wonderboom, the unique groups of trees growing on the outskirts of Pretoria. **1983** K.C. PALGRAVE *Trees of Sn Afr.* 113 *Ficus salicifolia* ... Wonderboom fig ... A spreading, medium sized tree, its height seldom exceeding 9 m.

wonderdruppels see DRUPPELS sense b ii.

wood-and-iron *adj.* Also **wood-an'-iron.** Of a building: consisting of a wooden frame and (usu. galvanized and) corrugated iron walls and roof. Used of two distinct types of building:
1. Dating from a previous era, esp. from Victorian times: usu. having wooden floors, often a verandah, and sometimes with wooden wall cladding instead of iron.

1871 E.J. DUGMORE Diary. 21 Nov., There are a few wood and iron stores to be seen. **1888** *Barberton Herald* 24 Jan., Tenders are invited for the two *Wood and Iron* Buildings Known as Bayly's Piano Depot, and Bayly's Stationery Store. **1982** *Weekend Post* 10 July 4 Mrs Vernon said the wood-and-iron houses found in the older parts of East London were the poor man's answer to his desire to have his own home ... In 1903, the building of these houses was restricted. **1991** S. DU TOIT in *Weekend Post* 9 Mar. (Leisure) 5 A tent town sprang up but these temporary homes were gradually replaced by wood-and-iron buildings. Today the old wood-and-iron houses and shops have been meticulously restored and no modern buildings spoil the Victorian atmosphere.

2. In recent times: small, owner-built, often ramshackle and without flooring, usu. forming part of an INFORMAL settlement; occas. applied to a sturdier dwelling built under government supervision in a township.

1948 A. PATON *Cry, Beloved Country* 222 The wood-and-iron building was like an oven. **1979** *Sunday Times* 12 Aug. (Extra) 1 Their wood and iron shanty .. was demolished. **1983** *Daily Dispatch* 12 May 7 Ciskei Public Works Department staff battled against the clock yesterday putting up wood and iron shacks to accommodate 70 families moved from Blue Rock squatter camp. **1986** *E. Prov. Herald* 19 July 2 Council officials .. asked them to pull down their shacks or have it done for them. One said when he saw how council officials had flattened one of the wood-and-iron structures earlier this week, he decided to pull down his own himself. **1990** R. GOOL *Cape Town Coolie* 166 A settlement of a dozen or so wood-an'-iron houses clustered anxiously around a trading store.

woolf var. WOLF *n.*[2]

woor-woor var. WOER-WOER.

Workers' Day *n. phr.* Initially the first Friday in May, and subsequently the first of May, celebrated as a public holiday in honour of employees, esp. manual labourers.

Before 1987 this holiday (elsewhere usu. referred to as 'May Day' or 'Labour Day') was not officially recognized in South Africa.

1987 *Proclamation* in *Govt Gaz.* Vol.262 No.10683 1, I hereby declare the first Friday of May as a public holiday throughout the Republic to be commemorated as Workers' Day. **1988** *Cape Times* 5 May 1 The Cape Times will appear as usual tomorrow, Workers' Day. **1988** *New Nation* 7 July 2 The IMF has called for May 1 to replace Workers Day as a paid public holiday. **1989** *E. Prov. Herald* 7 Oct. 1 The Government decided yesterday that, as from 1990, Workers' Day will fall on May 1. **1994** *E. Prov. Herald* 8 Sept. 1 It was accepted that Workers' Day would be on May 1 rather than on the first Friday of May.

wors /vɔːs, vɔrs/ *n.* [Afk., ad. Du. *worst* sausage.] **1.** Sausage, esp. BOEREWORS (sense 1). Also *attrib.* See also DROËWORS.

[1936 E. Rosenthal *Old-Time Survivals* 21 (*caption*) These women are .. disposing of a monster sausage, 700 feet long, in connection with a 'Worsbraaiaand', a kind of rural sausage picnic.] **1965** C. Van Heyningen *Orange Days* 11 Soap, candles, wors, biltong .. could not be bought and were made at home. **1976** [see graze]. **1983** in *Sunday Times* 21 Aug. 11 Shocked by the great wors scandal, self-styled boerewors king 'Morris the Butcher' got an expert to give him a clean bill of health. 'There's no gemors here,' pronounced .. braai champion Peter Klarie ... 'A good wors should have less than 10 percent fat otherwise you have to over-cook it. Wors should be pink on the inside.' **1990** [see perlemoen]. **1991** *Weekend Post* 6 Apr. 5 Braai fires lit, the aroma of wors and steak sizzling on the grill drew people to the entertainment area. **1991** [see pap *n.* sense 1]. **1994** *Sunday Times* 23 Jan. 28 (*advt*) Who knows who invented wors? Who cares?

2. *comb.* **worsmonger**, one who makes and sells sausages; **wors roll**, a bread roll served with boerewors enclosed in it.

  1981 *Cape Times* 22 Jan. 1 All is not well in the sausage industry ... Some unlikely things are becoming wors, according to the latest newsletter of the Housewives' League ... The newsletter's advice: Blow the whistle on any cunning **worsmonger** who is trying to dress up his soya mixture in steer's clothing. **1989** *Informant, Grahamstown* We will be selling light food (breyani & rice and **wors rolls**).

worst *adj. colloq.* [Special sense of general Eng., influenced by best.] Esp. in the language of children: least favourite. Cf. best.

  1991 *Sunday Times* 27 Jan. (K-TV Times) 12 'And your best and worst subject at school?' 'I like Drama & History but not Afrikaans.' **1994** *Ibid.* 17 Apr. 21 My worst thing is my parents checking up on me. They are not very understanding, refuse to negotiate. **1995** R.J. Silva *Informant, Grahamstown* Do you know what my worst plants are? Thorns and cactuses.

wortelbredie see bredie sense b.

wow var. wau.

‖**woza** /ˈwɔ(ː)za/ *v. intrans.* [Zulu, imperative formed on -*za* come.] Used esp. among Zulu speakers, always in the imperative or subjunctive: 'come', 'come here'.

  1949 O. Walker *Proud Zulu* (1951) 145 The umNdlunkulu girls .. emerged from their enclosure shouting: 'Wo-Za! Wo-Za-ke! Wo-Za-lapa! Come Come! Come here!' **1951** — *Shapeless Flame* 265 She .. put her head out of a side window and shouted down into the yard: 'Woza! Come 'ere, Daniel. Gijima!' **1983** N.S. Ndebele *Fools* 88 School is out ... Children .. are shouting: 'Woza weekend!' **1987** E. Makhanya in *Sowetan* 28 Dec. 8 Woza Monday, honey.

woza-woza /ˌwɔzaˈwɔːza/ *n. colloq.* [Zulu *iwozawoza* incentive, attraction, inducement; also transf. (in the sense which has passed into Eng.); formed on n. prefix i- + -*wozawoza*, a reduplication of *woza*, see woza.] In urban (esp. township) Eng.: a magical ingredient supposedly added to food or drink at a drinking establishment to cast a spell which will induce customers to return in future. Also *attrib.*

  1976 K.M.C. Motsisi in M. Mutloatse *Casey & Co.* (1978) 62 Kid Pancholla grabs the scale when it is brought and says he would like to take out the medicine or the woza-woza from out of the concoctional brew. **1982** M. Mzamane *Children of Soweto* 13 Shebeen queens were known to cast a spell on their customers with woza-woza and other potent concoctions to keep them hooked on their alcohol. **1987** *Learn & Teach* No.2, 14 Some people say I am using 'woza-woza' muti to bring customers to my backyard. But that is not true. People come because I cook well and my food is cheap.

wraggies /ˈvraxis, ˈvraxiːz/ *adv. colloq.* Also **wragties**. [Afk., as next.] wragtig.

  1963 [see beneukt]. **1974** *Informant, Bloemfontein* What a lovely taste — it was wraggies real butter. **1975** S. Roberts *Outside Life's Feast* 86 It was wraggies hard to believe those men were policemen.

wragtie /ˈvraxti/ *adv. colloq.* [Afk., formed on *wragtig* (see wragtig) + -ie.] wragtig.

  [**1873** *Standard & Mail* 31 July 3 When the Separation League set people by the ears throughout these parts, we heard a typical Midlander exclaim in the open street 'Grahamstad!!! Nie, wrachtie nie!'] **1973** Y. Burgess *Life to Live* 96 'Haai wragtie,' Roelie said. 'Now he looks jus' like a constipated fowl!' **1977** *Family Radio & TV* 19 Sept. 53 Now, *wragtie*, that thing gets hot. **1977** Fugard & Devenish *Guest* 46 Oom Doors: I'm beginning to lose my temper with you ... Louis: Then you must maar lose it, Pa, because wragtie I've had enough. **1980** *Daily Dispatch* 6 May 6 One female frog laid as many as 250 000 eggs at one sitting. Wragtie. **1987** L.B. Hall in *Style* May 12 I've searched for a long time for a small eaterie in the country ... And *wragtie*, I've found it.

wragties var. wraggies.

wragtig /ˈvraxtəx, ˈvraxtax/ *adv. colloq.* Also **vrachtig, vragtag, vragtig, wragtag**. [Afk., contraction of *waaragtig* truly, really, fr. Du. *waarachtig.*] Truly, really; used to emphasize a statement, and sometimes as an expletive; vrachter; wraggies; wragtie.

  [**1897** Schulz & Hammar *New Africa* 371 This call sounds much like the Dutch invocation, 'Ja Vrachtig, Ja Vrachtig!' an expression the Boers look upon as profane when applied in ordinary conversation.] **1936** C. Birkby *Thirstland Treks* 272 'Wragtig! We live in wonderful times!' ejaculated the astonished settlers of Thirstland. **1939** S. Cloete *Watch for Dawn* 159 Vragtig, truly, I say, .. those who have done this will reap what they have sown. **1959** J. Meiring *Candle in Wind* 30 You have only to look at her mother, .. to see that *she* is a Bushman. Look how fat she is! Wragtig! We Coloured people do not get fat like that! *c*1966 M. Jabour in *New S. Afr. Writing* 90 Wragtig, a man can't live without a woman. **1974** *Daily Dispatch* 2 Dec. 10 Well this is not on. I shudder to think what would happen to a firm if they had our publicity association members as their board of directors. Wragtig! **1980** A. Fugard *Tsotsi* 54 He's bad. Wragtig bad hey. **1987** L. Beake *Strollers* 16 She got in a fight with the police. Three of them laid out, big heavy ous too. Wragtig!

1987 [see ja-nee sense 3]. **1989** *Weekend Argus* 11 Nov. 20 He .. begged to be allowed to serve anywhere .. except near .. water .. and *wragtig* — in true military style with regard to choices — he ended up not only on the water but also in it! **1994** *Sunday Times* 23 Jan. 28 (*advt*) This deep fried twisted doughnut dipped and basted with lashings of syrup is wragtig a mooi ding.

write *v. trans.* and *intrans.* [Special sense of general Eng.] To sit or take (a written examination or series of examinations).

  The transitive use is not exclusively *S. Afr.* Eng., occurring also in the English of Barbados.

  1943 'J. Burger' *Black Man's Burden* 173 The examinations [at Fort Hare] are the same as those written by European students in the other constituent colleges of the University. **1958** *Cape Argus* 7 Nov. 3 Several women attended the course but Miss X— was the only one to write the course examinations. **1971** *Sunday Express* 28 Mar. (Home Jrnl Suppl.) 14 My daughter is writing Matric this year. **1984** [see matric sense 1 a]. **1991** [see re-classify]. **1993** *Race Rel. Survey* 1992–3 (S.A.I.R.R.) 607 While candidates writing under the auspices of the DET obtained an overall pass rate of 39%, those writing in the 'independent' homelands achieved a passrate of 53%. *Ibid.* 608 African pupils writing as private candidates achieved significantly better results than the national average in South Africa.

Wykmaster *n. obs.* [Part. tr. Du. *wykmeester*, see wykmeester.] wardmaster.

  1801 R. Curtis et al. in G.M. Theal *Rec. of Cape Col.* (1899) IV. 155 The Wykmasters, or Wardens of the several Wards of the Town, this day attended the Commission, and were invested with orders and full authority to make out a Capitation list of all the inhabitants of every description residing within their respective Wards.

Wykmeester /ˈveɪkmɪəstə(r)/ *n. Obs. exc. hist.* Also **Wijkmeester**, and with small initial. [Du. *Wykmeester, Wijkmeester, wyk* or *wijk* ward, district + *meester* master.] wardmaster.

  *c*1795 W.S. Van Ryneveld in G.M. Theal *Rec. of Cape Col.* (1897) I. 249 The Aldermen or Wykmeesters. The increase of the Cape Town rendered it necessary to divide it into several parts .., and two Aldermen were appointed to each district. **1799** F. Dundas in G.M. Theal *Rec. of Cape Col.* (1898) II. 332 In each ward or section of the Town, it shall be the duty of each Wykmeester to form a list of the number of Slaves each House can afford in case of need. **1806** *Gleanings in Afr.* (anon.) 252 Every street has its respective *wykmeester*, being a respectable house-holder, to act in cases of alarm as a constable, to maintain order, and prevent irregularities. *a*1878 J. Montgomery *Reminisc.* (1981) 71 He told us that he could not board us before we had reported ourselves to Mr Bremmer, the wijkmeester or field-cornet. **1926** P.W. Laidler *Tavern of Ocean* 107 Each man so appointed was required to have a board with his rank 'Wijkmeester' painted on it affixed to his house. **1975** [see wardmaster].

X

Xesibe /ǁe'si:be, ke'si:be, -bi/ *pl. n.* Also **Xesibes, Xesibi.** [Xhosa *amaXesibe* the Xesibe people, so named after an early leader.] (The) members of a people living in the northern part of the Transkei and now considered part of the Xhosa group (see XHOSA *n.* sense 1 a). Also *attrib.*

The Transkei is now a part of the province of the Eastern Cape.

As is the case with many names of peoples and groups in *S. Afr. Eng.*, this word has been found only in plural uses; however, it may be that it has also been used in unrecorded singular forms.
1884 *Cape Law Jrnl* I. 223 The Amaxosa Kafirs, Fingoes, Tembus, Amampondo, Xesibes, Zulus, [etc.]. **1901** *Natives of S. Afr.* (S. Afr. Native Races Committee) 14 The Xesibes in Matatiele. **1936** *Cambridge Hist. of Brit. Empire* VIII. 519 It [*sc.* the Cape Colony] .. incorporated the Xesibe district of Mount Ayliff in Griqualand East (October 1886). **1941** C.W. DE KIEWIET *Hist. of S. Afr.* 73 In Kafirland .. dwelt the Ama-Xosa, the Tembu, the Pondo, the Xesibe, and the Ama-Baca. **1954** W.D. HAMMOND-TOOKE *Nguni* [23 Xesibe, the founder of the tribe, is said to have been a full brother of the twins Mpondo and Mpondomise.] *Ibid.* 25 Today the Xesibe occupy an area of 240 square miles along the northern border of Pondoland. **1974** H. POTGIETER in *Std Encycl. of Sn Afr.* X. 397 It [*sc.* the Tabankulu district of the Transkei] .. is populated mainly by Pondos and descendants of the Xesibi and Amacwera. **1975** W.D. HAMMOND-TOOKE in *Std Encycl. of Sn Afr.* XI. 554 Bhaca and Xesibe women do not use ochre. *Ibid.* 555 Initiation of boys (circumcision) .. has fallen into disuse among the Bhaca, Xesibe and Mpondo.

Xhoisan var. KHOISAN.

Xhoi-Xhoi var. KHOIKHOI.

Xhosa /'kɔ(:)sə, ǁɔ(:)sa/ *n.* and *adj.* Pl. usu. -s, unchanged, or ama-. Forms: *sing.* isiXhosa, Kosa, Kósa, Khoza, Si-Xosa; *sing.* and *pl.* Ama-Xosa, Xhosa, Xosa; *pl.* Amakasa, Amakosa(e), Amakosas, Amakosoe, Amakosse, Aman Kozas, Amascosa, Ammakosae, AmaXhosa, Amokosa, Kaussas, Koos(s)as, Kosas, Kossa, Koussie, Koza(s), Magossees, X(h)osas. Also (occas.) with small initial. [Xhosa n. stem *-Xhosa*, found in words such as *isiXhosa* the Xhosa language and *amaXhosa* the Xhosa people (*sing.* umXhosa); origin disputed. For notes on singular and plural forms, see AMA-.

According to oral tradition the word is derived from the name of *uXhosa*, an early (but possibly mythical) leader; or from an unrecorded Nguni-language word rel. to Xhosa *xoza*, Zulu *xhoza* chip off, pare, and Zulu i(li)*xhoza* resister, deserter (also the term for a member of the Xhosa people). It is possible that the name has its origins in a split in the Nguni group, the splinter group or its leader being labelled 'deserter' or 'resister'. If the name from which *Xhosa* was derived was a label or nickname rather than a proper name, it would help explain the apparently mythical nature of uXhosa. Another theory is that *Xhosa* is related to Khoikhoi //kósab /'ǁosab/ 'a member of the Xhosa people', listed in J.G. Kroenlein's *Wortschatz der Khoi-Khoin (Namaqua-Hottentoten)*, Berlin, 1889 (p.215). Kroenlein gives no etymology for //kósab, but has entries for //khó rough, sharp, severe (p.214) and sàb 'subst. der Buschmann' (s.v. sá to pick up, to gather, p.293), this second element being the word used by the Khoikhoi for a member of the San, suggesting that //kósab may have been used by the Khoikhoi to distinguish the Xhosa from the San.]

The word KAFFIR (*n.* senses 1 b and c), now *offensive*, was in the past used in all these senses.

A. *n.*
1.a. A member of a people of the Nguni group descended from the clan of Phalo (d. 1775) and claiming descent from chief Xhosa, i.e., of the Gcaleka and Rharhabe peoples. See also GCALEKA sense 1, RHARHABE sense a. **b.** A member of a major sub-division of the Nguni group, comprising those peoples traditionally living in what is now the Eastern Cape Province, and including those described in sense a.

Forms in *isi-* and *Si-* are not used in this sense.

The ties among those of the larger group now called the Xhosa are based not on traditional political unity, but on geographical origin, common language, and similarities in traditional culture. Nguni people from those groups living south of the Zulus are considered Xhosas, and their language has been standardized for official purposes.
1801 J. BARROW *Trav.* I. 219 The Kaffers call themselves Koussie, which word is pronounced by the Hottentots with a strong palatal stroke of the tongue on the first syllable. **1809** R. COLLINS in G.M. Theal *Rec. of Cape Col.* (1900) VII. 37 The original apellation .. I have understood to be Kóza instead of Koussie. *Ibid.* 62 He said that Hinsa was the first of the Aman Kozas (Kaffer people). **1812** A. PLUMPTRE tr. *H. Lichtenstein's Trav. in Sn Afr.* I. 309 The tribe .. call themselves Koosas, or Kaussas. **1822** W.J. BURCHELL *Trav.* I. 268 The Kosas, or Caffres on the eastern side of the colony. **1837** J.E. ALEXANDER *Narr. of Voy.* I. 366 The so-called Kaffirs are divided into three great nations: the Amakosas, or the people of a chief Kosa, extending from the Keiskamma to the Bashee; the Amatembies, or Tambookies, between the upper Kye and Umtata; and the Amapondas, or people of the elephants' tooth, from the Umtata to the south of Port Natal. **1840** [see QUITRENT sense 2 b.] **1860** W. SHAW *Story of my Mission* 397 The people residing on the border of the Cape Colony call themselves Amaxosa. **1887** S.W. SILVER & Co.'s *Handbk to S. Afr.* 60 Extraordinary national suicide of the Amaxosa ... In 1857 .. the Amaxosa .. suffered themselves to be persuaded into an act of almost incredible folly. **1911** D.B. HOOK *'Tis but Yesterday* 18 He had thought it better to leave than be at the mercy of the unsubdued Amaxosa. **1932** J.H. SOGA *Ama-Xosa* 7 The next chief of importance after Mnguni was Xosa, from whom the tribe derives its name of Ama-Xosa. **1949** J. MOCKFORD *Golden Land* 77 The Xosas, the Kafirs, clashed with the Whiteman in the eastern regions of the Cape. **1964** *Drum* Nov. 22 Mr. Tsewu combines with his spiritualism a considerable knowledge of the tribal history of the Ama-Xhosa. **1975** *Std Encycl. of Sn Afr.* XI. 550 During the rule of Palo his two sons, Gcaleka .. and Rarabe, quarrelled and the AmaXhosa divided into two groups. **1981** J.B. PEIRES *House of Phalo* 13 There is every reason to believe that the word 'Xhosa' is derived from the Khoi '//kɔa', meaning 'angry men'. **1983** *Umso* Oct. 3 The first contact between the newly arrived British Settlers and the amaXhosa occurred on the 7th January 1821. **1987** D. TUTU in *E. Prov. Herald* 2 Apr. 10 It did strike us as odd that the history book always spoke of the white settlers capturing cattle from the Xhosas while the Xhosas always stole cattle from the whites. **1990** *Weekly Mail* 9 Mar. 8 According to apartheid theory, there should have been one homeland for the Xhosa. **1992** *Daily Dispatch* 11 Dec. 9 Her main interest was to research the culture and customs of the amaXhosa.

c. *comb.* **Xhosaland**, those areas of the Eastern Cape Province traditionally inhabited by the Xhosa peoples; AMAKOSINA.

See also the note at KAFFRARIAN.
1944 J. MOCKFORD *Here Are S. Africans* 82 They [*sc.* the Xhosa] meant .. to purge Xosaland of the Smits and Smiths. **1981** J.B. PEIRES *House of Phalo* 1 Xhosaland (emaXhoseni, lit. 'at the place where the Xhosa are') is most easily, if somewhat simplistically, conceived as comprising four adjacent belts running parallel to the coast. The northernmost of these .. was never permanently settled by the Xhosa ... The overwhelming majority of Xhosa lived in the 'highlands', the slopes of the smaller mountains such as the Winterberg and the Amatola, where innumerable streams and rivulets drain into the great rivers of Xhosaland, the Fish, the Keiskamma, the Buffalo and the Kei. **1986** B. MACLENNAN *Proper Degree of Terror* 50 The most common form of resistance was simply desertion ... They often headed into Xhosaland, where, according to Van Reenen, they 'enjoy the same privileges as the Kaffirs'. **1988** P. EDGAR in *Personality* 25 July 69 If it were not for these two men and myself, those cows would have ended up as karosses for some dusky maidens in Xhosaland.

2. [Xhosa *isiXhosa.*] The language of this people, a Sintu (Bantu) language of the Nguni group. Also *comb.* (objective) **Xhosa-speaking** *adj. phr.*, having Xhosa as one's home language.

Forms in *ama-* are not used in this sense. See also ISI-.
1857 J.L. DÖHNE *Zulu-Kafir Dict.* p.xvi, The Zulu .. sometimes differs considerably from the Xosa in respect to idiom ... The Xosa often differs from the Zulu in the clicks, and in compound consonants. **1883** R.N. CUST *Mod. Langs of Afr.* II. 302 The Xhosa is deemed to represent the oldest form of Bántu speech, being farthest removed from contact with the Negro, Hamitic or Semitic Languages. **1920** S.M. MOLEMA *Bantu Past & Present* 305 The oldest .. of the Bantu papers is the Imvo, edited and published at King William's Town by Mr. J. Tengo Jabavu in English and Sixosa (language of Ama-Xosa and Fingoes). **1931** J.H. SOGA *Ama-Xosa* 94 A number of tales .. have, within recent years, made their appearance in the vernacular (Si-Xosa). **1954** C.M. DOKE *Sn Bantu Languages* 91 Xhosa has produced a number of novelists, while recently .. poetry has been published. **1963** *Transkei Constitution Act* in *Statutes of Rep. of S. Afr.* 1963 546 Xhosa shall be recognised as an additional official language of the Transkei. c**1980** *S. Afr. 1979: Off. Yrbk* (Dept of Info.) 107 The languages of the various lan-

guage groups are: *Nguni*: Xhosa (3 912 680) spoken in the Republic of Transkei, the Ciskei and the Eastern Cape generally [etc.]. **1990** W. Smith *Golden Fox* 158 Michael spoke both Xhosa and Zulu.

B. *adj.*

Some of the uses quoted below might more correctly be seen as *attrib.* uses of the noun.

1. Designating the language of the Xhosas, a Sintu (or Bantu) language of the Nguni group; of, pertaining to, or in this language.

Forms in *ama-* are now seldom used in this sense.

1824 *Cape Chron.* in *S. Afr. Jrnl* I. 84 The first sheet of an elementary School Book, in the Amakosa tongue, (the dialect of the Frontier Caffers,) has reached Cape Town. **1838** J.E. Alexander *Exped. into Int.* II. 166 The Amakosa and Tembé languages .. are different dialects of the same language. **1857** J.L. Döhne *Zulu-Kafir Dict.* p.xii, In 1852, in the southern district of Natal .., I was surprised to find that the small tribe called Amambombo .., spoke the Amaxosa dialect. **1902** G.M. Theal *Beginning of S. Afr. Hist.* 37 The following words in the Xosa dialect will further illustrate. **1979** A. Gordon-Brown *Settlers' Press* 56 It was decided to ask the Revd Stephen Kay, then overseas .., to buy a press with type suitable for printing in the Xhosa language. **1982** C.M. Knox in *Fair Lady* 13 Jan. 79 She's producing Xhosa [programmes] for an independent production company. **1987** G. Silber in *Style* Nov. 53 *Pessimist*, Person taking Xhosa lessons.

2. Designating a person or group of the Xhosa-speaking peoples; RED *adj.* sense 2 b i; RED BLANKET *adj. phr.* sense 2.

Forms in *isi-* and *Si-* are not used in this sense.

1834 J.C. Chase in A. Steedman *Wanderings* (1835) II. 192 In 1797, Mr. Barrow .. furnished some very interesting information of the Amokosa nation. **1836** A.F. Gardiner *Journey to Zoolu Country* 9 During our progress through the Amakosa tribes we occasionally stopped at the traders' stations. **1847** M.C. Johnstone in *Imp. Blue Bks* Command Paper 912–1848, 64 It is not improbable, that there will be very great distress amongst the Amakosa Kafirs during the winter. **1860** A.W. Drayson *Sporting Scenes* 17 We were at war with the Amakosa tribes. **1882** C.L. Norris-Newman *With Boers in Tvl* 12 Troubles commenced .. between the Ngaika and other Amascosa chiefs. **1916** *Rand Daily Mail* 1 Nov. 3 Mr Doran yesterday sent a Xosa woman named Angelina to gaol for six weeks for forging an order for the supply of a bottle of brandy. **1961** T. Matshikiza *Choc. for my Wife* 58 We were on our way to meet Gibson Finca, a Xhosa refugee. **1971** *Daily Dispatch* 27 Nov. 14 (*letter*) The Xhosa nation consists of Pondos, Pondomise, Baca, Hlubi, Fingo, Gcaleka, Nguni, Ngqika (Gaika) and so on. **1980** J. Cock *Maids & Madams* 174 Dutch Farmers with Xhosa servants are reported as early as 1777. **1986** *City Press* 13 July 6 (*letter*) A black lady told me that because I am Xhosa I should apply for Transkei or Ciskei citizenship. **1994** *Weekly Mail & Guardian* 13 May 8 The *isikhakha*, the earth-coloured dress worn by Amaxhosa people, complete with handmade pipe.

3. Of or pertaining to Xhosas or their traditions, culture, or society; used or made mainly or originally by Xhosas; affecting or intended for Xhosas.

1858 B. Nicholson in J. Maclean *Compendium of Kafir Laws* (1906) 170 This latter part thus agreeing with the Xosa tradition. **1971** *Daily Dispatch* 2 Oct. (Suppl.) 13 (*advt*) Since 1969 we have been specialists in the manufacture of traditional xhosa garments. **1974** *Ibid.* 20 Dec. (Indaba) 3 Ten black women will be employed by the Xhosa Development Corporation to help in the manufacture of traditional Xhosa beer at its brewery. **1979** *E. Prov. Herald* 30 Oct. 1 White and coloured members of the party learnt Xhosa songs. **1981** *Sunday Tribune* 30 Aug. 5 Tobias was .. renamed 'Kojak' .. after having his hair closely cropped in the Xhosa style. **1982** *Sunday Times* 18 July 24 For the South African Government to subsidise two Xhosa states is a downright waste of money. **1988** M. Davies in *Style* July 105 Other pieces include .. Xhosa beadwork dating to the 1940s. **1990** A. Mpangase in M. Kentridge *Unofficial War* 57 He said .. that the only way to end violence in the area was to drive the UDF and COSATU from KwaZulu to Xhosa areas. **1992** R. Barnes in *Weekly Mail* 28 Aug. (Exclusive Communique) p.iv, It reflects the innard of Xhosa society.

Hence **Xhosadom** *n. rare*, collectively, the areas and people considered to belong to the Xhosa group.

1981 J.B. Peires *House of Phalo* 19 The limits of Xhosadom were not ethnic or geographic, but political: all persons or groups who accepted the rule of the Tshawe thereby became Xhosa.

Xhosastan see -STAN.

Y

ya var. JA.

yaabô var. YEBO.

ya(c)h, yag varr. JAG v.

yah var. JA.

ya(h)-nee var. JA-NEE.

yard n. [Special sense of general Eng. Perh. rel. to Jamaican Eng.: 'the Government yard' in Trenchtown, a poor part of Kingston, Jamaica, is a collection of government-owned buildings within a walled area, with small flats rented out as accommodation.]
A plot of land, or the grounds or courtyard of a building, accommodating a number of small, usu. insubstantial rooms which are rented out as living space. Also *attrib*.

   1915 *Transvaal Leader* in D.B. Coplan, *Urbanization of African Performing Arts*. (1980) 137 There are yards .. from which lead a labyrinth of passages, the haunt of the criminal, the passless native, the loafer. **1936** WILLIAMS & MAY *I Am Black* 103 He took Shabala down foul-smelling passages and into yards where women lived in rickety tin shacks and plied their trades. *Ibid.* 172 Evangi .. was selling beer again. He .. found her in a yard not far from the middle of the city. **1948** E. HELLMANN *Rooiyard* 7 Rooiyard consists of 107 rooms and a shop, which serves as a kind of concession store to the yard. The yard is roughly triangular in shape. *Ibid.* 20 The increasing difficulty of obtaining 'yard' accommodation is revealed by the fact that .. only 5 out of 109 found it possible to obtain accommodation in yards. **1982** J. MANGANYE in *Pace* Nov. 180, I found them burying their dead in the yard. I don't like it because .. his ghost may find it easy to give you problems because his grave is in the yard. **1987** P. LAURENCE in *Star* 24 Oct. 2 Unlike other townships, the lowest structure is the yard committee. **1992** D. NINA in *Focus on Afr.* Apr.-June 32 Mama Irene's grandchildren .. like to play with matches — threatening the security of the yard.

yarpie, yarpy varr. JAPIE.

yarwellnofine see JA *adv.* sense 3 f.

yassas var. YISSUS.

yaw var. JA.

yebo /ˈje(ː)bɔ/ *adv.* Also **yaabô, yearbo, yeh baw, yeh-bo.** [Zulu.] 'Yes', 'I agree'. ‖**a.** Quoting or representing the word as spoken in Zulu. **b.** *colloq.* As a general term of assent, agreement, or acknowledgement; hence **yebo** *int.* Cf. EHE.

   1836 A.F. GARDINER *Journey to Zoolu Country* 91 Baba — (Father) used in reply, as 'Yearbo Baba,' 'Yes, Father.' **1855** J.W. COLENSO *Ten Weeks in Natal* 134 There was a general assent of 'Yebo,' Yes, to this, expressing great satisfaction. **1875** D. LESLIE *Among Zulus* 80 He was greeted with a perfect storm of 'Bayete' and 'Yebo Baba.' **1898** B. MITFORD *Induna's Wife* 27 Yeh-bo — I see it all — the angry infuriated countenance of Umzilikazi, the dread anxiety on the faces of the other izinduna. **1923** G.H. NICHOLLS *Bayete!* 224 Those who are in favour of the strike must answer: 'Yebo!' Those .. against .. will answer 'Ca!' **1937** C. BIRKBY *Zulu Journey* 121 'Yebo, inkosi!' the old Zulu headman raised his right hand in courteous agreement with the Native Commissioner's words. **1952** *Drum* Mar. 7 For a moment nobody answered .. then some said 'Yebo Nkosi.' **1967** S.M.A. LOWE *Hungry Veld* 96 Nena ate well and said little ... 'Did you enjoy it?' Lucy asked of her. 'Yebo,' she answered, 'I was hungry.' **1982** W.O. KWAMTHETWA in *Staffrider* Vol.5 No.2, 7 'Yebo mfowethu,' responded Pikinini. **1985** H. PRENDINI in *Style* 39 You'll hear them (especially the Natal chaps) .. muttering 'aikona!' or 'yebo!' depending on whether they agree or not. **1991** *Personality* 18 Mar. 14 Let's get down to a bit of hard core ruggerbugger talk ... Everyone says 'yeh baw' a lot.

yellow *adj.* In special collocations.
a. In the names of fauna: **yellow-bill** [tr. Afk. *geelbek*], in full **yellow-bill(ed) duck**, the GEELBEK (sense 2), *Anas undulata*; **yellow cobra**, or (*obs.*) **- serpent, - snake** [tr. S. Afr. Du. *geelslang* fr. Du. *geel* yellow + *slang* snake], the *Cape Cobra* (see CAPE sense 2 a), *Naja nivea*; **yellow steenbras**, see STEENBRAS sense b.

   1906 STARK & SCLATER *Birds of S. Afr.* IV. 134 *Anas undulata*, Geelbec or Yellow Bill. **1967** E. ROSENTHAL *Encycl. of Sn Afr.* 158 Duck, .. Water bird well represented in South Africa. Varieties include *Yellowbill* (or *Geelbek*) [etc.]. **1972** [see GEELBEK sense 2]. **1920** F.C. CORNELL *Glamour of Prospecting* 80 (Swart), We saw .. an occasional geel capel (**yellow cobra**). **1786** G. FORSTER tr. A. *Sparrman's Voy. to Cape of G.H.* I. 200 The quivers .. are lined about the aperture with .. the skin of the **yellow serpent**, which is considered as the most venomous of any in that country. **1790** W. PATERSON *Narr. of Four Journeys* 75 We saw .. the **Yellow Snake**, or Covra [*sic*] Capel. **1819** G.M. KEITH *Voy.* 70 The yellow snake .. differs in colour only from the hooded snake of India, and being from four to eight feet in length, their size and bright yellow colour render it easy to avoid them. **1839** J.E. ALEXANDER *Exped. into Int.* I. 27 In clambering amongst the rocks we saw .. a yellow-snake. **1866** J. LEYLAND *Adventures* 23 A Cobra-de-capello, known as the Yellow Snake in the Colony, sprang out, erected itself and came after me. **1886** G.A. FARINI *Through Kalahari Desert* 451 We saw a large yellow snake, that was rapid in his movements, always disappearing into a katteah or meercat's hole whenever he could get near enough to dispatch it .. They called it a *Jill slange*, or yellow snake.
b. *Geology. Diamond-mining*. **yellow ground** or (less commonly) **yellow soil**, weathered layers of BLUE GROUND which is at surface level and has turned yellow as a result of oxidization.

   1887 J.W. MATTHEWS *Incwadi Yami* 179 The 'yellow ground' only extends to a certain depth; this is friable, and was easily broken by means of shovels and clubs. **1913** C. PETTMAN *Africanderisms* 568 *Yellow ground*, The ground in the Pipe .. of the Kimberley Diamond Mine lying on top of the Blue ground .. was so called by the diggers because of its colour. **1937** H. SAUER *Ex Afr.* 45 During the first couple of years the top friable yellow ground, was exclusively worked. **1946** S. CLOETE *Afr. Portraits* 136 After the bottom of the yellow ground had been struck .. the real wealth had been found to lie .. below it in the hard blue clay. **1968** J.T. McNISH *Rd to Eldorado* 241 This was the first known instance of yellow ground found on the diamond fields. **1973** A. HOCKING *Diamonds* 6 Gradually the diggers puzzled out the real character of the mines they had stumbled on: .. the yellow ground near the surface was in fact only weathered blue-ground. **1985** A.J.A. JANSE in Glover & Harris *Kimberlite Occurrence & Origin* 23 When diggers found that much harder compact blue ground underlay the yellow ground, many sold out. **1882** J. NIXON *Among Boers* 146 The **yellow-soil** .. is characteristic of the Diamond Fields region. **1897** F.R. STATHAM *S. Afr. as It Is* 190 The workers who had gone deepest — perhaps some sixty feet — suddenly found that the yellow soil from which they had been extracting diamonds came to a stop.
c. In cookery: **yellow rice**, rice prepared with turmeric and raisins, a feature of traditional Cape Malay and Afrikaner cookery; BEGRAFNISRYS; FUNERAL RICE; GEELRYS.

   1890 A.G. HEWITT *Cape Cookery* 55 Yellow Rice to be Eaten with Roast Meat. **1891** H.J. DUCKITT *Hilda's 'Where Is It?'* 204 Rice (Yellow). (Malay Recipe.) **1910** *S. Afr. 'Inquire Within'* (*Cape Times*) 34 Yellow Rice. One pound of washed rice, half a pound of currants washed and picked, quarter of an ounce of turmeric dissolved in a cupful of water, and a stick of cinnamon. **1930** M. RAUBENHEIMER *Tested S. Afr. Recipes* 84 Yellow or Curried Rice (Cape Dish). **1935** P. SMITH *Platkop's Children* 77 It was roasted hens an' roasted mutton .. an' yellow rice with raisin in it. **1964** J. MEINTJES *Manor House* 49 Peas, cauliflower, roast potatoes, yellow rice with raisins, [etc.]. **1977** F.G. BUTLER *Karoo Morning* 261 Your most typical dishes — yellow rice, sosaties and biltong — are Malay. **1979** *Weekend Argus* 10 Mar. Section 7 Bobotie ... Serve with yellow rice with raisins and a fruit chutney. **1990** S. GRAY in *Staffrider* Vol.9 No.1, 50 This trencher duly arrived .. : mounds of yellow rice.

yellowfish *n.* Pl. unchanged. [tr. Afk. *geelvis*, or formed in S. Afr. Eng., fr. Eng. *yellow* + *fish*.]
a. Any of several freshwater fishes of the genus *Barbus* (family Cyprinidae), so called because of the colouration of some species; GEELVIS; MOGGEL sense 2. See also BAARDMAN sense 1 b, KARPER sense 2, SCALY.

   1834 A. SMITH *Diary* (1939) I. 168 Fish in the pools of this river of two kinds, the flat head and bearded yellow fish. **1867** *Blue Bk for Col. 1866* FF19, Barber and yellow fish are caught in considerable quantities in the Orange and Kraai Rivers. **1880** P. GILLMORE *On Duty* 132 In the Mooi river good fishing is to be obtained. Yellow-fish, ... are abundant, and grow to a great size. **1913** W.W. THOMPSON *Sea Fisheries of Cape Col.* 138 The best species is the Geel-mogel (*Barbus holubi*) .. it is considered the best variety for eating, and in the Zak River is called Geel-visch or yellow-fish and grows to 4 or 5 lbs in weight. **1945** H. GERBER *Fish Fare* 79 Yellowfish .. Orange, Vaal & Limpopo River systems. Although these fish have rather prominent Y-shaped bones, the flesh is fairly palatable. **1964** V. POHL *Dawn & After* 39, I caught three yellow-fish in quick succession ... After treating the lot of us, the doctor informed our parents that yellow fish roe could be poisonous at certain times of the year. **1971** *Farmer's Weekly* 12 May 86, I later caught so many yellowfish that a young Bantu boy who served me as a gillie could not carry the bag of fish. **1982** M.N.

BRUTON et al. *Pocket Guide Freshwater Fishes* 43 Like most yellowfish, fights powerfully until completely exhausted. **1988** *S. Afr. Panorama* Dec. 36 The lightning-fast, strong and golden-bodied *yellowfish* (*Barbus* species) indigenous to the Vaal and Orange river systems.

b. With distinguishing epithet: **Clanwilliam yellowfish**, *B. capensis*; BARBER sense 1 a; see also GEELVIS; **large-mouth yellowfish**, *B. kimberleyensis*; **large-scaled yellowfish**, *B. marequensis*; **Lowveld yellowfish**, see *small-scaled yellowfish*; **small-mouth(ed) yellowfish**, *B. holubi*; **small-scaled yellowfish**, *B. polylepsis*.

1987 T.F.J. VAN RENSBURG *Intro. to Fynbos* 48 Ten species are regarded as endangered. They are: **Clanwilliam yellowfish** ... Olifants River. **1983** *Star* 15 Sept. 11 The **large-mouth yellow-fish** (Barbus kimberleyensis) .. spawns only at about the age of seven years. **1978** U. DE V. PIENAAR *Freshwater Fishes of Kruger Nat. Park* 36 **Large-scaled Yellow-fish** (Barbus marequensis) ... The cleaner the water, the more pronounced is the yellow colour of the fish. **1971** *Farmer's Weekly* 12 May 83 One of the most willing and easiest fish to be caught .. is the **Lowveld yellowfish** also known as 'Barbus polylepsis', or, commonly, the smallscaled yellowfish. *Ibid.* 85 Many anglers .. confuse it with the Vaal River **smallmouthed yellowfish**, 'Barbus holubi', because the two are alike. *c*1978 *Report No.34* (Dept of Nature & Environ. Conservation) 55 Recently attention has been given to the culture of the small-mouth yellowfish. **1971** [**smallscaled yellowfish**: see quot. at *Lowveld yellowfish* above].

yellow mellow *n. phr. Slang.* Inverted form of MELLOW YELLOW. Also *attrib.*

1987 N. MATHIANE in *Frontline* Feb. 24 There are many Casspirs and Ford Sierras and youths scuttle whenever the Yellow Mellow armoured police bus appears. **1988** B. SCHREINER in *Staffrider* Vol.7 No.2, The police .. retreated into their yellow mellow to wait it out.

yellowtail *n.* [Transf. use of general Eng. *yellowtail* (designating similar fishes elsewhere).] Any of several species of kingfish (family Carangidae) having yellow colouring on the caudal fin: **a.** *Seriola lalandi*; ALBACORE; HALF-CORD. **b.** *S. rivoliana*. **c.** *Alepes djedaba*.

In Smith and Heemstra's *Smiths' Sea Fishes* (1986), the name 'giant yellowtail' is used for *S. lalandi*, 'longfin yellowtail' for *S. rivoliana*, and 'shrimp scad' for *A. djedaba*.

1905 H.E.B. BROOKING in *E. London Dispatch* 18 Sept. 2 Cape salmon (elops saurus), shad (temnodon saltator), yellowtail (seriola lalandii), and such like fish. **1930** C.L. BIDEN *Sea-Angling Fishes* 69 Local names: America — Yellowtail; Amberjack ... South Africa — Albacore; Yellowtail. **1955** C. HORNE *Fisherman's Eldorado* 3 Yellowtail are not only found in Cape Peninsula waters. They are widely dispersed along both south and east coasts, they are the amberfish of America, they are known to Australian and New Zealand anglers. **1970** *Argus* 30 Jan. 8 *Yellowtail* suddenly became voracious around Cape Point. **1992** YELD & GUBB in *Afr. Wildlife* Vol.46 No.2, 201 They are entitled to take .. white steenbras, yellowtail, [etc.]. **1993** R. VAN DER ELST *Guide to Common Sea Fishes* 155 *Common names* SA — Cape yellowtail. Elsewhere — southern yellowtail, yellowtail amberjack ... The Cape yellowtail is a common, but seasonal, gamefish of great esteem.

yellowwood *n.* [tr. S. Afr. Du. *geelhout*, fr. Du. *geel* yellow + *hout* wood.]

In all senses also called GEELHOUT.

1. The fine-grained golden-yellow wood of any of several species of forest tree of the genus *Podocarpus* (see sense 2 below). See also KALANDER *n.*[2], OUTENIQUA sense 2 b, UPRIGHT YELLOWWOOD sense b. Also *attrib.*

1790 E. HELME tr. *F. Le Vaillant's Trav.* II. 288, I also remarked the *Geele-Houtt*, (yellow-wood) so called from its colour: which .. is very serviceable for planks, beams, and rafters. **1802** *Cape Town Gaz.* 16 Aug. 2 Yellow wood Beams, 22 feet long, 10 by 12 inches, 18 to 22 Rix Dollars each. **1821** C.I. LATROBE *Jrnl of Visit* 197 The furniture in Mr Meyer's house, made of stink-wood, yellow-wood, and other curious woods, does him great credit, both as to beauty and strength. **1832** *Graham's Town Jrnl* 14 Sept. 147 Butter Casks, made of the best or *real* Yellow Wood, constantly on hand. **1843** J. COLLETT Diary. II. 12 July, Slab of Yellow Wood bored. **1855** J.W. COLENSO *Ten Weeks in Natal* 188, I saw in a humble shed at Maritzburg handsome chairs of yellow-wood. **1861** LADY DUFF-GORDON *Lett. from Cape* (1925) 72 The floor of the zolder is made of yellow wood, and resting on beams, forms the ceiling of my room. **1870** *George Advertiser* 14 Apr., (*advt*) J.C. Truter, General Dealer ... Has always on hand .. Yellow-wood and stinkwood Planks. **1926** P. SMITH *Beadle* (1929) 18 The shovel, the chairs .., the meal-chest, the kneading trough, the bucket-rack .. were all, like the ceiling of the room and its doors and window-frames, made of yellow-wood grown rich in colour with age and beautiful with the constant use of years. **1952** G.M. MILLS *First Ladies of Cape* 75 The 'stinkwood' and 'yellow-wood' wardrobes have the characteristic gable outline which was quite traditional in furniture. **1964** J. MEINTJES *Manor House* 9 Precious yellowwood ... Isn't it beautiful? Those beams were cut in Knysna and brought here by ox-wagon, two hundred years ago. **1981** [see GEELHOUT]. **1988** H. DUGMORE in *Personality* 27 June 62 Stinkwood now goes for about R200 a cubic foot and yellowwood for about R75, and both are extremely difficult to come by.

2. In full *yellowwood tree*: any of several coniferous forest trees of the genus *Podocarpus* of the Podocarpaceae: **a.** *P. falcatus*, the largest of these trees, occurring naturally along the eastern and south-eastern seaboards and mountain ranges, and in the Eastern Transvaal; KALANDER *n.*[2]; OUTENIQUA sense 2 a. **b.** *P. latifolius*, a large tree occurring naturally along the eastern and southern seaboards and mountain ranges, and in the Eastern Transvaal; UPRIGHT YELLOWWOOD sense a. **c.** *P. elongatus*, the smallest of the southern African yellowwoods, occurring naturally only in the Western Cape; *Kaffrarian yew*, see KAFFRARIAN; SOUTH AFRICAN CEDAR. **d.** *P. henkelii*, a large tree occurring naturally in the mountain forests and coastal belt of KwaZulu-Natal. Also *attrib.*, as *yellowwood forest*.

In F. von Breitenbach's *Nat. List of Indigenous Trees* (1987), the name 'Outeniqua yellowwood' is used for *P. falcatus*, 'real yellowwood' for *P. latifolius*, 'Breede River yellowwood' for *P. elongatus*, and 'Henkel's yellowwood' for *P. henkelii*.

1810 G. BARRINGTON *Acct of Voy.* 326 The most common is that called the *geel hout* or yellow wood. These trees grow to the amazing size of ten feet in diameter. **1823** W. SHAW in B. Shaw *Memorials* (1841) 239 Our wagons were drawn up under the shade of one of the beautiful yellow wood trees. **1831** [see GEELHOUT]. **1835** T.H. BOWKER Journal. 6 May, We have been fireing Bullets & Balls amongst the yellow wood trees .. and spoiling the timber. **1856** R.E.E. WILMOT *Diary* (1984) 47 Plumbago bushes .. overhung by yellow-wood trees in their indescribably ghostly trappings of grey moss. **1865** 'A LADY' *Life at Natal* (1972) 101 A yellowwood tree is a tall, grey-stemmed veteran, standing straight and stately, and clear of branches until its tall crest, forty, fifty, sixty feet high, is crowned with dark foliage. **1871** E.J. DUGMORE Diary. 24 Oct., The sawyer told us of one fine old Yellowwood in the forest measuring 40 feet in circumference. **1882** T.B. JENKINSON *Amazulu* 196 The yellow-wood forests are like those .. in Griqualand. **1887** J.C. BROWN *Crown Forests* 305 Some of the noble yellowwood trees now being given away to refugee sawyers .. could not be produced under a couple of centuries. **1907** [see ASSEGAI sense 2]. **1910** [see ESSENWOOD]. **1928** [see VELDKOS]. **1961** PALMER & PITMAN *Trees of S. Afr.* 121 The yellowwoods of our high forests are the most magnificent of all our forest trees. Standing sometimes 150 feet high, with a trunk diameter up to 11 feet, these giants tower above the surrounding forest. **1976** *Weekend Argus* 29 May 8 The rarest type of yellowwood — the Breda River yellowwood — is to be found only in the South Western Cape. It is the smallest type, .. having [a] bushy shrub-like appearance. **1987** T.F.J. VAN RENSBURG *Intro. to Fynbos* 16 The Breede River yellowwood (*Podocarpus elongatus*) is often seen in the south. This tree, which seldom grows very high, has long, narrow leaves.

yerr(ah) var. YIRRA.

yes baas /ˈjes bɑːs/ *adj. phr.* and *n. phr. Colloq.* [Part. tr. Afk. *ja baas, ja* yes + *baas* boss, master.] **A.** *adj. phr.* JA BAAS *adj. phr.*

1963 K. MACKENZIE *Dragon to Kill* 134 He also thought of the yes-baas, touch-my-cap Africans he met in town. **1971** *Post* 28 Mar. 9 In the United States .. a full-scale campaign against the Yes Baas mentality is being mounted. **1974** M.A. MUTLOATSE in S. Gray *On Edge of World* 110 He wasn't a yes-baas muntu.

B. *n. phr.*

1. JA BAAS *n. phr.* sense 2.

1975 S. SEPAMLA in *New Classic* No.1, 12, I asked, what about my pass-book? Joe shook his head as if he really pitied me ... There's so much of the yes-baas in you that you can hardly see the difference between the paper you carry and the penis which is part of your body.

2. The utterance 'yes baas', seen as the epitome of the language and attitudes of a servile person; cf. JA BAAS *n. phr.* sense 1.

1971 *Post* 28 Mar. 9 A feeling of inferiority grows in him ... It makes him say: 'Yes Baas.' **1977** M.P. GWALA *Jol'iinKomo* 16 A man's irrational thoughts On his chained condition may get gripped: By the fear he may act rational And dance to the fuck-up tune of 'yes baas'. **1982** *Staffrider* Vol.4 No.4, 22 Put on your mask, son of Mendi. Remember to say 'Yes, baas,' 'No, baas.' It is a game; sometimes you win.

yes-no *adv.* [tr. Afk. *ja-nee*.] JA-NEE.

1900 H. BLORE *Imp. Light Horseman* 76 Yes-no, but I wanted to ask you whether dere was not an artery cut ... If this be your skill then need I not fear ... Yes-no; a Kaffir, even of my cunning, could do no better. **1948** [see JA-NEE sense 1]. **1970** *Informant, E. Cape* Yes-no, don't worry, I'll be fine. **1972** *Informant, E. Cape* Yes-no, rhenosterbos isn't a problem here thank goodness — it really can damage your veld. **1972** J. SMUTS *Informant, Grahamstown* Yes-no, this is the sort of thing where you wander about in the dark. **1980** J. SCOTT in *Het Suid-Western* 6 Aug. 'How goes it with you, Koos?' 'Yes no, cannot complain, Piet.' **1986** *Fair Lady* 5 Mar. 24 Is Wine an aphrodisiac? The answer is that South Africanism which floored me as a newcomer to this country: 'Yes-no' (followed by 'it depends').

yes(s)is, yessus varr. YISSUS.

yesslik var. JISLAAIK.

yho(o) var. YO.

yinna /ˈjɪnə, ˈjənə/ *int.* Also **yiina**, **yinne**. [As next.] YIRRA.

[**1970** N. CONWAY *Informant, Salisbury (Harare, Zimbabwe)* My hene. Carefully substituting an 'n' for an 'r' so as not to sound too blasphemous.] **1977** S. ROBERTS in E. Pereira *Contemp. S. Afr. Plays* 242 Men! Yinna, they drive you mad. **1983** A. WILLCOX in *Sunday Times* 28 Aug. (Mag. Sect.) 18 Who's that oke writing like mad over there? Have you come to steal my jokes again? Yiina. You okes. **1989** *Sunday Times* 29 Oct. 29 Yinne, man, this sudden switch to democracy is too fast for me.

yirra /ˈjərə, ˈjɪ-/ *int. colloq.* Also **jirr(a)**, **jirre**, **jurre**, **jur-ruh**, **yerr(ah)**, **yirrah**. [Englished form of Afk. *jere*, altered or disguised form of *Here* (see HERE).] An exclamation expressing amazement, shock, annoyance, exasperation, anger, or fear; YINNA. Cf. HERE *int.*

1963 K. MACKENZIE *Dragon to Kill* 151 *Yirra*, man, just when I had almost finished packing! **1974** *Drum* 22 Sept. 10 Jirr — that old tannie was saying, 'Ek weet nie waarom moet daai Mr Nehls altyd kom interfere nie.' 1977 F.G. BUTLER *Karoo Morning* 142 Bugger off home, Butler. Yerrah, man, do you want to break your blerry neck? 1979 J. GRATUS *Jo'burgers* 238 'Jirra!' Pienaar exploded. 'You're bloody mad.' 1980 *Sunday Times* 10 Feb., South Africans don't like to get too wordy. A vocabulary consisting of 'yirra' and 'shame', with any of up to 47 intonations ranging from sincerity to belligerence, is considered quite adequate for gracious and profound communication. 1984 A. DANGOR in *Staffrider* Vol.6 No.1, 17 Jurre, don't start that kak story again. 1985 P. SLABOLEPSZY *Sat. Night at Palace* 45 Ah, Jirre, man! One for one!! Bloody chicken, man! 1987 M. POLAND *Train to Doringbult* 11 We're going to have a hell of a drought. *Yirra* it's tough being a farmer! 1988 A. SHER *Middlepost* 87 You should see me and my chommies slup. Yells bells, jur-ruh!

yislaaik, -like varr. JISLAAIK.

yissus /ˈjəsəs, ˈjɪsəs/ *int. slang.* Also **jisses, jissus, jussis, jussus, jysis, yassas, yes(s)is, yessus, yissis.** [Representing the Afk. pronunciation of *Jesus* (normally pronounced /ˈjɪəsəs/) when used as an exclamation or oath.] JISLAAIK.

1942 U. KRIGE *Dream & Desert* (1953) 121 'Jysis!' Mostert whistled through his teeth. 'I had no idea they'd collect such a packet.' 1955 D.C. THEMBA in J. Crwys-Williams *S. Afr. Despatches* (1989) 320 Yessus! The Leech will never find us here. 1969 A. FUGARD *Boesman & Lena* 38 It was big! All the roads ... new ways, new places. *Yessus*! It made me drunk. 1971 *Drum* Aug. 52 Yessus, I'm surprised none of my children can sing. 1975 S. ROBERTS *Outside Life's Feast* 89 Bawling all night, her eyes swollen, red. Yesis, she mus' hate me! 1977 D. MULLER *Whitey* 100 'Yissis!' Achmet Smit gave a loud cry as he tumbled from the bench to land on all fours. 1979 M. MATSHOBA *Call Me Not a Man* 71 Jabu .. had been the wettest blanket: 'Yissis, sonny! What has gone wrong with you?' he would ask. 1982 C. HOPE *Private Parts* 9 Jissus, but it's hot. 1985 [see MAN *int.*] 1988 I. STEADMAN in *Weekly Mail* 9 Dec. 32 Yissus, that was funny. 1993 *Informant, Grahamstown* Jissus, Bonnie! ... That's lank rude, hey!

yo /jɔ(ː)/ *int.* Also **yho(o), jo.** [Xhosa.] An exclamation expressing any of a variety of emotions, esp. surprise, wonder, contempt, dismay, and disbelief.

1871 J. MACKENZIE *Ten Yrs* (1971) 444 Then followed the wild chorus, expressive of great anguish — 'Yo — yo — yo!' the mourners falling on their faces, tearing their hair, and beating their breasts. 1925 D. KIDD *Essential Kafir* 38 They have many very expressive exclamations, such as 'Yo!' when they wish to show contempt. 1953 D.C. THEMBA in *Drum* Apr. 48 They were all crying bitterly: 'Jo-o! Jo-o! Jo-nana-jo!' 1975 *E. Prov. Herald* 5 July 9 'Yo, food costs too much,' the women said, clicking their tongues and shaking their heads. 1979 *Staffrider* Vol.2 No.1, 26 'Maybe we're going to receive wage rises.' 'Yo, Maria. I wouldn't cling to that hope if I were you.' 1983 *Fair Lady* 1 June 45 As for training the children — yo! The homework to be done for school. 1990 J. ROSENTHAL *Wake Up Singing* 49 Yo! This is terrible.

yoiner var. JOINER.

yoke key *n. phr. Obs.* [Perhaps fr. a misinterpretation of YOKESKEY as *yoke's key* (see quot. 1839).] SKEY sense 1.

1832 *Graham's Town Jrnl* 30 Mar. 56 Diedericus Van der Kemp, for stealing four yoke keys, .. found guilty. 1839 [see YOKESKEY]. 1871 [see JUKSKEI sense 1]. 1962 F.C. METROWICH *Scotty Smith* 151 This led to an open fight, which Scotty abruptly ended by cracking his opponent over the head with a yoke key.

yokeskey /ˈjəʊkskeɪ, -kiː/ *n. obsolescent.* Also **yokeskei, yoke's key, yokeski, yokeskie.** Pl. **-s,** and (formerly) **-schegen.** [Calque formed on S. Afr. Du. *jukschei* (later *-skei*), *juk* yoke + *schei,* see SKEY. The two pronunciations are evidence of two different interpretations of the word's origin, as *yoke + skey* and *yoke's + key* (see prec.).]

1. SKEY sense 1.

1817 G. BARKER *Journal.* 29 May, Held school &c. Made yoke schegen. 1835 A. SMITH *Diary* (1939) I. 338 The woman .. took up a yokeskey. 1839 T. SHONE *Diary.* 9 Apr., I mended the sides of my waggon ..., after this I made some yoke's keys. 1850 R.G.G. CUMMING *Hunter's Life* 24 Passing through each end of the yoke, at distances of 18 inches from one another, are two parallel bars of tough wood about 18 inches in length; these are called yoke-skeys. 1864 T. BAINES *Explor. in S.-W. Afr.* 384 Plaiting goat-skins into wagon-whips, making yoke-skeis and training young oxen. 1882 C. DU VAL *With Show through Sn Afr.* II. 191 Two more bullocks added to the team, ox-yokes, and yokeskeys, and chains purchased. 1899 'S. ERASMUS' *Prinsloo* 17 Piet took up a yokeskei and beat them off the waggon. 1907 J.P. FITZPATRICK *Jock of Bushveld* (1909) 95 Often .. while trekking .. something goes wrong with the gear — a yokeskey or a nekstrop breaks. 1914 S.P. HYATT *Old Transport Rd* 270 Yokeskeys, the fifteen-inch-long pieces of wood which, passed through the yoke, go on each side of the bullocks' necks, were constantly breaking. 1934 B.I. BUCHANAN *Pioneer Days* 31 The straight yoke was placed across their necks and secured by the throat strap attached to the wooden yokeskeys. 1958 R.E. LIGHTON *Out of Strong* 78 The girls sat around, played hopscotch, or sometimes joined the boys in throwing yokeskeis. 1970 A.J. DU PREEZ *Informant, Misgund (W. Cape)* Yoke Skey. A flat notched piece of timber, to which is attached the strap or 'riem' with which the ox is inspanned.

2. *fig. rare.* In the idiomatic phr. *the extra yokeskey,* an unwanted or unneeded person, 'the fifth wheel on a wagon'.

1934 *Cape Argus* 19 May (Swart), 'I am the extra yokeskei in the political life of South Africa' said Mr Roos.

yong var. JONG.

Youth Day *n. phr.* [See quot. 1994.] The 16th of June, observed as a public holiday from 1995.

Until 1995 not an official holiday, but nevertheless observed by many. See also *Soweto Day* (SOWETO sense 3).

1994 *E. Prov. Herald* 8 Sept. 1 The anniversary of the Soweto uprising on June 16 would be renamed Youth Day. 1994 *Ibid.* 8 Dec. 2 The confusion that has existed over the past few months regarding the public holidays for 1995 ended today, by the publication of the Public Holiday Act 1994 in the Government Gazette ... The full list of public holidays is as follows: ... June 16 Youth Day, [etc.].

youth preparedness *n. phr. Hist.* Also with initial capitals. [tr. Afk. *jeugweerbaarheid, jeug* youth + *weerbaarheid* capability of bearing arms, military preparedness.] In the past, a compulsory subject in white state schools in certain areas, covering a wide range of topics and ostensibly aimed at preparing pupils for entry into the adult world. Also *attrib.*

As part of the 'Christian National Education' syllabus, the course was rejected by many as being a vehicle for pro-apartheid propaganda. See also CHRISTIAN-NATIONAL sense 1.

1972 *E. Prov. Herald* 12 Feb. 5 'Youth preparedness' is still a subject for which most Port Elizabeth high school heads are 'quite unprepared'. In 1973 it will be compulsory in all Cape schools. 1973 *Sunday Times* 18 Feb. 5 Their parents sent letters to the principal .. politely requesting that their children be excused from flag-saluting ceremonies, marching and shooting — part of the Youth Preparedness programme — and from singing the national anthem. 1988 *Informant, Grahamstown* We had a subject at school called Youth Preparedness. It was a period of about an hour and a half once a week ... We did all sorts of things: patchwork, marching — imagine it, a class of girls marching round the tennis courts! We learnt about tax and things, sex education — general sorts of things. 1990 *Projects pamphlet* (Nusas, Rhodes Univ.), She was blacklisted by the Transvaal Education Department for opposing youth preparedness (cadets), and is still not allowed to teach there.

‖**ystervark** /ˈeɪstəfɑːk, ˈeɪstərfark/ *n.* Also **ijzer vark, yzer-vark(e), yzer-varken, yzerwarké.** [Afk., earlier S. Afr. Du. *ijzervarken,* fr. Du. *ijzer* iron + *varken* hog, pig.] The porcupine *Hystrix africaeaustralis* of the Hystricidae, a large rodent with a protective covering of sharply pointed quills which are banded in black and white; IRON HOG.

Some early contexts may be referring to the southern African hedgehog *Atelerix frontalis* of the Erinaceidae.

1786 G. FORSTER tr. A. *Sparrman's Voy. to Cape of G.H.* I. 151 The *hystrix cristata* of Linnaeus, called by the colonists here *yzer-varken* (or the *iron-hog*), is the same animal as the Germans carry about for show in our country by the name of the *porcupine.* 1795 C.R. HOPSON tr. *C.P. Thunberg's Trav.* I. 283 The Porcupine, or Yzer-varken (*Hystrix*) whose usual food is the root of that beautiful plant, the *Calla Aethiopica,* will frequently deign to put up with cabbage and other vegetables. 1810 G. BARRINGTON *Acct of Voy.* 282 They have .. an animal that burrows in the ground, called the *yzer varke,* or iron hog, the flesh of which, when salted and dried, is esteemed by the Dutch as a great delicacy. Several of the farmers breed them; but it is so vicious, that it is not safe for strangers to approach them. [1835 A. STEEDMAN *Wanderings* I. 81 On returning we fell in with a porcupine, *hystrix cristata,* an animal which usually forages by night, and causes sad devastation among the crops of vegetables: the Dutch call it *yzer varke,* or the iron hog.] 1847 J. BARROW *Reflect.* 146 Here is also an animal that burrows in the ground, called the Yzerwarké, the iron-hog (hystrix cristata). 1950 H.C. BOSMAN in L. Abrahams *Bekkersdal Marathon* (1971) 43 All he had was book-learning and didn't know, for instance, a simple thing like that an ystervark won't roll himself up when he's tame. 1985 P. SLABOLEPSZY *Sat. Night at Palace* 17 An ystervark is a porcupine, I'm telling you.

yung var. JONG.

yusslaik, -lark varr. JISLAAIK.

yzer *n. obs.* [Ellipt. for YZER HOUT.] IRONWOOD sense a.

1847 J. BARROW *Reflect.* 162 Next in size was the *yzer,* or iron-wood (*sideroxylon*); *hassagai-hout* (*Curtisia faginea*).

yzer hout *n. phr. Obs.* Also **eysterhout.** [S. Afr. Du. *ysterhout, yster* (fr. Du. *ijzer*) iron + *hout* wood.] IRONWOOD sense a.

1821 C.I. LATROBE *Jrnl of Visit* 238 Here grows that valuable wood called eysterhout, or iron-wood, so hard, and likewise so tough, that an axle-tree made of it will bear more than an iron one of twice its thickness. 1822 W.J. BURCHELL *Trav.* I. 181 The pole we had now put in, being of Yzer hout (or iron wood), was not so tough as the other; but many degrees harder and heavier. The boors esteem the iron-wood to be, for this purpose, but little inferior to the hassagay-wood.

yzer-vark, yzerwarké varr. YSTERVARK.

Z

zaaidam var. SAAIDAM.

zakubona var. SAWUBONA.

zalie var. SALIE.

zambal var. SAMBAL.

zandkruiper var. SANDKRUIPER.

zand-mol *n. obs.* Also **zand moll**. [S. Afr. Du., fr. Du. *zand* sand + *mol* mole.] The SAND-MOLE, *Bathyergus suillus*.

   1786 G. FORSTER tr. A. *Sparrman's Voy. to Cape of G.H.* II. 196 The other species [of mole], which is called the *zand-mol*, is the mus Africanus of Mr. Pennant. **1822** W.J. BURCHELL *Trav.* I. 57 The animal which makes these hillocks is a very large kind of mole-rat, nearly as big as a rabbit... It is peculiar to this colony, and is called Zand Moll (Sand mole). **1912** *State* Sept. 231 (Pettman), The giant among these burrowing mole-like animals is known as the sand mole or *zand mol*.

zandveld var. SANDVELD.

ZAR /zed ei 'ɑː(r)/ *n. hist.* Also **Z.A.R.** [Initial letters of Du. *Zuid Afrikaansche Republiek.*] The South African (or Transvaal) Republic; BOER REPUBLIC sense a; SAR *n.*[1] Also *attrib.*

   Established in 1881, the ZAR came under British control in 1902, after the Anglo-Boer War.

   [**1881** G.F. AUSTEN *Diary* (1981) 37 Erasmus is.. a commissioner for the ZA Republic.] **1899** A. WERNER *Captain of Locusts* 27 The man had come unharmed for a thousand miles or more, and there were no more Z.A.R. police-posts to the south-east. **1973** *S. Afr. Panorama* Oct. 39 South Africa's explosives history dates back to 1887 when the Volksraad (parliament) of the Zuid Afrikaansche Republiek (ZAR) decided to allow explosives to be marketed by a single agent at a fixed price. **1975** [see GEREFORMEERDE]. **1979** T. GUTSCHE *There Was a Man* 143 The British Customs, confronted by a swarthy foreigner carrying Z.A.R. papers..., suspected gun-running. **1983** *Gold Jrnl* Vol.4 No.18, 4 ZAR Coins — Spectacular Growth. **1989** *Weekend Post* 26 Aug. 11 The SA Army is.. rooted in the ZAR's old Staatsartillerie.

Zarp /zɑːp/ *n. hist.* Also **Z.A.R.P.**, and with small initial. [The letters used on a badge worn by the members of this police force, being the initial letters of *Zuid-Afrikaansche Republiek* (or, according to some sources, *Rijdende*) *Politie* South African Republic (or Mounted) Police. The force included both mounted and foot police.] A member of the police force of the South African (Transvaal) Republic. Usu. in *pl.*: in *sing.*, a collective term for the force as a whole.

   1894 *Standard & Diggers' News* in G.N. Van den Bergh *Polisiediens in Zuid Afrikaansche Republiek* (1980) 161 Submit to the tyrannic bonds of these Zarps? Not much. God save the Queen... Down with the Boers. **1896** *Star* 14 Oct. 4, I had a conversation with a Zarp, stationed on Pretoria Bridge, and.. he assured me that a diligent search was made of the Park nightly. **1929** H.A. CHILVERS *Out of Crucible* 112 There was a house to house search for these arms. In one case a body of miners persuaded weary Zarps to dig all day under the foundations of a cyanide tank for rifles. [**1934** N. DEVITT *Mem. of Magistrate* 115 The father had been a sergeant in the Z.A.R.P.] **1955** T.V. BULPIN *Storm over Tvl* 217 The bulk of the personnel of the Republican Police Force, known as the Z.A.R.P.S. (Zuid Afrikaansche Republiek Polisie) consisted of rustics drawn from the country districts. **1969** A.A. TELFORD *Jhb.: Some Sketches* 13 Gambling houses, though forbidden by law, flourished everywhere, some with sentries posted outside them to warn of the approach of the 'Zarps', as the police were called. **1977** R.J. HAINES in R.J. Bouch *Infantry in S. Afr. 1652–1976* 25 The 'ZARPS', the Police of the South African Republic, numbered about 1 400 at the outbreak of war. **1987** W. STEENKAMP *Blockhouse* 16 Whelan.. had been in the Zarps, the republican police.

Hence **Zarpine** *adj. rare*, of this police force.

   1895 *Standard & Diggers' News* 23 Nov. 21 Jan.. resisted Zarpine authority, and even attempted to test the Zarpine probity by the bribe of a sixpence.

zaza see quot. 1821 at TSAA.

ZCC *n.* Also **Z.C.C.** [Initial letters of *Zion Christian Church.*] A large independent church which blends certain traditional African beliefs and practices with those of Christianity; *nonce*, a representative of this church. Also *attrib.* See also ZIONIST.

   1970 *Post* 19 July 2 The Bishop drove off at high speed — followed by his late father's Buick and a convoy of Z.C.C. cars. **1971** *Drum* May 10 Those ZCC people have treated me decently and I have nothing to say. I get whatever I want and my son is being well looked after, too, in Moria. **1985** *S. Afr. Panorama* June 5 Although Bishop Lekgangyane has visited Israel and the Holy Land, and his followers are adjured among other things not to eat pork, the ZCC has no affiliation with Zionism or Judaism. **1988** E. MALULEKE in *Drum* Apr. 37 She left the ZCC after two years when her car was broken into during a church service. **1992** P. STOBER in *Weekly Mail* 24 Apr. 21 The ZCC has a bursary scheme and is conducting a literacy campaign... In line with African traditions, the church is strongly patriarchal... 'There is no question of ladies officiating. Marriage and polygamy as of old is permitted,' explained the ZCC.

Zchoosch var. JEWISH.

zebŏngas pl. form of IMBONGI.

zebra *n.* [Transf. sense of general Eng. *zebra* the quadruped *Equus zebra*; so called for its similar black stripes.] In full **zebra fish**: the seabream *Diplodus cervinus hottentotus* of the Sparidae, a distinctively-coloured fish with a silver-gold body and vertical black stripes; BONTROK sense a; DASSIE sense 2 c; HANGBERGER sense 1; KARANTEEN sense 1 a; STREEPDASSIE; *wildepaard* sense (b), see WILDE sense b; *wildeperd*, see WILDE sense b.

   The name 'zebra' is used for this species in Smith and Heemstra's *Smiths' Sea Fishes* (1986).

   1905 H.E.B. BROOKING in *E. London Dispatch* 29 July 7 A few fish are being taken from the Buffalo.. silvers and grunters, and occasionally a small skate or zebra. **1913** C. PETTMAN *Africanderisms* 571 *Zebra fish, Sargus cervinus*. The name has reference to several well-defined stripes running across the body of this fish. **1930** [see *wildeperd* (WILDE sense b)]. **1951** L.G. GREEN *Grow Lovely* 91 Similarities to animals were responsible for the zebra, dassie and parrot fish. **1971** *Grocott's Mail* 30 July 3 Gordon.. caught a zebra of 1,36kg (3lb). Zebras are usually caught when the water temperature is low, but Doug said the temperature was average and the water a good fishing colour. **1974** *Daily Dispatch* 29 May 27 Mr Walter Pettit caught two cob, a jan bruin, a black steenbras, a zebra and a moonfish totalling 10,6 kg. **1980** *E. Prov. Herald* 31 July 15 When I used to go gully fishing.. I found a piece of crayfish lashed to the hook with a short piece of shirring elastic the best bait for fish such as hottentot, galjoen, zebra and the other fish found in our gullies.

zee bamboes, zee-bambos varr. SEEBAMBOES.

zee kat var. SEEKAT.

zeekoe /ˈsiːku, -kuɪ/ *n.* Also **seekoe(i), zee-coe**. Pl. unchanged, or **-s**. [S. Afr. Du. (later Afk. *seekoei*) hippopotamus, transf. use of Du. *zeekoe* seal, walrus.]

1. *obs.* SEA-COW sense 1.

   1822 W.J. BURCHELL *Trav.* I. 409 Had never seen a Zee-koe (Sea-Cow), as the colonists call the Hippopotamus. **1839** W.C. HARRIS *Wild Sports* 278 It was with the greatest difficulty.. that the perverse Hottentots could be induced to suspend hostilities against the *Zeekoes*. **1925** F.C. SLATER *Centenary Bk of S. Afr. Verse* 238 (Seekoei = sea-cow) — Hippopotamus. Formerly very common in all the rivers from the eastern districts of the Cape northwards; a few still remain in the Transvaal. **1957** L.G. GREEN *Beyond City Lights* 163 Hippo (zeekoe).. were found in the Diep River.

2. *comb.* **zeekoe gat** /- xat/, pl. **-s**, **-ten**, [Du., *gat* hole, pool], sea-cow hole (see SEA-COW sense 2); **zeekoe spek** *obs.* [Du., *spek* fat, bacon], SPEK sense a.

   1822 W.J. BURCHELL *Trav.* I. 263 These ponds, called **Zeekoe-gatten**, (Sea-cow holes,) are generally supposed to have been made by *Hippopotami*. **1827** G. THOMPSON *Trav.* I. 101 Large pools, or as the colonists call them, *Zeekoe-gats*, deep enough to float a man-of-war. **1883** M.A. CAREY-HOBSON *Farm in Karoo* 155 These deep places in the rivers here and there are called by the Dutch and other colonists, 'Zee Koe gaten' — hippopotamus holes — because when the huge river horses were still inhabitants of the country they lived and bred in these holes, where they continually rolled and plashed about in order to prevent sand from accumulating in them. **1905** G.W. STOW *Native Races of S. Afr.* 51 Instead of the deep chasms now found..., chains of deep *zeekoegats*, or hippopotamus' pools, occupied their place. **1920** F.C. CORNELL *Glamour of Prospecting* 111 Before us lay a broad, placid sheet of calm, unruffled water with a typical zee-coe-gat (hippo hole). **1941** A.G. BEE *Kalahari Camp Fires* (1943) 268 Below the drift was a 'zeekoegat' which means 'hippo hole', and is a whirlpool or strong current. **1971** *Daily Dispatch* 16 Dec. 10 A hippopotamus pool (seekoegat) which they sounded for depth by measuring with the long whiphandles. **1822** W.J. BURCHELL *Trav.* I. 411 The ribs are covered with a thick layer of fat, celebrated as the greatest delicacy; and known to the colonists as a rarity by the name of 'Zeekoe-spek' (Seacow-pork). **1843** J.C. CHASE *Cape of G.H.* 69 The salted and smoked flesh of the hippopotamus, or as it is called here Zee Koe spek (sea-cow pork), and from good pork it cannot be distinguished. **1852** A.W. COLE *Cape & Kafirs* 83 'I've had a little present given to me — it's a nice bit of zeekoe spek' (sea-cow, *alias* hippopotamus pork). **1913** C. PETTMAN *Africanderisms* 572 *Zeekoe spek*, The fat of the hippopotamus is considered a great delicacy, and in the earlier days of the Colony was an important article in Cape cookery.

zendeling var. SENDELING.

Zenzele /zen'zeːle/ *n.* Also **Zensele**, and with small initial. [See next.] The quality of self-reliance; a name used to designate self-help organizations and schemes, and practices intended to promote self-reliance in a variety of fields.

1952 M.H. XUMA in *Drum* Sept. 10 I've been running Zenzele (Do-It-Yourself) clubs for African women on the Rand for the past 11 years. **1977** *Daily Dispatch* 5 Sept. 7 A call to women to use their latent power to gain political and economic rights was made by Mrs Helen Suzman .. at the triennial conference of the Federation of Women of South Africa (Zenzele). **1986** *Drum* Feb. 21 As a trained diviner I want to do more research on modern and traditional healing methods. That is why I insist that we must inculcate a spirit of *zenzele*, do it yourself. **1989** *Grocott's Mail* 31 Jan. 5 Self-help Zenzele-type housing could be erected.

‖**zenzele** /zen'ze(ː)le/ *v. intrans.* [Xhosa and Zulu, 'be independent', 'be your own helper' (lit. 'do for yourself', reflexive concord *z(i)*- + *-enz(a)* do + *-ele*, subjunctive form of applicative suffix *-ela* for, on behalf of).] 'Be your own helper': used as a slogan.

1985 *S. Afr. Panorama* Oct. 21 Each organisation .. had the opportunity to tell the other groups about their activities, but it proved that in their efforts to help others they also saw the opportunity to help themselves. Zenzele! Help yourself! That was the cry which resounded time after time.

zevenjaartje var. SEWEJAARTJIE.

zhoozsh var. JEWISH.

zibi /'zi(ː)bi/ *n.* Also with initial capital. [fr. Zulu *izibi* refuse, rubbish (n. prefix *izi-* + adj. stem *-bi* bad, dirty); brought into S. Afr. Eng. by an anti-litter campaign which used the slogan *Zap it in the zibi can*.] Refuse; rubbish; rubbish bin; usu. *attrib.*, and *comb.* **zibi can**.

1983 S. JACOBS in *City Press* 9 Oct. 3 The consensus about certain programmes is that the sooner someone slips them from the shelves and zaps them in the Zibi can, the better. **1983** A. JOHNSON *Informant, Grahamstown* This is our little zibi bag ... Zap it in the Zibi. **1985** on Radio South Africa 24 Jan., *(advt)* Zap it in the zibi can.

ziekentrooster, **zieketroost** *n.*[1], **ziektetroos** varr. SIEKETROOSTER.

zieketroost *n.*[2], **ziekte troost** varr. SIEKETROOS.

zimboti var. UMZIMBEET.

Zim-Zim /'zɪmzɪm/ *n.* and *adj.* [Unknown; perh. fr. the pronunciation of *-sm* in AZASM, but see quot. 1990.]

For note on reduplication in *S. Afr. Eng.*, see NOW-NOW.

A. *n.*

1. An adherent of the philosophy of black consciousness. Also *attrib.*

1987 N. MATHIANE in *Frontline* Feb. 24 Azasm — known as the Zim-Zims — remain in the Azapo fold. **1990** R. MALAN *My Traitor's Heart* 258 In Soweto, youngsters who said Biko were dubbed Zim-zims, in honour of all the *-isms* in their ideological arsenal. Dhlamini 1 became a Zim-zim stronghold.

2. The name of a vigilante group.

1991 P. GARSON in *Weekly Mail* 20 Dec. (Suppl.) 11 The Zim-Zims — not Azapo or PAC-supporting youths as the name suggests, but who are mostly the sons of businessmen — were formed into a vigilante gang earlier this year to protect those whose enterprises were the target of boycotts by the community.

B. *adj.* Supportive of black consciousness.

1989 *Informant, Pietermaritzburg* They've accused SACHED in Maritzburg of being Zim-Zim, you know, Black Consciousness.

zinc *n.* Also **zink**. [Calque formed on S. Afr. Du. *zink* galvanized iron.] Galvanized iron, i.e. iron coated with zinc, used in the manufacture of baths, buckets, other household utensils, and flat or corrugated sheets for the roofs and walls of buildings. Also *attrib.* See also TIN.

Also used in this sense in *W. Indian Eng.*

Some of the earlier quots may be referring to true zinc.

1831 *S. Afr. Almanac & Dir.* 179 The upper part of the roof is covered with zinc, which has not been found to answer the high expectations formed of its suitability. **1833** *Graham's Town Jrnl* 24 Jan. 1 (*advt*) On Sale .. sheet Zinc for roofing. **1862** T. SHONE *Diary.* 25 Sept., Henry was helping .. Knight Roof his house with zink. **1876** F. BOYLE *Savage Life* 25 A crowbar, two zinc buckets, [etc.]. **1883** O.E.A. SCHREINER *Story of Afr. Farm* 18 The zinc roofs .. reflected the fierce sunlight. **1926** P. SMITH *Beadle* (1929) 66 On its flat, zinc roof yellow pumpkins were spread out for winter use. **1949** J. MOCKFORD *Golden Land* 69 The house-tops .. are frequently made of sheets of corrugated-iron — galvanised iron, as it is called, or, popularly, zinc. **1956** D. JACOBSON *Dance in Sun* 11 On the post there was a sheet of flattened zinc with the name of the farm painted in black upon it. **1959** K.M.C. MOTSISI in M. Mutloatse *Casey & Co.* (1978) 31, I don't take to the thought of being thrown out of my zinc-and-cardboard shanty easily. **1967** E.M. SLATTER *My Leaves Are Green* 160 There was a zinc bath which could be filled with water heated on the stove. **1973** *Evening Post* 19 May 20 (*advt*) Sale of 21 Prefabricated Timber and Iron (Zinc) Huts. **1978** [see PLATDAK]. **1986** D. CASE *Love, David* 40, I ran to the zinc fence and peered through one of the holes. **1989** H. McINDOE in *Sunday Times* 5 Mar. 14 The passport issue does not worry the 20 families living in a cluster of zinc shacks at Ariamsvlei township. **1990** [see PONDOK].

zinduna pl. form of INDUNA.

zinja pl. form of INJA.

zinkin(g)s var. SINKINGS.

zinkingsdruppels see DRUPPELS sense b i.

zintuna pl. form of INDUNA.

Zionist *adj.* and *n.* [fr. the name of the *Christian Catholic Apostolic Church in Zion*, the first such church in South Africa: see quot. 1968 at *Zionism* (below).]

A. *adj.* Of or pertaining to a group of independent southern African churches which practise a form of Christianity incorporating elements of traditional African beliefs. See also SHEMBE, ZCC.

1941 W.M.B. NHLAPO in *Bantu World* 1 Mar. 9, I have been fortunate to see two well-established churches; Shembe in Natal and Mahona in the Free State. All the other Zionist churches are but tiny and poor shadows of these two. **1959** L. LONGMORE *Dispossessed* 325 Sundkler discussing African separatist churches of the Zionist type points out that they are hostile to European techniques of education and medicine. They .. carry over into their doctrines and worship values and rituals derived from traditional religion. **1962** M. BRANDEL-SYRIER *Black Woman* 235 'Zionist' Churches are .. revivalistic, emotional, prophetic and visionary. Not so anti-European as the Ethiopians. **1968** COLE & FLAHERTY *House of Bondage* 152 Zionist prophets .. are believed .. to be invested by the Holy Spirit with a supernatural power to heal. **1980** M. MATSHOBA in M. Mutloatse *Forced Landing* 126 Converts wore their 'Zionist' uniforms of blue on snow-white and clutched their staffs and bibles to join other worshippers in the locations. **1990** *S. Afr. Panorama* Nov.-Dec. 4 The most important impetus for Zionist churches came from Zion City near Chicago in the USA.

B. *n.* A member of a Zionist church; in *pl.*, also used as a collective term for these churches and their members.

1948 B.G.M. SUNDKLER *Bantu Prophets* 55 Theologically the Zionists are now a syncretistic Bantu movement with healing, speaking with tongues, purification rites, and taboos as the main expressions of their faith. **1956** H. BLOOM *Episode* 318 Among the crowd were a number of .. location Zionists of various sects. **1968** COLE & FLAHERTY *House of Bondage* 151 Often you will hear this simple expression of faith: 'I was ill. The Zionists prayed for me and now I am well'. **1978** *Staffrider* Vol.1 No.4, 26 Sometimes the Zionists would march down the street with their khaki uniforms and the white, tyre-soled boots they wore, singing without accompaniment. **1980** J. COCK *Maids & Madams* 56 Preston-Whyte found that 20 per-cent of all domestic servants were Zionists. She attributed the popularity of this church to the community spirit among church members. **1990** J. KNAPPERT *Aquarian Guide to Afr. Mythology* 37 Among the Zionists, baptism has a central place.

Hence **Zionism** *n.*, the religious beliefs and practices of these churches; the churches collectively, described as a movement.

1968 COLE & FLAHERTY *House of Bondage* 151 African Zionism has no connection with any modern Jewish movement. It is based on a Christian sect founded .. in 1896 by John Alexander Doxie. By 1904, missionaries from Zion, Illinois, were carrying Doxie's teaching to a receptive African audience. **1980** D.B. COPLAN *Urbanization of African Performing Arts.* 183 In Zionism, African 'prophets' combined aspects of traditional African and Christian religious ritual, belief, and social organization.

zit-kamer var. SITKAMER.

zoepie var. SOPIE.

zoetdoorn var. SOETDORING.

zoet(e)koekie, **zoetenkoekje** varr. SOETKOEKIE.

zol, zoll /zɔl/ *n.* Pl. *-s*, **zolle** /'zɔlə/. [Unkn.; the word *zol* in the sense of 'marijuana cigarette' was recorded in Mexico in the 1950s (see article by H. Braddy in *American Speech* Vol.30 No.2, May 1955, p.88), but it is not known what the relationship is between that word and this.]

1.a. A hand-rolled marijuana cigarette; *boom-skuif*, see BOOM *n.* sense 2; PILL; SKYF *n.* sense a; STOP sense 1 b. **b.** A twist of paper containing the amount of marijuana required to make a cigarette. Cf. STOP sense 1 a.

1946 C.P. WITTSTOCK in E. Partridge *Dict. of Underworld* (1950) 399 Dagga .. : .. torpedo, aap, zol. **1949** H.C. BOSMAN *Cold Stone Jug* (1969) 45 The dagga cigarette is now ready (the 'zol', they call it), and the rookers gather round in a circle. **1959** J. MEIRING *Candle in Wind* 133 'Haven't you got a zoll for me?' he begged. 'Just one? I'll die if I can't have one!' **1967** *Drum* 27 Aug. 7 The customers in turn sell 'zols' — cigarette size — to their customers. **1974** *Evening Post* 28 Oct. 1 Police confiscated four bags of dagga and 964 dagga zolls after a car was stopped near Kinkelbos. **1975** [see STOP sense 2]. **1980** A. FUGARD *Tsotsi* 20 Tsotsi rocked gently on his chair. Boston asked no more questions, brooding into his glass while the zol passed between Butcher and Die Aap. **1992** S. BARTLETT in *Weekend Post* 13 June 3 The dagga is packed into 2g to 4g 'zols' or envelopes. **1993** *Sunday Nation*

8 Aug. 6 'It's this that's been my downfall,' he said, waving the bottle and puffing on his zol.

2. DAGGA *n.*² sense 1.

1952 'MR DRUM' in *Drum* Sept. 12 It is known in the slang as 'garnja,' .. 'zoll,' [etc.]. 1963 L.F. FREED *Crime in S. Afr.* 207 Dagga .. was known .. by a variety of names, such as .. 'zoll', 'tokwaan', [etc.]. 1978 *Darling* 8 Nov. 74 Once I tried mixing my zoll with hash ... I was holding this guitar, I kept on dropping it and the people were laughing. 1986 [see BUTTON sense a]. 1990 B. RONGE in *Sunday Times* 16 Dec. (Mag. Sect.) 6 Even microwaves and cheap little diamond rings are good in an exchange for mandrax buttons or some superior zol in Hillbrow.

3. A hand-rolled tobacco cigarette; SKYF *n.* sense b.

1968 A. FUGARD *Notebks* (1983) 176 He was the only source of the brown paper used for rolling zols (Horseshoe or Springbok tobacco). 1971 *Cape Times* 3 July (Mag. Sect.) 4 Boon makes us a *lekker* zol of BB tobacco and brown paper check. 1974 [see SKYF *n.*]. 1988 S.A. BOTHA in *Frontline* Oct.-Nov. 10 Our pockets bulged with the .. packs of BB tobacco, and strips of newspaper in which we rolled our zolle. Not even the dumbest novice in prison leaves his tobacco lying around untended.

Zola Budd /ˌzəʊlə ˈbʌd/ *n. phr.* Also Zolabud(d). [See quot. 1994.] **a.** A police vehicle, the HIPPO, esp. a slow one; cf. MARY DECKER sense a. **b.** A small bus, seating usu. between ten and fifteen passengers, and used for taxi shuttle services; also called TAXI (sense 1); cf. MARY DECKER sense b. Also *attrib.*

In sense b, this name was initially applied only to Toyota minibuses.

1985 H. PRENDINI in *Style* Oct. 41 'Johnnies' (soldiers), 'Zola Budds' (slow SADF hippos) and 'Mary Deckers' (fast hippos). [1987 Z. BUDD in *Flying Springbok* Aug. 22 I've heard Brenda Fassies's record (*Izolabudd*, in honour of the taxis running between Johannesburg and Soweto but I haven't seen the video or met her.] 1987 [see MARY DECKER]. 1987 G. MOKAE in *Pace* Oct. 60 Vusi [Maranatha] claims invention of the now popular name 'Zola Budd' for a Toyota taxi in 1985. 1988 *Learn & Teach* 18 There is a blue 'Zola Budd' taxi on the road. 1988 A. JACOT-GUILLARMOD *Informant*, Grahamstown The Kombi taxis which run all over the town have a new name, besides their old one of 'kwela-kwela'. They are now known as Zola Budds 'cos they run so fast! 1989 B. NTEMBO in *Pace* Feb. 44 Mr Cheapside .. bought five cars in one month — three Toyotas, two four-wheel-drive vehicles and two 'Zola Budds'. 1991 [see MARY DECKER]. 1994 P. HAWTHORNE in *Time* 19 Dec. 16 Hilary Sombela hailed a crowded 'Zola Budd' — a minibus taxi, so called by township residents because the vehicles are usually as reliably swift as South Africa's famed middle-distance runner.

Hence **Zola Budd it** *intrans. v. phr. nonce*, to travel in a minibus taxi.

1994 C. CURZON in *Flying Springbok* Sept. 44 During a recent hectic trip to Israel, 'Zolabudding' it through the country and four centuries of eventful history.

zolder var. SOLDER.

zoll see ZOL.

‖**Zondagshuis** /ˈzɔndaks ˌhœɪs, -ˌheɪs/ *n.* Pl. **-huise** /-ˈhœɪsə, -ˈheɪsə/, and (formerly) **-huizen**. [Afk. (now obs.), fr. Du. *Zondag* Sunday + linking phoneme -s- + *huis* house.] SUNDAY HOUSE. Also **zondagshuisje** [Du. *-je* see -IE].

1900 M. MARQUARD *Lett. from Boer Parsonage* (1967) 75 Zondagshuizen are being broken into and searched, — my heart is sore for many of our people with the terrible loss this will mean to them. Ibid. 78 Tomorrow is Ascension day: no church one. One of the elders promised to come on Sunday, though he'll find it *moeilijk* for his zondagshuis has been pillaged by the Soldiers of the Queen. 1967 L. MARQUARD in M. Marquard *Lett. from Boer Parsonage* 24 A feature of Winburg, as of any small Free State town, was the *Zondagshuisje* (little Sunday house) ... These houses were, as the name indicates, intended for week-end use only, but after the Boer War, when it sometimes became necessary to have children living in town for school, the *Zondagshuis* served that additional purpose.

zone *v. trans. Hist.* [Special sense of general Eng.] PROCLAIM. Usu. *passive*. See also UNZONED.

1966 *Survey of Race Rel.* 1965 (S.A.I.R.R.) 187 Albertville, the Coloured suburb which was zoned for Whites in 1956. 1970 *Daily Dispatch* 27 Mar. 9 This area, and another mainly residential, adjacent area in the North End, were zoned for White occupation. 1970 J. PACKER *Veronica* 32 God knows where we'll be living then ... Our area is zoned for white. 1971 *Argus* 5 June (Weekend Mag. Suppl.) 1 The area had not been zoned. 1979 *Indaba* 24 Aug.7 Fingo village is still officially zoned Coloured.

Hence **zoning** *vbl n.*, the proclamation of an area for the exclusive use of one ethnic group.

1970 *Daily News* 29 May, Black zoning has left a wake of dying 'White' villages. 1971 *Daily Dispatch* 2 Oct. 1 Zoning meant an area or portion being set aside to be owned by a race group.

Zoola(a), Zoolah, Zooler, Zooloo, Zoolu varr. ZULU.

zoopje var. SOPIE.

Zoulah, Zoulou varr. ZULU.

zoupie var. SOPIE.

zoutbos, zoute bosch varr. SOUTBOS.

zoute ribbetje, zout-ribbetje varr. SOUTRIBBETJIE.

zozo /ˈzɔzɔ/ *n.* Also with initial capital. [fr. *Zozo*, the registered trade name of a company supplying prefabricated parts for small 'do it yourself' houses. The company initially made playground equipment (the manufacture of houses beginning in the early 1970s), and was named after a monkey in a series of children's stories by H.A. Rey.] The proprietary name of a particular make of prefabricated building, esp. (esp. in township Eng.) applied loosely to any prefabricated or temporary building, esp. a small one. Also *attrib.*

1980 *Sunday Times* 3 Feb. 11 To boycott zozos (mealie-meal stalls) which are used as tuck shops at most schools. 1986 M. MANAKA in S. Gray *Market Plays* 61 Izwe: You will not be around when the roof of this zozo comes down. Jimi: Only the professors can close the zozo. 1987 *Learn & Teach* No.2, 34 Do you live in a Zozo and hate your landlord? Have you waited years and years for a house? 1987 *Pace* Sept. 49 Lesedi has grown phenomenally, exceeding the expectations of its planners to the extent that several 'Zozos' had to be erected on the premises for use as consulting rooms and offices. 1990 R. STENGEL *January Sun* 151 For R52, each person got a plot of three hundred square meters, a water tap, a toilet, and a Zozo house, which is a gleaming one-room tin shed.

ZP *n.* Pl. unchanged, or **-s**. [The lettering on the registration plates of motor vehicles belonging to the KwaZulu Police, being a short form of KZP (see KZP).] A policeman of the former KwaZulu Police Force; used collectively (*pl.* unchanged), the force as a whole. Also *attrib.* See also KZP.

1990 *Weekly Mail* 27 Apr. 7 Other organizations .. want the ZPs out of the townships. 1990 *New African* 11 June 3 A ZP member attempted to stop the memorial service, claiming that .. the gathering was illegal. 1990 Ibid. 18 June 1 The UDF/Cosatu Joint Working Committee .. kicked off their campaign to end the Natal violence by saturating stadiums with 'Scrap the ZP' stickers. 1990 Ibid. 9 July 3 The said ZP, who was in plainclothes, had been cornered and killed after he had opened fire indiscriminately. 1990 V. MVELASE in M. Kentridge *Unofficial War* 180 In those townships which have been handed over to the KwaZulu Police, the ZP, you find order .. because the ZP are so strict.

zuikerbekje see quot. 1923 at SUIKERBEKJE.

Zulu /ˈzuːluː(ː), ‖zʊːlʊ/ *n. and adj.* Formerly also Zoola(a), Zoolah, Zooler, Zooloo, Zoolu, Zoulah, Zoulou, Zula, Zulo(e), Zuloo, and (occas.) with small initial. [Zulu n. stem -Zulu, found in words such as *amaZulu* Zulus, the Zulu people or clan collectively (sing. *umZulu*), *isiZulu* the Zulu language, and *uZulu* the Zulu people; as int., uttered in praise of the Zulu king.

From the name of *uZulu* (dates unknown, prob. died c1709), the founding leader of the dominant *amaZulu* clan, the name of which was later assumed by the consolidated chiefdoms under it (see note at sense A 1). UZulu's name was derived fr. *izulu* sky, a word which later also came to mean 'heaven'. Through misunderstanding of its derivation, *amaZulu* has often been taken to mean 'sky people' or 'people of heaven', but a strictly correct interpretation would be 'people of uZulu (the clan founder)'.]

In addition to the senses given below, there are senses of 'Zulu' which have developed outside South Africa and which are used internationally; these will be found in general dictionaries of English.

A. *n.*

1.a. Pl. **-s, ama-,** or unchanged. A member of an African people of the Nguni group, living mainly in KwaZulu-Natal. See also VATUA sense b. Also *attrib.*

The Zulu people was formed by the unification, mainly from 1818 onwards, of a number of Nguni clans and chiefdoms living in what has become the northern half of KwaZulu-Natal. A major factor in this consolidation was the conquest of other groups by the amaZulu chiefdom led by Shaka, who became the first king of the unified group. See also MFECANE.

1824 in J.S. Christopher *Natal* (1850) 21 Chaka, king of the Zulus, to whom belongs the whole of the country from Natal to Dela Goa Bay. 1829 W. SHAW Diary. 16 May, Chaka's grandfather was called Zulu, which signifies High, or the Heavens .. from him the Nation is now called Amazulu, or people of Heaven. c1847 H.H. DUGMORE in J. Maclean *Compendium of Kafir Laws* (1906) 1 The Amampondo and the Amazulu are .. distinguished by their dress, mode of warfare, and other customs. 1850 H.F. FYNN Diary. (Killie Campbell Africana Library MS22895), We had proceeded seven days from Natal when we had slept in a bush on the Imbean Clola river and little expecting the Zuloes would follow us, were surprised an hour before daybreak by a violent noise which was the Zuloes stabbing many of our people, while we were all asleep. 1876 F. BOYLE *Savage Life* 31 He was a Zulu, but taller than the average of his race. 1887 J.W. MATTHEWS *Incwadi Yami* 187 The South African native, especially the Zulu, is .. naturally honest. 1908 *Rand Daily Mail* 11 Sept. 7 The gangs quickly gained adherents. A few Xosa, Zulu and Fingo of a very low type were admitted to membership. 1923 [see MOSOTHO]. 1931 G. BEET *Grand Old Days* 23 After the day's work, diggers in their hundreds were talking fortissimo ..; whole tribes of Zulus, Xosas and Bechuanas were booming out their chants of love and battle. 1949 O. WALKER *Proud Zulu* (1951) 9 At the beginning of the 19th Century .. the amaZulu, or 'Children of Heaven,' were a tiny pastoral African clan surrounded by scores of equally pastoral tribes. 1964 G. CAMPBELL *Old Dusty* 32, I was a soldier in the impis of the amaZulu. 1976 WEST & MORRIS *Abantu* 37 To many people the Zulu are the best-known African people on the continent, for their military exploits led to the rise of a great kingdom that made them feared for a long time. 1978 A. ELLIOTT *Sons of Zulu* 14 Since the pagan tribesman has no equivalent of heaven — nor any hell — I personally prefer to interpret 'Zulu' to mean the sky and 'amaZulu' to mean 'the people of the sky'. 1980 N. FERREIRA *Story of Afrikaner* 99 There is only one South Africa ... That does not mean you cannot be an Afrikaner or Zulu or Xhosa. **1990** *New African* 16 July 6 Zulu said the people have been told that the African National Congress .. is for AmaXhosa and there were no Zulus in it.

b. *comb.* **Zululand**, the area ruled by Zulus for much of the eighteenth century, roughly that area of KwaZulu-Natal to the north of the Tugela River; at one time the official name of this area, but usu. an informal name; also *attrib.*; hence **Zululander**, one (not necessarily a Zulu) who lives in Zululand.

1857 W.H.I. BLEEK in *Cape Monthly Mag.* I. Apr. 202 Known all over Kafirland and Zululand. **1865** F.S.C. COLENSO in W. Rees *Colenso Lett. from Natal* (1958) 93 Mr. Robertson, the Missionary in Zululand had said to him that the Bishop had given him his book. **1879** *Daily News* 22 Mar. 6 We intend to 'jump' Zululand if we can. **1885** H. RIDER HAGGARD *King Solomon's Mines* 48, I ran away from Zululand and came to Natal because I wanted to see the white man's ways. **1905** A.T. BRYANT *Zulu-Eng. Dict.* 66 He [*sc.* Dinuzulu] is now re-instated as a headman in the Nongoma district in the north of Zululand. **1913** [see PONDO sense b]. **1923** [see ORIBI]. **1948** A. PATON *Cry, Beloved Country* 269 The great tribe of Zululand. **1971** *Daily News* 26 Feb. 15 The departure .. reduces the number of South African born White priests in the Anglican Diocese of Zululand to two – and neither of these is a Zululander. **1974** *E. Prov. Herald* 4 Oct. 1 A large Swazi impi .. crossed the Swaziland border into Zululand .. on Monday. **1992** *Natal Mercury* 23 Nov. 15 New Zululand firm wins SBDC award.

c. *nonce.* ***The Zulu***: The area inhabited by the Zulus.

1875 D. LESLIE *Among Zulus* 31, I am now on my way home. This is my eighth Sunday in the Zulu. I don't know what sort of trip I have made.

2. Occas. also **isiZulu**. The language of this people, being a Sintu (Bantu) language of the Nguni group.

1839 W.C. HARRIS *Wild Sports* 150 Andries could stutter tolerably in Sichuana, and possessed a smattering of zooloo, and we thus hoped to be able to proceed without the aid of a sworn interpreter. **1850** J.E. METHLEY *New Col. of Port Natal* 38 If your waggon driver be a Hottentot, or Mulatto, he will be able to interpret your orders, as they can generally speak the Zoola. **1885** H. RIDER HAGGARD *King Solomon's Mines* 22 The people .. were a branch of the Zulus, speaking a dialect of Zulu. **1912** W. WESTRUP *Land of To-Morrow* 57 He leaned forward and spoke in Zulu to the puller. **1930** L. BARNES *Caliban in Afr.* 71 It is rare to find any phrase in, say, Zulu for which there is an exact verbal equivalent in English or Afrikaans. **1936** H.F. TREW *Botha Treks* 175 The general was talking Zulu. **1957** S.G. MILLIN in D. Wright *S. Afr. Stories* (1960) 152 Rosie and her sister .. knew English, Afrikaans and Zulu, no less than Sesuto. **1973** *Drum* 8 Jan. 14 Bill .. grew up in Natal and learned Zulu along with English. **1982** *Pace* June 16, I wasn't the best-qualified person for the job, but I got it because I speak Zulu. We're using local people on this project and without Zulu I would have had no chance. **1988** *New Nation* 10 Mar. 15, I would like to learn to speak Zulu and have purchased a set of cassettes and numerous books.

3. Pl. **-s**. An indigenous breed of cattle: NGUNI sense 3. See also sense B 3 below.

1852 C. BARTER *Dorp & Veld* 155 (Pettman), Oxen of the .. Fatherland breed, .. though highly prized are surpassed for all working purposes by the light and hardy Zulus. **1880** *Alice Times* 6 Feb., They are a kind of Zulu, and like all the cattle from the mainland are small, wiry, and active. *c***1963** B.C. TAIT *Durban Story* 4 A span of 16 *Zulus* (the term for small oxen) .. were harnessed to the cart.

B. *adj.*

Some of the uses cited below might more correctly be considered *attrib.* uses of the noun.

1. Also **Ama-**. Of or pertaining to the Zulu people, or their culture or traditions.

1827 G. THOMPSON *Trav.* II. 408, I accompanied Messrs. Farewell, Fynn, and several other seamen, with about forty natives, on a journey to King Chaka, of the Zoola nation. **1828** W. SHAW Diary. 30 June, A vacant country .. separates the Amapondo from the Amazooloo Nation. **1832** *Graham's Town Jrnl* 28 Sept. 152 You will have heard of the Zoola commando going out against the Mussellikats. **1835** G. CHAMPION *Jrnl* (1968) 11 The Zoolah chief, Dingaan. **1836** A.F. GARDINER (*title*) Narrative of a Journey to the Zoolu Country in South Africa. **1837** F. OWEN *Diary* (1926) 10 My two Zooloo men are able to give me some assistance in the pronunciation, and in the names of many external objects. **1843** J.C. CHASE *Cape of G.H.* 238 The Mantatees, the remnants of tribes broken up and dispersed by the Zoolah conquests in 1822 to 1824. **1846** [see NATIVE *adj.* sense 1]. **1857** D. LIVINGSTONE *Missionary Trav.* 86 The Matabele, a Caffre or Zulu tribe. **1878** T.J. LUCAS *Camp Life & Sport* 99 The Zulu Kaffirs are, I think, even taller than the Amakosa, not unfrequently reaching six feet three. **1895** [see UNKULUNKULU sense 1]. **1903** *Ilanga* 9 Oct. 4 As a herder of cattle the Zulu youth is kept at home. **1908** *Rand Daily Mail* 11 Sept. 7 The native police .., with the exception of about six, are Zulu ... The native constables, because of their Zulu blood, are the sworn foes of the Amalaita. **1936** H.F. TREW *Botha Treks* 177 An adaptation of the celebrated horns formation used by the Zulu impis. *c***1948** H. TRACEY *Lalela Zulu* p.v, Where the music is genuinely of Zulu origin, composed in the tradition of Zulu music, we have classified it as 'Country Zulu'. **1954** H. NXUMALO in J. Crwys-Williams *S. Afr. Despatches* (1989) 31 The fat Zulu warder said .. : 'He's mad, sir.' **1970** A. PATON *D.C.S. Oosthuizen Mem. Lecture No. 1* 5 Mr. Lubinda Mate, born in South Africa, married to a Zulu woman .. was told .. that he would have to leave South Africa. **1971** *Personality* 28 May 57 'Qash' decided to .. obey Zulu law. **1974** *S. Afr. Panorama* Sept. 2 (*caption*) They visited a Zulu kraal. **1976** M. THOLO in C. Hermer *Diary* (1980) 35 Swazis and Zulus have a way of saying 'Umuntu phe?' meaning 'Are you a person?' as if, if you are not Swazi or Zulu, you are not a person. **1977** *Fair Lady* 8 June (Suppl.) 28 Traditional English, Indian and Mauritian influences have married with .. indigenous Zulu dishes. **1980** D.B. COPLAN Urbanization of African Performing Arts. 46 Local African instruments fashioned on European models such as .. the *igqongwe*, a Zulu ramkie, have developed. **1982** *Pace* Nov. 100 In Zulu mythology the trusted aides of Zulu kings were said to have been buried with them. **1990** M. BADELA in *New African* 27 Aug. 1 Prince Mduduzi Zulu of the Zulu Royal Family and Chief Mwelo Nonkonyana told hostel residents .. that they were 'playing right into the hands of the enemy' by taking up clubs, spears, and guns. **1992** B. KELLER in *Scope* 13 Nov. 90 In their zeal to do away with Zulu values and Zulu discipline, they've trained their young to attack anyone who is Zulu.

2. Of, pertaining to, or in the language of the Zulu people.

1836 L. GROUT in D.J. Kotze *Lett. of American Missionaries* (1950) 102 We now have the prospect of entering immediately upon the work of reducing the Zoolah language to writing. **1871** J. MACKENZIE *Ten Yrs* (1971) 337 Mr. Sykes .. is a diligent and most successful student of the Zulu language. **1908** D. BLACKBURN *Leaven* 18 Mr Betts added a few mispronounced abusive epithets from his limited Zulu vocabulary. *a***1951** H.C. BOSMAN *Willemsdorp* (1977) 63 He laughed to hear the elderly black woman emit a long string of Zulu swear-words. **1968** J. LELYVELD in Cole & Flaherty *House of Bondage* 8 Soweto is not a Zulu or Xhosa word. **1987** G. SILBER in *Style* Nov. 53 Taking Zulu lessons. **1990** R. GOOL *Cape Town Coolie* 113 The translation of a Zulu poem .. kept recurring in Henry's mind.

3. Of or pertaining to an indigenous breed of cattle (see sense A 3 above).

1846 *Natal Witness* 27 Mar. (*advt*) Wanted, by the Undersigned, 30 to 40 Fat Zulu Oxen. P. Ferreira Pietermaritzburg. **1862** J.S. DOBIE *S. Afr. Jrnl* (1945) 5 Drawn by six pairs of tailless rats of oxen with immense upright horns – the Zulu breed. **1885** H. RIDER HAGGARD *King Solomon's Mines* 42, I bought a beautiful team of twenty salted Zulu oxen ... These Zulu oxen are small and light, not more than half the size of the Africander oxen .. ; but they will live where the Africanders will starve. **1897** 'F. MACNAB' *On Veldt & Farm* 134 When I was in Natal, I saw cattle called Zulu cattle. **1948** H.V. MORTON *In Search of S. Afr.* 184, I saw Zulu cattle for the first time, beasts with wide-spreading horns, their hides strangely flecked with black and white. **1968** S. CLOETE *Chetoko* 14 The bull belonged to a famous breed. It went back through generations of raids and capture to the royal Zulu cattle – white animals with black skins beneath the hair, and black noses and ears. **1979** C. ENDFIELD *Zulu Dawn* 177 They .. saw .. a herd of Zulu cattle grazing!

4. *comb.* **Zulu War**, any of the series of conflicts between British and Zulu forces resulting from the invasion of Zululand by the British in 1879.

1880 F.S.C. COLENSO in W. Rees *Colenso Lett. from Natal* (1958) 352 It will be painful to my dear Husband. But he has had much to suffer – this Zulu War with all its attendant horrors. **1898** J.F. INGRAM *Story of Afr. City* 77 A magnificent cluster of white marble figures has been placed to commemorate the names of those who fell in the Zulu War. **1971** J. MCCLURE *Steam Pig* (1973) 10 He secured a military contract on the eve of the first Zulu War and prospered exceedingly. **1987** L. CAPSTICKDALE in *S. Afr. Panorama* Aug. 45 Other rare items are .. books on the Zulu War of 1879; [etc.].

Hence **Zulu** *v. intrans. nonce*, in the phr. **Zulu it** [formed by analogy with general Eng. *lord it*], to dominate (an area) as the Zulus were seen to do; **Zuludom** *n.*, the area inhabited by Zulus; **Zuluize** *v. trans.*, to bring (a word) into a form suited to the Zulu language; so **Zuluization** *n.*, the act or an instance of bringing (a word) into a form suited to the Zulu language; **Zuluized** *ppl adj.*, (of a word) brought into such a form; (of a person) not Zulu in origin, but assimilated into Zulu society; **Zuluness** *n.*, the quality or state of being a Zulu.

1876 *Jrnl Soc. Arts* 28 Jan. 166 Into the heart of savage Zuludom. **1882** P. ROBINSON *Noah's Ark*, The lion .., they say, is King in Africa, yet the gorilla Zulus it over the forests within the lion's territory. **1895** *Pall Mall Gaz.* (U.K.) 6 Aug., Death of John Dunn. A Zuluized Englishman. **1949** O. WALKER *Proud Zulu* (1951) 33 They used his Zulu-ised name 'Jantoni'. **1987** C.T. MSIMANG in *S. Afr. Jrnl of Afr. Langs* Vol.7 No.3, 82 Certain loans from English are Zulu'ized in Tsotsitaal. *Ibid.* 85 *Irabaneka* is Zulu'ization of 'rubber neck' ... An English adjective, 'fond', has been Zulu'ized by suffixing a verbal formative *-za*. **1990** D. BECKETT in *Frontline* Sept. 30 Shaka embodies Zuluness, tradition, the beliefs of their fathers. **1990** M. KENTRIDGE *Unofficial War* 54 Ndlovu .. ascribes this unusual laissez faire attitude of the police to the essential 'Zuluness' of the Inkatha bands. **1992** B. NZIMANDE in *Natal Witness* 6 Nov. 1 How can Buthelezi say we must fight for Zuluness ... Zulus are fighting for freedom. Zuluness will not liberate them; the ideals of the Freedom Charter will.

Zulustan see -STAN.

zureveld(t) var. ZUURVELD.

zuring var. SURING.

zuurdeeg var. SUURDEEG.

zuurveld /ˈsyːrfɛlt, ˈsɪuəfelt/ *n. hist.* Also **suurveld(t)**, **zureveld(t)**, **zuur(e)-velden**, **zuurfeldt**, **zuurveldt**, and with initial capital. [S. Afr. Du., *zuur* unpalatable, sour + *veld* open, undeveloped countryside.] **a.** ***sourveld***, see SOUR sense 2. Also *attrib.* **b.** ***The Zuurveld***: A name given to the Albany area of the Eastern Cape.

1785 G. FORSTER tr. *A. Sparrman's Voy. to Cape of G.H.* I. 249 What are termed by the colonists *Zuurvelden* or *Sour-fields*, are such as lie somewhat higher and cooler than the shore, and thus are better supplied with rain than the other plains. **1821** [see PISANG sense 2 a]. **1827** T. PHILIPPS *Scenes & Occurrences* 119 The pasture is all zureveldt. **1835** [see PARTY sense 1]. **1850** R.G.G. CUMMING *Hunter's Life* (ed.2) I. 13 Black, zuurfeldt oxen. **1871** [see *sweetveld* (SWEET sense 2)]. **1875** [see GALLSICKNESS sense 1]. **1878** T.J. LUCAS *Camp Life & Sport* 208 The flats .. are covered with a wiry kind of grass, called 'Suur veldt' (sour grass). *a*1880 W.G. ATHERSTONE in *S.W. Silver & Co.'s Handbk to S. Afr.* 230 Kruisfontein, belonging to Mr. John Atherstone, is .. an unmitigated zuurfeldt farm, situated on a sandstone ridge. There is no limestone on the farm. **1887** *S.W. Silver & Co.'s Handbk to S. Afr.* 157 Amongst the herbs, bushes, and shrubs found on the Zuurveldt are the Kanna bush. *c*1936 *S. & E. Afr. Yr Bk & Guide* 179 'Zuurveld' or 'Sour Grass' is found in many parts of the country, especially in areas of high rainfall. **1976** A.R. WILLCOX *Sn Land* 156 They could use certain areas for grazing only seasonally. These were termed by the Dutch Zuurveld which .. means land producing grass that is sour i.e. unpalatable to stock, in winter, but good grazing in summer.

zwaarger var. SWAER.

zwarthaak var. SWARTHAAK.

Zwartland var. SWARTLAND.

zwart-wit-pens var. SWARTWITPENS.

SELECT BIBLIOGRAPHY

This is a list of those works which were most commonly used in compiling the dictionary, or about which it may be difficult to find information elsewhere. It is hoped that the bibliography will prove a useful tool for readers interested in South African texts.

Listing is strictly alphabetical, disregarding the initial definite or indefinite article. Abbreviations are explained in the list on page xxviii.

Publications quoted by title in the dictionary are listed by title, not by institution; where an exception is made, a cross-reference is provided. Translations are listed under the name of the translator (if known), with a cross-reference from the author's name; pseudonymous works are under the pseudonym, where the author's actual name is shown in brackets.

For published titles a place and date of publication is provided. Facsimile reprints are listed to facilitate access to older documents. For magazines, dates are not usually supplied. Many newspapers have complicated histories, and it has been necessary to rely on secondary sources for these details. The sources have not always been in agreement, and although every care has been taken to eliminate errors, some may have occurred.

Unpublished titles are not italicized. The precise location of unpublished material is generally given. In particular, reference is made to the following resource centres:

Albany Museum (Grahamstown)
Cory Library (Rhodes University, Grahamstown)
Dictionary Unit (Grahamstown)
Killie Campbell Africana Library (Durban)
National English Literary Museum (Grahamstown)
Private collections
South African Library (Cape Town)

Further information on material held by the Dictionary Unit, or in private collections, is available from the Unit.

SELECT BIBLIOGRAPHY

ABRAHAMS, L. *The celibacy of Felix Greenspan* Johannesburg 1977
—— ed. *A Bekkersdal marathon* Cape Town 1971
—— ed. *Bosman at his best* Cape Town 1965
—— 8th impression 1974
—— ed. *A cask of jerepigo* Johannesburg 1972
—— ed. *Jurie Steyn's post office* Cape Town 1971
—— ed. *Unto dust* Cape Town 1963
ABRAHAMS, P. *Mine boy* London 1954 (first publ. 1946)
—— *Return to Goli* London c.1953
—— *Tell freedom* London 1954
ACOCKS, J.P.H. *Veld types of South Africa* (Department of Agricultural Technical Services) Pretoria 1975
ADA see Art, Design and Architecture
ADAMS, B. *The narrative of Private Buck Adams* [written 1884] ed. by A. Gordon-Brown Cape Town 1941 (Van Riebeeck Society)
ADAMS, H. & SUTTNER, H. *William Street District Six* Cape Town 1988
ADAMS, J. *Wild flowers of the northern Cape* Cape Town 1976
ADAMS, T.P. *An eulogy on Dr Alexander Cowie and Mr Benjamin Green; who lost their lives on their return from Delagoa Bay to Graham's Town* Graham's Town 1830
ADAMSON, R.S. et al. *The botanical features of the south western Cape Province* Cape Town 1929
ADEY, D. *Under the Southern Cross: short stories from South Africa* Johannesburg 1988
Africa Contemporary Record 1986-7 London 1988
Africana Notes and News Johannesburg
(The) African court calendar (and directory) Cape Town 1801; 1807-26 (continued by *The South African almanac(k) and directory*)
African Drum see *Drum*
The African Journal Cape Town 1849-51 (continuation of *Sam Sly's African Journal*)
African Wildlife Cape Town
Africa South and East Johannesburg
Africa Today New York
The Agricultural Journal of the Cape of Good Hope Cape Town 1888-1910 (until 1903 with title *(The) Agricultural Journal*; continued by *The Agricultural Journal of the Union of South Africa*)
The Agricultural Journal of the Union of South Africa Pretoria 1911-14 (continuation of *The Agricultural Journal of the Cape of Good Hope* and *The Natal Agricultural Journal*)
The Albany Settlers 1824-36 (Society for the Relief of Distressed Settlers) Cape Town 1836
ALEXANDER, J.E. *An expedition of discovery into the interior of Africa through the hitherto undescribed countries of the Great Namaquas, Boschmans and Hill Damaras* 2 vols. London 1838
—— *Narrative of a voyage of observation among the colonies of Western Africa in the flagship 'Thalia', and of a campaign in Kaffir-land in 1835* 2 vols. London 1837
Alice Times (title varies) Adelaide, Eastern Cape 1874-
ALSTON, M. *Wanderings of a bird-lover in Africa* London 1937
The American heritage dictionary of the English language ed. by W. Morris New York 1969
ANDERSON, A.A. *Twenty-five years in a waggon in the gold regions of Africa* Vol. II London 1887
ANDERSON, H.J. ed. *Letters from the Cape 1861-2* see Duff-Gordon, L., Lady
—— ed. *South Africa a century ago (1797-1801)* see Barnard, Lady Anne
ANDERSSON, C.J. (Karl Johan Andersson) *Notes of travel in South Africa* ed. by L. Lloyd London 1875
ANDREWS, C. *Reminiscences of the Kafir War 1834-5*. 1877. Typescript. Dictionary Unit
ANGOVE, J. *In the early days: pioneer life on the South African diamond fields* Kimberley 1910
ANNESLEY, G. *Voyages and travels to India, Ceylon, the Red Sea, Abyssinia, and Egypt, in the years 1802, 1803, 1804, 1805, and 1806. By George, Viscount Valentia* 3 vols. London 1809
Annual report of the calendar year 1911 (Department of Justice) Cape Town 1912
Antiquity: a quarterly review of archaeology Gloucester, U.K. 1927-
APPLEYARD, J.W. *The War of the Axe and the Xosa Bible: the journal of the Revd J.W. Appleyard* [written 1841-59] ed. by J. Frye Cape Town 1971
ARBOUSSET, T. see Brown, J.C. tr.
Archeology and natural resources of Natal (University of Natal) Cape Town 1951
The Argus Cape Town 1969- (continuation of *The Cape Argus*; weekend ed. *Weekend Argus*)

The Argus annual and Cape of Good Hope directory... Cape Town 1888-97 (continuation of *The general directory and guide book to the Cape of Good Hope*; title varies)
ARMSTRONG, H.C. *Grey steel* London 1937
Art, Design and Architecture (ADA) Cape Town
ATCHERLEY, R.J. *A trip to Boerland* London 1879
ATKINS, J.B. *The relief of Ladysmith* London 1900
ATMORE, M.G. *Cape furniture* Cape Town 1965
AUSTEN, G.F. *The diary of G.F. Austen: my experiences in Potchefstroom during the First Boer War* Roodepoort 1981 (Human Sciences Research Council, Source Publication No. 73)
The Australian national dictionary ed. by W.S. Ramson Melbourne 1988
AYLIFF, J. *Journal, 1821-30*. Typescript ed. by P.B. Hinchliff. Private collection [publ. in 1971 as part of 'The Graham's Town Series']
—— *Journal of 'Harry Hastings' Albany settler* ed. by L.A. Hewson & F.G. Van der Riet Grahamstown 1963
AYLIFF, J. & WHITESIDE, J. *History of the Abambo generally known as Fingos* Butterworth 1912
—— facsimile reprint Cape Town 1962

BABE, J.L. *The South African diamond fields* New York 1872
BACKHOUSE, J. *A narrative of a visit to the Mauritius and South Africa* London 1844
BADEN-POWELL, R.S.S. *The Matabele Campaign* [written 1896] London 1897
BAGLEY, Mr *Letter from Bagley to his mother in Bloemfontein, written from Kimberley during Anglo-Boer War*. a.1902. Private collection
BAILLIE, F.D. *Mafeking: a diary of the siege* Westminster, U.K. 1900
BAIN, A.G. *Journals of Andrew Geddes Bain* [written 1826, 1829, 1835, 1836, 1838, & 1846] ed. by M.H. Lister Cape Town 1949 (Van Riebeeck Society)
BAINES, T. *Explorations in South-West Africa. Being an account of a journey in the years 1861 and 1862 from Walvisch Bay, ... to Lake Ngami and the Victoria Falls* London 1864
—— facsimile reprint Salisbury, Rhodesia [Harare, Zimbabwe] 1973
—— *Journal of residence in Africa 1842-53* [written 1850-53] Vol. II ed. by R.F. Kennedy Cape Town 1964 (Van Riebeeck Society)
BAKER, J.R. *Race* (Foundation for Human Understanding) Athens 1981
BALDWIN, W.C. *African hunting from Natal to the Zambesi, including Lake Ngami, the Kalahari Desert, etc., from 1852 to 1860* New York 1863
—— 3rd ed. London 1894
BALFOUR, A.B. *Twelve hundred miles in a waggon* London 1895
BALLANTYNE, R.M. *The settler and the savage* London 1877
BALLEN, R. *Dorps: small towns of South Africa* Cape Town 1986
BANCROFT, F. *The veldt dwellers* London 1912
BANKS, J. *Journal ... during Captain Cook's first voyage in H.M.S. 'Endeavour' in 1768-71* ed. by J.D. Hooker London 1896
—— see also Hawkesworth, J.
(The) Bantu World see *World*
BARAGWANATH, P. *The brave remain* Cape Town 1965
BARAITSER, M. & OBHOLZER, S. *Cape country furniture* Cape Town 1971
BARKER, B.J. *The fairest Cape* Cape Town 1991
BARKER, G. *Journal. 1815-28*. Cory Library MS14258
BARKER, M.A., Lady *A year's housekeeping in South Africa* London 1877
BARNARD, K.H. *A pictorial guide to South African fishes* Cape Town 1947
BARNARD, Lady Anne *The letters of Lady Anne Barnard to Henry Dundas: from the Cape and elsewhere together with her journal of a tour into the interior and certain other letters* ed. by A.M.L. Robinson Cape Town 1973
—— *South Africa a century ago: letters written from the Cape of Good Hope (1797-1801)* ed. by W.H. Wilkins Cape Town 1910
—— *South Africa a century ago (1797-1801)* ed. by H.J. Anderson 2 parts (Part I *Letters written from the Cape of Good Hope*, Part II *Extracts from a journal addressed to her sisters in England*) Cape Town 1924
—— see also Fairbridge, D. ed. *Lady Anne Barnard at the Cape of Good Hope*; also Lindsay, Lord
BARNES, A.R. *The South African household guide* 5th ed. rev. & enlarged by A. Glossop Cape Town 1913
BARNES, L. *Caliban in Africa* London 1930

BARNHART, C.L., STEINMETZ, S., & BARNHART, R.K. *The Barnhart dictionary of new English 1963-1972* London 1973
—— *The second Barnhart dictionary of new English* New York 1980
—— rev. ed. *Third Barnhart dictionary of new English* [no place] 1990
BARNOUW, A.J. *Language and race problems in South Africa* The Hague 1934
BARRINGTON, G. *An account of a voyage to New South Wales* London 1810 (first publ. 1803)
BARRIS, K. *Small change* Johannesburg 1988
BARROW, J. *An autobiographical memoir of Sir John Barrow, Bart., late of the Admiralty, including reflections, observations and reminiscences at home and abroad, from early life to advanced age* London 1847
—— *Travels into the interior of Southern Africa, in which are described the character and the condition of the Dutch colonists of the Cape of Good Hope and of the several tribes of natives beyond its limits* 2nd ed. 2 vols. London 1806
'BARTOLOMEO, FRA PAOLINO DA SAN' (J.P. Wesdin) see Johnston, W. tr.
BAUMANN, G. & BRIGHT, E. *The lost republic: the biography of a land-surveyor* London 1940
BEAK, G.B. *The aftermath of war* London 1906
BEAKE, L. *A cageful of butterflies* Cape Town 1989
—— *The strollers* Cape Town 1987
—— *Tjojo and the wild horses* Pretoria 1990
BEALE, P. ed. see Partridge, E.
BEAL PRESTON, D.M. see Preston, D.M.B.
BEATTIE, T.R. *Pambaniso: a Kaffir hero, or scenes from savage life* Cape Town 1891
—— *A ride through the Transkei* Kingwilliamstown 1891
BECK, H. *Meet the Cape wines* Cape Town 1955
BECKER, C.J. *Guide to the Transvaal* Dublin 1878
—— facsimile reprint Pretoria 1976
BECKER, J. *The virgins* Cape Town 1986 (first publ. 1976)
BECKER, P. *Path of blood* London 1962
—— *Sandy tracks to the kraals* Johannesburg 1956
—— *Tribe to township* St Albans, U.K. 1974
BEE, A.G. *Kalahari camp fires: retold from the manuscript of A.S. Poultney, pioneer* Durban 1941
—— 2nd ed. Durban 1943
BEE, D. *Children of yesterday* London 1961
BEET, G. *The grand old days of the diamond fields: memories of past times with the diggers of Diamondia* Cape Town 1931
BEKKER, S. & HUMPHRIES, R. *From control to confusion* Pietermaritzburg 1985
BELL, T. *Industrial decentralisation in South Africa* Oxford, U.K. 1973
BELL, W.H.S. *Bygone days: being reminiscences of pioneer life in the Cape Colony and the Transvaal* London 1933
BELLAIRS, B. St J., Lady ed. *The Transvaal war: 1880-81* Edinburgh 1885
—— facsimile reprint Cape Town 1972
'A BENGALI' *Notes on the Cape of Good Hope* Calcutta 1847
BENNETT, J. *The hawk alone* London 1965
—— *Jamie* London 1963
—— *Mister fisherman* London 1967 (first publ. 1964)
BENSE, J.F. *A dictionary of the Low-Dutch element in the English vocabulary* The Hague 1939
BENSON, M. *The African patriots: the story of the African National Congress of South Africa* London 1963
—— *At the still point* London 1988 (first publ. 1969)
BERGER, L.G. *Where's the madam?* Cape Town 1966
BERJAK, P. et al. *In the mangroves of Southern Africa* (Wildlife Society of Southern Africa, Natal Branch) Durban 1982
The best of South African Short Stories (Reader's Digest Association) ed. by A. Turner Cape Town 1991
BEWS, J.W. *The grasses and grasslands of South Africa* Pietermaritzburg 1918
BHANA, S. & PACHAI, B. eds. *A documentary history of Indian South Africans* Cape Town 1984
BIDEN, C.L. *Sea-angling fishes of the Cape (South Africa)* London 1930
BIERMANN, B. *Red wine in South Africa* Cape Town 1971
BINNS, C.T. *The warrior people: Zulu origins, customs and witchcraft* Cape Town 1974
BIRD, J. ed. *Annals of Natal 1495-1845* 2 vols. Pietermaritzburg 1888
BIRD, W.W. *State of the Cape of Good Hope, in 1822* [written anonymously] London 1823
BIRKBY, C. *Airman lost in Africa* Dassie ed. [Johannesburg] 1957
—— *Springbok victory* Johannesburg 1941
—— *Thirstland treks* London 1936
—— *Zulu journey* London 1937
BISSET, C.B. *Sport and war in Africa* London 1875

SELECT BIBLIOGRAPHY

BLACK, S. *The dorp* 2nd ed. London 1921
—— *Stephen Black: three plays* see Gray, S. ed.
BLACKBURN, D. *A burgher Quixote* London 1903
—— *Leaven* London 1908
—— another ed. Pietermaritzburg 1991
—— see also 'Erasmus, S.'
BLACKBURN, D. & CADDELL, W. *Secret service in South Africa* London 1911
Black Enterprise Johannesburg (continued by *Enterprise*)
The Black Sash Cape Town (from Dec. 1961 published in Johannesburg; continued by *Sash*)
BLAGDEN, C.O. *An English–Malay phrase book* London 1934
BLAMEY, J.C. Diary. 1851. Killie Campbell Africana Library MS6121
BLEEK, D. *A Bushman dictionary* New Haven, U.S.A. 1956
BLEEK, W.H.I. *A comparative grammar of South African languages* Cape Town 1862
BLERSCH, F. *Handbook of agriculture* Cape Town 1906
BLIGNAUT, A.J. *Dead end road* Cape Town 1980
BLONDEL, A. & LAMB, S. *The parrot's egg* Johannesburg 1985
The Bloody Horse Johannesburg 1980–81
BLORE, H. *An imperial light horseman* London 1900
Blue Book for Colony see *Colony of the Cape of Good Hope*
BOLD, J.D. *Dictionary, grammar and phrase book of Fanagalo* 4th rev. ed. [Johannesburg] 1957 (first publ. 1951)
—— 7th ed. (with title *Phrase-book, grammar and dictionary of Fanagalo*) Johannesburg 1968
Bolt: magazine of the Literary Society (University of Natal) Durban
Bona Durban
BOND, G. *Chaka the terrible* London 1961
BOONZAIER, E. & SHARP, J. eds. *South African keywords: the uses and abuses of political concepts* Cape Town 1988
BOOTH, A.B. ed. see Champion, G.
BOOYSEN, C.M. ed. *Tales of South Africa: an anthology of South African short stories* Cape Town 1963
BORCHERDS, P.B. *An auto-biographical memoir of Petrus Borchardus Borcherds* Cape Town 1861
BOSHOFF, P.E. & NIENABER, G.S. *Afrikaanse etimologieë* Pretoria 1967
BOSMAN, A.M. & BONSMA, F.N. *Essential ranch improvements* (Department of Agriculture & Forestry) Pretoria 1838
BOSMAN, H.C. *Almost forgotten stories* see Rosenberg, V. ed.
—— *A Bekkersdal marathon* see Abrahams, L. ed.
—— *Bosman at his best* see Abrahams, L. ed.
—— *A cask of jerepigo* see Abrahams, L. ed.
—— *Cold stone jug* Cape Town 1969 (first publ. 1949)
—— *Jurie Steyn's post office* see Abrahams, L. ed.
—— *Mafeking road* Cape Town 1969
—— *Makapan's caves* see Gray, S. ed.
—— *Uncollected essays* see Rosenberg, V. ed.
—— *Unto dust* see Abrahams, L. ed.
—— *Willemsdorp* [written a.1951] Cape Town 1977
—— see also Gray, S. *Theatre One*; also Sachs, B.
BOSMAN, J. *The rock of gold* Pretoria 1985
BOTHA, C.G. *Our South Africa past and present* Cape Town 1938
—— *Social life in the Cape Colony in the 18th century* Cape Town 1928
BOTHA, M.C. & BURGER, J.F. *Maskew Miller's grammar of Afrikaans* 5th ed. Cape Town [?1928]
BOTHMA, J. DU P. ed. *Game ranch management* Pretoria 1989
—— see also Hall-Martin, A., Walker, C., & Bothma, J. du P.
BOUCH, R.J. ed. *Infantry in South Africa 1652–1976* (Documentation Service, South African Defence Force) Pretoria 1977
BOUGH, W. Letter to Bishop Colenso. 1858. Killie Campbell Africana Library KCM48899
BOWER, L. *Zulu boy* London 1960
BOWKER, J.M. *Speeches, letters, and selections from important papers of the late John Mitford Bowker* Grahamstown 1864
BOWKER, T.H. Journal. 1834–35. Typescript. Cory Library MS915
BOWLER, L.P. *African nights: a mystery narrative of surprises* London [1929]
BOYLE, F. *The savage life: a second series of 'Camp notes'* London 1876
—— *To the Cape for diamonds* London 1873
BRADLOW, E. & F. eds. see Somerville, W.
BRANCH, M. *Explore the Cape flora and its animals* Cape Town 1988
BRAND, R.H. *The Union of South Africa* Oxford, U.K. 1909

BRANDEL-SYRIER, M. *Black woman in search of God* London 1962
BRANDT, J. *The petticoat commando* London 1913
BRANFORD, J. *A dictionary of South African English* Cape Town 1978
—— 3rd ed. rev. & enlarged 1987
—— 4th edition ed. by J. & W. Branford 1991
BREGIN, E. *The kayaboeties* Cape Town 1989
BRETT YOUNG, F. see Young, F.B.
BRIGGS, D.R. & WING, J. *The harvest and the hope* Johannesburg 1970
BRINK, A.P. *A chain of voices* London 1982
—— *A dry white season* London 1979
—— *The first life of Adamastor* London 1993
—— *An instant in the wind* London 1976
—— *Looking on darkness* London 1974
—— *Mapmakers: writing in a state of siege* London 1983
—— *Rumours of rain* London 1978
—— see also Stander, S. tr.
BRINK, A.P. & HEWITT, W.H. ad. Aristophanes's *The birds*. 1973. Unpubl. play. Dictionary Unit
BRINK, M. *Entertaining with potjiekos* Cape Town 1986
BRINKMAN, L.H. *The breath of the Karroo* London 1914
—— *The glory of the backveld* London 1924
BRITS, J.P. ed. see Du Toit, P.J.
BROOKS, H. *Natal; a history and description of the Colony, including its natural features, productions, industrial condition and prospects* London 1876
BROSTER, J.A. *Red blanket valley* Johannesburg 1967
BROWN, G. *Personal adventure in South Africa* London 1855
BROWN, J.A. *Gathering of the eagles* Cape Town 1970
—— *Journey to Mousanzia* Pretoria 1988
—— *One man's war: a soldier's diary* Cape Town 1980
—— *The return* Cape Town 1971
—— *The white locusts* Cape Town 1983
BROWN, J.C. ed. *Management of Crown forests at the Cape of Good Hope under the old regime and under the new* London 1887
—— tr. T. Arbousset's *Narrative of an exploratory tour to the north-east of the Colony of the Cape of Good Hope* Cape Town 1846
Brown's 'South Africa': a practical and complete guide ed. by A. Samler Brown Johannesburg 1893
—— see also *The South and East African year book and guide*
BRUCE, M.C. *The golden vessel* Johannesburg 1919
—— *The new Transvaal* London 1908
BRUNNER, E. DE S. *Problems and tensions in South Africa* New York 1955 (reprinted from *Political Science Quarterly* Vol. LXX. No. III., Sept. 1955)
BRUTON, M.N., JACKSON, P.B.N., & SKELTON, P.H. et al. *Pocket guide to the freshwater fishes of Southern Africa* Cape Town 1982
BRUWER, J.P. VAN S. *South West Africa: disputed land* Cape Town 1966
BRYANT, A.T. *An abridged English–Zulu word-book* Pinetown 1949
—— *A Zulu–English dictionary ... a synopsis of Zulu grammar and a concise history of the Zulu people* Pinetown 1905
—— *Zulu medicine and medicine-men* Cape Town 1966
—— *The Zulu people as they were before the white man came* Pietermaritzburg 1949
BRYDEN, H.A. *Gun and camera in Southern Africa* London 1893
—— *A history of South Africa* London 1904
—— *Kloof and Karroo* London 1889
—— *Nature and sport in South Africa* London 1897
—— *Tales of South Africa* London 1896
BUCHAN, J. *The four adventures of Richard Hannay* London 1930
—— *Memory hold-the-door* London 1940
—— *Prester John* Harmondsworth, U.K. 1961 (first publ. 1910)
BUCHANAN, B.I. *Pioneer days in Natal* Pietermaritzburg 1934
Bulletin (Centre for Science Development) Pretoria (continued by *CSD Bulletin*)
BULLOCK, C. *The Mashona and the Matabele* Cape Town 1950
—— *Rina: a story of Africa* Johannesburg 1949
BULLOCK, J.B. ed. *Peddie: settlers' outpost* by Donald, Kirby, et al. Grahamstown [1960]
BULPIN, T.V. *Lost trails of the Low Veld* Cape Town 1951
—— *Lost trails of the Transvaal* Cape Town 1956
—— new ed. London 1965
—— *Storm over the Transvaal* Cape Town 1955
—— *The white whirlwind* London 1961
BUNN, D. & TAYLOR, J. eds. *From South Africa* Chicago 1988

BUNTING, B. *The story behind the non-white press* [no place] 1959 (A New Age pamphlet)
BURCHELL, W.J. *Travels in the interior of Southern Africa* 2 vols. London 1822–24
'BURGER, J.' *The black man's burden* London 1943
BURGESS, Y. *A life to live* Johannesburg 1973
—— *Say a little mantra for me* Johannesburg 1979
BURKE, C. *Kimberley* London 1986
BURMAN, J. *Guide to the Garden Route* Cape Town 1973
BURMAN, S. & REYNOLDS, P. eds. *Growing up in a divided society* Johannesburg 1986
BURNETT, B. *A reply to the 'Report of the Commissioners of Inquiry at the Cape of Good Hope', upon the complaints addressed to the Colonial Government and to the Earl Bathurst* [written 1826] London 1827
BURNETT, B.B. *Anglicans in Natal* Durban [1955]
BURROW, J. *Travels in the wilds of Africa: being the diary of a young scientific assistant who accompanied Sir Andrew Smith in the expedition of 1834–1836* ed. by P.R. Kirby Cape Town 1971
BURTT-DAVY, J. *Maize: its history, cultivation, handling and uses* London 1914
BUTHELEZI, M.G. *Power is ours* New York 1979
BUTLER, F.G. (Guy) *Bursting world* Cape Town 1983
—— *Cape charade* Cape Town 1968
—— *The dove returns* Cape Town 1956
—— *Karoo morning* Cape Town 1977
—— *A local habitation* Cape Town 1991
—— *South of the Zambezi* London 1966
—— *Take root or die* Cape Town 1970 ('Albany Series')
—— *Tales from the old Karoo* Johannesburg 1989
—— ed. *When boys were men* Cape Town 1969
BUTLER, H. *South African sketches* London 1841
BUTTERWORTH, H. *Traveller tales of South Africa* Boston 1900

CALLAWAY, G. *A shepherd of the veld* London 1911
CALLAWAY, H. *The religious system of the Amazulu Izinyanga Zokubula or, divination, as existing among the Amazulu in their own words, with a translation into English and notes* Pietermaritzburg 1870
CALVERT, A.F. *South West Africa during the German occupation 1884–1914* London 1915
The Cambridge history of the British Empire Volume VIII: South Africa, Rhodesia and the Protectorates Cambridge, U.K. 1936
CAMERON, V.L. *Reverse the shield* London 1926
CAMPBELL, A.G. *The Echo: a literary, scientific and critical magazine* see *The Echo*
CAMPBELL, G. *Old Dusty of the Low Veld* Cape Town 1964
CAMPBELL, I.R.D. (Roy) *The mamba's precipice* London 1953
CAMPBELL, J. *Travels in South Africa, undertaken at the request of the Missionary Society* London 1815 [2 editions, with different pagination]
—— *Travels in South Africa undertaken at the request of the London Missionary Society; being a narrative of a second journey in the interior of that country* 2 vols. London 1822
CAMPBELL, Roy see Campbell, I.R.D.
CAMPBELL TAIT, B. see Tait, B.C.
CANA, F. *South Africa from the Great Trek to the Union* London 1909
CANDY, S. ed. *Natal coast gardening* (Durban & Coast Horticultural Society) Durban c.1968
The Cape Argus Cape Town 1857–1969 (continued by *The Argus*)
'A CAPE COLONIST' (E.G. Aspeling) *The Cape Malays* Cape Town 1883
Cape Herald Cape Town 1965–
Cape Illustrated Magazine Cape Town 1890–1900 (continued by *The South African Illustrated Magazine*)
The Cape Law Journal Grahamstown 1884–1900 (continued by *The South African Law Journal*)
The Cape Mercury and Weekly Magazine see *Cape Town Weekly Magazine*
The Cape Monitor Cape Town 1850–?1862
The Cape Monthly Magazine 11 vols. Cape Town 1857–62
—— new series 18 vols. 1870–79
—— new series 4 vols. 1879–81
—— see also Robinson, A.M.L. ed.
Cape of Good Hope Agricultural Journal see *Agricultural Journal of the Cape of Good Hope*
The Cape of Good Hope almanac and annual register Cape Town 1837–63 (continuation of *The South African almanac(k) and directory*; title varies; continued by *The Cape Town directory*)
Cape of Good Hope Government Gazette Cape Town 1826–1910 (continuation of *Cape Town Gazette, and African Advertiser*)
—— see also *Government Gazette/Staatskoerant*

SELECT BIBLIOGRAPHY

Cape of Good Hope Literary Gazette Cape Town 1830-35
Cape Punch Cape Town 1888
Cape Statutes see *Statute law of the Cape of Good Hope*
Cape Times (title varies) Cape Town 1876-
The 'Cape Times' 'Inquire within' for households Cape Town 1910
The Cape Town directory Cape Town 1865-68 (continuation of *The Cape of Good Hope almanac and annual register*; title varies; continued by *The general directory and guide book to the Cape of Good Hope*)
Cape Town Gazette, and African Advertiser Cape Town 1800-26 (continued by *Cape of Good Hope Government Gazette*)
Cape Town Weekly Magazine Cape Town 1859 (from Apr. with title *The Cape Mercury and Weekly Magazine*)
Capricorn School Magazine Pietersburg
CAREY-HOBSON, M.A. *At home in the Transvaal* London 1896
——*The farm in the Karoo* London 1883
CARMICHAEL, D. see Hooker, W.J.
CARSTENS, W.P. *The social structure of a Cape Coloured reserve* Cape Town 1966
CARTER, G.M. *The politics of inequality: South Africa since 1948* London 1958
CARTWRIGHT, A.P. *By the waters of the Letaba: a history of the Transvaal Lowveld* Cape Town 1974
——*The gold miners* Cape Town [preface dated 1962]
CASALIS, A. *English-Sotho vocabulary* Morija, Basutoland [Lesotho] 1977
CASE, D. *Love, David* Johannesburg 1986
CATO, G.C. *General history of Admirality Reserve.* c.1884. Typescript. Killie Campbell Africana Library MS1596a
——*Letter to Richards.* 1879. Typescript. Killie Campbell Africana Library MS1602b
——*Letter to William Shepstone.* 1873. Typescript. Killie Campbell Africana Library MS1599b
CENTLIVRES, S. VAN DE SANDT *Blundering into university apartheid* Cape Town 1959
A century of transport 1860-1960: a record of achievement of the Ministry of Transport of the Union of South Africa Johannesburg 1960
Chambers's etymological dictionary of the English language ed. by J. Donald London 1872
——another edition ed. by A.M. Macdonald London 1963
Chambers 20th century dictionary new edition ed. by E.M. Kirkpatrick et al. Edinburgh 1983
CHAMPION, G. *Journal of an American Missionary in the Cape Colony 1835* ed. by A.B. Booth Cape Town 1968
CHAPMAN, M. & DANGOR, A. eds. *Voices from within* Johannesburg 1982
CHAPMAN, M. & VOSS, T. eds. *Accents: an anthology of poetry from the English-speaking world* Cape Town 1986
CHASE, J.C. *The Cape of Good Hope and the Eastern Province of Algoa Bay* ed. by J.S Christophers London 1843
——facsimile reprint Cape Town 1967
CHATTERTON, J. *The return of the drums* Dassie ed. [Johannesburg] 1956
CHILD, D. *Portrait of a pioneer: the letters of Sidney Turner from South Africa 1864-1901* Johannesburg 1980
——*Yesterday's children* Cape Town 1969
——ed. see Churchill, J. & M.; also Drummond, J.H.
CHILVERS, H.A. *Out of the crucible: being the romantic story of the Witwatersrand goldfields; and of the great city which arose in their midst* London 1929
——*The yellow man looks on* London 1933
CHRISTENSEN, P.A. *South African snake venoms and antivenoms* Johannesburg 1955
CHRISTOPHERS, J.S. ed. see Chase, J.C.
Church and society: a testimony of the Dutch Reformed Church (General Synodical Commission) Bloemfontein 1987
CHURCHILL, J.F. *Diary.* 1850-52. 2 vols. Typescript. Killie Campbell Africana Library MS37 & MS37a
CHURCHILL, J. & M. *A merchant family in early Natal: diaries and letters of Joseph and Marianne Churchill 1850 to 1880* ed. by D. Child Cape Town 1979
CHURCHILL, W.S. *London to Ladysmith via Pretoria* London 1900
The Citizen Johannesburg 1976-
City Press Johannesburg 1983- (continuation of *Golden City Press*)
Clarion Call (Bureau of Communication, Department of the Chief Minister, Kwazulu) Benmore, Johannesburg
CLARK, P.M. *The autobiography of an old drifter* London 1936
CLARKE, S. ed. *'Vanity Fair' in Southern Africa 1896 to 1914* Johannesburg 1991
CLAYTON, C. ed. see Schreiner, Olive E.A.

CLEAVER, M.M. *A young South African: a memoir of F.R.M. Cleaver* Johannesburg 1913
CLOETE, S. *African portraits* London 1946
——*Canary pie* London 1976
——*Chetoko and other African stories* Glasgow 1976 (first publ. in 1968 as *The writing on the wall and other African stories*)
——*The company with the heart of gold* London 1973
——*The hill of doves* Boston 1942
——*Mask* London 1958
——*Rags of glory* London 1963
——*The soldier's peaches and other stories* London 1959
——*Turning wheels* London 1937
——*Watch for the dawn* London 1939
CLOUTS, S. *One life* Johannesburg 1966
COATES PALGRAVE, K. see Palgrave, K.C.
COATES PALGRAVE, W. see *Report of W. Coates Palgrave ...*
COCK, J. *Maids and madams* Johannesburg 1980
COETZEE, J.M. *Dusklands* Johannesburg 1974
——*In the heart of the country* Johannesburg 1979
COETZEE, R. *The South African culinary tradition* Cape Town 1979
COHEN, L. *Reminiscences of Johannesburg and London* London 1924
——*Reminiscences of Kimberley* London 1911
COLE, A.W. *The Cape and the Kafirs: or notes of five years' residence in South Africa* London 1852
——*Reminiscences of my life and of the Cape Bench and Bar* Cape Town 1896
COLE, E. & FLAHERTY, T. *House of bondage* London 1968
COLENSO, F. *Letter to Mrs Lyall.* 1871. Killie Campbell Africana Library KCM49645
COLENSO, J.W. *Letter.* 1855. Killie Campbell Africana Library KCM48894
——*Ten weeks in Natal: a journal of a first tour of visitation among the colonists and Zulu Kafirs of Natal* Cambridge, U.K. 1855
COLLETT, J. *Accounts I.* 1831, 1832. Albany Museum history division H582(a) [catalogued as 'Account book, 1831, 1832']
——*Accounts II.* see *Diary II.*
——*Diary I.* Albany Museum history division H582(b) [catalogued as 'Diary Dec. 1835, 1836, 1838']
——*Diary II.* Albany Museum history division H593 [catalogued as 'Diary 1839-47'; this text is referred to in quotations as 'Accounts II.' or 'Diary II.']
COLLINS, R. *The impassioned wind* London 1958
Collins Cobuild English language dictionary ed. by J. Sinclair et al. London 1987
Collins dictionary of the English language ed. by P. Hanks et al. London 1979
Collins gem dictionary Bahasa Malaysia-English, English-Bahasa Malaysia rev. ed. London 1975
Colony of the Cape of Good Hope 1866 (Cape of Good Hope) Cape Town 1867 [Note This text is referred to in quotations as *Blue Book for the Colony 1866*]
COMAROFF, J.L. ed. see Plaatje, S.T.
Commission of inquiry into the structure and functioning of the courts (Chairman: G.G. Hoexter) 3 vols. Parl. Paper R.P.78-1983
Compendium of the law of the Cape of Good Hope London 1868
The concise Oxford dictionary of current English ed. by J.B. Sykes Oxford, U.K. 1983
The concise Scots dictionary ed. by M. Robinson et al. Aberdeen, Scotland 1985
Concise Siswati dictionary compiled by D.K. Rycroft Pretoria 1982
Conserva (Department of Environmental Affairs) Pretoria
Contact Cape Town
Contrast: South African quarterly Cape Town
CONYNGHAM, J. *The arrowing of the cane* Johannesburg 1986
COOK, J. *Voyages of discovery* London 1908
——see also Hawkesworth, J.
COOK, M.A. *The Cape kitchen: a description of its position, lay-out, fittings and utensils* Cape Town 1973
COON, C.S. *The origin of races* London 1963
Co-operative Winegrowers' Association (Ko-operatieve Wijnbouwers Vereniging van Zuid-Afrika Beperkt) Paarl [no date]
COPE, J. *Alley cat and other stories* London 1973
——*The tame ox* Cape Town 1960
——ed. see Livingstone, Douglas
COPLAN, D.B. *The urbanization of African performing arts in South Africa.* Doctoral thesis, Indiana University, U.S.A., 1980
CORDINER, J. *A voyage to India* London 1820
CORNELL, F.C. *The glamour of prospecting* London 1920
CORY, G.E. ed. see Owen, F.

Cosmopolitan Cape Town
COTTON, R.J. *Ag, man* Cape Town 1986
COTTON, W.A. *The race problem in South Africa* London 1926
——*Racial segregation in South Africa: an appeal* London 1931
COUPER, J.R. *Mixed humanity: a story of camp life in South Africa* Cape Town [1892]
COURTENAY, B. *The power of one* London 1989
COWDEN, J. *For the love of an eagle* Cape Town 1973
COWEN, C. ed. *The South African exhibition 1886* Cape Town 1886
COWEN, D.V. *Constitution-making for a democracy: an alternative to apartheid* Johannesburg 1960 [issued as a supplement to *Optima*]
COWIN, K. *Bushveld, bananas and bounty* London 1954
CRAIG, A. & HUMMEL, C. eds. see Roberts, M. tr.
CRESWICKE, L. *The life of the Right Honourable Joseph Chamberlain* 4 vols. London [preface dated 1904]
CROMPTON-LOMAX, E. *The South African menu and kitchen dictionary* Cape Town 1988
CRONIN, J. *Inside* Johannesburg 1983
CROUDACE, G. *The black rose* London 1968
——*The secret of the rock* Cape Town 1988
——*The silver grass* London 1968
Crux: a journal on the teaching of English (Foundation for Education, Science & Technology) Pretoria
CRWYS-WILLIAMS, J. ed. *South African Despatches: two centuries of the best in South African journalism* Johannesburg 1989
CSD Bulletin (Centre for Science Development) Pretoria 1992- (continuation of *Bulletin*)
CUBITT, G. & RICHTER, J. *South West* Cape Town 1976
'CUMBERLAND, S.' (Charles Garner) *What I think of South Africa; its people and its politics* London 1896
CUMMING, R.G.G. (R.G. Gordon Cumming) *Five years of a hunter's life in the far interior of South Africa* 2 vols. London 1850
——8th popular ed. 1911

DACHS, A.J. ed. see Mackenzie, J.
The Daily Dispatch East London 1925- (continuation of *East London Dispatch*)
Daily News Durban 1878- (with title *Natal Mercantile Advertiser* 1878-9 July 1886, *Natal Advertiser* 10 July 1886-5 Mar. 1887, *The Natal Advertiser and South African Mining Journal* 7 Mar. 1887-Dec. 1894, and *Natal Daily News* Aug. 1937-24 Mar. 1962; absorbed *Sunday Tribune* 1939-47; weekend ed. *Saturday News* merged with *Weekend Mercury* to form *Natal on Saturday*)
Daily News London 1846-
Daily Representative Queenstown 1927-78 (continuation of *Queenstown Daily Representative and Border Chronicle*)
DAMPIER, W. *A new voyage round the world* London 1698
DANE, P. *The great houses of Constantia* Cape Town 1981
Darling Durban
DAVENPORT, T.R.H. *South Africa: a modern history* London 1977
——2nd ed. Johannesburg 1978
DAVENPORT, T.R.H. & HUNT, K.S. eds. *The right to the land* Cape Town 1974
DAVIDSON, B. *Old Africa rediscovered* London 1970
——*Report on Southern Africa* London 1952
DAVIES, H. *Great South African Christians* Cape Town [1951]
DAVIES, R., O'MEARA, D., & DLAMINI, S. *The struggle for South Africa* 2 vols. London 1984
DAVIS, J.G. (J. Gordon Davis) *Hold my hand I'm dying* London 1969
——*The land God made in anger* London 1990
DAY, D. *The encyclopedia of vanished species* Hong Kong 1989
DAY, J.H. *A guide to marine life on South African shores* Cape Town 1969
DEDERICK, S. *Tickey* London 1965
DE KIEWIET, C.W. *A history of South Africa, social and economic* London 1941 (first publ. 1940)
——2nd ed. 1966
DE KLERK, W.A. *The white wines of South Africa* Cape Town 1967
DE KOCK, V. *The fun they had* Cape Town 1955
——*Those in bondage* Cape Town 1950
DE KOK, W.D. tr. *E.N. Marais's The soul of the white ant* reprint Harmondsworth, U.K. 1973 (first publ. 1937)
DELIUS, A. *Border* Cape Town 1976
——*The day Natal took off* Cape Town 1963
——*The last division* Cape Town 1959
——*The young traveller in South Africa* London 1955
DE MIST, J.A.U. *Diary of a journey to the Cape of Good Hope and interior of Africa in 1802 and 1803* Cape Town 1954

SELECT BIBLIOGRAPHY

DE MOSENTHAL, J. & HARTING, J.E. *Ostriches and ostrich farming* London 1877
DENNISON, C.G. *A fight to the finish* London 1904
DENT, G.R. & NYEMBEZI, C.L.S. *Scholar's Zulu dictionary* Pietermaritzburg 1969
DE RIDDER, J. *Sad laughter memories: two novellas of old Sophiatown* Johannesburg 1983
DESAI, V.G. tr. *M.K. Gandhi's Satyagraha in South Africa* reprint Madras 1950
DESMOND, C. *The discarded people* Johannesburg [c.1970]
DEVEREUX, R. *Side lights on South Africa* London 1899
DE V. PIENAAR, U. see Pienaar, U. de V.
DE VILLIERS, H.H.W. *Rivonia: Operation Mayibuye* Johannesburg 1964
DE VILLIERS, M., SMUTS, J., & EKSTEEN, L.C. *Nasionale woordeboek* 3rd ed. rev. & enlarged Cape Town 1977
DE VILLIERS, S.A. *Robben Island: out of reach, out of mind* Cape Town 1971
DE VILLIERS, S.J.A. *Cook and enjoy it* Johannesburg 1969
DEVITT, N. *The blue lizard and other stories of native life in South Africa* Pretoria 1928
—— *Celebrated South African crimes* Durban 1941
—— *The concentration camps in South Africa during the Anglo-Boer war of 1899–1902* Pietermaritzburg 1941
—— *Memories of a magistrate, including twenty-five years on the South African Bench* London 1934
—— *People and places: sketches from South African history* Cape Town 1945
De Volks(s)tem see under 'V'
DE VOS HUGO, D. see Hugo, D. de Vos
DE WET, C.R. *Three years war* Westminster, U.K. 1902
DHLOMO, H.I.E. see Visser, N. & Couzens, T. eds.
DHLOMO, R.R.R. *An African tragedy* Lovedale, Eastern Cape [c.1928]
DICKE, B.H. *The bush speaks: border life in old Transvaal* Pietermaritzburg 1937
A dictionary of American English on historical principles ed. by W.A. Craigie & J.R. Hulbert 4 vols. Chicago 1938–44
A dictionary of Canadianisms on historical principles ed. by W.S. Avis et al. Toronto 1967
A dictionary of English usage in Southern Africa ed. by D.R. Beeton & H. Dorner Cape Town 1975
Dictionary of horticulture with plant names (National Terminology Services, Department of National Education) Pretoria 1991
Dictionary of Jamaican English ed. by F.G. Cassidy & R.B. Le Page London 1967
—— 2nd ed. 1980
Dictionary of Newfoundland English ed. by G.M. Story, W.J. Kirwin, & J.D.A. Widdowson Toronto 1982
Die Volkstem see under 'V'
Diggers' ditties: a selection from the literary scribblings of early Kimberley residents (compiled by Africana Library, Kimberley) Cape Town 1989
DIKE, F. *The first South African* Johannesburg 1979
DIKOBE, M. *The marabi dance*. 1970. Typescript. Dictionary Unit
Diseases and pests affecting sheep and goats in South Africa (Cooper & Nephews SA (Pty) Ltd) 5th ed. Johannesburg c.1929
DISTANT, W.L. *A naturalist in the Transvaal* London 1892
DIXIE, Lady Florence Caroline *In the land of misfortune* London 1882
DOBIE, J.S. *South African journal* ed. by A.F. Hattersley Cape Town 1945 (Van Riebeeck Society)
DODD, A.D. ed. *Anthology of short stories by South African writers* Cape Town [?1958]
DÖHNE, J.L. *A Zulu-Kafir dictionary* Cape Town 1857
—— facsimile reprint Farnborough, U.K. 1967
DOKE, C.M. & VILIKAZI, B.W. eds. *Zulu-English dictionary* 2nd ed. Johannesburg 1953 (first publ. 1948)
DOKE, J.J. *M.K. Gandhi: an Indian patriot in South Africa* London 1909
—— *The secret city* London 1913
DONALD, J.M. see Bullock, J.B. ed.
DOUGHTY, O. *Early diamond days: the opening of the diamond fields of South Africa* London 1963
DOUGLAS, R.G.S. ed. see Mazikana, P.C. & Johnstone, I.J.
DOUGLASS, A. *Ostrich farming in South Africa* London [preface dated 1881]
DOYLE, A.C. *The great Boer War* London 1900
—— 16th impression 1902
DOYLE, M. *Impala* London 1968
DRAYSON, A.W. *Sporting scenes amongst the Kaffirs of South Africa* London 1860
DRISCOLL, P. *Wilby Conspiracy* [?no place] 1972
DRIVER, C.J. *In the water-margins* Cape Town 1994
—— *Patrick Duncan: South African and Pan-African* London 1980

Drum Johannesburg 1951– (with title *African Drum* Mar. 1951–Jan. 1952)
DRUMMOND, E. *The burning land* Cape Town 1979
DRUMMOND, J. *The saboteurs* London 1967
DRUMMOND, J.H. *Diary. 1908*. Typescript ed. by D. Child, 1993. Private collection
DUCKITT, H.J. *Hilda's 'Where is it?' of recipes* London 1891
—— see also Kuttel, M. ed.
DUFF-GORDON, L., Lady *Letters from the Cape 1861-2* ed. by H.J. Anderson Cape Town [1925]
—— see also Galton, F. ed.
DUGGAN-CRONIN, A.M. *The Bantu tribes of South Africa* [photographic studies] 4 vols.
—— Vol. I Sect. I *The Bavenda* by G.P. Lestrade 1928; Vol. II *The Suto-Chuana Tribes* Sect. I *The Bechuana* by G.P. Lestrade 1929, Sect. II *The Bapedi (Transvaal Basotho)* by W. Eiselen 1931, Sect. III *The Southern Basotho* by G.P. Lestrade 1933; Vol. III *The Nguni* introd. by N.J. Van Warmelo, Sect. I *The Ciskei and Southern Transkei Tribes (Xhosa and Thembu)* by W.G. Bennie 1939, Sect. II *The Mpondo and Mpondomise* by M. Wilson 1949, Sect. III *The Zulu* by D. McK. Malcolm 1938, Sect. IV *The Swazi* by H. Beemer 1941, Sect. V *Baca, Hlubi, Xesibe* by W.D. Hammond-Tooke 1954; Vol. IV Sect. I *The Vathonga (the Thonga-Shangaan people)* by H.P. Junod 1935, Sect. II *The Vachopi of Portuguese East Africa* by H.P. Junod 1936 Cambridge, U.K. (Alexander McGregor Memorial Museum, Kimberley)
DUGMORE, E.J. Diary of Eliza Jane Dugmore, 1871. An account of a trip by ox wagon from Koonap to Vetberg in Albania. Private collection
DUGMORE, H.H. *Reminiscences of an Albany settler* Grahamstown 1871 [quotations are from a lecture delivered in May 1870]
—— *Reminiscences of an Albany settler ... together with his recollections of the Kaffir war of 1835* ed. by F.G. Van der Riet & L.A. Hewson Grahamstown 1958
—— see also Maclean, J.
DUMINY, A.H. & ADCOCK, L.J.G. eds. see Paver, R.
Dunell, Ebden & Co. Port Elizabeth price list [Port Elizabeth] Aug. 1919–July 1920
DU P. BOTHMA, J. see Bothma, J. du P. ed.
DU PLESSIS, I.D. *The Cape Malays* Cape Town 1944
DU PLESSIS, I.D. & LÜCKHOFF, C.A. *The Malay quarter and its people* Cape Town 1953
DU PLESSIS, J. *A thousand miles in the heart of Africa* Cape Town 1905
DU PLESSIS, M. *A state of fear* Cape Town 1983
DU TOIT, A. & GILIOMEE, H. *Afrikaner political thought 1780–1850* Vol. I Johannesburg 1983
DU TOIT, P.J. *Diary of a national scout* ed. by J.P. Brits Pretoria 1974
DUTTON, F.H. tr. *T. Mofolo's Chaka: an historical romance* London 1931
DU VAL, C. *With a show through Southern Africa* 2 vols. London 1882
Dynamic change in South Africa (Department of Foreign Affairs & Information) Pretoria 1980

Eastern Province Herald Port Elizabeth 1845– (until 1898 with title *The Eastern Province Herald and Port Elizabeth Commercial News*)
Eastern Province year book and annual register for 1861 Grahamstown 1861
The Eastern Star Grahamstown 1871–89 (publ. in Johannesburg from 1887; continued by *The Star*)
East London Dispatch East London 1872–1925 (with title *East London Daily Dispatch (and Frontier Advertiser)* from 1898; continued by *The Daily Dispatch*)
EATON, S.N. Journal from Sarah Norman Eaton from leaving London, June 22nd, 1818 and of a voyage to the Cape of Good Hope on board the 'Garland' ... and from her arrival at the Cape of Good Hope 26 September 1818. Mimeograph. South African Library
EBERSOHN, W. *A lonely place to die* London 1979
The Echo: a literary, scientific and critical magazine ed. by A.G. Campbell Grahamstown 1840
ECKLON, C.F. & ZEYHER, C. *Enumeratio Plantarum Africae, Australis Extratropicae quae exhibent, determinatae et expositae a Christiano Fredrico Ecklon et Carolo Zeyher* Hamburg 1837
The Economist measurement guide and reckoner London 1975
EDELSTEIN, M.L. *What do young Africans think?* (South African Institute of Race Relations) Johannesburg 1972
EDGECOMBE, D.R. Letters of Hannah Dennison 1820 Settler. M.A. thesis, Rhodes University, 1968
EDMONDS, H. & MARLOTH, R. *Elementary botany of South Africa, theoretical and practical* London 1897

EDMONSTONE, F.J. *Where mists still linger* Johannesburg [1952]
EDWARDS, D. *A plant-ecological survey of the Tugela river basin* (Town & Regional Planning Commission, Natal) [no place] 1967 (Botanical Survey of South Africa Memoir No. 36)
EGLINGTON, C. tr. *E. Leroux's One for the Devil* Boston 1968
The 1820 Johannesburg 1938–83 (continued by *The Settler*)
ELIOVSON, S. *Flowering shrubs and trees for South African gardens* Cape Town 1951
ELLIOTT, Arthur *South Africa through the centuries ... 1000 photographs* Cape Town 1930
ELLIOTT, Aubrey *Sons of Zulu* London 1978
ELLIS, A.B. *South African sketches* London 1887
ELPHICK, R. *Kraal and castle: Khoikhoi and the founding of white South Africa* Yale, U.S.A. 1977
EMSLIE, E. Diary. 1901. National English Literary Museum manuscript collection 091EMS
ENDFIELD, C. *Zulu dawn* London 1979
ENGELBRECHT, T. see Tweehuizen, M. tr.
The English Academy review (The English Academy of Southern Africa) Johannesburg
English Alive: an anthology for high schools – a selection of the best school writing of the year (South African Council for English Education) Constantia, Cape Town
The English dialect dictionary ed. by J. Wright 6 vols. London 1898–1905
English in Africa (Institute for the Study of English in Africa) Grahamstown
English usage in South Africa (University of South Africa) Pretoria 1970–
—— see also *A dictionary of English usage in Southern Africa*
Enterprise Johannesburg 1990– (continuation of *Black Enterprise*)
Entertaining with wines of the Cape (Ko-operatieve Wijnbouwers Vereniging van Zuid-Afrika Beperkt) Paarl 1968
'ERASMUS, S.' (D. Blackburn) *Prinsloo of Prinsloosdorp* London 1899
ESSOP, A. *The Hajji and other stories* Johannesburg 1978
ESSOP et al. *Challenge to the 25 Natal Moolvies on Palan Haggani* Durban 1969
Estcourt High School Magazine Estcourt 1990
ESTERHUYSE, C.J. *Protea species: tree of the year 1986* Pretoria 1986 (Department of Environment Affairs pamphlet 359)
EVANS, M.S. *Black and white in South East Africa* London 1911
'E.V.C.' *The promised land* London 1884
EVELEIGH, W. *South-West Africa* Cape Town 1915
Evening Post Port Elizabeth ?1947– (with Saturday ed. *Weekend Post* from 1963)
EWART, J. Journal covering his stay at the Cape of Good Hope 1811–14 with an introduction by A. Gordon-Brown Cape Town 1970
EYBERS, G.W. ed. *Select constitutional documents illustrating South African history* New York 1918

FAIRBRIDGE, D. *Gardens of South Africa* London 1924
—— *Piet of Italy* London 1913
—— *That which hath been* Cape Town 1913 (first publ. 1910)
—— *The torch bearer* Cape Town 1915
—— ed. *Lady Anne Barnard at the Cape of Good Hope* Oxford, U.K. 1924
Fair Lady Cape Town
FALLER, F. *Weather words* Johannesburg 1986
Family Radio & T.V. Durban (continued by *Personality*)
FARINI, G.A. *Through the Kalahari desert* London 1886
Farmers' Annual of South Africa Bloemfontein 1914
(*The*) *Farmer's Weekly* Durban 1911–
Farming in South Africa (Department of Agriculture) Pretoria
FARRAN, R. *Jungle chase* London 1957 (first publ. 1951)
FARRANT, J. *Mashonaland martyr: Bernard Mizeki and the Pioneer church* Cape Town 1966
FEBRUARY, V.A. *Mind your colour* London 1981
Femina Cape Town
FERREIRA, N. *The story of an Afrikaner* Johannesburg 1980
Fighting Forces of Rhodesia No. 4 Salisbury, Rhodesia [Harare, Zimbabwe] 1977
Financial Mail Johannesburg 1959–
FISH, R.L. *Rough diamond* London 1983
FITZPATRICK, J.P. *Jock of the bushveld* London 1909
—— *The outspan* London 1897
—— *The Transvaal from within* London 1899
FITZROY, V.M. *Cabbages and cream* London [1948]

―――*Dark bright land* Cape Town 1955
FITZSIMONS, V.F.M. *Snakes of Southern Africa* Cape Town 1962
FIVAZ, D. *Towards explanation in African linguistics* [inaugural lecture, Rhodes University] Grahamstown 1974
FLATHER, H. *Thaba Rau* Cape Town [c.1976]
FLEMING, F.P. see Flemyng, F.P.
FLEMMING, L.D. *A crop of chaff* 2nd ed. Pietermaritzburg 1925 (first publ. 1924)
―――*A fool on the veld* 5th ed. Bloemfontein 1933 (first publ. 1916)
―――*Fun on the veld* London 1928 (first publ. 1926)
―――*A settler's scribblings in South Africa* Pietermaritzburg 1921 (first publ. 1910)
FLEMYNG, F.P. (Francis Fleming) *Kaffraria, and its inhabitants* London 1853
―――*Southern Africa: a geography and natural history of the country, colonies, and inhabitants from the Cape of Good Hope to Angola* London 1856
FLINT, W. & GILCHRIST, J.D.F. eds. *Science in South Africa* Cape Town 1905
Flying Springbok (South African Airways) Johannesburg
Focus on Africa (British Broadcasting Corporation) London 1990-
FORBES, V.S. ed. *Carl Peter Thunberg travels at the Cape of Good Hope 1772-1775* with revised tr. by J. & I. Rudner Cape Town 1986 (Van Riebeeck Society)
FORD, E.B. *The waterfalls: a phantasy of Basutoland* [bardic gold medal poem, South African Eisteddfod 1924] Basutoland [Lesotho] c.1924
FORSTER, G. *A voyage round the world ... during the years 1772, 3, 4, & 5* London 1777
―――tr. *A. Sparrman's Voyage to the Cape of Good Hope from the year 1772, to 1776* [translated 1785] 2nd ed. 2 vols. London 1786 [acc. to some sources, this text was prob. tr. by C.R. Hopson]
FORSYTH INGRAM, J. see Ingram, J.F.
Forum (Students' Representative Council, Rhodes University) Vol. 6 No. 2 Grahamstown 1970
Forum (title varies as *The Forum: South Africa's first national review* and *The Forum: South Africa's independent weekly news-magazine*) Johannesburg
FOUCHE, L. ed. see Fuller, C.
FOUCHÉ, R. & CURREY, W.M. *Housecraft for primary schools* London 1941
FOURIE, L. see *The native tribes of South West Africa*
FOX, F.W. & NORWOOD YOUNG, M.E. *Food from the veld* Johannesburg 1982
FRACK, I. *A South African doctor looks backwards – and forward* Johannesburg 1943
A fragment of church history at the Cape of Good Hope see Jardine, A.J.
FRANKLIN, J.S. *This union* Cape Town 1949
FRANSEN, H. *The Stellenbosch museum* Stellenbosch 1967
FRANSEN, H. & COOK, M.A. *The old houses of the Cape* Cape Town 1965
FRASER, B. *Sunshine and lamplight* Cape Town [1957]
FRASER, M. ed. *Johannesburg pioneer journals 1888-1909* Cape Town 1985 (Van Riebeeck Society)
FREDERIKSE, J. *None but ourselves* Johannesburg 1982
FREED, L.F. *Crime in South Africa* Cape Town 1963
FREEMAN, J.J. *A tour in South Africa* London 1851
FREMANTLE, H.E.S. *The new nation* London 1909
FREWER, E.E. tr. *E. Holub's Seven years in South Africa* London 1881
The Friend Bloemfontein 1896-1900; 1902-85
FROES, T. *Kruger & Co., Limited, the Pretoria illicit gold buying firm and the Africander Bond's connexion therewith* Cape Town 1900
Frontline Johannesburg 1979-91
FRYE, J. ed. see Appleyard, J.W.
FRYKE, C. (or FRICK, C.) & SCHWEITZER, C. see 'S.L.' tr.
FUGARD, A. *The blood knot* Johannesburg 1968
―――*Boesman and Lena* Cape Town 1969
―――*Dimetos and two early plays* London 1977
―――*Hello and goodbye* Cape Town 1971 (first publ. 1966)
―――*Notebooks 1960-1977* Johannesburg 1983
―――*People are living there* Cape Town 1969
―――*Tsotsi* Johannesburg 1980
FUGARD, A. & DEVENISH, R. *The guest* Johannesburg 1977
FUGARD, A., KANI, J., & NTSHONA, W. *Statements* Cape Town 1974
FUGARD, S.M. *The castaways* Johannesburg 1972
―――*Rite of passage* Johannesburg 1976
FULLER, B. *Call back yesterday* Cape Town 1953
FULLER, C. *Louis Trigardt's trek across the Drakensberg 1837-8* ed. by L. Fouche Cape Town 1932 (Van Riebeeck Society)
FULTON, A. *The dark side of mercy* Cape Town 1968

―――*I swear to Apollo* Cape Town 1970
FYNN, H.F. Diary. 1850. Typescript. Killie Campbell Africana Library MS22895
―――Letters. 1846-61. [include correspondence with D. Erskine, G.W. Mackinnon, the Secretary to Government for Native Affairs, I.J. Smith, R.B. Struthers, & C.H. Williams] Killie Campbell Africana Library MS2288

GALSWORTHY, J. *The Forsyte saga* London 1922
GALTON, F. *The narrative of an explorer in tropical South Africa* London 1853
―――*Travels in South Africa. Narrative of an explorer in tropical South Africa (being an account of a visit to Damaraland in 1851) ...* London 1889
―――ed. *Vacation tourists and notes of travel* 3 vols. (Vol. III *Letters from the Cape* by Lady Duff-Gordon) London 1864
GANDHI, M.K. see Desai, V.G. tr.
GARDEN, R.J. Diary. 1851-53. Typescript. Killie Campbell Africana Library MS29081
Gardening questions answered see *Your gardening questions answered*
GARDINER, A.F. Fragments from family documents. 1838. Typescript. Killie Campbell Africana Library KCM8716
―――*A journey to the Zoolu country* London 1836
GARRETT, A.E.F. ed. *South African Methodism* Cape Town [no date]
GARSTIN, C. *The sunshine settlers* London 1918
GAUGAIN, P. Diary, copies of letters, etc. 1821-31. Albany Museum history division 2720
GEEN, M.S. *The making of the Union of South Africa* London 1946
The general directory and guide book to the Cape of Good Hope (and its dependencies ...) Cape Town 1869-87 (continuation of *The Cape Town directory*; continued by *The Argus annual and Cape of Good Hope directory ...*)
The George Advertiser George 1864-70
George and Knysna Herald George 1881-1971 (continued by *The South Western Herald*)
GERBER, H. *Cape cookery old and new* Cape Town 1950
―――*Fish fare for South Africans: being a comprehensive guide to the correct cookery of all fish found round our coasts* Cape Town 1945
GIBBON, P. *Margaret Harding* London 1911
―――*The vrouw Grobelaar's leading cases* London 1905
GIBBS, H. *Twilight in South Africa* London [1950]
GIBBS, P. *The history of the BSAP* 2 vols. (Vol. I *The first line of defence 1889-1903*, Vol. II *The right of line 1903-1939*) Salisbury, Rhodesia [Harare, Zimbabwe] 1972-74
GIBBS RUSSEL, G.E. et al. *Grasses of Southern Africa* (Botanical Research Institute, National Botanic Gardens) [Pretoria] 1991 (Memoirs of the Botanical Survey of South Africa No. 58)
GIBSON, G.F. *The story of the Imperial Light Horse in the South African War 1899-1902* Johannesburg 1937
GIBSON, J.M. *Wild flowers of Natal (coastal region)* Durban 1975
GIBSON, J.Y. *The Kap-tent wagon* Cape Town 1919 (reprinted from *South African Journal of Science*, July 1919)
GIFFARD, A. ed. see Montgomery, J.
GILL, E.L. *A first guide to South African birds* Cape Town 1936
GILLESPIE, A. *Gleanings and remarks: collected during many months of residence at Buenos Ayres ... with a prefatory account of the expedition from England, until the surrender of the Colony of the Cape of Good Hope* Leeds, U.K. 1818
GILLMORE, P. *The great thirst land* London [1878]
―――*The land of the boer* London [1881]
GLANVILLE, E. *A fair colonist* London 1894
―――*Tales from the veld* London 1897
Gleanings in Africa: exhibiting a faithful and correct view of the names and customs of the inhabitants of the Cape of Good Hope ... in a series of letters from an English officer (anon.) London 1806
GLOSSOP, A. ed. see Barnes, A.R.
GODBOLD, B. Autobiography. 1989. Private collection
GODFREY, D. *The enchanted door* Cape Town 1963
GODLEY, R.S. *Khaki and blue* London 1935
GODLONTON, R. *Memorials of the British settlers of South Africa* Grahamstown 1844
―――facsimile reprint Cape Town 1971
―――*Introductory remarks to a narrative of the irruption of the Kafir hordes into the Eastern Province of the Cape of Good Hope 1834-35* Cape Town 1836
―――*A narrative of the irruption of the Kaffir hordes into the Eastern Province of the Cape of Good Hope 1834-35* Grahamstown 1836

―――facsimile reprint Cape Town 1965
―――*Sketches of the Eastern districts of the Cape of Good Hope* Grahamstown 1842
Golden City Post see *Post*
Golden City Press Johannesburg 1982-83 (continued by *City Press*)
Golden Fleece/Goue Vag (South African Wool Board) Pretoria
GOLDIE, F. *Ostrich country* Cape Town [1968]
―――*River of gold* Cape Town 1969
GOLDSTUCK, A. *The rabbit in the thorn tree* Johannesburg 1990
GOLDSWAIN, J. *The chronicle of Jeremiah Goldswain Albany settler of 1820* ed. by U. Long 2 vols. Cape Town 1946-49 (Van Riebeeck Society)
GOOL, R. *Cape Town coolie* Oxford, U.K. 1990
GOOLD-ADAMS, R.J.M. *South Africa to-day and to-morrow* London 1936
GORDIMER, N. *A guest of honour* London 1971
GORDON, G. *Four people* London 1964
GORDON, G. & W. trs. *F.A. Venter's Dark pilgrim* London 1959
GORDON, R.J. see Raper, P.E. tr.
GORDON-BROWN, A. *An artist's journey* Cape Town 1972
―――*Guide to Southern Africa 1967* Cape Town 1966
―――*The settlers' press* Cape Town 1979
―――*South African heritage* 5 vols. Cape Town 1965
―――*South African yearbook and guide* London 1957
―――*The year book and guide to Southern Africa* London 1951
―――*The year book and guide to Southern Africa 1960* London 1959
―――*The year book and guide to Southern Africa 1965* London 1964
―――ed. see Adams, B.
―――see also Ewart, J.
GORDON CUMMING, R.G. see Cumming, R.G.G.
GORDON DAVIS, J. see Davis, J.G.
GOUGH, D. *Issues in the semantics and pragmatics of Xhosa questions* (Department of African Languages, Rhodes University) Grahamstown 1982
GOVENDER, R. *Lahnee's Pleasure* Johannesburg 1980
Government Gazette/Staatskoerant (Union of South Africa 1910-61; Republic of South Africa 1961-) Pretoria 1910-
―――see also *Cape of Good Hope Government Gazette*
The Graham's Town Journal, or, Cape of Good Hope Eastern Provincial Register see *The Journal*
Grahamstown Training College Magazine Grahamstown
The grasses and pastures of South Africa see Meredith, D. ed.
GRATUS, J. *The Jo'burgers* London 1979
GRAY, R. *A journal of the Bishop's visitation tour through the Cape Colony, in 1848* Part I London 1849
―――*A journal of the Bishop's visitation tour through the Cape Colony, in 1850* Part II London 1851
―――*A journal of a visitation to the diocese of Graham's Town, in July and August, 1856* London 1857
GRAY, S. *Caltrop's desire* Cape Town 1981
―――*Local colour* Johannesburg 1975
―――ed. *Makapan's caves* Harmondsworth, U.K. 1987
―――ed. *Market plays* Johannesburg 1986
―――ed. *Mhudi* see Plaatje, S.T.
―――ed. *On the edge of the world* Johannesburg 1974
―――ed. *Stephen Black: three plays* Johannesburg 1984
―――ed. *Theatre one* Johannesburg 1978 (includes *Paradise is closing down* by P-D. Uys, and works by H.C. Bosman, F. Dike, A. Fugard, & D. Livingstone)
―――ed. *Theatre two* (includes works by G. Aron, C. Hope, Junction Avenue Theatre Co., & P-D. Uys) Johannesburg 1981
―――ed. *Three plays* see *Stephen Black: three plays*
―――ed. *Writers' territory* Cape Town 1973
The greater dictionary of Xhosa ed. by H.W. Pahl, A.M. Pienaar, & T.A. Ndungane Vol. III Alice, Eastern Cape 1989
GREEN, G.A.L. *An editor looks back* Cape Town 1947
GREEN, L.G. *Beyond the city lights* Cape Town 1957
―――*Full many a glorious morning* Cape Town 1968
―――*A giant in hiding: the life story of Frank Armstrong Wightman* Cape Town 1970
―――*Grow lovely, growing old* Cape Town 1951
―――*I heard the old men say* Cape Town 1964
―――*In the land of afternoon* Cape Town 1959
―――*Karoo* Cape Town 1955
―――*Lords of the last frontier* Cape Town 1952
―――*Secret Africa* London 1936
―――reprint [Cape Town] 1974
―――*So few are free* Cape Town 1946
―――*South African beachcomber* Cape Town 1958
―――*Strange Africa* Cape Town 1938 (first publ. 1934)

SELECT BIBLIOGRAPHY

———A taste of South-Easter Cape Town 1971
———Tavern of the seas Cape Town 1947
———There's a secret hid away Cape Town 1956
———These wonders to behold Cape Town 1959
———To the river's end Cape Town 1948
———Under a sky like flame Cape Town 1954
———When the journey's over Cape Town 1972
———Where men still dream Cape Town 1945
GREENE, L.P. *The L. Patrick Greene adventure omnibus* London [1928]
GREENLEES, M. tr. *O.F. Mentzel's Life at the Cape in the mid-eighteenth century: being the biography of Rudolf Siegfried Allemann* Cape Town 1919 (Van Riebeeck Society)
GREGERSEN, E.A. *Language in Africa: an introductory survey* New York 1975
GRENFELL WILLIAMS, J. see Williams, J.G.
GRIFFITH, K. *Thank God we kept the flag flying: the siege and relief of Ladysmith 1899-1900* London 1974
GRIFFITHS, R. *Children of pride* London 1959
———*The grey about the flame* London [1951]
———*Man of the river* London 1968
———*This day's madness* London 1960
GRINDLEY, J.R. *Riches of the sea* Cape Town 1969
GRINNELL-MILNE, D. *Baden-Powell at Mafeking* London 1957
GROBLER, J. *A decisive clash: a short history of Black protest politics in South Africa 1875-1976* Pretoria 1988
Grocott's Mail Grahamstown 1870- (with title *Grocott's Free Paper* 1870-71, *Grocott's Penny Mail* 1872-Feb. 1899 and July 1901-Apr. 1920, and *Grocott's Daily Mail* Feb.-Dec. 1899 and May 1920-64; absorbed *The Journal* in 1920)
Groot Noord-Sotho woordeboek, Noord-Sotho, Afrikaans, Engels ed. by D. Ziervogel & P.C. Mokgokong Pretoria 1975
GROUT, L. *Zulu-land; or, life among the Zulu-Kafirs of Natal and Zulu-land, South Africa* London a.1864
The Guardian Weekly London 1968-
———Southern African ed. see *The Weekly Mail*
A guide to the vertebrate fauna of the Eastern Cape Province (Albany Museum) 2 parts (Part I *Mammals and birds*, Part II *Reptiles, amphibians, and freshwater fishes*) Grahamstown 1931-37
GUTSCHE, T. *There was a man* Cape Town 1979
GWALA, M.P. *Jol'iinkomo* Johannesburg 1977

HAAGNER, A. & IVY, R.H. *Sketches of South African bird life* Cape Town 1908
———3rd rev. ed. 1923
HACKSLEY, M.M. tr. *E. Van Heerden's Ancestral voices* London 1989
HAGGARD, H.R. (H. Rider Haggard) *Benita* London 1906
———*King Solomon's mines* London 1885
———another ed. Moscow 1972
———*Nada the lily* London 1895
———*Queen Sheba's ring* London 1910
———*She* London 1914
HAHN, C.H.L. see *The native tribes of South West Africa*
HAHN, T. *Tsuni-‖Goam: the Supreme Being of the Khoi-khoi* London 1881
HALL-MARTIN, A., WALKER, C., & BOTHMA, J. DU P. *Kaokoveld: the last wilderness* Johannesburg 1988
HALLS, J.J. *The life and correspondence of Henry Salt, esq. FRS* 2 vols. London 1834
HAMILTON, C.E. *Sketches of life and sport in South-Eastern Africa* London 1870
HAMMOND-TOOKE, W.D. *Bhaca society* Cape Town 1962
———see also Duggan-Cronin, A.M.
HANCOCK, J. Diary. 1820-37. Albany Museum history division SMD9 [catalogued as 'Journal']
HANCOCK, W.K. *Smuts* 2 vols. (Vol. I *The sanguine years 1870-1919*, Vol. II *The fields of force 1919-1950*) Cambridge, U.K. 1962-68
Handbook and Guide (Royal Automobile Club of South Africa) 1938
Handbook for farmers in South Africa (Department of Agriculture (& Forestry)) Pretoria 1929
———new ed. 1937
———new ed. 3 vols. 1957
Handbook of the Mines and Works Act of the Union ... and the Mines Works and Machinery Regulations Johannesburg 1954
A handbook on wine for retail licensees (Ko-operatieve Wijnbouwers Vereniging van Zuid-Afrika Beperkt) Paarl [no date]
HANKS, J. *Mammals of Southern Africa* Johannesburg 1976
Hansard see Republic of South Africa. Parliament. House of Assembly. Debates (1961-); also Union of South Africa. Parliament. House of Assembly. Debates (1910-61) [Note The name *Hansard* is used in quotations to refer to South African parliamentary debates since Union in 1910]
HARRIS, P. *Some small compassion* Cape Town 1964
HARRIS, W.C. *Wild sports of Southern Africa* London 1839
HART, R.C. *Plankton, fish and man: a triplet in limnology* [inaugural lecture, Rhodes University] Grahamstown 1986
HARTMANN, M. *Shadow of the leopard* London 1978
HARVEY, W.H. *The genera of South African plants* Cape Town 1868
H.A.T.: verklarende handwoordeboek van die Afrikaanse taal ed. by P.C. Schoonees, C.J. Swanepoel, S.J. Du Toit, & C.M. Booysen Johannesburg 1965
———2nd edition ed. by F.F. Odendal et al. Johannesburg 1983
HATTERSLEY, A.F. ed. see Dobie, J.S.
HATTINGH, A. *Wine: a guide for young people* (Ko-operatieve Wijnbouwers Vereniging van Zuid-Afrika Beperkt) Paarl 1975
HATTINGH, J.L. & BREDEKAMP, H.C. eds. *Coloured viewpoint: a series of articles in the Cape Times, 1958-1965 by R.E. van der Ross* (The Western Cape Institute for Historical Research, University of the Western Cape) Bellville 1984
HAWKESWORTH, J. *An account of the voyages undertaken ... for making discoveries in the southern hemisphere, and successively performed by Commodore Byron, Captain Wallis, Captain Carteret, and Captain Cook ... : drawn up from the journals which were kept by the several commanders and from the papers of Joseph Banks* 3 vols. London 1773
HEADLAM, C. ed. *The Milner papers South Africa 1897-9* [Vol. I] London 1931
———ed. *The Milner papers South Africa 1899-1905* Vol. II London 1933
HEALE, J. *Scowlers's luck: an adventure in the Fish River Canyon* Pretoria 1990
HEARD, V. & FAULL, L. *Our best traditional recipes* Cape Town 1979
HEATON NICHOLLS, G. see Nicholls, G.H.
HECKFORD, S. *A lady trader in the Transvaal* London 1882
Heinemann New Zealand dictionary ed. by H.W. Orsman et al. Auckland 1982
HELLER, D. *In search of VOC glass* Cape Town 1951
HELLMANN, E. *Rooiyard: a sociological study of an urban native slum yard* Cape Town 1948
———ed. *Handbook on race relations in South Africa* (South African Institute of Race Relations) Cape Town 1949
HELME, E. tr. *F. Le Vaillant's Travels from the Cape of Good-Hope, into the interior parts of Africa* 2 vols. London 1790
———see also Le Vaillant, F.
HEMINGWAY, E. *Green hills of Africa* St Albans, U.K. 1977 (first publ. 1936; quotations are taken from the 1977 ed., but dated simply 1895)
HENDERSON, M. & ANDERSON, J.G. *Common weeds in South Africa* (Department of Agricultural Technical Services) Pretoria 1966
HENNING, C.G. *Graaff-Reinet: a cultural history 1786-1886* Cape Town 1975
HENSHILWOOD, N. *A Cape childhood* Cape Town 1972
Herald: George and Knysna see *George and Knysna Herald*
The Herald Phoenix George 1979- (continuation of *The South Western Herald*)
HERMER, C. *The diary of Maria Tholo* Johannesburg 1980
HERRMAN, L. ed. see Isaacs, N.
Het Suid-Western see *Oudtshoorn Courant and Het Suid-Western*
HEWITT, A.G. *Cape cookery* Cape Town 1890
HEWSON, L.A. & VAN DER RIET, F.G. eds. see Ayliff, J.; also Dugmore, H.H.
HEYER, A.E. *A brief history of the Transvaal secret service system* Cape Town 1899
HICKS, B.M. *The Cape as I found it* London 1900
HIGHAM, M. *Household cookery for South Africa* 8th ed. Johannesburg 1939
———9th ed. Johannesburg 1941
HILLEGAS, H.C. *Oom Paul's people* New York 1900
HINCHLIFF, P.B. ed. see Ayliff, J.
HOBBS, J. *Thoughts in a makeshift mortuary* London 1989
HOBHOUSE, E. *The brunt of war and where it fell* London 1902
HOBMAN, D.L. *Olive Schreiner: her friends and times* London 1955
Hobson-Jobson: a glossary of Anglo-Indian colloquial words and phrases, and of kindred terms, etymological, historical, geographical and discursive ed. by H. Yule & A.C. Burnell London 1886
———new edition ed. by W. Crooke London 1903
———reprint London 1969

HOCKING, A. *Diamonds* Cape Town 1973 ('Pride of South Africa Series' No. 2)
HOCKLY, H.E. *The story of the British settlers of 1820 in South Africa* Cape Town 1948
HODSON, A.W. *Trekking the Great Thirst: travel and sport in the Kalahari desert* London 1912
HOERNLÉ, R.F.A. *South African native policy and the liberal spirit* Cape Town 1939
HOLDEN, W.C. *The past and future of the Kaffir races* London [preface dated 1866]
———facsimile reprint Cape Town 1963
HOLM, J.A. & SHILLING, A.W. *Dictionary of Bahamian English* New York 1982
HOLUB, E. see Frewer, E.E. tr.
The Homefinder Durban
HONE, M. *Sarah-Elizabeth* London 1945
HOOK, D.B. *'Tis but yesterday* London 1911
HOOKER, J.D. ed. see Banks, J.
HOOKER, W.J. *Botanical Miscellany* 3 vols. (Vols II & III include *Biographical notice of the late Captain Dugald Carmichael* by C. Smith) London 1831
HOOPER, C. *Brief authority* London 1960
HOPE, C. *Cape drives* London 1974
———*The Hottentot room* London 1987
———*Private parts* Johannesburg 1981
———new ed. London 1982
———another ed. London 1984 (quotations are mostly taken from the 1984 ed., but dated simply 1982)
———*A separate development* London 1983
HOPSON, C.R. tr. *C.P. Thunberg's Travels in Europe, Africa and Asia, made between the years 1770 and 1779* 2nd ed. 4 vols. London 1795
———3rd ed. 4 vols. London 1795-96
———see also Forster, G.
HORNE, C. *Fisherman's Eldorado* Cape Town [1955]
HORRELL, M. *Action, reaction, and counter-action: a brief review of non-white political movements in South Africa* (South African Institute of Race Relations) Johannesburg 1963
———*The African homelands of South Africa* (South African Institute of Race Relations) Johannesburg 1973
———*South Africa: basic facts and figures* (South African Institute of Race Relations) Johannesburg 1973
———*South African trade unionism* (South African Institute of Race Relations) Johannesburg 1961
House and Leisure Cape Town
'A HOUSEWIFE OF THE COLONY' *Colonial household guide* Cape Town 1889
HOYLE, J. *Some flowers of the bush* London 1953
HUDDLESTON, T. *Naught for your comfort* London 1956
HUDSON, M.B. *A feature in South African frontier life, based upon the wanderings of a frontier family* Port Elizabeth 1852
HUGHES, D., HANDS, P., & KENCH, J. *The complete book of South African wines* Cape Town 1983
———2nd ed. 1988
HUGO, D. DE VOS *In die Kerkhof* Cape Town 1906
HUME, M. *Sawdust heaven Dassie* ed. [Johannesburg ?1955]
HUNTER, L. *African dawn* Alice, Eastern Cape 1949
HUTCHEON, D. *Rinderpest in South Africa: a short description of its history, general characters and methods of treatment* Cape Town 1902 [Cory Library CAP630]
HUTCHINSON, Mrs (Mrs George William Hutchinson) *In tents in the Transvaal* London 1879
HYATT, S.P. *The old transport road* London 1914

Ikhwezi Lomso/Morning Star (title varies as *(I)kwezi Lomso*) Queenstown 1958-60
Ilanga Durban 1903- (until 1965 with title *Ilanga lase Natal*)
ILLSLEY, W. *Wagon on fire* London 1955
Imperial blue books see United Kingdom. Parliamentary papers
The Independent London 1986-
Indigenous trees and shrubs for your garden (Wildlife Society of Southern Africa, Natal Branch) Durban 1974
INGRAM, J.F. (J. Forsyth Ingram) *The story of an African city* Pietermaritzburg 1898
———*The story of a gold concession* Pietermaritzburg 1893
Inside South Africa Cape Town
INSKEEP, R.R. *The peopling of Southern Africa* Cape Town 1978
'THE INTELLIGENCE OFFICER' (L. James) *On the heels of De Wet* Edinburgh 1902
IRWIN, W.N. *Echoes of the past: an army surgeon's experiences in South Africa 1843-46* ed. by H.B. Newham London 1927 (reprinted from *Journal of the Royal Army Medical Corps*)

SELECT BIBLIOGRAPHY

ISAACS, N. *Travels and adventures in Eastern Africa, descriptive of the Zoolas, their manners, customs, etc.* 2 vols. London 1836
—— ed. by L. Herrman 2 vols. Cape Town 1936-37 (Van Riebeeck Society)
'I.W.' see Wauchope, I.W.

JACKSON, A. *Trader on the veld* Cape Town 1958
JACKSON, M.C. *A soldier's diary: South Africa 1899-1901* London 1913
JACOBSON, D. *A dance in the sun* London 1956
—— *A long way from London* London 1953
—— *The price of diamonds* London 1957
—— *Through the wilderness: selected stories* Harmondsworth, U.K. 1977 (first publ. as *Inklings* 1973)
JANSONIUS, H. *Nieuw groot Nederlands-Engels woordenboek* 3 vols. Leiden 1972-73
JARDINE, A.J. *A fragment of church history, at the Cape of Good Hope* [written anonymously] Cape Town 1827
JEFFREYS, K.M. tr. *The memorandum of Commissary J.A. de Mist containing recommendations for the form and administration of government at the Cape of Good Hope, 1802* Cape Town 1920 (Van Riebeeck Society)
JEFFREYS, M.D.W. [Note Some of the quotations used in these articles are cited verbatim in the dictionary, with Jeffreys acknowledged in parentheses]
—— *Africanderisms* (article publ. in *Africana Notes and News*, June 1964, Vol. 16 No. 2)
—— *Africanderisms III* (article publ. in *Africana Notes and News*, Mar. 1970, Vol. 19 No. 1)
—— *A vague equivalent* (article publ. in *Africana Notes and News*, Mar. 1967, Vol. 17 No. 5)
JENKINS, G. *A bridge of magpies* Glasgow 1977
—— *Scend of the sea* Glasgow 1971
JENKINSON, T.B. *AmaZulu* London 1882
JENNINGS, L.E. *The concise trilingual dictionary in English, Xhosa, Afrikaans* 2nd ed. Lovedale, Eastern Cape 1962
JEPPE, F. *Jeppe's Transvaal almanac and directory for 1889* Cape Town 1889
—— *Transvaal book almanac and directory for 1877* Pietermaritzburg 1877
—— facsimile reprint Pretoria 1976
JERMIESON, A. *Rosaletta* Cape Town 1988
JOHNSON, W.S. *Orangia: a geographical reader of the Orange River Colony* London 1906
JOHNSTON, H.H. *The opening up of Africa* London [1911]
JOHNSTON, W. tr. *'Fra Paolino da San Bartolomeo's' Voyage to the East Indies* London 1800
Joint operational dictionary (Directorate of Language Services, South African Defence Force) Pretoria 1977
JOLLIE, E.T. (E. Tawse Jollie) *The real Rhodesia* Bulawayo, Rhodesia [Zimbabwe] 1971 (first publ. 1924)
JONES, I. ed. *S.A.B.C.'s Woman's World cookbook: South African favourite recipes* Diep River 1989
JONKER, A. tr. *P. Pieterse's Day of the giants* Pretoria 1986
JOUBERT, E. *The long journey of Poppie Nongena* Johannesburg 1980
The Journal Grahamstown 1831-1920 (with title *The Graham's Town Journal, or, Cape of Good Hope Eastern Provincial Register* 1833-64; absorbed by *Grocott's Mail*)
The Journal of the Botanical Society of South Africa Parts XIV-XLIII Cape Town 1928-57
JUBB, R.A. *Freshwater fishes of Southern Africa* Cape Town 1967
JUNOD, H.P. & JAQUES, A.A. *Vutlhari bya Vatsonga (Machangana): the wisdom of the Tsonga-Shangana people* (Swiss Mission in South Africa) 2nd ed. Johannesburg 1957
—— see also Duggan-Cronin, A.M.
JUTA, H.H. *Reminiscences of the western circuit* Cape Town 1912
JUTA, J. *Look out for the ostriches* Dassie ed. [Johannesburg ?1933]
JUTA, R. *The Cape peninsula, being pen and colour sketches* Cape Town 1910
—— *The tavern* London 1920

The Kairos document: challenge to the church (Kairos theologians) rev. 2nd ed. Johannesburg 1986
KALLAWAY, P. & PEARSON, P. *Johannesburg: images and continuities* Johannesburg 1986
Kamus Harian Federal Malay-English-Malay dictionary ed. by M.S. Daud & A.H. Omar Kuala Lumpur 1977
KANTEY, M. *All tickets/alle kaartjies* Johannesburg 1991
KARODIA, F. *Daughters of the twilight* London 1986
Kathay's unabridged new Crown dictionary of national language: Malay-English English-Malay by S. Santoso & Y.K. Lee Singapore 1964
KAVANAGH, M. *We merry peasants* Cape Town 1963
KAY, S. *Travels and researches in Caffraria* London 1833
KEANE, A.H. *Africa* 2 vols. London 1895
—— 2nd ed. Vol. II (with title *South Africa*) London 1904
—— *The Boer states: land and people* London 1900
KEET, B.B. see Marquard, N.J. tr.
KEITH, G.M. *A voyage to South America and the Cape of Good Hope; in his Majesty's gun brig 'The Protector'* London 1819 (first publ. 1810)
KENCH, J. *Cape Dutch homesteads* with photographs by D. Goldblatt & M. Courtney-Clarke Cape Town 1981
—— *Cottage furniture in South Africa* Cape Town 1987
KENDALL, E.A. *The English boy at the Cape* 3 vols. London 1835
KENMUIR, D. *Song of the surf* Cape Town 1988
—— *The tusks and the talisman* Pretoria 1987
KENNEDY, R.F. ed. see Baines, T.
KENTRIDGE, M. *An unofficial war: inside the conflict in Pietermaritzburg* Cape Town 1990
KEPPEL-JONES, A. *South Africa: a short history* London 1949
—— 3rd ed. 1963
—— ed. see Philipps, T.
KESTELL, J.D. *Through shot and flame* London 1903
KIDD, D. *The essential kafir* London 1904
—— 2nd ed. London 1925
KIDD, M.M. *Cape Peninsula* (Botanical Society of South Africa) Cape Town 1983 (South African Wild Flower Guide No. 3)
—— *Wild flowers of the Cape Peninsula* Cape Town 1950
KIFT, E.L. *Letters to Alfred Jarvis in Port Elizabeth on business and personal topics. 1844-50.* Cory Library MS14,333
KILBURN, R. & RIPPEY, E. *Sea shells of Southern Africa* Johannesburg 1982
KINDERSLEY, Mrs (Mrs Nathaniel Edward Kindersley) *Letters from the island of Teneriffe, Brazil, the Cape of Good Hope, and the East Indies* London 1777
KING, N.L. *Tree-planting in South Africa* (reprinted from *Journal of the South African Forestry Association* No. 21, Oct. 1951)
KINGWILL, P. *Message of the black eagle* Cape Town 1988
KIPLING, R. *The five nations* New York 1903
KIRBY, P.R. *The musical instruments of the native races of South Africa* London 1934
—— 2nd ed. Johannesburg 1965
—— ed. see Burrow, J.; also Smith, A.
—— see also Bullock, J.B. ed.
KIRSTEIN, C. *Best South African braai recipes* Cape Town 1986
KLEIN, H. *Land of the silver mist* Cape Town 1952
—— *Stage coach dust* London 1937
KLEVANSKY, I.H. *The Kugel book* Cape Town 1982
KNAPPERT, J. *The Aquarian guide to African mythology* Northamptonshire, U.K. 1990
KNIGHT, E.F. *South Africa after the war* London 1903
KNOX, C.M. tr. *E. Van Heerden's Mad dog and other stories* Cape Town 1992
KOLB, P. see Medley, G. tr.
KOPS, H. *Veld, city and sea* Dassie ed. [Johannesburg 1956]
KOTZE, D.J. ed. *Letters of the American missionaries 1835-38* Cape Town 1950 (Van Riebeeck Society)
KRAMER, D. *Short back and sides* Cape Town 1982
KRAUSS, F. see Spohr, O.H. tr.
KRIEL, T.J. *The new Sesotho-English dictionary* Johannesburg 1950
KRIGE, E.J. *The social system of the Zulus* 2nd ed. Pietermaritzburg 1950 (first publ. 1936)
KRIGE, E.J. & J.D. *The realm of a rain-queen: a study of the pattern of Lovedu society* Oxford, U.K. 1943
—— reprint 1965
KRIGE, U. *The dream and the desert* London 1953
A Krio-English dictionary ed. by C.N. Fyle & E.D. Jones Oxford, U.K. 1980
KROENLEIN, J.G. *Wortschatz der Khoi-Khoin (Namaqua-Hottentotten)* Berlin 1889
—— facsimile reprint Farnborough, U.K. 1971
KUNENE, M. *Anthem of the decades* London 1981
—— *Zulu poems* New York 1970
KUPER, H. *A witch in my heart* London 1970
KUPER, L. *The college brew* Durban [1961]
KUTTEL, M. *Hildegonda Duckitt's book of recipes* Cape Town 1966
—— *Quadrilles and konfyt: the life and journal of Hildagonda Duckitt* Cape Town 1954
Kwazulu Natal joint executive authority (J.E.A.) (Bureau of Information) Pretoria [?1988]

LABAND, J. & HASWELL, R. eds. *Pietermaritzburg 1838-1988: a new portrait of an African city* Pietermaritzburg 1988
LABOV, T. *Language in Society* Vol. II Cambridge, U.K. 1983
'A LADY' (?Sir John Robinson) *Life at Natal a hundred years ago* Cape Town 1972
'A LADY' (?L.G. Ross) *Life at the Cape a hundred years ago* Cape Town 1963
LAFFEATY, C. *Far forbidden plains* London 1990
LAGDEN, G.Y. *The Basutos* 2 vols. London 1909
LAIDLER, P.W. *A tavern of the ocean: being a social and historical sketch of Cape Town from its earliest days* Cape Town 1926
LAKEMAN, S. *What I saw in Kaffir-land* London 1880
LAMONT, A.B. *A rural reader for South Africa* London 1910
LANHAM, P. & MOPELI-PAULUS, A.S. *Blanket boy's moon* London 1953
LARSON, J.K. ed. *The history and genealogy of the Talbots, Sweetnams, and Wiggills (including autobiographies on South African life).* [written in Utah, U.S.A.] 1953. Cory Library MS6658
LASKER, C. tr. *A. Small's Kanna he is coming home.* a.1985. Unpubl. translation. University of New York
LATROBE, C.I. *Journal of a visit to South Africa in 1815 and 1816, with some account of the missionary settlements of the United Brethren near the Cape of Good Hope* London 1821 (first publ. 1818)
LAU, B. *Southern and Central Namibia in Jonker Afrikaner's time* Windhoek, South West Africa [Namibia] 1987
LAUBSCHER, B.J.F. *Sex, custom and psychopathology* London 1937
LAUGHTON, F.S. *The sylviculture of the indigenous forests of the Union of South Africa* (Department of Agriculture & Forestry) Pretoria 1937
LAWRENCE, J. *Harry Lawrence* Cape Town 1978
LAYARD, E.L. *The birds of South Africa* London 1867
—— new ed. rev. by R.B. Sharpe London 1884
Leadership Cape Town (from 1982 to 1992 with title *Leadership South Africa*; also publ. in Johannesburg)
Learn and Teach Johannesburg 1990-94
LEES PRICE, E. see Price, E.L.
LEIPOLD, L. *Bushveld doctor* London 1937
LENNOX-SHORT, A. & LIGHTON, R.E. eds. *Stories South African* Johannesburg 1969
LEPPAN, H.D. *Agricultural policy in South Africa* Johannesburg 1931
LE ROUX, A. & SCHELPE, T. *Namaqualand* (Botanical Society of South Africa) Cape Town 1988 (South African Wild Flower Guide No. 1)
LEROUX, E. see Eglington, C. tr.
LESLIE, D. *Among the Zulus and AmaTongas* Glasgow 1875
LETCHER, O. *Africa unveiled* London 1931
LE VAILLANT, F. *Travels into the interior parts of Africa, by way of the Cape of Good Hope, in the years 1780, 1781, 1782, 1783, 1784 and 1785* [written in French, translator unknown] 2 vols. London 1790
—— 2nd ed. [translator unknown] 2 vols. London 1796 (quotations from this ed. have been incorrectly attributed to the translator Helme, E.)
LEVESON, M. ed. *Firetalk: selected short stories from the entries to the 1989 Sanlam Literary Award* Cape Town 1990
LEVIN, H., BRANCH, M., RAPPAPORT, S., & MITCHELL, D. *A field guide to the mushrooms of South Africa* Cape Town 1985
LEVINSON, O. *The ageless land* Cape Town 1961
—— *Story of Namibia* 2nd ed. rev. & enlarged Cape Town 1978 (first publ. in 1976 as *South West Africa*)
LEWCOCK, R. *Early 19th century architecture in South Africa 1795-1837* Cape Town 1963
LEWIN ROBINSON, A.M. see Robinson, A.M.L.
LEWINS, J.D. Diary. 1849-50. Private collection
LEWSEN, P. ed. see Wilmot, R.E.E.
LEYLAND, J. *Adventures in the far interior of South Africa including a journey to Lake Ngami and rambles in Honduras* Liverpool 1866
LICHTENSTEIN, M.H.K. (Hinrich) see Plumptre, A. tr.
LIGHTON, R.E. *Out of the strong* London 1958
—— see also Lennox-Short, A. & Lighton, R.E. eds.
Light years (Old Mutual) Pinelands, Cape Town
LINDSAY, Lord (Alexander William Crawford) *Lives of the Lindsays; or, a memoir of the Houses of Crawford and Balcarres* Vol. III London 1849
LINDSAY, K. *'Neath the Southern Cross* London 1931
LINDSAY, T.J. *The shadow* London 1990 (first publ. 1988)
LINDSEY-RENTON, R.H. *The 1920 diary of R.H. Lindsey-Renton* ed. by I.P. Lindsey-Renton Bryanston, Johannesburg 1979
LINES, G.W. *The Ladysmith siege* London 1900
LINNÉ, C. VON *A genuine and universal system of natural history; comprising the three kingdoms of animals, vegetables, and minerals* 14 vols. London c.1794-c.1813
A list of South African newspapers 1800-1982 Pretoria 1983

SELECT BIBLIOGRAPHY

LISTER, G. *Reminiscences of Georgina Lister* Johannesburg 1960
LISTER, M.H. ed. see Bain, A.G.
LITTLE, J.S. *South Africa: a sketchbook of men, manners and facts* 2 vols. London 1884
LIVINGSTONE, David *The last journals of David Livingstone ... continued by a narrative of his last moments and sufferings, obtained from his faithful servants Chuma and Susi by Horace Waller* 2 vols. London 1874
——*Missionary Travels* London 1857
LIVINGSTONE, Douglas *A rosary of bone* ed. by J. Cope Cape Town 1975
LLEWELLYN, E.C. *The influence of Low Dutch on the English vocabulary* London 1936
LLOYD, L. ed. see Andersson, C.J.
LLOYD, M. tr. *Diaries of the Jesuit missionaries of Bulawayo 1874-1881* Salisbury, Rhodesia [Harare, Zimbabwe] 1939
London Magazine: a monthly review of literature London 1954-
LONG, U. ed. see Goldswain, J.; also Price, E.L.
Longman dictionary of contemporary English ed. by P. Procter et al. Harlow, U.K. 1981
Longman new universal dictionary ed. by P. Procter et al. Harlow, U.K. 1982
LONGMORE, L. *The dispossessed* London 1959
LOUBSER, J.W. ed. *Africana short stories* Johannesburg 1970
LOUW, A.M. *20 days that autumn* Cape Town 1963
LOWE, S.M.A. *The hungry veld* Pietermaritzburg 1967
LOWNDES, E.E.K. *Every-day life in South Africa* London 1900
LUBKE, R., GESS, F.W., & BRUTON, M.N. *A field guide to the Eastern Cape coast* Grahamstown 1988
LUCAS, T.J. *Camp life and sport in South Africa* London 1878
LUDMAN, B. *The day of the kugel* Cape Town 1989
LUTHULI, A.J. *Let my people go* London 1962
LYALL, S. *Reminiscences.* c.1900. Killie Campbell Africana Library MS138
LYE, W.F. ed. see Smith, A.
LYE, W.F. & MURRAY, C. *Transformations on the Highveld: the Tswana and Southern Sotho* Cape Town 1980
LYNNE, S. *Glittering gold* London 1972
Lynx: contemporary South African writing (Time out of Time) Johannesburg 1990
LYSTER, L. *Ballads of the veld-land* London 1913

MAARTENS, M. *Ring around the moon* Pretoria 1987
MACDONALD, T. *Ouma Smuts* London 1946
——*Transvaal story* Cape Town 1961
MACDONALD, W. *The romance of the golden rand* London 1933
MACKENZIE, A. Journal. 1859. Typescript. Killie Campbell Africana Library Colenso Papers Block 7
MACKENZIE, J. *Papers of John Mackenzie* ed. by A.J. Dachs Johannesburg 1975
——*Ten years north of the Orange River: a story of everyday life and work among the South African tribes from 1859-1869* 2nd ed. with new introduction by C. Northcott London 1971
MACKENZIE, K. *The deserter* London 1965
——*A dragon to kill* London 1963
MACKRILL, J. Diary written in various places ... including Cape Town 1809 and Boschberg (Somerset East) 1816. 1806-16. Cory Library MS7336
MACLEAN, G.L. *Roberts' birds of Southern Africa* see Roberts, A.
MACLEAN, J. *A compendium of Kafir laws and customs with papers by H.H. Dugmore, and notes by J.C. Warner & C.P. Brownlee* reprint Grahamstown 1906 (first publ. 1858)
——facsimile reprint Pretoria 1968
MACLENNAN, B. *A proper degree of terror* Johannesburg 1986
MACLENNAN, D.A.C. In the dawn wind. 1970. Unpubl. play. [publ. as *The Great Wall of China* in Bolt No. 7, Mar. 1973]
——*Reckonings* Cape Town 1983
——The wake: a comedy in two acts. 1971. Unpubl. play. Dictionary Unit
'MACNAB, F.' (Agnes Fraser) *On veldt and farm* London 1897
MACNAB, R.M. ed. *Poets in South Africa* Cape Town 1958
Makanna, or the land of the savage (anon.) 3 vols. London 1834
MALAN, Rian *My traitor's heart* London 1990
MALAN, Robin *Ah big yaws* by 'Rawbone Malong' Cape Town 1972
MANDELA, N. *No easy walk to freedom* London 1965

MANDELBROTE, H.J. tr. *O.F. Mentzel's A geographical-topographical description of the Cape of Good Hope* Parts I & II Cape Town 1921-25 (Part III tr. by G.V. Marais & J. Hoge; whole work ed. by Mandelbrote) (Van Riebeeck Society)
MANDELBROTE, J.C. *The Cape Press 1838-50* Cape Town 1945
MANGOPE, L.M. *A place for all* Cape Town c.1979
MANLEY, M. tr. *L.M. Oosthuizen's Media policy and ethics* Cape Town 1989
MANSON, H.W.D. *Pat Mulholland's day* Cape Town 1964
MARAIS, D. *Ag, sis man!* Cape Town 1965
——*Europeans only* Cape Town 1960
——*Hey! Van der Merwe* Cape Town 1961
——*I got a licence* Cape Town 1962
——*I like it here* Cape Town 1964
MARAIS, E.C.G. tr. see Marais, E.N.
MARAIS, E.N. *My friends the baboons* [tr. unknown] [no place] 1939
——another ed. tr. by E.C.G. Marais Cape Town 1971
——*The road to Waterberg and other essays* Cape Town 1972
——*The soul of the ape* Harmondsworth, U.K. 1973
——*The soul of the white ant* see De Kok, W.D. tr.
MARAIS, G.V. & HOGE, J. tr. *O.F. Mentzel's A geographical-topographical description of the Cape of Good Hope* see Mandelbrote, H.J.
MARKHAM, V.R. *The South African scene* London 1913
MARKS, B. *Our South African army today* Cape Town 1977
MARLOTH, R. *Dictionary of the common names of plants* Cape Town 1917
——President's address, August 29, 1894 [in Transactions of the South African Philosophical Society Vol. VIII Part II, 1896]
——see also Edmonds, H. & Marloth, R.
MARQUARD, L. *Peoples and policies of South Africa* London 1952
——*The story of South Africa* London [1955]
MARQUARD, M. *Letters from a Boer parsonage* Cape Town 1967
MARQUARD, N.J. tr. *B.B. Keet's Whither - South Africa?* Stellenbosch 1956
MARTIN, A. *Home life on an ostrich farm* London 1890
MARTIN, A.C. *The concentration camps 1900-1902* Cape Town 1957
MARTIN, C.G.C. & FRIEDLAENDER, K.J. *History of surveying and land tenure in South Africa* collected papers Vol. I (Surveying and land tenure in the Cape 1652-1812) Cape Town 1984
MARTIN, H.J. & ORPEN, N. *South Africa at war* Cape Town 1979
MARTINIUS, M.E. *A sketch of the development of rural education (European) in the Cape Colony (1652-1910)* Grahamstown [preface dated 1922]
MASON, G.H. *Life with the Zulus of Natal South Africa* London 1855
——facsimile reprint London 1968
MASON, R. *Prehistory of the Transvaal* Johannesburg 1962
MASSON, M. *Birds of passage* London 1950
MATHEWS, B. *Consider Africa* London 1935
MATSHIKIZA, T. *Chocolates for my wife* London 1961
MATSHOBA, M. *Call me not a man* Johannesburg 1979 ('Staffrider Series' No. 2)
MATTHEE, D. *The mulberry forest* London 1989 (first publ. 1987)
MATTHEWS, J. *The park and other stories* Cape Town 1974
——new ed. Johannesburg 1983
MATTHEWS, J.W. *Incwadi Yami or twenty years' personal experience in South Africa* New York 1887
MAYLAM, P. *A history of the African people of South Africa: from the early iron age to the 1970s* Cape Town 1986
MAYSON, J.S. *The Malays of Capetown* Manchester 1861
MAZIKANA, P.C. & JOHNSTONE, I.J. *Zimbabwe epic* ed. by R.G.S. Douglas Harare, Zimbabwe 1982
MCALLEN, T. *Kyk daar: a rooinek's guide to South Africa* Durban 1983
MCALLISTER, P.A. Xhosa beer drinks and their oratory. 1986. Doctoral thesis, Rhodes University, Grahamstown, 1987
MCCLURE, J. *The caterpillar cop* London 1974 (first publ. 1972)
——*The gooseberry fool* Harmondsworth, U.K. 1976 (first publ. 1974)
——*Rogue eagle* London 1976
——*Snake* Harmondsworth, U.K. 1977 (first publ. 1975; quotations are taken from a 1981 reprint)
——*The steam pig* Harmondsworth, U.K. 1973 (first publ. 1971)
MCKAY, J. *Reminiscences of the last Kafir war* Grahamstown 1871

——reprint Cape Town 1970 (quotations are taken from the 1970 reprint, but dated simply 1871)
MCKIERNAN, G. *Narrative and journal of Gerald McKiernan in South West Africa, 1874-79* ed. by P. Serton Cape Town 1954 (Van Riebeeck Society)
MCLACHLAN, G.R. & LIVERSIDGE, R. *Roberts birds of South Africa* see Roberts, A.
MCLAREN, J. *A new concise Xhosa-English dictionary* Cape Town 1963
MCMAGH, K. *A dinner of herbs* Cape Town 1968
MCNISH, J.T. *The road to Eldorado* Cape Town 1968
MCRAE, A.G. *The hill called Grazing: the story of a Transvaal farm* London 1956
The Mediator Cape Town 1837-39 (continuation of *The Moderator, or, Cape of Good Hope Impartial Observer*)
MEDLEY, G. tr. *P. Kolb's The present state of the Cape of Good Hope* 2 vols. London 1731
Meet the South African Transport Services (Publicity & Travel Department, South African Transport Services) Johannesburg 1982
MEINTJES, J. *Manor House* New York 1964
——*Sandile: the fall of the Xhosa nation* Cape Town 1971
——*Sword in the sand* Cape Town 1969
——*The Voortrekkers: the story of the Great Trek and the making of South Africa* London 1973
MEIRING, J. *Candle in the wind* London 1959
MEKGOE, S.S. *Lindiwe* Johannesburg 1978
MELAMU, M. *Children of the twilight* Johannesburg 1987
Memorandum explaining the background and objects of the promotion of Bantu selfgovernment bill Parl. Paper W.P.3-1959
MENTZEL, O.F. see Greenlees, M. tr.; also Mandelbrote, H.J. tr.
MEREDITH, C. *Peggy of Cape Town* Cape Town 1910
MEREDITH, D. ed. *The grasses and pastures of South Africa* (Part I *A guide to the identification of grasses in South Africa* by L.K.A. Chippindall, Part II *Pasture management in South Africa* by J.D. Scott, J.J. Theron, Meredith, et al.) [Johannesburg] 1955
MERRETT, P. & BUTCHER, R. eds. see Struthers, R.B.
MERRIMAN, N.J. *The Cape journals of Archdeacon N.J. Merriman 1848-55* ed. by D.H. Varley & H.M. Matthew Cape Town 1957 (Van Riebeeck Society)
MESTHRIE, R. A lexicon of South African Indian English. Thesis, ?University of Durban-Westville. c.1986. Dictionary Unit
——*A lexicon of South African Indian English* Yorkshire, U.K. 1992
METCALFE, H. *Chronicle of Private Henry Metcalfe* ed. by F. Tuker London 1953
METELERKAMP, S. *George Rex of Knysna* Cape Town [?1955]
——3rd ed. 1963
The Meteor Grahamstown 1881-84
METHLEY, J.E. *The new colony of Port Natal with information for emigrants* London 1850
METROWICH, F.C. *Frontier flames* Cape Town 1968
——*Scotty Smith* Cape Town 1962
——*The valiant but once* Cape Town 1956
MEURANT, L.H. *Sixty years ago* Cape Town 1885
——facsimile reprint Cape Town 1963
MFUSI, M.J.H. Soweto Zulu slang: a sociolinguistic study of an urban vernacular in Soweto. Honours thesis, University of South Africa, 1990
MILLAR, C. ed. *Sixteen stories by South African writers* Cape Town 1964
MILLER, P. *Myths and legends of Southern Africa* Cape Town 1979
MILLIN, S.G. *Adam's rest* London 1922
——*God's step-children* London 1924
——*South Africa* London 1941
MILLS, G.M. *First ladies of the Cape* Cape Town [?1952]
Miner's companion in English, Afrikaans, Sesuto and Mine Kaffir (Prevention of Accidents Commission, Rand Mutual Assurance Co. Ltd) Johannesburg 1938
Miner's dictionary: English-Fanakalo, Afrikaans-Fanakalo (Chamber of Mines Services) Johannesburg 1981
Mining dictionary (Terminology Bureau, Department of Education) Pretoria 1983
Missionary Notices London
MITFORD, B. *Aletta: a tale of the Boer invasion* London 1900
——*The curse of Clement Waynflete* 3rd ed. London 1896 (first publ. 1894)
——*The induna's wife* London 1898
——*The weird of Deadly Hollow* London 1899
MOCKFORD, J. *The golden land* London 1949
——*Here are South Africans* London 1944
The Moderator, or, Cape of Good Hope Impartial Observer Cape Town Jan.-July 1837 (continued by *The Mediator*)

SELECT BIBLIOGRAPHY

MODISANE, B. *Blame me on history* Johannesburg 1986 (first publ. 1963)
MOFFAT, R. *Missionary labours and scenes in Southern Africa* London 1846
MOFOLO, T. *Chaka the Zulu* [translator unknown] Oxford, U.K. 1949
—— see also Dutton, F.H. tr.
MOLEMA, S.M. *The Bantu past and present* Edinburgh 1920
—— facsimile reprint Cape Town 1963
MOLLER, J.W.N. *What every housewife should know* Cape Town 1928
MOLLOY, B. *South African CB dictionary* Cape Town 1979
MOLTENO, P.A. *Selections from the correspondence of Percy Alport Molteno 1892–1914* ed. by V. Solomon Cape Town 1981 (Van Riebeeck Society)
The Monitor: the journal of the Human Rights Trust Port Elizabeth
MÖNNIG, H.O. & VELDMAN, F.J. *Handbook on stock diseases* Cape Town 1954
—— 2nd ed. 1976
MONTGOMERY, J. *The reminiscences of John Montgomery* ed. by A. Giffard Cape Town 1981 ('The Graham's Town Series')
MOODIE, D.C.F. *The history of the battles and adventures of the British, the Boers and the Zulus, etc., in Southern Africa, from the time of Pharoah Necho, to 1880* 2 vols. Cape Town 1888
MOODIE, J.W.D. *Scenes and adventures, as a soldier and settler* Montreal 1866
—— *Ten years in South Africa* 2 vols. London 1835
MOORE, D.M. ed. *Garden earth: an encyclopedia of plant life* Amsterdam 1991
MOORE, H. *Land of Good Hope* (London Society for the Propagation of the Gospel in Foreign Parts) London 1918
MORIARTY, A. *Outeniqua Tsitsikamma and eastern Little Karoo* (Botanical Society of South Africa) Cape Town 1982 (South African Wild Flower Guide No. 2)
MORRELL, B. *Narrative of a voyage to the south and west coast of Africa* London 1844
MORTON, H.V. *In search of South Africa* London 1948
The Motorist (Automobile Association of South Africa) Johannesburg
MOTSISI, K.M.C. (Casey 'Kid' Motsisi) see Mutloatse, M. ed.
MPHAHLELE, E. *Afrika my music: an autobiography 1957–1983* Johannesburg 1984
—— *Down Second Avenue* London 1959
—— educational ed. London 1965
—— *Renewal time* London 1988
MTSAKA, M.J. *Not his pride* Johannesburg 1978 (Raven Playscript 1)
MTSHALI, M.B. *Give us a break: diaries of a group of Soweto children* Johannesburg 1988
MULLER, D. *Whitey* Johannesburg 1977
MULLER, M. *Art, past and present* Cape Town 1960
—— *Cloud across the moon* London 1970
—— *Green peaches ripen* London 1968
MULLINS, R.J. *The diary of R.J. Mullins. 1854-57.* Cory Library MS 7111 & MS 7112
MUNDAY, J. *Grasses, grains and conservation* Johannesburg 1987
MUNITICH, B. *Ben's buddy* Pretoria 1987
MUNNIK, G.G. *Memoirs of Senator the Hon. G.G. Munnik* Cape Town [1934]
MUNRO, I. *A narrative of the military operations on the Coromandel coast ... from the year 1780 to the peace in 1784* London 1789
MURRAY, A.A. *The blanket* New York 1957
MURRAY, J. ed. *In mid-Victorian Cape Town: letters from Miss Rutherfoord* Cape Town 1953
—— *Young Mrs Murray goes to Bloemfontein* Cape Town 1954
MURRAY, M. *Under Lion's Head* Cape Town 1964
MURRAY, Y. *Choice maize dishes* (The Maize Board) Pretoria 1981
MURRAY-BOOYSON, C. *More tales of South Africa* Cape Town 1967
MUTLOATSE, M. ed. *Casey & Co.: selected writings of Casey 'Kid' Motsisi* Johannesburg 1978
—— ed. *Forced landing* Johannesburg 1980 ('Staffrider Series' No. 3)
MZAMANE, M. *Children of Soweto* Johannesburg 1982

NAIDOO, J. *Coolie location* London 1990
NAPIER, E.D.H.E. *Excursions in Southern Africa* 2 vols. London 1849
The Natal Agricultural Journal (from 1911 continued by *The Agricultural Journal of the Union of South Africa*)
Natal Daily News see *Daily News*
(*The*) *Natal Mercury* Durban 1852- (first publ. as *Natal Mercury and Commercial and Shipping Gazette*; weekend ed. *Weekend Mercury* merged with *Saturday News* to form *Natal on Saturday*)
Natal on Saturday Durban 1993-
The Natal Witness Pietermaritzburg 1846- (with title *Natal Witness, and Agricultural and Commercial Advertiser* ?1863-73)
NATHAN, M. *South Africa from within* London 1926
The National Geographic Magazine Washington 1888-
The Natives and their missionaries, by a Native Minister see Wauchope, I.W.
The natives of South Africa: their economic and social condition (The South African Native Races Committee) London 1901
The native tribes of South West Africa with contributions by C.H.L. Hahn, L. Fourie, & H. Vedder Cape Town 1928
The native tribes of the Transvaal London 1905
NAUDÉ, S.D. *Kaapse plakkaatboek deel V* Cape Town 1950
NDABA, S. ed. *One day in June: poetry and prose from troubled times* Johannesburg 1986
NDEBELE, N.S. *Fools and other stories* Johannesburg 1983
NEAME, L.E. *The history of apartheid* London 1962
—— *White man's Africa* Cape Town 1952
NEL, P.R.T. tr. *M.H. Trümpelmann's The Joint Matriculation Board* Cape Town 1991
New African Durban
The New African: the radical monthly Cape Town & London
New Classic Literary Journal Johannesburg 1975-78
New Coin Poetry (publ. by South African Poetry Society; later by Institute for the Study of English in Africa) Grahamstown 1965-
New dictionary of American slang ed. by R.L. Chapman London 1987
A new English dictionary on a historical basis: the compact edition of the Oxford English dictionary 2 vols. Oxford, U.K. 1971
A new English dictionary on historical principles; founded mainly on the material collected by the Philological Society ed. by J.A.H. Murray, H. Bradley, W.A. Craigie, & C.T. Onions 10 vols. Oxford, U.K. 1888-1928
—— see also *The Oxford English dictionary* 2nd ed.
NEWHAM, H.B. ed. see Irwin, W.N.
NEWMAN, K.B. *Birdlife in Southern Africa* Johannesburg 1979
—— *Newman's birds of Southern Africa* Johannesburg 1983
New Nation (South African Catholic Bishops Conference) Johannesburg ?1985- (with Sunday ed., *Sunday Nation*)
New Nation: the South African review of opinion and fact Pretoria 1967-73
News/Check Johannesburg
New South African Writing (South African Centre of the International P.E.N. Club) Cape Town c.1964-68 [series of 5 annual vols.]
—— see also *South African P.E.N. year book*
The New Statesman London 1913-
Newsweek New York
NEWTON-KING, S. & MALHERBE, V.C. *The Khoikhoi rebellion in the Eastern Cape (1799-1803)* Cape Town 1981 (Communications No. 5, Centre for African Studies, University of Cape Town)
NGUBANE, H. *Original peoples: Zulus of Southern Africa* Hove 1994
NGUGI, J. *The river between* London 1970
NICHOLLS, G.H. (G. Heaton Nicholls) *Bayete! 'Hail to the King!'* London 1923
NICHOLSON, G. *Fifty years in South Africa* London 1898
NICHOLSON, M. *A dictionary of American-English usage* New York 1958
NICOL, M. *The powers that be* London 1990
NICOLLS, J.A. & EGLINGTON, W. *The sportsman in South Africa* London 1892
NIENABER, G.S. *Hottentots* Pretoria 1963
NIENABER, G.S. & RAPER, P.E. see Rabie, P.S. tr.
NIXON, J. *Among the Boers* London 1882
NKOSI, L. *Mating birds* Johannesburg 1987
NKOSI, T. *The time of the comrades* Johannesburg 1987
NOBLE, J. *Descriptive handbook of the Cape Colony: its condition and resources* Cape Town 1875
—— *Illustrated official handbook of the Cape and South Africa* Cape Town 1893
—— *Official handbook. History, productions, and resources of the Cape of Good Hope* (with cover title *Cape of Good Hope: official handbook, 1886*) Cape Town 1886
—— *South Africa, past and present* London 1877
NOBLE, R. ed. *The Cape and its people* Cape Town 1869
Nongqai (Department of Justice) Pretoria 1913-61
NORRIS-NEWMAN, C.L. *With the Boers in the Transvaal and Orange Free State* London 1882
NOTCUTT, H.C. *How Kimberley was held for England* Bloemfontein [1900]
Now everyone is afraid (Catholic Institute for International Relations) London 1988
NTHODI, M. WA *From the calabash* Johannesburg 1978
Nusas talks to the ANC (National Union of South African Students) Cape Town c.1986
Nuwe junior Sepedi ed. by J.C. Grobbelaar Johannesburg 1978

OBERHOLZER, O. *Ariesfontein to Zuurfontein: a pictorial journey* [Johannesburg] 1988
O'CONNOR, J.K. *The Afrikander rebellion* Cape Town 1915
Official place names in the Union and South West Africa (Place Names Committee, Department of Education, Arts, & Science) Pretoria 1952
Official visitors' guide, Durban (Durban Publicity Association) Durban 1955
Official year book of the Union and of Basutoland, Bechuanaland Protectorate, and Swaziland (Union Office of Census & Statistics; later, Bureau of Census & Statistics) Pretoria c.1917-c.1961
—— see also *South Africa: official yearbook of the Republic of South Africa*
O'KEEFE, B. *Gold without glitter* Dassie ed. [Johannesburg] 1957
OLIVER, J.O. *A beginner's guide to our birds* (Wildlife Society of Southern Africa, Natal Branch) 2nd ed. Durban 1980
ONDERSTALL, J. *Transvaal Lowveld and Escarpment, including the Kruger National Park* (Botanical Society of South Africa) Cape Town 1984 (South African Wild Flower Guide No. 4)
'ONE WHO WAS IN IT' *Kruger's Secret Service* London 1900
OOSTHUIZEN, L.M. see Manley, M. tr.
Ophir Pretoria 1967-76
OPPERMAN, D.J. ed. *Spirit of the vine* Cape Town 1968
Optima (Anglo American Corporation & De Beer groups of companies) Johannesburg
ORPEN, J.M. *Reminiscences of life in South Africa from 1846 to the present day* Durban [1908]
—— another ed. [including further reminiscences written 1916] Cape Town 1964
ORPEN, N. *War in the desert* Cape Town 1983
ORPEN, N. & MARTIN, H.J. *Salute the sappers* 2 parts Johannesburg 1981-82 (Vol. VII of the series 'South African forces: World War II')
OSBORNE, O. *In the land of the Boers* London 1900
Oudtshoorn Courant and Het Suid-Western Oudtshoorn 1879-
Our land (United Tobacco Co.) Cape Town c.1937
Our living world (Southern African Nature Foundation) Stellenbosch
Outpost: stories of the police of Rhodesia with illustrations by P. Miller Cape Town 1970
The Outspan Bloemfontein 1927-57 (continued by *Personality*)
OVENSTONE, R. *Donna of High Noon* Cape Town c.1981
OVINGTON, J. *A voyage to Suratt in the year 1689* ed. by H.G. Rawlinson London 1929 (first publ. 1696; quotations are taken from the 1929 ed., but dated simply 1696)
OWEN, F. *Diary of the Reverend Francis Owen* ed. by G.E. Cory Cape Town 1926 (Van Riebeeck Society)
—— Letter to Church Missionary Society. 1838. Killie Campbell Africana Library KCM53500
The Oxford English dictionary 2nd ed. prepared by J.A. Simpson & E.S.C. Weiner 20 vols. Oxford, U.K. 1989
—— see also *A new English dictionary on historical principles*
Oxford English dictionary additions series ed. by J.A. Simpson & E.S.C. Weiner 2 vols. Oxford, U.K. 1993

Pace Johannesburg
PACKER, J. *Boomerang* London 1972
—— *The dark curtain* London 1977
—— *The high roof* London 1959
—— *Home from the sea* London 1963
—— *Veronica* London 1970
PAGE, J. *Captain Allen Gardiner, sailor and saint* London [1897]
PAKENHAM, T. *The Boer War* Bergvlei, Johannesburg [1982] (first publ. 1979)
PALGRAVE, K.C. (K. Coates Palgrave) *Trees of Southern Africa* Cape Town 1983
PALGRAVE, W.C. see *Report of W. Coates Palgrave ...*
PALMER, E. *A field guide to the trees of Southern Africa* Johannesburg 1977

SELECT BIBLIOGRAPHY

——*The plains of Camdeboo* London 1966
PALMER, E. & PITMAN, N. *Trees of South Africa* Cape Town 1961
——*Trees of Southern Africa* 3 vols. Cape Town 1972
PAMA, C. *The wine estates of South Africa* Cape Town 1979
Pan-African congress on prehistory see *Proceedings of the Pan-African congress on prehistory*
'PAOLINO, FRA' see Johnston, W. tr.
PAPPE, L. *Florae Capensis Medicae Prodromus; or an enumeration of South African plants used as remedies by the colonists of the Cape of Good Hope* 3rd ed. Cape Town 1868
——*Silva capensis or a description of South African forest trees and arborescent shrubs* 2nd ed. Cape Town 1862
——*Synopsis of the edible fishes at the Cape of Good Hope* 2nd ed. Cape Town 1866
Paratus (South African Defence Force) Pretoria
PARKES, M. *Wheatlands: the story of a family and a farm* Port Elizabeth 1979
PAROZ, R.A. ed. see *Southern Sotho-English dictionary*
PARTRIDGE, A.C. ed. *Lives, letters and diaries* Cape Town 1971 ('English literature in South Africa' series, Vol. I)
PARTRIDGE, E. *A dictionary of slang and unconventional English* 6th ed. New York 1967
——8th edition ed. by P. Beale London 1984
——*A dictionary of the underworld* London 1950
——ed. *A dictionary of forces' slang 1939-1945* London 1948
PATEL, E. *They came at dawn* Cape Town 1980
——ed. *The world of Can Themba* Johannesburg 1985
PATERSON, W. *A narrative of four journeys into the country of the Hottentots, and Caffraria, in the years 1777, 1778, and 1779* London 1789
——2nd ed. 1790
PATON, A. *Cry, the beloved country* London 1948
——*D.C.S. Oosthuizen memorial lectures Number One ... May 13th, 1970* (Academic Freedom Committee) Grahamstown 1970
——*Kontakion for you departed* London 1969
——*Too late the phalarope* London 1953
——*Towards the mountain* Cape Town 1980
PATON, A. & SHAH, K. *Sponono* Cape Town 1983
PATTERSON, R. *Reptiles of Southern Africa* Cape Town 1987
PAUL, N. *A child in the midst* London 1909
PAUW, J. *In the heart of the whore* Halfway House 1991
PAVER, R. *The reminiscences of Richard Paver* ed. by A.H. Duminy & L.J.G. Adcock Cape Town 1979 ('The Graham's Town Series')
PAYTON, C.A. *The diamond diggings of South Africa* London 1872
PEARSE, G.E. *Eighteenth century furniture in South Africa* Pretoria 1960
PEDERSEN, C. ed. *Down memory lane at Riet River* Grahamstown 1988
PEIRES, J.B. *The house of Phalo* Johannesburg 1981
P.E.N. 1960: new South African writing and a survey of fifty years of creative achievement (South African Centre of the International P.E.N. Club)
——see also *South African P.E.N. year book*
PERCIVAL, R. *An account of the Cape of Good Hope* London 1804
PEREIRA, E. ed. *Contemporary South African plays* Johannesburg 1977
Personality Durban 1957-197? (continuation of *The Outspan*)
Personality Durban ?1986- (continuation of *Family Radio & T.V.*)
PETENI, R.L. *Hill of fools* Cape Town 1976
PETTMAN, C. *Africanderisms: a glossary of South African colloquial words and phrases and of place and other names* London 1913 [Note Some of the quotations used in this book are cited verbatim in the dictionary, with Pettman acknowledged in parentheses]
——*Notes on South African place names* Kimberley 1914
PHILIP, M. *Caravan caravel* Cape Town 1973
PHILIPPS, T. *Philipps, 1820 settler* ed. by A. Keppel-Jones Pietermaritzburg 1960
——*Scenes and occurences in Albany and Caffer-land* [his letters, publ. anonymously] London 1827
PHILLIPS, D.S.F.A (Mrs Lionel Phillips) *Some South African recollections* London 1899
PHILLIPS, M. *Catchee Chinaman* Pretoria 1973
Philosophical transactions of the Royal Society London 1665-
PIENAAR, U. DE V. *The freshwater fishes of the Kruger National Park* (National Parks Board) Johannesburg 1978
Pietersburg English Medium School Magazine Pietersburg
PIETERSE, P. *Day of the giants* see Jonker, A. tr.

——*Shadow of the eagle* see Winter, J. tr.
PIGOT, E.S. *The journal of Eliza Sophia Pigot. 1819-21.* Typescript ed. by M. Rainier. Albany Museum history division [publ. in 1974 as part of 'The Graham's Town Series']
PINNOCK, D. *The brotherhoods* Cape Town 1984
PLAATJE, S.T. *The Boer War diary of Sol T. Plaatje: an African at Mafeking* ed. by J.L. Comaroff Johannesburg 1973
——*Mhudi* ed. by S. Gray Johannesburg 1975
——*Native life in South Africa* London 1917
——another ed. Johannesburg 1982
PLANT, R. *The Zulu in three tenses* Pietermaritzburg 1905
PLATZKY, L. & WALKER, C. *The surplus people* Johannesburg 1985
PLAYNE, S. *Cape Colony (Cape Province): its history, commerce, industries and resources* Cape Town c.1911
PLOMER, W. *The case is altered* London 1932
——*Turbott Wolfe* London 1965
PLUMPTRE, A. tr. *H. Lichtenstein's Travels in Southern Africa in the years 1803, 1804, 1805 and 1806* 2 vols. London 1812-15
——reprint Cape Town 1928-30 (Van Riebeeck Society)
POHL, V. *Adventures of a Boer family* Johannesburg 1946
——*Bushveld adventures* London 1940
——*The dawn and after* London 1964
POLAND, M. *Train to Doringbult* London 1987
POLLOCK, N.C. & AGNEW, S. *An historical geography of South Africa* London 1963
'POLSON, N.' (Peter Nicolson) *A subaltern's sick leave, or ... a visit in search of health to China and the Cape of Good Hope* Calcutta 1837
A Portuguese-English dictionary ed. by J.L. Taylor & P.C. Martin Stanford, U.S.A. 1970
Post Durban 1955- (with title *Golden City Post* 1955-60; numerous editions; Transvaal ed. (1977-80) absorbed *(The) Bantu World* in 1955, continued by *Sowetan*)
POYNTON, R.J. *Characteristics and uses of selected trees and shrubs cultivated in South Africa* (South African Forestry Research Institute) Pretoria 1984
A practical Ndebele dictionary ed. J.N. Pelling Harare, Zimbabwe 1985
PRANCE, C.R. *Antic memories* Umtata 1947
——*Tante Rebella's saga* London 1937
——*Under the blue roof: sketches of a settler's life in the Transvaal backveld* Bloemfontein 1944
Press Digest Johannesburg (1936-47; 1948-72)
PRESTON, D.M.B. (D.M. Beal Preston) *The story of a frontier town* Cathcart, Eastern Cape 1976
Pretoria News Pretoria 1898-99; 1902-
PRETORIUS, P.J. *Jungle man* London 1949
PRICE, E.L. (E. Lees Price) *The journals of Elizabeth Lees Price written in Bechuanaland, Southern Africa 1854-1906* ed. by U. Long London 1956
——Letters. Cory Library manuscript collection
PRICHARD, H.M. *Friends and foes in the Transkei* London 1880
PRINGLE, T. *African sketches* London 1834
——*Ephemerides; or, occasional poems, written in Scotland and South Africa* London 1828
——*Some account of the present state of the English settlers in Albany, South Africa* London 1824
Probe (National Union of South African Students, University of Cape Town) Cape Town 1953-61
Proceedings of, and evidence taken by, the Commission on Native Affairs (Cape of Good Hope) Grahamstown 1865
Proceedings of the Pan-African congress on prehistory ed. by L.S.B. Leakey [no place] 1947
——see also *Third Pan-African congress on prehistory*
PROZESKY, O. *The wrath of the lamb* Pretoria 1987
PROZESKY, O.P.M. *A field guide to the birds of Southern Africa* London 1970
PUDNEY, J. ed. *Pick of today's short stories* London 1961
PURCHAS, S. *Hakluytus posthumus, or Purchas his pilgrimes* 20 vols. Glasgow 1625
——reprint 1905
PURVIS, W.F. & BIGGS, L.V. *South Africa: its peoples, progress and problems* London 1896

QUAIL, E. *Papaniki* Johannesburg 1988
Quarry '76: new South African writing Johannesburg 1976
——*Quarry '77: new South African writing* Johannesburg 1977
——*Quarry '78-9: new South African writing* Pretoria 1979
Queenstown Daily Representative and Border Chronicle Queenstown 1865-1927 (merged with *Queenstown Free Press* to become *Queenstown Daily Representative and Free Press* 1901; title varies as *Daily Representative and Free Press* 1905-23, and *Queenstown Daily Representative and Free Press* 1923-27; continued by *Daily Representative*)
Queenstown Free Press Queenstown 1859-1901 (merged with *Queenstown Daily Representative and Border Chronicle*)
QUEST, J. *The burning river* Pretoria 1987
A question of colour: a study of South Africa [written anonymously] London 1906

RABIE, P.S. tr. *Nienaber & Raper's Hottentot (Khoekhoen) place names* Durban 1983
RABONE, A. ed. *The records of a pioneer family, being letters and diaries of Alfred Essex, William Rabone, and Harriet Rabone* Cape Town 1966
Race relations survey (South African Institute of Race Relations) Johannesburg 1946- (title varies as *(A) survey of race relations (in South Africa)*)
RAIDT, E.H. ed. *Beschryvinge van Kaap der Goede Hoope, met de zaaken daar toe behoorende, door François Valentyn, 1726* [with English translation by R. Raven-Hart, *Description of the Cape of Good Hope with the matters concerning it*] 2 vols. Cape Town 1971-73 (Van Riebeeck Society)
RAINIER, M. ed. see Pigot, E.S.
RALLS, A.M. & GORDON, R.E. *Daughter of yesterday* Cape Town 1975
RAMGOBIN, M. *Waiting to live* Cape Town 1986
Rand Daily Mail Johannesburg 1902-85
RAPER, P.E. *Dictionary of Southern African place names* Johannesburg 1989
——tr. *Robert Jacob Gordon's Cape travels, 1777 to 1786* ed. by Raper & M. Boucher Vol. I Johannesburg 1988
——see also Rabie, P.S. tr.
RAUBENHEIMER, M. *Tested South African recipes* Johannesburg 1930
RAVEN-HART, R. *Before Van Riebeeck* Cape Town 1967
——*Cape Good Hope 1652-1702: the first fifty years of Dutch colonisation as seen by callers* 2 vols. Cape Town 1971
——tr. *F. Valentyn's Description of the Cape of Good Hope with the matters concerning it* see Raidt, E.H. ed.
RAVENSTEIN, E.G. *The voyages of Diogo Cão and Bartholomeu Dias 1482-88* Pretoria 1987 (reprinted from *Geographical Journal* Vol. 16 No. 6, Dec. 1900)
'RAWBONE MALONG' see Malan, Robin
RAWLINSON, H.G. ed. see Ovington, J.
RAYMOND, H. *B.I. Barnato, a memoir* London 1897
The Reader: a step to better English Johannesburg 1979- (until Aug. 1979 with title — — : *a paper in easy English*)
Reader's Digest Cape Town
Reader's Digest family guide to the law in South Africa ed. by C. Walton Cape Town 1986
Reader's Digest gardening questions answered see *Your gardening questions answered*
Reader's Digest illustrated history of South Africa: the real story ed. by D. Oakes Cape Town 1989
The Red Wing: journal ... of the Natural History Society (St Andrew's College) Vol. V No. IV Grahamstown 1961
REED, D. *Somewhere south of Suez* London 1950
The regional services councils (Bureau for Information) Pretoria 1988
REITZ, C.L. *Poisonous South African snakes and snakebite* Pretoria 1978
REITZ, D. *Commando* London 1929
——*No outspan* London 1943
RENSHAW, R. *Voyage to the Cape of Good Hope and up the Red Sea* Manchester, U.K. 1804
Report by the Chief Commissioner of police, for the Union of South Africa, for the year 1911 Parl. Paper U.G.62-1912 [publ. 1913]
Report of the Administrator on the Bondelzwarts rising, 1922 Parl. Paper U.G.30-1922
Report of the Ciskei Commission [appointed in terms of Government Notice 14 in the *Ciskei Official Gazette* Vol. 6 No. 177 of 4 August 1978] (Chairman: G.P. Quail) Pretoria 1980
Report of the Commission appointed to enquire into acts of violence committed by Natives at Krugersdorp, Newlands, Randfontein and Newclare (Chairman: J. de V. Louw) Parl. Paper U.G.47-1950
Report of the Commission for socio-economic development see *Summary of the report of the Commission for socio-economic development*
Report of the Commission of Enquiry into South West Africa Affairs 1962-1963 (Chairman: F.H. Odendaal) Parl. Paper R.P.12-1964
Report of the Commission on Native education 1949-1951 (Chairman: W.M. Eiselen) Parl. Paper U.G.53-1951

Report of the director of nature and environmental conservation No. 34 1977–78 (Department of Nature & Environmental Conservation) Cape Town c.1978
Report of the National Road Board for the calendar year 1938 (Chairman: P.I. Hoogenhout) Parl. Paper U.G.19-1939
Report of the Natives Affairs Commission appointed to enquire into the working of the provisions of the Natives (Urban Areas) Act relating to the use and supply of Kaffir beer (Chairman: G.H. Nicholls) Parl. Paper [Commission of Enquiry] 1942
Report of the Natives Law Commission 1946–48 (Chairman: H.A. Fagan) Parl. Paper U.G.28-1948
Report of the proceedings of the Natives Representative Council held at Pretoria in November, 1938 (Chairman: D.L. Smit) Parl. Paper U.G.10-1939
Report of the Railways & Harbours Board for the year ended 31st December, 1937 Parl. Paper U.G.41-1938
Report of the Railways & Harbours Board for the year ended 31 December, 1938 Parl. Paper U.G.21-1939
Report of the Rehoboth Commission (Chairman: J. De Villiers) Parl. Paper U.G.41-1926
Report of W. Coates Palgrave, esq., special commissioner to the tribes north of the Orange River, of his mission to Damaraland and Great Namaqualand in 1876 [House of Assembly, Report of Select Committee] Cape Parl. Paper G.50-1877
The report of the Wesleyan-Methodist Missionary Society for the year ending April 1872 London 1872
Reports of the commissioners of inquiry on the Cape of Good Hope I. Upon the administration of the Government at the Cape of Good Hope; II. Upon the finances at the Cape of Good Hope Cape Town 1827
Republic of South Africa. Parliament. House of Assembly. Debates Cape Town 1961– [Note The name Hansard is used in quotations to refer to South African parliamentary debates since Union in 1910]
Republic of South Africa. Parliament. Statutes. 1961–
REUNERT, T. *Diamonds and gold in South Africa* Cape Town 1893
REYNOLDS, R. & B. *Grahamstown from cottage to villa* Cape Town 1974
Rhodeo (Students' Representative Council, Rhodes University) Grahamstown
RIDER HAGGARD, H. see Haggard, R.H.
RIDSDALE, B. *Scenes and adventures in Great Namaqualand* London 1883
RIP, C.M. *Contemporary social pathology* 2nd ed. Pretoria 1978
RITCHIE, J.E. *Brighter South Africa* London 1892
RITTER, E.A. *Shaka Zulu: the rise of the Zulu empire* Cape Town 1955
RIVE, R. ed. *Modern African prose* London 1964
ROBERTS, A. *The birds of South Africa* 6th impression London 1948 (first publ. 1940)
—— 2nd, 3rd, & 4th ed. *Roberts birds of South Africa* rev. by G.R. McLachlan & R. Liversidge Cape Town 1978
—— 5th ed. *Roberts' birds of Southern Africa* rewritten by G.L. Maclean Cape Town 1984
—— *The mammals of South Africa* ed. by R. Bigalke, V. FitzSimons, & D.E. Malan [Johannesburg] 1951
—— *Our South African birds* Cape Town 1941
ROBERTS, B. *Churchills in Africa* London 1970
—— *Kimberley: turbulent city* Cape Town 1976
ROBERTS, Margaret *Herbs for healing* Cape Town 1989
ROBERTS, Michael tr. *Johan August Wahlberg. Travel journals (and some letters) South Africa and Namibia/Botswana, 1838–1856* ed. by A. Craig & C. Hummel Cape Town 1994 (Van Riebeeck Society)
ROBERTS, S. *Jacks in corners* Johannesburg 1987
—— *Outside life's feast* Johannesburg 1975
ROBINSON, A.M.L. (A.M. Lewin Robinson) ed. *The letters of Lady Anne Barnard to Henry Dundas: from the Cape and elsewhere . . .* see Barnard, Lady Anne
—— ed. *Selected articles from the Cape Monthly Magazine* Cape Town 1978 (Van Riebeeck Society)
ROCHE, H.A. *On trek in the Transvaal; or, over berg and veldt in South Africa* 4th ed. London 1878
ROGERS, M. *The Black Sash: the story of the South African Women's Defence of the Constitution League* Johannesburg 1956
RONAN, B. *Forty South African years* London 1923
ROOKE, D. *Diamond Jo* London 1965
—— *A lover for Estelle* London 1961
—— *Margaretha de la Porte* London 1974
—— *The South African twins* London 1953
RORKE, M. *Melina Rorke: her amazing experiences in the stormy nineties of South Africa's story* London 1939
ROSCOE, A. *Uhuru's fire: African literature east to south* Cambridge, U.K. 1977
ROSE, C. *Four years in Southern Africa* London 1829

ROSE, F.H. *Kruger's wagon: a romance of adventure* London 1943
ROSE, W. *The reptiles and amphibians of Southern Africa* Cape Town 1950
ROSENBERG, V. *Sunflower to the sun* Cape Town 1976
—— ed. *Almost forgotten stories* Cape Town 1979
—— ed. *Uncollected essays* Cape Town 1981
ROSENTHAL, E. *Encyclopaedia of Southern Africa* London 1967
—— *General de Wet* Dassie ed. [Johannesburg a.1956] (first publ. 1946; quotations are taken from the Dassie ed., but dated simply 1946)
—— *Here are diamonds* London 1950
—— *The hinges creaked* Cape Town 1951
—— *Meet me at the Carlton: the story of Johannesburg's old Carlton Hotel* Cape Town 1972
—— *Old-time survivals in South Africa* Pretoria 1936
—— *River of diamonds* Cape Town [?1957]
—— *Rustenburg romance* Johannesburg 1979
ROSENTHAL, J. *Wake up singing* Cape Town 1990
ROSS, E. *Diary of the siege of Mafeking October 1899 to May 1900* ed. by B.P. Willan Cape Town 1980 (Van Riebeeck Society)
ROSS, R. *Adam Kok's Griquas* Cambridge, U.K. 1976
ROSTEN, L. *The joys of Yiddish* New York 1970
ROTHMAN, M. & E. *The Drostdy at Swellendam* Swellendam 1967
ROTHMANN, A. *The elephant shrew and company* Cape Town 1964
ROUX, E. *The veld and the future* Cape Town 1946
RSA policy review (Bureau for Information) Vol. I No. I Pretoria 1988
RUDNER, J. & I. tr. see Forbes, V.S. ed.
RUNCIE, J. *Idylls by two oceans* Cape Town 1910
RUSSELL, G.H. *Under the sjambok: a tale of the Transvaal* London 1899

SACHS, B. ed. *Herman Charles Bosman as I knew him: S.A. Opinion – Trek Anthology* Johannesburg 1971
The SA Consumer/Die SA Verbruiker (Consumer Council) Pretoria
SADLER, C. ed. *Never a young man: extracts from the letters and journals of the Rev. William Shaw* Cape Town 1967
SALT, H. *A voyage to Abyssinia, and travels into the interior of that country, executed under the orders of the British Government, in the years 1809 and 1810* London 1814
—— see also Halls, J.J.
SAMPSON, A. *Drum: a venture into the new Africa* London 1956
—— *The treason cage: the opposition on trial in South Africa* London 1958
SAMPSON, H.F. *The white-faced huts* Grahamstown 1961
SAMPSON, V. *Kom binne* Cape Town 1931
Sam Sly's African Journal: a register of facts, fiction, news, literature, commerce and amusement Cape Town 1843–49 (continuation of *The South African Advocate and Cape Town Spectator*; continued by *The African Journal*)
SANDEMAN, E.F. *Eight months in an ox-waggon* London 1880
SANDERSON, J. *Memoranda of a trading trip into the Orange River (Sovereignty) Free State, and the country of the Transvaal Boers* Pretoria 1981 (facsimile reprint of article in *Journal of the Royal Geographical Society*, Vol. XXX, 1860)
SARON, G. & HOTZ, L. eds. *The Jews in South Africa: a history* Cape Town 1955
Sash Johannesburg 1969– (continuation of *The Black Sash*)
Saspu National (South African Student Press Union) Johannesburg 1980–
Saturday News see *Daily News*
Saturday Star see *The Star*
SAUER, H. *Ex Africa* London 1937
—— facsimile reprint Bulawayo, Rhodesia [Zimbabwe] 1973
SAUL, C.D. *South African periodical publications 1800–1875* Cape Town 1949
SAUNDERS, C. *Historical dictionary of South Africa* Metuchen, U.S.A. 1983
SAVORY, T.W. *Diary. 1849.* Killie Campbell Africana Library MS1528a
SAYERS, C.O. *Looking back on George* George 1982
Scenes and occurences in Albany and Caffer-land see Philipps, T.
SCHÄFER, I.D. *The burgeoning family law and joint custody* [inaugural lecture, Rhodes University] Grahamstown 1986
SCHAPERA, I. ed. *David Livingstone: South African papers* Cape Town 1974 (Van Riebeeck Society)
SCHAPERA, Isaac *Bantu-speaking tribes* London 1937

—— *The KhoiSan peoples of South Africa* London 1930
SCHELPE, E. *An introduction to the South African orchids* London 1966
SCHIRMER, P. *The concise illustrated South African Encyclopaedia* Johannesburg 1980
SCHOLEFIELD, A. *Eagles of malice* London 1968
—— *The last safari* London 1988
—— *Wild dog running* London 1872
SCHOLTZ, C.H. & HOLM, E. eds. *Insects of Southern Africa* Durban 1986
SCHREINER, Olive E.A. *Closer Union* Cape Town 1960 (first publ. 1909)
—— *Diamond fields. 1882.* National English Literary Museum Pringle collection 471/20
—— *The story of an African farm* London 1883
—— *Thoughts on South Africa* London 1923 [preface dated 1896]
—— *The woman's rose* ed. by C. Clayton Johannesburg 1986
—— see also Hobman, D.L.
SCHREINER, Oliver D. *The nettle* (South African Institute of Race Relations) Johannesburg 1964
SCHWARZ, E.H.L. *The Kalahari and its native races* London 1928
—— *The Kalahari; or, Thirstland redemption* Cape Town [1920]
SCLATER, W.L. *The mammals of South Africa* 2 vols. London 1900-1 [part of the series 'The fauna of South Africa' ed. by Sclater]
—— see also Stark, A.C. & Sclater, W.L.
Scope Durban
SCULLY, W.C. *Between sun and sand* London 1898
—— *By veldt and kopje* London 1907
—— *Daniel Vananda: the life story of a human being* Cape Town 1923
—— *Further reminiscences of a South African pioneer* London 1913
—— *The harrow* Cape Town 1921
—— *Kaffir stories* London 1895
—— *Lodges in the wilderness* London 1915 [preface dated 1914]
—— *A vendetta of the desert* London 1898
SEARY, E.R. ed. *South African short stories* Cape Town 1947
SEED, J. *Ntombi's song* Johannesburg 1988
SEGAL, A. *Johannesburg Friday* London 1954
SEGAL, R. *The Tokolosh* Cape Town [1960]
Select Committee Report on Mission to Damaraland see *Report of W. Coates Palgrave . . .*
SELIGMAN, C.G. *Races of Africa* London 1930
—— 1st rev. ed. 1939
—— rev. ed. 1957
SELOUS, F.C. *Travel and adventure in South East Africa* London 1893
SELWYN, W. *Cape carols and miscellaneous verses* Cape Town 1891
SEMPLE, R. *Walks and sketches at the Cape of Good Hope* London 1805
SEPAMLA, S. *Third generation* Johannesburg 1986
SEROTE, M.W. *Behold Mama, flowers* Pretoria 1978
SERTON, P. ed. see McKiernan, G.
Setswana dictionary: Setswana-English and English-Setswana compiled by J.T. Brown 3rd ed. Johannesburg 1925 (first publ. c.1875)
—— reprint with new preface [dated 1965] by J.D. Jones 1982
The Settler Johannesburg 1983– (continuation of *The 1820*)
SEWELL, J.F. *The private diary of the village harbour-master 1875–97* Plettenberg Bay 1983
SEYMOUR, S.M. *Native law in South Africa* Cape Town 1953
SHAHANI, A.T. *The pocket English-Hindustani dictionary* Karachi [no date]
—— *The pocket Hindustani-English dictionary* Karachi [no date]
SHARPE, R.B. ed. see Layard, E.L.
SHAW, B. *Memorials of Southern Africa* London 1841
SHAW, G.B. *The adventures of the black girl in her search for God* London 1932
SHAW, W. *Diary. 1820–29.* Typescript. Cory Library MS1132
—— *Story of my mission in south-eastern Africa* London 1860
—— see also Sadler, C. ed.
SHEPHARD, J.B. *Land of the Tikoloshe* London 1955
SHER, A. *Middlepost* London 1989
SHERLOCK, C. *Hyena dawn* London 1990
SHIPP, J. *Memoirs of the extraordinary military career of John Shipp, late Lieut. in his Majesty's 87th regiment* London 1890 (first publ. 1828)

SELECT BIBLIOGRAPHY

SHONE, T. Diary, Clumber and Caffraria. 1838–67. Cory Library MS10548, MS10763, MS10764, & MS10765
SHOOTER, J. *The kafirs of Natal and the Zulu country* London 1857
SHORT, G. *The Trevor Goddard story* Durban 1965
SIDWELL, H.B. *Story of South Africa* 5th ed. Cape Town 1893
SIEGFRIED, W.R. ed. *Some protected birds of the Cape Province* (Department of Nature Conservation, Cape Provincial Administration) Cape Town 1962
—— another ed. 1967
Signature (Diners Club SA (Pty) Ltd) Johannesburg
SIKAKANE, J. *A window on Soweto* (International Defence & Aid Fund) London 1977
—— reprint 1980
SILBERBAUER, G.B. *Hunter and habitat in the central Kalahari desert* Cambridge, U.K. 1981
S.W. Silver & Co.'s handbook to South Africa London 1887
SIM, T.R. *The forests and forest flora of the Colony of the Cape of Good Hope* London 1907
SIMON, B. *Joburg, sis!* Johannesburg 1974
SISSON, J.J.L. *The South African judicial dictionary* Durban 1960
SKAIFE, S.H. *African insect life* Johannesburg 1979
—— *Animal life in South Africa* Cape Town [?1918]
—— *A naturalist remembers* Cape Town 1963
—— *South African nature notes* Cape Town [?1939]
Ski-Boat Durban
SKINNER, J.D. & SMITHERS, R.H.N. *The mammals of the Southern African subregion* Pretoria 1990
'S.L.' tr. *Fryke & Schweitzer's A relation of two several voyages made into the East-Indies by Christopher Fryke ... and Christopher Schewitzer* [sic] London 1700
SLABOLEPSZY, P. *Braait Laaities.* 1991. Unpubl. play. [script by courtesy of the Dramatic, Artistic, & Literary Rights Organisation]
—— *Saturday night at the Palace* Johannesburg 1985
The slang dictionary; or the vulgar words, street phrases, and 'fast' expressions of high and low society ed. by J.G. Hotten London 1872
SLATER, F.C. *The centenary book of South African verse* London 1925
—— *The new centenary book of South African verse* London 1945
—— *The secret veld* London 1931
—— *Selected poems of Francis Carey Slater* London 1947
—— *The sunburnt south* London 1908
—— *The trek* London 1938
SLATTER, E.M. *My leaves are green* Cape Town [1967]
SLINGSBY, P. *Tomas* Cape Town 1988
SLOVO, J. *Ties of blood* London 1990
SMALL, A. see Lasker, C. tr.
SMITH, A. *Andrew Smith's journal of his expedition into the interior of South Africa, 1834–6* ed. by W.F. Lye Cape Town 1975
—— *A contribution to South African materia medica, chiefly from plants in use among natives* Lovedale, Eastern Cape 1885
—— *The diary of Dr Andrew Smith* ed. by P.R. Kirby 2 vols. Cape Town 1939–40 (Van Riebeeck Society)
—— *Illustrations of the zoology of South Africa ... Reptilia* London 1849
—— see also Burrow, J.
SMITH, C.A. *Common names of South African plants* ed. by E.P. Phillips & E. Van Hoepen Pretoria 1966 (Botanical Survey Memoir No. 35)
SMITH, E.W. *The life and times of Daniel Lindley (1801–80)* London 1949
SMITH, J. *Streams to rivers* Cape Town 1988
SMITH, J.L.B. *High tide* Cape Town 1968
—— *Old Fourlegs: the story of the coelacanth* London 1957
—— *The sea fishes of Southern Africa* Johannesburg 1949
SMITH, J.L.B. & M.M. *Fishes of the Tsitsikama Coastal National Park* (National Parks Board of Trustees) Johannesburg 1966
SMITH, M.M. & HEEMSTRA, P.C. eds. *Smiths' Sea Fishes* Johannesburg 1986
SMITH, M.M. & JACKSON, P.B.N. *Common and scientific names of the fishes of Southern Africa* 2 parts (Part I *Marine fishes* by Smith, Part II *Freshwater fishes* by Jackson) Grahamstown 1975
SMITH, P. *The beadle* London 1929
—— *The Little Karoo* London 1936
—— *Platkop's children* London 1935
SMITH, R. *The great gold lands of South Africa* London 1891
SMITH, W. *The burning shore* London 1985
—— *The diamond hunters* London 1973
—— *Golden fox* London 1990
SMUTS, Danie *Folk remedies* Cape Town 1989

SMUTS, Dene & ALBERTS, P. *The forgotten highway through Ceres and the Bokkeveld* Johannesburg 1988
SNYMAN, L. & KLARIE, A. *Free from the sea* Cape Town 1979
SOGA, J.H. *The Ama-Xosa: life and customs* Alice, Eastern Cape [1931]
SOLOMON, V. ed. see Molteno, P.A.
Some protected birds of the Cape Province see Siegfried, W.R. ed.
Some protected wild flowers of the Cape Province (Department of Nature Conservation, Cape Provincial Administration) Cape Town 1967
SOMERVILLE, W. *William Somerville's narrative of his journeys to the Eastern Cape frontier and to Lattakoo 1799–1802* ed. by E. & F. Bradlow Cape Town 1979 (Van Riebeeck Society)
SOULE, A., DIXON, G., & RICHARDS, R. *The Wynand du Toit story* Johannesburg 1987
South Cape Town
South Africa: land of outdoor life (South African Railways & Harbours) [Cape Town] 1923
South Africa: last stronghold of steam (Publicity & Travel Department, South African Transport Services) Johannesburg 1982
The South African Advocate and Cape Town Spectator Cape Town 1843 (continued by *Sam Sly's African Journal*)
South African Agricultural Journal see *Agricultural Journal of the Union of South Africa*
The South African almanac(k) and directory Cape Town 1827–35 (continuation of *(The) African court calendar (and directory);* title varies; continued by *The Cape of Good Hope almanac and annual register*)
The South African Consumer see *The SA Consumer/Die SA Verbruiker*
South African Digest Pretoria
South African Garden and Home Durban
The South African Geographical Journal Johannesburg
The South African Illustrated Magazine Cape Town 1900–6 (continuation of *Cape Illustrated Magazine;* continued by *The South African Magazine*)
South African 'Inquire within' for households see *The 'Cape Times' 'Inquire within' for households*
South African Journal of Science Cape Town 1909
—— see also Gibson, J.Y.
South African Labour Bulletin Johannesburg (until 1982 publ. in Durban)
The South African Law Journal Cape Town 1901– (continuation of *The Cape Law Journal;* until 1910 publ. in Grahamstown)
The South African Magazine Cape Town 1867–69
The South African Magazine Cape Town 1906–7 (continuation of *The South African Illustrated Magazine*)
South African Panorama (Bureau for Information) Pretoria
South African P.E.N. year book 1954 (South African Centre of the International P.E.N. Club) [Johannesburg] 1954
South African P.E.N. year book 1956–1957 (South African Centre of the International P.E.N. Club) Cape Town 1957
—— see also *New South African Writing;* also *P.E.N. 1960: new South African writing*
The South African pocket Oxford dictionary ed. by W. Branford Cape Town 1987
South African Spectator Cape Town 1900–12
South Africa: official yearbook of the Republic of South Africa (Department of Information; later, Information Service of South Africa, Department of Foreign Affairs & Information, Bureau for Information) c.1975–
—— see also *Official year book of the Union and of Basutoland, Bechuanaland Protectorate, and Swaziland*
South Africa Speaks London 1962 ('Reports on the State of South Africa' No. 21)
The South and East African year book and guide with atlas and diagrams ed. by A. Samler Brown & G. Gordon Brown London c.1936
—— see also Brown's 'South Africa'
Southern Sotho–English dictionary reclassified, rev. & enlarged by R.A. Paroz Morija, Basutoland [Lesotho] 1961
The South Western Herald/Suidwestelike Herald George 1971–78 (continuation of *George and Knysna Herald;* continued by *The Herald Phoenix*)
SOWDEN, L. *The crooked bluegum* London 1955
—— *The Union of South Africa* New York 1943
Sowetan Johannesburg 1980– (continuation of the *Transvaal* ed. of *Post*)
SPARRMAN, A. see Forster, G. tr.
The Spectator: a weekly review of politics, etc. London 1828–
The Spectator and Mining Mail Port Elizabeth 1876–91
SPEIRS, R. Diary. 1852. Killie Campbell Africana Library KCM8681

SPENDER, E.H. *General Botha: the career and the man* London 1916
SPILHAUS, M.W. (M. Whiting Spilhaus) *Doorstep-baby* Cape Town 1969
—— *Under a bright sky* Cape Town 1959
SPOHR, O.H. tr. *Ferdinand Krauss's Travel journal Cape to Zululand: observations by a collector and naturalist 1838–40* Cape Town 1973
Spotlight (South African Institute of Race Relations) Johannesburg
SPOTTISWOODE, H. ed. *South Africa: the road ahead* Cape Town 1960
Staffrider Johannesburg
STAINBANK, D.L.W. Diary. 1857–79. Typescript. Killie Campbell Africana Library KCM8680
Standard encyclopaedia of Southern Africa 12 vols. Cape Town 1970–76
Standard hospital diets in use at the Groote Schuur Hospital, Cape Town (Groote Schuur Hospital) Cape Town 1943
Standard Shona dictionary ed. by M. Hannan Salisbury, Rhodesia [Harare, Zimbabwe] 1981
STANDER, S. *Flight from the hunter* London 1977
—— *The horse* London 1968
—— tr. A.P. Brink's *Brandy in South Africa* Cape Town 1973
The Star Johannesburg 1889–1900; 1901– (continuation of *The Eastern Star;* with title *Comet* 25 Mar.–13 Apr. 1897; weekend eds. *Saturday Star* and *Sunday Star*)
STARK, A.C. & SCLATER, W.L. *The birds of South Africa* 4 vols. [commenced by Stark, completed and ed. by Sclater; part of the series 'The fauna of South Africa' ed. by Sclater] London 1900–1906
—— see also Sclater, W.L.
State of the Cape of Good Hope, in 1822 see Bird, W.W.
State of South Africa: economic, financial and statistical year-book for the Republic of South Africa 1965 Johannesburg c.1965
State of South Africa: economic, financial and statistical year-book for the Republic of South Africa 1967 Johannesburg c.1967
State of the Union: economic, financial and statistical year-book for the Union of South Africa 1959–60 Johannesburg c.1960
STATHAM, F.R. *Blacks, Boers and British: a three-cornered problem* London 1881
—— *South Africa as it is* London 1897
Statute law of the Cape of Good Hope, comprising the placaats, proclamations and ordinances, enacted before the establishment of the colonial parliament and still wholly or in part in force Cape Town 1862
Statutes of the Cape of Good Hope passed by the first parliament during the sessions 1854–1858 Cape Town 1883
Statutes of the Cape of Good Hope passed by the second parliament during the sessions 1859–1863 Cape Town 1863
Statutes of the Cape of Good Hope passed by the third parliament during the sessions 1864–1868 Cape Town 1868
Statutes of the Cape of Good Hope passed by the fourth parliament during the sessions 1869–1873 Cape Town 1879
Statutes of the Cape of Good Hope passed by the fifth parliament during the sessions 1874–1878 Cape Town 1882
Statutes of Natal ... being a compilation of the statutes of the Colony of Natal from the years 1845 to 1899 compiled & ed. by R.L. Hitchins & G.W. Sweeney 3 vols. Pietermaritzburg 1900–2
Statutes of the Republic of South Africa see Republic of South Africa. Parliament. Statutes
Statutes of the Union of South Africa see Union of South Africa. Parliament. Statutes
STAVORINUS, J.S. see Wilcocke, S.H. tr.
STAYT, H.A. *The BaVenda* London 1931
STEEDMAN, A. *Wanderings and adventures in the interior of Southern Africa* 2 vols. London 1835
—— facsimile reprint Cape Town 1966
STEENKAMP, W. *Blake's woman* Cape Town 1986
—— *The blockhouse* Pretoria 1987
—— *Land of the thirst king* Cape Town 1975
STENGEL, R. *January sun* New York 1990
STEPHENS, E.L. *Some South African edible fungi* illustrated by M.M. Kidd Cape Town 1953
—— *Some South African poisonous and inedible fungi* Cape Town 1953
STEVENSON, N. *African harvest* London 1928
—— *The farmers of Lekkerbat* London 1930
STEVENSON-HAMILTON, J. *The Low-veld* London 1929
—— *South African Eden* London 1937
STEWART, J. *Outlines of Kaffir grammar* Alice, Eastern Cape 1906
STEYN, M.M. *The diary of a South African* Cape Town 1919
STOKES, C.S. & WILTER, B.A. *Veld trails: an anthology* Johannesburg 1934
STOKES, H. *What bird is that?* Cape Town 1965

SELECT BIBLIOGRAPHY

STONEMAN, B. *Plants and their ways in South Africa* London 1906
STORMBERG, R.Y. *Mrs Pieter de Bruyn* Cape Town 1920
—— *With love from Gwenno* Cape Town [1919]
The story of the Johannesburg stock exchange 1887-1947 (Committee of the Johannesburg Stock Exchange) Johannesburg 1948
STOUT, B. *Narrative of the loss of the ship 'Hercules', commanded by Captain Benjamin Stout, on the coast of Caffraria ...* London 1798
STRETCH, C.L. *Journal. His early life, notes on the 1819 war and detailed journal of the 1834-35 war. 1825-35.* Cory Library MS14,558
STRUTHERS, R.B. *Hunting journal 1852-1856 in the Zulu kingdom and the Tsonga regions* ed. by P. Merrett & R. Butcher Pietermaritzburg 1991
—— *St Lucia hunting diaries. 1852-56.* Killie Campbell Africana Library KCM55079
—— see also Fynn, H.F. *Letters.*
STRUTT, D.H. *Fashion in South Africa 1652-1900* Cape Town 1975
STUART, C. & T. *Field guide to the mammals of Southern Africa* Cape Town 1988
STUBBS, T. *Men I have known. 1868.* Appendix to M.A. thesis by R.T. McGeoch, Rhodes University, 1965
—— *Reminiscences of Thomas Stubbs. 1876.* Appendix to M.A. thesis by R.T. McGeoch, Rhodes University, 1965
Style Johannesburg (with regional editions *Cape Style*, *Highveld Style*, and *Natal Style*)
Het Suid-Western see *Oudtshoorn Courant and het Suid-Western*
Summary of the report of the Commission for socio-economic development of the Bantu areas within the Union of South Africa (Chairman: F.R. Tomlinson) Parl. Paper U.G.61-1955
Sunday Nation see *New Nation*
Sunday Star see *The Star*
Sunday Times Johannesburg 1906-
Sunday Tribune Durban 1935-39; 1947- (absorbed by *Natal Daily News* 1939-47; with title *Sunday Tribune and Sunday Post* 1951-69)
SUNDERMEIER, T. ed. *Church and nationalism in South Africa* Johannesburg 1975
A supplement to the Oxford English dictionary ed. by R.W. Burchfield 4 vols. Oxford, U.K. 1972-86
(A) survey of race relations (in South Africa) see *Race relations survey*
SUTHERLAND, J. *Memoir respecting the Kaffers, Hottentots, and Bosjemans, of South Africa* 2 vols. Cape Town 1845-46
SUTHERLAND, W.S. *South African sketches, parodies, and verses up-to-date* Cradock 1901
SWA/Namibia today (South West Africa/Namibia Information Service) Windhoek, South West Africa [Namibia] 1980
SWANSON, D. *Highveld, Lowveld and jungle* Dassie ed. [Johannesburg c.1957]
SWART, C.P. *A supplement to: the Rev. Charles Pettman's 'Glossary of South African colloquial words and phrases and of place and other names'.* M.A. thesis, University of South Africa, 1934 [Note Some of the quotations used in this thesis are cited verbatim in the dictionary, with Swart acknowledged in parentheses]
SYKES, F.W. *With Plumer in Matabeleland* Westminster, U.K. 1897
—— facsimile reprint Bulawayo, Rhodesia [Zimbabwe] 1972

TACHARD, G. *A relation of the voyage to Siam, performed by six Jesuits sent ... to the Indies and China, in the year 1685 ...* London 1688
TAIT, B.C. (B. Campbell Tait) *The Durban story* Durban [c.1963]
TAWSE JOLLIE, E. see Jollie, E.T.
TELFORD, A.A. *Johannesburg: some sketches of the golden metropolis* Cape Town 1969
—— *Yesterday's dress* Cape Town 1972
TERRY, E. *A voyage to East India; with a description of the large territories under the subjection of the Great Mogul* London 1777
THEAL, G.M. *The beginning of South African history* London 1902
—— *Notes on Canada and South Africa* Cape Town [1895]
—— *Records of the Cape Colony* 36 vols. London 1897-1905
The 1820 see under 'E'
THEMBA, C. see Patel, E. ed.
THÉRON, A. *More South African deep freezing* Cape Town 1970

THEROUX, P. *My secret history* London 1989
Third Pan-African congress on prehistory ed. by J.D. Clark London 1957
—— see also *Proceedings of the Pan-African congress on prehistory*
This is South Africa (Department of Foreign Affairs & Information) Pretoria 1980
THOLO, M. see Hermer, C.
THOM, H.B. ed. *Journal of Jan van Riebeeck* 3 vols. (Vol. I tr. by W.P.L. Van Zyl (pp. 315-83 tr. by L.C. Van Oordt), Vol. II tr. by J. Smuts, Vol. III tr. by C.K. Johnman & A. Ravenscroft) Cape Town 1952-58 (Van Riebeeck Society)
—— see also Van Riebeeck, J.
THOMAS, E.N. *How thankful we should be: comments on Natal* Cape Town 1894
THOMPSON, G. *Travels and adventures in Southern Africa* London 1827
—— 2nd ed. 2 vols. 1827
THOMPSON, K. *Richard's way* London 1965
THOMPSON, L.M. *Unification of South Africa 1902-1910* London 1960
THOMPSON, O.R. *The voice of the veld* London 1930
THOMPSON, W.W. *The sea fisheries of the Cape Colony* Cape Town 1913
THOMSON, W.R. *Poems, essays and sketches, with a memoir* Cape Town 1868
A thousand ways to die: the struggle for safety in the gold mines (National Union of Mineworkers) Johannesburg [introductory message dated 1986]
THUNBERG, C.P. see Forbes, V.S. ed.; also Hopson, C.R. tr.
The Times atlas of the world reprint of 7th ed. London 1987
TINDALL, J. *The journal of Joseph Tindall* ed. by B.A. Tindall Cape Town 1959 (Van Riebeeck Society)
TRACEY, H. *Lalela Zulu* Johannesburg [preface dated 1948]
TRAILL, A. ed. *Khoisan linguistic studies 3* (African Studies Institute, University of Witwatersrand) Johannesburg 1977
Transactions of the Missionary Society (London Missionary Society) Vol. I London 1803
Transactions of the South African Philosophical Society Cape Town 1878-1909
TREDGOLD, A. *Bay between the mountains* Cape Town 1985
TREW, H.F. *Botha treks* London 1936
Trial of Andries Botha Field-cornet of the Upper Blinkwater, in the Kat River Settlement, for high treason, in the Supreme Court ... on the 12th May, 1852 Cape Town 1852
—— facsimile reprint Cape Town 1969
Tribal natives and trade unionism: the policy of the Rand Gold Mining Industry (The Transvaal Chamber of Mines) Johannesburg 1946
Tribute Johannesburg
TROLLOPE, J. *The steps of the sun* London 1983
TROTTER, A.F. *Old Cape Colony* Cape Town 1903
TRÜMPELMANN, M.H. see Nel, P.R.T. tr.
Tsonga-English dictionary ed. by R. Cuenod Johannesburg 1985
TUCKER, H. *Our beautiful peninsula* Cape Town [1913]
TUKER, H.F. ed. see Metcalfe, H.
TULLEKEN, S. VAN H. *The practical cookery book for South Africa* 28th ed. Cape Town 1951
TURNER, L.C.F., GORDON-CUMMING, H.R., & BETZLER, J.E. *War in the southern oceans* Oxford, U.K. 1961
TURNER, S. see Child, D.
TUTU, D. *The voice of one crying in the wilderness* London 1982
TUTU, L.V. *Twilight of the struggle (and other articles)* Alice, Eastern Cape c.1986
'TWEDE IN BEVEL' *Piet Kolonel and his men* Durban 1944
TWEEHUIZEN, M. tr. T. Engelbrecht's *Boys of summer* Pretoria 1987
Tweetalige woordeboek/bilingual dictionary 8th rev. & enlarged edition ed. by P.A. Joubert & J.J. Spies Cape Town 1984
TYACK, M. *South Africa: land of challenge* Lausanne 1970
TYFIELD, T. & NICOL, K.R. eds. *The living tradition: an anthology of English verse from 1340-1940* Cape Town 1946
TYLDEN, G. *The rise of the Basuto* Cape Town 1950

UCT Studies in English (Department of English, University of Cape Town) Cape Town
Uniform Pretoria 1976-
Union list of South African newspapers Cape Town 1950 (Grey Bibliographies No. 3)

Union of South Africa. Parliament. House of Assembly. Debates Cape Town 1910-61 [Note The name *Hansard* is used in quotations to refer to South African parliamentary debates since Union in 1910]
Union of South Africa. Parliament. Statutes 1910-61
United Kingdom. Parliamentary papers. London [Note These are referred to collectively in quotations as *Imperial blue books*]
UYS, P.-D. *No one died laughing* London 1986
—— *Paradise is closing down* see Gray, S. ed.

VALBECK, M. *Headlong from heaven* Cape Town [c.1936]
VALENTIA, Viscount see Annesley, G.
VALENTYN, F. see Raidt, E.H. ed.
VAN ALPHEN, J.G. *Jan Venter, S.A.P.* Cape Town 1929
'Van Dale' groot woordenboek der Nederlandse taal ed. by C. Kruyskamp 's-Gravenhage, Netherlands 1961
VAN DEN BERGH, G.N. *Die polisiediens in die Zuid Afrikaansche Republiek* Pretoria 1980
VAN DER COLFF, J. *Bible route: Mozambique!* Roodepoort 1976
VAN DER ELST, R. *A guide to the common sea fishes of Southern Africa* 3rd ed. Cape Town 1993
VAN DER POST, L. *African cooking* New York 1970
—— *A bar of shadow* London 1954
—— *The seed and the sower* London 1963
—— *A story like the wind* London 1972
VAN DER RIET, B. *Letters from various individuals re botanical matters. 1920-38.* Cory Library PR3981
VAN DER RIET, F.G. & HEWSON, L.A. see Hewson, L.A. & Van der Riet, F.G. eds.
VAN DER ROSS, R.E. see Hattingh, J.L. & Bredekamp, H.C. eds.
VAN DER SPUY, U. *Ornamental shrubs and trees for gardens in Southern Africa* Cape Town 1954
VAN DE SANDT CENTLIVRES, S. see Centlivres, S. van de Sandt
VAN H. TULLEKEN, S. see Tulleken, S. van H.
VAN HEERDEN, E. see Hacksley, M.M. tr.; also Knox, C.M. tr.
VAN HEYNINGEN, C. *Orange days: memoirs of eighty years ago in the old Orange Free State* Pietermaritzburg 1965
VAN HEYNINGEN, C. & BERTHOUD, J. *Uys Krige* New York 1966
VAN ONSELEN, L.E. *Cape antique furniture* Cape Town 1959
—— *Trekboer* Cape Town 1961
VAN RENSBURG, T.F.J. *An introduction to fynbos* (Department of Environment Affairs) [Pretoria 1987]
VAN RIEBEECK, J. *Daghregister gehouden by den oppercoopman Jan Anthonisz van Riebeeck* ed. by D.B. Bosman with historical notes by H.B. Thom 3 vols. Cape Town 1952-57 (Van Riebeeck Society)
—— see also Thom, H.B. ed.
VAN RYNEVELD, W.S. *Before his Majesty in Council. Cape of Good Hope. Between William Brown, master, and Andrew Spooner, super-cargo of the American ship, the Five Brothers, appellants, and Willem Stephanus van Ryneveld, ex officio, Attorney-General, respondent. 1796.* South African Library
VAN S. BRUWER, J.P. see Bruwer, J.P. van S.
VAN WARMELO, D. *On commando* London 1902
VAN WYK, A. *The birth of a new Afrikaner* Cape Town 1991
VAN WYK, C. *A message in the wind* Cape Town 1982
VAN WYK, M. *Cooking the South African way* Johannesburg 1986
VARLEY, D.H. & MATTHEW, H.M. eds. see Merriman, N.J.
VAUGHAN, I. *The diary of Iris Vaughan* [Johannesburg] 1958
—— *Last of the sunlit years* Cape Town 1969
—— *These were my yesterdays* Cape Town 1966
VEDDER, H. see *The native tribes of South West Africa*
VENTER, F.A. see Gordon, G. & W. trs.
VENTER, P.C. *Soweto: shadow city* Johannesburg c.1977
VERBEEK, J. & A. *Victorian & Edwardian Natal* Pietermaritzburg 1982
Verbeterde drietalige woordebook: Venda-Afrikaans-Engels ed. by P.J. Wentzel & T.W. Muloiwa Pretoria 1982
Veterinary products handbook (I.C.I. Pharmaceuticals Ltd) Johannesburg [?1970]
VILJOEN, B.J. *My reminiscences of the Anglo-Boer War* London 1902
VILLA-VICENCIO, C. *The theology of apartheid* Cape Town [c.1978]
VINEY, G. *Colonial houses of South Africa* Cape Town 1987
VISSER, N. & COUZENS, T. eds. *H.I.E. Dhlomo collected works* Johannesburg 1985
VLADISLAVIĆ, I. *The folly* Cape Town 1993

―― *Missing persons* Cape Town 1989
The Voice Braamfontein, Johannesburg 1976– (with title – – *of the Voiceless* 1979–80)
Die Volkstem Pretoria 1873–80; 1881–1951 (first publ. as *De Volksstem*; with title *De Volkstem* 1914–15; from 1949 publ. in Johannesburg)
VON BREITENBACH, F. *National list of indigenous trees* (Dendrological Foundation) Pretoria 1987
VON LINNÉ, C. see Linné, C. von
Voorslag Durban 1926–27

WALKER, C. *Signs of the wild* 3rd ed. Cape Town 1985
―― see also Hall-Martin, A., Walker, C., & Bothma, J. du P.
WALKER, E. *A history of South Africa* London 1928
―― 3rd ed. *A history of Southern Africa* 1957
―― new impression with corrections 1968
WALKER, O. *The hippo poacher, in talks with Domenic Dunn* London 1967
―― *Kaffirs are lively* London 1948
―― *Proud Zulu Dassie* ed. [Johannesburg ?1951] (first publ. 1949)
―― *Shapeless flame* London 1951
―― *Wanton city* London 1949
WALL, M.A. *The dominee and the dom-pas or, the padre and the passes* Cape Town 1961
WALLACE, R. *Farming industries of the Cape Colony* London 1896
WALLER, H. see Livingstone, David
WANNENBURGH, A. *The natural wonder of Southern Africa* Cape Town 1984
WA NTHODI, M. see Nthodi, M. wa
WARD, H. *The Cape and the Kaffirs: a diary of five years' residence in Kaffirland* 3rd ed. London 1851
―― *Five years in Kaffirland* 2 vols. London 1848
―― *Jasper Lyle: a tale of Kaffirland* London 1852
WARD, R. *Records of big game* London 1896
―― *The sportsman's handbook to practical collecting, preserving, and artistic setting up of trophies and specimens* 6th ed. London 1891
WARWICK, P. *Black people and the South African war 1899–1902* Johannesburg 1983
WAUCHOPE, I.W. *The natives and their missionaries, by a native minister* [written by 'I.W.'] Lovedale, Eastern Cape [1908] (reprinted from *The Christian Express*)
WAUGH, E. *Black mischief* London 1932
WEBSTER, W.H.B. *Narrative of a voyage to the southern Atlantic Ocean, in the years 1828, 29, 30, performed in H.M. sloop Chanticleer* ... London 1834
Webster's third new international dictionary of the English language ed. by P.B. Gove et al. London 1961
WEDGEWOOD, J. *The last of the radicals* London 1951
Weekend Argus see *The Argus*
Weekend Mercury see *(The) Natal Mercury*
Weekend News and Sunday Magazine Port Elizabeth 1936–48
Weekend Post see *Evening Post*

The Weekly Mail Johannesburg 1985–93 (includes Southern African ed. of *The Guardian Weekly*; continued by *Weekly Mail & Guardian*)
Weekly Mail & Guardian Johannesburg 1993– (continuation of *The Weekly Mail*; publ. in association with *The Guardian Weekly*)
WERNER, A. *The captain of the locusts* London 1899
The Wesleyan-Methodist Magazine London
Wesleyan Missionary Reports see *The report of the Wesleyan-Methodist Missionary Society*
WEST, M. *Bishops and prophets in a black city: African independent churches in Soweto, Johannesburg* Cape Town 1975
WEST, M. & MORRIS, J. *Abantu: an introduction to the black people of South Africa* Cape Town 1976
WESTRUP, W. *The land of to-morrow* London 1912
WESTWOOD, G. *Ross of Silver Ridge* London 1975
WETHERELL, V. *The Indian question in South Africa* Cape Town 1946
Whitaker's almanack 1984 London 1983
WHITE, A.C. *The call of the bushveld* Bloemfontein 1948
WHITE, J.M. *The land God made in anger* London 1969
White wines (Ko-operatieve Wijnbouwers Vereniging van Zuid-Afrika Beperkt) Paarl [no date]
WHITING SPILHAUS, M. see Spilhaus, M.W.
WHITNEY, P.A. *Blue fire* London 1973
WICHT, H. *Road below me* Cape Town 1958
WIDDICOMBE, J. *In the Lesuto: a sketch of African mission life* 2nd ed. London 1895 (first publ. c.1892 as *Fourteen years in Basutoland*)
WILCOCKE, S.H. tr. *J.S. Stavorinus's Voyages to the East Indies* 3 vols. London 1798
WILES, J. *The moon to play with* London 1954
WILHELM, P. *The healing process* Johannesburg 1988
WILKES, G.A. *A dictionary of Australian colloquialisms* London 1978
WILKINS, W.H. ed. *South Africa a century ago: letters written from the Cape of Good Hope (1797–1801)* see Barnard, Lady Anne
WILLAN, B.P. ed. see Ross, E.
WILLCOX, A.R. *Southern land: the prehistory and history of Southern Africa* Cape Town 1976
WILLIAMS, F. *The Cape Malay cookbook* Cape Town 1988
WILLIAMS, J.G. (J. Grenfell Williams) *Moshesh, the man on the mountain* London 1950
WILLIAMS, J.G. (J. Grenfell Williams) & MAY, H.J. *I am black* London [1936]
WILMOT, A. *Diamonds and the South African diamond fields* Cape Town 1869
WILMOT, R.E.E. *A Cape traveller's diary, 1856* ed. by P. Lewsen Johannesburg 1984
WILSON, D.C. *Ten fingers for God* London 1965
WILSON, E. *Reminiscences of a Frontier armed & mounted police officer in South Africa* Grahamstown 1866
WILSON, H.C. *The two scapegoats* Pietermaritzburg 1914
WILSON, H.W. *With the flag to Pretoria* 2 vols. London 1900–1
WILSON, M.M. *The thousand years before Van Riebeeck* Johannesburg 1970 (Raymond Dart Lecture No. 6)
―― see also Duggan-Cronin, A.M.

WILSON, M.M. & MAFEJE, A. *Langa: a study of social groups in an African township* London 1963
WILSON, Lady Sarah Isabella Augusta *South African memories* London 1909
WILSON-MOORE, C. & A.P. *Diggers' doggerel* Cape Town 1890
Wines of origin (Ko-operatieve Wijnbouwers Vereniging van Zuid-Afrika Beperkt) Paarl [no date]
WINTER, J. tr. P. Pieterse's *Shadow of the eagle* Pretoria 1991
WINTERBOTTOM, J.M. *Common birds of the South-East Cape* Town 1953
WOLHUTER, H. *Memories of a game ranger* Johannesburg 1948
Woman's Value Cape Town
Wonderful South Africa Empire Exhibition ed. Johannesburg [1936]
Woordeboek van die Afrikaanse taal (Buro van die WAT) 8 vols. Pretoria 1950–91
The Workers' Herald (Industrial & Commercial Workers' Union of Africa) Johannesburg 1923–28
Work in Progress Johannesburg
World Johannesburg 1932–44; 1945–77 (as *(The) Bantu World*, 1932–55, absorbed by Transvaal ed. of *Post* and continued by *Sowetan*)
The world's best fairy tales (Reader's Digest Association) ed. by B.B. Sideman Cape Town 1969
WORMSER, M.F. *The ostrich industry in South Africa*. M.A. thesis, Transvaal University College (University of Pretoria), 1930
WRIGHT, D. ed. *South African stories* London 1960
WRIGHT, E. *Letters. 1849–94.* Typescript. Killie Campbell Africana Library KCM4224
WRIGHT, L. *Letter to C. Danby. 1856.* Typescript. Killie Campbell Africana Library KCM4224

Xhosa dictionary ed. by H. Nabe, P.W. Dreyer, & G.L. Kakana Johannesburg 1986

The year book and guide to Southern Africa 1951 see Gordon-Brown, A.
You Cape Town
YOUNG, F.B. (F. Brett Young) *City of gold* London 1940
―― *They seek a country* London 1937
YOUNG, F.E.M. *The bywoner* London 1916
Your gardening questions answered (Reader's Digest Association) ed. by A. Turner & V. Leroux Cape Town 1989

ZALOUMIS, E.A. & CROSS, R. *A field guide to the antelope of Southern Africa* (Wildlife Society of Southern Africa, Natal Branch) Durban 1979
ZEEDERBERG, H. *Veld express* Cape Town 1971
Zoo-Historical Gazetteer: annals of the Cape Provincial museums ed. by C.J. Skead (Albany Museum) Grahamstown 1973
ZURNAMER, B. *Locomotives of the South African Railways* Bloemfontein 1970

REF PE 3451 .D53 1996

REF PE 3451 .D53 1996